HARRAP'S

DICTIONARY

Spanish/English – Inglés/Español

HARRAP'S

DICTIONARY

Spanish/English – Inglés/Español

HARRAP

First published in Great Britain 2003
by Chambers Harrap Publishers Ltd
7 Hopetoun Crescent, Edinburgh EH7 4AY

ISBN 0245 60680 7 (UK)
ISBN 84-8332-369-9 (España)
ISBN 970-22-0664-2 (Latinoamérica)

Distribución en España: SPES EDITORIAL, S.L.
Aribau, 197-199, 3ª planta
08021 Barcelona

Distribución en Latinoamérica: Ediciones Larousse, S. A. de C. V.
Dinamarca núm. 81, México 06600, D.F.

Designed and typeset by Chambers Harrap Publishers Ltd, Edinburgh
Printed and bound in Italy by La Tipografica Varese SPA

CONTENTS/ÍNDICE

CONTRIBUTORS/COLABORADORES

CONTRIBUTORS/COLABORADORES

Publishing Manager / Dirección editorial

Patrick White

Managing Editor / Coordinación editorial

Teresa Álvarez

Editorial team / Equipo editorial

Joaquín Blasco
Talia Bugel
José A. Gálvez
Óscar Ramírez Molina
Liam Rodger

Pilar Bernal Macías
Harry Campbell
Juan Campbell-Rodger Vila
Daniela Delas
Débora Farji-Haguet
Roxana Fitch Romero
Paloma Gillard
Andrew Hastings
Christopher Langmuir
Heloïse McGuinness
Victoria Ordoñez Diví
Silvia Rebollo Condé
José María Ruiz Vaca
Alison Sadler
Ricardo Sampedro
Anna Stevenson
Mónica Tamariz
Eduardo Vallejo
Stephen Waller

Latin American Spanish / Español de América

Aaron Alboukrek
Talia Bugel

American English / Inglés norteamericano

SULA
John Wright

Proofreaders / Corrección de pruebas

Lola Busuttil
Anne Kansau
Irene Lakhani
Suzanne McCloskey
Alison Sadler
Megan Thomson

Prepress / Preimpresión

Marina Karapanovic
David Reid

INTRODUCTION

This completely new dictionary from Harrap has been designed and edited to provide the user, whether a student of language, a translator or someone using the dictionary for professional purposes, with an up-to-date and accurate reference work. It provides in-depth coverage of the vocabulary of Spanish and English, with a wide range of idiomatic usages and expressions.

As with all Harrap dictionaries, there is excellent coverage of slang (including Latin-American terms) and everyday language. This is supplemented by extensive treatment of terminology from the sciences to sports, and from business and law to journalism and politics. Particular emphasis has been given to computing terminology, including the language of the Internet – e.g. *cache memory, e-cash, hit* (on website); *casilla de verificación, dinero electrónico, octeto.*

English and Spanish are major world languages, and this is reflected in the coverage of regional varieties in the dictionary. The editors have been assisted by an international team of consultants from both sides of the Atlantic. Both Peninsular and the many varieties of Latin-American Spanish are covered in considerable detail. North American and British varieties of English are of course given detailed attention, but the user will also find words and expressions typical of Australian, Canadian, Scottish and Irish varieties of English.

A feature of this dictionary is the inclusion of false friend boxes, as well as a number of usage and grammar panels for both English and Spanish speakers that give clear and full explanations of important areas, such as the use of the subjunctive in Spanish, punctuation and other topics that can cause difficulties.

Further practical assistance is provided in the central colour supplement that features full and detailed communication guides for Spanish and English, covering a wide range of contexts and with lots of practical information.

The text is presented in an accessible way with blue used to pick out headwords and aid consultation. Long entries have been given extra prominence and have been treated in particular detail.

In sum, the new *Harrap's Spanish Dictionary* is a top-of-the-range dictionary that offers a fantastic breadth of coverage and level of detail in an attractive and accessible form.

Organization of entries

Headwords are presented in blue type in this dictionary and appear in alphabetical order. Note that it is the style in this dictionary to place a word beginning with an upper-case letter before one beginning with a lower-case one, thus March will precede march, and, on the Spanish-English side, to place the unaccented form of a word before the accented, thus cual precedes cuál.

Phrasal verbs, also presented in blue type, are listed together immediately after the relevant verb, regardless of alphabetical order, and are preceded by a single arrowhead.

> ▸ **cave in** *vi (ground, structure)* hundirse, ceder; *Fig (stop resisting)* rendirse, darse por vencido(a)

❑ Grammatical divisions

The grammatical classification of an entry is marked with an italic label, eg *n*, *vi*, or *prep*. All the abbreviated labels are included in the list of abbreviations at the front and back of the dictionary. When an entry has more than one part of speech, each part of speech is introduced by a bold Arabic numeral.

> **harpoon** [hɑːˈpuːn] **1** *n* arpón *m*
> **2** *vt* arponear

❑ Sub-headwords and pronominal verbs

Where the plural noun form of a headword has meaning(s) distinct from the main headword form, or where the headword forms a fixed prepositional, adverbial or adjectival phrase, these may be entered as separate grammatical divisions, preceded by a bold Arabic numeral on a new line, and with an appropriate grammatical label (eg *nmpl, loc adv*).

candileja 1 *nf* (**a**) *(parte del candil)* oil reservoir (**b**) *(candil pequeño)* small oil lamp (**c**) *(planta)* nigella
2 **candilejas** *nfpl* footlights

nylon ['naɪlɒn] 1 *n (textile)* nylon *m*, nailon *m*; **n. shirt/scarf** camisa/pañuelo de nailon
2 **nylons** *npl (stockings)* medias *fpl* de nylon; **a pair of nylons** unas medias de nylon

tienta 1 *nf Taurom* trial *(of the bulls)*
2 **a tientas** *loc adv* blindly; **andar a tientas** to grope along; **buscar algo a tientas** to grope about *o* around for sth

This presentation is also used for Spanish pronominal verbs, where the label *vpr* is given.

desafinar 1 *vi (instrumento)* to be out of tune; *(cantante)* to sing out of tune; *(músico)* to play out of tune
2 **desafinarse** *vpr (instrumento)* to go out of tune

❑ Semantic divisions

The different senses of a word are each introduced by a bracketed lower-case letter in bold type.

jirafa *nf* (**a**) *(animal)* giraffe (**b**) *(para micrófono)* boom

Nuances of senses, or semantic splits required to show different translations for the same sense, are shown within the same sense category by using indicating material in brackets. This material may consist of a synonym or typical collocating words, eg the objects of a transitive verb, or the nouns with which an adjective is commonly used.

constrict [kən'strɪkt] *vt* (**a**) *(make narrow) (blood vessels, intestine)* constreñir, contraer (**b**) *(restrict) (flow, breathing)* dificultar; *(person, economy)* constreñir; **to feel constricted (by sth)** sentirse constreñido(a) (por algo)

❑ Compounds

In this dictionary compounds of two or more words have been presented under the entry for the first word of the compound. They appear in bold italic type in alphabetical order at the end of the relevant semantic division. The block is introduced by the symbol ►►

electricity [ɪlek'trɪsɪtɪ] *n* (**a**) *(power)* electricidad *f*; **the e. (supply)** el suministro eléctrico; **to turn** *or* **to switch the e. off/on** conectar/desconectar la corriente; **to be without e.** estar sin suministro eléctrico ►► *esp Br* ***e. bill*** factura *f* de la luz; ***e. generator*** generador *m* eléctrico, grupo *m* electrógeno; ***e. pylon*** torre *f* de alta tensión
(**b**) *(tension, energy)* tensión *f*; **there was e. in the air** el ambiente estaba cargado

The rule of entering a compound under its first element means, for example, that *sedge warbler, melodious warbler* and *garden warbler* will be found under garden, melodious **and** sedge **respectively, and not at the entry** warbler.

Hyphenated words in both English and Spanish, however, appear as entries in their own right, in the relevant alphabetical order.

Grammatical information

❑ Plurals

When a Spanish noun has a plural which does not follow regular plural formation rules, as is common in the case of foreign loanwords, this is shown immediately after the headword (or after the phonetic transcription if this is included).

amateur [ama'ter] (*pl* **amateurs**) 1 *adj* amateur
2 *nmf* amateur

Similarly, English irregular plurals are also given after the headword and phonetic transcription, placed in brackets.

child [tʃaɪld] (*pl* **children** ['tʃɪldrən]) *n* niño(a) *m,f*; *(son)* hijo *m*; *(daughter)* hija *f*; **they have three children** tienen tres hijos; **children's literature** literatura infantil; **children's boutique** boutique infantil; [...]

Note that -ies plurals of words ending in -y are regarded as regular, and so these forms are not shown.

❑ English verb forms

Irregular forms of English verbs are given after the headword for that verb.

eat [i:t] (*pt* **ate** [et, eɪt], *pp* **eaten** ['i:tən]) 1 *vt* (**a**) *(food)* comer; **to e. (one's) breakfast/lunch/dinner** desayunar/almorzar/cenar; **I don't e. meat** no como carne; **they ate their way through a whole chicken** se zamparon un pollo entero
[...]

seek [si:k] (*pt & pp* **sought** [sɔ:t]) 1 *vt* (**a**) *(look for) (thing lost, job, solution)* buscar; *(friendship, promotion, approval)* buscar; **to s. one's fortune** buscar fortuna; **he sought revenge on them** buscaba vengarse de ellos; **we sought shelter in a shop doorway** nos guarecimos en la puerta de una tienda
[...]

The irregular verb forms (with the exception of those where the only irregularity is the doubling of the final consonant, such as equip or pad) are themselves given as entries in alphabetical order, with a cross-reference to the relevant verb entry, unless they would be immediately adjacent to the main verb entry.

eaten *pp of* **eat**

Note that -ied past tense and past participle forms of verbs ending in -y are regarded as regular, and so these forms are not shown.

❑ Spanish verb conjugations

A number in square brackets is given after each Spanish verb. Users should refer to the conjugation model indicated by this number in the list of Spanish conjugations at the end of the book to find the full conjugation of the verb.

afincarse [60] *vpr* to settle (**en** in)

The first person forms of irregular verbs are also entered as headwords and cross-referred to the infinitive in the following style:

desdigo *etc ver* **desdecir**

Pronunciation

Pronunciation information has been given for all English headwords using the International Phonetic Alphabet (IPA), except in the case of US spelling variants, and irregular plural and verb forms, which are given a cross-reference to the main entry, where the pronunciation is given.

tire[1] *US* = **tyre**

tyre, *US* **tire** ['taɪə(r)] *n* neumático *m*, *Am* llanta *f*, *Arg* goma *f* ►► ***t. chain*** cadena *f (para la nieve)*; ***t. gauge*** manómetro *m*; ***t. marks*** rodada *f*; ***t. pressure*** presión *f* de los neumáticos *or* de las ruedas; ***t. valve*** válvula *f* de neumático

A phonetic transcription has been given for all English abbreviations, unless they are only used in written language. Thus it will be clear whether the abbreviation is an acronym or its letters are pronounced individually.

> **MBO** [embiː'əʊ] (*pl* **MBOs**) *n Com* (*abbr* **management buyout**) = adquisición de una empresa por sus directivos

On the Spanish-English side of the dictionary a phonetic transcription is given in those cases where the word does not follow regular Spanish pronunciation norms – ie where the word is a foreign loanword. A phonetic transcription has been given for Spanish abbreviations only where they are true acronyms and pronounced as a word.

> **OMS** [oms] *nf* (*abrev de* **Organización Mundial de la Salud**) WHO

An explanation of the symbols used can be found in the pronunciation guides on pages xxi – xxvi.

Register

The register of all words and phrases in the source language is clearly indicated in this dictionary. Register labels are used to indicate the level of language – whether formal (*Formal*), informal (*Fam*), very informal (*very/muy Fam* – used with words and phrases which presuppose a greater degree of intimacy between speaker and audience, and which may shock some people), or vulgar (*Vulg* – used with vulgar words, especially taboo usages which are likely to shock in any context). As far as possible, the translations given match the register of the word in the source language and no register markers are therefore applied to translations.

> **gazuza** *nf Fam (hambre)* **tener g.** to be famished *o* ravenous
>
> **shithouse** ['ʃɪthaʊs] *n Vulg (toilet)* cagódromo *m*

They also indicate usage, showing whether a word is, for example, pejorative, ironic or euphemistic.

> **gentuza** *nf Pey* riffraff, rabble
>
> ▸ **pass away** *vi Euph* fallecer

All abbreviated labels are included in the list of labels on the inside and back covers of the book.

Register labels can occur in various combinations. A word can be either archaic or literary, old-fashioned or humorous, and so on. In such cases the presentation is as follows:

> **parlous** ['pɑːləs] *adj Formal or Hum* **to be in a p. state** estar en un estado precario
>
> **pate** [peɪt] *n Old-fashioned or Hum* calva *f*

A word which is simultaneously informal and old-fashioned, or informal and euphemistic, etc, will be presented as follows with the labels in sequence:

> **rubia** *nf* (**a**) *Fam Anticuado (moneda)* peseta (**b**) *ver también* **rubio**
>
> **well-padded** [wel'pædɪd] *adj Fam Euph* rellenito(a), rechoncho(a)

In instances where a term is given two translations, one technical and the other non-technical, the technical translation is placed second and preceded by the label *Spec* or *Espec* on the English-Spanish and Spanish-English sides respectively. The technical translation has been given in addition to the neutral one where the word being translated can be used in both technical and non-technical contexts.

> **halite** ['heɪlaɪt] *n* sal *f* gema, *Spec* halita *f*
>
> **masticar** [60] **1** *vt* (**a**) *(mascar)* to chew, *Espec* to masticate
> [...]

Specialist language

This dictionary features a large number of specialized items of vocabulary relating to areas as diverse as computing, finance, law, science and medicine. Many recently-coined terms have been included, particularly terminology created by the growth of the Internet or other new technologies.

A full list of the abbreviated field labels used to mark these specialist terms is to be found on the inside and back covers of the book. Field labels are used primarily to indicate specialist vocabulary, or to differentiate the various meanings of the headword. In cases where a word has several meanings in different domains, all with the same translation, field labels can be combined in sequence to show that the translation works for all the senses indicated.

> **palette** ['pælɪt] *n* (**a**) *Art* paleta *f* ►► ***p. knife*** espátula *f* (**b**) *Comptr* paleta *f*
>
> **indexación** *nf Econ & Informát* indexing

International coverage

This dictionary aims to give very full coverage of the international varieties of both English and Spanish. On the English-Spanish side of the dictionary, thorough treatment of English as it is used in Britain and in America is complemented by coverage of Australian, Irish and other forms of English. Thus, terms which the user might search for in vain in other bilingual dictionaries – such as bludger, galloot and rooinek (Australian, Scottish, and South African respectively) to cite but three – will be found within the pages of this dictionary.

Similarly, on the Spanish-English side, Latin-American Spanish is extensively covered. The editors of the dictionary have aimed at giving wide-ranging coverage of Latin-American Spanish, but also to be as precise as possible in indicating where given terms and expressions are used.

> **abalear** *vt Andes, CAm, Ven (tirotear)* to shoot at

On the Spanish-English side of the dictionary, British and American variant translations are shown where appropriate, marked as *Br* and *US* respectively.

> **damero** *nm* (**a**) *(tablero) Br* draughtboard, *US* checkerboard (**b**) *(pasatiempo)* double acrostic

On the English-Spanish side, variant translations are also shown where appropriate, and wherever possible a general translation is given first.

> **megabucks** ['megəbʌks] *npl Fam* una millonada, *Esp* un pastón, *Méx* un chingo de dinero, *RP* una ponchada de pesos

The following labels are used:

Austr	Australian English
Br	British English
Can	Canadian English
Irish	Irish English
NZ	New Zealand English
SAfr	South African English
Scot	Scottish English
US	American English

Am	Latin American Spanish
Andes	Andean Spanish (Bolivia, Chile, Colombia, Ecuador, Peru)
Arg	Argentinian Spanish
Bol	Bolivian Spanish
CAm	Central American Spanish
Carib	Caribbean Spanish (Cuba, Puerto Rico, Dominican Republic, Venezuela)
Chile	Chilean Spanish
Col	Colombian Spanish
CRica	Costa Rican Spanish
CSur	Cono Sur Spanish (Argentina, Chile, Uruguay, Paraguay)

Cuba	Cuban Spanish
Ecuad	Ecuadorian Spanish
Guat	Guatemalan Spanish
Hond	Honduran Spanish
Méx	Mexican Spanish
Nic	Nicaraguan Spanish
Pan	Panamanian Spanish
Par	Paraguayan Spanish
Perú	Peruvian Spanish
PRico	Puerto Rican Spanish
RDom	Dominican Spanish
RP	Spanish from Argentina, Uruguay, Paraguay
Salv	Salvadoran Spanish
Urug	Uruguayan Spanish
Ven	Venezuelan Spanish

Idioms and Proverbs

The label IDIOM will be found in the English-Spanish text before a fixed idiomatic expression. On the Spanish-English side the equivalent label EXPR is used. In certain cases (eg apple, activo) a whole subdivision of an entry may be given over to idiomatic expressions, in which case the label (modified to IDIOMS on English-Spanish) is given only once at the head of the sense division.

Proverbs are marked with the label PROV on both sides of the dictionary.

Glosses and Cultural Equivalents

Where it is not possible to give a proper translation equivalent, a gloss may be given. This is introduced by an equals sign. No gender information is included in glosses. Supporting glosses may also be given where a translation equivalent exists which is much less common than the item being translated.

easternized ['iːstənaɪzd] *adj US* = que adoptó las costumbres del este de los EE.UU. aunque proviene de otra zona del país

quesadilla *nf* (**a**) *CAm, Méx (salada)* quesadilla, = filled fried tortilla (**b**) *Ecuad (dulce)* = sweet, cheese-filled pasty

A cultural equivalent may be given, with or without a gloss, to indicate a rough equivalent in the target language culture. Cultural equivalents are introduced by ≃, and where a gloss is also given, the cultural equivalent will follow the gloss.

RACE ['rraθe] *nm* (*abrev de* **Real Automóvil Club de España**) = Spanish automobile association, *Br* ≃ AA, RAC, *US* ≃ AAA

venture ['ventʃə(r)] **1** *n* (**a**) *(undertaking)* aventura *f*, iniciativa *f*; **it's his first v. into politics/fiction** es su primera incursión en política/la literatura de ficción ▸▸ *Br* ***V. Scout*** = scout de entre 16 y 20 años, ≃ pionero(a) *m,f*

False Friend Boxes and Language Notes

To supplement the linguistic information already implicit in the entries, the dictionary contains several features intended to give additional assistance to the user. Each side of the dictionary has over 150 notes on false friends, drawing attention to potential translation pitfalls.

compromise ['kɒmprəmaɪz] 1 *n* solución *f* negociada *or* intermedia; **to reach a c.** alcanzar una solución intermedia; **there must be no c.** no estamos dispuestos a negociar
2 *vt* (**a**) *(principles)* traicionar (**b**) *(jeopardize)* poner en peligro; **to c. oneself** ponerse en un compromiso
3 *vi* (**a**) *(make concessions)* transigir, hacer concesiones; **to c. with sb (on sth)** transigir (con alguien) en algo, hacer concesiones (a alguien) en algo (**b**) *(be lax)* **we'll never c. on safety** nunca comprometeremos la seguridad

False friend: The Spanish noun **compromiso** is not a translation for the English word **compromise**. In Spanish **compromiso** means "commitment", "agreement" or "engagement".

Both sides of the dictionary also have language notes and panels which discuss problematic, interesting or otherwise noteworthy aspects of the two languages. Examples include panels on the role of the subjunctive in both languages, on the "split infinitive" in English, and Spanish "gentilicios".

INTRODUCCIÓN

Este diccionario Harrap de nueva planta está diseñado y editado para proporcionar al lector —sea éste estudiante de inglés, traductor o profesional— una obra de consulta de actualidad y precisión, en la que se recoge ampliamente el léxico inglés y el español, incluyendo una extensa selección de expresiones y usos idiomáticos.

Al igual que en el resto de los diccionarios Harrap, esta obra contiene numerosos términos de argot y expresiones cotidianas de los distintos países en los que se habla español o inglés, además de terminología especializada, de las ciencias a los deportes, del mundo de los negocios al derecho, el periodismo o la política. Se ha hecho hincapié en el vocabulario de informática e Internet, como por ejemplo: *cache memory, e-cash, hit* (en página web); *casilla de verificación, dinero electrónico, octeto.*

El inglés y el español son lenguas de gran relevancia en el mundo y esto se refleja en el esfuerzo hecho por el equipo editorial, con ayuda de expertos de ambos lados del Atlántico, por recoger las diversas variedades regionales. Se analizan de forma exhaustiva tanto el español peninsular como el hablado en los distintos países de América. En cuanto al inglés, se ha puesto lógicamente gran atención en las variantes británica y americana, pero también se encontrarán palabras y expresiones típicas de Australia, Canadá, Irlanda y Escocia.

Un elemento singular de este diccionario es la inclusión de notas y recuadros con información sobre falsos amigos, además de otros aspectos gramaticales y lingüísticos importantes que pueden causar dificultades a los hablantes de ambas lenguas, como el uso del subjuntivo en español o las diferencias de puntuación entre ambos idiomas.

Asimismo, el suplemento de las páginas centrales proporciona ayuda lingüística de tipo práctico, con dos completas guías para comunicarse en inglés y en español en medios escritos, telefónicos o electrónicos, que incluyen numerosos contextos y gran información práctica.

La presentación está diseñada para facilitar la labor de consulta, por lo que, por ejemplo, los lemas aparecen en azul. Las entradas más largas, a las que se ha dado una prominencia especial, se han estudiado en profundidad.

En suma, este nuevo diccionario es la obra más ambiciosa de la gama Harrap, que recoge ampliamente y con gran detalle el vocabulario de ambos idiomas, con una presentación clara y accesible.

Organización de las entradas

Los lemas, que aparecen en orden alfabético, están en azul. En el caso de que una palabra pueda escribirse con mayúscula y minúscula, aparecerá antes la escrita con mayúscula, es decir March precede a march. En la parte de español-inglés la forma no acentuada de una palabra precede a la acentuada; por ejemplo, cual precede a cuál.

Los verbos con partícula ingleses, también en azul y marcados con el símbolo ►, se incluyen directamente tras el verbo principal correspondiente, aún cuando siguiendo un estricto orden alfabético les hubiera correspondido un lugar posterior en el texto.

► **cave in** *vi (ground, structure)* hundirse, ceder; *Fig (stop resisting)* rendirse, darse por vencido(a)

❑ Divisiones gramaticales

La categoría gramatical de la entrada se muestra en cursiva, por ejemplo: *n, vi,* o *prep*. Se puede ver la lista completa de las abreviaturas utilizadas en este diccionario en el interior de la cubierta del libro. Cuando una entrada tiene más de una categoría gramatical, cada una de ellas aparece precedida de un número en negrita.

harpoon [hɑːˈpuːn] **1** *n* arpón *m*
2 *vt* arponear

❑ Subentradas y verbos pronominales

Cuando el plural de una palabra tiene un sentido especial, distinto del significado del singular, o cuando se ha considerado que una locución preposicional, adverbial o adjetiva merecía una nueva categoría gramatical, dicho plural o locución aparece también en azul, con su correspondiente marca gramatical (p. ej.: *nmpl, loc adv*).

candileja 1 *nf* (**a**) *(parte del candil)* oil reservoir (**b**) *(candil pequeño)* small oil lamp (**c**) *(planta)* nigella
2 **candilejas** *nfpl* footlights

nylon ['naɪlɒn] 1 *n (textile)* nylon *m*, nailon *m*; **n. shirt/scarf** camisa/pañuelo de nailon
2 **nylons** *npl (stockings)* medias *fpl* de nylon; **a pair of nylons** unas medias de nylon

tienta 1 *nf Taurom* trial *(of the bulls)*
2 **a tientas** *loc adv* blindly; **andar a tientas** to grope along; **buscar algo a tientas** to grope about *o* around for sth

Se usa también la misma presentación para los verbos pronominales en español.

desafinar 1 *vi (instrumento)* to be out of tune; *(cantante)* to sing out of tune; *(músico)* to play out of tune
2 **desafinarse** *vpr (instrumento)* to go out of tune

❑ Divisiones semánticas

Cuando una palabra tiene más de una acepción, esta viene precedida de una letra en minúscula entre paréntesis y en negrita.

jirafa *nf* (**a**) *(animal)* giraffe (**b**) *(para micrófono)* boom

Dentro de una misma acepción, los distintos matices y las divisiones semánticas necesarias para mostrar traducciones distintas vienen indicados con información en cursiva entre paréntesis. Esta información puede consistir en sinónimos o palabras que se combinan con frecuencia con el lema, por ejemplo los objetos directos en el caso de verbos transitivos, o los sustantivos a los que acompaña a menudo un adjetivo.

constrict [kən'strɪkt] *vt* (**a**) *(make narrow) (blood vessels, intestine)* constreñir, contraer (**b**) *(restrict) (flow, breathing)* dificultar; *(person, economy)* constreñir; **to feel constricted (by sth)** sentirse constreñido(a) (por algo)

❑ Compuestos de más de una palabra

Los compuestos o combinaciones estables de dos o más palabras que forman un sintagma nominal aparecen en la entrada correspondiente a la primera palabra de dicho sintagma, bajo la categoría semántica a la que pertenecen. Se les distingue por estar en negrita cursiva y además porque el primer compuesto de cada categoría viene precedido por el símbolo ▸▸

electricity [ɪlek'trɪsɪtɪ] *n* (**a**) *(power)* electricidad *f*; **the e. (supply)** el suministro eléctrico; **to turn** *or* **to switch the e. off/on** conectar/desconectar la corriente; **to be without e.** estar sin suministro eléctrico ▸▸ *esp Br* ***e. bill*** factura *f* de la luz; ***e. generator*** generador *m* eléctrico, grupo *m* electrógeno; ***e. pylon*** torre *f* de alta tensión
(**b**) *(tension, energy)* tensión *f*; **there was e. in the air** el ambiente estaba cargado

El hecho de que los compuestos aparezcan siempre en la entrada correspondiente a la primera palabra quiere decir que, por ejemplo, ***sedge warbler, melodious warbler*** y ***garden warbler*** se encontrarán en las entradas garden, melodious y sedge respectivamente, y no en la entrada warbler.

Los compuestos formados por dos palabras unidas por guión tienen su propia entrada, tanto en inglés como en español.

ear-hole ['ɪəhəʊl] *n* agujero *m* de la oreja

Información gramatical

❑ Plurales

En las palabras españolas cuyo plural no sigue las reglas generales de la formación del plural (como suele ocurrir a menudo en los préstamos extranjeros) el plural aparece tras el lema en la entrada correspondiente, o tras su transcripción fonética, si se da el caso.

amateur [ama'ter] (*pl* **amateurs**) **1** *adj* amateur
2 *nmf* amateur

De la misma forma, los plurales irregulares ingleses aparecen tras el lema y su transcripción fonética, entre paréntesis:

child [tʃaɪld] (*pl* **children** ['tʃɪldrən]) *n* niño(a) *m,f*; *(son)* hijo *m*; *(daughter)* hija *f*; **they have three children** tienen tres hijos; **children's literature** literatura infantil; **children's boutique** boutique infantil; [...]

Conviene tener en cuenta que los plurales en -ies, de palabras inglesas que terminan en -y, se consideran regulares, por lo que estas formas no se muestran.

❑ Las formas verbales inglesas

Las formas irregulares de pasado o participio de los verbos ingleses aparecen tras el lema y su transcripción fonética:

eat [iːt] (*pt* **ate** [et, eɪt], *pp* **eaten** ['iːtən]) **1** *vt* **(a)** *(food)* comer; **to e. (one's) breakfast/lunch/dinner** desayunar/almorzar/cenar; **I don't e. meat** no como carne; **they ate their way through a whole chicken** se zamparon un pollo entero
[...]

seek [siːk] (*pt & pp* **sought** [sɔːt]) **1** *vt* **(a)** *(look for) (thing lost, job, solution)* buscar; *(friendship, promotion, approval)* buscar; **to s. one's fortune** buscar fortuna; **he sought revenge on them** buscaba vengarse de ellos; **we sought shelter in a shop doorway** nos guarecimos en la puerta de una tienda
[...]

Estas mismas formas (con la excepción de aquellas cuya única irregularidad es que doblan la consonante final, como equip o pad) aparecen como entradas independientes donde les corresponda alfabéticamente, a no ser que sean adyacentes a la entrada del infinitivo.

eaten *pp of* **eat**

Las formas de pasado y participio acabadas en -ied, correspondientes a verbos que terminen en -y, se consideran regulares y por lo tanto no se muestran tras el lema.

❑ Las conjugaciones verbales del español

Los verbos que presentan alguna irregularidad con relación a las tres conjugaciones básicas del español contienen un número entre corchetes tras el lema. Este número corresponde a un modelo de conjugación determinado que puede consultarse en el suplemento de conjugaciones verbales al final del libro.

afincarse [60] *vpr* to settle (**en** in)

La primera persona de los verbos irregulares también aparece como entrada en su lugar correspondiente según el orden alfabético, con una remisión al infinitivo.

desdigo *etc ver* **desdecir**

Pronunciación

Todas las entradas inglesas contienen transcripción fonética, para la cual se ha usado el Alfabeto Fonético Internacional. Las excepciones son las variantes ortográficas estadounidenses, como tire en vez de tyre, las formas irregulares del plural y los verbos (que contienen una remisión a la forma base, en la que se da su transcripción fonética), y las abreviaturas que sólo se utilizan en inglés escrito, es decir, que nunca se pronuncian como tales.

tire[1] *US* = **tyre**

tyre, *US* **tire** ['taɪə(r)] *n* neumático *m*, *Am* llanta *f*, *Arg* goma *f* ►► ***t. chain*** cadena *f (para la nieve)*; ***t. gauge*** manómetro *m*; ***t. marks*** rodada *f*; ***t. pressure*** presión *f* de los neumáticos *or* de las ruedas; ***t. valve*** válvula *f* de neumático

Todas las siglas y acrónimos ingleses tienen transcripción fonética, dado que de esta forma queda más claro si se pronuncian letra por letra o como acrónimo.

MBO [embiː'əʊ] (*pl* **MBOs**) *n Com* (*abbr* **management buyout**) = adquisición de una empresa por sus directivos

En la sección de español–inglés se ha dado transcripción fonética a aquellas palabras cuya pronunciación puede desviarse de la norma española por ser préstamos de otras lenguas, además de a las siglas que se pronuncian como una palabra, no letra por letra.

OMS [oms] *nf* (*abrev de* **Organización Mundial de la Salud**) WHO

Se puede consultar la explicación de los símbolos fonéticos en las páginas xxi–xxiv.

Registro o nivel de uso

Las marcas de registro se usan para explicar el nivel de uso de las palabras y expresiones de la lengua origen: si se trata de una palabra o expresión propia del lenguaje culto o extremadamente educada (*Formal*), si se utiliza en situaciones informales o familiares (*Fam*), si da por hecha una mayor intimidad entre los interlocutores y puede llegar a molestar a algunos hablantes (*very/muy Fam*), o si es vulgar o tabú, pudiendo por lo tanto ofender en cualquier contexto (*Vulg*). En la medida de lo posible, las traducciones dadas corresponden al registro de la lengua origen, por lo que no llevan marcas de registro.

gazuza *nf Fam (hambre)* **tener g.** to be famished *o* ravenous

shithouse ['ʃɪthaʊs] *n Vulg (toilet)* cagódromo *m*

También se marca la intención del hablante al utilizar ciertas palabras: si una palabra o expresión es peyorativa, irónica o un eufemismo.

gentuza *nf Pey* riffraff, rabble

▸**pass away** *vi Euph* fallecer

La lista de abreviaturas usadas en el diccionario puede verse en el interior de la cubierta.

A veces aparece más de una marca, ya que una palabra puede ser arcaica o literaria, anticuada o humorística, etc. En estos casos la información aparece como se indica a continuación:

parlous ['pɑːləs] *adj Formal or Hum* **to be in a p. state** estar en un estado precario

pate [peɪt] *n Old-fashioned or Hum* calva *f*

Si una palabra es al mismo tiempo informal y anticuada, o bien es por ejemplo un eufemismo de registro familiar, la información aparece como sigue:

rubia *nf* (**a**) *Fam Anticuado (moneda)* peseta (**b**) *ver también* **rubio**

well-padded [wel'pædɪd] *adj Fam Euph* rellenito(a), rechoncho(a)

En casos en los que se dan dos traducciones, una de un nivel técnico usada en contextos especializados y otra usada de formal más general, la traducción especializada aparece en segundo lugar, precedida de la marca *Spec* en la parte de inglés–español y de *Espec* en la parte de español–inglés.

halite ['heɪlaɪt] *n* sal *f* gema, *Spec* halita *f*

masticar [60] **1** *vt* (**a**) *(mascar)* to chew, *Espec* to masticate [...]

Tecnicismos

Esta obra recoge numerosos términos especializados de campos como la informática, las finanzas, el derecho, la ciencia y la medicina. Se incluyen muchos términos de nuevo cuño, especialmente la terminología surgida a partir del desarrollo de Internet y las nuevas tecnologías

La lista de abreviaturas usadas como marcas de campos especializados aparece en el interior de la cubierta de esta obra. Estas marcas se usan fundamentalmente para indicar que se trata de vocabulario especializado, o para diferenciar distintas acepciones de una palabra. Cuando una palabra se usa en distintos campos especializados con una misma traducción estas marcas a menudo se combinan para indicar que la traducción funciona en los mismos.

> **palette** ['pælɪt] *n* (**a**) *Art* paleta *f* ►► ***p. knife*** espátula *f* (**b**) *Comptr* paleta *f*

> **indexación** *nf Econ & Informát* indexing

Variantes regionales

En esta obra se ha hecho un esfuerzo por recoger las variantes del inglés y el español hablado hoy día en el mundo. En la parte de inglés–español se incluyen palabras y expresiones del inglés británico, estadounidense, australiano o irlandés, además del escocés y el sudafricano. Por ello se pueden consultar términos como bludger (australiano) galloot (escocés) o rooinek (sudafricano).

De la misma forma, en la parte de español–inglés, están ampliamente representadas las variantes de español de América. Se ha intentado incluir una gran parte del vocabulario americano sin que ello fuera en detrimento de la precisión a la hora de indicar las regiones o países en los que se usa una determinada palabra o expresión.

> **abalear** *vt Andes, CAm, Ven (tirotear)* to shoot at

En lo que se refiere a las traducciones, en la parte de español-inglés se dan las variantes británica y estadounidense, marcadas como *Br* y *US* respectivamente.

> **damero** *nm* (**a**) *(tablero) Br* draughtboard, *US* checkerboard (**b**) *(pasatiempo)* double acrostic

En la parte de inglés-español, también se muestran las variantes regionales, dándose primero una traducción universal siempre que sea posible.

> **megabucks** ['megəbʌks] *npl Fam* una millonada, *Esp* un pastón, *Méx* un chingo de dinero, *RP* una ponchada de pesos

Se han usado las siguientes marcas:

Austr	inglés de Australia
Br	inglés británico
Can	inglés de Canadá
Irish	inglés de Irlanda
NZ	inglés de Nueva Zelanda
SAfr	inglés de Sudáfrica
Scot	inglés de Escocia
US	inglés estadounidense
Am	español de América
Andes	español andino (Bolivia, Chile, Colombia, Ecuador, Perú)
Arg	español de Argentina
Bol	español de Bolivia
CAm	español centroamericano
Carib	español caribeño (Cuba, Puerto Rico, República Dominicana, Venezuela)
Chile	español de Chile
Col	español de Colombia
CRica	español de Costa Rica
CSur	español del Cono Sur
Cuba	español de Cuba

Ecuad	español de Ecuador
Guat	español de Guatemala
Hond	español de Honduras
Méx	español de México
Nic	español de Nicaragua
Pan	español de Panamá
Par	español de Paraguay
Perú	español de Perú
PRico	español de Puerto Rico
RDom	español de República Dominicana
RP	español de los países ribereños del Río de la Plata
Salv	español de El Salvador
Urug	español de Uruguay
Ven	español de Venezuela

Modismos y refranes

La marca IDIOM precede a las expresiones idiomáticas o modismos en la parte de inglés–español. Cuando una categoría semántica solamente contiene expresiones idiomáticas, estas vienen precedidas de una única marca, IDIOMS, que abarca a toda la categoría.

En la parte de español–inglés la marca equivalente es EXPR.

Los refranes aparecen precedidos de la marca PROV en ambas partes del diccionario.

Glosas y equivalentes culturales

A veces no es posible dar una verdadera traducción para un término o expresión, por lo que en su lugar se da una explicación. En este diccionario, estas explicaciones, que no llevan marca de género, aparecen precedidas del signo igual (=). En ocasiones se dan también explicaciones de apoyo cuando sí existe una traducción, pero esta es mucho menos frecuente que el término equivalente en la lengua origen.

easternized ['iːstənaɪzd] *adj US* = que adoptó las costumbres del este de los EE.UU. aunque proviene de otra zona del país

quesadilla *nf* (**a**) *CAm, Méx (salada)* quesadilla, = filled fried tortilla (**b**) *Ecuad (dulce)* = sweet, cheese-filled pasty

A veces se da un equivalente cultural para explicar un concepto o institución paralelo en la cultura del idioma al que se traduce, precedido del símbolo ≃. Si se considera de utilidad, este equivalente cultural puede ir precedido de una explicación como las mencionadas en el párrafo anterior.

RACE ['rraθe] *nm* (*abrev de* **Real Automóvil Club de España**) = Spanish automobile association, *Br* ≃ AA, RAC, *US* ≃ AAA

venture ['ventʃə(r)] **1** *n* (**a**) *(undertaking)* aventura *f*, iniciativa *f*; **it's his first v. into politics/fiction** es su primera incursión en política/la literatura de ficción ►► *Br* ***V. Scout*** = scout de entre 16 y 20 años, ≃ pionero(a) *m,f*

Falsos amigos y notas gramaticales

Para complementar la información lingüística dada en las entradas, esta obra contiene además recuadros con información adicional. Cada parte del diccionario tiene más de 150 notas sobre falsos amigos, cuya finalidad es alertar sobre fallos muy fáciles de cometer en el otro idioma.

compromiso *nm* **(a)** *(obligación)* commitment; **me vi en el c. de tener que aceptar** I found myself obliged to accept; **adquirí el c. de ayudarlos** I undertook to help them; **cumplir un c.** to fulfil *o* honour a commitment; **no cumplieron el c. de entregar las armas** they did not honour their commitment to hand over their weapons; **sin c.** without obligation; **reciba información en su domicilio, sin ningún c.** let us send you our brochure without obligation
(b) *(acuerdo)* agreement; **patronal y sindicatos alcanzaron un c.** management and unions reached an agreement; **presentaron una propuesta de c.** they proposed a compromise
(c) *(cita)* engagement; **esta noche tengo un c. y no podré salir contigo** I'm busy this evening, so I won't be able to go out with you; **si no tienes ningún c., podríamos ir al cine** if you're not doing anything else, we could go to the cinema
(d) *(dificultad)* compromising *o* difficult situation; **poner a alguien en un c.** to put sb in a difficult *o* awkward position
(e) *(ideológico)* commitment; **ha dejado siempre claro su c. con la paz** he has always made clear his commitment to peace
(f) *(para casarse)* engagement; **han anunciado su c.** they have announced their engagement; **es una joven soltera y sin c.** she's young, free and single ►► ***c. matrimonial*** engagement
(g) *(encuentro deportivo)* fixture

Falso amigo: El sustantivo inglés **compromise** no es la traducción del español **compromiso**. En inglés, **compromise** significa "solución negociada" o "solución intermedia".

También se han creado notas y paneles con explicaciones sobre puntos problemáticos o dignos de interés en ambas lenguas, por ejemplo sobre el "split infinitive" en inglés o los gentilicios en español.

GUIDE TO SPANISH PRONUNCIATION

The pronunciation of most Spanish words is predictable as there is a close match between spelling and pronunciation. The table below gives an explanation of that pronunciation. In the dictionary text therefore, pronunciation is only given when the word does not follow these rules, usually because it is a word of foreign origin. In these cases, the IPA (International Phonetic Alphabet) is used (see column 2 of the tables below).

Letter in Spanish	*IPA Symbol*	*Example in Spanish*	*Pronunciation (example in English)*
Vowels			
Note that all vowel sounds in Spanish are shorter than in English			
a	[a]	ala	*Similar to the sound in* "father" *but more central*
e	[e]	eco	*Similar to the sound in* "met"
i	[i]	iris	*Like the vowel sound in* "meat" *but much shorter*
o	[o]	oso	off, on
u	[u]	uva	*Like the vowel sound in* "soon" *but much shorter*
Semiconsonants			
"i" *in the diphthongs*: ia, ie, io, iu	[j]	hiato, hielo, avión, viuda	yes
"u" *in the diphthongs*: ua, ue, ui, uo	[w]	suave, fuego, huida	win
Consonants			
b	[b]	bomba *(at beginning of word or after* "m"*)*	boom
	[β]	abajo, cabra *(all other contexts)*	*A* "b" *pronounced without quite closing the lips completely*
c	[θ] *(in Spain)*	ceño *(before* "e"*)* cinco *(before* "i"*)*	thanks *(in Spain)*
	[s] *(in Latin America and southern Spain)*		sun *(in Latin America and southern Spain)*
	[k]	casa, saco *(all other contexts)*	cat
ch	[tʃ]	caucho	arch
d	[d]	donde *(at beginning of word or after* "n"*)* aldea *(after* "l"*)*	day
	[ð]	adorno, arder *(all other contexts)*	*Similar to the sound in* "mother" *but less strong*
f	[f]	furia	fire

Letter in Spanish	*IPA Symbol*	*Example in Spanish*	*Pronunciation (example in English)*
g	[χ]	gema *(before "e")* girasol *(before "i")*	*Like an "*h*" but pronounced at the back of the throat (similar to Scottish "*loch*")*
	[g]	gato *(at beginning of word)* lengua *(after "*n*")*	goose
	[ɣ]	agua, rasgo *(all other contexts)*	*Like a "*w*" pronounced while trying to say "*g*"*
j	[χ]	jabalí, deje	*Like an "*h*" but pronounced at the back of the throat (similar to Scottish "*loch*")*
l	[l]	lado	lake
ll	[j]	lluvia	yellow
	[ʒ]		*In some regions (eg the Rio de la Plata area of South America) it is pronounced like the "*s*" in "*pleasure*"*
m	[m]	mano	man
n	[n]	nulo	no
ñ	[ŋ]	año	onion
p	[p]	papa	pool
r	[r]	dorado *(in between vowels)* hablar *(at end of syllable or word)*	*A rolled "*r*" sound (similar to Scottish "*r*")*
	[rr]	rosa *(at beginning of word)* alrededor *(after "*l*")* enredo *(after "*n*")*	*A much longer rolled "*r*" sound (similar to Scottish "*r*")*
rr	[rr]	arroyo	*A much longer rolled "*r*" sound (similar to Scottish "*r*")*
s	[s]	saco	sound
sh	[ʃ]	show	show
t	[t]	tela	tea
v	[b]	vaso, invierno *(at the beginning of word or after "*n*")*	boom
	[β]	ave *(all other contexts)*	*A "*b*" pronounced without quite closing the lips completely*
x	[ks]	examen	extra
y	[j]	ayer	yellow
	[ʒ]		*In some regions (eg the Rio de la Plata area of South America) it is pronounced like the "*s*" in "*pleasure*"*
z	[θ] *(in Spain)*	zapato	thanks *(in Spain)*
	[s] *(in Latin America and southern Spain)*		sun *(in Latin America and southern Spain)*

GUÍA DE LA PRONUNCIACIÓN INGLESA

Para ilustrar la pronunciación inglesa, en este diccionario utilizamos los símbolos del AFI (Alfabeto Fonético Internacional). En el siguiente cuadro, para cada sonido del inglés hay ejemplos de palabras en inglés y palabras en español donde aparece un sonido similar. En los casos en los que no hay sonido similar en español, ofrecemos una explicación de cómo pronunciarlos.

Carácter AFI	*Ejemplo en inglés*	*Ejemplo en español*

Consonantes

[b]	babble	bebé
[d]	dig	dedo
[dʒ]	giant, jig	*se pronuncia como* [ʒ] *en* "pleasure" *pero con una* "d" *adelante, o como* "gi" *en italiano:* Giovanna
[f]	fit, physics	faro
[g]	grey, big	gris
[h]	happy	"h" *aspirada*
[j]	yellow	*se pronuncia como* "y" *o* "ll" *en España*: yo, lluvia
[k]	clay, kick	casa
[l]	lip	labio
	pill	papel
[m]	mummy	mamá
[n]	nip, pin	nada
[ŋ]	sing	*se pronuncia como* "n" *antes de* "c": banco
[p]	pip	papá
[r]	rig, write	*sonido entre* "r" *y* "rr"
[s]	sick, science	sapo
[ʃ]	ship, nation	show
[t]	tip, butt	tela
[tʃ]	chip, batch	caucho
[θ]	thick	zapato *(como se pronuncia en España)*
[ð]	this	*se pronuncia como la* "d" *de* "hada" *pero más fuerte*
[v]	vague, give	*se pronuncia como* "v" *de* vida *en el pasado, es decir, con los dientes apoyados sobre el labio inferior*
[w]	wit, why	whisky
[z]	zip, physics	"s" *con sonido zumbante*
[ʒ]	pleasure	*se pronuncia como* "y" *o* "ll" *en el Río de la Plata*: yo, lluvia
[χ]	loch	jota

Diptongos

[aɪ]	why, high, lie	aire
[aʊ]	how	aura
[eə]	bear	"ea" *pronunciado muy brevemente y con sonido de* "e" *más marcado que el de* "a"
[eɪ]	day, make, main	reina
[əʊ]	show, go	"ou" *como en* COU
[ɪə]	here, gear	hielo *pronunciado con el sonido de* "i" *más marcado y alargado que el de* "e"
[ɔɪ]	boy, soil	voy

Carácter AFI	*Ejemplo en inglés*	*Ejemplo en español*

Vocales

En inglés, las vocales marcadas con dos puntos son mucho más alargadas

[æ]	rag	*se pronuncia "a" con posición bucal para "e"*
[ɑ:]	large, bath	*"a" muy alargada*
[ʌ]	cup	*"a" breve y cerrada*
[e]	set	*se pronuncia como "e" de* elefante *pero más corta*
[ɜ:]	curtain, were	*se pronuncia como una "e" larga con posición bucal entre "o" y "e"*
[ə]	utter	*se pronuncia como "e" con posición bucal para "o"*
[ɪ]	big, women	*"i" breve, a medio camino entre "e" e "i"*
[i:]	leak, wee	*"i" muy alargada*
[ɒ]	lock	*"o" abierta*
[ɔ:]	wall, cork	*"o" cerrada y alargada*
[ʊ]	put, look	*"u" breve*
[u:]	moon	*"u" muy alargada*

ALGUNOS APUNTES SOBRE LA PRONUNCIACIÓN INGLESA

1. La arbitrariedad ortográfica

A veces parece que la correlación entre la forma hablada y la escrita del inglés está regida por una cierta arbitrariedad. Esta es la impresión que puede llevarse el hablante de español que quiera abordar las reglas fonológicas del inglés, ya que en español la pronunciación de la mayoría de palabras es predecible a partir de su forma escrita. A continuación mostramos los casos más frecuentes en los que una sola grafía se pronuncia de diferentes maneras.

-ALLET

/æleɪ/	/ɒlɪt/	/ælɪt/
ballet	wallet	mallet

-AUGH-

/ɔ:/	/ɑ:f/
daughter	laughter

-EAR-

/ɑ:/	/ɪə/	/ɜ:/
heart	beard	heard

-EAK

/eɪk/	/i:k/
break	bleak

IE-

/i:/	/ɪ/	/e/
grieve	sieve	friend

-INGER

/ɪŋgə/	/ɪŋə/	/ɪndʒə/
finger	singer	ginger

-OMB

/u:m/	/ɒm/	/əʊm/
tomb	bomb	comb

-OOD

/ʌd/	/u:/	/ʊ/
blood	food	good

-OUGH

/ʌf/	/ɒf/	/əʊ/
enough	cough	though
/aʊ/	/u:/	/ʌp/
bough	through	hiccough

-OULD

/əʊld/	/ʊd/
shoulder	should

-OVER

/u:və/	/ʌvə/	/əʊvə/
mover	cover	clover

-URY

/jʊərɪ/	/erɪ/	/jʊrɪ/
fury	bury	penury

2. Los homógrafos

Una de las consecuencias de que una grafía pueda tener varias pronunciaciones es que una única forma escrita puede representar más de una palabra. Estas palabras se denominan homógrafos, y en la presente obra aparecen seguidas de un número en volada, por ejemplo, wind[1]. A continuación aparecen algunos ejemplos:

bass	/bæs/	cuando se refiere al pez	/beɪs/	para el tipo de voz
bow	/bəʊ/	cuando significa "arco"	/baʊ/	si quiere decir "reverencia"
buffet	/'bʌfɪt/	si significa "golpe, revés"	/'bʊfeɪ/	cuando se trata de "bufé"

close	/kləʊz/	si quiere decir "cerrar"	/kləʊs/	si significa "cerca"
lead	/li:d/	para "ventaja", "pista", "conducir", etc.	/led/	para el metal
live	/lɪv/	si significa "vivir"	/laɪv/	si quiere decir "vivo"
lower	/'ləʊə(r)/	para "bajar" o "rebajar"	/'laʊə(r)/	para "mirar amenazadoramente"
minute	/'mɪnɪt/	si significa "minuto"	/maɪ'nju:t/	si se trata de "diminuto"
refuse	/rɪ'fju:z/	para "rechazar"	/'refju:s/	si significa "basura"
row	/rəʊ/	para "fila" o "remar"	/raʊ/	si significa "discutir"
sow	/səʊ/	si significa "plantar"	/saʊ/	para "cerda"
tear	/teə(r)/	si significa "rasgar"	/tɪə(r)/	si se trata de "lágrima"
wind	/wɪnd/	cuando significa "viento"	/waɪnd/	si se trata de "enrollar"
wound	/wu:nd/	para "herida"	/waʊnd/	si significa "enrollado"

3. Las consonantes mudas

Algunas consonantes nunca se pronuncian cuando se encuentran en determinadas posiciones. Este hecho se debe habitualmente a los cambios fonéticos sufridos por la lengua inglesa a lo largo de los siglos, mientras que las grafías se han visto inalteradas. En la siguiente relación aparecen algunos de los casos más frecuentes de consonantes mudas.

b	comb, numb, thumb, debt, subtle
d	Wednesday, handkerchief
g	Las palabras que empiezan por "gn-" (como gnome), sigh, resign, reign, diaphragm
h	Las palabras que empiezan por "wh-" (como when), exhibition, honour, ghetto, ghost
k	Las palabras que empiezan por "kn-" (como knit y knife)
p	Las palabras que empiezan por "psy-" (como psychology), pneumonia, corps, cupboard, receipt
t	castle, chestnut, fasten, listen, mortgage

4. La pronunciación del inglés americano y del británico

Tanto en el inglés británico como en el americano existen diferentes acentos, que varían en función de la región y de la clase social. Aunque en Estados Unidos hay una gran homogeneidad, y es del todo legímito hablar de un "acento americano", existen variedades bien definidas en el sur y en el este. En el Reino Unido, por otra parte, no cuentan con acento general alguno. La variedad que se suele emplear como modelo para describir la pronunciación del inglés británico se conoce como "RP" (Received Pronunciation). Al ser usada por una minoría reducida de hablantes, no es equiparable a la variedad del inglés americano "general". De todas formas, como tiene la ventaja de no pertenecer a ninguna zona geográfica concreta del Reino Unido, esta pronunciación modelo es la que empleamos en las transcripciones fonéticas de la presente obra. Hoy en día el acento de los hablantes cultos de clase media se encuentra a medio camino entre dicha pronunciación modelo y la variedad de la región de la que procedan. Aunque resulta difícil hacer generalizaciones sobre las diferencias que existen entre el inglés americano y el británico, los puntos que aparecen a continuación pueden servir de guía práctica.

▸ La pronunciación de la "r" después de vocal

En la mayor parte de las variedades británicas, la "r" después de vocal no se pronuncia a no ser que preceda a otra vocal. En casi todas las variedades norteamericanas la "r" se pronuncia de forma muy suave (alófono conocido como "r colouring"). La ausencia de ese "r colouring" es uno de los rasgos que define la variedad de Nueva Inglaterra. Ambos sonidos se indican en este diccionario mediante /(r)/.

▸ La pronunciación de la "d" y la "t" intervocálicas

En las variedades norteamericanas, tanto la "d" como la "t" intervocálicas tienden a pronunciarse mediante un ligero y breve golpe de la lengua contra los alveolos (conocido como "flapped r"). Así pues, palabras como liter y leader o writer y rider pueden sonar de forma muy parecida, mientras que en inglés británico son claramente distintas.

▸ El sonido /uː/

En el Reino Unido el sonido /uː/ se convierte en /juː/ cuando va precedido de las consonantes "t, d, s, z" y "n", mientras que en Estados Unidos no cambia. Vocablos como duty, new, tulip, etc., son ejemplos de esta diferencia fonética.

▸ El sonido /əʊ/

La pronunciación de la primera parte de este diptongo en palabras como no, go, boat, etc., varía considerablemente. A oídos de un hablante británico puede sonar bastante afectado o pretencioso que este diptongo comience con un sonido semejante al de la vocal neutra /ə/. En Estados Unidos, y en la mayor parte del Reino Unido, el diptongo en cuestión comienza por un sonido vocálico que se aproxima bastante al de la "o" del español.

▸ El sonido /ɒ/

El sonido representado por la letra "o" en palabras como not, got, forgot, etc., se transcribe como /ɒ/ en la presente obra. En inglés británico es un sonido corto que se articula en la parte posterior de la cavidad bucal, mientras que en Estados Unidos es un sonido más largo cuyo punto de articulación no es tan posterior y se asemeja a la /ɑː/ de bar.

▸ El sonido /æ/

En inglés británico el sonido /æ/ de angry, hat, cattle, etc., es anterior en cuanto al punto de articulación y de duración breve, mientras que en inglés americano la duración es algo más larga y el sonido se asemeja más al de la /e/ de bell.

DICCIONARIO
DICTIONARY

Español-Inglés
Spanish-English

A, a

A, a [a] *nf (letra)* A, a; EXPR **si por a o por be...** if for any reason...

A (**a**) (*abrev de* **autopista**) *Br* M, *US* freeway (**b**) (*abrev de* **alfil**) *(en notación de ajedrez)* B

A *prep*

a combines with the article **el** to form the contraction **al** (e.g. **al centro** to the centre).

(**a**) *(indica dirección)* to; **voy a Perú** I'm going to Peru; **me voy al extranjero** I'm going abroad; **gira a la derecha/izquierda** turn right/left; **¡vete a casa!** go home!; **llegó a Caracas/a la fiesta** he arrived in Caracas/at the party; **se cayó al pozo** he fell into the well

(**b**) *(indica posición)* **está a la derecha/izquierda** it's on the right/left; **nos veremos a la salida del trabajo** we'll meet outside after work; **se encuentra al sur de la ciudad** it's to the south of the city; **vivimos al sur del país** we live in the south of the country; **a orillas del mar** by the sea; **escribe al margen** write in the margin; **sentarse a la mesa** to sit down at the table; **se puso a mi lado** she stood by my side

(**c**) *(indica distancia, tiempo)* **está a más de cien kilómetros** it's more than a hundred kilometres away; **está a cinco minutos de aquí** it's five minutes (away) from here; **está a tres días de viaje** it's a three-day journey away

(**d**) *(después de)* **a las pocas semanas** a few weeks later; **al mes de casados** a month after they were married; **a los quince minutos de juego** fifteen minutes into the game

(**e**) *(hasta)* to; **de Segovia a Madrid** from Segovia to Madrid; **abierto de lunes a viernes** open from Monday to Friday; **de aquí al día de la boda pueden pasar muchas cosas** a lot can happen between now and the wedding day

(**f**) *(momento preciso)* at; **a las siete** at seven o'clock; **a los 11 años** at the age of 11; **al caer la noche** at nightfall; **a la hora de la cena** at dinnertime; **al día siguiente** the following day; **a mediados de año** halfway through the year; *Arg* **a la mañana/tarde** in the morning/afternoon; *Arg* **a la noche** at night; *Arg* **ayer salimos a la noche** we went out last night; **¿a cuánto estamos? – a 15 de febrero** what is the date today? – (it's) 15 February; **al oír la noticia se desmayó** on hearing the news, she fainted; **al oirla la reconocí** when I heard her voice, I recognized her; **me di cuenta al volver** I realized when I returned; **iremos al cine a la salida del trabajo** we're going to the cinema after work

(**g**) *(indica frecuencia)* per, every; **40 horas a la semana** 40 hours per *o* a week; **tres veces al día** three times a day

(**h**) *(con complemento indirecto)* to; **dáselo a Juan** give it to Juan; **dile a Juan que venga** tell Juan to come; **les enseño informática a mis compañeros** I'm teaching my colleagues how to use computers; **se lo compré a un vendedor ambulante** I bought it from a hawker

(**i**) *(con complemento directo)* **busco a mi hermano** I'm looking for my brother; **quiere a sus hijos/a su gato** she loves her children/her cat; **me tratan como a un hijo** they treat me as if I was their son; **estudio a Neruda** I'm studying Neruda

(**j**) *(cantidad, medida, precio)* **a cientos/miles/docenas** by the hundred/thousand/dozen; **a... kilómetros por hora** at... kilometres per hour; **¿a cuánto están las peras?** how much are the pears?; **tiene las**

A

Personal "a"

Where the direct object of a verb is a specific person or group of people, or an animal regarded as an individual (such as a pet), Spanish requires this object to be preceded by the preposition **a**, which is not translated into English. Additionally, the definite article is required, unless the object is a proper name, or is already preceded by a possessive adjective:

apenas podía oír al orador *I could hardly hear the speaker*
quiero mucho a mi perro *I really love my dog*

Where a human object is not a specific individual, the preposition can be omitted:

están buscando otra persona *they're looking for someone else*

The personal **a** is also used with personal pronouns, even where they do not refer to specific individuals:

¿estás esperando a alguien? *are you waiting for someone?*
no teme a nadie *she's not afraid of anyone*

The personal **a** can also be used elsewhere to avoid the ambiguity which arises because of the more flexible word order permitted in Spanish than in English:

el pez rojo se comió al azul *the red fish ate the blue one*
es un delito que daña a la economía *it's a crime which damages the economy*

In other cases, the personal **a** is sometimes omitted precisely to distinguish the direct object from an indirect object preceded by the dative **a** (which is translated by English "to"):

presentó su novia a su familia *he introduced his girlfriend to his family*

When non-human nouns are personified or otherwise particularized they may also take the personal "a":

desafió a la muerte *she defied death*
no temo a su cólera *I'm not afraid of his rage*

Whether a non-human noun is particularized in this way depends on the subjective perception of the speaker and the effect they wish to make, so there is much variation in actual use.

peras a 2 euros she's selling pears for *o* at 2 euros; **tocamos a cinco por cabeza** we should get five each; **ganaron por tres a cero** they won three zero

(k) *(indica modo)* **lo hace a la antigua** he does it the old way; **a lo bestia** rudely; **al compás (de la música)** in time (with the music); **pagar al contado** to pay cash; **una camisa a cuadros/a lunares** a check/polka-dot shirt; **comieron a discreción** they ate as much as they wanted; **a escondidas** secretly; **a lo grande** in style; **a lo Mozart** after Mozart; **a oscuras** in the dark; **ir a pie/a caballo** to walk/ride, to go on foot/on horseback; **poner algo a remojo** to leave sth to soak; **cortar algo a rodajas** to cut sth in slices, to slice sth; **un folleto a todo color** a full-colour brochure; **a trompicones** in fits and starts; **merluza a la vasca/gallega** Basque-style/Galician-style hake; **pollo al ajillo** = chicken fried with garlic

(l) *(instrumento)* **escribir a máquina** to type; **a lápiz** in pencil; **a mano** by hand; **afeitarse a navaja** to shave wet, to shave with a razor; **pasar un documento a ordenador** to type a document (up) on the computer; **avión a reacción** jet (plane); **olla a presión** pressure cooker

(m) *(indica finalidad)* to; **aprender a nadar** to learn to swim; **a beneficio de los más necesitados** for the benefit of those most in need; *Fam* **¿a qué tanto ruido?** what's all this noise about?

(n) *(complemento de nombre)* **sueldo a convenir** salary to be agreed; **temas a tratar** matters to be discussed

(o) *(indica condición)* **a no ser por mí, hubieses fracasado** had it not been *o* if it hadn't been for me, you would have failed; **a decir verdad, no valió la pena** to tell the truth, it wasn't worth it; **a juzgar por lo visto...** judging from what I can see...; **a la luz de la información disponible** in the light of the available information

(p) *(en oraciones imperativas)* **¡a la cama!** go to bed!; **¡a callar todo el mundo!** quiet, everyone!; **¡a bailar!** let's dance!; **¡a trabajar!** let's get to work!

(q) *(en comparación)* **prefiero el té al café** I prefer tea to coffee; **prefiero pasear a ver la tele** I prefer going for walks to watching the TV

(r) *(indica contacto, exposición)* **ir con el pecho al aire** to go bare-chested; **se disuelve al contacto con el agua** it dissolves on (coming into) contact with water; **al influjo de** under the influence of; **al calor del fuego** by the fire; **a la sombra de un árbol** in the shade of a tree; **estar expuesto al sol** to be in the sun

(s) *(en busca de)* **ir a por pan** to go for bread; **voy a por el periódico** I'm going to go for *o* get the paper

(t) *(en cuanto a)* **a bruto no le gana nadie** he's as stupid as they come

(u) *(indica desafío)* **¿a que te caes?** be careful or you'll fall over; **¿a que no adivinas quién ha venido?** I bet you can't guess who has come, guess who has come; **¿a que no lo haces? – ¿a que sí?** I bet you can't do it! – bet I can!; **¿a que se han marchado sin esperarme?** don't tell me, they've left without waiting for me; **¿a que te llevas una bofetada?** do you want to get smacked?

AA *nmpl* (*abrev de* **Alcohólicos Anónimos**) AA

AA. EE. (*abrev de* **Asuntos Exteriores**) **Ministerio de A.** Ministry of Foreign Affairs, *Br* ≃ Foreign Office, *US* ≃ State Department

Aaiún *n* **(el) A.** Laayoune

ababol *nm* (a) *(amapola)* poppy (b) *Fam (simplón)* fool, idiot

abacá *nm* (a) *Bot* abaca (b) *Tex* Manila hemp

abacería *nf* grocery store

abacial *adj* **iglesia a.** abbey (church)

ábaco *nm* (a) *(para contar)* abacus (b) *Arquit* abacus

abad *nm* abbot

abadejo *nm* cod

abadesa *nf* abbess

abadía *nf* (a) *(iglesia)* abbey (b) *(territorio)* abbacy

abajeño, -a, abajero, -a *Am* 1 *adj* lowland; **la población abajeña** the lowland population, lowlanders

2 *nm,f* lowlander

ABAJO 1 *adv* (a) *(posición) (en general)* below; *(en edificio)* downstairs; **boca a.** face down; **de a.** bottom; **el estante de a.** the bottom shelf; **si no quieres subir hasta la cumbre, espérame a.** if you don't want to climb to the top, wait for me at the bottom; **tengo el coche a. en la calle** my car is parked down in the street; **vive (en el piso de) a.** she lives downstairs; **está aquí/allí a.** it's down here/there; **a. del todo** right at the bottom; **más a.** further down; **la parte de a.** the bottom; **Italia va dos puntos a.** Italy are two points down, Italy are losing by two points; **echar** *o* **tirar a.** *(pared)* to knock down; **venirse a.** *(proyecto, edificio)* to fall down, to collapse; *(persona)* to go to pieces

(b) *(dirección)* down; **ve a.** *(en edificio)* go downstairs; **hacia** *o* **para a.** down, downwards; **tirar hacia a.** to pull down; **calle/escaleras a.** down the street/the stairs; **cuesta a.** downhill; **tres portales más a.** three doors further along; **río a.** downstream

(c) *(en una escala)* **niños de diez años para a.** children aged ten or under; **de tenientes para a.** everyone of the rank of lieutenant and below; **a. de** less than

(d) *(en un texto)* below; **la dirección se encuentra más a.** the address is given below; **el a. citado...** the undermentioned...; **el a. firmante** the undersigned; **los a. firmantes** the undersigned

2 *interj* **¡a....!** down with...!; **¡a. la dictadura!** down with the dictatorship!

3 **abajo de** *loc prep Am* below, under; **el gato se escondió a. de la mesa** the cat hid under the table; **una fiesta así no te va a salir a. del millón de pesos** you won't be able to organize a party like that for under a million pesos

---

abalanzar [14] 1 *vt (lanzar)* to fling, to hurl

2 **abalanzarse** *vpr* (a) *(lanzarse)* to rush, to hurl oneself; **me abalancé hacia la salida** I rushed towards the exit; **el policía se abalanzó sobre el atracador** the policeman pounced on the robber; **los niños se abalanzaron sobre la comida** the children fell upon the food (b) *(precipitarse)* to rush in; **no te abalances, piensa antes de actuar** don't just rush in, think before doing anything

abaleado, -a *Andes, CAm, Ven* 1 *adj* **tres personas abaleadas** three people with bullet wounds

2 *nm,f* **los abaleados fueron trasladados al hospital** the gunshot victims were taken to hospital

abalear *vt Andes, CAm, Ven (tirotear)* to shoot at

abaleo *nm Andes, CAm, Ven (tiros)* shooting; *(intercambio de disparos)* shootout; **en el a. murieron dos personas** two people were killed in the shooting

abalizar [14] *vt Náut* to buoy, to mark with buoys

abalorio *nm* (a) *(cuenta)* glass bead (b) *(bisutería)* trinket

abancalar *vt* to terrace

abanderado, -a *nm,f* (a) *(quien lleva la bandera)* standard-bearer (b) *(defensor, portavoz)* champion; **un a. de los derechos de los inmigrantes** a champion of immigrant rights

abanderamiento *nm* (a) *Náut* registration (b) *(defensa)* championing

abanderar *vt* (a) *Náut* to register (b) *(defender)* to champion

abandonado, -a *adj* (a) *(desierto)* deserted; **una casa abandonada** *(desocupada)* a deserted house; *(en mal estado)* a derelict house; **viven en un cobertizo a.** they live in a disused shed

(b) *(niño, animal, vehículo)* abandoned

(c) *(descuidado) (persona)* unkempt; *(jardín, casa)* neglected; **es muy a.** he neglects *o* doesn't look after his appearance; **tiene muy abandonadas a sus plantas** she's been neglecting *o* hasn't been looking after her plants; **tiene la tesis muy abandonada** he has hardly done any work on his thesis (recently)

(d) *Perú (depravado)* depraved

ABANDONAR 1 *vt* (a) *(lugar)* to leave; *(barco, vehículo)* to abandon; **abandonó la sala tras el discurso** she left the hall after the speech; **abandonó su pueblo para trabajar en la ciudad** she left her home town for a job in the city; **a. el barco** to abandon ship; **¡abandonen el barco!** abandon ship!; **a. algo a su suerte** *o* **destino** to abandon sth to its fate; **los cascos azules abandonarán pronto la región** the UN peacekeeping troops will soon be pulling out of the region

(b) *(persona)* to leave; *(hijo, animal)* to abandon; **abandonó a su hijo** she abandoned her son; **a. a alguien a su suerte** *o* **destino** to abandon sb to their fate; **¡nunca te abandonaré!** I'll never leave you!

(c) *(estudios)* to give up; *(proyecto)* to abandon; **abandonó la carrera en el tercer año** she dropped out of university in her third year, she gave up her studies in her third year; **han amenazado con a. las negociaciones** they have threatened to walk out of the negotiations; **han amenazado con a. la liga** they have threatened to pull out of the league; **a. la lucha** to give up the fight

(d) *(sujeto: suerte, buen humor)* to desert; **lo abandonaron las fuerzas y tuvo que retirarse** his strength gave out and he had to drop out; **nunca la abandona su buen humor** she never loses her good humour

2 *vi* (a) *(en carrera, competición)* to pull out, to withdraw; *(en ajedrez)* to resign; *(en boxeo)* to throw in the towel; **abandonó en el primer asalto** his corner threw in the towel in the first round; **una avería lo obligó a a. en la segunda vuelta** a mechanical fault forced him to retire on the second lap

(b) *(rendirse)* to give up; **no abandones ahora que estás casi al final** don't give up now you've almost reached the end

3 **abandonarse** *vpr* (**a**) *(de aspecto)* to neglect oneself, to let oneself go (**b**) **abandonarse a** *(desesperación, dolor)* to succumb to; *(placer, sentidos)* to abandon oneself to; *(vicio)* to give oneself over to; **se abandona con facilidad a la desesperación** she is quick to despair

---

abandono *nm* (**a**) *(descuido) (de aspecto, jardín)* state of abandon; *(de estudios, obligaciones)* neglect; **la iglesia se encontraba en estado de a.** the church was derelict

(**b**) *(de lugar)* **los bomberos ordenaron el a. del edificio** the firemen instructed everyone to leave the building, the firemen had the building evacuated; **el a. de su puesto le costó un arresto al soldado** the soldier was placed in confinement for abandoning his post

(**c**) *(de hijo, proyecto)* abandonment; **el a. de animales se incrementa tras las Navidades** there is a rise in the number of animals abandoned after Christmas; **el movimiento defiende el a. de la energía nuclear** the movement is in favour of abolishing the use of nuclear energy; **han anunciado el a. de la violencia** they have announced that they are going to give up violence; **su desilusión lo llevó al a. de la profesión** he was so disillusioned that he left the profession ▸▸ *Der* ***a. de hogar*** desertion *(of family, spouse)*; *UE* ***a. de tierras:*** **el gobierno está fomentando el a. de tierras** the government is promoting land set-aside

(**d**) *(entrega)* abandon, abandonment; **se entregó con a. a su amante** she gave herself with abandon to her lover

(**e**) *(de competición, carrera)* withdrawal; **el a. se produjo en el kilómetro 10** he pulled out after 10 kilometres; **ganar por a.** to win by default

abanicar [60] 1 *vt* to fan

2 **abanicarse** *vpr* (**a**) *(con abanico)* to fan oneself; **se abanicó la cara** she fanned her face (**b**) EXPR *Chile Fam* **abanicarse con algo: el jefe se abanica con tus problemas** the boss couldn't care less about your problems

abanicazo *nm* **me dio un a. en la cabeza** she hit me on the head with her fan

abanico *nm* (**a**) *(para abanicarse)* fan; **hizo un a. con los naipes** he fanned out the cards; **los soldados se abrieron en a.** the soldiers fanned out

(**b**) *(gama)* range; **tenemos un amplio a. de modelos** we have a wide range of models; **un a. de precios** a range of prices; **se dieron cita un enorme a. de culturas** people from a vast diversity of cultures came together

(**c**) *Geol* ***a. aluvial*** alluvial fan

(**d**) *(en ciclismo)* **los ciclistas se movían haciendo abanicos** the cyclists fanned out

abanique *etc ver* **abanicar**

abaniqueo *nm (con abanico)* fanning

abarajar *vt RP Fam (agarrar)* to catch in flight

abaratamiento *nm* reduction *o* fall in price; **el a. de los precios** the reduction *o* fall in prices

abaratar 1 *vt (precio, coste)* to bring down, to reduce; *(artículo)* to reduce the price of

2 **abaratarse** *vpr (precio, coste)* to fall; *(artículo)* to go down in price, to become cheaper

abarca *nf* = type of sandal worn by country people

abarcar [60] *vt* (**a**) *(incluir)* to cover; **nuestra hacienda abarca un tercio de la comarca** our estate covers a third of the district; **este artículo intenta a. demasiado** this article tries to cover too much; **el libro abarca cinco siglos de historia de Latinoamérica** the book covers *o* spans five centuries of Latin American history; PROV **quien mucho abarca poco aprieta** don't bite off more than you can chew

(**b**) *(ver)* to be able to see, to have a view of; **desde la torre se abarca todo el valle** you can see the whole valley from the tower; **hasta donde abarca la vista** as far as the eye can see

(**c**) *(rodear)* **no consigo a. el tronco con los brazos** I can't get my arms around the tree trunk

abaritonado, -a *adj Mús* baritone

abarque *etc ver* **abarcar**

abarquillar 1 *vt (madera)* to warp

2 **abarquillarse** *vpr (madera)* to warp

abarrajar *Perú* 1 *vt (tirar)* to hurl, to throw

2 **abarrajarse** *vpr* (**a**) *(tropezarse)* to trip, to stumble (**b**) *(depravarse)* to become corrupt

abarrajo *nm Perú* fall, stumble

abarrotado, -a *adj* (**a**) *(lleno) (teatro, autobús)* packed (**de** with); *(desván, baúl)* crammed (**de** with) (**b**) *Ven* **estar a. de trabajo** to have a lot of work

abarrotar *vt* (**a**) *(teatro, autobús)* to pack (**de** *o* **con** with); *(desván, baúl)* to cram full (**de** *o* **con** of); **los curiosos abarrotaban la estancia** the room was packed with onlookers (**b**) *CAm, Méx Com* to monopolize, to buy up

abarrotería *nf CAm, Méx* grocer's (shop), grocery store

abarrotero, -a *nm,f CAm, Méx* grocer

abarrotes *nmpl Andes, CAm, Méx* (**a**) *(mercancías)* groceries (**b**) **(tienda de) a.** grocer's shop, grocery store

abastecedor, -ora *nm,f* supplier

abastecer [46] 1 *vt* to supply (**de** with); **a. de agua a la ciudad** to supply the city with water; **esa región nos abastece de materias primas** that region supplies *o* provides us with raw materials

2 **abastecerse** *vpr* to stock up (**de** on); **tienen problemas para abastecerse de combustible** they have problems in obtaining fuel; **se abastecen de agua en el pozo de la plaza** they get their water from the well in the square

abastecido, -a *adj* supplied, stocked (**de** with); **una tienda bien abastecida** a well-stocked store

abastecimiento *nm* supplying; **se ha interrumpido el a.** they've cut off the supply ▸▸ ***a. de aguas*** water supply

abastezco *etc ver* **abastecer**

abasto *nm* (**a**) *(provisión, suministro)* supply (**b**) *Ven (tienda)* grocer's (store) (**c**) EXPR **no dar a.** to be unable to cope; **no da a. con tanto trabajo** she can't cope with so much work

abatatar *RP Fam* 1 *vt (turbar, confundir)* to frighten, to scare

2 **abatatarse** *vpr (acobardarse, avergonzarse)* to become embarrassed

abate *nm* abbé *(title given to French or Italian priest)*

abatible *adj* **mesa a.** foldaway table; **asientos abatibles** *(en coche)* = seats that tip forwards or fold flat; *(en tren)* tip-up seats

abatido, -a *adj* dejected, downhearted; **está muy a. por la muerte de su padre** he's feeling very down because of his father's death; **"no me quiere", respondió a.** "she doesn't love me," he said dejectedly *o* downheartedly

abatimiento *nm (desánimo)* low spirits, dejection; **el a. se instaló en las almas de los soldados** an air of despondency set in amongst the soldiers; **con a.** dejectedly, downheartedly

abatir 1 *vt* (**a**) *(derribar) (muro)* to knock down; *(avión)* to shoot down; **el atracador fue abatido a tiros** the robber was gunned down (**b**) *(desanimar)* to depress, to dishearten; **no te dejes a. por tan poca cosa** don't let yourself be upset by something so trivial

2 **abatirse** *vpr* (**a**) *(caer)* **abatirse sobre algo/alguien** to pounce on sth/sb; **la desesperación se abatió sobre ellos** they were overcome by a feeling of despair; **la desgracia se abatió sobre la región** the region has been struck *o* hit by disaster; **el halcón se abatió sobre su presa** the falcon swooped down on its prey; **una tormenta de nieve se abatió sobre la cumbre** the summit was hit by a snowstorm

(**b**) *(desanimarse)* to become dejected *o* disheartened

abazón *nm Zool* cheek pouch

abdicación *nf (de monarca)* abdication

abdicar [60] 1 *vt (trono, corona)* to abdicate; **a. el trono (en alguien)** to abdicate the throne (in favour of sb)

2 *vi* (**a**) *(monarca)* to abdicate (**b**) **a. de** *(principios, ideales)* to renounce; **abdicó de su derecho a apelar** she gave up her right to appeal

abdomen *nm (de persona, insecto)* abdomen

abdominal *adj* abdominal; **dolores abdominales** abdominal pains

abdominales *nmpl* (**a**) *(ejercicios)* sit-ups (**b**) *(músculos)* stomach muscles

abducción *nf* abduction

abductor *nm Anat* abductor

abecé *nm* (**a**) *(abecedario)* ABC; **todavía no han aprendido el a.** she still hasn't learnt the alphabet *o* her ABC (**b**) *(fundamentos)* **no sabe ni el a. de lingüística** he doesn't know the first thing about linguistics; **esa obra es el a. de la jardinería** that book covers the basics of gardening

abecedario *nm* (**a**) *(alfabeto)* alphabet; **ya se sabe el a.** she already knows the *o* her alphabet (**b**) *(libro)* spelling book

abedul *nm* birch (tree) ▸▸ ***a. blanco*** silver birch

abeja *nf* bee ▸▸ ***a. obrera*** worker bee; ***a. reina*** queen bee

abejar *nm* apiary

abejarrón *nm* bumble-bee

abejaruco *nm* bee-eater

abejorro *nm* bumble-bee

Abel *n pr* Abel

abelmosco *nm* musk mallow

aberración *nf* (a) *(desviación de la norma)* **me parece una a.** I find it ridiculous; **echó gaseosa al champán, iqué a.!** he put lemonade in the champagne, that's sacrilege! ►► ***a. sexual*** sexual perversion (b) *Fot* aberration (c) *Fís* aberration

aberrante *adj* (a) *(absurdo)* ridiculous, idiotic (b) *(perverso)* perverse (c) *(anormal)* abnormal, aberrant

abertura *nf* (a) *(agujero)* opening; *(ranura)* crack (b) *Fot* aperture ►► ***a. del diafragma*** aperture

abertzale [aβer'tʃale], **aberzale** [aβer'θale] *Esp Pol* 1 *adj* = radical Basque nationalist
2 *nmf* = radical Basque nationalist

abeto *nm* fir ►► ***a. blanco*** silver fir; ***a. rojo*** Christmas tree, common spruce

abey *nm* jacaranda

abicharse *vpr CSur (fruta)* to become worm-eaten

abichón *nm* silverside

Abidjan = **Abiyán**

abiertamente *adv (claramente)* clearly; *(en público)* openly

ABIERTO, -A 1 *participio ver* **abrir**
2 *adj* (a) *(puerta, boca, tienda)* open; **dejar el grifo a.** to leave the tap on *o* running; **bien** *o* **muy a.** wide open; **a. de par en par** wide open; **a. de 9 a 5** *(en letrero)* opening hours: 9 to 5; **a. hasta tarde** open late; **a. al público** open to the public; **la cabaña está en pleno campo a.** the cabin is in the open country
(b) *(herida)* open
(c) *(desabrochado)* undone; **llevas abierta la camisa** your shirt is undone
(d) *Informát (archivo)* open
(e) *(cheque)* open
(f) *(claro)* open; **mostró su abierta oposición al proyecto** he was openly opposed to the project; **existe una abierta enemistad entre los dos políticos** the two politicians are quite openly enemies
(g) *Ling (vocal)* open
(h) *(liberal, tolerante)* open-minded; **tiene una mentalidad muy abierta** she's very open-minded; **estar a. a cualquier sugerencia** to be open to suggestions
(i) *(franco, sincero)* open; **es una persona muy abierta, nunca oculta nada** she's very open, she never hides anything
(j) *(sin decidir)* open; **promete ser una final muy abierta** it promises to be a very open *o* evenly contested final
(k) *TV* **un programa en a.** = on pay TV, a programme which is not scrambled so that non-subscribers may also watch it
(l) *Ven (generoso)* generous
3 *nm* (a) *Dep* open (tournament) ►► ***el a. británico*** the British Open; ***el a. USA*** the US Open
(b) *Col (terreno)* cleared land

abietácea *nf Bot* 1 *nf (planta)* fir
2 **abietáceas** *nfpl (familia)* **las abietáceas** the fir family

abietáceo, -a *adj Bot* of the fir family

abigarrado, -a *adj* (a) *(mezclado)* **la habitación está abigarrada** the room is a real jumble of different things (b) *(multicolor)* multi-coloured

abigeato *nm* cattle rustling

ab intestato, abintestato *adv Der (sin testamento)* intestate

abisal *adj* **fosa a.** ocean trough; **pez a.** abyssal fish; **las profundidades abisales** the depths of the ocean

Abisinia *n Antes* Abyssinia

abisinio, -a *Antes* 1 *adj* Abyssinian
2 *nm,f* Abyssinian

abismal *adj* (a) *(diferencia, distancia)* vast, colossal; **una caída a. de los precios** a huge *o* massive drop in prices (b) *(del abismo)* abyssal; **las profundidades abismales** the depths of the ocean

abismante *adj Andes, RP* dramatic

abismar 1 *vt Formal* **a. a alguien en la desesperación** to plunge sb into despair
2 **abismarse** *vpr* (a) **abismarse en** *(lectura)* to become engrossed in (b) *Andes, RP (sorprenderse)* to be amazed (c) *Carib (arruinarse)* to be ruined

abismo *nm* (a) *(profundidad)* abyss; EXPR **estar al borde del a.** to be on the brink of ruin *o* disaster (b) *(diferencia)* gulf; **entre su sueldo y el mío hay un a.** there's a huge difference between our salaries

Abiyán, Abidjan *n* Abidjan

abjuración *nf Formal* abjuration, renunciation

abjurar *Formal* 1 *vt (fe, creencias)* to abjure, to renounce
2 *vi* **a. de** *(fe, creencias)* to abjure, to renounce

ablación *nf Med (de tejido, órgano)* excision, surgical removal ►► ***a. del clítoris*** female circumcision

ablandador *nm* softener; **a. de carne** (meat) tenderizer

ablandamiento *nm* (a) *(de objeto, material)* softening (b) *(de persona)* softening

ablandar 1 *vt* (a) *(objeto, material)* to soften (b) *(persona)* to soften; **sus ruegos no lo ablandaron** her pleas were not sufficient to make him relent (c) *CSur, Cuba Aut* to run in; **hicimos 1.000 km para a. el auto nuevo** we drove for 1,000 km to run the new car in
2 **ablandarse** *vpr* (a) *(objeto, material)* to soften, to become softer (b) *(actitud, rigor)* to soften; **su padre se ablandó cuando la vio llorar** her father relented when he saw her crying

ablande *nm CSur, Cuba Aut* running in; **el auto está en a.** I'm/we're running the car in

ablativo *nm Gram* ablative ►► ***a. absoluto*** ablative absolute

ablución *nf Rel* **hizo sus abluciones** he performed his ablutions

ablusado, -a *adj (vestido, camisa)* loose, baggy

abnegación *nf* abnegation, self-denial; **trabajó toda su vida con a.** she worked selflessly all her life

abnegadamente *adv* selflessly

abnegado, -a *adj* selfless, unselfish

abnegarse [43] *vpr* to deny oneself

abobadamente *adv Fam* blankly, bewilderedly

abobado, -a *adj Fam* (a) *(estupefacto)* blank, uncomprehending; **se quedó a. al enterarse** he was astounded *o* speechless when he found out (b) *(estúpido)* stupid

abocado, -a *adj* (a) *(destinado)* **estar a. a** to be heading for; **este proyecto está a. al fracaso** this project is heading for failure (b) *(vino)* = blended from sweet and dry wines (c) *CSur (dedicado)* allocated (a to); **el presupuesto a. a la investigación** the research budget, the budgetary resources allocated to research

abocar [60] 1 *vt* **a. a alguien a algo** to lead sb to sth; **eso nos abocaría a la ruina** that would lead us to disaster
2 *vpr CSur, Ven* **a. a algo** *(dedicarse a)* to dedicate oneself to sth; **hace dos meses se abocó al estudio** she's been taking her studies seriously for the last two months; **tenemos que abocarnos a la promoción de las energías renovables** we have to seriously set about promoting renewable forms of energy

abocetar *vt* to sketch

abochornado, -a *adj* (a) *(avergonzado)* embarrassed (b) *Chile (tiempo)* stifling, muggy

abochornar 1 *vt* (a) *(avergonzar)* to embarrass (b) *(acalorar)* **ieste calor abochorna a cualquiera!** this heat is stifling!
2 **abochornarse** *vpr* (a) *(avergonzarse)* to get embarrassed (b) *(acalorarse)* to swelter (c) *Chile (tiempo)* to become stifling *o* muggy

abofetear *vt* to slap *(in the face)*; **el viento lo abofeteaba en la cara** the wind buffeted him in the face

abogacía *nf* legal profession; **ejercer la a.** to practise law; **estudiar a.** to study law

abogado, -a *nm,f* (a) *Der Br* lawyer, *US* attorney ►► ***a. criminalista*** criminal lawyer; ***a. defensor*** counsel for the defence; ***a. del Estado*** public prosecutor; ***a. de familia*** family lawyer; ***a. laboralista*** labour lawyer; ***a. matrimonialista*** divorce lawyer; ***a. de oficio*** legal aid lawyer
(b) *(intercesor)* intermediary; *(defensor)* advocate; **siempre ha sido un a. de los pobres** he has always stood up for the poor ►► ***a. del diablo*** devil's advocate; **hacer de a. del diablo** to play devil's advocate

abogar [38] *vi* (a) *Der* **a. por alguien** to represent sb (b) *(defender)* **a. por algo** to advocate *o* champion sth; **a. por alguien** to stand up for sb, to defend sb

abolengo *nm* lineage; **de (rancio) a.** of noble lineage

abolición *nf* abolition

abolicionismo *nm Hist* abolitionism

abolicionista *Hist* 1 *adj* abolitionist
2 *nmf* abolitionist

abolir *vt* to abolish

abollado, -a *adj* dented

abolladura *nf* dent; **el automóvil estaba lleno de abolladuras** the car was dented all over

abollar 1 *vt* to dent
2 **abollarse** *vpr* to get dented

abombado, -a 1 *adj* (**a**) *(hacia fuera)* buckled; **la lata está un poco abombada** the tin has buckled slightly outwards; **una pared abombada** a wall bulging outwards (**b**) *Andes, RP Fam (aturdido)* dopey
2 *nm,f Andes, RP Fam* hothead, scatterbrain

abombar 1 *vt* to buckle (outwards)
2 **abombarse** *vpr* (**a**) *(pared)* to buckle (outwards) (**b**) *Am (estropearse)* to spoil, to go off (**c**) *Andes, RP Fam (aturdirse)* to be dazed; **siempre se abomba cuando ocurre algo así** whenever something like that happens his brains get scrambled *o* he's all over the place

abominable *adj* abominable ►► ***el a. hombre de las nieves*** the abominable snowman

abominablemente *adv* abominably

abominación *nf* abomination

abominar 1 *vt (detestar)* to abhor, to abominate
2 *vi* **a. de** *(condenar)* to condemn, to criticize

abonable *adj (pagadero)* payable

abonado, -a *nm,f* (**a**) *(a revista, canal de televisión)* subscriber; *(a teléfono, de gas, electricidad)* customer (**b**) *(al fútbol, teatro, transporte)* season-ticket holder

abonar 1 *vt* (**a**) *(pagar)* to pay; **a. algo en la cuenta de alguien** to credit sb's account with sth; **¿cómo desea abonarlo?** how would you like to pay?; **¿desea a. con tarjeta o en efectivo?** would you like to pay by credit card or in cash?
(**b**) *(fertilizar)* to fertilize
(**c**) *(suscribir)* **a. a alguien a una revista** to get sb a subscription to a magazine
(**d**) *(acreditar)* **lo abona un brillante pasado** he brings with him an outstanding reputation
2 **abonarse** *vpr* (**a**) *(a revista)* to subscribe (**a** to) (**b**) *(al fútbol, teatro, transporte)* to buy a season ticket (**a** for)

abonaré *nm* promissory note

abonero, -a *nm,f Méx* hawker, street trader

abono *nm* (**a**) *(pase)* season ticket; **un a. de diez viajes** a ten-journey ticket ►► ***a. transporte*** season ticket *(for bus, train and underground)*
(**b**) *(fertilizante)* fertilizer ►► ***a. orgánico*** organic fertilizer; ***a. químico*** artificial *o* chemical fertilizer
(**c**) *(pago)* payment; **realizar un a.** to make a payment; **no existe cuota de a. mensual** there is no monthly fee
(**d**) *Com* credit entry
(**e**) *Méx (plazo)* instalment; **pagar en abonos** to pay by instalments

aboque *etc ver* **abocar**

abordable *adj (persona)* approachable; *(tema)* that can be tackled; *(tarea)* manageable

abordaje *nm Náut* boarding; **¡al a.!** attack!; **los piratas entraron al a.** the pirates boarded them

abordar *vt* (**a**) *(barco)* to board *(in attack)*
(**b**) *(persona)* to approach; **nos abordaron unos maleantes** we were accosted by some undesirables
(**c**) *(resolver)* to tackle, to deal with; **no saben cómo a. el problema** they don't know how to deal with *o* tackle the problem
(**d**) *(plantear)* to bring up; **el artículo aborda el problema del racismo** the article deals with the issue of racism
(**e**) *Méx, Ven (avión, barco)* to board; *(tren, autobús)* to get on; *(coche)* to get into

aborigen 1 *adj (indígena)* indigenous, native; *(de Australia)* Aboriginal
2 *nmf (población indígena)* native; *(de Australia)* Aborigine; **aborígenes** indigenous population, natives; *(de Australia)* Aborigines

aborrascarse [60] *vpr* to become stormy

aborrecer [46] *vt* (**a**) *(odiar)* to abhor, to loathe; **me hizo a. la comida picante** it really put me off spicy food; **aborrece la soledad** she loathes being on her own (**b**) *(crías)* to reject

aborrecible *adj* abhorrent, loathsome

aborrecido, -a *adj* loathed, hated

aborrecimiento *nm* loathing, hatred

aborregado, -a *adj* (**a**) *Fam (adocenado)* **estar a.** to be like sheep (**b**) **cielo a.** mackerel sky

aborregarse [38] *vpr* (**a**) *Fam (adocenarse)* to become like sheep (**b**) *(cielo)* to become covered with fleecy clouds

aborrezco *etc ver* **aborrecer**

abortar 1 *vt* (**a**) *(feto)* to abort (**b**) *(misión, aterrizaje)* to abort; *(atentado)* to foil; **abortaron la operación antes de que empezara** they called off the operation before it had started (**c**) *Informát (programa)* to abort
2 *vi (espontáneamente)* to have a miscarriage, to miscarry; *(intencionadamente)* to have an abortion

abortista 1 *adj* pro-abortion
2 *nmf* abortionist

abortivo, -a 1 *adj* abortifacient; **sustancia abortiva** abortifacient; **fue acusada de prácticas abortivas** she was accused of carrying out illegal abortions
2 *nm* abortifacient

aborto *nm* (**a**) *(espontáneo)* miscarriage; *(intencionado)* abortion; **tuvo un a.** she had a miscarriage; **le practicaron un a.** she had an abortion ►► ***a. clandestino*** backstreet abortion; ***a. eugénico*** therapeutic abortion; ***el a. libre*** abortion on demand; ***a. terapéutico*** therapeutic abortion (**b**) *(feto)* aborted foetus (**c**) *muy Fam (persona fea)* freak

abotagado, -a, abotargado, -a *adj* (**a**) *(hinchado)* swollen; *(cara)* puffy (**b**) *(atontado)* **tengo la mente abotargada** my mind has gone fuzzy

abotagarse [38], **abotargarse** [38] *vpr* (**a**) *(hincharse)* to swell (up) (**b**) *(atontarse)* to become dull

abotinado, -a *adj* **zapato a.** boot

abotonar 1 *vt* to button up
2 **abotonarse** *vpr* to do one's buttons up; **abotonarse la camisa** to button one's shirt up; **este vestido se abotona por detrás** this dress buttons up the back

abovedado, -a *adj* vaulted

abovedar *vt* to arch, to vault

abra *nf*

Takes the masculine articles **el** and **un**.

(**a**) *(bahía)* bay (**b**) *(valle)* valley (**c**) *(grieta)* fissure (**d**) *Col (de puerta)* leaf; *(de ventana)* pane (**e**) *RP (en bosque)* clearing

abracadabra *nm* abracadabra

abrace *etc ver* **abrazar**

Abraham, Abrahán *n pr* Abraham

abrasado, -a *adj* burned, scorched; **murió a.** he (was) burned to death

abrasador, -ora *adj* burning; **pasión abrasadora** burning passion

abrasar 1 *vt* (**a**) *(quemar) (casa, bosque)* to burn down; *(persona, mano, garganta)* to burn (**b**) *(desecar)* to scorch; **el sol abrasó los campos** the sun parched the fields (**c**) *(consumir)* to consume; **lo abrasaba el deseo** he was consumed by desire
2 *vi (café, sopa)* to be boiling hot; **este sol abrasa** the sun is really hot today
3 **abrasarse** *vpr (casa, bosque)* to burn down; *(persona)* to burn oneself; **me abrasé los brazos** I burnt my arms; **los campos se abrasaron con el calor** the heat parched the fields

abrasilerado, -a *RP* 1 *adj* influenced by Brazil, Brazilianized; **el habla abrasilerada de la frontera** the Brazilian-influenced border dialect; **los ritmos abrasilerados de su música** the Brazilianized rhythms of his music
2 *nm,f* **es un a.** he's adopted lots of Brazilian ways *o* habits

abrasión *nf* (**a**) *(fricción)* abrasion (**b**) *Med (por fricción)* abrasion; *(por agente corrosivo)* burn

abrasivo, -a 1 *adj* abrasive
2 *nm* abrasive

abrazadera *nf* (**a**) *Tec* brace, bracket (**b**) *(en carpintería)* clamp

abrazar [14] 1 *vt* (**a**) *(rodear con los brazos)* to hug, to embrace (**b**) *(doctrina)* to embrace (**c**) *(profesión)* to go into
2 **abrazarse** *vpr* to hug, to embrace; **abrazarse a alguien** to hug sb, to cling to sb; **se abrazó a un árbol** he clung to a tree; **se abrazaron con pasión** they embraced passionately

abrazo *nm* hug, embrace; **dar un a. a alguien** to hug sb, to give sb a hug; **nos fundimos en un a.** we fell into each other's arms; **un (fuerte) a.** *(en carta formal)* Yours, Best wishes; *(a un amigo)* Love; **Marina te manda un a.** Marina sends you her love; **dale un a. de mi parte** give her my love

abreboca *nm*, **abrebocas** *nm inv Andes, CAm, Carib, Méx* appetizer

abrebotellas *nm inv* bottle opener

abrecartas *nm inv* paper knife, letter opener

abrechapas *nm inv* bottle opener

abrecoches *nm inv* commissionaire, doorman

abrelatas *nm inv* can opener, *Br* tin opener

abrevadero *nm (construido)* drinking trough; *(natural)* watering place

abrevar 1 *vt* to water, to give water to
2 *vi* to drink

abreviación *nf* (**a**) *(de proceso, explicación)* shortening; *(de viaje, estancia)* cutting short (**b**) *(de texto)* abridgement (**c**) *(de palabra)* abbreviation

abreviadamente *adv* briefly, succinctly

abreviado, -a *adj (texto)* abridged

abreviar 1 *vt* (**a**) *(proceso, explicación)* to shorten; *(viaje, estancia)* to cut short (**b**) *(texto)* to abridge (**c**) *(palabra)* to abbreviate
2 *vi (darse prisa)* to hurry up; **para a.** *(al hacer algo)* to keep it quick; *(al narrar algo)* to cut a long story short; **¡venga, abrevia!** come on, keep it short!
3 **abreviarse** *vpr CAm* to hurry, to make haste

abreviatura *nf* abbreviation

abridor *nm* (**a**) *(abrebotellas)* (bottle) opener (**b**) *(abrelatas)* (can) opener, *Br* (tin) opener

abrigado, -a *adj* (**a**) *(persona)* well wrapped-up; **va muy bien a.** he's wrapped-up nice and warm; **si te metes en la cama estarás más a.** you'll be warmer if you get into bed (**b**) *(lugar)* sheltered (**de** from) (**c**) *Am (prenda)* warm

abrigador, -ora 1 *adj Andes, Méx (prenda)* warm
2 *nm,f Méx (cómplice)* accessory (after the fact)

abrigar [38] 1 *vt* (**a**) *(arropar)* to wrap up; *(calentar)* to keep warm (**b**) *(albergar) (esperanza)* to cherish; *(sospechas, malas intenciones)* to harbour
2 *vi (ropa, manta)* to be warm; **esta chaqueta no abriga nada** this jacket is useless at keeping you warm
3 **abrigarse** *vpr* (**a**) *(arroparse)* to wrap up; **abrígate más, así vas a tener frío** wrap up warmer, you'll be cold like that (**b**) *(resguardarse)* to shelter (**de** from)

abrigo 1 *nm* (**a**) *(prenda)* coat ►► ***a. de piel*** *o* ***pieles*** fur coat (**b**) *(defensa contra el frío)* **ropa de a.** warm clothing; **esta manta me es de mucho a.** this blanket keeps me nice and warm (**c**) *(refugio)* shelter; **al a. de** *(peligro, ataque)* safe from; *(lluvia, viento)* sheltered from; *(ley)* under the protection of; **creció al a. de sus abuelos** she was brought up in her grandparents' care
2 **de abrigo** *loc adj Esp Fam* **se organizó una pelea de a.** a real free-for-all broke out; **es un tipo de a.** he's a dodgy character; **es un niño de a.** he's a little scamp

abrigue *etc ver* **abrigar**

abril *nm* April; **tiene catorce abriles** he is fourteen (years of age); PROV **en a., aguas mil** March winds, April showers; *ver también* **septiembre**

abrillantado, -a 1 *adj RP (fruta)* glazed
2 *nm (acción)* polish; **a. de suelos** floor polishing

abrillantador *nm (sustancia)* polish

abrillantadora *nf (máquina)* polisher

abrillantar *vt* (**a**) *(zapatos, suelo)* to polish (**b**) *(piedra preciosa)* to cut

---

ABRIR 1 *vt* (**a**) *(en general)* to open; *(alas)* to spread; *(agua, gas)* to turn on; *(cerradura)* to unlock, to open; *Informát (archivo)* to open; *(cremallera)* to undo; *(melón, sandía)* to cut open; *(paraguas)* to open; *(cortinas)* to open, to draw; *(persianas)* to raise; *(frontera)* to open (up); **ella abrió la caja** she opened the box; **abre el grifo** turn the tap on; **a. un libro** to open a book; **a. la licitación/sesión** to open the bidding/session; EXPR **en un a. y cerrar de ojos** in the blink *o* twinkling of an eye
(**b**) *(túnel)* to dig; *(canal, camino)* to build; *(agujero, surco)* to make; **la explosión abrió un gran agujero en la pared** the explosion blasted a big hole in the wall; **le abrieron la cabeza de un botellazo** they smashed his head open with a bottle
(**c**) *(iniciar) (cuenta bancaria)* to open; *(investigación)* to open, to start
(**d**) *(inaugurar)* to open; **van a a. un nuevo centro comercial** they're going to open a new shopping centre
(**e**) *(apetito)* to whet; **la natación abre el apetito** swimming makes you hungry
(**f**) *(signo ortográfico)* to open; **a. comillas/paréntesis** to open inverted commas/brackets
(**g**) *(encabezar) (lista)* to head; *(manifestación, desfile)* to lead
(**h**) *(mentalidad)* to open; **viajar le ha abierto la mente** travelling has opened her mind *o* made her more open-minded
(**i**) *(posibilidades)* to open up; **el acuerdo abre una nueva época de co-operación** the agreement paves the way for a new era of co-operation; **la empresa intenta a. nuevos mercados en el exterior** the company is trying to open up new markets abroad
(**j**) *(comenzar)* to open; **el discurso del Presidente abrió el congreso** the President's speech opened the congress; **abrió su participación en el torneo con una derrota** she opened *o* started the tournament with a defeat
(**k**) **a. fuego (sobre** *o* **contra)** *(disparar)* to open fire (on)
(**l**) *también Fig* **a. paso** *o* **camino** to clear the way; **su dimisión abre paso a una nueva generación** his resignation clears the way for a new generation
(**m**) *Dep* **a. el juego** to play a more open *o* expansive game
(**n**) *Fam (operar)* **tuvieron que a. al paciente para sacarle la bala** they had to cut the patient open to remove the bullet
(**o**) *Col, Cuba (desbrozar)* to clear
2 *vi* (**a**) *(en general)* to open; **la tienda abre a las nueve** the shop opens at nine (o'clock); **abrimos también los domingos** *(en letrero)* also open on Sundays
(**b**) *(abrir la puerta)* to open the door; **abre, que corra un poco el aire** open the door and let a bit of air in here; **¡abra, policía!** open up, it's the police!
(**c**) *(en juego de cartas)* to open; **me toca a. a mí** it's my lead
(**d**) *Fam (en operación)* **será una intervención sencilla, no hará falta a.** it's a straightforward procedure, we won't need to cut her open
3 **abrirse** *vpr* (**a**) *(puerta, caja)* to open; *(cremallera, chaqueta)* to come undone; **este bote no se abre** this jar won't open; **la puerta se abre fácilmente** the door opens easily; **se te ha abierto la camisa** your shirt has come undone; **la pared se abrió a causa del terremoto** the earthquake caused a crack to appear in the wall
(**b**) *(empezar) (película, función)* to open, to begin; **el libro se abre con una escena muy violenta** the book opens with a very violent scene; **el debate se abrió con una intervención del ministro** the debate began with a speech by the minister
(**c**) *(periodo)* to begin; **cuando se abra el plazo para presentar solicitudes** when they start accepting applications
(**d**) *(sincerarse)* to open up; **abrirse a alguien** to open up to sb, to confide in sb; **tienes que abrirte más a la gente** you should be more open with people
(**e**) *(posibilidades)* to open up; **tras su marcha se abrieron nuevas posibilidades** after she left, new opportunities arose
(**f**) *(cielo)* to clear
(**g**) *(flores)* to blossom
(**h**) *(vehículo en una curva)* to go wide; **se abrió demasiado en la curva y se cayó de la bici** he went too wide on the bend and fell off his bike
(**i**) *Dep* **se abrió por la banda para esquivar a la defensa** he moved out onto the wing to get behind the defence
(**j**) *(rajarse)* to split open; **se cayó del caballo y se abrió la cabeza** she fell off her horse and split her head open
(**k**) *también Fig* **abrirse paso** *o* **camino** to make one's way
(**l**) *Fam (irse)* to clear off; **nosotros nos abrimos ya** it's time for us to be off
(**m**) *Am Fam (retirarse)* to back out

---

abrochador, -ora *nm,f RP (grapadora)* stapler

abrochar 1 *vt* (**a**) *(botones, camisa)* to do up; *(cinturón)* to fasten (**b**) *RP (grapar)* to staple
2 **abrocharse** *vpr (botones, camisa)* to do up; *(cinturón)* to fasten; **abrocharse la camisa** to do up one's shirt; **este vestido se abrocha por detrás** this dress does up at the back; **¡abróchate!** *(el abrigo)* do your coat up!; **abróchense los cinturones de seguridad** fasten your seat belts

abrogación *nf Der* abrogation, repeal

abrogar [38] *vt Der* to abrogate, to repeal

abrojo *nm* (**a**) *Bot* caltrop (**b**) *Náut* **abrojos** reefs, sharp rocks

abroncar [60] *vt* (**a**) *(reprender)* to tell off (**b**) *(abuchear)* to boo

abrótano *nm* **a. (macho)** southernwood ►► ***a. hembra*** santolina

abrumado, -a *adj (agobiado)* overwhelmed; *(molesto)* annoyed; **a. por el trabajo** overwhelmed *o* swamped with work

abrumador, -ora *adj (mayoría, superioridad)* overwhelming; *(victoria)* crushing; **sus productos dominan de forma abrumadora el mercado** their products completely dominate the market

abrumar *vt (agobiar)* to overwhelm; **lo abruma tanta responsabilidad** he is overwhelmed by all the responsibility; **tantas atenciones la abruman** she finds all that attentiveness overwhelming; **me abruma estar entre mucha gente** I find being in large crowds oppressive

abruptamente *adv* abruptly

abrupto, -a *adj* (**a**) *(escarpado)* sheer; *(accidentado)* rugged (**b**) *(brusco)* abrupt, sudden

ABS *nm (abrev de* **anti-lock braking system***)* ABS; **frenos A.** anti-lock brakes

absceso *nm Med* abscess

abscisa *nf Mat* x-axis

absenta *nf (bebida)* absinthe

absentismo *nm Esp* **(a)** *(de terrateniente)* absentee landownership **(b)** *(de trabajador, alumno)* ***a. escolar*** truancy; ***a. laboral*** *(justificado)* absence from work; *(injustificado)* absenteeism

absentista *Esp* 1 *adj* absentee
2 *nmf* absentee

ábside *nm* apse

absolución *nf* **(a)** *Der* acquittal **(b)** *Rel* absolution; **dar la a. a alguien** to give sb absolution

absolutamente *adv (completamente)* absolutely, completely; **es a. imprescindible acabar antes del viernes** it is absolutely essential to finish before Friday; **no me costó a. nada** it didn't cost me anything at all; **eso es a. falso** that's completely untrue

absolutismo *nm* absolutism

absolutista 1 *adj* absolutist
2 *nmf* absolutist

absoluto, -a 1 *adj* **(a)** *(no relativo)* absolute
(b) *(completo) (verdad, mayoría)* absolute; *(silencio)* total, absolute; *(reposo)* complete; **tengo una confianza absoluta en ellos** I have complete *o* every confidence in them; **es el campeón a. de este torneo** he's the overall winner of the tournament; **es un a. sinvergüenza** he's completely shameless
(c) *(monarca)* absolute
(d) *Ling (ablativo, superlativo)* absolute; **ablativo a.** ablative absolute
(e) *Filosofía* **lo a.** the absolute
2 **en absoluto** *loc adv* **nada en a.** nothing at all; **no me gustó en a.** I didn't like it at all; **¿te importa? – en a.** do you mind? – not at all

absolutorio, -a *adj* absolutory, absolving

absolver [41] *vt* **(a)** *Der* to acquit; **lo absolvieron de los cargos** he was acquitted of the charges **(b)** *Rel* **lo absolvió (de sus pecados)** he absolved him of his sins

absorbencia *nf* absorbency; **una tela de gran a.** a very absorbent cloth

absorbente 1 *adj* **(a)** *(esponja, material)* absorbent **(b)** *(persona, carácter)* demanding **(c)** *(actividad)* absorbing
2 *nm* absorbent

absorber *vt* **(a)** *(líquido, gas, calor)* to absorb; **esta aspiradora no absorbe el polvo muy bien** this vacuum doesn't pick up dust very well; **absorbió el refresco con la pajita** he sucked the soft drink through a straw; **esta crema se absorbe muy bien** this cream works into the skin very well
(b) *(consumir)* to take up, to soak up; **esta tarea absorbe mucho tiempo** this task takes up a lot of time
(c) *(atraer, dominar)* **este trabajo me absorbe mucho** this job takes up a lot of my time; **su mujer lo absorbe mucho** his wife is very demanding; **la televisión los absorbe** television dominates their lives
(d) *(empresa)* to take over; **Roma Inc. absorbió a su mayor competidor** Roma Inc. took over its biggest rival

absorbible *adj* absorbable

absorción *nf* **(a)** *(de líquido, gas, calor)* absorption; **con gran poder de a.** highly absorbent **(b)** *(de empresa)* takeover

absorto, -a *adj* absorbed **(en** in**)**; **se quedó a. en la contemplación de las llamas** he was absorbed in his contemplation of the flames

abstemio, -a 1 *adj* teetotal
2 *nm,f* teetotaller

abstención *nf* abstention; **hubo mucha a.** *(en elecciones)* there was a low turnout; **se espera un nivel de a. del 30 por ciento** 30 percent of the electorate are expected not to vote

abstencionismo *nm* abstentionism

abstencionista 1 *adj* abstentionist
2 *nmf* abstentionist

abstenerse [67] *vpr* **(a)** *(guardarse)* to abstain **(de** from**)**; **se abstuvo de mencionar su embarazo** she refrained from mentioning her pregnancy; **nos abstuvimos de beber** we didn't touch a drop; **el médico le recomendó que se abstuviera de fumar** the doctor advised her to refrain from smoking **(b)** *(en votación)* to abstain; **me abstuve en las últimas elecciones** I didn't vote in the last election

abstinencia *nf* abstinence

abstracción *nf* abstraction; **la capacidad de a.** the capacity for abstract thought; **el concepto de número es una a.** number is an abstract concept

abstraccionismo *nm* abstractionism

abstracto, -a 1 *adj* abstract
2 **en abstracto** *loc adv* in the abstract

abstraer [68] 1 *vt* to consider separately, to detach
2 **abstraerse** *vpr* to detach oneself **(de** from**)**

abstraídamente *adv* **miraba el paisaje a.** he gazed at the landscape, lost in thought

abstraído, -a *adj* lost in thought; **estaba a. en la lectura** he was engrossed in his reading

abstruso, -a *adj* abstruse

abstuviera *etc ver* **abstenerse**

absuelto, -a *participio ver* **absolver**

absuelvo *etc ver* **absolver**

absurdo, -a 1 *adj* absurd; **lo a. sería que no lo hicieras** it would be absurd for you not to do it
2 *nm* **decir/hacer un a.** to say/do something ridiculous *o* idiotic; **reducción al a.** reductio ad absurdum; **el teatro del a.** the Theatre of the Absurd

abubilla *nf* hoopoe

abuchear *vt* to boo

abucheo *nm* booing; **recibió un a. del público** she was booed by the audience

Abu Dabi, Abu Dhabi *n* Abu Dhabi

abuelito, -a *nm,f Fam* grandpa, *f* grandma

abuelo, -a *nm,f* **(a)** *(familiar)* grandfather, *f* grandmother; **abuelos** grandparents; EXPR *Fam* **¡cuéntaselo a tu abuela!** pull the other one!; EXPR *Fam* **éramos pocos y parió la abuela** that was all we needed; EXPR *Fam* **no necesitar abuela** to be full of oneself ▸▸ ***a. materno*** maternal grandfather; ***a. paterno*** paternal grandfather
(b) *(anciano) (hombre)* old man, old person; *(mujer)* old woman, old person; **tenga, a., siéntese aquí** here, have this seat

abuhardillado, -a *adj* **habitación abuhardillada** attic room

Abuja *n* Abuja

abulense 1 *adj* of/from Avila *(Spain)*
2 *nmf* person from Avila *(Spain)*

abulia *nf* apathy, lethargy; **hacer algo con a.** to do sth apathetically *o* lethargically

abúlico, -a 1 *adj* apathetic, lethargic
2 *nm,f* apathetic *o* lethargic person

abulón *nm* abalone

abultado, -a *adj* **(a)** *(paquete)* bulky; *(labios)* thick; *(frente)* prominent; **estómago a.** potbelly **(b)** *(beneficios, factura)* sizeable; **ganaron por una abultada mayoría** they won by a large majority; **sufrieron una abultada derrota** they suffered a heavy defeat

abultamiento *nm (bulto)* bulkiness

abultar 1 *vt* **(a)** *(mejillas)* to puff out **(b)** *(cifras, consecuencias)* to exaggerate
2 *vi* **(a)** *(ocupar mucho espacio)* to be bulky; **el equipaje abulta mucho** the luggage takes up a lot of room **(b)** *(formar un bulto)* to bulge; **la pistola le abulta debajo de la americana** you can see the bulge of his gun under his jacket

abundamiento *nm Formal* **la situación era difícil y, a mayor a., los nervios estaban a flor de piel** it was a difficult situation and, what is more, people's nerves were on edge; **a mayor a., presenté las cifras** I provided the figures for further clarification

abundancia *nf* **(a)** *(gran cantidad)* abundance; **la región posee petróleo en a.** the region is rich in oil; **teníamos comida en a.** we had plenty of food; **un área de gran a. biológica** an area rich in animal and plant life **(b)** *(riqueza)* plenty, prosperity; **una época de a.** a time of plenty; EXPR **nadar** *o* **vivir en la a.** to be filthy rich

abundante *adj* abundant; **teníamos comida a.** we had plenty of food; **una zona a. en petróleo** an area that is rich in oil; **luce una a. cabellera** she has a fine head of hair; **habrá nubosidad a. en el norte del país** there will be heavy cloud in the north

abundantemente *adv* abundantly; **comimos a.** we ate our fill

abundar *vi* **(a)** *(ser abundante)* to abound; **aquí abundan los camaleones** there are lots of chameleons here; **este año abundan las naranjas** the oranges have done very well this year
(b) a. en *(tener en abundancia)* to be rich in; **la región abunda en recursos naturales** the region is rich in natural resources
(c) a. en *(insistir)* to insist on; **en su discurso abundó en la**

necesidad de recortar gastos in her speech she insisted on the need to cut costs

(**d**) **a. en** *(estar de acuerdo con)* to agree completely with; **abundo en vuestra opinión** I entirely agree with you

abundoso, -a *adj Andes, CAm, Carib, Méx* abundant

aburguesado, -a *adj* bourgeois

aburguesamiento *nm* bourgeoisification

aburguesarse *vpr* to adopt middle-class ways; **se han aburguesado mucho desde que se casaron** they've become very bourgeois *o* middle-class since they married

aburrición *nf Col, Méx* boredom; **hasta la a.** to the point of boredom; **¡qué a.!, ¡vámonos!** this is so boring!, let's leave!; **¡qué a. de película!** what a boring film!

aburrido, -a 1 *adj* (**a**) *(harto, fastidiado)* bored; **estar a. de hacer algo** to be fed up with doing sth; **estoy a. de esperar** I'm fed up with *o* tired of waiting; **me tiene muy a. con sus constantes protestas** I'm fed up with her constant complaining; EXPR *Fam* **estar a. como una ostra** to be bored stiff

(**b**) *(que aburre)* boring; **este libro es muy a.** this book is very boring; **la fiesta está muy aburrida** it's a very boring party

2 *nm,f* bore; **¡eres un a.!** you're so boring!

aburridor, -ora *Am* **1** *adj* boring

2 *nm,f* bore; **¡es un a.!** he's so boring!

aburrimiento *nm* boredom; **hasta el a.** to the point of boredom; **¡qué a.!, ¡vámonos!** this is so boring!, let's leave!; **¡qué a. de película!** what a boring film!

aburrir 1 *vt* to bore; **este trabajo me aburre** this job is boring; **aburre a todo el mundo con sus batallitas** he bores everyone with his old stories; **me aburre tener que madrugar todos los días** it's really tiresome having to get up early every day

2 aburrirse *vpr* to get bored; **cuando no tengo nada que hacer me aburro** I get bored when I haven't got anything to do; **se aburrieron muchísimo en la fiesta** they were really bored at the party; EXPR *Fam* **aburrirse como una ostra** to be bored stiff

abusado, -a *Méx Fam* **1** *adj* smart, sharp; **esos niños son bien abusados, saben cómo sacarle dinero a sus padres** those kids are really smart, they know how to get money out of their parents; **si no te pones a. te quedarás sin comer** if you don't watch out there won't be anything left for you to eat

2 *interj* look out!; **¡abusada, fíjate en el tráfico antes de cruzar!** look out! watch what the traffic is doing before you start crossing the road!; **a. con el excusado, ¡no es basurero!** *(en letrero)* be careful how you use the toilet – it's not a *Br* dustbin *o US* trashcan!

abusar *vi* (**a**) *(excederse)* to go too far; **a. de algo** to abuse sth; **a. del alcohol** to drink to excess; **no le conviene a. de la bebida** he shouldn't drink too much; **puedes comer dulces, pero sin a.** you can eat sweets, but don't overdo it

(**b**) *(aprovecharse)* **a. de alguien** to take advantage of sb; **abusan de su generosidad** they take advantage of *o* abuse her generosity

(**c**) **a. (sexualmente) de alguien** *(forzar)* to sexually abuse sb

abusivamente *adv* improperly

abusivo, -a *adj* (**a**) *(trato)* **recibimos un trato a.** we were treated like dirt; **la policía infligió tratos abusivos a los detenidos** the police mistreated the detainees (**b**) *(precio)* extortionate

abuso *nm* (**a**) *(uso excesivo)* abuse (**de** of) ▸▸ ***a. de autoridad*** abuse of authority; ***a. de confianza*** breach of confidence; *Der* ***abusos deshonestos*** indecent assault; ***a. de poder*** abuse of power; *Com* ***a. de posición dominante*** abuse of a position of dominance; ***abusos sexuales*** sexual abuse (**b**) *(atropello)* scandal, outrage; **¡esto es un a.!** this is outrageous!

abusador, -ora *Am* **1** *adj* selfish; **no seas a., ya te presté plata ayer** don't push your luck, I already lent you some money yesterday

2 *nm,f* (**a**) *(caradura)* selfish person (**b**) *(matón)* bully

abusón, -ona *Esp Fam* **1** *adj* (**a**) *(caradura)* selfish; **no seas a., que los demás no han comido** don't be selfish *o* greedy, the others haven't eaten yet (**b**) *(matón)* bullying

2 *nm,f* (**a**) *(caradura)* selfish person (**b**) *(matón)* bully

abyección *nf Formal (bajeza)* vileness; **¿cómo se puede cometer una a. así?** how could anybody do something so vile?

abyecto, -a *adj Formal (despreciable)* vile; **un crimen a.** a heinous crime

a. C. *(abrev de* **antes de Cristo**) BC

A.C.A. ['aka] *nm (abrev de* **Automóvil Club Argentino**) = Argentinian automobile association, *Br* ≃ AA, RAC, *US* ≃ AAA

acá *adv* (**a**) *(lugar)* here; **de a. para allá** back and forth; **más a.** closer; **¡ven a.!** come (over) here!; **entra por a.** come in this way; **acércate un poco para a.** come a bit closer (**b**) *(tiempo)* **de una semana a.** during the last week; **de un tiempo a.** recently; **del año pasado a. han pasado muchas cosas** a lot has happened since last year

acabado, -a 1 *adj* (**a**) *(terminado)* finished (**b**) *(completo)* perfect, consummate (**c**) *(fracasado)* finished, ruined; **como ciclista está a.** he's finished as a cyclist, his career as a cyclist is over

2 *nm* (**a**) *(de producto)* finish ▸▸ ***a. mate*** matt finish; ***a. satinado*** satin finish (**b**) *(de piso)* décor

acabamiento *nm Ven* exhaustion

ACABAR 1 *vt (terminar)* to finish; **hemos acabado el trabajo** we've finished the work; **todavía no ha acabado el primer plato** he still hasn't finished his first course; **acabamos el viaje en Canadá** our journey ended in Canada; **la bufanda está sin a.** the scarf hasn't been finished yet; EXPR *RP Fam* **¡acabala!** that's enough!

2 *vi* (**a**) *(terminar)* to finish, to end; **el cuchillo acaba en punta** the knife ends in a point; **el asunto acabó mal** *o* **de mala manera** the affair finished *o* ended badly; **detesto las películas que acaban bien** I hate films that have a happy ending; **acabó sus días en el exilio** he ended his days in exile; **ése acabará en la cárcel** he'll end up in jail; **cuando acabes, avísame** tell me when you've finished; **a. de hacer algo** to finish doing sth; **a. de trabajar/comer** to finish working/eating; **a. con algo** to finish with sth; **¿has acabado con el martillo?** have *o* are you finished with the hammer?; **a. por hacer algo, a. haciendo algo** to end up doing sth; **acabarán por llamar** *o* **llamando** they'll call eventually *o* sooner or later; **para a. de arreglarlo** to cap it all; *Fam* **¡acabáramos!** so that's what it was!

(**b**) *(haber hecho recientemente)* **a. de hacer algo** to have just done sth; **acabo de llegar** I've just arrived

(**c**) **a. con** *(destruir) (enemigo)* to destroy; *(salud)* to ruin; *(violencia, crimen)* to put an end to; **a. con la paciencia de alguien** to exhaust sb's patience; **está acabando con mi paciencia** she's trying my patience; **acabaron con todas las provisiones** they used up all the provisions; **la droga acabó con él** drugs killed him; **¡ese niño va a a. conmigo!** that boy will be the death of me!

(**d**) *(volverse)* to end up; **a. loco** to end up (going) mad

(**e**) *(en construcciones con infinitivo)* **no acabo de entenderlo** I can't quite understand it; **no acaba de parecerme bien** I don't really think it's a very good idea; **no acaba de gustarme del todo** I just don't really like it; **el plan no me acaba de convencer** I'm not totally convinced by the plan

(**f**) *RP, Ven Fam (tener un orgasmo)* to come

(**g**) EXPR **de nunca a.** never-ending; **este proyecto es el cuento de nunca a.** this project just seems to go on and on

3 acabarse *vpr* (**a**) *(agotarse)* to be used up, to be gone; **se nos ha acabado la gasolina** we're out of petrol; **se ha acabado la comida** there's no more food left; **se ha acabado la leche** the milk has run out, we've run out of milk; **no corras tanto, se te acabarán las fuerzas** don't run so fast, you'll run out of energy

(**b**) *(terminar) (guerra, película)* to finish, to be over

(**c**) *(consumir) (comida)* to eat up; **¡acábatelo todo y no dejes ni una miga!** make sure you eat it all up!

(**d**) *RP, Ven Fam (tener un orgasmo)* to come

(**e**) EXPR **¡se acabó!** *(¡basta ya!)* that's enough!; *(se terminó)* that's it, then!; **¡te quedarás en casa y (san) se acabó!** you'll stay at home and that's that *o* that's the end of it!; **se acabó lo que se daba** that is/was the end of that; *Méx Fam* **no acabársela: no me la acabo con la cantidad de trabajo que hay** I can't deal with the amount of work we've got

acabóse *nm* **¡es el a.!** it really is the limit!

acachado, -a *adj Chile Fam* **estoy acachada de trabajo** I'm up to my eyes in work

acacia *nf* acacia ▸▸ ***a. espinosa*** mimosa thorn

academia *nf* (**a**) *(colegio)* school, academy ▸▸ ***a. de baile*** dance school; *RP* ***a. de choferes*** driving school; ***a. de idiomas*** language school; ***a. de informática*** = private institution offering courses in computing; **voy a una a. de informática** I'm doing a computer course; ***a. militar*** military academy (**b**) *(sociedad)* academy; **la A. de las Ciencias** the Academy of Science (**c**) *RP (universidad)* **la a.** university, academia

académicamente *adv* academically

academicismo *nm* academicism

académico, -a 1 *adj* (**a**) *(año, título)* academic (**b**) *(estilo)* academic (**c**) *(de la Academia)* of/from the Academy; **el diccionario a.** the Academy dictionary
2 *nm,f* academician ►► ***a. de número*** full academy member

acadio, -a 1 *adj* Akkadian
2 *nm,f (persona)* Akkadian
3 *nm (lengua)* Akkadian

acaecer [46] *vi Formal* to take place, to occur; **sucesos acaecidos años atrás** events which took place years ago; **el terremoto acaeció de madrugada** the earthquake occurred early in the morning

acahualillo *nm* Mexican tea, goosefoot

acalambrante *adj RP Fam* **hace un frío a.** it's freezing cold; **son de una ignorancia a.** they're unbelievably ignorant; **los precios ahí son acalambrantes** the prices there would make your hair stand on end

acalambrarse *vpr* to get cramp

acallar *vt (protestas, críticas, armas)* to silence; *(rumores)* to put an end to; *(miedos)* to calm; **una propuesta para a. a los rebeldes en el partido** a proposal designed to silence the party rebels

acaloradamente *adv (debatir)* heatedly; *(defender)* passionately, fervently

acalorado, -a *adj* (**a**) *(por calor)* hot (**b**) *(por esfuerzo)* flushed (with effort) (**c**) *(apasionado) (debate)* heated; *(persona)* hot under the collar; *(defensor)* fervent

acaloramiento *nm* (**a**) *(calor)* heat (**b**) *(pasión)* passion, ardour; **discutieron con a.** they argued heatedly

acalorar 1 *vt* (**a**) *(dar calor)* to (make) warm (**b**) **a. a alguien** *(excitar)* to make sb hot under the collar
2 **acalorarse** *vpr* (**a**) *(coger calor)* to get hot (**b**) *(excitarse)* to get hot under the collar

acampada *nf (acción)* camping; **ir/estar de a.** to go/be camping; **(zona de) a. libre** *(en letrero)* free campsite

acampanado, -a *adj (pantalones)* flared

acampar *vi* to camp; **prohibido a.** *(en letrero)* no camping

ácana *nm o nf* = hard, reddish Cuban wood

Takes the masculine articles **el** and **un**.

acanalado, -a *adj* (**a**) *(columna)* fluted (**b**) *(tejido)* ribbed (**c**) *(hierro)* corrugated

acanaladura *nf (en columna)* groove, fluting

acanalar *vt* (**a**) *(terreno)* to dig channels in (**b**) *(plancha)* to corrugate

acantilado *nm* cliff

acanto *nm* acanthus

acantonamiento *nm Mil* (**a**) *(acción)* billeting (**b**) *(lugar)* billet

acantonar *Mil* 1 *vt* to billet
2 **acantonarse** *vpr* to be billeted

acantopterigio, -a *adj Zool* acanthopterygian

acaparador, -ora 1 *adj* greedy
2 *nm,f* hoarder

acaparamiento *nm* (**a**) *(monopolio)* monopolization (**b**) *(en tiempo de escasez)* hoarding

acaparar *vt* (**a**) *(monopolizar)* to monopolize; *(mercado)* to corner; **acaparaba las miradas de todos** all eyes were upon her; **los atletas alemanes acapararon las medallas** the German athletes swept the board; **una vez más las elecciones acapararon el interés de la prensa** once more the newspapers were dominated by the elections (**b**) *(aprovisionarse de)* to hoard

acápite *nm* (**a**) *Am (párrafo)* paragraph (**b**) *CAm (título)* title

acapulquense *adj, nmf* = **acapulqueño**

acapulqueño, -a, 1 *adj* of/from Acapulco *(Mexico)*
2 *nm,f* person from Acapulco *(Mexico)*

acaramelado, -a *adj* (**a**) *Fam (pareja)* lovey-dovey; **los vi muy acaramelados en un banco del parque** I saw them being all lovey-dovey on one of the park benches (**b**) *Fam (afectado)* sugary (sweet) (**c**) *(con caramelo)* covered in caramel

acaramelar 1 *vt* to cover in caramel
2 **acaramelarse** *vpr Fam* to go *o* get (all) lovey-dovey

acariciador, -ora *adj* caressing

acariciar 1 *vt* (**a**) *(persona)* to caress; *(animal, pelo, piel)* to stroke; **la brisa acariciaba su piel** the breeze caressed her skin (**b**) *(idea, proyecto)* to cherish
2 **acariciarse** *vpr (mutuamente)* to caress (each other); **se acarició el pelo** she stroked her hair

ácaro *nm* mite

acarraladura *nf Perú (en la media)* run, *Br* ladder

acarreador *nm Chile (cargador)* porter

acarrear 1 *vt* (**a**) *(ocasionar)* to give rise to; **el abuso del medicamento acarrea problemas musculares** if this medicine is not used in the correct dosage it can give rise to muscular problems; **los hijos acarrean muchos gastos** bringing up children involves a lot of expense; **el cambio de ciudad le acarreó muchos problemas** moving to another city created a lot of problems for her; **un delito que puede a. penas de cárcel** a crime which can carry a prison sentence
(**b**) *(transportar)* to carry; *(carbón)* to haul
2 **acarrearse** *vpr Chile Fam* **acarrearse con algo** to run off with sth

acarreo *nm* (**a**) *(transporte)* transporting; **animales de a.** beasts of burden, draught animals (**b**) *Informát* carry

acarroñarse *vpr Col Fam (acobardarse)* to chicken out

acartonado, -a *adj* (**a**) *(piel)* wizened; **tengo la piel acartonada** my skin feels dry (**b**) *(tela)* stiff (**c**) *(estilo, personaje)* wooden (**d**) *Am (persona)* stiff

acartonar 1 *vt* (**a**) *(piel)* **los años le han acartonado la piel** the years have left her skin wizened (**b**) *(tela)* to make stiff
2 **acartonarse** *vpr* to become wizened

acaso 1 *adv* (**a**) *(quizá)* perhaps; **es a. su mejor película** it is perhaps his best film (**b**) *(en preguntas)* **¿a. no lo sabías?** are you trying to tell me you didn't know?; **¿no estoy haciendo a. lo que me pediste?** am I not doing what you asked me to?
2 **si acaso** *loc adv* **¿te traigo algo? – si a., una botella de vino** can I get you anything? – you could get me a bottle of wine, if you like; **no creo que vengan muchos, si a. algún amigo** I don't think many people will come, one or two friends, perhaps *o* maybe; **si a. lo vieras, dile que me llame** if you should see him, ask him to phone me
3 **por si acaso** *loc adv* just in case; **llévatelo por si a.** take it just in case; **por si a. no te veo mañana, toma la llave ahora** (just) in case I don't see you tomorrow, take the key now

acatamiento *nm* compliance (**de** with)

acatar *vt* (**a**) *(normas)* to respect, to comply with; *(órdenes)* to obey; **se negó a a. el fallo del tribunal** she refused to comply with *o* observe the court's decision; **a. la Constitución** to abide by the Constitution (**b**) *CAm (oír)* to hear

acatarrado, -a *adj* **estar a.** to have a cold

acatarrarse *vpr* to catch a cold

acaudalado, -a *adj* well-to-do, wealthy

acaudalar *vt* to accumulate, to amass

acaudillamiento *nm* leadership, command

acaudillar *vt (ejército, revuelta)* to lead

ACB *nf* (*abrev de* **Asociación de Clubes de Baloncesto**) = Spanish basketball association; **la Liga A.** = Spanish basketball premier league

acceder *vi* (**a**) *(consentir)* to agree; **a. a una petición** to grant a request; **accedió a venir** she agreed to come; **accedieron a las demandas de los secuestradores** they agreed to *o* acceded to the kidnappers' demands
(**b**) *(tener acceso)* **a. a algo** to enter sth, to gain entry to sth; *Informát* **a. a una base de datos** to access a database; **se puede a. directamente a la sala por la puerta trasera** there is direct access to the hall by the rear entrance; **por esa puerta se accede a la cripta** that door leads to the crypt; **desde la biblioteca se puede a. a Internet** you can log on to the Internet at the library; **las sillas de ruedas accederán por una rampa** there is wheelchair access via a ramp
(**c**) *(alcanzar)* **a. al trono** to accede to the throne; **a. al poder** to come to power; **accedió al cargo de presidente** he became president; **este título permite a. a los estudios de posgrado** this qualification enables you to go on to do postgraduate studies

accesibilidad *nf* accessibility; **mejorar la a. de los discapacitados a edificios públicos** to improve disabled access to public buildings

accesible *adj* (**a**) *(lugar)* accessible (**b**) *(persona)* approachable (**c**) *(texto, explicación)* accessible (**d**) *(precio)* affordable; **una oferta a. a los pequeños inversores** an offer which is affordable for small investors

accésit *nm inv* second prize *(in literary, artistic or scientific competition)*

acceso *nm* (**a**) *(entrada)* entrance (**a** to); **la policía vigila todos los accesos a la capital** the police are watching all the approaches to the capital
(**b**) *(paso)* access (**a** to); **un edificio con a. para sillas de ruedas** a building with wheelchair access; **esta escalera da a. a los pisos superiores** this staircase gives access to the upper floors; **tener a. a algo** to have access to sth; **tiene a. a información confidencial** she has access to confidential information; **quieren facilitar el a. de los**

jóvenes a la vivienda they want to make it easier for young people to find a place of their own (to live)
(**c**) *(a persona)* access; **es un profesor de fácil a.** he's a very accessible teacher
(**d**) *(ataque)* fit; *(de fiebre, gripe)* bout; **un a. de celos/de locura** a fit of jealousy/madness
(**e**) *Formal* ***a. carnal*** *(acto sexual)* sexual act
(**f**) *Informát* access; *(a página Web)* hit; **a. a Internet** Internet access ▸▸ ***a. aleatorio*** random access; ***a. directo*** direct access; ***a. remoto*** remote access; ***a. secuencial*** sequential access

accesorio, -a 1 *adj* incidental, of secondary importance
2 *nm (utensilio)* accessory
3 **accesorios** *nmpl (de moda, automóvil)* accessories

accidentado, -a 1 *adj* (**a**) *(vida)* turbulent; *(viaje, fiesta)* eventful (**b**) *(terreno, camino)* rough, rugged (**c**) *(vehículo)* **el avión a.** the plane involved in the crash
2 *nm,f* injured person; **los accidentados** the people injured in the accident

accidental[1] *adj* (**a**) *(circunstancial)* accidental; **tuvo una caída a.** she accidentally fell (**b**) *(no esencial)* incidental, of secondary importance (**c**) *(imprevisto)* chance, unforeseen

accidental[2] *nm Mús* accidental

accidentalmente *adv* accidentally, by accident

accidentarse *vpr* to be involved in *o* have an accident

accidente *nm* (**a**) *(suceso)* accident; **tener** *o* **sufrir un a.** to have an accident ▸▸ ***a. aéreo*** plane crash; ***a. de automóvil*** car crash; ***a. automovilístico*** car crash; ***a. de aviación*** plane crash; ***a. de avión*** plane crash; ***a. de carretera*** road *o* traffic accident; ***a. de circulación*** road *o* traffic accident; ***a. de coche*** car crash; ***a. ferroviario*** railway accident; ***a. laboral*** industrial accident; ***a. mortal*** fatal accident; ***a. nuclear*** nuclear accident; ***a. de trabajo*** industrial accident; ***a. de tráfico*** road *o* traffic accident
(**b**) **por a.** *(por casualidad)* by accident, accidentally; **es músico por a.** he became a musician by accident
(**c**) *(irregularidad)* **los accidentes del terreno** the unevenness of the terrain ▸▸ ***a. geográfico*** geographical feature
(**d**) *Gram* accidence
(**e**) *Mús* accidental

acción 1 *nf* (**a**) *(efecto de hacer)* action; **en a.** in action, in operation; **entrar** *o* **ponerse en a.** *(persona)* to go into action; **pasar a la a.** to take action; **puso la maquinaria en a.** she switched on the machinery; **películas de a.** action movies *o Br* films; **un hombre de a.** a man of action ▸▸ *Pol* ***a. directa*** direct action
(**b**) *(hecho)* deed, act; **una buena a.** a good deed ▸▸ *Rel* ***a. de gracias*** thanksgiving
(**c**) *(influencia)* effect, action; **la a. de la luz sobre los organismos marinos** the effect of sunlight on marine organisms; **rocas erosionadas por la a. del viento** rocks eroded by the wind ▸▸ ***a. detergente*** detergent effect; ***a. y reacción*** action and reaction
(**d**) *(combate)* action
(**e**) *(de relato, película)* action; **la a. tiene lugar en Venezuela** the action takes place in Venezuela
(**f**) *Fin* share; **acciones** *esp Br* shares, *esp US* stock ▸▸ ***acciones en cartera*** *Br* shares *o US* stock in portfolio; ***acciones liberadas*** paid-up *Br* shares *o US* stock; ***acciones ordinarias*** *Br* ordinary shares, *US* common stock; ***a. de oro*** golden share; ***a. al portador*** bearer share; ***acciones preferentes*** *Br* preference shares, *US* preferred stock; ***acciones de renta fija*** *Br* fixed-interest shares, *US* fixed-income stock
(**g**) *Der* ***a. civil*** civil action; ***a. legal*** lawsuit; **iniciar acciones legales contra alguien** to take legal action against sb; ***a. popular*** action brought by the People
2 *interj* action!; **¡luces!, ¡cámaras!, ¡a.!** lights!, camera!, action!

accionable *adj* **a. por control remoto** remote-controlled

accionamiento *nm* activation

accionar 1 *vt* (**a**) *(mecanismo, palanca)* to activate (**b**) *Am Der* to bring a suit against
2 *vi (gesticular)* to gesture, to gesticulate

accionariado *nm Fin Br* shareholders, *US* stockholders

accionarial, *Am* **accionario, -a** *adj Fin esp Br* share, *esp US* stock; **paquete** *o* **participación a.** *Br* shareholding *o US* stockholding

accionista *nmf Fin Br* shareholder, *US* stockholder; **a. mayoritario/minoritario** majority/minority *Br* shareholder *o US* stockholder

Accra *n* Accra

ace[1] [eis] *nm (en tenis)* ace

ace[2] *nm Perú* washing powder

acebo *nm (árbol)* holly bush *o* tree; **hojas de a.** holly

acebuche *nm* wild olive tree

acechanza *nf* observation, surveillance

acechar *vt* to watch, to spy on; **el cazador acechaba a su presa** the hunter was stalking his prey

acecho *nm* observation, surveillance; **estar al a. de** to lie in wait for; *Fig* to be on the lookout for

acecinar *vt* to cure

acedarse *vpr Méx Fam* to go off

acedera *nf* sorrel

acedía *nf* (**a**) *(pez)* little sole (**b**) *Med* heartburn

acéfalo, -a *adj* (**a**) *(sin cabeza)* headless (**b**) *(estado, organización)* leaderless

aceitada *nf* (**a**) *Am (lubricación)* **hay que darle una a. a esas bisagras** those hinges need oiling (**b**) *Chile Fam (soborno)* **dar una a. a alguien** to grease sb's palm

aceitar *vt* (**a**) *(motor)* to lubricate (**b**) *(comida)* to pour oil onto (**c**) *Chile Fam (sobornar)* **a. a alguien** to grease sb's palm

aceite *nm (para cocinar, lubricar)* oil; **este coche pierde a.** this car is leaking oil ▸▸ ***a. de ballena*** whale oil; ***a. de cacahuete*** peanut oil; ***a. de coco*** coconut oil; ***a. de colza*** rapeseed oil; ***a. esencial*** essential oil; ***a. de girasol*** sunflower oil; ***a. de hígado de bacalao*** cod-liver oil; ***a. de linaza*** linseed oil; *Am* ***a. de lino*** linseed oil; ***a. lubricante*** lubricating oil; ***a. de maíz*** corn oil; ***a. de oliva*** olive oil; ***a. de oliva virgen*** virgin olive oil; ***a. de oliva virgen extra*** extra virgin olive oil; ***a. de palma*** palm oil; ***a. de parafina*** paraffin oil; ***a. de ricino*** castor oil; ***a. de sésamo*** sesame oil; ***a. de soja*** soybean oil; ***a. para el sol*** suntan oil; ***a. vegetal*** vegetable oil

aceitera *nf* (**a**) *(para llevar aceite)* oil bottle *o* can *(for salad oil)* (**b**) **aceiteras** *(para servir aceite)* cruet set *(for oil and vinegar)* (**c**) *(empresa)* cooking oil company

aceitero, -a 1 *adj* cooking oil; **el sector a.** the cooking oil-producing industry; **una región aceitera** a cooking oil-producing region; **las exportaciones aceiteras** cooking oil exports
2 *nm (ave)* oilbird

aceitoso, -a *adj* oily

aceituna *nf* olive ▸▸ ***a. gordal*** queen olive, = type of large olive often used for marinating; ***a. negra*** black olive; ***a. rellena*** stuffed olive; ***a. verde*** green olive

aceitunado, -a *adj* olive; **piel aceitunada** olive skin

aceitunero, -a *nm,f* (**a**) *(recogedor)* olive picker (**b**) *(vendedor)* olive merchant

aceituno *nm* (**a**) *(árbol)* olive tree (**b**) *Esp Fam (Guardia Civil)* = informal name for member of the Guardia Civil

aceleración *nf* acceleration ▸▸ *Fís* ***a. centrípeta*** centripetal acceleration; *Fís* ***a. lineal*** linear acceleration

acelerada *nf Am (acelerón)* acceleration, burst of speed

aceleradamente *adv* at top speed

acelerado, -a *adj* (**a**) *(rápido)* rapid, quick (**b**) *Fís* accelerated (**c**) *Fam* **estar a.** *(persona)* to be hyper (**d**) *Aut* **el motor está a.** the engine is racing

acelerador, -ora 1 *adj* accelerating
2 *nm* (**a**) *(de automóvil)* accelerator; **pisar el a.** to step on the accelerator; *Fig* to step on it ▸▸ *Fís* ***a. lineal*** linear accelerator; *Fís* ***a. de partículas*** particle accelerator (**b**) *Informát* accelerator ▸▸ ***a. gráfico*** graphic accelerator; ***a. de vídeo*** video accelerator

aceleramiento *nm* acceleration, speeding up

acelerar 1 *vt* (**a**) *(proceso)* to speed up (**b**) *(vehículo)* to accelerate; *(motor)* to gun; **tendremos que a. la marcha si no queremos llegar tarde** we'll have to step up the pace if we don't want to be late (**c**) *Fam (persona)* to get hyper
2 *vi* (**a**) *(conductor)* to accelerate (**b**) *(darse prisa)* to hurry (up); **acelera, que llegamos tarde** hurry up, we're late!
3 **acelerarse** *vpr* (**a**) *(proceso)* to speed up (**b**) *(motor)* to accelerate (**c**) *Fam (persona)* to get hyper

acelerón *nm (de corredor, coche)* burst of speed; **no des tantos acelerones** stop accelerating suddenly like that; **el a. de la demanda ha hecho subir los precios** the sudden surge in demand has forced prices up

acelga *nf* chard

acendrado, -a *adj Formal* untarnished, pure

acendrar *vt Formal (cualidad, sentimiento)* to refine

acento *nm* (**a**) *(entonación)* accent; **tener a. andaluz** to have an Andalusian accent; **habla con a. colombiano** she speaks with a Colombian accent
(**b**) *(ortográfico)* accent; **mármol lleva a. en la a** "mármol" has an accent on the "a" ▸▸ ***a. agudo*** acute accent; ***a. circunflejo*** circumflex accent; ***a. grave*** grave accent; ***a. ortográfico*** written accent; ***a. primario*** primary stress; ***a. prosódico*** prosodic stress
(**c**) *(énfasis)* emphasis; **poner el a. en algo** to emphasize sth, to put the emphasis on sth

acentor *nm* dunnock ▸▸ ***a. alpino*** alpine accentor

acentuable *adj Gram* that should have an accent; **las mayúsculas son acentuables** capital letters should be accented *o* should have an accent

acentuación *nf* (**a**) *(de palabra, sílaba)* accentuation (**b**) *(intensificación)* intensification; *(de problema)* worsening; **una a. de las actitudes racistas** a rise in racist attitudes

acentuadamente *adv (marcadamente)* markedly, distinctly

acentuado, -a *adj* (**a**) *(sílaba)* stressed; *(vocal) (con tilde)* accented (**b**) *(marcado)* marked, distinct

acentuar [4] **1** *vt* (**a**) *(palabra, letra) (al escribir)* to accent, to put an accent on; *(al hablar)* to stress (**b**) *(intensificar)* to accentuate; **la inflación acentuó la crisis** inflation made the recession even worse; **el maquillaje acentúa su belleza** the make-up enhances her beauty (**c**) *(recalcar)* to stress, to emphasize; **a. la necesidad de hacer algo** to emphasize the need to do sth
2 acentuarse *vpr* (**a**) *(intensificarse)* to deepen, to increase (**b**) *(llevar acento)* **las consonantes nunca se acentúan** consonants never have an accent

aceña *nf* (**a**) *(rueda)* waterwheel (**b**) *(molino)* watermill

acepción *nf (de palabra, frase)* meaning, sense

aceptabilidad *nf* (**a**) *(de propuesta, explicación, comportamiento)* acceptability (**b**) *Gram* acceptability

aceptable *adj* (**a**) *(propuesta, explicación, comportamiento)* acceptable (**b**) *Gram* acceptable

aceptablemente *adv* acceptably, tolerably (well)

aceptación *nf* (**a**) *(aprobación)* acceptance (**b**) *(éxito)* success, popularity; **tener gran a. (entre)** to be very popular (with *o* among) (**c**) *Com & Fin* acceptance

aceptar *vt* (**a**) *(regalo)* to accept (**b**) *(admitir)* to accept; **no aceptaron sus condiciones** they didn't accept her conditions; **¿aceptas a Enrique como tu legítimo esposo?** do you take Enrique to be your lawful wedded husband?; **no aceptará un "no" por respuesta** he won't take no for an answer; **no se aceptan cheques** *(en letrero)* we do not take cheques; **se aceptan donativos** *(en letrero)* donations welcome

aceptor *nm* (**a**) *Fís* acceptor (**b**) *Quím* acceptor

acequia *nf* irrigation channel *o* ditch

acera *nf* (**a**) *(para peatones) Br* pavement, *US* sidewalk; EXPR *Fam* **ser de la otra a., ser de la a. de enfrente** *(ser homosexual)* to be one of them, to be queer (**b**) *(lado de la calle)* side of the street; **el colegio está en la a. de los pares/de la derecha** the school is on the even-numbered/right-hand side of the street

acerado, -a *adj* (**a**) *(con acero)* containing steel (**b**) *(fuerte, resistente)* steely, tough (**c**) *(mordaz)* cutting, biting

acerar *vt* (**a**) *(poner aceras)* to pave (**b**) *(convertir en acero)* to turn into steel

acerbidad *nf Formal (mordacidad)* caustic *o* cutting nature

acerbo, -a *adj Formal* (**a**) *(áspero)* bitter (**b**) *(mordaz)* caustic, cutting

acerca: acerca de *loc prep* about

acercamiento *nm* (**a**) *(a un lugar)* **reclaman el a. de los presos a su región de origen** they are calling for the prisoners to be moved nearer to their home region (**b**) *(entre países)* rapprochement; **se produjo un a. entre sus posturas** their positions moved closer to each other

acercar [60] **1** *vt* (**a**) *(aproximar)* to bring nearer; **acerca la mesa a la pared** *(sin tocar la pared)* move the table closer to the wall; *(tocando la pared)* push *o* move the table up against the wall; **acércame el pan** could you pass me the bread?
(**b**) *(llevar)* **la acercó a la estación en moto** he gave her a *Br* lift *o US* ride to the station on his bike; **¿te importaría acercarme a mi casa?** would you mind giving me a *Br* lift *o US* ride home?; **te acercaré el cortacésped mañana** I'll bring you the lawnmower over tomorrow
(**c**) *(personas, posturas)* **la desgracia común los acercó** shared misfortune brought them together; **han acercado posturas tras dos semanas de negociaciones** after two weeks of negotiations the two sides are now closer to each other
2 acercarse *vpr* (**a**) *(en el espacio)* to come closer, to approach; **acércate más, que no te oigo** come closer, I can't hear you; **acércate un poco más a la ventana** move a bit closer to the window; **acércate a ver esto** come and have a look at this; **no te acerques al precipicio** don't go near the edge; **se me acercó una mujer para preguntarme la hora** a woman came up to me and asked me the time; *Fig* **se acercó a él en busca de protección** she turned to him for protection
(**b**) *(ir)* to go; *(venir)* to come; **se acercó a la tienda a por pan** she popped out to the shops for some bread; **acércate por aquí un día de estos** come over and see us some time
(**c**) *(en el tiempo) (fecha, estación, elecciones)* to draw nearer, to approach; **se acerca la Navidad** Christmas is coming; **nos acercamos al verano** it will soon be summer
(**d**) *(parecerse)* **acercarse a** to resemble; **su estilo se acerca más a la poesía que a la prosa** his style is closer to poetry than to prose
(**e**) *(en negociaciones) (países, bandos)* to come closer; **sus posturas se han acercado mucho en las últimas semanas** the differences between them have narrowed considerably over recent weeks

ácere *nm* maple

acería *nf* steelworks *(singular)*

acerico *nm* pincushion

acero *nm* (**a**) *(metal)* steel; **nervios de a.** nerves of steel ▸▸ ***a. al carbono*** carbon steel; ***a. galvanizado*** galvanized steel; ***a. inoxidable*** stainless steel (**b**) *(espada)* blade

acerola *nf* haw

acerolo *nm* hawthorn

acerque *etc ver* **acercar**

acérrimamente *adv* staunchly, fervently

acérrimo, -a *adj (defensor)* diehard, fervent; *(enemigo)* bitter

acertadamente *adv* (**a**) *(correctamente)* correctly (**b**) *(oportunamente, adecuadamente)* wisely, sensibly

acertado, -a *adj* (**a**) *(certero) (respuesta)* correct; *(disparo)* on target; *(comentario)* appropriate (**b**) *(oportuno)* good, clever; **estuvo muy a. en su elección** he made a very clever choice

acertante 1 *adj* winning
2 *nmf* winner; **sólo ha habido dos acertantes de seis** only two people got all six numbers right; **los máximos acertantes** *(de lotería)* the entrants with the most right numbers; *(de quiniela)* the entrants with the highest number of score draws

acertar [3] **1** *vt* (**a**) *(adivinar)* to guess (correctly); **acerté dos respuestas** I got two answers right (**b**) *(blanco)* to hit
2 *vi* (**a**) *(al contestar, adivinar)* to be right; *(al escoger, decidir)* to make a good choice; **acerté a la primera** I got it right first time; **acertó al elegir esa profesión** she made the right decision when she chose that career; **acertaste con su regalo** you chose her present well, you chose just the right present for her; *Fam* **no a. una: a la hora de comprar regalos no acierta una** when it comes to buying presents she never gets it right
(**b**) *(en blanco)* **acertó en la diana** she hit the bull's-eye; **el disparo le acertó en la cabeza** the bullet hit him in the head
(**c**) *(conseguir)* **a. a hacer algo** to manage to do sth; **no acierto a entenderlo** I can't understand it at all
(**d**) *(ocurrir casualmente)* **acertaba a pasar por allí** she happened to pass that way; **acertó a nevar cuando llegamos al pueblo** it happened to start snowing when we reached the village
(**e**) **a. con** *(hallar)* to find; **acertamos con el desvío correcto** we found the right turn-off

acertijo *nm* riddle; **poner un a. a alguien** to ask sb a riddle

acervo *nm UE* ***a. comunitario*** acquis communautaire; ***a. cultural*** *(de una nación, región)* cultural heritage; ***a. genético*** gene pool; a. ***génico*** gene pool; ***a. popular*** popular culture

acetaldehído *nm Quím* acetaldehyde

acetato *nm Quím* acetate

acético, -a *adj Quím* acetic

acetilcolina *nf Bioquím* acetylcholine

acetileno *nm Quím* acetylene

acetilo *nm Quím* acetyl

acetona *nf* (**a**) *Quím* acetone (**b**) *(quitaesmaltes)* nail-polish remover

acevía *nf* yellow *o* eyed sole

achacable *adj* attributable (**a** to)

achacar [60] *vt* to attribute (**a** to); **achacó la intoxicación al marisco** she blamed the food poisoning on the seafood; **siempre achaca las culpas a los demás** she always blames everyone else

achacoso, -a, achaquiento, -a *adj* (**a**) *(persona)* **está muy a.** he's got a lot of aches and pains (**b**) *(cosa)* faulty, defective

achaflanar *vt* to chamfer, to bevel

achampañado, -a *adj* sparkling

achamparse *vpr Andes* **(a)** *(quedarse con)* to retain *(another's property)* **(b)** *(establecerse)* to settle, to put down roots

achanchar 1 *vt Chile (en damas)* to trap
2 **achancharse** *vpr* **(a)** *Am Fam (apoltronarse)* to get lazy **(b)** *Andes, RP Fam (engordar)* to get fat

achantado, -a *adj Fam* **(a)** *Ven (quedado)* **anda muy a.** he has no enthusiasm for anything **(b)** *RP (vulgar)* tacky; **esta calle está muy achantada** this street has really gone down-market

achantar *Fam* **1** *vt* to put the wind up; **a ese no lo achanta nada** nothing gets him scared
2 **achantarse** *vpr* to get the wind up; **no se achanta ante nada** she doesn't get frightened by anything

achaparrado, -a *adj* squat

achaparrarse *vpr* **(a)** *(árbol)* to grow squat **(b)** *(engordar)* to get chubby

achaplinado, -a *nm,f Chile Fam* faint-heart, waverer; **no invitemos a ese gallo, es un a.** let's not invite that guy, he's such a wet blanket

achaplinarse *vpr Chile Fam* to have second thoughts, to get cold feet

achaque 1 *ver* **achacar**
2 *nm* **achaques** aches and pains; **son los achaques propios de la vejez** they're just the usual aches and pains you get when you're old; **siempre tiene algún a.** she's always got something wrong with her

achaquiento, -a = **achacoso**

achatado, -a *adj* flattened; **la Tierra está achatada por los polos** the Earth is flattened at the poles

achatar 1 *vt* to flatten
2 **achatarse** *vpr* to level out

achicador *nm* bailer

achicar [60] **1** *vt* **(a)** *(empequeñecer)* to make smaller **(b)** *(acobardar)* to intimidate **(c)** *(agua) (de barco)* to bail out; *(de mina)* to pump out **(d)** *Méx (cubrir con miel)* to (cover in) honey
2 **achicarse** *vpr* **(a)** *(empequeñecer)* to grow smaller **(b)** *(acobardarse)* to be intimidated

achicharrado, -a *adj* **(a)** *(quemado)* burnt to a crisp **(b)** *(acalorado)* boiling (hot)

achicharrante *adj (calor, sol)* boiling, roasting

achicharrar 1 *vt* **(a)** *(quemar)* to burn **(b)** *(a preguntas)* to plague, to overwhelm (**a** with) **(c)** *Andes (aplastar, estrujar)* to squash
2 *vi (sol, calor)* to be boiling
3 **achicharrarse** *vpr Fam* **(a)** *(quemarse)* to fry, to get burnt **(b)** *(de calor)* to be boiling (hot) **(c)** *(volverse loco)* to go mad

achichincle, achichinque *nm Méx Fam Pey* lackey

achicopalar *Méx Fam* **1** *vt* **no te dejes a. por él** don't let him walk all over you
2 **achicopalarse** *vpr* to get down, to get the blues; **no quiere achicopalarse** he wants to stay upbeat; **¡no se achicopale!** don't get down in the dumps

achicoria *nf* **(a)** *(hierba)* chicory **(b)** *(infusión)* chicory **(c)** *RP Fam (pobreza)* poverty

achinado, -a *adj* **(a)** *(ojos)* slanting **(b)** *(persona)* Chinese-looking **(c)** *RP (aindiado) (facciones)* Indian-looking

achiote *nm* annatto

achiotillo *nm* achiotillo

achique 1 *ver* **achicar**
2 *nm* **(a)** *Náut* bailing out **(b)** *(en fútbol)* offside trap

achiquillado, -a *adj Méx* childish

achiquitar *Am Fam* **1** *vt* to diminish, to make smaller
2 **achiquitarse** *vpr* to become diminished, to get smaller

achís *interj (estornudo)* atchoo!, atishoo!

achispado, -a *adj Fam* tipsy

achispar *Fam* **1** *vt* to make tipsy
2 **achisparse** *vpr* to get tipsy

Achkabad *n* Ashkhabad

achoclonarse *vpr Andes Fam* to crowd round

achocolatado, -a *adj Am* **leche achocolatada** drinking chocolate

acholado, -a *adj* **(a)** *Bol, Chile, Perú Pey (mestizo) (físicamente)* Indian-looking, mestizo; *(culturalmente)* = who has adopted Indian ways **(b)** *Perú Fam Pey (ordinario)* common, vulgar **(c)** *Ecuad (avergonzado)* ashamed, red in the face; **no seas a., ¡cántanos algo!** don't be shy *o* embarrassed, give us a song!

acholamiento *nm Bol, Chile, Perú Fam Pey* **le preocupaba el a. progresivo de su familia** he was concerned by the way more and more of his family were marrying mestizos; **se mudaron cuando empezó el a. del barrio** they moved out when mestizos started to move into the neighbourhood

acholar 1 *vt Bol, Chile, Perú* to embarrass, to make blush
2 **acholarse** *vpr* **(a)** *Bol, Chile, Perú Fam Pey (acriollarse)* to go native; **te estás acholando en tus elecciones** you're getting a bit common, your tastes are going a bit down-market **(b)** *Ecuad (avergonzarse)* to be ashamed **(c)** *Bol, Chile, Perú (atemorizarse)* to get scared; *(acobardarse)* to get cold feet; **hay que estar muy seguro para no acholarse** you have to be very sure of yourself not to get scared

achorado, -a *adj Fam* **(a)** *Chile (valiente)* gutsy **(b)** *Perú (canalla)* loutish, *Br* yobbish

achorarse *vpr Fam* **(a)** *Chile (envalentonarse)* to pluck up courage **(b)** *Perú (encanallarse)* to turn into a lout *o Br* yob

achuchado, -a *adj* **(a)** *Esp Fam (difícil)* hard, tough; **la vida está muy achuchada** life is very hard, money is tight **(b)** *RP (con frío)* shivering; *(con fiebre)* feverish

achuchar *Fam* **1** *vt* **(a)** *(abrazar)* to hug **(b)** *(estrujar)* to push and shove, to jostle **(c)** *(presionar)* to be on at, to badger
2 **achucharse** *(abrazarse)* to hug, to cuddle; **se pasaron la tarde achuchándose en el sofá** they spent the afternoon cuddling on the sofa

achucharrar 1 *vt Col, Hond* to crush, to squash
2 **achucharrarse** *vpr* **(a)** *Méx (desanimarse)* to be disheartened, to be discouraged **(b)** *Col, Méx (quemarse) (carne)* to burn *o* get burnt; *(planta)* to wither (in the sun)

achuchón *nm Fam* **(a)** *(abrazo)* big hug; **me dio un a.** he gave me a big hug **(b)** *(estrujón)* push, shove; **había achuchones para entrar** there was pushing and shoving to get in **(c)** *(indisposición)* mild illness; **le dio un a.** he came over all funny

achucutar, achucuyar 1 *vt* **(a)** *CAm, Col, Cuba, Ecuad (abatir)* to dishearten **(b)** *CAm, Col, Cuba, Ecuad (humillar)* to humble **(c)** *Guat (marchitar)* to wither, to fade
2 **achucutarse, achucuyarse** *vpr* **(a)** *CAm, Col, Cuba, Ecuad (abatirse)* to be disheartened **(b)** *CAm, Col, Cuba, Ecuad (humillarse)* to humble oneself **(c)** *Guat (marchitarse)* to wither, to fade

achulado, -a *adj Esp* cocky

achunchado, -a *adj Andes Fam* **(a)** *(avergonzado)* embarrassed, red in the face **(b)** *(atemorizado, acobardado)* scared

achunchar *Andes Fam* **1** *vt* **(a)** *(avergonzar)* to shame **(b)** *(atemorizar, acobardar)* to frighten
2 **achuncharse** *vpr* **(a)** *(avergonzarse)* to be ashamed **(b)** *(atemorizarse, acobardarse)* to be frightened

achuntar *vi Chile Fam* **(a)** *(acertar)* to get it right **(b)** *(embocar)* **no le achunto nunca a la papelera** I never manage to get it in the wastepaper basket

achuñuscar *vt Chile Fam (papel)* to scrunch up; *(tela)* to crumple; **el clima seco te achuñusca la piel** the dry climate makes your skin wrinkly

achurar *vt RP Fam* **(a)** *(acuchillar)* to stab to death **(b)** *(animal)* to disembowel

achuras *nfpl Perú, RP* **(a)** *(asaduras)* offal **(b)** *(plato)* dish of offal

aciago, -a *adj Formal* black, fateful; **un día a.** a fateful day

aciano *nm* cornflower

acíbar *nm* **(a)** *(planta)* aloes **(b)** *(jugo)* bitter aloes **(c)** *Literario (amargura)* bitterness

acicalado, -a *adj* dapper

acicalar 1 *vt* to do up, to spruce up
2 **acicalarse** *vpr* to do oneself up, to spruce oneself up

acicate *nm* **(a)** *(espuela)* spur **(b)** *(estímulo)* incentive; **esto le servirá de a.** this will spur him on

acicatear *vt* to spur, to incite

acícula *nf Bot* needle, *Espec* acicula

acidez *nf* **(a)** *(química)* acidity; **grado de a.** degree of acidity ▸▸ ***a. del suelo*** soil acidity **(b)** *(de sabor)* acidity **(c)** **a. (de estómago)** heartburn **(d)** *(desagrado)* acidity, bitterness; **habló con a.** she spoke caustically *o* acidly

acid house ['asiðˈχaus] *nm* acid house

acidificar [60] **1** *vt* to acidify
2 **acidificarse** *vpr* to become acidic

ácido, -a 1 *adj* **(a)** *(bebida, sabor)* acid, sour **(b)** *Quím* acidic **(c)** *(desabrido)* caustic, acid; **habló con tono á.** she spoke caustically *o* acidly

2 *nm* (**a**) *Quím* acid ►► ***á. acético*** acetic acid; ***á. acetilsalicílico*** acetylsalicylic acid; ***á. ascórbico*** ascorbic acid; ***á. aspártico*** aspartic acid; ***á. bórico*** boric acid; ***á. carbónico*** carbonic acid; ***á. cítrico*** citric acid; ***á. clorhídrico*** hydrochloric acid; *Bioquím* ***á. desoxirribonucleico*** deoxyribonucleic acid; ***á. fénico*** carbolic acid; ***á. fólico*** folic acid; ***á. glutámico*** glutamic acid; ***á. graso*** fatty acid; ***á. láctico*** lactic acid; ***á. lisérgico*** lysergic acid; ***á. málico*** malic acid; ***á. nítrico*** nitric acid; ***á. nitroso*** nitrous acid; *Bioquím* ***á. nucleico*** nucleic acid; ***á. oxálico*** oxalic acid; ***á. palmítico*** palmitic acid; ***á. prúsico*** prussic acid; *Bioquím* ***á. ribonucleico*** ribonucleic acid; ***á. sulfhídrico*** hydrogen sulphide; ***á. sulfúrico*** sulphuric acid; ***á. úrico*** uric acid

(**b**) *Fam (droga)* acid

acidosis *nf inv Med* acidosis

acidular *vt* to acidulate

acídulo, -a *adj* acidulous

acientífico, -a *adj* unscientific

acierto 1 *ver* **acertar**

2 *nm* (**a**) *(a pregunta)* correct answer (**b**) *(en quinielas)* = correct prediction of results in football pools entry (**c**) *(habilidad, tino)* good *o* sound judgement; **dijo con a. que debíamos esperar** she wisely said we should wait; **fue un a. vender las acciones** it was a good *o* smart idea to sell the shares; **fue un a. invitarles a la fiesta** it turned out to be a great idea to invite them to the party

ácimo, -a *adj (pan)* unleavened

acimut (*pl* **acimutes**) *nm Astron* azimuth

acinturado, -a *adj Am (vestido)* with a narrow waist

ación *nf* stirrup strap

acitrón *nm* candied citron

acitronar *vt Méx* to fry until golden-brown

aclamación *nf* acclamation, acclaim; **por a.** unanimously; **fue declarado el mejor por a. popular** it was hailed as the best by public acclaim

aclamar *vt* (**a**) *(aplaudir)* to acclaim (**b**) *(proclamar)* **fue aclamado emperador** he was proclaimed emperor

aclaración *nf* clarification, explanation; **me gustaría hacer una a.** I'd like to clarify something; **los miembros del partido le pidieron una a.** the party members asked her for an explanation

aclarado *nm Esp (enjuague)* rinsing; **dar un a. a algo** to rinse sth, to give sth a rinse

aclarar 1 *vt* (**a**) *Esp (enjuagar)* to rinse

(**b**) *(explicar)* to clarify, to explain; **aclaremos una cosa** let's get one thing clear; **eso lo aclara todo** that explains everything; **¿me podría a. ese último punto?** could you clarify *o* explain that last point for me?

(**c**) *(color)* to make lighter; **el sol aclara el pelo** the sun makes your hair lighter

(**d**) *(lo espeso) (chocolate, sopa)* to thin (down); *(bosque)* to thin out; **aclaró la pintura con un poco de aguarrás** she thinned the paint with a little turpentine

2 *v impersonal* **ya aclaraba** *(amanecía)* it was getting light; *(se despejaba)* the sky was clearing; **la tarde se fue aclarando** it brightened up during the afternoon

3 **aclararse** *vpr* (**a**) *(entender)* **a ver si nos aclaramos** let's see if we can get this straight; **no me aclaro con este programa** I can't get the hang of this program; **con sus explicaciones no me aclaro** I don't find his explanations very helpful; **con tres monedas diferentes no hay quién se aclare** with three different currencies nobody knows where they are

(**b**) *(explicarse)* **se aclaró la situación** the situation became clear

(**c**) *(tener las cosas claras)* to know what one wants; **mi jefe no se aclara** my boss doesn't know what he wants; **aclárate, ¿quieres venir o no?** make up your mind! do you want to come or not?

(**d**) **aclararse la garganta** *o* **la voz** to clear one's throat

(**e**) *(pelo)* **el pelo se aclara con el sol** the sun makes your hair lighter; **se aclaró el pelo** she dyed her hair a lighter colour

aclaratoria *nf Ven* explanatory note

aclaratorio, -a *adj* explanatory

aclimatación *nf* acclimatization; **la a. al nuevo entorno laboral le llevó unos meses** it took her a few months to become accustomed to the new working environment

aclimatar 1 *vt (planta, animal)* to acclimatize (**a** to)

2 **aclimatarse** *vpr* (**a**) *(planta, animal)* to acclimatize (**a** to) (**b**) *(acostumbrarse)* to settle in; **aclimatarse a algo** to get used to sth

acné, acne *nm Med* **a. (juvenil)** acne

ACNUR [ak'nur] *nm (abrev de* **Alto Comisionado de las Naciones Unidas para los Refugiados***)* UNHCR

acobardamiento *nm* cowardice, cowardliness

acobardar 1 *vt* to frighten, to scare

2 **acobardarse** *vpr* to get frightened *o* scared; **acobardarse ante un reto** to shrink back from a challenge; **no se acobarda ante nada** nothing scares him

acodado, -a *adj* (**a**) *(persona)* leaning (on his/her elbows) (**b**) *(cañería)* elbowed

acodadura *nf (en tubo, varilla)* bend, angle

acodar 1 *vt* (**a**) *(tubo, varilla)* to bend (at an angle) (**b**) *Bot* to layer

2 **acodarse** *vpr* to lean (**en** on)

acodo *nm Bot* shoot, *Espec* layer

acogedor, -ora *adj* (**a**) *(país, persona)* friendly, welcoming (**b**) *(casa, ambiente)* cosy

acogedoramente *adv* hospitably

acoger [52] 1 *vt* (**a**) *(recibir) (persona)* to welcome; **nos acogieron en su propia casa** they welcomed us into their own home

(**b**) *(recibir) (idea, noticia)* to receive; **el plan fue acogido con mucho entusiasmo** the plan was very enthusiastically received; **los trabajadores acogieron con escepticismo el anuncio de la empresa** the workforce reacted sceptically to the company's announcement

(**c**) *(dar refugio a)* to take in; **Suecia acogió a los refugiados políticos** Sweden took in the political refugees; **que Dios la acoja en su seno** God rest her soul

2 **acogerse** *vpr* **acogerse a** *(recurrir a)* to invoke; **se acogió al artículo primero de la Constitución** she invoked Article 1 of the Constitution; **no te acojas a una excusa tan tonta** don't try and hide behind such a ridiculous excuse; **2.000 trabajadores se han acogido al nuevo plan de pensiones** 2,000 workers have signed up for the new pension scheme; **abortó acogiéndose a la nueva ley** she was able to have an abortion under the new law

acogida *nf* (**a**) *(recibimiento) (de persona)* welcome, reception; **el equipo recibió una calurosa a.** the team was warmly received

(**b**) *(recibimiento) (de idea, película)* reception; **el producto ha tenido una buena a. en el mercado** the product has been well received by the market; **la nueva ley tuvo una mala a.** the new law was not well received *o* didn't go down well

(**c**) *(protección, refugio) (de refugiado)* refuge; **un movimiento que da a. a diversas ideologías** a movement which embraces a number of different ideologies

acogido, -a 1 *nm,f (pobre)* poorhouse resident

2 *nm Agr* pasturing fee

acogotar *vt* (**a**) *(matar)* to kill *(with a blow to the neck)* (**b**) *Fam (derribar)* to knock down (**c**) *Fam (intimidar, agobiar)* to pester; **me acogotaba pidiéndome cosas todo el día** she was driving me mad asking me to do things all day (**d**) *CSur Fam (sobrecargar)* to overwhelm

acojo *ver* **acoger**

acojonado, -a *Esp muy Fam* 1 *adj* (**a**) *(asustado)* **está acojonada ante la entrevista del martes** she's crapping herself about her interview on Tuesday (**b**) *(impresionado)* **me quedé a. cuando me enteré** I was damn *o Br* bloody surprised when I found out

2 *nm,f* **es un a.** he's a damn *o Br* bloody chicken

acojonante *adj Esp muy Fam* (**a**) *(impresionante)* damn fine, *Br* bloody incredible; **una moto a.** *Br* a bloody incredible bike, *US* a mother of a bike (**b**) *(que da miedo)* damn *o Br* bloody scary; **les di un susto a.** I scared the crap out of them

acojonar *Esp muy Fam* 1 *vt* (**a**) *(asustar)* **a. a alguien** to scare the crap out of sb (**b**) *(impresionar)* **nos acojonó con su última película** we were damn *o Br* bloody impressed by his last film

2 *vi* (**a**) *(asustar)* to be damn *o Br* bloody scary (**b**) *(impresionar)* **hace un frío que acojona** it's damn *o Br* bloody freezing

3 **acojonarse** *vpr* **me acojoné y no se lo dije** I crapped out of telling her

acojone, acojono *nm Esp muy Fam* **me entró un a. terrible** I started crapping myself; **¡qué a. de película!** *Br* what a bloody amazing film!, *US* what a mother of a film!

acolchado, -a 1 *adj* (**a**) *(tela)* **tela acolchada** quilted material (**b**) *(puerta)* padded

2 *nm RP (edredón)* bedspread

acolchar *vt* (**a**) *(tela)* to quilt (**b**) *(puerta)* to pad

acólito *nm* (**a**) *(monaguillo)* altar boy (**b**) *(acompañante)* acolyte

acollar [64] *vt Agr* to earth up

acollarar *vt CSur (unir)* to tie together

acomedido, -a *adj Andes, CAm, Méx* accommodating, obliging

acomedirse [47] *vpr Andes, CAm, Méx* to offer to help, to volunteer

acometer 1 *vt* (**a**) *(atacar)* to attack (**b**) *(emprender)* to undertake; **acometió la tarea con ilusión** she took on the task with enthusiasm (**c**) *(sobrevenir)* **me acometió un dolor punzante** I was hit by a stabbing pain; **me acometió el sueño** I was overcome by sleepiness
2 *vi (embestir)* to attack; **a. contra** to attack, to charge at

acometida *nf* (**a**) *(ataque)* attack, charge (**b**) *(de luz, gas)* (mains) connection

acometimiento *nm (acción)* attacking; *(ataque)* attack

acomodación *nf* accommodation

acomodadamente *adv* (**a**) *(convenientemente)* conveniently (**b**) *(confortablemente)* comfortably

acomodadizo, -a *adj* accommodating, easy-going

acomodado, -a *adj* (**a**) *(rico)* well-off, well-to-do (**b**) *(instalado)* ensconced (**c**) *CSur, Méx Fam (colocado en un trabajo)* **es un a.** he got his job by pulling strings

acomodador, -ora *nm,f* usher, *f* usherette

acomodar 1 *vt* (**a**) *(instalar) (persona)* to seat, to instal; *(cosa)* to place; **acomodó a los niños en la habitación de invitados** she put the children in the guest room; **nos acomodaron en su casa lo mejor que pudieron** they put us up in their house as best they could; **el vehículo tiene capacidad para a. a siete adultos** the vehicle seats seven adults
(**b**) *(adaptar)* to fit; **acomodamos nuestro paso al del resto del grupo** we adjusted our pace to that of the rest of the group
(**c**) *CSur, Méx (colocar en un trabajo)* **a. a alguien** to get sb a job through connections *o* influence
2 **acomodarse** *vpr* (**a**) *(instalarse)* to make oneself comfortable; **se acomodó en el sillón** he settled down in the armchair
(**b**) *(adaptarse)* to adapt (**a** to); **el presupuesto deberá acomodarse a nuestras necesidades** our budget should meet our needs; **es una persona que se acomoda a todo** she's a very easy-going person; **el producto tendrá que acomodarse a los gustos del consumidor** the product will have to give the consumer what they want
(**c**) *CSur, Méx (colocarse en un trabajo)* to set oneself up through connections
(**d**) *RP (arreglarse)* to straighten; **acomodate el pelo antes de salir** give your hair a brush before you go out

acomodaticio, -a *adj (complaciente)* accommodating, easy-going

acomodo *nm* (**a**) *(alojamiento)* accommodation; *Fig* **dar a. a algo** to allow for sth, to take sth into account (**b**) *CSur, Méx (influencia)* string-pulling, influence (**c**) *Méx (empleo temporal)* seasonal job

acompañado, -a *adj* accompanied; **llegó a. de** *o* **por sus familiares** he arrived accompanied by *o* in the company of his relatives; **la foto va acompañada de un texto** the photo is accompanied by a caption; **pollo a. de una ensalada** chicken served with a salad; **el estreno irá a. de un debate** the première will be followed by a discussion

acompañamiento *nm* (**a**) *(comitiva) (en entierro)* cortège; *(de rey)* retinue (**b**) *(guarnición)* accompaniment; **pescado frito y de a. ensalada** fried fish served with a salad (**c**) *(musical)* accompaniment

acompañante *nmf* companion; **los acompañantes no pueden entrar al quirófano** anyone accompanying a patient may not be present in the operating *Br* theatre *o US* room; **acudió a la gala del brazo de su último a.** she arrived at the gala arm in arm with her latest companion; **aunque el conductor resultó herido sus acompañantes salieron ilesos** although the driver was injured the other people in the vehicle were unharmed

acompañar 1 *vt* (**a**) *(ir con)* to go with, to accompany; **a. a alguien a la puerta** to show sb out; **a. a alguien a casa** to walk sb home; **su esposa lo acompaña en todos sus viajes** his wife goes with him on all his trips
(**b**) *(hacer compañía)* **a. a alguien** to keep sb company; **la radio me acompaña mucho** I listen to the radio for company
(**c**) *(compartir emociones con)* **a. en algo a alguien** to be with sb in sth; **lo acompaño en el sentimiento** (you have) my condolences
(**d**) *(adjuntar)* to enclose; **acompañó la solicitud de** *o* **con su curriculum vitae** he sent his *Br* CV *o US* resumé along with the application
(**e**) *(con música)* to accompany; **ella canta y su hermana la acompaña al piano** she sings and her sister accompanies her on the piano
(**f**) *(añadir)* **a. la carne con verduras** to serve the meat with vegetables
2 *vi (hacer compañía)* to provide company; **una radio acompaña mucho** radios are very good for keeping you company; **fue una lástima que el tiempo no acompañara** it's a shame the weather didn't hold out
3 **acompañarse** *vpr* **canta y se acompaña con el piano** she sings and accompanies herself on the piano

acompasado, -a *adj* (**a**) *(crecimiento, desarrollo)* steady (**b**) *(pasos)* measured

acompasar *vt* to synchronize (**a** with)

acomplejado, -a 1 *adj* **está a. por su calvicie** he has a complex about his bald patch
2 *nm,f* **es un a.** he has got a complex

acomplejante *adj* **es a. ver tanta gente elegante** it makes you feel inadequate seeing so many well-dressed people

acomplejar 1 *vt* **no dejes que el triunfo de tu rival te acompleje** don't give yourself a complex about your rival winning
2 **acomplejarse** *vpr* (**a**) *Psi* to develop a complex (**b**) *Fam (preocuparse)* to get hung-up

Aconcagua *nm* **el A.** Aconcagua

aconcharse *vpr* (**a**) *Chile, Perú (sedimiento)* to settle (**b**) *Chile, Perú (situación)* to settle down, to calm down (**c**) *Chile (atemorizarse)* to take fright, to get scared

acondicionado, -a *adj (equipado)* equipped; **estar bien/mal a.** to be in a fit/no fit state; **con aire a.** air-conditioned

acondicionador *nm* (**a**) *(de aire)* air-conditioner (**b**) *(de pelo)* conditioner

acondicionamiento *nm* (**a**) *(reforma)* conversion, upgrading (**b**) ***a. de aire*** air-conditioning

acondicionar 1 *vt* (**a**) *(reformar)* to convert, to upgrade (**b**) *(preparar)* to prepare, to get ready; **acondicionaron la entrada para que pudieran pasar discapacitados** they adapted *o* modified the entrance to enable access to disabled people (**c**) *(pelo)* to condition
2 **acondicionarse** *vpr (aclimatarse)* to become accustomed

acondroplasia *nf Med* achondroplasia

aconfesional *adj* secular

aconfesionalidad *nf* secular nature

acongojadamente *adv* in distress, in anguish

acongojado, -a *adj* distressed, anguished

acongojar 1 *vt* to distress, to cause anguish to
2 **acongojarse** *vpr* to be distressed

acónito *nm* wolfsbane, *Espec* aconite

aconsejable *adj* advisable

aconsejado, -a *adj* sensible, prudent

aconsejar 1 *vt* (**a**) *(dar consejos)* to advise; **a. a alguien (que haga algo)** to advise sb (to do sth); **le pedí que me aconsejara (acerca de)** I asked him for advice (about); **la están aconsejando mal** they're giving her bad advice; **¿y tú qué me aconsejas que haga?** and what do you think I should do?, and what would your advice be?; **los expertos aconsejan beber 2 litros de agua al día** experts recommend that you drink 2 litres of water a day; **se aconseja mantener la planta alejada de la luz directa** it is advisable *o* recommended to keep the plant away from direct sunlight
(**b**) *(hacer aconsejable)* to make advisable; **la delicadeza de la situación aconseja actuar con prudencia** the delicacy of the situation makes caution advisable
2 **aconsejarse** *vpr* **se aconsejó de varios expertos** she went to a number of experts for advice

acontecer [46] **1** *vi* to take place, to happen
2 *nm* **el a. histórico de este siglo** the historical events of this century

acontecimiento *nm* event; **esto es todo un a.** this is quite an event!; **adelantarse a los acontecimientos** *(precipitarse)* to jump the gun; *(prevenir)* to take pre-emptive measures

acontezca *etc ver* **acontecer**

acopiar *vt* to stock up on

acopio *nm* stock, store; **hacer a. de** *(existencias, comestibles)* to stock up on; *(valor, paciencia)* to summon up

acoplable *adj* attachable (**a** to)

acoplado, -a 1 *adj* coupled, joined
2 *nm CSur* trailer

acoplador *nm Tec* ***a. direccional*** directional coupler

acopladura *nf* joint, connection

acoplamiento *nm* (**a**) *(de piezas)* attachment, connection (**b**) *(en el espacio)* docking (**c**) *(de micrófonos)* feedback

acoplar 1 *vt* (**a**) *(pieza)* to attach (**a** to) (**b**) *(persona)* to adapt, to fit
2 **acoplarse** *vpr* (**a**) *(piezas)* to fit together; **acoplarse a algo** to fit sth; **los módulos espaciales se acoplaron sin problemas** the two space modules docked without incident
(**b**) *(persona)* to adjust (**a** to); **se han acoplado muy bien el uno al otro** they get on well together; **se ha acoplado a la nueva situación**

sin ningún problema she has adjusted easily to the new situation
(**c**) *(micrófono)* to give feedback
(**d**) *(animales)* to mate
(**e**) *Fam (apoltronarse)* **se acopló en el sillón** he *Br* plonked *o US* plunked himself down in the armchair
(**f**) *RP (unirse)* to join in; **se acoplaron a la manifestación** they joined the demonstration

acoquinado, -a *adj Fam* timid, nervous

acoquinar *Fam* **1** *vt* to put the wind up
2 acoquinarse *vpr* to get the wind up

acorazado, -a 1 *adj* armour-plated; **cámara acorazada** strongroom, vault
2 *nm (buque)* battleship

acorazar [14] **1** *vt* to armour-plate, to armour
2 acorazarse *vpr* (**a**) *(protegerse)* **acorazarse (contra alguien)** to shield *o* protect oneself (against sb) (**b**) *(insensibilizarse)* to become hardened

acorazonado, -a *adj* heart-shaped

acordado, -a *adj* (**a**) *(con acuerdo)* agreed (upon); **lo a. fue que lo pagarían ellos** it was agreed that they would pay (**b**) *(sensato)* prudent, sensible

ACORDAR [64] **1** *vt* (**a**) *(ponerse de acuerdo en)* to agree (on); **a. hacer algo** to agree to do sth; **acordaron que lo harían** they agreed to do it; **el Consejo de Ministros acordó los nuevos precios de la gasolina** the Cabinet fixed *o* set the new petrol prices
(**b**) *Am (conceder)* to award
(**c**) *Am (recordar)* to remind; **acuérdame de llamar a mi madre,** *RP* **haceme a. que llame a mi madre** remind me to call my mother
2 *vi* to go together
3 acordarse *vpr* (**a**) *(recordar)* **acordarse (de algo/de hacer algo)** to remember (sth/to do sth); **ella no se acuerda de eso** she doesn't remember that; **si mal no me acuerdo** if I remember correctly, if my memory serves me right
(**b**) *(ponerse de acuerdo)* to agree, to come to an agreement; **no se acuerdan con nosotros** they don't agree with us; **se acordó que no harían declaraciones** it was agreed that they wouldn't make any statements
(**c**) *Fam (como amenaza)* **¡te vas a a.!** you're in for it!, you'll catch it!; **¡como rompas algo, te vas a a.!** if you break anything, you've had it!
(**d**) *Fam (como insulto)* **salió del campo acordándose de toda la familia del árbitro** he left the field calling the referee all the names under the sun; **cuando vi que la calefacción seguía sin funcionar, me acordé de toda la familia del fontanero** when I saw that the heating still wasn't working, I swore inwardly at the plumber

acorde 1 *adj* (**a**) *(conforme)* **todos se mostraron acordes con la decisión** everyone agreed with the decision; **estuvieron acordes en aplazar la reunión** they agreed to postpone the meeting; **tienen puntos de vista acordes** they see some things the same way
(**b**) *(en consonancia)* **a. a** *o* **con: recibirán una ayuda a. a sus necesidades** the aid they receive will be appropriate to their needs; **vestía un traje a. con la ceremonia** the dress she was wearing was appropriate for the ceremony; **una política energética a. con los nuevos tiempos** an energy policy for today's world
2 *nm Mús* chord; **desfilaron a los acordes del himno nacional** they marched to the strains of the national anthem

acordeón *nm* (**a**) *Mús* accordion (**b**) *Col, Méx Fam (en examen)* crib

acordeonista *nmf* accordionist

acordonado, -a *adj* (**a**) *(área)* cordoned off (**b**) *Méx (animal)* thin, lean

acordonamiento *nm (de área)* cordoning off

acordonar *vt* (**a**) *(área)* to cordon off (**b**) *(atar)* to do up, to lace up

acornear *vt* to gore

ácoro *nm* sweet flag, *Espec* calamus

acorralamiento *nm* cornering

acorralar *vt* (**a**) *(rodear)* to corner; **la policía acorraló a los fugitivos en una esquina** the police cornered the fugitives; **los visitantes acorralaron al equipo local en su área** the visitors penned the home team inside their penalty area
(**b**) *(intimidar)* **se siente acorralado** he feels cornered *o* trapped; **el ministro se vio acorralado por el entrevistador** the minister was backed into a corner by the interviewer
(**c**) *(ganado)* to pen, to corral

acortamiento *nm (de plazo, longitud, distancia)* shortening; *(de condena)* reduction; **se empieza a notar el a. de los días** the days are starting to get shorter

acortar 1 *vt* (**a**) *(longitud, cuerda)* to shorten (**b**) *(falda, pantalón)* to take up (**c**) *(reunión, viaje)* to cut short (**d**) *(condena)* to cut, to reduce
2 *vi* **por este camino acortaremos** we'll get there quicker this way
3 acortarse *vpr (días)* to get shorter

acosado, -a *adj* (**a**) *(por perseguidores)* hounded, pursued (**b**) *(por molestia)* plagued, beset; **a. por las dudas** plagued by doubts

acosador, -ora *adj* relentless, persistent

acosamiento *nm* harassment

acosar, *Méx* **acosijar** *vt* (**a**) *(perseguir)* to pursue relentlessly (**b**) *(hostigar)* to harass; **lo acosaron a** *o* **con preguntas** they fired questions at him; **fue acosada sexualmente en el trabajo** she was sexually harassed at work

acoso *nm* (**a**) *(persecución)* relentless pursuit (**b**) *(hostigamiento)* harassment ▸▸ ***a. y derribo*** = rural sport in which horsemen harry and bring down bulls; *Fig* **han denunciado una operación de a. y derribo contra el presidente** they have condemned the concerted attempt(s) to hound the president out of office; ***a. sexual*** sexual harassment

acostada *nf CSur Fam* **se pegó una a. con mi hermano** she went to bed with my brother

acostado, -a *adj (tumbado)* lying down; *(en la cama)* in bed

acostar [64] **1** *vt* (**a**) *(tumbar)* to lie down; *(en la cama)* to put to bed (**b**) *Náut* to bring alongside
2 *vi Náut* to reach the coast
3 acostarse *vpr* (**a**) *(irse a la cama)* to go to bed; **suele acostarse tarde** he usually goes to bed late (**b**) *(tumbarse)* to lie down (**en** on); **acuéstese boca arriba** lie face up (**c**) *Fam (tener relaciones sexuales)* **acostarse con alguien** to sleep with sb; **acostarse juntos** to sleep together

acostón *nm Méx Fam* **darse un a. con alguien** to go to bed with sb; **ser un buen a.** to be good in bed

acostumbrado, -a *adj* (**a**) *(habitual)* usual; **lo hizo con su acostumbrada tranquilidad** she did it with her customary calm; **la temporada comienza esta año antes de lo a.** the season begins earlier than usual this year
(**b**) *(habituado)* **estamos acostumbrados** we're used to it; **estar a. a algo** to be used to sth; **estoy a. a la lluvia** I'm used to the rain; **estar a. a hacer algo** to be used to doing sth; **está acostumbrada a madrugar** she's used to getting up early; **no está a. a que le den órdenes** he's not used to taking orders from people; **ya nos tiene acostumbrados a sus excentricidades** we're used to his eccentric behaviour by now

acostumbramiento *nm CSur* habit; **provocar a.** to be habit-forming

acostumbrar 1 *vt* **a. a alguien a algo** to get sb used to sth; **a. a alguien a hacer algo** to get sb used to doing sth
2 *vi* **a. (a) hacer algo** to be in the habit of doing sth; **acostumbra (a) trabajar los sábados** he usually works on Saturdays
3 acostumbrarse *vpr* **te acostumbrarás pronto** you'll soon get used to it; **acostumbrarse a algo/alguien** to get used to sth/sb; **no me acostumbro a la comida de aquí** I can't get used to the food here; **acostumbrarse a hacer algo** *(familiarizarse)* to get used to doing sth; *(adquirir el hábito)* to get into the habit of doing sth; **acostúmbrate a llegar puntual** you'd better get into the habit of arriving on time

acotación *nf* (**a**) *(nota)* note in the margin (**b**) *(en plano, mapa)* spot height (**c**) *Teatro* stage direction

acotado, -a *adj (terreno, campo)* enclosed

acotamiento *nm* (**a**) *(de terreno, campo)* enclosing, demarcation (**b**) *Méx (arcén) Br* hard shoulder, *US* shoulder

acotar *vt* (**a**) *(terreno, campo)* to enclose, to demarcate (**b**) *(texto)* to write notes in the margin of (**c**) *(plano, mapa)* to add spot heights to (**d**) *(tema, competencias)* to delimit

ACP *(abrev de* **África, el Caribe y el Pacífico**) ACP; **países A.** ACP countries

acracia *nf* anarchy

ácrata 1 *adj* anarchist
2 *nmf* anarchist

acre 1 *adj* (**a**) *(olor)* acrid, pungent; *(sabor)* bitter (**b**) *(brusco, desagradable)* caustic
2 *nm* acre

acrecencia *nf Der* accretion

acrecentamiento *nm* increase, growth

acrecentar [3] **1** *vt* to increase
2 acrecentarse *vpr* to increase

acrecer *vi Der* to accrue

acreditación *nf* (**a**) *(de periodista)* press card; *(de congresista, deportista)* pass (**b**) *(de diplomático)* credentials

acreditado, -a *adj* (a) *(periodista, deportista)* accredited; **los congresistas acreditados** the official conference delegates (b) *(embajador, representante)* accredited (c) *(reputado) (médico, abogado)* distinguished; *(marca)* reputable

acreditar *vt* (a) *(periodista, deportista)* to accredit
(b) *(certificar)* to certify; *(autorizar)* to authorize, to entitle; **un centro que ha sido acreditado para la docencia** an accredited *o* approved teaching centre; **los interesados deben a. que cumplen los requisitos** applicants must provide documentary evidence that they meet the requirements
(c) *(demostrar)* to prove, to confirm; **este diploma lo acredita como traductor jurado** this diploma certifies that he is an official translator; **el carnet lo acredita como miembro de la delegación** the ID card identifies him as a member of the delegation
(d) *(dar fama a)* to do credit to; **el premio lo acreditó como escritor** the award confirmed his status as a writer
(e) *(embajador)* to accredit
(f) *Fin* to credit

acreditativo, -a *adj* accrediting; **diploma a.** certificate; **¿tiene algún documento a. de que es el dueño del vehículo?** do you have any documents proving your ownership of the vehicle?; **un recibo a. del pago de una factura** a receipt confirming payment of an invoice

acreedor, -ora 1 *adj* **se ha hecho a. a** *o* **de la confianza de sus alumnos** he has earned his pupils' trust; **su dedicación la hace acreedora a un ascenso** she deserves a promotion because of her dedication
2 *nm,f Fin* creditor ▸▸ ***a. asegurado*** secured creditor; ***a. hipotecario*** mortgagee

acribillado, -a *adj* **a. a balazos** riddled with bullets; **a. por los mosquitos** bitten all over by mosquitos; **a. a preguntas** bombarded with questions

acribillar *vt* (a) *(llenar de agujeros)* to perforate, to pepper with holes; **a. a alguien a balazos** to riddle sb with bullets; **me han acribillado los mosquitos** the mosquitos have bitten me all over (b) *(molestar)* **a. a alguien a preguntas** to fire questions at sb; **los acribillaron a fotografías cuando salieron del hotel** they were caught in a blaze of flashbulbs as they left the hotel

acrílico, -a 1 *adj* acrylic
2 *nm* acrylic

acriminarse *vpr Chile* to disgrace oneself

acrimonia *nf (aspereza)* acrimony; **con a.** bitterly

acrimonioso, -a *adj* acrimonious

acriollado, -a *adj Am* **estar muy a.** to have adopted local ways; **la segunda generación ya estaba muy acriollada** the second generation was very much at home in the country

acriollarse *vpr Am* to adopt local ways

acrisolado, -a *adj* (a) *(irreprochable)* irreproachable (b) *(probado)* proven, tried and tested

acrisolar *vt* (a) *(metal)* to refine, to purify (b) *(purificar)* to clarify (c) *(verdad)* to prove

acristalado, -a *adj (terraza, galería)* glazed

acristalamiento *nm (acción)* glazing

acristalar *vt* to glaze

acrítico, -a *adj* uncritical

acritud *nf (aspereza)* acrimony; **con a.** bitterly

acrobacia *nf* (a) *(en circo)* **hacer acrobacias** to perform acrobatics; *Fig* **tuvo que hacer acrobacias con las cifras** he had to massage the figures (b) *(de avión)* aerobatic manoeuvre

acróbata *nmf* acrobat

acrobático, -a *adj (ejercicios, espectáculo)* acrobatic

acrofobia *nf* fear of heights, *Espec* acrophobia; **tener a.** to be afraid of heights

acromático, -a *adj* achromatic, colourless

acromatismo *nm* achromatism

acromatizar *vt* to achromatize

acromegalia *nf Med* acromegaly

acronimia *nf* **su nombre se forma por a.** its name is an acronym

acrónimo *nm* acronym

acrópolis *nf inv* acropolis; **la A.** *(en Atenas)* the Acropolis

acróstico *nm* acrostic

acta *nf*

Takes the masculine articles **el** and **un**.

(a) *(certificado)* certificate; **a. (de nombramiento)** certificate of appointment ▸▸ ***a. de defunción*** death certificate; ***a. de diputado*** = document certifying that the holder is a member of parliament; **no piensa renunciar a su a. de diputada** she has no plans to resign her seat in parliament; ***a. notarial*** affidavit
(b) **acta(s)** *(de junta, reunión)* minutes; **actas** *(de congreso)* proceedings; **constar en a.** to be recorded in the minutes; **levantar a.** to take the minutes
(c) **actas** *(educativas)* = official record of a student's marks
(d) *(acuerdo) UE* ***A. de Adhesión*** Act of Accession; ***a. fundacional*** founding treaty; *UE* ***A. Única (Europea)*** Single European Act

actina *nf Bioquím* actin

actinia *nf* sea anemone

actínido *nm Quím* actinide

actinio *nm Quím* actinium

actitud *nf* (a) *(disposición de ánimo)* attitude; **con esa a. no vamos a ninguna parte** we won't get anywhere with that attitude; **mostró una a. muy abierta a las sugerencias** she was very open to suggestions; **llegó en a. de criticar todo** he arrived ready to find fault with everything; **la a. ante la muerte** the way one faces one's death (b) *(postura)* **el león estaba en a. vigilante** the lion had adopted an alert pose

activación *nf* (a) *(de alarma, mecanismo)* activation; **la luz provoca la a. del dispositivo** the device is activated by light (b) *(estímulo)* stimulation; **medidas que pretenden la a. del consumo** measures designed to boost *o* stimulate consumption (c) *Quím* activation

activador, -ora 1 *adj* activator
2 *nm* activator

activamente *adv* actively

activar 1 *vt* (a) *(alarma, mecanismo)* to activate (b) *(explosivo)* to detonate (c) *(estimular)* to stimulate; **a. los intercambios comerciales** to boost *o* stimulate trade; **el ejercicio activa la circulación de la sangre** exercise stimulates your circulation
2 **activarse** *vpr* (a) *(alarma)* to go off; *(mecanismo)* to be activated; **el mecanismo se activa con la voz** the mechanism is voice-activated (b) *(explosivo)* to go off

actividad *nf* (a) *(trabajo, tarea)* activity; **mis numerosas actividades no me dejan tiempo para nada** I'm involved in so many different activities *o* things that I have no time for anything else; **empezó su a. como escritor en 1947** he started writing in 1947; **una ley que regula la a. de las agencias de viajes** a law that regulates the activities *o* operation of travel agencies ▸▸ ***a. económica*** economic activity; **tendrá un impacto negativo en la a. económica mundial** it will have a negative impact on world *o* global economic activity
(b) **actividades** *(acciones)* activities; **la policía investiga las actividades de la organización** the police are investigating the organization's activities
(c) *(comercial)* trading; **el mercado registraba una a. frenética** there was furious trading on the markets
(d) *(escolar)* activity; **un cuaderno de actividades** an activities book ▸▸ ***actividades extraescolares*** extra-curricular activities
(e) *(cualidad de activo)* activeness; **desplegar una gran a.** to be in a flurry of activity; **un volcán en a.** an active volcano

activismo *nm* activism

activista *nmf* activist

activo, -a 1 *adj* (a) *(dinámico)* active; **el principio a. de un medicamento** the active ingredient of a medicine; **es muy a., siempre está organizando algo** he's very active, he's always organizing something or other
(b) *(que trabaja)* **la población activa** the working population; **en a.** *(trabajador)* in employment; *(militar)* on active service; **todavía está en a.** he's still working
(c) *(eficaz) (veneno, medicamento)* fast-acting; **tiene un veneno poco a.** its poison is fairly weak
(d) *(volcán)* active
(e) *Fís (material)* active
(f) *Gram* active
(g) EXPR *Fam* **por activa y por pasiva: hemos tratado por activa y por pasiva de...** we have tried everything to...; **se lo he explicado por activa y por pasiva y no lo entiende** I've tried every way I can to explain but she doesn't understand
2 *nm Fin* assets ▸▸ ***activos de caja*** available assets, bank reserves; ***a. circulante*** current assets; ***a. disponible*** liquid assets; ***a. fijo*** fixed assets, ***a. financiero*** financial assets; ***a. inmaterial*** intangible assets; ***a. inmovilizado*** fixed assets; ***activos invisibles*** invisible assets; ***a. líquido*** liquid assets

acto 1 *nm* (a) *(acción)* act; **no es responsable de sus actos** she's not responsible for her actions; **lo acusaron de cometer actos terroristas** he was charged with committing acts of terrorism; **lo cazaron en el a.**

de huir con el dinero they caught him just as he was making off with the money ▸▸ ***a. de conciliación*** = formal attempt to reach an out-of-court settlement; ***a. de fe*** act of faith; *Ling* ***a. de habla*** speech act; *Ling* ***a. ilocutivo*** illocution, illocutionary act; *Ling* ***a. perlocutivo*** perlocution, perlocutionary act; ***a. de presencia:* hacer a. de presencia** to attend; ***a. reflejo*** reflex action; ***a. de servicio:* murió en a. de servicio** *(militar)* he died on active service; *(policía)* he was killed in the course of his duty; ***a. sexual*** sexual act; ***a. de solidaridad*** show of solidarity

(b) *(ceremonia)* ceremony; **un a. conmemorativo del Día de la Independencia** an Independence Day celebration, an event to mark Independence Day; **es responsable de la organización de actos culturales** she is responsible for organizing cultural events; **asistió a todos los actos electorales de su partido** he attended all his party's election rallies; **su último a. oficial fue la inauguración de un hospital** her last official engagement was the opening of a hospital

(c) *Teatro* act; **una comedia en dos actos** a comedy in two acts

2 **acto seguido** *loc adv* immediately after

3 **en el acto** *loc adv* on the spot, there and then; **reparaciones en el a.** repairs done while you wait; **murió en el a.** she died instantly

actor[1] *nm* actor ▸▸ ***a. de cine*** movie *o Br* film actor; ***a. cómico*** comic actor; ***a. de doblaje*** = actor who dubs voices in a foreign-language film; ***a. dramático*** stage *o* theatre actor; ***a. principal*** lead actor; ***a. de reparto*** supporting actor; ***a. secundario*** supporting actor; ***a. de teatro*** stage actor

actor[2], **-ora** *nm,f Der* plaintiff

actriz *nf* actress ▸▸ ***a. de cine*** movie *o Br* film actress; ***a. cómica*** comic actress; ***a. de doblaje*** = actress who dubs voices in a foreign-language film; ***a. dramática*** stage *o* theatre actress; ***a. principal*** leading actress; ***a. de reparto*** supporting actress; ***a. secundaria*** supporting actress; ***a. de teatro*** stage actress

actuación *nf* (a) *(conducta, proceder)* conduct, behaviour

(b) *(interpretación)* performance; **la a. del protagonista es excelente** the main character gives an excellent performance; **esta tarde vamos a una a. de unos cómicos** we're going to a comedy show this evening; **con la a. estelar de...** starring...; **tuvo una a. muy decepcionante** she gave a very disappointing performance

(c) *Der* **actuaciones** proceedings

(d) *Ling* performance

actual *adj* (a) *(del momento presente)* present, current; **las tendencias actuales de la moda** current fashion trends; **el a. alcalde de la ciudad** the city's present *o* current mayor; **el a. campeón del mundo** the current *o* reigning world champion; **el seis del a.** the sixth of this month

(b) *(de moda)* modern, up-to-date; **tiene un diseño muy a.** it has a very modern *o* up-to-date design

(c) *(de interés)* topical; **el desempleo es un tema muy a.** unemployment is a very topical issue

> **Falso amigo**: El adjetivo inglés **actual** no es la traducción del español **actual** en sus acepciones más frecuentes. En inglés **actual** significa "verdadero, real".

actualidad *nf* (a) *(momento presente)* current situation; **la a. política** the current political situation; **cuentan en la a. con más de un millón de socios** they currently have more than a million members; **estas piezas en la a. se fabrican en serie** these parts are mass-produced nowadays

(b) *(de asunto, noticia)* topicality; **una noticia de rabiosa a.** an extremely topical news item; **estar de a.** *(ser de interés)* to be topical; **poner algo de a.** to make sth topical; **una revista de a.** a current affairs magazine

(c) *(noticia)* news *(singular)*; **la a. informativa** the news; **la a. deportiva** the sports news; **ser a.** to be making the news

(d) *(vigencia)* relevance to modern society; **sus libros siguen teniendo gran a.** her books are still very relevant today; **una obra de teatro que no ha perdido a.** a play which is still relevant today

actualización *nf* (a) *(de información, datos)* updating (b) *(de tecnología, industria)* modernization (c) *Informát (de software, hardware)* upgrade (d) *Ling* actualization

actualizar [14] *vt* (a) *(información, datos)* to update (b) *(tecnología, industria)* to modernize (c) *Informát (software, hardware)* to upgrade

actualmente *adv* (a) *(en estos tiempos)* these days, nowadays; **a. casi nadie viaja en burro** hardly anyone travels by donkey these days *o* nowadays (b) *(en este momento)* at the (present) moment; **su padre está a. en paradero desconocido** his father's present whereabouts are unknown

> **Falso amigo**: El adverbio inglés **actually** no es la traducción del español actualmente. En inglés **actually** significa "en realidad" o "de hecho".

actuante *nmf* performer

actuar [4] *vi* (a) *(obrar, producir efecto)* to act; **actuó según sus convicciones** she acted in accordance with her convictions; **actúa de** *o* **como escudo** it acts *o* serves as a shield; **actúa de secretario** he acts as a secretary; **este tranquilizante actúa directamente sobre los centros nerviosos** this tranquilizer acts directly on the nerve centres; **los carteristas actúan principalmente en el centro de la ciudad** the pickpockets are mainly active in the city centre

(b) *Der* to undertake proceedings

(c) *(en película, teatro)* to perform, to act; **en esta película actúa Cantinflas** Cantinflas appears in this film

actuarial *adj* actuarial

actuario, -a *nm,f* (a) *Der* clerk of the court (b) *Fin* ***a. de seguros*** actuary

acuadrillar *vt Chile (atacar)* to gang up on

acuafortista *nmf* etcher

acualún *nm* aqualung

acuarela *nf* (a) *(técnica)* watercolour (b) *(pintura)* watercolour

acuarelista *nmf (pintor)* watercolourist

acuariano, -a *Am* 1 *adj* Aquarius; **ser a.** to be (an) Aquarius

2 *nm,f* Aquarius, Aquarian; **los acuarianos son...** Aquarians are...

acuario 1 *adj inv Esp (persona)* Aquarius; **ser a.** to be (an) Aquarius

2 *nm* (a) *(edificio, pecera grande)* aquarium; *(pecera)* fish tank (b) *(signo del zodiaco)* Aquarius; **los de A. son...** Aquarians are...

3 *nmf inv Esp (persona)* Aquarius, Aquarian; **los a. son...** Aquarians are...

acuartelado, -a *adj* (a) *Mil* quartered, billeted (b) *(escudo)* quartered

acuartelamiento *nm Mil* (a) *(acción)* confinement to barracks (b) *(lugar)* barracks

acuartelar 1 *vt Mil* (a) *(alojar)* to quarter (b) *(retener)* to confine to barracks

2 **acuartelarse** *vpr* to withdraw to barracks

acuático, -a *adj* aquatic; **deportes acuáticos** water sports

acuatinta *nf* (a) *(técnica)* aquatint (b) *(estampa)* aquatint

acuatizaje *nm* landing on water

acuatizar [14] *vi* to land on water

acuchillado, -a 1 *adj* (a) *(herido)* knifed, slashed (b) *(madera)* planed; *(suelo)* sanded

2 *nm (de suelos)* sanding

acuchillador *nm (de suelos)* floor sander

acuchillamiento *nm (apuñalamiento)* stabbing, slashing

acuchillar *vt* (a) *(apuñalar)* to stab (b) *(suelos)* to sand

acuciante *adj* urgent, pressing; **sentía un deseo a. de marcharse** she felt an urgent *o* pressing desire to leave; **éste es el problema más a. en estos momentos** this is the most urgent *o* pressing problem at the moment

acuciar *vt* (a) *(instar)* to goad; **el deseo me acuciaba** I was driven by desire; **está acuciada por problemas económicos** she is plagued by financial difficulties (b) *(ser urgente)* **le acucia encontrar un nuevo trabajo** he urgently needs to find a new job

acucioso, -a *adj* (a) *(diligente)* diligent, meticulous (b) *(deseoso)* eager

acuclillarse *vpr (agacharse)* to squat (down)

acudir *vi* (a) *(ir)* to go; *(venir)* to come; **a. a una cita/un mitin** to turn up for an appointment/at a rally; **a. en ayuda de alguien** to come to sb's aid *o* assistance; **nadie acudió a mi llamada de auxilio** no one answered my cry for help; **Sr. Pérez, acuda a recepción** could Mr Perez please come to reception?; **no es obligatorio a. a todas las clases** it isn't compulsory to attend all the classes; **a. a la mente** to come to mind; **a. a las urnas** to go to the polls

(b) *(frecuentar)* **a este restaurante acuden muchos personajes famosos** this restaurant is patronized by many celebrities

(c) *(recurrir)* **a. a alguien** to turn to sb; **si necesitas ayuda, puedes a. a mí** if you need help you can ask me *o* come to me; **amenazaron con a. a la violencia** they threatened to resort to violence; **piensan a. a la justicia** they intend to go to court

acueducto *nm* (a) *(para el agua)* aqueduct (b) *Esp Fam (vacacional)* = extra-long weekend, consisting of midweek public holiday, weekend, and the two days in between

ácueo, -a *adj* aqueous

acuerdo 1 *ver* **acordar**

2 *nm* (a) *(determinación, pacto)* agreement; **un a. verbal** a verbal agreement; **llegar a un a.** to reach (an) agreement; **tomar un a.** to

make a decision; **no hubo a.** they did not reach (an) agreement; **de común a.** by common consent ►► ***a. comercial*** trade agreement; ***A. General sobre Aranceles y Comercio*** General Agreement on Tariffs and Trade; *Informát* ***a. de licencia*** licence agreement; ***a. marco*** general *o* framework agreement; ***a. de paz*** peace agreement *o* deal; *Fin* ***a. de recompra*** repurchase agreement; ***a. tácito*** tacit agreement

(**b**) *Am (recuerdo)* **hazme a. de comprar pan** remind me to buy some bread

(**c**) *Méx (reunión)* staff meeting

3 de acuerdo *loc adv* (**a**) *(conforme)* **estar de a. (con algo/alguien)** to agree (with sth/sb); **estar de a. en algo** to agree on sth; **estamos de a. en que es necesario encontrar una solución** we agree that we have to find a solution; **ponerse de a. (con alguien)** to agree (with sb), to come to an agreement (with sb)

(**b**) *(bien, vale)* all right; **lo traeré mañana – de a.** I'll bring it tomorrow – all right *o* fine; **de a., me has convencido, lo haremos a tu manera** all right, you've convinced me, we'll do it your way

(**c**) **de a. con** *(conforme a)* in accordance with; **de a. con cifras oficiales...** according to official figures...

acuerpado, -a *adj CAm, Col, Méx* (**a**) *(corpulento)* burly (**b**) *(respaldado)* **a. por** backed up *o* supported by

acuesto *etc ver* **acostar**

acuícola *adj* aquatic

acuicultivo *nm* hydroponics *(singular)*

acuicultura *nf* (**a**) *(explotación de recursos)* aquiculture, aquaculture (**b**) *(de peces)* fish farming

acuífero, -a *Geol* **1** *adj* aquiferous, water-bearing

2 *nm* aquifer

acuilmarse *vpr CAm, Méx* to falter, to lose one's nerve

acuitar *vt (afligir)* to distress, to afflict

acullá *adv* (over) there, yonder; **aquí, allá y a.** here, there and yonder

acullico *nm Bol, Perú* (**a**) *(bolo)* = ball of chewed coca leaves kept in the mouth (**b**) *(cosecha)* coca harvest

aculturación *nf* acculturation

acumulable *adj* **el máximo a.** the maximum possible; **los puntos no son acumulables para la segunda ronda** points are not carried forward to the second round

acumulación *nf* (**a**) *(acción)* accumulation (**b**) *(montón)* accumulation, collection; **una a. peligrosa de residuos** a dangerous build-up of waste deposits

acumulador, -ora **1** *adj* **proceso a. de información** information-gathering process; **proceso a. de riqueza** process of enrichment

2 *nm* (**a**) *Elec* accumulator, storage battery ►► ***a. de calor*** storage heater (**b**) *Informát* accumulator

acumular **1** *vt* to accumulate; **le gusta a. recuerdos de sus viajes** she likes collecting souvenirs of her trips; **el tren fue acumulando retrasos en las diferentes paradas** the train got further and further delayed at every stop

2 acumularse *vpr* to accumulate, to build up; **se acumularon bolsas de basura en las calles** *Br* rubbish *o US* garbage bags piled up in the streets; **se me acumula el trabajo** work is piling up on me

acumulativo, -a *adj* cumulative

acunar *vt (en cuna)* to rock; *(en brazos)* to cradle

acuñación *nf* (**a**) *(de moneda)* minting (**b**) *(de palabra, expresión)* coining

acuñar *vt* (**a**) *(moneda)* to mint (**b**) *(palabra, expresión)* to coin

acuosidad *nf* wateriness

acuoso, -a *adj* (**a**) *(que contiene agua)* watery (**b**) *(jugoso)* juicy

acupuntor, -ora *nm,f* acupuncturist

acupuntura *nf* acupuncture

acurrucarse [60] *vpr (encogerse)* to crouch down; *(por frío)* to huddle up; *(por miedo)* to cower; **se acurrucó en un sillón** he curled up in an armchair; **se acurrucaron el uno contra el otro** they huddled up together

acusación *nf* (**a**) *(inculpación)* accusation; *Der* charge; **verter acusaciones (contra alguien)** to make accusations (against sb); **negó todas las acusaciones** she denied all the charges; **fueron juzgados bajo la a. de terrorismo** they were tried for having committed terrorist offences

(**b**) *Der (personas)* **la a.** the prosecution ►► ***a. particular*** private action; ***la a. popular*** = the prosecution which acts on behalf of pressure groups and other interested bodies in cases of public interest

acusadamente *adv* distinctly; **un clima a. continental** a distinctly continental climate

acusado, -a **1** *adj (marcado)* marked, distinct; **el cuadro tiene una acusada influencia cubista** the painting shows a marked Cubist influence; **tiene una acusada personalidad** she has a strong personality

2 *nm,f (procesado)* **el a.** the accused, the defendant

acusador, -ora **1** *adj* accusing

2 *nm,f* accuser

acusar **1** *vt* (**a**) *(culpar)* to accuse; **a. a alguien de algo** to accuse sb of sth; **siempre me acusan a mí de todo** they always blame me for everything

(**b**) *Der* to charge; **a. a alguien de algo** to charge sb with sth; **lo acusaron de asesinato** he was charged with murder

(**c**) *(mostrar, resentirse de)* **su rostro acusaba el paso del tiempo** the passage of time had taken its toll on his face; **los atletas acusaron el calor** the athletes were showing the effects of the heat; **cada vez acusa más el paso de los años** she is showing her age more and more; **su espalda acusó el esfuerzo** his back ached from the effort; **la bolsa ha acusado el golpe de las declaraciones del ministro** the stock exchange has registered the effects of the minister's statement

(**d**) *(recibo)* to acknowledge; **acusamos la recepción del paquete** we acknowledge the receipt of your package

2 acusarse *vpr* (**a**) *(mutuamente)* to blame one another (**de** for) (**b**) *(uno mismo)* **acusarse de haber hecho algo** to confess to having done sth; **¡padre, me acuso!** father, I confess

acusativo *nm Gram* accusative

acusatorio, -a *adj* accusatory

acuse *nm* ***a. de recibo*** acknowledgement of receipt; *Informát* acknowledgement

acusica, acusón, -ona *Fam* **1** *adj* **es muy a.** he's a real telltale

2 *nmf* telltale

acusón, -ona *adj, nm,f* = **acusica**

acústica *nf* (**a**) *(ciencia)* acoustics *(singular)* (**b**) *(de local)* acoustics

acústico, -a *adj* acoustic

acutángulo *adj* acute-angled

AD *nf* (*abrev de* **Acción Democrática**) = Venezuelan political party

ada *nm Informát* Ada

adagio *nm* (**a**) *(sentencia breve)* adage (**b**) *Mús* adagio

adalid *nm* champion, leader

adamascado, -a *adj* damask

adamantino, -a *adj* adamantine, diamond-like

Adán *n pr* Adam

adán *nm Fam (desaliñado)* ragamuffin, scruffy man; EXPR **ir hecho un a.** to be scruffily dressed, to go about in rags; EXPR **ir en traje de a.** to be in one's birthday suit, to be naked

adaptabilidad *nf* adaptability

adaptable *adj* adaptable

adaptación *nf* (**a**) *(acomodación)* adjustment (**a** to); **a. al medio** adaptation to the environment (**b**) *(modificación)* adaptation; **la película es una buena a. del libro** the film is a good adaptation of the book

adaptado, -a *adj* suited (**a** to); **una especie adaptada al clima desértico** a species which is adapted to the desert climate; **está bien a. a su nuevo colegio** he's quite at home in his new school now

adaptador *nm Elec* adaptor ►► ***a. de corriente*** transformer; *Informát* ***a. de vídeo*** video adaptor

adaptar **1** *vt* (**a**) *(modificar)* **un modelo adaptado a condiciones desérticas** a model adapted to suit desert conditions; **el edificio no ha sido aún adaptado a su nueva función** the building still hasn't been modified to suit its new function (**b**) *(libro, obra de teatro)* to adapt (**a** for); **adaptó la novela al cine** she adapted the novel for film *o* the screen

2 adaptarse *vpr* to adjust (**a** to); **no se ha adaptado al clima local** he hasn't adjusted *o* got used to the local climate; **se adaptó fácilmente a trabajar en equipo** she quickly adjusted to teamwork; **el nuevo local se adapta a las necesidades de la tienda** the new premises meet *o* are well suited to the shop's requirements

adaraja *nf Arquit* toothing (stone)

adarga *nf* = oval *o* heart-shaped leather shield

adarme *nm (pizca)* **no tiene un a. de sentido común** he hasn't got an ounce of common sense

addenda *nf,* **adenda** *nf,* **addendum** *nm* addendum

Addis Abeba *n* Addis Ababa

a. de C. (*abrev de* **antes de Cristo**) BC

adecentar 1 *vt* to tidy up; **van a a. la fachada del edificio** they're going to give the building a facelift
2 **adecentarse** *vpr* to smarten oneself up

adeco, -a *Ven* 1 *adj* = of/relating to the Acción Democrática party
2 *nm,f* = member/supporter of the Acción Democrática party

adecuación *nf* (**a**) *(idoneidad, conveniencia)* suitability (**b**) *(adaptación)* adaptation

adecuadamente *adv* appropriately, suitably

adecuado, -a *adj* appropriate, suitable; **muchos niños no reciben una alimentación adecuada** many children do not have a proper diet; **ponte un traje a. para la ceremonia** wear something suitable for the ceremony; **no es un hombre a. para ella** he's not the right sort of man for her; **el sistema actual no es el a.** the current system isn't the right one; **no creo que este sea el lugar más a. para discutir del tema** I don't think this is the best *o* right place to discuss the matter; **repartieron los fondos de forma adecuada** they shared out the funds appropriately

adecuar 1 *vt* to adapt; **hay que a. los medios a los fines** you have to adapt the means to the end
2 **adecuarse** *vpr (ser apropiado)* to be appropriate (**a** for); **las medidas se adecuan a las circunstancias** the measures are in keeping with the situation; **este apartamento se adecua a nuestras necesidades** this apartment is well suited to *o* meets our needs; **el programa puede adecuarse a las necesidades del cliente** the programme can be adapted to the customer's needs; **un producto que se adecua a todos los bolsillos** a product which is affordable for everyone

adefesio *nm Fam* (**a**) *(persona)* fright, sight; **iba hecho un a.** he looked a real sight (**b**) *(cosa)* eyesore, monstrosity; **ese sombrero es un a.** that hat is hideous

a. de J.C. *(abrev de* **antes de Jesucristo**) BC

Adelaida *n* Adelaide

adelantado, -a 1 *adj* (**a**) *(precoz)* advanced; **Galileo fue un hombre a. a su tiempo** Galileo was a man ahead of his time; **está muy a. para su edad** he's very advanced for his age
(**b**) *(avanzado)* advanced; **llevamos el trabajo muy a.** we're quite far ahead with the work; **una tecnología muy adelantada** a very advanced technology; **pago a.** advance payment; **le dio un pase a. al extremo** *(en fútbol)* he passed the ball forward for the winger to run on to
(**c**) *(reloj)* fast; **llevo el reloj a.** my watch is fast; **ese reloj va a.** that clock is fast
2 *nm,f Hist* = governor of a frontier province
3 *nm (en rugby)* knock-on
4 **por adelantado** *loc adv* in advance; **hay que pagar por a.** you have to pay in advance

adelantamiento *nm* (**a**) *(en carretera)* overtaking; **los adelantamientos en curva están prohibidos** overtaking on bends is prohibited; **un a. imprudente** a reckless overtaking manoeuvre (**b**) *(de fecha)* bringing forward; **el a. de la entrada en vigor del euro** the bringing forward of the date on which the euro comes into force

---

ADELANTAR 1 *vt* (**a**) *(vehículo, competidor)* to overtake; **me adelantó en la última vuelta** she overtook me on the final lap
(**b**) *(mover hacia adelante)* to move forward; *(pie)* to put forward; *(balón)* to pass forward; **adelantó su coche para que yo pudiera aparcar** she moved her car forward so I could park; **adelante dos casillas** *(en juego)* move forward *o* jump two squares; **habrá que a. los relojes una hora** we'll have to put the clocks forward (by) an hour
(**c**) *(en el tiempo) (reunión, viaje)* to bring forward; **adelantaron la fecha de la reunión** they brought forward the date of the meeting; **me quedaré en la oficina para a. el trabajo** I'm going to stay on late at the office to get ahead with my work
(**d**) *(dinero)* to pay in advance; **pedí que me adelantaran la mitad del sueldo de julio** I asked for an advance of half of my wages for July
(**e**) *(información)* to release; **el gobierno adelantará los primeros resultados a las ocho** the government will announce the first results at eight o'clock; **no podemos a. nada más por el momento** we can't tell you *o* say any more for the time being
(**f**) *(mejorar)* to promote, to advance; **¿qué adelantas con eso?** what do you hope to gain *o* achieve by that?; **con mentir no adelantamos nada** there's nothing to be gained by lying; **no adelanto nada en mis estudios de alemán** I'm not making any progress with my German; **adelantaron cinco puestos en la clasificación** they moved up five places in the table
2 *vi* (**a**) *(progresar)* to make progress; **la informática ha adelantado mucho en la última década** there has been a lot of progress in information technology over the past decade
(**b**) *(reloj)* to be fast; **mi reloj adelanta** my watch is fast
(**c**) *(en carretera)* to overtake; **prohibido a.** *(en señal)* no overtaking
(**d**) *(avanzar)* to advance, to go forward; **la fila adelanta con lentitud** the *Br* queue *o US* line is moving forward *o* advancing slowly
3 **adelantarse** *vpr* (**a**) *(en el tiempo)* to be early; *(frío, verano)* to arrive early; **la reunión se ha adelantado una hora** the meeting has been brought forward an hour; **este año se ha adelantado la primavera** spring has come early this year
(**b**) *(en el espacio)* to go on ahead; **se adelantó unos pasos** he went on a few steps ahead; **me adelanto para comprar el pan** I'll go on ahead and buy the bread
(**c**) *(reloj)* to gain; **mi reloj se adelanta cinco minutos al día** my watch is gaining five minutes a day
(**d**) *(anticiparse)* **adelantarse a alguien** to beat sb to it; **se adelantó a mis deseos** she anticipated my wishes; **se adelantaron a la competencia** they stole a march on their rivals; **no nos adelantemos a los acontecimientos** let's not jump the gun

---

ADELANTE 1 *adv* (**a**) *(movimiento)* forward, ahead; **echarse a.** to lean forward; **dar un paso a.** to step forward; **hacia a.** forwards; **no se puede seguir a. porque la carretera está cortada** we can't go on because the road is closed
(**b**) *(en el tiempo)* **(de ahora) en a.** from now on; **de este año en a.** from this year on; **en a., llame antes de entrar** in future, knock before coming in; **más a. ampliaremos el negocio** later on, we'll expand the business; **mirar a.** to look ahead
(**c**) *(posición)* **los asientos de a.** the front seats; **la parte de a.** the front; **más a. se encuentra el centro de cálculo** further on is the computer centre; **prefiero sentarme a.** *(en coche)* I'd rather sit in the front; *(en teatro, cine)* I'd rather sit towards the front; **más a.** *(en camino)* further on; *(en teatro, cine)* further forward; *(en texto)* below, later; **se encuentra camino a.** it's further along *o* down the road
2 **adelante de** *loc prep Am* in front of; **Pablo se sienta a. de mí** Pablo sits in front of me
3 *interj (¡siga!)* go ahead!; *(¡pase!)* come in!

---

adelanto *nm* (**a**) *(de dinero)* advance; **pidió un a. del sueldo** she asked for an advance on her wages
(**b**) *(técnico)* advance; **este descubrimiento supone un gran a.** this discovery is a great advance; **utilizan los últimos adelantos tecnológicos** they use the latest technological advances *o* developments
(**c**) *(de noticia)* advance notice; **un a. del programa de festejos** a preview of the programme of celebrations
(**d**) *(de reunión, viaje)* bringing forward; **el gobierno anunció el a. de las elecciones** the government announced that it was bringing forward the date of the elections
(**e**) *(anticipación)* **el tren llegó con (diez minutos de) a.** the train arrived (ten minutes) early; **el proyecto lleva dos días de a.** the project is two days ahead of schedule

adelfa *nf* oleander

adelfilla *nf* spurge laurel

adelgazamiento *nm* slimming; **plan de a.** slimming plan; **esa droga tiene como efecto un acusado a.** this drug causes considerable weight loss

adelgazante *adj* slimming

adelgazar [14] 1 *vt (kilos)* to lose; **esta faja te adelgaza la figura** that girdle makes you look slimmer
2 *vi* to lose weight, to slim; **ha adelgazado mucho** he has lost a lot of weight

ademán 1 *nm (gesto) (con las manos)* gesture; *(con la cara)* face, expression; **hizo a. de decir algo/de huir** he made as if to say sth/run away; **se acercó en a. de pegarle** she approached him as if to hit him
2 **ademanes** *nmpl (modales)* manners

ADEMÁS *adv* moreover, besides; *(también)* also; **es guapa y a. inteligente** she's beautiful, and clever too; **dijo, a., que no pensaba retirarse** she also said that she didn't intend to retire; **canta muy bien y a. toca la guitarra** not only does she sing very well, she also plays the guitar; **no sólo es demasiado grande, sino que a. te queda mal** it's not just that it's too big, it doesn't suit you either; **a. hay que tener en cuenta que...** it should, moreover, be remembered that...; **a. de** as well as; **a. de simpático es inteligente** as well as being nice, he's intelligent; **a. de perder el partido, enfadaron a la afición** on top of losing the match they upset their supporters

---

ADENA [a'ðena] *nf (abrev de* **Asociación para la Defensa de la Naturaleza**) = Spanish branch of the World Wildlife Fund

adenina *nf Bioquím* adenine

adenitis *nf inv Med* adenitis

adenoideo, -a *adj Med* adenoidal

adenoides *nfpl Med* adenoids

adenoma *nm Med* adenoma

adentrarse *vpr* (a) **a. en** *(jungla, barrio)* to go deep into; **se adentraron en el laberinto** they went further *o* deeper inside the labyrinth (b) **a. en** *(asunto)* to study in depth; **en su estudio intenta a. en la mentalidad del criminal** in her study she attempts to get inside the mind of the criminal; **prefiero no adentrarme en un asunto tan polémico** I'd rather not go into such a controversial issue

adentro 1 *adv* (a) *(movimiento)* inside; **pasen a.** come/go inside; **empújalo hacia a.** push it inside; **le clavó el cuchillo muy a.** she plunged the knife deep into him (b) *(en el interior)* **la parte de a.** the inside; **hoy comeremos a.** we'll eat inside *o* indoors today; **quédate a. y no salgas** stay inside *o* indoors and don't go out; **tierra a.** inland; **mar a.** out to sea

2 **adentro de** *loc prep Am* inside; **a. del armario** inside the cupboard

adentros *nmpl* **sonrió para sus a.** he smiled to himself; **"ésta me la pagará", pensó/se dijo para sus a.** "she'll pay for this," he thought/ said to himself

adepto, -a 1 *adj (partidario)* supporting; **ser a. a** to be a follower of

2 *nm,f* follower (**a** *o* **de** of); **el vegetarianismo tiene muchos adeptos** there are lots of people who are vegetarians; **un tipo de música que va ganando adeptos** a musical style that is getting an increasingly large following

> **Falso amigo**: La palabra inglesa **adept** no es la traducción del español **adepto**. En inglés **adept** significa "experto".

adequizar *vt Ven Pol* (a) *(persona)* to recruit as a member *o* supporter of the Acción Democrática party; **su familia lo adequizó desde pequeño** his family brought him up as a AD supporter (b) *(institución)* to fill with members or supporters of the Acción Democrática party; **adequizaron el comité** they packed the committee with AD supporters

aderezar [14] *vt* (a) *(sazonar) (ensalada)* to dress; *(comida)* to season (b) *(tejidos)* to size (c) *(conversación)* to liven up, to spice up

aderezo *nm* (a) *(aliño) (de ensalada)* dressing; *(de comida)* seasoning (b) *(adorno)* adornment

adeudar 1 *vt* (a) *(deber)* to owe (b) *Fin* to debit; **a. 5.000 pesos a una cuenta** to debit 5,000 pesos to an account

2 **adeudarse** *vpr* to get into debt

adeudo *nm* (a) *Fin* debit; **con a. a mi cuenta corriente** debited to my current account (b) *Méx (deuda)* debt

adherencia *nf* (a) *(de sustancia, superficie)* stickiness, adhesion (b) *(de neumáticos)* roadholding (c) *(parte añadida)* appendage (d) **adherencias** *(en herida)* adhesions

adherente *adj* adhesive, sticky

adherir [63] 1 *vt* to stick; **llevaba una bomba adherida al cuerpo** he had a bomb strapped to his body

2 **adherirse** *vpr* (a) *(pegarse)* to stick; **unos neumáticos que se adhieren muy bien al firme** tyres that hold the road very well (b) **adherirse a** *(opinión, idea)* to adhere to; **me adhiero a tu propuesta** I support your proposal; **varios sindicatos se adhirieron a la convocatoria de huelga** a number of unions supported the strike call (c) **adherirse a** *(partido, asociación)* to join

adhesión *nf* (a) *(a opinión, idea)* support (**a** of); **aplaudieron su a. a los principios democráticos** they applauded his commitment to democracy; **su propuesta recibió pocas adhesiones** her proposal found few supporters (b) *(a una organización)* entry (**a** into) (c) *Fís* adhesion

adhesivo, -a 1 *adj* adhesive

2 *nm* (a) *(pegatina)* sticker (b) *(sustancia)* adhesive

adhiero *etc ver* **adherir**

adhiriera *etc ver* **adherir**

ad hoc *adj inv* ad hoc; **una medida a.** an ad hoc measure

adiabático, -a *adj Fís* adiabatic

adianto *nm* maidenhair fern

adicción *nf* addiction (**a** to); **esa droga produce una fuerte a.** this drug is highly addictive

adición *nf* (a) *(suma)* addition; **hay que efectuar la a. de todos los gastos** we have to calculate the total cost (b) *(añadidura)* addition; **el garage es una a. reciente** the garage is a recent addition (c) *RP (cuenta) Br* bill, *US* check

adicional *adj* additional; **hubo que contratar a personal a. durante la temporada alta** we had to take on extra *o* additional staff during the high season

adicionalmente *adv* additionally, in addition

adicionar *vt* (a) *(añadir, sumar)* to add (b) *(alargar)* to extend, to prolong

adictivo, -a *adj* addictive

adicto, -a 1 *adj* (a) *(a droga, hábito)* addicted (a to); **es a. a la televisión** he's a TV addict (b) *(partidario)* **a. a** in favour of; **no soy muy a. a las reformas propuestas** I'm not greatly enamoured of the proposed reforms

2 *nm,f* (a) *(a droga, hábito)* addict; **un a. a la heroína/al tabaco** a heroin/nicotine addict; **un a. a la televisión** a TV addict (b) *(partidario)* supporter; **los adictos al régimen** the supporters of the regime

adiestrado, -a *adj* trained; **un perro a. para la caza** a dog trained for hunting

adiestrador, -ora *nm,f (de animales)* trainer

adiestramiento *nm* training

adiestrar *vt* to train; **a. a alguien en algo/para hacer algo** to train sb in sth/to do sth

adinerado, -a *adj* wealthy

ad infinitum *adv* ad infinitum

adiós (*pl* **adioses**) 1 *nm* goodbye; **decir a. a alguien** to say goodbye to sb; **decir a. a algo** to wave *o* kiss sth goodbye

2 *interj* (a) *(saludo) (al despedirse)* goodbye!; *(al cruzarse con alguien)* hello! (b) *(expresa disgusto)* blast!; **¡a., nos hemos quedado sin gasolina!** blast, we're out of petrol!

adiposidad *nf* fattiness

adiposo, -a *adj* fatty; **tejido a.** adipose tissue

aditamento *nm (complemento)* accessory; *(cosa añadida)* addition

aditivo *nm* additive ►► ***a. alimentario*** food additive

adivinable *adj* foreseeable

adivinación *nf* (a) *(predicción)* prophecy, prediction ►► ***a. del futuro*** fortune-telling; ***a. del pensamiento*** mind-reading (b) *(conjetura)* guessing

adivinador, -ora *nm,f* fortune-teller

adivinanza *nf* riddle; **jugar a las adivinanzas** to play at (guessing) riddles; **me puso una a.** she asked me a riddle

adivinar 1 *vt* (a) *(predecir)* to foretell; *(el futuro)* to tell

(b) *(acertar)* to guess; **¡adivina en qué mano está la moneda!** guess which hand the coin is in!; **adivinó el acertijo** he worked out the riddle; **¿a que no adivinas qué he comprado?** guess what I bought

(c) *(intuir)* to suspect; **adivino que le pasa algo** I've got the feeling something's wrong with him

(d) *(vislumbrar)* to spot, to make out; **la propuesta deja a. las verdaderas intenciones de los generales** this proposal reveals the generals' true intentions; **la madre adivinó la tristeza oculta bajo su sonrisa** her mother could see the sadness behind her smile

2 **adivinarse** *vpr (vislumbrarse)* to be visible; **el castillo apenas se adivinaba en la lejanía** the castle could just be made out in the distance

adivinatorio, -a *adj* prophetic; **las artes adivinatorias** the arts of prophecy

adivino, -a *nm,f* fortune-teller; **no soy a.** I'm not psychic

adjetivación *nf* adjectival use

adjetivado, -a *adj* used as an adjective

adjetival *adj* adjectival

adjetivar *vt* (a) *(calificar)* **a. algo/a alguien de** *o* **como** to describe sth/sb as (b) *Gram* to use adjectivally

adjetivo, -a 1 *adj* adjectival

2 *nm* adjective ►► ***a. atributivo*** attributive adjective; ***a. calificativo*** qualifying adjective; ***a. comparativo*** comparative adjective; ***a. demostrativo*** demonstrative adjective; ***a. especificativo*** = qualifying adjective which follows the noun; ***a. explicativo*** = adjective preceding the noun and usually denoting a conventional characteristic; ***a. indefinido*** indefinite adjective; ***a. numeral*** quantitative adjective; ***a. posesivo*** possessive adjective; ***a. superlativo*** superlative adjective

adjudicación *nf* awarding ►► *Com* ***a. por concurso público*** competitive tendering; ***a. de obras*** awarding of contracts *(for public works)*

adjudicador, -ora 1 *adj* adjudicating; **comité a.** adjudicating committee

2 *nm,f* adjudicator

adjudicar [60] 1 *vt (asignar)* to award; **el testamento les adjudicó los muebles** the furniture was left to them in the will; **les fue adjudicada la construcción del puente** they were awarded the contract to build the bridge
2 **adjudicarse** *vpr* (**a**) *(apropiarse)* to take for oneself (**b**) *(triunfo)* to win; **el equipo local se adjudicó la victoria** the home team won

adjudicatario, -a 1 *adj* **la empresa adjudicataria del contrato** the company awarded *o* which won the contract
2 *nm,f* **el a. del contrato** the winner of the contract, the person/ company awarded the contract; **el a. del premio** the winner of the prize

adjudique *etc ver* **adjudicar**

adjuntar *vt* (**a**) *(a carta)* to enclose; **le adjunto a esta carta una lista de precios** I am enclosing a price list with this letter, please find enclosed a price list (**b**) *Informát (a correo electrónico)* to attach; **a. un archivo a un mensaje** to attach a file to a message

adjunto, -a 1 *adj* (**a**) *(incluido)* enclosed; **ver mapa a.** see the enclosed map (**b**) *Informát (archivo)* attached (**c**) *(auxiliar)* assistant; **profesor a.** assistant lecturer
2 *nm,f (auxiliar)* assistant; **trabaja como a. al director** he's the director's assistant
3 *nm Gram* adjunct
4 *adv* enclosed; **a. le remito el recibo** please find a receipt enclosed

adlátere *nmf Pey* underling

adminículo *nm* gadget

administración *nf* (**a**) *(de empresa, finca)* administration, management; *(de casa)* running; **la a. de la justicia corresponde a los jueces** judges are responsible for implementing the law ▸▸ ***a. de empresas*** business administration; ***a. de fondos*** fund management; ***a. de recursos*** resource management
(**b**) *(oficina)* manager's office
(**c**) **la A.** *(los órganos del Estado)* the government ▸▸ ***a. autonómica*** regional government, government of an autonomous region; ***a. central*** central government; ***a. de justicia*** legal system; ***a. local*** local government; ***a. pública, administraciones públicas*** civil service
(**d**) **la A.** *(en EE.UU.)* the Administration; **la A. (de) Truman** the Truman Administration
(**e**) *(de medicamento)* administering; **a. por vía oral** *(en prospecto)* to be taken orally
(**f**) *(de sacramentos)* administering
(**g**) *Esp* ***a. de loterías*** lottery outlet

administrado, -a 1 *adj* **a. por la ONU** under UN administration
2 *nm,f* person under administration

administrador, -ora 1 *nm,f* (**a**) *(de empresa)* manager ▸▸ *Informát* ***a. de (sitio) web*** webmaster (**b**) *(de bienes ajenos)* administrator ▸▸ ***a. de fincas*** land agent
2 *nm Informát* ***a. de archivos*** file manager

administrar 1 *vt* (**a**) *(empresa, finca)* to manage, to run; *(casa)* to run; *(país)* to govern, to run; *(recursos)* to manage; **administra bien tu dinero** don't squander your money; **a. justicia** to administer justice (**b**) *(medicamento)* to administer (**c**) *(sacramentos)* to administer
2 **administrarse** *vpr (organizar dinero)* to manage one's finances

administrativamente *adv* administratively

administrativo, -a 1 *adj* administrative; **personal a.** administrative staff
2 *nm,f* office worker

admirable *adj* admirable

admirablemente *adv* admirably

admiración *nf* (**a**) *(respeto)* admiration; **digno de a.** admirable; **"¡eres la mejor!", dijo con a.** "you're the best!" he said admiringly; **siento mucha a. por él** I admire him greatly
(**b**) *(sorpresa)* amazement; **declaró, para a. de todos, que dimitía del cargo** he announced, to everyone's amazement, that he was resigning from the post; **causó a. con el traje que llevaba** she caused a sensation with her dress
(**c**) *(signo ortográfico) Br* exclamation mark, *US* exclamation point

admirado, -a *adj* (**a**) *(respetado)* **está con nosotros nuestro a. Sánchez** we have with us our very good friend Mr Sánchez; **como diría mi a. Federico...** as my dear friend Federico would say... (**b**) *(sorprendido)* amazed; **me quedé a. con sus conocimientos** I was amazed at how much she knew

admirador, -ora *nm,f* admirer; **soy un gran a. de su obra** I'm a great admirer of her work

admirar 1 *vt* (**a**) *(personaje, obra de arte)* to admire; **admiro su sinceridad** I admire her frankness; **lo admiro por su honradez** I admire his honesty; **ser de a.** to be admirable (**b**) *(sorprender)* to amaze; **me admira su descaro** I can't believe his cheek (**c**) *(contemplar)* to admire
2 **admirarse** *vpr* to be amazed; **admirarse de algo** to be amazed at sth

ADJETIVO

Position of adjectives: before or after the noun?

Certain Spanish adjectives always precede the noun. For example, possessive adjectives, ordinal numbers and words such as **otro**, **tanto**, **mucho**, and **poco** which specify quantity or identity rather than give a description:

mi libro favorito *my favourite book*
tanto ruido *so much noise*
la tercera vez *the third time*
mucho dinero *a lot of money*
otra aspirina *another aspirin*
poca suerte *little luck*

With the exception of a few fixed phrases such as **Extremo Oriente** (*Far East*) or **Oriente Próximo** (*Near East),* the basic rules for descriptive adjectives are as follows. If the adjective restricts the application of the noun, it comes after the noun. Adjectives are most obviously restrictive in this sense where they indicate a subcategory of the class of things referred to by the noun. Adjectives indicating nationality, origin and purpose, or which indicate a contrast (including an implicit one, as with colour adjectives) are also typically of this kind:

carne fresca *fresh meat* (as opposed to cooked, dried, rotten etc)
literatura contemporánea *contemporary literature*
la pasión latina *Latin passion*
la industria textil *the textile industry*
dame una toalla limpia *give me a clean towel*
es un empleado eficiente *he's an efficient employee*

If there is no such restriction, the adjective can come before or after the noun. Where the adjective precedes the noun this is usually to add emphasis:

tras sus sorprendentes palabras *after his surprising words*
una inesperada reacción del público *an unexpected reaction from the audience*

Adjectives can also precede the noun to give a more poetic tone to the language:

sus grandes ojos me miraban extrañados *she looked at me with her big eyes full of surprise*

admirativo, -a *adj (maravillado)* admiring; **una mirada admirativa** an admiring look

admisibilidad *nf* acceptability

admisible *adj* acceptable

admisión *nf* (**a**) *(de persona)* admission; *(de solicitudes)* acceptance; **reservado el derecho de a.** *(en letrero)* the management reserves the right to refuse admission; **mañana se abre el plazo de a. de solicitudes** applications may be made from tomorrow (**b**) *(de error, culpa)* admission (**c**) *Tec* induction

admitir *vt* (**a**) *(dejar entrar)* to admit, to allow in; **a. a alguien en** to admit sb to; **lo admitieron en la universidad** he was accepted by the university; **no se admiten perros** *(en letrero)* no dogs; **no se admite la entrada a menores de 18 años** *(en letrero)* no admittance for under-18s
(**b**) *(reconocer)* to admit; **admitió la derrota** she admitted defeat; **admito que estaba equivocado** I admit I was wrong
(**c**) *(aceptar)* to accept; **se admiten propinas** *(en letrero)* gratuities at your discretion; **admitimos tarjetas de crédito** we accept all major credit cards; **admitieron a trámite la solicitud** they allowed the application to proceed
(**d**) *(permitir, tolerar)* to allow, to permit; **no admite ni un error** he won't stand for a single mistake; **este texto no admite más retoques** there can be no more changes to this text; **es una situación que no admite comparación** this situation cannot be compared to others; **su hegemonía no admite dudas** their dominance is unquestioned
(**e**) *(tener capacidad para)* to hold; **este monovolumen admite siete pasajeros** this people mover seats seven passengers; **la sala admite doscientas personas** the room holds *o* has room for two hundred people

admón. *(abrev de* **administración***)* admin.

admonición *nf Formal* warning; **recibió una severa a.** she was severely admonished

admonitorio, -a *adj Formal* warning; **voz admonitoria** voice with a note of warning

ADN 1 *nm (abrev de* **ácido desoxirribonucleico***)* DNA
2 *nf (abrev de* **Acción Democrática Nacionalista***)* = Bolivian political party

ad nauseam *adv* ad nauseam

adobado, -a *adj* (**a**) *(alimentos) (para guiso)* marinated; *(para conserva)* pickled (**b**) *(pieles)* tanned

adobar *vt* (**a**) *(alimentos) (para guisar)* to marinate; *(para conservar)* to pickle (**b**) *(pieles)* to tan

adobe *nm* adobe

adobo *nm* (**a**) *(acción) (para guisar)* marinating; *(para conservar)* pickling (**b**) *(salsa) (para guisar)* marinade; *(para conservar)* marinade; **poner en a. durante dos horas** marinate for two hours (**c**) *(de pieles)* tanning

adocenado, -a *adj* mediocre, run-of-the-mill

adocenarse *vpr* to lapse into mediocrity

adoctrinamiento *nm* (**a**) *(de ideas)* indoctrination (**b**) *(enseñanza)* instruction

adoctrinar *vt* (**a**) *(inculcar ideas)* to indoctrinate (**b**) *(enseñar)* to instruct

adolecer [46] *vi* **a. de** *(enfermedad)* to suffer from; *(defecto)* to be guilty of; **adolece de falta de entusiasmo** she suffers from a lack of enthusiasm; **su análisis adolece de simplismo** his analysis is guilty of being simplistic

adolescencia *nf* adolescence; **se dedicó a la pintura desde la a.** she's been painting since she was a teenager

adolescente 1 *adj* adolescent; **tienen un hijo a.** they have a teenage son
2 *nmf* adolescent, teenager; **un ídolo de los adolescentes** a teen idol

adolezco *etc ver* **adolecer**

adonde 1 *adv* where; **la ciudad a. vamos** the city we are going to; **voy a. estuvimos ayer** I'm going where we went yesterday; *ver* **donde**
2 *prep Fam (a casa de)* **vamos a. la abuela** we're going to granny's

adónde *ver* **dónde**

adondequiera *adv* wherever; **a. que va, le siguen sus admiradores** his admirers follow him wherever he goes *o* everywhere

Adonis *n Mitol* Adonis

adonis *nm inv Fig* Adonis, handsome young man

adopción *nf* (**a**) *(de hijo)* adoption; **Uruguay es mi país de a.** Uruguay is my adopted country; **tomó a dos niños coreanos en a.** he adopted two Korean children (**b**) *(de moda, decisión)* adoption; **estoy en contra de la a. de medidas sin consultar al interesado** I'm against taking any steps without consulting the person involved

adoptado, -a *adj (hijo)* adopted

adoptante 1 *adj* adopting
2 *nmf* adopter, adoptive parent

adoptar *vt* (**a**) *(hijo)* to adopt
(**b**) *(nacionalidad)* to adopt
(**c**) *(medida, decisión)* to take; **adoptaron medidas para luchar contra el desempleo** they took measures to combat unemployment; **la policía adoptó la decisión de prohibir la manifestación** the police took the decision to ban the demonstration
(**d**) *(forma)* to take on; **el insecto adapta la forma de una bola para protegerse** the insect curls itself into a ball in order to protect itself; **su timidez adopta la forma de agresividad** his shyness manifests itself as aggressiveness

adoptivo, -a *adj* (**a**) *(hijo, país)* adopted (**b**) *(padre)* adoptive (**c**) *(país, nacionalidad)* adopted

adoquín *nm* (**a**) *(piedra)* cobblestone (**b**) *Fam (persona)* blockhead

adoquinado, -a 1 *adj* cobbled
2 *nm* (**a**) *(suelo)* cobbles (**b**) *(acción)* cobbling

adoquinar *vt* to cobble

adorable *adj (persona)* adorable; *(lugar, película)* wonderful

adorablemente *adv* adorably

adoración *nf* (**a**) *(de persona)* adoration; **"lo que tú quieras", dijo con a.** "whatever you want," he said adoringly; **sentir a. por alguien** to worship sb (**b**) *(de dios, ídolo)* adoration, worship; **se prohibió la a. de los dioses paganos** the worship of pagan gods was forbidden ▸▸ *Rel* ***la A. de los Reyes Magos*** the Adoration of the Magi

adorador, -ora 1 *adj* (**a**) *(enamorado)* adoring (**b**) *Rel* worshipping
2 *nm,f* (**a**) *(enamorado)* adorer (**b**) *Rel* worshipper

adorar *vt* (**a**) *(persona, comida)* to adore (**b**) *(dios, ídolo)* to worship

adoratriz *nf Rel* = nun belonging to the order of the Slaves of the Most Holy Sacrament

adormecedor, -ora *adj* soporific

adormecer [46] 1 *vt* (**a**) *(producir sueño)* to lull to sleep (**b**) *(entumecer)* to make numb (**c**) *(aplacar) (miedo, ira)* to calm; *(pena, dolor)* to alleviate, to lessen
2 **adormecerse** *vpr* to drift off to sleep

adormecido, -a *adj* (**a**) *(soñoliento)* sleepy, drowsy (**b**) *(entumecido)* numb, asleep

adormecimiento *nm* (**a**) *(sueño)* sleepiness, drowsiness (**b**) *(entumecimiento)* numbness (**c**) *(de pena, dolor)* alleviation, lessening

adormezco *etc ver* **adormecer**

adormidera *nf* poppy

adormilado, -a *adj* (**a**) *(dormido)* dozing; **se quedó a. en el sillón** he dozed off in the armchair (**b**) *(con sueño)* sleepy

adormilarse *vpr* to doze; **se adormiló en el sofa** she dozed off on the sofa

adornado, -a *adj* decorated (**con** with)

adornar 1 *vt* (**a**) *(decorar)* to decorate; **adornó la habitación con cuadros** she decorated *o* hung the room with paintings (**b**) *(aderezar)* to adorn (**con** with); **adornó el relato con florituras del lenguaje** she embellished the story with fancy language
2 *vi* to be decorative; **hace falta algo que adorne** we need to add some sort of decorative touch
3 **adornarse** *vpr* **se adornó el pelo con unas flores** she wore flowers in her hair as a decoration

adorno *nm (objeto)* ornament; **los adornos navideños** the Christmas decorations; **de a.** *(árbol, figura)* decorative; **es sólo de a.** *(no funciona)* it's just for show; EXPR *Fam Hum* **estar de a.: está aquí sólo de a.** he's just taking up space here; **no está aquí sólo de a.** he's not here just because he's a pretty face

adosado, -a 1 *adj* (**a**) *(pegado)* **un granero a. al edificio principal** a granary attached to the main building (**b**) *(casa)* terraced; **chalé a.** terraced villa (**c**) *(columna)* half-relief
2 *nm* terraced house

adosar *vt* **a. algo a algo** to push sth up against sth; **adosaron un almacén a la tienda** they built a warehouse on to the shop; **la bomba que adosaron a los bajos del vehículo** the bomb they attached to the underside of the car

adquiero *etc ver* **adquirir**

adquirible *adj* acquirable, obtainable

adquirido, -a *adj* acquired; **tener derecho a. sobre algo** to have acquired a right to sth

adquiriente, adquirente 1 *adj* **(a)** *(que obtiene algo)* acquiring **(b)** *(comprador)* buying
2 *nm,f* **(a)** *(que obtiene algo)* acquirer **(b)** *(comprador)* buyer

adquiriera *etc ver* **adquirir**

adquirir [5] *vt* **(a)** *(comprar)* to acquire, to purchase; **ya es posible a. pasajes de avión a través de Internet** you can now buy air tickets on the Internet; **adquirieron el 51 por ciento de las acciones de la empresa** they acquired a 51 percent shareholding in the company
(b) *(conseguir) (conocimientos, hábito, cultura)* to acquire; *(éxito, popularidad)* to achieve; *(libertad, experiencia)* to gain; *(fortuna)* to acquire, to come by; *(nacionalidad)* to obtain; **adquirió una reputación de inflexibilidad** he gained *o* acquired a reputation for inflexibility; **adquirieron el compromiso de ayudarse mutualmente** they committed themselves to helping each other

adquisición *nf* **(a)** *(compra)* purchase; **ayudas para la a. de viviendas** financial assistance for house buyers
(b) *(de empresa)* takeover
(c) *(cosa comprada)* purchase; **nuestra casa fue una excelente a.** our house was an excellent buy
(d) *(de hábito, cultura)* acquisition; **a. de conocimientos** acquisition of knowledge ►► *Ling* ***a. lingüística*** language acquisition
(e) *Fam (persona)* **el nuevo secretario es toda una a.** the new secretary is quite a find

adquisidor, -ora 1 *adj* **(a)** *(que obtiene algo)* acquiring **(b)** *(comprador)* buying
2 *nm,f* **(a)** *(que obtiene algo)* acquirer **(b)** *(comprador)* buyer

adquisitivo, -a *adj* **poder a.** purchasing power

adrede *adv* on purpose, deliberately

adrenalina *nf* **(a)** *(sustancia)* adrenalin **(b)** *Fam (excitación)* adrenalin; **le dio una subida de a.** it gave him a rush *o* buzz; **el disco es una descarga de a.** the record is like a shot of adrenalin

adrenérgico, -a *adj Biol* adrenergic

Adriano *n pr* Hadrian

adriático, -a 1 *adj* Adriatic; **el mar Adriático** the Adriatic Sea
2 *nm* **el Adriático** the Adriatic (Sea)

adrizar *vt Náut* to right

adscribir 1 *vt* **(a)** *(asignar)* to assign **(b)** *(destinar)* to appoint; **lo adscribieron a Guadalajara** they sent him to Guadalajara
2 adscribirse *vpr* **adscribirse a** *(grupo, partido)* to become a member of; *(ideología)* to subscribe to

adscripción *nf* **(a)** *(atribución)* attribution, ascription **(b)** *(destino laboral)* assignment, appointment

adscrito, -a 1 *participio ver* **adscribir**
2 *adj* assigned

ADSL *nm* (*abrev de* **asymmetric digital subscriber line**) ADSL

adsorber *vt Fís* to adsorb

adsorción *nf Fís* adsorption

aduana *nf* customs *(singular)*; **pasar por la a.** to go through customs; **derechos de a.** customs duty

aduanero, -a 1 *adj* customs; **controles aduaneros** customs controls
2 *nm,f* customs officer

aducir [18] *vt (motivo, pretexto)* to give, to furnish; **adujo insolvencia para evitar pagar a sus acreedores** he claimed insolvency to avoid paying his creditors; **"estaba muy cansado", adujo** "I was very tired," he explained

aductor *nm Anat* adductor

adueñarse *vpr* **(a) a. de** *(apoderarse de)* to take over, to take control of; **se adueñó de la mejor cama sin consultar a nadie** he claimed the best bed for himself without asking anyone **(b) a. de** *(dominar)* to take hold of; **el pánico se adueñó de ellos** panic took hold of them

adujar *vt Náut (cadena, cabo)* to coil

adujera *etc ver* **aducir**

adujo *etc ver* **aducir**

adulación *nf* flattery

adulador, -ora 1 *adj* flattering
2 *nm,f* flatterer

adulancia *nf Ven* flattery

adulante, -a *Ven* **1** *adj* flattering
2 *nm,f* flatterer

adular *vt* to flatter

adulón, -ona *nm,f* toady

adulteración *nf* **(a)** *(de sustancia)* adulteration **(b)** *(de información)* distortion

adúlteramente *adv* adulterously

adulterar *vt* **(a)** *(alimento)* to adulterate **(b)** *(información, verdad)* to doctor, to distort

adulterino, -a *adj* **hijo a.** illegitimate child

adulterio *nm* adultery

adúltero, -a 1 *adj* adulterous
2 *nm,f* adulterer, *f* adulteress

adulto, -a 1 *adj* **(a)** *(desarrollado)* adult; **la edad adulta** adulthood **(b)** *(maduro)* adult; **un comportamiento a.** adult behaviour
2 *nm,f* adult; **película para adultos** adult movie

adustamente *adv* dourly, severely

adustez *nf* dourness, severity; **con a.** dourly, severely

adusto, -a *adj* **(a)** *(persona, mirada, gesto)* dour, severe **(b)** *(terreno, paisaje)* harsh

aduzco *ver* **aducir**

ad valorem *adv Fin* ad valorem

advenedizo, -a 1 *adj* upstart; **un político a.** an upstart politician
2 *nm,f* upstart

advenimiento *nm* **(a)** *(llegada)* advent; **el a. de la democracia** the advent *o* coming of democracy **(b)** *(ascenso al trono)* accession

adventicio, -a *adj* **(a)** *(ocasional)* accidental, adventitious **(b)** *(raíz, tallo)* adventitious

adventismo *nm* Adventism

adventista 1 *adj* Adventist; **la Iglesia A. del Séptimo Día** the Seventh Day Adventist Church
2 *nmf* Adventist; **un a. del séptimo día** a Seventh Day Adventist

adverbial *adj Gram* adverbial

adverbio *nm Gram* adverb ►► ***a. de cantidad*** adverb of degree; ***a. de lugar*** adverb of place; ***a. de modo*** adverb of manner; ***a. de tiempo*** adverb of time

adversar *vt CAm, Ven* to oppose

adversario, -a *nm,f* adversary, opponent; **fueron adversarios en varios torneos** they played each other in several competitions; **los brasileños son un a. temible** the Brazilians are formidable adversaries *o* opponents

adversativo, -a *adj Gram* adversative

adversidad *nf* **(a)** *(dificultad)* adversity; **se enfrentó a todo tipo de adversidades** he faced up to all sorts of difficulties *o* adversities
(b) *(situación difícil)* **la a.** adversity; **no logró sobreponerse a la a.** she was unable to triumph over adversity; **puedes contar con él en la a.** you can count on him when things get difficult
(c) *(cualidad desfavorable)* adverse nature; **tuvieron que quedarse en casa ante la a. del clima** they had to stay at home because of the adverse weather conditions

adverso, -a *adj* **(a)** *(condiciones)* adverse; **incluso en las condiciones más adversas** even in the worst *o* most adverse conditions **(b)** *(destino)* unkind **(c)** *(suerte)* bad; **la suerte le fue adversa** fate was unkind to him **(d)** *(viento)* unfavourable

advertencia *nf* warning; **servir de a.** to serve as a warning; **hacer una a. a alguien** to warn sb; **los expertos han lanzado una a. preocupante** the experts have issued a worrying warning; **no hizo caso de mi a.** she ignored my warning

advertido, -a *adj* **(a)** *(avisado)* informed, warned; **¡estás** *o* **quedas a.!** you've been warned! **(b)** *(capaz)* capable, skilful

advertir [63] *vt* **(a)** *(notar)* to notice; **no he advertido ningún error** I didn't notice *o* spot any mistakes; **advirtió la presencia de un hombre extraño** she became aware of *o* noticed a strange man
(b) *(prevenir, avisar)* to warn; **la señal advierte del peligro de desprendimientos** the sign warns you that there is a danger of landslides; **me advirtió del peligro** he warned me of the danger; **¡te lo advierto por última vez!** I'm telling you for the last time!; **¡te lo advierto, si no te comportas te tendrás que marchar!** I'm warning you, if you don't behave you'll have to leave!; **te advierto que no estoy de humor para bromas** I should warn you, I'm not in the mood for jokes; **te advierto que no me sorprende** I have to say it doesn't surprise me

adviento *nm Rel* Advent

advierto *etc ver* **advertir**

advirtiera *etc ver* **advertir**

advocación *nf* **una catedral bajo la a. de la Virgen de Guadalupe** a church dedicated to the Virgin of Guadalupe

adyacencia *nf Formal* adjacency

adyacente *adj* adjacent; **viven en la casa a. a la nuestra** they live in the house next to ours
AEB *nf (abrev de* **Asociación Española de Banca)** = association of Spanish private banks
AEE *nf (abrev de* **Agencia Espacial Europea)** ESA
AENA [a'ena] *nf (abrev de* **Aeropuertos Españoles y Navegación Aérea)** = Spanish airports and air traffic control authority
Aenor *nf (abrev de* **Asociación Española para la Normalización y Certificación)** = Spanish body which certifies quality and safety standards for manufactured goods, *Br* ≃ BSI, *US* ≃ ANSI
aeración *nf* aeration
aéreo, -a *adj* **(a)** *(del aire)* aerial **(b)** *(de la aviación)* air; **base aérea** air base; **controlador a.** air traffic controller; **línea aérea** airline
aerobic, aeróbic *nm* aerobics *(singular)*
aeróbico, -a *adj* aerobic
aerobio, -a *Biol* 1 *adj* aerobic
2 *nm* aerobe
aerobismo *nm Am* aerobics *(singular)*
aerobús (*pl* **aerobuses**) *nm* airbus
aeroclub (*pl* **aeroclubes**) *nm* flying club
aerodeslizador *nm* hovercraft
aerodinámica *nf* **(a)** *(ciencia)* aerodynamics *(singular)* **(b)** *(línea)* **el nuevo prototipo tiene una a. avanzada** the new prototype has advanced aerodynamics
aerodinámico, -a *adj* **(a)** *Fís* aerodynamic **(b)** *(forma, línea)* streamlined
aerodinamismo *nm* aerodynamic properties
aeródromo *nm* airfield, aerodrome
aeroembolismo *nm Med* decompression sickness
aeroespacial, aerospacial *adj* aerospace
aerofagia *nf Med* aerophagia
aerofaro *nm Av* beacon
aerofobia *nf* fear of flying
aerófobo, -a *adj* scared of flying
aerofotografía *nf* **(a)** *(técnica)* aerial photography **(b)** *(fotografía)* aerial photograph
aerofreno *nm* aerobrake, air brake
aerogenerador *nm* wind turbine
aerógrafo *nm* airbrush
aerograma *nm* airmail letter, aerogram
aerolínea *nf* airline
aerolito *nm* aerolite
aeromarítimo, -a *adj* aeromarine
aerómetro *nm* aerometer
aeromodelismo *nm* airplane modelling
aeromodelista 1 *adj* model airplane; **club a.** model airplane club
2 *nmf* model airplane enthusiast
aeromozo, -a *nm,f Am* air steward, *f* air hostess
aeronauta *nmf* aeronaut
aeronáutica *nf* aeronautics *(singular)*
aeronáutico, -a *adj* aeronautic
aeronaval *adj* **una operación de rescate a.** an air-sea rescue operation; **una batalla a.** a battle fought in the air and at sea; **fuerzas aeronavales** air and sea forces
aeronave *nf* **(a)** *(avión, helicóptero)* aircraft **(b)** *(dirigible)* airship
aeroparque *nm Arg* small airport
aeroplano *nm* aeroplane, aircraft
aeropuerto *nm* airport
aerosilla *nf RP* chairlift
aerosol *nm* aerosol (spray); **también se encuentra en a.** it's also available in aerosol
aerospacial = **aeroespacial**
aerostación *nf* ballooning
aerostática *nf* aerostatics *(singular)*
aerostático, -a *adj* **globo a.** hot-air balloon
aeróstato, aerostato *nm* hot-air balloon
aerotaxi *nm Av* air taxi, light aircraft *(for hire)*
aeroterrestre *adj Mil* air-land, air-to-ground
aerotransportado, -a *adj (tropas, polen)* airborne
aerotransportar *vt* to airlift
aerotrén *nm* maglev
aerovía *nf* airway, air lane
AFA ['afa] *nf (abrev de* **Asociación de Fútbol Argentino)** = Argentinian Football Association
afabilidad *nf* affability; **con a.** affably
afable *adj* affable
afablemente *adv* affably
áfaca *nf* yellow vetchling
afamado, -a *adj* famous
afán *nm* **(a)** *(esfuerzo)* hard work; **con a.** energetically, enthusiastically; **pone mucho a. en el trabajo** she puts a lot of effort into her work
(b) *(anhelo)* urge; **a. de riquezas** desire for wealth; **su único a. es salir por televisión** his one ambition is to appear on television; **su a. de agradar llega a ser irritante** his eagerness to please can be positively irritating; **tienen mucho a. por conocerte** they're really keen to meet you; **lo único que le mueve es el a. de lucro** he's only interested in money; **una organización sin a. de lucro** *Br* a non-profit making *o US* not-for-profit organization; **lo hizo sin a. de lucro** she did it with no thought of personal gain
afanador, -ora *nm,f* **(a)** *Méx (empleado)* (office) cleaner **(b)** *Méx, RP Fam (ladrón)* crook, thief
afanar 1 *vt Fam (robar)* to pinch, to swipe
2 **afanarse** *vpr (esforzarse)* to work hard; **se afanó mucho por acabarlo a tiempo** he worked hard to finish it on time
afanosamente *adv* eagerly, zealously; **buscó a. el libro** she hunted high and low for the book
afanoso, -a *adj* **(a)** *(persona)* busy, hard-working **(b)** *(lucha)* determined, dedicated; *(búsqueda)* painstaking, thorough
afarolarse *vpr Andes, Cuba Fam* **(a)** *(exaltarse)* to get excited, to get worked up **(b)** *(enojarse)* to get angry
afasia *nf Med* aphasia
afásico, -a *Med* 1 *adj* aphasic
2 *nm,f* aphasic
AFE ['afe] *nf (abrev* **Asociación de Futbolistas Españoles)** = Spanish soccer players association
afear 1 *vt* **(a)** *(volver feo)* to make ugly; **ese peinado la afea** that hairstyle doesn't do her any favours; **las líneas de alta tensión afean el paisaje** power lines spoil the landscape **(b)** *(criticar)* **a. a alguien su conducta** to condemn sb's behaviour
2 **afearse** *vpr* to lose one's looks
afección *nf* complaint, disease; **una a. cutánea/del riñón** a skin/kidney complaint
afectación *nf* affectation; **con a.** affectedly
afectadamente *adv* affectedly
afectado, -a 1 *adj* **(a)** *(amanerado)* affected **(b)** *(afligido)* upset, badly affected **(c)** *RP (asignado)* assigned
2 *nm,f* victim; **los afectados por las inundaciones serán indemnizados** the people affected by the floods will receive compensation
afectar *vt* **(a)** *(incumbir)* to affect; **las medidas afectan a los pensionistas** the measures affect pensioners
(b) *(afligir)* to upset, to affect badly; **todo lo afecta** he's very sensitive; **lo afectó mucho la muerte de su hermano** his brother's death hit him hard
(c) *(producir perjuicios en)* to damage; **la sequía que afectó a la región** the drought which hit the region; **a esta madera le afecta mucho la humedad** this wood is easily damaged by damp
(d) *(simular)* to affect, to feign; **afectó enfado** he feigned *o* affected anger
(e) *RP (destinar, asignar)* to assign
afectísimo, -a *adj (en carta)* **suyo a.** *(si se desconoce el nombre del destinatario)* yours faithfully; *(si se conoce el nombre del destinatario)* yours sincerely
afectivamente *adv* emotionally
afectividad *nf* emotions; **la a. en el niño** the emotional world of the child
afectivo, -a *adj (emocional)* emotional; **tener problemas afectivos** to have emotional problems
afecto, -a 1 *adj* **(a)** *(aficionado)* keen (**a** on); **son afectos a la conversación** they are fond of talking **(b)** *(adepto)* sympathetic (**a** to); **un militar a. al antiguo régimen** a soldier who is sympathetic to the old regime **(c)** *(adscrito)* attached (**a** to); **un funcionario a. al departamento de contabilidad** a civil servant attached to the accountancy department

2 *nm* (**a**) *(cariño)* affection, fondness; **sentir a. por alguien** *o* **tener a. a alguien** to be fond of sb; **lo trata con a.** she's very affectionate towards him; **en poco tiempo le ha tomado mucho a.** she has quickly become very fond of him (**b**) *(sentimiento, emoción)* emotion, feeling

afectuosamente *adv* (**a**) *(cariñosamente)* affectionately (**b**) *(en carta)* (yours) affectionately

afectuoso, -a *adj* affectionate, loving

afeitada *nf Am (del pelo, barba)* shave; **se dio una a. rápida** he shaved himself quickly, he had a quick shave

afeitado *nm* (**a**) *(del pelo, barba)* shave; **se dio un a. rápido** he shaved himself quickly, he had a quick shave (**b**) *Taurom* = blunting of the bull's horns for safety reasons

afeitadora *nf* electric razor *o* shaver

afeitar 1 *vt* (**a**) *(barba, pelo, cabeza, persona)* to shave (**b**) *Taurom* = to blunt the bull's horns for safety reasons (**c**) *Fam (rozar)* to graze, to shave; **la bala pasó afeitándome la cara** the bullet whistled past my face

2 **afeitarse** *vpr (uno mismo)* to shave; **se afeitó la barba** he shaved his beard off; **se afeitó las piernas** she shaved her legs

afeite *nm Anticuado (cosmético)* make-up

afelpado, -a *adj* plush

afeminado, -a 1 *adj* effeminate

2 *nm* **es un a.** he's effeminate

afeminamiento *nm* effeminacy

afeminar 1 *vt* to make effeminate

2 **afeminarse** *vpr* to become effeminate

aferente *adj Anat* afferent

aféresis *nf Ling* apheresis

aferrar 1 *vt* (**a**) *(objeto)* to grab (hold of) (**b**) *(embarcación)* to moor

2 *vi (anclar)* to moor

3 **aferrarse** *vpr* (**a**) **aferrarse a algo** *(a objeto)* to cling to sth (**b**) *(a idea, opinión)* **se aferran a un plan que está condenado al fracaso** they are clinging on to a plan that is destined to fail; **se aferró a su familia para superar la crisis** she clung to her family to get through the crisis

affaire [a'fer] *nm* (**a**) *(asunto)* affair; **un a. político** a political scandal (**b**) *(sentimental)* affair

affmo., -a. (*abrev de* **afectísimo, -a**) *(en carta)* **suyo a.** *(si se desconoce el nombre del destinatario)* yours faithfully; *(si se conoce el nombre del destinatario)* yours sincerely

Afganistán *n* Afghanistan

afgano, -a 1 *adj* Afghan

2 *nm,f* Afghan

3 *nm (perro)* Afghan (hound)

AFI ['afi] *nm Ling* (*abrev de* **Alfabeto Fonético Internacional**) IPA

afianzamiento *nm* (**a**) *(de construcción)* reinforcement (**b**) *(de ideas, relaciones)* consolidation

afianzar [14] 1 *vt* (**a**) *(construcción)* to reinforce; **afianzaron los cimientos** they reinforced the foundations

(**b**) *(posición)* to make secure; *(relación)* to consolidate; **afianzó el pie en el escalón** he steadied his foot on the step; **la empresa ha afianzado su liderazgo en el sector** the company has consolidated its market leadership; **el tratado afianza las relaciones entre los dos países** the treaty consolidates relations between the two countries

2 **afianzarse** *vpr* (**a**) *(en lugar)* to steady oneself; **afianzarse en una posición** *(en organización)* to establish oneself in a position; **el puerto se ha afianzado como centro comercial de la zona** the port has established itself as the trading centre of the area

(**b**) *(idea, creencia)* to take root; *(relación)* to become stronger *o* closer; **se afianzó en su opinión** he became more convinced of his opinion

afiche *nm Am* poster

afición *nf* (**a**) *(interés)* interest, hobby; **su mayor a. es la lectura** his main interest is reading; **quieren fomentar la a. a la lectura** they want to encourage reading for pleasure; **siente mucha a. por la poesía** she has a great love of poetry; **tiene mucha a. por el marisco** he's very partial to seafood, he's a big fan of seafood; **su a. a la bebida acabó con su salud** his fondness of alcohol ruined his health; **lo hago por a.** I do it because I enjoy it

(**b**) **la a.** *(los aficionados)* the fans; **el juego del equipo no convenció a la a.** the fans were not impressed by the team's performance

aficionado, -a 1 *adj* (**a**) *(interesado)* keen; **ser a. a algo** to be keen on sth; **el público a. al cine** the cinema-going public (**b**) *(no profesional)* amateur

2 *nm,f* (**a**) *(interesado)* fan; **es un a. al cine** he's a keen cinema-goer; **un gran a. a la música clásica** a great lover of classical music; **los aficionados a los toros** followers of bullfighting, bullfighting fans (**b**) *(no profesional)* amateur; **un trabajo de aficionados** an amateurish piece of work

aficionar 1 *vt* **a. a alguien a algo** to make sb keen on sth; **un plan para a. a los niños a la poesía** a scheme designed to get children interested in poetry

2 **aficionarse** *vpr* to become keen (**a** on); **últimamente se está aficionando demasiado a la bebida** he's been getting a bit too fond of drink lately

afiebrado, -a *adj Am* feverish; **estar a.** to have a temperature

afiebrarse *vpr Am* to develop a temperature

afijo, -a *Gram* 1 *adj* affixed

2 *nm* affix

afilado, -a 1 *adj* (**a**) *(cuchillo, punta, lápiz)* sharp (**b**) *(dedos, rasgos)* pointed (**c**) *(comentario, crítica)* cutting; **tiene la lengua muy afilada** he has a very sharp tongue

2 *nm* sharpening

afilador, -ora 1 *adj* sharpening

2 *nm,f (persona)* knife grinder

3 *nm* (**a**) *(objeto)* sharpener; **a. de cuchillos** knife sharpener (**b**) *Chile (sacapunta)* pencil sharpener

afilalápices *nm inv* pencil sharpener

afilar 1 *vt (cuchillo, punta, lápiz)* to sharpen; **la envidia le afiló aún más la lengua** envy gave her an even sharper tongue

2 *vi* (**a**) *RP (flirtear)* to flirt (**b**) *Chile Vulg (copular)* to screw, to fuck

3 **afilarse** *vpr (hacerse puntiagudo)* to become pointed, to taper; **se le ha afilado mucho la lengua** he has become very sharp-tongued

afiliación *nf* (**a**) *(a organización) (de persona)* membership; *(de grupo)* affiliation; **conocía su a. al partido comunista** he knew she was a member of the communist party; **ha bajado el nivel de a. a los sindicatos** union membership has fallen; **se ha incrementado el número de afiliaciones a la Seguridad Social** the number of people registered with the social security system has risen

(**b**) *(a doctrina)* **sea cual sea su a. ideológica** whatever your ideological affiliation may be

afiliado, -a *nm,f* member (**a** of)

afiliar 1 *vt* **quieren a. el club a la federación** they want to affiliate the club to the federation; **me afilió al sindicato** he signed me up to the union; **el museo está afiliado a una red nacional** the museum belongs to *o* is a member of a national network

2 **afiliarse** *vpr* to join; **afiliarse a un partido** to join a party; **afiliarse a la Seguridad Social** to register with the social security system

afín *adj* similar; **su postura es a. a la nuestra** his opinion is close to ours; **ideas afines** similar ideas

afinación *nf (de instrumento)* tuning

afinador, -ora 1 *nm,f (de instrumentos)* tuner

2 *nm (electrónico)* (electronic) tuner; *(diapasón)* tuning fork

afinar 1 *vt* (**a**) *(instrumento)* to tune; **a. la voz** to sing in tune (**b**) *(perfeccionar, mejorar)* to fine-tune; **a. la puntería** to improve one's aim (**c**) *(pulir)* to refine

2 *vi (cantar)* to sing in tune

3 **afinarse** *vpr* (**a**) *(hacerse más delgado)* to become *o* get thinner (**b**) *(perfeccionarse)* **se ha afinado mucho en los últimos años** he's become quite sophisticated in recent years; **se le ha afinado el olfato** her sense of smell has become keener

afincarse [60] *vpr* to settle (**en** in)

afinidad *nf* (**a**) *(armonía, semejanza)* affinity; **sentir a. hacia alguien** to feel one has something in common with sb; **hay a. de gustos entre ellos** they share similar tastes (**b**) *(parentesco)* **por a.** by marriage (**c**) *Quím* affinity

afirmación *nf* (**a**) *(declaración)* statement, assertion; **esas afirmaciones son falsas** those statements are false (**b**) *(asentimiento)* affirmative response

afirmar 1 *vt* (**a**) *(decir)* to say, to declare; **afirmó que...** he said *o* stated that...; **afirmó haber hablado con ella** he said *o* stated that he had talked to her (**b**) *(reforzar)* to reinforce

2 *vi (asentir)* to agree, to consent; **afirmó con la cabeza** she nodded (in agreement)

3 **afirmarse** *vpr* (**a**) *(asegurarse)* **afirmarse en los estribos** to steady oneself in the stirrups (**b**) *(ratificarse)* **afirmarse en algo** to reaffirm sth

afirmativa *nf* affirmative

afirmativamente *adv* affirmatively; **responder a.** to reply in the affirmative, to say yes

afirmativo, -a *adj* affirmative; **una respuesta afirmativa** an affirmative answer

aflautado, -a *adj* high-pitched

aflicción *nf* suffering, sorrow

afligido, -a *adj (triste)* afflicted, distressed; *(rostro, voz)* mournful; **está muy a. por la tragedia** he's very upset by the tragedy

afligir [24] 1 *vt* (a) *(causar daño)* to afflict; **los males que afligen a la región** the problems afflicting the region (b) *(causar pena)* to distress; **su partida la afligió** she was saddened by his leaving
2 **afligirse** *vpr* to be distressed (**por** by); **no te aflijas, seguro que vuelve** don't get upset, he's bound to come back

aflojar 1 *vt* (a) *(presión, tensión)* to reduce; *(cinturón, corbata, tornillo)* to loosen; *(cuerda)* to slacken; EXPR **a. las riendas** to ease up; **a. el ritmo** to slow down, to slacken one's pace (b) *Fam (dinero)* to cough up; **por fin aflojó los 100 pesos que me debía** he finally coughed up the 100 pesos he owed me (c) EXPR *RP Fam* **a. la lengua** to let the cat out of the bag
2 *vi* (a) *(disminuir)* to abate, to die down; **por fin aflojó el viento** finally the wind died down (b) *(ceder)* to ease off; **el corredor aflojó en la última vuelta** the runner eased off on the final lap (c) *RP Fam (parar)* to stop; **aflojá** stop it!
3 **aflojarse** *vpr (tuerca)* to come loose; *(cuerda)* to slacken; **se aflojó la corbata** he loosened his tie; **aflójate el cinturón** loosen your belt

afloración *nf* (a) *(de mineral)* outcrop (b) *(de sentimiento)* surfacing

afloramiento *nm* (a) *(de mineral)* outcrop (b) *(de sentimiento)* outburst

aflorar *vi* (a) *(mineral)* to outcrop (b) *(río)* to come to the surface (c) *(sentimiento)* to surface, to show; **su talento para la música no afloró hasta la edad adulta** her musical talent became apparent only in adulthood; **están comenzando a a. las tensiones en el partido** the tensions within the party are starting to surface

afluencia *nf* (a) *(concurrencia)* influx; **hubo una gran a. de público** the attendance was high; **la a. a las urnas fue escasa** the turn-out was low; **la a. de turistas es constante durante el verano** there is a constant stream *o* influx of tourists throughout the summer (b) *(abundancia)* abundance

afluente 1 *adj (locuaz)* fluent
2 *nm* tributary

> **Falso amigo**: El adjetivo inglés **affluent** no es la traducción del español **afluente**. En inglés **affluent** significa "acomodado".

afluir [34] *vi* (a) *(gente)* to flock (**a** to) (b) *(río)* to flow (**a** into) (c) *(sangre, fluido)* to flow (**a** to)

aflujo *nm* (a) *(concurrencia)* influx; **un gran a. de turistas extranjeros** a huge influx of foreign tourists (b) *(de sangre, fluido)* **se produce un a. de sangre hacia la zona infectada** blood flows towards the infected area

afmo., -a. (*abrev de* **afectísimo, -a**) *(en carta)* **suyo a.** *(si se desconoce el nombre del destinatario)* yours faithfully; *(si se conoce el nombre del destinatario)* yours sincerely

afonía *nf* **tener a.** to have lost one's voice

afónico, -a *adj* **se quedó a.** he lost his voice; **estoy a.** I've lost my voice

aforado, -a *nm,f Der (parlamentario)* = person enjoying parliamentary immunity

aforar *vt* (a) *Tec* to gauge (b) *(mercancía)* to value, to assess the value of

aforismo *nm* aphorism

aforo *nm (de teatro, plaza de toros, estadio)* capacity; **la sala tiene un a. de 600 personas** the hall holds 600 people

afortunadamente *adv* fortunately, luckily

afortunado, -a 1 *adj* (a) *(persona)* lucky, fortunate; **el a. candidato que consiga el puesto** the candidate fortunate enough to obtain the position; **el a. ganador** the lucky winner; PROV **a. en el juego... (desafortunado en amores)** lucky in cards, unlucky in love (b) *(coincidencia, frase, decisión)* happy; **una sugerencia poco afortunada** an unfortunate suggestion
2 *nm,f (persona)* lucky person; *(en lotería)* lucky winner; **la afortunada que se llevó el mayor premio** the lucky person who won the first prize

afótico, -a *adj Biol* aphotic

afrancesado, -a 1 *adj* (a) *(costumbre, estilo)* Frenchified (b) *Hist* = who supported the French during the Peninsular War
2 *nm,f Hist* = supporter of the French during the Peninsular War

afrechillo *nm RP* bran

afrecho *nm* bran

afrenta *nf (ofensa, agravio)* affront; **ser una a. a algo** to be an affront to sth

afrentar *vt (ofender)* to affront

afrentoso, -a *adj (ofensivo)* offensive, insulting

África *n* Africa ▸▸ ***Á. central*** Central Africa; ***el Á. negra*** Black Africa; ***Á. del Norte*** North Africa; ***Á. occidental*** West Africa; ***Á. oriental*** East Africa; ***el Á. subsahariana*** sub-Saharan Africa; ***Á. del Sur*** Southern Africa

africada *nf Ling* affricate

africado, -a *adj Ling* affricative

africanismo *nm* Africanism

africanista *nmf* Africanist

africano, -a 1 *adj* African
2 *nm,f* African

afrikaans *nm (lengua)* Afrikaans

afrikáner (*pl* **afrikáners** *o* **afrikáner**) 1 *adj* Afrikaner
2 *nmf* Afrikaner

afro *adj inv* afro; **un peinado a.** an afro (hairstyle)

afroamericano, -a 1 *adj* Afro-American, African American
2 *nm,f* Afro-American, African American

afrodisiaco, -a, afrodisíaco, -a, 1 *adj* aphrodisiac
2 *nm* aphrodisiac

Afrodita *n Mitol* Aphrodite

afrontar *vt (hacer frente a)* to face; **a. las consecuencias** to face (up to) the consequences; **afrontó la situación con entereza** she faced up squarely to the situation

afrutado, -a *adj* fruity

afta *nf Med* mouth ulcer

> Takes the masculine articles **el** and **un**.

after shave ['afterʃeif] *nm* aftershave (lotion)

aftosa *nf* foot and mouth disease

afuera 1 *adv* (a) *(indicando lugar, posición)* outside; **por (la parte de) a.** on the outside; **he dejado la bicicleta a.** I've left my bicycle outside; **vamos a. a pasear** let's go out for a walk; **vengo de a.** I've just come in from outside; **desde a. no pude ver nada** I couldn't see anything from outside (b) *RP (interior del país)* the provinces; **pasamos el fin de semana a.** we spent the weekend away from the capital
2 **afuera de** *loc prep Am* outside; **a. de la casa** outside the house
3 *interj* get out!

afuerano, -a, afuereño, -a, afuerino, -a *nm,f Am* outsider

afueras *nfpl* **las a.** the outskirts; **en las a.** on the outskirts

afuereño, -a, afuerino, -a = **afuerano**

afusilar *vt Méx* to shoot

agachadiza *nf* snipe

agachar 1 *vt* to lower; **a. la cabeza** *(por vergüenza, deferencia)* to bow one's head; *(para evitar un puñetazo, pelota, bala)* to duck (one's head); **agacha la cabeza, que no me dejas ver** move your head down a bit, I can't see
2 **agacharse** *vpr (acuclillarse)* to crouch down; **se agachó a recoger el pañuelo** she bent down to pick up the handkerchief; **nos agachamos al empezar el tiroteo** we ducked down when the shooting began

agalla *nf* (a) *(de pez)* gill (b) *(de árbol)* gall, gallnut (c) **agallas** *(valentía)* guts; **tener agallas para hacer algo** to have the guts to do sth; **es una chica con agallas** she's a gutsy girl, she has guts (d) *Carib* **agallas** *(codicia)* greed

agalloso, -a, agalludo, -a *Carib Fam* 1 *adj* (a) *(codicioso, avaro)* grasping (b) *(ruin, mezquino)* mean
2 *nm,f (codicioso, avaro)* grasping person; PROV *Ven* **el agalludo come crudo** someone who tries to grab everything for himself won't make good choices

agamí *nm* (*pl* **agamíes**) trumpeter

agandallar *Méx Fam* 1 *vt* to steal, *Br* to nick; **Pepe le agandalló la novia a su hermano** Pepe stole his brother's girlfriend
2 *vi* to pilfer, *Br* to nick things

ágape *nm* banquet, feast

agar-agar *nm inv* agar

agárico *nm* scaly wood mushroom, agaric

agarrada *nf* (a) *Fam (pelea)* run-in, bust-up; **tuvo una a. con su jefe** she had a run-in *o* bust-up with her boss (b) *ver también* **agarrado**

agarradera *nf Am* handle

agarraderas *nfpl Fam* **tener buenas a.** to have friends in high places

agarradero *nm* (**a**) *(asa)* hold (**b**) *Fam (pretexto)* pretext, excuse

agarrado, -a 1 *adj* (**a**) *(asido)* **me tenía a. de un brazo/del cuello** he had me by the arm/the throat; **agarrados del brazo** arm in arm; **agarrados de la mano** hand in hand (**b**) *Fam (tacaño)* tight, stingy (**c**) *Fam (baile)* slow
2 *nm,f Fam (tacaño)* **ser un a.** to be tight *o* stingy
3 *nm Fam (baile)* slow dance
4 *adv Fam* **bailar a.** to dance cheek to cheek

agarrador *nm (pez)* bony-finned remora

AGARRAR 1 *vt* (**a**) *(asir)* to grab; **me agarró de la cintura** he grabbed me by the waist; **agarra bien al niño y no se caerá** hold onto the child tight and he won't fall
(**b**) *Fam (pillar) (ladrón)* to catch; **¡si la agarro, la mato!** if I catch her I'll kill her!; **me agarró desprevenido** he caught me off guard
(**c**) *Esp Fam (pillar) (enfermedad)* to catch
(**d**) EXPR *Fam* **agarrarla, a. una buena** to get sloshed; *Fam* **esta novela no hay por dónde agarrarla** I can't make head or tail of this novel; *Méx Fam* **a. patín** to have a good laugh; *RP Fam* **a. la mano a algo** to get to grips with sth; *RP Fam* **a. viaje** to accept an offer; *RP Fam* **a. viento en la camiseta** to really get going; **después de un comienzo accidentado, el proyecto agarró viento en la camiseta** after a shaky start the project really took off
2 *vi* (**a**) *Esp (asir)* **a. de** to take hold of; **¡agarra de la cuerda!** grab the rope!
(**b**) *(tinte)* to take
(**c**) *(planta)* to take root
(**d**) *(ruedas)* to grip
(**e**) *(clavo)* to go in; **el tornillo no ha agarrado** the screw hasn't gone in properly
(**f**) *Am (encaminarse)* **a. para** to head for; **agarró para la izquierda** he took a left; EXPR *RP Fam* **a. para el lado de los tomates** to get hold of the wrong end of the stick
(**g**) *(tomar costumbre)* **agarrarle a alguien por: le agarró por el baile** she took it into her head to take up dancing; **le agarró por cantar en medio de la clase** he got it into his head to start singing in the middle of the class; **le agarró por no tomar alcohol** she suddenly started not drinking alcohol; **¿está aprendiendo ruso? – sí, le agarró por ahí** is she learning Russian? – yes, that's her latest mad idea
(**h**) EXPR *Fam* **a. y hacer algo** to go and do sth; **agarró y se fue** she upped and went; **agarró y me dio una bofetada** she went and slapped me
3 **agarrarse** *vpr* (**a**) *(sujetarse)* to hold on; **¡agárrate bien!** hold on tight!; **agarrarse a** *o* **de algo** to hold on to sth; **este coche se agarra bien al firme** this car holds the road well; **se agarró de la mano de su madre** she held on to *o* gripped her mother's hand; EXPR *Fam* **¡agárrate!** guess what!; *Fam* **¡agárrate!, ¿a qué no sabes qué han hecho los niños?** are you sitting down?... guess what the children have done, prepare yourself for a shock when I tell you what the children have done
(**b**) *(pegarse)* to stick; **el arroz se ha agarrado a la cazuela** the rice has stuck to the pot; **se me han agarrado los macarrones** the macaroni have stuck together
(**c**) *Fam (pelearse)* to scrap, to have a fight; *Am* **agarrarse a golpes** to get into a fistfight
(**d**) *(pretextar)* **agarrarse a algo** to use sth as an excuse; **se agarra a su cansancio para no hacer nada** she uses tiredness as an excuse to do nothing
(**e**) *Am (contraer)* **se agarró una gripe** she caught a cold
(**f**) *Am (tomar)* to take; **me agarré un caramelo** I took a sweet
(**g**) EXPR *Am* **agarrársela con alguien** to pick on sb

agarre *nm* (**a**) *(acción de agarrar)* grabbing (**b**) *(de vehículo)* roadholding; *(de neumático)* grip (**c**) *(valor)* guts

agarrón *nm* (**a**) *(tirón)* pull, tug; **me torció un dedo del a. que me dio** she grabbed me so hard that she sprained my finger; **el árbitro señaló penalti por a. del defensa** the referee gave a penalty for shirt-pulling by the defender (**b**) *Am Fam (altercado)* scrap, fight

agarrotado, -a *adj* (**a**) *(rígido)* stiff, tense (**b**) *(mecanismo)* jammed

agarrotamiento *nm* (**a**) *(rigidez)* stiffness (**b**) *(de mecanismo)* **para evitar el a. del mecanismo** to prevent the mechanism seizing up *o* jamming (**c**) *(opresión)* tightness (**d**) *(ejecución)* garotting

agarrotar 1 *vt* (**a**) *(parte del cuerpo)* **estos ejercicios me agarrotan los músculos** these exercises make my muscles stiff (**b**) *(mecanismo)* to seize up, to jam (**c**) *(ejecutar con garrote)* to garotte
2 **agarrotarse** *vpr* (**a**) *(parte del cuerpo)* to go stiff; **se me ha agarrotado la pierna** my leg has gone stiff (**b**) *(mecanismo)* to jam, to seize up

agasajar *vt* to lavish attention on, to treat like a king; **a. a alguien con algo** to lavish sth upon sb; **lo agasajaron con una fiesta de bienvenida** they gave a welcoming party in his honour

agasajo *nm* lavish attention

ágata *nf* agate

Takes the masculine articles **el** and **un**.

agateador *nm* short-toed tree creeper ►► ***a. norteño*** tree creeper

agauchado, -a *adj RP* gaucho-like

agaucharse *vpr RP* = to adopt gaucho dress and ways

agave *nm* agave

agazapado, -a *adj* crouching

agazaparse *vpr* (**a**) *(para esconderse)* to crouch; **se agazapó tras unos arbustos** he crouched down behind some bushes (**b**) *(agacharse)* to bend down

agencia *nf* (**a**) *(empresa)* agency ►► ***a. de acompañantes*** escort agency; ***a. de aduanas*** customs agent's; *Fin* ***a. de calificación (de riesgos)*** credit rating agency; ***a. de colocación*** employment agency; ***a. de contactos*** dating agency; ***a. de contratación*** recruitment agency; ***a. de detectives*** detective agency *o* bureau; ***a. inmobiliaria*** *Br* estate agent's, *US* real estate office; ***a. matrimonial*** marriage bureau; ***a. de modelos*** modelling agency; ***a. de noticias*** news agency; ***a. de prensa*** press agency; ***a. de la propiedad*** *Br* estate agent's, *US* real estate office; ***a. de publicidad*** advertising agency; ***a. de seguros*** insurance company; *Bolsa* ***a. de valores*** stockbrokers; ***a. de viajes*** travel agency
(**b**) *(organismo)* agency ►► ***a. de ayuda humanitaria*** aid *o* relief agency; ***a. de cooperación*** development agency; ***A. Espacial Europea*** European Space Agency; ***A. de Protección de Datos*** Data Protection Agency; *Esp* ***la A. Tributaria*** *Br* ≃ the Inland Revenue, *US* ≃ the IRS
(**c**) *(sucursal)* branch ►► ***a. urbana*** high street branch

agenciar *Fam* 1 *vt* **a. algo a alguien** to wangle sb sth; **nos agenció entradas para el concierto** she got hold of some tickets for the concert for us, she wangled us some tickets for the concert
2 **agenciarse** *vpr* (**a**) *(conseguir)* to wangle, to get hold of; **me he agenciado un traje para la ceremonia** I've managed to wangle *o* get hold of a suit for the ceremony
(**b**) **agenciárselas: se las agencia muy bien para conseguir lo que quiere** she's very good at getting what she wants; **se las agenció para que le dieran permiso** he wangled it so that they gave him permission; **ahí te las agencies, yo no te voy a ayudar** sort things out for yourself, I'm not going to help you

agenda *nf* (**a**) *(de notas, fechas)* diary; *(de anillas)* Filofax®; *(de teléfonos, direcciones)* address book; **tener una a. muy apretada** to have a very busy schedule ►► ***a. electrónica*** electronic personal organizer (**b**) *(de trabajo, reunión)* agenda

agente 1 *nmf* (**a**) *(representante)* agent ►► ***a. artístico*** agent *(of artiste, actor)*; ***a. de bolsa*** stockbroker; ***a. de cambio*** stockbroker; ***a. comercial*** broker; ***a. inmobiliario*** *Br* estate agent, *US* real estate agent; ***a. libre de seguros*** insurance broker; ***a. literario*** literary agent; ***a. de patentes*** patent agent; ***a. de la propiedad*** *Br* estate agent, *US* real estate agent; ***a. de seguros*** insurance broker; ***a. teatral*** theatrical agent
(**b**) *(funcionario)* officer ►► ***a. de aduanas*** customs officer; ***a. doble*** double agent; ***a. de inmigración*** immigration officer; ***a. de policía*** police officer, policeman, *f* policewoman; ***a. secreto*** secret agent; ***a. de seguridad*** security officer; *RP* ***a. de tránsito*** traffic policeman
(**c**) *Econ* ***agentes económicos*** *o* ***sociales*** social partners
2 *nm* (**a**) *(causa activa)* agent ►► *Quím* ***a. oxidante*** oxidizing agent; *Biol* ***a. patógeno*** pathogen; *Quím* ***a. reductor*** reducing agent; *Quím* ***a. tensioactivo*** surfactant; *Informát* ***a. de usuario*** user agent (**b**) *Gram* agent

agérato *nm* ageratum

agigantado, -a *adj* (**a**) *(muy grande)* huge, gigantic; **avanzar a pasos agigantados** to come on by leaps and bounds (**b**) *(extraordinario)* extraordinary

agigantar 1 *vt* to blow up, to magnify
2 **agigantarse** *vpr (ciudad, problema)* to become gigantic; **sus diferencias se agigantan cada vez más** their differences are growing ever wider

ágil *adj* (**a**) *(movimiento, persona)* agile (**b**) *(estilo, lenguaje)* fluent; *(respuesta, mente)* nimble, sharp

agilidad *nf* agility; **moverse con a.** to move with agility, to be agile ►► ***a. mental*** mental agility

agilipollado, -a *adj Esp muy Fam* **estar a.** *(por drogas, cansancio)* to be out of it; **¿estás a. o qué?** are you on another planet or what?

agilipollarse *vpr Esp muy Fam* **se está agilipollando con tanta televisión** he's frying his brain with so much TV

agilización *nf* speeding up

agilizar [14] *vt (trámites, proceso)* to speed up

ágilmente *adv* agilely, nimbly

agio *nm Econ* agio, speculation

agiotaje *nm Econ* agiotage, speculation

agiotista *nmf Econ* stockjobber

agitación *nf* (a) *(intranquilidad)* restlessness, agitation; **respondió con a.** she answered agitatedly; **el café le provoca a.** coffee makes him nervous (b) *(jaleo)* racket, commotion (c) *(conflicto)* unrest; **la a. estudiantil ha crecido** there has been an increase in student unrest (d) *(del mar)* choppiness

agitadamente *adv* agitatedly

agitado, -a *adj* (a) *(persona)* worked up, excited (b) *(mar)* rough, choppy

agitador, -ora 1 *nm,f (persona)* agitator
2 *nm (varilla)* stirring rod; *(para cóctel)* swizzle-stick

agitanado, -a *adj* gypsy-like

agitar 1 *vt* (a) *(sacudir)* to shake; *(remover)* to stir; **a. los brazos/un pañuelo** to wave one's arms/a handkerchief; **agítese antes de usar** *(en etiqueta)* shake before use (b) *(poner nervioso a)* to get worked up (c) *(inquietar)* to worry, to upset (d) *(masas, pueblo)* to stir up
2 **agitarse** *vpr* (a) *(moverse)* to move, to shake (b) *(ponerse nervioso)* to get worked up (c) *(inquietarse)* to become agitated

agite *nm RP, Ven Fam* (a) *(desorden)* riot; **hubo un gran a. frente al palacio** there was a major riot outside the palace (b) *(fiesta)* party, *Br* knees-up; **mañana hay a. en casa de Ana** Ana's having a party tomorrow

aglomeración *nf (de objetos, sustancia)* build-up; *(de gente)* crowd; **se produjo una a.** a crowd formed; **se esperan grandes aglomeraciones en el centro** *(de gente)* huge crowds are expected in the centre; *(de tráfico)* a heavy build-up of traffic is expected in the centre ►► ***a. urbana*** urban sprawl

aglomerado *nm* (a) *(agregación)* agglomerate (b) *(de madera)* chipboard (c) *(combustible)* coal briquette

aglomerante *adj* agglomerative

aglomerar 1 *vt* to bring together
2 **aglomerarse** *vpr* to mass *o* gather together

aglutinación *nf* agglutination

aglutinante 1 *adj* (a) *(sustancia)* binding (b) *Ling* agglutinative
2 *nm* binder, binding agent

aglutinar 1 *vt (aunar, reunir) (personas)* to unite, to bring together; *(ideas, esfuerzos)* to pool
2 **aglutinarse** *vpr* (a) *(pegarse)* to bind (together) (b) *(agruparse)* to gather, to come together

agnosticismo *nm* agnosticism

agnóstico, -a 1 *adj* agnostic
2 *nm,f* agnostic

ago. *(abrev de* **agosto**) Aug.

agobiado, -a *adj* **están agobiados de trabajo** they're snowed under with work; **están agobiados de problemas** they're weighed down with problems; **está a. por las deudas** he's weighed down with debt, he's up to his ears in debt; **está a. por el éxito** the burden of his success is beginning to tell on him

agobiante *adj (presión, trabajo, persona)* overwhelming; *(calor)* stifling; *(ambiente)* oppressive; **problemas agobiantes** overwhelming problems; **trabajo a.** backbreaking work

agobiar 1 *vt* to overwhelm; **el trabajo la agobia** her work is getting on top of her; **agobia a todos con sus problemas** she drives everyone up the wall with her problems; **me agobia con sus gritos** his shouting really gets to me
2 **agobiarse** *vpr Fam* to feel overwhelmed; **¡no te agobies!** don't worry!; **se agobia mucho con el trabajo** she lets her work get on top of her

agobio *nm* (a) *(físico)* choking, suffocation; **las aglomeraciones me producen a.** I feel oppressed by crowds of people; **¡qué a.!** it's stifling! (b) *(psíquico)* pressure; **¡qué a.!** this is murder *o* a nightmare!

agolparse *vpr (gente)* to crowd; *(sangre)* to rush; **se le agolpaban los problemas** his problems were piling up

agonía 1 *nf* (a) *(del moribundo)* death throes; **su a. duró varios meses** he took several months to die (b) *(decadencia)* decline, dying days (c) *(sufrimiento)* agony; **tras varias semanas de a., por fin recibió la respuesta** after several weeks of agonized waiting, she finally received the reply
2 *nmf* **agonías** *Esp Fam* **¡qué agonías eres!** what a moaner *o Br* misery-guts you are!

agónico, -a *adj también Fig* dying; **una dictadura agónica** a crumbling dictatorship

agonista *adj Anat* agonistic

agonizante *adj (persona, institución)* dying; *(dictadura)* on its last legs; **tras quince días de a. espera** after two weeks of agonized waiting

agonizar [14] *vi* (a) *(morir) (persona)* to be dying; *(dictadura)* to be on its last legs (b) *(sufrir)* to be in agony

ágora *nf Hist* agora

Takes the masculine articles **el** and **un.**

agorafobia *nf* agoraphobia

agorar [6] *vt* to predict

agorero, -a 1 *adj (predicción)* ominous; **no seas a.** don't be such a prophet of doom
2 *nm,f* prophet of doom

agostado, -a *adj* parched

agostar *vt* 1 (a) *(secar)* to wither, to parch (b) *(debilitar)* to ruin
2 **agostarse** *vpr (campo)* to dry up; *(planta)* to wither, to shrivel

agosto *nm* (a) *(mes)* August; EXPR **hacer su a.** to line one's pockets (b) *(cosecha)* harvest (time); *ver también* **septiembre**

agotado, -a *adj* (a) *(persona, animal)* exhausted, tired out; **estar a. de hacer algo** to be tired out *o* exhausted from doing sth (b) *(producto) (libro, disco)* out of stock; *(entradas)* sold out; **agotadas las localidades** *(en cartel)* sold out (c) *(pila, batería)* flat

agotador, -ora *adj* exhausting

agotamiento *nm* (a) *(cansancio)* exhaustion; **caminaron hasta el a.** they walked until they could go no further (b) *(de producto)* selling out; *(de reservas)* exhaustion

agotar 1 *vt* (a) *(cansar)* to exhaust, to tire out; **este niño me agota** this child tires me out
(b) *(consumir) (producto)* to sell out of; *(agua)* to use up, to run out of; *(recursos)* to exhaust, to use up; **hemos agotado todas las copias** we've sold all the copies; **ya había agotado todos los pretextos** she had run out of excuses; **agotaron todas las vías legales para obtener la extradición** they exhausted all the legal channels for obtaining the extradition order; **piensa a. su mandato al frente del partido** she intends to serve her full term as party leader
(c) *(pila, batería)* to run down
2 **agotarse** *vpr* (a) *(cansarse)* to tire oneself out, to exhaust oneself; **se agotó con la caminata** the walk tired him out *o* exhausted him
(b) *(acabarse)* to run out; *(libro, disco, entradas)* to sell out; **se nos agotaron las provisiones** our provisions ran out; **las entradas se agotaron en seguida** the tickets sold out almost immediately; **se nos ha agotado ese modelo** that model has sold out; **se me está agotando la paciencia** my patience is running out *o* wearing thin
(c) *(pila, batería)* to go flat

agracejo *nm* barberry

agraciado, -a 1 *adj* (a) *(atractivo)* attractive, fetching (b) *(afortunado)* **resultó a. con un televisor** he won a television; **el número a. es el 13** the winning number is 13
2 *nm,f (ganador)* winner

agraciar *vt* (a) *(embellecer)* to make more attractive (b) *(conceder una gracia)* to pardon (c) *Formal (premiar)* to reward

agradable *adj* (a) *(persona)* pleasant; **son muy agradables** they're very pleasant; **es una persona de talante muy a.** he has a very pleasant disposition (b) *(clima, temperatura)* pleasant; *(olor, sabor, película, ciudad)* nice, pleasant; **es muy a. al tacto** it feels very nice; **¡qué sorpresa tan a.!** what a nice *o* pleasant surprise!

agradablemente *adv* agreeably, pleasantly; **estoy a. sorprendido** I'm pleasantly surprised

agradar 1 *vt* to please; **me agradó recibir tu carta** I was pleased to receive your letter
2 *vi* to be pleasant; **siempre trata de a.** she always tries to please

agradecer [46] *vt* (a) *(sujeto: persona)* **a. algo a alguien** *(dar las gracias)* to thank sb for sth; *(estar agradecido)* to be grateful to sb for sth; **quisiera agradecerles su presencia aquí** I would like to thank you for coming *o* being here; **te lo agradezco mucho** I'm very grateful to you; **le agradezco su interés** thank you for your interest; **te agradecería que te callaras** I'd be grateful *o* I'd appreciate it if you'd shut up
(b) *(sujeto: cosa)* **esa pared agradecería una mano de pintura** that wall could do with a lick of paint; **el campo agradecerá las lluvias** the rain will be good for the countryside

agradecido, -a *adj* (a) *(persona)* grateful; **estoy muy a. por tu ayuda** I'm very grateful for your help; **están muy agradecidos a mi familia** they're very grateful to my family (b) *(cosa)* **estas plantas son muy agradecidas** these plants don't need much looking after

agradecimiento *nm* gratitude; **le regalaron una placa como** *o* **en a. por su ayuda** she was presented with a plaque in recognition of *o* to thank her for her help; **en su discurso de a. dijo que...** in his thank-you speech he said that...

agradezco *etc ver* **agradecer**

agrado *nm (gusto)* pleasure; **esto no es de mi a.** this is not to my liking; **si algo no es de su a., háganoslo saber** if there is anything you are not happy with, please let us know; **su actuación fue del a. del público** her performance went down well with the audience; **no aceptó de buen a. la sugerencia** he didn't accept the suggestion with good grace; **vio con a. el nuevo nombramiento** she was pleased about the new appointment

agrafia *nf Psi* agraphia

agramatical *adj* ungrammatical

agramaticalidad *nf* ungrammatical nature

agrandamiento *nm* **para evitar el a. del agujero** to stop the hole getting bigger

agrandar 1 *vt* to make bigger; **ese maquillaje te agranda los ojos** that make-up makes your eyes look bigger
2 **agrandarse** *vpr (grieta)* to widen, to get bigger; *(diferencias)* to widen, to grow

agrario, -a *adj (reforma)* agrarian; *(producto, política, organización)* agricultural

agrarismo *nm Méx* agrarian reform movement

agrarista *nmf Méx* supporter of agrarian reform

agravamiento *nm*, **agravación** *nf* worsening

agravante 1 *adj* aggravating
2 *nm o nf* (**a**) *(problema)* additional problem (**b**) *Der* aggravating circumstance; **con el** *o* **la a. de embriaguez** aggravated by his drunkenness

agravar 1 *vt (situación, enfermedad)* to aggravate
2 **agravarse** *vpr* to get worse, to worsen

agraviado, -a *adj* offended; **sentirse a. (por algo)** to feel offended (by sth)

agraviar *vt* to offend

agravio *nm* (**a**) *(ofensa)* offence, insult; **sus palabras fueron un a. a la institución** her words were an insult to the institution (**b**) *(perjuicio)* wrong; **eso sería un a. comparativo** that would be unfair (treatment)

agraz *nm* (**a**) *(uva)* unripe grape (**b**) *(zumo)* sour grape juice

agredido, -a *nm,f* victim

agredir *vt* to attack

agregación *nf (acción de añadir)* addition

agregado, -a 1 *adj* (**a**) *(añadido)* added on (**b**) **profesor a.** *(de secundaria)* teacher *(with a permanent post)*
2 *nm,f* (**a**) *(profesor) (de secundaria)* teacher *(with a permanent post)* (**b**) *(diplomático)* attaché ▸▸ ***a. comercial*** commercial attaché; ***a. cultural*** cultural attaché; ***a. militar*** military attaché
3 *nm* (**a**) *(conjunto)* aggregate (**b**) *(añadido)* addition (**c**) *Geol* ***a. cristalino*** crystalline aggregate (**d**) *Econ* aggregate (**e**) *Chile (guarnición)* garnish

agregaduría *nf* (**a**) *(cargo)* position of attaché (**b**) *(oficina)* attaché's office

agregar [38] 1 *vt* (**a**) *(añadir)* to add (**a** to); **a. la leche poco a poco** add the milk a little at a time (**b**) *(a lo dicho)* to add; **"y estamos preparados para ello", agregó** "and we're ready for it," she added (**c**) *(a empleado)* to assign, to appoint (**a** to)
2 **agregarse** *vpr (unirse)* to join; **se nos han agregado varias personas** a number of people have joined us

agremiado, -a *Am* 1 *adj* unionized
2 *nm,f* trade unionist, union member

agremiar *Am* 1 *vt* to unionize
2 **agremiarse** *vpr* (**a**) *(unirse a un gremio)* to join a/the union (**b**) *(crear un gremio)* to form a union

agresión *nf (ataque)* act of aggression, attack; **sufrir una a.** to be the victim of an attack ▸▸ ***a. sexual*** sex attack

agresivamente *adv* aggressively

agresividad *nf* (**a**) *(violencia)* aggression; **un discurso lleno de a.** a very aggressive speech; **hacer/decir algo con a.** to do/say sth aggressively (**b**) *(osadía)* aggressiveness

agresivo, -a *adj* (**a**) *(violento)* aggressive (**b**) *(osado)* aggressive; **una publicidad muy agresiva** very aggressive advertising

agresor, -ora *nm,f* attacker, assailant

agreste *adj* (**a**) *(abrupto, rocoso)* rough, rugged (**b**) *(rudo)* coarse, uncouth

agria *nf Col Fam* beer, *US* brew

agriamente *adv (discutir)* bitterly

agriar [32] 1 *vt* (**a**) *(vino, leche)* to (turn) sour (**b**) *(carácter)* to sour, to embitter; **la úlcera le agrió el carácter** his ulcer made him bad-tempered
2 **agriarse** *vpr* (**a**) *(vino, leche)* to turn sour (**b**) *(carácter)* to become embittered

agrícola *adj (sector, política, producto)* agricultural; **región a.** farming region

agricultor, -ora *nm,f* farmer

agricultura *nf* agriculture ▸▸ ***a. biológica*** organic farming; ***a. ecológica*** organic farming; ***a. extensiva*** extensive farming; ***a. intensiva*** intensive farming; ***a. orgánica*** organic farming; ***a. de subsistencia*** subsistence farming

agridulce *adj* (**a**) *(sabor, plato)* sweet-and-sour (**b**) *(carácter, palabras)* bittersweet

agrietado, -a *adj* (**a**) *(muro, tierra, plato)* cracked, covered with cracks (**b**) *(labios, piel)* chapped

agrietamiento *nm* cracking

agrietar 1 *vt* (**a**) *(muro, tierra, plato)* to crack (**b**) *(labios, piel)* to chap
2 **agrietarse** *vpr* (**a**) *(muro, tierra, plato)* to crack (**b**) *(labios, piel)* to chap

agrimensor, -ora *nm,f* surveyor

agrimensura *nf* surveying

agringado, -a *Am Pey* 1 *adj* gringo-like, = like a North American or European
2 *nm,f* = person who behaves like a North American or European

agringarse *vpr Am Pey* = to become like a North American or European

agrio, -a 1 *adj* (**a**) *(ácido)* sour; *(naranja)* sour, sharp (**b**) *(discusión)* bitter
2 **agrios** *nmpl* citrus fruits

agripalma *nf* motherwort

agriparse *vpr Andes, Méx* to catch the flu

agro *nm (agricultura)* agricultural sector; **el a. español** Spanish agriculture

agroalimentación *nf* **(el sector de) la a.** the food and agriculture industry

agroalimentario, -a *adj* **el sector a.** the food and agriculture industry

agrobiología *nf* agrobiology

agroindustria *nf* agribusiness

agromercado *nm Cuba* farmers' market

agronomía *nf* agronomy

agronómico, -a *adj* agronomic

agrónomo, -a 1 *adj* agronomic; **ingeniero a.** agronomist
2 *nm,f* agronomist

agropecuario, -a *adj* **el sector a.** the agricultural and livestock sector

agróstide *nf* bent grass

agrotextil *adj* agrotextile

agroturismo *nm* rural tourism

agrumarse *vpr* to go lumpy

agrupación *nf* (**a**) *(asociación)* group, association (**b**) *(agrupamiento)* grouping

agrupamiento *nm (concentración)* grouping ▸▸ ***a. espontáneo*** *(en rugby)* ruck

agrupar 1 *vt* to group (together); **la red agrupa a veinte emisoras locales** the network brings together *o* is made up of twenty local radio stations; **la guía agrupa toda la información disponible sobre el tema** the guide brings together all the available information on the subject; **una asociación que agrupa a más de 10.000 médicos** an association of more than 10,000 doctors
2 **agruparse** *vpr* (**a**) *(congregarse)* to gather; **varios curiosos se agruparon en torno al accidentado** a crowd of onlookers gathered around the accident victim (**b**) *(unirse)* to form a group; **se agrupan en dos categorías diferentes** they fall into two different categories

AGUA 1 *nf*

Takes the masculine articles **el** and **un**.

(**a**) *(líquido)* water ▸▸ ***a. de azahar*** = drink made with orange blossom, used as a mild sedative; ***aguas bautismales*** baptismal waters; ***a. bendita*** holy water; ***a. blanda*** soft water; *RP* ***a. de la canilla*** tap water; ***a. de coco*** coconut milk; ***a. de colonia*** eau de Cologne; ***aguas continentales*** inland *o* continental waters; ***a. corriente*** running water; ***a. destilada*** distilled water; ***a. dulce*** fresh water; ***a. dura*** hard water; ***a. embotellada*** bottled water; ***a. fuerte*** nitric acid; ***a. del grifo*** tap water; *Chile, Col, Méx* ***a. de la llave*** tap water; ***a. de lluvia*** rainwater; *Euf* ***aguas mayores*** faeces; ***a. medicinal*** water with medicinal properties; *Euf* ***aguas menores*** urine; ***a. de mesa*** bottled water, table water; *Fam Dep* ***a. milagrosa*** ≃ magic sponge; ***a. mineral*** mineral water; *Cuba (agua con gas)* sparkling mineral water; ***a. mineral con gas*** sparkling mineral water; ***a. mineral sin gas*** still mineral water; *Cuba* ***a. natural*** still mineral water; ***aguas negras*** sewage; ***a. nieve*** sleet; **está cayendo a. nieve** it's sleeting; ***a. de nieve*** melt-water; ***a. oxigenada*** hydrogen peroxide; ***a. pesada*** heavy water; ***a. pluvial*** rainwater; ***a. potable*** drinking water; *Quím* ***a. regia*** aqua regia; ***aguas residuales*** sewage; ***a. de rosas*** rose-water; ***a. salada*** salt water; ***a. salobre*** salt water; ***a. de Seltz*** Seltzer (water); *Am* ***aguas servidas*** sewage; ***a. subterránea*** groundwater; ***aguas superficiales*** surface water; ***a. tónica*** tonic water; *Esp* ***a. de Valencia*** = cocktail of champagne, orange juice and Cointreau

(**b**) **aguas** *(de río, mar)* waters; **aguas arriba/abajo** upstream/downstream ▸▸ ***aguas bravas*** white water; ***aguas costeras*** coastal waters; ***aguas jurisdiccionales*** territorial waters; ***aguas territoriales*** territorial waters

(**c**) *(lluvia)* rain; **ha caído mucha a.** there has been a lot of rain

(**d**) *(grieta en barco)* leak; **hacer a.** *(barca)* to leak; *(negocio)* to go under; **este negocio hace a. por todas partes** this firm is on the point of going under

(**e**) *(manantial)* **aguas** waters, spring; **tomar las aguas** to take the waters ▸▸ ***aguas termales*** thermal *o* hot springs

(**f**) *(vertiente de tejado)* slope; **un tejado de dos aguas** a ridged roof; **cubrir aguas** to put the roof on

(**g**) *Med* **aguas** waters; **ha roto aguas** her waters have broken

(**h**) **aguas** *(en diamante, tela)* water

(**i**) *Perú Fam (dinero)* dough

(**j**) EXPR *Fam* **¡al a., patos!** *(en piscina)* in you jump!; *Fam* **bailarle el a. a alguien** to lick sb's boots; *Fam* **cambiar el a. al canario** to take a leak; **claro como el a.** as clear as day; **más claro, a.** nothing can be clearer than that; *Méx Fam* **como a. para chocolate** hopping mad, fizzing; **echar a. al mar** to carry coals to Newcastle; **entre dos aguas** in doubt, undecided; **estar con el a. al cuello** to be up to one's neck (in it); **hacerse a. en la boca** to melt in one's mouth; **se me hace la boca a.** it makes my mouth water; **se me hizo la boca a. al ver el pastel** when I saw the cake, my mouth started watering; **nadar entre dos aguas** to sit on the fence; **quedar en a. de borrajas** to come to nothing; **eso es a. pasada** that's water under the bridge; **sacar a. de las piedras** to make something out of nothing; **sin decir a. va ni a. viene** suddenly, unexpectedly; **venir como a. de mayo** to be a godsend; **las aguas volvieron a su cauce** things got back to normal; PROV **no digas nunca de esta a. no beberé** you should never say never; PROV **a. pasada no mueve molino** it's no use crying over spilt milk

2 *interj Méx Fam* **¡aguas!** look *o* watch out!, careful!

---

aguacate *nm* (**a**) *(fruto)* avocado (pear) (**b**) *(árbol)* avocado (tree) (**c**) *Andes, Guat, Ven (enclenque)* weakling, milksop

aguacatillo *nm* = tropical tree, related to the avocado

aguacero *nm* downpour; **cayó un a.** there was a downpour

aguachar *Chile* **1** *vt* (**a**) *(amansar)* to tame (**b**) *(separar de la madre)* to separate from its mother

2 aguacharse *vpr (encariñarse)* to become attached (**de** to)

aguachento, -a, aguachoso, -a *adj Am* watery

aguachirle *nf*

Takes the masculine articles **el** and **un**.

Esp Fam **este café es un a.** this coffee tastes like dishwater

aguachoso, -a = **aguachento**

aguacil *nm RP (libélula)* dragonfly

aguacioso *nm* smooth sand eel

aguacúa *nf Chile Fam* bleach

aguada *nf Arte* (**a**) *(técnica)* gouache (**b**) *(dibujo)* gouache

aguadilla *nf Esp* ducking; **hacer una a. a alguien** to give sb a ducking

aguado, -a *adj* (**a**) *(con demasiada agua)* watery (**b**) *(diluido a propósito)* watered-down (**c**) *Méx, RP, Ven (insípido)* tasteless (**d**) *Am (sin fuerzas)* weak (**e**) *CAm, Méx, Ven Fam (aburrido)* dull, boring

aguador, -ora *nm,f* (**a**) *(vendedor)* water vendor (**b**) *(en ciclismo)* = domestique who distributes water bottles to team members

aguafiestas *nmf inv* spoilsport

aguafuerte *nm o nf Arte* etching

aguaitada *nf Andes, Ven Fam* look-see; **echar una a. a algo** to have *o* take a look-see at sth

aguaitador, -ora *Andes, Ven Fam* **1** *adj* meddlesome

2 *nm,f* busybody

aguaitar *Fam* **1** *vt* (**a**) *Andes, Carib (acechar)* to keep a watch on (**b**) *Andes (mirar)* to look at (**c**) *Andes (vigilar)* to watch, to look after (**d**) *Ven (esperar)* to wait; **a. a alguien** to wait for sb

2 *vi Andes* (**a**) *(espiar)* to snoop (**b**) *(mirar)* to look; **nunca se le había ocurrido a. adentro de la caja** she'd never thought of taking a look in the box (**c**) *(curiosear)* to nose around

aguaje *nm* (**a**) *CAm (regañina)* reprimand, telling-off (**b**) *Andes, CAm (aguacero)* downpour (**c**) *Carib Fam (fanfarronería)* swaggering, boasting (**d**) *Ven Fam (aburrimiento)* pain in the neck

aguajero, -a *Carib Fam* **1** *adj* boastful

2 *nm,f* show-off

aguamala *nf Carib, Col, Ecuad, Méx* jellyfish

aguamanil *nm* ewer and basin

aguamarina *nf* aquamarine

aguamiel *nm o nf* (**a**) *Am (bebida)* = water mixed with honey or cane syrup (**b**) *Carib, Méx (jugo)* maguey juice

aguanieve *nf* sleet; **está cayendo a.** it's sleeting

aguantable *adj* bearable, tolerable

aguantaderas *nfpl Fam (paciencia)* **tener muchas a.** to have the patience of a saint

aguantador, -ora *adj Am* (**a**) *(persona)* very patient; **es a.** he has the patience of a saint (**b**) *(zapato, mesa)* hard-wearing, tough

---

AGUANTAR **1** *vt* (**a**) *(sostener)* to hold; **aguanta los libros mientras limpio la estantería** hold the books while I dust the shelf

(**b**) *(peso, presión)* to bear; **esa estantería no va a a. el peso de los libros** that shelf won't take the weight of the books; **la presa no aguantará otro terremoto** the dam won't withstand another earthquake; **está aguantando bien las presiones** she's holding *o* bearing up well under the pressure

(**c**) *(tolerar, soportar)* to bear, to stand; **esta plantas no aguantan bien el calor** these plants don't like the heat; **no aguantó el ritmo de sus rivales** she couldn't keep up with her rivals; **a tu hermana no hay quien la aguante** your sister's unbearable; **no puedo aguantarlo, no lo aguanto** I can't bear him; **no sé cómo la aguantas** I don't know how you put up with her; **ya no aguanto más este dolor** this pain is unbearable; **no sabe a. una broma** he doesn't know how to take a joke

(**d**) *(tiempo)* to hold out for; **aguantó dos meses en el desierto** he survived for two months in the desert; **no creo que aguante mucho tiempo fuera su país** I don't think he'll be able to last long abroad; **¿cuánto tiempo aguantas sin fumar un cigarillo?** how long can you go without smoking a cigarette?; **este abrigo me ha aguantado cinco años** this coat has lasted me five years

(**e**) *(contener) (respiración, mirada)* to hold; *(risa)* to contain; **debes a. la respiración para hacerte la radiografía** you'll have to hold your breath when you have the X-ray; **apenas pude a. la risa** it was all I could do not to laugh

(**f**) *Méx, RP Fam (esperar)* to wait for

2 *vi* (**a**) *(tiempo)* to hold on; **aguanta un poco más, en seguida nos vamos** hold on a bit longer, we'll be going soon; **no aguanto más – necesito un vaso de agua** I can't take any more, I need a glass of water; **¡ya no aguanto más, vámonos!** I've had enough, let's go!

(**b**) *(resistir)* to last; **estas botas aguantarán hasta al año que viene** these boots should last me till next year; **a. hasta el final** to stay the course *o* the distance; **a pesar de estar lesionado, aguantó hasta el final** despite his injury, he carried on until the end

(**c**) *Taurom* to stand firm

3 aguantarse *vpr* (**a**) *(contenerse)* to restrain oneself, to hold oneself back; **tuve que aguantarme la risa** I had to stop myself from laughing *o* contain my laughter; **aguanta un poco más, que ya llegamos** hold on a bit longer, we're nearly there

(**b**) *(resignarse)* **no quiere aguantarse** he refuses to put up with it; **si no les gusta la película, tendrán que aguantarse** if they don't like the film they'll just have to put up with it, if they don't like the film, too bad; **no quiero – ¡pues te aguantas!** I don't want to – too bad, you'll just have to!

---

aguante *nm* (**a**) *(paciencia)* tolerance; **tiene muy poco a., se enfada con cualquier comentario** she's not very tolerant, she's very quick to lose her temper (**b**) *(resistencia)* strength; *(de persona)* stamina

aguapé *nm* phlomis

aguar [11] 1 *vt* (**a**) *(mezclar con agua)* to water down; **a. el vino** to water the wine down (**b**) *(estropear)* to spoil, to ruin; **la noticia nos aguó la fiesta** the news spoiled our enjoyment (**c**) *Andes, CAm (abrevar)* to water
2 **aguarse** *vpr* (**a**) *(estropearse)* to be spoiled (**b**) *Ven (ojos)* to fill with tears; **al recordar la escena, se le aguaron los ojos** when she remembered the scene, her eyes filled with tears

aguará *nm* maned wolf

aguardar 1 *vt* to wait for, to await; **aguardaban a su padre** they were waiting for their father; **aguarda a que acabe** wait until I've finished
2 *vi* to wait; **¡aguarda aquí!** wait here!; **aguarda, lo mejor será que llamemos** hold on, it would be best if we called; **date prisa, que el vuelo no aguarda** hurry up or the plane will go without you

aguardentoso, -a *adj* (**a**) *(voz)* hoarse, gravelly (**b**) *Ecuad (persona)* drunk

aguardiente *nm* spirit, liquor ►► ***a. de caña*** cane spirit, rum

aguarrás *nm* turpentine

aguascalentense 1 *adj* of/from Aguascalientes *(Mexico)*
2 *nmf* person from Aguascalientes *(Mexico)*

aguatero, -a *Am* 1 *adj* water; **camión a.** = truck that delivers bottled water; **empresa aguatera** = company selling purified water in large bottles
2 *nm,f* water seller

aguatinta *nf* (**a**) *(técnica)* aquatint (**b**) *(estampa)* aquatint

aguaturma *nf* Jerusalem artichoke

aguavientos *nm inv* phlomis

aguaviva *nf RP* jellyfish

aguayo *nm Bol* (**a**) *(tela)* = traditional Bolivian multicoloured cloth (**b**) *(manta)* = multicoloured blanket in which babies are kept warm and carried

aguda *nf (palabra)* word stressed on the last syllable

agudeza *nf* (**a**) *(de vista, olfato)* keenness; **a. visual** keen-sightedness, sharp-sightedness (**b**) *(mental)* sharpness, shrewdness; **respondió con a.** she replied shrewdly (**c**) *(dicho ingenioso)* witticism (**d**) *(de filo, punta)* sharpness (**e**) *(de sonido)* high pitch

agudización *nf* (**a**) *(de sentido)* increase, intensification (**b**) *(de problema, crisis)* worsening, aggravation

agudizar [14] 1 *vt* (**a**) *(afilar)* to sharpen (**b**) *(sentido)* to make keener; *(mente)* to sharpen; **a. el ingenio** to sharpen one's wits (**c**) *(problema, crisis)* to exacerbate, to make worse; **el frío agudizó el dolor** the cold made the pain worse; **la sequía agudizó la hambruna** the drought exacerbated the famine
2 **agudizarse** *vpr* (**a**) *(problema, crisis)* to get worse; **la fiebre se agudiza por la noche** the fever gets worse at night; **su desesperanza se agudiza cada día** his despair grows with every passing day (**b**) *(ingenio)* to get sharper

agudo, -a 1 *adj* (**a**) *(filo, punta)* sharp
(**b**) *(vista, olfato)* keen
(**c**) *(crisis, problema, enfermedad)* serious, acute
(**d**) *(dolor)* intense; **sentí un dolor a. al mover el brazo** I felt a sharp pain when I moved my arm
(**e**) *(sonido, voz)* high, high-pitched
(**f**) *(perspicaz) (persona)* sharp, shrewd; *(ingenio)* keen, sharp
(**g**) *(ingenioso)* witty; **estás muy a.** you're on form *o* very witty today; *Irónico* **¡muy a.!** *(cuando algo no es gracioso)* very clever *o* funny!; *(cuando algo es evidente)* very observant!
(**h**) *Gram (palabra)* stressed on the last syllable
(**i**) *Gram (tilde)* acute
2 *nm* **agudos** *(sonidos)* treble

agüe *etc ver* **aguar**

agüero 1 *ver* **agorar**
2 *nm (presagio)* **ver un gato negro es un mal a.** it's bad luck if you see a black cat; **de mal a.** that bodes ill

aguerrido, -a *adj (experimentado)* veteran; **soldados/tropas aguerridas** battle-hardened soldiers/troops

agüevado, -a *adj Col Fam* dopey

agüevarse *vpr Col Fam* (**a**) *(acobardarse)* to chicken out, to get cold feet (**b**) *(aturdirse)* to be knocked all of a heap, *Br* to be gob-smacked

agüevonado, -a = **ahuevonado**

aguijada *nf* goad

aguijón *nm* (**a**) *(de insecto, escorpión)* sting (**b**) *(vara afilada)* goad (**c**) *(estímulo)* spur, stimulus

aguijonazo *nm* sting, prick

aguijonear *vt* (**a**) *(animal)* to goad on (**b**) *(estimular)* to drive on; **a. a alguien para que haga algo** to spur sb on to do sth (**c**) *(atormentar, fastidiar)* to torment

águila *nf*

Takes the masculine articles **el** and **un**.

(**a**) *(ave)* eagle; EXPR **ser un a.** *(ser vivo, listo)* to be sharp *o* perceptive; **es un a. para los negocios** he has a real head for business ►► ***a. caudal*** golden eagle; ***a. imperial*** Spanish imperial eagle; ***a. pescadora*** osprey, fish hawk; ***a. ratonera*** buzzard; ***a. real*** golden eagle
(**b**) *Méx (de moneda)* heads; **¿a. o sol?** heads or tails?

aguileña *nf (planta)* columbine

aguileño, -a *adj (nariz)* aquiline

aguilón *nm Andes (caballo)* slow horse

aguilucho *nm* (**a**) *(polluelo de águila)* eaglet (**b**) *(ave rapaz)* harrier ►► ***a. cenizo*** Montagu's harrier; ***a. lagartero*** laughing falcon; ***a. lagunero*** marsh harrier; ***a. pálido*** hen harrier

aguinaldo *nm* (**a**) *(propina)* = tip given at Christmas, *Br* Christmas box; **hay unos niños en la puerta pidiendo el a.** ≃ there are some carol singers at the door (**b**) *Am (paga extra)* = extra month's pay at Christmas; **medio a.** = extra half-month's pay at end of June (**c**) *Carib, Méx (planta)* aguinaldo (**d**) *Ven (canto)* Christmas carol

agüita *nf Chile* herbal tea

agüitado, -a *adj Méx Fam (triste)* sad, downhearted

agüitarse *vpr Méx Fam* (**a**) *(entristecerse)* **nos agüitamos por no poder ir a tu fiesta** we were really sorry we couldn't make it to your party (**b**) *(avergonzarse)* to be embarrassed; **quisiera pedirle prestado el carro, pero me agüito** I'd like to ask him if I can borrow the car, but I'm too embarrassed

agüite *nm Méx Fam* (**a**) *(tristeza)* sadness; **¡qué a.!** what a damn shame! (**b**) *(vergüenza)* **me da a. llegar tan tarde** I feel embarrassed *o* don't like arriving so late (**c**) *(molestia)* nuisance, pain; **es un a. tener que trabajar el sábado** it's a pain having to work on Saturday

aguja *nf* (**a**) *(de coser)* needle; *(de hacer punto)* knitting needle ►► ***a. de crochet*** crochet hook; ***a. de ganchillo*** crochet hook; ***a. de mechar*** larding needle; ***a. de punto*** knitting needle
(**b**) *(jeringuilla)* needle ►► ***a. hipodérmica*** hypodermic needle
(**c**) *(indicador) (de reloj)* hand; *(de brújula, balanza)* pointer ►► *Náut* ***a. de bitácora*** (ship's) compass; ***a. horaria*** hour hand; ***a. magnética*** compass needle; *Náut* ***a. de marear*** (ship's) compass
(**d**) *(de tocadiscos)* stylus, needle
(**e**) *(de iglesia)* spire
(**f**) *(de conífera)* needle
(**g**) *Ferroc* point
(**h**) *(de hojaldre)* = roll-shaped meat or fish pie
(**i**) **de a.** *(vino)* slightly sparkling, *Espec* pétillant
(**j**) *(pez)* garfish
(**k**) *(ave)* godwit ►► ***a. colinegra*** black-tailed godwit; ***a. colipinta*** bar-tailed godwit
(**l**) **agujas** *(de res)* ribs

agujereado, -a *adj* riddled with holes

agujerear 1 *vt* to make a hole/holes in
2 **agujerearse** *vpr* **se me han agujereado los pantalones** I've got a hole in my trousers; **se ha agujereado el ombligo** she's had her navel pierced

agujero *nm* (**a**) *(hueco, abertura)* hole ►► ***a. en la capa de ozono*** hole in the ozone layer; ***a. de ozono*** hole in the ozone layer (**b**) *(en oreja, ombligo)* **se hizo agujeros en las orejas** she had her ears pierced (**c**) *(deuda)* deficit; **hay un a. de cien millones de pesos** a hundred million pesos are unaccounted for (**d**) *Astron* ***a. negro*** black hole

agujetas *nfpl* (**a**) *Esp (en los músculos)* **tener a.** to feel stiff; **tanto ejercicio me ha dado a.** all that exercise has left me feeling stiff (**b**) *Méx (cordones)* shoelaces

agur *interj Fam* bye!

Agustín *n pr* **San A.** St Augustine (354-430 AD)

agustiniano, -a *adj (obra, pensamiento)* Augustinian

agustino, -a *Rel* 1 *adj* Augustinian
2 *nm,f* Augustinian

agutí (*pl* **agutíes**) *nm* agouti

aguzanieves *nf inv* pied wagtail

aguzar [14] *vt* (**a**) *(afilar)* to sharpen (**b**) *(apetito)* to whet (**c**) *(sentido, mente)* to sharpen; **a. el ingenio** to sharpen one's wits; **aguza el oído, a ver si oyes qué dicen** listen carefully and see if you can hear what they're saying

ah *interj (admiración)* ooh!; *(sorpresa)* oh!; *(pena)* ah!; **¡ah, ya sé a quién te refieres!** ah, now I know who you mean!

AHÍ *adv* (**a**) *(lugar determinado)* there; **a. arriba/abajo** up/down there; **desde a. no se ve nada** you can't see anything from there; **ponlo a.** put it over there; **vino por a.** he came that way; **¡a. están!** there they are!; **¡a. tienes!** here *o* there you are!; **a. vienen los niños** here *o* there come the children; **a. mismo** right there; **déjalo a. mismo** leave it (over) there; *Am* **a. nomás** right over there

(**b**) *(lugar indeterminado)* **a. es donde te equivocas** that's where you are mistaken; **la solución está a.** that's where the solution lies; **de a. a la fama hay muy poco** it's not far to go from there to being famous; **de a. a llamarle tonto hay poca distancia** there's little difference between saying that and calling him stupid; **andan por a. diciendo tonterías** they're going around talking nonsense; **está por a.** *(en lugar indeterminado)* she's around (somewhere); *(en la calle)* she's out; **se ha ido a pasear por a.** she's gone out for a walk; **las llaves están por a.** the keys are around there somewhere; *Fam* **andar por a. con los amigos** to hang out with one's friends; **por a.** *(aproximadamente eso)* something like that; **¿te costó 10 euros? – por a., por a.** it cost you 10 euros, did it? – yes, somewhere around that *o* more or less; **por a. va la cosa** you're not too far wrong; **por a. no paso** that's one thing I'm not prepared to do; EXPR *Am* **¡a. está!** (you) see!; **todavía no me contestaron – a. está, yo te dije** they still haven't answered – (you) see, I told you so; EXPR *CAm, Méx Fam* **¡a. muere!** forget it!; EXPR **¡a. es nada!: subió al Everest sin oxígeno, ¡a. es nada!** guess what, he only climbed Everest without any oxygen!; **ha vendido ya dos millones, ¡a. es nada!** she's sold two million already, not bad, eh?; *Fam* **¿cómo estás? -** *Andes, Carib, RP* **a.** *o CAm, Méx* **a. nomás** how are you? – so-so; EXPR **a. le duele: a pesar de su éxito, la crítica sigue sin aceptarlo, ¡a. le duele!** frustratingly for him, he still hasn't achieved critical acclaim despite his success; EXPR **¡a. me las den todas!** I couldn't care less!; EXPR *Méx Fam* **a. se va** (it's no) big deal; EXPR *Méx Fam* **hacer algo al a. se va** to do sth any old how

(**c**) **de a. que** *(por eso)* and consequently; **es un mandón, de a. que no lo aguante nadie** he's very bossy, that's why nobody likes him; **de a. su enfado** that's why she was so angry

(**d**) *(momento)* then; **de a. en adelante** from then on; **a. me di cuenta de que estaba mintiendo** that was when I realized he was lying

ahijado, -a *nm,f* (**a**) *(de padrinos)* godson, *f* goddaughter; **ahijados** godchildren (**b**) *(protegido)* protégé, *f* protégée

ahijar *vt* to adopt

ahijuna, aijuna *interj RP muy Fam (admiración)* son of a gun!; *(maldición) Br* bloody hell!, *US* godammit!

ahínco *nm* enthusiasm, devotion; **con a.** *(estudiar, trabajar)* hard, enthusiastically; *(solicitar)* insistently

ahíto, -a *adj* (**a**) *(saciado)* **estar a.** to be full (**b**) *(harto)* to be fed up (**de** with)

ahogadilla *nf* ducking; **hacer una a. a alguien** to give sb a ducking

ahogado, -a 1 *adj* (**a**) *(en el agua)* drowned; **murió a.** he drowned

(**b**) *(falto de aliento) (respiración)* laboured; *(persona)* out of breath; **sus palabras, ahogadas por el llanto, casi no se entendían** it was almost impossible to understand what he was saying through his sobs

(**c**) *(apagado) (grito, sonido)* muffled

(**d**) *(agobiado)* overwhelmed, swamped (**de** with); **a. de calor** stifling in the heat

(**e**) *Andes, Méx (estofado)* stewed

2 *nm,f* drowned person

3 *nm Andes, Méx (guiso)* stew; *(sofrito)* = mixture of onion, garlic, peppers etc fried together as base for stews

ahogador *adj Ven (de caballo)* throatlatch

ahogar [38] 1 *vt* (**a**) *(en el agua)* to drown

(**b**) *(cubriendo la boca y nariz)* to smother, to suffocate

(**c**) *(extinguir) (fuego)* to smother, to put out; **los gritos de protesta ahogaban el discurso** the cries of protest drowned out his speech

(**d**) *(dominar) (levantamiento)* to put down, to quell; *(pena)* to hold back, to contain; **ahogó sus penas** *(con la bebida)* he drowned his sorrows

(**e**) *Aut (coche)* to flood

(**f**) **a. el rey** *(en ajedrez)* to stalemate one's opponent

(**g**) *Andes, Méx (guisar)* to stew

2 **ahogarse** *vpr* (**a**) *(en el agua)* to drown; EXPR **ahogarse en un vaso de agua** to make a mountain out of a molehill (**b**) *(asfixiarse)* to suffocate; **el paciente se ahogó en su propio vómito** the patient choked on his own vomit (**c**) *(de calor)* to be stifled; **me estoy ahogando de calor** I'm suffocating in this heat (**d**) *(fuego, llama)* to go out (**e**) *Aut (motor)* to flood

ahogo *nm* (**a**) *(asfixia)* breathlessness, difficulty in breathing (**b**) *(angustia)* anguish, distress (**c**) *(económico)* financial difficulty (**d**) *Andes (salsa)* stewing sauce

ahondar 1 *vt (hoyo, túnel)* to deepen; **el paso del tiempo ahondó las diferencias entre los dos hermanos** the differences between the two brothers grew wider as time went by

2 *vi* **a. en** *(penetrar)* to penetrate deep into; *(profundizar)* to study in depth; **no quiero a. más en esta cuestión** I don't want to go into this matter any further

AHORA 1 *adv* (**a**) *(en el presente)* now; **a. los jóvenes se entretienen de otra manera** young people today have different forms of entertainment; **¿no has querido comer? a. te aguantas hasta la hora de la cena** so you didn't eat your lunch up? well, you're just going to have to wait until dinnertime now; **un territorio hasta a. inexplorado** a region as yet unexplored; **hasta a. sólo se han presentado dos voluntarios** so far only two people have volunteered; *Fam* **a. sí que la hemos fastidiado** we've really gone and blown it now; *Fam* **a. lo harás porque lo digo yo** you'll do it because I jolly well say so; **ya verás como a. lo consigues** just wait and see, you'll manage it this time; **¡a. caigo!** *(ahora comprendo)* now I understand!; *(ahora recuerdo)* now I remember!; **a. mismo** right now; **a. o nunca** it's now or never; **a. me entero** it's the first I've heard of it, that's news to me; **¿sabías que no hace falta hacer eso? – ¡a. me entero!** did you know you don't need to do that? – now you tell me!; **a partir de a., de a. en adelante** from now on; *RP* **de a. en más** from now on; **por a.** for the time being; **por a. no hemos tenido ningún problema** we haven't had any problems so far; **a. que lo pienso, no fue una película tan mala** come to think of it, it wasn't that bad a film

(**b**) *(pronto)* in a second; **a. cuando venga descubriremos la verdad** we'll find out the truth in a moment, when she gets here; **a. voy, déjame terminar** let me finish, I'm coming in a minute; **justo a. iba a llamarte** I was just about to ring you this minute; **lo voy a hacer a. mismo, en cuanto acabe de planchar** I'll do it just as soon as I've finished the ironing

(**c**) *(hace poco)* just now, a few minutes ago; **he leído tu mensaje a.** I've just read your message; **se acaban de marchar a. mismo** they just left a few moments ago, they've just left

2 *conj* (**a**) *(ya... ya)* **a. habla, a. canta** one minute she's talking, the next she's singing

(**b**) *(pero)* but, however; **éste es mi plan, a., no vengas si no quieres** that's my plan, but of course you don't have to come if you don't want to; **tienes razón, a., que la historia no está completa** you're right, mind you, the story isn't finished yet

3 **ahora bien** *loc conj* but; **ven cuando quieras; a. bien, tendrás que esperar a que acabemos** come whenever you like, although you'll have to wait until we've finished

ahorcado, -a 1 *nm,f (persona)* hanged man, *f* hanged woman

2 *nm* **el (juego del) a.** hangman

ahorcamiento *nm* hanging

ahorcar [60] 1 *vt* (**a**) *(colgar)* to hang (**b**) *(dejar)* **a. los hábitos** to give up the cloth, to leave the clergy

2 **ahorcarse** *vpr* to hang oneself

ahorita, ahoritica, ahoritita *adv Andes, CAm, Carib, Méx Fam* (**a**) *(en el presente)* (right) now; **a. voy** I'm just coming (**b**) *(pronto)* in a second; **a. le traeré su plato** your meal's coming right up (**c**) *(hace poco)* just now, a few minutes ago; **a. mismo terminé el trabajo** I just finished the job this minute

ahormar *vt* (**a**) *(en molde)* to mould, to fit (**b**) *(ropa, zapatos)* to break in (**c**) *(carácter)* to mould

ahorquillado, -a *adj* forked

ahorquillar *vt* (**a**) *Agr* to prop up with forks (**b**) *(dar forma)* to shape like a fork

ahorrador, -ora 1 *adj* thrifty, careful with money

2 *nm,f* (**a**) *(ahorrativo)* thrifty person (**b**) *Méx (en el banco)* saver

ahorrar 1 *vt* (**a**) *(dinero)* to save; **ahorró tres millones** she saved three million; **comprando a granel ahorras bastante dinero** you can save quite a lot of money by buying in bulk

(**b**) *(economizar) (energía)* to save; **es importante a. agua** it's important to save water; **por esta carretera ahorras tiempo** it's quicker if you take this road; **lo haremos aquí para a. tiempo** we'll do it here to save time

(**c**) *(evitar)* **gracias, me has ahorrado un viaje** thank you, you've saved me a journey; **ahórrame los detalles** spare me the details; **no**

ahorraremos esfuerzos para conseguir nuestro propósito we will spare no effort to achieve our aim; **no se lo voy a contar para ahorrarle un disgusto** I'm not going to tell him, so as not to upset him
2 *vi* to save; **es incapaz de a.** he doesn't know how to save (money)
3 **ahorrarse** *vpr* (**a**) *(dinero)* to save; **nos ahorramos 1.000 pesos** we saved (ourselves) 1,000 pesos (**b**) *(molestia)* **ahorrarse la molestia (de hacer algo)** to save oneself the trouble (of doing sth); **si lo haces con cuidado te ahorrarás tener que repetirlo** if you do it carefully you'll save yourself having to do it again; **me ahorré un viaje** I saved myself a journey

ahorrativo, -a *adj* (**a**) *(persona)* thrifty (**b**) *(medida)* money-saving

ahorrista *nmf RP* saver

ahorro *nm* (**a**) *(gasto menor)* saving; **esta medida supone un a. de varios millones** this measure means a saving of several millions; **medidas de a. energético** energy-saving measures; **una campaña para fomentar el a.** a campaign encouraging people to save; **este sistema es un a. de tiempo** this system saves (you) time *o* is a time-saver (**b**) **ahorros** *(cantidad)* savings

ahuecado, -a *adj* (**a**) *(vacío)* hollow, empty (**b**) *(mullido) (edredón)* plumped up; **quiero el pelo a.** I'd like my hair to have more body (**c**) *(voz)* deep

ahuecar [60] 1 *vt* (**a**) *(tronco)* to hollow out (**b**) *(manos)* to cup (**c**) *(mullir) (colchón)* to plump up; *(pelo)* to give body to; *(tierra)* to hoe (**d**) *(voz)* to deepen (**e**) EXPR *Fam* **a. el ala** to clear off
2 *vi Fam (irse)* to clear off
3 **ahuecarse** *vpr (engreírse)* to puff up *(with pride)*

ahuehuete *nm* Montezuma cypress

ahuesado, -a *adj Perú* in a rut

ahuesarse *vpr* (**a**) *Andes Com (artículo)* to become useless *o* worthless (**b**) *Guat (adelgazar)* to become very thin (**c**) *Perú (anquilosarse)* to get into a rut

ahuevado, -a *adj* (**a**) *(forma)* egg-shaped (**b**) *CAm, Ecuad, Perú Fam (cobarde)* chicken, gutless; **¡no seas a.!** don't be chicken! (**c**) *CAm, Ecuad, Perú Fam (tonto)* dopey

ahuevar 1 *vt* (**a**) *(forma)* to make egg-shaped (**b**) *(vino)* to clarify with egg white (**c**) *CAm, Ecuad, Perú Fam (volver tonto)* **a. a alguien** to leave sb lost for words, *Br* to leave sb gobsmacked (**d**) *CAm, Ecuad, Perú Fam (acobardar)* to scare, to put the wind up
2 **ahuevarse** *vpr CAm, Ecuad, Perú Fam* (**a**) *(atontarse)* to be lost for words, *Br* to be gobsmacked (**b**) *(acobardarse)* to chicken out, to get cold feet; **quise decírselo pero me ahuevé** I meant to tell him but I chickened out (of it)

ahuevonado, -a, agüevonado, -a *adj Ven Fam* dopey; **el a. de su hermano** his dope of a brother; **la noticia le dejó a.** the news knocked him all of a heap

ahumado, -a 1 *adj* (**a**) *(jamón, pescado)* smoked (**b**) *(cristal)* smoked; *(gafas)* tinted (**c**) *Fam (borracho)* drunk
2 *nm* smoking
3 **ahumados** *nmpl* = smoked fish and/or meat

ahumar 1 *vt* (**a**) *(jamón, pescado)* to smoke (**b**) *(lugar)* to make all smoky
2 **ahumarse** *vpr* (**a**) *(llenarse de humo)* to get all smoky (**b**) *(ennegrecerse de humo)* to become blackened with smoke (**c**) *Fam (emborracharse)* to get drunk

ahuyama = **auyama**

ahuyentar *vt* (**a**) *(espantar, asustar)* to scare away (**b**) *(mantener a distancia)* to keep away; **el fuego ahuyentaba a las fieras** the fire kept the wild animals away; **el elevado precio ahuyentó a los compradores** the high price put buyers off; **ahuyentó su mal humor** he shook off his bad mood (**c**) *(apartar)* to drive away; **ahuyenta los malos pensamientos** banish all evil thoughts from your mind

AID *nf (abrev de* **Asociación Internacional de Desarrollo**) IDA

AIEA *nf (abrev de* **Agencia Internacional de la Energía Atómica**) IAEA

aijuna = **ahijuna**

aikido *nm* aikido

ailanto *nm* tree of heaven

aimara = **aymara**

AIN *nf (abrev de* **Agencia de Información Nacional**) = Cuban national news agency

aindiado, -a *adj (facciones)* Indian-looking; **tiene un habla muy aindiada** he talks *o* sounds really like an Indian

airadamente *adv* angrily

airado, -a *adj* angry; **"¡eso nunca!", replicó a.** "never!" he replied angrily

airar 1 *vt* to anger, to make angry
2 **airarse** *vpr* to get angry

airbag ['erβaγ, air'βaγ] (*pl* **airbags**) *nm (en coche)* air bag ▸▸ ***a. frontal*** front air bag; ***a. lateral*** side air bag

---

AIRE 1 *nm* (**a**) *(fluido)* air; **al a.** *(al descubierto)* exposed; **con el pecho al a.** bare-chested; **con las piernas al a.** with bare legs, bare-legged; **si duermes con los pies al a. te enfriarás** if you sleep with your feet sticking out from under the covers, you'll catch cold; **el médico le aconsejó que dejara la quemadura al a.** the doctor advised him to leave the burn uncovered; **disparar al a.** to shoot into the air; **disparó al a.** she fired a shot into the air; **a.-a.** *(misil)* air-to-air; **a esta rueda le falta a.** this tyre is a bit flat; **al a. libre** in the open air; **un concierto al a. libre** an open-air concert; EXPR **a mi/tu/***etc.* **a.: prefiero hacerlo a mi a.** I'd rather do it my (own) way; **tú a tu a., si te aburres vete a casa** do whatever you like, if you're bored just go home; EXPR **cambiar de aires** to have a change of scene; **el médico le recomendó cambiar de aires** the doctor recommended a change of air; EXPR **dejar algo en el a.** to leave sth up in the air; EXPR **estar en el a.** *(sin decidir)* to be in the air; *Rad & TV* to be on the air; **el resultado todavía está en el a.** the result could still go either way; **el programa sale al a. los lunes a las nueve** the programme is broadcast on Mondays at nine o'clock; EXPR **saltar** *o* **volar por los aires: el automóvil saltó** *o* **voló por los aires** the car was blown into the air; EXPR **tomar el a.** to go for a breath of fresh air; EXPR *Fam* **vivir del a.** *(no tener nada)* to live on thin air; *(comer poco)* to eat next to nothing; *Fam* **sin trabajo ni casa, ¿es que piensa vivir del a.?** how does she expect to survive without a job or a home? ▸▸ ***a. acondicionado*** air-conditioning; ***a. comprimido*** compressed air; ***a. líquido*** liquid oxygen; ***a. del mar*** sea air; ***a. puro*** fresh air; ***a. viciado*** foul air
(**b**) *(viento)* wind; **hoy hace mucho a.** it's very windy today; **cierra la puerta que entra a.** close the door, there's a draught ▸▸ ***a. polar*** polar wind; ***a. tropical*** tropical wind
(**c**) *(aspecto)* air, appearance; **un vehículo de a. deportivo** a sporty-looking car; **tiene a. de haber viajado mucho** he looks like somebody who has done a lot of travelling; **tiene un a. distraído** she has an absent-minded air about her, she comes across as rather absent-minded; **su respuesta tenía un cierto a. de escepticismo** there was a touch of scepticism about her answer
(**d**) *(parecido)* **tiene un a. a su madre** she has something of her mother; **tiene un a. con alguien que conozco** he reminds me of someone I know
(**e**) *(vanidad)* **se da aires de lista** she makes out she's clever; **desde que es jefe se da muchos aires (de grandeza)** since he became the boss he's been giving himself airs
(**f**) *Fam (parálisis)* attack, fit; **le dio un a.** he had a fit
(**g**) *Mús (melodía)* air, tune; *(ritmo)* tempo ▸▸ ***a. lento*** slow tempo; ***a. popular*** folk song, traditional song; ***a. rápido*** fast *o* upbeat tempo
(**h**) *(ventosidad)* wind; **tener a.** to have wind
(**i**) *Méx Fam* **dar a. a alguien** *(despedir)* to sack sb; **dio a. a su novio** she dumped her boyfriend
2 *interj Fam* clear off!; **¡a., y no se te ocurra volver por aquí!** clear off and don't let me see you here again!

---

aireación *nf* ventilation

aireado, -a *adj* airy

airear 1 *vt* (**a**) *(ventilar)* to air (**b**) *(contar)* to air (publicly); **el periódico aireó el escándalo** the newspaper published details of the scandal
2 **airearse** *vpr* (**a**) *(persona)* to get a breath of fresh air (**b**) *(habitación)* **abre la ventana para que se airee el cuarto** open the window to let the room air *o* to air the room

airoso, -a *adj* (**a**) *(garboso)* graceful, elegant (**b**) *(triunfante)* **salir a. de algo: salió a. de la prueba** he passed the test with flying colours; **salió a. de la entrevista** he gave a good account of himself in the interview

aislacionismo *nm Pol* isolationism

aislacionista *Pol* 1 *adj* isolationist
2 *nmf* isolationist

aisladamente *adv* **considerado/tomado a.** considered/taken in isolation

aislado, -a *adj* (**a**) *(remoto)* isolated (**b**) *(incomunicado)* cut off; **nos quedamos aislados por la nieve** we were cut off by the snow; **vive a. del resto del mundo** he has cut himself off from the rest of the world (**c**) *(singular)* isolated (**d**) *(cable, pared)* insulated

aislamiento *nm* (**a**) *(de lugar)* isolation (**b**) *(de persona)* isolation (**c**) *(de virus)* isolation (**d**) *(de cable, vivienda)* insulation ►► ***a. acústico*** soundproofing; ***a. eléctrico*** electric insulation; ***a. térmico*** thermal insulation

aislante 1 *adj* insulating
2 *nm* (**a**) *(para camping)* camping mat (**b**) *(material)* insulating material ►► ***a. acústico*** soundproofing material; ***a. eléctrico*** electrical insulator; ***a. térmico*** thermal insulator

aislar 1 *vt* (**a**) *(persona)* to isolate (**b**) *(del frío, de la electricidad)* to insulate; *(del ruido)* to soundproof (**c**) *(incomunicar)* to cut off; **la nevada aisló la comarca del resto del país** the snow cut the area off from the rest of the country (**d**) *(virus)* to isolate
2 *vi* **estas ventanas aíslan muy bien del frío/ruido** these windows are very good at keeping the cold/noise out
3 **aislarse** *vpr* to isolate oneself, to cut oneself off (**de** from)

aizkolari *nm* = competitor in the rural Basque sport of chopping felled tree-trunks

ajá *interj (sorpresa)* aha!; *(asentimiento)* uh-huh

Ajaccio *n* Ajaccio

ajado, -a *adj (flor)* withered; *(piel)* wrinkled; *(colores)* faded; *(ropa)* worn; *(persona)* wizened

ajamonarse *vpr Fam (mujer)* to get a middle-aged spread

ajar 1 *vt (flores)* to wither, to cause to fade; *(piel)* to wrinkle; *(colores)* to cause to fade; *(ropa)* to wear out
2 **ajarse** *vpr (flores)* to fade, to wither; *(piel)* to wrinkle, to become wrinkled; *(belleza, juventud)* to fade

ajardinado, -a *adj* landscaped; **zonas ajardinadas** landscaped (green) areas

ajardinar *vt* to landscape

a. J.C. (*abrev de* **antes de Jesucristo**) BC

aje *nm* yam

ajedrea *nf* savory *(plant)*

ajedrecista *nmf* chess player

ajedrecístico, -a *adj* **dotes ajedrecísticas** chess-playing skills; **torneo a.** chess tournament

ajedrez *nm* (**a**) *(juego)* chess; **jugar al a.** to play chess (**b**) *(piezas y tablero)* chess set

ajedrezado, -a *adj* checked, check

ajenjo *nm* (**a**) *(planta)* wormwood, absinthe (**b**) *(licor)* absinthe

ajeno, -a *adj* (**a**) *(de otro)* of others; **jugar en campo a.** to play away from home; **no te metas en los problemas ajenos** don't interfere in other people's problems; **no le importa la miseria ajena** she doesn't care about the suffering of others; **recurrieron a capital a.** they turned to outside investors, they used borrowed capital
(**b**) *(no relacionado)* **es un problema a. a la sociedad de hoy** it's a problem that no longer exists in today's society; **todo eso me es a.** *(no me atañe)* all that has nothing to do with me; **esto es a. a nuestro departamento** our department doesn't deal with that; **por causas ajenas a nuestra voluntad** for reasons beyond our control; **un escándalo al que no es a. el presidente** a scandal in which the president is not uninvolved; **su plan es a. a cualquier intento partidista** their plan in no way seeks to gain party-political advantage; **una tradición ajena a nuestra cultura** a tradition which is alien to our culture
(**c**) *(ignorante)* **era ajena a lo que estaba ocurriendo** she had no knowledge of what was happening

ajerezado, -a *adj* sherry-like

ajete *nm* = green stalk of young garlic plant

ajetreado, -a *adj* busy; **he tenido un día muy a.** I've had a very busy day

ajetrearse *vpr (afanarse)* to bustle about

ajetreo *nm* **con tanto a. me olvidé de llamarle** things were so hectic that I forgot to phone him; **hoy hay mucho a. en la oficina** there's a lot going on *o* happening in the office today; **el a. de la ciudad** the hustle and bustle of the city

ají (*pl* **ajíes** *o* **ajís**) *nm* (**a**) *Andes, RP (pimiento)* chilli (pepper) (**b**) *Andes, RP (salsa)* = sauce made from oil, vinegar, garlic and chilli (**c**) *Ven* ***a. chirel*** = small, hot chilli pepper

ajiaceite *nm* = sauce made from garlic and olive oil

ajiaco *nm* (**a**) *Andes, Carib (estofado)* = chilli-based stew (**b**) *Méx (estofado con ajo)* = tripe stew flavoured with garlic (**c**) *Ven (sopa)* = vegetable soup which sometimes also contains meat (**d**) *Cuba Fam (alboroto)* rumpus, racket; **en la fiesta se formó tremendo a.** it was bedlam at the party (**e**) *Cuba Fam (problema)* mess

ajicero, -a *Ven* 1 *nm* (**a**) *(salsa)* = sauce made from oil, vinegar, garlic and chilli (**b**) *(envase)* "ajicero" bottle
2 *nm,f (persona)* "ajicero" maker

ajila *interj Cuba* clear off!, get lost!

ajilimójili, ajilmoje 1 *nm* = pepper, garlic and vinegar sauce
2 **ajilimójilis** *nmpl Fam* bits and pieces; **con todos sus ajilimójilis** with the works *o* all the trimmings

ajillo *nm* **al a.** = fried with lots of garlic; **champiñones/gambas al a.** garlic mushrooms/prawns

ajilmoje = **ajilimójili**

ajo[1] *nm (planta, condimento)* garlic; **un diente de a.** a clove of garlic; EXPR *Fam Euf* **¡a. y agua!** too bad!, tough!; EXPR *Fam* **en el a.: pregúntale a ella, que está en el a.** ask her, she's in on it *o* in the know; *Fam* **varios funcionarios están metidos en el a.** a number of civil servants are mixed up in the affair ►► ***a. blanco*** cold garlic soup; ***a. tierno*** = green stalk of young garlic plant

ajo[2], *RP* **ajó** *interj* goo-goo

ajoarriero *nm* **(bacalao al) a.** = stew of salt cod cooked with eggs and garlic

ajolote *nm (pez)* axolotl

ajonjolí (*pl* **ajonjolíes**) *nm (planta)* sesame; **semillas de a.** sesame seeds

ajorca *nf* bangle

ajotar *vt PRico* **a. a los perros contra alguien** to set the dogs on sb

ajuar *nm* (**a**) *(de novia)* trousseau (**b**) *(de casa)* furnishings

ajuiciar *vt* **a. a alguien** to bring sb to their senses

ajumado, -a *adj Carib Fam* tight, tipsy

ajumarse *vpr Carib Fam* to get tight *o* tipsy

ajuntar *Fam* 1 *vt (lenguaje infantil)* to be pals *o* friends with
2 **ajuntarse** *vpr* (**a**) *(lenguaje infantil) (ser amigos)* to be pals *o* friends (**b**) *(irse a vivir juntos)* to move in together

Ajuria Enea *n* = official residence of the president of the autonomous Basque government, used by extension to refer to the Basque government as a whole

ajustable *adj* adjustable; **sábana a.** fitted sheet; **un volante a. en altura** an adjustable steering-wheel

ajustado, -a 1 *adj* (**a**) *(ceñido) (ropa)* tight-fitting; **este vestido me queda muy a.** this dress is really tight on me; **le gustan los pantalones ajustados** she likes wearing tight-fitting trousers
(**b**) *(tuerca, pieza)* tight
(**c**) *(resultado, final)* close; **estos precios están muy ajustados, no le puedo hacer ningún descuento** my margin on these prices is very low, I can't give you a discount
(**d**) *(adaptado)* **a. a: presentaron un presupuesto a. a sus posibilidades** they proposed a budget in line with their resources; **un precio a. a la calidad del producto** a price in keeping with the quality of the product
2 *nm* fitting

ajustador, -ora 1 *adj* adjusting
2 *nm,f Imprenta* typesetter
3 **ajustadores** *nmpl Col, Cuba* bra

ajustamiento *nm (ajuste)* settlement

AJUSTAR 1 *vt* (**a**) *(encajar) (piezas de motor)* to fit; *(puerta, ventana)* to push to
(**b**) *(arreglar)* to adjust; **el técnico ajustó la antena** the engineer adjusted the aerial
(**c**) *(apretar)* to tighten; **ajusta bien la tapa** screw the lid on tight
(**d**) *(poner en posición) (retrovisor, asiento)* to adjust
(**e**) *(pactar) (matrimonio)* to arrange; *(pleito)* to settle; *(paz)* to negotiate; *(precio)* to fix, to agree; **hemos ajustado la casa en cinco millones** we have agreed a price of five million for the house
(**f**) *(adaptar)* to alter; **el sastre ajustó el vestido** the tailor altered the dress; **tendrás que a. tus necesidades a las nuestras** you'll have to adapt your needs to fit in with ours; **tenemos que a. los gastos a los ingresos** we shouldn't spend more than we earn; **a. las pensiones al índice de inflación** to index-link pensions
(**g**) *(asestar)* to deal, to give
(**h**) *Imprenta* to make up
(**i**) *(reconciliar)* to reconcile
(**j**) *(saldar)* to settle; EXPR **a. las cuentas a alguien** to settle a score with sb; EXPR **¡la próxima vez que te vea ajustaremos cuentas!** you'll pay for this the next time I see you!
2 *vi (venir justo)* to fit properly, to be a good fit; **la ventana no ajusta bien** the window won't close properly
3 **ajustarse** *vpr* (**a**) *(encajarse)* to fit; **el tapón no se ajusta a la**

botella the top won't fit on the bottle; *Fig* **tu relato no se ajusta a la verdad** your account is at variance with the truth, your account doesn't match the facts

(**b**) *(adaptarse)* to fit in (**a** with); **es un chico muy sociable, se ajusta a todo** he's a very sociable boy and fits in wherever he goes; **tu plan no se ajusta a nuestras necesidades** your plan doesn't meet our needs; **su arte no se ajusta al paladar europeo** his art doesn't appeal to European taste; **ajústate a lo que te han dicho** do as you've been told; **tenemos que ajustarnos al presupuesto del que disponemos** we have to keep within the limits of our budget; **su decisión no se ajusta a derecho** her decision does not have a sound legal basis; **ajustarse a las reglas** to abide by the rules

(**c**) *(ponerse de acuerdo)* to come to an agreement; **se ajustaron con sus acreedores** they came to an agreement with their creditors

---

ajuste *nm* (**a**) *(de pieza)* fitting; *(de mecanismo)* adjustment

(**b**) *(de salario)* agreement

(**c**) *(ecónomico)* **las medidas de a. económico propuestas por el gobierno** the economic measures proposed by the government; **ajustes presupuestarios** budget adjustments ►► ***a. de plantilla*** downsizing

(**d**) *RDom, Ven (pago único)* = agreed payment for a piece of work

(**e**) *Ven Fam (arreglo)* deal; **le va mal porque no hizo a. con los poderosos de turno** it's going badly for him because he didn't square things *o* do a deal with those in power at the time

(**f**) *Fig* ***a. de cuentas:*** **los ajustes de cuentas son frecuentes entre bandas rivales** the settling of scores is common amongst rival gangs; **murió en un a. de cuentas** he died in a tit-for-tat killing

ajustero, -a *nm,f RDom, Ven* = person who contracts to do work for a fixed payment

ajusticiado, -a *nm,f* executed criminal

ajusticiamiento *nm* execution

ajusticiar *vt* to execute

al *ver* **a, el**

Alá *nm* Allah

ala

Takes the masculine articles **el** and **un**.

1 *nf* (**a**) *(de ave, insecto)* wing; *(de avión)* wing; EXPR **cortar las alas a alguien** to clip sb's wings; EXPR **dar alas a** *(alentar)* to encourage; *(consentir)* to give a free hand to; EXPR *Fam* **está tocado del a.** he's soft in the head; EXPR *Fam* **del a: 5.000 pesetas del a.** a whopping 5,000 pesetas ►► ***a. delta*** *(aparato)* hang-glider; **hacer a. delta** to go hang-gliding; *Av* ***a. en delta*** delta wing

(**b**) *(de edificio)* wing

(**c**) *(de tejado)* eaves

(**d**) *(de partido)* wing

(**e**) *(de sombrero)* brim; **un sombrero de a. ancha** a wide-brimmed hat

(**f**) *(de compresa)* wing

(**g**) *(de nariz)* side

(**h**) *(de mesa)* leaf

(**i**) *Dep (posición)* wing

2 *nmf (en fútbol, rugby)* winger, wing; *(en baloncesto)* foward ►► ***a. delantero*** *(en rugby)* wing forward; ***a. pívot*** *(en baloncesto)* power forward

3 *interj* (**a**) *(para dar ánimo, prisa)* come on! (**b**) *(para expresar incredulidad)* no!, you're joking! (**c**) *(para expresar admiración, sorpresa)* wow!

alabanza *nf* praise; **decir algo en a. de alguien** to say sth in praise of sb; **su acción es digna de a.** she deserves praise for what she did; **un intento digno de a.** a praiseworthy attempt

alabar 1 *vt* to praise; EXPR *Fam* **¡alabado sea Dios!** *(expresa sorpresa)* good heavens!

2 alabarse *vpr* to boast; **se alaba de valiente** he's always boasting about how brave he is

alabarda *nf* halberd

alabardero *nm* (**a**) *(soldado)* halberdier (**b**) *Teatro* member of the claque

alabastro *nm* alabaster

alabear 1 *vt* to warp

2 alabearse *vpr* to warp

alabeo *nm* warping

alacena *nf* (**a**) *(mueble)* kitchen cupboard (**b**) *(en la pared)* wall cupboard

alacrán *nm* (**a**) *(escorpión)* scorpion (**b**) ***a. cebollero*** mole cricket

alacranera *nf (planta)* scorpiurus

alacridad *nf Literario* alacrity

aladares *nmpl* earlocks

ALADI [a'laði] *nf* (*abrev de* **Asociación Latinoamericana de Integración**) LAIA, = Latin American association promoting integration of trade

aladierno *nm* buckthorn

Aladino *n pr* Aladdin

alado, -a *adj (con alas)* winged

ALALC [a'lalk] *nf Antes* (*abrev de* **Asociación Latinoamericana de Libre Comercio**) LAFTA

alambicado, -a *adj (lenguaje, estilo)* (over-)elaborate, involved

alambicar [60] *vt* (**a**) *(destilar)* to distil (**b**) *(complicar)* to overcomplicate

alambique *nm* still

alambrada *nf* (**a**) *(cerca)* wire fence (**b**) *(material)* wire netting

alambrado *nm* (**a**) *(acción)* fencing off *(with wire netting)* (**b**) *Am (cerca)* wire fence

alambrar *vt* to fence off *(with wire netting)*

alambre *nm* (**a**) *(hilo metálico)* wire ►► *Arg* ***a. carril*** cable car; ***a. de espino*** barbed wire; ***a. de púas*** barbed wire (**b**) *Chile (cable)* cable, lead; EXPR **estar con los alambres pelados** to have got out of the wrong side of bed, to be like a bear with a sore head

alambrista *nmf* tightrope walker

alameda *nf* (**a**) *(sitio con álamos)* poplar grove (**b**) *(paseo)* tree-lined avenue

álamo *nm* poplar ►► ***á. blanco*** white poplar; ***á. negro*** black poplar; ***á. temblón*** aspen, trembling poplar

Al-Andalus *n Hist* = Arab empire in southern Spain (711–1492)

alano, -a 1 *adj Hist* Alani

2 *nm,f* (**a**) *(perro)* mastiff (**b**) *Hist* **los alanos** *(pueblo)* the Alani, = Germanic tribe which invaded Spain in the 5th century AD

alante *adv Fam (considerado incorrecto)* = **adelante**

alar *nm* (**a**) *(del tejado)* eaves (**b**) *Col (acera) Br* pavement, *US* sidewalk

alarde *nm* show, display; **hizo a. de su inteligencia** she showed off *o* flaunted her intelligence; **en un a. de generosidad, nos invitó a cenar** in a display of generosity he invited us to dinner

alardear *vi* **alardea de valiente** he preens himself on his bravery; **alardea de tener un yate** she makes quite a thing about having a yacht

alardeo *nm* showing off

alargadera *nf* extension lead

alargado, -a *adj* long; **tiene la cara alargada** he has a long face

alargador *nm* extension lead

alargamiento *nm* (**a**) *(de objeto)* lengthening (**b**) *(en el tiempo)* extension

alargar [38] **1** *vt* (**a**) *(ropa)* to lengthen (**b**) *(viaje, visita, plazo)* to extend; *(conversación)* to spin out; **el árbitro alargó el primer tiempo cinco minutos** the referee added five minutes' stoppage time to the end of the first half (**c**) *(brazo, mano)* to stretch out (**d**) *(pasar)* **a. algo a alguien** to pass sth (over) to sb; **alárgame el paraguas, por favor** could you pass me (over) the umbrella, please?

2 alargarse *vpr (hacerse más largo) (días)* to get longer; *(reunión)* to be prolonged; *(hacerse muy largo)* to go on for ages; **la reunión se alargó hasta el alba** the meeting went on *o* stretched on until dawn

alargue *nm RP* extension lead

alarido *nm* shriek, howl; **dar** *o* **pegar un a.** to let out a shriek *o* howl

alarma *nf* (**a**) *(señal)* alarm; **dar la a., dar la voz de a.** to raise the alarm

(**b**) *(dispositivo)* alarm ►► ***a. antirrobo*** *(en coche)* antitheft *o* car alarm; *(en casa)* burglar alarm; ***a. contra incendios*** fire alarm

(**c**) *(preocupación)* alarm; **cundió la a.** panic spread; **saltó la a. entre los responsables de la empresa** alarm bells started ringing among the company's management; **las propuestas del gobierno provocaron gran a. social** the government's proposals caused widespread alarm among the population

(**d**) *Mil* call to arms

alarmante *adj* alarming

alarmar 1 *vt* (**a**) *(avisar)* to alert (**b**) *(asustar)* to alarm

2 alarmarse *vpr (inquietarse)* to be alarmed

alarmismo *nm* alarmism

alarmista 1 *adj* alarmist

2 *nmf* alarmist

Alaska *n* Alaska

a látere *nmf Pey* underling

alauí (*pl* **alauíes**), **alauita** *adj (reino, monarca)* Moroccan, of Morocco

alavés, -esa 1 *adj* of/from Alava *(Spain)*
 2 *nm,f* person from Alava *(Spain)*

alazán, -ana 1 *adj* chestnut
 2 *nm,f* chestnut (horse)

alazor *nm* safflower

alba *nf*

Takes the masculine articles **el** and **un.**

(a) *(amanecer)* dawn, daybreak; **al a.** at dawn **(b)** *(vestidura)* alb

albacea *nmf Der* **a. (testamentario)** executor

albaceteño, -a 1 *adj* of/from Albacete *(Spain)*
 2 *nm,f* person from Albacete *(Spain)*

albacora *nf (pez)* long-finned tuna, albacore

albahaca *nf* basil

albanés, -esa 1 *adj* Albanian
 2 *nm,f (persona)* Albanian
 3 *nm (lengua)* Albanian

Albania *n* Albania

albañil *nm* bricklayer

albañilería *nf* **(a)** *(oficio)* bricklaying **(b)** *(obra)* brickwork

albanokosovar 1 *adj* Kosovo Albanian
 2 *nmf* Kosovo Albanian

albar *adj Literario* white

albarán *nm Esp Com* delivery note

albarca *nf* = type of sandal worn by country people

albarda *nf* **(a)** *(arreos)* packsaddle **(b)** *(tocino)* strip of bacon **(c)** *CAm, Méx (silla de montar)* saddle

albardilla *nf* **(a)** *(silla de montar)* training saddle **(b)** *(de tocino)* strip of bacon

albardín *nm* Spanish grasshemp, = type of esparto grass

albaricoque *nm Esp* apricot

albaricoquero *nm Esp* apricot tree

albariño *nm* = fruity Galician white wine

albatros *nm inv* **(a)** *(ave)* albatross ►► ***a. viajero*** wandering albatross **(b)** *(en golf)* albatross

albayalde *nm* white lead

albedo *nm Fís* albedo

albedrío *nm (antojo, elección)* fancy, whim; **a su a.** as takes his/her fancy; *Filosofía* **libre a.** free will; **a su libre a.** of his/her own free will

alberca *nf* **(a)** *(depósito)* water tank **(b)** *Col, Méx (piscina)* swimming pool **(c)** *Perú (cerca)* fence **(d)** *Col (pila)* sink

albérchigo *nm* peach tree

albergar [38] **1** *vt* **(a)** *(personas)* to accommodate, to put up; **nos albergaron en la habitación de invitados** they put us (up) in the guest room; **el polideportivo albergó a los damnificados** the sports centre provided temporary accommodation for the victims; **el partido alberga a comunistas y ecologistas** the party is a home to communists and greens
 (b) *(exposición)* **el centro cultural albergará la exposición de Picasso** the cultural centre will be the venue for the Picasso exhibition, the Picasso exhibition will be held in the cultural centre; **un antiguo palacio alberga el Museo Antropológico** the Museum of Anthropology is housed in a former palace
 (c) *(odio)* to harbour; **todavía albergamos esperanzas de conseguirlo** we still have hopes of achieving it
 2 albergarse *vpr* to stay; **¿en qué hotel se albergan?** what hotel are they staying in?

albergue *nm* **(a)** *(alojamiento)* accommodation, lodgings; **dar a. a alguien** to take sb in **(b)** *(hostal)* hostel ►► ***a. juvenil*** youth hostel; ***a. de juventud*** youth hostel; *RP* ***a. transitorio*** = hotel where rooms may be rented by the hour **(c)** *(de montaña)* shelter, refuge **(d)** *(establecimiento benéfico)* hostel

alberguista *nmf* youth hosteller

albinismo *nm* albinism

albino, -a 1 *adj* albino
 2 *nm,f* albino

Albion *n* Albion

albo, -a *adj Literario* white

albóndiga *nf* meatball

albor *nm* **(a)** *Literario (blancura)* whiteness **(b)** *Formal (luz del alba)* first light of day **(c)** **albores** *(principio)* dawn, earliest days; **los albores de la civilización** the dawn of civilization

alborada *nf* **(a)** *(amanecer)* dawn, daybreak **(b)** *Mús* = popular song sung at dawn **(c)** *Mil* reveille

alborear *v impersonal* **empezaba a a.** dawn was breaking

alboreo *nm Literario* daybreak, dawn

albornoz *nm* bathrobe

alborotadamente *adv* **(a)** *(desordenadamente)* excitedly **(b)** *(ruidosamente)* noisily, rowdily

alborotado, -a *adj* **(a)** *(agitado)* rowdy; **los niños están alborotados con la excursión** the children are all excited about the trip; **los ánimos están alborotados** feelings are running high **(b)** *(pelo)* dishevelled **(c)** *(mar)* rough **(d)** *Cuba (sexualmente)* sex-starved

alborotador, -ora 1 *adj* rowdy
 2 *nm,f* troublemaker; **los alborotadores atacaron a la policía** the rioters attacked the police

alborotar 1 *vt* **(a)** *(perturbar)* to disturb, to unsettle; EXPR *Fam* **a. el gallinero** to stir things up, to put the cat among the pigeons; **en cuanto se habla de sueldos, se alborota el gallinero** as soon as wages are mentioned, people get all worked up **(b)** *(amotinar)* to stir up, to rouse **(c)** *(desordenar)* to mess up; **el viento le alborotó el pelo** the wind messed up her hair
 2 *vi* to be rowdy; **¡niños, no alboroten!** calm down, children!
 3 alborotarse *vpr* **(a)** *(perturbarse)* to get worked up **(b)** *(mar)* to get rough **(c)** *Chile (encabritarse)* to rear up

alboroto 1 *nm* **(a)** *(ruido)* din; **había mucho a. en la calle** there was a lot of noise in the street **(b)** *(jaleo)* fuss, to-do; **se armó un gran a.** there was a huge fuss; **se produjeron alborotos callejeros** there were street disturbances
 2 alborotos *nmpl CAm* popcorn

alborozado, -a *adj* overjoyed, delighted

alborozar [14] **1** *vt* to delight
 2 alborozarse *vpr* to be overjoyed; **se alborozaron con la noticia de su embarazo** they were overjoyed at the news that she was pregnant

alborozo *nm* delight, joy; **la decisión causó a.** the decision was met with delight *o* joy; **celebraron el triunfo con a.** they celebrated their victory with jubilation

albricias *interj Anticuado* splendid!, first class!

albufera *nf* lagoon

álbum (*pl* **álbumes**) *nm* **(a)** *(cuaderno)* album ►► ***á. de fotos*** photo album; ***á. de sellos*** stamp album **(b)** *(de disco)* album

albumen *nm* **(a)** *Biol* albumen **(b)** *(clara)* egg white

albúmina *nf Quím* albumin

albuminoide *adj Quím* albuminoid

albur *nm* **(a)** *(pez)* bleak **(b)** *(azar)* chance; **dejar algo al a.** to leave something to chance **(c)** *Méx, RDom (juego de palabras)* pun; *(doble sentido)* double meaning **(d)** *PRico (mentira)* lie

albura *nf Literario (blancura)* whiteness

alburear *vi Méx Fam (decir albures)* to pun, to make a pun

alburero, -a *nm,f Méx Fam* = person fond of puns

alburno *nm* bleak

ALCA ['alka] *nf (abrev de* **Área de Libre Comercio de las Américas***)* FTAA, Free Trade Area of the Americas

alca *nf* razorbill

alcabala *nf* **(a)** *Col (peaje)* customs post **(b)** *Ven (garita)* guard post **(c)** *Hist* = tax on all sales and exchanges of goods **(d)** *Perú (impuesto)* = tax to fund municipal services, *Br* ≃ council tax

alcachofa *nf* **(a)** *(planta)* artichoke **(b)** *Esp (pieza) (de regadera)* rose, sprinkler; *(de ducha)* shower head

alcahuete, -a *nm,f* **(a)** *(mediador)* lovers' go-between **(b)** *(chismoso)* gossipmonger **(c)** *RP Fam (delator) (ante padres, maestra)* snitch, telltale; *(ante policía) Br* grass, *US* rat

alcahuetear 1 *vt RP Fam (delatar) (ante padres, maestra)* to snitch on; *(ante policía) Br* to grass on *o* up, *US* to rat on
 2 *vi* **(a)** *(intermediar en amoríos)* to act as a go-between **(b)** *(chismear)* to gossip

alcahuetería *nf* **(a)** *(acción)* **el antiguo oficio de la a.** the former calling of the go-between **(b)** *Fam (triquiñuela)* trick, scheme **(c)** *RP Fam (delación) (ante padres, maestra)* tale-telling, snitching; *(ante policía) Br* grassing, *US* ratting

alcaide, -esa *nm,f* prison governor

alcaldada *nf* abuse of power

alcalde, -esa *nm,f (presidente de ayuntamiento)* mayor, *f* mayoress ▸▸ ***a. de barrio*** = in major cities, person responsible for carrying out some of mayor's duties within a given district; ***a. pedáneo*** = mayor of a small village

alcaldesa *nf (mujer del alcalde)* mayoress, mayor's wife

alcaldía *nf* (**a**) *(cargo)* mayoralty; **el candidato del gobierno a la a.** the government's candidate for the post of mayor (**b**) *(sede)* mayor's office (**c**) *(término municipal)* municipality

álcali *nm Quím* alkali

alcalinidad *nf Quím* alkalinity

alcalino, -a *adj Quím* alkaline

alcaloide *nm Quím* alkaloid

alcamunero, -a *Ven Fam* **1** *adj* gossipy; **no seas a.** don't be a gossip
2 *nm,f* common gossip

alcance *nm* (**a**) *(de arma, misil, emisora)* range; **de corto/largo a.** short-/long-range; **una colisión por a.** *(por detrás)* a rear-end collision; *(angular)* a side-on collision
(**b**) *(de persona)* **a mi a.** within my reach; **utilizaron todos los medios a su a.** they used every means at their disposal; **al a. de mi bolsillo** within my means; **este restaurante sólo está al a. de los más pudientes** only the very wealthy can afford to eat at this restaurant; **esta tarea no está al a. de sus posibilidades** he's not up to this task, this task is beyond his capabilities; **la cuerda estaba casi al a. de la mano** the rope was almost within arm's reach; **tuvo la victoria al a. de la mano** she was within sight of victory, she had victory within her grasp; **al a. de la vista** within sight; **el castillo queda fuera del a. de nuestra vista** we can't see the castle from here; **dar a. a alguien** to catch up with sb; **el pelotón dio a. al ciclista escapado** the bunch caught (up with) the cyclist who had broken away from them; **fuera del a. de** beyond the reach of; **guardar fuera del a. de los niños** *(en etiqueta)* keep out of reach of *o* away from children
(**c**) *(de reformas, medidas)* scope, extent; **todavía no se han dado cuenta del a. del fallo judicial** the full implications of the verdict have still not become clear to them; **un cambio de a. universal** a change that affects everybody; **de a.** important
(**d**) **una noticia de a.** *(de última hora)* a piece of news that has just come in
(**e**) *(inteligencia)* **una persona de pocos alcances** a slow *o* dim-witted person
(**f**) *Chile (resto)* **este mes se quedó con un a.** he had a bit left over this month
(**g**) *Chile (comentario)* clarification; **estoy de acuerdo, pero debo hacerle un a.** I agree, but I must make one thing clear

alcancía *nf* (**a**) *esp Am (hucha)* moneybox; *(en forma de cerdo)* piggy bank (**b**) *Andes, RP (cepillo de limosnas)* collection box

alcanfor *nm* camphor

alcanforado, -a *adj (con alcanfor)* camphorated

alcanforero *nm* camphor tree

alcantarilla *nf* (**a**) *(de aguas residuales) (conducto)* sewer; *(boca)* drain (**b**) *Méx (de agua potable)* water tank

alcantarillado *nm* sewerage system, sewers

alcantarillar *vt* to build sewers in

alcantarillero, -a *nm,f CSur* sewerage worker

ALCANZAR [14] **1** *vt* (**a**) *(igualarse con)* to catch up with; **si estudias duro, alcanzarás a tu hermana** if you study hard you'll catch up with your sister; **¿a que no me alcanzas?** bet you can't catch me!; **vayan ustedes delante que ya los alcanzaré** you go on ahead, I'll catch you up
(**b**) *(llegar a)* to reach; *(autobús, tren)* to manage to catch; **a. el autobús** to catch the bus; **lo alcancé con una escalera** I used a ladder to reach it; **los termómetros alcanzarán mañana los 30 grados** the temperature tomorrow will reach *o* go as high as 30 degrees; **a. la mayoría de edad** to come of age; **a. la meta** to reach the finishing line; **a. un precio alto** *(en subasta)* to sell for *o* obtain a high price; **alcanzó la costa a nado** he swam to the coast; **su sueldo no alcanza el salario mínimo** she earns less than the minimum wage; **este coche alcanza los 200 km/h** this car can do up to *o* reach 200 km/h; **el desempleo ha alcanzado un máximo histórico** unemployment is at *o* has reached an all-time high
(**c**) *(lograr)* to obtain; **a. un objetivo** to achieve a goal; **alcanzó su sueño tras años de trabajo** after years of work, he achieved his dream; **el equipo alcanzó su segundo campeonato consecutivo** the team won *o* achieved their second championship in a row; **a. la fama/el éxito** to achieve fame/success; **a. la madurez** to come of age, to reach maturity
(**d**) *(entregar)* to pass; **alcánzame la sal** could you pass me the salt?; **alcánzame ese jarrón, que no llego hasta el estante** could you get that vase down for me, I can't reach the shelf
(**e**) *(golpear, dar)* to hit; **el proyectil alcanzó de lleno el centro de la ciudad** the shell exploded right in the city centre; **le alcanzaron dos disparos** he was hit by two shots; **el árbol fue alcanzado por un rayo** the tree was struck by lightning
(**f**) *(afectar)* to affect; **la epidemia no les alcanzó** they were unaffected by the epidemic; **la sequía no alcanza a esta provincia** this province has been untouched by the drought
2 *vi* (**a**) *(ser suficiente)* **a. para algo/alguien** to be enough for sth/sb; **el sueldo no me alcanza para llegar a fin de mes** my salary isn't enough to make ends meet; **no sé si alcanzará para todos** I don't know if there'll be enough for everyone
(**b**) *(poder)* **a. a hacer algo** to manage to do sth; **alcancé a verlo unos segundos** I managed to see him for a few seconds; **no alcanzo a comprender por qué** I can't begin to understand why; **no alcanzo a ver lo que quieres decir** I can't quite see what you mean
(**c**) *(llegar)* **está tan alto que no alcanzo** it's too high for me to reach, it's so high up I can't reach it; **hasta donde alcanza la vista** as far as the eye can see; **hasta donde alcanzo a recordar** as far back as I can remember

---

alcaparra *nf*, **alcaparrón** *nm* caper

alcaparro *nm* caper plant

alcaparrón = **alcaparra**

alcaraván *nm* stone curlew ▸▸ ***a. playero*** beach thick-knee

alcaravea *nf* caraway

alcatraz *nm* gannet ▸▸ ***a. atlántico*** northern gannet; ***a. pardo*** brown booby

alcaucil *nm RP* artichoke

alcaudón *nm* shrike ▸▸ ***a. dorsirrojo*** red-backed shrike; ***a. real*** great grey shrike

alcayata *nf* = L-shaped hook for hanging pictures etc

alcazaba *nf* citadel

alcázar *nm* (**a**) *(fortaleza)* fortress (**b**) *Náut* quarterdeck

alce **1** *ver* **alzar**
2 *nm (europeo)* elk; *(americano)* moose

alcista **1** *adj* (**a**) *(tendencia)* upward (**b**) *Bolsa (inversor)* bullish; **mercado a.** bull market; **valores alcistas** stocks whose price is rising
2 *nmf Bolsa (inversor)* bull, bullish investor

alcoba *nf* bedroom

> **Falso amigo**: El sustantivo inglés **alcove** no es la traducción del español **alcoba**. En inglés **alcove** significa "hueco".

alcohol *nm* (**a**) *Quím* alcohol ▸▸ ***a. de 96°*** surgical spirit; ***a. etílico*** ethanol, ethyl acohol; ***a. de grano*** grain alcohol; ***a. metílico*** methanol; ***a. de quemar*** methylated spirits, meths (**b**) *(bebida)* alcohol, drink; **tiene problemas con el a.** he has a drink problem; **si bebes a., no conduzcas** if you drink alcohol *o* have something to drink, don't drive

alcoholemia *nf* blood alcohol level; **prueba** *o* **test de a.** Breathalyser® test

alcohólico, -a **1** *adj* (**a**) *(bebida)* alcoholic; **una bebida no alcohólica** a non-alcoholic drink (**b**) *(persona)* **ser a.** to be an alcoholic
2 *nm,f* alcoholic ▸▸ ***Alcohólicos Anónimos*** Alcoholics Anonymous

alcoholímetro, alcohómetro *nm* (**a**) *(para bebida)* alcoholometer (**b**) *(para la sangre) Br* Breathalyser®, *US* drunkometer

alcoholismo *nm* alcoholism

alcoholizado, -a *adj* **estar a.** to be an alcoholic

alcoholizar [14] **1** *vt* to turn into an alcoholic
2 alcoholizarse *vpr* to become an alcoholic

alcohómetro = **alcoholímetro**

alcor *nm* hill, hillock

alcornocal *nm* grove of cork oaks

alcornoque *nm* (**a**) *(árbol)* cork oak; *(madera)* cork, corkwood (**b**) *Fam (persona)* idiot, fool; **¡pedazo de a.!** you idiot!

alcorque *nm* = hollow dug at base of tree to retain rainwater

alcotán *nm (ave)* hobby

alcotana *nf* pickaxe

alcurnia *nf* lineage, descent; **una familia de noble a.** a family of noble descent; **una dama de alta a.** a lady of noble birth *o* lineage

alcuza *nf* (**a**) *(aceitera)* oil bottle *o* jug (**b**) *Andes (vinagreras)* cruet set

aldaba *nf* (**a**) *(llamador)* doorknocker (**b**) *(pestillo)* latch (**c**) *muy Fam* **aldabas** *(pechos)* knockers

aldabilla *nf* latch, catch

aldabón *nm* (**a**) *(de puerta)* (large) doorknocker (**b**) *(de cofre, baúl)* (large) handle

aldabonazo *nm* (**a**) *(golpe)* loud knock *(with doorknocker)* (**b**) *(llamada de atención)* **la tragedia fue un a. en la conciencia de los ciudadanos** the tragedy was a wake-up call for the citizens

aldea *nf* small village ►► ***la a. global*** the global village

aldeano, -a 1 *adj* (**a**) *(de la aldea)* village; **las costumbres aldeanas** the village customs (**b**) *(pueblerino, rústico)* rustic
2 *nm,f* villager

aldehído *nm Quím* aldehyde

ale *interj* come on!

aleación *nf* (**a**) *(acción)* alloying (**b**) *(producto)* alloy

alear *vt* to alloy

aleatoriamente *adv* randomly, at random

aleatorio, -a *adj* random

alebrestado, -a *adj Fam* (**a**) *Méx (alborotado)* excited (**b**) *Méx (furioso)* furious, mad; **anda a. porque le robaron** he's mad because he was robbed (**c**) *Ven (alegre)* merry (**d**) *Ven (sobreexcitado)* overexcited, worked up (**e**) *Col (nervioso)* nervous

alebrestar *Fam* 1 *vt Méx* **a. a alguien** to get sb excited, to stir sb up; **no alebresten a los niños** don't get the children all excited; **lo arrestaron por a. a la tropa** he was arrested for inciting the troops; **andaban alebrestando a la gente en el estadio** they were going round stirring people up at the stadium
2 **alebrestarse** *vpr* (**a**) *Méx (alborotarse, entusiasmarse)* to get excited; **el bebé se alebresta a la hora de la comida** the baby gets all excited when dinnertime comes round
(**b**) *Méx, Ven (rebelarse, indisciplinarse)* to rebel; **se alebrestó la yegua** the horse reared up; **lo regañé y se me alebrestó** I told him off and he snapped back at me
(**c**) *Ven (animarse, alegrarse)* to get merry
(**d**) *Col (ponerse nervioso)* to get nervous

aleccionador, -ora *adj* (**a**) *(instructivo)* instructive (**b**) *(ejemplar)* exemplary

aleccionamiento *nm* instruction, training

aleccionar *vt* to instruct, to teach

alecrín *nm* tiger shark

aledaño, -a 1 *adj* adjacent
2 **aledaños** *nmpl* surrounding area; **en los aledaños del estadio** in the vicinity of the stadium

alegación *nf* (**a**) *(acusación)* allegation (**b**) *(argumento)* claim

alegador, -ora *adj Am* argumentative

alegar [38] 1 *vt (motivos, pruebas)* to put forward; **alegó cansancio para no participar** she claimed she was too tired to join in; **a. que** to claim (that); **¿tiene algo que a. en su defensa?** do you have anything to say in your defence?
2 *vi Am* (**a**) *(quejarse)* to complain; **a. por algo** to complain about sth (**b**) *(discutir)* to argue; **a. de algo** to argue about sth

alegato *nm* (**a**) *Der (escrito)* plea (**b**) *(argumento)* **la película es un a. contra la censura** the film is an attack on censorship; **el poeta hizo un a. a favor de la libertad de expresión** the poet argued in favour of freedom of expression (**c**) *Andes (disputa)* argument

alegoría *nf* allegory

alegóricamente *adv* allegorically

alegórico, -a *adj* allegorical

alegrar 1 *vt* (**a**) *(persona)* to cheer up, to make happy; *(fiesta)* to liven up; **me alegró el día** it made my day; **le alegró mucho su visita** his visit really cheered her up; **esas plantas alegran la vista** those plants brighten up the view; **¡alegra esa cara!** cheer up!, give us a smile!
(**b**) *(habitación, decoración)* to brighten up
(**c**) *(emborrachar)* to make tipsy
(**d**) *Taurom* **a. la embestida al toro** to incite the bull to charge
2 **alegrarse** *vpr* (**a**) *(sentir alegría)* to be pleased; **voy a poder ir a la fiesta – ¡me alegro!** I'm going to be able to come to the party – good!; **nos alegramos de su nombramiento** we are pleased that she has been appointed; **me alegro de que me hagas esa pregunta** I'm glad you asked me that; **me alegro de que les vaya bien** I'm glad to hear that they're all right; **¡no sabes cuánto me alegro!** I can't tell you how pleased I am!; **me alegro mucho por ellos** I'm very pleased for them
(**b**) *(emborracharse)* to get tipsy

alegre *adj* (**a**) *(persona)* happy, cheerful; **estás muy a.** you're very happy *o* cheerful today; **¡hay que estar a.!** cheer up!; **es una persona muy a.** she's a very happy *o* cheerful person (**b**) *(fiesta, día)* lively (**c**) *(habitación, decoración, color)* bright (**d**) *(irreflexivo)* happy-go-lucky; **hace las cosas de un modo muy a.** she's very happy-go-lucky (**e**) *(borracho)* tipsy, merry (**f**) *Euf* **una mujer de vida a.** a loose woman

alegremente *adv* (**a**) *(con alegría)* happily, joyfully (**b**) *(irreflexivamente)* blithely

alegreto, allegretto [ale'ɣreto] *Mús* 1 *nm* allegretto
2 *adv* allegretto

alegría *nf* (**a**) *(gozo)* happiness, joy; **llorar de a.** to weep with happiness *o* joy; **me dio una a. tremenda** it gave me great pleasure, it made me very happy; **¡qué a. volver a verte!** how lovely to see you again!; **ha sacado otro disco, para a. de sus seguidores** he has brought out a new record, to the delight of his fans ►► ***a. de vivir*** joie de vivre
(**b**) *(motivo de gozo)* joy; EXPR *Fam* **ser la a. de la huerta** to be the life and soul of the party
(**c**) *(irresponsabilidad)* rashness, recklessness; **gastaron el dinero con demasiada a.** they spent the money too freely
(**d**) ***a. de la casa*** *(planta)* busy Lizzie

alegro, allegro [a'leɣro] *Mús* 1 *nm* allegro
2 *adv* allegro

alegrón, -ona *Fam* 1 *adj Am (contento)* merry
2 *nm* thrill; **me dio un a. increíble verla tan feliz con su bebé** I was thrilled to see her so happy with her baby

alejado, -a *adj* (**a**) *(lugar)* distant (**de** from); **viven en una granja alejada** they live on a remote farm; **su casa está más alejada de aquí que la mía** her house is further *o* farther (away) from here than mine; **la enfermedad le obligó a permanecer a. de los escenarios durante dos meses** his illness kept him off the stage for two months
(**b**) *(distanciado)* **viven muy alejados el uno del otro** they live very far apart; **le acusaron de estar a. de la realidad** they accused him of being out of touch (with reality)

alejamiento *nm* (**a**) *(respecto a lugar)* distance; **el a. de la capital facilitaba la corrupción** being so far from the capital made it easier for corruption to flourish
(**b**) *(distanciamiento) (entre personas)* estrangement; **se produjo un a. gradual entre los dos hermanos** the two brothers gradually grew apart; **una crisis nerviosa le llevó a un a. temporal de la música** a nervous breakdown led her to give up music for a while; **se produjo un a. entre sus posturas** their positions grew apart

Alejandría *n* Alexandria

alejandrino, -a *Lit* 1 *adj* alexandrine
2 *nm* alexandrine

Alejandro *n pr* ***A. Magno*** Alexander the Great

alejar 1 *vt* (**a**) *(separar)* to move away; **aleja las plantas de la ventana** move the plants away from the window; **la policía alejó a los curiosos** the police moved the onlookers on; **nuestro objetivo es alejarlo del mundo de las drogas** our aim is to get him away from the drug culture
(**b**) *(ahuyentar) (sospechas, temores)* to allay; **las nuevas cifras alejan el fantasma de la crisis** the new figures mean that the spectre of a recession has receded
2 **alejarse** *vpr* (**a**) *(ponerse más lejos)* to go away (**de** from); *(retirarse)* to leave; **saldremos cuando las nubes se hayan alejado** we'll go out once the clouds have cleared up *o* gone; **no te alejes** don't wander off, don't go too far; **se alejaron demasiado del refugio** they strayed too far from the shelter; **¡aléjate de mí!** go away!; **aléjate de la bebida** stay away from the drink
(**b**) *(distanciarse)* to grow apart; **se fue alejando de sus amigos** he grew apart from his friends

alelado, -a *adj* **no te quedes ahí a. y haz algo** stop sitting around like an idiot and do something; **estoy a. hoy** I'm just not with it today; **me quedé a. cuando me contó lo de su embarazo** I was stunned *o* left speechless when she told me she was pregnant

alelamiento *nm* **tengo un a.** I'm not with it

alelar *vt* to daze, to stupefy; **la televisión lo alela** the television dulls his mind

alelí (*pl* **alelíes**) *nm* wallflower

alelo *nm Biol* allele

aleluya 1 *nm o nf* hallelujah
2 *interj* hallelujah!

alemán, -ana 1 *adj* German
2 *nm,f (persona)* German
3 *nm (lengua)* German

Alemania *n* Germany ►► *Antes* ***A. del Este*** East Germany; *Antes* ***A. Federal*** West Germany; *Antes* ***A. Occidental*** West Germany; *Antes* ***A. Oriental*** East Germany

alentado, -a *adj* (**a**) *Andes, Méx, Ven (recuperado)* better; **la veo muy alentada** she looks a lot better (**b**) *Chile (listo)* bright (**c**) *Chile (experimentado)* (sexually) experienced

alentador, -ora *adj (noticias, resultado)* encouraging; **palabras alentadoras** words of encouragement

alentar [3] 1 *vt* (**a**) *(animar)* to encourage; **los hinchas alentaban a su equipo** the fans cheered their team on; **la alentó para que siguiera estudiando** he encouraged her to keep on studying (**b**) *Col (palmotear)* to applaud

2 **alentarse** *vpr Andes, Méx, Ven (recuperarse)* to recover, to get better

aleonado, -a *adj Chile* mane-like

alerce *nm* larch ►► ***a. de Chile*** Patagonia cypress

alergeno, alérgeno *nm Med* allergen

alergia *nf* (**a**) *(médica)* allergy; **el marisco le produce a.** he's allergic to seafood; **tener a. a algo** to be allergic to sth ►► ***a. de contacto*** contact allergy; ***a. al polen*** hay fever; ***a. a la primavera*** hay fever (**b**) *Fam Hum (a personas, ideologías)* allergy; **les tiene a. a los políticos** she's allergic to politicians

alérgico, -a 1 *adj* (**a**) *(a sustancia)* allergic; **todas las personas alérgicas al polen** everyone who suffers from hay fever, all hay fever sufferers (**b**) *Fam Hum (a personas, ideologías)* allergic

2 *nm,f* allergy sufferer; *(al polen)* hay fever sufferer

alergista *nmf*, **alergólogo, -a** *nm,f* allergist

alergología *nf* = the study and treatment of allergies

alergólogo, -a = **alergista**

alero 1 *nm* (**a**) *(del tejado)* eaves; EXPR **estar en el a.** to be up in the air (**b**) *(de coche)* wing

2 *nmf Dep (en baloncesto)* forward

alerón *nm* (**a**) *(de avión)* aileron (**b**) *(de coche)* spoiler (**c**) *Esp Fam (axila)* armpit; **le cantan los alerones** he has smelly armpits

alerta 1 *adj o adj inv* alert

2 *nf* alert; **en estado de a.** on alert; **pusieron en a. a las tropas** they put the troops on standby; **el vigía dio la (voz de) a.** the lookout raised the alarm ►► ***a. roja*** red alert

3 *adv* on the alert; **estar a.** to be on the alert

4 *interj* watch *o* look out!

alertar *vt* to alert (**de** about *o* to); **alertaron a los esquiadores del peligro de aludes** they warned the skiers that there was a danger of avalanches

aleta *nf* (**a**) *(de pez)* fin ►► ***a. caudal*** caudal fin; ***a. dorsal*** dorsal fin; ***a. pectoral*** pectoral fin; ***a. pélvica*** pelvic fin (**b**) *(de foca)* flipper (**c**) *(de buzo)* flipper (**d**) *(de automóvil)* wing (**e**) *(de nariz)* flared part

aletargado, -a *adj* drowsy, lethargic

aletargamiento *nm* lethargy, drowsiness

aletargar [38] 1 *vt* to make drowsy, to send to sleep

2 **aletargarse** *vpr* (**a**) *(adormecerse)* to become drowsy (**b**) *(hibernar)* to hibernate

aletazo *nm* flap *(of fin or wing)*; **la ballena hundió el bote de un a.** the whale sank the boat with a single lash of its tail

aletear *vi* **el pájaro aleteó** *(con rapidez)* the bird fluttered its wings; *(con lentitud)* the bird flapped its wings

aleteo *nm (rápido)* flutter; *(lento)* flapping (of wings); **se distraía mirando el a. de los pájaros** he amused himself by watching the birds fluttering/flapping by

Aleutianas *npl* **las (Islas) A.** the Aleutian Islands, the Aleutians

alevín *nm* (**a**) *(cría de pez)* fry, young fish (**b**) *(persona)* novice, beginner (**c**) *Dep* **alevines** ≃ colts *(from ages 9 to 12)*

alevosía *nf* (**a**) *(premeditación)* premeditation; **con premeditación y a.** with malice aforethought (**b**) *(traición)* treachery

alevoso, -a *adj* (**a**) *(premeditado)* premeditated (**b**) *(traidor)* treacherous

alfa *nf* alpha; **A. y Omega** *(Cristo)* Alpha and Omega

Takes the masculine articles **el** and **un**.

alfabéticamente *adv* alphabetically

alfabético, -a *adj* alphabetical

alfabetización *nf* (**a**) *(de personas) (acción)* teaching to read and write; **cursos de a. para adultos** courses for teaching adults to read and write (**b**) *(de personas) (estado)* literacy (**c**) *(de palabras, letras)* alphabetization

alfabetizado, -a 1 *adj (persona)* literate

2 *nm,f* literate person

alfabetizar [14] *vt* (**a**) *(personas)* to teach to read and write (**b**) *(palabras, letras)* to put into alphabetical order

alfabeto *nm* alphabet ►► ***a. braille*** Braille alphabet; ***A. Fonético Internacional*** International Phonetic Alphabet; ***a. latino*** Roman alphabet; ***a. morse*** Morse code

alfaguara *nf* wellspring

alfajor *nm* (**a**) *(de ajonjolí)* = crumbly shortbread, flavoured with sesame seeds (**b**) *(en el Río de la Plata)* = biscuit made of two pieces of shortbread filled with creamy toffee (**c**) *(en Venezuela)* = diamond-shaped biscuit made with tapioca flour, cream cheese and sugar cane juice

alfalfa *nf* alfalfa, lucerne

alfanje *nm* scimitar

alfanumérico, -a *adj Informát* alphanumeric

alfanúmero *nm Informát* alphanumeric string

alfaque *nm* sandbank, bar

alfar *nm* potter's workshop, pottery

alfarería *nf* (**a**) *(técnica)* pottery (**b**) *(lugar)* potter's, pottery shop

alfarero, -a *nm,f* potter

alféizar *nm (de puerta)* embrasure, splay; **el a. de la ventana** the windowsill

alfeñique *nm Fam (persona)* wimp

alférez *nm Mil* second lieutenant ►► ***a. de fragata*** *(en la marina) Br* midshipman, *US* ensign; ***a. de navío*** *(en la marina)* sublieutenant

alfil *nm* bishop

alfiler *nm* (**a**) *(para coser)* pin; EXPR **no cabe ni un a.** it's jam-packed; EXPR **prendido con alfileres** sketchy; **lleva la asignatura prendida con alfileres** he has only a sketchy idea of the subject ►► *Cuba* ***a. de criandera*** safety pin; *Andes, RP, Ven* ***a. de gancho*** *(imperdible)* safety pin; *Col* ***a. de nodriza*** safety pin (**b**) *(joya)* brooch, pin ►► ***a. de corbata*** tie-pin

alfiletero *nm* (**a**) *(acerico)* pincushion (**b**) *(estuche)* pin box

alfombra *nf* (**a**) *(grande)* carpet; *(pequeña)* rug; **una a. de flores** a carpet of flowers ►► ***a. mágica*** magic carpet; ***a. persa*** Persian carpet; ***a. voladora*** magic carpet (**b**) *Andes, CAm, Carib, Méx (moqueta)* fitted carpet

alfombrado, -a 1 *adj* carpeted; **una calle alfombrada de flores** a street carpeted with flowers

2 *nm* carpets, carpeting

alfombrar *vt (habitación)* to carpet; **alfombraron la calle con flores** they carpeted the street with flowers

alfombrilla *nf* (**a**) *(alfombra pequeña)* rug (**b**) *(felpudo)* doormat; *(del baño)* bath mat (**c**) *Informát (para ratón)* mouse mat (**d**) *(enfermedad)* measles *(singular)*

alfóncigo *nm* pistachio tree

alfondega *nf* yellow gurnard

alfonsino, -a *adj* Alphonsine, = relating to one of the Spanish kings named Alfonso

alforfón *nm* buckwheat

alforja *nf* (**a**) *(de persona)* knapsack (**b**) *(de caballo)* saddlebag

alforza *nf CSur* tuck

alga *nf*

Takes the masculine articles **el** and **un**.

(**a**) *(planta de mar)* **algas (marinas)** seaweed; **un a.** a piece of seaweed; **la hélice se enredó en un a.** the propeller got caught in some seaweed (**b**) *Biol (microscópicas)* alga ►► ***algas verdeazuladas*** blue-green algae

algalia *nf* (**a**) *(planta)* abelmosk (**b**) *(animal)* civet (**c**) *(sustancia)* civet

algarabía *nf* (**a**) *(habla confusa)* gibberish (**b**) *(alboroto)* racket (**c**) *(ave)* fulvous whistling-duck

algarada *nf* disturbance

algarroba *nf* (**a**) *(planta)* vetch (**b**) *(fruto)* carob *o* locust bean

algarrobo *nm* carob *o* locust tree

algazara *nf* racket, uproar

algazul *nm* iceplant

álgebra *nf* algebra ►► ***a. de Boole*** Boolean algebra

Takes the masculine articles **el** and **un**.

algebraico, -a *adj* algebraic

algicida *nm* algicide

álgido, -a *adj* (**a**) *(culminante)* critical; **en el punto á. del conflicto** at the height of the conflict (**b**) *Formal (muy frío)* bitterly cold, freezing; *(sonrisa)* wintry, frosty

ALGO 1 *pron* (**a**) *(alguna cosa)* something; *(en interrogativas)* anything; **a. de comida/bebida** something to eat/drink; **a. para leer** something to read; **¿necesitas a. para el viaje?** do you need anything for your journey?; **¿te pasa a.?** is anything the matter?; **deben ser las diez y a.** it must be gone ten o'clock; **pagaron dos millones y a.** they paid over two million; EXPR **a. es a.** something is better than nothing; **a. así, a. por el estilo** something like that; **a. así como...** something like...; **por a. lo habrá dicho** he must have said it for a reason; **si se ofende, por a. será** if she's offended, there must be a reason for it

(**b**) *(cantidad pequeña)* a bit, a little; **a. de** some; **habrá a. de comer, pero es mejor que vengas cenado** there will be some food, but it would be best if you had dinner before coming; **¿has bebido cerveza? – a.** did you drink any beer? – a bit

(**c**) *Fam (ataque)* **te va a dar a. como sigas trabajando así** you'll make yourself ill if you go on working like that; **ia mí me va a dar a.!** *(de risa)* I'm going to do myself an injury (laughing)!; *(de enfado)* this is going to drive me mad!

(**d**) *(cosa importante)* something; **si quieres llegar a ser a.** if you ever want to be anybody, if you ever want to get anywhere; **se cree que es a.** he thinks he's something (special)

2 *adv (un poco)* a bit; **es a. más grande** it's a bit bigger; **estoy a. cansado de vuestra actitud** I'm rather *o* somewhat tired of your attitude; **se encuentra a. mejor** she's a bit *o* slightly better; **necesito dormir a.** I need to get some sleep

3 *nm* (**a**) **un a.** *(cosa indeterminada)* something; **esa película tiene un a. especial** that film has something special

(**b**) *Col (refrigerio)* refreshment; **tomar el a.** to have a snack *(between meals)*

algodón *nm* (**a**) *(planta)* cotton; EXPR **criado entre algodones** pampered ▸▸ ***a. hidrófilo*** *Br* cotton wool, *US* absorbent cotton; ***a. en rama*** raw cotton (**b**) *(tejido)* cotton; **una camisa de a.** a cotton shirt (**c**) *(porción)* **un a.** *(médico)* a cotton swab; *(cosmético) (bola)* cotton ball; *(plano)* cotton pad (**d**) ***a. dulce*** *Br* candyfloss, *US* cotton candy (**e**) ***a. pólvora*** gun cotton

algodonal *nm* cotton plantation

algodonero, -a 1 *adj* cotton; **la industria algodonera** the cotton industry

2 *nm* cotton plant

3 *nm,f* (**a**) *(productor)* cotton planter *o* grower (**b**) *(recolector)* cotton picker

algodonoso, -a *adj* fluffy; **nubes algodonosas** cotton-wool clouds

algol *nm Informát* Algol, ALGOL

algorítmico, -a *adj Mat* algorithmic

algoritmo *nm Mat* algorithm

alguacil *nm* (**a**) *(del ayuntamiento)* mayor's assistant (**b**) *(del juzgado)* bailiff (**c**) *RP (libélula)* dragonfly

alguacilillo *nm Taurom* = mounted official at bullfight

alguien *pron* (**a**) *(alguna persona)* someone, somebody; *(en interrogativas)* anyone, anybody; **a. tiene que habernos oído** someone *o* somebody must have heard us; **hay a. ahí?** is anyone *o* anybody there?; **¿cómo lo sabes?, ¿te lo ha contado a.?** how do you know, did someone *o* somebody tell you?; **si a. lo quiere, que lo diga** if anyone *o* anybody wants it, they should say so

(**b**) *(persona de importancia)* somebody; **se cree a.** she thinks she's somebody (special); **algún día llegará a ser a.** she'll be somebody (important) one day

ALGUNO, -A

algún is used instead of **alguno** before masculine singular nouns (e.g. **algún día** some day).

1 *adj* (**a**) *(indeterminado)* some; *(en frases interrogativas)* any; **¿tienes algún libro?** do you have any books?; **¿tiene algún otro color?** do you have any other colours?; **algún día** some *o* one day; **en algún lugar** somewhere; **tiene que estar en algún lugar** it must be somewhere or other; **compró algunas cosas** he bought a few things; **ha surgido algún (que otro) problema** the odd problem has come up; **si tuvieras alguna duda me lo dices** should you have any queries, let me know

(**b**) *(en frases negativas)* any; **no tiene importancia alguna** it's of no importance whatsoever; **no tengo interés a. (en hacerlo)** I'm not in the least (bit) interested (in doing it); **en modo a.** in no way; **no vamos a permitir que este contratiempo nos afecte en modo a.** we're not going to allow this setback to affect us in any way

2 *pron* (**a**) *(persona)* someone, somebody; *(plural)* some people; *(en frases interrogativas)* anyone, anybody; **¿ha llegado a.?** has anyone *o* anybody arrived?; **¿conociste a algunos?** did you get to know any?; **algunos de** some *o* a few of; **algunos de nosotros no estamos de acuerdo** some of us don't agree

(**b**) *(cosa)* the odd one; *(plural)* some, a few; *(en frases interrogativas)* any; **¿tienes a.?** have you got any?; **¿queda a.?** are there any left?; **me salió mal a.** I got the odd one wrong; **compraremos algunos** we'll buy some *o* a few; **algunos de** some *o* a few of

alhaja *nf* (**a**) *(joya)* jewel; *(objeto de valor)* treasure (**b**) *(persona)* gem, treasure; *Irónico* **¡menuda a.!** he's a right one!

alhajar *vt* (**a**) *(persona)* to bedeck with jewels (**b**) *(casa)* to furnish

alhajera *nf*, **alhajero** *nm Am* jewellery box

Alhambra *nf* **la A.** the Alhambra

alharaca *nf* fuss; **hacer alharacas** to kick up a fuss

alharma, alharmega *nf* harmala, harmel

alhelí (*pl* **alhelíes**) *nm* wallflower

alheña *nf* privet

alholva *nf* fenugreek

alhucema *nf* lavender

aliado, -a 1 *adj* allied

2 *nm,f* ally; *Hist* **los Aliados** the Allies

3 *nm Chile* (**a**) *(bebida)* = mixture of white wine and "chicha" (**b**) *(sandwich)* = ham and cheese toasted sandwich

alianza *nf* (**a**) *(pacto, parentesco)* alliance; **una a. contra natura** an unholy alliance ▸▸ ***la A. Atlántica*** NATO; ***a. matrimonial*** *(vínculo)* marriage bond; *(boda)* wedding (**b**) *(anillo)* wedding ring

aliar [32] 1 *vt* (**a**) *(naciones)* to ally (**con** with) (**b**) *(cualidades)* to combine (**con** with)

2 **aliarse** *vpr* to form an alliance (**con** with); **se aliaron todos contra mí** they all ganged up against me

aliaria *nf* garlic mustard, jack-by-the-hedge

alias 1 *adv* alias; **Pedro García, a. "el Flaco"** Pedro Garcia, alias *o* a.k.a. "el Flaco"

2 *nm inv* (**a**) *(apodo)* alias (**b**) *Informát* alias

álibi *nm Der* alibi

alicaído, -a *adj* (**a**) *(triste)* depressed (**b**) *(débil)* weak

alicantino, -a 1 *adj* of/from Alicante *(Spain)*

2 *nm,f* person from Alicante *(Spain)*

alicatado, -a *Esp* 1 *adj* tiled

2 *nm* tiling

alicatador, -ora *nm,f Esp* tiler

alicatar *vt Esp* to tile

alicate *nm* (**a**) **alicates** *(herramienta)* pliers (**b**) *Am (para uñas)* nail clippers

alicatero, -a *nm,f Chile Fam* electrician, *Br* sparks

aliciente *nm* (**a**) *(incentivo)* incentive; **esto le servirá de a.** that will act as an incentive to her (**b**) *(atractivo)* attraction; **con el a. adicional de un precio muy competitivo** with the added attraction of a very competitive price

alícuota *adj* (**a**) *Mat* aliquot (**b**) *(proporcional)* proportional

alienación *nf* (**a**) *(sentimiento)* alienation (**b**) *(trastorno psíquico)* derangement, madness ▸▸ ***a. mental*** mental derangement, insanity

alienado, -a 1 *adj* insane

2 *nm,f* insane person, lunatic

alienante *adj* alienating

alienar *vt* (**a**) *(volver loco)* to derange, to drive mad (**b**) *Filosofía* to alienate

alienígena 1 *adj* alien

2 *nmf* alien

aliento 1 *ver* **alentar**

2 *nm* (**a**) *(respiración)* breath; **cobrar a.** to catch one's breath; **nos dejó sin a.** it left us breathless *o* out of breath; **me falta el a.** I'm out of breath

(**b**) *(aire que sale de boca)* breath; **mal a.** bad breath; **le huele el a.** his breath smells; **le huele el a. a tabaco** his breath smells of cigarettes; **le olía el a. a whisky** he had whisky on his breath

(**c**) *(ánimo)* **el premio le dio a. para seguir con su trabajo** the prize encouraged her to continue with her work; **el a. del público impulsó al equipo** the crowd's enthusiastic support spurred the team on

(**d**) *(inspiración)* inspiration; **una novela de a. épico** a novel of epic sweep

aligátor *nm* alligator

aligeramiento *nm* (**a**) *(de carga)* lightening (**b**) *(alivio)* alleviation, easing

aligerar 1 *vt* (**a**) *(peso)* to lighten; **necesitamos a. el avión de peso** we need to make the plane lighter; **los compañeros me aligeran de trabajo** my colleagues take on some of my work themselves (**b**) *(pena)* to relieve, to ease; **aligeró su conciencia** she eased her conscience (**c**) *(ritmo)* to speed up; **a. el paso** to quicken one's pace
 2 *vi (darse prisa)* to hurry up; **aligera, que llegamos tarde** hurry up, or we'll be late

alígero, -a *adj Literario (rápido)* fleet-footed

aligote *nm* Spanish bream

aligustre *nm* privet ▸▸ ***a. de California*** Californian privet

alijar *vt (embarcación)* to unload

alijo *nm* consignment; **a. de drogas** consignment of drugs; **un a. de armas** an arms cache

alimaña *nf* pest *(animal)*

alimentación *nf* (**a**) *(acción)* feeding; **se encarga de la a. de los elefantes** she's in charge of feeding the elephants (**b**) *(comida)* food; **una tienda de a.** a grocery store; **el sector de la a.** the food industry (**c**) *(régimen alimenticio)* diet; **una a. equilibrada** a balanced diet; **una a. rica en proteínas** a protein-rich diet (**d**) *Tec* feed, input; **fuente de a.** power supply

alimentador, -ora 1 *adj Tec* feeding
 2 *nm Tec* feed, feeder ▸▸ ***a. de corriente*** power supply unit; *Informát* ***a. de papel*** paper feed

alimentar 1 *vt* (**a**) *(dar comida)* to feed; **alimentan a los tigres con carne** they feed the tigers meat; **tengo cinco hijos que a.** I've got five kids to feed; **el hijo mayor trabaja y alimenta a toda la familia** the eldest son goes to work so that the whole family can eat
 (**b**) *(dar energía, material)* to feed; **la lectura alimenta el espíritu** reading improves your mind; **esa actitud alimenta la intolerancia** that attitude fuels intolerance; **trabajar con él le ha alimentado el ego** working with him has boosted her ego
 (**c**) *(motor, coche)* to fuel; *(caldera)* to stoke; **a. una batería** to charge *o* recharge a battery
 2 *vi (nutrir)* to be nourishing; **los garbanzos alimentan mucho** chickpeas are very nutritious
 3 alimentarse *vpr (comer)* **alimentarse de** to live on; **sólo se alimenta de verduras** she lives on nothing but vegetables; **la calculadora se alimenta con dos pilas** the calculator is powered by two batteries

alimentario, -a *adj* food; **la industria alimentaria** the food industry; **una dieta alimentaria** a diet; **productos alimentarios** foodstuffs; **hábitos alimentarios** eating habits; **pensión alimentaria** maintenance

alimenticio, -a *adj* (**a**) *(nutritivo)* nourishing; **esta sopa es muy alimenticia** this soup is very nutritious; **un desorden a.** an eating disorder (**b**) *(alimentario)* food; **la industria alimenticia** the food industry; **una dieta alimenticia** a diet; **productos alimenticios** foodstuffs; **hábitos alimenticios** eating habits; **pensión alimenticia** maintenance

alimento *nm* (**a**) *(comestible)* food ▸▸ ***alimentos básicos*** basic foodstuffs; ***alimentos infantiles*** baby foods; ***alimentos transgénicos*** GM food (**b**) *(sostén)* **la lectura es un a. para el espíritu** reading improves your mind; **el desempleo es un a. para la delincuencia** unemployment fuels crime

alimoche *nm* Egyptian vulture

alimón: al alimón *loc adv Esp* jointly, together; **escribieron la novela al a.** they co-wrote the novel

alineación *nf* (**a**) *(colocación en línea)* alignment
 (**b**) *(de ruedas)* alignment
 (**c**) *Dep (composición de equipo)* line-up; **anunció la a. el día anterior a la final** he announced the team *o* line-up the day before the final; **fue excluido de la a. en el último momento** he was left out of the team at the last minute; **fueron sancionados por la a. de cuatro extranjeros** they were penalized for including four foreigners in their starting line-up

alineadamente *adv* in a straight line

alineado, -a *adj* (**a**) *(en línea recta)* lined up (**b**) *Dep (en equipo)* selected (**c**) *Pol* **países no alineados** non-aligned countries

alineamiento *nm* alignment; *Pol* **no a.** non-alignment

alinear 1 *vt* (**a**) *(colocar en línea)* to line up (**b**) *(ruedas)* to align (**c**) *Dep (seleccionar)* to include in the starting line-up
 2 alinearse *vpr* (**a**) *(colocarse en línea)* to line up; *(soldados)* to fall in (**b**) *Pol* to align (**con** with *o* alongside); **siempre se ha alineado con los más débiles** she has always sided with the underdog

aliñado, -a *adj (ensalada)* dressed; *(carne)* seasoned

aliñar *vt (ensalada)* to dress; *(carne)* to season

aliño *nm (para ensalada)* dressing; *(para carne)* seasoning

alío *etc ver* **aliar**

alioli *nm* = sauce made from garlic and olive oil

alionín *nm* long-tailed tit

aliquebrado, -a *adj Fam (abatido)* downhearted, depressed

alirón 1 *n* **cantar el a.** to sing a victory chant; *Fig* to cry victory
 2 *interj* hooray!

alisar 1 *vt (ropa, superficie)* to smooth (down)
 2 alisarse *vpr* **alisarse el pelo** to smooth (down) one's hair

aliscafo, alíscafo *nm RP* hydrofoil

aliseda *nf* alder grove

alisios *Meteo* **1** *adj* **vientos a.** trade winds
 2 *nmpl* trade winds

alisma *nf* water plantain

aliso *nm* alder

alistamiento *nm Mil* enlistment

alistar 1 *vt* (**a**) *(reclutar)* to recruit (**b**) *(inscribir en lista)* to list (**c**) *(preparar)* to prepare, to get ready
 2 alistarse *vpr* (**a**) *Mil* to enlist, to join up; **alistarse en el ejército/la marina** to join the army/navy (**b**) *Am (prepararse)* to get ready

alita *nf (de compresa)* wing

alitán *nm* larger spotted dogfish

aliteración *nf* alliteration

aliviadero *nm (de embalse)* overflow, spillway

alivianado, -a *adj Méx* easy-going, laid-back; **Juan es muy a., seguro te presta su auto** Juan is very laid-back, I'm sure he'll lend you his car; **ese profesor es a. con sus alumnos** that teacher is very easy-going with his pupils

alivianar *Fam* **1** *vt* (**a**) *Am (ayudar)* to help out, to give a hand; **aliviáname a poner la mesa mientras preparo la cena** give me a hand laying the table while I make dinner
 (**b**) *Méx (reconfortar)* to buck up; **hay que a. a Teresa, la veo muy preocupada** we need to buck Teresa up, she looks really worried to me
 (**c**) *Méx* **a. con** *(prestar)* to help out with; **lo alivianaron con algo de dinero** they helped him out with some money
 2 alivianarse *vpr* (**a**) *Am (tranquilizarse)* to take it easy; **¡aliviánate!, no te preocupes más** take it easy and stop worrying!
 (**b**) *Méx (comprender)* **muchos chavos de hoy se alivianan con el trabajo doméstico** a lot of guys *o Br* blokes today are cool about doing housework; **ya se alivianó y sí va a participar en la obra de teatro** he's come round and he WILL be taking part in the play; **los vecinos se alivianaron y compartiremos los gastos** the neighbours have come on side and we're going to share the cost

aliviane *nm Méx Fam* (**a**) *(relajamiento)* **¡tengo un a.!** I feel really relaxed!; **las vacaciones fueron un a. sensacional** the holiday was wonderfully relaxing (**b**) *(ayuda)* helping hand

aliviar *vt* (**a**) *(atenuar)* to relieve, to soothe; **una medicina para a. el dolor** a medicine to relieve the pain; **estas pastillas te aliviarán el dolor** these pills will relieve the pain
 (**b**) *(persona)* to relieve; **contarle tus penas a alguien te aliviará** it will help if you tell your troubles to someone; **me alivia saber que no soy el único** it's a relief *o* it helps to know I'm not the only one
 (**c**) *(carga)* to lighten
 (**d**) *Fam (robar)* to lift; **me aliviaron la cartera** someone has lifted my wallet

alivio 1 *nm* (**a**) *(de enfermedad)* relief; **con estas pastillas notarás un a. inmediato** when you take these pills you will feel instant relief *o* you will feel better immediately (**b**) *(de preocupación)* relief; **¡qué a.!** what a relief!; **fue un a. saber que había llegado bien** it was a relief to know that she had arrived safely
 2 de alivio *loc adj Fam* **agarró un resfriado de a.** she caught a stinker of a cold; **es un niño de a.** he's a little monster

aljaba *nf* quiver

aljama *nf Hist* (**a**) *(sinagoga)* synagogue; *(mezquita)* mosque (**b**) *(barrio) (judío)* Jewish quarter; *(árabe)* Moorish quarter (**c**) *(comunidad)* = self-governing community of Moors or Jews under Christian rule

aljibe *nm* (**a**) *(de agua)* cistern (**b**) *Náut* tanker

aljófar *nm (perla)* seed pearl

ALLÁ *adv* (**a**) *(indica espacio)* over there; **aquí no hay espacio para esos libros, ponlos a.** there's no room for these books here, put them over there; **no te pongas tan a., que no te oigo** don't stand so far away, I can't hear you; **a. abajo/arriba** down/up there; **a. donde sea**

away, I can't hear you; **a. abajo/arriba** down/up there; **a. donde sea posible** wherever possible; **a. lejos** right back there; **a. en tu pueblo se come muy bien** they eat well back in your home town; **hacerse a.** to move over *o* along; **hacia a.** that way, in that direction; **más a.** further on; **no dejes el vaso tan cerca del borde, ponlo más a.** don't leave the glass so near the edge, move it in a bit; **los trenes son un desastre, sin ir más a., ayer estuve esperando dos horas** trains are hopeless, you don't need to look far to find an example, only yesterday I had to wait for two hours; **más a. de** beyond; **no vayas más a. de la verja** don't go beyond the gate; **no se veía más a. de unos pocos metros** visibility was down to a few metres; **voy para a. mañana** I'm going there tomorrow; **échate para a.** move over; **por a.** over there, thereabouts

(**b**) *(indica tiempo)* **a. por los años cincuenta** back in the fifties; **a. para el mes de agosto** around August some time

(**c**) *(en frases)* **a. él/ella** that's his/her problem; **a. tú, a. te las compongas** that's your problem; **a. se las arreglen ellos** that's their problem, that's for them to worry about; **a. cada cual** each person will have to decide for themselves; **a. tú con lo que haces** it's up to you what you do; **los negocios no andan muy a.** business is rather slow at the moment; **no ser muy a.** to be nothing special; **no encontrarse** *o* **sentirse muy a.** to feel a bit funny; **hoy no estoy muy a.** I'm not quite myself today; **¡a. voy!** here I go *o* come!; **¿estamos todos listos? ¡vamos a.!** is everybody ready? then let's begin!; **¡vamos a., tú puedes!** go for it *o* go on, you can do it!

---

allacito *adv Andes (indica espacio)* over there; **¿dónde queda la iglesia? – a.** where's the church? – right there

allanamiento *nm* (**a**) *Esp (sin autorización judicial)* forceful entry ►► *Der* ***a. de morada*** breaking and entering (**b**) *Am (con autorización judicial)* raid

allanar *vt* (**a**) *(terreno)* to flatten, to level; *Fig* **a. el camino** *o* **terreno a alguien** to smooth the way for sb (**b**) *(dificultad)* to overcome; **consiguieron a. todas las diferencias** they managed to sort out all their differences (**c**) *(irrumpir en)* to break into; **las tropas allanaron la ciudad** the troops sacked the city (**d**) *Am (hacer una redada en)* to raid

allegado, -a **1** *adj (cercano)* close; **es una persona muy allegada a la familia** she's a close friend of the family; **fuentes allegadas a la cantante declararon que...** according to sources close to the singer...

2 *nm,f* (**a**) *(familiar)* relative; *(amigo)* close friend; **a la ceremonia acudieron la familia y allegados** the ceremony was attended by close friends and family; **sólo pueden entrar los allegados al difunto** only the close friends and family of the deceased may enter (**b**) *Chile (huésped)* guest (**c**) *Chile Fam (gorrón)* sponger

allegar [38] **1** *vt* (**a**) *(acercar)* to place near (**b**) *(añadir)* to add

2 allegarse *vpr (adherirse)* to conform

allegreto = **alegreto**

allegro = **alegro**

allende *prep Literario* beyond; **a. los mares** across the seas; **a. los montes** beyond the mountains

allí *adv* (**a**) *(en el espacio)* there; **a. abajo/arriba** down/up there; **a. mismo** right there; **está por a.** it's around there somewhere; **se va por a.** you go that way; **está a. dentro** it's in there; **a. donde vayas...** wherever you go... (**b**) *(en el tiempo)* then; **hasta a. todo iba bien** everything had been going well until then *o* up to that point

---

ALMA *nf*

Takes the masculine articles **el** and **un**.

(**a**) *(espíritu)* soul; **es un chico de a. noble** he's a noble-minded boy; **encomiendo mi a. a Dios** I commend my soul to God ►► ***a. en pena*** soul in purgatory; EXPR **como a. en pena** like a lost soul

(**b**) *(persona)* soul; **un pueblo de doce mil almas** a town of twelve thousand people; **no se ve un a.** there isn't a soul to be seen

(**c**) *(de negocio, equipo)* backbone; **son el a. de la compañía** they're the backbone *o* core of the company; **el a. de la fiesta** the life and soul of the party; **el a. del proyecto** the driving force behind the project; **el humor es el a. de este espectáculo** humour is at the heart of this show ►► ***a. máter*** driving force; **ser el a. máter de algo** to be the driving force behind sth

(**d**) *(de cañón)* bore

(**e**) *Mús (de instrumento)* soundpost

(**f**) *(de viga)* web

(**g**) EXPR **a. mía, mi a.** *(apelativo)* dearest, darling; **agradecer algo en el a.** to be deeply grateful for sth; **arrancarle el a. a alguien** *(matarlo)* to kill sb; *Fam* **se le cayó el a. a los pies** his heart sank; *Fam* **como a. que lleva el diablo** like a bat out of hell; **con toda mi/tu/***etc.* **a.** with all my/your/*etc* heart; **lo odia con toda su a.** she hates him with all her heart; **cantaba con toda su a.** he was singing his heart out, he was singing for all he was worth; **deseo con toda mi a. que seas feliz** I hope with all my heart that you'll be happy; **me da en el a. que no llamarán** I can feel it in my bones *o* deep down that they're not going to ring; **en el a.** truly, from the bottom of one's heart; **entregar el a.** to give up the ghost; **estar con el a. en un hilo** to be worried stiff; **llegar al a. a alguien** to touch sb's heart; **lo que dijo me llegó al a.** her words really struck home; *Fam* **no puedo con mi a.** I'm ready to drop, I'm completely worn out; **no tener a.** to be heartless; **partir el a. a alguien** to break sb's heart; **me salió del a. contestarle así** I didn't mean to answer him like that, it just came out that way; **sentirlo en el a.** to be truly sorry; **lo siento en el a. pero no puedo ayudarte** I'm truly sorry, but I can't help you; **ser el a. gemela de alguien** to be sb's soul mate; **ser un a. atravesada** *o* **de Caín** *o* **de Judas** to be a fiend *o* a villain; *Fam* **ser un a. de cántaro** to be a mug; **ser un a. de Dios** to be a good soul

---

Alma Ata *n* Alma-ata

almacén *nm* (**a**) *(para guardar)* warehouse ►► ***a. frigorífico*** refrigerated storehouse (**b**) *(tienda)* store, shop; **(grandes) almacenes** department store (**c**) *Andes, RP (de alimentos)* grocer's (shop), grocery store (**d**) *CAm (de ropa)* clothes shop

almacenaje *nm* storage

almacenamiento *nm* (**a**) *(de mercancías, información)* storage (**b**) *Informát* storage ►► ***a. masivo*** mass storage; ***a. permanente*** permanent storage; ***a. temporal*** temporary storage

almacenar *vt* (**a**) *(mercancías)* to store (**b**) *(reunir)* to collect; **en veinte años han almacenado éxitos y fracasos** over twenty years they have notched up both hits and flops (**c**) *Informát* to store

almacenero, -a *nm,f*, **almacenista** *nmf* (**a**) *(que almacena)* warehouse worker (**b**) *Andes, RP (que vende)* grocer

almáciga *nf* (**a**) *(resina)* mastic (**b**) *(masilla)* putty (**c**) *(semillero)* nursery, seedbed

almácigo *nm* (**a**) *(árbol)* mastic tree (**b**) *(semilla)* nursery seed (**c**) *(semillero)* nursery, seedbed

almádena *nf* sledgehammer

almadraba *nf* (**a**) *(pesca)* tuna fishing (**b**) *(red)* tuna-fishing net

almagre *nm* red ochre

almanaque *nm* (**a**) *(calendario)* calendar (**b**) *(publicación anual)* almanac

almazara *nf* olive-oil mill

almeja *nf* (**a**) *(molusco)* clam (**b**) *Vulg (vulva)* pussy

almena *nf* = upright part of castle battlement, *Espec* merlon; **almenas** battlements

almenado, -a *adj* crenellated

almenaje *nm* battlements

almenara *nf* (**a**) *(fuego)* beacon (**b**) *(candelero)* candelabrum, candelabra

almendra *nf* almond ►► ***a. amarga*** bitter almond; ***a. dulce*** almond; ***almendras fileteadas*** flaked almonds; ***almendras garrapiñadas*** = almonds covered in caramelized sugar

almendrado, -a **1** *adj* almond-shaped; **ojos almendrados** almond eyes

2 *nm* (**a**) *(pasta)* = crumbly biscuit made with almonds (**b**) *(helado)* almond-flavoured ice cream

almendro *nm* almond (tree)

almendruco *nm* green almond

almeriense **1** *adj* of/from Almería *(Spain)*

2 *nmf* person from Almería *(Spain)*

almez *nm* hackberry tree

almiar *nm* haystack

almíbar *nm* syrup; **en a.** in syrup

almibaradamente *adv (afectadamente)* cloyingly

almibarado, -a *adj* (**a**) *(con almíbar)* covered in syrup (**b**) *(afectado)* syrupy, sugary

almibarar *vt* to cover in syrup

almidón *nm* starch

almidonado, -a **1** *adj* starched

2 *nm* starching

almidonar *vt* to starch

alminar *nm* minaret

almirantazgo *nm* (**a**) *(dignidad)* admiralty (**b**) *(de la Armada)* Admiralty

almirante *nm* admiral

almirez *nm* mortar
almizclado, -a, almizcleño, -a *adj* musky
almizcle *nm* musk
almizcleño, -a = **almizclado**
almizclero *nm* musk deer
almohada *nf* pillow; EXPR **consultarlo con la a.** to sleep on it
almohade 1 *adj* Almohad(e)
2 *nmf* Almohad(e), = member of the Arab dynasty which ruled in North Africa and Muslim Spain in the 7th and 8th centuries
almohadilla *nf* (**a**) *(para sentarse)* cushion (**b**) *(de gato, perro)* pad (**c**) *(alfiletero)* pincushion (**d**) *(en béisbol)* bag (**e**) *Arquit* bolster (**f**) *RP (tampón)* ink pad (**g**) *Bol, Chile (borrador)* blackboard *Br* rubber *o US* eraser
almohadillado, -a *adj* padded
almohadillar *vt* (**a**) *(acolchar)* to pad (**b**) *Arquit* to decorate with bolsters
almohadón *nm* (**a**) *(cojín grande)* cushion (**b**) *(funda)* pillowcase
almohaza *nf* currycomb
almohazar *vt (caballo)* to curry
almoneda *nf* (**a**) *(subasta)* auction (**b**) *(local)* discount store
almorávide 1 *adj* Almoravid
2 *nmf* Almoravid, = member of the Berber dynasty which ruled in North Africa and Muslim Spain in the 6th and 7th centuries
almorejo *nm* green bristle-grass
almorranas *nfpl Fam* piles
almorta *nf* chickling vetch
almorzar [31] 1 *vt* (**a**) *(a mediodía)* to have for lunch; **los viernes almuerzan pescado** on Fridays they have fish for lunch (**b**) *(a media mañana)* to have as a mid-morning snack
2 *vi* (**a**) *(a mediodía)* to have lunch (**b**) *(a media mañana)* to have a mid-morning snack
almuecín, almuédano *nm* muezzin
almuerzo *nm* (**a**) *(a mediodía)* lunch; **a. de trabajo** working lunch (**b**) *(a media mañana)* mid-morning snack
aló *interj Andes, Carib (al teléfono)* hello!
alocadamente *adv* (**a**) *(locamente)* crazily (**b**) *(irreflexivamente)* rashly, recklessly
alocado, -a 1 *adj* (**a**) *(loco)* crazy; **lleva una vida alocada** she lives a wild life (**b**) *(irreflexivo)* rash, reckless; **fue una decisión alocada** it was a rash decision
2 *nm,f* (**a**) *(loco)* **es un a.** he's crazy (**b**) *(irreflexivo)* **es un a.** he's rash *o* reckless
alocución *nf* address, speech
aloe, áloe *nm* (**a**) *(planta)* common aloe (**b**) *(jugo)* aloes
alófono *nm Ling* allophone
alógeno, -a *adj* immigrant, incoming
alojado, -a *nm,f Andes, Méx* guest, lodger
alojamiento *nm* accommodation; **estoy buscando a.** I'm looking for accommodation; **el precio incluye el a.** the price includes accommodation; **dar a. a alguien** to put sb up
alojar 1 *vt* to put up; **alojaron a los supervivientes en un polideportivo** they put the survivors up in a sports centre; **cada tienda de campaña puede a. a treinta refugiados** each tent can house thirty refugees; *Informát* **a. páginas web** to host web pages
2 **alojarse** *vpr* (**a**) *(hospedarse)* to stay; **se alojaron en un hotel** they stayed at a hotel (**b**) *(introducirse)* to lodge; **la bala se alojó en el pulmón derecho** the bullet lodged in her right lung
alomorfo *nm Ling* allomorph
alón *nm* wing *(of bird, for eating)*
alondra *nf* skylark ▸▸ ***a. cornuda*** shore lark
alopatía *nf* allopathy
alopecia *nf* hair loss, *Espec* alopecia
alopécico, -a *adj* **ser a.** to suffer from hair loss *o Espec* alopecia
alpaca *nf* (**a**) *(metal)* alpaca, German *o* nickel silver (**b**) *(animal)* alpaca (**c**) *(tela)* alpaca
alpargata *nf* espadrille
alpargatería *nf* = shop selling espadrilles
Alpes *nmpl* **los A.** the Alps
alpestre *adj* alpine
alpinismo *nm* mountaineering, mountain climbing
alpinista *nmf* mountaineer, mountain climber
alpino, -a *adj* Alpine
alpiste *nm* (**a**) *(planta)* canary grass (**b**) *(semilla)* birdseed (**c**) EXPR *RP Fam* **estar al a.** *(alerta)* to keep one's ears *o* eyes open
alquequenje *nm* winter cherry
alquería *nf Esp* farmstead
alquilado, -a *adj (casa, oficina, televisor)* rented; *(coche, bicicleta, traje)* hired
alquilar 1 *vt* (**a**) *(dejar en alquiler) (casa, oficina)* to rent (out); *(televisor)* to rent (out); *(coche, bicicleta)* to hire out; *(traje)* to hire out; **le alquilamos nuestra casa** we rented our house (out) to him; **se alquila** *(en letrero)* to let; **se alquilan bicicletas** *(en letrero)* bicycles for hire; EXPR *RP Fam* **estuvo** *o* **fue de** *o* **para a. balcones** *(muy bueno)* it was amazing *o* awesome; *(muy divertido)* it was a scream
(**b**) *(tomar en alquiler) (casa, oficina)* to rent; *(televisor)* to rent; *(coche, bicicleta)* to hire; *(traje)* to hire
(**c**) *RP Fam (burlarse de)* **a. a alguien** to pull sb's leg, *Br* to take the mickey out of sb; **siempre me alquilan por la impuntualidad** they're always pulling my leg *o Br* taking the mickey out of me about being late
2 **alquilarse** *vpr (persona)* to sell oneself; **no se alquila por cualquier precio** he won't sell himself for any price
alquiler *nm* (**a**) *(acción) (de casa, oficina)* renting; *(de televisor)* renting; *(de coche, bicicleta)* hiring; **de a.** *(casa)* rented; **¿está en venta o en a.?** is it for sale or to let?; **coche de a.** hire car; **tenemos pisos de a.** we have *Br* flats *o US* apartments to let; **a. de bicicletas** *(en letrero)* bicycles for hire; **a. de coches** *(en letrero)* car hire *o* rental; **una madre de a.** a surrogate mother ▸▸ ***a. con opción a compra*** rental with option to buy
(**b**) *(precio) (de casa, oficina)* rent; *(de televisión)* rental; *(de coche)* hire charge; **han subido los alquileres de la vivienda** rents have gone up
alquimia *nf* alchemy
alquimista *nmf* alchemist
alquitara *nf* still
alquitrán *nm* (**a**) *(para asfaltar)* tar (**b**) *(en cigarrillo)* tar
alquitranado *nm* (**a**) *(acción)* tarring (**b**) *Náut* tarpaulin
alquitranar *vt* to tar
alrededor 1 *adv* (**a**) *(en torno)* around; **a. de la mesa** around the table; **las casas de a.** the surrounding houses (**b**) *(aproximadamente)* **a. de** around; **llegaremos a. de medianoche** we'll arrive around midnight; **tiene a. de treinta y cinco años** she's about thirty-five
2 *nm* **miré a mi a.** I looked around (me); **todo a su a. era desierto** she was surrounded by desert; **alrededores** surrounding area; **los alrededores de Guadalajara** the area around Guadalajara; **el apagón afectó a Nueva York y sus alrededores** the power cut affected New York and the surrounding area; **había mucha gente en los alrededores del estadio** there were a lot of people in the area around the stadium
Alsacia *nf* Alsace ▸▸ ***A.-Lorena*** Alsace-Lorraine
alsaciano, -a 1 *adj* Alsatian
2 *nm,f* Alsatian
álsine *nm* common chickweed
alta *nf*

Takes the masculine articles **el** and **un**.

(**a**) *(del hospital)* **a. (médica)** discharge; **dar de a. a alguien, dar el a. a alguien** to discharge sb (from hospital)
(**b**) *(documento)* certificate of discharge
(**c**) *(en una asociación)* membership; **el mes pasado se produjeron muchas altas** a lot of new members joined last month; **darse de a. (en)** *(club)* to become a member (of); *(Seguridad Social)* to register (with); **dar de a. a alguien** *(en club)* to enrol sb; **con fecha de hoy causa a. en el club** she is a member of the club as of today
(**d**) **dar de a. a alguien** *(en teléfono, gas, electricidad)* to connect sb
altamente *adv* highly, extremely; **a. satisfecho** highly *o* extremely satisfied
altanería *nf* (**a**) *(soberbia)* haughtiness; **con a.** haughtily (**b**) *Anticuado (cetrería)* falconry
altanero, -a *adj* haughty
altar *nm* altar; **conducir** *o* **llevar a alguien al a.** to lead sb down the aisle; EXPR **elevar a los altares a alguien** to canonize sb ▸▸ ***a. mayor*** high altar
altavoz *nm* (**a**) *(para anuncios)* loudspeaker; **la llamaron por el a.** they called her over the loudspeaker (**b**) *(de tocadiscos, ordenador)* speaker
alterable *adj* changeable

alteración *nf* (**a**) *(cambio)* alteration (**b**) *(excitación)* agitation; **se notaba su a. en mi presencia** she became clearly agitated in my presence (**c**) *(alboroto)* disturbance ►► ***a. del orden público*** breach of the peace

alterado, -a *adj* (**a**) *(cambiado)* altered, changed (**b**) *(perturbado)* disturbed, upset; **los niños están muy alterados con la llegada de las vacaciones** the children are rather overexcited with the holidays coming up (**c**) *(enfadado)* angry, annoyed

alterar 1 *vt* (**a**) *(cambiar)* to alter, to change; **a. el orden de las palabras** to change the order of the words; **esto altera nuestros planes** that changes our plans
(**b**) *(perturbar) (persona)* to agitate, to fluster; **le alteran mucho los cambios** the changes upset him a lot; **no le gusta que alteren sus costumbres** she doesn't like having her routine upset
(**c**) *(orden público)* to disrupt; **fue detenido por a. el orden público** he was arrested for causing a breach of the peace
(**d**) *(estropear)* **el calor alteró los alimentos** the heat made the food go off
2 **alterarse** *vpr* (**a**) *(perturbarse)* to get agitated *o* flustered (**b**) *(estropearse)* to go off

altercado *nm* argument, row; **tuvo un a. con el jefe** she had an argument *o* a row with the boss; **a. callejero** disturbance

altercar *vi* to argue

álter ego *nm* alter ego

alternadamente *adv* alternately

alternador *nm Elec* alternator

alternadora *nf CSur* = woman working in a "bar de alterne", *US* B-girl

alternancia *nf* alternation ►► ***a. de poder*** = alternation of different parties in government

alternar 1 *vt* to alternate; **alterna los ejercicios** alternate the exercises; **alterna el estudio con la diversión** she alternates studying with having fun; **el libro alterna escenas de ternura con momentos de violencia** the book alternates between scenes of violence and moments of tenderness
2 *vi* (**a**) *(relacionarse)* to socialize (**con** with); **no suelen a. mucho** they don't usually socialize much; **no me gusta la gente con la que alterna** I don't like the people she mixes with (**b**) *(sucederse)* **a. con** to alternate with; **la estación de lluvias alterna con la estación seca** the rainy season alternates with the dry season
3 **alternarse** *vpr* (**a**) *(en el tiempo)* to take turns; **se alternan para cuidar al niño** they take it in turns to look after the child; **los dos partidos se alternan en el poder** the two parties take turns in office; **se alternarán los claros y las nubes** there will be a mixture of clear spells and patches of cloud (**b**) *(en el espacio)* to alternate

alternativa *nf* (**a**) *(opción)* alternative; **no tenemos a.** we have no alternative; **no nos queda otra a. que aceptar** we have no alternative *o* choice but to accept; **nuestra mejor a. es...** our best bet is... ►► ***a. de poder*** alternative party of government
(**b**) *Taurom* = ceremony in which a bullfighter shares the kill with his novice, accepting him as a professional; **tomar la a.** = to become accepted as a professional bullfighter; EXPR **dar la a. a alguien** to give sb their first big break

alternativamente *adv* (**a**) *(con alternancia)* alternately (**b**) *(como segunda opción)* alternatively

alternativo, -a *adj* (**a**) *(movimiento)* alternating (**b**) *(posibilidad)* alternative (**c**) *(medicina, energía)* alternative; *(cine, teatro)* alternative

alterne *nm* **bar de a.** = bar where women encourage people to drink in return for a commission; **chica de a.** = woman working in a "bar de alterne", *US* B-girl

alterno, -a *adj* (**a**) *(en el tiempo)* alternate; **visita a sus abuelos en días alternos** she visits her grandparents every other day (**b**) *(en el espacio)* alternate (**c**) *Elec* alternating (**d**) *Col (persona, cargo)* acting; *(sala, edificio)* adjoining; **el secretario a.** the acting secretary; **el edificio a.** the annex

alteza *nf* (**a**) *(de sentimientos)* loftiness (**b**) **A.** *(tratamiento)* Highness; **Su A. Real** His/Her Royal Highness; **su A. el Príncipe** His Highness the Prince

altibajos *nmpl* (**a**) *(del terreno)* **la carretera estaba llena de a.** the road went up and down a lot (**b**) *(cambios repentinos)* ups and downs; **la economía está sufriendo continuos a.** the economy is undergoing a lot of ups and downs; **el paciente mejora a a.** the patient is getting better in fits and starts (**c**) *(de la vida)* ups and downs

altillo *nm* (**a**) *(desván)* attic, loft (**b**) *Esp (armario)* = small storage cupboard above head height, usually above another cupboard (**c**) *(cerro)* hillock

altilocuencia *nf* grandiloquence

altilocuente *adj* grandiloquent

altimetría *nf* altimetry

altímetro *nm* altimeter

altiplanicie *nf* high plateau

altiplánico, -a *adj Am* = of/relating to the "altiplano"

altiplano *nm* high plateau; **el A.** *(en Bolivia)* the Altiplano

altiro *adv Chile Fam* right away

Altísimo *nm Rel* **el A.** the Most High

altisonante, altísono, -a *adj* high-sounding

altitud *nf* altitude; **viven a más de 4.000 m de a.** they live at an altitude of over 4,000 m

altivamente *adv* haughtily

altivez, altiveza *nf* haughtiness; **con a.** haughtily

altivo, -a *adj* haughty

ALTO, -A 1 *adj* (**a**) *(persona, árbol, edificio)* tall; *(montaña)* high; **es más a. que su compañero** he's taller than his colleague; **el Everest es la montaña más alta del mundo** Everest is the world's highest mountain; **¡qué alta está tu hermana!** your sister's really grown!; **un jersey de cuello a.** *Br* a polo neck, *US* a turtleneck; **tacones** *o Andes, RP* **tacos altos** high heels; **lo a.** *(de lugar, objeto)* the top; *Fig (el cielo)* Heaven; EXPR **hacer algo por todo lo a.** to do sth in (great) style; **una boda por todo lo a.** a sumptuous wedding; **en lo a. de** at the top of; **el gato se escondió en lo a. del árbol** the cat hid up the tree ►► ***a. relieve*** high relief
(**b**) *(indica posición elevada)* high; *(piso)* top, upper; **tu mesa es muy alta para escribir bien** your desk is too high for writing comfortably; **¡salgan con los brazos en a.!** come out with your arms raised *o* your hands up; **aguántalo en a. un segundo** hold it up for a second; EXPR **mantener la cabeza bien alta** to hold one's head high; **tienen la moral muy alta** their morale is very high; EXPR **pasar algo por a.** *(adrede)* to pass over sth; *(sin querer)* to miss sth out; **esta vez pasaré por a. tu retraso** I'll overlook the fact that you arrived late this time; **el portero desvió el balón por a.** the keeper tipped the ball over the bar; **de alta mar** deep-sea; **en alta mar** out at sea; **le entusiasma la alta montaña** she loves mountaineering; **equipo de alta montaña** mountaineering gear
(**c**) *(cantidad, intensidad)* high; **de alta calidad** high-quality; **tengo la tensión muy alta** I have very high blood pressure; **tiene la fiebre alta** her temperature is high, she has a high temperature; *Informát* **un disco duro de alta capacidad** a high-capacity hard disk; **un televisor de alta definición** a high-resolution TV screen; **una inversión de alta rentabilidad** a highly profitable investment; **un tren de alta velocidad** a high-speed train ►► ***a. horno*** blast furnace; ***altos hornos*** *(factoría)* iron and steelworks; *Informát* ***alta resolución*** high resolution; ***alta temperatura*** high temperature; ***alta tensión*** high voltage; *Der* ***alta traición*** high treason; ***a. voltaje*** high voltage
(**d**) *(en una escala)* **la alta competición** *(en deporte)* competition at the highest level; **de a. nivel** *(delegación)* high-level; **un a. dirigente** a high-ranking leader ►► *Hist* ***la alta aristocracia*** the highest ranks of the aristocracy; ***a. cargo*** *(persona) (de empresa)* top manager; *(de la administración)* top-ranking official; *(puesto)* top position *o* job; **los altos cargos del partido** the party leadership; **los altos cargos de la empresa** the company's top management; ***alta cocina*** haute cuisine; ***A. Comisionado*** High Commission; ***alta costura*** haute couture; *Mil* ***a. mando*** *(persona)* high-ranking officer; *(jefatura)* high command; ***alta sociedad*** high society
(**e**) *(avanzado)* ***alta fidelidad*** high fidelity; ***altas finanzas*** high finance; *Informát* ***de a. nivel*** *(lenguaje)* high-level; ***alta tecnología*** high technology
(**f**) *(sonido, voz)* loud; **en voz alta** in a loud voice; **el que no esté de acuerdo que lo diga en voz alta** if anyone disagrees, speak up
(**g**) *(hora)* late; **a altas horas de la noche** late at night
(**h**) *Geog* upper; **un crucero por el curso a. del Danubio** a cruise along the upper reaches of the Danube; **el A. Egipto** Upper Egypt ►► *Hist* ***A. Perú*** = name given to Bolivia during the colonial era; *Antes* ***Alta Volta*** Upper Volta
(**i**) *Hist* High; **la alta Edad Media** the High Middle Ages
(**j**) *(noble, ideales)* lofty
(**k**) *(crecido, alborotado) (río)* swollen; *(mar)* rough; **con estas lluvias el río va a.** the rain has swollen the river's banks
2 *nm* (**a**) *(altura)* height; **mide 2 metros de a.** *(cosa)* it's 2 metres high; *(persona)* he's 2 metres tall
(**b**) *(lugar elevado)* height ►► ***los Altos del Golán*** the Golan Heights
(**c**) *(detención)* stop; **hacer un a.** to make a stop; **hicimos un a. en el**

camino para comer we stopped to have a bite to eat; **dar el a. a alguien** to challenge sb ►► ***a. el fuego*** *(cese de hostilidades)* ceasefire; **¡a. el fuego!** *(orden)* cease fire!

(**d**) *Mús* alto

(**e**) *(voz alta)* **no se atreve a decir las cosas en a.** she doesn't dare say out loud what she's thinking

(**f**) *Andes, Méx, RP (montón)* pile; **tengo un a. de cosas para leer** I have a pile *o* mountain of things to read

(**g**) *CSur, Perú* **altos** *(de casa)* upstairs *Br* flat *o US* apartment *(with its own front door)*; **vive en los altos de la tintorería** she lives in a separate *Br* flat *o US* apartment above the dry cleaner's

(**h**) *Méx (señal)* stop sign

3 *adv* (**a**) *(arriba)* high (up); **volar muy a.** to fly very high (**b**) *(hablar)* loud; **por favor, no hables tan a.** please, don't talk so loud

4 *interj* halt!, stop!; **¡a.! ¿quién va?** halt! who goes there?; **¡a. ahí!** *(en discusión)* hold on a minute!; *(a un fugitivo)* stop!

altocúmulo *nm Meteo* altocumulus

altoparlante *nm Am* loudspeaker

altorrelieve *nm* high relief

altozano *nm* hillock

altramuz *nm* (**a**) *(planta)* lupin (**b**) *(semilla)* lupin seed *(eaten as a snack)*

altruismo *nm* altruism; **con a.** altruistically

altruista 1 *adj* altruistic

2 *nmf* altruist

altruistamente *adv* altruistically

ALTURA *nf* (**a**) *(de persona, cosa)* height; **mide** *o* **tiene 2 metros de a.** *(persona)* he's 2 metres tall; *(cosa)* it's 2 metres high

(**b**) *(posición)* height; **pon los dos altavoces a la misma a.** put both speakers level with each other; **a la a. de los ojos** at eye level; **la serpiente le mordió a la a. del tobillo** the snake bit him on the ankle; **el tráfico está congestionado a la a. del ayuntamiento** there's a traffic jam in the area of the town hall; **¿a qué a. está la oficina de turismo?** how far along the road is the tourist information office?; **está a la a. de la estación** it's next to the station

(**c**) *(altitud)* height; **Viella está a 1.000 metros de a.** Viella is 1,000 metres above sea level; **ganar** *o* **tomar a.** *(avión)* to climb; **perder a.** *(avión)* to lose height; **volar a gran a.** to fly at altitude; **volaremos a 2.000 metros de a.** we'll be flying at an altitude of 2,000 metres; **se esperan nevadas en alturas superiores a los 800 metros** snow is forecast on high ground above 800 metres; *Fig* **las alturas** *(el cielo)* Heaven; **Gloria a Dios en las alturas** glory to God in the highest

(**d**) *(latitud)* latitude

(**e**) *Fig (nivel)* **a la a. de** on a par with; **comprarlo no estaba a la a. de mis posibilidades** it wasn't within my means to buy it; **su última novela no está a la a. de sus anteriores** her last novel isn't up to the standard of her previous ones; EXPR **estar a la a. de las circunstancias** to be worthy of the occasion, to be equal to the challenge; **ninguno de los dos equipos estuvo a la a. de las circunstancias** neither of the teams was able to rise to the occasion; **no está a la a. del puesto** he's not up to the job; **la película no estuvo a la a. de sus expectativas** the film didn't come up to *o* fell short of her expectations; EXPR *Fam* **a la a. del betún** *o RP* **del felpudo: nos dejó a la a. del betún** *o RP* **del felpudo** it left us looking really bad; *Fam* **hemos quedado a la a. del betún** *o RP* **del felpudo, teníamos que haberle comprado un regalo** it looks really bad that we didn't buy him a present; **la moda inglesa nunca se pondrá a la a. de la italiana** English fashion will never reach the standard of Italian fashion; **intentan ponerse a la a. de los líderes del mercado** they're trying to catch up with the market leaders; **al devolverle el insulto, se puso a su a.** by insulting him back, she showed herself to be no better than him; EXPR *Fam* **a la a. de los zapatos: como tenista, no le llega a la a. de los zapatos** he's nowhere near as good a tennis player as her; **rayar a gran a.** to excel, to shine; **jugaron a gran a. y ganaron el título** they played magnificently and won the title

(**f**) *Fig (de persona)* stature; *(de sentimientos, espíritu)* loftiness; **un escritor de gran a. moral** a writer with lofty morals

(**g**) *(tiempo)* **a estas alturas** this far on; **a estas alturas ya tendrían que saber lo que me gusta** by now, they ought to know what I like; **a estas alturas ya no se puede cambiar nada** it's too late to change anything now; **a estas alturas ya debías saber que eso no se hace** you should know better than that by now; **a estas alturas del año ya es muy tarde para ponerse a estudiar** it's a bit late in the year to start studying; **si a estas alturas no te has decidido...** if you haven't decided by now...; **no me digas que a estas alturas todavía tienes dudas sobre tu boda** don't tell me you still have doubts about getting married even at this late stage

(**h**) *(cumbre)* summit, top; **las grandes alturas alpinas** the great peaks of the Alps

(**i**) *Esp (piso)* floor; **una casa de dos alturas** a two-storey house

(**j**) *(salto de altura)* high jump

(**k**) *Mús* pitch

(**l**) *Náut* **de a.** *(buque)* ocean-going; **flota de a.** deep-sea fleet; **navegación de a.** ocean navigation; **pesca de a.** deep-sea fishing

(**m**) *Geom (de triángulo)* height

alturado, -a *adj Perú* calm; **un debate a.** a calm debate; **sus intervenciones siempre son alturadas** her contributions are always very measured

alu *nf Informát* alu

Takes the masculine articles **el** and **un**.

alubia *nf* bean ►► ***a. blanca*** cannellini bean; ***a. roja*** kidney bean

alucinación *nf* hallucination; **tener alucinaciones** to have hallucinations

alucinado, -a *adj* (**a**) *(con alucinaciones)* hallucinating (**b**) *Fam (sorprendido)* staggered, *Br* gobsmacked; **quedarse a. (con)** to be staggered (by) *o Br* gobsmacked (by); **estamos alucinados con la casa que se ha comprado** we can't believe the house she's bought (**c**) *Fam (encantado)* **estar a. con algo/alguien** to be wild *o* crazy about sth/sb

alucinamiento *nm* hallucination

alucinante *adj* (**a**) *(que provoca alucinaciones)* hallucinatory (**b**) *Fam (extraordinario)* amazing, awesome; **una película a.** an amazing *o* awesome film; **es a. lo bien que canta** she's a hell of a good singer

alucinantemente *adv Fam* amazingly

alucinar 1 *vi* (**a**) *(tener alucinaciones)* to hallucinate (**b**) *Fam (delirar)* **¡tú alucinas!** you must be dreaming!; **¡yo alucino!** I can't believe it!; **yo alucino con tu hermano** *(con enfado, admiración)* that brother of yours is incredible; **alucinó con todos los regalos que le hicieron** he was bowled over by all the presents they gave him

2 *vt Fam* (**a**) *(seducir)* to hypnotize, to captivate (**b**) *(gustar)* **le alucinan las motos** he's crazy about motorbikes

alucinatorio, -a *adj* hallucinatory

alucine *nm Fam* **¡qué a.!** that's amazing!; **un a. de moto** a humdinger of a bike, a totally amazing bike; **canta de a.** she's a hell of a singer; **es un a. de tía** *(físicamente)* she's absolutely gorgeous

alucinógeno, -a 1 *adj* hallucinogenic

2 *nm* hallucinogen

alud *nm* (**a**) *(de nieve)* avalanche (**b**) *(de solicitudes, protestas, personas)* avalanche; **un a. de preguntas** an avalanche *o* a flood of questions

aluda *nf* winged ant

aludido, -a 1 *adj* **alabaron el trabajo del jefe de personal, pero el a. seguía enojado** they praised the personnel manager's work, but he was still annoyed; **darse por a.** *(ofenderse)* to take it personally; **no se dio por a.** he didn't take the hint

2 *nm,f* **el a.** the aforesaid

aludir *vi* (**a**) **a. a algo/alguien** *(sin mencionar)* to allude to sth/sb (**b**) **a. a algo/alguien** *(mencionando)* to refer to sth/sb; **en el discurso evitó a. a los impuestos** he avoided mentioning taxes in his speech

alumbrado *nm* lighting ►► ***a. público*** street lighting

alumbramiento *nm* (**a**) *(parto)* delivery (**b**) *(con luz)* lighting

alumbrar 1 *vt* (**a**) *(iluminar)* to light (up); **alumbró el camino con una linterna** he lit the way with a torch; **las antorchas que alumbran la sala** the torches which light the hall; **el ayuntamiento ha decidido a. el parque** the town council has decided to install lighting in the park (**b**) *(dar a luz)* to give birth to (**c**) *Ven (hechizar)* to cast a spell on; **la visión los alumbró a todos** the vision cast a spell on everyone present

2 *vi* (**a**) *(iluminar)* to give light; **esa lámpara alumbra muy poco** that lamp doesn't give much light *o* isn't very bright (**b**) *(dar a luz)* to give birth

alumbre *nm* alum

alúmina *nf Quím Br* aluminium *o US* aluminum oxide

aluminio *nm Quím Br* aluminium, *US* aluminum ►► ***a. anodizado*** anodized *Br* aluminium *o US* aluminum

aluminosis *nf inv Constr* = structural weakness of buildings as a result of inadequate building materials containing aluminium

aluminoso, -a *adj* aluminous

alumnado *nm (de escuela)* pupils; *(de universidad)* students

alumno, -a *nm,f (de escuela, profesor particular)* pupil; *(de universidad)* student; **ex a.** *(de escuela)* ex-pupil, former pupil, *US* alumnus; *(de universidad)* former student, *US* alumnus ►► ***a. externo*** day pupil; ***a. de intercambio*** exchange student; ***a. interno*** boarder

alunado, -a *adj RP Fam* annoyed, in a bad mood

alunarse *vpr RP Fam (malhumorarse)* to get annoyed *o* in a bad mood

alunizaje *nm* (a) *(en la luna)* landing on the moon, lunar landing (b) *(robo)* ram-raiding

alunizar [14] *vi* to land on the moon

alusión *nf* (a) *(sin mencionar)* allusion; **hacer a. a** to allude to; **su discurso se entendió como una a. a la crisis** her speech was understood as referring to the crisis; **"es un motivo de orgullo", dijo en a. al reciente galardón** "it makes me proud," he said, referring to his recent award

(b) *(mencionando)* reference; **hacer a. a** to refer to; **en el discurso evitó hacer a. a los impuestos** he avoided mentioning taxes in his speech; **por alusiones, tiene derecho a responder** because he has been mentioned, he has the right to reply

alusivo, -a *adj* **a.** a alluding to; **un comentario a. al incidente** a comment alluding to the incident; **un estilo a.** an allusive style

aluvial *adj Geol* alluvial

aluvión *nm* (a) *(de agua)* flood (b) *(gran cantidad)* **un a. de insultos** a torrent of abuse; **un a. de preguntas** a flood *o* barrage of questions; **recibieron un a. de críticas en la redacción** the newspaper was flooded with complaints (c) *Geol (sedimento)* alluvium; **tierras de a.** alluvial deposits

alveolar 1 *adj* (a) *Anat* alveolar (b) *Ling* alveolar
2 *nf Ling* alveolar

alveolo, alvéolo *nm* (a) *(de panal)* cell (b) *Anat (dental)* alveolus; *(pulmonar)* alveolus

alverja *nf Am (considerado incorrecto)* pea

alverjilla *nf Am (considerado incorrecto)* sweet pea

alza *nf*

Takes the masculine articles **el** and **un**.

(a) *(subida)* rise; **el a. de las temperaturas** the rise in temperatures; **un a. en las cotizaciones** a rise in share prices; **al a.: los precios están al a.** prices are rising; **la previsión de la inflación ha sido revisada al a.** the forecast level of inflation has been revised upwards; **la evolución al a. de las acciones** the rising value of the shares; **la evolución al a. de los precios** the upward trend in prices; *Bolsa* **jugar al a.** to bull the market; **en a.: una empresa en a.** a company that is on its way up; **un cantante en a.** a singer who is gaining in popularity

(b) *(de zapato)* raised insole

(c) *(de arma)* sight

alzacristales *nm inv* **a. (eléctrico)** electric window

alzacuello *nm* dog collar

alzada *nf* (a) *(de caballo)* height (b) *Der* appeal

alzado, -a 1 *adj* (a) *(militar)* rebel (b) *(precio)* fixed; **a tanto a.** *(modo de pago)* in a single payment (c) *Am Fam (en celo) Br* on heat, *US* in heat (d) *Am Fam (insolente)* insolent (e) *Andes, RP Fam (salvaje)* wild (f) *Col Fam (borracho)* drunk
2 *nm* (a) *(proyección vertical)* elevation (b) *Cuba (estante)* shelf

alzamiento *nm* (a) *(hacia arriba)* raising, lifting (b) *(revuelta)* uprising, revolt; **un a. militar** a military uprising ►► *Hist* ***el A. Nacional*** = Francoist term for the 1936 rebellion against the Spanish Republican Government (c) *Der* ***a. de bienes*** = concealment of assets to avoid paying creditors

alzapaño *nm (cordón)* curtain tie

ALZAR [14] **1** *vt* (a) *(levantar)* to lift, to raise; *(voz)* to raise; *(vela)* to hoist; *(cuello de abrigo)* to turn up; *(mangas)* to pull up; *Am (bebé)* to pick up; **alzó la cabeza al oír el ruido** she looked up when she heard the noise; **a. la voz a alguien** to raise one's voice to sb; **¡a mí no me alzas la voz!** don't you talk to me like that!; **a. el vuelo** *(despegar) (pájaro)* to fly off; *(avión)* to take off; **a. un embargo** to lift an embargo

(b) *(aumentar)* to raise; **alzaron el precio del petróleo** they put up *o* raised the price of *Br* petrol *o US* gasoline; **alzaron la producción de coches** they increased *o* stepped up car production

(c) *(construir)* to erect; **han alzado un templete en el medio de la plaza** they've erected a shrine in the middle of the square

(d) *(sublevar)* to stir up, to raise; **alzaron a los campesinos contra los terratenientes** they encouraged the peasants to revolt against the landowners

(e) *(recoger)* to pick (up); **a. la ropa de invierno** to put away one's winter clothes; **a. los frutos** to gather fruit; **a. la mesa** to clear the table

(f) *Rel* to elevate

(g) *Imprenta* to collate

(h) *Méx Fam (plata)* to scrape together; **alzaron lo suficiente para unos tacos** they scraped together enough money to buy some tacos

2 *vi Rel* to elevate

3 alzarse *vpr* (a) *(levantarse)* to rise; **el monumento se alza majestuoso en mitad de la plaza** the monument rises up *o* stands majestically in the middle of the square; **las temperaturas se alzaron por encima de los 40 grados** temperatures rose above 40 degrees; **se cayó y nadie le ayudó a alzarse** she fell over and nobody helped her to get up *o* nobody helped her to her feet; **alzarse de hombros** to shrug (one's shoulders); *Fig* **su trabajo se alza muy por encima del resto** his work really stands out above everyone else's

(b) *(sublevarse)* to rise up, to revolt; **alzarse en armas** to take up arms; **los rebeldes se alzaron contra el gobierno** the rebels rose up *o* revolted against the government

(c) *(conseguir)* **alzarse con la victoria** to win, to be victorious; **se alzó con el premio Nobel** she won the Nobel Prize; **los ladrones se alzaron con un cuantioso botín** the thieves made off with a large sum; **el equipo holandés se alzó con el premio** the Dutch team walked away with *o* carried off the prize

(d) *Am (animal)* to run wild

(e) *Col (emborracharse)* to get drunk

Alzheimer *nm* **(mal** *o* **enfermedad de) A.** Alzheimer's (disease)

AM *nf (abrev de* **amplitude modulation***)* AM

a.m. *(abrev de* **ante meridiem***)* a.m.

ama *nf*

Takes the masculine articles **el** and **un**.

(a) *(dueña)* owner (b) *(de criado)* mistress ►► ***a. de casa*** housewife; ***a. de cría*** wet nurse; ***a. de llaves*** housekeeper (c) *(de animal)* mistress, owner (d) *Anticuado (cuidadora)* nanny, nurse

amabilidad *nf* kindness; **¿tendría la a. de...?** would you be so kind as to...?; **tuvo la a. de acompañarme** he was kind enough to accompany me; **siempre nos tratan con a.** they're always nice to us

amabilísimo, -a *superlativo ver* **amable**

amable *adj* (a) *(persona)* kind, nice; **es una persona de carácter a.** she's a kind *o* nice person; **un policía muy a.** a very nice policeman; **se mostró muy a. con nosotros** he was very kind *o* nice to us; **es muy a. de tu parte** it's very kind *o* nice of you; **¿sería tan a. de...?** would you be so kind as to...?; **la joven ministra representa la cara a. del régimen** the young woman minister is the acceptable face of the government

(b) *Andes, RP (rato)* nice, pleasant; **pasamos un rato muy a.** we had a very nice *o* pleasant time

amablemente *adv* kindly

amado, -a 1 *adj* **mis seres amados** my loved ones
2 *nm,f* loved one, beloved

amadrinar *vt* (a) *(niño)* to act as a godmother to (b) *(barco)* to christen (c) *Andes, RP (en equitación)* to train to follow the lead

amaestrado, -a *adj (animal)* trained; *(en circo)* performing

amaestrador, -ora *nm,f* trainer

amaestramiento *nm* training

amaestrar *vt* to train

amagar [38] **1** *vt* (a) *(mostrar la intención de)* to make as if to; **le amagó un golpe** he made as if to hit him; **amagó una sonrisa** she gave a hint of a smile (b) *Dep* to dummy; **amagó un pase y batió al portero** he dummied as if to pass and beat the goalkeeper
2 *vi* (a) **amaga tormenta** *(amenaza)* it looks like there's going to be a storm (b) *Dep* to dummy

amago *nm* (a) *(movimiento simulado)* **hizo a. de darle un puñetazo** she made as if to punch him; **hizo a. de salir corriendo** he made as if to run off (b) *(indicio)* sign, hint; **tuve un a. de gripe** I felt like I had a bout of flu coming on; **tuvo un a. de infarto** he suffered a mild heart attack (c) *Dep* dummy; *(en boxeo)* feint; **hacer un a.** to dummy; *(en boxeo)* to feint

amainar 1 *vt Náut* to take in
2 *vi* (a) *(temporal, lluvia, viento)* to abate, to die down (b) *(enfado, críticas)* to abate, to die down

amalgama *nf* (a) *Quím* amalgam (b) *(mezcla)* mixture, amalgam; **esa novela es una a. de estilos** that novel is written in a mixture *o* an amalgam of styles

amalgamación *nf* (a) *Quím* amalgamation (b) *(mezcla)* amalgamation, combination

amalgamar *vt* (**a**) *Quím* to amalgamate; (**b**) *(mezclar)* to combine; **su obra amalgama varios estilos** her work combines several styles

amamantar *vt* (**a**) *(animal)* to suckle (**b**) *(bebé)* to breastfeed

amancay *nm Andes* golden hurricane lily

amancebamiento *nm* living together, cohabitation

amancebarse *vpr* to live together, to cohabit

amanecer[1] [46] 1 *v impersonal* **amaneció a las siete** dawn broke at seven; **en invierno amanece más tarde** it gets light later in winter
 2 *vi* (**a**) *(persona)* **amanecimos en Estambul** *(tras dormir)* we awoke to find ourselves in Istanbul; *(sin dormir)* we saw the dawn in Istanbul; **el niño amaneció con fiebre** the child woke up with a temperature; *Am* **¿cómo amaneciste?** how did you sleep? (**b**) *(lugar)* **las calles amanecieron nevadas** the next morning, the streets were covered in snow
 3 **amanecerse** *vpr Andes, Carib, Méx* to stay up all night; **nos amanecimos conversando** we stayed up all night talking

amanecer[2] *nm* (**a**) *(alba)* dawn; **al a.** at dawn (**b**) *(comienzo)* dawn; **es el a. de una nueva era** it's the dawn of a new era

amanecida *nf* dawn, daybreak

amanecido, -a *adj* (**a**) *Andes, Carib, Méx (persona)* **estar a.** to have stayed up all night (**b**) *RP (pan)* stale

amanerado, -a *adj* (**a**) *(afeminado)* effeminate (**b**) *(afectado)* mannered, affected

amaneramiento *nm* (**a**) *(afeminamiento)* effeminacy; **con a.** effeminately (**b**) *(afectación)* affectation; **con a.** affectedly

amanerarse *vpr* (**a**) *(afeminarse)* to become effeminate (**b**) *(volverse afectado)* to become affected

amanezco *etc ver* **amanecer**

amanita *nf* amanita ►► ***a. faloides*** death cap; ***a. muscaria*** fly agaric

amansadora *nf RP Fam* tedious wait; **después de tres horas de a., conseguí el formulario** after hanging around for three hours, I finally got the form; **¿qué tal la compra de las entradas? – fue una a.** how did it go when you bought the tickets? – it took forever *o* I had to *Br* queue *o US* stand in line for hours

amansar 1 *vt* (**a**) *(animal)* to tame (**b**) *(persona)* to calm down (**c**) *(pasiones)* to calm (**d**) *Andes Fam (zapatos)* to break in
 2 **amansarse** *vpr* (**a**) *(animal)* to become tame (**b**) *(persona)* to calm down

amante 1 *adj* **es a. de su familia** he loves his family; **ser muy a. de la naturaleza/los animales** to be a great nature/animal lover; **es a. de la cocina francesa** he's very partial to French food; **no soy muy a. del jazz** I'm not a great jazz fan
 2 *nmf* (**a**) *(querido)* lover (**b**) *(aficionado)* **los amantes del arte/de la naturaleza** art/nature lovers

amanuense *nmf* scribe

amañado, -a *adj* (**a**) *(manipulado) (elecciones, resultado)* rigged; *(partido)* fixed (**b**) *(mañoso)* resourceful (**c**) *Col (adaptado)* acclimatized; **está perfectamente amañada** she's fully acclimatized

amañador, -ora *adj Col* pleasant

amañar 1 *vt* (**a**) *(elecciones, resultado)* to rig; *(partido)* to fix (**b**) *(documento)* to doctor
 2 **amañarse** *vpr* (**a**) *(arreglarse)* to manage; **se las amaña muy bien viviendo solo** he copes *o* manages fine living by himself (**b**) *Col (adaptarse)* to acclimatize; **¿ya te has amañado en esas tierras?** have you acclimatized yet?, have you got used to living here yet?

amaño *nm (treta)* ruse, dodge; **hizo un a. para no pagar el impuesto** he fixed things so he didn't have to pay the tax

amapola *nf* poppy ►► ***a. del opio*** poppy, opium poppy

amapuche *nm Ven* (**a**) *(caricia)* caress (**b**) *(brujería)* spell

amar 1 *vt* to love; EXPR **amarás a Dios sobre todas las cosas** thou shalt love God above all things; EXPR **ama a tu prójimo como a ti mismo** love thy neighbour as thyself
 2 **amarse** *vpr* (**a**) *(quererse)* **se aman** they love each other (**b**) *(hacer el amor)* to make love

amaraje *nm* (**a**) *(de hidroavión)* landing at sea (**b**) *(de vehículo espacial)* splashdown

amaranto *nm* amaranth

amarar *vi* (**a**) *(hidroavión)* to land at sea (**b**) *(vehículo espacial)* to splash down

amaretto *nm* amaretto

amargado, -a 1 *adj (resentido)* bitter; EXPR **estar a. de la vida** to be bitter and twisted
 2 *nm,f* bitter person; **ser un a.** to be bitter *o* embittered

amargamente *adv* bitterly

amargar [38] 1 *vt* (**a**) *(alimento)* to make bitter (**b**) *(día, vacaciones)* to spoil, to ruin; **a. la vida a alguien** to make sb's life a misery; EXPR **a nadie le amarga un dulce** everyone enjoys a treat
 2 **amargarse** *vpr* (**a**) *(alimento)* to become bitter (**b**) *(persona)* to become bitter; **no te amargues (la vida) por eso** don't let it bother you

amargo, -a 1 *adj* (**a**) *(sabor)* bitter (**b**) *(sin azúcar)* bitter (**c**) *(persona, recuerdo)* bitter
 2 *nm* (**a**) *RP (mate)* bitter maté (**b**) *Ven (aguardiente)* bitters

amargor *nm (sabor)* bitterness

amarguear *vi RP Fam* to drink bitter maté

amarguera *nf* thorow-wax, shrubby hare's-ear

amargura *nf (pena)* sorrow; **lloró con a.** he wept bitterly

amariconado, -a *Fam Pey* 1 *adj* (**a**) *(afeminado)* limp-wristed, *Br* poofy, *US* faggy (**b**) *(delicado)* wimpy, wimpish
 2 *nm (delicado)* wimp

amariconar *Fam Pey* 1 *vt* (**a**) *(volver afeminado)* to make limp-wristed (**b**) *(volver delicado)* to turn into a wimp
 2 **amariconarse** *vpr* (**a**) *(volverse afeminado)* to go limp-wristed (**b**) *(volverse delicado)* to turn into a wimp

amarilis *nf* amaryllis

amarillear 1 *vt* to turn yellow
 2 *vi* to (turn) yellow

amarillento, -a, *Col, Méx, Ven* **amarilloso, -a** *adj* yellowish

amarillez *nf* yellowness

amarillismo *nm (de prensa)* sensationalism

amarillista *adj (prensa)* sensationalist

amarillo, -a 1 *adj* (**a**) *(color)* yellow (**b**) *(raza)* yellow-skinned (**c**) *(pálido)* sallow; **te veo un poco a.** you're looking a bit pale (**d**) *(prensa)* sensationalist (**e**) *(sindicato)* yellow, = that leans towards the employers' interests
 2 *nm (color)* yellow; **el a. es mi color favorito** yellow is my favourite colour ►► ***a. limón*** lemon (yellow); **una camiseta a. limón** a lemon (yellow) T-shirt

amarilloso, -a = **amarillento**

amariposado, -a *adj Fam (afeminado)* effeminate

amarizaje *nm* (**a**) *(de hidroavión)* landing at sea (**b**) *(de vehículo espacial)* splashdown

amarizar *vi* (**a**) *(hidroavión)* to land at sea (**b**) *(vehículo espacial)* to splash down

amaro *nm* clary sage

amarra *nf Náut* mooring rope; **largar** *o* **soltar amarras** to cast off; EXPR *Fam* **tener amarras** to have connections, to have friends in high places

amarradero *nm Náut* (**a**) *(poste)* bollard; *(argolla)* mooring ring (**b**) *(sitio)* mooring

amarrado, -a *adj Col, Cuba, Méx Fam (tacaño)* stingy, mean

amarraje *nm Náut* mooring charge

amarrar 1 *vt* (**a**) *Náut* to moor (**b**) *(atar)* to tie (up); **a. algo/a alguien a algo** to tie sth/sb to sth
 2 **amarrarse** *vpr* (**a**) *Andes, CAm, Carib, Méx (pelo)* to tie up; **se amarró el pelo** she tied her hair up; **amarrarse los zapatos** *o* **los cordones** to tie one's shoes *o* shoelaces (**b**) *Ven Fam* **hay que amarrársela** *(apretarse el cinturón)* we have to tighten our belts

amarre *nm Náut* mooring; **el temporal hizo necesario el a. de la flota** the storm meant the fleet had to be tied up

amarrete, -a *Andes, RP Fam* 1 *adj* mean, tight
 2 *nm,f* mean person, miser

amarrocar *vt RP Fam* to hoard

amarronado, -a *adj* brownish

amartelado, -a *adj (ojos, mirada)* adoring; **siempre andan muy amartelados** they're always really lovey-dovey

amartelarse *vpr* to be lovey-dovey

amartillar *vt (arma)* to cock

amasado *nm* (**a**) *(de masa)* kneading (**b**) *(de yeso)* mixing

amasadora *nf* mixing machine *(in bakery)*

amasandería *nf Chile* bakery

amasar *vt* (**a**) *(masa)* to knead (**b**) *(yeso)* to mix (**c**) *(riquezas)* to amass

amasiato *nm* (**a**) *CAm, Chile, Méx (concubinato)* cohabitation, common-law marriage; **vivir en a.** to live together (**b**) *Méx (pacto)* **denunció el a. entre los dos partidos** he condemned the complicity between the two parties

amasijar *RP Fam* **1** *vt (pegar)* **lo amasijaron** they kicked his head in
2 *vi (amantes)* **a. (con alguien)** to neck (with sb), *Br* to snog (sb)

amasijo *nm* **(a)** *(masa de harina)* dough **(b)** *(mezcla)* **un a. de cables y trozos de metal** a tangle of cables and bits of metal; **el coche quedó convertido en un a. de hierros** all that remained of the car was a heap of mangled iron **(c)** *RP Fam (paliza)* thrashing, beating

amasio, -a *nm,f CAm, Méx* common-law husband, *f* common-law wife

amate *nm Méx* **(a)** *(árbol)* = type of Mexican fig tree **(b)** *(papel)* = paper made with "amate" bark, used for painting **(c)** *(pintura)* = painting on a sheet of "amate" paper

amateur [ama'ter] *(pl* **amateurs)** **1** *adj* amateur
2 *nmf* amateur

amateurismo [amate'rismo] *nm* amateurism

amatista *nf* amethyst

amatorio, -a *adj* love; **poesía amatoria** love poetry; **técnicas amatorias** love-making techniques

amazacotado, -a *adj* **(a)** *(comida)* stodgy **(b)** *(almohadón)* hard

amazona *nf* **(a)** *(jinete)* horsewoman **(b)** *Mitol* Amazon

Amazonas *nm (río)* **el A.** the Amazon

Amazonia *nf (región)* **la A.** the Amazon

amazónico, -a *adj (selva, región)* Amazon; *(tribu, cultura)* Amazonian

ambages *nmpl* **sin a.** without beating about the bush; **admitió sin a. que había mentido** she admitted without hesitation that she had lied

ámbar *nm* **(a)** *(resina)* amber **(b)** *(color)* amber; **el semáforo está (en) á.** the lights are amber

ambarino, -a *adj* amber

Amberes *n* Antwerp

ambición *nf* ambition; **su máxima a. era visitar la India** her greatest ambition was to go to India; **la a. de poder lo perdió** his burning desire for power was his undoing; **tener ambiciones** to be ambitious; **no tiene ambiciones** he's unambitious, he lacks ambition

ambicionar *vt* **ambiciona el puesto de presidente** it is his ambition to become president; **ambiciona un gran futuro para la empresa** she has big plans for the company's future

ambicioso, -a **1** *adj* **(a)** *(persona)* ambitious **(b)** *(proyecto, plan)* ambitious
2 *nm,f* ambitious person

ambidiestro, -a, ambidextro, -a **1** *adj* ambidextrous
2 *nm,f* ambidextrous person

ambientación *nf* **(a)** *(de película, obra)* setting **(b)** *(de radio)* sound effects **(c)** *(de persona)* acclimatization

ambientador *nm (de aire)* air freshener

ambiental *adj* **(a)** *(del medio ambiente)* environmental **(b)** *(música, luz)* background **(c)** *(físico, atmosférico)* ambient

ambientar **1** *vt* **(a)** *(situar)* to set; **la película está ambientada en el siglo XIX** the film is set in the 19th century **(b)** *(iluminar)* to light; *(decorar)* to decorate; **puso música suave para a.** she put on some soft music to give some atmosphere
2 ambientarse *vpr (en nuevo trabajo, lugar)* **tardó un poco en ambientarse** it was a while before he felt at home *o* settled in

ambientazo *nm Fam (gran ambiente)* **había un gran a.** there was a great atmosphere

AMBIENTE **1** *adj* ambient; **temperatura a.** room temperature
2 *nm* **(a)** *(aire)* air, atmosphere; **el a. de la capital es irrespirable** you can't breathe the air in the capital; **en el a. había un olor desagradable** there was an unpleasant smell (in the air); **abre la ventana, el a. está muy cargado** open the window, it's very stuffy in here; **el a. está enrarecido** *(cargado)* it's very stuffy; *(con tensión)* the atmosphere is highly charged; *Fig* **se respira una enorme tensión en el a.** the tension (in the atmosphere) is palpable
(b) *(entorno)* environment; *(profesional, universitario)* world, circles; **en su última película no consigue recrear el a. de la época** in his latest film, he fails to recreate the atmosphere of the period; **esta lámpara crea un a. muy íntimo** this lamp creates a very intimate atmosphere; **en esta oficina no hay a. para trabajar** the atmosphere in this office is not conducive to work; **creo que no iré a la fiesta, no me van esos ambientes** I don't think I'll go to the party, it's not my sort of crowd *o* it's not my scene; **su cese ha creado muy mal a. entre el personal** her dismissal has created a very bad atmosphere amongst the staff; **entre viejos manuscritos Julián se encuentra en su a.** Julián is in his element when he's surrounded by old manuscripts, Julián is never happier than when he's surrounded by old manuscripts
(c) *(animación)* life, atmosphere; **en esta discoteca no hay a.** there's no atmosphere in this disco; **un a. espectacular rodeó la celebración de los Juegos Olímpicos** the atmosphere during the Olympic Games was amazing; **los monarcas fueron recibidos con un a. de gala** the monarchs were received with great pomp
(d) *Esp Fam* **el a.** *(homosexual)* the gay scene; **bar de a.** gay bar
(e) *Andes, RP (habitación)* room; **alquila un apartamento de un a.** she's renting a studio *Br* flat *o US* apartment; **tres ambientes, baño y cocina** two bedrooms, living room, bathroom and kitchen

ambigú *(pl* **ambigúes** *o* **ambigú)** *nm (bufé)* buffet

ambiguamente *adv* ambiguously

ambigüedad *nf* ambiguity; **con a.** ambiguously

ambiguo, -a *adj* **(a)** *(lenguaje, respuesta)* ambiguous **(b)** *Ling (sustantivo, género)* common; **de género a.** that can be either masculine or feminine

ámbito *nm* **(a)** *(espacio, límites)* confines, scope; **un problema de á. nacional** a nationwide problem; **una ley de á. provincial** a law which is applicable at provincial level; **dentro del á. de** within the scope of; **fuera del á. de** outside the realm of; *Biol* **á. geográfico** *(de una especie)* geographic domain
(b) *(ambiente)* world, circles; **una teoría poco conocida fuera del á. científico** a theory which is little known outside scientific circles *o* the scientific world; **la violencia en el á. familiar** domestic violence

ambivalencia *nf* ambivalence

ambivalente *adj* ambivalent

ambo *nm CSur* two-piece suit

ambos, -as **1** *adj pl* both; **a. actores resultaron premiados** both actors received an award, the two actors both received an award
2 *pron pl* both (of them); **me gustan a.** I like both of them, I like them both

ambrosía *nf* **(a)** *Mitol* ambrosia **(b)** *(planta)* ambrosia

ambulancia *nf* ambulance

ambulanciero, -a *nm,f Fam* ambulance man, *f* ambulance woman

ambulantaje *nm Méx* peddling, hawking

ambulante *adj (circo, feria)* travelling; **vendedor a.** pedlar, hawker; **prohibida la venta a.** *(en letrero)* no hawking; **una biblioteca a.** a mobile library

ambulatorio, -a **1** *adj (tratamiento, clínica)* outpatient; **paciente a.** outpatient
2 *nm* clinic, health centre

ameba *nf* amoeba

amebiasis *nf inv* amoebiasis

amedrentador, -ora *adj* scary, frightening

amedrentar **1** *vt* to scare, to frighten
2 amedrentarse *vpr* to get scared *o* frightened

amén **1** *nm* amen; EXPR **en un decir a.** in the twinkling of an eye; EXPR **decir a. a** to accept unquestioningly
2 amén de *loc adv* **(a)** *(además de)* as well as; **acudieron varios amigos, a. de toda la familia** several friends came, as well as the whole family; **es altamente tóxico, a. de ser explosivo** as well as *o* in addition to being explosive, it's also highly toxic **(b)** *(excepto)* except for

amenaza *nf* threat; **proferir amenazas contra alguien** to threaten sb; **una a. para el medio ambiente** a threat to the environment, an environmental hazard; **lo hizo bajo a.** she did it under duress ►► ***a. de bomba*** bomb scare; ***a. de muerte*** death threat

amenazador, -ora *adj* threatening, menacing

amenazadoramente *adv* threateningly, menacingly

amenazante *adj* threatening, menacing

amenazar [14] **1** *vt* **(a)** *(persona)* to threaten; **a. a alguien con hacerle algo** to threaten to do sth to sb; **a. a alguien con hacer algo** to threaten sb with doing sth; **a. a alguien con el despido** to threaten to sack sb; **a. a alguien de muerte** to threaten to kill sb
(b) *(dar señales de)* **esos nubarrones amenazan lluvia** those dark clouds are threatening rain; **esa casa amenaza ruina** that house is in danger of collapsing
2 *vi* **(a)** *(persona)* **amenazó con su dimisión** she threatened to resign; **amenazaron con ejecutar a los rehenes** they threatened to execute the hostages
(b) **a. con** *(dar señales de)* to threaten to; **una huelga que amenaza con crear un caos de transporte** a strike which threatens to cause transport chaos; **una especie que amenaza con desaparecer** an

endangered species, a species which is in danger of extinction

3 *v impersonal* **amenaza lluvia/tormenta** it looks like it's going to rain/there's going to be a storm

amenidad *nf* (**a**) *(entretenimiento)* entertaining qualities; **la a. de sus clases atrae a muchos estudiantes** her classes are so entertaining that a lot of students attend them (**b**) *(agrado)* pleasantness

> **Falso amigo**: El sustantivo inglés **amenity** no es la traducción del español **amenidad**. En inglés **amenity** significa "servicio".

amenizar [14] *vt* to make pleasant; **los músicos amenizaron la velada** the musicians helped make it a pleasant evening; **amenizó la reunión con sus historias** he brightened up the meeting with his stories

ameno, -a *adj (libro, programa)* entertaining, enjoyable; *(paraje)* pleasant; **es una persona de trato muy a.** he's very pleasant company

amenorrea *nf Med* amenorrhoea

amento *nm (planta)* catkin

América *n (continente)* America, the Americas; *esp Esp (Estados Unidos)* America, the States; **un vocablo típico del español de A.** a word which is typical of Latin American Spanish; **el comercio de esclavos hacia A.** the slave trade with the Americas ►► ***A. Central*** Central America; ***A. Latina*** Latin America, ***A. del Norte*** North America; ***A. del Sur*** South America

americana *nf (chaqueta)* jacket

americanada *nf Fam Pey (película)* typical Hollywood film; **es una a.** it's terribly American

americanismo *nm* (**a**) *(carácter)* American character (**b**) *(palabra, expresión) (en español)* = Latin American word or expression; *(en inglés)* Americanism

americanista *nmf* Americanist, = person who studies native American language and culture

americanización *nf* Americanization

americanizar [14] **1** *vt* to Americanize

2 **americanizarse** *vpr* to become Americanized

americano, -a **1** *adj* (**a**) *(del continente)* American (**b**) *(de Estados Unidos)* American

2 *nm,f* (**a**) *(del continente)* American (**b**) *(de Estados Unidos)* American

americio *nm Quím* americium

amerindio, -a **1** *adj* American Indian, Amerindian

2 *nm,f* American Indian, Amerindian

ameritado, -a *adj Am* worthy; **es un estudiante muy a.** he's a hard-working student; **Diego Sánchez, el a. poeta** Diego Sanchez, the distinguished poet

ameritar *vt Am* to deserve; **tan buenos resultados ameritan un brindis** such excellent results deserve a toast; **la isla amerita una visita** the island is worth a visit

amerizaje *nm* (**a**) *(de hidroavión)* landing at sea (**b**) *(de vehículo espacial)* splashdown

amerizar [14] *vi* (**a**) *(hidroavión)* to land at sea (**b**) *(vehículo espacial)* to splash down

amestizado, -a *adj* mestizo-like, having mestizo features

ametralladora *nf* machine-gun

ametrallamiento *nm* machine-gunning

ametrallar *vt* (**a**) *(con ametralladora)* to machine-gun (**b**) *(con metralla)* to shower with shrapnel

amianto *nm* asbestos

amiba *nf* amoeba

amida *nf Quím* amide

amigable *adj* amicable

amigablemente *adv* amicably

amigarse *vpr* (**a**) *(hacerse amigos)* to become friends (**b**) *(reconciliarse)* to make up

amígdala *nf* tonsil; **amígdalas** tonsils

amigdalitis *nf inv* tonsillitis

amigo, -a **1** *adj* (**a**) *(no enemigo)* friendly; **México y otros países amigos** Mexico and other friendly nations; **un pintor a. me lo regaló** a painter friend of mine gave it to me; **se han hecho muy amigos** they've become good friends *o* very friendly

(**b**) *(aficionado)* **soy a. de la buena mesa** I'm partial to good food; **es a. de la verdad** he's someone who values the truth; **no soy a. de madrugar** I don't like getting up early; **es a. de salir todas las noches** he's a great one for going out every night

2 *nm,f* (**a**) *(persona)* friend; **un a. íntimo** a close friend; **un a. del colegio** a schoolfriend; **es un a. de mis padres** he's a friend of my parents; **hacerse a. de** to make friends with ►► *Fam Hum* ***los amigos de lo ajeno*** the light-fingered; ***a. por correspondencia*** pen friend *o* pal; ***a. invisible*** = form of gift-giving (for example at office Christmas parties or in a large family) where each person anonymously buys a present for another

(**b**) *Fam (compañero, novio)* partner

(**c**) *Fam (amante)* lover

(**d**) *(tratamiento)* **el a.** our friend; **lo que el a. quiere es un vaso de whisky** what our friend here wants is a glass of whisky

3 *interj* **ia., eso es otra cuestión!** that's another matter, my friend!

amigote, amiguete *nm Fam* pal, *Br* mate, *US* buddy

amiguismo *nm* **hay mucho a. en esta empresa** in this company it's not what you know, it's who you know; **la política de subvenciones está basada en el a.** grants are awarded on the basis of who knows who

amilanamiento *nm* **su a. le impedía hablar** he was so intimidated he couldn't speak

amilanar **1** *vt* to intimidate; **sus insultos la amilanaron** she felt intimidated by his insults

2 **amilanarse** *vpr* to be discouraged, to lose heart; **no se amilana ante nada** nothing daunts her

amina *nf Quím* amine

aminoácido *nm Biol* amino acid

aminoración *nf* reduction

aminorar **1** *vt* to reduce

2 *vi* to decrease, to diminish

amistad *nf* (**a**) *(relación)* friendship; **hacer** *o* **trabar a. (con)** to make friends (with); **las une una gran a.** they are great friends, they share a very close friendship; **lo hizo por a.** she did it out of friendship (**b**) **amistades** *(amigos)* friends

amistarse *vpr Col Fam* (**a**) *(hacer amigos)* to make friends (**b**) *(reconciliarse)* to make (it) up

amistosamente *adv* in a friendly way, amicably

amistoso, -a **1** *adj* friendly; *Dep* **un partido a.** a friendly

2 *nm Dep* friendly

Ammán *n* Amman

ammonites, amonites *nm inv* ammonite

amnesia *nf* amnesia

amnésico, -a **1** *adj* amnesic, amnesiac

2 *nm,f* amnesiac

amniocentesis *nf inv Med* amniocentesis

amnios *nm inv Anat* amnion

amnioscopia *nf Med* amnioscopy

amniótico, -a *adj* amniotic

amnistía *nf* amnesty; **conceder una a. a alguien** to grant sb an amnesty ►► ***a. fiscal*** = amnesty during which people guilty of tax evasion may pay what they owe without being prosecuted; ***a. general*** general amnesty

amnistiado, -a **1** *adj* amnestied

2 *nm,f* amnestied person

amnistiar [32] *vt* to grant amnesty to

amo *nm* (**a**) *(dueño)* owner (**b**) *(de criado)* master; EXPR *Fam* **ser el a. del cotarro** to rule the roost (**c**) *(de animal)* master, owner

amoblado *nm Andes* suite; **un a. de cocina** a kitchen suite

amoblar *vt Am* to furnish

amodorrado, -a *adj* drowsy

amodorramiento *nm* drowsiness

amodorrar **1** *vt* to make (feel) drowsy

2 **amodorrarse** *vpr* to get drowsy

amohinar **1** *vt* to irritate, to annoy

2 **amohinarse** *vpr* to become irritated *o* annoyed

amojamar **1** *vt (atún)* to dry and salt

2 **amojamarse** *vpr* to become wizened (with age)

amojonar *vt* to mark the boundaries of *(with boundary stones)*

amolar [64] **1** *vt* (**a**) *(afilar)* to grind, to sharpen (**b**) *Fam (molestar)* to irritate, to annoy (**c**) *Ven Fam (timar)* to rip off; **me han amolado 20 bolívares** they conned me out of 20 bolivars (**d**) *Méx Fam (estropear)* to ruin; **mi teléfono está amolado** my telephone's bust (**e**) *Méx Fam (hacer daño a)* to do in, to beat to a pulp

2 **amolarse** *vpr* (**a**) *Am (enojarse)* to become irritated *o* annoyed

(**b**) *Méx Fam (aguantarse)* to put up with it, to lump it; **si no te gusta, te amuelas** if you don't like it, you can lump it

(**c**) *Méx Fam (estropearse)* **los cables se amolaron** the cables are bust *o* ruined, the cables have had it; **mi asunto ya se amoló** that business of mine has had it *o Br* has gone pear-shaped; **llovió tanto que el partido de futbol se amoló** it rained so much the football match was a washout

amoldable *adj* adaptable; **ser a. a** to be able to adapt to

amoldamiento *nm* adaptation

amoldar 1 *vt* to adapt (**a** to)
2 amoldarse *vpr* to adapt (**a** to); **no se amoldó al nuevo horario** she couldn't adapt to *o* get used to the new hours; **este sombrero no se amolda a mi cabeza** this hat won't change to fit the shape of my head

amomo *nm* amomum, cardamom

amonal *nm* ammonal

amonedar *vt* to mint

amonestación *nf* (**a**) *(reprimenda)* reprimand (**b**) *(en fútbol)* warning (**c**) **amonestaciones** *(para matrimonio)* banns

amonestar *vt* (**a**) *(reprender)* to reprimand (**b**) *(en fútbol)* to caution (**c**) *(para matrimonio)* to publish the banns of

amoniacal *adj* with ammonia

amoniaco, amoníaco *nm* (**a**) *(gas)* ammonia (**b**) *(líquido)* (liquid) ammonia

amónico, -a *adj* **nitrato/cloruro a.** ammonium nitrate/chloride

amonio *nm Quím* ammonium

amonites = **ammonites**

amononar *CSur Fam* **1** *vt* to dress *o* smarten up
2 amononarse *vpr* to doll oneself up, to dress up

amontillado, -a 1 *adj* **vino a.** amontillado, = medium-dry sherry
2 *nm* amontillado, = medium-dry sherry

amontonamiento *nm* (**a**) *(apilamiento)* piling up; **el a. de personas a la salida impidió la normal evacuación** the crush of people at the exit prevented the evacuation from proceeding as planned (**b**) *(acumulación)* gathering (**c**) *(montón)* heap, pile

amontonar 1 *vt* (**a**) *(apilar)* to pile up (**b**) *(reunir)* to accumulate
2 amontonarse *vpr (personas)* to form a crowd; *(problemas, trabajo)* to pile up; *(ideas, solicitudes)* to come thick and fast

AMOR *nm* (**a**) *(sentimiento)* love; **el a. lo transforma todo** love changes everything; *Anticuado* **mantiene amores con un señor de Montevideo** she's having a liaison with a gentleman from Montevideo; **un a. imposible** a love that could never be; *Formal* **al a. de la lumbre** *o* **del fuego** by the fireside; **a. mío, mi a.** my love; **a. por algo** love of sth; **a. por alguien** love for sb; **siente un gran a. por los animales** she has a great love of animals, she really loves animals; **hacer el a.** *(físicamente)* to make love; *Anticuado (cortejar)* to court; **hacer el a. a** *o* **con alguien** to make love to *o* with sb; **por a.** for love; *Fam* **por a. al arte** for the love of it; **deme una limosna, por a. de Dios** for charity's sake *o* for the love of God, please spare me something; **¡por el a. de Dios, cállate!** for God's sake shut up!; EXPR **de mil amores** with pleasure; PROV **a. con a. se paga** one good turn deserves another ►► ***a. de adolescente*** puppy love; *Lit* ***a. cortés*** courtly love; ***a. libre*** free love; ***el a. de madre*** a mother's love; ***el a. materno*** a mother's love; ***a. platónico*** platonic love; ***a. propio*** pride; **tiene mucho/poco a. propio** she has high/low self-esteem; ***a. verdadero*** true love
(**b**) *(persona amada)* love; **un antiguo a.** an old flame; **Ana fue su primer a.** Ana was his first love; **el a. de mi vida** the love of my life
(**c**) *(esmero)* devotion; **escribe con a. su última novela** she's lovingly crafting her latest novel; **limpiaba con a. el valioso jarrón** he cleaned the valuable vase lovingly

amoral *adj* amoral

amoralidad *nf* amorality

amoratado, -a *adj* (**a**) *(de frío)* blue (**b**) *(por golpes)* black and blue

amoratar 1 *vt* (**a**) *(sujeto: el frío)* to turn blue (**b**) *(sujeto: persona)* to bruise
2 amoratarse *vpr* (**a**) *(por el frío)* to turn blue (**b**) *(por golpes)* to turn black and blue

amorcillo *nm (figura)* cupid

amordazar [14] *vt* (**a**) *(persona)* to gag; *(perro)* to muzzle (**b**) *(hacer callar)* to gag; **a. a la prensa** to gag the press

amorfo, -a *adj* (**a**) *(sin forma)* amorphous (**b**) *(débil de carácter)* lacking in character (**c**) *Fam (contrahecho)* misshapen

amorío *nm* love affair; **tuvo que dimitir al conocerse su amoríos con su secretaria** he had to resign when people found out about his affair with his secretary

amormío *nm (planta)* sea daffodil

amorocharse *vpr Ven Fam* to pal up (together)

amorosamente *adv* lovingly, affectionately

amoroso, -a *adj* (**a**) *(trato, sentimiento)* loving; **carta amorosa** love letter; **relación amorosa** love affair; **es muy a. con los niños** he's very affectionate with children (**b**) *RP (bonito)* charming

amortajar *vt (difunto)* to shroud

amortiguación *nf* (**a**) *(de ruido)* muffling; *(de luz)* dimming (**b**) *(de golpe)* softening, cushioning (**c**) *(de vehículo)* **la a.** the shock absorbers

amortiguado, -a *adj (ruido)* muffled; *(luz)* dimmed

amortiguador, -ora 1 *adj* (**a**) *(de ruido)* muffling; *(de luz)* dimming (**b**) *(de golpe)* softening, cushioning
2 *nm (de vehículo)* shock absorber

amortiguamiento *nm* (**a**) *(de ruido)* muffling; *(de luz)* dimming (**b**) *(de golpe)* cushioning, softening

amortiguar [11] **1** *vt* (**a**) *(ruido)* to muffle; *(luz)* to dim (**b**) *(golpe)* to soften, to cushion (**c**) *(color)* to tone down
2 amortiguarse *vpr* (**a**) *(ruido)* to die away; *(fuego)* to die down (**b**) *(golpe)* to be cushioned

amortizable *adj (bonos, acciones)* redeemable; **a. en el plazo de un año** redeemable in one year

amortización *nf* (**a**) *(de deuda, préstamo, hipoteca)* repayment, paying-off (**b**) *(de inversión, capital)* recouping; *(de bonos, acciones)* redemption; *(de bienes de equipo)* depreciation (**c**) *(de puesto de trabajo)* abolition; **este cambio implicará la a. de puestos de trabajo** this change will mean some jobs will be done away with

amortizar [14] *vt* (**a**) *(sacar provecho)* to get one's money's worth out of; **amortizamos la compra de la fotocopiadora muy rápidamente** the photocopier very soon paid for itself (**b**) *(deuda, préstamo, hipoteca)* to repay, to pay off (**c**) *(inversión, capital)* to recoup; *(bonos, acciones)* to redeem; *(bienes de equipo)* to depreciate (**d**) *(puesto de trabajo)* to abolish, to do away with

amosal *nm* = type of explosive

amoscarse [60] *vpr Fam* to get in a huff

amostazar [14] **1** *vi Fam* to irritate, to annoy
2 amostazarse *vpr* (**a**) *Fam (enfadarse)* to get irritated *o* annoyed (**b**) *Andes, CAm (avergonzarse)* to become embarrassed

amotinado, -a 1 *adj* rebel, insurgent
2 *nm,f* rebel, insurgent

amotinamiento *nm (de subordinados, población)* rebellion, uprising; *(de marineros)* mutiny

amotinar 1 *vt (a subordinados)* to incite to riot; *(a población)* to incite to rebellion; *(a marineros)* to incite to mutiny
2 amotinarse *vpr (subordinados)* to riot; *(población)* to rise up; *(marineros)* to mutiny

amovible *adj (cargo)* revocable

amparar 1 *vt* (**a**) *(proteger)* to protect; **la ley ampara a los consumidores** the law protects consumers; **ese derecho lo ampara la Constitución** that right is enshrined in the Constitution (**b**) *(dar cobijo a)* to give shelter to, to take in
2 ampararse *vpr* (**a**) *(en ley)* **ampararse en una ley** to have recourse to a law; **se amparó en su condición de diputado para no declarar** he used his parliamentary immunity to avoid making a statement; **se ampara en la excusa de que no sabía nada** she uses her ignorance as an excuse
(**b**) *(cobijarse)* **ampararse de** to (take) shelter from; **se ampararon de la lluvia en una cabaña** they sheltered from the rain in a hut; **cuando pasó por aquella crisis se amparó en su familia** her family were a great support to her at that difficult time

amparo *nm* protection; **su familia es su único a.** his family is his only place of refuge; **dar a. a** to give protection to, to protect; **al a. de** *(persona, caridad)* with the help of; *(ley)* under the protection of; **huyeron al a. de la oscuridad** they fled under cover of darkness

ampelis *nm inv* waxwing

amperaje *nm Elec* amperage

amperímetro *nm Elec* ammeter

amperio *nm Elec* amp, ampere

ampli *nm Fam (amplificador)* amp

ampliable *adj* (**a**) *(plazo)* extendible (**b**) *Informát* expandable

ampliación *nf* (**a**) *(de negocio)* expansion; **una a. de plantilla** an increase in staff numbers; **la a. de la Unión Europea** the enlargement of the European Union ►► *Informát* ***a. de memoria*** memory upgrade
(**b**) *(de local, vivienda)* extension; *(de aeropuerto)* expansion
(**c**) *Econ* ***a. de capital*** share issue

(**d**) *(de plazo)* extension; **la a. del horario de apertura de bares** the extension *o* lengthening of opening hours for bars
(**e**) *(de fotografía)* enlargement

ampliador, -ora *adj* extending, expanding

ampliadora *nf (de fotografía)* enlarger

ampliamente *adv* (**a**) *(con espacio)* easily; **aquí cabe todo a.** there's more than enough room for everything here; **batió el récord del mundo a.** she easily beat the world record, she beat the world record by some distance
(**b**) *(extensamente) (aceptado, debatido)* widely; **el público ha sido informado a.** the public has been fully informed; **la eficacia del método ha quedado a. demostrada** the method has clearly been shown to be effective
(**c**) *Fam (mucho)* **paso a. de hablar con ella** there's no way I'm talking to her

ampliar [32] *vt* (**a**) *(negocio)* to expand; **han ampliado el servicio a todo el país** they have extended the service to cover the whole country; **van a a. el catálogo de productos** they are going to expand *o* extend their product range; **ampliarán la plantilla del banco** they are going to take on additional staff at the bank, they are going to increase staff numbers at the bank; **no quieren a. más la Unión Europea** they don't want to enlarge the European Union any further
(**b**) *(local, vivienda)* to extend; *(aeropuerto)* to expand; **queremos a. el salón** we want to make the living-room bigger
(**c**) *Econ (capital)* to increase
(**d**) *(plazo)* to extend
(**e**) *(fotografía)* to enlarge, to blow up; *(fotocopia)* to enlarge
(**f**) *(estudios)* to further, to continue; *(conocimientos)* to increase, to expand

amplificación *nf* amplification

amplificador, -ora 1 *adj* amplifying
2 *nm* amplifier ►► ***a. de audio*** (audio) amplifier

amplificar [60] *vt* (**a**) *(efecto)* to amplify, to increase (**b**) *(onda, señal)* to amplify

amplio, -a *adj* (**a**) *(grande) (sala, maletero)* roomy, spacious; *(avenida)* wide; **una a. sonrisa** a broad smile
(**b**) *(ropa)* loose
(**c**) *(extenso) (explicación, cobertura)* comprehensive; *(ventaja, capacidad)* considerable; **en el sentido más a. de la palabra** in the broadest sense of the word; **ganaron por una amplia mayoría** they won with a large majority; **hubo un a. consenso** there was a broad consensus; **ofrecen una amplia gama de servicios** they offer a wide range of services; **gozan de una amplia aceptación** they enjoy widespread approval; **tiene una amplia experiencia** she has wide-ranging experience
(**d**) *(abierto)* **una persona de amplias miras** *o* **a. de miras** a broad-minded person

amplitud *nf* (**a**) *(espaciosidad) (de sala, maletero)* roominess, spaciousness; *(de avenida)* wideness; **aquí cabe todo con a.** there's more than enough room for everything here (**b**) *(de ropa)* looseness (**c**) *(extensión)* extent, comprehensiveness (**d**) **a. de miras** *(tolerancia)* broad-mindedness (**e**) *Fís* ***a. de onda*** amplitude

ampolla *nf* (**a**) *(en piel)* blister; **los zapatos nuevos me han hecho ampollas en el pie** my new shoes have given me blisters on my foot; EXPR **levantar ampollas** to cause bad feeling (**b**) *(frasco)* phial; *(para inyecciones)* ampoule

ampollarse *vpr* to blister; **se me han ampollado los pies** I've got blisters on my feet

ampolleta *nf Chile* light bulb

ampulosidad *nf* pomposity; **con a.** pompously

ampuloso, -a *adj* pompous

amputación *nf* (**a**) *(de miembro)* amputation (**b**) *(de libro, película)* mutilation *(by censor)*

amputado, -a 1 *adj* (**a**) *(miembro)* amputated (**b**) *(libro, película)* mutilated *(by censor)*
2 *nm,f* amputee

amputar *vt* (**a**) *(miembro)* to amputate; **le amputaron un brazo** one of his arms was amputated (**b**) *(libro, película)* to mutilate

Amsterdam ['amsterðam] *n* Amsterdam

amucharse *vpr Andes, RP Fam (juntarse, amontonarse)* to squeeze up, to make room

amueblado, -a 1 *adj (piso)* furnished
2 *nm RP* = room hired for sex

amueblar *vt* to furnish; **un apartamento sin a.** an unfurnished *Br* flat *o US* apartment

amuela *etc ver* **amolar**

amuermado, -a *adj Esp Fam* bored silly

amuermar *Esp Fam* **1** *vt* **el teatro me amuerma** the theatre just puts me to sleep *o* bores me silly
2 *vi* to be incredibly boring
3 amuermarse *vpr* **los niños se amuerman en el verano aquí** the kids get bored in the summer here; **nos amuermamos después de tanta comida** we were all a bit dopey after the huge meal

amulatado, -a *adj* mulatto-like

amuleto *nm (antiguo)* amulet; **a. (de la suerte)** lucky charm

amurallado, -a *adj* walled

amurallar *vt* to build a wall around

amurrarse *vpr Chile* to get depressed

Ana *n pr* **A. Bolena** Anne Boleyn; **A. Estuardo** Queen Anne (of England); **Santa A.** St Anne

anabaptismo *nm* Anabaptism

anabaptista 1 *adj* Anabaptist
2 *nmf* Anabaptist

anabólico, -a *adj Biol* anabolic

anabolismo *nm Biol* anabolism

anabolizante 1 *adj* anabolic
2 *nm* anabolic steroid

anacahuita *nf* pepper tree

anacarado, -a *adj* pearly

anacardo *nm* cashew nut

anaclítico *nm Ling* palindrome

anacoluto *nm Gram* anacoluthon

anaconda *nf* anaconda

anacoreta *nmf* anchorite, hermit

anacrónico, -a *adj* anachronistic

anacronismo *nm* anachronism

ánade *nm* duck ►► ***á. friso*** gadwall; ***á. rabudo*** pintail; ***á. real*** mallard; ***á. silbón americano*** American wigeon; ***á. sombrío*** black duck

anaeróbico, -a *adj Biol* anaerobic

anaerobio, -a *Biol* **1** *adj* anaerobic
2 *nm* anaerobe

anafe *nm* portable stove

anafiláctico, -a *adj Med* **choque a.** anaphylactic shock; **reacción anafiláctica** anaphylactic reaction

anáfora *nf* anaphora

anafrodisiaco, -a, anafrodisíaco, -a 1 *adj* anaphrodisiac
2 *nm* anaphrodisiac

anagálide *nf* water speedwell

anagrama *nm* (**a**) *(por cambio de letras)* anagram (**b**) *(símbolo de empresa)* logo (**c**) *(siglas)* acronym

anal *adj Anat* anal

anales *nmpl* (**a**) *(libro)* annual, yearbook (**b**) *(historia)* annals; **su actuación pasará a los a. del deporte** her performance will go down in the annals *o* history of the sport

analfabetismo *nm* illiteracy ►► ***a. funcional*** functional illiteracy

analfabeto, -a 1 *adj* illiterate
2 *nm,f* (**a**) *(que no sabe leer)* illiterate (**b**) *Fam (ignorante)* ignoramus

analgesia *nf* analgesia

analgésico, -a 1 *adj* analgesic
2 *nm* analgesic

análisis *nm inv* (**a**) *(de situación, problema)* analysis; **hacer un a. de algo** to analyse sth ►► *Com* ***a. del camino crítico*** critical path analysis; *Esp Econ* ***a. coste-beneficio*** cost-benefit analysis; *Econ* ***a. de costo-beneficio*** cost-benefit analysis; ***a. cualitativo*** qualitative analysis; ***a. cuantitativo*** quantitative analysis; *Ling* ***a. del discurso*** discourse analysis; ***a. de mercado*** market analysis
(**b**) *(médico)* analysis ►► ***a. clínico*** (clinical) test; ***a. de orina*** urine test; ***a. químico*** chemical analysis; ***a. de sangre*** blood test
(**c**) *Gram* analysis ►► ***a. gramatical*** sentence analysis; ***a. sintáctico*** syntactic analysis
(**d**) *Informát* analysis ►► ***a. de sistemas*** systems analysis
(**e**) *Mat* analysis
(**f**) *Psi* analysis

analista *nmf* (**a**) *(experto)* analyst ►► ***a. financiero*** investment analyst; ***a. de mercados*** market analyst; ***a. político*** political analyst (**b**) *(de laboratorio)* analyst (**c**) *Informát* (computer) analyst ►► ***a. de sistemas*** systems analyst (**d**) *(psiquiatra)* analyst

analítica *nf* (medical) tests; **una a. completa** = a full set of blood and/ or urine tests

analítico, -a *adj* analytical

analizar [14] *vt* (a) *(situación, problema)* to analyse (b) *(sangre, orina)* to test, to analyse (c) *Gram* to parse; **a. sintácticamente la siguiente oración** parse the following sentence

analmente *adv* anally

análogamente *adv* similarly

analogía *nf* similarity, analogy; **hizo una a. entre los dos casos** he drew an analogy between the two cases; **por a.** by analogy

analógico, -a *adj* (a) *(análogo)* analogous, similar (b) *(reloj, computador)* analogue

análogo, -a *adj* (a) *(semejante)* analogous, similar (a to) (b) *Biol (órgano)* analogous

ananá *nm*, **ananás** *nm inv RP* pineapple

anapesto *nm Lit* anapaest

ANAPO [a'napo] *nf (abrev de* **Alianza Nacional Popular**) = Colombian political party

anaquel *nm* shelf

anaranjado, -a 1 *adj* orangish, orangey
2 *nm* orangish colour

anarco *Fam* 1 *adj* anarchistic
2 *nmf* anarchist

anarcosindicalismo *nm Pol* anarcho-syndicalism

anarcosindicalista *Pol* 1 *adj* anarcho-syndicalist
2 *nmf* anarcho-syndicalist

anarquía *nf* (a) *(falta de gobierno)* anarchy (b) *(doctrina política)* anarchism (c) *(desorden)* chaos, anarchy; **en esta oficina reina la a.** this office is in a permanent state of chaos

anárquicamente *adv (desordenadamente)* anarchically, chaotically

anárquico, -a *adj* (a) *(de la anarquía)* anarchic (b) *(desordenado)* anarchic, chaotic

anarquismo *nm* anarchism

anarquista 1 *adj* anarchist
2 *nmf* anarchist

anarquizar [14] 1 *vt* to make anarchic
2 *vi* to propagate anarchism

anatema *nm* (a) *(excomunión)* excommunication, anathema (b) *(condena)* condemnation

anatematizar *vt* (a) *(excomulgar)* to excommunicate, to anathematize (b) *(condenar)* to condemn

anatomía *nf* (a) *(ciencia)* anatomy (b) *(estructura)* anatomy (c) *(cuerpo)* body

anatómicamente *adv* anatomically

anatómico, -a *adj* (a) *(de la anatomía)* anatomical (b) *(asiento, diseño, calzado)* orthopaedic

anca *nf* haunch ►► ***ancas de rana*** frogs' legs

Takes the masculine articles **el** and **un**.

ancestral *adj (costumbre)* age-old; *(miedo)* atavistic

ancestro *nm* ancestor

ANCHO, -A 1 *adj* (a) *(abertura, carretera, río)* wide; **mídelo a lo a.** measure it crosswise; **a lo a. de** across (the width of); **había rocas a lo a. de la carretera** there were rocks across the middle of the road; **es a. de hombros** he's broad-shouldered; **en este asiento se está muy a.** this seat is nice and wide; **venirle a. a alguien** to be too big for sb; **el puesto de director le viene a.** he doesn't have what it takes for the job of manager

(b) *(muro)* thick

(c) *(ropa)* loose-fitting; **te va** *o* **está a.** it's too big for you; **este vestido me viene a. de cintura** this dress is too big for me around the waist

(d) *(persona) (cómoda)* comfortable; **estaremos más anchos si nos vamos al jardín** we'll have more room if we go into the garden; **a mis/tus anchas** at ease; **ponte a tus anchas** make yourself at home

(e) *Esp (persona) (satisfecha, orgullosa)* smug, self-satisfied; *(desahogada)* relieved; **estar/ponerse muy a.** to be/become conceited; **yo tan preocupada y él, tan a.** I was so worried whereas he didn't seem at all bothered *o* the least bit concerned; EXPR **quedarse tan a.** not to care less; **lo dijo delante de todos y se quedó tan a.** he said it in front of everyone, just like that; **¡qué a. me he quedado después del examen!** I'm so relieved to have got the exam over with!; *Irónico* **¡se habrá quedado a. con la tontería que ha dicho!** he must be delighted with himself for making that stupid remark

2 *nm* width; **¿cuánto mide** *o* **tiene de a.?** how wide is it?; **tener 5 metros de a.** to be 5 metres wide ►► *Informát* ***a. de banda*** bandwidth; *Ferroc* ***a. de vía*** gauge

anchoa *nf* anchovy

anchura *nf* (a) *(de abertura, carretera, río)* width (b) *(de muro)* thickness

ancianidad *nf* old age

anciano, -a 1 *adj* old
2 *nm,f (hombre)* old man, old person; *(mujer)* old woman, old person; **los ancianos** the elderly
3 *nm (de tribu)* elder

ancla *nf*

Takes the masculine articles **el** and **un**.

anchor; **echar anclas** *o* **el a.** to drop anchor; **levar anclas** to weigh anchor

anclado, -a *adj* (a) *(barco)* at anchor (b) *(inmobilizado)* fixed; **está a. en su rechazo** he is absolutely determined in his refusal; **una aldea anclada en el pasado** a village stuck in the past

anclaje *nm* (a) *(de barco)* anchoring (b) *Tec* **los anclajes de una grúa** the moorings of a crane

anclar 1 *vt* to anchor
2 *vi* to (drop) anchor

ancón *nm Col, Méx (rincón)* corner

áncora *nf Literario* (a) *(ancla)* anchor (b) *(salvación)* sheet anchor

Takes the masculine articles **el** and **un**.

anda *interj* (a) *(indica sorpresa)* gosh!; **¡a., no fastidies!** you're kidding!, you don't say!; **¡a., qué coincidencia!** well, there's a coincidence!; EXPR **¡a. la osa!** well I never!, upon my word!

(b) *(por favor)* go on!; **¡a., déjame subirme a tu moto!** go on, let me have a go on your motorbike!; **¡a. y déjame en paz!** give me some peace, will you!

(c) *(venga)* come on!; **¡a., salta!** go on, jump!

(d) *(indica desprecio) muy Fam* **¡a. y que te den!** get stuffed!; *Vulg* **¡a. y que te jodan!** go fuck yourself!; **¡a. ya!** *(negativa despectiva)* get away!, come off it!

andadas *nfpl* EXPR *Fam* **volver a las a.** to return to one's bad old ways

andaderas *nfpl* baby-walker

andador, -ora 1 *adj* fond of walking; **es muy a.** he likes walking
2 *nm* (a) *(tacataca)* baby-walker (b) *(para adultos)* walking frame, Zimmer frame® (c) *Méx (camino)* walkway

andadura *nf* **la a. de un país** the evolution of a country; **su a. por Europa** his travels through Europe; **el Festival comenzó su a. en 1950** the Festival's history began in 1950; **un proyecto con sólo tres meses de a.** a project that has only been in existence for three months

ándale, ándele *interj CAm, Méx Fam* come on!; **vamos ya o llegaremos tarde, á.** come on, we have to go now or we'll be late!

Andalucía *n* Andalusia

andalucismo *nm* (a) *(palabra, expresión)* = Andalusian word or expression (b) *(ideología)* = doctrine favouring Andalusian autonomy

andalusí (*pl* **andalusíes**) *Hist* 1 *adj* Moorish
2 *nmf* Moor, = of or related to the Arab empire of Al-Andalus in southern Spain (711-1492)

andaluz, -uza 1 *adj* Andalusian
2 *nm,f* Andalusian

andamiaje *nm* (a) *(andamios)* scaffolding (b) *(estructura)* structure, framework

andamiar *vt* to put up scaffolding on

andamio *nm* **se cayó de un a.** he fell from some scaffolding; **andamios** scaffolding

andana *nf (fila)* row

andanada *nf* (a) *(disparos)* broadside (b) *(reprimenda)* broadside; **me soltó una a. de insultos** she hurled a torrent of abuse at me (c) *Taurom* = covered stand in a bullring

andando *interj (yo, nosotros)* come on!, let's get a move on!; *(tú, vosotros, ustedes)* come on!, get a move on!

andante[1] *adj (caballero)* errant

andante[2] *Mús* 1 *nm* andante
2 *adv* andante

andantino *nm Mús* andantino

andanzas *nfpl (peripecias)* adventures

ANDAR [7] 1 *vi* (a) *esp Esp (caminar)* to walk; *(moverse)* to move; **¿fuiste en autobús o andando?** did you go by bus or on foot?, did you go by bus or did you walk?; **a. por la calle** to walk in the street; **a. deprisa/despacio** to walk quickly/slowly; **a. a gatas** to crawl; **a. de puntillas** to tiptoe

(b) *(funcionar)* to work, to go; **la nueva moto anda estupendamente** the new motorbike is running superbly; **el reloj no anda** the clock has stopped; **las cosas andan mal** things are going badly; **los negocios andan muy bien** business is going very well

(c) *(estar)* to be; **¿qué tal andas?** how are you (doing)?; **no sabía que habían operado a tu padre – ¿qué tal anda?** I didn't know your father had had an operation, how is he (getting on *o* doing)?; **¿dónde anda tu hermano? no lo he visto desde hace meses** what's your brother up to these days? I haven't seen him for months; **creo que anda por el almacén** I think he's somewhere in the warehouse; **a. en boca de todos** to be on everyone's lips; **desde que tiene novia, a. muy contento** ever since he got a girlfriend he's been very happy; **ando muy ocupado** I'm very busy at the moment; **¿cómo andas de dinero?** how are you (off) for money?; **andamos muy mal de dinero** we're very short of money, we're very badly off for money; **idate prisa, que andamos muy mal de tiempo!** hurry up, we haven't got much time!, hurry up, we're late!; **a. detrás de** *o* **tras algo/alguien** to be after sth/sb; EXPR **de a. por casa** *(explicación, método)* basic, rough and ready; **mi ropa de a. por casa** my clothes for wearing around the house; **hice un apaño de a. por casa y ya funciona** I patched it up myself and it works again now; PROV **ande yo caliente, ríase la gente** I'm quite happy, I don't care what other people think; PROV **quien mal anda mal acaba** everyone gets their just deserts

(d) *(ocuparse)* **a. en** *(asuntos, líos)* to be involved in; *(papeleos, negocios)* to be busy with; **anda metido en pleitos desde el accidente** ever since the accident he's been busy fighting legal battles

(e) *(hurgar)* **a. en** to rummage around in; **¿quién ha andado en mis papeles?** who has been messing around with my papers?

(f) *(indica acción)* **a. haciendo algo** to be doing sth; **con esa chulería, David anda buscándose problemas** David's asking for trouble, always being so cocky; **en ese país andan a tiros** in that country they go round shooting one another; **andan a voces todo el día** they spend the whole day shouting at each other; EXPR **a. a vueltas con algo** to be having trouble with sth; **anda echando broncas a todos** he's going round telling everybody off; **anda explicando sus aventuras** he's talking about his adventures

(g) *(ir)* **a. con alguien** to go around *o* round with sb; **anda por ahí con una jovencita** he's running around with a young girl; **anda con gente muy poco recomendable** she mixes with *o* goes around with a very undesirable crowd; PROV **dime con quién andas y te diré quién eres** birds of a feather flock together

(h) **a. por** *(alcanzar, rondar)* to be about; **anda por los sesenta** he's about sixty; **debe de a. por el medio millón** it must be *o* cost about half a million

(i) *Fam (enredar)* **a. con algo** to play with sth

(j) EXPR *RP* **iandá a saber!** who knows!

2 *vt* (a) *(recorrer)* to go, to travel; **anduvimos 15 kilómetros** we walked (for) 15 kilometres

(b) *CAm (llevar puesto)* to wear

(c) *CAm (llevar)* to carry

3 *nm* (a) *(modo de caminar)* gait, walk; **andares** *(de persona)* gait; **tiene andares de modelo** she walks like a model (b) *(transcurso)* **con el a. del tiempo, comprenderás todo mejor** you'll understand everything better with the passing of time

4 **andarse** *vpr* (a) *(obrar)* **andarse con cuidado/misterios** to be careful/secretive; **andarse con rodeos, andarse por las ramas** to beat about the bush; **mi jefa no se anda con bromas, si cometes un error te despide** my boss isn't one to mess around, if you make a mistake, she sacks you

(b) *(recorrer)* to walk; **nos anduvimos todas las calles del centro** we walked up and down every street in the city centre

(c) **todo se andará** all in good time

(d) *Am (marcharse)* to go, to leave; **ándate o llegarás tarde** you'd better go or you'll be late; **iándate de una vez!** go away!

andariego, -a, andarín, -ina *adj* fond of walking; **es muy a.** he's a very keen walker

andarivel *nm Andes, RP (para corredor, nadador)* lane marker

andarríos *nm inv* ***a. bastardo*** wood sandpiper; ***a. chico*** sandpiper; ***a. grande*** green sandpiper ***a. maculado*** spotted sandpiper

andas *nfpl* = float carried on people's shoulders in religious procession; **llevar a alguien en a.** to give sb a chair-lift

ándele = **ándale**

andén *nm* (a) *(en estación)* platform (b) *Andes, CAm (acera) Br* pavement, *US* sidewalk (c) *Andes (bancal de tierra)* terrace

Andes *nmpl* **los A.** the Andes

andinismo *nm Am* mountaineering, mountain climbing

andinista *nmf Am* mountaineer, mountain climber

andino, -a 1 *adj* Andean
2 *nm,f* Andean

Andorra *n* Andorra ►► ***A. la Vieja*** Andorra la Vella

andorrano, -a 1 *adj* Andorran
2 *nm,f* Andorran

andrajo *nm* rag; **vestido con andrajos** dressed in rags

andrajosamente *adv* **vestido a.** dressed in rags

andrajoso, -a 1 *adj (ropa, persona)* ragged
2 *nm,f* person dressed in rags

Andrés *n pr* **San A.** St Andrew

androceo *nm Bot* androecium

androcracia *nf* patriarchy

androfobia *nf* androphobia

andrófobo, -a 1 *adj* man-hating
2 *nm,f* man-hater

andrógeno *nm* androgen

andrógino, -a 1 *adj* androgynous
2 *nm* hermaphrodite

androide *nm (autómata)* android

andrología *nf* andrology, = study of the male reproductive system and treatment of its disorders

andrólogo, -a *nm,f* = specialist in the treatment of disorders of the male reproductive system

Andrómeda *nf (galaxia)* Andromeda

andromorfo, -a *adj* andromorphous

andropausia *nf* male menopause

androsterona *nf* androsterone

andurriales *nmpl* remote place; **¿qué haces por estos a.?** what are you doing so far off the beaten track?

anduviera *etc ver* **andar**

anea *nf Br* bulrush, *US* cattail; **silla de a.** chair with a wickerwork seat

anécdota *nf* (a) *(historia)* anecdote; **nos contó una a. muy graciosa** he told us a very amusing anecdote *o* story (b) *(suceso trivial)* matter of little importance; **el incidente fue una mera a.** the incident was of no importance

anecdotario *nm* collection of anecdotes

anecdótico, -a *adj* (a) *(con historietas)* anecdotal; **un libro lleno de datos anecdóticos** a book full of anecdotal information (b) *(no esencial)* incidental; **eso es un detalle a.** that's just incidental

anegadizo, -a *adj* frequently flooded, subject to flooding

anegamiento *nm* flooding

anegar [38] 1 *vt* (a) *(inundar)* to flood (b) *(ahogar) (planta)* to drown
2 **anegarse** *vpr* (a) *(inundarse)* to flood; **anegarse en llanto** to burst into a flood of tears; **sus ojos se anegaron de lágrimas** tears welled up in his eyes (b) *(ahogarse)* to drown

anejo, -a 1 *adj* (a) *(edificio)* connected (**a** to) (b) *(documento)* attached (**a** to); **la información figura en la lista aneja** the information may be found on the attached list (c) *(inherente)* **esta técnica lleva a. cierto riesgo** this technique involves a certain risk; **un cargo que lleva anejas funciones de dirección** a post which carries with it some management responsibilities

2 *nm* (a) *(edificio)* annexe; **se vende casa de campo con todos sus anejos** farmhouse for sale with all its outhouses (b) *(libro)* supplement *(to specialist journal)*

anélido *nm Zool* annelid

anemia *nf* anaemia ►► *Med* ***a. (de célula) falciforme*** sickle-cell anaemia; ***a. perniciosa*** pernicious anaemia

anémico, -a 1 *adj* anaemic
2 *nm,f* anaemia sufferer

anemómetro *nm* anemometer, wind gauge

anémona *nf* (a) *(planta)* anemone ►► ***a. de los bosques*** wood anemone (b) *(actinia)* sea anemone

anestesia *nf (técnica)* anaesthesia; *(sustancia)* anaesthetic; **una intervención con a.** an operation under anaesthetic; **todavía está bajo los efectos de la a.** she's still under anaesthetic ►► ***a. epidural*** *(técnica)* epidural anaesthesia; *(sustancia)* epidural anaesthetic; ***a. general*** *(técnica)* general anaesthesia; *(sustancia)* general anaesthetic; ***a. local*** *(técnica)* local anaesthesia; *(sustancia)* local anaesthetic

anestesiar *vt* to anaesthetize, to place under anaesthetic; **me anestesiaron la pierna** they gave me a local anaesthetic in my leg

anestésico, -a 1 *adj* anaesthetic
2 *nm* anaesthetic ►► ***a. local*** local anaesthetic

anestesiología *nf* anaesthesiology

anestesiólogo, -a *nm,f* anaesthesiologist

anestesista *nmf* anaesthetist

aneurisma *nm Med* aneurysm

anexar *vt (documento)* to attach

anexión *nf* annexation

anexionar 1 *vt* to annex
2 **anexionarse** *vpr* to annex

anexionismo *nm Pol* annexationism

anexionista *Pol* 1 *adj* annexationist
2 *nmf* annexationist

anexo, -a 1 *adj* (**a**) *(edificio)* connected (**a** to) (**b**) *(documento)* attached (**a** to); **las cifras figuran en la lista anexa** the figures may be found on the attached list
2 *nm* (**a**) *(edificio)* annexe; **se vende casa de campo con todos sus anexos** farmhouse for sale with all its outhouses (**b**) *(libro)* appendix (**c**) *Anat* **anexos** adnexa

anfeta *nf Fam* tab of speed

anfetamina *nf* amphetamine

anfibio, -a 1 *adj* (**a**) *(animal)* amphibious (**b**) *(vehículo)* amphibious
2 *nm* amphibian

anfíbol *nm Geol* amphibole

anfibolita *nf Geol* amphibolite

anfibología *nf* amphibology, amphiboly

anfiteatro *nm* (**a**) *(en teatro)* circle; *(en cine)* balcony (**b**) *(en universidad)* lecture theatre (**c**) *(romano)* amphitheatre

anfitrión, -ona 1 *adj* host; **país a.** host country
2 *nm,f* host, *f* hostess
3 *nm Informát* host

ánfora *nf* (**a**) *(cántaro)* amphora (**b**) *Méx, Perú (electoral)* ballot box

Takes the masculine articles **el** and **un**.

anfótero, -a *adj Quím* amphoteric

anfractuoso, -a *adj Geol* uneven

angarillas *nfpl* (**a**) *(para enfermos)* stretcher (**b**) *(sobre animal)* pack-saddle with panniers (**c**) *(vinagreras)* cruet set

ángel *nm* (**a**) *(ser espiritual)* angel; EXPR **como los ángeles: canta como los ángeles** she has a divine voice, she sings like an angel; EXPR **ha pasado un á.** don't all talk at once! *(after lull in conversation)* ►► ***á. caído*** fallen angel; ***á. custodio*** guardian angel; ***á. de la guarda*** guardian angel
(**b**) *(persona buena)* angel; **¡eres un á.!** you're an angel!
(**c**) *(encanto, simpatía)* EXPR **tener á.** to have something special

Ángela *n* EXPR **¡Á. María!** *(denotando sorpresa)* goodness gracious!; **¡Á. María, ahora la recuerdo!** ah, now I remember her!

angélica *nf* angelica

angelical, angélico, -a *adj* angelic

angelín *nm* angelin, West Indian cabbage tree

angelino, -a 1 *adj* of/from Los Angeles *(USA)*
2 *nm,f* Angeleno, person from Los Angeles *(USA)*

angelito *nm* (**a**) *(ángel)* cherub; EXPR **¡que sueñes con los angelitos!** pleasant *o* sweet dreams! (**b**) *Fam (niño)* baby; **¡a.!** poor lamb!, poor little thing!

angelopolitano, -a 1 *adj (de Puebla)* of/from Puebla *(Mexico)*
2 *nm,f (de Puebla)* person from Puebla *(Mexico)*

angelote *nm* (**a**) *(estatua)* large figure of an angel (**b**) *Fam (niño)* chubby child (**c**) *Fam (persona apacible)* **es un a.** he's very good-natured (**d**) *(pez)* angel shark, angelfish

ángelus *nm inv Rel* angelus

angina *nf* (**a**) **anginas** *(amigdalitis)* sore throat; **tener anginas** to have a sore throat (**b**) ***a. de pecho*** angina (pectoris)

angiografía *nm Med* angiogram, = X-ray of circulatory system

angiología *nm Med* = study of the circulatory system and its disorders

angiosperma *nf Bot* angiosperm

anglicanismo *nm Rel* Anglicanism

anglicano, -a *Rel* 1 *adj* Anglican
2 *nm,f* Anglican

anglicismo *nm* Anglicism

anglo[1], -a *Hist* 1 *adj* Anglian
2 *nm* Angle; **los anglos** the Angles

anglo-[2] *pref* Anglo-; **a.-mexicano** Anglo-Mexican

angloamericano, -a 1 *adj* Anglo-American
2 *nm,f* Anglo-American

anglocanadiense 1 *adj* Anglo-Canadian
2 *nm,f* Anglo-Canadian

anglofilia *nf* anglophilia

anglófilo, -a 1 *adj* anglophile
2 *nm,f* anglophile

anglofobia *nf* anglophobia

anglófobo, -a 1 *adj* anglophobe
2 *nm,f* anglophobe

anglófono, -a, anglohablante 1 *adj* English-speaking, anglophone
2 *nm,f* English speaker, anglophone

anglonormando, -a 1 *adj* Anglo-Norman
2 *nm,f* Anglo-Norman

angloparlante 1 *adj* English-speaking, anglophone
2 *nm,f* English speaker, anglophone

anglosajón, -ona 1 *adj* Anglo-Saxon
2 *nm,f* Anglo-Saxon

Angola *n* Angola

angoleño, -a, angolano, -a 1 *adj* Angolan 2 *nm,f* Angolan

angora *nf* (**a**) *(de conejo)* angora (**b**) *(de cabra)* mohair

angosto, -a *adj* narrow

angostura[1] *nf (estrechez)* narrowness

angostura[2] *nf* (**a**) *(corteza)* angostura bark (**b**) *(extracto)* angostura

ángstrom (*pl* **ángstroms**) *nm* angstrom

anguila *nf* eel ►► ***a. eléctrica*** electric eel; ***a. de mar*** conger eel

angula *nf* elver

angular 1 *adj* angular
2 *nm Fot* **gran a.** wide-angle lens

ángulo *nm* (**a**) *(figura geométrica)* angle ►► ***á. agudo*** acute angle; ***á. de aproximación*** *(de avión)* angle of approach; *Mat* ***á. complementario*** complementary angle; ***á. crítico*** critical angle; *Fís* ***á. de incidencia*** angle of incidence; ***á. interno*** interior angle; ***á. llano*** straight angle; *Mil* ***á. de mira*** line of sight; ***á. muerto*** *(de espejo retrovisor)* blind spot; ***á. obtuso*** obtuse angle; ***á. rectilíneo*** plane angle; ***á. recto*** right angle; ***á. de reflexión*** angle of reflection; ***á. de refracción*** angle of refraction; *Mil* ***á. de tiro*** elevation
(**b**) *(rincón)* corner
(**c**) *(punto de vista)* angle; **visto desde este á.** seen from this angle

angulosidad *nf* angularity

anguloso, -a *adj* angular

angurria *nf Am* (**a**) *(hambre)* hunger (**b**) *(codicia, avidez)* greed

angurriento, -a *adj Am* (**a**) *(hambriento)* hungry, starved (**b**) *(codicioso, ávido)* greedy

angustia *nf* (**a**) *(aflicción)* anxiety; **vivieron las semanas de secuestro con a.** they were in a state of constant anxiety throughout the weeks of the kidnapping; **lloraba con a.** she was crying in distress
(**b**) *Psi* distress; **una sensación de a. existencial** a feeling of angst
(**c**) *(sensación física)* **siente una a. en el pecho** she feels short of breath *o* breathless
(**d**) *Fam (persona)* **¡qué a. de mujer!** what a worrier that woman is!

angustiadamente *adv* anxiously

angustiado, -a *adj (mirada)* anguished; **están cada día más angustiados por su futuro** they are more and more anxious about his future

angustiante *adj (situación)* distressing

angustiar 1 *vt* to distress; **lo angustiaba el haber engordado** he was distressed at having put on weight; **lo que más me angustia es la espera** the worst thing for me is the waiting
2 **angustiarse** *vpr* to get worried (**por** about); **se angustia por cualquier cosa** she gets worried at the slightest thing

angustiosamente *adv (esperar)* anxiously

angustioso, -a *adj (espera)* anxious; *(situación, noticia)* distressing

anhelante *adj* longing; **una mirada a.** a longing look; **estaba a. por verlo** she was longing to see him

anhelar *vt* to long for; **un político que anhela poder** a politician who is hungry for power; **anhela tener su propia casa** she longs to have a house of her own; **anhelan que acabe la guerra** they are longing for the war to end

anhelo *nm* longing; **su a. de libertad** her desire *o* longing for freedom; **esperamos con a. su llegada** we eagerly await their arrival

anheloso, -a *adj* longing; **están anhelosos por que termine** they can't wait for it to finish

anhídrido *nm Quím* anhydride ▸▸ ***a. carbónico*** carbon dioxide; ***a. sulfúrico*** sulphur trioxide; ***a. sulfuroso*** sulphur dioxide

aní *nm* ani

Aníbal *n pr* Hannibal

anidar *vi* (a) *(pájaro)* to nest (b) *(sentimiento)* **el odio anidaba en el pueblo** hatred had taken root in the village; **la esperanza anidó en su corazón** hope took root in her heart

anilina *nf* aniline

anilla *nf* (a) *(de llavero, cadena, cortina)* ring; **carpeta de anillas** ring binder (b) *(de lata)* ring pull (c) *(de puro)* band (d) *Dep* **anillas** rings

anillado *nm* (a) *(de aves)* ringing (b) *RP (encuadernado)* comb binding

anillar *vt* (a) *(sujetar)* to fasten with rings (b) *(aves)* to ring (c) *RP (encuadernar)* to put in a comb binding

anillo *nm* (a) *(aro)* ring; EXPR *Fam* **ese dinero me viene como a. al dedo** that money is just what I needed; **me vienes como a. al dedo, necesitaba un electricista** how lucky that you should have come, I was looking for an electrician!; EXPR *Fam* **caerse los anillos: por ayudarle no se te van a caer los anillos** there'd be no shame in giving him a helping hand, you know ▸▸ ***a. de boda*** wedding ring; ***a. de compromiso*** engagement ring; ***a. de émbolo*** piston ring; *Anat* ***a. pélvico*** pelvic girdle; ***a. de pistón*** piston ring

(b) *(en estadio)* ring

(c) *(de árbol)* ring ▸▸ ***a. de crecimiento*** growth ring

(d) *Zool* annulus

(e) *Astron (de planeta)* ring ▸▸ ***a. de asteroides*** asteroid belt; ***anillos de Saturno*** rings of Saturn

(f) *Arquit (en columna)* annulet; *(en cúpula)* circular base

(g) *Taurom* ring

ánima *nf* soul; **a. bendita** *o* **del Purgatorio** soul in purgatory

Takes the masculine articles **el** and **un**.

animación *nf* (a) *(alegría)* liveliness; **los desfiles callejeros dan mucha a. a las fiestas** the street parades make the celebrations very lively *o* really liven up the celebrations

(b) *(bullicio)* hustle and bustle, activity

(c) *Cine* animation ▸▸ *Am* ***a. por computadora*** computer animation; *Esp* ***a. por ordenador*** computer animation

(d) *(promoción)* **un curso de a. a la lectura** a course to encourage people to read more ▸▸ ***a. (socio)cultural*** = organization of social and cultural activities for young people or pensioners; ***a. turística*** = organization of games, outings and social activities for guests

animadamente *adv (discutir, hablar)* animatedly; **charlaban a.** they were having a lively conversation

animado, -a *adj* (a) *(con buen ánimo)* cheerful; **se encuentra muy a. después de la operación** he's in excellent spirits after the operation

(b) *(entretenido)* lively; **fue un partido muy a.** it was a very lively match

(c) *(con alma)* animate, living; **los objetos animados e inanimados** animate and inanimate objects

(d) *Cine* animated; **a. por** *Esp* **ordenador** *o Am* **computadora** computer-animated

animador, -ora 1 *adj* encouraging

2 *nm,f* (a) *(en espectáculo)* compere

(b) *(en hotel)* events co-ordinator, = organizer of games, outings and social activities for guests

(c) *(en fiesta de niños)* children's entertainer

(d) *(en centro cultural)* **a. (socio)cultural** = organizer of social and cultural activities for young people or pensioners

(e) *(en deporte)* cheerleader

(f) *Cine* animator

animadversión *nf* hostility; **con su actitud se ganó la a. de sus compañeros** her attitude made her unpopular with her colleagues; **sentir a. hacia algo** to be hostile towards sth; **sentir a. hacia alguien** to feel hostility towards sb

animal 1 *adj* (a) *(instintos, funciones)* animal; **el reino a.** the animal kingdom (b) *(persona) (basto)* rough (c) *(persona) (ignorante)* ignorant

2 *nm* animal; EXPR **como un a.: sudaba como un a.** he was sweating like a pig; **trabajamos como animales para acabar a tiempo** we worked like slaves to get it finished on time ▸▸ ***a. de bellota*** *(cerdo)* pig; *Fam (insulto)* ignoramus; ***a. de carga*** beast of burden; ***a. de compañía*** pet; ***a. doméstico*** *(de granja)* farm animal; *(de compañía)* pet; ***animales de granja*** farm animals; ***a. de laboratorio*** laboratory animal; ***a. político*** political animal; ***a. protegido*** protected species; ***a. racional*** rational being; ***a. de tiro*** draught animal; ***a. transgénico*** transgenic animal

3 *nmf* (a) *(persona basta)* animal, brute (b) *(persona ignorante)* (ignorant) brute

animalada *nf Fam* (a) *(dicho, hecho)* **su comportamiento fue una auténtica a.** he behaved like a complete animal; **siempre que va borracho dice animaladas** whenever he gets drunk he turns the air blue *o Br* starts effing and blinding (b) *(gran cantidad)* **prepararon una a. de sangría** they made tons of sangria

ANIMAR 1 *vt* (a) *(estimular)* to encourage; **los fans animaban a su equipo** the fans were cheering their team on; **a. a alguien a hacer algo** to encourage sb to do sth; **me animaron a aceptar la oferta** they encouraged me to accept the offer; **lo animó a que dejara la bebida** she encouraged him to stop drinking

(b) *(alegrar)* to cheer up; **tu regalo la animó mucho** your present really cheered her up; **los colores de los participantes animaban el desfile** the colourful costumes of the participants brightened up the procession, the costumes of the participants added colour to the procession

(c) *(fuego, diálogo, fiesta)* to liven up; *(comercio)* to stimulate; **el tanto del empate animó el partido** the equalizer brought the game to life, the game came alive after the equalizer; **las medidas del gobierno pretenden a. la inversión** the government's measures are aimed at stimulating *o* promoting investment

(d) *(mover)* **los artistas animaban los títeres** the puppeteers operated the puppets; **han utilizado la tecnología digital para a. las secuencias de acción** the action shots are digitally generated

(e) *(impulsar)* to motivate, to drive; **no le anima ningún afán de riqueza** she's not driven by any desire to be rich; **no me anima ningún sentimiento de venganza** I'm not doing this out of a desire for revenge

2 **animarse** *vpr* (a) *(persona)* to cheer up; *(fiesta, ambiente)* to liven up; **¡anímate!** cheer up!; **la reunión se animó con el reparto de premios** the gathering livened up when the prizes were handed out; **el negocio se va animando** business is picking up

(b) *(decidir)* to finally decide; **animarse a hacer algo** to finally decide to do sth; **se animó a ir al cine** she finally got round to going to the cinema; **¿quién se anima a subir hasta la cumbre?** who's up for climbing right to the top?; **no me animo a decírselo** I can't bring myself to tell her; **no cuentes con él para la excursión, nunca se anima a hacer nada** don't expect him to come along on the trip, he always wimps out

anime *nm* (a) *Am (árbol)* courbaril, West Indian locust tree (b) *Am Ven (espuma de poliuretano)* polyurethane foam

anímicamente *adv* emotionally

anímico, -a *adj* **estado a.** state of mind; **no está en la mejor situación anímica para ir de vacaciones** she's not in the best state of mind for going on holiday; **sufrió un decaimiento a.** he went into a bout of depression

animismo *nm* animism

animista 1 *adj* animistic

2 *nmf* animist

ÁNIMO 1 *nm* (a) *(valor)* courage; **me da muchos ánimos saber que contamos contigo** it's comforting to know that we have you with us; **cobrar á.** to take heart

(b) *(aliento)* encouragement; **dar ánimos a alguien** to encourage sb; **tienes que darle ánimos para que deje la bebida** you have to encourage him to stop drinking; **iremos al estadio para dar ánimos a nuestros jugadores** we'll go to the stadium to support *o* cheer on our team

(c) *(energía)* energy, vitality; *(humor)* disposition; **¡levanta ese á.!** cheer up!; **los ánimos estaban revueltos** feelings were running high; **estoy con el á. decaído** I'm feeling downhearted *o* gloomy; **apaciguar** *o* **calmar los ánimos** to calm things *o* people down; **cuando me enteré de su despido, se me cayeron los ánimos al suelo** when I heard of her dismissal, my heart sank; **tener ánimos para** to be in the mood for, to feel like; **no tiene ánimos para nada** she doesn't feel like doing anything; **trabajar con á.** to work energetically

(d) *(intención)* **con/sin á. de** with/without the intention of; **lo dijo con á. de herir** his remark was intended to be hurtful; **han realizado un estudio con á. de conocer mejor el problema** they've carried out a study with a view to achieving a better understanding of the problem; **sin á. de ofenderte, creo que...** no offence (intended), but I think...; **lo hice sin á. de ofenderte** I didn't mean to offend you; **una organización sin á. de lucro** a non-profit-making organization

(e) *(alma)* mind

2 *interj (¡adelante!)* come on!; *(¡anímate!)* cheer up!; **¡á., Zaragoza!** *Br* come on you Zaragoza!, *US* go Zaragoza!; **¡á., que no ha sido nada!** come (on) now, it was nothing

---

animosidad *nf* animosity; **existe una gran a. entre los dos equipos** there's a lot of animosity *o* bad feeling between the two teams; **siente a. contra los productos de ese país** she is ill-disposed towards products from that country

animoso, -a *adj* **(a)** *(valiente)* courageous **(b)** *(decidido)* undaunted

aniñado, -a *adj (comportamiento)* childish; *(voz, rostro)* childlike

aniñar 1 *vt (en aspecto)* **este corte de pelo te aniña** that haircut makes you look like a child

2 aniñarse *vpr (en carácter)* to become like a child

anión *nm Fís* anion

aniquilación *nf*, **aniquilamiento** *nm* annihilation

aniquilador, -ora *adj* destructive

aniquilamiento = **aniquilación**

aniquilar *vt* **(a)** *(destruir)* to annihilate, to wipe out; **los nazis aniquilaron a los judíos** the Nazis exterminated the Jews; **el candidato oficial aniquiló a la oposición** the official candidate annihilated *o* destroyed the opposition; **los tenistas suecos aniquilaron a sus rivales** the Swedish tennis players annihilated *o* thrashed their opponents

(b) *(abatir)* to destroy; **tres años en paro la aniquilaron moralmente** three years of unemployment had totally demoralized her

anís *(pl* **anises**) *nm* **(a)** *(planta)* anise **(b)** *(grano)* aniseed ►► ***a. estrellado*** star anise **(c)** *(licor)* anisette **(d) anises** *(confite)* = aniseed-flavoured boiled sweets

anisado, -a 1 *adj* aniseed-flavoured

2 *nm* = aniseed-flavoured liquor

anisete *nm* anisette

aniversario *nm (de muerte, fundación, suceso)* anniversary; *(cumpleaños)* birthday ►► ***a. de boda*** wedding anniversary

anjova *nf* bluefish

Ankara *n* Ankara

ano *nm* anus

anoche *adv* last night; **a. fui al cine** I went to the cinema last night *o* yesterday evening; **antes de a.** the night before last

anochecer [46] **1** *nm* dusk, nightfall; **al a.** at dusk *o* nightfall

2 *v impersonal* to get dark; **anochecía** it was getting dark; **llegamos cuando ya había anochecido** it was already dark when we arrived

3 *vi* **anochecimos en la frontera** we were at the border by nightfall

anochecida *nf* nightfall, dusk

anochezco *etc ver* **anochecer**

anodino, -a *adj* unremarkable

ánodo *nm Elec* anode

anofeles, anófeles *nm inv* anopheles

anomalía *nf* anomaly

anómalo, -a *adj* unusual, anomalous

anomia *nf Psi* anomie

anón *nm Am* sugar apple

anonadado, -a *adj* **(a)** *(sorprendido)* astonished, bewildered; **se quedó a. cuando nos vio entrar** he was totally astonished *o* taken aback when he saw us come in **(b)** *(abatido)* stunned

anonadamiento *nm* astonishment, bewilderment

anonadar 1 *vt* **(a)** *(sorprender)* to astonish, to bewilder; **anonadó al público con su comportamiento** her behaviour astonished *o* bewildered the audience, the audience was totally taken aback by her behaviour **(b)** *(abatir)* to stun

2 anonadarse *vpr* **(a)** *(sorprenderse)* to be astonished, to be bewildered **(b)** *(abatirse)* to be stunned

anónimamente *adv* anonymously

anonimato *nm* anonymity; **permanecer en el a.** to remain nameless; **se valió del a. para enviar las amenazas** he sent the threats anonymously; **vivir en el a.** to live out of the public eye; **salir del a.** to reveal one's identity

anónimo, -a 1 *adj (libro, obra)* anonymous; **un comunicante a. reivindicó el atentado** an anonymous caller claimed responsibility for the attack

2 *nm (escrito)* anonymous letter; *(cuadro)* unsigned painting

anorak *(pl* **anoraks**) *nm* anorak

anorexia *nf* anorexia ►► ***a. nerviosa*** anorexia nervosa

anoréxico, -a 1 *adj* anorexic

2 *nm,f* anorexic

anormal 1 *adj* **(a)** *(anómalo)* abnormal **(b)** *(subnormal)* subnormal **(c)** *Fam (como insulto)* moronic; **no seas a.** don't be such a moron

2 *nmf* **(a)** *(persona)* subnormal person **(b)** *Fam (como insulto)* moron

anormalidad *nf* **(a)** *(anomalía)* abnormality **(b)** *(defecto físico o psíquico)* handicap, disability

anormalmente *adv* abnormally

anotación *nf* **(a)** *(nota escrita)* note; **anotaciones al margen** *(de escritor, científico)* marginal notes; **hizo varias anotaciones al margen** she made several notes in the margin **(b)** *Com (en registro)* entry ►► ***a. contable*** book entry

anotador, -ora 1 *nm,f* **(a)** *Dep* scorer **(b)** *Cine* continuity person

2 *nm RP* loose-leaf notebook

anotar 1 *vt* **(a)** *(escribir)* to note down, to make a note of; **anotó la dirección en su agenda** she noted down *o* made a note of the address in her diary **(b)** *(libro)* to annotate; **el catedrático anotó una edición de "La Celestina"** the professor provided the notes for an edition of "La Celestina" **(c)** *Dep* to score

2 anotarse *vpr* **(a)** *(deporte)* to score; **nos anotamos un triunfo más** we scored another triumph

(b) *RP (apuntarse) (en curso)* to enrol (**en** for); *(para actividad)* to sign up (**en** for); **¿van al cine?, ¡me anoto!** are you going to the cinema? count me in!; **siempre se anota cuando vamos al cine** she always tags along when we go to the cinema; **¿con quién vino el pesado ese? – supongo que se anotó él solo** who brought that bore along? – I imagine he invited himself

anovulatorio, -a 1 *adj* anovulatory

2 *nm* anovulant

anoxia *nf Med* anoxia

anquilosado, -a *adj* **(a)** *(articulación) (paralizado)* paralysed; *(entumecido)* stiff **(b)** *(economía, ciencia)* stagnant

anquilosamiento *nm* **(a)** *(de articulación) (parálisis)* paralysis; *(entumecimiento)* stiffening **(b)** *(de economía, ciencia)* stagnation

anquilosar 1 *vt* **(a)** *(articulación) (paralizar)* to paralyse; *(entumecer)* to stiffen **(b)** *(economía, ciencia)* to cause to stagnate

2 anquilosarse *vpr* **(a)** *(articulación) (paralizarse)* to become paralysed; *(entumecerse)* to stiffen **(b)** *(economía, ciencia)* to stagnate

ANR *nf (abrev de* **Asociación Nacional Republicana**) = Paraguayan political party, better known as the "Colorados"

ánsar *nm* (greylag) goose ►► ***á. campestre*** bean goose; ***á. careto*** white-fronted goose; ***á. piquicorto*** pink-footed goose

ansarón *nm* gosling

anserina *nf* good-king-henry

ansia *nf*

> Takes the masculine articles **el** and **un**.

(a) *(afán)* longing, yearning; **tiene a. de poder** she is hungry for power; **bebía con a.** he drank thirstily; **las ansias de vivir** the will to live; **las ansias independentistas de la región** the region's desire for independence

(b) *(ansiedad)* anxiousness; *(angustia)* anguish; **esperan los resultados con a.** they are anxiously waiting for the results; **no pases a., todo saldrá bien** don't worry *o* be anxious, it will all turn out all right in the end

(c) ansias *(náuseas)* sickness, nausea

ansiar [32] *vt* **a. algo** to long for sth; **encontraron la felicidad que tanto ansiaban** they found the happiness that they had been longing for; **ansiaba regresar a su país** she longed to return to her country; **todos ansiamos llegar a un acuerdo** we are all anxious to reach an agreement; **ansían que el problema se resuelva lo antes posible** they are anxious for the problem to be solved as soon as possible

ansiedad *nf* **(a)** *(inquietud)* anxiety; **esperan los resultados con a.** they are anxiously waiting for the results **(b)** *Psi* nervous tension

ansina, asina *adv CSur Fam* = form of "así", used in rural areas

ansiolítico, -a 1 *adj* sedative, *Espec* anxiolytic

2 *nm* sedative, *Espec* anxiolytic

ansiosamente *adv* **(a)** *(con afán)* longingly, yearningly **(b)** *(con ansiedad)* anxiously; **esperan a. la resolución judicial** they are anxiously awaiting the judge's ruling

ansioso, -a *adj* **(a)** *(impaciente)* impatient; **estar a. por** *o* **de hacer algo** to be impatient to do sth; **está a. por acabar el trabajo** he can't wait to finish work; **está a. de reencontrarse con su familia** he can't wait *o* is impatient to be reunited with his family **(b)** *(angustiado)* in anguish; **esperan ansiosos noticias sobre sus familiares** they are waiting anxiously for news of their relatives

anta *nf (europeo)* elk; *(americano)* moose

Takes the masculine articles **el** and **un**.

antagónico, -a *adj* antagonistic

antagonismo *nm* antagonism

antagonista 1 *adj* **(a)** *Anat* **músculo a.** antagonist **(b)** *Med* **medicamento a.** antagonist
2 *nmf (contrario)* opponent, antagonist
3 *nm* **(a)** *Anat* antagonist **(b)** *Med* antagonist

antagonizar *vt (fármaco)* to counteract

antaño *adv* in days gone by; **los revolucionarios de a.** the revolutionaries of yesteryear *o* of days gone by

antara *nf Bol, Perú* = type of flute

antártico, -a 1 *adj* Antarctic; **el océano Glacial A.** the Antarctic Ocean
2 *nm* **el A.** the Antarctic

Antártida *nf* **la A.** the Antarctic

ante[1] *nm* **(a)** *(piel)* suede; **zapatos de a.** suede shoes **(b)** *(animal) (europeo)* elk; *(americano)* moose

ANTE[2] *prep* **(a)** *(delante de, en presencia de)* before; **se arrodilló a. el Papa** he kneeled before the Pope; **comparecer a. el juez** to appear before the judge, to appear in court; **apelar a. el tribunal** to appeal to the court; **es muy tímido y se encoge a. sus superiores** he's very timid and clams up in the presence of his superiors; **nos hicimos una foto a. la Esfinge** we took a photo of ourselves standing in front of the Sphinx; **estamos a. otro Dalí** this is another Dali, we have before us another Dali; **desfilar/marchar a. algo/alguien** to file/march past sth/sb
(b) *(frente a) (hecho, circunstancia)* in the face of; **a. una actitud tan intolerante, poco se puede hacer** there is little we can do in the face of such intolerance; **a. la insistencia de su hermano, accedimos a admitirla** at her brother's insistence, we agreed to take her on; **no se detendrá a. nada** she'll stop at nothing, nothing will stop her; **no se amilana a. nada** he isn't scared of anything; **¿cuál es tu postura a. el aborto?** what's your opinion about abortion?; **cerrar los ojos a. algo** *(ignorar)* to close one's eyes to sth; **a. la duda, mejor no intentarlo** if in doubt, it's best not to attempt it; **me descubro a. su esfuerzo** I take my hat off to him for his effort; **extasiarse a. algo** to go into ecstasies over sth; **se quedó solo a. el peligro** he was left to face the danger alone; **se crece a. las dificultades** she thrives in the face of adversity; **ser responsable a. alguien** to be accountable to sb; **retroceder a. el peligro** to shrink back from danger
(c) *(respecto de)* compared to; **su obra palidece a. la de su maestro** his work pales in comparison with that of his master; **su opinión prevaleció a. la mía** his opinion prevailed over mine
(d) a. todo *(sobre todo)* above all; *(en primer lugar)* first of all

anteanoche *adv* the night before last

anteayer *adv* the day before yesterday

antebrazo *nm* forearm

antecámara *nf* antechamber

antecedente 1 *adj* preceding, previous
2 *nm* **(a)** *(precedente)* precedent, **una derrota sin antecedentes** an unprecedented defeat; **una crisis que no tiene antecedentes en la historia reciente** a crisis which is unprecedented in recent history; **un paciente con antecedentes cardiacos** a patient with a history of heart trouble
(b) antecedentes *(de asunto)* background; **los antecedentes de un conflicto** the background to a conflict; **estar en antecedentes** to be aware of the background; **poner a alguien en antecedentes (de)** *(informar)* to fill sb in (on); **ya me han puesto en antecedentes** they've filled me in
(c) *Der* **antecedentes (penales** *o* **policiales)** criminal record
(d) *Gram* antecedent
(e) *Mat* antecedent

anteceder *vt* to come before, to precede; **el silencio que antecedió al comienzo del concierto** the silence which preceded the beginning of the concert

antecesor, -ora *nm,f* **(a)** *(predecesor)* predecessor **(b) antecesores** *(antepasados)* ancestors

antecocina *nf* = room off the kitchen used for storage

antedatar *vt (documento)* to antedate

antedicho, -a 1 *adj* aforementioned
2 *nm,f* **el a.** the aforementioned person

antediluviano, -a *adj* **(a)** *(anterior al diluvio)* antediluvian **(b)** *Hum (viejo)* antediluvian

antefirma *nf* **(a)** *(cargo)* title of the signatory **(b)** *(fórmula)* closing formula

antelación *nf* **con a. (a)** in advance (of); **con dos horas de a.** two hours in advance; **prepararon la fiesta con bastante a.** they got things ready for the party in plenty of time; **no me avisaron con la suficiente a.** they didn't give me enough notice; **el vuelo llegó con una hora de a.** the flight arrived one hour early

antelar 1 *vt Chile (anticipar)* to anticipate
2 *vi Méx (obrar con antelación)* to act ahead of time

antemano *adv* **de a.** beforehand, in advance; **el resultado se sabía de a.** the outcome was known in advance; **estaban en contra suya de a.** they were against him even before things started; **agradeciéndole de a. su cooperación...** *(en carta)* thanking you in advance for your cooperation...

antena *nf* **(a)** *(de radio, televisión)* aerial, antenna; **estar/salir en a.** to be/go on the air; EXPR *Fam* **poner la a.** *(escuchar)* to prick up one's ears; EXPR *Fam* **estar con** *o* **tener la a. puesta: siempre tiene la a. puesta** he's always listening in to other people's conversations ►► ***a. colectiva*** = aerial shared by all the inhabitants of a block of flats, *US* CATV; ***a. direccional*** directional aerial; ***a. directiva*** directional aerial; ***a. parabólica*** satellite dish; ***a. de radar*** radar dish; ***a. receptora*** receiving aerial *o* antenna
(b) *(de animal)* antenna

antenista *nmf* = person who installs, adjusts and repairs TV aerials

antenoche *adv Am* the night before last

anteojeras *nfpl Br* blinkers, *US* blinders

anteojo 1 *nm (telescopio)* telescope, spy-glass
2 **anteojos** *nmpl* **(a)** *(prismáticos)* binoculars **(b)** *(quevedos)* pince-nez **(c)** *Am (gafas)* spectacles, glasses ►► ***a. de aumento*** prescription glasses; ***a. de sol*** sunglasses

antepasado, -a *nm,f* ancestor

antepecho *nm* **(a)** *(de puente)* parapet **(b)** *(de ventana)* sill

antepenúltimo, -a 1 *adj* third (from) last; **es la antepenúltima carrera del campeonato** it's the third (from) last race of the championships; **"encefálico" se acentúa en la antepenúltima sílaba** "encefálico" has an accent on the third (from) last syllable
2 *nm,f* third from last; **llegó el a.** he came third from last

anteponer [50] **1** *vt* **(a)** *(poner delante)* **a. algo a algo** to put sth in front of sth; **antepuso una introducción a su traducción del libro** she prefaced her translation of the book with an introduction **(b)** *(dar más importancia a)* **a. algo a algo** to put sth before sth; **antepone su trabajo a todo lo demás** he puts his work before everything else
2 **anteponerse** *vpr* **anteponerse a algo** to come before sth; **su familia se antepone a lo demás** his family comes before everything else

anteproyecto *nm* preliminary draft ►► *Pol* ***a. de ley*** draft bill

antepuesto, -a *participio ver* **anteponer**

antera *nf Bot* anther

anterior *adj* **(a)** *(en el tiempo)* previous; **un modelo muy parecido al a.** a model which is very similar to the previous *o* last one; **el año a.** the year before, the previous year; **el día a. a la inauguración** the day before *o* prior to the opening; **los cinco años anteriores a la independencia** the five years before *o* prior to independence; **un jarrón a. a la época romana** a pre-Roman vase
(b) *(en el espacio)* front; **la parte a. de un edificio** the front of a building
(c) *(en una ordenación)* previous, last; **el problema señalado en el párrafo a.** the problem identified in the previous *o* last paragraph
(d) *(vocal)* front

anterioridad *nf* **con a.** beforehand, previously; **estaba todo planeado con a.** everything had been planned beforehand *o* in advance; **queremos llegar con suficiente a.** we want to get there in plenty of time; **con a. a** prior to, before; **con a. al embarque hay que pasar el control de pasaportes** you have to go through passport control prior to *o* before boarding

anteriormente *adv* previously; **como dije a....** as I said previously *o* before...; **a. a la llegada del presidente** prior to *o* before the president's arrival

ANTES 1 *adv* **(a)** *(en el tiempo)* before; *(antaño)* formerly, in the past; **lo he dicho a.** I've said it before; **no importa si venís a.** it doesn't matter if you come earlier; **me lo podías haber contado a.**

you could have told me earlier *o* before; **a. llovía más** it used to rain more often; **a. no había televisión y la gente se entretenía con la radio** in the past, there wasn't any television, so people used to listen to the radio; **ya no nado como a.** I can't swim as I used to; **desde el accidente, ya no es el mismo de a.** he hasn't been the same since the accident; **cuanto a.** as soon as possible; **mucho/poco a.** long/shortly before; **lo a. posible** as soon as possible; **a. de** before; **a. de entrar dejen salir** *(en letrero)* please let people off first before boarding; **no llegues a. de las cinco** don't get there before five, make sure you arrive no earlier than five; **tenlo preparado a. de medianoche** have it ready by midnight; **a. de hacer algo** before doing sth; **consúltame a. de añadir nada** consult me first before you add anything *o* before adding anything; **a. de que llegaras** before you arrived; **a. de anoche** the night before last; **a. de ayer** the day before yesterday; **a. de Cristo** before Christ, BC; **de a.** *(antiguo)* old; *(anterior)* previous; **el sistema de a. era muy lento** the old system was very slow; **esta cerveza sabe igual que la de a.** this beer tastes the same as the previous one *o* the one before

(**b**) *(en el espacio)* before; **me bajo dos pisos a.** I get off two floors before (you); **a. de** before; **el motel está a. del próximo cruce** the motel is before the next junction

(**c**) *(primero)* first; **esta señora está a.** this lady is first; **ten paciencia, este señor está a. que nosotros** be patient, this man is in front of us; **entraron a. que yo** they went in in front of me; **¿quién va a salir a.?** who's going to leave (the) first?

(**d**) *(expresa preferencia)* rather; **no quiero tener coche, a. me compraría una moto** I don't want a car, I'd rather buy a motorbike; **a.... que** rather... than; **prefiero la sierra a. que el mar** I prefer the mountains to the sea; **iría a la cárcel a. que mentir** I'd rather go to prison than lie; **a. de nada** first of all, before anything else; **a. que nada** *(expresando preferencia)* above all, first and foremost; **a. al contrario** on the contrary

2 *adj (previo)* previous; **la noche a.** the night before

3 **antes bien** *loc conj* on the contrary; **no le aburría, a. bien parecía agradarle** far from boring him, it appeared to please him

---

antesala *nf* (**a**) *(habitación)* anteroom; EXPR **estar en la a. de** to be on the verge of; **en la a. del poder** on the verge of coming to power; EXPR **hacer a.** to wait (**b**) *(cosa precedente)* prelude; **la matanza fue la a. de una guerra civil** the massacre was the prelude to a civil war; **el encuentro privado fue la a. de la reunión oficial** the private meeting was a prelude to the official one

antevíspera *nf* **la a. de la inauguración** two days before the opening

antiabortista 1 *adj* anti-abortion, pro-life

2 *nmf* anti-abortion *o* pro-life campaigner

antiaborto *adj inv* anti-abortion, pro-life

antiácido, -a 1 *adj* (**a**) *(medicamento)* antacid (**b**) *(anticorrosivo)* anticorrosive

2 *nm (medicamento)* antacid

antiadherente *adj* non-stick

antiaéreo, -a *adj* anti-aircraft

antialcohólico, -a *adj* **campaña antialcohólica** campaign against alcohol abuse; **liga antialcohólica** temperance league

antialérgico, -a 1 *adj* anti-allergenic

2 *nm* anti-allergenic

antiamericano, -a *adj* anti-American

antiarrugas *adj inv* (**a**) *(crema)* antiwrinkle (**b**) *(tejido, prenda)* non-iron

antiasmático, -a 1 *adj* anti-asthmatic

2 *nm* anti-asthmatic drug

antiatómico, -a *adj* antinuclear

antibacteriano, -a *adj* antibacterial

antibalas, antibala *adj inv* bullet-proof

antibiótico, -a 1 *adj* antibiotic

2 *nm* antibiotic

antibloqueo 1 *adj inv* **frenos a.** anti-lock brakes

2 *nm inv* anti-lock braking system

anticancerígeno, -a, anticanceroso, -a 1 *adj* **medicamento a.** cancer drug

2 *nm* cancer drug

anticarro *adj inv* antitank

anticaspa *adj* anti-dandruff; **champú a.** (anti-)dandruff shampoo

anticatarral 1 *adj* **medicamento a.** cold remedy

2 *nm* cold remedy

anticelulítico, -a *adj* anticellulite

antichoque *adj inv* shockproof

anticiclón *nm* area of high pressure, *Espec* anticyclone

anticiclónico, -a *adj* **frente a.** high-pressure front

anticipación *nf* earliness; **con a.** in advance; **compró las entradas con a.** she bought the tickets beforehand *o* in advance; **con un mes de a.** a month in advance; **con a. a** prior to; **llegó con a. a la hora prevista** he arrived before he was supposed to; **se recomienda reservarlo con la mayor a. posible** you are advised to book as early as possible

anticipadamente *adv* in advance, beforehand; **pagar a.** to pay in advance; **se jubiló a.** she took early retirement; **le agradecemos a. su colaboración** *(en carta)* thanking you in advance for your co-operation

anticipado, -a *adj (elecciones)* early; *(pago)* advance; **por a.** in advance, beforehand; **¿va a haber venta anticipada de entradas?** will tickets be on sale in advance?; **le agradezco por a. su ayuda** *(en carta)* thanking you in advance for your help

anticipar 1 *vt* (**a**) *(prever)* to anticipate; **él ya había anticipado la crisis económica** he had already anticipated the recession

(**b**) *(adelantar)* to bring forward; **el presidente anticipó las elecciones** the president brought forward the elections

(**c**) *(pago)* to pay in advance; **me anticiparon dos semanas de sueldo** they gave me an advance of two weeks' salary

(**d**) *(información)* to tell in advance; **no te puedo a. nada** I can't tell you anything just now

2 **anticiparse** *vpr* (**a**) *(suceder antes)* to arrive early; **se anticipó a su tiempo** he was ahead of his time; **este año se ha anticipado la llegada del invierno** winter has come early this year (**b**) *(adelantarse)* **anticiparse a alguien** to beat sb to it; **se anticipó al portero y marcó gol** he beat the goalkeeper to the ball and scored

anticipo *nm* (**a**) *(de dinero)* advance; **pedí un a. sobre mi sueldo** I asked for an advance on my salary; **recibió cien mil dólares como a. por su libro** she received a hundred thousand dollar advance for her book

(**b**) *(presagio)* foretaste; **esto es sólo un a. de lo que vendrá después** this is just a foretaste of what is to come; **presentó un par de temas como a. de su nuevo disco** she previewed a couple of tracks from her new record

anticlerical *adj* anticlerical

anticlericalismo *nm* anticlericalism

anticlímax *nm inv* (**a**) *(en teatro, cine)* aftermath *(of climax)* (**b**) *(en retórica)* anticlimax

anticlinal *nm Geol* anticline

anticoagulante *Med* 1 *adj* anticoagulant

2 *nm* anticoagulant

anticolesterol *adj (fármaco)* anticholesterol; *(dieta)* cholesterol-free

anticolonialismo *nm* anticolonialism

anticolonialista 1 *adj* anticolonialist

2 *nmf* anticolonialist

anticomunismo *nm* anti-Communism

anticomunista 1 *adj* anti-Communist

2 *nmf* anti-Communist

anticoncepción *nf* contraception

anticonceptivo, -a 1 *adj* contraceptive; **método a.** method of contraception; **píldora anticonceptiva** contraceptive pill

2 *nm* contraceptive ►► ***a. de barrera*** barrier method of contraception; ***a. oral*** oral contraceptive

anticonformismo *nm* non-conformism

anticonformista 1 *adj* nonconformist

2 *nmf* nonconformist

anticongelante 1 *adj* antifreeze

2 *nm* antifreeze

anticonstitucional *adj* unconstitutional

anticonstitucionalidad *nf* unconstitutionality

anticonstitucionalmente *adv* unconstitutionally

anticorrosión *adj inv* anticorrosive

anticorrosivo, -a 1 *adj* anticorrosive

2 *nm* anticorrosive substance

anticorrupción *adj inv* anticorruption

anticristo *nm* **el a.** the Antichrist

anticuado, -a 1 *adj (persona, ropa)* old-fashioned; **esa técnica está anticuada** that method is out of date; **mi módem se ha quedado a.** my modem is out of date
2 *nm,f* old-fashioned person; **mi madre es una anticuada** my mother is very old-fashioned

anticuario, -a 1 *nm,f* (a) *(comerciante)* antique dealer (b) *(experto)* antiquarian
2 *nm (establecimiento)* antique shop

anticuarse *vpr* to become old-fashioned

anticucho *nm Andes (brocheta)* kebab

anticuerpo *nm Med* antibody

antidemocráticamente *adv* undemocratically

antidemocrático, -a *adj (no democrático)* undemocratic; *(contra la democracia)* antidemocratic

antideportivamente *adv* unsportingly

antideportivo, -a *adj* unsporting, unsportsmanlike

antidepresivo, -a 1 *adj* antidepressant
2 *nm* antidepressant (drug)

antideslizante *adj (superficie)* non-slip; *(neumático)* non-skid

antideslumbrante *adj* anti-dazzle

antidetonante 1 *adj* antiknock
2 *nm* antiknock agent

antidiabético, -a 1 *adj* anti-diabetic
2 *nm* anti-diabetic drug

antidiarreico, -a 1 *adj* **medicamento a.** diarrhoea remedy
2 *nm* diarrhoea remedy

antidiftérico, -a 1 *adj* diphtheria; **vacuna antidiftérica** diphtheria vaccine
2 *nm* diphtheria medicine

antidisturbios 1 *adj inv* riot; **material a.** riot gear; **policía a.** riot police
2 *nmpl* **los a.** the riot police

antidopaje, antidoping [anti'ðopin] *Dep* 1 *adj inv* drugs; **prueba a.** drugs test; **control a.** drugs test
2 *nm* drugs test

antídoto *nm* (a) *(médico)* antidote; **es un buen a. contra el aburrimiento** it's an effective antidote to boredom (b) *Informát* antidote

antidroga *adj inv (campaña)* antidrug; **la lucha a.** the fight against drugs; **una redada a.** a drugs bust

antidumping [anti'ðumpin] *adj inv Econ (medidas, leyes)* antidumping

antieconómico, -a *adj* (a) *(caro)* expensive (b) *(no rentable)* uneconomic

antiemético, -a *Med* 1 *adj* antiemetic
2 *nm* antiemetic

antier *adv Am Fam* the day before yesterday

antiespasmódico, -a 1 *adj* antispasmodic
2 *nm* antispasmodic

antiestático, -a *adj* antistatic

antiestético, -a *adj* unsightly

antiestrés *adj inv* **una medida a.** a way to fight stress; **ejercicios a.** stress-reducing exercises, exercises to reduce stress

antifascista 1 *adj* antifascist
2 *nmf* antifascist

antifaz *nm* mask *(covering top half of face)*

antifeminista 1 *adj* antifeminist
2 *nmf* antifeminist

antifranquista 1 *adj* anti-Franco
2 *nmf* anti-Francoist, opponent of Franco

antifúngico, -a 1 *adj* antifungal
2 *nm* antifungal preparation

antigás *adj inv* gas; **careta a.** gas mask

antígeno *nm Med* antigen

antigripal 1 *adj* designed to combat flu; **un medicamento a.** a flu remedy
2 *nm* flu remedy

antigualla *nf Pey (cosa)* museum piece; *(persona)* old fogey, old fossil

antiguamente *adv* (a) *(hace mucho)* in the past; **a. se utilizaban las diligencias** they used to use stagecoaches in the past (b) *(previamente)* formerly; **más conocido a. como...** formerly better known as...

Antigua y Barbuda *n* Antigua and Barbuda

antigubernamental *adj* antigovernment

antigüedad *nf* (a) *(edad)* antiquity (b) *(veteranía)* seniority; **un plus de a.** a seniority bonus; **un trabajador de veinte años de a.** a worker who has been with the company for twenty years ►► ***a. laboral*** seniority *(in a post)* (c) *Hist* **la A. (clásica)** (Classical) Antiquity (d) *(objeto antiguo)* antique; **antigüedades** *(tienda)* antique shop

antiguo, -a 1 *adj* (a) *(viejo)* old; *(inmemorial)* ancient; **un a. amigo/enemigo** an old friend/enemy ►► ***a. alumno*** *(de colegio)* ex-pupil, former pupil, *US* alumnus; **una reunión de antiguos alumnos** a school reunion; ***el a. continente*** *(Europa)* Europe; ***la antigua Roma*** Ancient Rome; ***el A. Testamento*** the Old Testament
(b) *(anterior, previo)* former; **la antigua Unión Soviética** the former Soviet Union ►► ***el a. régimen*** the former regime; *Hist* the ancien régime
(c) *(veterano)* **los miembros/empleados más antiguos tienen preferencia** preference is given to the longest-serving members/employees; **los vecinos más antiguos** the neighbours who've been here longest
(d) *(pasado de moda)* old-fashioned; **a la antigua** in an old-fashioned way; **chapado a la antigua** stuck in the past, old-fashioned
2 *nm,f* (a) *(persona)* old-fashioned person; **su tío es un a.** her uncle is very old-fashioned (b) **los antiguos** *(de la Antigüedad)* the ancients

antihéroe *nm* antihero

antihielo *nm* de-icer

antihigiénico, -a *adj* unhygienic

antihipertensivo, -a 1 *adj* for high blood pressure
2 *nm* medicine for high blood pressure

antihistamina *nf* antihistamine

antihistamínico, -a 1 *adj* antihistamine
2 *nm* antihistamine

antiimperialismo *nm* anti-imperialism

antiimperialista 1 *adj* anti-imperialist
2 *nmf* anti-imperialist

antiincendios *adj inv (medida)* fire-prevention; **la normativa a.** the fire regulations; **alarma a.** fire alarm

antiinflacionista, antiinflacionario, -a *adj Econ* anti-inflationary

antiinflamatorio, -a 1 *adj* anti-inflammatory
2 *nm* anti-inflammatory drug

antijurídico, -a *adj* unlawful

antillano, -a 1 *adj* West Indian, of/from the Caribbean
2 *nm,f* West Indian, person from the Caribbean

Antillas *nfpl* **las A.** the West Indies ►► ***las A. Holandesas*** the Dutch Antilles

antilogaritmo *nm Mat* antilogarithm

antílope *nm* antelope

antimagnético, -a *adj Fís* antimagnetic

antimateria *nf Fís* antimatter

antimicrobiano, -a 1 *adj* antibacterial
2 *nm* antibacterial agent

antimilitarismo *nm* antimilitarism

antimilitarista 1 *adj* antimilitarist
2 *nm* antimilitarist

antimisil *adj Mil* antimissile

antimonárquico, -a 1 *adj* antimonarchist
2 *nm,f* antimonarchist

antimonio *nm Quím* antimony

antimonopolio *adj inv Econ* anti-trust

antimotines *Am* 1 *adj inv* riot; **material a.** riot gear; **policía a.** riot police
2 *nmpl* **los a.** the riot police

antinarcótico, -a *adj (campaña)* antidrug; **la lucha antinarcótica** the fight against drugs; **la policía antinarcótica** the drug squad

antinatural *adj* (a) *(contra natura)* unnatural (b) *(afectado)* artificial, affected

antiniebla *adj inv* **faros a.** fog lamps

antinomia *nf* (a) *Filosofía* antinomy (b) *Formal (entre leyes, principios)* conflict

antinorteamericano, -a *adj* anti-American

antinuclear *adj* antinuclear

antioqueño, -a 1 *adj* of/from Antioquia *(Colombia)*
2 *nm,f* person from Antioquia *(Colombia)*

Antioquia *n (en Colombia)* Antioquia

Antioquía *n (en Turquía)* Antioch

antioxidante 1 *adj* (**a**) *(contra el óxido)* anti-rust (**b**) *(contra la oxidación)* antioxidant
2 *nm* (**a**) *(contra el óxido)* rustproofing agent (**b**) *(contra la oxidación)* antioxidant

antipalúdico, -a *adj* antimalarial

antipapa *nm* antipope

antiparabólico, -a *adj Ven Fam* laid-back, easy-going

antiparasitario, -a 1 *adj (para perro, gato)* **collar a.** flea collar; **pastillas antiparasitarias** worming tablets
2 *nm* (**a**) *(para perro, gato) (collar)* flea collar; *(pastilla)* worming tablet (**b**) *Tel* suppressor

antiparras *nfpl* (**a**) *Esp Fam (gafas)* specs (**b**) *CSur (de esquiar, nadar, motociclismo)* goggles ►► ***a. protectoras*** protective goggles

antipartícula *nf Fís* antiparticle

antipasto *nm Am* antipasto

antipatía *nf* dislike; **tener a. a alguien** to dislike sb

antipáticamente *adv* unpleasantly

antipático, -a 1 *adj* unpleasant; **estuvo muy a. con sus primos** he was very unpleasant to *o* towards his cousins; **me resulta muy a.** I don't like him at all, I find him very unpleasant; **no seas a. y ven a saludar a mi madre** don't be so miserable and come and say hello to my mother; **limpiar el baño es un trabajo muy a.** cleaning the bathroom is a very unpleasant job
2 *nm,f* unpleasant person; **tu jefe es un a.** your boss is really unpleasant, your boss isn't very nice at all

antipatriótico, -a *adj* unpatriotic

antipedagógico, -a *adj* antipedagogical

antipersona, antipersonal *adj Mil* anti-personnel

antiperspirante *nm* antiperspirant

antipirético, -a 1 *adj* antipyretic
2 *nm* antipyretic

antípodas *nfpl* **las a.** the Antipodes; EXPR **estar en las a. de algo/alguien** *(ser contrario a)* to be diametrically opposed to sth/sb

antipolilla 1 *adj* antimoth
2 *nm* moth killer

antiproteccionista *Pol & Econ* 1 *adj* antiprotectionist
2 *nmf* antiprotectionist

antiprotón *nm Fís* antiproton

antiquísimo, -a *superlativo ver* **antiguo**

antirrábico, -a *adj* antirabies

antirracismo *nm* antiracism

antirracista 1 *adj* antiracist
2 *nmf* antiracist

antirreflectante *adj* non-reflective

antirreflejos *adj inv* antiglare

antirreglamentariamente *adv* **actuar a.** to break the rules

antirreglamentario, -a *adj* **ser a.** to be against the rules; **un procedimiento a.** a procedure which contravenes the rules; **una entrada antirreglamentaria** *(en fútbol)* a foul; **estar en posición antirreglamentaria** *(futbolista)* to be offside

antirreligioso, -a *adj* antireligious

antirrepublicano, -a 1 *adj* antirepublican
2 *nm,f* antirepublican

antirretroviral 1 *adj* antiretroviral
2 *nm* antiretrovirus

antirreumático, -a 1 *adj* antirheumatic
2 *nm* antirheumatic

antirrevolucionario, -a 1 *adj* antirevolutionary
2 *nm,f* antirevolutionary

antirrobo 1 *adj inv* antitheft; **dispositivo a.** antitheft device
2 *nm* (**a**) *(en coche)* antitheft device (**b**) *(en edificio)* burglar alarm

antisemita 1 *adj* antisemitic
2 *nmf* anti-semite

antisemítico, -a *adj* antisemitic

antisemitismo *nm* antisemitism

antisepsia *nf* antisepsis

antiséptico, -a 1 *adj* antiseptic
2 *nm* antiseptic

antisida *adj inv* anti-Aids

antisísmico, -a *adj* **materiales antisísmicos** = materials designed to resist earthquakes

antisocial 1 *adj* antisocial
2 *nmf Andes, RP (delincuente)* criminal

antisubmarino, -a *adj* antisubmarine

antisudoral 1 *adj* antiperspirant
2 *nm* antiperspirant

antisuero *nm* antiserum

antitabaco *adj inv* antismoking

antitanque *adj* antitank

antitaurino, -a *adj* anti-bullfighting

antiterrorismo *nm* fight against terrorism

antiterrorista *adj* antiterrorist

antítesis *nf inv* antithesis; **es la a. del ejecutivo agresivo** he's the complete opposite of the aggressive executive

antitetánica *nf* tetanus *o* anti-tetanus injection

antitetánico, -a *adj (suero, vacuna)* tetanus, anti-tetanus

antitético, -a *adj Formal* antithetical

antitoxina *nf Biol* antitoxin

antitrago *nm Anat* antitragus

antitranspirante 1 *adj* antiperspirant
2 *nm* antiperspirant

antitrust [anti'trus(t)] *adj Econ (medidas, leyes)* anti-trust

antitumoral 1 *adj* anti-tumour
2 *nm* anti-tumour drug

antitusígeno, -a 1 *adj* anti-cough, *Espec* antitussive
2 *nm* cough medicine, *Espec* antitussive

antivariólico, -a *adj* smallpox; **vacuna antivariólica** smallpox vaccine

antiviral *adj* antiviral

antivirus 1 *adj inv* antivirus
2 *nm inv Informát* antivirus system

antivuelco *adj inv Aut* anti-roll

antofagastino, -a 1 *adj* of/from Antofagasta *(Chile)*
2 *nm,f* person from Antofagasta *(Chile)*

antojadizo, -a *adj* capricious

antojarse *vpr* (**a**) *(por deseo)* **se le antojaron esos zapatos** she took a fancy to those shoes; **se le ha antojado comer ciruelas** he has a craving for plums; **cuando se me antoje** when I feel like it; **hace lo que se le antoja** he does whatever he feels like doing
(**b**) *Formal (parecer)* **se me antoja que está en lo cierto** it seems to me that he is right; **eso se me antoja poco probable** that seems far from likely to me
(**c**) *Méx (apetecer)* to feel like, to want

antojitos *nmpl Ecuad, Méx* snacks, appetizers

antojo *nm* (**a**) *(capricho)* whim; **a mi/tu a.: entraba y salía de la casa a su a.** she went in and out of the house just as she pleased; **maneja a la gente a su a.** she can twist people round her little finger (**b**) *(de embarazada)* craving; **tiene el a. de comer fresas** she has a craving for strawberries (**c**) *(lunar)* birthmark

antología *nf* (**a**) *(colección)* anthology (**b**) **de a.** *(inolvidable)* memorable, unforgettable; **un gol de a.** a spectacular *o* memorable goal

antológico, -a *adj* (**a**) *(recopilador)* anthological (**b**) *(inolvidable)* memorable, unforgettable; **un gol a.** a spectacular *o* memorable goal

antonimia *nf* antonymy

antónimo, -a 1 *adj* antonymous
2 *nm* antonym

Antonio *n pr* **San A.** St Anthony; **San A. de Padua** St Anthony of Padua

antonomasia *nf* antonomasia; **por a.** par excellence

antorcha *nf* torch ►► ***a. olímpica*** Olympic torch

antracita *nf* anthracite

ántrax *nm inv Med* (**a**) *(por estafilococo)* carbuncle (**b**) *(por bacilo)* anthrax

antro *nm Fam Pey* dive, dump; **ese bar es un a. de mala muerte** that bar is a dive *o* dump; *Hum* **un a. de perdición** a den of iniquity

antropocéntrico, -a *adj* anthropocentric

antropocentrismo *nm* anthropocentrism

antropofagia *nf* cannibalism, anthropophagy

antropófago, -a 1 *adj* man-eating, cannibalistic
2 *nm,f* cannibal

antropografía *nf* anthropography

antropoide 1 *adj* anthropoid
2 *nm* anthropoid

antropología *nf* anthropology ►► ***a. cultural*** cultural anthropology; ***a. social*** social anthropology

antropológicamente *adv* anthropologically

antropológico, -a *adj* anthropological

antropólogo, -a *nm,f* anthropologist

antropometría *nf* anthropometry

antropométrico, -a *adj* anthropometric

antropomórfico, -a *adj* anthropomorphic

antropomorfo, -a 1 *adj* anthropomorphous
2 *nm,f* anthropomorph

antroponimia *nf* anthroponymy

antropónimo *nm* proper name, *Espec* anthroponym

anual *adj* (a) *(que sucede cada año)* annual; **un festival que se celebra con carácter a.** a festival which is held annually; **la economía ha estado creciendo un 5 por ciento a.** the economy has been growing at 5 percent a year; **paga una cuota a. de 5.000 pesos** he pays an annual fee of 5,000 pesos (b) *(que dura un año)* **un pase a.** a year pass (c) *(planta)* annual

anualidad *nf* annuity, yearly payment

anualizar [14] *vt Econ* to annualize

anualmente *adv* annually, yearly; **la final se celebra a. en la capital** the final is held in the capital every year

anuario *nm* yearbook

anubarrado, -a *adj* cloudy, overcast

anudar 1 *vt (pañuelo)* to knot, to tie in a knot; *(corbata, cordones)* to tie
2 **anudarse** *vpr* **anudarse los cordones/la corbata** to tie one's shoelaces/one's tie

anuencia *nf Formal* consent, approval

anuente *adj Formal* approving, permissive

anulación *nf* (a) *(cancelación)* cancellation; *(de ley)* repeal; *(de matrimonio, contrato)* annulment (b) *Dep (de un partido)* calling-off; **no estaban de acuerdo con la a. del gol** they disagreed with the decision to disallow the goal; **anunciaron la a. del resultado** they announced that the result had been declared void

anular[1] 1 *adj (en forma de anillo)* ring-shaped; **dedo a.** ring finger
2 *nm (dedo)* ring finger

anular[2] 1 *vt* (a) *(cancelar)* to cancel; *(ley)* to repeal; *(matrimonio, contrato)* to annul (b) *Dep (partido)* to call off; *(gol)* to disallow; *(resultado)* to declare void (c) *(restar iniciativa)* **su marido la anula totalmente** she's totally dominated by her husband; **el defensa anuló a la estrella del equipo contrario** the defender marked the opposing team's star out of the game
2 **anularse** *vpr* (a) *(uno mismo)* **en su presencia, me anulo** I can't be myself when he's there (b) *(mutuamente) (efectos, fuerzas)* to cancel each other out; **se anulan el uno al otro** *(personas)* they stifle each other (c) *Mat* to cancel out

Anunciación *nf Rel* **la A.** the Annunciation

anunciador, -ora 1 *adj* (a) *(de publicidad)* advertising; **la empresa anunciadora** the advertiser (b) *(de noticia)* announcing
2 *nm,f* (a) *(de publicidad)* advertiser (b) *(de noticia)* announcer

anunciante *adj, nmf* = **anuciador**

anunciar 1 *vt* (a) *(notificar)* to announce; **hoy anuncian los resultados** the results are announced today; **me anunció su llegada por teléfono** he phoned to tell me that he would be coming; **anunció que no podría venir** she told us she wouldn't be able to come
(b) *(hacer publicidad de)* to advertise (c) *(presagiar)* to herald; **esas nubes anuncian tormenta** by the look of those clouds, it's going to rain; **los primeros brotes anunciaban la primavera** the first shoots heralded the spring
2 **anunciarse** *vpr* (a) *(con publicidad)* to advertise; **se anuncian en "El Sol"** they advertise in "El Sol"
(b) *(prometer ser)* **las elecciones se anuncian reñidas** the election promises to be a hard-fought one; **la nueva temporada se anuncia muy interesante** the new season promises to be very interesting
(c) *(persona)* to announce one's presence; **se anunció golpeando suavemente en la mesa** she announced her presence by knocking gently on the table

anuncio *nm* (a) *(de noticia)* announcement
(b) *(cartel, aviso)* notice; *(póster)* poster ►► ***a. luminoso*** illuminated sign
(c) *(publicitario) (en prensa)* advert; *(en televisión)* advert, commercial ►► ***anuncios breves*** classified ads *o* adverts; ***anuncios clasificados*** classified ads *o* adverts; ***anuncios por palabras*** classified ads *o* adverts; ***a. personal*** *(por palabras)* personal advert
(d) *(presagio)* sign, herald; **esas nubes son un a. de tormenta** those clouds mean a storm is on its way; **el enfrentamiento era el a. de una cruenta guerra civil** the clash was the prelude to a bloody civil war

anverso *nm* (a) *(de moneda)* head, obverse (b) *(de hoja)* front; **en el a. aparece la lista de participantes** the list of participants appears on the front

anzuelo *nm* (a) *(para pescar)* (fish) hook (b) *Fam (cebo)* bait; EXPR **echar el a. a alguien** to put out bait for sb; EXPR **morder** *o* **picar** *o* **tragarse el a.** to take the bait

añada *nf (de cosecha, vino)* year's harvest; **la a. del 1970 fue excelente** 1970 was an excellent year

añadido, -a 1 *adj* added (**a** to)
2 *nm* addition

añadidura *nf* addition; **por a.** in addition

añadir *vt* (a) *(sustancia)* to add; **a ese precio hay que a. el IVA** you have to add *Br* VAT *o US* sales tax to that price (b) *(comentario, información)* to add; **"y estará acabado el próximo año", añadió** and it will be finished next year, she added; **ese artículo añade muy poco a lo que ya sabía** that article adds very little to what I already knew

añagaza *nf* trick, ruse

añales *(considerado incorrecto)* = **añares**

añapero *nm* nighthawk

añares, añales *nmpl RP Fam* ages, years; **hace a. que no lo veo** I haven't seen him for ages *o* years

añejamiento *nm* maturing, ageing

añejar *vt* to mature, to age

añejo, -a *adj* (a) *(vino, licor, queso)* mature (b) *(costumbre)* long-established; **el sabor a. del pueblecito pesquero** the old-world charm of the little fishing village

añicos *nmpl* **hacer algo a.** to smash sth to pieces *o* smithereens; **la explosión hizo a. los cristales** the explosion smashed the windows to smithereens *o* shattered the windows; **el asesinato hizo a. el proceso de paz** the murder shattered the peace process; **hacerse a.** to shatter, to smash to pieces; **el jarrón se cayó y se hizo a.** the vase fell and smashed to pieces *o* shattered; **estoy hecho a.** I'm utterly exhausted

añil 1 *adj inv* indigo
2 *nm* (a) *(arbusto)* indigo (b) *(color)* indigo (c) *(sustancia)* blue, blueing

---

AÑO *nm* (a) *(periodo de tiempo)* year; **el a. pasado** last year; **el a. antepasado** the year before last; **el a. que viene** next year; **este a.** this year; **a. tras a.** year in year out, year after year; **se celebra cada a.** it's held every year; **durante muchos años** for several years; **en el a. 1939** in 1939; **los años treinta** the thirties; **ganar dos millones al a.** to earn two million a year; **lleva años al servicio de la compañía** he's been with the company for years; **mañana hará un a. que compramos la casa** it'll be a year tomorrow since we bought the house; **le cayeron dos años** *(sentencia)* she got two years; **con el paso de los años** over the years; **¡cómo pasan los años!** how time flies!; **¡hace años que no voy al teatro!** I haven't been to the theatre for years *o* ages!; EXPR *Fam* **está de buen a.** he's got plenty of meat on him; **Sara no era de mi a.** *(curso académico)* Sara wasn't in my year; **perder un a.** *(por suspender los exámenes)* to have to repeat a year; *(por enfermedad, viaje)* to lose a year; PROV **a. de nieves, a. de bienes** = if there's a lot of snow in winter, it will be a good year for the crops ►► ***a. académico*** academic year; ***a. bisiesto*** leap year; *Am* ***a. calendario*** calendar year; *Fam* ***el a. catapún*** the year dot; *Fam* **todavía utilizo una radio del a. catapún** I still use a really ancient radio; *Fam* **vive en Murcia desde el a. catapún** she's been living in Murcia for ages *o* donkey's years; *Rel* ***a. eclesiástico*** Church year; ***a. escolar*** school year; ***a. fiscal*** *Br* financial year, *US* fiscal year; *Anticuado* ***a. de gracia*** year of grace; **en el a. de gracia de 1812** in the year of grace *o* our Lord 1812; ***a. gregoriano*** Gregorian year; *Am Rel* ***a. jubilar*** Holy Year; *Rel* ***a. de jubileo*** Holy Year; ***a. judicial*** judicial year, = working year of Spanish judiciary; ***a. lectivo*** academic year; ***a. legislativo*** parliamentary year; *Astron* ***a. luz*** light year; EXPR **estar a años luz de** to be light years away from; ***a. natural*** calendar year; *Fam* ***el a. de Maricastaña*** the year dot; *Fam* **ese vestido parece del a. de Maricastaña** that dress looks ancient; *Fam* ***el a. de la nana*** the year dot; ***a. nuevo*** New Year; **¡feliz a. nuevo!** Happy New Year!; PROV **a. nuevo, vida nueva** the New Year is as good a moment as any to make a fresh start; *Chile Fam* ***el a. del ñauca*** the year dot; *RP Fam* ***el a. del ñaupa*** the year dot; **esa ropa es del a. de(l) ñaupa** those clothes are out of the ark; *Fam* ***el a. de la pera*** the year dot; *Fam* ***el a. de la polca*** the year dot; ***a. sabático*** sabbatical (year); *Rel* ***a. santo*** Holy Year; *Astron* ***a. sideral*** sidereal year; ***a. solar*** solar year; *RP, Ven Fam* ***el a. verde*** never; ***a. viejo*** New Year's Eve (**b**) **años** *(edad)* age; **¿cuántos años tienes? – tengo diecisiete años** how old are you? – I'm seventeen (years old); **cumplir años** to have one's birthday; **cumplo años el 25** it's my birthday on the 25th; **el bebé cumple hoy dos años** it's the baby's second birthday today, the baby's two (years old) today; **los niños aprenden a andar alrededor del a.** children learn to walk when they're about a year old *o* one; **a los once años** at the age of eleven; **bebía desde los doce años y acabó alcoholizado** he started drinking when he was twelve and became an alcoholic; **me fui de casa a los dieciséis años** I left home at sixteen; **en mis años mozos hubiera ido andando** when I was younger *o* in my youth I would have walked there; **a sus años, no debería trabajar tantas horas** she shouldn't be working such long hours at her age; **metido en años** elderly; **una persona metida en años** an elderly person; **estar entrado** *o* **metido en años** to be getting on; **quitarse años** *(mentir sobre la edad)* to lie about one's age; **te has quitado años de encima** *(rejuvenecer)* you look much younger; **por ti no pasan los años** you never seem to get any older

---

año-hombre (*pl* **años-hombre**) *nm Econ* man-year

añojo *nm* (**a**) *(animal)* yearling (**b**) *(carne de res)* veal *(from a yearling calf)*

añoranza *nf (de persona, pasado)* nostalgia (**de** for); *(de hogar, país)* homesickness (**de** for)

añorar *vt* to miss

añoso, -a *adj* old, aged

aorta *nf Anat* aorta

aórtico, -a *adj* aortic

aovado, -a *adj* egg-shaped

aovar *vi (aves, reptiles)* to lay eggs; *(peces)* to spawn

AP *nm* (*abrev de* **Acción Popular**) = centrist Peruvian political party

APA ['apa] *nf*

Takes the masculine articles **el** and **un**.

(*abrev de* **Asociación de Padres de Alumnos**) = Spanish association for parents of schoolchildren, ≃ PTA

apa 1 *interj Méx Fam (para expresar admiración, sorpresa)* wow!
2 **al apa** *loc adv Chile* **llevar a alguien al a.** to carry sb over one's shoulders *o* on one's back

apabullante *adj (victoria, éxito)* overwhelming; *(edificio, película)* stunning, breathtaking; *(rapidez, habilidad)* breathtaking, astonishing; **es de una simpatía a.** he's extremely friendly

apabullar 1 *vt* to overwhelm; **me apabulla tanta generosidad** I'm overcome *o* overwhelmed by so much generosity; **su respuesta me apabulló** her reply left me speechless; **los corredores keniatas apabullaron a sus rivales** the Kenyan runners crushed *o* overwhelmed their rivals; **nos apabulló con sus conocimientos de música antigua** she astonished *o* astounded us with her knowledge of early music
2 **apabullarse** *vpr* to be overwhelmed

apacentar [3] *vt* to (put out to) graze, to pasture

apache 1 *adj* Apache
2 *nmf* Apache

apachurrado, -a *adj Méx Fam (triste, desanimado)* downhearted

apachurrar *vt Fam* to squash, to crush

apacible *adj* (**a**) *(temperamento, trato, persona)* mild, gentle (**b**) *(lugar, ambiente, clima)* pleasant (**c**) *(sueño, muerte)* peaceful

apaciblemente *adv (dormir, morir)* peacefully

apaciento *etc ver* **apacentar**

apaciguador, -ora *adj* calming

apaciguamiento *nm* calming; **una política de a.** a policy of appeasement

apaciguar [11] 1 *vt* (**a**) *(persona)* to calm down; **su discurso apaciguó los ánimos de la gente** his speech calmed people down; **no consiguieron a. su ira** they were unable to calm her anger (**b**) *(dolor)* to soothe
2 **apaciguarse** *vpr* (**a**) *(persona)* to calm down; **los ánimos se han apaciguado** people have calmed down (**b**) *(dolor)* to abate; *(mar)* to calm down; *(viento)* to drop

apadrinamiento *nm (de proyecto)* sponsorship, patronage; *(de candidato, artista)* patronage

apadrinar *vt* (**a**) *(en bautizo) (sujeto: hombre o mujer)* to act as a godparent to; *(sujeto: hombre)* to act as a godfather to; **a. una boda** = to act as sponsor for a couple who are getting married, accompanying them at the ceremony (**b**) *(apoyar) (proyecto)* to sponsor; *(candidato)* to support; **apadrinó a varios artistas** he was a patron to various artists

apagado, -a 1 *adj* (**a**) *(luz, fuego)* out; *(aparato)* off; **asegúrate de que el coche esté a.** make sure the car's engine isn't running (**b**) *(color)* subdued (**c**) *(sonido)* dull, muffled; *(voz)* low, quiet (**d**) *(persona)* subdued; **estás muy a., ¿qué te pasa?** you seem very subdued, what's wrong?
2 *nm Informát* shutdown ►► ***a. automático*** automatic shutdown

apagador *nm* (**a**) *(para velas)* snuffer (**b**) *Méx (para luz)* light switch

apagar [38] 1 *vt* (**a**) *(luz)* to switch off; *(aparato)* to turn *o* switch off; **apaga el horno** turn *o* switch off the oven; *Informát* **a. equipo** *(en menú)* shut down (**b**) *(extinguir) (fuego, cigarrillo, vela)* to put out; **"por favor apaguen sus cigarrillos"** "please extinguish your cigarettes" (**c**) *(reducir) (sed)* to quench; *(dolor)* to get rid of; *(color)* to soften; *(sonido)* to muffle; *(brillo)* to dull
2 *vi* EXPR *Esp Fam* **¡apaga y vámonos!: si eso es lo mejor que sabes hacer, ¡apaga y vámonos!** if that's the best you can do we might as well forget it; **si no quieren ayudarnos, ¡apaga y vámonos!** if they don't want to help us, let's not waste any more time over it
3 **apagarse** *vpr* (**a**) *(luz)* to go out; **tarda un par de minutos en apagarse** *(aparato)* it takes a couple of minutes to switch itself off; **de repente se apagó la televisión** the TV suddenly went off, the TV screen suddenly went blank
(**b**) *(extinguirse) (fuego, vela, cigarrillo)* to go out
(**c**) *(reducirse) (sed)* to be quenched; *(dolor, rencor)* to die down; *(color)* to fade; *(sonido)* to die away; *(brillo)* to become dull; *(ilusión)* to die, to be extinguished; *(vida)* to come to an end; **todavía no se han apagado los ecos del escándalo** the furore surrounding the scandal has yet to die down

apagavelas *nm inv* snuffer

apagón *nm* power cut

apaisado, -a *adj (orientación)* landscape; **un cuadro/espejo a.** a painting/mirror which is wider than it is high

apalabrar *vt* **ya tenemos la venta apalabrada** we've got a verbal agreement on the sale; **he apalabrado que venga a reparar la lavadora la semana que viene** we've agreed he'll come and fix the washing machine next week; **tengo apalabrada una pista para las siete** I've got *o* booked a court for us at seven o'clock; **no cumplió lo apalabrado** she didn't do what she'd agreed to, she didn't do what she said she would

Apalaches *nmpl* **los A.** the Appalachians

apalancado, -a *adj Esp Fam* **se pasó la tarde apalancada delante del televisor** she spent the afternoon lounging in front of the television

apalancamiento *nm Econ* leverage

apalancar [60] 1 *vt (para abrir, mover)* to lever open
2 **apalancarse** *vpr Esp Fam (apoltronarse)* to install oneself, to settle down; **cuando se apalanca en el sofá no hay quien lo mueva** once he's installed himself *o* settled down on the sofa there's no moving him

apalanque *nm Esp Fam* **¡tengo un a.!** I feel like I've put down roots here!

apaleamiento *nm* beating, thrashing

apalear *vt* (**a**) *(golpear) (persona)* to beat up; *(alfombra)* to beat (**b**) *(varear)* **a. un aceituno** to beat olives off the branches of an olive tree

apanar *vt Andes* to coat in breadcrumbs

apandar *vt Fam* to swipe

apantallar *vt* (**a**) *Méx (sorprender, impresionar)* to impress (**b**) *RP (abanicar)* to fan

apañado, -a *adj Fam* (**a**) *(hábil, mañoso)* clever, resourceful; **es muy apañada para las reparaciones domésticas** she's very clever *o* good at repairing things around the house
(**b**) *(buen administrador)* **una mujercita muy apañada** a woman who is good at making ends meet
(**c**) *(útil) (herramienta, tienda)* handy; **este gorro es muy a. para los días de frío** this cap is great for when it's cold; EXPR *Fam* **estar a.: ¡y ahora se va de vacaciones? ¡pues estamos apañados!** and now he's off on holiday? well that's just what we need!; **¡estaríamos apañados si ahora tuviéramos que pagar la cena también!** it really would be the last straw if we had to pay for the meal as well!; **¡están apañados si se piensan que vamos a aceptar!** if they think we're going to accept, they've got another think coming!

apañar *Fam* 1 *vt* (**a**) *(reparar)* to mend (**b**) *(amañar)* to fix, to arrange (**c**) *Andes, CAm, RP (encubrir)* to cover up for, to protect
2 *vi (sustraer)* **apañó con todo lo que encontró** he nabbed *o* lifted

everything he could lay his hands on

3 **apañarse** *vpr* (a) *Esp (arreglarse)* to cope, to manage; **se apaña con muy poco dinero** she gets by on very little money; **se las apañó para que la invitaran** she wangled an invitation; **no sé cómo te las apañas para trabajar y cuidar a tus hijos** I don't know how you cope *o* manage with the job and the kids to look after; **¿no quiso que le ayudáramos?, ahora que se las apañe** she didn't want us to help her? well, she'll just have to shift for herself, then

(b) *Méx* **apañarse con algo** *(apropiarse de, quedarse con)* to manage to get one's hands on sth

apaño *nm Fam* (a) *(reparación)* temporary repair, patch-up job; **esto ya no tiene a.** it's beyond fixing, it's had it (b) *(chanchullo)* fix, shady deal (c) *(acuerdo)* compromise (d) *(amorío)* **tener un a. con alguien** to have a thing going with sb

apapachado, -a *adj Méx Fam* pampered, spoilt

apapachador, -ora *adj Méx Fam* comforting

apapachar *vt Méx Fam* (a) *(mimar)* to cuddle (b) *(consentir)* to spoil

apapacho *nm Méx Fam (mimo)* cuddle

aparador *nm* (a) *(mueble bajo)* sideboard; *(mueble alto)* dresser (b) *(escaparate)* shop window

aparataje *nm* (a) *Am Fam (aparatos)* gear (b) *Andes Pol* machinery (of state *o* government)

aparato *nm* (a) *(máquina)* machine; *(electrodoméstico)* appliance; **compró un a. para medir el viento** she bought a device to measure the wind speed ▸▸ ***a. de diálisis*** dialysis machine; ***aparatos eléctricos*** electrical appliances; ***aparatos electrónicos*** electronic devices; ***aparatos de laboratorio*** laboratory apparatus; ***a. de radio*** radio; ***a. de televisión*** television set; ***a. de vídeo*** video recorder

(b) *(teléfono)* **¿quién está al a.?** who's speaking?; **¡al a.!** speaking!

(c) *(avión)* plane

(d) *(prótesis)* aid; *(para dientes)* braces, *Br* brace ▸▸ ***a. para sordos*** hearing aid

(e) *(en gimnasia) (en competición, escuela)* piece of apparatus; *(en gimnasio privado)* exercise machine ▸▸ ***aparatos gimnásticos*** *(en competición, escuela)* apparatus; ***a. de remo*** rowing machine

(f) *Anat* ***a. circulatorio*** circulatory system; ***a. digestivo*** digestive system; ***a. excretor*** excretory system; ***a. genital*** genitalia, genitals; ***a. locomotor*** locomotor system; ***a. olfativo*** olfactory system; ***a. reproductor*** reproductive system; ***a. respiratorio*** respiratory system; ***a. urinario*** urinary tract; ***a. visual*** visual system

(g) *Pol* **el a. del Estado** the machinery of the State; **el a. del partido** *(altos mandos)* the party leadership; *(organización)* the party machinery; **el a. represivo** the machinery of repression

(h) *(ostentación)* pomp, ostentation; **una boda con gran a.** a wedding with a lot of pomp and ceremony

(i) *Meteo* ***a. eléctrico*** thunder and lightning; **una tormenta con impresionante a. eléctrico** a storm with an impressive display of thunder and lightning

(j) *Fam (genitales de hombre)* equipment, *Br* tackle

aparatoso, -a *adj* (a) *(ostentoso)* ostentatious, showy (b) *(espectacular)* spectacular; **el accidente fue muy a., pero no ocurrió nada grave** the accident looked very spectacular, but no one was seriously injured

aparcacoches *nmf inv Esp (en hotel, discoteca)* parking valet

aparcamiento *nm Esp* (a) *(acción)* parking ▸▸ ***a. en batería*** = parking at an angle to the *Br* pavement *o US* sidewalk; ***a. en cordón*** = parking end-to-end; ***a. en línea*** = parking end-to-end

(b) *(para muchos vehículos) Br* car park, *US* parking lot ▸▸ ***a. disuasorio*** park-and-ride; ***a. subterráneo*** underground car park; ***a. vigilado*** *Br* car park *o US* parking lot with an attendant

(c) *(hueco)* parking place; **tardamos una hora en encontrar a.** it took us an hour to find somewhere to park

aparcar [60] 1 *vt Esp* (a) *(estacionar)* to park (b) *(posponer)* to shelve (c) *Informát (cabezales)* to park

2 *vi* to park; **prohibido a.** *(en cartel)* no parking

aparcería *nf* sharecropping

aparcero, -a *nm,f* sharecropper

apareamiento *nm* mating

aparear 1 *vt* to mate

2 **aparearse** *vpr* to mate

APARECER [46] 1 *vt Méx (presentar)* to produce; **inesperadamente Pedro apareció mis llaves** Pedro quite unexpectedly produced my keys; **el mago apareció un conejo de un sombrero** the magician pulled a rabbit out of a hat

2 *vi* (a) *(ante la vista)* to appear; **el sol apareció detrás de las murallas** the sun appeared *o* came up from behind the city walls; **a. de repente** to appear from nowhere; **el mago hizo a. un conejo de su chistera** the magician pulled a rabbit out of his hat; **su número de teléfono no aparece en la guía** her phone number isn't (listed) in the phone book

(b) *(publicación)* to come out; **la revista aparece los jueves** the magazine comes out *o* is published on Thursdays

(c) *(algo perdido)* to turn up; **¿ya ha aparecido el perro?** has the dog been found yet?; **ha aparecido un cuadro inédito de Miró** a previously unknown Miró painting has turned up *o* been discovered

(d) *(persona)* to appear; **a. en público** to appear in public; **aparece en varias películas de Ford** she appears in several of Ford's films; *Fam* **a. por** *(lugar)* to turn up at; *Fam* **hace días que Antonio no aparece por el bar** we haven't seen Antonio in the bar for days, it's several days since Antonio showed his face in the bar; *Fam* **¡a buenas horas apareces, ahora que ya hemos terminado!** it's a bit late turning up now, we've already finished!; *Fam* **¡y no se te ocurra volver a a. por aquí!** and don't let me see your face round here again!

3 **aparecerse** *vpr* (a) *(aparición)* to appear; **se le aparecen espíritus en sus sueños** she sees ghosts in her dreams; **se le apareció la Virgen** the Virgin Mary appeared to him; *Fam Fig* he had a real stroke of luck; *Fam* **como no se me aparezca la Virgen, no sé cómo voy a aprobar el examen** it's going to take a miracle for me to pass the exam

(b) *Am Fam (persona)* to turn up; **a esta hora es mejor que ni me aparezca** it's so late it would be better if I didn't show my face; **siempre se aparecen despeinados y sucios** they always turn up dishevelled and dirty

---

aparecido, -a *nm,f* (a) *(fantasma)* ghost (b) *Andes Fam Pey (advenedizo)* upstart

aparejado, -a *adj* **llevar** *o* **traer a.** *(conllevar)* to entail; **una reforma que trae aparejada una subida de precios** a reform which will mean *o* entail a price rise; **una infracción que lleva aparejada una multa de dos millones de pesos** an offence that carries a penalty of two million pesos

aparejador, -ora *nm,f* = on-site architect, responsible for the implementation of the designing architect's plans

aparejar *vt* (a) *(preparar)* to get ready, to prepare (b) *(caballerías)* to harness (c) *Náut* to rig (out)

aparejo *nm* (a) *(de caballerías)* harness (b) *(de pesca)* tackle (c) *Tec (de poleas)* block and tackle (d) *Náut* rigging; **aparejos** equipment

aparentar 1 *vt* (a) *(parecer)* to look, to seem; **no aparenta más de treinta** she doesn't look more than thirty (b) *(fingir)* to feign; **aparentó estar enfadado** he pretended to be angry, he feigned anger

2 *vi (presumir)* to show off; **viste así sólo para a.** she just dresses like that to show off

aparente *adj* (a) *(falso, supuesto)* apparent; **con su a. simpatía se ganó el aprecio del jefe** he won the boss over with his apparent friendliness; **ganaron con a. facilidad** they won with apparent ease

(b) *(visible)* visible; **las huelgas son una manifestación a. del descontento social** the strikes are a visible sign of social unrest; **se rompió sin causa a.** it broke for no apparent reason

(c) *(vistoso)* elegant, smart; **es un vestido muy a.** it's a very elegant dress

aparentemente *adv* apparently, seemingly; **colecciona objetos a. inútiles** she collects apparently *o* seemingly useless objects; **a. es muy antipático, pero en realidad no lo es** he comes across as rather unpleasant at first, but he isn't really

aparezco *etc ver* **aparecer**

aparición *nf* (a) *(de persona, cosa)* appearance; **un libro de reciente a.** a recently published book; **hizo su a. en la sala** she made her entrance into the hall (b) *(de ser sobrenatural)* apparition

apariencia *nf* (a) *(aspecto)* appearance; **un príncipe con a. de mendigo** a prince who looks like a beggar; **en a.** apparently; **se llevaban bien sólo en a.** they only appeared to get on well together

(b) **apariencias** *(indicios)* signs, indications; **las apariencias indican que la situación mejorará** the signs are that the situation will improve; **guardar las apariencias** to keep up appearances; EXPR **las apariencias engañan** appearances can be deceptive

(c) *(falsedad)* illusion

apartadero *nm* (a) *(ferrocarril)* siding ▸▸ ***a. muerto*** dead-end siding (b) *(en carretera)* passing place

apartado, -a 1 *adj* (a) *(separado)* **a. de** away from; **hoy día vive a. del mundo del teatro** nowadays he has very little to do with the theatre (b) *(alejado)* remote; **nuestra casa está bastante apartada del centro** our house is quite far from the centre

2 *nm (párrafo)* paragraph; *(sección)* section ▸▸ ***a. de correos*** Post Office box, PO Box; ***a. postal*** Post Office box, PO Box

apartahotel = **aparthotel**

apartamento *nm* (**a**) *esp Am (departamento) Br* flat, *US* apartment (**b**) *Esp (piso pequeño)* apartment

apartamiento *nm (aislamiento)* remoteness, isolation

APARTAR 1 *vt* (**a**) *(alejar)* to move away; *(quitar)* to remove; **¡apártense de la carretera, niños!** come away from the road, children!; **aparta el coche, que no puedo pasar** move the car out of the way, I can't get past; **aparta de mí estos pensamientos** *(cita bíblica)* protect me from such thoughts; **el polémico ministro ha sido apartado de su cargo** the controversial minister has been removed from his office; **a. la mirada** to look away; **no apartó la mirada de nosotros** he never took his eyes off us; **sus ojos no se apartaban de ella** his eyes never left her; **aparté la vista de aquel espectáculo tan desagradable** I averted my gaze *o* I turned away from that unpleasant sight; **a. a alguien de un codazo** to elbow sb aside; **a. a alguien de un empujón** to push sb out of the way

(**b**) *(separar)* to separate; **aparta las fichas blancas de las negras** separate the white counters from the black ones; **nadie los apartó, y acabaron a puñetazos** nobody attempted to separate them and they ended up coming to blows

(**c**) *(escoger)* to take, to select; **ya he apartado la ropa para el viaje** I've already put out the clothes for the journey

(**d**) *(disuadir)* to dissuade; **lo apartó de su intención de ser médico** she dissuaded him from becoming a doctor

2 **apartarse** *vpr* (**a**) *(hacerse a un lado)* to move to one side, to move out of the way; **¡apártense, es una emergencia!** make way, it's an emergency!; **¿podría apartarse, por favor?** could you move out of the way, please?; **apártate a un lado, por favor** please move aside *o* to one side; **se apartó para dejarme pasar** he stood aside to let me pass; **¡apártate de mi vista!** get out of my sight!

(**b**) *(separarse)* to separate, to move away from each other; **apartarse de** *(grupo, lugar)* to move away from; *(tema)* to get away from; *(mundo, sociedad)* to cut oneself off from; **se fue apartando gradualmente de sus amigos** she gradually drifted apart from her friends; **el partido se ha apartado de la ortodoxia leninista** the party has moved away from orthodox Leninism; **nos apartamos de la carretera** we left the road; **nos estamos apartando del camino** we are straying from the path; **el velero se apartó de la ruta** the sailing ship went off course

APARTE 1 *adv* (**a**) *(en otro lugar, a un lado)* aside, to one side; **las cartas urgentes ponlas a.** put the urgent letters to one side; **dejando a. tu último comentario...** leaving aside your last comment...; **bromas a.** joking apart

(**b**) *(por separado)* separately; **este paquete vino a.** this parcel came separately; **poner a. el grano y la paja** to separate the grain from the chaff; **la bufanda envuélvala a., es para regalar** please wrap the scarf up separately, it's a gift

(**c**) *(además)* besides; **y a. tiene otro todoterreno** and she has another four-wheel drive besides *o* too; **y a. no tengo por qué hacerte caso** and anyway *o* besides, there's no reason why I should take any notice of you; **a. de** apart from, except for; **a. de esta pequeña errata, el resto está perfecto** apart from *o* except for this small mistake, the rest is perfect; **a. de feo...** besides being ugly...; **no encontré otra razón a. de la que te he explicado** I couldn't find any reason for it other than the one I've told you; **a. de eso, no hay nada más que decir** other than that, there's nothing more to say; **a. de que no es un goleador nato, ha costado muy caro** quite apart from the fact that he isn't an instinctive goal scorer, he cost a lot of money; **es mi mejor amigo, a. de ti, claro está** he's my best friend, apart from you *o* except for you, of course

2 *adj inv* separate; **lo guardaré en un cajón a.** I'll keep it in a separate drawer; **es un poeta a., tremendamente original** he's in a league *o* class of his own as a poet, he's incredibly original; **ser caso** *o* **capítulo a.** to be a different matter; **tu hermana es un caso a.** your sister's a special case; **constituir una clase a.** to be in a league *o* class of one's own

3 *nm* (**a**) *(párrafo)* new paragraph

(**b**) *Teatro* aside; *Fig* **se lo dijo en un a.** she told him when the others couldn't hear her

apartheid [apar'χeið] (*pl* **apartheids**) *nm* apartheid

aparthotel, apartahotel, apartotel *nm* hotel apartments

apartosuite *nf* luxury hotel apartment

apartotel = **aparthotel**

apasionadamente *adv* passionately

apasionado, -a 1 *adj (amante, defensa)* passionate; *(lector)* very keen

2 *nm,f* lover, enthusiast; **es un a. de la música clásica** he's a lover of classical music

apasionamiento *nm* passion, enthusiasm; **con a.** passionately

apasionante *adj (tema, debate, viaje)* fascinating; *(partido)* thrilling

apasionar 1 *vt* to fascinate; **lo apasiona la música** he's mad about music; **no es un deporte que me apasione** it's not a sport I'm particularly keen on, it's not a sport that does a lot for me

2 **apasionarse** *vpr* to get excited *o* enthusiastic; **apasionarse por** to develop a passion for; **luego se apasionó por el tango durante una época** then he was really keen on tango for a while

apatía *nf* apathy; **con a.** apathetically

apático, -a 1 *adj* apathetic

2 *nm,f* apathetic person

apátrida 1 *adj* stateless

2 *nmf* stateless person

apdo., aptdo. *nm (abrev de* **apartado***)* PO Box; **a. de correos 8000** PO Box 8000

apeadero *nm (de tren)* = minor train stop with no permanent buildings, *Br* halt

apear 1 *vt* (**a**) *(bajar)* to take down (**b**) *Fam (disuadir)* **a. a alguien de** to talk sb out of; **no pudimos apearle de la idea** we couldn't get him to give up the idea (**c**) *CAm (regañar)* to tell off

2 **apearse** *vpr* (**a**) *(bajarse)* **apearse de** *(tren)* to alight (from), to get off; *(coche, autobús)* to get out (of); *(caballo)* to dismount (from) (**b**) *Fam* **apearse de** *(idea)* to give up; EXPR **apearse del burro** to back down

apechugar [38] *vi Fam* **a. con: tuve que a. con la limpieza de la casa** I got lumbered with doing the housework; **ahora vas a tener que a. con las consecuencias** now you're going to have to suffer *o* pay the consequences

apedreamiento *nm* (**a**) *(acción)* stone-throwing (**b**) *(matanza)* stoning

apedrear *vt* (**a**) *(tirar piedras a) (persona, cosa)* to throw stones at (**b**) *(matar)* to stone

apegarse [38] *vpr* **a. a algo/a alguien** to become fond of sth/sb

apego *nm* attachment, fondness; **siente** *o* **tiene mucho a. hacia su ciudad natal** she feels *o* is very attached to her home town; **su personaje representa el a. a los valores materiales** his character represents people who are attached to material things; **su a. a la vida le ayudó a sobrevivir la enfermedad** her love of life helped her to survive her illness; **una nación con mucho a. a la religión** a deeply religious nation; **es conocido por su a. a la ley** he's known as a law-abiding citizen

apelable *adj Der* open to appeal

apelación *nf* (**a**) *Der* appeal; **interponer una a.** to lodge *o* make an appeal (**b**) *(llamado)* appeal; **hizo una a. al sentimiento nacionalista** she made an appeal to nationalist sentiment

apelar *vi* (**a**) *Der* to (lodge an) appeal; **a. ante un tribunal** to appeal to a court; **a. contra algo** to appeal against sth (**b**) *(recurrir)* **a. a** *(persona)* to go to; *(sentido común, bondad, generosidad)* to appeal to; *(violencia)* to resort to

apelativo *nm* (**a**) *(nombre)* name; **más conocido con el a. de...** better known by the name of..., better known as... (**b**) *Ling* form of address; **un a. cariñoso** an affectionate form of address, a term of endearment

apellidar 1 *vt (apodar)* to call

2 **apellidarse** *vpr* **se apellida Suárez** her surname is Suárez

apellido *nm* surname ►► ***a. de casada*** married name; ***a. de soltera*** maiden name

apelmazado, -a *adj* (**a**) *(pelo)* matted; **el jersey está todo a.** the jumper has lost its fluffiness (**b**) *(arroz)* stodgy (**c**) *(bizcocho)* stodgy

apelmazar [14] 1 *vt* (**a**) *(jersey, pelo)* to matt (**b**) *(arroz)* to make stodgy (**c**) *(bizcocho)* to make stodgy

2 **apelmazarse** *vpr* (**a**) *(jersey, pelo)* to get matted (**b**) *(arroz)* to go stodgy (**c**) *(bizcocho)* to go stodgy

apelotonar 1 *vt* to bundle up

2 **apelotonarse** *vpr* (**a**) *(gente)* to crowd together; **el público se apelotonaba a la entrada del teatro** the audience crowded round the entrance to the theatre (**b**) *(comida)* to go lumpy

apenadamente *adv* sadly, with sadness

apenado, -a *adj* (**a**) *(entristecido)* sad; **estaba muy apenada por su muerte** she was greatly saddened by his death (**b**) *Andes, CAm, Carib, Méx (avergonzado)* embarrassed; **está muy a. por lo que hizo** he's very embarrassed about what he did

apenar 1 *vt (entristecer)* to sadden; **me apena que te vayas** I'm really sorry that you're leaving

2 **apenarse** *vpr* (**a**) *(entristecerse)* to be saddened; **se apenó mucho al recibir la noticia** she was very sad to hear the news (**b**) *Andes, CAm, Carib, Méx (avergonzarse)* to be embarrassed; **no te apenes, pídeme lo que precises** don't be embarrassed *o* shy, just ask me for whatever you need

---

APENAS 1 *adv* (**a**) *(casi no)* scarcely, hardly; **a. duerme/descansa** she hardly sleeps/rests at all; **no estudia a.** he hardly studies at all; **a. te dolerá** it will scarcely *o* hardly hurt at all; **¿solías ir a la discoteca? – a.** did you use to go to the disco? – hardly ever; **a. (si) me puedo mover** I can hardly move; **sin que a. protestara, sin que protestara a.** almost without her protesting (at all), without her hardly protesting (at all); **sin a. dinero** without hardly any money (at all), with next to no money; **sin a. comer** without hardly eating, without eating almost anything

(**b**) *(tan sólo)* only; **en a. dos minutos** in only two minutes, in little under two minutes; **hace a. dos minutos** only two minutes ago; **a. llevo dos horas en este país** I've hardly been in this country for two hours, I haven't been in this country for more than two hours

(**c**) *Méx (no antes de)* **a. me pagan el lunes** I won't get paid till Monday

2 *conj (tan pronto como)* as soon as; **a. conocido el resultado, comenzaron a celebrarlo** as soon as they heard the result, they started celebrating; **a. llegaron, se pusieron a comer** no sooner had they arrived than they began eating; **a. acabes, dímelo** let me know as soon as you've finished

---

apencar [60] *vi Fam* **a. con** *(responsabilidad)* to shoulder; *(consecuencias, dificultad)* to live with; **siempre me toca a. con el trabajo sucio** I always get lumbered with the dirty work

apendejamiento *nm CAm, Méx, Ven Fam* halfwittedness

apendejar *Fam* 1 *vt CAm, Méx, Ven* (**a**) *(atontar)* to make halfwitted (**b**) *Méx (acobardar)* to put the wind up, to scare

2 **apendejarse** *vpr* (**a**) *CAm, Méx, Ven (atontarse)* to go halfwitted; **se apendeja cada vez que ve un bebé** she goes all soppy whenever she sees a baby (**b**) *Méx (acobardarse)* to turn chicken; **se apendejaron ante el primer fracaso** they chickened out after the first setback

apéndice *nm* (**a**) *(de libro, documento)* appendix; *Fig* **está harta de ser un a. de su marido** she's tired of being just an appendage of her husband (**b**) *Anat (de intestino)* appendix ►► ***a. cecal*** vermiform appendix; ***a. nasal*** nose; *Fam Hum* **imenudo a. nasal!** what a *Br* conk *o US* schnozz!; ***a. vermicular*** (vermiform) appendix

apendicectomía *nf Med* appendectomy

apendicitis *nf inv* appendicitis; **me han operado de a.** I had my appendix out

Apeninos *nmpl* **los A.** the Apennines

apepsia *nf Med* apepsia

aperar *vt* (**a**) *Andes, RP, Ven (caballos)* to harness (**b**) *Ven (persona)* to equip

apercibimiento *nm Der* warning, notice; **la amenaza de a. de cierre se cierne sobre el estadio** the stadium is threatened with closure

apercibir 1 *vt* (**a**) *(reprender, advertir)* to reprimand, to give a warning to (**b**) *Der* to issue with a warning

2 **apercibirse** *vpr* **apercibirse de algo** to notice sth

apercollar *vt Col* to hug tightly

apergaminado, -a *adj (piel, papel)* parchment-like

apergaminarse *vpr (piel)* to become parchment-like

aperitivo *nm (bebida)* aperitif; *(comida)* appetizer; *(pincho con la cerveza)* bar snack; **salimos a tomar el a. con ellos** we went out to have a pre-lunch drink with them; *Fig* **iy esto es sólo un a.!** and that's just for starters!

apero *nm* (**a**) *(utensilio)* tool; **aperos (de labranza)** farming implements (**b**) *Andes, RP* **aperos** *(arneses)* riding gear, trappings

apersonarse *vpr* (**a**) *RP (presentarse)* to appear in person; **se apersonó en mi casa a pedir explicaciones** she came in person to my house to demand an explanation (**b**) *Col* **a. de algo** *(ocuparse)* to take care of sth; **me apersonaré del almuerzo** I'll take care of lunch

apertura 1 *nf* (**a**) *(acción de abrir) (de caja, cuenta corriente, investigación, tienda)* opening; **se ha anunciado la a. de negociaciones con la guerrilla** it has been announced that negotiations with the guerrillas have been started; **han pedido la a. de un expediente disciplinario** they have requested that disciplinary action be taken

(**b**) *(inauguración) (de año académico, temporada)* start; **el Presidente acudió a la a. de la nueva fábrica** the President attended the opening of the new factory

(**c**) *Dep (pase)* through ball; *(saque)* kick-off

(**d**) *(en ajedrez)* opening (move)

(**e**) *(tolerancia)* openness, tolerance

(**f**) *(en política, economía)* **el nuevo ministro es partidario de la a. política** the new minister is in favour of a more open regime; **buscan la a. de mercados en Asia** they are seeking to open up markets in Asia ►► ***a. económica*** economic liberalization

(**g**) *Fot* ***a. de campo*** field aperture

2 *nmf (en rugby)* fly-half

aperturismo *nm* (**a**) *(político, económico)* **un ministro representante del a.** a minister in favour of a more open regime; **a. económico** policy of economic liberalization (**b**) *(tolerancia)* openness, tolerance

aperturista 1 *adj* (**a**) *(en política)* in favour of a more open regime; *(en economía)* in favour of economic liberalization (**b**) *(tolerante)* open, tolerant

2 *nmf (en política)* supporter of a more open regime; *(en economía)* supporter of economic liberalization

apesadumbradamente *adv* sorrowfully

apesadumbrado, -a *adj* grieving, sorrowful

apesadumbrar 1 *vt* to sadden

2 **apesadumbrarse** *vpr* to be saddened; **se apesadumbró por la noticia** she was saddened by the news

apestado, -a 1 *adj Fam* (**a**) *Méx (con mala suerte)* unlucky; **está a.** he's unlucky (**b**) *Andes, RP Fam (enfermo)* sick; **está a.** he's sick

2 *nm,f* plague victim

apestar 1 *vi* to stink (**a** of); **huele que apesta** it stinks to high heaven; **la calle apesta a basura** the street stinks of rubbish; **todo este asunto apesta a corrupción** this whole affair reeks of corruption

2 *vt* (**a**) *(por mal olor)* to stink out (**b**) *(por peste)* to infect with the plague

apestoso, -a *adj* (**a**) *(que huele mal)* foul (**b**) *(fastidioso)* annoying; **iqué niño más a.!** that child's an utter pest!

apetecer [46] 1 *vi Esp* **¿te apetece un café?** do you fancy a coffee?; **¿qué te apetecería hacer?** what would you like to do?; **me apetece salir** I feel like going out; **hace siempre lo que le apetece** he always does what he likes *o* as he pleases

2 *vt* **tenían todo cuanto apetecían** they had everything they wanted; **no apetezco poder** I do not seek power

apetecible *adj* (**a**) *(comida)* appetizing, tempting (**b**) *(vacaciones, empleo)* desirable; *(oferta)* tempting; **un soltero muy a.** a very eligible bachelor

apetencia *nf* desire; **no tengo a. de poder** I have no desire for power, I do not seek power

apetezca *etc ver* **apetecer**

apetito *nm* (**a**) *(ganas de comer)* appetite; **abrir el a.** to whet one's appetite; **perder el a.** to lose one's appetite; **tener a.** to be hungry; **este niño tiene buen apetito** this child has a good appetite; **comer con buen a.** to eat heartily

(**b**) *(impulso, apetencia)* desire; **tiene un gran a. de conocimiento** she has a great hunger *o* desire for knowledge; **una novela que apela a los más bajos apetitos** a novel that plays on our basest instincts ►► ***a. sexual*** sexual appetite

apetitoso, -a *adj* (**a**) *(comida)* appetizing, tempting (**b**) *(vacaciones, empleo)* desirable; *(oferta)* tempting

ápex *nm Bot* apex

Apia *n* Apia

apiadarse *vpr* to show compassion; **a. de alguien** to take pity on sb

apiario *nm Am* apiary

apical *adj Ling* apical

ápice *nm* (**a**) *(vértice) (de montaña)* peak; *(de hoja, lengua)* tip (**b**) *(punto culminante)* peak, height (**c**) *(pizca)* **ni un á.** not a single bit; **no cedió un á.** he didn't budge an inch; **su popularidad no ha descendido un á.** her popularity has not gone down in the slightest; **no se ha movido un á.** she hasn't moved an inch

apícola *adj* = related to beekeeping

apicultor, -ora *nm,f* beekeeper

apicultura *nf* beekeeping

apilable *adj (mesas, sillas, piezas)* stackable

apilamiento *nm* (**a**) *(acción)* piling up (**b**) *(montón)* pile, stack

apilar, *Ven* **apilonar** 1 *vt* to pile up

2 **apilarse** *vpr* to pile up; **se nos está apilando el trabajo** we've got a backlog of work building up

apiñado, -a *adj (apretado)* packed, crammed

apiñamiento *nm* cramming

apiñar 1 *vt* to pack
2 **apiñarse** *vpr (agolparse)* to crowd together; *(para protegerse, por miedo)* to huddle together; **apiñarse en torno a algo/alguien** to huddle round sth/sb

apiñonado, -a *adj Méx (piel)* bronze; *(persona)* bronze-skinned

apio *nm* celery

apiolar *Fam* 1 *vt* (**a**) *Esp (matar)* to bump off, *US* to whack (**b**) *(informar)* to fill in; **Pedro me apioló de cómo pagar menos luz** Pedro told me *o* filled me in on how to cut my electricity bill
2 **apiolarse** *vpr* to get clued up; **ya me apiolé del recorrido de los micros** I've already got clued up *o* found out about the bus routes

apirético, -a 1 *adj* antipyretic
2 *nm* antipyretic

apisonado, apisonamiento *nm* rolling, levelling

apisonadora *nf* (**a**) *(vehículo)* steamroller (**b**) *Fam (persona, equipo)* **los guerrilleros fueron incapaces de hacer frente a la a. militar francesa** the guerrillas were steamrollered by the French army

apisonamiento = **apisonado**

apisonar *vt (con vehículo apisonadora)* to roll; *(con apisonadora manual)* to tamp down

apitutado, -a *nm,f Chile Fam* = person who has got where they are through connections

apitutar *vt Chile Fam* **su padre lo apitutó en la compañía** his father got him a job in the company by pulling strings

aplacamiento *nm* calming

aplacar [60] 1 *vt* (**a**) *(persona, ánimos)* to placate; **aplacaron su ira** they appeased his anger (**b**) *(hambre)* to satisfy; *(sed)* to quench; *(dolor)* to ease
2 **aplacarse** *vpr* (**a**) *(persona, ánimos)* to calm down (**b**) *(dolor, tempestad)* to abate

aplanadora *nf Am (vehículo)* steamroller

aplanar 1 *vt* (**a**) *(superficie)* to level (**b**) *(desanimar)* **este calor me aplana** this heat really saps my energy
2 **aplanarse** *vpr* (**a**) *(superficie)* to level out (**b**) *(desanimarse)* to become apathetic

aplanchar *CAm, Col* 1 *vt* to iron
2 *vi* to do the ironing

aplasia *nf Med* aplasia

aplastamiento *nm* (**a**) *(por peso)* squashing, crushing; **murieron por a.** they were crushed to death (**b**) *CSur (falta de ánimo)* lack of enthusiasm; **se sentía un terrible a. entre los militantes** the party activists felt utterly deflated

aplastante *adj (victoria, derrota)* crushing, overwhelming; *(apoyo, mayoría, superioridad)* overwhelming; **esa argumentación es de una lógica a.** that line of reasoning is devastating in its logic

aplastar 1 *vt* (**a**) *(por peso)* to squash, to crush (**b**) *(equipo, revuelta)* to crush (**c**) *Fam (confundir)* to leave dumbfounded *o* speechless
2 **aplastarse** *vpr* (**a**) *(por el peso)* to get squashed *o* crushed (**b**) *Méx Fam (dejarse caer)* to collapse, to slump

aplatanado, -a *adj Esp, Méx Fam* **este calor me deja a.** I can't do anything in this heat; **allí están todos como aplatanados** they're so laid back there they're almost horizontal

aplatanamiento *nm Esp, Méx Fam* **por las tardes me entra un a. terrible** in the afternoons I feel like I can't lift a finger

aplatanar *Esp, Méx Fam* 1 *vt* **este calor me aplatana** I can't do anything in this heat
2 **aplatanarse** *vpr* **por las tardes se aplatanan** they're not up to doing a thing in the afternoons

aplaudir 1 *vt* (**a**) *(dar palmadas)* to applaud; **el público lo aplaudió a rabiar** the audience applauded him wildly (**b**) *(aprobar)* to applaud; **aplaudo su propuesta** I applaud your proposal
2 *vi* to applaud, to clap

aplauso *nm* (**a**) *(ovación)* round of applause; **aplausos** applause; **pido un a. para...** please put your hands together for..., could we have a big hand for...; **recibió un a. cerrado** she received rapturous applause (**b**) *(alabanza)* praise, acclaim; **su actitud merece nuestro a.** her attitude should be applauded by us; **recibir el a. de la crítica** to be praised by the critics

aplazable *adj* postponable

aplazado, -a 1 *adj* (**a**) *(viaje)* postponed; *(reunión, juicio) (antes de empezar)* postponed; *(ya empezado)* adjourned (**b**) *RP (en examen)* **hubo treinta alumnos aplazados en su clase y sólo dos en la mía** thirty pupils failed in his class and only two in mine
2 *nm,f RP* **los aplazados tienen que rendir otra vez el examen en febrero** those who failed have to resit the exam in February

aplazamiento *nm* (**a**) *(de viaje)* postponement; *(de reunión, juicio) (antes de empezar)* postponement; *(ya empezado)* adjournment; **el presidente ordenó el a. de la reunión** the chairman adjourned the meeting (**b**) *(de pago)* deferral

aplazar [14] *vt* (**a**) *(viaje)* to postpone; *(reunión, juicio) (antes de empezar)* to postpone; *(ya empezado)* to adjourn (**b**) *(pago)* to defer (**c**) *RP (en examen)* to fail

aplicabilidad *nf* applicability; **una ley con una a. estrictamente regional** a law which is only applicable at regional level

aplicable *adj* applicable (**a** to)

aplicación *nf* (**a**) *(de técnica, teoría)* application; *(de plan)* implementation; *(de sanciones)* imposition; **una ley de a. inmediata** a law that will take immediate effect; **exigen la a. del acuerdo de paz** they are demanding that the peace agreement should be implemented
(**b**) *(de pomada, vendaje, pintura)* application
(**c**) *(uso)* application, use; **las aplicaciones de la energía hidroeléctrica** the different applications *o* uses of hydroelectric power
(**d**) *(al estudio)* application; **su a. al trabajo** the application she shows in her work
(**e**) *(adorno)* appliqué
(**f**) *Informát* application
(**g**) *Mat* map, function
(**h**) *Andes (solicitud)* application

aplicado, -a *adj* (**a**) *(estudioso)* diligent (**b**) *(ciencia)* applied

aplicador *nm* applicator

aplicar [60] 1 *vt* (**a**) *(técnica, teoría)* to apply; *(plan)* to implement; *(sanciones)* to impose; *(nombre, calificativo)* to give, to apply (**b**) *(pomada, vendaje, pintura)* to apply; **aplicó alcohol en la herida** she cleaned the wound with alcohol
2 *vi Andes (postular)* to apply (**a** for)
3 **aplicarse** *vpr* (**a**) *(esmerarse)* to apply oneself; **se aplicó mucho en los estudios** he applied himself very hard to his studies
(**b**) *(concernir)* **aplicarse a** to apply to; **el artículo 28 se aplicará en los siguientes casos...** article 28 shall apply in the following cases...; **este recargo no se aplicará a los pensionistas** this extra charge does not apply to pensioners
(**c**) *(a uno mismo)* **... ¡y aplícate eso a ti también!** ... and that goes for you as well!

aplique *nm* (**a**) *(lámpara)* wall lamp (**b**) *(en ropa)* appliqué (**c**) *RP (de pelo)* hairpiece, hair extension

aplomado, -a *adj* (**a**) *(sereno)* self-assured, self-possessed (**b**) *(plomizo)* lead-coloured

aplomarse *vpr (serenarse)* to become self-assured *o* self-possessed

aplomo *nm* self-assurance, self-possession; **respondió con a.** she answered with aplomb; **actuó con a.** he acted with assurance

apnea *nf* (**a**) *Med* apnoea ►► ***a. del sueño*** sleep apnoea (**b**) *Dep (buceo)* free diving

apocado, -a *adj* timid

apocalipsis *nm inv* (**a**) **el A.** *(libro)* the Apocalypse, Revelations (**b**) **el A.** *(fin del mundo)* the end of the world (**c**) *(calamidad)* calamity

apocalíptico, -a *adj* apocalyptic

apocamiento *nm* timidity

apocar [60] 1 *vt (intimidar)* to intimidate, to make nervous
2 **apocarse** *vpr (intimidarse)* to be frightened *o* scared; *(humillarse)* to humble oneself

apocopado, -a *adj Gram* apocopated

apocopar *vt Gram* to apocopate

apócope *nf Gram* apocopation

apócrifo, -a *adj* apocryphal

apodar 1 *vt* to nickname
2 **apodarse** *vpr* to be nicknamed; **se apoda "el Flaco"** he's known as "el Flaco"

apoderado, -a *nm,f* (**a**) *Der* (official) representative (**b**) *(de torero, deportista)* agent, manager

apoderamiento *nm (apropiación)* appropriation, seizure

apoderar 1 *vt* (**a**) *(autorizar)* to authorize, to empower; *Der* to grant power of attorney to (**b**) *(torero, deportista)* **a. a alguien** to be/become sb's manager *o* agent
2 **apoderarse** *vpr* (**a**) **apoderarse de** *(adueñarse de)* to seize; **los sublevados se apoderaron del aeropuerto** the rebels took control of *o* seized the airport; **el atracador se apoderó de varios rehenes** the armed robber took several hostages; **los radicales se apoderaron del control del partido** the radicals took *o* seized control of the party; **la oscuridad se apoderaba de la casa** darkness was gradually taking over the house

(**b**) **apoderarse de** *(dominar)* to overcome; **el miedo se apoderó de él** he was overcome with *o* by fear; **después de comer la pereza se apodera de mí** after eating I feel extremely lethargic

apodo *nm* nickname

apófisis *nf inv Anat* apophysis, bony process

apogeo *nm* (**a**) *(cumbre)* height, apogee; **está en el a. de su carrera política** she's at the height of her political career; **el feudalismo estaba entonces en pleno a.** at that time feudalism was at its height, this time marked the apogee of the feudal system (**b**) *Astron* apogee

apolillado, -a *adj* (**a**) *(ropa)* moth-eaten (**b**) *(sin usar)* **tienes la máquina de coser apolillada** your sewing machine is just gathering dust; **tengo los logaritmos un poco apolillados** I'm a bit rusty on logarithms (**c**) *(anticuado)* **unos métodos apolillados** dusty old methods

apolillar 1 *vi RP Fam (dormir)* to snooze, to doze
2 **apolillarse** *vpr* (**a**) *(ropa)* to get moth-eaten (**b**) *(no usarse) (objetos)* to gather dust; *(método)* to get *o* become outdated

apolillo *nm RP Fam* sleepiness; **tener a.** to be sleepy

apolíneo, -a *adj* (**a**) *(en belleza)* **un joven a.** *o* **de una belleza apolínea** a young man who looks like a Greek god, a young Adonis (**b**) *Mitol* Apollonian

apolítico, -a *adj* apolitical

Apolo *n Mitol* Apollo

apologética *nf Rel* apologetics *(singular)*

apologético, -a *adj* apologetic

apología *nf* (**a**) *(defensa)* **hacer a. de algo** to defend *o* justify sth; **le acusaron de a. del terrorismo** they accused him of supporting o defending terrorism (**b**) *(texto)* apologia

apologista *nmf* apologist

apoltronarse *vpr* **a. en** *(sillón)* to make oneself comfortable in; **se ha apoltronado mucho desde que se casó** he's settled into an easy life since he (got) married; **se ha apoltronado en su puesto** she's settled into a cosy rut at work

aponeurosis *nf inv Anat* aponeurosis

apoplejía *nf Med* apoplexy

apopléjico, -a, apoplético, -a *adj* apoplectic

apoquinar *Esp Fam* 1 *vt* to fork out, to cough up
2 *vi* to cough up; **aquí hay alguien que no ha apoquinado** someone here hasn't paid their share

aporcar *vt Agr* to earth up

aporreado,-a 1 *adj (pobre, mísero)* wretched
2 *nm Cuba, Méx* = beef stew with tomato and garlic

aporrear *vt* (**a**) *(puerta)* to bang *o* hammer on; **a. el piano** to bang *o* plonk away on the piano (**b**) *(persona)* to beat; **lo aporreó a puñetazos** she beat him with her fists

aportación *nf* (**a**) *(contribución)* contribution; **su trabajo es una valiosa a. al estudio de la enfermedad** her work constitutes a valuable contribution to the study of the disease; **hacer una a.** to contribute; **hizo una a. de 10.000 pesos** she made a contribution of 10,000 pesos (**b**) *Fin (bien aportado)* investment

aportar 1 *vt (contribuir con)* to contribute; **cada empresa aportará cien millones** every company will contribute a hundred million; **todos los miembros del equipo aportaron ideas** all the members of the team contributed their ideas; **el campeón argentino aporta diez jugadores al equipo nacional** the Argentinian champions provide ten of the players in the national team; **el informe no aporta nada nuevo** the report doesn't say anything new
2 *vi* (**a**) *RP (a seguridad social)* to pay social security contributions (**b**) *CSur Fam (aparecer)* to turn up

aporte *nm* (**a**) *(aportación)* contribution ►► ***a. calórico*** calorie content; ***a. vitamínico*** vitamin content (**b**) *Geol* supply (**c**) *RP (a seguridad social)* social security contribution

aposentaduría *nf Chile* seat

aposentar 1 *vt* to put up, to lodge
2 **aposentarse** *vpr* (**a**) *(fijar su residencia)* to take up residence (**b**) *(residir)* to reside

aposento *nm* (**a**) *(habitación)* room; *Anticuado o Hum* **se retiró a sus aposentos** she withdrew (to her chamber) (**b**) *(alojamiento)* lodgings

aposición *nf Gram* apposition; **en a.** in apposition

apósito *nm* dressing

aposta *adv Esp* on purpose, intentionally

apostadero *nm Mil* naval station

apostante *nmf* (**a**) *(que apuesta) Br* better, *US* bettor (**b**) *(en lotería)* = person who plays a lottery

apostar [64] 1 *vt* (**a**) *(jugarse)* to bet; **te apuesto una cena a que gana el Madrid** I bet you (the price of) a dinner that Madrid will win; **te apuesto lo que quieras a que tengo razón** I bet you anything you like I'm right (**b**) *(emplazar)* to post
2 *vi* (**a**) *(confiar en)* **a. por: ¿quién crees que ganará? – yo apuesto por Rodriguez** who do you think will win? – my money is on Rodriguez; **la empresa apostó fuerte por Internet** the company has committed itself to the Internet in a big way; **el electorado ha apostado por el cambio** the electorate has opted for change; **apostó por su vicepresidente para llevar a cabo la reforma** he entrusted the implementation of the reform to the vice-president
(**b**) *(tener seguridad en)* **apuesto a que no viene** I bet he doesn't come
3 **apostarse** *vpr* (**a**) *(jugarse)* to bet; **apostarse algo con alguien** to bet sb sth; **¿qué te apuestas a que no viene?** how much do you bet he won't come? (**b**) *(colocarse)* to post oneself; **se apostó detrás de un árbol** she posted herself behind a tree

apostasía *nf* apostasy

apóstata *nmf* apostate

apostatar *vi (renegar)* to apostatize

a posteriori *loc adv* with hindsight; **habrá que juzgarlo a.** we'll have to judge it after the event

apostilla *nf* (**a**) *(nota)* note (**b**) *(comentario)* comment

apostillar *vt* (**a**) *(anotar)* to annotate (**b**) *(añadir)* to add

apóstol *nm* (**a**) *Rel* apostle (**b**) *(de ideales)* apostle

apostolado *nm Rel* (**a**) *(de apóstol)* apostolate (**b**) *(de ideales)* mission

apostólico, -a *adj Rel* (**a**) *(de los apóstoles)* apostolic (**b**) *(del papa) (bendición)* papal; *(iglesia católica)* apostolic

apóstrofe *nm o nf Lit* apostrophe

apóstrofo *nm (signo)* apostrophe

apostura *nf* dashing appearance

apoteósico, -a *adj* tremendous; **la ópera tiene un final a.** the opera has a tremendous finale; **lograron un triunfo a.** they achieved a famous victory

apoteosis *nf inv* (**a**) *(culminación)* crowning moment, culmination (**b**) *(final)* grand finale

apoyabrazos *nm inv* armrest

apoyacabezas *nm inv* headrest

apoyamuñecas *nm inv* wrist rest

apoyar 1 *vt* (**a**) *(inclinar)* to lean, to rest; **apoya la cabeza en mi hombro** rest your head on my shoulder; **apoyó la bicicleta contra la pared** she leant the bicycle against the wall; **apoyó los codos sobre la mesa** he leant his elbows on the table
(**b**) *(respaldar)* to support; **todos apoyaron su decisión** everyone supported her decision; **lo apoyó mucho durante su depresión** she gave him a lot of support when he was depressed; **los directivos los apoyaron en su protesta** management supported their protest
(**c**) *(basar)* to base; **apoya su teoría en datos concretos** her theory is based on *o* supported by concrete statistics
2 **apoyarse** *vpr* (**a**) *(sostenerse)* **apoyarse en** to lean on; **la anciana se apoyaba en un bastón** the old woman was leaning on a walking-stick; **hace el pino apoyándose sólo en una mano** he can do a handstand supporting his weight on only one hand; **la estatua se apoya sobre dos pilares** the statue is supported by two pillars
(**b**) *(basarse)* **apoyarse en** *(sujeto: tesis, conclusiones)* to be based on; *(sujeto: persona)* to base one's arguments on; **¿en qué te apoyas para hacer semejante afirmación?** what do you base that statement on?, what grounds do you have for making that statement?
(**c**) *(buscar respaldo)* **apoyarse en** to rely on; **cuando estuvo desempleado se apoyó en su familia** he relied on his family to support him while he was unemployed
(**d**) *(respaldarse mutuamente)* to support one another

apoyatura *nf Mús* appoggiatura

apoyo *nm* support; **salieron adelante con el a. de su familia** they got by with the support of her family; **me dio su a. moral** she gave me her moral support; **buscan apoyos económicos para el proyecto** they are seeking funding *o* financial support for the project; **anunciaron su a. a la iniciativa** they declared their support for the initiative; **presentó las pruebas en a. de su teoría** he presented the evidence to support his theory

apozarse *vpr Andes (rebalsarse)* to overflow

applet ['aplet] (*pl* **applets**) *nm Informát* applet

APRA ['apra] *nf*

Takes the masculine articles **el** and **un**.

(*abrev de* **Alianza Popular Revolucionaria Americana**) = Peruvian political party to the centre-right of the political spectrum

apreciable *adj* (**a**) *(perceptible) (diferencias, mejoría)* appreciable, perceptible (**b**) *(considerable) (cantidad)* appreciable, significant (**c**) *(estimable)* worthy

apreciación *nf* (**a**) *(estimación)* assessment, evaluation; **un error de a.** an error of judgement; **todos han coincidido en su a. negativa de las reformas** everyone agreed with his negative assessment *o* evaluation of the reforms (**b**) *(de moneda)* appreciation

apreciado, -a *adj* (**a**) *(querido)* esteemed, highly regarded (**b**) *(valorado)* prized (**por** by)

apreciar 1 *vt* (**a**) *(valorar)* to appreciate, to value; **aprecio mucho tu ayuda** I really appreciate your help; **aprecia demasiado las cosas materiales** she puts too high a value on material things; **un plato muy apreciado por los turistas** a dish that is very popular with tourists; **no sabe a. una buena obra de teatro** he doesn't know how to appreciate a good play

(**b**) *(sentir afecto por)* **aprecio mucho a tu hermana** I think a lot of your sister, I'm very fond of your sister

(**c**) *(percibir)* to detect, to notice; **han apreciado una mejora significativa** they have detected *o* noticed a significant improvement; **acércate si quieres a. mejor los detalles** come closer so you can see the detail better

2 apreciarse *vpr* (**a**) *(moneda)* to appreciate

(**b**) *(notarse)* to be noticeable; **no se apreciaba ninguna diferencia entre los dos** there was no noticeable difference between them; **el agujero se aprecia a simple vista** the hole can be seen with the naked eye; **en el gráfico se aprecia un incremento espectacular de los ingresos** in the graph we can see a spectacular growth in income, the graph shows a spectacular growth in income

apreciativo, -a *adj* (**a**) *(gesto)* appraising; **una mirada apreciativa** an appraising look (**b**) *(valor)* estimated; **un cálculo a.** an estimate

aprecio *nm* **sentir a. por alguien** to think highly of sb; **se ganó el a. de todos** he came to be highly regarded by everyone; **no gozó en vida del a. de la crítica** she did not enjoy critical acclaim during her lifetime

aprehender *vt* (**a**) *(coger) (persona)* to apprehend; *(alijo, mercancía)* to seize (**b**) *(comprender)* to take in

aprehensión *nf (de persona)* arrest, capture; *(de alijo, mercancía)* seizure

apremiante *adj* pressing, urgent

apremiar 1 *vt* (**a**) *(meter prisa)* **a. a alguien para que haga algo** to put pressure on sb to do sth; **nos apremian para que acabemos cuanto antes** they are putting pressure on us to finish as soon as possible (**b**) *(obligar)* **a. a alguien a hacer algo** to compel sb to do sth

2 *vi (ser urgente)* **el tiempo apremia** we're running out of time, time is short; **apremia que se tome una decisión** a decision urgently needs to be taken

apremio *nm* (**a**) *(urgencia)* urgency; **hacer algo con a.** *(con prisa)* to do sth hastily *o* in a rush (**b**) *Der (mandamiento)* writ; **reclamar algo por vía de a.** to issue a writ for sth (**c**) *RP* ***apremios físicos*** physical torture; ***apremios ilegales*** torture

aprender 1 *vt* to learn; **aprendí mucho de mi profesor** I learned a lot from my teacher; **a. a hacer algo** to learn to do sth; **a. algo de memoria** to learn sth by heart; *Fig* **parece que no han aprendido la lección** it seems like they haven't learned their lesson

2 *vi* to learn; **¡aprende de tu hermana!** learn from your sister!; **¡para que aprendas!** that'll teach you!; **¡así aprenderá!** that'll teach him!; **¡nunca aprenderán!** they'll never learn!

3 aprenderse *vpr* **aprenderse algo** to learn sth; **tengo que aprenderme la tabla de los elementos** I have to learn the periodic table; **aprenderse algo de memoria** to learn sth by heart

aprendiz, -iza *nm,f* (**a**) *(ayudante)* apprentice; **es a. de carpintero** he's an apprentice carpenter, he's a carpenter's apprentice (**b**) *(novato)* beginner

aprendizaje *nm* (**a**) *(adquisición de conocimientos)* learning; **el a. de un oficio** learning a trade ►► ***a. de idiomas*** language learning (**b**) *(para trabajo)* apprenticeship

aprensión *nf* (**a**) *(miedo)* apprehension (**por** about); **la decisión fue recibida con a.** people reacted apprehensively to the decision (**b**) *(escrúpulo)* squeamishness (**por** about); **me dan a. las lombrices** I'm squeamish about worms

aprensivo, -a *adj* (**a**) *(miedoso)* apprehensive (**b**) *(escrupuloso)* squeamish (**c**) *(hipocondríaco)* hypochondriac

apresamiento *nm* (**a**) *(de delincuente)* arrest, capture (**b**) *(de barco)* capture, seizure

apresar *vt* (**a**) *(delincuente)* to catch, to capture (**b**) *(barco)* to seize (**c**) *(presa)* to catch

apres-ski 1 *adj inv* après-ski

2 *nm* après-ski

aprestar 1 *vt* (**a**) *(preparar)* to prepare, to get ready (**b**) *(tela)* to size

2 aprestarse *vpr* **aprestarse a hacer algo** to get ready to do sth

apresto *nm* (**a**) *(rigidez de la tela)* stiffness; **el almidón da a. a las telas** starch is used to stiffen cloth (**b**) *(sustancia)* size

apresuradamente *adv* (**a**) *(con rapidez)* hurriedly; **evacuaron el edificio a.** they hurriedly evacuated the building; **tuvo que regresar a. a Caracas** she had to return to Caracas in a hurry (**b**) *(con precipitación)* hastily; **fue una decisión tomada a.** it was a hastily taken decision

apresurado, -a *adj (viaje)* hurried; *(decisión)* hasty; **se retiraron de forma apresurada** they hastily *o* hurriedly withdrew

apresuramiento *nm* haste; **hacer algo con a.** to do sth hurriedly *o* hastily

apresurar 1 *vt* (**a**) *(meter prisa a)* to hurry along, to speed up; **nos apresuró para que termináramos** he tried to get us to finish quicker; **no quiero a. las cosas** I don't want to rush things (**b**) *(acelerar)* **a. el paso** to quicken one's pace; **apresura la marcha o no llegaremos** hurry up or we won't arrive on time

2 apresurarse *vpr* to hurry; **¡apresúrate!** hurry up!; **apresurarse a hacer algo: se apresuró a aclarar que no sabía nada** she was quick to point out that she knew nothing; **los vecinos se apresuraron a ayudar** the neighbours rushed to help

apretadamente *adv (por poco, con justeza)* narrowly

apretado, -a 1 *adj* (**a**) *(ropa, nudo, tuerca)* tight; **estos pantalones me quedan apretados** these trousers are too tight for me

(**b**) *(estrujado)* cramped; **en esta oficina estamos muy apretados** we're very cramped in this office; **íbamos un poco apretados en el coche** it was a bit of a squeeze in the car

(**c**) *(caligrafía)* cramped

(**d**) *(triunfo)* narrow; *(esprint)* close

(**e**) *(de tiempo)* busy; **tengo unas tardes muy apretadas** my afternoons are very busy

(**f**) *(de dinero)* **vamos muy apretados** things are very tight at the moment, we're very short of money at the moment; **están pasando una época apretada** they're going through hard times

(**g**) *Fam (tacaño)* tight

(**h**) *Méx Fam (orgulloso)* stuck-up, snotty

(**i**) *Méx Fam Pey (reprimido)* strait-laced, uptight

(**j**) *Ven Fam (estricto)* strict

2 *nm,f Méx Fam Pey (reprimido)* strait-laced *o* uptight person

APRETAR [3] **1** *vt* (**a**) *(oprimir) (botón, tecla)* to press; *(gatillo)* to pull, to squeeze; *(acelerador)* to step on; **el zapato me aprieta** my shoe is pinching; **me aprietan las botas** my boots are too tight

(**b**) *(nudo, tuerca, cinturón)* to tighten; EXPR *Fam* **a. las clavijas** *o* **los tornillos a alguien** to put the screws on sb

(**c**) *(juntar) (dientes)* to grit; *(labios)* to press together; *(puño)* to clench; **tendrás que a. la letra** you'll have to squeeze your handwriting up

(**d**) *(estrechar)* to squeeze; *(abrazar)* to hug; **no me aprietes el brazo, me estás haciendo daño** stop squeezing my arm, you're hurting me; **la apretó contra su pecho** he held her to his chest; **a. la mano a alguien** to shake sb's hand

(**e**) *(acelerar)* **a. el paso** *o* **la marcha** to quicken one's pace; **como no apretemos el paso, no llegaremos nunca** if we don't hurry up, we'll never get there

(**f**) *(exigir)* to tighten up on; *(presionar)* to press; **a. la disciplina** to tighten up on discipline; **lo apretaron tanto que acabó confesando** they pressed him so hard that he ended up confessing; **no me gusta que me aprieten en el trabajo** I don't like to feel pressurized in my work; **lo están apretando para que acepte la oferta** they are pressing him *o* putting pressure on him to accept the offer

(**g**) *(ropa, objetos)* to pack tight

2 *vi* (**a**) *(calor, lluvia)* to get worse, to intensify; **salgo de casa a las dos, cuando más aprieta el calor** I leave home at two o'clock, when the heat is at its worst; **en agosto ha apretado mucho el calor** it got a lot hotter in August; **cuando la necesidad aprieta, se agudiza el ingenio** people become more resourceful when they really have to

(**b**) *(zapatos)* to pinch; *(ropa)* to be too tight

(**c**) *(esforzarse)* to push oneself; **tienes que a. más si quieres aprobar** you'll have to pull your socks up if you want to pass

(**d**) *Fam* **a. a correr** to run off; **el ladrón apretó a correr** the thief ran off

3 apretarse *vpr (agolparse)* to crowd together; *(acercarse)* to squeeze up; EXPR **apretarse el cinturón** to tighten one's belt; **si nos apretamos un poco cabremos todos** if we squeeze up a bit we can all fit in

apretón *nm (estrechamiento)* squeeze; **apretones** crush; **hubo apretones para entrar** there was a crush to get in ►► ***a. de manos*** handshake; **se dieron un cálido a. de manos** they shook hands warmly

apretujamiento *nm (de personas)* crush, squeeze

apretujar 1 *vt* (**a**) *(aplastar)* to squash (**b**) *(hacer una bola con)* to screw up
2 **apretujarse** *vpr* (**a**) *(en banco, autobús)* to squeeze together; **si nos apretujamos, cabemos todos** if we squeeze up, there will be room for everyone (**b**) *(por frío)* to huddle up

apretujón *nm (abrazo)* bear hug; **hubo apretujones para entrar en el cine** there was a crush to get into the cinema

apretura *nf* (**a**) *(apretujón)* crush (**b**) *(escasez)* **pasar apreturas** to be hard up

aprieto 1 *ver* **apretar**
2 *nm* fix, difficult situation; **estar en un a.** to be in a fix; **poner en un a. a alguien** to put sb in a difficult position; **salir de un a.** to get out of a fix *o* difficult situation

a priori *adv* (**a**) *(con antelación)* in advance; **es difícil saber a. qué va a pasar** it's difficult to know what will happen beforehand, it's difficult to know in advance what will happen (**b**) *Der & Filosofía* a priori

apriorístico, -a *adj* **hacer juicios apriorísticos** to prejudge things

aprisa *adv* fast, quickly; **ia.!** quick!; **tenemos que ir más a.** we need to go faster *o* more quickly; **tuvimos que hacer el equipaje a. y corriendo** we had to pack in a rush

aprisco *nm* fold, pen

aprisionamiento *nm* **el derrumbe ocasionó el a. de tres personas** three people were trapped when the building collapsed

aprisionar *vt* **a. a alguien con cadenas** to put sb in chains; **quedaron aprisionados bajo los escombros** they were trapped under the rubble; **la viga le aprisionaba la pierna** her leg was trapped under the beam

aprista 1 *adj* = of/relating to the Peruvian APRA party
2 *nmf* = member/supporter of the Peruvian APRA party

aprobación *nf* (**a**) *(de proyecto, medida)* approval; *(de ley, moción)* passing; **dio su a. al proyecto** he gave the project his approval, he approved the project (**b**) *(de comportamiento)* approval

aprobado, -a 1 *adj (aceptado)* approved
2 *nm Educ* = mark between 5 and 5.9 out of 10, ≃ (bare) pass; **un a. raso** *o* **raspado** a bare pass; **sacó un a. raso** *o* **raspado** he only scraped a pass

aprobar [64] 1 *vt* (**a**) *(proyecto, medida)* to approve; *(ley, moción)* to pass (**b**) *(examen, asignatura)* to pass; **me han aprobado en química** I passed my chemistry exam (**c**) *(comportamiento)* to approve of
2 *vi (estudiante)* to pass

aprobatorio, -a *adj (gesto, mirada)* approving

aproblemar *Chile* 1 *vt* to worry; **vuelve a casa temprano, no aproblemes a tu madre** come home early and don't go worrying your mother
2 **aproblemarse** *vpr* to worry; **es muy difícil convivir con ella, se aproblema por todo** she's very difficult to live with, she worries about everything *o* makes a problem out of everything

aprontar 1 *vt* (**a**) *(preparar)* to quickly prepare *o* get ready (**b**) *(entregar)* to hand over at once
2 **aprontarse** *vpr RP (prepararse)* to get ready; **aprontate, que a las ocho salimos** get ready, we're leaving at eight; **iaprontate para cuando llegue tu papá!** just you wait till your daddy gets here!

apronte *nm CSur Fam* preparation; **los aprontes para la fiesta nos llevaron toda la tarde** it took us all afternoon to get ready for the party

apropiación *nf (incautación, ocupación)* appropriation ►► *Der* ***a. indebida*** embezzlement

apropiadamente *adv* appropriately

apropiado, -a *adj* suitable, appropriate; **su comportamiento no fue muy a.** his behaviour was rather inappropriate; **estos zapatos no son apropiados para la playa** these shoes aren't very suitable for the beach; **no es la persona apropiada para el puesto** he's not the right person for the job

apropiar 1 *vt* to adapt (**a** to)
2 **apropiarse** *vpr* **apropiarse de** *(tomar posesión de)* to appropriate; **se ha apropiado de ese sillón** he treats that chair as if it belongs to him; **se apropió de mis ideas para redactar el proyecto** he stole my ideas for the plan

apropósito *nm* = comical sketch on a topical subject

aprovechable *adj* usable; **esa tela todavía es a.** we can still use that cloth

aprovechado, -a 1 *adj* (**a**) *(caradura)* **es muy a.** he's a real opportunist, he always has an eye for the main chance (**b**) *(bien empleado)* **el espacio en esta habitación está muy bien a.** they've made the most of the available space in this room (**c**) *(aplicado)* diligent
2 *nm,f* opportunist; **es un a.** he always has an eye for the main chance

aprovechador, -ora *CSur* 1 *adj* **es muy a.** he's a real opportunist, he always has an eye for the main chance
2 *nm,f* opportunist; **es un a.** he always has an eye for the main chance

aprovechamiento *nm* (**a**) *(utilización)* use; **la aridez de las tierras dificulta su a. agrícola** the aridity of the land means that it is not suitable for agricultural use; **el a. de la energía eólica** the exploitation of wind power (**b**) *(en el estudio)* progress, improvement

APROVECHAR 1 *vt* (**a**) *(tiempo, dinero)* to make the most of; *(oferta, ocasión)* to take advantage of; *(conocimientos, experiencia)* to use, to make use of; **han aprovechado todo el potencial del jugador brasileño** they have used the Brazilian player to his full potential; **me gustaría a. esta oportunidad para...** I'd like to take this opportunity to...; **a. que...** to make the most of the fact that...; **aprovechó que no tenía nada que hacer para descansar un rato** since she had nothing to do, she took the opportunity to have a rest; **aprovechó que sabía alemán para solicitar un traslado a Alemania** she used the fact that she knew German to ask for a transfer to Germany
(**b**) *(lo inservible)* to put to good use; **buscan una forma de a. los residuos** they're looking for a way of putting by-products to good use; **no tires los restos de la paella, los aprovecharé para hacer sopa** don't throw what's left of the paella away, I'll use it to make a soup; **el generador aprovecha la fuerza del agua para producir electricidad** the generator uses the power of the water to produce electricity
2 *vi* (**a**) *(mejorar)* to make progress; **desde que tiene un profesor particular aprovecha más en física** since he's had a private tutor he's made more progress in physics
(**b**) *(disfrutar)* **aprovecha mientras puedas** make the most of it *o* enjoy it while you can; **icómo aprovechas para comer chocolate, ahora que no te ve nadie!** you're really making the most of the opportunity to eat chocolate while nobody can see you!; EXPR **ique aproveche!** enjoy your meal!
3 **aprovecharse** *vpr* (**a**) *(sacar provecho)* to take advantage (**de** of); **nos aprovechamos de que teníamos coche para ir a la ciudad** we took advantage of the fact that we had a car to go to the city; **se aprovechó de que nadie vigilaba para salir sin pagar** she took advantage of the fact that nobody was watching to leave without paying; **aprovecharse de las desgracias ajenas** to benefit from other people's misfortunes
(**b**) *(abusar de alguien)* to take advantage (**de** of); **todo el mundo se aprovecha de la ingenuidad de Marta** everyone takes advantage of Marta's gullible nature; **fue acusado de aprovecharse de una menor** he was accused of child abuse

aprovisionador, -ora *nm,f* supplier

aprovisionamiento *nm* supplying; **problemas en el a. energético** problems with the energy supply

aprovisionar 1 *vt* to supply; **el río aprovisiona de agua a varios pueblos** the river supplies several towns with water
2 **aprovisionarse** *vpr* **aprovisionarse de algo** to stock up on sth

aprox. *(abrev de* **aproximadamente**) approx

aproximación *nf* (**a**) *(acercamiento)* approach; *(de países)* rapprochement; *(de puntos de vista)* converging; **ha habido una ligera a. de las dos partes** *(en negociación)* the two sides have come a little closer; **maniobra de a.** *(de avión)* approach (**b**) *(en cálculo)* approximation (**c**) *(en lotería)* = consolation prize given to numbers immediately before and after the winning number

aproximadamente *adv* approximately; **de altura, es a. como tu hermana** she's about your sister's height; **son a. las cinco** it's about five o'clock

aproximado, -a *adj (cifra, cantidad)* approximate; **tengo una idea aproximada del problema** I have a rough idea of the problem

aproximar 1 *vt (acercar) (objeto)* to move closer; *(países)* to bring closer together; **aproxima la mesa a la puerta** move the table closer to *o* over towards the door; **un intento de a. posturas** an attempt at a rapprochement *o* to bring the two sides closer together

2 **aproximarse** *vpr* (**a**) *(en el espacio)* to approach, to come closer; **el autobús se aproximaba a la parada** the bus was approaching the stop; **nos aproximamos a la capital** we are approaching the capital; **el déficit se aproxima a los seis millones** the deficit is close to six million

(**b**) *(en el tiempo)* **se aproximan las vacaciones** the holidays are drawing nearer *o* approaching

(**c**) *(parecerse)* to be similar; **un régimen que intenta aproximarse a un sistema democrático** a regime that is trying to become more like a democracy; **no hay ningún lenguaje que se le aproxime** there's no other language which resembles it

aproximativo, -a *adj* approximate, rough

apruebo *etc ver* **aprobar**

aptdo. = **apdo.**

áptero, -a *nm,f Zool* apterous insect

aptitud *nf* ability, aptitude; **tiene aptitudes para convertirse en una estrella del deporte** she has the ability to become one of the stars of the sport; **no tiene a. para la música** he has no musical ability, he has no aptitude for music; **tuvo que pasar unas pruebas de a. física** he had to undergo a number of fitness tests

apto, -a 1 *adj* (**a**) *(adecuado, conveniente)* suitable (**para** for); **apta/no apta para menores** *(película)* suitable/unsuitable for children; **apta para todos los públicos** *o CSur* **todo público** *(película) Br* ≃ U, *US* ≃ G; **a. para el consumo humano** suitable for human consumption

(**b**) *(capacitado) (físicamente)* fit; **lo declararon no a. para el servicio militar** he was declared unfit for military service; **no es a. para ocupar un puesto directivo** he's not suited to a managerial position

(**c**) *(candidato)* **los alumnos declarados aptos/no aptos** students who have passed/failed

2 *nm* pass; **saqué un a./no a.** I passed/failed

apuesta 1 *ver* **apostar**

2 *nf* (**a**) *(acción)* bet; **hacer una a. sobre algo** to have a bet on sth; **el partido ha hecho una fuerte a. por el liberalismo** the party has committed itself strongly to liberalism (**b**) *(cantidad de dinero)* bet; **las apuestas eran muy elevadas** the stakes were very high

apuesto, -a 1 *ver* **apostar**

2 *adj* dashing

apunado, -a *Andes* 1 *adj* **estar a.** to have altitude sickness

2 *nm,f* **los apunados se quedaron abajo** the people with altitude sickness didn't go up

apunamiento *nm Andes* altitude sickness

apunar *Andes* 1 *vt* to give altitude sickness

2 **apunarse** *vpr* to get altitude sickness

apuntado, -a *adj (arco)* pointed

apuntador, -ora 1 *nm,f Teatro* prompter; EXPR *Fam* **hasta el a.: lo sabía hasta el a.** the world and his wife knew it; EXPR *Fam* **no quedó ni el a.** there wasn't a soul left

2 *nm Informát* scrapbook

apuntalamiento *nm* **fue necesario el a. de la casa** the house had to be shored up

apuntalar *vt* (**a**) *(casa)* to shore up (**b**) *(idea)* to underpin

apuntamiento *nm Der* case summary

APUNTAR 1 *vt* (**a**) *(anotar)* to make a note of, to note down; **a. a alguien** *(en lista)* to put sb down (**en** on); *(en curso)* to put sb's name down (**en** *o* **a** for), to sign sb up (**en** *o* **a** for); **apunta en una lista todo lo que quieres que compre** jot down everything you want me to buy, make a list of the things you want me to buy; **tengo que a. tu número de teléfono** I must make a note of your phone number, I must write your phone number down somewhere; **he apuntado a mi hijo a clases de natación** I've put my son's name down for swimming lessons, I've signed my son up for swimming lessons; **apunté a mis padres para ir a la excursión** I put my parents down for the trip; **apúntamelo (en la cuenta)** put it on my account; **ya puedes ir con cuidado, que esto lo apunto** *(amenaza)* you'd better watch out, I'm not going to forget this

(**b**) *(dirigir) (dedo)* to point; *(arma)* to aim; **a. a alguien** *(con el dedo)* to point at sb; *(con un arma)* to aim at sb; **a. una pistola hacia alguien, a. a alguien con una pistola** to aim a gun at sb; **les apuntó con un rifle** he aimed *o* pointed a rifle at them; **apuntó al blanco y disparó** he took aim at the target and shot; **la brújula apunta al norte** the compass points (to the) north

(**c**) *Teatro* to prompt; *Fam* **fue expulsada de clase por a. las respuestas a un compañero** she was thrown out of the classroom for whispering the answers to a classmate

(**d**) *(sugerir)* to hint at; *(indicar)* to point out; **apuntó la posibilidad de subir los impuestos** he hinted that he might raise taxes; **la policía ha apuntado la posibilidad de que los secuestradores la hayan matado** the police have admitted that the kidnappers may have killed her; **el joven jugador apunta buenos conocimientos** the young player shows a lot of promise

(**e**) *(afilar)* to sharpen

(**f**) *Col (abotonar)* to button up

2 *vi* (**a**) *(vislumbrarse)* to appear; *(día)* to break; **en los árboles ya apuntaban las primeras hojas** the first leaves were appearing on the trees

(**b**) *(indicar)* **a. a** to point to; **todo apunta a que ganará Brasil** everything points to a win for Brazil; **todas las pruebas apuntan a su culpabilidad** all the evidence points to him being guilty; **las sospechas apuntan a un grupo separatista** a separatist group is suspected

(**c**) *Teatro* to prompt

(**d**) *(con un arma)* to aim; **¡carguen, apunten, fuego!** ready, take aim, fire!; EXPR **a. a lo más alto** to set one's sights very high

3 **apuntarse** *vpr* (**a**) *(en lista)* to put one's name down; *(en curso)* to enrol; **me he apuntado a** *o* **en un curso de alemán** I've enrolled on a German course; *Esp* **apuntarse al paro** *Br* to sign on, *US* ≃ to go on welfare

(**b**) *(participar)* to join in (**a hacer algo** doing sth); **nos vamos al cine, ¿te apuntas?** we're going to the cinema, do you want to come too?; **yo me apunto** I'm in; **no le digas nada sobre la fiesta, que se apuntará** don't say anything to her about the party or she'll want to come too; **¿quién se apunta a una partida de cartas?** does anyone fancy a game of cards?, who's up for a game of cards?; EXPR *Esp Fam* **ese se apunta a un bombardeo** he's game for anything; **se apunta a todas las celebraciones** she never misses a party

(**c**) *(tantos, éxitos)* to score, to notch up; **se apuntó la canasta de la victoria** he scored the winning basket; EXPR *Fam* **¡apúntate diez!** *(al acertar)* bingo!, bang on!; **apuntarse un éxito** to score a success; **apuntarse un tanto (a favor)** to earn a point in one's favour

(**d**) *(manifestarse)* **este cambio de política ya se apuntaba hace meses** this change of policy has been coming for months

(**e**) *Col (abotonarse)* to do one's buttons up; **apuntarse la camisa** to do (the buttons on) one's shirt up

apunte *nm* (**a**) *(nota)* note (**b**) **apuntes** *(en colegio, universidad)* notes; **tomar** *o Esp* **coger apuntes** to take notes (**c**) *(boceto)* sketch (**d**) *Com* entry (**e**) *Teatro* prompt (**f**) EXPR *CSur Fam* **llevar el a.** to pay attention; **hace tiempo que se lo digo, pero nunca me lleva el a.** I've been telling her for some time, but she never takes any notice of me

apuntillar *vt* (**a**) *Taurom* **a. al toro** = to kill the bull with a dagger when the bullfighter has repeatedly failed to finish it off (**b**) *(rematar)* to finish off

apuñalamiento *nm* stabbing

apuñalar *vt* to stab

apurada *nf* (**a**) *RP, Ven Fam* **si no nos hubiéramos dado esa a. habríamos llegado tarde** if we hadn't moved it like we did we'd have been late; **hacer algo a las apuradas** to rush sth; **se nota que este artículo lo escribió a las apuradas** you can tell she wrote this article in a rush (**b**) *ver también* **apurado**

apuradamente *adv Am* hurriedly

apurado, -a 1 *adj* (**a**) *(necesitado)* in need; **están apurados de dinero** they are short of money; **vamos muy apurados de tiempo** we've got very little time, we're very short of time

(**b**) *(avergonzado)* embarrassed

(**c**) *(difícil)* awkward, difficult; **una situación apurada** a tricky situation

(**d**) *(victoria)* narrow

(**e**) *Esp (afeitado)* smooth, close

(**f**) *Am (con prisa)* **estar a.** to be in a hurry

2 *nm Esp (afeitado)* **proporciona un a. perfecto** it gives a perfect shave

3 *nm,f Am* **ser un a.** to be in a hurry

apurar 1 *vt* (**a**) *(agotar)* to finish off; *(existencias, la paciencia)* to exhaust; **a. algo hasta la última gota** to finish sth down to the last drop; **apuró el vaso y se marchó** he drained his glass and left

(**b**) *(meter prisa)* to hurry

(**c**) *(preocupar)* to trouble

(**d**) *(avergonzar)* to embarrass

(**e**) EXPR **si me apuras: tardaré tres días, dos si me apuras** it'll take me three days, two if you push me; **había unos diez, doce si me**

apuras there were about ten, twelve at the most

2 *vi* (**a**) *Esp (afeitar)* to give a close *o* smooth shave (**b**) *Andes (urgir)* **es muy tranquilo, nunca nada le apura** he's very laid-back, he's never in a hurry

3 **apurarse** *vpr* (**a**) *Esp, Méx (preocuparse)* to worry (**por** about); **no te apures, ya encontraremos una solución** don't worry, we'll find a solution (**b**) *esp Am (darse prisa)* to hurry; **apúrate o perderemos el tren** hurry up or we'll miss the train

apuro *nm* (**a**) *(dificultad)* tight spot, difficult position; **estar en un a.** to be in a tight spot *o* difficult position; **poner a alguien en un a.** to put sb in a tight spot *o* difficult position; **me encontré en un a. cuando me preguntó por su mujer** I found myself in a difficult position when she asked me about his wife; **buscan a alguien que los saque del a. en el que están** they are looking for somebody to help them out of their predicament

(**b**) *(penuria)* **pasar apuros** to experience hardship; **pasaron muchos apuros económicos en la posguerra** they experienced a lot of financial hardship after the war

(**c**) *(vergüenza)* embarrassment; **me da a. (decírselo)** I'm embarrassed (to tell her); **¡qué a.!** how embarrassing

(**d**) *Am (prisa)* **tener a.** to be in a hurry

apurón *nm RP Fam* **en el a. no nos dimos cuenta y dejamos la luz prendida** we were in such a hurry *o* rush that we left the light on without realizing; **hacer algo a los apurones** to rush sth; **se nota que este artículo lo escribió a los apurones** you can tell she wrote this article in a rush

apurruñamiento *nm Ven Fam* crush

apurruñar *vt Ven Fam* (**a**) *(estrujar)* to scrunch up (**b**) *(abrazar)* to give a bear hug

apurruñón *nm Ven Fam* bear hug

aquaplaning [akwa'planin] *nm* aquaplaning

aquejado, -a *adj* **a. de algo** suffering from sth

aquejar *vt* to afflict; **le aquejan varias enfermedades** he suffers from a number of illnesses; **la crisis económica que aqueja a la región** the economic crisis afflicting the region

---

AQUEL, -ELLA (*pl* **aquellos, -ellas**) **1** *adj demostrativo* that; *(plural)* those; **las fotos aquellas que te enseñé** those photos I showed you

2 *nm* **no es guapa pero tiene su a.** she's not pretty, but she's got a certain something

---

AQUÉL, -ÉLLA (*pl* **aquéllos, -éllas**) *pron demostrativo*

Note that **aquél** and its various forms can be written without an accent when there is no risk of confusion with the adjective.

(**a**) *(ese)* that (one); *(plural)* those (ones); **este cuadro me gusta pero a. del fondo no** I like this picture, but I don't like that one at the back; **a. fue mi último día en Londres** that was my last day in London

(**b**) *(nombrado antes)* the former; **teníamos un coche y una moto, ésta estropeada y a. sin gasolina** we had a car and a motorbike, the former was out of *Br* petrol *o US* gas, the latter had broken down

(**c**) *(con oraciones relativas)* whoever, anyone who; **a. que quiera hablar que levante la mano** whoever wishes *o* anyone wishing to speak should raise their hand; **aquéllos que...** those who...

---

aquelarre *nm* coven

aquella *ver* **aquel**

aquélla *ver* **aquél**

AQUELLO *pron demostrativo* that; **¿has hecho a. que te pedí?** did you do what I asked you to?; **no consiguió saber si a. lo dijo en serio** he never found out whether she meant those words *o* that seriously; **a. de su mujer es una mentira** all that about his wife is a lie

---

aquellos, -as *ver* **aquel**

aquéllos, -as *ver* **aquél**

aquenio *nm* achene

aqueo *Hist* **1** *adj* Achaean

2 *nm* Achaean; **los aqueos** the Achaeans

aquerenciarse *vpr* **a. a algo** to become fond of *o* attached to sth

aqueste, -a *pron demostrativo Anticuado o Hum* this

AQUÍ *adv* (**a**) *(indica lugar)* here; **a. abajo/arriba** down/up here; **a. dentro/fuera** in/out here; **a. mismo** right here; **a. y ahora** here and now; **a. y allá** here and there; **¡a. tienes!** *(dando algo)* here you are!; *Fam* **a. Clara, una amiga** this is my friend Clara; *Fam* **a. el señor quería una cerveza** this gentleman wanted a beer; **los a. presentes** everyone here *o* present; **¡fuera de a.!** go away!; **¡ven a.!** come here!; **era muy desordenado y dejaba las cosas a. y allá** he was very untidy and left things lying around all over the place; **de a. en adelante** from here on; **de a. para allá** *(de un lado a otro)* to and fro; **va de a. para allá sin tener destino fijo** she travels around without really knowing where she's going; **por a.** over here; **vive por a.** she lives around here somewhere; **vengan todos por a., por favor** please all come this way; **por a. cerca** nearby, not far from here; **razón a.** *(en letrero)* enquire within; EXPR *Fam* **de aquí te espero: nos pilló una tormenta de a. te espero** we got caught in a mother of a storm; *Fam* **es un mentiroso de a. te espero** he tells lies like nobody's business, he's a liar through and through; *Fam* **se organizó un follón de a. te espero** all hell broke loose

(**b**) *(ahora)* now; **de a. a mañana** between now and tomorrow; **la traducción tiene que estar acabada de a. a mañana** the translation has to be ready by tomorrow; **de a. a poco** shortly, soon; **de a. a un mes** a month from now, in a month; **de a. en adelante** from now on

(**c**) *(en tiempo pasado)* **pasó a leer el manifiesto y a. todo el mundo se calló** he began reading the manifesto, at which point everyone went silent; **a. empezaron los problemas** that was when the problems started

(**d**) *(consecuencia)* **de a. que** *(por eso)* hence, therefore; **llegaba siempre tarde al trabajo, de a. que lo hayan despedido** he was always late for work, so they sacked him

(**e**) *Am (más o menos)* **¿cómo estás? - a.** how are you? - so-so

---

aquiescencia *nf Formal* acquiescence; **hacer algo con la a. de alguien** to do sth with sb's approval

aquiescente *adj Formal* acquiescent

aquietamiento *nm* calming

aquietar **1** *vt* to calm down; **su intervención aquietó los ánimos** her speech calmed things down

2 **aquietarse** *vpr (mar)* to calm down; **el calmante me aquietó el dolor** the painkiller relieved the pain

aquilatamiento *nm (valoración)* assessment

aquilatar *vt* (**a**) *(metales, joyas)* to assay (**b**) *(valorar)* to assess

Aquiles *n Mitol* Achilles

aquilino, -a *adj (nariz)* aquiline

Aquisgrán *n* Aachen

ar *interj* **¡presenten armas!, ¡a.!** present arms!; **¡derecha!, ¡a.!** right turn!

ara *nf*

Takes the masculine articles **el** and **un**.

Formal (losa) altar stone; *(altar)* altar; EXPR **en aras de: un sacrificio realizado en aras de la reconciliación** a sacrifice made in order to promote reconciliation; **simplificaron el procedimiento en aras de una mayor eficacia** they simplified the procedure in the interests of greater efficiency; **prohibieron su entrada en aras de la seguridad nacional** they refused him entry on the grounds that he posed a threat to national security

árabe **1** *adj* (**a**) *(países, mundo, dirigente)* Arab (**b**) *(lengua, literatura)* Arabic (**c**) *(de Arabia)* Arabian

2 *nmf (persona)* Arab

3 *nm (lengua)* Arabic

arabesco *nm* arabesque

Arabia Saudí, Arabia Saudita *n* Saudi Arabia

arábigo, -a *adj (de Arabia)* Arab, Arabian; *(numeración)* Arabic

arabismo *nm* Arabic word *o* expression

arabista *nmf* Arabist

arable *adj* arable

arácnido *Zool* **1** *nm* arachnid

2 **arácnidos** *nmpl (familia) Arachnida*; **de la clase de los arácnidos** of the *Arachnida* class

arada *nf* (**a**) *(acción)* ploughing (**b**) *(tierra labrada)* ploughed field

arado *nm* (**a**) *(apero)* plough; EXPR *Fam* **es más bruto** *o* **bestia que un a.** *(es un impetuoso)* he always charges ahead without thinking; *(es un torpe)* he always makes a mess of everything he does (**b**) *Col (huerto)* orchard

arador *nm* **a. de la sarna** scabies mite

Aragón *n* Aragon

aragonés, -esa **1** *adj* Aragonese

2 *nm,f* Aragonese

aragonesismo *nm (palabra, expresión)* = Aragonese word or expression

aragonito *nm Geol* aragonite

araguaney *nm* trumpet tree, tabebuia *(Venezuelan national tree)*

araguato *nm (mono)* howler monkey

Aral *nm* **el mar de A.** the Aral Sea

aralia *nf* fatsia japonica

arameo *nm (lengua)* Aramaic; EXPR *Fam* **jurar en a.** to swear, *Br* to eff and blind

arancel *nm Com* tariff ►► ***a. aduanero*** customs duty; *UE* ***a. externo común*** common external tariff

arancelario, -a *adj Com* tariff; **derechos arancelarios** customs duties; **barreras arancelarias** tariff barriers

arándano *nm* bilberry, blueberry

arandela *nf* (a) *(anilla) (de metal)* washer; *(de papel, plástico)* ring reinforcement (b) *CAm, Méx (de camisa)* frills, ruffle

araña *nf* (a) *(animal)* spider ►► ***a. corredora*** wolf spider; ***a. de mar*** spider crab (b) *(lámpara)* chandelier

arañar 1 *vt* (a) *(con uñas, objeto punzante)* to scratch (b) *(reunir)* to scrape together; **arañó los suficientes votos para salir elegido** he scraped together enough votes to get elected; **el equipo arañó un empate** the team scraped a draw
2 *vi (animal)* to scratch

arañazo *nm* scratch

arao *nm* guillemot ►► ***a. aliblanco*** black guillemot

arapaima *nm* arapaima

arapapá *nm* boatbill, boat-billed heron

araponga *nm* bellbird

arar *vt* to plough

arauaco, -a 1 *adj* Araucanian
2 *nm,f* Araucanian

araucano, -a 1 *adj* Araucanian
2 *nm,f (persona)* Araucanian
3 *nm (lengua)* Araucanian

araucaria *nf* monkey puzzle tree

arbitán *nm* Mediterranean ling

arbitraje *nm* (a) *(en fútbol, baloncesto)* refereeing; *(en tenis, voleibol)* umpiring (b) *Der* arbitration; **se sometieron al a. de la ONU** they agreed to UN arbitration; **buscan un a. amistoso del contencioso** they are seeking to resolve the dispute amicably (c) *Bolsa* arbitrage

arbitral *adj* (a) *(en deporte)* **una polémica decisión a.** a controversial decision by the referee/umpire (b) *Der* **procedimiento a.** arbitration process; **un laudo a.** = a binding judgement in arbitration

arbitrar 1 *vt* (a) *(en fútbol, baloncesto)* to referee; *(en tenis, voleibol)* to umpire (b) *(medidas)* to adopt; *(solución)* to find (c) *(recursos)* to obtain; *(dinero)* to raise (d) *Der* to arbitrate
2 *vi* (a) *(en fútbol, baloncesto)* to referee; *(en tenis, voleibol)* to umpire (b) *Der* to arbitrate

arbitrariamente *adv* arbitrarily

arbitrariedad *nf* (a) *(carácter subjetivo)* arbitrariness (b) *(carácter aleatorio)* arbitrariness (c) *(acción)* arbitrary action; **cometió una a. al negarnos el permiso** it was arbitrary and unfair of her to refuse us permission

arbitrario, -a *adj* (a) *(subjetivo)* arbitrary (and unfair) (b) *(aleatorio)* arbitrary

arbitrio *nm* (a) *(albedrío)* judgement; **dejar algo al a. de alguien** to leave sth to sb's discretion; **interpretó la ley a su a.** she interpreted the law as she pleased (b) **arbitrios** *(impuestos)* taxes

árbitro, -a *nm,f* (a) *(en deporte) (en fútbol, baloncesto)* referee; *(en tenis, voleibol)* umpire ►► ***á. asistente*** *(en fútbol)* assistant referee (b) *Der* arbitrator

árbol *nm* (a) *(planta leñosa)* tree; EXPR **los árboles le impiden ver el bosque** he can't see the wood for the trees; PROV **quien a buen á. se arrima (buena sombra le cobija)** it pays to have friends in high places ►► ***á. del caucho*** rubber tree; ***el á. de la ciencia*** the tree of knowledge; ***á. de la mirra*** myrrh; ***á. de Navidad*** Christmas tree; ***á. del pan*** breadfruit tree; ***á. del Paraíso*** oleaster; *Andes* ***á. de Pascua*** Christmas tree; ***á. de la quina*** cinchona; ***á. de la vida*** tree of life
(b) *(esquema)* tree diagram ►► ***á. genealógico*** family tree
(c) *Informát* tree
(d) *Náut* mast
(e) *Ling* tree
(f) *Tec* shaft ►► ***á. de levas*** camshaft; ***á. de transmisión*** transmission shaft
(g) *Anat* ***á. bronquial*** bronchial tree

arbolado, -a 1 *adj* (a) *(terreno)* wooded; *(calle)* tree-lined (b) *(mar)* = with waves between 6 and 9 metres in height
2 *nm* trees; **una zona de denso a.** a densely wooded area

arboladura *nf Náut* masts and spars

arbolar *vt* (a) *(plantar árboles en)* to plant with trees (b) *(barco)* to mast

arboleda *nf (bosque)* grove, small wood; **la a. que bordea el río** the trees beside the river

arbóreo, -a *adj* arboreal; **masa arbórea** area of forest

arborescencia *nf Bot* arborescence

arborescente *adj* tree-shaped

arboricida *nm* **es un a.** it kills trees

arborícola *adj Zool* arboreal

arboricultor, -ora *nm,f* nurseryman, *f* nurserywoman, *Espec* arboriculturist

arboricultura *nf* tree cultivation, *Espec* arboriculture

arborizar *vt* to plant trees on

arbotante *nm* (a) *Arquit* flying buttress (b) *Méx (poste) (de luz)* lamppost; *(de teléfono) Br* telegraph *o US* telephone pole (c) *Méx (en pared)* wall-mounted light fixture

arbustivo, -a *adj* shrub-like; **plantas arbustivas** shrubs

arbusto *nm* bush, shrub; **se escondió entre unos arbustos** he hid in some bushes; **arbustos ornamentales** shrubbery

arca *nf*

Takes the masculine articles **el** and **un**.

(a) *(arcón)* chest ►► ***el A. de la Alianza*** the Ark of the Covenant
(b) **arcas** *(fondos)* coffers; **las arcas públicas** the Treasury; **el dinero salió de las arcas comunitarias** the money came from the EU's coffers
(c) *(barco)* ***el a. de Noé*** Noah's Ark

arcabucero *nm (soldado)* arquebusier

arcabuz *nm* arquebus

arcada *nf* (a) *(de estómago)* **me dieron arcadas** I retched; **el olor le produjo arcadas** the smell made her retch (b) *(arcos)* arcade (c) *(de puente)* arch

arcaico, -a *adj* archaic

arcaísmo *nm* archaism

arcaizante *adj* archaizing

arcángel *nm* archangel; **el A. San Gabriel** the archangel Gabriel

arcano, -a 1 *adj* arcane
2 *nm* (a) *(misterio)* mystery (b) *(del tarot)* arcana

arce *nm* maple ►► ***a. blanco*** maple; ***a. sacarino*** sugar maple

arcén *nm Esp Br* hard shoulder, *US* shoulder

archi- *pref Fam* **el archifamoso cantante** the mega-famous singer; **son archienemigos** they are arch-enemies

archibebe *nm* redshank ►► ***a. claro*** greenshank

archiconocido, -a *adj* very well-known; **es a. su amor por los animales** his love for animals is very well-known; **la fiesta se celebró en su a. palacio** the party was held in her legendary palace

archidiácono *nm* dean *(of cathedral)*

archidiócesis *nf inv* archdiocese

archiducado *nm* archdukedom

archiduque, -esa *nm,f* archduke, *f* archduchess

archimillonario, -a *nm,f* multimillionaire

archipámpano *nm Fam Hum* **hablando con el, parece el a. de las Indias** to talk to him you'd think he was some kind of big shot

archipiélago *nm* archipelago; **el a. balear** the Balearic Islands; **el a. de las Antillas** the West Indies

archisabido, -a *adj* very well-known

archivador, -ora 1 *nm,f* archivist
2 *nm* (a) *(mueble)* filing cabinet (b) *(cuaderno)* ring binder

archivar *vt* (a) *(documentos)* to file (b) *Informát* to file (c) *(proyecto) (definitivamente)* to drop; *(temporalmente)* to shelve; **archivaron el caso por falta de pruebas** they dropped the case owing to a lack of proof

archivero, -a *nm,f*, **archivista** *nmf* archivist

archivística *nf* archiving

archivo *nm* (a) *(lugar)* archive; *TV* **imágenes de a.** library pictures (b) *(documentos)* archives (c) *Informát* file ►► ***a. adjunto*** attachment; ***a. ejecutable*** exe file; ***a. invisible*** invisible file; ***a. oculto*** hidden file; ***a. de texto*** text file

archivolta = **arquivolta**

arcilla *nf* clay

arcilloso, -a *adj* clay-like, clayey; **suelo arcilloso** clayey soil

arcipreste *nm* archpriest

arco *nm* (a) *(figura curva)* arch ►► ***a. apuntado*** Gothic arch; ***a. detector de metales*** security gate *(at airport, etc)*; ***a. formero*** supporting arch; ***a. de herradura*** horseshoe arch; ***a. iris*** rainbow; ***a. de medio punto*** semicircular arch; ***a. ojival*** Gothic arch; ***a. parlamentario:* partidos de todo el a. parlamentario** parliamentary parties from across the whole political spectrum; *Anat* ***a. superciliar*** superciliary arch; ***a. triunfal*** triumphal arch; ***a. de triunfo*** triumphal arch; ***el A. del Triunfo*** *(en París)* the Arc de Triomphe
(b) *(para flechas)* bow; **tiro con a.** archery
(c) *Mús (de instrumento de cuerda)* bow
(d) *Elec* ***a. eléctrico*** electric arc; ***a. voltaico*** electric arc
(e) *Geom* arc
(f) *esp Am Dep (portería)* goal, goalmouth

arcón *nm* large chest

Ardenas *nfpl* **las A.** the Ardennes

arder *vi* (a) *(quemarse) (bosque, casa)* to burn; **la iglesia está ardiendo** the church is burning *o* on fire; **ha ardido el granero** the barn has burnt down; **una antorcha que arde permanentemente** a torch that is always burning; **todavía arden los rescoldos de la hoguera** the bonfire is still smouldering; EXPR *Fam* **con eso va que arde** that's more than enough
(b) *(estar caliente) (café, sopa)* to be boiling hot; EXPR **¡está que arde!** *(persona)* he's fuming; *(reunión)* it's getting pretty heated
(c) *(sentir ardor)* **le arde la cara** her face is burning; **me arde el estómago** I've got heartburn; **tanto dinero le arde en sus manos** all that money is burning a hole in his pocket
(d) *(por deseos)* **a. de rabia** to burn with rage; **a. en deseos de hacer algo** to be dying to do sth
(e) *(por agitación)* **la ciudad ardía en fiestas** the city was one great party; **todavía arde la revuelta de mayo** the spirit of the May uprising is still alive

ardid *nm* ruse, trick

ardido, -a *adj Andes, Guat (enfadado, enojado)* irritated

ardiente *adj* (a) *(en llamas)* burning; *(líquido)* scalding (b) *(ferviente) (deseo)* burning; *(admirador, defensor)* ardent; **un a. discurso** a passionate speech

ardientemente *adv* ardently, fervently

ardilla *nf* squirrel ►► ***a. estriada*** chipmunk; ***a. gris*** grey squirrel; ***a. listada*** chipmunk; ***a. roja*** red squirrel; ***a. voladora*** flying squirrel

ardite *nm* **no vale un a.** it isn't worth a brass farthing

ardor *nm* (a) *(calor)* heat; *(quemazón)* burning (sensation); EXPR ***a. de estómago*** heartburn (b) *(entusiasmo)* fervour; *(pasión)* passion; **con a.** passionately, fervently

ardorosamente *adv (apasionadamente)* ardently, fervently

ardoroso, -a *adj* (a) *(caliente)* hot, burning (b) *(apasionado)* ardent, fervent

arduamente *adv* arduously, with great difficulty

arduo, -a *adj* arduous

área *nf*

Takes the masculine articles **el** and **un**.

(a) *(zona)* area ►► ***a. de descanso*** *(en carretera) Br* lay-by, *US* rest area; *Econ* ***a. (del) euro*** Euro zone; *Econ* ***a. de libre comercio*** free trade area; ***a. metropolitana*** metropolitan area; ***a. protegida*** protected area; ***a. de servicio*** *(en carretera)* service area
(b) *(ámbito)* area; **la investigación en áreas como la inteligencia artificial** research in areas such as artificial intelligence; **una carrera del a. de Ciencias** a university course in a science subject; **el responsable del a. económica del partido** the person in charge of the party's economic policy
(c) *(medida)* are, = 100 square metres
(d) *Geom (superficie)* area
(e) *Dep* **a. (de penalty** *o* **castigo)** (penalty) area ►► ***a. grande*** eighteen-yard box, penalty area; ***a. pequeña*** six-yard box

areca *nf (palmera)* areca, betel palm

ARENA [a'rena] *nf (abrev de* **Alianza Republicana Nacionalista**) = right wing Salvadoran political party

arena *nf* (a) *(de playa)* sand ►► ***a. para gatos*** cat litter; ***arenas movedizas*** quicksand (b) *(escenario de la lucha)* arena; **la a. política** the political arena (c) *Taurom* bullring

arenal *nm* area of sandy ground

arenero *nm Taurom* = boy who smooths the surface of the bullring with sand

arenga *nf* (a) *(discurso)* harangue (b) *Chile Fam (disputa)* quarrel, argument

arengar [38] *vt* to harangue

arenilla *nf* (a) *(polvo)* dust (b) **arenillas** *(cálculos)* stones

arenisca *nf* sandstone

arenoso, -a *adj (con arena)* sandy

arenque *nm* herring; **a. ahumado** kipper

areola, aréola *nf* areola

areometría *nf* hydrometry

areómetro *nm* hydrometer

areópago *nm Hist* Areopagus

arepa *nf Carib, Col* = pancake made of maize flour; EXPR *Ven* **buscar** *o* **ganarse la a.** to earn a living; EXPR *Ven* **el que no pila no come a.** you have to work for a living; EXPR *Ven* **está** *o* **se ha puesto la a. cuadrada** times are hard

arepera *nf Carib, Col* (a) *(tienda)* = stall selling maize pancakes (b) *muy Fam Pey (lesbiana)* dyke, lezzy

arepería *nf Carib, Col (tienda)* = stall selling maize pancakes

arepero, -a *nm,f Carib, Col* = person who sells maize pancakes

arequipe *nm* (a) *Col (dulce de leche)* = toffee pudding made with caramelized milk (b) *Ven (postre)* = rice pudding made with eggs, wine and cinnamon

arete *nm* (a) *(pez)* red gurnard (b) *Andes, Méx (pendiente)* earring; *Esp (en forma de aro)* hoop earring

argamasa *nf* mortar

Argel *n* Algiers

Argelia *n* Algeria

argelino, -a 1 *adj* Algerian
2 *nm,f* Algerian

argentado, -a *adj (de color plateado)* silver, silvery

argénteo, -a *adj (de plata)* silver

argentífero, -a *adj* silver-bearing

Argentina *n* **(la) A.** Argentina

argentinidad *nf* **un debate sobre la a.** a debate about what it means to be an Argentinian

argentinismo *nm* = word or expression peculiar to Argentinian Spanish

argentino, -a 1 *adj* (a) *(de Argentina)* Argentinian (b) *(sonido)* silvery
2 *nm,f* Argentinian

argolla *nf* (a) *(aro)* (large) ring (b) *Andes, Méx (alianza)* wedding ring (c) *Carib (pendiente)* hoop earring (d) *Andes, CAm Fam (camarilla)* **formar a.** to form a monopoly (e) *Ven Fam (homosexual)* queer, *Br* poof, *US* fag (f) EXPR *CAm Fam* **tener a.** to have friends in high places

argón *nm Quím* argon

argonauta *nm* (a) *Mitol* Argonaut (b) *(molusco)* paper nautilus

argot (*pl* **argots**) *nm* (a) *(popular)* slang (b) *(técnico)* jargon

argucia *nf* deceptive argument

argüende *nm Méx Fam* (a) *(chisme)* gossip (b) *(fiesta)* party, *Br* rave-up

argüendero, -a *nm,f Méx Fam* gossip

argüir [8] 1 *vt* (a) *(argumentar)* to argue; **arguyó como excusa que nadie le había informado** in her defence, she argued that nobody had told her (b) *(demostrar)* to prove, to demonstrate (c) *(deducir)* to deduce
2 *vi (argumentar)* to argue; **arguyó en contra de la propuesta** he argued against the proposal

argumentación *nf* line of argument

argumental *adj (de novela, película)* **hilo a.** plot; **tema a.** subject, theme

argumentar 1 *vt (alegar)* to argue (**que** that); **no argumentó bien su hipótesis** he didn't argue his theory very well; **se puede a. que...** it could be argued that...
2 *vi (discutir)* to argue

argumento *nm* (a) *(razonamiento)* argument (b) *(trama)* plot

arguyera *etc ver* **argüir**

arguyo *etc ver* **argüir**

aria *nf (de ópera)* aria

Takes the masculine articles **el** and **un**.

Ariadna *n Mitol* Ariadne

ariano, -a *Am* 1 *adj* Aries; **ser a.** to be (an) Aries
2 *nm,f* Aries; **los a. son...** Arians are...

arica *nf Ven (abeja)* bee

aridez *nf* (**a**) *(de terreno, clima)* aridity, dryness (**b**) *(de libro, tema)* dryness

árido, -a 1 *adj* (**a**) *(terreno, clima)* arid, dry (**b**) *(libro, tema)* dry
2 **áridos** *nmpl* dry goods; *Constr* **áridos de construcción** aggregate

aries 1 *adj inv Esp* Aries; **ser a.** to be (an) Aries
2 *nm (signo)* Aries, Arian; **los de A. son...** Arians are...
3 *nmf inv Esp (persona)* Aries, Arian; **los a. son...** Arians are...

ariete *nm* (**a**) *Mil* battering-ram (**b**) *Dep* centre-forward

ario, -a 1 *adj* Aryan
2 *nm,f* Aryan

ariqueño, -a 1 *adj* of/from Arica *(Chile)*
2 *nm,f* person from Arica *(Chile)*

arísaro *nm* friar's cowl

ariscamente *adv* surlily

arisco, -a *adj* surly

arista *nf* (**a**) *Geom* edge (**b**) *(en montaña)* arête (**c**) *(de trigo)* beard (**d**) *(dificultad)* **su imagen presentaba aún muchas aristas** there were still a lot of awkward problems with his image; **tenemos que limar muchas aristas para poder llegar a un acuerdo** there are a lot of problems that need to be ironed out before we have an agreement

aristocracia *nf* aristocracy ►► *Hist* ***a. obrera*** labour aristocracy

aristócrata *nmf* aristocrat

aristocrático, -a *adj* aristocratic

Aristóteles *n pr* Aristotle

aristotélico, -a 1 *adj* Aristotelian
2 *nm,f* Aristotelian

aritmética *nf* arithmetic; **a. parlamentaria** parliamentary arithmetic

aritmético, -a 1 *adj* arithmetic(al); **progresión aritmetica** arithmetic progression
2 *nm,f* arithmetician

arizónica *nf* Arizona cypress

arlequín *nm* harlequin

arma *nf*

Takes the masculine articles **el** and **un**.

(**a**) *(instrumento)* arm, weapon; **alzarse en armas** to rise up in arms; **pasar a alguien por las armas** to have someone shot (by a firing squad); **¡presenten armas!** present arms!; **rendir armas** to surrender arms; **tomar las armas** to take up arms; **velar las armas** to undertake the vigil of the arms; EXPR **ser un a. de doble filo** to be a double-edged sword; EXPR **ser de armas tomar** to be someone to be reckoned with ►► ***a. atómica*** nuclear weapon; ***a. bacteriológica*** bacteriological weapon; ***a. biológica*** biological weapon; ***a. blanca*** blade, = weapon with a sharp blade; ***a. convencional*** conventional weapon; ***a. de fuego*** firearm; ***a. homicida*** murder weapon; ***a. ligera*** light weapon; ***a. nuclear*** nuclear weapon; ***a. pesada*** heavy weapon; ***a. química*** chemical weapon; ***a. reglamentaria*** regulation firearm; *también Fig* ***a. secreta*** secret weapon
(**b**) *(medio)* weapon; **la mejor a. contra la arrogancia es la indiferencia** the best defence against arrogance is to ignore it; **renunciaron a la violencia como a. política** they renounced the use of violence as a political weapon; **la vacuna será una poderosa a. contra la malaria** the vaccine will be a powerful weapon against malaria
(**c**) *(cuerpo en ejército)* arm; **el a. de infantería** the infantry arm
(**d**) **las armas** *(profesión)* the military career, the Army; **eligió la carrera de las armas** he chose a career in the Army

armada *nf* (**a**) *(marina)* navy; **la A.** the Navy ►► *Hist* ***la A. Invencible*** the Spanish Armada (**b**) *(escuadra)* fleet

armadillo *nm* armadillo

armado, -a 1 *adj* (**a**) *(con armas)* armed; *Fig* **a. hasta los dientes** armed to the teeth (**b**) *(con armazón)* reinforced
2 *nm (pez)* armed gurnard

armador, -ora *nm,f* (**a**) *(dueño)* shipowner (**b**) *(constructor)* shipbuilder

armadura *nf* (**a**) *(de guerrero)* armour (**b**) *(de barco, tejado)* framework

armamentismo *nm* **el creciente a. en la región** the arms build-up in the region

armamentista, armamentístico, -a *adj* arms; **carrera a.** arms race

armamento *nm* (**a**) *(armas)* arms; **a. ligero/pesado** light/heavy weaponry; **el a. nuclear de un país** a country's nuclear arsenal (**b**) *(acción)* arming

armañac *nm* Armagnac

ARMAR 1 *vt* (**a**) *(montar) (mueble, modelo)* to assemble; *(tienda)* to pitch
(**b**) *(ejército, personas)* to arm; **armaron a los ciudadanos con fusiles** they armed the citizens with rifles; **a. caballero a alguien** to knight sb
(**c**) *(fusil, pistola)* to load
(**d**) *Fam (lío, escándalo)* to cause; **armarla** to cause trouble; **armó una buena con sus comentarios** she really went and did it with the comments she made; **¡buena la has armado!** you've really gone and done it now!; **a. bronca** *o* **bulla** to kick up a row *o* racket; **a. camorra** to pick a fight; EXPR **a. la gorda** to kick up a fuss *o* stink
(**e**) *(fundar, sentar)* to base, to found
(**f**) *Náut* to fit out
(**g**) *Am (cigarrillo)* to roll
(**h**) EXPR *Méx Fam* **armarla: ¿sabes algo de electrónica? – no, no la armo** do you know anything about electronics? – no, I'm no good in that department
2 **armarse** *vpr* (**a**) *(con armas)* to arm oneself; *Fig* **armarse hasta los dientes** to arm oneself to the teeth; *Fig* **armarse de** *(valor, paciencia)* to summon up; **se armó de valor y le contó la verdad** he plucked up his courage and told her the truth
(**b**) *Fam (organizarse)* **se armó un gran escándalo** there was a huge fuss; **con tantas instrucciones, me armé un lío tremendo** with all those instructions I got into a terrible muddle; **la que se va a a. cuando se entere tu padre** all hell's going to break loose when your father finds out; **si no paras de una vez se va a a. una buena** if you don't stop that at once, there'll be trouble; EXPR **se armó la gorda** *o* **la de San Quintín** *o* **la de Dios es Cristo** *o* **la de Troya** all hell broke loose
(**c**) *Andes (enriquecerse)* to strike it rich, to come into money
(**d**) *RP (consolidarse)* to do well for oneself

armario *nm* (**a**) *(para objetos)* cupboard; *(para ropa)* wardrobe; EXPR *Fam* **salir del a.** to come out of the closet ►► ***a. empotrado*** fitted cupboard/wardrobe; ***a. de luna*** wardrobe *(with mirrors on the doors)*; ***a. ropero*** wardrobe (**b**) *Fam (jugador, deportista) Br* donkey, carthorse, *US* goat

armatoste *nm* (**a**) *(mueble, objeto)* unwieldy object (**b**) *(máquina)* contraption

armazón *nm o nf* (**a**) *(de avión, coche)* chassis; *(de barco)* frame; *(de edificio)* skeleton (**b**) *(ideológico, argumental)* framework (**c**) *RP (de anteojos)* frame

armella *nf* eyebolt

Armenia *n* Armenia

armenio, -a 1 *adj* Armenian
2 *nm,f (persona)* Armenian
3 *nm (lengua)* Armenian

armería *nf* (**a**) *(depósito)* armoury (**b**) *(tienda)* gunsmith's (shop) (**c**) *(arte)* gunsmith's craft

armero *nm* (**a**) *(fabricante)* gunsmith (**b**) *Mil (soldado)* armourer

armiño *nm* (**a**) *(piel)* ermine (**b**) *(animal)* stoat

armisticio *nm* armistice

armonía, harmonía *nf* (**a**) *Mús* harmony (**b**) *(de colores, formas)* harmony (**c**) *(amistad)* harmony; **la falta de a. entre los miembros del gabinete** the lack of agreement within the cabinet; **vivir en a. con alguien** to live in harmony with sb

armónica *nf* harmonica, mouth organ

armónicamente *adv* harmoniously

armónico, -a 1 *adj* (**a**) *Mús* harmonic (**b**) *(colores, formas)* harmonious
2 *nm Mús* harmonic

armonio *nm* harmonium

armoniosamente *adv* harmoniously

armonioso, -a *adj* harmonious

armónium *nm* harmonium

armonización *nf* (**a**) *Mús* harmonization (**b**) *(de colores, formas)* harmonization; **la a. de políticas agrarias entre los miembros de la UE** the harmonization of agricultural policy among EU members

armonizar [14] 1 *vt* (**a**) *Mús* to harmonize (**b**) *(concordar)* to harmonize; **el objetivo es a. las políticas de los Estados miembros** the aim is to harmonize member states' policies; **necesitamos a. criterios** we need to make sure we're using the same criteria; **tratan de a. los**

ingresos con los gastos they are trying to balance their expenditure with their income

2 *vi (concordar)* **a. (con)** to match; **esas dos prendas no armonizan bien** those two garments don't go well together *o* don't match; **el nuevo edificio no armoniza con los alrededores** the new building doesn't fit into its surroundings

ARN *nm (abrev de* **ácido ribonucleico**) RNA

arnés (*pl* **arneses**) *nm* (**a**) *Hist* armour (**b**) *(para escalada)* harness (**c**) **arneses** *(de animales)* trappings, harness

árnica *nf* arnica

Takes the masculine articles **el** and **un**.

aro *nm* (**a**) *(círculo)* hoop; **los aros olímpicos** the Olympic rings; **un sostén de aros** an underwired bra; EXPR **pasar por el a.** to knuckle under ►► ***aros de cebolla*** onion rings (**b**) *(en gimnasia rítmica)* hoop (**c**) *Tec* ring (**d**) *Am (pendiente)* earring; *Esp (en forma de aro)* hoop earring (**e**) *Ven (alianza)* wedding ring ►► ***a. liso*** engagement ring (**f**) *Col (montura)* rim (**g**) *Bol (anillo)* ring

aroma *nm (de alimentos)* aroma; *(de rosas)* scent; *(de vino)* bouquet; **a. artificial** artificial flavouring

aromaterapia *nf* aromatherapy

aromático, -a *adj* aromatic

aromatizador *nm* air freshener

aromatizante *nm* flavouring

aromatizar [14] *vt* (**a**) *(con perfume)* to perfume (**b**) *(comida)* to flavour

aromatoterapia *nf* aromatherapy

arpa *nf*

Takes the masculine articles **el** and **un**.

harp; EXPR *RP Fam* **sonar como a. vieja: emprendió un nuevo proyecto, pero al poco tiempo sonó como a. vieja** she started a new project, but before long she screwed up *o Br* it all went pear-shaped; *RP Fam* **¿te fue bien en el examen? – no, soné como a. vieja** did the exam go well? – no, I made a real mess of it ►► ***a. de boca*** Jew's harp

arpegiar *vi Mús* to play arpeggios

arpegio *nm Mús* arpeggio

arpeo *nm* grappling-iron

arpía *nf* (**a**) *Mitol* harpy (**b**) *(mujer mala)* witch

arpillera, harpillera *nf* sacking, *Br* hessian, *US* burlap

arpista *nmf* harpist

arpón *nm (para pescar)* harpoon

arponear *vt* to harpoon

arquear 1 *vt* (**a**) *(madera)* to warp; *(vara, fusta)* to flex (**b**) *(cejas, espalda)* to arch; **el gato arqueó el lomo** the cat arched its back (**c**) *Náut (embarcación)* to gauge, to measure the tonnage of (**d**) *Am Com* to do the books

2 **arquearse** *vpr* (**a**) *(madera)* to warp (**b**) *(cejas, espalda)* to arch

arqueo *nm* (**a**) *(de cejas, espalda, lomo)* arching (**b**) *Com* cashing up (**c**) *Náut* registered tonnage

arqueolítico, -a *adj* Stone-age

arqueología *nf* archaeology ►► ***a. industrial*** industrial archaeology

arqueológico, -a *adj* archaeological

arqueólogo, -a *nm,f* archaeologist

arquería *nf (arcos)* arcade

arquero, -a 1 *nm Mil* archer

2 *nm,f* (**a**) *Dep (tirador)* archer (**b**) *(tesorero)* treasurer (**c**) *Am Dep (portero)* goalkeeper

arqueta *nf* casket

arquetípico, -a *adj* archetypal

arquetipo *nm* archetype; **es el a. de hombre de los 80** he's the archetypal 80s man

Arquímedes *n pr* Archimedes

arquitecto, -a *nm,f* architect; **fue el a. de la revolución** he was the architect of the revolution ►► ***a. técnico*** = on-site architect, responsible for the implementation of the designing architect's plans

arquitectónicamente *adv* architecturally

arquitectónico, -a *adj* architectural; **el patrimonio a. de Barcelona** the architectural heritage of Barcelona

arquitectura *nf* (**a**) *(arte, técnica)* architecture ►► ***a. civil*** = non-ecclesiastical architecture; ***a. funcional*** functional architecture; ***a. de interiores*** interior design; ***a. naval*** naval architecture; ***a. religiosa*** ecclesiastical *o* church architecture (**b**) *Informát* architecture ►► ***a. abierta*** open architecture

arquitectural *adj* architectural

arquitrabe *nm Arquit* architrave

arquivolta, archivolta *nf Arquit* archivolt

arr. (*abrev de* **arreglo de**) arr.

arrabal *nm* slum

arrabalero, -a 1 *adj* (**a**) *(de barrio pobre)* of/from the slums (**b**) *Esp (barriobajero)* rough, coarse

2 *nm,f* (**a**) *(persona de barrio pobre)* person from the slums (**b**) *Esp (barriobajero)* rough *o* coarse person

arrabio *nm Ind* pig iron

arracada *nf* drop *o* pendant earring

arracimarse *vpr* to cluster together

arraclán *nm* alder buckthorn

arraigado, -a *adj* (**a**) *(costumbre, idea)* deeply rooted; **el racismo está muy a. en la región** racism is endemic in the region (**b**) *(persona)* established

arraigar [38] 1 *vt* (**a**) *(establecer)* to establish (**b**) *Andes, Méx Der* to limit *o* restrict the movement of

2 *vi* (**a**) *(planta)* to take root (**b**) *(costumbre, idea)* to take root

3 **arraigarse** *vpr (establecerse)* to settle down (**en** in)

arraigo *nm* roots; **tener mucho a.** to be deeply rooted; **una costumbre de gran a. en el país** a custom which is deeply rooted in that country; **un candidato con mucho a. popular** a candidate with widespread popular support

arramblar *vi* (**a**) *(destruir)* **a. con** to sweep away (**b**) *Fam (arrebatar)* **a. con** to make off with; **fue el primero en llegar y arrambló con el poco champán que había** he was the first person to arrive and he nabbed what little champagne there was

arrancada *nf* (**a**) *(de vehículo)* start; **con una a. repentina dejó a sus rivales atrás** he put on a sudden spurt and left his rivals behind (**b**) *(en halterofilia)* snatch

ARRANCAR [60] 1 *vt* (**a**) *(sacar de su sitio) (árbol)* to uproot; *(malas hierbas, flor)* to pull up; *(cable, página, pelo)* to tear out; *(cartel, cortinas)* to tear down; *(muela)* to pull out, to extract; *(ojos)* to gouge out; *(botón, etiqueta)* to tear *o* rip off; **arranqué el póster de la pared** I tore the poster off the wall; **a. la cabellera a alguien** to scalp sb; **a. de cuajo** *o* **de raíz** *(árbol)* to uproot; *(brazo, pierna)* to tear right off; *Fig* **a. a alguien de un sitio** to shift sb from somewhere; *Fig* **a. a alguien de las drogas/del alcohol** to get sb off drugs/alcohol

(**b**) *(arrebatar)* **a. algo a alguien** to grab *o* snatch sth from sb; **a. algo de las manos de alguien** to snatch sth out of sb's hands; **tenía el bolso muy bien agarrado y no se lo pudieron a.** she was holding on very tight to her handbag and they couldn't get it off her; **el vigilante consiguió arrancarle el arma al atracador** the security guard managed to grab the robber's gun; **el Barcelona consiguió a. un punto en su visita a Madrid** Barcelona managed to take a point from their visit to Madrid; **la oposición arrancó varias concesiones al gobierno** the opposition managed to win several concessions from the government

(**c**) *(poner en marcha) (coche, máquina)* to start; *Informát* to start up, to boot (up)

(**d**) *(obtener)* **a. algo a alguien** *(confesión, promesa, secreto)* to extract sth from sb; *(sonrisa, dinero, ovación)* to get sth out of sb; *(suspiro, carcajada)* to bring sth from sb; **no consiguieron arrancarle ninguna declaración** they failed to get a statement out of him

2 *vi* (**a**) *(partir)* to leave; **¡corre, que el autobús está arrancando!** quick, the bus is about to leave; **el Tour ha arrancado finalmente** the Tour has finally got *o* is finally under way

(**b**) *(máquina, coche)* to start; **no intentes a. en segunda** you shouldn't try to start the car in second gear

(**c**) *(empezar)* to get under way, to kick off; **ya arrancó la campaña electoral** the election campaign is already under way; **el festival arrancó con un concierto de música clásica** the festival got under way *o* kicked off with a classical music concert; **empataron al poco de a. la segunda mitad** they equalized shortly after the second half had got under way *o* kicked off

(**d**) *Fam* **a. a hacer algo** *(persona)* to start doing *o* to do sth; **arrancó a llorar de repente** she suddenly started crying, she suddenly burst into tears

(**e**) *(provenir)* **la tradición arranca de la Edad Media** the tradition dates back to the Middle Ages; **el río arranca de los Andes** the river has its source in the Andes; **todos los problemas arrancan de una**

nefasta planificación all the problems stem from poor planning
3 **arrancarse** *vpr* (a) **arrancarse a hacer algo** to start doing *o* to do sth; **arrancarse a llorar** to start crying, to burst into tears (b) *Taurom* to charge off (c) *Chile (salir corriendo)* to rush off

arranchador, -ora *nm,f Andes* bag snatcher
arranchar *vt* (a) *Andes, CAm (arrebatar)* to seize, to snatch (b) *Andes, Cuba (aprehender)* to catch, to capture
arranque 1 *ver* **arrancar**
2 *nm* (a) *(comienzo)* start; **el equipo no ha tenido un buen a. liguero** the team has had a poor start to the season; **la película se proyectó en el a. del certamen** the festival kicked off with a screening of the film
(b) *Aut (motor)* starter (motor); **durante el a.** *(puesta en marcha)* while starting the car ►► ***a. eléctrico*** electrical starting
(c) *Informát* boot-up, start-up
(d) *(de arco)* base
(e) *(arrebato)* **en un a. de ira/generosidad** in a fit of anger/generosity; **¡tiene unos arranques!** he just flies off the handle without warning!
(f) *(decisión)* drive
arrapiezo *nm Fam* urchin, young scallywag
arras *nfpl* (a) *(fianza)* deposit (b) *(en boda)* = coins given by the bridegroom to the bride
arrasamiento *nm* destruction, razing
arrasar 1 *vt (destruir) (edificio, cosecha)* to destroy; *(zona)* to devastate; **el fuego arrasó el castillo** the fire destroyed the castle, the castle was burned to the ground in the fire
2 *vi* (a) **a. con** *(destruir)* to destroy; **el huracán arrasó con toda la cosecha** the hurricane destroyed the entire harvest; **los niños arrasaron con todos los pasteles** the children made short work of the cakes
(b) *Fam (triunfar)* to win overwhelmingly; **el equipo brasileño arrasó en la primera fase** the Brazilian team swept everything before it in the first stage; **la película arrasó en toda Europa** the movie was a massive success throughout Europe
arrastrado, -a 1 *adj* (a) *(miserable)* miserable, wretched; **lleva una vida arrastrada** she lives a miserable *o* wretched life (b) *(pronunciación, letra)* drawn out (c) *Méx, RP (servil)* grovelling
2 *nm,f Méx, RP (persona servil)* groveller
arrastrar 1 *vt* (a) *(objeto, persona)* to drag; *(carro, vagón)* to pull; *(remolque)* to tow; **el viento arrastró las hojas** the wind blew the leaves along; *Fig* **el presidente arrastró en su caída a varios ministros** the president took several ministers down with him; **la caída de la Bolsa neoyorquina arrastró al resto de mercados** the crash on the New York stock exchange pulled the other markets down with it; **a. los pies** to drag one's feet; EXPR *RP Fam* **a. el ala a alguien** to set one's cap at sb
(b) *Informát* to drag; **a. y soltar** to drag and drop
(c) *(convencer)* to win over, to sway; **a. a alguien a algo/a hacer algo** to lead sb into sth/to do sth; **dejarse a. por algo/alguien** to allow oneself to be swayed by sth/sb
(d) *(producir)* to bring; **la guerra arrastra ya 3.000 muertos** the war has already claimed 3,000 lives
(e) *(atraer)* to pull in; **un cantante que arrastra muchos seguidores** a singer who pulls in large crowds
(f) *(soportar)* **arrastra una vida miserable** she leads a miserable life; **arrastra muchas deudas/muchos problemas** he has a lot of debts/problems hanging over him; **arrastra esa dolencia desde hace varios años** she has been suffering from this complaint for several years
(g) *(al hablar)* to draw out; **arrastra las erres** he rolls his r's
2 *vi* (a) *(rozar el suelo)* to drag along the ground; **te arrastra el vestido** your dress is dragging on the ground; **estas cortinas arrastran** these curtains are touching the floor (b) *(en juegos de cartas)* **a. con tréboles** to lead with a club
3 **arrastrarse** *vpr* (a) *(por el suelo)* to crawl; **los soldados se arrastraban por el barro** the soldiers crawled through the mud (b) *(humillarse)* to grovel; **se arrastró ante ella** he grovelled to her
arrastre *nm* (a) *(acarreo)* dragging; EXPR *Fam* **estar para el a.** to have had it; *Fam* **el partido de tenis me ha dejado para el a.** the tennis match has done me in
(b) *(pesca)* trawling
(c) *Taurom* = dragging of the dead bull from the bullring
(d) *Geol* **de a.** alluvial
(e) *(atractivo)* pull, influence; **un político con mucho a.** a politician with a lot of pull; *RP Fam* **tener a.: esa chica tiene mucho a.** that girl is quite something *o* can really turn heads
(f) *Col, Méx (molino)* silver mill
arrastrero *nm* trawler
arrayán *nm* myrtle
arre *interj* gee up!; **¡a., caballo!** gee up!
arrea *interj* (a) *(caramba)* good grief *o* heavens! (b) *(vamos)* come on!, get a move on!; **¡a., que llegamos tarde!** come on *o* get a move on or we'll be late!
arreado, -a *adj Col Fam (a toda velocidad)* **pasaron arreados** they flew by; **en cuanto lo vieron, salieron arreados** they legged it as soon as they saw him
arrear 1 *vt* (a) *(azuzar)* to gee up (b) **¡arreando!** *(¡vamos!)* come on!, let's get a move on! (c) *(propinar)* to give; **a. una bofetada a alguien** to give sb a slap, to slap sb (d) *(poner arreos)* to harness (e) *Arg, Chile, Méx (robar)* to steal, to rustle
2 *vi* EXPR **el que venga después** *o* **detrás, que arree** let's leave that for someone else to sort out
arrebatado, -a *adj* (a) *(vehemente)* impassioned; **un a. visionario** an enraptured visionary (b) *(iracundo)* enraged (c) *(cara)* flushed; *(rojo)* deep
arrebatador, -ora *adj (personalidad, sonrisa)* captivating
arrebatamiento *nm* (a) *(apasionamiento)* passion, enthusiasm (b) *(furor)* fury, rage
arrebatar 1 *vt* (a) *(quitar)* **a. algo a alguien** to snatch sth from sb; **me arrebató el billete de las manos** she snatched the banknote out of my hands; **le arrebató el récord mundial** he took the world record off him; **arrebataron mercado a sus competidores** they won market share from their competitors; **les arrebataron sus tierras** their land was seized; **campos de cultivo arrebatados al desierto** farmland reclaimed from the desert
(b) *(cautivar)* to captivate
(c) *(quemar)* **la carne quedó arrebatada** the meat was burnt on the outside and not properly cooked on the inside
(d) *Ven (atropellar)* to knock down
2 **arrebatarse** *vpr* (a) *(enfurecerse)* to get furious (b) *(quemarse)* **se ha arrebatado la carne** the meat is burnt on the outside and not properly cooked on the inside
arrebato *nm* (a) *(arranque)* **lo tiró por la ventana de un a.** *o* **en un a. de cólera** he threw it out of the window in a fit of rage; **en un a. de generosidad** in an outburst of generosity; **un a. de amor** a crush (b) *(furia)* rage, fury; **con a.** in fury, enraged (c) *(éxtasis)* ecstasy (d) *RP (robo)* bag-snatching
arrebatón *nm Carib Fam* bag-snatching; **le dieron un a.** she had her bag snatched
arrebol *nm* (a) *(de cara)* rosiness, ruddiness (b) *(de nubes)* red glow
arrebolado, -a *adj* blushing
arrebolar 1 *vt (ruborizar)* to redden
2 **arrebolarse** *vpr (mejillas)* to redden, to blush
arrebujar 1 *vt* (a) *(amontonar)* to bundle (up) (b) *(arropar)* to wrap up (warmly)
2 **arrebujarse** *vpr (arroparse)* to wrap oneself up; *(encogerse)* to huddle up; **se arrebujó entre las mantas** he snuggled up under the blankets
arrechar *CAm, Col, Méx, Ven* 1 *vt Vulg* to make horny
2 **arrecharse** *vpr* (a) *Fam (enfurecerse)* to blow one's top (b) *Vulg (excitarse)* to get horny
arrechera *nf CAm, Col, Méx, Ven Fam (furia)* **le dio a.** she blew her top
arrecho, -a *adj* (a) *CAm, Col, Méx, Ven Vulg (excitado)* horny
(b) *CAm, Méx, Ven Fam (colérico)* crabby, *Br* stroppy; **es una persona difícil, muy arrecha** she's a difficult person to get on with, the least thing makes her blow her top
(c) *CAm, Méx, Ven Fam (furioso)* mad, furious; **la cuenta de luz altísima lo puso a.** he blew his top over the huge electricity bill
(d) *CAm, Col, Méx, Ven Fam (difícil)* hellish, hellishly difficult
(e) *CAm, Col, Méx, Ven Fam (valiente)* gutsy
(f) *Ven Fam (sensacional)* mega, wicked; **su último disco es arrechísimo** her latest record is mega *o* wicked
arrechucho *nm Fam* **me dio un a.** I was ill, I wasn't feeling too well
arreciar *vi* (a) *(temporal, lluvia)* to get worse; *(viento)* to get stronger, to pick up (b) *(críticas)* to intensify
arrecife *nm* reef ►► ***a. barrera*** barrier reef; ***a. de coral*** coral reef
arredrar 1 *vt* to put off, to intimidate; **las dificultades no le arredraban** he wasn't put off by the difficulties
2 **arredrarse** *vpr* **no se arredra ante nada** he's not easily put off; **se arredró con las amenazas que recibió** he was intimidated by the threats he received

arreglado, -a *adj* (**a**) *(reparado)* fixed, repaired
(**b**) *(ropa)* mended
(**c**) *(ordenado)* tidy
(**d**) *(solucionado)* sorted out; **¡y asunto a.!** that's that!; EXPR *Fam* **estar a.: ¿y ahora se va de vacaciones? ¡pues estamos arreglados!** and now he's off on holiday? well that's just what we need!; **¡estaríamos arreglados si ahora tuviéramos que pagar la cena también!** it really would be the last straw if we had to pay for the meal as well!; **¡están arreglados si se piensan que vamos a aceptar!** if they think we're going to accept, they've got another think coming!
(**e**) *(precio)* reasonable
(**f**) *(bien vestido)* smart; **le gusta ir a.** he likes to dress smartly

---

ARREGLAR 1 *vt* (**a**) *(reparar)* to fix, to repair; **me arreglarán la moto en una semana** they'll fix *o* repair my bike for me within a week; **están arreglando la autopista** they're repairing the motorway; *Fam* **me costó una fortuna arreglarme la boca** it cost me a fortune to have my teeth seen to
(**b**) *(ropa) (estrechar)* to take in; *(agrandar)* to let out
(**c**) *(ordenar)* to tidy (up); **a. la casa** to do the housework
(**d**) *(solucionar)* to sort out; **todo arreglado, podemos pasar** everything's been sorted out now, we can go in; **arreglaron los papeles para casarse** they got all the necessary papers together so that they could marry; **ya arreglaremos cuentas cuando hayas cobrado** we'll settle once you've been paid, we'll sort out who owes what once you've been paid
(**e**) *Mús* to arrange
(**f**) *(acicalar)* to smarten up; *(cabello)* to do; **arregla a los niños, que vamos a dar un paseo** get the children ready, we're going for a walk; **tengo que arreglarme el pelo para la fiesta** I have to get my hair done before the party
(**g**) *(adornar)* to decorate
(**h**) *(plato)* to season; **¿quieres que arregle la ensalada?** shall I put some dressing on the salad?
(**i**) *Am (planta)* to tend to
(**j**) *Am (votación)* to rig
(**k**) *Fam (escarmentar)* **¡ya te arreglaré yo!** I'm going to sort you out!
2 *vi Am (quedar)* **arreglé de ir al cine el sábado** I've arranged to go to the cinema on Saturday; **¿cómo vas a la fiesta? - ya arreglé con Silvia** how are you getting to the party? - I've already arranged to go with Silvia
3 **arreglarse** *vpr* (**a**) *(asunto, problema)* to sort itself out; **no llores, todo se arreglará** don't cry, it'll all sort itself out *o* work out in the end
(**b**) *(tiempo)* to improve, to get better; **si se arregla el día saldremos de excursión** if the weather improves *o* gets better we can go on a trip somewhere
(**c**) *(apañarse)* to make do (**con algo** with sth); **es muy austero, con poca cosa se arregla** he's very austere, he makes do with very little; **no me prepares nada especial, me arreglo con un café** don't make anything special for me, a coffee will do fine; EXPR **arreglárselas (para hacer algo)** to manage (to do sth); **nos las arreglamos como pudimos** we did the best we could; **¡arréglatelas como puedas!** that's your problem!; **siempre se las arregla para conseguir lo que quiere** she always manages to get what she wants; **no sé cómo te las arreglas para perder siempre** I don't know how you always manage to lose
(**d**) *(acicalarse)* to smarten up; **no he tenido tiempo para arreglarme** I didn't have time to get ready; **se pasa la mañana arreglándose** she spends all morning doing herself up
(**e**) *RP Fam (amigarse)* to make up; **¿no estaban peleadas? – sí, pero ya nos arreglamos** hadn't you fallen out? – yes, but we've made up now
(**f**) *RP Fam (empezar a salir)* to start going out; **hace dos meses que nos arreglamos** we started going out two months ago

---

arreglista *nmf Mús* (musical) arranger

arreglo *nm* (**a**) *(reparación)* repair; **la moto necesitará algunos arreglos** the motorbike will need a few repairs doing; **tras el a. del fallo el transbordador pudo despegar** after the fault had been fixed the shuttle was able to take off; EXPR **tener a.: este secador no tiene a.** this hairdryer is beyond repair; **¡ese niño no tiene arreglo!** that child's a hopeless case!; **¡todo tiene a.!** there's always a solution to everything!
(**b**) *(de ropa)* alteration; **hacer un a. a un vestido** to make an alteration to a dress
(**c**) *(acuerdo)* agreement; **llegar a un a.** to reach an agreement; **un a. pacífico de las diferencias** an amicable settlement of differences; **con a. a** in accordance with; **con a. al derecho internacional** in accordance with international law; **lo hice con a. a las instrucciones que recibí** I did it in accordance with the instructions I received
(**d**) ***a. de cuentas*** settling of scores
(**e**) *(aseo)* **a. personal** (personal) appearance
(**f**) *Mús* **a. (musical)** (musical) arrangement

arrejuntar *Fam* 1 *vt Am* (**a**) *(poner junto)* to put together; **arrejunta los pies** put your feet together (**b**) *(reunir)* **arrejuntó plata para comprar una moto** he got together enough money to buy a motorbike
2 **arrejuntarse** *vpr* (**a**) *(pareja)* to shack up together; **nuestros vecinos se han arrejuntado** our neighbours are shacked up together (**b**) *Am (grupo)* to get together; **nos arrejuntamos para construir la iglesia** we got together to build the church

arrellanarse *vpr* to settle back; **se arrellanó en el sofá** she settled back in the sofa

arremangado, -a = **remangado**

arremangar = **remangar**

arremeter *vi* **a. contra** to attack; **los soldados arremetieron contra las posiciones enemigas** the soldiers attacked *o* charged the enemy positions; **el portavoz de la oposición arremetió contra el proyecto** the opposition spokesman attacked the project

arremetida *nf* attack

arremolinar 1 *vt* **el viento arremolina las hojas** the wind swirled the leaves around
2 **arremolinarse** *vpr* (**a**) *(agua, hojas)* to swirl (about) (**b**) *(personas)* **los fans se arremolinaban a la salida del teatro** an excited crowd of fans was milling around outside the theatre; **arremolinarse alrededor de** *o* **en torno a** to mill round about, to crowd round

arrendador, -ora *nm,f* lessor

arrendajo *nm* jay ►► ***a. azul*** blue jay

arrendamiento, arriendo *nm* (**a**) *(acción de dar en arriendo)* renting, leasing; **estos terrenos están en a.** *(cedidos)* this land is being rented *o* leased; **contrato de a.** lease ►► ***a. financiero*** financial leasing (**b**) *(acción de tomar en arriendo)* renting, leasing; **tomar algo en a.** to rent *o* lease sth (**c**) *(precio)* rent

arrendar [3] *vt* (**a**) *(dar en arriendo)* to let, to lease; **me arrendó su casa** he let *o* rented his house to me (**b**) *(tomar en arriendo)* to rent, to lease; **arrendamos sus tierras desde hace años** we have leased his land for years; *Am* **se arrienda** *(en letrero)* for *o* to rent

arrendatario, -a 1 *adj* leasing
2 *nm,f (de alojamiento)* tenant, leaseholder; *(de local comercial)* leaseholder

arrendaticio, -a *adj* **condiciones arrendaticias** terms of lease

arreo *nm Am (recua)* herd, drove

arreos *nmpl* (**a**) *(de caballo)* harness (**b**) *(equipo)* accessories, equipment

arrepanchigarse [38] *vpr Fam* to stretch out, to sprawl

arrepentido, -a 1 *adj* repentant; **a. de sus acciones, pidió disculpas** he apologized remorsefully; **estoy muy a. de lo que hice** I'm deeply sorry for what I did, I very much regret what I did; **un terrorista a.** a reformed terrorist
2 *nm,f* (**a**) *Rel* penitent (**b**) *Pol* = person who has renounced criminal ways and helped the police

arrepentimiento *nm* (**a**) *(de pecado, crimen)* repentance (**b**) *(cambio de idea)* change of mind

arrepentirse [63] *vpr* (**a**) *(de acción)* to regret it; **a. de algo/de haber hecho algo** to regret sth/having done sth; **ven a Cuba, no te arrepentirás** come to Cuba, you won't regret it; **como no me hagas caso, te arrepentirás** you'll be sorry if you don't listen to me, if you don't listen to me you'll live to regret it
(**b**) *(de pecado, crimen)* to repent; **a. de algo/de haber hecho algo** to repent (of) sth/having done sth
(**c**) *(volverse atrás)* **al final, me arrepentí y no fui** in the end, I decided not to go; **no te arrepientas en el último momento** don't change your mind at the last minute

arrestado, -a 1 *adj* under arrest; **queda usted a.** you are under arrest
2 *nm,f* person under arrest; **llevaron los arrestados a la comisaría** they took those they had arrested to the police station

arrestar *vt* to arrest

arresto *nm* (**a**) *(detención)* arrest; **su a. se produjo en plena calle** he was arrested in broad daylight; **durante su a. lo torturaron** while under arrest he was tortured
(**b**) *(reclusión)* **al soldado le impusieron dos días de a.** the soldier was locked up for two days ►► ***a. domiciliario*** house arrest; ***a. mayor*** = prison sentence of between one month and a day and six months; ***a. menor*** = prison sentence of between one and thirty days

arrestos *nmpl (valor)* courage; **tener a. para hacer algo** to have the courage to do sth

arrianismo *nm Rel* Arianism, Arian heresy

arriano, -a *Rel* **1** *adj* Arian
2 *nm,f* Arian

arriar [32] *vt (velas, bandera)* to lower

arriate *nm* (flower-) bed

ARRIBA **1** *adv* **(a)** *(posición) (en general)* above; *(en edificio)* upstairs; **me he dejado el paraguas a.** I've left my umbrella up in the *Br* flat *o US* apartment; **te esperaremos a., en la cumbre** we'll wait for you up at the top; **de a.** top; **el estante de a.** the top shelf; **el apartamento de a.** *(el siguiente)* the upstairs *Br* flat *o US* apartment; *(el último)* the top *Br* flat *o US* apartment; **vive a.** she lives upstairs; **los vecinos de a.** the upstairs neighbours; **está aquí/allí a.** it's up here/there; **a. del todo** right at the top; **más a.** further up; **ponlo un poco más a.** put it a bit higher up; **el Estudiantes va dos puntos a.** Estudiantes are two points up, Estudiantes are winning by two points; *Am* **a. de** above
(b) *(dirección)* up; **ve a.** *(en edificio)* go upstairs; **hacia** *o* **para a.** up, upwards; **empujar hacia a.** to push upwards; **calle/escaleras a.** up the street/stairs; **cuesta a.** uphill; **río a.** upstream; **tres bloques más a.** three blocks further along *o* up
(c) *(en una escala)* **los de a.** *(los que mandan)* those at the top; **personas de metro y medio para a.** people of one and a half metres or over, people taller than one and a half metres; **de sargentos para a.** everyone above the rank of sergeant; **a. de** more than
(d) *(en un texto)* above; **más a.** above; **el a. mencionado** the above-mentioned
(e) EXPR *Fam* **estar hasta a. de trabajo** to be up to one's neck in work; **de a. abajo** *(cosa)* from top to bottom; *(persona)* from head to toe; **inspeccionar algo de a. abajo** to inspect sth thoroughly; **mirar a alguien de a. abajo** *(con desdén)* to look sb up and down; *RP Fam* **tener algo para tirar para a.** to have loads of sth
2 *prep Am* **a. (de)** *(encima de)* on top of
3 de arriba *loc adv RP Fam* free; **a esa disco siempre entro de a.** I always get into that disco for free; **suele fumar de a.** she's always scrounging cigarettes off people
4 *interj* up you get!; **¡a., que se hace tarde!** come on, get up, it's getting late!; **¡a....!** up (with)...!; **¡a. la república!** long live the republic!; **¡a. los mineros!** up (with) the miners!; **¡a. las manos!** hands up!

arribada *nf Náut* arrival, entry into port

arribar *vi* **(a) a. a** *(lugar)* to reach; **a. a puerto** to reach port; *Fig* **el proceso de paz arribó a buen puerto** the peace process came to a successful conclusion **(b) a. a** *(conclusión, acerdo)* to arrive at

arribazón *nf* = arrival of large numbers of turtles or seaweed on the shore

arribeño, -a *Am* **1** *adj* highland
2 *nm,f* highlander

arribismo *nm* **(a)** *(oportunismo)* opportunism **(b)** *(ambición)* social climbing

arribista **1** *adj* opportunist, careerist
2 *nmf* arriviste

arribo *nm (llegada)* arrival

arriende *etc ver* **arrendar**

arriendo = **arrendamiento**

arriero, -a *nm,f* muleteer

arriesgado, -a *adj* **(a)** *(peligroso) (decisión, operación)* risky **(b)** *(osado)* daring; **es una persona muy arriesgada** she's a very daring person

arriesgar [38] **1** *vt* **(a)** *(exponer a peligro)* to risk; **arriesgó la vida por sus ideales** she risked her life for her beliefs **(b)** *(proponer)* to venture, to suggest
2 arriesgarse *vpr* to take risks/a risk; **no quiero arriesgarme** I don't want to risk it; **no se arriesgó a participar** she didn't risk taking part; **si no te vas ahora te arriesgas a perder el tren** if you don't go now you risk missing the train; **se arriesga a que le descubran** he's running the risk of being found out

arrimado *nm Col, Méx, Ven Fam* scrounger; **está de a. en mi casa** he's living off me

arrimar **1** *vt* **(a)** *(acercar)* to move *o* bring closer; **a. algo a** *o* **contra algo** *(pared, mesa)* to move sth up against sth; EXPR *Fam* **a. el hombro** to lend a hand, to muck in; EXPR **a. el ascua a su sardina** to look after number one **(b)** *(arrinconar)* to put away
2 arrimarse *vpr* **(a)** *(acercarse)* to move closer; **arrímate, que no cabemos** move up or we won't all fit in; **arrimarse a algo** *(acercándose)* to move closer to sth; *(apoyándose)* to lean on sth; **arrímate más a la mesa** move in closer to the table; **el barco se arrimó al muelle** the boat pulled alongside the quay; EXPR **arrimarse al sol que más calienta: siempre se arrima al sol que más calienta** she'll change her loyalties whenever it suits her own interests
(b) *(ampararse)* **arrimarse a alguien** to seek sb's protection
(c) *Fam (pareja)* to shack up together
(d) *Ven Fam (en casa)* **se arrimaron en casa de sus padres cuando se inundó su casa** her parents took them in when they were flooded out
(e) *Taurom* to get close to the bull

arrimo *nm (amparo)* protection; **al a. de** under the protection of

arrinconado, -a *adj* **(a)** *(abandonado)* discarded, forgotten; **tenían el baúl a. en una esquina** the trunk was lying discarded *o* forgotten in a corner **(b)** *(acorralado)* cornered

arrinconamiento *nm (abandono)* **la guerra causó el a. del asunto** the issue was shelved because of the war

arrinconar *vt* **(a)** *(apartar)* to put in a corner **(b)** *(dar de lado)* **a. a alguien** to leave sb out in the cold **(c)** *(abandonar)* to discard; **el proyecto fue arrinconado** the project was shelved **(d)** *(acorralar)* to (back into a) corner; **el presidente arrinconó con sus preguntas al candidato** the president backed the candidate into a corner with his questions

arriscado, -a *adj* **(a)** *(atrevido)* daring, bold **(b)** *(peñascoso)* craggy

arriscar [60] **1** *vt Andes, CAm, Méx (remangar)* to roll up
2 *vi Col (osar)* to dare; **a que usted no arrisca con un bulto de cemento** I bet you can't lift a bag of cement
3 arriscarse *vpr* **(a)** *Andes, CAm, Méx (remangarse)* to roll up; **arriscarse los pantalones** to roll up one's trouser legs **(b)** *Perú, Salv (engalanarse)* to dress up

arritmia *nf Med* arrhythmia

arrítmico, -a *adj (irregular)* irregular

arrizar *vt Náut* **(a)** *(vela)* to reef **(b)** *(atar)* to lash down

arroba *nf* **(a)** *(unidad de peso)* = 11.5 kg; *Fig* **por arrobas** by the sackful **(b)** *(unidad de volumen) (para vino)* = approx 16 litres; *(para aceite)* = approx 12 litres **(c)** *Informát (símbolo)* at, @ sign; **"juan, a. mundonet, punto, es"** "juan, at mundonet, dot, es"

arrobado, -a *adj* enraptured

arrobar **1** *vt* to captivate
2 arrobarse *vpr* to go into raptures

arrobo, arrobamiento *nm* rapture; **la miraba con a.** he looked at her in rapture

arrocero, -a **1** *adj* rice; **la producción arrocera** rice production; **una región arrocera** a rice-growing region
2 *nm,f (agricultor)* rice grower

arrodillar **1** *vt* to force to kneel
2 arrodillarse *vpr* **(a)** *(ponerse de rodillas)* to kneel down (**ante** in front of *o* before) **(b)** *(someterse)* to go down on one's knees, to grovel (**ante** to)

arrogación *nf Der* adoption

arrogancia *nf* arrogance; **con a.** arrogantly

arrogante *adj* arrogant

arrogantemente *adv* arrogantly

arrogar [38] **1** *vt (adoptar)* to adopt
2 arrogarse *vpr (poderes)* to assume, to arrogate to oneself

arrojadizo, -a *adj* **utilizar algo como arma arrojadiza** *(botella, ladrillo)* to use sth as a missile; *Fig* **servirá como arma arrojadiza contra el gobierno** it will be used as a stick to beat the government

arrojado, -a *adj* bold, fearless

arrojar **1** *vt* **(a)** *(lanzar)* to throw; *(con violencia)* to hurl, to fling; **arrojaron piedras contra la embajada** they hurled *o* flung stones at the embassy; **prohibido a. basuras** *(en letrero)* no dumping; **prohibido a. objetos a la vía** *(en letrero)* do not throw objects onto the track
(b) *(despedir) (humo)* to send out; *(olor)* to give off; *(lava)* to spew out; *Fig* **a. luz sobre algo** to throw light on sth
(c) *(echar)* **a. a alguien de** to throw *o* kick sb out of; **lo arrojaron de casa** they threw *o* kicked him out
(d) *(resultado)* **el censo arrojó la cifra de 50 millones de habitantes** the census arrived at a figure of 50 million inhabitants; **las cuentas arrojaban un déficit de 5.000 millones** the accounts showed a deficit of five billion; **el resultado arroja dudas sobre la popularidad del gobierno** the result casts doubt on the government's popularity; **las cifras arrojan perspectivas optimistas para la economía** the figures offer room for optimism about the future of the economy; **la gestión del gobierno arroja un saldo positivo** on balance, the

government's performance has been good
(e) *(vomitar)* to throw up
2 *vi (vomitar)* to throw up
3 **arrojarse** *vpr* to hurl oneself; **arrojarse en los brazos de alguien** to fling *o* throw oneself at sb; **se arrojó por la borda** she threw herself *o* jumped overboard; **se arrojaron al río** they threw themselves *o* jumped into the river; **se arrojó sobre el asaltante** she hurled herself at her attacker

arrojo *nm* courage, fearlessness; **con a.** courageously, fearlessly

arrolladito *nm RP* ***a. primavera*** spring roll

arrollado *nm RP (dulce) Br* swiss roll, *US* jelly roll; *(salado)* = roll of sponge cake with a savoury filling ►► ***a. primavera*** spring roll

arrollador, -ora *adj (victoria)* crushing, overwhelming; *(superioridad)* overwhelming; *(éxito)* resounding, overwhelming; *(belleza, personalidad)* dazzling; **es de una simpatía arrolladora** she's an incredibly nice person

arrollamiento *nm Am* **la cantidad de arrollamientos aumenta año tras año** more people get run over every year; **es increíble que haya sobrevivido al a.** it's amazing that she survived being run over like that

arrollar 1 *vt* (a) *(atropellar)* to knock down, to run over; **lo arrolló un coche** he was knocked down *o* run over by a car (b) *(tirar) (sujeto: agua, viento)* to sweep away (c) *(vencer)* to crush (d) *(enrollar)* to roll (up)
2 *vi (ganar todos los premios)* to sweep the board; *(vencer claramente)* to achieve a crushing victory

arropar 1 *vt* (a) *(con ropa)* to wrap up (b) *(en cama)* to tuck up (c) *(proteger)* to support; **arropado por su familia, consiguió superar su depresión** with his family's support, he was able to come through his depression
2 **arroparse** *vpr* to wrap oneself up

arrope *nm* (a) *(de mosto)* grape syrup (b) *(de miel)* honey syrup

arrorró *(pl* **arrorroes***) nm Andes, RP Fam* lullaby

arrostrar *vt (penalidad, peligro)* to endure

arroyada *nf* (a) *(crecida)* flood, freshet (b) *(cauce)* channel

arroyo *nm* (a) *(riachuelo)* stream (b) *(de la calle)* gutter; EXPR **plantar a alguien en la mitad del a.** to throw *o* kick sb out; EXPR **sacar a alguien del a.** to drag sb out of the gutter; EXPR **terminar en el a.: terminaron las dos en el a.** they both ended up in the gutter (c) *Cuba (calzada)* road (surface), *US* pavement

arroz *nm (cereal)* rice; EXPR *Fam* **¡que si quieres a., Catalina!** for all the good that did!; EXPR *Carib Fam* **a. con mango** *(lío)* chaos, mayhem; *Carib Fam* **la fiesta se convirtió en un a. con mango** the party got pretty wild ►► ***a. blanco*** boiled rice; ***a. a la cubana*** = boiled rice topped with a fried egg and tomato sauce, served with fried banana or plantain; ***a. de grano largo*** long-grain rice; ***a. integral*** brown rice; ***a. con leche*** rice pudding; ***a. salvaje*** wild rice; ***a. silvestre*** wild rice; ***a. vaporizado*** easy-cook rice

arrozal *nm* paddy field

arruga *nf* (a) *(en ropa, papel)* crease; **tenía el traje lleno de arrugas** his suit was all creased (b) *(en piel)* wrinkle, line; **con arrugas** wrinkled (c) *Andes, Pan (estafa)* trick, swindle

arrugado, -a *adj* (a) *(ropa, papel)* creased, crumpled (b) *(piel)* wrinkled, lined

arrugamiento *nm (de ropa, papel)* creasing, crumpling

arrugar [38] 1 *vt* (a) *(ropa, papel)* to crease, to crumple (b) *(piel)* to wrinkle (c) **a. el ceño** to frown
2 **arrugarse** *vpr* (a) *(ropa, papel)* to get creased (b) *(piel)* to get wrinkled; **se le arrugaron las yemas de los dedos** *(en el baño)* his fingertips wrinkled up (c) *Fam (acobardarse)* to chicken out; **iba a reclamar pero al final se arrugó** he was going to complain, but in the end he chickened out

arruinado, -a *adj (persona)* ruined, bankrupt; *(empresa)* failed, bankrupt; **una familia arruinada** a family that has seen better days

arruinar 1 *vt* (a) *(financieramente)* to ruin (b) *(estropear)* to ruin; **el pedrisco arruinó la cosecha** the hail ruined the crop; **el alcohol le arruinó la salud** alcohol ruined his health; **el mal tiempo arruinó la ceremonia** the bad weather ruined *o* spoiled the ceremony
2 **arruinarse** *vpr* (a) *(financieramente)* to go bankrupt, to be ruined; *Irónico* **porque pages una ronda no te vas a a.** buying a round won't exactly bankrupt you (b) *(estropearse)* to be ruined; **esta piel se ha arruinado con la lluvia** the rain ruined this leather

arrullar 1 *vt* (a) *(para dormir)* to lull to sleep; **arrullaron al niño para que se durmiera** they sang the child to sleep (b) *(palomas)* to coo at *o* to (c) *Fam (personas)* to whisper sweet nothings to
2 **arrullarse** *vpr (palomas)* to coo

arrullo *nm* (a) *(de palomas)* cooing (b) *(nana)* lullaby (c) *(de agua, olas)* murmur; **se quedó dormido al a. de las olas** he was lulled to sleep by the murmur of the waves

arrumaco *nm Fam* **hacerse arrumacos** *(amantes)* to kiss and cuddle; **hacer arrumacos a** *(bebé)* to coo at

arrumaje *nm Náut* stowage

arrumar *vt* (a) *Náut* to stow (b) *Andes, Ven (amontonar)* to pile up

arrumbar *vt* **viejos libros arrumbados en un cajón** old books stored *o* packed away in a box; **arrumbaron los viejos odios que había entre ellos** they buried the long-standing hatred that had existed between them

arrume *nm Andes, Ven* pile

arrurruz *nm (fécula)* arrowroot

arsenal *nm* (a) *(de armas)* arsenal (b) *(de cosas, pruebas)* array; **utilizó todo el a. teórico del marxismo para rebatir el argumento** he used the entire armoury of Marxist theory to refute the argument (c) *Esp (de barcos)* shipyard

arsénico *nm Quím* arsenic

art *nm Arte* ***a. decó*** art deco; ***a. nouveau*** art nouveau, modern style

art. *(abrev de* **artículo***)* art.

arte *nm o nf*

Usually masculine in the singular and feminine in the plural.

(a) *(creación estética)* art; **una obra de a.** a work of art; **el a. gótico/barroco** Gothic/baroque art; EXPR **como por a. de birlibirloque** *o* **de magia** as if by magic ►► ***a. abstracto*** abstract art; ***artes audiovisuales*** audiovisual arts; ***a. conceptual*** conceptual art; ***artes decorativas*** decorative arts; ***a. dramático*** drama; ***artes escénicas*** performing arts; ***a. figurativo*** figurative art; ***artes gráficas*** graphic arts; ***artes interpretativas*** performing arts; ***artes liberales*** liberal arts; ***artes marciales*** martial arts; ***a. naïf*** naive art; ***artes y oficios*** arts and crafts; ***artes plásticas*** plastic arts; ***a. religioso*** religious art; ***a. rupestre*** cave paintings
(b) *(habilidad, estilo)* artistry; **con (buen) a.** with (great) style; **tiene mucho a. para recitar** she's got a real talent for reciting poetry
(c) *(astucia)* artfulness, cunning; **emplearon todas sus artes para timarla** they used all their cunning *o* wiles to cheat her; **malas artes** trickery; EXPR **no tener a. ni parte en algo** to have nothing whatsoever to do with sth
(d) **artes (de pesca)** *(instrumentos)* fishing tackle
(e) *Lit (verso)* **de a. mayor** = comprising lines of more than eight syllables; **de a. menor** = comprising lines of eight syllables or fewer

artefacto *nm* (a) *(aparato)* device; *(máquina)* machine; **a. explosivo/incendiario** explosive/incendiary device ►► *CSur* ***artefactos de baño*** bathroom fixtures; *RP* ***a. eléctrico*** electrical household appliance; *RP* ***artefactos de iluminación*** light fittings and fixtures; *CSur* ***artefactos sanitarios*** bathroom fixtures (b) *(armatoste)* contraption

artejo *nm Zool* article

artemisa, artemisia *nf* mugwort, *Espec* artemisia

arteramente *adv* cunningly, slyly

arteria *nf* (a) *(vaso sanguíneo)* artery ►► ***a. aorta*** aortic artery; ***a. carótida*** carotid artery; ***a. celíaca*** coeliac artery; ***a. coronaria*** coronary artery; ***a. femoral*** femoral artery; ***a. iliaca*** ileac artery; ***a. ilíaca*** ileac artery; ***a. pulmonar*** pulmonary artery; ***a. subclavia*** subclavian artery (b) *(calle, carretera)* artery; **una de las principales arterias de la capital** one of the capital's main arteries

artería *nf* cunning, slyness

arterial *adj* arterial

arterioesclerótico, -a, arterioesclerósico, -a *adj Med* arteriosclerotic

arterioesclerosis, arteriosclerosis *nf inv Med* arteriosclerosis

arteriola *nf Anat* arteriole

artero, -a *adj* cunning, sly

artesa *nf* (a) *(para amasar pan)* kneading trough (b) *Geol* **un valle en a.** a U-shaped valley

artesanado *nm* (a) *(artesanos)* craftsmen (b) *(arte)* artisanship, artisanry

artesanal *adj (zapatos, bomba)* handcrafted; *(queso, miel)* produced using traditional methods, handmade; *(pesca, agricultura)* traditional; **de fabricación a.** *(zapatos, bomba)* handcrafted; *(queso, miel)* produced using traditional methods, handmade; **métodos artesanales** traditional methods; **pan a.** traditionally baked bread; **el sector a.** traditional industries; **el pueblo es un importante centro a.** the village is an important centre for traditional industries; **encontraron una solución a. al problema** they found a solution to the problem using traditional methods

artesanalmente *adv* **fabricado a.** made using traditional methods

artesanía *nf* (**a**) *(arte)* craftsmanship; **un taller de a.** a crafts workshop; **objetos de a.** crafts, handicrafts (**b**) *(productos)* crafts, handicrafts; **feria de a.** craft fair

artesano, -a 1 *adj (zapatos, bomba)* handcrafted; *(queso, miel)* produced using traditional methods; *(pesca, agricultura)* traditional; **métodos artesanales** traditional methods
2 *nm,f* craftsman, *f* craftswoman

artesiano, -a *adj* **pozo a.** artesian well

artesón *nm* (**a**) *Arquit (techo)* coffered ceiling (**b**) *Arquit (adorno)* coffer (**c**) *(para fregar)* washtub

artesonado, -a *Arquit* 1 *adj* coffered
2 *nm* coffered ceiling

ártico, -a 1 *adj* Arctic; **el océano Glacial Á.** the Arctic Ocean
2 *nm* **el Á.** the Arctic

articulación *nf* (**a**) *Anat* joint ►► ***a. de la cadera*** hip joint; ***a. de la rodilla*** knee joint (**b**) *Tec* joint (**c**) *Ling* articulation (**d**) *(estructuración)* co-ordination; **los problemas de a. de un estado federal** the problems of co-ordinating a federal state; **la a. del relato es muy sencilla** the story has a very simple structure

articulado, -a 1 *adj* (**a**) *(brazo, hueso)* articulated (**b**) *(vehículo, grúa, robot)* articulated
2 *nm* articles

articular 1 *adj Med* articular; **tiene problemas articulares** she has problems with her joints
2 *vt* (**a**) *(piezas)* to articulate
(**b**) *(palabras)* to articulate; **no pude a. palabra** I couldn't utter *o* say a word
(**c**) *(ley, contrato)* to break down into separate articles
(**d**) *(plan, política)* to develop, to produce; **la necesidad de a. una fiscalidad única para toda europa** the need to develop a single European taxation system; **esta reforma está articulada en torno a tres principios** this reform is structured around *o* built on three principles
3 *vi (pronunciar)* to articulate; **a. bien** to articulate clearly
4 **articularse** *vpr* **el informe se articula en tres partes** the report is structured in three parts

articulista *nmf* feature writer; **según el a.** according to the author *o* writer (of the article)

artículo *nm* (**a**) *Gram* article ►► ***a. definido*** definite article; ***a. determinado*** definite article; ***a. indefinido*** indefinite article; ***a. indeterminado*** indefinite article; ***a. neutro*** neuter article *(in Spanish, refers to the article "lo")*
(**b**) *(periodístico)* article ►► ***a. de fondo*** editorial
(**c**) *(de diccionario)* entry
(**d**) *(en ley, reglamento)* article ►► *Rel* ***a. de fe*** article of faith; **tomar algo como a. de fe** to take sth as gospel
(**e**) *(objeto, mercancía)* article, item; **han rebajado todos los artículos** all items have been reduced; EXPR *Fam* **hacer el a. a alguien** to give sb a sales pitch ►► ***a. básico*** basic product; ***artículos de fumador*** smokers' requisites; ***a. de importación*** import; ***artículos de limpieza*** *(objetos)* cleaning accessories; *(productos)* cleaning products; ***a. de primera necesidad*** basic commodity; ***artículos de regalo*** gift items; ***artículos de viaje*** travel accessories
(**f**) *Formal* **in a. mortis** *(confesar, casarse)* on one's deathbed

artífice *nmf* (**a**) *(creador, responsable)* architect; **el a. del proceso de paz** the architect of the peace process; **el a. de esta técnica quirúrgica** the inventor of this surgical technique, the man who developed this surgical technique (**b**) *(artesano)* craftsman, *f* craftswoman

artificial *adj* (**a**) *(hecho por el hombre) (flor, lago)* artificial; *(material)* man-made, artificial (**b**) *(no espontáneo) (persona, sonrisa, amabilidad)* artificial

artificialidad *nf* artificiality

artificialmente *adv* artificially

artificiero *nm (experto)* explosives expert; *(desactivador)* bomb disposal officer

artificio *nm* (**a**) *(aparato)* device (**b**) *(falsedad)* **se comporta con mucho a.** he has a very artificial manner; **un estilo sin a.** a very natural style (**c**) *(artimaña)* trick

artificiosidad *nf* artificiality; **con a.** unnaturally, artificially

artificioso, -a *adj (no natural)* contrived

artillado, -a *adj* **helicóptero a.** helicopter gunship

artillería *nf* (**a**) *Mil* artillery ►► ***a. antiaérea*** anti-aircraft guns; ***a. de campaña*** field artillery; ***a. ligera*** light artillery; ***a. pesada*** heavy artillery (**b**) *(recursos)* **desplegaron toda la a. diplomática para evitar la guerra** they used every diplomatic means at their disposal to avoid war (**c**) *Dep (delantera)* attack, forward line

artillero, -a 1 *adj* artillery; **ataque a.** artillery attack
2 *nm* (**a**) *Mil (soldado)* artilleryman (**b**) *(especialista en explosivos)* explosives expert (**c**) *Dep (goleador)* marksman, goal-scorer

artilugio *nm* (**a**) *(objeto)* contraption (**b**) **artilugios** *(herramientas)* equipment; **los artilugios de pesca** fishing tackle (**c**) *(artimaña, engaño)* trick, ruse

artimaña *nf* trick, ruse; **se sirvió de todo tipo de artimañas para conseguir su objetivo** she used all kinds of trickery to get what she wanted

artiodáctilo *Zool* 1 *nm (animal)* artiodactyl
2 **artiodáctilos** *nmpl (familia) Artiodactyla*; **del orden de los artiodáctilos** of the order *Artiodactyla*

artista *nmf* (**a**) *(creador)* artist; **los grandes artistas del siglo** the great artists of the 20th century ►► ***a. gráfico*** graphic artist
(**b**) *(de teatro, circo)* artiste; *(cantante)* artist; **un a. de cine** a movie actor ►► ***a. invitado*** guest artist; ***a. de variedades*** cabaret artist
(**c**) *Fam (maestro, habilidoso)* **es una a. en la cocina** she is a superb cook; **es un a. arreglando televisores** he's got a real knack for fixing televisions, *Br* he's a dab hand at fixing televisions

artísticamente *adv* artistically

artístico, -a *adj* artistic

artrítico, -a 1 *adj* arthritic
2 *nm,f* arthritic

artritis *nf inv Med* arthritis ►► ***a. reumatoide*** rheumatoid arthritis

artrópodo *Zool* 1 *nm (animal)* arthropod
2 **artrópodos** *nmpl (familia) Arthropoda*; **del tipo de los artrópodos** of the phylum *Arthropoda*

artroscopia *nm Med* arthroscopy

artrosis *nf inv Med* arthrosis

Arturo *n pr* **el rey A.** King Arthur

aruco *nm* horned screamer

arúspice *nm Hist* haruspex

arveja *nf RP* pea

arzobispado *nm* archbishopric

arzobispal *adj* archiepiscopal

arzobispo *nm* archbishop

arzolla *nf* knapweed, centaury

arzón *nm* saddle tree

as *nm* (**a**) *(carta)* ace; **el a. de picas** the ace of spades; EXPR **tener** *o* **llevar** *o* **guardar un a. en la manga** to have an ace up one's sleeve (**b**) *(en dado)* ace (**c**) *(campeón)* **ser un a.** to be brilliant; **un a. del volante** an ace driver; **un a. de la informática** a computer whizzkid (**d**) *Náut* ***a. de guía*** *(nudo)* bowline

ASA *n* (*abrev de* **American Standards Association**) ASA

asa *nf* (**a**) *(mango)* handle (**b**) ***a. fétida*** asafoetida

Takes the masculine articles **el** and **un**.

asadera *nf CSur* roasting tin

asadero *nm Fam* furnace; **esta habitación es un a.** this room is a furnace, it's boiling in this room

asado, -a 1 *adj* (**a**) *(en el horno) (carne)* roast; *(papa o patata) (en trozos)* roast; *(entera con piel)* baked; **castañas asadas** roast chestnuts (**b**) *(a la parrilla) (pescado, chorizo)* grilled
2 *nm* (**a**) *(carne)* roast (**b**) *Col, CSur (barbacoa)* barbecue (**c**) *Col, CSur (reunión)* barbecue (**d**) *RP* ***a. de tira*** *Br* thin flank, *US* plate

asador, -ora 1 *nm* (**a**) *(aparato)* roaster (**b**) *(varilla)* spit (**c**) *(restaurante)* grill, grillroom; **a. de pollos** = shop selling ready-roast chicken
2 *nm,f RP (persona)* = person who does the cooking at a barbecue

asaduras *nfpl (de cordero, ternera)* offal; *(de pollo, pavo)* giblets

asaetear, asaetar *vt* (**a**) *(disparar)* to shoot arrows at; *(matar)* to kill with arrows; **murió asaeteado** he was shot to death by archers (**b**) *(molestar)* **lo asaetearon a preguntas** they bombarded him with questions

asafétida *nf* asafoetida

Takes the masculine articles **el** and **un**.

asalariado, -a 1 *adj* salaried
2 *nm,f* salaried employee

asalariar *vt* to take on

asalmonado, -a *adj* (**a**) *(color)* salmon (**b**) **trucha asalmonada** salmon trout

asaltacunas *nmf inv Fam Hum* cradle-snatcher

asaltante *nmf* (**a**) *(agresor)* attacker; **no consiguió ver bien a su a.** she was unable to get a good view of her attacker; **los asaltantes del palacio presidencial** the people who stormed the presidential palace (**b**) *(atracador)* robber

asaltar *vt* (**a**) *(atacar)* to attack; *(castillo, ciudad)* to storm; **la policía asaltó el avión** the police stormed the plane
(**b**) *(robar)* to rob; **lo asaltaron con una navaja** he was robbed *o* mugged at knifepoint
(**c**) *(sujeto: dudas, pánico)* to seize; **iba a ir pero al final le asaltaron las dudas** he was going to go, but he was seized by doubts at the last minute; **me asalta una duda, ¿me llegará el dinero?** I have one doubt, will I have enough money?; **le asaltó el pánico** he was overcome by *o* seized with panic
(**d**) *(importunar)* **los periodistas asaltaron al actor a preguntas** the journalists bombarded the actor with questions; **los pabellones se vieron asaltados por visitantes** the pavilions were overrun with visitors

asalto *nm* (**a**) *(ataque)* attack; *(de castillo, ciudad)* storming; **un fusil de a.** an assault rifle; **tomar algo por a.** to storm sth; **las empresas europeas preparan su a. al mercado asiático** European companies are preparing for their assault on the Asian market
(**b**) *(robo)* robbery; **un a. a mano armada** an armed robbery
(**c**) *(en boxeo)* round
(**d**) *(en esgrima)* bout
(**e**) *(en disputa)* round
(**f**) *Arg (fiesta)* = party where guests bring a bottle and something to eat
(**g**) *CAm (fiesta sorpresa)* surprise party

asamblea *nf* (**a**) *(reunión)* meeting; **una a. de vecinos** a meeting of local residents; **los trabajadores, reunidos en a., votaron a favor de la huelga** the workers voted for strike action at a mass meeting; **convocar una a.** to call a meeting ►► ***a. de accionistas*** shareholders' meeting; ***a. general anual*** annual general meeting; ***a. plenaria*** plenary assembly
(**b**) *(cuerpo político)* assembly ►► ***a. constituyente*** constituent assembly; ***A. General*** *(de la ONU)* General Assembly; ***a. nacional*** parliament

asambleario, -a *adj* **reunión asamblearia** full meeting; **decisión asamblearia** decision taken by a meeting

asambleísta *nmf* (**a**) *(en reunión)* **los asambleístas** the people at the meeting (**b**) *(en cuerpo político)* assembly member; *(en asamblea nacional)* member of parliament

asar **1** *vt* (**a**) *(alimentos) (al horno)* to roast; *(a la parrilla)* to grill (**b**) *Fam* **a. a alguien a preguntas** *(importunar)* to plague sb with questions; *(acosar)* to grill sb (with questions)
2 asarse *vpr* (**a**) *(alimentos) (en horno)* to roast; *(en parrilla)* to grill; **necesita más tiempo para asarse bien** it needs more time to cook properly (**b**) *Fam (persona)* to be boiling (hot); **me estoy asando de calor** I'm boiling (hot); **si no te quitas el abrigo te vas a a.** if you don't take your coat off, you'll melt

asaz *adv Anticuado Literario* exceedingly; **un comportamiento a. extraño** exceedingly strange behaviour

asbesto *nm* asbestos

asbestosis *nf inv Med* asbestosis

ascendencia *nf* (**a**) *(linaje)* descent, ancestry; *(extracción social)* extraction; **de a. aristocrática** of aristocratic ancestry; **soy de a. mexicana** I'm of Mexican extraction (**b**) *(influencia)* ascendancy

ascendente **1** *adj (entonación, trayectoria)* rising; *(movimiento, curva)* upward
2 *nm (en astrología)* ascendant

ascender [66] **1** *vi* (**a**) *(subir)* to climb, to go up; **el avión ascendió rápidamente** the plane climbed rapidly; **ascendieron a la cima** they climbed to the summit; **la carretera asciende hasta el lago** the road goes up to the lake; **la carretera asciende hasta los 3.000 m** the road climbs to 3,000 m
(**b**) *(aumentar, elevarse) (precios, temperaturas)* to rise, to go up
(**c**) *(en empleo, deportes)* to be promoted (**a** to); **ascendió a jefe de producción** he was promoted to production manager; **el equipo ascendió a segunda división** the team was promoted *o* went up to the second division; **a. al trono** to ascend the throne; **a. al poder** to come to power
(**d**) **a. a** *(totalizar)* to come to; **¿a cuánto asciende el total?** what does the total come to?; **la facturación ascendió a 5.000 millones** turnover came to *o* totalled five billion; **el número de desaparecidos asciende ya a 37** the number of missing has now reached 37
2 *vt* **a. a alguien (a)** to promote sb (to); **fue ascendida al puesto de subdirectora** she was promoted to the position of deputy director; **lo ascendieron a coronel** he was promoted to the rank of colonel

ascendiente **1** *nmf (antepasado)* ancestor
2 *nm (influencia)* influence; **tener a. sobre alguien** to have influence over sb

ascensión *nf* (**a**) *(a montaña)* ascent (**b**) *(de precios, temperaturas)* rise (**c**) *(al trono)* ascent; **tras su a. al poder** after she came to power (**d**) *Rel* **la A.** *(subida a los cielos)* the Ascension; *(festividad)* Ascension Day

ascensional *adj (movimiento, fuerza)* upward

ascenso *nm* (**a**) *(a montaña)* ascent
(**b**) *(de precios, temperaturas)* rise; **se espera un a. de las temperaturas** temperatures are expected to rise; **el uso de Internet continúa en a.** Internet use continues to rise *o* is still on the rise
(**c**) *(de político, rey)* **tras su a. al poder** after she came to power
(**d**) *(en empleo, deportes)* promotion; **consiguieron el a. del equipo a primera división** the team achieved promotion to the first division

ascensor *nm Br* lift, *US* elevator; **yo subo en a.** I'm taking the *Br* lift *o US* elevator

ascensorista *nmf* (**a**) *(en ascensor) Br* lift attendant, *US* elevator attendant (**b**) *(mecánico) Br* lift mechanic, *US* elevator mechanic

ascesis *nf inv Formal* ascesis

asceta *nmf* ascetic; **lleva vida de a.** she lives an ascetic lifestyle

ascética *nf* asceticism

ascético, -a *adj* ascetic

ascetismo *nm* asceticism

asciendo *etc ver* **ascender**

ASCII ['asθi] *nm Informát (abrev de* **American Standard Code for Information Interchange**) ASCII

asco *nm* (**a**) *(sensación)* disgust, revulsion; **¡qué a.!** how disgusting!; **lo miró con cara de a.** she looked at him in disgust; **me da a.** I find it disgusting; **las anguilas me dan a.** I find eels disgusting; **da a. ver cómo trata a su mujer** it's sickening to see how he treats his wife; **¡me das a.!** you make me sick!; **tener a. a algo** to find sth disgusting; EXPR *Fam* **morirse de a.: en clase nos morimos de a.** we're bored to death in class; **está muerto de a. esperando que le llamen** he's fed up to the back teeth waiting for them to call; **tienes la bici ahí muerta de a.** you've got that bike just gathering dust there; EXPR **hacer ascos a** to turn one's nose up at, to turn down; **no le hace ascos a nada** he won't turn anything down; **no le haría ascos a una cervecita fría** I wouldn't say no to a cold beer
(**b**) *Fam (persona, cosa)* **esta sopa es un a.** this soup is disgusting *o* revolting; **es un a. de persona** he's scum; **es un a. de lugar** it's a hole; **un a. de tiempo** rotten weather; **¡qué a. de vida!** what a life!; EXPR **hecho un a.: este cuarto está hecho un a.** this room is a tip; **después de la tormenta llegó a casa hecho un a.** he arrived back home after the storm in a real state; **la enfermedad lo dejó hecho un a.** the illness left him a total wreck

ascórbico, -a *adj Quím* ascorbic

ascua *nf*

Takes the masculine articles **el** and **un**.

ember; EXPR **estar en** *o* **sobre ascuas** to be on tenterhooks; **tener a alguien en** *o* **sobre ascuas** to keep sb on tenterhooks; EXPR **como sobre ascuas: el presidente pasó por el asunto como sobre ascuas** the president skated over the issue

aseado, -a *adj* (**a**) *(limpio)* clean (**b**) *(arreglado)* smart

aseador, -ora *nm,f CAm, Chile, Col, Ven, Méx* cleaner

ASEAN [ase'an] *nf (abrev de* **Asociación de Naciones del Asia Sudoriental**) ASEAN

asear **1** *vt* (**a**) *(limpiar)* to clean (**b**) *(arreglar)* to wash and dress
2 asearse *vpr* to get washed and dressed

asechanza *nf* snare

asediar *vt* (**a**) *(ciudad)* to lay siege to, to besiege (**b**) *(persona)* **los fans la asediaban pidiéndole autógrafos** she was besieged by fans asking for autographs; **el equipo visitante asedió la portería rival** the away team laid siege to their opponents' goal; **lo asediaron a preguntas** he was bombarded with questions

asedio *nm* (**a**) *(de ciudad)* siege; **estar bajo a.** to be under siege (**b**) *(de persona)* **la prensa lo sometía a un a. constante** he was hounded by the press; **en la segunda parte el equipo local sufrió un a. constante** the home team was under siege for the whole of the second half

asegurado, -a 1 *adj* insured; **está a. en cinco millones** it's insured for five million; **está a. a todo riesgo** it's fully insured
2 *nm,f* policy-holder

asegurador, -ora 1 *adj* insurance; **compañía aseguradora** insurance company
2 *nm,f (persona)* insurer

aseguradora *nf (compañía)* insurance company

asegurar 1 *vt* **(a)** *(fijar)* to secure; **asegúralo con una cuerda** secure it with a rope; **asegura las piezas con pegamento** fix the pieces together with glue; **aseguró la puerta con el cerrojo** she bolted the door (shut)
(b) *(garantizar)* to assure; **te lo aseguro** I assure you; **a. a alguien que...** to assure sb that...; **el gobierno aseguró que no subiría los impuestos** the government promised it would not increase taxes; **¿y quién me asegura que no me está mintiendo?** and what guarantee do I have he isn't lying to me?; **con él de coordinador el conflicto está asegurado** with him as co-ordinator, conflict is assured *o* a certainty; **tienes que trabajar más si quieres a. tu ascenso** you'll have to work harder if you want to make certain you get promoted
(c) *(contra riesgos)* to insure (**contra** against); **a. algo a todo riesgo** to take out comprehensive insurance on sth; **a. en** *(cantidad)* to insure sth for
(d) *Méx (decomisar)* to confiscate, to seize
2 asegurarse *vpr* **(a)** *(agarrarse)* **asegúrate bien a la roca o te caerás** hold on tight to the rock or you'll fall
(b) *(cerciorarse)* **asegurarse de que...** to make sure that...; **asegúrate de cerrar la puerta** make sure you close the door
(c) *(garantizar)* to make sure of; **con la victoria se aseguraron el ascenso** they made sure of promotion with that win
(d) *Com* to insure oneself, to take out an insurance policy

asemejar 1 *vt* **ese peinado lo asemeja a su padre** that hairstyle makes him look like his father
2 *vi* **a. a** to be similar to, to be like
3 asemejarse *vpr* to be similar; **las dos historias se asemejan mucho** the two stories are very similar; **se asemeja a su madre** she resembles her mother; **no se asemeja en nada a un árbol** it's nothing like a tree, it bears no resemblance to a tree

asenso *nm Formal* assent; **dieron su a. al nuevo plan** they assented to the new plan

asentaderas *nfpl Fam (nalgas)* behind, buttocks

asentado, -a *adj* **(a)** *(localizado)* located, situated; **una central nuclear asentada cerca de la capital** a nuclear power station located *o* situated close to the capital; **un español a. en Argentina** a Spaniard living in Argentina; **una ciudad asentada sobre un antigua población romana** a city built on an ancient Roman settlement
(b) *(establecido)* settled, established; **una tradición muy asentada entre los católicos** a long-established tradition amongst Catholics; **está muy a. en su nuevo trabajo** he has settled into his new job very well
(c) *(sensato)* sensible, mature; **es un chico muy a.** he's a very sensible *o* mature young man

asentador, -ora 1 *nm,f (mercader)* wholesale dealer
2 *nm Méx (en imprenta)* planer

asentamiento *nm* **(a)** *(acción)* settlement ►► *Perú* ***a. humano*** shanty town; *Am* ***a. ilegal*** illegal settlement **(b)** *(lugar)* settlement

asentar [3] **1** *vt* **(a)** *(instalar) (empresa, campamento)* to set up; *(comunidad, pueblo)* to settle
(b) *(asegurar)* to secure; *(cimientos)* to lay
(c) *(afianzar) (conocimientos)* to consolidate; **toma un té, te asentará el estómago** have a cup of tea, it will settle your stomach
(d) *(golpe)* **le asentó una bofetada** she slapped him, she gave him a slap; **le asentaron dos puñaladas** he was stabbed twice
(e) *(apuntar) (entrada)* to make; *(cifras)* to enter; *(firma)* to affix
2 asentarse *vpr* **(a)** *(instalarse) (comunidad, pueblo)* to settle; **se asentaron a la orilla de un río** they settled on the banks of a river; **no tardaron mucho en asentarse en el poder** it didn't take them long to get used to holding the reins of government **(b)** *(sedimentarse)* to settle; **espera a que se asiente el polvo** wait until the dust settles **(c)** *(madurar) (persona)* to settle down

asentimiento *nm* approval, assent

asentir [63] *vi* **(a)** *(estar conforme)* to agree; **a. a algo** to agree to sth **(b)** *(afirmar con la cabeza)* to nod; **asintió con la cabeza** she nodded in agreement

asentista *nmf (abastecedor)* supplier

aseo *nm* **(a)** *(limpieza) (acción)* cleaning; *(cualidad)* cleanliness; **a. personal** personal cleanliness *o* hygiene **(b)** *Esp (habitación)* bathroom; **aseos** *Br* toilets, *US* rest room

asepsia *nf* **(a)** *(higiene)* asepsis **(b)** *(indiferencia)* detachment

asépticamente *adv* **(a)** *(higiénicamente)* aseptically **(b)** *(con indiferencia)* with detachment

aséptico, -a *adj* **(a)** *(desinfectado)* sterilized **(b)** *(indiferente)* lacking in emotion, emotionless

asequible *adj* **(a)** *(razonable) (precio, producto)* affordable; *(objetivo)* attainable; **un precio a. para el consumidor medio** a price within reach of the average consumer **(b)** *(comprensible) (concepto)* accessible **(c)** *(sencillo) (persona)* approachable

aserción *nf* assertion

aserradero *nm* sawmill

aserrar [3] *vt* to saw (up)

aserrín *nm* sawdust

aserruchar *vt CSur* to saw with a hand saw

aserto *nm* assertion

asesinar *vt (persona)* to murder; *(rey, jefe de Estado)* to assassinate; *Fam (canción, obra teatral)* to murder; **lo asesinaron a sangre fría** he was murdered in cold blood

asesinato *nm (de persona)* murder; *(de rey, jefe de Estado)* assassination

asesino, -a 1 *adj* **(a)** *(que mata)* **el arma asesina** the murder weapon **(b)** *(mirada, instinto)* murderous; **le lanzó una mirada asesina** she looked daggers at him, she gave him a murderous look
2 *nm,f (de persona)* murderer, *f* murderess, killer; *(de rey, jefe de Estado)* assassin ►► ***a. profesional*** professional killer; ***a. en serie*** serial killer; ***a. a sueldo*** contract killer

asesor, -ora 1 *adj* advisory
2 *nm,f* adviser ►► ***a. científico*** *(de gobierno)* scientific adviser; *(de programa televisivo)* scientific consultant; ***a. financiero*** financial adviser; ***a. fiscal*** tax adviser; *Chile* ***asesora del hogar*** maid; ***a. de imagen*** image consultant; ***a. jurídico*** legal adviser; ***a. militar*** military adviser

asesoramiento *nm (de político)* advice; *(de empresario)* consultancy; **esta empresa proporciona a. de imagen a varios políticos** this company acts as image consultant to several politicians

asesorar 1 *vt (a político)* to advise; *(a empresario)* to act as a consultant to
2 asesorarse *vpr* to seek advice; **asesorarse con** *o* **de alguien** to consult sb; **me asesoré de los requisitos necesarios** I sought advice regarding what was necessary

asesoría *nf* **(a)** *(oficio)* consultancy **(b)** *(oficina)* consultant's office ►► ***a. financiera*** financial consultant's; ***a. fiscal*** *(oficina)* financial adviser's office; ***a. de imagen y comunicación*** PR company; ***a. jurídica*** legal adviser's; ***a. legal*** legal adviser's

asestar *vt* **le asestó un golpe en la cabeza** she struck him on the head; **le asestó un tiro en la rodilla** he shot her in the knee; **los rebeldes asestaron un duro golpe a las tropas gubernamentales** the rebels dealt a severe blow to the government troops

aseveración *nf* assertion

aseverar *vt* to assert

asexuado, -a *adj* asexual

asexual *adj* asexual

asexualmente *adv* asexually

asfaltado, -a 1 *adj* asphalt; **un camino a.** an asphalt road
2 *nm* **(a)** *(acción)* asphalting, surfacing **(b)** *(asfalto)* asphalt, (road) surface

asfaltadora *nf* (road) surfacer

asfaltar *vt* to asphalt, to surface

asfáltico, -a *adj* asphalt; **una superficie asfáltica** an asphalt surface

asfalto *nm* **(a)** *(sustancia)* asphalt **(b)** *(carretera)* **50 personas han perdido la vida en el a. este fin de semana** 50 people lost their lives on the roads this weekend

asfixia *nf* **(a)** *(por falta de oxígeno)* asphyxiation, suffocation; **murió por a.** she suffocated **(b)** *(agobio)* suffocation; **este calor me produce a.** I'm suffocating in this heat **(c)** *(económica)* **la alta fiscalidad produce la a. de las empresas** the high taxes are crippling business

asfixiante *adj* **(a)** *(humo, aire)* asphyxiating **(b)** *(calor)* stifling; **hace un calor a.** it's stiflingly hot **(c)** *(relación, ambiente)* stifling; **una inflación a. para la pequeña empresa** a level of inflation crippling to small businesses

asfixiar 1 *vt* **(a)** *(ahogar)* to asphyxiate, to suffocate; **murieron asfixiados** they suffocated
(b) *(agobiar)* to stifle; **este calor asfixia a cualquiera** it's stiflingly hot
(c) *(económicamente)* to cripple; **tuvo que cerrar porque las deudas**

lo asfixiaban he had to close down because he was crippled by debt; **las nuevas medidas van a a. a la pequeña empresa** the new measures will cripple small businesses

2 **asfixiarse** *vpr* (**a**) *(ahogarse)* to asphyxiate, to suffocate (**b**) *(agobiarse)* to suffocate; **¡aquí me asfixio (de calor)!** I'm suffocating in here!

asgo *etc ver* **asir**

ASÍ 1 *adv (de este modo)* this way, like this; *(de ese modo)* that way, like that; **ellos lo hicieron a.** they did it this way; **a. es la vida** that's life; **yo soy a.** that's just the way I am; **¿a. me agradeces todo lo que he hecho por ti?** is this how you thank me for everything I've done for you?; **a. no vamos a ninguna parte** we're not getting anywhere like this *o* this way; **¿eso le dijo? – a., como te lo cuento** did she really say that to him? – (yes) indeed, those were her very words; **a. a.** *(no muy bien)* so-so; **¿cómo te ha ido el examen? – a. a.** how did the exam go? – so-so; **algo a.** *(algo parecido)* something like that; **tiene seis años o algo a.** she is six years old or something like that; **algo a. como** *(algo igual a)* something like; **el apartamento les ha costado algo a. como 20 millones** the *Br* flat *o US* apartment cost them something like 20 million; **a. como** *(también)* as well as; *(tal como)* just as; **las inundaciones, a. como la sequía, son catástrofes naturales** both floods and droughts are natural disasters; **a. como para los idiomas no vale, para las relaciones públicas nadie la supera** whilst she may be no good at languages, there is no one better at public relations; **a. como a.** *(como si nada)* as if it were nothing; *(irreflexivamente)* lightly; *(de cualquier manera)* any old how; **¡no puedes marcharte a. como a.!** you can't leave just like that!; **a. cualquiera gana** anyone could win that way *o* like that; **subimos hasta la cumbre en teleférico – ¡a. cualquiera!** we reached the summit by cable car – anyone could do that!; **a. de... so...**; **no seas a. de celoso** don't be so jealous; **era a. de largo** it was this/that long; **es a. de fácil** it's as easy as that; **no hace nada de ejercicio – a. de gordo está** he doesn't do any exercise – it's no wonder he's so fat; *Irónico* **me ha costado muy barato – a. de bueno será** it was very cheap – don't expect it to be any good, then; **a. es/fue como...** that is/was how...; **a. es** *(para asentir)* that is correct, yes; **¡a. me gusta!** that's what I like (to see)!; **¡a. me gusta, sigue trabajando duro!** excellent, keep up the hard work!, that's what I like to see, keep up the hard work!; *Fam* **a. o asá** either way, one way or the other; **el abrigo le quedaba pequeño, a. es que se compró otro** the coat was too small for her, so she bought another one; **a. sea** so be it; *Esp* **a. sin más,** *Am* **a. no más** *o* **nomás** just like that; **a. y todo** even so; **se ha estado medicando mucho tiempo y, a. y todo, no se encuentra bien** he's been taking medication for some time and even so he's no better; **aun a.** even so; **o a.** *(más o menos)* or so, or something like that; **y a.** thus, and so; **y a. sucesivamente** and so on, and so forth; **y a. todos los días** and the same thing happens day after day

2 *conj* (**a**) *(aunque)* even if; **te encontraré a. tenga que recorrer todas las calles de la ciudad** I'll find you even if I have to look in every street in the city

(**b**) *Am (aun si)* even if; **no nos lo dirá, a. le paguemos** he won't tell us, even if we pay him

3 *adj inv (como éste)* like this; *(como ése)* like that; **no seas a.** don't be like that; **con un coche a. no se puede ir muy lejos** you can't go very far with a car like this one; **una situación a. es muy peligrosa** such a situation is very dangerous

4 *interj* I hope...; **¡a. no vuelva nunca!** I hope he never comes back!; **¡a. te parta un rayo!** drop dead!

5 **así pues** *loc conj* so, therefore; **no firmaron el tratado, a. pues la guerra era inevitable** they didn't sign the treaty, so war became inevitable

6 **así que** *loc conj (de modo que)* so; **la película empieza dentro de media hora, a. que no te entretengas** the film starts in half an hour, so don't be long; **¿a. que te vas a presentar candidato?** so you're going to stand as a candidate, are you?

7 **así que** *loc adv (tan pronto como)* as soon as; **a. que tengamos los resultados del análisis, le citaremos para la visita** as soon as we have the results of the test we'll make an appointment for you

Asia *n* Asia ▸▸ ***A. Menor*** Asia Minor

asiático, -a 1 *adj* Asian, Asiatic; **el sudeste a.** Southeast Asia

2 *nm,f* Asian, Asiatic

asidero *nm* (**a**) *(asa)* handle (**b**) *(punto de apoyo)* handhold (**c**) *(apoyo)* support; **la familia es su único a.** her family is her only source of comfort and support (**d**) *(pretexto)* excuse; **su enfermedad le sirve de a. para no colaborar** he is using his illness as an excuse not to participate

asiduamente *adv* frequently, regularly

asiduidad *nf* frequency; **con a.** frequently, regularly

asiduo, -a 1 *adj* regular; **son asiduos visitantes de este museo** they visit this museum regularly, they are regular visitors to this museum

2 *nm,f* regular; **es un a. de este tipo de acontecimientos** he's a regular at this type of event

asiento 1 *ver* **asentar**

2 *ver* **asentir**

3 *nm* (**a**) *(silla, butaca)* seat; **ceder el a. a alguien** to let sb have one's seat; **reservar un a. a alguien** to save a seat for sb; **tomar a.** to sit down; **a. delantero/trasero** front/back seat; **a. de pasillo/de ventana** *(en avión)* aisle/window seat ▸▸ ***a. abatible*** *(en coche)* = seat that tips forwards or folds flat; *(en tren)* tip-up seat; ***a. anatómico*** orthopaedic seat; ***a. plegable*** folding chair; *RP* ***a. rebatible*** *(en auto)* = seat that tips forwards or folds flat; *(en tren)* tip-up seat, = seat that tips forward or folds flat; ***a. reclinable*** reclining seat

(**b**) *(de silla, butaca)* seat

(**c**) *(base) (de vasija, botella)* bottom

(**d**) *(emplazamiento)* **la ciudad tiene su a. en una montaña** the city is located *o* situated on a mountain

(**e**) *(poso)* sediment

(**f**) *Com* entry ▸▸ ***a. contable*** book entry

(**g**) *Constr (de edificio)* settling

(**h**) *Méx (zona minera)* mining district *o* area

asierro *etc ver* **aserrar**

asignación *nf* (**a**) *(atribución) (de dinero, productos)* allocation; **defienden un modelo de a. de recursos más justo** they are in favour of a fairer allocation *o* distribution of resources; **él se encarga de la a. de prioridades** he is in charge of setting *o* establishing priorities

(**b**) *(cantidad asignada)* allocation; **tenemos una a. anual de cinco millones de dólares** we have an annual allocation of five million dollars; **todas las familias reciben una a. económica por cada hijo** all families receive an allowance for each child they have ▸▸ *CSur* ***a. familiar*** = state benefit paid to families for every child, *Br* ≃ child benefit

(**c**) *(sueldo)* salary; **le dan una a. semanal de 10 euros** they give him *Br* pocket money *o US* an allowance of 10 euros a week

(**d**) *(de empleado)* **anunciaron su a. a un nuevo destino** they announced that she was being assigned to a new post

(**e**) *CAm (deber)* homework

asignar *vt* (**a**) *(atribuir)* **a. algo a alguien** to assign *o* allocate sth to sb; **le han asignado una oficina en el último piso** he has been allocated an office on the top floor; **le asignan siempre los trabajos más difíciles** they always give her the hardest jobs; **a. importancia a algo** to place importance on sth

(**b**) *(destinar)* **a. a alguien a** to assign sb to; **la asignaron al departamento de relaciones públicas** she was assigned to the public relations department

asignatario, -a *nm,f Am Der (de herencia)* heir; *(de legado)* legatee

asignatura *nf* subject; **me queda una a. del año pasado** I have to resit one subject that I failed last year ▸▸ ***a. optativa*** optional subject; ***a. pendiente*** = subject in which a pupil or student has to retake an exam; *Fig* unresolved matter

asilado, -a *nm,f* (**a**) *(huérfano, anciano)* = person living in an old people's home, convalescent home etc (**b**) *(refugiado)* **a. (político)** person who has been granted political asylum

asilar 1 *vt* (**a**) *(huérfano, anciano)* to put into a home (**b**) *(refugiado político)* to grant political asylum to

2 **asilarse** *vpr (refugiado político)* to obtain (political) asylum

asilo *nm* (**a**) *(hospicio)* home ▸▸ ***a. de ancianos*** old people's home (**b**) *(refugio)* refuge, sanctuary; *(amparo)* asylum ▸▸ ***a. político*** political asylum; **solicitar a. político** to seek (political) asylum

asilvestrado, -a *adj* feral

asilvestrarse *vpr* to become feral

asimetría *nf* asymmetry

asimétricamente *adv* asymmetrically

asimétrico, -a *adj* asymmetric, asymmetrical

asimilable *adj (alimentos, nutrientes)* assimilable; **resumieron el texto para hacerlo más a.** they summarized the text to make it easier to take in

asimilación *nf* (**a**) *(de conocimientos, información)* assimilation

(**b**) *(de alimentos)* assimilation

(**c**) *(equiparación)* granting of equal rights; **reivindican la a. salarial con el resto de funcionarios** they are demanding that their salaries be brought into line with those of other public sector employees

(**d**) *Ling* assimilation

(**e**) *Biol* assimilation

(**f**) *(integración)* assimilation

asimilado, -a *adj Am* **médico a.** = doctor attached to the army

asimilar 1 *vt* (**a**) *(idea, conocimientos)* to assimilate (**b**) *(alimentos)* to assimilate (**c**) *(asumir)* to take in; **todavía no han asimilado la derrota** they still haven't taken in the defeat (**d**) *(equiparar)* to grant equal rights to; **asimilaron los profesores al resto de funcionarios** teachers' pay was brought into line with that of other public sector employees (**e**) *Ling* to assimilate

2 asimilarse *vpr* (**a**) *Ling* to become assimilated (**b**) *(parecerse)* **asimilarse a algo** to resemble sth

asimismo *adv*

An alternative but less common spelling is **así mismo**.

(también) also; *(a principio de frase)* likewise; **el éxito depende, a., de la preparación de los participantes** success also depends on the participants being properly prepared; **se declaró a. convencido de...** he also said that he was convinced of...; **creo a. importante recalcar que...** in the same way I feel it important to emphasize that...

asina = **ansina**

asíncrono, -a *adj Informát* asynchronous

asíndeton *nm Ling* asyndeton

asintiera *etc ver* **asentir**

asintomático, -a *adj Med* asymptomatic

asíntota *nf Geom* asymptote

asir [9] **1** *vt* to grasp, to grab; **asió a su hermano de los pantalones** she grabbed her brother by the trousers

2 asirse *vpr* **se asió con fuerza a la cuerda** she clung tightly to the rope; **se asió del brazo de su novia** he clung to his girlfriend's arm; **se asía a los recuerdos del pasado** she clung to past memories

Asiria *n Hist* Assyria

asirio, -a *Hist* **1** *adj* Assyrian

2 *nm,f (persona)* Assyrian

3 *nm (lengua)* Assyrian

asistemático, -a *adj* unsystematic

asistencia *nf* (**a**) *(ayuda)* assistance; **prestar a. a alguien** to give assistance to sb ►► ***a. en carretera*** breakdown service; ***a. domiciliaria*** *(de médico, enfermera)* home visits; ***a. a domicilio*** *(de médico, enfermera)* home visits; ***a. jurídica*** legal advice; ***a. jurídica de oficio*** legal aid; ***a. letrada*** legal advice; ***a. médica*** medical attention; ***a. pública*** social security; ***a. sanitaria*** health care; ***a. social*** social work; ***a. técnica*** technical assistance

(**b**) *(presencia) (acción)* attendance; *(hecho)* presence; **la a. a las prácticas de química es obligatoria** attendance at chemistry practicals is compulsory; **el rey ha confirmado su a. a la ceremonia** the king has confirmed that he will be attending the ceremony; **se ruega confirme su a. al acto** *(en invitación)* please let us know whether you will be able to attend

(**c**) *(afluencia)* attendance; **la a. a la manifestación fue muy pequeña** the demonstration was very poorly attended, very few people turned out for the demonstration; **no se tienen datos precisos de a.** we do not have an exact attendance figure

(**d**) *Dep* assist

(**e**) **las asistencias** *(en estadio)* the paramedics, *Br* ≃ the St John Ambulance; *(en rally)* the technical staff

(**f**) *Col, Méx (pensión)* guesthouse

asistencial *adj (sanitario)* health care; **servicios asistenciales** health care services

asistenta *nf Esp* cleaning lady

asistente 1 *adj* **el público a. aplaudió a rabiar** the audience *o* everyone present applauded wildly; **los científicos asistentes a un congreso** the scientists attending a congress

2 *nmf* (**a**) *(ayudante)* assistant, helper ►► ***a. social*** social worker (**b**) *(presente)* **los asistentes** those present; **cada a. recibirá un regalo** everyone who attends will receive a free gift; **se espera una gran afluencia de asistentes** a high attendance is expected (**c**) *Dep (árbitro)* assistant referee

3 *nm* (**a**) *Mil* batman, orderly (**b**) *Informát (software)* wizard ►► ***a. personal*** *(de bolsillo)* personal assistant

asistido, -a *adj (respiración, reproducción)* assisted; *(fecundación)* artificial

asistir 1 *vt* (**a**) *(ayudar)* to attend to; **en este centro asisten a los sin techo** this centre provides care for the homeless; EXPR **¡Dios nos asista!** God above!, good heavens!

(**b**) *(paciente, enfermo)* to attend; **los heridos fueron asistidos en un hospital cercano** the injured were treated *o* attended at a nearby hospital; **le asiste el doctor Jiménez** he is being attended by Dr Jiménez; **la comadrona que me asistió en el parto** the midwife who helped me give birth

(**c**) *(acompañar)* to accompany

(**d**) *(amparar, apoyar)* **le asiste la razón** she has right on her side; **el derecho les asiste** they have the law on their side

2 *vi* (**a**) *(acudir)* to attend; **a. a un acto** to attend an event; **asisten a misa todos los domingos** they go to church *o* attend mass every Sunday (**b**) *(limpiar)* to work as a cleaner (**c**) *(presenciar)* to witness; **estamos asistiendo a cambios históricos** we are witnessing historic changes (**d**) *(en juegos de cartas)* to follow suit

asistolia *nf Med* asystole

askenazi = **asquenazi**

asma *nf* asthma

Takes the masculine articles **el** and **un**.

asmático, -a 1 *adj* asthmatic

2 *nm,f* asthmatic

asno, -a 1 *adj Fam (necio)* stupid, dim

2 *nm,f* (**a**) *(animal)* ass (**b**) *Fam (necio)* ass

asociación *nf* (**a**) *(acción)* association; **en a. con la ONU** in association with the UN ►► ***a. de ideas*** association of ideas; ***a. libre*** free association

(**b**) *(grupo, colectivo)* association; **una a. cultural** a cultural association; **una a. ecologista** an environmental group ►► ***a. de consumidores*** consumer association; ***A. Europea de Libre Comercio*** European Free Trade Association; ***a. gremial*** trade association; ***a. de padres de alumnos*** = Spanish association for parents of schoolchildren, ≃ PTA; ***a. de vecinos*** residents' association

asociacionismo *nm* **una época caracterizada por el a.** a period which saw the formation of many grass-roots organizations; **una medida destinada a fomentar el a. entre los jóvenes** a measure aimed at encouraging young people to join together in defence of their interests

asociado, -a 1 *adj* (**a**) *(relacionado)* associated; **un problema a. a la falta de proteínas** a problem associated with a lack of protein; **se lo asocia con el descubrimiento del teléfono** he is associated with the invention of the telephone (**b**) *(miembro)* associate; **director a.** associate director; **profesor a.** associate lecturer

2 *nm,f* (**a**) *(miembro)* associate, partner (**b**) *(profesor)* associate lecturer

asocial *adj* asocial

asociar 1 *vt* (**a**) *(relacionar)* to associate; **asocia el verano a** *o* **con la playa** she associates summer with the seaside (**b**) *Com* **asoció a sus hijos a la empresa** he made his sons partners in the firm

2 asociarse *vpr* (**a**) *(relacionarse)* to be associated; **una dolencia que se asocia con el** *o* **al exceso de ejercicio** a complaint that is associated with excessive exercise

(**b**) *(unirse)* to join together; **se asociaron con otros científicos europeos** they joined together *o* collaborated with other European scientists; **se asociaron para defender sus derechos** they joined together to defend their rights

(**c**) *Com* to form a partnership; **se asoció con varios amigos** he formed *o* entered a partnership with some friends

asociativo, -a *adj* (**a**) *(de asociación)* **las formas asociativas de nuestra sociedad** the forms of association in our society (**b**) *Mat* associative

asocio *nm Col* association; **en a. de** in association with

asolado, -a *adj* devastated

asolador, -ora *adj (destructor)* ravaging, devastating

asolamiento *nm* devastation

asolar [64] *vt* to devastate

asoleada *nf Andes, RP* **salimos a darnos una a.** we went outside to get a bit of sunshine

asolear 1 *vt* to expose to the sun, to put in the sun

2 asolearse *vpr* (**a**) *Andes, Méx, RP (tomar el sol)* to bask in the sun, to sun oneself (**b**) *CAm, Méx (insolarse)* to get sunstroke (**c**) *Méx Fam (trabajar)* to work, to slave

asomado, -a *Ven* **1** *adj (entrometido)* interfering, meddlesome

2 *nm,f (entrometido)* meddler

ASOMAR 1 *vt* **a. la cabeza por la ventana** to stick one's head out of the window; **asomaron el bebé al balcón** they took the baby out onto the balcony; **prohibido a. la cabeza por la ventanilla** *(en letrero)* do not lean out of the window; **el humor asoma en su última película** there are signs of humour in his most recent film; **con los malos resultados empezaron a a. las críticas** criticism started to surface after the poor results; *Fig* **a. la cabeza** to show one's face

2 *vi* (**a**) *(sobresalir)* to peep up; *(del interior de algo)* to peep out; **la sábana asoma por debajo de la colcha** the sheet is peeping out from under the bedspread; **el lobo asomaba por detrás del árbol** the wolf was peeping out from behind the tree; **sus zapatos asoman por detrás de las cortinas** her shoes are showing below *o* peeping out from below the curtains; **te asoma la camisa por debajo de la chaqueta** your shirt is sticking out from under your jacket; **el castillo asomaba en el horizonte** the castle could be made out on the horizon

(b) *(salir)* **ya le asoman los primeros dientes** his first teeth are coming through already, he's already cutting his first teeth; **las flores asoman ya** the flowers are already starting to come out

(c) *(empezar)* **asoma el día** day is breaking

3 asomarse *vpr* **(a)** *(sacar la cabeza)* **asomarse a la ventana** *(abierta)* to stick one's head out of the window; *(cerrada)* to go/come to the window; **asomarse al balcón** to go out onto the balcony, to appear on the balcony; **prohibido asomarse por la ventanilla** *(en letrero)* do not lean out of the window; *Fig* **nos vamos a a. ahora a un tema polémico** we are now going to touch upon a controversial subject

(b) *(mostrarse)* to show oneself, to appear; **después de una recepción tan hostil, no se volverá a a. por aquí en mucho tiempo** after such a hostile reception, she won't show her face *o* herself round here again for a while

---

asombrar 1 *vt* to amaze, to astonish; **el tenor volvió a a. a todos con su maestría** once again the tenor amazed *o* astonished everyone with his masterful performance; **el colorido del paisaje nunca deja de asombrarme** it never ceases to amaze *o* astonish me how colourful the landscape is; **me asombra oír sus quejas** I'm surprised to hear her complain

2 asombrarse *vpr* to be amazed *o* astonished; **me asombro con** *o* **de lo que sabe sobre aves** I'm amazed *o* astonished at how much she knows about birds; **no sé de qué te asombras** I don't know why you're so surprised

asombro *nm* amazement, astonishment; **no salía de su a.** she couldn't get over her amazement *o* astonishment; **miraba a los niños con a.** she watched the children in amazement *o* astonishment; **ante el a. de los asistentes, se puso a cantar** to the amazement *o* astonishment of everyone present, she started singing

asombrosamente *adv* amazingly, astonishingly; **salió a. ileso del accidente** amazingly *o* astonishingly, he was not injured in the accident

asombroso, -a *adj* amazing, astonishing

asomo *nm (indicio)* trace, hint; *(de esperanza)* glimmer; **habló sin el menor a. de orgullo** he spoke without the slightest trace *o* hint of pride; **un edificio horrible, sin a. de buen gusto** a horrible building without the slightest trace *o* hint of good taste; **su actuación no deja el menor a. de duda** her performance leaves absolutely no room for doubt; **no pudo evitar un a. de llanto** she couldn't prevent tears from welling up in her eyes; EXPR **ni por a.: las previsiones de ventas no se alcanzarán ni por a.** there is no way *o* there isn't the slightest chance that the sales forecasts will be met; **no se parece a su madre ni por a.** he doesn't look the least bit like his mother; **ése no es el problema ni por a.** that's not what the problem is at all

asonada *nf* **(a)** *(protesta)* protest demonstration **(b)** *(intentona golpista)* attempted coup

asonancia *nf (de rima)* assonance

asonante *adj (rima)* assonant

asorochar *Andes* **1** *vt* to cause to have altitude sickness

2 asorocharse *vpr* **(a)** *(por la altitud)* to get altitude sickness **(b)** *(sonrojarse)* to blush

aspa *nf*

> Takes the masculine articles **el** and **un**.

(a) *(figura)* X-shaped cross **(b)** *(de molino)* arm; *(de ventilador)* blade **(c)** *RP (cuerno)* horn

aspado, -a *adj (con forma de cruz)* cross-shaped

aspar *vt* **(a)** *(hilo)* to reel, to wind **(b)** *(crucificar)* to crucify **(c)** *Fam (mortificar)* to mortify **(d)** *(ofender)* to vex, to annoy **(e)** EXPR *Fam* **¡que me aspen si lo entiendo!** I'll be damned if I understand it

aspartamo *nm (edulcorante)* aspartame

aspaventero, -a *adj (persona)* theatrical; *(gesto)* theatrical, exaggerated

aspaviento *nm* **aspavientos** *(con gestos)* furious gesticulations; **¡deja de hacer aspavientos!** *(con gestos)* stop waving your arms around like that!; *(con palabras)* stop making such a fuss!; **intenta nadar sin hacer aspavientos** try and swim without thrashing around so much

aspecto *nm* **(a)** *(apariencia)* appearance; **un adulto con a. de niño** an adult who looks like a child, an adult with a childlike appearance; **tener buen a.** *(persona)* to look well; *(comida)* to look nice *o* good; **tiene mal a.** *(persona)* she doesn't look well; *(comida)* it doesn't look very nice; **tenía a. de vagabundo** he looked like a tramp; **la casa ofrecía un a. horrible después de la fiesta** the house looked a real mess after the party

(b) *(faceta)* aspect; **bajo este a.** from this angle; **en ese a.** in that sense *o* respect; **en todos los aspectos** in every respect; **en cuanto al a. económico del plan,...** as far as the financial aspects of the plan are concerned,...; **hay que destacar como a. negativo que...** one negative aspect *o* point is that...

(c) *Gram* aspect

(d) *Astrol* aspect

ásperamente *adv (responder, criticar)* harshly

aspereza *nf* **(a)** *(al tacto)* roughness **(b)** *(de terreno)* ruggedness, roughness **(c)** *(de sabor)* sharpness, sourness **(d)** *(de clima)* harshness **(e)** *(de voz)* harshness **(f)** *(rudeza) (de persona)* abruptness; **decir algo con a.** to say something sharply *o* abruptly

asperilla *nf* woodruff

asperjar *vt* **(a)** *(rociar)* **a. algo con** to sprinkle sth with **(b)** *Rel* to sprinkle with holy water

áspero, -a *adj* **(a)** *(rugoso)* rough **(b)** *(terreno)* rugged, rough **(c)** *(sabor)* sharp, sour **(d)** *(de clima)* harsh **(e)** *(de voz)* rasping, harsh **(f)** *(persona, carácter)* abrupt, surly; **una áspera disputa** *(entre grupos)* a bitter dispute

asperón *nm* sandstone

aspersión *nf (de jardín)* sprinkling; *(de cultivos)* spraying; **riego por a.** sprinkling

aspersor *nm (para jardín)* sprinkler; *(para cultivos)* sprayer

áspic *nm Culin* **un á. de pollo** chicken in aspic

áspid *nm* asp

aspidistra *nf* aspidistra

aspillera *nf (abertura)* loophole, crenel

aspiración *nf* **(a)** *(pretensión)* aspiration; **su máxima a. era encontrar un trabajo** his greatest ambition was to find a job; **un político con aspiraciones** an ambitious politician **(b)** *(de aire) (por una persona)* breathing in **(c)** *(de aire) (por una máquina)* suction **(d)** *Ling* aspiration

aspirado, -a *adj Ling* aspirated

aspirador *nm*, **aspiradora** *nf* vacuum cleaner, *Br* Hoover®; **pasar el a.** to vacuum, *Br* to hoover

aspirante 1 *adj* **(a)** *(persona)* aspiring **(b)** *(objeto)* **bomba a.** suction pump

2 *nmf (candidato)* candidate **(a** for); *(en deportes, concursos)* contender **(a** for); **un a. al trono** an aspirant to the throne; **los dos aspirantes a la presidencia** the two presidential candidates

aspirar 1 *vt* **(a)** *(aire) (sujeto: persona)* to breathe in, to inhale **(b)** *(aire) (sujeto: máquina)* to suck in **(c)** *(limpiar con aspirador)* to vacuum, *Br* to hoover; **tengo que limpiar el polvo y a. toda la casa** I have to dust and vacuum *o Br* hoover the whole house **(d)** *Ling* to aspirate

2 *vi* **a. a algo** *(ansiar)* to aspire to sth; **aspira a (ser) ministro** he aspires to become a minister; **aspira a ganar el concurso** she hopes to win the contest

aspirina *nf* aspirin

asqueado, -a *adj* sick; **estar a. de (hacer) algo** to be sick of (doing) sth; **está a. de su trabajo** he's sick of his job

asqueante *adj* disgusting, sickening

asquear *vt* to disgust, to make sick; **ese olor me asquea** that smell is disgusting; **le asquea su trabajo** she loathes her job

asquenazi, askenazi 1 *adj* Ashkenazi

2 *nm,f* Ashkenazi

asquerosamente *adv* **se comporta a.** his behaviour is disgusting; **me cae a. mal** I can't stand the sight of her

asquerosidad *nf* **¡qué a. de bebida!** what a disgusting *o* revolting drink!; **una a. de película** *(repugnante)* a disgusting *o* revolting movie; *(pésima)* an appallingly bad movie; **me puse hecho una a.** I got absolutely filthy; **esta oficina está hecha una a.** this office is a tip

asqueroso, -a 1 *adj* **(a)** *(que da asco)* disgusting, revolting; **una película asquerosa** a revolting movie; **tu cuarto está a.** your room is filthy; **es un cerdo a.** he's a disgusting pig **(b)** *(malo)* mean; **no seas a. y devuélvele el juguete** don't be so mean and give her the toy back

2 *nm,f* **(a)** *(que da asco)* disgusting *o* revolting person; **es un a.** he's disgusting *o* revolting **(b)** *(mala persona)* mean person; **es un a., no me quiso prestar dinero** he's so mean, he wouldn't lend me any money

asta *nf*

Takes the masculine articles **el** and **un**.

(**a**) *(de bandera)* flagpole, mast; **a media a.** at half-mast (**b**) *(de lanza)* shaft; *(de brocha)* handle (**c**) *(cuerno)* horn

astabandera *nf Méx* flagpole

astado, -a 1 *adj* horned
2 *nm (toro)* bull

Astana *n* Astana

astato, ástato *nm Quím* astatine

astenia *nf* fatigue, *Espec* asthenia

asténico, -a *adj* easily fatigued, *Espec* asthenic

áster *nf* aster

asterisco *nm* asterisk

asteroide *nm* asteroid

astigmático, -a *adj* astigmatic

astigmatismo *nm* astigmatism

astil *nm* (**a**) *(de hacha, pico)* haft; *(de azada)* handle (**b**) *(de balanza)* beam (**c**) *(de pluma)* shaft

astilla *nf* splinter; **me he clavado una a. en el brazo** I've got a splinter in my arm; **hacer astillas** to smash to smithereens

astillar 1 *vt (mueble)* to splinter; *(tronco)* to chop up
2 **astillarse** *vpr (mueble, hueso)* to splinter

astillero *nm* (**a**) *(de barcos)* shipyard (**b**) *Méx (en monte)* lumbering site

astilloso, -a *adj* splintery

astracán *nm* astrakhan

astracanada *nf Pey* farce; **al final la película se convierte en una a.** at the end, the film degenerates into farce

astrágalo *nm* (**a**) *Anat* ankle bone, *Espec* astragalus (**b**) *Arquit* astragal

astral *adj* astral

astrancia *nf* Hadspen Blood, greater masterwort

astringencia *nf (capacidad astringente)* binding qualities

astringente *adj (alimento)* binding; *(loción)* astringent

astringir [24] *vt (contraer)* to astringe, to contract

astro *nm* (**a**) *(cuerpo celeste)* heavenly body ►► ***el a. rey*** the Sun (**b**) *(persona famosa)* star

astrocito *nm Biol* astrocyte

astrofísica *nf* astrophysics *(singular)*

astrofísico, -a 1 *adj* astrophysical
2 *nm,f* astrophysicist

astrolabio *nm* astrolabe

astrología *nf* astrology

astrológico, -a *adj* astrological

astrólogo, -a *nm,f* astrologer

astronauta *nmf* astronaut

astronáutica *nf* astronautics *(singular)*

astronave *nf* spacecraft, spaceship

astronavegación *nf* space navigation

astronomía *nf* astronomy

astronómico, -a *adj* (**a**) *(de la astronomía)* astronomical (**b**) *(cantidad)* astronomical

astrónomo, -a *nm,f* astronomer

astroquímica *nf* astrochemistry

astroso, -a *adj (andrajoso)* shabby, ragged

astucia *nf* (**a**) *(del ladino, tramposo)* cunning (**b**) *(del sagaz, listo)* astuteness; **con a.** astutely (**c**) *(trampa)* ruse; **eso fue una a. para no pagar** that was just a ruse to get out of paying

astur 1 *adj* (**a**) *Hist* Astorgan, = of/relating to the pre-Roman people of Astorga (**b**) *(asturiano)* Asturian
2 *nmf* (**a**) *Hist* Astorgan (**b**) *(asturiano)* Asturian

asturiano, -a 1 *adj* Asturian
2 *nm,f* Asturian

Asturias *n* Asturias

astutamente *adv* (**a**) *(con trampas)* cunningly (**b**) *(con sagacidad)* astutely

astuto, -a *adj* (**a**) *(ladino, tramposo)* cunning (**b**) *(sagaz, listo)* astute

asuelo *etc ver* **asolar**

asueto *nm* break, rest; **unos días de a.** a few days off

asumir *vt* (**a**) *(hacerse cargo de) (puesto)* to take up; *(papel)* to take on; **a. la responsabilidad de algo** to take on responsibility for sth; **a. el mando/control (de)** to take charge/control (of); **cuando murió su padre, él asumió el papel de cabeza de familia** when his father died he took over as head of the family; **el general asumió la presidencia del país** the general took over the presidency of the country; **el presidente asumió el compromiso de ayudar a las víctimas** the president gave a commitment to help the victims; **asumieron el riesgo de viajar sin mapa** they took the risk of travelling without a map; **el Estado asumirá las pérdidas de la empresa** the State will cover the company's losses
(**b**) *(adquirir)* to take on; **el descontento asumió caracteres alarmantes** the discontent began to take on alarming proportions; **el incendio asumió proporciones descontroladas** the fire got out of control
(**c**) *(aceptar)* to accept; **el equipo ha asumido su papel de favorito** the team has accepted the mantle *o* role of favourites; **asumieron su reacción como algo normal** they accepted her reaction as something that was to be expected; **no asume la muerte de su esposa** he can't come to terms with his wife's death; **eso lo tengo completamente asumido** I've fully come to terms with that

asunceno, -a, asunceño, -a 1 *adj* of/from Asunción; **las calles asuncenas** the streets of Asunción
2 *nm,f* person from Asunción

Asunción *n* Asunción

asunción *nf* (**a**) *(de puesto)* taking up; *(de papel)* taking on; **reunió a las tropas tras la a. del mando** he assembled his troops after taking over command; **no es partidario de la a. de riesgos** he does not like taking risks (**b**) *Rel* **la A.** *(subida a los cielos)* the Assumption; *(festividad)* the Feast of the Assumption

asuntar *vi RDom (prestar atención)* to pay attention

asunto *nm* (**a**) *(tema)* matter; *(problema)* issue; **necesitamos hablar de un a. importante** we need to talk about an important matter; **quieren llegar al fondo del a.** they want to get to the bottom of the matter; **anda metido en un a. turbio** he's mixed up *o* involved in a dodgy affair; **no quiero hablar del a. ese del divorcio** I don't want to talk about that divorce business; **no es a. tuyo** it's none of your business; **¡métete en tus asuntos!** mind your own business!; **el a. es que...** the thing is that...; **te han llamado de Hacienda – mal a.** you've had a call from the tax man – that doesn't sound very good!; **¡y a. concluido** *o* **arreglado!** and that's that! ►► ***asuntos de Estado*** affairs of state; ***asuntos exteriores*** foreign affairs; ***a. pendiente:*** **tenemos un a. pendiente que tratar** we have some unfinished business to attend to; **asuntos pendientes** *(en orden del día)* matters pending; ***asuntos a tratar*** agenda
(**b**) *(de obra, libro)* theme
(**c**) *(romance)* affair; **tener un a. con alguien** to have an affair with sb
(**d**) *Col, Ven* **poner el a.** to watch one's step

asustadizo, -a *adj* easily frightened

asustado, -a *adj (con miedo)* frightened, scared; *(preocupado)* worried

asustar 1 *vt (dar miedo)* to frighten, to scare; *(preocupar)* to worry; **se escondió detrás del sofá para asustarme** she hid behind the sofa so she could jump out and frighten me *o* give me a fright; **¡me has asustado!** you gave me a fright!; **le asustan las arañas** he's scared of spiders; **me asusta pensar que pueda tener razón** the scary thing is she may be right
2 **asustarse** *vpr (tener miedo)* to be frightened (**de** of); *(preocuparse)* to get worried; **me asusté al verlo** I got a shock when I saw him; **no te asustes, seguro que no le ha pasado nada grave** don't be worried, I'm sure nothing bad has happened to him

AT *(abrev de* **Antiguo Testamento***)* OT

atabal *nm* kettledrum

atacado, -a *adj RP, Ven Fam* grumpy; **no le hagas caso, hace días que está a.** don't mind him, he's been in that bad mood for days

atacador *nm* tamper

atacama 1 *adj* Atacaman
2 *nm,f* Atacaman Indian

atacante 1 *adj* (**a**) *(que agrede)* attacking (**b**) *Dep (equipo, jugador)* attacking
2 *nmf* (**a**) *(agresor)* attacker (**b**) *Dep* forward

atacar [60] 1 *vt* (**a**) *(acometer)* to attack
(**b**) *Dep* to attack
(**c**) *(criticar)* to attack; **su propuesta fue atacada por los asistentes** her proposal was attacked by those present
(**d**) *(afectar)* **le atacó la risa/fiebre** he had a fit of laughter/a bout of fever; **me atacó el sueño** I suddenly felt very sleepy
(**e**) *(poner nervioso)* **ese ruido me ataca** that noise gets on my nerves;

su impuntualidad me ataca los nervios his unpunctuality gets on my nerves

(**f**) *(acometer)* to launch into; **el tenor atacó el aria con entusiasmo** the tenor launched into the aria with gusto; **los ciclistas atacaron la última subida con gran energía** the cyclists attacked the final climb energetically

(**g**) *(corroer)* to corrode; **la humedad ataca los metales** humidity corrodes metal

(**h**) *(dañar)* to attack; **esta enfermedad ataca el sistema respiratorio** this disease attacks the respiratory system

(**i**) *Ven Fam (cortejar)* to try to *Br* get off with *o US* make out with; **no es el primer chico que la ataca** he isn't the first boy to try to *Br* get off with *o US* make out with her

2 *vi* (**a**) *(tropas, animal)* to attack (**b**) *Dep* to attack

atache *nm RP* briefcase

atacón, -ona *Ven Fam* 1 *adj* **me gustan las mujeres ataconas** I like women who are not afraid to make the first move

2 *nm,f* **es un a.** he's a bit of a wolf

atado *nm* (**a**) *(conjunto, montón)* bundle; EXPR *CSur* **ser un a. de nervios** *(permanentemente)* to be hyperactive; *(temporalmente)* to be a bundle of nerves (**b**) *Arg (cajetilla)* packet

atadura *nf* (**a**) *(con cuerda)* tie; **consiguió romper las ataduras y escaparse** she managed to free *o* untie herself and get away (**b**) *(vínculo)* tie; **rompió las ataduras familiares** he cut his ties with his family

ataguía *nf* cofferdam

atajada *nf Am (parada)* save

atajador *nm Chile, Méx (arriero)* cattle driver

atajar 1 *vt* (**a**) *(contener)* to put a stop to; *(hemorragia, inundación)* to stem; **a. un problema** to nip a problem in the bud; **las medidas pretenden a. el problema de la evasión de impuestos** the measures are intended to put a stop to the problem of tax evasion

(**b**) *(salir al encuentro de)* to cut off, to head off; **la policía atajó a los terroristas en la frontera** the police cut off *o* headed off the terrorists at the border

(**c**) *(interrumpir)* to cut short, to interrupt; **no me atajes cuando estoy hablando** don't interrupt me *o* butt in when I'm speaking

(**d**) *(interceptar) (pase)* to cut off, to intercept

(**e**) *Am (agarrar)* to catch; **tírame las llaves que las atajo** throw me the keys, I'll catch them; **el portero atajó la pelota** the goalkeeper stopped the ball

2 *vi (acortar)* to take a short cut (**por** through); **atajaremos por el puente** we can take a short cut via the bridge; **si bajas por aquí atajas** it's quicker if you go down this way

3 **atajarse** *vpr RP Fam* to get all defensive

atajo *nm* (**a**) *(camino corto)* short cut; **tomar** *o Esp* **coger un a.** to take a short cut ►► *Informát* ***a. de teclado*** keyboard short cut (**b**) *(medio rápido)* short cut (**c**) *Esp Pey (panda)* **¡a. de cobardes/ladrones!** you bunch of cowards/thieves!; **soltó un a. de disparates** he came out with a pack of nonsense

atalaya 1 *nf* (**a**) *(torre)* watchtower (**b**) *(altura)* vantage point

2 *nmf (persona)* lookout

atañer [67] *vi* to concern; **en lo que atañe a este asunto** as far as this subject is concerned; **ese asunto atañe a nuestro departamento** that matter is the responsibility of our department; **ese problema no te atañe** that problem doesn't concern you

atapuzado, -a *Ven Fam adj (cuarto)* crammed; *(persona)* stuffed

atapuzar *Ven Fam* 1 *vt (cuarto, maleta)* to cram (**de** with); *(persona)* to stuff (**de** with)

2 **atapuzarse** *vpr* to stuff one's face

ataque 1 *ver* **atacar**

2 *nm* (**a**) *(acometida)* attack; **¡al a.!** charge! ►► ***a. aéreo*** *(sobre ciudad)* air raid; *(sobre tropas)* air attack; *Bolsa* ***a. especulativo*** dawn raid; ***a. preventivo*** pre-emptive strike

(**b**) *Dep* attack; **una jugada de a.** an attack, an attacking move

(**c**) *(crítica)* attack; **lanzó duros ataques contra el presidente** she launched several harsh attacks on the president

(**d**) *(acceso)* fit; **en un a. de celos la mató** he killed her in a fit of jealousy; *Fam* **como no se calle me va a dar un a.** if he doesn't shut up I'm going to have a fit ►► ***a. cardíaco*** heart attack; ***a. al corazón*** heart attack; ***a. epiléptico*** epileptic fit; ***a. de nervios*** attack of hysteria; ***a. de pánico*** panic attack; ***a. de risa:* le dio un a. de risa** he had a fit of the giggles

(**e**) *(de sustancia)* corrosive effect

atar 1 *vt* (**a**) *(unir) (nudo, cuerda)* to tie; **ata la cuerda firmemente** tie the rope securely; EXPR **a. cabos** to put two and two together; EXPR **a. los cabos sueltos** to tie up all the loose ends; EXPR **dejar todo atado y bien atado** to make sure everything is settled

(**b**) *(con cuerdas) (persona)* to tie up; *(caballo)* to tether; **lo ataron de pies y manos** they tied his hands and feet; **ató el caballo a la verja** she tethered the horse to the gate; EXPR **tengo las manos atadas, estoy atado de pies y manos** my hands are tied; **esa cláusula nos ata las manos** our hands are tied by that clause

(**c**) *(constreñir)* to tie down; **su trabajo la ata mucho** her work ties her down a lot; **no me siento atado a nadie** I don't feel tied to anybody; EXPR **a. corto a alguien** to keep a tight rein on sb

2 *vi* **un bebé ata mucho** having a baby ties you down a lot

3 **atarse** *vpr* (**a**) *(uno mismo)* **se ató por la cintura para descender el barranco** she tied a rope round her waist in order to go down into the ravine (**b**) *(pelo)* to tie up; **se ató el pelo** she tied her hair up; **atarse los zapatos** *o* **los cordones** to tie one's shoes *o* shoelaces

atarantado, -a *adj Am Fam* (**a**) *(tonto)* dim, slow; **ese niño siempre fue medio a.** that boy was always a bit dim *o* slow (**b**) *(aturdido)* stunned, dazed; **la noticia lo dejó a.** he was stunned by the news

atarantar *vt Am Fam (aturdir)* to daze; **la sorpresa lo atarantó** the surprise left him dazed

atarazana *nf* shipyard

atardecer [46] 1 *nm* dusk; **al a.** at dusk; **contemplaron el a. desde la playa** they watched the sun go down from the beach

2 *v impersonal* to get dark; **está atardeciendo** it's getting dark

atareado, -a *adj* busy

atarearse *vpr* to busy oneself, to occupy oneself

atarjea *nf Perú (depósito)* water supply

atascado, -a *adj* blocked (up)

atascar [60] 1 *vt* to block (up)

2 **atascarse** *vpr* (**a**) *(tubería)* to get blocked up; **se ha atascado el retrete** the toilet is blocked

(**b**) *(mecanismo)* to get stuck *o* jammed; **se atascó la puerta y no pudimos abrirla** the door got stuck *o* jammed and we couldn't get it open

(**c**) *(detenerse)* to get stuck; **el camión quedó atascado en la carretera** the truck got stuck on the road

(**d**) *(al hablar)* **recitó toda la lista sin atascarse** she reeled off the whole list without hesitating once; **se atascó al pronunciar mi nombre** he got his tongue tied in a knot when he tried to say my name

(**e**) *Fam (asunto, proyecto)* to get bogged down

(**f**) *Méx Fam (atiborrarse)* to stuff oneself; **nomás vinieron a la fiesta a atascarse** they only came to the party to stuff themselves

(**g**) *Méx Fam (ensuciarse)* to get in a mess; **siempre que comen espaguetis, los escuincles se atascan** whenever they eat spaghetti, the kids get into a real mess

atasco *nm* (**a**) *(obstrucción)* blockage (**b**) *(de vehículos)* traffic jam; *Fig* **se ha producido un a. en las negociaciones** the negotiations have stalled

ataúd *nm* coffin

ataurique *nm Arquit* ataurique, = plaster decoration using plant motifs typical of Islamic art

ataviar [32] 1 *vt* to dress up; **a. a alguien con algo** to dress sb up in sth

2 **ataviarse** *vpr* to dress up; **se atavió mucho para salir** she got all dressed up to go out; **se atavió con sus mejores galas** she dressed herself up in all her finery

atávico, -a *adj* atavistic

atavío *nm* (**a**) *(adorno)* adornment (**b**) *(indumentaria)* attire; **vestía un elegante a.** she was elegantly attired

atavismo *nm* (**a**) *(herencia arcaica)* **el racismo es un a. que hay que erradicar** racism is an atavistic instinct which we have to root out (**b**) *Biol* atavism

ataxia *nf Med* ataxia

ate *nm Méx* quince jelly

ateísmo *nm* atheism

atemorizado, -a *adj* frightened; **tienen a la región atemorizada con sus ataques** they have been terrorizing the region with their attacks; **vivir a.** to live in fear

atemorizar [14] 1 *vt* to frighten; **quieren atemorizarnos con sus atrocidades** they want to intimidate us with their barbaric acts

2 **atemorizarse** *vpr* to get *o* be frightened; **me atemorizo con los truenos** I get very frightened when there's thunder

atemperar *vt (críticas, protestas)* to temper, to tone down; *(ánimos, nervios)* to calm

atemporal *adj* timeless

Atenas *n* Athens

atenazar [14] *vt (sujetar)* to clench; **el miedo la atenazaba** she was gripped by fear

ATENCIÓN 1 *nf* (a) *(interés)* attention; **tienes que dedicar más a. a tus estudios** you've got to put more effort into your studies, you've got to concentrate harder on your studies; **miraremos tu expediente con mucha a.** we'll look at your file very carefully; **aguardaban el resultado con a.** they were listening attentively for the result; **escucha con a.** listen carefully; **a la a. de** for the attention of; **llamar la a.** *(atraer)* to attract attention; **lo que más me llamó la a. fue la belleza del paisaje** what struck me most was the beauty of the countryside; **su belleza llama la a.** her beauty is striking; **al principio no me llamó la a.** at first I didn't notice anything unusual; **llamar la a. a alguien** *(amonestar)* to tell sb off; **le llamé la a. sobre el coste del proyecto** I drew her attention to the cost of the project; **con sus escándalos, andan llamando la a. todo el tiempo** they are always attracting attention to themselves by causing one scandal or another; **le gusta llamar la a.** she likes to be noticed; **el desastre electoral fue una llamada** *o* **toque de a. al partido gobernante** the disastrous election results were a clear message to the governing party; **a los niños pequeños les cuesta mantener la a.** small children find it difficult to stop their attention from wandering; **poner** *o* **prestar a.** to pay attention; **si no pones** *o* **prestas a., no te enterarás de lo que hay que hacer** if you don't pay attention, you won't know what to do

(b) *(cortesía)* attentiveness; **atenciones** attentiveness; **tenía demasiadas atenciones con el jefe** she was overly attentive towards the boss; **nos colmaron de atenciones** they waited on us hand and foot; **deshacerse en atenciones con** to lavish attention on; **en a. a** *(teniendo en cuenta)* out of consideration for; *(en honor a)* in honour of; **en a. a sus méritos** in honour of her achievements; **organizaron una cena en a. al nuevo embajador** they held a dinner in honour of the new ambassador; **le cedió el asiento en a. a su avanzada edad** he let her have his seat because of her age

(c) *(servicio)* **la a. a los ancianos** care of the elderly; **horario de a. al público** opening hours ►► *Com* ***a. al cliente*** customer service; ***a. domiciliaria*** *(de médico)* home visits; **para la a. domiciliaria, llamar al...** if you wish to call a doctor out, ring this number...; ***a. hospitalaria*** hospital care; ***a. primaria*** *(en ambulatorio)* primary health care; ***a. sanitaria*** health care

2 *interj (en aeropuerto, conferencia)* your attention please!; *Mil* attention!; **¡a., van a anunciar el ganador!** listen, they're about to announce the winner!; **¡a.!** *(en letrero)* danger!; **¡a., peligro de incendio!** *(en letrero) (con materiales inflamables)* (warning!) fire hazard; *(en bosques)* danger of forest fires in this area

ATENDER [66] 1 *vt* (a) *(satisfacer) (petición, ruego)* to agree to; *(consejo, instrucciones)* to heed; **no pudieron a. sus súplicas** they couldn't answer her pleas; **a. las necesidades de alguien** to meet sb's needs

(b) *(cuidar de) (necesitados, invitados)* to look after; *(enfermo)* to care for; *(cliente)* to serve; **el doctor que atendió al accidentado** the doctor who treated the accident victim; **¿qué médico te atiende normalmente?** which doctor do you normally see?; **atiende la farmacia personalmente** she looks after the chemist's herself; **vive solo y sin nadie que lo atienda** he lives alone, without anyone to look after him; **¿me puede a. alguien, por favor?** could somebody help *o* serve me, please?; **¿lo atienden?, ¿lo están atendiendo?** are you being served?; **en esta tienda te atienden muy bien** the service in this shop is very good; **me temo que el director no puede atenderlo en este momento** I'm afraid the manager isn't available just now; **la operadora atiende las llamadas telefónicas** the operator answers the phone calls

(c) *(tener en cuenta)* to keep in mind

(d) *Anticuado (esperar)* to await, to wait for

2 *vi* (a) *(estar atento)* to pay attention (**a** to); **lo castigaron porque no atendía en clase** he was punished for not paying attention in class; **¡cállate y atiende de una vez!** shut up and pay attention *o* listen!; **no atiendes a las explicaciones que te hacen tus invitados** you're not paying attention to what your guests are saying

(b) *(considerar)* **atendiendo a...** taking into account...; **atendiendo a las circunstancias, aceptaremos su candidatura** under the circumstances, we will accept your candidacy; **atendiendo a las encuestas, necesitamos un cambio radical de línea** if the opinion polls are anything to go by, we need a radical change of policy; **la clasificación atiende únicamente a criterios técnicos** the table only takes into account technical specifications, the table is based purely on technical specifications; **le enviamos la mercancía atendiendo a su petición** following your order, please find enclosed the goods requested; EXPR **a. a razones: cuando se enfada, no atiende a razones** when she gets angry, she refuses to listen to reason

(c) *(ocuparse)* **no puedo a. a todo** I can't do everything (myself); **en esta tienda atienden muy mal** the service in this shop is very poor; **¿quién atiende aquí?** who's serving here?

(d) *(llamarse) (animal)* **a. por** to answer to the name of; **el perro atiende por el nombre de Chispa** the dog answers to the name of Chispa; **su nombre es Manuel, pero en la cárcel atiende por Manu** his real name is Manuel, but they call him Manu in jail

3 **atenderse** *vpr Am* **se atiende con la doctora Rodríguez** Doctor Rodríguez normally sees her, her doctor is Doctor Rodríguez

atendible *adj (razón)* worthy of consideration

Atenea *n Mitol* Athena, Athene

ateneo *nm (literario)* literary society; *(científico)* scientific society

atenerse [67] *vpr* (a) **a. a** *(seguir, cumplir) (promesa, orden)* to stick to; *(ley, normas)* to observe, to abide by; **atente a las instrucciones que se te han dado** stick to *o* follow the instructions you have been given; **el gobierno se atendrá a la decisión del tribunal** the government will abide by the court's decision; **con tantas versiones diferentes de lo que pasó, no sabemos a qué atenernos** there are so many different versions of what happened that we don't know what to believe; **a. a las consecuencias** to accept the consequences

(b) *(remitirse)* **me atengo a lo dicho por mi colega** I would agree with what my colleague has said

(c) *(limitarse)* **si nos atenemos a lo que sabemos...** if we stick to what we know...; **a. a la verdad** to stick to the truth

atenido, -a *nm,f Col Fam* lazybones, *Br* layabout

ateniense 1 *adj* Athenian

2 *nmf* Athenian

atentado *nm* (a) *(ataque violento)* **a. (terrorista)** terrorist attack; **sufrir un a.** *(persona)* to be the victim of a terrorist/Mafia/*etc* attack; **un a. con bomba** a bomb attack, a bombing; **un a. contra el presidente** an attempt on the president's life

(b) *(afronta)* crime; **la construcción de la cementera es un a. contra el medio ambiente** the building of the cement factory is a crime against the environment; **la ley es un a. contra la libertad de expresión** the law constitutes an attack on freedom of expression

atentamente *adv* (a) *(con atención, cortesía)* attentively; **mire a.** watch carefully (b) *(en cartas)* **(se despide) a.** *(si se desconoce el nombre del destinatario)* Yours faithfully; *(si se conoce el nombre del destinatario)* Yours sincerely

atentar *vi* **a. contra (la vida de) alguien** to make an attempt on sb's life; **atentaron contra la sede del partido** there was an attack on the party headquarters; **a. contra algo** *(principio)* to be a crime against sth; **esta decoración atenta contra el buen gusto** this décor is an offence against good taste

atentatorio, -a *adj* **es una ley atentatoria a la intimidad de las personas** it's a law which invades people's privacy; **la conducta del gobierno es atentatoria contra los derechos humanos** the government's behaviour constitutes an attack on human rights

atenti *interj RP Fam* (a) *(atención)* hey!; **¡a.!, ¿a que no sabés qué hice ayer?** hey, I bet you can't guess what I did yesterday!; **¡a. con la bicicleta ahí!** look *o* watch out for that bicycle! (b) *(cuidado)* **¡a. con el tránsito!** *(a conductor)* drive carefully!; *(a peatón)* watch out for the traffic!

atento, -a 1 *adj* (a) *(pendiente)* attentive; **un alumno muy a.** a very attentive pupil; **una lectura atenta de la ley permite ver que...** careful reading of the law shows that...; **estar a. a** *(explicación, programa, lección)* to pay attention to; *(ruido, sonido)* to listen out for; *(acontecimientos, cambios, avances)* to keep up with; **escucha a. lo que te voy a decir** listen carefully to what I'm going to tell you; **se manifestaron bajo la atenta mirada de la policía** they demonstrated under the watchful eye of the police

(b) *(cortés)* **es tan atenta con todo el mundo** she's so friendly and kind to everyone; **tienes que ser más a. con los invitados** you should pay more attention to your guests; **¡qué chico más a.!** what a nice young man!

2 *interj RP Fam* watch out!, be careful!; **¡a. a la señal!** wait for the signal

atenuación *nf* (a) *(de dolor)* easing, alleviation; *(de sonido, luz)* attenuation (b) *Der (de responsabilidad)* extenuation, mitigation

atenuante *Der* 1 *adj* **circunstancia a.** extenuating circumstance

2 *nm* extenuating circumstance; **eso no puede ser un a.** that cannot be considered an extenuating circumstance

atenuar [4] 1 *vt* (a) *(disminuir, suavizar)* to diminish; *(dolor)* to ease, to alleviate; *(sonido, luz)* to attenuate (b) *Der (responsabilidad)* to extenuate, to mitigate

2 **atenuarse** *vpr (disminuir, suavizarse)* to lessen, to diminish

ateo, -a 1 *adj* atheistic
2 *nm,f* atheist

aterciopelado, -a *adj* velvety

aterido, -a *adj* freezing; **a. de frío** shaking *o* shivering with cold

aterirse *vpr* to be freezing

aterosclerosis, ateroesclerosis *nf inv Med* atherosclerosis

aterrado, -a *adj* terror-stricken

aterrador, -ora *adj* terrifying

aterrar 1 *vt* to terrify; **me aterran las tormentas** I'm terrified of storms; **me aterra pensar que hayan podido tener un accidente** I'm terrified that they might have had an accident
2 **aterrarse** *vpr* to be terrified

aterrizado, -a *adj Andes Fam* down-to-earth

aterrizaje *nm (de avión)* landing ▸▸ ***a. de emergencia*** emergency landing; ***a. forzoso*** emergency landing

aterrizar [14] *vi* (a) *(avión)* to land
(b) *(caer) (objeto, persona)* to land; **el tapón aterrizó en mi plato** the cork landed on my plate; **tropezó y aterrizó con violencia en el suelo** she tripped up and clattered to the ground
(c) *Fam (aparecer)* **estábamos tan tranquilos en casa cuando aterrizaron mis tíos** we were relaxing at home when my uncle and aunt landed on us out of the blue
(d) *Fam (tomar contacto)* **todavía estoy aterrizando en el nuevo trabajo** I'm still finding my feet in my new job

aterrorizador, -ora *adj* terrifying

aterrorizar [14] 1 *vt* to terrify; **me aterrorizan las arañas** I'm terrified of spiders; **el atracador aterrorizaba a sus víctimas** the robber terrorized his victims
2 **aterrorizarse** *vpr* to be terrified

atesoramiento *nm* hoarding

atesorar *vt* (a) *(riquezas)* to hoard (b) *(virtudes)* to be blessed with

atestación *nf Der* affidavit, statement

atestado, -a 1 *adj* packed; **la discoteca estaba atestada** the disco was packed; **el museo estaba a. de turistas** the museum was packed with tourists; **mi mesa está atestada de libros** my desk is covered in books
2 *nm* official report; **levantar un a.** to write an official report

atestar 1 *vt* (a) *(llenar)* to pack, to cram (**de** with); **los manifestantes atestaban la plaza** the square was packed with demonstrators (b) *Der* to testify to
2 **atestarse** *vpr (llenarse)* to get *o* become packed (**de** with)

atestiguar [11] 1 *vt* (a) *(declarar)* **a. que** to testify that (b) *(demostrar, probar)* **a. algo** to bear witness to sth; **diversos estudios atestiguan la validez de su teoría** various studies bear witness to *o* bear out the validity of her theory; **la economía sigue creciendo, así lo atestiguan las estadísticas** the economy continues to grow, as is borne out by the statistics
2 *vi (declarar)* to testify

atezado, -a *adj* tanned

atiborrar *Fam* 1 *vt* **los aficionados atiborraban el estadio** the stadium was packed to the rafters with fans; **las cajas atiborraban el almacén** the warehouse was crammed full of crates; **atiborró el coche de maletas** he stuffed the car full of suitcases; **mis padres nos atiborraron de comida** my parents stuffed us with food; **las calles estaban atiborradas de coches** the streets were packed with cars
2 **atiborrarse** *vpr* to stuff one's face; **se atiborraron de pasteles** they stuffed their faces with cakes

ático *nm* (a) *(piso)* = attic *Br* flat *o US* apartment, usually with a roof terrace (b) *(desván)* attic

atiendo *etc ver* **atender**

atiene *etc ver* **atener**

atierre *nm Méx (cubrimiento)* covering with earth

atigrado, -a *adj* (a) *(gato)* tabby (b) *(estampado)* striped *(like tiger)*

atildado, -a *adj* smart, spruce

atildar 1 *vt* to smarten up
2 **atildarse** *vpr* to smarten oneself up

atinadamente *adv (calificar, denominar)* rightly, justly; **actuó muy a.** she acted very wisely

atinado, -a *adj (respuesta, comentario)* to the point; **estuvo muy a. en sus críticas** his criticisms were very telling *o* very much to the point; **tomaron una decisión muy atinada** they took a very wise *o* sensible decision

atinar *vi* (a) *(adivinar)* to guess correctly; **atinaron en sus previsiones** their predictions turned out to be correct
(b) *(golpear)* **a. en: la flecha atinó en el blanco** the arrow hit the target; **el misil atinó en el puente** the missile made a direct hit on the bridge
(c) *(encontrar)* **a. con: atinó con el libro que buscaba** she found the book she had been looking for; **siguió revisando el texto hasta a. con las palabras exactas** he continued to revise the text until he hit on exactly the right words
(d) *(conseguir, lograr)* **a. a hacer algo: no atinaba a abrir la cerradura** she couldn't manage to open the lock; **sólo atinaba a mirarla boquiabierto** all he could do was stare at her in astonishment; **cuando la veía no atinaba a decir palabra** when he saw her he could never manage to say anything

atinente, atingente *adj Formal* **a.** pertaining to

atingencia *nf* (a) *Arg, CAm, Chile, Méx (relación)* connection
(b) *Chile, Méx (adecuación)* appropriateness; **la Cámara está estudiando la a. de esa ley** the House is investigating whether the law is appropriate *o* acceptable; **actuar con a. e imparcialidad** to act appropriately and with impartiality
(c) *Méx (tino)* good sense; **tuvo la a. de comprar ahí cuando el terreno era muy barato** he had the good sense to buy when the land there was very cheap
(d) *Perú (acotación)* comment, observation

atingente = **atinente**

atípico, -a *adj* atypical

atiplado, -a *adj* high-pitched

atirantar *vt* to make tense, to tighten

atisbar 1 *vt* (a) *(vislumbrar)* to make out; **se atisbaba un castillo en el horizonte** a castle could (just) be made out on the horizon; **se atisba un principio de acuerdo** the first signs of an agreement are becoming apparent; **no atisbaban ninguna salida a la crisis** they could not see any way out of the crisis
(b) *(acechar)* to watch, to spy on; **atisbaba por un agujero lo que ocurría en la otra habitación** he was spying on *o* watching what was happening in the other room through a hole
2 *vi* to peep

atisbo *nm (indicio)* trace, hint; *(de esperanza)* glimmer; **su declaración ha disipado cualquier a. de duda** her statement has removed any trace of doubt; **negó cualquier a. de veracidad en lo publicado** he denied that there was even a hint of truth to what had been published; **mientras quede un a. de vida** as long as there is still a flicker *o* the slightest sign of life

atiza *interj* my goodness!, by golly!

atizador *nm* poker

atizar [14] 1 *vt* (a) *(fuego)* to poke, to stir
(b) *(sospechas, discordias)* to stir up; **el asesinato atizó odios ancestrales** the murder fanned the flames of *o* stirred up ancient hatreds
(c) *Esp (persona)* **me atizó bien fuerte** *(un golpe)* he hit me really hard; *(una paliza)* he gave me a good hiding; **le atizó una bofetada** she slapped him, she gave him a slap; **me atizó una patada en la pierna** he kicked me in the leg
2 **atizarse** *vpr Esp Fam* **atizarse algo** *(comer)* to guzzle sth; *(beber)* to knock sth back

atlante *nm Arquit* atlas, telamon

atlántico, -a 1 *adj* Atlantic; **el océano A.** the Atlantic (Ocean)
2 *nm* **el A.** the Atlantic (Ocean)

Atlántida *n* **la A.** Atlantis

atlantismo *nm Pol* pro-NATO stance

atlantista *adj Pol* pro-NATO

atlas *nm inv* (a) *(mapa)* atlas ▸▸ ***a. de anatomía*** anatomical atlas; ***a. lingüístico*** linguistic atlas *o* map (b) *Anat (vértebra)* atlas (c) *Geog* **el A., los A.** the Atlas Mountains

atleta *nmf* athlete

atlético, -a *adj* (a) *(competición, club)* athletics; **prueba atlética** athletics event (b) *(cuerpo, persona)* athletic (c) *(del Atlético de Madrid)* = of/relating to Atlético de Madrid Football Club

atletismo *nm* athletics *(singular)* ▸▸ ***a. en pista cubierta*** indoor athletics

atmósfera *nf* (a) *(capa gaseosa)* atmosphere ▸▸ ***a. superior*** upper atmosphere
(b) *(de habitación)* atmosphere; **la a. de esta sala está muy cargada** this room is very stuffy, the atmosphere in this room is very stale
(c) *(ambiente)* atmosphere; **hay una a. muy mala en el trabajo** the atmosphere at work is very bad; **reinaba una a. de desconfianza** an

atmosphere of distrust prevailed; **recrea muy bien la a. del periodo** it very successfully recreates the atmosphere *o* ambience of the period **(d)** *(unidad de presión)* atmosphere

atmosférico, -a *adj* atmospheric

atochamiento *nm Chile* **(a)** *(de autos)* traffic jam **(b)** *(de personas)* crush; **la gran cantidad de usuarios provocó un a. en la red** the large number of users jammed the network

atocinado, -a *adj Fam (persona)* porky, fat

atole, atol *nm* **(a)** *CAm, Méx (con maíz)* = thick hot drink made of corn meal; EXPR **dar a. con el dedo a alguien** to take sb in, to fool sb **(b)** *Ven (con arroz, cebada)* = thick drink made with boiled rice, barley or sago and variously flavoured

atolladero *nm* **(a)** *(apuro)* fix, jam; **estamos en un a.** we are in a fix *o* jam; **se metió en un a.** he got himself into a fix *o* jam; **meter en/sacar de un a. a alguien** to put sb in/get sb out of a tight spot **(b)** *(lodazal)* mire

atollarse *vpr* **(a)** *(en lodazal)* to get stuck; **el autobús se atolló en el barro** the bus got stuck in the mud **(b)** *(en obstáculo)* to get stuck; **me he atollado en la tercera lección y no consigo seguir** I'm stuck on the third lesson and can't seem to get any further

atolón *nm* atoll

atolondrado, -a 1 *adj* **(a)** *(precipitado)* foolish, thoughtless **(b)** *(aturdido)* bewildered, confused

2 *nm,f (precipitado)* **es un a.** he's rather foolish, he's a bit of a fool

atolondramiento *nm* **(a)** *(precipitación)* foolishness, thoughtlessness **(b)** *(aturdimiento)* bewilderment

atolondrar 1 *vt* to bewilder; **me atolondra tanto griterío** all this shouting is making my head spin

2 atolondrarse *vpr (por golpe)* to be stunned; *(por griterío, confusión)* to be bewildered; **se atolondró con el golpe** she was stunned by the blow

atomicidad *nf* atomicity

atómico, -a *adj (energía, armas)* atomic, nuclear; *(central)* nuclear; **núcleo a.** (atomic) nucleus

atomismo *nm Filosofía* atomism

atomista *nmf Filosofía* atomist

atomización *nf* **(a)** *(de líquido)* atomization **(b)** *(de mercado, industria)* fragmentation

atomizado, -a *adj (mercado, industria)* fragmented

atomizador *nm* atomizer, spray; **un perfume con a.** a spray perfume

atomizar [14] *vt* **(a)** *(líquido)* to atomize **(b)** *(de mercado, industria)* to fragment

átomo *nm* **(a)** *(de elemento químico)* atom ►► ***á. gramo*** gram atom **(b)** *(pequeña cantidad)* **en sus declaraciones no hay un á. de verdad** there isn't a grain of truth in what she said; **sin un á. de humildad, declaró que se lo merecía** without even the faintest suggestion of humility, he said he deserved it; **no tenemos ni un á. de esperanza de que esto vaya a cambiar** we haven't the slightest hope of this changing

atonal *adj Mús* atonal

atonalidad *nf Mús* atonality

atonía *nf (de mercado, economía)* sluggishness

atónito, -a *adj* astonished, astounded; **me quedé a. con lo que me contó** I was astonished *o* astounded by what he told me; **miraba con ojos atónitos** she watched wide-eyed

átono, -a *adj* atonic

atontadamente *adv* foolishly, stupidly

atontado, -a 1 *adj* **(a)** *(aturdido)* dazed, stunned; **el golpe lo dejó a.** the blow stunned *o* dazed him **(b)** *(alelado)* **por las mañanas estoy un poco a.** I'm not really with it in the mornings

2 *nm,f* idiot, half-wit

atontamiento *nm* **(a)** *(aturdimiento)* confusion, bewilderment **(b)** *(alelamiento)* **¡tengo un a. hoy!** I really can't think straight today!

atontar 1 *vt* **(a)** *(aturdir)* to daze, to stun **(b)** *(volver tonto)* to dull the mind of; **la televisión atonta a los niños** television dulls children's minds

2 atontarse *vpr* to become stupefied

atontolinado, -a *adj Fam* **(a)** *(atontado)* dazed **(b)** *(despistado)* **estar a.** to have one's head in the clouds

atontolinar *Fam* **1** *vt (aturdir)* to daze, to stun

2 atontolinarse *vpr* to go off in a world of one's own

atorado, -a *Ven Fam* **1** *adj* rash

2 *nm,f* rash person; **es un a.** he's very rash

atoramiento *nm* obstruction, blockage

atorar 1 *vt* to obstruct, to clog

2 atorarse *vpr* **(a)** *(atragantarse)* to choke (**con** on) **(b)** *(cortarse)* to become tongue-tied **(c)** *Am (atascarse)* to get blocked, to get clogged up **(d)** *Am (meterse en un lío)* to get into a mess

atore *nm Ven Fam* **¿y por qué ese a.?** what's the rush?; **está siempre en un a.** she's always in a rush

atormentadamente *adv* tormentedly

atormentado, -a *adj* tormented

atormentar 1 *vt* **(a)** *(torturar)* to torture **(b)** *(sujeto: sentimiento, dolor)* to torment; **ese dolor de cabeza la está atormentando** she's in agony with that headache; **la atormenta la culpa** she is plagued *o* tormented by guilt

2 atormentarse *vpr* to torment *o* torture oneself (**con** about)

atornillador *nm CSur* screwdriver

atornillar *vt* to screw; **a. algo a algo** to screw sth to sth

atorón *nm Méx* traffic jam

atorrante, -a *Fam* **1** *adj* **(a)** *RP (perezoso)* lazy **(b)** *RP (sinvergüenza)* crooked **(c)** *RP (vagabundo)* good-for-nothing **(d)** *Ecuad (antipático)* boorish

2 *nm,f* **(a)** *RP (perezoso)* layabout **(b)** *RP (sinvergüenza)* twister, crook **(c)** *RP (vagabundo)* good-for-nothing **(d)** *Ecuad (antipático)* boor

atortolarse *vpr Fam* **(a)** *(enamorarse)* to fall in love **(b)** *(en actitud cariñosa)* **dos enamorados se atortolaban en un banco** two lovers were whispering sweet nothings to each other on a bench

atosigamiento *nm* **ante el a. de su familia, accedió a cambiar la fecha** she gave in to pressure from her family and agreed to change the date

atosigar [38] **1** *vt* **(a)** *(con prisas)* to harass; **no me atosigues, que estaré listo en un instante** stop rushing *o* harassing me, I'll be ready in a moment **(b)** *(con exigencias)* to pester, to badger; **los periodistas lo atosigaban con preguntas** the journalists badgered him with questions

2 atosigarse *vpr RP Fam (de comida)* to stuff one's face

ATP *nf Dep* (*abrev de* **Asociación de Tenistas Profesionales**) ATP

atrabiliario, -a *adj* foul-tempered, bilious

atracada *nf Carib, Méx, PRico Fam* **darse una a. de algo** to stuff one's face with sth

atracadero *nm* mooring

atracador, -ora *nm,f (de banco)* bank robber; *(en la calle)* mugger

atracar [60] **1** *vt* **(a)** *(banco)* to rob; *(persona)* to mug; **nos atracaron en el parque** we got mugged in the park **(b)** *Chile (golpear)* to beat, to hit

2 *vi (barco)* to dock (**en** at)

3 atracarse *vpr* **(a)** *(comer)* to eat one's fill (**de** of) **(b)** *CAm, Carib (pelearse)* to fight, to quarrel **(c)** *Andes, RP (trabarse)* to get stuck *o* jammed

atracción *nf* **(a)** *(física)* attraction ►► ***a. gravitacional*** gravitational pull; ***a. gravitatoria*** gravitational pull

(b) *(atractivo)* attraction; **sentir a. por** *o* **hacia alguien** to feel attracted to sb; **la ciudad ejercía una gran a. sobre ella** the city fascinated her

(c) *(espectáculo)* act

(d) *(centro de atención)* centre of attention; **con ese vestido vas a ser la a. de la fiesta** you'll be the centre of attention at the party in that dress ►► ***a. turística*** tourist attraction

(e) *(de feria)* (fairground) attraction; **nos montamos en todas las atracciones** we went on all the rides; **parque de atracciones** amusement park

atraco *nm (a banco)* robbery; *(a persona)* mugging; **¡esto es un a.!** this is a stick-up!; *Fam Fig* **¿1.000 euros por eso? ¡menudo a.!** 1,000 euros for that? that's daylight robbery! ►► ***a. a mano armada*** armed robbery

atracón *nm Fam* **(a)** *(comilona)* **darse un a. de algo** *(de comida)* to stuff one's face with sth; *(de películas, televisión)* to overdose on sth **(b)** *Ven (embotellamiento)* traffic jam

atractivamente *adv* attractively

atractivo, -a 1 *adj* attractive

2 *nm (de persona)* attractiveness, charm; *(de cosa)* attraction; **tener a.** to be attractive; **su rostro tiene un a. especial** her face has a special charm; **tu plan tiene muchos atractivos** your plan has a lot of points in its favour; **tiene el a. añadido de ser gratis** it has the added attraction *o* advantage of being free ►► ***a. sexual*** sex appeal

atraer [68] **1** *vt* (**a**) *(causar acercamiento)* to attract; **lo atrajo hacia sí tirándole de la corbata** she pulled him towards her by his tie

(**b**) *(atención, gente)* to attract, to draw; **la asistencia de personajes famosos atrajo a gran cantidad de público** the presence of the famous drew huge crowds; **la miel atrae a las moscas** honey attracts flies; **su ambición le atrajo la antipatía de mucha gente** he was disliked by many because of his ambitious nature

(**c**) *(gustar)* to attract; **me atrae tu hermana** I'm attracted to your sister, I find your sister attractive; **no me atrae mucho la comida china** I'm not too keen on Chinese food; **no me atrae mucho la idea** the idea doesn't appeal to me much

2 atraerse *vpr (mutuamente)* to attract one another; **los extremos se atraen** opposites attract

atragantarse *vpr* (**a**) *(ahogarse)* to choke; **te vas a atragantar** you'll choke; **se atragantó con una espina** she got a fish bone stuck in her throat (**b**) *Fam (no soportar)* **se me ha atragantado ese libro/tipo** I can't stand that book/guy

atraigo *etc ver* **atraer**

atrajo *etc ver* **atraer**

atrancar [60] **1** *vt* (**a**) *(cerrar)* to bar (**b**) *(obstruir)* to block

2 atrancarse *vpr* (**a**) *(encerrarse)* to lock oneself in (**b**) *(atascarse)* to get blocked (**c**) *(al hablar, escribir)* to dry up; **se atranca con las palabras largas** he stumbles over the long words

atrapamoscas *nf inv (planta)* Venus flytrap

atrapar *vt* (**a**) *(agarrar, alcanzar)* to catch; **la policía atrapó a los atracadores** the police caught the bank robbers; **el portero atrapó la pelota** the goalkeeper caught the ball (**b**) *Fam (contraer)* to come down with; **he atrapado un resfriado** I've come down with a cold

atraque *nm* docking

atrás 1 *adv* (**a**) *(movimiento)* backwards; **echarse para a.** to move backwards; **dar un paso a.** to take a step backwards; **hacia a.** backwards; EXPR *Méx Fam* **estar hasta a.** *(borracho)* to be plastered

(**b**) *(en el tiempo)* earlier; **se casaron tres años a.** they had married three years earlier; **cuarenta años a. pocos tenían televisores** not many people had televisions forty years ago

(**c**) *(posición)* **está allá a.** it's back there; **el asiento de a.** the back seat; **la parte de a.** the back; **la falda es más larga por a.** the skirt is longer at the back; **prefiero sentarme a.** I'd rather sit at the back; EXPR *CSur* **saberse algo de a. para adelante** to know sth back to front

(**d**) *Am* **a. de** behind; **me escondí a. de un árbol** I hid behind a tree; **hace meses viene enfrentando un problema a. de otro** he's had one problem after another over the past few months

2 *interj* get back!

atrasado, -a *adj* (**a**) *(en el tiempo)* delayed; **vamos atrasados en este proyecto** we're behind schedule on this project; **tengo mucho trabajo a.** I've got a big backlog of work; **va muy a. en los estudios** he's very behind with his studies; **número a.** back number; *Am* **llegó a.** he arrived late; *Am* **mi vuelo salió a.** my flight was delayed, my flight departed late

(**b**) *(reloj)* slow; **mi reloj va a.** my watch is slow; **llevas el reloj a.** your watch is slow

(**c**) *(pago)* overdue, late

(**d**) *(en evolución, capacidad)* backward; **las regiones más atrasadas del país** the most backward regions of the country

atrasar 1 *vt* (**a**) *(poner más atrás)* to move (further) back (**b**) *(en el tiempo) (reunión, viaje, reloj)* to put back; **atrasaron la fecha de la reunión** they put back the date of the meeting (**c**) *Dep (balón)* to pass back

2 *vi (reloj)* to be slow

3 atrasarse *vpr* (**a**) *(en el tiempo)* to be late; *(frío, verano)* to come *o* arrive late; **este año se ha atrasado el verano** summer has been late in coming this year

(**b**) *(quedarse atrás)* to fall behind; **se están atrasando en los pagos** they are falling behind with their payments

(**c**) *(reloj)* to lose time; **mi reloj se atrasa cinco minutos al día** my watch loses five minutes a day

(**d**) *(llegar tarde)* to be delayed; **su vuelo se atrasó** her flight was delayed; **se atrasaron media hora** they were delayed by half an hour; **nos atrasamos hablando con mi tía** we got held up talking to my aunt

(**e**) *Andes (no crecer)* to be stunted

atraso *nm* (**a**) *(demora)* delay; **llegar con (quince minutos de) a.** to be (fifteen minutes) late; **los trenes circulan hoy con (una hora de) a.** the trains are running (an hour) late today; **el proyecto lleva mucho a.** the project is a long way behind schedule

(**b**) *(del reloj)* slowness

(**c**) *(de evolución, desarrollo)* backwardness; **no tener móvil me parece un a.** not having a mobile is so backward!

(**d**) **atrasos** *(de pagos)* arrears; **todavía no me han pagado los atrasos del año pasado** they still haven't paid me their arrears *o* the money they owe me from last year

atravesado, -a *adj* (**a**) *(cruzado)* **hay un árbol a. en la carretera** there's a tree lying across the road; **el barco había quedado a. a la entrada del puerto** the ship had blocked the entrance to the harbour; EXPR *Fam* **tener a. a algo/a alguien: tengo a. a Manolo** I can't stand Manolo

(**b**) *(bizco)* cross-eyed, cock-eyed

(**c**) *Fam (malintencionado)* nasty

(**d**) EXPR *RP Fam* **andar a.** to be grumpy, *Br* to have the hump

atravesar [3] **1** *vt* (**a**) *(interponer)* to put across; **los manifestantes atravesaron un camión en la carretera** the demonstrators blocked the road with a truck; **atravesó un madero para que no pudieran abrir la puerta** she barred the door with a plank of wood

(**b**) *(ir al otro lado de)* to cross; **atravesó el río a nado** she swam across the river; **atravesó la calle corriendo** he ran across the street; **han atravesado el ecuador de la carrera** they have passed the halfway stage in their university course

(**c**) *(traspasar)* to pass *o* go through; **la bala le atravesó un pulmón** the bullet went through one of his lungs; **el río atraviesa el pueblo** the river goes *o* runs through the village

(**d**) *(pasar)* to go through, to experience; **a. una mala racha** to be going through a bad patch; **atraviesan un buen momento** things are going well for them at the moment

2 *vi* **atraviesan por dificultades** they are having problems, they're going through a difficult patch

3 atravesarse *vpr (interponerse)* to be in the way; **se nos atravesó una moto** a motorbike crossed in front of us; **la desgracia se atravesó en su camino** ill fortune crossed her path; **se le atravesó una espina en la garganta** he got a fish bone caught in his throat; *Fam* **se me ha atravesado la vecina** I can't stand my neighbour; *Fam* **se me atravesó el latín** Latin and me just didn't get on together

atrayente *adj* attractive

atrechar *vi PRico Fam* to take a short cut

atreverse *vpr* to dare; **a. a hacer algo** to dare to do sth; **a. a algo** to be bold enough for sth; **a. con alguien** to take sb on; **no me atrevo a entrar ahí** I daren't go in there, I'm scared to go in there; **¿a que no te atreves a saltar desde ahí?** I bet you're too scared to jump from there!; **¡atrévete y verás!** just you dare and see what happens!; **¿cómo te atreves a decir eso?** how dare you say that!

atrevidamente *adv* (**a**) *(osadamente)* daringly (**b**) *(descaradamente)* cheekily

atrevido, -a 1 *adj* (**a**) *(osado)* daring; **es muy a., le encantan los deportes de riesgo** he's very daring, he loves dangerous sports; **un escote a.** a daring neckline; **una película/escultura atrevida** a bold film/sculpture (**b**) *(caradura)* cheeky

2 *nm,f* (**a**) *(osado)* daring person (**b**) *(caradura)* cheeky person; **¡qué a., contestar así a tu madre!** what a cheek, answering your mother back like that!

atrevimiento *nm* (**a**) *(osadía)* **el a. de sus diseños** the daring of his designs; **perdona mi a., ¿estás casada?** if you don't mind me asking, are you married? (**b**) *(insolencia)* cheek; **tuvo el a. de gritarle** she had the cheek *o* nerve to shout at him; **¡qué a.!** what a cheek!

atrezo, atrezzo *nm Teatro & Cine* props

atribución *nf* (**a**) *(imputación)* attribution; **no está confirmada la a. del atentado a los separatistas** it has not been confirmed that the separatists were responsible for the attack; **la a. del cuadro a Vermeer es polémica** the attribution of the painting to Vermeer is controversial

(**b**) *(asignación)* **es responsable de la a. de contratos a otras empresas** the person in charge of awarding contracts to other firms

(**c**) **atribuciones** *(competencias)* powers; **cumplir con sus atribuciones constitucionales** to fulfil one's constitutional duties; **no tengo atribuciones para tomar esa decisión** I do not have the authority to take that decision

atribuible *adj* attributable; **un accidente a. al mal estado de la carretera** an accident that can be put down to the poor condition of the road

atribuir [34] **1** *vt* (**a**) *(imputar)* **a. algo a** to attribute sth to; **un cuadro atribuido a Goya** a painting attributed to Goya; **atribuyen la autoría del delito al contable** they believe the accountant committed the crime; **le atribuyen la responsabilidad del accidente** they believe he is responsible for the accident; **le atribuyen una gran paciencia** she is said to be very patient

(**b**) *(asignar) (función, gestión)* to assign; **las competencias que les atribuye la constitución** the powers conferred on *o* vested in them by the constitution

2 **atribuirse** *vpr (méritos)* to claim to have; *(poderes)* to assume for oneself; *(culpa)* to take, to accept; *(atentado)* to claim responsibility for; **se atribuye el éxito de la película** she is claiming the credit for the film's success; **se atribuyó la autoría del secuestro** he admitted to having carried out the kidnapping

atribulado, -a *adj Formal* distressed

atribular *Formal* 1 *vt* to distress

2 **atribularse** *vpr* to get distressed; **se atribula con el más mínimo problema** the slightest problem distresses her

atributivo, -a *adj Gram (adjetivo)* predicative; *(verbo)* copulative

atributo *nm* (a) *(cualidad)* attribute (b) *(símbolo)* symbol; **la corona y el cetro son los atributos de la monarquía** the crown and sceptre are the symbols of royal power (c) *Gram (término)* predicate

atribuyo *etc ver* **atribuir**

atril *nm (para libros)* lectern; *(para partituras)* music stand; *(para hojas)* document stand

atrincherado, -a *adj* (a) *(en trinchera)* entrenched, dug in (b) *(en postura, actitud)* entrenched

atrincheramiento *nm* entrenchment

atrincherar 1 *vt* to entrench, to surround with trenches

2 **atrincherarse** *vpr* (a) *(en trinchera)* to entrench oneself, to dig oneself in (b) *(en postura, actitud)* **se atrincheró en su oposición a la propuesta** he persisted in his opposition to the proposal; **se atrincheraron en su postura** *(en negociación)* they dug their heels in and refused to give up their position

atrio *nm* (a) *(pórtico)* portico (b) *(patio interior)* atrium

atrocidad *nf* (a) *(cualidad)* barbarity (b) *(acción)* atrocity (c) *Fam (horror)* **su último libro es una a.** his latest book is atrocious *o* the pits; **me parece una a. que no tengan calefacción** I think it's terrible *o* awful that they don't have heating

atrofia *nf* (a) *(de músculo, función orgánica)* atrophy (b) *(deterioro)* atrophy, deterioration

atrofiado, -a *adj* (a) *(músculo, función orgánica)* atrophied (b) *(deteriorado)* atrophied

atrofiar 1 *vt* (a) *(músculo, función orgánica)* to atrophy (b) *(deteriorar)* to weaken

2 **atrofiarse** *vpr* (a) *(músculo, función orgánica)* to atrophy (b) *(deteriorarse)* to deteriorate, to become atrophied

atronador, -ora *adj (ruido)* deafening; *(voz)* thunderous

atronar 1 *vt* **el ruido del tráfico atronaba las calles** the streets resounded with the deafening noise of the traffic

2 *vi* **los ruidos de los manifestantes atronaban en las calles** the streets resounded with the deafening noise of the demonstrators; **las ovaciones atronaban en el estadio** the stadium rang with the cheers of the crowd

atropelladamente *adv* **todo fue preparado a.** it was all prepared in a great rush; **en la película, las imágenes se suceden a.** the film is a jumble *o* flurry of images; **hablaba a. y sin pronunciar bien** she was gabbling and not pronouncing her words properly; **el corazón le latía a.** her heart was pounding furiously; **corrieron a. hacia el tren** they ran helter-skelter towards the train

atropellado, -a *adj (acciones)* rushed; *(explicación)* garbled; **una sucesión de imágenes atropelladas** a jumble *o* flurry of images

atropellamiento *nm* **ha habido un a. con dos víctimas mortales** two people were run over and killed in an accident; **fui testigo del a. de mi tía** I saw my aunt get run over

atropellar 1 *vt* (a) *(sujeto: vehículo)* to run over, to knock down; **lo atropelló un coche** he was run over *o* knocked down by a car; **murió atropellado** he was run over and killed

(b) *(sujeto: persona)* to trample on; **salió atropellando a todo el que se le puso por delante** he trampled right over everyone who got in his way

(c) *(derechos)* to ride roughshod over; **la ley atropella los derechos de los inmigrantes** the law rides roughshod over immigrants' rights

2 **atropellarse** *vpr* (a) *(al hablar)* to trip over one's words; **tranquilo, no te atropelles** slow down, you're gabbling (b) *(al avanzar)* **la muchedumbre se atropellaba a la salida** there was a lot of pushing and shoving among the crowd on the way out

atropello *nm* (a) *(por vehículo)* **ha habido un a. con dos víctimas mortales** two people were run over and killed in an accident; **fui testigo del a. de mi tía** I saw my aunt get run over

(b) *(moral)* abuse; **denunciaron el a. a los derechos humanos por parte del régimen** they condemned the government for human rights abuses; **¡esto es un a.!** this is an outrage!

(c) *(precipitación)* **con a.** in a rush; **habla con mucho a.** she gabbles a lot

atropina *nf* atropin, atropine

atroz *adj* (a) *(cruel) (crimen, tortura)* horrific, barbaric (b) *(enorme)* **hace un frío a.** it's terribly *o* bitterly cold; **es de una fealdad a.** he's terribly *o* incredibly ugly (c) *(muy malo)* atrocious, awful

atrozmente *adv* (a) *(cruelmente)* barbarically (b) *(como intensificador)* terribly; **lo hizo a. mal** he did it atrociously, he did it terribly badly

atruena *etc ver* **atronar**

ATS *nmf Esp (abrev de* **ayudante técnico sanitario**) qualified nurse

attaché [ata'tʃe] *nm* attaché case

atte. *(abrev de* **atentamente**) **(se despide) a.** *(si se desconoce el nombre del destinatario)* Yours faithfully; *(si se conoce el nombre del destinatario)* Yours sincerely

atuendo *nm* clothes; **acudió a la fiesta con un a. informal** she wore a casual outfit to the party

atufar *Fam* 1 *vt* to stink out; **atufó toda la habitación con humo** she stank the room out with smoke

2 *vi* to stink (**a** of)

3 **atufarse** *vprAndes (aturdirse)* to become dazed *o* confused

atún *nm* tuna ▸▸ ***a. listado*** skipjack tuna

atunero, -a 1 *adj* tuna

2 *nm,f (barco)* tuna-fishing boat; *(persona)* tuna-fisherman

aturdido, -a *adj* dazed

aturdimiento *nm* (a) *(por ruido, luz)* bewilderment, confusion; **el golpe le produjo a.** he was stunned by the blow (b) *(por noticia)* **la noticia le produjo tal a. que no nos oyó** she was so stunned by the news that she didn't hear us

aturdir 1 *vt* (a) *(sujeto: ruido, luz)* to confuse, to bewilder (b) *(sujeto: golpe, noticia)* to stun; **la noticia lo dejó aturdido** he was stunned by the news

2 **aturdirse** *vpr* (a) *(con ruido, luz)* to get confused (b) *(por golpe, noticia)* to be stunned

aturullar *Fam* 1 *vt* to fluster

2 **aturrullarse** *vpr* to get flustered

atusar 1 *vt* (a) *(recortar) (pelo)* to trim, to cut; *(planta)* to prune, to trim (b) *(alisar)* to smooth, to slick back

2 **atusarse** *vpr* (a) *(arreglarse)* to do oneself up in one's finery (b) *(alisarse)* **atusarse el bigote/pelo** to smooth one's moustache/hair (c) *PRico (enfadarse)* to get angry

aucuba *nf* Japan laurel

audacia *nf* (a) *(valentía)* daring, boldness; **con a.** daringly, boldly (b) *(descaro)* audacity

audaz *adj* (a) *(valiente)* daring, bold (b) *(descarado)* audacious

audazmente *adv* (a) *(con valentía)* daringly, boldly (b) *(con descaro)* audaciously

audible *adj* audible

audición *nf* (a) *(acción de oír)* hearing (b) *(de música)* concert; *(de poesía)* reading, recital (c) *(selección de artistas)* audition (d) *RP (programa)* programme

audiencia *nf* (a) *(recepción)* audience; **dar** *o* **conceder a.** to grant an audience; **recibir a alguien en a.** to grant sb an audience

(b) *(público)* audience

(c) *(de programa de TV, radio)* **la a. del programa ha caído mucho** the programme has lost a lot of viewers/listeners; **un horario de máxima a.** a peak viewing/listening time

(d) *Der (tribunal, edificio)* court ▸▸ ***A. Nacional*** = court in Madrid dealing with cases that cannot be dealt with at regional level; ***a. provincial*** provincial court; ***a. territorial*** regional court

(e) *Der (juicio)* hearing ▸▸ ***a. pública*** public hearing

audífono *nm* (a) *(para sordos)* hearing aid (b) *Am* **audífonos** *(cascos)* headphones

audímetro, audiómetro *nm* (a) *Tec* audiometer (b) *TV* audiometer, audience-monitoring device

audio *nm* audio

audiofrecuencia *nf* audio frequency

audiolibro *nm* talking book, book on tape

audiometría *nf* audiometry

audiómetro = **audímetro**

audiovisual 1 *adj* audiovisual

2 *nm* (a) *(montaje, presentación)* audiovisual presentation (b) **audiovisuales** *(recursos)* audiovisual aids

auditar *vt* to audit

auditivo, -a *adj (canal)* aural; *(nervio)* auditory; **tener problemas auditivos** to have hearing problems

auditor, -ora 1 *adj* **empresa auditora** auditor(s)
2 *nm,f* auditor ►► ***a. externo*** external auditor

auditora *nf* auditor(s)

auditoría *nf* (**a**) *(profesión)* auditing (**b**) *(despacho)* auditor's, auditing company (**c**) *(balance)* audit ►► ***a. de cuentas*** audit; ***a. externa*** external audit; ***a. interna*** internal audit

auditorio *nm* (**a**) *(público)* audience (**b**) *(lugar)* auditorium

auditórium *nm* auditorium

auge *nm* (**a**) *(apogeo)* **estar en (pleno) a.** to be booming; **el turismo está en un momento de a.** tourism is booming; **una idea que está cobrando a.** an idea that is becoming more popular (**b**) *(ascenso)* **el a. del fascismo en la primera mitad de siglo** the rise of fascism during the first half of the century; **el a. de la economía** the growth of the economy

augur *nm Hist* augur

augurar *vt (sujeto: suceso)* to augur; *(sujeto: persona)* to predict; **el resultado de las elecciones no augura un futuro estable** the result of the elections does not augur well for future stability; **esas nubes no auguran nada bueno** those clouds don't look too promising

augurio *nm* (**a**) *(señal)* omen, sign; **un comienzo así es buen a.** a start like that augurs well (**b**) *(pronóstico)* prediction; **no se cumplieron los augurios** the predictions did not come true

augusto, -a *adj* august

aula *nf*

Takes the masculine articles **el** and **un**.

(de escuela) classroom; *(de universidad)* lecture room; **con la vuelta a las aulas** when school/university starts again ►► ***a. magna*** = main hall in a university used for ceremonial purposes

aulaga *nf* gorse

áulico, -a *adj* court; **poeta á.** court poet

aullador *nm (mono)* howler monkey

aullar *vi* to howl; **aullaba de dolor** she was howling with pain

aullido *nm* howl; **se oía el a. de un lobo** you could hear a wolf howling; **lanzó un a. de miedo** she gave a shriek of fear

aumentar 1 *vt* to increase; **a. la producción** to increase production; **los enfrentamientos aumentaron la tensión en la zona** the clashes increased the tension in the zone; **me han aumentado el sueldo** my salary has been increased *o* raised; **la lente aumenta la imagen** the lens magnifies the image; **aumentó casi 10 kilos** he put on almost 10 kilos
2 *vi (temperatura, precio, gastos, tensión)* to increase, to rise; *(velocidad)* to increase; **a. de tamaño** to increase in size; **a. de precio** to go up *o* increase in price; **el desempleo aumentó en un 4 por ciento** unemployment rose *o* increased by 4 percent; **con lo que come, no me sorprende que haya aumentado de peso** it doesn't surprise me that he's put on weight, considering how much he eats

aumentativo, -a 1 *adj* augmentative
2 *nm* augmentative

aumento *nm* (**a**) *(de temperatura, precio, gastos, sueldo, tensión)* increase, rise; *(de velocidad)* increase; **un a. del 10 por ciento** a 10 percent increase; **un a. de los precios** a price rise; **las temperaturas experimentarán un ligero a.** temperatures will rise slightly; **ir** *o* **estar en a.** to be on the increase ►► ***a. lineal*** *(de sueldo)* across-the-board pay rise; ***a. de sueldo*** pay rise; **pedir un a. de sueldo** to ask for a (pay) *Br* rise *o US* raise
(**b**) *(en óptica)* magnification; **una lente de 20 aumentos** a lens of magnification x 20
(**c**) *Méx (posdata)* postscript

AUN 1 *adv* even; **a. los más fuertes lloran** even the strongest people cry
2 *conj* even; **a. estando cansado, lo hizo** even though he was tired, he did it; **a. sin dinero, logró sobrevivir** she managed to survive even without any money; **ni a. puesta de puntillas logra ver** she can't see, even on tiptoe; **a. cuando** *(a pesar de que)* even though, although; *(incluso si)* even if; **es muy pesimista, a. cuando todos los pronósticos le son favorables** she's very pessimistic, even though all the predictions seem to favour her; **a. cuando nos cueste, tenemos que hacerlo** even if it's difficult, we have to do it; **a. así** even so; **a. así, deberías decirle algo** even so, you ought to say something to her; **ni a. así lograron la victoria** even then they still didn't manage to win

AÚN *adv* (**a**) *(con afirmación)* still; *(con negación)* yet, still; **a. respira** he's still breathing; **están a. aquí** they are still here; **a. no lo he recibido** I still haven't got it, I haven't got it yet; **¿se lo has preguntado? – a. no** have you asked her? – no, not yet; **¿a. no has terminado?** haven't you finished yet?; **¿y a. quieres que te haga caso?** and you still expect me to listen to you?; **si nos sobrara el tiempo, a., pero no nos sobra** if we had plenty of time, maybe, but we don't
(**b**) *(incluso)* even; **a. más** even more; **es a. más alto que ella** he's even taller than her; **si ganamos, lo pasaremos a. mejor que ayer** if we win, we'll have an even better time than yesterday; **¡jugad con más pasión a.!** play with even more passion!

aunar 1 *vt* to join, to pool; **a. esfuerzos** to join forces; **su talento, aunado a su dedicación, dio excelentes resultados** her talent combined with her dedication achieved excellent results
2 **aunarse** *vpr (aliarse)* to unite

AUNQUE *conj* (**a**) *(a pesar de que)* even though, although; *(incluso si)* even if; **tendrás que venir a. no quieras** you'll have to come, even if you don't want to; **a. quisiera no podría** even if I wanted to, I wouldn't be able to; **a. es caro, me lo voy a comprar** although it's expensive I'm going to buy it, I'm going to buy it even though it's expensive; **a. me cae bien, no me fío de él** much as I like him, I don't trust him; **a. no te lo creas llegó el primero** believe it or not, he came first; **a. parezca mentira** strange as it may seem, believe it or not; **a. parezca raro** oddly enough, odd though it may seem; **cómprale a. sea una caja de bombones** buy her something, even if it is only a box of chocolates; *RP* **decime la verdad a. más no sea** at least tell me the truth

AUMENTATIVO

Spanish has a range of augmentative suffixes (eg **-azo(a)**, **-ón(ona)** or **-ote(a)**) which are used to create new nouns and adjectives. These suffixes can be used merely to indicate greater size or intensity, but they often add an emotional or dramatic edge:

¡qué ojazos tiene! *what big eyes she has!*
está bien sanote *he's the picture of health*
¡qué memorión! *what an amazing memory!*
es ya una mujerona más alta que su padre *she's already a big woman taller than her father*

These suffixes can often add a pejorative note to the base word:

casa (*house*)	**casucha** (*hovel*)
pájaro (*bird*)	**pajarraco** (*big ugly bird*)

On occasion, a new word with a distinct sense evolves from the use of an augmentative suffix:

culebra (*snake*)	**culebrón** (*TV soap opera*)
cabeza (*head*)	**cabezota** (*pigheaded person*)
cuchara (*spoon*)	**cucharón** (*ladle*)

Other cases are less fixed, but still frequently encountered:

voz (*voice*)	**vozarrón** (*loud voice*)

(b) *(pero)* although; **es lista, a. un poco perezosa** she's clever, although *o* if a little lazy; **aquellos cuadros no están mal, a. éstos me gustan más** those paintings aren't bad, but I like these (ones) better

aúpa *Esp* 1 *interj* **(a)** *(¡levántate!)* get up!; *(al coger a un niño en brazos)* ups-a-daisy! **(b)** *(¡viva!)* **ia. (el) Atleti!** up the Athletic!

2 **de aúpa** *loc adj Fam (tremendo)* **una comida de a.** a brilliant meal; **un susto de a.** a hell of a fright; **hacía un frío de a.** it was perishing; **mis padres son de a.** my parents are unreal *o* unbelievable

au pair [o'per] (*pl* **au pairs**) *nmf* au pair

aupar 1 *vt* **(a)** *(subir)* to help up; *(levantar en brazos)* to lift up in one's arms; **aúpame, que no llego** lift me up, I can't reach

(b) *(a posición social, económica)* **la película que lo aupó a la fama** the film that catapulted him to fame; **auparon la empresa al liderazgo del sector automovilístico** they made the company the number one car manufacturer; **una coalición lo aupó a la presidencia** a coalition brought him to the presidency

(c) *(animar)* to cheer on; **consiguió el oro aupado por un público enfervorecido** he was cheered on to the gold medal by a frenzied crowd

2 **auparse** *vpr* to climb up; **se aupó a la valla para poder ver mejor** she climbed up onto the fence to get a better view

aura *nf*

Takes the masculine articles **el** and **un**.

(a) *(halo)* aura **(b)** *Med* aura **(c)** *(viento)* gentle breeze **(d)** *Am (ave)* turkey buzzard

áureo, -a *adj (de oro)* gold; *(dorado)* golden

aureola, auréola *nf* **(a)** *Astron* halo **(b)** *Rel* halo **(c)** *(fama)* aura

aurícula *nf Anat (del corazón)* auricle, atrium

auricular 1 *adj* auricular

2 *nm* **(a)** *(de teléfono)* receiver **(b)** **auriculares** *(de arco)* headphones; *(de botón)* earphones

aurífero, -a *adj* gold-bearing

auriga *nm* charioteer

auriñaciense *Geol* 1 *adj* Aurignacian

2 *nm* **el A.** the Aurignacian period

aurora *nf* **(a)** *(alba)* dawn; **al despuntar** *o* **romper la a.** at dawn **(b)** *(comienzo)* dawning; **la a. de una nueva época** the dawning of an new era **(c)** *(fenómeno atmosférico)* ***a. austral*** aurora australis, southern lights; ***a. boreal*** aurora borealis, northern lights; ***a. polar*** aurora **(d)** *(planta)* flower-of-an-hour

auscultación *nf* auscultation

auscultar *vt* **(a)** *Med* **a. a alguien** to listen to sb's chest; **le auscultó el pecho** she listened to his chest **(b)** *(sondear)* to sound out

ausencia *nf* **(a)** *(de persona, cosa)* absence; **se notó su a.** she was missed, her absence was noticed; **lo acabaron durante su a.** they finished it during *o* in his absence; **si llama alguien en mi a., toma el recado** if anyone calls while I'm away, take a message; **la jornada se caracterizó por la a. de incidentes** the day passed off without incident; **habrá a. de nubes en todo el norte del país** there will be clear skies across the whole of the north of the country

(b) *(falta de asistencia)* absence; **hay varias ausencias** there are several people who couldn't attend

(c) *Med* absence, petit mal

ausentarse *vpr* to go away; **se ausentará durante el fin de semana** she will be away for the weekend; **se ausentó de su país durante varios años** he lived abroad for several years; **el trabajo lo obliga a a. de su familia** his work means he has to spend a lot of time away from his family

ausente 1 *adj* **(a)** *(no presente)* absent; **los alumnos ausentes al examen tendrán que hacer un trabajo** pupils who miss the exam will have to write an essay; **estará a. todo el día** he'll be away all day; **está a. por enfermedad** he's off sick; **estuvo a. de su país durante una larga temporada** she lived abroad for some time

(b) *(distraído)* **un joven de mirada a.** a young man with a faraway look in his eyes; **estaba a., pensando en sus cosas** she was wrapped up in her own thoughts

2 *nmf* **(a)** *(no presente)* **criticó a los ausentes** she criticized the people who weren't there; **Rusia fue la gran a. de la cumbre** Russia was the most notable absentee from the summit **(b)** *Der* missing person

ausentismo *nm* **(a)** *(de terrateniente)* absentee landownership **(b)** *(de trabajador, alumno)* ***a. escolar*** truancy; ***a. laboral*** *(justificado)* absence from work; *(injustificado)* absenteeism

ausentista 1 *adj* absentee

2 *nmf* absentee

auspiciar *vt* **(a)** *(apoyar, favorecer)* to back, to support; **una campaña auspiciada por las autoridades** a campaign backed *o* supported by the authorities; **una fundación auspiciada por la patronal italiana** a foundation sponsored by Italian employers; **un grupo que auspicia una política de tolerancia** a group that advocates a policy of tolerance **(b)** *(pronosticar)* to predict; **a. el futuro** to predict the future

auspicio *nm* **(a)** *(protección)* protection; **bajo el a.** *o* **los auspicios de...** under the auspices of... **(b)** **auspicios** *(señales)* omens; **el día se inició con buenos auspicios** the day got off to a promising start

auspicioso, -a *adj* auspicious, promising; **se han dado avances muy auspiciosos** some very promising progress has been made; **los resultados hasta la fecha no han sido muy auspiciosos** the results so far haven't been very auspicious *o* promising

austeramente *adv* austerely

austeridad *nf* **(a)** *(de costumbres, vida)* austerity; **con a.** austerely **(b)** *(de estilo)* austerity; **viste con a.** she dresses very plainly

austero, -a *adj* **(a)** *(costumbres, vida)* austere; **adoptar un presupuesto a.** to limit budgetary expenditure **(b)** *(de estilo)* austerity; *(de ropa)* plainness

austral 1 *adj* southern

2 *nm Antes (moneda)* austral, = former Argentinian unit of currency

Australia *n* Australia

australiano, -a 1 *adj* Australian

2 *nm,f* Australian

australopiteco *nm* Australopithecus

Austria *n* Austria

austriaco, -a, austríaco, -a 1 *adj* Austrian

2 *nm,f* Austrian

Austrias *nmpl* **los A.** the Hapsburgs

austro *nm Literario* south

austrohúngaro, -a, austro-húngaro, -a *adj Hist* Austro-Hungarian

autarquía *nf* **(a)** *(económica)* autarky, self-sufficiency **(b)** *(política)* autarchy

autárquico, -a *adj* **(a)** *(económicamente)* autarkic, self-sufficient **(b)** *(políticamente)* autarchical

autenticación *nf* **(a)** *Der (de firma, documento)* authentication **(b)** *Informát* authentication

auténticamente *adv* truly, genuinely; **un parlamento a. representativo** a truly representative parliament; **un sabor a. francés** an authentically French taste

autenticar *vt* **(a)** *Der (firma, documento)* to authenticate **(b)** *Informát* to authenticate **(c)** *RP (compulsar)* to check against the original; **una fotocopia autenticada** a certified copy

autenticidad *nf* authenticity

auténtico, -a *adj* **(a)** *(cuadro)* genuine; *(diamante)* real; *(documento)* authentic **(b)** *(persona)* genuine; *(sentimiento)* genuine, real **(c)** *(como intensificador)* **es un a. imbécil** he's a real idiot; **eso es un a. disparate** that's completely crazy; **fue un a. desastre** it was a total disaster

autentificación *nf* **(a)** *Der (de firma, documento)* authentication **(b)** *Informát* authentication

autentificar [60] *vt* **(a)** *Der (firma, documento)* to authenticate **(b)** *Informát* to authenticate

autillo *nm* scops owl ►► ***a. americano*** eastern screech owl; ***a. cariblanco*** white-faced owl

autismo *nm* autism

autista 1 *adj* autistic

2 *nmf* autistic person

autístico, -a *adj* autistic

autito *nm CSur* ***autitos chocadores*** Dodgems®, bumper cars

auto *nm* **(a)** *esp CSur (coche)* car ►► *CSur* ***a. de alquiler*** hire car; *CSur* ***a. antiguo*** *(de antes de 1930)* vintage car; *(más moderno)* classic car; *CSur* ***a. bomba*** car bomb; *CSur* ***a. de carreras*** racing car; ***autos de choque*** Dodgems®, bumper cars; *CSur* ***a. deportivo*** sports car; *CSur* ***a. de época*** *(de antes de 1930)* vintage car; *(más moderno)* classic car; *Chile* ***autos locos*** Dodgems®, bumper cars; *CSur* ***a. sport*** sports car

(b) *Der (resolución)* judicial decree ►► ***a. judicial*** judicial decree; ***a. de prisión*** arrest warrant; ***a. de procesamiento*** committal for trial order; **dictar a. de procesamiento contra alguien** to commit sb for trial

(c) *Der* **autos** *(documentos)* case documents; **constar en autos** to be recorded in the case documents; **la noche de autos** the night of the crime; **poner a alguien en autos** *(en antecedentes)* to inform sb of the background

(**d**) *Hist* ***a. de fe*** auto-da-fé, = public punishment of heretics by the Inquisition

(**e**) *Lit* = short play with biblical or allegorical subject, ≃ mystery play ►► ***a. de Navidad*** Nativity play; ***a. navideño*** Nativity play; ***a. sacramental*** = allegorical play celebrating the Eucharist

autoabastecerse *vpr (ser autosuficiente)* to be self-sufficient; **a. de algo** to be self-sufficient in sth

autoabastecimiento *nm* self-sufficiency; **el a. energético** energy self-sufficiency

autoadhesivo, -a, autoadherente *adj* self-adhesive

autoafirmación *nf* assertiveness

autoalimentación *nf Informát* automatic paper feed

autoaprendizaje *nm* self-directed learning; **un libro de a.** a teach-yourself book

autoayuda *nf* self-help

autobanco *nm* drive-in cash machine

autobiografía *nf* autobiography

autobiográfico, -a *adj* autobiographical

autobomba *nm esp RP* fire engine

autobombo *nm Fam* self-glorification; **darse a.** to blow one's own trumpet

autobronceador *nm* self-tanning cream

autobús (*pl* **autobuses**) *nm* bus ►► ***a. de dos pisos*** double-decker (bus); ***a. escolar*** school bus; ***a. de línea*** (inter-city) bus, *Br* coach; ***a. urbano*** city bus

autobusero, -a 1 *adj Am* bus; **una ruta autobusera** a bus route; **sindicato a.** bus drivers' union

2 *nm,f Fam* bus driver

autocar *nm Esp* bus, *Br* coach ►► ***a. de línea*** (inter-city) bus, *Br* coach

autocaravana *nf Esp* motor home, *US* RV

autocarril *nm Bol, Chile, Nic (automotor)* railcar *(with own power unit)*

autocartera *nf Fin Br* bought-back shares, *US* treasury stock

autocensura *nf* self-censorship

autocine *nm* drive-in (cinema)

autoclave *nm Med* autoclave, sterilizing unit

autocomplacencia *nf* self-satisfaction

autocomplaciente *adj* self-satisfied

autocontrol *nm* self-control

autocracia *nf* autocracy

autócrata *nmf* autocrat

autocrático, -a *adj* autocratic

autocrítica *nf* self-criticism

autocrítico, -a *adj* self-critical

autóctono, -a 1 *adj (cultura, lengua)* indigenous, native; *(lengua)* indigenous; **una especie autóctona de la isla** a species that is indigenous *o* native to the island; **la población autóctona** the indigenous *o* native population

2 *nm,f* native

autocuración *nf* self-healing

autodefensa *nf* self-defence

autodefinido *nm* = type of crossword

autodefinirse *vpr* to describe oneself

autodenominado, -a *adj* self-proclaimed

autodestrucción *nf* self-destruction

autodestructivo, -a *adj* self-destructive

autodestruirse *vpr* to self-destruct

autodeterminación *nf* self-determination; **el derecho a la a.** the right to self-determination

autodiagnóstico *nm Informát* self-test

autodidacta 1 *adj* self-taught

2 *nmf* self-taught person

autodidacto, -a *adj, nm,f* = **autodidacta**

autodirigido, -a *adj* guided

autodisciplina *nf* self-discipline

autodisolución *nf* **tras la a. del parlamento** after parliament voted to dissolve itself

autodominio *nm* self-control

autódromo *nm* motor racing circuit

autoedición *nf Informát* desktop publishing, DTP

autoeditar *vt Informát* to produce using DTP

autoeditor, -ora *nm,f Informát* DTP operator

autoempleo *nm* self-employment

autoencendido *nm Aut* automatic ignition

autoescuela *nf* driving school

autoestima *nf* self-esteem

autoestop *nm* hitchhiking; **hacer a.** to hitchhike; **viajó por todo el país en a.** she hitchhiked round the country

autoestopista *nmf* hitchhiker

autoevaluación *nf* self-assessment

autoexcluirse *vpr* to exclude oneself

autoexec [auto'eksek] (*pl* **autoexecs**) *nm Informát* autoexec file

autoexilio *nm* voluntary exile

autoexploración *nf* self-examination

autoexposición *nf Fot* automatic exposure

autofagia *nf Med* autophagia, autophagy

autofecundación *nf (de planta)* self-fertilization, self-pollination

autofinanciación *nf* self-financing

autofinanciar 1 *vt* to self-finance

2 **autofinanciarse** *vpr* to be self-financed

autofoco *nm*, **autofocus** *nm inv* autofocus

autógeno, -a *adj (soldadura)* autogenous

autogestión *nf* (**a**) *(de empresa)* self-management (**b**) *(de región, país)* self-government

autogestionar 1 *vt* **autogestionan sus fondos** they manage their own finances

2 **autogestionarse** *vpr* (**a**) *(empresa)* to manage itself (**b**) *(región, país)* to govern itself

autogiro *nm* autogiro

autogobierno *nm Pol* self-government, self-rule

autogol *nm Dep* own goal

autogolpe *nm Pol* = coup staged by the government to gain extra-constitutional powers

autografiar [32] *vt* to autograph

autógrafo *nm* autograph

autoguardado *nm Informát* automatic backup

autoinculpación *nf* self-incrimination

autoinculparse *vpr* **a. de algo** to incriminate oneself of sth

autoinducción *nf Elec* self-induction

autoinjerto *nm Med* autograft

autoinmune *adj Med* autoimmune

autoinmunidad *nf* autoimmunity

autoinyectable *adj* self-injectable

autolavado *nm* car wash

automarginación *nf* self-exclusion from society

autómata *nm* (**a**) *(robot)* automaton, robot (**b**) *Fam (persona)* automaton, robot

automáticamente *adv* automatically

automático, -a 1 *adj* (**a**) *(mecanismo, dispositivo)* automatic (**b**) *(gesto, reacción)* automatic; **la derrota provocó su cese a.** he was automatically sacked after the defeat

2 *nm* (**a**) *(cierre)* press stud (**b**) *Elec* trip switch (**c**) *Am (carro, auto)* automatic

automatismo *nm* automatism

automatización *nf* automation

automatizado, -a *adj* automated

automatizar [14] *vt* to automate

automedicación *nm* self-medication

automedicarse [60] *vpr* **es peligroso a.** it's dangerous to take medicines that have not been prescribed by a doctor

automercado *nm Ven* supermarket

automoción *nf* (**a**) *(sector)* car industry (**b**) *(ciencia)* self-propulsion

automotor, -triz 1 *adj* (**a**) *(autopropulsado)* self-propelled (**b**) *(del automóvil)* car; **industria automotriz** car *o Br* motor *o US* automobile industry; **piezas automotrices** car parts

2 *nm* railcar *(with own power unit)*

automóvil 1 *adj* **un vehículo a.** a motor vehicle
2 *nm Br* car, *US* automobile; **salón del a.** motor show ►► ***a. club*** automobile association *o* club

automovilismo *nm* (a) *(actividad)* motoring (b) *Dep* motor racing

automovilista *nmf* motorist, driver

automovilístico, -a *adj* motor; **industria automovilística** car *o Br* motor *o US* automobile industry; **carrera automovilística** motor race; **accidente a.** car accident

autonomía *nf* (a) *(de estado, región)* autonomy; *(de persona, empresa)* independence; **no tiene a. para tomar decisiones** she is not authorized to take decisions; **la ley otorga amplia a. a la región** the act devolves wide-ranging powers on the region
(b) *(de vehículo)* range; *(de computadora portátil, teléfono móvil)* battery life; *(de videocámara)* recording time ►► ***a. de vuelo*** *(de avión)* range
(c) *Pol (territorio)* autonomous region, = largest administrative division in Spain, with its own Parliament and a number of devolved powers

autonómico, -a *adj Pol (administración, parlamento)* autonomous; **elecciones autonómicas** elections to the autonomous (regional) parliaments

autonomismo *nm Pol* autonomy movement

autonomista *Pol* 1 *adj* autonomist
2 *nmf* autonomist

autónomo, -a 1 *adj* (a) *(independiente)* autonomous (b) *(trabajador)* self-employed; *(traductor, periodista)* freelance (c) *Pol (región, parlamento)* autonomous
2 *nm,f (trabajador)* self-employed person; *(traductor, periodista)* freelance, freelancer

autopalpación *nf* self-examination

autoparte *nf Méx* car part

autopase *nm Dep* **se hizo un a.** he ran on to his own pass

autopista *nf Br* motorway, *US* freeway ►► *Méx* ***a. de cuota*** *Br* toll motorway, *US* turnpike; *Informát* ***autopista(s) de la información*** information superhighway; ***a. de peaje*** *Br* toll motorway, *US* turnpike

autoplastia *nf Med* autoplasty

autoproclamado, -a *adj* self-proclaimed; **el a. defensor de los pobres** the self-proclaimed champion of the poor

autoproclamarse *vpr* to proclaim oneself

autopropulsado, -a *adj* self-propelled

autopropulsión *nf* self-propulsion

autoprotección *nf* self-protection

autopsia *nf* autopsy, postmortem; **hacer** *o* **practicar la a. a alguien** to carry out an autopsy *o* postmortem on sb

autopullman [auto'pulman] (*pl* **autopullmans**) *nm Esp* luxury bus *o Br* coach

autor, -ora *nm,f* (a) *(de libro, estudio)* author; *(de cuadro)* painter; *(de canción)* writer; *(de película)* maker; *(de sinfonía)* composer; *(de ley)* instigator; **el a. de la propuesta** the person who made the proposal; **el a. del paisaje** the artist who painted the landscape; **de a. anónimo** *o* **desconocido** anonymous
(b) *(de crimen, fechoría)* perpetrator; **fue encarcelado como a. de un delito de robo** he was sent to prison for committing a robbery; **el a. material de un secuestro** the person responsible for carrying out a kidnapping; **la autora intelectual del crimen** the woman who masterminded the crime
(c) *(de gol, canasta)* scorer; **el a. del gol** the goalscorer

autoría *nf* (a) *(de obra)* authorship (b) *(de crimen)* responsibility; **un grupo separatista ha reivindicado la a. del atentado** a separatist group has claimed responsibility for the attack; **se le atribuye la a. del asesinato** he is said to have committed the murder

autoridad *nf* (a) *(poder)* authority; **no tienes a. para hacer eso** you have no authority to do that; **impusieron su a.** they imposed their authority; **le falta ejercer más a. sobre sus empleados** he needs to exercise more authority over the people who work for him ►► ***a. moral*** moral authority
(b) *(persona al mando)* **las autoridades militares/religiosas** the military/religious authorities; **entregarse a las autoridades** *(a la policía)* to give oneself up; **la a.** the authorities
(c) *(eminencia)* authority; **es una a. en historia** he is an authority on history
(d) *(control, dominio)* authority; **habla siempre con mucha a.** she always talks with great authority
(e) *(autor citado)* authority; *(texto citado)* quotation

autoritariamente *adv* in an authoritarian way

autoritario, -a 1 *adj* (a) *(persona)* authoritarian (b) *(gobierno)* authoritarian
2 *nm,f* authoritarian

autoritarismo *nm* authoritarianism

autorización *nf* authorization; **entraron en el edificio con a. judicial** they had a warrant allowing them to enter the building; **dar a. a alguien (para hacer algo)** to authorize sb (to do sth); **pedir a. para hacer algo** to request authorization to do sth; **pidieron a. para aterrizar** they requested clearance to land; **tenemos a. para usar la sala** we have been authorized *o* we have permission to use the hall; **necesitan la a. de sus padres** they need their parents' consent

autorizado, -a *adj* (a) *(permitido)* authorized; **un distribuidor a.** an authorized *o* official distributor; **una película no autorizada para menores** a film passed as unsuitable for children; **autorizada para mayores de 18 años** *(en letrero) Br* ≃ 18, *US* ≃ R; **una manifestación no autorizada** an unauthorized demonstration; **una biografía no a.** an unofficial biography (b) *(digno de crédito)* authoritative

autorizar [14] *vt* (a) *(pago, crédito, manifestación)* to authorize; **autorizaron la publicación del informe** they authorized *o* sanctioned the publication of the report; **autoricé a mi hermano para que recogiera el paquete** I authorized my brother to collect the package; **nos autorizó para controlar el presupuesto** she authorized us to monitor the budget
(b) *(documento)* to authorize; **autorizó el documento con su firma** she authorized the document with her signature
(c) *(dar derecho a)* **su cargo no lo autoriza para insultarme** his position doesn't give him the right to insult me; **este título nos autoriza para ejercer en Europa** this qualification allows us to practise in Europe

autorradio *nm o nf* car radio

autorrebobinado *nm Fot* auto rewind

autorregulable *adj (pieza, dispositivo)* self-adjusting

autorregulación *nf* self-regulation

autorregularse *vpr (organización)* to be self-regulating

autorretorno *nm Informát* word wrap

autorretrato *nm* self-portrait

autorreverse *nm* auto-reverse

autorreversible *adj* auto-reverse; **un casete a.** a cassette recorder with auto-reverse

autoservice *nm RP* self-service shop, small supermarket

autoservicio *nm* (a) *(restaurante)* self-service restaurant (b) *(supermercado)* supermarket

autostop *nm* hitchhiking; **hacer a.** to hitchhike; **viajó por todo el país en a.** she hitchhiked round the country

autostopista *nmf* hitchhiker

autosuficiencia *nf* (a) *(orgullo, soberbia)* smugness (b) *(económica)* self-sufficiency

autosuficiente *adj* (a) *(orgulloso, soberbio)* smug (b) *(económicamente)* self-sufficient

autosugestión *nf* auto-suggestion

autosugestionarse *vpr* to convince oneself (**de** of)

autotest *nm Informát* self-test

autotransplante *nm* autotransplantation

autótrofo, -a *adj Biol* autotrophic

autovacuna *nf Med* autoinoculation

autovía *nf Br* dual carriageway, *US* divided highway

auxiliar[1] 1 *adj* (a) *(material)* auxiliary; *(mesa)* occasional (b) *(personal)* ancillary, auxiliary (c) *Gram* auxiliary
2 *nmf* assistant ►► ***a. administrativo*** administrative assistant; ***a. de laboratorio*** lab assistant; ***a. de vuelo*** flight attendant
3 *nm Gram* auxiliary
4 *nf RP (rueda de recambio)* spare wheel

auxiliar[2] *vt* (a) *(socorrer)* to assist, to help (b) *(moribundo)* to attend

auxilio 1 *nm* (a) *(socorro)* assistance, help; **una llamada de a.** a call for help; *Av & Náut* a distress call; **grité pidiendo a.** I shouted for help; **pedir/prestar a.** to call for/give help; **acudir en a. de alguien** to come to sb's assistance; **primeros auxilios** first aid (b) *RP (grúa)* breakdown truck
2 *interj* help!

auyama, ahuyama *nf Carib, Col* pumpkin

Av., av. (*abrev de* **avenida**) Ave

aval *nm* **(a)** *(documento)* guarantee, reference ►► ***a. bancario*** bank guarantee **(b)** *(respaldo)* backing; **un proyecto con el a. de la ONU** a UN-backed project; **se incorporó a la empresa con el a. del éxito obtenido en otros trabajos** he came to the company with a record of success in other jobs

avalancha *nf* **(a)** *(de nieve)* avalanche **(b)** *(de solicitudes, protestas, personas)* avalanche

avalar *vt* **(a)** *(préstamo, crédito)* to guarantee

(b) *(respaldar) (oficialmente)* to endorse; **una resolución avalada por la ONU** a resolution endorsed by the UN; **una propuesta avalada por miles de firmas** a proposal backed *o* supported by thousands of signatures; **su eficacia está avalada por ensayos clínicos rigurosos** its effectiveness has been demonstrated in strict clinical trials; **su reputación lo avala** his reputation speaks for itself

avalista *nmf* guarantor

avaluar *vt Am* to value; **avaluaron la mansión en tres millones** the mansion was valued at three million

avalúo *nm Am* valuation

avance 1 *ver* **avanzar**

2 *nm* **(a)** *(movimiento hacia delante)* advance; **el a. a través de la selva fue dificultoso** making progress through the jungle was not easy ►► *Informát* ***a. de línea*** *(de impresora)* line feed; *Informát* ***a. de página*** *(de impresora)* form feed

(b) *(adelanto, progreso)* advance; **avances científicos/tecnológicos** scientific/technological advances *o* progress; **los avances en la lucha contra el cáncer** advances in the fight against cancer

(c) *(anticipo de dinero)* advance payment

(d) *(de película)* trailer

(e) *Rad & TV (de futura programación)* preview ►► ***a. informativo*** *(resumen)* news summary; *(por noticia de última hora)* newsflash

avante *interj* forward!; **¡a. a toda vela!** full speed *o* steam ahead!

avanzada 1 *nf* **(a)** *Mil* advance patrol **(b)** *(grupo)* advance party

2 de avanzada *loc adj Am (avanzado)* **tecnología de a.** cutting-edge technology; **ideas de a.** avant-garde ideas

avanzadilla *nf* **(a)** *Mil* advance patrol **(b)** *(grupo)* advance party; **son la a. del arte del futuro** they are the advance guard of the art of the future

avanzado, -a 1 *adj* **(a)** *(en desarrollo, proceso) (alumno, curso, tecnología, país)* advanced; **una persona de avanzada edad** *o* **de edad avanzada** a person advanced in years; **tiene un cáncer muy a.** she is in the advanced stages of cancer **(b)** *(progresista) (ideas)* advanced **(c)** *(hora)* late; **a avanzadas horas de la noche** late at night; **acabamos avanzada ya la tarde** we finished late in the afternoon

2 *nm,f* person ahead of his/her time

avanzar [14] **1** *vi* **(a)** *(moverse)* to advance; **las tropas continúan avanzando** the troops are still advancing; **el tráfico no avanzaba** the traffic wasn't moving

(b) *(progresar)* to make progress; **está avanzando mucho en sus estudios** she's making very good progress with her studies; **esta tecnología avanza a gran velocidad** this technology is developing very quickly

(c) *(tiempo)* to pass; **el tiempo avanza muy deprisa** time passes very quickly; **a medida que avanza el siglo** as the century draws on

(d) *(carrete)* to wind on

2 *vt* **(a)** *(adelantar)* to move forward; **las tropas avanzaron sus posiciones** the troops advanced their position; **avanzaron varias posiciones en la clasificación de liga** they moved up several places in the league

(b) *(noticias)* **a. algo a alguien** to inform sb of sth in advance; **les avanzó los resultados del estudio** she informed them of the results of the study before it was published

(c) *(carrete)* to wind on

avaricia *nf (codicia)* greed; *(tacañería)* avarice; EXPR **la a. rompe el saco** greed doesn't pay; EXPR *Fam* **con a.: es feo/pesado con a.** he isn't half ugly/boring

avariciosamente *adv (con codicia)* greedily; *(con tacañería)* avariciously

avaricioso, -a 1 *adj (codicioso)* greedy; *(tacaño)* avaricious, miserly

2 *nm,f (codicioso)* greedy person; *(tacaño)* miser

avariento, -a 1 *(codicioso)* greedy; *(tacaño)* avaricious, miserly

2 *nm,f (codicioso)* greedy person; *(tacaño)* miser

avaro, -a 1 *adj (codicioso)* greedy; *(tacaño)* miserly, mean

2 *nm,f (codicioso)* greedy person; *(tacaño)* miser

avasallador, -ora 1 *adj* overwhelming

2 *nm,f* slave-driver

avasallamiento *nm (de pueblo)* subjugation

avasallar 1 *vt* **(a)** *(arrollar)* to overwhelm; **el equipo visitante avasalló al local** the away team overwhelmed the home side **(b)** *(dominar)* **dejarse a.** to let oneself be pushed *o* ordered around; **va por la vida avasallando a todo el mundo** he'll trample over people to get what he wants **(c)** *(someter)* to subjugate

2 *vi (arrollar)* **va por la vida avasallando** he'll trample over people to get what he wants

avatar *nm* **(a)** *(cambio)* vagary, sudden change; **los avatares de la vida** the ups and downs of life **(b)** *Informát* avatar

Avda., avda. *(abrev de* **avenida***)* Ave

AVE ['aβe] *nm (abrev de* **Alta Velocidad Española***)* = Spanish high-speed train

ave[1] *nf*

Takes the masculine articles **el** and **un**.

(animal) bird; *Culin* **caldo de a.** ≃ chicken stock ►► ***a. acuática*** waterfowl, water bird; ***a. agorera*** bird of ill omen; ***aves de corral*** poultry; *también Fig* ***el A. Fénix*** the phoenix; ***a. fría*** lapwing; ***a. lira*** lyre-bird; ***a. lira real*** superb lyre-bird; ***a. marina*** sea bird; ***a. migratoria*** migratory bird; ***a. nocturna*** nocturnal bird; ***a. del paraíso*** bird of paradise; ***a. de paso*** migratory bird; EXPR **ser un a. de paso** to be a rolling stone; ***a. de presa*** bird of prey; ***a. rapaz*** bird of prey; ***a. de rapiña*** bird of prey; ***a. sol*** sun bittern; ***a. zancuda*** wader

ave[2] *interj* **¡a., César!** Hail, Caesar!; EXPR **¡a. María Purísima!** *(indica sorpresa)* saints preserve us!; *(en confesión)* Hail Mary, full of grace

avecinarse *vpr* to be on the way; **se avecina una tormenta** there's a storm coming *o* on the way; **¡la que se nos avecina!** we're really in for it!

avecindarse *vpr* to take up residence

avefría *nf* lapwing

Takes the masculine articles **el** and **un**.

avejentado, -a *adj (persona, cuero)* aged; **está muy a. para su edad** he looks a lot older than he is

avejentar 1 *vt* to age, to put years on

2 avejentarse *vpr* to age

avellana *nf* hazelnut

avellanal, avellanar *nm* grove of hazel trees

avellano *nm* hazel (tree)

avemaría *nf*

Takes the masculine articles **el** and **un**.

(a) *(oración)* Hail Mary; **reza cuatro avemarías** say four Hail Marys **(b)** *Mús* Ave Maria

avena *nf* **(a)** *(planta)* oat ►► ***a. loca*** wild oats **(b)** *(grano)* oats

avenencia *nf (acuerdo)* compromise

avengo *etc ver* **avenir**

avenida *nf* **(a)** *(calle)* avenue **(b)** *(crecida de río)* flood, freshet

avenido, -a *adj* **bien/mal avenidos** on good/bad terms

avenimiento *nm* **(a)** *(reconciliación)* reconciliation, conciliation **(b)** *(acuerdo)* agreement, accord

avenir [71] **1** *vt* to reconcile, to conciliate

2 avenirse *vpr* **(a)** *(llevarse bien)* to get on (well); **se aviene muy bien con todo el mundo** she gets on very well with everyone **(b)** *(ponerse de acuerdo)* **avenirse a hacer algo** to agree to do sth; **se avinieron a entrevistarse** they agreed to be interviewed; **se avendrá a lo que decida la mayoría** she'll go along with whatever the majority decides

aventado, -a *Méx Fam* **1** *adj* daring

2 *nm,f* dare-devil

aventajado, -a *adj (adelantado)* outstanding

aventajar 1 *vt* **(a)** *(rebasar)* to overtake **(b)** *(estar por delante de)* to be ahead of; **a. a alguien en algo** to surpass sb in sth

2 aventajarse *vpr (mejorar)* to improve, to get better

aventar [3] **1** *vt* **(a)** *(abanicar)* to fan

(b) *Agr* to winnow

(c) *Andes, CAm, Méx Fam (tirar)* to throw; **me aventó la pelota** she threw me the ball; **le aventé una bofetada** I slapped him; **nos aventaron ahí, y no volvieron hasta tres horas más tarde** they dumped us there, and didn't come back till three hours later

(d) *Andes, CAm, Méx Fam (dirigir)* **me aventó una mirada amenazadora** she shot me a threatening look, she glared at me threateningly

(e) *Andes, CAm, Méx (empujar)* to push, to shove

2 aventarse *vpr Méx* **(a)** *(tirarse)* to throw oneself; **se aventó por el balcón** he threw himself off the balcony **(b)** *(atreverse)* to dare;

aventarse a hacer algo to dare to do sth (**c**) *Fam (beberse)* to down; *(comerse, beberse)* to guzzle, to down; **aviéntate una cervecita** have a beer (**d**) *Fam (pasar)* **me aventé dos años en la tesis** I spent two years on my thesis

aventón *nm CAm, Méx, Perú* (**a**) *(en vehículo)* **dar a. a alguien** to give sb a lift; **pedir a.** to hitch a lift; **nos fuimos de a. hasta Puebla** we hitched *o* hitchhiked as far as Puebla (**b**) *(empujón)* push, shove; **lo sacaron a la calle a aventones** they pushed *o* shoved him out into the street

aventura *nf* (**a**) *(suceso, empresa)* adventure; **una película/un libro de aventuras** an adventure film/story; **deportes de a.** adventure sports; **embarcarse en una a.** to set off on an adventure; **me pasaron mil aventuras en mi viaje a la capital** I had a very eventful time on my visit to the capital; **conseguir las entradas fue una a.** it was quite an adventure getting hold of the tickets

(**b**) *(relación amorosa)* affair; **tener una a. con alguien** to have an affair with sb

aventurado, -a *adj* risky

aventurar 1 *vt* (**a**) *(dinero, capital)* to risk, to venture (**b**) *(opinión, conjetura)* to venture, to hazard; **no me atrevo a a. un resultado** I wouldn't like to hazard a guess at what the result will be; **me aventuré a sugerir el aplazamiento de la reunión** I ventured to suggest that the meeting should be postponed

2 **aventurarse** *vpr* to take a risk/risks; **tendrán que aventurarse más que nunca** they'll have to take more risks than ever; **se aventuraron por la selva** they ventured through the jungle; **aventurarse a hacer algo** to dare to do sth; **como llovía mucho no nos aventuramos a salir** as it was raining heavily, we didn't venture out

aventurerismo, aventurismo *nm* adventurism

aventurero, -a 1 *adj* adventurous

2 *nm,f* adventurer, *f* adventuress

aventurismo = **aventurerismo**

average *nm* **(gol) a.** goal average

avergonzado, -a *adj* (**a**) *(humillado, dolido)* ashamed (**b**) *(abochornado)* embarrassed; **está a. de** *o* **por lo que hizo** he's embarrassed about what he did

avergonzar [10] 1 *vt* (**a**) *(deshonrar, humillar)* to shame (**b**) *(abochornar)* to embarrass; **el comportamiento de mi marido me avergüenza** I feel embarrassed by my husband's behaviour

2 **avergonzarse** *vpr (por remordimiento, deshonra)* to be ashamed (**de** of); *(por timidez, bochorno)* to be embarrassed (**de** about); **me avergüenzo de haberla insultado** I'm ashamed to have insulted her

avería *nf* (**a**) *(de máquina)* fault; *(de vehículo)* breakdown; **el tren sufrió una a. en la locomotora** the train's engine developed a fault; **tuvimos** *o* **sufrimos una a. en la carretera** we broke down on the road; **llamar a averías** *(para vehículo)* to call the garage; *(para aparato)* to call the repair service; *Fam* **hacerse una a.** *(herida)* to hurt oneself (**b**) *Náut (de mercancía)* average ▸▸ ***a. gruesa*** general average

averiado, -a *adj* (**a**) *(máquina)* out of order; *(vehículo)* broken down; **mi moto está averiada** my motorbike has broken down (**b**) *(mercancías)* damaged

averiar [32] 1 *vt* to damage

2 **averiarse** *vpr (máquina, vehículo)* to break down; **se ha averiado la radio** the radio isn't working

averiguación *nf* (**a**) *(indagación)* investigation; **hacer averiguaciones** to make inquiries; **tras muchas averiguaciones, descubrí que estaba casado** after making several inquiries, I discovered that he was married (**b**) *CAm, Méx (discusión)* argument, dispute

averiguar [11] 1 *vt (indagar)* to find out

2 *vi CAm, Méx (discutir)* to argue, to quarrel

averno *nm Mitol* **el a.** the underworld

averroísmo *nm Filosofía* Averroism

averroísta *Filosofía* 1 *adj* Averroistic

2 *nmf* Averroist

aversión *nf* aversion; **tener a. a algo, sentir a. hacia algo** to feel aversion towards sth; **tomar a. a algo** to take a dislike to sth

avestruz *nm* ostrich; EXPR **la política del a.** burying one's head in the sand

avetorillo *nm* little bittern

avetoro *nm* bittern ▸▸ ***a. lentiginoso*** American bittern

avezado, -a *adj* seasoned; **un a. submarinista** a seasoned scuba diver

aviación *nf* (**a**) *(navegación)* aviation; **un accidente de a.** a plane crash ▸▸ ***a. civil*** civil aviation; ***a. comercial*** commercial aviation (**b**) *(militar)* air force

aviador, -ora *nm,f* (**a**) *(piloto)* pilot (**b**) *Méx Fam* = person listed as an employee in a government office and who is paid but who never comes to work

aviar[1] [32] 1 *vt* (**a**) *(preparar)* to prepare (**b**) *Fam (apañar)* **¡estamos aviados!** we've had it!; **estás aviado si te crees que te lo va a dar** you're kidding yourself if you think he's going to give it to you; **¡estaríamos aviados!** that would be the absolute end!, that would be all we need!

2 **aviarse** *vpr Fam (manejarse)* to manage; **se las avía muy bien solo** he manages very well on his own

aviar[2] *adj* **especie a.** bird species; **producción a.** poultry production

aviario, -a 1 *adj* **especie aviaria** bird species; **producción aviaria** poultry production

2 *nm* collection of birds

avícola *adj* poultry; **granja a.** poultry farm

avicultor, -ora *nm,f* poultry breeder, poultry farmer

avicultura *nf* poultry breeding, poultry farming

ávidamente *adv (ansiosamente)* avidly, eagerly; *(codiciosamente)* greedily, avariciously

avidez *nf (ansia)* eagerness; *(codicia)* greed; **leyó el horóscopo con a.** she avidly *o* eagerly read the horoscope; **devoró el postre con a.** he greedily *o* hungrily devoured the dessert

ávido, -a *adj (lector)* avid; *(coleccionista)* keen; **es una persona ávida de información** he's someone with a thirst for information; **un artista á. de fama** an artist who is hungry for fame

aviene *etc ver* **avenir**

aviento *etc ver* **aventar**

avieso, -a *adj (persona)* evil, twisted; *(mirada)* baleful; **se acercó a ella con aviesas intenciones** he approached her with evil intent

avifauna *nf* bird life

avinagrado, -a *adj* (**a**) *(vino, alimento)* sour (**b**) *(persona, carácter)* sour

avinagrar 1 *vt* (**a**) *(vino, alimento)* to sour, to make sour (**b**) *(persona, carácter)* to turn sour

2 **avinagrarse** *vpr* (**a**) *(vino, alimento)* to go sour (**b**) *(persona, carácter)* to become sour; **se le avinagró el carácter** she became bitter

Aviñón *n* Avignon

avío *nm* (**a**) *(preparativo)* preparation; **yo me encargo del a. de la habitación** I'll get the room ready (**b**) *(utilidad)* **esta cazuela me hace muy buen a.** I find this pot extremely useful (**c**) **avíos** *(equipo)* things ▸▸ ***avíos de pesca*** fishing tackle (**d**) *Méx (préstamo)* agricultural loan

avión *nm* (**a**) *(aeronave)* plane, *Br* aeroplane, *US* airplane; **en a.** by plane; **por a.** *(en sobre)* airmail ▸▸ ***a. de carga*** cargo plane; ***a. de caza*** fighter plane; ***a. cisterna*** tanker (plane); ***a. comercial*** commercial aircraft; ***a. de despegue vertical*** jump jet; ***a. espía*** spy plane; ***a. de espionaje*** spy plane; ***a. invisible*** stealth plane; ***a. militar*** military aircraft; ***a. nodriza*** refuelling plane; ***a. de papel*** paper aeroplane; ***a. de pasajeros*** passenger aircraft; ***a. a reacción*** jet; ***a. de reconocimiento*** reconnaissance *o* spotter plane; ***a. de transporte*** transport plane

(**b**) *(pájaro)* house martin ▸▸ ***a. purpúreo*** purple martin; ***a. zapador*** sand martin

avionazo *nm Méx* plane crash

avioneta *nf* light aircraft

aviónica *nf* avionics *(singular)*

avisado, -a *adj* prudent, discreet

avisador, -ora *nm,f RP* advertiser

avisar 1 *vt* (**a**) *(informar)* **a. a alguien de algo** to let sb know sth, to tell sb sth; **llamó para a. que llegaría tarde** she called to say she would be late (**b**) *(advertir)* to warn (**de** of); **yo ya te había avisado** I did warn you; **estás avisado** you've been warned (**c**) *(llamar)* to call, to send for; **hay que a. al electricista** we'll have to call the electrician; **corre, avisa a la policía** go and get the police

2 *vi* **entró sin a.** she came in without knocking; **avisa cuando acabes** let me/us/*etc* know when you've finished; EXPR **el que avisa no es traidor** don't say I didn't warn you

aviso *nm* (**a**) *(advertencia, amenaza)* warning; **andar sobre a.** to be on the alert; **estar sobre a.** to be forewarned; **poner sobre a. a alguien** to warn sb; **¡que te sirva de a.!** let that be a warning to you! ▸▸ ***a. de bomba*** bomb warning

(**b**) *(notificación)* notice; *(en teatros, aeropuertos)* call; **hasta nuevo a.** until further notice; **último a. para los pasajeros del vuelo IB 257** last call for passengers for flight IB 257; **sin previo a.** without notice; **llegó sin previo a.** he arrived without warning ▸▸ *Com* ***a. de***

vencimiento due-date reminder
(**c**) *Taurom* = warning to matador not to delay the kill any longer
(**d**) *Am (anuncio)* advertisement, advert; EXPR **no te deja pasar un a.** she doesn't let you get a word in edgeways ▸▸ ***a. clasificado*** classified advertisement; ***a. fúnebre*** death notice; ***a. publicitario*** advertisement, advert

avispa 1 *nf (insecto)* wasp; EXPR *Ven Fam* **comer a.** to be on one's toes
2 *nmf Ven (persona)* sharp *o* quick-witted person; **es un a.** he's very sharp *o* quick-witted

avispado, -a *adj Fam* sharp, quick-witted

avispar 1 *vt Chile* to frighten
2 **avisparse** *vpr Fam* to wise up

avispero *nm* (**a**) *(nido)* wasps' nest; EXPR *Fam* **alborotar el a.** to stir up a hornet's nest (**b**) *Fam (lío)* mess; **meterse en un a.** to get into a mess

avispón *nm* hornet

avistamiento *nm* sighting; **el a. de ballenas es poco frecuente** whales are rarely sighted

avistar *vt* to sight, to make out

avitaminosis *nf inv Med* vitamin deficiency

avituallamiento *nm* (**a**) *(de tropas)* provisioning; **se encargaron del a. de los refugiados** they took charge of providing the refugees with food (**b**) *(en ciclismo) (lugar)* feeding station; **se produjo una caída durante el a.** one of the competitors fell while taking on food

avituallar *vt (tropas)* to provision; *(refugiados, hambrientos)* to provide with food

avivado, -a, avivato, -a *nm,f CSur Fam* smart alec *o* aleck

avivar 1 *vt* (**a**) *(fuego)* to stoke up
(**b**) *(color)* to brighten
(**c**) *(sentimiento)* to intensify; **el asesinato avivó los odios entre las dos comunidades** the murder served to fuel the hatred between the two communities
(**d**) *(polémica)* to stir up; *(debate)* to liven up
(**e**) *(acelerar)* **a. el paso** *o* **ritmo** to quicken one's pace, to go faster
(**f**) *RP Fam* **a. a alguien** *(despabilar)* to wise sb up; *(informar)* to fill sb in
2 **avivarse** *vpr* (**a**) *(sentimiento)* to be rekindled
(**b**) *(color)* to brighten
(**c**) *(fuego)* to flare up
(**d**) *(polémica)* to be stirred up; **la discusión se fue avivando** the discussion got more and more animated
(**e**) *RP Fam (persona)* to wise up

avivato, -a = **avivado**

avizor *adj* **estar ojo a.** to be on the lookout

avizorar *vt* to watch, to spy on; **el vigía avizoraba el horizonte** the lookout was scanning the horizon

avoceta *nf* avocet

avutarda *nf* great bustard

axial *adj* axial

axila *nf* (**a**) *(sobaco)* armpit (**b**) *Bot* axil

axilar *adj* underarm; **zona a.** armpit

axioma *nm* axiom

axiomático, -a *adj* axiomatic

axis *nm inv Anat* axis

axón *nm Anat* axon

ay *interj* (**a**) *(expresando dolor físico)* ouch!; *(expresando sorpresa, pena)* oh!; **¡ay de mí!** woe is me!; **¡ay, qué cuadro tan lindo!** (gosh,) what a lovely painting! (**b**) *(como amenaza)* **¡ay de ti si te cojo!** heaven help you if I catch you!

aya *nf* governess

Takes the masculine articles **el** and **un**.

ayate *nm Méx* sisal

ayatolá, ayatola *nm* ayatollah

ayer 1 *adv* (**a**) *(el día anterior)* yesterday; **a. era lunes** yesterday was Monday, it was Monday yesterday; **a. a mediodía** at midday yesterday; **a. por la noche, a. noche** last night; **a. por la tarde, a. tarde** yesterday afternoon/evening; **a. por la mañana,** *Arg* **a. a la mañana** yesterday morning; **parece que fue a.** it seems like yesterday
(**b**) *(en el pasado)* **a. nadie había oído su nombre, y hoy es una estrella** only a short while ago no one had heard of her and now she's a star; **un político de los de a.** a politician of the old school
2 *nm* **el a.** yesteryear; **no puedes vivir siempre del a.** you can't live your whole life in the past

ayllu *nm Andes* = rural Indian settlement

aymara, aimara 1 *adj* Aymara
2 *nmf (persona)* Aymara
3 *nm (lengua)* Aymara

ayo *nm (tutor)* tutor

ayotete *nm* bryony

ayte. (*abrev de* **ayudante**) asst.

ayuda 1 *nf* (**a**) *(asistencia)* help, assistance; **acudir en a. de alguien** to come/go to sb's assistance; **nos fuiste de gran a.** you were a great help to us; **no me sirvió de mucha a.** it wasn't much help to me; **prestar a.** to help, to assist ▸▸ ***a. en carretera*** breakdown service; *Informát* ***a. en línea*** on-line help; *Informát* ***a. en pantalla*** onscreen help
(**b**) *(económica, alimenticia)* aid; **un paquete de ayudas a la pequeña empresa** a package of measures to help small businesses ▸▸ ***a. al desarrollo*** development aid; ***a. exterior*** foreign aid; ***a. extranjera*** foreign aid; ***a. humanitaria*** humanitarian aid; **un convoy de a. humanitaria** a relief convoy
(**c**) *(limosna)* **una a., por favor** could you spare me some change, please?
(**d**) *(enema)* enema
2 *nm Hist* ***a. de cámara*** royal valet

ayudado *nm Taurom* = pass made with the cape held in both hands

ayudanta *nf* assistant

ayudante 1 *adj* assistant
2 *nmf* assistant ▸▸ *Mil* ***a. de campo*** aide-de-camp; *Cine* ***a. de dirección*** director's assistant; *Cine* ***a. del electricista*** best boy; ***a. de investigación*** research assistant; ***a. de laboratorio*** laboratory assistant; *Esp* ***a. técnico sanitario*** qualified nurse

ayudantía *nf (en universidad)* assistantship

ayudar 1 *vt* to help; **a. a alguien a hacer algo** to help sb (to) do sth; **me ayudaron a subir el piano** they helped me carry the piano up; **una profesora particular le ayuda en los estudios** a private tutor is helping him with his studies; **necesito que me ayuden con este problema** I need your help with this problem; **¿en qué puedo ayudarle?** how can I help you?
2 *vi* to help; **¿puedo a.?** can I help?
3 **ayudarse** *vpr* **ayudarse de** *o* **con** to make use of; **caminaba ayudándose de un bastón** he walked with the help of a stick

ayunas *nfpl* **en a.: son las doce y todavía estoy en a.** it's twelve o'clock and I still haven't eaten; **venga en a. para hacerse el análisis de sangre** don't eat anything before you come for your blood test; EXPR **estar/quedarse en a.** *(sin enterarse)* to be/to be left in the dark

ayuno *nm* fast; **hacer a.** to fast

ayuntamiento *nm* (**a**) *(corporación) Br* town council, *US* city council (**b**) *(edificio) Br* town hall, *US* city hall (**c**) *Anticuado* **a. (carnal)** sexual congress

ayuntarse *vpr Anticuado* to enjoy sexual congress

azabache *nm* jet; **negro como el a.** jet-black

azada *nf* hoe

azadón *nm* (large) hoe

azafata *nf* (**a**) *(en avión)* air stewardess, *Br* air hostess ▸▸ ***a. de tierra*** ground stewardess; **azafatas de tierra** ground crew; ***a. de vuelo*** air stewardess, *Br* air hostess (**b**) *(en feria, congreso)* hostess ▸▸ ***a. de exposiciones y congresos*** (conference) hostess; ***a. de ferias y congresos*** (conference) hostess

azafate *nm CAm, Carib, Méx, Perú* tray

azafrán *nm* saffron

azafranado, -a *adj* saffron(-coloured)

azagaya *nf* assegai, light spear

azahar *nm* (**a**) *(del naranjo)* orange blossom (**b**) *(del limonero)* lemon blossom

azalea *nf* azalea

azar *nm* (**a**) *(casualidad)* chance; **juego de a.** game of chance; **al a.** at random; **dos concursantes elegidos al a.** two randomly chosen contestants; **no dejaron nada al a.** they left nothing to chance; **por a.** by (pure) chance; **si por algún a. no puedes venir, llámanos** if by any chance you should be unable to come, give us a ring; **quiso el a. que pasara yo por allí en ese preciso instante** fate decreed that I should be passing that way at that very moment
(**b**) *(suceso, vicisitud)* **los azares de la vida** the ups and downs of life

azaramiento *nm* embarrassment

azarar 1 *vt (avergonzar)* to embarrass, to fluster; **a. a alguien** *(ruborizar)* to make sb blush
2 **azararse** *vpr (avergonzarse)* to be embarrassed, to be flustered; *(ruborizarse)* to blush

azaroso, -a *adj* (**a**) *(peligroso)* hazardous, risky (**b**) *(con aventuras)* eventful; **un periodo a. de la historia francesa** an eventful period in French history

Azerbaiyán *n* Azerbaijan

azerbaiyano, -a 1 *adj* Azerbaijani
2 *nm,f* Azerbaijani

azerí (*pl* **azeríes**) 1 *adj* Azeri
2 *nm,f* Azeri

ázimo *adj (pan)* unleavened

azimut (*pl* **azimutes**) *nm Astron* azimuth

azogar [38] *vt* to quicksilver, to silver

azogue *nm* quicksilver, mercury

azolve *nm Méx* (**a**) *(suciedad)* sludge (**b**) *(sedimento)* alluvium

azor *nm* goshawk

azoradamente *adv* in embarrassment

azorado, -a *adj* (**a**) *(turbado)* embarrassed, flustered (**b**) *CSur, Méx (asombrado)* amazed

azoramiento *nm* embarrassment

azorar 1 *vt* (**a**) *(turbar)* to embarrass (**b**) *CSur, Méx (asombrar)* to amaze
2 **azorarse** *vpr (turbarse)* to be embarrassed

Azores *nfpl* **las (islas) A.** the Azores

azotacalles *nm inv Fam* loafer, idler

azotado, -a *adj Chile (atigrado)* striped

azotador *nm Méx* caterpillar

azotaina *nf Fam* **dar una a. a alguien** to give sb a good smacking

azotar 1 *vt* (**a**) *(en el trasero)* to smack, to slap (**b**) *(con látigo)* to whip (**c**) *(viento, olas)* to lash; **el viento le azotaba la cara** the wind lashed her face (**d**) *(devastar)* to devastate; **la epidemia azotó la región** the region was devastated by the epidemic; **una región azotada por las guerras** a war-torn region (**e**) *Méx (cerrar bruscamente)* to slam
2 **azotarse** *vpr* (**a**) *(persona)* to flog oneself (**b**) *Bol (lanzarse)* to throw oneself

azote *nm* (**a**) *(utensilio para golpear)* whip, scourge; *Fig* **se ha convertido en el a. de los liberales** she has become the scourge of liberals
(**b**) *(en el trasero)* smack, slap; **dar un a. a alguien** to smack sb
(**c**) *(latigazo)* lash
(**d**) *(de viento, olas)* **la casa sufría el a. de las olas** the house was lashed by the waves
(**e**) *(calamidad)* scourge; **el pueblo sufrió el a. de las inundaciones** the town was severely hit by floods

azotea *nf* (**a**) *(de edificio)* terraced roof (**b**) *Fam (cabeza)* **estar mal de la a.** to be funny in the head

AZT *nm Farm* (*abrev* **azidothymidine**) AZT

azteca 1 *adj* (**a**) *(precolombino)* Aztec (**b**) *Fam (mexicano)* **el equipo a.** the Mexican team
2 *nmf (persona)* Aztec
3 *nm (lengua)* Nahuatl, Aztec

azúcar *nm o nf* sugar; **sin a.** sugar-free ►► ***a. blanquilla*** white sugar; ***a. cande*** *o* ***candi*** sugar candy, rock candy; ***a. de caña*** cane sugar; *Chile* ***a. flor*** *Br* icing *o US* confectioner's sugar; *Esp, Méx* ***a. glas*** *Br* icing *o US* confectioner's sugar; *RP* ***a. impalpable*** *Br* icing *o US* confectioner's sugar; *Esp* ***a. de lustre*** *Br* icing *o US* confectioner's sugar; ***a. moreno*** brown sugar; *RP* ***a. en pancitos*** sugar lumps; *Col* ***a. polvo*** *Br* icing *o US* confectioner's sugar; ***a. en terrones*** sugar lumps

azucarado, -a *adj* (**a**) *(endulzado)* sweet, sugary (**b**) *Pey (suavizado)* sugary sweet

azucarar 1 *vt* (**a**) *(endulzar)* to sugar-coat, to sugar (**b**) *Pey (suavizar)* to make sugary sweet
2 **azucararse** *vprAm (cristalizar)* to crystallize

azucarera *nf* (**a**) *(fábrica)* sugar refinery (**b**) *(recipiente)* sugar bowl

azucarero, -a 1 *adj* sugar; **la industria azucarera** the sugar industry
2 *nm* sugar bowl

azucarillo *nm* (**a**) *(terrón)* sugar lump (**b**) *(dulce)* lemon candy

azucena *nf* white lily ►► ***a. atigrada*** tiger lily

azud *nm (presa)* dam

azufaifa *nf* jujube fruit

azufaifo *nm* common jujube

azufre *nm Quím* sulphur

azufroso, -a *adj* sulphurous

azul 1 *adj* (**a**) *(color)* blue; *Méx Fam* **los de a.** *(la policía)* the cops, *Br* the boys in blue (**b**) *(pescado)* oily
2 *nm* (**a**) *(color)* blue; **el a. es mi color favorito** blue is my favourite colour ►► ***a. acero*** steel blue; ***a. celeste*** sky blue; ***a. (de) cobalto*** cobalt blue; ***a. eléctrico*** electric blue; *RP* ***a. Francia*** royal blue; ***a. marino*** navy blue; ***a. de metileno*** methylene blue; ***a. de Prusia*** Prussian blue; ***a. turquesa*** turquoise; ***a. de ultramar*** ultramarine
(**b**) *Am (azulete)* blue
3 **azules** *nmpl Méx Fam* **los azules** *(la policía)* the cops, *Br* the boys in blue

azulado, -a *adj* bluish

azulejo, -a 1 *adj (azulado)* bluish
2 *nm* (**a**) *(baldosín)* (glazed) tile (**b**) *Ven (pájaro)* = type of bluebird

azulete *nm (para lavar)* blue

azulgrana 1 *adj inv Dep* = of/relating to Barcelona Football Club
2 *nmpl* **los a.** = Barcelona Football Club

azulón, -ona 1 *adj* deep blue
2 *nm (pato)* mallard

azuloso, -a *adj* bluish

azúmbar *nm* bryony

azur *Literario* 1 *adj* azure
2 *nm* azure

azurita *nf* azurite

azuzar [14] *vt* (**a**) *(animal)* **a. a los perros contra alguien** to set the dogs on sb (**b**) *(persona)* to egg on

B, b

B, b [*Esp* be, *Am* be('larga)] *nf (letra)* B, b

baba *nf* **(a)** *(saliva) (de niño)* dribble; *(de adulto)* spittle, saliva; EXPR *Fam* **caérsele la b. a alguien: se le cae la b. con su nieta** she absolutely dotes on her granddaughter; **se le cae la b. escuchando a Mozart** he's in heaven when he's listening to Mozart; EXPR *Fam* **tener mala b.** to be a nasty piece of work **(b)** *(saliva) (de animal)* slobber **(c)** *(de caracol)* slime **(d)** *(de planta)* sap

babaco *nm* babaco, = seedless variety of papaya

babalao *nm Cuba Fam* = priest in Afro-Cuban "santería" religion

babear *vi* **(a)** *(niño)* to dribble; *(adulto)* to slobber **(b)** *(animal)* to slobber **(c)** *Fam (de gusto)* to drool (**con** over)

babel *nm o nf Fam* **el debate se convirtió en una b.** the debate degenerated into noisy chaos

babeo *nm* **(a)** *(de niño)* dribbling; *(de adulto)* slobbering **(b)** *(de animal)* slobbering

babero *nm* bib

babi *nm Esp Fam* = child's overall

Babia *nf* EXPR **estar** *o* **quedarse en B.** to have one's head in the clouds

babieca *Fam* **1** *adj* simple, stupid
2 *nmf* fool, idiot

babilla *nf* **(a)** *(de res)* stifle **(b)** *(rótula)* kneecap **(c)** *(caimán)* Rio Apaporis caiman

Babilonia *n Hist (ciudad)* Babylon; *(región)* Babylonia

babilónico, -a, babilonio, -a *adj* **(a)** *Hist* Babylonian **(b)** *(fastuoso)* lavish

bable *nm* = Asturian dialect

babor *nm* port; **girar a b.** to turn to port; **¡iceberg a b.!** iceberg to port!

babosa *nf* **(a)** *(animal)* slug **(b)** *ver también* **baboso**

babosada *nf CAm, Méx Fam (disparate)* daft thing; **¡no digas babosadas!** don't talk *Br* rubbish *o US* bull!

babosear 1 *vt* **(a)** *(llenar de babas)* to slobber on *o* all over **(b)** *RP Fam (burlarse de)* **b. a alguien** to mess sb about
2 *vi CAm, Méx Fam (decir tonterías)* to talk *Br* rubbish *o US* bull

baboseo *nm* **(a)** *(de babas)* dribbling **(b)** *(molestia, insistencia)* **me irrita con su b.** I hate the way he sucks up to me

baboso, -a 1 *adj* **(a)** *(niño)* dribbling; *(adulto)* slobbering **(b)** *(animal)* slobbering **(c)** *Fam (despreciable)* slimy **(d)** *Am Fam (tonto)* daft, stupid
2 *nm,f Fam* **(a)** *(persona despreciable)* creep **(b)** *Am (tonto)* twit, idiot

babucha *nf (zapatilla)* slipper; *(árabe)* Moorish slipper; EXPR *RP Fam* **llevar a alguien a b.** to carry sb on one's shoulders

babuino *nm* yellow baboon

baby doll [beiβi'ðol] *nm Am* baby-doll nightdress

baby fútbol [beiβi'futbol] *nm* **(a)** *Chile (fútbol sala)* five-a-side soccer **(b)** *Ecuad, Urug (fútbol infantil)* junior soccer *(for pre-teens)*

baca *nf* roof rack

bacaladera *nf Esp Fam* = manual credit card imprinter, *US* knuckle buster

bacaladero, -a 1 *adj* cod-fishing; **la flota bacaladera** the cod-fishing fleet
2 *nm* cod-fishing boat

bacaladilla *nf* blue whiting

bacalao *nm* cod; EXPR *Esp Fam* **cortar** *o* **partir el b.** to call the shots ►► ***b. al pil-pil*** = Basque dish of salt cod cooked with olive oil and garlic; ***b. salado*** salt *o* salted cod; ***b. a la vizcaína*** = Basque dish of salt cod cooked in a tomato and red pepper sauce

bacán, -ana 1 *adj Fam* **(a)** *Cuba, Perú (bueno)* cool, wicked **(b)** *RP (caro)* steep
2 *nm,f RP Fam (rico)* toff; **como un b.** like a real gentleman
3 *nm Cuba (empanada)* tamale

bacanal *nf* **(a)** *(orgía)* orgy **(b)** *Hist* bacchanal

bacante *nf Hist* bacchante

bacará, bacarrá *nm* baccarat

bachata *nf Cuba, PRico (juerga, jolgorio)* rave-up, binge; **estar de b.** to have a noisy party

bache *nm* **(a)** *(en carretera)* pothole
(b) *(en un vuelo)* air pocket
(c) *(dificultades)* bad patch; **el sector atraviesa un profundo b.** the industry is going through hard times
(d) *CSur Fam (olvido)* **me olvidé de apagar la estufa, ¡qué b.!** how silly of me, I forgot to switch the stove off!; **a la tercera pregunta me dio un b.** I drew a blank on the third question
(e) *RP Fam (trauma)* hang-up
(f) *RP Fam (de conocimientos)* gap

bachicha *Chile Fam* **1** *adj* Eyetie, = pejorative term meaning "Italian"
2 *nmf* Eyetie, = pejorative term referring to an Italian

bachiche *Perú Fam* **1** *adj* Eyetie, = pejorative term meaning "Italian"
2 *nmf* Eyetie, = pejorative term referring to an Italian

bachiller *nmf* **(a)** *(en secundaria)* = person who has passed the "bachillerato" **(b)** *Perú (licenciado)* (university) graduate

bachillerato *nm* **(a)** *(en secundaria)* = academically orientated school course for pupils in the final years of secondary education ►► *Esp Antes* ***b. elemental*** = first two years of the "bachillerato"; *Esp Antes* ***b. superior*** = final years of the "bachillerato"; *Esp Antes* ***b. unificado polivalente*** = academically orientated Spanish secondary school course for pupils aged 14-17
(b) *Perú (licenciatura)* degree

bacía *nf* barber's bowl

bacilar *adj* bacillary

baciliforme *adj* bacillary, bacilliform

bacilo *nm* bacillus ►► ***b. de Koch*** tubercle bacillus

bacín *nm* chamberpot

bacinica, bacinilla *nf* chamberpot

backgammon [bak'ɣamon] *nm* backgammon

backup [ba'kap] *(pl* **backups***)* *nm Informát* backup

Baco *n Mitol* Bacchus

bacon ['beikon] *nm inv Esp* bacon ►► ***b. entreverado*** streaky bacon

bacoreta *nf (pez)* little tunny

bacteria *nf* bacterium; **bacterias** bacteria; **el aire está lleno de bacterias** the air is full of germs

bacteriano, -a *adj* bacterial

bactericida 1 *adj* bactericidal
2 *nm* bactericide

bacteriófago *nm Med* bacteriophage

bacteriología *nf* bacteriology

bacteriológico, -a *adj* bacteriological; **guerra bacteriológica** germ *o* bacteriological warfare

bacteriólogo, -a *nm,f* bacteriologist

báculo *nm* **(a)** *(de obispo)* crosier ►► ***b. pastoral*** crosier **(b)** *(sostén)* support; **ella será el b. de mi vejez** she'll comfort me in my old age

badajada *nf (golpe de campana)* stroke, chime

badajo *nm* clapper *(of bell)*

badana *nf (piel)* basan, sheepskin leather; *(de sombrero)* basan hatband

badén *nm* (**a**) *(de carretera) (depresión)* dip (**b**) *(en un terreno)* channel (**c**) *(vado)* lowered kerb; **b. permanente** *(en letrero)* keep clear at all times

badil *nm*, **badila** *nf* fire shovel

bádminton *nm inv* badminton

badulaque 1 *adj* idiotic
2 *nm* idiot

bafle[1] (*pl* **bafles**), **baffle** ['bafle] (*pl* **baffles**) *nm* (loud)speaker

bafle[2] *nm Am* waffle

bagaje *nm (profesional)* experience; **el candidato tiene b. político suficiente** the candidate has plenty of political experience; **el b. conceptual del Renacimiento** the philosophical heritage of the Renaissance; **tener un amplio b. cultural** to be very cultured

bagatela *nf* (**a**) *(cosa insignificante)* trifle; **no quiero perder tiempo en bagatelas** I don't want to waste time on minor *o* insignificant details (**b**) *Mús* bagatelle

bagayero, -a *nm,f RP Fam* smuggler

bagayo *nm RP Fam* (**a**) *(contrabando)* contraband (**b**) *(bulto)* bag; **¿traés muchos bagayos? – no, sólo una valija** have you got a lot of stuff? – no, just one case (**c**) *(mujer fea)* hag, dog

bagazo *nm* (**a**) *(de caña de azúcar)* bagasse, sugarcane pulp (**b**) *(de linaza)* linseed pulp (**c**) *(de frutas)* marc, waste pulp

Bagdad *n* Baghdad

bagre *nm* (**a**) *(pez)* catfish (**b**) *Andes, RP Fam Pey (mujer)* hag, dog; *Andes (hombre)* face-ache, ugly mug (**c**) *CRica Pey (prostituta)* prostitute (**d**) *CAm (persona astuta)* astute person (**e**) *Andes (persona desagradable)* fool, idiot

bagual, -ala *Bol, RP* 1 *adj (feroz)* wild, untamed
2 *nm (caballo)* wild horse

baguala *nf* = traditional Argentinian song

baguette [ba'ɣet] *nf* baguette

bah *interj* bah!

Bahamas *nfpl* **las B.** the Bahamas

bahamés, -esa (*pl* **bahameses**) 1 *adj* of/from the Bahamas
2 *nm,f* person from the Bahamas

bahía *nf* bay

bahiano, -a 1 *adj* of/from Bahia *(Brazil)*
2 *nm,f* person from Bahia *(Brazil)*

Bahrein, Bahréin *n* Bahrain

Baikal *nm* **el (lago) B.** Lake Baikal

baila *nf* sea bass

bailable *adj (canción)* danceable; **música b.** music you can dance to

bailaor, -ora, bailador, -ora *nm,f* flamenco dancer

bailar 1 *vt* (**a**) *(música)* to dance; **b. una rumba** to dance a rumba; **es difícil b. esta música** it's difficult to dance to this music; EXPR *Fam* **que me quiten lo bailado: aunque nos pusimos perdidos, que nos quiten lo baila(d)o** even though we got lost, it didn't spoil our enjoyment
(**b**) *(peonza)* to spin
2 *vi* (**a**) *(danzar)* to dance; **¿bailas?** would you like to dance?; **b. agarrado** to dance cheek to cheek; **sacar a alguien a b.** *(bailar)* to dance with sb; *(pedir)* to ask sb to dance *o* for a dance; EXPR *Fam* **es otro que tal baila** he's just the same, he's no different; *Fam* **el padre era un mujeriego y el hijo es otro que tal baila** the father was a womanizer and his son's a chip off the old block; EXPR **b. con la más fea: siempre me toca a mí b. con la más fea** I always seem to get the short straw; EXPR **b. al son que tocan: ése baila al son que le tocan los de arriba** he does whatever his bosses tell him to do
(**b**) *(no encajar)* to be loose; **le baila un diente** he has a loose tooth; **los pies me bailan (en los zapatos)** my shoes are too big; **esta falda me baila** this skirt is loose on me *o* too big for me
(**c**) *(peonza)* to spin
(**d**) *(variar) (cifras)* to fluctuate; **los resultados de las encuestas bailan entre el 5 y el 15 por ciento** the results of the polls range from 5 to 15 percent

bailarín, -ina 1 *adj* **ser muy b.** to be a very keen dancer
2 *nm,f (profesional)* dancer; *(de ballet)* ballet dancer

baile *nm* (**a**) *(arte)* dance, dancing ►► ***b. clásico*** ballet; ***b. flamenco*** flamenco dancing; ***b. popular*** folk dancing; ***b. regional*** regional folk dancing; ***bailes de salón*** ballroom and Latin dance *o* dancing; ***b. de San Vito*** *(enfermedad)* St Vitus' dance; EXPR *Fam* **tener el b. de San Vito** *(no estar quieto)* to have ants in one's pants
(**b**) *(pieza)* dance; **¿me concede este b.?** may I have the pleasure of this dance?
(**c**) *(fiesta)* ball ►► ***b. de disfraces*** fancy-dress ball; *Am* ***b. de fantasía*** fancy-dress ball; ***b. de gala*** gala ball; ***b. de máscaras*** masked ball
(**d**) *(movimiento rítmico)* **el b. de las olas** the swaying of the waves
(**e**) *(cambios)* **pese al b. de nombres, emerge un claro favorito** despite all the different names being bandied about, a clear favourite is emerging; **hubo un frenético b. de entrenadores** managers came and went in quick succession; **el constante b. de fronteras en el Báltico** the constant redrawing of borders in the Baltic

bailón, -ona *Fam* 1 *adj* **ser muy b.** to love dancing
2 *nm,f* **ser un b.** to love dancing

bailongo *nm Fam* bop

bailotear *vi Fam* to bop, to boogie

bailoteo *nm Fam* bopping

BAJA *nf* (**a**) *(descenso)* drop, fall; **una b. en las temperaturas** a drop in temperature; **no se descarta una b. en los tipos de interés** a cut in interest rates isn't being ruled out; **redondear el precio a la b.** to round the price down; **el precio del cacao sigue a la b.** the price of cocoa is continuing to fall, the slump in the price of cocoa is continuing; **la bolsa de Madrid sigue a la b.** share prices on the Madrid stock exchange are continuing to fall; **tendencia a la b.** downward trend; **las eléctricas cotizaron ayer a la b.** share prices for the electricity companies fell yesterday; *Fin* **jugar a la b.** to bear the market
(**b**) *(cese)* redundancy; **han anunciado veinte bajas** *(forzadas)* they have announced twenty redundancies; **la empresa ha sufrido bajas entre sus directivos** *(voluntarias)* a number of managers have left the firm; **la pérdida de las elecciones provocó cientos de bajas en el partido** the election defeat caused hundreds of people to leave the party; **dar de b. a alguien** *(en una empresa)* to lay sb off; *(en un club, sindicato)* to expel sb; **darse de b. (de)** *(dimitir)* to resign (from); *(salirse)* to drop out (of); **pedir la b.** *(de un club, organización)* to ask to leave; *(del ejército)* to apply for a discharge ►► ***b. incentivada*** voluntary redundancy; ***b. por jubilación*** retirement; ***b. retribuida*** paid leave; ***b. no retribuida*** unpaid leave; ***b. con sueldo*** paid leave; ***b. sin sueldo*** unpaid leave
(**c**) *Esp (por enfermedad) (permiso)* sick leave; *(documento)* sick note, doctor's certificate; **estar/darse de b.** to be on/take sick leave ►► ***b. por enfermedad*** sick leave; ***b. por maternidad*** maternity leave; ***b. por paternidad*** paternity leave
(**d**) *Mil* loss, casualty; **se registraron numerosas bajas en el combate** they suffered heavy casualties in the battle, a number of people were lost in the battle
(**e**) *Dep (por lesión)* casualty, injured player; *(por sanción)* suspended player; **al no haberse recuperado todavía, el brasileño causa** *o* **es b. para el próximo encuentro** as he still hasn't recovered from injury, the Brazilian is out of the next game; **acudieron a la final con varias bajas importantes** they went into the final with a number of important players missing

---

bajá *nm* pasha, bashaw

bajacaliforniano, -a 1 *adj* of/from Baja California *(Mexico)*
2 *nm,f* person from Baja California *(Mexico)*

bajada *nf* (**a**) *(descenso)* descent; **cuando veníamos de b.** on our way (back) down ►► ***b. de aguas*** *(tubo)* drainpipe; ***b. de bandera*** *(de taxi)* minimum fare (**b**) *(pendiente)* (downward) slope; **está al final de la b. de la escuela** it's at the bottom of the road that leads down to the school (**c**) *(disminución)* decrease, drop; **una b. de los precios** *(caída)* a drop *o* fall in prices; *(rebaja)* a price cut

bajamar *nf* low tide

bajante *nf (tubo)* drainpipe

bajaquillo *nm* groundsel tree

BAJAR 1 *vt* (**a**) *(poner abajo) (libro, cuadro)* to take/bring down; *(telón, persiana)* to lower; *(ventanilla)* to wind down, to open; **he bajado la enciclopedia de la primera a la última estantería** I've moved the encyclopedia down from the top shelf to the bottom one; **ayúdame a b. la caja** *(desde lo alto)* help me get the box down; *(al piso de abajo)* help me carry the box downstairs
(**b**) *(ojos, cabeza, mano)* to lower; **bajó la cabeza con resignación** she lowered *o* bowed her head in resignation
(**c**) *(descender) (montaña, escaleras)* to go/come down; **bajó las escaleras a toda velocidad** she ran down the stairs as fast as she could; **bajó la calle a todo correr** he ran down the street as fast as he could
(**d**) *(reducir) (inflación, hinchazón)* to reduce; *(precios)* to lower, to cut; *(música, volumen, radio)* to turn down; *(fiebre)* to bring down; **b. el fuego (de la cocina)** to reduce the heat; **b. el tono** to lower one's voice; **b. la moral a alguien** to cause sb's spirits to drop; **b. los bríos** *o* **humos a alguien** to take sb down a peg or two
(**e**) *(hacer descender de categoría)* to demote

(**f**) *Fam Informát* to download
(**g**) *Carib Fam (pagar)* to cough up, to pay up
2 *vi* (**a**) *(apearse) (de coche)* to get out; *(de moto, bicicleta, tren, avión)* to get off; *(de caballo)* to dismount; *(de árbol, escalera, silla)* to get/come down; **b. de** *(de coche)* to get out of; *(de moto, bicicleta, tren, avión)* to get off; *(de caballo)* to get off, to dismount; *(de árbol, escalera, silla, mesa)* to get/come down from; **es peligroso b. de un tren en marcha** it is dangerous to jump off a train while it is still moving; **b. a tierra** *(desde barco)* to go on shore; **bajo en la próxima parada** I'm getting off at the next stop
(**b**) *(descender)* to go/come down; **¿podrías b. aquí un momento?** could you come down here a minute?; **tenemos que b. a sacar la basura** we have to go down to put the *Br* rubbish *o US* trash out; **bajo enseguida** I'll be down in a minute; **b. corriendo** to run down; **b. en ascensor** to go/come down in the *Br* lift *o US* elevator; **b. por la escalera** to go/come down the stairs; **b. (a) por algo** to go down and get sth; **ha bajado a comprar el periódico** she's gone out *o* down to get the paper; **b. a desayunar** to go/come down for breakfast; **el río baja crecido** the river is high; **está bajando la marea** the tide is going out; **el jefe ha bajado mucho en mi estima** the boss has gone down a lot in my estimation
(**c**) *(disminuir)* to fall, to drop; *(fiebre, hinchazón)* to go/come down; *(cauce)* to go down, to fall; **los precios bajaron** prices dropped; **bajó la gasolina** the price of *Br* petrol *o US* gasoline fell; **el euro bajó frente a la libra** the euro fell against the pound; **bajó la Bolsa** share prices fell; **las acciones de C & C han bajado** C & C share prices have fallen; **han bajado las ventas** sales are down; **este modelo ha bajado de precio** this model has gone down in price, the price of this model has gone down; **el coste total no bajará del millón** the total cost will not be less than *o* under a million; **no bajará de tres horas** it will take at least three hours, it won't take less than three hours
(**d**) *Fam (ir, venir)* to go/come down; **bajaré a la capital la próxima semana** I'll be going down to the capital next week; **¿por qué no bajas a vernos este fin de semana?** why don't you come down to see us this weekend?
(**e**) *(descender de categoría)* to be demoted (**a** to); *Dep* to be relegated, to go down (**a** to); **el Atlético bajó de categoría** Atlético went down
3 bajarse *vpr* (**a**) *(apearse) (de coche)* to get out; *(de moto, bicicleta, tren, avión)* to get off; *(de caballo)* to dismount; *(de árbol, escalera, silla)* to get/come down; **bajarse de** *(de coche)* to get out of; *(de moto, bicicleta, tren, avión)* to get off; *(de caballo)* to get off, to dismount; *(de árbol, escalera, silla)* to get/come down from; **nos bajamos en la próxima** we get off at the next stop; **¡bájate de ahí ahora mismo!** get/come down from there at once!; EXPR *Fam* **bajarse del burro** to back down
(**b**) *Fam (ir, venir)* to go/come down; **bájate a la playa conmigo** come down to the beach with me
(**c**) *(agacharse)* to bend down, to stoop; **¡bájate un poco, que no veo nada!** move your head down a bit, I can't see!
(**d**) *(medias, calcetines)* to pull down; **bajarse los pantalones** to take one's trousers down; EXPR *Fam* to climb down
(**e**) *Fam Informát* to download; **me he bajado un juego estupendo** I downloaded an excellent game

bajativo *nm Andes, RP* (**a**) *(licor)* digestive liqueur (**b**) *(tisana)* herbal tea

bajel *nm Literario* vessel, ship

bajera *nf* (**a**) *RP (de cabalgadura)* saddle blanket (**b**) *CAm, Col, Méx (tabaco)* bad tobacco

bajero, -a *adj (sábana)* bottom

bajeza *nf* (**a**) *(cualidad)* baseness; **actuó con b.** she behaved basely *o* vilely (**b**) *(acción)* vile deed

bajial *nm Méx, Perú* lowland

bajini(s): por lo bajini(s) *loc adv Fam* **me contó el secreto por lo b.** she whispered the secret to me; **iba quejándose por lo b.** he was muttering complaints under his breath

bajío *nm* (**a**) *(de arena)* sandbank (**b**) *(terreno bajo)* low-lying ground

bajista 1 *adj Bolsa (inversor)* bearish; **mercado b.** bear market; **un valor b.** a share whose price is falling
2 *nmf* (**a**) *(músico)* bass player, bassist (**b**) *Bolsa (inversor)* bear

BAJO, -A 1 *adj* (**a**) *(objeto, cifra)* low; *(persona, estatura)* short; **es más b. que su amigo** he's shorter than his friend; **el pantano está muy b.** the water (level) in the reservoir is very low; **tengo la tensión baja** I have low blood pressure; **tener la moral baja, estar b. de moral** to be in low *o* poor spirits; **estar en baja forma** to be off form; **han mostrado una baja forma alarmante** they have shown worryingly poor form, they have been worryingly off form; **los precios más bajos de la ciudad** the lowest prices in the city; **tirando** *o* **calculando por lo b.** at least, at the minimum; **de baja calidad** poor(-quality); **b. en calorías** low-calorie; **b. en nicotina** low in nicotine (content) ▸▸ *Elec* ***baja frecuencia*** low frequency; *Arte* ***b. relieve*** bas-relief; *Informát* ***baja resolución*** low resolution
(**b**) *(cabeza)* bowed; *(ojos)* downcast; **paseaba con la cabeza baja** she was walking with her head down
(**c**) *(poco audible)* low; *(sonido)* soft, faint; **en voz baja** softly, in a low voice; **pon la música más baja, por favor** turn the music down, please; **por lo b.** *(en voz baja)* in an undertone; *(en secreto)* secretly; **reírse por lo b.** to snicker, to snigger
(**d**) *(grave)* deep
(**e**) *Geog* lower; **el b. Amazonas** the lower Amazon
(**f**) *Hist* lower; **la baja Edad Media** the late Middle Ages
(**g**) *(pobre)* lower-class ▸▸ ***los bajos fondos*** the underworld
(**h**) *(vil)* base
(**i**) *(soez)* coarse, vulgar; **se dejó llevar por bajas pasiones** he allowed his baser instincts to get the better of him
(**j**) *(metal)* base
(**k**) *Perú* ***baja policía*** street cleaners
2 *nm* (**a**) *(dobladillo)* hem; **meter el b. de una falda** to take up a skirt
(**b**) *(planta baja) (piso) Br* ground floor flat, *US* first floor apartment; *(local) Br* premises on the ground floor, *US* premises on the first floor; **los bajos** *Br* the ground floor, *US* the first floor
(**c**) *Mús (instrumento, cantante)* bass; *(instrumentista)* bassist
(**d**) *Mús (sonido)* bass
(**e**) *Aut* **bajos** *(de vehículo)* underside
(**f**) *(hondonada)* hollow
(**g**) *(banco de arena)* shoal, sandbank
3 *adv* (**a**) *(hablar)* quietly, softly; **ella habla más b. que él** she speaks more softly than he does; **¡habla más b., vas a despertar al bebé!** keep your voice down or you'll wake the baby up!
(**b**) *(caer)* low; *Fig* **¡qué b. has caído!** how low you have sunk!
(**c**) *(volar)* low
4 *prep* (**a**) *(debajo de)* under; **b. su apariencia pacífica se escondía un ser agresivo** beneath his calm exterior there lay an aggressive nature; **b. cero** below zero; *Fig* **b. cuerda** *o* **mano** secretly, in an underhand manner; **le pagó b. mano para conseguir lo que quería** he paid her secretly to get what he wanted; **b. este ángulo** from this angle; **b. la lluvia** in the rain; **b. techo** under cover; **dormir b. techo** to sleep with a roof over one's head *o* indoors
(**b**) *(sometido a)* **b. coacción** under duress; **b. control** under control; **b. el régimen de Franco** under Franco's regime; **fue encarcelado b. la acusación de...** he was jailed on charges of...; *Der* **b. fianza** on bail; **b. mando de** under the command of; **prohibido aparcar b. multa de 100 euros** no parking – penalty 100 euros; **b. observación** under observation; **b. palabra** on one's word; **el trato se hizo b. palabra** it was a purely verbal *o* a gentleman's agreement; **b. pena de muerte** on pain of death; **b. tratamiento médico** receiving medical treatment; **b. la tutela de** in the care of

bajón[1] *nm* (**a**) *(bajada)* slump; **las ventas han dado un b.** sales have slumped; **se produjo un b. de las temperaturas** there was a substantial fall in temperatures; **el año pasado dio un b. en los estudios** last year his schoolwork really went downhill
(**b**) *(físico)* **su salud ha dado un b.** her health has taken a turn for the worse; **sufrió un b. en el último kilómetro de la carrera** he ran out of steam in the last kilometre of the race
(**c**) *Fam (desánimo)* downer; **le dio un b.** he had a downer

bajón[2] *nm Mús* dulcian

bajonazo *nm Taurom* = thrust with a sword to the bull's neck that pierces its lungs

bajonear *RP Fam* **1** *vt (abatir, deprimir)* **b. a alguien** to get sb down
2 bajonearse *vpr* to get down

bajorrelieve *nm* bas-relief

bajuno, -a *adj* low, vile

bajura *nf* **pesca de b.** coastal fishing

bakala *Esp Fam* **1** *adj* **ser b.** to be into raves
2 *nmf* raver

bakaladero, -a *Esp Fam* **1** *adj (música)* rave
2 *nm,f* raver

bakalao *Esp Fam* **1** *adj inv* rave
2 *nm (música)* rave music

Bakú *n* Baku

bala 1 *nf* (a) *(proyectil)* bullet; **fue herido de b.** he was wounded by a gunshot; **recibió cinco impactos de b.** she received five bullet wounds; EXPR *Fam* **como una b.: entró como una b.** she rushed in; **salió como una b.** he shot off; EXPR *Col, Méx Fam* **ni a b.** no way; EXPR *CSur Fam* **no le entran ni las balas** nothing will get through to him; EXPR **tirar con b.** to snipe, to make snide remarks ▸▸ ***b. de fogueo*** blank cartridge, blank; ***b. de goma*** rubber bullet; ***b. perdida*** stray bullet; ***b. de plástico*** plastic bullet
(b) *(fardo)* bale
(c) *Am Dep* shot; **lanzamiento de b.** shot put
(d) *Am Fam (persona inteligente)* **es una b. para la física** she's a whizz at physics
2 *nmf Fam* ***b. perdida*** good-for-nothing, ne'er-do-well; ***b. rasa*** good-for-nothing, ne'er-do-well

balacear *vt Am (tirotear)* to shoot

balacera *nf Am* (a) *(tiroteo)* shoot-out (b) *(lluvia de balas)* hail of bullets

balada *nf* ballad

baladí *(pl* **baladíes***) adj* trivial

baladre *nm* oleander

baladrón, -ona *nm,f* braggart

baladronada *nf* boast; **echar baladronadas** to boast, to brag

bálago *nm* (a) *(paja)* grain stalk (b) *(espuma)* soapsuds

balalaika, balalaica *nf* balalaika

balance *nm* (a) *Com (operación)* balance; *(documento)* balance sheet ▸▸ ***b. de comprobación*** trial balance; ***b. consolidado*** consolidated balance sheet; ***b. de inventario*** stock check; *Am* ***b. de pagos*** balance of payments
(b) *(resultado)* outcome; **el b. de la experiencia fue positivo** on balance, the experience was a positive one; **el accidente tuvo un b. de seis heridos** a total of six people were wounded in the accident; **el b. de muertos** the death toll
(c) *(análisis, reflexión)* assessment; **han hecho un b. positivo de la gestión del nuevo presidente** their assessment of the new president's performance is positive; **al acabar la temporada, hicieron b. de los resultados** at the end of the season they took stock of *o* reflected on their results
(d) *(en equipo de música)* balance
(e) *Cuba (balancín)* rocking chair

balancear 1 *vt (cuna)* to rock; *(columpio)* to swing
2 **balancearse** *vpr* (a) *(en columpio, hamaca)* to swing; *(de pie)* to sway; *(en cuna, mecedora)* to rock; **el borracho bajaba por la calle balanceándose** the drunk was swaying from side to side as he walked down the street (b) *(barco)* to roll

balanceo *nm* (a) *(de columpio, hamaca)* swinging; *(de cuna, mecedora)* rocking (b) *(de barco)* rolling; **el b. del barco me marea** the rolling motion of the boat makes me feel sick (c) *Am Aut* wheel balance

balancín *nm* (a) *(mecedora)* rocking chair (b) *(en el jardín)* swing hammock (c) *(columpio)* seesaw (d) *Aut* rocker arm

balandra *nf (embarcación)* sloop

balandrismo *nm* yachting

balandrista *nmf* yachtsman, *f* yachtswoman

balandro *nm* yacht

balano, bálano *nm* (a) *(del pene)* glans penis (b) *(bellota de mar)* acorn barnacle

balanza 1 *nf* (a) *(báscula)* scales; **la b. se inclinó a nuestro favor** the balance *o* scales tipped in our favour ▸▸ ***b. de cocina*** kitchen scales; ***b. de cruz*** beam balance scale(s); ***b. de precisión*** precision balance
(b) *Com* ***b. comercial*** balance of trade; ***b. por cuenta corriente*** current accounts balance; ***b. de pagos*** balance of payments; ***b. de pagos por cuenta corriente*** balance of payments on current account
2 *nf inv (signo)* Libra
3 *nmf inv (persona)* Libra

balanzón *nm Méx (de balanza)* pan

balar *vi* to bleat

balarrasa *nm Fam* good-for-nothing, ne'er-do-well

balasto *nm* (a) *Ferroc* ballast (b) *Col (en carreteras)* gravel bed

balata *nf Chile, Méx Aut* brake lining

balaustrada *nf* (a) *Arquit* balustrade (b) *(de escalera)* banister

balaustre, balaústre *nm (de barandilla)* baluster, banister

balay *(pl* **balays** *o* **balayes***) nm* (a) *Am (cesta)* wicker basket (b) *Carib (para arroz)* = wooden bowl for washing rice

balazo *nm* (a) *(disparo)* shot; **recibió un b. en la pierna** he was shot in the leg, he received a bullet wound to the leg; EXPR *RP Fam* **ser un b.** to be a whizz (b) *(herida)* bullet wound

balboa *nm* balboa

balbucear, balbucir 1 *vt (por nerviosismo, vergüenza)* to stammer out; **ya balbucea sus primeras palabras** he's saying his first words; **"ya casi hemos llegado", balbuceó jadeante** "we're almost there," she panted
2 *vi* to babble; **el bebé ya balbucea** the baby already babbles away to himself

balbuceo *nm* (a) *(al hablar)* **se oye el b. del bebé** you can hear the baby babbling to himself; **sus balbuceos denotaban nerviosismo** you could tell he was nervous by the way he was stammering (b) **balbuceos** *(inicios)* early stages; **los balbuceos del cine** the earliest days of cinema

balbuciente *adj* (a) *(palabras)* faltering, hesitant (b) *(incipiente)* **una democracia b.** a fledgling democracy

balbucir [74] = **balbucear**

Balcanes *nmpl* (a) **los B.** *(región)* the Balkans (b) **los B.** *(cordillera)* the Balkan Mountains, the Balkans

balcánico, -a *adj* Balkan

balcanización *nf Pol* Balkanization

balcón *nm* (a) *(terraza)* balcony; **b. corrido** long balcony *(along front of building)* (b) *(mirador)* vantage point

balconada *nf (balcón corrido)* long balcony *(along front of building)*

balconcillo *nm Taurom* = balcony above the tunnel through which the bull enters the ring, or above one of the entrances to the seating area for the spectators

balconear *Fam* 1 *vt* (a) *RP (evaluar)* to size up, *Br* to suss out (b) *Méx (poner en evidencia)* to show up, to make a fool of
2 *vi RP (curiosear)* to gossip from the balcony
3 **balconearse** *vpr Méx (hacerse propaganda)* to sell oneself, to steal the limelight

balconera *nf Urug* = political banner hung from a balcony

balda *nf Esp* shelf

baldado, -a *adj* (a) *(tullido)* crippled (b) *Esp Fam (exhausto)* shattered

baldaquino, baldaquín *nm* (a) *(de tela)* canopy (b) *Arquit (sobre altar)* baldachin

baldar 1 *vt* (a) *(tullir)* to cripple (b) *Fam (agotar)* to exhaust, to shatter
2 **baldarse** *vpr Fam (agotarse)* to get exhausted, to get worn out

balde *nm* (a) *(cubo)* pail, bucket ▸▸ *CSur* ***b. de hielo*** ice bucket
(b) EXPR **de b.** *(gratis)* free (of charge); **yo no trabajo de b.** I don't work for nothing *o* for free; EXPR **estar de b.** *(estar sin hacer nada)* to be hanging around doing nothing; EXPR **en b.: hice un viaje en b.** I made a journey for nothing, it was a wasted journey; **intentaron llamarlo en b.** they tried unsuccessfully to call him; **los años no pasan en b.** I'm not getting any younger; **no en b. es considerado el mejor hospital del país** it's not for nothing that it's considered the finest hospital in the country

baldear *vt* to sluice down

baldeo *nm* sluicing down

baldíamente *adv (inútilmente)* fruitlessly, for nothing

baldío, -a 1 *adj* (a) *(sin cultivar)* uncultivated; *(no cultivable)* barren; **un terreno b.** an area of wasteland (b) *(inútil)* fruitless; **sus esfuerzos resultaron baldíos** her efforts came to nothing
2 *nm* (a) *(terreno sin cultivar)* uncultivated land (b) *Méx, RP (solar)* vacant lot

baldón *nm* **ser un b. para** to bring shame upon

baldosa *nf (en casa, edificio)* tile; *(en la acera)* paving stone

baldosín *nm* tile

balduque *nm* red tape *(for binding official documents)*

baleado *nm Am* **el saldo fue de tres baleados** three people suffered bullet wounds

balear[1] 1 *adj* Balearic; **el archipiélago b., las islas Baleares** the Balearic Islands, the Balearics
2 *nmf* person from the Balearic Islands *(Spain)*

balear[2] 1 *vt* (a) *Am (disparar)* to shoot (b) *CAm (estafar)* to swindle
2 **balearse** *vpr Am* **balearse con alguien** to have a shoot-out with sb

Baleares *nfpl* **las B.** the Balearic Islands, the Balearics

baleárico, -a *adj* Balearic

baleo *nm Am* shoot-out

balero *nm* **(a)** *Méx, RP (juguete)* cup and ball *(toy)* **(b)** *Méx (articulación)* bearing **(c)** *RP Fam (cabeza)* nut, head; **no le da el b. para la física** she hasn't got a head *o* brain for physics **(d)** *RP Fam (persona inteligente)* **es un b.** he's jolly clever *o* a bright spark

Bali *n* Bali

balido *nm* bleat, bleating

balín *nm* pellet

balística *nf* ballistics *(singular)*

balístico, -a *adj* ballistic

baliza *nf* **(a)** *Náut* marker buoy **(b)** *Av* beacon ▸▸ ***b. de radar*** radar beacon; ***b. de seguimiento*** tracking buoy; ***b. sonora*** sonar beacon **(c)** *Aut* warning light *(for roadworks)* **(d)** *RP (intermitente) Br* indicator, *US* turn signal

balizamiento, balizado *nm* **(a)** *Náut* marker buoys **(b)** *Av* beacons **(c)** *Aut* warning lights *(for roadworks)*

balizar *vt* **(a)** *Náut* to mark out with buoys **(b)** *Av* to mark out with beacons **(c)** *Aut* to mark out with warning lights

ballena *nf* **(a)** *(animal)* whale ▸▸ ***b. azul*** blue whale; ***b. franca*** right whale; ***b. gris*** grey whale; ***b. vasca*** right whale **(b)** *(varilla) (de corsé)* stay; *(de paraguas)* spoke

ballenato *nm* whale calf

ballenero, -a 1 *adj* whaling; **barco b.** whaler, whaling ship
 2 *nm,f (pescador)* whaler
 3 *nm (barco)* whaler, whaling ship

ballesta *nf* **(a)** *Hist* crossbow **(b)** *Aut* (suspension) spring

ballestero *nm Hist* crossbowman

ballet [ba'le] (*pl* **ballets**) *nm* ballet

ballico *nm* ryegrass ▸▸ ***b. perenne*** perennial ryegrass

balneario, -a 1 *adj Am* **ciudad balnearia** seaside resort
 2 *nm* **(a)** *(de baños medicinales)* spa **(b)** *Am (centro turístico)* seaside resort, spa town

balneoterapia *nf* balneotherapy

balompédico, -a *adj* soccer, *Br* football; **un encuentro b.** a soccer game *o* match, *Br* a football match

balompié *nm* soccer, *Br* football

balón *nm* **(a)** *(pelota)* ball; **b. de fútbol** soccer ball, *Br* football; **b. de rugby** rugby ball; EXPR *Fam* **echar balones fuera** to evade the issue ▸▸ ***b. medicinal*** medicine ball; *Fig* ***b. de oxígeno*** shot in the arm **(b)** *(bombona)* cylinder **(c)** *Arg (vaso)* large beer glass

balonazo *nm* **rompió la ventana de un b.** he smashed the window with the football; **me dio un b. en la cara** he hit me right in the face with the ball

baloncestista *nmf* basketball player

baloncestístico, -a *adj* basketball; **tácticas baloncestísticas** basketball tactics

baloncesto *nm* basketball

balonmanista *nmf* handball player

balonmanístico, -a *adj* handball; **tácticas balonmanísticas** handball tactics

balonmano *nm* handball

balonvolea *nm* volleyball

balota *nf Perú* = numbered ball used in bingo, lotteries, or for random selection of examination subjects etc

balotaje *nm Am* run-off, = second round of voting

balsa *nf* **(a)** *(embarcación)* raft **(b)** *(estanque)* pond, pool; EXPR **ser una b. de aceite** *(mar)* to be as calm as a millpond; *(reunión)* to go smoothly **(c)** *(árbol)* balsa; *(madera)* balsa-wood

balsámico, -a *adj* balsamic

balsamina *nf* balsamine

bálsamo *nm* **(a)** *(medicamento)* balsam **(b)** *(alivio)* balm; **sus palabras fueron como un b. para nosotros** her words were a balm to us **(c)** *CSur (para pelo)* conditioner

balsero, -a *nm,f (de Cuba)* = refugee fleeing Cuba on a raft

Baltasar *n pr* Balthazar

báltico, -a 1 *adj (país)* Baltic; **el mar B.** the Baltic Sea
 2 *nm* **el B.** the Baltic

baluarte *nm* **(a)** *(fortificación)* bulwark **(b)** *(bastión)* bastion, stronghold; **es uno de los principales baluartes del sindicalismo en el país** it is one of the main trade union strongholds in the country; **el portero volvió a ser el b. del equipo** the goalkeeper was once again the mainstay of the team

baluma, balumba *nf* **(a)** *(desorden)* mess **(b)** *Cuba, Ecuad (alboroto)* row, din

balurdo, -a *adj Ven Fam* **(a)** *(ropa)* tacky **(b)** *(persona)* square; **sus padres son muy balurdos** her parents are dead square

bamba 1 *nf* **(a)** *(composición musical)* bamba **(b)** *(bollo)* cream bun **(c)** *Esp* **bambas** *(zapatillas de deporte) Br* plimsolls, *US* sneakers
 2 **de bamba** *loc adv Cuba Fam* **me lo encontré de b.** it was a fluke that I found it

bambalina *nf* backdrop; EXPR **entre bambalinas** *(en teatro)* backstage; **se entera de todo lo que pasa entre bambalinas** she knows everything that's going on behind the scenes

bambi *nm Fam* baby deer

bambolear 1 *vt* to shake
 2 **bambolearse** *vpr* **(a)** *(árbol, persona)* to sway; *(mesa, silla)* to wobble **(b)** *(tren, autobús)* to judder

bamboleo *nm* **(a)** *(de árbol, persona)* swaying; *(de mesa, silla)* wobbling **(b)** *(de tren, autobús)* juddering

bambolla *nf (bombo)* fuss; *(ostentación)* show; **se hizo mucha b. sobre el tema** a lot of fuss was made about it

bambú (*pl* **bambúes** *o* **bambús**) *nm* bamboo

bambuco *nm* bambuco, = traditional Colombian dance

bambula *nf* cheesecloth

banal *adj* banal

banalidad *nf* banality

banalizar [14] *vt* to trivialize

banana *nf* banana ▸▸ ***b. split*** *(postre)* banana split

bananal, bananar *nm* **(a)** *(plantío)* banana grove **(b)** *(plantación)* banana plantation

bananero, -a 1 *adj* banana; **república bananera** banana republic
 2 *nm (árbol)* banana tree

banano *nm* **(a)** *(árbol)* banana tree **(b)** *(fruta)* banana

banasta *nf* large wicker basket, hamper

banasto *nm* round basket

banca *nf* **(a)** *(actividad)* banking ▸▸ ***b. electrónica*** electronic banking; ***b. telefónica*** telephone banking
 (b) **la b.** *(institución)* the banks, the banking sector; **la b. privada** the private (sector) banks
 (c) **la b.** *(en juegos)* the bank; **hacer saltar la b.** to break the bank
 (d) *(asiento)* bench
 (e) *Andes, RP (escaño)* seat
 (f) *RP* **tener b.** to have influence *o* pull

bancada *nf* **(a)** *(asiento)* stone bench **(b)** *(mesa)* large table **(c)** *Náut* rower's bench **(d)** *Tec* bedplate, bed **(e)** *Andes, RP Pol* parliamentary group

bancal *nm* **(a)** *(para cultivo)* terrace **(b)** *(parcela)* plot

bancar *RP Fam* 1 *vt* **(a)** *(aguantar, soportar)* to put up with, to stand; **no lo banco más** I'm not putting up with it any longer **(b)** *(pagar)* to pay for, to fork out for
 2 **bancarse** *vpr (aguantar, soportar)* to put up with, to stand; **no me banco más este trabajo** I can't stand this job any longer

bancario, -a 1 *adj* bank; **crédito b.** bank loan; **cuenta bancaria** bank account; **entidad bancaria** bank; **sector b.** banking sector
 2 *nm,f CSur (empleado)* bank clerk

bancarrota *nf* bankruptcy; **declararse en b.** to declare oneself bankrupt; **estar en b.** to be bankrupt; **ir a la b.** to go bankrupt

banco *nm* **(a)** *(asiento)* bench; *(de iglesia)* pew ▸▸ *Pol* ***b. azul*** = seats in Spanish parliament where government ministers sit; ***b. público*** public bench; ***b. de remo*** rowing machine
 (b) *(institución financiera)* bank ▸▸ ***b. central*** central bank; *UE* ***B. Central Europeo*** European Central Bank; ***b. comercial*** commercial bank; ***b. emisor*** issuing bank; ***B. Europeo de Inversiones*** European Investment Bank; ***B. Europeo de Reconstrucción y Desarrollo*** European Bank for Reconstruction and Development; ***b. hipotecario*** mortgage bank, *Br* ≃ building society, *US* ≃ savings and loan association; ***b. industrial*** industrial bank; ***B. Interamericano de Desarrollo*** Inter-American Development Bank; ***b. de inversiones*** investment bank; ***b. mercantil*** merchant bank; ***el B. Mundial*** the World Bank; ***b. de negocios*** merchant bank
 (c) *(de peces)* shoal ▸▸ ***b. de peces*** shoal of fish; ***b. de pesca*** fishing ground, fishery
 (d) *(depósito)* bank ▸▸ *Informát* ***b. de datos*** data bank; ***b. de órganos*** organ bank; ***b. de sangre*** blood bank; ***b. de semen*** sperm bank
 (e) *(de carpintero, artesano)* workbench
 (f) *Tec* ***b. de pruebas*** test bench; *Fig* testing ground; **servir de b. de pruebas para algo** to be a testing ground for sth
 (g) ***b. de arena*** sandbank; ***b. de hielo*** pack ice; ***b. de niebla*** fog bank

banda *nf* (**a**) *(cuadrilla)* gang ►► ***b. armada*** terrorist organization
(**b**) *(de música) (de viento y percusión)* (brass) band; *(de rock, pop)* band; **una b. de gaiteros** a pipe band
(**c**) *(faja)* sash ►► ***b. presidencial*** presidential sash
(**d**) *(para el pelo)* hairband
(**e**) *(cinta)* ribbon ►► ***b. magnética*** magnetic strip; ***b. de Möbius*** Möbius strip; ***b. sonora*** *(de película)* soundtrack; ***b. transportadora*** *(para bultos, mercancía)* conveyor belt; *(para peatones)* moving walkway
(**f**) *(franja)* stripe; **una camisa con bandas blancas** a T-shirt with white stripes ►► ***b. sonora*** *(en carretera)* rumble strip
(**g**) *(escala)* band ►► *Fin* ***b. de fluctuación*** fluctuation *o* currency band; ***b. de precios*** price range *o* band; ***b. salarial*** wage bracket, salary band
(**h**) *Rad* waveband; **ancho de b.** bandwidth ►► ***b. ancha*** broadband; ***b. estrecha*** narrow band; ***b. de frecuencia(s)*** frequency band
(**i**) *(en fútbol)* **línea de b.** touchline; **el balón salió por la b.** the ball went out of play; **avanzar por la b.** to go down the wing
(**j**) *(en billar)* cushion
(**k**) *(pez)* dealfish
(**l**) *Hist* ***la B. Oriental*** = name of former Spanish territories comprising the present-day Republic of Uruguay and southern Brazil
(**m**) *Méx (grupo de jóvenes)* gang, crowd; **se descolgó toda la b. al concierto de rock** the whole gang went to the rock concert
(**n**) EXPR **cerrarse en b.** to dig one's heels in; **se han cerrado en b. a cualquier reforma** they have flatly refused to accept any reforms; *Esp Fam* **agarrar** *o* **coger a alguien por b.** *(para reñirle)* to have a little word with sb; *(atrapar)* to buttonhole sb; **jugar a dos bandas** to play a double game; *RP Fam* **estar/quedar en b.** to be/be left at a loss

bandada *nf (de aves)* flock; *(de peces)* shoal

bandazo *nm (de barco, avión)* lurch; **dar bandazos** *(barco, avión)* to lurch; **dar un b.** *(con el volante)* to swerve violently; **el borracho bajaba por la calle dando bandazos** the drunk was lurching from side to side as he walked down the street; **su estilo da continuos bandazos** he is constantly chopping and changing his style

bandear 1 *vt* to buffet
2 bandearse *vpr* to look after oneself, to cope; **se bandea muy bien sin su familia** she is coping very well without her family; **nos bandeamos muy bien en el mundo de los negocios** we are getting along just fine in the world of business

bandeja *nf* (**a**) *(para servir, trasladar)* tray; EXPR **pasar la b.** *(en iglesia)* to pass the collection plate round; *(en la calle)* to pass the hat round; EXPR **servir** *o* **poner algo a alguien en b. (de plata)** to hand sth to sb on a plate
(**b**) *(para comida)* serving dish, platter
(**c**) *(de horno)* tray
(**d**) *(en coche)* rear shelf
(**e**) *(en caja de herramientas)* tray
(**f**) *(de impresora, fotocopiadora)* **b. (de papel)** (paper) tray
(**g**) *(en baloncesto)* lay-up
(**h**) *Chile (en avenida)* = tree-lined promenade that goes down the centre of a wide avenue
(**i**) *Méx (palangana)* washbowl

bandejón *nm Chile* = tree-lined promenade that runs down the centre of a wide avenue

bandera 1 *nf* (**a**) *(de país, organización)* flag; **bajar la b.** to lower the flag; **izar la b.** to raise the flag; **jurar b.** to swear allegiance to the flag; **las banderas estaban a media asta** the flags were at half-mast; EXPR *Fam* **hasta la b.** *(lleno)* chock-a-block ►► *UE* ***b. azul*** *(en la playa)* blue flag, = flag designating a clean beach, used within the European Union; ***b. blanca*** white flag; ***b. de conveniencia*** flag of convenience; *Dep* ***b. a cuadros*** chequered flag; *Dep* ***b. de llegada*** chequered flag *(at end of race)*; ***la b. pirata*** the Jolly Roger; ***b. roja*** *(señal de peligro)* red flag; *Dep* ***b. de salida*** chequered flag *(at start of race)*
(**b**) *(nacionalidad de buque)* flag; **un barco de b. panameña** a ship sailing under a Panamanian flag
(**c**) *(de taxi)* flag; **bajada de b.** minimum fare
(**d**) *(ideología, causa)* cause; **la b. de los derechos humanos** the cause of human rights
(**e**) *(en ejército)* company
2 de bandera *loc adj Esp Fam (magnífico)* fantastic, terrific

banderazo *nm* (**a**) *Dep* **señaló con un b. que la pelota había salido** he raised his flag to signal that the ball had gone out of play ►► ***b. de llegada:*** **recibió el b. de llegada** he took the chequered flag; ***b. de salida*** starting signal; **dio el b. de salida** he raised the chequered flag
(**b**) *Ven (en taxi)* minimum fare

banderilla *nf* (**a**) *Taurom* banderilla, = barbed dart thrust into bull's back (**b**) *Esp (aperitivo)* = hors d'oeuvre of pickles and olives on a cocktail stick

banderillear *vt Taurom* **b. al toro** to stick "banderillas" into the bull's back

banderillero, -a *nm,f Taurom* banderillero, = bullfighter who sticks "banderillas" into the bull

banderín *nm* (**a**) *(bandera)* pennant; *Dep* **b. (de córner)** corner flag (**b**) *Mil* pennant-bearer (**c**) *Mil* ***b. de enganche*** *(oficina)* recruitment office

banderita *nf* flag, charity sticker; **día de la b.** flag day

banderola *nf* (**a**) *(bandera)* pennant (**b**) *RP (de puerta)* transom; *(en el techo)* skylight

bandidaje *nm* banditry

bandido, -a *nm,f* (**a**) *(delincuente)* bandit (**b**) *(granuja)* rascal, rogue; **el muy b. se ha llevado mi paraguas** that rascal has stolen my umbrella; **ese tendero es un b.** that shopkeeper is a bit of a twister

bando *nm* (**a**) *(facción)* side; **el b. republicano** the republicans, the republican side; **pasarse al otro b.** to change sides; EXPR *Fam* **ser del otro b.** *(ser homosexual)* to be one of them, to be queer (**b**) *(edicto)* edict

bandola *nf* mandolin

bandolera *nf* (**a**) *(correa)* bandoleer; **en b.** slung across one's chest (**b**) *Esp (bolso)* shoulder bag (**c**) *RP (cartera)* shoulder pouch (**d**) *ver también* **bandolero**

bandolerismo *nm* banditry

bandolero, -a *nm,f* bandit

bandolina *nf* mandolin

bandoneón *nm* bandoneon, = musical instrument, similar to the accordion, used in tango music

bandoneonista *nmf* bandoneon player

bandurria *nf* (**a**) *(guitarra)* = small 12-stringed guitar (**b**) *(ave)* black-faced ibis

Bangkok *n* Bangkok

Bangladesh [bangla'ðeʃ] *n* Bangladesh

Bangui *n* Bangui

banjo ['banjo] *nm* banjo

Banjul [ban'jul] *n* Banjul

banner ['baner] *nm Informát* banner ►► ***b. publicitario*** advertising banner

banquero, -a *nm,f* banker

banqueta *nf* (**a**) *(asiento)* stool (**b**) *(para los pies)* footstool (**c**) *CAm, Méx (acera) Br* pavement, *US* sidewalk

banquete *nm (comida)* banquet; **dar un b.** to have *o* hold a banquet; **se dieron un b. de marisco** they had a wonderful meal of seafood ►► ***b. de boda(s)*** wedding breakfast; ***b. eucarístico*** holy communion

banquetero, -a *nm,f Chile, Méx* caterer *(for weddings, large parties etc)*

banquillo *nm* (**a**) *(asiento)* low stool (**b**) *Der* **el b. (de los acusados)** the dock; **estas acusaciones llevarán al b. a muchos políticos** these accusations will land many politicians in the dock (**c**) *Dep* bench

banquina *nf RP (arcén) Br* hard shoulder, *US* shoulder

banquisa *nf* ice field

banquito *nm RP* stool

bantú (*pl* **bantúes**) *nm (pueblo africano)* Bantu

bañadera *nf* (**a**) *Arg (bañera)* bath (**b**) *RP (vehículo)* = old-fashioned school bus

bañado *nm Bol, RP (terreno)* marshy area

bañador *nm Esp (de mujer)* swimsuit; *(de hombre)* swimming trunks

bañar 1 *vt* (**a**) *(asear)* to bath; *Med (paciente)* to bathe
(**b**) *(revestir)* to coat; **baña el bizcocho con chocolate** pour chocolate over the sponge, cover the sponge in chocolate; **bañado en oro/plata** gold-/silver-plated; **bañado en sudor** bathed in sweat
(**c**) *(sujeto: río)* to flow through; **el Índico baña las costas del país** the Indian Ocean washes the coast of the country
(**d**) *(sujeto: sol, luz)* to bathe; **el sol bañaba el patio** the courtyard was bathed in sunlight
(**e**) *Ven Fam (superar)* **su prima la baña en simpatía** her cousin is a million times nicer than she is
2 bañarse *vpr* (**a**) *(en el baño)* to have *o* take a bath
(**b**) *(en playa, piscina)* to go for a swim; **¿nos bañamos?** shall we go for a swim?; **me bañé durante una hora** I was in the water for an hour;

prohibido bañarse *(en letrero)* no bathing
(c) *Am (ducharse)* to have a shower; EXPR *CSur Fam* **mandar a alguien a bañarse** to tell sb to get lost; *CSur Fam* **¡andá a bañarte!** get lost!

bañera *nf* bathtub, bath ►► ***b. de hidromasaje*** whirlpool bath, Jacuzzi®

bañero, -a *nm,f Arg* lifeguard

bañista *nmf* bather

baño *nm* (a) *(acción) (en bañera)* bath; *(en playa, piscina)* swim; **darse un b.** *(en bañera)* to have *o* take a bath; *(en playa, piscina)* to go for a swim; EXPR *Esp Fam* **dar un b. a alguien** to take sb to the cleaners ►► ***b. de asiento*** hip bath; ***b. de espuma*** bubble bath; ***b. (de) María*** bain-marie; **calentar algo al b. (de) María** to heat sth in a bain-marie; *Fig* ***b. de sangre*** bloodbath; ***b. de sol*:** **tomar baños de sol** to sunbathe; ***b. turco*** Turkish bath; ***b. de vapor*** steam bath
(b) *(cuarto de aseo)* bathroom; **una casa con tres baños** a three-bathroom house
(c) *(servicios) Br* toilet, *US* bathroom, washroom; **necesito ir al b.** I need to go to the *Br* toilet *o US* bathroom; **¿dónde está el b.?** where's the *Br* toilet *o US* bathroom? ►► *Am* ***b. público*** *Br* public toilet, *US* washroom
(d) **baños** *(balneario)* spa; **tomar los baños** to go to a spa ►► ***baños termales*** thermal baths
(e) *Am (ducha)* shower; **darse un b.** to have a shower
(f) *(bañera)* bathtub, bath
(g) *(vahos)* inhalation
(h) *(capa)* coat; **un reloj con un b. de oro** a gold-plated watch

bao *nm Naut* beam

baobab *nm* baobab (tree)

baptista 1 *adj* Baptist
2 *nmf* Baptist

baptisterio, bautisterio *nm* baptistery

baqueano, -a, baquiano, -a *Am* 1 *adj Fam* **ese hombre es muy b.** that guy knows this place like the back of his hand; **estar muy b. en algo** to be well up on sth
2 *nm,f (conocedor de una zona)* guide

baquelita *nf* Bakelite®

baqueta *nf* (a) *(de fusil)* ramrod; EXPR *Fam* **tratar** *o* **llevar a alguien a la b.** to push sb around (b) *Mús* drumstick

baquetazo *nm Fam* (a) *(golpe)* thump; EXPR **tratar a alguien a baquetazos** to treat sb like dirt (b) *(caída)* fall; **darse** *o* **pegarse un b.** to give oneself a real thump, to have a nasty fall

baqueteado, -a *adj Fam* **estar muy b.** to have been to the school of hard knocks; **está muy b. en cuestiones de Bolsa** he's an old hand when it comes to the stock market

baquetear *Fam* 1 *vt (maltratar, molestar)* to push around
2 *vi (equipaje)* to bump up and down

baqueteo *nm Fam (molestias)* stresses and strains, hassle

baquetón, -ona *Méx Fam* 1 *adj* **es muy b.** he's a selfish pig
2 *nm,f* selfish pig, heel

baquiano, -a = **baqueano**

báquico, -a *adj* bacchic, bacchanalian

báquiro *nm Col, Ven* peccary

bar *nm* (a) *(establecimiento)* bar; **ir de bares** to go out drinking, to go on a pub crawl ►► ***b. de copas*** bar; ***b. restaurante*** = bar with a restaurant attached; ***b. terraza*** = stand selling alcoholic and soft drinks, surrounded by tables and chairs for customers (b) *(unidad)* bar

baraca *nf* (a) *(suerte)* luck (b) *(don divino)* gift of divine protection

barahúnda, baraúnda *nf* racket, din

baraja *nf* (a) *(conjunto de naipes) Br* pack *o US* deck (of cards); EXPR **jugar con dos barajas** to play a double game ►► ***b. española*** = Spanish deck of cards; ***b. francesa*** = standard 52-card deck (b) *Am (naipe individual)* (playing) card

barajadura *nf (de cartas)* shuffling

barajar *vt* (a) *(cartas)* to shuffle; **b. a la americana** to riffle
(b) *(posibilidades)* to consider; **la policía baraja tres teorías diferentes** the police are looking at *o* considering three different theories; **se barajan varios nombres para el puesto** various names are being mentioned in connection with the post
(c) *Chile (golpe)* to parry
(d) *RP Fam (agarrar)* to grab, to snatch; **barajé la taza a pocos centímetros del piso** I grabbed the cup just before it hit the floor

barajita *nf Ven* picture card

baranda[1] *nf* (a) *(valla) (al borde de algo)* rail; *(en escalera)* banister (b) *(pasamanos)* handrail (c) *(de mesa de billar)* rail

baranda[2] *nf RP Fam* stink; **¡qué b. hay aquí!** it stinks in here!

barandal *nm, Esp* **barandilla** *nf* (a) *(valla) (al borde de algo)* rail; *(en escalera)* banister (b) *(listón)* handrail

barata *nf* (a) *Méx (rebaja)* sale (b) *Chile (insecto)* cockroach

baratero, -a *nm,f Am (comerciante)* = owner of a shop selling cheap goods

baratija *nf* trinket, knick-knack; **baratijas** junk

baratillo *nm* (a) *(género)* junk (b) *(tienda)* junk shop; *(mercadillo)* flea market

barato, -a 1 *adj* (a) *(objeto)* cheap; **ser muy b.** to be very cheap; **los tomates están muy baratos** tomatoes are very cheap at the moment; EXPR **lo b. sale caro** buying cheap is a false economy (b) *(sentimentalismo)* cheap; *(literatura)* trashy; **déjate de filosofía barata** cut the half-baked philosophizing
2 *adv* cheap, cheaply; **me costó b.** it was cheap, I got it cheap; **vender algo b.** to sell sth cheaply; **en este bar se come muy b.** you can eat very cheaply in this bar, the food's very cheap in this bar

baraúnda = **barahúnda**

barba 1 *nf* (a) *(pelo)* beard; **barbas** beard; **un hombre con b. de dos/tres/varios días** a man with stubble; **apurarse la b.** to shave close; **dejarse (la) b.** to grow a beard; **le está saliendo (la) b.** he's starting to get hairs on his chin *o* a beard; EXPR *Méx* **hacer la b. a alguien** to butter sb up; EXPR **lo hizo en sus (propias) barbas** he did it right under her nose; EXPR **reírse de alguien en sus propias barbas** to laugh in sb's face; EXPR **un hombre con toda la b.** a real man; EXPR **subirse a las barbas de alguien** to be cheeky to sb; PROV **cuando las barbas de tu vecino veas cortar** *o* **pelar, pon las tuyas a remojar** = when the trouble reaches next door, you'd better watch out for yourself ►► ***b. cerrada*** thick beard; ***b. de chivo*** goatee
(b) *(barbilla)* chin
(c) *Esp Fam* **por b.** *(por persona)* each; **la comida nos ha salido a 20 euros por b.** the meal cost us 20 euros each
(d) *(de ballena)* whalebone
(e) **barbas** *(de pez)* barbel; *(de mejillón perro, cabra)* beard; *(de ave)* wattle
(f) **barbas** *(de papel)* uneven edge; *(de tela)* frayed edge
2 *nm inv* **barbas** *Fam (barbudo)* beardy; **el barbas que está sentado a la derecha** the guy with the beard sitting on the right

barbacana *nf* (a) *(de defensa)* barbican (b) *(saetera)* loophole, embrasure

barbacoa *nf* (a) *(utensilio)* barbecue (b) *(asado, carne)* barbecue; **hacer una b.** to have a barbecue (c) *Bol (baile)* tap dance

barbada *nf* (a) *(pez)* four-bearded rockling (b) *(en caballo)* curb (chain)

barbadejo *nm (arbusto)* wayfaring tree

barbadense 1 *adj* Barbadian
2 *nmf* Barbadian

barbado, -a *adj* bearded

Barbados *n* Barbados

barbaján, -ana *Méx* 1 *nm,f* boor, lout
2 *adj* boorish, loutish

bárbaramente *adv* (a) *(de forma bárbara)* barbarically, cruelly (b) *Fam (extraordinariamente)* brilliantly, fantastically

barbárico, -a *adj* barbaric, barbarian

barbaridad *nf* (a) *(cualidad)* cruelty
(b) *(disparate)* **lo que dijo/hizo es una b.** what he said/did is ridiculous; **no cometamos la b. de decir que sí** let's not be so foolish as to say yes; **¡qué b., ya son las once!** oh my God, it's eleven o'clock already!; **¡qué b., ha vuelto a subir la gasolina!** can you believe it, the price of petrol has gone up again!
(c) *(insulto)* **salió del campo diciendo barbaridades** he left the pitch swearing
(d) *Fam (montón)* **una b.: se gastó una b.** she spent a fortune; **bebe una b.** he drinks like nobody's business *o* like a fish; **llovió una b.** it poured with rain, *Br* it chucked it down; **te quiero una b.** I love you like crazy; **trajo una b. de regalos** she brought loads of presents

barbarie *nf* (a) *(crueldad) (cualidad)* cruelty, savagery; *(acción)* atrocity (b) *(incultura)* barbarism

barbarismo *nm* (a) *(extranjerismo)* = foreign word that has not yet been fully accepted as part of the language (b) *(incorrección)* substandard usage, barbarism

bárbaro, -a 1 *adj* (a) *Hist* barbarian
(b) *(cruel)* barbaric, cruel
(c) *(bruto)* uncouth, coarse; **no seas b., desconecta primero el enchufe** don't be such an idiot, take the plug out first
(d) *Fam (excelente)* fantastic, great; **su último disco es b.** her latest

record is fantastic *o* great; **con esa falda estás bárbara** you look fantastic *o* great in that skirt; **es una persona bárbara** she's a wonderful person; **conseguí las entradas – ¡b.!** I got the tickets – great *o* fantastic!
(e) *Fam (como intensificador)* **hacía un frío b.** it was dead cold; **tengo una sed bárbara** I'm dead thirsty
2 *nm,f* (a) *Hist* barbarian; **los bárbaros** the barbarians
(b) *(persona bruta)* brute, animal; **el b. de su marido la pega** her brute of a husband beats her; **unos bárbaros destrozaron la cabina telefónica** some animals *o Br* yobs destroyed the phone box
3 *adv Fam (magníficamente)* **pasarlo b.** to have a wild time

barbear *vt CAm, Méx (adular)* to flatter, to butter up

barbechar *vt Agr* (a) *(no cultivar)* to leave fallow (b) *(arar)* to plough for sowing

barbecho *nm Agr* (a) *(sistema)* land set-aside; **tierras en b.** fallow land; **dejar un campo en b.** to set aside a field (b) *(campo)* fallow field

barbería *nf* barber's (shop)

barbero, -a 1 *adj Méx Fam* **ser muy b.** to be a real bootlicker
2 *nm* barber

barbilampiño, -a 1 *adj* smooth-faced, beardless
2 *nm* beardless man

barbilla *nf* chin

barbitúrico 1 *adj* barbituric
2 *nm* barbiturate

barbo *nm* barbel ►► ***b. de mar*** red mullet

barbón *nm* (a) *(hombre)* man with a beard (b) *(cabra)* billy-goat

barboquejo *nm* chinstrap

barbotar 1 *vi* to mutter
2 *vt* to mutter

barbudo, -a 1 *adj* bearded; **la mujer barbuda** *(en circo)* the bearded woman
2 *nm* man with a beard

barbullar *vi* to jabber

barca *nf* dinghy, small boat; **b. de remos** rowing boat

Barça ['barsa] *nm Dep* = informal name for Barcelona Football Club

barcada *nf* (a) *(carga)* boatload (b) *(viaje)* crossing

barcaje *nm (tarifa)* ferry fare

barcarola *nf* barcarole, gondolier's song

barcaza *nf* barge, lighter

Barcelona *n* Barcelona

barcelonés, -esa 1 *adj* of/from Barcelona *(Spain, Venezuela)*
2 *nm,f* person from Barcelona *(Spain, Venezuela)*

barcelonismo *nm Dep (apoyo)* = support for Barcelona Football Club; *(seguidores)* = Barcelona Football Club supporters

barcelonista *Dep* 1 *adj* = of/relating to Barcelona Football Club
2 *nmf* = supporter or member of Barcelona Football Club

barchilón, -ona *nm,f Ecuad, Perú (enfermero)* nurse

barcia *nf* chaff

barcino, -a *adj* white and reddish-brown

barco *nm (pequeño)* boat; *(de gran tamaño)* ship; **recorrieron la región en b.** they travelled round the region by boat; **¡abandonen el b.!** abandon ship! ►► ***b. ballenero*** whaler, whaling ship; ***b. de carga*** cargo boat *o* ship; ***b. cisterna*** tanker; ***b. deportivo*** sailing boat *(for sport or pleasure sailing)*; ***b. de guerra*** warship; ***b. mercante*** merchant ship; ***b. nodriza*** refuelling ship; ***b. de pasajeros*** passenger ship; ***b. de pesca*** fishing boat; ***b. pesquero*** fishing boat; ***b. pirata*** pirate ship; ***b. de recreo*** pleasure boat; ***b. de vapor*** steamer, steamboat; ***b. de vela*** sailing ship; ***b. velero*** sailing ship

barda *nf Méx* fence; EXPR *Fam* **volarse una b.** *(beisbolista)* to hit a home run

bardaguera *nf* willow

bardana *nf* burdock

bardo *nm* bard

baremar *vt* to mark using a scale

baremo *nm* (a) *(escala)* scale (b) *(norma)* yardstick

Barents *n* **el mar de B.** the Barents Sea

bareto *nm Esp Fam (bar)* boozer

bargueño *nm* = carved-wood cabinet with many small drawers

baria *nf Fís* barye

bario *nm Quím* barium

barión *nm Fís* baryon

barisfera *nf Geol* barysphere

barita *nf Geol* barium sulphate

baritina *nf Geol* barytine

barítono *nm* baritone

barloventear *vi Náut* to tack to windward

barlovento *nm Náut* windward (side)

barman (*pl* **barmans**) *nm* barman

barnacla *nf* ***b. canadiense*** Canada goose; ***b. cariblanca*** barnacle goose; ***b. carinegra*** brent goose; ***b. cuelliroja*** red-breasted goose

barniz *nm (para madera)* varnish; *(para cerámica)* glaze; *Fig* **bajo un b. de progresismo se oculta un candidato reaccionario** a reactionary is hidden under the candidate's progressive veneer ►► ***b. de uñas*** nail varnish

barnizado, -a 1 *adj (madera)* varnished; *(cerámica)* glazed
2 *nm (acción) (de madera)* varnishing; *(de cerámica)* glazing

barnizador, -ora *nm,f* French polisher

barnizar [14] *vt (madera)* to varnish; *(cerámica)* to glaze

barométrico, -a *adj* barometric

barómetro *nm* (a) *(instrumento)* barometer (b) *(indicador)* barometer; **este índice es un b. del estado de la Bolsa** this index is a barometer of the situation on the stock market; **esta revista es un buen b. de lo que piensan los empresarios** this magazine is a good gauge of the current thinking of businessmen (c) *(sondeo de opinión)* (public opinion) poll *o* survey

barón *nm* (a) *(noble)* baron (b) *Pol* **los barones del partido** the party's power-brokers

baronesa *nf* baroness

barquero, -a *nm,f* boatman, *f* boatwoman

barqueta *nf (bandeja)* tray

barquía *nf* = small eight-oar fishing boat

barquilla *nf* (a) *(de globo)* basket (b) *Carib (helado)* ice-cream cone

barquillera *nf (caja)* = metal container for wafers, carried by a "barquillero"

barquillero, -a *nm,f* = street vendor selling wafers

barquillo *nm (plano)* wafer; *(cono)* cone, *Br* cornet; *(enrollado)* rolled wafer

barquisimetano, -a 1 *adj* of/from Barquisimeto *(Venezuela)*
2 *nm,f* person from Barquisimeto *(Venezuela)*

barra 1 *nf* (a) *(pieza alargada)* bar; *(redonda)* rod; *(de bicicleta)* crossbar; **b. (de pan)** French stick; EXPR **no se para en barras** nothing stops him ►► *Aut* ***b. antivuelco*** anti-roll bar; ***b. espaciadora*** space bar; *Aut* ***barras laterales*** side (impact) bars; *Tec* ***b. del pistón*** piston rod
(b) *(bloque) (de hielo)* block; *(de chocolate)* bar ►► ***b. de labios*** lipstick
(c) *(de bar, café)* bar *(counter)* ►► ***b. americana*** = bar where hostesses chat with clients; ***b. libre*** = unlimited drink for a fixed price
(d) *(en escudo, bandera)* bar
(e) *(para bailarines)* barre ►► ***b. fija*** barre
(f) *Dep* ***barras asimétricas*** asymmetric bars; ***b. de equilibrios*** balance beam; ***b. fija*** horizontal bar, high bar; ***barras paralelas*** parallel bars
(g) *Mús* bar (line)
(h) *(signo gráfico)* slash, oblique ►► ***b. invertida*** backslash; ***b. oblicua*** slash, oblique
(i) *Informát* ***b. de desplazamiento*** scroll bar; ***b. de herramientas*** tool bar; ***b. de menús*** menu bar; ***b. de tareas*** task bar
(j) *(tribunal)* **llevar a alguien a la b.** to take sb to court
(k) *(de arena)* bar, sandbank
(l) *CSur (desembocadura)* mouth
(m) *Andes, RP Fam (grupo de amigos)* gang; **tiene una b. muy linda** she hangs out with a very nice crowd
(n) *Andes, RP Fam (público)* crowd, spectators; **los chiflidos de la b.** *o* **las barras eran ensordecedores** the fans' whistles were deafening ►► ***b. brava*** = group of violent soccer fans
2 *nmf RP Fam (en fútbol)* = member of a group of violent soccer fans

Barrabás *n pr* Barabbas; **¡ese niño es más malo que B.!** that child is a little devil!

barrabás *nm (adulto)* devil, brute; *(niño)* rogue, scamp

barrabasada *nf Fam* (a) *(jugarreta)* **aquello fue una b.** that was outrageous; **hacer una b. a alguien** to do something nasty to sb (b) *(travesura)* **hacer barrabasadas** to get up to mischief *o* no good (c) *(disparate)* **¿cómo se te pudo ocurrir semejante b.?** whatever put such a stupid idea into your head?; **sus declaraciones han sido una verdadera b.** what she said was utter nonsense

barraca *nf* (**a**) *(chabola)* shack (**b**) *(de feria) (caseta)* booth; *(puesto)* stall (**c**) *(en Valencia y Murcia)* thatched farmhouse (**d**) *RP (tienda)* builders' merchant's (shop)

barracón *nm* barrack hut

barracuda *nf (pez)* barracuda

barrado, -a *adj (con listas)* barred

barragana *nf (concubina)* concubine

barranca *nf* (**a**) *(precipicio)* precipice; *(hondonada)* ravine; *(menos profunda)* gully (**b**) *RP (cuesta)* hill; **ir(se) b. abajo** to go downhill; **después del divorcio se fue b. abajo** she went downhill after the divorce; **el sistema de seguridad social va b. abajo** the social security system is going downhill

barranco *nm*, **barranquera** *nf (precipicio)* precipice; *(hondonada)* ravine; *(menos profunda)* gully

barranquismo *nm Dep* canyoning

barranquista *nmf Dep* canyoner, canyoning enthusiast

barraquismo *nm* **erradicar el b.** to deal with the shanty town problem

barreminas *nm inv* minesweeper

barrena *nf* (**a**) *(herramienta)* drill (**b**) **entrar en b.** *(avión)* to go into a spin; **la economía ha entrado en b.** the economy has gone into free fall; **sus índices de popularidad siguen cayendo en b.** his popularity ratings continue on their downward spiral

barrenador *nm (insecto)* woodworm

barrenar *vt* (**a**) *(taladrar)* to drill (**b**) *(frustrar)* to scupper

barrendero, -a *nm,f* street sweeper

barrenero, -a *nm,f* driller

barrenillo *nm* (**a**) *(insecto)* boring insect, borer (**b**) *Cuba (manía)* mania, obsession

barreno *nm* (**a**) *(instrumento)* large drill (**b**) *(agujero) (para explosiones)* blast hole

barreño *nm Esp* washing-up bowl

barrer 1 *vt* (**a**) *(con escoba)* to sweep

(**b**) *(sujeto: viento, olas)* to sweep away; **el huracán barrió todo a su paso** the hurricane destroyed everything in its path

(**c**) *(con escáner)* to scan

(**d**) *(con la vista)* to scan

(**e**) *(llevarse)* **los ladrones barrieron la casa** the thieves cleaned out the house; **el público barrió su última novela** the public snapped up every last copy of his latest novel

(**f**) *Fam (derrotar)* to thrash, to annihilate

2 *vi* (**a**) *(con escoba)* to sweep; EXPR **b. para adentro** *o* **casa** to look after number one; **ese árbitro siempre barre para casa** that referee always favours the home team

(**b**) *(llevarse)* **b. con: los invitados barrieron con todas las bebidas** the guests made short work of the drink; **el público barrió con su última novela** the public snapped up every last copy of his latest novel

(**c**) *Fam (arrasar)* to sweep the board; **el candidato oficial barrió en las urnas** the government candidate swept the board in the election; **el atleta keniata barrió en la final** the Kenyan athlete trounced his rivals *o Br* walked it in the final

barrera *nf* (**a**) *(para controlar acceso)* barrier; *(de campo, casa)* fence ►► ***barreras arancelarias*** tariff barriers; ***barreras no arancelarias*** non-tariff barriers; ***barreras arquitectónicas*** *(para silla de ruedas)* obstructions for wheelchair users; ***barreras comerciales*** trade barriers

(**b**) *Ferroc* crossing gate

(**c**) *(dificultad, obstáculo)* barrier; **la b. del idioma le impedía integrarse** the language barrier made it difficult for her to integrate; **el índice bursátil superó la b. psicológica de los 1.000 puntos** the stock market index crossed the psychological barrier of 1,000 points; **superaron la b. del millón de discos vendidos** sales of their album went over the million mark; **poner barreras a algo** to erect barriers against sth, to hinder sth; **se casaron saltándose las barreras sociales** they married despite the huge difference in their social backgrounds ►► ***b. del sonido*** sound barrier

(**d**) *Dep (de jugadores)* wall

(**e**) *Taurom (valla)* = barrier around the edge of a bullring; *(localidad)* = front row of seats immediately behind the barrier around the edge of the bullring

barreta *nf Méx (piqueta)* pick, pickaxe

barretina *nf* = traditional Catalan cap, made of red wool and similar to a nightcap in shape

barriada *nf* (**a**) *(barrio popular)* working-class district *o* neighbourhood *o* area (**b**) *Am (barrio de chabolas)* shanty town

barrial *Am* **1** *adj* neighbourhood; **las tiendas barriales** the local shops

2 *nm (barrizal)* quagmire; **la calle terminó siendo un b.** the street was reduced to a quagmire

barrica *nf* keg

barricada *nf* barricade; **levantar barricadas** to put up barricades

barrida *nf (con escoba)* **dar una b. a algo** to give sth a sweep, to sweep sth

barrido *nm* (**a**) *(con escoba)* **dar un b. a algo** to give sth a sweep, to sweep sth; **a esta cocina le hace falta un b.** this kitchen could do with a sweep; EXPR **servir** *o* **valer tanto para un b. como para un fregado** *(persona)* to be a jack-of-all-trades (**b**) *(de escáner)* scan (**c**) *(con la vista)* scan; **di un b. a los titulares del periódico** I scanned the newspaper headlines (**d**) *Cine* pan, panning

barriga *nf* (**a**) *Fam (vientre)* stomach; *(especialmente en lenguaje infantil)* tummy; **me duele la b.** my stomach *o* tummy hurts; EXPR **rascarse** *o* **tocarse la b.** to twiddle one's thumbs, to laze around; EXPR *RP Fam* **ser una b. resfriada** to be a blabbermouth

(**b**) *Fam (abultamiento del vientre)* paunch; **echar b.** to get a paunch; **tener b.** to have a paunch; EXPR **hacer una b. a alguien** to get sb up the spout *o Br* duff

(**c**) *(de cántaro, vasija)* belly

barrigazo *nm Fam* **darse un b.** to fall flat on one's face

barrigón, -ona *Fam* **1** *adj* paunchy; **te estás poniendo muy b.** you're getting quite a paunch; PROV *RP* **al que nace b. es al ñudo que lo fajen** you can't make a leopard change his spots

2 *nm,f* (**a**) *(persona)* person with a paunch; **es un b.** he has a paunch (**b**) *Carib (niño)* tot, nipper

3 *nm (barriga)* big belly

barrigudo, -a *Fam* **1** *adj* paunchy; **se puso muy b.** he got quite a paunch

2 *nm,f (persona)* person with a paunch; **es un b.** he has a paunch

barril *nm* barrel; **cerveza de b.** draught beer; EXPR *Am Fam* **ser un b. sin fondo** to be a bottomless pit ►► ***b. de petróleo*** oil barrel; ***b. de pólvora*** powder keg; EXPR **ser un b. de pólvora** to be a powder keg

barrila *nf* EXPR *Fam* **dar la b. (a alguien)** *(hablando)* to go on and on (to *o* at sb); **me estuvo dando la b. con lo de hacerme miembro del club** he went on and on at me about joining the club; **¿por qué no te vas a dar la b. con la guitarra a otro sitio?** why don't you go and annoy people with your music somewhere else?

barrilero, -a *nm,f* cooper

barrilete *nm* (**a**) *(de revólver)* chamber (**b**) *(de carpintero)* clamp (**c**) *Arg (cometa)* kite

barrilla *nf* saltwort, barilla

barrillo *nm* spot

barrio *nm* (**a**) *(vecindario)* area, district, neighbourhood; **un b. acomodado** a well-to-do area *o* neighbourhood; **vive en un b. céntrico** she lives centrally; **la gente del b. nos conocemos todos** everyone knows everyone else round here; **la contaminación afecta más al centro que a los barrios** the pollution is worse in the centre of the city than further out; **una tienda/un cine de b.** a local shop/ cinema; EXPR *Esp Fam Hum* **irse al otro b.** to kick the bucket, to snuff it; EXPR *Esp Fam Hum* **mandar a alguien al otro b.** to bump sb off ►► ***los barrios bajos*** the rough parts of town; ***b. chino*** *(de chinos)* Chinatown; *Esp (de prostitución)* red-light district; ***b. comercial*** shopping district; *Col* ***b. de invasión*** shanty town; ***b. latino*** Latin Quarter; ***b. marginal*** deprived area *o* district; ***b. obrero*** working-class area *o* district *o* neighbourhood; ***b. periférico*** outlying area *o* district; ***b. residencial*** residential area *o* district *o* neighbourhood; *Andes* ***b. de tolerancia*** red-light district

(**b**) *Ven (de chabolas)* shanty town

barriobajero, -a *Pey* **1** *adj* **ese acento es muy b.** that accent is very common *o* vulgar; **unos tipos con aspecto b.** some rough-looking types; **un chico b.** a lout, *Br* a yob

2 *nm,f* lout, *Br* yob

barrista *nmf Perú Dep* supporter, fan

barritar *vi (elefante)* to trumpet

barrito *nm Am* spot

barrizal *nm* quagmire; **la calle terminó siendo un b.** the street was reduced to a quagmire

barro *nm* (**a**) *(fango)* mud; EXPR **arrastrarse por el b.** to abase oneself (**b**) *(arcilla)* clay; **una figurita de b.** a clay figure ►► ***b. cocido*** terracotta (**c**) *(grano)* spot (**d**) *Cuba Fam (peso)* peso (**e**) *Chile* ***barros jarpa*** *(ropa)* morning coat; *(sandwich)* toasted ham and cheese sandwich; ***barros luco*** *(sandwich)* toasted beef and cheese sandwich

barrocamente *adv* baroquely

barroco, -a 1 *adj* (**a**) *Arte* baroque (**b**) *(recargado)* ornate
2 *nm Arte* baroque

barrón *nm* marram grass

barroquismo *nm* (**a**) *Arte* baroque style (**b**) *(recargamiento)* ornate style

barroso, -a *adj* muddy

barrote *nm* bar; **estar entre barrotes** *(en prisión)* to be behind bars

barruntamiento = **barrunto**

barruntar *vt (presentir)* to suspect; **el perro barruntaba el peligro** the dog could scent danger

barrunto, barruntamiento *nm* (**a**) *(presentimiento)* suspicion; **tengo el b. de que va a pasar algo malo** I have a feeling something bad is going to happen (**b**) *(indicio)* sign, indication

bartola *nf* EXPR *Fam* **echarse** *o* **tenderse** *o* **tumbarse a la b.** to lounge around; EXPR *Fam* **hacer algo a la b.** to do sth any old how

bartolillo *nm Esp (pastel)* = small turnover filled with confectioner's custard

Bartolomé *n pr* **San B.** St Bartholomew

bártulos *nmpl* things, bits and pieces; **recoge todos los b. y nos vamos** get all your things *o* bits and pieces together and we'll be off; **está preparando los b. de pesca** he's getting his fishing gear together; EXPR *Fam* **liar los b.** to pack one's bags

barullento, -a *adj RP Fam* noisy

barullo *nm Fam* (**a**) *(ruido)* din, racket; **el b. del tráfico no me deja dormir** the din of the traffic is keeping me awake; **armar b.** to make a racket
(**b**) *(desorden)* mess; **hay un b. de papeles encima de la mesa** there are papers all over the desk; **se armó un b. con los números** he got into a real mess *o* muddle with the figures; **con tanta información tengo un b. en la cabeza** my head is in a muddle with so much information

basa *nf Arquit* base

basal *adj Fisiol* basal

basáltico, -a *adj* basaltic

basalto *nm* basalt

basamento *nm Arquit* base, plinth

basar 1 *vt* **b. algo en** to base sth on
2 **basarse** *vpr* (**a**) **basarse en** *(persona)* to base one's argument on; **¿en qué se basa usted (para decir eso)?** what basis do you have for saying that?; **¿en qué te basas (para decir eso)?** what makes you say that?; **me baso en lo que he oído** I'm going by what I've heard (**b**) **basarse en** *(teoría, obra)* to be based on

basáride *nf* ringtail

basca 1 *nf Esp Fam (de amigos)* crowd; **vino toda la b.** the whole crew *o* crowd came along
2 *nfpl* **bascas** *(náuseas)* nausea; *(ganas de vomitar)* retching

bascosidad *nf Ecuad (obscenidad)* obscenity, rude word

báscula *nf* scales ▸▸ ***b. de baño*** bathroom scales; ***b. para camiones*** weighbridge; ***b. de precisión*** precision scales

basculador *nm* dumper truck

bascular *vi* (**a**) *(péndulo)* to swing (**b**) *(volquete)* to tilt (**c**) *Esp (variar)* to swing, to oscillate; **bascula entre la alegría y la tristeza** her moods swing *o* oscillate between happiness and sadness

BASE 1 *nf* (**a**) *(parte inferior)* base; *(de edificio)* foundations; **colocaron un ramo de flores en la b. del monumento** they placed a bunch of flowers at the foot of the monument ▸▸ ***b. de maquillaje*** foundation (cream)
(**b**) *(fundamento, origen)* basis; **el respeto al medio ambiente es la b. de un desarrollo equilibrado** respect for the environment is *o* forms the basis of balanced development; **el petróleo es la b. de su economía** their economy is based on oil; **salí de la universidad con una sólida b. humanística** I left university with a solid grounding in the humanities; **ese argumento se cae por su b.** that argument is built on sand; **esta teoría carece de b.** this theory is unfounded, this theory is not founded on solid arguments; **partimos de la b. de que...** we assume that...; **se parte de la b. de que todos ya saben leer** we're starting with the assumption that everyone can read; **sentar las bases para** to lay the foundations of; **sobre la b. de esta encuesta se concluye que...** on the basis of this opinion poll, it can be concluded that...
(**c**) *(conocimientos básicos)* grounding; **habla mal francés porque tiene mala b.** she doesn't speak French well because she hasn't learnt the basics properly
(**d**) **las bases** *(de partido, sindicato)* the grass roots, the rank and file; **afiliado de las bases** grassroots member
(**e**) *(militar, científica)* base ▸▸ ***b. aérea*** air base; ***b. espacial*** space station; ***b. de lanzamiento*** launch site; ***b. naval*** naval base; ***b. de operaciones*** operational base
(**f**) *Quím* base
(**g**) *Geom* base
(**h**) *Mat* base
(**i**) *Ling* base (form)
(**j**) *Informát* ***b. de datos*** database; ***b. de datos documental*** documentary database; ***b. de datos relacional*** relational database
(**k**) *Fin* ***b. imponible*** taxable income
(**l**) *Com* ***b. de clientes*** customer base
(**m**) **bases** *(para prueba, concurso)* rules
(**n**) *(en béisbol)* base; *Méx* **dar b. por bola a alguien** to walk sb
(**o**) EXPR *Esp Fam* **a b. de bien: nos humillaron a b. de bien** they really humiliated us; **lloraba a b. de bien** he was crying his eyes out; **los niños disfrutaron a b. de bien** the children had a great time
2 *nmf (en baloncesto)* guard
3 **a base de** *loc prep* by (means of); **me alimento a b. de verduras** I live on vegetables; **el flan está hecho a b. de huevos** crème caramel is made with eggs; **a b. de no hacer nada** by not doing anything; **a b. de trabajar duro fue ascendiendo puestos** she moved up through the company by working hard; **aprender a b. de equivocarse** to learn the hard way; *Fig* **se sacó la carrera a b. de codos** she got her degree by sheer hard work
4 **en base a** *loc prep (considerado incorrecto)* on the basis of; **en b. a lo visto hasta ahora, no creo que puedan ganar** from what I've seen so far, I don't think they can win; **el plan se efectuará en b. a lo convenido** the plan will be carried out in accordance with the terms agreed upon

baseball ['beisβol] *nm Am* baseball

BASIC, Basic ['beisik] *nm Informát* BASIC, Basic

básica *nf Antes Educ* = stage of Spanish education system for pupils aged 6-14

básicamente *adv* basically

basicidad *nf Quím* alkalinity

básico, -a *adj* (**a**) *(fundamental)* basic; **tiene conocimientos básicos de informática** she has some basic knowledge of computers; **el arroz es su alimentación básica** rice is their staple food; **lo b. de** the basics of (**b**) *Quím* basic, alkaline

Basilea *n* Basle, Basel

basílica *nf* basilica

basilisco *nm* (**a**) *Mitol* basilisk; EXPR *Fam* **hecho(a) un b.: ponerse hecho un b.** to go mad, to fly into a rage; **salió de la habitación hecho un b.** he came out of the room in a towering rage (**b**) *(lagarto)* basilisk

basket *nm* basketball ▸▸ ***b. average*** basket average

basketball ['basketbol] *nm Am* basketball

basquear *vi Méx Fam* to puke up

básquet *nm Am* basketball

básquetbol, basquetbol *nm Am* basketball

basquetbolero, -a *Am* 1 *adj* **ser muy b.** to be mad about basketball; **en el mundo b.** in the basketball world, in basketball circles
2 *nm,f (seguidor)* basketball fan *o* fanatic; *(jugador)* basketball player

basquetbolista *nmf Am* basketball player

basquiña *nf* (outer) skirt

basset ['baset] *nm* basset hound

basta 1 *nf Chile* hem
2 *interj* **¡b. (ya)!** that's enough!; **he dicho que no, ¡y b.!** I said no, and that's that!; **¡b. de chistes/tonterías!** that's enough jokes/of this nonsense!

bastante 1 *adj* (**a**) *(suficiente)* enough; **no tengo dinero b.** I haven't got enough money; **no es lo b. ancha para que entre el piano** it's not wide enough to get the piano through
(**b**) *(mucho)* **tengo b. frío** I'm quite *o* pretty cold; **tienen b. dinero** they're quite *o* pretty well off; **bastantes libros** quite a lot of books, a fair number of books; **tenemos b. tiempo** we have quite a lot of time
2 *adv* (**a**) *(suficientemente)* **es lo b. lista para...** she's smart enough to...; **ya has hablado b., ahora cállate** you've done enough talking, be quiet now
(**b**) *(considerablemente) (con adjetivos, adverbios)* quite; *(con verbos)* quite a lot; **es b. fácil** it's pretty *o* quite easy; **es una práctica b. común** it's quite a common practice, it's a pretty common practice; **b. mejor** quite a lot better; **me gustó b.** I enjoyed it quite a lot; **he cenado b.** I had a pretty big dinner; **desde que le operaron ha**

mejorado b. he's quite a lot better *o* he's improved quite a lot since he had the operation

(**c**) *(con frecuencia)* quite a lot; **voy b. por ahí** I go there quite a lot; **¿viajas mucho? – b.** do you do much travelling? – yes, quite a lot *o* a fair bit

3 *pron* **éramos bastantes** there were quite a few *o* a lot of us; **hay bastantes que piensan así** there are quite a few people who share the same opinion; **queda b.** there's quite a lot left

bastanteo *nm Der* = validation of a power of attorney

bastar 1 *vi* to be enough; **estos dos me bastan, con estos dos me basta** these two are enough for me, these two will do me; **con ocho basta** eight will be enough; **basta con que se lo digas** all you have to do is tell her; **un pavo de ese tamaño basta y sobra para seis personas** a turkey that size will be more than enough for six people; **basta con que se encuentre una pequeña dificultad para que se desanime** the minute he comes across the slightest problem, he loses heart; **basta que salga a la calle para que se ponga a llover** all I have to do is go out into the street for it to start raining

2 **bastarse** *vpr* **él solo se basta para terminar el trabajo** he'll be able to finish the work himself; **ella se basta sola para cuidar de toda la familia** she manages to look after the whole family by herself; **yo me basto y me sobro para hacer este trabajo** I'm more than capable of doing this job on my own

bastardear *vt* to bastardize

bastardía *nf* bastardy

bastardilla 1 *adj* **letra b.** italics

2 *nf* italics; **en b.** in italics

bastardo, -a 1 *adj* (**a**) *(hijo)* bastard (**b**) *Bot* bastard, hybrid

2 *nm,f* (**a**) *(hijo)* bastard (**b**) *muy Fam* bastard, swine

bastedad, basteza *nf* coarseness

bastidor *nm* (**a**) *(armazón)* frame (**b**) *(para bordar)* embroidery frame (**c**) *Esp Aut* chassis (**d**) *Teatro* **bastidores** wings; **entre bastidores** *(en el teatro)* offstage; *(en privado)* behind the scenes (**e**) *Chile (de ventana)* lattice window

bastilla *nf* (**a**) *(dobladillo)* hem; **se me ha descosido la b.** my hem is coming down (**b**) *Hist* **la B.** the Bastille; **la toma de la B.** the storming of the Bastille

bastión *nm también Fig* bastion

basto, -a 1 *adj* (**a**) *(grosero, vulgar)* coarse (**b**) *(tejido)* rough, coarse (**c**) *(madera)* unfinished, unpolished

2 *nm* (**a**) *(naipe)* = any card in the "bastos" suit (**b**) **bastos** *(palo)* = suit in Spanish deck of cards, with the symbol of a wooden club

bastón *nm* (**a**) *(para andar)* walking stick; **usar b.** to walk with a stick (**b**) *(de mando)* baton; EXPR **empuñar el b.** to take the helm ►► ***b. de mando*** ceremonial mace (**c**) *(para esquiar)* ski stick (**d**) *Anat (de la retina)* rod

bastonazo *nm* blow (with a stick); **me dio un b. en la cabeza** he hit me on the head with a stick

bastoncillo *nm* (**a**) *(para los oídos) Br* cotton bud, *US* Q-tip® (**b**) *Anat (de la retina)* rod

bastonear *vt* to beat with a stick

bastonera *nf* umbrella stand

bastonero *nm* (**a**) *(fabricante)* cane maker (**b**) *(vendedor)* cane seller (**c**) *(en baile)* caller

basura 1 *adj inv* **comida b.** junk food; **contrato b.** short-term contract *(with poor conditions)*

2 *nf* (**a**) *(desechos) Br* rubbish, *US* garbage, trash; *(en la calle)* litter; **no te olvides de sacar la b.** don't forget *Br* to put the rubbish out *o US* to take out the garbage; **el parque estaba lleno de b.** the park was full of litter ►► ***b. espacial*** space junk; ***b. orgánica*** organic waste; ***b. radiactiva*** radioactive waste

(**b**) *(recipiente) Br* rubbish bin, dustbin, *US* garbage *o* trash can; **tirar algo a la b.** to throw sth away

(**c**) *(bazofia) Br* rubbish, *US* garbage, trash; **este artículo es una b.** this article is *Br* a load of rubbish *o US* trash

(**d**) *(persona)* scum, filth

basural *nm CSur Br* rubbish dump, *US* garbage dump

basurear *vt Perú, RP Fam (despreciar, tratar mal)* to treat like dirt; **no me gusta que me basureen** I don't like being treated like dirt

basurero, -a 1 *nm,f (persona) Br* dustman, refuse collector, *US* garbage man, garbage collector

2 *nm* (**a**) *(vertedero) Br* rubbish dump, *US* garbage dump (**b**) *RP, Ven (contenedor) Br* dustbin, *US* garbage *o* trash can

bat *nm Méx Dep* bat; **al b.** at bat

bata *nf* (**a**) *(de casa)* housecoat; *(al levantarse)* dressing gown ►► *Am* ***b. de baño*** bathrobe; *Am* ***b. de playa*** beach robe

(**b**) *(de alumno, trabajo, profesor)* overall; *(de médico)* white coat; *(de laboratorio)* lab coat

(**c**) *RP Fam* **batas** *(ropa)* gear; **Juan gasta mucho en batas** Juan spends a lot on his gear *o* clothes

(**d**) EXPR *RP Fam* **volar la b.: Luisa sale de viaje mañana, está que le vuela la b.** Luisa's going off tomorrow, so she hasn't got the time or inclination to think about anything else; **su último disco me vuela la b.** I think her latest album is wicked; **a Juana le vuela la b.** Juana's off her head, Juana doesn't know what she's doing

batacazo *nm* (**a**) *(golpe)* bump, bang; **darse un b.** to bump *o* bang oneself (**b**) *(fracaso)* **los resultados representan un nuevo b. para el partido** the results are another blow for the party; **se dieron** *o* **pegaron un b. con su último disco** their last album was a flop (**c**) *CSur Fam (triunfo inesperado)* surprise victory; **dar un b.** to pull off a surprise victory

bataclana *nf RP* cabaret artist(e)

batahola, bataola *nf esp Am Fam* row, rumpus; **se armó una b.** there was a row *o* rumpus

batalla 1 *nf* (**a**) *(con armas)* battle; **una b. de bolas de nieve** a snowball fight; **presentar b.** to give battle ►► *también Fig* ***b. campal*** pitched battle; ***b. naval*** naval *o* sea battle

(**b**) *(por una cosa)* battle; **la b. contra el crimen/la inflación** the battle *o* fight against crime/inflation; **una b. legal** a legal battle; EXPR **presentar b.** to put up a fight; EXPR **presentar b. a algo/alguien** to tackle sth/sb, to take sth/sb on

(**c**) *(esfuerzo)* struggle; **aceptar su muerte le supuso una dura b.** it was a real struggle for her to come to terms with his death

(**d**) *Aut* wheelbase

2 **de batalla** *loc adj (de uso diario)* everyday

batallador, -ora *adj* **es muy b.** he's a real fighter

batallar *vi* (**a**) *(con armas)* to fight (**b**) *(por una cosa)* to battle; **batalló duramente para conseguir que la aceptaran** she battled *o* struggled hard to gain acceptance; **ya estoy harto de b. contra este sistema operativo** I'm fed up of battling with this operating system

batallita *nf Fam* **el abuelo siempre está contando batallitas** granddad's always going on about the old times

batallón *nm* (**a**) *Mil* battalion (**b**) *Fam (grupo numeroso)* flock; **un b. de periodistas la esperaba a la salida** a flock of journalists was waiting for her at the exit

batán *nm (máquina)* fulling mill

bataola = **batahola**

batasuno, -a, batasunero, -a *Fam Antes Pol* 1 *adj* = of/related to the militant Basque nationalist party Herri Batasuna

2 *nm,f* = member of Herri Batasuna

batata *nf Esp, Arg, Col, Ven* sweet potato

batazo *nm Dep* hit ►► ***b. de base*** base hit

bate *nm Dep* bat ►► ***b. de béisbol*** baseball bat

batea *nf* (**a**) *(embarcación)* flat-bottomed boat (**b**) ***b. mejillonera*** = raft for farming mussels (**c**) *Am (artesa)* trough *(for washing clothes)*; EXPR *Ven* **ni lava ni presta la b.** he's a dog in the manger

bateador, -ora *nm,f Dep (en béisbol)* batter; *(en críquet)* batsman, *f* batswoman

batear *Dep* 1 *vt* to hit

2 *vi* to bat

batel *nm* small boat

batelero, -a *nm,f* boatman, *f* boatwoman

batería 1 *nf* (**a**) *(de coche)* battery

(**b**) *Elec & Informát* battery ►► ***b. solar*** solar cell

(**c**) *Mil* battery

(**d**) *Mús* drums; **tocar la b.** to play the drums

(**e**) *Teatro* footlights

(**f**) *(conjunto)* set; *(de preguntas)* barrage ►► ***b. de cocina*** cookware set; ***b. de pruebas*** battery of tests

(**g**) **aparcar en b.** to park at an angle to the *Br* pavement *o US* sidewalk

2 *nmf* drummer

baterista *nmf Am* drummer

batial *adj* bathyal

batiburrillo, batiborrillo *nm Fam* **este estudio es un b. de diferentes teorías** this study is a mishmash of different theories; **tengo un b. de ideas en la cabeza** my head is a jumble of ideas; **se ocupa de un b. de actividades diversas** she deals with all sorts of different activities

baticabeza *nm* click beetle

baticola *nf (correa)* crupper

batida *nf* (**a**) *(de caza)* beat; **hacer una b. (en la zona)** to beat the area (**b**) *(de policía)* search; **la policía hizo una b. en la zona para encontrar a los terroristas** the police combed the area in search of the terrorists

batido, -a 1 *adj* (**a**) *(nata)* whipped; *(claras)* whisked (**b**) *(senda, camino)* well-trodden (**c**) *(seda)* shot (**d**) **tierra batida** *(en tenis)* clay
 2 *nm* (**a**) *(acción de batir)* beating (**b**) *(bebida)* milk shake; **b. de chocolate/fresa** chocolate/strawberry milk shake

batidor, -ora 1 *nm* (**a**) *(aparato manual)* whisk (**b**) *(eléctrico)* mixer (**c**) *(en caza)* beater (**d**) *Mil* scout
 2 *nm,f RP Fam (denunciante) Br* grass, *US* rat

batidora *nf (de brazo, vaso)* blender; *(con aspas, para amasar)* mixer

batiente 1 *adj* **reír a mandíbula b.** to laugh one's head off, to laugh oneself silly
 2 *nm* (**a**) *(de puerta)* jamb; *(de ventana)* frame (**b**) *(costa)* shoreline (**c**) *Mús* damper

batifondo *nm RP Fam* racket, uproar; **no armen mucho b.** don't make too much of a racket; **el b. actual sobre Internet** the current hoo-ha about the Internet

batik *nm* batik

batín *nm* dressing gown, robe

batintín *nm* gong

batir 1 *vt* (**a**) *(mezclar) (huevos, mezcla líquida)* to beat, to whisk; *(nata)* to whip; *(mantequilla)* to cream
 (**b**) *(golpear)* to beat against; **las olas batían las rocas** the waves beat against the rocks; **el viento batía las ventanas** the windows were banging in the wind; **b. palmas** to clap
 (**c**) *(alas)* to flap, to beat
 (**d**) *(metal)* to beat
 (**e**) *(moneda)* to mint
 (**f**) *(derrotar)* to beat; **b. al portero** *(superarlo)* to beat the goalkeeper
 (**g**) *(récord)* to break
 (**h**) *(explorar) (sujeto: policía)* to comb, to search
 (**i**) *(explorar) (sujeto: cazador)* to beat
 (**j**) *RP Fam (denunciar)* to report, to turn in
 (**k**) *RP Fam* **b. la justa: preguntale a Santi que te bate la justa** ask Santi, he can give you the goods; **te lo digo yo que acabo de volver, te bato la justa** I've just come back from there, so I know what I'm talking about
 2 *vi (sol, lluvia)* to beat down
 3 batirse *vpr* (**a**) *(luchar)* to fight; **batirse en duelo** to fight a duel (**b**) *(puerta)* to slam shut
 (**c**) EXPR *Fam* **batirse el cobre** to break one's back, to bust a gut; **batirse en retirada** to beat a retreat; *RP Fam* **batirse el parche** to blow one's own trumpet

batiscafo *nm* bathyscaphe

batisfera *nf* bathysphere

batista *nf* batiste, cambric

batita *nf RP* baby jacket

bato *nm Méx Fam* guy

batón *nm RP* dressing gown

batracio *Zool* **1** *nm (animal)* batrachian
 2 batracios *nmpl (clase) Batrachia*; **de la clase de los batracios** of the *Batrachia* class

Batuecas *nfpl* EXPR *Fam* **estar en las B.** to have one's head in the clouds

batuque *nm RP Fam* = noisy street party with drum music

baturro, -a 1 *adj* Aragonese
 2 *nm,f* (**a**) *(del campo)* Aragonese peasant (**b**) *(de Aragón)* person from Aragon *(Spain)*

batuta *nf* baton; **la Orquesta Filarmónica, bajo la b. de Karajan** the Philharmonic Orchestra, conducted by Karajan; EXPR **llevar la b.** to call the tune *o* shots

baudio *nm Informát* baud

baúl *nm* (**a**) *(cofre)* trunk (**b**) *Arg, Col (maletero) Br* boot, *US* trunk

baulera *nf Arg Br* boxroom, *US* trunk room

bauprés *(pl* **baupreses**) *nm Náut* bowsprit

bautismal *adj* baptismal

bautismo *nm* (**a**) *(sacramento)* baptism ►► *Fig* ***b. de fuego*** baptism of fire (**b**) *RP (ceremonia)* baptism, christening (**c**) *RP (fiesta)* christening party

Bautista *nm* **el B.** St John the Baptist

bautisterio = **baptisterio**

bautizar [14] *vt* (**a**) *(administrar sacramento a)* to baptize, to christen (**b**) *(denominar)* to christen; **bautizaron al gato con el nombre de "Sam"** they christened the cat "Sam"; **bautizaron el yate "la Intrépida"** they named the yacht "la Intrépida"
 (**c**) *(poner mote a)* to nickname; **en el colegio bautizan con mote a todos los profesores** they give all the teachers at school nicknames
 (**d**) *Fam (aguar)* to dilute

bautizo *nm* (**a**) *(ceremonia)* baptism, christening (**b**) *(fiesta)* christening party (**c**) *(de barco)* naming

bauxita *nf Geol* bauxite

bávaro, -a 1 *adj* Bavarian
 2 *nm,f* Bavarian

Baviera *n* Bavaria

baya *nf* berry

bayeta *nf* (**a**) *(tejido)* flannel (**b**) *(para limpiar)* cloth; **b. de gamuza** chamois

bayo, -a 1 *adj* bay
 2 *nm* bay (horse)

bayón *nm* = type of sandalwood

bayonesa *nf (bollo)* = pastry filled with strands of crystallized pumpkin

bayoneta *nf* (**a**) *(arma)* bayonet (**b**) **bombilla de b.** light bulb with bayonet fitting

bayonetazo *nm* (**a**) *(golpe)* bayonet thrust (**b**) *(herida)* bayonet wound

baza *nf* (**a**) *(en naipes)* trick; **hacer una b.** to make a trick; EXPR **jugar una b.: jugó bien sus bazas** she played her cards right; **están jugando su última b.** they're playing their last card; EXPR *Fam* **meter b.: no pude meter b. (en la conversación)** I couldn't get a word in edgeways; **siempre trata de meter b. (en la conversación)** she's always trying to butt in; **intentan meter b. en la gestión de la empresa** they are trying to elbow in on the management of the company
 (**b**) *(ventaja)* advantage; **la gran b. del producto es su reducido precio** the product's great advantage is its low price; **presentaron como b. electoral la educación** they played the education card in the election; **el delantero ruso es la gran b. del equipo** the Russian forward is the team's main weapon

bazar *nm* (**a**) *(tienda)* bazaar, = shop selling electrical goods, trinkets etc (**b**) *(mercado)* bazaar

bazo *nm* spleen

bazofia *nf* (**a**) *(comida)* pigswill (**b**) *(libro, película)* **ser (una) b.** to be *Br* rubbish *o US* garbage

bazuca, bazooka *nm* bazooka

BBS *nf Informát* (*abrev de* **Bulletin Board Service**) BBS

BCE *nm* (*abrev de* **Banco Central Europeo**) ECB

BCN (*abrev de* **Barcelona**) = Barcelona

be *nf* (**a**) *Esp (letra)* = name of the letter "b"; EXPR **be por be** down to the last detail; EXPR **tener las tres bes** to be the perfect buy (**b**) *Am* **be alta** *o* **grande** *o* **larga** b *(to distinguish from "v")*

bearnesa 1 *adj* béarnaise
 2 *nf* béarnaise sauce

beat [bit] *nm* (**a**) *(música)* beat (music) (**b**) *(unidad)* beat

beatería *nf* (**a**) *(piedad)* devoutness (**b**) *(santurronería)* sanctimoniousness

beatificación *nf* beatification

beatificar [60] *vt* to beatify

beatífico, -a *adj* beatific

beatísimo *adj* **el B. Padre** the Most Holy Father

beatitud *nf* beatitude

beatnik ['bitnik] *nm* beatnik

beato, -a 1 *adj* (**a**) *(beatificado)* blessed (**b**) *(piadoso)* devout (**c**) *(santurrón)* sanctimonious
 2 *nm,f* (**a**) *(beatificado)* beatified person (**b**) *(piadoso)* devout person (**c**) *(santurrón)* sanctimonious person

bebe, -a *nm,f Andes, RP* baby

bebé *nm* baby ►► ***b. probeta,*** *Am* ***b. de probeta*** test-tube baby

bebedero *nm* (**a**) *(de jaula)* water dish (**b**) *(abrevadero)* drinking trough (**c**) *Guat, Perú (bar)* refreshment stand (**d**) *Méx, RP (fuente)* drinking fountain

bebedizo *nm* (**a**) *(brebaje)* potion; *(de amor)* love potion (**b**) *(veneno)* poison

bebedor, -ora *nm,f (borrachín)* heavy drinker; **ser un gran b.** to drink a lot; **es un b. empedernido** he's a hardened drinker

beber 1 *vt* (a) *(líquido)* to drink; **¿qué quieres b.?** what would you like to drink?
(b) *(absorber) (palabras, consejos)* to lap up; *(sabiduría, información)* to draw, to acquire; EXPR **b. los vientos por alguien** to be head over heels in love with sb
2 *vi* (a) *(tomar líquido)* to drink; **b. de una fuente** to drink from a fountain; *Fam* **b. a morro** to swig straight from the bottle; **dar de b. a alguien** to give sb something to drink; **me dio de b. un poco de agua** she gave me a little water to drink
(b) *(tomar alcohol)* to drink; **no sabe b.** he doesn't know his limit where alcohol's concerned; **bebí más de la cuenta** I had one too many; **si bebes, no conduzcas** don't drink and drive
(c) *(brindar)* **b. a la salud de alguien** to drink to sb's health; **b. por algo** to drink to sth
3 *nm* drinking; **cuida mucho el b.** he's very careful how much he drinks
4 **beberse** *vpr* to drink; **bébetelo todo** drink it all up; **se bebió casi un litro de agua** he drank almost a litre of water

bebercio *nm Esp Fam Hum* **nosotros nos encargamos del b.** we'll take care of the liquid refreshment; **tu amigo le da mucho al b.** your friend's very fond of the bottle

bebestible *nm RP Fam* **ellos llevan los comestibles y nosotros los bebestibles** they're bringing the eats and we're bringing the drinks

bebible *adj* drinkable

bebida *nf* (a) *(líquido)* drink ►► ***b. sin alcohol*** *(fría o caliente)* non-alcoholic drink; *(refresco)* soft drink; ***b. alcohólica*** alcoholic drink; ***b. carbónica*** carbonated drink; ***b. isotónica*** isotonic drink; ***b. refrescante*** soft drink (b) *(acción)* drinking; **darse** *o* **entregarse a la b.** to take to drink *o* the bottle; **el problema de la b.** the problem of alcoholism *o* drinking

bebido, -a *adj* drunk

bebistrajo *nm Fam Pey* concoction, brew

beca *nf (del gobierno)* grant; *(de organización privada)* scholarship ►► *UE* ***b. Erasmus*** Erasmus scholarship; ***b. de investigación*** research scholarship

becabunga *nf* brooklime

becada *nf* woodcock

becado, -a 1 *adj* **alumno b.** *(por el gobierno)* grant holder; *(por organización privada)* scholarship holder
2 *nm,f esp Am (del gobierno)* grant holder; *(de organización privada)* scholarship holder

becar [60] *vt (sujeto: gobierno)* to give *o* award a grant to; *(sujeto: organización privada)* to award a scholarship to

becario, -a *nm,f (del gobierno)* grant holder; *(de organización privada)* scholarship holder

becerrada *nf* = bullfight with young bulls

becerrillo *nm* calfskin

becerro, -a 1 *nm,f (animal)* calf ►► ***el b. de oro*** the golden calf
2 *nm (piel)* calfskin

bechamel *nf* béchamel *o* white sauce

becuadro *nm Mús* natural sign

bedao *nm* zebra sea bream

bedel, -ela *nm,f* janitor

beduino, -a 1 *adj* Bedouin
2 *nm,f* Bedouin

beee *interj (balido)* baa

befa *nf* jeer; **hacer b. de** to make fun of

befar 1 *vt* to make fun of
2 **befarse** *vpr* **befarse de** to make fun of

befo, -a 1 *adj (de labios gruesos)* thick-lipped; **labios befos** thick lips
2 *nm* thick lower lip

begonia *nf* begonia

BEI ['bei] *nm UE (abrev de* **Banco Europeo de Inversiones)** EIB

beicon *nm Esp* bacon

beige [beis] *(pl* **beiges)** 1 *adj* beige
2 *nm* beige

Beijing [bei'jin] *n* Beijing

Beirut *n* Beirut

beis *Esp* 1 *adj inv* beige
2 *nm inv* beige

béisbol, *Cuba, Méx* **beisbol** *nm* baseball

beisbolero, -a 1 *adj* baseball; **liga beisbolera** baseball league
2 *nm,f* baseball player

beisbolista *nmf* baseball player

beisbolístico, -a *adj* baseball; **un encuentro b.** a baseball game

bejel *nm* red gurnard

bejuco *nm* (a) *(en América)* liana (b) *(en Asia)* rattan

bel 1 *nm Fís* bel
2 *adj Mús* **el b. canto** bel canto

Belcebú *n pr* Beelzebub; *Anticuado* **¡por B.!** gadzooks!

beldad *nf Literario* (a) *(belleza)* fairness, beauty (b) *(mujer bella)* beauty

belemnita *nf,* **belemnites** *nm inv Geol* belemnite

Belén *n* Bethlehem

belén *nm* (a) *(de Navidad)* crib, Nativity scene (b) *Fam (desorden)* bedlam (c) *Fam (embrollo)* mess; **meterse en belenes** to get mixed up in trouble

beleño *nm* henbane

belesa *nf* common plumbago, leadwort

belfo *nm* lip *(of horse)*

belga 1 *adj* Belgian
2 *nmf* Belgian

Bélgica *n* Belgium

Belgrado *n* Belgrade

Belice *n* Belize

beliceño, -a 1 *adj* Belizean
2 *nm,f* Belizean

belicismo *nm* warmongering

belicista 1 *adj* belligerent
2 *nmf* warmonger

bélico, -a *adj* **conflicto b.** military conflict; **esfuerzo b.** war effort; **espiral bélica** spiral towards war

belicosamente *adv* aggressively

belicosidad *nf* aggressiveness

belicoso, -a *adj* (a) *(guerrero)* bellicose, war-like (b) *(agresivo)* aggressive

beligerancia *nf* belligerence; **con b.** belligerently

beligerante 1 *adj* belligerent
2 *nmf* belligerent

belinún, -una *RP Fam* 1 *adj* dopey
2 *nm,f* dope

belio *nm Fís* bel

bellaco, -a 1 *adj* (a) *Literario (bribón)* villainous, wicked (b) *RP (caballo)* spirited, hard to control (c) *Ecuad, Pan (valiente)* brave
2 *nm,f Literario* villain, scoundrel

belladona *nf* belladonna, deadly nightshade

bellaquería *nf Literario* (a) *(cualidad)* wickedness, villainy (b) *(acto)* **hacerte eso fue una b.** that was a dastardly thing for him to do to you

belle époque [bele'pok] *nf* belle époque

belleza *nf* (a) *(cualidades)* beauty; **productos de b.** beauty products (b) *(objeto, animal)* **es una b. de edificio/caballo** it's a beautiful building/horse (c) *(persona)* beauty; **llegó acompañado de varias bellezas** he arrived in the company of several beautiful women

bello, -a *adj* beautiful ►► ***bellas artes*** fine arts; ***el b. sexo*** the fair sex

bellota *nf* (a) *(de árbol)* acorn (b) ***b. de mar*** acorn barnacle

beluga *nf* beluga, white whale

bemba *nf Andes, Carib Fam* thick lips

bembo, -a *nm,f Méx (tonto)* fool, idiot

bembón, -ona *adj Andes, Carib Fam* thick-lipped

bemol *Mús* 1 *adj* flat
2 *nm (nota)* flat; *(signo)* flat (sign); **doble b.** double flat; EXPR *Fam* **tener (muchos) bemoles** *(ser difícil)* to be tricky; *(tener valor)* to have guts; **tiene bemoles que ahora él se adjudique el mérito** it's a bit rich him claiming the credit

benceno *nm Quím* benzene

bencina *nf* (a) *Quím* benzine (b) *Chile (gasolina) Br* petrol, *US* gas

bencinera *nf Chile Br* petrol station, *US* gas station

bencinero, -a *Chile* 1 *adj* **la producción bencinera** oil production; **un motor bencinero** a *Br* petrol *o US* gasoline engine
2 *nm,f Br* (petrol) pump attendant, *US* gas station attendant

bendecir [51] *vt* (a) *(agua, fieles, edificio)* to bless; **b. la mesa** to say grace; **que Dios te bendiga** God bless you (b) *(agradecer)* **bendigo el día en que la conocí** I bless the day I met her

bendición *nf* (a) *(religiosa)* blessing; EXPR **ser una b. (de Dios)** to be wonderful; **canta que es una b.** she sings divinely ►► ***b. urbi et orbe*** urbi et orbe blessing (b) **bendiciones (nupciales)** *(boda)* wedding (c) *(consentimiento)* blessing; **lo hicieron sin la b. de sus padres** they did it without their parents' blessing

bendigo *etc ver* **bendecir**

bendijera *etc ver* **bendecir**

bendito, -a 1 *adj* (a) *(santo)* holy; *(alma)* blessed; EXPR *Fam* **¡b. sea Dios!** *(expresando gratitud)* thank God *o* the Lord!; *(expresando preocupación)* good Lord o heavens!
(b) *(dichoso)* lucky; **¡bendita la hora en que llegaste!** thank heavens you arrived!
(c) *(para enfatizar)* blessed; **ya está otra vez con esa bendita historia** there she goes again with the same blessed story!; **ya llegó el b. autobús** the blessed bus has finally arrived
2 *nm,f* simple soul; EXPR **dormir como un b.** to sleep like a baby

benedictino, -a *Rel* 1 *adj* Benedictine
2 *nm,f* Benedictine

benefactor, -ora 1 *adj* beneficent
2 *nm,f* benefactor, *f* benefactress

benéficamente *adv (caritativamente)* charitably

beneficencia *nf* (a) *(ayuda)* charity; **casa de b.** poorhouse (b) *(institución)* charity

beneficiar 1 *vt* (a) *(favorecer)* to benefit; **con esta medida todos nos veremos beneficiados** that measure will benefit all of us; **yo fui el que salió más beneficiado** I was the one who benefited the most; **ese comportamiento no te beneficia** behaving like that won't do you any good
(b) *Esp Fam* **beneficiarse a alguien** to have sb, *Br* to have it away with sb
(c) *Min (extraer)* to extract
(d) *Carib, Chile (res)* to butcher
2 **beneficiarse** *vpr* to benefit; **beneficiarse de** *o* **con algo** to benefit from sth; **20 presos políticos se beneficiaron de la amnistía** 20 political prisoners benefited from the amnesty; **el dólar se benefició de la debilidad del euro** the dollar benefited *o* profited from the weakness of the euro; **muchos ciudadanos se beneficiarán con el cambio** many citizens will benefit *o* profit from the change

beneficiario, -a *nm,f* (a) *(de seguro)* beneficiary (b) *(de cheque)* payee

beneficio *nm* (a) *(bien)* benefit; **a b. de** *(gala, concierto)* in aid of; **en b. de** for the good of; **ello redundó en b. nuestro** it was to our advantage; **en b. de todos** in everyone's interest; **en b. propio** for one's own good; **sólo buscan el b. propio** they're only interested in what's in it for them
(b) *(ganancia)* profit; **la tienda ya está dando beneficios** the shop is already making a profit ►► ***b. bruto*** gross profit; ***beneficios antes de impuestos*** pre-tax profits; ***b. neto*** net profit
(c) *Min (extracción)* extraction
(d) *Carib, Chile (de res)* slaughter

beneficioso, -a *adj* beneficial (**para** to)

benéfico, -a *adj* (a) *(favorable)* beneficial (**para** to) (b) *(de caridad)* charity; **una entidad benéfica** a charity, a charitable organization; **un concierto b.** a charity *o* benefit concert; **un partido b.** a charity *o* benefit match

Benelux *nm* **el B.** Benelux

Benemérita *nf Esp* **la B.** = name given to the "Guardia Civil"

benemérito, -a *adj (causa, institución)* worthy; *(persona)* distinguished ►► *Am* ***b. de la patria*** = title bestowed on men and women deemed to have done great services for their country

beneplácito *nm* consent; **dio su b.** she gave her consent; **cuentan con el b. de las autoridades** they have the authorities' consent

benévolamente *adv* benevolently, kindly

benevolencia *nf* benevolence, kindness; **lo trataron con b.** they treated him kindly

benevolente, benévolo, -a *adj (persona)* benevolent, kind; **se mostró b. con la propuesta** he looked kindly on the proposal; **su actitud b. con sus empleados** her indulgent attitude towards her employees

Bengala *n* Bengal

bengala *nf* (a) *(de señalización)* flare (b) *(de fiesta)* sparkler

bengalí (*pl* **bengalíes** *o* **bengalís**) 1 *adj* Bengali
2 *nmf* Bengali

benignidad *nf* (a) *(de persona, carácter)* benign nature (b) *(de enfermedad, tumor)* benign nature (c) *(de clima, temperatura)* mildness

benigno, -a *adj* (a) *(enfermedad, tumor)* benign (b) *(clima, temperatura)* mild (c) *(persona, carácter)* benevolent, kind

benimerín *nm Hist* = member of the Berber dynasty which ruled in North Africa and Muslim Spain in the 13th and 14th centuries

Benín *n* Benin

beninés, -esa 1 *adj* Beninese
2 *nm,f* Beninese; **los benineses** the Beninese

benjamín, -ina *nm,f* (a) *(hijo menor)* youngest child (b) *Dep* **benjamines** ≃ colts *(aged 8–9)*

benjuí (*pl* **benjuís** *o* **benjuíes**) *nm (resina)* benzoin, benjamin

benteveo *nm* great kiskadee

béntico, -a, bentónico, -a *adj Biol* benthic, benthonic

bentonita *nf* bentonite

benzoato *nm Quím* benzoate

benzoico, -a *adj Quím* benzoic

benzol *nm Quím* benzol

beodez *nf Formal* inebriation, drunkenness

beodo, -a 1 *adj* drunk, inebriated
2 *nm,f* drunkard

beque *etc ver* **becar**

berberecho *nm* cockle

Berbería *n Anticuado* Barbary

berberisco, -a 1 *adj* Berber
2 *nm,f* Berber

berbiquí (*pl* **berbiquíes** *o* **berbiquís**) *nm* brace and bit

berceo *nm* (giant) feather grass

BERD *nm (abrev de* **Banco Europeo de Reconstrucción y Desarrollo**) EBRD

bereber, beréber, berebere 1 *adj* Berber
2 *nmf (persona)* Berber
3 *nm (lengua)* Berber

berenjena *nf Br* aubergine, *US* eggplant

berenjenal *nm Fam (enredo)* mess; **meterse en un b.** to get oneself into a right mess; **no sé cómo vamos a salir de este b.** I don't know how we're going to get out of this mess *o* one

bergamota *nf* bergamot

bergante *nm* scoundrel, rascal

bergantín *nm* brigantine

beriberi *nm Med* beriberi

berilio *nm Quím* beryllium

berilo *nm Geol* beryl

Bering *n* **el mar de B.** the Bering Sea; **el estrecho de B.** the Bering Strait

berkelio, berquelio *nm Quím* berkelium

Berlín *n* Berlin; *Antes* **B. Este** East Berlin; *Antes* **B. Occidental** West Berlin; *Antes* **B. Oriental** East Berlin

berlina *nf* (a) *(automóvil)* four-door saloon (b) *(coche de caballos)* berlin

berlinés, -esa 1 *adj* of/from Berlin; **las calles berlinesas** the Berlin streets, the streets of Berlin
2 *nm,f* Berliner

berma *nf* (a) *Andes (arcén) Br* hard shoulder, *US* shoulder (b) *Perú (isleta central)* traffic island

bermejo, -a *adj* reddish

bermejuela *nf* roach

bermellón 1 *adj inv* vermilion
2 *nm* (a) *(sustancia)* vermilion (b) *(color)* vermilion

bermuda *nf (planta)* Bermuda grass

Bermudas *nfpl* **las B.** Bermuda

bermudas *nfpl o nmpl* Bermuda shorts

Berna *n* Berne

bernia *nmf Hond (haragán)* loafer, idler

berquelio = **berkelio**

berrea *nf* rut

berrear *vi* (a) *(animal)* to bellow (b) *(niño)* to howl (c) *Fam (cantar mal)* to screech, to howl

berreo *nm* (**a**) *(de animal)* bellow; **los berreos de la vaca** the cow's bellowing (**b**) *(de niño)* howl; **los berreos del niño** the child's howling *o* howls

berrera *nf* narrowleaf cattail

berreta *adj inv RP Fam* cheapo, crappy

berretada *nf RP Fam* **sólo venden berretadas** they only sell tat *o* cheap rubbish

berretín *nm RP Fam* **son gente llena de berretines** they're full of fads and fancies; **tiene el b. de que su familia era noble** she's got this big thing about how he comes from a noble family

berrido *nm* (**a**) *(de animal)* **dar berridos/un b.** to bellow (**b**) *(de niño)* howl; **oímos el b. de un niño** we heard a child's cry; **dar berridos** to howl (**c**) *Fam* **dar berridos** *(cantar mal)* to screech

berrinche *nm Fam* tantrum; *Esp* **coger** *o Am* **hacer un b.** to throw a tantrum

berro *nm* watercress; **una ensalada de berros** a watercress salad

berrocal *nm* rocky place

berrueco *nm (roca)* granite rock

berruenda *nf* ling

bertorella *nf* shore rockling

berza *nf* cabbage; EXPR *Esp Fam* **estar con la b.: hoy está con la b.** *(atontado)* he's not with it today

berzal *nm* cabbage patch

berzas, berzotas *nmf inv Esp Fam* thickhead

besamanos *nm inv* (**a**) *(recepción)* = audience in which people pay their respects to a monarch or other dignitary (**b**) *(saludo)* **saludar a alguien con un b.** to kiss sb's hand in greeting

besamel *nf* béchamel *o* white sauce

besar 1 *vt* (**a**) *(con los labios)* to kiss; **le besó la mano** he kissed her hand; **lo besó en la cara** she kissed his face (**b**) *Literario (acariciar)* to caress; **la brisa les besaba el rostro** the breeze caressed their faces

2 **besarse** *vpr* to kiss; **se besaron en la boca** they kissed each other on the lips

Besarabia *n* Bessarabia

beso *nm* kiss; **dar un b. a alguien** to give sb a kiss, to kiss sb; **le dio un b. en los labios** he kissed her on the lips; **un b., muchos besos** *(en carta)* love; **Marisa te manda besos** Marisa sends her love; **tirar un b. a alguien** to blow sb a kiss; EXPR **comerse a besos a alguien** to smother sb with kisses ►► ***b. francés*** French kiss; ***b. de Judas*** Judas' kiss; ***b. con lengua*** French kiss; *Esp Fam* ***b. de tornillo*** French kiss

bestia 1 *adj Fam* (**a**) *(bruto)* **es tan b. que quería meter el piano por la ventana** he's such an oaf, he wanted to try and get the piano in through the window; **un chiste muy b.** a really gross joke

(**b**) *(violento)* **es muy b. con su mujer** he's a real brute to his wife; **¡qué tipo más b.!** what a brute *o* thug!

(**c**) *(ignorante)* thick; **¡qué b., no sabe quién descubrió América!** he's so thick he doesn't even know who discovered America!

(**d**) *(extraordinario)* amazing; **¡qué b., regateó a seis jugadores él solito!** wow *o* that's amazing, he beat six players all by himself!

(**e**) **a lo b.: conduce siempre a lo b.** he always drives like a maniac; **comer a lo b.** to stuff one's face; **cerró la puerta a lo b.** he slammed the door shut; **si metes el clavo a lo b. se va a doblar** if you just bash the nail in like that it'll get bent; **trata a su mujer a lo b.** he treats his wife like dirt

2 *nmf Fam* (**a**) *(bruto)* oaf; **yo no le dejo mi coche al b. de tu hermano** I'm not going to let your oaf of a brother have my car

(**b**) *(ignorante)* brute

(**c**) *(violento)* brute

3 *nf (animal)* beast; *Fam* **ese tipo es una mala b.** that guy's a really nasty piece of work ►► ***b. de carga*** beast of burden; *Fig* ***b. negra*** bête noire

bestiada *nf Esp Fam* (**a**) *(barbaridad)* **lo que dijo/hizo fue una b.** what he said/did was just outrageous; **me pareció una b. que nos pidieran tanto dinero** I thought it was way out of order for them to ask us for so much money (**b**) **una b. de** *(muchos)* tons *o* stacks of

bestial *adj* (**a**) *(brutal)* animal, brutal (**b**) *Fam (enorme)* **tengo un cansancio/un apetito b.** I'm dead tired/hungry; **tengo unas ganas bestiales de ir** I'm absolutely dying to go (**c**) *Fam (estupendo)* terrific; **su último disco es b.** her latest album is terrific

bestialidad *nf* (**a**) *(brutalidad)* brutality (**b**) *Fam (barbaridad)* **lo que dijo/hizo fue una b.** what he said/did was just outrageous; **me parece una b. que los dejes solos tanto tiempo** I think it's a scandal that you leave them on their own such a lot (**c**) *Fam (montón)* **una b. de** tons *o* stacks of

bestialismo *nm* bestiality

bestialmente *adv* brutally, savagely

bestiario *nm Lit* bestiary

best-seller, best-séller [bes'seler] (*pl* **best-sellers**) *nm* bestseller

besucón, -ona *Fam* 1 *adj* **está muy b.** he's being very kissy; **tiene una madre muy besucona** her mother is a great one for kissing people

2 *nm,f* **es un b.** he's a great one for kissing people

besugo *nm* (**a**) *(pez)* sea bream (**b**) *Esp Fam (persona)* idiot

besuguera *nf* = oval casserole for cooking fish

besuquear *Fam* 1 *vt* to smother with kisses

2 **besuquearse** *vpr* to smooch

besuqueo *nm Fam* smooching

beta *nf* (**a**) *(letra griega)* beta (**b**) *Informát* beta

betabel *nm Méx Br* beetroot, *US* beet

betabloqueante, betabloqueador *nm Farm* beta-blocker

betadine® *nm* = type of antiseptic

betamax® *nf Perú* (Betamax) video (recorder)

betarraga, beterraga *nf Andes Br* beetroot, *US* beet

betel *nm* betel (pepper)

beterava *nf Bol Br* beetroot, *US* beet

beterraga = **betarraga**

bético, -a *adj* (**a**) *(andaluz)* Andalusian (**b**) *Hist* = of/relating to Roman province of Betica in southern Spain (**c**) *Dep* = of/relating to Real Betis Football Club

betonera *nf Chile* concrete mixer

betulácea *nf Bot* member of the *Betulaceae* family, betulaceous tree/shrub

betuláceo, -a *adj Bot* betulaceous

betún *nm* (**a**) *(para calzado)* shoe polish (**b**) *Quím* bitumen ►► ***b. asfáltico*** asphalt; ***b. de Judea*** asphalt

betunero *nm* shoeshine, *Br* bootblack

bezo *nm* thick lip

bi *Fam* 1 *adj* bi

2 *nmf* bi

bi- *pref* bi-

biaba *nf RP Fam* (**a**) *(tortazo)* hiding; **darle una b. a alguien** to give sb a hiding (**b**) *(paliza)* beating; **darle una b. a alguien** to beat sb up (**c**) *(derrota)* thrashing; **el equipo uruguayo les dio una b.** Uruguay thrashed them

bianual *adj* (**a**) *(dos veces al año)* biannual, twice-yearly (**b**) *(cada dos años)* biennial

bianualmente *adv* (**a**) *(dos veces al año)* biannually, twice-yearly (**b**) *(cada dos años)* every two years, biennially

biatlón *nm* biathlon

biatómico, -a *adj Quím* diatomic

bibelot *nm* bibelot, trinket

biberón *nm* (**a**) *(botella)* (baby's) bottle (**b**) *(alimento)* **dar el b. a** to bottle-feed; **toma un b. cada cuatro horas** we give her her bottle once every four hours

biblia *nf* Bible; EXPR *Fam* **la B. en verso: ser la B. en verso** to be endless; **me contó la B. en verso** she told me a story that went on and on; **vinieron mis tíos y primos, la B. en verso** all my uncles and cousins came, the whole crowd turned up

bíblico, -a *adj* biblical

bibliobús (*pl* **bibliobuses**) *nm Esp* mobile library

bibliofilia *nf* bibliophile

bibliófilo, -a *nm,f* (**a**) *(coleccionista)* book collector (**b**) *(lector)* book lover

bibliografía *nf* bibliography

bibliográfico, -a *adj* bibliographic

bibliógrafo, -a *nm,f* bibliographer

bibliología *nf* bibliology

bibliomanía *nf* bibliomania

bibliómano, -a *nm,f* bibliomaniac

bibliorato *nm RP* lever arch file

biblioteca *nf* (**a**) *(lugar)* library ►► ***b. ambulante*** mobile library; ***b. de consulta*** reference library; ***b. de préstamo*** lending library; ***b. pública*** public library (**b**) *(conjunto de libros)* library (**c**) *Chile, Perú, RP (mueble)* bookcase

bibliotecario, -a *nm,f* librarian

bibliotecología *nf* library science

biblioteconomía *nf* librarianship, *US* library science

Bic® *nm o nf* Biro®

bicameral *adj Pol* bicameral, two-chamber; **sistema b.** two-chamber *o* bicameral system

bicameralismo *nm Pol* two-chamber system, bicameralism

bicampeón, -ona *nm,f* two-times *o* twice champion

bicarbonato *nm* (a) *(medicamento)* **b. (sódico)** bicarbonate of soda (b) *Quím* bicarbonate ►► ***b. sódico*** sodium bicarbonate; ***b. de sodio*** sodium bicarbonate

bicéfalo, -a *adj* bicephalic, bicephalous

bicentenario *nm* bicentenary

bíceps *nm inv* biceps

bicha *nf Fam* (a) *(culebra)* snake (b) *Ven (mujer)* floozy

bichada = **vichada**

bichar = **vichar**

bicharraco *nm Fam* (a) *(animal)* beast, creature; *(insecto)* creepy-crawly, bug; **iqué b. más raro!** what a bizarre creature! (b) *(persona) (mala)* nasty piece of work; *(pilla)* little terror

biche *adj Col* unripe

bichero *nm Náut* boat hook

bichi *adj Méx Fam* stark naked, *Br* starkers; **siempre anda b. por la casa** he always goes round the house stark naked

bichicome *nmf Urug* tramp, *US* bum

bicho *nm* (a) *(insecto)* bug, creepy-crawly; **lo picó un b.** he was bitten by an insect; EXPR *Fam* **¿qué b. le ha picado?** *Br* what's up with him?, *US* what's eating him? ►► *RP* ***b. bolita*** *(cochinilla)* woodlouse; *RP* ***b. de luz*** *(gusano de luz)* glow-worm

(b) *Fam (animal)* beast, creature

(c) *Fam (persona)* **(mal) b.** nasty piece of work; *(pillo)* little terror; **b. raro** weirdo ►► ***b. viviente:*** **siempre está intentado ligar con todo b. viviente** he'll try to *Br* get off with *o US* hit on anything that moves; **no hay b. viviente que se coma esto** there isn't a creature alive that would eat that

(d) *RP Fam (apelativo)* honey

(e) *Perú Fam (envidia, despecho)* spite, envy; **de puro b.** out of pure spite

bichoco, -a *adj CSur (animal)* old, decrepit

bici *nf Fam* bike

bicicleta *nf* bicycle, bike; **andar** *o* **ir en b.** to go by bicycle; **montar en b.** to ride a bicycle ►► ***b. de carreras*** racing bike; ***b. estática*** exercise bike; ***b. de montaña*** mountain bike; ***b. todo terreno*** mountain bike

bicicletear *vi RP Fam* (a) *(especular)* = to speculate using money owed to someone else (b) *(no pagar)* to put off paying

biciclo *nm* penny farthing

bicicross *nm* cyclocross

bicilíndrico, -a *adj* two-cylinder

bicla *nf CAm, Méx Fam* bike

bicoca *nf Fam* (a) *(compra, alquiler)* bargain (b) *Esp (trabajo)* cushy number; **es una b. trabajar aquí** this job's a cushy number (c) *Chile (capirotazo)* flick

bicolor *adj* two-coloured

bicóncavo, -a *adj* biconcave

biconvexo, -a *adj* biconvex

bicromía *nf* two-colour print

bicúspide *adj* bicuspid

BID *nm* (*abrev de* **Banco Interamericano de Desarrollo**) IDB, Inter-American Development Bank

bidé, bidet (*pl* **bidets**) *nm* bidet

bidimensional *adj* two-dimensional

bidireccional *adj* bidirectional

bidón *nm* (a) *(barril)* drum (b) *(lata)* (jerry) can (c) *(de plástico)* plastic jerry can (d) *(en bicicleta)* water bottle

biela *nf Tec* connecting rod ►► ***b. del pistón*** piston rod

bieldo *nm*, **bielda** *nf Agr* winnowing fork

Bielorrusia *n* Belarus

bielorruso, -a 1 *adj* Belorussian, Byelorussian

2 *nm,f* Belorussian, Byelorussian

biempensante, bienpensante 1 *adj* right-thinking; **la sociedad b.** respectable society

2 *nmf* **los biempensantes** right-thinking *o* respectable people

BIEN 1 *adj inv (respetable)* **una familia b.** a good family; **un barrio b.** a good area; *Pey* a posh area; **un restaurante b.** a posh restaurant; *Pey* **niño b.** rich kid; **gente b.** well-to-do people

2 *nm* (a) *(concepto abstracto)* good; **el b. y el mal** good and evil; **se cree que está por encima del b. y del mal** she thinks ordinary moral laws don't apply to her; **hacer el b.** to do good (deeds); **un hombre de b.** a good man

(b) *(provecho)* good; **los padres desean el b. de los hijos** parents desire the good of their children; **esto te hará b.** this will do you good; **si se marcha, nos hará un b. a todos** if she leaves, she'll be doing us all a favour; **espero que el cambio sea para b.** I hope the change is for the best, I hope the change works out well; **por el b. de** for the sake of; **lo hice por tu b.** I did it for your own good; **han trabajado muy duro por el b. de todos** they have worked very hard for the good of everyone

(c) *(nota)* = mark between 6 and 6.9 out of 10, ≃ pass, ≃ C

3 **bienes** *nmpl* (a) *(patrimonio)* property ►► ***bienes de capital*** capital assets; ***bienes comunales*** common property; ***bienes fungibles*** perishables; ***bienes gananciales*** shared possessions; ***bienes inmateriales*** intangible assets; ***bienes inmuebles*** real estate, *US* real property; ***bienes muebles*** personal property; ***bienes públicos*** public property; ***bienes raíces*** real estate

(b) *(productos)* goods ►► ***bienes de consumo*** consumer goods; ***bienes de consumo duraderos*** consumer durables, *US* hard goods; ***bienes de equipo*** capital goods; ***bienes de producción*** industrial goods; ***bienes terrenales*** worldly goods

4 *adv* (a) *(debidamente, adecuadamente)* well; **¿cómo estás? – b., gracias** how are you? – fine, thanks; **habla inglés b.** she speaks English well; **iagárrate b.!** hold on tight!; **cierra b. la puerta** shut the door properly; **conoce b. el tema** she knows a lot about the subject, she knows the subject well; **¿vamos b. de gasolina?** are we doing all right for *Br* petrol *o US* gas?, have we got plenty of *Br* petrol *o US* gas?; **b. mirado** *(bien pensado)* if you look at it closely; *(bien visto)* well-regarded; **b. pensado** on reflection; **contestar b.** *(correctamente)* to answer correctly; *(cortésmente)* to answer politely; **escucha b.,...** listen carefully,...; **estar b. relacionado** to have good connections; **le está b. empleado** he deserves it, it serves him right; **hacer algo b.** to do sth well; **has hecho b.** you did the right thing; **hiciste b. en decírmelo** you were right to tell me; **pórtate b.** be good, behave yourself; **salir b. librado** to get off lightly; **todo salió b.** everything turned out well; **vivir b.** *(económicamente)* to be well-off; *(en armonía)* to be happy

(b) *(expresa opinión favorable)* well; **imuy b.!** very good!, excellent!; **ib. hecho!** well done!; **me cayó muy b.** I liked her a lot; **me han hablado b. de él** they have spoken well of him to me; **en Portugal se come muy b.** the food is very good in Portugal; **estar b.** *(de aspecto)* to be nice; *(de salud)* to be *o* feel well; *(de calidad)* to be good; *(de comodidad)* to be comfortable; **iestá b.!** *(bueno, vale)* all right then!; *(es suficiente)* that's enough!; **este traje te está b.** this suit looks good on you; **la tienda está b. situada** the shop is well situated; **está b. que te vayas, pero antes despídete** it's all right for you to go, but say goodbye first; **tal comportamiento no está b. visto** such behaviour is frowned upon; **encontrarse b.** *(de salud)* to feel well; **no se encuentra nada b.** she doesn't feel at all well; **oler/saber b.** to smell/taste nice *o* good; **iqué b. huele en esta cocina!** it smells nice *o* good in this kitchen!; **opinar b. de alguien** to think highly of sb; **no acaba de parecerme b.** I don't really think it's a very good idea; **no me parece b. que no la saludes** I think it's wrong of you not to say hello to her; **¿te parece b. así?** is it O.K. like this?, is this all right?; **pasarlo b.** to have a good time; **iqué b., mañana no trabajo!** great, I don't have to go to work tomorrow!; *Irónico* **iqué b., ahora dice que no me puede pagar!** isn't that just great, now she says she can't pay me!; **salir b.** to turn out well; **iqué b. sales en la foto!** you look great in the photo!; **sentar b. a alguien** *(ropa)* to suit sb; *(comida)* to agree with sb; *(comentario)* to please sb; **el rojo no te sienta nada b.** red doesn't suit you at all; **come tan rápido que no le puede sentar b.** she eats so quickly she's bound to get indigestion; **algunos consideran que una copita de vino sienta b.** some people think a glass of wine is good for you; **no le sentó nada b. que lo criticaras en público** he didn't like you criticizing him in public at all, he was none too impressed by you criticizing him in public; **tu ayuda va a venir muy b.** your help will be very welcome; **no me viene nada b. salir esta tarde** it's not very convenient for me *o* it doesn't really suit me to go out this afternoon; PROV **b. está lo que b. acaba** all's well that ends well

(c) *(muy)* **quiero el filete b. hecho** I want my steak well done; **b. abierto** wide open; **abre b. la boca** open wide

(d) *(uso enfático)* pretty; **un regalo b. caro** a pretty expensive present; **vamos a llegar b. tarde** we're going to be pretty late; **estoy b. cansado** I'm pretty tired; **hoy me he levantado b. temprano** I got up nice and early today; **quiero un vaso de agua b. fría** I'd like a nice cold glass of water

(**e**) *(vale, de acuerdo)* all right, O.K.; **¿nos vamos? – b.** shall we go? – all right

(**f**) *(de buena gana, fácilmente)* quite happily; **ella b. que lo haría, pero no le dejan** she'd be happy to do it *o* she'd quite happily do it, but they won't let her

(**g**) *(expresa protesta)* **¡b. podrías haberme avisado!** you could at least have told me!; **¡b. podrías pagar tú esta vez!** it would be nice if you paid for once *o* for a change!

(**h**) *(en frases)* **b. es verdad que...** it's certainly true that...; **¡b. por...!** three cheers for...!; **¡ya está b.!** that's enough!; **¡ya está b. de hacer el vago!** that's enough lazing around!; **estar a b. con alguien** to be on good terms with sb; **¡pues (sí que) estamos b.!** that's all we needed!; **tener a b. hacer algo** to be good enough to do sth; **le rogamos tenga a b. pasarse por nuestras oficinas** we would ask you to (be good enough to) come to our offices

5 *conj* **b. ... b.** either... or; **puedes venir b. por avión, b. por barco** you can come by plane or by boat; **dáselo b. a mi hermano, b. a mi padre** give it to either my brother or my father

6 *interj* (**a**) *(aprobación)* good!, great!; *(fastidio)* oh, great!; **hoy saldréis al recreo media hora antes – ¡b.!** break time will be half an hour earlier today – great!; **se acaba de estropear la televisión – ¡b., lo que nos faltaba!** the television has just broken down – oh great, that's all we needed!

(**b**) *(enlazando)* **y b., ¿qué te ha parecido?** well *o* so, what did you think of it?; **y b., ¿a qué estás esperando?** well, what are you waiting for?

7 más bien *loc conj* rather; **no estoy contento, más b. estupefacto** I'm not so much happy as stunned; **más b. creo que no vendrá** I rather suspect she won't come, I think it's unlikely that she'll come

8 no bien, *RP* **ni bien** *loc conj* no sooner, as soon as; **no b. me había marchado cuando empezaron a...** no sooner had I gone than they started...

9 si bien *loc conj* although, even though

---

bienal 1 *adj* biennial
2 *nf* biennial exhibition

bienalmente *adv* every two years, biennially

bienaventurado, -a *Rel* 1 *adj* blessed; **bienaventurados los pobres de espíritu** blessed are the poor in spirit
2 *nm,f* blessed person

bienaventuranza *nf* (**a**) *Rel* divine vision; **las bienaventuranzas** the Beatitudes (**b**) *(felicidad)* happiness

bienestar *nm* wellbeing ►► ***b. económico*** economic wellbeing; *Col* ***B. Familiar*** = family welfare authority; ***b. social*** social welfare

biengranada *nf* small red goosefoot

bienhablado, -a *adj* polite

bienhechor, -ora 1 *adj* beneficial
2 *nm,f* benefactor, *f* benefactress

bienintencionadamente *adv* with good intentions

bienintencionado, -a *adj* well-intentioned

bienio *nm* (**a**) *(periodo)* two years (**b**) *(aumento de sueldo)* two-yearly increment

bienpensante = **biempensante**

bienquisto, -a *adj* popular, well-liked

bienvenida *nf* welcome; **dar la b. a alguien** to welcome sb; **demos un aplauso de b. a nuestro próximo invitado** let's have a warm round of applause to welcome our next guest

bienvenido, -a *adj* welcome; **¡b.!** welcome!; **en este país serás siempre b.** you will always be welcome in this country

bies *nm inv* bias binding; **al b.** *(costura, corte)* on the bias; *(sombrero)* at an angle

bifásico, -a *adj Elec* two-phase; **sistema b.** AC system

bife *nm* (**a**) *Andes, RP (bistec)* steak ►► *RP* ***b. ancho*** entrecôte (**b**) *Andes, RP (bofetada)* slap

bífido, -a *adj* forked

bífidus *nm* bifidus

bifocal 1 *adj* bifocal
2 **bifocales** *nfpl (gafas)* bifocals

bifurcación *nf* (**a**) *(de carretera, río, ferrocarril)* fork; **toma la primera b. a la derecha** go right at the first fork in the road (**b**) *Fís & Mat* bifurcation

bifurcado, -a *adj* forked

bifurcarse [60] *vpr* (**a**) *(carretera, río, ferrocarril)* to fork (**b**) *Fís & Mat* to bifurcate

bigamia *nf* bigamy

bígamo, -a 1 *adj* bigamous
2 *nm,f* bigamist

bígaro *nm* winkle

Big Bang *nm* Big Bang

bigote 1 *nm* (**a**) *(de persona)* moustache; EXPR *Fam* **menear el b.** to chomp away; **es hora de menear el b.** grub's up!, it's chow time! ►► ***b. retorcido*** handlebar moustache

(**b**) *(de gato)* whiskers; *(de langosta)* antennae, feelers

(**c**) *(mancha)* moustache; **el helado te ha dejado b.** you've got an ice-cream moustache; **límpiale los bigotes al bebé** wipe the baby's mouth

2 de bigote(s) *loc adj Esp Fam* **me llevé un susto de bigotes** I got a hell of a fright; **hacía un frío de bigote(s)** it was *Br* bloody *o US* goddamn cold

bigotera *nf (compás)* bow compass

bigotudo, -a 1 *adj* with a big moustache
2 *nm (ave)* bearded tit

bigudí (*pl* **bigudís** *o* **bigudíes**) *nm* curler

bija *nf* (**a**) *(planta)* annatto (**b**) *(tintura)* annatto (dye)

bijao *nm* balisier heliconia

bijouterí [biʒute'ri] (*pl* **bijouteries**) *nf RP* imitation jewellery

bikini = **biquini**

bilabial *Ling* 1 *adj* bilabial
2 *nf* bilabial

bilateral *adj* bilateral

bilbaíno, -a 1 *adj* of/from Bilbao *(Spain)*
2 *nm,f* person from Bilbao *(Spain)*

bilet *nm Méx* lipstick

bilharziosis *nf inv Med* bilharzia

biliar *adj Anat* bile; **cálculo b.** gallstone

bilingüe *adj* bilingual

bilingüismo *nm* bilingualism

bilioso, -a *adj* (**a**) *(con bilis)* bilious (**b**) *(con mal genio)* bilious

bilirrubina *nf Bioquím* bilirubin

bilis *nf inv* (**a**) *(líquido)* bile; EXPR **tragar b.** to grin and bear it (**b**) *(mal genio)* **desahogar la b. con alguien** to vent one's spleen on sb

billar *nm* (**a**) *(juego)* billiards *(singular)* ►► ***b. americano*** pool; ***b. francés*** billiards; ***b. romano*** bar billiards; ***b. a tres bandas*** = form of billiards using only three cushions (**b**) *(mesa)* billiard table (**c**) **billares** *(sala)* billiard hall

billetaje *nm* tickets

billete *nm* (**a**) *(de banco) Br* note, *US* bill; **un b. pequeño** *o Am* **chico** a small (denomination) *Br* note *o US* bill; **un b. grande** a large (denomination) *Br* note *o US* bill; *Chile* **un b. largo** a large (denomination) *Br* note *o US* bill ►► ***b. de banco*** banknote

(**b**) *Esp (de transporte)* ticket ►► ***b. abierto*** open ticket; ***b. de ida*** *Br* single (ticket), *US* one-way ticket; ***b. de ida y vuelta*** *Br* return (ticket), *US* round-trip (ticket); ***b. kilométrico*** = ticket to travel a set distance; ***b. sencillo*** *Br* single (ticket), *US* one-way (ticket)

(**c**) *Esp, Cuba (de cine, teatro)* ticket; **no hay billetes** *(en letrero)* sold out

(**d**) *(de rifa, lotería)* ticket ►► ***b. de lotería*** lottery ticket

(**e**) *Andes, Méx Fam (dinero)* dough; **sólo le interesa el b.** she's only interested in money; **esa familia tiene mucho b.** that family's loaded (with money) *o Br* not short of a bob or two

(**f**) *Am (mensaje)* note

billetera *nf* wallet, *US* billfold

billetero, -a 1 *nm* wallet, *US* billfold
2 *nm,f Carib, Méx (lotero)* lottery ticket vendor

billón *núm* **un b.** a trillion, a million million

billonario, -a 1 *adj* **pérdidas billonarias** losses running into trillions
2 *nm,f* trillionaire

bimembre *adj* two-limbed

bimensual *adj* twice-monthly

bimestral *adj* (**a**) *(cada dos meses)* two-monthly (**b**) *(que dura dos meses)* two-month

bimestre *nm* two months

bimetálico, -a *adj Econ* bimetallic

bimetalismo *nm Econ* bimetallism

bimilenario, -a 1 *adj* two-thousand-year-old, bimillenary
2 *nm* two-thousandth anniversary, bimillenary

bimodal *adj* bimodal

bimotor 1 *adj* twin-engine(d); **avión b.** twin-engine(d) plane
2 *nm* twin-engine(d) plane

binario, -a *adj* binary

binarismo *nm Ling* binarism

bingo 1 *nm* (**a**) *(juego)* bingo (**b**) *(sala)* bingo hall (**c**) *(premio)* (full) house; **hacer b.** to get a full house; **¡b.!** (full) house!
2 *interj Fam* bingo!; **¡b., éste es el que me faltaba!** bingo, this is the one I needed!

binguero, -a *nm,f* bingo caller

binocular 1 *adj* binocular
2 **binoculares** *nmpl (prismáticos)* binoculars; *(de ópera, teatro)* opera glasses

binóculo 1 *nm (gafas)* pince-nez
2 **binóculos** *nmpl Am (prismáticos)* binoculars

binomio *nm* (**a**) *Mat* binomial ►► ***b. de Newton*** binomial theorem (**b**) *(de personas)* pairing; **forman un b. perfecto** they are a perfect pairing

binza *nf* (**a**) *(de cebolla)* skin (**b**) *(de huevo)* skin

biocarburante *nm* biofuel

biocatalizador *nm Biol* biocatalyst

biocenosis *nf Biol* biocoenosis

bioclimático, -a *adj* bioclimatological

bioclimatología *nf* bioclimatology

biocombustible *nm* biofuel

biocompatibilidad *nf* biocompatibility

biocompatible *adj* biocompatible

biodegradabilidad *nf* biodegradability

biodegradable *adj* biodegradable

biodegradación *nf*, **biodeterioro** *nm* biodegradation

biodiversidad *nf* biodiversity

bioelemento *nm* bioelement

bioensayo *nm* bioassay

bioestadística *nf* biostatistics *(singular)*

bioestratigrafía *nf* biostratigraphy

bioética *nf* bioethics *(singular)*

biofísica *nf* biophysics *(singular)*

biofísico, -a *adj* biophysical

biogás *nm* biogas

biogénesis *nf* biogenesis

biogenética *nf* genetics *(singular)*

biografía *nf* biography

biografiar [32] *vt* to write the biography of

biográfico, -a *adj* biographical

biógrafo, -a 1 *nm,f (escritor)* biographer
2 *nm CSur Anticuado (cine)* cinema, *US* movie theater

bioindicador *nm* bioindicator

bioingeniería *nf* bioengineering

biología *nf* biology ►► ***b. celular*** cell biology; ***b. marina*** marine biology; ***b. molecular*** molecular biology

biológicamente *adv* biologically

biológico, -a *adj* (**a**) *(de la biología)* biological (**b**) *(agricultura, productos)* organic

biólogo, -a *nm,f* biologist ►► ***b. marino*** marine biologist

bioluminescencia *nf* bioluminescence

bioma *nm* biome

biomasa *nf Biol* biomass

biomaterial *nm* biomaterial

biombo *nm* (folding) screen

biometría *nf* biometry

biónica *nf* bionics *(singular)*

biónico, -a *adj* bionic

biopsia *nf* biopsy

bioquímica *nf (ciencia)* biochemistry

bioquímico, -a 1 *adj* biochemical
2 *nm,f (persona)* biochemist

biorritmo *nm* biorhythm

BIOS ['bios] *nm o nf Informát* (*abrev de* **Basic Input/Output System**) BIOS

biosensor *nm Biol* biosensor

biosfera *nf* biosphere

biosíntesis *nf inv* biosynthesis

biosintético, -a *adj* biosynthetic

biota *nf Biol* biota

biotecnología *nf* biotechnology

biotecnológico, -a *adj* biotechnological; **industria biotecnológica** biotechnology industry

bioterrorismo *nm* bioterrorism

bioterrorista 1 *nmf* bioterrorist
2 *adj* bioterrorist

biotipo *nm* biotype

biotita *nf Geol* biotite

biotopo, biótopo *nm Biol* biotope

bióxido *nm Quím* dioxide ►► ***b. de carbono*** carbon dioxide

bip *nm (pitido)* beep

bipartición *nf* splitting (into two parts)

bipartidismo *nm Pol* two-party system

bipartidista *adj Pol* **sistema b.** two-party system

bipartito, -a *adj* bipartite

bípedo, -a 1 *adj* two-legged
2 *nm,f* biped

biplano *nm* biplane

biplaza 1 *adj* **vehículo b.** two-seater; **avioneta b.** two-seater
2 *nm* two-seater

bipolar *adj* bipolar

biquini, bikini *nm, Am nm o nf* (**a**) *(bañador)* bikini; **ir en b.** to wear a bikini (**b**) *Esp (sandwich)* toasted cheese and ham sandwich

BIRD *nm* (*abrev* **Banco Internacional para la Reconstrucción y el Desarrollo**) IBRD

birdie ['berδi] *nm (en golf)* birdie; **hacer b. en un hoyo** to birdie a hole

BIRF *nm* (*abrev* **Banco Internacional de Reconstrucción y Fomento**) IBRD

birlar *vt Fam* to pinch, *Br* to nick; **me han birlado la calculadora** someone's pinched *o Br* nicked my calculator

birlibirloque *nm* EXPR *Esp* **como por arte de b.** as if by magic

birlocha *nf* kite

Birmania *n* Burma

birmano, -a *Antes* 1 *adj* Burmese
2 *nm,f (persona)* Burmese; **los birmanos** the Burmese
3 *nm (lengua)* Burmese

birome *nf RP* Biro®, ballpoint (pen)

birra *nf Fam* beer, *US* brew

birreactor *nm* twin-jet aircraft

birreta *nf* biretta

birrete *nm* (**a**) *(de clérigo)* biretta (**b**) *(de catedrático, abogado, juez)* = square tasselled hat worn by university professors, lawyers and judges on formal occasions

birria *nf Fam* (**a**) *(persona)* drip; **una b. de jugador** a useless player; **me encuentro hecho una b.** I'm in a bad way (**b**) *(cosa)* junk, *Br* rubbish, *US* garbage; **esta película es una b.** this movie is a load of *Br* rubbish *o US* garbage; *Col* **jugar de b.** to play half-heartedly (**c**) *Méx (comida)* stew ►► ***b. de cabra*** goat-meat stew

birrioso, -a *adj Fam* (**a**) *(malo)* crummy; **el examen me quedó b.** I made a mess of the exam (**b**) *(escaso)* measly

biruji *nm Fam* **entra mucho b. por esa ventana** there's a hell of a draught coming through that window; **¡qué b. hace!** it's freezing cold!

bis (*pl* **bises**) 1 *adj inv* **viven en el 150 b.** they live at 150a
2 *nm* encore; **hicieron dos bises** they did two encores
3 *adv Mús (para repetir)* bis

bisabuelo, -a *nm,f* great-grandfather, *f* great-grandmother; **bisabuelos** great-grandparents

bisagra *nf (de puerta, ventana)* hinge

bisbisar, bisbisear *vt* to mutter

bisbiseo *nm* muttering

bisbita *nm* meadow pipit ►► ***b. arbóreo*** tree pipit; ***b. campestre*** tawny pipit; ***b. dorado*** golden pipit; ***b. gorgirrojo*** red-throated pipit; ***b. ribereño alpino*** water pipit; ***b. ribereño costero*** rock pipit

biscote *nm Esp* piece of Melba toast; **biscotes** Melba toast
bisecar [60] *vt Mat* to bisect
bisección *nf Mat* bisection
bisector, -triz *adj Mat* bisecting
bisectriz *nf Mat* bisector
bisel *nm* bevel
biselado, -a 1 *adj* bevelled
2 *nm* bevelling
biselar *vt* to bevel
bisemanal *adj* twice-weekly
bisexual 1 *adj* bisexual
2 *nmf* bisexual
bisexualidad *nf* bisexuality
bisiesto *adj* **año b.** leap year
bisílabo, -a, bisilábico, -a *adj* two-syllable
bisíncrono, -a *adj Informát* bisync, bisynchronous
bismuto *nm Quím* bismuth
bisnes *nm inv Esp Fam* deal; **me ofrecieron un b. muy legal** they offered me a really good deal
bisnieto, -a, biznieto, -a *nm,f (varón)* great-grandson, great-grandchild; *(hembra)* great-granddaughter, great-grandchild; **bisnietos** great-grandchildren
bisojo, -a *adj* **un niño b.** a child with a squint
bisonte *nm* bison
bisoñada *nf (acción)* **eso fue una b.** that was typical of a beginner
bisoñé *nm* toupee
bisoñería *nf* (**a**) *(cualidad)* inexperience (**b**) *(acción)* **eso fue una b.** that was typical of a beginner
bisoño, -a 1 *adj* (**a**) *(inexperto)* inexperienced (**b**) *(soldado)* raw
2 *nm,f* (**a**) *(inexperto)* novice, beginner (**b**) *(soldado)* raw recruit
bísquet *nm Méx* breakfast muffin
Bissau [bi'sau] *n* Bissau
bistec, bisté *nm* steak
bisteque *nm Chile* steak; **b. a caballo** = steak with two fried eggs on top
bistorta *nf* bistort, snakeweed
bisturí (*pl* **bisturíes**) *nm* scalpel
bisulfato *nm Quím* bisulphate
bisutería *nf* imitation jewellery
bit [bit] (*pl* **bits**) *nm Informát* bit ►► ***b. de paridad*** parity bit
bita *nf Náut* bitt
bitácora *nf Náut* binnacle; **cuaderno de b.** logbook
bitensión *adj inv* dual-voltage
bíter, bitter ['biter] *nm* bitters *(singular)*
bitoque *nm* (**a**) *(de tonel)* bung, plug (**b**) *Am (de jeringa)* cannula
bitter = **bíter**
bituminoso, -a *adj* bituminous
biunívoco, -a *adj* one-to-one
biuret *nm Quím* biuret
bivalente *adj Quím* bivalent
bivalvo, -a *Zool* 1 *adj* bivalve
2 *nm* bivalve
bividí (*pl* **bividís** *o* **bividíes**) *nm Perú Br* vest, *US* undershirt
biyección *nf Mat* bijection
Bizancio *n* Byzantium
bizantino, -a 1 *adj* (**a**) *Hist* Byzantine (**b**) *(discusión, razonamiento)* hair-splitting
2 *nm,f* Byzantine
bizarría *nf* (**a**) *(valor)* bravery; **con b.** bravely, valiantly (**b**) *(generosidad)* generosity
bizarro, -a *adj* (**a**) *(valiente)* brave, valiant (**b**) *(generoso)* generous
bizco, -a 1 *adj* (**a**) *(estrábico)* cross-eyed (**b**) *(pasmado)* **dejar a alguien b.** to dumbfound sb, to flabbergast sb; **se quedó b. con los juegos del mago** the magician's tricks astounded him
2 *nm,f* cross-eyed person
bizcocho *nm* (**a**) *(pastel grande)* sponge (cake); **hizo un b. para merendar** he made a sponge cake for tea (**b**) *(pastelillo)* sponge finger ►► ***b. borracho*** = sponge cake soaked in alcohol, ≃ rum baba (**c**) *(cerámica)* bisque, biscuit (**d**) *RP (repostería)* bun
bizcochuelo *nm RP* sponge (cake)
biznieto, -a = **bisnieto**
bizquear *vi* to squint
bizquera *nf* squint
blablablá, bla bla bla *nm Fam* blah, empty talk
black-bass [blak'bas] *nf* black bass
blackjack [blak'jak] *nm* blackjack
blanca *nf* (**a**) *Mús Br* minim, *US* half note (**b**) *(moneda)* = old Spanish coin made from copper and silver; EXPR *Esp Fam* **estar** *o* **quedarse sin b.** to be flat broke (**c**) *(en ajedrez, damas)* white (piece); **las blancas tienen ventaja** white is winning ►► ***la b. doble*** *(en dominó)* double blank (**d**) *ver también* **blanco**
Blancanieves *n pr* Snow White; **B. y los siete enanitos** Snow White and the Seven Dwarfs

BLANCO, -A 1 *adj* (**a**) *(color)* white; **página/verso en b.** blank page/verse; **votar en b.** to return a blank ballot paper; **dejé cuatro respuestas en b.** I left four answers blank, I didn't answer four questions; **se quedó con la mente en b.** his mind went blank; **una noche en b.** *(sin dormir)* a sleepless night
(**b**) *(pálido)* white, pale; **estás muy b.** you're so white; **nunca se pone moreno porque es muy b.** he never tans because he's very fair-skinned; **se quedó b. del susto** *(pálido)* she turned white *o* pale with fear
(**c**) *(raza)* white
(**d**) *Urug Pol* = of/relating to the Partido Nacional
2 *nm,f* (**a**) *(persona)* white; **los blancos** whites (**b**) *Urug Pol* = member/supporter of the Partido Nacional
3 *nm* (**a**) *(color)* white; **el b. es mi color favorito** white is my favourite colour; **calentar algo al b.** to make sth white-hot; **una televisión en b. y negro** a black-and-white television; **filmado en b. y negro** filmed in black and white; **prefiero el b. y negro al color** I prefer black-and-white to colour ►► *Quím* ***b. (de) España*** whiting; ***b. del ojo*** white of the eye; ***b. de la uña*** half-moon
(**b**) *(diana, objetivo)* target; *(de miradas)* object; **se convirtió en el b. de la crítica** he became the target of the criticism; **dar en el b.** to hit the target; *Fig* to hit the nail on the head; **la campaña publicitaria dio en el b.** the advertising campaign struck a chord; **has dado en el b. con tu último artículo** your last article was spot-on ►► ***b. fácil*** sitting duck; ***b. móvil*** moving target
(**c**) *(espacio vacío)* blank (space); **ha dejado muchos blancos en el examen** she left a lot of things blank in the exam
(**d**) *(vino)* white (wine)
(**e**) *PRico (formulario)* blank form

blancor *nm* whiteness
blancura *nf* whiteness
blancuzco, -a *adj* off-white
blandengue 1 *adj Fam* (**a**) *(material)* soft; **la tarta ha quedado muy b.** the cake has turned out a bit soggy (**b**) *(persona)* weak, wimpish
2 *nmf Fam* softie; *Pey* wimp
blandir *vt* to brandish
blando, -a 1 *adj* (**a**) *(material, superficie)* soft (**b**) *(carne)* tender (**c**) *(agua)* soft (**d**) *Econ* **crédito b.** soft loan (**e**) *(persona) (débil)* weak (**f**) *(persona) (indulgente)* lenient, soft; **es muy b. con sus subordinados** he's very lenient with *o* soft on his subordinates
2 *nm,f* (**a**) *(persona débil)* weak person; **es un b.** he's so weak (**b**) *(persona indulgente)* lenient person; **eres una blanda** you're so lenient

> **Falso amigo**: El adjetivo inglés **bland** no es la traducción del español **blando**. En inglés **bland** significa "soso" o "insulso".

blandón *nm* (**a**) *(de cera)* wax taper (**b**) *(candelero)* candlestick
blanducho, -a *adj Fam* (**a**) *(galleta)* soggy (**b**) *(músculo)* flabby
blandura *nf* (**a**) *(de material, superficie)* softness (**b**) *(de carne)* tenderness (**c**) *(de agua)* softness (**d**) *(de persona) (debilidad)* weakness (**e**) *(de persona) (indulgencia)* leniency
blanduzco, -a *adj Fam* softish
blanqueado = **blanqueo**
blanqueador, -ora 1 *adj* **líquido b.** whitener
2 *nm* (**a**) *(líquido)* whitener (**b**) *Col, Méx (lejía)* bleach
blanquear *vt* (**a**) *(ropa)* to whiten; *(con lejía)* to bleach (**b**) *(dinero)* to launder (**c**) *(con cal)* to whitewash
blanquecino, -a *adj* off-white
blanqueo, blanqueado *nm* (**a**) *(de ropa)* whitening; *(con lejía)* bleaching (**b**) ***b. de dinero*** money laundering (**c**) *(encalado)* whitewashing

blanquiazul *Méx Pol* 1 *adj* = of/relating to the Partido de Acción Nacional
2 *nmf* = member/supporter of the Partido de Acción Nacional

blanquillo *nm* (**a**) *(árbol)* toothed spurge (**b**) *CAm, Méx (huevo)* egg (**c**) *Andes (melocotón)* white peach

blanquinegro, -a *adj* black-and-white

blasfemar *vi* (**a**) *Rel* to blaspheme (**contra** against) (**b**) *(maldecir)* to swear, to curse; **blasfemaba de todos los que le habían traicionado** he cursed everyone who had betrayed him

blasfemia *nf* (**a**) *Rel* blasphemy (**b**) *(injuria)* **es una b. hablar así de...** it's sacrilege to talk like that about...

blasfemo, -a 1 *adj* blasphemous
2 *nm,f* blasphemer

blasón *nm* (**a**) *(escudo)* coat of arms (**b**) *(orgullo)* honour, glory; **hacer b. de** to flaunt

blasonería *nf* heraldry

blastocisto *nm Biol* blastocyst

blastocito *nm Biol* blastocyte

blastodermo *nm Biol* blastoderm

blástula *nf Biol* blastula

blaugrana 1 *adj inv Dep* = of/relating to Barcelona Football Club
2 *nmpl* **los b.** the Barcelona football team

blazer ['bleiser] *nm* blazer

bledo *nm* EXPR *Fam* **me importa un b.** I don't give a damn, I couldn't care less

blef *nm CSur* bluff; **mi vecina es un b.** my neighbour's all hot air; **su libro es un b.** his book's a case of style over substance

blenda *nf Geol* blende

blenorragia *nf Med* blennorrhagia

blenorrea *nf Med* blennorrhoea

blindado, -a 1 *adj* (**a**) *(puerta)* armour-plated; **coche b.** bullet-proof car; *Mil* **vehículo b.** armoured vehicle; *Mil* **columna blindada** armoured column (**b**) *(reactor nuclear)* shielded
2 *nm Mil (vehículo)* armoured vehicle

blindaje *nm* (**a**) *(de puerta)* armour-plating; *(de vehículo)* armour (**b**) *(de reactor nuclear)* shielding

blindar *vt* (**a**) *(puerta, vehículo)* to armour-plate (**b**) *(reactor nuclear)* to shield

blíster 1 *adj* **cobre b.** blister copper
2 *nm* blister pack, bubble pack

bloc (*pl* **blocs**) *nm* pad ►► ***b. de dibujo*** sketch pad; ***b. de notas*** notepad

blocaje *nm (en fútbol)* bodycheck

blocar [60] *vt Dep* to block; *(en fútbol)* to bodycheck; **el portero blocó la pelota** the goalkeeper grabbed the ball

blof *nm Cuba, Méx* bluff; **mi vecina es un b.** my neighbour's all hot air; **sus obras famosas son un b.** her most famous works are a case of style over substance

blofeador, -ora *nm,f Méx* **es un b.** he's full of hot air

blofear *vi Cuba, Méx* to talk hot air

blofero, -a *nm,f Cuba* **es un b.** he's full of hot air

blonda *nf* (**a**) *(encaje)* blond lace (**b**) *Esp (para tartas)* doily

blondo, -a *adj Literario* blond, *f* blonde

bloody mary ['bloði'meri] *nm* bloody Mary

bloomer ['blumer] (*pl* **bloomers**) *nm Cuba* panties, *Br* knickers

bloque 1 *ver* **blocar**
2 *nm* (**a**) *(pieza)* block
(**b**) *(edificio)* block; **un b. de apartamentos** *Br* a block of flats, *US* an apartment block; **un b. de oficinas** an office block
(**c**) *(de noticias, anuncios)* section
(**d**) *Informát* block
(**e**) *Pol* bloc; **en b.** en masse ►► *Hist* ***el b. del Este*** the Eastern bloc
(**f**) *Tec* **b. (de cilindros)** cylinder block
(**g**) *Dep (equipo)* unit; **dieron una pobre impresión de b.** they didn't play as a unit

bloqueado, -a *adj Informát* locked

bloqueador, -ora 1 *adj (crema)* blocking; *(fuerzas, naves)* blockading
2 *nm Farm* blocker

bloquear 1 *vt* (**a**) *(comunicaciones, carreteras) (por nieve, inundación)* to block; **los manifestantes bloqueaban la salida de la fábrica** the demonstrators were blocking the exit to the factory
(**b**) *(mecanismo)* to jam; **la centralita del ministerio está bloqueada** the ministry's switchboard is jammed
(**c**) *(acuerdo)* to block; **bloqueó todo avance en este asunto durante la reunión** she blocked *o* prevented any progress on this issue during the meeting
(**d**) *Fin (cuentas)* to freeze
(**e**) *(con ejército, barcos)* to blockade
(**f**) *Aut* to lock
(**g**) *Dep (jugador)* to block; *(en baloncesto)* to block out, to screen
(**h**) *Informát (disquete)* to lock
2 **bloquearse** *vpr* (**a**) *(atascarse)* to be stuck; *Aut (dirección)* to lock; **se me bloquearon los frenos** my brakes jammed
(**b**) *(persona) (en situación violenta)* to freeze; **cuando está estresado se bloquea** he just freezes when he's under stress; **me bloqueé en el examen** my mind went blank in the exam
(**c**) *Informát (pantalla)* to freeze

bloqueo *nm* (**a**) *(con ejército, barcos)* blockade; ►► ***b. naval*** naval blockade
(**b**) *Econ* blockade; **violar el b.** to break the blockade ►► ***b. económico*** economic blockade
(**c**) *(de comunicaciones, accesos) (por nieve, inundación)* **debido al b. de la zona** owing to the fact that the area is cut off
(**d**) *(de mecanismo)* jamming
(**e**) *Fin (de cuentas)* freeze, freezing
(**f**) *Aut* locking
(**g**) *Dep (de jugador)* block; *(en baloncesto)* screen
(**h**) *(de persona)* ***b. mental*** mental block

blues [blus] *nm inv Mús* blues

blufeador, -ora *nm,f CSur* **es un b.** he's full of hot air

blufear *vi CSur* to talk hot air

blúmer (*pl* **blúmers** *o* **blúmeres**), **blume** (*pl* **blumes** *o* **blúmenes**) *nm CAm, Carib* panties, *Br* knickers

blusa *nf* blouse ►► ***b. camisera*** (plain) blouse

blusón *nm* smock

bluyín *nm*, **bluyines** *nmpl Andes, Ven* jeans

BM *nm* (*abrev de* **Banco Mundial**) World Bank

BMV *nf* (*abrev de* **Bolsa Mexicana de Valores**) = Mexican stock exchange

boa 1 *nf (serpiente)* boa ►► ***b. constrictor*** boa constrictor
2 *nm (de plumas)* (feather) boa

boardilla = **buhardilla**

boatiné *nm* padded fabric; **un bata de b.** a quilted dressing gown

boato *nm* show, ostentation

bobada, bobería *nf* (**a**) *(estupidez)* stupid thing; **decir una b.** to say something stupid; **decir bobadas** to talk nonsense; **hacer una b.** to do something stupid; **hacer bobadas** to mess about; **no voy a cometer la b. de decírselo** I'm not going to be so stupid as to tell her
(**b**) *(cosa sin importancia)* silly little thing; **se enfada por bobadas** she gets angry over silly little things; **no te gastes mucho, cómprale alguna b.** don't go spending a lot, just get him a little something

bobalicón, -ona *Fam* 1 *adj* simple
2 *nm,f* simpleton

bobera *nf RP* silliness; **creo que le atacó la b.** I think he's gone daft *o* nuts; **la edad de la b.** that silly age

bobería = **bobada**

bobi *nm* gudgeon

bóbilis: de bóbilis (bóbilis) *loc adv Esp Fam (de balde)* for free, for nothing; *(sin esfuerzo)* without trying; **no te creas que vas a aprobar el examen de b.** don't go thinking you can just breeze through the exam

bobina *nf* (**a**) *(de cordel, cable, papel)* reel; *(en máquina de coser)* bobbin (**b**) *Elec* coil ►► ***b. de encendido*** ignition coil; ***b. de inducción*** induction coil

bobinado *nm* reeling

bobinar *vt* to wind

bobo, -a 1 *adj* (**a**) *(tonto)* stupid, daft (**b**) *(ingenuo)* naive, simple
2 *nm,f* (**a**) *(tonto)* fool, idiot; **hacer el b.** to act *o* play the fool (**b**) *(ingenuo)* simpleton
3 *nm* (**a**) *Teatro* = rustic simpleton (**b**) *CAm, Méx (pez)* threadfin

bobsleigh ['boβslei] (*pl* **bobsleighs**) *nm* bobsleigh

bobtail ['boβteil] *nm* Old English sheepdog

BOCA *nf* (**a**) *(de persona, animal)* mouth; **una b. más para alimentar** one more mouth to feed; **me he arreglado la b. por muy poco dinero** I had my teeth seen to for a very reasonable price; **te huele la b. a tabaco** your breath smells of tobacco; **b. abajo** face down; **no es aconsejable poner a los bebés b. abajo** it's best not to lie babies on their stomachs; **b. arriba** face up; **ronca más cuando duerme b. arriba** he snores more when he sleeps on his back; **poner**

las cartas b. arriba to turn one's cards face up; **este paseo me ha abierto b.** this walk has whetted my appetite; *Fig* **no abrió la b.** he didn't open his mouth, he didn't say a word; **será mejor que no abras la b.** it would be best if you didn't say anything; EXPR **andar** *o* **correr** *o* **ir de b. en b.** to be on everyone's lips; EXPR **andar** *o* **estar en b. de todos** to be on everyone's lips; EXPR **buscar la b. a alguien** to draw sb out; *Fam* **icállate** *o* **cierra la b.!** shut up!; **siempre que hay problemas calla la b.** whenever there are problems, she keeps very quiet; **apareció en público para cerrar la b. a quienes lo daban por muerto** he appeared in public in order to silence everyone who thought he was dead; **de b. promete mucho, pero luego no hace nada** he's all talk, he makes a lot of promises, but then he never keeps them; **es muy valiente, pero de b.** he's all mouth; **sorprendió escuchar insultos de b. de un obispo** it was surprising to hear insults from the lips of a bishop; **lo escuchamos de b. de los protagonistas** we heard it (straight) from the horse's mouth; EXPR *Fam* **lo dice con la b. chica** she doesn't really mean it; EXPR **hablar por b. de ganso** to repeat what one has heard; EXPR **hacer b.: dimos un paseo para hacer b.** we went for a walk to work up an appetite; EXPR **se me hace la b. agua,** *Am* **se me hace agua la b.** it makes my mouth water; **cuando paso delante de una pastelería, se me hace la b. agua** whenever I go past a bakery, my mouth starts to water; EXPR **irse de la b.** to let the cat out of the bag; **se fue de la b.** he let the cat out of the bag; **lo han detenido porque su cómplice se ha ido de la b.** he has been arrested because his accomplice gave him away; EXPR **meterse en la b. del lobo** to put one's head into the lion's mouth; EXPR **este cuarto está oscuro como la b. del lobo** this room is pitch-black; EXPR **no decir esta b. es mía** not to open one's mouth; **no tienen nada que llevarse a la b.** they don't have a crust to eat; *Fam* **partir la b. a alguien** to smash sb's face in; EXPR **salir/ir a pedir de b.** to turn out/to go perfectly; **si te hace falta algo, pide por esa b.** if you need anything, just say so *o* ask; EXPR **poner algo en b. de alguien** to attribute sth to sb; **el gobierno, por b. de su portavoz...** the government, through its spokesperson...; EXPR **quedarse con la b. abierta** to be left speechless; EXPR **me lo has quitado de la b.** you took the words right out of my mouth; EXPR **tapar la b. a alguien** to silence sb; EXPR **su nombre no me viene ahora a la b.** I can't think of her name right now; **siempre dice lo primero que le viene a la b.** he always says the first thing that comes into his head; PROV **en b. cerrada no entran moscas** silence is golden; PROV **por la b. muere el pez** silence is golden; PROV **quien tiene b. se equivoca** to err is human, everybody makes mistakes ►► ***b. a b.*** mouth-to-mouth resuscitation; **hacer el b. a b. a alguien** to give sb mouth-to-mouth resuscitation, to give sb the kiss of life; ***b. de fuego*** firearm

(**b**) *(entrada)* opening; *(de botella, túnel)* mouth; *(de buzón)* slot; *(de cañón)* muzzle; *(de escenario)* stage door; *(de puerto)* entrance; **las bocas del Danubio** the mouth of the Danube; *Fam* **a b. de jarro** point-blank ►► ***b. del estómago*** pit of the stomach; *RP* ***b. de expendio*** outlet; ***b. de gol*** goalmouth; ***b. de incendios*** hydrant; ***b. de metro*** *Br* tube *o* underground entrance, *US* subway entrance; ***b. de riego*** hydrant; *RP* ***b. de subte*** *Br* tube *o* underground entrance, *US* subway entrance; *RP* ***b. de tormenta*** drain

(**c**) *Zool (pinza)* pincer

(**d**) *(filo)* cutting edge

(**e**) *(del vino)* flavour

(**f**) *Bot* ***b. de dragón*** snapdragon

(**g**) *CAm (aperitivo)* snack

---

bocacalle *nf* (**a**) *(entrada)* entrance *(to a street)* (**b**) *(calle)* side street; **gire en la tercera b.** take the third turning; **vivo en una b. de la calle Independencia** I live in a street off calle Independencia

bocadillería *nf Esp* sandwich shop

bocadillo *nm* (**a**) *Esp (comida)* filled roll *(made with a baguette)* (**b**) *(en cómic)* speech bubble, balloon (**c**) *Ven (postre)* = dessert of fruit jelly in banana leaves

bocadito *nm* (**a**) ***b. de nata*** *(pastel)* profiterole (**b**) *RP (canapé)* titbit, canapé (**c**) *Cuba (sandwich)* filled roll *(made with a baguette)*

bocado *nm* (**a**) *(comida)* **mastica cuidadosamente cada b.** chew every mouthful carefully; **se comió el pastel de un b.** she ate the whole cake in one go; **le di un b. pero no me gustó** I had *o* took a bite of it, but I didn't like it; **nos marchamos con el b. en la boca** we left as soon as we had finished eating; **tomé un b. en el avión** I had something to eat on the plane; **no probar b.: el niño no quiso probar b.** the child didn't touch his food; **no he probado b. en todo el día** I haven't had a bite to eat all day; EXPR *Fam* **no tener para un b.** to be broke *o* penniless ►► ***b. de cardenal*** choice morsel

(**b**) *(mordisco)* bite; **el perro me dio un b. en la pierna** the dog bit my leg

(**c**) *(en caballería)* bit

(**d**) ***b. de Adán*** Adam's apple

(**e**) EXPR *Fam* **buen b.: la empresa es considerada un buen b. por las grandes del sector** the industry's leading companies are eager to gobble up this firm; **su novio es un buen b.** her boyfriend's a real looker

bocajarro: a bocajarro *loc adv* (**a**) *(a quemarropa)* point-blank; **le dispararon varias veces a b.** he was shot several times at point-blank range; **el portero rechazó el remate a b.** the goalkeeper made a point-blank save (**b**) *(de improviso)* **se lo dije a b.** I told him straight out; **el médico le dio la noticia a b.** the doctor gave him the news straight out *o* without preparing him for it

bocal *nm* jug

bocallave *nf* keyhole

bocamanga *nf* cuff

bocamina *nf (de mina)* pithead, mine entrance

bocana *nf* (**a**) *(canal)* entrance channel (**b**) *Nic* mouth *(of river)*

bocanada *nf* (**a**) *(de líquido)* mouthful (**b**) *(de humo)* puff; **el humo salía a bocanadas de la chimenea** puffs of smoke were coming out of the chimney (**c**) *(de viento)* gust; **su llegada a la oficina supuso una b. de aire fresco** her arrival at the office came as a breath of fresh air

boca-oreja *nm* **por el b.** by word of mouth

bocarte *nm Esp* (fresh) anchovy

bocasucia *nmf RP* **ser un b.** to be foul-mouthed

bocata *nm Esp Fam* filled roll *(made with a baguette)*

bocatería *nf Esp Fam* sandwich shop

bocatoma *nf Am* sluice *(in an irrigation ditch)*

bocazas *Fam* **1** *adj* **ser b.** to be a bigmouth *o* blabbermouth

2 *nmf inv* bigmouth, blabbermouth

bocel *nm Arquit* torus

boceto *nm* (**a**) *(dibujo)* sketch, rough outline (**b**) *(de proyecto)* outline

bocha *nf* (**a**) *(bolo)* bowl (**b**) **bochas** *(juego)* bowls *(singular)* (**c**) *RP Fam (cabeza)* nut, bonce

bochar *vt RP Fam* (**a**) *(en examen)* to fail; **lo bocharon en física** he failed physics, *US* he flunked physics (**b**) *(rechazar)* to dismiss; **siempre bocha mis propuestas** she always throws out *o* dismisses my proposals

boche *nm Andes Fam* (**a**) *(barullo)* uproar, tumult; *(lío)* mess, muddle (**b**) *(riña, disputa)* fight, quarrel

bochear *vi Bol Fam* to kick up a fuss

bochinche *nm Fam* (**a**) *Am (ruido)* racket; **armar b.** to make a racket (**b**) *Am (alboroto)* fuss; **hizo mucho b. para ir a la fiesta y después no fue** she kicked up a real fuss about going to the party and then she didn't go (**c**) *PRico (chisme)* gossip (**d**) *Méx (fiesta)* party

bochinchear *vi Am Fam* to make a racket

bochinchero, -a, bochinchoso, -a *Fam* **1** *adj* (**a**) *Am (alborotador)* rowdy; **estos niños son muy bochincheros** these children are very rowdy (**b**) *PRico (chismoso)* gossipy

2 *nm,f* (**a**) *Am (alborotador)* rowdy, brawler (**b**) *PRico (chismoso)* gossip

bocho *nm Fam* (**a**) *Méx (auto)* Beetle (**b**) *RP (sabio)* egghead; *(en escuela)* brainbox

bochorno *nm* (**a**) *(calor)* stifling *o* muggy heat (**b**) *(vergüenza)* embarrassment; **iqué b.!** how embarrassing!

bochornoso, -a *adj* (**a**) *(tiempo)* stifling, muggy (**b**) *(vergonzoso)* embarrassing

bocina *nf* (**a**) *(claxon)* horn; *(de faro)* foghorn; **tocar la b.** to sound *o* toot one's horn; *Dep* **sobre la b.** on the hooter (**b**) *(megáfono)* megaphone; *(de gramófono)* horn; **colocó las manos en forma de b.** she cupped her hands round her mouth (**c**) *Méx (altavoz)* loudspeaker; *(del teléfono)* mouthpiece

bocinazo *nm* hoot; **dar un b.** to toot *o* honk one's horn

bocio *nm Med* goitre

bock [bok] (*pl* **bocks**) *nm* stein

bocón, -ona 1 *adj Am Fam* (**a**) *(bocazas)* **ser b.** to be a bigmouth *o* blabbermouth (**b**) *(fanfarrón)* **ser b.** to be a bigmouth *o* show-off

2 *nm,f Am Fam* (**a**) *(bocazas)* bigmouth, blabbermouth (**b**) *(fanfarrón)* bigmouth, show-off

3 *nm Carib (pez)* Pacific anchoveta

bocoy (*pl* **bocoyes**) *nm* barrel, cask

boda *nf* wedding ►► ***bodas de diamante*** *(de matrimonio)* diamond wedding; *(de organización, evento)* diamond jubilee; ***bodas de oro*** *(de matrimonio)* golden wedding; *(de organización, evento)* golden jubilee; ***bodas de plata*** *(de matrimonio)* silver wedding; *(de organización, evento)* silver jubilee

bodega *nf* (**a**) *(cava)* wine cellar (**b**) *(tienda de vino)* wine shop; *(taberna)* bar *(mainly selling wine)* (**c**) *(en buque, avión)* hold (**d**) *(en casa)* cellar (**e**) *CAm, Carib (colmado)* small grocery store (**f**) *Méx (almacén)* store

bodegaje *nm Andes, CAm* storage

bodegón *nm* (**a**) *Arte* still life (**b**) *(taberna)* tavern, inn

bodeguero, -a *nm,f* (**a**) *(de tienda de vino)* = owner of a wine cellar (**b**) *CAm, Carib (de colmado)* small grocery store owner

bodoque *nm* (**a**) *(en bordado)* tuft (**b**) *Fam (persona torpe)* blockhead, dunce (**c**) *Guat, Méx (chichón)* lump, swelling

bodorrio *nm Fam Pey* **el b. al que fuimos el sábado pasado** that sorry excuse for a wedding we went to last Saturday

bodrio *nm* (**a**) **ser un b.** *(película, novela, cuadro)* to be *Br* rubbish *o US* trash; **¡qué b.!** what a load of *Br* rubbish *o US* trash!; **¡qué b. de libro!** what a dreadful book! (**b**) *Fam (comida)* slop, pigswill

body ['boði] (*pl* **bodies**) *nm* body *(garment)* ►► ***b. building*** body building; ***b. milk*** body milk

BOE ['boe] *nm* (*abrev de* **Boletín Oficial del Estado**) official Spanish gazette, = daily state publication, giving details of legislation etc

bóer 1 *adj* Boer
2 *nmf* Boer

bofe 1 *adj Am (desagradable)* disagreeable, unpleasant
2 *nm* lights; EXPR *Fam* **echar el b.** *o* **los bofes** to puff and pant

bofetada *nf* (**a**) *(golpe)* slap (in the face); **dar una b. a alguien** to slap sb (in the face); **emprenderla a bofetadas con alguien** to punch sb, to begin hitting sb; EXPR *Esp* **darse de bofetadas con algo** *(no armonizar)* to clash with sth; EXPR *Fam* **no tener ni media b.** to be a wimp (**b**) *(afrenta)* slap in the face

bofetón *nm* hard slap (in the face); **dar un b. a alguien** to give sb a hard slap in the face, to slap sb hard in the face

bofia *nf Esp Fam* **la b.** the pigs, the cops

boga *nf* (**a**) *(moda)* **estar en b.** to be in vogue (**b**) *(pez fluvial)* Iberian nase (**c**) *(pez marino)* bogue

bogar [38] *vi* (**a**) *(remar)* to row (**b**) *(navegar)* to sail

bogavante *nm* lobster

bogey, bogui ['boɣi] *nm (en golf)* bogey; **hacer b. en un hoyo** to bogey a hole; **doble b.** double bogey

Bogotá *n* Bogota

bogotano, -a 1 *adj* of/from Bogota; **las calles bogotanas** the streets of Bogota
2 *nm,f* person from Bogota

bogui = **bogey**

bohardilla *nf* (**a**) *(habitación)* attic (**b**) *(ventana)* dormer (window)

bohemia *nf* bohemian lifestyle

bohemio, -a 1 *adj* (**a**) *(aspecto, vida, barrio)* bohemian (**b**) *(de Bohemia)* Bohemian
2 *nm,f* (**a**) *(artista, vividor)* bohemian (**b**) *(de Bohemia)* Bohemian

bohío *nm Carib* hut

boicot (*pl* **boicots**) *nm* boycott

boicotear *vt* (**a**) *(no asistir, no comprar)* to boycott (**b**) *(interrumpir, impedir) (acto, actividad)* to disrupt; **boicotearon la admisión en el colegio de los tres estudiantes** they tried to prevent the three students enrolling at the school; **dos estados continúan boicoteando el avance hacia el mercado común** two states continue to impede progress towards a common market

boicoteo *nm* boycott

bóiler *nm Méx* boiler

boina *nf* beret

boiserie [bwase'ri] *nm* = wooden panelling including built-in shelving, cupboards etc

boîte [bwat] (*pl* **boîtes**) *nf* nightclub

boj (*pl* **bojes**) *nm* (**a**) *(árbol)* box (**b**) *(madera)* boxwood

bojar *vt Náut (medir)* to measure the perimeter of

bojote *nm Andes, CAm, Carib (paquete)* parcel, package

bol (*pl* **boles**) *nm* bowl

BOLA *nf* (**a**) *(esfera)* ball; *(de helado)* scoop; **tengo una b. en el estómago** my stomach feels bloated; **si sigues comiendo pasteles te pondrás como una b.** if you carry on eating cakes, you'll get fat; EXPR **dejar rodar la b.** to let it ride ►► ***b. de alcanfor*** mothball; ***b. de cristal*** crystal ball; ***b. de fuego*** fireball; ***b. del mundo*** globe; ***b. de naftalina*** mothball; ***b. de nieve*** snowball; *Fig* **convertirse en una b. de nieve** to snowball

(**b**) *(pelota)* ball; *(canica)* marble; EXPR *Esp Fam* **no tocar** *o* **rascar b.: se pasó el partido entero sin tocar** *o* **rascar b.** he didn't do a single thing in the whole match; EXPR **no dio pie con b.** he didn't do *o* get a thing right ►► ***b. de billar*** billiard ball; ***b. de break*** *(en tenis)* break point; *Ven* ***bolas criollas*** bowls *(singular)*; ***b. de juego*** *(en tenis)* game point; ***b. jugadora*** *(en billar)* cue ball; ***b. de partido*** *(en tenis)* match point; ***b. de set*** *(en tenis)* set point

(**c**) *Fam (mentira)* fib; **contar bolas** to fib, to tell fibs; **me intentó meter una b.** she tried to tell me a fib; **esa b. no me la trago** I'm not going to fall for that one

(**d**) *Fam (rumor)* **corre la b. por ahí de que te has echado novio** they say you've got yourself a boyfriend; **¡corre la b.!, nos van a poner un examen mañana** they're going to give us an exam tomorrow, pass it on!

(**e**) *Fam (músculo)* **sacar b.** to make one's biceps bulge

(**f**) ***b. de nieve*** *(planta)* snowball tree

(**g**) *muy Fam* **bolas** *(testículos)* balls; *Fam* **en bolas** *(desnudo)* stark naked, *Br* starkers; EXPR *Ven Fam* **echarle bolas: tienes que echarle bolas al asunto** you really need to put some oomph *o* guts into it; EXPR *RP muy Fam* **hinchar** *o* **romper las bolas** *(molestar)* to be a pain in the *Br* arse *o US* butt; EXPR *Fam* **pillar a alguien en bolas** *(sin nada, desprevenido)* to catch sb out; **¡me has pillado en bolas!, ¡no tengo ni idea!** you've got me there, I haven't a clue!; **el profesor nos pilló en bolas** the teacher caught us unprepared

(**h**) *Am (betún)* shoe polish

(**i**) *Chile (cometa)* kite *(large and round)*

(**j**) *Méx Fam (grupo de gente)* crowd; **en b.** *(en grupo)* in a crowd, as a group

(**k**) *Méx (riña)* tumult, uproar

(**l**) *Cuba, Chile* **bolas** croquet

(**m**) *Fam* EXPR *Esp* **a mi/tu/su b.: nosotros trabajando y él, a su b.** we were working and there he was, just doing his own thing; *Bol, RP* **andar como b. sin manija** to wander around; *Ven* **de b. que sí** sure, you bet your life; *Méx* **estar** *o* **meterse en b.** to participate; *Méx* **hacerse bolas** to get muddled up; *RP* **estar hecho b.** to be shattered *o Br* knackered; *Andes, Ven* **parar** *o RP* **dar b. a alguien** to pay attention to sb; *RP* **nadie le da b. al nuevo compañero** nobody takes any notice of our new colleague; *RP* **nunca le dio b. a su hijo** she never showed any interest in her son; *RP* **tener bolas** *(ser valiente)* to have guts; *(ser lento)* to be slow *o* thick

(**n**) *ver también* **bolo**²

bolacear *vi RP Fam (decir tonterías)* to talk rubbish; *(mentir)* to tell whoppers

bolacero, -a *nm,f RP Fam* **es un b.** *(dice tonterías)* he talks a load of rubbish; *(miente)* he tells such whoppers

bolada *nf Fam* (**a**) *RP (oportunidad)* opportunity; **aprovechar la b.: ¿por qué no aprovechás la b. y te vas hasta los Alpes?** why don't you make the most of the opportunity and go to the Alps as well? (**b**) *Perú Fam (rumor)* rumour, piece of gossip

bolardo *nm Náut* bollard

bolazo *nm* (**a**) *(golpe)* blow with a ball; **recibió un b. en la cara** the ball hit him in the face (**b**) *RP Fam (tontería)* **decir bolazos** to talk nonsense (**c**) *RP Fam (mentira)* whopper, fib

bolchevique 1 *adj* Bolshevik
2 *nmf* Bolshevik

bolchevismo, bolcheviquismo *nm* Bolshevism

boldo *nm (infusión)* boldo, = type of herbal tea

boleada *nf Méx* shine, polish

boleado, -a *adj RP Fam* in a daze

boleador, -ora *nm,f Méx* shoeshine, *Br* bootblack

boleadoras *nfpl* bolas, = set of three ropes weighted at the ends, used by Indians as a weapon or by gauchos of the River Plate area for capturing cattle by entangling their legs

bolear *vt* (**a**) *(cazar)* to bring down with bolas (**b**) *Méx (sacar brillo)* to shine, to polish (**c**) *RP Fam (marear)* to daze; **tiene un olor que te bolea** the smell knocks you back

bolera *nf* (**a**) *(local)* bowling alley (**b**) *ver también* **bolero**¹, **bolero**²

bolería *nf Méx* shoeshine store

bolero¹**, -a 1** *adj Fam (mentiroso)* **no seas b.** stop telling stories
2 *nm,f Fam (mentiroso)* fibber
3 *nm (baile)* bolero

bolero²**, -a** *nm,f Méx (limpiabotas)* shoeshine, *Br* bootblack

boleta[1] *nf* **(a)** *Cuba, Méx, RP (para votar)* ballot, voting slip **(b)** *CSur (comprobante) (de venta, de depósito bancario)* receipt **(c)** *CAm, CSur (multa)* parking ticket **(d)** *Méx (de calificaciones) Br* (school) report, *US* report card **(e)** *Col (entrada)* ticket **(f)** *Col Fam (cosa linda)* **¡qué b. de zapatos!** what a lovely *o* gorgeous pair of shoes!

boleta[2] *adj Col Fam* garish, freakish; **mire esa vieja tan b.** look at that woman, she looks a real fright

boletaje *nm CAm, Méx* ticket sales

boletear *RP Fam* **1** *vt* to bump off, to do in
2 boletearse *vpr* to do oneself in, *Br* to top oneself

boletería *nf Am (de cine, teatro)* box office; *(de estación)* ticket office

boletero, -a *nm,f Am* box office attendant

boletín *nm* **(a)** *(publicación)* journal, periodical ►► ***b. de calificaciones*** *Br* (school) report, *US* report card; ***b. de evaluación*** *Br* (school) report, *US* report card; ***B. Oficial del Estado*** official Spanish gazette, = daily state publication, giving details of legislation etc; ***b. de prensa*** press release
(b) *(en radio, televisión)* bulletin ►► ***b. informativo*** news bulletin; ***b. meteorológico*** weather forecast; ***b. de noticias*** news bulletin
(c) *(impreso)* form ►► ***b. de suscripción*** subscription form
(d) *Cuba (de tren)* ticket

boleto 1 *nm* **(a)** *(de lotería, rifa)* ticket
(b) *(de quinielas)* coupon ►► ***b. de apuestas*** betting slip
(c) *Am (para medio de transporte)* ticket ►► ***b. de ida*** *Br* single (ticket), *US* one-way ticket; ***b. de ida y vuelta*** *Br* return (ticket), *US* round-trip (ticket); *Méx* ***b. redondo*** *(de ida y vuelta) Br* return (ticket), *US* round trip (ticket)
(d) *Col, Méx (para espectáculo)* ticket
(e) *(seta)* boletus
(f) *Méx Fam (asunto, problema)* **tú no te metas, este es mi b.** don't poke your nose in, this is my business; **si me endeudo, es mi b.** if I get into debt, that's my problem *o Br* lookout
(g) *RP Der* ***b. de compra-venta*** contract of sale; ***b. de venta*** contract of sale
(h) EXPR *RP Fam* **ser un b.** to be a piece of cake
2 de boleto *loc adv Méx Fam* **lo que sea, él te lo trae de b.** whatever it is, he'll get it for you in no time; **¡trae unas pinzas, de b.!** get me some pliers, and make it snappy!

boletus *nm inv (seta)* boletus

boli *nm Esp Fam* pen, Biro®

boliche *nm* **(a)** *(en petanca)* jack **(b)** *(bolos)* ten-pin bowling **(c)** *(bolera)* bowling alley **(d)** *Arg (discoteca)* disco **(e)** *CSur Fam (bar)* cheap bar; *(tienda)* small-town store

bolichero, -a *CSur Fam* **1** *adj* **es muy b.** he's usually to be found propping up the bar somewhere, *US* he's a barfly
2 *nm,f* **(a)** *(cliente)* **es un b.** he's usually to be found propping up the bar somewhere, *US* he's a barfly **(b)** *(propietario) (de bar)* bar owner; *(de tienda)* store owner

bólido *nm* **(a)** *(automóvil)* racing car; EXPR **ir como un b.** to go at a rate of knots, *Br* to go like the clappers **(b)** *(meteorito)* meteor

bolígrafo *nm* ballpoint pen, Biro®

bolilla *nf RP (en sorteo)* = small numbered ball used in lotteries; *Antes (en examen)* subject; EXPR **darle b. a alguien** to pay attention to sb; **acá nadie me da b.** nobody here takes any notice of me

bolillo *nm* **(a)** *(en costura)* bobbin; **hacer (encaje de) bolillos** to make (bobbin *o* pillow) lace **(b)** *Méx (panecillo)* bread roll **(c)** *CRica, Pan Mús* drumsticks **(d)** *Col (porra)* truncheon

bolina *nf Náut* bowline; **ir** *o* **navegar de b.** to sail close to the wind

bolinga *Esp Fam* **1** *adj (borracho)* plastered, *Br* legless
2 *nm (persona)* boozer
3 *nf* **agarrar una b.** to get plastered *o Br* legless

bolita 1 *nf CSur* **(a)** *(bola)* marble **(b) las bolitas** *(juego)* marbles; **jugar a la b.** *o* **las bolitas** to play marbles
2 *nmf Arg Fam* = sometimes pejorative term referring to a Bolivian person

bolívar *nm* bolivar

Bolivia *n* Bolivia

boliviano, -a 1 *adj* Bolivian
2 *nm,f (persona)* Bolivian
3 *nm (moneda nacional)* boliviano, Bolivian peso

bollera *nf Esp muy Fam* dyke

bollería *nf* **(a)** *(tienda)* cake shop **(b)** *(productos)* cakes ►► ***b. industrial*** factory-made cakes and pastries

bollicao *nmf Esp Fam (adolescente)* tasty young thing

bollo *nm* **(a)** *(para comer) (de pan)* (bread) roll; *(dulce)* bun; EXPR *RP Fam* **ser un b.** *(ser fácil)* to be a piece of cake
(b) *(abolladura)* dent
(c) *Esp (abultamiento)* bump
(d) *Esp Fam (embrollo)* fuss, to-do; **armar un b.** to kick up a fuss
(e) *Esp muy Fam (acto sexual)* **hacer un b.** *Br* to have it off, *US* to get it on *(of lesbians)*
(f) *RP (bola)* ball; **tirá ese b. de papel a la basura** throw that ball of paper away
(g) *CSur Fam (puñetazo)* punch
(h) *Col (tamal)* tamale
(i) *Col (dificultad)* trouble, difficulty
(j) *Col Fam (caca)* turd; EXPR **me siento como un b.** I feel crap

bolo[1] *nm* **(a)** *(pieza)* bowling pin **(b) los bolos** *(juego)* (tenpin) bowling; **jugar a los bolos** to bowl, to go bowling **(c)** ***b. alimenticio*** bolus **(d)** *Esp Fam (actuación)* gig; **hacer bolos** to tour **(e)** *Ven Fam (bolívar)* bolivar

bolo[2]**, -a** *CAm Fam* **1** *adj (borracho)* sloshed
2 *nm,f (borracho)* boozer

Bolonia *n* Bologna

boloñesa *nf* bolognese sauce

bolován *nm Am* vol-au-vent

BOLSA[1] *nf* **(a)** *(recipiente)* bag; **una b. de** *Esp* **patatas** *o Am* **papas fritas** a bag of *Br* crisps *o US* chips ►► ***b. de agua caliente*** hot-water bottle; ***b. de aire*** air pocket; ***b. de aseo*** toilet bag; ***b. de (la) basura*** rubbish *o US* garbage bag; ***b. de la compra*** shopping bag; ***b. de deportes*** holdall, sports bag; *Am* ***b. de dormir*** sleeping bag; *CSur Fam* ***b. de gatos:*** **la oficina es una b. de gatos** it's pandemonium in the office; ***b. de golf*** golf bag; ***b. de hielo*** ice pack; ***b. de mano*** (piece *o* item of) hand luggage; ***b. de marginación*** = underprivileged social group *o* area; *Zool* ***b. marsupial*** pouch; ***b. del pan*** = bag hung on outside of door for delivery of fresh bread; ***b. de papel*** paper bag; ***b. de plástico*** *(en tiendas)* carrier *o* plastic bag; ***b. de playa*** beach bag; ***b. de pobreza*** deprived area; ***b. de viaje*** travel bag
(b) *(mercado financiero)* **b. (de valores)** stock exchange, stock market; **ha habido un atentado en la B. de Madrid** there has been a terrorist attack on the Madrid Stock Exchange; **la b. ha subido/bajado** share prices have gone up/down; **jugar a la b.** to speculate on the stock market ►► ***b. alcista*** bull market; ***b. bajista*** bear market; ***b. de comercio*** commodity exchange; ***b. de materias primas*** commodities exchange; *Chile, Cuba* ***b. negra*** black market; ***b. de trabajo*** *(en universidad, organización)* = list of job vacancies and situations wanted; *(en periódico)* appointments section
(c) *(bolso) (de dinero)* purse, pocketbook; EXPR **¡la b. o la vida!** your money or your life!; EXPR *Fam* **aflojar la b.** to put one's hands in one's pocket, to fork out; *Fam* **afloja la b. e invítame a una copa** fork out and buy me a drink
(d) *(premio)* purse, prize money
(e) *Educ (beca)* ***b. de estudios*** (study) grant; ***b. de viaje*** travel grant
(f) *Min (de mineral, aire)* pocket
(g) *Anat* sac; *(de testículos)* scrotum ►► ***b. de aguas*** amniotic sac; ***b. sinovial*** synovial bursa
(h) *(arruga, pliegue) (en ojos)* bag; **le están saliendo bolsas debajo de los ojos** she's getting bags under her eyes; **esos pantalones te hacen bolsas en la rodilla** those trousers are loose at the knees
(i) ***b. de pastor*** *(planta)* shepherd's purse
(j) *CAm, Méx, Perú (bolsillo)* pocket
(k) *Méx (bolso) Br* handbag, *US* purse
(l) EXPR *Chile* **de b.** at someone else's expense; *Fam* **hacer b.** *Chile (abusar)* to abuse; *RP (destruir)* to ruin, *Br* to knacker; *RP Fam* **el vaso se cayó al suelo y se hizo b.** the glass fell to the ground and shattered; *RP Fam* **la muerte de su gato lo dejó hecho b.** he was bummed out *o Br* gutted about his cat dying

bolsa[2] *adj Ven Fam* dimwit, *Br* thicko

bolsada *nf Col Fam* **una b. de algo** a bag *o* bagful of sth

bolsear *CAm, Méx Fam vt* **(a)** *(robar)* **b. a alguien** to pick sb's pocket **(b)** *(registrar)* **b. a alguien** to search sb's pockets

bolsillo *nm* **(a)** *(en ropa)* pocket; **pañuelo de b.** pocket handkerchief; **calculadora de b.** pocket calculator; **edición de b.** pocket edition; EXPR **meterse a alguien en el b.** to have sb eating out of one's hand **(b)** *(lugar con dinero)* pocket; **lo pagué de mi b.** I paid for it out of my own pocket; EXPR *Fam* **llenarse los bolsillos** to fill one's pockets; EXPR *Fam* **rascarse el b.** to fork out

bolsín *nm Bolsa* local stock exchange, *US* curb market

bolsista *nmf* **(a)** *Bolsa* stockbroker **(b)** *CAm, Méx (carterista)* pickpocket

bolsístico, -a *adj Bolsa* stock market; **actividad bolsística** activity on the stock market

bolsita *nf* ***b. de té*** tea bag

bolso *nm* **(a)** *Esp (de mujer) Br* handbag, *US* purse ►► ***b. de bandolera*** shoulder bag **(b)** *(de viaje)* bag ►► ***b. de mano*** (piece *o* item of) hand luggage

bolsón, -ona 1 *nm* **(a)** *Andes (de colegial)* school bag **(b)** *RP (de deporte)* holdall, sports bag; *(de viaje)* travel bag ►► ***b. de pobreza*** deprived area **(c)** *Bol (de mineral)* pocket **(d)** *Méx (laguna)* lagoon **(e)** *Arg, Méx (de tierra)* hollow
2 *nm,f Andes, RDom Fam (tonto)* dunce, ignoramus

boludear *vi RP Fam* **(a)** *(hacer tonterías)* to mess about *o* around **(b)** *(decir tonterías)* to talk nonsense **(c)** *(perder el tiempo)* to mess about *o* around

boludez *nf RP Fam* **(a)** *(acto, dicho)* damn stupid thing; **eso que hiciste es una b.** that was a damn stupid thing (of you) to do; **hacer boludeces** to act like an idiot; **decir una b.** to say something really stupid; **no digas boludeces** stop talking nonsense
(b) *(cosa insignificante)* silly little thing; **se pelearon por una b.** they had a row over nothing *o* some silly little thing
(c) *(pereza)* **ayer no hice nada, me dio un ataque de b.** I didn't do anything yesterday, I just couldn't be bothered *o Br* fagged

boludo, -a *RP Fam* 1 *adj* **(a)** *(estúpido)* damn stupid **(b)** *(perezoso)* bone idle; **yo no contaría con ella, es muy b.** I wouldn't count on her helping, she's bone idle
2 *nm,f* **(a)** *(estúpido) Br* prat, *US* jerk **(b)** *(perezoso)* lazybones; **acá no hay lugar para boludos** there's no room for slackers here **(c)** **hacerse el b.** to act dumb, to pretend one hasn't heard/seen *etc*

bomba 1 *nf* **(a)** *(explosivo)* bomb; **poner** *o* **colocar una b.** to plant a bomb; **paquete/coche b.** parcel/car bomb; EXPR **caer como una b.** to be a bombshell ►► ***b. atómica*** atom *o* nuclear bomb; ***b. de cobalto*** cobalt bomb; ***b. de dispersión*** cluster bomb; ***b. fétida*** stink bomb; ***b. de fragmentación*** fragmentation bomb, cluster bomb; ***b. H*** H bomb; ***b. de hidrógeno*** hydrogen bomb; ***b. de humo*** smoke bomb; ***b. incendiaria*** incendiary (bomb), fire-bomb; ***b. lacrimógena*** tear-gas grenade; ***b. lapa*** = bomb affixed to underside of vehicle; ***b. de mano*** (hand) grenade; ***b. de neutrones*** neutron bomb; *también Fig* ***b. de relojería*** time bomb; ***b. teledirigida*** remote-controlled bomb; ***b. termonuclear*** thermonuclear bomb
(b) *(de agua, de bicicleta)* pump ►► ***b. aspirante*** suction pump; ***b. hidráulica*** hydraulic pump; ***b. de mano*** stirrup pump; ***b. neumática*** pneumatic pump; ***b. de pie*** foot pump; ***b. rotativa*** rotary pump; ***b. de succión*** suction pump; ***b. de vacío*** vacuum pump
(c) *(acontecimiento)* bombshell; *Fam* **la fiesta de anoche fue la b.** the party last night was something else
(d) *(con chicle)* bubble; **hacer bombas** to blow bubbles
(e) *(en piscina)* **tirarse en b.** to do a bomb
(f) *Chile, Ecuad, Ven (gasolinera) Br* petrol station, *US* gas station; **b. (de gasolina)** *(surtidor) Br* petrol pump, *US* gas pump
(g) *Col, Hond, RDom (burbuja)* bubble
(h) *Andes Fam (borrachera)* drinking bout; **estar en b.** to be drunk
(i) *Am (cometa)* circular kite
(j) *RP (dulce)* choux pastry puff
(k) *Chile (camión)* fire engine
(l) *Chile (estación)* fire station
(m) *Chile (cuerpo) Br* fire brigade, *US* fire department
2 *adj inv Esp Fam* **una noticia b.** a bombshell
3 *adv Esp Fam* **pasarlo b.** to have a great time

bombacha *nf RP* **(a)** *(braga) Br* knickers, *US* panties **(b)** **bombachas** *(pantalones)* = loose trousers worn by gauchos

bombachos *nmpl (pantalones)* baggy *Br* trousers *o US* pants; *(para golf)* plus fours

bombardear *vt* **(a)** *(con bombas)* to bomb; *(con artillería)* to bombard **(b)** *(átomo)* to bombard **(c)** *(con preguntas, peticiones)* to bombard; **la televisión bombardea a los niños con publicidad** television bombards children with adverts

bombardeo *nm* **(a)** *(con bombas)* bombing; *(con artillería)* bombardment ►► ***b. aéreo*** *(ataque)* air raid; *(serie de ataques)* aerial bombardment **(b)** *(de átomo)* bombardment ►► ***b. atómico*** bombardment in a particle accelerator **(c)** *(con preguntas, peticiones)* bombardment; **la película es un constante b. de imágenes** the film bombards you with an uninterrupted stream of images

bombardero *nm (avión)* bomber ►► ***b. invisible*** stealth bomber

bombardino *nm Mús* saxhorn

bombástico, -a *adj* bombastic

bombazo *nm* **(a)** *(explosión)* explosion, blast **(b)** *Fam (noticia)* bombshell

bombear *vt* **(a)** *(líquido)* to pump **(b)** *(pelota)* to float; **el extremo bombeó el balón al área** the forward floated the ball into the box

bombeo *nm* **(a)** *(de líquido)* pumping **(b)** *(abombamiento)* bulge

bombero, -a *nm,f* **(a)** *(de incendios)* fire fighter, fireman, *f* firewoman; **coche de bomberos** fire engine; **cuerpo de bomberos** *Br* fire brigade, *US* fire department; EXPR *Esp* **tener ideas de b.** to have wild *o* crazy ideas **(b)** *Ven (de gasolinera) Br* petrol-pump *o US* gas-pump attendant

bombilla *nf* **(a)** *Esp (de lámpara)* light bulb; EXPR *Fam* **se le encendió la b.** he had a flash of inspiration **(b)** *(en baloncesto)* key **(c)** *RP (para mate)* = tube for drinking maté **(d)** *Méx (cucharón)* ladle

bombillo *nm CAm, Carib, Col, Méx* light bulb

bombín *nm* **(a)** *(sombrero)* bowler **(b)** *(inflador)* bicycle pump

bombita *nf RP* light bulb

bombo[1] *nm* **(a)** *(instrumento musical)* bass drum; EXPR *Fam* **tengo la cabeza como un b.** my head is throbbing
(b) *(músico)* bass drum (player)
(c) *(para sorteo)* drum
(d) *Fam (elogio)* hype; **le están dando mucho b. a la nueva película** the new film is getting a lot of hype, they're really hyping the new film; **le gusta mucho darse b.** he's always blowing his own trumpet; EXPR **a b. y platillo** with a lot of hype
(e) *Tec* drum
(f) *Fam (embarazo)* **estar con b.** to be up the spout, *Br* to be up the duff; **ya se le nota el b.** she's already got a bulge; **le ha hecho un b. a su novia** he's got his girlfriend up the spout *o Br* up the duff
(g) EXPR *RP Fam* **irse al b.** to fail, to come to nothing; *Fam* **mandar a alguien al b.** to bump sb off

bombo[2]**, -a** *adj Cuba* **(a)** *(tibio)* lukewarm **(b)** *(insípido)* weak

bombón *nm* **(a)** *(golosina)* chocolate ►► ***b. helado*** = chocolate-coated ice cream **(b)** *Fam (persona) Br* stunner, *US* tomato; **es un b.** she's *Br* a stunner *or US* a tomato

bombona *nf* **(a)** *(contenedor)* cylinder ►► ***b. de butano*** (butane) gas cylinder; ***b. de gas*** gas cylinder; ***b. de oxígeno*** oxygen bottle *o* cylinder **(b)** *Ven (botella)* bottle *(of liquor)*

bombonera *nf (caja)* sweet tin

bombonería *nf Br* sweet shop, *US* candy store

bómper *nm Col Br* bumper, *US* fender

bonachón, -ona 1 *adj* good-natured
2 *nm,f* good-natured person; **es un b.** he's very good-natured

bonachonería *nf* good nature

bonaerense 1 *adj* of/from Buenos Aires; **las calles bonaerenses** the streets of Buenos Aires
2 *nmf* person from Buenos Aires

bonancible *adj (tiempo)* fair; *(mar)* calm

bonanza *nf* **(a)** *(de tiempo)* fair weather; *(de mar)* calm at sea **(b)** *(prosperidad)* prosperity **(c)** *Náut* **ir en b.** to have a favourable wind

bonchar, bonchear *vi Fam* **(a)** *Ven (divertirse)* to have a good time **(b)** *Cuba (bromear)* to joke around

bonche *nm* **(a)** *Ven Fam (fiesta)* bash, *Br* knees-up **(b)** *Carib Fam (broma)* joke **(c)** *Méx (montón)* bunch

bonchear = **bonchar**

bondad *nf* **(a)** *(cualidad)* goodness; **la b. del clima** the mildness of the climate **(b)** *(amabilidad)* kindness; **¿tendrías la b. de acercarme esa silla?** would you be so kind as to pass me that chair?; **tenga la b. de entrar** do please come in

bondadosamente *adv* with kindness, good-naturedly

bondadoso, -a *adj* kind, good-natured

bonete *nm* **(a)** *(eclesiástico)* biretta **(b)** *(universitario)* mortarboard

bonetería *nf Méx, RP* haberdashery

bonetero *nm* spindle tree

bongo *nm* **(a)** *(animal)* bongo **(b)** *CAm, Carib (canoa)* dugout canoe

bongó *nm* bongo (drum)

boniato *nm* **(a)** *Esp, Cuba, Urug (batata)* sweet potato **(b)** *Esp Fam (billete)* thousand-peseta note; **costó cinco boniatos** it cost five thousand pesetas

bonificación *nf* **(a)** *(aumento)* bonus; *(descuento)* discount; **me hacen una b. del 15 por ciento** they give me a 15 percent discount **(b)** *(en ciclismo)* time bonus

bonificar [60] *vt* (a) **me bonificaron con el diez por ciento** *(descuento)* they gave me a ten percent discount; *(aumento)* they gave me a ten percent bonus
(b) *(apoyar)* to subsidize; **el gobierno bonificará la contratación de trabajadores mayores de 50 años** the government will offer subsidies to companies who take on workers over the age of 50
(c) *(en ciclismo)* **b. a alguien** to give sb a time bonus

bonito[1] *nm* bonito ►► ***b. de altura*** skipjack tuna; ***b. del norte*** long-finned tuna, albacore

bonito[2], **-a** 1 *adj* (a) *(lindo)* pretty; *(agradable)* nice; **tu hermana es bastante bonita** your sister is quite pretty; **salió un día muy b.** it turned out to be a nice day; **es la canción más bonita del disco** it's the most beautiful song on the album
(b) *Fam (grande)* **recibió una bonita suma de sus padres** she got a tidy sum of money from her parents
(c) *Irónico* **¡muy b.!** great!, wonderful!; **¿te parece b. lo que has hecho?** are you proud of what you've done, then?
2 *adv Am* (a) *(bien)* well; **baila muy b.** she's a very good dancer
(b) *(mucho)* a lot; **ha crecido b.** he's really grown

Bonn [bon] *n* Bonn

bono *nm* (a) *(vale)* voucher ►► ***b.-restaurante*** *Br* luncheon voucher, *US* meal ticket (b) *Fin* bond ►► ***b. de ahorro*** savings bond; ***b. basura*** junk bond; ***b. de caja*** short-term bond; ***b. convertible*** convertible bond; ***b. del Estado*** government bond; ***b. al portador*** bearer bond; ***b. del tesoro*** treasury bond

bonobús *(pl* **bonobuses**) *nm Esp* = multi-journey bus ticket

bonoloto *nm* = Spanish state-run lottery

bonotrén *nm Esp* = multiple-journey railway ticket

bonsái *nm* bonsai

bonus-malus *nm Com* no-claims bonus clause

bonzo *nm* (a) *(budista)* Buddhist monk, bonze (b) **quemarse a lo b.** to set oneself alight

boñiga *nf (de vaca)* cowpat; *(de caballo)* piece of horse dung

booleano, -a *adj Mat* Boolean

boom [bum] *nm* boom

boomerang [bume'ran] *(pl* **boomerangs**) *nm* boomerang

boqueada *nf* gasp; EXPR *Fam* **dar las últimas boqueadas** *(persona)* to be on one's death bed; *(vacaciones, proceso)* to be nearly over; **cuando el imperio daba las últimas boqueadas** in the dying days of the empire

boquear *vi* (a) *(persona)* to be on one's death bed (b) *(vacaciones, proceso)* to be nearly over; **cuando el imperio boqueaba** in the dying days of the empire

boquera *nf* = cracked lip in the corner of one's mouth

boqueras *nmf inv Esp Fam (en cárcel)* screw

boquerón *nm* (fresh) anchovy ►► ***boquerones en vinagre*** pickled anchovy fillets

boquete *nm* hole; **abrir** *o* **hacer un b. en** to make a hole in

boquetero, -a *nm,f RP* = thief who breaks into the building he robs by making a hole through the wall from a neighbouring building

boquiabierto, -a *adj* (a) *(con boca abierta)* open-mouthed (b) *(embobado)* astounded, speechless; **se quedó b. contemplando la escena** he watched the scene in bewilderment; **su respuesta me dejó boquiabierta** her answer left me speechless

boquilla 1 *nf* (a) *(para fumar)* cigarette holder (b) *(de pipa)* mouthpiece; *(de cigarrillo)* roach *(made of cardboard)* (c) *(de instrumento musical)* mouthpiece (d) *(de tubo, aparato)* nozzle (e) *Ecuad (rumor)* rumour, gossip
2 **de boquilla** *loc adj Fam* **todo lo dice de b.** he's all talk; **es un revolucionario de b.** he's an armchair revolutionary

boquita *nf Guat* snack

borato *nm Quím* borate

bórax *nm* borax

borbollar *vi (líquido)* to bubble, to boil

borbollón *nm* **hablar a borbollones** to gabble

Borbón *n* Bourbon; **los Borbones** the Bourbons

borbónico, -a *adj* Bourbon

borborigmo *nm* tummy rumble, *Espec* borborygmus; **el estómago me hace borborigmos** my stomach is rumbling

borbotear, borbotar *vi* to bubble

borboteo *nm* bubbling

borbotones *nmpl* **salir a b.** *(líquido)* to gush out; **la herida sangraba a b.** blood was gushing out of the wound; **déjelo hervir 20 minutos a b.** keep it at a rolling boil for 20 minutes; **hablar a b.** to gabble

borceguí *(pl* **borceguíes**) *nm* half boot

borda *nf* (a) *Náut* gunwale; **un fuera b.** *(barco)* an outboard motorboat; *(motor)* an outboard motor; EXPR **tirar** *o* **echar algo por la b.** to throw sth overboard (b) *Esp (cabaña)* hut

bordada *nf Náut* tack; **dar bordadas** to tack

bordado, -a 1 *adj* (a) *(tela)* embroidered (b) *Esp (perfecto)* perfect; **el discurso/examen le salió b.** his speech/the exam went like a dream
2 *nm* embroidery

bordador, -ora *nm,f* embroiderer

bordadura *nf* embroidery

bordar *vt* (a) *(coser)* to embroider; **b. algo a mano** to hand-embroider sth (b) *(hacer bien)* to do excellently; **bordó el examen** she did excellently in the exam; **la selección bordó su actuación** the team gave an excellent performance; **la actriz borda el papel de Cleopatra** the actress is outstanding in the role of Cleopatra

borde[1] *nm (límite)* edge; *(de carretera)* side; *(de río)* bank; *(de vaso, botella)* rim; **lleno hasta el b.** full to the brim; **al b. del mar** by the sea; **no dejes que se acerquen al b. de la piscina** don't let them go near the edge of the swimming pool; **el delantero fue derribado al b. del área** the forward was brought down on the edge of the area; **estoy al b. de un ataque de nervios** I'm going to go off my head in a minute; **el proceso de paz está al b. del colapso** the peace process is on the brink of collapse; EXPR **estar al b. del abismo** to be on the brink of ruin *o* disaster

borde[2] *Esp Fam* 1 *adj (antipático)* **eres muy b.** you're a real *Br* ratbag *o US* s.o.b.; **no seas b. y deja que venga ella también** don't be such *Br* a ratbag *o US* an s.o.b., and let her come too; **no te pongas b. que casi no te he tocado** there's no need to get in a huff *o Br* strop, I hardly touched you
2 *nmf (antipático) Br* ratbag, *US* s.o.b.; **si encuentro al b. que me ha robado la bicicleta lo mato** if I find the rat that stole my bike, I'll kill him

bordeado, -a *adj* **b. de** lined with; **un camino b. de árboles** a tree-lined path

bordear *vt* (a) *(estar alrededor de)* to border; **cientos de árboles bordean el camino** hundreds of trees line the way
(b) *(moverse alrededor de)* to skirt (round); **tuvimos que b. el lago** we had to skirt (round) the lake; **bordearon la costa** they hugged the coast
(c) *(rozar)* to be close to; **bordea los ochenta años** she's nearly eighty years old; **su insistencia bordea lo impertinente** his insistence is verging *o* bordering on the impertinent

bordeaux [bor'ðo] 1 *adj inv* burgundy
2 *nm inv* burgundy

bordelés, -esa *adj* of/from Bordeaux *(France)*

bordería *nf Esp Fam* **soltar una b.** to come out with something really rude

bordillo *nm Br* kerb, *US* curb

bordo *nm* (a) *Náut & Av* **a b.** on board; **un avión con 100 pasajeros a b.** a plane carrying 100 passengers; **diario de a b.** logbook; **bienvenidos a b.** welcome aboard; **viajamos a b. de un transatlántico de lujo** we travelled on a luxury liner (b) *Guat, Méx (presa)* dam, dike

bordó *RP* 1 *adj inv* burgundy
2 *nm* burgundy

bordón *nm* (a) *(estribillo)* chorus, refrain (b) *(cuerda)* bass string (c) *Ven (benjamín)* youngest child

boreal *adj* northern

bóreas *nm inv Literario (viento)* Boreas, north wind

borgiano, -a *adj* Borgesian, = of/relating to the Argentinian writer Jorge Luis Borges (1899-1986)

Borgoña *n* Burgundy

borgoña *nm (vino)* burgundy

bórico, -a *adj* boric

boricua 1 *adj* Puerto Rican
2 *nmf* Puerto Rican

borincano, -a, borinqueño, -a 1 *adj* Puerto Rican
2 *nm,f* Puerto Rican

borla *nf* (a) *(de flecos)* tassel (b) *(pompón)* pompom (c) *(para maquillaje)* powder puff

borlote *nm Méx Fam* (a) *(alboroto)* racket, din (b) *(desorden)* commotion, row

borne *nm Elec* terminal

bornear 1 *vt (torcer)* to twist
2 *vi Náut* to swing *o* turn on its moorings
3 **bornearse** *vpr* to warp, to become warped

Borneo *n* Borneo

boro *nm Quím* boron

borona *nf* (**a**) *(mijo)* millet (**b**) *(maíz)* maize, *US* corn (**c**) *(pan)* corn bread (**d**) *CAm, Col, Ven (migaja)* breadcrumb

borra *nf* (**a**) *(lana basta)* flock (**b**) *(pelusa)* fluff (**c**) *(sedimento) (del café, vino)* dregs (**d**) *RP* ***b. de vino:*** **una camisa b. de vino** a burgundy shirt

borrachera *nf* (**a**) *(embriaguez)* drunkenness; **tener una b.** to be drunk; **agarrarse** *o Esp* **cogerse una b.** to get drunk; **aún no se me ha pasado la b.** I still haven't sobered up (**b**) *(entusiasmo)* **estaba en plena b. creativa** he was in the grip of artistic inspiration; **está experimentando la b. del éxito** she's drunk *o* dizzy with success

borrachín, -ina *nm,f Fam* boozer

borracho, -a 1 *adj* (**a**) *(ebrio)* drunk; EXPR *Fam* **b. como una cuba** blind drunk; EXPR *Fam* **ini b.!** (absolutely) no way!; **ino lo haría ni b.!** there's no way you'd get me doing that! (**b**) *(emocionado)* **b. de** *(poder, éxito)* drunk *o* intoxicated with; **está b. de ideas** he's overflowing with ideas; **estaba b. de alegría** he was wild with joy
2 *nm,f (persona)* drunk
3 *nm (bizcocho)* = sponge cake soaked in alcohol, ≃ rum baba

borrachuzo, -a *nm,f Fam* boozer

borrado *nm Informát* clearing

borrador *nm* (**a**) *(escrito)* rough draft; **hacer un b. de** to draft; **hazlo en b. y luego pásalo a limpio** do a rough version first and then do a neat version (**b**) *(dibujo)* sketch (**c**) *(para pizarra)* board duster (**d**) *(goma de borrar) Br* rubber, *US* eraser

borraja *nf* borage

borrajear 1 *vt* to scribble
2 *vi* to scribble

borrar 1 *vt* (**a**) *(hacer desaparecer) (con goma) Br* to rub out, *US* to erase; *(en casete)* to erase; EXPR **b. a algo/alguien del mapa** to wipe sth/sb off the map
(**b**) *(la pizarra)* to wipe, to dust
(**c**) *(tachar)* to cross out
(**d**) *(de lista)* to take off; **sus padres la borraron de clase de piano** her parents stopped sending her to piano classes
(**e**) *Informát (archivo)* to delete
(**f**) *(olvidar)* to erase; **el tiempo borró el recuerdo de aquel desastre** with time, she was able to erase the disaster from her memory; **intenta borrarla de tu cabeza** try and put her out of your mind
(**g**) *Méx, RP Fam (no hacer caso a)* to ignore; **me peleé con ella porque siempre me borraba** I fell out with her because she always ignored me
2 **borrarse** *vpr* (**a**) *(desaparecer)* to disappear; **las huellas se borraron con la marea alta** the tide washed the tracks away; **se bloqueó el ordenador y se borraron algunos documentos** when the computer crashed, certain files were lost; EXPR **se borró del mapa** he dropped out of sight, he disappeared from circulation
(**b**) *(de lista)* to take one's name off; **me he borrado de las clases** I've stopped going to those classes; **me he borrado del viaje porque no me quedan vacaciones** I've pulled out of the trip because I haven't got any holidays left
(**c**) *(olvidarse)* to be wiped away; **se le borró de la mente** he forgot all about it
(**d**) *Méx, RP Fam (irse)* to split; **nosotros nos borramos** we're off; **ibórrate!** *(piérdete)* get lost!

borrasca *nf* (**a**) *Meteo (baja presión)* area of low pressure (**b**) *(tormenta)* thunderstorm (**c**) *(riña)* flaming row

borrascoso, -a *adj* (**a**) *(tiempo)* stormy (**b**) *(vida, reunión, relación)* stormy, tempestuous

borrego, -a 1 *adj Fam Pey* sheep-like
2 *nm,f* (**a**) *(animal)* lamb (**b**) *Fam Pey (persona)* sheep; **todos lo siguen como borregos** they all follow him like sheep (**c**) **borregos** *(nubes)* fleecy clouds (**d**) **borregos** *(olas)* white horses, *US* white caps (**e**) *RP Fam (chico)* kid (**f**) *Cuba, Méx (noticia falsa)* hoax; **soltar un b.** to start a rumour

borreguil *adj Fam Pey* sheep-like

borreguillo *nm* fleece

borreguismo *nm Fam Pey* sheep-like behaviour

borrico, -a 1 *adj Fam* (**a**) *(tonto)* dim-witted, dim (**b**) *(testarudo)* pigheaded
2 *nm,f* (**a**) *(burro)* donkey (**b**) *Fam (tonto)* dimwit, dunce (**c**) *Fam (testarudo)* **ser un b.** to be pigheaded

borriquero, -a *adj* **cardo b.** cotton thistle

borriqueta *nf*, **borriquete** *nm* trestle

borrón *nm* (**a**) *(de tinta)* blot (**b**) *(tachón)* **el examen estaba lleno de borrones** the exam paper was covered in crossings out; EXPR **hacer b. y cuenta nueva** to wipe the slate clean (**c**) *(hecho)* blot; **aquel escándalo fue un b. en su carrera** that scandal was a blot on his career (**d**) *(deshonor)* blemish

borronear *vt* (**a**) *(garabatear)* to scribble on (**b**) *(escribir deprisa)* to scribble

borroso, -a *adj* (**a**) *(foto, visión)* blurred; **lo veo todo b.** everything is a blur (**b**) *(escritura, texto)* smudgy (**c**) *(recuerdo)* hazy

borujo *nm (de papel)* ball; *(de cabello, hilo)* tangle

bos *nm Esp Fam (jefe)* boss

boscaje *nm (bosque)* thicket, copse

boscoso, -a *adj* wooded, woody

Bósforo *nm* **el B.** the Bosphorus

Bosnia *n* Bosnia ▸▸ ***B. y Herzegovina*** Bosnia-Herzegovina

bosniaco, -a 1 *adj* Bosnian Muslim
2 *nm,f* Bosnian Muslim

bosnio, -a 1 *adj* Bosnian
2 *nm,f* Bosnian

bosque *nm (pequeño)* wood; *(grande)* forest; *Fig* **un b. de jugadores** a crowd of players ▸▸ ***b. tropical*** tropical forest

bosquejar *vt* (**a**) *(esbozar)* to sketch (out) (**b**) *(dar una idea de)* to give a rough outline of

bosquejo *nm* (**a**) *(esbozo)* sketch (**b**) *(de idea, tema, situación)* rough outline

bosquete *nm* copse

bosquimano, -a 1 *adj* Bushman
2 *nm,f* Bushman

bossa-nova [bosa'noβa] *nf* bossa nova

bosta 1 *adj RP muy Fam* crap; **un libro b.** a crap book
2 *nf* (**a**) *(excremento) (de vaca)* cowpat; *(de caballo)* piece of horse dung (**b**) *RP muy Fam (cosa mal hecha)* load of crap; **este texto es una b.** this text is a load of crap; **este teléfono es una b.** this telephone is crap

bostezar [14] *vi* to yawn; **b. de aburrimiento** to yawn with boredom

bostezo *nm* yawn

bota *nf* (**a**) *(calzado)* boot; EXPR **morir con las botas puestas** to die with one's boots on; EXPR **colgar las botas** to hang up one's boots; EXPR *Fam* **ponerse las botas** *(comiendo)* to stuff one's face; **con este negocio nos vamos a poner las botas** we're going to make a fortune with this business; EXPR *Am* **los tiene a todos abajo de la b.** he has everyone under his thumb ▸▸ ***botas de agua*** gumboots, *Br* wellingtons; ***botas camperas*** cowboy boots; ***botas de caña alta*** knee-length boots; *Méx, Ven* ***botas de caucho*** gumboots, *Br* wellingtons; ***botas de esquí*** *o* ***esquiar*** ski boots; ***botas de fútbol*** soccer *o Br* football boots; ***botas de goma*** gumboots, *Br* wellingtons; ***botas de montaña*** climbing boots; ***botas de montar*** riding boots; ***botas de senderismo*** hiking *o* walking boots
(**b**) *(de vino)* = small leather container for wine

botadero *nm Andes, Ven Br* rubbish tip *o* dump, *US* garbage dump

botado, -a *adj Andes Fam* (**a**) *(fácil)* easy, simple; **eso está b.** that's easy *o* simple (**b**) *(barato)* **los CDs andan** *o* **están botados** the CDs cost peanuts *o* are dirt cheap

botadura *nf* launching

botafumeiro *nm* censer

botalón *nm Col, Ven (poste)* post, stake

botamanga *nf Andes, RP (de pantalón) Br* turn-up, *US* cuff

botana *nf Méx* (**a**) *(tapa)* snack, appetizer (**b**) *Fam (charla)* **echar b.** to have a laugh

botanear *Méx* 1 *vi* (**a**) *(tapear)* to have a snack, to snack (**b**) *Fam (charlar)* to have a laugh
2 **botanearse** *vpr Fam* **botaneársela: yo me la botaneo mucho cuando hablo con ella** I have a real laugh when I talk to her

botánica *nf* botany

botánico, -a 1 *adj* botanical
2 *nm,f* botanist

botanista *nmf* botanist

botar 1 *vt* (**a**) *(barco)* to launch
(**b**) *(pelota)* to bounce
(**c**) *Fam (despedir)* to throw *o* kick out; **lo botaron del trabajo** he was sacked; *Andes* **su novio la botó** her boyfriend dumped her
(**d**) *Dep (córner)* to take

(**e**) *Andes, CAm, Carib, Méx (tirar)* to throw away; **bótalo a la basura** throw it away; **b. la basura** *(sacar)* to put the *Br* rubbish *o US* garbage out

(**f**) *Andes, CAm, Carib, Méx (malgastar)* to waste, to squander; **b. el dinero** to throw one's money away

(**g**) *(derribar, volcar)* to knock over

2 *vi* (**a**) *Esp (saltar)* to jump; **botaba de contento** I was jumping for joy; EXPR *Fam* **está que bota** he is hopping mad

(**b**) *(pelota)* to bounce

3 botarse *vpr Andes, CAm, Carib, Méx (tirarse)* to jump; **botarse al agua** to jump into the water; *(de cabeza)* to dive into the water

botarate *nm Fam* fool

botarel *nm Arquit* buttress

botavara *nf Náut* boom

bote *nm* (**a**) *(envase) (tarro)* jar; *Esp (lata)* tin, can; *(de champú, pastillas)* bottle; **los guisantes ¿son naturales o de b.?** are the peas fresh or tinned? ►► *Am* ***b. de la basura*** *Br* rubbish bin, *US* garbage can, trash can; ***b. de humo*** smoke canister

(**b**) *(barca)* boat ►► ***b. de remos*** rowing boat; ***b. salvavidas*** lifeboat

(**c**) *(caja para propinas)* tips box; **el cambio, para el b.** keep the change

(**d**) *(salto)* jump; **dar botes** *(saltar)* to jump up and down; *(vehículo)* to bump up and down; **pegar un b.** *(de susto)* to jump, to give a start; **dio un b. de alegría** she jumped for joy

(**e**) *(de pelota)* bounce; **tienes que dejar que dé un b.** you have to let it bounce; **dar botes** to bounce; **a b. pronto** on the half volley

(**f**) *(en lotería)* rollover jackpot

(**g**) *Méx, Ven Fam (cárcel) Br* nick, *US* joint

(**h**) *Ven (escape)* leak

(**i**) EXPR **a b. pronto** *(sin pensar)* off the top of one's head; *Esp Fam* **chupar del b.** to feather one's nest; *Fam* **darse el b.** *Br* to scarper, *US* to split; **de b. en b.** chock-a-block; *Esp* **meter en el b. a alguien** to win sb over; *Esp* **tener en el b. a alguien** to have sb eating out of one's hand; *Fam* **¡tonto del b.!** stupid halfwit!

botear *vi Méx Fam* **salir a b.** to go out rattling (collecting) tins

botella *nf* (**a**) *(recipiente)* bottle; **una b. de champán/leche** *(recipiente)* a champagne/milk bottle; *(contenido)* a bottle of champagne/milk; **en b.** bottled; EXPR **darle a la b.** *(beber alcohol)* to be a heavy drinker ►► ***b. de oxígeno*** oxygen cylinder (**b**) *Cuba (autoestop)* **dar b. a alguien** to give sb a ride *o esp Br* lift; **hacer b.** to hitchhike

botellazo *nm* **recibió un b. en la cabeza** he was hit over the head with a bottle

botellero *nm* (**a**) *(accesorio)* wine rack (**b**) *RP (persona)* = person who collects bottles for resale

botellín *nm (de cerveza)* small bottle *(0.2 l)*

botellón *nm Esp Fam* = informal street gathering where young people meet to drink and socialize

botepronto *nm (en rugby)* drop kick

botica *nf Anticuado* pharmacy, *Br* chemist's (shop), *US* drugstore; EXPR **aquí hay de todo como en b.** there's a bit of everything here

boticario, -a *nm,f Anticuado* pharmacist, *Br* chemist, *US* druggist

botija 1 *nf (vasija)* earthenware jar

2 *nmf Urug Fam (muchacho)* kid

botijear *vt Urug Fam* **b. a alguien** to treat sb like a kid

botijo *nm* = earthenware vessel with a spout used for drinking water

botillería *nf Chile (de vino, licor)* liquor store

botín[1] *nm (calzado)* ankle boot ►► *Am* ***b. de fútbol*** football boot

botín[2] *nm* (**a**) *(de guerra)* plunder, booty; EXPR **repartirse el b.** to share out the spoils (**b**) *(de atraco)* loot

botina *nf* ankle boot

botiquín *nm* (**a**) *(caja)* first-aid kit; *(mueble)* first-aid cabinet ►► ***b. de primeros auxilios*** *(caja)* first-aid kit; *(mueble)* first-aid cabinet (**b**) *(enfermería)* sick bay (**c**) *Ven (taberna)* bar

boto *nm* (**a**) *(bota)* riding boot (**b**) *(para vino)* wineskin

botón[1] *nm* (**a**) *(para abrochar)* button; EXPR *RP Fam* **al divino** *o* **santo b.** for nothing ►► ***b. de muestra:*** **esto es sólo un b. de muestra** this is just one example; **la cena no fue más que un b. de muestra de la cocina local** the meal was no more than a taster *o* sample of the local cuisine

(**b**) *(de aparato)* button; *(de timbre)* buzzer; **el b. de pausa/de rebobinado** the pause/rewind button; **darle al b.** to press the button

(**c**) *(de planta)* bud, gemma ►► ***b. de oro*** buttercup

(**d**) *(en esgrima)* button

botón[2], -ona *RP Fam* **1** *adj* (**a**) *(delator)* telltale (**b**) *(estricto)* pernickety, *US* persnickety

2 *nm* (**a**) *(policía)* cop (**b**) *(delator)* telltale (**c**) *(persona estricta)* nit-picker, *US* fussbudget

botonadura *nf* buttons

botonera *nf (planta)* santolina, lavender-cotton

botones *nmf inv (de hotel)* bellboy, *US* bellhop; *(de oficina)* errand boy, *f* errand girl

Botsuana, Botswana *n* Botswana

botsuanés, -esa 1 *adj* of/relating to Botswana *(Africa)*

2 *nm,f* person from Botswana *(Africa)*

Botswana = **Botsuana**

botulismo *nm* botulism

botuto *nm Carib* giant sea snail

bouquet [bu'ke] (*pl* **bouquets**) *nm* (**a**) *(del vino)* bouquet (**b**) *(de flores)* bouquet

bourbon ['burβon] (*pl* **bourbons**) *nm* bourbon

boutique [bu'tik] *nf* boutique ►► ***b. infantil*** children's boutique; ***b. de novia*** bridal shop; ***b. de señora*** fashion boutique

bóveda *nf* (**a**) *Arquit* vault ►► ***b. de arista*** groin vault; ***b. de cañón*** barrel vault; ***la b. celeste*** the firmament; ***b. de crucería*** ribbed vault; *Am* ***b. de seguridad*** *(en banco)* vault (**b**) *Anat* ***b. craneal*** cranial vault

bóvido *Zool* **1** *nm (animal)* bovid

2 bóvidos *nmpl (familia) Bovidae*; **de la familia de los bóvidos** of the *Bovidae* family

bovino, -a 1 *adj* bovine; **ganado b.** cattle *(plural)*

2 *nm* bovine

3 bovinos *nmpl (subfamilia)* cattle *(plural)*

box (*pl* **boxes**) *nm* (**a**) *(de caballo)* stall (**b**) *(de coches)* pit; **entrar en boxes** to make a pit stop (**c**) *Am (boxeo)* boxing

boxcalf *nm* box-calf

boxeador, -ora *nm,f* boxer

boxear *vi* to box

boxeo *nm* boxing

bóxer (*pl* **boxers**) *nm* (**a**) *(perro)* boxer (**b**) *(calzoncillo)* boxer shorts

boya *nf* (**a**) *(en el mar)* buoy ►► ***b. de campana*** bell buoy (**b**) *(de una red)* float

boyada *nf* drove of oxen

boyante *adj* (**a**) *(feliz)* happy (**b**) *(próspero) (empresa, negocio)* prosperous; *(economía, comercio)* buoyant

boyar *vi* to float

boyero, -a 1 *nm,f (pastor)* oxherd

2 *nm (ave)* oxpecker

boy scout [bojes'kaut] (*pl* **boy scouts**) *nm* boy scout

boza *nf Náut* painter

bozal *nm* (**a**) *(para perro)* muzzle (**b**) *Am (cabestro)* halter

bozo *nm (bigote)* down *(on upper lip)*

bps *Informát* (*abrev de* **bits por segundo**) bps

braceada *nf (movimiento)* swing of the arms; **dar braceadas** to wave one's arms about

braceaje *nm* depth (in fathoms)

bracear *vi* (**a**) *(mover los brazos)* to wave one's arms about (**b**) *(nadar)* **braceaba con energía** he swam with strong arm strokes

braceo *nm* arm strokes; **sé que mi b. deja mucho que desear** I know my arm strokes could be a lot better

bracero *nm* (**a**) *(jornalero)* day labourer (**b**) *Am* wetback, = illegal Mexican immigrant in the US

bracista *nmf Dep* breaststroker

bráctea *nf Bot* bract

braga *nf* (**a**) *Esp (prenda interior) Br* knickers, *US* panties; **una b., unas bragas** a pair of *Br* knickers *o US* panties; EXPR *Fam* **estar hecho una b.** to be whacked; EXPR *Fam* **pillar** *o* **coger en bragas: ¿la capital de Chad? ¡me pillas** *o* **coges en bragas!** the capital of Chad? you've really got me there!; **el profesor me pilló en bragas, no me sabía la lección** the teacher caught me out, I hadn't learnt the lesson ►► ***b.-pañal*** disposable *Br* nappy *o US* diaper

(**b**) *Fam (cosa de mala calidad)* **esta novela es una b.** this novel is dire *o Br* pants

(**c**) *(para el cuello)* snood

(**d**) *Ven (ropa)* boiler suit

bragado, -a *adj (firme, resuelto)* tough, determined

bragadura *nf (de persona, prenda)* crotch

bragazas *Fam* 1 *adj* henpecked
2 *nm inv* henpecked man
braguero *nm* truss
bragueta *nf Br* flies, *US* zipper
braguetazo *nm Esp Fam* marriage for money; **dar el b.** to marry for money
Brahma *n pr* Brahma
brahmán, bramán *nm* Brahman
brahmanismo, bramanismo *nm* Brahmanism
Brahmaputra *nm* **el B.** the Brahmaputra
braille ['braile] *nm* Braille
brainstorming [brein'stormin] (*pl* **brainstormings**) *nm* brainstorming session
brama *nf* rut, rutting season
bramadera *nf* (**a**) *(juguete)* bull-roarer (**b**) *Mús* reed pipes
bramadero *nm Am (poste)* tethering post
bramán = **brahmán**
bramanismo = **brahmanismo**
bramante *nm* twine
bramar *vi* (**a**) *(animal)* to bellow (**b**) *(persona) (de dolor)* to groan; *(de ira)* to roar (**c**) *(viento)* to howl; *(mar)* to roar
bramido *nm* (**a**) *(de animal)* bellow (**b**) *(de persona) (de dolor)* groan; *(de ira)* roar; **dar un b. de cólera** to give a furious roar (**c**) *(del viento)* howling; *(del mar)* roar
brandy *nm* brandy
branquial *adj* branchial
branquias *nfpl* gills
branquiosaurio *nm* branchiosaur
braña *nf* mountain pasture
braquial *adj Anat* brachial
braquicefalia *nf Anat* brachycephalism
braquicéfalo, -a *adj Anat* brachycephalic
braquiocefálico, -a *adj Anat* brachiocephalic
braquiuro *nm* bald uakari
brasa 1 *nf* (**a**) *(tizón)* ember; **a la b.** barbecued (**b**) EXPR *Esp Fam* **dar la b.** to go on and on; **¡deja de dar la b.!** stop going on and on!, give it a rest!
2 *nmf Esp Fam* **ser un b.** to be deadly boring
brasear *vt* to barbecue
brasero *nm* brazier; **b. eléctrico** electric heater
brasier *nm Carib, Col, Méx* bra
Brasil *nm* **(el) B.** Brazil
brasil *nm (árbol)* brazilwood tree; *(madera)* brazil(wood)
brasileño, -a, *RP* **brasilero, -a** 1 *adj* Brazilian
2 *nm,f* Brazilian
Brasilia *n* Brasilia
brasuca *RP Fam* 1 *adj* = pejorative term meaning "Brazilian"
2 *nmf* = pejorative term referring to a Brazilian person
Bratislava *n* Bratislava
bravata *nf* (**a**) *(amenaza)* threat (**b**) *(fanfarronería)* piece of bravado; **estoy cansado de sus bravatas** I'm tired of his bravado
braveza *nf* (**a**) *(de persona)* bravery (**b**) *(de animal)* wildness (**c**) *(del viento, mar)* fierceness, fury
bravío, -a *adj* (**a**) *(persona)* free-spirited (**b**) *(animal)* spirited (**c**) *(mar)* choppy, rough
bravo, -a 1 *adj* (**a**) *(persona) (valiente)* brave (**b**) *(persona) (violento)* fierce (**c**) *Andes, CAm, Carib, Méx (persona) (airado)* angry; **ponerse b.** to get angry (**d**) *(animal)* wild (**e**) *(planta)* wild (**f**) *(mar)* rough; **el mar se ha puesto b.** the sea has got rough (**g**) *RP (difícil)* difficult
2 *interj* bravo!
3 **a la brava** *loc adv Méx Fam (con descuido)* in a slapdash way; **limpiaste tu cuarto a la brava** you didn't do *o* make a very good job of cleaning your room
4 **a las bravas, por las bravas** *loc adv* by force
bravucón, -ona 1 *adj* loudmouthed; **es muy b.** he's a real loudmouth, he's all talk; **su comportamiento b.** his bravado
2 *nm,f* loudmouth
bravuconada *nf* show of bravado
bravuconear *vi* to brag
bravuconería *nf* bravado
bravura *nf* (**a**) *(de persona)* bravery (**b**) *(de animal)* ferocity (**c**) *(de mar)* roughness

braza *nf* (**a**) *Esp (en natación)* breaststroke; **nadar a b.** to do the breaststroke; **los 100 metros b.** the 100-metres breaststroke (**b**) *(medida)* fathom (**c**) *Náut (cabo)* brace
brazada *nf* (**a**) *(en natación)* stroke (**b**) *(cantidad)* armful
brazado *nm* armful
brazal *nm* (**a**) *(insignia)* armband (**b**) *(de escudo)* handle
brazalete *nm* (**a**) *(en la muñeca)* bracelet (**b**) *(en el brazo, para nadar)* armband
brazo *nm* (**a**) *(de persona)* arm; **paseaba del b. de su novio** she was walking arm in arm with her boyfriend; **agárrate de mi b.** hold on to my arm; **en brazos** in one's arms; **llevaba al nene en brazos** he was carrying the child in his arms; EXPR **echarse en brazos de alguien** to throw oneself at sb; EXPR **luchar a b. partido** *(con empeño)* to fight tooth and nail; EXPR **con los brazos abiertos** with open arms; EXPR **quedarse de brazos cruzados, cruzarse de brazos** to sit back and do nothing; EXPR **no dio su b. a torcer** he didn't budge an inch, he didn't allow himself to be persuaded; EXPR **ser el b. derecho de alguien** to be sb's right-hand man (*f* right-hand woman)
(**b**) *(de animal)* foreleg
(**c**) *(de sillón)* arm
(**d**) *(de árbol, río, candelabro)* branch
(**e**) *(de grúa)* boom, jib
(**f**) *(de balanza)* arm
(**g**) *(rama)* wing; **el b. político de ETA** the political wing of ETA; **el b. secular** *(no eclesiástico)* the secular arm
(**h**) *(trabajador)* hand
(**i**) ***b. de gitano*** *Br* swiss roll, *US* jelly roll
(**j**) *Geog* ***b. de mar*** inlet, arm of the sea
brazuelo *nm* shoulder
Brazzaville [bratsa'βil] *n* Brazzaville
brea *nf* (**a**) *(sustancia)* tar (**b**) *(para barco)* pitch
break [breik] *nm Dep* break; **punto de b.** break point
break dance [breik'dans] *nm* break dance
brear *vt Esp Fam* **b. a alguien** to beat sb up; **b. a preguntas** to bombard with questions
brebaje *nm* concoction, foul drink
breca *nf (pez)* pandora
brecha *nf* (**a**) *(abertura)* hole, opening; **la b. entre ricos y pobres** the gulf *o* gap between rich and poor
(**b**) *(herida)* gash; **hacerse una b. en la cabeza** to cut one's head, to split one's head open
(**c**) *Mil* breach
(**d**) *Méx* **camino de b.** dirt track
(**e**) EXPR **abrir b. en un mercado** to break into a market; **los jóvenes del partido están abriendo b. con propuestas vanguardistas** the young members of the party are blazing the trail with groundbreaking proposals; **no le asusta estar en b.** he's not afraid to take the rough with the smooth; **lleva veinte años en la b.** he's been in the thick of it for twenty years
brechtiano, -a *adj* Brechtian
brécol *nm* broccoli
brega *nf* (**a**) *(lucha)* struggle, fight (**b**) EXPR **andar a la b.** to toil, to work hard
bregar [38] *vi* (**a**) *(luchar)* to struggle, to fight (**b**) *(trabajar)* to work hard (**c**) *(reñir)* to quarrel (**con** with)
brejetero, -a, brertero, -a *adj Carib Fam* mischievous
breña *nf* rugged scrubland *o* brush
breque *nm* (**a**) *(pez)* bleak (**b**) *CAm (freno)* brake
brertero = **brejetero**
Bretaña *n* Brittany
brete *nm* (**a**) *(apuro)* fix, difficulty; EXPR **estar en un b.** to be in a fix; EXPR **poner a alguien en un b.** to put sb in a difficult *o* awkward position (**b**) *Ven Fam (ajetreo)* commotion, stew; **está siempre en un b.** she's always in a flap (**c**) *Cuba Fam (enredo)* mess
bretel *nm CSur* strap; **un vestido sin breteles** a strapless dress
bretón, -ona 1 *adj* Breton
2 *nm,f (persona)* Breton
3 *nm (lengua)* Breton
breva *nf* (**a**) *(fruta)* early fig; EXPR *Esp Fam* **¡no caerá esa b.!** some chance (of that happening)! (**b**) *(cigarro)* flat cigar (**c**) *Esp (pastel)* = long cream-filled doughnut (**d**) *CAm, Cuba, Méx (tabaco de mascar)* chewing tobacco
breve 1 *adj* (**a**) *(corto)* brief; **en b.** *(pronto)* shortly; *(en pocas palabras)* in short; **seré b.** I shall be brief; **en breves instantes** in a few moments; **anuncios breves** classified ads *o* adverts (**b**) *(sílaba, vocal)*

short (c) *(pie)* dainty; *(cintura)* slender
2 *nf Mús* breve
3 **breves** *nmpl (anuncios)* classified ads *o* adverts; *(noticias)* news in brief

brevedad *nf* (a) *(en el tiempo)* shortness; **la b. de su discurso sorprendió** her speech was surprisingly brief; **a** *o* **con la mayor b.** as soon as possible; **se ruega b.** please be brief (b) *(de pie)* daintiness; *(de cintura)* slenderness

brevemente *adv* (a) *(durante poco tiempo)* briefly (b) *(en breve)* shortly, soon

brevet *nm* (a) *Chile (de avión)* pilot's licence (b) *Bol, Ecuad, Perú (de automóvil) Br* driving licence, *US* driver's license (c) *RP (de velero)* sailing licence

brevete *nm Bol, Ecuad, Perú (de automóvil) Br* driving licence, *US* driver's license

breviario *nm* (a) *Rel* breviary (b) *(compendio)* compendium

brezal *nm* moorland, moors

brezo *nm* heather

briaga *nf Méx Fam (borrachera)* piss-up; **agarrar una b.** to get plastered *o* blitzed

briago, -a *adj Méx Fam* plastered, blitzed

bribón, -ona 1 *adj (pícaro)* roguish
2 *nm,f* scoundrel, rogue

bribonada *nf* **ser una b.** to be a roguish thing to do; **estoy harto de sus bribonadas** I'm fed up with him always getting up to mischief

bricolage, bricolaje *nm Br* DIY, do-it-yourself, *US* home improvement

brida *nf* (a) *(de caballo)* bridle (b) *(de tubo)* bracket, collar (c) *Med* adhesion

bridge [britʃ] *nm* bridge

brie [bri] *nm* brie

brigada 1 *nm Mil* warrant officer
2 *nf* (a) *Mil* brigade ►► *Hist* ***las Brigadas Internacionales*** the International Brigades; *Hist* ***las Brigadas Rojas*** the Red Brigades (b) *(equipo)* squad, team ►► ***b. anti corrupción*** fraud squad; ***b. antidisturbios*** riot squad; ***b. antidroga*** drug squad; ***b. de delitos económicos*** fraud squad; ***b. de estupefacientes*** drug squad; ***b. de explosivos*** bomb squad

brigadier *nm* (a) *(en el ejército)* brigadier (b) *(en la marina)* rear admiral

brigadista *nmf Hist* = member or veteran of the International Brigades during the Spanish Civil War

brik (*pl* **briks**) *nm* tetrabrik®; **un b. de leche** a carton of milk

brillante 1 *adj* (a) *(reluciente) (luz, astro)* shining; *(metal, zapatos, pelo)* shiny; *(ojos, sonrisa, diamante)* sparkling (b) *(magnífico)* brilliant; **el pianista estuvo b.** the pianist was outstanding; **el joven escritor tiene un futuro b.** the young writer has a brilliant future ahead of him
2 *nm* diamond, *Espec* brilliant

brillantemente *adv* brilliantly

brillantez *nf* (a) *(luminosidad) (de metal, zapatos, pelo)* shininess, shine; *(de ojos, sonrisa, diamante)* sparkle (b) *(éxito)* brilliance; **hacer algo con b.** to do sth outstandingly

brillantina *nf (gomina)* hair cream, Brylcreem®

brillar *vi* (a) *(luz, astro, metal, zapatos, pelo)* to shine; *(ojos, diamante)* to sparkle (b) *(sobresalir)* to shine; **brilla por su simpatía** she's remarkable for her kindness; EXPR **b. por su ausencia** to be conspicuous by its/one's absence; **la higiene brilla por su ausencia** there is a notable lack of hygiene; EXPR **b. con luz propia** to be outstanding

brillo *nm* (a) *(resplandor) (de luz, astro)* brightness; *(de metal, zapatos, pelo)* shine; *(de ojos, diamante)* sparkle; *(de monitor, televisor)* brightness; **sacar b. a** to polish, to shine; **¿en b. o en mate?** *(fotos)* would you like gloss photos or matt ones? (b) *(lucimiento)* splendour, brilliance (c) ***b. de labios*** lip gloss; ***b. de uñas*** clear nail varnish

brilloso, -a *adj Am* shining

brincar [60] *vi* (a) *(saltar)* to skip (about); **b. de alegría** to jump for joy; *Esp Fam* **está que brinca** *(enfadado)* he's hopping mad (b) *Ven Fam (pagar)* to cough up

brinco *nm* jump; **se levantó del asiento de un b.** she jumped up from her seat; **pegar** *o* **dar un b.** to jump, to give a start; **daba brincos de alegría** she was jumping for joy; **el corazón me dio un b. cuando oí su voz** my heart skipped a beat when I heard his voice; EXPR **en un b.** in a second, quickly; EXPR *Méx Fam* **ponerse al b.: mi padre se me puso al b. porque anoche llegué muy tarde** my father came down on me like a ton of bricks because I came in late last night; EXPR *Ven* **quitar los brincos a alguien** to bring sb down a peg

brindar 1 *vi* to drink a toast; **b. por algo/alguien** to drink to sth/sb; **b. a la salud de alguien** to drink to sb's health
2 *vt* (a) *(ofrecer)* to offer; **me brindó su casa** he offered me the use of his house; **el ayuntamiento brindó todos los medios a su disposición** the town council made available all the means at its disposal; **quiero agradecer la confianza que me brindan** I would like to thank you for the confidence you are showing in me; **su visita me brindó la ocasión de conocerlo mejor** his visit gave me the opportunity to get to know him better
(b) *Taurom* to dedicate; **b. el triunfo a alguien** *(en deportes, competiciones)* to dedicate one's victory to sb
3 **brindarse** *vpr* **brindarse a hacer algo** to offer to do sth; **se brindó a ayudarme** she offered to help me

brindis *nm inv* toast; **hacer un b. (por)** *(proponerlo)* to propose a toast (to); *(beber)* to drink a toast (to)

brío *nm* (a) *(energía, decisión)* spirit; **con b.** spiritedly; **trabajaba con mucho b.** she was a very energetic worker (b) *(de caballo)* spirit

brioche *nm* brioche

briofita *nf Bot* bryophyte

briosamente *adv* spiritedly

brioso, -a *adj* (a) *(con energía, decisión)* spirited, lively (b) *(caballo)* spirited

briqueta *nf (de carbón)* briquette

brisa *nf* breeze ►► ***b. del mar*** sea breeze; ***b. marina*** sea breeze

brisca *nf* = card game where each player gets three cards and one suit is trumps

británico, -a 1 *adj* British
2 *nm,f* British person, Briton; **los británicos** the British

brizna *nf* (a) *(filamento) (de hierba)* blade; *(de tabaco)* strand (b) *(un poco)* trace, bit; **no soplaba ni una b. de viento** there wasn't even a breath of wind (c) *Ven (llovizna)* drizzle

briznar *v impersonal Ven (lloviznar)* to drizzle

broca *nf* (drill) bit ►► ***b. helicoidal*** twist drill

brocado *nm* brocade

brocal *nm (de pozo)* parapet, curb

brocearse *vpr Andes, Arg* **el filón se ha broceado** the seam has been exhausted

broceo *nm Andes, Arg* exhaustion, depletion

brocha *nf (de pintor)* brush; *(de maquillaje)* make-up brush; **de b. gorda** *(basto)* broad, vulgar; **pintor de b. gorda** painter and decorator ►► ***b. de afeitar*** shaving brush

brochazo *nm*, **brochada** *nf* brushstroke

broche *nm* (a) *(en collar, pulsera)* clasp, fastener ►► *Am* ***b. de presión*** snap fastener
(b) *(joya)* brooch
(c) *(cierre, conclusión)* **el concierto puso el b. final a las fiestas** the concert rounded off the celebrations ►► ***b. de oro*** final flourish; **el recital puso el b. de oro a la velada** the recital was the perfect end to the evening
(d) *Méx, Urug (para el pelo) Br* slide, *US* barrette
(e) *Arg (para la ropa)* peg, *US* clothespin
(f) *RP (grapa)* staple
(g) *Chile (clip)* paperclip
(h) *Ecuad* **broches** cuff links

brocheta, *RP* **brochette** [broˈʃet] *nf* (a) *(varilla)* skewer (b) *(plato)* kebab; **b. de carne/de pollo** shish/chicken kebab

brócoli, bróculi *nm* broccoli

bróder *nm Esp, Andes, CAm Fam* (a) *(hermano)* bro (b) *(amigo) Br* mate, *US* bro

broderí (*pl* **broderíes** *o* **broderís**) *nm* broderie anglaise

bróker *nmf* broker

broma[1] *nf* (a) *(ocurrencia, chiste)* joke; *(jugarreta)* prank, practical joke; **gastar una b. a alguien** to play a joke *o* prank on sb; **en** *o* **de b.** as a joke; **tomar algo a b.** not to take sth seriously; **no estar para bromas** not to be in the mood for jokes; **estás de broma, ¿no?** you must be joking!; **hoy estoy con ganas de b.** I'm in a mischievous mood today; EXPR **entre bromas y veras** half-jokingly; EXPR **fuera de b., bromas aparte** joking apart; **ni en** *o* **de b.** no way, not on your life; **no se lo digas ni en b.** don't you even think about telling her; **no aceptaremos ni en b.** no way will we accept ►► ***b. de mal gusto*** bad joke; ***b. pesada*** nasty practical joke
(b) *Fam Irónico (cosa cara)* **me salió la b. por 400 euros** that little business set me back 400 euros
(c) *Fam (contrariedad)* pain; **el aeropuerto estaba cerrado y no pudimos salir – ¡menuda b.!** the airport was closed and we were stranded – what a pain!

(**d**) *Ven Fam (objeto)* thing, *Br* effort; **¿para qué sirve esa b.?** *(en aparato)* what's that thing for?; **me gusta esa b. que llevas puesta** that's a very nice little affair you're wearing

broma[2] *nf (molusco)* shipworm

bromato *nm Quím* bromate

bromatología *nf* nutrition

bromatológico, -a *adj* nutritional

bromatólogo, -a *nm,f* nutritionist

bromear *vi* to joke; **con la religión no se bromea** religion isn't something to be taken lightly

bromelia *nf* bromeliad

bromeliácea 1 *nf (planta)* bromeliad
2 bromeliáceas *nfpl (familia)* bromeliads

bromeliáceo, -a *adj* bromeliaceous

bromista 1 *adj* **ser muy b.** to be a real joker
2 *nmf* joker

bromo *nm Quím* bromine

bromuro *nm Quím* bromide

bronca 1 *nf* (**a**) *(jaleo)* row; **armar (una) b.** to kick up a row; **se armó una b. increíble** there was an almighty row; **buscar b.** to look for trouble
(**b**) *Esp (regañina)* scolding, telling-off; **echar una b. a alguien** to give sb a row, to tell sb off; **me echaron la b. por llegar tarde** I got a row for being late; **el equipo fue recibido con una b.** the team were booed when they came out onto the pitch
(**c**) *RP Fam (rabia)* **me da b.** it hacks me off; **¡estoy con una b.!** I'm really hacked off!; **el jefe le tiene b.** the boss has got it in for her; **está que vuela de (la) b.** she's foaming at the mouth
(**d**) *Méx Fam (problema)* **tengo una b. de dinero** I'm in a fix over money
(**e**) *Méx Fam (dificultad)* snag, problem; **fue una b. poder mudarme** moving was no picnic
(**f**) *ver también* **bronco**
2 *nmf Esp Fam* **ser un bronca(s)** to be a troublemaker, to be trouble

bronce *nm* (**a**) *(aleación)* bronze (**b**) *(estatua)* bronze (statue) (**c**) *Dep (medalla)* bronze (medal); **Bulgaria se llevó el b.** Bulgaria took the bronze

bronceado, -a 1 *adj* (**a**) *(moreno)* tanned (**b**) *(de color bronce)* bronze
2 *nm* tan

bronceador, -ora 1 *adj* **crema bronceadora** suntan cream
2 *nm (loción)* suntan lotion; *(crema)* suntan cream

broncear 1 *vt* (**a**) *(piel)* to tan (**b**) *(cubrir de bronce)* to bronze
2 broncearse *vpr* to get a tan

broncíneo, -a *adj* bronze

bronco, -a 1 *adj* (**a**) *(grave) (voz)* harsh; *(tos)* throaty (**b**) *(brusco)* gruff, surly (**c**) *(tosco)* rough; *(paisaje, peñascos)* rugged (**d**) *Méx Fam (huraño)* unsociable
2 *nm,f Méx Fam* unsociable person, loner

broncodilatador, -ora *Farm* **1** *adj* **un medicamento b.** a bronchodilator
2 *nm* bronchodilator

bronconeumonía *nf Med* bronchopneumonia

broncopulmonar *adj Med* bronchopulmonary

broncoscopia *nf Med* bronchoscopy

bronquedad *nf* (**a**) *(de voz)* harshness (**b**) *(brusquedad)* gruffness, surliness (**c**) *(tosquedad)* roughness; *(de paisaje, peñascos)* ruggedness

bronquial *adj* bronchial

bronquio *nm* bronchial tube; **tiene problemas de bronquios** she has a chest complaint

bronquiolo *nm Anat* bronchiole

bronquítico, -a *adj* bronchitic

bronquitis *nf inv* bronchitis

brontosaurio *nm* brontosaurus

broquel *nm* (**a**) *(escudo)* small shield (**b**) *(amparo)* shield

broqueta *nf* (**a**) *(varilla)* skewer (**b**) *(plato)* kebab; **b. de carne/de pollo** shish/chicken kebab

brotar 1 *vi* (**a**) *(planta)* to sprout, to bud; *(semilla)* to sprout; **ya le están brotando las flores al árbol** the tree is already beginning to flower; **las lechugas están brotando muy pronto este año** the lettuces are sprouting very early this year
(**b**) *(agua, sangre) (suavemente)* to flow; *(con violencia)* to spout; **b. de** to well up out of; **brotaba humo de la chimenea** smoke billowed from the chimney; **le brotaron las lágrimas** tears welled up in her eyes; **la sangre brotaba a borbotones de la herida** blood was gushing from the wound
(**c**) *(enfermedad)* **le brotó el sarampión** she came down with measles; **le brotó un sarpullido** he came out in a rash
(**d**) *(esperanza, pasiones)* to stir; **entre los dos brotó una profunda amistad** a deep friendship sprang up between them; **brotaron sospechas de que hubiera habido un fraude** suspicions of fraud started to emerge
2 brotarse *vpr* (**a**) *Am (salir sarpullidos)* to come out in a rash; **se brotó toda** she came out in a rash all over her body
(**b**) *RP Fam (disgustarse)* **no me hagas acordar de ese día, que me broto** don't remind me of that day, the very thought of it makes me ill; **María se brota cada vez que ve a Pedro** María can't stand the sight of Pedro

brote *nm* (**a**) *(de planta)* bud, shoot; *(de semilla)* sprout ►► ***brotes de soja*** beansprouts (**b**) *(estallido) (de enfermedad)* outbreak; **se produjeron varios brotes de violencia** there were several outbreaks of violence

broza *nf* (**a**) *(maleza)* brush, scrub (**b**) *(hojarasca)* dead leaves (**c**) *Fig (relleno)* waffle

brucelosis *nf inv Med* brucellosis

bruces: de bruces *loc adv* face down; **se cayó de b.** he fell headlong, he fell flat on his face; EXPR **darse de b. con algo/alguien** to find oneself face-to-face with sth/sb

bruja *nf* (**a**) *(hechicera)* witch, sorceress (**b**) *Fam (mujer fea)* hag (**c**) *Fam (mujer mala)* witch (**d**) *CAm, Carib, Méx Fam* **andar** *o* **estar b.** *(sin dinero)* to be broke *o Br* skint

Brujas *n* Bruges

brujería *nf* witchcraft, sorcery

brujo, -a 1 *adj* (**a**) *(hechicero)* enchanting, captivating (**b**) *Méx Fam* broke
2 *nm* wizard, sorcerer

brújula *nf* compass ►► ***b. giroscópica*** gyrocompass

brujulear *vi Esp Fam* (**a**) *(dar vueltas)* to mooch around (**b**) *(actuar con habilidad)* to manoeuvre

brulote *nm Am (palabrota)* swear-word

bruma *nf (niebla)* mist; *(en el mar)* sea mist

brumoso, -a *adj* misty

Brunei *n* Brunei

bruno, -a *adj* dark brown

bruñido, -a 1 *adj* polished
2 *nm* polishing

bruñir *vt (piedra, metal)* to polish

bruscamente *adv* (**a**) *(de repente)* suddenly, abruptly; **las temperaturas disminuyeron b.** temperatures fell suddenly *o* plummeted; **frenó b.** she braked sharply (**b**) *(toscamente)* brusquely

brusco, -a 1 *adj* (**a**) *(repentino, imprevisto)* sudden, abrupt; **un cambio b. de las temperaturas** a sudden change in temperature; **dio un frenazo b.** she braked sharply (**b**) *(tosco, grosero)* brusque; **me contestó de forma brusca** he answered me brusquely
2 *nm,f* brusque person

Bruselas *n* Brussels

bruselense 1 *adj* of/from Brussels; **las calles bruselenses** the streets of Brussels
2 *nmf* person from Brussels

brusquedad *nf* (**a**) *(imprevisión)* suddenness, abruptness; **con b.** suddenly, abruptly (**b**) *(grosería)* brusqueness; **los trata con mucha b.** she's very brusque with them

brut 1 *adj* brut
2 *nm inv* brut

brutal *adj* (**a**) *(violento)* brutal (**b**) *Fam (extraordinario)* wicked, brutal; **un libro/una película b.** a wicked *o* brutal book/film; **tengo un cansancio b.** I'm dead tired, I'm bushed; **conseguí entradas para el concierto – ¡b.!** I got hold of some tickets for the concert – wicked *o* brutal!

brutalidad *nf* (**a**) *(cualidad)* brutality; **con b.** brutally (**b**) *(acción)* atrocity; **las brutalidades cometidas por el ejército** the atrocities committed by the army (**c**) *(tontería)* stupid thing; **decir brutalidades** to talk nonsense (**d**) *Fam (gran cantidad)* **una b. (de)** loads (of)

brutalizar [14] *vt* to brutalize, to maltreat

brutalmente *adv* brutally

Bruto *n pr* Brutus

bruto, -a 1 *adj* (a) *(violento)* rough
(b) *(torpe)* clumsy
(c) *(ignorante)* thick, stupid
(d) *(maleducado)* rude
(e) *(sin tratar)* **en b.** *(diamante)* uncut; *(petróleo)* crude
(f) *(sueldo, peso)* gross; **gana 1.000 pesos brutos al mes** she earns 1,000 pesos a month gross
(g) **a lo b.**, *Am* **a la bruta** roughly, crudely
(h) *RP Fam (grande)* enormous; **agarrarse bruta gripe** to get a stinker of a cold; **se llevó b. susto** she got a hell of a fright
(i) *Ven Fam (mucho)* **sabe en b.** she's a real brain; **nos divertimos en b.** we had a really great time
2 *nm,f* (a) *(violento)* brute (b) *(torpe)* clumsy person; **es un b.** he's really clumsy (c) *(ignorante)* idiot (d) *(maleducado)* rude person; **es un b.** he's really rude

Bs.As. *(abrev de* **Buenos Aires**) Buenos Aires

B.S.O. *nf (abrev de* **Banda Sonora Original**) OST

BTT *nf (abrev de* **bicicleta todo terreno**) mountain bike

bu *(pl* **búes**) *nm Fam* bogeyman

buaa *interj* boo-hoo!

buba *nf Med (en ganglio linfático)* bubo

bubón *nm Med* bubo

bubónico, -a *adj* **peste bubónica** bubonic plague

bucal *adj (higiene, salud)* oral; *(cavidad)* buccal

bucanero *nm* buccaneer

Bucarest *n* Bucharest

búcaro *nm* (a) *(florero)* ceramic vase (b) *(botijo)* clay water jug

buceador, -ora *nm,f* diver ►► ***b. de aguas profundas*** deep-sea diver; ***b. de profundidad*** deep-sea diver

bucear *vi* (a) *(en agua)* to swim underwater, to dive (b) *(investigar)* **b. en** to delve into

buceo *nm* diving

buche *nm* (a) *(de ave)* crop (b) *(de animal)* maw (c) *Fam (de persona)* belly; **llenar el b.** to fill one's belly (d) *(trago)* **tomó un b. de agua** he took *o* drank a mouthful of water; **hacer buches** to rinse one's mouth (out) (e) *Ecuad (sombrero)* top hat (f) *Guat, Méx (bocio)* goitre

bucle *nm* (a) *(de pelo)* curl, ringlet (b) *(en hilo, cable)* loop (c) *(en carretera)* loop (d) *Informát* loop

bucodental *adj* oral (and dental); **higiene b.** oral hygiene

bucólica *nf Lit* pastoral poem, bucolic

bucólico, -a *adj* (a) *(campestre)* **un paisaje b.** a charmingly rural landscape; **la vida bucólica** country life (b) *Lit* pastoral, bucolic

bucolismo *nm* pastoralism; **el b. de un paisaje** the bucolic nature of a landscape

Buda *n pr* Buddha

Budapest *n* Budapest

budare *nf Ven* = round griddle for making maize pancakes and roasting coffee

budín *nm* (a) *(dulce)* pudding ►► *RP* ***b. inglés*** fruitcake; *Am* ***b. de pan*** bread pudding (b) *(salado)* terrine ►► ***b. de carne*** meat loaf; ***b. de salmón*** salmon terrine

budismo *nm* Buddhism ►► ***b. zen*** Zen Buddhism

budista 1 *adj* Buddhist
2 *nmf* Buddhist

buen *ver* **bueno**

buenamente *adv* (a) *(dentro de lo posible)* **hice lo que b. pude** I did what I could, I did as much as I could; **prepáralo como b. puedas** prepare it as best you can; **que cada uno dé lo que b. pueda** everyone should give whatever they can comfortably afford (b) *(por las buenas)* willingly

buenas *ver* **bueno**

buenaventura *nf* (a) *(adivinación)* fortune; **leer** *o* **decir la b. a alguien** to tell sb's fortune (b) *(suerte)* good luck

buenazo, -a *Fam* 1 *adj* (a) *(bondadoso)* good-natured, kind-hearted (b) *(ingenuo)* naive
2 *nm,f* (a) *(bondadoso)* good-natured *o* kind-hearted soul (b) *(ingenuo)* **es un b.** he's really naive

buenmozura *nf Am* good looks; **¡Pedro era de una b.!** Pedro was so good-looking!

BUENO, -A

buen is used instead of **bueno** before masculine singular nouns (e.g. **buen hombre** good man). The comparative form of **bueno** is **mejor** (better), and the superlative form is **el mejor** (masculine) or **la mejor** (feminine) (the best).

1 *adj* (a) *(en general)* good; **tu hijo es muy buen estudiante** your son's a very good student; **hacer ejercicio es b. para la salud** exercise is good for your health; **la cena estaba muy buena** the meal was very good; **una buena oportunidad** a good opportunity; **los buenos tiempos** the good times; **¿tienes hora buena?** do you have the right time?; **el juez de silla señaló que la bola fue/no fue buena** the umpire said the ball was good/called the ball out; **golpeó la pelota con la pierna buena** he struck the ball with his stronger foot; **tener buena acogida** to be well received; **tener buen aspecto** *(persona)* to look well; *(cosa)* to look good; **ir por buen camino** to be on the right track; **tener buen concepto de** to think highly of; **creo que éste no es un buen momento para decírselo** I don't think this is a good time to tell her; PROV **lo b. si breve dos veces b.** you can have too much of a good thing ►► ***el buen salvaje*** the noble savage; ***el buen samaritano*** the Good Samaritan
(b) *(bondadoso, amable)* kind, good; **ser b. con alguien** to be good to sb; **¡sé b.!** be good!
(c) *(curado, sano)* well, all right; **ya estoy b.** I'm all right now; **todavía no estoy b. del todo** I'm not completely better *o* recovered yet; **ponerse b.** to get well
(d) *(apacible)* nice, fine; **buen tiempo** good *o* fine weather; **hizo buen tiempo** the weather was good; *Esp* **¿hace b. ahí fuera?** is it nice out?
(e) *(aprovechable)* all right; *(comida)* fresh; **esta lecha no está buena** this milk is bad *o* off
(f) *(uso enfático)* **ese buen hombre** that good man; **una buena cantidad de comida** a good *o* considerable amount of food; **tiene una buena cantidad de libros** she has a large amount of books, she has quite a few books; **un buen susto** a real fright; **un buen lío** a real *o* fine mess; **un buen día se va a llevar un disgusto** one of these days she's going to get a nasty shock; **le cayó una buena reprimenda** he got a stern ticking-off; **le pegó un puñetazo de los buenos** he punched her really hard, he gave her an almighty punch
(g) *Fam (atractivo)* **estar b.** to be a bit of all right, to be tasty; **¡qué b. está tu vecino!** your neighbour's gorgeous *o* a real hunk!
(h) *Irónico (muy malo)* fine; **¡b. es lo b.!** enough's enough!; **¡b. está!** that's enough!; **¡buen amigo te has echado!** some friend he is!; **¡buen granuja estás hecho!** you rascal!, you're a real rascal!; **¡buena la has armado** *o* **hecho!** you've really gone and done it now!; **librarse de una buena** to have a lucky *o* narrow escape; **de buena te libraste** you had a lucky *o* narrow escape; **¡si te pillo no te librarás de una buena!** if I catch you, you'll be in for it!; **estaría b.** that would really cap it all; **si te crees que va a aceptar, estás b.** you're kidding yourself if you think she's going to accept; **estamos buenos como tengamos que esperarle** if we have to wait for him we've had it; **te has metido en una buena** this is a fine mess you've got *o* gotten yourself into!; **poner b. a alguien** to criticize sb harshly
(i) *(en saludos)* **¡buenas!** hello!; **¡buenas!, ¿qué tal?** hi *o* hello, how are you?; **¡buenos días!**, *RP* **¡buen día!** good morning!; **¡buenas tardes!** *(hasta las cinco)* good afternoon!; *(después de las cinco)* good evening!; **¡buenas noches!** good night!; **no me dio ni los buenos días** she didn't even say good morning to me
(j) *(en frases)* **¡buen provecho!** enjoy your meal!; **¡buen viaje!** have a good trip!; **de buen ver** good-looking, attractive; **de buena gana** willingly; **¡me comería un bocadillo de buena gana!** I really fancy a sandwich!; **lo hizo, y de buena gana** he did it willingly; **lo haría de buena gana, pero estoy ocupado** I'd be pleased *o* more than happy to do it, but I'm busy; **dar algo por b.** to approve sth; *Am Fam* **estar en la buena** to be on a roll; **lo b. es que...** the best thing about it is that...; **prueba este pastel y verás lo que es b.** try this cake, it's excellent; *Irónico* **como no me lo des, verás lo que es b.** if you don't give it to me, you'll be in for it
2 *nm,f* (a) *Cine* **el b.** the goody; **los buenos siempre ganan** the good guys always win
(b) *(bonachón)* **el b. de tu hermano** your good old brother
3 *adv* (a) *(vale, de acuerdo)* all right, O.K.; **¿te acompaño hasta la esquina? – b.** would you like me to walk up to the corner with you? – O.K.; **le pregunté si quería ayuda y me dijo que b.** I asked her if she needed any help and she said all right; **¿quieres venir con nosotros? – b.** do you want to come with us? – if you like *o* sure; **b., yo ya me voy** right, I'm off now; **¡te has equivocado! – b. ¿y qué?** you were wrong – yeah, so what?
(b) *(pues)* well; **b., el caso es que...** well, the thing is...
(c) *Am (bien)* **¡qué b.!** (that's) great!; **¡qué b. que vinieron!** I'm so glad that you could come!
4 *interj* (a) *(expresa sorpresa)* **¡b.!, ¡qué alegría verte por aquí!** hey, how nice to see you!; **¡b., mira quien está aquí!** well, look who's here!
(b) *(expresa irritación)* **¡b.!, ¡lo que faltaba!** great, that's just what we needed!
(c) *Col, Méx (al teléfono)* hello

5 buenas *nfpl* EXPR **estar de buenas** *(bien dispuesto)* to be in a good mood; **de buenas a primeras** *(de repente)* all of a sudden; *(a simple vista)* at first sight, on the face of it; **así, de buenas a primeras, no sé qué decir** I'm not sure I know what to say without thinking about it first; **por las buenas** willingly; **lo hará por las buenas o por las malas** she'll do it whether she likes it or not; **intentamos persuadirlo por las buenas** we tried to convince him the nice way; **¿quieres hacerlo por las buenas o por las malas?** do you want to do it the easy or the hard way?

Buenos Aires *n* Buenos Aires

buey (*pl* **bueyes**) **1** *nm* **(a)** *(mamífero)* ox; EXPR **trabajar como un b.** to work like a slave; EXPR *RP* **hablar de bueyes perdidos** to chatter about nothing in particular; EXPR *RP* **saber con qué bueyes se ara** to know what sort of people one is dealing with; PROV *RP* **entre bueyes no hay cornadas** birds of a feather stick together ►► ***b. almizclero*** musk ox
(b) *(crustáceo)* edible crab, *Br* brown crab ►► ***b. de mar*** edible crab, *Br* brown crab
(c) *Méx Fam (hombre)* guy; **siempre vienen los mismos bueyes** it's always the same guys who come
2 *interj Méx Fam* **¿qué tal estás, b.?** how are you doing, man *o Br* my son?; **¡espérame, b.!** hang on, man *o Br* mate!

búfalo *nm* buffalo ►► ***b. de agua*** water buffalo

bufanda *nf* **(a)** *(prenda)* scarf **(b)** *Esp Fam (gratificación)* bonus

bufar *vi* **(a)** *(toro, caballo)* to snort; *(gato)* to hiss **(b)** *Fam (persona)* **está que bufa** he's foaming at the mouth

bufé (*pl* **bufés**), **buffet** (*pl* **buffets**) *nm* **(a)** *(comida)* buffet ►► ***b. frío*** cold buffet; ***b. libre*** = buffet where you can eat as much as you like for a set price **(b)** *(restaurante)* buffet restaurant **(c)** *Andes (mueble)* sideboard

búfer, buffer ['bafer] (*pl* **buffers**) *nm Informát* buffer ►► ***b. de impresión*** print buffer

bufete *nm* **(a)** *(despacho)* lawyer's practice **(b)** *(mueble)* writing desk

buffer = **búfer**

buffet = **bufé**

bufido *nm* **(a)** *(de toro, caballo)* snort; *(de gato)* hiss **(b)** *Fam (de persona)* snarl of anger

bufo, -a 1 *adj* **(a)** *(grotesco)* comic **(b)** *Mús* comic
2 *nm RP Fam* fairy, nancy (boy)

bufón *nm* **(a)** *(en la corte)* jester **(b)** *(gracioso)* clown; **hacer el b.** to act the clown, to clown around

bufonada, bufonería *nf* jape; **estamos cansados de sus bufonadas** we're tired of him always acting the clown *o* clowning around

bufonesco, -a *adj* comical, clownish

bufoso *nm RP Fam* rod, piece

bug [buɣ] (*pl* **bugs**) *nm Informát* bug

buga *nm Fam* **(a)** *Esp (coche)* wheels, *Br* motor **(b)** *Méx* straight (person)

buganvilla *nf* bougainvillea

buggy ['buɣi] *nm* beach buggy

bugle *nm* bugle

bugui *nm (baile)* boogie

bugui-bugui *nm (baile)* boogie-woogie

buhardilla, boardilla *nf* **(a)** *(habitación)* attic **(b)** *(ventana)* dormer (window)

búho *nm* owl ►► ***b. chico*** long-eared owl; ***b. nival*** snowy owl; ***b. pescador*** brown fish owl; ***b. real*** eagle owl

buhonería *nf* pedlar's wares

buhonero, -a *nm,f* hawker, pedlar

buitre 1 *adj Fam* **es muy b.** *(con la comida)* he's a greedy pig; *(con los amigos, padres)* he's a real scrounger; *(con las chicas)* he's a real lech
2 *nm* **(a)** *(ave)* vulture ►► ***b. leonado*** griffon vulture; ***b. monje*** black vulture **(b)** *(persona) (con la comida)* greedy pig; *(con los amigos, padres)* scrounger; *(con las chicas)* lech

buitrear *vt Fam* to scrounge; **siempre va buitreando tabaco a sus amigos** she's always scrounging cigarettes off her friends

buitrera *nf* **(a)** *(nido)* vulture's nest **(b)** *(comedero)* vultures' feeding ground

buitrero, -a 1 *adj* vulturine
2 *nm* vulture hunter

buitrón *nm* **(a)** *(para pescar)* fish trap **(b)** *(red)* game-hunting net **(c)** *(trampa)* snare, trap **(d)** *(ave)* fan-tailed warbler **(e)** *Andes (horno)* silver-smelting furnace

bujarra, bujarrón *nm Esp muy Fam Pey (homosexual) Br* poof, *US* faggot

buje *nm Tec* axle box, bushing

bujía *nf* **(a)** *Aut* spark plug **(b)** *(vela)* candle

Bujumbura *n* Bujumbura

bula *nf (documento)* (papal) bull; EXPR **tener b.** to receive special treatment; **tiene b. para entrar y salir a sus anchas** he has special dispensation to come and go just as he pleases

bulbo *nm* **(a)** *Bot* bulb **(b)** *Anat* bulb ►► ***b. raquídeo*** medulla oblongata

bulboso, -a *adj* bulbous

buldog (*pl* **buldogs**) *nm* bulldog

buldózer (*pl* **buldozers**) *nm* bulldozer

bulerías *nfpl* = popular Andalusian song and dance

bulevar (*pl* **bulevares**) *nm* **(a)** *(avenida)* boulevard **(b)** *Urug (isleta)* traffic island

Bulgaria *n* Bulgaria

búlgaro, -a 1 *adj* Bulgarian
2 *nm,f (persona)* Bulgarian
3 *nm (lengua)* Bulgarian

bulimia *nf* bulimia

bulímico, -a *adj* bulimic

bulín *nm Fam* **(a)** *RP (picadero)* bachelor pad **(b)** *RP (casa)* little place **(c)** *Perú (burdel)* whorehouse, *Br* knocking shop

bulla *nf* **(a)** *Fam (ruido)* racket, uproar; **armar** *o* **meter b.** to kick up a racket; EXPR *Chile* **ser quitado de b.** to shy away from the limelight **(b)** *Esp Fam (prisa)* **meter b. a alguien** to hurry sb up; **tener b.** to be in a hurry **(c)** *RP Fam (aspavientos)* **te voy a contar lo que hice, pero no hagas b.** I'll tell you what I did, but don't go blabbing it around **(d)** *Ven (minería)* = gold or diamond deposit

bullabesa *nf* bouillabaisse

bullanga *nf* merrymaking

bullanguero, -a 1 *adj* **ser muy b.** to love a good time, to love partying
2 *nm,f* **es un b.** he loves a good time *o* loves partying

bullaranga *nf Carib, Col Fam* racket, uproar

bulldog [bul'doɣ] (*pl* **bulldogs**) *nm* bulldog

bulldozer [bul'doθer] (*pl* **bulldozers**) *nm* bulldozer

bullicio *nm* **(a)** *(de ciudad, mercado)* hustle and bustle **(b)** *(de multitud)* hubbub

bullicioso, -a 1 *adj* **(a)** *(agitado) (reunión, multitud)* noisy; *(calle, mercado)* busy, bustling **(b)** *(inquieto)* rowdy, boisterous
2 *nm,f* boisterous person

bullir *vi* **(a)** *(hervir)* to boil; *(burbujear)* to bubble; **me bulle la sangre cuando veo injusticias así** it makes my blood boil to see injustices like that
(b) *(multitud)* to bustle; *(ratas, hormigas)* to swarm; *(mar)* to boil; **la calle bullía de gente** the street was swarming with people; **los pasillos bullían de actividad** the corridors were a hive of activity
(c) *(surgir)* to bubble up; **le bullían muchas ideas en la cabeza** her head was bubbling over with ideas

bullterrier [bul'terjer] (*pl* **bullterriers**) *nmf* bull terrier

bulo *nm Esp* false rumour; **hicieron correr el b. de que estaba casado** they spread the false rumour that he was married

bulón *nm RP (tornillo)* = large round-headed screw

bulto 1 *nm* **(a)** *(volumen)* bulk, size; **hacer mucho b.** to take up a lot of space; EXPR **hacer b.** to make up the numbers; **viene a hacer b.** he's just here to make up the numbers; EXPR **de b.: un error de b.** a glaring error
(b) *(abombamiento) (en rodilla, superficie)* bump; *(en maleta, bolsillo)* bulge; **me ha salido un b. en el brazo** I've got a lump on my arm
(c) *(forma imprecisa)* blurred shape; **dos bultos se movían en la oscuridad** two shapes were moving in the darkness
(d) *(paquete)* package; *(maleta)* item of luggage; *(fardo)* bundle; **¿dónde puedo dejar mis bultos?** where can I put my luggage *o* bags?; **un b. sospechoso obligó a evacuar el edificio** a suspicious package forced them to evacuate the building ►► ***b. de mano*** piece *o* item of hand luggage
(e) b. (redondo) *(estatua)* statue
(f) *CAm, Col, Méx, Ven (cartapacio)* briefcase, satchel
(g) *Méx Fam* **de b.: esas cajas sólo están de b.** *(de sobra)* those boxes are just taking up space
2 a bulto *loc adv* approximately, roughly; **hacer un cálculo a b.** to make a rough estimate

bululú (*pl* **bululúes**) *nm Ven Fam (alboroto)* racket, commotion

bum *interj (explosión)* boom!; *(golpe)* bang!

bumerán (*pl* **bumeranes**) *nm* boomerang

bungaló, bungalow [bunga'lo] (*pl* **bungalows**) *nm* chalet

búnker (*pl* **bunkeres**) *nm* (**a**) *(refugio)* bunker (**b**) *Esp Pol* reactionary forces (**c**) *(en golf)* bunker

buñolería *nf* = stand or store selling doughnuts

buñueliano, -a *adj* Bunuelian, = typical of the macabre surrealistic style of the Spanish film director Luis Buñuel (1900-83)

buñuelo *nm* (**a**) *(dulce)* doughnut ►► ***b. de viento*** doughnut *(filled with cream)* (**b**) *(salado)* dumpling

BUP [bup] *nm Antes* (*abrev de* **Bachillerato Unificado Polivalente**) = academically orientated Spanish secondary school course for pupils aged 14-17

buque *nm* ship; EXPR *RP Fam* **tomarse el b.** *Br* to play truant, *US* to play hookey ►► ***b. de cabotaje*** coastal vessel, coaster; ***b. de carga*** cargo ship; ***b. cisterna*** tanker; ***b. escuela*** training ship; ***b. factoría*** factory ship; ***b. de guerra*** warship; *también Fig* ***b. insignia*** flagship; ***b. mercante*** merchant ship; ***b. nodriza*** refuelling ship; ***b. oceanográfico*** oceanographical ship; ***b. de pasajeros*** passenger ship, liner

buqué *nm* bouquet *(of wine)*

buraco *nm RP Fam* hole

burbuja *nf* bubble; **hacer burbujas** to bubble; **con burbujas** *(bebida)* fizzy; **sin burbujas** *(bebida)* still

burbujeante *adj* (**a**) *(agua hirviendo)* bubbling (**b**) *(champán, sidra)* fizzy

burbujear *vi* (**a**) *(agua hirviendo)* to bubble (**b**) *(champán, sidra)* to fizz

burbujeo *nm* (**a**) *(agua hirviendo)* bubbling (**b**) *(champán, sidra)* fizzing

burda: burda de *loc adv Ven Fam* **¿qué tal estuvo la excursión? – b. de chévere** how was the trip? – dead cool; **cuenta unos chistes b. de buenos** she tells some dead good jokes

burdamente *adv* crudely

burdel *nm* brothel

Burdeos *n* Bordeaux

burdeos 1 *adj inv* burgundy

2 *nm inv* (**a**) *(color)* burgundy (**b**) *(vino)* Bordeaux

burdo, -a *adj* (**a**) *(lenguaje, modales)* crude, coarse (**b**) *(tela)* coarse (**c**) *(imitación, copia)* cheap, crude; *(manipulación, mentira)* blatant

bureo *nm Esp Fam (juerga)* knees-up; **salir de b.** to go out on the town

bureta *nf* burette

burgalés, -esa 1 *adj* of/from Burgos *(Spain)*

2 *nm,f* person from Burgos *(Spain)*

búrger ['buryer] (*pl* **búrgers**), **búrguer** (*pl* **búrguers**) *nm Fam* burger bar *o* restaurant

burgo *nm Hist* borough, town

burgomaestre *nm* burgomaster, mayor

búrguer = **búrger**

burgués, -esa 1 *adj* (**a**) *Hist & Pol* bourgeois (**b**) *(de la clase media)* middle-class

2 *nm,f* (**a**) *Hist & Pol* member of the bourgeoisie; **pequeño b.** petit bourgeois (**b**) *(de la clase media)* member of the middle class

burguesía *nf* (**a**) *Hist & Pol* bourgeoisie; **alta b.** haute bourgeoisie (**b**) *(clase media)* middle class; **alta b.** upper middle class

buril *nm* burin, engraver's tool

burilar *vt* to engrave

Burkina Faso *n* Burkina Faso

burla *nf* (**a**) *(mofa)* taunt; **hacer b. de** to mock; **fue el blanco de las burlas de sus compañeros** he was the butt of his companions' jokes; **fue la b. de todo el mundo** everyone made fun of her; **esa sentencia es una b. a la justicia** that sentence is a travesty of justice (**b**) *(broma)* joke; EXPR **entre burlas y veras** half-jokingly (**c**) *(engaño)* trick

burladero *nm Taurom* = wooden board behind which the bullfighter can hide from the bull

burlador *nm Literario* Casanova, Don Juan

burlar 1 *vt (esquivar)* to evade; *(ley)* to flout; **consiguió b. a sus perseguidores** she managed to outwit her pursuers; **el ladrón burló los sistemas de seguridad** the thief found a way round the security systems; EXPR **burla burlando** without anyone noticing

2 **burlarse** *vpr* to mock; **burlarse de algo/alguien** to mock sth/sb, to make fun of sth/sb; **burlarse de las leyes** to flout the law

burlesco, -a *adj* (**a**) *(tono)* jocular (**b**) *Lit* burlesque

burlete *nm* draught excluder

burlón, -ona 1 *adj (con malicia)* mocking; *(sin malicia)* jokey, waggish; **una risa burlona** a mocking laugh; **es muy b.** he's a real joker *o* wag; **no seas tan b. conmigo** stop teasing me, don't be such a tease

2 *nm,f (bromista)* joker, wag; *(que toma el pelo)* tease

burlonamente *adv* (**a**) *(en broma)* jokingly (**b**) *(con sarcasmo)* mockingly

buró *nm* (**a**) *(escritorio)* bureau, writing desk (**b**) *Pol* executive committee (**c**) *Méx (mesa de noche)* bedside table

burocracia *nf* bureaucracy; **ya no hay tanta b. para sacarse el pasaporte** there isn't so much red tape involved in getting a passport any more

burócrata *nmf* bureaucrat

burocrático, -a *adj* bureaucratic

burocratismo *nm* bureaucracy

burocratización *nf* bureaucratization

burocratizar [14] *vt* to bureaucratize

burra *nf* (**a**) *Esp Fam* bike (**b**) *ver también* **burro**

burrada *nf* (**a**) *(tontería)* **decir/hacer una b.** to say/do something stupid; **decir burradas** to talk nonsense; **hacer burradas** to act stupidly (**b**) *Esp Fam (cantidad)* **una b. de** loads of, masses of; **había una b. de gente** there were loads *o* masses of people there (**c**) *Esp Fam (muchísimo)* **me gustó una b.** I thought it was dead brilliant; **bebí una b.** I had loads to drink

burrera *nf Bol Fam* (**a**) *(dicho)* **decir burreras** to talk nonsense (**b**) *(cosa)* trifle

burrero, -a *nm,f* (**a**) *CSur (aficionado a la hípica)* horse-racing fan (**b**) *Méx (arriero)* muleteer

burrito *nm CAm, Méx* burrito

burro, -a 1 *adj Fam* (**a**) *(necio)* thick, dumb

(**b**) *(tosco)* rough, oafish; **¡eres más b.!** you're such an oaf!

(**c**) *(terco)* pigheaded; **se puso b. y no pudimos convencerle** he dug his heels in and we couldn't convince him

2 *nm,f* (**a**) *(animal)* donkey; EXPR *Fam* **apearse** *o* **bajarse del b.** to back down; EXPR *Fam* **no ver tres en un b.** to be as blind as a bat; **con estas gafas no veo tres en un b.** I can't see a thing with these glasses; EXPR *Fam Hum* **¡la carne de b. no es transparente!** we can't see through you, you great lump! PROV *Fam* **b. grande, ande o no ande** big is best ►► ***b. de carga*** workhorse

(**b**) *Fam (necio)* ass, dimwit; **hacer el b.** to behave like an idiot

(**c**) *Fam (bruto)* oaf

(**d**) *Fam (terco)* stubborn mule; **es un b.** he's as stubborn as a mule, he's really pigheaded

(**e**) *Fam (trabajador)* **b. (de carga)** workhorse; EXPR **trabaja como una burra** she works like a slave

3 *nm* (**a**) *Esp (juego de cartas)* ≃ old maid

(**b**) *CSur (caballo de carreras)* racehorse

(**c**) *Carib (banco)* improvised bench

(**d**) *Arg* ***b. de arranque*** starter motor

(**e**) *Carib, Méx (escalera)* stepladder

(**f**) *Méx (tabla de planchar)* ironing board

(**g**) *Am Fam (transportador de drogas)* mule

(**h**) *RP Fam (caballo con arcos)* pommel horse

burro-taxi *nm* = donkey hired out for sight-seeing tours

bursátil *adj* stock market; **actividad b.** stock market trading; **crisis b.** stock market crisis; **mercado b.** stock market; **valores bursátiles** *Br* shares *o US* stocks (quoted on the stock exchange)

bursitis *nf inv Med* bursitis ►► ***b. de rodilla*** housemaid's knee

burujo *nm (de papel)* ball; *(de cabello, hilo)* tangle

burundés, -esa 1 *adj* of/from Burundi

2 *nm,f* person from Burundi

Burundi *n* Burundi

bus (*pl* **buses**) *nm* (**a**) *Informát* bus ►► ***b. de datos*** data bus; ***b. de direccionamiento*** address bus (**b**) *Fam (autobús)* bus; **en b.** by bus

busaca *nf Carib* bag, satchel

busca 1 *nf* search; **(ir) en b. de** (to go) in search of; **a la b. de algo** in search of sth; **orden de b. y captura** arrest warrant; **en b. y captura** on the run (from the police)

2 *nm Esp (buscapersonas)* pager

buscabullas = **buscapleitos**

buscador, -ora 1 *nm,f* hunter; **b. de oro** gold prospector
2 *nm Informát (en Internet)* search engine

buscapersonas *nm inv* pager

buscapiés *nm inv* firecracker, jumping jack

buscapleitos, *Méx* **buscabullas** *nmf inv Fam* troublemaker

BUSCAR [60] 1 *vt* (**a**) *(para encontrar)* to look for, to search for; *(provecho, beneficio propio, fortuna)* to seek; **busco apartamento en esta zona** I am looking for a *Br* flat *o US* apartment in this area; **estoy buscando trabajo** I'm looking for work; **la policía busca a los terroristas** the police are searching *o* hunting for the terrorists; **lo busqué, pero no lo encontré** I looked *o* hunted for it, but I didn't find it; **¿me ayudas a b. las llaves?** would you mind helping me to look for the keys?; **se fue a b. fortuna a América** he went to seek his fortune in America; **fui a b. ayuda** I went in search of help; **ive a b. ayuda, rápido!** quick, go for *o* and find help!; EXPR **es como b. una aguja en un pajar** it's like looking for a needle in a haystack; EXPR *CSur Fam* **b. la vuelta a algo** to (try to) find a way of doing sth
(**b**) *(recoger)* to pick up; **vino a b. sus libros** he came to pick up his books; **voy a b. el periódico** I'm going for the paper *o* to get the paper; **ir a b. a alguien** to pick sb up; **ya iré yo a b. a los niños al colegio** I'll go and pick the children up from school; **pasará a buscarnos a las nueve** she'll pick us up at nine
(**c**) *(en diccionario, índice, horario)* to look up; **buscaré la dirección en mi agenda** I'll look up the address in my address book
(**d**) *(intentar conseguir)* **siempre busca quedar bien con todos** she always tries to please everybody; **no sé qué está buscando con esa actitud** I don't know what he is hoping to achieve with that attitude; **con estas medidas buscan reducir la inflación** these measures are intended to reduce inflation, with these measures they are seeking to reduce inflation; *Fam* **ése sólo busca ligar** he's only after one thing
(**e**) *Informát* to search for
(**f**) *Fam (provocar)* to push, to try the patience of; **no me busques, que me voy a enfadar** don't push me *o* it, I'm about to lose my temper; **b. bronca** *o* **camorra** to look for trouble
2 *vi* to look; **busqué bien pero no encontré nada** I had a thorough search, but didn't find anything; **buscamos por toda la casa** we looked *o* searched throughout the house, we searched the house from top to bottom
3 **buscarse** *vpr* (**a**) *Fam (castigo, desgracia)* **se está buscando problemas** she's asking for trouble; **buscarse la ruina** to bring about one's own downfall; **buscársela** to be asking for it; **no sigas así, te la estás buscando** you're asking for it if you carry on like that
(**b**) EXPR *Fam* **buscarse la vida** *(ganarse el sustento)* to seek one's fortune; *(arreglárselas uno solo)* to look after oneself; **búscate la vida, pero el trabajo tiene que estar acabado hoy** I don't care how you do it, but the work has to be finished today
(**c**) *(en letrero)* **se busca (vivo o muerto)** wanted (dead or alive); **se busca: pastor alemán** lost: German shepherd; **se busca camarero** waiter wanted

buscarla *nf (ave)* warbler ▸▸ ***b. pintoja*** grasshopper warbler

buscavidas *nmf inv Fam* (**a**) *(desenvuelto)* go-getter (**b**) *(entrometido)* nosy person, *Br* nosy parker

buscón, -ona *nm,f (estafador)* swindler

buscona *nf Fam (prostituta)* whore

buseca *nf RP* tripe stew

buseta *nf Col, CRica, Ecuad, Ven* minibus

busilis *nm inv Esp Fam* (**a**) *(clave)* crux (**b**) *(dificultad)* hitch, snag; **ahí está el b.** that's the catch

búsqueda *nf* search; **a la b. de algo** in search of sth; *Esp* **(ir) en b. de** (to go) in search of

busquillas *nmf inv Andes Fam* go-getter

bustier *nm* strapless top

busto *nm* (**a**) *(pecho)* chest (**b**) *(senos)* bust (**c**) *(escultura)* bust

butaca *nf* (**a**) *(mueble)* armchair (**b**) *(localidad)* seat ▸▸ *Esp* ***b. de entresuelo*** seat in the dress circle; ***b. de patio*** *Br* seat in the stalls, *US* orchestra seat

butacón *nm* large easy chair

Bután *n* Bhutan

butanero, -a *nm,f* = person who delivers gas cylinders

butanés, -esa 1 *adj* Bhutanese
2 *nm,f* Bhutanese

butano 1 *adj Esp (color)* bright orange
2 *nm (gas)* butane (gas)

buten: de buten *loc adv Esp Fam* fantastic, ace; **nos lo pasamos de b.** we had a fantastic *o* an ace time

butifarra *nf* (**a**) *(embutido)* = type of Catalan pork sausage (**b**) *Perú (bocadillo)* ham, lettuce and onion sandwich

butileno *nm Quím* butylene

butrón *nm Esp* **método del b.** = method of robbery by breaking into a building via a hole made from inside an adjoining building

butronero, -a *nm,f Esp* = robber who breaks in through a hole made from inside an adjoining building

buu *interj* boo!

buxácea 1 *nf (planta)* member of the *Buxaceae* family
2 **buxáceas** *nfpl (familia) Buxaceae*

buxáceo, -a *adj Bot* of/from the *Buxaceae* family

buzamiento *nm Geol* dip ▸▸ ***b. de falla*** fault dip

buzar [14] *vi Geol* to dip

buzo *nm* (**a**) *(persona)* diver (**b**) *Arg (sudadera)* sweatshirt (**c**) *Arg (chándal)* tracksuit (**d**) *Col, Urug (jersey)* sweater, *Br* jumper

buzón *nm* (**a**) *(para cartas)* post box, *Br* letter box, *US* mailbox; **echar algo al b.** to post sth, *US* to mail sth; EXPR *RP Fam* **comprar un b.: Lucía es increíble, capaz de comprar un b.** Lucía is incredibly gullible; EXPR *RP Fam* **vender un b.: no lo mandes a hacer las compras, que igual le venden un b.** don't send him shopping, he'll probably get ripped off ▸▸ ***b. de sugerencias*** suggestions box; ***b. de voz*** voice mail
(**b**) *Informát (de correo electrónico)* (electronic) mailbox, e-mail address
(**c**) *Fam (boca)* big mouth

buzonear *vi* to deliver leaflets

buzoneo *nm* leafleting

bypass [bai'pas] (*pl* **bypasses**) *nm Med* heart bypass operation

byte [bait] (*pl* **bytes**) *nm Informát* byte

C, c

C, c [θe] *nf (letra)* C, c

C[1] *nf (número romano)* C

C[2] (**a**) (*abrev de* **Celsius** *o* **centígrado**) C (**b**) *Esp* (*abrev de* **carretera comarcal**) minor road, *Br* ≃ B road (**c**) (*abrev de* **caballo**) *(en notación de ajedrez)* Kt

c/ (**a**) (*abrev de* **cuenta**) a/c (**b**) (*abrev de* **calle**) St

C++ [θemas'mas, θeplus'plus] *nm Informát* C++

C1 *nm* (*abrev de* **Canadian canoe 1**) C1

C2 *nm* (*abrev de* **Canadian canoe 2**) C2

CA *nf* (**a**) (*abrev de* **corriente alterna**) AC (**b**) *Esp* (*abrev de* **Comunidad Autónoma**) = autonomous Spanish region

ca *interj Fam (no)* no way!

cabal 1 *adj* (**a**) *(honrado)* upright, honest (**b**) *(exacto)* exact; *(completo)* complete; **a los nueve meses cabales** at exactly nine months
2 **cabales** *nmpl* EXPR **no está en sus cabales** he's not in his right mind

cábala *nf* (**a**) *(doctrina)* cabbala (**b**) **hacer cábalas** *(conjeturas)* to speculate, to guess

cabalgada *nf Esp* **hay una larga c. hasta el pueblo** it's a long ride to the village; **tres días de c.** three days on horseback

cabalgadura *nf* mount

cabalgamiento *nm Geol* overthrust (fault)

cabalgar [38] 1 *vi (jinete)* to ride
2 *vt* (**a**) *(caballo)* to ride (**b**) *(semental)* to cover, to mate with

cabalgata *nf* (**a**) *Esp (desfile)* cavalcade, procession ▸▸ ***la c. de Reyes, la c. de los Reyes Magos*** = procession to celebrate the journey of the Three Kings, on 5 January (**b**) *Am (paseo)* **ir de c.** to go for a ride

cabalista *nmf* (**a**) *(estudioso)* cabbalist (**b**) *(intrigante)* intriguer

cabalístico, -a *adj* (**a**) *(de la cábala)* cabbalistic (**b**) *(oculto)* mysterious

caballa *nf* mackerel

caballada *nf* (**a**) *(manada)* herd (**b**) *Am Fam (animalada)* stupid thing; **hacer caballadas** to make a fool of oneself

caballar *adj* equine, horse; **ganado c.** horses

caballerango *nm CRica, Méx* groom, stable lad

caballeresco, -a *adj* (**a**) *(persona, modales)* chivalrous (**b**) *(literatura)* chivalric

caballería *nf* (**a**) *(animal)* mount, horse (**b**) *(cuerpo militar) (a caballo)* cavalry; *(en vehículos motorizados)* motorized troops ▸▸ ***c. ligera*** light cavalry (**c**) *(institución feudal)* **la c. medieval** medieval knights; **novela de caballería(s)** tale of chivalry ▸▸ ***c. andante*** knight errantry

caballeriza *nf* stable

caballerizo, -a *nm,f* groom, stable lad, *f* stable girl

caballero 1 *adj (cortés)* gentlemanly
2 *nm* (**a**) *(hombre cortés)* gentleman; **ser todo un c.** to be a real gentleman
(**b**) *(señor, varón)* gentleman; *(al dirigir la palabra)* sir; **¿qué desea el c.?** can I help you, sir?; **caballeros** *(en letrero) (en aseos)* gents; *(en grandes almacenes)* menswear; *Esp* **el servicio de caballeros** the men's toilet *o US* washroom; **zapatos de c.** men's shoes; **peluquería de caballeros** barber's, *Br* men's hairdresser's, *US* barbershop
(**c**) *(miembro de una orden)* knight; **armar c. a alguien** to knight sb ▸▸ ***c. andante*** knight errant
(**d**) *(noble)* nobleman
(**e**) *Fin* ***c. blanco*** white knight

caballerosamente *adv* like a gentleman, chivalrously

caballerosidad *nf* gentlemanliness, chivalry; **con c.** like a gentleman, chivalrously

caballeroso, -a *adj* chivalrous, gentlemanly

caballete *nm* (**a**) *(de pintor)* easel (**b**) *(de mesa)* trestle (**c**) *(de nariz)* bridge (**d**) *(de tejado)* ridge

caballista *nmf* (**a**) *(experto)* expert on horses (**b**) *(jinete)* expert rider

caballito *nm* (**a**) *(caballo pequeño)* small horse, pony; **llevar a alguien a c.** to give sb a piggy-back; EXPR *Fam* **hacer el c.** *(con moto)* to do a wheelie ▸▸ ***c. del diablo*** dragonfly; ***c. de mar*** seahorse (**b**) *(de juguete) (balancín)* rocking horse; *(palo)* hobbyhorse (**c**) **caballitos** *(de feria)* merry-go-round, *US* carousel

caballo *nm* (**a**) *(animal)* horse; **a c.** on horseback; **montar** *o Am* **andar a c.** to ride; EXPR *Chile* **estar a c. en algo** *(materia)* to have mastered sth; EXPR **a c. entre: estar a c. entre dos cosas** to be halfway between two things; **vive a c. entre Madrid y Bruselas** she lives part of the time in Madrid and part of the time in Brussels; EXPR **a mata c.** at breakneck speed; EXPR *Fam Hum* **ser más lento que el c. del malo** to be a real *Br* slowcoach *o US* slowpoke; PROV **a c. regalado no le mires el diente** don't look a gift horse in the mouth ▸▸ *Fig* ***c. de batalla*** *(dificultad, escollo)* bone of contention; *(objetivo, obsesión)* hobbyhorse; ***c. de carga*** packhorse; ***c. de carreras*** racehorse; *Fig* ***c. ganador*** front runner; ***c. de tiro*** workhorse, carthorse; *Fig* ***c. de Troya*** Trojan horse
(**b**) *(pieza de ajedrez)* knight
(**c**) *(naipe)* = card in Spanish deck with picture of knight, equivalent to queen in standard deck
(**d**) *Tec* ▸▸ ***c. de fuerza*** cheval-vapeur; ***c. de fuerza métrico*** cheval-vapeur ***c. de vapor*** cheval-vapeur; ***c. de vapor inglés*** horsepower; ***c. de vapor métrico*** cheval-vapeur
(**e**) *Fam (heroína)* smack, horse
(**f**) *Dep* horse ▸▸ ***c. con arcos*** pommel horse; ***c. sin arcos*** vaulting horse
(**g**) *CRica* **caballos** *(pantalones)* trousers
(**h**) *Carib Fam (persona hábil)* **ser un c. (para algo)** to be a whizz *o* an ace (at sth)
(**i**) *Carib Fam (tonto)* dope, thicko

caballón, -ona 1 *adj Méx, Ven Fam (alto)* huge
2 *nm Agr* ridge
3 *nm,f Méx, Ven Fam (persona alta)* giant

caballuno, -a *adj (cara, risa)* horsy, horsey

cabalmente *adv* (**a**) *(totalmente)* totally, fully (**b**) *(exactamente)* exactly, precisely (**c**) *(justamente)* fairly

cabaña *nf* (**a**) *(choza)* hut, cabin; **una c. de pastores** a shepherd's hut (**b**) *(ganado)* livestock; **la c. bovina de Gales** the national herd of Welsh cattle (**c**) **c. (de salida)** *(en billares)* baulk (**d**) *RP (finca)* cattle ranch (**e**) *Méx (portería de fútbol)* goal

cabañero *nm (pastor)* shepherd

cabaré, cabaret (*pl* **cabarets**) *nm* (**a**) *(espectáculo)* cabaret (**b**) *(lugar)* cabaret, nightclub

cabaretera *nf (artista)* cabaret artist(e)

cabás (*pl* **cabases**) *nm* = plastic or metal case with handle, used by schoolgirls for carrying lunch etc

cabe 1 *nm Perú* trip; **meter c. a alguien** to trip sb up
2 *prep Arcaico* near, next to

cabeceada *nf Am* (**a**) *(de sueño)* nod (**b**) *(en fútbol)* header

cabecear 1 *vi* (**a**) *(dormitar)* to nod (off) (**b**) *(persona) (negando)* to shake one's head (**c**) *(caballo)* to toss its head (**d**) *(en fútbol)* to head the ball (**e**) *(balancearse) (barco, avión)* to pitch
2 *vt Carib (tabaco)* to bind

cabeceo *nm* (**a**) *(de sueño)* nodding (**b**) *(de caballo)* tossing (**c**) *(de barco, avión)* pitching

cabecera *nf* (**a**) *(de fila, de mesa)* head
(**b**) *(de cama)* top end; **estar a la c. de (la cama de) alguien** to be at sb's bedside
(**c**) *Esp (de texto)* heading; *(de periódico)* masthead
(**d**) *(de programa televisivo)* title sequence

(e) *(principio) (de río)* source; *(de manifestación)* head; *(de tren)* front; *(de pista de aterrizaje)* start; **la c. del autobús 38 está aquí** the 38 bus starts from here

(f) *Esp (de organización)* **ocupa la c. de la organización desde 1995** he has headed the organization since 1995

(g) *Esp* ***c. de comarca*** = administrative centre of a Spanish "comarca", *Br* ≃ county town, *US* ≃ county seat

cabecero *nm (de cama)* headboard

cabecilla *nmf* ringleader; **el c. rebelde** the rebel leader

cabecita *nmf Arg Fam* **c. (negra)** = pejorative term for lower-class person of mixed race and/or rural origins

cabellera *nf* **(a)** *(melena)* head of hair; *(como trofeo)* scalp; **cortar la c. a** to scalp **(b)** *(de cometa)* tail

cabello *nm (melena)* hair; **tiene el c. rubio** he has blond hair; **c. graso/seco** greasy/dry hair; EXPR **se le pusieron los cabellos de punta** her hair stood on end ►► ***c. de ángel*** *(dulce)* = preserve consisting of strands of pumpkin in syrup

cabelludo, -a *adj* hairy; **cuero c.** scalp

CABER [12] *vi* **(a)** *(entrar, pasar)* to fit (**en** in *o* into); **los libros no caben en la estantería** the books won't fit on the bookshelves *o* in the bookcase; **caben cinco personas** there is room for five people; **¿cuánta gente cabe en este estadio?** how many people can this stadium hold?; **el vino no cabrá en ese vaso** that glass won't hold the wine, that glass is too small for the wine; **no me cabe en el dedo** it won't fit (on) my finger; **no quiero postre, no me cabe nada más** I don't want a dessert, I couldn't eat another thing; **esta falda ya no me cabe** I can't get into this skirt any more; **c. por** to go through; **el armario no cabe por la puerta** the wardrobe won't go through the door; EXPR **no cabía ni un alfiler** the place was packed out; EXPR **no caberle a alguien en la cabeza: no me cabe en la cabeza que se haya ido sin llamar** I simply can't understand her leaving without calling; EXPR **no c. en sí de alegría** to be beside oneself with joy

(b) *(en divisiones)* **nueve entre tres caben a tres** three into nine goes three (times); **tres entre cinco no caben** five into three won't go

(c) *(ser posible)* to be possible; **cabe la posibilidad de que no pueda venir** (it is possible that) he might not come; **sólo cabe una solución, aplazar la conferencia** there is only one solution (available to us), to postpone the conference; **cabe añadir que...** one might add that...; **cabe decir...** it is possible to say...; **cabe destacar que...** it's worth pointing out that...; **cabe esperar que...** it is to be hoped that...; **cabe mencionar que...** it's worth mentioning that..., it should be mentioned that...; **cabe preguntarse si...** one might ask whether...; **cabe recordar que...** it should be remembered that...; **el nuevo modelo todavía es mejor, si cabe** the new model is even better, difficult though it may be to imagine; **sus declaraciones han añadido más tensión, si cabe, a la situación** his remarks have made the situation more tense, if that were possible; EXPR **dentro de lo que cabe** *(en cierto modo)* up to a point, to some extent; **dentro de lo que cabe, no nos ha ido tan mal** all things considered, it didn't go that badly for us

(d) *(corresponder)* **c. a alguien** to be sb's duty *o* honour, to fall to sb; **me cupo a mí darle las noticias** it fell to me to give him the news; **me cabe la satisfacción de ser el que anuncie el resultado** it is my honour to announce the result, I am delighted to have the honour of announcing the result

cabestrante *nm (de ancla, de arrastre)* capstan; *(en el que se enrolla cable)* winch

cabestrillo *nm* sling; **tenía el brazo en c.** she had her arm in a sling

cabestro *nm* **(a)** *(cuerda)* halter **(b)** *(buey)* leading ox **(c)** *Esp, CRica Fam (persona torpe)* clumsy oaf **(d)** *Esp, CRica Fam (persona bruta)* halfwit, moron; **¡pero qué c. eres!** how could you be so stupid?

CABEZA 1 *nf* **(a)** *(de persona, animal)* head; **me duele la c.** I've got a headache; **bajar** *o* **doblar la c.** to bow one's head; **de c.** *(en fútbol)* with a header; **marcó de c.** he scored with his head *o* with a header, he headed a goal; **tirarse de c. (al agua)** to dive (into the water); **se tiró de c. a la piscina** she dived into the pool; *Am* **en c.** *(sin sombrero)* bareheaded; **le lleva una c. a su madre** she's a head taller than her mother; *Fam* **le abrieron la c. de un ladrillazo** they split his skull with a brick; **lavarse la c.** to wash one's hair; EXPR *Fam* **alzar** *o* **levantar c.** to get back on one's feet, to recover; **desde que perdieron la final, no han conseguido alzar** *o* **levantar c.** they still haven't recovered from losing the final, they still haven't managed to pick themselves up after losing the final; **no hay manera de que alce** *o* **levante c.** it's hard to see her recovering *o* getting over it; EXPR *Fam* **calentar** *o* **hinchar la c. a alguien** to drive sb mad; **no te calientes más la c., no hay nada que hacer** stop getting worked up *o Br* het up about it, there's nothing we can do; EXPR **con la c. (bien) alta** with one's head held high; EXPR *Fam* **la c. me da vueltas** my head's spinning; EXPR **darse de c. en la pared: se dio de c. en la pared por haber actuado tan torpemente** she kicked herself for behaving so stupidly; EXPR *RP Fam* **jugarse la c.** to be absolutely sure; **¿te parece que al final se van a casar? – ¡me juego la c.!** do you think that they'll end up getting married? – you can bet on it!; **me juego la c. que hoy gana Nacional** I'll give you any odds Nacional wins today; EXPR **meter la c.** to get one's foot in the door; EXPR **meterse de c. en algo** to plunge into sth; EXPR *Fam* **tengo la c. como un bombo** my head is throbbing; *Fam* **me estás poniendo la c. como un bombo con tantas preguntas estúpidas** you're making my head spin *o* hurt with all those stupid questions; EXPR *Fam* **rodar cabezas: si no se producen resultados, rodarán cabezas** if things don't get better, heads will roll; EXPR *Fam* **romperse** *o* **quebrarse la c.** to *Br* rack *o US* cudgel one's brains; **la amenazó con romperle la c.** he threatened to smash her head in *o* to bash her brains in; EXPR **sacar la c.** *(aparecer)* to show one's face; *(atreverse)* to speak up; EXPR *Fam* **subirse a la c.: se le subió a la c.** it went to his head; **el vino se le subió a la c.** the wine went to her head; **se le ha subido a la c. el ascenso** his promotion has gone to his head; EXPR *Fam* **tener la c. a pájaros** *o* **llena de pájaros** to have one's head in the clouds; EXPR *Fam* **tener la c. como una olla de grillos** to be round the bend; EXPR *Fam* **tenía la c. en otra parte** my mind was wandering, my thoughts were elsewhere; EXPR *Fam* **tener la c. en su sitio** *o* **bien puesta** to have a sound head on one's shoulders, to have one's head screwed on (properly); EXPR **volver la c.** *(negar el saludo)* to turn away; PROV **más vale ser c. de ratón que cola de león** it's better to reign in Hell than to serve in Heaven ►► *Culin* ***c. de jabalí*** *Br* brawn, *US* headcheese

(b) *(mente)* **tiene buena c. para los números** she has a (good) head for numbers; EXPR *Fam* **andar** *o* **estar mal de la c.,** *RP* **estar de la c.** to be funny in the head; EXPR **no me cabe en la c.** I simply can't understand it; **no me cabe en la c. que haya sido él** I can't believe it was him; EXPR *Fam* **se me va la c.** *(me mareo)* I feel dizzy; EXPR **se me ha ido completamente de la c.** it's gone clean out of my mind *o* head; **no consigo que el accidente se me vaya de la c.** I can't get the accident out of my mind; EXPR **meter algo en la c. a alguien** to get sth into sb's head; **métete en la c. que no vas a poder ir** get it into your head that you're not going to be able to go; **se le ha metido en la c. que...** he has got it into his head that...; EXPR **se me pasó por la c.** it crossed my mind; EXPR **venir a la c.** to come to mind; **ahora no me viene a la c.** I can't think of it right now; EXPR **tener mala c.** *(poco juicio)* to act foolishly; **me he olvidado, ¡qué mala c. tengo!** how silly of me to forget! EXPR **tener mucha c.** to have brains

(c) *(juicio)* sense; **tener poca c.** to have no sense; **obrar con c.** to use one's head; **perder la c.** to lose one's head; **Pedro ha perdido la c. por esa chica** Pedro has lost his head over that girl; **¿has perdido la c. o qué?** are you out of your mind?

(d) *(persona)* **por c.** per head; **costará 500 por c.** it will cost 500 per head; **pagamos diez euros por c.** we paid ten euros each

(e) *(de clavo, alfiler, fémur, cometa)* head ►► ***c. de ajo*** head of garlic; ***c. atómica*** nuclear warhead; *Aut* ***c. de biela*** big end; *Informát & TV* ***c. de borrado*** erase head; ***c. buscadora*** *(en misil)* homing device; ***c. de combate*** warhead; ***c. grabadora*** *(en vídeo, casete)* recording head; ***c. de guerra*** warhead; ***c. lectora*** *(en vídeo, casete)* (read) head; *Informát* ***c. lectora-grabadora*** read-write head; ***c. magnética*** magnetic head; ***c. nuclear*** nuclear warhead; ***c. reproductora*** *(en vídeo, casete)* (playback) head

(f) *(animal cuadrúpedo)* **c. (de ganado)** head (of cattle)

(g) *(población)* ***c. de partido*** *Br* ≃ county town, *US* ≃ county seat

(h) *(posición)* front, head; **c. abajo** upside down; **c. arriba** the right way up; **a la** *o* **en c.** *(en competición)* in front, in the lead; *(en lista)* at the top *o* head; **el equipo francés está a la c. de la clasificación** the French team is top of the league; **está situado en (la) c. del pelotón** he's at the front of the pack, he's amongst the leaders of the pack; **a la c. de** *(delante de)* at the head of; *(al cargo de)* in charge of; **estar a la c. de la empresa** to run the company; **Juan está a la c. de la expedición** Juan is the leader of the expedition; **la c. visible del movimiento** the public face of the movement ►► ***c. de mina*** coalface; *Mil* ***c. de playa*** beachhead; *Mil & Fig* ***c. de puente*** bridgehead; *Dep* ***c. de serie*** seed; **el primer c. de serie se enfrenta al segundo** the top *o* number one seed will play the second *o* number two seed

(i) EXPR *Esp Fam* **andar** *o* **ir de c.** *(muy atareado)* to be snowed under; **esta semana voy de c. y no he tenido tiempo de llamar a nadie** I'm really snowed under this week and I haven't had time to call anyone; *Esp* **escarmentar en c. ajena** to learn from another's mistakes; *RP* **darle por la c. a alguien** to really lay *o* slang into sb; *Fam* **ir de c. a** to head straight for; *Esp Fam* **ir de c. con alguien** *(enamorado)* to be head over heels in love with sb; *Esp Fam* **llevar a alguien de c.: los hijos la llevan de c.** the children drive her up the wall; *Fam* **sentar la c.** to settle down; *Fam* **(estar) tocado de la c.** (to be) touched; *Esp*

Fam **traer de c. a alguien** to drive sb mad
 2 *nmf Fam* ***c. de chorlito*** *(despistado)* scatterbrain; *(estúpido)* airhead; *Fam* ***c. cuadrada:*** **es un c. cuadrada** he's got his ideas and he won't listen to anyone else; *Fam* ***c. dura:*** **es un c. dura** he's got his ideas and he won't listen to anyone else; ***c. de familia*** head of the family; *Fam* ***c. hueca*** airhead; *Pol* ***c. de lista*** = person who heads a party's list of candidates; **va como c. de lista por Salamanca** he's the head of the party list for Salamanca; *Fam* ***c. loca*** airhead; *RP* ***c. de novia*** airhead; ***c. pensante:*** **las cabezas pensantes de la derecha venezolana** the policy-makers of the Venezuelan right; **las cabezas pensantes de la organización** the brains behind the organization; ***c. rapada*** skinhead; ***c. de turco*** scapegoat

---

cabezada *nf* **(a)** *(de sueño)* **dar cabezadas** to nod off; **echar** *o* **dar una c.** to have a nap
 (b) *(golpe)* **se dio una c. con** *o* **contra la puerta** he banged his head against the door; **dar una c. a alguien** to head-butt sb
 (c) *(de barco, avión)* **dar cabezadas** to pitch; **me mareé con las cabezadas que daba el barco** I got seasick from the way the boat was pitching about
 (d) *(de caballo)* bridle
 (e) *Andes, RP (de silla de montar)* saddlebow

cabezal *nm* **(a)** *(de aparato, maquinilla de afeitar)* head; **c. basculante** swivel head **(b)** *(de magnetoscopio, disco duro, casete)* head **(c)** *(almohada)* bolster **(d)** *Chile, Méx (travesaño)* lintel

cabezazo *nm* **(a)** *(golpe) (con la cabeza)* head-butt; *(en la cabeza)* blow *o* bump on the head; **dar un c. a alguien** to head-butt sb; **se dio un c. con** *o* **contra la lámpara** she banged her head on the light **(b)** *Dep* header; **marcar de un c.** to score with a header, to head a goal ▸▸ ***c. en plancha*** diving header

cabezo *nm* **(a)** *(cumbre)* summit, peak **(b)** *(cerro alto)* high hill; *(montecillo)* small hill, hillock **(c)** *(escollo)* reef

cabezón, -ona 1 *adj* **(a)** *(persona) (de cabeza grande)* **ser c.** to have a big head **(b)** *(terco)* **ser c.** to be pigheaded *o* stubborn; **¡qué c. eres!** how pigheaded *o* stubborn you are! **(c)** *Fam* **este vino es muy c.** this wine will give you a nasty hangover
 2 *nm,f (terco)* pigheaded *o* stubborn person
 3 *nm Col (remolino)* eddy

cabezonada *nf Fam* **el ir a la playa fue una c. de tu padre** going to the beach was something your father got into his head that we just had to do

cabezonería *nf Fam* **(a)** *(cualidad)* pigheadedness, stubbornness; **con c.** pigheadedly, stubbornly; **se niega a ayudarnos por c.** she refuses to help us out of sheer pigheadedness **(b)** *(acción)* **el ir a la playa fue una c. de tu padre** going to the beach was something your father got into his head that we just had to do

cabezota *Fam* 1 *adj* pigheaded
 2 *nmf* pigheaded person

cabezudo, -a 1 *adj Fam* pigheaded, stubborn
 2 *nm,f Fam* pigheaded *o* stubborn person
 3 *nm (en fiestas)* = giant-headed papier-mâché carnival figure

cabezuela *nf Bot* capitulum

cabida *nf* capacity; **un auditorio con c. para cinco mil espectadores** an auditorium which has room for *o* holds five thousand people; **el edificio da c. a** *o* **tiene c. para veinte familias** there is room for twenty families in the building, the building is big enough for twenty families; **ampliarán la oficina para dar c. a más trabajadores** they'll make the office bigger to make room for more workers; **un movimiento que da c. a** *o* **en el que tienen c. diferentes ideologías** a movement which has room for different ideologies; **ese comportamiento no tiene c. en una democracia** such behaviour has no place in a democracy; **medidas para dar c. a imprevistos** measures to allow for the unpredictable

cabila *nf* = tribe of Bedouins or Berbers

cabildante *nmf* councillor

cabildear *vi Pol* to lobby

cabildo *nm* **(a)** *(municipio)* ≃ district council **(b)** *(de eclesiásticos)* chapter **(c)** *(sala)* chapterhouse **(d)** *(en Canarias)* ***c. insular*** = organization in the Canary Islands comprising representatives from all the towns of an island

cabina *nf* **(a)** *(cuartito)* booth; *(de ascensor) Br* lift, *US* car; *(de teleférico)* car; *(en laboratorio de idiomas)* booth; *(de peaje)* tollbooth ▸▸ ***c. de comentaristas*** *(en estadio)* commentary box; ***c. electoral*** polling booth, voting booth; ***c. de interpretación*** interpreters' booth; ***c. de proyección*** projection *Br* room *o US* booth; ***c. telefónica*** *(con puerta)* phone box, *US* phone booth; ***c. de traducción*** interpreters' booth
 (b) *(vestuario) (en playa)* bathing hut; *(en piscina)* changing cubicle
 (c) *(de avión) (de piloto de avioneta)* cockpit; *(de piloto de aeronave, bombardero)* flight deck, cockpit; *(de los pasajeros)* (passenger) cabin ▸▸ ***c. de mandos*** flight deck; ***c. presurizada*** pressurized cabin
 (d) *(de camión, grúa)* cab; *(de coche de carreras)* cockpit ▸▸ ***c. espacial*** space capsule

cabinero, -a *nm,f Col* air hostess

cabio *nm Constr* **(a)** *(madero)* joist **(b)** *(del tejado)* rafter

cabizbajo, -a *adj* **caminaba c.** he was walking with his head bowed; **volvieron a casa cabizbajos tras la derrota** they went home crestfallen *o* downcast after the defeat

cable *nm* **(a)** *(de puente, ascensor, teleférico, ancla)* cable; EXPR *Fam* **echar** *o* **lanzar** *o* **tender un c.** to help out, to lend a hand ▸▸ ***c. aéreo*** overhead cable; ***c. submarino*** submarine *o* undersea cable
 (b) *(conductor eléctrico) (para conectar)* cable, lead; *(dentro de aparato)* wire; EXPR *Fam* **se le cruzaron los cables** *(se confundió)* he got mixed up; EXPR *RP Fam* **andar** *o* **estar con los cables pelados** to have got out of the wrong side of bed, to be like a bear with a sore head; EXPR *Fam* **se le cruzaron los cables y la pegó** in a moment of madness, he hit her ▸▸ ***c. coaxial*** coaxial cable; ***c. de serie*** serial cable
 (c) *(de fibra óptica)* cable; **una red de c.** a cable network; **un operador de c.** a cable company; **televisión por c.** cable television ▸▸ ***c. de fibra óptica*** fibre optic cable; ***c. óptico*** optical cable
 (d) *(telegrama) Br* telegram, *US* cable; **poner** *o* **enviar a alguien un c.** to send sb a *Br* telegram *o US* cable, to cable sb
 (e) *Náut (medida)* cable

cableado, -a *Informát* 1 *adj* hardwired
 2 *nm* **(a)** *(colocación de cables)* wiring **(b)** *(conjunto de cables)* cabling, cables

cablear *vt (casa, habitación)* to wire (up)

cablegrafiar [32] *vt* to cable

cablegráfico, -a *adj* **mensaje c.** *Br* telegram, *US* cable

cablegrama *nm Br* telegram, *US* cable; **poner** *o* **enviar a alguien un c.** to send sb a *Br* telegram *o US* cable, to cable sb

cableoperador *nm*, **cableoperadora** *nf* cable company

cablero *nm Náut* cable ship

cablevisión *nf* cable television

cablista *nmf* cable layer

cabo 1 *nm* **(a)** *(en ejército)* corporal ▸▸ ***c. primero*** = military rank between corporal and sergeant
 (b) *(accidente geográfico)* cape ▸▸ ***el C. de Buena Esperanza*** the Cape of Good Hope; ***C. Cañaveral*** Cape Canaveral; ***el C. de Hornos*** Cape Horn; ***C. Kennedy*** Cape Kennedy; ***C. Verde*** *(país)* Cape Verde
 (c) *(trozo) (de cuerda)* bit, piece
 (d) *(extremo, punta) (de vela)* stub, stump; *(de cuerda)* end; EXPR **de c. a rabo** from beginning to end; EXPR **atar cabos** to put two and two together ▸▸ ***c. suelto*** loose end; EXPR **no dejar ningún c. suelto, atar los cabos sueltos** to tie up all the loose ends
 (e) *(hebra de cuerda)* strand; **lana de cuatro cabos** four-ply wool
 (f) *Náut (cuerda)* rope
 (g) EXPR **al fin y al c.** after all; **estar al c. de la calle** to be well informed; **llevar algo a c.** to carry sth out; **el secuestrador llevó a c. sus amenazas** the kidnapper carried out his threat; **he conseguido llevar a c. mis planes** I've managed to carry out my plans
 2 **al cabo de** *loc prep* **al c. de una semana** after a week, a week later; **al c. de varios días** after a few days, a few days later

cabotaje *nm* **(a)** *(navegación)* coastal shipping **(b)** *RP* **vuelo de c.** *(en avión)* internal flight

caboverdiano, -a 1 *adj* Cape Verdean
 2 *nm,f* Cape Verdean

cabra *nf* **(a)** *(animal)* goat; EXPR *Fam* **estar como una c.** to be off one's head; PROV **la c. siempre tira al monte** you can't make a leopard change its spots ▸▸ ***c. de angora*** angora goat; ***c. montés*** wild goat, ibex; ***c. montés de los Pirineos*** Spanish ibex **(b)** *Chile (carruaje)* gig, cabriolet **(c)** *Carib, Col (dado cargado)* loaded dice **(d)** *Carib, Col (trampa)* = cheat in game of dice or dominoes **(e)** *ver también* **cabro**

cabrales *nm inv* = Asturian cheese similar to Roquefort

cabré *etc ver* **caber**

cabreado, -a *adj muy Fam* pissed off, *US* pissed (**con** with); **andar** *o* **estar c.** to be pissed off *o US* pissed

cabrear *muy Fam* 1 *vt* **c. a alguien** to piss sb off; **me cabrea su actitud** his attitude really gets my goat *o Br* gets up my nose
 2 **cabrearse** *vpr* to get really pissed off *o US* pissed (**con** with); **no te cabrees, sólo era una broma** keep your hair on, I was only joking; **se ha cabreado con Ana** he's really pissed off *o US* pissed with Ana

cabreo *nm muy Fam* **agarrar** *o Esp* **coger un c.** to get really pissed off *o US* pissed; **lleva un c. tremendo** she's really pissed off *o US* pissed; **ya se le pasará el c.** he'll calm down again soon enough

cabrerizo, -a *nm,f* goatherd

cabrero, -a 1 *adj RP Fam* **estar c.** to be in a foul mood
2 *nm,f* goatherd

cabrestante *nm (de ancla, de arrastre)* capstan; *(en el que se enrolla cable)* winch

cabria *nf* derrick, crane

cabría *etc ver* **caber**

cabrilla *nf* **(a)** *(pez)* spotted grouper, cabrilla **(b) cabrillas** *(olas)* white horses, foam-crested waves **(c)** *(juego)* **hacer cabrillas** to play ducks and drakes

cabrillear *vi* **(a)** *(formarse olas)* to form whitecaps, to break into foam **(b)** *(resplandecer)* to glimmer, to sparkle

cabrio *nm Constr* rafter

cabrío *adj* **macho c.** billy-goat

cabriola *nf (brinco)* prance; *(de caballo)* capriole; **hacer cabriolas** *(caballo)* to prance about; *(niño)* to caper around

cabriolar *vi (caballo)* to prance about; *(niño)* to caper around

cabriolé *nm* **(a)** *(automóvil)* convertible, cabriolet **(b)** *(carruaje)* cabriolet **(c)** *(capote)* = short sleeveless cape

cabritada *nf muy Fam* **no invitarle ha sido una c.** it was *Br* bloody *o US* goddamn mean not to invite him; **tendremos que hacerlo otra vez – ¡qué c.!** we'll have to do it over again – what a *Br* bloody *o US* goddamn pain!

cabritas *nfpl*, **cabritos** *nmpl Chile* popcorn

cabritilla *nf (piel)* kid, kidskin

cabrito, -a 1 *nm (animal)* kid (goat)
2 *nm,f Fam Euf (insulto) Br* basket, *US* son of a gun

cabritos = **cabritas**

cabro, -a *Chile Fam* **1** *adj* wet behind the ears
2 *nm,f* kid

cabrón, -ona 1 *adj* **(a)** *Vulg (como insulto)* **¡qué c. eres!** you bastard!; **mi profesor de inglés es muy c.** my English teacher is a real bastard *o US* asshole **(b)** *Méx muy Fam (difícil) Br* bloody *o US* goddamn difficult; **el examen estuvo bien c.** the exam was a bitch
2 *nm,f* **(a)** *Vulg (insulto)* bastard, *f* bitch, *US* asshole **(b)** *Méx Fam (genio)* whizz, ace; **es un c. para la física** he's a whizz at physics **(c)** *Méx muy Fam (tío)* guy; **¿adónde irá ese c.?** where the hell is that guy going?
3 *nm* **(a)** *Vulg (cornudo)* **es un c.** his wife's screwing around behind his back **(b)** *(animal)* billy-goat **(c)** *CAm, Méx muy Fam (como apelativo)* **hola c., ¿qué tal estás?** how are you, you old bastard? **(d)** *Esp muy Fam* **trabajó/estudió como un c.** he worked/studied his *Br* arse *o US* ass off
4 a lo cabrón *loc adv Méx Fam* by force; **entraron a la casa a lo c.** they broke into the house

cabronada *nf Am Fam, Esp Vulg* **(a)** *(mala jugada)* **hacerle una c. a alguien** to do a nasty thing to sb; **lo que te han hecho es una c.** that was a really nasty thing they did to you **(b)** *(fastidio)* pain in the bottom; **¡qué c., vamos a tener que trabajar el domingo!** what a pain in the bottom! we're going to have to work on Sunday!

cabronazo *nm* **(a)** *Vulg (persona)* bastard **(b)** *Méx Fam (golpe)* punch, thump; **dar un c. a alguien** to punch sb

cabroncete *nm Vulg Br* git, *US* son of a bitch

cabruno, -a *adj* goat; **ganado c.** goats

cabujón *nm (piedra)* cabochon

cabuya *nf* **(a)** *(planta)* agave **(b)** *(fibra)* hemp fibre **(c)** *CAm, Col, Ven (cuerda)* rope; **dar c.** *(atar)* to moor; EXPR *Ven* **darle c. a alguien** *(alentar)* to encourage sb; EXPR *Fam* **ponerse en la c.** to catch the drift

caca *nf Fam* **(a)** *(excremento) Br* poo, *US* poop; **hacer c.** to do a *Br* poo *o US* poop; **hacerse c. encima** to make a mess in one's pants, to mess one's pants; **el niño tiene c.** the baby needs to have his *Br* nappy *o US* diaper changed; *Esp* **una c. de vaca** a cowpat; *Esp* **¿que si te dejo el dinero? ¡una c. de vaca!** will I lend you the money? that'll be the day *o Br* that'll be right!; **(una) c. de perro** (a piece of) dog *Br* poo *o US* poop
(b) *(cosa sucia)* nasty *o* dirty thing; **no toques eso, es c.** don't touch that, it's dirty
(c) *(cosa mala)* **este libro es una c.** this book is *Br* rubbish *o US* garbage

cacahual *nm* cacao plantation

cacahuete, *CAm, Méx* **cacahuate** *nm* **(a)** *(fruto)* peanut, *Br* groundnut **(b)** *(planta)* peanut, *Br* groundnut

cacalote *nm* **(a)** *CAm, Méx (de maíz)* popcorn **(b)** *Méx (cuervo)* crow

cacao *nm* **(a)** *(polvo)* cocoa, cocoa powder; *(bebida) (caliente)* cocoa; *(fría)* chocolate milk ►► ***c. en polvo*** cocoa powder
(b) *(árbol)* cacao
(c) *(semilla)* cocoa bean
(d) *Esp (para labios)* lip salve
(e) *Fam (confusión)* chaos, mess; *(jaleo)* fuss, rumpus; **se armó un c.** there was total chaos; **se han metido en un buen c.** they've got themselves in a real mess ►► ***c. mental:*** **tiene un c. mental terrible** his head's in a real muddle
(f) EXPR *Ven Fam* **ser un gran c.** to be rich and powerful; **pedir c.** *Ven Fam (ayuda)* to ask for help; *Nic Fam (perdón)* to say sorry

cacaotal *nm* cacao plantation

cacarear 1 *vt Fam* **(a)** *(jactarse de)* to boast about **(b)** *(pregonar)* to blab about; **la tan cacareada precisión de los ataques resultó ser un mito** the accuracy of the attacks, which so much was made of, turned out to be a myth
2 *vi (gallina)* to cluck, to cackle; *(gallo)* to crow

cacareo *nm (de gallina)* cluck, clucking; *(de gallo)* cock-a-doodle-doo

cacatúa *nf* **(a)** *(ave)* cockatoo **(b)** *Fam (mujer vieja)* old bat

cacera *nf* irrigation ditch

cacereño, -a 1 *adj* of/from Cáceres *(Spain)*
2 *nm,f* person from Cáceres *(Spain)*

cacería *nf (a caballo)* hunt; *(con fusiles)* shoot; **la c. del zorro** fox-hunting; **salieron** *o* **fueron de c.** they went hunting

cacerola *nf* pot, pan

cacerolada *nf*, **cacerolazo** *nm* = protest in which demonstrators bang on pots and pans to complain about food shortages

cacerolear *vi RP* = to protest (against government economic policy) by banging on pots and pans to complain about food shortages

caceroleo *nm RP* = protest in which demonstrators bang on pots and pans to complain about food shortages

cacha *nf* **(a)** *Fam (muslo)* thigh **(b)** *(mango) (de cuchillo)* handle; *(de pistola)* butt **(c)** *Andes, CAm (engaño)* trick, deceit **(d)** *Col (cuerno)* horn

cachachá *nm* EXPR *Ven Fam* **coger el c.** to up and go, *Br* to scarper

cachaco, -a *Fam* **1** *adj Col* **(a)** *(de Bogotá)* of/from Bogotá *(Colombia)* **(b)** *(del páramo)* = relating to the Andean upland region
2 *nm,f* **(a)** *Col (de Bogotá)* person from Bogotá *(Colombia)* **(b)** *(del páramo)* = person from the Andean upland region **(c)** *Bol, Perú Fam Pey (policía)* cop **(d)** *Perú Fam Pey (militar)* soldier

cachada *nf* **(a)** *Am Taurom* goring **(b)** *RP (broma)* mockery, taunt

cachador, -ora *nm,f RP* joker

cachalote *nm* sperm whale

cachanilla 1 *adj* of/from Baja California *(Mexico)*
2 *nmf* person from Baja California *(Mexico)*

cachar 1 *vt* **(a)** *CAm, Ecuad, RP (burlarse de)* to tease; **lo cachan por el corte de pelo** they're teasing him about his haircut
(b) *Am (cornear)* to gore
(c) *Am (atrapar)* to catch; **¡cachen a ese hombre, acaba de robarme la cartera!** stop that man! he's stolen my wallet!
(d) *Nic, RP Fam (agarrar)* to grab; **cachá una cerveza si tenés sed** help yourself to a beer if you're thirsty
(e) *Am Fam (sorprender)* to catch; **cacharon a Silvina besándose con su jefe** Silvina was caught kissing her boss
(f) *CAm Fam (robar)* to swipe, to pinch
(g) *CSur Fam (entender)* to understand, to get; **no cacho nada de japonés** I can't understand a word of Japanese
2 cacharse *vpr* EXPR *RP Fam Euf* **¡me cacho!** *Br* sugar!, *US* shoot!

cacharpa *nf Méx Fam (monedas)* small change

cacharpas *nfpl Am* junk

cacharrazo *nm Fam* thump; **me di** *o* **pegué un c.** *(al caer)* I had a nasty fall; *(en la cabeza, rodilla)* I gave myself a real thump *o* bang; *(en automóvil)* I had a crash

cacharrería *nf* = shop selling terracotta cookware, flowerpots etc

cacharrero, -a *nm,f* = person who sells terracotta cookware, flowerpots etc

cacharro *nm* **(a)** *(recipiente)* pot; **fregar los cacharros** to do the dishes **(b)** *Fam (trasto)* piece of junk; **tendremos que tirar todos estos cacharros** we'll have to throw all this junk *o Br* rubbish out **(c)** *Fam (máquina)* crock; *(automóvil)* heap, banger **(d)** *Fam (aparato, chisme)* gadget, gizmo; **aprietas este c. y sale agua** press this thing *o* gizmo here and water comes out

cachas *Esp Fam* 1 *adj (fuerte)* well-built, beefy; **estar c.** to be well-built; **ponerse c.** to put on muscle
2 *nm inv (hombre fuerte)* he-man, muscleman

cachaza *nf* (**a**) *Fam (calma)* **tener c.** to be laid-back (**b**) *(aguardiente)* = type of cheap rum

cachazudo, -a 1 *adj* (**a**) *(lento)* sluggish (**b**) *(flemático)* calm, placid
2 *nm,f* (**a**) *(lento) Br* slowcoach, *US* slowpoke (**b**) *(flemático)* phlegmatic person (**c**) *Cuba (paciente)* **es un c.** he's the soul of patience
3 *nm Cuba, Méx (gusano)* tobacco worm

cache *adj Am* sloppy, slovenly

caché[1] *nm Informát* **(memoria) c.** cache memory

caché[2], **cachet** [ka'tʃe] (*pl* **cachets**) *nm* (**a**) *(tarifa de artista)* fee (**b**) *Fam (distinción)* cachet; **estos invitados dan mucho c. al programa** these guests add a real touch of class to the programme

cachear *vt* (**a**) *(registrar)* to frisk; **los cachearon a la entrada** they were frisked as they went in (**b**) *Chile (cornear)* to gore

cachemir *nm*, **cachemira** *nf* (**a**) *(tejido)* cashmere (**b**) *(estampado)* **una corbata/un pañuelo de c.** a Paisley (pattern) tie/headscarf

Cachemira *n* Kashmir

cachemira = **cachemir**

cacheo *nm* **someter a alguien a un c.** to frisk sb

cácher *nmf (en béisbol)* catcher

cachet = **caché**[2]

cachetada *nf*, *Arg* **cachetazo** *nm (en la cara)* slap; *(en el trasero)* slap, smack

cachete *nm* (**a**) *(moflete)* chubby cheek (**b**) *(bofetada) (en la cara)* slap; *(en el trasero)* slap, smack

cachetear *vt* to slap

cachetero *nm* (**a**) *(puñal)* dagger *(for killing cattle)* (**b**) *Taurom (torero)* = bullfighter who finishes off the bull with a dagger

cachetón, -ona 1 *adj* (**a**) *Am Fam (mofletudo)* chubby-cheeked (**b**) *Méx Fam (despreocupado)* heartless, selfish (**c**) *Chile Fam (presumido)* bigheaded
2 *nm,f Méx Fam* selfish, heartless person

cachetudo, -a *adj (mofletudo)* chubby-cheeked

cachicamo *nm Ven* armadillo

cachifo, -a *nm,f Ven Fam Pey (mujer)* maid, *Br* skivvy; *(hombre)* flunkey

cachila *nf RP (automóvil)* vintage car

cachilo *nm RP Fam* heap, banger

cachimba *nf* (**a**) *(pipa)* pipe (**b**) *RP (pozo)* well

cachimbo *nm Am* pipe

cachiporra *nf* (**a**) *(garrote)* club, cudgel; *(de policía)* truncheon (**b**) *Cuba (ave)* blacknecked stilt

cachiporrazo *nm* (**a**) *(con cachiporra)* blow with a club; **darle** *o* **pegarle un c. a alguien** to club sb (**b**) *Fam* **me di** *o* **pegué un c.** *(al caer)* I had a nasty fall; *(en la cabeza, rodilla)* I gave myself a real thump *o* bang; *(en automóvil)* I had a crash

cachirul *nm* (**a**) *Méx Fam (trampa)* trick, *Br* wheeze, fiddle (**b**) *Méx Fam (tramposo)* **hay dos cachirules en el equipo** there are two players in the team who aren't eligible (**c**) *CRica (avión de papel)* paper aeroplane

cachirulo *nm* (**a**) *(chisme)* thingumajig (**b**) *(pañuelo)* = headscarf worn by men as part of traditional Aragonese costume (**c**) *Par (permanente)* perm

cachivache *nm Fam* (**a**) *(chisme)* thingummy, thingumajig; **tiene el cuarto lleno de cachivaches** his room is full of stuff (**b**) *(trasto)* piece of junk; **tira los cachivaches que no sirvan** throw out anything that's just junk

cacho[1] *nm* (**a**) *Fam (pedazo)* piece, bit; **el plato se rompió en tres cachos** the plate broke into three bits; **sólo vi el c. final del partido** I only saw the end of the game; EXPR **ser un c. de pan** *(ser muy bueno)* to have a heart of gold (**b**) *Esp Fam (como intensificador)* **¡c. tonto!** you idiot!; *Vulg* **¡c. cabrón!** you bastard!; **me di un c. tortazo increíble** I gave myself one hell of a thump

cacho[2] *nm* (**a**) *Andes, Ven (asta)* horn; EXPR *CAm, Ven Fam* **montarle cachos a alguien** to be unfaithful to sb; *(a un hombre)* to cuckold sb
(**b**) *Col, Ven Fam (de drogas)* joint
(**c**) *Andes (cubilete)* dice cup
(**d**) *Andes, Guat, Ven (cuento)* story; **no me vengan a contar cachos, que sé lo que pasó** don't start telling me stories, I know what happened
(**e**) *Andes, Guat, Ven (burla)* joke; **le hicieron un c. a Raúl y lo hicieron enojar mucho** they played a joke on Raúl and he got really angry
(**f**) *RP* ***c. de banana*** *(racimo)* hand *o* large bunch of bananas

cachón, -ona *adj CAm, Col (animal)* with large horns

cachondearse *vpr Esp Fam* **no te cachondees, le puede pasar a cualquiera** don't laugh, it could happen to anyone; **c. de alguien** to make fun of sb, *Br* to take the mickey out of sb

cachondeo *nm Esp Fam* (**a**) *(diversión)* **ser un c.** to be a laugh; **irse de c.** to go out on the town; **ya está bien de c., vamos a ponernos a estudiar** that's enough fooling *o* larking about, let's get down to some studying; **se llevan un c. enorme con sus nuevos vecinos** they get on like a house on fire with their new neighbours; **se llevan mucho c. con mi nuevo sombrero** they think my new hat is a great laugh; **no le hagas caso, está de c.** *(de broma)* don't pay any attention to him, he's having you on; **me voy a vivir a Nepal, y no estoy de c.** I'm going to live in Nepal, and I'm not kidding you (**b**) *Pey (cosa poco seria)* joke; **¡este gobierno es un c.!** this government is a joke!; **tomarse algo a c.** to treat sth as a joke

cachondo, -a 1 *adj* (**a**) *Esp Fam (divertido)* **es un tío muy c.** he's a really good laugh; **fue una fiesta muy cachonda** the party was a scream *o* a real gas (**b**) *Esp, Méx muy Fam (excitado)* **estar c.** to be horny *o* randy; **poner c. a alguien** to get sb horny *o* randy; **ponerse c.** to get horny *o* randy
2 *nm,f Esp Fam* **es una cachonda, nos reímos un montón con ella** she's great fun, we always have a good laugh with her; **es un c. (mental)** he's always the life and soul of the party

cachorro, -a *nm,f* (**a**) *(de perro)* pup, puppy; *(de gato)* kitten; *(de león, lobo, oso)* cub
(**b**) *(de ideología, grupo social)* **en esa escuela de negocios se educan los cachorros del capitalismo** that business school is teaching the next generation of capitalists; **a pesar de ser un c. de la dictadura, mostró gran capacidad de diálogo** despite being a product of the dictatorship, he showed himself to be open to dialogue

cachucha *nf* (**a**) *Andes, CAm, Méx (gorra)* cap (**b**) *Chile (bofetón)* slap

cachuela *nf Andes (río)* rapids

cachumbo *nm* (**a**) *Am (cáscara)* gourd (**b**) *Col Fam (rizo)* curl

cachurrera *nf* spiny cocklebur *o* clotbur

cachuso, -a, cachuzo, -a *adj RP Fam (roto, desvencijado)* broken-down, *Br* clapped-out

cacicada *nf Pey* **ya estamos hartos de sus cacicadas** we've had enough of his high-handed decisions

cacicazgo, cacicato *nm* (**a**) *(dignidad)* chieftainship (**b**) *(territorio)* = territory of a "cacique"

cacique *nm* (**a**) *Pey (jefe local)* local political boss (**b**) *Pey (déspota)* petty tyrant (**c**) *(jefe indio)* chief, cacique

caciquil *adj Pey* despotic

caciquismo *nm Pey* caciquism, = domination of the affairs of a town or district by a local political boss through power and influence rather than legitimate constitutional means

cacle *nm Méx Fam (zapato)* shoe

caco *nm Fam* thief

cacofonía *nf Ling* cacophony

cacofónico, -a *adj Ling* cacophonous

cacografía *nf* spelling mistake

cacomite *nm* tiger flower

cacoquimia *nf Med* cachexia

cactácea *Bot* 1 *nf (planta)* cactus
2 **cactáceas** *nfpl (familia) Cactaceae*; **de la familia de las cactáceas** of the *Cactaceae* family

cactáceo, -a *Bot adj* **planta cactácea** plant of the cactus family

cacto *nm*, **cactus** *nm inv* cactus ▸▸ ***c. de Navidad*** Christmas cactus

cacuí = **cacui**

cacumen *nm Fam (ingenio)* brains, wits; **tener buen c.** to be a smart cookie, to have brains

cacuy, cacuí *nm (ave)* potoo

CAD [kað] *nm* (*abrev de* **computer-aided design**) CAD

CADA *adj inv* (**a**) *(indicando correspondencia)* each; **nos tocan 1.000 pesos a c. (uno)** it comes to 1,000 pesos each *o* apiece; **c. cosa a su tiempo** one thing at a time; **c. cual** each one, everyone; **c. cual que haga lo que le parezca** everyone do as they see fit; **c. uno de** each of; **c. uno** *o* **cual a lo suyo** everyone should get on with their own business; **c. uno es c. uno, c. uno es como es** everyone's different; **c. vez** every time, each time; **c. vez que viene, me pide algo prestado**

every time *o* each time *o* whenever he comes, he asks to borrow something

(b) *(con números, tiempo)* every; **c. tres segundos nace un niño** a child is born every three seconds; **tres de c. diez personas** three out of every ten people; **cinco televisores por c. cien habitantes** five televisions per hundred inhabitants; **c. dos meses** every two months; **c. cierto tiempo** every so often; **¿c. cuánto?** how often?; **a c. momento** *o Am* **rato** all the time, constantly; **a c. momento** *o Am* **rato me preguntan algo, así no puedo trabajar** people are constantly asking me things, so I can't get any work done

(c) *(valor progresivo)* **me gusta c. vez más** I like it more and more; **sus discursos son c. vez más largos** his speeches get longer and longer; **el tema me interesa c. vez menos** I'm getting less and less interested in the subject; **esta revista es c. vez peor** this magazine gets worse and worse; **c. día más** more and more each day

(d) *(valor enfático)* such; **¡se pone c. sombrero!** she wears such hats!; **¡tiene c. cosa!** the things he comes up with!; **¡mis vecinos arman c. escándalo!** my neighbours are always kicking up a fuss *o* row about something!

---

cadalso *nm* scaffold

cadarzo *nm* floss

cadáver *nm (de persona)* corpse, (dead) body; *(de animal)* carcass; **ingresó c.** *(en hospital)* he was dead on arrival; EXPR **por encima de mi c.** over my dead body

cadavérico, -a *adj* (a) *(de cadáver)* cadaverous (b) *(pálido)* deathly pale

caddy, caddie ['kaði] *(pl* **caddies***)* *nm* caddie

cadejo *nm CAm Fam (animal fantástico)* = imaginary animal that comes out at night

cadena 1 *nf* (a) *(de eslabones, piezas)* chain; **una c. de oro/de plata** a gold/silver chain; *Aut* **cadenas** *(para el hielo)* (tyre) chains, snow chains; *Fig* **rompió sus cadenas** he broke out of his chains ►► ***c. alimentaria*** food chain; ***c. alimenticia*** food chain; ***c. antirrobo*** anti-theft chain; ***c. humana*** human chain; *Fisiol* ***c. respiratoria*** respiratory chain; *Biol* ***c. trófica*** food chain

(b) *(de lavabo)* chain; **tirar de la c.** to pull the chain, to flush the toilet

(c) *(red de establecimientos)* chain ►► ***c. hotelera*** hotel chain; ***c. de supermercados*** supermarket chain; ***c. de tiendas*** chain of stores

(d) *(red de emisoras)* station ►► ***c. radiofónica*** radio station; ***c. de televisión*** television station; ***c. televisiva*** television station

(e) *(canal televisivo)* channel; **¿en qué c. dan la película?** what channel is the movie on?

(f) *(de montañas)* range ►► ***c. de montañas*** mountain range; ***c. montañosa*** mountain range

(g) *(de proceso industrial)* line ►► *Méx* ***c. de ensamblaje*** assembly line; ***c. de montaje*** assembly line; ***c. de producción*** production line

(h) *Informát* string ►► ***c. de bits*** bit chain; ***c. de caracteres*** character string; ***c. SCSI*** SCSI chain

(i) *Quím* chain

(j) *(de presidiarios)* chain gang

(k) *(musical)* **c. (de música** *o* **musical)** sound system

(l) *Ling* string

(m) ***c. perpetua*** life imprisonment; **condenar a alguien a c. perpetua** to sentence sb to life imprisonment

2 **en cadena** *loc adj* **accidente en c.** pile-up; **reacción en c.** chain reaction; **trabajo en c.** assembly-line working

cadencia *nf* (a) *(ritmo)* rhythm (b) *Mús (de pieza musical)* rhythm (c) *(frecuencia)* frequency (d) *Ling* falling intonation *(at end of utterance)*

cadencioso, -a *adj* rhythmical

cadeneta *nf* (a) *(bordado)* chain stitch (b) *(de papel)* paper chain

cadera *nf* (a) *(parte)* hip (b) *(hueso)* hip, *Espec* coxa

caderamen *nm Fam* **¡fíjate que c. tiene esa chica!** get her! talk about broad *o* wide in the beam!

cadete, -a 1 *nm* (a) *(en ejército)* cadet (b) *Dep* = sports player aged 14-15

2 *nm,f RP (chico de los recados)* office junior

cadi *nm* caddie

cadí *(pl* **cadíes***)* *nm* cadi, = judge in a Muslim community

cadmio *nm Quím* cadmium

caducado, -a *adj* (a) *(carné, pasaporte)* out-of-date (b) *(alimento, medicamento)* past its use-by date; **un yogur c.** a yoghurt that's past its use-by date

caducar [60] *vi* (a) *(carné, ley, contrato)* to expire; **me ha caducado el pasaporte** my passport has run out *o* expired (b) *(alimento, medicamento)* to pass its use-by date; **este yogur caduca mañana** this yoghurt's use-by date is tomorrow; **caduca a las dos semanas** it will be past its use-by date in two weeks

caduceo *nm* Mercury's staff *o* rod *(symbol of medicine and commerce)*

caducidad *nf* (a) *(de carné, pasaporte)* expiry; **fecha de c.** expiry date (b) **fecha de c.** *(de alimento, medicamento)* use-by date (c) *(cualidad)* finite nature

caducifolio, -a *adj Bot* deciduous

caduco, -a *adj* (a) *(persona)* decrepit (b) *(idea, moda)* outmoded (c) *(perecedero)* perishable (d) *Bot* **de hoja caduca** deciduous

caedizo, -a 1 *adj* (a) *(que cae)* in danger of falling (b) *Bot* deciduous

2 *nm CAm, Col, Méx (saliente)* overhang

CAER [13] 1 *vi* (a) *(hacia abajo)* to fall; **cuando caen las hojas** when the leaves fall; **c. de un tejado/árbol** to fall from a roof/tree; **c. en un pozo** to fall into a well; **el avión cayó al mar** the plane crashed into the sea; **tropezó y cayó al suelo** she tripped and fell (over *o* down); **cayó en brazos de su madre** she fell into her mother's arms; **cayó por la ventana a la calle** he fell out of the window into the street; **cayó de bruces/de cabeza** she fell flat on her face/headlong; **cayó redondo** he slumped to the ground, he collapsed in a heap; **cayó rodando por la escalera** she fell down the stairs; **dejar c. algo** *(objeto)* to drop sth; **dejar c. que...** *(comentar)* to let drop that...; **dejó c. la noticia de su renuncia como si no tuviera importancia** she casually mentioned the fact that she was resigning as if it were a matter of no importance; **hacer c. algo** to knock sth down, to make sth fall

(b) *(lluvia, nieve)* to fall; **caerá nieve por encima de los 1.000 metros** snow is expected in areas over 1,000 metres; **cayeron cuatro gotas** there were a few spots of rain; **cayó una helada** there was a frost; **está cayendo un diluvio** it's pouring down; *Fam* **está cayendo una buena** it's pouring down, *Br* it's chucking it down; **cayó un rayo a pocos metros del edificio** a bolt of lightning struck only a few metres from the building

(c) *(sol)* to go down, to set; **al c. el día** *o* **la tarde** at dusk; **al c. el sol** at sunset; **la noche cayó antes de que llegaran al refugio** night fell before they reached the shelter

(d) *(colgar)* to fall, to hang down; **el cabello le caía sobre los hombros** her hair hung down to *o* fell over her shoulders

(e) *(ciudad, gobierno)* to fall; **el aeropuerto cayó en poder de los insurgentes** the airport fell to the rebels, the airport was taken by the rebels; **el Imperio Romano cayó en el siglo V** the Roman Empire fell in the 5th century; **el escándalo hizo c. al Primer Ministro** the scandal brought the Prime Minister down; **han caído los líderes del comando terrorista** the leaders of the terrorist unit have been captured

(f) *(morir) (soldado)* to fall, to be killed; EXPR **c. como moscas** to drop like flies; **los soldados caían como moscas ante las ametralladoras enemigas** the soldiers were dropping like flies under the fire from the enemy machine-guns

(g) *(decrecer) (interés)* to decrease, to subside; *(precio)* to fall, to go down; **ha caído bastante el interés por estos temas** interest in these subjects has fallen away *o* subsided quite a lot; **ha caído el precio del café** the price of coffee has gone down *o* fallen; **los precios cayeron súbitamente** prices fell suddenly; **la libra ha caído frente al marco** the pound has fallen *o* dropped against the mark

(h) *(incurrir)* **siempre cae en los mismos errores** she always makes the same mistakes; *Rel* **no nos dejes c. en la tentación** lead us not into temptation; **tu actitud cae en lo patético** your attitude is nothing less than pathetic; **no debemos c. en la provocación** we shouldn't allow ourselves to be provoked

(i) *(picar) (en broma)* to fall for it; **me gastaron una broma, pero no caí** they played a trick on me, but I didn't fall for it; **c. en una trampa** to fall into a trap

(j) *(tocar, ir a parar a)* **me cayó el premio** I won the prize; **nos cayó la mala suerte** we had bad luck; **me cayó el tema que mejor me sabía** I got a question on the subject I knew best; **le cayeron dos años (de cárcel)** he got two years (in jail); **la desgracia cayó sobre él** he was overtaken by misfortune; **¿cómo me ha podido c. a mí un trabajo así?** how did I end up getting a job like this?; **procura que el informe no caiga en sus manos** try to avoid the report falling into her hands

(k) *Esp (estar, quedar)* **cae cerca de aquí** it's not far from here; **¿por dónde cae la oficina de turismo?** where's *o* whereabouts is the tourist information centre?; **los baños caen a la izquierda** the toilets are on the left; **cae en el segundo capítulo** it's in the second chapter; **eso cae fuera de mis competencias** that is *o* falls outside my remit

(l) *(darse cuenta)* **no dije nada porque no caí** I didn't say anything because it didn't occur to me to do so; **c. (en algo)** *(recordar)* to be able to remember (sth); **¡ahora caigo!** *(lo entiendo)* I see it now!; *(lo recuerdo)* now I remember!; **ahora caigo en lo que dices** now I see what you are saying; *Esp* **no caigo** I give up, I don't know; EXPR **c. en la cuenta** to realize, to understand; **cuando cayó en la cuenta del error, intentó subsanarlo** when she realized her mistake, she tried to correct it

(m) *(coincidir) (fecha)* **c. en** to fall on; **cae en domingo** it falls on a Sunday; **¿en qué día cae Navidad este año?** what day (of the week) is Christmas this year?

(n) *(abalanzarse)* **c. sobre** to fall *o* descend upon; **c. sobre alguien** *(ladrón)* to pounce *o* fall upon sb; **cayeron sobre la ciudad para saquearla** they fell upon the city and pillaged it

(o) *(en situación)* **c. enfermo** to fall ill, to be taken ill; **cayó en cama** he took to his bed; **c. en desuso** to fall into disuse; **c. en el olvido** to fall into oblivion; **c. en la desesperación** to fall into despair; **c. en desgracia** to fall into disgrace

(p) *(sentar)* **c. bien/mal** *(comentario, noticia)* to go down well/badly; **su comentario no cayó nada bien** her comment didn't go down well; **c. bien/mal a alguien** *(comida, bebida)* to agree/disagree with sb; *Esp (ropa)* to suit/not to suit sb; *Esp* **los pantalones ajustados no te caen nada bien** tight trousers don't suit you at all; EXPR **c. como un jarro de agua fría** to come as a real shock

(q) *(causar una impresión)* **me cae bien** I like him, he seems nice; **me cae mal** I can't stand him; **tu hermano me cae muy mal** I can't stand your brother; **me cayó mal** I didn't like him at all; **cae mal a todo el mundo** he doesn't get on with anyone; *Fam* **tu jefe me cae gordo** I can't stand your boss

(r) *Esp Fam (en examen)* to fail; **la mitad de la clase cayó en el primer examen** half the class failed the first exam; **¿cuántas te han caído?** how many did you fail?

(s) *Fam (decaer)* to go downhill; **el equipo ha caído mucho en el último mes** the team has gone seriously off the boil over the last month

(t) *Com (pago)* to fall due

(u) *Am (visitar)* to drop in

(v) EXPR **c. (muy) bajo** to sink (very) low; **parece mentira que hayas caído tan bajo** I can hardly believe that you would sink so low; **¡qué bajo has caído!** I never thought you'd sink so low!; **c. por su propio peso** to be self-evident; **todos mis consejos cayeron en saco roto** all my advice fell on deaf ears; **dejarse c. por casa de alguien** to drop by sb's house; **estar al c.** to be about to arrive; **ya son las cinco, así que deben de estar al c.** it's five o'clock, so they should be arriving any minute now; **el anuncio debe de estar al c.** the announcement should be made any minute now; **se proseguirá con la investigación caiga quien caiga** the investigation will proceed no matter who might be implicated *o* even if it means that heads will roll; *RP Fam* **c. parado** to fall on one's feet

2 caerse *vpr* **(a)** *(persona)* to fall over *o* down; **el chico resbaló y se cayó** the boy slipped and fell over; **¡ten cuidado o te caerás!** be careful or you'll fall (over)!; **no me caí de milagro** it's a miracle I didn't fall (over); **caerse de algo** to fall from sth; **se cayó de la moto** she fell off her motorbike; **se cayó de bruces/cabeza** she fell flat on her face/headlong; *Fam* **se cayó de culo** he fell flat on his backside; **se cayó de espaldas** he fell over backwards; **se cayó redonda** she slumped to the ground, she collapsed in a heap; **estoy que me caigo** *(de cansancio)* I'm ready to drop; *Fam* **casi me caigo del susto** I nearly fell over with fright; EXPR *Fam* **no tiene dónde caerse muerto** he hasn't got a penny to his name

(b) *(objeto)* to drop, to fall; *(árbol)* to fall; **se me cayó el libro** I dropped the book; **agárralo bien, que no se te caiga** hold onto it tight so you don't drop it; **¡se le ha caído la cartera!** you've dropped your *Br* wallet *o US* billfold!

(c) *(desprenderse) (diente, pelo)* to fall out; *(botón, hojas)* to fall off; *(cuadro)* to fall down; **las hojas están empezando a caerse** the leaves are starting to fall; **se me ha caído un diente** one of my teeth has fallen out; **no quiere aceptar que se le esté cayendo el pelo** he refuses to accept that he's going bald *o* that his hair is starting to fall out; *Fam* **este coche se cae en pedazos** this car is falling to pieces; *Fam* **esta casa se cae de vieja** this house is falling apart with age, this house is so old it's falling apart; *Fam* **el polémico prólogo se ha caído de la nueva edición del libro** the controversial preface has been dropped from the new edition of the book; *Fam* **el famoso catedrático se cayó de la lista de ponentes en el último momento** the famous professor withdrew from the list of speakers at the last moment

(d) *(falda, pantalones)* to fall down; **se te caen los pantalones** your trousers are falling down

(e) *Informát (red, servidor)* to go down; **la red se ha caído** the network is down

Cafarnaúm *n* Capernaum

café 1 *nm* **(a)** *(bebida)* coffee; **¿quieres un c.?** would you like a (cup of) coffee? ►► ***c. americano*** large black coffee; ***c. cortado*** = coffee with a dash of milk; ***c. exprés*** expresso; ***c. expreso*** expresso; ***c. de filtro*** filter coffee; ***c. instantáneo*** instant coffee; ***c. irlandés*** Irish coffee; ***c. con leche*** white coffee; ***c. molido*** ground coffee; *Am* ***c. negro*** black coffee; *Méx* ***c. de olla*** = coffee boiled with cinnamon and raw sugar; *Andes* ***c. perfumado*** coffee with alcohol; *Esp* ***c. solo*** expresso; ***c. soluble*** instant coffee; *Andes, Ven* ***c. tinto*** black coffee; *RP* ***c. torrado*** high-roast coffee; ***c. torrefacto*** high-roast coffee; ***c. turco*** Turkish coffee; ***c. vienés*** = coffee topped with whipped cream

(b) *(cultivo)* coffee; **una plantación de c.** a coffee plantation

(c) *(establecimiento)* café, coffee shop ►► ***c. bar*** = café where alcohol is also sold

(d) *Fam (humor, genio)* **tener mal c.** to be bad-tempered; **estar de mal c.** to be in a bad mood

(e) *RP Fam (rezongo)* telling-off

2 *adj inv (color)* coffee-coloured; *Am (marrón)* brown

café-cantante (*pl* **cafés-cantantes** *o* **cafés-cantante**) *nm* = café with resident singer

café-concierto (*pl* **cafés-concierto**) *nm* = café with live music

cafeína *nf* caffeine; **sin c.** caffeine-free

cafelito *nm Esp Fam* (cup of) coffee

cafesero, -a *adj Carib Fam* **es muy c.** he's a big coffee drinker

cafetal *nm* coffee plantation

cafetalero, -a 1 *adj* coffee; **industria cafetalera** coffee industry

2 *nm,f* coffee grower

café-teatro (*pl* **cafés-teatro**) *nm* = café with live entertainment

cafetera *nf* **(a)** *(para preparar café) (italiana)* = stove-top coffee percolator; *(eléctrica)* (filter) coffee machine; *(de émbolo)* cafetière; *(en bares)* expresso machine; *(para servir café)* coffee pot; EXPR *Fam* **estar como una c.** to be nuts *o* batty ►► ***c. de émbolo*** cafetière **(b)** *Fam (aparato viejo)* old crock; *(coche)* boneshaker, jalop(p)y **(c)** *ver también* **cafetero**

cafetería *nf (establecimiento)* café, snack bar; *(en facultad, hospital, museo)* cafeteria; *(en empresa)* canteen

cafetero, -a 1 *adj* **(a)** *(de café)* coffee; *(país)* coffee-producing; **producción cafetera** coffee production **(b)** *(bebedor de café)* **es muy c.** he's a big coffee drinker

2 *nm,f (cultivador)* coffee grower; *(comerciante)* coffee merchant

cafetín *nm* small café *o* coffee shop

cafeto *nm* coffee bush

cafiche *nm Andes Fam (proxeneta)* pimp

caficultor, -ora *nm,f CAm, Col, Méx* coffee grower

cafiolo, cafisho *nm RP Fam (proxeneta)* pimp

cafre 1 *adj* **(a)** *(bruto)* brutish **(b)** *Méx Fam (dominguero)* **¡qué c. eres!** you're a terrible driver!

2 *nmf* **(a)** *(bruto)* brute, boor **(b)** *Méx Fam (dominguero)* Sunday driver

caftán *nm* caftan, kaftan

cafúa *nf RP Fam* clink, slammer

cagaaceite *nm* mistle thrush

cagada *nf* **(a)** *Fam (excremento)* shit; **una c.** a piece of shit, a turd; **pisé una c. de perro** I stood in some dog shit; **el parque estaba lleno de cagadas** the park was full of dog shit

(b) *muy Fam (equivocación) Br* cock-up, *US* foul-up; **ha sido una c. haber aceptado su propuesta** accepting her proposal was a dumbass idea

(c) *muy Fam (cosa de mala calidad)* **este libro es una c.** this book is (a load of) crap

(d) *ver también* **cagado**

cagadera = **cagalera**

cagadero *nm muy Fam Br* bog, *US* john

cagado, -a *muy Fam* **1** *adj* shit-scared

2 *nm,f (cobarde)* yellow-belly, chicken

cagalera, *Am* **cagadera** *nf Fam (diarrea)* the runs; **le entró c.** he got the runs

cagar [38] **1** *vt muy Fam* **(a)** *(fastidiar, estropear)* **cagué la segunda pregunta del examen** I *Br* cocked *o US* balled up the second question in the exam; EXPR **cagarla** *(estropear)* to *Br* cock *o US* ball (it) up; **¡la hemos cagado, ahora tendremos que repetirlo otra vez!** we've *Br* cocked *o US* balled it up!, now we're going to have to do it again!; **no voy a permitir que llegue él y la cague** I'm not going to let him come along and *Br* cock *o US* ball it all up; **¡la has cagado!** *(estás en un lío)* you're in deep shit *o* up shit creek!

(b) *RP (traicionar)* to screw, to shaft; **confió en sus amigos y lo cagaron** he trusted his friends and they screwed him

(c) *RP (vencer)* to wipe the floor with, to slaughter; **en el ajedrez siempre me caga** he always wipes the floor with *o* slaughters me at chess

2 *vi* **(a)** *Fam (defecar)* to have *o* take a dump

(b) *RP muy Fam (fastidiarse)* to be screwed; **si mañana llueve, cagamos** if it rains tomorrow, we're screwed

3 cagarse *vpr Fam* to crap oneself; **se cagó de miedo al oír la explosión** he crapped himself when he heard the explosion; **fue expulsado por cagarse en la familia del árbitro** he was sent off for calling the referee every name under the sun; **va por ahí cagándose en todo el mundo** she goes around insulting everybody; **icágate, hemos vendido todas las entradas!** *Br* bloody hell *o US* goddamn it, if we haven't sold all the tickets!; EXPR *Hum* **icágate, lorito! me han subido el sueldo** would you believe it *o* well stone me!, they've given me a raise!; EXPR *RP Vulg* **me cago en la diferencia** it doesn't make any fucking difference; EXPR *Vulg* **ime cago en la hostia!** fucking hell!; EXPR *muy Fam* **ime cago en diez** *o* **en la mar** *o* **en la leche!** *Br* bleeding hell!, *US* goddamn it!; EXPR *Vulg* **ime cago en tu puta madre!** you motherfucker!; EXPR *muy Fam* **que te cagas: hace un frío que te cagas ahí fuera** it's *Br* bloody *o US* goddamn freezing out there!; **me he comprado una moto que te cagas** I've bought a shit-hot new motorbike; **tu amiga está que te cagas** your friend is *Br* bloody *o US* goddamn gorgeous; EXPR *muy Fam Hum* **este pastel está que se caga la perra** this cake is *Br* bloody *o US* goddamn delicious; EXPR *muy Fam* **de cagarse: marcó un golazo de cagarse** he scored a *Br* bloody *o US* goddamn brilliant goal

cagarruta *nf* dropping

cagódromo *nm muy Fam* shithouse

cagón, -ona *Fam* **1** *adj* **(a)** *(que caga)* **este bebé es muy c.** this baby is forever dirtying its *Br* nappy *o US* diaper **(b)** *(miedica)* chicken, cowardly

2 *nm,f* **(a)** *(que caga)* **este bebé es un c.** this baby is forever dirtying its *Br* nappy *o US* diaper **(b)** *(miedica)* chicken, coward

cague 1 *ver* **cagar**

2 *nm Fam (miedo)* **ime entró un c.!** I was scared as hell!, *Br* I was bricking it!; **las alturas me dan mucho c.** heights really give me the willies

cagueta *Fam* **1** *adj* chicken, cowardly

2 *nmf* chicken, coward

caída *nf* **(a)** *(de persona)* fall; **sufrir una c.** to have a fall; **se rompió la cadera por una mala c.** he fell badly and broke his hip

(b) *(de hojas, lluvia, nieve)* fall; *(de diente, pelo)* loss; **en la época de la c. de la hoja** when the leaves fall off the trees; EXPR *RP Fam* **ser la c. de la estantería** to be out of this world ▸▸ ***c. de agua*** waterfall; ***c. libre*** free fall; ***c. de ojos:*** **tiene una atractiva c. de ojos** she has an attractive way of lowering her eyelashes; ***c. en picado*** *(de avión)* crash dive

(c) *(de imperio, ciudad, dictador)* fall; **la c. del Imperio Romano** the fall of the Roman Empire; **la c. del muro (de Berlín)** the fall of the Berlin Wall

(d) *(de paro, precios)* drop **(de** in); **se espera una c. de las temperaturas** temperatures are expected to drop; **se ha registrado una c. del desempleo** there has been a fall in unemployment, unemployment has gone down ▸▸ ***c. en picado*** *(de la economía)* free fall; *(de precios)* nose-dive; ***c. de tensión*** voltage drop

(e) *(de sol)* **a la c. del sol** at sunset; **a la c. de la tarde** at nightfall

(f) *(de terreno)* drop **(de** in); **una c. muy pronunciada del terreno** a steep incline *o* slope

(g) *(de tela, vestido)* drape

(h) *Fam Informát (de red)* crash

(i) *Náut (de velas)* drop, hoist

(j) *(en golf)* break

caído, -a 1 *adj* **(a)** *(árbol, hoja)* fallen **(b)** *(decaído)* low **(c)** *(pechos)* saggy; *(ears, eyes)* droopy; *(shoulders)* round, sloping; **es caída de hombros** she's round-shouldered **(d) c. del cielo** *(oportuno)* heaven-sent; *(inesperado)* out-of-the-blue; **tu ayuda nos viene como caída del cielo** your help is like manna from heaven

2 *nmpl* **los caídos** the fallen; **un monumento a los caídos (en la guerra)** a war memorial

caigo *ver* **caer**

caigua *nf* achocha

caimán *nm* alligator, cayman; **las islas C.** the Cayman Islands

caimito *nm CAm, Carib* **(a)** *(árbol)* caimito **(b)** *(fruto)* star apple, caimito

Caín *n pr* Cain; EXPR *Fam* **pasar las de C.** to have a hell of a time

Cairo *n* **El C.** Cairo

caite *nm CAm* = type of cheap sandal, with soles made from recycled tyres

caja *nf* **(a)** *(recipiente)* box; *(para transporte, embalaje)* box, crate; **una c. de zapatos** a shoe box; **una c. de cervezas** a crate of beer; **una c. de bombones** *(vacía)* a chocolate box; **compré una c. de bombones** I bought a box of chocolates ▸▸ ***c. acústica*** loudspeaker; *Fam* ***la c. boba*** *(televisión)* the box, *Br* the telly, *US* the boob tube; ***c. de cambios*** gearbox; ***c. de cerillas*** matchbox; *Col, RDom* ***c. de dientes*** false teeth; *Elec* ***c. de empalmes*** junction box; ***c. de fusibles*** fuse box; ***c. de herramientas*** tool box; ***c. de música*** music box; ***c. negra*** *(en avión)* black box, flight recorder; ***c. nido*** nesting box; *Fig* ***la c. de Pandora*** Pandora's box; ***c. de pinturas*** paintbox; ***c. de resonancia*** sound-box; *Fig* sounding board; ***c. de ritmos*** drum machine; ***c. sorpresa*** jack-in-the-box; *Fam* ***la c. tonta*** *(televisión)* the box, *Br* the telly, *US* the boob tube; ***c. torácica*** ribcage

(b) *(de reloj)* case; *(de engranajes)* housing

(c) *(de violín, guitarra)* sound-box

(d) *(tambor)* drum; EXPR **echar** *o* **despedir a alguien con cajas destempladas** to send sb packing

(e) *(de camión, furgoneta)* back

(f) *(ataúd)* coffin

(g) *(hueco) (de escalera)* well; *(de chimenea, ascensor)* shaft ▸▸ ***c. de la escalera*** stairwell

(h) *(para el dinero)* cash box ▸▸ *Esp* ***c. de ahorros*** savings bank; *Com* ***c. B*** = parallel illegal system of book-keeping; ***c. de caudales*** safe, strongbox; ***c. fuerte*** safe, strongbox; ***c. registradora*** cash register; ***c. de resistencia*** strike fund; ***c. rural*** agricultural credit bank; ***c. de seguridad*** safe-deposit box

(i) *(en tienda, supermercado)* till; *(mostrador)* checkout; *(en banco)* cashier's desk; **horario de c.** *(en banco)* banking hours; **para pagar, pasen por la c. número dos** please pay at till number two ▸▸ ***c. rápida*** express checkout

(j) *(dinero recaudado)* takings; *Com* **hacer (la) c.** to cash up; **hacer una c. de 1.000 euros** to have takings of *o* to take in 1,000 euros

(k) *Imprenta* case ▸▸ ***c. alta*** upper case; ***c. baja*** lower case

(l) *(en armas)* gun stock

(m) *Mil* **entrar en c.** to be called up ▸▸ ***c. de reclutamiento*** recruiting office; ***c. de reclutas*** recruiting office

(n) *Perú (depósito)* water tank

(o) *Chile (de río)* dry riverbed

cajamarquino, -a, cajamarqueño, -a 1 *adj* of/from Cajamarca *(Peru)*

2 *nm,f* person from Cajamarca *(Peru)*

cajearse *vpr Méx Fam* **se cajeó con 50.000 pesos de multa** he was landed with a 50,000-peso fine

cajero, -a 1 *nm,f (en tienda)* cashier; *(en supermercado)* checkout assistant; *(en banco)* teller, cashier

2 *nm* cash machine, cash dispenser ▸▸ ***c. automático*** cash machine, cash dispenser; ***c. nocturno*** = safe built into outside wall of a bank where deposits can be made when bank is closed, *Br* night safe

cajeta *nf* **(a)** *CAm, Méx (dulce de leche)* = toffee pudding made with caramelized milk **(b)** *PRico (turrón)* = type of nougat

cajetilla *nf (de cigarrillos)* packet

cajetín *nm* **(a)** *(en imprenta)* box **(b)** *Elec* moulding

cajilla *RP* **1** *nf (de cigarrillos)* packet

2 *nm Fam Anticuado (persona)* moneybags *(singular)*

cajista *nmf Imprenta* typesetter, compositor

cajón *nm* **(a)** *(de mueble)* drawer ▸▸ *Fig* ***c. de sastre:*** **su mesa es un c. de sastre** he's got everything but the kitchen sink on his desk; **esa revista es un c. de sastre en el que caben todo tipo de artículos** that magazine has articles about everything under the sun; **el concepto de medicina oriental es un c. de sastre** oriental medicine is a catch-all category

(b) *(caja grande)* box, crate; *(de mudanza)* packing case

(c) *(ataúd) Br* coffin, *US* casket

(d) *Méx (de estacionamiento)* parking space *o* bay

(e) *RP (para botellas)* crate

(f) EXPR *Fam* **eso es de c.** that goes without saying

cajonera *nf* **(a)** *(mueble)* chest of drawers **(b)** *(en pupitre)* = shelf under desk for books, papers etc **(c)** *Ecuad (vendedora)* itinerant saleswoman

cajuela *nf CAm, Méx (maletero) Br* boot, *US* trunk

cajuelita *nf CAm, Méx (guantera)* glove compartment

cal *nf (en polvo)* lime; *(pintura)* whitewash; **el agua tiene mucha c.** the water is very hard; EXPR **cerrar a c. y canto** to shut tight *o* firmly; EXPR **una de c. y otra de arena: con este hombre, es una de c. y otra de arena** you never know with that man, he's nice one minute and horrible the next; **el equipo está dando una de c. y otra de arena** the team are good one minute, awful the next ►► ***c. apagada*** slaked lime; ***c. viva*** quicklime

cala *nf* (**a**) *(bahía pequeña)* cove (**b**) *Náut (parte sumergida)* hold (**c**) *(de melón, sandía)* sample piece (**d**) *(planta)* arum lily (**e**) *(perforación)* test boring (**f**) *Esp Fam (peseta)* peseta

calabacera *nf* pumpkin, gourd

calabacín *nm, Méx* **calabacita** *nf Br* courgette, *US* zucchini

calabaza *nf* (**a**) *(planta, fruto)* pumpkin, gourd; EXPR *Fam* **dar calabazas a alguien** *(a pretendiente)* to turn sb down, *Br* to knock sb back ►► ***c. de peregrino*** bottle gourd (**b**) *Fam (suspenso)* fail, *US* failing grade; **una c. en inglés** a fail *o US* failing grade in English; **dar calabazas a alguien** to fail *o US* flunk sb

calabobos *nm inv* drizzle

calabozo *nm (celda)* cell; **los calabozos del castillo** the castle dungeon *o* dungeons

calaca *nf Méx* skeleton *(as symbol of death)*

calada *nf* (**a**) *(inmersión)* soaking (**b**) *Esp Fam (de cigarrillo)* drag, puff; **dar una c.** to take a drag, to have a puff

caladero *nm* fishing grounds, fishery

calado, -a 1 *adj* (**a**) *(empapado)* soaked; EXPR **c. hasta los huesos** soaked to the skin

(**b**) *(en costura)* embroidered *(with openwork)*

2 *nm* (**a**) *(de barco)* draught; **un buque de gran c.** a deep-draughted vessel

(**b**) *(profundidad)* depth; **un puerto de poco c.** a shallow port

(**c**) *(bordado)* openwork

(**d**) *Esp (de automóvil)* stall; **el c. se produce al cambiar de marcha** the engine stalls when you change gear

(**e**) *(importancia)* significance, importance; **reformas de gran c.** reforms of great significance; **países del c. de Francia y Alemania** countries of the importance *o* stature of France and Germany; **un nombramiento de gran c. político** an appointment of great political significance

calador *nm Am (para grano)* grain sampler

calafate *nmf Náut* caulker

calafatear *vt Náut* to caulk

calafateo *nm Náut* caulking

calamar *nm* squid; **calamares a la romana** squid rings fried in batter; **calamares en su tinta** squid cooked in its own ink

calambrazo *nm Fam* jolt, (electric) shock

calambre *nm* (**a**) *(descarga eléctrica)* (electric) shock; **le dio un c. al tocar el enchufe** he got a shock when he touched the plug; **ese enchufe da c.** that plug will give you an electric shock

(**b**) *(contracción muscular)* cramp; **me dio un c. en la pierna** I got cramp *o US* a cramp in my leg

(**c**) EXPR *RP Fam* **dar c.: las cuentas que me llegaron dan c.** the bills they sent are astronomical; **la situación de los refugiados da c.** the refugees' plight is harrowing

calambuco *nm (árbol)* calaba tree

calamento *nm* basil thyme, calamint

calamidad *nf* (**a**) *(catástrofe)* disaster, calamity; **pasar calamidades** to suffer great hardship; **¡qué c.!** how awful! (**b**) *(persona)* **ser una c.** to be a dead loss

calamina *nf* (**a**) *(silicato de cinc)* zinc ore, *Espec* smithsonite, *US* calamine (**b**) *(cinc fundido)* zinc (**c**) *Chile, Perú (para techos)* corrugated zinc

calamita *nf (imán)* lodestone

calamitoso, -a *adj* calamitous

cálamo *nm* (**a**) *(planta)* calamus, sweet flag (**b**) *(pluma)* pen (**c**) *(caña)* reed, stalk (**d**) *(flauta)* = type of ancient reed flute

calamoco *nm* icicle

calamón *nm (ave)* purple gallinule

calancho, -a *adj Bol Fam* in the raw, *Br* starkers

calandra *nf* radiator grille

calandraca *adj RP Fam Pey* doddery

calandrar *vt (papel, ropa)* to calender

calandria *nf* (**a**) *(pájaro)* calandra lark (**b**) *Tec* calender (**c**) *Méx (carroza)* open carriage *(for tourists)*

calaña *nf Pey* **de esa c.** of that ilk; **no me junto con los de su c.** I don't mix with people of his sort; **gente de la peor c.** people of the worst sort, the worst sort of people

cálao *nm* hornbill

calapié *nm* toe-clip

calar 1 *vt* (**a**) *(empapar)* to soak

(**b**) *Esp (motor)* to stall

(**c**) *(persona, asunto)* to see through, *Br* to suss out; **lo calé nada más verlo** I had him worked out as soon as I set eyes on him; **no consigo c. sus intenciones** I can't work out what she's after

(**d**) *(sombrero)* to jam on

(**e**) *(melón, sandía)* to cut a sample of

(**f**) *(tela)* to do openwork embroidery on

(**g**) *(perforar)* to perforate, to pierce

(**h**) *Náut (velas)* to lower, to let down; *(redes)* to cast

(**i**) *(bayoneta)* to fix

(**j**) *Am (grano)* to sample

2 *vi* (**a**) *Náut* to draw

(**b**) *(ser permeable)* **estos zapatos calan** these shoes let in water

(**c**) *(penetrar)* **c. (hondo) en** to strike a chord with; **un producto que ha calado (hondo) entre los consumidores** a product that has struck a chord among consumers

3 **calarse** *vpr* (**a**) *(empaparse)* to get soaked; EXPR **me he calado hasta los huesos** I got soaked to the skin, I got drenched to the bone

(**b**) *(sombrero)* to pull down

(**c**) *Esp (motor)* to stall

calato, -a *adj Perú Fam (desnudo)* naked

calavera 1 *nf* (**a**) *(cráneo)* skull (**b**) *Méx Aut* **calaveras** tail lights (**c**) *Méx (dulce)* sugar skull

2 *nm (libertino)* rake

calcado, -a *adj* (**a**) *(dibujo, figura)* traced

(**b**) *(muy parecido)* **ser c. a alguien** to be the spitting image of sb; **ser c. a algo** to be practically identical to sth; **un programa político c. al del partido en el gobierno** a political programme which is practically identical to *o* simply a copy of the government's; **ese cuadro está c. del que pintó Goya** this painting is a copy of the one painted by Goya

calcamonía *nf Fam* transfer, *US* decal

calcáneo *nm Anat* heel bone, *Espec* calcaneum

calcañal, calcañar *nm* heel

calcar [60] *vt* (**a**) *(dibujo)* to trace (**b**) *(imitar)* to copy

calcáreo, -a *adj (terreno)* chalky, *Espec* calcareous; **aguas calcáreas** hard water

calce 1 *ver* **calzar**

2 *nm* (**a**) *(cuña)* wedge (**b**) *Guat, Méx, PRico Der* footnote

calcedonia *nf Geol* chalcedony

calcemia *nf Med* calcaemia

calceta *nf (labor)* knitting; **hacer c.** to knit

calcetar *vi* to knit

calcetín *nm* sock ►► ***calcetines cortos*** ankle socks, short socks; ***c. de ejecutivo*** = man's thin heelless sock

cálcico, -a *adj* calcic

calcificación *nf* calcification

calcificar [60] 1 *vt* to calcify

2 **calcificarse** *vpr* to calcify

calcinación *nf*, **calcinamiento** *nm* burning

calcinado, -a *adj (material)* burnt, scorched; *(edificio)* burnt-out; *(cuerpo)* charred

calcinamiento = **calcinación**

calcinar *vt* to burn, to scorch

calcio *nm Quím* calcium

calcita *nf Geol* calcite

calco *nm* (**a**) *(reproducción)* tracing (**b**) *(imitación)* carbon copy; **es un c. del original** it's a carbon copy of the original; **un c. de lo que pasó en la guerra de Bosnia** a carbon copy of what happened in the Bosnian conflict (**c**) *Ling* calque, loan translation

calcografía *nf* (**a**) *(técnica)* (copper/brass) engraving, *Espec* chalcography (**b**) *(imagen)* (copper/brass) engraving

calcolítico, -a 1 *adj* chalcolithic

2 *nm* **el Calcolítico** the Chalcolithic

calcomanía *nf* transfer, *US* decal

calcopirita *nf Geol* chalcopyrite

calculable *adj* calculable

calculador, -ora *adj* calculating; **una persona fría y calculadora** a cold and calculating person

calculadora *nf* calculator ►► ***c. de bolsillo*** pocket calculator; ***c. científica*** scientific calculator; ***c. programable*** programmable calculator; ***c. solar*** solar-powered calculator

calcular *vt* (a) *(cantidades)* to calculate; **c. la raíz cuadrada de un número** to calculate *o* extract the square root of a number; **c. un puente/una bóveda** to do the calculations involved in building a bridge/a vault; **c. mal** to miscalculate, to misjudge; **c. a ojo** to judge by eye; **calculando por lo alto, costará unos 2 millones** it will cost about 2 million at the most *o* the outside; **¿podrías c. por lo bajo cuánto tiempo haría falta?** could you work out the minimum amount of time it would take?; **su fortuna se calcula en $20 millones** he is estimated to be worth $20 million
(b) *(pensar, considerar)* **está todo cuidadosamente calculado** everything has been carefully worked out; **no calculó las consecuencias de sus actos** she didn't foresee the consequences of her actions; **no calcularon bien el impacto de sus acciones** they misjudged the effect their actions would have
(c) *(suponer)* to reckon; **le calculo sesenta años** I reckon *o* guess he's about sixty; **calculo que estará listo mañana** I reckon *o* think it will be ready tomorrow
(d) *(imaginar)* to imagine; **calcula la sorpresa que se llevó cuando se lo dijimos** just imagine how surprised he was when we told him; **¿y se enfadó? – ¡calcula!** was he angry? – well, what do you think?

calculista *nmf Com* planner

cálculo *nm* (a) *(operación)* calculation; **c. aproximado** estimate; **hacer un c. aproximado** to estimate, to make an estimate; **hacer cálculos** to do some calculations; **estamos haciendo cálculos para saber cuánta gente vendrá** we're trying to work out how many people are going to come ▸▸ *Com* ***c. de costos*** costing; ***c. mental:*** **hacer cálculos mentales** to do mental arithmetic
(b) *(ciencia)* calculus ▸▸ ***c. diferencial*** differential calculus; ***c. infinitesimal*** infinitesimal calculus; ***c. integral*** integral calculus
(c) *(evaluación)* estimate; **si no me fallan los cálculos,...** if my calculations are correct,...; **según mis cálculos, llegaremos a las cinco** by my reckoning, we'll arrive at five o'clock ▸▸ ***c. de probabilidades*** probability theory
(d) *Med* stone, *Espec* calculus ▸▸ ***c. biliar*** gallstone; ***c. renal*** kidney stone

Calcuta *n* Calcutta

caldas *nfpl* hot springs

caldeado, -a *adj (habitación, edificio)* heated; **los ánimos están muy caldeados** tempers *o* feelings are running high

caldeamiento *nm* (a) *(calentamiento)* warming, heating (b) *(excitación)* excitement; **se notaba un c. entre el público** there was growing excitement among the audience; **la decisión del árbitro provocó el c. de los espectadores** the referee's decision angered the crowd

caldear 1 *vt* (a) *(calentar)* to heat (up) (b) *(excitar)* to warm up, to liven up; **las declaraciones del presidente caldearon el ambiente** the president's statements really stirred things up
2 **caldearse** *vpr* (a) *(calentarse)* to heat up, to warm up; **la casa se caldeó en pocos minutos** the house warmed up in a few minutes (b) *(excitarse)* to get heated; **los ánimos se han caldeado** people have got themselves worked up; **la disputa comercial ha comenzado a caldearse** the trade dispute has begun to heat up

caldén *nm* = type of mesquite found in Argentina

caldeo, -a *Hist* 1 *adj* Chaldean
2 *nm,f (persona)* Chaldean
3 *nm (lengua)* Chaldean

caldera *nf* (a) *(industrial)* boiler ▸▸ ***c. de vapor*** steam boiler (b) *(olla)* cauldron ▸▸ *Fam Hum* ***las calderas de Pedro Botero*** *(el infierno)* (the nethermost depths of) hell (c) *Geol* caldera (d) *Urug (hervidor)* kettle

calderada *nf* (a) *(en caldera)* cauldron; **una c. de cocido** a cauldron of stew (b) **una c. de** *(mucho)* heaps of

calderería *nf* (a) *(oficio)* boilermaking (b) *(tienda)* boilermaker's shop

calderero, -a *nm,f* boilermaker

caldereta *nf* (a) *(de pescado)* fish stew (b) *(de carne)* meat stew

calderilla *nf (monedas)* small change

calderita *adj RP Fam* short-tempered; **es muy c.** he's got a short fuse

caldero *nm* cauldron

calderón *nm* (a) *Mús* pause (b) *Imprenta* paragraph mark (c) *(animal)* long-finned pilot whale

calderoniano, -a *adj* Calderonian, = typical of the style of the dramatist Pedro Calderón de la Barca (1600-1681)

caldillo *nm* liquid *(on plate of food)*

caldo *nm* (a) *(para cocinar)* stock; *(sopa)* clear soup, broth; **c. de pollo** *(para cocinar)* chicken stock; *(sopa)* chicken soup *o* consommé; EXPR *Fam Hum* **cambiar el c. a las aceitunas** to take a leak; EXPR *Esp Fam* **poner a alguien a c.** *(criticar)* to slate sb; *(reñir)* to give sb a ticking-off ▸▸ ***c. de cultivo*** culture medium; *Fig (condición idónea)* breeding ground
(b) *(aderezo)* dressing
(c) *(vino)* wine
(d) *Méx (de caña)* sugarcane juice

caldoso, -a *adj (comida)* with lots of stock; **estar demasiado c.** to be watery; **arroz c.** soggy rice

calé 1 *adj* gypsy
2 *nmf* gypsy

caledoniano, -a *adj Geol* Caledonian; **plegamiento c.** Caledonian fold

calefacción *nf* heating ▸▸ ***c. central*** central heating; ***c. eléctrica*** electric heating; ***c. por inducción*** induction heating; ***c. por suelo (radiante)*** underfloor heating

calefaccionar *vt CSur (calentar)* to heat (up), to warm (up)

calefactor, -ora 1 *nm (aparato)* heater
2 *nm,f (persona)* heating engineer

calefón *nm CSur (calentador)* water heater

caleidoscópico, -a *adj* kaleidoscopic

caleidoscopio *nm* kaleidoscope

calendario *nm* (a) *(sistema)* calendar ▸▸ ***c. del contribuyente*** = timetable for making annual tax returns; ***c. eclesiástico*** ecclesiastic calendar; ***c. escolar*** school calendar; ***c. gregoriano*** Gregorian calendar; ***c. juliano*** Julian calendar; ***c. laboral*** = officially stipulated working days and holidays for the year; ***c. lunar*** lunar calendar; ***c. perpetuo*** perpetual calendar; ***c. solar*** solar calendar
(b) *(objeto)* calendar; **un c. de mesa** a desk calendar
(c) *(programa)* schedule, programme; **la cita más importante en el c. musical de la ciudad** the most important event in the city's theatrical calendar; **los participantes en el congreso tienen un c. muy apretado** the conference participants have a busy programme; **programaron el c. de actividades para el festival** they drew up the schedule *o* programme of activities for the festival

calendas *nfpl* calends ▸▸ ***c. griegas:*** **las obras terminarán en las c. griegas** hell will freeze over before the work is finished; **te recibirá en las c. griegas** hell will freeze over before he'll see you

caléndula *nf* calendula, pot marigold

calentada *nf Am Fam* **dale una c. al arroz** heat the rice up again

calentador *nm* (a) *(de agua)* heater ▸▸ ***c. de agua*** water heater; ***c. de gas*** gas heater; ***c. de inmersión*** immersion heater (b) *(de cama)* warming pan, bed warmer (c) **calentadores** *(prenda)* legwarmers

calentamiento *nm* (a) *(subida de temperatura)* heating; **el c. del planeta** global warming ▸▸ ***c. global*** global warming (b) *(de la economía)* overheating; *(de debate)* heating up (c) *(ejercicios)* warm-up; **realizar un c. adecuado** to warm up properly; **ejercicios de c.** warm-up exercises; **sufrió un tirón durante el c.** he pulled a muscle while he was warming up

calentar [3] 1 *vt* (a) *(subir la temperatura de)* to heat (up), to warm (up); *(motor, máquina)* to warm up; **calienta un poco la leche** warm the milk up a bit; EXPR *Fam Dep* **c. banquillo** to sit on the bench; EXPR **c. motores** to warm up; EXPR **calentarle la cabeza a alguien** to pester sb
(b) *(músculos)* **c. los músculos** to limber up, to warm up
(c) *(animar)* to liven up; **sus declaraciones han calentado la campaña electoral** his statements have turned the heat up in the election campaign
(d) *Fam (pegar)* to hit, to strike; **¡te voy a c.!** you'll feel the back of my hand!
(e) *Fam (sexualmente)* to turn on
(f) *(agitar)* to make angry, to annoy; **¡me están calentando con tanta provocación!** all their provocation is getting me worked up!
2 *vi* (a) *(dar calor)* to give off heat; **esta estufa no calienta** this heater doesn't give off much heat
(b) *(entrenarse)* to warm up
3 **calentarse** *vpr* (a) *(por calor) (persona)* to warm oneself, to get warm; *(cosa)* to heat up
(b) *Fam (pegarse)* **se calentaron a base de bien** they really laid into one another
(c) *Fam (sexualmente)* to get horny *o* randy
(d) *(agitarse)* to get angry *o* annoyed; EXPR **calentarse la cabeza** to worry, to get worked up

calentito, -a *adj Fam* (a) *(cuerpo, ambiente)* (nice and) warm; *(comida)* piping hot (b) *(noticia)* hot off the press

calentón, -ona 1 *adj RP* short-tempered; **es muy c.** he's got a short fuse
2 *nm* **dale un c. al arroz** heat up the rice; **el coche ha sufrido un c.** the car has overheated

calentorro, -a *Esp Fam* 1 *adj* **estar c.** to be horny *o* randy
2 *nm,f* **ser un c.** to be a horny *o* randy little devil

calentura *nf* (a) *(fiebre)* fever, temperature (b) *(herida)* cold sore; **me ha salido una c.** I've got a cold sore (c) *Fam (sexual)* **le entró una c.** he got the hots, he got horny *o* randy (d) *Chile (tisis)* tuberculosis, consumption (e) *Carib (planta)* = type of milkweed (f) *Carib (descomposición)* fermentation

calenturiento, -a *adj* (a) *(con fiebre)* feverish (b) **tener una imaginación calenturienta** *(incontrolada)* to have a wild imagination; *(sexualmente)* to have a dirty mind (c) *Chile (tísico)* tubercular, consumptive

caleño, -a 1 *adj* of/from Cali *(Colombia)*
2 *nm,f* person from Cali *(Colombia)*

calera *nf* limekiln

calesa *nf* = open-topped horse-drawn carriage

calesita *nf RP* merry-go-round, *US* carousel

caleta *nf* (a) *(bahía)* cove, inlet (b) *PRico (calle)* = short road leading to the sea (c) *Col, Ven (escondite)* hiding place

caletear *vi Andes* to dock at all ports

caletero *nm Ven (descargador)* docker, stevedore

calibración *nf*, **calibrado** *nm* (a) *(medida)* calibration (b) *(de arma)* boring (c) *(corrección)* gauging ►► *Imprenta* ***c. de color*** colour correction

calibrador *nm (para medir)* gauge; *(de mordazas)* calliper

calibrar *vt* (a) *(medir)* to calibrate, to gauge (b) *(dar calibre a) (arma)* to bore (c) *(juzgar)* to gauge, to size up; **tenemos que c. cuidadosamente los pros y los contras** we must carefully weigh up the pros and cons

calibre *nm* (a) *(de arma)* calibre; **una bala del c. 9** a 9-mm bullet (b) *(de alambre)* gauge; *(de tubo)* bore (c) *(instrumento)* gauge (d) *(tamaño)* size; *(importancia)* importance, significance; **un actor del c. de Cary Grant** an actor of the calibre of Cary Grant; **una sequía de tal c. que se han secado los ríos** a drought so severe that the rivers have dried up

caliche *nm Andes* (a) *(salitre)* sodium nitrate, Chile saltpetre (b) *(terreno)* = ground rich in nitrates

calichera *nf Andes* = ground rich in nitrates

caliciforme *adj* tulip-shaped

calicó *nm* calico

calidad *nf* (a) *(de producto, servicio)* quality; **una casa de c.** a luxury house; **una edición de c.** a deluxe edition; **un género de (buena) c.** a quality product; **de primerísima c.** highest quality; **una buena relación c.-precio** good value (for money) ►► *Informát* ***c. borrador*** draft quality; ***c. de imagen*** image quality; ***c. de vida*** quality of life
(b) *(clase)* class
(c) *(condición)* **me lo dijo en c. de amigo** he told me as a friend; **acudió en c. de testigo** he was present as a witness; **fue contratado en c. de experto jurídico** he was employed as a legal expert; **no le revisan el equipaje por su c. de diplomático** his luggage isn't searched due to his diplomatic status

cálidamente *adv* warmly

calidez *nf (de persona, recibimiento)* warmth

cálido, -a *adj* (a) *(frente)* warm; *(clima, país)* warm, hot (b) *(recibimiento)* warm (c) *(tono)* warm

calidoscópico, -a *adj* kaleidoscopic

calidoscopio *nm* kaleidoscope

calientabraguetas *nf inv muy Fam* cocktease(r), pricktease(r)

calientahuevos *nf inv Col, Ven Vulg* cocktease(r), pricktease(r)

calientapiernas *nmpl* legwarmers

calientapiés *nm inv* foot-warmer

calientapija *nf RP Vulg* cocktease(r), pricktease(r)

calientaplatos *nm inv* hotplate

calientapollas *nf inv Esp Vulg* cocktease(r), pricktease(r)

caliente 1 *ver* **calentar**
2 *adj* (a) *(a alta temperatura)* hot; *(templado)* warm; **un café c.** a hot coffee; **de sangre c.** hot-blooded; *Fig* **en c.** in the heat of the moment
(b) *(que da calor)* warm; **esta chaqueta es muy c.** this jacket is really warm *o* keeps you really warm
(c) *(acalorado)* heated; **el debate se puso c.** the debate became rather heated
(d) *(conflictivo)* **la situación se está poniendo c.** the situation is hotting up; **se presenta un otoño c. para el gobierno** it looks like the government is in for a long hot autumn; **la zona más c. de la frontera entre los dos países** the real hot spot on the border between the two countries
(e) *(tono, color)* warm
(f) *(reciente)* hot off the press; **noticias calientes: Norma va a tener un niño** here's the latest: Norma's going to have a baby
(g) *Fam (cercano)* **no llegó a encontrarlo, pero anduvo muy c.** he didn't manage to find it, but he was very close
(h) *Fam (película, novela)* raunchy
(i) *Fam (excitado)* horny, randy
(j) *RP Fam (enojado) US* pissed, *Br* narked
3 *interj (al buscar algo)* you're warm!

caliento *etc ver* **calentar**

califa *nm* caliph

califato *nm* caliphate

calificación *nf* (a) *(atribución de cualidades)* classification (b) *(escolar) Br* mark, *US* grade (c) *Fin* rating ►► ***c. crediticia*** credit rating; ***c. financiera*** financial rating; ***c. de solvencia*** credit rating

calificado, -a *adj* (a) *(importante)* eminent (b) *(apto)* qualified (c) *(trabajador)* skilled

calificador, -ora *adj* (a) *(que evalúa)* assessing (b) *(que clasifica)* classifying, grading (c) *(de examen)* grading, marking (d) *Gram* qualifier

calificar [60] 1 *vt* (a) *(denominar)* **c. a alguien de algo** to call sb sth, to describe sb as sth; **su comportamiento fue calificado de heroico** his behaviour was described as heroic
(b) *(examen, trabajo)* to mark; **c. a alguien con un suspenso** to fail sb, *US* to give sb a failing grade
(c) *Gram* to qualify
(d) *(propiedad)* to classify; **han calificado el terreno como urbanizable** *Br* the land has been designated as a brownfield site, *US* the land has been zoned for construction
(e) *(personalidad)* **su gesto lo califica de caballero** his gesture shows him to be a gentleman
2 **calificarse** *vpr* **con esa acción se califica de cobarde** by that action he shows himself to be a coward; **esos comentarios se califican por sí solos** we all know what to make of remarks like that, there's no need to comment on remarks like that

calificativo, -a 1 *adj (adjetivo)* qualifying
2 *nm* epithet; **no merece el c. de corrupto** he doesn't deserve to be called corrupt; **calificativos elogiosos/insultantes** glowing/insulting terms

califón *nm Chile (calentador)* water heater

California *n* California

californiano, -a 1 *adj* Californian
2 *nm,f* Californian

californio *nm Quím* californium

cáliga *nf* Roman sandal

calígine *nf Literario* (a) *(niebla)* mist (b) *(oscuridad)* dark, gloom

caliginoso, -a *adj Literario* (a) *(neblinoso)* misty (b) *(oscuro)* dark, gloomy

caligrafía *nf* (a) *(arte)* calligraphy (b) *(letra)* handwriting; **los niños empiezan a hacer (ejercicios de) c. a los cuatro años** children start writing (exercises) at four years old; **un cuaderno de c.** a handwriting workbook

caligrafiar *vt* to pen, to write *(with elegant handwriting)*

caligráfico, -a *adj* handwriting; **hicieron un estudio c. de los candidatos** they had the candidates' handwriting analysed

calígrafo, -a *nm,f* calligrapher

caligüeba, caligüeva *nf Ven Fam* **estar con c.** to be feeling down

calima, calina *nf* haze, mist

calimocho *nm Esp Fam* = drink comprising red wine and cola

calina = **calima**

calipso *nm* calypso

calistenia *nf* callisthenics *(singular)*

cáliz *nm* (a) *Rel* chalice (b) *Bot* calyx

caliza *nf* limestone

calizo, -a *adj* chalky

callada *nf* EXPR **nos dio la c. por respuesta** he answered us with silence

calladamente *adv* silently

callado, -a *adj* **estar c.** to be quiet *o* silent; **¿quieres estar callada, por favor?** would you please be *o* keep quiet!; **ser c.** to be quiet *o* reserved; **tener algo c.** to keep sth quiet *o* a secret; **¡qué c. lo tenías!** you certainly kept that quiet *o* a secret!

callampa *nf Chile* (**a**) *(seta)* mushroom; EXPR **no vale c.** it isn't worth a bean (**b**) *(chabola)* shack (**c**) **callampas** *(barrio)* shanty town

callamperío *nm Chile* shanty town

callampero, -a *nm,f Chile* shanty dweller

callana *nf Andes, RP (cazuela)* = earthenware dish for roasting corn

callandito *adv Fam* on the quiet; **c., c., ha ido acumulando una fortuna** he's been building up a fortune on the quiet

callar 1 *vi* (**a**) *(no hablar)* to keep quiet, to be silent; EXPR **quien calla otorga** silence signifies consent

(**b**) *(dejar de hablar)* to be quiet, to stop talking; **mandar c. a alguien** to tell sb to shut up; **hacer c. a alguien** to silence sb; **¡calla!** shut up!; **¡calla, si eso me lo dijo a mí también!** guess what!, he said that to me, too!; **¡calla, que me he dejado el paraguas en el tren!** gosh! I've left my umbrella on the train!; **los cañones callaron tras tres días de combate** after three days of battle the guns fell silent

2 *vt* (**a**) *(ocultar)* to keep quiet about; **calló la verdad para no inculpar a su amigo** she withheld the truth so as not to incriminate her friend

(**b**) *(acallar)* to silence

3 **callarse** *vpr* (**a**) *(no hablar)* to keep quiet, to be silent

(**b**) *(dejar de hablar)* to stop talking, to fall silent; **no se calló hasta que no terminó de contar sus vacaciones** he didn't stop talking until he had told everyone all about his *Br* holidays *o US* vacation; **¡cállate!** shut up!; **¿te quieres c.?** would you keep quiet?

(**c**) *(ocultar)* to keep quiet about; *(secreto)* to keep; **esa no se calla nada** she always says what she thinks

calle *nf* (**a**) *(en población)* street, road; **cruzar la c.** to cross the street *o* road; **c. arriba/abajo** up/down the street *o* road; **tres calles más abajo** three blocks further down; EXPR *Fam* **echar** *o* **tirar por la c. de en medio** to go ahead regardless; EXPR **hacer la c.** *(prostituta)* to walk the streets; EXPR **llevarse a alguien de c.** to win sb over; EXPR **traer** *o* **llevar a alguien por la c. de la amargura** to put sb through hell, to make sb's life hell; EXPR *RP Fam* **tener c.** to know what's what, to be street smart ►► *Ven* ***c. ciega*** dead end, blind alley; ***c. cortada:*** **hay cuatro calles cortadas en el centro** four streets in the city centre are closed to traffic; **c. cortada (por obras)** *(en letrero)* road closed (for repairs); *CSur* ***c. cortada*** dead end, blind alley; ***c. de dirección única*** one-way street; ***c. de doble dirección*** two-way street; ***c. mayor*** high street, *US* main street; ***c. peatonal*** pedestrian street; ***c. principal*** main street; *RP* ***c. de una mano*** one-way street; *Col* ***c. de una vía*** one-way street

(**b**) *(lugar en el exterior)* **la c.** the street; **se pasa el día en la c.** she is always out; **salgo un momento, ¿quieres algo de la c.?** I'm just popping out, can I get you anything (from the shops)?; **no grites, te puede oír toda la c.** don't shout, the whole neighbourhood can hear you; **dejar** *o* **poner a alguien en la c.** *(sin trabajo)* to put sb out of a job; *(sin casa)* to throw sb out; **echar a alguien a la c.** *(de un trabajo)* to sack sb; *(de un lugar público)* to kick *o* throw sb out; **echarse a la c.** *(manifestarse)* to take to the streets; **el asesino está en la c. tras pasar años en la cárcel** the murderer is out after spending years in prison; **salir a la c.** *(salir de casa)* to go out

(**c**) *(ciudadanía)* **la c.** the public; **¿qué se opina en la c.?** what does the man in the street think?; **el lenguaje de la c.** everyday language

(**d**) *Esp (en atletismo, natación)* lane; **la c. de dentro/de fuera** the inside/outside lane

(**e**) *(en golf)* fairway

calleja *nf* sidestreet, alley

callejear *vi* to wander the streets

callejero, -a 1 *adj (perro, gato)* stray; **hace mucha vida callejera** he likes going out a lot; **disturbios callejeros** street riot; **un puesto c.** a street stall

2 *nm (guía)* street map, A-Z

callejón *nm* (**a**) *(calle)* alley ►► ***c. sin salida*** dead end, blind alley; *Fig* blind alley, impasse; **la OTAN se ha metido en un c. sin salida** NATO has got itself into a blind alley, NATO is at an impasse (**b**) *Taurom* = barricaded passage between the edge of the bullring and the seats

callejuela *nf* backstreet, sidestreet

callicida *nm* corn remover

callista *nmf* chiropodist

callo *nm* (**a**) *(dureza)* callus; *(en el pie)* corn; EXPR **tener c.** *(estar acostumbrado)* to be hardened; EXPR *Fam* **dar el c.** *(trabajar)* to slog (**b**) *Med (en fractura)* callus (**c**) *Fam (persona fea)* sight, fright; **ser un c.** to look a real sight (**d**) *Esp* **callos** tripe ►► ***callos a la madrileña*** = tripe cooked with ham, pork sausage, onion and peppers

callosidad *nf* callus; **callosidades** calluses, hard skin

calloso, -a *adj* calloused

calma *nf* (**a**) *(sin ruido o movimiento)* calm, stillness; **en c.** calm; **se vivía una c. tensa** there was an uneasy calm ►► ***c. chicha*** dead calm

(**b**) *(sosiego)* calm, tranquility; **un llamamiento a la c.** an appeal for calm; **el orador pidió c. a los asistentes** the speaker appealed to the audience to be calm; **con c.** calmly; **mantener la c.** to keep calm *o* one's composure; **perder la c.** to lose one's composure; **tener c.** *(tener paciencia)* to be patient; **tómatelo con c.** take it easy

calmante 1 *adj* sedative, soothing

2 *nm* sedative, painkiller

calmar 1 *vt* (**a**) *(mitigar)* to relieve; *(dolor)* to relieve, to ease; *(hinchazón)* to relieve; *(quemadura)* to soothe; *(sed)* to quench; *(hambre)* to take the edge off (**b**) *(tranquilizar) (persona)* to calm (down), to soothe; *(situación)* to defuse; **tómate esto para c. los nervios** take this to calm your nerves

2 **calmarse** *vpr* (**a**) *(persona, ánimos, situación)* to calm down, to quieten down (**b**) *(dolor, tempestad)* to abate; *(fiebre)* to subside; *(wind)* to die down

calmo, -a *adj (tranquilo)* calm

calmoso, -a *adj* calm

caló *nm* (**a**) *Esp (gitano)* = Spanish gypsy dialect (**b**) *Méx (argot)* = working-class Mexico City slang

calor *nm* (**a**) *(temperatura alta)* heat; *(tibieza)* warmth; **el c. dilata los cuerpos** heat causes bodies to expand; **al c. de la lumbre** by the fireside; **asarse de c.** to be roasting, to be boiling hot; **este abrigo da mucho c.** this coat is very warm; **entrar en c.** to get warm; *(público, deportista)* to warm up; **hace c.** it's warm *o* hot; **¡qué c. (hace)!** it's so hot!; **tener c.** to be warm *o* hot; **voy a abrir la ventana, tengo c.** I'm going to open the window, I'm too hot ►► ***c. animal*** body heat; ***c. blanco*** white heat; *Fís* ***c. específico*** specific heat; ***c. latente*** latent heat; ***c. negro*** electric heating; ***c. radiante*** radiant heat

(**b**) *(afecto, entusiasmo)* warmth; **la emocionó el c. del público** she was moved by the warmth of the audience ►► ***c. humano*** human warmth

(**c**) *RP Fam (vergüenza)* embarrassment; **me da c. hablar en público** I get embarrassed if I have to speak in public

(**d**) *RP* **calores** *(de la menopausia)* hot flushes *o US* flashes

caloría *nf* calorie; **bajo en calorías** low-calorie

calórico, -a *adj* caloric; **contenido/gasto c.** caloric content/expenditure

calorífero, -a *adj (que da calor)* heat-producing

calorífico, -a *adj* calorific

calorímetro *nm* calorimeter

calorro, -a *nm,f Fam* = term, usually offensive, used to refer to a Spanish gypsy

calostro *nm* colostrum

calote 1 *adj Méx Fam* beefy

2 *nm RP Fam* swindle

calumnia *nf (oral)* slander, calumny; *(escrita)* libel, calumny

calumniador, -ora 1 *adj (declaraciones)* slanderous; *(escrito)* libellous

2 *nm,f (oralmente)* slanderer; *(por escrito)* libeller

calumniar *vt (oralmente)* to slander; *(por escrito)* to libel

calumnioso, -a *adj (de palabra)* slanderous; *(por escrito)* libellous

calurosamente *adv (con afecto) (elogiar, recibir)* warmly; *(aplaudir)* warmly, enthusiastically

caluroso, -a *adj* (**a**) *(excesivamente)* hot; *(agradablemente)* warm; **una camisa muy calurosa** a very warm shirt (**b**) *(afectuoso)* warm (**c**) *Fam (sensible al calor)* **es muy c.** he can't take the heat, he really feels the heat

calva *nf* (**a**) *(en la cabeza)* bald patch (**b**) *(en tejido, terreno)* bare patch (**c**) *ver también* **calvo**

calvados *nm inv* Calvados

calvario *nm* (**a**) *(Vía Crucis)* Calvary, Stations of the Cross (**b**) *(sufrimiento)* ordeal, trial; **pasar un c.** to go through an ordeal

calvero *nm* (**a**) *(claro)* clearing, glade (**b**) *(terreno)* clay pit

calvicie *nf* baldness

calvinismo *nm* Calvinism

calvinista *adj* Calvinist

Calvino *n pr* Calvin

calvo, -a 1 *adj* bald; **quedarse c.** to go bald; EXPR *Fam Hum* **¡te vas a quedar c.!** *(de tanto pensar)* too much thinking's bad for you!
2 *nm,f* bald person

calvorota *Fam* 1 *adj* bald
2 *nmf* baldy

calza *nf* (a) *(cuña)* wedge; *(para avión, coche)* chock (b) *Anticuado (media)* stocking (c) *Col (empaste)* filling (d) *RP* **c., calzas** *(pantalón)* ski pants

calzada *nf* (a) *(de calle)* road (surface), *US* pavement (b) *(de autopista)* carriageway, roadway (c) *(camino)* road ►► ***c. romana*** Roman road

calzado, -a 1 *adj (con zapatos)* shod
2 *nm* footwear; **tienda de c.** shoe shop; **fabricantes de c.** shoe manufacturers ►► ***c. deportivo*** sports shoes; ***c. ortopédico*** orthopaedic footwear

calzador *nm (para calzarse)* shoehorn; *Fig* **tuvieron que meternos en el autobús con c.** we had to be shoehorned onto the bus

calzar [14] 1 *vt* (a) *(zapato, bota)* to wear; **calzaba zapatos de ante** she was wearing suede shoes; **¿qué número calza?** what size (shoe) do you take?; **calzo el 43** I take a (size) 43
(b) *(proveer de calzado)* to provide shoes for
(c) *(poner calzado)* **calza al bebé** put shoes on the baby, put the baby's shoes on
(d) *(puerta)* to wedge open; **calzó la mesa** he put a wedge under one of the table legs
(e) *(rueda)* to put a wedge under
(f) *Col (muela)* to fill
2 **calzarse** *vpr* (a) *(ponerse zapatos)* to put one's shoes on; **¡cálzate!** put your shoes on!; **la familia real se calza en esa zapatería** this shoemaker's is supplier to the royal family
(b) *(zapato)* to put on; **se calzó las botas** he put on his boots

calzo *nm (cuña)* wedge; *(para avión, coche)* chock

calzón *nm* (a) *Esp Dep* shorts
(b) *Andes, Méx, RP (bragas)* panties, *Br* knickers; **un c., unos calzones** a pair of panties; *RP* **en calzones** *(en ropa interior)* in one's underwear; EXPR *RP Fam* **se le cayeron los calzones** she was staggered *o Br* gobsmacked
(c) *Bol, Méx (calzoncillos) Br* underpants, *US* shorts; **un c., unos calzones** a pair of *Br* underpants *o US* shorts; EXPR *Fam* **se le cayeron los calzones** he was scared witless ►► *Méx* ***c. de baño*** swimming trunks
(d) *Bol (guiso)* pork stew

calzonarias *nfpl Col Br* braces, *US* suspenders

calzonarios *nmpl Ecuad* panties, *Br* knickers

calzonazos *nm inv, Am* **calzonudo** *nm Fam* henpecked husband; **ser un c.** to be henpecked *o US* whipped

calzoncillo *nm*, **calzoncillos** *nmpl (slip)* briefs, *Br* (under)pants, *US* shorts; *(bóxer)* boxer shorts ►► ***calzoncillos largos*** long johns

calzoneta *nf CAm* swimming trunks

calzonudo = **calzonazos**

CAM [kam] 1 *nm* (*abrev de* **computer-aided manufacturing**) CAM
2 *nf* (*abrev de* **Comunidad Autónoma de Madrid**) autonomous region of Madrid, = Madrid and the surrounding province

cama *nf* (a) *(mueble)* bed; **estar en** *o* **guardar c.** to be confined to bed; **el médico le ha dicho que tiene que estar en** *o* **guardar c.** the doctor told her to stay in bed; *Am Fam* **estar** *o* **quedar de c.** to be wrecked *o Br* knackered; **hacer la c.** to make the bed; **irse a la c.** to go to bed; **meterse en la c.** to get into bed; **saltar de la c.** to jump *o* leap out of bed; EXPR **hacerle** *o* **ponerle la c. a alguien** to plot against sb; EXPR *Dep* **hacerle la c. a alguien** to make a back for sb, to upend sb; PROV **a la c. no te irás sin saber una cosa más** you learn something new every day ►► ***c. de agua*** water bed; *RP* ***camas cameras*** twin beds; ***c. doble*** double bed; *Am* ***c. de dos plazas*** double bed; ***c. elástica*** trampoline; ***camas gemelas*** twin beds; ***c. individual*** single bed; *RP* ***c. marinera*** truckle bed, = bed with another pull-out bed underneath; ***c. de matrimonio*** double bed; ***c. nido*** truckle bed, = bed with another pull-out bed underneath; ***c. de rayos UVA*** sunbed; ***c. redonda*** group sex; *RP* ***c. solar*** sunbed; ***c. turca*** divan bed; *Am* ***c. de una plaza*** single bed; ***c. de uno*** single bed
(b) *(plaza hospitalaria)* (hospital) bed ►► ***c. de hospital*** hospital bed

camachuelo *nm* bullfinch ►► ***c. carminoso*** scarlet bullfinch; ***c. picogrueso*** pine grosbeak; ***c. trompetero*** trumpeter finch

camada *nf* litter

camafeo *nm* cameo

camagüeyano, -a 1 *adj* of/from Camagüey *(Cuba)*
2 *nm,f* person from Camagüey *(Cuba)*

camal *nm Andes (matadero)* slaughterhouse

camaleón *nm* (a) *(reptil)* chameleon (b) *(persona cambiante)* chameleon (c) *PRico (ave)* falcon

camaleónico, -a *adj (persona)* chameleon-like

camalero *nm Perú* slaughterer, butcher

camalotal *nm Am* water hyacinth bed

camalote *nm Am* water hyacinth

camambú *nm* grape ground-cherry

cámara 1 *nf* (a) *(de fotos, cine)* camera ►► ***c. cinematográfica*** movie *o Br* cine camera; ***c. de control de velocidad*** speed camera; ***c. digital*** digital camera; ***c. fotográfica*** camera; ***c. lenta*** slow motion; *también Fig* **a c. lenta** in slow motion; **si miras la repetición de la jugada a c. lenta podrás fijarte en todos los detalles** if you watch the slow-motion replay, you'll be able to see all the details; *TV* ***c. oculta*** candid camera; ***c. oscura*** camera obscura; ***c. réflex*** reflex *o* SLR camera; ***c. de televisión*** television camera; ***c. de vídeo*** *o Am* ***video*** *(profesional)* video camera; *(de aficionado)* camcorder
(b) *(sala)* chamber ►► ***c. acorazada*** strongroom, vault; ***c. de gas*** gas chamber; ***c. mortuoria*** funeral chamber; ***c. de torturas*** torture chamber
(c) *(receptáculo)* chamber; **c. (de aire)** *(de balón)* bladder; *(de neumático)* inner tube ►► ***c. de combustión*** combustion chamber; ***c. de descompresión*** decompression chamber; ***c. frigorífica*** cold-storage room; **un camión con c. frigorífica** a refrigerated *Br* lorry *o US* truck; *Fís* ***c. de niebla*** cloud chamber; ***c. de resonancia*** echo chamber; *RP* ***c. séptica*** septic tank; ***c. de vacío*** vacuum chamber
(d) *(de arma)* chamber, breech
(e) *(asamblea)* chamber ►► ***c. alta*** upper house; *Esp* ***c. autonómica*** autonomous regional parliament; ***c. baja*** lower house; ***C. de los Comunes*** House of Commons; ***c. legislativa*** legislative chamber; ***C. de los Lores*** House of Lords; ***C. de Representantes*** House of Representatives; ***c. territorial*** = chamber of parliament where members represent a region, rather than electoral constituencies of roughly equal size
(f) *Com (entidad, organismo)* chamber ►► ***c. agrícola*** farmers' association; ***c. de Comercio*** Chamber of Commerce; ***c. de compensación*** clearing house; ***c. de la propiedad*** property owners' association
(g) **de c.** *(del rey)* court, royal; **pintor de c.** court painter
2 *nmf (persona)* cameraman, *f* camerawoman

camarada *nmf* (a) *(en partido político)* comrade; **el c. Gómez** comrade Gómez (b) *(compañero)* colleague; **c. de trabajo** workmate, colleague

camaradería *nf* camaraderie; **en la oficina reina la c.** everyone's very friendly in the office; **se tratan con c.** they're very friendly to one another

camarera *nf Am (azafata)* air hostess

camarero, -a *nm,f* (a) *(de restaurante, bar)* waiter, *f* waitress (b) *(de hotel)* chamberperson, *f* chambermaid (c) *(de barco)* steward (d) *(de rey)* chamberlain, *f* lady-in-waiting

camareta *nf* (a) *Náut* small cabin (b) *Andes, Arg (cañón)* = small mortar used in firework displays

camarilla *nf Pey* clique, cabal; **el ministro llegó acompañado de su c.** the minister arrived with his hangers-on

camarín *nm* (a) *(en teatro)* dressing room (b) *(capilla)* niche, alcove

camarina *nf* broom crowberry

camarista *nmf* (a) *Arg (juez)* appeal court judge (b) *Méx (en hotel)* chamberperson, *f* chambermaid

camarógrafo, -a *nm,f* cameraman, *f* camerawoman

camarón *nm* (a) *(quisquilla) Br* shrimp, *US* prawn (b) *CAm, Col (propina)* tip (c) *Perú (persona)* turncoat (d) *Ven Fam (siesta)* nap

camarote *nm* cabin

camarotero *nm Am (en barco)* steward

camastro *nm* ramshackle bed

camata *nmf Esp Fam Br* barman, *US* bartender, *f* barmaid

camba *Bol Fam* 1 *adj* of/from the forested lowland region of Bolivia
2 *nmf* person from the forested lowland region of Bolivia

cambado, -a *adj RP* bowlegged

cambalache *nm* (a) *Fam (trueque)* swap; **hacer un c.** to make *o* do a swap, to swap (b) *RP (tienda)* junk shop (c) *RP (gran desorden)* chaos

cambalachear *vt Fam* to swap

cambalachero, -a *Am* 1 *adj* swapping
2 *nm,f* (a) *(trocador)* swapper (b) *(vendedor)* second-hand dealer, *Br* junk dealer

cámbaro *nm* = small edible crab

cambiable *adj* (a) *(alterable)* changeable (b) *(canjeable)* exchangeable

cambiadizo, -a *adj* changeable, variable

cambiado, -a *adj* **está muy c.** he's changed a lot, he's very changed

cambiador, -ora 1 *adj* changing
2 *nm,f* moneychanger
3 *nm* (a) *(mando)* control switch ►► ***c. de calor*** heat exchanger (b) *Andes, Méx Ferroc Br* pointsman, *US* switchman (c) *(colchón)* changing mat

cambiante *adj (tiempo)* changeable; *(situación)* constantly changing, unstable; *(temperamento)* volatile, unpredictable

CAMBIAR 1 *vt* (a) *(alterar, modificar)* to change; **han cambiado la fecha de salida** they've changed *o* altered the departure date; **quiere c. su imagen** she wants to change her image; **el divorcio lo ha cambiado por completo** the divorce has changed him completely, he has changed completely since the divorce; **cambió su sonrisa en llanto** her smile turned to tears; **tus disculpas no cambian nada** your apologies don't change anything
(b) *(trasladar)* to move; **tenemos que c. las sillas de lugar** we have to move the chairs; **cambiaron la sede central a Buenos Aires** they moved their headquarters to Buenos Aires; **lo van a c. a otro colegio** they're going to move him to another school
(c) *(reemplazar) (rueda, sábanas)* to change; **tenemos que c. la lavadora** we have to get a new washing machine; **tengo que c. el agua del acuario** I have to change the water in the aquarium, I have to put some fresh water in the aquarium; **c. un artículo defectuoso** to exchange a faulty item; **si no está satisfecho, lo puede c.** if you're not satisfied with it, you can change it; **tuve que cambiarle una rueda al coche** I had to change one of the wheels on the car; **cambiaré este tornillo por otro más largo** I'll swap this screw for a longer one; EXPR *Fam* **icambia el disco** *o* **rollo, que ya aburres!** you're getting boring! can't you talk about anything else?
(d) *(intercambiar)* to swap; **c. cromos/sellos** to swap picture cards/stamps; **c. impresiones** to compare views; **c. algo por algo** to exchange sth for sth; **cambié mi reloj por el suyo** I swapped watches with him; **he cambiado mi turno con un compañero** I swapped shifts with a colleague; **¿te importa si te cambio el sitio?** would you mind swapping *o* changing places with me?
(e) *(dinero)* to change; **en aquel banco cambian dinero** they change money at that bank; **¿me podría c. este billete en monedas, por favor?** could you give me change for this note in coins, please?; **c. dólares en euros** to change dollars into euros
(f) *(bebé)* to change
2 *vi* (a) *(alterarse)* to change; **ha cambiado mucho desde el accidente** she has changed a lot since the accident; **la situación no ha cambiado mucho** there has been little change in the situation; **algunas personas no cambian nunca** some people never change; **ya crecerá y cambiará** she'll change as she gets older; **c. a mejor/peor** to change for the better/worse; **en ese caso, la cosa cambia** that's different, that changes everything; **le ha cambiado la voz** his voice has broken
(b) **c. de** to change; **c. de autobús/tren** to change buses/trains; *Fig* **c. de camisa/chaqueta** to change one's shirt/jacket; **c. de canal** *(de TV)* to turn over, to change channels; **c. de casa** to move (house); **c. de color** to change colour; **c. de dueño** to change hands; **c. de idea/intención** to change one's mind/plans; **c. de manos** *(dinero, vehículo)* to change hands; **c. de ritmo** to change pace; **c. de rumbo** to change course; **c. de sexo** to have a sex change; **c. de sitio** to change place, to move; **c. de táctica** to change one's tactics; **c. de trabajo** to move *o* change jobs
(c) *Aut (de marchas)* **c. (de marcha)** to change gear; **c. a segunda** to change into second gear
(d) *Meteo* to change, to shift; **el viento cambió** the wind changed
3 **cambiarse** *vpr* (a) *(mudarse)* to change; **cambiarse (de ropa)** to change (one's clothes), to get changed; **cambiarse de vestido** to change one's dress; **cambiarse de casa** to move (house); **se cambió de nombre** he changed his name
(b) *(intercambiarse)* to swap; **se cambiaron los cuadernos** they swapped exercise books; **ino me cambiaría por él!** I wouldn't be in his shoes!; **¿te importaría cambiarme el sitio?** would you mind swapping *o* changing places with me?

cambiario, -a *adj Fin (mercado)* currency, foreign exchange

cambiavía 1 *nmf (persona) Col, Cuba, Méx Br* pointsman, *f* pointswoman, *US* switchman, *f* switchwoman
2 *nm (mecanismo) Br* points, *US* switch

cambiazo *nm Fam* (a) *(cambio grande)* radical change; **esa chica ha dado un c.** that girl has really changed (b) *(sustitución)* switch *(in order to steal bag etc)*; **dar el c.** to do a switch

CAMBIO 1 *nm* (a) *(alteración, modificación)* change; **vivimos una época de grandes cambios** we live in times of great change; **c. de actitud** change in attitude; **c. de gobierno** change of government; **c. radical** turnabout, turnround; **c. de tiempo** change in the weather; **ha ganado con el c. de trabajo** he has benefited from changing jobs; **con el c. de política hemos perdido todos** we have all lost out as a result of the change in policy; **se ha producido un c. de situación** the situation has changed, there has been a change in the situation; **el c. al sistema métrico ha sido muy sencillo** the changeover to the metric system has been very straightforward; **tu hijo ha pegado un c. tremendo** your son has really changed; **a las primeras de c.** at the first opportunity; **abandonó la carrera a las primeras de c.** she dropped out of the race almost as soon as it had started *o* shortly after it had started; **cayeron eliminados a las primeras de c.** they fell at the first hurdle ►► ***c. climático*** climate change; *Ling* ***c. de código*** code switching; ***c. de domicilio*** change of address; ***c. de escena*** *Teatro* scene change; *Fig* change of scene; ***c. generacional:*** **el partido necesita un c. generacional urgente** the party is in urgent need of a new generation of leaders; **este joven pintor es un ejemplo del c. generacional en marcha** this young man is one of the new generation of painters who are coming to dominate the artistic scene; ***c. de guardia*** *(ceremonia)* changing of the guard; ***c. horario*** *(bianual)* = putting clocks back or forward one hour; ***c. hormonal*** hormonal change; ***c. de imagen*** image change; ***el c. de milenio*** the end of the millennium; ***c. de rasante*** brow of a hill; ***c. de sentido*** U-turn; ***c. de sexo*** sex change; *Der* ***c. de tribunal*** change of venue; *Ferroc* ***c. de vía*** *Br* points, *US* switch
(b) *(reemplazo, trueque)* exchange; **(oficina de) c.** *(en letrero)* bureau de change; **durante las rebajas no se admiten cambios** while the sales are on, goods may not be exchanged; **a c. (de)** in exchange *o* return (for); **no pido nada a c.** I'm not asking for anything back *o* in return; **se admite su vieja lavadora a c.** we will take your old washing machine in part exchange; **te dejo el coche a c. de que lo laves** I'll let you use my car if you wash it for me ►► *Aut* ***c. de aceite*** oil change; ***c. de impresiones*** exchange of opinions; *Quím* ***c. iónico*** ion exchange; ***c. de papeles*** role reversal
(c) *(monedas, billetes)* change; **¿tiene c.?** have you got some change?; **¿tiene c. de 50?** have you got change for *o* of 50?; **nos hemos quedado sin cambio(s)** we're out of change; **quédese con el c.** keep the change; **me ha dado el c. incorrecto** she gave me the wrong change
(d) *Fin (de acciones)* price; *(de divisas)* exchange rate; **ha bajado el c. del peso** the (exchange rate of the) peso has fallen; **los valores eléctricos han mantenido el c.** share prices in the electricity companies have remained steady; **¿a cuánto está el c. de la libra?** what's the exchange rate for the pound? ►► ***c. base*** base rate; ***c. extranjero*** foreign exchange; ***c. medio*** average exchange rate; ***c. oficial*** official exchange rate
(e) *Aut* **el c. es muy duro** the gears are rather stiff ►► ***c. automático*** automatic transmission; ***c. de marchas*** *(acción)* gear change; *(palanca) Br* gear stick, *US* gear shift; ***c. sincronizado*** *(en bicicleta)* indexed gear; ***c. de velocidades*** *(acción)* gear change; *(palanca) Br* gear stick, *US* gear shift
(f) *Dep (sustitución)* substitution, change; **hacer un c.** to make a substitution *o* change; **el equipo visitante ha pedido (hacer un) c.** the away team want to make a substitution *o* change; **el jugador lesionado pidió el c. al entrenador** the injured player signalled to the manager that he wanted to come off
2 *interj Rad* **ic. (y corto)!** over!; **ic. y cierro!** over and out!
3 **en cambio** *loc adv (por otra parte)* on the other hand, however; *(en su lugar)* instead; **ellos no pueden ayudarnos, en c. tú sí** they can't help us, but *o* whereas you can; **éste me gusta, en c. este otro es feo** I like this one, but this other one is horrible

cambista *nmf* (a) *(de dinero)* moneychanger (b) *RP Ferroc Br* pointsman, *f* pointswoman, *US* switchman, *f* switchwoman

Camboya *n* Cambodia

camboyano, -a 1 *adj* Cambodian
2 *nm,f* Cambodian

cambray (*pl* **cambrayes**) *nm* cambric

cámbrico, -a *Geol* 1 *adj* Cambrian
2 *nm* **el c.** the Cambrian (period)

cambuche *nm Col Fam* hovel, dump

cambur *nm Ven* (**a**) *(empleo)* job (**b**) *(empleado)* clerk (**c**) *(plátano)* banana

camedrio *nm* wall germander

camelar *vt Fam* (**a**) *(convencer)* to butter up, to win over; **me cameló para que lo ayudara** he sweet-talked me into helping him (**b**) *(enamorar)* to win the heart of; **la cameló rápidamente** he quickly set her heart aflutter (**c**) *Méx (observar)* to watch, to observe

camelia *nf* camellia

camélido *Zool* **1** *nm* camel, member of the camel family
 2 camélidos *nmpl (familia) Camelidae*; **de la familia de los camélidos** of the *Camelidae* family

camelina *nf* gold of pleasure

camelista *Fam* **1** *adj* wheedling, flattering
 2 *nmf* flatterer

camellar *vi Col, Ecuad Fam* to work

camellero, -a *nm,f* camel driver

camello, -a 1 *nm,f (animal)* camel ►► ***c. bactriano*** Bactrian camel
 2 *nm* (**a**) *Fam (traficante)* drug pusher *o* dealer (**b**) *Col, Ecuad Fam (empleo)* job (**c**) *Náut* caisson (**d**) *Cuba (autobús)* bus *(converted truck)*

camellón *nm* (**a**) *Agr* ridge (**b**) *Col, Méx (en avenida) Br* central reservation, *US* median (strip)

camelo *nm Fam* (**a**) *(engaño)* con; **esas pastillas para adelgazar son un c.** those slimming pills are a con; **es puro c.** it's just humbug; **nos contó un c. para que le prestáramos dinero** he told us a lie so we'd lend him money (**b**) *(noticia falsa)* hoax

camembert ['kamember] (*pl* **camemberts**) *nm* Camembert

camerino *nm Teatro* dressing room

camero, -a *adj* **cama camera** three-quarter bed

Camerún *n* **(el) C.** Cameroon

camerunés, -esa 1 *adj* Cameroonian, of/from Cameroon
 2 *nm,f* Cameroonian

camilla 1 *nf (sin ruedas)* stretcher; *(con ruedas)* trolley
 2 *adj inv* **mesa c.** = round table, often with a heater underneath

camillero, -a *nm,f* stretcher-bearer

caminante *nmf* walker

CAMINAR 1 *vi* (**a**) *(andar)* to walk; **me gusta c.** I like walking; **nosotros iremos caminando** we'll walk, we'll go on foot; **c. por la acera** to walk on the *Br* pavement *o US* sidewalk; **c. de un lado para otro** to walk up and down, to walk to and fro; **c. derecho** *o* **erguido** to walk with a straight back; **¡camina derecho!** don't slouch!; *Fig* **es difícil c. siempre derecho** it's not easy always to keep to the straight and narrow; **c. de puntillas** to tiptoe
 (**b**) *(seguir un curso)* **el río camina por el valle hacia la desembocadura** the river passes *o* flows through the valley on its way to the sea
 (**c**) *(encaminarse)* **c. hacia** to head for; **c. hacia el desastre** to be heading for disaster; **caminamos hacia una nueva época** we are entering a new era
 (**d**) *Am Fam (funcionar)* to work
 (**e**) *Am Fam (progresar)* to progress; **si no conoces a nadie, no caminas** if you don't know the right people, you won't get anywhere
 2 *vt* to walk; **caminamos 20 kilómetros** we walked 20 kilometres

---

caminata *nf* long walk; **se pegaron una buena c.** they had a long walk; **hay una buena c. hasta el centro** it's quite a step *o* trek to the centre

---

CAMINO *nm* (**a**) *(sendero)* path, track; *(carretera)* road; **han abierto un c. a través de la selva** they've cleared a path through the jungle; **acorté por el c. del bosque** I took a shortcut through the forest; EXPR **la vida no es un c. de rosas** life is no bed of roses; PROV **todos los caminos llevan a Roma** all roads lead to Rome ►► ***c. de acceso*** access road; *Fam Fig* ***c. de cabras*** rugged path; ***c. forestal*** forest track; ***c. de grava*** gravel path; ***c. de herradura*** bridle path; ***c. de hierro*** railway; *Am* ***c. de mesa*** table runner; *Hist* ***c. real*** king's highway; ***C. de Santiago*** *Rel* = pilgrimage route to Santiago de Compostela; *Astron* Milky Way; ***c. de sirga*** towpath; *Fig* ***c. trillado*** well-trodden path; *Fig* **tiene el c. trillado** the hard work has already been done for him; ***c. vecinal*** country lane
 (**b**) *(ruta, vía)* way; **el c. de la estación** the way to the station; **equivocarse de c.** to go the wrong way; **indicar el c. a alguien** to show sb the way; **no recuerdo el c. de vuelta** I can't remember the way back; **iremos por el c. más corto** we'll go by the shortest route, we'll go the quickest way; **está c. de la capital** it's on the way to the capital; **me encontré a Elena c. de casa** I met Elena on the way home; **van c. del éxito** they're on their way to success; **en el** *o* **de c.** *(de paso)* on the way; **ve a comprar el periódico, y de c. sube también la leche** go for the newspaper and bring the milk up while you're at it; **me pilla de c.** it's on my way; **a estas horas ya estarán en c.** they'll be on their way by now; **por este c.** this way
 (**c**) *(viaje)* journey; **nos espera un largo c.** we have a long journey ahead of us; **se detuvieron tras cinco horas de c.** they stopped after they had been on the road for five hours; **estamos casi a mitad de c.** we're about halfway there; **pararemos a mitad de c.** we'll stop halfway; **hicimos un alto en el c. para comer** we stopped (along the way) to have a bite to eat; *también Fig* **todavía nos queda mucho c. por delante** we've still got a long way to go; **el c. se me ha hecho eterno** the journey seemed to last forever; **ponerse en c.** to set off
 (**d**) *Univ* **Caminos(, Canales y Puertos)** *(ingeniería)* civil engineering
 (**e**) *(medio)* way; **el c. para conseguir tus propósitos es la honestidad** the way to get what you want is to be honest
 (**f**) EXPR **abrir c. a** to clear the way for; **el hermano mayor ha abierto c. a los pequeños** the older brother cleared the way for the younger ones; **dos jinetes abrían c. a la procesión** two people rode ahead to clear a path for the procession; **abrirse c.** to get on *o* ahead; **se abrió c. entre la maraña de defensas** he found a way through the cluster of defenders; **abrirse c. en el mundo** to make one's way in the world; **le costó mucho abrirse c., pero ahora tiene una buena posición** it wasn't easy for him to get on, but he's got a good job now; **allanar el c.** to smooth the way; **atravesarse** *o* **cruzarse** *o* **interponerse en el c. de alguien** to stand in sb's way; **no permitiré que nadie se cruce en mi c.** I won't let anyone stand in my way; *Fam* **tienen un bebé en c.** they've got a baby on the way; **ir por buen c.** to be on the right track; **ir por mal c.** to go astray; **con su comportamiento, estos alumnos van por mal c.** the way they are behaving, these pupils are heading for trouble; **fueron cada cual por su c.** they went their separate ways; **van c. del desastre/éxito** they're on the road to disaster/success; **va** *o* **lleva c. de convertirse en estrella** she's on her way to stardom; **a medio c.** halfway; **siempre deja todo a medio c.** she always leaves things half-done; **estar a medio c.** to be halfway there; **está a medio c. entre un delantero y un centrocampista** he's somewhere between a forward and a midfielder; **quedarse a medio c.** to stop halfway through; **el proyecto se quedó a medio c. por falta de presupuesto** the project was left unfinished *o* was abandoned halfway through because the funds dried up; **iba para estrella, pero se quedó a mitad de c.** she looked as if she would become a star, but never quite made it; **traer a alguien al buen c.** to put sb back on the right track

---

camión *nm* (**a**) *(de mercancías)* truck, *Br* lorry; **recibieron tres camiones de ayuda humanitaria** they received three truckloads of humanitarian aid; EXPR *Fam* **estar como un c.** to be gorgeous ►► ***c. articulado*** *Br* articulated lorry, *US* semitrailer; ***c. de la basura*** *Br* dustcart, *US* garbage truck; ***c. cisterna*** tanker; ***c. frigorífico*** refrigerated truck *o Br* lorry; ***c. de mudanzas*** removal van, furniture van
 (**b**) *CAm, Méx (autobús)* bus

camionada *nf Andes, RP* truckload, *Br* lorry-load

camionaje *nm* haulage

camionero, -a 1 *adj CAm, Méx* bus; **central camionera** bus station; **paro c.** bus strike
 2 *nm,f* (**a**) *(de camión)* truck driver, *Br* lorry driver, *US* trucker (**b**) *CAm, Méx (de autobús)* bus driver

camioneta *nf* van; *(con la parte de atrás abierta)* pick-up (truck)

camisa *nf* (**a**) *(prenda)* shirt ►► ***c. de dormir*** nightshirt; ***c. de fuerza*** straitjacket; *Hist* ***c. negra*** Blackshirt
 (**b**) *(de serpiente)* slough, skin; **cambiar** *o* **mudar de c.** to shed its skin
 (**c**) *Tec* lining ►► ***c. de agua*** water jacket
 (**d**) EXPR **jugarse hasta la c.** to stake everything; **meterse en c. de once varas** to complicate matters unnecessarily; **mudar(se)** *o* **cambiar(se) de c.** to change sides; **no le llega la c. al cuerpo** she's scared stiff; **perder hasta la c.** to lose one's shirt

camisería *nf (tienda)* shirt shop, outfitter's

camisero, -a 1 *adj (blusa, vestido)* shirtwaist
 2 *nm,f* (**a**) *(fabricante)* shirtmaker (**b**) *(vendedor)* outfitter
 3 *nm Chile (camisa de mujer)* blouse

camiseta *nf* (**a**) *(interior) Br* vest, *US* undershirt (**b**) *(de manga corta)* T-shirt (**c**) *(de deportes) (de tirantes)* vest; *(con mangas)* shirt; *Fig* **defender la c. del Lugo** to play for Lugo; EXPR **sudaron la c.** they played their hearts out; EXPR *RP Fam* **ponerse la c.: se puso la c. de la empresa** he became a real company man

camisilla *nf Col, Urug Br* vest, *US* undershirt

camisola *nf* (**a**) *(prenda interior)* camisole (**b**) *(de deportes)* sports shirt (**c**) *Am (de mujer)* woman's blouse

camisón *nm* (**a**) *(de noche)* nightdress, nightgown (**b**) *Andes, Carib (de mujer)* chemise

camomila *nf* camomile

camorra *nf* (**a**) *Fam (riña)* **armar c.** to cause trouble; **buscar c.** to look for trouble (**b**) *(organización mafiosa)* **la C.** the Camorra

camorrero, -a *adj, nm,f* = **camorrista**

camorrista *Fam* **1** *adj* belligerent, quarrelsome
2 *nmf* troublemaker

camote *nm* (**a**) *Andes, CAm, Méx (batata)* sweet potato
(**b**) *Méx (dulce)* = confection made with sweet potato
(**c**) *Andes, CAm, Méx (bulbo)* tuber, bulb
(**d**) *Andes Fam (enamoramiento)* **estar c. por** *o* **de alguien** to be madly in love with sb; EXPR *Perú* **donde camotes se asaron, cenizas quedaron** love will never die
(**e**) *Perú Fam (novio)* lover, sweetheart
(**f**) *Méx Fam (complicación)* mess; **meterse en un c.** to get into a mess *o* pickle
(**g**) *Perú (juego)* piggy-in-the-middle
(**h**) *Méx Fam* EXPR **estar camotes** to be wrecked *o Br* knackered; **hacerse c.** to get into a muddle; **poner a alguien como c.** to make mincemeat of sb; **tragar c.** *(balbucir)* to stammer; *(andar con rodeos)* to beat about the bush; *(pagar consecuencias)* to pay the price; **ese bocón tendrá que tragar c. con sus palabras** that bigmouth will have to pay for what he said

camotero, -a *adj Ecuad Fam* **es muy c.** he falls in love very easily

camotillo *nm* (**a**) *Andes (dulce)* = sweet made of mashed sweet potatoes (**b**) *Méx (madera)* = type of violet-coloured wood streaked with black (**c**) *CAm (cúrcuma)* turmeric

camotudo, -a *adj Perú Fam* **es muy c.** he falls in love very easily

camp [kamp] *adj inv (estilo, moda)* retro

campal *adj también Fig* **batalla c.** pitched battle

campamento *nm* (**a**) *(lugar)* camp; *(acción)* camping; **los niños se van de c. este año** the children are going to summer camp this year ►► ***c. avanzado*** *(en montañismo)* advance camp; ***c. base*** *(en montañismo)* base camp; ***c. nudista*** nudist camp
(**b**) *(grupo de personas)* camp; **todo el c. colaboró en la búsqueda** the whole camp joined in the search
(**c**) *Mil (periodo de instrucción)* training camp

campana *nf* (**a**) *(de iglesia)* bell; EXPR **echar las campanas al vuelo: no queremos echar las campanas al vuelo antes de tiempo** we don't want to start celebrating prematurely; **es pronto para echar las campanas al vuelo** let's not count our chickens before they're hatched; EXPR *Fam* **oír campanas y no saber dónde** not to know what one is talking about; EXPR **te ha salvado la c.** (you were) saved by the bell ►► ***c. de buzo*** diving bell; ***c. extractora (de humos)*** extractor hood; *Mat* ***c. de Gauss*** normal distribution curve, *US* bell curve; ***c. de salvamento*** diving bell (**b**) *(de chimenea)* chimney breast (**c**) *(para alimentos)* **c. (de cristal)** glass cover

campanada *nf* (**a**) *(de campana)* peal (**b**) *(de reloj)* stroke, chime; **al dar las doce campanadas...** on the stroke of twelve... (**c**) *(suceso)* sensation; EXPR **dar la c.** to make a big splash, to cause a sensation

campanario *nm* belfry, bell tower

campanear *vi RP Fam* to act as lookout *(during robbery)*

campanero, -a *nm,f* (**a**) *(persona que toca)* bell-ringer (**b**) *(fabricante)* bell founder (**c**) *Ven (ave)* bellbird

campaniforme *adj* bell-shaped

campanil *nm* campanile

campanilla *nf* (**a**) *(campana pequeña)* (small) bell; *(con mango)* handbell; *Fam* **la suya fue una boda de campanillas** their wedding was a lavish affair (**b**) *Anat* uvula (**c**) *(flor)* campanula, bellflower ►► ***c. de invierno*** snowdrop

campanilleo *nm* tinkle, tinkling sound

campanología *nf* bellringing, *Espec* campanology

campante *adj* **le dije que estaba despedido, y se quedó tan c.** I told him he was fired, and he didn't turn a hair; **perdió todo lo que tenía, pero estaba tan c.** he lost everything he had, but it was like water off a duck's back; **llevaba un vestido ridículo, pero iba tan c.** he was dressed ridiculously, but it didn't seem to concern him in the least

campanudo, -a *adj* (**a**) *(acampanado)* bell-shaped (**b**) *(grandilocuente)* high-flown; **retórica campanuda** high-flown rhetoric

campánula *nf* campanula, bellflower

campanulácea *nf Bot* campanula

campaña *nf* (**a**) *(acción organizada)* campaign; **una c. de recogida de firmas** a petition campaign; **una c. contra el tabaco** an anti-smoking campaign; **una c. de defensa de los bosques** a campaign to defend the forests; **hacer c. (de/contra)** to campaign (for/against) ►► ***c. de descrédito*** dirty tricks campaign; ***c. de difamación*** smear campaign; ***c. electoral*** election campaign; ***c. informativa*** information campaign; ***c. de marketing*** marketing campaign; ***c. publicitaria*** advertising campaign; ***c. de reclutamiento*** recruitment campaign *o* drive
(**b**) *(periodo) (deportivo)* season; *(de pesca)* (fishing) season; **la c. del atún** the tuna-fishing season; **la producción de aceite en la c. 2003-2004** the production of oil in the year 2003-2004; **los bancos han incrementado sus beneficios con respecto a la c. anterior** the banks have increased their profits compared to last (financial) year
(**c**) *RP (campo)* countryside
(**d**) *(expedición militar)* campaign; **la c. de Rusia** the Russian campaign; **hospital/ambulancia de c.** field hospital/ambulance; **uniforme de c.** combat uniform

campar *vi* EXPR **campa por sus respetos** he follows his own rules, he does things his own way; EXPR **c. a sus anchas** to be at (one's) ease, to feel at home

campear *vi* (**a**) *(pacer)* to graze (**b**) *CSur (buscar en el campo)* to search *o* scour the countryside

campechana *nf* (**a**) *Cuba, Méx (bebida)* cocktail (**b**) *ver también* **campechano²**

campechanamente *adv (reír)* good-naturedly, heartily

campechanía *nf* good-natured *o* down-to-earth character

campechano¹, -a *adj* good-natured, down-to-earth

campechano², -a **1** *adj (de Campeche)* of/from Campeche *(Mexico)*
2 *nm,f (de Campeche)* person from Campeche *(Mexico)*

campeche *nm* logwood

campeón, -ona *nm,f* (**a**) *(en campeonato)* champion; **el c. mundial** the world champion; *Fam* **es todo un c. sacando fotos** he's very good at taking photos ►► ***c. de invierno*** = league leader halfway through the season (**b**) *(de causa)* champion, defender; **el c. de los derechos de los inmigrantes** the champion *o* defender of the rights of immigrants

campeonato *nm* championship; EXPR *Fam* **de c.** *(bueno)* terrific, great; *(malo)* terrible; **hace un frío de c.** it's absolutely freezing; **un susto de c.** a fright and a half, a terrible fright; **un idiota de c.** a prize idiot ►► ***c. de liga*** league championship; ***c. mundial*** world championship; ***c. del mundo*** world championship

campeonísimo, -a *nm,f Dep* supreme champion

campera *nf* (**a**) *Esp* **camperas** *(botas)* cowboy boots (**b**) *RP (chaqueta)* jacket; **c. de cuero** leather jacket; **c. de duvet** feather-lined anorak; **c. vaquera** denim jacket

campero, -a **1** *adj* (**a**) *Esp* **botas camperas** cowboy boots (**b**) *CSur (persona)* = expert at ranching or farming
2 *nm Andes* Jeep®

campesinado *nm* peasants, peasantry

campesino, -a **1** *adj (del campo)* rural, country; *(en el pasado, en países pobres)* peasant; **las labores campesinas** farmwork
2 *nm,f (persona del campo)* country person; *(en el pasado, en países pobres)* peasant

campestre *adj* country; **comida c.** picnic; **fiesta c.** open-air country festival

camping, cámping ['kampin] (*pl* **campings**) *nm* (**a**) *(actividad)* camping; **ir de c.** to go camping ►► ***c. gas*** portable gas stove (**b**) *(terreno)* campsite, *US* campground

campiña *nf* countryside

campista *nmf* camper

CAMPO *nm* (**a**) *(terreno, área)* field; **un c. de tomates** a field of tomatoes; EXPR **dejar el c. libre a algo/alguien** to leave the field clear for sth/sb ►► ***c. de acogida*** *(de refugiados)* provisional refugee camp; ***c. de aterrizaje*** landing-field; ***c. de aviación*** airfield; *también Fig* ***c. de batalla*** battlefield; ***c. de concentración*** concentration camp; ***los Campos Elíseos*** *(en París)* the Champs Élysées; ***el c. enemigo*** enemy territory; ***c. de exterminio*** death camp; ***el C. de Gibraltar*** = the area of Spain at the border of Gibraltar; ***c. de hielo*** ice field; ***campos de maíz*** cornfields; *también Fig* ***c. minado*** minefield; ***c. de minas*** minefield; ***c. de nieve*** snowfield; ***c. petrolífero*** oilfield; ***c. de prisioneros*** prison camp; ***c. de pruebas*** testing ground, proving-ground; ***c. de refugiados*** refugee camp; ***c. de tiro*** *(para aviones)* bombing range; *(para policías, deportistas)* firing

range, shooting range; ***c. de trabajo*** *(de vacaciones)* work camp; *(para prisioneros)* labour camp
(**b**) *(campiña)* **el c.** the country, the countryside; **una casa en el c.** a house in the country; **en mitad del c.** in the middle of the country *o* countryside; **la emigración del c. a la ciudad** migration from rural areas to cities ▸▸ ***c. abierto*** open countryside; *Dep* ***c. a través*** cross-country running; **a través** cross-country
(**c**) *Esp Dep (de fútbol, hockey)* pitch; *(de tenis)* court; *(de golf)* course; **el c. de fútbol del Barcelona** the Barcelona football ground; **el c. contrario** the opponents' half; **jugar en c. propio/contrario** to play at home/away (from home) ▸▸ ***c. atrás*** *(en baloncesto)* backcourt violation; ***c. de deportes*** sports ground; ***c. de entrenamiento*** training ground; ***c. de juego*** playing field
(**d**) *(área, ámbito)* field; **el c. de las ciencias** the field of science; **un c. del saber** a field *o* an area of knowledge; **no entra en su c. de actuación** it's not one of his responsibilities ▸▸ *Ling* ***c. léxico*** lexical field
(**e**) *Informát* field
(**f**) **de c.** *(sobre el terreno)* in the field; **trabajo de c.** fieldwork
(**g**) *Fís* field ▸▸ ***c. eléctrico*** electric field; ***c. electromagnético*** electromagnetic field; ***c. de fuerza*** force field; ***c. gravitatorio*** gravitational field; ***c. magnético*** magnetic field; ***c. magnético terrestre*** terrestrial magnetic field; ***c. visual*** visual field, field of vision
(**h**) *(partido, bando)* camp, side; **el c. rebelde** the rebels
(**i**) *Andes (sitio)* room, space; **hazme c. para que me siente** make some room so I can sit down
(**j**) *RP (hacienda)* farm, ranch

---

camposanto *nm* cemetery, graveyard

campus *nm inv* campus ▸▸ ***c. universitario*** university campus

camuflado, -a *adj (oculto)* hidden; *(soldado, tanque)* camouflaged; **un vehículo c. de la policía** an unmarked police vehicle

camuflaje *nm* camouflage; **ropa de c.** camouflage clothes; **soldados de c.** soldiers wearing camouflage

camuflar 1 *vt (tropas, tanque)* to camouflage; *(intenciones)* to disguise, to conceal; **camufló el maletín robado entre el resto del equipaje** he concealed the stolen briefcase among the rest of the luggage
2 **camuflarse** *vpr* to camouflage oneself; **el camaleón se camufla cambiando de color** the chameleon camouflages itself by changing colour

CAN [kan] *nf (abrev de* **Comunidad Andina de Naciones**) Andean Community, = organization for regional cooperation formed by Bolivia, Colombia, Ecuador, Peru and Venezuela

can *nm* (**a**) *(perro)* dog, canine ▸▸ ***C. Mayor*** *(constelación)* Canis Major; ***C. Menor*** *(constelación)* Canis Minor (**b**) *Arquit* modillion (**c**) *(gatillo)* trigger

cana 1 *nf* (**a**) *(pelo blanco)* grey *o* white hair; **tiene bastantes canas** she has quite a lot of grey hair; EXPR *Fam* **echar una c. al aire** to let one's hair down; EXPR *Fam* **peinar canas** to be getting on, to be old; EXPR *RP Fam Hum* **salir canas verdes: estos niños me van a hacer salir canas verdes** these kids will be the death of me
(**b**) *Andes, Cuba, RP Fam (cárcel) Br* nick, *US* joint
(**c**) *RP Fam (policía)* **la c.** the cops
2 *nmf RP Fam (agente de policía)* cop

Caná *n* Cana; **las bodas de C.** the wedding feast at Cana

Canadá *n* **(el) C.** Canada

canadiense 1 *adj* Canadian
2 *nmf* Canadian

canal 1 *nm* (**a**) *(cauce artificial)* canal ▸▸ ***c. de riego*** irrigation channel
(**b**) *(entre dos mares)* channel, strait ▸▸ ***el c. de Beagle*** the Beagle Channel; ***el c. de la Mancha*** the (English) Channel; ***el c. de Panamá*** the Panama Canal; ***el c. de Suez*** the Suez Canal
(**c**) *(de radio, televisión)* channel; **cambiar de c.** to switch channels ▸▸ ***c. autonómico*** = regional TV channel in Spain; *TV* ***c. generalista*** general-interest channel; ***c. de pago*** subscription channel
(**d**) *Informát* channel
(**e**) *Anat* canal, duct
(**f**) *(medio, vía)* channel; **se enteró por varios canales** she found out through various channels ▸▸ *Com* ***c. de comercialización*** distribution channel; *Com* ***c. de venta(s)*** sales channel
2 *nm o nf* (**a**) *(de tejado)* (valley) gutter
(**b**) *(res)* carcass; **abrir en c.** to slit open; *Fig* to tear apart
(**c**) *Arquit* groove, fluting
(**d**) *(de libro)* edge

canalé *nm* ribbed knitwear

canaleta *nf Bol, CSur (canal)* gutter

canalete *nm* paddle

canalización *nf* (**a**) *(de agua)* piping; **todavía no tienen c. de agua** they're not yet connected to the water mains (**b**) *(de río)* canalization (**c**) *(de recursos, esfuerzos)* channelling

canalizar [14] *vt* (**a**) *(territorio)* to canalize; *(agua)* to channel (**b**) *(río)* to canalize (**c**) *(recursos, esfuerzos)* to channel

canalla 1 *nmf (persona)* swine, dog
2 *nf* **la c.** the rabble, the riffraff

canallada *nf* despicable action, vile thing to do

canallesco, -a *adj (acción, intención)* despicable, vile; *(sonrisa)* wicked, evil

canalón *nm (de tejado)* gutter; *(en la pared)* drainpipe

canana *nf* (**a**) *(para cartuchos)* cartridge belt (**b**) *Col (camisa de fuerza)* straitjacket (**c**) *CRica (bocio)* goitre (**d**) *Col* **cananas** *(esposas)* handcuffs

cananeo, -a *nm,f* Canaanite

canapé *nm* (**a**) *(para comer)* canapé (**b**) *(sofá)* sofa, couch (**c**) *(debajo del colchón)* bed base

Canarias *nfpl* **las (islas) C.** the Canary Islands, the Canaries

canario, -a 1 *adj* (**a**) *(de las Canarias)* of/from the Canary Islands, Canary (**b**) *Urug (de Canelones)* = relating to the Canelones department (**c**) *Urug Fam Pey (del interior)* up-country
2 *nm,f* (**a**) *(de las Canarias)* Canary Islander (**b**) *Urug (de Canelones)* person from the Canelones department (**c**) *Urug Fam Pey (del interior)* country bumpkin, *US* hick
3 *nm* (**a**) *(pájaro)* canary (**b**) *Chile (silbato)* clay whistle

canasta *nf* (**a**) *(cesto)* basket ▸▸ *RP* ***c. familiar:*** **el precio de la c. familiar** the cost of the average week's shopping (**b**) *(juego de naipes)* canasta (**c**) *(en baloncesto) (aro)* basket (**d**) *(en baloncesto) (anotación)* basket; **anotar** *o* **meter una c.** to score a basket ▸▸ ***c. de dos puntos*** two-pointer; ***c. de tres puntos*** three-pointer (**e**) *Col, Méx (baca)* roof rack

canastera *nf* pratincole

canastero, -a *nm,f* (**a**) *(fabricante de cestas)* basket weaver (**b**) *Chile (vendedor ambulante)* street vendor

canastilla *nf* (**a**) *(cesto pequeño)* basket (**b**) *(de bebé)* layette

canasto 1 *nm (cesta)* large basket
2 *interj Anticuado o Hum (expresa enfado)* for heaven's sake!; *(expresa sorpresa)* good heavens!

Canberra *n* Canberra

cáncamo *nm (en barco)* ringbolt; *(en cuadro)* ring-headed screw ▸▸ ***c. de argolla*** ringbolt

cancán 1 *nm* (**a**) *(baile)* cancan (**b**) *(enagua)* frilly petticoat
2 **cancanes** *nmpl o nfpl RP (leotardos) Br* tights, *US* pantihose *(plural)*

cáncana *nf Col (persona)* thin person

cancanear *vi CAm, Méx (tartamudear)* to stutter, to stammer

cancaneo *nm CAm, Méx (tartamudeo)* stuttering, stammering

cancel *nm* (**a**) *(puerta)* storm door (**b**) *(reja)* ironwork screen (**c**) *Guat, Méx, PRico (mampara)* folding screen

cancela *nf* wrought-iron gate

cancelación *nf* (**a**) *(de contrato, vuelo, reunión)* cancellation (**b**) *(de deuda)* payment, settlement (**c**) *Informát* cancellation

cancelar 1 *vt* (**a**) *(contrato, vuelo, reunión)* to cancel (**b**) *(deuda)* to pay, to settle (**c**) *Informát* to cancel (**d**) *Chile, Ven (compra)* to pay for
2 *vi Chile, Ven (pagar)* to pay

Cáncer 1 *adj inv (persona)* Cancer; *Esp* **ser C.** to be (a) Cancer
2 *nm (signo del zodiaco)* Cancer; **los de C. son...** Cancerians are...
3 *nm,f inv (persona)* Cancer, Cancerian; *Esp* **los C. son...** Cancerians are...

cáncer *nm* (**a**) *(enfermedad)* cancer; **un paciente con c.** a patient with cancer ▸▸ ***c. cervical*** cervical cancer; ***c. de colon*** cancer of the colon; ***c. de mama*** breast cancer; ***c. de ovario*** ovarian cancer; ***c. de piel*** skin cancer; ***c. de próstata*** prostate cancer; ***c. de pulmón*** lung cancer
(**b**) *Fig (mal)* cancer; **la droga es el c. de nuestra sociedad** drugs are the cancer of our society

cancerbero *nm (en fútbol)* goalkeeper

canceriano, -a *Am* 1 *adj* Cancer; **ser c.** to be (a) Cancer
2 *nm,f* Cancer, Cancerian; **los c. son...** Cancerians are...

cancerígeno, -a *Med* 1 *adj* carcinogenic
2 *nm* carcinogen

cancerología *nf Med* oncology

cancerológico, -a *adj Med* oncological

cancerólogo, -a *nm,f Med* cancer specialist, oncologist

canceroso, -a *Med* **1** *adj (tejido, tumor)* cancerous; *(enfermo)* suffering from cancer
2 *nm,f (enfermo)* cancer patient

cancha *nf* **(a)** *(de tenis, baloncesto, balonmano)* court; *Am (de fútbol, rugby)* field, pitch; *Am (de golf)* course; *Am (de polo)* field; *CSur (de esquí)* slope; EXPR *RP* **está en su c.** he's in his element ►► *Am* ***c. de carreras*** racetrack
(b) *Chile (para aviones)* ***c. de aterrizaje*** runway; **una c. de aterrizaje en mitad de la selva** a landing strip in the middle of the jungle
(c) *Am (descampado)* open space, open ground
(d) *Am (corral)* fenced yard
(e) *Andes, PRico Fam (maíz)* toasted maize *o US* corn
(f) EXPR **dar c. a alguien** *(darle una oportunidad)* to give sb a chance; *RP Fam* **¡abran c.!** make way!; *RP Fam* **tener c.** to be streetwise *o* savvy

canchero, -a **1** *adj RP Fam* **(a)** *(desenvuelto)* savvy, streetwise; **ya estoy más c. en el tema** I know my way about the subject a lot better now **(b)** *(moderno)* trendy, stylish; **tiene ropa muy c.** he has really trendy clothes
2 *nm,f* **(a)** *RP Fam (desenvuelto)* savvy *o* streetwise person; **es un c. con las mujeres** he really has a way with women **(b)** *Am (cuidador)* groundsman, *f* groundswoman

cancho *nm Chile (retribución)* fee

canciller *nm Pol* **(a)** *(de gobierno)* chancellor **(b)** *(de asuntos exteriores)* foreign minister **(c)** *(de embajada)* chancellor

cancillería *nf Pol* **(a)** *(de gobierno)* chancellorship **(b)** *(de asuntos exteriores)* foreign ministry **(c)** *(de embajada)* chancellery, *Br* chancery

canción *nf* song; *Fig* **¡no me vengas con canciones!** I don't want to hear any of your excuses!; *Fig* **otra vez con la misma c.** here it comes, the same old story ►► ***c. de amor*** love song; ***c. de cuna*** lullaby; *Lit* ***c. de gesta*** chanson de geste, = medieval heroic narrative poem (e.g. "El Cid"); ***c. popular*** folk song; ***c. protesta*** protest song

cancionero *nm* **(a)** *(colección de canciones)* songbook **(b)** *Lit* anthology, collection

cancro *nm Med* cancer

candado *nm* padlock; **estar con c.** to be padlocked; **echar** *o* **poner el c. a algo** to padlock sth, to put a padlock on sth; **me olvidé de poner el c.** I forgot to padlock it *o* to put a padlock on it ►► ***c. de combinación*** combination lock

candanga *adj Ven Fam* **ser c.** *(situación)* to be nasty; *(persona)* to be a pain

candeal *adj* **pan c.** white bread *(of high quality, made from durum wheat)*

candela *nf* **(a)** *(vela)* candle
(b) *Fam (lumbre)* light; **¿me das c.?** have you got a light?
(c) *Fís (unidad)* candle
(d) *Carib (fuego)* fire; *(llama)* flame; **el sillón se prendió c.** the armchair caught fire
(e) *Col, Ven (quemador)* burner
(f) *Col Fam (ron)* rum
(g) EXPR *Esp, Col Fam* **darle c. a alguien** to thump sb, to beat sb up; *Ven Fam* **echar c. por la boca** to curse and swear; *Carib Fam* **eso está c.** *(eso está que arde)* things are pretty hot

candelabro *nm* **(a)** *(para velas)* candelabra **(b)** *(cactus)* (barrel) cactus

candelaria *nf* **(a)** *(planta)* great mullein **(b)** *Rel* **la C.** Candlemas

candelero *nm (para velas)* candlestick; EXPR **estar en el c.** to be in the limelight

candelilla *nf* **(a)** *(planta)* euphorbia **(b)** *Arg, Chile (fuego fatuo)* will-o'-the-wisp **(c)** *Am (luciérnaga)* firefly, glowworm **(d)** *Am (en costura)* hemstitch **(e)** *Cuba (insecto)* = insect which attacks leaves of tobacco plant

candente *adj* **(a)** *(incandescente)* red-hot **(b)** *(actual)* highly topical; **de c. actualidad** highly topical; **un tema c.** a burning issue; **un problema c.** an urgent *o* a pressing problem

cándidamente *adv* innocently, naively

candidatear *Am* **1** *vt* to nominate
2 candidatearse *vpr* **(a)** *(a elecciones)* to stand (for election) **(b)** *(a trabajo)* to apply

candidato, -a *nm,f* candidate; **un c. a la alcaldía/al Premio Nobel** a candidate for mayor/the Nobel Prize

candidatura *nf* **(a)** *(para un cargo)* candidacy; **presentar su c. a** to put oneself forward as a candidate for; **su c. para el puesto fue rechazada** she was not chosen for the position **(b)** *(lista)* list of candidates; **una c. de derechas** a list of candidates for a right-wing party

candidez *nf* ingenuousness, naivety; **con c.** innocently, naively

candidiasis, candidosis *nf inv Med* thrush, *Espec* candidiasis

cándido, -a *adj* ingenuous, naive

> **Falso amigo**: El adjetivo inglés **candid** no es la traducción del español **cándido**. En inglés **candid** significa "sincero, franco".

candidosis = **candidiasis**

candil *nm* **(a)** *(lámpara de aceite)* oil lamp **(b)** *Méx (candelabro)* chandelier

candileja **1** *nf* **(a)** *(parte del candil)* oil reservoir **(b)** *(candil pequeño)* small oil lamp **(c)** *(planta)* nigella
2 candilejas *nfpl* footlights

candombe *nm (danza)* = Uruguayan dance of African origin

candongas *nfpl Andes (pendientes)* hoop earrings

candongo, -a *Fam* **1** *adj* **(a)** *(zalamero)* smarmy **(b)** *(astuto)* sly, cunning **(c)** *(holgazán)* lazy
2 *nm,f* **(a)** *(zalamero)* smooth talker **(b)** *(astuto)* sly person **(c)** *(holgazán)* layabout, idler

candor *nm* innocence, naivety

> **Falso amigo**: El sustantivo inglés **candour** no es la traducción del español **candor**. En inglés **candour** significa "sinceridad, franqueza".

candorosamente *adv* innocently, naively

candoroso, -a *adj* innocent, naive

caneca *nf* **(a)** *Cuba (petaca)* hip flask **(b)** *Col (para basura) Br* rubbish bin, *US* trash can

canela *nf* cinnamon; EXPR *Fam* **ser c. fina** to be sheer class ►► ***c. en polvo*** ground cinnamon; ***c. en rama*** stick cinnamon

canelo, -a **1** *adj (caballo, perro)* golden brown
2 *nm* **(a)** *(árbol)* cinnamon tree **(b)** EXPR *Fam* **¡hemos hecho el c.!** *(nos han engañado)* we've been had!; **ayudándoles no haces más que el c. porque no te lo van a agradecer** helping them is a waste of time because you won't get any thanks for it; **¡deja de hacer el c. y ponte a trabajar!** stop acting the fool and get down to work!

canelón *nm* **(a)** *(plato)* **canelones** cannelloni **(b)** *Guat, Ven (rizo)* corkscrew curl

canesú *nm* **(a)** *(de vestido)* bodice **(b)** *(de blusa)* yoke

cangilón *nm (cubo)* bucket, scoop

cangrejo *nm* **(a)** *(animal)* crab; EXPR **ponerse como un c.** *(tomando el sol)* to go as red as a lobster ►► ***c. cacerola*** king crab, horseshoe crab; ***c. ermitaño*** hermit crab; ***c. de mar*** crab; ***c. de río*** crayfish **(b)** *(constelación)* **el C.** the Crab

canguelo, canguis *nm Fam* **le entró c.** she got the wind up, she freaked out

cangüeso *nm* blenny

canguis = **canguelo**

cangurera *nf Méx Br* bum bag, *US* fanny pack

canguro **1** *nm (animal)* kangaroo
2 *nmf Esp Fam (persona)* babysitter; **hacer de c.** to babysit

caníbal **1** *adj* cannibalistic
2 *nmf* cannibal

canibalismo *nm* **(a)** *(de seres vivos)* cannibalism **(b)** *Mktg* cannibalization

canibalización *nf Mktg* cannibalization

canibalizar *vt Mktg* to cannibalize

canica *nf* **(a)** *(bola)* marble **(b)** **las canicas** *(juego)* marbles; **jugar a las canicas** to play marbles

caniche *nm* poodle

canicie *nf* grey hair

canícula *nf* dog days, high summer

canicular *adj* **calor c.** blistering heat

cánido, -a **1** *adj* canine
2 *nm* canine

canijo, -a **1** *adj* **(a)** *(pequeño)* tiny; *(enfermizo)* sickly **(b)** *Méx Fam (terco)* pigheaded **(c)** *Méx Fam (intenso)* **hace un frío c.** it's freezing cold
2 *nm,f (pequeño)* shorty, small person; *(enfermizo)* sickly person

canilla *nf* **(a)** *Fam (espinilla)* shinbone **(b)** *Esp (bobina)* bobbin **(c)** *RP (grifo) Br* tap, *US* faucet **(d)** *Méx Fig (fuerza)* strength; **a c.** by force **(e)** *Perú (juego)* = type of dice game

canillera *nf* **(a)** *Am (temblor de piernas)* **tenía c.** his legs were trembling *o* shaking **(b)** *Am (espinillera)* shin pad

canillita *nm RP* newspaper vendor

canino, -a 1 *adj* canine; **exposición canina** dog show; **comida canina** dog food; **residencia canina** kennels
 2 *nm (diente)* canine (tooth)

canje *nm* exchange

canjeable *adj* exchangeable; **un vale c. por un regalo** a gift voucher

canjear *vt (objeto)* to exchange; *(vale, cupón)* to redeem; **si no le gusta, lo puede c. por otro del mismo precio** if you don't like it, you can change it for another one of the same price

cannabis *nm inv* cannabis

cano, -a *adj (blanco)* white; *(gris)* grey *(hair)*

canoa *nf* **(a)** *(india)* canoe, dugout **(b)** *(deportiva)* canoe, kayak ►► ***c. canadiense*** Canadian canoe

canódromo *nm* greyhound stadium *o* track

canon *nm* **(a)** *(norma)* norm, canon; EXPR **como mandan** *o* **según los cánones: todos iban vestidos como mandan** *o* **según los cánones** everybody was dressed in the traditional manner; **si la auditoría se hubiera hecho como mandan** *o* **según los cánones...** if they had done the audit properly...
 (b) *(modelo)* ideal; **el c. griego de belleza** the Greek ideal of beauty
 (c) *(impuesto)* tax
 (d) *Mús* canon
 (e) *Rel* **cánones** canon law

canónico, -a *adj* canonical; **derecho c.** canon law

canónigo *nm* canon

canonista *nmf* expert in canon law

canonización *nf* canonization

canonizar [14] *vt* to canonize

canonjía *nf* **(a)** *Rel* canonry **(b)** *Fam (trabajo fácil)* cushy number

canoro, -a *adj* **ave canora** songbird

canoso, -a *adj (persona)* grey-haired, white-haired; *(cabellera, barba)* grey, white

canotier [kano'tje] *(pl* **canotiers**) *nm (sombrero)* (straw) boater

cansado, -a *adj* **(a)** *(fatigado)* tired; **tener cara de c.** to look tired; **estar c. de algo/de hacer algo** to be tired of sth/of doing sth **(b)** *(harto)* tired, sick; **estoy c. de decirte que apagues la luz al salir** I'm tired *o* sick of telling you to turn off the light when you go out **(c)** *(pesado, cargante)* tiring; **es muy c. viajar cada día en tren** it's very tiring travelling on the train every day

cansador, -ora *adj Andes, RP* **(a)** *(que cansa)* tiring **(b)** *(que aburre)* boring

cansancio *nm* **(a)** *(fatiga)* tiredness; **muerto de c.** dead tired **(b)** *(hastío)* boredom; **hasta el c.** over and over again

cansar 1 *vt* **(a)** *(producir cansancio)* to tire (out); **me cansa mucho leer sin gafas** I get very tired if I read without my glasses **(b)** *(tierra)* to exhaust
 2 *vi* to be tiring; **esta tarea cansa mucho** it's a very tiring job *o* task; **la misma música todos los días acaba por c.** the same music every day gets a bit wearying, you get tired of hearing the same music every day
 3 **cansarse** *vpr también Fig* to get tired (**de** of); **los niños se cansan muy pronto de todo** children get tired of things very quickly; **¡ya me he cansado de repetirlo! ¡cállense ahora mismo!** I'm sick of repeating it! be quiet this minute!; **no se cansa nunca de escribirme** she's always writing to me

cansinamente *adv (caminar)* wearily, sluggishly

cansino, -a *adj (gesto, paso)* weary, lethargic

cansón, -ona *Col, Ecuad, Ven Fam* **1** *adj* **(a)** *(que cansa)* tiring **(b)** *(que aburre)* boring
 2 *nm,f* bore, pain

Cantabria *n* Cantabria

Cantábrico, -a 1 *adj* **la cordillera Cantábrica** the Cantabrian Mountains; **la cornisa Cantábrica** the Cantabrian coast; **el mar C.** the Cantabrian Sea
 2 *nm* **el C.** the Cantabrian Sea

cántabro, -a 1 *adj* Cantabrian
 2 *nm,f* Cantabrian

cantada *nf Dep Fam* blunder, goalkeeping error

cantado, -a *adj Fam* **el resultado está c.** the result is a foregone conclusion; **estaba c. que no iba a aceptar** he was never going to accept; **su nombramiento estaba c.** her appointment was a foregone conclusion; **le dio un pase c.** he telegraphed his pass to him

cantador, -ora *nm,f* traditional folk singer

cantaleta *nf Am* **la misma c.** the same old story

cantamañanas *nmf inv Fam* **es un c.** you can't depend on him for anything

cantante 1 *adj* singing
 2 *nmf* singer; **c. de rock/de ópera** rock/opera singer; **c. pop** pop singer

cantaor, -ora *nm,f* flamenco singer

cantar[1] *nm* poem; EXPR *Fam* **eso es otro c.** that's another story ►► ***el C. de los C. es*** *(en la Biblia)* the Song of Songs; ***c. de gesta*** chanson de geste, = medieval heroic narrative poem (e.g."El Cid")

cantar[2] **1** *vt* **(a)** *(canción)* to sing
 (b) *(bingo, línea, el gordo)* to call (out); **cántame los números y yo los escribo** you call out the numbers and I'll write them down; EXPR *Fam* **c. a alguien las cuarenta** to give sb a piece of one's mind; EXPR *RP Fam* **c. algo a alguien: te canté que tu madre no te dejaría ir** I TOLD you your mother wouldn't let you go; EXPR *RP Fam* **c. la justa a alguien** to give it to sb straight up; EXPR **c. victoria** to claim victory
 (c) *Fam (confesar)* to confess
 (d) *(alabar)* to praise; **no se cansa de c. la belleza del lugar** he never tires of singing the praises of the beauty of the place
 2 *vi* **(a)** *(persona)* to sing
 (b) *(ave)* to sing; *(gallo)* to crow; *(insecto)* to chirp
 (c) *Fam (confesar)* to confess, to talk; EXPR **c. de plano** to make a full confession
 (d) *Esp Fam (apestar)* to stink; **le cantan los pies** he has smelly feet
 (e) *Esp Fam (llamar la atención)* to stick out like a sore thumb; **ese traje rojo canta mucho** that red suit really draws attention to you; **canta un montón que estás nervioso** it's really obvious that you're nervous; **Carlos y yo cantábamos en una fiesta tan elegante** Carlos and I really stood out at that posh party
 (f) *Esp Fam (portero)* **les metieron un gol porque el portero cantó** they conceded a goal because the goalkeeper blundered
 (g) *(alabar)* **c. a** to sing the praises of
 (h) *Am Fam (escoger)* **¡canté primero para la ducha!** *Br* bags I get the first shower!, *US* dibs on the first shower!

cantárida *nf* Spanish fly

cantarín, -ina *adj* **(a)** *(persona)* fond of singing **(b)** *(voz)* singsong

cántaro *nm* large pitcher; **a cántaros** in torrents; EXPR **llover a cántaros** to rain cats and dogs

cantata *nf* cantata

cantautor, -ora *nm,f* singer songwriter

cante *nm* **(a)** *(arte)* = Andalusian folk song ►► ***c. flamenco*** flamenco singing; ***c. hondo*** = traditional flamenco singing; ***c. jondo*** = traditional flamenco singing **(b)** EXPR *Esp Fam* **dar el c.** *(llamar la atención)* to stick out a mile

cantear 1 *vt Chile (piedra)* to cut
 2 **cantearse** *vpr Esp Fam (ponerse bravucón)* to get uppity, to try it on; **como se cantee, le daré un puñetazo** if he tries anything smart, I'll thump him

cantegril *nm Urug* shanty town

cantera *nf* **(a)** *(de piedra)* quarry; *(mina)* open-cut mining **(b)** *(de jóvenes promesas)* **un jugador de la c.** a home-grown player; **el instituto es una buena c. de lingüistas** the institute produces many linguists **(c)** *ver también* **cantero**

canterano, -a 1 *adj* home-grown
 2 *nm,f* home-grown player

cantería *nf* **(a)** *(arte)* stonecutting **(b)** *(obra)* stonework

cantero, -a 1 *nm,f (picapedrero)* quarry worker, quarryman; *(masón)* stonemason, mason
 2 *nm Cuba, RP (parterre)* flowerbed

cántico *nm* **(a)** *(canto)* **cánticos** singing **(b)** *(en estadio)* chant **(c)** *(poema)* canticle

cantidad 1 *nf* **(a)** *(medida)* quantity, amount; **la c. de energía que se emite** the amount of energy given off; **¿qué c. de pasta hará falta?** how much pasta will we need?
 (b) *(abundancia)* abundance, large number; *Fam* **había c. de colegas míos allí** there were lots of my colleagues there; **en c.** in abundance; *Fam* **prepararon comida en cantidades industriales** they made food in industrial quantities
 (c) *(número)* number; **sumar dos cantidades** to add two numbers *o* figures together

(**d**) *(suma de dinero)* sum (of money)
(**e**) *Fís* ***c. de movimiento*** momentum
(**f**) *Ling (de vocal, sílaba)* quantity
2 *adv Esp Fam* really; **me gusta c.** I really like it a lot; **corrimos c.** we did a lot of running; **me duele c.** it really hurts

cantidubi *adv Esp Fam* really; **me gustó c.** I really liked it a lot, I liked it heaps

cantiga, cántiga *nf* ballad

cantil *nm* (**a**) *(escalón)* shelf, ledge (**b**) *Am (borde de acantilado)* cliff edge

cantilena *nf* **la misma c.** the same old story

cantimplora *nf* water bottle

cantina *nf* (**a**) *(de soldados)* mess (**b**) *(en fábrica, colegio)* canteen (**c**) *(en estación de tren)* buffet (**d**) *Andes, CAm, Méx (bar)* bar (**e**) *RP (de comida italiana)* Italian restaurant

cantinela *nf* **la misma c.** the same old story

cantinero, -a *nm,f* canteen manager, *f* canteen manageress

canto[1] *nm* (**a**) *(acción, arte)* singing; **estudia c.** she studies singing ►► ***c. gregoriano*** Gregorian chant; ***c. llano*** plainchant, plainsong
(**b**) *(canción)* song ►► ***c. fúnebre*** funeral chant; ***c. guerrero*** war song; *Fig* ***c. de sirena*** wheedling
(**c**) *(de ave)* song ►► *Fig* ***c. de(l) cisne*** swan song; *Fig* ***c. del gallo*** daybreak; *Fig* **al c. del gallo** at daybreak
(**d**) *(exaltación, alabanza)* hymn; **su discurso fue un c. a la violencia** his speech was a hymn to violence
(**e**) *Lit (poema heroico)* = short heroic poem
(**f**) *Lit (parte de poema)* canto

canto[2] *nm* 1 (**a**) *(lado, borde)* edge; *(de cuchillo)* blunt edge; *(de libro)* front edge; **de c.** edgeways; EXPR *Fam* **por el c. de un duro** by a hair's breadth; EXPR **faltó el c. de un duro para que tuviera un accidente** they missed having an accident by a hair's breadth
(**b**) *(guijarro)* pebble; EXPR *Fam* **darse con un c. en los dientes** to count oneself lucky, to be happy with what one has got ►► ***c. rodado*** pebble
2 **al canto** *loc adv* for sure; **cada vez que viene, (hay) pelea al c.** every time she comes, you can be sure there'll be a fight; **tenemos tormenta al c.** we're definitely in for a storm

Cantón *n* Canton

cantón *nm* (**a**) *(en Suiza)* canton (**b**) *Méx Fam (casa)* place

cantonal *adj* cantonal

cantonalismo *nm* cantonalism

cantonalización *nf Pol* = division of a region into cantons

cantonera *nf (de esquina, libro)* corner piece

cantonés, -esa 1 *adj* Cantonese
2 *nm (lengua)* Cantonese

cantor, -ora 1 *adj* singing; **ave cantora** songbird
2 *nm,f* singer

cantora *nf Andes Fam* chamber pot

cantoral *nm* choir book

cantueso *nm* lavender

canturrear *Fam* 1 *vt* to sing softly, to croon
2 *vi* to sing softly, to croon

canturreo *nm Fam* quiet singing, crooning

cánula *nf Med* cannula

canutas *nfpl* EXPR *Esp Fam* **pasarlas c.** to have a rough time; **las pasamos c. para encontrar alojamiento** we had a hell of a time finding somewhere to stay

canutillo *nm* (**a**) *(para encuadernar)* plastic binding *(for comb binding machine)* (**b**) *(en tela)* ribbing

canuto[1] *nm* (**a**) *(tubo)* tube (**b**) *Fam (de droga)* joint

canuto[2]**, -a** *Ven Fam* 1 *adj (tonto)* thick
2 *nm,f (tonto)* **es un c.** he's really thick

caña *nf* (**a**) *(planta)* cane ►► ***c. de azúcar*** sugar cane; ***c. dulce*** sugar cane
(**b**) *(de río, de estanque)* reed
(**c**) *(tallo)* cane
(**d**) *Esp (de cerveza)* = small glass of beer; **nos tomamos unas cañas con unos amigos** we had a few beers with some friends
(**e**) *(para pescar)* **c. (de pescar)** (fishing) rod
(**f**) *(de barco)* **la c. del timón** the helm
(**g**) *(de bota, calcetín)* leg; **bota de c. alta** knee-length boot; **bota de media c.** calf-length boot
(**h**) *(tuétano)* bone marrow; *(hueso)* shank
(**i**) *Andes, Cuba, RP (aguardiente)* caña, = type of rum made using sugar cane spirit
(**j**) *Fam* EXPR **dar c. a alguien** *(pegar)* to give sb a beating; **hay que darle más c. para que trabaje** *(presionarle)* you have to really breathe down his neck to get him to work; **meter c.: métele c.** *(a vehículo)* step on it; **me están metiendo c. para que acepte** they're putting pressure on me to accept

cañabrava *nf Cuba, RP* = reed used for building roofs and walls

cañacoro *nm Bot* Indian shot

cañada *nf* (**a**) *(camino para ganado)* cattle track (**b**) *RP (arroyo)* creek, stream (**c**) *Cuba (valle)* valley

cañadón *nm RP* ravine

cañadonga *nf Ven muy Fam* booze-up, *Br* piss-up

cañaduz *nf Andes* sugar cane

cañafístula *nf* cassia

cañaheja *nf* giant fennel

cañal *nm* (**a**) *(cañaveral)* reedbed (**b**) *(de azúcar)* sugar cane plantation

cañamazo *nm* (**a**) *(tela)* hessian (**b**) *(para bordar)* (embroidery) canvas

cañamera *nf* rough marshmallow

cáñamo *nm* hemp ►► ***c. índico*** Indian hemp; ***c. indio*** Indian hemp

cañamón *nm* hempseed

cañavera *nf* reed-grass

cañaveral *nm* (**a**) *(juncos)* reedbed (**b**) *Am (de azúcar)* sugar cane plantation

cañazo *nm Am (aguardiente)* rum

cañería *nf* pipe; **las cañerías** the plumbing

cañero, -a 1 *adj Esp Fam (música)* heavy
2 *nm Méx (almacén)* sugar mill storeroom
3 *nm,f Am* (**a**) *(trabajador)* sugar plantation worker (**b**) *(propietario)* sugar plantation owner

cañí *adj* (**a**) *Fam (folclórico, popular)* = term used to describe the traditional folklore and values of Spain (**b**) *(gitano)* gypsy

cañizal, cañizar *nm* reedbed

cañizo *nm* wattle

caño *nm* (**a**) *(tubo)* tube, pipe; *(of fountain)* spout; EXPR *RP Fam* **dar con un c. a algo/alguien** to lay into sth/sb, to lambast sth/sb ►► *RP* ***c. de escape*** exhaust (pipe) (**b**) *(en fútbol)* nutmeg; **hacer un c. a alguien** to nutmeg sb (**c**) *(canal)* narrow channel (**d**) *Col (río)* stream (**e**) *Perú (grifo) Br* tap, *US* faucet

cañón 1 *adj* (**a**) *Esp Fam* **estar c.** *(guapo)* to be gorgeous
(**b**) *Méx Fam* **estar c.: está c. que pases el examen** I don't give much for your chances of passing the exam
2 *nm* (**a**) *(arma)* gun; *Hist* cannon ►► ***c. de agua*** water cannon; ***c. antiaéreo*** antiaircraft gun; ***c. anticarro*** antitank gun; ***c. antitanque*** antitank gun; ***c. de campaña*** field gun; *Fís* ***c. de electrones*** electron gun; *Fís* ***c. electrónico*** electron gun; ***c. de nieve*** snow cannon
(**b**) *(tubo) (de fusil, pistola)* barrel; *(de órgano)* pipe; **una escopeta de dos cañones** a double-barrelled shotgun
(**c**) *(de chimenea)* flue; *(de escalera)* stairwell
(**d**) *(foco)* spotlight
(**e**) *Geog* canyon
(**f**) *(de pluma)* pin feather
(**g**) *(de barba)* stubble
(**h**) *RP (dulce)* = pastry filled with cream or runny toffee
(**i**) *Col (tronco)* tree trunk
(**j**) *Perú (sendero)* path
(**k**) *Méx (paso estrecho)* defile
(**l**) *CSur Fam* **ni a c.** no way; **con esta lluvia, no salgo de casa ni a c.** there's no way I'm going out in this rain
3 *adv Esp Fam* **pasarlo c.** *(genial)* to have a fantastic time

cañonazo *nm* (**a**) *(disparo de cañón)* gunshot (**b**) *Fam (en fútbol)* powerful shot

cañonear *vt* to shell

cañoneo *nm* shelling

cañonera *nf* gunboat

cañonero, -a *nm,f (en fútbol)* **es un c.** he has a powerful shot

cañota *nf* common reed

caoba 1 *adj* mahogany; **color c.** mahogany
2 *nf* (**a**) *(árbol, madera)* mahogany (**b**) *(color)* mahogany, reddish-brown (**c**) *CAm, Chile (caño)* gutter (**d**) *Chile, Nic (artesa)* trough

caobo *nm Am* mahogany

caolín *nm* kaolin, china clay

caos *nm inv* chaos; **ser un c.** to be in chaos; **el c. en el transporte público** the chaotic state of public transport

caóticamente *adv* chaotically

caótico, -a *adj* chaotic

CAP [kap] *nm (abrev de* **Certificado de Aptitud Pedagógica**) = Spanish teaching certificate needed to teach in state secondary education

cap. (*abrev de* **capítulo**) ch.

capa *nf* (**a**) *(manto)* cloak, cape; EXPR *Fam* **andar de c. caída** *(persona)* to be in a bad way; *(negocio)* to be struggling; EXPR **hacer de su c. un sayo** to do as one pleases ►► ***c. pluvial*** *(de sacerdote)* cope
(**b**) *(baño) (de barniz, pintura)* coat; *(de chocolate)* coating, layer; **hay que dar una segunda c.** it needs a second coat
(**c**) *(para encubrir)* veneer; **bajo una c. de bondad se esconde su carácter malvado** her evil nature is concealed behind a veneer of kindness
(**d**) *(estrato)* layer ►► ***c. atmosférica*** atmosphere; *Geol* ***c. freática*** aquifer; ***c. de hielo*** ice sheet; ***c. de nieve*** layer of snow; ***c. de ozono*** ozone layer
(**e**) *(grupo social)* stratum, class; **las capas altas de la sociedad** the upper classes, the upper strata of society; **las capas marginales** the marginalized strata of society
(**f**) *Taurom* cape
(**g**) *ver también* **capo**

capacete *nm* (**a**) *(de armadura)* casque (**b**) *Carib, Méx (de automóvil) Br* bonnet, *US* hood

capacha *nf* (**a**) *(cesta)* basket (**b**) *Chile Fam (cárcel) Br* nick, *US* joint

capacho *nm* basket

capacidad *nf* (**a**) *(cabida)* capacity; **unidades de c.** units of capacity; **c. máxima** *(en ascensor)* maximum load; **con c. para 500 personas** with a capacity of 500; **este teatro tiene c. para 1.200 espectadores** this theatre can seat 1,200 people ►► *Informát* ***c. de almacenamiento*** storage capacity; ***c. de carga*** cargo capacity; ***c. eléctrica*** *(de condensador)* capacitance; *Informát* ***c. de memoria*** memory capacity; ***c. pulmonar*** lung capacity
(**b**) *(aptitud, talento, potencial)* ability; **no tener c. para algo/para hacer algo** to be no good at sth/at doing sth ►► ***c. adquisitiva*** purchasing power; ***c. de aprendizaje*** ability to learn; ***c. de concentración*** ability to concentrate; *Fin* ***c. de endeudamiento*** borrowing capacity *o* power; ***c. de fabricación*** manufacturing capacity; ***c. de gestión*** managerial skills; ***c. ofensiva*** fire power; ***c. de producción*** production capacity; ***c. de reacción*** ability to react *o* respond; ***c. de respuesta*** ability to react *o* respond
(**c**) *Der* capacity

capacitación *nf* (**a**) *(habilitación)* enabling, empowerment (**b**) *(formación)* training; **cursos de c. profesional** professional training courses

capacitado, -a *adj* qualified; **estar c. para algo** to be qualified for sth

capacitador, -ora *Am* **1** *adj* **curso c.** training course
2 *nm,f* trainer

capacitancia *nf Elec* capacitance

capacitar 1 *vt* (**a**) **c. a alguien para hacer algo** *(habilitar)* to entitle sb to do sth; **un título que capacita para pilotar helicópteros** a certificate which entitles *o* qualifies you to fly helicopters (**b**) **c. a alguien para hacer algo** *(formar)* to train sb to do sth
2 capacitarse *vpr (formarse)* to train

capacitor *nm Elec* electric capacitor

capado *adj* castrated, gelded

capadura *nf (castración)* castration

capar *vt* (**a**) *(animal)* to castrate, to geld; *muy Fam* **si se enteran, me capan** if they find out, they'll skin me alive *o Br* have my guts for garters (**b**) *Andes, Carib (podar)* to prune (**c**) *Col Fam* **c. clase** *(faltar)* to play *Br* truant *o US* hookey

caparazón *nm* (**a**) *(de animal)* shell, *Espec* carapace (**b**) *(psicológico)* shell

caparrosa *nf Quím* copperas

capataz, -aza *nm,f* foreman, *f* forewoman

capaz 1 *adj* (**a**) *(apto)* capable, able; **es un profesor muy c.** he's a very skilled *o* gifted teacher
(**b**) *(de hacer algo)* capable; **c. de algo** capable of sth; **es c. de todo con tal de conseguir lo que quiere** she's capable of anything to get what she wants; **c. de hacer algo** capable of doing sth; **una noticia c. de conmover a todo el mundo** a news story that would move anyone; **es muy c. de robarle a su propia madre** he would be quite capable of stealing from his own mother; **¡no serás c. de dejarme sola!** surely you wouldn't leave me all alone!; **no me siento c. de subir hasta la cumbre** I don't think I can make it to the top
(**c**) *(espacioso)* **muy/poco c.** with a large/small capacity; **c. para** with room for
(**d**) *Der* competent
2 *adv Andes, RP Fam (tal vez)* maybe; **¿vendrás esta noche? – c.** are you coming tonight? – maybe; **c. (que) viene Pedro** Pedro might come

capazo *nm* (**a**) *(cesta)* large wicker basket (**b**) *(para bebé)* Moses basket, *Br* carrycot

capcioso, -a *adj* disingenuous; **pregunta capciosa** trick question

capea *nf Taurom* = amateur bullfight with young bulls

capear 1 *vt* (**a**) *Taurom* to make passes at with a cape (**b**) *(eludir) (persona)* to avoid; *(situación)* to get out of; EXPR **c. el temporal** to ride out *o* weather the storm (**c**) *Chile, Guat Fam (clase)* to skip
2 *vi Chile, Guat Fam* to play *Br* truant *o US* hookey

capella, cappella [ka'pela]: **a capella** *Mús* **1** *loc adj* a cappella
2 *loc adv* a cappella

capellán *nm* chaplain

capellanía *nf* chaplaincy

capelo *nm* (**a**) *(sombrero)* **c. (cardenalicio)** cardinal's hat (**b**) *(dignidad)* **obtuvo el c. (cardenalicio)** he was given a cardinal's hat

Caperucita Roja *n* (Little) Red Riding Hood

caperuza *nf* (**a**) *(gorro)* hood (**b**) *(capuchón)* top, cap

capibara *nf* capybara

capicúa 1 *adj inv* palindromic; **una matrícula c.** a registration number that's the same back to front as forward
2 *nm inv* number that's the same back to front as forward

capilar 1 *adj* (**a**) *(del cabello)* hair; **loción c.** hair lotion (**b**) *Fís* capillary (**c**) *Anat* capillary
2 *nm Anat* capillary ►► ***c. sanguíneo*** capillary

capilaridad *nf Fís* capillary action, capillarity

capilla *nf* (**a**) *(iglesia)* chapel; EXPR **estar en c.** *(condenado a muerte)* to be awaiting execution; *Fam (en ascuas)* to be on tenterhooks ►► ***c. ardiente*** funeral chapel (**b**) *Imprenta* proof sheet, running sheet

capirotada *nf Méx* = bread pudding with nuts and raisins

capirotazo *nm* flick

capirote *nm* (**a**) *(gorro)* pointed hood; EXPR *Fam* **ser tonto de c.** to be a complete idiot (**b**) *(en cetrería)* hood

Capirucha *n Méx Fam* = colloquial name for Mexico City

capisayo *nm Col (camiseta) Br* vest, *US* undershirt

capiscar *Fam* **1** *vt* to get; **no te capisco** I don't get you
2 *vi* to get it

cápita *ver* **per cápita**

capitación *nf Fin* capitation

capital 1 *adj* (**a**) *(importante)* supreme, prime; *(error)* serious, grave; **es de c. importancia que vengan** it is of prime *o* the utmost importance that they come; **una obra c. de la literatura universal** one of the great works of world literature
(**b**) *(pecado)* deadly
2 *nm Econ* capital; **el c. público/privado** public/private capital; **he invertido un pequeño c. en el negocio de mi hermano** I've invested a small sum in my brother's business; **el c. y los trabajadores** Capital and Labour ►► ***c. activo*** active capital; ***c. circulante*** floating capital; ***c. disponible*** working capital; ***c. escriturado*** share capital, *US* capital stock; ***c. especulativo*** hot money; ***c. fijo*** fixed capital; ***c. flotante*** floating capital; *Am* ***capitales golondrina*** = speculative capital invested internationally wherever the highest returns are available; ***c. inicial*** starting capital; ***c. inmovilizado*** tied-up capital; ***c. invertido*** capital invested; ***c. líquido*** liquid assets; ***c. productivo*** active capital; ***c. (de) riesgo*** venture capital, risk capital; ***c. social*** share capital, shareholders' equity; ***c. suscrito*** subscribed capital
3 *nf* (**a**) *(de país, región)* capital (city); **soy de Teruel c.** I'm from the city of Teruel (**b**) *(centro)* capital; **París es la c. mundial del arte** Paris is the artistic capital of the world ►► ***c. europea de la cultura*** European city of culture

capitalidad *nf* capital status; **ostentar la c. de** to be the capital of

capitalino, -a 1 *adj* of the capital (city), capital; **la vida capitalina** life in the capital (city)
2 *nm,f* citizen of the capital

capitalismo *nm* capitalism

capitalista 1 *adj* capitalist
2 *nmf* capitalist

capitalizable *adj Fin* capitalizable

capitalización *nf Fin* capitalization

capitalizar [14] *vt* (a) *Fin* to capitalize (b) *(sacar provecho de, acaparar)* to capitalize on; **la casa de discos capitalizó el triunfo del grupo** the record company cashed in on the group's success

capitán, -ana *nm,f* (a) *(en ejército de tierra)* captain; *(en aviación) Br* flight lieutenant, *US* captain; *(en marina)* lieutenant ▸▸ ***c. de corbeta*** lieutenant commander; ***c. de fragata*** commander; ***c. general*** *Br* field marshal, *US* general of the army
(b) *(de transatlántico)* captain; *(de pesquero)* captain, skipper ▸▸ ***c. de puerto*** harbourmaster
(c) *(de equipo deportivo)* captain
(d) *CAm, Méx, Ven (restaurante)* head waiter, maitre d'

capitana *nf (buque)* flagship

capitanear *vt* (a) *(ejército)* to captain (b) *(transatlántico)* to captain; *(pesquero)* to captain, to skipper (c) *(equipo deportivo)* to captain (d) *(dirigir)* to head, to lead

capitanía *nf Mil* (a) *(empleo)* captaincy (b) *(oficina)* military headquarters ▸▸ ***c. general*** Captaincy General (c) *(territorio)* military region

capitel *nm Arquit* capital ▸▸ ***c. corintio*** Corinthian capital; ***c. dórico*** Doric capital; ***c. jónico*** Ionic capital

capitolio *nm* (a) *(edificio)* capitol; **el C.** *(en Estados Unidos)* the Capitol (b) *(acrópolis)* acropolis

capitoste *nmf Fam* top dog, bigwig; **los capitostes del partido** the party bosses *o* bigwigs

capitulación *nf* (a) *(rendición)* capitulation, surrender (b) ***capitulaciones matrimoniales*** marriage contract

capitular[1] *adj* **sala c.** chapterhouse

capitular[2] *vi* to capitulate, to surrender

capítulo *nm* (a) *(de libro)* chapter; *(de serie)* episode; *Fig* **un c. negro en la historia del país** a shameful chapter in our history ▸▸ *UE* ***C. Social*** Social Chapter
(b) *(tema)* subject; **en el c. de inversiones, el gobierno ha anunciado...** as for investments, the government has announced...; **por sectores, destaca el c. de agricultura** agriculture stands out among the other areas of the economy; EXPR **ser c. aparte** to be another matter (altogether)
(c) *Rel* assembly, chapter; EXPR **llamar a alguien a c.** to call sb to account

capo, -a 1 *adj RP Fam (bueno)* great, *US* neat
2 *nm* (a) *(de la mafia)* mafia boss, capo ▸▸ ***c. de la droga*** drug baron; ***c. mafioso*** mafia boss (b) *Fam (de empresa, sindicato)* boss, chief
3 *nm,f RP Fam (prodigio)* ace, whizz; **es una capa en física** she's a real ace *o* whizz at physics

capó *nm Br* bonnet, *US* hood

capomo *nm* breadnut (tree)

capón[1] 1 *adj* castrated
2 *nm (animal)* capon

capón[2] *nm Fam (golpe)* rap on the head; **me dio un c.** he rapped me on the head

caporal *nm* (a) *Mil* corporal (b) *Am (capataz)* foreman, supervisor

capota *nf* (a) *(de vehículo) Br* convertible roof, *US* convertible top (b) *(sombrero)* bonnet

capotar *vi* (a) *(automóvil)* to overturn (b) *(avión)* to nosedive

capotazo *nm Taurom* = pass with the cape

capote *nm* (a) *(capa)* cape with sleeves; *(militar)* greatcoat
(b) *Taurom* cape ▸▸ ***c. de brega*** = short red cape used in bullfighting; ***c. de paseo*** = short embroidered silk bullfighter's cape
(c) EXPR **decir para su c.** *(para sí)* to say to oneself; *Méx* **de c.** *(a escondidas)* secretly; **echar un c. a alguien** to give sb a (helping) hand; *RP Fam* **hacer c.: su última puesta en escena hizo c.** his last production was a great success

capotear *vt Taurom* to distract with the cape

cappella = **capella**

capricho *nm* (a) *(deseo)* whim, caprice; **a mi c.** at my whim; **darse un c.** to treat oneself; **se compró el yate por c.** he bought the yacht on a whim; **este caballo es su último c.** this horse is his latest whim; **tener dos casas es un c. al alcance de muy pocos** having two houses is a luxury few can afford (b) *Arte* caprice (c) *Mús* capriccio

caprichoso, -a *adj* capricious, impulsive; **actuar de forma caprichosa** to act capriciously *o* impulsively

capricorniano, -a *Am* 1 *adj* Capricorn; **ser c.** to be (a) Capricorn
2 *nm,f* Capricorn; **los c. son...** Capricorns are...

Capricornio 1 *adj inv* Capricorn; *Esp* **ser C.** to be (a) Capricorn
2 *nm (signo)* Capricorn; **los de C. son...** Capricorns are...
3 *nmf inv (persona)* Capricorn; *Esp* **los C. son...** Capricorns are...

cápsula *nf* (a) *(recipiente, envoltorio)* capsule (b) *(tapón)* cap (c) *(píldora)* capsule (d) *(de nave espacial)* **c. (espacial)** space capsule (e) *Anat* capsule ▸▸ ***c. suprarrenal*** adrenal gland (f) *(en planta)* capsule (g) *(de proyectil)* ***c. fulminante*** percussion cap

capsular *adj* capsular

captación *nf* (a) *(de adeptos)* recruitment; **la c. de clientes** winning *o* attracting (new) clients (b) *(percepción, entendimiento)* understanding (c) *(de radio, televisión)* reception (d) *(de aguas)* **un sistema de c. de aguas** a system for collecting water (e) ***c. de fondos*** fundraising

captar 1 *vt* (a) *(atraer) (simpatía)* to win; *(interés)* to gain, to capture; *(adeptos)* to recruit, to attract; *(clientes)* to win, to attract; **esa secta ha captado a muchos jóvenes de la zona** that sect has recruited *o* attracted many young people from the area
(b) *(percibir)* to detect; **no captó la ironía que había en su voz** she didn't detect the irony in his voice; **c. una indirecta** to take a hint
(c) *(entender)* to grasp; **c. las intenciones de alguien** to understand sb's intentions
(d) *(sintonizar)* to pick up, to receive
(e) *(aguas)* to collect
2 **captarse** *vpr (atraer)* to win, to attract

captor, -ora *nm,f* captor

captura *nf* (a) *(de persona, animal)* capture ▸▸ *Informát* ***c. de pantalla*** screen capture *o* dump (b) *(en pesca)* catch

capturar *vt (persona, animal)* to capture

capturista *nmf Méx* typist, keyboarder

capucha *nf* (a) *(de prenda)* hood; **con c.** hooded (b) *(de bolígrafo)* cap, top

capuchina *nf* nasturtium

capuchino, -a 1 *adj* Capuchin
2 *nm* (a) *(fraile)* Capuchin (b) *(café)* cappuccino (c) *(mono)* capuchin (monkey) (d) *Carib (cometa)* = small paper kite

capucho *nm* hood

capuchón *nm* (a) *(de prenda)* hood; **con c.** hooded (b) *(de bolígrafo, pluma)* cap, top

capullo, -a 1 *adj Esp muy Fam* **ser muy c.** to be a real jerk *o Br* dickhead
2 *nm* (a) *(de flor)* bud ▸▸ ***c. de rosa*** rosebud (b) *(de gusano)* cocoon (c) *Esp Vulg (glande)* head
3 *nm,f Esp muy Fam (persona despreciable)* jerk, *Br* dickhead

caquexia *nf Med* cachexia

caqui 1 *adj inv (color)* khaki
2 *nm* (a) *(color)* khaki (b) *(árbol)* kaki (c) *(fruto)* kaki, sharon fruit

CARA[1] *nf* (a) *(rostro)* face; **tiene una c. muy bonita** she has a very pretty face; **me ha salido un grano en la c.** I've got a spot on my face; **esa c. me suena de algo** I remember that face from somewhere, I've seen that face somewhere before; **los atracadores actuaron a c. descubierta** the robbers didn't bother covering their faces; **castigar a alguien de c. a la pared** to make sb stand facing the wall (as a punishment); **arrugar la c.** to screw up one's face; *también Fig* **asomar la c.** to show one's face; **¡mira quién asoma la c.!** look who's here!; **c. a c.** face-to-face; **un (encuentro) c. a c. entre los dos candidatos** a head-to-head (debate) between the two candidates
(b) *(expresión, aspecto)* **¡alegra esa c., ya es viernes!** cheer up *o* don't look so miserable, it's Friday!; **cuando se enteró de la noticia, puso muy buena c.** when she heard the news, her face lit up; **no supe qué c. poner** I didn't know how to react; **¡no pongas mala c.!** don't look so miserable!; **cuando le contamos nuestro plan, puso muy mala c.** when we told her our plan, she pulled a face; **tener buena/mala c.** *(persona)* to look well/awful; **tiene c. de buena persona** she has a kind face, she looks like a nice person; **tener c. de enfadado** to look angry; **tienes c. de no haber dormido** you look like you haven't slept; **tiene c. de querer comer** she looks as if she'd like something to eat; **esta comida tiene buena c.** this meal looks good; **tiene c. de ponerse a llover** it looks as if it's going to rain ▸▸ *Esp Fam* ***c. de acelga:* tener c. de acelga** to have a pale face; ***c. de ángel:* tener c. de ángel** to look like an angel; ***c. de asco:* poner c. de asco** to pull a face, to look disgusted; *Fam* ***c. de circunstancias:* puso c. de circunstancias** his face took on a serious expression *o* turned serious; *RP Fam* ***c. de culo:* tener c. de culo** to look really *Br* hacked off *o US* pissed; *Fam* ***c. de hereje:* tener c. de hereje** to have an ugly mug; *Fam* ***c. larga:* poner c. larga** to pull a long face; *Esp Fam* ***c. de pascua:* tener c. de pascua** to have a happy face; *Fam* ***c. de perro:* no pongas esa c. de perro** don't look so miserable; **tiene c. de perro** he has an unfriendly

face; **un enfrentamiento a c. de perro** a crunch match; ***c. de pocos amigos:*** **tener c. de pocos amigos** to have an unfriendly face; *Esp Fam* ***c. de póquer:*** **tener/poner c. de póquer** to have/pull a poker face; ***c. de tonto:*** **tener/poner c. de tonto** to have/pull a stupid face; *Fam* ***c. de viernes:*** **tener c. de viernes** to have a long face; *Fam* ***c. de vinagre:*** **tener c. de vinagre** to have a sour face

(**c**) *(persona)* face; **acudieron muchas caras famosas** a lot of famous faces were there; **veo muchas caras nuevas** I see a lot of new faces here

(**d**) *(lado)* side; **c. A** *(de disco)* A side

(**e**) *Geom* face

(**f**) *(parte frontal)* front

(**g**) *(de moneda)* heads; *Fig* **la otra c. de la moneda** the other side of the coin; **c. o cruz** *o Andes, Ven* **sello** *o RP* **ceca** heads or tails; **echar algo a c. o cruz** to toss (a coin) for sth, *US* to flip a coin for sth; **si sale c., elijo yo** if it's heads, I get to choose

(**h**) *(indicando posición)* **c. a** facing; **quiero un apartamento c. al mar** I want an apartment that looks out on to the sea; **c. al futuro** with regard to the future, in future; **c. arriba/abajo** face up/down; *Esp* **de c.** *(sol, viento)* in one's face; **los ciclistas tenían el viento de c.** the cyclists were riding into the wind

(**i**) **de c. a** *(indicando objetivo)* with a view to; **de c. a mejorar** with a view to improving

(**j**) EXPR **se le cayó la c. de vergüenza** she blushed with shame; **¡no sé cómo no se te cae la c. de vergüenza al hablar así a tu madre!** you should be ashamed of yourself, talking to your mother like that!; **dar c. a algo** to face *o* confront sth; **dar la c.** *(responsabilizarse)* to face up to the consequences; **siempre que quiere mandar un mensaje me manda a mí, en vez de dar la c. él** whenever he has a message to deliver, he always sends me instead of doing it himself; **ya estoy harto de ser yo el que siempre dé la c.** I'm fed up of always being the one who takes the flak; **dar la c. por alguien** *(disculpar)* to make excuses for sb; *(defender)* to stick up for sb; *RP* **dar vuelta la c. a alguien** to look away from sb; *Fam* **decir algo a alguien** *Esp* **a la c.** *o Am* **en la c.** to say sth to sb's face; **si tiene algo que decir, que me lo diga** *Esp* **a la c.** *o Am* **en la c.** if she has something to say to me, she can say it to my face; *Fam* **echar algo en c. a alguien** to reproach sb for sth; *Esp Fam* **es lo más grosero/estúpido que me he echado a la c.** he's the rudest/most stupid person I've ever met; *Fam* **hacer c. a** to stand up to; **lavar la c. a algo** to make cosmetic changes to sth; **mirar a alguien a la c.** to look sb in the face; *Fam* **partir la c. a alguien** to smash sb's face in; *Esp* **plantar c. a alguien** to confront sb; *Andes, RP* **poner la c.** *(responsabilizarse)* to face up to the consequences; *Esp Fam* **por la c.: entrar por la c.** *(sin pagar)* to get in without paying; *(sin ser invitado)* to gatecrash; *Fam* **por su c. bonita, por su linda c.: le dieron el trabajo por su c. bonita** *o* **por su linda c.** she got the job because her face fitted; **reírse de alguien en su c.** to laugh in sb's face; **en mi c. no se me ríe nadie** nobody laughs at me to my face; *Fam* **romper la c. a alguien** to smash sb's face in; **sacar la c. por alguien** to stick up for sb; **saltar a la c.** to be blindingly obvious; **tener dos caras** to be two-faced; **verse las caras** *(pelearse)* to have it out; *(enfrentarse)* to fight it out; *Andes* **voltear la c. a alguien** to look away from sb

---

CARA[2] *Fam* 1 *nf (desvergüenza)* cheek, nerve; **tener la c. de hacer algo** to have the nerve to do sth; **tener mucha c., tener la c. muy dura** to have a lot of cheek *o* nerve, *Br* to have a real brass neck; **¡qué c. más dura!** what a cheek *o* nerve!; **¡qué c., ahora me echa las culpas a mí!** the cheek of it! now he's trying to put the blame on me!; **¡hay que tener c. para decir eso!** what a cheek *o* nerve to say a thing like that!; EXPR *Esp* **tener más c. que espalda** to have a cheek *o* nerve

2 *nmf Fam* **ser un(a) c. (dura)** to have a lot of cheek *o* nerve, *Br* to have a real brass neck

---

carabao *nm* water buffalo

carabela *nf* caravel

carabina *nf* (**a**) *(arma)* carbine, rifle (**b**) *Fam (acompañante)* chaperone; **ir de c.** *Br* to play gooseberry, *US* to be like a fifth wheel

carabinero *nm* (**a**) *(en España)* customs policeman (**b**) *(en Italia)* carabiniere (**c**) *(marisco)* scarlet shrimp, = type of large red prawn (**d**) *Chile (policía)* military policeman

cárabo *nm (búho)* tawny owl

caracará *nm* caracara

Caracas *n* Caracas

caracha *nf*, **carache** *nm Andes* scab

caracol 1 *nm* (**a**) *(animal)* snail (**b**) *(concha)* shell (**c**) *(del oído)* cochlea (**d**) *(rizo)* curl

2 *interj* **¡caracoles!** good grief!

caracola *nf* (**a**) *(animal)* conch (**b**) *(concha)* conch (**c**) *(bollo)* = spiral-shaped bun

caracolada *nf* = stew made with snails

caracolear *vi (caballo)* to prance about

caracolillo 1 *nm* (**a**) *(planta)* Australian pea (**b**) *(café)* pea-bean coffee (**c**) *(caoba)* veined mahogany (**d**) *(en la cara)* kiss curl

2 *nm Teatro* make-up assistant

caracolitos *nmpl RP (pasta)* shell-shaped noodles

carácter (*pl* **caracteres**) *nm* (**a**) *(personalidad, modo de ser)* character; **tener buen c.** to be good-natured; **tener mal c.** to be bad-tempered

(**b**) *(genio)* character, personality; **una mujer de c.** a woman of character; **tener mucho c.** to have a strong personality; **tener poco c.** not to have much personality

(**c**) *(índole, naturaleza)* character; **una reunión de c. privado/oficial** a private/an official meeting; **un artículo de c. satírico** a satirical article; **el c. accidentado del terreno** the ruggedness of the terrain; **solicitaron ayuda con c. de urgencia** they requested urgent assistance

(**d**) *(de imprenta)* character; **escriba en caracteres de imprenta** *(en impreso)* please print ▸▸ ***caracteres alfanuméricos*** alphanumeric characters

(**e**) *Biol* ***c. adquirido*** acquired characteristic; ***c. dominante*** dominant character; ***c. heredado*** inherited characteristic; ***c. ligado al sexo*** sex-linked characteristic; ***c. recesivo*** recessive characteristic

caracteriología = **caracterología**

caracteriológico = **caracterológico**

característica *nf* (**a**) *(rasgo)* characteristic, feature (**b**) *Mat* characteristic (**c**) *Am (prefijo)* area code

característico, -a *adj* characteristic; **este gesto es c. de ella** this gesture is typical *o* characteristic of her

caracterización *nf* (**a**) *(descripción)* description (**b**) *(de personaje)* characterization (**c**) *(maquillaje)* make-up

caracterizador, -ora *nm,f* make-up artist

caracterizar [14] 1 *vt* (**a**) *(definir)* to characterize; **un rasgo que caracteriza a la especie** a trait which characterizes the species; **con la amabilidad que lo caracteriza** with the kindness so typical of him (**b**) *(representar)* to portray; **c. a alguien** to portray sb (**c**) *(maquillar)* to make up

2 **caracterizarse** *vpr* to be characterized (**por** by); **se caracteriza por su bajo consumo de energía** it is notable for its low energy consumption; **una economía que se caracteriza por su alta inflación** an economy characterized by high inflation; **unas declaraciones que se caracterizan por su ambigüedad** statements of an ambiguous nature

caracterología, caracteriología *nf* psychological study of character

caracterológico, -a, caracteriológico, -a *adj* **estudio c.** psychological profile

caracú (*pl* **caracús** *o* **caracúes**) *nm Andes, RP* bone marrow

caracul *nm* karakul

caraculo *nm muy Fam Br* pillock, *US* butthead

caradura *Fam* 1 *adj* **ser muy c.** to have a lot of cheek *o* nerve, *Br* to have a real brass neck

2 *nmf* **ser un(a) c.** to have a lot of cheek *o* nerve, *Br* to have a real brass neck

caradurez *nf RP Fam* cheek

caradurismo *nm Fam* cheek

carajada *nf* (**a**) *Méx Fam (gran cantidad)* **una c. de** masses *o US* scads of (**b**) *Col Fam (tontería)* **¡no digas carajadas!** don't talk nonsense!; **siempre compra carajadas** she's always buying junk

carajal *nm Fam* (**a**) *Am (caos)* madhouse; **esta oficina es un c.** this office is a madhouse (**b**) *Méx (gran cantidad)* load, heap; **me dijo un c. de mentiras** he told me a pack of lies

carajillo *nm* = small black coffee with a dash of spirits

carajito, -a *nm,f CAm, Col, Ven Fam (niño)* kid

carajo 1 *nm* (**a**) *Vulg (pene)* prick, cock

(**b**) *Ven Vulg Pey (persona) Br* arsehole, *US* asshole

(**c**) *muy Fam* EXPR **¡al c. con el examen!** to hell with the exam!, *Br* bugger the exam!; **mandar a alguien al c.** to tell sb to go to hell; **mandó todo al c.** he chucked everything; **me importa un c.** I couldn't give a shit; **irse al c.** *(plan, proyecto)* to go down the tubes; **¡qué c.!** damn it!, hell!; **¡tengo un frío/hambre del c.!** I'm *Br* bloody *o US* goddamn freezing/starving!; **no vale un c.** it isn't worth a damn; **¡vete al c.!** go to hell!

2 *interj muy Fam* damn it!; **¡c., qué frío hace!** it's *Br* bloody *o US* goddamn freezing!

caramba *interj* **¡(qué) c.!** *(sorpresa)* good heavens!, *Br* blimey!, *US* jeez!; *(enfado)* for heaven's sake!; **¡c. con la que no sabía nada!** so she's the one who didn't know anything, eh?; **¡c. qué listo es tu hijo!** gee but your son's smart!

carámbano *nm* icicle; EXPR *Fam* **estar hecho un c.** to be frozen stiff

carambola 1 *nf* **(a)** *(en billar)* cannon **(b)** *Fam (casualidad)* **de** *o* **por c.** by a (lucky) fluke **(c)** *(fruto)* star fruit, carambola
2 *interj* good heavens!

carambolo *nm (árbol)* carambola

caramelizar [14] *vt (bañar)* to cover with caramel

caramelo *nm* **(a)** *(golosina) Br* (boiled) sweet, *US* candy; **un c. de limón** a lemon drop; **un c. de menta** a mint ►► ***c. para la tos*** cough sweet *o* drop **(b)** *(azúcar fundido)* caramel; **calentarlo a punto de c.** heat it until it is about to caramelize; EXPR **estar a punto de c.: creo que lo voy a convencer, está a punto de c.** I'll think I'll manage to convince him, he's on the point of agreeing; **su nuevo álbum está a punto de c.** his new album is about to hit the shops ►► ***c. hilado*** spun sugar **(c)** *(algo apetitoso)* plum

caramillo *nm* shepherd's flute

carancho *nm* **(a)** *(halcón)* caracara ►► ***c. moñudo*** crested caracara **(b)** *Perú (búho)* owl

carantoñas *nfpl* EXPR **hacer c. a alguien** to butter sb up

caraota *nf Ven* bean

carapacho *nm* carapace

carapálida *Am Fam Hum* **1** *adj* paleface
2 *nmf* paleface

carapulcra *nf Perú* = chicken and pork stew in a potato and ground peanut sauce

caraqueño, -a 1 *adj* of/from Caracas *(Venezuela)*
2 *nm,f* person from Caracas *(Venezuela)*

carátula *nf* **(a)** *(de libro)* front cover; *(de disco)* sleeve; *(de vídeo, CD)* cover **(b)** *(máscara)* mask **(c)** *Méx (de reloj)* dial, face **(d)** *Am (portada)* front page

caratular *vt RP* to put a cover on

caraú *nm* limpkin

caravana *nf* **(a)** *(remolque) Br* caravan, *US* trailer **(b)** *(de camellos)* caravan; *(de carromatos)* wagon train; **la c. presidencial** the presidential motorcade; **una c. humanitaria** an aid convoy **(c)** *(atasco) Br* tailback, *US* backup; **había mucha c.** there was a huge *Br* tailback *o US* backup **(d)** *Urug (aro, pendiente)* earring

caravaning [kara'βanin] *(pl* **caravanings***) nm* caravanning; **hacer c.** to go caravanning

caray *interj* **¡(qué) c.!** *(sorpresa)* good heavens!, *Br* blimey!, *US* jeez!; *(enfado)* damn it!; **¡c. con la que no sabía nada!** so she's the one who didn't know anything, eh?; **¡c. qué listo es tu hijo!** gee but your son's smart!

carbohidrato *nm* carbohydrate

carbón *nm* **(a)** *(para quemar)* coal; EXPR **negro como el c.** *(negro)* black as coal; *(bronceado)* brown as a berry ►► ***c. animal*** animal charcoal; ***c. de leña*** charcoal; ***c. mineral*** coal; ***c. de piedra*** coal; ***c. vegetal*** charcoal **(b)** *(para dibujar)* charcoal

carbonada *nf* = barbecued *Br* mince *o US* mincemeat patties

carbonara *nf* carbonara

carbonatado, -a *adj* carbonated

carbonato *nm Quím* carbonate ►► ***c. cálcico*** calcium carbonate

carboncillo *nm* charcoal; **un dibujo al c.** a charcoal drawing

carbonera *nf* **(a)** *(lugar)* coal bunker **(b)** *ver también* **carbonero**

carbonería *nf* coal merchant's

carbonero, -a 1 *adj* coal; **industria carbonera** coal industry
2 *nm,f (comerciante)* coal merchant ►► *Fig* ***la fe del c.*** blind faith
3 *nm* **(a)** *(ave)* great tit ►► ***c. capirotado*** black-capped chickadee; ***c. garrapinos*** coal tit; ***c. palustre*** marsh tit; ***c. sibilino*** willow tit **(b)** *(pez)* coley, coalfish

carbónico, -a *adj* **(a)** *Quím* carbonic **(b)** *(bebida)* carbonated

carbonífero, -a 1 *adj* **(a)** *(que contiene carbón)* coal-bearing; **una cuenca carbonífera** a coalfield **(b)** *Geol* carboniferous
2 *nm Geol* **el c.** the Carboniferous (period)

carbonilla *nf* **(a)** *(ceniza)* cinder **(b)** *RP (carboncillo)* charcoal

carbonización *nf* carbonization

carbonizado, -a *adj (cuerpo)* charred; *(mueble)* burnt; *(edificio)* burnt-out

carbonizar [14] **1** *vt* to char, to carbonize; **morir carbonizado** to burn to death
2 carbonizarse *vpr (cuerpo)* to be charred *o* burnt; *(muebles)* to be reduced to ashes; *(edificio)* to be burnt-out

carbono *nm Quím* carbon ►► ***c. 14*** carbon 14

carbonoso, -a *adj* carbonaceous

carborundo *nm Quím* carborundum®

carbunco, carbunclo *nm* **(a)** *Geol* carbuncle **(b)** *Med* anthrax

carbúnculo *nm* carbuncle

carburación *nf* carburation

carburador *nm* carburettor

carburante *nm* fuel

carburar 1 *vt* to carburate
2 *vi Fam* to work, to go; **esta moto ya no carbura** this motorbike doesn't work *o* go any more; **mi abuelo ya no carbura** my grandad isn't all there any more

carburo *nm* carbide

carca 1 *adj Fam Pey* old-fashioned
2 *nmf* **(a)** *Fam Pey (persona)* old fogey **(b)** *Andes Fam (suciedad)* filth, muck

carcacha, carcancha *nf* **(a)** *Andes, Méx Fam (auto viejo)* old banger **(b)** EXPR *Perú Fam* **estar hecho una c.** to be a bag of bones

carcaj *(pl* **carcajes***) nm* quiver

carcajada *nf* guffaw; **reír a carcajadas** to roar with laughter, to laugh uproariously; **soltar una c.** to burst out laughing

carcajearse *vpr* **(a)** *(reírse)* to roar with laughter **(b)** *(burlarse)* to make fun **(de** of)

carcajeo *nm* roars of laughter

carcamal, *Méx, RP* **carcamán** *Fam Pey* **1** *adj* decrepit; **un viejo c.** a decrepit old man
2 *nmf* old crock

carcancha = **carcacha**

carcasa *nf (armazón, estructura)* framework; *(de moto)* frame; *(de ordenador)* case; *(de máquina)* casing

cárcava *nf* **(a)** *(zanja)* gully **(b)** *(foso)* pit

cárcel *nf* **(a)** *(prisión)* prison, jail; **meter a alguien en la c.** to put sb in prison; **lo metieron en la c.** he was put in prison ►► ***c. de alta seguridad*** *Br* top security prison, *US* maximum security prison *o* jail; ***c. de régimen abierto*** open prison **(b)** *(herramienta)* clamp

carcelario, -a *adj* prison; **la vida carcelaria** prison life; **régimen c.** prison conditions

carcelero, -a *nm,f* warder, jailer

carcinógeno, -a 1 *adj* carcinogenic
2 *nm* carcinogen

carcinoma *nm Med* carcinoma, cancerous tumour

carcocha *nf Perú Fam Pey* old banger

carcoma *nf* **(a)** *(insecto)* woodworm **(b)** *(polvo)* wood dust **(c)** *(preocupación)* anxiety, grief

carcomer 1 *vt* **(a)** *(madera)* to eat away at **(b)** *(persona)* to eat away at; **la enfermedad está carcomiendo su salud** the sickness is eating away at his health; **le carcome la envidia** he's eaten up with envy; **me carcome una duda** there's a doubt niggling away at me
2 carcomerse *vpr* to be eaten up *o* consumed **(de** with)

carcomido, -a *adj (madera)* worm-eaten

carda *nf* **(a)** *(acción)* carding **(b)** *(instrumento)* card

cardado, -a 1 *adj* **(a)** *(lana)* carded **(b)** *(pelo)* backcombed
2 *nm* **(a)** *(de lana)* carding **(b)** *(del pelo)* backcombing

cardador, -ora *nm,f* carder

cardamomo *nm* cardamom

cardán *nm Tec* cardan joint, universal joint

cardar *vt* **(a)** *(lana)* to card **(b)** *(pelo)* to backcomb

cardenal[1] *nm* **(a)** *Rel* cardinal **(b)** *(pájaro)* cardinal ►► ***c. de Virginia*** Northern cardinal **(c)** *Chile (planta)* geranium

cardenal[2] *nm (hematoma)* bruise

cardenalato *nm* rank of cardinal, cardinalate

cardenalicio, -a *adj* **colegio c.** college of cardinals *(group)*; **manto c.** cardinal's robe

cardenillo *nm* verdigris

cárdeno, -a *adj* purple

cardiaco, -a, cardíaco, -a 1 *adj* cardiac; **parada cardiaca, paro c.** cardiac arrest; **insuficiencia cardiaca** heart failure; *Fam* **está c.** *(está muy nervioso)* he's a bag of nerves
2 *nm,f* person with a heart condition; *Fam* **un final de partido no apto para cardiacos** a heart-stopping finale to the match

cardias *nm inv Anat* cardia

cárdigan *nm* cardigan

cardillo *nm* golden thistle

cardinal 1 *adj* (a) *(principal)* cardinal; **consideramos de c. importancia que asista a la reunión** we think it is of cardinal importance that she attends the meeting (b) *(número)* cardinal (c) *(punto)* cardinal
2 *nm (número)* cardinal number

cardiocirujano, -a *nm,f* heart surgeon

cardiogénico, -a *adj* cardiogenic

cardiografía *nf* cardiography

cardiógrafo *nm* cardiograph

cardiograma *nm* cardiogram

cardiología *nf* cardiology

cardiólogo, -a *nm,f* cardiologist

cardiomegalia *nf Med* cardiomegaly

cardiópata 1 *adj* **ser c.** to have a heart condition
2 *nmf* person with a heart condition

cardiopatía *nf* heart condition; **padece una c.** he suffers from *o* has a heart condition

cardiopulmonar *adj* cardiopulmonary

cardiorrespiratorio, -a *adj* cardiopulmonary

cardiovascular *adj* cardiovascular

carditis *nf inv Med* carditis

cardo *nm* (a) *(planta)* thistle ►► ***c. borriquero*** cotton thistle (b) *Esp Fam (persona fea)* **c. (borriquero)** ugly mug, face-ache; **es un c. borriquero** he's as ugly as sin, *Br* he has a face like the back end of a bus (c) *Esp Fam (persona arisca)* **c. (borriquero)** prickly customer

cardón *nm* (a) *Arg (cacto)* = type of giant cactus (b) *CRica, Méx, Perú (pita)* = type of agave cactus

cardume, cardumen *nm* (a) *(de peces)* school, shoal (b) *Andes, RP, Ven (abundancia) (de gente, insectos)* swarm

carear *vt (testigos, acusados)* to bring face to face; **el juez careó a los dos testigos** the judge confronted the two witnesses with each other

carecer [46] *vi* **c. de algo** to lack sth; **una casa que carece de agua corriente** a house with no running water; **unas declaraciones que carecen de interés** statements of no interest

carel *nm Náut* edge

carenado *nm*, **carena** *nf* (a) *(de moto)* fairing (b) *Náut (reparación)* **el c. de un barco** the repairing of the hull of a ship

carenar *vt Náut* to repair the hull of

carencia *nf* (a) *(ausencia)* lack; *(defecto)* deficiency; **sufrir carencias afectivas** to be deprived of love and affection; **sufrir muchas carencias** to suffer great need (b) *(en la dieta)* deficiency ►► ***c. vitamínica*** vitamin deficiency

carenciado, -a *Am* 1 *adj* deprived
2 *nm,f* deprived person

carente *adj* **c. de** lacking (in); **c. de lógica** lacking in logic, illogical; **c. de sentido** nonsensical; **un libro c. de interés** a book devoid of interest

careo *nm (de testigos, acusados)* confrontation; **someter a un c.** to bring face to face

carero, -a *Fam* 1 *adj* pricey
2 *nm,f (tendero)* = shopkeeper who charges high prices; **el pescadero es un c.** the fishmonger is pretty pricey

carestía *nf* (a) *(alto precio)* high cost *o* price; **la c. de la vida** the high cost of living (b) *(escasez)* shortage

careta *nf* (a) *(para cubrir)* mask ►► ***c. antigás*** gas mask (b) *(fachada)* front; **quitarle a alguien la c.** to unmask sb

careto *nm Esp Fam* **¡qué c. tienes! ¿no has dormido?** you look terrible! weren't you able to sleep last night?; **no pongas ese c.** don't pull a face like that

carey *nm* (a) *(material)* tortoiseshell (b) *(tortuga)* sea turtle (c) *Cuba (planta)* rough-leaved liana

carezco *etc ver* **carecer**

carga *nf* (a) *(acción)* loading; **zona de c. y descarga** loading and unloading area
(b) *(cargamento) (de avión, barco)* cargo; *(de tren)* freight; **la c. va en la bodega** the cargo goes in the hold
(c) *(peso)* load; **no sé si esta viga aguantará tanta c.** I don't know if this beam will be able to take such a heavy load ►► ***c. máxima autorizada*** maximum authorized load; ***c. útil*** *(de vehículo)* payload
(d) *(responsabilidad)* burden; **representa una enorme c. para sus hijos** she is a great burden on her children; **llevar la c. de algo** to be responsible for sth; **una persona con cargas familiares** a person with family responsibilities
(e) *(ataque)* charge; **¡a la c.!** charge!; **volver a la c.** *(atacar de nuevo)* to go back on the offensive; *(insistir)* to insist ►► ***c. policial*** baton charge
(f) *(explosivo)* charge ►► ***c. explosiva*** explosive charge; ***c. de profundidad*** depth charge
(g) *(de mechero, pluma)* refill
(h) *(de obra, declaraciones)* **un poema con una fuerte c. erótica** a highly erotic poem; **una estatua con una c. simbólica** a statue that is very symbolic; **una película con gran c. emocional** a movie that has a real emotional punch
(i) *(impuesto)* tax ►► ***cargas administrativas*** administrative costs; ***c. financiera*** financial cost; ***c. fiscal*** *(impuesto)* tax; *(presión fiscal)* tax burden; ***c. impositiva*** *(impuesto)* tax; *(presión fiscal)* tax burden; ***cargas sociales*** social security contributions; ***c. tributaria*** levy
(j) *(eléctrica) (de partícula)* charge; *(de circuito)* load
(k) *(en fútbol)* push *(with one's body)*; *(en rugby, hockey)* shoulder charge ►► ***c. reglamentaria*** bodycheck; **hacer una c. reglamentaria a alguien** to bodycheck sb (l) EXPR *RP Fam* **llevar la c. a alguien** *Br* to chat sb up, *US* to hit on sb

cargada *nf RP Fam (broma)* practical joke

cargadero *nm (para carga)* loading bay

cargado, -a *adj* (a) *(lleno)* loaded (**de** with); **estar c. de deudas** to be weighed down with debt; **un calendario muy c.** a heavy schedule; **una madre cargada de preocupaciones** a mother burdened with worries
(b) *(arma)* loaded
(c) *(bebida)* strong
(d) *(eléctricamente)* charged
(e) *(bochornoso) (ambiente, atmósfera)* oppressive; *(habitación)* stuffy; *(tiempo)* sultry, close; *(cielo)* overcast
(f) *(tenso) (ambiente, atmósfera)* tense; **una reunión cargada de tensión** an extremely tense meeting
(g) *Fam (borracho)* **está** *o* **va c.** he's had a few too many

cargador, -ora 1 *nm,f (persona)* loader ►► ***c. de muelle*** docker, stevedore
2 *nm* (a) *(de arma de fuego)* magazine; **el asaltante vació el c. contra su víctima** the attacker emptied his gun into his victim (b) *(de pilas, baterías)* charger (c) *Col (tirantes) Br* braces, *US* suspenders

cargamento *nm* (a) *(de buque)* cargo; *(de camión)* load; **un c. de drogas** a shipment of drugs (b) *Fam* **un c. de** *(muchos)* a load of, loads of

cargante *adj Fam* annoying

CARGAR [38] 1 *vt* (a) *(vehículo)* to load; **c. algo de** to load sth with; **c. algo en un barco/camión** to load sth onto a ship/lorry; **cargaron la furgoneta con cajas** they loaded the van up with boxes; **c. algo demasiado** to overload sth
(b) *(arma, cámara)* to load; *(pluma, mechero)* to refill; *RP (tanque)* to fill (up); **ha cargado el guiso de sal** he's put too much salt in the stew, he's overdone the salt in the stew; EXPR **c. las tintas** to exaggerate, to lay it on thick
(c) *(peso encima)* to throw over one's shoulder; **cargué la caja a hombros** I carried the box on my shoulder
(d) *Elec* to charge
(e) *Esp Fam (molestar)* to bug; **me carga su pedantería** his pretentiousness really gets on my nerves; **me carga tener que aguantarlo** it bugs the hell out of me that I have to put up with him
(f) *(adeudar) (importe, factura, deuda)* to charge (**a** to); **c. un impuesto a algo/alguien** to tax sth/sb; **c. algo a alguien en su cuenta** to charge sth to sb's account; **no me han cargado todavía el recibo de la luz** the payment for the electricity bill still hasn't gone through; **c. de más** to overcharge; **c. de menos** to undercharge
(g) *(responsabilidad, tarea)* to give; **siempre lo cargan de trabajo** they always give him far too much work to do; **le cargaron la culpa a ella** they laid *o* put the blame on her
(h) *(producir pesadez) (sujeto: olor)* to make stuffy; *(sujeto: comida)* to bloat; **el humo ha cargado la habitación** the atmosphere in the room is thick with smoke
(i) *Informát* to load
(j) *Náut (velas)* to furl, to take in
(k) *Méx Fam (matar)* to bump off, *US* to ice
(l) *RP Fam (bromear)* **José se casó – ¡me estás cargando!** José got

married – you're having me on *o* you're kidding!

(**m**) *RP Fam (intentar seducir)* **c. a alguien** to come on to sb, *Br* to try to get off with sb, *US* to hit on sb

(**n**) *Ven Fam (llevar encima)* to carry, to tote; *(llevar puesto)* to wear, to have on; **c. una pistola** to carry a gun; **c. anteojos** to wear specs; **c. un niño** *(en brazos)* to carry a child; *(de la mano)* to lead a child by the hand; **no cargo carro hoy** I haven't got my wheels today; **aún cargo aquella imagen conmigo** I can still picture the scene; **carga siempre una cara triste** he always has a sad face on him; **carga una gran pena** he's sick at heart; **carga dolor de espalda** she has a bad back; **cargamos fama de deshonestos** we have a name for being dishonest

(**o**) *Chile, Perú (atacar)* to attack

2 *vi* (**a**) **c. con** *(paquete, bulto)* to carry; **cargué con todos los paquetes** I carried all the packages

(**b**) **c. con** *(coste, responsabilidad)* to bear; *(consecuencias)* to accept; *(culpa)* to get; **hoy me toca a mí c. con los niños** it's my turn to look after the children today

(**c**) *(atacar)* to charge; **la policía cargó contra los alborotadores** the police charged (at) the rioters; **el pelotón cargó sobre la posición enemiga** the platoon charged the enemy position

(**d**) *(toro)* to charge

(**e**) *(recaer)* **c. sobre alguien** to fall on sb

(**f**) *(acento)* **c. sobre** to fall on

(**g**) *Dep* **c. contra alguien** to brush sb aside, to push sb *(with one's body)*

(**h**) *Arquit* **c. en** *o* **sobre** to lean *o* rest on; **la bóveda carga sobre cuatro pilares** the vault is supported by four pillars

(**i**) *(tormenta)* to turn, to veer

(**j**) *Elec* to charge; **esta batería ya no carga** this battery won't charge any more

(**k**) *RP Fam (bromear)* **se murió el gato – ¡estás cargando!** the cat died – you're kidding *o* joking!

(**l**) *RP Fam (intentar seducir)* **se pasó la noche cargando** he spent the night *Br* trying to get off with someone *o US* hitting on people

3 cargarse *vpr* (**a**) *Fam (romper)* to break; **se cargó el jarrón** she broke the vase; **se cargó la empresa** he ruined the company; **con ese horrible edificio se han cargado el paisaje** they've ruined *o* spoilt the landscape with that horrible building

(**b**) *Fam (suspender)* to fail; **el profesor se cargó a la mitad de la clase** the teacher failed half the class

(**c**) *Fam (matar) (persona)* to bump off; *(animal)* to kill

(**d**) *Fam (eliminar, prescindir de)* to get rid of; **se han cargado a nuestro representante** they've got rid of our representative

(**e**) *(por olor)* to get stuffy; *(por humo)* to get smoky

(**f**) *(colmarse)* **cargarse de** to be loaded down with; **cargarse de deudas** to get up to one's neck in debt; **se cargó de hijos** she had a lot of children; **los ojos se le cargaban de lágrimas** his eyes filled with tears; **se cargó de responsabilidades** she took on a lot of responsibilities

(**g**) *Esp Fam* **¡te la vas a c.!** you're in for it!; **si no me lo devuelves, te la vas a c.** if you don't give it back to me, there'll be trouble

(**h**) *(parte del cuerpo)* **se me han cargado las piernas** my legs are tired; **se me ha cargado la cabeza con tanto ruido** my head's throbbing from all this noise

(**i**) *Elec* to charge; **aún no se ha cargado la batería** the battery still hasn't charged

(**j**) *Meteo* to cloud over; **el cielo se cargó desde primeras horas de la mañana** the sky *o* it clouded over very early in the morning

(**k**) *Méx Fam (matar)* to rub out, to do in

(**l**) *RP Fam (intentar seducir)* **Pedro se (la) carga a María** *Br* Pedro is trying to get off with Maria, *US* Pedro is hitting on Maria

---

cargazón *nf (malestar físico)* heaviness

CARGO *nm* (**a**) *(empleo)* post, position; **ocupa** *o* **es un c. muy importante** she holds a very important position *o* post; **desempeña un c. de ministro** he is a minister; **tomar posesión del c.** to take up office ►► ***c. directivo*** manager; ***c. público:*** **ostenta** *o* **es un c. público** she holds public office; **varios cargos públicos se han visto involucrados en el escándalo** several people holding public office have been implicated in the scandal

(**b**) *(cuidado)* charge; **los niños han quedado a mi c.** the children have been left in my care; **una producción a c. del Teatro Nacional** a National Theatre production; **está a c. de la seguridad de la empresa, tiene a su c. la seguridad de la empresa** he is in charge of *o* responsible for company security; **hacerse c. de** *(asumir el control de)* to take charge of; *(ocuparse de)* to take care of; *(comprender)* to understand; **se hizo c. de la gestión de la empresa** she took over the running of the company; **el ejército se hizo c. del poder** the army took power *o* over; **no te preocupes, yo me hago c. de los niños** don't worry, I'll look after the children; **me hago c. de la difícil situación** I am aware of *o* I realize the difficulty of the situation; **tenemos que ir al entierro y llegaremos tarde – sí, me hago c.** we have to go to the funeral, so we'll be late – OK, I understand

(**c**) *Econ* charge; **con c. a** charged to; **han asignado una nueva partida con c. a los presupuestos del estado** they have created a new budget heading; **correr a c. de** to be borne by; **todos los gastos corren a c. de la empresa** all expenses will be borne by the company; **la comida corre a c. de la empresa** the meal is on the company; **la organización corre a c. del Municipio** the organization will be carried out by the town council, the town council will be organizing the event; **sin c. adicional** for *o* at no extra charge

(**d**) *(acusación)* charge; **formular graves cargos contra alguien** to bring serious charges against sb; **se declaró inocente de todos los cargos que se le imputaban** he said he was innocent on all counts ►► ***c. de conciencia:*** **tener c. de conciencia** to feel pangs of conscience, to feel remorse; **me da c. de conciencia dejarle pagar** I feel bad about letting him pay; **comprar productos de este país me representa un c. de conciencia** I feel guilty about buying this country's products

(**e**) *(buque de carga)* cargo ship, freighter

---

cargosear *vt CSur* to annoy, to pester

cargoso, -a *adj CSur* annoying

carguero *nm* (**a**) *(barco)* cargo ship, freighter (**b**) *RP (animal)* beast of burden

cariacontecido, -a *adj* crestfallen

cariado, -a *adj (diente, muela)* decayed

cariar *vt* **1** to cause decay in; **el azúcar caria las muelas** sugar causes tooth decay

2 cariarse *vpr* to decay; **las muelas se carian si no se cepillan** your back teeth decay if you don't brush them

cariátide *nf* caryatid

caribe 1 *adj (pueblo)* Carib

2 *nmf (persona)* Carib

3 *nm* (**a**) **el (mar) C.** the Caribbean (Sea) (**b**) **el C.** *(región)* the Caribbean (**c**) *(lengua)* Carib

caribeño, -a 1 *adj* Caribbean

2 *nm,f* person from the Caribbean

caribú (*pl* **caribús** *o* **caribúes**) *nm* caribou

caricato *nm* (**a**) *(actor)* comedian (**b**) *Am (caricatura)* caricature

caricatura *nf* (**a**) *(de personaje)* caricature (**b**) *(imitación burda)* caricature; **su análisis de la situación es una c. de la realidad** her analysis of the situation is a caricature of the facts (**c**) *Méx (dibujos animados)* cartoon

caricaturesco, -a *adj* (**a**) *(ilustración)* **un retrato c.** a caricature portrait (**b**) *(ridículo)* **un retrato c. de la situación** a caricature of the situation; **un ejemplo c. de las desigualdades sociales del país** a grotesque example of the social inequalities in the country

caricaturista *nmf* caricaturist

caricaturización *nf* caricature

caricaturizar [14] *vt* to caricature

caricia *nf (a persona)* caress, stroke; *(a animal)* stroke; **hacer caricias/una c. a alguien** to caress sb

Caricom [kari'kom] *nm o nf* (*abrev de* **Comunidad (Económica) del Caribe**) Caricom

caridad *nf* charity; **¡una limosnita, por c.!** can you spare some change?; **le ayudó por c.** she helped him out of pity; **hacer obras de c.** to do charitable works; **vivir de la c.** to live on charity; EXPR **la c. bien entendida empieza** *Esp* **por uno mismo** *o Am* **por casa** charity begins at home

caries *nf inv* (**a**) *(proceso)* **c. (dental)** tooth decay, *Espec* (dental) caries; **el problema de la c.** the problem of tooth decay (**b**) *(infección)* cavity; **tengo tres c.** I have three cavities

carilanco *nm* white-lipped peccary

carilla *nf* (**a**) *(página)* page, side (**b**) *(de colmenero)* beekeeper's mask

carillo, -a *adj Fam* pricey

carillón *nm* (**a**) *(reloj)* grandfather clock (**b**) *(instrumento) (con tubos)* tubular bells; *(con planchas)* glockenspiel

cariñena *nm* = red wine from Cariñena, in the province of Zaragoza

cariño *nm* (**a**) *(afecto)* affection; **una demostración de c.** a display of affection; **habla con mucho c. de sus padres** she speaks very fondly of her parents; **se le recuerda con c.** he is remembered fondly *o* with affection; **tratar algo con c.** to treat sth with loving care; **tratar a alguien con c.** to be loving *o* affectionate to *o* towards sb; **tener c. a** to be fond of; **tomar c. a** to grow fond of; **tratar a alguien con c.** to be affectionate to *o* towards sb

(**b**) *(muestra de afecto)* sign of affection; **le hizo unos cariños a los niños** he kissed/cuddled the children

(**c**) *(cuidado)* loving care

(**d**) *(apelativo)* dear, love, *US* honey

(**e**) *CAm, Chile (regalo)* gift

(**f**) *RP* **cariños** *(en carta)* love

cariñosamente *adv* affectionately

cariñoso, -a *adj* affectionate, tender; **es muy c.** he's very affectionate; **ha estado muy c. conmigo últimamente** he's been very affectionate towards me recently; **un saludo muy c.** *(en carta)* love, with love

carioca 1 *adj* of/from Rio de Janeiro

2 *nmf* person from Rio de Janeiro

carisma *nm* charisma; **tener mucho c.** to have lots of charisma, to be very charismatic

carismático, -a *adj* charismatic

Cáritas *nf* = charitable organization run by the Catholic Church

caritativo, -a *adj* charitable

cariz *nm* look, appearance; **la ciudad tiene un marcado c. colonial** the city has a very colonial aspect; **nos preocupa el c. que pueda tomar el conflicto** we are concerned about how the conflict may develop; **tomar mal/buen c.** to take a turn for the worse/better

carlanca *nf* (**a**) *(para mastín)* spiked collar (**b**) *Chile, Hond (molestia, fastidio)* annoyance

carlinga *nf Av (para piloto)* cockpit; *(para pasajeros)* cabin

carlismo *nm Hist* Carlism, = support for the claim to the Spanish throne of Don Carlos de Borbón and his descendants after the death of his brother Fernando VII in 1833

carlista *Hist* 1 *adj* Carlist

2 *nmf* Carlist, = supporter of the claim to the Spanish throne of Don Carlos de Borbón and his heirs

Carlomagno *n pr* Charlemagne

Carlos *n pr* **C. I de España y V de Alemania** Charles V *(Holy Roman Emperor and King of Spain)*

carmelita 1 *adj* (**a**) *(religioso)* Carmelite (**b**) *Cuba (color)* brown

2 *nmf (religioso)* Carmelite

3 *nm Cuba (color)* brown

carmesí (*pl* **carmesíes**) 1 *adj* crimson

2 *nm* crimson

cármica® *nf Urug* ≃ Formica®

carmín 1 *adj (color)* carmine

2 *nm* (**a**) *(color)* carmine (**b**) *(lápiz de labios)* lipstick

carnada *nf también Fig* bait

carnal 1 *adj* (**a**) *(lujurioso)* carnal; **amor c.** physical love; **deseos carnales** desires of the flesh; **tener una relación c. con alguien** to have sexual relations with sb (**b**) *(parientes)* **primo c.** first cousin; **tío c.** uncle *(not by marriage)*

2 *nm Méx Fam (amigo)* friend, *Br* mate, *US* buddy

carnalidad *nf* carnality

carnalmente *adv* carnally

carnaval *nm* (**a**) *(fiesta)* carnival (**b**) *Rel* Shrovetide

carnavalada *nf Fam* farce

carnavalesco, -a *adj* carnival; **ambiente c.** carnival atmosphere

carnaza *nf también Fig* bait

carne *nf* (**a**) *(de persona)* flesh; **tenía el codo en c. viva** his elbow was raw; *Fig* **tengo la ofensa en c. viva** I'm still smarting from the insult ►► *Fig* ***c. de cañón*** cannon fodder; ***c. de gallina*** gooseflesh, goose pimples, goose bumps; **se me pone la c. de gallina al ver esas imágenes** it sends a shiver down my spine when I see those pictures

(**b**) *(de fruta)* flesh

(**c**) *(alimento)* meat ►► ***c. asada al horno*** roast (meat); ***c. asada a la parrilla*** *Br* grilled meat, *US* broiled meat; ***c. blanca*** white meat; ***c. de carnero*** mutton; ***c. de cerdo*** pork; *Andes* ***c. de chancho*** pork; ***c. de cordero*** lamb; *Ven Culin* ***c. desmechada*** shredded meat; *Culin* ***c. sin hueso*** boned meat; EXPR **ser c. sin hueso** to be a cushy job; ***c. magra*** lean meat; *Culin* ***c. mechada*** = joint of beef or pork stuffed and roasted; *Esp* ***c. de membrillo*** quince jelly; *Am* ***c. molida*** *Br* mince, *US* ground beef; *Esp, RP* ***c. picada*** *Br* mince, *US* ground beef; ***c. de porcino*** pork; *Méx* ***c. de puerco*** pork; *Méx* ***c. de res*** beef; ***c. roja*** red meat; ***c. de ternera*** veal; ***c. de vaca*** beef; ***c. de vacuno*** beef; ***c. de venado*** venison

(**d**) *(sensualidad)* flesh; **los placeres de la c.** the pleasures of the flesh

(**e**) EXPR **se me abren las carnes al ver esas imágenes/oír su llanto** it breaks my heart to see those pictures/hear her crying; *Fam* **¡córrete a un lado, que la c. de burro no es transparente!** move over, I can't see through you, you know!; **cobrar** *o* **criar** *o* **echar carnes** to put weight on; **echar** *o* **poner toda la c. en el asador** to go for broke; **en carnes** naked; **en c. y hueso** in person; **nos visitó el Presidente, en c. y hueso** the President himself visited us, the President visited us in person; **en c. propia: te entiendo perfectamente, he vivido tus sufrimientos en c. propia** I know exactly what you're talking about, I've suffered the same experiences as you myself; **entrado** *o* **metido en carnes** plump; **no ser ni c. ni pescado** to be neither fish nor fowl; **perder carnes** to lose weight; **ser de c. y hueso** to be human; **le temblaban las carnes** he was very frightened

carné (*pl* **carnés**), **carnet** (*pl* **carnets**) *nm* (**a**) *(documento)* card ►► ***c. de afiliado*** membership card; ***c. de alberguista*** youth hostel card; ***c. de biblioteca*** library card; *RP* ***c. de calificaciones*** *Br* (school) report, *US* report card; ***c. de conducir*** *Br* driving licence, *US* driver's license; *RP* ***c. de conductor*** *Br* driving licence, *US* driver's license; ***c. de donante*** donor card; ***c. de estudiante*** student card; ***c. de identidad*** identity card; ***c. joven*** young person's discount card; *Chile* ***c. de manejar*** *Br* driving licence, *US* driver's license; *RP* ***c. de notas*** *Br* (school) report, *US* report card; ***c. de socio*** membership card; *RP* ***c. de vacunación*** vaccination certificate

(**b**) *(agenda)* notebook

carneada *nf Andes, RP (acción)* slaughtering, butchering

carnear *vt* (**a**) *Andes, RP (sacrificar)* to slaughter, to butcher (**b**) *Chile (engañar)* to deceive, to take in

cárneo, -a *adj CSur* meat; **el sector c.** the meat industry

carnero, -a 1 *nm* (**a**) *(animal)* ram (**b**) *(carne)* mutton

2 *nm,f Andes, RP Fam Pey* (**a**) *(persona débil)* weak-willed person (**b**) *(esquirol)* scab, *Br* blackleg

carnestolendas *nfpl* carnival, = the week preceding the beginning of Lent, marked by public festivities in some cities and regions of Spain and Latin America

carnet = **carné**

carnicería *nf* (**a**) *(tienda)* butcher's (shop) (**b**) *(masacre)* massacre, bloodbath; **fue una c.** it was carnage

carnicero, -a 1 *adj (animal)* carnivorous

2 *nm,f* (**a**) *(que vende carne)* butcher (**b**) *(persona sanguinaria)* butcher

3 *nm (animal)* carnivore

cárnico, -a *adj* meat; **industrias cárnicas** meat industry; **productos cárnicos** meat products

carnitas *nfpl Méx* = small pieces of braised pork

carnívoro, -a 1 *adj* (**a**) *(animal)* carnivorous (**b**) *(planta)* carnivorous

2 *nm* carnivore

carnosidad *nf* fleshy part

carnoso, -a *adj (persona)* fleshy; *(parte)* fleshy, meaty; *(labios)* full

caro, -a 1 *adj* (**a**) *(costoso)* expensive; **ser muy c.** to be very expensive *o* dear; **la vida está muy cara** everything is so expensive (**b**) *Formal (querido)* cherished

2 *adv* **costar c.** to be expensive; **este televisor nos salió muy c.** this television cost us a lot; EXPR **pagar c. algo** to pay dearly for sth; EXPR **salir c.: un día te va a salir cara tu conducta** you'll pay dearly for this behaviour one day; EXPR **vender c. algo** not to give sth up easily; **vendieron cara su derrota** their enemy paid a high price for their victory

caroba *nf* jacaranda

Carolina *n* ***C. del Norte*** North Carolina; **C. del Sur** South Carolina

Carolinas *npl* **las C.** the Caroline Islands

carolingio, -a *Hist* 1 *adj* Carolingian

2 *nm,f* Carolingian

carón, -ona *adj Am Fam* big-faced

Caronte *n Mitol* Charon

carota *Esp Fam* 1 *adj* **ser muy c.** to have a lot of cheek *o* nerve, *Br* to have a real brass neck

2 *nmf* **ser un(a) c.** to have a lot of cheek *o* nerve, *Br* to have a real brass neck

caroteno *nm*, **carotina** *nf* carotene

carótida 1 *adj* carotid

2 *nf* carotid

carotina = **caroteno**

carozo *nm RP (de fruta, aceituna)* stone, *US* pit

carpa[1] *nf (pez)* carp

carpa[2] *nf* (**a**) *(de circo)* big top; *(en parque, la calle)* marquee (**b**) *Am (tienda de campaña)* tent ▸▸ ***c. de oxígeno*** oxygen tent

carpanta *nf Esp Fam* ravenous hunger; **tener una c.** to be ravenous *o* starving

Cárpatos *nmpl* **los C.** the Carpathians

carpe *nm* hornbeam

carpelo *nm Bot* carpel

carpeta *nf* (**a**) *(archivador)* file, folder ▸▸ ***c. de anillas*** ring binder (**b**) *(de disco)* sleeve (**c**) *Informát* folder ▸▸ ***c. del sistema*** system folder (**d**) *RP (blonda)* crochet mat (**e**) *Perú (pupitre)* desk

> **Falso amigo**: El sustantivo inglés **carpet** no es la traducción del español **carpeta**. En inglés **carpet** significa "alfombra".

carpetazo *nm* **dar c. a una discusión** to bring a discussion to an end; **dar c. a un proyecto** to shut down a project

carpetovetónico, -a *adj* deeply Spanish

carpiano, -a *adj Anat* carpal

carpincho *nm* capybara

carpintería *nf* (**a**) *(oficio) (de muebles y utensilios)* carpentry; *(de puertas y ventanas)* joinery ▸▸ *Am* ***c. de obra*** joinery (**b**) *(taller)* carpenter's/joiner's shop (**c**) *(marcos)* ***c. de aluminio*** aluminium window frames and doorframes; ***c. PVC*** PVC window frames and doorframes

carpintero, -a *nm,f (de muebles y utensilios)* carpenter; *(de puertas y ventanas)* joiner ▸▸ *Náut* ***c. de ribera*** shipwright

carpir *vt Am (tierra)* to hoe

carpo *nm Anat* carpus

carraca[1] *nf* (**a**) *(instrumento)* rattle (**b**) *(ave)* roller

carraca[2] *nf Fam (cosa vieja) (máquina)* crock; *(automóvil)* heap, banger

carrasca *nf* Evergreen oak

carrascal *nm* = hill covered in Evergreen oaks

carraspear *vi* to clear one's throat

carraspeo *nm* cough, clearing of one's throat

carraspera *nf* **tener c.** to have a frog in one's throat

carrasposo, -a *adj* (**a**) *(con carraspera)* hoarse (**b**) *Am (áspero)* rough

CARRERA *nf* (**a**) *(acción de correr)* **me acerqué a la tienda en una c.** I ran down to the shop; **tuve que dar una c. para atrapar el autobús** I had to run to catch the bus; **me di** *o* **pegué una c. y lo alcancé** I ran and managed to catch it; **a c. abierta** *o* **tendida** at full speed; **a la c.** *(corriendo)* running, at a run; *(rápidamente)* fast, quickly; *(alocadamente)* hastily; **ir a un sitio de una c.** to run somewhere; **tomar c.** to take a run-up

(**b**) *(competición)* race; **carreras** races, racing; **un caballo de carreras** a racehorse; **un coche de carreras** a racing car; **sólo quedan diez motos en c.** only ten motorbikes are left in the race; **echaron una c. hasta la puerta** they raced each other to the door; **¿echamos una c.?** shall we race each other?; **varias empresas han entrado en la c. por ganar el concurso** a number of firms have joined the race to win the competition ▸▸ ***c. armamentística*** arms race; ***c. de armamentos*** arms race; ***c. de caballos*** horse race; **me gustan las carreras de caballos** I like horseracing; ***c. ciclista*** cycle race; ***c. de coches*** motor race; ***c. contrarreloj*** *(en ciclismo)* time trial; *Fig* race against the clock; *RP* ***c. de embolsados*** sack race; *Méx* ***c. de encostalados*** sack race; ***la c. espacial*** the space race; ***c. por etapas*** *(en ciclismo)* stage race; ***c. de fondo*** long-distance race; ***c. de fondo en carretera*** *(en ciclismo)* road race; ***c. de galgos*** greyhound race; ***c. hípica*** horse race; ***c. de medio fondo*** middle-distance race; ***c. de motos*** motorcycle race; **me gustan las carreras de motos** I like motorcycle racing; ***c. de obstáculos*** steeplechase; *Fig* **este proyecto se ha convertido en una c. de obstáculos** it has been one problem after another with this project; ***c. popular*** fun run; ***c. de relevos*** relay (race); ***c. de sacos*** sack race; ***c. de vallas*** hurdles race; ***c. de velocidad*** *(en atletismo)* sprint

(**c**) *(en béisbol, críquet)* run ▸▸ ***c. completa*** home run

(**d**) *(estudios)* university course; **hacer la c. de derecho/físicas** to study law/physics (at university); **tengo la c. de Medicina** I'm a medicine graduate, I have a degree in medicine; **¿qué piensas hacer cuando acabes la c.?** what do you want to do when you finish your studies?; **dejar** *o* **abandonar la c. a medias** to drop out of university *o US* college; **darle (una) c. a alguien** to pay for sb's studies; *Fam Fig* **¡vaya c. lleva tu hijo!** your son's got quite a record! ▸▸ ***c. media*** = three-year university course (as opposed to normal five-year course); ***c. superior*** = university course lasting five or six years; ***c. técnica*** applied science degree

(**e**) *(profesión)* career; **eligió la c. de las armas** she decided to join the army; **de c.** *(de profesión)* career; **es diplomático/militar de c.** he's a career diplomat/soldier; **hacer c.** *(triunfar)* to get on; **está haciendo c. en el mundo periodístico** she's carving out a career for herself as a journalist; *Esp* **con estos niños tan rebeldes no se puede hacer c.** you can't do anything with these badly behaved children

(**f**) EXPR *Fam* **hacer la c.** *(prostituirse)* to walk the streets

(**g**) *(trayecto)* route

(**h**) *(de taxi)* ride; **¿cuánto es la c. a la estación?** what's the fare to the station?

(**i**) *(en medias) Br* ladder, *US* run; **tener una c.** to have a *Br* ladder *o US* run

(**j**) *(calle)* street, = name of certain streets

(**k**) *Náut* route

(**l**) *Astron* course

(**m**) *(hilera)* row, line; *(de ladrillos)* course

(**n**) *Tec (de émbolo)* stroke ▸▸ ***c. ascendente*** upstroke; ***c. de compresión*** compression stroke; ***c. descendente*** downstroke

(**o**) *Arquit* girder, beam

(**p**) *Col, Méx, Ven (en el pelo)* parting

(**q**) *RP (tejido)* row

(**r**) *ver también* **carrero**

---

carreraje *nm (en béisbol)* = calculation of the number of runs

carrerilla *nf* (**a**) *(carrera breve)* **tomar** *o Esp* **coger c.** to take a run-up; **decir algo de c.** to reel sth off (**b**) *Mús* run

carrero, -a *nm,f RP* cart driver

carreta *nf* (**a**) *(carro)* cart; EXPR *RP* **poner la c. adelante de los bueyes** to put the cart before the horse (**b**) *Guat (carrito)* trolley, *US* cart (**c**) *RP Fam (transporte lento)* **ese tren/ómnibus es una c.** that train/bus goes at a crawl (**d**) *Col Fam (labia)* smooth talk; **tener c.** *(tener labia)* to have the gift of the gab; **hablar** *o* **echar mucha c.** *(decir tonterías)* to talk nonsense

carretada *nf* (**a**) *(carga)* cartload (**b**) *Fam (gran cantidad)* cartload

carrete *nm* (**a**) *(de hilo)* bobbin, reel; *(de alambre)* coil (**b**) *(de pesca)* reel; EXPR **dar c. a alguien** to draw sb out (**c**) *(de película)* (roll of) film

carretear 1 *vt Chile* (**a**) *(transportar)* to cart, to haul (**b**) *(conducir)* to drive

2 *vi Am (avión)* to taxi

carretel *nm* (**a**) *(para pesca)* reel (**b**) *Náut* winch (**c**) *RP (de hilo)* bobbin, reel

carretera *nf* road; **por c.** by road; **mapa de carreteras** road map ▸▸ ***c. de circunvalación*** *Br* ring road, *US* beltway; ***c. comarcal*** minor road; ***c. costera*** coast road; *Méx* ***c. de cuota*** toll road; ***c. general*** main road; ***c. litoral*** coast road; ***c. nacional*** *Br* ≃ A road, *US* ≃ state highway; ***c. de peaje*** toll road; ***c. secundaria*** side road; ***c. troncal*** *Br* trunk road, *US* highway

carretero, -a 1 *adj Am* road; **un accidente c.** a road accident; **tráfico c.** road traffic

2 *nm,f* wheelwright; **fumar como un c.** to smoke like a chimney; **jurar como un c.** to swear like a trooper

carretilla *nf* (**a**) *(para transportar)* wheelbarrow ▸▸ ***c. elevadora*** fork-lift truck (**b**) EXPR *Fam* **de c.: se sabía la lista de c.** she knew the list off by heart (**c**) *Guat (tontería)* nonsense

carretón *nm (carro)* dray

carricerín *nm* sedge warbler ▸▸ ***c. cejudo*** aquatic warbler; ***c. real*** moustached warbler

carricero *nm* reed warbler ▸▸ ***c. agrícola*** paddyfield warbler; ***c. picogordo*** thick-billed warbler; ***c. políglota*** marsh warbler; ***c. tordal*** great reed warbler

carricoche *nm Anticuado* jalopy, *Br* old banger

carril *nm* (**a**) *(de carretera)* lane ▸▸ ***c. de aceleración*** *Br* acceleration lane, *US* on-ramp; ***c. bus*** bus lane; ***c. de deceleración*** *Br* deceleration lane, *US* off-ramp; ***c. de incorporación*** *Br* acceleration lane, *US* on-ramp; ***c. lento*** slow lane; ***c. de salida*** *Br* deceleration lane, *US* off-ramp (**b**) *(de vía de tren)* rail (**c**) *(de ruedas)* rut (**d**) *(guía)* rail

carril-bici (*pl* **carriles-bici**) *nm Br* cycle lane, *US* bikeway

carrilero, -a *nm,f (en fútbol)* wing back

carrillera *nf* (**a**) *(quijada)* jaw (**b**) *(de casco)* strap

carrillo *nm* cheek; EXPR **comer a dos carrillos** to cram one's face with food

carriola *nf* (**a**) *(cama)* truckle bed (**b**) *Méx (coche de bebé) Br* pram, *US* baby carriage

carrito *nm* (**a**) *(para equipaje)* trolley, *US* cart ►► ***c. de golf*** *(para los palos)* golf trolley; *(para desplazarse)* golf buggy (**b**) *(de supermercado)* trolley, *US* cart (**c**) *RP, Ven (ambulante)* food stand *(that can be towed)* (**d**) *Méx, Ven* ***carritos chocones*** Dodgems®, bumper cars

carrizal *nm* reedbed

carrizo 1 *nm Bot* reed
2 *interj Méx, Ven Fam (sorpresa) Br* blimey!, *US* jeez!; *(enfado)* for heaven's sake!; **¡c. con la que no sabía nada!** so she's the one who didn't know anything, eh?; **¡c. qué listo es tu hijo!** gee but your son's smart!

carro *nm* (**a**) *(vehículo)* cart; *(en batallas)* chariot; **un c. de trigo** a cartload of wheat; *Fig* **apuntarse** *o* **subirse al c. de la tecnología** to sign up for the new technology; EXPR **¡para el c.!** *(espera un momento)* hang on a minute!; EXPR **aguantar carros y carretas** to put up with a lot; EXPR *Fam* **parar el c. a alguien** to get sb to cool it; **mi madre me está encima para que me case con ella – tienes que pararle el c.** my mother is on at me to marry her – you'll have to get her to back off there; EXPR **poner el c. delante del caballo** *o* **de las mulas** to put the cart before the horse; EXPR **tirar del c.** to do all the donkey work ►► *Andes, CSur, Méx* ***c. alegórico*** carnival float; *Chile* ***c. de arrastre*** trailer; ***c. blindado*** armoured vehicle; *Col* ***c. bomba*** car bomb; *Andes, CSur, Méx* ***c. de bomberos*** fire engine; *Méx* ***c. de carga*** goods wagon *o* van; ***c. de combate*** tank; *Andes, CAm, Carib, Méx* ***c. sport*** sports car
(**b**) *(carrito)* trolley, *US* cart; *(de bebé) Br* pram, *US* baby carriage ►► ***c. de la compra*** shopping trolley *(two-wheeled)*
(**c**) *(de máquina de escribir)* carriage
(**d**) *(para diapositivas)* magazine
(**e**) *Andes, CAm, Carib, Méx (automóvil)* car ►► *Col* ***carros locos*** Dodgems®, bumper cars
(**f**) *Méx (vagón)* car ►► ***c. comedor*** dining car; ***c. dormitorio*** sleeper

carrocería *nf* bodywork

carrocero, -a *nm,f* coachbuilder

carromato *nm* wagon

carroña *nf* (**a**) *(carne)* carrion (**b**) *(persona ruin)* **los narcotraficantes no son más que c.** drug traffickers are just scum

carroñero, -a *adj (animal)* carrion-eating

carrotanque *nm Col, Méx (cisterna)* tanker

carroza[1] *nf* (**a**) *(carruaje)* carriage (**b**) *(en cabalgata)* float (**c**) *CSur (coche fúnebre)* hearse

carroza[2] *Fam* **1** *adj* (**a**) *(viejo)* doddery; **ser c.** to be doddery (**b**) *(anticuado)* **ser c.** to be an old fogey *o* a square; **tiene ideas carrozas** he's got fuddy-duddy ideas
2 *nmf* (**a**) *(persona vieja)* old crock (**b**) *(persona anticuada)* old fogey, square; **está hecho un c.** he's turned into an old fogey *o* a square

carruaje *nm* carriage

carrusel *nm* (**a**) *(tiovivo)* merry-go-round, *US* carousel (**b**) *(de caballos)* dressage, display of horsemanship

carst *nm Geol* karst

cárstico, -a *adj Geol* karstic; **región cárstica** karstic region

CARTA *nf* (**a**) *(escrito)* letter; **echar una c.** to *Br* post *o US* mail a letter ►► ***c. abierta*** open letter; ***c. de agradecimiento*** letter of thanks, thank you letter; ***c. de amor*** love letter; ***c. blanca*** carte blanche; **dar c. blanca a alguien** to give sb carte blanche *o* a free hand; **tiene c. blanca para conceder un crédito** she is solely responsible for deciding whether or not to give somebody a loan; ***c. bomba*** letter bomb; ***c. certificada*** *Br* recorded *o US* certified letter; ***c. pastoral*** pastoral letter; ***c. de pésame*** letter of condolence; *Am* ***c. postal*** postcard; ***c. de presentación*** *(para un tercero)* letter of introduction; *(con un currículum) Br* covering letter, *US* cover letter; ***c. de recomendación*** reference (letter); ***c. urgente*** express letter
(**b**) *(naipe)* (playing) card; **baraja de cartas** pack *o* deck of cards; **jugar a las cartas** to play cards; **echar las cartas a alguien** to tell sb's fortune *(with cards)*; **voy a ir a que me echen las cartas** I'm going to have my fortune told; EXPR **c. sobre la mesa, pesa** once you've played a card, you can't change your mind; EXPR **enseñar las cartas** to show one's hand; EXPR **jugar a cartas vistas** *(con honradez)* to act openly; *(con certeza)* to act with certainty; EXPR **jugar bien sus cartas** to play one's cards right; EXPR **jugarse la última c.** to play one's last card; EXPR **jugarse todo a una c.** to put all one's eggs in one basket; EXPR **no saber a qué c. quedarse** to be unsure; EXPR **poner las cartas boca arriba** *o* **sobre la mesa** to put one's cards on the table ►► ***c. falsa*** low card
(**c**) *(menú)* menu; **a la c.** *(menú)* à la carte; *(televisión, programación)* pay-per-view; **comer a la c.** to eat à la carte; **no tienen menú del día y hay que comer a la c.** they don't have a set menu, you have to choose from the à la carte menu; **un servicio a la carta** a tailor-made service ►► ***c. de vinos*** wine list
(**d**) *(mapa)* map; *Náut* chart ►► ***c. astral*** star chart, astrological chart; ***c. de marear*** sea chart; ***c. marina*** sea chart; ***c. meteorológica*** weather map
(**e**) *(documento)* charter ►► *Náut* ***c. de contramarca*** letter of reprisal; ***cartas credenciales*** letters of credence; *Com* ***c. de crédito*** letter of credit; *Com* ***c. de crédito documentaria*** documentary letter of credit; *Náut* ***c. de fletamento*** charter party; ***c. fundacional*** founding charter; ***c. general*** form letter; ***c. de hidalguía*** letters patent of nobility; *Dep* ***c. de libertad:*** **dar la c. de libertad a alguien** to give sb a free transfer; ***C. Magna*** *(constitución)* constitution; *Náut* ***c. de marca*** letters-of-marque; ***c. de naturaleza*** naturalization papers; *Com* ***c. de pago*** receipt; *Com* ***c. de pedido*** order; ***la C. Social*** the Social Charter; ***c. de trabajo*** work permit; *Com* ***c. de venta*** bill of sale; ***c. verde*** green card *(for international car insurance)*
(**f**) *TV* ***c. de ajuste*** *Br* test card, *US* test pattern
(**g**) EXPR **a c. cabal** through and through; **es un hombre íntegro a c. cabal** he's honest through and through; **adquirir** *o* **tomar c. de naturaleza** *(costumbre, práctica)* to become widely accepted; **tomar cartas en un asunto** to intervene in a matter

---

cartabón *nm* (**a**) *(regla)* set square *(with angles of 30°, 60° and 90°)* (**b**) *Am (para medir personas)* measuring stick

cartagenero, -a 1 *adj* of/from Cartagena *(Spain or Colombia)*
2 *nm,f* person from Cartagena *(Spain or Colombia)*

cartaginense *adj, nmf* = **cartaginés**

cartaginés, -esa *Hist* **1** *adj* Carthaginian
2 *nm,f* Carthaginian

Cartago *n Hist* Carthage

cártamo *nm* safflower

cartapacio *nm* (**a**) *(carpeta)* folder (**b**) *(cuaderno)* notebook

cartearse *vpr* **nos seguimos carteando** we still write to each other; **se cartea con otros científicos** she corresponds with other scientists

cartel[1] *nm* (**a**) *(anuncio)* poster; **prohibido fijar carteles** *(en letrero)* post *o* stick no bills; **estar en c.** *(película, obra de teatro)* to be on, to be showing (**b**) *(fama)* **tener buen/mal c.** to be popular/unpopular; **un actor de c.** a well-known actor

cartel[2]**, cártel** *nm* (**a**) *(de empresas)* cartel (**b**) *(de droga, crimen)* cartel, syndicate; **el c. de Cali/Medellín** the Cali/Medellín cartel

cartela *nf (tarjeta)* card

cartelera *nf* (**a**) *(tablón)* billboard, *Br* hoarding (**b**) *(lista de espectáculos)* entertainments page; **estar en c.** to be showing; **lleva un año en c.** it has been running for a year (**c**) *Am (de anuncios) Br* noticeboard, *US* bulletin board

cartelero, -a *adj* popular, big-name

cartelista *nmf* poster artist

carteo *nm* correspondence

cárter *nm Aut* housing; *(del cigüeñal)* crankcase

cartera *nf* (**a**) *(para dinero)* wallet, *US* billfold
(**b**) *(para documentos)* briefcase; *(sin asa)* portfolio; *(de colegial)* satchel; EXPR **tener algo en c.** to have sth in the pipeline
(**c**) *Com & Fin* portfolio ►► ***c. de acciones*** share portfolio; ***c. de clientes*** client portfolio; ***c. de inversiones*** investment portfolio; ***c. de pedidos*** *(pedidos pendientes)* orders in hand; *(pedidos atrasados)* backlog; ***c. de valores*** investment portfolio
(**d**) *Pol (de ministro)* portfolio; **ocupa la c. de Defensa** he is the Minister of Defence, he has the Defence portfolio
(**e**) *Andes, RP (bolso) Br* handbag, *US* purse
(**f**) *ver también* **cartero**

carterear *vt Chile* to pickpocket

carterista *nmf* pickpocket

cartero, -a *nm,f Br* postman, *f* postwoman, *US* mailman, *f* mailwoman

cartesiano, -a 1 *adj* Cartesian
2 *nm,f* Cartesian

cartilaginoso, -a *adj* cartilaginous

cartílago *nm* cartilage

cartilla *nf* (**a**) *(documento)* book ►► ***c. de ahorros*** savings book, passbook; ***c. militar*** = booklet to say one has completed one's military service; ***c. del paro*** = registration card issued to the unemployed, *Br* ≃ UB40; ***c. de racionamiento*** ration book; ***c. de la seguridad social*** = card bearing national insurance number, doctor's address and other personal details

(**b**) *(para aprender a leer)* primer; EXPR *Fam* **leerle la c. a alguien** to read sb the riot act; *Fam* **no saberse la c.** not to have a clue

cartografía *nf* cartography ►► ***c. aérea*** aerocartography

cartográfico, -a *adj* cartographic

cartógrafo, -a *nm,f* cartographer

cartomancia *nf* fortune-telling *(with cards)*

cartón *nm* (**a**) *(material)* cardboard ►► ***c. piedra*** papier-mâché (**b**) *(de cigarrillos)* carton (**c**) *(de leche, zumo)* carton ►► ***c. de huevos*** eggbox (**d**) *Arte* cartoon (**e**) *Méx (tira cómica)* comic strip

cartoné *nm* **en c.** bound in boards

cartonista *nmf Méx* comic strip artist

cartuchera *nf* (**a**) *(para cartuchos)* cartridge belt (**b**) *Fam (grasa acumulada)* saddlebag (**c**) *RP (para lápices)* pencil box (**d**) *Chile (para lentes)* glasses case

cartucho *nm* (**a**) *(de arma)* cartridge; EXPR **quemar el último c.** to play one's last card ►► ***c. de dinamita*** stick of dynamite; ***c. de fogueo*** blank cartridge (**b**) *(de tinta, videojuego)* cartridge ►► ***c. de tóner*** toner cartridge (**c**) *(envoltorio) (de monedas)* roll; *(cucurucho)* paper cone

cartuja *nf* charterhouse

cartujo, -a 1 *adj* Carthusian

2 *nm* (**a**) *(religioso)* Carthusian (**b**) *(persona retraída)* hermit

cartulina *nf* (**a**) *(cartón)* card, thin cardboard; **una carpeta de c.** a cardboard folder (**b**) *(en deporte)* card ►► ***c. amarilla*** yellow card; ***c. roja*** red card

carúncula *nf Anat* ***c. lacrimal*** *o* ***lagrimal*** lacrimal caruncle

CASA *nf* (**a**) *(edificio)* house; *(apartamento) Br* flat, *US* apartment; **vivo en una c. de tres plantas** my house has got three floors; **vivimos en una c. de alquiler** we live in rented accommodation; **buscar c.** to look for somewhere to live; **cambiarse** *o* **mudarse de c.** to move (house); **de c. en c.** house-to-house; **se le cae la c. encima** *(se deprime)* it's the end of the world for him; EXPR *Fam* **como una c.** *(enorme)* massive; **dijo un disparate como una c.** he made a totally ludicrous remark; **una mentira como una c.** a whopping great lie; **un fuera de juego como una c.** a blindingly obvious offside; EXPR **echar** *o* **tirar la c. por la ventana** to spare no expense; **para comprarse un coche tan caro, tiró la c. por la ventana** he spared no expense when he bought that car; EXPR **empezar la c. por el tejado** to put the cart before the horse; ►► ***c. adosada*** *Br* terraced house, *US* row house; ***c. de altos*** *Andes, CAm, Carib, Méx (edificio)* multistorey building; *CSur, Perú (casa de arriba)* upstairs *Br* flat *o US* apartment; ***c. de apartamentos*** *Br* block of flats, *US* apartment building; ***C. Blanca*** *(en Estados Unidos)* White House; ***c. de campo*** country house; ***c. y comida*** board and lodging; *Esp* ***c. cuartel*** *(de la Guardia Civil)* = police station also used as living quarters by Guardia Civil; *Arg* ***c. de departamentos*** *Br* block of flats, *US* apartment building; *Am* ***c. habitación*** residential building; *RP* ***c. de inquilinato*** = communal dwelling where poor families each live in a single room and share bathroom and kitchen with others; ***c. de labor*** farmhouse; ***c. de labranza*** farmhouse; *Méx* ***c. llena:* con c. llena** *(en béisbol)* with the bases loaded; ***C. de la Moneda*** *(en Chile)* = Chile's presidential palace; ***c. de muñecas*** *Br* doll's house, *US* dollhouse; ***c. natal:* la c. natal de Goya** the house where Goya was born; ***c. parroquial*** priest's house, presbytery; ***c. piloto*** show house; ***c. de postas*** posthouse, inn; ***c. prefabricada*** prefab; *RP* ***c. rodante*** *Br* caravan, *US* trailer; ***C. Rosada*** *(en Argentina)* = Argentinian presidential palace; ***c. semiadosada*** semi-detached house; ***c. solariega*** ancestral home, family seat; ***c. unifamiliar*** = house, usually detached, on an estate; ***c. de vecindad*** tenement house

(**b**) *(hogar)* home; **bienvenido a c.** welcome home; **en c.** at home; **¿está tu hermano en c.?** is your brother at home?; **me quedé en c. leyendo** I stayed at home and read a book; **en c. se cena pronto** we have dinner early at home; **estar de c.** to be casually dressed; **unas zapatillas de ir por c.** slippers for wearing around the house; **pásate por (mi) c.** come round, come over to my place; **estar fuera de c.** to be out; **ir a c.** to go home; **irse de c.** to leave home; **me fui de c. a los dieciséis años** I left home at sixteen; **franquear la c. a alguien** to open one's home to sb; **generalmente es la mujer la que lleva la c.** it's usually the woman who runs the household; **no para en c.** he's hardly ever at home; **no tener c. ni hogar** to be homeless; **ponte como en tu c., estás en tu c.** make yourself at home; **sin c.** homeless; **había varios sin c. durmiendo a la intemperie** there were several homeless people sleeping rough; **hemos recogido a un niño sin c.** we've taken in a child from a broken home; *Esp* **quiere poner c. en Valencia** she wants to go and live in Valencia; **sentirse como en c.** to feel at home; **ser (uno) muy de su c.** to be a homebody; EXPR *Fam* **como Pedro por su casa: entra y sale como Pedro por su c.** she comes in and out as if she owns the place; EXPR **todo queda en c.: nadie se enterará de tu despiste, todo queda en c.** no one will find out about your mistake, we'll keep it between ourselves; **el padre y el hijo dirigen el negocio, así que todo queda en c.** the business is run by father and son, so it's all in the family; EXPR *Esp Fam* **los unos por los otros y la c. sin barrer** everybody said they'd do it and nobody did; EXPR *Esp Fam* **esto parece la c. de tócame Roque** everyone just does whatever they want in here, it's like Liberty Hall in here; PROV **cada uno en su c., y Dios en la de todos** = you should mind your own business; PROV **en c. del herrero cuchillo de palo** the shoemaker's wife is always worst shod ►► ***c. mortuoria*** home of the deceased; ***c. paterna*** parental home

(**c**) *(familia)* family; *(linaje)* house; **procede de una de las mejores casas de la ciudad** she comes from one of the most important families in the city ►► *Hist* ***la c. de Austria*** the (Spanish) Hapsburgs; *Hist* ***la c. de Borbón*** the Bourbons; ***c. real*** royal family

(**d**) *(establecimiento)* company; **este producto lo fabrican varias casas** this product is made by several different companies; **por la compra de un televisor, la c. le regala una radio** buy one television and we'll give you a radio for free; **¡invita la c.!** it's on the house!; **especialidad/vino de la c.** house speciality/wine ►► ***c. de apuestas*** betting shop; *Méx* ***c. de asistencia*** boarding house; ***c. de banca*** banking house; *Com* ***c. central*** head office; ***c. de citas*** brothel; ***c. de comidas*** = cheap restaurant serving simple meals; ***c. discográfica*** record company; ***c. editorial*** publishing house; ***c. de empeño*** pawnshop; ***c. de empeños*** pawnshop; ***c. exportadora*** exporter; ***c. de huéspedes*** *Br* ≃ guesthouse, *US* ≃ rooming house; ***c. importadora*** importer; ***c. de lenocinio*** house of ill repute; *Com* ***c. matriz*** *(de empresa)* head office; *(de grupo de empresas)* parent company; ***c. de préstamo*** pawnshop; ***c. pública*** brothel; *Vulg* ***c. de putas*** whorehouse; ***c. de subastas*** auction house, auctioneer's; *Am* ***c. de tolerancia*** brothel

(**e**) *(institución, organismo)* *RP* ***c. bancaria*** savings bank; ***c. de baños*** public bathhouse; ***c. de beneficencia*** poorhouse; *Fin* ***c. de cambio*** bureau de change; ***c. de caridad*** poorhouse; ***c. consistorial*** town *o US* city hall; ***c. de correos*** post office; ***c. cuna*** *(orfanato)* foundling home; *(guardería)* nursery; ***c. de Dios*** house of God; *CSur* ***c. de estudios*** educational establishment; ***c. de fieras*** zoo; *Am* ***c. de gobierno*** = workplace of the head of state, governor, mayor etc; ***c. de locos*** madhouse; *Fig* **¡esto es una c. de locos!** this place is a madhouse!; ***c. de la moneda*** *(fábrica)* mint; ***c. del pueblo*** = village social club run by local council; ***c. rectoral*** rectory; ***c. regional*** = social club for people from a particular region (in another region or abroad); ***c. religiosa*** *(de monjas)* convent; *(de monjes)* monastery; *RP* ***c. de reposo*** rest home; *RP* ***c. de salud*** rest home; ***c. del Señor*** house of God; ***c. de socorro*** first-aid post; ***c. de la villa*** town hall

(**f**) *CSur* **las casas** *(en estancia, hacienda)* the farmstead

(**g**) *Dep* home; **jugar en c.** to play at home; **jugar fuera de c.** to play away (from home); **el equipo de c.** the home team

(**h**) *(en juegos de mesa)* home

(**i**) *(casilla de ajedrez, damas)* square

(**j**) ***c. celeste*** *(en astrología)* house

casabe *nm* (**a**) *(pez)* amberfish (**b**) *(planta)* cassava (**c**) *Col, Ven (torta)* cassava bread

casaca *nf (de chaqué)* frock coat; *(chaquetón)* jacket

casación *nf Der* annulment

casadero, -a *adj* marriageable; **estar en edad casadera** to be of marriageable age

casado, -a 1 *adj* married (**con** to)

2 *nm,f* married man, *f* married woman; **los casados no entienden que los solteros podamos ser felices** married people can't understand how single people can be happy; **los recién casados** the newly-weds; **la vida de c.** married life; PROV **el c. casa quiere** = when you're married, you want your own place

casamata *nf* casemate

casamentero, -a 1 *adj* matchmaking

2 *nm,f* matchmaker

casamiento *nm* wedding, marriage

Casandra *n Mitol* Cassandra

casanova *nm* Casanova, lady-killer

casar 1 *vt* (**a**) *(en matrimonio)* to marry; **los casó el cura del pueblo** they were married by the village priest; **ya ha casado a todos sus hijos** all his children are married; **llevan años intentando c. a su hijo** they've been trying to marry off their son *o* get their son married off for years (**b**) *(unir)* to fit together

2 *vi* (**a**) *(armonizar)* to match; **el tapizado del sofá y el de las sillas**

no casan the sofa and the chairs don't match (**b**) *(cuadrar)* to balance, to tally; **las cuentas no casan** the accounts don't tally

3 **casarse** *vpr* to get married (**con** to); **se casan mañana** they're getting married tomorrow; **se casó con una mujer diez años mayor que él** he married a woman ten years his senior; **casarse en segundas nupcias** to remarry; **casarse por interés** to marry for money; **casarse por la iglesia** to have a church wedding; **casarse por lo civil** to have a *Br* registry office wedding *o US* civil wedding; EXPR **casarse de penalti** to have a shotgun wedding; EXPR **no se casa con nadie** he maintains his independence, he ploughs his own furrow; **en cuestiones de política, no se casa con nadie** when it comes to politics, she's totally impartial

cascabel *nm* (small) bell; EXPR **poner el c. al gato** to bell the cat, to dare to go ahead

cascabela *nf CRica* rattlesnake

cascabelear *vi Fam* (**a**) *(estar atolondrado)* to act in a scatterbrained manner (**b**) *Méx (criticar)* to moan (**c**) *Chile (refunfuñar)* to grumble

cascabeleo *nm* tinkle, jingle

cascada *nf* (**a**) *(de agua)* waterfall (**b**) *(gran cantidad)* **una c. de preguntas** a deluge of questions; **una c. de imágenes** a riot of images; **en c.** one after another

cascadismo *nm* ice climbing

cascado, -a *adj* (**a**) *(ronco)* rasping; **tener la voz cascada** to be hoarse (**b**) *Esp Fam (estropeado)* bust, *Br* clapped-out; *(persona)* worn-out

cascajo *nm* (**a**) *(cascote)* rubble (**b**) EXPR *Fam* **estar hecho un c.** to be a wreck

cascanueces *nm inv* (**a**) *(utensilio)* nutcracker (**b**) *(ave)* nutcracker

cascar [60] 1 *vt* (**a**) *(romper)* to crack; **c. un huevo** to crack an egg (**b**) *Esp Fam (dañar)* to damage, to harm (**c**) *Esp Fam* **cascarla** *(morir)* to kick the bucket (**d**) *Fam (voz)* to make croaky (**e**) *Fam (pegar)* to thump; *Esp Vulg* **como no te calles, te casco una hostia** if you don't shut up, I'll smash your face in

2 *vi Esp Fam* (**a**) *(hablar)* to chat, to natter; **no pararon de c. en toda la tarde** they were chatting *o* nattering away all afternoon (**b**) *(morir)* to kick the bucket

3 **cascarse** *vpr* (**a**) *(romperse)* to crack (**b**) *Esp Fam* **se le cascó la voz** his voice went croaky (**c**) *Esp muy Fam* **cascársela** *(masturbarse)* to jerk off, *Br* to wank

cáscara *nf* (**a**) *(de almendra, huevo, gamba)* shell; *(de limón, naranja)* peel, rind (**b**) *Méx Fam* **echar una c.** *(un partido)* to have a game

cáscaras *interj* wow!

cascarilla *nf* husk

cascarón *nm* (**a**) *(cáscara)* eggshell; **romper el c.** to hatch; EXPR **salir del c.** *(independizarse)* to leave the nest; *(abrirse)* to come out of one's shell (**b**) *Fam (embarcación)* tub

cascarrabias *Fam* 1 *adj inv* grouchy, cranky; **un viejo c.** an old grouch, an old misery-guts

2 *nmf inv* grouch, misery-guts

cascarudo *nm RP* beetle

casco 1 *nm* (**a**) *(para la cabeza)* helmet; *(de albañil)* hard hat; *(de motorista)* crash helmet ►► ***cascos azules*** UN peacekeeping troops, blue berets

(**b**) *(de barco)* hull

(**c**) *(de ciudad)* ***c. antiguo*** old (part of) town; ***c. histórico*** old (part of) town; ***c. de población*** city centre; ***c. urbano*** city centre; ***c. viejo*** old (part of) town

(**d**) *(de caballo)* hoof

(**e**) *Esp, Méx (de botella)* (empty) bottle

(**f**) *(pedazo)* fragment, piece

(**g**) *Méx, RP (en estancia, hacienda)* farmstead

(**h**) *Andes, Cuba, RP (gajo)* segment

(**i**) EXPR **calentarse** *o* **romperse los cascos** to *Br* rack *o US* cudgel one's brains; **ser alegre** *o* **ligero de cascos** *(irresponsable)* to be irresponsible; *(mujer)* to be flighty

2 **cascos** *nmpl Fam (auriculares)* headphones

cascote *nm* piece of rubble; **cascotes** rubble

caseína *nf* casein

caserío *nm* (**a**) *(aldea)* hamlet (**b**) *(casa de campo)* country house

caserna *nf Mil* bombproof bunker

casero, -a 1 *adj* (**a**) *(hecho en casa)* *(comida)* home-made; **un explosivo de fabricación casera** a home-made explosive; **un vídeo c.** a home video

(**b**) *(trabajos)* domestic

(**c**) *(celebración)* family

(**d**) *(hogareño)* home-loving; **es muy c.** he's a real homebody

(**e**) *(árbitro)* **un árbitro conocidamente c.** a referee known to favour the home team; **el árbitro estuvo muy c.** the referee blatantly favoured the home team

2 *nm,f* (**a**) *(propietario)* landlord, *f* landlady

(**b**) *(encargado)* house agent

(**c**) *Andes, Cuba (cliente)* customer

caserón *nm* large, rambling house

caseta *nf* (**a**) *(casa pequeña)* hut ►► *Méx* ***c. de cobro*** tollbooth; ***c. de feria*** *(de tiro)* booth; *(de artesanía, libros, comida)* stall; ***c. de salida*** *(en esquí)* start hut; *Méx* ***c. telefónica*** phone box, *US* phone booth (**b**) *(en la playa)* bathing hut (**c**) *Dep (vestuario)* changing room; EXPR **mandar a un jugador a la c.** to send a player off, *Br* to send a player for an early bath (**d**) *(para perro)* kennel

casete 1 *nf (cinta)* cassette

2 *nm (magnetófono)* cassette *o* tape recorder

cash-flow ['kaʃflou] *nm* cash flow

casi *adv* (**a**) *(faltando poco)* almost; **c. me muero** I almost *o* nearly died; **c. me caigo** I almost *o* nearly fell; **c. no dormí** I hardly slept at all; **el c. millón de refugiados** the refugees, who number almost a million; **no llegamos hasta la cumbre pero c., c.** we didn't quite get to the top, but almost; **no comió c. nada** she hardly ate anything; **c. nunca** hardly ever; **c. siempre** almost *o* nearly always; **está c. olvidado – sin el c.** it's all but forgotten – leave out the "all but"

(**b**) *(expresando indecisión)* **c. me voy a quedar con el rojo** I think I'll probably go for the red one; **c. c. preferiría dormir en un albergue que en una pensión** I'd almost prefer to sleep in a youth hostel rather than a guesthouse

(**c**) EXPR *Irónico* **c. nada: ¿qué te pasa? – ¡c. nada! que me ha dejado mi mujer** what's up? – my wife's only gone and left me, that's all!; **lo venden por 3 millones – ¡c. nada!** they're selling it for 3 million – what a snip!

casilla *nf* (**a**) *(de caja, armario)* compartment; *(para cartas)* pigeonhole ►► *Andes, RP* ***c. de correos*** PO Box; *CAm, Carib, Méx* ***c. postal*** PO Box

(**b**) *(en un impreso)* box ►► *Informát* ***c. de verificación*** checkbox

(**c**) *(de tablero de juego, crucigrama)* square ►► ***c. de salida*** start; **volver a la c. de salida** to go back to the start

(**d**) *Ecuad (retrete)* toilet

(**e**) *Méx (de votación)* voting booth

(**f**) *Fam* EXPR **sacar a alguien de sus casillas** to drive sb mad; **salir** *o* **salirse de sus casillas** to fly off the handle

casillero *nm* (**a**) *(mueble)* set of pigeonholes (**b**) *(casilla)* pigeonhole (**c**) *(marcador)* scoreboard (**d**) *(en formulario)* box

casimir *nm* (**a**) *(tejido)* cashmere (**b**) *(estampado)* **una corbata/un pañuelo de c.** a Paisley (pattern) tie/headscarf

casino *nm* (**a**) *(para jugar)* casino (**b**) *(asociación)* (social) club (**c**) *Chile (en empresa, institución)* canteen

Casiopea *n* Cassiopeia

casís *nm inv* (**a**) *(arbusto)* blackcurrant bush (**b**) *(fruto)* blackcurrant (**c**) *(licor)* cassis

casitas *nfpl Chile* public lavatory

casiterita *nf Geol* cassiterite

CASO *nm* (**a**) *(situación, circunstancias, ejemplo)* case; **un c. especial** a special case; **un c. límite** a borderline case; **voy a contarles un c. curioso que pasó aquí** I'm going to tell you about something strange that happened here; **les expuse mi c.** I made out my case to them; **el c. es que** *(el hecho es que)* the thing is (that); *(lo importante es que)* what matters is (that); **el c. es que a pesar de la aparatosidad del accidente nadie resultó herido** despite the spectacular nature of the accident, the fact remains that no one was injured; **el c. es que no sé qué hacer** basically, I don't know what to do; **cuando llegue el c., hablaremos del asunto** if it should ever come to that, we'll discuss it then; **darse el c.: rara vez se da el c. de que dos candidatos obtengan el mismo número de votos** it is very rare for two candidates to receive the same number of votes; **si se da el c., tomaremos las medidas necesarias** if that should happen, we'll take the necessary steps; **en c. afirmativo/negativo** if so/not; **en c. contrario** otherwise; **en c. de** in the event of; **en c. de emergencia** in case of emergency; **en c. de incendio** in the event of a fire; **en c. de no haber mayoría...** should there be no majority...; **en c. de necesidad** if necessary; **en c. de no poder venir, comuníquenoslo** should you be unable to come, please let us know; **en c. de que** if; **(en) c. de que venga** should she come, if she comes; **en cualquier** *o* **todo c.** in any event *o* case; **dijo que en todo c. nos avisaría** she said she'd let us know, whatever; **no tenemos dinero para un hotel, en todo c. una pensión** we certainly haven't got enough money for a hotel, so it'll have to be a guesthouse, if anything; **en el c. de Bosnia, la situación es más complicada** in the case of Bosnia, the situation is more complicated; **en el mejor/peor de los casos** at best/worst; **en el peor de los casos, llegaremos un poco tarde** the worst that can happen is that we'll be a few minutes late; **en tal** *o* **ese c.** in that case; **yo en tu c. no iría** I wouldn't go if I were you; **en último c., en c. extremo** as a last resort; **hablar al c.** to keep to the point; **ir al c.** to get to the point; **llegado** *o* **si llega el c., ya veremos qué hacemos** we'll cross that bridge when we come to it; **cuando llegue el c., se lo diremos** we'll tell you when the time comes; **lo mejor del c.** the best thing (about it); **poner por c. algo/a alguien** to take sth/sb as an example; **pongamos por c. que...** let's suppose (that)...; **ponerse en el c. de alguien** to put oneself in sb's position; **según (sea) el c., según los casos** as *o* whatever the case may be; **eso no viene** *o* **hace al c.** that's irrelevant; **tu comportamiento no viene** *o* **hace al c.** your behaviour is out of place; **verse en el c. de hacer algo** to be obliged *o* compelled to do sth

(b) *(atención)* attention; **hacer c. a** to pay attention to; **tuve que gritar para que me hicieran c.** I had to shout to attract their attention; **¡maldito el c. que me hacen!** they don't take the blindest bit of notice of me!; **hacer c. omiso de** to ignore; **¡ni c.!, ¡no hagas c.!** don't take any notice!; **se lo dije, pero ella, ni c.** I told her, but she didn't take any notice; **no me hace ni c.** she doesn't pay the slightest bit of attention to me; **creo que su cumpleaños es el viernes, pero no me hagas mucho c.** I think her birthday is on Friday, but don't take my word for it

(c) *(médico, legal)* case; **el c. Dreyfus** the Dreyfus affair; **el c. Watergate** Watergate, the Watergate affair; **se han dado varios casos de intoxicación** there have been several cases of poisoning; EXPR *Fam* **ser un c. perdido** to be a lost cause ►► ***c. clínico:*** **un c. clínico muy interesante** a very interesting case; EXPR *Fam* **ser un c. (clínico)** to be a case, to be a right one; ***c. de conciencia*** matter of conscience; *Der* ***c. fortuito*** act of God; ***c. de fuerza mayor*** force of circumstance(s); **fue un c. de fuerza mayor** it was due to force of circumstance(s); ***c. de honra*** question of honour; ***c. judicial*** court case; *Der* ***c. de prueba*** test case

(d) *Gram* case

(e) EXPR *Méx* **no tiene c.,** *RP* **no hay c.** *(no tiene solución)* nothing can be done about it

---

casona *nf* large house, mansion

casorio *nm Fam* **(a)** *(boda)* wedding **(b)** *Esp (boda inconveniente)* unwise marriage

caspa *nf* **(a)** *(en el pelo)* dandruff **(b)** *Esp Fam* **la c.** *(famosos)* C-list celebs

Caspio *nm* **el (mar) C.** the Caspian Sea

cáspita *interj Anticuado o Hum (sorpresa)* my word!; *(enfado)* dash it!

casposo, -a *adj* **(a)** *(que tiene caspa)* covered in dandruff; **ser c.** to have dandruff **(b)** *Esp Fam (asqueroso)* disgusting **(c)** *Esp Fam (música, película)* cheesy; **los famosos casposos** people who are famous for being famous

casquería *nf* **(a)** *(tienda)* = shop selling offal **(b)** *(productos)* offal **(c)** *Fam* **en esa película sale demasiada c.** that movie is too gory

casquete *nm* **(a)** *(gorro)* skullcap **(b)** *(en esfera)* ***c. esférico*** segment of a sphere; ***c. glacial*** icecap; ***c. polar*** polar icecap **(c)** *muy Fam* **echar un c.** to have a screw *o Br* shag

> **Falso amigo**: El sustantivo inglés **casket** no es la traducción del español **casquete**. En inglés, **casket** significa "cofre" o "ataúd".

casquijo *nm* gravel, broken stone

casquillo *nm* **(a)** *(cartucho de bala)* case **(b)** *(de lámpara)* socket *(for light bulb)* **(c)** *CAm (herradura)* horseshoe

casquivano, -a *adj* **(a)** *Fam (irresponsable)* irresponsible **(b)** *(mujer)* flighty

cassette [ka'sete, ka'set] **1** *nf (cinta)* cassette
2 *nm (magnetófono)* cassette *o* tape recorder

casta *nf* **(a)** *(linaje)* caste; EXPR **de c. le viene al galgo** it runs in the family; EXPR **él y todos los de su c.** him and all his sort *o* ilk **(b)** *(especie, calidad)* breed; **un toro de c.** a pedigree bull; **es de buena c.** *(persona)* he's from good stock **(c)** *(en la India)* caste

castaña *nf* **(a)** *(fruto)* chestnut; EXPR *Fam* **sacarle a alguien las castañas del fuego** to get sb out of trouble; EXPR *Fam* **¡toma c.!** so there! ►► ***c. de agua*** water chestnut; *RP* ***c. de cajú*** cashew nut; ***c. de Indias*** horse chestnut; *RP* ***c. de Pará*** Brazil nut; ***c. pilonga*** dried chestnut

(b) *Esp Fam (golpe)* bash; **darse** *o* **pegarse una c.** *(golpe)* to give oneself a bump; *(con vehículo)* to have a crash

(c) *Esp Fam (borrachera)* **agarrarse una c.** to get plastered *o* legless; **llevar una c.** to be plastered *o* legless

(d) *Esp Fam (cosa aburrida)* bore; **este libro es una c.** this book is boring

(e) *Esp Fam* **castañas:** *(años)* **tiene cuarenta castañas** he's forty

(f) *(moño)* bun

(g) *Méx (barril pequeño)* keg

castañar *nm* chestnut grove

castañazo *nm Fam* bash; **darse** *o* **pegarse un c.** *(golpe)* to give oneself a bump; *(con vehículo)* to have a crash

castañero, -a *nm,f* roast chestnut seller

castañeta *nf Taurom* = bullfighter's ornamental pigtail

castañetear *vi (dientes)* to chatter; **me castañetean las rodillas** my knees are knocking

castañeteo *nm* **(a)** *(de castañuelas)* clacking **(b)** *(de dientes)* chattering

castaño, -a 1 *adj (color)* brown, chestnut; **ojos castaños** brown eyes
2 *nm* **(a)** *(color)* chestnut; EXPR **pasar de c. oscuro** to be beyond a joke **(b)** *(árbol)* chestnut (tree) ►► ***c. de Indias*** horse chestnut (tree) **(c)** *(madera)* chestnut

castañuela *nf (instrumento)* castanet; EXPR **estar como unas castañuelas** to be over the moon

castellanizar [14] *vt* to hispanicize

castellano, -a 1 *adj* Castilian
2 *nm,f (person)* Castilian
3 *nm (lengua)* (Castilian) Spanish; **las variedades del c. habladas en América** the varieties of Spanish spoken in Latin America

castellanohablante 1 *adj* Spanish-speaking
2 *nmf* Spanish speaker

castellano-leonés, -esa 1 *adj* of/from Castile and León *(Spain)*
2 *nm,f* person from Castile and León *(Spain)*

castellano-manchego, -a 1 *adj* of/from Castile and La Mancha *(Spain)*
2 *nm,f* person from Castile and La Mancha *(Spain)*

castellanoparlante 1 *adj* Spanish-speaking
2 *nmf* Spanish speaker

casticismo *nm* purism

casticista *nmf* purist

castidad *nf* chastity

castigador, -ora *Fam* **1** *adj* seductive
2 *nm,f* lady-killer, *f* man-eater

castigar [38] **1** *vt* **(a)** *(imponer castigo a)* to punish; **castigaron a los niños sin cena** they punished the children by sending them to bed without dinner; **lo castigaron con la pena capital** he was given the death penalty; **los castigaron a copiar la lección diez veces** they had to write out the lesson ten times as a punishment

(b) *Dep* to penalize; **el árbitro castigó la acción con penalti** the referee awarded a penalty for the foul

(c) *(dañar) (piel, salud)* to damage; *(sujeto: sol, viento, epidemia)* to devastate; **una zona castigada por las inundaciones** a region severely hit by the floods; **las nuevas medidas castigan a los pequeños inversores** the new measures are prejudicial to small investors

(d) *(enamorar)* to seduce

(e) *(caballo) (con espuelas)* to spur; *(con látigo)* to whip

(f) *Taurom* to wound

2 castigarse *vpr* to be hard on oneself; **no te castigues así** don't be so hard on yourself

castigo *nm* **(a)** *(sanción)* punishment; **una expedición militar de c.** a punitive military expedition; **nos levantaron el c. por buen comportamiento** we were let off the rest of our punishment for good behaviour ►► ***c. corporal*** corporal punishment; ***c. ejemplar*** exemplary punishment

(b) *Dep* **máximo c.** penalty; **el árbitro señaló el máximo c.** the referee pointed to the spot

(c) *(daño)* damage; **infligir un duro c. a** to inflict severe damage on

(d) *Fam (molestia, suplicio)* **¡qué c. de niño/hombre!** what a pain that child/man is!

(e) *Taurom* wound

Castilla *n* Castile; EXPR **¡ancha es C.!: tú haz lo que te apetezca, ¡ancha es C.!** you do what you want, it's Liberty Hall!; **se han gastado 5 millones en la boda – ¡ancha es C.!** they spent 5 million on the wedding – well, it's all right for some people! ►► ***C. y León*** Castile and León; ***C. la Nueva*** New Castile; ***C. la Vieja*** Old Castile

Castilla-La Mancha *n* Castile and La Mancha

castillo *nm* (a) *(edificio)* castle; EXPR **hacer castillos en el aire** to build castles in the air ►► ***c. de arena*** sandcastle; ***c. de fuegos artificiales*** firework display; ***c. hinchable*** bouncy castle; ***c. de naipes*** house of cards; EXPR **hacer castillos de naipes** to build castles in the air (b) *Náut* ***c. de popa*** quarterdeck; ***c. de proa*** forecastle

casting ['kastin] *(pl* **castings***)* *nm (de actores)* audition; **hacer un c.** to hold an audition

castizo, -a *adj* (a) *(lenguaje, palabra)* = derived from popular usage and considered linguistically pure (b) *(típico) (barrio, taberna)* typical; **es un andaluz c.** he's an Andalusian through and through

casto, -a *adj* (a) *(persona)* chaste (b) *(sonrisa, mirada)* chaste

castor *nm* (a) *(animal)* beaver (b) *(piel)* beaver fur

castración *nf (de persona)* castration; *(de animal)* castration, gelding; *(de gato)* neutering; **la c. de gatos es una práctica común hoy en día** neutering cats is common practice nowadays

castrado, -a 1 *adj* (a) *(persona)* castrated; *(animal)* castrated, gelded; *(gato)* neutered (b) *(apocado)* emasculated
2 *nm* (a) *(hombre)* eunuch (b) *(caballo)* gelding

castrador, -ora *adj Fig* **una madre castradora** a domineering *o* dominant mother

castrar *vt* (a) *(persona)* to castrate; *(animal)* to castrate, to geld; *(gato)* to neuter (b) *(debilitar)* to sap, to impair (c) *(anular)* to weaken, to impair

castrense *adj* military; **la vida c.** army life, life in the army

castrismo *nm* Castroism

castrista 1 *adj* Castroist
2 *nmf* Castroist

castro *nm* = pre-Roman fort

casual 1 *adj* accidental; **un encuentro c.** a chance encounter
2 *nm Fam* **por un c.** by any chance

casualidad *nf* coincidence; **la c. hizo que nos encontráramos** chance brought us together; **dio la c. de que...** it so happened that...; **¡qué c.!** what a coincidence!; **no es c. que...** it's no coincidence that...; **de c.** by chance; **me encuentras aquí de c., porque hoy no pensaba venir** I'm only here by chance, I hadn't intended to come today; **por c.** by chance; **me he enterado por c. de que estás buscando apartamento** I happened to hear that you're looking for an apartment *o Br* flat; **¿no llevarás por c. un paraguas?** you wouldn't happen to have an umbrella with you, would you?

> **Falso amigo**: El sustantivo inglés **casualty** no es la traducción del español **casualidad**. En inglés, **casualty** significa "víctima".

casualmente *adv* (a) *(por casualidad)* by chance (b) *(precisamente)* as it happens; **c., es vecino mío** as it happens, he's a neighbour of mine; **c., iba buscando uno parecido** as it happens, I was looking for something like that myself

casuario *nm* (Southern) cassowary

casucha *nf* (a) *Pey (para gente)* hovel, dump (b) *Chile (para perro)* kennel

casuística *nf (conjunto de casos)* **la c. no permite sacar conclusiones definitivas** no definite conclusions can be drawn from the previous cases

casulla *nf* chasuble

casus belli *nm inv* casus belli

cata *nf* (a) *(de vino)* tasting ►► ***c. de vinos*** wine tasting (b) *Col (secreto)* hidden *o* secret thing (c) *CSur (ave)* parakeet

catabolismo *nm Bioquím* catabolism

cataclismo *nm* cataclysm; **su dimisión provocó un c. en el partido** her resignation threw the party into chaos

catacumbas *nfpl* catacombs

catadióptrico *nm* reflector

catador, -ora *nm,f* taster ►► ***c. de vinos*** wine taster

catadura *nf* (a) *(prueba)* tasting (b) *(aspecto)* look, appearance

catafalco *nm* catafalque

catáfora *nf Ling* cataphora

catafórico, -a *adj Ling* cataphoric

catalán, -ana 1 *adj* Catalan, Catalonian
2 *nm,f (persona)* Catalan
3 *nm (lengua)* Catalan

catalanismo *nm* (a) *(palabra, expresión)* = word or expression of Catalan origin (b) *(ideología)* Catalan nationalism

catalanista 1 *adj* Catalan nationalist
2 *nmf* Catalan nationalist

catalejo *nm* telescope

catalepsia *nf* catalepsy

cataléptico, -a 1 *adj* (a) *(enfermo)* cataleptic; **en estado c.** in (a state of) suspended animation (b) *Fam (atontado)* half asleep
2 *nm,f (enfermo)* cataleptic

Catalina *n pr* **C. de Aragón** Catherine of Aragon; **C. la Grande** Catherine the Great

catálisis *nf inv* catalysis

catalítico, -a *adj Quím* catalytic

catalizador, -ora 1 *adj* (a) *Quím* catalytic (b) **el principio c. del cambio** *(impulsor)* the catalyst of change
2 *nm* (a) *Quím* catalyst (b) *Aut* catalytic converter (c) *(persona)* catalyst

catalizar [14] *vt* (a) *Quím* to catalyse (b) *(impulsar)* to provoke

catalogación *nf* cataloguing; **dos expertos se encargarán de la c. de los objetos** two experts will be in charge of cataloguing the objects; **su c. entre los tres mejores me parece injusta** I think it's unfair to rank him among the top three; **no admitir c.** *(ser extraordinario)* to be hard to categorize

catalogar [38] *vt* (a) *(en catálogo)* to catalogue (b) *(clasificar)* **c. a alguien de** *o* **como** to class sb as; **el consumo de cannabis no está catalogado como delito grave** the use of cannabis is not an arrestable offence; **una empresa catalogada entre las primeras del sector** a company ranked among the leaders in its field

catálogo *nm* catalogue

catalpa *nf* catalpa

catalufo, -a *nm,f Esp Fam Pey (catalán)* = pejorative term for a Catalan

Cataluña *n* Catalonia

catamarán *nm* catamaran

cataplasma *nf* (a) *Med* poultice (b) *Fam (pesado)* bore

cataplines *nmpl Fam (testículos)* nuts, *Br* goolies

cataplum, cataplún *interj* crash!, bang!

catapulta *nf* (a) *(arma)* catapult (b) *(en portaaviones)* catapult

catapultar *vt* (a) *(con catapulta)* to catapult (b) *(lanzar)* **salió catapultado del asiento** he was catapulted out of the seat; **c. a alguien a la fama** to shoot sb to fame

catapún *Fam* 1 *interj* crash!, bang!; **abrí la puerta y ¡c.!, me encontré con Juanita** I opened the door and who should I see but Juanita!
2 *adj* **el año c.** the year dot; **todavía utilizo una radio del año c.** I still use a really ancient radio; **vive en Murcia desde el año c.** she's been living in Murcia for ages *o* donkey's years

catar *vt* to taste

catarata *nf* (a) *(de agua)* waterfall ►► ***las cataratas del Iguazú*** the Iguaçú Falls; ***las cataratas del Niágara*** Niagara Falls (b) *Med* cataract; **lo van a operar de cataratas** he's going to have a cataract operation

cátaro, -a *Hist* 1 *adj* Cathar
2 *nm,f* Cathar

catarral *adj* catarrhal

catarro *nm* (a) *(constipado)* cold; **coger** *o* **agarrar un c.** to catch a cold (b) *(inflamación)* catarrh

catarsis *nf inv* catharsis

catártico, -a *adj* cathartic

catastral *adj* **registro c.** land register; **valor c.** = value of a property recorded in the land register, *Br* ≃ rateable value, *US* ≃ assessed value

catastro *nm* land registry

catástrofe *nf (calamidad)* catastrophe; *(accidente de avión, tren)* disaster ►► ***c. ecológica*** environmental disaster *o* catastrophe; ***c. natural*** natural disaster

catastróficamente *adv* disastrously, catastrophically

catastrófico, -a *adj* disastrous, catastrophic

catastrofismo *nm (pesimismo)* scaremongering, alarmism

catastrofista 1 *adj* alarmist
2 *nmf* alarmist

catatónico, -a *adj* (a) *(paciente)* catatonic (b) *Fam (alterado)* flabbergasted, *Br* gobsmacked

catavientos *nm inv* wind sleeve, wind cone

catavino *nm* wine-tasting glass

catavinos *nmf inv* wine taster

catch ['katʃ] *nm (lucha libre)* catch

catcher *(pl* **catchers***)* *nmf (en béisbol)* catcher

catchup (*pl* **catchups**) *nm* ketchup, *US* catsup

cate *nm Fam* fail; **me han puesto un c.** they failed me

cateador, -ora *nm,f Andes, RP* prospector

catear *vt* (**a**) *Esp Fam (suspender)* to fail, *US* to flunk; **he cateado** *o* **me han cateado la física** I failed *o US* flunked physics (**b**) *Andes, RP (mina)* to prospect (**c**) *Am (casa)* to search

catecismo *nm* catechism

catecumenado *nm* religious instruction; **un grupo de c.** a religious study group

catecúmeno, -a *nm,f* = member of a religious study group

cátedra *nf* (**a**) *(en universidad)* chair; **ocupa la c. de Historia antigua** she holds the chair of Ancient History; EXPR **sentar c.** to lay down the law (**b**) *(en instituto)* post of head of department (**c**) *(departamento)* department

catedral *nf (edificio)* cathedral; EXPR *Fam* **una mentira como una c.** a whopping great lie

catedralicio, -a *adj* cathedral; **ciudad catedralicia** cathedral city

catedrático, -a *nm,f* (**a**) *(de universidad)* professor (**b**) *(de instituto)* head of department

categoría *nf* (**a**) *(clase)* category; **un hotel de primera c.** a top-class hotel; **en su c. de presidente,...** as president,... ►► ***c. gramatical*** part of speech

(**b**) *(calidad)* quality; **de (primera) c.** first-class; **un discurso de c.** a first-class *o* an excellent speech; **se enfrenta a dos rivales de c.** she faces two opponents of the first rank

(**c**) *(posición social)* standing; **de c.** important

(**d**) *Dep (división)* division; **perder la c.** to be relegated ►► ***la c. reina*** *(en motociclismo)* 500 cc category; *(en automovilismo)* Formula One

(**e**) *(en lógica)* category

categóricamente *adv* categorically, absolutely

categórico, -a *adj* categorical; **respondió con un "no" c.** he replied with a most emphatic "no"

catenaria *nf Ferroc* catenary

cateo *nm* (**a**) *Am (registro)* (police) search (**b**) *Andes, RP (mina)* mine

catequesis *nf inv* catechism lesson, ≃ Sunday school; **c. de confirmación** = religious instruction in preparation for confirmation

catequizar [14] *vt* (**a**) *(enseñar religión a)* to instruct in Christian doctrine (**b**) *(adoctrinar)* to convert

catering, cátering ['katerin] (*pl* **caterings, cáterings**) *nm* catering

caterva *nf* **una c. de vagos** a shower of layabouts; **una c. de trastos inútiles** a heap of useless junk

catéter *nm* catheter

cateterismo *nm* catheterization

cateto, -a 1 *adj Pey* uncultured, uncouth

2 *nm,f Pey* country bumpkin

3 *nm Geom* = either of the two short sides of a right-angled triangle, *Espec* cathetus

catgut (*pl* **catguts**) *nm Med* catgut

catilinaria *nf* diatribe

catinga *nf Am (olor)* foul smell

catión *nm Fís* cation

catire, -a *Carib* **1** *adj (rubio)* blond, *f* blonde

2 *nm,f Fam (como apelativo)* blondie; **¡venga para acá, c.!** come here, blondie!

catódico, -a *adj* cathodic, cathode

cátodo *nm* cathode

catolicidad *nf* catholicity

catolicismo *nm* Catholicism

católico, -a 1 *adj* Catholic; EXPR *Fam* **no estar muy c.** to be under the weather ►► ***c. romano*** Roman Catholic

2 *nm,f* Catholic

catón *nm (libro)* primer

catorce *núm* fourteen; *ver también* **tres**

catorceavo, -a, catorzavo, -a *núm (fracción)* fourteenth; **la catorceava parte** a fourteenth

catre *nm (cama)* camp bed, *US* cot; *Fam* **irse al c.** to hit the sack, *US* to hit the hay

catrín, -ina *nm,f CAm, Méx Fam* moneybags *(singular)*, *Br* toff

catsup (*pl* **catsups**) *nm Méx* ketchup, *US* catsup

caucásico, -a, caucasiano, -a 1 *adj* Caucasian

2 *nm,f* Caucasian

Cáucaso *nm* **el C.** the Caucasus

cauce *nm* (**a**) *(de río, canal)* bed; **seguir el c. del río** to follow the course of the river; **el c. del río no es navegable** the river isn't navigable; EXPR **ya han vuelto las aguas a su c.** things have returned to normal

(**b**) *(camino, forma)* course; **esta solicitud hay que hacerla siguiendo los cauces reglamentarios** this application has to be made following the correct procedure; **las negociaciones siguen por los cauces habituales** the negotiations are continuing on the same course; **volver a su c.** to return to normal; **abrir nuevos cauces de diálogo** to open new channels for talks

(**c**) *(acequia)* channel

cauchal *nm* rubber plantation

cauchera *nf* (**a**) *(planta)* rubber plant (**b**) *Ven (tienda)* tyre centre

cauchero, -a 1 *adj* rubber; **la industria cauchera** the rubber industry; **una región cauchera** a rubber-producing area

2 *nm,f* (**a**) *(en plantación)* rubber gatherer *o* worker (**b**) *Ven (en gomería)* tyre fitter

cauchito *nm Col (goma elástica)* rubber band, *Br* elastic band

caucho *nm* (**a**) *(sustancia)* rubber ►► ***c. sintético*** synthetic rubber; ***c. vulcanizado*** vulcanized rubber (**b**) *(planta)* rubber tree (**c**) *Ven (impermeable) Br* mac, *US* slicker (**d**) *Ven (neumático)* tyre

caución *nf* (**a**) *(precaución)* caution (**b**) *Der* bail; **bajo c.** on bail ►► ***c. de indemnidad*** bond of indemnity

caucionar *vt* (**a**) *(precaver)* to caution (**b**) *Der* to put up *o* to post bail for

caucus *nm inv Pol* caucus

cauda *nf Am Astron* tail *(of comet)*

caudal[1] *nm* (**a**) *(cantidad de agua)* flow, volume (**b**) *(capital, abundancia)* wealth

caudal[2] *adj Zool* caudal

caudalosamente *adv* torrentially

caudaloso, -a *adj* (**a**) *(río)* with a large flow (**b**) *(persona)* wealthy, rich

caudillaje *nm* leadership

caudillismo *nm* = tendency for politics, either national or within a party, to be dominated by a strong leader

caudillo *nm* (**a**) *(en la guerra)* leader, head (**b**) *Hist* **el C.** *(en España)* = title used to refer to Franco (**c**) *(en América Latina) (de partido político)* party boss; *(dictador)* strongman

causa *nf* (**a**) *(origen)* cause; **la c. última** the ultimate cause *o* reason; **el tabaco es la c. de muchas enfermedades respiratorias** smoking is the cause of many respiratory diseases; **él es la c. directa de todos mis problemas** he is directly responsible for all my problems; **la relación c.-efecto** the relationship between cause and effect ►► ***c. final*** final cause; ***c. primera*** first cause

(**b**) *(razón, motivo)* reason; **se desconocen las causas del accidente** it is not known what caused the accident; **por esta c. mueren al año muchos niños** every year many children die as a result of this; **a** *o* **por c. de** because of; **llegaron tarde a** *o* **por c. del intenso tráfico** they arrived late because of the heavy traffic; **ello no es c. suficiente para dejar de asistir a clase** that isn't a good enough reason for stopping going to school; **por c. mayor** for reasons beyond my/our/*etc* control

(**c**) *(ideal, objetivo)* cause; **una c. humanitaria** a humanitarian cause; **es todo por una buena c.** it's all for *o* in a good cause; **abrazar una c.** to embrace a cause; **dieron su vida por la c.** they gave their lives for the cause; EXPR **hacer c. común con alguien** to make common cause with sb; EXPR **ser una c. perdida** to be a lost cause

(**d**) *Der* case; **una c. contra alguien** a case against sb ►► ***c. civil*** lawsuit; ***c. criminal*** criminal case

(**e**) *Andes (comida ligera)* light meal, snack

(**f**) *Perú (guiso)* = dish of mashed potatoes mixed with cheese, olives, sweetcorn and lettuce, eaten cold

causahabiente *nm Der* assignee

causal *adj* (**a**) *(relación, encadenamiento)* causal (**b**) *Gram* causal

causalidad *nf* causality

causante 1 *adj* **la razón c.** the cause

2 *nmf* **el c. del accidente** the person responsible for *o* who caused the accident; **eres el c. de todos mis males** you're the cause of all my problems

causar *vt (daños, problemas)* to cause; *(placer, satisfacción)* to give; **el huracán causó estragos en la costa** the hurricane wreaked havoc on the coast; **el terremoto causó dos mil muertos** two thousand people died in the earthquake, the earthquake killed two thousand people; **el accidente le causó graves lesiones** he was seriously injured in the accident; **c. (una) buena/mala impresión** to make a good/bad impression; **me causa mucha felicidad saber que se hayan reconciliado**

it makes me very happy to know they've made up with one another; **esta crema a veces causa una sensación de picor** this cream sometimes causes an itching sensation

causativo, -a *adj* causative

causeo *nm Andes (comida ligera)* light meal, snack

causticidad *nf* (a) *(de sustancia)* causticity (b) *(de comentarios)* causticity

cáustico, -a *adj* (a) *(sustancia)* caustic (b) *(comentario)* caustic

cautela *nf* caution, cautiousness; **obrar con c.** to act cautiously

cautelar *adj (medida)* precautionary, preventive; *(detención)* preventive

cautelosamente *adv* cautiously

cauteloso, -a 1 *adj* cautious, careful
2 *nm,f* cautious person

cauterio *nm Med* cauterization

cauterización *nf* cauterization

cauterizar [14] *vt* to cauterize

cautivador, -ora 1 *adj* captivating, enchanting
2 *nm,f* charmer

cautivante *adj Am* captivating, enchanting

cautivar *vt* (a) *(seducir)* to captivate, to enchant; **su simpatía me cautiva** I find her friendly manner quite captivating (b) *(apresar)* to capture

cautiverio *nm* captivity; **pasó cinco años de c. en Argel** he spent five years in prison in Algiers

cautividad *nf* captivity; **vivir en c.** to live in captivity

cautivo, -a 1 *adj* captive
2 *nm,f* captive

cauto, -a *adj* cautious, careful

cava[1] *nf* (a) *(bodega)* wine cellar (b) *(faena agrícola)* = action of hoeing the soil in a vineyard to break it up

cava[2] *nm (bebida)* cava, = Spanish sparkling wine

cavador, -ora *nm,f* digger

cavar 1 *vt (hoyo)* to dig; *(con azada)* to hoe; **c. un pozo** to sink a well; EXPR **está cavando su propia tumba** she is digging her own grave
2 *vi (hacer hoyo)* to dig; *(con azada)* to hoe

cavatina *nf Mús* cavatina

caverna *nf (cueva)* cave; *(más grande)* cavern

cavernícola 1 *adj* (a) *(animal, hombre)* cave-dwelling (b) *Pey (retrógrado)* reactionary
2 *nmf* (a) *(de las cavernas)* caveman, *f* cavewoman (b) *Pey (retrógrado)* reactionary

cavernoso, -a *adj* (a) *(con cavernas)* cavernous, with caves (b) *(voz, tos)* hollow

caviar *nm* caviar

cavidad *nf* cavity ▸▸ *Anat* ***c. abdominal*** abdominal cavity; *Anat* ***c. bucal*** oral *o* buccal cavity; *Anat* ***c. nasal*** nasal cavity; *Anat* ***c. peritoneal*** peritoneal cavity; *Anat* ***c. torácica*** thoracic cavity

cavilación *nf* deep thought, pondering; **tras muchas cavilaciones, decidió entregarse** after much thought, he decided to give himself up

cavilar *vi* to think deeply, to ponder; **estuvo cavilando sobre qué modelo comprar** he was debating with himself *o* pondering which model to buy

caviloso, -a *adj* thoughtful, pensive

cayado *nm* (a) *(de pastor)* crook (b) *(de obispo)* crozier (c) *Anat* **c. de la aorta** aortic arch

cayena *nf (especia)* cayenne pepper

cayera *etc ver* **caer**

cayo *nm (isla)* cay, key

cayopollín *nm* four-eyed opossum

cayuco *nm* = Indian canoe

caz *nm* ditch, canal

caza 1 *nf* (a) *(acción de cazar)* hunting; **la c. del zorro** fox hunting; **ir de c.** to go hunting; *también Fig* **dar c. a** to hunt down ▸▸ ***c. submarina*** underwater fishing
(b) *(animales, carne)* game ▸▸ ***c. mayor*** big game; ***c. menor*** small game
(c) *(búsqueda)* hunt; **ir a la c. de algo** to go hunting for sth; **ir a la c. de un trabajo** to go job-hunting ▸▸ *Fig* ***c. de brujas*** witch-hunt; ***c. y captura:*** **prometió dar c. y captura al asesino** he promised to track the terrorist down; **un millonario que va a la c. y captura de esposa** a millionaire who is hunting for a wife; ***c. del tesoro*** treasure hunt
(d) *Fam (en ciclismo)* chase
2 *nm (avión)* fighter (plane)

cazabe *nm Am* cassava bread

cazabombardero *nm* fighter-bomber

cazadero *nm* **este prado es un c. de conejos** this meadow is a good place to hunt rabbits

cazador, -ora 1 *adj* hunting
2 *nm,f (persona)* hunter ▸▸ ***c. de autógrafos*** autograph hunter; ***c. de cabezas*** headhunter; ***c. de firmas*** autograph hunter; ***c. furtivo*** poacher; ***c. de pieles*** fur trapper; ***c.-recolector*** hunter-gatherer; ***c. de recompensas*** bounty hunter

cazadora *nf (prenda)* jacket ▸▸ ***c. de aviador*** bomber jacket; ***c. vaquera*** denim jacket

cazadotes *nm inv* fortune hunter

cazafortunas *nmf inv* fortune hunter

cazalla *nf (bebida)* = aniseed-flavoured spirit

cazaminas *nm inv* minesweeper

cazanazis *nmf inv* Nazi hunter

cazar [14] *vt* (a) *(animales)* to hunt
(b) *Fam (pillar, atrapar)* to catch; *(en matrimonio)* to trap; **cazó a una rica heredera** he landed himself a rich heiress; **he conseguido c. dos entradas para el concierto** I managed to get hold of two tickets for the concert; **cazó un buen trabajo** she landed herself a good job; EXPR **cazarlas al vuelo** to be quick on the uptake
(c) *Fam (sorprender)* to catch; **me has cazado despistado** you've caught me on the hop
(d) *Fam (entender)* to catch, to get; **cuando me hablan rápido en inglés, no cazo una** when people speak English quickly to me, I can't understand a word
(e) *Fam (hacer una falta a)* to hack down; **el portero cazó al delantero** the goalkeeper brought down the forward
(f) *Fam (en ciclismo)* to chase down

cazarrecompensas *nmf inv* bounty hunter

cazasubmarino *nm* submarine hunter-killer

cazatalentos *nmf inv* (a) *(de artistas, deportistas)* talent scout (b) *(de ejecutivos)* headhunter

cazatorpedero *nm* = small fast boat designed for use against torpedo boats

cazo *nm* (a) *(cacerola)* saucepan (b) *(cucharón)* ladle (c) *Fam (persona fea)* pig (d) EXPR *Fam* **meter el c.** *(meter la pata)* to put one's foot in it

cazoleta *nf* (a) *(recipiente)* pot (b) *(de pipa)* bowl (c) *(de espada)* guard

cazón *nm* dogfish

cazuela *nf* (a) *(recipiente)* pot, saucepan; *(de barro)* earthenware cooking pot (b) *(guiso)* casserole, stew; **c. de marisco** seafood casserole; **pollo a la c.** chicken casserole

cazurro, -a 1 *adj (bruto)* stupid
2 *nm,f (bruto)* idiot, fool

CC (a) *(abrev de* **código civil***)* civil code (b) *(abrev de* **código de circulación***)* highway code (c) *(abrev de* **cuerpo consular***)* consular staff (d) *(abrev de* **corriente continua***)* DC

cc *(abrev de* **centímetros cúbicos***)* cc

c/c *(abrev de* **cuenta corriente***)* c/a

CC. AA. *nfpl (abrev de* **Comunidades Autónomas***)* = autonomous regions (of Spain)

CC. OO. *nfpl (abrev de* **Comisiones Obreras***)* = Spanish left-wing trade union

CD 1 *nm (abrev de* **compact disc***)* CD ▸▸ ***C. interactivo*** interactive CD
2 (a) *(abrev de* **Club Deportivo***)* sports club; *(en fútbol)* FC (b) *(abrev de* **Cuerpo Diplomático***)* CD

CD-I *nm (abrev de* **compact disc interactivo***)* CD-I

CD-ROM ['θeðe'rrom] *nm (abrev de* **compact disc-read only memory***)* CD-ROM

CE 1 *nm (abrev de* **Consejo de Europa***)* CE
2 *nf* (a) *Antes (abrev de* **Comunidad Europea***)* EC (b) *(abrev de* **Comisión Europea***)* EC

ce *nf* (a) **ce por be** *(detalladamente)* in great detail (b) **por ce o por be** *(por una razón u otra)* one way or another; **si por ce o por be no pudiera acudir, te llamaría** if I couldn't be there for one reason or another, I'd call you

cebada *nf* barley ▸▸ ***c. perlada*** pearl barley

cebadal *nm* barley field

cebado, -a 1 *adj (gordo)* huge
2 *nm (de tubo, bomba)* priming

cebador, -ora 1 *nm* (**a**) *(de fluorescente)* starter (**b**) *(de pólvora)* primer
2 *nm,f RP* (**a**) *Aut* starter (**b**) *(de mate)* = person who prepares a drink of maté

cebadura *nf RP (de mate)* = measure of maté

cebar 1 *vt* (**a**) *(engordar)* to fatten (up) (**b**) *(fuego, caldera)* to stoke, to fuel; *(máquina, arma)* to prime (**c**) *(anzuelo)* to bait (**d**) *(sentimiento)* to feed, to arouse (**e**) *RP (mate)* to prepare, to brew
2 **cebarse** *vpr* **la policía se cebó con los manifestantes** the police dealt with the demonstrators brutally; **siempre se ceba en** *o* **con los más débiles** she always really takes it out on the weakest ones

cebichada *nf* = dinner party at which "cebiche" is served

cebiche, ceviche *nm* = raw fish marinated in lemon juice

cebo *nm* (**a**) *(para pescar)* bait; **c. de pesca** fishing bait (**b**) *(para explosivo, pistola)* primer (**c**) *(para atraer)* bait; **usó el dinero como c.** she used the money as a bait

cebolla *nf* onion ►► *RP* ***c. de verdeo*** *Br* spring onion, *US* scallion

cebollazo *nm Esp Fam (borrachera)* **agarrar un c.** to get plastered

cebolleta *nf* (**a**) *(planta) Br* spring onion, *US* scallion (**b**) *(en vinagre)* (small) pickled onion, silverskin onion

cebollino *nm* (**a**) *(planta)* chive (**b**) *(cebolleta) Br* spring onion, *US* scallion (**c**) *Fam (necio)* idiot

cebollita *nf RP* ***c. de verdeo*** *Br* spring onion, *US* scallion

cebón, -ona 1 *adj* (**a**) *(animal)* fattened (**b**) *Fam (persona)* fat
2 *nm* pig

cebra *nf* zebra

cebú (*pl* **cebúes**) *nm* zebu

ceca *nf Hist* mint; EXPR *Fam* **ir de la C. a la Meca** to go here, there and everywhere; EXPR *RP* **cara o c.** heads or tails

cecear *vi* (**a**) *(como defecto)* to lisp (**b**) *(como fenómeno lingüístico)* = to pronounce the letter "s" as "th"

ceceo *nm* (**a**) *(defecto)* lisp (**b**) *(fenómeno lingüístico)* = the pronunciation of the letter "s" as "th"

cecina *nf* = dried, salted meat

cedazo *nm* sieve; **pasar algo por un c.** to sieve sth

ceder 1 *vt* (**a**) *(traspasar, transferir)* to hand over; **las tierras fueron cedidas a los campesinos** the land was handed over to the peasants; **el gobierno central cederá a los ayuntamientos el control de la política cultural** central government will hand control of cultural policy to the town halls
(**b**) *(conceder)* to give up; **c. el paso** to give way; **me levanté para c. mi asiento a una anciana** I stood up and gave my seat to an old lady; **el actual campeón cedió dos segundos con respecto al ganador** the reigning champion was two seconds slower than the winner
(**c**) *(pelota)* to pass
2 *vi* (**a**) *(venirse abajo)* to give way; **la puerta finalmente cedió** the door finally gave way; **el suelo del escenario cedió por el peso del decorado** the stage floor gave way under the weight of the scenery
(**b**) *(rendirse)* to give up; **cedió a sus ruegos** he gave in to their pleading; **no cederemos a las amenazas** we won't give in to threats; **cedió ante las presiones de la comunidad internacional** he gave way to international pressure; **no deben c. a la tentación de tomarse la justicia por su mano** they mustn't give in to the temptation to take the law into their own hands; **c. en** to give up on; **cedió en lo esencial** he gave in on the important issues
(**c**) *(destensarse)* to give; **el jersey ha cedido** the jersey has gone baggy
(**d**) *(disminuir)* to abate, to ease up; **por fin cedió la tormenta** at last the storm eased up; **la fiebre ha cedido** the fever has gone down

cederrón *nm* CD-ROM

cedilla *nf (letra)* cedilla; **ce (con) c.** c cedilla

cedro *nm* cedar ►► ***c. del Atlas*** Atlas cedar; ***c. del Líbano*** Cedar of Lebanon

cédula *nf* document ►► ***c. de citación*** summons *(singular)*; ***c. de habitabilidad*** = certificate stating that a place is habitable; ***c. hipotecaria*** mortgage bond; *Am* ***c. de identidad*** identity card; ***c. de vecindad*** identity card

CEE *nf Antes* (*abrev de* **Comunidad Económica Europea**) EEC

cefalalgia *nf* headache, *Espec* cephalalgia

cefalea *nf* headache

cefálico, -a *adj Anat* cephalic

cefalópodo *Zool* 1 *nm (animal)* cephalopod, member of the order *Cephalopoda*
2 **cefalópodos** *nmpl (orden) Cephalopoda*; **del orden de los cefalópodos** of the order *Cephalopoda*

cefalorraquídeo, -a *adj Fisiol (líquido)* cerebrospinal

cefalotórax *nm inv Zool* cephalothorax

céfiro *nm (viento)* zephyr

cefo *nm* moustached monkey

cegador, -ora *adj* blinding

cegar [43] 1 *vt* (**a**) *(dejar ciego)* to blind; **esa luz tan intensa me ciega** that very bright light is blinding me (**b**) *(obnubilar)* to blind; **la avaricia lo ciega** he is blinded by greed (**c**) *(tapar) (ventana)* to block off; *(tubo)* to block up
2 *vi* to be blinding
3 **cegarse** *vpr* (**a**) *(quedarse ciego)* to be blinded (**b**) *(obnubilarse)* to be blinded

cegato, -a *Fam* 1 *adj* short-sighted
2 *nm,f* short-sighted person

cegesimal *adj* = of/relating to CGS units

ceguera *nf* (**a**) *(invidencia)* blindness ►► ***c. nocturna*** night blindness; ***c. parcial*** partial blindness; ***c. total*** total blindness (**b**) *(obcecación)* blindness

CEI ['θei] *nf* (*abrev de* **Confederación de Estados Independientes**) CIS

ceiba *nf* kapok tree

ceibo *nm* ceiba, silk-cotton tree

Ceilán *n Antes* Ceylon

ceilandés, -esa 1 *adj* Sinhalese
2 *nm,f (persona)* Sinhalese
3 *nm (lengua)* Sinhalese

ceja *nf* (**a**) *(en la cara)* eyebrow; EXPR *Fam* **hasta las cejas: está endeudado hasta las cejas** he's up to his ears in debt; *Fam* **nos pusimos hasta las cejas de vodka** we pickled ourselves in vodka, we drank ourselves silly on vodka; EXPR *Fam* **quemarse las cejas** to burn the midnight oil; EXPR *Fam* **entre c. y c.: se le metió entre c. y c. que tenía que hacerlo** he got it into his head that he had to do it; **tiene a mi hermano entre c. y c.** he can't stand the sight of my brother
(**b**) *(mástil)* bridge
(**c**) *(cejilla)* capo

cejar *vi* to let up; **no cejó hasta conseguir su objetivo** she didn't let up until she had achieved her aim; **al final cejó en su esfuerzo** in the end he gave up in his attempt; **no cejaremos en nuestro empeño (por...)** we will not let up in our efforts (to...)

cejijunto, -a *adj* (**a**) *(persona)* **es c.** his eyebrows meet in the middle (**b**) *(gesto)* **estar c.** to frown, to be frowning

cejilla *nf* (**a**) *(de guitarra)* capo (**b**) *(colocación del dedo)* bar, barré; **hacer la c.** to bar

cejudo, -a *adj* bushy-browed, thick-browed

celacanto *nm (pez)* coelacanth

celada *nf* (**a**) *(emboscada)* ambush (**b**) *(trampa)* trick, trap (**c**) *(pieza de armadura)* helmet

celador, -ora *nm,f (de colegio) Br* caretaker, *US & Scot* janitor; *(de hospital)* porter, orderly; *(de prisión)* warder; *(de museo)* attendant

celaje *nm* (**a**) *(claraboya)* skylight (**b**) *Carib, Perú (fantasma)* ghost

CELAM [θe'lam] *nm* (*abrev de* **Consejo Episcopal Latinoamericano**) = Latin American bishops' conference

celar 1 *vt* (**a**) *(encubrir)* to hide, to conceal (**b**) *(vigilar)* to make sure, to ensure; **c. que algo se cumpla** to make sure *o* ensure that sth is done
2 *vi* **c. por** *o* **sobre** to watch out for, to take care of

celda *nf* (**a**) *(de convento)* cell (**b**) *(de cárcel)* cell ►► ***c. de aislamiento*** solitary confinement cell; ***c. de castigo*** solitary confinement cell (**c**) *(de panal)* cell (**d**) *Informát* cell

celdilla *nf* cell *(of honeycomb)*

celebérrimo, -a *adj* extremely famous

celebración *nf* (**a**) *(festejo)* celebration; **las celebraciones duraron hasta el día siguiente** the festivities went on until the next day; **estar de c.** to be celebrating
(**b**) *(de ceremonia, reunión)* holding; **la c. de unos Juegos Olímpicos** the holding of the Olympic Games; **la oposición exige la c. de elecciones anticipadas** the opposition is calling for early elections to be held
(**c**) *(religiosa)* celebration; **tras la c. de la misa, el párroco salió a dar un paseo** after he had finished saying mass, the priest went out for a walk

celebrante 1 *adj* celebrating
2 *nmf* participant (in a celebration)
3 *nm (sacerdote)* celebrant

celebrar 1 *vt* (**a**) *(festejar)* to celebrate; **esta victoria hay que celebrarla** this victory calls for a celebration
(**b**) *(llevar a cabo)* to hold; **celebraremos la reunión esta tarde** we'll hold the meeting this afternoon
(**c**) *(oficio religioso)* to celebrate; *(boda)* to officiate at; **¿quién va a c. vuestra boda?** who will be the priest at your wedding?; **celebró una misa en memoria del difunto** he said *o* celebrated a mass in memory of the deceased
(**d**) *(alegrarse de)* **celebro tu ascenso** I'm delighted by your promotion; **celebro que hayas podido venir** I'm delighted you were able to come
(**e**) *(alabar)* to praise, to applaud
2 *vi (decir misa)* to say mass
3 **celebrarse** *vpr* (**a**) *(festejarse)* to be celebrated; **esa fiesta se celebra el 25 de julio** that holiday falls on 25 July; **el fin del asedio se celebró por todo lo alto** the end of the siege was celebrated in style
(**b**) *(llevarse a cabo)* to take place, to be held; **las elecciones se celebrarán dentro de dos meses** the elections will take place *o* be held within two months; **la entrevista se celebró a puerta cerrada** the meeting took place behind closed doors

célebre *adj* famous, celebrated

celebridad *nf* (**a**) *(fama)* fame (**b**) *(persona famosa)* celebrity

celemín *nm* = dry measure equivalent to 4.625 litres

celentéreo *Zool* 1 *nm* coelenterate, member of the order *Coelenterata*
2 **celentéreos** *nmpl (orden) Coelenterata*; **del orden de los celentéreos** of the order *Coelenterata*

celeridad *nf* speed; **con c.** rapidly

celesta *nf* celeste

celeste 1 *adj* (**a**) *(del firmamento)* celestial, heavenly; **bóveda c.** firmament (**b**) *(color)* **azul c.** sky blue
2 *nm* sky blue

celestial *adj* (**a**) *(del cielo, paraíso)* celestial, heavenly (**b**) *(delicioso)* heavenly; **esto me suena a música c.** *(a falsa promesa)* that sounds like a lot of hot air; *(maravillosamente)* that's music to my ears

celestina *nf (persona)* lovers' go-between

celibato *nm* celibacy

célibe 1 *adj* celibate
2 *nmf* celibate

celidonia *nf* celandine

celinda *nf* syringa, mock-orange

cellisca *nf* sleet

celo *nm* 1 (**a**) *(esmero)* zeal, keenness; **con c.** zealously (**b**) *(devoción)* devotion (**c**) *(de hembra)* heat; *(de ciervo)* rut; **nuestra perra está en c.** our dog is *Br* on *o US* in heat (**d**) *Esp (cinta adhesiva) Br* Sellotape®, *US* Scotch® tape
2 **celos** *nmpl* jealousy; **dar celos a alguien** to make sb jealous; **tener celos de alguien** to be jealous of sb

celofán *nm* Cellophane®

celoma *nm Anat* coelom

celosamente *adv* conscientiously, zealously

celosía *nf* lattice window, jalousie

celoso, -a 1 *adj* (**a**) *(con celos)* jealous; **está c. del profesor de tenis** he's jealous of the tennis coach (**b**) *(cumplidor)* conscientious; **es muy c. en lo que hace** he's very conscientious
2 *nm,f (con celos)* jealous person

Celsius *adj* Celsius; **grado C.** degree Celsius; **escala C.** Celsius (temperature) scale

celta 1 *adj* Celtic
2 *nmf (persona)* Celt
3 *nm (lengua)* Celtic

celtibérico, -a *adj* Celtiberian

celtíbero, -a, celtibero, -a 1 *adj* Celtiberian
2 *nm,f* Celtiberian

céltico, -a *adj* Celtic

célula *nf* (**a**) *(en biología)* cell ▸▸ ***c. madre*** mother cell; ***c. T*** T-cell (**b**) *Elec* cell ▸▸ ***c. fotoeléctrica*** photocell, photoelectric cell; ***c. fotovoltaica*** photovoltaic cell (**c**) *(grupo de personas)* cell

celular 1 *adj* (**a**) *(de la célula)* cellular (**b**) **coche c.** *(de la policía) Br* police van, *US* police wagon (**c**) *Tel* **telefonía c.** cellphones; **el mercado de la telefonía c.** the cellphone market
2 *nm Am* mobile (phone)

celulitis *nf inv* (**a**) *(acumulación de grasa)* cellulite (**b**) *Med (inflamación)* cellulitis

celuloide *nm* (**a**) *Quím* celluloid (**b**) *(cine)* **la industria del c.** the movie *o Br* film industry; **el mundo del c.** the world of the movies, *Br* the world of film; **llevar una novela al c.** to bring a novel to the screen; **las estrellas del c.** the stars of the silver screen

celulosa *nf* cellulose

cementar *vt (metal)* to face-harden

cementera *nf* (**a**) *(fábrica)* cement factory (**b**) *(empresa)* cement company

cementerio *nm* (**a**) *(de muertos)* cemetery (**b**) *(de objetos, productos)* ***c. de automóviles*** scrapyard; ***c. de coches*** scrapyard; ***c. nuclear*** nuclear dumping ground; ***c. radiactivo*** nuclear dumping ground

cemento *nm* (**a**) *(material)* cement; *(hormigón)* concrete ▸▸ ***c. armado*** reinforced concrete; ***c. Portland*** Portland cement (**b**) *(de dentista)* cement (**c**) *Am (pegamento)* glue

cemita *nf Arg (pan)* bran bread

cena *nf* dinner; **dar una c.** to give a dinner party; **¿qué quieres de c.?** what would you like for dinner?; *Rel* **la Última C.** the Last Supper ▸▸ ***c. de despedida*** farewell dinner; ***c. de gala*** gala dinner; ***c. de homenaje*: dieron una c. de homenaje al presidente** they gave a dinner in honour of the president; ***c. oficial*** official dinner

cenáculo *nm* (**a**) *Formal (grupo)* circle (**b**) *Rel* Cenacle, = room in which the Last Supper took place

cenador *nm* (**a**) *(en jardín)* arbour, bower (**b**) *(adosado a casa)* conservatory

cenaduría *nf Méx* (cheap) restaurant

cenagal *nm* (**a**) *(zona)* bog, mire (**b**) *(situación)* **meterse en un c.** to get into deep water

cenagoso, -a *adj* muddy

cenar 1 *vt* to have for dinner; **c. una sopa/un plato de verduras** to have some soup/vegetables for dinner
2 *vi* to have dinner; **¿qué hay para c.?** what's for dinner? **c. fuera, salir a c.** to go out for dinner, to eat out; **invitar a alguien a c.** to invite sb to dinner; **quédate a c.** stay for dinner; **en ese restaurante dan muy bien de c.** they serve an excellent dinner in that restaurant

cencerro *nm (campana)* cowbell; EXPR *Fam* **estar como un c.** to be as mad as a hatter

cendal *nm* sendal

cenefa *nf* (**a**) *(en vestido)* border (**b**) *(en pared)* frieze

cenestesia *nf Psi* coenaesthesia

cenetista 1 *adj* = relating to the CNT
2 *nmf* member of the CNT

cenicero *nm* ashtray

cenicienta *nf* (**a**) **(la) C.** *(personaje)* Cinderella (**b**) *(persona, equipo)* **es la c. de la casa** she's the person who does all the work in the house; **la selección coreana es la c. del grupo** the Korean squad are regarded as the makeweights *o* minnows of the group

ceniciento, -a *adj* ashen, ash-grey

cenit *nm* (**a**) *Astron* zenith (**b**) *(punto culminante)* zenith, peak; **ha llegado al c. de su carrera** she is at the peak of her career

cenital *adj (posición)* zenithal; **luz c.** light from above

ceniza *nf* (**a**) *(de cigarrillo, madera)* ash; **reducir algo a c.** to reduce sth to ashes; **tomar la c.** = to be marked on the forehead with ashes on Ash Wednesday ▸▸ ***c. volcánica*** volcanic ash (**b**) **cenizas** *(de cadáver)* ashes

cenizo, -a 1 *adj* ashen, ash-grey
2 *nm,f Fam (gafe)* jinxed person; **ser un c.** to be jinxed
3 *nm* (**a**) *(planta)* fat hen, *US* pigweed (**b**) *Fam (mala suerte)* bad luck; **tener el c.** to have bad luck, to be unlucky

cenobio *nm* monastery

cenobita *nmf* coenobite

cenotafio *nm Arte* cenotaph

cenote *nm CAm, Méx* natural water well

cenozoico, -a *Geol* 1 *adj* Cenozoic
2 *nm* **el c.** the Cenozoic

censal *adj* **error c.** error in the census

censar *vt* to take a census of

censista *nmf* census enumerator *o* taker

censo *nm* (**a**) *(de población, agrario)* census; **c. de aves amenazadas/de joyeros** list of endangered birds/jewellers ▸▸ ***c. de población*** (population) census (**b**) *Esp (electoral)* electoral roll *o* register; **estar inscrito en el c.** to be on the electoral roll *o* register ▸▸ ***c. electoral*** electoral roll *o* register (**c**) *(tributo)* tax (**d**) *Der* lease

censor, -ora 1 *nm,f* (**a**) *(funcionario)* censor; **c. de cine** movie *o Br* film censor (**b**) *(crítico)* critic (**c**) *Esp Econ* ***c. de cuentas*** auditor; ***c. jurado de cuentas*** *Br* chartered accountant, *US* certified public accountant
2 *nm Hist (en Roma)* censor

censura *nf* (**a**) *(prohibición)* censorship (**b**) **la c.** *(organismo)* the censors (**c**) *(reprobación)* censure, severe criticism; **decir algo en tono de c.** to say something censoriously *o* in a tone of censure (**d**) *Esp Econ* ***c. de cuentas*** inspection of accounts, audit

censurable *adj* blameworthy, reprehensible

censurar *vt* (**a**) *(prohibir)* to censor; **censuraron dos escenas de la película** two scenes in the movie were censored (**b**) *(reprobar)* to criticize severely, to censure; **siempre censura mi comportamiento** she always criticizes my behaviour

centauro *nm* centaur

centavo, -a 1 *núm* hundredth; **la centava parte** a hundredth; *ver también* **octavo**
2 *nm (moneda) (en países anglosajones)* cent; *(en países latinoamericanos)* centavo; EXPR **sin un c.: estar sin un c.** to be flat broke; **murió sin un c.** he died penniless

centella *nf* (**a**) *(rayo)* flash (**b**) *(chispa)* spark (**c**) **es una c.** *(persona)* he's like lightning; EXPR **rápido como una c.** quick as a flash

centelleante *adj* (**a**) *(luz)* sparkling; *(estrella)* twinkling (**b**) *(ojos) (de entusiasmo)* sparkling; *(de ira)* flashing

centellear *vi* (**a**) *(luz)* to sparkle; *(estrella)* to twinkle (**b**) *(joya)* to sparkle (**c**) *(ojos) (con entusiasmo)* to sparkle; *(con ira)* to flash

centelleo *nm* (**a**) *(de luz, estrella)* twinkle, twinkling (**b**) *(de joya)* sparkle (**c**) **el c. de sus ojos** *(con entusiasmo)* the sparkle in her eyes; *(con ira)* her flashing eyes

centena *nf* hundred; **una c. de coches** a hundred cars

centenal *nm* rye field

centenar *nm* hundred; **un c. de** a hundred; **a centenares** by the hundred

centenario, -a 1 *adj (persona)* over a hundred; *(institución, edificio, árbol)* century-old
2 *nm,f (persona)* centenarian
3 *nm* (**a**) *(fecha)* centenary; **quinto c.** five hundredth anniversary; **hoy se cumple el primer c. de su nacimiento** today is the centenary of his birth (**b**) *Méx (moneda)* = gold 50-peso coin, legal tender 1916-30

centeno *nm* rye

centesimal *adj* centesimal

centésimo, -a 1 *núm* hundredth; *ver también* **octavo**
2 *nm* cent *(of Uruguayan peso)*

centiárea *nf* square metre

centígrado, -a *adj* centigrade; **veinte grados centígrados** twenty degrees centigrade

centigramo *nm* centigram

centilitro *nm* centilitre

centímetro *nm* centimetre

céntimo *nm (de euro, peseta, bolívar)* cent; EXPR **sin un c.: estar sin un c.** to be flat broke; **murió sin un c.** he died penniless

centinela *nm* sentry; **estar de c.** to be on sentry duty

centollo *nm*, **centolla** *nf* European spider crab

centón *nm* (**a**) *Lit* cento (**b**) *(manta)* crazy quilt

centrado, -a *adj* (**a**) *(situado en el centro)* centred (**b**) *(concentrado)* concentrated; **está muy c. en su trabajo** he's very focused on his work (**c**) *(equilibrado)* stable, balanced; **desde que tiene trabajo está más c.** he's more stable *o* balanced since he's been working (**d**) *(basado)* **c. en** based on

central 1 *adj* (**a**) *(en el centro)* central (**b**) *(principal)* central, main (**c**) *Ling (articulación)* central
2 *nf* (**a**) *(oficina)* headquarters, head office; *(de correos, comunicaciones)* main office
(**b**) *(de energía)* power station ▸▸ ***c. atómica*** nuclear power station; ***c. de biomasa*** biomass power plant *o* station; ***c. eléctrica*** power station; ***c. eólica*** wind farm; ***c. geotérmica*** geothermal power station; ***c. heliotérmica*** solar power plant *o* station, solar farm; ***c. hidráulica*** hydraulic generator; ***c. hidroeléctrica*** hydroelectric power station; ***c. maremotriz*** tidal power station *o* plant; ***c. nuclear*** nuclear power station; ***c. solar*** solar power plant *o* station, solar farm; ***c. térmica*** power station *(coal- or oil-fired)*
(**c**) **c. (sindical)** *(sindicato) Br* trade union, *US* labor union
(**d**) ***c. telefónica*** telephone exchange
(**e**) *Carib, CAm (de azúcar)* sugar mill
(**f**) *Méx* ***c. camionera*** bus station
3 *nm Dep* central defender

centralismo *nm Pol* centralism

centralista *Pol* 1 *adj* centralist
2 *nmf* centralist

centralita *nf* switchboard

centralización *nf* centralization

centralizado, -a *adj* centralized; *Aut* **cierre c.** central locking

centralizar [14] *vt* to centralize

centrar 1 *vt* (**a**) *(colocar en el centro)* to centre
(**b**) *(persona)* to steady, to make stable; **el nuevo trabajo lo ha centrado mucho** the new job has really helped him settle down
(**c**) *(interés, atención)* **la reunión de los dos presidentes centró la atención de todo el mundo** the meeting between the two presidents caught the attention of the whole world; **centró su intervención en las causas del calentamiento global** her remarks focused on the causes of global warming; **una medida económica centrada en reducir el desempleo** an economic measure aimed at reducing unemployment; **centraba todas las miradas** all eyes were on her
(**d**) *Dep* to centre, to cross
2 *vi Dep* to centre, to cross
3 **centrarse** *vpr* (**a**) **centrarse en algo** *(tener como objeto)* to concentrate *o* focus on sth; **la historia se centra en la lucha de una familia por sobrevivir** the story revolves around a family's struggle for survival
(**b**) *(concentrarse)* to concentrate; **con tanto ruido no consigo centrarme** I can't concentrate with so much noise; **necesitas centrarte más en lo que estás haciendo** you need to concentrate more on what you're doing
(**c**) *(equilibrarse)* to find one's feet; **se ha centrado mucho desde que tiene el nuevo trabajo** he's settled down a lot since he's been in his new job

céntrico, -a *adj* central; **una calle muy céntrica** a street right in the centre of town; **¿cuál es la sucursal más céntrica?** which is the most central branch?

centrifugación *nf* centrifugation

centrifugado *nm (de ropa)* spin

centrifugadora *nf* (**a**) *(para secar ropa)* spin-dryer (**b**) *Tec* centrifuge

centrifugar [38] *vt* (**a**) *(ropa)* to spin-dry (**b**) *Tec* to centrifuge

centrífugo, -a *adj* centrifugal

centrípeto, -a *adj* centripetal

centrismo *nm* centrism

centrista 1 *adj* centre, centrist; **un partido c.** a party of the centre
2 *nmf* centrist; **los centristas propusieron una reforma** the centre proposed a reform

CENTRO *nm* (**a**) *(área, punto central)* centre; **en el c. de la vía** in the middle of the track; **estaba en el c. de la muchedumbre** she was in the middle of the crowd; **las lluvias afectarán al c. del país** the rain will affect the central region *o* centre of the country; **la jardinería es el c. de su existencia** her life revolves around gardening ▸▸ ***c. de atención*** centre of attention; ***c. de atracción*** centre of attraction; **las playas son el c. de atracción para el turismo** beaches are the main tourist attraction; ***c. de gravedad*** centre of gravity; ***c. de interés*** centre of interest; *Fís* ***c. de masa*** centre of mass; ***c. de mesa*** centrepiece; ***c. nervioso*** nerve centre; *también Fig* ***c. neurálgico*** nerve centre; *Fís* ***c. óptico*** optical centre
(**b**) *(de ciudad)* town centre; **me voy al c.** I'm going to town; **tengo una casa en pleno c.** I have a house right in the town centre; **c. ciudad** *o* **urbano** *(en letrero)* city/town centre ▸▸ ***c. histórico*** = old (part of) town
(**c**) *(económico, administrativo)* centre; **un importante c. financiero/cultural** an important financial/cultural centre ▸▸ ***c. turístico*** tourist resort
(**d**) *(establecimiento, organismo)* centre; *(planta)* plant, factory; *(tienda)* branch; *(colegio)* school ▸▸ *Esp* ***c. de acogida*** reception centre; *Esp* ***c. de acogida para mujeres maltratadas*** refuge for battered women; ***c. asistencial de día*** day care centre; ***c. de atención telefónica*** call centre; ***c. de cálculo*** computer centre; ***c. cívico*** community centre; ***c. comercial*** shopping centre *o US* mall; *Am* ***c. comunal*** community centre; *Am* ***c. comunitario*** community centre; ***c. concertado*** state-subsidized (private) school; ***c. de control*** control centre; ***c. cultural*** cultural centre; ***c. demográfico*** centre of

population; ***c. deportivo*** sports centre; ***c. de desintoxicación*** detoxification centre *o* clinic; ***c. de detención*** detention centre; ***c. docente*** educational institution; ***c. educativo*** educational institution; ***c. de enseñanza*** educational institution; ***c. espacial*** space centre; ***c. de estudios*** academy, school; ***c. excursionista*** hill-walking club; ***c. hospitalario*** hospital; ***c. de información*** information centre; ***c. de investigación*** research institute; ***c. de llamadas*** call centre; *Mil* ***c. de mando*** command centre; ***c. médico*** (private) clinic; ***c. meteorológico*** weather centre; ***c. de negocios*** business centre; ***c. penitenciario*** prison, *US* penitentiary; ***c. de planificación familiar*** family planning clinic; ***c. regional*** regional office; ***c. de rehabilitación*** rehabilitation centre; ***c. de salud*** clinic, *Br* health centre; ***c. sanitario*** clinic, *Br* health centre; ***c. social*** community centre; ***c. de trabajo*** workplace; *Am* ***c. de tratamiento intensivo*** intensive care unit

(**e**) *(en política)* centre; **un partido de c.** a centre party; **ser de c.** to be at the centre of the political spectrum

(**f**) *Dep (posición)* **c. del campo** midfield; **juega en el c. del campo** he plays in midfield

(**g**) *Dep (pase)* cross, centre; **envió un c. al área contraria** he crossed the ball into the opposition's penalty area; **consiguió un espectacular gol con un c. chut** he scored a spectacular goal with what was intended more as a cross than a shot

(**h**) *Méx (traje)* suit

(**i**) *Hond (chaleco) Br* waistcoat, *US* vest

(**j**) *Cuba (enaguas)* underskirt

---

centroafricano, -a 1 *adj* central African
2 *nm,f* central African

Centroamérica *n* Central America

centroamericano, -a 1 *adj* Central American
2 *nm,f* Central American

centrocampista *nmf* midfielder

centroderecha *nm* centre right

centroeuropeo, -a 1 *adj* Central European
2 *nm,f* Central European

centroizquierda *nm* centre left

centuplicar [60] *vt* to increase a hundredfold

céntuplo 1 *adj* hundredfold
2 *nm* hundredfold

centuria *nf* (**a**) *(siglo)* century (**b**) *Hist (en Roma)* century

centurión *nm Hist* centurion

cenutrio, -a *Fam* 1 *adj (estúpido)* stupid, *US* dumb
2 *nm,f (estúpido)* idiot, fool

cenzontle *nm* mockingbird

ceñido, -a *adj* tight

ceñidor *nm* belt

ceñir [47] 1 *vt* (**a**) *(ajustar, apretar)* to take in

(**b**) *(poner)* to put on; **le ciñó una banda de honor** a sash of honour was placed around him

(**c**) *(abrazar)* to embrace; **el vestido le ceñía el talle** the dress hugged her figure

(**d**) *(rodear)* to surround; **las colinas ciñen la ciudad** the hills surround the city

2 **ceñirse** *vpr* (**a**) *(apretarse)* to tighten; **se ciñó la espada** he girded *o* put on his sword

(**b**) *(limitarse)* **nos debemos c. al presupuesto** we have to keep within the budget; **cíñete a contestar a lo que te han preguntado** restrict yourself to answering the questions you have been asked; **me ciño a lo que dicta la ley** I'm sticking to the letter of the law; **la retrospectiva no se ciñe a sus cuadros más conocidos** the retrospective does not restrict itself to her best-known works

ceño *nm* frown, scowl; **fruncir el c.** to frown, to knit one's brow; **entró con el c. fruncido** he came in with furrowed brow

ceñudo, -a *adj* frowning, scowling

CEOE ['θeo'e] *nf (abrev de* **Confederación Española de Organizaciones Empresariales**) = Spanish employers' association, *Br* ≃ CBI

cepa *nf* (**a**) *(de vid)* vine, stock (**b**) *(de vino)* variety (**c**) *(linaje)* stock; EXPR **de pura c.** *(auténtico)* real, genuine; **es un argentino de pura c.** he's an Argentinian through and through; **es un delantero centro de pura c.** he's a thoroughbred centre forward (**d**) *(de virus, células)* strain

CEPAL [θe'pal] *nf (abrev de* **Comisión Económica para América Latina**) ECLAC, Economic Commission for Latin America and the Caribbean

cepellón *nm* root-ball

cepillado *nm* (**a**) *(con cepillo)* brush, brushing (**b**) *(en carpintería)* planing (**c**) *Ven (refresco)* = drink of flavoured crushed ice

cepillar 1 *vt* (**a**) *(ropa, pelo)* to brush; *(dientes)* to brush, to clean (**b**) *(madera)* to plane (**c**) *Fam (robar)* to pinch; **c. algo a alguien** to pinch sth from sb (**d**) *Esp, Col Fam (adular)* to butter up, to flatter

2 **cepillarse** *vpr* (**a**) *(pelo, ropa)* to brush; *(dientes)* to brush, to clean; **cepillarse el pelo** to brush one's hair (**b**) *Fam (comida, trabajo)* to polish off (**c**) *Fam (suspender)* to flunk; **se lo cepillaron** they flunked him (**d**) *Fam* **cepillarse a alguien** *(matarlo)* to bump sb off (**e**) *muy Fam* **cepillarse a alguien** *(copular con él)* to screw sb

cepillo *nm* (**a**) *(para limpiar)* brush; **pasar el c. por algo** to give sth a brush; **lleva el cabello cortado a c.** he has a crew cut ▸▸ ***c. de dientes*** toothbrush; ***c. del pelo*** hairbrush; ***c. de uñas*** nailbrush (**b**) *(de carpintero)* plane (**c**) *(para barrer)* brush; **pasar el c.** to brush the floor (**d**) *(de donativos)* collection box, poor box

cepo *nm* (**a**) *(para cazar)* trap (**b**) *(para vehículos)* wheel clamp; **poner el c. a un coche** to clamp a car (**c**) *(para sujetar)* clamp (**d**) *(para presos)* stocks

ceporro *Fam* 1 *adj* thick, dim
2 *nm* (**a**) *(torpe)* idiot, blockhead (**b**) EXPR **dormir como un c.** to sleep like a log

cera *nf* (**a**) *(sustancia)* wax; **hacerse la c.** *(depilarse)* to wax; EXPR **no hay más c. que la que arde** what you see is what you get ▸▸ ***c. de abeja*** beeswax; ***c. depilatoria*** hair-removing wax; ***c. virgen*** pure wax (**b**) *(para dibujar)* crayon (**c**) *(del oído)* earwax (**d**) *Andes, Méx (vela)* candle (**e**) EXPR *Fam* **dar c.: el equipo visitante dio mucha c.** the visiting team played really dirty; **recibir c.** to get stick

cerafolio *nm* chervil

cerámica *nf* (**a**) *(arte)* ceramics *(singular)*, pottery (**b**) *(objeto)* piece of pottery; **un jarrón de c.** a ceramic *o* pottery vase; **una colección de c. precolombina** a collection of pre-Colombian pottery *o* ceramics

cerámico, -a *adj* ceramic

ceramista *nmf* potter

cerapio *nm Esp Fam* zilch; **me han puesto un c. en el examen** I got zilch *o* a big zero in the exam

cerbatana *nf* blowpipe

CERCA 1 *nf (valla)* fence; *(muro)* wall ▸▸ ***c. eléctrica*** electric fence; ***c. viva*** hedge

2 *adv* (**a**) *(en el espacio)* near, close; **¿está** *o* **queda c.?** is it near *o* nearby?; **no me hace falta un taxi porque voy c.** I don't need a taxi, because I'm not going far; **c. de** near, close to; **la tienda está c. del metro** the shop's near the *Br* underground *o US* subway; **está c. de mí** it's near me; **estuvo c. de ganar el premio** she came close to winning the prize; **de c.** *(examinar, mirar)* closely; *(afectar)* deeply; *(vivir)* first-hand; **vivió de c. el problema de las drogas** she had first-hand experience of drug addiction; **no ve bien de c.** he's long-sighted; **ver algo/a alguien de c.** to see sth/sb close up; **por aquí c.** nearby

(**b**) *(en el tiempo)* **el verano ya está c.** summer is nearly here, summer isn't far away; **c. del principio** close to *o* near the beginning; **son c. de las ocho** it's about eight (o'clock); **los hechos ocurrieron c. de las seis de la tarde** the events in question took place at around six o'clock in the evening; **estamos c. del final del festival** we are nearing *o* approaching the end of the festival

(**c**) *(indica aproximación)* **c. de** nearly, about; **acudieron c. de mil manifestantes** there were nearly *o* about a thousand demonstrators there; **si no costó 2 millones, andará c.** it can't have cost much less than 2 million

---

cercado *nm* (**a**) *(valla)* fence; *(muro)* wall (**b**) *(terreno)* enclosure (**c**) *Bol, Perú (división territorial)* district, = provincial capital and surrounding towns

cercanía 1 *nf (proximidad)* nearness, closeness; **la c. de su destino los animó** they were spurred on by the fact that they were so close to their destination; **la c. entre los dos países favorece los intercambios comerciales** the proximity of the two countries favours trade between them; **ante la c. de las elecciones, la campaña se intensificó** as the elections drew closer, the campaign heated up

2 **cercanías** *nfpl (lugar)* **en las cercanías de Buenos Aires** in the area around Buenos Aires; **el accidente ocurrió en las cercanías de un hospital** the accident happened near a hospital; **las tropas están estacionadas en las cercanías de la frontera** the troops are stationed close to *o* near the border; **tren de cercanías** local train, suburban train

3 **cercanías** *nm inv* local train, suburban train

cercano, -a *adj* (**a**) *(en el espacio)* nearby; **c. a** near, close to; **el C. Oriente** the Near East
(**b**) *(en el tiempo)* near; **c. a** near, close to
(**c**) *(con cifras)* close; **pagaron un precio c. a los 2 millones** they paid close to *o* nearly 2 million
(**d**) *(pariente, amigo, colaborador)* close; **según fuentes cercanas a la familia real,...** according to sources close to the royal family,...
(**e**) *(en contenido)* **una obra más cercana a la tragedia que a la comedia** a play that is closer to tragedy than to comedy

cercar [60] *vt* (**a**) *(vallar)* to fence (off) (**b**) *(ciudad, fortaleza)* to besiege, to lay siege to; *(atracador, fugitivo)* to surround

cercenamiento *nm (de libertades)* restriction, curtailment

cercenar *vt* (**a**) *(amputar)* to amputate; **se cercenó una mano con una sierra eléctrica** he cut one of his hands off with a power saw (**b**) *(restringir)* to cut back, to curtail; **un gobierno que cercena las libertades individuales** a government which restricts *o* curtails personal freedom; **quieren c. los gastos** they want to cut back *o* reduce expenses

cerceta *nf* teal ►► ***c. aliazul*** blue-winged teal; ***c. carretona*** garganey

cercha *nf* (**a**) *(para medir)* = flexible rule for measuring curved surfaces (**b**) *(para esculpir)* curved template (**c**) *Náut* outer rim

cerciorar 1 *vt* to convince
2 cerciorarse *vpr* to make sure (**de** of); **cerciórate de que apagas todas las luces cuando te vayas** make sure you turn off all the lights when you leave; **enviaron a una delegación para cerciorarse de lo que estaba ocurriendo** they sent a delegation to find out exactly what was going on

cerco *nm* (**a**) *(marca)* circle, ring; **el vaso ha dejado un c. en la mesa** the glass has left a ring on the table
(**b**) *(de astro)* halo
(**c**) *(asedio)* siege; **poner c. a** to lay siege to; **la policía ha estrechado el c. en torno a los presos fugados** the police have tightened the net around the escaped prisoners; **el gobierno estableció un c. sanitario** the government established a cordon sanitaire
(**d**) *(de ventana, puerta)* frame
(**e**) *Am (valla)* fence ►► ***c. vivo*** hedge

cercoleto *nm* kinkajou, honey bear

cerda *nf* (**a**) *(pelo) (de cerdo, jabalí)* bristle; *(de caballo)* horsehair (**b**) *ver también* **cerdo**

cerdada *nf Fam* (**a**) *(porquería)* mess; **esta habitación es una c.** this room is a pigsty
(**b**) *(acción sucia)* disgusting habit; **¡no hagas cerdadas!** stop being so disgusting!
(**c**) *(jugarreta)* dirty trick; **fue una c. que cancelaran el viaje en el último momento** it was really mean of them to cancel the trip at the last moment; **sus compañeros le hacen cerdadas constantemente** his colleagues are always playing nasty practical jokes on him

Cerdeña *n* Sardinia

cerdo, -a 1 *adj Fam* (**a**) *(sucio)* filthy (**b**) *(malintencionado)* mean
2 *nm,f* (**a**) *(animal)* pig, *f* sow; EXPR *Fam* **comer como un c.** *(mucho)* to eat a lot; *(sin modales)* to eat like a pig; EXPR *Fam* **estar como un c.** *(gordo)* to be a fat pig; PROV **a cada c. le llega su San Martín** = everyone gets their come-uppance at some point (**b**) *Fam (sucio)* dirty *o* filthy pig (**c**) *Fam (persona malintencionada)* pig, swine
3 *nm (carne)* pork

cereal *nm* cereal; **cereales** *(de desayuno)* (breakfast) cereal

cerealero, -a *Am* **1** *adj (región)* cereal-growing; **producción cerealera** cereal production
2 *nm,f* cereal-grower

cerealista 1 *adj (región)* cereal-growing; **producción c.** cereal production
2 *nmf* cereal-grower

cerebelo *nm Anat* cerebellum

cerebral *adj* (**a**) *(del cerebro) (derrame)* cerebral, brain; *(tumor, muerte, cirugía)* brain; *(parálisis, embolia, corteza)* cerebral; **lesión c.** cerebral lesion (**b**) *(racional)* cerebral

cerebro *nm* (**a**) *(órgano)* brain; EXPR **lavar el c. a alguien** to brainwash sb ►► ***c. electrónico*** electronic brain (**b**) *(cabecilla)* brains *(singular)* ►► ***c. gris*** éminence grise (**c**) *(inteligencia)* brains; **¡qué poco c. tienes!** you're so stupid! (**d**) *(persona inteligente)* brains *(singular)*; **es todo un c.** he's brainy

cerebrovascular *adj Med* cerebrovascular

ceremonia *nf* (**a**) *(acto)* ceremony; **c. de apertura/de clausura** opening/closing ceremony; *Am* **c. de transmisión de mando** ceremonial handover of power
(**b**) *(pompa, boato)* ceremony, pomp; **recibieron a los reyes con gran c.** they welcomed the king and queen with great pomp; **se casaron sin c. ni formalidades de ningún tipo** their wedding was a very quiet and modest affair

ceremonial 1 *adj* ceremonial
2 *nm* (**a**) *(reglas)* ceremonial (**b**) *(libro)* ceremonial

ceremoniosamente *adv* ceremoniously

ceremonioso, -a *adj* ceremonious

céreo, -a *adj* wax, waxen; **brillo c.** waxy sheen

cerería *nf (negocio)* candlemaker's shop

Ceres *n Mitol* Ceres

cereza *nf* (**a**) *(fruta)* cherry (**b**) *Am (del café)* coffee bean

cerezal *nm* cherry orchard

cerezo *nm* (**a**) *(árbol)* cherry tree ►► ***c. japonés*** flowering cherry (**b**) *(madera)* cherry (wood)

cerilla *nf* (**a**) *Esp (fósforo)* match (**b**) *(cerumen)* earwax

cerillero, -a 1 *nm,f (vendedor)* match vendor
2 *nm (recipiente, caja)* matchbox

cerillo *nm CAm, Ecuad, Méx* match

cerio *nm Quím* cerium

cerner [66], **cernir** [25] **1** *vt* to sieve, to sift
2 cernerse *vpr* (**a**) *(ave, avión)* to hover (**b**) *(amenaza, peligro)* to loom, to hover; **una grave amenaza se cernía sobre la ciudad** a grave threat loomed *o* hovered over the city

cernícalo *nm* (**a**) *(ave)* kestrel ►► ***c. americano*** American kestrel; ***c. primilla*** lesser kestrel (**b**) *Fam (bruto)* brute

cernidor *nm* sieve

cernir = **cerner**

cero 1 *adj inv* zero
2 *núm* zero; *ver también* **tres**
3 *nm* (**a**) *(número)* nought, zero; **la reserva está a c.** the fuel gauge is at empty; **cortarse el pelo al c.** to shave one's head, to cut all one's hair off; **partir** *o* **empezar de c.** to start from scratch; **sacó un c. en física** he got zero in physics; **acelera de c. a cien en seis segundos** it goes from nought *o* zero to a hundred in six seconds; **la inflación experimentó un crecimiento c.** there was no increase in the rate of inflation; EXPR **ser un c. a la izquierda** *(un inútil)* to be useless; *(un don nadie)* to be a nobody
(**b**) *(cantidad)* nothing; *(en fútbol, hockey, rugby) Br* nil, *US* zero; *(en tenis)* love; **el marcador es tres (a) c.** the score is three-nothing *o Br* three-nil *o US* three-zero; **el marcador es empate a c.** the score is nothing-nothing *o Br* nil-nil *o US* zero-zero; **llevan tres empates a c. consecutivos** they have had three goalless *o* scoreless draws in a row
(**c**) *(temperatura)* zero; **sobre/bajo c.** above/below zero; **hace 5 grados bajo c.** it's minus 5 ►► ***c. absoluto*** absolute zero
(**d**) *RP Fam* ***c. kilómetro*** *(auto)* brand-new car; **un video c. kilómetro** a brand-new video; *muy Fam* **una mujer c. kilómetro** a cherry

cerote *nm CAm, Méx muy Fam* turd

cerquillo *nm Am Br* fringe, *US* bangs

cerquita *adv* very near

CERRADO, -A **1** *participio ver* **cerrar**
2 *adj* (**a**) *(puerta, boca, tienda)* closed, shut; *(con llave, pestillo)* locked; *(puño)* clenched; *(sobre)* closed; **la botella no está bien cerrada** the top of the bottle isn't on properly; **todos los grifos están cerrados** all the *Br* taps *o US* faucets are (turned) off; **en esta habitación huele a c.** this room smells stuffy; **la puerta estaba cerrada con llave** the door was locked; **c. por obras/vacaciones** *(en letrero)* closed for alterations/holidays; **c. los fines de semana** *(en letrero)* closed at weekends
(**b**) *(curva)* sharp, tight
(**c**) *(circuito)* closed
(**d**) *(aplauso, ovación)* rapturous
(**e**) *(lucha)* bitter; **una cerrada lucha por el liderazgo** a bitter leadership struggle
(**f**) *Ling (vocal)* close
(**g**) *(acento, deje)* broad, thick; **habla con un acento gallego c.** she speaks with a broad *o* thick Galician accent
(**h**) *(mentalidad, sociedad)* closed (**a** to); **tiene una actitud muy cerrada** she has a very closed mentality; **es muy c.** he's very narrow-minded; **está c. al cambio** he is not open to change
(**i**) *(tiempo, cielo)* overcast; **la noche era cerrada** it was a dark night
(**j**) *(rodeado)* surrounded; *(por montañas)* walled in; **no se adaptan a espacios cerrados** they aren't suited to living in confined spaces; **una terraza cerrada** a glazed balcony
(**k**) *(vegetación, bosque)* thick, dense; *(barba)* thick

(l) *(poco claro, difícil)* abstruse; **su estilo es muy c.** his style is very abstruse
(m) *(introvertido, tímido)* reserved; **le cuesta hacer amigos porque es muy c.** he finds making friends difficult because he's very reserved
(n) *(estricto)* strict; **el colegio tiene criterios muy cerrados de admisión** the school has very strict entrance requirements
(o) *(torpe)* dense, stupid; **es un poco c., hay que explicarle todo varias veces** he's rather dense *o* stupid, you have to explain everything to him over and over again; EXPR *Fam* **ser c. de mollera** to be thick in the head
(p) *(obstinado)* obstinate, stubborn
3 *nm* fenced-in garden

---

cerradura *nf* lock ►► ***c. de combinación*** combination lock; ***c. de seguridad*** security lock

cerraja *nf* **(a)** *(cerradura)* lock **(b)** *(planta)* sow thistle

cerrajería *nf* **(a)** *(oficio)* locksmithery **(b)** *(local)* locksmith's (shop)

cerrajero, -a *nm,f* locksmith

CERRAR **1** *vt* **(a)** *(en general)* to close; *(puerta, cajón, boca, tienda)* to shut, to close; *Informát (archivo)* to close; *(con llave)* to lock; *(grifo, llave de gas)* to turn off; *(botella)* to put the top on; *(tarro)* to put the lid *o* top on; *(carta, sobre)* to seal; *(cortinas)* to draw, to close; *(persianas)* to pull down; *(agujero, hueco)* to fill, to block (up); *(puños)* to clench; **c. una puerta con llave** to lock a door; **cierra el gas cuando salgas** turn the gas off when you leave; **una corriente de aire cerró la puerta** a draught blew the door shut; EXPR *Fam* **¡cierra el pico!** shut your trap!
(b) *(negocio, colegio) (a diario)* to close; *(permanentemente)* to close down; **el gobierno cerrará dos centrales nucleares** the government is to close down two nuclear power stations
(c) *(vallar)* to fence (off), to enclose; **cerraron el balcón para convertirlo en comedor** they closed *o* walled off the balcony and converted it into a dining room
(d) *(carretera, calle)* to close off; *también Fig* **c. el paso a alguien** to block sb's way; **una valla les cerraba la salida** a fence blocked their way out
(e) *(manifestación, desfile)* to bring up the rear of; **c. la marcha** *(ir en última posición)* to bring up the rear; **la orquesta cerraba el desfile** the orchestra closed the procession
(f) *(gestiones, acuerdo)* to finalize; **han cerrado un trato para...** they've reached an agreement *o* made a deal to...; **cerraron el trato ayer** they wrapped up the deal yesterday; **cerraron las conversaciones sin ningún acuerdo** they ended the talks without reaching an agreement
(g) *(cicatrizar)* to heal, to close up
(h) *Elec (circuito)* to close
(i) *(circunferencia, círculo)* to complete; **cerraron la carretera de circunvalación** they completed the *Br* ring road *o US* beltway
(j) *(signo ortográfico)* to close; **c. comillas/paréntesis** to close inverted commas/brackets
(k) *(posibilidades)* to put an end to; **el último atentado cierra cualquier esperanza de acuerdo** the most recent attack puts an end to any hopes of an agreement
(l) *(terminar)* to close; **el discurso del Presidente cerró el año legislativo** the President's speech brought the parliamentary year to a close; **esta corrida cierra la temporada taurina** this bullfight rounds off the bullfighting season; **cerró su participación en el torneo con una derrota** they lost their last game in the tournament
(m) *(plegar)* to close up; **cerró el paraguas** he closed his umbrella
(n) *Prensa* **el periódico cerró la edición más tarde de lo normal** the newspaper went to press later than usual
2 *vi* **(a)** *(en general)* to close; *(tienda)* to close, to shut; *(con llave, pestillo)* to lock up; **este cajón no cierra bien** this drawer doesn't shut properly; **la Bolsa cerró con pérdidas** the stock market closed down several points; EXPR *RP Fam* **¡cerrá y vamos!: si no quieren ayudarnos, ¡cerrá y vamos!** if they don't want to help us, let's not waste any more time over this
(b) *(persona)* to close the door; **¡cierra, que entra frío!** close the door, you're letting the cold in!; **me olvidé de c. con llave** I forgot to lock the door
(c) *(negocio, colegio) (a diario)* to close; *(definitivamente)* to close down; **¿a qué hora cierra?** what time do you close?; **la biblioteca cierra a las ocho** the library closes at eight; **cerramos los domingos** *(en letrero)* closed on Sundays
(d) *(en juego de cartas)* to go out; *(en dominó)* to block
(e) *(herida)* to close up, to heal
3 cerrarse *vpr* **(a)** *(al exterior)* to close, to shut; **la puerta se cerró accidentalmente** the door closed *o* shut accidentally
(b) *Fig (incomunicarse)* to clam up; **cerrarse a** to close one's mind to; **no te cierres tanto a la gente** don't close yourself off to other people so much
(c) *(cielo)* to cloud over; **la tarde se está cerrando** it's clouding over this afternoon
(d) *(acabar)* to end; **el plazo de inscripción ya se ha cerrado** the deadline for registration is up; **la representación se cierra con una escena muy dramática** the play ends with a very dramatic scene; **el congreso se cerró con un discurso del rey** the conference closed *o* ended with a speech from the king
(e) *(vehículo en una curva)* to take the bend tight; **se cerró demasiado** he took the bend too tight
(f) *Dep* **tras el gol, el equipo se cerró en su área** after the goal the team sat back and defended
(g) *(herida)* to heal, to close up
(h) *(acto, debate, discusión)* to (come to a) close

---

cerrazón *nf* **(a)** *(obstinación)* stubbornness, obstinacy **(b)** *(falta de inteligencia)* dim-wittedness **(c)** *RP (niebla)* heavy mist

cerrejón *nm* hillock

cerrero, -a *adj* **(a)** *(libre)* wandering, roaming **(b)** *(cabezota)* wild, untamed **(c)** *Am (bruto)* rough, coarse

cerril *adj* **(a)** *(animal)* wild **(b)** *(obstinado)* stubborn, obstinate **(c)** *(tosco, grosero)* coarse

cerrilmente *adv (obstinadamente)* stubbornly, obstinately

cerro *nm* hill; EXPR *Esp Fam* **irse por los cerros de Úbeda** to go off at a tangent, to stray from the point

cerrojazo *nm* **dar c. a** *(puerta)* to bolt shut; *(conversación, reunión, proyecto)* to put an end to, to bring to a halt

cerrojo *nm (para cerrar)* bolt; **echar el c.** to bolt the door; *Fam (en fútbol)* to close the game down

certamen *nm* competition, contest; **c. literario** literary competition; **c. cinematográfico** movie awards

certero, -a *adj* **(a)** *(tiro)* accurate **(b)** *(comentario, respuesta)* appropriate

certeza, certidumbre, certitud *nf* certainty; **tener la c. de que** to be certain (that); **lo digo con la c. del que ha estudiado el tema** I say this with some confidence as I have studied the matter; **no se sabe con c. qué causó la explosión** it is not known for certain what caused the explosion

certificación *nf* **(a)** *(hecho)* certification **(b)** *(documento)* certificate

certificado, -a **1** *adj (documento)* certified; *(carta, paquete)* registered; **enviar un paquete por correo c.** to send a parcel by registered *Br* post *o US* mail
2 *nm* certificate ►► ***c. de ahorro*** savings certificate; ***c. de buena conducta*** certificate of good conduct; ***c. de calidad*** quality guarantee; ***c. de defunción*** death certificate; *Fin* ***c. de depósito*** certificate of deposit; ***c. de estudios*** academic record; ***c. de garantía*** guarantee certificate; ***c. de matrimonio*** marriage certificate; ***c. médico*** medical certificate; *Com* ***c. de origen*** certificate of origin; ***c. de residencia*** = official document confirming one's residence in a country, city etc

certificar [60] *vt* **(a)** *(constatar)* to certify **(b)** *(en correos)* to register **(c)** *(sospechas, inocencia)* to confirm

certificatorio, -a *adj* certifying

certitud = **certeza**

cerúleo, -a *adj Literario* azure, cerulean

cerumen *nm* earwax

cerval *adj* **miedo c.** terror; **le tiene un miedo c. a las serpientes** he's absolutely terrified of snakes

cervantino, -a, cervantesco, -a *adj* Cervantine

cervantista *nmf* Cervantes specialist

cervatillo *nm* (small) fawn

cervato *nm* fawn

cervecera *nf* **(a)** *(fábrica)* brewery **(b)** *ver también* **cervecero**

cervecería *nf* **(a)** *(fábrica)* brewery **(b)** *(bar)* bar *(specializing in beer)*

cervecero, -a **1** *adj* **(a)** *(de la fabricación)* brewing; **fábrica cervecera** brewery; **industria cervecera** brewing industry **(b)** *(aficionado)* **Mario es muy c.** Mario really likes his beer
2 *nm,f (fabricante)* brewer

cerveza *nf* beer; **dos cervezas, por favor** two beers, please ►► ***c. sin alcohol*** alcohol-free beer, non-alcoholic beer; ***c. de barril*** draught beer; *Am* ***c. clara*** lager; ***c. negra*** stout; ***c. rubia*** lager; ***c. sin*** alcohol-free beer, non-alcoholic beer

cervical 1 *adj* (**a**) *(del cuello del útero)* cervical (**b**) *(del cuello)* neck; **lesión c.** neck injury; **vértebra c.** cervical vertebra
2 **cervicales** *nfpl* neck vertebrae

cérvido *nm* animal with antlers, *Espec* cervid

cerviz *nf (nuca)* nape, back of the neck; EXPR **bajar** *o* **doblar la c.** *(humillarse)* to bow down, to submit; EXPR **ser duro de c.** to be stiff-necked *o* stubborn

cesación *nf (cese)* stopping, ceasing ▸▸ *RP* ***c. de pagos*** suspension of payments

cesante 1 *adj* (**a**) *(destituido)* dismissed, sacked (**b**) *CSur, Méx (parado)* unemployed
2 *nmf* dismissed civil servant *(after change of government)*

cesantía *nf (destitución)* sacking

cesar 1 *vt (destituir)* to sack; *(alto cargo)* to remove from office
2 *vi* (**a**) *(parar)* to stop *o* cease; **c. de hacer algo** to stop *o* cease doing sth; **cesó de nevar** it stopped snowing; **sin c.** non-stop, incessantly; **no cesó de hacer preguntas** she kept asking questions (**b**) *(dimitir)* to resign, to step down; **cesó como presidente de la empresa** he resigned *o* stepped down as company chairman

César *n pr Hist* Caesar; **C. Augusto** Augustus (Caesar); EXPR **dar (a Dios lo que es de Dios y) al C. lo que es del C.** to render unto Caesar the things which are Caesar's (and to God the things which are God's)

cesárea *nf* caesarean (section); **le hicieron la** *o* **una c.** she had a caesarean; **nació mediante** *o* **por c.** he was a caesarean, he was born by caesarean

cese *nm* (**a**) *(detención, paro)* stopping, ceasing; **la ONU pidió un c. del embargo económico** the UN called for an end to the economic embargo; **la guerrilla anunció el c. definitivo de sus acciones** the guerrillas announced they were giving up violence; **liquidación por c. de negocio** *(en letrero)* closing-down sale ▸▸ *Am* ***c. del fuego*** cease-fire
(**b**) *(destitución)* sacking; *(de alto cargo)* removal from office; **su apoyo a los huelguistas le costó el c.** her support for the strikers cost her her job; **le comunicaron el c. por teléfono** he was informed of his sacking by telephone; **dar el c. a alguien** to dismiss sb

Cesid [θe'sið] *nm (abrev de* **Centro Superior de Investigación de la Defensa**) = Spanish military intelligence and espionage service

cesio *nm Quím* caesium

cesión *nf (de derechos, territorios, jugadores)* transfer ▸▸ *Der* ***c. de bienes*** surrender of property; *UE* ***c. de cuotas*** *(pesqueras)* quota hopping; *Dep* ***c. al portero*** *(en fútbol)* back pass

cesionario, -a *nm,f* transferee, assignee

cesionista *nmf Der* transferor, assignor

césped *nm* (**a**) *(hierba)* lawn, grass; *Am (en tenis)* grass court; *Am* **cancha de c.** grass court; **cortar el c.** to mow the lawn, to cut the grass; **prohibido pisar el c.** *(en letrero)* keep off the grass (**b**) *Dep* field, pitch; **saltan al c. los dos equipos** the two teams are coming out onto the field *o* pitch

cesta *nf* (**a**) *(canasta)* basket; *Econ* **(el precio de) la c. de la compra** the cost of the average week's shopping; *Informát* **c. (de la compra** *o* **de pedidos)** *(en página web)* shopping basket *o US* cart ▸▸ *Econ* ***c. de monedas*** basket of currencies; ***c. de Navidad*** Christmas hamper
(**b**) *(en baloncesto) (aro)* basket
(**c**) *(en baloncesto) (tanto)* basket
(**d**) *(deporte)* ***c. punta*** jai alai, pelota *(played with basket-like rackets)*

cestería *nf* (**a**) *(oficio)* basket making (**b**) *(tienda)* basket shop

cestero, -a *nm,f* basket weaver

cesto *nm* (**a**) *(cesta)* (large) basket ▸▸ ***c. de los papeles*** wastepaper basket; ***c. de la ropa sucia*** laundry basket, linen basket (**b**) *(en baloncesto) (aro, tanto)* basket

cesura *nf* caesura

cetáceo *nm* cetacean

cetaria *nf* shellfish farm

Cetes *nmpl Méx* treasury bond

cetme *nm* = light automatic rifle used by Spanish army

cetona *nf Quím* ketone

cetrería *nf* falconry

cetrero *nm (cazador)* falconer

cetrino, -a *adj Formal* sallow

cetro *nm* (**a**) *(vara)* sceptre (**b**) *(reinado)* reign; **bajo el c. de...** in the reign of... (**c**) *(superioridad)* **ostentar el c. de** to hold the crown of; **competirán por el c. mundial de la categoría** they will compete for the crown of world champion in their class

ceugma *nf Ling* zeugma

Ceuta *n* Ceuta

ceutí *(pl* **ceutíes**) 1 *adj* of/from Ceuta *(Spain)*
2 *nmf* person from Ceuta *(Spain)*

ceviche = **cebiche**

cf., cfr. *(abrev de* **confróntese**) cf

CFC *nmpl (abrev de* **clorofluorocarbonos**) CFC

cfr. = **cf.**

cg *(abrev de* **centigramo**) cg

CGA *nm Informát (abrev de* **colour graphics adaptor**) CGA

Ch, ch [tʃe] *nf* = ch digraph, traditionally considered a separate character in the Spanish alphabet

ch/ *(abrev de* **cheque**) cheque

chabacanada *nf* vulgar thing; **ser una c.** to be vulgar

chabacanería *nf* (**a**) *(acción, comentario)* **lo que hizo/dijo fue una c.** what he did/said was vulgar; **no tengo por qué aguantar sus chabacanerías** I don't have to put up with his vulgarity (**b**) *(cualidad)* vulgarity, tastelessness; **viste con c.** she dresses without taste

chabacano, -a 1 *adj* vulgar
2 *nm* (**a**) *(lengua)* = Spanish creole spoken in some parts of the Philippines (**b**) *Méx (fruto)* apricot (**c**) *Méx (árbol)* apricot tree

chabola *nf Esp* shack; **barrio de chabolas** shanty town

chabolismo *nm Esp* **erradicar el c.** to deal with the shanty town problem; **el crecimiento del c.** the growing number of people living in shanty towns

chabolista *nmf Esp* shanty town dweller

chacal *nm* jackal

chácara *nf* (**a**) *Am Anticuado (granja)* farm (**b**) *Col, Pan, Ven (portamonedas) Br* purse, *US* wallet

chacarero, -a *nm,f Andes, RP* farmer

chacha *nf Fam* maid

chachachá *nm* cha-cha

cháchara *nf Fam* chatter, *Br* nattering; **estar de c.** to chat, *Br* to natter

chacharear *vi Fam* (**a**) *(hablar)* to chatter (**b**) *(chismosear)* to gossip

chacharero, -a *Fam* 1 *adj* **es muy c.** he's a real chatterbox
2 *nm,f (charlatán)* chatterbox

chachi *Esp Fam* 1 *adj inv* cool, neat; **c. piruli** really neat, *Br* way cool
2 *adv* **lo pasamos c.** we had a really cool *o Br* a brilliant time
3 *interj* cool!, neat!, *Br* brilliant!

chacho *nm* (**a**) *Esp Fam (niño)* son; **c., ¡cómo me alegro de verte!** it's great to see you, my son! (**b**) *Col (valiente)* he-man

chacina *nf* cured *o* prepared pork

chacinería *nf (tienda)* pork butcher's

chacinero, -a *nm,f* pork butcher

Chaco *nm* **el (Gran) C.** the Chaco, = vast region of scrubland and swamp shared by Argentina, Bolivia and Paraguay

chacolí *(pl* **chacolís**) *nm* = light wine from the Basque Country

chacota *nf* EXPR *Fam* **tomar algo a c.** to take sth as a joke

chacotero, -a *CSur Fam* 1 *adj* **es un tipo muy c.** he likes a good laugh
2 *nm,f* **es un c.** he likes a good laugh

chacra *nf Andes, RP* farm

Chad *n* **(el) C.** Chad

chadiano, -a 1 *adj* Chadian
2 *nm,f* Chadian

chador *nm* chador

chafalonía *nf* = scrap silver or gold

chafar 1 *vt* (**a**) *(aplastar) (pastel)* to squash; *(pelo, hierba, flor)* to flatten; *(plátano)* to mash; *(uva)* to tread
(**b**) *(arrugar)* to crease
(**c**) *(estropear)* to ruin; **el robo nos chafó las vacaciones** the robbery ruined our holiday; **me has chafado la sorpresa que les iba a dar** you've ruined the surprise I had for them
(**d**) *Esp Fam (abrumar)* to crush, to floor; **su respuesta me dejó chafado** I felt crushed by her reply, her reply floored me
2 **chafarse** *vpr* (**a**) *(aplastarse) (pastel)* to get squashed; *(pelo, hierba, flor)* to get flattened
(**b**) *Fam (estropearse)* to be ruined

chaflán *nm* **(a)** *(de edificio)* corner *(cut off at an angle, rather than at 90 degrees)*; **la tienda hace c.** the store is on the corner of the building **(b)** *Geom* bevel

chaira *nf* **(a)** *(cilindro)* sharpening steel **(b)** *Fam (navaja)* blade

chajá *nm* **(a)** *(pájaro)* crested screamer **(b)** *Urug (postre)* = meringue filled with peaches, served with whipped cream

chal *nm* shawl

chala *nf* **(a)** *Andes, RP (de mazorca)* maize *o US* corn husk **(b)** *Chile (sandalia)* leather sandal

chalado, -a *Fam* **1** *adj* crazy, mad; **estar c. por algo/alguien** to be crazy about sth/sb

2 *nm,f* loony

chaladura *nf Fam* **(a)** *(locura)* craziness, madness **(b)** *(enamoramiento)* crazy infatuation

chalán, -ana *nm,f (comerciante)* horse-dealer

chalana *nf (embarcación)* barge

chalanear **1** *vi (regatear)* to haggle

2 *vt Am (adiestrar)* to break

chalar *Fam* **1** *vt* to drive round the bend

2 chalarse *vpr* **chalarse por** to be crazy about

chalé *(pl* **chalés***)*, **chalet** *(pl* **chalets***)* *nm (casa)* detached house (with garden); *(campestre)* cottage; *(de alta montaña)* chalet ►► *Esp* ***c. adosado*** terraced villa; *Esp* ***c. pareado*** semi-detached house

chaleco *nm Br* waistcoat, *US* vest; *(de punto)* tank top; EXPR *Méx Fam* **a c.** *(a la fuerza)* **me hacían estudiar a c.** they forced me to study ►► ***c. antibalas*** bullet-proof vest; ***c. antifragmentación*** flak jacket; *Am* ***c. de fuerza*** straitjacket; ***c. salvavidas*** life jacket

chalet = **chalé**

chalina *nf Am (chal)* narrow shawl

chalona *nf Andes, Arg* jerked *o* salted mutton

chalota, chalote *nf* shallot

chalupa *nf* **(a)** *(embarcación)* = small two-masted boat **(b)** *Méx (torta)* = small tortilla with a raised rim to contain a filling

chama *nm Cuba Fam* kid

chamaco, -a *nm,f Méx Fam* **(a)** *(muchacho)* kid **(b)** *(novio)* boyfriend; *(novia)* girlfriend

chamal *nm Bol, Chile, RP (de mujer)* = blanket-like shawl; *(de hombre)* = garment similar to gaucho's "chiripá"

chamamé *nm* = Argentinian and Paraguayan dance related to the polka

chamán *nm* shaman

chamanismo *nm* shamanism

chamarasca *nf* **(a)** *(leña)* brushwood **(b)** *(llama)* brushfire

chamarilear *vi* to deal in second-hand goods

chamarileo *nm* dealing in second-hand goods

chamarilero, -a *nm,f* second-hand dealer

chamarra *nf* jacket

chamarreta *nf* bomber jacket

chamba *nf* **(a)** *Esp Fam (suerte)* **lo encontré de** *o* **por c.** it was a fluke that I found it; **¡vaya c. que tienes!** you flukey thing! **(b)** *CAm, Méx, Perú, Ven Fam (trabajo)* job **(c)** *Col, Ven (zanja)* ditch

chambelán *nm* chamberlain

chambergo *nm* **(a)** *(chaquetón)* short coat **(b)** *RP (sombrero)* wide-brimmed hat

chambero, -a *nm,f Andes, Méx* scavenger *(on rubbish tip)*

chambismo *nm Méx Fam* moonlighting

chambista *nmf Méx Fam* moonlighter

chambón, -ona *nm,f Am Fam* sloppy *o* shoddy worker

chamboneada *nf*, **chambonada** *nf*, **chamboneo** *nm Am Fam* botch, botched job

chambonear *vi Am Fam* to bungle, to botch things up

chamboneo = **chamboneada**

chamiza *nf* **(a)** *(hierba)* thatch **(b)** *(leña)* brushwood

chamizo *nm* **(a)** *(choza)* thatched hut **(b)** *Fam Pey (lugar)* hovel, dive

champa *nf* **(a)** *CAm (tienda de campaña)* tent **(b)** *CAm (cobertizo)* shed

champán *nm* **(a)** *(bebida)* champagne **(b)** *(sampán)* sampan

champaña *nm o nf* champagne

champear *vt Andes* to fill in with turf

champiñón *nm* mushroom ►► ***c. pequeño*** button mushroom

champión *nm Urug Br* sports shoe, trainer, *US* sneaker

champola *nf* **(a)** *CAm, Carib (refresco de guanábana)* soursop milkshake **(b)** *Chile (refresco de chirimoya)* = drink made from custard apple

champú *(pl* **champús** *o* **champúes***)* *nm* shampoo ►► ***c. anticaspa*** dandruff shampoo

champús *(pl* **champuses***)*, **champuz** *(pl* **champuces***)* *nm Andes* = cornmeal porridge flavoured with orange juice and sugar

chamuchina *nf Andes, Cuba, Hond (populacho)* mob, rabble

chamuco *nm Méx Fam* Old Nick, the Devil

chamullar *vt Esp Fam* to speak badly; **chamullo algo de inglés** I can speak a few words of English

chamuscado, -a *adj (pelo, plumas)* singed; *(tela, papel)* scorched; *(tostada)* burnt

chamuscar [60] **1** *vt (pelo, plumas)* to singe; *(tela, papel)* to scorch; *(tostada)* to burn

2 chamuscarse *vpr (pelo, plumas)* to get singed; *(tela, papel)* to get scorched; *(tostada)* to burn, to get burnt; **se chamuscó el bigote** he singed his moustache, he got his moustache singed

chamusquina *nf (quemado)* scorching, singeing; EXPR *Fam* **me huele a c.** it smells a bit fishy to me, I don't like the look of this

chamuyar *RP Fam* **1** *vt* **(a)** *(susurrar)* to mutter, to whisper; **le chamuyó algo al oído** she muttered something in his ear **(b)** *(engañar)* to take in, to diddle

2 *vi* to mutter, to whisper; **dos enamorados chamuyaban en un rincón** two lovers were muttering *o* whispering to each other in a corner

chancar [60] *vt Andes* to crush, to grind

chance **1** *nm o nf Am* opportunity, chance; **me dio una segunda c.** he gave me a second chance; **aprovechar la c.** to seize the opportunity; **en** *o* **a la primera c.** at the first opportunity; **tener c. de hacer algo** to have the chance to do sth; **¿me das un c.?** can I have a go?

2 *adv Méx* maybe; **iré al cine hoy, c. mañana** I'm going to the movies *o Br* cinema today, or maybe tomorrow

chancearse *vpr* **c. de** to make fun of

chancero, -a *adj Am* funny

chanchada *nf Am* **(a)** *(porquería)* disgusting habit; **¡no hagas chanchadas!** stop being so disgusting! **(b)** *Fam (jugarreta)* dirty trick

chanchita *nf CSur* piggy bank

chancho, -a *Am* **1** *adj Fam (sucio)* filthy

2 *nm,f* **(a)** *(animal)* pig, *f* sow; EXPR *Fam* **comer como un c.** *(mucho)* to eat a lot; *(sin modales)* to eat like a pig; EXPR *Fam* **estar gordo como un c.** to be a fat pig; EXPR *RP Fam* **estar** *o* **ser como chanchos** *(ser amigos)* to be bosom buddies *o* pals; EXPR *Chile, Col, RP Fam Hum* **c. limpio no engorda** a little bit of dirt never hurt anyone; EXPR *RP Fam* **querer la chancha y los cuatro reales** to want to have one's cake and eat it; PROV **a cada c. le llega su San Martín** = everyone gets their come-uppance at some point

(b) *Fam (persona sucia)* dirty *o* filthy pig

3 *nm (carne)* pork

chanchullero, -a *Fam* **1** *adj* crooked, dodgy

2 *nm,f* trickster, crook

chanchullo *nm Fam* fiddle, racket; **siempre anda metido en chanchullos** he's always on the fiddle, he's always got some racket going; **hicieron un c. para evitar pagar** they worked some fiddle to avoid paying

chancla *nf (sandalia)* backless sandal; *(para la playa) Br* flip-flop, *US & Aus* thong

chancleta *nf* **(a)** *(sandalia)* backless sandal; *(para la playa) Br* flip-flop, *US* thong **(b)** *Andes, RP Fam (bebé)* baby girl

chanclo *nm* **(a)** *(de madera)* clog **(b)** *(de plástico)* galosh

chancro *nm (enfermedad)* chancre

chándal *(pl* **chandals***)* *nm Esp* tracksuit

chanfaina *nf Col Fam* cushy number *(obtained through connections)*

changa *nf* **(a)** *Bol, RP (trabajo temporal)* odd job **(b)** *Andes, Cuba (chiste)* joke **(c)** *ver también* **chango**

changador *nm RP (cargador)* porter

changarro *nm Méx (tienda)* small store; *(puesto)* stand

chango, -a **1** *adj* **(a)** *Carib (bromista)* playful, joking **(b)** *Chile (fastidioso)* tedious, annoying **(c)** *Méx, PRico* **estar c.** to be cheap and plentiful

2 *nm,f* **(a)** *Carib (bromista)* joker, prankster **(b)** *Chile (fastidioso)* tedious person **(c)** *Arg, Bol, Méx (muchacho)* youngster

3 *nm* **(a)** *Méx (mono)* monkey **(b)** *Ven* **changos** *(harapos)* rags

changuear *vi Ven* to joke, to jest

changuito *nm* (**a**) *Arg (de la compra)* shopping *Br* trolley *o US* cart (**b**) *Arg (para bebé) Br* pushchair, *US* stroller

changurro *nm* = typical Basque dish of dressed crab

chanquete *nm* = small translucent fish similar to whitebait

chantaje *nm* blackmail; **hacer c. a alguien** to blackmail sb; **le hicieron un c.** he was blackmailed ►► ***c. emocional*** emotional blackmail

chantajear *vt* to blackmail; **lo chantajearon con unas fotos comprometedoras** they blackmailed him with some compromising photos

chantajista *nmf* blackmailer

chantillí *nm* whipped cream

chanza *nf* joke; **estar de c.** to be joking

chañar *nm Andes, RP* (**a**) *(árbol)* Chilean palo verde (**b**) *(fruto)* = fruit of the Chilean palo verde

chao *interj Fam* bye!, see you!

chapa *nf* (**a**) *(lámina) (de metal)* sheet, plate; *(de madera)* board ►► ***c. ondulada*** corrugated iron
(**b**) *(de vehículo)* bodywork; **taller de c. y pintura** body shop
(**c**) *(de botella)* top, cap; **juego de las chapas** = children's game played with bottle tops
(**d**) *(insignia) (de policía)* badge; **el perro lleva una c. identificativa en el collar** the dog has an identity tag *o* disc on its collar
(**e**) *RP (de matrícula) Br* numberplate, *US* license plate
(**f**) *Col, Cuba, Méx (cerradura)* lock
(**g**) *Esp Fam* EXPR **no ha dado** *o* **pegado ni c.** he hasn't done a stroke (of work); **no tener ni c.** *(ni idea)* not to have a clue; *(dinero)* to be flat broke

chapado, -a *adj* (**a**) *(recubierto) (con metal)* plated; *(con madera)* veneered; **c. en oro** gold-plated; *Fig* **c. a la antigua** stuck in the past, old-fashioned (**b**) *Esp Fam (cerrado)* shut, closed

chapalear *vi (chapotear)* to splash

chapar **1** *vt* (**a**) *(recubrir) (con metal)* to plate; *(con madera)* to veneer (**b**) *Esp Fam (cerrar)* to shut, to close (**c**) *Perú (agarrar)* to grab (hold of); **c. a alguien del brazo** to grab sb by the arm, to grab sb's arm
2 *vi Esp Fam* (**a**) *(cerrar)* to shut, to close; **¿a qué hora chapa este garito?** what time does this joint shut *o* close? (**b**) *(estudiar)* to cram, *Br* to swot; **estuvo chapando toda la noche** I was up cramming *o Br* swotting all night

chaparral *nm* chaparral, = thicket of kermes oaks

chaparro, -a **1** *adj* short and squat
2 *nm,f (persona)* short, squat person
3 *nm (arbusto)* kermes oak

chaparrón *nm* (**a**) *(lluvia)* downpour; **cayó un c.** there was a downpour (**b**) *Fam (gran cantidad)* **su novela ha recibido un c. de premios** she has been showered with prizes for her novel; **recibió un c. de críticas** he received a barrage of criticism; **recibieron un c. de solicitudes** they received a flood of applications

chapata *nf* = flat crusty loaf

chapear *vt (con metal)* to plate; *(con madera)* to veneer

chapela *nf* (Basque) beret

chapero *nm Fam* male prostitute, *Br* rent boy

chapín, -ina *CAm, Méx Fam* **1** *adj* Guatemalan
2 *nm,f* Guatemalan

chapista *nmf* panel beater

chapistería *nf (taller)* body shop

chapita *nf RP (del tacón)* heel

chapitel *nm Arquit* (**a**) *(de torre)* spire (**b**) *(de columna)* capital

chapó *interj (¡bien hecho!)* well done!, bravo!; **se merece un c. por el esfuerzo realizado** he deserves a pat on the back for all the effort he's put in; **¡c.!, te comportaste como un caballero** bravo! you behaved like a gentleman

chapola *nf Col* butterfly

chapopote *nm Carib, Méx* bitumen, pitch

chapotear *vi* to splash about

chapoteo *nm* splashing

chapucear *vt* to botch (up)

chapucería *nf* botch, botched job; **esta reparación es una auténtica c.** this repair is a real botched job; **tu examen es una c.** you've made a real botch *o* mess of your exam

chapucero, -a **1** *adj (trabajo)* shoddy, sloppy; *(persona)* bungling
2 *nm,f* sloppy *o* shoddy worker; **no seas un c. y pon más cuidado al pintar** don't be so sloppy and be more careful when you're painting

chapulín *nm CAm, Méx* (**a**) *(saltamontes)* grasshopper (**b**) *Fam (niño)* kid

chapurrar, chapurrear *vt* to speak badly; **chapurrea el francés** she speaks broken *o* bad French

chapurreo *nm* jabbering

chapuza **1** *nf* (**a**) *(trabajo mal hecho)* botch, botched job; **esta reparación es una auténtica c.** this repair is a real botched job; **tu examen es una c.** you've made a real botch *o* mess of your exam (**b**) *(trabajo ocasional)* odd job; **vive de las chapuzas** he makes his living by doing odd jobs
2 **chapuzas** *nmf inv (persona)* sloppy *o* shoddy worker; **no seas un c. y pon más cuidado al pintar** don't be so sloppy and be more careful when you're painting

chapuzón *nm* dip; **darse un c.** to go for a dip

chaqué *nm* morning coat

chaqueño, -a **1** *adj* of/from the Chaco *(South America)*
2 *nm,f* person from the Chaco *(South America)*

chaqueta *nf (de traje, de cuero)* jacket; *(de punto)* cardigan; EXPR **cambiar(se)** *o* **mudarse de c.** to change sides ►► *Esp* ***c. de chándal*** tracksuit top

chaquetear *vi Esp Fam (cambiar de bando)* to change sides

chaqueteo *nm Esp Fam* changing sides

chaquetero, -a *Esp Fam* **1** *adj* **es un político c.** he's a political opportunist; **es muy c.** he will change his loyalties at the drop of a hat if it suits his own ends
2 *nm,f* turncoat

chaquetilla *nf* short jacket ►► ***c. torera*** bolero

chaquetón *nm* short coat ►► ***c. tres cuartos*** three-quarter-length coat

charada *nf* = newspaper puzzle in which a word must be guessed, with its meaning and certain syllables given as clues

charanga *nf* (**a**) *(banda)* brass band (**b**) *Fam (fiesta)* party (**c**) *Fam (ruido)* racket

charango *nm* = small South American guitar

charca *nf* pool, pond

charco *nm* (**a**) *(de líquido)* puddle; **un c. de sangre** a pool of blood (**b**) *Fam (océano Atlántico)* **cruzar** *o* **pasar el c.** to cross the Pond *o* Atlantic

charcutería *nf (tienda)* = shop selling cold meats, sausages etc

charcutero, -a *nm,f* pork butcher

charla *nf* (**a**) *(conversación)* chat; **estar de c.** to chat (**b**) *(conferencia)* talk (**sobre** about *o* on); **dar una c.** to give a talk (**c**) *Informát* chat ►► ***c. en tiempo real*** real time chat

charla-coloquio (*pl* **charlas-coloquio**) *nm* talk followed by a question-and-answer session

charlar *vi* to chat (**sobre** about); **c. con alguien** to chat with sb, to have a chat with sb

charlatán, -ana **1** *adj* talkative
2 *nm,f* (**a**) *(hablador)* chatterbox (**b**) *Pey (mentiroso)* trickster, charlatan (**c**) *(indiscreto)* gossip (**d**) *(vendedor)* hawker, pedlar
3 *nm (ave)* bobolink

charlatanería *nf* (**a**) *(locuacidad)* talkativeness (**b**) *Pey (palabrería)* spiel

charlestón *nm* Charleston

charleta *nmf RP Fam* chatterbox

Charlot *n pr* Charlie Chaplin

charlotada *nf Fam* (**a**) *(payasada)* **deja de hacer charlotadas** stop clowning around (**b**) *Taurom* slapstick bullfight

charlotear *vi* to chat

charloteo *nm* chatting; **estar de c.** to be chatting *o* having a chat

charnego, -a *nm,f Fam Pey* = term referring to an immigrant to Catalonia from another part of Spain

charnela *nf* hinge

charol *nm* (**a**) *(piel)* patent leather (**b**) *(barniz)* varnish (**c**) *Andes (bandeja)* tray

charola *nf Bol, CAm, Méx* tray

charolar *vt* to varnish

charque, charqui *nm Andes, RP* jerked *o* salted beef

charquear *vt Andes, RP (carne)* to dry, to cure

charqui = **charque**

charquicán *nm Andes, Arg* = stew made from salted meat, potatoes, beans and seasoning

charrán *nm* tern ►► ***c. ártico*** arctic tern; ***c. inca*** Inca tern; ***c. patinegro*** sandwich tern

charrancito *nm* little tern

charreada *nf Méx (espectáculo)* display of horseriding skills by "charros", ≃ rodeo

charrería *nf Méx* = horseriding skills as practised by "charros"

charretera *nf* epaulette

charro, -a **1** *adj* **(a)** *(recargado)* gaudy, showy **(b)** *Esp (salmantino)* Salamancan **(c)** *Méx (líder)* = in league with the bosses **(d)** *Méx Fam (tonto)* dim
2 *nm,f* **(a)** *Esp (salmantino)* Salamancan **(b)** *Méx (con traje típico)* = Mexican cowboy/cowgirl in traditional dress **(c)** *Méx (jinete)* horseman, *f* horsewoman **(d)** *Méx Fam (tonto)* dimwit **(e)** *Méx (líder)* = union leader in league with the bosses

charrúa **1** *adj* **(a)** *(indio)* Charrua **(b)** *(uruguayo)* Uruguayan
2 *nmf* **(a)** *(indio)* Charrua **(b)** *(uruguayo)* Uruguayan

chárter *(pl* **chárter** *o* **chárteres)** **1** *adj* **vuelo c.** charter flight; **¿este vuelo es c. o regular?** is this a charter or a scheduled flight?
2 *nm* charter flight

chas *interj* pow!, wham!

chasca *nf* **(a)** *Fam (hoguera)* campfire **(b)** *(leña)* brushwood **(c)** *Andes (greña)* mop of hair

chascar [60] **1** *vt* **(a)** *(lengua)* to click **(b)** *(dedos)* to snap **(c)** *(látigo)* to crack
2 *vi* **(a)** *(lengua)* to click **(b)** *(madera)* to crack

chascarrillo *nm Fam* funny story

chasco *nm* **(a)** *(decepción)* disappointment; **llevarse un c.** to be disappointed **(b)** *(burla)* trick; **dar un c. a alguien** to play a trick on sb

chasis *nm inv* **(a)** *(de vehículo)* chassis **(b)** *Fot* dark slide **(c)** *Fam (esqueleto)* body

chasque, chasqui *nm* = Inca messenger or courier

chasqueado, -a *adj (decepcionado)* disappointed

chasquear **1** *vt* **(a)** *(lengua)* to click **(b)** *(dedos)* to snap **(c)** *(látigo)* to crack **(d)** *(dar un chasco a)* to play a trick on, to fool
2 *vi* **(a)** *(lengua)* to click **(b)** *(madera, hueso)* to crack

chasqui = **chasque**

chasquido *nm* **(a)** *(de lengua)* click **(b)** *(de dedos)* snap, click **(c)** *(de látigo)* crack **(d)** *(de madera, hueso)* crack **(e)** *(de arma)* click

chasquilla *nf Chile (flequillo) Br* fringe, *US* bangs

chat *nm Informát (charla)* chat; *(sala)* chat room

chata *nf* **(a)** *(orinal)* bedpan **(b)** *ver también* **chato**

chatarra *nf* **(a)** *(metal)* scrap (metal) **(b)** *(objetos, piezas)* junk **(c)** *Fam (joyas)* cheap and nasty jewellery; **este anillo es pura c.** this ring is a piece of tat **(d)** *Fam (condecoraciones)* brass, medals; **un general cargado de c.** a general weighed down with medals **(e)** *Fam (monedas)* small change **(f)** *Méx Fam (comida)* junk food

chatarrería *nf* scrapyard

chatarrero, -a *nm,f* scrap (metal) dealer

chatear *vi Fam* **(a)** *Esp (beber)* to have a few glasses of wine **(b)** *Informát* to chat

chateo *nm Esp Fam* **ir de c.** to go out for a few glasses of wine

chato, -a **1** *adj* **(a)** *(nariz)* snub **(b)** *(persona)* snub-nosed **(c)** *(superficie, objeto)* flat **(d)** *PRico, RP Fam (sin ambiciones)* commonplace; **una vida chata** a humdrum existence
2 *nm,f* **(a)** *(persona)* snub-nosed person **(b)** *Fam (apelativo)* love, dear
3 *nm Esp Fam* **c. (de vino)** = small glass of wine

chau *interj Bol, CSur, Perú Fam* bye!, see you!

chaucha **1** *adj RP Fam* dull, boring; **la fiesta estuvo bastante c.** the party was pretty dull *o* boring
2 *nf* **(a)** *Bol, RP (judía verde)* green bean **(b)** *Andes (patata)* early potato **(c)** *Andes, RP (moneda)* = coin of little value; EXPR **costar chauchas y palitos** to cost next to nothing

chauvinismo [tʃoβi'nismo] *nm* chauvinism

chauvinista [tʃoβi'nista] **1** *adj* chauvinistic
2 *nmf* chauvinist

chaval, -ala *nm,f Fam* **(a)** *(persona)* kid; **está hecho un c.** he's like a young kid **(b)** *(apelativo) (para chicos)* son; *(para chicas)* young lady; **chavala, acércame esa silla** bring me over that chair, will you, young lady?; **¿tú quién te has creído que eres, c.?** who do you think you are, sonny *o Br* sunshine?

chavalería *nf Fam* kids

chavea *nmf Fam* kid

chaveta *nf* **(a)** *(clavija)* cotter pin **(b)** *Fam (cabeza)* nut, head; EXPR **estar mal de la c.** to be funny in the head; EXPR **perder la c.** *(volverse loco)* to go off one's rocker; **ha perdido la c. por una compañera de clase** he's gone nuts about one of the girls in his class **(c)** *Andes (navaja)* penknife

chavo, -a *Fam* **1** *nm,f Méx* **(a)** *(chico)* guy; *(chica)* girl **(b)** *(novio)* boyfriend; *(novia)* girlfriend
2 *nm (dinero)* **no tener un c.** to be broke; **quedarse sin un c.** to be left broke

chayote *nm CAm, Méx* chayote

Che *n pr* **(el) C.** Che (Guevara)

che **1** *interj* **(a)** *(¡oye!)* hey!
(b) *RP Fam (como muletilla)* **¿cómo andás, c.?** hey, how's it going?; **¿por qué no te venís al cine con nosotros, c.?** hey, why don't you come to the cinema with us?; **c. Diego, ¿tendrás el auto mañana?** hey, Diego, will you have the car tomorrow?; **c., ¿y ahora qué hacemos?** well, what are we supposed to do now, then?; **¡pero qué hacés, c.!** oi, what do you think you're doing?; **c., ¡vení para acá!** hey, over here, you!; **¡callate, c.!** shut it, you!
2 *nmf Chile Fam* Argentinian, *Br* Argie

checa *nf* **(a)** *Hist (en la Unión Soviética)* Cheka **(b)** *(en otros países)* secret police **(c)** *(local)* secret police headquarters *(singular)* **(d)** *ver también* **checo**

checada *nf Andes, CAm, Méx* checkup

checar *vt Andes, CAm, Méx* **(a)** *(comprobar)* to check; **c. el nivel de aceite** to check the oil; **el veterinario checó a mi perro** the vet gave my dog a checkup; EXPR *Fam* **¡chécalo bien!** check it out!
(b) *(vigilar)* to check up on, to monitor; **hace meses que la policía viene checando sus actividades** the police have been checking up on what he's been doing for months
(c) *(marcar)* **c. tarjeta** *(en fábrica) (a la entrada)* to clock in; *(a la salida)* to clock out; EXPR *Fam* **tengo que ir a c., tengo que c. tarjeta** *(en casa de la novia)* I have to see my girlfriend

chechén, -ena, checheno, -a **1** *adj* Chechen
2 *nm,f* Chechen

Chechenia *n* Chechnya

checheno = **chechén**

chécheres *nmpl Col* junk

checo, -a **1** *adj* Czech
2 *nm,f (persona)* Czech
3 *nm (lengua)* Czech

checoslovaco, -a, checoeslovaco, -a *Antes* **1** *adj* Czechoslovakian, Czechoslovak
2 *nm,f* Czechoslovakian, Czechoslovak

Checoslovaquia, Checoeslovaquia *n Antes* Czechoslovakia

chef [tʃef] *(pl* **chefs)** *nm* chef

Chejov *n pr* Chekhov

chela *nf Méx Fam (cerveza) Br* jar, *US* brewski

chele, -a *CAm* **1** *adj* **(a)** *(rubio)* blond, *f* blonde **(b)** *(de piel blanca)* fair-skinned
2 *nm,f* **(a)** *(rubio)* blond, *f* blonde **(b)** *(de piel blanca)* fair-skinned person

cheli *nm Fam* = slang typical of Madrid

chelín *nm Antes* **(a)** *(en Austria)* schilling **(b)** *(en el Reino Unido)* shilling

chelo *nm* cello

chencha *adj Méx* lazy, idle

chepa *nf Fam* hump; EXPR **subírsele a alguien a la c.: al menor descuido se te suben a la c.** if you don't watch your step they'll walk all over you

cheposo, -a, chepudo, -a *Fam* **1** *adj* hunchbacked
2 *nm,f* hunchback

cheque *nm Br* cheque, *US* check; **pagar con c.** to pay by cheque; **cobrar un c.** to cash a cheque; **cruzar un c.** to cross a cheque; **extender un c. (a alguien)** to make out a cheque (to sb) ▸▸ ***c. bancario*** banker's cheque; ***c. barrado*** crossed cheque; ***c. en blanco*** blank cheque; EXPR **dar** *o* **extender a alguien un c. en blanco** to give sb a blank cheque; ***c. cruzado*** crossed cheque; ***c. sin fondos*** bad cheque; ***c. (de) gasolina*** *Br* petrol *o US* gas voucher; ***c. nominativo*** = cheque made out to a specific person; **un c. nominativo a favor de Carla Gimeno** a cheque made out to Carla Gimeno; ***c. al portador*** cheque payable to the bearer; ***c. de ventanilla*** counter cheque; ***c. de viaje*** traveller's cheque

chequeada *nf Andes* checkup

chequear *vt (comprobar)* to check; **c. a un paciente** to examine a patient, to give a patient a checkup; **c. las cuentas de una empresa** to go over the accounts *o* do the books of a business; *Informát* **c. el disco duro** to check the hard drive

chequeo *nm* (a) *(médico)* checkup, medical; **hacerse un c.** to have a checkup ▸▸ ***c. médico*** checkup, medical (b) *(comprobación)* check; **tuvo que pasar un c. policial** the police ran a check on him; **hacer un c. (de algo)** to check (sth)

chequera *nf Br* chequebook, *US* checkbook

cherembeco *nm Col Fam* thingumajig, whatsit

cheroqui 1 *adj* Cherokee
2 *nmf* Cherokee

cheto, -a = **concheto**

chetumaleño, -a 1 *adj* of/from Chetumal *(Mexico)*
2 *nm,f* person from Chetumal *(Mexico)*

cheve *nf Méx Fam (cerveza) Br* jar, *US* brewski

chévere *Andes, CAm, Carib, Méx Fam* 1 *adj (estupendo)* great, fantastic; **una fiesta muy c.** a really great *o* fantastic party; **tu compañera me ha parecido muy c.** I thought your girlfriend was really great; **ese vestido rojo te queda c.** you look great *o* fantastic in that red dress
2 *interj* great!, fantastic!; **¿vamos al cine mañana? – ¡c.!** shall we go to the movies tomorrow? – that would be great!

cheviot (*pl* **cheviots**) *nm* cheviot

chía *nf Méx* (a) *(semilla)* sage seed (b) *(refresco)* = drink made from sage seeds, lemon juice and sugar

chiapaneco, -a 1 *adj* of/from Chiapas *(Mexico)*
2 *nm,f* person from Chiapas *(Mexico)*

chibcha 1 *adj* Chibchan, Chibcha
2 *nmf* Chibcha

chibolo *nm Andes, CAm* swelling, bump

chic 1 *adj inv* chic
2 *nm* chic; **Juan tiene mucho c.** Juan is really chic

chica *nf* (a) *(criada)* maid ▸▸ ***c. de alterne*** = girl who works in bars on a commission basis, encouraging customers to drink, *US* B-girl (b) *ver también* **chico**

chicane [tʃi'kan] *nf Dep* chicane

chicano, -a 1 *adj* Chicano, Mexican-American
2 *nm,f (persona)* Chicano, Mexican-American
3 *nm (lengua)* Chicano

chicarrón, -ona *nm,f Fam* strapping lad, *f* strapping girl

chicha *nf* (a) *Esp Fam (para comer)* meat; EXPR *Fam* **de c. y nabo** lousy; **un reloj de c. y nabo** a lousy watch
(b) *Esp Fam (de persona)* flesh; **tiene pocas chichas** *(está flaco)* he's as thin as a rake
(c) *(bebida alcohólica)* = alcoholic drink made from fermented maize; EXPR *Fam* **no ser ni c. ni limonada** *o* **limoná** to be neither one thing nor the other, to be neither fish nor fowl
(d) *(bebida refrescante)* = thick, sweet drink made from rice, condensed milk and vanilla

chícharo *nm CAm, Méx* pea

chicharra *nf* (a) *(insecto)* cicada (b) *Méx (timbre)* electric buzzer

chicharrero, -a *Fam* 1 *adj* of/from Tenerife *(Spain)*
2 *nm,f* person from Tenerife *(Spain)*

chicharro *nm (pez)* horse mackerel

chícharro *nm Am (guisante)* pea

chicharrón 1 *nm (frito)* pork crackling
2 **chicharrones** *nmpl (embutido)* = cold processed meat made from pork

chiche 1 *adj Andes, RP (delicado)* fine, delicate
2 *nm* (a) *Andes, RP Fam (juguete)* toy (b) *Andes, RP (adorno)* delicate ornament (c) *CAm, Méx muy Fam (pecho)* tit

chichería *nf Andes* "chicha" shop

chichi *nm* (a) *muy Fam (vulva) Br* fanny, *US* beaver (b) *Guat, Méx (nodriza)* wet nurse (c) *Méx muy Fam (pecho)* tit

chichí *nm Col Fam* pee, *Br* wee-wee

chichigua *nf CAm, Méx (nodriza)* wet nurse

chichinabo: de chichinabo *loc adj Fam (de poca calidad)* **un reloj de c.** a lousy watch

chichón *nm* bump (on the head); **me di un golpe y me salió un c.** I hit myself on the head and it came up in a bump

chichonear *vi RP* to play jokes

chichonera *nf (para niños)* = protective headband to prevent toddlers hurting themselves when they bang into something; *(para ciclistas)* hairnet, = soft protective headgear for cyclists

chicle *nm* chewing gum; **¿me das un c.?** can I have a piece of chewing gum?; **mascar c.** to chew gum ▸▸ *Urug* ***c. globero*** bubble gum

chiclé, chicler *nm Aut* jet

chico, -a 1 *adj esp Am* (a) *(joven)* small, young; **este perro es demasiado c. para separarlo de su madre** this dog is too small *o* young to be taken away from its mother
(b) *(de poco tamaño)* small; **este apartamento es muy c.** this *Br* flat *o* *US* apartment is very small; EXPR **lo bueno viene en frasco c.** good things come in small packages
2 *nm,f* (a) *(joven)* boy, *f* girl; **no es mala chica** she isn't a bad girl
(b) *(hijo)* son, boy; *(hija)* daughter, girl; **mi chica mayor ya se ha casado** my eldest daughter *o* girl is already married; **los chicos han ido a pasar el fin de semana con sus abuelos** the children have gone to their grandparents for the weekend
(c) *(empleado)* boy, *f* girl; **la compra se la llevará el c.** the delivery boy will bring your shopping home for you ▸▸ *RP* ***c. de los mandados*** *(en oficina)* office boy; *(en tienda)* errand boy; ***c. de los recados*** *(en oficina)* office boy; *(en tienda)* errand boy
(d) *(novio)* boyfriend; *(novia)* girlfriend; **a ver si nos presentas a tu c.** why don't you introduce us to your boyfriend *o* young man?
(e) *(tratamiento)* **c., ponme un café** waiter, could I have a coffee, please?; **¡chica, no sé qué decirte!** well, what can I say?; **¡c., qué suerte has tenido!** you lucky thing!; **chica, haz lo que quieras** look, you can do what you want; **¡vamos c., no te pongas así!** come on, don't be like that!

chicotazo *nm Am* crack, whipcrack; EXPR **como c.: salir como c.** to shoot off, to be off like a shot; **los autos iban como c.** the cars were zooming along

chicote *nm Am* whip

chicuelina *nf Taurom* = pass made by the bullfighter, holding the cape at chest height in front of him

chido, -a *adj Méx Fam* cool, *US* neat; **un auto c.** a really cool car

chifla *nf Fam* **tomarse algo a c.** to treat sth as a joke; **tomarse las cosas a c.** to treat everything as a joke

chiflado, -a *Fam* 1 *adj* crazy, mad; **está c. por la música étnica** he's crazy *o* mad about ethnic music; **está c. por una compañera de clase** he's really fallen for one of his classmates
2 *nm,f* loony

chifladura *nf (locura)* madness; **ese plan es una c.** that plan's insane *o* crazy; **su última c. son las motos** his latest craze is for motorbikes; **todos conocemos su c. por el rock psicodélico** we all know how crazy she is about psychedelic rock

chiflar 1 *vt Fam (encantar)* **me chifla el pescado frito** I just love fried fish; **me chifla ese jugador** I'm mad *o* crazy about that player
2 *vi (silbar)* to whistle; EXPR *RP* **no se puede c. y comer gofio** you can't have your cake and eat it
3 **chiflarse** *vpr Fam* **se chifla por las novelas policíacas** he's crazy *o* mad about detective novels; **se ha chiflado por un compañero del trabajo** she's really fallen for someone at her work

chifle *nm* (a) *(para pólvora)* powder horn (b) *(silbato)* whistle

chiflete *nm RP Fam Br* draught, *US* draft; **en esta habitación hay mucho c.** this room is very draughty

chiflido *nm* whistling

chiflón *nm Méx Fam Br* draught, *US* draft; **en esta habitación hay mucho c.** this room is very draughty

chifonier *nm (mueble)* tallboy

chigüín, -ina *nm,f CAm Fam* kid

chihuahua *nm* chihuahua

chihuahuense 1 *adj* of/from Chihuahua *(Mexico)*
2 *nmf* person from Chihuahua *(Mexico)*

chií (*pl* **chiíes**), **chiíta** 1 *adj* Shi'ite
2 *nmf* Shi'ite

chijete *nm RP Fam Br* draught, *US* draft; **en esta habitación hay mucho c.** this room is very draughty

chilaba *nf* jellaba

chilango, -a *Méx Fam* 1 *adj* of/from Mexico City
2 *nm,f* person from Mexico City

chilapastroso, -a *adj Méx Fam* 1 *adj* scruffy, shabby
2 *nm,f* scruff

chilaquiles *nmpl Méx* = dish made with fried pieces of tortilla baked in a chilli and tomato sauce, usually containing chicken or pork

chilatole, chileatole *nm Méx (guiso)* = pork stew with sweetcorn and chilli

chilca *nf* = type of tropical shrub

chilco *nm Arg, Chile* hardy fuchsia

Chile *n* Chile

chile *nm* (**a**) *CAm, Méx (pimiento)* chilli ►► ***c. ancho*** = dried poblano chilli; ***c. chipotle*** = dried and smoked or pickled jalapeño chilli; ***c. habanero*** = small, extremely hot, fresh chilli, ≃ Scotch bonnet pepper; ***c. jalapeño*** = small hot fresh green chilli; ***c. pasilla*** = long dark-brown or black dried chilli; ***c. poblano*** = large fresh mild chilli, similar to a green pepper; ***c. serrano*** = small hot fresh green or red chilli; ***c. verde*** = small hot fresh green chilli
(**b**) *CAm Fam (mentira)* fib
(**c**) *Méx Fam (pene)* willy, *US* peter

chileatole = **chilatole**

chilena *nf* (**a**) *Dep* (overhead) scissors kick (**b**) *ver también* **chileno**

chilenismo *nm* Chilean word/expression

chilenitis *nf inv Chile Fam* = stomach upset suffered by tourists in Chile

chileno, -a 1 *adj* Chilean
2 *nm,f* Chilean

chilindrón *nm Culin* = seasoning made of tomatoes and peppers

chillanejo, -a 1 *adj* of/from Chillán *(Chile)*
2 *nm,f* person from Chillán *(Chile)*

chillante *adj Méx* loud, gaudy; **una blusa de color amarillo c.** a loud yellow blouse

chillar 1 *vi* (**a**) *(gritar) (personas)* to scream, to yell; *(aves, monos)* to screech; *(cerdo)* to squeal; *(ratón)* to squeak (**b**) *(hablar alto)* to shout; **chilla más, que aquí atrás no se te oye** speak up, we can't hear you at the back; **¡no chilles, que no somos sordos!** don't shout, we're not deaf! (**c**) *(chirriar)* to screech; *(puerta, madera)* to creak; *(bisagras)* to squeak
2 *vt Fam (reñir)* to yell *o* shout at; **siempre le chilla al niño** she's always yelling *o* shouting at the child; **a mí no me chilla nadie** no one shouts at me

chillería *nf (alboroto)* screaming, yelling

chillido *nm* (**a**) *(de persona)* scream, yell; **pegar** *o* **dar un c.** to scream, to yell (**b**) *(de animal) (de ave, mono)* screech; *(de cerdo)* squeal; *(de ratón)* squeak

chillo *nm* (**a**) *(en carpintería)* lath (**b**) *CAm (deuda)* debt

chillón, -ona 1 *adj* (**a**) *(voz)* piercing, screeching (**b**) *(persona)* **es muy c.** he has a really loud voice (**c**) *(color)* loud, gaudy; **una blusa de color amarillo c.** a loud yellow blouse
2 *nm,f* **es un c.** he has a really loud voice

chilote[1] *nm Méx (bebida)* = drink made of chilli and pulque

chilote[2]**, -a** 1 *adj* of/from Chiloé *(Chile)*
2 *nm,f* person from Chiloé *(Chile)*

chilpancingueño, -a 1 *adj* of/from Chilpancingo *(Mexico)*
2 *nmf* person from Chilpancingo *(Mexico)*

chilpayate, -a *nm,f Méx Fam* kid

chilpotle *nm Méx* = smoked or pickled jalapeño chile

chimango *nm (ave)* chimango

chimba *nf Andes (de río)* opposite bank

chimbo, -a *adj Col, Ven Fam* (**a**) *(de mala calidad)* lousy (**b**) *(complicado)* screwed-up; **la cosa está chimba** things are really screwed-up

chimenea *nf* (**a**) *(tubo) (de casa)* chimney; *(de locomotora, fábrica)* chimney, smokestack; *(de barco)* funnel, smokestack; **entrar/salir por la c.** *(humo, viento)* to come down/go up the chimney
(**b**) *(hogar)* fireplace; **encender la c.** to light the fire
(**c**) *Geol (en volcán)* vent
(**d**) *(de paracaídas)* apex
(**e**) *(en montaña, glaciar)* chimney
(**f**) *Min* ***c. de aire*** air shaft
(**g**) *Fam (cabeza)* nut, *Br* bonce; **no te calientes la c.** don't worry your head about it

chimento *nm RP* rumour, piece of gossip

chimichurri *nm RP* = barbecue sauce made from garlic, parsley, oregano and vinegar

chimpancé *nm* chimpanzee

chimpún *nm Perú* soccer *o Br* football boot

chin *interj* (**a**) **¡c. c.!** *(al brindar)* cheers! (**b**) *Méx (¡ay!)* blast!, drat!

China *n* **(la) C.** China ►► ***la C. comunista*** Communist China; ***la C. nacionalista*** Nationalist China

china *nf* (**a**) *(piedra)* small stone, pebble; **se me ha metido una c. en el zapato** I've got a stone in my shoe; EXPR *Fam* **le tocó la c.** he drew the short straw (**b**) *Fam (droga)* deal *(small amount of cannabis)* (**c**) *Am Pey (india)* Indian woman (**d**) *Am Pey (criada)* Indian servant (**e**) *Méx (mujer del charro)* = charro's wife (**f**) *RP (mujer del gaucho)* = gaucho's wife (**g**) *ver también* **chino**

> **Falso amigo**: El sustantivo inglés **china** no es la traducción del español **china**. En inglés, **china** significa "loza" o "porcelana".

chinampa *nf Méx* = man-made island for growing flowers, fruit and vegetables, in Xochimilco, near Mexico City

chinchar *Fam* 1 *vt* to pester, to bug
2 **chincharse** *vpr* to put up with it; **¡tú no tienes, para que te chinches!** you haven't got any, so there!; **si no te gusta, te chinchas** if you don't like it, you can lump it

chincharrero *nm Andes* = small fishing boat

chinche 1 *adj Fam* annoying
2 *nm o nf (insecto)* bedbug; EXPR *Fam* **caer** *o* **morir como chinches** to drop *o* die like flies
3 *nf Am Br* drawing pin, *US* thumbtack
4 *nmf Fam (persona)* pest, pain

chincheta *nf Esp Br* drawing pin, *US* thumbtack

chinchilla *nf* (**a**) *(animal)* chinchilla (**b**) *(piel)* chinchilla fur

chinchín 1 *nm* (**a**) *(ruido)* = noise of a brass band (**b**) *CAm (sonajero)* rattle
2 *interj* cheers!

chinchón *nm* (**a**) *(bebida)* = aniseed liqueur (**b**) *(juego de cartas)* = card game similar to rummy

chinchorro *nm* (**a**) *Méx (red)* net (**b**) *Chile, Ven (hamaca)* hammock

chinchoso, -a *Fam* 1 *adj* annoying
2 *nm,f* pest, pain

chinchudo, -a *adj RP* prickly, touchy

chinchulín *nm*, **chinchulines** *nmpl Andes, RP (plato)* = piece of sheep or cow intestine, plaited and then roasted

chinela *nf (zapatilla)* slipper

chinero *nm* china cabinet

chinesco, -a *adj* Chinese

chinga *nf* (**a**) *CAm, Ven (colilla)* cigar end (**b**) *Ven (borrachera)* drunkenness (**c**) *CAm, Ven (en el juego)* = fee paid by gamblers (**d**) *Méx muy Fam (paliza)* **me dieron una c.** they kicked the shit out of me (**e**) *Méx muy Fam (trabajo duro)* **es una c.** it's a bitch of a job (**f**) *Méx muy Fam (fastidio)* pain in the *Br* arse *o US* ass

chingada *nf Méx Vulg* **¡vete a la c.!** fuck off!; **de la c.** *(muy difícil)* fucking hard; **en la casa de la c.** *(muy lejos)* in the back of beyond, away to hell and gone

chingadazo *nm Méx muy Fam (golpe)* thump

chingadera *nf Méx Fam* (**a**) *(contravención)* **¡deja de hacer chingaderas!** stop mucking about! (**b**) *(porquería)* **siempre está comprando chingaderas** he's always buying *Br* rubbish *o US* garbage

chingado, -a 1 *adj* (**a**) *Esp, Méx muy Fam (estropeado)* bust, *Br* knackered (**b**) *Méx Vulg (como intensificador)* fucking; **te devuelvo tu c. carro** here's your fucking car back
2 *interj Méx Vulg* fucking hell!

chingana *nf Andes Fam* = cheap bar or café

chingar [38] 1 *vt* (**a**) *Esp, Méx muy Fam (estropear)* to bust, *Br* to knacker
(**b**) *Esp, Méx muy Fam* **c. a alguien** *(molestar)* to get up sb's nose, to piss sb off
(**c**) *Esp, Méx Vulg (copular con)* to screw, to fuck; EXPR *Méx* **¡chingas a tu madre!** like fuck!, *Br* bollocks!
(**d**) *Méx muy Fam (engañar)* **¡no me chingues!** pull the other one!, *Br* stop taking the piss!
(**e**) *Méx muy Fam (beber)* to drink a lot of; **anoche me chingué dos botellas de tequila yo solo** last night I downed two bottles of tequila on my own
(**f**) *Méx muy Fam (robar)* to pinch, *Br* to nick
(**g**) *Méx muy Fam (suspender)* **me chingaron en el examen** I flunked the exam
(**h**) *Méx muy Fam (estafar)* **chingarle a alguien plata** to screw sb out of some money; **trataron de chingarme 10 pesos en la cuenta del restaurante** they tried to do me out of 10 pesos when I paid the restaurant *Br* bill *o US* check
(**i**) *Méx muy Fam (para apurar a alguien)* **¡chíngale!, ¡chínguenle!** put your back into it!
2 *vi* (**a**) *Esp, Méx Vulg (copular)* to screw, to fuck
(**b**) *Méx muy Fam (molestar)* **¡deja de c.!** stop pissing me off!
3 **chingarse** *vpr Méx muy Fam* (**a**) *(estropearse)* to pack in, to conk out; **se nos chingó la televisión justo cuando empezaba el juego** the

TV packed in on us just as the game was about to start
(**b**) *(jorobarse)* **¡ya me chingué! ya lo habían vendido** of all the stinking luck! they'd already sold it
(**c**) *(comerse)* to scoff, to wolf down; **nos chingamos todo lo que había en el refrigerador** we scoffed everything that was in the fridge
(**d**) *(esforzarse)* **nos chingamos para terminar el trabajo a tiempo** we slogged our guts out to finish the work on time

chingo, -a 1 *adj* (**a**) *CAm, Ven (persona)* snub-nosed (**b**) *CAm (ropa)* short; *(persona)* in one's underwear (**c**) *CAm (animal)* bobtailed
2 *nm Méx muy Fam* **un c. de** *(un montón de)* a shitload of; **tengo un c. de hambre** I'm *Br* bloody *o US* goddamn starving
3 **chingos** *nmpl CAm* underwear

chingolo *nm* rufous-collared sparrow

chingón, -ona *Méx muy Fam* 1 *adj (muy bueno)* fantastic, great, *US* neat; **¡qué carro más c.!** what a great car!
2 *nm,f (persona)* big shot

chinguero *nm Méx muy Fam* shitload; **tengo un c. de trabajo** I've got a shitload of work to do

chinita *nf* (**a**) *Am (criada)* maid (**b**) *Chile (animal) Br* ladybird, *US* ladybug

chino, -a 1 *adj* (**a**) *(de China)* Chinese
(**b**) *Am (mestizo)* of mixed ancestry
(**c**) *Méx (rizado)* curly
2 *nm,f (persona)* Chinese person; **un c.** a Chinese man; **una china** a Chinese woman; **los chinos** the Chinese; EXPR **engañar a alguien como a un c.** to take sb for a ride; EXPR **trabajar como un c.** to slave away; EXPR **ser un trabajo de chinos** *(minucioso)* to be a fiddly *o* finicky job; *(pesado)* to be hard work
3 *nm* (**a**) *(lengua)* Chinese; EXPR *Fam* **me suena a c.** *(no lo conozco)* I've never heard of it; *(no lo entiendo)* it's all Greek to me; EXPR *Méx Fam* **está en c. que pase eso** no way is that going to happen
(**b**) *(pasapuré)* hand-operated food mill
(**c**) *Andes, RP (mestizo)* = person of mixed ancestry
(**d**) *Andes, Ven (niño)* child
4 **chinos** *nmpl* (**a**) *(juego)* = game in which each player must guess the number of coins or pebbles in the others' hand
(**b**) *(pantalones)* chinos
5 **chino chano** *loc adv (poco a poco)* bit by bit, little by little; **caminaron sin detenerse y, c. chano, llegaron a su destino** they walked on steadily and eventually got where they were going

chintz [tʃinθ] *nm* chintz

chip (*pl* **chips**) *nm Informát* chip; EXPR *Fam* **cambiar el c.** to get into the right frame of mind ►► ***c. de silicio*** silicon chip

chipa *nf Col* (**a**) *(cesto)* straw basket (**b**) *(rodete)* = roll of cloth formed into a circular pad to support a vessel carried on one's head

chipé, chipén *Fam* 1 *adj inv* brilliant, terrific; **me parece c.** I think it's brilliant *o* terrific; **ser de c.** to be brilliant *o* terrific
2 *adv* **se lo pasaron c.** they had a brilliant *o* terrific time

chipendi *adv Fam* **nos lo pasamos c. (lerendi)** we had an ace time

chipirón *nm* baby squid

chipocle = **chipotle**

chipote, chipotazo *nm* (**a**) *Guat (golpe)* slap (**b**) *Méx (chichón)* lump

chipotle, chipocle *nm Méx* = smoked jalapeño chilli

Chipre *n* Cyprus

chipriota 1 *adj* Cypriot
2 *nmf* Cypriot

chiqueado, -a *adj Méx Fam* spoilt; **a Pepito no lo aguanto porque lo tienen demasiado c.** I can't stand Pepito because he's a real spoilt brat

chiqueadores *nmpl Méx (remedio)* = home remedy for headaches

chiquear *vt Méx Fam* to spoil

chiqueo *nm Méx Fam* show of affection; **hacerle chiqueos a alguien** to kiss and cuddle sb

chiquero *nm Taurom* bull-pen

chiquicientos, -as *adj RP Fam* hundreds (and hundreds) of, umpteen

chiquilicuatro, chiquilicuatre *nm Fam* nobody; **ser un c.** to be a nobody

chiquillada *nf (cosa de niños)* childish thing; *(travesura)* childish prank; **se enfadaron por una c.** they got angry about nothing; **hacer una c. (a alguien)** to play a childish prank (on sb)

chiquillería *nf* kids

chiquillo, -a 1 *adj (infantil)* childish; **¡no seas c.!** don't be childish!
2 *nm,f* kid; **se comporta como un c.** he behaves like a child

chiquitín, -ina 1 *adj* tiny
2 *nm,f* tiny tot

chiquito, -a 1 *adj* (**a**) *(pequeño)* tiny (**b**) *(muy joven)* little, young; **todavía es muy c. para viajar solo** he's still very little *o* young to be travelling on his own
2 *nm* (**a**) *Esp (de vino)* = small glass of wine (**b**) *RP Fam (instante)* minute; **espere un c.** wait a minute (**c**) *RP Fam (pequeño pedazo)* small piece; **¿me das un c. de tarta?** can I have just a tiny piece of tart?
3 *nm,f Am Fam* kid
4 **chiquitas** *nfpl* EXPR **no andarse con chiquitas** not to mess about

chiribita *nf (chispa)* spark; EXPR *Fam* **echar chiribitas** *(de enfado)* to be furious; EXPR *Fam* **le hacían chiribitas los ojos al verlo** her eyes lit up when she saw him; EXPR *Fam* **ver chiribitas** to see spots in front of one's eyes

chiribitil *nm Fam (cuarto)* tiny room

chirigota *nf Fam (broma)* joke; **se toma todo a c.** he treats everything as a joke

chirimbolo *nm Fam* thingumajig, whatsit; **¿para qué sirve este c.?** what's this thing here for?

chirimiri *nm Esp* drizzle

chirimoya *nf* custard apple

chirimoyo *nm* custard apple tree

chiringa *nf PRico* kite

chiringuito *nm* (**a**) *(bar)* refreshment stall (**b**) *Fam (negocio)* **montarse un c.** to set up a little business

chiripa *nf Fam* fluke; **¡qué c. has tenido!** you lucky thing!, you really lucked out there!; **me enteré de** *o* **por c.** I found out by a fluke

chiripá (*pl* **chiripaes**) *nm Bol, CSur (para gaucho)* = garment worn by gauchos over trousers

chirivía *nf* parsnip

chirla *nf* luttleneck

chirle *adj RP (masa)* sticky; *(salsa)* watery, runny

chirola *nf Fam* (**a**) *RP (poco dinero)* **costar chirolas** to cost next to nothing (**b**) *CAm, Carib Fam* clink, slammer; **en c.** in the clink *o* slammer

chirona *nf Esp Fam* clink, slammer; **en c.** in the clink *o* slammer

chirote *nm Andes* (**a**) *(pájaro)* linnet (**b**) *(tonto)* fool, idiot

chirriante *adj (ruidoso)* screeching; *(puerta, madera)* creaking; *(bisagra, muelles)* squeaking

chirriar [32] *vi (sonar)* to screech; *(puerta, madera)* to creak; *(bisagra, muelles)* to squeak

chirrido *nm (ruido)* screech; *(de puerta, madera)* creak; *(de bisagra, muelles)* creak, squeak; **la bisagra dio un c.** the hinge creaked *o* squeaked

chirrión *nm Am (látigo)* horsewhip

chiruca® *nf* lightweight hiking boot

chis *interj* ssh!

chischás *nm inv (de espadas)* clash

chiscón *nm Pey* poky little room

chisgarabís (*pl* **chisgarabises**) *nm Fam* busybody

chisme *nm* (**a**) *(cotilleo)* rumour, piece of gossip; **no hace más que contar chismes** all she does is spread gossip (**b**) *Fam (objeto desconocido)* thingumajig, thingy; **¿para qué sirve este c.?** what's this thing here for? (**c**) *Fam (objeto inútil)* piece of junk; **tienes el cuarto lleno de chismes** your room is full of junk

chismear, chusmear *Am Fam* 1 *vt (contar, chismorrear)* **me chismearon que...** I heard that...
2 *vi (contar chismes)* to gossip

chismografía *nf Fam* (**a**) *(afición al chisme)* fondness for gossip (**b**) *(conjunto de chismes)* gossiping

chismorrear *vi* to spread rumours, to gossip

chismorreo *nm* gossip; **se pasaron la tarde de c.** they spent the afternoon gossiping

chismoso, -a 1 *adj* gossipy; **no seas tan c.** don't be such a gossip
2 *nm,f* gossip, scandalmonger

chispa 1 *nf* (**a**) *(de fuego)* spark; EXPR *Fam* **echar chispas** to be hopping mad; EXPR *Fam* **está que echa chispas** she's hopping mad, she's fuming
(**b**) *(de electricidad)* spark; **si juntas los cables, saltan chispas** if you put the cables together, you get *o* it throws off sparks; *Fig* **saltaron chispas entre los asistentes al debate** sparks flew among the participants in the debate
(**c**) *(pizca)* bit; **añade una c. de sal** add a pinch of salt
(**d**) *(agudeza, gracia)* sparkle; **esa novela tiene c.** that novel has

really got something; **cuenta los chistes con mucha c.** he tells jokes really well
(e) **están cayendo chispas** *(lluvia ligera)* it's spitting (with rain)
2 *interj Méx* **¡chispas!** good heavens!, *Br* blimey!, *US* jeez!

chispazo *nm* (a) *(de fuego, electricidad)* spark; **dar un c.** to give off a spark, to spark (b) *(suceso aislado)* **se caracteriza por sus chispazos de inspiración** he's noted for his flashes of inspiration; **aquella manifestación fue el primer c. de la revolución** that demonstration was what sparked off the revolution; **sus discursos contienen chispazos de humor** his speeches have flashes of wit

chispeante *adj* (a) *(que chispea)* that gives off sparks (b) *(conversación, ojos)* sparkling; **posee un c. sentido del humor** she has a lively sense of humour

chispear 1 *vi* (a) *(chisporrotear)* to spark (b) *(relucir)* to sparkle; **un talento que chispea ocasionalmente** a talent with occasional flashes of genius
2 *v impersonal (llover)* to spit (with rain); **empezó a c.** a few spots of rain started to fall

chisporrotear *vi* (a) *(fuego, leña)* to crackle (b) *(aceite)* to splutter (c) *(comida)* to sizzle

chisporroteo *nm* (a) *(de fuego, leña)* crackling (b) *(de aceite)* spluttering (c) *(de comida)* sizzling

chisquero *nm* (cigarette) lighter

chist *interj* ssh!

chistar 1 *vi* (a) *(llamar)* to hiss *(to catch sb's attention)* (b) *(replicar)* **¡cómete la sopa, y sin c.!** keep quiet and finish your soup!; **hizo lo que le pidieron sin c.** he did what they asked without a murmur *o* a word of protest
2 *vt* (a) *(llamar)* **c. a alguien** = to attract sb's attention by hissing; **tuvimos que c. al camarero para que viniera** we had to hiss to get the waiter to come over to us (b) *(replicar)* **¡a mí no me chistes!** don't you answer me back!

chiste *nm* (a) *(cuento)* joke; **contar chistes** to tell jokes; **¡lo que cuentas suena a c.!** it sounds like a joke!; *Fig* **no tiene ningún c.** there's nothing special about it ▸▸ *Méx* ***c. colorado*** dirty joke; *Am* ***c. de gallegos*** ≃ Irish joke, *US* ≃ Polish joke; *Esp* ***c. de Lepe*** *Br* ≃ Irish joke, *US* ≃ Polish joke; ***c. verde*** dirty joke
(b) *Andes, Méx, RP (broma)* joke, prank; **hacerle un c. a alguien** to play a joke *o* prank on sb; **la pelea era** *CSur* **en** *o Méx* **de c.** the fight was just for fun; **no es c., perdió las dos piernas en un accidente** I'm not kidding, he lost both his legs in an accident; *CSur* **ni en c.,** *Méx* **ni de c.: ¿vas a la fiesta? – ni en c.** are you going to the party? – no way! *o* you must be joking!; *Méx* **no vuelvas a hacer eso ni de c.** don't even think about doing that again
(c) *Andes, Méx, RP Irónico (cosa cara)* **adivina cuánto salió el c. de su fiesta de Navidad** guess how much it cost for their little Christmas party?; **acaban de volver de China, ¿sabes cuánto les salió el c.?** they've just got back from China, how much do you think that little jaunt set them back?
(d) *Andes, Méx, RP (gracia)* **el c. es aprobar sin matarse estudiando** the really clever thing is passing without studying too hard
(e) *Méx (truco)* knack; **esto parece fácil, pero tiene su c.** this looks easy, but there's a knack to it
(f) *RP* **revistas de chistes** comics

chistera *nf (sombrero)* top hat

chistido *nm (llamada)* hiss *(to attract sb's attention)*

chistorra *nf* = type of cured pork sausage, typical of Aragon and Navarre

chistoso, -a 1 *adj* funny; **hoy estás muy c.** you're on form today
2 *nm,f* amusing *o* funny person

chistu *nm* = Basque flute

chistulari *nmf* = "chistu" player

chita *nf* EXPR *Esp Fam* **a la c. callando** quietly, on the quiet

chital *nm* axis deer, chital

chitón, chito *interj* quiet!; *Cine* **¡c., se rueda!** quiet on the set!; *Fam* **de esto que os acabo de contar, ¡c.!** don't say a word (to anyone) about what I've just told you!

chiva 1 *nf* (a) *CAm (manta)* blanket (b) *RP (barba)* goatee (c) *ver también* **chivo**
2 **chivas** *nfpl* (a) *Méx (pertenencias)* odds and ends (b) *Ven (ropa usada)* second-hand clothes

chivar *Fam* 1 *vt Esp* to whisper, to tell secretly
2 **chivarse** *vpr* (a) *Esp (niños)* to tell, *Br* to split (**de** on); *(delincuentes)* to squeal, *Br* to grass (**de** on); **si no me ayudas, me chivaré al profesor** if you don't help me, I'll tell the teacher on you; **alguien se ha chivado a la policía** someone has squealed *o Br* grassed to the police (b) *Am (enfadarse)* to become *o* get angry

chivatazo *nm Esp Fam Esp* tip-off; **dar el c.** to squeal, *Br* to grass

chivatear *vi Fam* (a) *Esp (delatar)* to squeal, *Br* to grass (b) *Andes (jugar)* to lark about

chivateo *nm Fam* (a) *Esp (de delincuente)* squealing, *Br* grassing (b) *Andes (juego)* larking about

chivato, -a 1 *nm,f Esp Fam* (a) *(delator) Br* grass, *US* rat (b) *(acusica)* telltale
2 *nm* (a) *(luz)* warning light; **el c. de la gasolina** the fuel warning light (b) *(alarma)* alarm bell (c) *Ven Fam (pez gordo)* big cheese

chivito *nm* (a) *Arg (carne)* roast kid (b) *Urug (sandwich)* steak sandwich *(containing cheese and salad)*

chivo, -a 1 *nm,f* kid, young goat; EXPR *Fam* **estar como una chiva** to be off one's head ▸▸ ***c. expiatorio*** scapegoat
2 *nm Méx Fam* pay, wages; **día del c.** payday

choc (*pl* **chocs**) *nm* shock

chocante *adj* (a) *(raro)* odd, strange; *(sorprendente)* startling; *(escandaloso)* shocking, scandalous; **viste con colores muy chocantes** she wears really loud colours; **me resulta c. verle tan contento** I'm astonished to see him looking so happy; **resulta c. oír hablar de derechos humanos a un sangriento dictador** it's rather a shock to hear a bloodstained dictator talking about human rights; **lo c. es que no lo descubriéramos antes** the most worrying thing is that we didn't find out about it earlier
(b) *RP (impropio)* inappropriate, unsuitable
(c) *Am Fam (antipático)* **no la invitaron por c.** she wasn't invited because she's such a pain

chocantería *nf Am (comentario)* annoying *o* unpleasant remark

---

CHOCAR [60] 1 *vi* (a) *(colisionar)* to crash, to collide (**con** *o* **contra** with); **chocaron dos autobuses** two buses crashed *o* collided; **el taxi chocó con una furgoneta** the taxi crashed into *o* collided with a van; **la moto chocó contra un árbol** the motorbike hit a tree; **iba despistado y chocó contra una farola** he wasn't concentrating and drove into a lamppost; **la pelota chocó contra la barrera** the ball hit the wall; **c. de frente con** to have a head-on collision with; **los dos vehículos chocaron frontalmente** *o* **de frente** the two vehicles collided head-on
(b) *(enfrentarse)* to clash; **la policía chocó con los manifestantes a las puertas del congreso** the police clashed with the demonstrators in front of the parliament; **el proyecto chocó con la oposición del ayuntamiento** the project ran into opposition from the town hall; **mis opiniones siempre han chocado con las suyas** he and I have always had different opinions about things; **tenemos una ideología tan diferente que chocamos constantemente** we have such different ideas that we're always disagreeing about something; **esta política económica choca con la realidad del mercado de trabajo** this economic policy goes against *o* is at odds with the reality of the labour market
(c) *(extrañar, sorprender) (ligeramente)* to puzzle, to surprise; *(mucho)* to shock, to astonish; **me choca que no haya llegado ya** I'm surprised *o* puzzled that she hasn't arrived yet; **le chocó su actitud tan hostil** she was taken aback *o* shocked by how unfriendly he was; **es una costumbre que choca a los que no conocen el país** it's a custom which comes as a surprise to those who don't know the country
(d) *Col, Méx, Ven Fam (molestar)* to annoy, to bug; **me choca que esté siempre controlándome** it really annoys me how she's always watching me
2 *vt* (a) *(manos)* to shake; EXPR *Fam* **¡chócala!, ¡choca esos cinco!** put it there!, give me five!
(b) *(copas, vasos)* to clink; **¡choquemos nuestros vasos y brindemos por los novios!** let's raise our glasses to the bride and groom!

---

chocarrería *nf* vulgar joke

chocarrero, -a *adj (chiste, lenguaje)* crude, vulgar

chochaperdiz *nf* woodcock

chochear *vi* (a) *(viejo)* to be senile; **el abuelo ya chochea** my grandad has gone senile (b) *Fam (de cariño)* **c. por alguien** to dote on sb; **siempre que habla de sus nietos, chochea** he goes all mushy when he talks about his grandchildren

chochera, chochez *nf* (a) *(vejez)* senility (b) *(dicho, hecho)* **decir/hacer chocheces** to say/do senile things

chochín *nm* wren ▸▸ ***c. de los cactos*** cactus wren; ***c. casero*** house wren

chocho, -a 1 *adj* (a) *(viejo)* senile; **estar c.** to be senile; **es un viejo c. que no sabe lo que dice** he's a senile old man who doesn't know what he's saying (b) *Fam (encariñado)* **está c. con su novia** he dotes on his girlfriend; **está c. con su nueva casa** he's over the moon about his new house

2 *nm* (a) *Esp, Méx muy Fam (vulva) Br* fanny, *US* beaver (b) *Fam (altramuz)* lupin seed *(for eating)*

choclo *nm Andes, RP* (a) *(mazorca)* corncob, ear of maize *o US* corn (b) *(granos)* sweetcorn (c) *(cultivo)* maize, *US* corn

choclón *nm Chile Fam* crowd

choco, -a 1 *adj CAm, Chile, Méx (persona) (cojo)* one-legged; *(manco)* one-armed

2 *nm* (a) *(sepia)* cuttlefish (b) *Andes (perro)* spaniel (c) *Andes (de pelo rizado)* curly-haired person; **chocos** curls

3 *nm,f* (a) *Col (persona morena)* dark-skinned person (b) *Bol (persona rubia)* blond, *f* blonde, fair-haired person (c) *CAm, Chile, Méx (tullido) (cojo)* one-legged person; *(manco)* one-armed person

chocolatada *nf* = afternoon party where thick drinking chocolate is served

chocolatado, -a *adj Am* **leche chocolatada** chocolate milk

chocolate *nm* (a) *(alimento)* chocolate; **una tableta de c.** a bar of chocolate; EXPR *Fam* **ser el c. del loro** *(ser insignificante)* to be a drop in the ocean ▸▸ *RP* ***c. amargo*** dark *o* plain chocolate; ***c. blanco*** white chocolate; ***c. con leche*** milk chocolate; ***c. negro*** dark *o* plain chocolate

(b) *(bebida)* **c. (a la taza)** thick drinking chocolate ▸▸ ***c. con churros*** = thick drinking chocolate and "churros"

(c) *Esp Fam (hachís)* hash

(d) EXPR *RP Fam* **c. por la noticia** you don't say!

chocolatera *nf* (a) *(vasija)* = pot for making drinking chocolate (b) *ver también* **chocolatero**

chocolatería *nf* (a) *(fábrica)* chocolate factory (b) *(establecimiento)* = café where drinking chocolate is served

chocolatero, -a 1 *adj* **ser muy c.** to love chocolate

2 *nm,f* (a) *(aficionado al chocolate)* chocaholic (b) *(oficio)* chocolate maker/seller

chocolatina *nf, RP* **chocolatín** *nm* chocolate bar

chofer *(pl* **choferes***) nmf Am* (a) *(como oficio) (de automóvil)* chauffeur (b) *(conductor)* driver

chófer *(pl* **chóferes***) nmf Esp (de automóvil)* chauffeur; *(de autobús)* driver

chola *nf* (a) *Esp Fam* nut; EXPR **estar mal de la c.** to have a screw loose, to be funny in the head (b) *ver también* **cholo**

cholla *nf CAm Fam (flema)* sluggishness

chollo *nm Esp Fam* (a) *(producto, compra)* bargain; **por ese precio, esa casa es un c.** the house is a bargain at that price (b) *(trabajo, situación)* cushy number; **tiene un c. de trabajo** he has a really cushy job; **con el cambio de la ley, se les ha acabado el c. a los contrabandistas** the change in the law has brought an end to the good times for smugglers

cholo, -a 1 *adj* (a) *Am (mestizo)* mestizo, half-caste (b) *Chile (cobarde)* cowardly (c) *Ven (querido)* dear, darling (d) *Ecuad (ordinario)* poor, common; **¡qué c.!** how common!

2 *nm,f* (a) *Andes* = sometimes pejorative term for mestizo who moves to the city from a rural area (b) *Am (mestizo)* half-caste, mestizo (c) *Am (indio)* educated *o* westernized Indian (d) *Chile (cobarde)* coward

chololo *nm Perú Fam* honey

choloque *nm Am* soapberry tree

chomba *nf* (a) *Arg (polo)* polo shirt (b) *Chile, Perú (suéter)* sweater

chompa *nf Andes* sweater, pullover

chompipe *nm CAm, Méx* turkey

chonchón *nm Chile* lamp

chones *nmpl Méx Fam* (a) *(calzoncillos) Br* underpants, *US* shorts (b) *(braga)* panties, *Br* knickers

chongo, -a 1 *adj RP Fam (vestido, auto)* tacky; *(persona)* tacky, tasteless

2 *nm* (a) *Méx (moño)* bun (b) *Méx Fam (broma)* joke (c) **chongos zamoranos** *(dulce)* = Mexican dessert made from milk curds, served in syrup (d) *RP Fam (horterada)* tacky thing

chonta *nf CAm, Perú (palmera)* = type of palm tree

chop, chopp [ʃop] *(pl* **chops, chopps***) nm CSur* (a) *(jarra)* beer mug (b) *(cerveza)* (mug of) beer

chóped *nm* = type of luncheon meat

chopera *nf* poplar grove

chopito *nm* baby squid

chopo *nm* poplar

chopp = **chop**

choque 1 *ver* **chocar**

2 *nm* (a) *(impacto)* impact; *(de automóvil, avión)* crash; **ha habido un c. de trenes** there's been a train crash ▸▸ ***c. frontal*** head-on collision

(b) *(enfrentamiento)* clash; **el c. entre los ejércitos produjo numerosas bajas** there were many casualties when the armies clashed; **tuvieron un c. sobre el reparto de poderes** they clashed over how power was to be shared out

(c) *(impresión)* shock; **la muerte de su marido le produjo un gran c. emocional** she was traumatized by her husband's death, her husband's death was a terrible shock to her ▸▸ ***c. cultural*** culture shock

(d) *Med* shock ▸▸ ***c. anafiláctico*** anaphylactic shock

(e) *Dep (partido)* clash

chorbo, -a *nm,f Esp Fam* (a) *(persona desconocida) (chico)* kid; *(adulto)* guy, *Br* bloke, *f* woman (b) *(novio)* guy, *Br* fella, *Br* bloke

chorcha *nf* (a) *(pájaro)* woodcock (b) *Méx (grupo)* get-together

chordón *nm* raspberry

chorear *vi Fam* (a) *Chile (refunfuñar)* to grumble, to moan (b) *Chile, Col, Perú, RP (robar)* to pilfer

choricear = **chorizar**

choriceo *nm Esp Fam* (a) *(robo)* robbery (b) *(timo)* rip-off

chorizar [14], **choricear** *vt Esp Fam* to swipe, to pinch; **me han vuelto a c. la cartera** I've had my *Br* wallet *o US* billfold pinched *o* swiped again

chorizo *nm* (a) *(embutido)* chorizo, = cured pork sausage, flavoured with paprika (b) *Esp Fam (ladrón)* thief (c) *Esp Fam (persona corrupta)* crook; **dice que todos los políticos son unos chorizos** she says all politicians are crooks (d) *muy Fam (excremento)* turd

chorlitejo *nm* ***c. chico*** little ringed plover; ***c. grande*** ringed plover

chorlito *nm* (a) *(ave)* plover ▸▸ ***c. cangrejero*** crab plover; ***c. carambolo*** dotterel; ***c. dorado*** golden plover; ***c. dorado chico*** American golden plover; ***c. gris*** grey plover; ***c. piquivuelto*** wrybill; ***c. terrestre*** least seedsnipe (b) *Fam* **cabeza de c.** scatterbrain

choro *nm Andes (marisco)* mussel

chorote *nm* (a) *Col (recipiente)* = unglazed pot for making chocolate (b) *Cuba (bebida)* thick chocolate drink

chorra *Esp Fam* 1 *nmf (tonto) Br* wally, *US* jerk; **hacer el c.** to muck about

2 *nf* (a) *(suerte)* **¡qué c. has tenido!** you flukey thing!; **ganaron de c.** it was a fluke that they won (b) *ver también* **chorro**[2]

chorrada *nf Fam* (a) *Esp (dicho, hecho)* **decir una c.** to say something stupid; **chorradas** *Br* rubbish, *US* garbage; **decir chorradas** to talk *Br* rubbish *o US* bull; **¡deja de hacer chorradas!** stop mucking about!

(b) *Esp (cosa insignificante)* **se gasta la paga en chorradas** he spends his wages on *Br* rubbish *o US* garbage; **cómprale alguna c. y ya está** just get him any old thing and be done with it; **tiene el coche lleno de chorradas** his car is full of stupid *Br* rubbish *o US* garbage; **se pelearon por una c.** they fell out over nothing

(c) *RP (cantidad)* **una c. de** stacks *o* heaps of; **el profesor nos dio una c. de artículos para leer** the teacher gave us stacks of articles to read

(d) *RP (robo)* **¡$5 por un café es una c.!** $5 for a cup of coffee is daylight robbery!

chorreado, -a *adj Am* stained (**de** with)

chorreadura *nf (mancha)* stain

chorrear 1 *vi* (a) *(gotear) (gota a gota)* to drip; *(en un hilo)* to trickle; **estar chorreando** *(estar empapado)* to be soaking *o* wringing wet; **esa cafetera chorrea** that coffee pot leaks; **el helado le chorreaba por la cara** he had ice cream running down his face (b) *(brotar)* to spurt *o* gush (out) (c) *RP Fam (robar)* to pinch, *Br* to nick; **c. algo a alguien** to pinch *o Br* nick sth off sb

2 *vt* (a) *(sujeto: prenda)* to drip; *(sujeto: persona)* to drip with; **ese tubo chorrea aceite** that pipe drips oil; **acabó la carrera chorreando sudor** he was dripping with sweat when he finished the race (b) *CSur (derramar)* to spill

3 **chorrearse** *vpr* **cuidado, no te chorrees helado en la blusa** careful you don't get ice cream on your blouse

chorreo *nm* (a) *(goteo) (gota a gota)* dripping; *(en un hilo)* trickling; *Fig* **un c. de dinero** a steady drain on funds; *Fig* **un c. de ofertas** a steady stream of offers (b) *(brote)* spurting, gushing

chorrera *nf* **(a)** *(canal)* channel, gully **(b)** *(adorno, volante)* frill; **chorreras** frill **(c)** *Am Fam (de gente, preguntas)* stream **(d)** *RP Fam* **una c. de** *(mucho)* loads of, a load of; **me gusta una c.** I love it

chorretón *nm* **(a)** *(chorro)* spurt **(b)** *(mancha)* stain

chorro[1] **1** *nm* **(a)** *(de líquido) (borbotón)* jet, spurt; *(hilo)* trickle; **sale un c. muy fino de agua** a thin trickle of water is coming out; **añade un c. de aceite a la ensalada** drizzle some oil over the salad; **salir a chorros** to spurt *o* gush out; **está sangrando a chorros** he's bleeding heavily; **la sangre se escapaba a chorros de la herida** blood was gushing from the wound; EXPR *Fam* **como los chorros del oro** as clean as a new pin

(b) *(de luz, gente, preguntas)* stream; **cayó un c. de monedas de la máquina tragaperras** coins poured out of the slot machine ►► ***c. de voz:*** **tener un c. de voz** to have a powerful voice

(c) *Méx Fam* **un c.** *(mucho)* a load, loads; **nos queda un c. de tiempo** we've got loads of time; **me provoca un c. ir al concierto** I really want to go to the concert

(d) *Méx Fam (diarrea)* the runs

2 *adv Méx Fam* loads; **me gusta c.** I love it; **me duele c.** it hurts like hell

chorro[2]**, -a** *nm,f RP Fam (ladrón)* thief

chotacabras *nm inv* nightjar ►► ***c. abanderado*** standard-winged nightjar; ***c. gris*** nightjar; ***c. pardo*** red-necked nightjar

chotearse *vpr Fam* **c. de** to make fun of

choteo *nm Fam* kidding; **estar de c.** to be kidding; **tomarse algo a c.** to treat sth as a joke

chotis *nm inv* = dance typical of Madrid; EXPR *Esp Fam Hum* **ser más agarrado que un c.** to be a real skinflint *o* tightwad

choto, -a **1** *adj Col (dócil, domesticado)* tame

2 *nm,f* **(a)** *(cabrito)* kid, young goat; EXPR *Fam* **estar como una chota** to be crazy, to be off one's rocker **(b)** *(ternero)* calf **(c)** *RP Fam (bobo)* twit, idiot

3 *nm RP (comida)* = small intestine, roasted as part of a "parrillada"

chova *nf* ***c. piquigualda*** alpine chough; ***c. piquirroja*** chough

chovinismo *nm* chauvinism

chovinista **1** *adj* chauvinistic

2 *nmf* chauvinist

choza *nf* **(a)** *(cabaña)* hut **(b)** *Esp Fam (vivienda)* pad

christma ['krisma] *nm*, **christmas** ['krismas] *nm inv* Christmas card

chubasco *nm (lluvia)* shower

chubasquero *nm* cagoule

chúcaro, -a *adj Andes, CAm, RP* **(a)** *(animal)* wild **(b)** *Fam (persona)* **ser c.** to be shy *o* withdrawn

chucha *nf* **(a)** *Col (animal)* opossum **(b)** *Arg, Chile Vulg (vulva)* cunt

chuchería *nf* **(a)** *(golosina) Br* sweet, *US* candy **(b)** *(objeto)* trinket

chucho *nm* **(a)** *Fam (perro)* mutt; **¡largo, c. asqueroso!** shoo, you horrible mutt! **(b)** *Cuba* **dar c.** *(dar golpes)* to lash **(c)** *RP Fam* ***c. de frío*** *(escalofrío)* shiver **(d)** *RP Fam (susto)* fright **(e)** *Chile (cárcel)* jail

chuchumeco *nm PRico Fam* jerk

chucrut (*pl* **chucruts**) *nm Culin* sauerkraut, choucroute

chueco, -a **1** *adj* **(a)** *Am (torcido)* twisted **(b)** *Am (patizambo)* bowlegged **(c)** *Méx, Ven Fam (cojo)* lame

2 *nm,f* **(a)** *Am (patizambo)* bowlegged person; **ser un c.** to have bow legs **(b)** *Méx, Ven Fam (cojo)* lame person

chufa *nf* **(a)** *(planta)* chufa **(b)** *(tubérculo)* tiger nut **(c)** *Esp Fam (golpe)* **se dio una c. con la moto** he had a smash-up on the bike; **como lo rompas te daré una c.** break it and I'll clobber you one

chufla *nf Fam* joke; **estar de c.** to be kidding; **tomarse las cosas a c.** to treat everything as a joke, not to take things seriously

chuico *nm Chile* demijohn

chulada *nf* **(a)** *Esp (bravuconada)* piece of bravado; **chuladas** bravado **(b)** *Fam (cosa bonita)* delight, gorgeous thing; **es una c. de foto** it's a lovely photo; **¡qué c. de zapatillas!** what lovely *o* gorgeous shoes!

chulapo, -a, chulapón, -ona *nm,f* = lower-class native of 18th-19th century Madrid

chulear *Fam* **1** *vt* **(a)** *Esp (explotar)* **c. a una mujer** to live off a woman **(b)** *Méx (elogiar)* **chulearon mucho a Ema con su nuevo vestido** Ema got lots of compliments in her new dress; **su actuación fue muy chuleada por la crítica** her performance won bouquets from the critics

2 chulearse *vpr Esp (fanfarronear)* to be cocky (**de** about); **se está chuleando de que aprobó el examen** he's making a big deal about how he passed the exam; **conmigo no te chulees** don't you get cocky with me

chulería *nf* **(a)** *Esp (bravuconería)* cockiness; **tratan al nuevo profesor con mucha c.** they really try it on with the new teacher; **lo de no presentarse a la reunión fue una c. del director** the fact that the manager didn't turn up at the meeting just shows how superior he thinks he is to everyone else **(b)** *(salero)* charm, winning ways

chulesco, -a *adj* = relating to lower-class Madrid life of the 18th-19th centuries

chuleta **1** *adj Esp Fam (chulo)* cocky

2 *nf* **(a)** *(de carne)* chop; **c. de cerdo/cordero** pork/lamb chop **(b)** *Esp, Ven Fam (en exámenes)* crib **(c)** *Chile (patilla)* sideboard, sideburn

3 *nmf Fam (chulo)* cocky person

chuletada *nf* barbecue *(with chops as the main ingredient)*

chuletón *nm* large chop

chuli *adj Esp Fam* cool, *Br* fabby; **¡qué habitación más c.!** what a cool *o Br* fabby little room!

chulla *adj Andes* single, unmarried

chullo *nm Andes* woollen cap

chulo, -a **1** *adj* **(a)** *Esp (descarado)* cocky; **ponerse c.** to get cocky

(b) *Esp, Méx Fam (bonito)* cool, *Br* top, *US* neat; **se ha comprado una moto muy chula** she's bought a really cool *o Br* top *o US* neat bike; **esta es la canción más chula del disco** this is the coolest song on the record; **lo más c. del verano es que los días son más largos** the coolest thing about summer is that the days are longer; EXPR *Fam* **ir más c. que un ocho** to have one's glad rags on

(c) *Esp Fam (lesionado)* **tengo la pata chula** I've done my leg in

2 *nm,f Esp* **(a)** *(descarado)* cocky person; *Vulg* **es un c. de mierda** he's a cocky little bastard

(b) *(madrileño)* = lower-class native of 18th-19th century Madrid

3 *nm Esp (proxeneta)* pimp

chumacera *nf* **(a)** *Tec* axle bearing **(b)** *Náut* rowlock

chumbar *RP* **1** *vt (disparar)* to shoot

2 *vi (ladrar)* to bark

chumbe *nm* **(a)** *Col, Ven (faja)* sash **(b)** *Andes, Arg (sulfato)* zinc sulphide

chumbera *nf* prickly pear cactus

chumbo, -a **1** *adj* **higo c.** prickly pear

2 *nm RP* lead

chuminada *nf Fam* **(a)** *(dicho, hecho)* **eso que ha dicho es una c.** what he said is a load of nonsense; **deja de hacer chuminadas** stop messing around **(b)** *(cosa insignificante)* silly thing, trifle; **me regalaron una c.** they gave me a stupid little present

chumino *nm Esp muy Fam Br* fanny, *US* beaver; EXPR *Vulg* **no me sale del c.** I can't be fucking well bothered, *Br* I can't be arsed

chunchules *nmpl Chile* tripe

chunchullo *nm Col* = piece of sheep or cow intestine, plaited and then roasted

chunga *nf Esp Fam* **tomarse algo a c.** to take sth as a joke, not to take sth seriously

chungo, -a *adj Esp Fam* **es un tío c.** he's a nasty piece of work; **la cosa está chunga** it's a real bitch; **veo muy c. que nos dejen entrar** I don't fancy our chances of getting in; **ha estado muy c. desde el accidente** he's been in a bad way since the accident; **es una situación muy chunga** it's a pretty sticky situation

chunguearse *vpr Fam* **c. de** to make fun of, to have a laugh about

chuño *nm Andes, RP* potato starch

chupa *nf* **(a)** *Esp Fam (cazadora)* coat; EXPR **poner a alguien como c. de dómine** to give sb a row, to lay into sb ►► ***c. de cuero*** leather jacket; ***c. vaquera*** denim jacket **(b)** *Ven Fam (chupón) Br* dummy, *US* pacifier

Chupa Chups® *nm inv Esp* lollipop *(spherical)*

chupacirios *nmf inv Fam Pey* holy Joe

chupada *nf (de helado) (con la lengua)* lick; *(con los labios)* suck; *(de cigarrillo)* puff, drag; **dale una c. al helado** have a lick of the ice cream; **le di una c. al cigarrillo** I had a puff at *o* drag on the cigarette

chupado, -a *adj* **(a)** *(delgado)* skinny **(b)** *Fam (fácil)* **estar c.** to be dead easy *o* a piece of cake; EXPR *Hum* **estar más c. que la pipa de un indio** to be as easy as falling off a log, to be like taking candy from a baby **(c)** *Esp, RP Fam (borracho)* plastered

chupador, -ora *adj* sucking

chupaflor *nm Am* hummingbird

chupamedias *nmf inv Andes, RP, Ven Fam* toady

chupamirto *nm Méx* hummingbird

chupar 1 *vt* (**a**) *(succionar)* to suck; *(lamer)* to lick; *(fumar)* to puff at; *Vulg* **chuparle la polla a alguien** to go down on sb, to give sb a blow-job; EXPR *Fam Dep* **c. banquillo** to be confined to the bench
(**b**) *(absorber)* to soak up; **esta bayeta chupa el agua muy bien** this cloth really soaks up the water
(**c**) *Fam (quitar)* **chuparle algo a alguien** to milk sb for sth; **esa mujer le está chupando la sangre** that woman is bleeding him dry
(**d**) *Fam (en deportes)* **c. la pelota** to hog the ball
(**e**) *Fam (abusar)* **cuando fue presidente, chupó lo que pudo** when he was president, he feathered his own nest as much as he could; **le gusta c. cámara** he likes to hog the camera; EXPR *Fam* **c. del bote** to feather one's nest
(**f**) *Esp Fam (aguantar)* to put up with; **me tuve que c. un viaje en autobús de cuatro horas** I was stuck with a four-hour bus journey
(**g**) *Am Fam (beber)* to booze on, to tipple
2 *vi Fam* (**a**) *(en deportes)* to hog the ball
(**b**) *Am (beber)* to booze, to tipple
3 **chuparse** *vpr* (**a**) *(succionar)* to suck; **chuparse el dedo** to suck one's thumb; EXPR *Fam* **¿te crees que me chupo el dedo?** do you think I was born yesterday?; EXPR **estar para chuparse los dedos** to be mouthwatering; EXPR *Fam* **¡chúpate esa!** take that!
(**b**) *Esp (adelgazar)* to get thinner
(**c**) *Esp Fam (aguantar)* to put up with; **se chupó una conferencia de tres horas** she had to sit through a three-hour lecture

chupasangre *nmf CSur Fam* leech, bloodsucker

chupatintas *nmf inv Pey* pen pusher

chupe *nm* (**a**) *Andes, Arg (comida)* stew (**b**) *Méx, RP Fam (bebida)* booze

chupeta *nf Col (dulce)* lollipop

chupete *nm* (**a**) *(para bebé) Br* dummy, *US* pacifier (**b**) *Col (dulce)* lollipop (**c**) *Bol (helado) Br* ice lolly, *US* Popsicle®

chupetear *vt* to suck on, to suck away at

chupeteo *nm* sucking

chupetín *nm* (**a**) *RP (piruleta)* lollipop (**b**) *Bol (helado) Br* ice lolly, *US* Popsicle®

chupetón *nm* (**a**) *(con la lengua)* lick; *(con los labios)* suck; **dar un c. a algo** to lick sth (**b**) *Esp Fam (moradura en la piel)* love bite, *US* hickey

chupi[1] *Esp Fam* 1 *adj* great, brill; **es una falda c.** that's a neat *o Br* fab skirt
2 *adv* **lo pasamos c.** we had a great *o Br* fab time
3 *interj* cool!, neat!, *Br* brilliant!

chupi[2] *nm RP Fam (bebida)* booze

chupín *nm RP* = fish and vegetable stew, cooked in white wine

chupinazo *nm* (**a**) *(cañonazo)* cannon shot (**b**) *(disparo de cohete)* firing of a rocket *(to mark the start of a festival)* (**c**) *Fam Dep (patada)* hard kick; *(a puerta)* screamer, hard shot

chupito *nm* shot

chupón, -ona 1 *adj Fam* (**a**) *(gorrón)* **es muy c.** he's a real sponger *o* scrounger (**b**) *(en deportes)* **un jugador c.** a hog
2 *nm,f Fam* (**a**) *(gorrón)* sponger, scrounger (**b**) *(en deportes)* hog
3 *nm* (**a**) *Bot* sucker (**b**) *Méx, Ven (chupete) Br* dummy, *US* pacifier (**c**) *Andes, CAm, Méx (del biberón)* teat (**d**) *RP Fam (en la boca)* sloppy kiss (**e**) *RP Fam (en la piel)* love bite, *US* hickey

chupóptero, -a *nm,f Fam Hum* parasite

churo *nm Col, Ecuad* (**a**) *(rizo)* curl (**b**) *(escalera)* spiral staircase

churra *nf* (**a**) EXPR *Fam Hum* **mezclar churras con merinas** to get two completely different things muddled up (**b**) *ver también* **churro**[2]

churrasco *nm* barbecued *o* grilled meat

churrasqueada *nf RP (asado)* barbecue

churrasquear *vi RP* to have a barbecue

churrasquera *nf RP* grill, *US* griddle

churrasquería *nf RP* steakhouse

churre *nm Fam* grease

churrera *nf* (**a**) *(maquina)* = machine for making "churros" (**b**) *ver también* **churrero**

churrería *nf* = shop or stall selling "churros"

churrero, -a *nm,f* "churros" seller

churrete *nm (chorro)* spurt; *(mancha)* stain

churria *nf Carib, Col, Guat (diarrea)* diarrhoea

churrigueresco, -a *adj Arte* churrigueresque

churrinche *nm* vermilion flycatcher

churro[1] *nm* (**a**) *(para comer)* = stick or ring of dough fried in oil and sprinkled with sugar; EXPR *Fam* **¡vete a freír churros!** get lost! (**b**) *Fam (chapuza)* botch; **ese dibujo es un c.** that drawing is awful; **esto es un c. de reparación** they've made a real botch of this repair (**c**) *Fam (suerte)* **¡tuviste mucho c.!** you flukey thing!; **lo encontraron de c.** it was a fluke that they found it

churro[2], **-a** *Andes, RP Fam* 1 *adj* stunning; **¡estás muy churra con ese vestido nuevo!** you look stunning in that new dress!
2 *nm,f* looker; **¡tu hermano es un c. bárbaro!** your brother is a real looker!

churruscado, -a *adj (quemado)* burnt; *Fam (crujiente)* crispy

churruscar [60] 1 *vt* to burn
2 **churruscarse** *vpr* to burn; **se me churruscaron las costillas** I burnt the chops

churrusco *nm Fam (tostada)* piece of burnt toast

churumbel *nm Esp Fam* kid

chusco, -a 1 *adj (gracioso)* funny
2 *nm (de pan)* crust of stale bread

chusma 1 *adj RP (chismoso)* gossipy
2 *nmf RP (chismoso)* gossip
3 *nf* rabble, mob

chusmear = **chismear**

chusmerío *nm RP (chisme)* piece of gossip

chuspa *nf Andes, RP* knapsack

chusquero, -a *adj Mil* **un sargento c.** a sergeant who has risen through the ranks

chut (*pl* **chuts**) *nm Dep (patada)* kick; *(a puerta)* shot

chuta *nf Esp Fam* syringe

chutar 1 *vi* (**a**) *(lanzar la pelota)* to kick the ball; *(a puerta)* to shoot (**b**) *Esp Fam (funcionar)* to work; **esto va que chuta** it's going great; **con eso va que chuta** that's more than enough
2 **chutarse** *vpr Esp Fam* to shoot up

chute *nm Esp Fam* fix

chuza *nf Méx (en bolos)* strike

chuzar [14] *vt Col* to prick

chuzo *nm Fam* EXPR **caer chuzos de punta, llover a chuzos** to pour down, *Br* to bucket down

CI *nm* (*abrev de* **cociente de inteligencia**) IQ

CIA ['θia] *nf* (*abrev de* **Central Intelligence Agency**) CIA

cía., Cía. (*abrev de* **compañía**) *Com* Co

cián 1 *adj* cyan
2 *nm* cyan

cianato *nm Quím* cyanate

cianhídrico, -a *adj* **ácido c.** hydrocyanic acid

cianosis *nf inv Med* cyanosis

cianótico, -a *adj Med* cyanotic

cianotipo *nm* blueprint, cyanotype

cianuro *nm* cyanide

ciar *vi* to back water

ciática *nf* sciatica

ciático, -a *adj* sciatic

cibercafé *nm Informát* Internet café, cybercafé

cibercultura *nf Informát* cyberculture

ciberdelito *nm Informát* cybercrime

ciberespacio *nm Informát* cyberspace

cibernauta *nmf Informát* Nettie, Net user

cibernética *nf Informát* cybernetics *(singular)*

cibernético, -a *adj Informát* cybernetic

ciberokupa *nmf Informát* cybersquatter

ciberpunk *nm Informát* cyberpunk

cibersexo *nm Informát* cybersex

ciberterrorismo *nm Informát* cyberterrorism

ciborg (*pl* **ciborgs**) *nm Informát* cyborg

cica *nf* cycas

cicatería *nf* stinginess, meanness

cicatero, -a 1 *adj* stingy, mean
2 *nm,f* skinflint, miser

cicatriz *nf* (**a**) *(física)* scar; **la operación le dejó c.** the operation left him with a scar (**b**) *(emocional)* scar

cicatrización *nf* scarring

cicatrizante 1 *adj* healing
2 *nm* healing substance

cicatrizar [14] 1 *vi* to form a scar, to heal (up); **la herida no ha cicatrizado bien** the wound hasn't healed properly
2 *vt* to heal

cícero *nm Imprenta* cicero

Cicerón *n pr* Cicero

cicerón *nm* eloquent speaker, orator

cicerone *nmf* guide

ciceroniano, -a *adj* Ciceronian

Cícladas *nfpl* **las C.** the Cyclades

ciclamato *nm* cyclamate

ciclamen *nm* cyclamen

ciclamor *nm* Judas tree

cíclicamente *adv* cyclically

cíclico, -a *adj* cyclical

ciclismo *nm* cycling; **hacer c.** to go cycling, to cycle ►► ***c. en pista*** track cycling; ***c. en ruta*** road racing

ciclista 1 *adj* cycling; **equipo c.** cycling team; **prueba c.** cycle race; **vuelta c.** tour
2 *nmf* cyclist

ciclo *nm* (a) *(periodo)* cycle ►► ***c. económico*** trade cycle; ***c. menstrual*** menstrual cycle; ***c. vital*** life cycle (b) *(de conferencias, actos)* series; *(de películas, conciertos)* season (c) *(de una onda)* cycle (d) *Educ* **el primer/segundo c.** *(en colegio)* primary/secondary school; **el c. de doctorado dura dos años** the PhD course lasts two years; **el primer c. de la carrera** = first phase in a university degree, where all students study the same subjects (e) *Lit* cycle; **el c. artúrico/troyano** the Arthurian/Trojan cycle (f) *Cuba (bicicleta)* bicycle

ciclocross, ciclocrós *nm* cyclo-cross

cicloide *nm Geom* cycloid

ciclomotor *nm* moped

ciclón *nm* (a) *(viento)* cyclone; EXPR *Fam* **como un c.: el actor pasó por la capital como un c.** the actor made a whirlwind visit to the capital ►► ***c. tropical*** tropical cyclone (b) *(persona)* human whirlwind

cíclope *nm* Cyclops

ciclópeo, -a *adj (enorme)* colossal, massive

ciclorama *nm Teatro* cyclorama

ciclostil, ciclostilo *nm* cyclostyle

ciclotimia *nf PSI* cyclothymia

ciclotrón *nm Fís* cyclotron

cicloturismo *nm* bicycle touring

cicloturista *nmf* = person on cycling holiday

cicloturístico, -a *adj* **ruta cicloturística** tourist cycling route; **vacaciones cicloturísticas** cycling holidays

ciclovía *nf Am Br* cycle lane, *US* bikeway

CICR *nm (abrev de* **Comité Internacional de la Cruz Roja**) IRCC

cicuta *nf* hemlock

CIDH *nf (abrev de* **Comisión Interamericana de Derechos Humanos**) ICHR

cidra *nf* citron

cidro *nm* citron (tree)

ciegamente *adv* blindly

ciego, -a 1 *ver* **cegar**
2 *adj* (a) *(invidente)* blind; **Juan es c. de nacimiento** Juan was born blind; **quedarse c.** to go blind
(b) *(ante algo)* blind; **el amor lo ha vuelto c.** love has made him blind
(c) *(enloquecido)* blinded (**de** by); **entonces, c. de ira, lo mató** then, blind with rage, he killed him; **está c. por el esquí** he's mad about skiing
(d) *(pozo, tubería)* blocked (up)
(e) *(total) (fe, confianza)* blind; **tengo una confianza ciega en él** I trust him unconditionally
(f) *Esp muy Fam (borracho)* blind drunk, *Br* pissed; *muy Fam (drogado)* stoned; **nos pusimos ciegos de cerveza** we got blind drunk *o Br* pissed on beer
3 *nm,f (invidente)* blind person; **los ciegos** the blind
4 *nm* (a) *Anat* caecum
(b) *Esp Fam (de droga)* trip; **tener/cogerse un c.** *(de alcohol)* to be/get blind drunk *o* plastered *o Br* pissed; **llevo un c. que no me tengo** I'm totally plastered, *Br* I'm pissed out of my mind
(c) **los ciegos** *(sorteo de la ONCE)* = lottery organized by Spanish association for the blind
(d) *RP (en naipes)* = player who has no trump cards in their hand
5 **a ciegas** *loc adv* blindly; **andar a ciegas** to grope one's way; **no hagas las cosas a ciegas** don't act without knowing what you are doing

ciegue *etc ver* **cegar**

cielo 1 *nm* (a) *(atmósfera)* sky; **c. despejado/con nubes** clear/cloudy sky; **mira hacia el c.** look upwards; **a c. abierto** *(a la intemperie)* in the open; *(mina)* opencast
(b) *Rel* heaven; **los que se portan bien van al c.** if you're good you'll go to heaven; **¡c. santo!** good heavens!; **ganarse el c.** to win salvation, to win a place in heaven; **pido al c. que nos ayude** may heaven *o* God help us
(c) *(tratamiento)* darling, my love, my dear; **c. (mío), ¿podrías ayudarme un momento?** could you help me a moment, darling?
(d) *(parte superior)* ***c. del paladar*** roof of the mouth; ***c. raso*** ceiling
(e) EXPR **me viene bajado del c.** it's a godsend (to me); **como llovido del c.** *(inesperadamente)* out of the blue; *(oportunamente)* at just the right moment; **estar en el séptimo c.** to be in seventh heaven; **se le juntó el c. con la tierra** he lost his nerve; **mover c. y tierra** to move heaven and earth; **ser un c.** to be an angel; **ver el c. abierto** to see one's way out
2 **cielos** *interj* good heavens!; **¡cielos, no me había dado cuenta de lo tarde que era!** good heavens! I hadn't realized how late it was!

ciempiés *nm inv* centipede

cien *núm* a *o* one hundred; **c. mil** a *o* one hundred thousand; **por c.** percent; **c. por c.** a hundred percent; EXPR *Fam* **poner a c. alguien: esa musiquilla me está poniendo a c.** that tune's getting on my nerves; EXPR *Fam* **dar c. mil vueltas a algo/alguien: mi moto le da c. vueltas a la tuya** my motorbike's miles better than yours; *ver también* **treinta**

ciénaga *nf* marsh, bog

ciencia 1 *nf* (a) *(método, estudio)* science; **la c. ya no puede hacer nada para salvar al enfermo** science is unable to do anything more to help the patient; **la astronomía es la c. que estudia los cuerpos celestes** astronomy is the science in which heavenly bodies are studied ►► ***ciencias aplicadas*** applied sciences; ***ciencias biológicas*** life sciences; ***c. del conocimiento*** cognitive science; ***ciencias económicas*** economics *(singular)*; ***ciencias empresariales*** business studies; ***ciencias exactas*** mathematics *(singular)*; ***c. ficción*** science fiction; ***ciencias físicas*** physical sciences; ***ciencias de la información*** media studies; ***ciencias naturales*** natural sciences; ***ciencias ocultas*** occultism; ***ciencias políticas*** political science; ***ciencias de la salud*** medical sciences; ***ciencias sociales*** social sciences; ***ciencias de la Tierra*** earth sciences
(b) *(sabiduría)* learning, knowledge; EXPR *Fam* **tener poca c.** to be straightforward; **la cocina tiene poca c., pero requiere mucho sentido común** cooking doesn't require a lot of skill, but you do need to use common sense; EXPR *Hum* **por c. infusa** through divine inspiration
(c) *Educ* **ciencias** science; **soy de ciencias** I studied science ►► ***ciencias mixtas*** = secondary school course comprising mainly science subjects but including some arts subjects; ***ciencias puras*** = secondary school course comprising science subjects only
2 **a ciencia cierta** *loc adv* for certain; **no se conoce a c. cierta el número de víctimas** the number of victims isn't known for certain

cienciología *nf* Scientology

cieno *nm* mud, sludge

científicamente *adv* scientifically

cientificismo, cientifismo *nm* = over-emphasis on scientific ideas

científico, -a 1 *adj* scientific
2 *nm,f* (a) *(investigador)* scientist (b) *Méx Pol* = one of the group of Europeanizing intellectuals influential during the rule of Porfirio Díaz (1876-1911)

cientifismo = **cientificismo**

cientista *nmf CSur* ***c. social*** social scientist

ciento *núm* a *o* one hundred; **c. cincuenta** a *o* one hundred and fifty; **cientos de** hundreds of; **por c.** percent; EXPR *Fam* **darle c. y raya a alguien** to run rings around sb; EXPR *Fam* **eran c. y la madre** everybody and his dog *o* the world and his wife was there; *ver también* **treinta**

ciernes *nmpl* **estar en c.** to be in its infancy; **una campeona en c.** a budding champion; **tenemos un viaje en c.** we're planning a journey

cierno *etc ver* **cerner**

cierre *nm* (a) *(de fábrica, tienda, colegio) (permanente)* closure; **se encarga del c. de la tienda al final del día** he locks up the shop at the end of each day; **el horario de c. de las tiendas** the shops' closing times; EXPR **echar el c.** *(a tienda)* to close up ►► *Ind* ***c. patronal*** lockout

(**b**) *(de herida)* closing up

(**c**) *(de fronteras)* closing

(**d**) *Rad & TV (de emisión)* closedown; **la hora de c.** closedown

(**e**) *Prensa* **al c. de la edición** as we were going to press

(**f**) *Bolsa (de sesión)* close (of trading); **precio de c.** closing price

(**g**) *(administrativo)* closure; **el juez ordenó el c. del bar** the judge ordered the closure of the bar, the judge ordered the bar to be closed

(**h**) *(finalización)* end; **las elecciones supusieron el c. de una época oscura en el país** the elections brought to an end *o* a close a dark chapter in the country's history; **al c. del plazo se habían presentado cinco candidaturas** by the closing date, five candidates had put their names forward; **según los datos del c. del ejercicio 1998...** according to the figures for the end of the 1998 *Br* financial *o US* fiscal year...

(**i**) *(mecanismo)* fastener ►► *Aut* ***c. centralizado*** central locking; ***c. de combinación*** combination lock; ***c. metálico*** *(de tienda)* metal shutter

(**j**) *Andes, Méx, RP (cremallera) Br* zip (fastener), *US* zipper; *Andes, Méx* **c. relámpago,** *Chile* **c. eclair,** *Urug* **c. metálico** *Br* zip, *US* zipper

cierro *etc ver* **cerrar**

ciertamente *adv* (**a**) *(con certeza)* certainly; **déjame que lo consulte y te lo diré c.** let me check it out and I'll tell you for certain; **es un problema c. complejo** it certainly is a complex problem; **c., estamos en una situación crítica** we are definitely in a critical situation

(**b**) *(sí enfático)* of course; **¿vendrás? – ¡c.!** are you coming? – of course!; **¿estás cansado? – ¡c. que sí!** are you tired? – I certainly am!

cierto, -a 1 *adj* (**a**) *(verdadero)* true; **estar en lo c.** to be right; **lo c. es que...** the fact is that...; **es c. que...** it's true (that...); **no es c. (que...)** it is not true (that...); **es el hijo de Javier, ¿no es c.?** he's Javier's son, isn't he?; **si bien es c. que...** while it is true that...; **¿qué hay de c. en las declaraciones del presidente?** what truth is there in the president's statement?

(**b**) *(seguro)* certain, definite; **es una señal cierta de su nerviosismo** it's a sure sign that they're nervous; **todavía no es c. que vaya a poder participar** it's still not certain that she'll be able to take part

(**c**) *(algún)* certain; **c. hombre** a certain man; **en cierta ocasión** once, on one occasion; **c. día, iba caminando por la calle, cuando...** I was walking down the street one day, when...; **hemos recibido un c. número de quejas** we have received a certain number of *o* some complaints; **tuvo un c. éxito con su primer disco** his first record was a moderate success; **me da c. reparo preguntárselo** I'm a bit reluctant to ask her; **en c. modo, han hecho lo que han podido** in a way, they did what they could; **hasta c. punto es verdad** it's true up to a point

2 *adv* right, certainly; **¿lo hizo usted? – c.** did you do it? – that's right; **por c.** by the way; **por c., ¿no te habrás acordado de comprar las entradas?** by the way, did you remember to buy the tickets?; **si la ves, por c., dile que la estoy buscando** by the way, if you see her tell her I'm looking for her

3 de cierto *loc adv* for certain, for sure; **lo sé de c.** I know for certain *o* for sure

ciervo, -a *nm,f* (**a**) *(macho)* deer, stag; *(hembra)* deer, hind (**b**) ***c. volante*** *(insecto)* stag beetle

cierzo *nm* north wind

CIF [θif] *nm Esp* (*abrev de* **código de identificación fiscal**) = number identifying company for tax purposes

cifra *nf* (**a**) *(signo)* figure; **un código de cuatro cifras** a four-digit code; **mi número de teléfono consta de siete cifras** my telephone number has seven digits

(**b**) *(cantidad)* number, total; *(de dinero)* sum; **ingresó la c. de 100.000 euros** he deposited the sum of 100,000 euros; **la c. de desempleados sigue subiendo** the number of unemployed continues to rise; **¿cuánto me darías? – di una c.** how much would you give me? – give me a number, name a price; **tuvo que pagar una c. muy alta** he had to pay a very large sum (of money) ►► *Econ* ***c. de negocios*** turnover; *Econ* ***c. de ventas*** sales figures

(**c**) *(código)* **en c.** coded, in code; **el mensaje estaba en c.** the message was coded *o* in code

cifrado, -a *adj* coded, in code

cifrar 1 *vt* (**a**) *(codificar)* to code (**b**) *(resumir, reducir)* to summarize; **cifran todas sus aspiraciones en llegar a la final** their one aim is to get to the final (**c**) *(tasar)* to evaluate, to estimate; **cifró las pérdidas en varios millones de pesos** he estimated the losses at several million pesos

2 cifrarse en *vpr* (**a**) *(ascender a)* to come to, to amount to; **las pérdidas se cifran en millones de dólares** the losses amount to millions of dollars (**b**) *(resumirse en)* to be summarized by

cigala *nf* Dublin Bay prawn, scampi

cigarra *nf* cicada

cigarrera *nf* (**a**) *(caja)* cigar case (**b**) *ver también* **cigarrero**

cigarrería *nf Am* tobacconist's (shop)

cigarrero, -a *nm,f (persona)* cigar maker

cigarrillo *nm* cigarette ►► ***c. con filtro*** filter (tip) cigarette, filter-tipped cigarette; ***c. mentolado*** menthol cigarette

cigarro *nm* (**a**) *(puro)* cigar (**b**) *(cigarrillo)* cigarette (**c**) *Ecuad (insecto)* dragonfly

cigomático, -a *adj Anat* zygomatic

cigoñino *nm* young stork

cigoto *nm Biol* zygote

ciguato, -a *Carib, Méx* **1** *adj* suffering from fish poisoning

2 *nm,f (enfermo)* fish poisoning victim

cigüeña *nf* stork; EXPR *Fam* **estar esperando a la c.** to be expecting ►► ***c. blanca*** white stork; ***c. negra*** black stork

cigüeñal *nm* crankshaft

cigüeñuela *nf* black-winged stilt

cilantro *nm* coriander

ciliado, -a *adj* ciliated

cilicio *nm (faja, cordón)* spiked belt *(of penitent)*; *(vestidura)* hair shirt

cilindrada *nf* cylinder capacity; **una moto de gran c.** a motorbike with a big engine

cilíndrico, -a *adj* cylindrical

cilindro *nm* (**a**) *(figura)* cylinder (**b**) *Aut* cylinder; **un motor de cuatro cilindros** a four-cylinder engine (**c**) *(de imprenta)* roller (**d**) *CAm, Méx (organillo)* barrel organ

cilio *nm Biol* cilium

cilla *nf (granero)* granary

cima *nf* (**a**) *(de montaña)* peak, summit (**b**) *(de árbol)* top (**c**) *(apogeo)* peak, high point; **ha alcanzado la c. de la popularidad** his popularity has reached an all-time high; **el artista está en la c. de su creatividad** the artist is at the peak of his creativity; EXPR **dar c. a algo** to round sth off (**d**) *Bot* cyme

cimarra *nf Chile Fam* **hacer la c.** to play *Br* truant *o US* hookey

cimarrón, -ona 1 *adj* (**a**) *(animal, planta, fruta)* wild (**b**) *Am (campo)* unimproved (**c**) *Am Hist (esclavo)* runaway, escaped

2 *nm,f* (**a**) *Am Hist (esclavo)* runaway slave (**b**) *Arg* unsweetened maté

cimbalero, -a *nm,f,* **cimbalista** *nmf Mús* cymbalist

címbalo *nm* cymbal

cimbel *nm* (**a**) *(señuelo)* decoy (**b**) *muy Fam (pene) Br* chopper, *US* johnson

cimborrio, cimborio *nm Arquit* cupola

cimbra *nf Arquit* (**a**) *(armazón)* form, centring (**b**) *(curvatura)* = interior face of an arch

cimbrar, cimbrear 1 *vt* (**a**) *(vara)* to wave about (**b**) *(caderas)* to sway (**c**) *Arquit* to erect the centring for

2 cimbrearse *vpr* to sway

cimbreante *adj* swaying

cimbrear = **cimbrar**

cimbreo *nm* (**a**) *(de vara)* waving (**b**) *(de caderas)* swaying

cimbronazo *nm* (**a**) *Am (estremecimiento)* shock; **la devaluación de la moneda fue un c. para toda la región** the devaluation of the currency sent shock waves throughout the region; **el c. que supuso la muerte de su padre** the severe shock of his father's death (**b**) *Am (temblor de tierra)* earth tremor

cimentación *nf* (**a**) *(acción)* laying of the foundations (**b**) *(cimientos)* foundations

cimentar [3] **1** *vt* (**a**) *(edificio)* to lay the foundations of (**b**) *(ciudad)* to found, to build (**c**) *(idea, paz, fama)* to cement, to consolidate; **intentan c. la situación de la empresa** they are trying to consolidate the company's position; **la victoria cimentó su amistad** the victory cemented their friendship

2 cimentarse *vpr (basarse)* **cimentarse en** to be based on; **su éxito se cimenta en la calidad de sus novelas** her success is built *o* based on the quality of her novels

cimera *nf (de casco, de escudo)* crest

cimero, -a *adj (alto)* topmost; *Fig (sobresaliente)* foremost, most outstanding

cimiento *etc ver* **cimentar**

cimientos *nmpl* (**a**) *(de edificio)* foundation; **echar los c.** to lay the foundations
(**b**) *(base)* basis *(singular)*; **los c. de una amistad** the basis of a friendship; **la crisis bursátil sacudió los c. del sector financiero** the stock market crisis shook the financial sector to its foundations *o* sent shock waves through the financial sector; **en el siglo XVIII se pusieron los c. del estado moderno** the foundations of the modern state were laid in the 18th century

cimitarra *nf* scimitar

cinabrio *nm* cinnabar

cinamomo *nm* cinnamon tree

cinc (*pl* **cines**) *nm Quím* zinc

cincel *nm* chisel

cincelado *nm (de piedra)* chiselling; *(de metal)* engraving

cincelar *vt (piedra)* to chisel; *(metal)* to engrave

cincha *nf* girth

cinchar *vt (ceñir)* to girth

cincho *nm* (**a**) *(cinturón)* belt (**b**) *(aro de hierro)* hoop (**c**) *Am (de caballo)* girth, cinch

cinco 1 *núm* five; **los c. continentes** the five continents *(= Europe, Asia, Africa, America and Oceania)*; *Antes* **el C. Naciones** *(en rugby)* the Five Nations; EXPR *Fam* **¡choca esos c.!** put it there!, give me five!; EXPR *Fam* **no tener ni c.** to be broke; *ver también* **tres**
2 *nm* (**a**) ***c. puertas*** *(vehículo)* four-door hatchback (**b**) *Carib (guitarra)* five-string guitar

cincuenta *núm* fifty; **los (años) c.** the fifties; *ver también* **treinta**

cincuentavo, -a *núm* fiftieth; *ver también* **octavo**

cincuentena *nf* fifty; **andará por la c.** he must be about fifty; **una c. de personas** fifty people

cincuentenario *nm* fiftieth anniversary

cincuentón, -ona *Fam* **1** *adj* **un señor c.** a man in his fifties
2 *nm,f* person in their fifties; **es un c.** he's in his fifties

cine 1 *nm* (**a**) *(arte)* cinema; **me gusta el c.** I like cinema *o* movies *o Br* films; **hacer c.** to make movies *o Br* films; **el mundo del c.** the movie *o Br* film world ►► ***c. de autor*** art cinema; ***c. comercial*** commercial cinema; ***c. cómico*** comedy movies *o Br* films; **Keaton fue uno de los grandes del c. cómico** Keaton was one of the big screen comedy greats; ***c. fórum*** film with discussion group; ***c. de género*** genre cinema; ***c. independiente*** independent cinema *o* movies *o Br* films; ***c. mudo*** silent movies *o Br* films; ***c. negro*** film noir; ***c. sonoro*** talking pictures, talkies
(**b**) *(edificio)* cinema, *US* movie theater; **ir al c.** to go to the cinema *o* the movies *o Br* films ►► ***c. de arte y ensayo*** art house (cinema), *US* art theater; ***c. de barrio*** local cinema *o US* movie theater; ***c. de estreno*** first-run cinema *o US* movie theater; ***c. de verano*** open-air cinema
2 de cine *loc adj Fam (muy bueno)* **se ha comprado una casa de c.** he's bought an amazing house
3 de cine *loc adv Fam (muy bien)* **cocina de c.** he's a fantastic *o* brilliant cook; **el equipo jugó de c.** the team played brilliantly

cineasta *nmf* movie maker *o* director, *Br* film maker *o* director

cineclub *nm* (**a**) *(asociación)* film society (**b**) *(sala)* club cinema

cinéfilo, -a 1 *adj* **es muy c.** *(que va al cine)* he's a keen moviegoer *o Br* filmgoer; *(entiende de cine)* he's a real movie *o Br* film buff; **los más cinéfilos recordarán aquella película** movie *o Br* film buffs will remember that film
2 *nm,f (que va al cine)* (keen) moviegoer *o Br* filmgoer; *(que entiende de cine)* movie *o Br* film buff

cinegética *nf* hunting

cinegético, -a *adj* hunting; **asociación cinegética** hunting club; **deporte c.** blood sport

cinemascope® *nm* Cinemascope®

cinemateca *nf* (**a**) *(colección)* film library (**b**) *(sala)* film theatre, cinematheque

cinemática *nf Fís* kinematics *(singular)*

cinematografía *nf* (**a**) *(arte)* movie-making, *Br* film-making (**b**) *(conjunto de películas)* movies, *Br* films; **un certamen dominado por la c. europea** a competition dominated by European movies *o Br* films

cinematografiar [32] *vt* to film

cinematográfico, -a *adj* movie, *Br* film; **guión c.** movie *o Br* film script

cinematógrafo *nm* (**a**) *(aparato)* movie *o Br* film projector (**b**) *(local)* cinema, *US* movie theater

cinerama® *nm* Cinerama®

cinética *nf* kinetics *(singular)*

cinético, -a *adj* kinetic

cingalés, -esa 1 *adj* Sinhalese
2 *nm,f (persona)* Sinhalese; **los cingaleses** the Sinhalese
3 *nm (lengua)* Sinhalese

cíngaro, -a 1 *adj* Tzigane
2 *nm,f* Tzigane

cinglar *vt Náut* to scull

cínico, -a 1 *adj (desvergonzado)* shameless
2 *nm,f (desvergonzado)* shameless person; **es un c.** he's shameless, he has no shame

cinismo *nm (desvergüenza)* shamelessness

cinta *nf* (**a**) *(de plástico, papel)* strip, band; *(de tela, en gimnasia rítmica)* ribbon ►► ***c. adhesiva*** adhesive *o* sticky tape; *RP (esparadrapo)* surgical tape; *CSur* ***c. aisladora*** insulating tape; ***c. aislante*** insulating tape; *Andes, CAm, Carib, Méx* ***c. durex***® adhesive *o* sticky tape; *RP* ***c. engomada*** adhesive *o* sticky tape; ***c. de impresora*** printer ribbon; ***c. de llegada*** *(en carrera)* finishing tape; ***c. métrica*** tape measure; ***c. perforada*** punched tape; *RP* ***c. scotch***® adhesive *o* sticky tape
(**b**) *(de imagen, sonido, ordenadores)* tape ►► ***c. de audio*** audio cassette; ***c. digital*** digital tape; ***c. digital de audio*** digital audio tape; ***c. limpiadora*** head cleaner, head-cleaning tape; ***c. magnética*** magnetic tape; ***c. magnetofónica*** recording tape; ***c. de*** *Esp* ***vídeo*** *o Am* ***video*** videotape; ***c. virgen*** blank tape
(**c**) *(mecanismo)* belt ►► ***c. transportadora*** conveyor belt
(**d**) *(película)* movie, *Br* film; **la última c. de Lynch** Lynch's latest movie *o Br* film
(**e**) *(planta)* spider plant

cinto *nm* belt

cintra *nf Arquit* (**a**) *(armazón)* form, centring (**b**) *(curvatura)* = interior face of an arch

cintura *nf* (**a**) *(de cuerpo)* waist; **de c. para abajo/arriba** from the waist down/up ►► ***c. de avispa*** wasp waist (**b**) *(de vestido)* waist; **le queda demasiado holgado de c.** the waist is too big for her, it's too big in the waist for her; EXPR *Fam* **meter en c. a alguien** to make sb toe the line, to bring sb into line

cinturilla *nf* waistband

cinturón *nm* (**a**) *(cinto)* belt; EXPR **apretarse el c.** to tighten one's belt ►► ***c. de asteroides*** asteroid belt; ***c. de castidad*** chastity belt; ***c. de seguridad*** *(en coche, avión)* seat *o* safety belt
(**b**) *(en artes marciales)* belt ►► *Dep* ***c. negro*** black belt; **ser c. negro** to be a black belt
(**c**) *(de ciudad)* belt ►► ***c. industrial*** industrial belt; ***c. metropolitano*** metropolitan area; **el c. metropolitano de Barcelona** greater Barcelona; *Am* ***c. de miseria*** = slum or shanty town area round a large city; ***c. verde*** green belt
(**d**) *(carretera) Br* ring road, *US* beltway

ciñera *etc ver* **ceñir**

ciño *etc ver* **ceñir**

cipayo *nm (soldado indio)* sepoy

cipo *nm* (**a**) *(lápida)* memorial stone (**b**) *(hito)* milestone

cipolino *nm* cipolin

cipote[1] *nm* (**a**) *Vulg (pene)* prick, cock (**b**) *Fam (bobo)* dimwit, moron

cipote[2]**, -a** *nm,f CAm* kid

ciprés (*pl* **cipreses**) *nm* cypress

circadiano, -a *adj* circadian

circense *adj* circus; **artista c.** circus performer; **espectáculo c.** circus show

circo *nm* (**a**) *(espectáculo)* circus (**b**) *Hist (en Roma)* circus (**c**) *Geol* **c. (glaciar)** cirque, corrie (**d**) *Fam (alboroto)* fuss, *Br* palaver; **vaya c. se ha organizado** what a fuss *o Br* palaver there's been

circón *nm (piedra preciosa)* zircon

circonio *nm Quím* zirconium

circuitería *nf Informát* circuitry

circuito *nm* (**a**) *(eléctrico)* circuit ►► ***c. abierto*** open circuit; *Elec* ***c. de alimentación*** power circuit; ***c. cerrado*** closed circuit; ***c. cerrado de televisión*** closed circuit television; ***c. eléctrico*** electric circuit; ***c. impreso*** printed circuit; ***c. integrado*** integrated circuit; ***c. lógico*** logic circuit; ***c. en paralelo*** parallel circuit
(**b**) *(de carreras) (en automovilismo)* circuit; *(en ciclismo)* course; **el c. de Jerez** the Jerez circuit ►► ***c. de entrenamiento*** fitness circuit; **c. urbano** city circuit
(**c**) *(de exposición, obra teatral)* circuit; **la película pasará por el c.**

de los cines de arte y ensayo the movie *o Br* film will be shown on the art house circuit
(**d**) *(de competiciones deportivas)* circuit; **el c. europeo/americano** *(de golf)* the European/American Tour; **la mejor tenista del c. femenino** the best tennis player on the ladies' circuit
(**e**) *(contorno)* belt
(**f**) *(viaje)* tour; **un c. por los países escandinavos** a tour of the Scandinavian countries

circulación *nf* (**a**) *(movimiento)* movement; **la libre c. de personas** the free movement of people ▸▸ ***la c. atmosférica*** atmospheric circulation
(**b**) *(de la sangre)* circulation; **tiene problemas de c.** he has bad circulation ▸▸ ***c. de la sangre*** circulation of the blood; ***c. sanguínea*** circulation of the blood
(**c**) *(de vehículos)* traffic ▸▸ ***la c. rodada*** vehicular traffic
(**d**) *(de moneda, valores, revista)* circulation; **fuera de c.** out of circulation; **poner en c.** to put into circulation; **retirar de la c.** to withdraw from circulation ▸▸ *Fin* ***c. de capitales*** circulation of capital; *Fin* ***c. fiducitaria*** paper currency; *Fin* ***c. monetaria*** paper currency

circulante *adj Fin* **capital c.** working capital

circular 1 *adj* circular
2 *nf* circular
3 *vi* (**a**) *(líquido)* to flow, to circulate (**por** through); *(aire)* to circulate; **abre la ventana para que circule el aire** open the window to let some air in
(**b**) *(persona)* to move, to walk (**por** around); **¡por favor, circulen!** move along, please!
(**c**) *(vehículos)* to drive (**por** along); **este autobús no circula hoy** this bus isn't running today; **el tren de alta velocidad circula a 200 km/h** the high-speed train travels at 200 km/h; **en el Reino Unido se circula por la izquierda** they drive on the left in the United Kingdom
(**d**) *(moneda)* to be in circulation
(**e**) *(capital, dinero)* to circulate
(**f**) *(difundirse)* to go round; **circula el rumor de que ha muerto** there's a rumour going round that he's died; **la noticia circuló rápidamente** the news quickly got round
4 *vt (de mano en mano)* to circulate; **hicieron c. un documento secreto entre los periodistas** they had a secret document circulated among the press

circulatorio, -a *adj* (**a**) *(de la sangre)* circulatory; **aparato** *o* **sistema c.** circulatory system (**b**) *(del tráfico)* traffic; **caos c.** traffic chaos

círculo *nm* (**a**) *(figura)* circle; **pusieron las sillas en c.** they put the chairs in a circle ▸▸ *Dep* ***c. central*** centre circle; ***c. polar*** polar circle; ***el C. Polar Antártico*** the Antarctic Circle; ***el C. Polar Ártico*** the Arctic Circle; ***c. vicioso*** vicious circle (**b**) *(grupo de personas)* circle; **invitó a todo el c. de sus amistades** she invited all her friends; **círculos económicos/políticos** economic/political circles ▸▸ ***c. de lectores*** book club (**c**) *(asociación)* club, association; **C. de Empresarios** businessmen's association

circuncidar *vt* to circumcise

circuncisión *nf* circumcision ▸▸ ***c. del clítoris*** female circumcision

circunciso *adj* circumcised

circundante *adj* surrounding

circundar *vt* to surround

circunferencia *nf* circumference

circunflejo *adj* **acento c.** circumflex

circunlocución *nf*, **circunloquio** *nm* circumlocution; **andarse con circunlocuciones** to be evasive

circunnavegación *nf* circumnavigation

circunnavegar [38] *vt* to circumnavigate, to sail round

circunscribir 1 *vt* (**a**) *(limitar)* to restrict, to confine (**a** to) (**b**) *Geom* to circumscribe
2 **circunscribirse** *vpr* to confine *o* restrict oneself (**a** to); **en mi discurso me circunscribiré a aspectos políticos** in my speech I will confine *o* restrict myself to the political side of things; **el paludismo se circunscribe a unas zonas muy bien definidas** malaria is confined *o* restricted to clearly defined areas; **un fenómeno que no se circunscribe al mundo rural** a phenomenon not confined to rural areas; **sus competencias se circunscriben a los asuntos económicos** his responsibilities are confined *o* limited to financial matters

circunscripción *nf* (**a**) *(limitación)* limitation (**b**) *(distrito)* district; *(militar)* division; **c. (electoral)** electoral district, *Br* constituency

circunscrito, -a 1 *participio ver* **circunscribir**
2 *adj* restricted, limited; **un plan de ayuda c. a los directamente afectados** an aid plan restricted *o* limited to those directly affected

circunspección *nf Formal* (**a**) *(comedimiento)* circumspection (**b**) *(seriedad)* graveness, seriousness

circunspecto, -a *adj Formal* (**a**) *(comedido)* circumspect (**b**) *(serio)* grave, serious

circunstancia *nf* (**a**) *(situación, condición)* circumstance; **¿en qué circunstancias se encuentra la empresa?** what state is the company in?; **en estas circunstancias, dadas las circunstancias** under *o* given the circumstances; **debido a circunstancias ajenas a nuestra voluntad** due to circumstances beyond our control; **las circunstancias me obligaron a ir** circumstances made it necessary for me to go; **se dan todas las circunstancias para una recuperación rápida** circumstances *o* conditions are favourable to a rapid recovery; **se da la c. de que ya le pasó lo mismo el año pasado** it so happens that the same thing happened to him last year; **las circunstancias no le son favorables** circumstances *o* conditions are not in her favour; **bajo ninguna c. se lo digas** under no circumstances must you tell her; **no supo estar a la altura de las circunstancias** he wasn't able to rise to the occasion
(**b**) *Der* circumstance ▸▸ ***c. agravante*** aggravating circumstance; ***c. atenuante*** extenuating circumstance; ***c. eximente*** exonerating circumstance

circunstancial *adj* (**a**) *(del momento)* chance; **un hecho c.** a chance occurrence; **una decisión c.** an ad hoc decision (**b**) *Gram* **complemento c.** adjunct

circunstante *nm* **los circunstantes** those present

circunvalación *nf* (**a**) *(acción)* going round (**b**) *(carretera) Br* ring road, *US* beltway

circunvalar *vt* to go round

circunvolar *vt* to fly round, to circle

circunvolución *nf* (**a**) *(vuelta)* circumvolution (**b**) *Anat* ***c. cerebral*** cerebral convolution

cirial *nm* processional candlestick

cirílico, -a 1 *adj* Cyrillic
2 *nm* Cyrillic

cirio *nm* (**a**) *(vela)* (wax) candle ▸▸ ***c. pascual*** paschal candle (**b**) *Fam (alboroto)* row, rumpus; **montar un c.** to kick up a row; **se armó un c.** there was an almighty row

cirquero, -a *nm,f Méx (artista)* circus performer

cirrípedo, cirrópodo *nm Zool* cirripede

cirro *nm* (**a**) *Meteo* cirrus (**b**) *Med* scirrhus

cirrocúmulo *nm Meteo* cirrocumulus

cirrópodo = **cirrípedo**

cirrosis *nf inv* cirrhosis ▸▸ ***c. hepática*** cirrhosis of the liver

cirrostrato *nm Meteo* cirrostratus

cirrótico, -a 1 *adj* cirrhotic; *Fam Fig* **estar c.** to be an alcoholic
2 *nm,f* = person suffering from cirrhosis; *Fam Fig* **ser un c.** to be an alcoholic

ciruela *nf* plum ▸▸ ***c. claudia*** greengage; ***c. pasa*** prune; *CSur* ***c. seca*** prune

ciruelo *nm* plum tree

cirugía *nf* surgery; **hacerse la c.** *(estética)* to have cosmetic surgery ▸▸ ***c. cardíaca*** heart surgery; ***c. correctiva*** corrective surgery; ***c. endoscópica*** keyhole surgery; ***c. estética*** cosmetic surgery; ***c. exploratoria*** exploratory surgery; ***c. facial*** facial surgery; ***c. invasiva*** invasive surgery; ***c. laparoscópica*** keyhole *o Espec* laparoscopic surgery; ***c. con láser*** laser surgery; ***c. maxilofacial*** facial *o Espec* maxillofacial surgery; ***c. plástica*** plastic surgery; ***c. reconstructiva*** reconstructive surgery; ***c. de trasplantes*** transplant surgery

ciruja *nmf Arg Fam* scavenger *(on rubbish tip)*

cirujano, -a *nm,f* surgeon ▸▸ ***c. plástico*** plastic surgeon

cirujear *vi Arg Fam* to scavenge *(on rubbish tips)*

cirujeo *nm Arg Fam* scavenging *(on rubbish tips)*

cisandino, -a *adj* on this side of the Andes

ciscar 1 *vt* (**a**) *Esp Fam (ensuciar)* to dirty, to soil (**b**) *Cuba, Méx (fastidiar)* to bother, to distract
2 **ciscarse** *vpr Esp Fam* to dirty oneself, *US* to fill one's pants; **ciscarse de miedo** to brick it, to crap oneself (with fear)

cisco *nm* (**a**) *(carbón)* slack; *Fam* **estoy hecho c.** I'm shattered; *Fam* **la moto quedó hecha c.** the motorbike was a write-off (**b**) *Fam (alboroto)* row, rumpus; EXPR **armar un c.** to kick up a row

Cisjordania *nf* the West Bank
cisjordano, -a *adj* of/from the West Bank
cisma *nm Rel* schism; *(escisión)* split
cismático, -a 1 *adj* schismatic
2 *nm,f* schismatic
cisne *nm* swan ►► ***c. cantor*** whooper swan; ***c. chico*** Bewick's swan; ***c. trompetero*** trumpeter swan; ***c. vulgar*** mute swan
Císter *nm* **el C.** the Cistercian order, the Cistercians
cisterciense 1 *adj* Cistercian
2 *nmf* Cistercian
cisterna *nf* (**a**) *(aljibe, tanque)* tank (**b**) *(de retrete)* cistern (**c**) *(camión)* tanker
cistitis *nf inv Med* cystitis
cistoscopia *nf Med* cystoscopy
cisura *nf* fissure
cita *nf* (**a**) *(entrevista) (con amigo, doctor, abogado)* appointment; *(de novios)* date; **una c. de negocios** a business appointment; **la próxima c. del equipo lo enfrentará a Paraguay** the team's next match will be against Paraguay; **no piensa faltar a la c. anual con los accionistas** he fully intends to be at the annual shareholders' meeting; **acordar una c.** to arrange an appointment; **darse c.** *(quedar)* to arrange to meet; *(encontrarse)* to meet; **decenas de directores se dan c. anualmente en Cannes** scores of directors come together *o* meet up in Cannes every year; **faltar a una c.** to miss an appointment; **pedir c.** to ask for an appointment; **tener una c.** to have an appointment ►► ***c. a ciegas*** blind date; ***c. electoral*** election; ***c. con las urnas:*** **tener una c. con las urnas** to go to the polls; **en la última c. con las urnas** in the last election
(**b**) *(referencia)* quotation
citación *nf Der* summons *(singular)*
citadino, -a *Am* 1 *adj* city; **es c.** he's from the city
2 *nm,f* city dweller
citar 1 *vt* (**a**) *(convocar)* to make an appointment with; **el jefe convocó una reunión y citó a todos los empleados** the boss called a meeting to which he invited all his workers; **me citó a la salida del cine** he arranged to meet me at the exit of the cinema
(**b**) *(aludir a)* to mention; **el jefe de la oposición citó algunos ejemplos de corrupción** the leader of the opposition cited several cases of corruption; **China y Japón, por c. sólo a dos países** China and Japan, to mention *o* name only two countries; **no quiero c. nombres, pero hay varias personas que no han pagado todavía** I'm mentioning no names, but there are several people who haven't paid yet
(**c**) *(textualmente)* to quote; **le gusta c. a Marx** he likes to quote (from) Marx
(**d**) *Der* to summons; **el juez citó a declarar a los procesados** the judge summonsed the defendants to give evidence
(**e**) *Taurom* to incite
2 **citarse** *vpr* **citarse (con alguien)** to arrange to meet (sb); **nos citamos a las ocho y media** we arranged to meet at half past eight
cítara *nf* zither
citatorio *nm Der* citation, summons *(singular)*
citófono *nm Andes* intercom, buzzer, *Br* entryphone
citología *nf* (**a**) *(análisis)* smear test; **hacerse una c.** to have a smear test (**b**) *Biol* cytology
citoplasma *nm Biol* cytoplasm
citotoxicidad *nf Biol* cytotoxicity
citotóxico, -a *adj Biol* cytotoxic
citrato *nm* citrate
cítrico, -a 1 *adj* citric
2 **cítricos** *nmpl* citrus fruits
CiU ['θiu] *nf (abrev de* **Convergència i Unió**) = Catalan coalition party to the right of the political spectrum
ciudad *nf* (**a**) *(localidad) (grande)* city; *(pequeña)* town; **la emigración del campo a la c.** migration from the countryside to the city; **la gente de la c.** people who live in cities, city folk ►► *Am* ***c. balnearia*** *(en la costa)* seaside resort; *(estación thermal)* spa town; ***C. del Cabo*** Cape Town; ***la C. Condal*** Barcelona; ***c. dormitorio*** commuter town, dormitory town; ***c.-estado*** city-state; ***c. fantasma*** ghost town; ***C. de Guatemala*** Guatemala City; ***c. jardín*** garden city; ***C. de México*** Mexico City; ***c. natal*** home town; *Méx* ***c. perdida*** shanty town; ***la C. Santa*** the Holy City; ***c. satélite*** satellite town; ***C. del Vaticano*** Vatican City
(**b**) *(instalaciones)* complex ►► ***c. deportiva*** sports complex; ***c. sanitaria*** hospital complex; ***c. universitaria*** university campus

ciudadanía *nf* (**a**) *(nacionalidad)* citizenship (**b**) *(población)* public, citizens (**c**) *(civismo)* public-spiritedness, good citizenship
ciudadano, -a 1 *adj (deberes, conciencia)* civic; *(urbano)* city; **seguridad ciudadana** public safety; **vida ciudadana** city life
2 *nm,f* citizen; **un c. de Buenos Aires** a citizen of Buenos Aires; **el c. de a pie** the man in the street
ciudadela *nf* (**a**) *(fortificación)* citadel, fortress (**b**) *Náut* bridge
ciudadrealeño, -a 1 *adj* of/from Ciudad Real *(Spain)*
2 *nm,f* person from Ciudad Real *(Spain)*
ciuredano, -a *nm,f Informát* netizen
civeta *nf* civet *(cat)*
civeto *nm* civet *(used in perfumes)*
cívicamente *adv* civically
cívico, -a *adj* (**a**) *(deberes, conciencia)* civic (**b**) *(conducta)* public-spirited (**c**) *(de la ciudad)* civic
civil 1 *adj* (**a**) *(derecho, sociedad, arquitectura)* civil (**b**) *(no militar)* civilian; **ir vestido de c.** to be in civilian clothes (**c**) *(no religioso)* civil; **una boda c.** a civil marriage; **casarse por lo c.** to get married in a *Br* registry office *o US* civil ceremony
2 *nmf* (**a**) *(no militar, no religioso)* civilian (**b**) *Esp Fam (Guardia Civil)* = member of the "Guardia Civil"
3 *nm RP (boda)* civil marriage ceremony; **¿fueron al c.? – no, sólo nos invitaron a la iglesia** did you go to the registry office ceremony? – no, we were only invited to the church ceremony
civilidad *nf* civility, courtesy
civilismo *nm Am* antimilitarism
civilista *nmf (juriconsulto)* = person versed in civil law
civilización *nf* civilization
civilizado, -a *adj* civilized
civilizador, -ora *adj* civilizing
civilizar [14] 1 *vt* (**a**) *(pueblo)* to civilize (**b**) *(persona)* **ese muchacho necesita que alguien lo civilice** that boy needs someone to teach him how to behave
2 **civilizarse** *vpr* (**a**) *(pueblo)* to become civilized (**b**) *(persona)* to learn how to behave properly
civilmente *adv* civilly
civismo *nm* (**a**) *(urbanidad)* public-spiritedness, good citizenship (**b**) *(cortesía)* civility, politeness
cizalla *nf* (**a**) *(tijeras)* shears, metal cutters (**b**) *(guillotina)* guillotine
cizaña *nf (planta)* darnel; EXPR **meter** *o* **sembrar c. (en)** to sow discord (among); EXPR **separar la c. del buen grano** to separate the wheat from the chaff
cl *(abrev de* **centilitro**) cl
clac *(pl* **claques**) *nf* (**a**) *(en teatro)* claque (**b**) *(camarilla)* clique
clamar 1 *vt (exigir)* to cry out for; **c. justicia** to cry out for justice
2 *vi* (**a**) *(implorar)* to appeal; **los agricultores claman por más ayudas** farmers are appealing for more help (**b**) *(protestar)* to cry out; EXPR **es como c. en el desierto** it's like talking to a brick wall; EXPR **c. al cielo: clama al cielo que no nos haya llamado todavía** it's disgraceful that he hasn't called us yet; **la decisión del juez clama al cielo** the judge's decision is outrageous
clámide *nf Hist* chlamys
clamor *nm* clamour; **un c. de voces pedía la dimisión del presidente** a chorus of voices called on the president to resign; **hay un c. popular en favor de la subida de las pensiones** people are clamouring for an increase in pensions
clamoroso, -a *adj* (**a**) *(victoria, éxito)* resounding (**b**) *(protesta, llanto)* loud, clamorous (**c**) *(acogida)* rapturous
clan *nm* (**a**) *(tribu, familia)* clan (**b**) *(banda)* faction
clandestinamente *adv* clandestinely
clandestinidad *nf* secrecy; **en la c.** underground; **pasar a la c.** to go underground
clandestino, -a 1 *adj (actividad)* clandestine; *(publicación, asociación)* underground; *(inmigrante)* illegal
2 *nm,f (persona)* illegal immigrant
claque *nf* (**a**) *(en teatro)* claque (**b**) *(camarilla)* clique
claqué *nm* tap dancing
claqueta *nf* clapperboard
clara *nf* (**a**) *(de huevo)* white (**b**) *Esp (bebida)* shandy
claraboya *nf* skylight
claramente *adv* clearly
clarasol® *nm Méx* bleach

clarear 1 *vt* to light up
2 *v impersonal* (**a**) *(amanecer)* **empezaba a c.** dawn was breaking (**b**) *(despejarse)* to clear up, to brighten up; **saldremos cuando claree** we'll go out when it clears up
3 **clarearse** *vpr (transparentarse)* to be see-through; **esta blusa se clarea mucho** you can see right through this blouse

clareo *nm (de bosque)* clearing

clarete 1 *adj* **vino c.** light red wine
2 *nm* light red wine

claretiano, -a 1 *adj* Claretian
2 *nm* Claretian

claridad *nf* (**a**) *(del aire, agua)* clearness
(**b**) *(luz)* light; **una c. cegadora** a blinding light
(**c**) *(luminosidad)* brightness; **una habitación con mucha c.** a very bright room, a room with a lot of light
(**d**) *(de voz, sonido)* clarity
(**e**) *(franqueza)* candidness; **habló con mucha c.** he was very candid, he spoke very candidly
(**f**) *(lucidez, orden, precisión)* clarity; **expresarse con c.** to express oneself clearly; **respondió con c. a todas las preguntas** she answered all the questions clearly; **ser de una c. meridiana** to be crystal clear; **las normas fueron definidas con c. meridiana** the rules were very clearly defined

claridoso, -a *adj Méx Fam* plain-spoken

clarificación *nf* clarification

clarificador, -ora *adj* clarifying

clarificar [60] 1 *vt* (**a**) *(aclarar)* to clarify; *(misterio)* to clear up (**b**) *(purificar)* to refine
2 **clarificarse** *vpr (situación)* to become clearer

clarín 1 *nm (instrumento)* bugle
2 *nmf (persona)* bugler

clarinete 1 *nm (instrumento)* clarinet
2 *nmf (persona)* clarinettist

clarinetista *nmf* clarinettist

clarisa *nf Rel* nun of the Order of St Clare

clarividencia *nf* (**a**) *(perspicacia)* far-sightedness, perception (**b**) *(facultad sobrenatural)* clairvoyance

clarividente 1 *adj* (**a**) *(perspicaz)* far-sighted, perceptive (**b**) *(que predice el futuro)* clairvoyant
2 *nmf* (**a**) *(persona perspicaz)* perceptive person (**b**) *(persona que predice el futuro)* clairvoyant

---

CLARO, -A 1 *adj* (**a**) *(luminoso)* bright; **una habitación clara** a bright *o* light room
(**b**) *(color)* light; **verde c.** light green
(**c**) *(sonido)* clear; **hablaba con una voz clara** she spoke in a clear voice
(**d**) *(sin nubes)* clear; **un día/cielo c.** a clear day/sky
(**e**) *(diluido) (té, café)* weak; *(salsa, sopa)* thin; **no me gusta el chocolate c.** I don't like my hot chocolate thin
(**f**) *(poco tupido)* thin, sparse
(**g**) *(persona, explicación, ideas, libro)* clear; **hablaba con un lenguaje c.** she spoke in clear terms; **dejar algo c.** to make sth clear; **poner algo en c.** to get sth clear, to clear sth up; **que quede (bien) c. que no fue idea mía** I want to make it (quite) clear that it wasn't my idea; **sacar algo en c. (de)** to make sth out (from); **después de escuchar su explicación no saqué nada en c.** after listening to her explanation, I was none the wiser; **tengo c. que no puedo contar con él** one thing I'm quite sure about is that I can't rely on him, one thing's for sure, I can't rely on him; **verlo c.** *(estar seguro)* to be sure; EXPR **pasar una noche en c.** to have a sleepless night; EXPR *Esp Fam* **llevarlo** *o* **tenerlo c.: ¡lo lleva** *o* **tiene c. si piensa que lo vamos a ayudar!** if he thinks we're going to help him, he can think again!; **si no vienen ellos, lo tenemos c.** if they don't come, we've had it
(**h**) *(obvio, evidente)* clear; **el resultado fue c.** the result was clear; **¿está c.?** is that clear?; **está c. que van a ganar** it's clear they're going to win; **está c. que te quieren engañar** it's obvious that they are trying to deceive you, they are obviously trying to deceive you; **está c.** *o* **c. está que si no quieres, no estás obligado a participar** of course *o* obviously, you're not obliged to participate if you don't want to; **a no ser, c., que tengas una idea mejor** unless, of course, you have a better idea; EXPR **está más c. que el agua** it's perfectly *o* crystal clear; **allí no vuelvo, eso está más c. que el agua** I'm not going there again, that's for certain
2 *nm* (**a**) *(en bosque)* clearing; *(en multitud)* space, gap; **vi un c. en la fila** I saw a gap in the row
(**b**) *(en cielo nublado)* break in the clouds; **se esperan nubes y claros** it will be cloudy with some bright spells; **en cuanto haya un c. salimos** we'll go out as soon as it brightens up
(**c**) *(calvicie, calva)* bald patch
(**d**) *(en pintura)* highlight
(**e**) *Arquit* skylight
(**f**) ***c. de luna*** moonlight
3 *adv* clearly; **hablar c.** to speak clearly; **dilo c., ¿te interesa o no?** tell me straight, are you interested or not?; **¡c.!** of course!; **¡c. que sí!, ¡pues c.!** of course!; **¡c. que no!** of course not!; **¡c. que me gusta!** of course I like it!; *Irónico* **¿me ayudarás? – c., no pensaba en otra cosa** will you help me? - oh sure, I wouldn't dream of doing anything else; *Irónico* **ve tú primero – c., así si hay algún agujero me caigo yo** you go first - oh great *o* thanks a lot, that way if there's a hole I'll be the one to fall into it; **c., con un jugador más ya se puede** of course, with an extra player it's hardly surprising; **la obra no tuvo éxito, c. que conociendo al director no me sorprende** the play wasn't a success, but then again that's hardly surprising knowing the director
4 *loc adv* **a las claras** clearly

---

claroscuro *nm* chiaroscuro

CLASE *nf* (**a**) *(grupo, categoría)* class; **de primera c.** first-class; **de segunda c.** second-class; **una mercancía de primera c.** a first-class *o* top-class product
(**b**) *(en medio de transporte)* class; **primera/segunda c.** first/second class; **viajar en primera/segunda c.** to travel first/second class ▸▸ ***c. económica*** economy class; ***c. ejecutiva*** business class; ***c. preferente*** club class; *Andes* ***c. salón*** *(en tren)* first class; ***c. turista*** tourist class
(**c**) *(grupo social, profesional, institucional)* class; **la c. médica** the medical profession; **la c. política** the political class, politicians ▸▸ ***c. alta*** upper class; ***c. baja*** lower class; ***la c. dirigente*** the ruling class; ***c. media*** middle class; ***c. media alta*** upper middle class; ***c. media baja*** lower middle class; ***c. obrera*** working class; ***c. ociosa*** the idle classes; ***clases pasivas*** = pensioners and people on benefit; ***c. social*** social class; ***c. trabajadora*** working class
(**d**) *(tipo)* sort, kind; **no me gusta esa c. de bromas** I don't like that kind of joke; **toda c. de** all sorts *o* kinds of; **les deseamos toda c. de felicidad** we wish you every happiness; **de toda c.** of all sorts *o* kinds; **sin ninguna c. de dudas** without a (shadow of a) doubt
(**e**) *Zool* class
(**f**) *Ling* class
(**g**) *(asignatura, lección) (en colegio)* class; *(en universidad)* lecture; **una c. de historia** a history class/lecture; **iremos al cine después de c.** *(en colegio)* we're going to the cinema after school; *(en universidad)* we're going to the cinema after class; **me voy a c., nos veremos luego** I'm going to my lecture, see you later; **el profesor no lo puede recibir ahora, está en c.** the teacher can't see you now, he's teaching *o* he's giving a class; **dar clases** *(en colegio)* to teach; *(en universidad)* to lecture; **da clases de español a un grupo de franceses** she teaches Spanish to a group of French people; **doy c. con el Sr. Vega** Mr Vega is my teacher; **faltar a c.** to miss school; **faltó una semana a c. por enfermedad** she was off school for a week because she was ill; **hoy tengo c.** *(en colegio)* I have to go to school today; *(en universidad)* I've got lectures today ▸▸ *Esp* ***clases de conducir*** driving lessons; ***c. magistral*** lecture; *Am* ***clases de manejar*** driving lessons; ***c. nocturna*** evening class; ***clases particulares*** private tuition; ***clases de recuperación*** = extra lessons for pupils who have failed their exams
(**h**) *(alumnos)* class; **me encontré a una compañera de c.** I met a classmate
(**i**) *(aula) (en colegio)* classroom; *(en universidad)* lecture room *o* hall
(**j**) *(estilo)* **tener c.** to have class; **una mujer con mucha c.** a very classy woman; **con ese gol demostró su c.** he showed his class with that goal

---

clasemediero, -a *Méx* 1 *adj* middle-class
2 *nm,f* middle-class person

clásica *nf* (**a**) *Dep (carrera)* classic (**b**) *Educ* **clásicas** classics (**c**) *ver también* **clásico**

clasicismo *nm* (**a**) *(en arte, literatura)* classicism (**b**) *(carácter de obra, autor)* classical nature

clasicista 1 *adj* classicist
2 *nmf* classicist

clásico, -a 1 *adj* (**a**) *(de la Antigüedad)* classical; **lenguas clásicas** classical languages (**b**) *(ejemplar, prototípico)* classic (**c**) *(peinado, estilo)* classical; **tiene unos gustos muy clásicos** she has very classical tastes (**d**) *(música)* classical (**e**) *(habitual)* customary; **es muy c. en**

estos casos it's very typical in these cases (**f**) *(peculiar)* **c. de** typical of
2 *nm* (**a**) *(escritor, músico)* classic (**b**) *(obra)* classic; **un c. de la música moderna** a classic of modern music (**c**) *Am Dep* big game

clasificación *nf* (**a**) *(ordenación)* classification ►► *Econ* ***c. de solvencia*** credit rating
(**b**) *(de animal, planta)* classification
(**c**) *(de película)* classification
(**d**) *Dep (lista) (en liga)* (league) table; *(en carrera, torneo)* classification; **encabezar la c.** *(en liga)* to be at the top of the league; *(en carrera, torneo)* to lead the classification ►► ***c. combinada*** combined event; ***c. por equipos*** team classification; ***c. general*** (general) classification; ***c. de la regularidad*** points classification
(**e**) *Dep (para competición)* qualification; **no consiguieron lograr la c. para las semifinales** they didn't manage to qualify for the semifinals

clasificado *nm Am* classified ad

clasificador, -ora 1 *adj* classifying
2 *nm (mueble)* filing cabinet

clasificadora *nf (máquina)* sorter

clasificar [60] **1** *vt* (**a**) *(datos, documentos)* to classify; **c. algo por orden alfabético** to put sth in *o* into alphabetical order
(**b**) *(animal, planta)* to classify
(**c**) *(película)* to certificate; **una película clasificada para mayores de 18 años** a film with an "18" certificate
(**d**) *Dep (para competición)* **c. a alguien** to enable *o* allow sb to qualify; **sólo la victoria clasificaría al equipo** the team needed to win to qualify
2 *vi Am Dep* to qualify (**para** for)
3 clasificarse *vpr* (**a**) *Dep (ganar acceso)* to qualify (**para** for); **se clasifican sólo los dos primeros** only the first two qualify; **nos hemos clasificado para los cuartos de final** we've got through to *o* qualified for the quarterfinals
(**b**) *Dep (llegar)* **se clasificó en segundo lugar** she came second

clasificatorio, -a *adj* qualifying

clasismo *nm* class discrimination

clasista 1 *adj* class-conscious; *Pey* snobbish
2 *nmf* class-conscious person; *Pey* snob

claudia *adj* **ciruela c.** greengage

claudicación *nf (cesión, rendición)* capitulation, surrender; **el acuerdo representa la c. de todos sus principios** the agreement represents a complete abandonment of all his principles

claudicar [60] *vi (ceder, rendirse)* to capitulate, to give up; **nunca claudicó de sus ideas** she never renounced her ideas; **se niegan a c. ante el chantaje** they refuse to give in to blackmail

Claudio *n pr* Claudius

claustral 1 *adj* (**a**) *(del claustro conventual)* **la restauración c.** the restoration of the cloisters; **la vida c.** *(de monjes)* monastic life; *(de monjas)* convent life (**b**) *(del claustro universitario)* senate; **elecciones claustrales** elections to the senate
2 *nmf* member of the senate

claustro *nm* (**a**) *(de convento)* cloister (**b**) *(en universidad)* senate (**c**) *(en instituto, colegio) (profesores)* teaching staff, *US* faculty; *(reunión)* ≃ staff meeting, *US* faculty meeting (**d**) ***c. materno*** *(matriz)* womb

claustrofobia *nf* claustrophobia; **en los ascensores me entra c.** I get claustrophobia *o* claustrophobic in *Br* lifts *o US* elevators

claustrofóbico, -a *adj* claustrophobic

cláusula *nf* (**a**) *(acto solemne)* clause ►► *Com* ***c. escala móvil*** *(de salarios)* escalator clause; ***c. de escape*** escape clause, get-out clause; *Econ* ***c. de nación más favorecida*** most-favoured nation clause; *Com* ***c. de penalización*** penalty clause; ***c. de rescisión (de contrato)*** *(en fútbol)* = buy-out clause in footballer's contract; *Com* ***c. de salvaguardia*** escape clause, get-out clause
(**b**) *Gram* clause; **una c. de relativo** a relative clause

clausura *nf* (**a**) *(acto solemne)* closing ceremony; **ceremonia de c.** closing ceremony; **el presidente pronunció el discurso de c.** the president gave the closing speech
(**b**) *(cierre)* closing down, closure; **el ayuntamiento ordenó la c. de varias discotecas** the council ordered the closing down *o* closure of several discotheques
(**c**) *(aislamiento)* enclosed life, enclosure; **convento/monja de c.** convent/nun of an enclosed order

clausurar *vt* (**a**) *(acto)* to close, to conclude; **el concierto clausuró el festival** the concert closed the festival *o* brought the festival to a close; **el Premio Nobel clausuró el congreso** the Nobel prizewinner closed the conference (**b**) *(local)* to close down; **las autoridades clausuraron el estadio por dos encuentros** the authorities closed the stadium for two matches

clava *nf (porra)* club, cudgel

clavada *nf Esp Fam (precio abusivo)* rip-off; **me pegaron una c. por este disco** they charged me way too much *o Br* well over the odds for this record

clavadista *nmf CAm, Méx* diver

clavado, -a *adj* (**a**) *(con clavos)* nailed
(**b**) *Fam (en punto)* **a las cuatro clavadas** at four o'clock on the dot; **llegaron clavados a la hora** they arrived (right) on the dot
(**c**) *(parecido)* almost identical; **es clavada a su madre** she's the spitting image of her mother; **esos zapatos son clavados a los que te regalé yo** those shoes are virtually identical to the ones I gave you
(**d**) *(fijo)* fixed; **tenía la vista clavada en la torre** his eyes were fixed on the tower; **el exhausto corredor se quedó c. a 100 metros de la meta** the exhausted runner stopped dead 100 metres from the finishing line

clavar 1 *vt* (**a**) *(clavo, estaca)* to drive (**en** into); *(cuchillo)* to thrust (**en** into); *(chincheta, alfiler)* to stick (**en** into); **le clavó los dientes en la oreja** she sank her teeth into his ear
(**b**) *(letrero, placa)* to nail, to fix; **clavó la suela de la bota** he nailed on the sole of the boot
(**c**) *(mirada, atención)* to fix, to rivet; **c. los ojos en** to stare at; **clavó su mirada en la de ella** he stared at her right in the eyes
(**d**) *Fam (cobrar)* **me han clavado 50 euros** they stung me for 50 euros; **en esa tienda te clavan** they charge you an arm and a leg in that shop
(**e**) *RP, Ven muy Fam (copular con)* to do it with, *Br* to have it off with
2 *vi RP, Ven muy Fam (copular)* to do it, *Br* to have it off
3 clavarse *vpr* (**a**) *(hincarse)* **me clavé una astilla en el pie** I got a splinter in my foot; **me clavé una chincheta en el dedo** I got a *Br* drawing pin *o US* thumbtack in my finger; **se clavó con un alfiler** he stuck a pin into himself
(**b**) *Méx Fam (dedicarse intensamente)* **clavarse a estudiar** to study hard
(**c**) *Méx Fam* **clavarse de alguien** *(enamorarse)* to fall head over heels in love with sb
(**d**) *RP Fam (estar confinado)* **clavarse en casa** to be stuck at home
(**e**) *RP Fam (decepcionarse)* **anoche nos clavamos con esa película** that movie we saw last night was a dead loss *o* a real turkey
(**f**) *RP muy Fam (hacer el amor)* **clavarse a alguien** to do it with sb, *Br* to have it off with sb

clave 1 *adj inv (fundamental, esencial)* key; **es una fecha c. para la empresa** it's a crucial date for the company; **el factor c. de la política económica** the key factor in economic policy
2 *nm Mús* harpsichord
3 *nf* (**a**) *(código)* code; **en c.** in code; **nos mandaron los mensajes en c.** they sent us the messages in code, they sent us coded messages ►► ***c. de acceso*** access code
(**b**) *(de sistema informático)* password; *(de caja fuerte)* combination
(**c**) *(solución)* key; **la c. del éxito está en una buena planificación** the key to success is good planning
(**d**) *(interpretación)* **un estudio en c. política de la situación** a study of the situation from a political standpoint; **interpreta la obra en c. sociológica** she interprets the work from a sociological point of view *o* perspective; **analiza en c. de humor la realidad del país** he puts a humorous slant on his analysis of the country's situation
(**e**) *Mús* clef ►► ***c. de fa*** bass clef; ***c. de sol*** treble clef
(**f**) *Arquit* keystone

clavecín *nm* spinet

clavel *nm* carnation

clavelito *nm* sweet william

clavellina *nf* small carnation, pink

clavelón *nm* Aztec marigold

clavero *nm (árbol)* clove tree

clavete *nm Mús* plectrum

claveteado *nm* studding

clavetear *vt* (**a**) *(adornar con clavos)* to stud (with nails) (**b**) *(poner clavos en)* to nail *(roughly)*

clavicémbalo *nm* harpsichord

clavicordio *nm* clavichord

clavícula *nf* collarbone, *Espec* clavicle

clavicular *adj (lesión, fractura)* of the collarbone, *Espec* clavicular

clavija *nf* (**a**) *(de enchufe)* pin; *(de auriculares, teléfono)* jack; EXPR **apretar las clavijas a alguien** to put the screws on sb (**b**) *Mús* peg

clavijero *nm* (**a**) *Mús* pegbox (**b**) *(percha)* clothes hook *o* peg (**c**) *Agr* clevis (**d**) *Elec* plug

clavillo *nm* pin, pivot *(of scissors, fan)*

clavo *nm* (**a**) *(pieza metálica)* nail; EXPR *Fam* **agarrarse a un c. ardiendo: Julián se agarra a su novia como a un c. ardiendo** Julian clings to his girlfriend as if he were terrified of losing her; **está tan desesperado por encontrar trabajo que se agarraría a un c. ardiendo** he's so desperate to find work he'd take on anything; EXPR **como un c.: estaré allí como un c.** I'll be there on the dot; **me extraña que no haya llegado, normalmente es como un c.** it's strange that she hasn't arrived yet, she's normally here on the dot; EXPR *Fam* **dar en el c.** to hit the nail on the head; EXPR **un c. saca otro c.** new cares/pleasures drive old ones away; EXPR *Fam* **no pega ni c.** he doesn't do a stroke of work; **llevas tres meses sin pegar ni c.** you haven't done a thing for three months; EXPR *Fam* **no tener ni un c., estar sin un c.** *(estar arruinado)* to be flat broke
(**b**) *Med (para huesos)* pin
(**c**) *(especia)* clove
(**d**) *(callo)* corn
(**e**) *Fam (precio abusivo)* rip-off

claxon (*pl* **cláxones**) *nm* horn; **tocar el c.** to sound the horn

clemátide *nf* traveller's joy

clembuterol *nm* clenbuterol

clemencia *nf* mercy, clemency; **actuar con c.** to show mercy, to be merciful; **suplicar c.** to beg for mercy

clemente *adj (persona)* merciful, clement; *(invierno)* mild

clementina *nf* clementine

Cleopatra *n pr* Cleopatra

clepsidra *nf* water clock

cleptomanía *nf* kleptomania

cleptomaníaco, -a, cleptomaniaco, -a *nm,f* kleptomaniac

cleptómano, -a *nm,f* kleptomaniac

clerecía *nf* (**a**) *(clero)* clergy (**b**) *(oficio)* priesthood

clerical 1 *adj* clerical
2 *nmf* clericalist

clericalismo *nm* clericalism

clericó *nm RP* = drink made of white wine and fruit

clérigo, -a 1 *nm (católico)* priest
2 *nm,f (anglicano)* clergyman, *f* clergywoman

clero *nm* clergy ▸▸ ***c. regular*** regular clergy *(belonging to religious orders)*; ***c. secular*** secular clergy

clic, click (*pl* **clics, clicks**) *nm Informát* click; **hacer c.** to click; **hacer doble c.** to double-click

clicar *Informát* 1 *vt* to click on
2 *vi* to click

cliché *nm* (**a**) *Fot* negative (**b**) *Imprenta* plate (**c**) *(tópico)* cliché

click = **clic**

cliente, -a 1 *nm,f (de tienda, garaje, bar)* customer; *(de banco, abogado)* client; *(de hotel)* guest; **perder/ganar un c.** to lose/gain a customer/client; **un c. habitual** a regular customer/client/guest; **el c. siempre tiene razón** the customer is always right
2 *nm Informát* client

clientela *nf (de tienda, garaje)* customers; *(de banco, abogado)* clients; *(de hotel)* guests; *(de bar, restaurante)* clientele

clientelismo *nm Pol* = practice of giving preferential treatment to a particular interest group in exchange for its support

clima *nm* (**a**) *(atmosférico)* climate ▸▸ ***c. de alta montaña*** high mountain climate; ***c. árido*** arid climate; ***c. continental*** continental climate; ***c. desértico*** desert climate; ***c. ecuatorial*** equatorial climate; ***c. marítimo*** maritime climate; ***c. mediterráneo*** Mediterranean climate; ***c. de montaña*** mountain climate; ***c. polar*** polar climate; ***c. subtropical*** subtropical climate; ***c. tropical*** tropical climate
(**b**) *(ambiente)* atmosphere; **las negociaciones se desarrollaron en un c. de distensión** the talks took place in a relaxed atmosphere; **un c. de nerviosismo dominó la reunión** there was a tense atmosphere throughout the meeting; **se detecta un c. de euforia** there is a palpable mood of euphoria

climatérico, -a *adj* **el periodo c. de la mujer** the female menopause

climaterio *nm* menopause

climático, -a *adj* climatic

climatización *nf* air conditioning

climatizado, -a *adj* air-conditioned; **piscina climatizada** heated swimming pool

climatizador *nm Aut* air-conditioning unit, climate control system; **un coche con c.** a car with air-conditioning *o* climate control

climatizar [14] *vt* to air-condition

climatología *nf* (**a**) *(ciencia)* climatology (**b**) *(tiempo)* climate

climatológico, -a *adj* climatological

clímax *nm inv* climax

clínic *nm Dep (reunión)* clinic

clínica *nf* (**a**) *(hospital)* clinic ▸▸ ***c. de adelgazamiento*** slimming clinic; ***c. capilar*** hair restoration clinic; ***c. dental*** dental surgery; ***c. de estética*** cosmetic surgery clinic; ***c. oftalmológica*** eye clinic; ***c. psiquiátrica*** psychiatric hospital; ***c. veterinaria*** veterinary surgery
(**b**) *(especialidad)* clinical medicine (**c**) *Med (síntomas)* symptoms (**d**) *ver también* **clínico**

clínicamente *adv* clinically; **c. muerto** clinically dead

clínico, -a 1 *adj* clinical; **análisis c.** (clinical) test; **caso c.** symptoms; **historial c.** medical *o* case history
2 *nm,f (médico)* doctor; *RP (médico general)* general practitioner
3 *nm (hospital)* teaching hospital

clip (*pl* **clips**) *nm* (**a**) *(para papel)* paperclip (**b**) *(para el pelo)* hairclip (**c**) *(cierre)* fastener; **pendientes de c.** clip-on earrings (**d**) *(videoclip)* (pop) video

clíper (*pl* **clípers**) *nm* (**a**) *(avión)* clipper (**b**) *(barco)* clipper

clisé *nm* (**a**) *Fot* negative (**b**) *Imprenta* plate (**c**) *(tópico)* cliché

clítico, -a *adj Ling* clitic

clitoriano, -a, clitoridiano, -a *adj* clitoral

clitoridectomía *nf* clitoridectomy

clitoridiano = **clitoriano**

clítoris *nm inv* clitoris

Cll *Col* (*abrev de* **calle**) St

cloaca *nf* (**a**) *(alcantarilla)* sewer (**b**) *(lugar sucio)* pigsty; **esta habitación es una c.** this room is a pigsty *o* tip (**c**) *Zool* cloaca

clocar [69] *vi* to cluck

cloch, cloche (*pl* **cloches**) *nm Méx, Ven* clutch

clon *nm* (**a**) *Biol* clone (**b**) *Fam (imitador)* clone

clonación *nf* cloning

clonar *vt* to clone

clónico, -a 1 *adj* cloned
2 *nm Informát (ordenador)* clone

cloquear *vi* to cluck

cloración *nf* chlorination

clorado, -a *adj* chlorinated

cloral *nm Quím* chloral

clorar *vt* to chlorinate

clorato *nm Quím* chlorate

clorhidrato *nm Quím* hydrochlorate

clorhídrico *adj Quím* **ácido c.** hydrochloric acid

clórico, -a *adj Quím* chloric

cloro *nm* (**a**) *Quím* chlorine (**b**) *CAm, Chile, Méx (lejía)* bleach

clorofila *nf* chlorophyll

clorofluorcarbono, clorofluorocarbono *nm* chlorofluorocarbon

cloroformizar [14], *Am* **cloroformar** *vt* to chloroform

cloroformo *nm* chloroform

cloroplasto *nm Bot* chloroplast

cloruro *nm Quím* chloride ▸▸ ***c. de cal*** bleaching powder; ***c. de hidrógeno*** hydrogen chloride; ***c. de polivinilo*** polyvinyl chloride; ***c. potásico*** potassium chloride; ***c. sódico*** sodium chloride; ***c. de sodio*** sodium chloride

clóset (*pl* **clósets**) *nm Am* fitted cupboard, *US* closet

clown ['klaun, 'kloun] (*pl* **clowns**) *nm* clown

club (*pl* **clubs** *o* **clubes**) *nm* (**a**) *(sociedad)* club ▸▸ ***c. deportivo*** sports club; ***c. de fans*** fan club; ***c. de fútbol*** football *o Br* soccer club; ***c. de golf*** golf club; ***c. juvenil*** youth club; ***c. náutico*** yacht club; ***c. de tenis*** tennis club (**b**) *(local social)* club (**c**) ***c. nocturno*** nightclub

clueca *adj* broody

clueque *etc ver* **clocar**

cluniacense 1 *adj* Cluniac; **monasterio c.** Cluniac monastery
2 *nm* Cluniac monk

cluster *nm Informát* cluster

clutch ['klutʃ] (*pl* **clutches**) *nm CAm, Carib, Méx* clutch

cm (*abrev de* **centímetro**) cm

CMAN *Imprenta* (*abrev de* **Cián Magenta Amarillo Negro**) CMYK

CNMV *nf Esp Fin* (*abrev de* **Comisión Nacional del Mercado de Valores**) *Br* ≃ SIB, *US* ≃ SEC

CNT *nf* (*abrev de* **Confederación Nacional del Trabajo**) = Spanish anarchist trade union federation created in 1911

CNV *nf Arg Fin* (*abrev de* **Comisión Nacional de Valores**) *Br* ≃ SIB, *US* ≃ SEC

Co. (*abrev de* **compañía**) Co.

coa *nf* (**a**) *Méx, Pan, Ven (apero)* hoe (**b**) *Chile (argot carcelero)* prison slang

coacción *nf* coercion; **actuaron bajo c.** they were acting under duress, they were coerced into it

coaccionar *vt* to coerce; **nos coaccionaron para que aceptáramos** they forced *o* coerced us into accepting

coactivo, -a *adj* coercive

coadjutor, -ora 1 *adj* coadjutant
2 *nm,f* coadjutor

coadyuvante *adj* helping, assisting

coadyuvar *vi Formal* **c. en algo/a hacer algo** to contribute to sth/to doing sth

coagulación *nf* clotting, coagulation

coagulante 1 *adj* clotting
2 *nm* clotting agent

coagular 1 *vt (sangre)* to clot, to coagulate; *(líquido)* to coagulate
2 **coagularse** *vpr (sangre)* to clot; *(líquido)* to coagulate

coágulo *nm* clot

coahuilense 1 *adj* of/from Coahuila *(Mexico)*
2 *nmf* person from Coahuila *(Mexico)*

coalescencia *nf* coalescence

coalición *nf* coalition; **formar (una) c. con** to form a coalition with

coaligar [38] 1 *vt* to ally, to unite
2 **coaligarse** *vpr* to unite, to join together

coandú *nm* tree porcupine, prehensile-tailed porcupine

coartada *nf* alibi

coartar *vt* to limit, to restrict

coaseguro *nm* coinsurance

coatí (*pl* **coatís** *o* **coatíes**) *nm (animal)* coati

coautor, -ora *nm,f* coauthor

coaxial *adj* coaxial

coba *nf Esp, Méx Fam (halago)* flattery; **dar c. a alguien** *(hacer la pelota)* to suck up *o* crawl to sb; *(aplacar)* to soft-soap sb

cobalto *nm Quím* cobalt

cobarde 1 *adj* cowardly
2 *nmf* coward

cobardía *nf* cowardice

cobardica *Fam* 1 *adj* **no seas c.** don't be a scaredy-cat
2 *nmf* scaredy-cat

cobaya *nmf también Fig* guinea pig

cobertera *nf* (**a**) *(cubierta, tapa)* lid (**b**) *(planta)* white water lily

cobertizo *nm* (**a**) *(tejado adosado)* lean-to (**b**) *(caseta)* shed

cobertor *nm* bedspread

cobertura *nf* (**a**) *(cubierta)* cover; **una tarta con c. de chocolate** a cake with chocolate *Br* icing *o US* frosting
(**b**) *(amparo)* **los acusaron de dar c. a un delincuente** they were accused of covering for a criminal; **aquel negocio servía de c. para el blanqueo de dinero** that business was a front *o* cover for money laundering
(**c**) *(de un servicio)* coverage; **mi teléfono móvil no tiene c. aquí** my mobile network doesn't cover this area; **c. nacional/regional** national/regional coverage; **miles de parados sin c. social** thousands of unemployed people who are not receiving benefit ►► ***c. informativa*** news *o* media coverage; ***c. periodística*** press coverage; ***c. sanitaria*** health cover
(**d**) *(de un seguro)* cover
(**e**) *Fin* security; **c. para un crédito/una hipoteca** security for a loan/ a mortgage

cobija *nf* (**a**) *Am (manta)* blanket (**b**) *PRico (techo)* = roof made from thatched palm leaves

cobijar 1 *vt* (**a**) *(albergar)* to house (**b**) *(proteger)* to shelter (**c**) *PRico (techar)* to thatch
2 **cobijarse** *vpr* to shelter, to take shelter; **se cobijaron debajo de un árbol** they took shelter *o* sheltered under a tree

cobijo *nm* (**a**) *(refugio)* shelter (**b**) *(protección)* protection, shelter; **dar c. a alguien** to give shelter to sb, to take sb in

cobista *nmf Fam* creep

COBOL, Cobol *nm Informát* COBOL, Cobol

cobra *nf* cobra ►► ***c. real*** king cobra

cobrable *adj* cashable

cobrador, -ora *nm,f* (**a**) *(de autobús)* conductor, *f* conductress (**b**) *(de deudas, recibos)* collector ►► ***c. de morosos*** debt collector

cobranza *nf (de pago)* collection

COBRAR 1 *vt* (**a**) *Com (dinero)* to charge; *(cheque)* to cash; *(deuda)* to collect; **cantidades por c.** amounts due; **¿me cobra, por favor?** how much do I owe you?; **nos cobra 1.000 euros de alquiler al mes** she charges us 1,000 euros rent a month, we pay her 1,000 euros rent a month; **cobran 10 euros por página** they charge 10 euros per page; **te cobrarán un mínimo de 10 euros por arreglarte los zapatos** it'll cost you at least 10 euros to get your shoes mended; **me cobró 1.000 pesos de más** he overcharged me by 1,000 pesos; **me cobraron 200 pesos de menos** they undercharged me by 200 pesos; **nos cobró por adelantado** we had to pay her in advance; **no me cobraron el IVA** they didn't charge me *Br* VAT *o US* ≃ sales tax; **cóbrelo todo junto** put it all together, we'll pay for it all together; **no nos cobró la mano de obra** he didn't charge us for labour; **la cobrarán en aquella ventanilla** you can pay at that counter over there; **el lechero vino a c. la factura mensual** the milkman came with the monthly bill
(**b**) *(un sueldo)* to earn, to be paid; **cobra un millón al año** she earns a million a year; **en junio cobraremos una prima** we'll be paid a bonus in June; **cobro mi pensión por el banco** my pension is paid straight into the bank; **está cobrando el paro** he's receiving unemployment benefit; **sobrevive cobrando diferentes subsidios** she lives by claiming a number of different benefits; **tengo que ir a c. la jubilación** I have to go and draw my pension; **no cobro nada, lo hago porque me gusta** I don't get paid for it, I do it because I enjoy it
(**c**) *(adquirir)* to take on, to acquire; **con su último disco ha cobrado fama universal** with her latest record she has achieved worldwide fame *o* she has become a household name; **cada día cobran más importancia los temas medioambientales** the environment is an issue which is becoming more and more important *o* which is gaining in importance; **cobró aliento y prosiguió la marcha** he paused to get his breath back and continued walking; **c. velocidad** to gather *o* gain speed
(**d**) *(sentir)* **cobrarle afecto** *o* **cariño a algo/alguien** to take a liking to sth/sb; **le cobró miedo al perro y no se atrevió a acercársele** she got scared of the dog and didn't dare go near it
(**e**) *(recuperar)* to retrieve, to recover; **las tropas cobraron el aeropuerto** the troops regained control of the airport
(**f**) *(en caza) (matar a tiros)* to shoot; *(recoger)* to retrieve, to fetch; **cobraron doscientas aves en un solo día** they came back with two hundred birds in just one day
(**g**) *CSur (señalar)* **el juez cobró penal/falta** the referee gave a penalty/foul
2 *vi* (**a**) *(en el trabajo)* to get paid; **cobrarás el día 5 de cada mes** you'll be paid on the 5th of every month; **llevan un año sin c.** they haven't had any wages for a year; **c. en efectivo** to be *o* get paid (in) cash
(**b**) *Fam (recibir una paliza)* **ivas a c.!** you'll catch it!; **el niño cobró por portarse mal** the child got a beating for being naughty
3 **cobrarse** *vpr* (**a**) *(causar)* **el accidente se cobró nueve vidas** nine people were killed in the crash; **el terremoto se cobró una elevada cantidad de muertos** there was a high death toll as a result of the earthquake
(**b**) *(consumición)* **cóbrese un café, ¿se cobra un café?** could I have the *Br* bill *o US* check, please? I had a coffee

---

cobre *nm Quím* copper; EXPR *Am Fam* **no tener un c.** to be flat broke

cobrizo, -a *adj (pelo, piel)* copper

cobro *nm (de talón)* cashing; *(de pago)* collection; **llamar a alguien a c. revertido** *Br* to make a reverse-charge call to sb, *US* to call sb collect ►► ***c. de comisiones*** *(delito)* acceptance of bribes *o* (illegal) commissions

coca *nf* (**a**) *(planta)* coca (**b**) *Fam (cocaína)* coke (**c**) *Col (boliche)* cup and ball

cocacho *Andes* 1 *adj (frijol)* hard
2 *nm* rap *o* blow on the head

Coca-Cola® *nf* Coca-Cola®, Coke®

cocada *nf* (**a**) *CAm, Carib (galleta)* = *Br* biscuit *o US* cookie made with shredded coconut (**b**) *Méx (postre)* coconut custard

cocaína *nf* cocaine

cocainismo *nm* cocaine addiction

cocainomanía *nf* cocaine addiction

cocainómano, -a *nm,f* cocaine addict

cocal *nm* (**a**) *Am (cocotal)* coconut grove (**b**) *Perú (plantación de coca)* coca plantation

cocalero, -a *Bol, Perú* **1** *adj* **región cocalera** coca-producing area; **productor c.** coca farmer *o* producer
2 *nm,f* coca farmer *o* producer

cocción *nf* (**a**) *(de alimentos)* cooking; *(en agua)* boiling; *(en horno)* baking (**b**) *(de cerámica, ladrillos)* firing

cóccix *nm inv* coccyx

cocear *vi* to kick

cocedero *nm* **c. (de marisco)** seafood restaurant

cocer [15] **1** *vt* (**a**) *(alimentos) (cocinar)* to cook; *(hervir)* to boil; *(en horno)* to bake
(**b**) *(cerámica, ladrillos)* to fire
2 cocerse *vpr* (**a**) *(alimentos) (cocinar)* to cook; *(hervir)* to boil; *(en horno)* to bake; **esta pasta tarda diez minutos en cocerse** this pasta cooks in ten minutes, this pasta takes ten minutes to cook
(**b**) *Fam (achicharrarse)* to be boiling *o* roasting; **me estoy cociendo (de calor)** I'm boiling *o* roasting
(**c**) *Fam (tramarse)* **me parece que se está cociendo algo gordo** I think something really big is brewing; **¿qué se cuece por aquí?** what's cooking?, what's going on here?
(**d**) *Fam (emborracharse)* to get plastered

cocha *nf* (**a**) *Perú (pampa)* pampa, plain (**b**) *Andes (charco)* pool

cochabambino, -a **1** *adj* of/from Cochabamba *(Bolivia)*
2 *nm,f* person from Cochabamba *(Bolivia)*

cochambre *nf Fam* (**a**) *(suciedad)* filth; **la habitación está llena de c.** the room is absolutely filthy (**b**) *(cosa de mala calidad) Br* rubbish, *US* garbage; **una c. de moto** a useless bike

cochambroso, -a *adj Fam* filthy

cochayuyo *nm Chile, Perú* seaweed

coche *nm* (**a**) *(automóvil)* car, *US* automobile; **ir en c.** *(montado)* to go by car; *(conduciendo)* to drive; **no me gusta ir en c. al centro** I prefer not to drive into town; **viajar en c.** to travel by car; EXPR *Fam* **ir en el c. de San Fernando** to go on *o* by Shanks's *Br* pony *o US* mare ▸▸ ***c. de alquiler*** hire car; ***c. antiguo*** *(de antes de 1930)* vintage car; *(más moderno)* classic car; ***c. automático*** automatic; ***c. bomba*** car bomb; ***c. de bomberos*** fire engine, *US* fire truck; ***c. de carreras*** racing car; ***c. celular*** police van; ***coches de choque*** Dodgems®, bumper cars; ***c. deportivo*** sports car; ***c. eléctrico*** electric car; ***c. de empresa*** company car; ***c. de época*** *(de antes de 1930)* vintage car; *(más moderno)* classic car; ***c. escoba*** *(en carrera)* sweeper van; ***c. familiar*** estate car; ***c. fúnebre*** hearse; ***c. grúa*** *Br* breakdown truck, *US* tow truck; ***c. patrulla*** patrol car; ***c. de policía*** police car
(**b**) *(autobús)* bus ▸▸ ***c. de línea*** bus *(between towns)*
(**c**) *(de caballos)* carriage
(**d**) *(de niño) Br* pram, *US* baby carriage
(**e**) *(de tren)* coach, *Br* carriage, *US* car ▸▸ ***c. cama*** sleeping car, sleeper; ***c. restaurante*** restaurant *o* dining car

cochecito *nm (de niño) Br* pram, *US* baby carriage

cochera *nf* (**a**) *(de autobuses, tranvías)* depot (**b**) *Am (garaje)* garage

cochería *nf Arg* undertaker's, *US* mortician's, funeral parlour *o US* home

cochero *nm* coachman

cochifrito *nm (de cabrito)* kid stew; *(de cordero)* lamb stew

cochinada *nf* (**a**) *(cosa sucia)* filthy thing; **es una c.** it's filthy; **hacer cochinadas** *(porquerías)* to be disgusting (**b**) *(grosería)* dirty word; **decir cochinadas** to use foul language; **hacer cochinadas** *(sexuales)* to be naughty; **esa revista es una c.** that magazine is disgusting *o* filthy (**c**) *(mala jugada)* dirty trick; **hacer una c. a alguien** to play a dirty trick on sb

cochinilla *nf* (**a**) *(crustáceo)* woodlouse (**b**) *(insecto)* cochineal

cochinillo *nm* suckling pig

cochino, -a **1** *adj* (**a**) *(sucio)* filthy (**b**) *(grosero) (chiste, revista)* dirty, filthy (**c**) *(malintencionado)* dirty (**d**) *Fam (maldito)* lousy, blasted; **eso es envidia cochina** it's sheer jealousy; **¿por qué no dejas de una vez los cochinos cigarrillos?** why don't you just give up those blasted cigarettes once and for all?
2 *nm,f* (**a**) *(animal)* pig, *f* sow (**b**) *(persona sucia)* dirty *o* filthy pig (**c**) *(persona grosera)* dirty *o* filthy pig (**d**) *(persona malintencionada)* swine
3 *nm Cuba (pez)* triggerfish

cochiquera *nf Fam* pigsty

cocho *nm Chile (maíz)* = mixture of corn meal and carob

cocido, -a **1** *adj* (**a**) *(alimentos)* cooked; *(hervido)* boiled (**b**) *(barro)* fired (**c**) *Esp Fam (borracho) Br* pissed, *US* loaded; **iba completamente c.** *Br* he was pissed as a newt, *US* he was totally loaded
2 *nm* stew ▸▸ ***c. madrileño*** = chickpea stew, containing meat, sausage and potatoes

cociente *nm* quotient ▸▸ ***c. intelectual*** IQ, intelligence quotient

cocimiento *nm (cocción)* cooking; *(en horno)* baking

cocina *nf* (**a**) *(habitación)* kitchen; **muebles/utensilios de c.** kitchen furniture/utensils
(**b**) *(electrodoméstico)* cooker, stove ▸▸ ***c. eléctrica*** electric cooker; ***c. de gas*** gas cooker
(**c**) *(arte)* cooking; **c. española/mexicana** Spanish/Mexican cuisine *o* cooking; **clase de c.** cookery class; **libro de c.** cookery book, cookbook ▸▸ ***c. casera*** home cooking; ***c. de mercado*** = cooking using fresh market produce; ***c. rápida*** fast food; **el microondas hace más fácil la c. rápida** the microwave makes it easier to prepare food quickly

cocinar **1** *vt* to cook
2 *vi* to cook; **le encanta c.** he loves cooking
3 cocinarse *vpr* (**a**) *(alimentos)* to cook (**b**) *(tramarse)* **¿qué se cocina por aquí?** what's cooking?, what's going on here?

cocinero, -a *nm,f* cook; EXPR **ha sido c. antes que fraile** he's got experience on the subject

cocinilla *nf* **1** *(infiernillo)* portable *o* camp stove
2 *nm Fam (persona)* **es un c.** he's great in the kitchen

cocker ['koker] *(pl* **cockers***)* *nm* cocker spaniel

coclea *nf Anat* cochlea

coclearia *nf* scurvy grass

coco *nm* (**a**) *(fruto)* coconut
(**b**) *Fam (cabeza)* nut, head; **ese chico está mal del c.** that boy is soft *o* isn't right in the head; **por más vueltas que le doy al c. no consigo entenderlo** I've *Br* racked *o US* cudgeled my brains, but I still can't understand it; EXPR *Fam* **comer el c.: le están comiendo el c. para que los ayude** they're going on at him to help them; *Fam* **no te comas el c., no ha sido él** don't worry yourself about it, it wasn't him; EXPR *Fam* **tener mucho c.** *(ser inteligente)* to be really brainy
(**c**) *Fam (fantasma)* bogeyman; **si no te portas bien vendrá el c.** if you're not good, the bogeyman will come and get you
(**d**) *Fam (persona fea)* ugly person; **es un c. de chico** he's an ugly devil
(**e**) *Biol (bacteria)* coccus
(**f**) *Cuba (ave)* white ibis
(**g**) *CSur muy Fam* **cocos** *(testículos)* balls; EXPR **romper los cocos** *(molestar)* to be a pain in the *Br* arse *o US* butt

cocoa *nf Am* cocoa (powder)

cocobolo *nm* rosewood (tree)

cococha *nf* = fleshy underside of the head of a cod or hake, considered a delicacy

cocodrilo *nm* crocodile

cocol *nm Méx* (**a**) *(pan)* = sweet bun covered in sesame seeds and flavoured with aniseed (**b**) *Fam* **del c.** *(muy mal)* awful, terrible; **¿cómo estuvo el viaje? – del c.** how was your trip? – it was awful *o* terrible

cocoliche *nm RP Fam* = pidgin Spanish spoken by Italian immigrants

cocorota *nf Fam* nut, *Br* bonce

cocotal *nm* coconut grove

cocotero *nm* coconut palm

cóctel, coctel *nm* (**a**) *(bebida)* cocktail
(**b**) *(comida)* cocktail ▸▸ *CAm* ***c. de frutas*** fruit salad, fruit cocktail; ***c. de gambas*** prawn cocktail; ***c. de mariscos*** seafood cocktail
(**c**) ***c. molotov*** petrol bomb, Molotov cocktail
(**d**) *(reunión)* cocktail party
(**e**) *(mezcla)* **los excursionistas forman un c. variado de nacionalidades** the people on the trip are a mixed bag of nationalities; **un c. de música latina y celta** a blend of Latin and Celtic music; **sequía y pobreza, un c. explosivo** drought and poverty, an explosive combination

coctelera *nf* cocktail shaker

coctelería *nf* cocktail bar

cocuyo *nm Carib* (**a**) *(insecto)* firefly (**b**) *(árbol)* bustic

coda *nf Mús* coda

codal *nm (de armadura)* elbow armour piece

codaste *nm Náut* sternpost

codazo *nm (suave)* nudge; *(violento)* jab *(with one's elbow)*; **abrirse paso a codazos** to elbow one's way through; **dar un c. a alguien** *(suave)* to nudge sb; *(violento)* to elbow sb; **pegar un c. a alguien** to elbow sb; **le rompieron la nariz de un c.** he got his nose broken by someone's elbow

codeador, -ora *Andes* **1** *adj* scrounging, sponging
2 *nm,f* scrounger, sponger

codear 1 *vi Andes* to wheedle, to cajole
2 codearse *vpr* to rub shoulders (**con** with)

CODECA [ko'ðeka] *nf* (**a**) *(abrev de* **Corporación de Desarrollo Económico del Caribe**) Caribbean Economic Development Corporation (**b**) *(abrev de* **Confederación de Estados Centroamericanos**) Confederation of Central American States

codecisión *nf UE* codecision

codeína *nf* codeine

codeo *nm Andes (insistencia)* wheedling, cajoling

codera *nf* (**a**) *(remiendo, refuerzo)* elbow patch (**b**) *(protección)* elbow pad (**c**) *Náut* (stern) mooring cable

codeso *nm* (common) laburnum

códice *nm* codex

codicia *nf* (**a**) *(de riqueza)* greed (**b**) *(de aprender, saber)* thirst (**de** for)

codiciar *vt* to covet

codicilo *nm Der* codicil

codiciosamente *adv* greedily

codicioso, -a *adj* greedy

codificación *nf* (**a**) *(de norma, ley)* codification (**b**) *(de mensaje en clave)* encoding (**c**) *Informát* coding

codificado, -a *adj (emisión de TV)* scrambled

codificador, -ora 1 *adj* codifying
2 *nm (aparato)* scrambler *(for pay TV)*

codificar [60] *vt* (**a**) *(ley)* to codify (**b**) *(mensaje)* to encode (**c**) *Informát* to code

código *nm* (**a**) *(de leyes, normas)* code ►► ***c. de circulación*** highway code; ***c. civil*** civil code; ***c. de comercio*** commercial law; ***c. de conducta*** code of conduct; ***c. mercantil*** commercial law; ***c. militar*** military law; ***c. penal*** penal code
(**b**) *(de señales, signos)* code ►► ***c. de barras*** bar code; ***c. genético*** genetic code; *Esp* ***c. de identificación fiscal*** = number identifying company for tax purposes; ***c. morse*** Morse code; ***c. postal*** *Br* postcode, postal code, *US* zip code; ***c. de señales*** signal code; ***c. telefónico*** *Br* dialling code, *US* area code; ***c. territorial*** *Br* dialling code, *US* area code
(**c**) *Informát* code ►► ***c. de acceso*** access code; ***c. alfanumérico*** alphanumeric code; ***c. ASCII*** ASCII (code); ***c. binario*** binary code; ***c. de error*** error code; ***c. fuente*** source code; ***códigos de fusión*** merge codes; ***c. máquina*** machine code

codillo *nm* (**a**) *(en un cuadrúpedo)* upper foreleg; *(plato)* knuckle of pork (**b**) *(de jamón)* shoulder (**c**) *(de un tubo)* elbow, bend

codirección *nf* co-direction, joint direction

codirector, -ora *nm,f* co-director, joint director

codirigir *vt* to co-direct

codo[1] *nm* (**a**) *(de brazo)* elbow; **tenía los codos sobre la mesa** she was leaning (with her elbows) on the table; **c. con c., c. a c.** side by side; *Fam* **se sacó la carrera a base de codos** she got her degree by sheer hard work; EXPR *Fam* **empinar el c.** to bend the elbow; EXPR *Fam* **hablar por los codos** to talk nineteen to the dozen, to be a chatterbox; EXPR *Fam* **hincar** *o* **romperse los codos** *(estudiar)* to study hard; **si quieres aprobar, vas a tener que hincar** *o* **romperte los codos** if you want to pass, you're going to have to roll your sleeves up and do some serious studying; EXPR *RP Fam* **no tener c.** to be stingy, to be tight-fisted ►► *Med* ***c. de tenista*** tennis elbow
(**b**) *(de prenda)* elbow
(**c**) *(en tubería)* bend; *(pieza)* elbow joint
(**d**) *(medida)* cubit

codo[2]**, -a** *adj Méx Fam* stingy, tight-fisted

codorniz *nf* quail ►► ***c. de California*** California quail

COE ['koe] *nm (abrev de* **Comité Olímpico Español**) Spanish Olympic Committee

coedición *nf* joint publication

coeditar *vt* to publish jointly

coeficiente *nm* (**a**) *(índice)* rate ►► *Fin* ***c. de caja*** cash ratio; ***c. de goles*** goal difference; ***c. intelectual*** intelligence quotient, IQ; ***c. de inteligencia*** intelligence quotient, IQ; *Fin* ***c. de liquidez*** liquidity ration (**b**) *Mat & Fís* coefficient ►► *Fís* ***c. de dilatación*** coefficient of expansion

coendú *nm* coendou

coenzima *nf Biol* coenzyme

coercer [40] *vt* to restrict, to constrain

coerción *nf* coercion

coercitivo, -a *adj* coercive

coetáneo, -a 1 *adj* contemporary
2 *nm,f* contemporary

coexistencia *nf* coexistence ►► ***c. pacífica*** peaceful coexistence

coexistente *adj* coexisting

coexistir *vi* to coexist

cofa *nf Náut* lower mast top ►► ***c. para el vigía*** crow's nest

cofia *nf (de enfermera, camarera)* cap; *(de monja)* coif

cofinanciación *nf* co-financing, joint financing

cofinanciar *vt* to co-finance, to finance jointly

cofrade *nmf* (**a**) *(de cofradía religiosa)* brother, *f* sister (**b**) *(de cofradía no religiosa)* member

cofradía *nf* (**a**) *(religiosa) (de hombres)* brotherhood, *(de mujeres)* sisterhood (**b**) *(profesional)* guild

cofre *nm* (**a**) *(arca)* chest, trunk; **c. del tesoro** treasure chest (**b**) *(para joyas)* jewel box (**c**) *Méx (capó) Br* bonnet, *US* hood (**d**) *Ecuad (maletero) Br* boot, *US* trunk

cofundador, -ora *nm,f* co-founder

cogedor, -ora 1 *nm,f (persona)* picker, gatherer
2 *nm (para carbón, ceniza)* shovel

COGER [52]

Although the word **coger** is accepted in educated use throughout Latin America, in many places its principal meaning is the taboo sense indicated at **2(f)**. For this reason it tends to be avoided in other contexts, and is usually replaced by **agarrar**.

1 *vt* (**a**) *(tomar, agarrar)* to take; **c. a alguien de la mano** to take sb by the hand; **pasear cogidos de la mano** to walk hand in hand; **c. a alguien en brazos** to take sb in one's arms; **coge la tetera por el asa** take *o* hold the teapot by the handle; **coge esta bolsa un momento** hold this bag a moment; **¿puedes c. el teléfono, por favor?** could you pick the phone up *o* answer the phone, please?; *Fam* **éste no ha cogido un libro en su vida** he's never picked up a book in his life; EXPR *Fam* **no haber por dónde cogerlo: esta película no hay por dónde cogerla** I couldn't make head or tail of this movie *o Br* film; **tu hermano es muy raro, no hay por dónde cogerlo** your brother's very strange, it's hard to know what to make of him; **se sabe todas las respuestas, no hay por dónde cogerlo** he knows all the answers, it's impossible to catch him out
(**b**) *(quitar)* to take; **c. algo a alguien** to take sth from sb; **¿quién me ha cogido el lápiz?** who's taken my pencil?; **te he cogido la calculadora un momento** I've just borrowed your calculator for a moment
(**c**) *(recoger) (objeto caído)* to pick up; *(frutos, flores)* to pick; **se me ha caído el bolígrafo, ¿me lo puedes c.?** I've dropped my pen, could you pick it up for me?; **nos gusta mucho c. setas** we really enjoy picking mushrooms *o* going mushrooming; **cogimos a un autoestopista muy simpático** we picked up a very friendly hitchhiker
(**d**) *(atrapar) (ladrón, pez, pájaro, pelota)* to catch; **¿a que no me coges?** bet you can't catch me!; *Fam* **isi te cojo, te la cargas!** if I catch you, you'll be in for it!
(**e**) *(sorprender)* **c. a alguien haciendo algo** to catch sb doing sth; **c. a alguien desprevenido** to take sb by surprise; **c. a alguien in fraganti** to catch sb red-handed *o* in the act; **la tormenta me cogió cerca de casa** the storm broke when I was nearly home; **el terremoto nos cogió en la capital** the earthquake happened while we were in the capital; **lo cogí de buen humor** I caught him in a good mood
(**f**) *(alcanzar) (persona, vehículo)* to catch up with; **aceleró para c. al corredor que llevaba delante** she ran faster to try and catch up with the runner in front of her; **cogió la delantera tras la segunda vuelta** she went into *o* took the lead after the second lap
(**g**) *(tren, autobús)* to take, to catch; **no me gusta c. el avión** I don't like flying; **prefiero c. el coche** I'd rather drive
(**h**) *(sacar, obtener)* to get; **he cogido hora con el dentista** I've made an appointment with the dentist; **¿has cogido las entradas?** have you got the tickets?
(**i**) *(quedarse con) (propina, empleo, apartamento)* to take; **ha cogido**

un trabajo de mecanógrafo he has taken a job as a typist; **llegaremos pronto para c. buen sitio** we'll get there early to get a good seat; **están tan ocupados que ya no cogen más encargos** they're so busy they've stopped taking on *o* accepting orders

(**j**) *(contratar, admitir) (personal)* to take on; **hemos cogido a una secretaria nueva** we've taken on a new secretary; **el colegio ya no coge más alumnos para este curso** the school has stopped taking pupils for this year

(**k**) *(contraer) (gripe, resfriado)* to catch, to get; **c. frío** to get cold; **c. una insolación** to get sunstroke; **c. el sarampión** to get *o* catch (the) measles; **c. una borrachera** to get drunk; **c. un berrinche** to throw a tantrum

(**l**) *(absorber)* to absorb, to soak up; **este tipo de esponja coge mucha agua** this type of sponge absorbs a lot of water; **esta mesa coge mucho polvo al lado de la ventana** this table gets very dusty *o* gathers a lot of dust next to the window

(**m**) *(sentir) (odio, afecto)* to start to feel; **c. cariño/miedo a** to become fond/scared of

(**n**) *(adquirir) (costumbre, vicio, acento)* to pick up; **los hijos cogen los hábitos de los padres** children pick up the habits of their parents; **ha cogido la costumbre de cantar por las mañanas** she has taken to singing in the mornings; EXPR *Fam* **cogerle el truco** *o* **tranquillo a algo** to get the knack of sth; EXPR *Fam* **cogerla con alguien: la ha cogido con nosotros, y no deja de molestarnos** she's got it in for us and never leaves us alone

(**o**) *(sintonizar) (canal, emisora)* to get, to receive

(**p**) *(entender)* to get; *(oír)* to catch; **¿coges lo que te digo?** do you get *o* understand what I'm saying to you?; **no cogió la indirecta** she didn't take the hint; **no cogió el chiste** he didn't get the joke; **cogí su comentario a mitad** I only half heard what she said, I only caught half of what she said

(**q**) *(cobrar)* **c. fuerzas** to build up one's strength; **c. velocidad** to gather *o* gain speed

(**r**) *(sujeto: vehículo)* to knock over, to run over; *(sujeto: toro)* to gore; **me cogió un coche, y ando con muletas** I was run over *o* hit by a car, and I'm on crutches now; **lo cogió un toro** he was gored by a bull

(**s**) *(abarcar) (espacio)* to cover, to take up; **estas oficinas cogen tres plantas del edificio** these offices take up *o* occupy three floors of the building

(**t**) *(elegir)* to choose; **cogió un mal momento para anunciar el resultado** she chose a bad moment to announce the result

(**u**) *Am Vulg (tener relaciones sexuales con)* to screw, to fuck; **c. a alguien** to screw *o* fuck sb

2 *vi* (**a**) *(situarse)* to be; **coge muy cerca de aquí** it's not very far from here

(**b**) *(dirigirse)* **c. a la derecha/la izquierda** to turn right/left; **coge por la calle de la iglesia** take the church road

(**c**) *(enraizar)* to take; **los rosales han cogido** the roses have taken

(**d**) *(contestar al teléfono)* to answer; **llevo un rato llamando, pero no cogen** I've been calling for a while now, but there's no answer *o* they don't answer

(**e**) *(indicando acción repentina)* **cogió y se fue** she upped and went; **de pronto cogió y me insultó** he turned round and insulted me; **si seguimos así, cojo y me marcho** if we carry on like this, I'm off

(**f**) *Am Vulg (tener relaciones sexuales)* to screw, to fuck; **c. con alguien** to screw *o* fuck sb

3 cogerse *vpr* (**a**) *(asirse)* **cogerse de** *o* **a algo** to cling to *o* clutch sth; **el anciano se coge del brazo de la enfermera** the old man is clutching the nurse's arm; **cógete bien** hold on tight; **se cogieron de las manos** they held each other's hands

(**b**) *(pillarse)* **cogerse los dedos/la falda con la puerta** to catch one's fingers/skirt in the door; *Fig* **han calculado por lo alto para no cogerse los dedos** their estimate is on the high side, just to be safe; *Fam* **cogerse un cabreo** to throw a fit; **cogerse una gripe** to catch the flu

(**c**) *(sintonizarse) (canal, emisora)* to get; **desde mi casa no se coge el Canal 5** you can't get Channel 5 from my house

(**d**) *Am Vulg (tener relaciones sexuales)* to screw, to fuck; **cogerse a alguien** to screw *o* fuck sb

---

cogestión *nf* joint management, co-management

cogida *nf (de torero)* goring

cogido *nm* gather

cogitabundo, -a *adj Formal* pensive, meditative

cognac [ko'ɲak] (*pl* **cognacs**) *nm* brandy, cognac

cognado *nm Ling* cognate

cognición *nf* cognition

cognitivo, -a *adj* cognitive

cognoscible *adj* knowable

cognoscitivo, -a *adj* cognitive

cogollo *nm* (**a**) *(de lechuga)* heart ►► ***c. de Tudela*** gem lettuce (**b**) *(brote)* shoot (**c**) *Fam (meollo)* heart, crux; **el c. de la cuestión** the heart *o* crux of the matter

cogorza *nf Fam* **agarrar una c.** to get smashed, to get blind drunk; **tendrías que ver la c. que lleva** you should see him, he's totally smashed

cogotazo *nm* rabbit punch

cogote *nm Esp Fam* nape, back of the neck

cogujada *nf* crested lark

cogulla *nf Rel* habit

cohabitación *nf* (**a**) *(convivencia)* cohabitation (**b**) *Pol* coexistence

cohabitar *vi* (**a**) *(convivir)* to cohabit, to live together (**b**) *Pol* to coexist

cohechar *vt (sobornar)* to bribe

cohecho *nm* bribery

coheredero, -a *nm,f* coheir, *f* coheiress

coherencia *nf* (**a**) *(de conducta, estilo)* consistency; **actuar con c.** to be consistent; **en c. con su postura, se negó a utilizar la violencia** in accordance with his position, he refused to use violence (**b**) *(de razonamiento)* coherence; **falta de c.** lack of coherence (**c**) *Fís* cohesion

coherente *adj* (**a**) *(conducta, estilo)* consistent (**b**) *(razonamiento)* logical, coherent; **ser c. con algo** to accord with sth, to be in line with sth

cohesión *nf* (**a**) *(de personas, cosas)* cohesion; **la c. del partido** party unity (**b**) *Fís* cohesion

cohesionado, -a *adj* united

cohesionar 1 *vt* to unite

2 cohesionarse *vpr* to unite

cohesivo, -a *adj* cohesive

cohete *nm* (**a**) *(proyectil)* rocket; **cohetes** *(fuegos artificiales)* fireworks; EXPR *Fam* **escapar** *o* **salir como un c.** to be off like a shot; EXPR *Fam* **no ser como para tirar cohetes** to be nothing to write home about (**b**) *(vehículo propulsado)* rocket ►► ***c. espacial*** space rocket; ***c. multietapa*** multi-stage rocket (**c**) *Méx (pistola)* pistol (**d**) *Méx (agujero)* blasting hole (**e**) *RP Fam* **al c.** *(en vano)* in vain

cohetería *nf (taller)* fireworks factory

cohibición *nf* inhibition

cohibido, -a *adj* inhibited

cohibir 1 *vt* to inhibit; **su presencia me cohíbe** her presence inhibits me

2 cohibirse *vpr* to become inhibited; **¡no te cohíbas!** don't be shy *o* embarrassed!

cohombro *nm* (**a**) *(planta)* cucumber (**b**) *(fruto)* cucumber (**c**) ***c. de mar*** sea cucumber

cohonestar *vt Formal* to present as justified, to (attempt to) legitimize

cohorte *nf* cohort

COI ['koi] *nm* (*abrev de* **Comité Olímpico Internacional**) IOC

coihué *nm* coigue, coihue

coima *nf Andes, RP Fam* bribe, *Br* backhander

coimear *vt Andes, RP Fam* to bribe

coimero, -a *nm,f Andes, RP Fam* bribe-taker

coincidencia *nf* (**a**) *(casualidad)* coincidence; **¡qué c. que yo también pasara por ahí!** what a coincidence that I happened to be passing by there too!; **se da la c. de que no es la primera vez que sale elegido** it so happens it's not the first time he's been elected; **cualquier parecido es pura c.** any similarity is purely coincidental

(**b**) *(en el tiempo)* **la c. de un partido de fútbol obligó a aplazar el debate** the debate had to be postponed because it clashed with a football match

(**c**) *(conformidad, parecido)* agreement; **hubo c. a la hora de valorar los resultados** there was agreement *o* people agreed when it came to assessing the results

coincidente *adj* (**a**) *(igual, parecido)* **un resultado c. con el obtenido hace dos años** a result that coincides with the one obtained two years ago (**b**) *(líneas)* coincident

coincidir *vi* (**a**) *(superficies, líneas)* to coincide (**con** with); **estas dos piezas no coinciden** these two pieces don't go together *o* match up

(**b**) *(versiones, gustos)* to coincide; **coincidimos en nuestras aficiones** we have *o* share the same interests

(**c**) *(estar de acuerdo)* to agree (**con** with); **su versión de los hechos no coincide con la de otros testigos** her version of events doesn't coincide *o* agree with that of other witnesses; **coincidimos en lo fundamental** we agree on the basic points; **coincidimos en opinar que...** we both agreed that...; **coincido contigo en que...** I agree with you that..., I am in agreement with you that...
(**d**) *(en un sitio)* **coincidimos en la fiesta** we were both at the party; **coincidí con ella en un congreso** I met her at a conference
(**e**) *(en el tiempo)* to coincide (**con** with); **mi cumpleaños coincide con el primer día de clase** my birthday falls on the first day of classes; **han coincidido tres accidentes en menos de dos meses** there have been three accidents in less than two months

coipo *nm* coypu

coito *nm* (sexual) intercourse

coitus interruptus *nm inv* coitus interruptus

cojear *vi* (**a**) *(persona, animal) (ser cojo)* to be lame; *(temporalmente)* to limp; **cojea desde el accidente** she's had a limp since the accident; **el perro cojea de una pata** the dog is lame in one leg; EXPR **ya sé de qué pie cojea** I know his weak points; EXPR **los dos cojean del mismo pie** they both have the same problem
(**b**) *(mueble)* to wobble
(**c**) *(razonamiento, frase)* to be faulty; **su teoría cojea en varios puntos** his theory has several weak points

cojera *nf* (**a**) *(acción)* limp (**b**) *(estado)* lameness

cojín *nm* cushion

cojinete *nm* (**a**) *(en eje)* bearing ►► ***c. de bolas*** ball bearing (**b**) *(en un riel de ferrocarril)* chair (**c**) *Col, Méx, Ven* **cojinetes** *(alforjas)* saddle-bags

cojo, -a 1 *ver* **coger**
2 *adj* (**a**) *(persona, animal)* lame; **el perro está c. de una pata** the dog is lame in one leg (**b**) *(mueble)* wobbly (**c**) *(razonamiento)* faulty; **tu explicación está un poco coja** your explanation doesn't quite ring true
3 *nm,f* cripple

cojón *Esp Vulg* 1 *nm* (**a**) *(testículo)* ball; **¿qué cojones haces tú aquí?** what the fuck are YOU doing here?; **¿quién cojones se ha creído que es?** who the fuck does he think he is?; **¡qué resfriado ni qué cojones!** don't give me that crap about having a cold!; EXPR **como una patada en los cojones: tu comentario le cayó** *o* **sentó como una patada en los cojones** she was well fucked off about your remark; EXPR **de los cojones: ya está llorando otra vez el niño de los cojones** that fucking child is crying again; EXPR **de cojones: esta comida está de cojones** this meal is *Br* bloody *o US* goddamn delicious; **es bueno/malo de cojones** it's *Br* bloody *o US* goddamn marvellous/awful; **hace un frío de cojones** it's fucking freezing; **esas gafas te sientan de cojones** those glasses look *Br* bloody *o US* goddamn brilliant on you; EXPR **de c. de mico: este asado está de c. de mico** this roast is *Br* bloody *o US* goddamn delicious; EXPR **hasta los cojones: estoy hasta los (mismísimos) cojones de nuestros vecinos** I've fucking well had it up to here with our neighbours; EXPR **no haber más cojones: era muy tarde y no hubo más cojones que pillar un taxi** it was late and we had no *o Br* bugger-all choice but to get a taxi; EXPR **manda cojones: ¡manda cojones que estando enfermo tenga que hacerlo yo!** fucking great *o* can you fucking believe it! I'm the one who has to do it, even though I'm ill!; EXPR **tus opiniones me las paso por el forro de los cojones** I couldn't give a shit *o Br* toss about what you think; EXPR **se le pusieron los cojones de corbata cuando se enteró** he nearly shat himself when he found out; EXPR **por cojones: ¡ahora lo vas a hacer por cojones!** you *Br* bloody *o US* goddamn well ARE going to do it!; EXPR **¡no me sale de los cojones!** I can't be *Br* bloody *o US* goddamn bothered!, *Br* I can't be arsed!; EXPR **¡no me toques** *o* **hinches los cojones y déjame en paz!** why can't you just fucking well leave me alone?; EXPR **tocarse los cojones: ahí está todo el día tocándose los cojones mientras nosotros trabajamos** he just sits around doing zilch *o Br* bugger-all all day long while we're busy working
(**b**) *(valor)* **tener cojones** *o* **un par de cojones** to have balls; **sí que tiene los cojones bien puestos, atreverse a contestar al jefe** he's certainly got balls, answering back to the boss; **le echó cojones al asunto, y le confesó la verdad** he screwed up every last fucking ounce of courage and confessed the truth to her; **¡qué cojones tiene, insultarme delante de todos!** what a fucking nerve, insulting me in front of everyone!; EXPR *Hum* **tiene más cojones que el caballo de Espartero** he's really got balls, that guy
2 *interj* **¡cojones!** *(expresa enfado)* for fuck's sake!; **¡que no voy a ir, cojones!** I'm not fucking going, all right?

cojonazos *nm inv Esp Vulg* **ser un c.** to be pussy-whipped

cojonudo, -a *adj muy Fam* (**a**) *Esp (estupendo) Br* bloody *o US* goddamn brilliant; **tus amigos son cojonudos** your friends are *Br* bloody *o US* goddamn brilliant guys; **me parece c., pero ahora no puedo ir** it sounds like *Br* bloody *o US* goddamn brilliant fun, but I can't go just now; *Irónico* **¡c., ahora no funciona la lavadora!** that's just *Br* bloody *o US* goddamn brilliant! now the washing machine isn't working!
(**b**) *RP muy Fam (valiente)* gutsy

cojudear *Andes* 1 *vt Fam (engañar)* to trick
2 *vi (hacer tonterías)* to piss about, to muck about

cojudez *nf Andes muy Fam* **¡qué c.!** *(acto)* what a *Br* bloody *o US* goddamn stupid thing to do!; *(dicho)* what a *Br* bloody *o US* goddamn stupid thing to say!; **decir/hacer una c.** to say/do something *Br* bloody *o US* goddamn stupid; **decir cojudeces** to talk a load of *Br* bloody *o US* goddamn nonsense; **hacer cojudeces** to act like a *Br* bloody *o US* goddamn idiot

cojudo, -a *adj Andes muy Fam Br* bloody *o US* goddamn stupid

cok *nm* coke

col *nf* cabbage; EXPR *Fam* **entre c. y c., lechuga** variety is the spice of life ►► ***c. de Bruselas*** Brussels sprout; ***c. lombarda*** red cabbage; ***c. rizada*** curly kale

cola *nf* (**a**) *(de mamífero, pez)* tail
(**b**) *(de ave)* tail
(**c**) *(de avión, cometa)* tail; EXPR *Bol, RP* **tener c. de paja** to be feeling guilty
(**d**) *(de vestido de novia)* train
(**e**) *(parte final) (de clase, lista)* bottom; *(de desfile)* end; **el país está a la c. del mundo civilizado en cuanto a inversiones educativas** the country has the worst record in the civilized world as regards investment in education; EXPR **ir a la c. del pelotón** to bring up the rear
(**f**) *(fila) Br* queue, *US* line; **hay mucha c.** there's a long *Br* queue *o US* line; **hacer** *o* **guardar c.** *Br* to queue (up), *US* to stand in line; **saltarse la c.** *Br* to jump the queue, *US* to cut in line; **llegué el último y me tuve que poner a la c.** I was the last to arrive, so I had to join the end of the *Br* queue *o US* line; **¡a la c.!** go to the back of the *Br* queue *o US* line! ►► *Informát* ***c. de impresión*** print queue
(**g**) *(pegamento)* glue; EXPR *Fam* **no pegan ni con c.: esa chaqueta y esos pantalones no pegan ni con c.** that jacket and those trousers clash horribly; **esos pantalones no pegan ni con c. en una fiesta tan formal** those trousers are totally inappropriate for such a formal do ►► ***c. de pescado*** fish glue
(**h**) *Fam (consecuencias)* EXPR **tener** *o* **traer c.** to have serious consequences *o* repercussions; **sus declaraciones tendrán** *o* **traerán c.** his statement won't be the end of it *o* won't be the last we hear of it; *RP* **comer c.** to suffer a setback
(**i**) *(peinado)* **c. (de caballo)** ponytail
(**j**) *(árbol)* cola tree
(**k**) *(sustancia excitante)* cola; **una bebida de c.** a cola drink
(**l**) *Fam (pene) Br* willy, *US* peter
(**m**) ***c. de caballo*** *(planta)* horse-tail
(**n**) ***c. de milano*** *(en carpintería)* dovetail; **ensamblar a** *o* **con c. de milano** to dovetail
(**o**) *Am Fam (nalgas) Br* bum, *US* fanny
(**p**) *Arg (de película)* trailer
(**q**) *Ven (autoestop)* **dar la c. a alguien** to give sb a lift; **pedir c.** to hitchhike

colaboración *nf* (**a**) *(cooperación)* collaboration; **hacer algo en c. con alguien** to do sth in collaboration with sb; **necesito tu c. para escribir el artículo** I need your help to write this article; **fue acusado de c. con banda armada** he was accused of collaborating with *o* helping a terrorist organization (**b**) *(de prensa)* contribution, article

colaboracionismo *nm Pey* collaborationism

colaboracionista *Pey* 1 *adj* collaborationist
2 *nmf* collaborator

colaborador, -ora 1 *adj* cooperative
2 *nm,f* (**a**) *(compañero)* associate, colleague (**b**) *(de prensa)* contributor, writer (**c**) ***c. externo*** freelancer

colaborar *vi* (**a**) *(cooperar)* to collaborate (**con** with); **algunos maridos se niegan a c. en las tareas domésticas** some husbands refuse to help with the housework; **muchas personas colaboraron en el rescate** many people helped in the rescue; **que cada uno colabore con lo que pueda** let everyone contribute what they can; **colaboró en la campaña con un donativo de 3 millones** she made a donation of 3 million to the campaign
(**b**) *(en prensa)* **c. en** *o* **con** to write for, to work for
(**c**) *(contribuir)* to contribute; **una dieta que colabora a controlar el**

nivel colesterol a diet which helps to control cholesterol levels; **los robots colaboran a incrementar la productividad** robots help to increase productivity, robots contribute to increased productivity

colación *nf* (**a**) *(para comer)* snack (**b**) *Am (dulce) Br* sweet, *US* candy (**c**) EXPR *Fam* **sacar** *o* **traer algo a c.** *(tema)* to bring sth up; **salir a c.** to come up

colada *nf* (**a**) *Esp (lavado)* laundry, washing; **echar algo a la c.** to put sth in the washing; **hacer la c.** to do the washing (**b**) *Esp (ropa limpia)* washing (**c**) *Geol* **c. (de lava)** lava flow (**d**) *(en alto horno)* tapping (**e**) *Dep Fam (internada)* run

coladera *nf* (**a**) *Am (colador)* colander (**b**) *Méx (alcantarilla)* sewer

coladero *nm Fam* (**a**) *(lugar)* easy way through; **la frontera del país se ha convertido en un c.** it has become very easy to get across the border; **la defensa del equipo es un c.** the team's defence is full of holes (**b**) *(colegio, universidad)* **ese colegio es un c.** anyone can pass the exams in that school

colado, -a *adj* (**a**) *(líquido)* strained (**b**) *Fam (enamorado)* **estar c. por alguien** to have a crush on sb

colador *nm (para líquidos)* strainer; *(para verdura)* colander; EXPR *Fam* **dejar como un c.** *(con agujeros)* to leave full of holes; *(a balazos)* to riddle with bullets

coladura *nf* (**a**) *(acción de colar)* straining (**b**) *Fam (chifladura)* crazy idea (**c**) *Fam (equivocación)* clanger; **fue una c. del gerente** it was the manager who slipped up

colage = **collage**

colágeno *nm* collagen

colapsado, -a *adj* (**a**) *(de actividad)* paralysed; *(de tráfico)* congested; **la oferta tuvo como consecuencia varias centralitas colapsadas** the offer led to several switchboards being jammed with calls (**b**) *(pulmón)* collapsed

colapsar 1 *vt* (**a**) *(actividad)* to bring to a halt, to stop; **el tráfico ha colapsado las calles** traffic has blocked the streets (**b**) *(pulmón)* to cause to collapse

2 **colapsarse** *vpr (mercado)* to collapse; **se ha colapsado el tráfico** traffic has ground to a halt; **la centralita se colapsó con llamadas de clientes** the switchboard was jammed with calls from customers

colapso *nm* (**a**) *Med (desvanecimiento)* collapse, breakdown; **sufrir un c.** to collapse (**b**) *(de pulmón)* collapse (**c**) *(de actividad)* collapse; **estar al borde del c.** to be on the brink of collapse; **la manifestación produjo el c. del tráfico** the demonstration brought traffic to a standstill

colar [64] 1 *vt* (**a**) *(leche, té, pasta)* to strain; *(café)* to filter

(**b**) *Fam (dinero falso)* to pass off as genuine; **han intentado colarme un billete falso** they tried to pass me a counterfeit *Br* note *o US* bill

(**c**) *Fam (mentira)* **les coló la excusa de que estaba enfermo** he gave them some story about being ill

(**d**) *(en cola)* **me coló** he let me *Br* jump the queue *o US* cut in line

(**e**) *(en sitio)* **nos coló en la fiesta** he got us into the party

(**f**) *(introducir)* to slip, to squeeze (**por** through); **coló el balón entre las piernas del portero** he slipped the ball through the goalkeeper's legs

2 *vi Fam (pasar por bueno)* **esto no colará** this won't wash; **mi historia coló y no me hicieron más preguntas** they swallowed my story and didn't ask me any more questions

3 **colarse** *vpr* (**a**) *(líquido, gas)* **colarse por** to seep through; **el aire se cuela por esta rendija** air passes through this crack; **las llaves se colaron por la alcantarilla** the keys dropped down the drain; **el balón se coló por la portería sin que ningún jugador pudiera detenerlo** the ball just slipped into the goal and no one could stop it

(**b**) *(en cola)* to *Br* jump the queue *o US* cut in line; **¡eh, no te cueles!** *Br* oi, don't jump the queue!, *US* hey, don't cut in line!

(**c**) *(en sitio)* to slip, to sneak (**en** into); **se colaron en el tren** they slipped *o* sneaked onto the train without paying; **colarse en una fiesta** to gatecrash a party; **nos colamos por la puerta de atrás** we sneaked in (by) the back door

(**d**) *Fam (equivocarse)* to slip up; **te has colado, no es mi hermana** you've got it wrong, she's not my sister

(**e**) *Fam (enamorarse)* **colarse por alguien** to fall for sb

colateral *adj* (**a**) *(efecto)* collateral, secondary; **un medicamento sin efectos colaterales** a medicine with no side effects; **daños colaterales** *(en guerra)* collateral damage (**b**) *(a ambos lados)* on either side (**c**) *(línea, recta)* collateral (**d**) *(pariente)* collateral

colcha *nf* bedspread

colchón *nm* (**a**) *(de cama)* mattress ►► ***c. de agua*** waterbed mattress; ***c. hinchable*** air bed; ***c. inflable*** air bed; ***c. de muelles*** spring mattress; ***c. neumático*** air bed (**b**) *(en asunto, negociación)* cushion, buffer (**c**) *Fin* cushion (**d**) *Informát* buffer (**e**) ***c. de aire*** *(en aerodeslizador)* air cushion

colchonero, -a 1 *nm,f* upholsterer, mattress-maker

2 *adj Fam Dep* = of/relating to Atlético de Madrid Football Club

colchoneta *nf (hinchable)* air bed, lilo®; *(en gimnasio)* mat; *(colchón fino)* narrow mattress

cole *nm Fam* school

colear 1 *vt* (**a**) *Col, Méx, Ven (res)* to throw down by the tail (**b**) *Chile (examen)* to fail (**c**) *Col, Méx Fam (molestar)* to bother, to annoy

2 *vi* (**a**) *(animal)* to wag its tail (**b**) *(asunto, problema)* to drag on; **todavía colea el escándalo** the scandal is still dragging on

3 **colearse** *vpr Arg, Ven (patinar)* to skid

colección *nf* (**a**) *(de sellos, objetos)* collection ►► ***la c. permanente*** *(de museo)* the permanent collection (**b**) *Fam (gran cantidad)* **tiene una c. de primos** he has loads of cousins; **cometió una c. de errores** he made a whole series of mistakes; **no dijo más que una c. de tonterías** he talked a load of nonsense (**c**) *(de moda)* collection; **la c. de primavera** the spring collection

coleccionable 1 *adj* collectable

2 *nm* = special supplement in serialized form

coleccionar *vt* to collect

coleccionismo *nm* collecting

coleccionista *nmf* collector

colecta *nf* (**a**) *(de dinero)* collection; **hacer una c.** to collect money, to organize a collection (**b**) *Rel* collect

colectar *vt* to collect

colectivamente *adv* collectively, together

colectivero, -a *nm,f Arg* bus driver

colectividad *nf* community

colectivismo *nm Pol* collectivism

colectivista *Pol* 1 *adj* collectivist

2 *nmf* collectivist

colectivización *nf* collectivization

colectivizar [14] *vt* to collectivize

colectivo, -a 1 *adj* (**a**) *(responsabilidad)* collective; *(iniciativa)* joint; *(suicidio, despidos)* mass; **el interés c.** collective interests; **transporte c.** public transport

(**b**) *Ling* collective

2 *nm* (**a**) *(grupo)* group; *(en estadística)* collective, population; **es miembro de un c. pacifista** she is a member of a pacifist group; **una reforma que afecta especialmente al c. médico** a reform which affects the medical community in particular

(**b**) *Ling (nombre)* collective noun

(**c**) *Andes (taxi)* collective taxi *(with a fixed rate and that travels a fixed route)*

(**d**) *Arg, Bol (autobús)* bus

(**e**) *RP (regalo)* = money from a whipround deposited by friends in a bank account or at a shop as a wedding present

colector, -ora 1 *adj* collecting

2 *nm,f (persona)* collector

3 *nm* (**a**) *(sumidero)* sewer ►► ***c. de basuras*** garbage chute (**b**) *Tec (de motor)* manifold ►► ***c. solar*** solar collector (**c**) *Elec (de transistor)* collector

colega *nmf* (**a**) *(compañero profesional)* colleague, *US* co-worker (**b**) *(homólogo)* counterpart, opposite number (**c**) *Esp Fam (amigo)* pal, *Br* mate, *US* buddy; **voy a salir con mis colegas** I'm going out with my pals *o Br* mates *o US* buddies; **¿te puedo ayudar, c.?** can I help you, pal *o Br* mate *o US* buddy?

colegiación *nf* = membership of a professional association

colegiado, -a 1 *adj* = who belongs to a professional association

2 *nm,f* (**a**) *(profesional)* = member of a professional association (**b**) *Dep (árbitro)* referee

colegial[1] 1 *adj* (**a**) *(de colegio)* school; **las instalaciones colegiales** the school premises (**b**) *(de colegio profesional)* **el estatuto c.** the association's statutes; **una organización c.** a professional association

colegial[2]**, -ala** *nm,f* schoolboy, *f* schoolgirl; **cartera/uniforme de c.** school bag/uniform

colegiarse *vpr* to join a professional association

colegiata *nf* collegiate church

colegiatura *nf* (**a**) *Andes, CAm, Méx (matrícula)* tuition fees (**b**) *Chile, Col, RP (colegiación)* = membership of a professional association

colegio *nm* (**a**) *(escuela)* school; **ir al c.** to go to school; **mañana no hay c.** there's no school tomorrow; **durante mis años de c.** while I was at school ►► *Esp* ***c. concertado*** state-subsidized (private) school; ***c. de curas*** school run by priests, Catholic boys' school; ***c. de educación especial*** special school; ***c. estatal*** *Br* state school, *US* public school; ***c. homologado*** officially approved school; ***c. de monjas*** convent school; ***c. nacional*** state primary school; ***c. de pago*** fee-paying school; ***c. de párvulos*** infant school; ***c. privado*** private school; ***c. público*** *Br* state school, *US* public school; ***c. universitario*** college
(**b**) *(de profesionales)* **c. (profesional)** professional association ►► ***c. de abogados*** bar association; ***c. cardenalicio*** college of cardinals; ***c. de médicos*** medical association
(**c**) *Pol* ***c. electoral*** *(lugar)* polling station; *(votantes)* ward
(**d**) *Esp* ***c. mayor*** hall of residence

colegir [55] *vi* to infer, to gather (**de** from); **de ahí se puede c. que...** it can thus be inferred that...

colegislador, -ora *adj (asamblea)* joint legislative

colegui *nmf Esp Fam (amigo)* pal, *Br* mate, *US* buddy

cóleo *nm* coleus

coleóptero *Zool* **1** *nm* coleopteran, member of the order *Coleoptera*
2 coleópteros *nmpl (orden) Coleoptera*; **del orden de los coleópteros** of the order *Coleoptera*

cólera 1 *nm (enfermedad)* cholera
2 *nf (ira)* anger, rage; **descargar la c. en alguien** to vent one's anger on sb; **montar en c.** to get angry, to fly into a temper *o* rage; **dejarse llevar por la c.** to lose one's temper

colérico, -a *adj* (**a**) *(furioso)* furious; **estar c.** to be furious (**b**) *(irritable) (gesto)* bad-tempered; **ser c.** *(persona)* to be quick-tempered

colesterol *nm* cholesterol; **tener el c. alto** *o* **elevado** to have a high cholesterol level

coleta *nf* (**a**) *(de pelo)* pigtail; EXPR **cortarse la c.** *(torero)* to retire (from bullfighting); **si este fin de semana no ganamos, me corto la c.** if we don't win this weekend, I'm going to call it a day *o* pack it in
(**b**) *Ven (paño)* floor cloth

coletazo *nm* (**a**) *(golpe)* flick *o* swish of the tail; **un c. de la ballena hundió la embarcación** a blow from the whale's tail sank the boat (**b**) *(de crisis, régimen)* **está dando los últimos coletazos** it's in its death throes

coletilla *nf (de discurso, escrito)* closing comment

coleto *nm* (**a**) *(vestidura)* jerkin (**b**) *Fam (adentros)* inner self; **decir para su c.** to say to oneself; **echarse algo al c.** *(comida)* to put sth away; *(bebida)* to knock sth back; **echarse un libro al c.** to read a book right through (**c**) *Ven (paño)* floor cloth

colgado, -a 1 *adj* (**a**) *(cuadro, jamón, camisa)* hanging (**de** from)
(**b**) *(teléfono)* on the hook; **deben tener el teléfono mal c.** they can't have put the receiver back properly
(**c**) *Fam (atontado, loco)* crazy, daft
(**d**) *Fam (abandonado)* **dejar c. a alguien** to leave sb in the lurch; **cancelaron la excursión y me quedé c. todo el fin de semana** they cancelled the trip and I was left with nothing to do all weekend
(**e**) *Fam (enganchado)* **quedarse c. (con)** to get hooked (on); **está c. de María** he's stuck on Maria; **está c. del alcohol** he can't stay off the drink; **se pasa el día c. del teléfono** he's on the phone all day long
(**f**) *Fam (pendiente)* **tengo c. el inglés del curso pasado** I have to resit the exam for last year's English course
(**g**) *Fam (drogado)* stoned
2 *nm,f Fam* (**a**) *(atontado, loco)* loony, *Br* nutter
(**b**) *(desamparado)* drip
(**c**) *(drogadicto)* junkie

colgador *nm* (**a**) *(percha)* hanger, coat hanger (**b**) *(gancho)* hook

colgadura *nf* (wall) hanging; **pusieron colgaduras en los balcones** they hung banners from the balconies

colgajo *nm* (**a**) *(tela)* hanging piece of material; *(hilo)* loose thread; **le gusta llevar colgajos al cuello** she likes to wear dangly necklaces (**b**) *(de piel)* flap

colgante 1 *adj* hanging
2 *nm* pendant

colgar [16] **1** *vt* (**a**) *(suspender)* to hang; **colgó el cuadro** she hung (up) the picture; **colgó la camisa en la percha** he hung the shirt on the coat hanger; **colgaron el anuncio en el tablón** they put the notice on the board; **cuelga el reloj de ese clavo** hang the clock on that nail
(**b**) *(ahorcar)* to hang; **lo colgaron por asesino** he was hanged for murder
(**c**) *(teléfono)* **c. el teléfono** to hang up; **me colgó en mitad de la frase** she hung up on me when I was in mid-sentence
(**d**) *(abandonar)* to give up; **c. los hábitos** to give up the cloth, to leave the clergy; *(renunciar)* to give up one's job; **c. las botas** to hang up one's boots; **c. los estudios** to abandon one's studies; **c. los guantes** to hang up one's gloves
(**e**) *(imputar)* **c. algo a alguien** to pin the blame for sth on sb; **le colgaron un robo que no había cometido** they pinned a robbery on him that he hadn't committed
(**f**) *(endilgar)* **le colgaron ese apodo en la escuela** he got that nickname at school; **le colgaron el sambenito de despistado** he got a name for being absent-minded
(**g**) *Informát (ordenador, computador)* to crash
2 *vi* (**a**) *(pender)* to hang (**de** from); **hay un cable que cuelga** there's a cable hanging loose
(**b**) *(tela, prenda de vestir)* to hang down; **el abrigo cuelga por atrás** the coat hangs down at the back
(**c**) *(hablando por teléfono)* to hang up, to put the phone down; **no cuelgue, por favor** hold the line, please
3 colgarse *vpr* (**a**) *(suspenderse)* to hang (**de** from); **no te cuelgues de esa rama o se romperá** don't hang from that branch, or it will break; **se colgó del cuello de su abuelo** he threw his arms round his grandfather's neck (**b**) *(ahorcarse)* to hang oneself (**de** from) (**c**) *Informát (ordenador, computador)* to crash; **se me ha colgado el ordenador** my computer has crashed

colibrí (*pl* **colibrís** *o* **colibríes**) *nm* hummingbird ►► ***c. gallardete*** streamertail

cólico *nm* colic ►► ***c. biliar*** biliary colic; ***c. hepático*** biliary colic; ***c. nefrítico*** renal colic; ***c. renal*** renal colic

colicorto *nm* short-tailed opossum

colíder *nmf* joint leader

coliflor *nf* cauliflower

coligación *nf* alliance

coligar [38] **1** *vt* to ally, to unite
2 coligarse *vpr* to unite, to join together

colijo *ver* **colegir**

colilla *nf* cigarette butt *o* stub

colimba *nf Arg Fam* military service

colimbo *nm (ave)* diver ►► ***c. ártico*** black-throated diver; ***c. chico*** red-throated diver; ***c. grande*** great northern diver

colimense 1 *adj* of/from Colima *(Mexico)*
2 *nmf* person from Colima *(Mexico)*

colín *nm* (**a**) *Esp (de pan)* breadstick (**b**) *(ave)* ***c. de Virginia*** (northern) bobwhite

colina *nf* hill

colinabo *nm* kohlrabi

colindante *adj* neighbouring, adjacent

colindar *vi* to be adjacent, to adjoin; **el edificio colinda con dos parques** the building is adjacent to two parks

colirio *nm* eyewash, eye-drops

colirrojo *nm* ***c. americano*** American redstart; ***c. real*** redstart; ***c. tizón*** black redstart

colisa *nf Chile (sombrero)* straw hat

coliseo *nm* coliseum

colisión *nf* (**a**) *(de vehículos)* collision, crash; *(de placas tectónicas, asteroides)* collision ►► ***c. frontal*** head-on collision; ***c. múltiple*** pile-up (**b**) *(de ideas, intereses)* clash; **sus planes están en abierta c. con los de la dirección** his plans are in direct conflict with those of management

colisionar *vi* (**a**) *(vehículo)* to collide, to crash (**con** *o* **contra** into); *(placas tectónicas, asteroides)* to collide (**b**) *(ideas, intereses)* to clash

colista 1 *adj* bottom, at the bottom; **el equipo c.** the bottom team
2 *nmf (en liga)* bottom team; *(en carreras)* tailender

colistero, -a *nm,f Fam Informát* list member

colitigante *nmf* joint litigant

colitis *nf inv* (**a**) *(inflamación del colon)* colitis (**b**) *(diarrea)* **tener c.** to have an upset stomach

colla *Bol* **1** *adj* of/from the altiplano
2 *nmf* = indigenous person from the altiplano

collado *nm* (**a**) *(colina)* hill (**b**) *(entre montañas)* saddle

collage, colage [ko'laʃ] *nm* collage

collalba *nf* (**a**) *(ave)* wheatear ►► ***c. gris*** wheatear; ***c. negra*** black wheatear; ***c. rubia*** black-eared wheatear (**b**) *(mazo)* mallet

collar *nm* (**a**) *(para personas)* necklace; **un c. de diamantes** a diamond necklace ►► ***c. ortopédico*** surgical collar (**b**) *(para animales)* collar ►► ***c. antiparasitario*** flea collar (**c**) *(abrazadera)* collar, ring

collarín *nm* surgical collar

collarino *nm Arquit* necking, gorgerin

colleja *nf* (**a**) *(golpe)* **darle una c. a alguien** to slap sb *o* give sb a slap on the back of the neck (**b**) *(planta)* campion

collera *nf* (**a**) *Andes (gemelo)* cufflink (**b**) *Andes (yunta)* brace, yoke

collie ['koli] *nm* collie

colmado, -a 1 *adj* full to the brim (**de** with); **está c. de problemas** he is loaded down with problems
2 *nm (tienda)* grocer's (shop)

colmar *vt* (**a**) *(recipiente)* to fill (to the brim) (**b**) *(aspiración, deseo)* to fulfil; **c. a alguien de regalos/elogios** to shower sb with gifts/praise; **este premio colma con creces mis aspiraciones** this prize is more than I'd ever hoped for; **el bebé colmó de felicidad a la familia** the baby brought so much happiness into the family's lives

colmatación *nf Geol* silting (up)

colmena *nf* beehive

colmenar *nm* apiary

colmenero, -a *nm,f* beekeeper

colmenilla *nf* morel (mushroom)

colmillo *nm* (**a**) *(de persona)* canine, eye tooth; *(de perro)* fang; *Fig* **enseñar los colmillos** to show one's teeth (**b**) *(de elefante, morsa)* tusk

colmo *nm* height; **el c. de la estupidez** the height of stupidity; **es el c. de la locura** it's sheer madness; **¡es el c. de la desfachatez!** what a cheek *o* nerve!; **lo suyo es el c. de la mala suerte** what happened to her was really bad luck; **para c.** to crown it all; **para c. de males, llovió** to make matters worse, it rained; **¡eso es el c.!** that's the last straw!; **¡es el c., es la tercera vez que llamo y no me hacen caso!** it's getting beyond a joke! this is the third time I've called and they're not paying any attention!

colocación *nf* (**a**) *(acción)* placing, positioning; **yo me encargaré de la c. de los cuadros** I'll see to the hanging of the paintings (**b**) *(posición)* place, position; **se encontraba en una c. inmejorable** she was in a perfect position (**c**) *(empleo)* position, job; **oficina de c.** employment agency (**d**) *Bolsa* placing, placement; **c. de acciones** placing *o* placement of shares (**e**) *Ling* collocation

colocado, -a 1 *adj* (**a**) *(en lugar)* placed; **marcó gol con un tiro raso y c.** he scored with a very low, well-placed shot (**b**) **estar muy bien c.** *(en empleo)* to have a very good job; **todavía no tiene al hijo c.** he hasn't found his son a job yet (**c**) *(en carreras de caballos)* **Capirote llegó c.** Capirote finished second (**d**) *Fam (drogado)* high, stoned; *(borracho)* blind drunk, smashed
2 *nm (en rugby)* place kick

colocador *nm Ling* collocate, collocator

colocar [60] 1 *vt* (**a**) *(en un sitio)* to place, to put; **c. una bomba** to plant a bomb; **el acomodador coloca a los espectadores en sus asientos** the usher shows the audience to their seats; **vuelve a c. ese libro donde estaba** put that book back where it was; **nos colocaron en la parte de atrás del avión** they put us in the rear section of the plane
(**b**) *(en una posición)* **c. los brazos en alto** to raise one's arms; **hay que c. bien ese cuadro, pues está torcido** that picture needs to be hung properly, it isn't straight
(**c**) *(en un empleo)* to find a job for; **colocó a su hijo de abogado en su empresa** he found his son a job as a lawyer in his own firm
(**d**) *(casar)* to marry off
(**e**) *Bolsa (acciones)* to place; *(dinero)* to invest; **coloqué mis ahorros en acciones** I invested my savings in shares; **colocaron un millón de títulos** they placed a million in bonds
(**f**) *(endilgar)* to palm off (**a** on); **le colocaron una moto que no funciona** they palmed a motorbike off on him that doesn't work; **el vendedor me intentó c. un modelo más caro** the salesman tried to get me to buy a more expensive model
(**g**) *Fam (sujeto: droga)* to give a high to; **¿a ti te coloca la marihuana?** does marihuana give you a high?
2 *vi Fam (droga, alcohol)* **este costo coloca cantidad** this hash gives you a real high; **este ponche coloca mucho** this punch is strong stuff
3 **colocarse** *vpr* (**a**) *(en una posición, en un lugar) (de pie)* to stand; *(sentado)* to sit; **colócate en tu asiento** sit in your seat; **oiga, colóquese en la fila** hey, *Br* get in the queue *o US* get in line; **el equipo se ha colocado en cabeza de la clasificación** the team tops the league; **con esta victoria se coloca entre los mejores tenistas del mundo** this win puts him among the world's top tennis players; **colócate boca arriba** lie face upwards, lie on your back
(**b**) *(en un empleo)* to get a job; **me he colocado de guardia jurado** I've got a job as a security guard
(**c**) *Fam (emborracharse)* to get smashed *o* blind drunk; *(drogarse)* to get high *o* stoned; **con dos cervezas ya se coloca** two beers and he's well away

colocolo *nm Chile* pampas cat

colocón *nm Fam* **llevar un c.** *(de droga)* to be high; *(de bebida)* to be *Br* pissed *o US* loaded; **pillar un c.** *(de droga)* to get high; *(de bebida)* to get *Br* pissed *o US* loaded

colofón *nm* (**a**) *(remate, fin)* climax, culmination; **como c. a la ceremonia** as a coda to the ceremony, to round off the ceremony; **aquel triunfo fue un excelente c. a una larga carrera** that win was a fitting end to a long career (**b**) *(de libro)* colophon

colofonia, colofonía *nf* rosin

coloidal, coloideo, -a *adj* colloidal

coloide *adj* colloid

coloideo = **coloidal**

Colombia *n* Colombia

colombianismo *nm* = word or expression peculiar to Colombian Spanish

colombiano, -a 1 *adj* Colombian
2 *nm,f* Colombian

colombicultura *nf* pigeon breeding

colombina *nf Col (dulce)* lollipop

colombino, -a *adj* = relating to Christopher Columbus

Colombo *n* Colombo

colombofilia *nf* pigeon-fancying

colombófilo, -a 1 *adj* pigeon-fancying
2 *nm,f* pigeon fancier

colon *nm Anat* colon ▸▸ ***c. irritable*** irritable bowel syndrome

Colón *n pr* **Cristóbal C.** Christopher Columbus

colón, -ona 1 *nm,f Fam (que se cuela) Br* queue-jumper, *US* line-jumper; **¡eh, no seas c.!** *Br* hey, there's a queue here!, *US* hey, don't cut in line!
2 *nm (moneda)* colon

colonense 1 *adj* of/from Colón *(Panama)*
2 *nmf* person from Colón *(Panama)*

Colonia *n* Cologne

colonia *nf* (**a**) *(estado dependiente)* colony
(**b**) *(campamento)* **c. (de verano)** (summer) camp; **ir de colonias** to go on a summer camp ▸▸ ***c. nudista*** nudist camp *o* colony
(**c**) *(de animales)* colony; **una c. de focas** a seal colony
(**d**) *(de personas)* community; **la c. mexicana en Argentina** the Mexican community in Argentina
(**e**) *(perfume)* eau de Cologne; **me gusta la c. que usa tu novio** I like your boyfriend's aftershave
(**f**) *(urbanización)* housing development
(**g**) *Méx (barrio)* district ▸▸ ***c. proletaria*** working-class district, working-class estate
(**h**) *Carib (hacienda)* sugarcane plantation

coloniaje *nm Am* (**a**) *(época)* colonial period (**b**) *(gobierno)* colonial government

colonial 1 *adj* colonial
2 **coloniales** *nmpl Esp* **(tienda de) coloniales** (fancy) grocery, delicatessen

colonialismo *nm* colonialism

colonialista 1 *adj* colonialist
2 *nmf* colonialist

colonización *nf* colonization

colonizador, -ora 1 *adj* colonizing
2 *nm,f* colonizer, colonist

colonizar [14] *vt* to colonize

colono *nm* (**a**) *(colonizador)* settler, colonist (**b**) *(agricultor)* tenant farmer

colopatía *nf Med* colonopathy, colopathy

coloquial *adj* colloquial

coloquialmente *adv* colloquially

coloquio *nm* (**a**) *(conversación)* conversation (**b**) *(debate)* discussion, debate (**c**) *Am (simposio)* conference, symposium

COLOR *nm* (**a**) *(que se ve)* colour; **lápices de colores** coloured pencils; **un vestido de colores** a colourful *o* brightly coloured dress; **¿de qué c.?** what colour?; **c. azul** blue; **c. rojo** red; **es de c. azul** it's blue; **pintó las sillas de c. verde** she painted the chairs green; **a todo c.** in full colour; **nos dieron un folleto con fotos a todo c.** they gave us a full-colour brochure; **ha agarrado un c. muy bueno durante sus**

vacaciones she's got a nice tan on her *Br* holiday *o US* vacation; **cambiar** *o* **mudar de c.** to change colour; *Fig (palidecer)* to turn pale; *Fig (sonrojarse)* to blush; **dar c. a algo** to colour sth in; *Fig* to brighten *o* liven sth up; **de c.** *(persona)* coloured; **voy a hacer una colada con ropa de c.** I'm going to wash the coloureds; **fotos en c.** colour photos; **televisión en c.** colour television; **deja el pollo en el horno hasta que comience a tomar c.** leave the chicken in the oven until it starts to brown ►► *Imprenta* ***c. aditivo*** additive colour; ***colores complementarios*** complementary colours; *Imprenta* ***c. directo*** spot colour; *Imprenta* ***c. plano*** spot colour; ***c. primario*** primary colour; ***c. sólido*** fast colour

(**b**) *(para pintar)* paint; **colores** *(lápices)* coloured pencils; **le gusta darse un poco de c. en la cara antes de salir** she likes to put a bit of colour *o* rouge on her cheeks before going out

(**c**) *(aspecto)* tone; **no tienes muy buen c.** you look a bit off-colour; **la situación adquirió un c. trágico** the situation took on tragic overtones

(**d**) *(ideología)* **se le nota su c. político** you can tell his political persuasion; **la televisión pública tiene un claro c. gubernamental** the state-run television channels are clearly biased in favour of the government

(**e**) *(raza)* colour; **sin distinción de credo ni c.** regardless of creed or colour

(**f**) *(animación)* colour; **las fiestas de mi pueblo han ido perdiendo c.** the festivals in my home town have lost a lot of their colour; **el carnaval es una fiesta llena de c.** carnival is a colourful festival ►► ***c. local*** local colour

(**g**) *(en los naipes)* suit

(**h**) *(bandera, camiseta)* **los colores nacionales** the national colours; **defender los colores del Académico** *(el equipo)* to play for Académico; **el equipo defendió con orgullo sus colores** the players showed great pride in fighting for their team

(**i**) *Formal (pretexto)* **so c. de** under the pretext of

(**j**) EXPR *Esp* **no hay c.** it's no contest; **entre tu modelo y el mío, no hay c.** there's no comparison between my model and yours; *Fam* **ponerse de mil colores: la descubrieron copiando y se puso de mil colores** she went bright red *o* as red as a beetroot when they caught her copying; **sacar los colores (a la cara) a alguien** to make sb blush; **subido de c.** *(chiste etc)* risqué, *esp US* off-colour; **ver las cosas de c. de rosa** to see things through rose-coloured *o* rose-tinted spectacles

---

coloración *nf* (**a**) *(acción)* colouring (**b**) *(color)* coloration, colouring (**c**) *(de animal)* markings ►► ***c. defensiva*** protective markings

colorado, -a **1** *adj* (**a**) *(color)* red; **ponerse c.** to blush, to go red; **tenía la cara colorada** his face was flushed; **me vas a poner c. con tantos elogios** I'm going to blush *o* go red with so much praise (**b**) *Andes, RP (pelirrojo)* red-haired

2 *nm (color)* red

3 *nm,f* (**a**) *Andes, RP (pelirrojo)* red-haired person, redhead (**b**) *Par, Urug Pol* = member of the Colorado party

Falso amigo: El adjetivo **coloured** no es la traducción del español **colorado**. En inglés, **coloured** significa "coloreado" o "de color".

colorante **1** *adj* colouring

2 *nm* (**a**) *(aditivo alimentario)* colouring; **sin colorantes ni conservantes** *(en etiqueta)* no artificial colourings or preservatives (**b**) *(tinte)* dye, colorant

coloratura *nf Mús* (**a**) *(pasaje)* coloratura, coloratura passage (**b**) *(cantante)* coloratura, coloratura soprano

colorear *vt* to colour (in)

colorete *nm* (**a**) *(en las mejillas)* **tener coloretes** to be red in the face (**b**) *(maquillaje) (de mejillas)* rouge, blusher (**c**) *Andes (maquillaje) (de labios)* lipstick

colorido *nm* (**a**) *(color)* colourfulness; **un cuadro con un c. estridente** a luridly coloured painting; **el c. del pez atrae a sus víctimas** the fish's colouring attracts its victims; *Fig* **una fiesta de gran c.** a very colourful local festival (**b**) *(brillo)* verve, style; **el ensayo tiene poco c.** the essay has a rather poor style

colorín *nm* (**a**) *(color fuerte)* bright colour; **de colorines** brightly coloured (**b**) **y c. colorado, este cuento se ha acabado** and that's the end of the story (**c**) *(jilguero)* goldfinch

colorismo *nm* (**a**) *(de pintor)* colourist style (**b**) *(del lenguaje)* floridity

colorista **1** *adj* colouristic

2 *nmf* colourist

colosal *adj* (**a**) *(estatura, tamaño)* colossal (**b**) *(extraordinario)* enormous; *(descaro)* incredible; **el tenor estuvo c.** the tenor was amazing *o* sensational

coloso *nm* (**a**) *(estatua)* colossus (**b**) *(cosa, persona)* giant

colostomía *nf Med* colostomy

cólquico *nm* meadow saffron

colt® [kolt] (*pl* **colts**) *nm* Colt®; **un c. del 45** a Colt 45

coludir *vi Der* to collude

columbrar *vt* (**a**) *(divisar)* to make out (**b**) *(conjeturar)* to guess

columna *nf* (**a**) *(en edificio)* column, pillar ►► ***c. corintia*** Corinthian column; ***c. dórica*** Doric column: ***c. jónica*** Ionic column; ***c. salomónica*** = twisted architectural column, *Espec* Solomonic column

(**b**) *(apoyo)* pillar ►► ***c. vertebral*** spinal column, spine; *Fig* **este tratado es la c. vertebral de la organización** this treaty is the backbone of the organization

(**c**) *(de texto)* column; **un artículo a cuatro columnas** a four-column article; **la c. de opinión** the opinion column

(**d**) *(de soldados, tanques)* column; **marchar en c. de a dos** to march two abreast *o* two by two

(**e**) *(de humo, mercurio)* column

(**f**) *(altavoz)* loudspeaker

(**g**) *Aut* ***c. de dirección*** steering column

columnata *nf* colonnade

columnista *nmf* columnist

columpiada *nf Fam (equivocación)* blunder

columpiar **1** *vt* to push *(on a swing)*

2 columpiarse *vpr* (**a**) *(mecerse)* to swing (**b**) *Fam (equivocarse)* to make a blunder, to put one's foot in it

columpio *nm* swing; **los columpios** the children's playground

colusión *nf* collusion

colutorio *nm* mouthwash, gargle

colza *nf* rape; **aceite de c.** rapeseed oil

coma[1] *nf* (**a**) *(signo ortográfico)* comma; *Fig* **sin faltar una c.** word for word (**b**) *Mat* $\simeq$ decimal point; **tres c. cuatro** *(escrito 3,4)* three point four ►► ***c. decimal*** decimal point (**c**) *Informát* ***c. flotante*** floating point (**d**) *Mús* comma

coma[2] *nm (médico)* coma; **estar en (estado de) c.** to be in a coma; **entrar en c.** to go *o* fall into a coma ►► ***c. etílico*** = coma caused by alcoholic poisoning; ***c. profundo*** deep coma

comadre *nf* (**a**) *(pariente)* **es mi c.** *(madrina de mi hijo)* she's godmother to my son; *(madre de mi ahijado)* I'm godmother to her son (**b**) *Pey (mujer chismosa)* gossip, gossipmonger (**c**) *(vecina)* neighbour (**d**) *Fam (amiga) Br* mate, *US* buddy

comadrear *vi* to gossip

comadreja *nf* weasel

comadreo *nm* gossiping; **le encanta el c.** she loves gossiping *o* to gossip; **se pasaron toda la tarde de c.** they spent the whole afternoon gossiping

comadrona *nf* midwife

comal *nm CAm, Méx* = flat clay or metal dish used for baking "tortillas"

comanche **1** *adj* Comanche

2 *nmf* Comanche

comandancia *nf* (**a**) *(rango)* command (**b**) *(edificio)* command headquarters (**c**) *Méx (comisaría)* police station

comandante *nmf* (**a**) *(en ejército) (rango)* major ►► ***c. en jefe*** commander-in-chief (**b**) *(en ejército) (de un puesto)* commander, commandant (**c**) *(de avión)* captain; **les habla el c.** this is your captain speaking (**d**) *Méx (comisario) Br* superintendent, *US* captain

comandar *vt* (**a**) *Mil* to command (**b**) *Dep (clasificación)* to lead, to head; **comandan la clasificación con 53 puntos** they are top of the table with 53 points

comandita: en comandita *loc adv Fam* **hacer algo en c.** to do something all together

comanditar *vt Com* to finance as a silent partner

comanditario, -a *Com* **1** *adj* silent

2 *nm,f* silent partner

comando *nm* (**a**) *(grupo armado)* commando ►► ***c. legal*** = terrorist cell, the members of which have no criminal records; ***c. suicida*** suicide squad; ***c. terrorista*** terrorist cell (**b**) *(miembro de grupo)* commando (**c**) *Informát* command ►► ***c. externo*** external command; ***c. interno*** internal command

comarca *nf* = administrative unit smaller than a region and larger than a municipality, ≃ district; **una c. arrocera** a rice-growing area

comarcal *adj* local; **un problema de ámbito c.** a local problem; **carretera c.** minor road

comarcano, -a *adj* nearby, neighbouring

comatoso, -a *adj* comatose

comay *nf Cuba Fam (vecina)* neighbour; **mi c. María** my friend Maria

comba *nf* (**a**) *Esp (juego)* skipping; **jugar** *o* **saltar a la c.** *Br* to skip, *US* to jump rope; EXPR *Fam* **no perder c.: no pierde c. para decir lo que siente** she never misses an opportunity to say what she feels; **tu amigo no pierde c., se entera de todo lo que pasa** your friend never misses a trick, he always knows what's going on

(**b**) *Esp (cuerda) Br* skipping rope, *US* jump rope

(**c**) *(de madera)* warp; *(de alambre, barra)* bend; *(de pared)* bulge; *(de viga)* sag

combado, -a *adj* warped

combadura *nf (de madera)* warp; *(de alambre, barra)* bend; *(de pared)* bulge; *(de viga)* sag

combar 1 *vt (alambre, barra, viga de metal)* to bend; *(pared)* to cause to bulge; *(puerta, viga de madera)* to warp

2 combarse *vpr (alambre, barra, viga de metal)* to bend; *(pared)* to bulge; *(puerta, viga de madera)* to warp

combate *nm* (**a**) *(militar)* combat; **el c. se produjo por la noche** the battle took place during the night; **caer** *o* **morir en c.** to die in combat *o* battle ►► ***c. cuerpo a cuerpo*** hand-to-hand combat

(**b**) *(lucha)* fight; **el c. contra las drogas/el desempleo** the fight against drugs/unemployment; **un c. desigual** an uneven contest; *también Fig* **dejar a alguien fuera de c.** to knock sb out; **este coche ha quedado fuera de c.** this car has had it

(**c**) *(en boxeo, artes marciales)* fight, contest; **deporte de c.** combat sport ►► ***c. de boxeo*** boxing match; ***c. de lucha libre*** wrestling match; ***c. por el título*** title fight

combatiente 1 *adj (ejército)* **los ejércitos combatientes** the armies involved in the conflict

2 *nmf (de ejército)* soldier; *(de guerrilla)* fighter; **ex c.** veteran

3 *nm (ave)* ruff

combatir 1 *vt* (**a**) *(ejércitos)* to combat, to fight; **c. al enemigo** to fight the enemy (**b**) *(problemas)* to combat, to fight; **c. el frío** to combat the cold; **combatieron todos los intentos de aprobar la ley** they fought against all attempts to pass the law; **un producto para c. la caries** a product which fights tooth decay

2 *vi* to fight (**contra** against); **combatió junto a los aliados** he fought with the allies; **combatió por la república** he fought for the republic

combatividad *nf* fighting spirit

combativo, -a *adj* (**a**) *(agresivo)* aggressive, combative; **un animal muy c.** a very aggressive *o* fierce animal (**b**) *(que no se desanima)* spirited, combative; **tiene un carácter c. y nunca abandona** she is very spirited *o* combative and never gives up

combi *nm* (**a**) *Esp (frigorífico)* fridge-freezer (**b**) *Am (microbús)* minibus

combinación *nf* (**a**) *(unión, mezcla)* combination; **una c. explosiva** an explosive combination; **la perfecta c. entre juventud y experiencia** the perfect combination *o* mix of youth and experience; **no tomar en c. con otros analgésicos** *(en etiqueta)* not to be taken with other painkillers

(**b**) *(de bebidas)* cocktail

(**c**) *(de caja fuerte)* combination; **la c. ganadora fue...** *(en lotería)* the winning numbers were...

(**d**) *(prenda)* slip

(**e**) *(plan)* scheme

(**f**) *Mat* permutation

(**g**) *Quím* compound

(**h**) *(de medios de transporte)* connections; **no hay buena c. para ir de aquí allí** there's no easy way of getting there from here; **hay muy buena c. para llegar al aeropuerto** there's a very good connection to the airport

(**i**) *Dep (pases)* pass; **una perfecta c. entre los dos jugadores acabó en gol** the two players combined perfectly to score a goal

combinada *nf Dep* combined event

combinado, -a 1 *adj (con distintos elementos)* combined

2 *nm* (**a**) *(bebida)* cocktail (**b**) *Dep (para un solo partido)* scratch team; **el c. nacional** the national team

combinar 1 *vt* (**a**) *(unir, mezclar)* to combine; **combina lo práctico con lo barato** it is both practical and cheap (**b**) *(bebidas)* to mix (**c**) *(colores)* to match (**d**) *(planificar)* to arrange, to organize; **combinan sus horarios para que siempre haya alguien en casa** they arrange the hours they work so there's always somebody at home (**e**) *Mat* to permute (**f**) *Quím* to combine

2 *vi (colores, ropa)* **c. con** to go with; **no tengo nada que combine con estos pantalones** I haven't got anything to go *o* that goes with these trousers

3 combinarse *vpr* (**a**) *(ponerse de acuerdo)* **nos combinamos para cuidar del bebé** we arrange things between us to look after the baby (**b**) *Quím* to combine

combinatoria *nf Mat* combinatorial analysis

combinatorio, -a *adj* combinatorial

combo *nm* (**a**) *Esp Fam (grupo musical)* combo, band (**b**) *Andes (mazo)* sledgehammer (**c**) *Chile (puñetazo)* punch, blow

combustibilidad *nf* combustibility

combustible 1 *adj* combustible

2 *nm* fuel ►► ***c. fósil*** fossil fuel; ***c. líquido*** liquid fuel; ***c. mineral*** mineral fuel; ***c. nuclear*** nuclear fuel; ***c. sólido*** solid fuel

combustión *nf* combustion ►► ***c. espontánea*** spontaneous combustion; ***c. lenta*** slow combustion; ***c. nuclear*** nuclear combustion

comecocos *nm inv* (**a**) *Fam (para convencer)* **este panfleto es un c.** this pamphlet is designed to brainwash you; **la televisión es un c.** television dulls your brain (**b**) *Fam (cosa difícil de comprender)* teaser, puzzler (**c**) *(juego)* pac-man®

comedero *nm* (**a**) *(para animales)* trough (**b**) *Am Fam (para personas)* greasy spoon, *US* hash house

comedia *nf* (**a**) *(obra humorística)* comedy; *(obra dramática)* play; **no me vengas con comedias** don't start your play-acting; EXPR **hacer (la) c.** to put on an act ►► *Lit* ***c. de capa y espada*** = play about chivalry, typical of Spanish 17th century theatre; ***c. costumbrista*** comedy of manners; ***c. de enredo*** comedy of intrigue; ***c. musical*** musical (comedy); ***c. romántica*** romantic comedy

(**b**) *(película)* comedy; *(serie televisiva)* comedy series ►► ***c. de situación*** situation comedy, sitcom

(**c**) *(género)* comedy

(**d**) *(engaño)* farce; **su cansancio es pura c.** her tiredness is just an act

(**e**) *Am (telenovela, radionovela)* soap opera

comediante, -a *nm,f* (**a**) *(actor)* actor, *f* actress (**b**) *(farsante)* fraud

comedido, -a *adj* (**a**) *Esp (moderado)* moderate, restrained (**b**) *Am (servicial)* obliging

comedieta *nf* light comedy

comedimiento *nm* moderation, restraint; **actuar con c.** to exercise *o* show restraint

comediógrafo, -a *nm,f* playwright, dramatist

comedirse [47] *vpr* (**a**) *Esp (moderarse)* to restrain oneself (**b**) *Am (ofrecerse)* to volunteer oneself

comedón *nm* blackhead

comedor, -ora 1 *adj* **es muy c.** he's a big eater, he likes his food

2 *nm* (**a**) *(habitación)* dining room (**b**) *(muebles)* dining-room suite (**c**) *(establecimiento) (de fábrica)* canteen ►► ***c. escolar*** dining hall; ***c. universitario*** refectory

comedura *nf Fam* **ese programa es una c. de coco** that programme is trying to brainwash you; **tiene muchas comeduras de coco** she has lots of things bugging her

comehostias *nmf inv muy Fam Pey* creeping Jesus

comején *nm* termite

comelón = **comilón**

comendador *nm* (**a**) *(de orden militar)* knight commander (**b**) *(de orden religiosa)* prelate

comendadora *nf (superiora)* mother superior

comensal *nmf* (**a**) *(en comida)* fellow diner; **los comensales charlaban animadamente** the diners were having a lively conversation; **una cena con veinte comensales** a dinner for twenty (people) (**b**) *Biol* commensal

comensalismo *nm Biol* commensalism

comentar *vt* (**a**) *(opinar sobre)* to comment on; **comentaron un poema de Quevedo** they commented on a poem by Quevedo

(**b**) *(hablar de)* to discuss; **estuvimos comentando lo que había pasado en la oficina** we were talking about *o* discussing what had happened in the office

(**c**) *(retransmisión)* to commentate on; **c. un partido de fútbol** to commentate on a soccer match

(**d**) *(considerado incorrecto) (decir)* to tell; **me han comentado que**

te interesa la filatelia they tell me you're interested in stamp-collecting; **no se lo comentes a nadie** don't tell anyone, don't mention it to anyone

comentario *nm* (a) *(observación)* comment, remark; **hizo un c. muy acertado** she made a very apt remark; **ahórrate tus comentarios** keep your remarks to yourself; **sólo era un c. personal, no te lo tomes a mal** it was just a remark between the two of us, don't take it the wrong way; **el presidente no quiso hacer comentarios** the president did not wish to (make any) comment; **sin comentarios** no comment; **y, sin más comentarios, se marchó** and, without another word, she left; **sobran comentarios** what can you say?
(b) *(crítica)* commentary ►► ***c. de texto*** literary commentary, textual analysis
(c) *(televisivos, radiofónicos)* commentary
(d) **comentarios** *(murmuraciones)* gossip; **siempre hace comentarios a mis espaldas** he's always talking about me behind my back
(e) *Ling* predicate

comentarista *nmf* commentator ►► ***c. deportivo*** sports commentator

comenzar [17] **1** *vt* to start, to begin; **c. diciendo que...** to start *o* begin by saying that...
2 *vi* to start, to begin; **c. a hacer algo** to start doing *o* to do sth; **c. por hacer algo** to begin by doing sth; **"hiena" comienza por hache** "hyena" starts with an "h"; **el partido comenzó tarde** the game started late

COMER **1** *vt* (a) *(alimentos)* to eat; **no come carne casi nunca** she hardly ever eats meat; **¿quieres c. algo?** would you like something to eat?
(b) *Esp, Méx (al mediodía)* to have for lunch; *esp Andes (a la noche)* to have for dinner; **hoy hemos comido pescado** we had fish today
(c) *(en los juegos de tablero)* to take, to capture; **me comió un alfil** he took one of my bishops
(d) *(consumir)* to eat up; **tus gastos me comen casi todo el sueldo** your expenses eat up almost all of my salary; **esta estufa come mucha leña** this stove uses *o* gets through a lot of wood; **los come la envidia** they're eaten up with envy; **eso me come mucho tiempo** that takes up a lot of my time; **me están comiendo los mosquitos** the mosquitoes are eating me alive
(e) EXPR **ni come ni deja c.** he's a dog in the manger; **no tengas miedo, nadie te va a c.** don't be afraid, nobody's going to eat you; *Fam* **c. el coco** *o* **tarro a alguien** *(convencer)* to brainwash sb; *Vulg* **c. el coño a alguien** to go down on sb; *Vulg* **c. la polla a alguien** to give sb a blowjob, to go down on sb; **sin comerlo ni beberlo: sin comerlo ni beberlo, le hicieron jefe** he became boss through no merit of his own; **sin comerlo ni beberlo, nos encontramos en la bancarrota** through no fault of our own, we went bankrupt
2 *vi* (a) *(ingerir alimentos)* to eat; **ahora no tengo ganas de c.** I don't feel like eating *o* I'm not hungry right now; **c. fuera, salir a c.** to eat out; **yo llevaré la bebida, tú compra las cosas de c.** I'll get the drink, you buy the food; **c. a la carta** to eat à la carte; **¡a c., chicos!** lunch is/dinner's/*etc* ready, children!; **¡come y calla!** shut up and eat your dinner!; **dar de c. al perro** to feed the dog; **no sé qué darles de c. a mis hijos esta noche** I don't know what to give the children to eat this evening; **en ese restaurante dan de c. muy bien** the food is very good in that restaurant; *Fam* **ser de buen c.** to have a healthy appetite; *Fig* **tener qué c.** to have enough to live on; EXPR *Fam* **c. a dos carrillos** to stuff one's face; EXPR **c. como una lima** *o* **un regimiento** to eat like a horse; EXPR **comimos como curas** *o* **reyes** we ate like kings; EXPR **c. y callar** beggars can't be choosers; EXPR *Fam* **dar** *o* **echar de c. aparte a alguien: a mi profesor hay que darle** *o* **echarle de c. aparte** you have to be careful how you deal with my teacher, because you never know how he's going to react; EXPR **donde comen dos comen tres** there's always room for one more at the table
(b) *Esp, Méx (al mediodía)* to have lunch; **¿qué hay de c.?** what's for lunch?; **en casa comemos a las tres** we have lunch at three o'clock at home; **hemos quedado para c.** we've arranged to meet for lunch; **c. fuera, salir a c.** to go out for lunch
(c) *esp Andes (a la noche)* to have dinner
3 comerse *vpr* (a) *(alimentos)* to eat; **en mi casa se come a las dos** we have lunch at two o'clock at home; **en ese restaurante se come muy bien** the food is very good at that restaurant; **se comió los tres platos** he had all three courses; **cómetelo todo** eat it all up; **comerse las uñas** to bite one's nails; *Fam* **como descubra al que ha hecho esto, me lo como vivo** when I find out who did this, I'll have their guts for garters; *Fam* **tu amigo está para comérselo** your friend's gorgeous; EXPR **comerse a alguien con los ojos** *o* **con la mirada** to be unable to keep one's eyes off sb; EXPR **comerse a alguien a besos** to cover sb with kisses; EXPR *Fam* **no te comas el coco** *o* **el tarro** don't worry your head about it; EXPR *Fam* **comerse un marrón: me ha tocado a mí comerme el marrón de limpiar la casa tras la fiesta** I got lumbered with having to clean the house after the party; EXPR *Esp Fam* **comerse un rosco: presume mucho, pero la realidad es que no se come un rosco** he's always bragging, but the truth of the matter is he never gets off with anyone; EXPR **¿y eso cómo se come?** and what are we/am I/*etc* supposed to make of that?
(b) *(consumirse)* to eat up; **se la comen los celos, se come de celos** she's consumed *o* eaten up with jealousy
(c) *(desgastar) (colores)* to fade; *(metal)* to corrode; **el sol se comió los colores de la ropa** the sun made the clothes fade; **la humedad se come el hierro** moisture causes iron to rust
(d) *(en los juegos de tablero)* to take, to capture; **se me comió la reina** she took my queen
(e) *(palabras, texto)* to swallow; **se comió un párrafo** she missed out a paragraph; **te has comido todos los acentos** you've missed out all the accents; **se come las palabras al hablar** he swallows his words when speaking; *Fam Fig* **se va a c. sus palabras** she'll have to eat her words
(f) *RP (saltarse)* **comerse una luz roja** to go through a red light
(g) *(ser mejor que)* to beat; **mi trabajo se come al tuyo** my job beats yours
(h) *Am muy Fam (fornicar)* **comerse a alguien** to get into sb's *Br* knickers *o US* panties
4 *nm* **cuida mucho el c.** she's very careful about what she eats; **es muy sobrio en el c.** he eats very frugally

comercial **1** *adj* (a) *(de empresas)* commercial; *(embargo, disputa)* trade; **relaciones comerciales** trade relations; **aviación c.** civil aviation; **política c.** trade policy; **gestión c.** business management; **déficit c.** trade deficit (b) *(que se vende bien)* commercial; **una película muy c.** a very commercial film
2 *nmf (vendedor, representante)* sales rep
3 *nm Am* commercial, *Br* advert

comercialismo *nm* commercialism

comercialización *nf* (a) *(de producto)* marketing (b) *(de cultura, deporte)* commercialization

comercializar [14] **1** *vt* (a) *(producto)* to market (b) *(cultura, deporte)* to commercialize
2 comercializarse *vpr (cultura, deporte)* to become commercialized

comercialmente *adv* commercially

comerciante *nmf* (a) *(negociante)* tradesman, *f* tradeswoman (b) *(tendero)* shopkeeper; **pequeños comerciantes** small businessmen

comerciar *vi* to trade, to do business; **c. con armas/pieles** to deal *o* trade in arms/furs; **c. en especies** to deal *o* trade in kind; **comerciamos principalmente con los países mediterráneos** we mainly trade *o* do business with the Mediterranean countries

comercio *nm* (a) *(de productos)* trade; **c. de aceite/esclavos** oil/slave trade; **libre c.** free trade ►► *Informát* ***c. electrónico*** e-commerce; ***c. exterior*** foreign trade; ***c. interior*** domestic trade; ***c. internacional*** international trade; ***c. justo*** fair trade
(b) *(actividad)* business, commerce ►► ***c. mayorista*** wholesale trade; ***c. minorista*** retail trade
(c) *(tienda)* shop, store
(d) *(conjunto de tiendas) Br* shops, *US* stores; **el c. cierra mañana por ser festivo** the *Br* shops *o US* stores are closed tomorrow because it's a holiday

comestible **1** *adj* edible, eatable
2 comestibles *nmpl* food; **tienda de comestibles** grocer's (shop), grocery store

cometa **1** *nm Astron* comet ►► ***el c. Halley*** Halley's comet
2 *nf* kite

cometer *vt (crimen)* to commit; *(error, falta de ortografía)* to make; *(pecado)* to commit

cometido *nm* (a) *(objetivo)* mission, task (b) *(deber)* duty

comezón *nf* (a) *(picor)* **tener c.** to have an itch; **tengo c. en la nariz** I've got an itchy nose (b) *(remordimiento)* twinge; *(deseo)* urge, itch; **sentía una c. por triunfar** she felt the urge to win

comible *adj Fam* just about edible

cómic (*pl* **cómics**), **comic** (*pl* **comics**) *nm* (a) *(viñetas)* comic strip (b) *(revista)* (adult) comic

comicial *adj* election; **jornada c.** election day

comicidad *nf* humorousness

comicios *nmpl Pol* elections

cómico, -a 1 *adj* (a) *(de la comedia)* comedy, comic; **actor c.** comedy actor; **cine c.** comedy movies *o Br* films (b) *(gracioso)* comic, comical
2 *nm,f* (a) *(actor de teatro)* actor, *f* actress (b) *(humorista)* comedian, comic, *f* comedienne

comida *nf* (a) *(alimento)* food; **la c. francesa/mexicana** French/Mexican food; **c. para perros/gatos** dog/cat food ►► ***c. basura*** junk food; ***c. casera*** home cooking; *Méx* ***c. chatarra*** junk food; *Méx* ***c. corrida*** set meal; *Méx* ***c. corriente*** set meal; ***comidas a domicilio*** = home delivery of food; ***comidas para empresas*** business catering; ***c. para llevar*** takeaway food; ***c. preparada*** ready meals; ***c. rápida*** fast food
(b) *(acto de comer)* meal; **se sirven comidas** *(en letrero)* food served
(c) *Esp, Méx (al mediodía)* lunch; **dar una c.** to have a lunch party; **una c. de negocios** *o* **de trabajo** a business lunch; **una c. campestre** a picnic
(d) *esp Andes (a la noche)* dinner

comidilla *nf Fam* **es la c. del barrio** it's the talk of the neighbourhood; **su divorcio se ha convertido en la c. de la prensa británica** the British press are having a field day with their divorce

comidió *etc ver* **comedirse**

comido, -a 1 *ver* **comedirse**
2 *adj* fed; **estar c.** to have eaten; **llegó ya c.** he had already eaten before he came; EXPR *Fam* **ser lo c. por lo servido** *(no merecer la pena)* to be unprofitable; *Fam* **le he ayudado, pero él me había ayudado antes, así que lo c. por lo servido** I helped him, but he'd helped me before, so fair's fair

comienzo 1 *ver* **comenzar**
2 *nm* start, beginning; **lo sabían desde el c.** they knew from the start *o* beginning; **y esto es sólo el c.** and this is just the start; **tuvo unos comienzos poco prometedores** it got off to an inauspicious start; **a comienzos del siglo XX** at the beginning of the 20th century; **al c.** in the beginning, at first; **dar c. (a algo)** to start (sth), to begin (sth); **la función dio c. a las siete y media** the performance started at half past seven; **el secretario dio c. a la reunión** the secretary began *o* opened the meeting

comillas *nfpl* inverted commas, quotation marks; **abrir/cerrar c.** to open/close quotation marks; **poner algo entre c.** to put sth in inverted commas; **un "proceso democrático", entre c., vigilado de cerca por los generales** a, quote, "democratic process", unquote, closely supervised by the generals ►► ***c. tipográficas*** curly quotes

> Nowadays most of the world's Spanish-language newspapers use "English" inverted commas, whether double (" ") or single (' '), when indicating quotations. However, the traditional method was to use "Latin" or "Spanish" commas (« »), and this form of punctation is still preferred in literary works.

comilón, -ona, *CAm, Méx* **comelón, -ona** *Fam* 1 *adj* greedy
2 *nm,f (persona)* greedy pig, glutton

comilona *nf Fam (festín)* blow-out, *Br* slap-up meal; **darse una c.** to have a blow-out *o Br* a slap-up meal

comino *nm* (a) *(planta)* cumin, cummin (b) *Fam (niño)* titch (c) EXPR *Fam* **me importa un c.** I don't give a damn; **no vale un c.** it isn't worth tuppence

comiquita *nf Ven Fam* comic strip, cartoon

comisaría *nf* **c. (de policía)** police station, *US* precinct, station house; **pasó la noche en c.** he spent the night in the police station

comisariado *nm* commission

comisario, -a *nm,f* (a) *(de policía) Br* superintendent, *US* captain ►► ***c. jefe*** *Br* chief superintendent, *US* chief (b) *(delegado)* commissioner ►► ***c. de carrera*** course steward; *UE* ***c. europeo*** European Commissioner; ***c. político*** political commissar (c) *(de muestra)* organizer; *(de exposición)* organizer, curator

comiscar [60] *vt* to nibble

comisión *nf* (a) *(delegación)* committee, commission; *UE* **la C. (Europea** *o* **de las Comunidades Europeas)** the (European) Commission ►► ***c. de control*** monitoring committee; ***c. disciplinaria*** disciplinary committee; ***c. ejecutiva*** executive committee; ***c. de investigación*** committee of inquiry; ***c. investigadora*** committee of inquiry; ***c. mixta*** joint committee; ***Comisiones Obreras*** = Spanish left-wing trade union; ***c. parlamentaria*** parliamentary committee; ***c. permanente*** standing committee; ***c. rogatoria*** rogatory commission
(b) *Com* commission; **(trabajar) a c.** (to work) on a commission basis; **recibe** *o* **se lleva una c. del 5 por ciento** she gets 5 percent commission ►► ***c. bancaria*** bank charges; *Econ* ***c. fija*** flat fee
(c) *(de un delito)* perpetration
(d) *(encargo)* assignment ►► ***c. de servicio(s):*** **trabajó seis meses de profesora, en c. de servicio** she was seconded to the school for six months

comisionado, -a *nm,f* committee member

comisionar *vt* to commission

comisionista *nmf* commission agent

comisquear 1 *vt* to nibble
2 *vi* to nibble

comisura *nf* corner *(of mouth, eyes)*; **se limpió el helado de la c. de los labios** he wiped the ice cream from the corner of his mouth

comité *nm* committee ►► ***c. central*** central committee; ***c. consultivo*** consultative committee; *Dep* ***c. de competición*** disciplinary committee; ***c. de disciplina*** disciplinary comittee; *UE* ***C. Económico y Social*** Economic and Social Committee; ***c. ejecutivo*** executive committee; *Ind* ***c. de empresa*** works council; *Ind* ***c. intercentros*** coordinating *o* joint committee *(of trade unions)*; ***c. olímpico*** Olympic Committee; ***c. permanente*** standing committee; *UE* ***C. de las Regiones*** Committee of the Regions

comitiva *nf* entourage; **la c. presidencial/real** the president's/royal entourage

Como *nm* **el lago C.** Lake Como

COMO 1 *adv* (a) *(comparativo)* **tan... c....** as... as...; **ser c. algo** to be like sth; **habla c. tú** he speaks like you (do); **vive c. un rey** he lives like a king; **lo que dijo fue c. para ruborizarse** his words were enough to make you blush; **es c. para no volver a dirigirle la palabra** I feel I never want to speak to him again; **nadie escribe c. él (escribe)** no one writes like him *o* like he does; **¿qué hace alguien c. tú en este lugar?** what's a person like you doing in a place like this?; EXPR **es (tan) negro c. el carbón** it's as black as coal
(b) *(de la manera que)* as; **lo he hecho c. es debido** I did it as *o* the way it should be done; **lloviendo c. llovía, decidimos no salir** seeing as it was raining so hard, we decided not to go out; **nevó c. nunca** it snowed like it had never snowed before; **teniendo tanto dinero c. tiene, no sé cómo puede ser tan avaro** I don't know how he can be so mean with all the money he has, I don't know how someone with all that money can be so mean; **hazlo c. te dé la gana** do it whatever way *o* however you like; **lo haga c. lo haga, no le va a dar tiempo** it doesn't matter how he does it, he won't have enough time; **se encuentra c. hacía mucho tiempo no se encontraba** she feels like she hasn't felt in a long time
(c) *(según)* as; **c. te decía ayer...** as I was telling you yesterday...; **c. de costumbre, llegó tarde** she was late, as usual
(d) *(aproximadamente)* about; **me quedan c. diez euros** I've got about ten euros left; **estamos c. a mitad de camino** we're about halfway there; **tiene un sabor c. a naranja** it tastes a bit like an orange, it has a slight taste of orange; **llegaré c. a las cinco** I'll get there about five
(e) *(por ejemplo)* such as, like; **me gustan deportes c. el tenis y el golf** I like sports such as tennis and golf; **para algunos países, c. Perú o Bolivia,...** for some countries, such as Peru or Bolivia,...
(f) *(en que)* **por la manera c. hablaba supe que era extranjero** I knew he was foreign from the way he talked
2 *prep (en calidad de, en concepto de)* as; **c. presidente que es, tiene que asistir** as president, he must attend; **trabaja c. bombero** he works as a fireman; **dieron el dinero c. anticipo** they gave the money as an advance; **c. pintor, no es muy bueno** he's not very good as a painter; **en esta lista aparece c. emigrado** he appears on this list as an emigrant
3 *conj* (a) *(ya que)* as, since; **c. no llegabas, nos fuimos** as *o* since you didn't arrive, we left; **c. no hablo inglés, no entendí nada** as *o* since I don't speak English, I didn't understand anything
(b) *Esp (si)* if; **c. no me hagas caso, lo pasarás mal** if you don't listen to me, there'll be trouble; **c. no se lo preguntes, nunca lo sabrás** you'll never know unless you ask her; **c. no te des prisa, llegaremos tarde** if you don't hurry (up) we'll be late
(c) *(que)* that; **después de tantas veces c. te lo he explicado** after all the times (that) I've explained it to you
(d) *Esp (expresa posibilidad)* **¿quién se olvidó de pagar? – c. no fuera yo...** who forgot to pay? – it could have been me...; **vengo a despedirme de Clara – pues c. no te des prisa, ya no la ves** I've come to say goodbye to Clara – well, if you don't hurry you'll miss her
(e) *(expresa consecuencia)* **es c. para no hablarle nunca más** it's enough to make you never want to talk to her again; **es c. para matarlo** I could kill him
4 **como que** *loc conj* (a) *(que)* that; **le pareció c. que lloraban** it seemed to him (that) they were crying
(b) *(expresa causa)* **pareces cansado – c. que he trabajado toda la**

noche you seem tired – well, I've been up all night working; **esta leche sabe rara – c. que está cortada** this milk tastes funny – that's because it's off

(**c**) *(expresa incredulidad)* **¡c. que te voy a creer a ti que eres un mentiroso!** as if I'd believe a liar like you!; **voy a darle una lección – c. que te vas a atrever** I'm going to teach him a lesson – you'd never dare *o* as if you'd dare

(**d**) *(como si)* as if; **haz c. que buscas algo** make as if *o* pretend you're looking for something

5 como quiera que *loc adv (de cualquier modo que)* whichever way, however; **c. quiera que elijas** whichever way *o* however you choose; **c. quiera que sea** whatever the case may be; **Alcazarquivir o c. quiera que se llame** Alcazarquivir, or whatever it's called

6 como quiera que *loc conj (dado que)* since, given that; **c. quiera que la mayoría parece estar a favor...** since *o* given that the majority seems to be in favour...

7 como si *loc conj* as if; **tú, c. si nada, no le hagas ni caso** just ignore it, don't take any notice of him

8 como ser *loc adv Am (es decir)* such as, like; **precisamos profesionales, c. ser médicos, abogados, etc.** we need professional people, such as doctors, lawyers, etc

---

CÓMO 1 *adv* (**a**) *(de qué manera)* how; **¿c. estás?,** *Andes, Ven* **¿c. andas?,** *RP* **¿c. andás?** how are you?; **¿c. te encuentras?** how are you feeling?; **¿c. te llamas?** what's your name?; **¿c. dices que se llama?** what did you say she was called?; **¿c. lo has hecho?** how did you do it?; **¿c. son?** what are they like?; **¿c. se escribe?** how do you spell it?; **¿c. es de alto?** how tall is he?; **me encanta c. bailas** I love the way you dance; **explícame c. se hace** tell me how you do it, tell me how it's done

(**b**) *(por qué motivo)* how; **¿c. te dejas tratar de esa manera?** how can you allow yourself to be treated like that?; **¿c. no vinieron a la fiesta?** why didn't they come to the party?; **pero, ¡c. no lo has dicho antes!** but why didn't you say so earlier?; **no sé c. has podido decir eso** I don't know how you could say that

(**c**) *(exclamativo)* how; **¡c. pasan los años!** how time flies!; **¡c. me alegro!** I'm so pleased!; **¡c. ha crecido tu hijo!** your son has really grown!; **¡c. ilumina esta lámpara!** this lamp's really bright!; **¡c.! ¿no te has enterado?** what! you mean you haven't heard?; **¡c. es posible que no quede café!** how can it be that there's no coffee left?; **han vuelto a mandar el recibo de la luz – ¡c.!, si ya lo hemos pagado** they've sent us another electricity bill – what? but we've already paid it!; **está lloviendo, ¡y c.!** it's raining like crazy!, *Br* it isn't half raining!; **¡c. llueve!** it's raining like crazy!, *Br* it isn't half raining!; **¡hay que ver c. toca el violín!** you wouldn't believe how well she plays the violin!; **¡c. no!** of course!

(**d**) *(interrogativo)* **¿c.?, ¿c. dices?** *(¿qué dices?)* sorry?, what?; **¿c. dices?, ¿no piensa pagar?** *(expresa sorpresa)* what do you mean, she's not going to pay?; *Fam* **¿c. es eso?** *(¿por qué?)* how come?; **¿c. que no la has visto nunca?** what do you mean you've never seen her?; **no piensa ayudarnos – ¿c. que no?** he doesn't want to help us – how come? *o* what do you mean he doesn't?; *Esp* **¿a c. están los tomates?** how much are the tomatoes?

2 *nm* **el c. y el porqué** the whys and wherefores

3 a cómo de lugar *loc adv CAm, Carib, Méx (sea como sea)* come what may; **tenemos que terminar este texto hoy, a c. de lugar** we've got to finish this text today, come what may

---

cómoda *nf* chest of drawers

cómodamente *adv* (**a**) *(confortablemente)* comfortably (**b**) *(de forma conveniente)* conveniently

comodidad 1 *nf* (**a**) *(estado, cualidad)* comfort; **el equipo ganó con c.** the team won comfortably *o* easily; **un vehículo en el que caben con toda c. 7 personas** a vehicle which seats 7 comfortably

(**b**) *(conveniencia)* convenience; **para su c.** for your convenience; **tener las tiendas tan cerca supone una c.** it's convenient *o* handy having the shops so close

(**c**) *(interés propio)* convenience; **no acompaño a su hijo por c.** I'm not going with her son because it doesn't suit me to

2 comodidades *nfpl* comforts; **una habitación con todo tipo de comodidades** a room equipped with everything you could need

> **Falso amigo**: El sustantivo inglés **commodity** no es la traducción del español **comodidad**. En inglés, **commodity** significa "bien de consumo" o "materia prima".

comodín 1 *adj Am (comodón)* comfort-loving

2 *nm* (**a**) *(naipe)* joker (**b**) *(persona)* Jack of all trades; **una palabra c.** an all-purpose word (**c**) *Informát* wild card (**d**) *Am (comodón)* comfort lover

cómodo, -a 1 *adj* (**a**) *(confortable)* comfortable; **estar c.** to feel comfortable; **ponte c.** *(como en casa)* make yourself at home; **no me siento c. delante de ellos** I don't feel comfortable *o* I feel uncomfortable in their company; **con estos zapatos voy muy c.** I'm very comfortable in these shoes

(**b**) *(conveniente)* convenient; **es muy c. que te traigan la compra a casa** it's very convenient *o* handy having the shopping delivered to your home

(**c**) *(oportuno, fácil)* easy; **es muy c. dejar que los demás decidan todo por ti** it's very easy to let others make all the decisions for you

(**d**) *(vago)* lazy

2 *nm,f* **ser un c.** to be lazy

> **Falso amigo**: El adjetivo inglés **commodious** no es la traducción del español **cómodo**. En inglés, **commodious** significa "amplio, espacioso".

comodón, -ona 1 *adj* (**a**) *(amante de la comodidad)* comfort-loving (**b**) *(vago)* laid-back; **no seas c.** don't be so lazy

2 *nm,f* (**a**) *(amante de la comodidad)* comfort-lover (**b**) *(vago)* laid-back person

comodoro *nm* (**a**) *(de buque)* commodore (**b**) *Arg (de avión) Br* group captain, *US* colonel

comoquiera: comoquiera que 1 *loc adv (de cualquier manera que)* whichever way, however; *(dado que)* since, seeing as

2 *loc conj (dado que)* since, given that; **c. que la mayoría parece estar a favor...** since *o* given that the majority seems to be in favour...

Comoras, Comores *nfpl* **las (islas) C.** the Comoros (Islands)

compa *nmf Fam* pal, *Br* mate, *US* buddy

compact ['kompak] (*pl* **compacts**) *nm inv* compact disc, CD

compactación *nf Informát* compression; **c. de ficheros** file compression

compactar *vt* to compress

compact disk, compact disc ['kompak'ðis(k)] (*pl* **compact disks** *o* **discs**) *nm* (**a**) *(aparato)* compact disc player (**b**) *(disco)* compact disc, CD

compacto, -a 1 *adj* compact

2 *nm* (**a**) *(aparato)* compact disc player (**b**) *(disco)* compact disc, CD

compactoteca *nf* compact disc *o* CD collection

compadecer [46] 1 *vt* to pity, to feel sorry for; **compadezco al que tenga que tratar contigo** I pity *o* feel sorry for anyone who has to have anything to do with you

2 compadecerse *vpr* **compadecerse de** to pity, to feel sorry for; **¿te ha tocado don Florentino de profesor de matemáticas? ¡te compadezco!** you've got Mr Florentino for maths? I feel sorry for you!

compadraje, compadreo *nm* (**a**) *(amistad)* companionship, close friendship (**b**) *(acuerdo)* conspiracy, plot

compadre *nm* (**a**) *(pariente)* **es mi c.** *(padrino de mi hijo)* he's godfather to my son; *(padre de mi ahijado)* I'm godfather to his son (**b**) *Fam (amigo) Br* mate, *US* buddy

compadrear *vi RP* to brag, to boast

compadreo = **compadraje**

compaginable *adj* **no ser c. con algo** to be incompatible with sth

compaginación *nf* (**a**) *(combinación)* reconciling; **es difícil lograr la c. de nuestros horarios de trabajo** it's difficult to get our working hours to fit in together (**b**) *Imprenta* page make-up

compaginar 1 *vt* (**a**) *(combinar)* to reconcile, to combine; **compagina muy bien las tareas del hogar con su trabajo** he combines the household chores with his job very well (**b**) *Imprenta* to make up

2 compaginarse *vpr* **compaginarse con** to square with, to go together with

compaña *nf Fam* **llegó con toda la c.** he arrived with the whole crew in tow

compañerismo *nm* comradeship

compañero, -a *nm,f* (**a**) *(pareja, acompañante)* partner; **la actriz asistió junto a su actual c.** the actress was accompanied by her current partner

(**b**) *(colega)* colleague; **c. (de clase)** classmate; **c. (de trabajo)** colleague, workmate, *US* co-worker; **fue c. mío en la universidad** he was at university at the same time as me; **hemos sido compañeros de aventuras** we've done lots of things together ►► ***c. de apartamento*** *Br* flatmate, *US* roommate; ***c. de armas*** comrade-in-arms; ***c. de casa*** housemate; ***c. de cuarto*** roommate; ***c. de equipo*** team-mate; *Esp* ***c. de piso*** *Br* flatmate, *US* roommate; ***c. de viaje*** travelling companion

(**c**) *(en juegos por parejas)* partner

(**d**) *(par)* **el c. de este guante/calcetín** the glove/sock that goes with this one
(**e**) *(camarada)* comrade; **el c. Rodríguez** comrade Rodríguez

compañía *nf* (**a**) *(cercanía)* company; **en c. de** accompanied by, in the company of; **hacer c. a alguien** to keep sb company
(**b**) *(acompañante)* company; **andar en malas compañías** to keep bad company; **ahora tienen c., volveré más tarde** they've got company just now, I'll come back later; **¿quiénes han sido? – Fernando y c., como de costumbre** who was it? – Fernando and co., as usual
(**c**) *(empresa)* company; **Fernández y C.** Fernández and Company ▸▸ ***c. aérea*** airline; ***c. discográfica*** record company; ***c. eléctrica*** electricity company; ***c. ferroviaria*** railway *o US* railroad company; ***c. naviera*** shipping company; ***c. petrolera*** oil company; ***c. de seguros*** insurance company; ***c. telefónica*** telephone company
(**d**) *(de teatro, danza)* company ▸▸ ***c. de repertorio*** repertory company
(**e**) *(en ejército)* company
(**f**) ***la C. de Jesús*** the Society of Jesus, the Jesuits

comparable *adj* comparable (**a** *o* **con** to *o* with)

comparación *nf* (**a**) *(entre personas, cosas)* comparison; **no es conveniente establecer comparaciones entre hermanos** it's not a good idea to compare brothers and sisters; **en c. con** in comparison with, compared to; **las comparaciones son odiosas** comparisons are odious; **no admite c., no hay punto de c.** there's no comparison; **sin c.** by far (**b**) *Gram* comparison

comparado, -a *adj* **c. con** compared to; **c. con el tuyo, el mío es increíble** compared to yours, mine is incredible; **gramática comparada** comparative grammar

comparar 1 *vt* to compare; **c. algo/a alguien con algo/alguien** to compare sth/sb with sth/sb; **c. precios** to compare prices, to shop around
2 *vi* to compare, to make a comparison; **¡no compares, ésta es mucho más bonita!** don't compare, this one's much nicer!

comparativamente *adv* comparatively

comparativo, -a 1 *adj* comparative
2 *nm* comparative

comparecencia *nf*, **comparecimiento** *nm (ante el juez, la prensa)* appearance

comparecer [46] *vi* to appear; **c. ante alguien** to appear before sb

compareciente *Der* **1** *adj* appearing
2 *nmf* person appearing

comparecimiento = **comparecencia**

comparsa 1 *nf* (**a**) *Teatro* extras (**b**) *(en carnaval)* = group of people at carnival in same costume and with masks
2 *nmf* (**a**) *Teatro* extra (**b**) *(en carreras)* also-ran; *(en competiciones)* minnow; **no es más que un c.** he's just there to make up the numbers

compartido, -a *adj (casa, habitación)* shared

compartimentación *nf* compartmentalization

compartimentar *vt* to compartmentalize

compartimento, compartimiento *nm* (**a**) *(en tren)* compartment (**b**) *(de armario)* part, section; *(de nevera)* compartment ▸▸ ***c. estanco*** watertight compartment

compartir *vt* (**a**) *(ganancias, gastos)* to share (out); **lo compartieron entre los familiares** they shared it (out) among their relations (**b**) *(casa, vehículo)* to share; **c. algo con alguien** to share sth with sb (**c**) *(ideas, pesimismo)* to share; **no comparto tu opinión** I don't share your opinion

compás (*pl* **compases**) *nm* (**a**) *(instrumento)* pair of compasses
(**b**) *Mús (ritmo)* rhythm, beat; **al c. (de la música)** in time (with the music); **llevar el c.** to keep time; **marcar el c.** to beat time; **perder el c.** to lose the beat ▸▸ *Mús* ***c. de cuatro por cuatro*** four-four time; ***c. ternario*** triple time
(**c**) *Mús (periodo)* bar; **tocaron unos compases de esa canción** they played a few bars of that song
(**d**) *Náut (brújula)* compass
(**e**) ***c. de espera*** pause, interlude; **las negociaciones se hallan en un c. de espera** negotiations have been temporarily suspended

compasillo *nm Mús* four-four time

compasión *nf* compassion, pity; **mover a la c.** to move to pity; **trata a todo el mundo sin c.** she has no sympathy for anyone; **disparó sin c. contra los prisioneros** he shot at the prisoners without pity; **tener c. de** to feel sorry for; **¡por c.!** for pity's sake!

compasivamente *adv* compassionately, sympathetically

compasivo, -a *adj* compassionate, sympathetic

compatibilidad *nf* (**a**) *(entre personas, proyectos)* compatibility; **entre ellos no hay c. de caracteres** they don't get on with each other at all (**b**) *Informát* compatibility

compatibilizar [14] *vt* to make compatible; **compatibiliza el trabajo con los estudios** she combines work and study, she fits her studies in with her job

compatible 1 *adj* (**a**) *(personas, proyectos)* compatible; **no son compatibles el uno con el otro** they are not compatible with each other; **su cargo no es c. con el de presidente** he cannot stay in his present post and be president at the same time (**b**) *Informát* compatible; **c. con versiones anteriores** backward compatible
2 *nm Informát* compatible computer

compatriota *nmf (hombre)* compatriot, fellow countryman; *(mujer)* compatriot, fellow countrywoman

compay *nm Cuba Fam (amigo)* friend, *Br* mate, *US* buddy

compeler *vt* to compel, to force; **lo compelieron a pagar** he was compelled *o* forced to pay

compendiar *vt* (**a**) *(cualidades, características)* to epitomize (**b**) *(libro, historia)* to abridge

compendio *nm* (**a**) *(libro)* compendium; **un c. de gramática** a short guide to grammar (**b**) *(síntesis)* epitome, essence; **esta muchacha es un c. de virtudes** this girl is a paragon of virtue, this girl is virtue itself

compenetración *nf* mutual understanding

compenetrado, -a *adj* **están muy compenetrados** they understand each other very well; **es un equipo muy c.** they work very well as a team

compenetrarse *vpr* (**a**) *(personas)* to understand each other; **se compenetra muy bien con su compañera de trabajo** she has reached a good understanding with her workmate (**b**) *Quím (partículas)* to interpenetrate

compensación *nf* (**a**) *(indemnización)* compensation; **en c. (por)** in return (for); **recibió 10 millones en c. por el fallecimiento de su marido** she received 10 million in compensation for the death of her husband; **solicitan una c. económica por los daños sufridos** they are seeking financial compensation for the damage
(**b**) *Fin* clearing ▸▸ ***c. bancaria*** bank clearing
(**c**) *Psi* compensation

compensar 1 *vt* (**a**) *(contrarrestar)* to make up for; **su talento compensa la falta de educación formal** her talent makes up for the fact that she lacks a formal education; **compensaron las pérdidas con las ganancias** the profit they made cancelled out their losses
(**b**) *(indemnizar)* **c. a alguien (de** *o* **por)** to compensate sb (for); **la compensaron con 2 millones** she got 2 million in compensation; **te compensaré por el esfuerzo** I'll make it worth your while
2 *vi* to be worthwhile; **no compensa** it's not worth it; **no me compensa (perder tanto tiempo)** it's not worth my while (wasting all that time); **compensa más comprarlo a granel** it pays *o* it's more economical to buy it in bulk
3 compensarse *vpr* **el mal estado del local se compensa con su excelente situación** the poor condition of the place is offset *o* compensated for by its excellent location; **la baja mortalidad se compensa con una baja natalidad** low mortality is offset by a low birth rate

compensatorio, -a *adj* compensatory

competencia *nf* (**a**) *(entre personas, empresas)* competition; **hay mucha c. por conseguir ese contrato** there's a lot of competition for that contract; **hacer la c. a alguien** to compete with sb ▸▸ *Com* ***c. desleal*** unfair competition
(**b**) *(persona, empresa)* **la c.** the competition; **trabaja para la c.** he works for the competition
(**c**) *(incumbencia)* field, province; **no es de mi c.** it's not my responsibility; **ese asunto es c. de la policía** that is a matter for the police; **los casos de terrorismo no son c. de ese tribunal** that court is not responsible for dealing with terrorism cases
(**d**) *(atribuciones)* **competencias** powers; **tienen competencias en materia de educación** they have authority over educational matters
(**e**) *(aptitud)* competence, ability; **un profesional de una gran c.** a very able *o* competent professional
(**f**) *Ling* competence ▸▸ ***c. comunicativa*** communicative competence; ***c. lingüística*** linguistic competence
(**g**) *Am (deportiva)* competition

competente *adj* (**a**) *(capaz)* competent (**b**) *(responsable)* **c. en materia de** responsible for

competer *vi* **c. a** *(incumbir)* to be up to, to be the responsibility of; *(a una autoridad)* to come under the jurisdiction of; **la protección del medio ambiente compete al gobierno de la nación** environmental protection is the reponsibility of the government; **es un asunto que no nos compete** it's not our responsibility *o* it's not up to us to deal with this matter

competición *nf* **(a)** *(deportiva)* competition ►► ***c. deportiva*** sports competition; *Dep* ***c. por puntos*** points competition **(b)** *(entre empresas, grupos)* competition; **la c. electoral** the electoral contest; **hay una dura c. por obtener un ascenso** there is fierce competition for promotion

competidor, -ora 1 *adj* rival, competing
2 *nm,f* **(a)** *(en concurso)* competitor **(b)** *Com (compañía)* competitor, rival; *(producto)* competitor, rival (product)

competir [47] *vi* **(a)** *(contender)* to compete **(con/por** with/for); **varios grupos compiten por la obtención del contrato** several groups are competing for the contract; **nos es muy difícil c. con las importaciones chinas** we find it very difficult to compete with Chinese imports; **exigen c. en pie de igualdad con otros países europeos** they are demanding to compete on an equal footing with other European countries
(b) *(igualar)* **c. (con)** to be on a par (with); **compiten en belleza** they rival each other in beauty; **un producto que puede competir con los importados** a product that can compete with foreign imports

competitivamente *adv* competitively

competitividad *nf* **(a)** *(de persona)* competitiveness **(b)** *(de producto, empresa)* competitiveness

competitivo, -a *adj* **(a)** *(persona)* competitive **(b)** *(producto, empresa)* competitive; **productos a precios muy competitivos** products at very competitive prices

compilación *nf* **(a)** *(acción)* compiling **(b)** *(colección)* compilation **(c)** *Informát* compiling

compilador, -ora 1 *adj* compiling
2 *nm,f (persona)* compiler
3 *nm Informát* compiler

compilar *vt* **(a)** *(libros, información)* to compile **(b)** *Informát* to compile

compincharse *vpr* **c. para hacer algo** to gang together to do sth

compinche *nmf Br* mate, *US* buddy; **detuvieron al ladrón y a sus compinches** they arrested the robber and his accomplices

compita *nmf Nic* **(a)** *(guerrillero)* = Nicaraguan guerrilla **(b)** *(tratamiento)* comrade

compitiera *etc ver* **competir**

compito *etc ver* **competir**

complacencia *nf* **(a)** *(agrado)* pleasure, satisfaction; **enseñaba el trofeo con c.** he proudly displayed the trophy **(b)** *(indulgencia)* indulgence; **tener complacencias con alguien** to be indulgent towards *o* with sb

> **Falso amigo**: El sustantivo inglés **complacency** no es la traducción del español **complacencia**. En inglés, **complacency** significa "autocomplacencia".

complacer [42] **1** *vt* to please; **me complace anunciar que...** I am pleased to announce (that)...
2 complacerse *vpr* **complacerse en hacer algo** to take pleasure in doing sth

complacido, -a *adj* pleased; **está muy c. con el esfuerzo realizado** he's very pleased with the efforts that have been made

complaciente *adj* **(a)** *(amable)* obliging, helpful **(b)** *(indulgente)* indulgent

complazco *etc ver* **complacer**

complejidad *nf* complexity

complejo, -a 1 *adj* **(a)** *(complicado, difícil)* complex; **es una situación muy compleja** it's a very complex *o* complicated situation
(b) *(número)* complex
2 *nm* **(a)** *(psicológico)* complex; **tiene c. de gorda** she's got a complex about being fat; **le va a entrar c.** he'll get a complex ►► ***c. de culpabilidad*** guilt complex; ***c. de Edipo*** Oedipus complex; ***c. de inferioridad*** inferiority complex; ***c. de superioridad*** superiority complex
(b) *(zona construida)* complex ►► ***c. deportivo*** sports complex; ***c. hospitalario*** hospital (complex); ***c. hotelero*** hotel complex; ***c. industrial*** industrial park; ***c. residencial*** private housing estate; ***c. turístico*** tourist development
(c) *(estructura)* complex ►► ***c. vitamínico*** vitamin complex

complementar 1 *vt* to complement
2 complementarse *vpr* to complement each other; **se complementan a la perfección** they complement each other perfectly, they are the perfect complement to each other

complementariedad *nf* complementarity; **es vital que haya un alto grado de c. entre las organizaciones** it is essential for the roles carried out by the different organizations to be complementary; **entre ambas empresas existe una eleveda c. geográfica** the two companies complement each other geographically

complementario, -a 1 *adj* **(a)** *(persona, cosa)* complementary **(b)** *(ángulo)* complementary **(c)** *(color)* complementary
2 *nm Esp (en la lotería)* = complementary number, *Br* ≃ bonus ball

complemento *nm* **(a)** *(añadido)* complement; **la fruta es el c. ideal de una dieta equilibrada** fruit is the ideal complement to a balanced diet ►► ***c. salarial*** bonus, wage supplement; ***c. vitamínico*** vitamin supplement
(b) *Gram* object, complement ►► ***c. agente*** agent; ***c. circunstancial*** adjunct; **c. circunstancial de tiempo/modo** adverbial of time/manner; ***c. directo*** direct object; ***c. indirecto*** indirect object
(c) *(de un ángulo)* complement
(d) complementos *(accesorios)* accessories; **complementos de novia** bridal accessories
(e) *Urug (segundo tiempo)* second half

completamente *adv* completely, totally; **estoy c. seguro/lleno** I'm completely sure/full; **el plan fracasó c.** the plan was a total failure

completar 1 *vt* **(a)** *(acabar)* to complete; **completaron la reparación en dos horas** they completed the repair in two hours; **esta obra completa la trilogía** this work completes the trilogy **(b)** *(impreso)* to fill out *o* in
2 completarse *vpr* to be completed; **la jornada se completó con una conferencia** the day ended *o* was rounded off with a lecture

completas *nfpl Rel* compline

completo, -a 1 *adj* **(a)** *(entero)* complete; **nombre c.** full name; **las obras completas de un autor** the complete works of an author; **vino toda la familia al c.** the entire family came
(b) *(lleno)* full; **el vagón está** *o* **va c.** the *Br* carriage *o US* car is full; **todos los hoteles de la ciudad están al c.** all the hotels in town are full; **completo** *(hotel)* no vacancies; *(aparcamiento)* full; *(en taquilla)* sold out
(c) *(perfecto)* complete; **un deportista muy c.** an all-round sportsman; **un espectáculo muy c.** a very well-rounded production
(d) *(rotundo)* complete; **un c. silencio** complete *o* total silence; **fue un c. éxito/fracaso** it was a complete success/a complete *o* total failure; **es un c. caballero** he's an absolute *o* the complete gentleman; **es un c. mentiroso** he's a complete liar
(e) *CSur (café, té, chocolate)* = served with toast, butter, cakes and pastries
2 *nm Chile* = hot dog with all the trimmings
3 por completo *loc adv* completely; **han desaparecido por c.** they have completely disappeared; **se dedica por c. a la música** she devotes herself full-time to music

complexión *nf* build; **ser de c. atlética/robusta** to be athletically built/well-built

> **Falso amigo**: El sustantivo inglés **complexion** no es la traducción del español **complexión**. En inglés **complexion** significa "tez" o "cariz".

complicación *nf* **(a)** *(proceso)* complication; **así sólo se consigue la c. de la situación** that will only complicate matters
(b) *(complejidad)* complexity; **un problema de gran c.** a very complex problem
(c) *(contratiempo)* problem, complication; **es una c. con la que no contábamos** it's a problem *o* complication we hadn't counted on; **han surgido varias complicaciones** several problems *o* complications have arisen
(d) *(en enfermedad)* complication; **si no hay complicaciones, le dan el alta mañana** if there are no problems *o* complications, he'll be discharged tomorrow

complicado, -a *adj* **(a)** *(situación, problema)* complicated **(b)** *(sistema, procedimiento)* complicated **(c)** *(carácter)* complex; **es un niño muy c.** he's a very complex child

complicar [60] **1** *vt* **(a)** *(dificultar)* to complicate; **esas declaraciones complican la obtención de un acuerdo** that statement will make it more difficult to reach an agreement; **complicarle la vida a alguien** to make life difficult for sb **(b)** *(comprometer)* **c. a alguien (en)** to involve sb (in)
2 complicarse *vpr* **(a)** *(problema)* to become *o* get complicated; **se**

están complicando las cosas things are getting complicated; **la reunión se complicó y terminamos a las once** complications arose at the meeting and we finished at eleven; **¡no te compliques la vida!** don't complicate matters (unnecessarily)!
(**b**) *(enfermedad)* to get worse
(**c**) *(comprometerse)* **se ha complicado en un asunto turbio** he has got mixed up *o* involved in some shady business

cómplice 1 *adj* conspiratorial; **una sonrisa/un silencio c.** a conspiratorial smile/silence
2 *nmf* accomplice; **ser c. de un delito** to be an accomplice to *o* in a crime

complicidad *nf* complicity; **fue acusado de c. en el robo** he was accused of being an accomplice to the robbery; **una mirada de c.** a conspiratorial look, a look of complicity

complot (*pl* **complots**), **compló** (*pl* **complós**) *nm* plot, conspiracy

complotar *vi* to plot

complutense 1 *adj* of/from Alcalá de Henares *(Spain)*
2 *nmf* person from Alcalá de Henares *(Spain)*

componedor, -ora *nm,f* (**a**) *(de texta)* typesetter (**b**) *Am (de huesos)* bonesetter

componenda *nf* shady deal

componente 1 *adj* component, constituent
2 *nm* (**a**) *(pieza)* component (**b**) *(de sustancia)* constituent (**c**) *Gram* component
3 *nmf (persona)* member
4 *nf* **viento de c. este/sur** easterly/southerly wind

componer [50] 1 *vt* (**a**) *(formar, ser parte de)* to make up; **los miembros que componen el tribunal** the members who make up the tribunal; **el turismo compone el 20 por ciento de los ingresos del país** tourism accounts for 20 percent of the country's income, 20 percent of the country's income comes from tourism
(**b**) *(música, versos)* to compose
(**c**) *(reparar)* to repair
(**d**) *(adornar) (cosa)* to deck out, to adorn; *(persona)* to smarten up
(**e**) *(en imprenta)* to set, to compose
(**f**) *Am (hueso)* to set
2 *vi (músico)* to compose
3 **componerse** *vpr* (**a**) *(estar formado)* **componerse de** to be made up of, to consist of; **el consejo se compone de diez miembros** the council is made up of *o* consists of ten members; **la colección se compone de veinte libros** there are twenty books in the set
(**b**) *(engalanarse)* to dress up
(**c**) **componérselas (para hacer algo)** *(arreglárselas)* to manage (to do sth); **allá se las compongan** that's their problem
(**d**) *Am (persona)* to get better; **cuando te compongas** when you're better
(**e**) *Am (tiempo)* to clear up, to improve

compongo *etc ver* **componer**

comportamiento *nm* (**a**) *(de personas)* behaviour (**b**) *(uso crítico) (de vehículo, acciones)* performance; **el c. de la inflación ha sido muy irregular este año** inflation has fluctuated considerably this year

comportar 1 *vt* to involve, to entail; **una casa comporta muchos gastos** a house involves *o* entails a lot of expense; **el riesgo que comporta la no utilización del casco** the risk involved in not wearing a helmet
2 **comportarse** *vpr* to behave; **comportarse bien** to behave (oneself); **comportarse mal** to behave badly, to misbehave; **se comporta como una madre** she acts *o* behaves like a mother; **compórtate o tendré que castigarte** behave yourself or I'll have to punish you

composición *nf* (**a**) *(de sustancia, producto)* composition ►► ***c. química*** chemical composition
(**b**) *(de equipo, comité)* composition, make-up
(**c**) *(obra literaria)* work; *(obra musical)* composition, work ►► ***c. musical*** composition; ***c. poética*** poetic composition, poem
(**d**) *(técnica musical)* composition
(**e**) *(redacción)* essay, composition (**sobre** on)
(**f**) *(en fotografía, pintura)* composition; EXPR **hacerse una c. de lugar** to size up the situation; **no me hago una c. de lugar, ¿cómo es la casa?** I can't quite visualize it, what's the house like?
(**g**) *Ling* compounding, combination
(**h**) *(en imprenta)* typesetting

compositor, -ora *nm,f* (**a**) *(de música)* composer (**b**) *RP (de caballos)* trainer (**c**) *Chile (de huesos)* bonesetter

> **Falso amigo**: El sustantivo inglés **compositor** no es la traducción del español **compositor**. En inglés, **compositor** significa "cajista".

compost *nm* compost

compostaje *nm* composting

compostelano, -a 1 *adj* of/from Santiago de Compostela *(Spain)*
2 *nm,f* person from Santiago de Compostela *(Spain)*

compostura *nf* (**a**) *(en comportamiento)* restraint; **guardar la c.** to show restraint; **perder la c.** to lose one's composure (**b**) *(reparación)* repair

compota *nf* compote, stewed fruit

compotera *nf* dessert bowl *o* dish

compra *nf* (**a**) *(adquisición)* purchase; **están considerando la c. de un automóvil** they are thinking about *o* considering buying a car; **por la c. de una enciclopedia te regalan un televisor** if you buy an encyclopedia, they'll give you a television free; **hacer** *Esp* **la c.** *o Am* **las compras** to do the shopping; **hago** *Esp* **la c.** *o Am* **las compras los viernes** I do the shopping on Fridays; **ir de compras** to go shopping ►► ***c. apalancada*** leverage buyout; ***c. al contado*** *(en efectivo)* cash purchase; *Am* ***c. en cuotas*** *Br* hire-purchase, *US* installment plan; ***c. al por mayor*** bulk buying; ***c. a plazos*** *Br* hire-purchase, *US* installment plan
(**b**) *(objeto adquirido)* purchase, buy; **esta impresora fue una excelente c.** this printer was a really good buy; **algunos supermercados te llevan la c. a casa** some supermarkets deliver your shopping to your home; **deja la c. sobre la mesa** leave the shopping on the table

comprador, -ora 1 *adj (que compra)* **fiebre compradora** buying frenzy; **la parte compradora** the buyer
2 *nm,f (adquiriente)* buyer, purchaser; *(en una tienda)* shopper, customer

comprar *vt* (**a**) *(adquirir)* to buy, to purchase; **se lo compré a un vendedor ambulante** I bought it from a street vendor *o* seller; **se lo compraron a Ignacio como regalo de despedida** they bought it for Ignacio as a leaving present; **se lo compraron para Navidades** they bought it for her for Christmas; **c. algo al contado** *(en metálico)* to pay cash for sth; *(en un plazo)* to pay for sth all at once *o Br* on the nail; **c. a plazos** *o Am* **cuotas** to buy on *Br* hire purchase *o US* an installment plan; **c. al por mayor** to buy wholesale; EXPR *Fam* **¡cómprate un bosque y piérdete!** go and play in the traffic!, take a hike!
(**b**) *(sobornar)* to buy (off), to bribe; **¡el árbitro está comprado!** they've bribed the referee!

compraventa, compra-venta *nf* (**a**) *(intercambio comercial)* trading (**de** in); **se dedican a la c. de viviendas** they buy and sell houses ►► ***c. de armas*** arms dealing; ***c. de acciones*** share dealing
(**b**) *(venta)* sale

comprender 1 *vt* (**a**) *(incluir)* to include, to comprise; **el grupo comprende varias empresas** the group comprises several companies; **el país comprende tres regiones bien diferenciadas** the country consists of three quite distinct regions; **el gasto de instalación no está comprendido** the cost of installation is not included; **la exposición comprende 500 cuadros** the exhibition consists of 500 paintings; **el periodo comprendido entre 1995 y 1999** the period between 1995 and 1999 *o* from 1995 to 1999
(**b**) *(entender)* to understand; **como comprenderás, me enfadé muchísimo** I don't have to tell you I was absolutely furious; **te comprendo perfectamente** I quite understand; **no comprendo tu actitud** I don't understand your attitude; **no comprendo cómo puede gustarte Carlos** I don't know what you see in Carlos; **comprendo que estés triste** I can understand that you're unhappy; **¿comprendes?, si no se lo decimos se va a enfadar** look, if we don't tell him, he's going to get angry
2 **comprenderse** *vpr (personas)* to understand each other; **nos comprendemos de maravilla** we understand each other really well

comprensible *adj* understandable, comprehensible; **es c. que pidan una subida de sueldo** it's understandable that they're asking for a pay increase

comprensiblemente *adv* understandably

comprensión *nf* (**a**) *(acción)* understanding; **las fotografías ayudan a la c. del texto** the photographs help you to understand the text; **un niño con problemas de c. oral** a child with problems understanding speech; **de fácil/difícil c.** easy/difficult to understand (**b**) *(actitud)* understanding; **tienes que mostrar más c. con él** you have to be more understanding with him

comprensivo, -a *adj* understanding; **mostrarse c. (con alguien)** to be understanding (with sb)

> **Falso amigo**: El adjetivo inglés **comprehensive** no es la traducción del español **comprensivo**. En inglés **comprehensive** significa "detallado, completo" o " rotundo".

compresa *nf* (**a**) *(femenina)* **c. (higiénica)** sanitary *Br* towel *o US* napkin (**b**) *(para herida)* compress

compresible *adj* compressible

compresión *nf* (**a**) *(acción)* compression (**b**) *(de motor)* compression (**c**) *Informát* compression ►► ***c. de archivos*** file compression; ***c. de datos*** data compression

compresor, -ora 1 *adj* compressing
2 *nm* compressor

comprimido, -a 1 *adj* compressed
2 *nm* pill, tablet

comprimir 1 *vt* (**a**) *(reducir el volumen)* to compress (**b**) *Informát* to compress
2 comprimirse *vpr (apretarse)* to squash up *o* together; **se comprimieron para que se pudiera sentar otra persona** they squashed up *o* together so someone else could sit down

comprobable *adj* verifiable, provable

comprobación *nf* checking

comprobante *nm* (**a**) *(documento)* supporting document, proof (**b**) *(recibo)* receipt ►► ***c. de compra*** proof of purchase, receipt; ***c. de gastos*** proof of expenditure, receipt

comprobar [64] *vt* (**a**) *(revisar)* to check; **comprueba los frenos antes de salir de viaje** check your brakes before setting out on a journey
(**b**) *(averiguar)* to check; **¿podrías c. a qué hora sale el tren?** could you check what time the train leaves?; **tengo que c. si lo tengo** I have to check *o* see if I've got it; **he comprobado en carne propia que estabas en lo cierto** I found out *o* discovered through personal experience that you were right
(**c**) *(demostrar)* to prove; **esto comprueba que yo tenía razón** this proves that I was right; **se ha comprobado que la vacuna es efectiva** the vaccine has been proved to be effective

comprometedor, -ora *adj* compromising

comprometer 1 *vt* (**a**) *(poner en peligro) (éxito, posibilidades)* to jeopardize; *(persona, inversión)* to compromise; **los documentos comprometen la seguridad del estado** the documents jeopardize *o* endanger state security
(**b**) *(avergonzar)* to embarrass; **publicaron unas fotos que lo comprometen** they published some compromising photos of him
(**c**) *(obligar)* **c. a alguien (a hacer algo)** to oblige *o* compel sb (to do sth); **el acuerdo no nos compromete a nada** the agreement doesn't commit us to anything
2 comprometerse *vpr* (**a**) *(asumir un compromiso)* to commit oneself; **se comprometió a hacerlo** she promised to do it; **me comprometí a acabarlo cuanto antes** I promised to finish it as soon as possible; **se han comprometido a cumplir el acuerdo de paz** they have committed themselves to fulfilling the peace agreement
(**b**) *(ideológicamente, moralmente)* to become involved (**en** in); **se comprometió en la defensa de los derechos humanos** she got involved in campaigning for human rights
(**c**) *(para casarse)* to get engaged (**con** to)

comprometido, -a *adj* (**a**) *(con una idea)* committed; **es un intelectual c.** he is a politically committed intellectual; **está c. con la defensa del medio ambiente** he is committed to the defence of the environment (**b**) *(situación)* compromising, awkward (**c**) *(para casarse)* engaged; **estar c. con alguien** to be engaged to sb

compromisario *nm Pol* delegate, representative *(in an election)*

compromiso *nm* (**a**) *(obligación)* commitment; **me vi en el c. de tener que aceptar** I found myself obliged to accept; **adquirí el c. de ayudarlos** I undertook to help them; **cumplir un c.** to fulfil *o* honour a commitment; **no cumplieron el c. de entregar las armas** they did not honour their commitment to hand over their weapons; **sin c.** without obligation; **reciba información en su domicilio, sin ningún c.** let us send you our brochure without obligation
(**b**) *(acuerdo)* agreement; **patronal y sindicatos alcanzaron un c.** management and unions reached an agreement; **presentaron una propuesta de c.** they proposed a compromise
(**c**) *(cita)* engagement; **esta noche tengo un c. y no podré salir contigo** I'm busy this evening, so I won't be able to go out with you; **si no tienes ningún c., podríamos ir al cine** if you're not doing anything else, we could go to the cinema
(**d**) *(dificultad)* compromising *o* difficult situation; **poner a alguien en un c.** to put sb in a difficult *o* awkward position
(**e**) *(ideológico)* commitment; **ha dejado siempre claro su c. con la paz** he has always made clear his commitment to peace
(**f**) *(para casarse)* engagement; **han anunciado su c.** they have announced their engagement; **es una joven soltera y sin c.** she's young, free and single ►► ***c. matrimonial*** engagement
(**g**) *(encuentro deportivo)* fixture

> **Falso amigo**: El sustantivo inglés **compromise** no es la traducción del español **compromiso**. En inglés, **compromise** significa "solución negociada" o "solución intermedia".

compruebo *etc ver* **comprobar**

compuerta *nf* floodgate, sluicegate

compuesta *nf Bot* composite

compuesto, -a 1 *participio ver* **componer**
2 *adj* (**a**) *(formado)* **c. de** composed of, made up of (**b**) *(múltiple)* compound; *(número)* compound; **interés c.** compound interest; **ojo c.** compound eye (**c**) *(oración, tiempo)* compound (**d**) *(flor, hoja)* composite (**e**) *(acicalado)* dressed up (**f**) EXPR **quedarse c. y sin novio(a)** *(en boda)* to be abandoned at the altar; *(perder algo)* to be left high and dry
3 *nm Quím* compound ►► ***c. orgánico*** organic compound; ***c. químico*** chemical compound

compulsa *nf* (**a**) *(de documento)* **hacer la c. de una fotocopia** to check a photocopy against the original (**b**) *(copia)* certified copy

compulsar *vt (documento)* to check against the original; **una fotocopia compulsada** a certified copy

compulsión *nf* (**a**) *(impulso obsesivo)* compulsion (**b**) *Der (obligación)* compulsion, duress

compulsivamente *adv* compulsively

compulsivo, -a *adj* compulsive, urgent

compungido, -a *adj (arrepentido)* contrite, remorseful; *(triste)* sorrowful

compungir [24] **1** *vt (entristecer)* to sadden
2 compungirse *vpr* **compungirse (por)** *(arrepentirse)* to feel compunction *o* remorse (about); *(entristecerse)* to feel sad (about)

compusiera *etc ver* **componer**

computable *adj* **gastos computables a efectos fiscales** expenditure taken into account for tax purposes

computación *nf* (**a**) *(cómputo)* calculation, computation (**b**) *Am (informática)* computing

computacional *adj* computational, computer

computadora *nf*, **computador** *nm esp Am* computer; **pasar un trabajo a la c.** to key up a piece of work on the computer ►► ***c. analógica*** analogue computer; ***c. de a bordo*** onboard computer; ***c. central*** central computer; ***c. compatible*** compatible computer; ***c. digital*** digital computer; ***c. doméstico*** home computer; ***c. personal*** personal computer; ***c. portátil*** laptop computer; ***c. de sobremesa*** desktop computer

computadorización *nf* computerization

computadorizar [14] *vt* to computerize

computar *vt* (**a**) *(calcular)* to compute, to calculate (**b**) *(considerar)* to count, to regard as valid

computarizar [14], **computerizar** [14] *vt* to computerize

cómputo *nm (recuento)* calculation; *(de votos)* count; **llevar el c. de algo** to calculate *o* count sth

comulgante *nmf* communicant

comulgar [38] *vi* (**a**) *Rel* to take communion (**b**) *(estar de acuerdo)* **c. con algo** to share sth; **no comulgo con sus principios** I don't share her principles; EXPR **no me van a hacer c. con ruedas de molino** I'm not going to fall for that

comulgatorio *nm* communion rail

común 1 *adj* (**a**) *(compartido) (amigo, interés)* mutual; *(bienes, pastos)* communal; **el bien c.** the common good; **el motociclismo es nuestra afición c.** we both like motorcycling; **¿cómo llevan la vida en c.?** how are they finding living together?; **hacer algo en c.** to do sth together; **hacer algo de c. acuerdo** to do sth by mutual consent *o* agreement; **es un rasgo c. a todos los reptiles** it's a characteristic shared by *o* common to all reptiles; **pusimos nuestros recursos en c.** we pooled our resources; **realizaron una puesta en c. de lo observado** they pooled their observations; **tener algo en c.** to have sth in common; **no tengo nada en c. con ella** I have nothing in common with her
(**b**) *(habitual, normal)* common; **una enfermedad muy c. en regiones tropicales** a disease very common in tropical regions; **es c. que llueva en primavera** it's normal for it to rain in spring, it often rains in spring; **fuera de lo c.** out of the ordinary; **poco c.** unusual; **por lo c.** generally; **c. y corriente** *o Am* **silvestre** run-of-the-mill; **es una persona c. y corriente** he's a perfectly ordinary person
(**c**) *(ordinario, vulgar)* ordinary, average; **un vino c.** an average *o*

ordinary wine; **una madera c.** a common type of wood

2 *nm* **como el c. de los mortales** like any ordinary person *o* common mortal

comuna *nf* **(a)** *(colectividad)* commune **(b)** *Am (municipalidad)* municipality

comunal *adj* communal

comunero, -a *nm,f* **(a)** *Hist (en Castilla)* = supporter of the uprisings in Castile during the reign of Carlos I **(b)** *Hist (en Colombia, Paraguay)* = supporter of independence **(c)** *Perú, Méx (indígena)* = member of an indigenous village community

comunicación *nf* **(a)** *(contacto, intercambio de información)* communication; **estar en c. con alguien** to be in contact with sb; **ponerse en c. con alguien** to get in touch with sb; **durante todas las negociaciones mantuvieron una c. intensa** they were in constant contact throughout the negotiations; **los medios de c. (de masas)** the (mass) media ►► ***c. no verbal*** nonverbal communication

(b) *(por teléfono)* **se cortó la c. mientras hablábamos** we were cut off

(c) *(escrito oficial)* communiqué

(d) *(ponencia)* paper (**sobre** on); **presentar una c.** to give a paper

(e) *(transporte)* communication; **hay muy buena c. con la capital** the capital is easily accessible by public transport or by car; **comunicaciones** communications; **las comunicaciones quedaron cortadas debido a las inundaciones** all communications were cut off as a result of the floods; **las comunicaciones aéreas con el continente son insuficientes** there are not enough flights to the continent

comunicado, -a 1 *adj* **bien c.** *(lugar)* well-served, with good connections

2 *nm* announcement, statement ►► ***c. oficial*** official communiqué; ***c. a la prensa, c. de prensa*** press release

comunicador, -ora *nm,f* communicator; **es un buen c.** he's a good communicator

comunicante 1 *adj* communicating

2 *nmf* informant; **un c. anónimo anunció la colocación del explosivo** an anonymous caller informed them that an explosive device had been planted

comunicar [60] 1 *vt* **(a)** *(sentimientos, ideas)* to convey; **c. optimismo/miedo** to convey *o* communicate optimism/fear; **le comuniqué que deseaba irme** I let him know *o* informed him that I wanted to leave

(b) *(movimiento, virus, calor)* to transmit

(c) *(información)* **c. algo a alguien** to inform sb of sth, to tell sb sth; **le comunicaron su despido por escrito** he was informed in writing of his dismissal; **lamentamos tener que comunicarle que...** we regret to inform you that...

(d) *(conectar)* to connect; **esta carretera comunica los dos pueblos** this road connects the two towns; **es una ciudad muy bien comunicada** it is a city with very good transport connections

(e) *Am (al teléfono)* to call, to telephone

2 *vi* **(a)** *(estar conectado)* **c. con** to lead to; **nuestras habitaciones comunican** there's a door between our two rooms; **el vestíbulo comunica con el salón** the hall leads to the living room

(b) *Esp (teléfono) (estar ocupado) Br* to be engaged, *US* to be busy; **está comunicando, comunica** the line's *Br* engaged *o US* busy

(c) *RP (teléfono) (estar sonando)* to ring

(d) *(hablar)* to get through; **no consigo c. con él** I can't get through to him

3 **comunicarse** *vpr* **(a)** *(hablarse)* to communicate (with each other); **se comunican por señas** they communicate by signs; **se comunican por correo electrónico** they communicate by e-mail; **le cuesta mucho comunicarse con sus compañeros** he finds it very difficult to communicate with his colleagues

(b) *(dos lugares)* to be connected; **las islas se comunican a través de un puente** the islands are connected by a bridge

(c) *(propagarse)* to spread; **el incendio se comunicó a los apartamentos contiguos** the fire spread to neighbouring *Br* flats *o US* apartments

comunicatividad *nf* communicativeness

comunicativo, -a *adj* communicative, open

comunicología *nf* communication theory

comunidad *nf* **(a)** *(grupo)* community; **la c. científica/educativa/judía** the scientific/education/Jewish community; **vivir en c.** to live in a community ►► ***C. Andina*** Andean Community, = organization for regional cooperation formed by Bolivia, Colombia, Ecuador, Peru and Venezuela; ***c. autónoma*** autonomous region, = largest administrative division in Spain, with its own Parliament and a number of devolved powers; ***c. de base*** *(religiosa)* base community, = lay Catholic community independent of church hierarchy; *Antes* ***C. Económica Europea*** European Economic Community; ***la C. Europea, las Comunidades Europeas*** the European Community; ***la c. internacional*** the international community; ***c. lingüística*** speech community; ***c. de propietarios*** residents' association; ***c. de vecinos*** residents' association

(b) *(de ideas, bienes)* communion ►► ***c. de bienes*** co-ownership *(between spouses)*

(c) *Am (colectividad)* commune; **vive en una c. anarquista** she lives in an anarchist commune

comunión *nf* **(a)** *(sacramento)* communion; **dar la c.** to give *o* administer communion; **recibir la c.** to receive *o* take communion; **hacer la primera c.** to take one's First Communion **(b)** *(unión)* communion

comunismo *nm* communism

comunista 1 *adj* communist

2 *nmf* communist

comunitario, -a *adj* **(a)** *(de la comunidad)* community; **espíritu c.** community spirit **(b)** *UE* Community, of the European Union; **política comunitaria** EU *o* Community policy; **los países comunitarios** the EU countries, the Community members **(c)** *Antes (de la CEE)* Community, EEC

comúnmente *adv* **(a)** *(generalmente)* commonly, generally; **c. se lo conoce como papel de plata** it is commonly known as silver paper **(b)** *(usualmente)* usually, ordinarily

CON *prep* **(a)** *(indica modo, manera o instrumento)* with; **se cortó c. un cuchillo** she cut herself with a knife; **chocó c. una farola** he bumped into a lamppost; **vino c. un taxi** she came by taxi; **voy cómodo c. estas botas/este jersey** I'm comfortable in these boots/this sweater; **iré a la boda c. un traje negro** I'm going to the wedding in a black suit; **un joven c. muy buenos modales** a very polite young man; **andar c. la cabeza alta** to walk with one's head held high; **ir c. prisa** to be in a hurry; **actuar c. timidez** to behave timidly; **llover c. fuerza** to rain hard; **lo ha conseguido c. su esfuerzo** he has achieved it through his own efforts; **se lo puedes decir c. toda confianza** you needn't worry about telling her; **trátalo c. mucho cariño** treat him with a lot of affection *o* very affectionately; **lo haré c. mucho gusto** it will be a pleasure for me to do it, I'll be delighted to do it; **c. arreglo a la ley** in accordance with the law

(b) *(indica compañía, relación o colaboración)* with; **vive c. sus padres** she lives with her parents; **se escribe c. gente de varios países** he corresponds with people from a number of different countries; **¿c. quién vas?** who are you going with?; **está muy enfadado c. su madre** he's very angry with his mother; **está casada c. mi hermano** she's married to my brother; **estoy de acuerdo c. ellos** I agree with them; **habló c. todos** he spoke to everybody; **un acuerdo de colaboración c. el Caribe** a cooperation agreement with the Caribbean

(c) *(indica contenido o cualidad)* **una persona c. carácter** a person of character; **un hombre c. bigote** a man with a moustache; **una bolsa c. patatas** a bag of potatoes; **una cartera c. varios documentos** a briefcase containing several documents

(d) *(indica unión o adición)* **un helado c. nueces** an ice cream with nuts; **un pastel c. nata** a cream cake; **el mío c. leche, por favor** I'd like milk in mine, please, I'd like mine white, please; **el total c. el IVA alcanza un millón** the total is a million including *Br* VAT *o US* (sales) tax; **tiene cuarenta c. dos décimas de fiebre** her temperature is 40.2 degrees

(e) *(indica estado o situación)* **c. buena salud** in good health; **está en cama c. gripe** she's in bed with flu; **está c. un enfado tremendo** he's really angry; **el niño está c. ganas de ir al baño** the child wants to go to the *Br* toilet *o US* bathroom; **corría c. ellos pisándome los talones** I ran with them hot *o* hard on my heels

(f) *(indica causa)* **el hielo se derrite c. el calor** ice melts when heated; **me desperté c. la música del vecino** I was woken up by our neighbour playing music; **c. este tiempo no se puede ir de excursión** we can't go out on a trip in this weather; **c. el tiempo lo olvidé** in time I forgot it; **c. todo el trabajo que hemos tenido hoy, se me ha olvidado llamarla** with all the work we've had today, I've forgotten to call her; **se entristeció c. las noticias** she was sad when she heard the news; **cómprales el libro, ¡c. lo que les gusta leer!** buy them the book, they like reading so much they'll be delighted!

(g) *(a pesar de)* in spite of; **c. todo** despite everything; **c. todo lo raro que es, me encantan sus películas** he may be weird, but I love his films, for all his weirdness, I love his films; **c. lo que hemos caminado hoy, y no estoy cansado** despite the fact that we've walked so far today, I'm still not tired; **c. lo estudioso que es, lo suspendieron** for all his hard work, they still failed him

(h) *(hacia)* **para c.** towards; **es amable para c. todos** she is friendly towards *o* with everyone (**i**) *(seguido de infinitivo) (para introducir una condición)* by; **c. hacerlo así** by doing it this way; **c. llamar ya quedarás bien** you'll make a good impression just by phoning; **c. llorar no consigues nada** it's no good crying, crying won't get you anywhere; **c. no decírselo a nadie, el secreto está garantizado** if we don't tell anyone, secrecy will be guaranteed; **c. salir a las diez es suficiente** if we leave at ten, we'll have plenty of time

(**j**) *(a condición de que)* **c. que, c. tal de que** as long as; **c. que llegue a tiempo me conformo** I don't mind as long as he arrives on time; **te dejo el gato c. tal de que le des de comer** I'll let you look after the cat as long as you feed it

(**k**) *(para expresar queja o decepción)* **mira que perder, ¡c. lo bien que jugaste!** you were unlucky to lose, you played really well!; **c. lo agradable que es, y casi no tiene amigos** considering how nice he is, he has surprisingly few friends

(**l**) *Am (donde)* **fue a quejarse c. su madre** he complained to his mother; **se hace los zapatos c. Ardaches** she has her shoes made at Ardaches; **los domingos comen c. su padre** on Sundays they eat at her father's

(**m**) *Méx (tras)* after; **ha trabajado día c. día** she's worked day after day *o* day in day out

---

conato *nm* attempt; **un c. de incendio** the beginnings of a fire; **un c. de robo** an attempted robbery; **hubo un c. de golpe de estado** there was a failed coup attempt

CONAVI [ko'naβi] *nf (abrev de* **Corporación Nacional de Ahorro y Vivienda**) = major Colombian savings and loan corporation

CONCACAF [konka'kaf] *nf (abrev de* **Confederación Norte-Centroamericana y del Caribe de Fútbol**) CONCACAF, = American soccer association, including USA, Canada, Central America and the Caribbean

concadenar = **concatenar**

CONCAMIN [konka'min] *nf (abrev de* **Confederación Nacional de Cámaras Industriales**) = Mexican national confederation of chambers of industry

CONCANACO [konka'nako] *nf (abrev de* **Confederación de Cámaras Nacionales de Comercio**) = Mexican national confederation of chambers of commerce

concatenación *nf* (**a**) *(de sucesos)* chain, succession; **una c. de imágenes/fenómenos** a series *o* succession of images/phenomena (**b**) *Informát* concatenation

concatenar, concadenar *vt* to link together

concavidad *nf* (**a**) *(cualidad)* concavity (**b**) *(lugar)* hollow

cóncavo, -a *adj* concave

concebible *adj* conceivable, imaginable

concebir [47] **1** *vt* (**a**) *(imaginar)* to imagine; *(plan)* to conceive; **sus palabras me hicieron c. esperanzas** her words gave me hope; **no concibas ilusiones porque no hay nada seguro por el momento** don't get your hopes up, there's nothing certain yet

(**b**) *(creer)* to believe; **no concibe que le hayan tratado de engañar** he can't believe that they tried to deceive him; **no concibo cómo pudiste contestarle así** I can't believe you answered him back like that

(**c**) *(sentir)* to begin to feel; **c. una antipatía por** to take a dislike to

(**d**) *(hijo)* to conceive

2 *vi* to conceive

conceder *vt* (**a**) *(dar)* to grant; *(premio)* to award; *(beca)* to give, to award; *(préstamo, subvención)* to give, to grant; *(asilo, indulto, extradición)* to grant; **le concedí el beneficio de la duda** I gave him the benefit of the doubt; **me concedió un deseo** he granted me a wish; **no concede entrevistas** she doesn't give interviews; **¿me concede cinco minutos?** could you give *o* spare me five minutes?; **le han concedido un permiso para acudir al congreso** he's been given *o* granted permission to attend the conference

(**b**) *(asentir)* to admit, to concede; **concedo que están en lo cierto** I admit that you're right

(**c**) *(atribuir) (importancia)* to give, to attach; **no concede ningún valor al dinero** money doesn't matter to her at all

concejal, -ala *nm,f* (town) councillor

concejalía *nf* (**a**) *(departamento)* department (**b**) *(puesto)* = seat on the town council

concejo *nm* (**a**) *(ayuntamiento)* (town) council (**b**) *(municipio)* municipality

concelebrar *vt Rel* to concelebrate

concentración *nf* (**a**) *(mental)* concentration; **capacidad de c.** powers of concentration, ability to concentrate; **me falta c.** I lack concentration

(**b**) *(agrupamiento)* concentration ►► ***c. de capital*** concentration of capital; *Econ* ***c. parcelaria*** land consolidation; ***c. urbana*** conurbation

(**c**) *(reunión)* gathering

(**d**) *Quím* concentration

(**e**) *Dep* get-together *(to prepare for an important match or tournament)*

concentrado, -a **1** *adj* concentrated

2 *nm* concentrate ►► ***c. de tomate*** tomato purée

concentrar **1** *vt* (**a**) *(atención, esfuerzos)* to concentrate

(**b**) *(gente)* to bring together; *(tropas)* to assemble; **esta zona concentra el 80 por ciento de los casos** 80 percent of the cases occurred in this region; **la organización concentra a los principales productores mundiales** the organisation brings together the principal world producers; **es la zona de la ciudad que concentra más cafés y restaurantes** it's the area of the city with the highest concentration of cafes and restaurants

(**c**) *(disolución)* to concentrate, to make more concentrated

(**d**) *Dep* to bring together, to assemble

2 concentrarse *vpr* (**a**) *(mentalmente)* to concentrate; **no consigue concentrarse en los estudios** she can't concentrate on her studies

(**b**) *(localizarse)* to be concentrated; **la mayor parte de la industria se concentra en la zona costera** most industrial activity is concentrated along the coast

(**c**) *(reunirse)* to gather, to congregate

(**d**) *(disolución)* to become more concentrated

(**e**) *Dep* to come together, to assemble

concéntrico, -a *adj* concentric

concepción *nf* (**a**) *(fecundación)* conception (**b**) *(de idea, novela)* conception (**c**) *(interpretación, visión)* conception, understanding; **tiene una c. de la historia muy particular** her conception *o* understanding of history is a very individual one

concepcionero, -a **1** *adj* of/from Concepción *(Chile or Paraguay)*

2 *nm,f* person from Concepción *(Chile or Paraguay)*

conceptismo *nm Lit* = literary style of 17th century Spain characterized by puns and conceits

conceptista *nmf Lit* = exponent of "conceptismo"

concepto *nm* (**a**) *(idea)* concept; **el c. del bien/de la justicia** the concept of good/of justice; **se expresa con conceptos claros y precisos** she expresses her ideas clearly and concisely; **ya me he formado un c. del asunto** I've got an idea of it now

(**b**) *(opinión)* opinion; **tener buen c. de alguien** to have a high opinion of sb; **lo tengo en muy buen c.** I think very highly of him, I have a very high opinion of him

(**c**) *(motivo)* **no lo conseguirán bajo ningún c.** there's no way they'll ever manage it; **bajo ningún c. se lo cuentes a tu hermana** on no account *o* under no circumstances must you tell your sister

(**d**) *(de una cuenta)* heading, item; **los ingresos por este c. crecieron un 5 por ciento** income under this heading increased by 5 percent; **pagar algo en c. de adelanto** to pay sth in advance; **en c. de dietas** by way of *o* as expenses; **recibió 2 millones en c. de derechos de autor** he received 2 million in royalties

conceptual *adj* conceptual

conceptualismo *nm* conceptualism

conceptualista **1** *adj* conceptualistic

2 *nmf* conceptualist

conceptualización *nf* conceptualization

conceptualizar *vt* to conceptualize

conceptuar [4] *vt* to consider, to judge

concerniente *adj* **c. a** concerning, regarding; **el importe c. a inversiones** the total for investment; **es un asunto c. a la policía** this is a police matter *o* a matter for the police; **en lo c. a la fiesta, no voy a poder ir** regarding the party, I won't be able to go

concernir [25] *v impersonal* to concern; **en lo que concierne a** as regards; **por lo que** *o* **en lo que a mí concierne** as far as I'm concerned; **eso a nosotros no nos concierne** that doesn't concern us

concertación *nf* settlement ►► *Ind* ***c. social*** = process of employer-trade-union negotiations, *Br* ≃ social contract

concertado, -a **1** *adj* (**a**) *(acordado)* arranged (**b**) *Esp (colegio)* state-assisted

2 *nm,f CRica, Ven* servant

concertar [3] **1** *vt* (**a**) *(acordar) (precio)* to agree on; *(cita, entrevista)* to arrange; *(pacto)* to reach; **concertaron la celebración de un congreso extraordinario** they agreed to hold a special conference (**b**) *(coordinar)* to coordinate (**c**) *Mús (voces)* to harmonize

2 *vi* (**a**) *(concordar)* to tally, to agree (**con** with); **las dos versiones de los hechos no conciertan** the two accounts of what happened don't agree *o* tally (**b**) *Gram* to agree (**con** with); **sustantivo y adjetivo conciertan en género y número** nouns and adjectives agree in gender and number

concertina *nf* concertina

concertino *nm* first violin

concertista *nmf* soloist; **c. de piano/guitarra** concert pianist/guitarist

concesión *nf* (**a**) *(de préstamo, licencia)* granting; *(de premio)* awarding; *(de indulto, asilo, visado)* granting

(**b**) *(cesión)* concession; **una casa en la que no hay la menor c. al lujo** a house without the least concession to luxury; **hacer concesiones (a)** to make concessions (to); **fue un debate duro y sin concesiones** it was a tough debate, with no quarter given on either side

(**c**) *Com (franquicia)* franchise, licence; *(within store)* concession; **tienen la c. exclusiva del producto en ese país** they have the exclusive franchise for the product in that country; **el servicio de limpieza fue dado en c. a una empresa privada** the contract for cleaning services was awarded to a private company

concesionario, -a *Com* **1** *adj* concessionary

2 *nm,f (persona con derecho exclusivo de venta)* licensed dealer; *(titular de una concesión)* concessionaire, licensee ►► ***c. de automóviles*** car dealer *(of particular make)*

concesivo, -a *adj Gram* **oración/conjunción concesiva** concessive clause/conjunction

concha *nf* (**a**) *(de molusco)* shell ►► ***c. de peregrino*** scallop (**b**) *(carey)* tortoiseshell (**c**) *Teatro (del apuntador)* prompt box (**d**) *Andes, RP Vulg (vulva)* cunt; EXPR **¡c. de su madre!** motherfucker! (**e**) *Ven (de árbol)* bark; *(de semilla)* husk; *(de manzana, pera)* peel; *(de naranja)* rind; *(de plátano)* peel, skin; *(del pan)* crust; *(de huevo)* shell

conchabar 1 *vt* (**a**) *(unir)* to join (**b**) *(mezclar)* to mix, to blend (**c**) *CSur Fam (contratar)* to hire

2 conchabarse *vpr Fam (conspirar)* **conchabarse para hacer algo** to gang up to do sth

cónchale *interj Ven Fam Euf* (**a**) *(expresando sorpresa) Br* blimey!, *US* jeez! (**b**) *(expresando disgusto)* for heaven's sake!

concheto, -a, cheto, -a *RP Fam* **1** *adj* posh; **tu vestido/auto es muy c.** that's a very snazzy dress/flash car

2 *nm,f* rich kid; **allí veranean los conchetos del país** all the rich kids spend the summer there; **siempre se viste a la última moda, es una concheta** she always dresses in the latest fashions, she's a real glamour girl

concho *nm Andes* (**a**) *(de café, vino)* dregs ►► ***c. de vino*** burgundy (**b**) **conchos** *(de comida)* leftovers

conchudo, -a 1 *adj* (**a**) *Bol Fam (afortunado)* lucky, *Br* jammy

(**b**) *Andes, Méx, Ven Fam (desfachatado)* shameless

(**c**) *Andes, Méx, Ven Fam (cómodo)* lazy

(**d**) *Bol Fam (homosexual)* queer, *Br* poofy

(**e**) *Méx, Ven Fam (oportunista)* **es muy c.** he always has an eye for the main chance, *Br* he's a chancer

(**f**) *Perú, RP muy Fam (persona despreciable)* **ser muy c.** to be a real jerk *o Br* dickhead

2 *nm,f* (**a**) *Bol Fam (afortunado)* lucky *o Br* jammy devil

(**b**) *Andes, Méx, Ven Fam (desfachatado)* **ser un c.** to be shameless, *Br* to have a brass neck

(**c**) *Andes, Méx, Ven Fam (cómodo)* lazybones, layabout

(**d**) *Bol Fam (homosexual)* queer, *Br* poof

(**e**) *Méx, Ven Fam (oportunista)* **es un c.** he always has an eye for the main chance, *Br* he's a chancer

(**f**) *Perú, RP muy Fam (persona despreciable)* jerk, *Br* dickhead

concibiera *etc ver* **concebir**

concibo *etc ver* **concebir**

conciencia, consciencia *nf* (**a**) *(física)* consciousness; **perder la c.** to lose consciousness, to faint

(**b**) *(mental)* awareness; **tener/tomar c. de** to be/become aware of; **tenía la c. de que lo dejé allí** I was pretty sure I'd left it there ►► ***c. de clase*** class consciousness; ***c. colectiva*** collective consciousness

(**c**) *(moral, integridad)* conscience; **la voz de la c.** the voice of conscience; **me remuerde la c.** I have a guilty conscience; **trabajar para ellos me causa problemas de c.** working for them doesn't sit easy with my conscience; **hacer algo a c.** *(con esmero)* to do sth conscientiously; **en c., no puedo decir que su trabajo sea bueno** in all conscience, I can't say that his work is good; **en c., creo que debo quedarme con ella** I really feel I should stay with her; **en c., no puedo ayudarte** I don't really feel it would be right of me to help you; **obrar en c.** to act in good conscience, to act according to one's conscience; **tener la c. limpia** *o* **tranquila** to have a clear conscience; **tener mala c.** to have a guilty conscience

concienciación, *Am* **concientización** *nf* **el objetivo básico de la campaña es la c. medioambiental** the basic aim of the campaign is to raise public awareness of environmental issues; **existe una falta de c. pública sobre el problema** there is insufficient public awareness of the problem

concienciar, *Am* **concientizar 1** *vt* **c. a alguien de algo** to make sb aware of sth

2 concienciarse, *Am* **concientizarse** *vpr* to become aware (**de** of); **todavía no se han concienciado de que tienen que tener más cuidado** they haven't yet realized that they have to be more careful

concientización = **concienciación**

concientizar = **concienciar**

concienzudo, -a *adj (persona)* conscientious; *(investigación, trabajo, tratamiento)* thorough

concierna *etc ver* **concernir**

concierto 1 *ver* **concertar**

2 *nm* (**a**) *(actuación)* concert; **un c. de música clásica/de rock** a classical music/rock concert (**b**) *(composición)* concerto; **c. para piano/viola** piano/viola concerto (**c**) *(acuerdo)* agreement; **llegarse a un c.** to reach an agreement ►► ***c. económico*** economic agreement *o* accord (**d**) *(orden)* order; **poner c. en algo** to bring order to sth; **hacer algo sin orden ni c.** to do sth haphazardly

conciliable *adj* reconcilable

conciliábulo *nm (reunión secreta)* secret meeting

conciliación *nf (en un litigio)* reconciliation; *(en un conflicto laboral)* conciliation

conciliador, -ora *Ind* **1** *adj* conciliatory

2 *nm,f* conciliator

conciliar 1 *adj* conciliar

2 *vt* (**a**) *(personas)* to reconcile

(**b**) *(compatibilizar)* **me resulta difícil c. los estudios con el trabajo** I find it difficult to fit my studies in with my work *o* to combine working and studying; **intentan c. los intereses públicos con los privados** they are trying to reconcile public and private interests; **en esta obra se concilian varios estilos diferentes** several different styles are effectively combined in this work

(**c**) **c. el sueño** to get to sleep

conciliatorio, -a *adj* conciliatory

concilio *nm* council; **convocar un c.** to convene a council ►► ***c. ecuménico*** ecumenical council

concisión *nf* conciseness; **con c.** concisely

conciso, -a *adj* concise; **le agredeceríamos que fuera c. en su respuesta** we would be grateful if you could keep your answer concise

concitar *vt Formal* to stir up, to arouse; **concitó al pueblo contra el gobierno** he incited the people against the government; **concitó la antipatía de sus compañeros** he earned *o* incurred the dislike of his colleagues

conciudadano, -a *nm,f* (**a**) *(de la misma ciudad)* fellow citizen (**b**) *(del mismo país)* fellow countryman, *f* fellow countrywoman

cónclave, conclave *nm* (**a**) *(de cardenales)* conclave (**b**) *(reunión)* meeting

concluir [34] **1** *vt* (**a**) *(acabar) (concierto, película, reunión)* to end, to conclude; *(trabajo, obras)* to finish, to complete; **una ovación concluyó su discurso** his speech got an ovation; **al c. 1999 todavía quedaban varias pueblos sin teléfono** at the end of 1999, several villages were still not connected to the telephone network; **"este incidente no se volverá a repetir", concluyó** "this incident will not be repeated," he concluded

(**b**) *(deducir)* to conclude; **acabó concluyendo que se había equivocado** he finally concluded that he had made a mistake; **de su respuesta concluyo que no le interesa** from her answer I gather that she's not interested; **de lo que se concluye que...** from which we can conclude that...

2 *vi* to (come to an) end; **el plazo concluye hoy** the time limit expires today, the deadline is today; **la manifestación concluyó con la lectura de un poema** the demonstration ended with the reading of a poem; **este año las clases concluyen en junio** terms ends in June this year; **c. haciendo** *o* **por hacer algo** to end up doing sth

conclusión *nf* (**a**) *(finalización) (de concierto, película, reunión)* end, conclusion; *(de trabajo, obras)* completion; **todos celebraron la feliz c. del secuestro** everyone was very pleased at the happy outcome of the kidnapping
(**b**) *(deducción)* conclusion; **llegar a una c.** to come to *o* reach a conclusion; **sacar conclusiones** to draw conclusions; **yo no te voy a decir nada, saca tus propias conclusiones** I'm not saying anything, you can draw your own conclusions; **lo que saqué en c. es que...** I came to *o* reached the conclusion that...; **en c.** in conclusion; **en c., no sabemos qué causó el accidente** in short, we don't know what caused the accident
(**c**) *Der* **conclusiones** *(del fiscal, la defensa)* summing up

conclusivo, -a *adj* conclusive, final

concluyente *adj (prueba)* conclusive; *(decisión)* final; *(estudio)* definitive; **no han conseguido probar de forma c. su culpabilidad** they haven't been able to prove his guilt conclusively; **el presidente fue c.: no va a dimitir** the president was quite definite *o* categorical: he is not going to resign

concluyo *etc ver* **concluir**

concomerse *vpr* **se concome no sabiendo qué va a pasar** not knowing what's going to happen is driving him crazy; **c. de envidia** to be green with envy; **c. de arrepentimiento** to be consumed with remorse; **c. de impaciencia** to be itching with impatience

concomitancia *nf* concomitance

concomitante *adj* concomitant

concordancia *nf* (**a**) *(acuerdo)* agreement; **sus actos no están en c. con sus ideas** his actions are not consistent with his ideas; **no hubo c. de pareceres** no one could agree; **no hay c. entre lo que dices tú y lo que dice tu hermano** what you say doesn't tally *o* agree with what your brother says (**b**) *Gram* agreement, concord (**c**) *Mús* harmony

concordar [64] **1** *vi* (**a**) *(estar de acuerdo)* to agree *o* tally (**con** with); **sus actos no concuerdan con sus ideas** his actions are not consistent with his ideas; **lo que me cuentas concuerda con lo que ya sabía** what you tell me fits in with what I knew already; **nuestras opiniones no concuerdan** our opinions differ
(**b**) *Gram* to agree (**con** with); **sustantivo y adjetivo concuerdan en género y número** nouns and adjectives agree in gender and number
2 *vt* to reconcile; **intentaremos c. las fechas** we'll try and make the dates coincide

concordato *nm* (**a**) *(acuerdo)* concordat (**b**) *Col, Urug Econ (expediente de crisis)* = statement of the economic difficulties of a company, presented to the authorities to justify redundancies

Concorde *nm* **el C.** Concorde

concorde *adj* in accord, in agreement; **no estamos concordes con la decisión** we do not agree with the decision; **estamos concordes en la necesidad de hacer algo** we agree *o* we're in agreement on the need to do something

concordia *nf* harmony; **en la oficina reina la c.** there's a very harmonious atmosphere in the office

concreción *nf* (**a**) *(de idea, medida)* specificity; **alabaron la c. de su discurso** his speech was praised for being concise and to the point (**b**) *Geol (de partículas)* concretion (**c**) *Med (cálculo)* stone, *Espec* calculus ►► ***c. biliar*** gallstone

concretamente *adv* specifically; **la mayoría de los niños, c. cuatro de cada cinco, prefieren...** the majority of children, four out of five to be precise, prefer...; **me estoy refiriendo c. a los países del Mediterráneo** I am referring specifically to the Mediterranean countries; **le preocupa la evolución de la economía y, más c., el crecimiento del paro** he is worried about the way the economy is going, and, more specifically *o* in particular, the increase in unemployment

concretar **1** *vt* (**a**) *(precisar)* to specify, to state exactly; **todavía no han concretado su oferta** they haven't made a firm offer yet; **¿podrías c. a qué te refieres?** could you be more specific about what you're referring to?, could you explain exactly what you're referring to?; **sin c. las cifras, prometió ayudas a la región** he promised aid for the region, although without mentioning specific figures
(**b**) *(concertar)* to settle on; **finalmente concretaron una fecha para el inicio de las negociaciones** they finally fixed *o* agreed on a starting date for the negotiations
(**c**) *(reducir a lo esencial)* to summarize
2 concretarse *vpr* (**a**) *(limitarse)* **concretarse a hacer algo** to confine *o* limit oneself to doing sth; **se concretó a lo que le habían preguntado** he confined himself to answering the question
(**b**) *(materializarse)* to take shape; **la prometida subvención nunca llegó a concretarse** the promised subsidy never materialized

concretizar [14] *vt* to specify, to state exactly

concreto[1], -a *adj* (**a**) *(no abstracto)* concrete; **un concepto c.** a concrete concept
(**b**) *(determinado)* specific, particular; **aún no tenemos una fecha concreta** we don't have a definite date yet; **estoy buscando un disco c., no me vale cualquiera** I'm looking for a particular *o* specific record, not just any one; **si no me das los detalles concretos no te podré ayudar** if you don't give me the specific *o* precise details I won't be able to help you; **en el caso c. de Nicaragua,...** in the specific case of Nicaragua,...; **en c., todavía no sabemos nada** in short, we don't know anything yet; **piensa volver a Europa, en c. a Francia** she's thinking of coming back to Europe, to France to be precise; **es un experto en economía, y más en c., en gestión de empresas** he's an expert in economics, more specifically in business management; **nada en c.** nothing definite; **la culpa no se le puede atribuir a nadie en c.** there is no one person who is to blame; **en ningún sitio en c.** nowhere in particular, not in any one place

concreto[2] *nm Am* concrete ►► ***c. armado*** reinforced concrete

concubina *nf (históricamente)* concubine; *Der* common-law wife

concubinato *nm (históricamente)* concubinage; *Der* cohabitation

concuerdo *ver* **concordar**

conculcación *nf Formal* infringement, violation

conculcar [60] *vt Formal* to infringe, to break

concuñado, -a *nm,f* (**a**) *(hermano del cuñado)* = brother or sister of one's brother-in-law or sister-in-law (**b**) *(cónyuge del cuñado)* = spouse of one's brother-in-law or sister-in-law

concupiscencia *nf* lustfulness, concupiscence

concupiscente *adj* lascivious, lustful

concurrencia *nf* (**a**) *(asistencia)* attendance; *(espectadores)* crowd, audience (**b**) *(de sucesos)* concurrence (**c**) *Com* competition; *Der* **no c.** non-competition clause

concurrente **1** *adj* (**a**) *(circunstancia)* concurrent (**b**) *(participante)* **el público c. aclamó al cantante** the audience applauded the singer; **los proyectos concurrentes a un concurso** the projects competing *o* entered in a competition
2 *nmf* person present; **los concurrentes aprobaron la moción** the motion was approved by those present

concurrido, -a *adj (bar, calle, exposición)* crowded, busy; *(espectáculo)* well-attended; **es un restaurante muy c.** there are always lots of people in that restaurant

concurrir *vi* (**a**) *(reunirse)* **c. a algo** to go to sth, to attend sth; **concurrieron a la reunión muchos vecinos** many residents went to *o* attended the meeting
(**b**) *(coincidir)* to coincide; **concurrieron varias circunstancias que agravaron el problema** a number of factors coincided to make the problem worse; **en él concurren todos los requisitos necesarios para optar a la beca** he meets all the requirements needed to apply for the scholarship; **en la película concurren varios géneros diferentes** the film combines several different genres; **en su persona concurren la amabilidad y la inteligencia** she is both kind and intelligent
(**c**) *(contribuir)* to combine; **varios factores concurrieron al éxito de la actuación** several factors contributed to *o* combined to ensure the success of the performance
(**d**) *(líneas, carreteras)* to meet, to converge; **las calles concurren en la plaza mayor** the streets meet in *o* converge on the main square
(**e**) *(participar)* **c. a** *(concurso)* to take part in, to compete in; *(examen)* to take, *Br* to sit; **varias empresas concurren al concurso** several companies are taking part in the competition; **el partido de los verdes concurre a las elecciones en coalición** the green party is running *o* standing in the election as part of a coalition; **los candidatos que concurren al Premio Nobel** the candidates for the Nobel prize
(**f**) *(estar de acuerdo)* to agree; **concurrimos en todos los puntos** we agree *o* are in agreement on all the points

concursado, -a *nm,f Der* insolvent debtor

concursante *nmf* (**a**) *(en concurso)* competitor, contestant (**b**) *(en oposiciones)* candidate

concursar **1** *vi* (**a**) *(competir)* to compete, to participate (**b**) *(en oposiciones)* to be a compete; **concursó a una plaza de médico** he competed for a doctor's post *(in public competitive examination)*
2 *vt Der* to declare insolvent *o* bankrupt

concurso *nm* (**a**) *(literaria, deportiva)* competition; **un c. de disfraces/de piano** a fancy dress/piano competition; **presentarse a un c.** to enter a competition; **presentar una película a c.** to enter a movie *o Br* film in competition ►► ***c. de belleza*** beauty contest; ***c. hípico*** horse show; ***c. de saltos*** show-jumping event
(**b**) *(de televisión)* game show; *(de preguntas y respuestas)* quiz show

(**c**) *(oposición)* **c.(-oposición)** = public competitive examination ►► ***c. de méritos*** merit-based selection process

(**d**) *(para una obra)* tender; **adjudicar un c.** to award a contract; **convocar un c.** to call for tender, to invite tenders; **salir a c. público** to be put out to tender ►► ***c. de adjudicación*** tendering process

(**e**) *(colaboración)* cooperation; **con el c. de todos, saldremos del apuro** if everyone helps *o* cooperates, we can get ourselves out of this mess

(**f**) *(concurrencia)* **el enorme c. de visitantes desbordó a los organizadores** the organizers couldn't cope with the huge number of visitors

> **Falso amigo**: El sustantivo inglés **concourse** no es la traducción del español **concurso**. En inglés, **concourse** significa "vestíbulo" o "concurrencia".

condado *nm* (**a**) *(territorio)* county (**b**) *(título)* earldom, countship

condal *adj* **el palacio c.** the count's palace; **la ciudad c.** Barcelona

conde, -esa *nm,f* count, *f* countess

condecoración *nf* (**a**) *(distinción)* decoration (**b**) *(insignia)* medal, decoration

condecorar *vt* to decorate

condena *nf* (**a**) *(castigo)* sentence; **cumplir c.** to serve a sentence; **cumplir una c. de diez años** to serve a ten-year sentence ►► ***c. a muerte*** death penalty

(**b**) *(sentencia)* sentence; **el juez dictó c.** the judge pronounced sentence

(**c**) *(reprobación, crítica)* condemnation (**por** of); **el presidente expresó su c. más enérgica por el atentado** the president condemned the attack in the strongest terms

condenable *adj* condemnable

condenación *nf* (**a**) *(desaprobación)* condemnation (**b**) *Rel* damnation

condenadamente *adv Fam* damn; **este programa es c. malo** this programme is absolute *Br* rubbish *o US* garbage

condenado, -a **1** *adj* (**a**) *(destinado)* doomed; **un proyecto c. al fracaso** a project doomed to failure; **un libro c. al olvido** a book destined to be forgotten

(**b**) *(a una pena)* sentenced; *(a un sufrimiento)* condemned

(**c**) *Fam (maldito)* damned, wretched; **ia ver si para de una vez esta condenada lluvia!** I wish this damned rain would stop!; **ino seas c. y devuélveme la llave!** don't be such a pig and give me the key back!

2 *nm,f* (**a**) *(a una pena)* convicted person; *(a muerte)* condemned person; EXPR *Fam* **como un c.: correr como un c.** to run like the blazes *o Br* the clappers; **estudiar como un c.** to study like mad *o* crazy; **trabajar como un c.** to work like a slave

(**b**) **los condenados** *(al infierno)* the damned

(**c**) *Fam (maldito)* wretch; **esa condenada se niega a pagarme** that wretched woman refuses to pay me

condenar **1** *vt* (**a**) *(declarar culpable)* to convict

(**b**) *(castigar)* **c. a alguien a algo** to sentence sb to sth; **fue condenado a muerte** he was sentenced *o* condemned to death; **fue condenado a tres años de prisión** he was sentenced to three years in prison; **fue condenado a pagar una multa de 15.000 pesos** he was ordered to pay a fine of 15,000 pesos; **la condenaron a no salir de casa durante los fines de semana** they punished her by grounding her at weekends

(**c**) *(predestinar)* **estar condenado a** to be doomed to; **esa iniciativa está condenada al fracaso** that initiative is doomed to failure; **los supervivientes están condenados a morir de hambre** the survivors are condemned to die of starvation

(**d**) *(reprobar)* to condemn; **todos los partidos condenaron el atentado** all parties condemned the attack

(**e**) *(tapiar) (con ladrillos)* to brick up, to wall up; *(con tablas)* to board up

2 condenarse *vpr* to be damned

condenatorio, -a *adj* condemnatory; **sentencia condenatoria** conviction

condensación *nf* condensation

condensado, -a *adj* condensed

condensador, -ora **1** *adj* condensing

2 *nm* condenser ►► ***c. eléctrico*** electric capacitor

condensar **1** *vt* (**a**) *(aire, vapor)* to condense (**b**) *(texto, conferencia)* to condense; **condensó su discurso en diez minutos** she condensed her speech into ten minutes

2 condensarse *vpr* to condense, to become condensed

CONDEPA [kon'depa] *nf (abrev de* **Conciencia de Patria**) = right-wing populist Bolivian political party

condesa *ver* **conde**

condescendencia *nf* (**a**) *(benevolencia)* graciousness, kindness; **tratar a alguien con c.** to treat sb with kindness and understanding (**b**) *(altivez)* condescension; **su tono de c. me resulta inaguantable** I find his condescending tone unbearable, I can't stand *o* bear his condescending tone

condescender [66] *vi* (**a**) *(con amabilidad)* **c. a** to consent to, to accede to; **condescendió en acompañarme** he kindly agreed to *o* consented to go with me (**b**) *(con desprecio, altivez)* **c. a** to deign to, to condescend to

condescendiente *adj* (**a**) *(amable)* obliging (**b**) *(altivo)* condescending

condestable *nm Hist* constable

CONDICIÓN *nf* (**a**) *(término, estipulación)* condition; **para votar es c. ser mayor de edad** in order to vote you have to be of age; **poner condiciones** to set conditions; **con la** *o* **a c. de que** on condition that; **con una sola c.** on one condition; **sin condiciones** unconditional; **las condiciones de un contrato** the terms of a contract; **condiciones acostumbradas/convenidas** usual/agreed terms ►► ***condiciones de entrega*** terms of delivery; ***condiciones de pago*** payment terms, terms of payment; ***c. sine qua non*** prerequisite; **tener experiencia con** *Esp* **ordenadores** *o Am* **computadores es c. sine qua non para obtener este trabajo** a knowledge of computers is essential for this job; ***condiciones de venta*** conditions of sale

(**b**) *(estado)* condition; **en buenas/malas condiciones** in good/bad condition; **tiró la leche porque estaba en malas condiciones** she threw the milk away because it was off; **deseamos participar en condiciones de igualdad** we want to participate on equal terms; **estar en condiciones de** *o* **para hacer algo** *(físicamente)* to be in a fit state to do sth; *(por la situación)* to be in a position to do sth; **no estar en condiciones** *(carne, pescado)* to be off; *(vivienda)* to be unfit for living in; *(instalaciones)* to be unfit for use; **no están en condiciones de exigir demasiado** they are not in a position to make too many demands; **la sala no reúne las condiciones necesarias para que se celebre el concierto** the hall does not meet the necessary requirements for the concert to be held there; **en tres días me dejaron la moto en condiciones** they fixed my motorbike for me in just three days; **no estaba en condiciones de jugar** he wasn't fit to play

(**c**) **condiciones** *(circunstancias)* conditions ►► ***condiciones atmosféricas*** weather conditions; ***condiciones de trabajo*** working conditions; ***condiciones de vida*** living conditions

(**d**) *(clase social)* social class; **de c. humilde** of humble circumstances; **en la manifestación había gente de toda c.** there were people of every description at the demonstration

(**e**) *(naturaleza)* nature; **la c. femenina/humana** the feminine/human condition; **un adolescente de c. rebelde** a rebellious youth; **mi c. de mujer...** the fact that I am a woman...

(**f**) *(calidad)* capacity; **en su c. de abogado** in his capacity as a lawyer; **en su c. de parlamentario, tiene derecho a un despacho** as an MP, he has the right to an office; **su c. de monarca no le permite opinar sobre ese asunto** as the monarch, he is not permitted to express an opinion on this matter

(**g**) *(aptitud)* **es un abogado de excelentes condiciones** he's an extremely able lawyer; **tiene condiciones para la pintura** she has a gift for painting; **no tiene condiciones para estudiar medicina** he's not good enough to study medicine

---

condicionado, -a *adj* conditioned; **c. a** subject to, dependent upon

condicional **1** *adj* conditional

2 *nm Gram* conditional (tense)

condicionamiento *nm* conditioning

condicionante **1** *adj* determining

2 *nm* determinant

condicionar *vt* (**a**) *(hacer dependiente de)* **c. algo a algo** to make sth dependent on sth (**b**) *(influir)* to influence

cóndilo *nm Anat* condyle

condimentación *nf* seasoning

condimentar *vt* to season

condimento *nm (aderezo)* seasoning; *(hierba)* herb; *(especia)* spice

condiscípulo, -a *nm,f (en la universidad)* fellow student; **fueron condiscípulos en la escuela** they were contemporaries at school

condolencia *nf* condolence; **expresó sus condolencias a la viuda** he offered his condolences to the widow

condolerse [41] *vpr* to feel pity (**de** for)

condominio *nm* (**a**) *Der (de un territorio)* condominium; *(de una cosa)* joint ownership (**b**) *(territorio)* condominium (**c**) *Am (edificio) Br* block of flats, *US* condominium

condón *nm* condom ►► ***c. femenino*** female condom

condonación *nf (de deuda)* cancellation, writing off; *(de pena)* remission, lifting

condonar *vt* (**a**) *(deuda)* to cancel, to write off; *(pena)* to remit, to lift (**b**) *(violencia, terrorismo)* to condone

cóndor *nm* (**a**) *(ave)* condor ►► ***c. de California*** California condor (**b**) *(en Colombia, Chile y Ecuador)* condor

condorito *nm Chile (sandalia de playa)* beach sandal

conducción *nf* (**a**) *Esp (de vehículo)* driving ►► ***c. temeraria*** careless *o* reckless driving (**b**) *(de calor, electricidad)* conduction (**c**) *(por tubería)* piping; *(por cable)* wiring (**d**) *(conducto) (de agua, gas)* pipe; *(de electricidad)* wiring (**e**) *(dirección) (de empresa)* management, running; *(de investigación)* running

conducente *adj* conducive, leading (**a** to); **unas medidas conducentes a la resolución de la crisis** measures which may provide a solution to the crisis

conducir [18] **1** *vt* (**a**) *(vehículo)* to drive (**b**) *(por tubería, cable) (calor)* to conduct; *(líquido)* to convey, to carry; *(electricidad)* to carry (**c**) *(dirigir) (empresa)* to manage, to run; *(ejército)* to lead; *(asunto)* to handle (**d**) *(programa televisivo)* to present, to host (**e**) *(persona)* to lead; **el guía nos condujo a la salida** the guide led us to the exit

2 *vi* (**a**) *(en vehículo)* to drive (**b**) *(a sitio, situación)* **c. a** to lead to; **esas discusiones no conducen a nada** those discussions won't achieve anything; **este plan conduce al desastre** this plan is a recipe for disaster; **una cifra que puede c. a error** a figure which could be misleading *o* lead to mistakes

3 conducirse *vpr* to behave

conducta *nf* behaviour, conduct

conductancia *nf Fís* conduction

conductibilidad *nf Fís* conductivity

conductismo *nm Psi* behaviourism

conductista *nmf Psi* behaviourist

conductividad *nf Fís* conductivity

conductivo, -a *adj Fís* conductive

conducto *nm* (**a**) *(de fluido)* pipe

(**b**) *(vía)* channel; **por c. de** through; **la resolución se comunicará por c. oficial** the decision will be made known through official channels; **me enteré de la boda por c. de tu hermana** I found out about the wedding through *o* from your sister

(**c**) *Anat* duct, channel ►► ***c. auditivo*** ear canal, *Espec* auditory meatus; ***c. biliar*** bile duct; ***c. deferente*** sperm duct, *Espec* vas deferens; ***c. hepático*** hepatic duct; ***c. lacrimal*** tear duct; ***c. semicircular*** semicircular canal

conductor, -ora 1 *adj (de electricidad, calor)* conductive

2 *nm,f* (**a**) *(de vehículo)* driver ►► ***c. en prácticas*** learner driver (**b**) *(de un programa televisivo)* presenter, host

3 *nm* conductor ►► ***c. eléctrico*** conductor

conductual *adj Psi* behavioural

conduela *etc ver* **condolerse**

condueño, -a *nm,f* joint owner, co-owner

conduje *etc ver* **conducir**

conduzco *etc ver* **conducir**

conectado, -a *adj* connected (**a** to); *Informát* **la impresora está conectada a la red** the printer is connected to the network; *Informát* **estar c. a Internet** to be on-line, to be on the Internet

conectar 1 *vt* (**a**) *(aparato, mecanismo) (con cables)* to connect (**a** *o* **con** (up) to); **conecta la lavadora a la red eléctrica** connect the washing machine to the electricity supply

(**b**) *(encender) (radio, calefacción)* to turn on, to switch on

(**c**) *(unir, comunicar)* to connect, to link; **el puente conecta la isla con el continente** the bridge connects *o* links the island to the mainland

(**d**) *(asociar)* to link, to connect; **la policía ha conectado el robo con las mafias locales** the police have linked *o* connected the robbery to the local mafia

(**e**) *Dep (disparo)* to strike

2 *vi* (**a**) *Rad & TV* **c. con** to go over to; **conectamos con nuestro enviado especial en la zona** and now over to our special correspondent in the area

(**b**) *(persona)* **c. con alguien** *(ponerse en contacto)* to get in touch with sb; *(entenderse)* to relate to sb; **una escritora que conecta con los más jóvenes** a writer who knows how to relate to younger readers; **al partido le ha fallado c. con los sectores más desfavorecidos** the party has failed to reach *o* get through to the most disadvantaged groups

(**c**) *(vuelo)* to connect; **necesito c. con el vuelo de las 9** I have to be there for a connecting flight at 9 o'clock

(**d**) *Informát* **c. y funcionar** plug and play

3 conectarse *vpr* to switch (itself) on; **las luces se conectan solas** the lights switch themselves on; **conectarse a Internet** *(por primera vez)* to get connected to the Internet, to go on-line; *(regularmente)* to go on the Internet, to go on-line

conectividad *nf Informát* connectivity

conectivo, -a *adj Ling* connective

conector *nm* (**a**) *(clavija, enchufe)* connector ►► ***c. hembra*** female connector; ***c. macho*** male connector; ***c. universal*** universal connector (**b**) *(cable)* cable, lead

conejar *nm* rabbit hutch

conejera *nf* (**a**) *(madriguera)* (rabbit) warren (**b**) *(conejar)* rabbit hutch

conejillo *nm también Fig* ***c. de Indias*** guinea pig

conejo, -a 1 *nm,f* rabbit, *f* doe; *muy Fam* **esa mujer es una coneja** that woman just has one *Br* bloody or *US* goddamn baby after another; EXPR *Fam* **reproducirse como conejos** to breed like rabbits ►► ***c. de angora*** angora rabbit; ***c. a la cazadora*** *(plato)* = rabbit cooked in olive oil with chopped onion, garlic and parsley

2 *nm Esp muy Fam (vulva)* pussy, *US* beaver

conexión *nf* (**a**) *(vínculo)* connection; **no hay c. entre los dos accidentes** there's no connection between the two accidents; **está siendo investigado en c. con el robo** he is being investigated in connection with the robbery; **una ciencia en íntima c. con la biología** a science very closely linked with biology

(**b**) *(eléctrica, informática)* connection; **la c. a la red eléctrica/telefónica no funciona** the mains/telephone connection doesn't work; **un hogar con c. a Internet** a home with an Internet connection, a home connected to the Internet

(**c**) *Rad & TV* link-up; **devolvemos la c. a nuestros estudios centrales** and now, back to the studio ►► ***c. vía satélite*** satellite link

(**d**) **tener conexiones** *(amistades influyentes)* to have connections; **consiguió el trabajo gracias a sus conexiones** she got the job thanks to her connections

(**e**) *(vuelo)* connection

conexo, -a *adj* related, connected

confabulación *nf* conspiracy

confabularse *vpr* to plot *o* conspire (**para** to); **se confabuló con sus enemigos para derrotar al invasor** he conspired with his enemies to defeat the invader

confección *nf* (**a**) *(de ropa)* tailoring, dressmaking; **el ramo de la c.** the clothing *o US* garment industry; **un traje/vestido de c.** a ready-to-wear *o* ready-made *o esp Br* an off-the-peg suit/dress

(**b**) *(de comida)* preparation, making; *(de lista)* drawing up; *(de estadística)* production, preparation; **productos de c. artesanal** handicrafts; **la c. de las listas electorales** the drawing up of the parties' lists of candidates

> **Falso amigo**: El sustantivo inglés **confection** no es la traducción del español **confección**. En inglés, **confection** significa "dulce" o "creación".

confeccionar *vt* (**a**) *(ropa)* to make (up) (**b**) *(plato)* to prepare; *(lista)* to draw up; *(estadística)* to produce, to prepare

confeccionista *nmf (fabricante)* clothing manufacturer; *(vendedor)* clothing retailer

confederación *nf (de estados, personas, bancos)* confederation ►► ***C. de Estados Independientes*** Confederation of Independent States; ***C. Helvética*** Switzerland, Swiss Confederation; ***c. hidrográfica*** = state organization responsible for overseeing the use of the water resources of a particular area

confederado, -a 1 *adj* confederate

2 *nm Hist* Confederate

confederarse *vpr* to confederate, to form a confederation

conferencia *nf* (**a**) *(charla)* talk, lecture (**sobre** on); **dar una c.** to give a talk *o* lecture ►► ***c. de prensa*** press conference

(**b**) *(reunión)* conference; **celebrar una c.** to hold a conference ►► ***c. episcopal*** bishops' conference

(**c**) *(por teléfono)* (long-distance) call; **poner una c.** to make a long-distance call ►► ***c. a cobro revertido*** *Br* reverse-charge call, *US* collect call

conferenciante *nmf* speaker

conferenciar *vi* to have a discussion

conferencista *nmf Am* speaker

conferir [63] *vt* (**a**) *(cualidad)* to give, to lend; **la asistencia del monarca confiere más importancia al acto** the presence of the monarch gives more importance to the ceremony; **el brillante colorido confiere gran dramatismo al cuadro** the brilliant colours give the painting a very dramatic effect *o* make the painting very dramatic
(**b**) **c. algo a alguien** *(honor, dignidad)* to confer *o* bestow sth upon sb; *(responsabilidades)* to give sth to sb, to confer sth on sb; **la nueva ley confiere el poder ejecutivo al presidente** the new law confers executive power on *o* gives executive power to the president

confesar [3] **1** *vt* (**a**) *(pecado)* to confess (to); **confieso que he pecado** I confess that I have sinned
(**b**) *(falta)* to confess (to); *(culpabilidad)* to confess, to admit; *(sentimientos)* to confess (to); **le confesó su amor** he confessed *o* declared his love to her; **confieso que te mentí** I admit I lied to you; **c. de plano** to make a full confession, to confess to everything; **si quieres que te confiese la verdad, desconozco la respuesta** to tell you the truth, I don't know the answer
(**c**) *(persona)* **el cura confesó al moribundo** the priest heard the dying man's confession
2 confesarse *vpr* (**a**) *(ante sacerdote)* to go to confession; **confesarse de algo** to confess sth; **confesarse con alguien** to confess one's sins to sb
(**b**) *(declararse)* **se confesó culpable del asesinato** she confessed to (being guilty of) the murder; **me confieso admirador de su música** I admit to being an admirer of her music, I confess I'm an admirer of her music

confesión *nf* (**a**) *(de pecado)* confession; **oír a alguien en c.** to hear sb's confession (**b**) *(de falta, culpabilidad, sentimientos)* confession; **hacer una c.** to confess; **extraer una c. de alguien** to extract a confession from sb, to get a confession out of sb (**c**) *(credo)* religion, (religious) persuasion, denomination; **de c. protestante** Protestant, of the Protestant faith

confesional *adj* denominational; **estado c.** = country with an official state religion

confesionario, confesonario *nm* confessional

confeso, -a 1 *adj* (**a**) *(reo)* self-confessed; **un c. republicano** a self-confessed republican (**b**) *Hist (judío)* converted
2 *nm,f Hist (judío)* converted Jew

confesonario = **confesionario**

confesor *nm* confessor

confeti *nm* confetti

confiabilidad *nf Am (fiabilidad)* reliability

confiable *adj Am (fiable)* reliable

confiado, -a *adj* (**a**) *(seguro)* confident; **estar c.** to be confident; **estar demasiado c.** to be overconfident; **estoy c. en que todo acabará bien** I'm confident everything will turn out all right; **se mostró c.** he was confident (**b**) *(crédulo)* trusting; **ser c.** to be trusting

confianza *nf* (**a**) *(seguridad)* confidence (**en** in); **c. en uno mismo** self-confidence; **tengo plena c. en su trabajo** I have the utmost confidence in her work; **tengo c. en que lo conseguirán** I'm confident they'll achieve it; **deposito toda mi c. en él** I'm putting all my faith *o* trust in him; **hace las cosas con mucha c.** she does things very confidently; **todavía no ha adquirido la suficiente c.** he hasn't acquired enough confidence yet; **no me inspira la más mínima c.** I have no confidence *o* faith in him whatsoever
(**b**) *(fe)* trust; **de c.** trustworthy; **una marca de toda c.** a very reliable brand; **uno de sus colaboradores de c.** one of his most trusted associates
(**c**) *(familiaridad)* familiarity; **amigo de c.** close *o* intimate friend; **en c.** in confidence; **te cuento todo esto en c.** I'm telling you all this in confidence; **tengo mucha c. con él** I am very close to him; **pregúntaselo tú, que tienes más c. con él** you ask him, you're closer to him; **una cosa te voy a decir con toda c....** let me be frank...; **puedes hablar con toda c.** you can talk quite freely; **entre nosotros hay c.** we're good friends; **se toma demasiadas confianzas** she's too familiar, she takes too many liberties; EXPR *Fam* **donde hay c. da asco** familiarity breeds contempt

confianzudo, -a *Am Fam* **1** *adj* forward, fresh
2 *nm,f* **es un c.** he's very forward *o* fresh

confiar [32] **1** *vt* (**a**) *(secreto)* to confide; **me confió que estaba muy nervioso** he confided to me that he was very nervous
(**b**) *(responsabilidad, persona, asunto)* **c. algo a alguien** to entrust sth to sb; **te confío el cuidado de las plantas** I'm relying on you to look after the plants; **le han confiado la dirección del partido** he has been entrusted with the leadership of the party
2 *vi (tener fe)* **c. en** to trust; **c. en la suerte** to trust to luck; **confía demasiado en los demás** he is too trusting of others; **no confío en sus intenciones** I don't believe his intentions are honest; **confiamos en el triunfo** we are confident of winning; **confío en que Dios nos ayudará** I have faith *o* am confident that God will help us; **confío en poder conseguirlo** I am confident of being able to achieve it
3 confiarse *vpr* (**a**) *(despreocuparse)* to be too sure (of oneself), to be overconfident; **yo de ti no me confiaría demasiado** I wouldn't be so sure of myself *o* so confident if I were you; **no se confió y preparó el examen concienzudamente** he didn't feel too confident so he studied hard for the exam
(**b**) *(sincerarse)* **confiarse a** to confide in; **me confié a mi amigo** I confided in my friend

confidencia *nf* confidence, secret; **hacer confidencias a** to confide in

confidencial *adj* confidential

confidencialidad *nf* confidentiality; **se garantiza la más estricta c.** the strictest confidentiality is guaranteed

confidencialmente *adv* confidentially

confidenciar *vt Am* **c. algo a alguien** to confide sth to sb, to tell sb sth in confidence; **le confidenció detalles del proyecto** she told him details of the project in confidence

confidente *nmf* (**a**) *(amigo)* confidant, *f* confidante (**b**) *(soplón)* informer

confiero *etc ver* **conferir**

confieso *etc ver* **confesar**

configuración *nf* (**a**) *(formación)* shaping, forming; **la c. de un nuevo orden mundial** the shaping *o* forming of a new world order (**b**) *(disposición)* configuration; *(de la costa)* outline, shape; *(de ciudad)* layout; **la c. del terreno** the lie *o* lay of the land (**c**) *Informát* configuration

configurar 1 *vt* (**a**) *(formar)* to shape, to form (**b**) *Informát* to configure
2 configurarse *vpr (constituirse)* **un paisaje que se ha configurado a través de las eras** a landscape which has been formed *o* taken shape over the ages; **hoy en día se configura como una de las empresas líderes del sector** these days it is one of the leading companies in the field

confín *nm* (**a**) *(límite)* border, boundary (**b**) *(extremo) (del reino, universo)* outer reaches; **en los confines de** on the very edge of; **el castillo se vislumbraba en los confines del horizonte** you could just make out the castle on the distant horizon; **viajó por todos los confines del mundo** he travelled to the four corners of the globe

confinamiento *nm*, **confinación** *nf* (**a**) *(de un detenido)* confinement (**en** to) (**b**) *(de un desterrado)* banishment (**a** *o* **en** to)

confinar 1 *vt* (**a**) *(detener, limitar)* to confine (**en** to); **el accidente lo confinó a una silla de ruedas** the accident left him in a wheelchair, he was confined to a wheelchair after the accident (**b**) *(desterrar)* to banish (**a** *o* **en** to)
2 *vi* **c. con algo** to border on, to adjoin
3 confinarse *vpr* to shut *o* hide oneself away; **se confinó en un pueblo aislado** he hid himself away in an isolated village

confiriera *etc ver* **conferir**

confirmación *nf* (**a**) *(de noticia, sospecha)* confirmation (**b**) *(de billete, reserva)* confirmation (**c**) *Rel* confirmation

confirmar 1 *vt* (**a**) *(noticia, sospecha)* to confirm; **esto sólo confirma mis sospechas** this simply confirms my suspicions (**b**) *(billete, reserva)* to confirm; **el ministro ha sido confirmado en el cargo** the minister has been confirmed in his post (**c**) *Rel* to confirm
2 confirmarse *vpr* (**a**) *(reafirmarse)* **se confirmó en su opinión** his opinion was confirmed; **me confirmo en mis temores** that confirms my fears (**b**) *Rel* to be confirmed

confirmativo, -a, confirmatorio, -a *adj* confirmatory

confiscación *nf* confiscation, appropriation

confiscar [60] *vt* to confiscate

confitado, -a *adj* candied; **frutas confitadas** crystallized fruit

confitar *vt* to candy

confite *nm Br* sweet, *US* candy

confitería *nf* (**a**) *(tienda)* confectioner's (**b**) *RP (café)* cafe ►► ***c. bailable*** disco

confitero, -a *nm,f* confectioner

confitura *nf* preserve, jam

conflagración *nf* (**a**) *(guerra)* conflict, war (**b**) *(incendio)* conflagration

conflictividad *nf* (**a**) *(cualidad)* controversial nature (**b**) *(conflicto)* conflict; **en las últimas semanas ha aumentado la c. en la zona** in recent weeks there has been increasing unrest in the area ►► ***c. laboral*** industrial unrest; ***c. social*** social unrest

conflictivo, -a *adj* (**a**) *(polémico)* controversial (**b**) *(época, país)* troubled; **una zona conflictiva de Europa** a trouble spot *o* an area of conflict in Europe (**c**) *(persona)* difficult

conflicto *nm* (**a**) *(combate, lucha)* conflict; *(de opiniones, ideas)* clash; **entrar en c. con** to come into conflict with; **los bandos en c.** the sides involved in the conflict ►► ***c. armado*** armed conflict; ***c. bélico*** armed conflict; ***c. generacional*** generation gap; ***c. de intereses*** conflict of interests; ***c. laboral*** industrial dispute
(**b**) *Psi* conflict; **se encuentra en c. consigo mismo** he is in conflict with himself

confluencia *nf (de ríos)* confluence; *(de caminos)* junction; *(de culturas, factores, intereses)* convergence; **en la c. entre la calle Rozas y la calle Paz** at the junction *o* intersection of Rozas and Paz

confluente *adj (río)* confluent; *(camino)* convergent; *(cultura, factor, interés)* converging

confluir [34] *vi* (**a**) *(ríos)* to flow into each other, to meet (**en** at); *(caminos)* to converge, to meet (**en** at); *(culturas, factores, intereses)* to converge (**b**) *(personas)* to come together, to gather (**en** in)

conformación *nf (configuración)* shape

conformar 1 *vt* (**a**) *(configurar)* to shape; **conformó una organización moderna y disciplinada** he built up a modern and disciplined organization; **los países que conforman la OPEP** the countries which make up *o* form OPEC; **los alimentos que conforman la dieta mediterránea** the foods that make up the Mediterranean diet
(**b**) *(contentar)* **c. a alguien** to keep sb happy
(**c**) *(cheque)* to endorse, to authorize
2 **conformarse** *vpr* **conformarse con** *(suerte, destino)* to resign oneself to; *(apañárselas con)* to make do with; *(contentarse con)* to settle for; **no se conforma con nada** she's never satisfied; **no se conforma con cualquier cosa** he won't settle for just anything; **me conformo con lo que tengo** I'm quite happy with what I've got; **me conformo con el tercer puesto** I'll settle for third place

conforme 1 *adj* (**a**) *(acorde)* **c. a** in accordance with; **c. al reglamento** in accordance with the rules; **el juez dictaminó que la decisión era c. a la ley** the judge ruled that the decision was in accordance with the law
(**b**) *(de acuerdo)* in agreement, happy; **estar c. con algo/alguien** to be happy with sth/sb; **si no estás c., protesta** if you don't agree, say so, if you're not happy, say so; **estoy c. en que vengas, pero no llegues tarde** I'm happy for you to come *o* it's all right by me if you come, but don't be late
(**c**) *(contento)* happy; **no estoy muy c. con la reparación efectuada** I'm not very happy with the repair they did
2 *adv* (**a**) *(a medida que)* as; **c. envejecía** as he got older
(**b**) *(como)* exactly as; **te lo cuento c. lo vi** I'm telling you exactly what I saw
(**c**) *(en cuanto)* as soon as; **c. amanezca, me iré** I'll leave as soon as it gets light
3 *nm* authorization; **todavía no ha dado su c.** he hasn't authorized it yet

conformidad *nf* (**a**) *(aprobación)* approval; **dio su c.** she gave her consent (**b**) *(acuerdo)* **de** *o* **en c. con** in accordance with

conformismo *nm* conformity, conformism

conformista 1 *adj* conformist
2 *nmf* conformist

confort (*pl* **conforts**) *nm* (**a**) *(comodidad)* comfort; **todo c.** *(en anuncio)* all mod cons (**b**) *Chile (papel higiénico)* toilet paper

confortabilidad *nf* comfort

confortable *adj* comfortable

confortablemente *adv* comfortably

confortante *adj* comforting, consoling

confortar *vt* (**a**) *(fortalecer)* **esta sopa te confortará** this soup will do you good (**b**) *(alentar, consolar)* to console, to comfort

confraternidad *nf* (**a**) *(hermandad)* brotherhood (**b**) *(entre personas, países)* fraternity

confraternizar [14] *vi* **c. con el enemigo** to fraternize with the enemy; **confraternizaron con los jugadores del otro equipo después del partido** they socialized with the players from the other team after the match

confrontación *nf* (**a**) *(enfrentamiento)* confrontation; *(deportivo)* clash (**b**) *(comparación)* comparison

confrontar *vt* (**a**) *(comparar)* to compare (**b**) *(encarar)* **confrontaron a los dos testigos** the two witnesses were brought face to face (**c**) *(enfrentar)* to confront, to face; **c. un problema** to confront *o* face a problem

confucianismo, confucionismo *nm* Confucianism

confuciano, -a *adj* Confucian

Confucio *n pr* Confucius

confucionista *adj* Confucian

confundible *adj* **las dos cosas son fácilmente confundibles** the two things are easily confused

confundido, -a *adj* (**a**) *(avergonzado)* embarrassed (**b**) *(equivocado)* confused

confundir 1 *vt* (**a**) *(trastocar)* **c. una cosa con otra** to mistake one thing for another; **c. dos cosas** to get two things mixed up; **siempre lo confundo con su hermano gemelo** I always mistake him for his twin brother; **creo que me está confundiendo con otro** I think you're confusing me with someone else; EXPR *Fam Hum* **c. la velocidad con el tocino** to mix up two completely different things
(**b**) *(desconcertar)* to confuse; **me confundes con tanta información** you're confusing me with all that information
(**c**) *(mezclar)* to mix up
(**d**) *(abrumar)* to overwhelm; **tanta simpatía me confunde** I'm overwhelmed by all this friendliness, all this friendliness is overwhelming
2 **confundirse** *vpr* (**a**) *(equivocarse)* to make a mistake; **confundirse de piso/tren** to get the wrong floor/train; **me confundí en los cálculos** I made a mistake in the figures, I got the figures wrong; **se ha confundido** *(al teléfono)* (you've got the) wrong number; **no te confundas... yo no soy un mentiroso** don't get the wrong idea... I'm no liar
(**b**) *(liarse)* to get confused; **me confundo con tanta información** I get confused by all that information
(**c**) *(mezclarse) (colores, siluetas)* to merge (**en** into); **confundirse entre la gente** *(personas)* to lose oneself in the crowd; **se han confundido las maletas** the suitcases have got mixed up; **se confundió en la multitud para poder escapar** he mingled with the crowd to make his escape

confusamente *adv* (**a**) *(con turbación)* confusedly (**b**) *(en desorden)* in confusion, in disorder; **me lo explicó c.** she gave me a muddled explanation of it; **lo recuerdo todo muy c.** my recollection of it all is very vague

confusión *nf* (**a**) *(desorden, lío)* confusion; **la c. aumentó con la llegada del cantante** the singer's arrival added to the confusion; **los ladrones actuaron aprovechando la c.** the thieves took advantage of the confusion; **hubo una gran c.** there was great confusion; **en su habitación reina la c.** her room is in chaos; **existe cierta c. acerca de lo que realmente quiso decir** there is some confusion as to what he really meant
(**b**) *(desconcierto)* **la noticia me llenó de c.** I was disconcerted by the news
(**c**) *(error)* mix-up; **ha habido una c.** there has been a bit of a mix-up; **esa frase puede llevar a c.** that phrase could lead to confusion *o* be misinterpreted

confusionismo *nm* confusion

confuso, -a *adj* (**a**) *(poco claro) (clamor, griterío)* confused; *(contorno, forma, imagen)* blurred; *(explicación)* confused (**b**) *(turbado)* confused, bewildered; **estar c.** to be confused *o* bewildered

conga *nf* (**a**) *(baile)* conga; **bailar la c.** to dance the conga (**b**) *Arg (juego de naipes)* = card game similar to rummy (**c**) *Cuba, Perú (tambor)* conga (drum) (**d**) *Col (hormiga)* = large poisonous ant

congelación *nf* (**a**) *(de alimento, líquido)* freezing
(**b**) *(de persona)* freezing; *(de dedos, miembro)* frostbite; **morir por c.** to freeze to death
(**c**) *(de precios, salarios)* freeze; *(de cuenta bancaria)* freezing; *(de negociaciones)* deadlock, impasse; **el gobierno anunció la c. inmediata de los sueldos de los funcionarios** the government announced an immediate wage freeze for public sector workers
(**d**) *TV & Cine* ***c. de imagen*** freeze-frame function

congelado, -a 1 *adj* (**a**) *(alimento, líquido)* frozen (**b**) *(persona, cadáver)* frozen; *(dedos, miembro)* frostbitten; **morir c.** to freeze to death (**c**) *(precios, salarios)* frozen; *(cuenta bancaria)* frozen; *(negociaciones)* deadlocked, at a standstill (**d**) *TV & Cine* **imagen congelada** freeze-frame
2 **congelados** *nmpl* frozen foods

congelador *nm* freezer

congelante *adj* freezing

congelar 1 *vt* (a) *(alimento, líquido)* to freeze (b) *(persona, cadáver)* to freeze; **el frío le congeló los dedos** he got frostbite in his fingers as a result of the cold (c) *(precios, salarios)* to freeze; *(cuenta bancaria)* to freeze; *(negociaciones)* to deadlock, to bring to a standstill (d) *TV & Cine (imagen)* to freeze

2 **congelarse** *vpr* (a) *(alimento, líquido)* to freeze; **¡me congelo de frío!** I'm freezing! (b) *(dedos, miembro)* to get frostbitten; **se le congelaron los pies y las manos** she got frostbite in her feet and hands

congénere *nmf* **me avergüenzo de mis congéneres** I am ashamed of my kind; **el cachorro fue devorado por sus congéneres** the cub was eaten by other lions; **el virus afecta más a los varones de más de 60 que a sus congéneres más jóvenes** the virus tends to affect males over the age of 60 more than their younger counterparts

congeniar *vi* to get on (**con** with); **congeniamos muy bien** we got on very well with each other, we hit it off really well

congénito, -a *adj* (a) *(enfermedad)* congenital (b) *Fam (talento, estupidez)* innate

congestión *nf* (a) *(de nariz, pulmones)* congestion; **tengo c. nasal** I've got a blocked nose (b) *(de tráfico)* congestion

congestionado, -a *adj* (a) *(nariz)* blocked; **tener la nariz congestionada** to have a blocked nose (b) *(cara)* flushed (c) *(tráfico)* congested

congestionar 1 *vt* to block

2 **congestionarse** *vpr* (a) *(cara)* to flush, to turn purple; **su cara se congestionó con el enfado** his face went purple with rage (b) *(tráfico)* to become congested

congestivo, -a *adj* congestive

conglomeración *nf* conglomeration

conglomerado *nm* (a) *(conjunto, mezcla)* combination; **un c. de problemas** a combination of problems (b) *(de madera)* chipboard (c) *Geol* conglomerate (d) *(de hoteles, empresas)* conglomerate

conglomerante 1 *adj* agglutinative

2 *nm* agglutinant, bonding *o* adhesive material

conglomerar 1 *vt* (a) *(intereses, tendencias)* to unite (b) *(sustancias)* to conglomerate

2 **conglomerarse** *vpr (sustancia)* to conglomerate

Congo *nm* (a) **el C.** *(río) Br* the (River) Congo, *US* the Congo (River) (b) **el C.** *(país)* (the) Congo ►► *Antes* ***el C. belga*** the Belgian Congo

congo *nm* (a) *Am (de tabaco)* second crop tobacco leaf (b) *CAm (mono)* howler monkey (c) *Cuba (baile)* congo

congoja *nf* anguish; **la ausencia de padre le producía una profunda c.** the lack of a father caused him great anguish; **pasaron horas de c. esperando que concluyera el rescate** they spent anxious hours waiting for the rescue to be completed

congoleño, -a 1 *adj* Congolese

2 *nm,f* Congolese

congosto *nm* gorge

congraciar 1 *vt* to win over

2 **congraciarse** *vpr* **congraciarse con alguien** to win sb over, to get on sb's good side

congratulación *nf Formal* **congratulaciones** congratulations; **recibió la c. del ministro** he received the minister's congratulations; **mis más sinceras congratulaciones** my wholehearted *o* warmest congratulations to you

congratular *Formal* 1 *vt* to congratulate; **c. a alguien por algo** to congratulate sb on sth

2 **congratularse** *vpr* to be pleased (**por** about); **se congratularon por el triunfo obtenido** they congratulated themselves on their victory; **nos congratulamos de que todo haya salido bien** we're pleased that everything turned out all right

congratulatorio, -a *adj Formal* congratulatory

congregación *nf* (a) *(junta)* gathering, assembly (b) *(de laicos)* order ►► ***la c. de los fieles*** the Roman Catholic Church (c) *(en el Vaticano)* congregation

congregante *nmf* = member of a Roman Catholic lay brotherhood/sisterhood

congregar [38] 1 *vt* to assemble, to bring together; **la fiesta congregó a miles de personas** thousands of people came to *o* gathered for the fiesta

2 **congregarse** *vpr* to assemble, to gather

congresista, *Arg, Chile* **congresal** *nmf* (a) *(en un congreso)* delegate (b) *(político)* congressman, *f* congresswoman

congreso *nm* (a) *(de una especialidad)* conference, congress (b) *(asamblea nacional)* **el C. (de los Diputados)** *(en España)* = the lower house of Spanish Parliament, *Br* ≃ the House of Commons, *US* ≃ the House of Representatives; **el C.** *(en Estados Unidos)* Congress ►► *Pol* ***el C. Nacional Africano*** the African National Congress (c) *(edificio)* parliament building

congrí *nm Cuba (plato)* rice and beans

congrio *nm* conger eel

congruencia *nf* (a) *(coherencia)* consistency; **no hay c. entre el planteamiento y la conclusión** there is no consistency between the initial presentation of the subject and the conclusion; **lo que dice no guarda c. con lo que hace** there's no consistency between what he says and what he does (b) *Der* congruence, cohesion (c) *Mat* congruence

congruente *adj* (a) *(coherente)* consistent, coherent; **sus palabras no son congruentes con sus actos** his words are not consistent with his actions (b) *Mat* congruent

cónica *nf Geom* conic

cónico, -a *adj* conical

conidio *nm Bot* conidium

conífera *nf* conifer

conífero, -a *adj* coniferous

conjetura *nf* conjecture; **todo eso no son más que conjeturas** all that is pure speculation *o* conjecture; **hacer conjeturas, hacerse una c.** to conjecture

conjeturar *vt* to conjecture about, to make predictions about; **puedo c. que el futuro se presenta brillante** I can predict a brilliant future ahead

conjugación *nf* (a) *Gram* conjugation; **un verbo de la 1ª/2ª/3ª c.** a verb ending in -ar/-er/-ir (b) *(combinación)* combination; *(de ideas)* pooling; *(de esfuerzos)* pooling, combining (c) *Biol* conjugation

conjugado, -a *adj* (a) *Gram* conjugated (b) *(combinado)* combined

conjugar [38] 1 *vt* (a) *Gram* to conjugate (b) *(combinar)* to combine; **un modelo que conjuga la estética con la funcionalidad** a model that combines good looks with functionality; **es muy difícil c. los intereses de todos** it's very difficult to find a balance between everybody's interests

2 **conjugarse** *vpr Gram* to conjugate

conjunción *nf* (a) *Gram* conjunction ►► ***c. adversativa*** adversative conjunction; ***c. coordinante*** coordinating conjunction; ***c. copulativa*** copulative conjunction; ***c. disyuntiva*** disjunctive conjunction; ***c. subordinante*** subordinating conjunction (b) *Astron* conjunction (c) *(de circunstancias, hechos)* combination

conjuntado, -a *adj* coordinated

conjuntamente *adv* jointly, together (**con** with); **dos productos que van a ser lanzados al mercado c.** two products that are to be launched together; **el gobierno, c. con la Cruz Roja, va a organizar la ayuda humanitaria** the government will be organizing humanitarian aid jointly with the Red Cross

conjuntar *vt (coordinar)* to coordinate; **un pintor que conjunta muy bien los colores** a painter who combines colours very well

conjuntiva *nf Anat* conjunctiva

conjuntivitis *nf inv* conjunctivitis

conjuntivo, -a *adj* (a) *Anat* conjunctive; **tejido c.** connective tissue (b) *Gram* conjunctive

conjunto, -a 1 *adj (acción, esfuerzo)* joint; **cuenta conjunta** joint account

2 *nm* (a) *(agrupación)* collection, group; **un c. de circunstancias** a number of factors; **un c. de maletas** a set of suitcases; **se enfrenta el c. local contra el líder** the local team is playing the leaders

(b) *(de ciudad)* ***c. histórico-artístico:*** **la ciudad de Cartagena es un c. histórico-artístico de gran interés** the historical and artistic attributes of Cartagena combine to form a highly interesting whole; ***c. monumental*** historical buildings and monuments; ***c. urbanístico:*** **un c. urbanístico muy heterógeno** a cityscape of great variety

(c) *(de ropa)* outfit; **llevaba un c. de camisa y pantalón** she was wearing matching shirt and trousers; **un c. primaveral** a spring outfit

(d) *(de música)* group, band; **un c. de jazz** a jazz band; **un c. de música clásica** a classical music group

(e) *(totalidad)* whole; **la media en el c. de Latinoamérica es de 5,4** in Latin America as a whole, the average is 5.4; **la calidad, en c., es buena, pero le falla algún detalle** overall the quality is good, but it falls down on the occasional detail; **los socios, en su c., están en contra de la venta** the whole membership is against the sale

(f) *Mat* set ►► ***c. vacío*** empty set

conjura, conjuración *nf* conspiracy, plot

conjurado, -a *nm,f* plotter, conspirator

conjurar 1 *vt* (**a**) *(exorcizar)* to exorcize; *Fig* **sus palabras conjuraron mi miedo** his words dispelled my fears (**b**) *(un peligro)* to ward off, to avert; **las medidas intentan c. la crisis económica** the measures are an attempt to avert an economic crisis

2 *vi (conspirar)* to conspire, to plot; **conjuraron para derrocar al gobierno** they conspired *o* plotted to overthrow the government

3 conjurarse *vpr (conspirar)* to conspire, to plot; **se conjuraron contra la dictadura** they conspired *o* plotted against the dictatorship; **cree que todos se han conjurado contra él** he thinks everyone has conspired against him

conjuro *nm* (**a**) *(encantamiento)* spell, incantation (**b**) *(exorcismo)* exorcism

conllevar *vt* (**a**) *(implicar)* to involve, to entail; **el cargo conlleva muchas responsabilidades** the post involves *o* entails many responsibilities; **esa decisión conlleva muchos peligros** the decision involves *o* entails a great deal of risk (**b**) *(soportar)* to bear; **estas pastillas le ayudarán a c. el dolor** these tablets will help you put up with *o* bear the pain

conmemoración *nf* (**a**) *(de batalla, muerte)* commemoration; *(de independencia, victoria)* celebrations (**b**) *(recuerdo)* commemoration; **en c. de** in commemoration of

conmemorar *vt* to commemorate

conmemorativo, -a *adj* commemorative; **un monumento c. de la independencia del país** a monument commemorating the country's independence

conmensurable *adj* quantifiable

conmigo *pron personal* with me; **no quiere ir c.** he doesn't want to go with me; **c. mismo/misma** with myself; **llevo siempre el pasaporte c.** I always carry my passport on me; **es muy amable c.** he's very kind to me; **estaba hablando c. mismo** I was talking to myself; EXPR **no las tengo todas c.** I am not too sure about it

conmilitón *nm* fellow soldier

conminación *nf* (**a**) *(amenaza)* threat (**b**) *Der* order

conminar *vt* (**a**) *(amenazar)* **c. a alguien (con hacer algo)** to threaten sb (with doing sth) (**b**) *Der (forzar)* **c. a alguien a hacer algo** *o* **a que haga algo** to instruct *o* order sb to do sth

conminativo, -a, conminatorio, -a *adj* threatening, menacing

conmiseración *nf* compassion, pity; **sentir c. por alguien** to feel compassion for sb, to pity sb

conmiserativo, -a *adj* compassionate

conmoción *nf* (**a**) *(física)* shock ►► ***c. cerebral*** concussion; **la caída le produjo una c. cerebral** he suffered concussion as a result of the fall (**b**) *(psíquica)* shock; **su muerte causó c. a la familia** his death left the family in a state of shock (**c**) *(tumulto)* upheaval (**d**) *(sísmica)* shock

conmocionar *vt* (**a**) *(psíquicamente)* to shock, to stun; **su asesinato conmocionó al país** his assassination shocked the country (**b**) *(físicamente)* to concuss

conmovedor, -ora *adj* moving, touching

conmover [41] **1** *vt* (**a**) *(emocionar)* to move, to touch; **nada le conmueve** nothing moves him, he isn't moved by anything; **su historia conmovió a todos** everyone was moved *o* touched by the story (**b**) *(sacudir)* to shake; EXPR **c. los cimientos de algo** to shake the foundations of sth

2 conmoverse *vpr* (**a**) *(emocionarse)* to be moved, to be touched; **los asistentes se conmovieron con su discurso** the audience was moved by his speech (**b**) *(sacudirse)* to be shaken; **la ciudad se conmovió por el terremoto** the city was shaken *o* rocked by the earthquake

conmuevo *etc ver* **conmover**

conmutación *nf* (**a**) *Der* commutation (**b**) *Elec* switching (**c**) *Ling* commutation (**d**) *Informát* ***c. de paquetes*** packet switching

conmutador *nm* (**a**) *(interruptor)* switch ►► ***c. basculante*** rocker switch (**b**) *Am (centralita)* switchboard

conmutar *vt* (**a**) *Der* to commute; **le conmutaron la pena de diez meses por una multa** his ten-month sentence was commuted to a fine (**b**) *(intercambiar)* to switch; **conmutó su horario con el de un compañero** he switched shifts with a colleague (**c**) *(convalidar) (estudios, título, asignaturas)* **c. algo por algo** to recognize sth as equivalent to sth

conmutativo, -a *adj* (**a**) *Der* commutative (**b**) *Mat* commutative

connatural *adj* innate; **una característica c. a las jirafas** an innate *o* inherent characteristic in giraffes

connivencia *nf* **fue acusado de c. con la mafia local** he was accused of colluding with the local mafia; **actuaron en c. con los dueños de la fábrica** they acted in collusion *o* connivance with the owners of the factory

connotación *nf* connotation; **una c. irónica** a hint of irony

connotado, -a *adj Am* noted, famous; **el c. autor** the noted author

connotar *vt* to suggest, to have connotations of

connubio *nm Formal (matrimonio)* matrimony, marriage

cono *nm* (**a**) *(figura)* cone ►► *Geol* ***c. de deyección*** debris cone; ***el C. Sur*** = Chile, Argentina, Paraguay and Uruguay; ***c. truncado*** truncated cone; ***c. volcánico*** volcanic cone (**b**) **(de señalización)** *(en carretera)* traffic cone (**c**) *(de la retina)* cone

conocedor, -ora *nm,f* expert; **es un gran c. de los vinos franceses** he is a connoisseur of French wine

CONOCER [19] **1** *vt* (**a**) *(saber cosas acerca de)* to know; **conoce la mecánica del automóvil** he knows a lot about car mechanics; **conoce el ruso a la perfección** he's fluent in Russian; **conocen todo lo que pasa en el pueblo** they know (about) everything that goes on in the village; **¿conoces alguna forma más rápida de hacerlo?** do you know a quicker way to do it?; **no conozco bien este tema** I'm not familiar with this subject; *Fam* **conoce el tema al dedillo** she knows the subject inside out; **c. algo a fondo** to know sth well; **dieron a c. la noticia a través de la prensa** they announced the news through the press; **Juan enseguida se dio a c. a mi amiga** Juan immediately introduced himself to my friend; **su segunda película lo dio a c.** *o* **se dio a c. con su segunda película como el gran director que es** his second movie *o Br* film achieved recognition for him as the great director that he is; **fue, como es de todos conocido, una difícil decisión** it was, as everyone knows, a difficult decision; **su amabilidad es de todos conocida** everyone knows how kind he is, he is well-known for his kindness

(**b**) *(lugar, país) (descubrir)* to get to know, to visit for the first time; *(desde hace tiempo)* to know; **no conozco Rusia** I've never been to Russia; **me gustaría c. Australia** I'd like to go to *o* visit Australia; **conoce la región como la palma de su mano** she knows the region like the back of her hand; **a los veinte años se marchó a c. mundo** at the age of twenty he went off to see the world; **¿te acompaño? – no hace falta, conozco el camino** shall I go with you? – there's no need, I know the way

(**c**) *(a una persona) (por primera vez)* to meet; *(desde hace tiempo)* to know; **¿conoces a mi jefe?** do you know *o* have you met my boss?; **lo conocí cuando era niño** I first met him when he was a child; **lo conozco de cuando íbamos al colegio** I know him from school; **tienes que c. a mi hermana** I must introduce you to my sister; **c. a alguien a fondo** to know sb well; **c. a alguien de nombre** to know sb by name; **c. a alguien de oídas** to have heard of sb; **c. a alguien de vista** to know sb by sight; **¿de qué la conoces?** how do you know her?; **no la conozco de nada** I've never met her before, I don't know her at all

(**d**) *(reconocer)* **c. a alguien (por algo)** to recognize sb (by sth); **lo conocí por su forma de andar** I recognized him by the way he walked

(**e**) *(experimentar)* **ésta es la peor sequía que ha conocido África** this is the worst drought Africa has ever had *o* known; **el último conflicto que ha conocido la región** the latest conflict witnessed by the region; **la empresa ha conocido un crecimiento espectacular** the company has seen *o* experienced spectacular growth

(**f**) *Anticuado o Hum (sexualmente)* **c. carnalmente a** to have carnal knowledge of; **hasta los treinta años no conoció varón** she had never been with a man until she was thirty

(**g**) *Der (causa)* to try; **el tribunal que conoce el caso se pronunciará mañana** the court trying the case will announce its verdict tomorrow

2 *vi* (**a**) **c. de** *(saber)* to know about; **no te preocupes, que conoce del tema** don't worry, he knows (about) the subject

(**b**) *Der* **c. de** to try; **c. de una causa** to try a case; **será juzgado por el tribunal que conoce de casos de terrorismo** he will be tried by the court that deals with cases relating to terrorism

3 conocerse *vpr* (**a**) *(a uno mismo)* to know oneself; **él se conoce mejor que nadie** he knows himself better than anyone

(**b**) *(dos o más personas) (por primera vez)* to meet, to get to know each other; *(desde hace tiempo)* to know each other; **nos conocimos en la recepción de la embajada** we met at the ambassador's reception; **no me engañes, nos conocemos demasiado** you can't fool me, we know each other too well; **se conocen de vista** they know each other by sight; **se conocen de oídas** they have heard of each other; EXPR *RP* **somos pocos y nos conocemos** we know each other too well

(**c**) *(saber en detalle)* to know; **se conoce todos los trucos del oficio** she knows all the tricks of the trade; **se conoce todas las calles de la ciudad** he knows every street in the city

(**d**) *(haberse descubierto)* **no se conoce ninguna cura para el cáncer** no cure for cancer is known; **no se le conoce ninguna debilidad** he is

not known to have any weaknesses, he has not been found to have any weaknesses
(e) *(reconocerse)* **se conoce su tristeza por los rasgos de su rostro** you can tell of her sadness by looking at her face
4 *v impersonal (parecer)* **se conoce que...** apparently...; **se conoce que hacía tiempo que estaba enfermo** apparently, he had been ill for some time; **se conoce que cambió de opinión en el último momento** apparently she changed her mind at the last minute; **¿no sabes quién es? se conoce que no ves la televisión** don't you know who she is? you can tell you never watch television

---

conocido, -a 1 *adj* (a) *(famoso)* well-known (b) *(sabido)* known; **su último domicilio c.** her last known address; **ese nombre me resulta c.** that name sounds familiar
2 *nm,f* acquaintance; **un c. mío** an acquaintance of mine, someone I know

conocimiento *nm* (a) *(saber)* knowledge; **hablar/actuar con c. de causa** to know what one is talking about/doing; **puso el robo en c. de la policía** she informed the police of the burglary; **ponemos en su c. que se ha detectado un error en el programa** this is to inform you that an error has been detected in the program; **no teníamos c. de su dimisión** we were not aware that he had resigned; **al tener c. del accidente, acudió inmediatamente al hospital** when she found out about the accident she immediately went to the hospital; **ha llegado a mi c. que estás insatisfecho** it has come to my attention that you are not happy
(b) **conocimientos** *(nociones)* knowledge; **tengo algunos conocimientos de informática** I have some knowledge of computers, I know a bit about computers; **nuestros conocimientos acerca de la enfermedad son muy limitados** our knowledge of the disease is very limited, we know very little about the disease
(c) *(sentido, conciencia)* consciousness; **perder el c.** to lose consciousness; **recobrar el c.** to regain consciousness; **estaba tumbado en el suelo, sin c.** he was lying unconscious on the floor
(d) *(juicio)* (common) sense; **no tiene todavía c. para saber lo que es peligroso** he doesn't yet have a sense of danger
(e) *Com* ***c. de embarque*** bill of lading

conoidal *adj Geom* conoidal, conoid

conozco *ver* **conocer**

conque *conj* so; **¿c. te has cansado?** so you're tired, are you?; **¿c. ésas tenemos?** so that's what you're up to?

conquense 1 *adj* of/from Cuenca *(Spain)*
2 *nmf* person from Cuenca *(Spain)*

conquista *nf* (a) *(de tierras)* conquest; *(de castillo)* capture; **la c. del poder** the winning of power; **la c. de nuevos clientes** the winning of new customers; **la c. del Aconcagua** the conquest of Aconcagua ▸▸ ***la c. del espacio*** the conquest of space
(b) *(de libertad, derecho)* winning; **la c. del voto** the winning of the vote; **una de las grandes conquistas de los sindicatos** one of the great achievements of the trade unions
(c) *(premio, medalla, título)* victory; **lucharon por la c. del segundo puesto** they battled for second place; **una nueva c. del Libertadores** another victory for Libertadores
(d) *(amorosa)* conquest; **va presumiendo de sus conquistas amorosas** he goes around boasting about his conquests; **llegó a la fiesta con su última c.** he arrived at the party with his latest conquest

conquistador, -ora 1 *adj* (a) *(ejército)* conquering (b) *(seductor)* seductive; **tiene fama de c.** he's got a reputation as a Casanova *o* a lady-killer
2 *nm,f (de tierras)* conqueror; *Hist (en América)* conquistador
3 *nm (seductor)* Casanova, lady-killer

conquistar *vt* (a) *(tierras)* to conquer; *(castillo)* to capture; *(poder)* to take, to win; *(clientes)* to win; *(montaña)* to conquer
(b) *(libertad, derechos)* to win
(c) *(premio, medalla, título)* to win; **conquistaron el título de campeones** they won the championship, they earned the title of champions; **conquistó la fama cuando sólo tenía diez años** she became famous when she was only ten years old
(d) *(a público, audiencia)* to win over; **conquistó a todos los asistentes con su simpatía** he won over everyone there with his friendliness
(e) *(a hombre, mujer)* to win the heart of; **le llevó tres semanas c. su amor** it took him three weeks to win her heart

consabido, -a *adj* (a) *(conocido)* well-known; **el c. asunto de la subida de sueldo** the all-too-familiar subject of pay rises (b) *(habitual)* usual; **tras la reunión se celebró la consabida cena** after the meeting there was the usual *o* customary dinner

consagración *nf* (a) *Rel (de pan, vino, templo)* consecration (b) *(dedicación)* dedication; **su c. al trabajo es admirable** her dedication to her work is admirable (c) *(reconocimiento)* recognition; **esta obra supuso la c. del joven escritor** this work gained recognition for the young writer

consagrado, -a *adj* (a) *Rel (pan, vino, templo)* consecrated (b) *(dedicado) (tiempo, espacio)* devoted; *(monumento, lápida)* dedicated (c) *(reconocido)* recognized, established

consagrar 1 *vt* (a) *Rel (pan, vino, templo)* to consecrate
(b) *(dedicar) (tiempo, espacio)* to devote; *(monumento, lápida)* to dedicate; **consagró su vida a la literatura** he devoted *o* dedicated his life to literature; **consagraron el monumento a los caídos en la guerra** they dedicated the monument to those who died in the war
(c) *(acreditar, confirmar)* to confirm, to establish; **la obra que lo consagró como escritor** the work that confirmed *o* established him as a writer
2 **consagrarse** *vpr* (a) *(dedicarse)* to devote *o* dedicate oneself (a to)
(b) *(alcanzar reconocimiento)* to establish oneself

consanguíneo, -a 1 *adj* related by blood; **hermano c.** half-brother *(of same father)*
2 *nm,f* blood relation

consanguinidad *nf* consanguinity; **relación de c.** blood relationship

consciencia = **conciencia**

consciente *adj* (a) *(despierto)* conscious; **estar c.** to be conscious (b) **ser c. de** *(darse cuenta de)* to be aware of; **no era c. de lo que hacía** he was not aware of what he was doing

conscientemente *adv* deliberately, consciously

conscripción *nf Andes, Arg* conscription

conscripto *nm Andes, Arg* conscript

consecución *nf (de deseo)* realization; *(de objetivo)* attainment; *(de premio)* winning

consecuencia *nf* (a) *(resultado)* consequence; **la crisis es c. de una mala gestión** the crisis is a consequence *o* result of bad management; **a** *o* **como c. de** as a consequence *o* result of; **atenerse a las consecuencias** to accept the consequences; **y, en c., anunció su dimisión** consequently, she announced her resignation; **tener consecuencias** to have consequences; **traer como c.** to result in; **anunció que defenderá sus ideas hasta las últimas consecuencias** she announced she will defend her beliefs whatever it takes
(b) *(coherencia)* consistency; **actuar en c.** to act accordingly; **cuando supo que estaba embarazada actuó en c.** when he found out that she was pregnant he did the decent thing; **actuó en c. con sus ideas** he acted in accordance with his beliefs; **tu propuesta no guarda c. con lo que acordamos ayer** your proposal is not consistent with *o* in accordance with what we agreed yesterday

consecuente *adj* (a) *(coherente)* consistent; **una persona c. (con sus ideas)** a person of principle, a person who acts according to his/her beliefs; **un cambio de estrategia c. con la nueva situación** a change of strategy in line with the new situation (b) *(consiguiente)* resulting; **su dimisión y la c. crisis de gobierno** his resignation and the resulting government crisis

consecuentemente *adv* (a) *(por consiguiente)* consequently, as a result (b) *(con coherencia)* consistently

consecutivamente *adv* consecutively; **entraron los tres hermanos c.** the three brothers came in one after the other

consecutivo, -a *adj* consecutive; **tres victorias consecutivas** three consecutive victories, three victories in a row; **siete semanas consecutivas** seven consecutive weeks, seven weeks on end

conseguido, -a *adj (logrado)* accomplished

conseguir [62] *vt (obtener)* to obtain, to get; *(un objetivo)* to achieve; **c. un premio Nobel/dos Oscars** to win *o* get a Nobel Prize/two Oscars; **consiguieron un aumento de sueldo** they got a pay rise; **consiguió la mayoría absoluta** he won *o* got an absolute majority; **consiguió todo lo que se propuso** she achieved everything she set out to do; **con esa actitud no conseguirás nada** you won't get anywhere with that attitude; **c. hacer algo** to manage to do sth; **tras un disputado esprint consiguió alzarse con el triunfo** she won a very closely contested sprint; **no consiguieron encontrar el camino** they didn't manage to find the way; **no consiguió que me enfadara** she didn't (manage to) get me annoyed; **al menos conseguimos que nos escucharan** at least we got them to listen to us

consejería *nf* (a) *(en embajada)* section, department; **la c. de cultura** the cultural section *o* department (b) *Esp (de comunidad autónoma)* department

consejero, -a *nm,f* **(a)** *(en asuntos personales)* adviser, counsellor; *(en asuntos técnicos)* adviser, consultant; **es buena/mala consejera** she gives sound/bad advice ►► ***c. matrimonial*** marriage guidance counsellor

(b) *(de un consejo de administración)* member of the board, director ►► *Com* ***c. delegado*** chief executive, *esp Br* managing director, *US* chief executive officer

(c) *(en embajada)* **el c. de cultura** the cultural attaché; **el c. de prensa** the press officer

(d) *Esp (de comunidad autónoma)* minister

consejo *nm* **(a)** *(advertencia)* advice; **dar un c.** to give some advice *o* a piece of advice; **te voy a dar un c.** I've got a piece of advice for you; **dar consejos** to give (some) advice; **pedir c. a alguien** to ask sb for advice, to ask (for) sb's advice

(b) *(organismo)* council; *(reunión)* meeting ►► ***c. de administración*** board (of directors); *(reunión)* board meeting; ***c. de dirección*** board (of directors); *(reunión)* board meeting; ***c. escolar*** board of governors, *Br* school board; ***c. de estado*** Council of State; ***C. de Europa*** Council of Europe; ***C. de Ministros*** *(de gobierno)* cabinet; *(reunión)* cabinet meeting; *UE* Council of Ministers; ***C. de Seguridad*** Security Council

(c) ***c. de guerra*** court martial

conseillería *nf* department, ministry *(in Galician regional government)*

conselleiro, -a *nm,f* minister *(in Galician regional government)*

conseller, -era *nm,f* minister *(in Catalan, Balearic or Valencian regional government)*

consellería *nf* department, ministry *(in Catalan, Balearic or Valencian regional government)*

consenso *nm* **(a)** *(acuerdo)* consensus; **llegar al** *o* **alcanzar el c.** to reach a consensus; **romper el c.** to destroy the consensus; **no hay c. sobre lo que hay que hacer** there is no consensus about what should be done; **buscan el c. de todos los participantes** they are seeking to achieve a consensus among all the participants **(b)** *(consentimiento)* consent

consensuado, -a *adj* approved by consensus

consensual *adj* consensual

consensuar [4] *vt* to reach a consensus on; **el comité al final consensuó la propuesta del presidente** the committee eventually agreed to approve the president's proposal

consentido, -a 1 *adj* spoilt

2 *nm,f* spoilt brat

consentidor, -ora 1 *adj (que malcría)* pampering, spoiling

2 *nm,f (persona que malcría)* indulgent person

consentimiento *nm* consent

consentir [63] **1** *vt* **(a)** *(tolerar)* to allow, to permit; **no te consiento que lo insultes delante de mí** I won't tolerate *o* have you insulting him in front of me **(b)** *(malcriar, mimar)* to spoil; **le consienten demasiado** they let him have his own way too much

2 *vi* **c. en algo/en hacer algo** to agree to sth/to do sth; **consintió en que se quedaran** he agreed to let them stay

conserje *nmf* **(a)** *(de bloque de viviendas) Br* caretaker, *US* superintendent, *US* supervisor **(b)** *(de colegio, ministerio)* doorman, *Br* porter **(c)** *(de hotel)* concierge

conserjería *nf* **(a)** *(en bloque de viviendas) Br* caretaker's office, *US* superintendent's *o* supervisor's office **(b)** *(en colegio, ministerio)* porter's lodge **(c)** *(en hotel)* concierge's desk

conserva *nf* **conservas** canned food, *Br* tinned food; **en c.** canned, *Br* tinned; **latas de c.** cans *o Br* tins of food; **c. de carne/pescado** tinned meat/fish; **conservas vegetales** canned *o Br* tinned vegetables

conservación *nf* **(a)** *(de alimentos)* preservation **(b)** *(de costumbres, patrimonio)* conservation; *(de bosques, animales)* conservation ►► ***c. de la energía*** energy conservation; ***c. del medio ambiente*** environmental conservation; ***c. de la naturaleza*** nature conservation **(c)** *(mantenimiento)* maintenance; **en buen/mal estado de c.** in good/bad condition

conservacionista 1 *adj* conservation, conservationist

2 *nmf* conservationist

conservador, -ora 1 *adj* **(a)** *(tradicionalista)* conservative; **es un entrenador muy c.** he's a very conservative manager **(b)** *(del partido conservador)* Conservative

2 *nm,f* **(a)** *(tradicionalista)* conservative **(b)** *(miembro del partido conservador)* Conservative **(c)** *(de museo)* curator; *(de biblioteca)* librarian; *(de parque natural)* keeper

conservadurismo *nm* conservatism

conservante *nm* preservative

conservar 1 *vt* **(a)** *(mantener) (alimento)* to preserve; *(amistad)* to sustain, to keep up; *(salud)* to look after; *(calor)* to retain; **c. algo en formol** to preserve sth in formalin; **conserva su buen humor** she keeps her spirits up; **conservaron el poder durante quince años** they remained in power for fifteen years; **la ciudad todavía conserva la muralla medieval** the city still has *o* retains its medieval wall

(b) *(guardar) (libros, cartas, secreto)* to keep; **todavía conserva sus primeras zapatillas de ballet** she still has her first ballet shoes; **consérvese en el frigorífico** *(en etiqueta)* keep refrigerated

2 conservarse *vpr* **(a)** *(alimento)* to keep; **si lo metes en el frigorífico se conservará perfectamente** if you put it in the fridge it will keep perfectly well

(b) *(persona)* **se conserva bien** he's keeping well; **se conserva muy joven** she keeps herself looking very young

(c) *(subsistir)* to survive; **no se conserva ningún escrito de esa época** there are no surviving documents from that time, no document has survived from that time

conservatismo *nm Am* conservatism

conservatorio *nm* conservatoire

conservero, -a *adj* canning; **la industria conservera** the canning industry

considerable *adj (grande) (diferencias, aumento)* considerable; *(avance)* significant; *(oferta)* substantial; *(desperfectos)* considerable, extensive; **supone un c. ahorro** it means a substantial saving; **llegó primero, a c. distancia del segundo** he arrived first, a long way ahead of the person who came second

considerablemente *adv* considerably

consideración *nf* **(a)** *(reflexión)* consideration, factor; **debemos tener en cuenta estas consideraciones** we must take these factors into consideration; **tomar en c.** to take into consideration *o* account; **estas cifras no tienen en c. el año 1999** these figures do not take 1999 into account

(b) *(respeto)* consideration; **te tengo en mucha c.** I think very highly of you; **tratar algo con c.** to treat sth with respect; **tratar a alguien con c.** to show sb consideration; **falta de c.** lack of consideration; **no tiene ninguna c. con su madre** he is very inconsiderate to his mother, he shows his mother no consideration; *Am* **de mi (mayor) c.** *(en carta)* Dear Sir/Madam

(c) *(atención)* consideration; **en c. a algo** in recognition of sth; **por c. a** *o* **hacia alguien** out of consideration for sb; **tuvieron con él muchas consideraciones** they were very considerate to him, they showed him great consideration

(d) *(importancia)* **de c.** serious; **hubo varios heridos de c.** several people were seriously injured; **hubo veinte heridos de diversa c.** there were twenty people with injuries of varying degrees of seriousness

considerado, -a *adj* **(a)** *(atento)* considerate, thoughtful; **es muy c. con sus padres** he is very considerate to his parents **(b)** *(respetado)* respected, highly regarded; **está muy bien considerada entre sus colegas** she is very highly-regarded by her colleagues

considerando *nm Der* legal reason *(for a judge's decision)*

considerar 1 *vt* **(a)** *(pensar en)* to consider; **hay que c. que es la primera vez que lo intentamos** you should take into account that this is the first time we've tried to do it; **consideré la posibilidad de presentarme, pero al final desistí** I thought about applying but in the end I gave up the idea

(b) *(juzgar, estimar)* to believe, to think; **no quiso c. mi propuesta** she wouldn't consider my proposal; **bien considerado, creo que tienes razón** on reflection, I think you're right; **considero que se han equivocado** I believe they've made a mistake

(c) *(respetar)* to esteem, to treat with respect; **sus compañeros lo consideran mucho** his colleagues have a high regard for him *o* think highly of him

2 considerarse *vpr (uno mismo)* to consider oneself; **me considero feliz** I consider myself happy; **no me considero preparado para realizar este trabajo** I don't feel qualified to do this job

consiento *etc ver* **consentir**

consigna *nf* **(a)** *(orden)* order, instruction; **recibieron la c. de detenerse** they were ordered *o* instructed to stop; **su c. era "divide y vencerás"** his motto was "divide and rule" **(b)** *(frase)* slogan; **los manifestantes gritaban consignas contra el gobierno** the demonstrators were shouting anti-government slogans **(c)** *(para el equipaje) Br* left-luggage office, *US* checkroom

consignación *nf* **(a)** *Com* consignment, shipment **(b)** *(asignación)* allocation **(c)** *Col (en banco)* deposit

consignador *nm Com* consignor

consignar *vt* (**a**) *(poner por escrito)* to record, to write down; **debes c. la fecha de nacimiento** you must record the date of birth; **no consignó correctamente la dirección y le devolvieron la carta** he didn't write the address correctly so they returned the letter to him
(**b**) *(asignar)* to allocate; **consignaron 3 millones para proyectos educativos** they allocated 3 million to educational projects
(**c**) *(mercancía)* to consign, to dispatch
(**d**) *(equipaje)* to deposit in the *Br* left-luggage office *o US* baggage room
(**e**) *Col (dinero)* to deposit

consignatario, -a *nm,f* (**a**) *(de una mercancía)* consignee (**b**) *Der (de depósito)* trustee (**c**) *(representante)* **c. (de buques)** shipping agent

consigo 1 *ver* **conseguir**
2 *pron personal (con él)* with him; *(con ella)* with her; *(con ellos, ellas)* with them; *(con usted, ustedes)* with you; *(con uno mismo)* with oneself; **c. mismo/misma** with himself/herself; **lleva siempre el pasaporte c.** she always carries her passport on her; **habla c. mismo** he talks to himself; **llevar** *o* **traer c.: el acuerdo de paz trajo c. la prosperidad a la región** the peace agreement brought prosperity to the region; **los riesgos que lleva c. una operación de este tipo** the risks involved in this type of operation; EXPR **no las tiene todas c.** he is not too sure about it

consiguiente *adj* resulting; **con la c. decepción** with the resulting disappointment; **el boom económico y la c. inflación** the economic boom and the resulting inflation; **por c.** consequently, therefore

consiguientemente *adv* consequently

consiguiera *etc ver* **conseguir**

consintiera *etc ver* **consentir**

consistencia *nf* (**a**) *(de masa, crema, salsa)* consistency; **batir la mezcla hasta que adquiera c.** beat the mixture until it thickens (**b**) *(de argumento)* soundness; **su tesis no tiene c.** his arguments are unsound

consistente *adj* (**a**) *(masa)* solid; *(crema, salsa)* thick (**b**) *(coherente) (argumento)* sound, convincing (**c**) *(compuesto)* **c. en** consisting of

> **Falso amigo**: El adjetivo inglés **consistent** no es la traducción del español **consistente**. En inglés, **consistent** significa "coherente" o "invariable, constante".

consistir *vi* (**a**) **c. en** *(ser, componerse de)* to consist of; **la oferta consiste en una impresora y un escáner** the offer consists of a printer and a scanner; **¿en qué consiste su problema?** what exactly is your problem?; **¿en qué consiste esta revisión médica?** what does this medical involve?; **su tarea consiste en atender el teléfono** her job simply involves *o* entails answering the phone
(**b**) **c. en** *(radicar, basarse en)* to lie in, to be based on; **su encanto consiste en su diseño** its appeal lies in the design; **el secreto consiste en añadir un chorro de vino** the secret lies in adding a dash of wine

consistorial *adj* (**a**) *(del ayuntamiento)* of the town *o US* city council; **casa c.** town *o US* city hall (**b**) *Rel* consistorial

consistorio *nm* town *o US* city council

consola *nf* (**a**) *(tablero de mandos)* console (**b**) *Informát* console ►► ***c. de videojuegos*** video games console (**c**) *(mesa)* console table (**d**) *(de órgano)* console

consolación *nf* **final** *o* **partido de c.** third place play-off; **premio de c.** consolation prize

consolador, -ora 1 *adj* consoling, comforting
2 *nm* dildo

consolar [64] **1** *vt* to console; **me consuela pensar que podría haber sido peor** it's some consolation to reflect that it could have been worse; **consuela saber que no somos los únicos** it's some consolation to know we're not the only ones; **no consiguió consolarla con sus palabras** his words failed to console *o* comfort her
2 consolarse *vpr* to console oneself, to take comfort; **¡consuélate! al menos no has suspendido** look on the bright side! at least you didn't fail; **se consuela contándoles sus penas a los amigos** she takes comfort in *o* from telling her troubles to her friends

consolidación *nf* (**a**) *(de proyecto, democracia)* consolidation; *(amistad)* strengthening; **su tercera novela supuso su c. como un gran escritor** his third novel confirmed him as a great writer (**b**) *Fin* consolidation

consolidado, -a 1 *adj* (**a**) *(proyecto, amistad, democracia)* established (**b**) *Fin* consolidated
2 *nm Fin* consolidated annuity

consolidar 1 *vt* (**a**) *(proyecto, democracia)* to consolidate; *(amistad)* to strengthen; **esa victoria la consolidó como una gran atleta** that victory confirmed her as a great athlete (**b**) *Fin* to consolidate
2 consolidarse *(amistad, democracia)* to grow stronger; *(reputación)* to be consolidated; *(precios)* to strengthen; **un proyecto político que se está consolidando** a political programme which is becoming consolidated

consomé *nm* consommé

consonancia *nf* (**a**) *(armonía)* harmony; **unos precios en c. con la realidad del mercado** prices that reflect the market situation; **obró en c. con sus ideas** he acted in accordance with his beliefs; **su actuación no guardó c. con su calidad** her performance was not a true reflection of her ability (**b**) *Mús* harmony (**c**) *Ling* consonance

consonante 1 *adj* (**a**) *(rima, sonido)* consonant (**b**) *(acorde)* **sus modales son consonantes con su condición social** her manners are in keeping with her social status
2 *nf* consonant

consonántico, -a *adj (sonido)* consonant, consonantal

consonar [64] *vi* (**a**) *Mús* to harmonize (**b**) *(rimar)* to rhyme

consorcio *nm* consortium ►► ***c. bancario*** bankers' consortium

consorte *nmf (cónyuge)* spouse; *(príncipe)* consort

conspicuo, -a *adj* (**a**) *(evidente)* conspicuous (**b**) *(ilustre)* eminent

conspiración *nf* plot, conspiracy

conspirador, -ora *nm,f* conspirator, plotter

conspirar *vi* to conspire, to plot; **c. contra alguien** to conspire *o* plot against sb; **conspiraron para derribar al presidente** they conspired *o* plotted to overthrow the president

constancia *nf* (**a**) *(perseverancia) (en una empresa)* perseverance; *(en las ideas, opiniones)* steadfastness; **hacer algo con c.** to persevere with sth; **es una persona con c.** she's the sort of person who always perseveres
(**b**) *(testimonio)* record; **dejar c. de algo** *(registrar)* to put sth on record; *(probar)* to demonstrate sth; **quiero dejar c. de mi desacuerdo** I want it to go on record that I disagree; **tengo c. de que estuvo aquí** I know for a fact that she was here; **no he tenido c. de su nombramiento** I haven't had confirmation of his appointment
(**c**) *Am (certificado)* certificate; ***c. de estudios*** academic record, *US* transcript

constante 1 *adj* (**a**) *(persona) (en una empresa)* persistent; *(en ideas, opiniones)* steadfast; **se mantuvo c. en su esfuerzo** he persevered in his efforts
(**b**) *(lluvia, atención)* constant, persistent; *(temperatura)* constant
(**c**) *(que se repite)* constant
2 *nf* (**a**) *(rasgo)* constant; **las desilusiones han sido una c. en su vida** disappointments have been a constant feature in her life; **las tormentas son una c. en sus cuadros** storms are an ever-present feature in his paintings; **la violencia es una c. histórica en la región** the region has known violence throughout its history
(**b**) *Mat* constant
(**c**) ***constantes vitales*** vital signs; **mantener las constantes vitales de alguien** to keep sb alive

constantemente *adv* constantly

Constantinopla *n Antes* Constantinople

constar *vi* (**a**) *(una información)* to appear, to figure (**en** in); **su nombre no consta en esta lista** his name is not on *o* does not appear on this list; **hacer c. algo** to put sth on record; **yo no he sido, que conste** let's get one thing clear, it wasn't me; **que conste que ya le había avisado** you can't say I didn't warn you; **llegó el primero, y que conste que casi no se había entrenado** he came first, and with practically no training at that; **que conste en acta la protesta** *(en juicio)* let the objection go on record; **que no conste en acta** *(en juicio)* strike it from the record; **y para que así conste, expido este certificado** = official formula which effectively means "I formally issue this certificate"
(**b**) *(saber con certeza)* **me consta que se lo pasaron muy bien** I know for a fact they had a very good time; **me consta que está casado** I know for a fact that he's married
(**c**) *(estar constituido por)* **c. de** to consist of; **la serie consta de cuatro episodios** the series consists of four episodes; **cada partido consta de cuatro tiempos** each game consists of four quarters

constatación *nf* (**a**) *(observación)* confirmation (**b**) *(comprobación)* verification

constatar *vt* (**a**) *(observar)* to confirm (**b**) *(comprobar)* to check

constativo, -a *adj Ling* constative

constelación *nf* constellation; **una c. de estrellas del baloncesto** a galaxy of basketball stars

constelado, -a *adj* starry, full of stars

consternación *nf* consternation, dismay; **sus declaraciones causaron c.** his statements caused consternation *o* dismay

consternado, -a *adj* dismayed, extremely upset

consternar 1 *vt* to dismay; **su muerte consternó a sus compañeros** his colleagues were extremely upset by his death
2 **consternarse** *vpr* to be dismayed; **me consterno al ver tanta miseria en esta región** I am dismayed to see so much poverty in the region

constipación *nf* **c. *de vientre*** constipation

constipado, -a 1 *adj* **estar c.** to have a cold
2 *nm* (**a**) *(resfriado)* cold; **agarrar un c.** to catch a cold (**b**) *Méx (estreñido)* constipated

> **Falso amigo**: El adjetivo inglés **constipated** no es la traducción del español **constipado**. En inglés **constipated** significa "estreñido".

constiparse *vpr* to catch a cold

constitución *nf* (**a**) *(naturaleza)* constitution; **tener una c. fuerte/débil** to have a strong/weak constitution; **ser de c. robusta** to have a strong constitution (**b**) *(de un estado)* constitution (**c**) *(creación)* creation, forming; **la c. de un grupo empresarial** the creation *o* setting up of a business group (**d**) *(composición)* composition, make-up

constitucional *adj* constitutional

constitucionalidad *nf* constitutionality

constitucionalista *nmf* constitutional expert

constitucionalmente *adv* constitutionally

constituir [34] 1 *vt* (**a**) *(componer)* to make up; **estas cinco secciones constituyen el primer capítulo** these five sections make up the first chapter; **la junta directiva está constituida por cinco miembros** the board of directors has five members
(**b**) *(ser)* to be, to constitute; **constituye una falta grave** it is *o* constitutes a serious misdemeanour; **no creo que constituya ningún obstáculo** I don't think it constitutes an obstacle, I don't see it as an obstacle
(**c**) *(crear)* to set up, to constitute
2 **constituirse** *vpr* (**a**) *(reunirse)* **el tribunal se constituirá mañana** the court will be in session from tomorrow
(**b**) **constituirse en** *(erigirse)* to set oneself up as; **constituirse en sociedad anónima** to become a limited company; **se constituyó en defensor de los emigrantes** he became a defender of the immigrants

constitutivo, -a *adj* constituent; **elemento c.** constituent element; **ser c. de algo** to constitute sth; **la apropiación de fondos es c. de delito** embezzling funds constitutes a crime

constituyente 1 *adj* (**a**) *(elemento)* constituent (**b**) *(asamblea)* constituent
2 *nm* (**a**) *(elemento)* constituent (**b**) *Ling* constituent
3 *nf* constituent assembly

constreñimiento *nm* constraint, compulsion

constreñir *vt* (**a**) *(obligar)* **c. a alguien a hacer algo** to compel *o* force sb to do sth; **se ven constreñidos a vivir en condiciones miserables** they are forced *o* obliged to live in wretched conditions (**b**) *(oprimir, limitar)* to restrict; **la nueva ley constriñe la libertad de asociación** the new law restricts freedom of association (**c**) *Med* to restrict

constricción *nf (opresión)* constriction

construcción *nf* (**a**) *(acción)* construction; *(de edificio, muro)* construction, building; *(de buque)* building; *(de automóvil, aeronave)* manufacture; *(de mueble)* making, building; **la c. sólida del vehículo** the vehicle's solid build; **en c.** *(edificio, página web)* under construction; **la c. del teatro llevará dos años** the theatre will take two years to build; **una fase clave en la construcción europea** a key phase in the development of the EU; **trabajamos en la c. de oportunidades para todos** we are working to create opportunities for everyone
(**b**) *(sector)* construction *o* building industry; **trabajadores de la c.** construction *o* building workers; **una empresa de la c.** a construction company ►► ***c. naval*** shipbuilding
(**c**) *(edificio, estructura)* building
(**d**) *Gram* construction

constructivismo *nm* constructivism

constructivista 1 *adj* constructivist
2 *nmf* constructivist

constructivo, -a *adj* constructive

constructo *nm Ling* **c. (teórico)** (theoretical) construct

constructor, -ora 1 *adj* building, construction; **empresa constructora** construction company *o* firm, building company
2 *nm,f* (**a**) *(de edificios)* builder (**b**) *(de automóviles, aeronaves)* maker, manufacturer; **c. naval** *o* **de buques** shipbuilder

construir [34] *vt* (**a**) *(edificio, muro)* to build; **construyó un mueble para su biblioteca** she made a piece of furniture for her library; **intentan c. una sociedad más justa** they are trying to build a fairer society (**b**) *(automóviles, aeronaves)* to manufacture; *(buque)* to build (**c**) *(frase, teoría)* to construct

> **Falso amigo**: El verbo inglés **to construe** no es la traducción del español **construir**. En inglés **to construe** significa "interpretar".

consubstanciación = **consustanciación**

consubstancial = **consustancial**

consuegro, -a *nm,f (hombre)* = father-in-law of one's son or daughter; *(mujer)* = mother-in-law of one's son or daughter

consuelo 1 *ver* **consolar**
2 *nm* consolation, solace; **su familia es su único c.** his family is his only solace *o* comfort; **es un c. saber que están bien** it's a comfort to know that they're all right; **dar c. a alguien** to comfort *o* console sb; **si te sirve de c., a mí me pasó lo mismo** if it's any consolation, the same thing happened to me

consuetudinario, -a *adj* customary; **derecho c.** common law

cónsul *nm* (**a**) *(diplomático)* consul ►► ***c. general*** consul general (**b**) *Hist* consul

consulado *nm* (**a**) *(oficina)* consulate ►► ***c. general*** consulate general (**b**) *(cargo)* consulship (**c**) *Hist* consulship, consulate

consular *adj* consular

consulta *nf* (**a**) *(petición de consejo) (acción)* consultation; *(pregunta)* query, enquiry; **hacer una c. a alguien** to ask sb's advice
(**b**) *(búsqueda de información)* consultation; **la c. del manual aclaró nuestras dudas** consulting the manual cleared up our doubts; **hacer una c. a alguien** to ask sb's advice; **libros de c.** reference books ►► ***c. electoral*** election(s); ***c. popular*** referendum, plebiscite
(**c**) *(de médico) (consultorio) Br* surgery, *US* office
(**d**) *(de médico) (visita)* appointment; **horas de c.** surgery hours; **pasar c.** to hold surgery; **tengo c. con el médico a las seis** I've got an appointment with the doctor at six; **c. previa petición de hora** *(en letrero)* appointments only, consultation by appointment only
(**e**) **llamar a consultas** *(diplomático)* to recall

consultar 1 *vt* (**a**) *(pidiendo consejo) (persona)* to consult; **consulte el manual antes de comenzar el montaje** *(en instrucciones)* read the manual before assembling; **lo tengo que c. con mi abogado** I have to talk to *o* consult my lawyer about it; **me consultó antes de hacerlo** *(me pidió consejo)* he consulted me before doing it; *(me pidió permiso)* he asked me before he did it; EXPR **consultarlo con la almohada** to sleep on it
(**b**) *(buscando información) (dato, fecha)* to look up; *(libro)* to consult; **consúltalo en el diccionario** look it up in the dictionary
2 *vi* **c. con** to consult, to seek advice from; **consulté con mis colegas el asunto del que me hablaste** I asked my colleagues about the matter you mentioned

consulting [kon'sultin] (*pl* **consultings**) *nm* consultancy (firm)

consultivo, -a *adj* consultative, advisory

consultor, -ora 1 *adj* consulting
2 *nm,f* consultant ►► ***c. (en administración) de empresas*** management consultant; ***c. fiscal*** tax consultant; ***c. jurídico*** legal adviser; ***c. medioambiental*** environmental consultant; ***c. de medio ambiente*** environmental consultant; ***c. de recursos humanos*** human resources consultant

consultora *nf* (**a**) *(empresa)* consultancy firm (**b**) *RP (de trabajadores)* recruitment consultancy

consultoría *nf* (**a**) *(empresa)* consultancy firm ►► ***c. de empresas*** business consultancy; ***c. fiscal*** tax consultancy; ***c. jurídica*** legal consultancy; ***c. medioambiental*** environmental consultancy; ***c. de medio ambiente*** environmental consultancy; ***c. de recursos humanos*** human resources consultancy (**b**) *(actividad)* consultancy, consulting

consultorio *nm* (**a**) *(de un médico) Br* surgery, *US* office (**b**) *(en periódico)* problem page; *(en radio)* = programme answering listeners' questions ►► ***c. sentimental*** *(en radio)* = phone-in where people get advice on their personal problems; *(en publicación)* agony column (**c**) *(asesoría)* advice bureau

consumación *nf (realización)* completion; *(de matrimonio)* consummation; *(de proyecto)* completion; *(de un crimen)* perpetration

consumado, -a *adj* consummate, perfect; **un actor c.** a consummate actor; **es un granuja c.** he's a real rascal

consumar *vt (realizar completamente)* to complete; *(matrimonio)* to consummate; *(proyecto)* to complete; *(crimen)* to perpetrate

consumibles *nmpl* consumables; **c. de informática** computer consumables

consumición *nf* (**a**) *(acción)* consumption (**b**) *(bebida, comida)* **pagué mi c. y me fui** I paid (for what I'd had) and left; **son diez euros la entrada con c.** it costs ten euros to get in, including the first drink

consumido, -a *adj (flaco)* emaciated

consumidor, -ora 1 *adj* **el primer país c. de electricidad** the country with the highest consumption of electricity
2 *nm,f (de producto)* consumer; *(en bar, restaurante)* patron, customer; **es un gran c. de comida rápida** he eats a lot of fast food

consumir 1 *vt* (**a**) *(producto)* to consume; **en casa consumimos mucho aceite de oliva** we use a lot of olive oil at home; **consumieron sus refrescos en el bar** they had their drinks at the bar; **está prohibido c. bebidas alcohólicas en los campos de fútbol** the consumption of alcohol is forbidden in football grounds; **fue acusado de c. drogas** he was accused of taking drugs; **c. preferentemente antes de...** *(en envase)* best before...
(**b**) *(gastar)* to use, to consume; **esta estufa consume mucha electricidad** this heater uses a lot of electricity; **esta moto consume muy poco** this motorbike uses very little *Br* petrol *o US* gas; **mi coche consume 7 litros a los cien** ≃ my car does 41 miles to the gallon
(**c**) *(desgastar)* to wear out; **el rozamiento consume los neumáticos** friction wears down the tyres
(**d**) *(destruir) (sujeto: fuego)* to destroy
(**e**) *(destruir) (sujeto: enfermedad)* to eat away at; **el cáncer lo va consumiendo poco a poco** the cancer is making him gradually waste away; **los celos lo consumen** he is eaten up by *o* consumed with jealousy; **este calor me consume** this heat is killing me *o* is too much for me
2 *vi* to consume
3 **consumirse** *vpr* (**a**) *(persona)* to waste away; **se fue consumiendo lentamente** she slowly wasted away; **se consume de envidia** he is eaten up *o* consumed with envy
(**b**) *(fuego)* to burn out; *(cigarro)* to burn down
(**c**) *(líquido, perfume)* to evaporate

consumismo *nm* consumerism

consumista 1 *adj* consumerist, materialistic
2 *nmf* **es un c.** he's a shopaholic

consumo *nm* consumption; **el c. de energía** energy consumption; **se ha disparado el c. de agua mineral** sales of mineral water have shot up; **c. de drogas** drug-taking; **le parece bien el c. moderado de alcohol** he thinks drinking in moderation is acceptable; **bienes de c.** consumer goods; **sociedad de c.** consumer society ►► *Econ* ***c. privado*** private consumption, consumer spending; *Econ* ***c. público*** public *o* government consumption

consunción *nf Formal* **murió por c.** she wasted away and died

consuno: de consuno *loc adv Formal* by mutual consent

consustanciación, consubstanciación *nf Rel* consubstantiation

consustancial, consubstancial *adj* **ser c. a algo** to be an integral part of sth; **la inteligencia es c. a los seres humanos** intelligence is an innate characteristic of human beings

contabilidad *nf* (**a**) *(oficio)* accountancy (**b**) *(de persona, empresa)* bookkeeping, accounting; **llevar la c.** to do the accounts; **doble c.** double-entry bookkeeping ►► *Fin* ***c. de costos*** *o Esp* ***costes*** cost accounting; *Fin* ***c. de gestión*** management accounting

contabilización *nf* (**a**) *(en contabilidad)* entering (**b**) *(cuenta)* counting; **la contabilización de los votos llevó varias horas** it took several hours to count the votes

contabilizar [14] *vt* (**a**) *(en contabilidad)* to enter (**b**) *(contar)* to count; **llevo contabilizadas veinte vacas** I've counted twenty cows

contable 1 *adj* countable
2 *nmf Esp* accountant ►► ***c. de gestión*** management accountant

contactar 1 *vt (comunicarse con)* to contact
2 *vi* **c. con alguien** to contact sb

contacto *nm* (**a**) *(entre dos cosas, personas)* contact; **entrar en c. con algo/alguien** to come into contact with sth/sb; **establecer c. con alguien** to make contact with sb; **mantener el c., seguir en c.** to keep in touch *o* contact; **perder el c.** to lose touch; **su primer c. con la política tuvo lugar en 1978** his first encounter with politics was in 1978; **ponerse en c. con** to get in touch with ►► ***c. visual*** eye contact
(**b**) *(persona)* contact
(**c**) *Fam* **contactos** *(amistades)* contacts; **tiene contactos en el ministerio** he has contacts at the ministry
(**d**) *Esp* **contactos** *(sección en prensa)* lonely hearts
(**e**) *Aut* ignition; **dale al c.** switch the engine on
(**f**) *Méx (enchufe)* power point, socket
(**g**) *Elec* contact; **hacer** *o* **establecer c.** to make contact; **el cortocircuito se produjo por un mal c.** the short circuit was caused by a faulty contact
(**h**) *Fot* contact (print)

contactología *nf* = contact lens design and manufacture

contactólogo, -a *nm,f* contact lens specialist

contada *nf CSur* counting-up

contado, -a 1 *adj* (**a**) *(raro)* rare, infrequent; **en contadas ocasiones** very rarely, on very few occasions; **son contadas las veces en las que viene a visitarnos** he very rarely comes to visit us (**b**) EXPR **mal c.: había diez personas mal contadas** there were no more than ten people
2 **al contado** *loc adj* **precio al c.** cash price
3 **al contado** *loc adv* **pagar algo al c.** *(en un plazo)* to pay for sth all at once *o* on the nail; *(en metálico)* to pay for sth in cash, to pay cash for sth

contador, -ora 1 *nm,f* (**a**) *Am (contable)* accountant ►► ***c. público*** *Br* chartered accountant, *US* certified public accountant; ***c. de gestión*** management accountant (**b**) ***c. de historias*** storyteller
2 *nm* (**a**) *(aparato)* meter; **el c. del gas/de la luz** the gas/electricity meter (**b**) *Fís* counter ►► ***c. Geiger*** Geiger counter

contaduría *nf* (**a**) *(oficina)* accountant's office (**b**) *(departamento)* accounts office (**c**) *Am (profesión)* accountancy ►► *Am* ***c. general*** audit office

contagiar 1 *vt* (**a**) *(persona)* to infect; *(enfermedad)* to transmit; **me has contagiado el resfriado** you've given me your cold (**b**) *(risa, entusiasmo)* **contagió su entusiasmo a sus compañeros** he infected his companions with his enthusiasm; **contagiado por el buen ambiente reinante, decidió salir a bailar** caught up in the general happy atmosphere, he decided to have a dance
2 **contagiarse** *vpr* (**a**) *(enfermedad)* to be contagious; *(persona)* to become infected; **una enfermedad que se contagia con rapidez** a disease that spreads quickly; **me contagié de mi hermano** I caught it from my brother (**b**) *(risa, entusiasmo)* to be infectious; **se contagió de su optimismo** he infected her with his optimism

contagio *nm (por contacto directo)* contagion; *(por contacto indirecto)* infection; **para prevenir el c. de la enfermedad** to prevent the spread of the disease

contagioso, -a *adj* (**a**) *(enfermedad) (por contacto directo)* contagious; *(por contacto indirecto)* infectious (**b**) *(risa, entusiasmo)* infectious

contáiner *(pl* **contáiners***) nm (para mercancías)* container

contaminación *nf* (**a**) *(acción)* contamination (**b**) *(de agua potable, alimentos)* contamination; *(de río)* pollution (**c**) *(del medio ambiente)* pollution ►► ***c. acústica*** noise pollution; ***c. ambiental*** environmental pollution; ***c. atmosférica*** air *o* atmospheric pollution; ***c. radiactiva*** radioactive contamination *o* pollution (**d**) *(de lengua)* corruption

contaminado, -a *adj* (**a**) *(alimento)* contaminated (**b**) *(medio ambiente)* polluted (**c**) *(lengua)* corrupted; **un texto muy c. por el inglés** a text full of imported English expressions

contaminante 1 *adj* contaminating, polluting
2 *nm* pollutant

contaminar 1 *vt* (**a**) *(alimento)* to contaminate (**b**) *(medio ambiente)* to pollute (**c**) *(pervertir)* to corrupt (**d**) *(texto)* to corrupt
2 *vi* to pollute; **el que contamine que pague** the polluter pays
3 **contaminarse** *vpr (agua potable, alimentos)* to become contaminated; *(río)* to become polluted; **el río se contaminó con los residuos tóxicos de la fábrica** the river was polluted by toxic waste from the factory

contante *adj* **dinero c. y sonante** hard cash

CONTAR [64] **1** *vt* (**a**) *(enumerar)* to count; **contaron doscientos manifestantes en la marcha del domingo** the number of demonstrators at Sunday's march was estimated at two hundred; **se pueden c. con los dedos de una mano** you can count them on (the fingers of) one hand
(**b**) *(incluir)* to count; **cuenta también los gastos de desplazamiento** count *o* include travel costs too; **somos cincuenta y siete sin c. a los niños** there are fifty-seven of us, not counting the children; **la economía, sin c. el desempleo, parece recuperarse** the economy, with the exception of the unemployment situation, seems to be recovering
(**c**) *(narrar)* to tell; **no me cuentes el final** don't tell me what happens; **ya me contarás qué tal te va por la capital** let me know how you get on in the capital; **me han contado maravillas sobre ese restaurante** I've heard great things about that restaurant; *Fam* **¿qué**

cuentas? how are you doing?; **¿qué me cuentas? ¡no me lo puedo creer!** never! I can't believe it!; *Fam* **cuéntame, ¿cómo te va la vida?** tell me, how are things?; *Irónico* **¿me lo cuentas a mí?** you're telling me!; EXPR *Fam* **¡cuéntaselo a tu abuela!** pull the other one!, come off it!; EXPR *Fam* **no me cuentes tu vida** I don't want to hear your life story

(**d**) *(tener una cantidad de)* **la población contaba mil habitantes** the village had a thousand inhabitants; **cuenta ya diez años** she's ten years old now; **el equipo cuenta ya dos victorias** the team has already achieved two wins, the team already has two wins under its belt

(**e**) *(considerar)* **te contaba como una persona seria** I thought you were a serious person; **cuenta que la próxima semana estoy de vacaciones** remember that I'm on holiday next week; **a él lo cuento como uno más del grupo** I consider *o* see him as just another member of the group

2 *vi* (**a**) *(hacer cálculos)* to count; **sabe c. hasta diez** she can count to ten; **c. con los dedos** to count on one's fingers; **un perro, dos gatos y para de c.** a dog, two cats and that's it

(**b**) *(importar)* to count; **lo que cuenta es que te pongas bien** the important thing is for you to get better, what matters is for you to get better; **en esta casa no cuento para nada** I count for nothing in this household; **para él lo único que cuenta es ganar dinero** the only thing that matters to him is making money; **los dos peores resultados no cuentan para el resultado final** the worst two scores aren't taken into account when calculating the final total; **es tan fuerte que cuenta por dos** he has the strength of two men

(**c**) **c. con** *(confiar en)* to count on, to rely on; **es un buen amigo, siempre se puede c. con él** he's a good friend, you can count on *o* rely on him; **¡no cuentes con ellos!** don't count on *o* rely on them!; **no cuentes conmigo, no voy a venir** don't expect me, I won't be coming; **cuenta con ello, estaré allí para ayudarte** I'll be there to help you, you can count on it, rest assured, I'll be there to help you

(**d**) **c. con** *(tener, poseer)* to have; **cuenta con dos horas para hacerlo** she has two hours to do it; **las minorías contarán con representación en el nuevo parlamento** minority parties will be represented in the new parliament

(**e**) **c. con** *(tener en cuenta)* to take into account; **con esto no contaba** I hadn't reckoned with that; **no contaban con que se acabara la cerveza tan rápidamente** they hadn't expected the beer to run out so quickly

3 **contarse** *vpr* (**a**) *(incluirse)* **estoy muy orgulloso de contarme entre sus amigos** I am very proud to number myself among her friends; **las películas europeas se cuentan entre las favoritas** the European films are among the favourites

(**b**) *Fam* **¿qué te cuentas?** how are you doing?

---

contemplación *nf* (**a**) *(observación)* contemplation
(**b**) *(meditación)* contemplation
(**c**) **contemplaciones** *(consideración)* consideration; **no andarse con contemplaciones** not to beat about the bush; **tratar a alguien sin contemplaciones** not to take sb's feelings into account; **nos echaron sin contemplaciones** they threw us out unceremoniously; **tratar a alguien con demasiadas contemplaciones** to be too lenient *o* soft with sb

contemplar *vt* (**a**) *(paisaje, monumento)* to look at, to contemplate
(**b**) *(opción, posibilidad)* to contemplate, to consider; **la ley contempla varios supuestos** the law provides for *o* covers various cases; **esta propuesta no contempla los ingresos por publicidad** this proposal doesn't take into account income from advertising; **el proyecto no contempla hacer excepciones** the project makes no provision for exceptions; **contemplamos el futuro con esperanza** we are hopeful about the future, we look to the future with hope; **está contemplando presentar la dimisión** she is considering handing in her resignation
(**c**) *(consentir)* to spoil

contemplativo, -a *adj* contemplative

contemporaneidad *nf* contemporaneity, contemporaneousness

contemporáneo, -a 1 *adj* (**a**) *(de la misma época)* contemporary; **fue c. de Colón** he was a contemporary of Columbus (**b**) *(de la época actual)* contemporary; **el arte c.** contemporary art
2 *nm,f* contemporary

contemporizador, -ora 1 *adj* accommodating
2 *nm,f* **es un c.** he's very accommodating

contemporizar [14] *vi* to be accommodating; **c. con alguien** to be accommodating towards sb

contención *nf* (**a**) *(detención)* **persigue la c. de la inflación/los salarios** he is intent on keeping inflation/wages down; **pusieron una venda para lograr la c. de la hemorragia** they put on a bandage to stop *o* staunch the bleeding; **muro de c.** retaining wall (**b**) *(de pasión, deseo)* restraint

contencioso, -a 1 *adj* (**a**) *(tema, cuestión)* contentious (**b**) *Der* litigious
2 *nm* dispute, conflict ▸▸ ***c. administrativo*** = court case brought against the state

contender [66] *vi (competir)* to contend; *(pelear)* to fight

contendiente 1 *adj (en una competición)* competing; **las partes contendientes** *(en una guerra)* the opposing sides; **los ejércitos contendientes** the opposing armies
2 *nmf (en una competición)* opponent; *(en una pelea)* opponent, adversary; *(en una guerra)* opponent, opposing side

contenedor, -ora 1 *adj* containing
2 *nm (recipiente grande)* container; **c. (de escombros)** *Br* skip, *US* Dumpster® ▸▸ ***c. de basura*** large wheelie bin; ***c. de vidrio*** bottle bank

contener [67] 1 *vt* (**a**) *(encerrar)* to contain; **¿qué contiene esa maleta?** what's in this suitcase?; **la novela contiene elementos diversos** the novel has many different aspects; **no contiene CFC** *(en etiqueta)* does not contain CFCs
(**b**) *(detener, reprimir) (epidemia)* to contain; *(respiración)* to hold; *(conflicto, crisis)* to contain; *(éxodo)* to contain, to stem; *(inflación, salarios)* to keep down; **no pudo c. la risa/el llanto** he couldn't help laughing/crying; **tuvieron que contenerlo para que no agrediera al fotógrafo** he had to be restrained from attacking the photographer
2 **contenerse** *vpr* to restrain oneself, to hold oneself back; **estuve a punto de insultarlo, pero conseguí contenerme** I was about to insult him, but I managed to restrain myself

contengo *ver* **contener**

contenido *nm* (**a**) *(de recipiente, libro)* contents; **una bebida con un alto c. alcohólico** a drink with a high alcohol content (**b**) *(de discurso, redacción)* content; **un programa con alto c. de violencia** a programme containing a lot of violence (**c**) *Ling* content

contentar 1 *vt* to please, to keep happy; **es muy fácil de c.** she's very easy to please
2 **contentarse** *vpr* **contentarse con** to make do with, to be satisfied with; **no se contenta con nada** she's never satisfied with anything; **me contentaría con una simple disculpa** I'd be happy with a simple apology; **me contentaría con quedar entre los tres primeros** I'd settle for being among the first three, I'd be happy if I got into the first three; **no se contentó con insultarle, además le golpeó** not content with insulting him, he hit him

contento, -a 1 *adj* (**a**) *(alegre)* happy; **está muy contenta** she is very happy; **se puso muy c. al ver a sus nietos** he was very happy to see his grandchildren; **estamos contentos de poder ayudar** we're happy *o* glad to be able to help; **han hecho un gran esfuerzo por tener contentos a sus huéspedes** they've made a big effort to keep their guests happy; **está muy contenta en el trabajo** she is very happy in her job
(**b**) *(satisfecho)* pleased; **la decisión no dejó c. a nadie** the decision didn't satisfy anyone; **no estoy nada contenta con la reparación** I'm not at all happy with the repair; **no c. con insultarlo, le pegó una bofetada** not content with insulting him, he slapped his face; *Fam* **pagamos cada uno la mitad y todos tan contentos** we paid half each and that was us; *Fam* **se llevó las llaves y se quedó tan c.** he took the keys just like that *o* as cool as you like
(**c**) *Fam (achispado)* tipsy, merry
2 *nm* happiness, joy; **el c. del público era evidente** you could see that the audience was happy; EXPR **no caber en sí de c.** to be beside oneself with joy

conteo *nm* counting-up

contera *nf (de bastón, paraguas)* ferrule; *(de espada)* chape

contertulio, -a *nm,f* = fellow member of a "tertulia"

contestación *nf* (**a**) *(respuesta)* answer; **en c. a su pregunta...** to answer your question...; **emitió un gruñido por c.** his only answer was a grunt; **se ruega c.** *(en invitación)* RSVP (**b**) *(protesta)* protest, opposition; **la nueva ley suscitó una c. universal** the new law gave rise to universal protest *o* opposition; **c. social/sindical** social/trade union protest *o* opposition

contestador 1 *adj CSur* cheeky
2 *nm* **c. (automático)** answering machine

contestadora *nf Méx, Ven* **c. (automática)** answering machine

contestar 1 *vt* (**a**) *(responder)* to answer; **c. a una pregunta** to answer a question; **c. a una carta** to reply to *o* answer a letter; **contestó que sí/que no** he said yes/no; **contestó que no podía** she replied *o* said that she couldn't
(**b**) *(oponerse a)* to oppose; **contestaron las medidas del gobierno** they opposed the government's measures; **contestaron la idoneidad del candidato** they questioned the candidate's suitability

2 *vi* (**a**) *(responder)* to answer; **no contestan** *(al teléfono)* there's no reply *o* answer
(**b**) *(con insolencia)* to answer back; **¡no contestes a tu madre!** don't answer back to your mother!

contestatario, -a 1 *adj* anti-establishment
2 *nm,f* anti-establishment person

contestón, -ona *adj Fam* cheeky; **es muy c.** he's always answering back

contexto *nm* (**a**) *(de texto)* context (**b**) *(circunstancias)* context; **en/fuera de c.** in/out of context

contextual *adj* contextual

contextualizar [14] *vt (problema, situación)* to put into perspective *o* context

contextura *nf* (**a**) *(estructura)* structure (**b**) *(de persona)* build

contienda 1 *ver* **contender**
2 *nf (competición, combate)* contest; *(guerra)* conflict, war; *(encuentro deportivo)* match, game; **una c. electoral** an election

contiene *ver* **contener**

contigo *pron personal* with you; **no quiere ir c.** she doesn't want to go with you; **es muy amable c.** he's very nice to you; **c. mismo/misma** with yourself; **¿estás hablando c. mismo?** are you talking to yourself?

contigüidad *nf* adjacency

contiguo, -a *adj* adjacent; **estar c. a** to adjoin

continencia *nf* continence, self-restraint

continental *adj* continental

continente *nm* (**a**) *Geog* continent (**b**) *(recipiente)* container

contingencia *nf* (**a**) *(eventualidad)* eventuality (**b**) *Formal (posibilidad)* possibility (**c**) *Méx* **c. (ambiental)** traffic restrictions *(to reduce pollution)*

contingente 1 *adj Formal* possible; **es un hecho c.** it's not impossible
2 *nm* (**a**) *(grupo)* contingent (**b**) *Com* quota (**c**) *(fuerza militar)* contingent; **el c. australiano en Timor** the Australian troops in Timor

continuación 1 *nf (de acción, estado)* continuation; *(de novela, película)* sequel; **es imprescindible dar c. al proyecto** it is essential that the project carries on, it is essential to keep the project going; **acaba de publicar la c. a su anterior novela** she has just published the sequel to her previous novel; **defienden la c. de la misma política económica** they are in favour of carrying on *o* continuing with the same economic policy
2 **a continuación** *loc adv* next; **a c. añada una pizca de sal** next, add a pinch of salt; **saludó al presidente y a c. se fue** she greeted the president and then left; **pasaremos a c. a abordar el problema del transporte público** we shall now pass on to address the problem of public transport; **¡a c., para todos ustedes, la gran cantante...!** and now, we bring you the great singer...!
3 **a continuación** *loc prep* after, following; **a c. de México se sitúa Argentina** Argentina is after Mexico

continuado *nm CSur* cinema, *US* movie theater *(with continuous performance)*

continuador, -ora 1 *adj* continuing
2 *nm,f* continuator; **es un c. de la obra de su maestro** he is carrying on *o* continuing the work of his teacher

continuamente *adv* (**a**) *(con repetición)* continually; **protesta c.** she never stops complaining, she complains all the time (**b**) *(sin interrupción)* continuously; **la información es c. actualizada** the information is constantly updated; **los siguieron c. durante dos semanas** they followed them continuously for two weeks

continuar [4] 1 *vt* to continue, to carry on with; **los peregrinos continuaron su camino** the pilgrims went *o* continued on their way; **continuarán el partido suspendido mañana** the abandoned match will be continued tomorrow
2 *vi* to continue, to go on; **c. haciendo algo** to continue doing *o* to do sth; **continúa lloviendo** it's still raining; **¿continúas viviendo en Brasil?** are you still living in Brazil?, do you still live in Brazil?; **continuamos trabajando en el mismo proyecto** we are still working on the same project; **continúan con el proyecto** they are carrying on with *o* continuing with the project; **todavía continúa en la empresa** she's still with *o* working for the company; **continúen en sus puestos hasta nueva orden** stay at your posts until you receive fresh orders; **continuará** *(historia, programa)* to be continued; **la finca continúa hasta el río** the farm extends as far as the river; **el camino continúa por la costa** the road continues *o* carries on along the coast
3 **continuarse** *vpr* to continue; **la carretera se continúa con la autopista** the road becomes the *Br* motorway *o US* freeway from there onwards

continuidad *nf* (**a**) *(en una sucesión)* continuity; **su última película representa la c. de un estilo iniciado hace tiempo** his latest film shows him continuing in the style he adopted some time ago
(**b**) *(permanencia)* continuation; **es necesaria su c. al frente del partido para garantizar la estabilidad** he must continue as party leader to guarantee stability; *Formal* **sin solución de c.** without stopping
(**c**) *Cine & TV* continuity

continuismo *nm* perpetuation of the status quo; **ha practicado el c. en lo económico** his economic policy has been no different to that of the previous government

continuista 1 *adj* **el sector c. del partido** the wing of the party that supports the status quo
2 *nmf* supporter of the status quo

continuo, -a 1 *adj* (**a**) *(ininterrumpido)* continuous; **las continuas lluvias obligaron a suspender el partido** the constant *o* continual rain forced them to call off the match (**b**) *(perseverante)* continual; **me irritan sus continuas preguntas** her continual questioning irritates me (**c**) *(unido)* continuous; **papel c.** continuous stationery
2 *nm* (**a**) *(sucesión)* succession, series (**b**) *Fís* continuum (**c**) *Ling* continuum
3 **de continuo** *loc adv* continually

contonearse *vpr (hombre)* to swagger; *(mujer)* to swing one's hips

contoneo *nm (de hombre)* swagger; *(de mujer)* sway of the hips

contornear *vt* (**a**) *(seguir el contorno de) (lago, isla)* to go round; *(río)* to follow the course of (**b**) *(perfilar)* to outline

contorneo *nm Informát* **c. de texto** text wrap

contorno *nm* (**a**) *(línea)* outline; **c. de cintura** waist (measurement); **c. de pecho** bust (measurement); **el c. accidentado de la isla** the ragged coastline of the island (**b**) **contornos** *(vecindad)* neighbourhood; *(de una ciudad)* outskirts

contorsión *nf* contortion

contorsionarse *vpr (retorcerse)* to do contortions; *(de dolor)* to writhe

contorsionista *nmf* contortionist

Contra *Pol* 1 *nf* **la C.** the Contras
2 *nmf* Contra (rebel)

contra 1 *prep* (**a**) *(indicando oposición)* against; **un antídoto c. el veneno** an antidote to the poison; **una cura c. el cáncer** a cure for cancer; **unas medidas c. la inflación** measures to combat inflation; **un jarabe c. la tos** a cough syrup; **jugaré c. él** I'll be playing against him; **están todos c. mí** they're all against me; **en c.** against; **todos se le pusieron en c.** everyone turned against him; **estar en c. de algo, estar c. algo** to be opposed to sth; **eso va c. el reglamento** that's against regulations; **tienen diez goles a favor y once en c.** they've scored ten goals and conceded eleven; **van 89-99 en c. de los Lakers** the Lakers are losing 89-99, the Lakers are 89-99 down
(**b**) *(indicando dirección)* against; **se estrelló c. una farola** he crashed into a lamppost; **nadar c. corriente** to swim against the current; *Am* **en c.** *(sol, viento)* in one's face; *Am* **los ciclistas tenían el viento en c.** the cyclists were riding into the wind
(**c**) *(enfrente, apoyado en)* against; **se apoyó c. el muro** she leant against the wall; **ponte c. la pared** stand (up) against the wall
(**d**) *(a cambio de)* **entrega c. reembolso** cash on delivery; **c. presentación de la entrada se entregará un regalo** receive a free gift when you show this ticket
2 *nm* **los pros y los contras** the pros and cons
3 *nf* EXPR *Am Fam* **llevar la c.** to be awkward *o* contrary; **¡siempre me está llevando la c.!** *(verbalmente)* she's always contradicting me!; *(con acciones)* she always does the opposite of what I tell her!
4 **en contra de** *loc conj (a diferencia de)* contrary to

contraalisios *Meteo* 1 *adj* **vientos c.** antitrades, antitrade winds
2 *nmpl* antitrades

contraalmirante, contralmirante *nm Mil* rear admiral

contraanálisis *nm inv (de orina, sangre)* **el jugador pidió un c.** the player asked for the second sample to be tested

contraatacar [60] *vi* to counterattack

contraataque *nm* (**a**) *(reacción)* counterattack (**b**) *Dep* counterattack; *(en baloncesto)* fast break

contraaviso *nm* **si no hay c.** unless information is provided to the contrary

contrabajista *nmf* double-bass player, double-bassist

contrabajo 1 *nm* (**a**) *(instrumento)* double bass (**b**) *(voz)* basso profundo, deep bass
2 *nmf (instrumentista)* double-bass player

contrabalancear *vt* to counterbalance

contrabalanza *nf* counterbalance

contrabandear *vi* to smuggle

contrabandista *nmf* smuggler

contrabando *nm* (**a**) *(acto)* smuggling; **c. de armas** gunrunning; **c. de alcohol/tabaco** alcohol/cigarette smuggling; **tabaco de c.** contraband cigarettes; **pasar algo de c.** to smuggle sth in (**b**) *(mercancías)* contraband ►► ***c. de guerra*** contraband of war

contrabarrera *nf Taurom* second row *(of seats in the uncovered area next to the barrier)*

contracción *nf* (**a**) *(de economía)* downswing, downturn (**b**) *Med* contraction ►► ***c. muscular*** muscular contraction (**c**) *Ling* contraction

contracepción *nf* contraception

contraceptivo, -a *adj* contraceptive

contrachapado, -a 1 *adj* (made of) plywood
2 *nm* plywood

contracifra *nf* key

contraconcepción *nf* contraception

contraconceptivo, -a *adj* contraceptive

contracorriente *nf* countercurrent; **ir a c.** to go against the current *o* tide

contráctil *adj* contractile

contractilidad *nf* contractility

contracto, -a *adj Gram* contracted

contractual *adj* contractual

contractura *nf (contracción)* spasm; *(dolor)* stiffness; **una c. muscular** a muscle spasm

contracturado, -a *adj RP* **tiene la espalda contracturada** she's got a stiff back

contracubierta *nf* (**a**) *(parte interior)* inside front cover (**b**) *(contraportada)* back cover

contracultura *nf* counter-culture

contracultural *adj* counter-culture; **una corriente c.** a counterculture movement

contracurva *nf* **una carretera llena de curvas y contracurvas** a road that twists one way and then the other

contradanza *nf* contredanse

contradecir [51] 1 *vt* to contradict
2 **contradecirse** *vpr* to contradict oneself; **se contradice continuamente** he's always contradicting himself; **sus palabras se contradicen con sus actos** his actions contradict his words

contradicción *nf* contradiction; **estar en c. con** to be in (direct) contradiction to; **¿una agresión pacífica? ¡eso es una c.!** a peaceful attack? that's a contradiction in terms!

contradice *etc ver* **contradecir**

contradicho, -a *participio ver* **contradecir**

contradictorio, -a *adj* contradictory; **ser c. con algo** to contradict sth, to be in contradiction with sth

contradigo *etc ver* **contradecir**

contradique *nm* outer harbour wall

contraer [68] 1 *vt* (**a**) *(enfermedad)* to catch, to contract (**b**) *(vicio, costumbre, deuda, obligación)* to acquire (**c**) **c. matrimonio (con)** to get married (to) (**d**) *(material)* to cause to contract (**e**) *(músculo)* to contract (**f**) *Informát (subdirectorios)* to collapse
2 **contraerse** *vpr* (**a**) *(material)* to contract; **algunos metales se contraen con el frío** some metals contract when cooled (**b**) *(músculo, pupila)* to contract (**c**) *Ling (sonidos)* to contract

contraespionaje *nm* counterespionage

contrafuerte *nm* (**a**) *Arquit* buttress (**b**) *(del calzado)* heel reinforcement (**c**) *Geog* spur

contragolpe *nm* counter-attack

contragolpear *vi* to counter-attack

contrahecho, -a *adj* deformed

contrahuella *nf* riser

contraincendios *adj inv* **sistema c.** fire-prevention system; **alarma c.** fire alarm

contraindicación *nf (en medicamento)* contraindication; **lea primero las contraindicaciones** read the enclosed leaflet first; **contraindicaciones: embarazo, diabetes** not to be taken during pregnancy or by diabetics; **este producto no tiene contraindicaciones de ningún tipo** this product can be safely used by all patients

contraindicado, -a *adj* **este medicamento está c. en pacientes diabéticos** this medicine should not be taken by diabetic patients

contraindicar *vt (sujeto: médico)* to advise against

contrainsurgente 1 *adj* counterinsurgent
2 *nmf* counterinsurgent

contraintuitivo, -a *adj* counterintuitive

contralmirante = **contraalmirante**

contralor *nm* (**a**) *Am (en institución, empresa)* comptroller (**b**) *Col (en instituciones del Estado)* government watchdog

contraloría *nf* (**a**) *Am (oficina)* comptroller's office (**b**) *Col (de instituciones del Estado)* government watchdog's office

contralto 1 *nm (voz)* contralto
2 *nmf (cantante)* counter tenor, *f* contralto

contraluz *nm (iluminación)* back lighting; **a c.** against the light; **vista a c., parece un león** in silhouette it looks like a lion; **pintó un c. de los árboles al atardecer** she painted the trees silhouetted against the sunset

contramaestre *nm* (**a**) *(en buque)* boatswain; *(en la armada)* warrant officer (**b**) *(capataz)* foreman

contramano: a contramano *loc adv* the wrong way; **esta puerta se abre a c.** this door opens the wrong way round; **no creo que vaya porque me cae a c.** I don't think I'll be going because it clashes with something else that's on; **lo multaron por circular a c.** *(en carril contrario)* he was fined for driving on the wrong side of the road; *(en dirección única)* he was fined for driving the wrong way down a one-way street

contramarcha *nf Mil* countermarch

contramedida *nf* countermeasure

contraofensiva *nf* counteroffensive

contraoferta *nf* counter offer

contraorden *nf* countermand

contrapartida *nf* (**a**) *(compensación)* compensation; **como c.** to make up for it (**b**) *Cont* balancing entry, cross entry

contrapelo: a contrapelo *loc adv (acariciar)* the wrong way; **afeitarse a c.** to shave against the direction of one's beard growth; **cepillar a c.** to brush against the nap; **su intervención iba a c. del resto** his remarks went against the general opinion; **vivir a c.** to have an unconventional lifestyle

contrapesar *vt* (**a**) *(físicamente)* to counterbalance (**b**) *(contrarrestar)* to compensate for

contrapeso *nm* (**a**) *(en ascensores, poleas)* counterweight (**b**) *(de equilibrista)* balancing pole (**c**) *(fuerza que iguala)* counterbalance; **su rapidez sirve de c. a su pequeño tamaño** her speed compensates for *o* makes up for her small stature

contraplano *nm Cine* reverse shot

contraponer [50] 1 *vt* (**a**) *(oponer)* **a su postura intransigente contrapusimos una más flexible** we responded to his intransigence by suggesting greater flexibility (**b**) *(cotejar)* to compare
2 **contraponerse** *vpr* to be opposed; **su intransigencia se contrapone al deseo de paz de la población** his unyielding attitude contrasts with the nation's desire for peace

contraportada, *Chile, Perú, RP* **contratapa** *nf (de periódico)* back page; *(de revista, de libro)* back cover; *(de disco)* back

contraposición *nf* (**a**) *(oposición)* conflict; **en c. con** in contrast to (**b**) *(comparación)* comparison; **en c. con** in comparison with

contraprestación *nf* **no pido ninguna c.** I'm not asking for anything in return; **como c. por algo** in return for sth

contraproducente *adj* counterproductive

contraprogramación *nf TV* competitive scheduling

contraprogramar *vi TV* to set competitive schedules

contrapropuesta *nf* counterproposal

contraproyecto *nm* counterproposal

contrapuerta *nf* (**a**) *(cancel)* storm door (**b**) *(en fortificación)* second *o* inner door

contrapuesto, -a 1 *participio ver* **contraponer**
2 *adj* conflicting

contrapuntear 1 *vt Mús* to sing in counterpoint
2 *vi* (a) *Andes, RP, Ven (cantar)* to sing improvised verses (b) *Carib, RP (rivalizar)* to compete
3 **contrapuntearse** *vpr Andes, Carib (enfadarse)* to quarrel, to argue

contrapunteo *nm* (a) *Mús* counterpoint (b) *Andes, Carib (disputa)* quarrel, argument

contrapunto *nm* (a) *Mús* counterpoint (b) *(contraste)* contrast (c) *Andes, RP, Ven (desafío poético)* = contest in which poetry is improvised to a musical accompaniment

contraria *nf* EXPR **llevar la c.** to be awkward *o* contrary; **¡siempre me está llevando la c.!** *(verbalmente)* she's always contradicting me!; *(con acciones)* she always does the opposite of what I tell her!

contrariado, -a *adj* upset

contrariamente: contrariamente a *loc adv* contrary to

contrariar [32] *vt* (a) *(dificultar)* to go against; **el mal tiempo contrarió nuestros planes** the bad weather thwarted our plans (b) *(disgustar)* to upset

contrariedad *nf* (a) *(dificultad)* setback; **surgió una c.** a problem came up (b) *(disgusto)* annoyance; **¡qué c.!** how annoying! (c) *(oposición)* contrary *o* opposing nature

---

CONTRARIO, -A 1 *adj* (a) *(opuesto) (dirección, sentido, idea)* opposite; *(opinión)* contrary; **soy c. a las corridas de toros** I'm opposed to bullfighting; **mientras no se demuestre lo c., es inocente** she's innocent until proved otherwise; **de lo c.** otherwise; **respeta a tu madre o de lo c. tendrás que marcharte** show your mother some respect, otherwise you'll have to go; **todo lo c.** quite the contrary; **¿estás enfadado con él? – todo lo c., nos llevamos de maravilla** are you angry with him? – quite the contrary *o* not at all, we get on extremely well; **ella es muy tímida, yo soy todo lo c.** she's very shy, whereas I'm the total opposite
(b) *(desfavorable, perjudicial)* **es c. a nuestros intereses** it goes against our interests; **el abuso de la bebida es c. a la salud** drinking is bad for your health
(c) *(rival)* opposing; **el equipo c. no opuso resistencia** the opposing team *o* opposition didn't put up much of a fight; **el diputado se pasó al bando c.** the MP left his party and joined their political opponents, *Br* the MP crossed the floor of the House
2 *nm,f (rival)* opponent
3 *nm (opuesto)* opposite; **gordo es el c. de flaco** fat is the opposite of thin
4 **al contrario** *loc adv* on the contrary; **al c. de lo que le dijo a usted** contrary to what he told you; **no me disgusta, al c., me encanta** I don't dislike it, quite the contrary in fact, I like it; **al c. de mi casa, la suya tiene calefacción central** unlike my house, hers has central heating; **no me importa, antes al c., estaré encantado de poder ayudar** I don't mind, on the contrary *o* indeed I'll be delighted to be able to be of help
5 **por el contrario** *loc adv* **no queremos que se vaya, por el c., queremos que se quede** we don't want her to go, on the contrary, we want her to stay; **este modelo, por el c., consume muy poco** this model, by contrast, uses very little; **este año, por el c., no hemos tenido pérdidas** this year, on the other hand, we haven't suffered any losses

---

Contrarreforma *nf Hist* **la C.** the Counter-Reformation

contrarreloj 1 *adj inv Dep* **etapa c.** time trial; **trabajar a c.** to work against the clock
2 *nf Dep* time trial ►► ***c. por equipos*** team time trial; ***c. individual*** individual time trial

contrarrelojista *nmf Dep* time trial specialist

contrarrembolso *nm* cash on delivery

contrarréplica *nf* reply; **en su c., el ministro dijo que...** the minister countered that...

contrarrestar *vt (neutralizar)* to counteract

contrarrevolución *nf* counterrevolution

contrarrevolucionario, -a 1 *adj* counterrevolutionary
2 *nm,f* counterrevolutionary

contrasentido *nm* **hacer/decir eso es un c.** it doesn't make sense to do/say that; **es un c. que quieras comprarte una casa y que estés despilfarrando el dinero** it doesn't make sense squandering your money when you want to buy a house

contraseña *nf* (a) *Mil* password (b) *Informát* password

contrastar 1 *vi* to contrast (**con** with)
2 *vt* (a) *(comprobar)* to check, to verify; **c. algo con algo** to check sth against sth; **c. opiniones** to compare opinions (b) *(objetos de oro, plata)* to assay (c) *(pesas)* to check

contraste *nm* (a) *(diferencia)* contrast; **los contrastes entre el norte y el sur** the contrasts between the north and the south; **en c. con** *(a diferencia de)* in contrast with *o* to; *(comparado con)* in comparison with (b) *(comprobación)* verification, checking; **tras un c. de opiniones...** after canvassing people's opinions... (c) *(en monitor, televisión)* contrast (d) *(marca)* hallmark (e) *Med* contrast medium

contrastivo, -a *adj Ling* contrastive

contrata *nf Der* (fixed-price) contract

contratación *nf* (a) *(de personal)* hiring; **es urgente la c. de un abogado** we urgently need to hire a lawyer; **la ley contempla diferentes modalidades de c.** the law provides *o* allows for different forms of recruitment; **c. indefinida** *o* **fija/temporal** permanent/temporary contracts; **ha bajado la c. indefinida** the number of (people in) permanent jobs has gone down; **una empresa de c. artística** a theatrical agency
(b) *(de servicio, mercancías) (de hotel)* hiring; *(de vuelo)* chartering ►► ***c. de obras*** (building) contracting
(c) *Bolsa (de valores)* trading, *Br* dealing

contratante 1 *adj* contracting; **la parte c.** the contracting party
2 *nmf* contracting party

contratapa = **contraportada**

contratar *vt* (a) *(obreros, personal, detective)* to hire; *(deportista)* to sign (b) *(servicio, obra, mercancía)* **c. algo a alguien** to contract for sth with sb

contratenor *nm* counter-tenor

contraterrorismo *nm* counterterrorism

contraterrorista *adj* counterterrorist

contratiempo *nm (accidente)* mishap; *(dificultad)* setback; **me ha surgido un c. y no voy a poder acudir** a problem has come up and I won't be able to attend; **el fallo judicial supone un enorme c.** the court's ruling means an enormous setback

contratista *nmf* contractor ►► ***c. de obras*** building contractor

contrato *nm* contract; **firmar un c.** to sign a contract; **romper un c.** to break (the terms of) a contract; **incumplimiento de c.** breach of contract; **bajo c.** under contract; **por c.** contractually ►► ***c. administrativo*** administrative contract; ***c. de alquiler*** lease, tenancy agreement; ***c. de aprendizaje*** apprentice contract; ***c. de arrendamiento*** lease; ***c. basura*** short-term contract *(with poor conditions)*; ***c. blindado*** golden parachute, cast-iron contract; ***c. de compraventa*** contract of sale; ***c. de exclusividad*** exclusive agreement; ***c. fijo*** permanent contract; ***c. indefinido*** permanent contract; ***c. laboral*** work contract; ***c. de licencia*** licensing agreement; ***c. de mantenimiento*** maintenance contract; ***c. matrimonial*** marriage contract; ***c. mercantil*** commercial contract; ***c. en prácticas*** work-experience contract; ***c. social*** social contract; ***c. temporal*** temporary *o* short-term *o* fixed-term contract; ***c. a tiempo parcial*** part-time contract; ***c. de trabajo*** work contract; ***c. verbal*** verbal contract

contravención *nf* contravention, violation; **en c. de** in contravention *o* violation of

contraveneno *nm* antidote

contravenir [71] *vt* to contravene

contraventana *nf* shutter

contraventor, -ora *nm,f Der* contravener, violator

contravía: en contravía *loc adv Col* **circulaba en c.** he was driving on the wrong side of the road

contrayente *nmf Formal* bridegroom, groom, *f* bride; **los contrayentes** the bride and groom

contribución *nf* (a) *(aporte)* contribution (b) *(impuesto)* tax; **c. directa/indirecta** direct/indirect tax; **contribuciones** taxes, taxation; **exento de contribuciones** tax-exempt ►► ***c. urbana*** = tax for local services, *Br* ≃ council tax

contribuir [34] *vi* (a) *(aportar dinero)* to contribute; **contribuyó con 100 millones** he contributed 100 million (b) *(colaborar)* to contribute; **todos contribuyeron al triunfo** everyone contributed to the victory; **sus declaraciones contribuyeron a enrarecer el ambiente** his words served to make the atmosphere tense (c) *(pagar impuestos)* to pay taxes

contribuyente *nmf* taxpayer

contrición *nf* contrition

contrincante *nmf* rival, opponent

contristar 1 *vt* to sadden
2 **contristarse** *vpr* to become sad *o* unhappy

contrito, -a *adj* (a) *(arrepentido)* contrite (b) *(triste, compungido)* downcast

control *nm* (**a**) *(dominio)* control; **bajo c.** under control; **fuera de c.** out of control; **perder el c.** *(de vehículo)* to lose control; *(perder la calma)* to lose one's temper; **bebe/fuma sin c.** he drinks/smokes an enormous amount ►► *Econ* ***c. de cambios*** exchange control; *Econ* ***c. de costos*** *o Esp* ***costes*** cost control; *Fin* ***c. crediticio*** credit control; *Fin* ***c. de crédito*** credit control; *Econ* ***c. de gestión*** management control; ***c. de (la) natalidad*** birth control; *Econ* ***c. de precios*** price control

(**b**) *(comprobación, verificación)* examination, inspection; **todos los productos pasan un riguroso c.** all the products are rigorously inspected *o* examined; **(bajo) c. médico** (under) medical supervision; **él se encarga del c. del gasto** he is the person in charge of controlling expenditure; **efectúan un c. continuo de su tensión** his blood pressure is being continuously monitored ►► *Informát* ***c. de acceso*** access control; **el c. de acceso al edificio** the system controlling access to the building; ***c. de alcoholemia*** breath test, *Br* Breathalyser® *o US* Breathalyzer® test; ***c. antidoping*** drugs test; ***c. de armamento*** arms control; ***c. de calidad*** quality control; *Com* ***c. de existencias*** stock control; ***c. financiero*** financial control; *Av* ***c. de tierra*** ground control; ***c. del tráfico aéreo*** air-traffic control

(**c**) *(vigilancia)* examination; **un edificio sometido a un fuerte c.** a building with very heavy security

(**d**) *(de policía)* checkpoint; *(en rally)* checkpoint ►► ***c. de pasaportes*** passport control; ***c. de velocidad por radar*** radar speed trap

(**e**) *(examen)* test, *US* quiz

(**f**) *Dep (del balón)* control; **tiene un buen c.** he's got good control

(**g**) *(mando)* control; **el c. del encendido/apagado** the on/off switch ►► ***c. remoto*** remote control; **activar algo por c. remoto** to activate sth by remote control

(**h**) *Rad* **en los controles estuvo Sandra** the show was produced by Sandra

controlado, -a *adj* controlled; **está todo c.** everything is under control

controlador, -ora *nm,f* (**a**) *(persona, aparato)* controller ►► ***c. aéreo*** air-traffic controller (**b**) *Informát* driver ►► ***c. de disco*** disk driver; ***c. de impresora*** printer driver

controlar 1 *vt* (**a**) *(dominar)* to control; **c. la situación** to be in control of the situation; **la empresa controla el 30 por ciento del mercado** the company controls 30 percent of the market; **los bomberos todavía no han conseguido c. el incendio** firefighters have still not managed to bring the fire under control; **medidas para c. los precios** measures to control prices

(**b**) *(comprobar, verificar)* to check; **controla el nivel del aceite** check the oil level; **controlan continuamente su tensión arterial** they are continuously monitoring his blood pressure

(**c**) *(vigilar)* to watch, to keep an eye on; **la policía controla todos sus movimientos** the police watch his every move; **nos controlan la hora de llegada** they keep a check on when we arrive; **controla que no se cuele nadie** see *o* make sure that no one *Br* jumps the queue *o US* cuts in line

2 *vi Fam (saber)* to know; **Rosa controla un montón de química** Rosa knows loads about chemistry

3 **controlarse** *vpr* to control oneself; **tuve que controlarme para no pegarle** I had to make an effort to stop myself hitting him

controversia *nf* controversy; **un resultado que generó** *o* **provocó c.** a controversial result, a result that caused controversy

controvertido, -a *adj* controversial; **es un pintor muy c.** he's a very controversial painter

controvertir [63] 1 *vt* to question, to dispute

2 *vi* to argue; **c. sobre algo** to argue about sth, to discuss sth

contubernio *nm Pey (alianza)* conspiracy, ring

contumacia *nf* (**a**) *(obstinación)* obstinacy, stubbornness (**b**) *Der* contempt (of court)

contumaz *adj* (**a**) *(obstinado)* stubborn, obstinate (**b**) *Der* in contempt (of court)

contumazmente *adv* stubbornly, obstinately

contundencia *nf* (**a**) *(de golpes)* force (**b**) *(de palabras, argumentos)* forcefulness; **"eso es falso", afirmó con c.** "that's not true," he said forcefully

contundente *adj* (**a**) *(arma, objeto)* blunt; **lanzaron objetos contundentes contra la policía** they threw heavy objects at the police

(**b**) *(golpe)* heavy; **recibió un puñetazo c.** he was punched hard

(**c**) *(razonamiento, argumento)* forceful, convincing; *(prueba)* conclusive, convincing; *(victoria)* comprehensive, resounding; **la empresa dio una respuesta c. a los huelguistas** the company dealt with the strikers decisively; **se mostró c. al exigir la dimisión del secretario general** he was quite categorical in demanding the resignation of the general secretary

contundentemente *adv* (**a**) *(golpear)* hard (**b**) *(responder, argumentar)* convincingly; *(derrotar)* comprehensively; **la policía disolvió c. la manifestación** the police forcefully broke up the demonstration

conturbar *vt Formal* to trouble, to perturb

contusión *nf* bruise, *Espec* contusion; **sufrió múltiples contusiones como resultado del accidente** he suffered severe bruising *o Espec* multiple contusions as a result of the accident

contusionar *vt* to bruise

contuso, -a 1 *adj* bruised

2 *nm,f* injured person

contuviera *etc ver* **contener**

conuco *nm Carib (parcela)* small plot of land

conurbación *nf* conurbation

conurbano *nm RP* suburbs

convalecencia *nf* convalescence

convalecer [46] *vi* to convalesce; **estar convaleciendo de una enfermedad** to be convalescing *o* recovering from an illness

convaleciente *adj* convalescent

convalidación *nf (de estudios, título)* recognition; *(de asignaturas)* validation

convalidar *vt (estudios, título)* to recognize; *(asignaturas)* to validate

convección *nf Fís* convection

convecino, -a *nm,f Br* neighbour, *US* neighbor

convector *nm* convector ►► ***c. de aire caliente*** convection heater

---

CONVENCER [40] 1 *vt* (**a**) *(persuadir)* to convince; **si convenzo a mi hermano, iré con su moto** I'll take my brother's motorbike, if I can persuade him to lend me it *o* if I can talk him into lending me it; **c. a alguien de algo** to convince sb of sth; **no la convencieron de que era la mejor idea** they were unable to convince *o* persuade her that it was the best idea; **lo convencí para que me dejara ir a la fiesta** I convinced *o* persuaded him to let me go to the party; **quisimos animarle a que viniera con nosotros, pero no se dejó c.** we tried to encourage him to come with us but were unable to convince him

(**b**) *(satisfacer)* **me convence esta lavadora, la voy a comprar** I like the sound of this washing machine, I'm going to buy it; **su última película no ha convencido a la crítica** her latest movie *o Br* film didn't impress the critics, the critics didn't think much of her latest movie *o Br* film; **esta manera de hacer las cosas no me convence lo más mínimo** I'm not at all sure that this is the right way to go about it; **es barato, pero no me acaba de c.** *o* **no me convence del todo** it's certainly cheap, but I'm not too sure about it; **tus amigos no me convencen** I'm not too keen on your friends

2 *vi* **su explicación no convenció** his explanation wasn't convincing; **allá donde va, convence** wherever she goes, she creates a good impression; **a pesar de ganar, el equipo no convenció** although they won, the team failed to impress

3 **convencerse** *vpr* (**a**) *(estar seguro)* **convencerse de** to become convinced of; **me convencí de que decía la verdad** I became convinced *o* I came to believe that she was telling the truth

(**b**) *(aceptar)* **a pesar de haberlo leído en la prensa, no quiere convencerse** despite having read it in the press, she still refuses to believe it; **convéncete, no conseguirás nada actuando así** believe (you) me, you won't get anywhere behaving like that; **convencerse de** to become convinced of; **finalmente se convenció de que tenía que dejar de fumar** he finally came to accept that he had to give up smoking; **me convencí de mi error** I realized my mistake

---

convencido, -a 1 *adj* convinced; **estoy c. de que va a salir perfectamente** I'm sure everything will be fine

2 *nm,f RP* believer; **soy una convencida de las ventajas de la medicina homeopática** I'm a believer in the benefits of homeopathic medicine; **es un c. de que el ejercicio es esencial para la salud** he's convinced that exercise is essential to good health

convencimiento *nm* (**a**) *(certeza)* conviction; **llegar al c. de algo** to become convinced of sth; **tener el c. de algo** to be convinced of sth (**b**) *(acción)* convincing

convención *nf* (**a**) *(acuerdo)* convention ►► ***la C. de Ginebra*** the Geneva Convention (**b**) *(asamblea)* convention (**c**) *(norma, costumbre)* convention

convencional *adj* (**a**) *(ideas, gustos, persona)* conventional (**b**) *(armas)* conventional

convencionalismo *nm* conventionality

convencionalmente *adv* conventionally

convenible *adj* (**a**) *(persona)* easy-going, accommodating (**b**) *(precio)* fair, reasonable

convenido, -a *adj* agreed; **hicieron lo c.** they did what they'd agreed

conveniencia *nf* (**a**) *(utilidad)* usefulness; *(oportunidad)* suitability (**b**) *(interés)* convenience; **sólo mira su c.** he only looks after his own interests; **un matrimonio de c.** a marriage of convenience

conveniente *adj* (**a**) *(útil)* useful; *(oportuno)* suitable, appropriate; *(lugar, hora)* convenient (**b**) *(aconsejable)* advisable; **sería c. asistir** it would be a good idea to go; **sería c. aclarar que este sistema no siempre funciona** it should be made clear that this system does not always work; **creer** *o* **juzgar c.** to think *o* see fit

convenio *nm* agreement ▸▸ *Ind* ***c. colectivo*** collective agreement; ***c. salarial*** wage agreement *o* settlement

convenir [70] **1** *vi* (**a**) *(venir bien)* to be suitable; **me conviene ir en tren** it suits me to go by train; **este horario me conviene** these hours suit me; **te convendría dormir unas horas** you would do well to get a few hours sleep; **sólo hace lo que le conviene** he only does what suits him

(**b**) *(ser aconsejable)* **conviene analizar la situación** it would be a good idea to analyse the situation; **no conviene que nos vean juntos** it wouldn't be a good idea for us to be seen together, it would be better if we weren't seen together; **no le conviene que le dé el sol** it's not good for it to be in the sun; **conviene aclarar que...** it should be made clear that...

(**c**) *(acordar)* **c. en** to agree (on); **convinieron en el precio** they agreed (on) the price; **convenimos en volver a reunirnos** we agreed to meet again

2 *vt* to agree (on); **convenimos un precio muy rápidamente** we quickly agreed (on) a price; **sueldo a c.** salary negotiable

conventilleo *nm Andes, RP* gossip

conventillero, -a *Andes, RP Fam Pey* **1** *adj* gossipy; **no seas c.** don't be such a gossip

2 *nm,f* common gossip

conventillo *nm Andes, RP* tenement house

convento *nm (de monjas)* convent; *(de monjes)* monastery

conventual *adj* **la vida c.** *(de monjas)* convent life; *(de monjes)* monastic life

convenzo *etc ver* **convencer**

convergencia *nf* (**a**) *(de líneas, carreteras)* convergence; **esta plaza es punto de c. de varias calles** several streets converge on *o* meet at this square (**b**) *(de ideas)* convergence (**c**) *Fís (de lente)* power (**d**) *Econ* convergence

convergente 1 *adj* (**a**) *(líneas)* converging, convergent; **dos carreteras convergentes** two roads that meet (**b**) *(ideas)* **tienen ideas convergentes** their ideas are very close (**c**) *Esp Pol* = of Convergència i Unió, a right-wing Catalan nationalist party

2 *nmf Esp Pol* = member or supporter of Convergència i Unió, a right-wing Catalan nationalist party

converger [52] *vi* (**a**) *(líneas, carreteras)* to converge (**en** on); **está donde convergen la autopista y el ferrocarril** it's where the motorway and the railway *o US* railroad meet up *o* converge (**b**) *(ideas)* **nuestras ideas convergen** we are very close in our thinking

conversa *nf Am Fam* chat; **estuvieron de c. toda la tarde** they were chatting all afternoon

conversable *adj Am Fam (precio)* negotiable

conversación *nf* (**a**) *(acción de hablar)* conversation; **una c. telefónica** a telephone conversation; **fue uno de los principales temas de c.** it was one of the main topics *o* subjects of conversation; **dar c. a alguien** to keep sb talking; **cambiar de c.** to change the subject; **trabar c.** to strike up a conversation

(**b**) *(manera de hablar)* conversation; **una persona de c. fácil** a person who is easy to talk to

(**c**) **conversaciones** *(contactos)* talks; **conversaciones de paz** peace talks

conversada *nf Am Fam* chat

conversador, -ora 1 *adj* talkative; **es muy poco c.** he doesn't talk much

2 *nm,f* conversationalist; **es una buena conversadora** she's a good conversationalist

conversar *vi* to talk, to converse; **conversaron de** *o* **sobre política durante dos horas** they talked about o discussed politics for two hours

conversión *nf* (**a**) *Rel* conversion; **su c. al catolicismo lo transformó** his conversion to Catholicism transformed him (**b**) *(transformación)* conversion (**en** into) (**c**) *(de medidas)* **la c. de millas en kilómetros** the conversion of miles (in)to kilometres (**d**) *Informát* ***c. de archivos*** file conversion; ***c. de datos*** data conversion

converso, -a 1 *adj* converted

2 *nm,f* convert to Catholicism

convertibilidad *nf Econ* convertibility

convertible 1 *adj* convertible

2 *nm (automóvil)* convertible

convertidor *nm Elec* converter ▸▸ ***c. de frecuencia*** frequency charger

convertir [25] **1** *vt* (**a**) *Rel* to convert (**a** to)

(**b**) *(transformar)* **c. algo/a alguien en** to convert sth/sb into, to turn sth/sb into; **convirtió la tienda en bar** she converted the shop into a bar; **convirtió al príncipe en rana** she turned the prince into a frog

(**c**) *(medidas)* **c. millas en kilómetros** to convert miles (in)to kilometres; **c. dólares en pesos** to convert dollars into pesos

(**d**) *Informát (archivos)* to convert

2 convertirse *vpr* (**a**) *Rel* to convert; **se convirtió al judaísmo** she converted to Judaism

(**b**) *(transformarse)* **convertirse en** to become, to turn into; **la zona se convirtió en un desierto** the area turned into *o* became a desert; **se ha convertido en el favorito para ganar** he has become the favourite to win; **el agua se convirtió milagrosamente en vino** the water miraculously turned into wine

convexidad *nf* convexity

convexo, -a *adj* convex

convicción *nf* (**a**) *(convencimiento)* conviction; **actuaba sin c.** he lacked conviction in what he was doing; **consiguió persuadirlos gracias a su fuerte c.** he managed to persuade them because he was so convinced of himself; **tener la c. de que** to be convinced that; **expresó su c. de que pronto se hallaría una solución al conflicto** he said he was convinced that a solution to the conflict would soon be found

(**b**) **convicciones** *(principios)* convictions, principles; **un político de profundas convicciones católicas** a politician with strongly-held Catholic beliefs, a staunchly Catholic politician

convicto, -a *adj* convicted; **c. de robo** convicted of robbery; **c. y confeso** guilty in fact and in law

convidado, -a *nm,f* guest ▸▸ ***c. de piedra:*** **estuvo en la cena como el c. de piedra** he sat through the whole meal without saying a word; **la oposición no quiere ser el c. de piedra en el debate** the opposition does not want to be a mere token participant in the debate

convidar 1 *vt* (**a**) *(invitar)* to invite; **c. a alguien a una copa** to stand *o* buy sb a drink; **me convidaron a comer en su casa** they invited me round for a meal (**b**) *Am (compartir)* **¿me convidás?** can I have some?; EXPR **al que come y no convida le sale un sapo en la barriga** = a curse on anyone who eats without inviting others to share

2 *vi (mover, incitar)* **el buen tiempo convida a salir** this good weather makes you want to get out; **la ocasión convidaba a la alegría** the occasion made you feel happy

conviene *etc ver* **convenir**

convierto *etc ver* **convertir**

convincente *adj* convincing

convincentemente *adv* convincingly

conviniera *etc ver* **convenir**

convite *nm* (**a**) *(invitación)* invitation (**b**) *(fiesta)* banquet

convivencia *nf* (**a**) *(de grupos sociales, culturas, lenguas)* coexistence; **tras veinte años de c. se separaron** they separated after twenty years of living together; **la c. dentro del equipo es muy buena** the members of the team get on very well together

(**b**) **convivencias** *(de estudiantes)* = period of a few days with no lectures when students take part in activities to get to know each other and learn how to get on

conviviente *nmf* partner

convivio *nm Méx* get-together, gathering; **estuvieron de c. el fin de semana** they had a get-together at the weekend

convivir *vi (personas)* to live together; *(grupos sociales)* to coexist, to live side by side; **c. con** to live with; **aquí conviven dos sistemas informáticos distintos** we have two different computer systems running side by side here

convocante 1 *adj* **las organizaciones convocantes de la manifestación** the organizations that organized the demonstration

2 *nmf (de protesta)* organizer; **los convocantes de la huelga** the people who called the strike

convocar [60] *vt* (a) *(reunión)* to convene; **convocaron a los accionistas a junta** the shareholders were called to a meeting, a shareholders' meeting was convened
(b) *(huelga, elecciones)* to call; *(manifestación)* to organize; **c. a alguien a una manifestación** to call on sb to demonstrate *o* to attend a demonstration; **c. a alguien a la huelga** to call sb out on strike; **el seleccionador ha convocado a cinco nuevos jugadores** the manager has called up five new players
(c) *(premio, examen)* to announce

convocatoria *nf* (a) *(anuncio, escrito)* notice; **la c. de un concurso** the announcement of a competition; **llamar a c.** to summon
(b) *(llamamiento)* **una c. de huelga** a strike call; **hacer una c. de huelga** to call a strike; **han anunciado la c. de elecciones** they've called an election; **el partido ganador en la c. electoral** the party which won the election; **no hubo novedades en la c. de la selección nacional** there were no surprises when the national squad was announced
(c) *(de examen)* **la c. de junio/septiembre** the June/September exams; **tengo el inglés en cuarta c.** I have to retake my English exam for the third time
(d) *(de reunión)* announcement, notification

convocatorio, -a *adj* convening, summoning

convólvulo *nm* leafroller moth

convoy *(pl* **convoyes***)* *nm* (a) *(de barcos, camiones)* convoy (b) *(tren)* train (c) *(vinagreras)* cruet set

convoyarse *vpr Ven (confabularse)* to conspire, to connive

convulsión *nf* (a) *(de músculos)* convulsion (b) *(de tierra)* tremor (c) *(política, social)* **un periodo de convulsiones** a period of upheaval; **la subida del dinero produjo convulsiones en la bolsa** the rise in interest rates caused chaos *o* turmoil on the stock exchange; **las convulsiones sociales del periodo de entreguerras** the social upheaval between the wars

convulsionar *vt (sociedad)* to throw into upheaval

convulsivo, -a *adj* convulsive

convulso, -a *adj* convulsed

conyugal *adj* conjugal, marital; **el hogar c.** the marital home; **vida c.** married life

cónyuge *nmf* spouse; **los cónyuges** husband and wife

coña *nf Esp muy Fam* (a) *(guasa)* **está de c.** she's just pissing around; **se lo toma todo a c.** he treats everything as a *Br* bloody *o US* goddamn joke; **no le hagas caso, que va de c.** don't mind him, he's just pissing around; **¡ni de c.!** no *Br* bloody *o US* goddamn way!; **no te lo va a dejar ni de c.** no *Br* bloody *o US* goddamn way is he going to let you have it; **se lo pasaron de c. en la playa** they had a *Br* bloody *o US* goddamn brilliant time at the beach
(b) *(casualidad)* **acertó de c.** it was a total fluke that he got it right
(c) *(molestia)* drag, pain; **tener que trabajar el domingo es una c.** it's a real drag *o* pain having to work on Sundays; **¡deja de dar la c.!** stop being such a pain!; **me está dando la c. para que vayamos con ella** she's going on and on about us going with her
(d) *ver también* **coño**[2]

coñac, coñá *(pl* **coñacs***)* *nm* brandy, cognac

coñazo *nm Esp muy Fam* pain, drag; **ese libro es un c.** that book's *Br* bloody *o US* goddamn boring; **¡qué c. de película!** what a *Br* bloody *o US* goddamn boring film!; **estoy harto de tanto c. con los teléfonos móviles** I'm fed up with those *Br* bloody *o US* goddamn mobile phones; **tu compañero es un c.** your mate's a real pain *o* drag; **¡deja de dar el c.!** stop being such a pain!; **me está dando el c. para que le deje ver el fútbol** he's going on and on at me to let him watch the football

coño[1] *esp Esp Vulg* 1 *nm* (a) *(vulva)* cunt; **comer el c. a alguien** to go down on sb, to eat sb out; EXPR **no me sale del c.** I can't be fucking bothered, *Br* I can't be arsed; **lo hago porque me sale del c.** I'm doing it because I fucking well feel like it; EXPR **estoy hasta el mismísimo c. de este ruido** I've fucking well had it with this noise; EXPR **vive en el quinto c.** she lives *Br* bloody *o US* goddamn miles from anywhere; EXPR **el c. de la Bernarda: me toman por el c. de la Bernarda** they think they can just treat me like shit; **esta casa es como el c. de la Bernarda** this household is fucking chaotic
(b) *(para enfatizar)* **¿dónde/qué c....?** where/what the fuck...?; **¿con quién c. estará hablando?** who the fuck is he talking to?; **¿qué c.?, salimos a cenar a un restaurante y ya está** what the fuck! we'll just go and have dinner in a restaurant, problem solved
2 *interj* (a) *(enfado)* for fuck's sake!; **¡cállate ya, c.!** shut the fuck up!
(b) *(sorpresa)* fucking hell!; **¡c., hacía tiempo que no te veía!** fucking hell, I haven't seen you for ages!; **¡c., nos hemos olvidado de contar a mi hermano!** fucking hell, we forgot to count my brother!

coño[2], **-a** *nm,f Vulg* (a) *Chile (español)* = offensive term for a Spaniard (b) *Ven (persona)* fucker; **¿quién es ese c. del abrigo verde?** who's the fucker in the green coat?

cooperación *nf* co-operation

cooperador, -ora *adj* co-operative

cooperante 1 *adj* co-operating
2 *nmf* (overseas) volunteer worker

cooperar *vi* (a) *(trabajar)* to co-operate; **cooperó con nosotros en nuestro primer proyecto** he worked with us on our first project; **cooperaron con la policía en la investigación** they co-operated with the police in the investigation, they helped the police with their enquiries; **tenemos que c. para hacer desaparecer la violencia** we must work together to put an end to violence
(b) *(contribuir)* to contribute; **cooperaron con dos hospitales de campaña** the contributed two field hospitals
(c) *(influir)* to contribute; **el mal tiempo cooperó al fracaso** the bad weather contributed to their failure

cooperativa *nf* (a) *(sociedad)* co-operative ►► ***c. agrícola*** farming co-operative; ***c. de crédito*** credit union; ***c. de viviendas*** housing co-operative (b) *(establecimiento)* co-operative

cooperativismo *nm* co-operative movement

cooperativista 1 *adj* **economía c.** economy based on co-operatives; **movimiento c.** co-operative movement
2 *nmf* (a) *(miembro de cooperativa)* member of a co-operative (b) *(partidario de cooperativa)* supporter of the co-operative movement

cooperativo, -a *adj* co-operative

cooptar *vt* to co-opt

coordenada *nf* co-ordinate ►► *Mat* ***coordenadas cartesianas*** Cartesian co-ordinates; ***coordenadas polares*** polar co-ordinates

coordinación *nf* (a) *(de esfuerzos, medios)* co-ordination (b) *(de movimientos, gestos)* co-ordination (c) *Gram* co-ordination

coordinado, -a *adj* co-ordinated

coordinador, -ora 1 *adj* co-ordinating
2 *nm,f* co-ordinator

coordinadora *nf (organización)* co-ordinating committee; **la c. de las ONG en España** the body that co-ordinates NGOs in Spain

coordinar 1 *vt* (a) *(esfuerzos, medios)* to co-ordinate; **la Cruz Roja coordina el envío de ayuda humanitaria** the Red Cross is co-ordinating the sending of humanitarian aid; **se encarga de c. los diferentes departamentos de la empresa** she is in charge of co-ordinating the different departments of the company; **ella coordina los intercambios universitarios** she is in charge of university exchanges; **coordina tres proyectos de investigación diferentes** he is co-ordinating three different research projects
(b) *(movimientos, gestos)* to co-ordinate
2 *vi Fam* to think straight; **cuando me pongo nervioso no coordino** I can't think straight when I get nervous

copa *nf* (a) *(recipiente)* glass ►► ***c. alta*** tall glass; ***c. de champán*** champagne glass; ***c. de coñac*** brandy glass
(b) *(contenido)* glass; **una c. de vino** a glass of wine; **beber una c. de más** to have a drink too many; **ir de copas** to go out drinking; **¿quieres (tomar) una c.?** would you like (to have) a drink? ►► ***c. de helado*** ice cream *(as dessert in restaurant)*
(c) *(de árbol)* top; EXPR **como la c. de un pino: una mentira como la c. de un pino** a whopper (of a lie); **un penalti como la c. de un pino** a blatant penalty
(d) *(trofeo, competición)* cup ►► ***la C. América*** *(en fútbol)* = international soccer championship held every two years between South American nations; ***la C. de Europa*** the European Cup; ***la C. Libertadores*** = South American club soccer competition; ***la C. del Mundo*** the World Cup; ***la C. del Rey*** = Spanish club soccer competition, *Br* ≃ the FA Cup; ***la C. de la UEFA*** the UEFA Cup
(e) *(de sombrero)* crown
(f) *(de sostén)* cup
(g) *(naipe)* = any card in the "copas" suit
(h) **copas** *(palo)* = suit in Spanish deck of cards, with the symbol of a goblet

copado, -a *adj RP Fam* (a) *(encantado)* over the moon; **está copada con su casa nueva** she's over the moon with her new house (b) *(muy bueno)* brilliant, fantastic; **¿no leíste este libro? ¡está c.!** haven't you read this book? it's brilliant *o* fantastic!

copaiba *nf* (a) *(bálsamo)* copaiba (balsam *o* resin) (b) *(árbol)* copaiba tree

copal *nm* (a) *(árbol)* West Indian locust-tree (b) *(resina)* copal resin

copante *adj RP Fam* brilliant, fantastic; **vimos un atardecer c.** we saw a fantastic sunset; **ese escritor es c.** he's a brilliant *o* fantastic writer

copar 1 *vt* (a) *(ocupar)* to fill; **los amigos del presidente han copado todos los puestos** all the positions have been filled by the president's friends; **las mejores horas están ya copadas** the best times are already taken; **los corredores keniatas coparon el podio** the Kenyan runners took all three medals
(b) *(atención, interés)* to capture; **la visita papal copó la atención de la prensa** the papers were full of the Pope's visit
(c) **c. la banca** *(en juegos)* to break the bank
(d) *RP Fam (encantar)* **le copa el chocolate/bailar** she loves *o* adores chocolate/dancing; **le copa Mario** she's crazy *o* mad about Mario; **esa película me copó** I thought that movie was brilliant, I just loved that movie
2 **coparse** *vpr RP Fam* **se copa con la salsa** he's crazy *o* mad about salsa

coparticipación *nf* copartnership

copartícipe *nmf (en empresa)* partner; *(en actividad)* participant; **son copartícipes en las acciones de la empresa** they are both shareholders in the company

copazo *nm Fam* **se metió un c. de coñac** he knocked back a brandy

cope *nm RP Fam* **ser un c.** to be brilliant *o* fantastic; **tener un c. con algo/alguien** to be crazy about sth/sb

copear *vi Fam* to have a few (drinks)

cópec *(pl* **copecs***)* *nm* kopeck

COPEI [ko'pei] *nm (abrev de* **Comité de Organización Política Electoral Independiente***)* = Venezuelan Christian-Socialist party

Copenhague *n* Copenhagen

copeo *nm Fam* boozing; **ir de c.** to go out boozing

copera *nf* (a) *RP* (nightclub) hostess (b) *ver también* **copero**

copernicano, -a *adj* Copernican

Copérnico *n pr* Copernicus

copero, -a 1 *adj Dep* **un equipo c.** a good cup team; **partido c.** cup game, cup tie
2 *nm,f Chile* waiter

copete *nm* (a) *(de ave)* crest (b) *(de pelo)* tuft (c) EXPR *Fam* **de alto c.** posh; *RP* **estoy hasta el c. de** *(harto)* I've had it up to here with, I'm sick of; *RP* **estoy hasta el c. de trabajo** I'm up to my eyes in work

copetín *nm RP (bebida)* aperitif; *(comida)* appetizer; **salimos a tomar el c. con ellos** we went out to have a pre-lunch drink with them

copetón, -ona 1 *adj* (a) *Am (ave)* tufted, crested (b) *Col Fam (achispado)* tipsy
2 *nm Col (ave)* crested sparrow

copetona *nf Méx* elegant woman

copetuda *nf* (a) *(ave)* skylark (b) *Cuba (planta)* marigold

copeyano, -a *Ven Pol* 1 *adj* relating to "COPEI"
2 *nm,f* member/supporter of "COPEI"

copia *nf* (a) *(reproducción)* copy; **hacer una c. de algo** to duplicate sth; **sacar una c.** to make a copy ▸▸ ***c. certificada*** certified copy; *Informát* ***c. impresa*** printout; ***c. en limpio*** fair copy
(b) *(de disco, libro, software)* copy; **han vendido 20.000 copias de su último disco** they've sold 20,000 copies of their latest record ▸▸ ***c. de evaluación*** *(libro) Br* inspection *o US* examination copy; *(software)* evaluation copy; ***c. maestra*** master copy; *Informát* ***c. de seguridad*** backup (copy); **hacer una c. de seguridad de algo** to back sth up, to make a backup of sth
(c) *(imitación)* copy; **es una c. de un cuadro de Monet** it's a copy of a painting by Monet
(d) *(acción)* copying
(e) *(persona)* (spitting) image
(f) *(de fotografía)* copy; **quería dobles copias de este carrete, por favor** I'd like an extra set of prints of this film, please ▸▸ *Fot* ***c. de contacto*** contact print

copiada *nf Fam (en examen)* **nos pegamos una c. increíble** we copied loads off each other

copiador, -ora *adj* copying

copiadora *nf (máquina)* photocopier

copiante *nmf* copyist

copiapino, -a 1 *adj* of/from Copiapó *(Chile)*
2 *nm,f* person from Copiapó *(Chile)*

copiar 1 *vt* (a) *(transcribir)* to copy; **copie este texto a máquina** type up (a copy of) this text (b) *(anotar)* to copy; **copió lo que yo iba diciendo** he took down what I was saying (c) *(imitar)* to copy; **copia siempre todo lo que hago** she always copies everything I do (d) *(en examen)* to copy; **copió la respuesta** she copied the answer (e) *Informát* to copy; **c. y pegar algo** to copy and paste sth
2 *vi (en examen)* to copy; **lo expulsaron por c.** he was thrown out of the exam for copying
3 **copiarse** *vpr* to copy; **copiarse de alguien** to copy sb

copichuela *nf Fam* drink

copihue *nm* Chilean bellflower *(national flower of Chile)*

copiloto *nmf (en avión)* co-pilot; *(en automóvil)* co-driver

copión, -ona *nm,f Fam* (a) *(imitador)* copycat (b) *(en examen)* cheat

copiosamente *adv (llover)* heavily; *(sudar)* profusely; **comer c.** to eat a lot; **llorar c.** to cry one's eyes out

copiosidad *nf* copiousness

copioso, -a *adj (lluvia)* heavy; *(sudor)* profuse; *(comida)* plentiful; *(ganancias)* substantial; **cayó una copiosa nevada** there was a heavy snowfall

copista *nmf* copyist

copistería *nf (tienda)* copy shop

copla *nf* (a) *(estrofa)* verse, stanza (b) *(canción)* folk song, popular song; EXPR **ya está otra vez con la misma c.** he's back on his hobby-horse; EXPR **no me vengas otra vez con la misma c.** don't give me that old story again

copo *nm* (a) *(de nieve)* flake ▸▸ ***c. de nieve*** snowflake (b) *(de cereales)* ***copos de avena*** rolled *o* porridge oats; ***copos de maíz*** cornflakes (c) *(de algodón)* ball (d) *RP (de nubes)* bank (e) *Col, Ven (de árbol)* top

copón *nm* (a) *Rel* ciborium (b) *(en naipes)* = ace of the "copas" suit in a Spanish deck of cards (c) *Esp muy Fam (como intensificador)* **un lío del c.** a hell of a mess; **nos lo pasamos del c.** we had a hell of a good time; **hace un frío del c.** it's *Br* bloody *o US* goddamn freezing; **jugaron un partido del c.** they played a hell of a good match *o* game

copra *nf* copra

coprocesador *nm Informát* coprocessor ▸▸ ***c. matemático*** maths coprocessor

coproducción *nf* coproduction, joint production

coproducir *vt* to coproduce

coprofagia *nf* coprophagy

coprófago, -a *adj* dung-eating, *Espec* coprophagic

coprolito *nm* coprolite

copropiedad *nf (de empresa)* joint ownership, co-ownership; *(multipropiedad)* timesharing

copropietario, -a *nm,f* co-owner, joint owner

coprotagonista *nmf* co-star

coprotagonizar *vt* to co-star in

copto, -a 1 *adj* Coptic
2 *nm,f (persona)* Copt
3 *nm (lengua)* Coptic

cópula *nf* (a) *(sexual)* copulation (b) *Gram* copula

copular *vi* to copulate

copulativo, -a *adj Gram* copulative

copyright [kopi'rrait] *(pl* **copyrights***)* *nm* copyright

coque *nm* coke

coquear *vi Andes, Arg* to chew coca leaves

coquero, -a *nm,f* (a) *Col (cultivador)* coca farmer *o* producer (b) *Am Fam (consumidor)* cokehead

coqueta *nf (tocador)* dressing table

coquetear *vi* (a) *(con persona)* to flirt (**con** with) (b) *(con actividad, ideología)* to flirt

coqueteo *nm* (a) *(con persona)* flirting; **le gusta mucho el c. con hombres jóvenes** she loves flirting with young men (b) *(con actividad, ideología)* flirtation

coquetería *nf* coquetry

coqueto, -a *adj* (a) *(persona) (que flirtea)* flirtatious (b) *(persona) (que se arregla mucho)* **es muy c.** he's very fussy about his appearance (c) *(habitación, adorno, detalle)* charming, delightful

coquetón, -ona *adj Fam (agradable)* attractive, charming

coquina *nf* lumachelle

coquito *nm* (a) *Méx (ave)* turtledove (b) *CAm, Méx (árbol)* coquito palm (c) ***c. del Brasil*** Brazil nut

coquizar *vt* to coke, to convert into coke

coracero *nm (soldado)* cuirassier

coraje *nm* (**a**) *(valor)* courage; **tener c.** to be brave, to have courage; **no tuvo el c. de admitir que estaba equivocado** he didn't have the courage to admit that he was wrong (**b**) *(rabia)* anger; **me da mucho c.** it makes me furious

corajudo, -a *adj (valiente)* brave

coral 1 *adj* choral
2 *nm* (**a**) *(animal)* coral ►► ***c. blanco*** white coral; ***c. rojo*** red coral (**b**) *(en joyería)* coral (**c**) *(color)* coral (**d**) *(composición)* chorale (**e**) *Cuba (arbusto)* coral tree
3 *nf* (**a**) *(coro)* choir (**b**) *(serpiente)* coral snake

coralífero, -a = **coralino**

coralillo *nm o nf* coral snake

coralino, -a, coralífero, -a *adj* coral

corambre *nf (conjunto de cueros)* hides, skins

Corán *nm Rel* **el C.** the Koran

coránico, -a *adj Rel* Koranic

coraza *nf* (**a**) *(de soldado)* cuirass (**b**) *(de buque, tanque)* armour (**c**) *(de tortuga)* shell (**d**) *(protección)* shield; **se protege bajo una c. de indiferencia** she protects herself with a wall of indifference

corazón *nm* (**a**) *(órgano)* heart; **a c. abierto** *(operación)* open-heart; **padecer del c.** to have heart trouble; EXPR **con el c. en la mano** frankly, openly; EXPR **con el c. en un puño** on tenterhooks; **estuvimos con el c. en un puño esperando el resultado del análisis** we were on tenterhooks waiting for the results of the test; EXPR **se me encoge el c. al ver...** it breaks my heart to see...; EXPR **romper** *o* **partir el c. a alguien** to break sb's heart; EXPR **no tener c.** to have no heart, to be heartless; EXPR **tener buen c.** to be kindhearted; EXPR **tener un c. de oro** to have a heart of gold; EXPR **tener un c. de piedra** to have a heart of stone ►► ***c. artificial*** artificial heart
(**b**) *(sentimientos)* heart; **sus comentarios me llegaron al c.** I was deeply touched by what he said; **se deja llevar por el c.** she lets her heart rule her head; **me dice el c. que todo va a salir bien** I have this feeling inside that everything will turn out all right; **se lo agradezco de todo c.** I thank you with all my heart *o* from the bottom of my heart; **te pido de todo c. que les dejes marchar** I'm begging you to let them go
(**c**) *(apelativo)* sweetheart; **¡Ana de mi c.!** Ana, sweetheart!
(**d**) *(parte central)* heart; **en pleno c. de la ciudad** right in the heart of the city
(**e**) *(de frutas)* core; *(de alcachofa)* heart; **sácale el c. a la manzana** core the apple
(**f**) **(dedo) c.** middle finger
(**g**) *(naipe)* heart
(**h**) **corazones** *(palo)* hearts

corazonada *nf* (**a**) *(presentimiento)* feeling, hunch; **tengo la c. de que va a venir** I have a feeling *o* hunch she'll come (**b**) *(impulso)* sudden impulse

corbata *nf* tie; **hacer el nudo a la c.** to tie one's tie; EXPR *muy Fam* **tenerlos de** *o* **por c.** to be scared stiff, *Br* to be bricking it ►► *Chile* ***c. de humita*** bow tie; *Ven* ***c. de lacito*** bow tie; ***c. de lazo*** bow tie; *Urug* ***c. moñita*** bow tie; *Arg* ***c. (de) moñito*** bow tie; *Méx* ***c. de moño*** bow tie; *Esp* ***c. de pajarita*** bow tie

corbatín *nm CAm, Carib, Col (corbata de pajarita)* bow tie

corbeta *nf* corvette

Córcega *n* Corsica

corcel *nm Literario* steed

corchea *nf Mús Br* quaver, *US* eighth note

corchera *nf* (**a**) *(en piscina)* lane marker (**b**) *(para anuncios) Br* noticeboard, *US* bulletin board *(made of cork)*

corchero, -a *adj* cork; **la industria corchera** the cork industry

corcheta *nf* eye *(of a hook and eye)*

corchete *nm* (**a**) *(broche)* hook and eye (**b**) *(signo ortográfico)* square bracket (**c**) *Chile (grapa)* staple

corchetear *vt Chile* to staple

corchetera *nf Chile* stapler

corcho 1 *nm* (**a**) *(material)* cork (**b**) *(tapón)* cork; **sacar el c. a una botella** to uncork a bottle (**c**) *(para pescar)* float
2 *interj Esp (expresando sorpresa)* good heavens!; *(expresando enfado)* for heavens' *o* goodness' sake!

corcholata *nf Méx* (metal) bottle top

córcholis *interj (expresando sorpresa)* good heavens!; *(expresando enfado)* for heavens' *o* goodness' sake!

corcova *nf* hump

corcovado, -a 1 *adj* hunchbacked
2 *nm,f* hunchback

corcovear *vi* to buck

corcovo, *CSur* **corcoveo** *nm* buck

cordada *nf* = roped party of mountaineers

cordado *Zool* **1** *adj* chordate
2 *nm* chordate

cordaje *nm* (**a**) *(de guitarra, raqueta)* strings (**b**) *Náut* rigging

cordal *nm Mús* tailpiece

cordel *nm* cord; **a c.** in a straight line

cordelería *nf* (**a**) *(tienda)* = shop selling rope, string etc (**b**) *(oficio)* ropemaking (**c**) *Náut* rigging

cordelero, -a *nm,f (fabricante)* rope maker

cordera *nf muy Fam (mujer)* babe

cordero, -a *nm,f* (**a**) *(animal)* lamb; EXPR *Fam* **mirar con cara** *o* **ojos de c. degollado** to look with mournful eyes (**b**) *(carne)* lamb ►► ***c. lechal*** suckling lamb (**c**) *(piel)* lambskin (**d**) *Rel* lamb ►► ***c. de Dios*** Lamb of God (**e**) *Fam (persona)* **su marido es un manso c.** her husband is as meek as a lamb, her husband wouldn't say boo to a goose

corderoy, corduroy *nm Andes, RP* corduroy

cordial 1 *adj* cordial; **fue una reunión c.** it was a friendly meeting, there was a good atmosphere in the meeting; **recibieron una c. acogida** they were given a warm welcome; **estuvo muy c. con sus invitados** he was very friendly to his guests; **quiero darles mi más c. bienvenida** I'd like to welcome you most warmly; **(reciba) un c. saludo** *(en carta)* best *o* kind regards
2 *nm* cordial, tonic

cordialidad *nf* cordiality

cordialmente *adv (afectuosamente)* cordially; *(en una carta)* sincerely

cordillera *nf* (**a**) *(montañosa)* mountain range ►► ***la c. de los Andes*** the Andes; ***la c. Andina*** the Andes; ***la C. Cantábrica*** the Cantabrian Mountains; ***la c. Pirenaica*** the Pyrenees (**b**) *RP* **la C.** *(los Andes)* the southern Andes

cordillerano, -a 1 *adj* Andean
2 *nm,f* Andean

córdoba *nm (moneda)* cordoba

cordobán *nm* cordovan

cordobés, -esa 1 *adj* of/from Cordoba *(Spain or Argentina)*
2 *nm,f* person from Cordoba *(Spain or Argentina)*

cordón *nm* (**a**) *(cuerda)* lace (**b**) *(de zapato)* lace (**c**) ***c. umbilical*** umbilical cord (**d**) *(cable eléctrico)* flex (**e**) *Náut* strand (**f**) *(para protección, vigilancia)* cordon ►► ***c. policial*** police cordon; ***c. sanitario*** cordon sanitaire (**g**) **aparcar en c.** to park end-to-end (**h**) *CSur, Cuba (de la vereda) Br* kerb, *US* curb

cordoncillo *nm* (**a**) *(de tela)* rib, cord (**b**) *(de una moneda)* milling

cordura *nf* (**a**) *(juicio)* sanity (**b**) *(sensatez)* sense

corduroy = **corderoy**

Corea *n* Korea ►► ***C. del Norte*** North Korea; ***C. del Sur*** South Korea

corea *nf Med* chorea ►► ***c. de Huntington*** Huntington's chorea

coreana *nf (abrigo)* parka

coreano, -a 1 *adj* Korean
2 *nm,f (persona)* Korean
3 *nm (lengua)* Korean

corear *vt (exclamando)* to chorus; *(cantando)* to sing; **los manifestantes coreaban consignas contra la guerra** the demonstrators were chanting anti-war slogans

coreografía *nf* choreography

coreográfico, -a *adj* choreographic

coreógrafo, -a *nm,f* choreographer

coriandro *nm* coriander

corifeo *nm* (**a**) *(director del coro)* coryphaeus (**b**) *(portavoz)* leader

corimbo *nm Bot* corymb

corindón *nm* corundum

corintio, -a 1 *adj* Corinthian
2 *nm,f* Corinthian

corista 1 *nmf (en coro)* chorus singer
2 *nf (en cabaret)* chorus girl

coriza *nm o nf Med* coryza

cormorán *nm* cormorant ►► ***c. grande*** great cormorant; ***c. moñudo*** shag

cornada *nf Taurom* = wound from bull's horns; **el torero recibió tres cornadas** the bullfighter was gored three times

cornalina *nf* carnelian

cornamenta *nf* (**a**) *(de toro)* horns; *(de ciervo)* antlers (**b**) *Fam (de marido engañado)* cuckold's horns

cornamusa *nm* (**a**) *(trompeta)* hunting horn (**b**) *(gaita)* bagpipes (**c**) *Náut* cleat

córnea *nf* cornea

cornear *vt* to gore

corneja *nf* crow ►► ***c. americana*** American crow; ***c. cenicienta*** hooded crow; ***c. negra*** carrion crow

cornejo *nm* dogwood

córneo, -a *adj* horny

córner *(pl* **córners***) nm Dep* corner (kick); **botar** *o* **lanzar un c.** to take a corner

corneta 1 *nf* (**a**) *(instrumento)* bugle (**b**) *Ven (claxon)* horn
2 *nmf (persona)* bugler

cornetazo *nm Ven* hoot

cornete *nm* (**a**) *(helado)* cornet, cone (**b**) *Anat* turbinate bone

cornetín 1 *nm (instrumento)* cornet
2 *nmf (persona)* cornet player

cornezuelo *nm (hongo)* **c. (del centeno)** (rye) ergot

cornflakes® ['konfleks] *nmpl* cornflakes®

corniforme *adj* horn-shaped

cornisa *nf* (**a**) *(moldura, saliente)* cornice (**b**) *Geog* ledge, lead ►► ***la C. Cantábrica*** the Cantabrian coast

corno *nm* (**a**) **c. (inglés)** *(instrumento)* cor anglais, English horn (**b**) *(árbol)* dogwood tree

cornucopia *nf* (**a**) *(espejo)* = small decorative mirror (**b**) *(cuerno)* cornucopia, horn of plenty

cornudo, -a 1 *adj* (**a**) *(animal)* horned (**b**) *Fam (marido)* cuckolded
2 *nm Fam (marido)* cuckold

coro *nm* (**a**) *(parte de iglesia)* choir (**b**) *(grupo de voces)* choir; *(en musical)* chorus; **se oyó un c. de protestas** there was a chorus of protest; **contestar a c.** to answer all at once; *Fig* **hacer c. a** to back up (**c**) *(pasaje musical)* chorus (**d**) *(en la tragedia griega)* chorus

coroides *nf inv Anat* choroid

corola *nf Bot* corolla

corolario *nm* corollary

corona *nf* (**a**) *(de monarca)* crown; **el heredero de la c.** the crown prince ►► ***c. de espinas*** crown of thorns
(**b**) *(deportiva)* crown
(**c**) **la c.** *(la monarquía)* the Crown
(**d**) *(estado)* **la C. de España/Inglaterra** the Spanish/English Crown
(**e**) *(de flores)* wreath ►► ***c. fúnebre*** funeral wreath; ***c. de laurel*** laurel wreath
(**f**) *(de santo)* halo
(**g**) *(coronilla)* crown
(**h**) *(moneda)* crown
(**i**) *(en diente)* crown
(**j**) *(solar)* corona ►► ***c. solar*** (solar) corona
(**k**) *(rueda dentada)* crown wheel

coronación *nf* (**a**) *(de monarca)* coronation
(**b**) *(de montaña, puerto de montaña)* **la c. de la montaña se produjo a las 7 de la tarde** they reached the summit of the mountain at 7 in the evening; **tras la c. del puerto los ciclistas iniciaron el descenso** after reaching the top of the pass, the cyclists began their descent
(**c**) *(remate)* culmination; **el galardón supuso la c. de su carrera** the award was the crowning point *o* culmination of his career

coronamiento *nm (culminación)* culmination; **esta novela es el c. de su obra** this novel is the culmination *o* crowning glory of her work

coronar 1 *vt* (**a**) *(persona)* to crown
(**b**) *(cima)* to reach; *(puerto de montaña)* to reach the top of; **coronaron el Everest** they reached the summit of Mount Everest; **coronó el puerto con cinco minutos de ventaja sobre el pelotón** he reached the top of the pass five minutes ahead of the pack
(**c**) *(cubrir)* **las montañas están coronadas de nieve** the mountains are capped with snow; **la tarta está coronada con dos muñequitos** the cake is topped with two little figures, there are two little figures on top of the cake
(**d**) *(terminar)* to complete; *(culminar)* to crown, to cap; **con el puesto de ministro corona su trayectoria profesional** being made a minister is the crowning point *o* culmination of his career
2 *vi (en damas)* to crown a piece; *(en ajedrez)* to queen a pawn
3 **coronarse** *vpr (bebé)* to crown

coronario, -a *adj Anat* coronary

coronel *nm Mil* colonel ►► ***c. de aviación*** *Br* group captain, *US* colonel

coronilla *nf* crown (of the head); EXPR *Fam* **ando** *o* **voy de c.** I'm at full stretch; EXPR *Fam* **estar hasta la c. de algo/alguien** to be fed up to the back teeth with sth/sb

corotos *nmpl Carib Fam (objetos)* things, whatnots

corpachón *nm* big body, big frame

corpiño *nm* (**a**) *(de vestido, top)* bodice (**b**) *Arg (sostén)* bra

corporación *nf* (**a**) *(organismo público)* corporation, authority ►► ***corporaciones locales*** local authorities (**b**) *(empresa)* corporation

corporal 1 *adj (trabajo, daño)* physical; *(castigo)* corporal; **calor c.** body heat
2 *nm Rel (lienzo)* corporal

corporativismo *nm* (**a**) *(doctrina)* corporatism (**b**) *Pey (de médicos, abogados)* = self-interested behaviour, especially of professional groups

corporativo, -a *adj* corporate

córpore insepulto *loc adv* **misa c., funeral de c.** funeral mass *(before the body is buried or cremated)*

corpóreo, -a *adj* corporeal

corpulencia *nf* heavy build, burliness; **un animal de gran c.** a very bulky animal

corpulento, -a *adj (persona)* heavily built, burly; *(animal)* bulky

corpus *(pl inv o* **corpora***) nm* (**a**) *(de datos, textos)* corpus (**b**) *(Rel)* **el C.** Corpus Christi

Corpus Christi ['korpus'kristi] *nm Rel* Corpus Christi

corpuscular *adj* corpuscular

corpúsculo *nm* corpuscle

corral *nm* (**a**) *(para aves)* run; *(para cerdos, ovejas)* pen; **pollo/huevos de c.** free-range chicken/eggs (**b**) *Hist (para teatro)* = open-air theatre in courtyard (**c**) *(para niños)* playpen

corrala *nf* = building with several floors of small flats on running balconies round a central courtyard

corralito *nm Fam* = freezing of bank accounts by government to prevent panic withdrawals

corralón *nm* (**a**) *Méx (depósito)* police car pound (**b**) *Perú (vivienda)* = communal urban dwelling for poor families (**c**) *RP (solar)* enclosed plot ►► ***c. de materiales*** builder's yard

correa *nf* (**a**) *(de bolso, reloj)* strap; *(cinturón)* belt; *(de perro)* lead, leash (**b**) *Tec* belt ►► ***c. de transmisión*** drive belt; ***c. del ventilador*** fan belt

correaje *nm* (**a**) *(de caballo)* harness (**b**) *(de soldado)* equipment belts

correcalles *nmf inv Fam (holgazán)* loafer

correcaminos *nm inv (ave)* roadrunner

corrección *nf* (**a**) *(de error)* correction; *(de examen)* marking; *(de texto)* revision ►► *Informát* ***c. de color*** colour correction; ***c. de pruebas*** proofreading
(**b**) *(cambio, enmienda)* correction; **el texto sólo tenía tres correcciones** the text only had three corrections
(**c**) *(perfección)* correctness
(**d**) *(de comportamiento)* courtesy; **se comportó distantemente con nosotros pero con mucha c.** he was distant but very correct in the way he behaved towards us ►► ***c. política*** political correctness
(**e**) *(reprimenda)* reprimand

correccional *nm* reformatory, reform school

correctamente *adv* (**a**) *(contestar)* correctly (**b**) *(comportarse)* courteously; **se comportó distantemente con nosotros pero c.** he was distant but very correct in the way he behaved towards us

correctivo, -a 1 *adj* corrective
2 *nm* (**a**) *(castigo)* punishment; **aplicar un c. a alguien** to punish sb (**b**) *(derrota abultada)* crushing defeat

correcto, -a 1 *adj* (**a**) *(resultado, texto, respuesta)* correct; **habla un c. francés** she speaks correct French (**b**) *(persona, conducta)* courteous; **el agente de policía fue muy c. con nosotros** the police officer treated us very correctly; **estos niños son muy correctos en la mesa** these children have very good table manners
2 *interj* right!, ok!

corrector, -ora 1 *adj* corrective
2 *nm,f* **c. (de pruebas)** proofreader ►► ***c. de estilo*** copy editor
3 *nm Informát* **c. de estilo** stylechecker; ***c. de gramática*** grammar checker; ***c. ortográfico*** spell-checker

corredera *nf* (**a**) *(ranura)* runner (**b**) *Arg Fam* **la c.** *(diarrea)* the runs

corredero, -a *adj* sliding; **puerta corredera** sliding door

corredizo, -a *adj* **nudo c.** slipknot; **puerta corrediza** sliding door

corredor, -ora 1 *adj Zool* **ave corredora** flightless bird
2 *nm,f* (a) *(deportista)* runner ▸▸ ***c. de fondo*** long-distance runner, distance runner; EXPR **ser un c. de fondo** to have staying power; ***c. de Fórmula 1*** Formula 1 racing driver; ***c. de maratón*** marathon runner
(b) *Com (intermediario)* ***c. de apuestas*** bookmaker; ***c. de bolsa*** stockbroker; ***c. de comercio*** registered broker; ***c. de fincas*** land agent; ***c. de seguros*** insurance broker
3 *nm* (a) *(pasillo)* corridor, passage; **un c. aéreo** an air corridor
(b) *(galería)* = passage surrounding an inner courtyard
(c) *(ave)* courser ▸▸ ***c. sahariano*** cream-coloured courser

corredora *nf Zool* flightless bird

correduría *nf Com (de bolsa)* brokerage ▸▸ ***c. de seguros*** *(oficina)* insurance broker's

corregible *adj* **es un problema c.** it's a problem that can be solved; **un error que no es fácilmente c.** a mistake which isn't easy to correct

corregidor, -ora *nm,f Hist* = magistrate appointed by the king, especially in former Spanish colonies

corregir [55] 1 *vt* (a) *(error)* to correct; **corrígeme si me equivoco, pero creo que...** correct me if I'm wrong, but I think...; **estas gafas corregirán la visión** these glasses will correct your vision (b) *(pruebas, galeradas)* to proofread (c) *(examen)* to mark (d) *(rumbo)* to correct (e) *(reprender)* to reprimand
2 **corregirse** *vpr* to change for the better; **se ha corregido mucho de su falta de puntualidad** he has done a lot to improve his punctuality

correlación *nf* correlation

correlacionar *vt* to correlate

correlativamente *adv* **veinte billetes numerados c.** twenty notes numbered in numerical sequence

correlativo, -a *adj* correlative

correlato *nm Ling* correlate

correligionario, -a *nm,f (en política, ideología)* person of the same ideological persuasion; *(en religión)* fellow believer; **Churchill y sus correligionarios** Churchill and his fellow conservatives

correlimos *nm inv* dunlin ▸▸ ***c. chico*** long-toed stint; ***c. gordo*** knot; ***c. menudillo*** least sandpiper; ***c. menudo*** little stint; ***c. oscuro*** purple sandpiper; ***c. tridáctilo*** sanderling; ***c. zarapitín*** curlew sandpiper

correntada *nf Andes, RP (de río)* strong current

correntoso, -a *adj Andes, RP (río)* swift, rapid

correo 1 *adj* **tren c.** mail train
2 *nm* (a) *(sistema, cartas) Br* post, *US* mail; **a vuelta de c.** by return (of post); **echar algo al c.** to *Br* post *o US* mail sth; **mandar algo por c.** to send sth by *Br* post *o US* mail ▸▸ ***c. aéreo*** airmail; *Informát* ***c. basura*** junk mail; ***c. certificado*** registered *Br* post *o US* mail; ***c. comercial*** direct mail; *Informát* ***c. electrónico*** electronic mail, e-mail; **me envió un c. (electrónico)** she e-mailed me, she sent me an e-mail; **me mandó la información por c. electrónico** she sent me the information by e-mail; ***c. postal*** ordinary mail; **enviar algo por c. postal** to send sth by *Br* post *o US* mail; *Am* ***c. recomendado*** registered *Br* post *o US* mail; ***c. urgente*** special delivery; *Informát* ***c. de voz*** voice mail
(b) *(persona)* messenger; **actuar como c. para alguien** to act as a messenger for sb; **los correos de la droga** drug couriers
(c) *Am (organismo)* the Post Office; **tengo que ir al c.** I have to go to the post office

Correos *nm inv Esp (organismo)* the Post Office; **tengo que ir a C.** I have to go to the post office

correoso, -a *adj (carne)* leathery, tough; *(pan)* chewy

CORRER 1 *vi* (a) *(persona, animal)* to run; **me gusta c. todas las mañanas** I like to go for a run every morning; **se fue corriendo** he ran off *o* away; **miles de fans corrieron al encuentro del cantante** thousands of fans ran to greet *o* meet the singer; **¡corre a pedir ayuda!** run for help!; **varias personas corrieron tras el asaltante** several people ran after the robber; **echar a c.** to start running; EXPR *Fam* **corre que se las pela** she runs like the wind; EXPR *Fam* **el que no corre, vuela** you've got to be on your toes *o* quick around here
(b) *(apresurarse)* **¡corre, que vamos a perder el autobús!** hurry up, we're going to miss the bus!; **no corras, que te vas a equivocar** don't rush yourself, or you'll make a mistake; **cuando me enteré del accidente, corrí a visitarla** when I heard about the accident I went to visit her as soon as I could *o* I rushed to visit her; **estoy agotado, toda la mañana corriendo de aquí para allá** I'm exhausted, I've been rushing *o* running around all morning; **corre, que va a empezar la película** quick, the film's about to start; EXPR **a todo c.: hay que acabar este trabajo a todo c.** we have to finish this job as quickly as possible; **cuando se enteró de la noticia, vino a todo c.** when she heard the news she came as quickly as she could
(c) *(participar en una carrera) (atleta, caballo)* to run; *(ciclista)* to ride; **corre con una moto japonesa** he rides a Japanese motorbike; **corre con un coche italiano** he drives an Italian car
(d) *(conductor)* to drive fast; **no corras tanto, que vamos a tener un accidente** slow down *o* stop driving so fast, we're going to have an accident
(e) *(vehículo)* **el nuevo modelo corre todavía más** the new model is *o* goes even faster; **esta moto no corre nada** this motorbike can't go very fast at all
(f) *(río)* to flow; *(agua del grifo)* to run; *(camino)* to run; **la sangre corre por las venas** blood flows through the veins; **deja c. el agua (del grifo)** leave the *Br* tap *o US* faucet running; **la vía del tren corre junto al lago** the railway *o US* railroad track runs alongside the lake
(g) *(viento)* to blow; **corría una ligera brisa** there was a gentle breeze, a gentle breeze was blowing
(h) *(el tiempo, las horas)* to pass, to go by; **esta última semana ha pasado corriendo** this last week has flown by
(i) *(transcurrir)* **corría el principio de siglo cuando...** it was around the turn of the century when...; **en los tiempos que corren nadie tiene un trabajo seguro** no one is safe in their job these days *o* in this day and age
(j) *(noticia)* to spread; **corre el rumor de que...** there's a rumour going about that...
(k) *(encargarse de)* **c. con** *(los gastos)* to bear; *(la cuenta)* to pay; **la organización de la cumbre corrió a cargo de las Naciones Unidas** the United Nations organized the summit, the United Nations took care of the organization of the summit; **la comida corre a cargo de la empresa** the meal is on the company; **esta ronda corre de mi cuenta** this round is on me, this is my round
(l) *(moneda)* to be legal tender
(m) *(sueldo, renta)* to be payable; **el alquiler corre desde principios de cada mes** the rent is payable at the beginning of each month
(n) *(venderse)* to sell; **este vino corre a diez euros la botella** this wine sells for ten euros a bottle
(o) *Informát (uso crítico)* to run; **el nuevo sistema operativo no correrá en modelos antiguos** the new operating system won't run on older models
2 *vt* (a) *(prueba, carrera) (a pie, a caballo)* to run; *(en coche, moto)* to take part in; **corrió los 100 metros** he ran the 100 metres; **correrá el Tour de Francia** he will be riding in the Tour de France
(b) *(mover) (mesa, silla)* to move *o* pull up; **corre la cabeza, que no veo** move your head out of the way, I can't see
(c) *(cerrar) (cortinas)* to draw, to close; *(llave)* to turn; **c. el cerrojo** *o* **pestillo** to bolt the door/gate/*etc*
(d) *(abrir) (cortinas)* to draw, to open
(e) *(experimentar)* **c. aventuras** to have adventures; **c. peligro** to be in danger; **si dejas la caja ahí, corre el peligro de que alguien tropiece con ella** if you leave the box there, (there's a danger *o* risk that) someone might trip over it; **c. el riesgo de (hacer) algo** to run the risk of (doing) sth; **no quiero c. ningún riesgo** I don't want to take any risks; **no sabemos la suerte que correrá el proyecto** we don't know what is to become of the project, we don't know what the project's fate will be; **no se sabe todavía qué suerte han corrido los desaparecidos** the fate of the people who are missing is still unknown
(f) *(noticia)* to spread; **corrieron el rumor sobre su dimisión** they spread the rumour of her resignation; **c. la voz** to pass it on
(g) *(pintura, colores)* **la lluvia corrió la capa de pintura** the rain made the paint run
(h) *Informát (uso crítico) (programa, aplicación)* to run; **no consigo c. este programa** I can't get this program to run properly
(i) *Com* to auction, to sell at auction
(j) *Taurom (torear)* to fight
(k) *Fam* **correrla** to go out on the town
(l) *Am Fam (despedir)* to throw out
(m) *Am Fam (ser válido)* to be in use; **las ideas progresistas allá no corren** progressive ideas don't get much of a hearing there
(n) *Am (perseguir)* to chase (after); **los perros iban corriendo a la liebre** the dogs chased after the hare
(o) *Méx, Ven (funcionar)* to be running; **hoy no corren los trenes** the trains aren't running today
(p) EXPR *RP Fam* **c. la coneja** to scrimp and save
3 **correrse** *vpr* (a) *(desplazarse) (persona)* to move over; *(cosa)* to slide; **córrete hacia la derecha** move over to the right a bit; **el cargamento se corrió con el movimiento del barco** the cargo slid to one side as the boat rocked
(b) *(pintura, colores)* to run; **se me ha corrido el rímel** my mascara

has run; **se corre al lavarlo** it runs in the wash

(c) *Andes, Esp muy Fam (tener un orgasmo)* to come; *Esp* **correrse de gusto (con algo)** *(disfrutar)* to get off (on sth)

(d) *Fam* **correrse una juerga** to go out on the town

(e) *Fam (avergonzarse)* to be embarrassed

(f) *Cuba, Guat, Méx (escaparse)* to run away, to escape

correría *nf* (a) *(incursión)* incursion, raid (b) *(aventura)* **son famosas sus correrías nocturnas** he is famous for his nocturnal expeditions *o* exploits

correspondencia *nf* (a) *(relación)* correspondence; **no hay c. entre la calidad y el precio** there is no relation between the quality and the price

(b) *(correo)* correspondence; **mantengo c. con ella** she and I write to each other; **¿te importaría recogerme mi c.?** would you mind picking up my *Br* post *o US* mail for me?

(c) *(de metro, tren)* connection; **este tren tiene c. con el de las 8 horas** this train connects with the one at 8 o'clock; **próxima estación, Sol, c. con línea 3** next stop Sol, change here for line 3

(d) *Mat* correspondence

corresponder 1 *vi* (a) *(compensar)* **c. (con algo) a algo/alguien** to repay sth/sb (with sth); **ella nunca correspondió a mi amor** she never returned my love, she never felt the same way about me; **amor no correspondido** unrequited love

(b) *(tocar)* **les corresponden 5 millones a cada uno** they get *o* they're due 5 million each; **a mí me correspondió encargarme de la comida** it was my job to take care of *o* organize the food

(c) *(coincidir, encajar)* to correspond **(a/con** to/with); **esta historia no corresponde con la realidad** this story doesn't tally *o* agree with the facts

(d) *(competer)* **corresponderle a alguien hacer algo** to be sb's responsibility to do sth; **no me corresponde a mí enjuiciar su trabajo** it's not my place to judge his work

(e) *(ser adecuado)* to be right *o* fitting; **voy a darle las gracias como corresponde** I'm going to thank him, as is only right; **estuvo genial, tal y como corresponde a un cantante de su talla** she was brilliant, just as you would expect from a singer of her stature

2 *vt (sentimiento)* to repay; **ella no le correspondía** she didn't feel the same way about him

3 **corresponderse** *vpr* (a) *(escribirse)* to correspond; **se corresponden con unos amigos en Australia** they have some friends in Australia who they keep in touch with by post

(b) *(amarse)* to love each other

(c) *(ser proporcional o adecuado)* to correspond **(con/a** with/to); **lo que ha dicho no se corresponde con lo que ocurrió en realidad** what she said doesn't tally *o* agree with what really happened

correspondiente *adj* (a) *(perteneciente, relativo)* corresponding **(a** to); **trajo todos los documentos correspondientes al tema** he brought all the documents relevant to the subject; **el presupuesto c. al ejercicio de 2001** the budget for 2001

(b) *(respectivo)* respective; **cada uno tomó su parte c.** each person took their own share; **yo me encargaré de limpiar mi parte c.** I'll make sure I clean my bit

(c) *(lógico)* **llegó tarde, con el c. disgusto de sus padres** he arrived late, to the understandable annoyance of his parents; **obtuvo el premio, con la c. alegría de sus amigos** she won the prize, much to the delight of her friends; **reaccionó con el c. enfado** unsurprisingly, he reacted angrily

corresponsabilidad *nf* joint responsibility

corresponsable *adj* jointly responsible (**de** for)

corresponsal *nmf* (a) *Prensa* correspondent ▸▸ ***c. de guerra*** war correspondent (b) *Com* agent

corresponsalía *nf* post of correspondent

corretaje *nm Com* brokerage

corretear 1 *vi* (a) *(correr)* to run about; **los niños estaban correteando por el parque** the children were running about in the park (b) *Fam (vagar)* to hang about

2 *vt* (a) *Méx (adelantar)* to overtake (b) *Andes (perseguir)* to chase, to pursue (c) *CAm (ahuyentar)* to drive away

correteo *nm* **el c. de los niños** the children's running about

correveidile *nmf Fam* gossip

corrida *nf* (a) *(acción de correr)* run; *Fam* **darse** *o* **pegarse una buena c.** to run like mad (b) *Taurom* **c. (de toros)** bullfight (c) *Esp muy Fam (orgasmo)* **en el momento de la c.** as he/she was coming (d) *Méx (viaje)* trip, run (e) *RP Fam* **hacer algo a las corridas** *(apresuradamente)* to do sth in a rush; **siempre como a las corridas** I always eat in a rush, I always rush my meals

corrido, -a 1 *adj* (a) *(cortinas)* drawn (b) *(avergonzado)* embarrassed (c) *(experimentado)* wordly-wise (d) *(continuo)* continuous; **balcón c.** long balcony *(along front of building)*; **banco c.** long bench; **dos páginas de texto c.** two pages of continuous *o* unbroken text; **se lo sabe de c.** she knows it by heart; **recitar algo de c.** to recite sth parrot-fashion

2 *nm (canción)* = Mexican ballad

CORRIENTE 1 *adj* (a) *(normal)* ordinary, normal; *(frecuente)* common; **es un alumno c.** he's an average pupil; **es un problema muy c.** it's a very common problem; **un reloj normal y c.** an ordinary watch; **una moto de lo más c.** a perfectly ordinary motorbike; **lo c. es comerlo con palillos** it's usually eaten with chopsticks; **lo c. es recibir una respuesta a los pocos días** it's normal *o* usual to receive a reply within a few days; **en Australia es c. ver koalas por las calles** in Australia you often see *o* it's not uncommon to see koala bears on the streets; **salirse de lo c.** to be out of the ordinary; EXPR *Fam* **c. y moliente** run-of-the-mill

(b) *(agua)* running

(c) *(cuenta)* current

(d) *(mes, año)* current; **en mayo del año c.** in May of this year

2 *nf* (a) *(de río)* current; **c. abajo** downstream; **c. arriba** upstream; EXPR **dejarse llevar de** *o* **por la c.** to follow the crowd; EXPR **llevar** *o* **seguir la c. a alguien** to humour sb; EXPR **ir** *o* **nadar** *o* **navegar contra c.** to go against the tide; EXPR **nadar a favor de la c.** to go with the flow ▸▸ ***c. de convección*** convection current; ***la c. del Golfo*** the Gulf Stream; ***la C. de Humboldt*** the Humboldt Current; ***c. de lava*** lava flow; ***c. marina*** ocean current; ***c. oceánica*** ocean current; ***c. de sangre*** bloodstream; ***c. sanguínea*** bloodstream; ***c. submarina*** underwater current

(b) *(de aire) Br* draught, *US* draft; **en esta habitación hay mucha c.** this room is very draughty ▸▸ *Meteo* ***c. en chorro*** jet stream

(c) ***c. migratoria*** migratory current

(d) *(de electricidad)* current; **toma de c.** socket; **media ciudad se quedó sin c.** half the city was left without electricity; **le dio la c. al tocar el enchufe** she got an electric shock when she touched the socket ▸▸ ***c. alterna*** alternating current; ***c. continua*** direct current; ***c. eléctrica*** electric current; ***c. trifásica*** three-phase current

(e) *(tendencia)* trend, current; *(de opinión)* tide; **las corrientes de la moda** fashion trends; **las corrientes de pensamiento que llegan de Europa** the schools of thought that are coming across from Europe; *Bolsa* **una c. alcista/bajista** an upward/downward trend; **el representante de la c. socialdemócrata en el partido** the representative of the social democratic tendency in the party

3 *nm (mes en curso)* **el 10 del c.** the 10th of this month

4 **al corriente** *loc adv* **estoy al c. del pago de la hipoteca** I'm up to date with my mortgage repayments; **estoy al c. de la marcha de la empresa** I'm aware of how the company is doing; **ya está al c. de la noticia** she has already heard the news; **mantener** *o* **tener a alguien al c. de algo** to keep sb informed about sth; **me mantengo al c. de lo que ocurre en mi país** I keep informed about what's going on in my country; **el profesor puso al c. de las clases a su sustituto** the teacher filled his replacement in on the classes; **tenemos que poner al c. nuestras bases de datos** we have to bring our databases up to date; **ponerse al c.** to bring oneself up to date

corrientemente *adv* (a) *(comúnmente)* commonly, usually; **el sistema que se emplea más c.** the most commonly used system (b) *(con normalidad)* unremarkably; **viste c.** he wears ordinary clothes

corrigió *ver* **corregir**

corrijo *ver* **corregir**

corrillo *nm* knot *o* small group of people

corrimiento *nm* shift, slipping ▸▸ *Astron* ***c. hacia el rojo*** redshift; ***c. de tierras*** landslide

corro *nm* (a) *(círculo)* circle, ring; **en c.** in a circle; **hacer c.** to form a circle; **se formó un c. en torno al accidentado** a circle of people formed around the injured person

(b) *(juego infantil)* **jugar al c. (de la patata)** = to hold hands in a circle, moving round and singing a song

(c) *Bolsa* ring, *US* pit; **el ambiente en los corros bursátiles madrileños era de pesimismo** traders in the Madrid stock exchange were in a pessimistic mood

corroboración *nf* corroboration

corroborar *vt* to corroborate

corroborativo, -a *adj* corroborative

corroer [58] **1** *vt* (**a**) *(desgastar)* to corrode; *(madera)* to rot; *(roca)* to erode (**b**) *(consumir)* to consume, to eat away at; **lo corroe la envidia** he's consumed with envy
2 corroerse *vpr (desgastarse)* to corrode; *(madera)* to rot; *(roca)* to erode

corromper 1 *vt* (**a**) *(madera)* to rot; *(alimentos)* to turn bad, to spoil (**b**) *(pervertir)* to corrupt (**c**) *(sobornar)* to bribe (**d**) *Informát (archivo)* to corrupt
2 corromperse *vpr* (**a**) *(pudrirse)* to rot (**b**) *(pervertirse)* to become corrupted (**c**) *Informát (archivo)* to become corrupted

corrosión *nf (desgaste)* corrosion; *(de metal)* rust

corrosivo, -a *adj* (**a**) *(sustancia, líquido)* corrosive (**b**) *(persona, comentario)* caustic

corrugación *nf* corrugation

corrugado, -a *adj* corrugated

corrugar *vt* to corrugate

corrupción *nf* (**a**) *(delito, decadencia)* corruption; **brigada anti c.** fraud squad ►► *Der* ***c. de menores*** corruption of minors (**b**) *(soborno)* bribery (**c**) *(de una sustancia)* decay

corruptela *nf (corrupción)* corruption; **denunciaron las corruptelas en la administración** they condemned the corruption in the government; **lo han acusado de una serie de pequeñas corruptelas** he has been accused of a number of misdemeanours

corrupto, -a *adj* corrupt

corruptor, -ora 1 *adj* corrupting
2 *nm,f* corrupter ►► *Der* ***c. de menores*** corruptor of minors

corrusco *nm* hard crust

corsario, -a 1 *adj (pirata)* pirate; **un buque c.** a pirate ship
2 *nm (pirata)* corsair, pirate

corsé *nm* corset

corsetería *nf* ladies' underwear shop

corso, -a 1 *adj* Corsican
2 *nm,f* Corsican
3 *nm* (**a**) *(dialecto)* Corsican (**b**) *Hist* **hacer el c.** to operate as a privateer

corta *nf* **a la c. o a la larga** sooner or later

cortaalambres *nm inv* wirecutters

cortacésped (*pl* **cortacéspedes**) *nm* lawnmower

cortacigarros *nm inv* cigar cutter

cortacircuitos *nm inv Elec (en circuito)* circuit breaker; *(fusible)* fuse wire, fusible

cortacorriente *nm Elec* switch

cortada *nf* (**a**) *Arg (calle)* side street, close (**b**) *Am (atajo)* shortcut (**c**) *Am (corte)* cut; **se dio una c. en la mano** she cut her hand

cortadera *nf* (**a**) *(planta)* = type of bulrush with sharp leaves (**b**) *(mata gramínea)* pampas grass

cortado, -a 1 *adj* (**a**) *(labios, manos)* chapped (**b**) *(leche)* curdled; *(mayonesa)* off (**c**) *(carretera)* closed; **c. por obras** *(en letrero)* road closed for repairs (**d**) **café c.** = small coffee with just a little milk (**e**) *Fam (persona)* **estar c.** to be inhibited; **quedarse c.** to be left speechless; **ser c.** to be shy; EXPR **estar cortados por el mismo patrón** *o Am* **con la misma tijera** to be cast in the same mould
2 *nm* (**a**) *(café)* = small coffee with just a little milk (**b**) *Fam (persona)* **ser un c.** to be shy

cortador, -ora 1 *adj* cutting
2 *nm (de césped)* lawnmower

cortadora *nf* cutter ►► ***c. de césped*** lawnmower

cortadura *nf* (**a**) *(corte)* cut (**b**) *Geog (garganta)* gorge

cortafrío, *RP* **cortafierro** *nm* cold chisel

cortafuego *nm,* **cortafuegos** *nm inv* (**a**) *(en monte)* firebreak (**b**) *(en edificio)* fire wall (**c**) *Informát* firewall

cortante *adj* (**a**) *(afilado)* sharp (**b**) *(viento)* biting; *(frío)* bitter (**c**) *(tajante) (frase, estilo)* cutting

cortapapel *nm,* **cortapapeles** *nm inv* paperknife, letter opener

cortapichas *nm inv Fam Hum* earwig

cortapicos *nm inv* earwig

cortapisa *nf* limitation, restriction; **quiere tener poder de decisión, sin ninguna c.** he wants complete freedom *o* a free hand to make decisions; **poner cortapisas a** to hinder, to put obstacles in the way of; **le pusieron cortapisas por ser mujer** they put obstacles in her way *o* made things difficult for her because she was a woman

cortaplumas *nm inv* penknife

cortapuros *nm inv* cigar cutter

CORTAR 1 *vt* (**a**) *(seccionar)* to cut; *(en pedazos)* to cut up; *(escindir) (rama, brazo, cabeza)* to cut off; *(talar)* to cut down; **c. el césped** to mow the lawn, to cut the grass; **hay que c. leña para el hogar** we have to chop some firewood for the hearth; **siempre corta el pavo** he always carves the turkey; **c. una rebanada de pan** to cut a slice of bread; **c. el pan a rodajas** to slice the bread, to cut the bread into slices; **c. algo en pedazos** to cut sth into pieces; **corta la tarta en cinco partes** divide the cake in five, cut the cake into five slices; **corta esta cuerda por la mitad** cut this string in half; **corta la cebolla muy fina** chop the onion very finely; **le cortaron la cabeza** they chopped her head off; **le cortaron dos dedos porque se le habían gangrenado** they amputated *o* removed two of his fingers that had gone gangrenous; **cortarle el pelo a alguien** to cut sb's hair
(**b**) *(recortar) (tela, figura de papel)* to cut out
(**c**) *(interrumpir) (retirada, luz, teléfono)* to cut off; *(carretera)* to close; *(hemorragia)* to stop, to staunch; *(discurso, conversación)* to interrupt; *Dep (pase, tiro)* to block; **c. la luz** to cut off the electricity supply; **nos han cortado el teléfono** our telephone has been cut off *o* disconnected; **la nieve nos cortó el paso** we were cut off by the snow; **cortaron el tráfico para que pasara el desfile** they closed the road to traffic so the procession could pass by; **la falta cortó el ataque del equipo visitante** the foul stopped the away team's attack; **cortada por obras** *(en letrero)* road closed for repairs; **en esta cadena de televisión no cortan las películas con anuncios** on this television channel they don't interrupt the films with adverts; EXPR *CSur Fam* **¡cortála!** shut it!, shut up!
(**d**) *(atravesar) (recta)* to cross, to intersect; *(calle, territorio)* to cut across; **el río corta la región de este a oeste** the river runs right across *o* bisects the region from east to west
(**e**) *(labios, piel)* to crack, to chap
(**f**) *(hender) (aire, olas)* to slice through
(**g**) *Fam (droga)* to cut
(**h**) *(baraja)* to cut
(**i**) *(leche)* to curdle; **el calor corta la mayonesa** heat makes mayonnaise go off
(**j**) *(recortar) (gastos)* to cut back
(**k**) *(poner fin a) (beca)* to cut; *(relaciones diplomáticas)* to break off; *(abusos)* to put a stop to; **c. un problema de raíz** *(impedirlo)* to nip a problem in the bud; *(erradicarlo)* to root a problem out; EXPR **c. algo por lo sano: tenemos que c. este comportamiento por lo sano** we must take drastic measures to put an end to this behaviour
(**l**) *(avergonzar)* **este hombre me corta un poco** I find it hard to be myself when that man's around
(**m**) *(película) (escena)* to cut; *(censurar)* to censor
(**n**) *RP (comunicación)* **c. la comunicación** to hang up; **me cortó en mitad de la frase** she hung up on me when I was in mid-sentence
(**o**) *Informát* to cut; **c. y pegar** cut and paste
2 *vi* (**a**) *(producir un corte)* to cut; **estas tijeras no cortan** these scissors don't cut (properly); **corte por la línea de puntos** cut along the dotted line; EXPR **c. por lo sano** *(aplicar una solución drástica)* to resort to drastic measures; **decidió c. por lo sano con su pasado** she decided to make a clean break with her past; EXPR *Esp Fam Hum* **corta y rema, que vienen los vikingos** give it a rest!, *Br* put a sock in it!
(**b**) *(atajar)* to take a short cut (**por** through); **corté por el camino del bosque** I took a short cut through the forest
(**c**) *(terminar una relación)* to split up (**con** with); **corté con mi novio** I've split up with my boyfriend
(**d**) *(en juego de cartas)* to cut
(**e**) *(ser muy intenso)* **hace un frío que corta** it's bitterly cold
(**f**) *Cine* **¡corten!** cut!
(**g**) *Rad* **¡corto y cambio!** over!; **¡corto y cierro!** over and out!
(**h**) *RP (hablando por teléfono)* to hang up, to put the phone down; **no corte, por favor** hold the line, please
3 cortarse *vpr* (**a**) *(herirse)* to cut oneself; **cortarse el pelo** to have a haircut, to have one's hair cut; **cortarse las uñas** to clip *o* cut one's nails; **cortarse las venas** to slit one's wrists; **cortarse (en) la cara** to cut one's face; **cortarse con un cristal** to cut oneself on a piece of glass; **me corté al afeitarme** I cut myself shaving; *Fam* **si no apruebo, me corto el cuello** I'm going to kill myself if I fail; *muy Fam* **si no me dan el trabajo, me la corto** I'm going to kill myself if they don't give me the job
(**b**) *(labios, piel)* to become chapped *o* cracked
(**c**) *(leche)* to curdle; *(mayonesa)* to go off
(**d**) *(interrumpirse)* **se cortó la comunicación** I was/we were/*etc* cut off; **la comunicación telefónica se cortó por culpa de la tormenta** the phone lines went down because of the storm; **se te va a c. la digestión** you'll get stomach cramps
(**e**) *Geom* **dos rectas que se cortan** two intersecting straight lines, two straight lines that intersect

(**f**) *(separarse)* to divide, to split; **el pelotón se cortó en dos grupos** the pack split into two groups
(**g**) *Fam (turbarse)* to become tongue-tied; **no se corta a la hora de criticar** he doesn't mince his words *o* hold back when it comes to criticizing; **no te cortes, sírvete lo que te apetezca** don't be shy *o* polite, take whatever you want; **no se cortó un pelo y vino a la fiesta sin haber sido invitado** he didn't worry about what people might think and came to the party without having been invited
(**h**) *Andes, RP (separarse)* to be left behind
(**i**) *Chile (caballo)* to catch a chill

cortas *nfpl (luces) Br* dipped headlights, *US* low beams
cortaúñas *nm inv* nail clippers
cortavientos *nm inv* windbreak

CORTE 1 *nm* (**a**) *(raja)* cut; *(en pantalones, camisa)* tear; **tiene un c. en la mano** she has cut her hand; **se hizo un c. en la rodilla** he cut his knee ►► ***c. y confección*** *(para mujeres)* dressmaking; *(para hombres)* tailoring; ***c. de pelo*** haircut
(**b**) *(retal de tela)* length
(**c**) *(interrupción)* **mañana habrá c. de agua de nueve a diez** the water will be cut off tomorrow between nine and ten; **la sequía ha obligado a imponer cortes de agua** the drought has forced the authorities to cut off the water supply for a number of hours each day; **c. de corriente** *o* **luz** power cut ►► ***c. de digestión*** stomach cramps
(**d**) *(sección)* section; **c. longitudinal** lengthways section, *Espec* longitudinal section; **c. transversal** cross-section
(**e**) *(concepción, estilo)* style; **una chaqueta de c. clásico** a jacket with a classic cut; **una novela de c. fantástico** a novel with an air of fantasy about it; **un gobierno de c. autoritario** a government with authoritarian tendencies
(**f**) *(pausa)* break ►► ***c. publicitario*** commercial break
(**g**) *Esp (filo)* (cutting) edge; **este c. está muy afilado** this blade is very sharp
(**h**) *(en golf)* cut; **meterse en** *o* **pasar el c.** to make the cut
(**i**) *(en ciclismo)* breakaway (group); **meterse en el c.** to join the breakaway group
(**j**) *(helado) Br* wafer, *US* ice-cream sandwich
(**k**) *(en baraja)* cut
(**l**) *Am (reducción)* cut, cutback ►► ***c. presupuestario*** budget cut; ***c. salarial*** wage *o* pay cut
(**m**) *Cine (por la censura)* cut
(**n**) *Fam (vergüenza)* embarrassment; **me da c. decírselo** I feel embarrassed to tell him; **¡qué c. tener que hablar con ella!** how embarrassing having to talk to her!
(**o**) *Fam (respuesta ingeniosa)* put-down; **dar** *o* **pegar un c. a alguien** to cut sb dead; **le di un buen c. y dejó de molestarme** my put-down made him stop annoying me
(**p**) ***c. de mangas*** = obscene gesture involving raising one arm with a clenched fist and placing one's other hand in the crook of one's elbow; **hacer un c. de mangas a alguien** ≃ to stick two fingers up at sb
(**q**) *Fam (de disco)* track
2 *nf* (**a**) *(del rey)* court; **la c. celestial** the Heavenly Host
(**b**) *(galanteo)* **hacer la c. a alguien** to court sb
(**c**) *(comitiva)* entourage, retinue; **vino el ministro con toda su c.** the minister arrived with his entourage
(**d**) *Esp* **las Cortes (Generales)** *(cámara legislativa)* the Spanish parliament ►► ***Cortes Constituyentes*** constituent assembly
(**e**) *Am (tribunal)* court ►► ***C. Penal Internacional*** International Criminal Court; ***C. Suprema de Justicia*** Supreme Court

cortedad *nf* (**a**) *(de longitud)* shortness; *(de duración)* shortness, brevity (**b**) *(timidez)* shyness; **c. de miras** short-sightedness
cortejar *vt* (**a**) *Anticuado (galantear)* to court, to woo (**b**) *(entre animales)* to court, to attract
cortejo *nm* (**a**) *(comitiva)* retinue ►► ***c. fúnebre*** funeral cortège *o* procession (**b**) *Anticuado (galanteo)* courtship (**c**) *(entre animales)* courtship
cortés *adj* polite, courteous; EXPR **lo c. no quita lo valiente** there's no harm in being polite
cortesana *nf (prostituta)* courtesan
cortesano, -a 1 *adj (modales)* courtly; **la vida cortesana** life at court
2 *nm,f (personaje de la corte)* courtier
cortesía *nf* (**a**) *(gentileza)* courtesy; **una fórmula de c.** a polite expression; **una visita de c.** a courtesy call; **las trataron con c.** they were treated courteously *o* politely; **por c. de** courtesy of; **tuvo la c. de llamarme** he was kind enough to phone me; **no tuvo la c. de mandar una felicitación** he didn't have the courtesy to send a card; **le daremos diez minutos de c.** we'll give him ten minutes
(**b**) *(obsequio)* **el vino es c. del restaurante** the wine comes with the compliments of the house
cortésmente *adv* courteously, politely
córtex *nm inv Anat* cortex
corteza *nf* (**a**) *(del árbol)* bark (**b**) *(de pan)* crust; *(de queso, tocino, limón)* rind; *(de naranja)* peel ►► ***cortezas de cerdo*** pork scratchings (**c**) *Geol (terrestre)* crust ►► ***la c. terrestre*** the earth's crust (**d**) *Anat* cortex ►► ***c. cerebral*** cerebral cortex
cortical *adj* cortical
corticoide *nm Bioquím* corticoid
cortijero, -a *nm,f* (**a**) *(dueño)* estate *o* farm owner (**b**) *(asalariado)* estate *o* farm manager
cortijo *nm* (**a**) *(finca)* farm *(typical of Andalusia and Extremadura)* (**b**) *(casa)* farmhouse
cortina *nf* curtain ►► ***c. de agua*** sheet of water; **cayó una c. de agua** there was a downpour; *RP* ***c. de enrollar*** rolling shutter; *Am* ***c. de hierro*** steel shutter; *Am Hist* ***la c. de hierro*** the Iron Curtain; *también Fig* ***c. de humo*** smoke screen; *CSur* ***c. musical*** theme tune/song
cortinaje, *RP* **cortinado** *nm* curtains
cortisona *nf* cortisone
corto, -a 1 *adj* (**a**) *(de poca longitud)* short; **las mangas me están cortas** my sleeves are too short; **estos pantalones se me han quedado cortos** these trousers are too short for me now; **hace varias semanas que no se viste de c.** *(futbolista)* he hasn't been in the squad for several weeks; **luces cortas** *Br* dipped headlights, *US* low beams
(**b**) *(de poca duración)* short; **el paseo se me ha hecho muy c.** the walk seemed to go very quickly
(**c**) *(escaso) (raciones)* small, meagre; *(disparo)* short of the target; **el lanzamiento se quedó c.** the throw fell short; **estoy c. de dinero** I'm short of money; **andamos muy cortos de tiempo** we're very short of time, we haven't got very much time; *Fig* **c. de miras** short-sighted; **c. de vista** short-sighted
(**d**) *(tonto)* **c. (de alcances)** dim, simple; EXPR *Fam Hum* **ser más c. que las mangas de un chaleco** to be as thick as two short planks
(**e**) EXPR **ni c. ni perezoso** just like that; **quedarse c.** *(al calcular)* to underestimate; **nos quedamos cortos al comprar pan** we didn't buy enough bread; **decir que es bueno es quedarse c.** it's an understatement to call it good; **este programa se queda c. para nuestras necesidades** this program doesn't do all the things we need
2 *nm* (**a**) *(cortometraje)* short (movie *o Br* film)
(**b**) *(bebida)* **un c. de vino/cerveza** a small wine/beer
(**c**) *Am* **los cortos de una película** *(los avances)* the trailer for a movie *o Br* film
cortocircuito *nm* short circuit
cortometraje *nm* short (movie *o Br* film)
cortón *nm* mole cricket
coruñés, -esa 1 *adj* of/from La Coruña *(Spain)*
2 *nm,f* person from La Coruña *(Spain)*
coruscante *adj Literario* coruscating
corva *nf* back of the knee
corvadura *nf (torcedura)* curvature, bend
corvallo *nm (pez)* brown meagre
corvejón *nm* (**a**) *(articulación)* hock (**b**) *(ave)* cormorant
córvido *Zool* 1 *nm* member of the crow family
2 **córvidos** *nmpl (familia) Corvidae*; **de la familia de los córvidos** of the *Corvidae* family
corvina *nf (pez)* meagre
corvo, -a *adj (curvado)* curved; *(nariz)* hooked
corzo, -a *nm,f* roe buck, *f* roe deer
cos *Mat* (*abrev de* **coseno**) cos

COSA *nf* (**a**) *(objeto, idea)* thing; **comprar unas cosas en el mercado** to buy a few things at the market; **alguna c.** anything; **¿quieres alguna c.?** is there anything you want?; **¿quiere usted alguna otra c.** *o* **alguna c. más?** do you want anything else?; **cualquier c.** anything; **venden recuerdos, postales y cosas así** they sell souvenirs, postcards and so on *o* and the like; **una c., ¿podrías venir mañana?** by the way, could you come tomorrow?; **escucha, una c., ¿por qué no te quedas esta noche?** listen, I've an idea, why don't you stay here tonight?; **tengo que decirte una c.** I've got something to tell you; **dime una c., ¿qué opinas de ella?** tell me (something), what do you think of her?; **es la c. más natural del mundo** it's the most natural thing in the world, it's completely normal; **¡esas cosas no se dicen!**

you mustn't say things like that!; **¡esas cosas no se hacen!** it just isn't done!; **no te preocupes, no es gran c.** don't worry, it's not important *o* it's no big deal; **este cuadro no vale gran c.** this painting isn't up to much; **te han dejado poca c.** they haven't left you much, they've hardly left you anything; **un bocadillo es poca c. para un chico tan voraz como él** a sandwich is very little for a hungry boy like him; **nos hemos comprado un apartamento, muy poquita c.** we've bought *Br* a flat *o US* an apartment, but it's nothing fancy; **es guapo, pero muy poquita c.** he's good-looking, but he hasn't got much of a body; **este vino es c. fina** this wine is good stuff; **fue una c. nunca vista** it was really out of the ordinary; **¡habráse visto c. igual!** have you ever seen the like of it!; **no hay tal c.** on the contrary; **¡qué c.!** how strange!; **¡qué c. más *o* tan extraña!** how strange!; EXPR **decir cuatro cosas a alguien: cuando lo vea le voy a decir cuatro cosas** when I next see him I'm going to give him a piece of my mind; EXPR **llamar a las cosas por su nombre** *(hablar sin rodeos)* to call a spade a spade; **llamemos a las cosas por su nombre...** let's be honest about it...

(b) *(asunto)* **tengo muchas cosas que hacer** I've got a lot (of things) to do; **la c. es que ahora no quiere firmar el contrato** the thing is she doesn't want to sign the contract any more; **está muy enfadada, y la c. no es para menos, le han robado el coche** she's very angry and with good reason, she's had her car stolen; **cada c. a su tiempo** one thing at a time; **ser c. de: no me preguntes por qué no queda comida, es c. de los niños** don't ask me why there's no food left, ask the children; **esto es c. de magia, estoy seguro de que ayer lo dejé aquí** this is most strange, I could swear I left it here yesterday; **no es c. de risa** it's no laughing matter; **eso de cambiar de trabajo es c. de pensárselo** changing jobs is something you need to think about carefully; **es c. de tener paciencia** it's a question of being patient; **no era c. de presentarse sin avisar** you couldn't just turn up without warning; **con el ambiente de seriedad que había, no era c. de contar un chiste** given the seriousness of the atmosphere, it was neither the time nor the place to tell a joke; **eso es c. mía** that's my affair *o* business; **no te metas en la discusión, que no es c. tuya** you keep out of the argument, it's none of your business; **eso es c. fácil** that's easy; **convencerle no será c. fácil** it won't be easy *o* it'll be no easy task to convince him; **esto es c. seria** this is a serious matter; **eso es otra c.** that's another matter; **¡eso es otra c.!, esa camisa te sienta mucho mejor** that's more like it, that shirt suits you much better!; **entre unas cosas y otras** what with one thing and another; **por unas cosas o por otras, no nos quedó tiempo de escribirte** for one reason or another we didn't have time to write to you

(c) *(situación)* **las cosas no van muy bien últimamente** things haven't been going very well recently; **...y así es como están las cosas** ...and that's how things are at the moment; **¿cómo van las cosas?** how are *o* how's things?; **estas cosas no pasarían si fuéramos más cuidadosos** these things wouldn't happen if we were more careful; EXPR *Fam* **la c. se pone fea** things are getting ugly, there's trouble brewing; EXPR *Fam* **está la c. que arde** things are reaching boiling point

(d) *(ocurrencia)* funny remark; **se le ocurren cosas graciosísimas** she comes out with some really funny stuff *o* remarks; **¡qué cosas tienes!** you do say some funny things!

(e) *(comportamiento)* **son cosas de mamá** that's just the way Mum is, that's just one of Mum's little idiosyncrasies; **no les riñas, son cosas de niños** don't tell them off, children are like that; **tenemos que aceptar su muerte, son cosas de la vida** we have to accept her death, it's one of those things (that happen)

(f) **cosas** *(pertenencias, utensilios)* things; **tras su muerte, metieron sus cosas en un baúl** after his death, they put his things *o* belongings in a trunk; **¿dónde guardas las cosas de pescar?** where do you keep your fishing things *o* tackle?

(g) *(en frases negativas) (nada)* **no hay c. peor que la hipocresía** there's nothing worse than hypocrisy; **no hay c. que me reviente más que su falta de interés** there's nothing (that) annoys me more than her lack of interest, what annoys me most is her lack of interest; *Fam (reparo)* **me da c. decírselo** I'm a bit uneasy about telling him; **el olor a hospital me da c.** the smell of hospitals makes me feel uneasy

(h) EXPR **o c. así: tendrá treinta años o c. así** he must be thirty or thereabouts; *Fam* **las cosas claras y el chocolate espeso** stop beating around the bush, tell me things as they are; **a c. hecha: se presentó al examen a c. hecha** he sat the exam although he knew he was certain to pass; **(como) c. de** *(aproximadamente)* about; **tardará (como) c. de tres semanas** it'll take about three weeks; **hacer algo como quien no quiere la c.** *(disimuladamente)* to do sth innocently; *(sin querer)* to do sth almost without realizing it; **como si tal c.** as if nothing had happened; **las cosas como son, nunca vas a aprobar ese examen** let's face it, you're never going to pass that exam; *Fam* **las cosas de palacio van despacio** these things usually take some time; **ni c. que se le parezca** nor anything of the kind; **ser c. de oír/ver: las declaraciones del ganador son c. de oír** the winner's remarks are worth hearing; **esta exposición es c. de ver** this exhibition is really worth seeing; *Esp Fam* **c. mala: me apetece ver esa película c. mala** I'm dying to see that movie *o Br* film, *Br* I want to see that film something chronic; **está lloviendo c. mala** it's pouring down, *Br* it's chucking it down; **me gusta c. mala** I fancy the pants off her, *Br* I fancy her something chronic; *Fam* **a otra c., mariposa** that's enough about that, let's change the subject; **es c. rara que se equivoque** it's very rare for her to make a mistake; **no ha llegado todavía, c. rara porque siempre es muy puntual** he hasn't arrived yet, which is strange, as he's usually very punctual; **¡lo que son las cosas!** it's a funny old world!; **no ser c. del otro mundo *o* del otro jueves** to be nothing special; **no sea c. que: ten cuidado, no sea c. que te vayas a caer** be careful or you'll fall; **se lo diré yo, no sea c. que se vaya a enterar por otra persona** I'll tell him because I wouldn't want him to find out from somebody else

---

cosaco, -a 1 *adj* Cossack
2 *nm,f* Cossack; EXPR *Fam* **beber como un c.** to drink like a fish

coscarse [60] *vpr Fam* (a) *(darse cuenta de)* to notice, to realize (b) *(entender)* to understand

coscoja *nf* kermes oak

coscorrón *nm (golpe)* bump on the head; *(con los nudillos)* rap on the head; **se dio un c.** he bumped his head

cosecante *nf Mat* cosecant

cosecha *nf* (a) *(recogida, época)* harvest; **es de la c. del 79** it's the 1979 vintage; **hacer la c.** to harvest; EXPR **ser de la (propia) c. de alguien** to be made up *o* invented by sb
(b) *(producto)* crop; **la c. de vid de este año ha sido muy buena** the grape harvest has been very good this year; **se ha perdido toda la c.** the entire crop *o* harvest has been lost
(c) *(de títulos, premios)* tally; **este último galardón se añade a su c. personal** this latest award adds one more to his personal tally

cosechadora *nf* combine harvester

cosechar 1 *vt* (a) *(recolectar) (cereales)* to harvest; *(frutos)* to pick
(b) *(cultivar)* to grow
(c) *(obtener)* to win, to reap; **su última novela ha cosechado muchos éxitos** his latest novel has been a great success; **cosechó numerosas críticas por sus declaraciones** he received a lot of criticism for his statement; **el equipo cubano cosechó veinte medallas en los campeonatos** the Cuban team picked up twenty medals at the championships; **su última película ha cosechado los aplausos de la crítica** his latest film has won critical acclaim
2 *vi* to (bring in the) harvest

cosechero, -a *nm,f (de cereales)* harvester, reaper; *(de frutos)* picker

cosedora *nf Col (grapadora)* stapler

coseno *nm Mat* cosine

coser 1 *vt* (a) *(ropa, vestido)* to sew; **c. un botón** to sew on a button (b) *(herida)* to stitch (up) (c) *(con grapas)* to staple (together) (d) EXPR **c. a alguien a balazos** to riddle sb with bullets; **c. a alguien a cuchilladas** to stab sb repeatedly
2 *vi* to sew; EXPR *Fam* **ser c. y cantar** to be child's play *o* a piece of cake

cosido *nm* stitching

cosificar *vt* to treat like an object

cosmética *nf* cosmetics *(singular)*

cosmético, -a 1 *adj* (a) *(sustancia)* cosmetic; **productos cosméticos** cosmetics (b) *(cambio, reforma)* cosmetic
2 *nm* cosmetic

cosmetología *nf* cosmetology

cosmetólogo, -a *nm,f* beautician

cósmico, -a *adj* cosmic

cosmogonía *nf* cosmogony

cosmografía *nf* cosmography

cosmógrafo, -a *nm,f* cosmographer

cosmología *nf* cosmology

cosmológico, -a *adj* cosmological

cosmonauta *nmf (astronauta)* astronaut; *(ruso)* cosmonaut

cosmonáutica *nf* astronautics *(singular)*

cosmopolita 1 *adj* cosmopolitan
2 *nmf* cosmopolitan

cosmopolitismo *nm* cosmopolitanism

cosmorama *nm (aparato)* peepshow *(of views etc)*

cosmos *nm inv* cosmos

cosmovisión *nf* world view

coso *nm* (a) *Taurom (plaza)* **c. (taurino)** bullring
(b) *(calle)* main street
(c) *CSur Fam (objeto)* whatnot, thing; **¿para qué sirve ese c.?** *(en aparato)* what's this thing *o* thingumajig for?; **comprame este c.** buy that for me; **¿me trajiste el c. que te pedí?** did you bring that thing I asked you for?; **me tenés que prestar veinte cosos** you've got to lend me twenty; **me gusta mucho el c. que llevas puesto** I really like what you're wearing
(d) *Andes, RP Fam (persona)* **¿otra vez vas a salir con... c.?** you're going out with... what's-his-face again?

cospel *nm Arg (ficha)* phone token

cosque *etc ver* **coscarse**

cosquillas *nfpl* **hacer c.** to tickle; **tener c.** to be ticklish; EXPR **buscarle las c. a alguien** to wind sb up, to irritate sb

cosquillear *vt* to tickle

cosquilleo *nm* tickling sensation; **siento un c. en la nariz** I've got a tickly feeling in my nose; *Fig* **noto un c. en el estómago** I've got butterflies in my stomach

cosquilloso, -a, cosquilludo, -a *adj Am Fam* ticklish

costa *nf* (a) *(marina)* coast; **pasan las vacaciones en la c.** they spend their holidays on the coast ►► ***la C. Azul*** the Côte d'Azur
(b) *(coste)* **a c. de** at the expense of; **lo hizo a c. de grandes esfuerzos** he did it by dint of much effort; **aún vive a c. de sus padres** he's still living off his parents; **a toda c.** at all costs ►► *Der* ***costas (judiciales)*** (legal) costs
(c) ***C. de Marfil*** Ivory Coast; ***C. Rica*** Costa Rica

costado *nm* side; **llevaba una bolsa al c.** he had a bag over his shoulder; **de c.** sideways; EXPR **por los cuatro costados: a la casa le da el sol por los cuatro costados** the house gets the sun all day; **es cubano por los cuatro costados** he's Cuban through and through

costal 1 *adj Med* rib, costal; **tiene una fractura c.** he has a fractured rib
2 *nm* sack

costalada *nf*, **costalazo** *nm* heavy fall *(backwards)*; **darse una c.** to fall over backwards

costalero *nm* (a) *(mozo de cuerda)* porter (b) *Rel* = bearer in Holy Week processions

costanera *CSur* 1 *adj* **rambla c.** promenade
2 *nf* promenade
3 **costaneras** *nfpl* rafters

costanero, -a *adj* (a) *(de la costa)* coastal (b) *(inclinado)* sloping

costar [64] *vi* (a) *(dinero)* to cost; **¿cuánto cuesta?** how much is it?; **me costó 300 pesos** it cost me 300 pesos; **costó muy barato** it was very cheap; EXPR **c. un ojo de la cara** *o* **un riñón** to cost an arm and a leg; EXPR **c. caro: esa broma le va a c. caro** he's going to pay dearly for that joke
(b) *(tiempo)* to take; **nos costó seis horas llegar** it took us six hours to get there; **nos costó tres horas de cola** we had to *Br* queue *o US* stand in line for three hours; **rellenar ese impreso no te costará ni cinco minutos** it won't take you five minutes to fill in that form
(c) *(resultar difícil, penoso)* **me costó decírselo** I found it difficult to tell him; **a este niño le cuesta dormirse** this child has difficulty getting to sleep; **no le habría costado nada ayudarme** it wouldn't have cost him anything to help me; **c. trabajo** to be difficult, to take a lot of work; **me costó (trabajo) acostumbrarme** it took me a while to get used to it; **cuesta (trabajo) abrir esa puerta** this door is difficult to open; **le costó mucho tiempo olvidarse de ella** it took him a long time to forget her; **cueste lo que cueste** whatever the cost; **le costó la vida/el trabajo** it cost him his life/his job; **me costó lo mío convencerles** I had a real job persuading them, they took a lot of persuading; EXPR **me costó sangre, sudor y lágrimas terminarlo** I sweat blood to get it finished; EXPR **nos costó Dios y ayuda** it took a huge effort

costarricense 1 *adj* Costa Rican
2 *nmf* Costa Rican

costarriqueño, -a 1 *adj* Costa Rican
2 *nm,f* Costa Rican

coste *nm Esp (de producción)* cost; *(de un objeto)* price; **cuatro semanas de prueba sin c. alguno** four weeks on approval free of charge; **la relación c.-beneficio** the cost-benefit ratio; **el c. humano de la guerra** the human cost of the war; *Com* **al c.** at cost ►► *Com* ***c. diferencial*** marginal cost; *Com* ***c. directo*** direct cost; *Com* ***c. de distribución*** distribution cost; *Com* ***c. efectivo*** actual cost; *Com* ***costes de explotación*** operating costs; *Com* ***c. de fabricación*** manufacturing cost; *Com* ***c. fijo*** fixed cost; *Com* ***c. financiero*** financial cost; *Com* ***c. indirecto*** indirect cost; *Com* ***c. de mano de obra*** labour cost; *Com* ***c. de mantenimiento*** running cost; *Com* ***c. marginal*** marginal cost; *Econ* ***c. de oportunidad*** opportunity cost; *Com* ***c. de producción*** cost of production; *Com* ***c. de reposición*** replacement cost; *Com* ***c., seguro y flete*** cost, insurance and freight; *Com* ***c. unitario*** unit cost; ***c. de la vida*** cost of living

costear 1 *vt* (a) *(pagar)* to pay for (b) *Náut (la costa)* to hug, to sail close to
2 *vi Náut* to hug *o* sail close to the coast
3 **costearse** *vpr* **costearse algo** *(pagarse)* to pay for sth oneself; **trabaja para costearse los estudios** she's working to pay for her studies

costeño = **costero**

costera *nf Méx* promenade

costero, -a, costeño, -a 1 *adj* coastal; **un pueblo c.** a seaside town
2 *nm,f Am* = person from the coast

costilla *nf* (a) *(de persona, animal)* rib ►► ***c. falsa*** false rib; ***c. flotante*** floating rib; ***c. verdadera*** true rib
(b) *Fam* **costillas** *(espalda)* back
(c) *(de cerdo)* chop; *RP (de vaca)* T-bone steak; **costillas de cerdo** pork chops
(d) *Fam (cónyuge)* better half
(e) *Náut* rib
(f) *RP Fam (coste)* **a c. de alguien** at sb's expense; **siempre se divierten a c. mío** they always have fun at my expense; **aún vive a c. de sus padres** he still lives off his parents

costillar *nm* (a) *(de persona)* ribs, ribcage (b) *(de carne)* side

costo *nm* (a) *(de producción)* cost; *(de un objeto)* price; **cuatro semanas de prueba sin c. alguno** four weeks on approval free of charge; **la relación c.-beneficio** the cost-benefit ratio; **el c. humano de la guerra** the human cost of the war; *Com* **al c.** at cost ►► *Com* ***c. diferencial*** marginal cost; *Com* ***c. directo*** direct cost; *Com* ***c. de distribución*** distribution cost; *Com* ***c. efectivo*** actual cost; *Com* ***costos de explotación*** operating costs; *Com* ***c. de fabricación*** manufacturing cost; *Com* ***c. fijo*** fixed cost; *Com* ***c. financiero*** financial cost; *Com* ***c. indirecto*** indirect cost; *Com* ***c. de mano de obra*** labour cost; *Com* ***c. de mantenimiento*** running cost; *Com* ***c. marginal*** marginal cost; *Econ* ***c. de oportunidad*** opportunity cost; *Com* ***c. de producción*** cost of production; *Com* ***c. de reposición*** replacement cost; *Com* ***c., seguro y flete*** cost, insurance and freight; *Com* ***c. unitario*** unit cost; ***c. de la vida*** cost of living
(b) *Esp Fam (hachís)* hash

costoso, -a *adj* (a) *(caro)* expensive (b) *(trabajo)* exhausting; *(triunfo)* costly; *(error)* costly

costra *nf* (a) *(de suciedad, de tierra)* layer, crust (b) *(de pan)* crust (c) *(de herida)* scab

costumbre *nf* (a) *(de persona)* habit; **tomar/perder la c. de hacer algo** to get into/out of the habit of doing sth; **tener la c. de** *o* **tener por c. hacer algo** to be in the habit of doing sth; **costumbres** habits; **el hombre es un animal de costumbres** man is a creature of habit; **no hay que perder las buenas costumbres** we don't want to break with tradition; **como de c.** as usual; **la cantidad de c.** the usual amount; **nos vemos a las ocho, en el sitio de c.** I'll see you at eight, in the usual place
(b) *(de país, cultura)* custom

costumbrismo *nm* = literary genre that deals with typical regional or national customs

costumbrista 1 *adj (novela)* = describing the customs of a country or region
2 *nmf* = author whose work portrays the customs of a country or region

costura *nf* (a) *(labor)* sewing, needlework (b) *(en tela)* seam; **sin costuras** seamless (c) *(oficio)* dressmaking; **alta c.** haute couture (d) *(cicatriz)* scar

costurera *nf* dressmaker, seamstress

costurero *nm (caja)* sewing box

cota *nf* (a) *(altura)* altitude, height above sea level; **volar a baja c.** to fly low; **la expedición ha alcanzado la c. de los 8.000 metros** the expedition has reached an altitude of 8,000 metres
(b) *(en mapa)* spot height
(c) *(nivel)* **alcanzar altas cotas de popularidad** to become very popular; **la participación alcanzó la c. del 90 por ciento** there was a 90 percent turnout
(d) *(armadura)* ***c. de malla(s)*** coat of mail
(e) *Mat* bound

cotangente *nf Mat* cotangent

cotarro *nm Fam* **le gusta meterse en todos los cotarros** he likes to be involved in everything; **pusieron algo de música para animar el c.** they put on some music to liven things up; **alborotar el c.** to stir up trouble; **dirigir el c.** to rule the roost, to be the boss

cotejar *vt* to compare (**con** with); **c. una copia con el original** to compare a copy with the original; **cotejaremos tus datos con los míos** let's compare your information with mine, let's check your information against mine

cotejo *nm* comparison

cotelé *nm Chile* corduroy

coterráneo, -a 1 *adj* compatriot
2 *nm,f* compatriot, fellow countryman, *f* fellow countrywoman

cotidianamente *adv* daily, every day

cotidianidad *nf (vida cotidiana)* everyday life; *(frecuencia)* commonness

cotidiano, -a *adj* daily; **el trabajo c.** day-to-day tasks; **ser algo c.** to be an everyday occurrence

cotiledón *nm* cotyledon

cotilla *Esp Fam* 1 *adj* gossipy; **es muy c.** he's a real gossip
2 *nmf* gossip, busybody

cotillear *vi Esp Fam* (**a**) *(cotillear)* to gossip (**b**) *(curiosear)* to pry; **no me gusta que cotillees en mi cuarto** I don't like you poking around in my room

cotilleo *nm Esp Fam* gossip, tittle-tattle; **tengo que contarte un c.** I've got a bit of gossip to tell you

cotillón *nm* = party on New Year's Eve or 5th of January

cotiza *nf Col, Ven* sandal; EXPR **ponerse las cotizas** to take shelter

cotizable *adj* quotable

cotización *nf* (**a**) *(valor)* value (**b**) *Bolsa (de producto, bienes, valores)* price; **la c. de apertura/al cierre** the opening/closing price; **ha mejorado la c. del euro** the euro has strengthened; **el barril de petróleo alcanzó una c. de 19 dólares** the price of oil reached 19 dollars a barrel (**c**) *(a la seguridad social)* contribution

cotizado, -a *adj* (**a**) *Bolsa* quoted (**b**) *(persona)* sought-after; **es una dentista muy cotizada** she's a very highly regarded dentist

cotizante 1 *adj* contributing
2 *nmf* contributor; **los cotizantes a la seguridad social** people who pay national insurance contributions

cotizar [14] 1 *vt* (**a**) *(valorar)* to quote; **las acciones de la empresa cotizan cinco enteros menos que ayer** the company's shares are five points down on yesterday
(**b**) *(pagar)* to pay; **cotiza un 5 por ciento de su salario a la seguridad social** she pays 5 percent of her salary in national insurance contributions
2 *vi* (**a**) *(pagar)* to contribute; **los trabajadores tienen que c. a la seguridad social** employees have to pay Social Security contributions (**b**) *Bolsa* **c. en bolsa** to be quoted *o* listed on the Stock Exchange; **sus acciones cotizan a 10 euros** their shares are quoted at 10 euros
3 **cotizarse** *vpr* (**a**) *(estimarse)* to be valued *o* prized; **el conocimiento de idiomas se cotiza mucho** a knowledge of foreign languages is considered extremely important (**b**) **cotizarse a 20 euros** *(producto)* to sell for 20 euros, to fetch 20 euros; *(bonos, valores)* to be quoted at 20 euros; **el dólar se cotiza a un euro** one dollar is worth one euro

coto *nm* (**a**) *(vedado)* preserve; *Fig* **poner c. a** to put a stop to ►► ***c. de caza*** game preserve; ***c. de pesca*** fishing preserve; ***c. privado*** *(en letrero)* private property (**b**) *Andes, CAm, Carib, RP (bocio)* goitre

cotón *nm Am* (**a**) *(tela)* cotton (**b**) *(camisa)* = coarse cotton shirt

cotona *nf* (**a**) *Am (camisa)* = coarse cotton shirt (**b**) *Méx (chaqueta)* chamois jacket

cotonete *nm Méx Br* cotton bud, *US* Q-tip®

cotorra *nf* (**a**) *(ave)* parrot; EXPR *Fam* **hablar como una c.** to talk nineteen to the dozen (**b**) *Fam (persona)* chatterbox

cotorrear *vi Fam* to chatter

cotorreo *nm Fam* chatter

cotorro *adj Méx* **¡qué c.!** *(¡qué curioso!)* how odd!, how strange!

cotoso, -a, cotudo, -a *adj Andes, RP* goitrous

cotufa *nf* (**a**) *(aguaturma)* Jerusalem artichoke (**b**) *(chufa)* tiger nut; EXPR *Fam* **pedir cotufas en el golfo** to ask for the moon (**c**) *Ven* **cotufas (de maíz)** popcorn

coturno *nm* buskin

COU [kou] *nm Antes* (*abrev de* **Curso de Orientación Universitaria**) = one-year course which prepared pupils aged 17-18 for Spanish university entrance examinations

couché [ku'tʃe] *adj* **papel c.** coated (magazine) paper

country[1] ['kauntri] 1 *adj inv* **estilo c.** country (and western) style
2 *nm (música)* country (and western) music

country[2] (*pl* **countries**) *nm Arg (barrio)* = luxury suburban housing development

coupé [ku'pe] *nm (automóvil)* coupé

courier ['kurjer] (*pl* **couriers**) *nm* courier

covacha *nf* hovel

covalencia *nf Quím* covalency, *US* covalence

covalente *adj Quím* covalent

coxal 1 *adj* hip; **fractura c.** hip fracture
2 *nm (hueso)* hip bone

coxalgia *nf Med* coxalgia

coxis *nm inv* coccyx

coyol *nm CAm, Méx* wine palm

coyotaje *nm Méx Fam* wheeling and dealing

coyote *nm* (**a**) *(animal)* coyote (**b**) *Méx Fam (en la frontera)* = person who guides illegal immigrants across the border into the USA (**c**) *Méx Fam (intermediario)* fixer, middleman

coyotear *vi Méx Fam* to wheel and deal

coyotero *nm Méx (perro)* = dog trained to hunt coyotes

coyunda *nf* (**a**) *(correa)* = strap for yoking oxen (**b**) *Fam (matrimonio)* yoke

coyuntura *nf* (**a**) *(situación)* situation; **la c. económica** the economic situation; **en la c. actual no es posible hablar de expansión** the way things are at the moment, it's impossible to talk of expanding; **aprovechó la c. para solicitar un préstamo** he took advantage of the opportunity to ask for a loan (**b**) *(articulación)* joint

coyuntural *adj* temporary, provisional

coz *nf* (**a**) *(patada)* kick; **dar** *o* **pegar** *o* **tirar coces** to kick; EXPR *Fam* **tratar a alguien a coces** to treat sb like dirt (**b**) *(pulla)* rude *o* nasty remark; **soltar una c. a alguien** to be rude *o* nasty to sb

C.P., cp (*abrev de* **código postal**) *Br* postcode, *US* zip code

CPI *nf* (*abrev de* **Corte Penal Internacional**) ICC

cps *Informát* (*abrev de* **caracteres por segundo**) cps

CPU *nf Informát* (*abrev de* **Central Processing Unit**) CPU

Cra., cra. (*abrev de* **carrera**) street, = name of certain streets

crac (*pl* **cracs**) *nm Fin* crash

crack [krak] (*pl* **cracks**) *nm* (**a**) *(estrella)* star, superstar (**b**) *Fin* crash ►► *Hist* ***el c. del 29*** the Wall Street Crash (**c**) *(droga)* crack

cracker ['kraker] (*pl* **crackers**) *nmf Fam Informát* cracker

Cracovia *n* Cracow, Krakow

crampón *nm* crampon

craneal, craneano *adj* cranial

cráneo *nm* skull, *Espec* cranium; EXPR *Fam* **ir de c.** to be at full stretch; EXPR *Fam* **romperse el c.** *(pensando)* to rack one's brains

craneoencefálico, -a *adj Med* **traumatismo c.** (severe) head injuries

craneofacial *adj Med* craniofacial

craneología *nf* craniology

crápula 1 *nmf* (**a**) *(libertino)* libertine (**b**) *Am (mala persona)* scoundrel, swine
2 *nf (libertinaje)* dissipation, debauchery

crapuloso, -a *adj (libertino)* debauched

craquear *vt Quím* to crack

craqueo *nm Quím* cracking

crash [kraʃ] *nm inv Fin* crash ►► *Hist* ***el c. del 29*** the Wall Street Crash

craso, -a *adj* (**a**) *(grave) (error)* serious; *(ignorancia)* astonishing (**b**) *(grueso)* fat

cráter *nm* crater ►► ***c. lunar*** lunar crater

crawl [krol] *nm Dep* crawl; **nadar a c.** to do the crawl

crayola® *nf Urug* crayon

crayón *nm Méx, Arg* crayon

creación *nf* (**a**) *(acción)* creation; **la c. de empleo** job creation; **la c. de riqueza** the creation of wealth; **la c. artística** artistic creativity; **c. literaria** *(materia)* creative writing; **su objetivo es la c. a largo plazo de una sociedad más justa** their long-term aim is to create a fairer society (**b**) *(resultado)* creation; **una de las últimas creaciones del escultor belga** one of the Belgian sculptor's latest creations

(**c**) **la C.** *(el mundo)* Creation

creacionismo *nm* creationism

creacionista 1 *adj* creationist
2 *nmf* creationist

creador, -ora 1 *adj* creative
2 *nm,f* creator; **fue uno de los grandes creadores de este siglo** he was one of the great creative geniuses of this century ▸▸ ***c. gráfico*** creator *(of cartoon etc)*; *Bolsa* ***c. de mercado*** market maker; ***c. de moda*** fashion designer
3 *nm Rel* **el C.** the Creator

crear 1 *vt* (**a**) *(hacer, producir, originar)* to create; **c. empleo/riqueza** to create jobs/wealth; **han creado un nuevo ministerio para él** they have created a new ministry for him; **me crea muchos problemas** it gives me a lot of trouble, it causes me a lot of problems; **Picasso creó escuela** Picasso's works have had a seminal influence
(**b**) *(inventar)* to invent; *(poema, sinfonía)* to compose, to write; *(cuadro)* to paint
(**c**) *(fundar)* to found
2 crearse *vpr (inventarse)* **se ha creado un mundo de fantasía** he lives in his own little world; **se crea problemas él solo** he imagines problems where there aren't any

creatina *nf* creatine

creatividad *nf* creativity

creativo, -a 1 *adj* creative
2 *nm,f* **c. (de publicidad)** copywriter, creative

crecepelo *nm* hair tonic *o* restorer

crecer [46] **1** *vi* (**a**) *(persona, planta, pelo, ciudad)* to grow (**b**) *(días, noches)* to grow longer (**c**) *(río, marea)* to rise (**d**) *(aumentar) (desempleo, inflación)* to rise, to increase; *(valor)* to increase; *(rumores)* to spread; *(descontento, interés)* to grow (**e**) *(la luna)* to wax
2 crecerse *vpr* to become more self-confident; **crecerse ante las dificultades** to thrive on adversity; **el equipo se creció tras marcar el gol** the team grew in confidence after scoring the goal; **el artista se creció con los aplausos del público** the artist grew in confidence in response to the audience's applause

creces: con creces *loc adv* **le devolvieron con c. el dinero que les prestó** they paid back the money he lent them with interest; **los italianos nos superan con c.** the Italians are a lot better than us; **es el mejor con c.** he is by far the best; **la oferta supera con c. a la demanda** supply far exceeds demand; **las temperaturas sobrepasaron con c. los 40 grados** temperatures soared into the 40s; **cumplió con c. el trabajo que se le encargó** he more than fulfilled the task he had been given; **superó con c. el examen de ingreso** she sailed through the entrance exam

crecida *nf* **la c. desbordó el cauce del río** the rise in the water level caused the river to burst its banks; **las crecidas anuales del Nilo** the annual flooding of the Nile

crecido, -a *adj* (**a**) *(cantidad)* large (**b**) *(hijo)* **tu hijo está muy c.** *(físicamente)* hasn't your son grown!; *(maduro)* your son's so grown-up now! (**c**) *(río)* high; **el río baja muy c. a la altura del puente** the river is very high where the bridge is

creciente *adj* (**a**) *(seguridad, confianza)* growing (**b**) *(luna)* crescent, waxing

crecimiento *nm* (**a**) *(de persona, planta, pelo)* growth (**b**) *(de empleo, inflación)* rise, increase; *(de valor)* increase; *(de precios)* rise; *(de descontento, interés)* growth; **un c. del 15 por ciento** a 15 percent increase ▸▸ ***c. cero*** zero growth; ***c. económico*** economic growth; ***c. de la población*** population growth; ***c. sostenible*** sustainable growth; ***c. vegetativo*** population growth

credencial 1 *adj* accrediting
2 *nf* (**a**) *(documento identificador)* pass; **credenciales (diplomáticas)** credentials (**b**) *Arg, Chile, Méx (carné)* card ▸▸ ***c. de socio*** membership card

credibilidad *nf* credibility

crediticio, -a *adj* credit; **entidad crediticia** credit institution, lender

crédito *nm* (**a**) *(préstamo)* loan; **pedir un c.** to ask for a loan; **(comprar algo) a c.** (to buy sth) on credit ▸▸ *Méx* ***c. de avío*** agricultural loan; ***c. bancario*** bank loan; ***c. blando*** soft loan; ***c. comercial*** business loan; ***c. al consumo*** consumer credit; ***c. de empalme*** bridging loan; ***c. a la exportación*** export credit; ***c. hipotecario*** mortgage (loan); ***c. oficial*** official credit; ***c. personal*** personal loan; ***c. preferencial*** preferential credit; ***c. provisional*** bridging loan; ***c. puente*** bridging loan; ***c. renovable*** revolving credit; ***c. vivienda*** mortgage
(**b**) *(cantidad de dinero)* credit
(**c**) *(plazo de préstamo)* credit
(**d**) *(en tienda)* credit; **en esta tienda tengo c.** they give me credit in this shop
(**e**) *(confianza)* trust, belief; **digno de c.** trustworthy; **dar c. a algo** to believe sth; **¡no doy c. a mis oídos!** I can't believe my ears!
(**f**) *(fama)* standing, reputation
(**g**) *(en universidad)* credit
(**h**) *Cine* **créditos** credits

credo *nm* (**a**) *(religioso)* **el c.** the Creed (**b**) *(ideológico, político)* credo, creed

credulidad *nf* credulity

crédulo, -a 1 *adj* credulous, gullible
2 *nm,f* credulous *o* gullible person

creencia *nf* belief; **cada cual es libre de tener sus creencias** everyone is entitled to their own opinion; **es una c. popular** it's a commonly held belief

---

CREER [37] **1** *vt* (**a**) *(estar convencido de)* to believe; **no te creo** I don't believe you; **no creas nada de lo que te cuenten** don't believe a word they say; **créeme, sólo quería ayudar** believe me *o* honestly, I only wanted to help; **no puedo c. lo que ven mis ojos** I can't believe my eyes; **no puedo c. lo que estoy oyendo** I can't believe my ears *o* what I'm hearing; **hay que verlo para creerlo** it has to be seen to be believed; **¡ya lo creo que iré!** of course I'll go!, you bet I'll go!; *Irónico* **¿nos puedes ayudar a subir el piano? – ¡ya lo creo!** could you help us carry the piano upstairs? – oh sure, I'd just love to!; EXPR **c. algo a pies juntillas** to believe sth blindly
(**b**) *(suponer, pensar)* to think; **creo que sí** I think so; **creo que no** I don't think so; **no creo que pueda ir con vosotros** I don't think I can go with you; **¿vendrás a la fiesta? – no creo** are you going to the party? – I don't think so; **creo que va a hacer calor** I think it's going to be hot; **creo que te equivocas** I think you're mistaken; **creo no equivocarme** I believe I'm right, I don't think I'm wrong; **creí oír un llanto** I thought I heard someone crying; **creo que ha sido Sara** I think it was Sara; **creo que está vivo** I think he's alive, I believe him to be alive; **¿crees que lo conseguiremos?** do you think we'll achieve it?, do you expect us to achieve it?; **creo recordar que no es la primera vez que lo hace** I seem to remember it's not the first time she's done it; **no te vayas a c. que soy siempre así** don't think *o* imagine I'm always like this; **no la creía tan simpática** I didn't think she was so nice; **¡quién lo hubiera creído!** who would have thought it!; **se llama Juan, creo** he's called Juan, I think; **están muy afectados, ¿no crees?** they seem very upset, don't you think?
(**c**) *(estimar)* to consider, to regard; **le creo capaz** I consider him competent; **c. a alguien capaz de hacer algo** to believe sb to be capable of doing sth
2 *vi* to believe (**en** in); **no cree, es ateo** he's not a believer, he's an atheist; **c. en Dios** to believe in God; **no cree en la monarquía** he doesn't believe in monarchy; **mis hijos no creen en Papá Noel** my children don't believe in Father Christmas; **creo en tu honestidad** I believe you're being honest; **según creo** to the best of my knowledge; **debe ser bastante interesante – no creas** it must be very interesting – far from it *o* don't you believe it
3 creerse *vpr* (**a**) *(considerarse)* to believe oneself to be; **se cree Dios** he thinks he's God; **se creen muy inteligentes** they think they're very intelligent; **¿qué te has creído, que soy tu esclava?** do you think I'm your slave or something?; **¿pero tú quién te has creído que eres?** just who do you think you are?; **invítame a una cerveza – ¡que te lo has creído** *o* **que te crees tú eso!** buy me a beer – get real *o* you must be joking!; *Fam* **es un buen jugador pero se lo cree mucho** he's a good player but he's very full of himself *o* *Br* he really fancies himself
(**b**) *(dar por cierto)* to believe completely; **no me lo creo** *o* **puedo c.** I can't *o* don't believe it; **aunque no te lo creas, es una buena persona** she's a good person, whatever you think, you may not think so, but she's a good person; **no te creas, parece travieso pero es un buen chaval** not really, I know he seems naughty, but he's a good lad; **se cree todo lo que lee** he believes *o* swallows everything he reads; **eso no te lo crees ni tú** surely even you can't believe that; **no te creas que es tan fácil** don't imagine it's as easy as that, it isn't that simple; **¡no te vas a c. quién nos visitó ayer!** you'll never guess *o* believe who visited us yesterday!

---

creíble *adj* credible, believable

creído, -a *Fam* **1** *adj* conceited; **se lo tiene muy c.** he's very full of himself, *Br* he really fancies himself
2 *nm,f* **es un c.** he's a bighead

crema 1 *nf* (**a**) *(sustancia pastosa)* cream ▸▸ ***c. de afeitar*** shaving cream; ***c. dental*** toothpaste; ***c. depilatoria*** hair remover; ***c. facial*** face cream; ***c. hidratante*** moisturizer; ***c. de manos*** hand cream; ***c.***

para la piel skin cream; ***c. solar*** sun cream; ***c. para zapatos*** shoe polish
(**b**) *(sopa)* cream ►► ***c. de espárragos*** cream of asparagus (soup); ***c. de marisco*** seafood bisque
(**c**) *(dulce)* **c. (pastelera)** confectioner's custard ►► ***c. de cacahuete*** peanut butter; ***c. catalana*** = custard dessert covered with caramelized sugar, ≃ crème brûlée
(**d**) *(de leche)* cream ►► *Am* ***c. agria*** sour cream; *Am* ***c. batida*** whipped cream; *Am* ***c. chantillí*** *o* ***chantilly*** whipped cream; *Am* ***c. doble*** single cream; *Am* ***c. líquida*** single cream; *Urug* ***c. rusa*** sour cream
(**e**) **la c. de...** *(lo mejor de)* the cream of...; **la c. del mundo literario** the cream of the literary world
2 *adj inv* cream; **color c.** cream(-coloured)

cremación *nf* cremation
cremallera *nf* (**a**) *(para cerrar) Br* zip (fastener), *US* zipper (**b**) *Tec* rack
cremar *vt* to cremate
crematístico, -a *adj* financial
crematorio, -a 1 *adj* **horno c.** crematorium (furnace), cremator
2 *nm* crematorium
crémor *nm* **c. (tártaro)** cream of tartar
cremosidad *nf* creaminess
cremoso, -a *adj* creamy
creosota *nf* creosote
creosotar *vt* to creosote
crepa *nf Méx (torta)* crêpe
crepe, crêpe, crepé 1 *nm* (**a**) *(tela)* crêpe ►► ***c. de la China*** crêpe de Chine (**b**) *(goma)* crêpe (rubber) (**c**) *Am (papel)* crêpe paper
2 *nf (torta)* crêpe
crepería *nf* creperie, pancake house
crepitación *nf (chasquido)* crackling; *(de huesos)* crepitus
crepitar *vi* to crackle
crepuscular *adj* crepuscular, twilight; **luz c.** twilight
crepúsculo *nm (al amanecer)* first light; *(al anochecer)* twilight, dusk; **en el c. de su vida** in his twilight years
crescendo [kre'ʃendo] *nm* crescendo; **in c.** growing; **la tensión sigue in c.** tension continues to mount
creso *Formal* **1** *adj* **rico y c.** extremely wealthy
2 *nm* **ser un c.** to be extremely wealthy
crespo, -a *adj* tightly curled, frizzy
crespón *nm* (**a**) *(tela)* crepe ►► ***c. de la China*** crêpe de Chine (**b**) *(en señal de luto) (brazalete)* mourning band; *(en bandera)* = piece of black cloth on a flag as a sign of mourning
cresta *nf* (**a**) *(de ave)* crest; *(de gallo)* comb (**b**) *(peinado punk)* Mohican (**c**) *(de ola, montaña)* crest; EXPR **estar en la c. (de la ola)** to be riding high (**d**) ***c. de gallo*** *(planta)* cockscomb
crestería *nf Arquit (de un edificio)* cresting; *(de una fortificación)* crenellations, battlements
Creta *n* Crete
creta *nf* chalk
cretáceo, -a, cretácico, -a *Geol* **1** *adj* Cretaceous
2 *nm* **el c.** the Cretaceous (period)
cretense 1 *adj* Cretan
2 *nmf* Cretan
cretinismo *nm (enfermedad)* cretinism
cretino, -a 1 *adj* (**a**) *Fam (necio)* cretinous (**b**) *(enfermo)* cretinous
2 *nm,f* (**a**) *Fam (necio)* cretin (**b**) *(enfermo)* cretin
cretona *nf (tejido)* cretonne
creyente 1 *adj* **ser c.** to be a believer
2 *nmf* believer; **no c.** nonbeliever
creyera *etc ver* **creer**
creyó *etc ver* **creer**
crezco *etc ver* **crecer**
cría *nf* (**a**) *(hijo del animal)* **crías** young; **c. de ave** chick; **c. de león** lion cub (**b**) *(camada)* litter (**c**) *(crianza) (de animales)* breeding; *(de plantas)* growing
criadero *nm* (**a**) *(de animales)* farm *(breeding place)*; *(de árboles, plantas)* nursery; **un c. de ratas** a breeding ground for rats ►► ***c. canino*** kennels, dog breeders; ***c. de ostras*** oyster bed (**b**) *Min* mine
criadilla *nf* (**a**) *(testículo)* testicle (**b**) ***c. de tierra*** truffle
criado, -a *nm,f* servant, *f* maid
criador, -ora *nm,f (de animales)* breeder; *(de plantas)* grower
críalo *nm* great spotted cuckoo
criandera *nf Andes, CAm, Carib* wet nurse
crianza *nf* (**a**) *(de bebé)* nursing, breastfeeding (**b**) *(de animales)* breeding, rearing (**c**) *(del vino)* ageing; **vino de c.** vintage wine (**d**) *(educación)* breeding
criar [32] **1** *vt* (**a**) *(amamantar) (sujeto: mujer)* to breast-feed; *(sujeto: animal)* to suckle
(**b**) *(animales)* to breed, to rear; *(flores, árboles)* to grow
(**c**) *(producir) (musgo, humedad)* **el muro ha criado mucho musgo** there's a lot of moss growing on the wall
(**d**) *(vino)* to mature
(**e**) *(educar)* to bring up; **niño mal criado** spoilt child; PROV **cría cuervos (y te sacarán los ojos): con todo lo que lo he ayudado, ahora no quiere ayudarme a mí – sí, cría cuervos (y te sacarán los ojos)** after all the times I've helped him, now he won't help me – yes, some people are just so ungrateful
2 criarse *vpr* (**a**) *(crecer)* to grow up; *(educarse)* to be educated; **el cachorro se crió en cautividad** the cub was reared in captivity; **nos criaron en el respeto a los demás** we were brought up to respect others
(**b**) *(reproducirse)* to breed
criatura *nf* (**a**) *(niño)* child; *(bebé)* baby; **la ecografía no permitió determinar el sexo de la c.** they weren't able to determine the sex of the baby from the scan (**b**) *(ser vivo)* creature (**c**) *(ser fántastico)* creature
criba *nf* (**a**) *(tamiz)* sieve; EXPR *Fam* **estar hecho una c.** to be full of holes (**b**) *(selección)* **en la primera c. eliminaron a diez candidatos** they weeded out ten candidates in the first round of the selection process; **hicieron una c. de los proyectos y eligieron el suyo** they sifted through the projects and chose his
cribado *nm* sieving
cribar *vt* (**a**) *(con tamiz)* to sieve (**b**) *(seleccionar)* to screen out, to select
cric *(pl* **crics***) nm* jack ►► ***c. de tornillo*** screw jack, jackscrew
cricket ['kriket] *nm* cricket
crimen *nm* (**a**) *(delito)* crime *(serious)*; **el autor del c.** *(de asesinato)* the murderer; **cometer un c.** to commit a crime ►► ***c. de Estado*** state crime; ***c. de guerra*** war crime; ***c. contra la humanidad*** crime against humanity; ***c. organizado*** organized crime; ***c. pasional*** crime of passion
(**b**) *Fam (cosa horrible)* **es un c. derrochar tanto dinero en una fiesta** it's criminal to spend so much money on a party; **¡ese corte de pelo es un c.!** that haircut is awful *o* criminal!; **sería un c. dejar al bebé solo** it would be criminal *o* a crime to leave the baby on its own
criminal 1 *adj* (**a**) *(del crimen)* criminal (**b**) *Fam (horrible)* criminal
2 *nmf* criminal ►► ***c. de guerra*** war criminal
criminalidad *nf* (**a**) *(cualidad)* criminality (**b**) *(número de crímenes)* crime rate; **se ha producido un descenso de la c.** the crime rate has gone down; **medidas para combatir la c.** measures to combat *o* fight crime
criminalista 1 *adj* criminal; **abogado c.** criminal lawyer
2 *nmf* criminal lawyer
criminalizar *vt* to criminalize
criminología *nf* criminology
criminólogo, -a *nm,f* criminologist
crin *nf* (**a**) *(pelo)* mane; **las crines de un caballo** a horse's mane; **cepillo de c.** horsehair brush (**b**) *(material)* esparto; **guante de c.** loofah mitt
crinolina *nf* crinoline
crío, -a *nm,f (niño)* kid; **esperan el c. para diciembre** the baby is due in December; **mi abuelo está hecho un c.** my grandfather doesn't look his age at all; **no te preocupes, son cosas de críos** don't let it bother you, it's not worth worrying about; **¡no seas c.!** don't be such a baby!, don't be so childish!
criobiología *nf* cryobiology
criocirugía *nf* cryosurgery
crioconservación *nf* cryopreservation
criodeshidratación *nf* freeze-drying, *Espec* lyophilization
criogenia *nf* cryogenics *(singular)*
criogénico, -a *adj* cryogenic
criogenización *nf* cryogenic freezing
criogenizar *vt* to freeze cryogenically
criollismo *nm (vocablo)* = word or expression indigenous to Latin America
criollo, -a 1 *adj* (**a**) *(persona)* born in Latin America to European parents; **sus dos hijas menores son criollas** her two younger daughters were born in Latin America (**b**) *(objeto, cultura)* local *(native to*

Latin America as opposed to foreign); **al poco tiempo de llegar adoptaron las costumbres criollas** shortly after arriving, they began to adopt the local customs (**c**) *(comida, lengua)* creole

2 *nm,f* (**a**) *(persona)* = person born in Latin America to European parents (**b**) EXPR *Perú, PRico, RP* **hacer algo a la criolla** to do sth informally

3 *nm (idioma)* creole; EXPR *Am* **hablar en c.** to speak plainly, to speak in plain Spanish

criónica *nf* cryonics *(singular)*

criopreservación *nf* cryopreservation

crioterapia *nf* cryotherapy

cripta *nf* crypt

crípticamente *adv* cryptically

críptico, -a *adj (mensaje, comentario)* cryptic; **no me gusta su manera críptica de hablar** I don't like the way he never says exactly what he means

criptoanálisis *nm inv* cryptanalysis

criptografía *nf* cryptography

criptográfico, -a *adj* cryptographic

criptógrafo, -a *nm,f* cryptographer

criptograma *nm* cryptogram

criptón *nm Quím* krypton

críquet *nm* cricket

crisálida *nf* chrysalis

crisantemo *nm* chrysanthemum

crisis *nf inv* (**a**) *(situación difícil)* crisis; **la c. del petróleo** the oil crisis; **la c. del matrimonio** the crisis affecting the institution of marriage; **la c. en el mercado de valores** the stock market crisis; **estar en c.** to be in crisis; **atravesar una crisis** to go through a crisis; **entrar en una época de c.** to go into crisis, to enter a period of crisis ►► ***c. económica*** economic crisis, recession; ***c. energética*** energy crisis; ***c. financiera*** financial crisis; ***c. de identidad*** identity crisis; ***c. ministerial*** cabinet crisis; *Hist* **la c. de los misiles** *(en Cuba)* the Cuban Missile Crisis

(**b**) *(médica)* crisis ►► ***c. cardiaca*** cardiac arrest; ***c. epiléptica*** epileptic attack; ***c. nerviosa*** nervous breakdown

crisma[1] *nf (cabeza) Fam* nut, *Br* bonce; **romperle la c. a alguien** to smash sb's face in; **romperse la c.** to bash one's head

crisma[2] *nm (bálsamo)* chrism

crisma[3], **crismas** *nm inv Esp* Christmas card

crisol *nm* (**a**) *(de metales)* crucible (**b**) *(lugar donde se mezclan cosas)* melting pot

crisólito *nm* chrysolite

crispación *nf*, **crispamiento** *nm* (**a**) *(de nervios)* tension; **se le nota su c.** you can see her nerves are on edge; **las negociaciones se desarrollaron en un clima de c.** the talks took place in an atmosphere of tension (**b**) *(de músculo)* tenseness

crispado, -a *adj (músculo)* tense; *(puño)* clenched

crispante *adj* nerve-racking

crispar 1 *vt* (**a**) *(nervios)* to set on edge; **este trabajo me crispa los nervios** this work sets my nerves on edge; **su actitud crispa a los que la rodean** her attitude gets on the nerves of everyone around her (**b**) *(músculos)* to tense; *(puño)* to clench

2 crisparse *vpr* (**a**) *(persona)* to get annoyed (**b**) *(músculo)* to become tense; **se le crisparon las manos** he clenched his fists

crispetas *nfpl Col* popcorn

cristal *nm* (**a**) *Esp (material)* glass; **el suelo está lleno de cristales** there's glass all over the floor ►► ***c. ahumado*** smoked glass; ***c. blindado*** bullet-proof glass; ***c. esmerilado*** ground glass; ***c. inastillable*** splinter-proof glass; ***c. labrado*** cut glass; ***c. tintado*** tinted glass

(**b**) *(vidrio fino)* crystal ►► ***c. de Murano*** Venetian glass; ***c. tallado*** cut glass

(**c**) *(de gafas)* lens; *Esp (lámina) (de ventana)* (window) pane; *Esp* **bajar el c.** *(ventanilla)* to open *o* roll down the window; EXPR **todo depende del c. con el que se mire** it all depends how you look at it ►► ***c. de aumento*** magnifying lens

(**d**) *(mineral)* crystal ►► ***c. de cuarzo*** quartz crystal; ***c. líquido*** liquid crystal; ***c. de roca*** rock crystal

(**e**) *Esp (espejo)* mirror

cristalazo *nm Méx* (**a**) *(de auto)* **le dieron un c. al carro y se robaron la radio** they smashed the car window and stole the stereo (**b**) *(de tienda)* smash-and-grab raid

cristalera *nf* (**a**) *(puerta)* French window (**b**) *(ventana)* large window (**c**) *(armario)* display cabinet (**d**) *ver también* **cristalero**

cristalería *nf* (**a**) *(vasos, copas)* set of glasses (**b**) *(tienda)* glazier's (shop) (**c**) *(fábrica)* glassworks *(singular)*

cristalero, -a 1 *nm,f* glazier

2 *nm RP* display cabinet

cristalino, -a 1 *adj* crystalline

2 *nm* crystalline lens

cristalización *nf* (**a**) *(compuesto)* crystallization (**b**) *(de plan, negociaciones)* coming to fruition

cristalizar [14] **1** *vi* (**a**) *(compuesto)* to crystallize (**b**) *(plan, negociaciones)* to come to fruition; **un proyecto que no llegó a c.** a project that never resulted in anything concrete; **c. en** to result in

2 cristalizarse *vpr* (**a**) *(compuesto)* to crystallize (**b**) **cristalizarse en** *(plan, negociaciones)* to develop into

cristalografía *nf* crystallography

cristaloide *nm* crystalloid

cristero, -a *Méx* **1** *adj* Cristero, = relating to the "Cristero" rebellion

2 *nm,f* Cristero, = supporter of the conservative Catholic rural rebellion (1926-9) against the Mexican government's secular policies

cristianamente *adv* as a good Christian, in a Christian way

cristiandad *nf* Christianity

cristianismo *nm* Christianity

cristianización *nf* Christianization, conversion to Christianity

cristianizar [14] *vt* to Christianize, to convert to Christianity

cristiano, -a 1 *adj* Christian

2 *nm,f* (**a**) *(religioso)* Christian; EXPR *Fam* **esto no hay c. que lo soporte** this is more than flesh and blood can stand; EXPR *Fam* **hablar en c.** *(en castellano)* to speak (proper) Spanish; *(en lenguaje comprensible)* to speak clearly; EXPR **no estar** *o* **andar muy c.** *(estar de mal humor)* not to be in the best of moods; *(encontrarse mal)* to be a bit out of sorts ►► *Hist* ***c. nuevo*** person converted to Christianity as an adult; *Hist* ***c. viejo*** = person with no Moorish, Jewish or non-Christian ancestry

(**b**) *CAm (bonachón)* good soul

Cristo *nm* (**a**) *(Jesucristo)* Christ; EXPR **armar un C.** to kick up a fuss; EXPR *Fam* **donde C. dio las tres voces** *o* **perdió el gorro** in the back of beyond; EXPR *Fam* **estar hecho un C.** to be a pitiful sight; *Fam* **se cayó de la bici y se puso como un C.** he fell off his bike and ended up looking a real mess; *Fam* **ni C.** *(nadie)* absolutely nobody, not a soul; *Fam* **todo C.** *(todo el mundo)* absolutely everyone

(**b**) *(crucifijo)* crucifix

Cristóbal *n pr* **C. Colón** Christopher Columbus

cristofué *nm* great kiskadee

criterio[1] *nm* (**a**) *(norma)* criterion; **¿con qué c. se efectuó esa selección?** on what basis was this selection made?; **celebraron una reunión para unificar criterios** they held a meeting to agree on their criteria ►► *UE* ***criterios de convergencia*** convergence criteria

(**b**) *(juicio)* judgement; **es una persona de mucho c.** she has very good *o* sound judgement; **decidió con buen c. no seguir con el experimento** he wisely decided not to continue with the experiment

(**c**) *(opinión)* opinion; **según mi c., no ha hecho un buen trabajo** in my opinion, he has not done a good job; **sus diferencias de c. son evidentes** they have clear differences of opinion

criterio[2], **critérium** *nm Dep* criterium

crítica *nf* (**a**) *(juicio, análisis)* review; **esa novela ha recibido muy buenas críticas** that novel has had very good reviews ►► ***c. cinematográfica*** film *o* movie criticism; ***c. literaria*** literary criticism

(**b**) *(conjunto de críticos)* **la c.** the critics

(**c**) *(ataque)* criticism; **le han llovido muchas críticas** he has received a barrage of criticism; **lanzó duras críticas contra el proyecto** she severely criticized the project

(**d**) *ver también* **crítico**

criticable *adj* **la actitud del gobierno es c.** the government's attitude is open to criticism; **difícilmente c.** hard to criticize

criticar [60] *vt* (**a**) *(censurar)* to criticize (**b**) *(enjuiciar) (literatura, arte)* to review

criticastro, -a *nm,f Fam Pey* hack critic

crítico, -a 1 *adj* (**a**) *(estudio, análisis, actitud)* critical; **es un informe muy c. con la policía** the report is very critical of the police (**b**) *(decisivo)* critical; **el enfermo está en estado c.** the patient is in a critical condition; **está en una edad crítica** he is at a critical age

2 *nm,f (persona)* critic ►► ***c. de arte*** art critic; ***c. de cine*** movie *o Br* film critic; ***c. cinematográfico*** movie *o Br* film critic; ***c. literario*** literary critic; ***c. teatral*** theatre critic; ***c. de teatro*** theatre critic

criticón, -ona 1 *adj* nit-picking, hypercritical; **no seas tan c.** don't be so nit-picking, stop criticizing all the time
2 *nm,f* nit-picker; **es un c.** he finds fault with everything, he does nothing but criticize

Croacia *n* Croatia

croar 1 *vi* to croak
2 *nm* croaking

croata 1 *adj* Croatian
2 *nmf* Croat, Croatian

CROC [krok] *nf (abrev de* **Confederación Revolucionaria Obrera y Campesina**) = Mexican peasants federation

crocante 1 *adj RP* crunchy
2 *nm (guirlache)* almond brittle

crocanti *nm (helado)* = ice cream covered in chocolate and nuts

croché, crochet [kro'tʃe] *(pl* **crochets**) *nm* (**a**) *(labor)* crochet; **hacer c.** to crochet; **una colcha de c.** a crocheted bedspread (**b**) *(en boxeo)* hook

croissant [krwa'san] *(pl* **croissants**) *nm* croissant

croissantería [krwasante'ria] *nf* = shop selling filled croissants

crol *nm Dep* crawl; **nadar a c.** to do the crawl

cromado 1 *adj* chromium-plated
2 *nm* chromium-plating

cromar *vt* to chrome, to chromium-plate

cromático, -a *adj* (**a**) *(de los colores)* chromatic (**b**) *(en óptica)* chromatic (**c**) *Mús* chromatic

cromatismo *nm* (**a**) *(de artista)* use of colour (**b**) *(en óptica)* chromaticity (**c**) *Mús* chromaticism

cromatografía *nf Quím* chromatography ►► ***c. de gases*** gas chromatography

crómlech, crónlech *(pl* **crómlechs, crónlechs**) *nm* stone circle

cromo *nm* (**a**) *(metal)* chrome (**b**) *Esp (estampa)* picture card; **un c. repetido** a swap; EXPR *Fam* **ir hecho un c.** *(desaliñado)* to look a real mess; *(muy arreglado)* to be dressed up to the nines

cromolitografía *nf* (**a**) *(arte)* chromolithography (**b**) *(estampa)* chromolithograph

cromosfera *nf* chromosphere

cromosoma *nm* chromosome ►► ***c. sexual*** sex chromosome

cromosómico, -a *adj* chromosomal

cromoterapia *nf* colour therapy

crónica *nf* (**a**) *(de la historia)* chronicle (**b**) *(de un periódico)* column; *(de la televisión)* feature, programme; **la c. deportiva** the sports news *o* report; *Am* **la c. roja** the crime reports

crónico, -a *adj* (**a**) *(enfermedad, problema)* chronic (**b**) *Fam (vicio)* ingrained; **es un perezoso/mentiroso c.** he's a hopeless layabout/liar

cronicón *nm* = brief, usually anonymous, chronicle

cronista *nmf* (**a**) *(historiador)* chronicler (**b**) *(en periódico)* writer; *(en televisión)* reporter

crónlech = **crómlech**

crono *nm Esp Dep* (**a**) *(tiempo)* time; **hizo el mejor c. de todos los participantes** she did the best time of all the competitors (**b**) *(cronómetro)* stopwatch

cronoescalada *nf Dep* time-trial climb

cronología *nf* chronology

cronológicamente *adv* chronologically, in chronological order

cronológico, -a *adj* chronological; **en orden c.** in chronological order

cronólogo, -a, *nm,f,* **cronologista** *nmf* chronologist

cronometrador, -ora *nm,f* timekeeper

cronometraje *nm* timekeeping

cronometrar *vt* to time

cronométrico, -a *adj* **es de una puntualidad cronométrica** he's extremely punctual

cronómetro *nm* (**a**) *Dep* stopwatch (**b**) *Tec* chronometer

cróquet *nm* croquet

croqueta *nf* croquette

croquis *nm inv* sketch

cross [kros] *nm inv Dep* (**a**) *(carrera)* cross-country race (**b**) *(deporte)* cross-country (running)

crótalo *nm* (**a**) *(serpiente)* rattlesnake (**b**) **crótalos** *(castañuelas)* castanets

croto, -a *nm,f RP Fam* twit, idiot

croupier [kru'pjer] *(pl* **croupiers**) *nm* croupier

cruasán *nm* croissant

cruasantería *nf* = shop selling filled croissants

cruce 1 *ver* **cruzar**
2 *nm* (**a**) *(de líneas)* crossing, intersection; *(de carreteras)* crossroads *(singular)*; **gira a la derecha en el próximo c.** turn right at the next junction
(**b**) *(paso)* crossing; **pasa al otro lado por el c.** use the crossing to cross the road; **un c. fronterizo** a border crossing
(**c**) *(de animales, plantas)* cross; **un c. de fox-terrier y chihuahua** a cross between a fox terrier and a chihuahua
(**d**) *(de teléfono)* crossed line; **hay un c. en la línea** we've got *o* there's a crossed line
(**e**) *(en fútbol)* crossfield ball *o* pass
(**f**) *(en competición deportiva)* round *(in knockout competition)*; **les tocó el c. más difícil** they got the toughest draw

cruceiro *nm Antes (moneda)* cruzeiro

crucero *nm* (**a**) *(viaje)* cruise; **hacer un c.** to go on a cruise (**b**) *(barco)* (battle) cruiser (**c**) *(de iglesias)* crossing (**d**) *(cruz de piedra)* stone cross (**e**) *Méx (cruce) (viario)* crossroads; *(férreo) Br* level crossing, *US* grade crossing

cruceta *nf* (**a**) *(de una cruz)* crosspiece (**b**) *(en fútbol)* angle *(of crossbar and goalpost)* (**c**) *Náut* crosstree

crucial *adj* crucial

crucífero, -a *adj Formal* cruciferous

crucificado, -a 1 *adj* crucified
2 *nm Rel* **el C.** Jesus Christ

crucificar [60] *vt* (**a**) *(en una cruz)* to crucify (**b**) *(atormentar)* to torment

crucifijo *nm* crucifix

crucifixión *nf* crucifixion

cruciforme *adj* cruciform

crucigrama *nm* crossword (puzzle) ►► ***c. críptico*** cryptic crossword

crucigramista *nmf* crossword compiler

cruda *nf Guat, Méx Fam* hangover

crudeza *nf* (**a**) *(de clima)* harshness; **con c.** harshly (**b**) *(de descripción, imágenes)* brutality, harsh realism; **describe la c. de la guerra con gran realismo** she describes the brutality of war very realistically; **le contestó con una c. inesperada** he replied with unexpected harshness

crudo, -a 1 *adj* (**a**) *(seda, algodón)* raw
(**b**) *(alimentos) (sin cocinar)* raw; *(sin cocer completamente)* undercooked
(**c**) *(petróleo)* crude
(**d**) *(clima, tiempo)* harsh
(**e**) *(realidad)* harsh; *(novela)* harshly realistic, hard-hitting
(**f**) *(cruel)* cruel
(**g**) *(color)* beige
(**h**) *Fam (difícil)* **en estos momentos está muy c. encontrar trabajo** it's really tough to find a job just now; **lo tiene c. si piensa que lo voy a invitar** he's in for a big disappointment if he thinks I'm inviting him
(**i**) *Guat, Méx Fam (con resaca)* hung over
2 *nm* (**a**) *(petróleo)* crude (oil)
(**b**) *Perú (arpillera)* sacking

cruel *adj* (**a**) *(persona, acción)* cruel; **fuiste muy c. con ella** you were very cruel to her (**b**) *(dolor)* excruciating, terrible (**c**) *(clima)* harsh (**d**) *(duda)* terrible

crueldad *nf* (**a**) *(de persona, acción)* cruelty; **mostró una c. inusitada** he displayed extraordinary cruelty (**b**) *(acción cruel)* act of cruelty; **es una c. abandonar animales** it's cruel to abandon animals (**c**) *(del clima)* harshness

cruelmente *adv* cruelly

cruento, -a *adj* bloody

crujía *nf* (**a**) *(pasillo)* passage, corridor (**b**) *Arquit (entre muros)* space *(between two load-bearing walls)* (**c**) *Náut* midship gangway

crujido *nm (de madera)* creaking; *(de hojas secas)* crackling; *(de papel)* scrunching; *(de hueso)* cracking; **un c.** *(de madera)* a creak; *(de hojas secas)* a crackle; *(de papel)* a scrunch; *(de hueso)* a crack; **el c. de sus pisadas** the crunch of his footsteps

crujiente *adj (patatas fritas, nieve)* crunchy; *(madera)* creaky; *(hojas secas)* rustling; *(pan)* crusty

crujir *vi (patatas fritas, nieve)* to crunch; *(madera)* to creak; *(hojas secas)* to crackle; *(papel)* to scrunch; *(hueso)* to crack; *(dientes)* to grind

crup *nm* croup

crupier *nm* croupier

crustáceo *nm* crustacean

cruz *nf* (**a**) *(forma)* cross; **ponga una c. en la casilla correspondiente** put a cross in the appropriate box; **la señal de la c.** the sign of the cross; **con los brazos en c.** with one's arms stretched out to the sides; EXPR *Fam* **hacerse cruces: todavía me hago cruces, ¿cómo pudo ganar?** I still can't get over it, how did he win?; EXPR *Fam* **hacer c. y raya** to break off relations; **él y yo, c. y raya** we're through (with each other) ▸▸ ***c. celta*** Celtic cross; ***c. gamada*** swastika; ***c. griega*** Greek cross; ***c. latina*** Latin cross; ***c. de Malta*** Maltese cross; ***la C. Roja*** the Red Cross; ***c. de San Andrés*** St Andrew's Cross; ***c. de Santiago*** cross of Santiago; ***la C. del Sur*** *(constelación)* the Southern Cross
(**b**) *(condecoración)* cross; **c. al mérito militar** military cross
(**c**) *(de una moneda)* tails *(singular)*
(**d**) *Fam (aflicción)* burden, torment; **¡tener que madrugar es una c. para mí!** having to get up early is absolute torture for me!; **¡qué c.!** what a life!
(**e**) *Zool* withers

cruza *nf Am* cross, crossbreed

cruzada *nf* (**a**) *Hist* crusade; **las Cruzadas** the Crusades (**b**) *(lucha)* crusade; **una c. contra el terrorismo** a crusade against terrorism

cruzado, -a 1 *adj* (**a**) *(cheque, piernas, brazos)* crossed (**b**) *(atravesado)* **hay un árbol c. en la carretera** there's a tree lying across the road; **se vieron atrapados en el fuego c.** they were caught in the crossfire (**c**) *(animal)* crossbred (**d**) *(abrigo, chaqueta)* double-breasted
2 *nm* (**a**) *Hist* crusader (**b**) *(en lucha)* crusader

cruzamiento *nm* (**a**) *(acción)* crossing (**b**) *(de animales)* crossbreeding

cruzar [14] **1** *vt* (**a**) *(calle, río)* to cross; **cruzó el Atlántico en velero** he sailed across the Atlantic; **nos cruzó al otro lado del río en su barca** he took us across to the other side of the river in his boat; **cruzó el río a nado** she swam across the river; **cruzó la calle corriendo** he ran across the street; **esta carretera cruza varios pueblos** this road goes through several towns; **un río que cruza todo el país** a river that flows the length of the country
(**b**) *(interponer)* **cruzaron un autobús para detener el tráfico** they put a bus across the road to stop the traffic
(**c**) *(piernas, brazos)* to cross; EXPR **crucemos los dedos** let's keep our fingers crossed
(**d**) *(unas palabras)* to exchange
(**e**) *(en fútbol)* **marcó cruzando la pelota** he scored with a cross-shot; **cruzó demasiado la pelota** he pulled his shot wide
(**f**) *(animales, plantas)* to cross
(**g**) *(cheque)* to cross
(**h**) EXPR *Fam* **c. la cara a alguien** to slap sb across the face; **como no te estés quieto te voy a c. la cara** if you don't keep still I'm going to slap you
2 cruzarse *vpr* (**a**) *(atravesarse)* to cross; **la A1 no se cruza con la A6** the A1 doesn't meet the A6 at any point; **se cruzaron un guiño** they winked at each other; **se está cruzando una línea** we're getting a crossed line; **sus caminos se cruzarían varias veces más** their paths were to cross again on several occasions; **cruzarse de brazos** to fold one's arms; *Fig (no hacer nada)* to stand back and do nothing; EXPR *Fam* **se le cruzaron los cables** he went mad *o* crazy
(**b**) *(interponerse)* **se me cruzó un perro y no pude esquivarlo** a dog ran out in front of me and I couldn't avoid it; **una mujer se cruzó entre ellos y acabó con su amistad** a woman came between them and that was the end of their friendship
(**c**) *(personas)* **cruzarse con alguien** to pass sb; **ayer me crucé con tu mujer camino trabajo** I saw *o* met your wife yesterday on the way to work; **si salimos a la misma hora nos cruzaremos en la frontera** if we leave at the same time we'll meet (up) at the border

CSTAL *nf* (*abrev de* **Confederación Sindical de los Trabajadores de América Latina**) = Latin-American trade union confederation

cta. (*abrev de* **cuenta**) a/c

CTC *nf* (*abrev de* **Central de Trabajadores de Cuba**) = Cuban trade union

cte. (*abrev de* **corriente**) inst.

CTI [sete'i] *nm Am* (*abrev de* **centro de tratamiento intensivo**) ICU

ctra. (*abrev de* **carretera**) Rd

c/u (*abrev de* **cada uno**) per item

cuac *interj (graznido)* quack!

cuachalote *adj Méx Fam* scruffy

cuaderna *nf Náut* rib

cuadernillo *nm* (**a**) *(de periódico)* supplement (**b**) *Imprenta (papel)* quinternion

cuaderno *nm (libreta)* notebook; *(de colegial)* exercise book ▸▸ ***c. de actividades*** activity book; ***c. de anillas*** ring binder; *Náut* ***c. de bitácora*** logbook; ***c. de dibujo*** sketch pad; ***c. de espiral*** spiral-bound notebook; ***c. de notas*** notebook

cuadra *nf* (**a**) *(establo)* stable (**b**) *(conjunto de caballos)* stable (**c**) *Fam (lugar sucio)* pigsty (**d**) *Am (en calle)* block (**e**) *Perú (recibidor)* reception room

cuadrada *nf Mús* breve

cuadrado, -a 1 *adj* (**a**) *(figura)* square (**b**) *Mat* square; **metro/kilómetro c.** square metre/kilometre (**c**) *Fam (musculoso)* muscly; **estar c.** to be muscly (**d**) *Am (estricto, cerrado)* narrow-minded (**e**) *Am (torpe)* thick, dumb
2 *nm* (**a**) *(figura)* square (**b**) *Mat* square; **tres (elevado) al c.** three square(d)

cuadrafonía *nf* quadraphonics

cuadrafónico, -a *adj* quadraphonic

cuadragésima *nf* Quadragesima Sunday *(first Sunday in Lent)*

cuadragésimo, -a *núm* fortieth; *ver también* **octavo**

cuadrangular 1 *adj* (**a**) *(forma)* quadrangular (**b**) *Dep* **un torneo c.** a quadrangular tournament, a tournament involving four teams
2 *nm Am (en béisbol)* home run

cuadrángulo *nm* quadrangle

cuadrante *nm* (**a**) *(de círculo)* quadrant (**b**) *(instrumento)* quadrant (**c**) *(reloj de sol)* sundial

cuadrar 1 *vi* (**a**) *(información, hechos)* to square, to agree (**con** with); **hay algo en su explicación que no cuadra** there's something about his explanation that doesn't add up
(**b**) *(números, cuentas)* to tally, to add up; **estas cuentas no cuadran** these accounts don't balance; **tus cálculos no cuadran con los míos** your calculations don't tally with mine
(**c**) *(armonizar)* **no le cuadra esa ropa** those clothes don't suit him; **ese color no cuadra con la decoración** that colour doesn't go with the decor
(**d**) *(convenir)* to suit; **si te cuadra, te recojo a las seis** if it suits you, I'll pick you up at six; *Ven* **c. con alguien** to arrange to meet sb
2 *vt* (**a**) *(dar forma de cuadrado a)* to make square, to square off
(**b**) *(cuentas)* to balance; **tenemos que c. los números** we need to make the numbers add up *o* tally; **están intentado c. el presupuesto** they're trying to balance the budget
(**c**) *Andes (auto)* to park
3 cuadrarse *vpr* (**a**) *(soldado)* to stand to attention
(**b**) *Taurom (toro)* to stand square
(**c**) *Esp (ponerse firme)* to stand firm, to take a firm stand; **se cuadró y dijo que no iba a seguir tolerando ese comportamiento** he took a firm stand and said he would no longer tolerate such behaviour
(**d**) *Perú, Ven Fam (enfrentarse)* **cuadrarse a alguien** to stand up to sb
(**e**) *Andes (estacionarse)* to park
(**f**) *CSur (solidarizarse)* **cuadrarse con alguien** to stand by sb
(**g**) *Ven Fam (alinearse)* to toe the line; **el partido se cuadró inmediatamente** the party immediately fell into line

cuadratín *nm Imprenta* quad

cuadratura *nf Geom* quadrature; **la c. del círculo** squaring the circle

cuádriceps *nm inv* quadriceps

cuadrícula *nf* grid

cuadriculado, -a *adj* (**a**) *(papel)* squared (**b**) *Fam (rígido)* **ser muy c.** to be very inflexible; **tiene una mente cuadriculada** he's very narrow-minded

cuadricular *vt* to divide into squares

cuadrienio *nm* four-year period; **el c. 1994-1997** the four years from 1994 to 1997

cuadriga, cuádriga *nf Hist* four-in-hand

cuadril *nm* (**a**) *(cadera)* hipbone (**b**) *RP (carne)* rump (steak)

cuadrilátero *nm* (**a**) *Geom* quadrilateral (**b**) *(en boxeo)* ring

cuadrilongo, -a 1 *adj* rectangular, oblong
2 *nm* rectangle, oblong

cuadrilla *nf* (**a**) *(de amigos, trabajadores)* group; *(de maleantes)* gang (**b**) *Taurom* team of helpers

cuadrivio *nm Hist* quadrivium

CUADRO *nm* (a) *(pintura)* painting; **un c. de Miró** a Miró, a painting by Miró; **c. al óleo** oil painting
(b) *(escena)* scene, spectacle; **después del terremoto, la ciudad presentaba un c. desolador** after the earthquake, the city was a scene of devastation; **¡vaya (un) c. ofrecíamos tras la tormenta!** we were in a sorry state after we got caught in the storm!
(c) *(descripción)* portrait ▸▸ ***c. de costumbres*** = scene portraying regional customs
(d) *(cuadrado)* square; *(de flores)* bed; **una camisa a cuadros** a checked shirt; **un diseño a cuadros** a checked pattern; **una camisa de cuadros verdes** a green checked shirt ▸▸ ***c. de saque*** *(en squash)* service box
(e) *(equipo)* team; **el c. visitante** the away team; **en este hospital hay un buen c. médico** *o* **facultativo** the medical staff in this hospital are good; **el c. directivo de una empresa** the management of a company; **los cuadros medios** *o* **intermedios de la administración** middle-ranking government officials ▸▸ ***c. flamenco*** flamenco group; ***cuadros de mando*** *(en ejército)* commanding officers; *(en organización)* highest-ranking officials; *(en empresa)* top management
(f) *(gráfico)* chart, diagram ▸▸ ***c. sinóptico*** tree diagram
(g) *(de bicicleta)* frame
(h) *(de aparato)* panel ▸▸ ***c. de distribución*** switchboard; ***c. eléctrico*** fuse box; ***c. de instrumentos*** *(en avión)* control panel; *(en automóvil)* dashboard; ***c. de mandos*** *(en avión)* control panel; *(en automóvil)* dashboard
(i) *Teatro* scene ▸▸ ***c. vivo*** tableau vivant
(j) *Med* **c. (clínico)** symptoms; **presenta un c. de extrema gravedad** her symptoms are extremely serious
(k) *(armazón)* framework
(l) *Mil* square formation
(m) *Informát* box ▸▸ ***c. de cierre*** close box; ***c. de diálogo*** dialog box
(n) *Am (matadero)* slaughterhouse
(o) EXPR **en c.: la empresa está en c. tras la marcha del equipo directivo** the company has been caught seriously short after its entire management team left; **con la lesión de siete jugadores, el equipo se queda en cuadros** the team has been seriously weakened after the injuries to seven of its players; *Fam* **quedarse a cuadros: cuando me dijo que yo era el padre del bebé, me quedé a cuadros** I was completely floored when she told me that I was the father of the baby

cuadros *nmpl Chile (braga)* panties, *Br* knickers

cuadrumano, -a 1 *adj* = having feet specialized for use as hands (like monkeys), *Espec* quadrumanous
2 *nm,f* quadrumanous animal

cuadrúpedo *nm* quadruped

cuádruple, cuádruplo 1 *adj* quadruple, fourfold
2 *nm* **el c. de gente/libros** four times as many people/books; **las exportaciones han aumentado el c.** exports have quadrupled, there has been a fourfold increase in exports; **me costó el c. que a él** it cost me four times what he paid

cuadruplicación *nf* quadruplication

cuadruplicado *nm* **por c.** in quadruplicate; **las solicitudes deberán presentarse por c.** you should provide four copies of your application

cuadruplicar [60] **1** *vt* to quadruple
2 cuadruplicarse *vpr* to quadruple, to increase fourfold

cuádruplo = **cuádruple**

cuajada *nf* curd (cheese)

cuajado, -a *adj* (a) *(leche)* curdled (b) *(lleno)* **c. de** full of; *(de lágrimas)* filled with; *(de estrellas)* studded with

cuajar[1] *nm Zool* fourth stomach, *Espec* abomasum

cuajar[2] **1** *vt* (a) *(solidificar) (leche)* to curdle; *(sangre)* to clot, to coagulate
(b) **c. de** *(llenar)* to fill with; *(cubrir)* to cover with
2 *vi* (a) *(lograrse) (acuerdo)* to be settled; *(negocio)* to take off, to get going; **era un jugador que prometía pero no llegó a c.** he was a player with promise but he never really achieved his potential
(b) *(ser aceptado) (persona)* to fit in; *(moda)* to catch on; **las propuestas no cuajaron** the proposals never came to anything; **un estilo arquitectónico que no cuajó en Inglaterra** an architectural style that didn't catch on in England
(c) *(nieve)* to settle
3 cuajarse *vpr* (a) *(leche)* to curdle; *(sangre)* to clot, to coagulate
(b) *(llenarse)* **cuajarse de** to fill (up) with

cuajo 1 *nm* (a) *(fermento)* rennet (b) *(árbol)* dali
2 de cuajo *loc adv* **arrancar de c.** *(árbol)* to uproot; *(brazo, cabeza)* to tear right off

CUAL 1 *pron relativo* (a) **el c./la c./los cuales/las cuales** *(de persona) (sujeto)* who; *(complemento)* who, *Formal* whom; *(de cosa)* which; **conoció a una española, la c. vivía en Buenos Aires** he met a Spanish girl who lived in Buenos Aires; **le extirparon el apéndice, el c. se había inflamado** they removed her appendix, which had become inflamed; **hablé con dos profesores, los cuales me explicaron la situación** I spoke to two teachers who explained the situation to me; **me encontré con Sandra, a la c. hacía tiempo que no veía** I met Sandra, who *o Formal* whom I hadn't seen for some time; **son dos personas con las cuales me llevo muy bien** they're two people (who) I get on very well with, *Formal* they're two people with whom I get on very well; **hablé con la persona a la c. escribí la semana pasada** I spoke with the person *Formal* whom I had written to *o Formal* to whom I had written last week; **la compañía para la c. trabajo** the company I work for, the company for which I work; **un problema para el c. no hay solución** a problem to which there is no solution; **una norma según la c. no se puede entrar a mitad de espectáculo** a rule stating that you may not enter the auditorium while the show is in progress; **estoy muy cansado, razón por la c. no saldré esta noche** I'm very tired, which is why I'm not going out tonight
(b) **lo c.** which; **está muy enfadada, lo c. es comprensible** she's very angry, which is understandable; **ha tenido mucho éxito, de lo c. me alegro** she's been very successful and I'm very pleased for her; **...de lo c. concluimos que...** ...from which we can conclude that...; **estaba de muy mal humor, en vista de lo c. no le dije nada** seeing as *o* in view of the fact that she was in a very bad mood, I didn't say anything to her; **por todo lo c. hemos decidido...** as a result of which we have decided...; **todo lo c. me hace pensar que no vendrá** all of which makes me think he won't come
(c) *(en frases)* **cada c. tiene sus gustos propios** everyone has his/her own tastes; **que cada c. extraiga sus conclusiones** you may all draw your own conclusions; **sea c. sea** *o* **fuere su decisión** whatever his decision (may be); **le conté lo que había pasado y se quedó tal c.** I told her what had happened and she didn't bat an eyelid
2 *adv Literario (como)* like; **se revolvió c. fiera herida** he writhed around like a wounded beast; EXPR **c. padre, tal hijo** like father, like son

CUÁL *pron* (a) *(interrogativo)* what; *(en concreto, especificando)* which (one); **¿c. es tu nombre?** what's your name?; **¿c. es la diferencia?** what's the difference?; **no sé cuáles son mejores** I don't know which are best; **dinos c. te gusta más** tell us which (one) you like best; **¿c. prefieres?** which (one) do you prefer?; **¿c. de estos dos te gusta más?** which of these two do you like best?; **¿de c. me hablas?** which (one) are you talking about?
(b) *(exclamativo)* **¡c. no sería mi sorpresa al conocer el resultado!** imagine my surprise when I heard the result!
(c) *(en oraciones distributivas)* **todos contribuyeron, c. más, c. menos** everyone contributed, although some more than others; **los tres son a c. más inteligente** all three are equally intelligent; **tiene dos casas a c. más lujosa** she has two houses, both of which are equally luxurious, she has two houses, the one as luxurious as the other; **a c. más deprisa** each as fast as the other

> In conversational English a preposition is frequently placed at the end of a sentence beginning with an interrogative pronoun. In Spanish the preposition must always come at the beginning of the sentence before the interrogative pronoun:
> **¿a cuál te referías?**
> *which one were you referring to?*
> The same contrast is found in the use of relative pronouns in the two languages:
> **es algo de lo cual prefiero no hablar**
> *it's something (that/which) I prefer not to talk about*

cualesquiera *ver* **cualquiera**

cualidad *nf* (a) *(característica)* characteristic, quality; **su c. más destacada es la conductividad** its most notable characteristic *o* property is its conductivity (b) *(virtud)* quality; **tiene buenas cualidades para la música** she has an aptitude for music

cualificación *nf* degree of skill *(of a worker)*; **debemos mejorar la c. de los obreros** we have to get a more highly skilled workforce

cualificado, -a *adj* skilled

cualificar [60] *vt* to qualify

cualitativamente *adv* qualitatively

cualitativo, -a *adj* qualitative

cualquier *ver* **cualquiera**

CUALQUIERA (*pl* **cualesquiera**)

Note that **cualquier** is used before singular nouns (e.g. **cualquier hombre** any man).

1 *adj* any; **no es un escritor c.** he's no ordinary writer; **cualquier día vendré a visitarte** I'll drop by one of these days; **cualquier cosa vale** anything will do; **a cualquier hora** any time; **hazlo de cualquier manera** do it any old how; **hace las cosas de cualquier manera** he does things any old how *o* carelessly; **de cualquier manera** *o* **modo, no pienso ayudar** I've no intention of helping, anyway *o* in any case; **en cualquier momento** at any time; **en cualquier lado/lugar** anywhere

2 *pron* anyone; **c. te lo dirá** anyone will tell you; **c. haría lo mismo** anyone would do the same; **¡c. se lo cree!** if you believe that, you'll believe anything!; **que lo haga c., pero rápido** I don't care who does it as long as it's done quickly; **¡c. lo sabe!** who knows!; **¡c. se lo come!** nobody could eat that!; **¡c. entiende a tu madre!** I don't think anyone understands your mother!; **con el mal humor que tiene, ¡c. se lo dice!** it's a brave man who would tell her in that mood!; **c. que** *(persona)* anyone who; *(cosa)* whatever; **c. que te vea se reiría** anyone who saw you would laugh; **c. que sea la razón** whatever the reason (may be); **avísame, c. que sea la hora a la que llame** let me know, whatever time she calls; **cualesquiera que sean las razones** whatever the reasons (may be)

3 *nmf Pey (don nadie)* nobody; **ser un c.** to be a nobody

4 *nf Fam Pey (prostituta)* tart

cuan *adv (todo lo que)* **se desplomó c. largo era** he fell flat on the ground

cuán *adv* how

CUANDO 1 *adv* when; **c. llegue el verano iremos de viaje** when summer comes we'll go travelling; **c. me agacho, me duele la espalda** when *o* whenever I bend down, my back hurts; **se marchó c. mejor lo estábamos pasando** she left just when we were having a really good time; **acababa de cerrar la puerta, c. estalló la bomba** I had just closed the door when the bomb went off; **fue entonces c. comprendí el problema** it was then that I realized the problem; **para c. llegamos, la fiesta ya había acabado** by the time we arrived the party was already over; **ven a visitarnos c. quieras** come and stay with us whenever you like; **cambia mucho de c. está de buen humor a c. está enfadado** he's very different when he's in a good mood to when he's angry; **¿te acuerdas de c. nos dieron el premio?** do you remember when *o* the time they gave us the prize?; **apenas se marchó el profesor, c. todos los alumnos se pusieron a hablar** no sooner had the teacher left than all the pupils started talking; **de c. en c., de vez en c.** from time to time, now and again; **c. más, c. mucho** at (the) most; **c. más, te ayudaré un rato** I'll help you for a short while, but no longer; **c. menos** at least; **nos harán falta c. menos cinco personas** we'll need at least five people; **c. quiera que me lo encuentro, siempre me sonríe** whenever I meet him he smiles at me

2 *conj* (**a**) *(si)* if; **c. tú lo dices será verdad** it must be true if you say so; **c. no te ha llegado la invitación, será porque no te quieren ver** if you haven't received an invitation, it must be because they don't want to see you; **no será tan malo c. ha vendido tantas copias** it can't be that bad if it's sold so many copies

(**b**) *(después de "aun") (aunque)* **no mentiría aun c. le fuera en ello la vida** she wouldn't lie even if her life depended on it

(**c**) *(indica contraste)* **no tiene muchos amigos, c. en realidad es una persona muy agradable** he doesn't have a lot of friends, even though he's actually a very nice person

(**d**) *(introduce valoración negativa)* when, even though; **siempre está protestando, c. es el que más oportunidades recibe** he's always complaining even though *o* when he's the one who gets more chances than anyone else

3 *prep* **quemaron ese colegio c. la guerra** that school was burned down during the war; **son restos de c. los romanos** they are remains from Roman times; **c. niño, solía bañarme en este río** when I was a boy I used to swim in this river

CUÁNDO 1 *adv* when; **¿c. vas a venir?** when are you coming?; **quisiera saber c. sale el tren** I'd like to know when *o* at what time the train leaves; **¡c. se dará cuenta de su error!** when will she realize her mistake?; **¿de c. es este periódico?** when's this paper from?; **¿desde c. vives en Lima?** how long have you been living in Lima?; **¿desde c. puedes llegar a casa a las dos de la madrugada?** since when were you allowed to get home at two in the morning?; **¿para c. estará arreglado?** when will it be ready?; *Am* **¡c. no!** so what's new!; **los empleados se quejan de los sueldos bajos – ¡c. no!** the employees are complaining about their wages being low – so what's new!

2 *nm* **ignorará el cómo y el c. de la operación** he won't know how or when the operation will take place

In conversational English a preposition is frequently placed at the end of a sentence beginning with an interrogative pronoun. In Spanish the preposition must always come at the beginning of the sentence before the interrogative pronoun:
¿para cuándo lo quieres?
when do you want it for?

cuantía *nf* (**a**) *(suma)* amount, quantity; **todavía no se conoce la c. de los daños causados por el terremoto** the final cost of the damage caused by the earthquake is not yet known; **van a conceder una ayuda de una c. sin precisar todavía** they are going to grant an as yet unspecified amount of aid; **recibió la c. íntegra del premio** he received the full amount of the prize money; **va a subir la c. del subsidio de desempleo** unemployment benefit is set to rise

(**b**) *(alcance)* extent; **ése es un problema de menor c.** that is a relatively insignificant *o* minor problem

(**c**) *Der* claim, amount claimed

cuántica *nf* quantum mechanics *(singular)*

cuántico, -a *adj* quantum; **mecánica/teoría cuántica** quantum mechanics/theory

cuantificable *adj* quantifiable

cuantificación *nf* (**a**) *(contabilización)* quantification (**b**) *Fís* quantization (**c**) *Filosofía* quantification

cuantificar [60] *vt* (**a**) *(contabilizar)* to quantify (**b**) *Fís* to quantize (**c**) *Filosofía* to quantify

cuantioso, -a *adj (daños, pérdidas)* substantial, considerable; *(fortuna, inversión)* substantial, large; *(oferta, recursos)* substantial

cuantitativamente *adv* quantitatively

cuantitativo, -a *adj* quantitative

CUANTO[1], -A 1 *adj* (**a**) *(todo)* **despilfarra c. dinero gana** he squanders all the money he earns; **soporté todas cuantas críticas me hizo** I put up with every single criticism he made of me; **todos cuantos intentos hicimos fracasaron** every single one of our attempts met with failure

(**b**) *(algunos)* **unos cuantos chicos** some *o* a few boys; **necesitaré unas cuantas hojas** I'm going to need a few sheets of paper

(**c**) *(antes de adv) (expresa correlación)* **cuantas más mentiras digas, menos te creerán** the more you lie, the less people will believe you; **cuantos más amigos traigas, tanto mejor** the more friends you bring, the better

2 *pron relativo* (**a**) *(todo lo que)* everything, as much as; **come c. quieras** eat as much as you like; **comprendo c. dice** I understand everything he says; **heredarás todo c. tengo** you will inherit everything I have; **esto es todo c. puedo hacer** this is as much as *o* all I can do

(**b**) **cuantos** *(todos) (personas)* everyone who; *(cosas)* everything (that); **cuantos fueron alabaron el espectáculo** everyone who went said the show was excellent; **dio las gracias a todos cuantos le ayudaron** he thanked everyone who helped him

(**c**) **unos cuantos** *(algunos)* some, a few; **no tengo todos sus libros, sólo unos cuantos** I don't have all of her books, only some *o* a few of them

3 *adv (expresa correlación)* **c. más se tiene, más se quiere** the more you have, the more you want; **cuantos menos vayamos, más barato saldrá** the fewer of us who go, the cheaper it will be; **c. más come, más gordo está** the more he eats, the fatter he gets; **c. más lo pienso, menos lo entiendo** the more I think about it, the less I understand it; **c. menos nos distraigas, mejor** the less you distract us, the better; **c. antes llegues, antes empezaremos** the sooner you arrive, the sooner we'll start

4 **cuanto antes** *loc adv* as soon as possible; **hazlo c. antes** do it as soon as possible *o* as soon as you can

5 **en cuanto** *loc prep (en calidad de)* as; **en c. cabeza de familia** as head of the family

6 **en cuanto** *loc conj (tan pronto como)* as soon as; **en c. acabe** as soon as I've finished; **la reconocí en c. la vi** I recognized her as soon as I saw her *o* instantly

7 **en cuanto a** *loc prep* as regards; **en c. a tu petición** as regards your request, as far as your request is concerned; **en c. a temas de literatura, nadie sabe más que él** no one knows more about literature than he does, when it comes to literature, no one knows more than he does

cuanto[2] *nm Fís* quantum

CUÁNTO, -A 1 *adj* (**a**) *(interrogativo) (singular)* how much; *(plural)* how many; **¿c. pan quieres?** how much bread do you want?; **¿cuántas manzanas tienes?** how many apples do you have?; **¿cuántos años tiene?** how old is she?; **¿cuántos kilos pesa?** how many kilos does it weigh?; **¿c. dinero cuesta?** how much money does it cost?; **¿cuánta gente acudió a la fiesta?** how many people came to the party?; **¿con cuántos voluntarios contamos?** how many volunteers do we have?; **no sé cuántos hombres había** I don't know how many men were there; **pregúntale c. dinero tiene** ask her how much money she has

(**b**) *(exclamativo)* what a lot of; **¡cuánta gente (había)!** what a lot of people (were there)!; **¡cuántos problemas da esta televisión!** this television has been one problem after another!, we've had so many problems with this television!; **¡c. tiempo hace que no la veo!** it's been so long *o* ages since I saw her!; **¡cuánta falta hacía esta tormenta!** we really needed that storm!, that storm was long overdue!; **¡cuánta carne ha quedado!** look at all the meat that's left over!; **¡c. aprovechado hay por ahí!** there's a lot of scroungers about!

2 *pron* (**a**) *(interrogativo) (singular)* how much; *(plural)* how many; **¿c. quieres?** how much do you want?; **¿c. es?** how much is it?; **¿c. mide?** how tall is she?; **¿c. pesa?** how much *o* what does it weigh?; **¿c. cobra?** how much *o* what does he earn?; **¿c. vale?** how much is it *o* does it cost?; **¿c. falta para las vacaciones?** how long (is there) to go until the *Br* holidays *o US* vacation?; **¿c. queda para el final?** how long (is there) to go until the end?; **¿c. hay hasta la frontera?** how far is it to the border?; **¿cuántos han venido?** how many came?; **¿cada c. hay una gasolinera?** how often is there a *Br* petrol *o US* gas station?; **¿a c. están los tomates?** how much are the tomatoes?; **¿a c. estamos hoy?** what's the date today?; **¿por c. me saldrá la reparación?** how much will the repairs come to?; **dime cuántas quieres** tell me how many you want; **dime c. te ha costado** tell me how much it cost you; **me gustaría saber c. te costarán** I'd like to know how much they'll cost you; **no sé cuántos acudirán** I don't know how many people will come; **no te imaginas c. lo siento** I can't tell you how sorry I am, I'm so sorry

(**b**) *(exclamativo)* **¡c. han cambiado las cosas!** how things have changed!; **¡c. me gusta!** I really like it!; **¡cuántos han venido!** so many people have come!; **¡c. tardaste, pensaba que ya no venías!** you were so late, I thought you weren't coming!; **¡c. me gustaría ir contigo!** I'd really love to go with you!

(**c**) *Fam* **hablé con un tal Martín no sé cuántos** I spoke to a Martín something or other

> In conversational English a preposition is frequently placed at the end of a sentence beginning with an interrogative pronoun. In Spanish the preposition must always come at the beginning of the sentence before the interrogative pronoun:
> **¿a cuánto ascienden las deudas?**
> *how much do the debts amount to?*

cuáquer® *nm Arg, Perú* (**a**) *(avena)* porridge oats (**b**) *(desayuno)* porridge

cuáquero, -a 1 *adj* Quaker
2 *nm,f* Quaker

cuarcita *nf* quartzite

cuarenta *núm* forty; **los (años) c.** the forties; *ver también* **treinta**

cuarentavo, -a *núm* fortieth; *ver también* **octavo**

cuarentena *nf* (**a**) *(por epidemia)* quarantine; **poner en c.** *(enfermos)* to (put in) quarantine; *(noticia)* to put on hold (**b**) *(cuarenta unidades)* forty; **andará por la c.** he must be about forty; **una c. de...** *(unos cuarenta)* about forty...; *(cuarenta)* forty...

cuarentón, -ona *Fam* 1 *adj* **un señor c.** a man in his forties
2 *nm,f* person in their forties; **es un c.** he's in his forties

cuaresma *nf Rel* Lent

cuaresmal *adj Rel* Lenten

cuark (*pl* **cuarks**) *nm Fís* quark

cuarta *nf* (**a**) *(palmo)* span (**b**) *Mús* perfect fourth (**c**) *(marcha)* fourth (gear); **meter (la) c.** to go into fourth (gear) (**d**) *Méx (para caballo de tiro)* riding crop

cuarteamiento *nm (resquebrajamiento)* cracking

cuartear 1 *vt* (**a**) *(agrietar)* to crack (**b**) *(partir, dividir)* to cut *o* chop up
2 **cuartearse** *vpr* to crack

cuartel *nm* (**a**) *Mil* barracks ►► *RP* ***c. de bomberos*** fire station; ***c. general*** *(de ejército, organización)* headquarters; ***cuarteles de invierno*** winter quarters (**b**) *(buen trato)* **dar c.** to give quarter, to show mercy; **guerra sin c.** all-out war; **lucha sin c.** fight to the death; **lanzaron una lucha sin c. contra la corrupción** they declared an all-out war on corruption

cuartelazo *nm*, **cuartelada** *nf* military uprising, revolt

cuartelero, -a *adj* (**a**) *Mil* barracks; **vida cuartelera** life in barracks (**b**) *(lenguaje)* vulgar, coarse

cuartelillo *nm Esp* (**a**) *(de la Guardia Civil)* = Guardia Civil post (**b**) *Fam (de droga)* = share of drugs retained by the dealer for personal consumption

cuarteo *nm* cracking

cuarterón, -ona 1 *adj* = having one Spanish and one half-caste parent
2 *nm,f* = person with one Spanish and one half-caste parent

cuarteta *nf Lit* quatrain *(with lines of up to eight syllables)*

cuartetista *nmf Mús* member of a quartet

cuarteto *nm* (**a**) *Mús* quartet ►► ***c. de cuerda*** string quartet (**b**) *Lit* quatrain *(with lines of eleven syllables)*

cuartilla *nf* (**a**) *Imprenta* sheet of quarto (**b**) *(hoja de papel)* sheet of paper

cuarto, -a 1 *núm* fourth; **la cuarta parte** a quarter; *RP Fam* **de cuarta** fourth-rate ►► ***c. árbitro*** *(en fútbol)* fourth official; ***la cuarta dimensión*** the fourth dimension; ***el c. poder*** *(la prensa)* the Fourth Estate; *ver también* **octavo**

2 *nm* (**a**) *(parte)* quarter; **póngame un c. de merluza** (I'd like) a quarter kilo of hake, please; EXPR *Fam* **ni qué ocho cuartos: ¡qué fiesta ni qué ocho cuartos, tú te quedas en casa!** I don't care whether there's a party or not, you're staying at home!; EXPR *Fam* **ser tres cuartos de lo mismo** to be exactly the same *o* no different; **uno es aburrido, y el otro tres cuartos de lo mismo** one is a bore and the other one is not much better ►► ***c. creciente*** first quarter *(of moon)*; *Dep* ***cuartos de final*** quarter finals; ***c. menguante*** last quarter *(of moon)*

(**b**) *(de hora)* quarter; **un c. de hora** a quarter of an hour; **tres cuartos de hora** three quarters of an hour; **son las dos y c.** it's a quarter *Br* past *o US* after two; **son las dos menos c.,** *Am* **es un c. para las dos** it's a quarter to two; **una hora y c.** an hour and a quarter; EXPR *Am* **ya pasó su c. de hora** he's had his time in the sun, his glory days are over

(**c**) *(curso universitario)* fourth year

(**d**) *(curso escolar)* = fourth year of primary school, *US* ≃ fourth grade

(**e**) *(de animal)* quarter; **los cuartos delanteros/traseros** front quarters/ hindquarters

(**f**) *(habitación)* room ►► ***c. de aseo*** washroom, small bathroom; ***c. de baño*** bathroom; *Col* ***c. de chécheres*** junk *o* lumber room; ***c. de estar*** living room; ***c. de huéspedes*** guest room; ***c. de juegos*** playroom, *US* rumpus room; ***c. oscuro*** *(para revelar fotografía)* darkroom; *RP* ***c. secreto*** *(cabina electoral)* voting booth; ***c. trastero*** lumber room

(**g**) *(dinero)* **estar sin un c.** to be broke; *Fam* **cuartos** dough, cash

(**h**) *Dep (periodo)* quarter

(**i**) *RP* ***c. intermedio*** *(receso)* recess, adjournment; **la asamblea pasó a c. intermedio** the meeting adjourned *o* went into recess; **discutieron tres temas y pasaron a c. intermedio** they discussed three topics and then adjourned

cuartofinalista *nmf* quarterfinalist

cuartucho *nm* dingy room

cuarzo *nm* quartz

cuásar *nm Astron* quasar

cuasicontrato *nm Der* quasi contract

cuasidelito *nm Der* quasi delict

cuate *CAm, Ecuad, Méx* 1 *adj* (**a**) *(gemelo)* twin; **hermano c.** twin brother; **torres cuates** twin towers (**b**) *(semejante)* similar; **no tener c.** to be unique (**c**) *Fam (buena gente)* **su hermano es muy c.** her brother is a great guy

2 *nmf* (**a**) *(gemelo)* twin (**b**) *Fam (amigo)* pal, *US* buddy; **se fue al bar con sus cuates** he went to the bar with his pals; **pásate por casa, c.** come round to my place (**c**) *Fam (persona) (hombre)* guy, *Br* bloke; *(mujer)* woman; **el tren venía repleto de cuates** the train was full of people (**d**) *(par)* **¿dónde está el c. de mi zapato?** where's my other shoe?

cuaternario, -a *Geol* 1 *adj* Quaternary
2 *nm* **el Cuaternario** the Quaternary (era)

cuatrerear *vt RP (ganado)* to rustle, to steal; *(caballos)* to steal

cuatrero, -a *nm,f (de caballos)* horse thief; *(de ganado)* cattle rustler

cuatricromía *nf Imprenta* four-colour process

cuatrienal *adj* four-year, *Formal* quadrennial

cuatrienio *nm* four-year period; **el c. 1994-1997** the four years from 1994 to 1997

cuatrillizo, -a *nm,f* quadruplet, quad

cuatrimestral *adj* **(a)** *(en frecuencia)* four-monthly **(b)** *(en duración)* four-month, lasting four months; *Educ* **asignatura c.** = four-month course in a given subject

cuatrimestre *nm* (period of) four months; **las previsiones económicas para el primer c. del año** the economic forecast for the first four months of the year

cuatrimotor 1 *adj* four-engined
2 *nm* four-engined plane

cuatripartito, -a *adj* four-part

cuatro 1 *núm* four; EXPR *Méx Fam* **meter las c.** *(meter la pata)* to (really) put one's foot in it; EXPR *Méx Fam* **ponerle** *o* **tenderle a alguien un c.** to set a trap for sb ►► ***c. por c.*** *(todoterreno)* four-wheel drive (vehicle); *ver también* **tres**
2 *adj (poco)* a few; **hace c. días** a few days ago; *Fam* **cuando lo vea le voy a decir c. cosas** when I see him I'm going to give him a piece of my mind; *Fam* **c. gatos** hardly a soul; *Fam* **éramos c. gatos** there were only a handful of us; **cayeron c. gotas** there were a few spots of rain; EXPR **más de c.: más de c. querrían tu trabajo** quite a few people would like your job, there's no shortage of people who'd like your job; EXPR **proclamar algo a los c. vientos** to shout sth from the rooftops ►► *Méx Fam* ***c. lámparas*** *(persona)* four-eyes; *Fam* ***c. latas*** *(coche)* Renault 4; *Fam* ***c. ojos*** four-eyes
3 *nm* **(a)** *(en remo)* ***c. con timonel*** coxed four; ***c. sin timonel*** coxless four **(b)** *Carib (guitarra)* = four-stringed guitar

cuatrocientos, -as *núm* four hundred; *ver también* **treinta**

Cuauhtémoc *n pr* Cuauhtemoc (1500-25), last Aztec king of Mexico, executed by Cortes

Cuba *n* Cuba; EXPR *Fam* **más se perdió en C.** it's not the end of the world

cuba *nf* **(a)** *(para vino)* barrel, cask; EXPR *Fam* **estar como una c.** to be legless *o* blind drunk **(b)** *(en camión)* tank **(c)** *(de alto horno)* blast-furnace shaft **(d)** *Col (hijo menor)* youngest child

cubalibre *nm (de ron)* rum and cola; *(de ginebra)* gin and cola

cubano, -a 1 *adj* Cuban
2 *nm,f* Cuban

cubata *nm Fam (de ron)* rum and cola; *(de ginebra)* gin and cola

cubero *nm* EXPR **a ojo de buen c.** roughly

cubertera *nf RP (cajón)* cutlery drawer; *(bandeja)* cutlery tray

cubertería *nf* (set of) cutlery; **una c. de plata** a set *o* canteen of silver cutlery

cubeta *nf* **(a)** *(balde, cubo)* bucket, pail **(b)** *(recipiente rectangular)* tray **(c)** *(de barómetro)* bulb **(d)** *(cubitera)* ice (cube) tray **(e)** *Geol* basin, basin fold

cubetera *nf CSur, Perú* ice (cube) tray

cubicaje *nm Aut* cubic *o* cylinder capacity; **una moto de gran c.** a motorbike with a big *o* powerful engine

cubicar [59] *vt* **(a)** *Mat* to cube **(b)** *(habitación, árbol)* = to determine the volume or capacity of

cúbico, -a *adj* **(a)** *(con forma de cubo)* cubic **(b)** *(metro, centímetro)* cubic; **cincuenta metros cúbicos** fifty cubic metres

cubierta *nf* **(a)** *(de mesa, cama)* cover ►► ***c. vegetal*** vegetation **(b)** *(de libro, revista)* cover **(c)** *(de neumático)* tyre **(d)** *(de barco)* deck ►► ***c. inferior*** lower deck; ***c. de popa*** poop deck; ***c. de proa*** foredeck; ***c. superior*** upper deck

cubierto, -a 1 *participio ver* **cubrir**
2 *adj* **(a)** *(tapado, recubierto)* covered (**de** with); **estar a c.** *(protegido)* to be under cover; *(con saldo acreedor)* to be in the black; **durmieron a c.** they slept with a roof over their heads; **ponerse a c.** to take cover **(b)** *(cielo)* overcast **(c)** *(vacante)* filled
3 *nm* **(a)** *(pieza de cubertería)* piece of cutlery; **cubiertos** cutlery; **mis cubiertos están sucios** my knife and fork (and spoon) are dirty **(b)** *(para cada persona)* place setting; **pon un c. más en la mesa** set another place at (the) table **(c)** *(comida)* set menu

cubil *nm* **(a)** *(de animales)* den, lair **(b)** *(de personas)* poky room

cubilete *nm* **(a)** *(en juegos)* cup **(b)** *(molde)* mould

cubismo *nm* cubism

cubista 1 *adj* cubist
2 *nmf* cubist

cubitera *nf* **(a)** *(bandeja)* ice (cube) tray **(b)** *(cubo)* ice bucket

cubito *nm (de hielo)* ice cube ►► ***c. de caldo*** stock cube

cúbito *nm Anat* ulna

cubo *nm* **(a)** *(recipiente)* bucket ►► ***c. de la basura*** *(en la cocina) Br* rubbish bin, *US* garbage can; *(en la calle) Br* rubbish *o* litter bin, *US* garbage can; ***c. de la ropa (sucia)*** laundry basket
(b) *(figura)* cube ►► ***c. de caldo*** stock cube
(c) *Mat* cube; **elevar al c.** to cube; **3 elevado al c.** 3 cubed; **¿cuál es el c. de 9?** what's the cube of 9?, what's 9 cubed?
(d) *(de rueda)* hub
(e) *(de bayoneta)* socket, holder
(f) *(de molino)* millpond
(g) *(torreón)* round tower

cubrecama *nm* bedspread

cubreobjetos *nm inv* slide cover

cubrimiento *nm* covering

cubrir 1 *vt* **(a)** *(tapar, recubrir)* to cover (**con** with); **cubrió la moto con una lona** he covered the motorbike with a tarpaulin; **cubrieron la pared con una mano de pintura** they gave the wall a coat of paint; **c. algo de algo** to cover sth with *o* in sth; **c. a alguien de insultos/alabanzas** to heap insults/praise on sb; **Ana cubrió de besos a su padre** Ana covered her father with kisses
(b) *(proteger)* to protect; **esta póliza nos cubre contra cualquier accidente** this policy covers us against all accidents
(c) *(a policía, soldado)* to cover; **c. la retirada** to cover the retreat
(d) *(ocultar)* to cover up, to hide
(e) *(puesto, vacante)* to fill; **hay veinte solicitudes para c. tres plazas** there are twenty applications for three jobs
(f) *(gastos)* to cover; **el presupuesto no cubre todos los gastos** the budget doesn't cover all the expenses; **c. gastos** *(exactamente)* to break even
(g) *(noticia)* to cover; **cubrió la guerra del Golfo** he covered the Gulf War
(h) *(recorrer)* to cover; **el ganador cubrió los 100 metros en 9 segundos** the winner did the 100 metres in 9 seconds
(i) *(el macho a la hembra)* **c. a** to mate with
(j) *Dep (marcar)* to cover; **se encarga de c. la banda derecha** he covers the right wing
2 cubrirse *vpr* **(a)** *(taparse)* to become covered (**de** with); EXPR **cubrirse las espaldas** to cover oneself; EXPR **cubrirse de gloria** *(triunfar)* to cover oneself in *o* with glory; *Irónico* to land oneself in it; EXPR *muy Fam* **se ha cubierto de mierda** he's made a complete *Br* arse *o US* ass of himself
(b) *(protegerse)* to shelter (**de** from)
(c) *(con sombrero)* to put one's hat on
(d) *(con ropa)* to cover oneself (**de** with)
(e) *(cielo)* to cloud over

cuca *nf* **(a)** *Esp Fam (peseta)* peseta **(b)** *Chile (ave)* = type of heron **(c)** *Col, Ven Vulg (vulva)* pussy, *Br* fanny

cucamonas *nfpl Fam* sweet talk

cucaña *nf* greasy pole

cucaracha *nf* cockroach

cucarrón *nm Am* beetle

cucha *nf RP* kennel; *Fam* **¡a la c.!** *(a niño)* off to bed!

cuchara *nf* **(a)** *(para comer)* spoon; EXPR *Fam* **meter la c.** to stick one's oar in ►► ***c. de café*** coffee spoon; ***c. de madera*** wooden spoon; **la c. de madera** *(en rugby)* the wooden spoon; ***c. de palo*** wooden spoon; ***c. sopera*** soup spoon **(b)** *(cucharada)* spoonful **(c)** *(de grúa, pala)* bucket, scoop **(d)** *(ave)* shoveler **(e)** *Am (de albañil)* trowel

cucharada *nf* spoonful ►► ***c. colmada*** heaped spoonful; ***c. rasa*** level spoonful; ***c. sopera*** tablespoonful

cucharadita *nf* teaspoon, teaspoonful

cucharilla, *Am* **cucharita** *nf* **(a)** *(cuchara)* teaspoon ►► ***c. de café*** teaspoon; ***c. de moka*** coffee spoon **(b)** *(para pescar)* spinner

cucharón *nm* ladle

cuché *adj* **papel c.** coated (magazine) paper

cucheta *nf RP Náut* berth

cuchichear *vi* to whisper

cuchicheo *nm* whispering

cuchilla *nf* **(a)** *(de guillotina)* blade **(b)** *(de carnicero)* cleaver **(c) c. (de afeitar)** razor blade **(d)** *(de navaja, espada)* blade **(e)** *Am (de montañas)* range (of hills) **(f)** *Andes, Carib (cortaplumas)* pocketknife

cuchillada *nf* **(a)** *(golpe)* stab; **dar una c. a alguien** to stab sb; **la emprendieron a cuchilladas con él** they started stabbing him **(b)** *(herida)* stab wound

cuchillería *nf* **(a)** *(oficio)* cutlery, knifemaking **(b)** *(taller)* cutler's shop

cuchillero, -a *nm,f (persona)* cutler

cuchillo *nm* (a) *(instrumento)* knife; EXPR **pasar a c.** to put to the sword ▸▸ ***c. de cocina*** kitchen knife; ***c. eléctrico*** electric carving knife; ***c. de monte*** hunting knife; ***c. del pan*** bread knife; ***c. de trinchar*** carving knife (b) *(en vestido)* gore (c) *Arquit* truss

cuchipanda *nf Fam* blow-out

cuchitril *nm* hovel

cuchufleta *nf Fam* joke; **estar de c.** to be joking

cuchumbí *nm* kinkajou, honey bear

cuclillas: en cuclillas *loc adv* squatting; **ponerse en c.** to squat (down)

cuclillo *nm* cuckoo

cuco, -a 1 *adj Fam* (a) *(bonito)* pretty (b) *Esp (astuto)* crafty, canny; **el muy c. nos ha conseguido engañar a todos** the crafty devil managed to take us all in

2 *nm* (a) *(ave)* cuckoo (b) *Esp (astuto)* crafty devil (c) *CSur (personaje imaginario)* bogeyman

cucos *nmpl Col (braga)* panties, *Br* knickers

cucú *nm* (a) *(canto)* cuckoo (b) *(reloj)* cuckoo clock

cucufato *nm* (a) *Bol, Perú (beato)* sanctimonious person (b) *CSur Fam (chiflado)* loony, nut

cucurucho *nm* (a) *(de papel)* paper cone; **un c. de palomitas** a paper cone filled with popcorn (b) *(para helado)* cornet, cone (c) *(gorro)* pointed hat

cudú *nm* kudu

cueca *nf* = Chilean national dance

cuece *ver* **cocer**

cuelga *nf* (a) *(de frutas)* = bunch of fruit hung out to dry (b) *(regalo)* birthday present

cuelgo *etc ver* **colgar**

cuelgue *nm Fam* (a) *(por la droga)* high; **el c. le durará varias horas** the high will last several hours, he'll be high for several hours

(b) *(enamoramiento)* **tiene un c. total por Sofía** he's absolutely crazy about Sofía, he's totally hooked on Sofía

(c) *(frustración)* drag; **¡que c. si nos tenemos que quedarnos en casa este fin de semana!** what a drag if we have to stay in this weekend!

(d) *Informát* crash

cuellicorto, -a *adj* short-necked

cuellilargo, -a *adj* long-necked

cuello *nm* (a) *(de persona, animal)* neck; **al c.** around one's neck; **le cortaron el c.** they cut *o* slit his throat; EXPR **estar con el agua** *o* **la soga al c.** to be in deep water *o* deep trouble; EXPR **estar hasta el c. de algo** to be up to one's eyes in sth; EXPR **jugarse el c.: me juego el c. a que no lo hace** I bet you anything you like he doesn't do it; EXPR **salvar el c.** to save one's skin

(b) *(de prendas)* collar; EXPR **habla para el c. de la camisa** she mumbles ▸▸ ***c. alto*** turtleneck, *Br* polo neck; *RP* ***c. a la base*** round neck; *RP* ***c. bebé*** Peter Pan collar; ***c. de cisne*** turtleneck, *Br* polo neck; *RP* ***c. palomita*** wing collar; ***c. de pico*** V-neck; ***c. redondo*** round neck; *Am* ***c. tortuga*** turtleneck, *Br* polo neck; *RP* ***c. volcado*** cowl neck; ***c. vuelto*** polo neck

(c) *(de botella)* neck ▸▸ *Fig* ***c. de botella*** bottleneck

(d) *Anat* ***c. uterino*** cervix; ***c. del útero*** cervix

cuelo *etc ver* **colar**

cuenca *nf* (a) *(de río, mar)* basin; **la c. del Amazonas** the Amazon basin ▸▸ ***c. hidrográfica*** *(de río)* river basin; ***c. oceánica*** oceanic basin; ***c. sedimentaria*** sedimentary basin (b) *(del ojo)* (eye) socket (c) *(región minera)* **c. (minera)** mining area *o* region

cuenco *nm* (a) *(recipiente)* bowl; *(de barro)* earthenware bowl (b) *(concavidad)* hollow; **llevaba las fresas en el c. de la mano** she carried the strawberries in her cupped hands

CUENTA 1 *ver* **contar**

2 *nf* (a) *(acción de contar)* count; *(cálculo)* sum; **el niño está aprendiendo a hacer cuentas** the child is learning to do sums; **voy a hacer cuentas de los gastos** I'm going to tot up *o* work out what we've spent; **vamos a echar cuentas de cuánto te debo** let's work out how much I owe you; **espera un momento, que saco la c.** wait a minute, I'll tot it up for you; **¿está llevando alguien la c.?** is anyone keeping count?; **he perdido la c., tendré que empezar de nuevo** I've lost count, I'll have to start again; EXPR *Fam* **hacer las cuentas de la lechera** to count one's chickens before they are hatched; EXPR *Fam* **hacer las cuentas del Gran Capitán** to be overoptimistic in one's calculations; EXPR *Fam* **hacer la c. de la vieja** to count on one's fingers ▸▸ ***c. atrás*** countdown

(b) *(depósito de dinero)* account; **abrir/cerrar una c.** to open/close an account; **abónelo/cárguelo en mi c., por favor** please credit/debit *o* charge it to my account; **me han abonado el sueldo en c.** they've paid my wages into my account; **he cargado el recibo en tu c.** I've charged the bill to your account; **ingresó el cheque en su c.** she paid the cheque into her account; **póngalo en mi c.** put it on my account ▸▸ ***c. abierta*** active account; ***c. acreedora*** credit account; *Esp* ***c. de ahorros*** savings account; *Esp* ***c. de ahorro vivienda*** = tax-exempt savings account used for paying deposit on a house; ***c. bancaria*** bank account; ***c. de caja*** cash account; ***c. comercial*** business account; ***c. conjunta*** joint account; ***c. corriente*** *Br* current account, *US* checking account; ***c. de crédito*** = current account with an overdraft facility; ***c. de depósito*** deposit account; ***c. deudora*** overdrawn account; ***c. de explotación*** operating statement; ***c. de giros*** giro account; ***c. indistinta*** joint account; ***c. de inversiones*** investment account; ***c. de pérdidas y ganancias*** profit and loss account; ***c. a plazo fijo*** deposit account; ***c. de resultados*** profit and loss account; ***c. transitoria*** suspense account; ***c. a la vista*** instant access account; *Esp* ***c. vivienda*** = tax-exempt savings account used for paying deposit on a house

(c) **cuentas** *(ingresos y gastos)* accounts; **las cuentas de esta empresa no son nada transparentes** this company's books *o* accounts are not very transparent; **él se encarga de las cuentas de la casa** he deals with the financial side of things in their household; **llevar las cuentas** to keep the books

(d) *(factura)* bill; *(en restaurante)* *Br* bill, *US* check; **la c. del supermercado/teléfono** the shopping/phone bill; **¡la c., por favor!** could I have the *Br* bill *o US* check, please?; **le pedí la c. al camarero** I asked the waiter for the *Br* bill *o US* check; **domiciliar una c.** to pay an account by direct debit; **pagar 10 euros a c.** to pay 10 euros down; **cuentas por cobrar/pagar** accounts receivable/payable; **pasar la c.** to send the bill; **tarde o temprano te pasará la c. de los favores que te ha hecho** sooner or later she'll want something in return for *o* she'll call in the favours she's done for you ▸▸ ***c. de gastos*** expenditure account; ***c. pendiente*** outstanding account; **tengo unas cuentas pendientes con él** I've a few scores to settle with him

(e) *Com (cliente, negocio)* account; **se encarga de las grandes cuentas de la empresa** she looks after the company's most important accounts

(f) *Informát* account ▸▸ ***c. con acceso telefónico*** dial-up account; ***c. de correo (electrónico)*** e-mail account; ***c. por línea conmutada*** dial-up account

(g) *(obligación, cuidado)* responsibility; **esa tarea es c. mía** that task is my responsibility; **el vino corre de mi c.** the wine's on me; **déjalo de mi c.** leave it to me; **investigaré esto por mi c., no me fío de la policía** I'll look into this matter myself, I don't trust the police; **lo tendrás que hacer por tu c., nadie te va ayudar** you'll have to do it yourself *o* on your own, no one's going to help you; **cualquier daño al vehículo corre por c. del conductor** the driver is liable for any damage to the vehicle; **tomas esa decisión por tu c. y riesgo, yo no te apoyo** on your head be it, I don't agree with your decision; **por su c. y riesgo decidió aprobar la operación** he decided to approve the operation without consulting anyone; **por la c. que le trae, más vale que llegue pronto** if he's got any sense at all, he'll arrive early; **lo haré bien, por la c. que me trae** I'm going to have to do it well, there's a lot riding on it; **trabajar por c. propia/ajena** to be self-employed/an employee; **ha crecido el número de trabajadores por c. propia** the number of self-employed has risen

(h) *(explicación, justificación)* **dar c. de algo** to give a report on sth; **no tengo por qué dar cuentas de mis acciones a nadie** I don't have to explain myself *o* answer to anybody; **no tengo por qué rendirle cuentas de mi vida privada** I don't have to explain to her what I do in my private life; **el jefe nos convocó para darnos cuentas de la situación** the boss called us in to explain the situation to us; **pedir cuentas a alguien** to call sb to account; **rendir cuentas de algo ante alguien** to give an account of sth to sb; **en resumidas cuentas, el futuro es prometedor** in short, the future looks good; **¿a c. de qué?** why on earth?, for what earthly reason?

(i) *(cálculos, planes)* **no entra en mis cuentas cambiarme de casa** I'm not planning to move house; **ese gasto no entraba en nuestras cuentas** we hadn't reckoned with that expense

(j) *(consideración)* **tener en c. algo** to bear sth in mind; **ten paciencia, ten en c. que es nuevo en el trabajo** be patient, you have to remember that *o* bear in mind that he's new to the job; **eso, sin tener en c. el dinero que hemos perdido ya** without, of course, taking into account *o* counting the money we've lost so far; **un factor a tener en c. es la reacción del público** one factor that has to be taken into account *o* borne in mind is the public's reaction; **habida c. de** considering; **habida c. de todo esto...** bearing all this in mind...; **habida c. de que...** bearing in mind that...

(k) *(de collar, rosario)* bead

(l) EXPR **ajustar** *o* **arreglar cuentas: ¡ya le ajustaré** *o* **arreglaré las cuentas cuando le vea!** I'll get my own back on him next time I see him!; **caer en la c.: ¡ahora caigo en la c.!** now I see *o* understand!; **no cayó en la c. de su error hasta una semana después** she didn't realize her mistake until a week later; **caí en la c. de que había que hacer algo** I realized that something had to be done; **dar c. de: en menos de cinco minutos dio c. de todos los pasteles** it took him less than five minutes to account for *o* polish off all the cakes; **dieron c. del rival con gran facilidad** they easily disposed of the opposition; **darse c. de algo** to realize sth; **lo hice sin darme c.** I did it without realizing; **¿te das c.?, ya te dije que no era ella** you see, I told you it wasn't her; **no se dio c. de que necesitaba ayuda** she didn't realize that she needed help; **no sé si te habrás dado c., pero parece muy nervioso** I don't know if you've noticed, but he seems very nervous; **es muy insensible, no se da c. de nada** he's very insensitive, he never notices *o* picks up what's going on; **¿te das c.? no me ha dado las gracias** can you believe it? he didn't even say thank you; **a fin de cuentas: no te preocupes, a fin de cuentas es mi problema** don't you worry about it, after all, it's my problem; **más de la c.: bebí más de la c.** I had one too many, I had too much to drink; **siempre habla más de la c.** he always talks too much, he always has to open his mouth; **salir a c.: sale a c. comprar las patatas en sacos de 10 kilos** it works out cheaper to buy potatoes in 10 kilo sacks; **salir de cuentas, estar fuera de cuentas** to be due (to give birth)

---

cuentacorrentista *nmf Br* current account holder, *US* checking account holder

cuentagotas *nm inv* dropper; EXPR **a** *o* **con c.: los espectadores fueron entrando a c.** the spectators trickled in; **nos han ido dando la subvención a c.** they've been giving us the grant money in dribs and drabs

cuentahílos *nm inv Imprenta* linen tester

cuentakilómetros *nm inv Aut* (a) *(de distancia recorrida) Br* ≃ mileometer, *US* ≃ odometer (b) *(de velocidad)* speedometer

cuentapropista *nmf Am (trabajador autónomo)* self-employed person

cuentarrevoluciones *nm inv Aut* tachometer, rev counter

cuentear *vi Am Fam* to gossip

cuentero, -a *Am Fam* 1 *adj* (a) *(chismoso)* gossipy (b) *(mentiroso)* **es muy c.** he's always telling fibs
2 *nm,f* (a) *(chismoso)* gossip, gossipmonger (b) *(mentiroso)* fibber

cuentista 1 *adj Fam (mentiroso)* **no seas c.** don't tell fibs
2 *nmf* (a) *(escritor)* short story writer (b) *Fam (mentiroso)* fibber; **es un c., se cayó él solo, yo no lo toqué** he's telling fibs *o* he's fibbing, he fell by himself, I never touched him

cuentitis *nf inv Fam* **lo del dolor de cabeza es c.** he just pretended to have a headache

cuento 1 *ver* **contar**
2 *nm* (a) *(narración)* short story; *(fábula)* tale; **un libro de cuentos** a storybook; **contar un c.** to tell a story; EXPR **venir a c.** to be relevant; **sin venir a c.** for no reason at all; **y eso, ¿a c. de qué?** what's all this in aid of?; EXPR *Fam* **ser el c. de nunca acabar** to be a never-ending story *o* an endless business; EXPR *Fam* **ir con el c. a alguien** to go and tell sb; EXPR **aplicarse el c.: ¿ves lo que le ha pasado? pues aplícate el c.** see what happened to him? well you just have a good think about that ►► ***c. de hadas*** fairy tale; *Fam* ***el c. de la lechera:*** **es el c. de la lechera** that's pie in the sky
(b) *Fam (mentira, exageración)* story, lie; **¡déjate de cuentos!** stop making things up!, don't give me that!; **ése tiene mucho c.** he's always putting it on; **venir con cuentos** to tell fibs *o* stories; EXPR *CSur* **hacerle a alguien el c. del tío** to pull a scam on sb, to con sb; EXPR *Esp* **tener más c. que Calleja** to be a big fibber; EXPR **vivir del c.** to live by one's wits ►► ***c. chino:*** **lo del final del mundo es c. chino** that stuff about the end of the world is a load of *Br* rubbish *o US* bull; **a mí no me vengas con cuentos chinos** don't give me that (*Br* rubbish *o US* bull)

cuerazo *nm* (a) *Am (golpe)* lash (b) EXPR *muy Fam* **ser un c.** *Méx (hombre o mujer)* to be hot stuff *o* really something; *Chile (mujer)* to be a real stunner *o* looker

cuerda *nf* (a) *(para atar) (fina)* string; *(más gruesa)* rope; **saltar a la c.** to skip; **los ataron con cuerdas** they tied them up with ropes; *Ven Fam* **una c. de idiotas/cobardes** a bunch of idiots/cowards; EXPR **estar contra las cuerdas** to be on the ropes; EXPR *Fam* **tirar de la c.** to go too far, to push it ►► ***c. floja*** tightrope; EXPR **estar en la c. floja** to be hanging by a thread
(b) *(de instrumento)* string; **instrumento de c.** string instrument
(c) *(en orquesta)* string section, strings; **la sección de c.** the string section, the strings; **cuarteto de c.** string quartet
(d) *(de mecanismo)* spring; **un juguete de c.** a clockwork toy; **un reloj de c.** a wind-up watch; **dar c. a** *(reloj, juguete)* to wind up; EXPR *Fam* **dar c. a alguien** *(para que siga hablando)* to encourage sb; EXPR *Fam* **este conferenciante todavía tiene c. para rato** this speaker looks like he's going to go on for a while yet; **el partido en el poder tiene c. para rato** the party in power looks as if it will be there for some time to come
(e) *Geom* chord
(f) *Anat* ***cuerdas vocales*** vocal cords
(g) *Dep (de pista)* curb; **una pista con una c. de 400 metros** a 400 metre track
(h) *(en gimnasia rítmica)* rope
(i) EXPR **bajo c.** secretly, in an underhand manner; *Fam* **de la misma c.** of the same opinion; **tocar a alguien la c. sensible** to strike a chord with sb
(j) *ver también* **cuerdo**

cuerdamente *adv* sensibly

cuerdo, -a 1 *adj* (a) *(sano de juicio)* sane; **no está c.** he's insane, he's not in his right mind (b) *(sensato)* sensible
2 *nm,f* sane person

cuereada *nf Ven (zurra)* beating, thrashing

cuerear *vt* (a) *Am (azotar)* to whip, to lash (b) *RP (desollar)* to skin, to flay (c) *RP Fam (criticar)* to slate

cuerina *nf RP* imitation leather

cuerito *nm Am* washer

cueriza *nf Andes Fam* beating, leathering

cuerna *nf* (a) *(vasija)* drinking horn (b) *(cornamenta)* horns; *(de ciervo)* antlers (c) *(trompa)* hunting horn

cuernavaquense 1 *adj* of/from Cuernavaca *(Mexico)*
2 *nmf* person from Cuernavaca *(Mexico)*

cuernavaqueño, -a *adj, nm,f* = **cuernavaquense**

cuerno *nm* (a) *(de animal)* horn; *(de ciervo)* antler; *(de caracol)* horn, feeler; EXPR *Fam* **¡y un c.!** you must be joking!, in your dreams!; EXPR *Fam* **mandar al c. a alguien** to send sb packing; EXPR *Fam* **irse al c.: nuestros planes se fueron al c.** our plans fell through; **¡vete al c.!** get lost!; EXPR *Fam* **poner (los) cuernos a alguien** to be unfaithful to sb; *(a un hombre)* to cuckold sb; EXPR *Fam* **oler a c. quemado** to smell/sound/look fishy; EXPR *Fam* **saber a c. quemado: sus comentarios me supieron a c. quemado** I thought his comments were really off; EXPR **romperse los cuernos** to break one's back ►► ***el c. de la abundancia*** the horn of plenty, cornucopia; *Geog* ***el C. de África*** the Horn of Africa
(b) *(de bicicleta)* bar end
(c) *(instrumento)* horn
(d) *Méx (bizcocho)* croissant

cuero 1 *adj Méx Fam* gorgeous; **Jaime está bien c.** Jaime's dead gorgeous
2 *nm* (a) *(en el animal)* skin; EXPR **en cueros (vivos)** stark naked; EXPR *CSur Fam* **no le da el c. para eso** *(no tiene fuerzas)* he's not up to it; *(no tiene dinero)* he can't afford it; EXPR *CSur Fam* **sacarle el c. a alguien** to tear sb to pieces ►► ***c. cabelludo*** scalp
(b) *(material)* leather; *(curtido)* hide; **una chamarra de c.** a leather jacket ►► *Am* ***c. de chancho*** pigskin; *CSur* ***c. de cocodrilo*** crocodile skin; *Am* ***c. de foca*** sealskin; *Am* ***c. de lobo marino*** sealskin
(c) *(para vino)* wineskin
(d) *(balón)* ball
(e) *Ecuad, Ven Pey (mujer) Br* bird, *US* broad
(f) *Am (látigo)* whip; **arrimar** *o* **dar c. a alguien** to whip sb, to flog sb
(g) *Méx Fam* EXPR **ser un c.** to be gorgeous

cuerpear *vi RP (esquivar)* to swerve, to dodge

CUERPO *nm* (a) *(objeto material)* body ►► *Astron* ***c. celeste*** heavenly body; *Quím* ***c. compuesto*** compound; ***c. extraño*** foreign body; *Náut* ***c. muerto*** mooring buoy; *Fís* ***c. negro*** black body; *Quím* ***c. simple*** element
(b) *(de persona, animal)* body; **el c. humano** the human body; **tiene un c. estupendo** he's got a great body; **¡c. a tierra!** hit the ground!, get down!; **luchar c. a c.** to fight hand-to-hand; **de medio c.** *(retrato, espejo)* half-length; **de c. entero** *(retrato, espejo)* full-length; EXPR *Fam* **a c. (gentil)** without a coat on; EXPR **a c. descubierto** *o* **limpio: se enfrentaron a c. descubierto** *o* **limpio** they fought each other hand-to-hand; EXPR **dar con el c. en la tierra** to fall down; EXPR *Fam* **dejar mal c.: la comida le dejó muy mal c.** the meal disagreed with him; **la discusión con mi padre me dejó muy mal c.** the argument with my father left a bad taste in my mouth; EXPR **en c. y alma: se dedicó en c. y alma a ayudar a los necesitados** he devoted himself

body and soul to helping the poor; **se entrega en c. y alma a la empresa** she gives her all for the company; EXPR *Fam* **demasiado para el c.: ¡esta película es demasiado para el c.!** this movie *o Br* film is just great!, *Br* this film is the business!; EXPR **echarse algo al c.: se echó al c. dos botellas de vino** he downed two bottles of wine; EXPR *Fam Euf* **hacer de c.** to relieve oneself; EXPR **le metieron el miedo en el c.** they filled her with fear, they scared her stiff; EXPR *Fam* **pedir algo el c.: esta noche el c. me pide bailar** I'm in the mood for dancing tonight; **no bebas más si no te lo pide el c.** don't have any more to drink if you don't feel like it; EXPR *Am Fam* **sacarle el c. a algo** to get out of (doing) sth; EXPR *RP Fam* **suelto de c.** as cool *o* nice as you like *o* please; **a pesar de todo lo que le dije, después se me acercó muy suelto de c.** despite everything I said to him, he came up to me later as cool *o* nice as you like; EXPR *Fam* **tratar a alguien a c. de rey** to treat sb like royalty *o* like a king; EXPR *Fam* **vivir a c. de rey** to live like a king

(**c**) *(tronco)* trunk

(**d**) *(parte principal)* main body; **el c. del libro** the main part *o* body of the book

(**e**) *(densidad, consistencia)* thickness; **la tela de este vestido tiene mucho c.** this dress is made from a very heavy cloth; **un vino con mucho c.** a full-bodied wine; **dar c. a** *(salsa)* to thicken; **tomar c.: mover hasta que la mezcla tome c.** stir until the mixture thickens; **están tomando c. los rumores de remodelación del gobierno** the rumoured cabinet reshuffle is beginning to look like a distinct possibility; **el proyecto de nuevo aeropuerto va tomando c.** the new airport project is taking shape

(**f**) *(cadáver)* corpse; **de c. presente** (lying) in state

(**g**) *(corporación consular, militar)* corps; **el agente fue expulsado del c. por indisciplina** the policeman was thrown out of the force for indiscipline ►► ***c. de baile*** dance company; ***c. de bomberos*** *Br* fire brigade, *US* fire department; ***c. diplomático*** diplomatic corps; ***c. del ejército*** army corps; ***c. expedicionario*** expeditionary force; ***c. médico*** medical corps; ***c. de policía*** police force

(**h**) *(conjunto de informaciones)* body; **c. de doctrina** body of ideas, doctrine; **c. legal** body of legislation

(**i**) *(parte de armario, edificio)* section

(**j**) *(parte de vestido)* body, bodice

(**k**) *(en carreras)* length; **el caballo ganó por cuatro cuerpos** the horse won by four lengths

(**l**) *Der* ***c. del delito*** corpus delicti, = evidence of a crime or means of perpetrating it

(**m**) *Imprenta* point; **letra de c. diez** ten point font

cuerudo, -a *adj Andes, CAm* (**a**) *(caballo)* slow, sluggish (**b**) *(persona)* shameless, brazen

cuervo *nm (término genérico)* crow; *(especie)* raven ►► ***c. marino*** cormorant; ***c. merendero*** rook

cuesco *nm* (**a**) *Fam (pedo)* (loud) fart (**b**) *Chile* stone *(of fruit)*

cuesta 1 *ver* **costar**

2 *nf (pendiente)* slope; **una calle/un camino en c.** a street/road on a hill; **c. arriba** uphill; EXPR *Fam* **hacerse c. arriba: trabajar los viernes se me hace muy c. arriba** I find working on Fridays heavy going; *también Fig* **c. abajo** downhill ►► ***la c. de enero*** = lack of money in January due to Christmas spending

3 a cuestas *loc adv* on one's back, over one's shoulders; **tuvo que llevar los sacos a cuestas** he had to carry the sacks on his back *o* over his shoulders; **lleva a cuestas la enfermedad de su marido** she has to bear the burden of her husband's illness

cuestación *nf* collection *(for charity)*

cuestión *nf* (**a**) *(pregunta)* question

(**b**) *(problema)* problem; **no es c. de tamaño sino de peso** it's a question *o* matter of weight not size

(**c**) *(asunto)* matter, issue; **una c. de honor/de principios** a matter of honour/principle; **los investigadores quieren llegar al fondo de la c.** the investigators want to get to the bottom of the matter; **la c. es que no he tenido tiempo** the thing is, I haven't had time; **en c.** in question; **el candidato en c. es venezolano** the candidate in question is Venezuelan; **tenemos que discutir el tema en c.** we must discuss the matter at hand; **en c. de** *(en materia de)* as regards; **en c. de una hora** in no more than an hour; **el edificio se hundió en c. de segundos** the building collapsed in a matter of seconds; **es c. de un par de días** it is a matter of a couple of days; **ya acabo, es c. de cinco minutos** I'm nearly finished, I'll only be five minutes; **es c. de trabajar más** it's a question of working harder; **será c. de ir yéndose** it's time we were on our way; **será c. de esforzarnos más** we'll just have to work harder; **no es c. de que el abuelo se ponga a hacerlo** there's no need for grandad to have to do it

(**d**) **poner algo en c.** to call sth into question

cuestionable *adj* questionable, debatable

cuestionar 1 *vt* to question

2 cuestionarse *vpr (plantearse)* to think about; *(dudar de)* to wonder about

cuestionario *nm* questionnaire

cuesto *etc ver* **costar**

cuestor *nm Hist* quaestor

cuete 1 *adj Méx Fam Br* pissed, *US* loaded; **estar c.** *Br* to be pissed, *US* to be loaded; **había un viejo c.** there was an old man there who was *Br* pissed *o US* loaded

2 *nm* (**a**) *Am (nave espacial)* (space) rocket; EXPR **salir como c.: se levantaron muy tarde, así que salieron como c.** they got up very late, so they had to shoot off

(**b**) *Am* **cuetes** *(fuegos artificiales)* fireworks

(**c**) *Méx, RP Fam (borrachera)* **estar en c.** *Br* to be pissed, *US* to be loaded; **tenía un c. muy grande** he was totally *Br* pissed *o US* loaded

(**d**) *RP Fam (pedo)* (loud) fart

(**e**) *Chile Fam (puñetazo)* **le dio un c. en la boca** he socked him one in the mouth

(**f**) *Perú Fam (pistola)* shooter, *US* piece

3 al cuete *loc adv RP Fam (inútilmente)* for nothing

cueva *nf* cave

cuévano *nm* pannier, large basket

cuezo 1 *ver* **cocer**

2 *nm Fam* EXPR **meter el c.** *(meter la pata)* to put one's foot in it, to drop a clanger; *(ser un entrometido)* to poke *o* stick one's nose in

cuico, -a 1 *adj Chile Fam* tasteless, tacky

2 *nm,f* (**a**) *Méx Fam (policía)* cop (**b**) *Chile Fam (hortera)* **es un c.** he has no taste, he's really tacky

CUIDADO, -A 1 *adj* **una edición cuidada** a beautifully produced edition; **es muy c. con su trabajo** he takes great care over his work

2 *nm* (**a**) *(precaución)* care; **con c.** *(con esmero)* carefully; *(con cautela)* cautiously; **hazlo con mucho c.** do it very carefully; **puso mucho c. en sus respuestas** she chose her answers very carefully; **ten c. o te harás daño** be careful or you'll hurt yourself; **ten c. al cruzar la calle** take care when crossing the road; **ten c. con el perro, que muerde** mind the dog doesn't bite you; **tuve c. de no decirles nada** I took care *o* was careful not to tell them anything; **hace las cosas sin ningún c.** she does things in a careless way; **¡c. con la cabeza!** mind your head!; **c. con el perro** *(en letrero)* beware of the dog; **c. con el escalón** *(en letrero)* mind the step; **(mucho) c. con lo que vas contando por ahí** you'd better watch what you tell people; EXPR **tener** *o* **traer sin c.: me tiene** *o* **trae sin c. lo que hagas** I couldn't care less what you do

(**b**) *(atención) (de personas, objetos)* care; **el c. de la piel/del cabello** skin/hair care; **todo sobre el c. de su gato** everything you need to know about looking after *o* caring for your cat; **el c. de la casa es mi responsabilidad** I'm responsible for doing the housework; **estoy al c. de la contabilidad de la empresa** I'm in charge of the company's accounts; **yo trabajo mientras él está al c. de los niños** I work while he looks after the children; **se quedó al c. de la casa mientras sus padres estaban de viaje** she looked after the house while her parents were away; **dejamos al perro al c. de los vecinos** we left the dog with the neighbours

(**c**) **cuidados** *(asistencia médica)* care; **a pesar de los cuidados recibidos, falleció en el lugar del accidente** despite the medical attention she received, she died at the scene of the accident; **necesitará los cuidados de un veterinario** it will need to be looked at by a vet ►► ***cuidados intensivos*** intensive care

(**d**) *(miedo, preocupación)* concern, apprehension; **no pases c.** *o Am* **pierde c., que me encargo yo de todo** don't worry, I'll take care of everything

(**e**) *(uso enfático)* **¡c. que es listo este niño!** this boy's really clever!; **¡c. que llegas a ser tonto!** you can be really stupid sometimes!

3 de cuidado *loc adj* **tuvo un accidente de c.** she had a nasty accident; **fue un accidente/una fiesta de (mucho) c.** it was some accident/party; **es un niño de c., es muy travieso** he's a little terror, he's so naughty; **es un criminal de c.** he's a dangerous criminal

4 *interj* careful!, look out!; **¡c.!, ¡mira antes de cruzar!** (be) careful, you should look before you cross the road!

cuidador, -ora *nm,f* (**a**) *(de anciano)* carer; *(de niño)* childminder; **el c. de los monos** the person who looks after the monkeys (**b**) *(de parque)* attendant (**c**) *Dep* trainer

cuidadosamente *adv* carefully

cuidadoso, -a *adj* careful; **es muy cuidadosa con lo que hace** she's very careful *o* takes a lot of care in what she does; **sé muy c. con lo que dices** be very careful what you say, you'd better watch what you say; **es muy poco c.** he's very careless, he doesn't take much care

cuidar **1** *vt* (**a**) *(niño, animal, casa)* to look after; *(enfermo)* to look after, to care for; *(plantas)* to look after, to tend

(**b**) *(aspecto)* to take care over; *(ropa)* to take care of, to look after; **si no cuidas esos zapatos no te durarán** if you don't look after those shoes they won't last; **cuida mucho su aspecto físico** he takes a lot of care over his appearance

(**c**) *(detalles)* to pay attention to; **tienes que c. más la ortografía** you must pay more attention to *o* take more care over your spelling

2 *vi* **c. de** to look after; **cuida de que no lo haga** make sure she doesn't do it; **cuida de que no se caiga** (be) careful he doesn't fall

3 cuidarse *vpr* (**a**) *(uno mismo)* to take care of oneself, to look after oneself; **está tan joven porque se cuida mucho** she looks so young because she takes good care of herself; **si no se cuida más acabará mal** he'll come to a bad end if he doesn't watch out; **¡cuídate!** take care!

(**b**) *(tener cuidado)* **cuidarse de algo** to be careful about sth, to take care about sth; **se cuidó mucho de que no la vieran** she took great care to ensure that no one saw her; **cuídate mucho de contarles que te lo dije yo** don't you dare tell them I told you, you'd better not tell them I told you

(**c**) *(ocuparse)* to take care of, to look after; **cuídate de tus asuntos** mind your own business

cuitas *nfpl Literario* cares, woes

cuitlacoche *nm CAm, Méx* corn smut, = edible fungus which grows on maize

cuja *nf Am (cama)* bed

culamen *nm Esp Fam Br* bum, *US* butt

culantrillo *nm* maidenhair (fern)

culantro *nm* coriander

culata *nf* (**a**) *(de arma)* butt (**b**) *(de motor)* cylinder head (**c**) *(de animal)* hindquarters

culatazo *nm* (**a**) *(golpe)* blow with a rifle butt; **le dieron un c.** they hit him with a rifle butt (**b**) *(retroceso)* recoil, kick

culé *Fam Dep* **1** *adj* = relating to Barcelona Football Club

2 *nmf* = supporter of Barcelona Football Club

culebra *nf* (**a**) *(reptil)* snake (**b**) *Ven Fam (telenovela)* TV soap (opera)

culebrear *vi* to zigzag

culebrón *nm Esp Fam* (**a**) *(televisivo)* soap opera (**b**) *(historia interminable)* saga; **el c. de las pensiones** the pensions saga

culera *nf (remiendo)* patch

culero, -a **1** *adj Méx muy Fam* (**a**) *(cobarde)* yellow-belly (**b**) *(traidor)* scumbag, *Br* git

2 *nm,f Fam (de drogas)* = person who smuggles drugs by hiding them in their rectum

culiacanense **1** *adj* of/from Culiacán *(Mexico)*

2 *nmf* person from Culiacán *(Mexico)*

culinario, -a *adj* culinary

culmen *nm* high point; **en el c. de su carrera** at the peak of her career

culminación *nf* (**a**) *(llegada al clímax)* culmination; **el premio supone la c. de su carrera como escritor** the prize is the culmination *o* crowning moment of his career as a writer; **este triunfo es la c. de un sueño** this victory is the fulfilment of a dream (**b**) *(terminación)* end; **ganaron el partido que suponía la c. del torneo** they won the final game of the tournament (**c**) *Astron* culmination

culminante *adj* culminating; **momento** *o* **punto c.** high point

culminar **1** *vt (terminar)* **las elecciones culminaron la transición democrática en el país** the elections completed the country's transition to democracy; **con el galardón culminó cincuenta años de dedicación a la medicina** the award was the culmination *o* crowning moment of fifty years dedicated to medicine

2 *vi* (**a**) *(terminar)* to end, to culminate; **las negociaciones culminaron con un acuerdo** the negotiations ended in (the signing of) an agreement (**b**) *(llegar al clímax)* **la tensión culminaba en el último capítulo del libro** the tension came to a head *o* reached its climax in the final chapter of the book (**c**) *Astron* to culminate

culo *nm*

> Note that in some regions of Latin America this term is vulgar in register.

Fam (**a**) *(nalgas) Br* bum, *US* butt; **le di una patada en el c.** I gave him a kick up the backside, *US* I kicked his butt; **c. firme** firm buttocks; **c. respingón** pert bottom; **¡vaya c. tiene!** she's got a nice *Br* arse *o US* ass!; **me caí de c.** I fell flat on my backside *o Br* bum; *Fig* **cuando vi su moto me caí de c.** I was flabbergasted *o Br* gobsmacked when I saw his motorbike; EXPR **con el c. al aire: su confesión dejó a sus compinches con el c. al aire** his confession left his accomplices up the creek; EXPR *muy Fam* **vive en el c. del mundo** she lives *Br* bloody *o US* goddamn miles from anywhere; EXPR *muy Fam* **estoy hasta el c. de trabajo** I've got so much *Br* bloody *o US* goddamn work to do!; EXPR *muy Fam* **ir de c.: el equipo va de c. este año** the team's doing shit *o* crap this year; **con esa estrategia vas de c.** that strategy's a load of crap; **esta última semana hemos ido de c., sin parar ni un minuto** this last week has been a *Br* bloody *o US* goddamn nightmare, we haven't had a minute's rest; EXPR *muy Fam* **lamer el c.: siempre está lamiéndole el c. al jefe** he's always licking the boss's *Br* arse *o US* ass, he's always sucking up to *o* brown-nosing the boss; EXPR *muy Fam* **éste no se moja el c. por nadie** he wouldn't lift a *Br* bloody *o US* goddamn finger to help anyone; EXPR *muy Fam* **partirse el c.: con este tío te partes el c.** that guy's a *Br* bloody *o US* goddamn hoot; EXPR *muy Fam* **pensar con el c.: ¡qué estupideces dice!, parece que piense con el c.** what a load of nonsense, she's just talking out of her *Br* arse *o US* ass; EXPR *muy Fam* **perder el c.: ha perdido el c. por una compañera de clase** he's madly in love with a girl in his class; EXPR *muy Fam* **ponerse hasta el c.: nos pusimos hasta el c. de cerveza** we got wasted on beer; EXPR **ser un c. inquieto** *o* **de mal asiento** *(enredador)* to be fidgety; *(errante)* to be a restless soul

(**b**) *(ano) Br* arsehole, *US* asshole; EXPR *RP muy Fam* **como el c.: me siento como el c.** I feel like shit; **esa muchacha me cae como el c.** I hate that girl's *Br* bloody *o US* goddamn guts; EXPR *Vulg* **dar por el c. a alguien** *(sodomizar)* to give it to sb up the *Br* arse *o US* ass; EXPR *Esp Vulg* **¡que te den por c.!, ¡vete a tomar por c.!** fuck off!; **no quiere ayudar – ¡que le den por c.!** he doesn't want to help – well fuck him, then!; EXPR *Esp Vulg* **tomar por c.: le pedí dinero prestado, y me mandó a tomar por c.** I asked her to lend me some money and she told me where to stick it *o* to fuck off; **estoy harto, voy a mandar todo a tomar por c.** fuck this *o Br* fuck this for a lark, I've had enough of it; **todo lo que habíamos hecho se fue a tomar por c. con el apagón** the power cut completely fucked up everything we'd done; EXPR *Esp muy Fam* **está a tomar por c.** it's *Br* bloody *o US* goddamn miles from anywhere; EXPR *Vulg* **meterse algo por el c.: te puedes meter tu propuesta por el c.** you can stick your proposal up your *Br* arse *o US* ass

(**c**) *(de vaso, botella)* bottom; *Esp* **gafas de c. de vaso,** *Am* **lentes de c. de botella** pebble-glasses

(**d**) *(líquido)* **queda un c. de vino** there's a drop (or two) of wine left in the bottom

(**e**) *(zurcido)* **me has hecho un c. de pollo en el calcetín** you've made a mess of darning my sock

(**f**) *RP Fam (suerte)* **me gané la lotería – ¡qué c.!** I won the lottery – you lucky *o Br* jammy thing!

culombio *nm Fís* coulomb

culón, -ona *adj Fam* **ser muy c.** to have a big backside, to be broad in the beam

culote *nm* cycling shorts

culpa *nf* (**a**) *(responsabilidad)* **un sentimiento de c.** a feeling of guilt; **todos tenemos algo de c.** we are all partly to blame; **echar la c. a alguien (de)** to blame sb (for); **por c. de** because of; **tener la c. de algo** to be to blame for sth; **la lluvia tuvo la c. del accidente** the rain was what caused the accident; **¿qué c. tengo yo de que te hayas caído?** it's hardly my fault you fell over, is it?; *Fam* **yo no tengo la c. de que seas tan distraído** it's not my fault you're so absent-minded

(**b**) *Rel* **culpas** sins; **el que esté libre de c. que tire la primera piedra** let him who is without sin cast the first stone

culpabilidad *nf* guilt

culpabilizar [14] **1** *vt* to blame; **c. a alguien (de)** *(atribuir la culpa)* to blame sb (for); *(acusar)* to accuse sb (of)

2 culpabilizarse *vpr* to accept the blame (**de** for)

culpable **1** *adj* guilty; **declarar c. a alguien** to find sb guilty; **declararse c. (de algo)** to plead guilty (to sth); **es c. de varios robos** he is responsible for *o* has committed several robberies; **me siento c. de lo que pasó** I feel responsible for what has happened

2 *nmf* culprit; **la policía busca al c. del robo** the police are looking for the person responsible for the robbery; **tú eres el c.** you're to blame

culpar **1** *vt* to blame; **c. a alguien (de)** *(atribuir la culpa)* to blame sb (for); *(acusar)* to accuse sb (of)

2 culparse *vpr* to blame oneself; **se culpa de lo que ocurrió** she blames herself for what happened

culteranismo *nm Lit* = highly elaborate literary style typical of 17th century Spanish writers such as Góngora

culterano, -a *Lit* 1 *adj* = related to "culteranismo"
2 *nm,f* = exponent of "culteranismo"

cultismo *nm* literary *o* learned word

cultivable *adj* cultivable, arable

cultivado, -a *adj* (a) *(terreno)* cultivated (b) *(persona)* cultivated, cultured

cultivador, -ora *nm,f (persona)* grower; **c. de naranjas** orange grower; **c. de trigo** wheat farmer

cultivadora *nf (máquina)* cultivator

cultivar 1 *vt* (a) *(tierra)* to farm, to cultivate; *(plantas)* to grow; **dejó sus tierras sin c.** he left his land uncultivated (b) *(amistad, inteligencia)* to cultivate (c) *(arte)* to practise (d) *(germen)* to culture
2 **cultivarse** *vpr (persona)* to improve oneself

cultivo *nm* (a) *(de tierra)* farming, cultivation; *(de plantas)* growing
(b) *(plantación)* crop ►► ***c. extensivo*** extensive farming; ***c. hidropónico*** hydroponics; ***c. intensivo*** intensive farming; ***c. de regadío*** irrigated crop; ***c. de secano*** dry-farmed crop; ***c. de subsistencia*** subsistence crop; ***c. transgénico*** GM crop
(c) *(de gérmenes)* culture ►► ***c. celular*** cell culture; ***c. de tejidos*** tissue culture
(d) *(de las artes)* promotion

culto, -a 1 *adj* (a) *(persona)* cultured, educated; *(estilo)* refined (b) *(palabra)* literary, learned
2 *nm* (a) *(devoción)* worship (a of); **el c. al diablo** devil worship; **el c. al cuerpo** the cult of the body beautiful; **c. a la personalidad** personality cult; **rendir c. a** *(dios)* to worship; *(persona, valentía)* to pay homage *o* tribute to; **un grupo/una película de c.** a cult movie/group (b) *(religión)* cult

cultura *nf* (a) *(de sociedad)* culture; **es especialista en la c. inca** she is a specialist in Inca culture ►► ***c. empresarial*** corporate culture; ***c. de masas*** mass culture; ***la c. del ocio*** leisure culture
(b) *(sabiduría)* **tiene mucha c.** she's very educated, she's very cultured; **tiene mucha c. teatral** she knows a lot about the theatre ►► ***c. general*** general knowledge; ***la c. popular*** popular culture

cultural *adj* cultural; **una actividad c.** a cultural activity; **la diversidad c.** cultural diversity

culturalmente *adv* culturally

cultureta *nmf Fam Pey* culture vulture

culturismo *nm* body-building

culturista *nmf* bodybuilder

culturización *nf* **la c. de los indígenas por los conquistadores** the way in which the conquistadors taught their culture to the indigenous population

culturizar [14] 1 *vt* **c. a las masas** to educate the masses
2 **culturizarse** *vpr* to educate oneself

cuma *Chile Fam* 1 *adj* terribly tacky
2 *nmf* **ser un c.** to be terribly tacky

cumanés, -esa, cumanagoto, -a 1 *adj* of/from Cumaná *(Venezuela)*
2 *nm,f* person from Cumaná *(Venezuela)*

cumbia *nf* cumbia

cumbiamba *nf Col, Perú (fiesta)* "cumbia" party

cumbiambero, -a 1 *adj* (a) *(bailarín)* = related to "cumbia" dancer (b) *Col, Perú Fam (de persona alegre)* fun-loving
2 *nm,f* (a) *(bailarín)* "cumbia" dancer (b) *Col, Perú Fam (persona alegre)* party animal, fun-loving person

cumbre 1 *adj inv* **el momento c. de su carrera** the peak *o* high point of his career; **su obra c.** her most outstanding work
2 *nf* (a) *(de montaña)* summit (b) *(punto culminante)* peak, high point (c) *(política)* summit (conference) ►► ***la C. de la Tierra*** the Earth Summit

cumbrera *nf (cumbre)* summit

cum laude *loc adj* cum laude; **obtuvo un sobresaliente c.** she passed summa cum laude

cumple *nm Fam* (a) *(aniversario)* birthday (b) *(fiesta)* birthday party *o* do

cumpleaños *nm inv* (a) *(aniversario)* birthday; **¡feliz c.!** happy birthday!; **¡c. feliz!** *(en canción)* happy birthday to you! (b) *(fiesta)* birthday party

cumplido, -a 1 *adj* (a) *(completo, lleno)* full, complete (b) *(cortés)* polite, courteous; **es muy c. con todo el mundo** he's very polite to everyone
2 *nm* compliment; **hacer un c. a alguien** to pay sb a compliment; **lo dijo como c.** she said it out of politeness

cumplidor, -ora 1 *adj* reliable, dependable
2 *nm,f* reliable *o* dependable person

cumplimentar *vt* (a) *(saludar)* to greet (b) *(felicitar)* to congratulate (c) *(cumplir) (orden)* to carry out; *(contrato)* to fulfil (d) *(impreso)* to fill in *o* out

cumplimiento *nm* (a) *(de un deber)* performance, carrying out; *(de contrato, obligaciones)* fulfilment; *(de la ley)* observance; *(de órdenes)* carrying out; **murió en el c. de su deber** he died in the course of *o* while carrying out his duty; **en c. del artículo 34** in compliance with article 34; **una disposición de obligado c.** a compulsory regulation
(b) *(de promesa)* fulfilment; *(de amenaza)* carrying out; **lo hizo en c. de una promesa** he did it to keep a promise
(c) *(de condena)* **comenzará el c. de su condena el próximo lunes** he will begin serving his sentence next Monday; **durante el c. del servicio militar** while he was doing his military service; **han solicitado el c. íntegro de las condenas para los narcotraficantes** they have demanded that the drug traffickers serve their full sentences
(d) *(de plazo)* expiry
(e) *(de objetivo)* achievement, fulfilment

CUMPLIR 1 *vt* (a) *(deber)* to do, to carry out, to perform; *(contrato, obligaciones)* to fulfil; *(ley)* to observe; *(orden)* to carry out; **c. los mandamientos** to keep *o* obey the commandments; **cumplí las instrucciones al pie de la letra** I followed the instructions to the letter; **esta máquina cumple todos los requisitos técnicos** this machine complies with *o* meets all the technical requirements; **los candidatos deben c. los siguientes requisitos** the candidates must meet *o* satisfy the following requirements; **los que no cumplan las normas serán sancionados** anyone failing to comply with *o* abide by the rules will be punished; **el ministerio no está cumpliendo su cometido de fomentar el empleo** the ministry is failing in its task of creating jobs, the ministry is not carrying out its brief of creating jobs
(b) *(promesa)* to keep; *(amenaza)* to carry out; **cumplió su deseo de subir al Aconcagua** she fulfilled her wish of climbing Aconcagua
(c) *(años)* to reach; **mañana cumplo veinte años** I'm twenty *o* it's my twentieth birthday tomorrow; **cumple años la próxima semana** it's her birthday next week, she has her birthday next week; **cuando cumplas los dieciocho te regalaremos una moto** we'll give you a motorbike when you're eighteen *o* for your eighteenth (birthday); **¡que cumplas muchos más!** many happy returns!; **tal y como está de salud, el abuelo no cumplirá los ochenta** in his current state of health, it's unlikely that grandad will see his eightieth birthday; **la Feria del Automóvil cumple este año su décimo aniversario** the Motor Show celebrates its tenth anniversary this year
(d) *(condena)* to serve; *(servicio militar)* to do
2 *vi* (a) *(plazo, garantía)* to expire; **el plazo de matriculación ya ha cumplido** the deadline for registration is already up *o* has already expired
(b) *(realizar el deber)* to do one's duty; **c. con alguien** to do one's duty by sb; **c. con el deber** to do one's duty; **c. con la palabra** to keep one's word; **yo me limito a c. con mi trabajo** I'm just doing my job
(c) *(con norma, condición)* to comply; **este producto no cumple con la normativa europea** this product doesn't comply with *o* meet European standards; **varios países cumplen con los requisitos para acceder al mercado único** several countries fulfil the criteria *o* meet the terms for joining the single market
(d) *(por cortesía)* **cumpla usted por mí** pay my respects; **lo dijo por c.** she said it because she felt she had to *o* out of politeness; **acudió a la boda por c. con su hermano** she went to the wedding out of a sense of duty to her brother; **con el ramo de flores que le enviamos ya cumplimos** I think we've done our duty *o* all that's expected of us by sending her a bunch of flowers
(e) *(servicio militar)* to do one's military service
(f) *Fam Euf (satisfacer sexualmente)* **acusó a su marido de no c.** she accused her husband of failing to fulfil his marital *o* conjugal duties
3 **cumplirse** *vpr* (a) *(hacerse realidad)* **finalmente se cumplió su deseo** finally her wish was fulfilled, she finally got her wish; **se cumplieron las predicciones y cayó una intensa tormenta** the predictions were proved right *o* came true and there was a violent storm; **se cumplieron las amenazas y una bomba estalló en el centro de la ciudad** the threats were carried out when a bomb exploded in the city centre
(b) *(plazo)* **mañana se cumple el plazo de presentación de solicitudes** the deadline for applications expires tomorrow; **el próximo año se cumple el primer centenario de su muerte** next year will be the hundredth anniversary of his death

---

cumulativo, -a *adj Der* cumulative

cúmulo *nm* (a) *(nube)* cumulus (b) *Astron* ***c. de estrellas*** star cluster; ***c. de galaxias*** galaxy cluster (c) *(de objetos)* pile, heap (d) *(de circunstancias, asuntos)* accumulation, series; **dijo un c. de tonterías** he said a lot of nonsense; **cometieron un c. de errores** they made a series of errors

cumulonimbo *nm (nube)* cumulonimbus

cuna *nf* (a) *(de niño)* cot, cradle ►► *Méx* ***c. viajera*** *Br* carrycot, *US* portacrib (b) *(de movimiento, civilización)* cradle; *(de persona)* birthplace (c) *(linaje)* **es de c. noble/humilde** he is of noble/humble birth

cundir *vi* (a) *(propagarse)* to spread; **cundió el pánico** the panic spread, there was widespread panic; **¡que no cunda el pánico!** keep calm, everyone!; **al oírse la noticia, cundió la alarma rápidamente** when people heard the news panic quickly started to spread

(b) *Esp (dar de sí) (comida, reservas)* to go a long way; *(trabajo, estudio)* to go well; **me cundió mucho el tiempo** I got a lot done; **esta pintura cunde muy poco** this paint doesn't go very far

cunear 1 *vt* to rock

2 **cunearse** *vpr* to rock, to sway

cuneiforme *adj* cuneiform

cunero, -a *adj* **candidato c.** carpetbagger

cuneta *nf* (a) *(de una carretera)* ditch (b) *(de una calle)* gutter

cunicultura *nf* rabbit-breeding

cunilinguo *nm*, **cunnilingus** *nm inv* cunnilingus

cuña *nf* (a) *(pieza)* wedge (b) *(de publicidad)* commercial break ►► ***c. informativa*** brief news item, space-filler (c) *(orinal)* bedpan (d) *Meteo* ridge, band ►► ***c. anticiclónica*** ridge *o* band of high pressure (e) *(en esquí)* snowplough; **frenar haciendo la c.** to slow down using a snowplough (f) *Andes, RP Fam (enchufe)* **tener c.** to have friends in high places

cuñado, -a *nm,f* brother-in-law, *f* sister-in-law

cuño *nm* (a) *(troquel)* die (b) *(sello, impresión)* stamp (c) EXPR **ser de nuevo c.** to be a new coinage; **un término de nuevo c.** a newly coined term; **un cargo de nuevo c.** a recently created post

cuota *nf* (a) *(contribución) (a entidad, club)* membership fee, subscription; *(a Hacienda)* tax (payment); *(a sindicato)* dues ►► ***c. de abono*** *(de teléfono)* line rental; ***c. de admisión*** admission fee; *Informát* ***c. de conexión*** set-up charge *o* fee; ***c. de ingreso*** entrance fee; ***c. de inscripción*** *(en congreso)* registration fee; ***cuotas de la seguridad social*** social security contributions, *Br* ≃ National Insurance contributions

(b) *Am (plazo)* instalment; **comprar en cuotas** to buy on *Br* hire purchase *o US* an installment plan; **pagar en cuotas** to pay in instalments ►► ***c. inicial*** down payment

(c) *(cupo)* quota; *UE* **las cuotas lácteas/pesqueras** milk/fishing quotas ►► *Econ* ***c. de mercado*** market share; ***c. de pantalla*** *(en televisión)* audience share; **la c. de pantalla del cine español ha crecido hasta el 10 por ciento** the number of Spanish movies being shown has risen to 10 percent; ***c. de producción*** production quota

(d) *Méx (importe)* toll; **autopista de c.** *Br* toll motorway, *US* turnpike

cupe *ver* **caber**

cupé *nm* coupé

Cupido *n Mitol* Cupid

cupido *nm (representación del amor)* cupid

cupiera *etc ver* **caber**

cuplé *nm* = saucy popular song

> **Falso amigo**: El sustantivo inglés **couplet** no es la traducción del español **cuplé**. En inglés, **couplet** significa "pareado".

cupletista *nmf* "cuplé" singer

cupo 1 *ver* **caber**

2 *nm* (a) *(cantidad máxima)* quota (b) *(cantidad proporcional)* share; *(de una cosa racionada)* ration (c) *Méx, Ven (cabida)* capacity, room

cupón *nm* (a) *(vale)* coupon ►► *Fin* ***c. cero*** zero coupon (b) *(de lotería, rifa)* ticket

cuprero, -a *adj Chile* copper; **la producción cuprera** copper production

cupresácea *nf Bot* = tree of the cypress family

cúprico, -a *adj Quím* copper; **óxido/sulfato c.** copper oxide/sulphate

cuprífero, -a *adj (yacimiento)* copper; *(mineral)* copper-bearing, *Espec* cupriferous

cuprita *nf* cuprite

cuproníquel *nm* cupronickel

cuproso, -a *adj Quím* copper, *Espec* cuprous

cúpula *nf* (a) *(bóveda)* dome, cupola (b) *(mandos)* leaders; **la c. del partido** the party leadership; **la c. militar** the top-ranking officers in the armed forces, the heads of the armed forces; **el presidente ha anunciado cambios en la c. de la organización** the *Br* chairman *o US* president has announced changes at top management level in the organization (c) *Mil (torre)* turret

cupulino *nm Arquit* lantern

cuquillo *nm* cuckoo

cura[1] *nm* priest; **meterse c.** to become a priest, to enter the priesthood; EXPR *Fam Hum* **como a un c. dos pistolas: ese sombrero te sienta como a un c. dos pistolas** that hat looks awful on you ►► ***c. obrero*** worker priest; ***el c. párroco*** the parish priest

cura[2] *nf* (a) *(curación)* cure; **todavía no se ha encontrado una c. para esa enfermedad** no cure has yet been found for that disease; **tener c.** to be curable; **no tener c.** *(ser incurable)* to be incurable; *Fam (ser incorregible)* to be incorrigible ►► *Rel* ***la c. de almas*** the cure of souls

(b) *(tratamiento)* treatment, cure; **me tienen que hacer una c. en la herida** *(tratar)* I need to get this wound treated; *(con venda)* I need to get this wound dressed ►► ***c. de adelgazamiento*** diet; ***c. de descanso*** rest cure; ***c. de humildad:*** **lo que necesita es una c. de humildad** she needs bringing down a peg or two; ***c. milagrosa*** miracle cure; ***c. de reposo*** rest cure; ***c. de sueño:*** **lo que necesitas es una c. de sueño** what you need is a good sleep

(c) *Chile (borrachera)* drunkenness

curable *adj* curable

curaca *nm Hist* = chief of an adminstrative region of the Inca empire

curación *nf* (a) *(de un enfermo) (recuperación)* recovery; **te deseamos una pronta c.** get well soon, we wish you a speedy recovery (b) *(de un enfermo) (tratamiento)* treatment; **una herida de difícil c.** a wound that won't heal easily; **la c. del cáncer** cancer treatment; **tener c.** to be treatable (c) *(de alimento)* curing

curado, -a 1 *adj* (a) *(enfermo)* cured; **ya está c. de la hepatitis** he's recovered from his hepatitis; EXPR *Fam* **estar c. de espanto** to have seen it all before (b) *(alimento)* cured (c) *(pieles)* tanned (d) *Chile Fam (borracho)* sloshed

2 *nm* (a) *(de alimentos)* curing (b) *(de pieles)* tanning (c) *Méx (bebida)* = drink of flavoured "pulque"

curador, -ora *nm,f* (a) *Der* guardian (b) *RP (en museo)* curator

curadoría *nf Der* guardianship

cural *adj* **la casa c.** the priest's house, the presbytery

curalotodo *nm Fam* cure-all

curandería *nf* (a) *(medicina popular)* traditional *o* folk medicine (b) *Fam Pey (medicina falsa)* quackery

curandero, -a *nm,f* (a) *(que utiliza magia)* witch doctor; *(que utiliza remedios naturales)* traditional healer (b) *Fam Pey (médico falso)* quack

curanto *nm Chile* = stew of meat and shellfish

curar 1 *vt* (a) *(sanar)* to cure (b) *(herida) (tratar)* to treat; *(con vendas)* to dress (c) *(alimentos)* to cure (d) *(pieles)* to tan (e) *RP (mate)* to cure, to season *(before using for the first time)*

2 *vi (enfermo)* to get well, to recover; *(herida)* to heal up

3 **curarse** *vpr* (a) *(sanar)* to recover (**de** from); EXPR **curarse de espanto: se curó de espanto durante la guerra** after living through the war, nothing could shock him; EXPR **curarse en salud** to play safe, to cover one's back (b) *(alimento)* to cure

curare *nm* curare

Curasao *n* Curaçao

curasao *nm* curaçao

curativo, -a *adj* curative

curato *nm (parroquia)* parish

curazao [kura'sao] *nm* curaçao

cúrcuma *nf* turmeric

curcuncho, -a *Andes Fam* 1 *adj* hunchbacked

2 *nm* (a) *(joroba)* hump (b) *(jorobado)* hunchback

curda *Fam* 1 *adj RP (de alcohol)* plastered

2 *nmf RP (borracho)* boozer

3 *nf* (a) *Esp, RP* **agarrar** *o Esp* **coger una c.** to get plastered; *RP* **estar en c.** to be plastered (b) *Ven (bebida)* booze

curdo, -a 1 *adj* (a) *(de Curdistán)* Kurdish (b) *Ven Fam (de alcohol o drogas)* off one's face; **siempre lo ven c.** whenever they see him he's off his face

2 *nm,f (persona)* Kurd

3 *nm (lengua)* Kurdish

cureña *nf* gun carriage

curia *nf* (a) *Hist* curia (b) *Rel* curia ►► ***la c. pontificia*** the papal curia; ***la c. romana*** the papal curia (c) *Der (abogacía)* legal profession

curiara *nf Ven* dugout canoe

curio *nm Quím* curium

curiosamente *adv* curiously, strangely; **c., el hielo no se fundió** curiously *o* strangely enough, the ice didn't melt

curiosear 1 *vi* (a) *(fisgonear)* to nose around (b) *(en tienda)* to browse round; **estuvo curioseando por el almacén** he was browsing around the store

2 *vt (libros, revistas)* to browse through

curiosidad *nf* (a) *(deseo de saber)* curiosity; **sentir** *o* **tener c. por** to be curious about; **te lo pregunto por c.** I'm just asking out of curiosity (b) *(cosa rara)* curiosity, curio; **trajo varias curiosidades de sus viajes** he brought back several interesting things *o* objects from his travels (c) *(limpieza)* neatness, tidiness

curioso, -a 1 *adj* (a) *(por saber, averiguar)* curious, inquisitive (b) *(raro)* odd, strange; **iqué c.!** how odd!, how strange!; **lo más c. es que...** the oddest *o* strangest thing is that...; **es c. que...** it's odd *o* strange that... (c) *(limpio)* neat, tidy; *(cuidadoso)* careful (d) *(fisgón)* inquisitive, nosy

2 *nm,f* (a) *(espectador)* onlooker (b) *(fisgón)* inquisitive *o* nosy person

curita *nf Am Br* (sticking-)plaster, *US* Band-aid®

curling ['kurlin] *nm Dep* curling

currante *Esp Fam* 1 *adj* **es muy c.** she's a hard worker; **hoy está muy c.** he's working very hard today

2 *nmf* worker

currar *Fam* 1 *vt* (a) *Esp (pegar)* to beat up (b) *RP (estafar)* to rip off

2 *vi Esp (trabajar)* to work

3 **currarse** *vpr Esp* **se curró mucho el examen** she really worked hard for the exam; **me curré muchísimo ese dibujo** I slaved over that drawing

curre *nm Esp Fam* work

currelar *vi Esp Fam* to work

currele, currelo *nm Esp Fam* work

curricular *adj Educ* curriculum; **diseño c.** curriculum design, design of the curriculum

currículo *nm* (a) *(currículum vitae)* curriculum vitae, *Br* CV, *US* résumé (b) *Educ* curriculum

currículum (vitae) [ku'rrikulum('bite)] (*pl* **currícula** *o* **currículums (vitae)**) *nm* curriculum vitae, *Br* CV, *US* résumé

currito, -a *nm,f Esp Fam* (ordinary) worker; **no soy más que un c.** I'm just a menial employee

curro *nm Fam* (a) *Esp (tarea, actividad, práctica)* work; **tengo mucho c. que hacer** I've got a lot of work to do (b) *Esp (empleo)* job; **buscar/encontrar c.** to look for/find work *o* a job; **estoy sin c.** I've got no job, I haven't got a job (c) *Esp (lugar)* work; **ir al c.** to go to work; **¿quieres que pase a recogerte al c.?** do you want me to pick you up from your work? (d) *RP (timo)* swindle, rip-off

curruca *nf* ***c. capirotada*** blackcap; ***c. carrasqueña*** subalpine warbler; ***c. mosquitera*** garden warbler; ***c. rabilarga*** Dartford warbler; ***c. zarcera*** whitethroat; ***c. zarcerilla*** lesser whitethroat

currusco *nm (punta de pan)* end *(of baguette)*

currutaco, -a *adj Andes, Guat, Ven (rechoncho)* tubby

curry *nm (especias)* curry powder; **pollo al c.** chicken curry

cursar *vt* (a) *(estudiar)* to study; **c. estudios de medicina** to study medicine; **cursaba segundo** she was in her second year (b) *(enviar)* to send (c) *(ordenar)* to give, to issue (d) *(tramitar)* to submit

cursi 1 *adj* (a) *(vestido, canción)* tacky, *Br* naff; **se puso un sombrero muy c.** she put on this really tacky *o Br* naff hat; **a mi abuela le gustan esas cortinas tan cursis** my grandmother likes those twee curtains

(b) *(modales, persona)* **es un escritor muy c.** he's such a corny writer; **camina de una manera muy c.** she has a very affected way of walking; **no seas c., cómete el plátano con las manos** don't be so prissy, eat the banana with your hands

2 *nmf* affected person; **es un c.** he's so affected; **no seas un c., cómete el plátano con las manos** don't be so prissy, eat the banana with your hands

cursilada *nf* **ser una c.** *(acto, comportamiento)* to be affected; *(comentario)* to be stupid *o Br* naff; *(decoración, objeto)* to be tacky *o Br* naff; **esas cortinas que le gustan a mi abuela son una c.** those curtains my grandmother likes are really twee; **es una c. comer el plátano con cuchillo y tenedor** it's really prissy to eat bananas with a knife and fork

cursilería *nf* (a) **ser una c.** *(acto, comportamiento)* to be affected; *(comentario)* to be stupid *o Br* naff; *(decoración, objeto)* to be tacky *o Br* naff; **esas cortinas que le gustan a mi abuela son una c.** those curtains my grandmother likes are really twee; **es una c. comer el plátano con cuchillo y tenedor** it's really prissy to eat bananas with a knife and fork

(b) *(cualidad)* tackiness, *Br* naffness

cursillista *nmf* student *(on a short course)*

cursillo *nm* (a) *(curso)* short course; **un c. de socorrismo/de esquí** a first-aid/skiing course; **un c. de formación** a training course (b) *(conferencias)* series of lectures

cursiva 1 *adj (letra)* italic; **en c.** in italics

2 *nf* italics

cursivo, -a *adj* cursive

curso *nm* (a) *(año académico)* year; **¿en qué c. estás?** what year are you in? ►► ***c. académico*** academic year; ***c. escolar*** school year

(b) *(lecciones)* course; **un c. de inglés/informática** an English/computing course ►► ***c. por correspondencia*** correspondence course; ***c. intensivo*** crash course; *Educ* ***c. puente*** = intermediate course which enables a university student to change degree courses

(c) *(grupo de alumnos)* class

(d) *(texto, manual)* textbook

(e) *(evolución) (de acontecimientos)* course; *(de la economía)* trend; **el c. de la enfermedad es positivo** he has taken a turn for the better; **dar c. a algo** *(dar rienda suelta)* to give free rein to sth; *(tramitar)* to process sth, to deal with sth; **en el c. de una semana ha habido tres accidentes** there have been three accidents in the course of a week; **la situación comenzará a mejorar en el c. de un año** the situation will begin to improve within a year; **en c.** *(mes, año)* current; *(trabajo)* in progress; **seguir su c.** to go on, to continue

(f) *(circulación)* **billete/moneda de c. legal** legal tender

(g) *(de río)* course; **el c. alto/medio** the upper/middle reaches

cursor *nm Informát* cursor

curtido, -a 1 *adj* (a) *(cuero)* tanned (b) *(piel)* tanned, weather-beaten (c) *(experimentado)* seasoned

2 *nm* (a) *(acción)* tanning (b) *(piel)* tanned hide

curtidor, -ora *nm,f* tanner

curtiduría *nf* tannery

curtiembre *nf Andes, RP* tannery

curtir 1 *vt* (a) *(cuero)* to tan (b) *(piel)* to weather (c) *(persona)* to harden

2 **curtirse** *vpr* (a) *(piel)* to become tanned *o* weather-beaten (b) *(persona)* to become hardened

curucutear *vi Ven Fam* to root about *o* around, to rummage about *o* around; **está siempre curucuteando en mis cajones** she's always rooting *o* rummaging about in my drawers

curul *nf Col, Méx* seat *(in parliament)*

curva *nf* (a) *(línea, forma, gráfico)* curve; **una c. de temperatura/producción** a temperature/production curve ►► ***c. de aprendizaje*** learning curve; *Fam* ***c. de la felicidad*** *(barriga)* paunch; ***c. de nivel*** contour line

(b) *(de carretera, río)* bend; **una carretera con muchas curvas** a winding road; **c. abierta** slight *o* shallow bend; **c. cerrada** sharp bend; **tomar** *o Esp* **coger una c.** to take a bend

(c) **curvas** *(de mujer)* curves

curvado, -a *adj (forma)* curved; *(espalda)* bent

curvar 1 *vt (doblar)* to bend; *(espalda, cejas)* to arch

2 **curvarse** *vpr* to become bent, to bend; **la estantería se curvó por el peso** the shelves bent *o* sagged under the weight

curvatura *nf* curvature

curvilíneo, -a *adj* (a) *(en geometría)* curved (b) *(silueta del cuerpo)* curvaceous

curvo, -a *adj (forma)* curved; *(doblado)* bent

cuscurro *nm* (a) *(pan frito)* crouton (b) *(punta de pan)* end *(of baguette)*

cuscús *nm inv* couscous

cuscuta *nf* common dodder

cusicusí, cusicusá *adv Andes, RP Fam* so-so

cusma *nf Andes* = sleeveless woollen shirt worn by Indians

cúspide *nf* (a) *(de montaña)* summit, top (b) *(de torre)* top (c) *(de organización)* leadership (d) *(apogeo)* peak, height; **en la c. de su carrera** at the peak of her career (e) *Geom* apex

custodia 1 *nf* (a) *(de cosas)* safekeeping; **se encargan de la c. de las joyas de la corona** they are the keepers of the crown jewels; **el edificio está bajo c. de dos policías** the building is guarded by two police officers

(b) *(de personas)* custody; **se disputan la c. de los hijos** they are in dispute over the custody of the children; **estar bajo la c. de** to be in the custody of; **la policía mantiene a los detenidos bajo c.** those arrested are in police custody
(c) *Rel* monstrance
(d) *Chile (consigna) Br* left-luggage office, *US* checkroom
(e) *RP (escolta)* bodyguard; **integra la c. del presidente** he's a member of the president's bodyguard
2 *nmf RP (guardia)* guard

custodiar *vt* **(a)** *(vigilar)* to guard **(b)** *(proteger)* to look after

custodio *nm* guard

cutáneo, -a *adj* skin; **enfermedad cutánea** skin disease; **erupción cutánea** rash

cúter *(pl* **cúters** *o* **cúter)** *nm* **(a)** *(cuchilla)* craft knife, Stanley knife® **(b)** *(barco)* cutter

cutí *nm* ticking

cutícula *nf* cuticle

cutirreacción *nf Med* skin test

cutis *nm inv* skin, complexion; **tiene el c. muy fino** she has very delicate skin; **una crema para el c.** a skin cream; **hacer a alguien una limpieza de c.** to cleanse sb's skin

cutre *adj Esp Fam* **(a)** *(de bajo precio, calidad)* cheap and nasty, crummy **(b)** *(sórdido)* shabby, dingy; **un garito c.** a sleazy nightclub **(c)** *(tacaño)* tight, stingy

cutrería, cutrez *nf Esp Fam* **(a)** *(cosa de bajo precio, calidad)* **me regaló una c.** he gave me a cheap and nasty present **(b)** *(sordidez)* shabbiness, dinginess; **este hotel es una c.** this hotel is a dump

cuy *(pl* **cuyes)** *nm Andes, RP (conejillo de Indias)* guinea pig

cuyo, -a *adj (posesión) (por parte de personas)* whose; *(por parte de cosas)* of which, whose; **ésos son los amigos en cuya casa nos hospedamos** those are the friends in whose house we spent the night; **ese señor, c. hijo conociste ayer** that man, whose son you met yesterday; **un equipo cuya principal estrella...** a team, the star player of which *o* whose star player...; **en c. caso** in which case

Cuzco *n* Cuzco, Cusco

cuzco *nm RP (animal)* small mongrel

cuzqueño, -a 1 *adj* of/from Cuzco *(Peru)*
2 *nm,f* person from Cuzco *(Peru)*

CV *nm* **(a)** *(abrev de* **currículum vitae)** *Br* CV, *US* résumé **(b)** *(abrev de* **caballo de vapor)** *(métrico)* CV; *(inglés)* HP

D, d

D, d [de] *nf (letra)* D, d
D (a) (*abrev de* **dama**) *(en notación de ajedrez)* Q (b) (*abrev de* **domingo**) Sun
D. (*abrev de* **don**) ≃ Mr
Da. (*abrev de* **doña**) *(casada)* ≃ Mrs; *(soltera)* ≃ Miss
dabuten, dabuti *adj Esp Fam* fantastic, ace; **nos lo pasamos d.** we had a fantastic *o* an ace time; **este vino es** *o* **está d.** this wine's great; **¿nos tomamos una copa? – ¡d., colega!** what about a drink? – sure thing, pal!
daca *nm Fam* **toma y d.** give and take
da capo *adv Mús* da capo
Dacca *n* Dacca
dacha *nf* dacha
dacio, -a *Hist* **1** *adj* Dacian
2 *nm,f* Dacian
dacrón® *nm* Dacron®
dactilar *adj* **huella d.** fingerprint
dáctilo *nm Lit* dactyl
dactilografía *nf* typing
dactilógrafo, -a *nm,f* typist
dactilología *nf* sign language
dactiloscopia *nf* study of fingerprints, *Espec* dactylography
dactiloscópico, -a *adj* fingerprint; **pruebas dactiloscópicas** fingerprint evidence
dadá *Arte* **1** *adj* Dadaist
2 *nm* Dada, Dadaism
dadaísmo *nm Arte* Dada, Dadaism
dadaísta *Arte* **1** *adj* Dadaist
2 *nmf* Dadaist
dádiva *nf Formal (regalo)* gift; *(donativo)* donation
dadivosidad *nf* generosity
dadivoso, -a *adj* generous
dado[1], -a **1** *adj* (a) *(concreto, determinado)* given; **en un momento d.** *(en el tiempo)* at a certain *o* given point
(b) *(teniendo en cuenta)* given, in view of; *Mat (en problemas, ejercicios)* given; **dadas las circunstancias, me veo obligada a dimitir** in view of the circumstances, I am forced to resign; **dada su edad** in view of *o* given his age; *Mat* **d. un punto A en el eje X...** given a point A on axis X...
(c) **ser d. a** *(ser proclive a)* to be inclined *o* given to; **los niños son muy dados a inventar historias** children are always making up stories; **es muy d. a viajar** he's a keen traveller; **somos dados a la conversación** we chat a lot
(d) *RP* **ser muy d.** *(extrovertido)* to be very outgoing
(e) EXPR *Esp Fam* **ir d.: vas d. si crees que te voy a ayudar** if you think I'm going to help you, you can think again; **con el nuevo jefe vamos dados** we're in for it with this new boss; **voy d. como no me eches una mano** if you don't give me a hand, I've had it
2 dado que *loc conj* since, seeing as; **d. que somos tan pocos, se suspende la reunión** seeing as there are so few of us here, the meeting is adjourned
dado[2] *nm* (a) *(para jugar)* dice, die; **echar** *o* **lanzar** *o* **tirar los dados** to throw the dice; **jugar a los dados** to play dice (b) *(de comida)* cube; **cortar en dados** *(patatas, zanahorias)* to dice; **una vez tostado el pan, córtelo en dados** once the bread is toasted, cut it into cubes (c) *Archit* dado
dador, -ora *nm,f* (a) *(de letra de cambio)* drawer (b) *(de carta)* bearer
daga *nf* (a) *(espada)* short sword, dagger (b) *Am (puñal)* dagger
daguerrotipia *nf* daguerreotype
daguerrotipo *nm* (a) *(aparato)* daguerreotype camera (b) *(imagen)* daguerreotype (c) *(técnica)* daguerreotype, daguerreotypy
Daguestán *n* Dagestan
daguestano, -a **1** *adj* Dagestani
2 *nm,f* Dagestani
daiquiri, *Am* **daiquirí** *nm* daiquiri
dajao *nm* mountain mullet
Dakar *n* Dakar
dal (*abrev de* **decalitro**) dal
Dalai-lama, Dalái-lama *nm* **el D.** the Dalai Lama
dalia *nf* dahlia
daliniano, -a *adj* (a) *(de Dalí)* **la obra daliniana** Dalí's works (b) *(como Dalí)* Daliesque; **tiene un estilo muy d.** she has a very Daliesque style
dalle *nm* scythe
dálmata **1** *adj* Dalmatian
2 *nmf (persona)* Dalmatian
3 *nm* (a) *(perro)* Dalmatian (b) *(antigua lengua)* Dalmatian
dalmática *nf Rel* dalmatic
dalmático, -a **1** *adj* Dalmatian
2 *nm,f* Dalmatian
daltónico, -a, daltoniano, -a **1** *adj* colour-blind
2 *nm,f* person with colour blindness; **los daltónicos** the colour-blind, colour-blind people
daltonismo *nm* colour blindness
dam (*abrev de* **decámetro**) dam
dama **1** *nf* (a) *(mujer)* lady; **su mujer es toda una d.** his wife is a real lady; **damas y caballeros** ladies and gentlemen; **primera d.** *Teatro* leading lady; *(esposa del presidente)* first lady ▸▸ ***d. de honor*** *(de novia)* bridesmaid; *(de reina)* lady-in-waiting
(b) *(en juego de damas)* king; **hacer d.** to make a king
(c) *(en ajedrez)* queen; **alfil/torre/caballo de d.** queen's bishop/rook/knight; **hacer d.** to queen a pawn
(d) *(en naipes)* queen; **la d. de corazones** the queen of hearts
(e) *Arcaico Lit (amada)* mistress
(f) ***d. de noche*** moonflower
2 damas *nfpl (juego) Br* draughts *(singular), US* checkers *(singular)*; **jugar a las damas** to play draughts ▸▸ ***damas chinas*** Chinese checkers
damajuana *nf* demijohn
damán *nm* hyrax, rock badger
damasceno, -a **1** *adj* Damascan
2 *nm,f* Damascan
Damasco *n* Damascus
damasco *nm* (a) *(tela)* damask (b) *Andes, RP (albaricoque)* apricot (c) *Andes, RP (albaricoquero)* apricot tree
damasquinado *nm* damascene
damasquinar *vt* to damascene
damasquino, -a **1** *adj* Damascan
2 *nm,f* Damascan
damero *nm* (a) *(tablero) Br* draughtboard, *US* checkerboard (b) *(pasatiempo)* double acrostic
damerograma *nm* double acrostic
damisela *nf Anticuado* damsel
damnificado, -a **1** *adj* affected, damaged; **un envío de ayuda urgente para la población damnificada por el terremoto** an urgent consignment of aid for the people affected by the earthquake
2 *nm,f* victim; **los damnificados por el huracán Mitch** the victims of hurricane Mitch
damnificar [60] *vt (cosa)* to damage; *(persona)* to harm, to injure
dan *nm (en artes marciales)* dan
dandi, dandy *nm* dandy

dandismo *nm* dandyism, foppishness

dandy = **dandi**

danés, -esa 1 *adj* Danish
2 *nm,f (persona)* Dane
3 *nm* (**a**) *(lengua)* Danish (**b**) **gran d.** *(perro)* Great Dane

danta *nf* (**a**) *(anta)* elk (**b**) *Andes, Carib, RP (tapir)* tapir

dantesco, -a *adj* (**a**) *(horroroso)* horrific, grotesque (**b**) *Lit* Dantesque, Dantean

danto *nm* (**a**) *(ave)* bare-necked umbrella bird (**b**) *CAm, Carib (tapir)* tapir

Danubio *nm* **el D.** the (River) Danube

danza *nf* (**a**) *(actividad)* dancing; **una compañía de d.** a dance company; **hacer d.** to go to dancing classes ►► ***d. clásica*** classical ballet; ***d. española*** Spanish dance; ***d. moderna*** modern dance
(**b**) *(baile)* dance ►► ***d. de guerra*** war dance; ***d. de los siete velos*** dance of the seven veils; ***d. del vientre*** belly dance
(**c**) *Lit* ***d. de la muerte*** dance of death
(**d**) EXPR **estar en d.** *(en movimiento, en actividad)* to be on the go *o* doing something; **estamos** *o* **llevamos en d. desde las cinco de la mañana** we've been on the go since five this morning; **estar metido en d.** to be up to no good

danzante 1 *adj* dancing
2 *nmf (bailarín)* dancer

danzar [14] *vi* (**a**) *(bailar)* to dance (**b**) *(ir de un sitio a otro)* to run about; **llevo todo el día danzando de acá para allá** I've been running about from one place to another all day

danzarín, -ina 1 *adj* active, lively
2 *nm,f* dancer

danzón *nm* = Cuban music and dance derived from the "habanera"

dañado, -a *adj (objeto, vehículo)* damaged

dañar 1 *vt* (**a**) *(persona)* to hurt; *(vista)* to harm, to damage; **el tabaco daña la salud** tobacco damages your health (**b**) *(pieza, objeto, edificio, carretera)* to damage; *(cosecha)* to harm, to damage; *(fruta, mercancía)* to damage, to spoil (**c**) *(prestigio, reputación)* to damage, to harm
2 **dañarse** *vpr* (**a**) *(sujeto: persona) (la espalda, la rodilla)* to injure, to hurt; **se dañó el codo jugando al squash** he hurt his elbow playing squash (**b**) *(pieza, objeto, cosecha)* to be *o* get damaged; *(fruta, mercancía)* to be *o* get damaged, to be *o* get spoilt

dañino, -a *adj* (**a**) *(sustancia, hábito, plaga)* harmful; **d. para la salud** harmful to health (**b**) *(persona)* evil; **es un tipo muy d.** he's a nasty piece of work

daño *nm* (**a**) *(dolor)* pain, hurt; **hacer d. a alguien** to hurt sb; **me hacen d. los zapatos** my shoes are hurting me; **hacerse d.** to hurt oneself; **cuidado, no te vayas a hacer d. con las tijeras** mind you don't hurt yourself with the scissors; **me hice d. en el tobillo** I hurt my ankle; **¿te has hecho d.?** have you hurt yourself?, are you hurt?
(**b**) *(perjuicio) (a algo)* damage; *(a alguien)* harm; **daños estructurales** structural damage; **los daños se calculan en miles de euros** the damage may run to thousands of euros; **daños y perjuicios** damages
(**c**) *Méx, RP Fam (mal de ojo)* evil eye

dañoso, -a *adj Der* injurious, damaging

DAR [20] 1 *vt* (**a**) *(entregar, otorgar)* to give; **d. algo a alguien** to give sth to sb, to give sb sth; **da parte de sus ingresos a los necesitados** she gives *o* donates part of her income to the poor; **dame el azúcar, por favor** could you pass *o* give me the sugar, please?; **daría cualquier cosa por saber lo que piensa** I'd give anything to know what he's thinking; **¡dámelo!** give it to me!, give me it!; **se lo di a mi hermano** I gave it to my brother
(**b**) *(pagar)* to give; *(ofrecer en pago)* to offer; **¿cuánto te dieron por la casa?** how much did they give you for the house?; **el concesionario me da 2.000 euros por la moto vieja** the dealer's offering 2,000 euros for my old motorbike; **300 dólares, ¿quién da más?** *(en subasta)* is there any advance on 300 dollars?
(**c**) *(proporcionar)* to give, to provide with; **la salsa le da un sabor muy bueno** the sauce gives it a very pleasant taste, the sauce makes it taste very nice; **este color le da un aspecto diferente a la habitación** this colour makes the room look different; **le di instrucciones de cómo llegar a casa** I gave her directions for getting to my house; **no nos dio ninguna explicación sobre su ausencia** he didn't give us *o* provide us with any explanation for his absence; **le dimos ánimos para que siguiera con su trabajo** we encouraged her to continue with her work; **su familia hizo un gran esfuerzo por darle estudios universitarios** his family went to a great deal of effort to enable him to go to university
(**d**) *(conceder)* to give; **le han dado el Premio Nobel** she has been awarded *o* given the Nobel Prize; **le dieron una beca** he was awarded *o* given a grant; **yo no le daría demasiada importancia** I wouldn't attach too much importance to it; **al final me dieron la razón** in the end they accepted that I was right; **le dieron una semana más para presentar el informe** they gave *o* allowed him one more week to hand in the report; **me dieron permiso para ir al médico** I got *o* was allowed time off work to go to the doctor; **¿da su permiso para entrar?** may I come in?; **nos dieron facilidades de pago** they offered us easy payment terms; **los médicos no le dan más de seis meses de vida** the doctors don't give him more than six months (to live); **¿qué interpretación das a este descubrimiento?** how would you interpret this discovery?
(**e**) *(decir)* **d. los buenos días** to say hello; **d. la bienvenida a alguien** to welcome sb; **le di las gracias por su ayuda** I thanked her for her help; **fuimos a darles el pésame** we went to offer them our condolences; **dale recuerdos de mi parte** give him my regards, say hello to him from me; **dale la enhorabuena** give her my congratulations; **me dio su opinión al respecto** he gave me his opinion on the matter; **¿quién le dará la noticia?** who's going to tell *o* give her the news?
(**f**) *(producir)* to give, to produce; *(frutos, flores)* to bear; *(beneficios, intereses)* to yield; **estas vacas dan mucha leche** these cows produce a lot of milk; **esta cuenta da un 5 por ciento de interés** this account offers a 5 percent interest rate, this account bears interest at 5 percent; **esta lámpara da mucha luz** this light is very bright; **le dio tres hijos** she bore him three children
(**g**) *(luz, agua, gas) (encender)* to turn *o* switch on; *(suministrar por primera vez)* to connect; *(suministrar tras un corte)* to turn back on
(**h**) *(provocar)* to give; **me da vergüenza/pena** it makes me ashamed/sad; **me da risa** it makes me laugh; **me da miedo** it frightens me; **¡me da una rabia que me traten así!** it infuriates me that they should treat me in this way!; **me dio un susto tremendo** she gave me a real fright; **el viaje me dio mucho sueño** the journey made me really sleepy; **da gusto leer un libro tan bien escrito** it's a pleasure to read such a well-written book; **los cacahuetes dan mucha sed** peanuts make you very thirsty; **este paseo me ha dado hambre** this walk has made me hungry *o* given me an appetite; **estas botas dan mucho calor** these boots are very warm
(**i**) *(fiesta, cena)* to have, to hold; **d. una cena en honor de alguien** to hold *o* give a dinner in sb's honour; **darán una recepción antes de la boda** there will be a reception before the wedding
(**j**) *(repartir) (en naipes)* to deal
(**k**) *(sujeto: reloj)* to strike; **el reloj dio las doce** the clock struck twelve
(**l**) *Cine, Teatro & TV* to show; *(concierto, interpretación)* to give; **¿qué dan esta noche en la tele? – dan una película del oeste** what's on the TV tonight? – they're showing a western *o* there's a western on; **dieron la ceremonia en directo** they broadcast the ceremony live
(**m**) *(propinar)* **le di una bofetada** I slapped him, I gave him a slap; **dio una patada a la pelota** he kicked the ball; **darle un golpe/una puñalada a alguien** to hit/stab sb
(**n**) *(untar con, aplicar)* **d. una capa de pintura al salón** to give the living room a coat of paint; **d. barniz a una silla** to varnish a chair
(**o**) *(señales, indicios)* to show; **d. pruebas de sensatez** to show good sense; **d. señales de vida** to show signs of life
(**p**) *(enseñar)* to teach; *(conferencia)* to give; **d. inglés/historia** to teach English/history; **dio una clase muy interesante** she gave a very interesting class; **mañana no daremos clase** there won't be a class tomorrow
(**q**) *Esp (recibir) (clase)* to have; **doy clases de piano con una profesora francesa** I have piano classes with a French piano teacher; **doy dos clases de francés a la semana** I have two French classes a week
(**r**) *(expresa acción)* **d. un grito** to give a cry; **d. un suspiro** to sigh, to give a sigh; **d. un vistazo a** to have a look at; **dio lectura a los resultados de la elección** she read out the election results; **cuando se enteró de la noticia, dio saltos de alegría** when he heard the news, he jumped for joy; **voy a d. un paseo** I'm going (to go) for a walk
(**s**) *Esp Fam (fastidiar)* to ruin; **es tan pesado que me dio la tarde** he's so boring that he ruined my afternoon for me; **el bebé nos da las noches con sus lloros** the baby never lets us get a decent night's sleep
(**t**) *(considerar)* **d. algo por** to consider sth as; **eso lo doy por hecho** I take that for granted; **doy por sentado que vendrás a la fiesta** I take it for granted that *o* I assume you'll be coming to the party; **doy por explicado este periodo histórico** that's all I want to say about this period of history; **doy esta discusión por terminada** I consider this discussion to be over; **d. a alguien por muerto** to give sb up for dead
(**u**) *Fam (presentir)* **me da que no van a venir** I have a feeling they're not going to come
(**v**) *RP (inyección)* to give

(w) EXPR **donde las dan las toman** you get what you deserve; **no d. una** to get everything wrong

2 *vi* (a) *(repartir) (en naipes)* to deal; **me toca d. a mí** it's my deal

(b) *(entregar)* **dame, que ya lo llevo yo** give it to me, I'll carry it

(c) *(horas)* to strike; **dieron las tres** three o'clock struck

(d) *(golpear)* **le dieron en la cabeza** they hit him on the head; **la piedra dio contra el cristal** the stone hit the window; **como no te portes bien, te voy a d.** if you don't behave, I'll smack you

(e) *(accionar)* **d. a** *(llave de paso)* to turn; *(botón, timbre)* to press; **dale al control remoto** hit the remote control; **dale al pedal** press down on the pedal; *Informát* **dale a la tecla de retorno** hit *o* press return; **dale a la manivela** turn the handle

(f) *(estar orientado)* **d. a** *(sujeto: ventana, balcón)* to look out onto, to overlook; *(sujeto: pasillo, puerta)* to lead to; *(sujeto: casa, fachada)* to face; **todas las habitaciones dan al mar** all the rooms look out onto *o* face the sea

(g) *(sujeto: luz, viento)* **el sol daba de lleno en la habitación** the sunlight was streaming into the room; **la luz me daba directamente en la cara** the light was shining directly in my face; **aquí da mucho viento** it's very windy here

(h) *(encontrar)* **d. con algo/alguien** to find sth/sb; **he dado con la solución** I've hit upon the solution

(i) *(proporcionar)* **d. de beber a alguien** to give sb something to drink; **da de mamar a su hijo** she breast-feeds her son

(j) *(ser suficiente)* **d. para** to be enough for; EXPR **d. ni para pipas: ¡eso no te da ni para pipas!** that's not even enough to buy a bag of peanuts!

(k) *(motivar)* **esta noticia va a d. mucho que hablar** this news will set people talking; **aquello me dio que pensar** that made me think

(l) *(importar)* **¡y a ti qué más te da!** what's it to you?; **me da igual** *o* **lo mismo** it's all the same to me, I don't mind *o* care; **no vamos a poder ir al cine – ¡qué más da!** we won't be able to go to the cinema – never mind!; **y si no lo conseguimos, ¿qué más da?** if we don't manage it, so what?; **¡qué más da quién lo haga con tal de que lo haga bien!** what does it matter *o* what difference does it make who does it as long as they do it properly?; **lo siento, no voy a poder ayudar – da igual, no te preocupes** I'm sorry but I won't be able to help – it doesn't matter, don't worry; **¿vamos o nos quedamos? – da lo mismo** should we go or should we stay? – it doesn't make any difference

(m) *(acertar)* **dio en el blanco** she hit the target; **diste en el blanco, hay que intentar reducir las pérdidas** you hit the nail on the head, we have to try and reduce our losses

(n) *(tomar costumbre)* **le ha dado por el yoga** he's decided to go in for yoga; **ahora le ha dado por no comer fruta** now she's decided not to eat fruit; **le dio por ponerse a cantar en medio de la clase** he took it into his head to start singing in the middle of the class; **¿está aprendiendo ruso? – sí, le ha dado por ahí** is she learning Russian? – yes, that's her latest thing; *Formal* **d. en hacer algo** to take to doing sth; **el viejo dio en leer libros de caballería** the old man took to reading books of chivalry

(o) *(expresa repetición)* **le dieron de palos** they beat him repeatedly with a stick

(p) *(afectar)* **le dio un infarto** he had a heart attack

(q) **d. de sí** *(ropa, calzado)* to give, to stretch; **no d. más de sí** *o* **para más** *(persona, animal)* not to be up to much any more; **este sueldo da mucho de sí** this salary goes a long way; **estos zapatos no dan para más** these shoes have had it; **es un poco tonto, no da para más** he's a bit stupid, he's not up to anything else

(r) *(expresa enfado)* **te digo que pares y tú, ¡dale (que dale)!** I've told you to stop, but you just carry on and on!; **¡y dale con la música!** there he goes again, playing loud music!; **te hemos dicho que no menciones el tema, y tú, dale que te pego** we've told you not to mention the subject, but you just carry on regardless *o* but here you are, bringing it up again; **¡y dale! te lo he dicho bien claro, no voy a ir** how many times do I have to tell you? I've said it once and I'll say it again, I'm not going

(s) *RP (comunicar)* **¿me darías con tu madre?** could I speak to your mother?, could you put your mother on?; **le doy con el Sr. Hualde** I'll put you through to Mr Hualde

(t) EXPR *Fam* **para d. y tomar: había cerveza para d. y tomar** there was loads of beer; *Fam* **darle a: ¡cómo le da a la cerveza!** he certainly likes his beer!; *Fam* **darle algo a alguien: si no se calla me va a d. algo** if he doesn't shut up soon, I'll go mad; **si sigues trabajando así te va a d. algo** you can't go on working like that; *Esp muy Fam* **¡que le den!: ¿que no quiere cooperar? ¡que le den!** he doesn't want to cooperate? well stuff him!

3 darse *vpr* (a) *(suceder)* to occur, to happen; **se da pocas veces** it rarely happens; **se dio la circunstancia de que un médico pasaba por allí en ese momento** it so happened that a doctor was passing that way at the time; **este fenómeno se da en regiones tropicales** this phenomenon occurs *o* is seen in tropical regions; **si se diera el caso, ven en taxi** if necessary *o* if need be, get a taxi

(b) *(entregarse)* **darse a la bebida** to take to drink; **se ha dado a cuidar niños abandonados** she has devoted herself to caring for abandoned children

(c) *(golpearse)* **darse contra** *o* **con** to hit; **se dieron contra una farola** they crashed into *o* hit a lamppost; **se dio de narices en la puerta** she bumped *o* walked into the door

(d) *(tener aptitud)* **se me da bien/mal el latín** I'm good/bad at Latin; **se me da muy bien jugar al baloncesto** I'm good at basketball; **¿qué tal se te da la química?** are you any good at chemistry?, how are you at chemistry?

(e) *(considerarse)* **darse por** to consider oneself (to be); **darse por vencido** to give in; **me doy por satisfecho con tu disculpa** I'm satisfied with your apology; **me doy por satisfecho con que acabemos entre los tres primeros** I'll be satisfied *o* happy if we finish in the first three; **con estos resultados me doy por contento** I'm quite happy with these results, I'll settle for these results; **nos dirigíamos a él, pero no se dio por enterado** our remarks were aimed at him, but he pretended not to notice

(f) *(uso recíproco)* **se dieron los regalos** they exchanged presents, they gave each other their presents; **se dieron de puñetazos a la salida del bar** they had a fight outside the bar

(g) *(uso reflexivo)* **darse una ducha/un baño** to have a shower/bath; **date prisa, que no llegamos** hurry up, we're late

(h) *RP (tratarse)* **no se da con sus primos** he doesn't have much to do with his cousins

(i) EXPR *Esp Fam* **dársela a alguien: tiene buenos modales y cara de inocente, pero a mí no me la da** she's well-mannered and has an innocent face, but she can't fool me; **dárselas de algo: se las da de intelectual/elegante** he fancies himself as an intellectual/a dandy; **se las da de listo** he makes out (that) he's clever; **se las da de interesante, pero es aburridísimo** he reckons he's interesting, but he's actually really boring

---

dardo *nm* (a) *(para jugar)* dart; **jugar a los dardos** to play darts (b) *(dicho satírico)* caustic remark; **lanzó varios dardos envenenados a la oposición** she directed several caustic remarks at the opposition

dársena *nf* (a) *(en puerto)* dock (b) *(en estación de autobuses)* bay

darviniano, -a, darwiniano, -a *adj* Darwinian

darvinismo, darwinismo *nm* Darwinism

darvinista, darwinista 1 *adj* Darwinian
2 *nmf* Darwinian

dasicerco *nm* mulgara

dasiuro *nm* quoll

DAT [dat] *nf Informát* (*abrev de* **digital audio tape**) DAT

data *nf* (a) *(fecha)* date (b) *Prensa* dateline (c) *Informát* data

datación *nf (de restos arqueológicos)* dating ▸▸ ***d. por carbono 14*** radiocarbon dating

datáfono *nm* dataphone

datagrama *nm Informát* datagram

datar 1 *vt* (a) *(carta, documento, manuscrito)* to date (b) *(restos arqueológicos)* to date; **los arqueólogos dataron los restos en la época prerromana** the archaeologists dated the remains to the pre-Roman period
2 *vi* **d. de** to date back to, to date from; **este cuadro data de poco antes de la guerra** this painting dates from just before the war; **su afición por la música data de la época universitaria** his love of music goes back to his university days

datear *vt Chile, Ven Fam* to tip off

datero, -a *nm,f Chile, Ven Fam* informer

dátil *nm* (a) *(fruto seco)* date (b) *(animal)* **d. (de mar)** date mussel (c) *Fam* **dátiles** *(dedos)* fingers

datilera 1 *adj* **palmera d.** date palm
2 *nf* date palm

dativo *nm Gram* dative

dato *nm* (a) *(hecho, cifra)* piece of information, fact; **lo que necesitamos son datos concretos** what we need is hard facts; **el alto desempleo es un d. que hay que tener en cuenta** the high level of unemployment is a factor which has to be borne in mind; **datos** *(información)* information, data; **si no me das más datos, no voy a poderte aconsejar** unless you give me more information, I won't be able to advise you; **el ministerio aún no cuenta con todos los datos** the ministry does not yet have all the information at its disposal; **datos (personales)** (personal) details; **déjenos sus datos y nos**

pondremos en contacto con usted leave us your details and we will get in touch with you ►► ***datos bancarios*** bank details; ***datos estadísticos*** statistical data
(b) **datos** *Informát* data

dB *nm* (*abrev de* **decibelio**) dB

DC *nf* (*abrev de* **Democracia Cristiana**) Christian Democracy

d. C. (*abrev de* **después de Cristo**) AD

dcha. (*abrev de* **derecha**) rt.

DD *Informát* (*abrev de* **doble densidad**) double density

d. de JC. (*abrev de* **después de Jesucristo**) AD

DDT *nm* (*abrev de* **diclorodifeniltricloroetano**) DDT

DE *prep*

de combines with the article **el** to form the contraction **del** (e.g. **del hombre** of the man).

1 (a) *(posesión, pertenencia)* of; **el automóvil de mi padre/mis padres** my father's/parents' car; **es de ella** it's hers; **la maleta es de Eva** the suitcase is Eva's *o* belongs to Eva; **el padre de la niña** the girl's father; **el director de la empresa** the manager of the company, the company's manager; **la boda** *o* **el casamiento de un amigo de mi hermano** the wedding of a friend of my brother's, a friend of my brother's wedding; **un equipo de segunda división** a second division team; **la comida del gato** the cat's food; **el título de la novela** the novel's title, the title of the novel; **la pata de la mesa** the table leg; **una subida de precios** a price rise; **los señores de Navarro** Mr and Mrs Navarro
(b) *(procedencia, distancia)* from; **salir de casa** to leave home; **soy de Bilbao** I'm from Bilbao; **no soy de aquí** I'm not from round here; **de la playa al apartamento hay 100 metros** it's 100 metres from the beach to the apartment; **estamos a 10 kilómetros de Buenos Aires** we're 10 kilometres away from Buenos Aires; **el rey de España** the king of Spain; **tuvo dos hijos de su primera esposa** he had two children by his first wife; **b de Barcelona** *(deletreando)* b for Barcelona
(c) *(en razonamiento)* **de su sonrisa se deduce que todo ha ido bien** you can tell from *o* by her smile that it all went well; **del resultado del experimento concluyo que la fórmula no funciona** I infer from the result of the experiment that the formula doesn't work
(d) *(con nombre en aposición)* **la ciudad de Caracas** the city of Caracas; **el túnel del Canal** the Channel Tunnel; **el signo de tauro** the sign of Taurus; **el puerto de Cartagena** the port of Cartagena
(e) *(en descripciones)* **una película de terror** a horror film; **la señora de verde** the lady in green; **el chico de la coleta** the boy with the ponytail; **una actriz de veinte años** a twenty-year-old actress; **¿de qué tamaño?** what size?; **un político de fiar** a trustworthy politician
(f) *(materia)* (made) of; **un vaso de plástico** a plastic cup; **un reloj de oro** a gold watch; **una mesa de madera** a wooden table
(g) *(contenido)* **un vaso de agua** a glass of water; **un plato de lentejas** a plate of lentils
(h) *(precio)* **he comprado las peras de 80 céntimos el kilo** I bought the pears that were 80 cents a kilo; **un sello de 50 céntimos** a 50-cent stamp
(i) *(uso)* **una bici de carreras** a racing bike; **ropa de deporte** sportswear; **una máquina de escribir** a typewriter; **una máquina de coser** a sewing machine; **esta sartén es la del pescado y ésta la de las tortillas** this frying pan's for fish and this one's for omelettes
(j) *(asunto)* about; **hablábamos de ti** we were talking about you; **libros de historia** history books
(k) *(en calidad de)* as; **trabaja de bombero** he works as a fireman; **aparece de cosaco** he appears as a Cossack, he plays a Cossack; **estás muy guapa de uniforme** you look very pretty in uniform; **al desfile de carnaval iré de Napoleón** I'll go as Napoleon in the carnival parade
(l) *(tiempo) (desde)* from; *(durante)* in; **trabaja de nueve a cinco** she works from nine to five; **vivió en Bolivia de 1975 a 1983** she lived in Bolivia between 1975 and 1983, she lived in Bolivia from 1975 to 1983; **de madrugada** early in the morning; **a las cuatro de la tarde** at four in the afternoon; **trabaja de noche y duerme de día** he works at night and sleeps during the day; **es de día** it's daytime; **de niño solía jugar en la calle** as a child I used to play in the street; **¿qué quieres ser de mayor?** what do you want to be when you grow up?; **un compañero del colegio** a friend from school; *Urug* **de mañana/tarde** in the morning/afternoon; *Urug* **de noche** at night; *Urug* **ayer salimos de noche** we went out last night
(m) *(causa)* with; **morirse de hambre** to die of hunger; **llorar de alegría** to cry with joy; **temblar de miedo** to tremble with fear; **eso es de fumar tanto** that's what comes from smoking so much
(n) *(manera, modo)* with; **de una patada** with a kick; **rompió el cristal de una pedrada** he shattered the window with a stone; **de una sola vez** in one go; **lo bebió de un trago** he drank it down in one go; **de tres en tres/cuatro en cuatro/***etc.* three/four/*etc* at a time; *CSur* **de a tres/cuatro/***etc.* in threes/fours/*etc*; **de fácil manejo** user-friendly; **ponerse de rodillas** to kneel down
(o) *(con valor partitivo)* of; **uno de los nuestros** one of ours; **varios de nosotros** several of us; **¿quién de ellos sabe la respuesta?** which of them knows the answer?
(p) *Literario (sobre)* **de la paz y la guerra** of war and peace
(q) *(en valoración)* **lo tacharon de vulgar** they branded him as vulgar, they accused him of being vulgar
(r) *(en lugar de)* **yo de ti no lo haría** I wouldn't do it if I were you; **yo de Eduardo le pediría perdón** if I were Eduardo, I'd say sorry to her
(s) *(en comparaciones)* **más/menos de...** more/less than...; *(con superlativos)* **el mejor de todos** the best of all; **el más importante del mundo** the most important in the world; **la peor película del año** the worst film this year *o* of the year; **la impresora más moderna del mercado** the most up-to-date printer on the market
(t) *(antes de infinitivo) (condición)* if; **de querer ayudarme, lo haría** if she wanted to help me, she'd do it; **de no ser por ti, me hubiese hundido** if it hadn't been for you, I wouldn't have made it; **de ir a verte, sería este domingo** if I do visit you, it'll be this Sunday
(u) *(después de adjetivo y antes de sustantivo) (enfatiza cualidad)* **el idiota de tu hermano** your stupid brother; **la buena de Susana** good old Susana; **¡pobre de mí!** poor me!
(v) *(después de adjetivo y antes de infinitivo)* **es difícil de creer** it's hard to believe; **una velada imposible de olvidar** an unforgettable evening
(w) *(después del verbo "haber") (obligación)* **he de trabajar más** I have to work harder; **has de gastar menos** you should spend less
(x) *(antes de complemento agente)* **una película de Buñuel** a film by Buñuel, a Buñuel film; **vino acompañado de su familia** he was accompanied by his family
(y) *(antes de adverbio de lugar)* **el apartamento de abajo** the downstairs *Br* flat *o US* apartment; **la fila de delante** the front row
2 **de no** *loc conj Am* otherwise; **dime la verdad, de no te castigaré** tell me the truth, otherwise I'm going to punish you

dé *etc ver* **dar**

dealer ['diler] (*pl* **dealers**) *nm (de automóviles, informática)* dealer

deambular *vi* to wander (about *o* around); **d. por el centro de la ciudad** to wander round the city centre; **deambulaba por la casa sin saber qué hacer** he wandered around the house without knowing what to do

deambulatorio *nm* ambulatory

deán *nm* dean

debacle *nf* debacle; **trató de explicar la d. electoral** he tried to explain the election debacle; **la reunión fue la d.** the meeting was a disaster

DEBAJO *adv* (a) *(en un lugar, posición)* underneath; **d. vive un pianista** a pianist lives downstairs; **el de d.** the one underneath; **el mío es el de d.** mine is the one below; **el de d. del todo** the one right at the bottom; **el vecino/la oficina de d.** the downstairs neighbour/office; **llevo una camiseta (por) d.** I've got a vest on underneath; **d. de** underneath, under; **el gato se escondió d. de la mesa** the cat hid under the table; **d. del sótano hay un pasadizo secreto** there's a secret passageway underneath the basement; **¿qué llevas d. del abrigo?** what have you got on under your coat?; **sacó el botín de d. de la cama** she took out the loot from under the bed; **pasamos por d. del puente** we went under the bridge; **vuelven a llevarse las faldas por d. de la rodilla** skirts are being worn below the knee again
(b) *(en jerarquías, escalas)* **d. de** below, under, underneath; **d. de mí** underneath/below me; **tengo a muchos empleados por d. de mí** I have several employees under me; **por d. de lo normal** below normal; **García estuvo por d. de sus posibilidades** García was below form *o* below par *o* beneath his best

debate *nm* debate; **se necesita un d. abierto sobre el tema** the issue needs to be discussed openly; **un d. electoral televisado** a televised electoral debate; **el d. sobre el estado de la nación** the state-of-the nation debate; **un d. público** a public debate; **someter un tema a d.** to discuss *o* debate a subject

debatir 1 *vt* to debate; **la ley se debate hoy en el Parlamento** the bill is being debated in Parliament today; **en nuestro próximo programa debatiremos el tema "moda y anorexia"** in our next programme we'll be discussing "fashion and anorexia"
2 *vi* to debate; **d. sobre algo** to discuss *o* debate sth
3 **debatirse** *vpr (luchar)* to struggle; **debatirse entre la vida y la muerte** to hover between life and death; **el país se debate en medio de una fuerte crisis política y financiera** the country is struggling in the

midst of a serious political and financial crisis; **me debatía entre mis miedos y las ganas de aventura** I was torn between my fears and my thirst for adventure

debe *nm* debit; **d. y haber** debit and credit; **anotar algo en el d. de una cuenta** to enter sth on the debit side of an account; **los reintegros se reflejan en el d. de su cuenta** withdrawals are shown in the debit column; *Fam* **este gobierno tiene en su d. el fracaso de la reforma sanitaria** on the debit side is the failure of this government's health reforms

---

DEBER 1 *nm (obligación)* duty; **mi d. es ayudar** it is my duty to help; **es mi d. intentar detenerle** it is my duty to try to stop him; **cumplir con el d.** to do one's duty; **faltarás a tu d. si no acudes a la reunión** you will be failing in your duty if you don't come to the meeting; **los derechos y los deberes de los ciudadanos** citizens' rights and duties; **mantener la ciudad limpia es d. de todos** keeping the city tidy is everyone's responsibility; **tiene un gran sentido del d.** she has a great sense of duty; **tengo el triste d. de comunicarles la aparición del cuerpo de su hijo** it is my sad duty to inform you that your son's body has been found

2 **deberes** *nmpl (trabajo escolar)* homework; **hacer los deberes** to do one's homework; **nos han mandado muchos deberes para el fin de semana** they've set *o* given us a lot of homework for the weekend

3 *vt* (**a**) *(adeudar)* to owe; **d. algo a alguien** to owe sb sth, to owe sth to sb; **¿qué** *o* **cuánto le debo?** how much is it?, how much does it come to?; **¿qué se debe?** how much is it?, how much does it come to?; **¿qué te debo del pan y la leche?** what do I owe you for the bread and milk?; **me deben medio millón de pesos** they owe me half a million pesos; **me debes una cena** you owe me a meal out

(**b**) *(moralmente)* to owe; **te debo la vida** I owe you my life; **este éxito se lo debo a mis compañeros** I owe this success to my colleagues, I have my colleagues to thank for this success; **creo que te debo una explicación** I think I owe you an explanation; **debemos mucho a nuestros padres** we owe our parents a lot; **no le debo nada a nadie** I don't owe anybody anything; *Formal* **¿a qué debemos el honor de su visita?** to what do we owe the pleasure of your visit?; EXPR *Fam* **d. una a alguien** to owe sb one; **te debo una, compañero** I owe you one, mate

4 *vi* (**a**) *(antes de infinitivo) (expresa obligación)* **debo hacerlo** I have to do it, I must do it; **deberían abolir esa ley** they ought to *o* should abolish that law; **debes dominar tus impulsos** you must *o* should control your impulses; **debería darles vergüenza** they ought to be ashamed; **no deberías fumar tanto** you shouldn't smoke so much; **no debes decir mentiras** you mustn't *o* shouldn't tell lies; **no debiste insultarle** you shouldn't have insulted her; *Fam* **una película como debe ser** a proper film, a film like films were meant to be

(**b**) *(expresa posibilidad)* **el tren debe de llegar alrededor de las diez** the train should arrive at about ten; **deben de haber llegado ya a casa** they must *o* should be home by now; **deben de ser las diez** it must be ten o'clock; **no debe de ser muy mayor** she can't be very old; **no debe de hacer mucho frío** it can't be very *o* that cold; **debe de ser extranjero** he must be a foreigner; **debes de estar cayéndote de sueño** you must be exhausted; **debo haberlo dejado en casa** I must have left it at home

5 **deberse** *vpr* (**a**) **deberse a** *(ser consecuencia de)* to be due to; **su mal humor se debe a su precario estado de salud** her bad mood is due to her poor health; **su ausencia puede deberse a que salieron con retraso** their absence could be down to *o* due to the fact that they left late; **y eso, ¿a qué se debe?** and what's the reason for that?; **¿a qué se debe tanta amabilidad?** what's with all this friendliness?, what's the reason for all this friendliness?; **todo se debió a un malentendido** it was all the result of a misunderstanding

(**b**) **deberse a** *(dedicarse a)* to have a duty *o* responsibility towards; **me debo a mi empresa** I have a duty to my company; **el escritor se debe a sus lectores** writers have a duty *o* a responsibility towards their readers

---

debidamente *adv* properly; **devuelva la solicitud d. cumplimentada a esta dirección** return the application form, properly completed, to this address; **ya fueron d. informados de los trámites que debían seguir** they were duly informed of the procedures to follow

debido, -a 1 *adj* (**a**) *(adeudado)* owing, owed

(**b**) *(justo, conveniente)* due, proper; **a su d. tiempo** in due course; **el tema se abordará en su d. momento** the subject will be dealt with in due course; **con el d. respeto, creo que se equivoca** with all due respect, I think you're mistaken; **creo que he comido más de lo d.** I think I've had a bit too much to eat; **como es d.** properly; **¡pórtate como es d.!** behave yourself!; **no saben cocinar una paella como es d.** they don't know how to cook a proper *o* real paella

2 **debido a** *loc prep* **d. a su enfermedad** owing to *o* because of his illness; **esto es d. a la falta de previsión** this is due to lack of foresight; **llegó tarde d. a que no sonó su despertador** she arrived late because her alarm clock didn't go off

débil 1 *adj* (**a**) *(persona) (sin fuerzas)* weak; *(condescendiente)* lax, lenient; **de constitución d.** prone to illness, sickly; **d. de carácter** of weak character

(**b**) *(voz, sonido)* faint; *(luz)* dim, faint; **una d. mejoría** a slight improvement; **una d. brisa movía las cortinas** a slight breeze moved the curtains

(**c**) *(país, gobierno, moneda)* weak; *(argumento, teoría)* weak, lame

(**d**) *(sílaba)* unstressed

(**e**) *(vocal)* weak *(i, u)*

2 *nmf* weak person; **ser un d.** to be weak; **una enfermedad que ataca a los más débiles** a disease which attacks the weakest *o* most vulnerable

debilidad *nf* (**a**) *(flojedad)* weakness; **siento d. en las piernas** my legs feel tired

(**b**) *(condescendencia)* laxness; **d. de carácter** weakness of character

(**c**) *(falta de solidez) (de gobierno, moneda, economía)* weakness

(**d**) *(inclinación)* **sus nietos son su d.** he dotes on his grandchildren; **tener** *o* **sentir d. por** to have a soft spot for; **el chocolate es su d.** he has a weakness for chocolate; **todos tenemos nuestras debilidades** we all have our weaknesses

(**e**) *Fam (hambre)* **siento d.** I feel as if I need something to eat

debilitación = **debilitamiento**

debilitador, -ora *adj* debilitating

debilitamiento *nm*, **debilitación** *nf* (**a**) *(de enfermo, organismo, salud)* weakening; **el enfermo sufrió un d.** the patient grew weaker (**b**) *(de gobierno, moneda, economía)* weakening; **el d. de la moneda supone un aumento del precio del petróleo** a weaker currency means higher oil prices

debilitante *adj* debilitating

debilitar 1 *vt* (**a**) *(enfermo, organismo)* to weaken; *(salud)* to weaken, to undermine (**b**) *(voluntad, moral)* to weaken, to undermine (**c**) *(gobierno, moneda, economía)* to weaken, to debilitate; **este escándalo puede d. al ministro** this scandal could weaken the minister's position

2 **debilitarse** *vpr* (**a**) *(enfermo, organismo)* to grow weaker; *(salud)* to deteriorate (**b**) *(voluntad, moral)* to grow weaker, to weaken (**c**) *(gobierno, moneda, economía)* to become *o* grow weak (**d**) *(voz, sonido)* to grow fainter; *(luz)* to grow dimmer *o* fainter

débilmente *adv* weakly; **la mariposa aleteaba d.** the butterfly fluttered its wings weakly; **hablaba d. y apenas podía incorporarse** he spoke in a weak voice and could hardly sit up; **las calles d. iluminadas** the dimly lit streets; **"bueno", contestó d.** "okay," he answered half-heartedly

debilucho, -a *Fam* 1 *adj* weak

2 *nm,f* weakling

debitar *vt* to debit

débito *nm (debe)* debit; *(deuda)* debt ►► *Am* ***d. bancario*** direct debit

debut (*pl* **debuts**) *nm (de persona)* debut; *(de obra)* premiere; **hizo su d. como actriz en este teatro** she made her debut as an actress in this theatre; **su d. en sociedad fue brillante** her entry into society was impressive

debutante 1 *adj* making his/her debut, appearing for the first time; **un país d. en los Juegos Olímpicos** a country taking part in its first Olympic Games

2 *nmf* = person making his/her debut; **está muy nervioso porque es un d.** he's very nervous because it's his first time

3 *nf (en sociedad)* debutante, deb; **baile de (las) debutantes** debutantes' ball

debutar *vi (actor, cantante)* to make one's debut; **debutó contra el Boca Juniors** he made his footballing debut against Boca Juniors; **el equipo colombiano debutará mañana en el campeonato** the Colombian team play their opening match in the championship tomorrow; **la obra debuta en Madrid el día 4** the play opens in Madrid on the 4th

década *nf* decade; **la d. de los noventa** the nineties

decadencia *nf (en estado físico, en importancia, en calidad)* decline; *(moral, espiritual)* decadence; **en d.** *(moda)* on the way out; *(cultura, sociedad)* in decline; **entrar en d.** *(moda)* to be on the way out; *(cultura, sociedad)* to go into decline, to become decadent; **la d. del imperio** the decline of the empire

decadente *adj* (**a**) *(ambiente, estilo, gustos)* decadent (**b**) *(economía)* in decline, declining; *(cultura, sociedad)* decadent (**c**) *Lit (del decadentismo)* Decadent

decadentismo *nm Lit* Decadence

decaedro *nm* decahedron

decaer [13] *vi* (a) *(debilitarse)* to decline; *(actividad, ritmo, trabajo)* to fall off, to slacken; *(entusiasmo, ánimos, energías)* to flag; *(interés, fama)* to decline, to wane; **su belleza no ha decaído con los años** her beauty has not faded with age; **¡que no decaiga!** don't lose heart! (b) *(imperio, sociedad)* to decline; *(empresa, establecimiento, zona)* to go downhill; **la fiesta fue decayendo** the party gradually fizzled out (c) *(enfermo)* to get weaker; *(salud)* to fail

decágono *nm* decagon

decagramo *nm* decagram

decaído, -a *adj (desalentado)* gloomy, downhearted, dispirited; **está muy d. desde que lo despidieron** he's been very low since he was sacked

decaigo *etc ver* **decaer**

decaimiento *nm* (a) *(desaliento)* gloominess (b) *(falta de fuerzas)* weakness (c) *(decadencia)* decline; **un d. de la actividad en el sector turístico** a decline in business in the tourist sector

decalcificación *nf* (a) *Med* loss of calcium (b) *(del agua)* softening

decalcificar [60] 1 *vt* (a) *Med* to decalcify (b) *(agua)* to soften
2 **decalcificarse** *vpr* to become decalcified, to lose calcium

decalitro *nm* decalitre

decálogo *nm* (a) *Rel* Decalogue, Ten Commandments (b) *(normas)* ten golden *o* basic rules

decámetro *nm* decametre

decanato *nm* (a) *(cargo)* deanship (b) *(despacho)* dean's office

decano, -a *nm,f* (a) *(de facultad)* dean; *(de colegio profesional)* secretary, chairman, *f* chairwoman (b) *(veterano) (hombre)* senior member, doyen; *(mujer)* senior member, doyenne; **el d. de la prensa escrita española** the elder statesman of the Spanish press

decantación *nf* (a) *(de líquidos)* decanting, settling (b) *(inclinación, tendencia)* shift (**hacia** towards) (c) *(elección, predilección)* preference (**por** for)

decantar 1 *vt* to decant
2 **decantarse** *vpr* (a) *(inclinarse)* to lean (**hacia** towards); **el partido se decantaba hacia posiciones más radicales** the party was leaning towards more radical positions; **la eliminatoria terminó decantándose a favor de Sampras** the qualifying round ended up going Sampras' way
(b) **decantarse por** *(optar por)* to opt for, to choose; **el público parece decantarse por el cine nacional** the public seems to be opting for home-grown movies

decapado *nm* (a) *(de pintura)* stripping (b) *(de herrumbre)* removal

decapante 1 *adj* **gel d.** paint stripper
2 *nm* paint stripper

decapar *vt (pintura)* to strip; *(herrumbre)* to remove

decapitación *nf* decapitation, beheading

decapitar *vt* to decapitate, to behead

decápodo, -a *Zool* 1 *adj* decapodal, decapodous
2 *nm* decapod, member of the order *Decapoda*
3 **decápodos** *nmpl (orden) Decapoda*; **del orden de los decápodos** of the order *Decapoda*

decasílabo, -a 1 *adj* decasyllabic
2 *nm* decasyllable

decatleta *nmf* decathlete

decatlón *nm* decathlon

decatloniano, -a 1 *adj* decathlon; **especialista d.** decathlon specialist
2 *nm,f* decathlete

decayera *etc ver* **decaer**

decé *Chile* 1 *adj* relating to the Christian Democrat party
2 *nmf* Christian Democrat

deceleración *nf* deceleration

decelerar 1 *vt* to decelerate, to slow down
2 *vi* to decelerate, to slow down

decena *nf* ten; **una d. de...** *(unos diez)* about ten...; *(diez)* ten...; **decenas de fans lo aguardaban a la salida** scores of fans were waiting for him at the exit; **cuestan 30 pesos la d.** they cost 30 pesos for ten; **las víctimas se cuentan por decenas** there have been dozens of casualties; **estos tornillos se venden por decenas** these screws are sold in tens

decenal *adj* **un plan d.** a ten-year plan; **un premio d.** a prize awarded every ten years

decencia *nf* (a) *(decoro)* decency; *(en el vestir)* modesty; **vestir con d.** to dress modestly (b) *(honradez)* decency

decenio *nm* decade

decente *adj* (a) *(digno, satisfactorio)* decent; **un sueldo d.** a decent salary *o* wage; **has hecho un examen bastante d.** you've done a decent enough exam
(b) *(en el comportamiento)* proper, respectable; *(en el vestir)* decent; **no vayas así, ponte algo d.** don't go like that, put on something decent; **este es un establecimiento d.** this is a respectable establishment; **una persona d. no se comportaría así** a respectable person wouldn't behave like that
(c) *(limpio)* clean

decentemente *adv* (a) *(dignamente)* decently; **este sueldo nos permite vivir d.** we can live a decent life on this salary (b) *(en comportamiento)* properly, decently; *(en el vestir)* respectably (c) *(pulcramente)* neatly, tidily

decepción *nf* disappointment; **llevarse una d.** to be disappointed, to suffer a disappointment; **me llevé una gran d. al oír la noticia** I was really disappointed when I heard the news; **su nueva película ha sido una d.** her new film is disappointing *o* a disappointment

> **Falso amigo**: El sustantivo inglés **deception** no es la traducción del español **decepción**. En inglés **deception** significa "engaño".

decepcionado, -a *adj* disappointed; **estoy muy d. con su comportamiento** I'm very disappointed by his behaviour

decepcionante *adj* disappointing

decepcionantemente *adj* disappointingly

decepcionar *vt* to disappoint; **su última novela me ha decepcionado** I was disappointed by her last novel; **tenemos plena confianza en ti, no nos decepciones** we have full confidence in you, do not disappoint us

deceso *nm Formal* decease, death

dechado *nm* **ser un d. de perfecciones** *o* **virtudes** to be a paragon of virtue

decibelio, *Am* **decibel** *nm* decibel

decididamente *adv* (a) *(con decisión)* resolutely, with determination; **hay que obrar d.** decisive action is called for (b) *(sin duda)* definitely; **d., es una buena idea** it's definitely a good idea

decidido, -a *adj (persona, gesto, modo de andar)* determined, purposeful; **camina con paso d.** he walks with a purposeful stride; **¿estás d.? mira que luego no puedes echarte atrás** is your mind made up? there's no going back later on, you know; **estar d. a hacer algo** to be determined to do sth; **están decididos a terminar con la corrupción** they are determined to put an end to corruption

---

DECIDIR 1 *vt* (a) *(tomar una decisión sobre)* to decide; **el juez decidirá si es inocente o no** the judge will decide *o* determine whether or not he is innocent; **no hay nada decidido por el momento** nothing has been decided for the moment; **todo está aún por d.** everything's still up in the air, nothing's been decided yet; **d. hacer algo** to decide to do sth; **he decidido cambiar de apartamento** I've decided to move *Br* flat *o US* apartment; **decidió que no valía la pena arriesgarse** she decided (that) it wasn't worth the risk; **han decidido que no van a tener más hijos** they've decided not to have any more children
(b) *(determinar)* to decide; **el voto de la clase media decidió la elección** the middle-class vote decided *o* swung the election; **el gol de Márquez decidió el partido** Márquez' goal decided *o* settled the game
(c) *(persuadir)* to persuade, to convince; **lo decidí a quedarse** I convinced him to stay; **su madre le decidió a dejar de fumar** his mother persuaded him to stop smoking; **¿qué te decidió a seguir con el negocio?** what made you decide to carry on with the business?
2 *vi* to decide, to choose; **¿a qué restaurante vamos? – tú decides** which restaurant shall we go to? – you decide; **d. entre dos cosas** to choose between two things; **ellos decidieron por mí** they decided for me, they took the decision for me; **tenemos que d. sobre la decoración del dormitorio** we have to decide how we're going to decorate the bedroom, we have to take a decision on the décor for the bedroom
3 **decidirse** *vpr* to decide, to make up one's mind; **aún no se ha decidido** he still hasn't decided *o* made up his mind; **¡decídete de una vez!** make up your mind!; **decidirse a hacer algo** to decide to do sth; **al final, me decidí a estudiar inglés** in the end, I decided to study English; **si te decides a venir, llámame** if you decide to come, give me a ring; **decidirse por** to decide on, to choose; **no sabía por qué color decidirme** I couldn't decide which colour to go for; **me decidí por el más barato** I decided on *o* decided to go for the cheapest

---

decigramo *nm* decigram

decilitro *nm* decilitre

décima *nf* (**a**) *(en medidas)* tenth; **una d. de segundo** a tenth of a second; **ganó por décimas de segundo** he won by tenths of a second; **tiene unas décimas de fiebre** she has a slight fever (**b**) *Lit (estrofa)* = ten-line stanza

decimal 1 *adj* decimal
2 *nm (cifra total)* decimal; *(cada dígito)* decimal place

decímetro *nm* decimetre

décimo, -a 1 *núm* tenth; **la décima parte** a tenth; **el siglo d.** *(escrito "siglo X")* the tenth century; *ver también* **octavo**
2 *nm* (**a**) *(fracción)* tenth (**b**) *(en lotería)* = ticket giving a tenth share in a number entered in the Spanish "Lotería Nacional" (**c**) *Am (moneda)* 10-cent coin

decimoctavo, -a *núm* eighteenth; *ver también* **octavo**

decimocuarto, -a *núm* fourteenth; *ver también* **octavo**

decimonónico, -a *adj* (**a**) *(del siglo XIX)* nineteenth-century (**b**) *Pey (anticuado)* old-fashioned, antiquated

decimonono, -a *núm Formal* nineteenth; *ver también* **octavo**

decimonoveno, -a *núm* nineteenth; *ver también* **octavo**

decimoquinto, -a *núm* fifteenth; *ver también* **octavo**

decimoséptimo, -a *núm* seventeenth; *ver también* **octavo**

decimosexto, -a *núm* sixteenth; *ver también* **octavo**

decimotercero, -a *núm* thirteenth; *ver también* **octavo**

Decimotercer is used instead of **decimotercero** before singular masculine nouns (e.g. **el decimotercer participante** the thirteenth entrant).

DECIR [21] 1 *vt* (**a**) *(en general)* to say; **siempre digo lo que pienso** I always say what I think; **es muy callado, nunca dice nada** he's very quiet, he never says anything *o* a word; **¿qué dice la etiqueta?** what does the label say?; **no digas tonterías** don't talk nonsense; **no digas tacos delante de los niños** don't swear in front of the children; **lo dijo en broma** she meant it as a joke; **¿quién te lo ha dicho?** who told you that?; **me da igual lo que diga la gente** I don't care what people say; **al d. esto, se marchó** with these words *o* with that, he left; **no sabía qué d.** I didn't know what to say, I was lost for words; **d. que sí/no** to say yes/no; **dice que no viene** she says (that) she's not coming; **como dice el refrán,...** as the saying goes,...; **dicen que va a ser un verano muy seco** they say it's going to be a very dry summer; EXPR **¡díjolo Blas, punto redondo!** sure, whatever!, yes, sure!; EXPR **donde dije digo, digo Diego: ayer dijiste que me lo dejarías – sí, pero no puedo – ya, donde dije digo, digo Diego** yesterday you told me you'd lend it to me – yes, but I can't now – you're always saying one thing one minute and another the next
(**b**) *(contar)* to tell; **se lo voy a d. a la profesora** I'm going to tell the teacher; **no se lo digas a nadie** don't breathe a word of it to anyone; **¿qué quieres que te diga?** what do you want me to say?, what can I say?; **ya te lo había dicho yo, es demasiado caro** I told you it's too expensive; **d. la verdad** to tell the truth; **d. mentiras** to tell lies; **pregunta si le dejas salir – dile que sí/no** she wants to know if she can go out – tell her she can/can't; **quiere saber si hemos terminado – dile que sí/no** he wants to know if we've finished – tell him we have/haven't; **dile que estoy ocupado** tell him I'm busy; **dígame lo que pasó** tell me what happened; **eso no es lo que me dijo a mí** that's not what she told me; **tengo que hacerte una pregunta – dime** I need to ask you a question – go ahead; **dígame en qué puedo ayudarle** what can I do for you?
(**c**) *(ordenar)* to tell; **la ley dice que es obligatorio el uso del casco** according to the law, it is compulsory to wear a crash helmet, the law says that it is compulsory to wear a crash helmet; **d. a alguien que haga algo** to tell sb to do sth; **haz lo que te digan y no protestes** do as you're told and don't complain; **dile que venga** tell her to come; **nos dijeron que nos fuéramos** they told us to go away; **lo vas a hacer porque lo digo yo** you'll do it because I say so
(**d**) *(recitar) (de memoria)* to recite; *(leyendo)* to read
(**e**) *(revelar)* to tell, to show; **eso lo dice todo** that says it all; **d. mucho (en favor) de** to say a lot for; **sus ropas dicen bastante sobre su situación económica** her clothes say a lot about her financial situation; **su violenta reacción dice mucho sobre su personalidad** his violent reaction tells us *o* reveals a lot about his personality
(**f**) *(llamar)* to call; **me dicen Paco** they call me Paco; **le dicen la carretera de la muerte** they call it the road of death
(**g**) *(asegurar)* to tell, to assure; **te digo que ella no está mintiendo** I tell you *o* assure you (that) she isn't lying; **dice que llegará mañana sin falta** she says (that) she'll definitely arrive tomorrow
(**h**) *(en frases)* **a d. verdad, no me apetece nada ir a la boda** to tell (you) the truth *o* to be honest, I don't really feel like going to the wedding; **como quien no dice nada** as if it were nothing; **olvídalo, como si no hubiera dicho nada** forget I ever mentioned it; **con decirte que me marché a los diez minutos, te puedes imaginar como fue la fiesta** if I tell you that I left after ten minutes, you can imagine what the party was like; **cualquiera diría que no le dan de comer en casa** anyone would *o* you'd think she never gets fed at home; **d. para sí** to say to oneself; **d. por d.** to talk for the sake of talking; **no te lo tomes en serio, lo dijo por d.** don't take it seriously, she didn't really mean it; **decirle a alguien cuatro verdades** to tell sb a few home truths; **es d.** that is, that's to say; **aracnofobia, es d. miedo a las arañas** arachnophobia, that is *o* that's to say, fear of spiders; **tengo otra cita – es d., que no vendrás a la inauguración** I've got another engagement – you mean *o* in other words you're not coming to the opening ceremony; **encantado de conocerte – lo mismo digo** pleased to meet you – likewise; **tu primer examen estaba muy mal, y lo mismo digo del segundo** you did very poorly in your first exam, and the same goes for the second one; **ni que d. tiene** needless to say; **yo no digo** *o* **no quiero d. nada, pero...** it's not for me to say, but...; **¿sabías que Santiago se ha casado? – ¡no me digas!** did you know that Santiago got married? – no! *o* never!; **¡no me digas que no te gusta!** don't tell me you don't like it!; **el tenis/este cuadro no me dice nada** tennis/this picture doesn't do anything for me; **no hay más que d.** that's all there is to it, that's that; **(o) mejor dicho** or rather; **por más que digas, no le veo nada especial a esta ciudad** whatever you say, I don't see what's so special about this city; **por decirlo así, por así decirlo** in other words, so to speak; *RP Fam* **¿qué decís?** how are you doing?, how are things?; **preocuparse por el qué dirán** to worry about what people will say; **no está lloviendo mucho que digamos** it's not exactly raining hard; **él no es muy inteligente que digamos** he isn't what you'd call intelligent; **ha sufrido un infarto – ¡qué me dices!** she's had a heart attack – no! *o* surely not!; **¡quién lo diría! tan rico y sin embargo tan humilde** who would have thought it, such a rich person and yet so humble!; **tardarán en construirlo cinco años, ¡se dice pronto!** they're going to take five years, no less, to build it!; **yo lo hago en cinco minutos – eso se dice pronto, no sabes lo difícil que es** I'll have it done in five minutes – that's easily said, you've no idea how difficult it is; **si tú lo dices** if you say so; **¡tú lo has dicho!** you said it!; *Esp* **¡y que lo digas!** you can say that again!; **y no digamos,** *Am* **ya no se diga,** *Am* **ni se diga** to say nothing of; **no le gusta el pescado y no digamos el pollo** she doesn't like fish, to say nothing of chicken
2 *vi* **como quien dice, como si dijéramos** so to speak; **es, como si dijéramos, una mezcla de danza y teatro** it's a sort of mixture of dance and theatre; **es, como quien dice, el alma de la empresa** he is, so to speak, the soul of the company; *Esp* **¿diga?, ¿dígame?** *(al teléfono)* hello?; *Fam* **¡digo!** *(¡ya lo creo!)* of course!; *(¡madre mía!)* I say!; **tenemos muchas ganas de ir de vacaciones, y nuestros hijos, no digamos** we can't wait to go on holiday, and as for our children...
3 **decirse** *vpr* (**a**) *(reflexionar)* to say to oneself; **a veces me digo, tengo que trabajar menos** sometimes I say to *o* tell myself I have to work less, sometimes I think I ought to work less; **me dije, cállate, no digas nada** I said to myself *o* I thought it's better not to say anything
(**b**) *(uso impersonal)* **¿cómo se dice "estación" en inglés?** how do you say "estación" in English?; **no se dice "cocreta" sino "croqueta"** it isn't "cocreta", it's "croqueta"; **se dice que...** they *o* people say (that)...; **se dice que subirán los impuestos** it's said they're going to raise taxes; **como se dice vulgarmente...** as they say...; EXPR **¡que no se diga que las fiestas de Valdelapeña son aburridas!** let no one say *o* let it not be said that the festivals in Valdelapeña are boring!
(**c**) *(uso recíproco)* **se dijeron de todo** they called each other everything under the sun
4 *nm* (**a**) *(refrán)* saying
(**b**) *(ocurrencia)* witticism, witty remark
(**c**) *(en frases)* **a d. de todos, según el d. general** by all accounts; **a d. de todos, no parece que vaya a tener mucho éxito** by all accounts, it seems unlikely that she'll have much success; **es un d. que todos tengamos las mismas oportunidades** it's not really true that we all have the same chances in life; **imaginemos, es un d., que...** let us suppose for one moment *o* for the sake of argument that...; **es un d., ¡claro que no estoy embarazada!** it's just a manner of speaking, of course I'm not pregnant!

decisión *nf* (**a**) *(dictamen, resolución)* decision; **la d. está en nuestras manos** the decision is in our hands; **la d. de expulsarlo no depende de mí** whether he should be expelled or not is not my decision; **llegar a** *o* **alcanzar una d.** to arrive at *o* reach a decision; **tomar una d.** to make *o* take a decision; **tomó la d. de no ir** she decided not to go
(**b**) *(firmeza de carácter)* determination, resolve; *(seguridad, resolución)* decisiveness; **actuar con d.** to act decisively; **es una persona con muy poca d.** he's a very indecisive person

decisivamente *adv* decisively

decisivo, -a *adj* (a) *(que decide)* decisive; **su intervención fue decisiva a la hora de llegar a un acuerdo** his intervention was decisive in reaching an agreement; **fue la batalla decisiva que cambió el curso de la guerra** that was the decisive battle which changed the course of the war; **Vázquez marcó el gol d.** Vázquez scored the decider *o* the deciding goal

(b) *(muy importante)* crucial, vital; **tu apoyo es d.** your support is crucial *o* vital

decisorio, -a *adj* decision-making

declamación *nf* (a) *(arte)* declamation (b) *(recitación)* recital, recitation

declamar 1 *vt* to declaim, to recite

2 *vi* to declaim, to recite

declamatorio, -a *adj* declamatory

declaración *nf* (a) *(manifestación) (ante la autoridad)* statement; **prestar d.** to give evidence; **tomar d. (a)** to take a statement (from) ▸▸ ***d. de impacto ambiental*** environmental impact statement; ***d. del impuesto sobre la renta*** income tax return; ***d. jurada*** sworn statement; ***d. del patrimonio*** = inventory of property, drawn up for tax purposes; ***d. de la renta*** income tax return; **hacer la d. de la renta** to *Br* send in *o US* file one's tax return

(b) *(afirmación)* declaration; **han pedido la d. de zona catastrófica para la región** they've requested that the region be declared a disaster area; **en sus declaraciones a la prensa, el ministro dijo que...** in his statement to the press, the minister said that...; **no hizo declaraciones a los medios de comunicación** he didn't make any statement to the media ▸▸ ***d. de amor*** declaration of love; ***d. de guerra*** declaration of war; ***d. de independencia*** declaration of independence; ***d. de principios*** statement of principles

(c) *(documento)* declaration ▸▸ ***d. universal de los derechos humanos*** universal declaration of human rights

(d) *(comienzo) (de incendio, epidemia)* outbreak

declaradamente *adv* clearly, manifestly

declarado, -a *adj (manifiesto)* open, professed; **es un homosexual d.** he is openly gay; **un d. defensor de los derechos humanos** an outspoken defender of human rights; **hay un odio d. entre ellos** there is open hostility between them

declarante *nmf* witness

declarar 1 *vt* (a) *(manifestar) (ante la autoridad)* to declare; **d. la verdad** to tell the truth; **d. el patrimonio** to declare one's property; **d. culpable/inocente a alguien** to find sb guilty/not guilty; **¿algo que d.?** *(en aduana)* anything to declare?; **¿tú declaras (a Hacienda) todo lo que ganas?** do you declare all your earnings (to the Tax Inspector)?

(b) *(afirmar)* to state, to say; **declaró a la prensa sus próximos proyectos** he informed the press of his future plans/projects; **el monarca declaró su apoyo al nuevo gobierno** the monarch expressed his support for the new government; **el secretario declaró abierta la sesión** the secretary declared the session open; **la región fue declarada zona catastrófica** the region was declared a disaster area; **ha sido declarado candidato a la presidencia** his candidacy for the presidency has been announced

2 *vi Der* to testify, to give evidence; **d. ante un tribunal** to testify before a tribunal; **lo llamaron a d.** he was called to give evidence

3 **declararse** *vpr* (a) *(incendio, epidemia, motín)* to break out; **se ha declarado un incendio forestal en la Sierra de Gredos** a forest fire has broken out in the Sierra de Gredos

(b) *(confesar el amor)* to declare one's feelings *o* love; **se le ha declarado Fernando** Fernando has declared his love to her

(c) *(manifestarse)* **el presidente se declaró enemigo de las privatizaciones** the president declared *o* stated that he was opposed to privatizations; **declararse a favor de algo** to say that one supports sth; **declararse en contra de algo** to say one is opposed to sth; **declararse culpable/inocente** to plead guilty/not guilty; **declararse en huelga** to go on strike; **declararse en quiebra** to declare oneself bankrupt

declarativo, -a, declaratorio, -a *adj* declarative, declaratory

declinación *nf* (a) *(caída)* decline (b) *Gram* declension (c) *Geog* declination (d) *Astron* declination

declinar 1 *vt* (a) *(rechazar) (ofrecimiento)* to decline; **declinó amablemente la invitación** he politely declined the invitation; **declinó toda responsabilidad en este asunto** he disclaimed any responsibility in this affair; **declinó hacer ningún comentario** he declined to make any comment (b) *Gram* to decline

2 *vi* (a) *(fiebre)* to subside, to abate; *(economía, imperio)* to decline; *(carrera profesional)* to decline, to go into a decline; *(fuerzas, energías, ganas, entusiasmo)* to wane; *(estado de salud)* to deteriorate; **su interés por la caza ha declinado** his interest in hunting has waned (b) *(día, tarde)* to draw to a close; **al d. el día** as the day drew to a close

declive *nm* (a) *(decadencia)* decline, fall; **un imperio en d.** an empire in decline; **entrar en d.** to go into decline (b) *(pendiente)* slope; **un terreno en d.** an area of sloping ground

decodificación = **descodificación**

decodificador = **descodificador**

decodificar = **descodificar**

decol *nm Col (lejía)* bleach

decolaje *nm Am* take-off

decolar *vi Am* to take off

decoloración *nf (pérdida de color)* discoloration, fading; *(de pelo)* bleaching

decolorante 1 *adj* bleaching

2 *nm* bleaching agent

decolorar 1 *vt* to bleach

2 **decolorarse** *vpr* to fade; **decolorarse el pelo** to bleach one's hair

decomisar *vt* to confiscate, to seize

decomiso *nm* (a) *(acción)* confiscation *(by customs)* (b) *(objeto)* = an item, such as a camera or radio, confiscated by customs; **tienda de decomisos** = shop selling goods confiscated by customs

decoración *nf* (a) *(acción)* decoration ▸▸ ***d. de escaparates*** window-dressing; ***d. de interiores*** interior design (b) *(conjunto de adornos)* décor; **me gusta mucho la d. de esta habitación** I really like the way this room is decorated (c) *(arte, técnica)* decorative arts (d) *(adornos)* decorations (e) *(decorado)* scenery, set

decorado *nm* set; **decorados** sets, scenery; EXPR **formar** *o* **ser parte del d.** to be part of the furniture

decorador, -ora *nm,f* interior designer; *Cine & Teatro* set designer ▸▸ ***d. de interiores*** interior designer

decorar 1 *vt (piso, paredes, tarta)* to decorate; *(escaparate)* to dress

2 *vi* to be decorative

decorativo, -a *adj* decorative

decoro *nm* (a) *(pudor)* decency, decorum; **guardar el d.** to maintain one's decorum; **saber guardar el d.** to know how to behave properly *o* appropriately; **hablar con d.** to speak with propriety (b) *(dignidad)* dignity; **vivir con d.** to live decently

decorosamente *adv* (a) *(con pudor, recato)* respectably, decently (b) *(aceptablemente)* respectably; **nuestro equipo actuó d. en el campeonato** our team gave a respectable performance in the championship

decoroso, -a *adj* (a) *(decente)* decent; **un vestido poco d.** a very revealing dress (b) *(correcto)* seemly, proper (c) *(aceptable)* decent, respectable; **un sueldo d.** a decent salary

decrecer [46] *vi* (a) *(disminuir) (en intensidad, importancia)* to decrease, to decline; *(en tamaño, cantidad)* to fall, to drop; **decreció el interés por la política** interest in politics declined; **el desempleo decreció en un 2 por ciento** unemployment has fallen by 2 percent; **la luna está decreciendo** the moon is on the wane; **los días decrecen conforme se acerca el invierno** the days grow shorter as winter approaches

(b) *(caudal del río, nivel de las aguas)* to go down, to fall

decreciente *adj (tasa, porcentaje, tipo)* declining, decreasing, falling; **una tendencia d.** a downward trend; **anote estas cantidades por** *o* **en orden d.** note down these quantities in descending order

decrecimiento *nm* decline, decrease, fall

decremento *nm* (a) *(decrecimiento)* decrease (b) *Informát* decrement

decrépito, -a *adj Pey* (a) *(anciano)* decrepit (b) *(civilización, industria)* decadent, declining (c) *(automóvil, tren, edificio)* dilapidated; *(coche) Br* clapped-out, *US* beat-up

decrepitud *nf Pey* (a) *(de anciano)* decrepitude (b) *(de civilización, industria)* decline (c) *(de edificio, automóvil, tren)* sorry state

decretar *vt (mediante ley)* to decree; *(mediante orden)* to order; **se decretó la libertad del acusado** the accused was ordered to be released; **el ayuntamiento ha decretado el cierre del bar** the town council has ordered the bar to be closed down

decretazo *nm Esp Fam Pey* diktat

decreto *nm* decree ▸▸ ***d. ley*** government decree

decrezco *etc ver* **decrecer**

decúbito *nm Formal* ***d. lateral:*** **en d. lateral** lying on one's side, *Espec* in lateral decubitus; ***d. prono*** prone position, *Espec* ventral decubitus; ***d. supino*** supine position, *Espec* supine decubitus

decuplar *vt* to multiply tenfold

décuplo, -a 1 *adj* decuple
2 *nm* **ser el d. de algo** to be tenfold sth

decurso *nm* **en el d. del tiempo** in the course of time; **en el d. de los siglos** over the centuries

dedal *nm* thimble

dedalera *nf (planta)* foxglove

dédalo *nm* labyrinth, maze

dedazo *nm* (a) *Am (designación arbitraria)* arbitrary appointment; **¿y él cómo llegó hasta ahí? – por d.** how did HE get the job? – they just gave it to him (b) *Méx (en política)* = direct designation of a successor by the president in office, bypassing democratic procedure

dedeo *nm Mús* dexterity

dedeté *nm Am* DDT

dedicación *nf* dedication (**a** to); **con d. exclusiva** *o* **plena** full-time; **los funcionarios tienen d. exclusiva** civil servants are not allowed to have any other job; **trabaja con d.** he works with real dedication

dedicado, -a *adj Informát* dedicated

dedicar [60] 1 *vt* (a) *(tiempo, dinero, energía)* to devote (**a** to); **he dedicado todos mis esfuerzos a esta novela** I've put all my effort into this novel; **dedicó sus ahorros a comprar una nueva casa** he used his savings to buy a new house
(b) *(espacio, cuarto, solar)* to use; **dedicaron la bodega a almacén** they used the wine cellar as a storeroom; **este solar se dedicará a viviendas** this land will be used for housing
(c) *(libro, monumento)* to dedicate; **tengo una copia dedicada de su libro** I have a signed copy of his book; **dedicó al público unas palabras de agradecimiento** he addressed a few words of thanks to the audience
(d) *(templo, ofrenda)* to dedicate
2 **dedicarse** *vpr* (a) **dedicarse a** *(una profesión)* **¿a qué se dedica usted?** what do you do for a living?; **se dedica a la enseñanza** she works as a teacher
(b) **dedicarse a** *(actividad, persona)* to spend time on; **los domingos me dedico al estudio** I spend Sundays studying; **dejé la empresa para dedicarme a mi familia** I left the company so that I could spend more time with my family; **se dedica a perder el tiempo** he spends his time doing nothing useful; **se dedica a quejarse sin aportar soluciones** all she does is complain without offering any constructive suggestions

dedicatoria *nf* dedication

dedicatorio, -a *adj* dedicatory

dedil *nm* fingerstall

dedillo: al dedillo *loc adv Fam* **conozco la Patagonia al d.** I know Patagonia inside out *o* like the back of my hand; **cumplir las instrucciones al d.** to carry out instructions to the letter; **saber(se) algo al d.** to know sth off by heart

dedo *nm* (a) *(de la mano)* finger; *(del pie)* toe; **meterse el d. en la nariz** to pick one's nose; **¡no señales con el d.!** don't point!; **contar con los dedos** to count on one's fingers ►► ***d. anular*** ring finger; ***d. corazón*** middle finger; ***d. gordo*** *(de la mano)* thumb; *(del pie)* big toe; ***d. índice*** index finger; ***d. medio*** middle finger; ***d. meñique*** little finger; ***d. pequeño*** *(del pie)* little toe; ***d. pulgar*** thumb
(b) *(medida)* **sólo un d. de whisky** just a drop of whisky; **había dos dedos de agua en el suelo** there was an inch of water on the floor; **estuvo a dos dedos de** *o* **le faltó un d. para morir en el accidente** he came within an inch of being killed in the accident; EXPR *Fam* **no tiene dos dedos de frente** *(es tonto)* he's as thick as two short planks; *(es imprudente)* he hasn't got the sense he was born with; **si tuvieras dos dedos de frente, no harías una cosa así** if you had the least bit of sense, you wouldn't do a thing like that
(c) EXPR *Fam* **nombrar** *o* **elegir a alguien a d.** to appoint sb without due regard to procedure; **se me escapó de entre los dedos** it slipped through my fingers; *Fam* **hacer d., ir a d.** to hitch; *Fam* **fuimos hasta Guadalajara a d.** we hitched to Guadalajara; *Fam* **nadie movió un d. para ayudarme** nobody lifted a finger to help me; *Esp Fam* **pillarse** *o* **cogerse los dedos** to get one's fingers burnt; *Fam* **poner el d. en la llaga** to put one's finger on it; *Méx* **no quitar el d. del renglón** *(no ceder)* not to give way; *(insistir)* to insist; *Fam* **señalar a alguien con el d.** *(criticar a alguien)* to criticize sb; *Méx Fam* **ser d.** to be a sneak

dedocracia *nf Fam* = situation where appointments are made at the whim of those in power

deducción *nf* (a) *(razonamiento)* deduction; **llegar a la d. de que...** to come to the conclusion that...; **¿cómo lo adivinaste? – por d.** how did you guess? – it was the logical conclusion
(b) *(en lógica)* deduction
(c) *(descuento)* deduction; **hacer una d. de algo** to make a deduction from sth; **hacemos una d. de 150 euros del precio original** we'll deduct 150 euros from the original price ►► ***d. fiscal*** tax deduction

deducible *adj* (a) *(idea)* deducible; **ser d. de algo** to follow from sth (b) *(dinero, gastos)* deductible

deducir [18] *vt* (a) *(inferir)* to guess, to deduce; **por la luz dedujo que debía de ser tarde** he could tell by the light that it must be late; **dedujo quién era el asesino** he worked out who the killer was; **¿qué se puede d. de todo esto?** what does all this tell us?, what can be deduced from all this?; **de aquí se deduce que...** from this one concludes *o* infers that...
(b) *(descontar)* to deduct (**de** from); **me deducen del sueldo la seguridad social** national insurance is deducted from my salary

deductivo, -a *adj* deductive

dedujera *etc ver* **deducir**

deduzco *etc ver* **deducir**

de facto *adj* de facto

defecación *nf* defecation

defecar [60] *vi* to defecate

defección *nf* defection (**a** to)

defectivo, -a *adj Gram* defective

defecto *nm* 1 (a) *(físico)* defect (**en** in); **no le veo ningún d. a esta casa** I can't see anything wrong with this house; **siempre le saca defectos a todo** he's always finding fault with everything ►► ***d. de fábrica*** manufacturing defect; ***d. de fabricación*** manufacturing defect; ***d. físico*** physical handicap; *Der* ***d. de forma*** procedural error; ***d. de pronunciación*** speech defect
(b) *(moral)* fault, shortcoming; **su único d. es la soberbia** his only fault *o* flaw is his pride; **tenía el d. de llegar siempre tarde** she had the bad habit of always being late
2 **en su defecto** *loc adv* **el arzobispo o, en su d., el obispo oficiará la ceremonia** the ceremony will be conducted by the archbishop or, in the absence of the archbishop, by the bishop; **acuda a la embajada o, en su d., al consulado más cercano** go to the embassy or, alternatively, to the nearest consulate
3 **por defecto** *loc adv* (a) *Informát & Tec (automáticamente)* by default; **la letra que te sale por d. es Arial** the default typeface is Arial
(b) *(tirando por lo bajo)* **más vale pecar por exceso que por d.** too much is better than not enough

defectuoso, -a *adj (mercancía)* defective, faulty; *(trabajo)* inaccurate

defender [66] 1 *vt* (a) *(país, ideas)* to defend; *(amigo)* to stand up for; *Dep (contrario, delantero)* to mark; **d. a alguien de algo** to defend sb from *o* against sth; **d. los derechos/intereses de alguien** to defend sb's rights/interests; **defendió su teoría con sólidos argumentos** he supported his theory with sound arguments; **d. la tesis** *(en universidad)* *Br* ≃ to have one's viva, *US* ≃ to defend one's dissertation; *Dep* **d. el título** to defend the title; EXPR **d. algo a capa y espada** to defend sth tooth and nail
(b) *(reo, acusado)* to defend
(c) *(proteger) (del frío, calor)* to protect (**de** against)
2 *vi Dep* to mark; **d. al hombre** to mark man for man, to man-mark; **d. en zona** to use a zone defence
3 **defenderse** *vpr* (a) *(protegerse)* to defend oneself (**de** against); **me defendí como pude de sus ataques** I defended myself from his attacks as best I could; **¡defiéndete, cobarde!** defend yourself, you coward!
(b) *(apañarse)* to get by; **se defiende bien en su trabajo** he's getting along okay at work; **se defiende en inglés** he can get by in English; **¿qué tal dibujas? – me defiendo** how are you at drawing? – I'm not too bad; **¿qué tal te defiendes en** *o* **con la cocina?** how good are you at cooking?; **sé defenderme sola** I can look after myself

defendible *adj* (a) *(castillo, ciudad)* defensible (b) *(actitud)* defensible, justifiable; *(argumento, hipótesis)* defensible

defendido, -a *nm,f (de abogado)* defendant

defenestración *nf Fig* sacking, unceremonious removal

defenestrar *vt* (a) *(lanzar por la ventana)* to throw out of a window (b) *(destituir)* to oust, to dismiss

defensa 1 *nf* (a) *(protección)* defence; **la d. del medio ambiente** the protection of the environment; **lleva siempre una pistola como d.** she always carries a gun to defend herself; **en su d. cabe decir que él ignoraba lo sucedido** in his defence, it has to be said that he didn't

know what had happened; **acudir en d. de algo/alguien** to come to the defence of sth/to sb's defence; **salir en d. de algo/alguien** to come out in defence of sth/sb ►► ***d. antiaérea*** anti-aircraft defences; ***la d. nacional*** national defence; ***d. pasiva*** passive resistance; ***d. personal*** self-defence
(b) (el Ministerio de) D. *Br* ≃ the Ministry of Defence, *US* ≃ the Defense Department
(c) *(legal)* defence; **basó su d. en la falta de pruebas** he based his defence on the lack of evidence; **en d. propia, en legítima d.** in self-defence; **la d.** *(parte en un juicio)* the defence; **la d. tiene la palabra** *(en juicio)* it is the turn of the defence to speak
(d) defensas *(sistema inmunitario)* defences; **tiene las defensas muy bajas** his body's defences are very low
(e) *(jugadores, parte del juego)* defence ►► ***d. al hombre*** man-to-man defence; ***d. hombre*** man-to-man defence; ***d. en zona*** *(en baloncesto)* zone defence
(f) *Méx (parachoques) Br* bumper, *US* fender
(g) *Aut* **d. (delantera)** *(en todoterrenos)* bull bars
2 *nmf (jugador)* defender; **la línea de defensas** the back line, the defence ►► ***d. central*** *(en fútbol)* central defender, centre back; ***d. de cierre*** *(en rugby)* fullback; *Fam* ***d. escoba*** *(en fútbol)* sweeper

defensiva *nf* defensive; **ponerse/estar a la d.** to go/be on the defensive; **jugar a la d.** to play defensively

defensivo, -a *adj* defensive; **área** *o* **zona defensiva** *(en fútbol)* defence; **estrategia defensiva** defensive strategy

defensor, -ora 1 *adj* **(a)** *(en tribunal)* **abogado d.** counsel for the defence
(b) *(partidario)* **siempre fue d. de una legislación más dura** he always advocated tougher legislation; **asociaciones defensoras de los consumidores** consumer *o* consumers' associations
2 *nm,f* **(a)** *(de ideal, persona)* defender; *(adalid)* champion; **un gran d. de la paz** a great campaigner for peace ►► ***d. del lector*** *(en periódico)* = person who represents the readership of a newspaper and deals with their complaints against the newspaper; ***d. de oficio*** court-appointed defence lawyer; *Esp* ***d. del pueblo*** ombudsman; ***d. del soldado*** = public body created to defend the rights of soldiers, especially young soldiers doing military service
(b) *(abogado)* counsel for the defence

defeño, -a *nm,f Méx* person from the "Distrito Federal" *(Mexico)*

deferencia *nf* deference; **tuvo la d. de llevarme al aeropuerto** she was kind enough to take me to the airport; **por d. a** in deference to

deferente *adj (cortés)* deferential

deferir [63] **1** *vt Der* to refer
2 *vi* to defer (**a** to)

deficiencia *nf* **(a)** *(defecto)* deficiency, shortcoming; **grandes deficiencias en el servicio de correos** serious deficiencies in the postal service; **deficiencias técnicas** technical faults; **el plan presenta notables deficiencias** the plan has major shortcomings *o* flaws
(b) *(insuficiencia)* lack; **d. de medios** insufficient means ►► ***d. inmunológica*** immunological deficiency; ***d. mental*** mental deficiency

deficiente 1 *adj* **(a)** *(defectuoso) (producto)* deficient; *(audición, vista)* defective **(b)** *(insuficiente) (cantidad)* insufficient, inadequate; *(nutrición, dieta, aporte vitamínico)* deficient, inadequate **(c)** *(persona)* handicapped; **las personas deficientes** the handicapped **(d)** *(mediocre)* poor, unsatisfactory; **el d. estado de las instalaciones** the unsatisfactory state of the facilities
2 *nmf* **d. (mental)** mentally handicapped person
3 *nm (nota)* **muy d.** very poor, E

déficit (*pl* **déficits**) *nm* **(a)** *(económico)* deficit ►► ***d. de la balanza comercial*** trade gap; ***d. comercial*** trade deficit; ***d. presupuestario*** budget deficit; ***d. público*** public deficit **(b)** *(falta)* lack, shortage (**de** of); **d. democrático** lack of democracy ►► ***d. hídrico*** shortfall in water supply

deficitario, -a *adj (empresa, operación)* loss-making; *(saldo, presupuesto)* negative; **la balanza comercial este año ha sido deficitaria** the trade balance this year has been negative; **zonas deficitarias en agua** areas prone to water shortages

defiendo *etc ver* **defender**

defiera *etc ver* **deferir**

definición *nf* **(a)** *(de un término)* definition; **por d.** by definition **(b)** *(en aparatos ópticos)* definition; *(en televisión)* resolution **(c)** *(concreción)* clarity; **el electorado exige una mayor d. de posturas** the electorate wants to know exactly what each candidate stands for

definido, -a *adj* **(a)** *(límite, idea)* (clearly) defined **(b)** *(trazo, línea)* sharp, well-defined **(c)** *Gram* **artículo d.** definite article

definir 1 *vt* **(a)** *(explicar, precisar)* to define; **debes d. tu postura** you must define your position, you must say where you stand **(b)** *(describir)* to describe; **la generosidad define su carácter** generosity typifies his character; **se define a sí mismo como de derechas** he describes himself as right-wing
2 definirse *vpr* to take a clear stance; **no se quiere d. políticamente** he doesn't want to make his political position clear; **no se definió por ninguno de los dos bandos** he took neither side; **el plan no acababa de definirse** the plan had not yet taken any definite shape

definitivamente *adv* **(a)** *(sin duda)* definitely; **d., el picante no me sienta bien** hot food definitely doesn't agree with me
(b) *(finalmente)* **nos tienes que decir d. si vas a venir o no** you have to tell us whether you're definitely coming or not; **hasta que no se solucione d. la avería no habrá electricidad** there won't be any electricity until the problem is properly fixed
(c) *(para siempre)* for good; **queremos quedarnos a vivir aquí d.** we want to come and live here for good; **la banda se separó d. en 1969** the band finally broke up in 1969; **la corte se instaló d. en Madrid** the court moved to Madrid, where it remained

definitivo, -a 1 *adj* **(a)** *(concluyente, final)* final, definitive; **la versión definitiva** *(de un texto)* the definitive version; **los resultados definitivos** the final results; **el Supremo emitirá el dictamen d. sobre el caso** the Supreme Court will make the definitive judgement in the case
(b) *(permanente, para siempre)* definitive, final; **la sede definitiva de la empresa estará en Buenos Aires** the company's definitive headquarters will be in Buenos Aires; **su despedida definitiva de los campos de fútbol** his final departure from the soccer pitch
(c) *(decisivo)* decisive; **su intervención fue definitiva para resolver el conflicto** his intervention was decisive in resolving the conflict
2 en definitiva *loc adv* **en definitiva, el futuro es prometedor** all in all, the future looks promising; **ésta es, en definitiva, la única alternativa que nos queda** this is, in short, the only alternative we have left

definitorio, -a *adj* defining

deflación *nf Econ* deflation

deflacionario, -a *adj Econ* deflationary

deflacionista *adj Econ* deflationary

deflagración *nf Formal* deflagration

deflagrar *vi Formal* to deflagrate

deflector *nm* baffle-board, baffle-plate, deflector

defoliación *nf* defoliation

defoliante 1 *adj* defoliant
2 *nm* defoliant

deforestación *nf* deforestation

deforestar *vt* to deforest

deformación *nf* **(a)** *(de huesos, objetos)* deformation; **lávese en agua fría para evitar la d. de la prenda** wash in cold water to prevent the garment from losing shape ►► ***d. física*** (physical) deformity **(b)** *(de imágenes, figuras)* distortion **(c)** *(de la verdad, la realidad)* distortion **(d) tener d. profesional** to be always acting as if one were still at work

deformado, -a *adj* **(a)** *(cuerpo, figura, miembro)* deformed **(b)** *(objeto)* misshapen **(c)** *(imagen)* distorted **(d)** *(verdad, realidad)* distorted

deformar 1 *vt* **(a)** *(cuerpo, figura, miembro)* to deform; *(prenda)* to pull out of shape; *(metal)* to twist; *(madera)* to warp **(b)** *(imagen)* to distort **(c)** *(la verdad, la realidad)* to distort
2 deformarse *vpr* **(a)** *(hueso, cuerpo, miembro)* to become deformed; *(prenda)* to go out of shape; *(metal)* to get twisted out of shape; *(madera)* to warp; **se me ha deformado el jersey al lavarlo** my jumper lost its shape when I washed it **(b)** *(imagen)* to become distorted

deforme *adj (cuerpo)* deformed, disfigured; *(imagen)* distorted; *(objeto)* misshapen

deformidad *nf* deformity

defraudación *nf (fraude fiscal)* tax evasion

defraudador, -ora 1 *adj (de impuestos)* tax-evading
2 *nm,f (de impuestos)* tax evader

defraudar 1 *vt* **(a)** *(decepcionar)* to disappoint; **su última película me defraudó mucho** I was very disappointed by his last film; **creí que podría contar contigo, pero me has defraudado** I thought I could count on you, but you've let me down **(b)** *(estafar)* to defraud; **d. al fisco, d. a Hacienda** to practise tax evasion
2 *vi (decepcionar)* to be disappointing, to disappoint; **reapareció Carreras y no defraudó** Carreras made a reappearance and did not disappoint

defunción *nf* decease, death; **cerrado por d.** *(en letrero)* closed due to bereavement

degeneración *nf* degeneration

degenerado, -a 1 *adj* degenerate
 2 *nm,f* degenerate

degenerar *vi* **(a)** *(degradarse)* to degenerate; **este lugar ha degenerado mucho** this place has really gone downhill **(b)** *(convertirse)* to degenerate (**en** into); **el debate degeneró en una discusión tensa** the debate degenerated into an argument

degenerativo, -a *adj (proceso, enfermedad)* degenerative

deglución *nf* swallowing

deglutir 1 *vt* to swallow
 2 *vi* to swallow

degolladero *nm* slaughterhouse

degollar [64] *vt* **(a)** *(cortar la garganta a)* to cut *o* slit the throat of; *(decapitar)* to behead; **¡como lo pille, lo degüello!** I'll kill him if I get my hands on him! **(b)** *Fam (interpretar mal)* to murder

degollina *nf Esp Fam (matanza)* bloodbath; **el examen fue una d.** droves of students failed the exam

degradable *adj* degradable

degradación *nf* **(a)** *(moral)* degradation **(b)** *(física) (de medio ambiente, naturaleza)* degradation; *(de calidad, servicio, producto)* deterioration **(c)** *(de mando militar, cargo)* demotion

degradado *nm Informát* blend ►► ***d. lineal*** gradient *o* graduated fill

degradante *adj* degrading

degradar 1 *vt* **(a)** *(moralmente)* to degrade, to debase; **el alcohol la ha degradado** she's been ruined by drink **(b)** *(físicamente) (medio ambiente, naturaleza)* to degrade; *(calidad, servicio, producto)* to cause to deteriorate; **la contaminación degrada el medio ambiente** pollution degrades the environment **(c)** *(de mando militar, cargo)* to demote, to downgrade
 2 degradarse *vpr* **(a)** *(moralmente)* to degrade *o* lower oneself **(b)** *(medio ambiente, naturaleza)* to deteriorate, to be degraded; *(calidad, servicio, producto)* to deteriorate

degüello 1 *ver* **degollar**
 2 *nm (degolladura)* slaughter; *(decapitación)* beheading; EXPR **entrar a d.** to storm in ruthlessly

degustación *nf* tasting *(of wines, food)*; **d. de vinos** wine tasting

degustar *vt* to taste *(wines, food)*

dehesa *nf* meadow

deicida 1 *adj* deicidal
 2 *nmf* deicide

deíctico, -a *Ling* **1** *adj* deictic
 2 *nm* deictic

deidad *nf* deity

deificación *nf* deification

deificar [60] *vt* to deify

deísmo *nm* deism

deísta 1 *adj* deist
 2 *nmf* deist

de iure, de jure *adj* de jure

deíxis *nf inv Ling* deixis

dejación *nf Formal Der* **(a)** *(de derechos, bienes)* abdication **(b)** *(de responsabilidades)* abdication **(c)** *(de deberes, funciones)* dereliction

dejada *nf* **(a)** *(en tenis)* drop shot; **hacer una d.** to play a drop shot **(b)** *ver también* **dejado**

dejadez *nf* **(a)** *(abandono)* neglect; *(en aspecto)* slovenliness; **viven en la más absoluta d.** they live in utter squalor **(b)** *(pereza)* laziness; *(falta de cuidado)* carelessness: **no lo hizo por d.** he didn't do it, because he couldn't be bothered

dejado, -a 1 *adj* **(a)** *(desaseado)* slovenly, slobbish; **¡no seas tan d. y dúchate más a menudo!** don't be such a slob, and have a shower more often!; **podías ser menos d. y limpiar la cocina de vez en cuando** you could try not to be such a slob and clean the kitchen occasionally
 (b) *(descuidado)* careless, sloppy; *(perezoso)* lazy; **no seas tan d. y escríbenos de vez en cuando** don't be so lazy and write to us occasionally
 2 *nm,f* **(a)** *(desaseado)* slovenly person, slob; **¡eres un d.!** you're so slovenly!
 (b) *(descuidado)* careless person

DEJAR 1 *vt* **(a)** *(poner)* to leave, to put; **dejó los papeles en la mesa** he put *o* left the papers on the table; **deja el abrigo en la percha** put your coat on the hanger; **he dejado la moto muy cerca** I've left *o* parked my motorbike nearby; **deja el jarrón, que lo vas a romper** put that vase down or you'll break it; **su compañero le dejó un balón perfecto y sólo tuvo que rematar a gol** his team-mate played a perfect ball for him and all he had to do was tap it in
 (b) *(olvidar)* to leave; **dejé el paraguas en el cine** I left my umbrella at the movies
 (c) *(encomendar)* **dejarle algo a alguien** to leave sth with sb; **le dejé los niños a mi madre** I left the children with my mother
 (d) *Esp (prestar)* **d. algo a alguien** to lend sb sth, to lend sth to sb; **¿me dejas un paraguas?** could you lend me an umbrella?; **¿nos dejarás tu casa el próximo verano?** will you let us use your house next summer?
 (e) *(abandonar) (casa, trabajo, país)* to leave; *(tabaco, estudios)* to give up; *(familia)* to abandon; **dejé la fiesta a medianoche** I left the party at midnight; **dejó el tenis cuando empezó la universidad** she gave up tennis when she started university; **dejó lo que estaba haciendo para ayudarla** he stopped *o* dropped what he was doing to help her; **te dejo, que si no pierdo el autobús** I have to leave you now, or I'll miss the bus; **su marido la ha dejado** her husband has left her; **lo dejó por un hombre más joven** she left him for a younger man; **d. a alguien en algún sitio** *(con el coche)* to drop sb off somewhere; **el avión dejó a treinta pasajeros en la primera escala** thirty passengers got off (the plane) at the first stopover; **d. atrás a alguien** to leave sb behind; **es muy inteligente y ha dejado atrás al resto de la clase** she's very intelligent and has left the rest of the class behind (her), she's very intelligent and is way ahead of the rest of the class; **dejó atrás al resto de corredores** he left the other runners behind *o* in his wake; **d. algo por imposible** to give sth up as a lost cause
 (f) *(posponer)* to leave; **dejemos esto para la próxima reunión** let's leave this matter until the next meeting; **dejamos el viaje para diciembre** we put off the journey until December; EXPR **no dejes para mañana lo que puedas hacer hoy** don't put off till *o* leave for tomorrow what you can do today
 (g) *(permitir)* **d. a alguien hacer algo** to let sb do sth, to allow sb to do sth; **no me dejan salir, estoy castigado** I'm being kept in as a punishment; **d. entrar/salir a alguien** to let sb in/out; **sus gritos no me dejaron dormir** his cries prevented me from sleeping; **déjame a mí, que tengo más experiencia** let me do it, I'm more experienced; **déjame a mí, yo me encargo de preparar la comida** leave it to me, I'll get dinner; **deja que tu hijo venga con nosotros** let your son come with us; **¿me dejas ir?** will you let me go?, can I go?; **d. correr algo** to leave sth be; **d. pasar** *o* **escapar algo** to let sth slip; **dejó pasar tres semanas** he let three weeks go by; **el resultado final no deja lugar a dudas** the final result leaves no room for doubt
 (h) *(reservar)* **deja algo de café para mí** leave some coffee for me; **deja algo para los demás** leave some for the others; **deja tus críticas para una mejor ocasión** save your criticisms for another time
 (i) *(reportar)* to bring; **el negocio les deja varios millones al año** the business brings them several million a year
 (j) *(legar)* to leave; **d. algo a alguien** to leave sth to sb; **dejó todos sus ahorros a varias instituciones benéficas** she left all her savings to charity
 (k) *(omitir)* to leave out; **la cocina déjala de momento, ahora hay que limpiar el baño** leave the kitchen for the moment, I want you to clean the bathroom now; **dejemos aparte las introducciones y comencemos la negociación** let's dispense with the introductions and get straight down to the negotiations; **d. algo por** *o* **sin hacer** to fail to do sth; **dejó lo más importante por resolver** he left the most important question unresolved
 (l) *(en imperativo) (olvidar)* to forget (about); **déjalo, no importa** forget it, it doesn't matter
 (m) *(en imperativo) (no molestar)* to leave alone *o* in peace; **¡déjame, que tengo trabajo!** leave me alone, I'm busy!; **déjame tranquilo** *o* **en paz** leave me alone *o* in peace; **¡deja a tu padre, está durmiendo!** leave your father alone *o* in peace, he's sleeping!; **déjalo estar** leave it as it is, let it be
 (n) *(seguido de infinitivo)* **dejó adivinar sus intenciones** she allowed her intentions to be guessed; **lo dejó caer** she dropped it; **dejó caer que no se presentaría a las próximas elecciones** he let it drop that he wouldn't be standing at the next election; **dejó escapar una magnífica oportunidad** she missed an excellent opportunity, she allowed an excellent opportunity to slip by
 (o) *(indica resultado)* to leave; **deja un sabor agridulce** it has a bittersweet aftertaste; **la lejía ha dejado marcas en la ropa** the bleach has left stains on the clothes; **el examen me dejó agotado** I was left exhausted by the exam; **¡no me dejes así, cuéntame qué pasó!** don't leave me guessing, tell me what happened!; **yo dejaría la pared tal y como está** I'd leave the wall as it is; **tu comportamiento deja bastante/mucho que desear** your behaviour leaves quite a lot/a lot to

be desired; **d. algo hecho** to get sth done; **te lo dejaré hecho para el lunes** I'll get it done for you by Monday; **d. algo como nuevo** to leave sth as good as new

(**p**) *(esperar a)* **d. que** to wait until; **dejó que acabara de llover para salir** he waited until it had stopped raining before going out; **retirar del fuego y d. enfriar** *o* **que se enfríe** remove from the heat and allow to cool; **deja que se calme un poco, y entonces háblale** wait until she calms down a bit before you talk to her

2 *vi* (**a**) *(parar)* **d. de hacer algo** to stop doing sth; **dejó de llover** it stopped raining, the rain stopped; **ha dejado de fumar/beber** he's stopped smoking/drinking; **no deja de venir ni un solo día** he never fails to come; **poco a poco dejaron de llamarse** they gradually stopped phoning one another; **no deja de ser extraño que haga tanto calor en esta época del año** it really is most strange for it to be so hot at this time of year

(**b**) *(en negativa) (indica promesa)* **no d. de** to be sure to; **¡no dejes de escribirme!** be sure to write to me!; **no dejes de avisarnos si tienes algún problema** be sure to tell us if you have any problem

(**c**) *(en imperativo) (indica negación)* **deja, ya subo yo las maletas** leave the cases, I'll bring them up; **deje, señora, ya lo hago yo** allow me, madam, I'll do it; **¿vas a volver a correr la maratón? – ¡deja, deja! ya tuve suficiente con la del año pasado** are you going to run the marathon again? – don't! last year was more than enough

3 dejarse *vpr* (**a**) *(olvidar)* **dejarse algo en algún sitio** to leave sth somewhere; **me he dejado la cartera en casa** I've left my *Br* wallet *o US* billfold at home

(**b**) *(permitir)* **dejarse engañar** to allow oneself to be taken in; **se dejaron ganar** they lost on purpose; *Am* **no te dejes** stand up for yourself; **no te dejes tomar el pelo** don't let them make fun of you; **le quisimos ayudar, pero no se dejó** we wanted to help him, but he wouldn't let us

(**c**) *(no cortarse)* **dejarse (la) barba/(el) bigote** to grow a beard/moustache; **dejarse el pelo largo** to grow one's hair long

(**d**) *(cesar)* **dejarse de hacer algo** to stop doing sth; **¡déjate de holgazanear y ponte a trabajar!** stop lazing around and do some work!; **¡déjate de tonterías!** don't talk nonsense!

(**e**) *(descuidarse)* to let oneself go; **se ha dejado mucho desde que perdió el trabajo** she's really let herself go since she lost her job

(**f**) EXPR **dejarse caer por: se dejó caer por la fiesta, aunque no había sido invitado** he turned up at the party even though he hadn't been invited; **a lo mejor nos dejamos caer por vuestra casa este fin de semana** we may drop by your house this weekend; **dejarse llevar** to get carried away; **me dejé llevar por la emoción del momento** I got carried away with the excitement of the moment; **se deja llevar por sus impulsos** she allows her impulses to get the better of her; **dejarse ver** to be seen; **se dejan ver mucho por lugares de moda** they are often to be seen *o* they like to be seen in the most fashionable places

---

deje, dejo *nm* (**a**) *(acento)* accent; **tiene un d. mexicano, habla con d. mexicano** he has a slight Mexican accent

(**b**) *(tono)* undertone; **había un d. de resentimiento en sus palabras** there was an undertone of resentment in her words

(**c**) *(sabor)* aftertaste; **tiene un d. a curry** it has a slight taste of curry

(**d**) *CSur (parecido)* slight resemblance; **tiene un d. a su padre** there's something of her father about her

de jure = **de iure**

del *ver* **de**

delación *nf* denunciation

delantal *nm* (**a**) *(mandil)* apron (**b**) *RP (bata)* white coat

---

DELANTE *adv* (**a**) *(en primer lugar, en la parte delantera)* in front; *(enfrente)* opposite; **d. hay una fábrica** there's a factory opposite; **¿dónde has aparcado? – d.** where have you parked? – opposite; **ve tú d., yo me sentaré detrás** you go in the front, I'll sit at the back; **nos sentamos d. para ver mejor** we sat at the front so we could see better; **el de d.** the one in front; **las luces/el asiento de d.** *(en automóvil)* the front lights/seat; **está sentado en el asiento de d.** *(en el inmediatamente anterior)* he's sitting in the seat in front of me; **d. de** in front of; **d. de mí/ti** in front of me/you; **lo tienes d. de las narices** it's right in front of *o* under your nose; **pasamos por d. de la catedral** we passed in front of the cathedral; **hay que acortar el vestido por d.** the dress needs taking up at the front; **visto por d. resulta impresionante** it's very impressive (seen) from the front; **la avalancha se llevó a los esquiadores por d.** the avalanche engulfed the skiers; **tenemos un mes entero por d.** we have a whole month ahead of us

(**b**) *(presente)* present; **cuando no está d., todos hablan mal de él** everyone speaks ill of him behind his back, whenever he's not there, everyone speaks ill of him; **d. de** *(en presencia de)* in front of; **se desnudó d. de todo el mundo** she undressed in front of everyone; **comparecer d. de un tribunal** to appear before a court

---

delantera *nf* (**a**) *(en deporte)* forwards, forward line

(**b**) *(ventaja)* **nos llevan tres minutos de d.** they're three minutes ahead of us; **su hermano le lleva la d. en los estudios** his brother is doing better than him at school

(**c**) *(primer puesto)* lead; **coger** *o* **tomar la d.** to take the lead; **coger** *o* **tomar la d. a alguien** to beat sb to it; **llevar la d.** to be in the lead

(**d**) *(parte frontal)* front

(**e**) *Teatro (primera fila)* front row

(**f**) *Fam (de mujer)* boobs

delantero, -a 1 *adj* front; **las patas delanteras** the front legs

2 *nm,f* forward ►► ***d. centro*** centre forward; *(en rugby)* lock (forward)

3 *nm (de vestido)* front

delatar 1 *vt* (**a**) *(denunciar)* to denounce; **lo delaté a la policía** I reported him to the police (**b**) *(sujeto: sonrisa, ojos)* to betray, to give away; **esa risita nerviosa te delata** that nervous giggle gives you away

2 delatarse *vpr* to give oneself away

delator, -ora *adj* **1** *(sonrisa, mirada)* telltale

2 *nm,f* informer

delco *nm Esp Aut* distributor

deleble *adj* erasable

delectación *nf Formal* delight, great pleasure; **con d.** with delight, delightedly

delegación *nf* (**a**) *(autorización)* delegation; **asumió la gestión de la empresa por d. de su padre** his father entrusted him with the running of the company

(**b**) *(comisión)* delegation ►► ***d. comercial*** *(de un país)* trade delegation

(**c**) *Esp (sucursal)* office ►► ***d. regional*** regional office, area office

(**d**) *(oficina pública)* local office ►► *Esp* ***D. del Gobierno*** = office representing central government in each province; *Esp* ***d. de Hacienda*** = head tax office *(in each province)*; *Méx* ***d. de policía*** police station

(**e**) *Chile, Ecuad, Méx (distrito)* municipal district

delegado, -a *nm,f* (**a**) *(representante)* delegate; **el d. de Educación** the representative from the Ministry of Education ►► *Esp* ***d. del Gobierno*** = person representing central government in each province; ***d. sindical*** shop steward (**b**) *(en colegio, universidad)* class representative ►► ***d. de curso*** class representative (**c**) *Esp (de empresa)* representative

delegar [38] **1** *vt* (**a**) *(funciones)* to delegate; **el gobierno central se resiste a d. ciertos poderes** central government is reluctant to delegate certain powers; **d. algo en alguien** to delegate sth to sb (**b**) *(representante)* to delegate; **d. a alguien para hacer algo** *o* **para que haga algo** to delegate sb to do sth

2 *vi* to delegate; **hay que saber d.** you have to know how to delegate; **d. en alguien para hacer algo** to delegate sth to sb

deleitar 1 *vt* to delight; **la música clásica nos deleita** we love classical music; **me deleitaba escucharla cantar** I loved listening to her sing

2 deleitarse *vpr* **deleitarse con** *o* **en algo** to take pleasure in sth; **deleitarse con la vista** to enjoy the view; **deleitarse haciendo algo** to take pleasure in *o* enjoy doing sth; **me deleitaba escuchándola cantar** I took great pleasure in listening to her sing

deleite *nm* delight; **el público escuchaba la música con d.** the audience listened to the music with delight; **para d. de todos los asistentes** to the delight of those present

deleitoso, -a *adj* delightful

deletéreo, -a *adj Formal o Literario* deleterious

deletrear *vt* to spell (out); **¿me puede d. su apellido, por favor?** could you spell your surname for me, please?

deletreo *nm (de palabras, sílabas)* spelling

deleznable *adj* (**a**) *(considerado incorrecto) (clima, libro, actuación)* appalling; *(excusa, razón)* contemptible; *(individuo, conducta, acto)* contemptible (**b**) *(material)* crumbly

delfín[1] *nm (animal)* dolphin ►► ***d. mular*** bottlenose dolphin

delfín[2] *nm* (**a**) *Hist* dauphin (**b**) *(sucesor)* successor

delfinario *nm* dolphinarium

delgadez *nf* (**a**) *(de persona) (tono neutro o negativo)* thinness; *(esbeltez)* slimness (**b**) *(de animal)* thinness (**c**) *(de cable, lámina, tabique)* thinness

delgado, -a *adj* **(a)** *(persona) (tono neutro o negativo)* thin; *(esbelto)* slim; **un tipo alto y d.** a tall, thin guy **(b)** *(animal)* thin **(c)** *(cable, tela, lámina, tabique)* thin; *(hilo)* thin, fine

delgaducho, -a *adj* skinny

deliberación *nf* deliberation; **someter algo a d.** to deliberate about *o* on sth; **tras largas deliberaciones** after much deliberation

deliberadamente *adv* deliberately, on purpose

deliberado, -a *adj* deliberate

deliberante *adj (reunión)* empowered to take decisions

deliberar *vi* **(a)** *(discutir)* to deliberate (**sobre** about *o* on); **el jurado se reunió a d.** the jury assembled to deliberate **(b)** *(meditar, pensar)* to deliberate; **después de mucho d., decidió actuar** after much deliberation, she decided to act

delicadamente *adv* delicately

delicadeza *nf* **(a)** *(cuidado)* care; **trata al bebé con d.** treat the baby very gently
(b) *(cortesía)* kindness, attentiveness; **tuvo la d. de invitarnos a cenar** he very kindly invited us to dinner; **¡podías tener la d. de llamar a la puerta!** don't you think it would be polite to knock?
(c) *(tacto, discreción)* tact; **le dio la noticia con d.** he broke the news to her tactfully *o* gently; **una falta de d.** a lack of tact; **¡qué falta de d.!** how tactless!; **tuvo la d. de no mencionar el tema** he was tactful enough not to mention the subject
(d) *(finura) (de aroma, gesto, material, objeto)* delicacy; *(de persona)* sensitivity
(e) *(de asunto, situación)* delicacy

delicado, -a *adj* **(a)** *(aroma, gesto, manos)* delicate; **un perfume muy d.** a very delicate perfume
(b) *(material, objeto)* delicate; **piel delicada** sensitive *o* delicate skin; **loción hidratante para pieles delicadas** moisturizing lotion for sensitive skin; **detergente para ropa delicada** *o* **prendas delicadas** detergent for delicates
(c) *(asunto, situación)* delicate, tricky; **una situación delicada** a delicate *o* tricky situation
(d) *(persona) (débil, enfermizo)* weak, delicate; **su estado (de salud) es d.** his condition is delicate; **estar d. de salud** to have delicate health; **estar d. del corazón** to have a weak heart
(e) *(persona) (sensible)* sensitive
(f) *(educado) (persona)* polite; *(lenguaje, modales)* refined
(g) *(persona) (tiquismiquis)* fussy, choosy, picky; **es demasiado d. para ir de camping** he likes his creature comforts too much to go camping; **¡no seas d., hay que comérselo todo!** don't be so picky, you've got to eat all of it!

delicia *nf* **(a)** *(placer)* delight; **estos pasteles son una d.** these cakes are delicious; **es una d. escucharle** it's a delight to listen to him; **hacer las delicias de alguien** to delight sb **(b)** *(pescado congelado)* fish finger; **delicias de merluza** hake fish fingers

deliciosamente *adv* **(a)** *(con encanto)* delightfully **(b)** *(sabrosamente)* deliciously

delicioso, -a *adj* **(a)** *(comida, bebida)* delicious; *(aroma, sabor)* delicious **(b)** *(persona, sonrisa, lugar, clima)* lovely, delightful

delictivo, -a *adj* criminal

delictual *adj Am* criminal

delimitación *nf* **(a)** *(de terreno, zona)* fixing of the boundaries, delimitation **(b)** *(de funciones, tareas, responsabilidades)* delimitation, demarcation

delimitador *nm Informát* delimiter

delimitar *vt* **(a)** *(terreno, zona)* to fix the boundaries of, to delimit, to demarcate **(b)** *(funciones, tareas, responsabilidades)* to define, to demarcate

delinco *etc ver* **delinquir**

delincuencia *nf* crime; **la d. aumentó durante el último año** crime increased last year ▸▸ ***d. informática*** computer crime; ***d. juvenil*** juvenile delinquency; ***d. organizada*** organized crime

delincuente *nmf* criminal; **pequeños delincuentes** petty criminals ▸▸ ***d. común*** common criminal; ***d. habitual*** habitual offender; ***d. juvenil*** juvenile delinquent *o* offender

delineación *nf* **(a)** *(trazado)* delineation, outlining **(b)** *(profesión, disciplina)* technical drawing *o* drafting

delineador, -ora *adj* delineating, outlining

delineamiento *nm (trazado)* delineation, outlining

delineante *nmf Br* draughtsman, *f* draughtswoman, *US* draftsman, *f* draftswoman

delinear *vt* **(a)** *(plano)* to draw **(b)** *(proyecto)* to outline

delinquir [22] *vi* to commit a crime; **son muchos los que vuelven a d.** many of them reoffend; **para él robar en una tienda no es d.** for him shoplifting is not a crime

delirante *adj* **(a)** *(por la fiebre)* delirious **(b)** *(enloquecido) (idea, fiesta)* wild, crazy; *(situación)* crazy; *(fans, público)* ecstatic, wild

delirar *vi* **(a)** *(enfermo, borracho)* to be delirious; **la fiebre lo hizo d.** the fever made him delirious **(b)** *(decir disparates)* to talk nonsense; **¡tú deliras!** you're off your head!

delirio *nm* **(a)** *(por fiebre, borrachera)* delirium; *(de un enfermo mental)* ravings ▸▸ ***delirios de grandeza*** delusions of grandeur **(b)** *(disparate)* crazy idea **(c)** *(pasión desatada)* **tras el gol de la victoria, el campo fue un d.** after the winning goal, the whole stadium went crazy; **lo quiere con auténtico d.** she loves him to distraction

delírium tremens *nm inv* delirium tremens

delito *nm* crime, offence; **cometer un d.** to commit a crime *o* an offence; **lo cogieron en flagrante d.** he was caught in the act; **no es ningún d. criticar al profesor** it's no crime to criticize the teacher; *Der* **ser constitutivo de d.** to constitute an offence; *Fam* **el corte de pelo que te han hecho es un d.** that haircut you've got is criminal; EXPR *Fam* **tener d.** *(ser el colmo) (persona)* to be an absolute disgrace; *(cosa, hecho)* to be an outrage ▸▸ ***d. común*** common crime; ***d. ecológico*** ecological crime; ***d. financiero*** financial crime; ***d. fiscal*** tax offence; ***d. informático*** computer crime; ***d. menor*** minor offence; ***d. político*** political crime; ***d. contra la propiedad*** crime against property; ***d. contra la salud pública*** crime against public health; ***d. de sangre*** violent crime

delta 1 *nm (desembocadura)* delta; **el d. del Nilo** the Nile delta
2 *nf (letra griega)* delta

deltoides *Anat* **1** *adj inv* deltoid
2 *nm inv* deltoid (muscle)

demacrado, -a *adj* gaunt, haggard

demacrar 1 *vt* to make gaunt *o* haggard
2 demacrarse *vpr* to become gaunt *o* haggard

demagogia *nf* demagoguery; **acusan a ambos partidos de hacer d.** both parties have been accused of being populist

demagógico, -a *adj* demagogic

demagogo, -a *nm,f* demagogue

demanda *nf* **(a)** *(petición)* request; *(reivindicación)* demand; **atender las demandas de los trabajadores** to respond to the workers' demands; **en d. de** asking for; **irán a la huelga en d. de una mejora salarial** they will go on strike in support of their demands for better pay ▸▸ ***d. de ayuda*** request for help; ***d. de empleo*** *(solicitud)* job application; ***d. de extradición*** extradition request; ***d. salarial*** wage claim
(b) *(en economía)* demand; **hay mucha d. de informáticos** there is a great demand for computer specialists; **ha crecido la d. de productos reciclables** there has been an increase in demand for recyclable products; **la d. de trabajo en el sector turístico es muy alta** jobs in the tourist industry are in high demand; **la oferta y la d.** supply and demand
(c) *(en derecho)* lawsuit; *(por daños y perjuicios)* claim; **interponer** *o* **presentar una d. contra** to take legal action against; **presenté una d. contra la constructora por daños y perjuicios** I sued the builders for damages; **una d. por difamación** a libel suit

demandado, -a 1 *nm,f* defendant
2 *adj* **la parte demandada** the defendant

demandante 1 *nmf* **(a)** *(en juicio)* plaintiff **(b)** *(solicitante)* ***d. de empleo*** job applicant
2 *adj* **la parte d.** *(en juicio)* the plaintiff

demandar *vt* **(a)** *(legalmente)* **d. a alguien (por)** to sue sb (for); **d. a alguien por daños y perjuicios** to sue sb for damages; **d. a alguien por difamación** to sue sb for libel; **los demandaremos ante el juez** we'll take them to court
(b) *(pedir, requerir)* to ask for, to seek; **los sindicatos demandan una mejora salarial** the unions are demanding a wage rise; **este deporte demanda mucha disciplina** this sport calls for *o* requires a lot of discipline

demarcación *nf* **(a)** *(señalización)* demarcation **(b)** *(territorio)* area **(c)** *(jurisdicción)* district **(d)** *(en deporte)* = area of playing field assigned to a player; **siempre juega en una d. adelantada** he always plays in an advanced position

demarcar *vt* to demarcate, to mark out

demarraje *nm Dep* burst of speed, spurt

demarrar *vi Dep* to put on a burst of speed, to put on a spurt; **demarró en las primeras rampas del puerto** he put on a burst of speed as they began the climb up to the pass

demás 1 *adj* (**a**) *(resto)* other; **los d. invitados** the other *o* the remaining guests; **las ranas y d. anfibios** frogs and other amphibians
(**b**) *RP Fam (sensacional)* great, cool, ace; **tu auto es d.** your car's really cool; **la fiesta estuvo d.** the party was great; **la casa le pareció d.** she thought the house was fab
2 *pron* (**a**) *(otras personas)* **los/las d.** the others, the rest; **entramos ella y yo, los d. se quedaron fuera** just she and I went in, the others stayed outside; **no te metas en los problemas de los d.** don't stick your nose in other people's business; **se bebió su cerveza y las de los d.** he drank his own beer and everyone else's
(**b**) *(otras cosas)* **lo d.** the rest; **sólo dejó la zanahoria, lo d. se lo comió todo** she only left the carrot, she ate all the rest; **deja fuera tres filetes y congela los d.** leave three fillets out and freeze the rest; **por lo d.** apart from that, otherwise; **por lo d. me encuentro bien** apart from that I feel fine; **todo lo d.** everything else; **todo lo d. viene en otro camión** all the rest will be coming along in another lorry; **la casa tiene lavadora, lavaplatos y todo lo d.** the house has a washing machine, a dishwasher and all the rest of it; **y d.** and so on; **planetas, estrellas, asteroides y d.** planets, stars, asteroids and so on
3 **por demás** *loc adv* (**a**) *(demasiado)* **come por d.** he eats too much *o* to excess; **me hacían regalos por d.** they showered me with gifts; **es reservado por d.** he's too reserved (**b**) *(en vano)* unsuccessfully, in vain

demasía: en demasía *loc adv* in excess, too much; **el vino, en d., es malo para la salud** wine, if drunk to excess, is bad for your health

demasiado, -a 1 *adj (en exceso)* too much; *(plural)* too many; **demasiada comida** too much food; **demasiados niños** too many children; **aquí hay d. niño** there are too many kids in here, this place is too full of kids; **tiene demasiada estatura** she's too tall; **hay d. ruido** it's too noisy; **¡esto es d.!** *(el colmo)* this is too much!
2 *adj inv Esp Fam (genial)* great, cool; **esta discoteca es d.** this club is something else; **¿que te has casado? ¡qué d.!** you're married? too much!
3 *adv (en exceso)* too much; *(antes de adj o adv)* too; **habla d.** she talks too much; **la quiere d. (como) para abandonarla** he loves her too much to want to leave her; **iba d. rápido** he was going too fast; **d. bien le fue en el examen, con lo poco que estudió** she did better in the exam than she deserved to, considering how little work she did for it
4 *pron* **éramos demasiados** there were too many of us; **demasiados se ven obligados a emigrar para subsistir** all too many are forced to emigrate to survive; **has metido d. en la maleta** you've packed too much into the case

demasié *Esp Fam* 1 *adj (genial)* great, cool, something else; **fue una fiesta d.** the party was something else; **¿de vacaciones a Cuba? ¡qué d.!** you're going to Cuba on holiday? cool!
2 *adv* **nos lo pasamos d.** we had a great *o* wicked time!

demencia *nf* madness, insanity ▸▸ ***d. senil*** senile dementia

demencial *adj (disparatado)* crazy, mad; **¡es d.!** it's insane *o* madness!

demente 1 *adj* mad
2 *nmf* (**a**) *(que padece demencia)* mental patient (**b**) *(loco)* lunatic

demeritar *vt Am* to belittle, to disparage

demérito *nm Formal (desprestigio, tacha)* blot, black mark; *(desventaja)* disadvantage; **los méritos y deméritos de algo** the merits and demerits of sth

demiurgo *nm* demiurge

demo *Informát* 1 *adj* demo; **una versión d.** a demo version
2 *nf* demo

democracia *nf* (**a**) *(forma de gobierno)* democracy; **la transición a la d.** the transition to democracy ▸▸ ***la d. cristiana*** Christian Democracy; ***d. parlamentaria*** parliamentary democracy; ***d. popular*** people's democracy (**b**) *(país)* democracy

demócrata 1 *adj* democratic
2 *nmf* democrat

democratacristiano, -a 1 *adj* Christian Democrat
2 *nm,f* Christian Democrat

democráticamente *adv* democratically; **miembros elegidos d.** democratically elected members

democrático, -a *adj* democratic

democratización *nf* democratization

democratizador, -ora *adj* democratizing; **proceso d.** process of democratization

democratizar [14] 1 *vt* to democratize, to make democratic
2 **democratizarse** *vpr* to become (more) democratic

democristiano, -a 1 *adj* Christian Democrat
2 *nm,f* Christian Democrat

demodé *adj inv Fam* unfashionable, *Br* untrendy

demodulador *nm Elec* demodulator

demografía *nf* demography

demográficamente *adv* demographically

demográfico, -a *adj (estudio, instituto)* demographic; **crecimiento d.** population increase

demógrafo, -a *nm,f* demographer

demoledor, -ora *adj* (**a**) *(huracán, terremoto, inundaciones)* devastating; *(energía, empuje, fuerza)* overwhelming, overpowering (**b**) *(crítica, ataque, declaración)* devastating (**c**) *(argumento)* overwhelming, crushing

demoler [41] *vt* (**a**) *(edificio)* to demolish, to pull down (**b**) *(organización, sistema)* to destroy (**c**) *(argumentos, teorías)* to demolish

demolición *nf* (**a**) *(de edificio)* demolition (**b**) *(de organización, sistema)* destruction (**c**) *(de argumentos, teorías)* demolition

demonche *interj Fam Euf* blast!, damn!

demoniaco, -a, demoníaco, -a *adj* devilish, diabolic

demonio *nm* (**a**) *(diablo)* devil
(**b**) *(persona traviesa)* devil; **este niño es el mismísimo d.** that child is a little devil
(**c**) *(persona hábil)* fiend; **es un d. con las motos** he's a fiend with motorbikes
(**d**) *Fam (para enfatizar)* **¿qué d.** *o* **demonios...?** what the hell...?; **¿quién/dónde demonios...?** who/where the blazes...?; **¡demonios!** damn (it)!; **¡demonios, no esperaba verte por aquí!** good heavens, I didn't expect to see you here!; **¡d. de ruido!** what a blasted racket!; **¡d. de crío!** confounded child!
(**e**) EXPR *Fam* **saber/oler a demonios** to taste/smell disgusting; *Fam* **como un d.: pesar como un d.** to weigh a ton; *Fam* **del d.: hoy hace un frío del d.** it's absolutely freezing today; **de mil demonios: tengo una gripe de mil demonios** I've got the most awful flu; **tiene un humor de mil demonios** she has a foul temper; **se lo llevaban todos los demonios** *(estaba muy enfadado)* he was hopping mad; *Fam* **ni qué demonios: ¡qué cansancio ni qué demonios! ¡a trabajar todo el mundo!** tired be damned! get to work everyone!; *Fam* **tener el d. en el cuerpo** to have ants in one's pants; *Fam* **¡vete al d.!** get lost!

demonizar *vt* to demonize

demontre *interj Fam Euf* blast!, damn!; **¡d. de niño, no para de comer!** that blasted child never stops eating!; **¿qué/quién/dónde demontres...?** what/who/where the blazes...?

demora *nf (retraso)* delay; **el vuelo sufre una d. de una hora** the flight has been delayed by one hour; **la d. en el pago conlleva una sanción** delay in payment will entail a penalty; **disculpen la d.** we apologize for the delay; **sin d.** without delay, immediately

demorar 1 *vt* (**a**) *(retrasar)* to delay; **el tráfico me demoró** I was held up by the traffic (**b**) *Am (tardar)* to take; **demoraron tres días en pintar la casa** it took them *o* they took three days to paint the house
2 *vi Am* to be late; **¡no demores!** don't be late!; **siempre demora en bañarse** he always takes ages in the bathroom; **este quitamanchas demora en actuar** this stain remover takes a while to work
3 **demorarse** *vpr* (**a**) *(retrasarse)* to be delayed (**b**) *(detenerse)* to stop (somewhere); **nos demoramos viendo escaparates** we stopped to look at the shops (**c**) *esp Am (tardar)* to be late; **no se demoren** don't be late

demorón, -ona *Andes, RP Fam* 1 *adj* slow
2 *nm,f* slowcoach

demoroso, -a *adj Arg, Chile Fam* (**a**) *(persona)* slow (**b**) *(proceso)* slow, time-consuming

demoscopia *nf* public opinion research

demoscópico, -a *adj* public opinion research; **una empresa demoscópica** a public opinion research organization

demostrable *adj* demonstrable

demostración *nf* (**a**) *(muestra)* demonstration; **una d. de cariño** a demonstration of affection
(**b**) *(exhibición)* display; **la policía hizo una d. de fuerza ante los manifestantes** the police made a show of force in front of the demonstrators
(**c**) *(del funcionamiento)* demonstration; **hacer una d.** *(de cómo funciona algo)* to demonstrate, to give a demonstration; **me hizo una d. de cómo preparar una paella** he showed me how to make a paella
(**d**) *(matemática)* proof

demostrar [64] *vt* (**a**) *(mostrar, exhibir)* to show, to display; **demuestra tener mucho interés (en)** he shows a lot of interest (in); **demostró ser lo suficientemente responsable para el puesto** she showed herself to be responsible enough for the post; **el tenista australiano demostró ser uno de los mejores** the Australian tennis player proved himself to be one of the best in the game; **demostraba no tenerle miedo a nadie** she showed that she was afraid of nobody

(**b**) *(probar)* to demonstrate, to prove; **¿me quieres? ¡pues demuéstramelo!** you love me, do you? well, prove it!; **...lo cual demuestra que estabas equivocado** ...which goes to show that you were wrong

(**c**) *(funcionamiento, procedimiento)* to demonstrate, to show; **¿nos podría d. cómo funciona?** would you mind showing us how it works?

demostrativo, -a 1 *adj* (**a**) *(representativo)* representative (**b**) *Gram* demonstrative (**c**) *Am (persona)* demonstrative

2 *nm Gram* demonstrative

demudado, -a *adj* **tenía el rostro d.** his face was pale; **estaba completamente demudada** *(angustiada)* she looked grief-stricken

demudar 1 *vt* to change, to alter; **la noticia le demudó el rostro** her expression changed when she heard the news

2 **demudarse** *vpr (persona, rostro)* to change; *(tejido)* to change colour; **se le demudó el rostro al oír la noticia** her expression changed when she heard the news

demuelo *etc ver* **demoler**

demuestro *etc ver* **demostrar**

denantes *adv Chile Fam* just now, just a moment ago

denario *nm (moneda)* denarius

dendrita *nf Anat* dendrite

dendrocronología *nf* dendrochronology

denegación *nf* refusal, rejection ►► *Der* ***d. de auxilio*** = failure to assist the victims of an accident, punishable by law

denegar [43] *vt* to turn down, to reject; **le ha sido denegado el visado** her visa application has been turned down; **me han denegado el crédito** they turned down my loan application; *Der* **denegada la protesta** objection overruled

dengue *nm* (**a**) *(melindre)* affectation; **no me vengas con dengues** stop putting on airs (**b**) *(enfermedad)* dengue

deniego *etc ver* **denegar**

denigración *nf* (**a**) *(humillación)* denigration (**b**) *(insulto)* insult

denigrante *adj* (**a**) *(humillante)* degrading (**b**) *(insultante)* insulting

denigrar *vt* (**a**) *(humillar)* to denigrate, to vilify (**b**) *(insultar)* to insult

denodadamente *adv* (**a**) *(con esfuerzo y decisión)* determinedly; **trabajar d.** to work tirelessly (**b**) *(con valentía)* bravely, intrepidly

denodado, -a *adj* (**a**) *(decidido)* determined; **realizaron un esfuerzo d. por convencerle** they made a sustained and determined effort to convince him (**b**) *(valiente)* brave, intrepid

denominación *nf* (**a**) *(nombre)* name ►► ***d. de origen*** = certification that a product (e.g. wine) comes from a particular region and conforms to certain quality standards (**b**) *(confesión religiosa)* denomination (**c**) *Am (valor)* low denomination note

denominador *nm* denominator ►► *Mat* ***d. común*** common denominator; **el d. común de todos los candidatos es su juventud** the thing the candidates have in common is that they are all young

denominar 1 *vt* to call; **esto es lo que denominamos un mapa de bits** this is what is termed a bitmap; **el comúnmente denominado mal de las vacas locas** mad cow disease, as it is popularly dubbed

2 **denominarse** *vpr* to be called; **este proceso se denomina fotosíntesis** this process is called photosynthesis; **se denominan a sí mismos demócratas** they call themselves democrats

denostar [64] *vt Formal* to insult

denotación *nf Ling* denotation

denotar *vt* (**a**) *(indicar)* to indicate, to show; **su sudor denotaba nerviosismo** his sweating indicated his extreme nervousness (**b**) *Ling* to denote

densamente *adv* densely; **zonas d. pobladas** densely populated areas

densidad *nf* (**a**) *(concentración)* density ►► ***d. de población*** population density; ***d. de tráfico*** traffic density (**b**) *Fís* density ►► ***d. absoluta*** true specific gravity; ***d. de flujo*** flux density; ***d. de radiación*** radiation flux (**c**) *Informát* density; **alta/doble d.** high/double density

denso, -a *adj* (**a**) *(vegetación, humo, líquido)* dense, thick (**b**) *(tráfico, programa de actividades)* heavy (**c**) *(libro)* dense; *(película, conferencia)* heavy-going

dentado, -a *adj* (**a**) *(rueda)* cogged, toothed; *(filo, cuchillo)* serrated; *(sello)* perforated (**b**) *Bot (hojas)* dentate

dentadura *nf* teeth ►► ***d. postiza*** false teeth, dentures

dental 1 *adj* (**a**) *(de los dientes)* dental; **hilo** *o* **seda d.** dental floss (**b**) *Ling* dental

2 *nf Ling* dental consonant

dentario, -a *adj* dental

dente: al dente *loc adv Culin* al dente

dentellada *nf* (**a**) *(mordisco)* bite; *(movimiento)* snap of the jaws; **dar dentelladas** to bite; **a dentelladas** with one's teeth (**b**) *(herida, marca)* tooth mark

dentellar *vi* **hacía mucho frío y el niño dentellaba** it was very cold and the child's teeth were chattering

dentellear *vt* to nibble

dentera *nf* **dar d. a alguien** to set sb's teeth on edge

dentición *nf* (**a**) *(proceso)* teething (**b**) *(dentadura)* teeth, *Espec* dentition ►► ***d. definitiva*** adult teeth, *Espec* permanent dentition; ***d. de leche*** milk teeth, *Espec* lacteal dentition; ***d. primaria*** milk teeth, *Espec* lacteal dentition; ***d. secundaria*** adult teeth, *Espec* permanent dentition

dentífrico, -a 1 *adj* **pasta dentífrica** toothpaste

2 *nm* toothpaste

dentina *nf* dentine

dentista *nmf* dentist; **ir al d.** to go to the dentist *o* dentist's

dentistería *nf CAm, Col, Ecuad, Ven* (**a**) *(odontología)* dentistry (**b**) *(consultorio)* dental surgery, dentist's

dentística *nf Chile, Ecuad* dentistry

dentón *nm (pez)* dentex

DENTRO *adv* (**a**) *(en el espacio)* inside; **espera aquí d.** wait in here; **está ahí d.** it's in there; **de d.** inside; **el bolsillo de d.** the inside pocket; **sacamos unas mesas de d.** we brought some tables out from indoors *o* inside; **el abrazo me salió de d.** I hugged her spontaneously; **d. de** in; **d. del coche** in *o* inside the car; **guardo mucho rencor d. de mí** I feel very resentful inside; **consiguió abrir la puerta desde d.** she managed to open the door from the inside; **hacia/para d.** inwards; **por d.** *(de un recipiente)* on the inside; *(de un lugar)* inside; *(de una persona)* inside, deep down; **está muy limpio por d.** it's very clean inside; **le dije que sí, pero por d. pensaba lo contrario** I said yes, but actually I was thinking the opposite

(**b**) *(en el tiempo)* **d. de** in, within; **el curso se acaba d. de tres días** the term ends in three days *o* in three days' time *o* three days from now; **d. de un año terminaré los estudios** I'll have finished my studies within a year; **d. de los próximos meses** within the next few months; **d. de nada** *(dentro de un rato)* in a minute, in a moment; *(pronto)* before you know it, before long; **la cena estará lista d. de nada** dinner will be ready in a moment; **d. de poco** in a while, before long; **d. de poco no quedarán máquinas de escribir** it won't be long before there are no typewriters left

(**c**) *(en posibilidades)* **d. de lo posible** as far as possible; **d. de lo que cabe, no ha sido un mal resultado** all things considered, it wasn't a bad result; **esta situación no está prevista d. del reglamento** this situation isn't covered by the regulations; **comprar una nueva casa no está d. de mis posibilidades** buying a new house would be beyond my means

---

dentudo, -a 1 *adj* large-toothed, toothy

2 *nm Cuba (pez)* shortfin mako (shark)

denuedo *nm* (**a**) *(esfuerzo)* resolve, determination; **trabajar con d.** to work determinedly (**b**) *(valor)* courage; **pelear con d.** to fight courageously

denuesto[1] *etc ver* **denostar**

denuesto[2] *nm Literario* insult

denuncia *nf* (**a**) *(acusación)* accusation; *(condena)* denunciation (**b**) *(a la policía)* report; **hacer** *o* **poner** *o* **presentar una d. contra alguien** to report sb to the police; **presentó una d. contra su esposo por malos tratos** she reported her husband to the police for ill-treatment; **presentar una d. por** *o* **de robo** to report a robbery *o* theft

denunciante *nmf* = person who reports a crime

denunciar *vt* (**a**) *(delito, delincuente)* to report; **han denunciado el robo de la moto (a la policía)** they have reported the theft of the motorbike (to the police); **ha denunciado a su esposo por malos tratos** she has reported her husband to the police for ill-treatment

(**b**) *(acusar, reprobar)* to condemn; **la prensa denunció la situación** the situation was condemned in the press

(**c**) *(delatar, revelar)* to indicate, to reveal; **goteras que denuncian el estado de abandono de la casa** leaks that betray the state of abandon the house is in

(**d**) *Pol* **d. un tratado** = to announce one is no longer bound by a treaty, *Espec* to denounce a treaty

denuncio *nm Andes (a la policía)* report

deontología *nf* ethics, *Espec* deontology; **la d. médica** medical ethics *(singular)*

deontológico, -a *adj* **código d.** code of ethics

D. E. P. (*abrev de* **descanse en paz**) RIP

deparar *vt* (**a**) *(traer)* **¿qué nos deparará el futuro?** what will the future bring?, what does the future have in store for us?; **la excursión nos deparó muchas sorpresas** the outing provided us with many surprises (**b**) *(ofrecer)* **d. la ocasión** *o* **posibilidad de hacer algo** to provide the opportunity to do sth

departamental *adj* departmental

departamento *nm* (**a**) *(en empresa, organización)* department ▸▸ ***d. de atención al cliente*** customer service department; ***d. de compras*** purchasing department; ***d. de contabilidad*** accounting *o* accounts department; ***d. financiero*** finance department; ***d. jurídico*** legal department; ***d. de personal*** personnel department; ***d. de ventas*** sales department
(**b**) *(en tienda)* department; **d. de caballeros** menswear department
(**c**) *(en universidad, centro de secundaria)* department; **D. de Historia Antigua** Department of Ancient History
(**d**) *(ministerio)* ministry, department ▸▸ ***D. de Estado*** State Department
(**e**) *(de cajón, maleta)* compartment
(**f**) *(de tren)* compartment
(**g**) *(provincia, distrito)* department
(**h**) *Arg (apartamento) Br* flat, *US* apartment

departir *vi* to talk, to converse; **d. con alguien de algo** to converse with sb about sth

> **Falso amigo**: El verbo inglés **to depart** no es la traducción del español **departir**. En inglés **to depart** significa "salir" o "desviarse".

depauperación *nf* (**a**) *(física)* weakening, enfeeblement (**b**) *(económica)* impoverishment

depauperado, -a *adj* (**a**) *(físicamente)* enfeebled, debilitated (**b**) *(económicamente)* impoverished

depauperar 1 *vt* (**a**) *(físicamente) (persona)* to debilitate, to weaken; *(salud)* to undermine (**b**) *(económicamente)* to impoverish
2 depauperarse *vpr* (**a**) *(físicamente) (persona)* to become debilitated; *(salud)* to be undermined (**b**) *(económicamente)* to become poorer

dependencia *nf* (**a**) *(de una persona, país)* dependence (**de** on) (**b**) *(de drogas)* dependency; **d. del tabaco** tobacco addiction *o* dependency (**c**) *(departamento)* section; *(sucursal)* branch (**d**) *(habitación)* room (**e**) *(edificación)* building; *(adosado)* annexe; *(independiente)* outbuilding; **en dependencias policiales** on police premises

depender *vi* (**a**) *(económicamente, psicológicamente, físicamente) (sujeto: persona)* **d. de algo** to depend on sth; **d. de alguien** to be dependent on sb; **depende de la caridad para sobrevivir** he/it survives on charity; **económicamente, aún depende de su familia** she's still financially dependent on her family; **lleva la moto para no d. de nadie a la hora de volver** go on your motorbike so you don't have to depend on anybody else to get back
(**b**) *(políticamente, administrativamente) (sujeto: nación, territorio, asunto)* **un territorio que depende de España** a territory that is a Spanish dependency; **la política educativa depende del gobierno central** educational policy is in the hands of central government
(**c**) *(en jerarquías, escalafones) (sujeto: persona, departamento)* **nosotros dependemos de la jefatura de Educación** we come under the Department of Education
(**d**) *(sujeto: decisión, resultado, consecuencias)* to depend; **¿vas a venir? – depende** are you coming? – it depends; **todo depende de lo que decida el juez** everything depends on what the judge decides; **depende de ti** it's up to you; **si de mí dependiera, el trabajo sería tuyo** if it was up to me, the job would be yours

dependiente[1] *adj* dependent (**de** on); **áreas dependientes del Ministerio de Cultura** areas coming under the Ministry of Culture

dependiente[2], -a *nm,f Br* sales assistant, shop assistant, *US* salesclerk

depilación *nf* hair removal ▸▸ ***d. a la cera*** waxing; ***d. eléctrica*** electrolysis

depiladora *nf* ladies' shaver

depilar 1 *vt (piernas, axilas)* to remove the hair from; *(cejas)* to pluck; *(con maquinilla)* to shave; *(con cera)* to wax
2 depilarse *vpr* **depilarse las piernas/axilas** *(con maquinilla)* to shave one's legs/armpits; *(con cera)* to wax one's legs/armpits; **depilarse las cejas** to pluck one's eyebrows

depilatorio, -a 1 *adj* hair-removing; **crema depilatoria** hair-removing cream
2 *nm* hair-remover

deplorable *adj (comportamiento, espectáculo, estado)* deplorable; *(aspecto)* sorry, pitiful

deplorablemente *adv* deplorably

deplorar *vt* (**a**) *(lamentar)* to regret deeply; **deploramos la actitud de nuestro hijo** we deeply regret our son's attitude (**b**) *(desaprobar)* to deplore; **todas las fuerzas políticas deploraron el hecho** all the political parties deplored the incident

deponente *Gram* **1** *adj* deponent
2 *nm* deponent verb

deponer [50] **1** *vt* (**a**) *(abandonar) (actitud)* to drop, to set aside; *(armas)* to lay down; **le conminaron a d. su actitud inmediatamente** they ordered him to modify his behaviour immediately; **el grupo rebelde depuso las armas** the rebel group laid down their arms
(**b**) *(destituir) (ministro, secretario, presidente)* to remove from office; *(líder, rey)* to depose; **d. a alguien de su cargo** to strip sb of his/her office
(**c**) *CAm, Méx (vomitar)* to vomit
2 *vi* (**a**) *Formal Med (defecar)* to defecate
(**b**) *Formal Der (declarar)* to testify, to give evidence; **d. ante el juez** to testify before a judge
(**c**) *CAm, Méx (vomitar)* to vomit

deportación *nf* deportation

deportado, -a 1 *adj* deported
2 *nm,f* deportee

deportar *vt* to deport

deporte *nm (ejercicio, actividad de competición)* sport; **hacer** *o* **practicar d.** to do sports; **hacer d. es bueno para la salud** sport is good for your health; **practicar un d.** to do a sport; EXPR **hacer algo por d.** to do sth for fun; **no cobro nada, lo hago por d.** I don't get paid for it, I do it for fun ▸▸ ***deportes acuáticos*** water sports; ***d. de aventura*** adventure sport; ***el d. blanco*** skiing; ***d. de combate*** combat sport; ***d. de competición*** competitive sport; ***deportes ecuestres*** equestrian sports; ***d. extremo*** extreme sport; ***deportes de invierno*** winter sports; ***d. de masas*** spectator sport; ***deportes náuticos*** water sports; ***el d. rey*** *(fútbol)* football; **el béisbol es el d. rey en Cuba** in Cuba baseball is the king of sports; ***d. de riesgo*** extreme sport

deportista 1 *adj* sporty, sports-loving; **es muy d.** she's very sporty
2 *nmf* sportsman, *f* sportswoman

deportivamente *adv* sportingly

deportividad *nf* sportsmanship

deportivo, -a 1 *adj* (**a**) *(de deportes) (ropa, calzado, centro, club)* sports; **coche** *o* **auto d.** sports car; **instalaciones deportivas** sports facilities; **periódico d.** sports (news)paper (**b**) *(informal)* casual; **un jersey d.** a casual sweater (**c**) *(conducta, espíritu, gesto)* sportsmanlike
2 *nm (automóvil)* sports car
3 deportivos *nmpl (zapatillas) Br* trainers, *US* sneakers

deposición *nf* (**a**) *(destitución) (de ministro, secretario, presidente)* removal from office; *(de líder, monarca)* overthrow (**b**) *Formal Med (defecación)* defecation; **deposiciones** *(heces)* stools (**c**) *Formal Der (declaración)* testimony, deposition

depositante 1 *adj* depositing
2 *nmf* depositor

depositar 1 *vt* (**a**) *(colocar)* to place; **depositaron al herido en el suelo** they put the wounded man on the floor; **deposite la moneda en la ranura** *(en letrero)* put the coin in the slot
(**b**) *(dejar)* to place; **pueden d. el equipaje en la consigna de la estación** you may leave your luggage in the left-luggage lockers in the station; **deposite aquí sus pilas usadas** *(en letrero)* dispose of dead batteries here
(**c**) *(sentimientos)* to place (**en** in); **depositaron su confianza en ella** they placed their trust in her; **había depositado sus ilusiones en su hijo** he had placed all his hopes on his son; **habían depositado todas sus esperanzas en aquella quiniela** they had pinned all their hopes on that pools coupon
(**d**) *(en el banco)* to deposit
2 depositarse *vpr (asentarse)* to settle

depositario, -a 1 *adj (de dinero)* depository
2 *nm,f* (**a**) *(de dinero)* trustee (**b**) *(de confianza)* repository (**c**) *(de mercancías)* depositary

depósito *nm* (**a**) *(almacén) (de mercancías)* store, warehouse; *(de armas)* dump, arsenal; **dejar algo en d.** to leave sth as security; **el Prado tiene numerosos cuadros en d.** the Prado Museum has a large number of paintings in storage ▸▸ ***d. de automóviles (municipal)*** *Br* car pound, *US* impound lot, *US* tow lot; ***d. de cadáveres*** morgue,

mortuary; ***d. de equipaje*** *Br* left luggage office, *US* baggage room; ***d. franco*** bonded warehouse; ***d. de municiones*** ammunition dump
(**b**) *(recipiente)* tank ▸▸ ***d. de agua*** reservoir, water tank; ***d. compresor*** pressure tank; ***d. de gasolina*** *Br* petrol tank, *US* gas tank; ***d. lanzable*** drop tank
(**c**) *(fianza)* deposit; **dejar una cantidad en d.** to leave a deposit; **dejamos un d. de 10.000 pesos** we left a deposit of 10,000 pesos
(**d**) *(en cuenta bancaria)* deposit; **hacer un d. en una cuenta bancaria** to pay money into an account ▸▸ ***d. disponible*** demand deposit; ***d. en efectivo*** cash deposit; ***d. indistinto*** joint deposit; ***d. a plazo fijo*** *Br* fixed-term deposit, *US* time deposit; *Col* ***d. a término fijo*** *Br* fixed-term deposit, *US* time deposit; ***d. a la vista*** demand deposit
(**e**) *(de polvo, partículas, sedimentos)* deposit ▸▸ ***depósitos minerales*** mineral deposits
(**f**) ***d. legal*** copyright deposit, legal deposit

depravación *nf* depravity

depravado, -a 1 *adj* depraved
2 *nm,f* depraved person; **ser un d.** to be depraved *o* degenerate

depravar 1 *vt* to corrupt, to deprave
2 **depravarse** *vpr* to become depraved

depre *Fam* 1 *adj* **estar d.** to be feeling down
2 *nf* **tener la d., estar con la d.** to be feeling down; **le ha entrado una d.** he's on a real downer

deprecación *nf Formal* entreaty

depreciación *nf* depreciation ▸▸ ***d. de la moneda*** currency depreciation

depreciar 1 *vt* to (cause to) depreciate
2 **depreciarse** *vpr* to depreciate

depredación *nf* (**a**) *(entre animales)* hunting, preying (**b**) *(daño)* depredation, pillaging

depredador, -ora 1 *adj* predatory
2 *nm,f* predator

depredar *vt* (**a**) *(sujeto: animal)* to prey on (**b**) *(sujeto: piratas, invasores)* to pillage

depresión *nf* (**a**) *(anímica)* depression ▸▸ ***d. nerviosa*** nervous breakdown; ***d. posparto*** postnatal *o* postpartum depression; ***d. puerperal*** postnatal *o* postpartum depression (**b**) *(económica)* depression (**c**) *(en superficie, terreno)* hollow, depression (**d**) *Meteo* ***d. atmosférica*** atmospheric depression; ***d. barométrica*** atmospheric depression (**e**) *Náut* **d. del horizonte** dip of the horizon

depresivo, -a 1 *adj* (**a**) *(propenso a la depresión)* depressive; **tiene un carácter d.** he's the depressive type (**b**) *(deprimente)* depressing (**c**) *(fármaco)* depressant
2 *nm,f (propenso a la depresión)* depressive
3 *nm (fármaco)* depressant

depresor, -ora 1 *adj* depressant
2 *nm* depressor

deprimente *adj* depressing

deprimido, -a *adj* (**a**) *(persona)* depressed; **se le veía un poco d.** he seemed a bit low *o* down (**b**) *(economía)* depressed (**c**) *(barrio, zona)* depressed (**d**) *(terreno)* depressed

deprimir 1 *vt* to depress
2 **deprimirse** *vpr* to get depressed; **¡no te deprimas!** don't let things get you down!, cheer up!

deprisa *adv* fast, quickly; **¡no conduzcas tan d.!** don't drive so fast!; **volveré lo más d. que pueda** I'll be back as quickly as I can; **¡d.!** quick!; **tenemos que ir más d.** we need to go faster *o* more quickly; EXPR **hacer algo d. y corriendo** to do sth in a rush, to rush sth; **tuvimos que hacer el equipaje d. y corriendo** we had to pack in a rush

depuesto, -a 1 *participio ver* **deponer**
2 *adj (destituido) (ministro, secretario, presidente)* removed from office; *(líder, rey)* deposed

depuración *nf* (**a**) *(de agua)* purification, treatment; *(de metal, gas)* purification (**b**) *(de partido, organismo, sociedad)* purge (**c**) *(de estilo)* refinement (**d**) *Informát* debugging

depurado, -a *adj (estilo)* refined, polished; *(lenguaje, técnica)* finely honed; *(sistema)* finely tuned; *(gustos)* refined; *(diseño, líneas)* sleek, elegant

depurador, -ora 1 *adj* purifying
2 *nm* (**a**) *(de agua, gas)* purifier (**b**) *Informát* debugger

depuradora *nf (en río)* treatment plant; *(de piscina)* filter system ▸▸ ***d. de aguas*** water purification plant

depurar *vt* (**a**) *(agua) (de río)* to purify, to treat; *(de piscina)* to filter (**b**) *(metal, gas)* to purify (**c**) *(partido, organismo)* to purge (**d**) *(estilo, gusto)* to refine; *(lenguaje, técnica)* to hone; *(sistema)* to fine-tune (**e**) *Informát* to debug

depusiera *etc ver* **deponer**

dequeísmo *nm Gram* = incorrect use of "de que" instead of "que" after a verb

derbi, derby *nm* (**a**) *(en hípica)* derby (**b**) *(en fútbol, baloncesto, balonmano)* (local) derby

derecha 1 *nf* (**a**) *(contrario de izquierda)* right, right-hand side; **el de la d. es mi primo** the one on the right is my cousin; **a la d. (de)** to the right (of); **la primera bocacalle a la d.** the first street on the right; **a mi/vuestra d.** on my/your right(-hand side); **girar a la d.** to turn right; **prohibido girar a la d.** *(en letrero)* no right turn; EXPR *Esp* **no hacer nada a derechas** to do nothing right
(**b**) *(en política)* right (wing); **la d.** the right; **un partido de** *Esp* **derechas** *o Am* **d.** a right-wing party; **ser de** *Esp* **derechas** *o Am* **d.** to be right-wing
(**c**) *(mano)* right hand; *(pierna)* right leg; **marcó con la d.** he scored with his right foot
(**d**) *(en tenis)* forehand
(**e**) *(puerta)* **el segundo d.** the right-hand *Br* flat *o US* apartment on the *Br* second *o US* third floor
(**f**) *ver también* **derecho**
2 *interj (orden militar)* right wheel!

derechazo *nm* (**a**) *(en fútbol)* powerful right-foot shot (**b**) *(en boxeo)* right (**c**) *Taurom* = pass with the cape held in the right hand

derechismo *nm (en política)* right-wing views

derechista 1 *adj* right-wing
2 *nmf* right-winger

derechización *nf (en política)* move to the right

DERECHO, -A 1 *adj* (**a**) *(vertical)* upright; *(recto)* straight; **este cuadro no está d.** this picture isn't straight; **recogió la lámpara del suelo y la puso derecha** she picked the lamp up off the floor and stood it upright; **siéntate** *o* **ponte d. o te dolerá la espalda** sit straight or you'll get backache; **siempre anda muy derecha** she always walks with a very straight back
(**b**) *(de la derecha)* right; **mano/pierna derecha** right hand/leg; **el margen d.** the right-hand margin; **a mano derecha** on the right, on the right-hand side
2 *nm* (**a**) *(leyes, estudio)* law; **un estudiante de d.** a law student; **estudiar d.** to study *o* read law; **una licenciada en d.** a law graduate; **la Facultad de D.** the Faculty of Law; **voy a D. a una conferencia** I'm going to a lecture in the Faculty of Law; **el d. me asiste** the law is on my side; **conforme** *o* **según d.** according to the law ▸▸ ***d. administrativo*** administrative law; ***d. canónico*** canon law; ***d. civil*** civil law; ***d. constitucional*** constitutional law; ***d. consuetudinario*** common law; ***d. financiero*** financial law; ***d. fiscal*** tax law; ***d. foral*** = ancient regional laws still existing in some parts of Spain; ***d. internacional*** international law; ***d. internacional público*** public international law; ***d. laboral*** labour law; ***d. marítimo*** maritime law; ***d. mercantil*** commercial law; ***d. natural*** natural law; ***d. penal*** criminal law; ***d. privado*** private law; ***d. procesal*** procedural law; ***d. público*** public law; ***d. romano*** Roman law; ***d. de sociedades*** *Br* company law, *US* corporation law; ***d. del trabajo*** labour law
(**b**) *(prerrogativa)* right; **el d. al voto** the right to vote; **los derechos de la mujer** women's rights; **los derechos y obligaciones del consumidor** the rights and responsibilities of the consumer; *Fam* **me queda el d. al pataleo** all I can do now is complain; **¿con qué d. entras en mi casa sin llamar?** what gives you the right to come into my house without knocking?; **con d. a dos consumiciones** *(en entrada)* this ticket entitles the holder to two free drinks; **esta tarjeta me da d. a un 5 por ciento de descuento** this card entitles me to a 5 percent discount; **el que sea el jefe no le da d. a tratarnos así** just because he's the boss doesn't mean he can *o* doesn't give him the right to treat us like this; **si quiere abstenerse, está en su d.** if she wants to abstain, she's perfectly within her rights to do so; **hizo valer sus derechos** he exercised his rights; **¡no hay d.!** it's not fair!; **¡no hay d. a que unos tengan tanto y otros tan poco!** it's not fair that some people should have so much and others so little!; **es de d. que consiga la indemnización que reclama** it is only right that she should receive the compensation she is claiming; **miembro de pleno d.** full member; **ha entrado, por d. propio** *o* **por propio d., en la historia de la literatura** she's gone down in literary history in her own right; **reservado el d. de admisión** *(en letrero)* the management reserves the right of admission; **reservados todos los derechos** all rights reserved; **tener d. a algo** to have a right to sth, to be entitled to sth;

tener d. a hacer algo to have the right to do sth, to be entitled to do sth; **tengo d. a descansar, ¿no?** I'm entitled to be able to rest now and then, aren't I?; **no tienes ningún d. a insultarme** you have no right to insult me ►► ***derechos de antena*** broadcasting rights; ***d. de asilo*** right of asylum; ***derechos de autor*** *(potestad)* copyright; ***derechos civiles*** civil rights; ***derechos especiales de giro*** special drawing rights; ***d. de gracia*** right to show clemency; ***derechos humanos*** human rights; ***d. de paso*** right of way; *Hist* ***d. de pernada*** droit du seigneur; ***derechos de propiedad*** proprietary rights; ***d. de réplica*** right to reply; ***d. de respuesta*** right to reply; ***d. de reunión*** right of assembly; ***d. de visita (a los hijos)*** *(de divorciado)* visiting rights, right of access

(**c**) **derechos** *(tasas)* duties, taxes; *(profesionales)* fees ►► ***derechos de aduana*** customs duty; ***derechos de autor*** *(dinero)* royalties; ***derechos de entrada*** import duties; ***derechos de examen*** examination fees; ***derechos de importación*** import duty; ***derechos de inscripción*** membership fee; ***derechos de matrícula*** matriculation fee; ***derechos de puerto*** harbour dues; ***derechos reales*** death duty; *Econ* ***d. de retención*** right of retention

(**d**) *(contrario de revés)* right side; **me puse el jersey del d.** I put my jumper on the right way round *o* properly; **cose los botones del d.** sew the buttons on the right side

3 *adv* (**a**) *(en línea recta)* straight; **fue d. a su despacho** she went straight to her office; **se fue d. a casa** she went straight home; **todo d.** straight ahead; **siga todo d. para llegar al museo** carry on straight ahead and you'll come to the museum

(**b**) *(sin rodeos)* straight; **iré d. al asunto** I'll get straight to the point; *RP* **decir** *o* **hacer algo d. viejo** to say sth straight out, to come right out with sth

---

deriva *nf* (**a**) *(de embarcación)* drift; **a la d.** adrift; **ir a la d.** *(embarcación, objeto flotante)* to drift; *(empresa, organización)* to be adrift; **el gobierno va a la d.** the government has lost its bearings (**b**) *Geol* ***d. continental*** continental drift

derivación *nf* (**a**) *(cable, canal, carretera)* branch (**b**) *Elec (conexión)* shunt; *(pérdida de fluido)* leakage (**c**) *Gram* derivation (**d**) *Mat* derivation

derivada *nf Mat* derivative

derivado, -a **1** *adj Gram* derived

2 *nm* (**a**) *(producto)* product; **la gasolina es un d. del petróleo** petrol is obtained from oil (**b**) *Gram* derivative (**c**) *Bolsa* derivative

derivar **1** *vt* (**a**) *(desviar)* to divert (**a** *o* **hacia** to *o* towards); **derivó el debate hacia otro tema** he steered the debate onto another topic; **su médico de cabecera lo derivó a un especialista** his GP referred him to a specialist

(**b**) *Mat* to derive

(**c**) *Ling* to derive

2 *vi* (**a**) *(desviarse)* to move, to drift (**a** *o* **hacia** to *o* towards); **el barco derivaba sin rumbo fijo** the ship was drifting out of control; **la tertulia derivaba hacia derroteros políticos** the discussion was drifting onto politics

(**b**) *(proceder)* **d. de** to derive from; **la crisis deriva de una mala gestión** the crisis was caused by bad management

(**c**) *(acabar)* **d. en** to end in; **la tensa situación familiar derivó en tragedia** the highly charged domestic situation ended in tragedy; **la rivalidad entre ellos derivó en abierta hostilidad** the rivalry between them ended in open hostility

(**d**) *Ling* **d. de** to be derived from, to derive from, to come from

3 derivarse *vpr* **derivarse de** to be derived from, to come from; **palabras que se derivan del griego** words which come from Greek; **problemas que se derivan de una infancia difícil** problems stemming from a troubled childhood

dermatitis *nf inv (inflamación)* dermatitis ►► ***d. seborreica*** seborrhoeic dermatitis

dermatoesqueleto *nm Zool* exoskeleton

dermatología *nf* dermatology

dermatológico, -a *adj* dermatological

dermatólogo, -a *nm,f* dermatologist

dermatosis *nf inv* dermatosis

dérmico, -a *adj* skin; **tejido d.** skin tissue

dermis *nf inv Anat* dermis

dermoprotector, -ora *adj* skin-protecting; **crema dermoprotectora** skin cream

dermorreacción *nf* skin test

derogación *nf (de ley)* repeal

derogar [38] *vt (ley)* to repeal

derogatorio, -a *adj* (**a**) *(ley)* repealing (**b**) *(contrato)* rescinding

> **Falso amigo**: El adjetivo inglés **derogatory** no es la traducción del español **derogatorio**. En inglés, **derogatory** significa "despectivo".

derrama *nf* (**a**) *(de impuesto, gasto)* apportionment (**b**) *(impuesto extraordinario)* special *o* additional tax

derramadero *nm (aliviadero)* spillway, wasteway

derramamiento *nm* spilling ►► ***d. de sangre*** bloodshed; **un golpe de estado sin d. de sangre** a bloodless coup

derramar **1** *vt* (**a**) *(por accidente)* to spill; **d. lágrimas/sangre** to shed tears/blood (**b**) *(verter)* to pour (**c**) *(favores, elogios)* to lavish; *(generosidad, simpatía)* to overflow with (**d**) *(gasto, impuesto)* to apportion (**e**) *Méx Fam* **derramarla** *(meter la pata)* to put one's foot in it

2 derramarse *vpr (por accidente)* to spill

derrame *nm* (**a**) *Med* discharge; **tuvo un d. en un ojo** she burst a blood vessel in her eye ►► ***d. cerebral*** stroke; ***d. sinovial*** water on the knee (**b**) *(de líquido)* spilling; *(de sangre)* shedding

derrapaje *nm* skid

derrapar *vi* to skid; EXPR *Fam* **le derrapan las neuronas** he's gone crazy

derrape *nm* skid

derredor: al derredor, en derredor *loc adv* around

derrelicto *nm Náut* derelict

derrengado, -a *adj Fam (agotado)* exhausted

derrengar *vt (agotar)* to exhaust, to tire out

derretir [47] **1** *vt (licuar) (mantequilla, metal, nieve)* to melt; *(hielo)* to thaw, to melt

2 derretirse *vpr* (**a**) *(mantequilla, nieve, metal)* to melt; *(hielo)* to thaw, to melt; **la nieve se derrite con el sol** the snow melts in the sunshine (**b**) *Fam (enamorarse)* to be madly in love (**por** with); **se derrite cada vez que ella lo mira** *(se emociona)* his heart misses a beat whenever she looks at him

derribar *vt* (**a**) *(construcción, edificio, muro, pared)* to knock down, to demolish; *(puerta)* to break down, to smash down; **derribó el castillo de naipes** she knocked down the house of cards

(**b**) *(árbol) (sujeto: leñador)* to cut down, to fell; *(sujeto: viento, tormenta)* to uproot

(**c**) *(avión, jugador, res)* to bring down; *(púgil, luchador)* to knock down, to floor; *(jinete)* to unseat

(**d**) *(gobierno, gobernante)* to overthrow

(**e**) *(en equitación) (obstáculo)* to knock over *o* down

derribo *nm* (**a**) *(de construcción, edificio)* demolition; **material de d.** rubble

(**b**) *(de árbol) (mediante tala)* felling; *(por el viento, la tormenta)* uprooting

(**c**) *(de avión, jugador, res)* bringing down; **el árbitro sancionó el d. con penalti** the referee gave a penalty after the man was brought down

(**d**) *(de gobierno, gobernante)* overthrow

(**e**) *(en equitación) (de obstáculo)* knocking down

derritiera *etc ver* **derretir**

derrito *etc ver* **derretir**

derrocamiento *nm (de gobierno)* toppling, overthrow; *(de rey)* overthrow

derrocar [60] *vt (gobierno)* to topple, to overthrow; *(rey)* to overthrow

derrochador, -ora **1** *adj* wasteful

2 *nm,f* spendthrift

derrochar **1** *vt* (**a**) *(malgastar) (dinero, fortuna)* to squander, to fritter away; *(gas, agua, electricidad)* to waste; *(fuerzas, energías)* to squander, to waste (**b**) *(rebosar de)* to ooze, to be full of; **siempre derrocha simpatía** he's always incredibly friendly; **derrochaba vitalidad** she was bursting with vitality

2 *vi* to waste

derroche *nm* (**a**) *(despilfarro)* waste, squandering; **iqué d.!** what an awful waste!; **todos esos campos de golf son un d. de agua** all these golf courses are a terrible waste of water

(**b**) *(abundancia)* profusion; **el concierto fue un d. de técnica, sensibilidad y talento** the concert was a fine display of technique, sensitivity and talent; **la película es todo un d. de imaginación** the film is prodigiously imaginative

derrota *nf* (**a**) *(fracaso)* defeat; **infligir una d. a alguien** to inflict a defeat on *o* upon sb; **sufrieron una seria d.** they suffered a serious defeat (**b**) *Náut (rumbo)* course

derrotado, -a *adj* (**a**) *(vencido)* defeated (**b**) *(deprimido)* in low spirits, depressed (**c**) *Fam (muy cansado)* worn out, dead tired

derrotar 1 *vt* to defeat; **los derrotaron por tres a cero** they were beaten three nil
2 *vi Taurom* = to make an upward thrust with the horns while swerving from the line of charge

derrote *nm Taurom* = unpredictable upward thrust the bull makes with its horns, accompanied by a swerve of its body

derrotero *nm* (**a**) *(camino)* direction; **un cambio de d. en la política exterior** a change of direction in foreign policy; **tu hijo no va por buenos derroteros** your son is going astray; **la Bolsa ha seguido por los mismos derroteros que la semana pasada** the stock market has continued the same trend as last week; **tomar otros** *o* **diferentes derroteros** to follow a different course
(**b**) *Náut (rumbo)* course
(**c**) *Náut (guía)* pilot book, navigation track

derrotismo *nm* defeatism

derrotista 1 *adj* defeatist
2 *nmf* defeatist

derrubio *nm* (**a**) *(desgaste)* erosion, washing away (**b**) *(tierra)* alluvium, sediment deposit

derruido, -a *adj (edificio, ciudad)* ruined

derruir [34] *vt (demoler)* to demolish, to knock down

derrumbadero *nm* cliff, precipice

derrumbamiento *nm* (**a**) *(de puente, edificio) (por accidente)* collapse; *(intencionado)* demolition; *(de pared, muro, techo)* collapse ►► ***d. de tierra*** landslide (**b**) *(de imperio)* fall; *(de empresa)* collapse; *(de persona)* devastation

derrumbar 1 *vt* (**a**) *(puente, edificio)* to demolish; *(muro, pared)* to knock down; **las fuertes nevadas derrumbaron muchos árboles** the heavy snowfalls brought down many trees (**b**) *(moralmente)* to destroy, to devastate
2 **derrumbarse** *vpr* (**a**) *(venirse abajo) (puente, edificio, muro, pared)* to collapse; *(techo)* to fall in, to cave in; **se derrumbó extenuado sobre la cama** he collapsed on the bed exhausted
(**b**) *(despeñarse)* to fall (**por** down)
(**c**) *(imperio)* to fall, to collapse; *(empresa)* to collapse, to founder; *(persona)* to go to pieces; **en la segunda parte el equipo se derrumbó** the team went to pieces in the second half
(**d**) *(esperanzas)* to be shattered

derrumbe *nm* (**a**) *(desplome)* collapse (**b**) *(demolición)* demolition, knocking down (**c**) *(de imperio)* fall, collapse; *(de empresa, economía, sector)* collapse; *(de persona)* breakdown

derruyo *etc ver* **derruir**

derviche *nm* dervish

desabastecer [46] *vt* **d. a alguien de** to leave sb short of

desabastecido, -a *adj* without supplies; **d. de** *(con pocas reservas)* short of; *(sin reservas)* out of; **una ciudad desabastecida de luz y agua** a city without electricity or water

desabastecimiento, *Méx* **desabasto** *nm* shortage of supplies

desabollador, -ora *nm,f Chile* panel beater

desabolladuría *nf Chile (taller)* body shop

desabollar *vt* to beat the dents out of

desaborido, -a *Esp Fam* 1 *adj* (**a**) *(comida)* tasteless, bland (**b**) *(persona) (aburrido)* boring, dull; *(desagradable)* unpleasant; **¡mira que eres d.!** you're so dull!
2 *nm,f (aburrido)* bore; *(borde, maleducado)* unpleasant person, sourpuss

desabotonar 1 *vt* to unbutton
2 **desabotonarse** *vpr* (**a**) *(persona)* to undo one's buttons; **desabotonarse la camisa** to unbutton one's shirt (**b**) *(sujeto: ropa)* to come undone

desabrido, -a *adj* (**a**) *(tiempo)* unpleasant, bad; **el día está d.** the weather is bad today (**b**) *(alimento, comida)* tasteless, insipid (**c**) *Esp (hosco) (persona, carácter, manera de ser)* surly; *(tono)* harsh (**d**) *Am (soso) (persona)* wet, bland, dull

desabrigado, -a *adj* (**a**) *(descubierto) (lugar)* unprotected, exposed (**b**) *(con poca ropa)* **no salgas tan d. a la calle** don't go out without some warmer clothes on; **ponle un abrigo al niño, que va muy d.** put a coat on that child or he'll freeze (**c**) *Fig (desamparado)* unprotected, defenceless

desabrigarse *vpr* (**a**) *(en la calle)* **¡no te desabrigues!** make sure you wrap up warmly! (**b**) *(en la cama)* to throw off the covers

desabrimiento *nm* (**a**) *(del tiempo)* unpleasantness (**b**) *(de alimento, comida)* lack of flavour (**c**) *(de persona)* surliness, unfriendliness; *(de carácter, manera de ser)* surliness; *(del tono)* harshness

desabrochar 1 *vt* to undo
2 **desabrocharse** *vpr* (**a**) *(persona)* to undo one's buttons; **desabróchese, por favor** unbutton *o* undo your shirt, please; **se desabrochó el cuello de la camisa** he unbuttoned his shirt collar (**b**) *(ropa)* to come undone; **se te ha desabrochado la bragueta** your fly has come undone

desacatado, -a *adj RP Fam* wild, out of control; **suele ser muy discreta, pero ayer estaba de lo más desacatada** she's usually very quiet, but she really let herself go yesterday; **ayer estaba d. y terminó tirándosele encima** yesterday he got right out of order and ended up throwing himself on top of her

desacatar *vt (ley, regla, orden)* to disobey; *(costumbre, persona)* not to respect

desacato *nm* (**a**) *(falta de respeto)* lack of respect, disrespect (**a** for) (**b**) *Der (al juez, tribunal)* contempt of court; **lo juzgaron por d. (al tribunal)** he was tried for contempt of court ►► ***d. a la autoridad*** = refusal to obey a legitimate authority

desaceleración *nf* (**a**) *(de vehículo)* slowing down, deceleration (**b**) *(de proceso, cambio)* slowing (down); **una d. del crecimiento económico** a slowdown in economic growth

desacelerar *vt* (**a**) *(vehículo)* to slow down (**b**) *(proceso, cambio)* to slow down

desacertadamente *adv* mistakenly

desacertado, -a *adj (inoportuno)* unwise, ill-considered; *(erróneo)* mistaken, wrong; **estuvo muy d. en sus comentarios** *(inoportuno)* her comments were ill-judged *o* unwise; *(erróneo)* her comments were very wide of the mark

desacertar *vi (equivocarse)* to be mistaken *o* wrong

desacierto *nm (error)* mistake, error; **fue un d. discutir con el jefe** it was a mistake to argue with the boss; **me parece una teoría llena de desaciertos** the theory seems to me to be full of mistakes

desacomodado, -a *adj RP (desordenado)* untidy, messy

desacomodar *vt RP* to make untidy

desacomodo *nm (molestia)* inconvenience, trouble

desacompasado, -a = **descompasado**

desaconsejable *adj (poco recomendable)* inadvisable, not advisable, unwise; **es d. tomar el sol sin la debida protección** it is not advisable to sunbathe without suitable protection

desaconsejado, -a 1 *adj* unwise; **está d. fumar durante el embarazo** you are advised not to smoke during pregnancy
2 *nm,f* unwise *o* imprudent person

desaconsejar *vt* **d. algo (a alguien)** to advise (sb) against sth; **me lo ha desaconsejado mi abogado** my lawyer has advised me against it; **d. a alguien que haga algo** to advise sb not to do sth; **se desaconseja salir durante la tormenta** you are advised not to go out during the storm

desacoplar *vt Elec* to disconnect; *Tec* to uncouple

desacorde *adj* (**a**) *(opiniones)* differing, conflicting (**b**) *(sonidos, notas musicales)* discordant; *(instrumentos)* out of tune (with one another)

desacostumbrado, -a *adj* (**a**) *(extraño, inusual)* unusual, uncommon; **la puntualidad es algo d. en él** it's unusual for him to be punctual (**b**) *(deshabituado)* **estar d. a hacer algo** not to be used to doing sth any more, to be out of the habit of doing sth; **está d. a este ritmo de entrenamiento** he's not used to this level of training any more

desacostumbrar 1 *vt* to get out of the habit; **han desacostumbrado al niño a dormir por la tarde** they have got the child out of the habit of sleeping in the afternoon
2 **desacostumbrarse** *vpr* to get out of the habit; **me he desacostumbrado a vivir en el campo** I'm not used to living in the country any more; **se había desacostumbrado a los rigores invernales** he'd forgotten what the harsh winters were like

desacralizar *vt* **la Navidad se ha desacralizado** Christmas has become very secular

desacreditado, -a *adj* discredited; **ha quedado d. ante la opinión pública** he has been discredited in the eyes of the public

desacreditar 1 *vt* to discredit; **hubo una campaña para desacreditarla** there was a campaign to discredit her; **este nuevo fracaso lo desacredita como político** this latest failure has destroyed his credibility as a politician; **su actuación ha desacreditado al partido** his behaviour has brought the party into disrepute

2 desacreditarse *vpr* to become discredited; **con su actitud intransigente se desacreditó él solo** he brought discredit on himself through his intransigent attitude

desactivación *nf* (**a**) *(de bomba, explosivo)* defusing, deactivation (**b**) *(de mecanismo, alarma)* disconnection (**c**) *(de situación peligrosa)* defusing; *(conflicto)* pacification; *(de plan de emergencia)* cancellation

desactivado, -a 1 *adj* (**a**) *(bomba, explosivo)* defused (**b**) *(mecanismo, alarma)* disconnected (**c**) *(situación peligrosa)* defused; *(conflicto)* pacified; *(de plan de emergencia)* cancelled
2 *nm (de bomba, explosivo)* defusing, deactivation

desactivador, -ora 1 *adj* **equipo d. de explosivos** bomb disposal team
2 *nm,f* **d. (de explosivos)** bomb disposal expert

desactivar *vt* (**a**) *(bomba, explosivo)* to defuse (**b**) *(mecanismo, alarma)* to disconnect (**c**) *(situación peligrosa)* to defuse; *(plan de emergencia)* to call off (**d**) *Informát* to disable, to deactivate

desacuerdo *nm* disagreement (**con** with); **varios miembros del equipo manifestaron su d. con el entrenador** various members of the team openly disagreed with the coach; **mostró su d. con el proyecto** he made clear his opposition to the project; **hay d. sobre varios puntos de la negociación** there is disagreement on various points in the negotiation; **estar en d.** *(personas)* to disagree; **estar en d. con algo/alguien** to disagree *o* not to agree with sth/sb; **estoy en d. con la política del gobierno** I don't agree with *o* I'm opposed to the government's policy; **no estoy en d. con ella** I don't disagree with her

desadaptación *nf Am* maladaptation

desadaptado, -a 1 *Am adj* (**a**) *(desacostumbrado)* no longer accustomed; **después de tantos años sin estudiar, está d. a la universidad** after not studying for so long, he feels out of place at university (**b**) *(inadaptado)* maladjusted
2 *nm,f Fam* misfit

desaduanar *vt Am* to release from customs

desafanarse *vpr Méx Fam* to get out of it; **siempre encuentra un pretexto para d.** she always finds a way to get out of it

desafección *nf* (**a**) *(falta de afecto, indiferencia)* **d. hacia** *o* **por algo** aversion to sth; **d. hacia** *o* **por alguien** coldness towards sb (**b**) *(oposición)* disaffection (**a** with)

desafecto, -a 1 *adj (opuesto)* hostile (**a** to), disaffected (**a** with); **sectores desafectos al régimen** sectors hostile to the regime
2 *nm (falta de afecto, indiferencia)* **d. hacia** *o* **por algo** indifference to *o* towards sth; **d. hacia** *o* **por alguien** coldness towards sb

desafiante *adj (gesto, mirada, actitud, tono, palabras)* defiant; **me miró d.** she stared at me defiantly

desafiantemente *adv* defiantly

desafiar [32] *vt* (**a**) *(persona)* to challenge; **d. a alguien a algo** to challenge sb to sth; **lo desafió a un duelo** he challenged him to a duel; **d. a alguien a hacer algo** to challenge sb to do sth; **te desafío a subir la cima de esta montaña** I challenge you to climb that mountain; **lo desafió a que acudiera a los tribunales** she challenged him to take the matter to court
(**b**) *(peligro, ley, autoridad, normas)* to defy; **d. a la muerte** to defy death; **desafió las órdenes de sus superiores** he disobeyed superior orders

desafilado, -a *adj* blunt

desafilar *vt* **1** to blunt, to dull
2 desafilarse *vpr* to get blunt

desafinado, -a *adj (instrumento)* out of tune

desafinar 1 *vi (instrumento)* to be out of tune; *(cantante)* to sing out of tune; *(músico)* to play out of tune
2 desafinarse *vpr (instrumento)* to go out of tune

desafío *nm* (**a**) *(reto)* challenge; **aceptar el d. de alguien** to take up *o* accept sb's challenge; **la curación del cáncer supone un d. para la comunidad médica** finding a cure for cancer is a challenge for the medical profession; **el d. tecnológico** the technological challenge
(**b**) *(duelo)* duel
(**c**) *(oposición, contradicción)* **d. a** *(peligro, ley, autoridad, normas)* defiance of; **el d. a la muerte del trapecista** the trapeze artist's death-defying feats

desaforadamente *adv (correr, cantar, bailar)* wildly, like crazy; *(comer, beber)* as if there was no tomorrow; *(ambicionar, codiciar, desear)* wildly; **gritó d.** he screamed his head off

desaforado, -a 1 *adj (gritos, baile, carrera)* wild; *(ambición, codicia, deseo)* unbridled, wild; *(celebración, fiesta)* wild; *(comilona, borrachera)* enormous, gargantuan
2 *nm,f* **los hinchas gritaban como desaforados** the fans screamed wildly; **bailaba/comía como un d.** he danced/ate like a man possessed

desafortunadamente *adv* unfortunately

desafortunado, -a 1 *adj* (**a**) *(desgraciado)* unfortunate; **el d. suceso ocurrió ayer** the unfortunate event occurred yesterday; **un día d. en las carreteras** a black day on the roads
(**b**) *(desacertado)* unfortunate; **un comentario d.** an unfortunate remark; **el equipo tuvo una desafortunada actuación** the team performed below par; **el ministro estuvo bastante d.** the minister made some unfortunate remarks
(**c**) *(sin suerte)* unlucky; **fue muy desafortunada en amores** she was very unlucky in love
2 *nm,f* unlucky person

desafuero *nm* (**a**) *(abuso)* outrage, atrocity; **cometer un d.** to commit an outrage (**b**) *Der (violación de leyes)* infringement, violation

desagotar *vt RP* to drain

desagradable 1 *adj* (**a**) *(sensación, tiempo, escena)* unpleasant; **no voy a salir, la tarde está muy d.** I'm not going to go out, the weather's turned quite nasty this afternoon; **una d. sorpresa** an unpleasant *o* a nasty surprise
(**b**) *(persona, comentario, contestación)* unpleasant; **está muy d. con su familia** he's very unpleasant to his family; **no seas d. y ven con nosotros al cine** don't be unsociable, come to the cinema with us
2 *nmf* **son unos desagradables** they're unpleasant people

desagradar *vi* to displease; **me desagrada su actitud** I don't like her attitude; **me desagradó tener que levantarme tan pronto** I didn't like having to get up so early; **créame, me desagrada mucho tener que decirle esto** believe me, I really don't like to have to say this to you; **a nadie le desagradan los elogios** nobody minds being praised; **¿qué es lo que tanto te desagrada de él?** what is it you dislike about him?; **¿qué te parece este bar? – no me desagrada** how do you like this bar? – it's not bad

desagradecido, -a 1 *adj* (**a**) *(persona)* ungrateful; **ha sido muy d. con su familia** he's been very ungrateful to his family (**b**) *(trabajo, tarea)* thankless
2 *nm,f* ungrateful person; **es un d.** he's so ungrateful

desagradecimiento *nm* ingratitude

desagrado *nm* displeasure, disapproval; **todos mostramos nuestro d.** we all showed our displeasure; **una mueca de d.** a look of disapproval; **con d.** reluctantly; **levantó el trapo mugriento con d.** she lifted the filthy cloth with evident distaste

desagraviar *vt* **d. a alguien por algo** *(por una ofensa)* to make amends to sb for sth; *(por un perjuicio)* to compensate sb for sth

desagravio *nm* **en señal de d.** (in order) to make amends; **pagó una cantidad en d. por el mal causado** she paid a sum to make up for the harm she'd done

desagregar [38] *vt* to disintegrate, to break up

desaguadero, desaguador *nm* drain

desaguar [11] **1** *vi* (**a**) *(bañera, lavadora)* to empty, to drain; *(agua)* to drain (**b**) *(río)* **d. en** to flow into
2 *vt (lugar inundado)* to get *o* pump the water out of

desagüe *nm* (**a**) *(vaciado)* draining, emptying (**b**) *(de bañera, fregadero, lavabo, lavadora)* waste outlet; *(de patio, calle, terraza)* drain; **el pendiente cayó por el d.** the earring fell down the drain ►► ***d. de azotea*** roof drain

desaguisado *nm Fam (desorden)* shambles *(singular)*; *(destrozo)* mess; **la inauguración fue un verdadero d.** the opening was a shambles; **hacer un d.** to make a mess; **¡vaya d. que te han hecho en la peluquería!** what a mess they've made of your hair!

desahogadamente *adv* comfortably; **vivir d.** to be comfortably off

desahogado, -a *adj* (**a**) *(de espacio)* spacious, roomy; **corre la mesa, así estaremos más desahogados** move the table, we'll have more room that way
(**b**) *(de dinero)* well-off, comfortable; **ahora estamos más desahogados** we're better-off now; **llevan una vida bastante desahogada** they're quite comfortably off
(**c**) *(de tiempo)* **tengo un trabajo muy d.** there's no rush in my job; **vamos muy desahogados de tiempo** we have more than enough time

desahogar [38] **1** *vt* (**a**) *(ira)* to vent; *(pena)* to relieve, to ease; **desahogó su enfado en su mejor amiga** she took out her annoyance on her best friend
(**b**) *(habitación, lugar, armario)* to clear, to make some space in; *(estantería)* to make some space on
2 desahogarse *vpr* (**a**) *(contar penas)* **desahogarse con alguien** to pour out one's woes to sb, to tell one's troubles to sb; **necesito alguien**

con quien me pueda d. I need somebody to talk to

(**b**) *(desfogarse)* to let off steam; **se desahogaba haciendo pesas en el gimnasio** he let off steam pumping iron in the gym; **se desahogan insultando al árbitro** they let off steam insulting the referee; **llora, si quieres desahogarte** cry if you want to let it all out

desahogo *nm* (**a**) *(alivio)* relief, release; **llorar le sirvió de d.** crying gave him some relief (**b**) *(de espacio)* space, room; **en esta oficina podremos trabajar con más d.** we'll have more room to work in this office (**c**) *(económico)* ease; **vivir con d.** to be comfortably off

desahuciar *vt* (**a**) *(inquilino)* to evict (**b**) *(enfermo)* **d. a alguien** to give up all hope of saving sb

desahucio *nm* (**a**) *(de inquilino)* eviction; **un aviso** *o* **una notificación de d.** an eviction notice (**b**) *Andes (de trabajador)* dismissal

desairado, -a *adj* (**a**) *(poco airoso) (actuación)* unimpressive, unsuccessful (**b**) *(humillado)* spurned

desairar *vt (persona)* to snub, to slight

desaire *nm (desprecio)* snub, slight; **sería un d. por tu parte no acudir** it will be seen as a snub if you don't go; **hacer un d. a alguien** to snub sb; **sufrir un d.** to receive a rebuff

desajustar 1 *vt (aparato, motor, máquina)* to put out of kilter; *(pieza, tuerca)* to loosen; **el golpe desajustó los tornillos** the blow loosened the screws

2 **desajustarse** *vpr (aparato, motor, máquina)* to go out of kilter, to stop working properly; *(pieza, tuerca, tornillo)* to come loose; **el mecanismo se ha desajustado** the mechanism isn't working properly

desajuste *nm* (**a**) *(de piezas)* misalignment; *(de aparato, motor, máquina)* malfunction, fault (**b**) *(de declaraciones, versiones)* inconsistency (**c**) *(económico)* imbalance

desalado, -a *adj* (**a**) *(sin la sal)* desalted (**b**) *(apresurado)* hurried (**c**) *(ansioso)* anxious, eager

desalador, -ora *adj* **planta desaladora de agua** desalination plant

desalar *vt (quitar la sal a)* to remove salt from; *(agua)* to desalinate

desalentador, -ora *adj* discouraging, disheartening

desalentar [3] 1 *vt* to dishearten, to discourage; **un resultado así desalienta a cualquiera** a result like this would dishearten anyone; **no dejes que eso te desaliente** don't let it discourage you

2 **desalentarse** *vpr* to be discouraged, to lose heart; **no se desalienta con facilidad** she isn't easily discouraged

desaliento *nm* dismay, dejection; **cundió el d. al conocerse el resultado** dismay spread as the result became known; **reaccionaron con d.** they reacted with dismay

desalineación *nf (de ruedas)* misalignment

desalinearse *vpr* to go out of line

desalinización *nf* desalination

desalinizador, -ora *adj* **planta desalinizadora** desalination plant

desalinizadora *nf* desalination plant

desalinizar *vt* to desalinate

desaliñado, -a *adj (persona, aspecto)* scruffy; **un tipo de aspecto d.** a scruffy-looking guy

desaliñar 1 *vt* (**a**) *(desarreglar)* to make untidy (**b**) *(arrugar)* to crease

2 **desaliñarse** *vpr* to become untidy

desaliño *nm (de persona, aspecto)* scruffiness

desalmado, -a 1 *adj* heartless

2 *nm,f* heartless person; **es un d.** he's completely heartless

desalojar *vt* (**a**) *(por emergencia) (edificio, personas)* to evacuate

(**b**) *(por la fuerza) (ocupantes)* to eject, to remove; *(inquilinos)* to evict; **la policía los desalojó de la sala por la fuerza** the police forcibly removed them from the hall

(**c**) *(por propia voluntad)* to abandon, to move out of; **los huelguistas desalojaron la factoría pacíficamente** the strikers left the factory peacefully; **¡desalojen la sala!** *(orden del juez)* clear the court!

(**d**) *(contenido, gas)* to expel

desalojo *nm* (**a**) *(por emergencia) (de edificio, personas)* evacuation (**b**) *(por la fuerza) (de ocupantes)* ejection, removal; *(de inquilinos)* eviction; **una orden de d.** an eviction order (**c**) *(de contenido, gas)* expulsion

desalquilar 1 *vt* (**a**) *(lo alquilado)* to stop renting (**b**) *(mudarse de)* to move out of, to vacate

2 **desalquilarse** *vpr* to become vacant

desamarrar 1 *vt* to cast off

2 **desamarrarse** *vpr* to come untied

desambientado, -a *adj (persona)* out of place

desambiguar *vt* to disambiguate

desamor *nm (falta de afecto)* indifference, coldness; *(odio)* dislike

desamortización *nf (de propiedades)* disentailment, alienation

desamortizar [14] *vt (propiedades)* to disentail, to alienate

desamparado, -a 1 *adj* (**a**) *(persona)* helpless (**b**) *(lugar)* desolate, forsaken

2 *nm,f* helpless person; **los desamparados** the needy, the helpless

desamparar *vt (persona)* to abandon

desamparo *nm (abandono)* abandonment; *(aflicción)* helplessness; **niños que viven en el más absoluto d.** children who live in a state of total neglect

desamueblado, -a *adj* unfurnished

desamueblar *vt* to remove the furniture from

desandar [7] *vt (camino)* to go back over; **tuve que d. 2 kilómetros** I had to go back 2 kilometres; **d. lo andado** to retrace one's steps; *Fig* to go back to square one

desangelado, -a *adj* (**a**) *(casa, barrio, ciudad)* soulless; *(acto, celebración)* dull, uninspiring (**b**) *(persona)* charmless

desangramiento *nm* heavy bleeding

desangrar 1 *vt* (**a**) *(animal, persona)* to bleed; **murió desangrado** he bled to death (**b**) *(económicamente)* to bleed dry

2 **desangrarse** *vpr* (**a**) *(animal, persona)* to lose a lot of blood (**b**) *(económicamente)* to be bled dry

desanidar *vi* to leave the nest

desanimado, -a *adj* (**a**) *(persona)* downhearted (**b**) *(fiesta, lugar)* quiet, lifeless

desanimar 1 *vt* to discourage; **los comentarios de sus amigos lo han desanimado** he has been put off *o* discouraged by his friends' comments

2 **desanimarse** *vpr* to get downhearted *o* discouraged; **no te desanimes** don't lose heart, don't be discouraged

desánimo *nm (desaliento)* dejection; **el d. cundía entre la población** there was widespread despondency among the population

desanudar *vt* to untie

desapacible *adj* (**a**) *(tiempo, clima)* unpleasant (**b**) *(carácter)* unpleasant, disagreeable

desaparecer [46] 1 *vi* (**a**) *(de la vista)* to disappear (**de** from); **desapareció tras las colinas** it dropped out of sight behind the hills; **me ha desaparecido la pluma** my pen has disappeared; **hizo d. una paloma y un conejo** he made a dove and a rabbit vanish; **será mejor que desaparezcas de escena durante una temporada** you'd better make yourself scarce for a while; **d. de la faz de la tierra** to vanish from the face of the earth; **¡desaparece de mi vista ahora mismo!** get out of my sight this minute!

(**b**) *(dolor, síntomas, mancha)* to disappear, to go; *(cicatriz)* to disappear; *(sarpullido)* to clear up

(**c**) *(en guerra, accidente)* to go missing, to disappear; **muchos desaparecieron durante la represión** many people disappeared during the crackdown

2 *vt Am (persona)* = to detain extrajudicially during political repression and possibly kill

desaparecido, -a 1 *adj* (**a**) *(extraviado)* missing (**b**) *(fallecido)* **el d. Jack Lemmon** the late Jack Lemmon; **un soldado d. en combate** a soldier missing in action (**c**) *(extinto)* **la desaparecida Sociedad de Naciones** the now defunct League of Nations

2 *nm,f* (**a**) *(en catástrofe)* missing person; **ha habido veinte muertos y tres desaparecidos** twenty people have been killed and three are missing (**b**) *(en represión política)* missing person *(kidnapped and possibly murdered by the authorities)* (**c**) *(en guerra)* **d. en combate** person missing in action

desaparición *nf* (**a**) *(de objeto, animal, persona)* disappearance; **especies/tradiciones en vías de d.** endangered species/traditions; **la d. de este ministerio perjudicó a muchos** many people were adversely affected by the closure of the ministry; **los represores practicaron la d. de militantes** the instigators of the repression were responsible for the disappearance of activists

(**b**) *Euf (muerte)* death

desapasionadamente *adv* dispassionately

desapasionado, -a *adj (relato de acontecimientos, crítica)* impartial; *(estilo, tono)* neutral, objective; *(observador, crítico, actitud)* impartial, unbiased

desapasionarse *vpr* to lose interest

desapego *nm* (**a**) *(indiferencia)* indifference (**por** towards); **siente gran d. por lo material** she's totally indifferent to material things (**b**) *(falta de afecto)* coldness (**por** towards)

desapercibido, -a *adj* (**a**) *(inadvertido)* unnoticed; **pasar d.** to go unnoticed; **su original obra no pasó desapercibida a los expertos** the originality of her work didn't go *o* pass unnoticed by the critics (**b**) *(desprevenido)* unprepared, unready

desapolillarse *vpr Fam* to shake off the cobwebs, to get out and about

desaprender *vt* to unlearn

desaprensión *nf (falta de escrúpulos)* unscrupulousness

desaprensivo, -a 1 *adj* (**a**) *(sin escrúpulos)* unscrupulous (**b**) *(gamberro)* reckless, heedless

2 *nm,f (gamberro)* reckless delinquent; **un grupo de desaprensivos quemó las papeleras** a group of vandals set fire to the *Br* litter bins *o US* litter baskets

desapretar [3] **1** *vt (tornillo, nudo)* to loosen

2 desapretarse *vpr* (**a**) *(tornillo, nudo)* to become loose; **se te ha desapretado el cordón del zapato** your shoelace is loose (**b**) *(uso reflexivo) (corbata, correa, cordón)* to loosen; **me desapreté los cordones de los zapatos** I loosened my shoelaces

desaprobación *nf* disapproval; **la miró con d.** he looked at her disapprovingly *o* with disapproval

desaprobador, -ora *adj* disapproving

desaprobar [64] *vt* (**a**) *(actitud, comportamiento)* to disapprove of (**b**) *(propuesta, plan)* to reject

desaprovechado, -a *adj* (**a**) *(desperdiciado) (tiempo, ocasión, talento)* wasted (**b**) *(mal aprovechado) (espacio, recursos, terreno)* not put to the best use; **tierras desaprovechadas** land not being put to good use

desaprovechamiento *nm* (**a**) *(de tiempo, ocasión, talento)* waste (**b**) *(de espacio, recursos, terreno)* failure to exploit fully

desaprovechar *vt* (**a**) *(desperdiciar) (tiempo, ocasión, talento)* to waste; **desaprovechó la ocasión de empatar el partido** he missed his chance to tie the match; **no desaproveches el agua** don't waste water (**b**) *(aprovechar mal) (espacio, recursos, terreno)* to underuse, to fail to exploit fully

desapruebo *etc ver* **desaprobar**

desapuntar *vt Col* to unbutton

desarbolar *vt* (**a**) *Náut* to dismast, to strip of masts (**b**) *Fam (destartalar)* to mess up, to make a mess of; **desarboló toda la defensa contraria** he ran rings round the opposing defence; **desarboló la argumentación del fiscal** she demolished the *Br* public prosecutor's *o US* district attorney's line of argument

desarmable *adj (mueble)* that can be dismantled

desarmado, -a *adj* (**a**) *(sin armas)* unarmed; **ir d.** not to carry arms *o* guns (**b**) *(desmontado)* dismantled

desarmador *nm Méx* (**a**) *(herramienta)* screwdriver (**b**) *(cóctel)* screwdriver

desarmar *vt* **1** (**a**) *(quitar las armas a)* to disarm (**b**) *(desmontar)* to take apart, to dismantle; **d. una tienda de campaña** to take down a tent (**c**) *(desconcertar)* to disarm; **intento reñirla, pero su sonrisa me desarma** I try to tell her off, but her smile disarms me

2 desarmarse *vpr* (**a**) *(país)* to disarm; *(guerrilla)* to disarm, to give up one's arms (**b**) *(desmontarse)* to come apart; **¿cómo se desarma esto?** how do you dismantle this?

desarme *nm (reducción de armamentos)* disarmament ►► *Econ* ***d. arancelario*** removal of tariff barriers; ***d. nuclear*** nuclear disarmament

desarraigado, -a *adj (persona)* uprooted, rootless

desarraigar [38] *vt* (**a**) *(vicio, costumbre)* to root out (**b**) *(persona, pueblo)* to banish, to drive out (**de** from)

desarraigo *nm* (**a**) *(de vicio, costumbre)* rooting out (**b**) *(de persona, pueblo)* rootlessness; **emigrantes víctimas del d.** emigrants beset by feelings of rootlessness

desarrapado, -a = **desharrapado**

desarreglado, -a *adj* (**a**) *(cuarto, armario, aspecto, persona)* untidy; *(pelo)* dishevelled (**b**) *(vida)* disorganized

desarreglar 1 *vt* (**a**) *(cuarto, armario)* to mess up, to make untidy; *(pelo, peinado)* to mess up (**b**) *(planes, horario)* to upset

2 desarreglarse *vpr* (**a**) *(pelo, peinado)* to get messed up (**b**) *(planes, horario)* to be upset

desarreglo *nm* (**a**) *(de cuarto, persona)* untidiness (**b**) *(de vida)* disorder; *(de planes, horario)* disruption; **me siento rara, debo de tener un d. hormonal** I'm feeling a bit funny, it must be my hormones ►► ***desarreglos menstruales*** menstrual irregularities

desarrendar [3] *vt* (**a**) *(dejar de arrendar)* to stop leasing (**b**) *(dejar de alquilar)* to stop renting

desarrollado, -a *adj* (**a**) *(país, proyecto)* developed; **una sociedad desarrollada** a developed society (**b**) *(niño)* well-developed

desarrollador, -ora *nm,f Informát* developer ►► ***d. de software*** software developer

desarrollar 1 *vt* (**a**) *(mejorar) (crecimiento, país)* to develop; *(economía, sector, comercio)* to develop; *(capacidades, talento, musculatura)* to develop; **desarrolló un sexto sentido para las finanzas** she developed *o* acquired a sixth sense for money

(**b**) *(exponer) (tema)* to explain, to develop; *(teoría)* to expound, to develop; **¿podrías d. esa idea un poco más?** could you expand on that idea a little more?

(**c**) *(realizar) (actividad, trabajo, proyecto)* to carry out

(**d**) *(crear) (prototipos, técnicas, estrategias)* to develop

(**e**) *(velocidad)* **esta moto desarrolla los 200 kilómetros por hora** this bike can reach a speed of 200 kilometres an hour

(**f**) *Mat (término)* to expand; *(ecuación, problema)* to solve, to work out

2 desarrollarse *vpr* (**a**) *(crecer, mejorar)* to develop; **la proteína es imprescindible para desarrollarse** protein is essential for development *o* growth

(**b**) *(suceder) (reunión, encuentro, manifestación)* to take place; *(película, obra, novela)* to be set; **la manifestación se desarrolló sin incidentes** the demonstration went off without incident; **la acción de la novela se desarrolla en el siglo XIX** the novel is set in the 19th century

(**c**) *(evolucionar)* to develop; **¿cómo se desarrollarán los acontecimientos?** how will events develop?

desarrollismo *nm* = policy of economic development at all costs

desarrollista *adj* **una concepción d. del progreso** a concept of progress based solely on economic development

desarrollo *nm* (**a**) *(mejora)* development; **el d. económico** economic development; **países en vías de d.** developing countries; **el pleno d. de las capacidades intelectuales** the full development of intellectual abilities

(**b**) *(crecimiento)* growth; **el d. del ser humano** human development; **la edad del d.** (the age of) puberty

(**c**) *(exposición) (de tema, teoría, idea)* explanation

(**d**) *(transcurso) (de negociaciones, conferencia)* course; **no hubo incidentes en el d. de la manifestación** there were no incidents in the course of the demonstration

(**e**) *(realización) (de actividad, trabajo, proyecto)* carrying out

(**f**) *(creación) (de prototipos, técnicas, estrategias)* development; **investigaciones encaminadas al d. de una vacuna contra el sida** research aimed at developing a vaccine against AIDS

(**g**) *(en bicicleta)* gear ratio; **mover un gran d.** to turn a big gear

(**h**) *Mat (de término)* expansion; *(de ecuación, problema)* solving, working out

desarropar 1 *vt* to uncover

2 desarroparse *vpr* **se desarropa durante la noche** he kicks off the bedclothes during the night

desarrugar [38] **1** *vt (alisar)* to smooth out; *(planchar)* to iron out the creases in

2 desarrugarse *vpr (sujeto: ropa)* to become uncreased; **las cortinas se desarrugarán solas, no hace falta plancharlas** the creases will come out of the curtains by themselves, you don't need to iron them

desarticulación *nf* (**a**) *(de huesos, miembros)* dislocation (**b**) *(de organización, banda)* breaking up; *(de plan)* foiling

desarticular 1 *vt* (**a**) *(huesos, miembros)* to dislocate (**b**) *(organización, banda)* to break up; *(plan)* to foil (**c**) *(máquina, artefacto)* to take apart, to dismantle

2 desarticularse *vpr* (**a**) *(huesos, miembros)* to be dislocated (**b**) *(uso reflexivo) (dislocarse)* to dislocate; **se desarticuló la mandíbula** he dislocated his jaw

desaseado, -a *adj* (**a**) *(sucio)* dirty (**b**) *(desarreglado)* untidy

desaseo *nm* (**a**) *(suciedad)* dirtiness (**b**) *(desarreglo)* untidiness, messiness

desasir [9] **1** *vt* to release, to let go

2 desasirse *vpr* (**a**) *(desatarse)* to get loose; **desasirse de** to free oneself of; **logró desasirse de las ataduras** he managed to free himself from the ties which bound him (**b**) *(desprenderse)* **desasirse de** to part with; **nunca me desasiré del anillo de mi abuela** I'll never part with my grandmother's ring

desasistido, -a *adj (enfermo, población, barrio)* neglected; **un barrio marginal d. por la administración** a deprived district neglected *o* abandoned by the authorities; **el único delantero se halla totalmente d.** the only striker has no support whatsoever; **dejar a alguien d.** to leave sb unattended (to)

desasistir *vt* to neglect, to abandon

desasnar *vt Fam* to teach, to civilize

desasosegado, -a *adj* uneasy, nervous

desasosegar [43] 1 *vt* to disturb, to make uneasy; **su penetrante mirada me desasosegaba** her penetrating gaze unnerved me
2 **desasosegarse** *vpr* to become uneasy; **empezó a desasosegarse** she began to feel uneasy

desasosiego *nm* unease; **reina un gran d. entre los aficionados** there is great unease among the fans; **algunas escenas producen bastante d.** some scenes are rather disturbing

desastrado, -a *adj (desaseado)* scruffy; **¿cómo puedes ir siempre tan d.?** how can you always go about looking so scruffy?

desastre *nm* (**a**) *(catástrofe)* disaster ►► ***d. aéreo*** air disaster; ***d. ecológico*** ecological disaster
(**b**) *(persona inútil)* disaster; **su madre es un d.** her mother is hopeless; **soy un d. para los negocios** I'm hopeless at business; **es un d. contando chistes** he's useless at telling jokes
(**c**) *Fam (fracaso)* disaster; **fue un d. de fiesta** the party was a flop; **estar hecho un d.** *(roto, sucio, desordenado)* to be a real disaster, to be in a mess; **el mundo está hecho un d.** the world's in a complete mess; **vas hecho un d., arréglate un poco** you look a right mess, tidy yourself up a bit; **¡vaya d.!** what a shambles!

desastrosamente *adv* disastrously

desastroso, -a *adj* (**a**) *(castastrófico)* disastrous; **la helada fue desastrosa para la cosecha** the frost had a disastrous effect on the harvest (**b**) *(muy malo)* disastrous; **esta comida es desastrosa** this food is appalling *o* awful

desatado, -a *adj* (**a**) *(atadura, animal)* loose; **llevas los cordones desatados** your laces are undone; **no lleves al perro d.** don't let the dog off its leash (**b**) *(descontrolado)* out of control, uncontrollable; **estar d.** to be wild; **últimamente tiene los nervios desatados** her nerves have been very frayed lately

desatar 1 *vt* (**a**) *(nudo, lazo)* to untie; *(paquete)* to undo
(**b**) *(animal)* to unleash; *(persona)* to untie
(**c**) *(tormenta, ira, pasión)* to unleash; *(entusiasmo)* to arouse; *(motín, disturbios, protestas)* to spark off, to trigger; *(lengua)* to loosen; **la decisión desató una ola de manifestaciones** the decision set off *o* triggered a wave of demonstrations; **su dimisión desató la crisis de gobierno** his resignation triggered *o* precipitated the governmental crisis
2 **desatarse** *vpr* (**a**) *(nudo, lazo)* to come undone; *(paquete)* to come undone *o* untied
(**b**) *(animal)* to get loose *o* free
(**c**) *(persona)* **¿puedes desatarte?** can you get free?; **desátese los zapatos** undo your shoes
(**d**) *(desencadenarse) (tormenta)* to break; *(ira, cólera, pasión)* to erupt; *(motín, disturbios, protestas)* to break out; *(polémica, crisis)* to flare up; **se desató en insultos contra sus adversarios** she showered a stream of insults on her opponents

desatascador *nm* (**a**) *(instrumento)* (sink) plunger (**b**) *(producto químico)* = chemical used to unblock sinks and drains

desatascar [60] 1 *vt* (**a**) *(tubería)* to unblock (**b**) *(negociaciones)* to break the deadlock in (**c**) *(tráfico, carreteras, calles)* to clear
2 **desatascarse** *vpr* (**a**) *(tubería)* to unblock (**b**) *(negociaciones)* to get moving again (**c**) *(tráfico, carreteras, calles)* to clear

desatención *nf* (**a**) *(falta de atención)* lack of attention (**b**) *(descortesía)* discourtesy, impoliteness

desatender [66] *vt* (**a**) *(obligación, persona)* to neglect (**b**) *(ruegos, consejos)* to ignore (**c**) *(puesto, tienda, mostrador)* to leave unattended

desatendido, -a *adj* (**a**) *(obligación, persona)* neglected (**b**) *(puesto, tienda, mostrador)* left unattended; *(maleta, paquete)* unattended (**c**) *(ruego, consejo)* ignored

desatento, -a *adj* (**a**) *(distraído)* inattentive; **siempre está d. en clase** he never pays attention in class (**b**) *(descortés)* impolite; **no seas tan d., ayuda al señor con las bolsas** try to be a little more helpful, help the gentleman with his bags; **has estado muy d. con tu abuela** you've been very impolite to your grandmother

desatiendo *etc ver* **desatender**

desatinado, -a *adj* (**a**) *(necio)* foolish, silly (**b**) *(imprudente)* rash, reckless

desatinar *vi (al actuar)* to act foolishly; *(al hablar)* to say stupid things; **¿una bicicleta nueva? ¡tú desatinas!** a new bicycle? are you *Br* mad *o US* crazy?

desatino *nm* (**a**) *(error)* mistake, error; **tratar de hacer el viaje en barco era un d.** attempting the journey by boat was a mistake (**b**) *(comentario estúpido o absurdo)* foolish remark; **no decía más que desatinos** he talked nothing but nonsense

desatornillador *nm Andes, CAm, Méx* screwdriver

desatornillar 1 *vt* to unscrew
2 **desatornillarse** *vpr* to become unscrewed *o* loose

desatracar [60] *Náut* 1 *vt* to cast off
2 *vi* to steer away from the coast

desatrancar [60] *vt* (**a**) *(puerta, ventana)* to unbolt (**b**) *(tubería, desagüe)* to unblock

desautorización *nf* withdrawal of authority

desautorizado, -a *adj* (**a**) *(falto de autoridad)* unauthorized (**b**) *(desmentido)* denied (**c**) *(prohibido)* banned

desautorizar [14] 1 *vt* (**a**) *(desmentir) (noticia)* to deny; **el ministro desautorizó las declaraciones del portavoz** the minister contradicted the statement made by the spokesperson
(**b**) *(prohibir) (manifestación, huelga)* to ban, to declare illegal
(**c**) *(desacreditar)* to discredit; **sus prejuicios racistas lo desautorizan como político** his racist ideas undermine his credentials as a politician; **desautorizaba a los profesores delante de sus alumnos** she undermined the teachers' authority in front of their pupils
2 **desautorizarse** *vpr (desacreditarse)* to be discredited; **desautorizarse ante la opinión pública** to be discredited in public opinion

desavenencia *nf (desacuerdo)* friction, tension; *(riña)* quarrel (**entre/con** between/with); **tuvo alguna d. con su novia** he had a row or two with his girlfriend; **desavenencias matrimoniales** marital disagreements

desavenido, -a *adj (enemistado)* at odds (**con** with); **dos familias desavenidas** two families at odds with each other

desavenirse [71] *vpr* to fall out (**con** with)

desaventajado, -a *adj* disadvantaged

desayunado, -a *adj* **salió ya d.** he went out after having breakfast

desayunar 1 *vi* to have breakfast; **tomo tostadas para d.** I have toast for breakfast; **cuando hayas acabado de d., llámame** call me when you've finished (having) breakfast
2 *vt* to have for breakfast; **siempre desayuno cereales** I always have cereal for breakfast
3 **desayunarse** *vpr* (**a**) *(tomar desayuno)* **se desayunaron con café y tostadas** they had coffee and toast for breakfast; **mañana todos los españoles se desayunarán con la gran noticia** tomorrow the whole of Spain will wake up to the news (**b**) *Fam (enterarse)* **¿ahora te desayunas?** have you only just found out?

desayuno *nm* breakfast; **a la hora del d.** at breakfast time; **¿qué tomaste de d.?** what did you have for breakfast?; **durante el d., en el d.** at *o* over breakfast; **tomar el d.** to have breakfast ►► ***d. continental*** continental breakfast; ***d. inglés*** English breakfast

desazolvar *vt Méx* to unblock

desazolve *nm Méx* unblocking

desazón *nf* (**a**) *(ansiedad)* unease, anxiety; **sintió cierta d. al oír aquel nombre** she felt rather uneasy when she heard that name (**b**) *(molestia)* annoyance (**c**) *(picazón)* **siento d. en todo el cuerpo** I feel itchy all over

desazonado, -a *adj* (**a**) *(soso)* tasteless, insipid (**b**) *(inquieto)* uneasy, nervous (**c**) *(enfermo)* unwell

desazonar *vt (causar ansiedad a)* to worry, to cause anxiety to

desbancar [60] *vt* (**a**) *(ocupar el puesto de)* to replace, to take the place of; **fue desbancado de la presidencia de la compañía** he was ousted *o* removed as president of the company; **Boca desbancó a River del primer puesto** Boca displaced River at the top of the table; **el ferrocarril terminó desbancando al caballo** the railway ended up replacing the horse
(**b**) *(en el juego)* to take the bank from

desbandada *nf, RP* **desbande** *nm (huida desordenada)* breaking up, scattering; **el disparo provocó la d. de los pájaros** the shot sent the birds flying in all directions; **los atracadores huyeron en d.** the assailants fled in disarray; **se oyó una sirena de policía y hubo d. general** a police siren was heard and everyone scattered

desbandarse *vpr (pájaros, muchedumbre, ejército)* to scatter

desbande = **desbandada**

desbarajustar *vt* **d. algo** to throw sth in disarray

desbarajuste *nm* disorder, confusion; **el banquete de boda fue un auténtico d.** the wedding reception was complete chaos; **¡vaya d.!** what a mess!

desbaratado, -a *adj (roto)* wrecked, broken down

desbaratar 1 *vt* (**a**) *(romper)* to ruin, to wreck; **el temporal desbarató el tendido eléctrico** the storm brought down the power lines (**b**) *(estropear, arruinar)* to spoil; **la lluvia desbarató nuestros planes** the rain spoiled *o* put paid to our plans; **la defensa desbarató el contraataque alemán** the defence broke up the German counterattack

2 **desbaratarse** *vpr (planes)* to be spoiled

desbarrancadero *nm Col, Méx, Ven* precipice; **estamos al borde del d.** we're on the verge of the abyss

desbarrancarse *vpr Am (vehículo)* to plunge; **la Bolsa se desbarrancó un 7,3 por ciento** the stock market plunged 7.3 percent

desbarrar *vi Esp* to talk nonsense

desbastador *nm (en carpintería)* plane

desbastar *vt (en carpintería)* to plane

desbaste *nm (en carpintería)* planing

desbeber *vi Fam* to pee

desbloquear 1 *vt* (**a**) *(carretera, redes de comunicaciones, líneas telefónicas)* to unblock, to clear (**b**) *(mecanismo, dispositivo, seguro)* to release, to free (**c**) *(cuenta, fondos)* to unfreeze (**d**) *(negociación, proceso de paz)* to end *o* break the deadlock in, to get moving

2 **desbloquearse** *vpr* (**a**) *(carretera, redes de comunicaciones, líneas telefónicas)* to clear (**b**) *(mecanismo, dispositivo, seguro)* to come free (**c**) *(negociación, proceso de paz)* to get over a deadlock, to start moving again

desbloqueo *nm* (**a**) *(de carretera, camino)* unblocking; *(de redes de comunicaciones, líneas telefónicas)* clearing (**b**) *(de mecanismo, dispositivo, seguro)* freeing (**c**) *(de cuenta)* unfreezing; *(de fondos)* release (**d**) *(de negociación)* ending *o* breaking of a deadlock; **contactos para el d. del proceso de paz** contacts for breaking the deadlock in the peace process

desbocado, -a *adj* (**a**) *(caballo)* runaway (**b**) *(inflación, tasa de desempleo)* soaring, rampant (**c**) *(actitud, comportamiento)* impudent; *(persona)* foul-mouthed (**d**) *(prenda de vestir)* stretched around the neck; *(mangas, cuello, escote)* loose, wide

desbocamiento *nm* (**a**) *(de un caballo)* bolting (**b**) *(de inflación, tasa de desempleo)* dramatic rise

desbocarse [60] *vpr* (**a**) *(caballo)* to bolt (**b**) *(inflación, tasa de desempleo)* to soar, to get out of control (**c**) *(persona)* to let out a stream of abuse (**d**) *(prenda de vestir)* to pull out of shape

desbolado, -a *RP Fam* 1 *adj* (**a**) *(desprolijo)* messy, untidy (**b**) *(informal)* feckless

2 *nm,f* (**a**) *(desprolijo)* untidy person (**b**) *(informal)* feckless person

desbolar *RP Fam* 1 *vt* to mess up; **tratá de no d. mucho la casa** try not to make the house too untidy

2 **desbolarse** *vpr* to undress, to strip

desbole *nm RP Fam* mess, chaos

desbordamiento *nm* (**a**) *(de río, embalse)* overflowing (**b**) *(de sentimiento, pasión)* loss of control (**c**) *Informát* overflow

desbordante *adj (sentimiento, pasión)* boundless, unrestrained; *(entusiasmo, amor, alegría)* boundless; **tiene una imaginación d.** he has a rich imagination

desbordar 1 *vt* (**a**) *(cauce, ribera)* to overflow, to burst; *(recipiente)* to brim over; **el río desbordó el dique** the river burst the flood bank; **procura que la leche no desborde el cazo** be careful not to let the milk spill over; **la basura desbordaba los contenedores** the bins were overflowing with rubbish

(**b**) *(límites)* to break through; **los manifestantes desbordaron el cordón policial** the demonstrators broke through the police cordon

(**c**) *(previsiones, capacidad)* to exceed; *(paciencia)* to push beyond the limit; **la respuesta del público desbordó todas nuestras previsiones** the public's response exceeded all our forecasts; **la cantidad de pedidos nos desborda** we can't cope with the number of orders; **estamos desbordados de trabajo** we're overwhelmed *o* swamped with work; **¡la ineptitud de este gobierno es algo que me desborda!** this government's ineptitude is just beyond belief!

(**d**) *(pasión, sentimiento)* to brim with, to overflow with; **todos desbordábamos felicidad** we were all brimming with happiness; **el artículo desborda elogios** the article is overflowing with praise; **su rostro desbordaba amor y ternura** her face shone with love and tenderness

(**e**) *(contrario, defensa)* to get past, to pass; **desbordó al portero en su salida** he beat the goalkeeper as he was coming out

2 *vi* **d. de** to overflow with

3 **desbordarse** *vpr* (**a**) *(río)* to flood, to burst its banks; *(lago, embalse)* to flood, to overflow; *(bañera, olla, líquido, contenido)* to overflow; **llena el vaso hasta arriba sin que se desborde** fill the glass to the brim without it overflowing; **la leche comenzó a desbordarse** the milk started to spill over

(**b**) *(pasión, sentimiento)* to erupt; **sueña que le toca la lotería y su imaginación se desborda** she dreams she's won the lottery and her imagination runs away with her

desborde *nm RP (de río)* overflowing

desboronar *vt Col, Ven (hacer migas)* to crumble

desbravar *vt (ganado)* to tame, to break in

desbriznar *vt Culin (judías verdes)* to string

desbrozar [14] *vt* **d. un terreno** to clear a piece of land of weeds/undergrowth; **d. un texto de información innecesaria** to remove the waffle from a text; **d. el camino para sacar adelante el proceso de paz** to clear the way to advance the peace process

desbrozo *nm* (**a**) *(eliminación de maleza)* clearing *(of undergrowth)* (**b**) *(maleza)* undergrowth; *(ramas podadas)* prunings, garden débris

descabalar 1 *vt* (**a**) *(quitar una parte a)* to leave incomplete (**b**) *(desorganizar)* to spoil, to upset

2 **descabalarse** *vpr* (**a**) *(perder una parte de)*; **se ha descabalado la cristalería, en la fiesta se rompieron dos copas** we haven't got a complete set of glasses any more, two got broken at the party

(**b**) *(desorganizarse)* to become disorganized, to be thrown into confusion; **la red ferroviaria se descabaló totalmente a consecuencia de la huelga** the rail network was thrown into utter confusion as a result of the strike; **todos mis planes se descabalaron** all my plans were messed up

descabalgar [38] *vi* to dismount

descabellado, -a *adj* crazy

descabellar *vt Taurom* to give the coup de grâce to

descabello *nm Taurom* coup de grâce

descabezado, -a *adj (sin cabeza)* headless

descabezamiento *nm* (**a**) *(decapitación)* decapitation, beheading (**b**) *(de árbol)* topping

descabezar [14] *vt* (**a**) *(quitar la cabeza a) (persona)* to behead; *(pollo, gallina, sardina)* to cut the head off; *(cosa)* to break the head off; **descabezaron al grupo terrorista** they left the terrorist group leaderless (**b**) *(quitar la punta a) (planta, árbol)* to top (**c**) **d. un sueño** to have a nap

descachalandrado, -a *adj Ven Fam* scruffy

descacharrado, -a *adj Fam Br* knackered, *US* bust

descacharrante *adj Fam* hilarious

descacharrar *vt Fam Br* to knacker, *US* to bust

descafeinado, -a 1 *adj* (**a**) *(sin cafeína)* decaffeinated (**b**) *(sin fuerza)* watered down

2 *nm* decaffeinated coffee

descafeinar *vt* (**a**) *(quitar cafeína a)* to decaffeinate (**b**) *(quitar fuerza a)* to water down

descalabrar, escalabrar 1 *vt* (**a**) *(herir)* to wound in the head; **lo descalabraron de una pedrada** he was hit on the head and injured by a stone (**b**) *Fam (perjudicar)* **la caída de la bolsa descalabró el proyecto** the fall on the stock market really messed up the project

2 **descalabrarse** *vpr* to hurt one's head, to brain oneself

descalabro *nm* major setback, disaster; **el d. electoral de la ultraderecha** the electoral rout of the far right; **sufrir** *o* **tener un d.** to suffer a major setback

descalcificación *nf* (**a**) *Med* decalcification (**b**) *(del agua)* water softening, *Espec* decalcification

descalcificador, -ora *nm,f (aparato)* water softener

descalcificar [60] 1 *vt* (**a**) *Med* to decalcify (**b**) *(agua)* to soften, *Espec* to decalcify

2 **descalcificarse** *vpr* to decalcify, to lose calcium

descalificación *nf* (**a**) *(de competición)* disqualification (**b**) *(ofensa)* dismissive insult; **lanzar descalificaciones contra alguien** to sling insults at sb; **una guerra de descalificaciones** a slanging match

descalificar [60] *vt* (**a**) *(en competición)* to disqualify; **d. a alguien por (hacer) algo** to disqualify sb for (doing) sth (**b**) *(desprestigiar)* to discredit; **descalificó con saña a su oponente** he viciously attacked his opponent; **una actitud que lo descalifica como político** an attitude which discredits him as a politician

descalzar [14] 1 *vt* **d. a alguien** to take sb's shoes off

2 **descalzarse** *vpr* to take off one's shoes

descalzo, -a *adj* barefoot; **caminar** *o* **andar d.** to walk barefoot; **ir d.** to go barefoot; **en casa siempre estoy d.** I never wear shoes at home; **no se puede decir que estén descalzos** *(no son pobres)* you would hardly call them poverty-stricken

descamación *nf (de piel)* flaking, peeling

descamar 1 *vt (pescado)* to scale
2 **descamarse** *vpr (piel)* to flake

descambiar *vt Esp Fam* to take/bring back *(for refund or exchange)*; **si no le gusta, lo puede d.** if you don't like it, you can bring it back; **¿quiere d. los pantalones por otra prenda?** would you like to exchange the trousers for something else?

descambio *nm Esp Fam* **no se admiten descambios** *(en letrero)* no refunds or returns

descaminado, -a = **desencaminado**

descaminar = **desencaminar**

descamisado, -a 1 *adj* **(a)** *(sin camisa)* barechested **(b)** *(con la camisa por fuera)* with one's shirt outside one's trousers; *(con la camisa desabotonada)* with one's shirt unbuttoned **(c)** *(pobre)* wretched
2 *nm,f* **(a)** *(pobre)* poor wretch **(b)** *Arg (de Evita)* = working-class supporter of General Perón and his wife Evita

descampado *nm* piece of open ground; **juegan al fútbol en un d.** they play football on an area *o* a patch of waste ground

descangallado, -a *adj RP (desaliñado)* shabby

descansado, -a *adj* **(a)** *(actividad, trabajo, tarea)* undemanding; *(vida, ritmo de vida)* restful, quiet **(b)** *(persona)* **estar d.** to be rested *o* refreshed

descansar 1 *vt* **(a)** *(reposar)* to rest, to lie; **descansó la cabeza en mi hombro** he laid *o* rested his head on my shoulder
(b) *(relajar)* to rest; **dormir descansa la vista** sleep gives your eyes *o* eyesight a rest; **al final de la jornada doy un paseo para d. la mente** at the end of the day I go for a walk to take my mind off work
(c) *Mil* **¡descansen armas!** order arms!
2 *vi* **(a)** *(reposar)* to rest; **descansó un rato antes de seguir** he rested for a while before continuing; **después de tanto trabajo necesito d.** I need a rest after all that work; **¿paramos a** *o* **para d.?** how about stopping for a rest?; **descansaremos en una hora** we'll take a break in an hour; **llevo cuatro horas trabajando sin d.** I've been working for four hours non-stop *o* without a break; **d. de algo** *(algo molesto)* to have a rest *o* break from sth; **necesitas d. de tantas preocupaciones** you need a break from all these worries; **no d. hasta conseguir algo** not to rest until one has achieved sth
(b) *(dormir)* to sleep; **¿has conseguido d. con este ruido?** did you manage to sleep with that noise?; **¡que descanses!** sleep well!
(c) *(estar enterrado)* to lie; **sus restos descansan en el cementerio local** she lies buried in the local cemetery; **aquí descansan los caídos en la batalla** here lie those fallen in the battle; **que en paz descanse** may he/she rest in peace
(d) d. en *o* **sobre algo** *(sujeto: viga, cúpula, tejado)* to rest on sth, to be supported by sth; *(sujeto: teoría, hipótesis, argumento)* to rest on sth, to be based on sth
(e) *(tierra de cultivo)* to lie fallow
(f) *Mil* **¡descansen!** at ease!

descansillo *nm* landing

descanso *nm* **(a)** *(reposo)* rest; **tomarse un d.** to take a rest; **necesito un d., me hace falta un d.** I need a rest; **día de d.** day off; **los lunes cerramos por d. semanal** we don't open on Mondays; **sin d.** without a rest *o* break; **trabajar/luchar sin d.** to work/fight tirelessly
(b) *(pausa)* break; *(en cine)* intermission; *(en teatro) Br* interval, *US* intermission; *(en deporte) (cualquier intermedio)* interval; *(a mitad del partido)* half-time; **en la escuela hacemos un d. de veinte minutos** at school our break lasts twenty minutes; **el resultado en el d. es de una a cero** the score at half-time is one-nil
(c) *(alivio)* relief; **ya no tengo que preocuparme por los exámenes, iqué d.!** I don't have to worry about my exams any more, thank God!
(d) *Mil* **adoptar la posición de d.** to stand at ease; **¡d.!** at ease!
(e) *Méx, RP (descansillo)* landing

descapitalización *nf Fin* undercapitalization

descapitalizado, -a *adj Fin* undercapitalized

descapitalizar [14] *Fin* 1 *vt* to undercapitalize
2 **descapitalizarse** *vpr* to be undercapitalized

descapotable 1 *adj* convertible
2 *nm* convertible

descaradamente *adv* **(a)** *(con desvergüenza)* cheekily; **me guiñó el ojo d.** he winked at me cheekily **(b)** *(flagrantemente)* blatantly; **estaba d. de parte del otro equipo** he was blatantly on the side of the other team; **mentir d.** to tell barefaced lies

descarado, -a 1 *adj* **(a)** *(desvergonzado) (persona)* cheeky, impertinent; **¡no seas (tan) d.!** don't be (so) cheeky!; **¡el muy d. se ha atrevido a burlarse de mí!** the cheeky devil had the nerve to make fun of me! **(b)** *(flagrante)* barefaced, blatant; **una mentira descarada** a barefaced lie; **¡es un robo d.!** it's daylight robbery!; **¡ha sido un penalti d.!** there's no way that wasn't a penalty!
2 *adv Esp Fam (por supuesto, seguro)* you bet!; **no lo conseguirá, d.** there's no way she'll manage to do it; **¡d. que iremos!** too right we're going to go!
3 *nm,f* cheeky devil; **eres un d. mirando** you are awful the way you stare at people

descararse *vpr* to be cheeky *o* insolent; **conmigo no te descares** don't try to be cheeky with me

descarga *nf* **(a)** *(de mercancías)* unloading; **zonas de carga y d.** loading and unloading areas **(b)** *(de electricidad)* shock; **le dio una d. eléctrica** he got an electric shock **(c)** *(disparos)* firing, shots; **se oyó una potente d.** a loud burst of gunfire was heard **(d)** *(liberación brusca)* **una d. de adrenalina** a rush *o* surge of adrenalin

descargable *adj Informát* downloadable

descargadero *nm* wharf, unloading dock

descargador, -ora *nm,f (en mercado)* porter; *(en puerto)* docker

descargar [38] 1 *vt* **(a)** *(vaciar) (cargamento, camión, barco)* to unload; **las nubes descargaron varios litros en pocas horas** it rained several inches in a few minutes
(b) *(desahogar) (ira, agresividad)* to vent; *(tensiones)* to relieve; **juega al squash para d. el estrés** he plays squash to work off the stress; **descargó su cólera sobre mí** he took his anger out on me; **descargó su conciencia en mí** he unburdened his conscience to me
(c) *(arma) (disparar)* to fire (**sobre** at); *(vaciar)* to unload; **la escopeta estaba descargada** the shotgun was unloaded
(d) *(puntapié, puñetazo)* to deal, to land; **descargó un golpe contra la mesa** he thumped his fist on the table
(e) *(pila, batería)* to run down
(f) *(exonerar)* **d. a alguien de algo** to free *o* release sb from sth; **lo descargaron de responsabilidades por estar convaleciente** they relieved him of some of his responsibilities as he was convalescing
(g) *Der (absolver)* **d. a alguien de algo** to clear sb of sth; **el juez los ha descargado de toda culpa** the judge cleared them of all blame
(h) *Informát* to download; **d. un programa de la Red** to download a program from the Net
2 *vi (nubarrón)* to burst; **la tormenta descargó en el norte de la ciudad** the storm broke over the north of the city
3 *v impersonal* to pour down; **tiene pinta de que va a d.** it looks as if it's going to pour down
4 **descargarse** *vpr* **(a)** *(desahogarse)* **descargarse con** *o* **en alguien** to take it out on sb
(b) *Der* to clear oneself (**de** of)
(c) *(pila, batería)* to go flat
(d) *Informát* to download; **el programa tarda muchísimo en descargarse** this program takes ages to download

descargo *nm* **(a)** *(excusa)* **en d. de alguien** in sb's defence; **cabe decir en su d. que todo lo hizo con la mejor intención** it should be said in his defence that he acted with the best of intentions **(b)** *Der* **en su d.** in her defence; **alegó la ausencia de mala fe en d. de su defendido** he claimed in his client's defence that she had acted without malice **(c)** *Com (de deuda)* discharge; *(recibo)* receipt

descarnadamente *adv (describir)* baldly; *(narrar, contar)* starkly

descarnado, -a *adj* **(a)** *(descripción, narración)* bald; *(realismo, estilo)* stark **(b)** *(persona, animal)* scrawny

descarnar *vt* **(a)** *(hueso, piel)* to scrape the flesh from **(b)** *(desmoronar)* to eat away

descaro *nm* cheek, impertinence; **iqué d.!, acudir sin ser invitados** what a cheek, coming without being invited!; **se dirigió a su profesor con mucho d.** he spoke to his teacher very cheekily; **mienten con todo el d.** they lie quite shamelessly *o* brazenly

descarozado, -a *adj Andes, RP* pitted, stoned

descarozar [14] *vt Andes, RP* to pit, to stone

descarriado, -a *adj* **(a)** *(animal)* stray **(b)** *(moralmente)* **anda d. a causa de las malas compañías** he's gone astray because of the bad company he's been keeping; **una mujer descarriada** a fallen woman

descarriarse [32] *vpr* **(a)** *(ovejas, ganado)* to stray **(b)** *(pervertirse)* to lose one's way, to go astray

descarrilamiento *nm* **(a)** *(de tren, vagón)* derailment **(b)** *(de proceso de paz, negociaciones)* breakdown (**de** of *o* in); **temen un d. de su política exterior** they fear that their foreign policy may go off the rails

descarrilar *vi* **(a)** *(tren, vagón)* to be derailed, to come off the rails; **alguien lo hizo d.** someone made it come off the rails, someone derailed it **(b)** *(proceso, política, negociaciones)* to derail; **los violentos no harán d. el proceso de paz** the men of violence will not derail the peace process

descarrío *nm* straying

descartable *Am* **1** *adj (pañal, jeringuilla, envase)* disposable
2 *nm (pañal)* disposable
3 *nf (jeringuilla)* disposable

descartar 1 *vt* **(a)** *(posibilidad, idea)* to rule out; *(plan)* to reject; *(persona)* to reject, to rule out; *(ayuda)* to refuse, to reject; **no descartamos un pacto con la izquierda moderada** we don't rule out a pact with the moderate left; **ha quedado descartado que el tumor sea maligno** any possibility that the tumour might be malignant has been ruled out
(b) *Am (tirar)* to throw out, to discard; **habrá que d. todos los libros viejos** all the old books will have to be thrown out
2 descartarse *vpr (en naipes)* to get rid of *o* discard cards; **me descarté de un cinco** I got rid of *o* discarded a five

descarte *nm* **(a)** *(en naipes)* discard **(b)** *(de posibilidad, idea, persona)* rejection; **el entrenador tendrá que hacer varios descartes** the manager will have to get rid of several players

descasarse *vpr Fam (divorciarse)* to get divorced

descascarar *vt* **1** **(a)** *(almendra, huevo)* to shell **(b)** *(limón, naranja)* to peel
2 descascararse *vpr* to peel (off)

descascarillado, -a *adj (mueble, pintura, loza)* chipped; **la pared estaba muy descascarillada** most of the paint/plaster had come off the wall

descascarillar 1 *vt (pelar)* to shell
2 descascarillarse *vpr (loza, pintura)* to chip, to get chipped; *(mueble)* to get chipped; **la pared se está descascarillando** the paint/plaster is flaking off the wall

descastado, -a 1 *adj* ungrateful
2 *nm,f* **ser un d.** to be ungrateful *(towards family or friends)*

descatalogado, -a *adj (disco)* discontinued; **está d.** *(disco)* it's been discontinued; *(libro)* it's no longer published; **la mayoría de sus novelas están descatalogadas** most of his novels are out of print

descatalogar *vt (libro, disco)* **lo han descatalogado** they've dropped it from their catalogue

descendencia *nf* **(a)** *(hijos)* offspring; *(hijos, nietos)* descendants; **morir sin (dejar) d.** to die without issue; **tener d.** *(hijos)* to have offspring/descendants **(b)** *(linaje)* lineage, descent

descendente *adj (número, temperatura)* falling; *(movimiento, línea, trayectoria)* downward, descending

descender [66] **1** *vi* **(a)** *(temperatura, nivel, precios)* to fall, to drop; **ha descendido el interés por la política** there is less interest in politics; **desciende el número de desempleados** *(en titulares)* unemployment down
(b) *(de una altura)* to descend; **descendimos por la cara este** we made our descent by the east face; **d. al interior de una mina** to go down (into) a mine; **el halcón descendió en picado** the falcon swooped down; **el río desciende por el valle** the river runs down the valley; **la niebla descendió sobre el valle** the mist descended on the valley
(c) *(de vehículo)* **d. de un avión** to get off a plane; **d. de un coche** to get out of a car; **d. de un tren** to get off a train
(d) *(en el trabajo)* to be demoted
(e) *(en competición deportiva)* to be relegated; **d. a segunda** to be relegated to the second division; **d. de categoría** to be relegated
(f) *(de antepasado)* **d. de** to be descended from; **desciende de aristócratas** she's of aristocratic descent; **el hombre desciende de los simios** man is descended from the apes
(g) *(en estimación)* to go down; **su prestigio como cantante descendió mucho** his reputation as a singer plummeted
2 *vt* **(a)** *(bajar)* **descendieron al paciente de la ambulancia** they took the patient out of the ambulance; **descendió las escaleras rápidamente** she ran down the stairs **(b)** *(en el trabajo)* to demote; **lo han descendido de categoría en el trabajo** he's been demoted at work

descendiente *nmf* descendant; **no dejó descendientes** she left no children, she died without issue; **es d. directo de los Stroganoff** he's a direct descendant of the Stroganoffs

descendimiento *nm Arte* **el D. (de la Cruz)** the Deposition (from the Cross)

descendista *nmf (en esquí)* downhill skier, downhiller; *(en ciclismo)* descender

descenso *nm* **(a)** *(de una altura)* descent; **los ciclistas iniciaron el d.** the cyclists began the descent; **sufrieron un accidente en el d.** they had an accident on the way down ▸▸ ***d. de aguas bravas*** white water rafting; ***d. de barrancos*** canyoning
(b) *(de precio, temperatura, nivel)* fall, drop; **el fuerte d. de las temperaturas** the sharp drop in temperatures; **la tasa de desempleo experimentó un espectacular d.** there was a spectacular drop in the unemployment rate; **ir en d.** to be decreasing *o* on the decline
(c) *(prueba de esquí)* downhill
(d) *(en competición deportiva)* relegation; **estar en las posiciones de d.** to be in the relegation zone

descentrado, -a *adj* **(a)** *(geométricamente)* off-centre **(b)** *(mentalmente)* unsettled, disorientated

descentralización *nf* decentralization

descentralizar [14] **1** *vt* to decentralize
2 descentralizarse *vpr* to become decentralized

descentrar 1 *vt* **(a)** *(geométricamente)* to knock off-centre **(b)** *(desconcentrar)* to distract; **el ruido me descentra** noise distracts me
2 descentrarse *vpr* **(a)** *(geométricamente)* to be knocked off centre **(b)** *(desconcentrarse)* to lose one's concentration; **se descentra fácilmente** he loses his concentration easily, he's easily distracted

desceñir [47] *vt* to unbelt

descepar *vt (planta)* to uproot, to pull up by the roots

descerebrado, -a *Esp, Andes, RP Fam* **1** *adj* moronic, brainless
2 *nm,f* moron, halfwit

descerebrarse *vpr Andes, RP Fam* to knock oneself out, *Br* to do one's head in

descerrajar *vt* **(a)** *(disparo)* to fire; **le descerrajó varios tiros** he fired several shots at her **(b)** *(puerta)* to force the lock on

deschavetado, -a *adj Am Fam* crazy, loony

deschavetarse *vpr Am Fam* to go crazy, to go off one's rocker

desciendo *etc ver* **descender**

descifrable *adj (mensaje, jeroglífico)* decipherable; *(letra)* legible

descifrar *vt* **(a)** *(clave, código)* to decipher, to crack; *(mensaje, jeroglífico)* to decipher; **¿has descifrado las instrucciones?** have you managed to make sense of the instructions?; **cuesta d. su letra** it's difficult to make out *o* decipher her handwriting
(b) *(motivos, intenciones)* to work out; *(misterio)* to solve; *(problemas)* to puzzle out; **no consigo d. lo que quiere decir** I can't make out what he's trying to say
(c) *Informát* to decrypt

desciña, desciñera *etc ver* **desceñir**

desclasado, -a *nm,f* **es un d.** *(pérdida de clase social)* he's come down in the world; *(traición de clase social)* he's a traitor to his class

desclasificar *vt* to declassify

desclavar *vt* to unnail

descoagulante *adj* liquefying, dissolving

descocado, -a *adj Fam* outrageous; **anoche estaba completamente d.** he was totally outrageous last night

descocarse *vpr Fam* to get carried away, *Br* to go OTT

descoco *nm Fam* **¡qué d.!** that's outrageous!

descodificación, decodificación *nf* decoding

descodificador, -ora, decodificador, -ora 1 *adj* decoding
2 *nm (aparato)* decoder; *(para televisión)* unscrambler

descodificar [60], **decodificar** *vt (mensaje)* to decode; *(emisión televisiva, acústica)* to unscramble

descojonante *adj muy Fam* **un chiste d.** a screamingly funny joke; **ser d.** to be a scream, to make one wet oneself

descojonarse *vpr muy Fam* **(a)** *(reír)* to piss oneself laughing (**de** at); **una película para d. de risa** a film that will have you wetting yourself **(b)** *(estropearse)* to pack up *o* in; **se me ha descojonado la radio** my radio's kaput *o Br* knackered

descojone, descojono *nm muy Fam* **ser un d.** to be a scream, to make one wet oneself; **la actriz que hace de madre era un d.** the actress who plays the mother had me wetting myself; **¡qué d. de película!** what a screamingly funny film!

descolgar [16] **1** *vt* **(a)** *(cosa colgada)* to take down; **d. la ropa** to take down the washing
(b) *(teléfono) (para hablar)* to pick up, to take off the hook; **descolgamos el teléfono para que no nos molestara nadie** we left the phone off the hook so nobody would disturb us
(c) *(en una carrera) (adelantarse)* **d. a alguien** to pull ahead of sb
2 *vi (para hablar por teléfono)* to pick up (the receiver); **para efectuar una llamada descuelgue y espere tono** to make a call, lift the receiver and wait for the dialling tone
3 descolgarse *vpr* **(a)** *(cosa colgada) (cortinas)* to come loose *o* unhooked; **el póster se ha descolgado** the poster has fallen off the wall
(b) *(bajar)* **descolgarse (por algo)** to let oneself down *o* to slide down (sth); **se descolgaron por la fachada con una cuerda** they lowered themselves down the front of the building on a rope

(**c**) *(corredor) (quedarse atrás)* to fall back *o* behind; **descolgarse del pelotón** to fall behind the pack

(**d**) *Fam (mencionar)* **descolgarse con algo** to come out with sth; **se descolgó con unas declaraciones sorprendentes** he came out with some surprising statements

(**e**) *Fam (presentarse)* to drop in *o* by, to turn up; **Manuel se descolgó un rato en el billar porque estaba harto de estudiar** Manuel dropped in at the billiard hall for a while because he was fed up of studying

descollante *adj (sobresaliente)* outstanding; **una de las figuras descollantes del régimen** one of the key figures of the regime

descollar *vi (sobresalir)* to stand out; **descuella entre la clase por su inteligencia** he stands out among his classmates for his intelligence

descolocación *nf (de jugadores, defensa)* **la d. de la defensa facilitó el gol** the goal was scored because the defenders were out of position

descolocado, -a *adj* (**a**) *(objeto)* out of place; *(jugador, defensa)* out of position; **pillar d. al portero** to catch the goalkeeper out of position (**b**) *Fam (confuso)* confused; **su respuesta me dejó un poco d.** her reply threw me a little

descolocar **1** *vt* (**a**) *(objeto)* to put out of place, to disturb; *(jugador, defensa)* to force out of position (**b**) *Fam (persona)* to confuse; **me descolocó totalmente con esa pregunta** I didn't know what to say in reply to his question

2 descolocarse *vpr (objeto)* **se te ha descolocado la pajarita** your bow tie isn't straight

descolonización *nf* decolonization

descolonizador, -ora *adj* **proceso d.** decolonization process

descolonizar [14] *vt* to decolonize

descolorante **1** *adj* (**a**) *(de color)* fading (**b**) *(de pelo)* bleaching

2 *nm* bleaching agent

descolorar **1** *vt* to fade

2 descolorarse *vpr* to fade

descolorido, -a *adj* (**a**) *(tela, alfombra)* faded; *(papel, manuscrito)* yellowing (**b**) *(rostro, piel)* pale

descolorir **1** *vt* to fade, to discolour

2 descolorirse *vpr* to discolour

descomedido, -a *adj Esp Formal* (**a**) *(exagerado)* excessive, uncontrollable (**b**) *(descortés)* discourteous, impolite

descomedirse [47] *vpr Esp Formal* to be discourteous, to be impolite

descompaginar *vt* (**a**) *(manuscrito)* **me has descompaginado el tesis** you've got the pages of my thesis out of order (**b**) *(rutina)* to disrupt; **el nacimiento de su primer hijo les ha descompaginado los horarios** the birth of their first child has played havoc with their timetable

descompasado, -a, desacompasado, -a *adj (música, ritmo)* jerky, uneven; *(aplausos)* disorganized, unsynchronized; **los bailarines y la música van descompasados** the dancers aren't in time with the music; **llevaban un ritmo d.** they weren't playing in time; **vamos totalmente descompasados** we're completely out of step (with each other)

descompensación *nf* imbalance

descompensado, -a *adj* unbalanced

descompensar **1** *vt* to unbalance

2 descompensarse *vpr* to become unbalanced

descomponer [50] **1** *vt* (**a**) *(pudrir) (fruta, comida, cuerpo)* to rot; **un organismo que descompone los cadáveres** an organism that causes bodies to decompose *o* rot; **la humedad descompone ciertos alimentos** dampness makes some foods rot

(**b**) *(dividir) (sustancia, molécula)* to break down; *(luz)* to split up; *(átomo)* to split; **d. algo en** to break sth down into

(**c**) *(desordenar)* to mess up

(**d**) *(estropear) (aparato, motor)* to break

(**e**) *(indisponer)* **la cena le descompuso el vientre** the dinner gave him an upset stomach; **creo que comí algo que me descompuso (el cuerpo)** I think I ate something that didn't agree with me

(**f**) *(turbar, alterar)* to disturb, to upset; **algo que dije pareció descomponerlo** something I said seemed to upset him

(**g**) *(enojar)* to annoy; **su pasividad me descompone** his passivity annoys me

(**h**) *Mat* **d. en factores (primos)** to factorize

2 descomponerse *vpr* (**a**) *(pudrirse) (fruta, comida)* to rot; *(cadáver)* to decompose, to rot

(**b**) *(dividirse) (sustancia, molécula)* to break down; *(luz)* to split (up); *(átomo)* to split; **la luz se descompone en un espectro** light splits up into a spectrum

(**c**) *(desordenarse)* to get messed up; **se me ha vuelto a d. el peinado** my hairdo has got messed up again

(**d**) *(estropearse) (aparato, máquina)* to break down

(**e**) *(estómago)* **se me descompuso el estómago** I had an attack of diarrhoea

(**f**) *(turbarse, alterarse)* **se le descompuso el rostro** he looked distraught; **no se descompone por nada** nothing seems to upset him

(**g**) *(irritarse)* to get (visibly) annoyed; **se descompuso al oír tus palabras** he got annoyed when he heard what you said

(**h**) *Am (tiempo)* to turn nasty

descomposición *nf* (**a**) *(en elementos)* breaking down; *(de luz)* splitting; *(de átomo)* splitting; *(de sustancia, molécula)* breaking down

(**b**) *(putrefacción) (de fruta, comida)* rotting; *(de cadáver)* decomposition, rotting; **en avanzado estado de d.** in an advanced state of decomposition; **la d. del régimen político es ya imparable** the decline of the regime is now irreversible

(**c**) *(alteración)* distortion

(**d**) *Esp (diarrea)* diarrhoea

(**e**) *Mat* ***d. factorial*** factorization

descompostura *nf* (**a**) *(falta de mesura)* lack of respect, rudeness (**b**) *Am (malestar)* unpleasant *o* nasty turn (**c**) *Am (diarrea)* diarrhoea (**d**) *Méx, RP (avería)* breakdown

descompresión *nf* (**a**) *(de cuerpo, gas, líquido)* decompression (**b**) *Informát* decompression; **un programa de d. de ficheros** a decompression programme

descompresor *nm Tec* decompression valve

descomprimir *vt* (**a**) *(cuerpo, gas, líquido)* to decompress (**b**) *Informát* to decompress

descompuesto, -a **1** *participio ver* **descomponer**

2 *adj* (**a**) *(putrefacto) (fruta, comida)* rotten; *(cadáver)* decomposed (**b**) *(alterado) (rostro)* distorted, twisted (**c**) *(con diarrea)* **estar d.** to have diarrhoea (**d**) *Andes, CAm, PRico (borracho)* tipsy (**e**) *Méx, RP (averiado) (máquina)* out of order; *(vehículo)* broken down; **mi moto está descompuesta** my motorbike has broken down

descomunal *adj* enormous, tremendous; **un d. edificio** a huge *o* an enormous building; **era un tipo d.** he was a huge guy; **tengo un hambre d.** I'm absolutely starving; **tuvieron una bronca d.** they had a tremendous argument

descomunalmente *adv* enormously, tremendously

desconcentrar **1** *vt* to distract; **la música me desconcentra** the music is distracting me; **¡calla, que me desconcentras!** be quiet, you're putting me off!

2 desconcentrarse *vpr* to get distracted; **cuando estás al volante no te puedes d. ni un momento** when you're behind the wheel you can't lose concentration *o* allow yourself to be distracted for a moment

desconcertado, -a *adj* disconcerted; **estar d.** to be disconcerted *o* thrown; **quedarse d.** to be taken aback

desconcertante *adj* disconcerting

desconcertar [3] **1** *vt* **su respuesta lo desconcertó** her answer threw him; **su comportamiento me desconcierta** I find his behaviour disconcerting

2 desconcertarse *vpr* to be thrown *o* bewildered (**ante** *o* **por** by)

desconchado *nm* (**a**) *(de pintura, loza, vajilla)* **hay que cubrir los desconchados de la pared** we'll have to cover the places where the paint has peeled off the wall; **el plato tenía un d.** the plate was chipped (**b**) *Chile (pelado)* shelling

desconchar **1** *vt (pintura)* to cause to flake; *(loza, vajilla)* to chip; **al colgar el cuadro desconchó la pared** he took a chunk out of the wall when he was nailing up the picture

2 desconcharse *vpr (pintura)* to flake off; *(loza)* to chip; **la pared se había desconchado en varios sitios** the plaster had come off the wall in several places

desconche *nm Ven* shelling

desconchinflar *Méx Fam* **1** *vt* to wreck, to bust

2 desconchinflarse *vpr* to pack up *o Br* in

desconchón *nm* **la pared tenía varios desconchones** the plaster had come off the wall in several places; **el plato tenía un d.** the plate was chipped

desconcierto **1** *ver* **desconcertar**

2 *nm* (**a**) *(desorden)* disorder (**b**) *(desorientación, confusión)* confusion; **su decisión causó gran d. en las filas del partido** his decision caused bewilderment among the rank and file of the party; **entre los trabajadores reina el d.** there is widespread confusion among the workforce

desconectado, -a *adj* (**a**) *(aparato)* unplugged (**b**) *(persona)* **está muy d. de su familia** he isn't in touch with his family very often; **está muy d. de la actualidad del país** he's very out of touch with what's going on in the country

desconectar 1 *vt (aparato)* to switch off; *(línea)* to disconnect; *(desenchufar)* to unplug; **desconecta la televisión del enchufe** unplug the television; **acuérdate de d. la alarma** remember to disconnect the alarm

2 *vi Fam (persona)* to switch off; **se va al campo para d.** she goes off to the country to get away from it all; **en cuanto ella se pone a hablar, yo desconecto** as soon as she starts talking I switch off; **d. de la realidad** to cut oneself off from reality; **vive desconectada de la realidad** she lives in a world of her own

3 **desconectarse** *vpr* (a) *(aparato)* **el radiador se desconecta solo** the radiator switches *o* turns itself off automatically; **se desconectó la línea en mitad de conversación** we were cut off in the middle of the conversation; **la televisión se desconectó de repente** the TV suddenly went dead

(b) *(aislarse, olvidarse)* to forget about one's worries; **desconectarse de algo** to shut sth out, to forget (about) sth; **me he desconectado de mis compañeros de universidad** I've lost touch with the people I was at university with

desconexión *nf* (a) *(de aparato, alarma)* switching off; *(línea telefónica)* disconnection (b) *(falta de relación)* gulf; **la d. del gobierno con los sindicatos** the gulf between the government and the unions

desconfiadamente *adv* distrustfully

desconfiado, -a 1 *adj* distrustful; **no seas tan desconfiado** don't be so distrustful; **un pueblo de gente huraña y desconfiada** a town with unsociable and mistrustful inhabitants

2 *nm,f* distrustful person; **es un d.** he's very distrustful

desconfianza *nf* distrust; **la miró con d.** he looked at her with distrust; **los animales salían de sus jaulas con d.** the animals emerged warily from their cages; **todavía me tienen cierta d.** they're still a little wary of me, they still don't trust me completely

desconfiar [32] *vi* (a) **d. de** *(sospechar de)* to distrust; **desconfío de él** I don't trust him; **¿desconfías de mí?** don't you trust me?; **no es que desconfíe de usted, pero...** it's not that I don't trust you, but...; **desconfiaban de sus constantes halagos** they mistrusted his constant flattery; **desconfíe de las imitaciones** beware of imitations

(b) **d. de** *(no confiar en)* to have no faith in; **siempre desconfié de los políticos y de lo que prometían** I never had any faith in politicians and their promises; **desconfío de que venga** I doubt whether he'll come; **desconfío de poder obtener un ascenso** I'm not sure if I'll be able to get a promotion

descongelación *nf* (a) *(de alimento)* thawing; *(de nevera)* defrosting (b) *(de precios, salarios, cuentas bancarias)* unfreezing; *(de negociaciones)* unblocking

descongelador *nm* **d. (de parabrisas)** de-icer

descongelar 1 *vt* (a) *(alimento)* to thaw; *(nevera)* to defrost (b) *(precios, salarios, cuentas bancarias)* to unfreeze; **d. las negociaciones** to restart the negotiations, to get the negotiations moving again

2 **descongelarse** *vpr* (a) *(alimento)* to thaw, to defrost; *(nevera)* to defrost (b) *(negociaciones)* to start moving again

descongestión *nf* (a) *(de nariz, vías respiratorias)* clearing, decongestion (b) *(del tráfico)* **las nuevas medidas facilitarán la d. del tráfico** the new measures will help to relieve traffic congestion

descongestionante *adj* decongestive

descongestionar 1 *vt* (a) *(nariz, vías respiratorias)* to clear (b) *(calle, centro de ciudad)* to make less congested; **d. el tráfico** to reduce congestion

2 **descongestionarse** *vpr* (a) *(nariz, vías respiratorias)* to clear (b) *(tráfico)* to become less congested; **el centro se ha descongestionado bastante** the centre has become much less congested

descongestivo, -a 1 *adj* decongestive

2 *nm* decongestant

desconocedor, -ora *adj* unaware **(de** of**)**; **era d. de sus intenciones** he was unaware of what her intentions were

desconocer [19] *vt* (a) *(ignorar)* not to know; **desconocemos sus motivos** we do not know his motives; **desconocía que fueran amigos** I was unaware they were friends; **se desconoce su paradero** her whereabouts are unknown; **se desconoce la identidad de los secuestradores** the identity of the kidnappers has yet to be established; **por causas que aún se desconocen** for reasons as yet unknown *o* which are still unknown; **sus libros se desconocen fuera de Latinoamérica** his books are unknown outside Latin America

(b) *(no reconocer)* to fail to recognize; **con ese peinado te desconozco** I can hardly recognize you with that hairstyle

desconocido, -a 1 *adj* (a) *(no conocido)* unknown; **su cine es del todo d. en Europa** his movies are totally unknown in Europe; **elementos químicos entonces desconocidos** chemical elements then unknown; **una enfermedad hasta ahora desconocida** a hitherto unknown illness; **por causas todavía desconocidas** for reasons as yet unknown *o* which are still unknown; **nació en 1821, de padre d.** he was born in 1821, and it is not known who his father was; **el mundo de lo d.** the world of the unknown; **su nombre no me es del todo d.** his name rings a bell

(b) *(extraño)* **no dé su teléfono o dirección a personas desconocidas** don't give your telephone number or address to strangers

(c) *(sin fama)* unknown; **escritores jóvenes, casi desconocidos** young, almost unknown, writers

(d) *(muy cambiado)* **estar d.** to have changed beyond all recognition; **¿ya no fumas ni bebes? ¡chico, estás d.!** you don't smoke or drink any more? well, well, you're a changed man!; **el viejo bar estaba d.** the old bar was unrecognizable; **así, sin gafas, estás d.** like that, with no glasses, you're unrecognizable

2 *nm,f* (a) *(extraño)* stranger; **hablar con un d.** to talk to a stranger; **no le abras la puerta a desconocidos** don't open the door to strangers

(b) *(persona sin fama)* unknown; **le dieron el premio a un (perfecto) d.** they gave the prize to a complete unknown

(c) *(persona sin identificar)* unidentified person; **un d. le disparó un tiro en la cabeza** he was shot in the head by an unknown assailant; **tres desconocidos prendieron fuego a varias tiendas** several shops were set on fire by three unidentified persons

desconocimiento *nm* ignorance, lack of knowledge; **tiene un d. total de la situación** he has absolutely no idea what the situation is; **el d. de la ley no exime de su cumplimiento** ignorance of the law does not exempt one from obeying it

desconozco *etc ver* **desconocer**

desconsideración *nf* thoughtlessness; **me parece una d. por su parte** I think it is rather thoughtless of him

desconsiderado, -a 1 *adj* thoughtless, inconsiderate

2 *nm,f* thoughtless *o* inconsiderate person; **es un d.** he's really thoughtless *o* inconsiderate

desconsoladamente *adv (llorar)* inconsolably; *(mirar, quejarse)* disconsolately

desconsolado, -a *adj (persona, rostro)* disconsolate; *(llanto)* inconsolable; **su desconsolada viuda no quiso hablar con la prensa** his heartbroken widow did not want to speak to the press; **me miraba d.** he looked at me disconsolately

desconsolar [64] *vt* to distress

desconsuelo *nm* distress, grief; **vive sumido en el d.** he's in the depths of despair

descontado, -a 1 *adj (rebajado)* discounted

2 **por descontado** *loc adv* obviously, needless to say; **¿vendrás a la fiesta? – ¡por d.!** are you going to the party? – but of course! **por d. que no revelaré el secreto** of course I won't tell anyone the secret; **dar algo por d.** to take sth for granted; **di por d. que serías discreto con este tema** I took it for granted you would be discreet about this matter; **doy por d. que te quedarás a cenar** now, you will be staying for dinner, won't you?; **¿nos apoyarás? – eso dalo por d.** will you support us? – you can count on it

descontaminación *nf* decontamination

descontaminar *vt* to decontaminate, to clean up

descontar [64] *vt* (a) *(una cantidad)* to deduct; **me lo descontarán de mi sueldo** it will be deducted from my salary; **facturaré 5.000 euros brutos, pero a eso habrá que descontarle gastos** I'll make 5,000 euros gross, but I'll have to take off the costs from that

(b) *(hacer un descuento de)* to discount; **me han descontado 1.000 pesos** they gave me a discount of 1,000 pesos; **me descontaron el 5 por ciento del precio de la lavadora** they gave me a 5 percent discount on the (price of the) washing machine

(c) *(exceptuar)* **siete, descontando a los profesores** seven, not counting the teachers; **si descuentas los días de vacaciones...** if you leave out the holidays...

(d) *(en deporte)* **el árbitro descontó tres minutos** the referee added three minutes to injury time

(e) *Fin (letra de cambio)* to discount

descontentar *vt* to upset, to make unhappy

descontento, -a 1 *adj* unhappy, dissatisfied; **estar d. con algo/alguien** to be dissatisfied *o* unhappy with sth/sb; **dijo estar d. con la decisión de los tribunales** he said he was unhappy with the court's decision

2 *nm* dissatisfaction; **los sindicatos expresaron su d. con la nueva ley** the unions expressed their dissatisfaction with the new law; **entre la población cundió el d.** discontent was spreading among the population

descontextualización *nf* decontextualization

descontextualizar *vt* to decontextualize

descontón *nm Méx (golpe)* blow, setback

descontrol *nm* (**a**) *(pérdida de control)* lack of control (**b**) *Fam (caos)* chaos; **en el despacho reinaba el d.** everything was in total chaos in the office; **la fiesta fue un d.** the party was rather wild; **su vida es un d.** he leads a very disorganized life

descontrolado, -a 1 *adj (automóvil, inflación)* runaway; *(persona)* out of control; **tengo a la clase descontrolada** I can't keep order in my class; **el tren circulaba d.** the train was running out of control; **estar d.** to be out of control

2 *nm,f* **un grupo de descontrolados interrumpió la reunión** a rowdy group disrupted the meeting

descontrolar 1 *vt Fam* to confuse; **¡no me descontroles!** stop confusing me!; **el cambio de horario me ha descontrolado** the change in timetable has got me all mixed up

2 *vi Esp Fam* **ese tío descontrola mucho** that guy's completely out of it

3 descontrolarse *vpr* (**a**) *(automóvil, inflación)* to go out of control (**b**) *(persona)* to lose control; *Fam (desmadrarse)* to go wild, to go over the top

desconvocar [60] *vt (huelga, manifestación, reunión)* to call off, to cancel

desconvocatoria *nf (de huelga, manifestación, reunión)* calling off, cancellation

descoordinación *nf* lack of coordination

descorazonado, -a *adj* disheartened

descorazonador, -ora *adj* discouraging

descorazonamiento *nm* discouragement

descorazonar 1 *vt* to discourage

2 descorazonarse *vpr* to be discouraged, to lose heart

descorchador *nm Andes, RP* corkscrew

descorchar *vt* to uncork

descorche *nm* (**a**) *(de botella)* uncorking (**b**) *(de árbol)* bark stripping

descornar [64] **1** *vt* to dehorn

2 descornarse *vpr Esp Fam* (**a**) *(emplearse a fondo)* **se descornaba a trabajar para pagar la casa** he worked himself into the ground to pay for the house (**b**) *(golpearse en la cabeza)* to brain *o* crown oneself

descorrer *vt* (**a**) *(cortinas)* to draw back, to open (**b**) *(cerrojo, pestillo)* to draw back

descortés (*pl* **descorteses**) *adj (persona, conduca, detalle)* rude, discourteous; **no seas tan d.** don't be so rude; **fue muy d. de** *o* **por su parte no estrecharnos la mano** it was very ill-mannered of him not to shake hands with us; **no quisiera parecer d., pero ya es muy tarde** I don't want to seem impolite *o* rude, but it's getting very late

descortesía *nf* (**a**) *(falta de cortesía)* rudeness, discourtesy; **se dirigió a nosotros con d.** he addressed us rather rudely (**b**) *(gesto poco cortés)* **fue una d. no saludarlos** it was impolite not to say hello to them

descortésmente *adv* rudely

descortezar *vt* (**a**) *(árbol)* to strip the bark from (**b**) *(pan)* to take the crust off

descoser 1 *vt* to unstitch

2 descoserse *vpr* to come unstitched; **se me ha descosido un botón** one of my buttons has come off; **se me descosió la camisa por las costuras** my shirt came apart at the seams

descosido, -a 1 *adj* unstitched

2 *nm,f* EXPR *Fam* **como un d.** *(hablar)* non-stop, nineteen to the dozen; *(trabajar, estudiar)* like crazy; *(beber, comer)* like there was no tomorrow; **gritar/reír como un d.** to shout/laugh one's head off

3 *nm (roto)* burst seam; **tengo un d. en el pantalón** the seam of my trousers is coming apart

descostillarse *vpr RP Fam* **d. de (la) risa** to split one's sides laughing

descoyuntado, -a *adj Fam (cansadísimo)* shattered

descoyuntar 1 *vt* to dislocate; *Fam* **no hagas eso, que te vas a d.** don't do that, you'll do yourself an injury *o* a mischief

2 descoyuntarse *vpr* (**a**) *(sujeto: articulación, huesos)* to become dislocated; **se le descoyuntó el hombro** he dislocated his shoulder (**b**) *(sujeto: persona)* **me descoyunté el codo** I put my elbow out of joint; EXPR *Fam* **descoyuntarse de (la) risa** to split one's sides laughing

descrédito *nm* discredit; **caer en el d.** to fall into disrepute; **ir en d. de algo/alguien** to count against sth/sb; **estar en d.** to be discredited

descreído, -a 1 *adj* unbelieving

2 *nm,f* non-believer

descreimiento *nm* unbelief

descremado, -a *adj* skimmed

descremar *vt* to skim

describir *vt* (**a**) *(con palabras)* to describe; **descríbanos al individuo que la atacó** describe the man who attacked you (**b**) *(trazar) (trayectoria, curva, órbita)* to describe

descripción *nf* description; **una d. de los hechos** an account of what happened

descriptible *adj* describable

descriptivo, -a *adj* descriptive

descrito, -a, descripto, -a *participio ver* **describir**

descuajaringado, -a, descuajeringado, -a *adj Fam* (**a**) *(roto) (mueble)* rickety; **estar d.** *(automóvil, aparato)* to be falling to bits; *(libro)* to be coming *o* falling apart (**b**) *(cansado)* shattered

descuajaringar [38], **descuajeringar** [38] *Fam* **1** *vt (mueble, aparato)* to break *o* bust into pieces; *(libro)* to tear apart *o* to pieces

2 descuajaringarse, descuajeringarse *vpr* (**a**) *(romperse)* to fall to bits; **la moto se está descuajaringando** the bike is falling to bits (**b**) *(troncharse de risa)* to fall about (laughing)

descuartizamiento *nm* (**a**) *(de res)* carving up, quartering (**b**) *(de persona)* dismemberment

descuartizar [14] *vt* (**a**) *(res)* to carve up, to quarter (**b**) *(persona)* to dismember; **un cuerpo descuartizado** a dismembered body

descubierto, -a 1 *participio ver* **descubrir**

2 *adj* (**a**) *(sin techo, tejado) (terraza, patio)* uncovered; *(vehículo, carroza)* open-top; *(piscina, polideportivo)* open-air (**b**) *(sin cubrir)* **decir/hacer algo a cara descubierta** to say/do sth openly; **atracaron el banco a cara descubierta** they held up the bank without wearing masks (**c**) *(cielo)* clear (**d**) *(naipes)* face up (**e**) *(zona, lugar)* open, exposed (**f**) *(sin sombrero)* bareheaded

3 *nm Fin (de empresa)* deficit; *(de cuenta bancaria)* overdraft; **tengo un d. de 2.000 euros** I have an overdraft of 2,000 euros; **al** *o* **en d.** overdrawn; **tener la cuenta al** *o* **en d.** to be overdrawn

4 al descubierto *loc adv* (**a**) *(a la luz pública)* **poner al d.** to reveal; **la policía puso al d. una red de prostitución infantil** the police uncovered a child prostitution ring; **quedar al d.** to be exposed *o* uncovered; **sus turbios negocios quedaron al d.** his shady dealings came out into the open *o* were exposed (**b**) *(al raso)* in the open

descubridor, -ora *nm,f* discoverer; **él fue el d. de los Beatles** he was the one who discovered the Beatles

descubrimiento *nm* (**a**) *(hallazgo) (de nuevas tierras, artista)* discovery; **este restaurante ha sido todo un d.** this restaurant was a real find

(**b**) *(avance técnico o científico)* discovery; **el d. de los agujeros negros** the discovery of black holes; **publicaron su d. en la revista "Nature"** they published their discovery in "Nature"

(**c**) *(de estatua, placa, busto)* unveiling

(**d**) *(de complot)* uncovering; *(de asesinos)* detection

descubrir 1 *vt* (**a**) *(hallar)* to discover; *(petróleo)* to strike, to find; *(oro, plutonio)* to find; *(nuevas tierras, artista, novedad científica)* to discover; **no han descubierto la causa de su enfermedad** they haven't discovered the cause of his illness; **callejeando descubrimos un bar irlandés** we came across an Irish bar as we wandered about the streets; **la policía descubrió al secuestrador** the police found the kidnapper; EXPR *Fam Hum* **¡has descubierto América!** you've reinvented the wheel

(**b**) *(destapar) (estatua, placa)* to unveil; *(complot, parte del cuerpo)* to uncover; *(cualidades, defectos)* to reveal; **los periodistas descubrieron un caso de estafa** the reporters uncovered a case of fraud; **la entrevista nos descubrió otra faceta de su personalidad** the interview revealed another aspect of his character; EXPR **d. el pastel** to let the cat out of the bag, to give the game away

(**c**) *(enterarse de)* to discover, to find out; **¿qué has conseguido d.?** what have you managed to find out?; **descubrió que su mujer lo engañaba** he discovered *o* found out that his wife was cheating on him

(**d**) *(vislumbrar)* to spot, to spy

(**e**) *(delatar)* to give away; **una indiscreción la descubrió** an indiscreet remark gave her away

2 descubrirse *vpr* (**a**) *(quitarse el sombrero)* to take one's hat off (**b**) *(mostrar admiración)* to take one's hat off; **ante una hazaña así no puedo sino descubrirme** I can only take my hat off to such a feat; **me descubro ante tu victoria** I salute your victory

(**c**) *(delatarse)* to give oneself away; **se descubrió con lo que dijo** she gave herself away with what she said

(**d**) *(parte del cuerpo)* to uncover; **no se les permite descubrirse el rostro** they aren't allowed to uncover their faces

(**e**) *(en boxeo)* to lower one's guard

descuelgo *etc ver* **descolgar**

descuento 1 *ver* **descontar**

2 *nm* (**a**) *(rebaja)* discount; **un d. del 5 por ciento** 5 percent off; **con d.** at a discount; **vendemos todo con d.** we sell everything at a discount; **artículos con d.** discounted items; **con el d. se le queda en 5.000** with the discount it comes to 5,000; **hacer d.** to give a discount; **nos hicieron un d. del 10 por ciento** they gave us a 10 percent discount; **llevar d.** to be on special offer; **los trajes no llevan d.** there are no discounts on suits ►► *Com* ***d. comercial*** trade discount; ***d. duro*** hard discount

(**b**) *(en fútbol)* **(tiempo de) d.** injury time; **marcaron en el tiempo de d.** they scored in injury time

(**c**) *(de remuneración, salario)* deduction

(**d**) *Fin (de letra de cambio)* discount

descuerar *vt Chile Fam* to slam, to criticize

descuerno *etc ver* **descornar**

descueve *nm Chile Fam* **el d.: lo pasamos el d.** we had a fantastic *o Br* brilliant time; **esa película es el d.** that movie *o Br* film is ace *o Br* the business

descuidadamente *adv (conducir, actuar)* carelessly; *(vestir)* untidily

descuidado, -a *adj* (**a**) *(desaseado) (persona, aspecto)* untidy; **arréglate un poco, no vayas tan d.** tidy yourself up a bit, don't be so slovenly

(**b**) *(abandonado) (jardín, casa)* neglected; *(habitación)* untidy; *(barrio, ciudad)* run-down; **un paraje bellísimo, pero muy d.** a lovely spot, but very poorly looked after

(**c**) *(negligente)* careless; **es muy d. con sus cosas** he's very careless with his things

(**d**) *(distraído)* **estaba d.** he wasn't paying attention

descuidar 1 *vt* to neglect; **descuidó su aspecto** he neglected his appearance; **descuidas mucho tu habitación** you never tidy your room; **han descuidado mucho el barrio** they've let the area get very rundown; **no descuides tu vida social** don't let your social life go by the board

2 *vi (no preocuparse)* **descuida, que yo me encargo** don't worry, I'll take care of it; **apaga la luz cuando te marches – descuida** turn off the light when you leave – don't worry, I will

3 descuidarse *vpr* (**a**) *(abandonarse)* to neglect one's appearance, to let oneself go

(**b**) *(despistarse)* not to be careful, to be careless; **me descuidé un instante y se me fue la bici a la cuneta** I let my attention wander for an instant and the bicycle went into the ditch; **como te descuides, ya no hay entradas** if you're not careful there won't be any tickets left; **no te puedes d. ni un momento** you've got to be alert all the time, you can't let your attention wander for a second; **como me descuide, llegaré tarde al examen** if I'm not careful, I'll be late for the exam

(**c**) EXPR **en cuanto te descuidas, se pone a llover** it rains all the time; **en cuanto te descuidas se pone a cantar** he'll break into song at the drop of a hat

descuidero, -a *nm,f Fam* sneak thief

descuido *nm* (**a**) *(falta de aseo) (en personas)* untidiness, slovenliness; *(de jardín, casa)* neglect; *(en habitación)* untidiness

(**b**) *(olvido)* oversight; *(error)* slip; **al menor d.** if you let your attention wander for even a moment; **en un d. se me fue la bici a la cuneta** my attention wandered for a moment and the bicycle went into the ditch; **en un d., borré el fichero** I deleted the file by mistake; *RP* **en un d.** *(cuando menos se espera)* when least expected

DESDE 1 *prep* (**a**) *(indica tiempo)* since; **no lo veo d. el mes pasado/d. ayer** I haven't seen him since last month/yesterday; **d. aquel día, nada volvió a ser igual** from that day on, things were never the same again; **d. ahora** from now on; **¿d. cuándo?** since when?; **¿d. cuándo se conocen?** how long *o* since when have you known each other?; **¿d. cuándo no hay que llamar para entrar?** since when has it been all right to come in without knocking?; **d. entonces** since then; **no la veo d. hace un año** I haven't seen her for a year, it's a year since I last saw her; **d. hace dos días no come** she hasn't eaten for two days; **¿d. cuánto hace que no come?** how long has she not been eating?; **d. hace mucho/un mes** for ages/a month; **trabaja para ellos d. hace poco** she recently started working for them; **te espero d. hace más de una hora** I've been waiting for you for more than an hour; *Fam* **id. hace que no la veo!** *(en tono enfático)* I haven't seen her for AGES!; **d.... hasta...** from... until...; **d. el lunes hasta el viernes** from Monday till Friday; **d. el 1 hasta el 15 de septiembre** from 1 to 15 September; **d. niño** *o* **d. pequeño me enseñaron a dar las gracias** I was brought up to say thank you to people from an early age; **d. el principio supe que no iba a salir bien** I knew from the very beginning *o* from the word go it wasn't going to turn out well; **d. que** since; **d. que la vi en el teatro, no he vuelto a saber nada de ella** I haven't heard from her since (the day) I saw her at the theatre; **d. que murió mi madre** since my mother died; **d. ya** *(inmediatamente)* right now; **ponte a ordenar esta habitación d. ya** start tidying this room this instant

(**b**) *(indica espacio)* from; **d. mi ventana se ve el puerto** you can see the harbour from my window; **vinieron a vernos d. Santiago** they came from Santiago to visit us; **¿d. dónde nos disparan?** where are they shooting at us from?; **d. arriba/abajo** from above/below; **visto d. arriba, parece más grande** seen from above, it looks bigger; **se ve d. lejos** it can be seen from a long way away; **d.... hasta...** from... to...; **d. aquí hasta el centro** from here to the centre; **d. un punto de vista jurídico...** from a legal point of view...; **afrontemos el proceso de paz d. la democracia y el respeto** let us enter the peace process in a spirit of democracy and respect

(**c**) *(indica cantidad mínima)* from; **d. 10.000 euros** from 10,000 euros

(**d**) *(indica lo que se abarca)* **d.... hasta...** from... to...; **se encargan de todo, d. el viaje hasta el alojamiento** they take care of everything, from the travel arrangements to the accommodation; **sabe hacer de todo, d. cambiar un fusible hasta arreglar una moto** she can do all sorts of things, from changing a fuse to repairing a motorbike

2 desde luego *loc adv* (**a**) *(por supuesto)* **id. luego (que sí)!** of course!; **id. luego que me gusta!** of course I like it!; **id. luego que no os ayudaré!** no way am I going to help you!, I'm certainly not going to help you!

(**b**) *(en tono de reproche)* **id. luego!** for goodness' sake!; **id. luego! ¡no te creía capaz de una cosa así!** I certainly didn't think you were capable of something like this!; **id. luego, tienes cada idea!** you really come out with some funny ideas!

---

desdecir [51] **1** *vi* **d. de** *(desmerecer)* to be unworthy of; *(no cuadrar con)* not to go with, to clash with; **una decoración que desdice de un local con tanta solera** a decor that's hardly appropriate in a place of such character

2 desdecirse *vpr* to go back on one's word; **desdecirse de** to go back on; **rápidamente se desdijo de sus críticas** he quickly withdrew his criticisms

desdén *nm* disdain, contempt; **la miró con d.** he looked at her disdainfully *o* with contempt; **tratar a alguien con d.** to treat sb with contempt

desdentado, -a 1 *adj* (**a**) *(persona, boca)* toothless (**b**) *Zool* edentate

2 *nm Zool* edentate, member of the order *Edentata*

3 desdentados *nmpl Zool (orden)* Edentata; **del orden de los desdentados** of the order *Edentata*

desdeñable *adj* insignificant; **una cantidad nada d.** a far from negligible *o* not inconsiderable amount; **un resultado d.** a result that can be ignored

desdeñar *vt* (**a**) *(despreciar)* to scorn; **desdeñó a varios pretendientes** she spurned several suitors; **desdeña a la gente que no es de su clase** he looks down on anyone not of his class (**b**) *(desestimar)* to dismiss; **no conviene d. las posibilidades del equipo inglés** the English team's chances should not be ruled out

desdeñosamente *adv* scornfully, disdainfully

desdeñoso, -a *adj* scornful, disdainful

desdibujado, -a *adj* (**a**) *(perfil, imagen)* blurred; *(recuerdo)* hazy (**b**) *(mediocre)* **se ha convertido en un equipo d.** the team has lost its way

desdibujar 1 *vt* to blur; **la neblina desdibujaba los rostros de la gente** the mist made people's faces look blurry

2 desdibujarse *vpr* to blur, to become blurred

desdice *etc ver* **desdecir**

desdicha *nf* (**a**) *(infelicidad)* unhappiness, misery; **nada consolaba su d.** nothing could console him in his unhappiness (**b**) *(suceso desgraciado)* misfortune; **pasamos toda clase de desdichas** we suffered all sorts of calamities; **tuvo la d. de caer muy enfermo** she had the misfortune to fall seriously ill; **iqué d. la suya!** what an unfortunate fellow!

desdichadamente *adv (vivir)* unhappily; **d., no fue posible** unfortunately, it wasn't possible

desdichado, -a 1 *adj* (**a**) *(decisión, situación, momento)* unfortunate; **aquel d. día en que la conocí** the fateful *o* unlucky day on which I met her (**b**) *(persona) (sin suerte)* unlucky; *(sin felicidad)* unhappy; **d. en amores** unlucky in love

2 *nm,f* poor wretch; **no es más que un pobre d.** he's just a poor wretch

desdicho, -a *participio ver* **desdecir**

desdigo *etc ver* **desdecir**

desdijera *etc ver* **desdecir**

desdoblamiento *nm* (**a**) *(de objeto)* unfolding (**b**) *(división)* splitting; **sufre d. de personalidad** she has a split personality (**c**) *(carretera)* conversion into a *Br* dual carriageway *o US* divided highway; *(ferrocarril)* conversion into a two-track (line)

desdoblar 1 *vt* (**a**) *(desplegar) (mantel, pañuelo, periódico)* to unfold; *(alambre)* to straighten out (**b**) *(dividir)* to split; **desdoblaron el antiguo ministerio en dos nuevas carteras** they divided the old ministry into two portfolios (**c**) *(carretera)* to make into a *Br* dual carriageway *o US* divided highway; *(ferrocarril)* to make into a two-track (line)

2 desdoblarse *vpr* (**a**) *(desplegarse) (mantel, periódico)* to unfold; *(alambre)* to straighten out (**b**) *(dividirse)* to divide (**c**) *(carretera)* to turn into a *Br* dual carriageway *o US* divided highway; *(ferrocarril)* to turn into a two-track (line) (**d**) *Fam (multiplicarse)* to be in two places at once

desdoble *nm Econ* split

desdolarización *nf* de-dollarization

desdolarizar *vt* to de-dollarize

desdoro *nm Formal* disgrace, cause of shame; **no es ningún d. servir en la barra de un bar** there's nothing to be ashamed of in working behind a bar

desdramatizar [14] *vt* to play down

desduanar = **desaduanar**

deseable *adj* desirable; **sería d. un mayor diálogo** greater dialogue would be welcome

deseado, -a *adj* (**a**) *(ansiado)* desired; **la tan deseada primera cita** the longed-for first date (**b**) *(embarazo)* planned; *(hijo)* wanted; **un embarazo no d.** an unwanted pregnancy

desear *vt* (**a**) *(querer)* to want; *(anhelar)* to wish; **siempre he deseado visitar Australia** I've always wanted to go to Australia; **desearía estar allí** I wish I was there; **por fin, la bici que tanto había deseado** at last, the bicycle I'd wanted so much; **desearía agradecerle su apoyo** I would like to thank you for your help; **si desea mayor información, llame al 900 1234** if you would like more information, please ring 900 1234; **desearíamos que nos informara sobre su disponibilidad** we would be grateful if you could inform us whether or not you would be available; **en nuestra empresa deseamos ofrecer lo mejor a nuestros clientes** in our company we want to offer our clients the best; **¿qué desea?** *(en tienda)* what can I do for you?; **¿desea algo más?** *(en tienda)* would you like anything else?, is that everything?; **¿desea que le enseñe más modelos?** *(en tienda)* would you like me to show you some other models?; **si lo desea, se lo enviamos a su domicilio** if you wish, we will deliver it to your home; **aquí estamos para lo que desee** *(a cliente)* we are at your entire disposal; **estar deseando hacer algo** to be looking forward to doing sth; **estaba deseando salir de allí** I couldn't wait to get out of there; **estoy deseando que lleguen las vacaciones** I'm really looking forward to the holidays; **¿te hace ilusión lo de ir en barco? – ¡estoy deseando!** are you looking forward to going by boat? – you bet I am! *o* am I ever!; **ser de d.** to be desirable; **es de d. que las negociaciones terminen pronto** a quick end to the negotiations would be desirable; **dejar mucho/no dejar nada que d.** to leave much/nothing to be desired

(**b**) *(felicidad, éxito, parabienes)* to wish; **d. algo a alguien** to wish sb sth; **te deseo mucha suerte** I wish you the best of luck; **¡deséame suerte!** wish me luck!; **me deseó lo mejor/un buen viaje** he wished me all the best/a pleasant journey; **me deseó buenas noches** he said goodnight (to me); **todos deseamos que te mejores pronto** we all wish you a speedy recovery

(**c**) *(sexualmente)* to desire; **te deseo, no puedo vivir sin ti** I want you, I can't live without you; **no desearás a la mujer de tu prójimo** thou shalt not covet thy neighbour's wife

desecación *nf* (**a**) *(de alimentos, plantas, flores)* drying, *Espec* desiccation (**b**) *(de humedal, marisma)* draining; **la d. de los pozos** the drying up of the wells

desecar [60] **1** *vt* (**a**) *(alimentos, plantas, flores)* to dry (**b**) *(humedal, marisma)* to drain; **la sequía ha desecado los pozos** the drought has dried up the wells

2 desecarse *vpr* (**a**) *(alimentos, plantas, flores)* to dry (**b**) *(humedal, marisma)* to dry up

desechable *adj (pañal, jeringuilla)* disposable; *(envase)* disposable, non-returnable

desechar *vt* (**a**) *(tirar)* to throw out, to discard

(**b**) *(rechazar) (ayuda, oferta)* to refuse, to turn down; *(idea, pensamiento)* to reject; *(posibilidad, sospecha)* to dismiss; *(propuesta, sugerencia)* to reject, to turn down; **pensó ir a pie, pero luego desechó la idea** he thought of going on foot but then dropped the idea; **no desecho la posibilidad de que haya sido ella** I don't rule out the possibility that it was her

desecho *nm* (**a**) *(objeto usado)* unwanted object; *(ropa)* cast-off; **material de d.** *(residuos)* waste products; *(metal)* scrap

(**b**) *(escoria)* dregs; **desechos** *(basura) Br* rubbish, *US* garbage, trash; *(residuos)* waste products; **no era más que un d. humano** he was a contemptible creature ►► ***desechos industriales*** industrial waste; ***desechos nucleares*** nuclear waste; ***desechos radiactivos*** radioactive waste

(**c**) *CAm, Carib (tabaco)* class A tobacco

desembalaje *nm* unpacking

desembalar *vt (caja, paquete)* to unpack; *(discos, libros, cubertería)* to unwrap

desembalsar *vt* to drain, to empty

desembalse *nm* draining, emptying

desembarazar [14] **1** *vt (habitación, camino)* to clear; **d. a alguien de algo** to rid sb of sth

2 desembarazarse *vpr* **desembarazarse de algo/alguien** to get rid of sth/sb

desembarazo *nm* ease, self-confidence; **actuar con d.** to behave self-confidently *o* with assurance

desembarcadero *nm* pier, landing stage

desembarcar [60] **1** *vt (pasajeros)* to disembark (**de** from); *(mercancías)* to unload (**de** from)

2 *vi* (**a**) *(de barco, avión)* to disembark (**de** from); **desembarcarán por la puerta C** you will disembark through gate C; **el 6 de junio las fuerzas aliadas desembarcan en Normandía** the allied forces land in Normandy on 6 June

(**b**) *(introducirse, establecerse)* **d. en** to move into; **la multinacional desembarcó en el sector inmobiliario** the multinational moved into the real estate sector

(**c**) *Am (de autobús, tren)* **d. (de)** to get off

3 desembarcarse *vprAm* to disembark (**de** from)

desembarco *nm* (**a**) *(de mercancías)* unloading; *(de pasajeros)* disembarkation (**b**) *(militar)* landing

desembargar *vt (bienes, casa)* to release, *Espec* to release from distraint; *(cuenta bancaria)* to unfreeze

desembargo *nm (de bienes, casa)* lifting of a distraining order on; *(de cuenta bancaria)* unfreezing

desembarque *nm (de mercancías)* unloading; *(de pasajeros)* disembarkation

desembarrancar [60] *vt* to refloat

desembarrar *vt* to clear of mud

desembocadura *nf* (**a**) *(de río)* mouth (**b**) *(de calle)* opening

desembocar [60] *vi* (**a**) **d. en** *(río)* to flow into; *(calle)* to lead onto; **¿dónde desemboca esta calle/este río?** where does this street/river come out?

(**b**) *(asunto, sucesos, situación)* **d. en** to lead to, to result in; **la manifestación desembocó en graves disturbios** the demonstration led to serious disturbances; **no sabemos en qué desembocará todo esto** we don't know where all this will end up *o* what all this will lead to

desembolsar *vt* to pay out

desembolso *nm* payment; **la operación supuso un d. de 100 millones** the operation cost 100 million; **hacer un d. de un millón de pesos** to pay (out) a million pesos ►► ***d. inicial*** down payment

desembozar [14] **1** *vt* (**a**) *(rostro)* to unmask, to uncover (**b**) *(cañería)* to unblock

2 desembozarse *vpr (descubrir el rostro)* to take off one's mask, to reveal oneself

desembragar [38] *Aut* **1** *vt* **d. el motor** to declutch

2 *vi* to disengage the clutch, to declutch

desembrollar *vt Fam* (**a**) *(lío, malentendido)* to straighten out; *(historia, lo ocurrido)* to unravel, to untangle (**b**) *(ovillo)* to disentangle

desembuchar 1 *vi Fam* to spit it out; **¡venga, desembucha!** come on, out with it!

2 *vt* (**a**) *Fam (revelar)* to come out with (**b**) *(sujeto: ave)* to regurgitate

desemejanza *nf* dissimilarity

desempacar [60] **1** *vt* to unpack

2 *vi (deshacer las maletas)* to unpack

desempacho *nm* self-confidence

desempalmar *vt* to disconnect

desempañar 1 *vt (quitar el vaho a) (con trapo)* to wipe the steam off; *(electrónicamente)* to demist

2 **desempañarse** *vpr (cristales)* to clear; **con este dispositivo se desempaña la luneta trasera** this device demists the rear window

desempapelar *vt (pared, habitación)* to strip the wallpaper from

desempaquetar *vt (paquete)* to unwrap; *(discos, libros, cubertería)* to unpack

desemparejar 1 *vt (guantes, calcetines)* **siempre acabo desemparejando los calcetines** I always end up with odd socks

2 **desemparejarse** *vpr (guantes, calcetines)* to become unpaired *o* odd; **se me han vuelto a d. los calcetines** my socks have got all mixed up again

desempatar 1 *vt* **su voto desempató la votación** he gave the casting vote; **desempató el partido en el último minuto** he scored the winning goal in the last minute

2 *vi* **todavía no han desempatado** it's still a draw; **jugaron una prórroga para d.** they played extra time to get a winner

desempate *nm* **el d. llegó en el minuto treinta con un gol del Barcelona** Barcelona took the lead in the thirtieth minute; **terminaron el concurso igualados y habrán de jugar un d.** they were level at the end of the competition and will have to play a decider; **marcó el gol del d.** he scored the goal which put them into the lead; **un partido de d.** a decider; **una votación de d.** *(en elección)* a run-off

desempeñar 1 *vt* (**a**) *(función, misión)* to carry out; *(puesto, cargo)* to hold, to have; *(papel)* to play; **desempeñó la misión de tener informada a la prensa** her mission was to keep the press informed; **desempeña el cargo de tesorero** he holds the post of treasurer; **le tocó d. un papel decisivo en el proceso de paz** it fell to him to play a key role in the peace process; **desempeñó en muchas ocasiones el papel de Drácula** he played (the part of) Dracula many times

(**b**) *(objetos, joyas, reloj)* to redeem

2 **desempeñarse** *vpr* (**a**) *(saldar deudas)* to get oneself out of debt

(**b**) *Am (trabajar)* to work; **desempeñarse como** to work as

desempeño *nm* (**a**) *(de función, misión)* carrying out; *(de papel)* performance; **falleció en el d. de sus funciones** he died in the performance of his duties; **se le acusa de cometer irregularidades en el d. de su cargo** he is accused of irregularities in the carrying out of his duties; **el d. del cargo de ministro no es tarea fácil** carrying out the job of a minister is no easy task; **reúne las condiciones para el d. del cargo** he has all the qualifications for the post

(**b**) *(de objeto, joyas, reloj)* redemption

desempleado, -a 1 *adj* unemployed

2 *nm,f* unemployed person; **lo peor para un d. es el aislamiento** the worst thing for someone who is out of work is the isolation; **los desempleados** the unemployed; **el número creciente de desempleados** the growing number of unemployed people ►► ***los desempleados de larga duración*** the long-term unemployed

desempleo *nm* (**a**) *(falta de empleo)* unemployment; **una de las tasas de d. más altas de Europa** one of the highest unemployment rates in Europe; **estar en el d.** to be unemployed ►► ***d. de larga duración*** long-term unemployment (**b**) *(subsidio)* unemployment benefit; **cobrar el d.** to receive unemployment benefit

desempolvar *vt* (**a**) *(mueble, jarrón)* to dust (**b**) *(recuerdos)* to revive, to reawaken; *(conocimientos)* to refresh; **un día decidió d. su violín** one day he decided to take up the violin again; **voy a tener que d. mi francés** I'm going to have to brush up (on) my French; **voy a d. los libros de física** I'm going to dig out my physics books

desenamorarse *vpr* to fall out of love (**de** with)

desencadenamiento *nm* (**a**) *(de tormenta)* breaking (**b**) *(de polémica, conflicto)* triggering; **causar el d. de algo** *(accidente, crisis)* to bring sth about; *(conflicto)* to trigger *o* spark off sth

desencadenante 1 *adj* **los factores desencadenantes de...** the factors which brought about...

2 *nm* **el d. de la tragedia/guerra** what brought about the tragedy/war

desencadenar 1 *vt* (**a**) *(preso, perro)* to unchain

(**b**) *(viento, tormenta)* to unleash

(**c**) *(accidente, polémica)* to give rise to; *(pasión)* to unleash; *(conflicto)* to trigger, to spark off; **la medida desencadenó fuertes protestas** the measure triggered furious protests

2 **desencadenarse** *vpr* (**a**) *(preso)* to unchain oneself, to get out of one's chains

(**b**) *(pasiones)* to erupt; *(polémica, guerra)* to break out; **se desencadenó una crisis entre ambos países** a crisis broke out between the two countries; **el conflicto se desencadenó con el descubrimiento de petróleo** the conflict arose when oil was discovered

(**c**) *(viento)* to blow up; *(tormenta)* to burst; *(terremoto)* to strike

desencajado, -a *adj* (**a**) *(mal ajustado) (mecanismo, pieza)* out of position; *(hueso, mandíbula)* dislocated; **el cajón está d.** the drawer is off its runners; **la puerta está desencajada** the door isn't on its hinges properly

(**b**) *(rostro)* contorted; **tenía el semblante d. por el miedo** his face was contorted with fear; **el corredor cruzó la meta con el rostro d.** the runner was grimacing as he crossed the finishing line

desencajar 1 *vt* (**a**) *(desajustar) (sin querer)* to knock out of place; *(intencionadamente)* to take apart; *(hueso)* to dislocate; **has desencajado el cajón** you've knocked the drawer off its runners; **el viento desencajó las ventanas/puertas** the wind jammed the windows/doors in their frames (**b**) *(rostro)* **el terror le desencajó el rostro** his face was contorted with fear

2 **desencajarse** *vpr* (**a**) *(desajustarse) (piezas, mecanismo)* to come out of place; *(hueso)* to dislocate; **se le ha desencajado la mandíbula** he's dislocated his jaw; **el cajón se ha desencajado** the drawer has come off its runners; **la puerta se ha desencajado** the door doesn't fit properly in its frame (**b**) *(rostro)* to become contorted, to contort

desencajonar *vt* to take out of a box

desencallar *vt* to refloat

desencaminado, -a, descaminado, -a *adj (equivocado)* **estás d. si piensas que voy a ceder** you're very much mistaken if you think I'm going to give in; **andar** *o* **ir d.** *(caminante, excursionista)* to be heading in the wrong direction; *(estar equivocado)* to be on the wrong track; **pues no andas muy d.** you're not far off

desencaminar, descaminar 1 *vt* (**a**) *(sujeto: malas compañías)* to lead astray (**b**) *(sujeto: guía)* **los desencaminó** he took them the wrong way

2 **desencaminarse, descaminarse** *vpr* (**a**) *(por malas compañías)* to go astray (**b**) *(en una excursión)* to go the wrong way

desencantado, -a *adj (desilusionado)* disenchanted (**con** with)

desencantar 1 *vt* (**a**) *(decepcionar)* to disappoint (**b**) *(romper el hechizo a)* to disenchant

2 **desencantarse** *vpr* to be disappointed (**con** with *o* by)

desencanto *nm* disappointment

desencapotarse *vpr (cielo)* to clear

desencarcelar *vt* to set free, to release

desenchufar *vt (quitar el enchufe de)* to unplug; *(apagar)* to switch off

desencolar 1 *vt* to unstick

2 **desencolarse** *vpr* to come unglued *o* unstuck

desencontrarse *vpr CSur* **casi nos desencontramos** we almost missed each other

desencuadernar *vt* 1 to unbind

2 **desencuadernarse** *vpr* to come apart from the binding

desencuentro *nm* (**a**) *(en una cita)* failure to meet up (**b**) *(desacuerdo)* disagreement; **tener un d.** to have a disagreement

desenfadadamente *adv (actuar)* in a relaxed *o* easy-going manner; *(vestir)* casually

desenfadado, -a *adj (persona, actitud)* relaxed, easy-going; *(reunión, charla)* relaxed; *(comedia, programa de TV)* light-hearted; *(estilo)* light; *(vestimenta)* casual; **ser d. en el vestir** to be a casual dresser

desenfado *nm (desenvoltura)* ease; *(desparpajo)* forwardness, uninhibited nature; **se comporta con mucho d.** he's very relaxed *o* easy-going; **viste con d.** she dresses casually

desenfocado, -a *adj (imagen)* out of focus; *(visión)* blurred; **la foto ha salido desenfocada** the photo's out of focus; **has salido d.** you're out of focus; **ver d.** to have blurred vision

desenfocar [60] 1 *vt* (**a**) *(con cámara)* to get out of focus (**b**) *(distorsionar)* to distort

2 **desenfocarse** *vpr* to go out of focus

desenfoque *nm* lack of focus

desenfrenadamente *adv (bailar)* wildly, in a frenzy; *(vivir, divertirse, comportarse)* wildly; *(beber, comer)* to excess

desenfrenado, -a *adj (ritmo, baile, carrera)* frantic, frenzied; *(fiesta, juerga, diversión)* wild; *(vida)* wild, riotous; *(comportamiento)* uncontrolled; *(deseo, pasión, entusiasmo)* unbridled; *(apetito)* insatiable; **el público bailaba d.** the audience were dancing in a frenzy

desenfrenar 1 *vt (caballo)* to unbridle

2 **desenfrenarse** *vpr (persona)* to lose one's self-control

desenfreno *nm* (a) *(descontrol)* lack of restraint; **bailaba con d.** he was dancing wildly *o* in a frenzy; **beber/comer con d.** to drink/eat to excess (b) *(vicio)* excess; **llevar una vida de juerga y d.** to lead a life of partying and excess

desenfundar 1 *vt (pistola)* to draw; *(mueble)* to uncover; *(máquina de escribir, raqueta)* to take the cover off; **desenfundó el violín** he took the violin out of its case; *Vulg* **desenfundarla** to whip it out

2 *vi* (a) *(sacar la pistola)* to draw (one's gun) (b) *Vulg (sacar el pene)* to whip it out

desenganchar 1 *vt* (a) *(vagón)* to uncouple; *(remolque)* to unhitch (b) *(caballo)* to unhitch (c) *(pelo, jersey)* to free, to unsnag (d) *(cortinas)* to unhook

2 **desengancharse** *vpr* (a) *(vagón)* to become uncoupled; *(remolque, tráiler, caravana)* to become unhitched (b) *(cortinas)* to become unhooked (c) *Fam (de drogas)* to kick the habit; **se ha desenganchado de la heroína** he has kicked his heroin habit

desenganche *nm* (a) *(de vagones)* uncoupling; *(de remolque)* unhitching (b) *(de caballos)* unhitching

desengañado, -a 1 *adj* disillusioned (**de** with)

2 *nm,f* person who has been disillusioned *(with life or love)*; **ser un d.** to have lost one's illusions

desengañar 1 *vt* (a) *(a una persona equivocada)* to reveal the truth to (b) *(a una persona esperanzada)* to disillusion

2 **desengañarse** *vpr* (a) *(perder la ilusión)* to become disillusioned (**de** with); **se desengañó de los estudios** he could no longer see any point in his studies

(b) *(dejar de engañarse)* **desengáñate** stop kidding yourself; **desengáñate, no te quiere** don't fool yourself, he doesn't love you; **desengáñese, los bancos lo que buscan es su dinero** don't delude yourself, what the banks are after is your money

desengaño *nm* disappointment; **he sufrido** *o* **me he llevado muchos desengaños en la vida** I've had a lot of disappointments in my life; **sufrí un gran d. cuando me contaron lo ocurrido** it was a big disappointment when they told me what had happened; **llevarse** *o* **sufrir un d. con alguien** to be disappointed in sb; **¡vaya d. que me he llevado contigo!** you've no idea how disappointed I am in you!; **llevarse** *o* **sufrir un d. con algo** to be disappointed with sth; **nos llevamos un buen d. con Venecia** we found Venice a real let-down ►► ***d. amoroso:*** **sufrir** *o* **tener un d. amoroso (con alguien)** to be let down in love (by sb)

desengarzar [14] *vt (perlas)* to unstring

desengranar 1 *vt (máquina)* to disengage

2 **desengranarse** *vpr (ruedas, mecanismo)* to disengage

desengrasante *nm* grease remover

desengrasar *vt (sartenes, cocina)* to remove the grease from

desenlace *nm (de obra, narración)* denouement, ending; *(de suceso, aventura)* result, outcome; **el secuestro tuvo un trágico d.** the kidnapping ended tragically

desenlazar [14] *vt (nudo)* to undo; *(pelo)* to let down, to untie; *(brazos)* to unlink; **desenlazó las manos** he unclasped his hands

desenmarañar *vt* (a) *(ovillo, pelo)* to untangle (b) *(asunto, historia, enredo)* to sort out; *(problema, enigma)* to resolve

desenmascarar *vt (descubrir)* to unmask; **un empleado del banco logró d. al atracador** a bank employee managed to remove the robber's mask; **d. al culpable** to unmask *o* expose the culprit

desenmohecer [46] *vt* (a) *(de moho)* to remove the mildew from (b) *(de óxido)* to remove the rust from

desenojar *vt* to calm, to pacify

desenredar 1 *vt* (a) *(hilos, ovillo, pelo)* to untangle (b) *(asunto, historia, lío)* to sort out; *(problema)* to resolve

2 **desenredarse** *vpr* (a) *(soltarse, desembarazarse)* to extricate oneself (**de algo** from sth) (b) *(quitar enredos de)* **desenredarse el pelo** to untangle one's hair

desenredo *nm* (a) *(de hilos, ovillo, pelo)* untangling (b) *(aclaración)* straightening out (c) *(de obra)* denouement

desenrollar 1 *vt (hilo, cinta, cable)* to unwind; *(persiana)* to roll down; *(alfombra, papel, póster)* to unroll

2 **desenrollarse** *vpr (hilo, cinta, cable)* to unwind; *(persiana)* to roll down; *(alfombra, papel, póster)* to unroll; *(serpiente)* to uncoil

desenroscar [60] **1** *vt (tapón, tuerca, tornillo)* to unscrew

2 **desenroscarse** *vpr* (a) *(tapón, tuerca, tornillo)* to unscrew (b) *(serpiente)* to uncoil

desensamblar *vt* to take apart, to disassemble

desensillar *vt* to unsaddle

desentenderse [66] *vpr* **yo me desentiendo** I want nothing to do with it; **cuando algo no le interesa, se desentiende por completo** when something doesn't interest him, he'll have nothing to do with it; **d. de algo/alguien** to want nothing to do with sth/sb; **nos desentendimos del asunto** we want nothing to do with this business; **¡es un caradura!, le dices que haga algo y se desentiende de ti** he's got a nerve!, you tell him to do something and he pretends he hasn't heard you

desentendido, -a *nm,f* **hacerse el d.** to pretend one hasn't noticed/heard; **¡no te hagas el d., te toca limpiar a ti!** don't pretend you don't know it's your turn to do the cleaning!; **cuando llegó su turno, se hizo el d.** when his turn came round, he pretended he hadn't noticed

desenterrar [3] *vt* (a) *(cadáver)* to disinter; *(tesoro, restos arqueológicos)* to dig up; EXPR **d. el hacha de guerra (contra)** to declare war (on) (b) *(recordar)* to recall, to revive (c) *(sacar a la luz)* **d. viejos rencores** to rake up old quarrels; **un sello discográfico dedicado a d. viejos éxitos** a record label which specializes in reviving old hits

desentiendo *etc ver* **desentenderse**

desentierro *etc ver* **desenterrar**

desentonación *nf* dissonance

desentonar *vi* (a) *(cantante)* to sing out of tune; *(instrumento)* to be out of tune

(b) *(color, cortinas, edificio)* to clash (**con** with); **esa falda desentona con este jersey** that skirt doesn't go *o* clashes with this jersey

(c) *(persona)* to be out of place; **en aquel sitio desentonábamos bastante** we were quite out of place there; **para no d., llevó un traje** so as not to look out of place, he wore a suit

desentono *nm (de voz, sonido)* dissonance

desentorpecer [46] **1** *vt* (a) *(tráfico)* to speed up, to ease the flow of; *(trámites, proceso)* to speed up, to facilitate (b) *(músculo, cuerpo)* **d. las piernas** to get rid of the stiffness in one's legs

2 **desentorpecerse** *vpr* (a) *(tráfico)* to speed up, to flow more freely; **las negociaciones se desentorpecerán con el nuevo mediador** the negotiations should go more smoothly with the new mediator (b) *(músculo, cuerpo)* to loosen up

desentrañar *vt* (a) *(enigma)* to unravel; *(problema)* to figure out, to get to the bottom of; *(clave)* to decipher, to break; *(significado, sentido)* to make out (b) *(destripar) (aves, reses, conejos)* to disembowel; *(pescado)* to gut

desentrenado, -a *adj (bajo de forma)* out of training; *(falto de práctica)* out of practice

desentrenarse *vpr (bajar de forma)* to get out of training

desentubar *vt Fam* **d. a un enfermo** to remove a tube/tubes from a patient

desentumecer [46] **1** *vt (músculos)* to loosen up, to get rid of the stiffness in; **acercó las manos al fuego para desentumecerlas** he held his hands near the fire to get the blood flowing again; **calentaban en la banda para d. los músculos** they warmed up on the touchline to loosen up

2 **desentumecerse** *vpr* **se le desentumecieron las piernas con el ejercicio** the exercise had loosened up his legs

desenvainar *vt (espada)* to draw

desenvoltura *nf (al moverse, comportarse)* ease; *(al hablar)* fluency; **ya nada con mucha d.** she can already swim with great ease; **me manejo en mi nuevo trabajo con mucha d.** I'm getting along fine in my new job; **tiene bastante d. con el inglés** he speaks English quite fluently; **les sorprendió su d. ante el auditorio** they were surprised by how at ease he was in front of the audience

desenvolver [41] **1** *vt (regalo, paquete)* to unwrap, to open

2 **desenvolverse** *vpr* (a) *(asunto, proceso)* to progress; *(trama)* to unfold; *(entrevista)* to pass off; **la reunión se desenvolvió con cordialidad** the meeting passed off very amicably

(b) *(persona)* to cope, to manage; **desenvolverse en la vida** to cope with *o* get along in life; **no te preocupes, sabe desenvolverse ella sola** don't worry, she can cope *o* manage by herself; **se desenvuelve muy bien en su nuevo trabajo** she's getting along fine in her new job; **se sabe d. bastante bien en inglés** he can get along pretty well in English

desenvuelto, -a 1 *participio ver* **desenvolver**

2 *adj* (a) *(comportamiento)* natural; *(movimiento)* natural, easy (b) *(persona)* self-assured; *(al hablar)* fluent; **es una joven muy desenvuelta** she's a very self-assured young woman; **se le ve muy d. con las mujeres** he seems very much at ease in the company of women

desenvuelvo *etc ver* **desenvolver**

deseo *nm* (**a**) *(pasión)* desire; **no sentía ningún d. por él** she felt no desire for him
(**b**) *(anhelo)* wish; **piensa un d. y sopla las velas** think of a wish and blow out the candles; **expresó su d. de paz para la región** he expressed his desire for peace in the region; **buenos deseos** good intentions; **con mis/nuestros mejores deseos** *(en carta, obsequio)* (with my/our) best wishes; **conceder un d.** to grant a wish; **se cumplió mi d.** my wish came true, I got my wish; **formular un d.** to make a wish; **pedir un d.** to ask for a wish; *Formal* **por d. expreso de...** at the express wish of...; **su último d. fue...** his last wish was...; **su último d. fue que la casa nunca se vendiera** her last *o* dying wish was that the house should never be sold; EXPR **tus deseos son órdenes** your wish is my command

deseoso, -a *adj* **estar d. de algo/de hacer algo** to long for sth/to do sth; **grupos jóvenes deseosos de éxito** young bands eager for success; **están deseosos de volver** they are longing to *o* they really want to come back; **se muestra d. de colaborar** he seems eager to help; **está d. de que apruebes el examen** he really wants you to pass the exam

desequilibrado, -a 1 *adj* (**a**) *(persona)* unbalanced (**b**) *(balanza, eje)* off-centre
2 *nm,f* madman, *f* madwoman

desequilibrante *adj* **es un jugador d.** he's a match winner

desequilibrar 1 *vt* (**a**) *(psicológicamente) (persona, mente)* to unbalance (**b**) *(físicamente) (objeto)* to knock off balance, to unbalance; *(balanza, eje)* to put out of balance; *(persona)* to throw *o* knock off balance (**c**) *(economía)* to upset
2 **desequilibrarse** *vpr* (**a**) *(psicológicamente) (persona, mente)* to become unbalanced (**b**) *(físicamente) (objeto)* to become unbalanced; *(balanza, eje)* to get out of balance; *(persona)* to lose one's balance (**c**) *(economía)* to become unbalanced

desequilibrio *nm* (**a**) *(mental)* mental instability (**b**) *(mecánico, en la dieta)* lack of balance (**c**) *(en la economía)* imbalance; **el fuerte d. entre inflación y salarios** the marked imbalance between inflation and wages

deserción *nf* desertion; **las numerosas deserciones en las filas socialistas** the numerous defections from the socialist ranks ►► *Am* ***d. escolar*** dropping out of school; **hubo más de cuatrocientas deserciones escolares en primaria** more than four hundred pupils dropped out of primary school

desertar *vi* (**a**) *(soldado)* to desert; **desertó de su compañía** he deserted from his company (**b**) *(político)* to defect; **muchos desertaron del partido comunista** many people defected from the Communist party (**c**) *(abandonar)* **d. de** to abandon; **desertó de sus obligaciones** she neglected her duties

desértico, -a *adj* (**a**) *(del desierto)* desert; **clima d.** desert climate; **zonas desérticas** desert areas (**b**) *(despoblado)* deserted

desertificación *nf* desertification

desertización *nf (del terreno)* desertification; *(de la población)* depopulation

desertizar 1 *vt* to turn into a desert
2 **desertizarse** *vpr* to turn into a desert

desertor, -ora *nm,f (del ejército)* deserter; **los desertores del partido** those who have left *o* abandoned the party

desescolarización *nf* lack of schooling

desescombrar *vt* to clear the rubble from

desescombro *nm* clearing (away) of rubble; **comenzaron las tareas de d.** the task of clearing away the rubble has started

desesperación *nf* (**a**) *(falta de alternativa)* desperation; *(desesperanza)* despair; **su d. era tal que pidió ayuda a un curandero** he was so desperate he asked a witch doctor's help; **pedía con d. que la ayudaran** she made desperate pleas for help; **se echó a llorar de d.** she burst into tears of despair; **me entra la d. cuando pienso en el poco tiempo que nos queda** I start getting *o* feeling desperate when I think of how little time we have left; **se suicidó presa de la d.** despair drove him to suicide; **vivir sumido en la d.** to be sunk in despair
(**b**) *(enojo)* **ime entra una d. cuando veo estas injusticias!** it makes me mad when I see injustices like these!; **es una d. lo lento que van los trenes** it's maddening how slow the trains are

desesperadamente *adv (falta de alternativa)* desperately, in desperation; *(sin esperanza)* despairingly

desesperado, -a 1 *adj* desperate; **estar d.** *(sin alternativa)* to be desperate; *(sin esperanza)* to be in despair; **lo hice porque estaba d.** I did it out of desperation; **gritaba d. que lo ayudaran** he was screaming frantically for them to help him; **en un intento d. por huir del incendio** in a desperate attempt to escape from the fire; **el estado de la población es d.** the people are in a desperate state; **(hacer algo) a la desesperada** (to do sth) in desperation
2 *nm,f* EXPR *Fam* **como un d.** like mad *o* crazy; **comer como un d.** to eat as if one were half-starved

> **Falso amigo**: El término inglés **desperado** no es la traducción del español **desesperado**. En inglés, **desperado** significa "forajido".

desesperante *adj* infuriating; **resulta d. oírle hablar** he's infuriating to listen to; **el balón rodaba por el barro con lentitud d.** the ball rolled through the mud infuriatingly *o* maddeningly slowly

desesperanza *nf* lack of hope; **cuando la vio besar a Rodrigo, la d. se apoderó de él** when he saw her kiss Rodrigo he gave up hope

desesperanzar [14] 1 *vt* to cause to lose hope
2 **desesperanzarse** *vpr* to give up hope, to lose hope

desesperar 1 *vt* (**a**) *(quitar la esperanza a)* to drive to despair (**b**) *(irritar, enojar)* to exasperate, to drive mad; **me desespera cuando se pone a hablar así** it makes me mad when he starts talking like that; **si hay algo que me desespera es la desorganización** if there's one thing that exasperates me *o* drives me mad, it's lack of organization
2 *vi* to despair, to give up hope; **no desesperes, aún se puede hacer algo** don't despair *o* give up hope, something can still be done; **d. de hacer algo** to give up all hope of doing sth; **desesperan ya de encontrar supervivientes** they have given up hope of finding survivors
3 **desesperarse** *vpr* (**a**) *(perder la esperanza)* to give up *o* lose hope, to despair; **no hay que desesperarse, aún pueden encontrarlos** we mustn't give up hope, they might still find them (**b**) *(irritarse, enojarse)* to get mad *o* exasperated; **es tan lento que me desespero con él** he's so slow he drives me mad

desespero *nm Andes, RP, Ven Fam (falta de alternativa)* desperation; *(desesperanza)* despair

desestabilización *nf* destabilization

desestabilizador, -ora *adj* destabilizing

desestabilizar [14] 1 *vt* to destabilize
2 **desestabilizarse** *vpr* to become destabilized

desestatización *nf Am* privatization, sell-off

desestatizar *vt Am* to privatize, to sell off

desestima, desestimación *nf* low opinion, lack of respect

desestimar *vt* (**a**) *(rechazar)* to reject, to turn down; **el Supremo desestimó el recurso** the Supreme Court rejected the appeal (**b**) *(despreciar)* to turn one's nose up at

desexilio *nm CSur* return from exile; **los problemas del d.** the problems encountered by returning exiles

desfachatado, -a *adj Fam* cheeky

desfachatez *nf Fam* cheek; **iqué d.!** the cheek of it!; **actúa con mucha d.** he behaves really brazenly *o* without shame

desfalcar [60] *vt* to embezzle

desfalco *nm* embezzlement; **hacer un d.** to embezzle (money)

desfallecer [46] *vi* (**a**) *(debilitarse)* to begin to flag; **no desfallezcas, queda poco para llegar** don't give up, we're almost there; **desfallecíamos de hambre** we were faint *o* fainting with hunger; **sin d.** without flagging (**b**) *(desmayarse)* to faint; **me sentía d.** I felt that I was going to faint

desfallecido, -a *adj* exhausted, faint

desfallecimiento *nm* (**a**) *(desmayo)* fainting fit; **sufrir un d.** to faint (**b**) *(debilidad)* faintness

desfallezco *etc ver* **desfallecer**

desfasado, -a *adj* (**a**) *(desincronizado)* out of synch *o* sync (**b**) *(persona)* out of touch; *(libro, moda)* old-fashioned; *(ideas)* old-fashioned, out of date

desfasar 1 *vt Elec* to phase out
2 *vi Esp Fam (desmadrarse)* to go wild *o* over the top

desfase *nm* (**a**) *(diferencia)* gap; **llevamos un d. de diez años con respecto a Suecia** we are ten years behind Sweden; **hay un d. entre la oferta y la demanda** supply is out of step with demand ►► ***d. horario*** *(tras vuelo)* jet lag (**b**) *Fís* phase lag (**c**) *Com* slippage

desfavorable *adj* unfavourable; **en condiciones desfavorables** in unfavourable *o* adverse conditions; **navegar con tiempo d.** to sail in unfavourable *o* adverse weather conditions; **la reacción de la crítica le fue d.** the critics' reaction was largely negative

desfavorablemente *adv* unfavourably

desfavorecer [46] *vt* (**a**) *(perjudicar)* to go against the interests of; **la reforma fiscal desfavorece a los más pobres** the tax reform will have a negative impact on the poorest sections of society; **han acusado al**

gobierno de d. a ciertas regiones they've accused the government of neglecting certain regions in favour of others; **la suerte nos ha desfavorecido** fortune has not been kind to us

(**b**) *(sentar mal a)* not to suit; **esa falda te desfavorece** that skirt doesn't suit you

desfavorecido, -a *adj* (**a**) *(desaventajado)* disadvantaged (**b**) *(feo)* **salí muy d. en la foto** I came out very badly in the photo

desfibrilador *nm Med* defibrillator

desfiguración *nf* (**a**) *(de rostro, cuerpo)* disfigurement (**b**) *(de la verdad)* distortion

desfigurado, -a *adj* disfigured; **el accidente lo dejó d.** the accident left him disfigured; **el rostro d. por el pánico** her face contorted with *o* in panic

desfigurar 1 *vt* (**a**) *(aspecto físico)* to disfigure; **el accidente le desfiguró la cara** his face was disfigured in the accident; **el espeso humo desfiguraba las siluetas de los bomberos** the thick smoke blurred the outline of the firemen's figures; **los chalets adosados han desfigurado el viejo pueblo** the semi-detached houses have ruined the look of the old town

(**b**) *(realidad, verdad)* to distort

2 desfigurarse *vpr* to become disfigured; **se le desfiguró el cuerpo** his body was disfigured; **se le desfiguró la cara al ver al asesino** her face contorted when she saw the killer

desfiladero *nm* gorge

desfilar *vi* (**a**) *(soldados)* to parade, to march past; **las tropas desfilaron ante el monarca** the troops paraded in front of *o* marched past the king

(**b**) *(personas)* to file; **miles de personas desfilaron ante la tumba del presidente** thousands of people filed past the president's tomb; **cientos de oficinistas desfilan por esta calle todos los días** hundreds of office workers pass along this street every day; **por este despacho han desfilado hombres muy ilustres** illustrious men have passed through this office; **imágenes horrendas desfilaban por su mente** horrific images passed through his mind

(**c**) *(modelos)* to parade; **d. por la pasarela** to parade *o* walk down the catwalk

(**d**) *Fam (marcharse)* to head off, to leave; **¡vamos, desfilando (de aquí)!** come on, out of here!

desfile *nm* (**a**) *(de soldados)* parade, march past ►► ***d. militar*** military parade (**b**) *(de personas)* **hubo un d. constante de personas ante la tumba** there was a constant stream of people filing past the tomb (**c**) *(de carrozas)* procession ►► ***d. de Carnaval*** carnival procession (**d**) ***d. de moda*** fashion show *o* parade; ***d. de modelos*** fashion show *o* parade

desfinanciado, -a *adj Am* **la institución está totalmente desfinanciada** the organization has absolutely no funds *o* money

desfinanciar *Am* **1** *vt* **la pésima administración terminó desfinanciando a esa empresa** incompetent management led to the company being left without sufficient funds *o* money

2 desfinanciarse *vpr* **las cooperativas eficientes corren poco riesgo de desfinanciarse** efficient cooperatives run little risk of ending up without sufficient funds *o* money

desfloración *nf*, **desfloramiento** *nm* deflowering

desflorar *vt* to deflower

desfogar [38] **1** *vt (ira, frustraciones)* to vent; **desfogó su cólera con su hermano** he took out *o* vented his anger on his brother

2 desfogarse *vpr* to let off steam; **se desfogaba dando golpes a la puerta** he vented his anger by hitting the door; **se desfogó llorando** she got some relief by crying

desfogue *nm* (**a**) *(desahogo)* **la violencia fue su d.** violence was his way of getting things out of his system (**b**) *Am (caño)* outlet

desfondamiento *nm* (**a**) *(ruptura)* **para evitar el d. de la caja** to prevent the bottom of the box falling out; **el impacto provocó el d. de la embarcación** the impact breached the hull of the boat (**b**) *(agotamiento)* **sufrió un d.** he was overcome by exhaustion

desfondar 1 *vt* (**a**) *(silla, asiento)* to break the seat of; *(vasija)* to break the bottom of; *(embarcación)* to breach the hull of; **vas a d. la caja/bolsa si la llenas más** the bottom will fall out of that box/bag if you put any more in it; **el golpe contra el suelo desfondó la maleta** the suitcase burst open when it hit the floor (**b**) *(agotar)* to wear out

2 desfondarse *vpr* (**a**) *(perder el fondo)* **la caja/bolsa se desfondó** the bottom fell out of the box/bag; **la silla se desfondó** the seat of the chair gave way (**b**) *(persona)* to become completely exhausted, to run out of steam

desforestación *nf* deforestation

desforestar *vt* to deforest

desgaire *nm (desaliño)* slovenliness, sloppiness; **vestir con d.** to dress sloppily; **al d.** nonchalantly, casually

desgajar 1 *vt (página)* to tear out (**de** of); *(libro, periódico)* to rip up; *(naranja)* to split into segments; **desgajó la rama (del árbol)** he broke the branch off (the tree)

2 desgajarse *vpr* to break off; **unas hojas se habían desgajado del libro** some pages had come loose from the binding (of the book); **una gran compañía que se ha desgajado en pequeñas empresas** a major company that has split up into small firms; **varios grupúsculos se desgajaron del partido** several factions split off *o* broke away from the party

desgana *nf*, *Am* **desgano** *nm* (**a**) *(falta de apetito)* lack of appetite; **comer con d.** to eat with little appetite (**b**) *(falta de ánimo)* lack of enthusiasm; **con d.** unenthusiastically, reluctantly; **trabajar con d.** to work with little enthusiasm

desganado, -a *adj* (**a**) *(sin apetito)* **estar d.** to be off one's food (**b**) *(sin ganas)* listless, apathetic

desganar 1 *vt* to take away the desire of

2 desganarse *vpr* (**a**) *(perder apetito)* to lose one's appetite (**b**) *(cansarse)* to lose interest

desgano = **desgana**

desgañitarse *vpr* to scream oneself hoarse

desgarbado, -a *adj* ungainly; **sus andares desgarbados** his ungainly walk

desgarrado, -a *adj* (**a**) *(roto)* torn, ripped (**b**) *(terrible, descarnado) (estilo)* bleak, uncompromising; *(relato, poema)* harrowing, heart-rending (**c**) *(rasgado) (grito)* piercing; *(voz)* gravelly, rasping

desgarrador, -ora *adj (grito)* piercing; *(llanto)* heart-rending; *(noticia)* harrowing; *(tragedia)* terrible

desgarrar 1 *vt* to rip; **el clavo me ha desgarrado la chaqueta** the nail has torn my jacket; EXPR **verles sufrir desgarra el corazón** it's heart-breaking to see them suffer

2 desgarrarse *vpr* (**a**) *(sujeto: ropa)* to get torn *o* ripped; **se me desgarró la camiseta** my T-shirt has got torn *o* ripped; EXPR **se me desgarra el corazón (cuando...)** it breaks my heart (when...) (**b**) *(músculo)* to tear; **se desgarró un músculo entrenando** she tore a muscle while training

desgarriate *nm Méx* mess; **es el responsable del d. en materia educativa** he is responsible for the mess education is in

desgarro *nm* (**a**) *(en tejido)* tear (**b**) *(en fibra, músculo)* **sufrió un d.** he tore a muscle ►► ***d. muscular*** torn muscle; **tiene un d. muscular en la pierna** he's torn a muscle in his leg

desgarrón *nm* big tear

desgastado, -a *adj* worn

desgastar 1 *vt* (**a**) *(suela, neumático)* to wear down; *(puño, cuerda)* to fray; *(roca)* to wear away; **han desgastado la tapicería del sofá con sus juegos** they've caused a lot of wear on the upholstery of the sofa with their playing on it (**b**) *(persona)* to wear out; *(organización)* to weaken

2 desgastarse *vpr* (**a**) *(suela, neumático)* to wear down; *(puño, cuerda)* to fray; *(roca)* to wear away; *(tela)* to become worn (**b**) *(persona)* to become worn out; *(organización)* to become ineffective

desgaste *nm* (**a**) *(de tela, muebles)* wear and tear; *(de roca)* wearing away; *(de pilas)* running down; *(de cuerda)* fraying; **el d. de las ruedas** the wear on the tyres

(**b**) *(de persona, organización)* wear and tear; **el d. de los años** the wear and tear of the years; **presenta todos los síntomas del d. que produce el poder** it displays all the symptoms of having been in power too long; **d. físico/psicológico** physical/mental wear and tear

desglosar *vt* to break down; **una factura desglosada** an itemized bill

desglose *nm* breakdown

desgobernar [3] *vt (país)* to govern badly

desgobierno *nm (de país)* misgovernment, misrule; *(de empresa, hogar)* mismanagement, bad management

desgoznar 1 *vt (arrancar)* to unhinge; *(desmontar)* to remove the hinges from

2 desgoznarse *vpr* to come off its hinges

desgracia *nf* (**a**) *(mala suerte)* misfortune; **le persigue la d.** he is dogged by bad luck; **bastante d. tengo ya con haber perdido mi trabajo** it's bad enough having lost my job; **ha tenido la d. de sufrir dos accidentes aéreos** she's had the misfortune to be in two plane crashes; **por d.** unfortunately; **¿le llegaste a conocer? – por d. para mí** did you ever meet him? – unfortunately for me, I did

(**b**) *(catástrofe)* disaster; **ha ocurrido una d.** something terrible has happened; **le persiguen las desgracias** bad things keep happening to him; **una vida llena de desgracias** a life full of misfortune; **¡qué d.!**

how awful!; **es una d. que...** it's a terrible shame that...; EXPR **las desgracias nunca vienen solas** it never rains but it pours ▸▸ ***desgracias personales:*** **no hubo que lamentar desgracias personales** there were no casualties, fortunately

(**c**) EXPR **caer en d.** to fall from grace *o* into disgrace; **caer en d. de alguien** to fall out of favour with sb; **es la d. de la familia** he's the shame of the family

desgraciadamente *adv* unfortunately; **d. para mí, no puedo asistir** unfortunately for me, I can't go

desgraciado, -a 1 *adj* (**a**) *(desafortunado) (día)* ill-fated; *(suceso, accidente, casualidad)* unfortunate

(**b**) *(desacertado) (intervención, elección)* unfortunate, unhappy

(**c**) *(sin suerte)* unlucky; **ser d. en el amor** to be unlucky in love

(**d**) *(infeliz)* unhappy; **es muy d. en su trabajo** he's very unhappy in his work; **llevar una vida desgraciada** to lead an unhappy *o* a miserable life

(**e**) *(canalla)* rotten, nasty

(**f**) *(sin atractivo)* unprepossessing, unattractive; **tiene un físico d.** she is physically unattractive

2 *nm,f* (**a**) *(persona sin suerte)* born loser

(**b**) *(infeliz)* wretch; **es un pobre d.** he's a poor wretch

(**c**) *(canalla)* swine; **ieres un d.!** you're a swine!; **el muy d. me robó el dinero** the swine stole my money

desgraciar 1 *vt* (**a**) *Fam (cosa)* to ruin, to wreck (**b**) *(deshonrar)* to demean (**c**) *Fam (herir)* **d. a alguien** to do sb a mischief

2 **desgraciarse** *vpr* (**a**) *(plan, proyecto)* to be a complete disaster, to fall through (**b**) *Fam (herirse)* to do oneself a mischief

desgranar *vt* (**a**) *(oración)* **d. las cuentas del rosario** to tell one's beads (**b**) *(ideas, argumentos)* to reel off; **d. insultos** to hurl *o* sling insults (**c**) *(trigo)* to thresh; *(maíz)* to remove from the cob; *(guisantes, habas)* to shell

desgravable *adj* tax-deductible

desgravación *nf* deduction; **las desgravaciones por hijo o familiar a cargo** the allowances for a dependent child or relative; **una inversión con derecho a d.** a tax-deductible investment; **una d. del 15 por ciento** a reduction in your tax of 15 percent ▸▸ ***d. fiscal*** tax relief

desgravar 1 *vt* (**a**) *(sujeto: persona)* to deduct from one's tax bill; **yo desgravo los gastos de papelería** I deduct the cost of stationery for tax purposes (**b**) *(sujeto: gastos)* **los alquileres desgravan un 5 por ciento** 5 percent of rent can be claimed against tax

2 *vi* to be tax-deductible; **¿las minusvalías físicas desgravan?** are there any tax allowances for physical disabilities?

3 **desgravarse** *vpr* (**a**) *(sujeto: gastos)* to be tax-deductible (**b**) *(sujeto: persona)* **se desgrava todo el dinero que puede** he claims as much as he can against tax

desgreñado, -a *adj* dishevelled

desgreñar 1 *vt* to dishevel, to tousle

2 **desgreñarse** *vpr (despeinarse)* to become dishevelled *o* tousled

desguace *nm* (**a**) *(acción) (de automóviles)* scrapping; *(de buques)* breaking (up); **esa camioneta está para el d.** this van is for the scrapheap; **material de d.** scrap (**b**) *(depósito)* scrapyard

desguañangado, -a, desguañingado, -a *adj Méx, Ven Fam (mueble)* rickety; *(vehículo)* beat-up, broken-down

desguañangar, desguañingar *vt Méx, Ven Fam* to wreck

desguarnecer [46] *vt* (**a**) *(quitar los adornos de)* to strip (**b**) *(dejar sin protección)* to withdraw the troops from; **quedar desguarnecido** to be left unprotected; **el portero dejó su meta desguarnecida** the goalkeeper left his goal undefended (**c**) *(caballo)* to unharness

desguazar [14] *vt (automóvil)* to scrap; *(buque)* to break up

deshabillé *nm* negligée

deshabitado, -a *adj (casa, edificio)* empty, unoccupied; *(región, pueblo, ciudad)* uninhabited

deshabitar *vt* (**a**) *(casa, edificio)* to leave, to vacate (**b**) *(territorio)* to depopulate; *(pueblo)* to empty (of people)

deshabituar [4] 1 *vt* **d. a alguien (de)** to get sb out of the habit (of)

2 **deshabituarse** *vpr* to break the habit, to get out of the habit (**de** of); **le costaba deshabituarse del café** she found it hard to do without her coffee

DESHACER [33] 1 *vt* (**a**) *(nudo, paquete)* to undo; *(maleta)* to unpack; *(costura)* to unpick; **d. las maletas** to unpack (one's bags); **el aire le deshizo el peinado** the wind messed up her hair; **la cama estaba sin d.** the bed hadn't been stripped; **tuvo que d. todo el camino porque se había olvidado las llaves en casa** she had to go all the way back because she had left her keys at home

(**b**) *Informát* to undo

(**c**) *(disolver) (helado, mantequilla)* to melt; *(pastilla, terrón de azúcar)* to dissolve; **d. un comprimido en agua** to dissolve a tablet in water

(**d**) *(desarmar, despedazar)* to take apart; *(libro)* to tear up; *(res, carne)* to cut up; *(roca)* to break up; *(castillo de arena)* to destroy; **d. un puzzle** to pull apart a jigsaw; **la tormenta deshizo el techo de la vivienda** the storm caused serious damage to the roof of the house

(**e**) *(desgastar)* to wear out; **te vas a d. la vista, tan cerca de la televisión** you'll ruin your eyesight by sitting so near the television; **el ejercicio excesivo deshace las articulaciones** excessive exercise wears down your joints; **tiene los nervios deshechos** his nerves are in shreds

(**f**) *(destruir) (enemigo)* to rout; *(matrimonio)* to ruin; **tres años de guerra deshicieron al país** three years of war devastated the country; **deshicieron al equipo rival** they destroyed *o* dismantled the opposition

(**g**) *(poner fin a) (contrato, negocio)* to cancel; *(pacto, tratado)* to break; *(plan, intriga)* to foil; *(organización)* to dissolve; **tenemos que d. este lío** we have to sort this problem out

(**h**) *(afligir)* to devastate; **la noticia de su asesinato deshizo a la familia** the news of his murder devastated his family

2 **deshacerse** *vpr* (**a**) *(costura)* to come undone *o* unstitched; *(trenza, moño)* to come undone; *(peinado)* to get messed up

(**b**) *(disolverse) (helado, mantequilla, nieve)* to melt; *(pastilla, terrón de azúcar)* to dissolve; *(niebla)* to lift; **el azúcar se deshace al contacto con el agua** sugar dissolves when it comes into contact with water; **los caramelos se van deshaciendo en la boca** the sweets gradually melt in your mouth; **la organización se deshizo tras la guerra** the organization broke up after the war; **la concentración se deshizo antes de que llegara la policía** the crowd dispersed before the police arrived

(**c**) *(desarmarse)* to fall apart; **el jarrón se deshizo en pedazos** the vase smashed to pieces

(**d**) **deshacerse de** *(librarse de)* to get rid of; **salió por una puerta trasera para deshacerse del detective** he left by a back door to lose the detective; **nos costó mucho deshacernos de él** it wasn't easy to get rid of him

(**e**) **deshacerse de** *(desprenderse de)* to get rid of; **se resiste a deshacerse de sus joyas** she's reluctant to part with her jewels; **se deshicieron de un sofá viejo** they got rid of an old sofa

(**f**) **deshacerse en** *(prodigarse en)* **se deshizo en elogios con** *o* **hacia su anfitrión** she lavished praise on her host; **se deshizo en lágrimas al enterarse** he cried his heart out when he found out; **siempre se deshace en atenciones con nosotros** she is always extremely attentive towards us

(**g**) **deshacerse por alguien** *(desvivirse)* to bend over backwards for sb; *(estar enamorado)* to be madly in love with sb; **se deshace por la empresa, y nadie se lo reconoce** he does everything he can for the company, and no one appreciates it; **está que se deshace por** *o* **con su nietecilla** he absolutely dotes on his little granddaughter; **deshacerse por hacer/conseguir algo** to go out of one's way to do/get sth

desharrapado, -a, desarrapado, -a 1 *adj* ragged; **¿cómo puedes ir siempre tan d.?** how can you go around dressed in those rags all the time?

2 *nm,f* person dressed in rags; **los desharrapados** *(los pobres)* the dispossessed

deshecho, -a 1 *participio ver* **deshacer**

2 *adj* (**a**) *(nudo, paquete)* undone; *(cama)* unmade; *(maleta)* unpacked

(**b**) *(destruido) (enemigo)* destroyed; *(tarta, matrimonio)* ruined

(**c**) *(derretido) (pastilla, terrón de azúcar)* dissolved; *(helado, mantequilla)* melted

(**d**) *(anulado) (contrato, negocio)* cancelled; *(pacto, tratado)* broken; *(plan, intriga)* foiled; *(organización)* dissolved

(**e**) *(afligido)* devastated; **d. en lágrimas** in floods of tears

(**f**) *(cansado)* exhausted; **la carrera lo dejó d.** the run left him exhausted; **vengo d.** I'm wrecked *o* exhausted

3 *nm Am (atajo)* short cut

deshelar [3] 1 *vt (nieve, lago, hielo)* to thaw, to melt; *(parabrisas)* to de-ice

2 **deshelarse** *vpr* to thaw, to melt

desheredado, -a 1 *adj* (**a**) *(excluido de herencia)* disinherited (**b**) *(indigente)* deprived

2 *nm,f (indigente)* deprived person; **los desheredados** the dispossessed

desheredar *vt* to disinherit

deshice *etc ver* **deshacer**

deshidratación *nf* dehydration

deshidratado, -a *adj* dehydrated; **llegó d. al hospital** he was suffering from dehydration when he arrived at the hospital; **piel deshidratada** dry skin

deshidratante 1 *adj* dehydrating
2 *nm* dehydrating agent

deshidratar 1 *vt* to dehydrate
2 **deshidratarse** *vpr* to become dehydrated

deshidrogenar *vt* to dehydrogenate, to dehydrogenize

deshiela *ver* **deshelar**

deshielo *nm* (**a**) *(de nieve, lagos, ríos)* thaw; **con la llegada del d.** when it starts to thaw, with the onset of the thaw; **aguas de d.** meltwater (**b**) *(de relaciones)* thaw

deshierra *etc ver* **desherrar**

deshijar *vt CAm, Carib, Col (planta)* to remove the suckers from

deshilachado, -a *adj* frayed

deshilachar 1 *vt* to unravel
2 **deshilacharse** *vpr* to fray

deshilado *nm* openwork embroidery

deshilar *vt* to unravel

deshilvanado, -a *adj* (**a**) *(tela)* untacked (**b**) *(discurso, guión)* disjointed; *(ideas)* confused, incoherent; **el juego del equipo fue bastante d.** the team's playing wasn't very coordinated

deshilvanar *vt* to untack

deshinchar 1 *vt* (**a**) *(globo, neumático)* to let down, to deflate (**b**) *(hinchazón)* to reduce; *(parte del cuerpo)* to reduce the swelling on; **d. el bulto** to make the lump go down
2 **deshincharse** *vpr* (**a**) *(globo, neumático)* to go down; **a la moto se le deshinchó una rueda** the motorbike got a *Br* puncture *o US* flat (**b**) *(hinchazón, bulto)* to go down; **ya se te deshinchó el tobillo** the swelling on your ankle has gone down (**c**) *(perder fuerza)* to run out of steam; **el equipo se deshinchó en el segundo tiempo** the team ran out of steam in the second half

deshipoteca *nf* paying off of the mortgage

deshipotecar [60] *vt* to pay off the mortgage on

deshizo *ver* **deshacer**

deshojar 1 *vt (flor)* to pull the petals off; *(árbol)* to strip the leaves off; *(libro, cuaderno)* to tear the pages out of; EXPR **d. la margarita** *(amante, enamorado)* = to pull the petals off a daisy saying "she loves me, she loves me not"; **el líder socialista sigue deshojando la margarita** the socialist leader is still debating what to do
2 **deshojarse** *vpr (flor)* to drop its petals; *(árbol)* to shed its leaves

deshoje *nm* falling of leaves

deshollejar *vt* to peel

deshollinador, -ora 1 *nm,f (persona)* chimney sweep
2 *nm (instrumento) (para chimeneas)* chimney brush; *(para techos y paredes)* ceiling brush

deshollinar *vt* to sweep

deshonestamente *adv (sin honradez)* dishonestly

deshonestidad *nf (falta de honradez)* dishonesty; **actuó con d.** she acted dishonestly

deshonesto, -a *adj* (**a**) *(sin honradez)* dishonest (**b**) *(sin pudor)* indecent, immoral

deshonor *nm*, **deshonra** *nf* (**a**) *(pérdida de la honra)* dishonour (**b**) *(cosa deshonrosa)* dishonour; **su comportamiento es un d. para su familia** his behaviour brings shame *o* disgrace on his family; **eres un d. para este colegio** you are a disgrace to this school; **no es ningún d. trabajar de barrendero** there's no shame in being a street sweeper, being a street sweeper is nothing to be ashamed of

deshonrar *vt* (**a**) *(injuriar)* to dishonour; **con su conducta deshonra a toda la familia** his behaviour is bringing disgrace upon the entire family (**b**) *(mujer)* to dishonour

deshonroso, -a *adj* dishonourable, shameful

deshora: a d., a deshoras *loc adv (en momento inoportuno)* at a bad time; *(en horas poco habituales)* at an unearthly hour; **siempre da su opinión a d.** she always gives her opinion when it's not asked for; **no es bueno comer a d.** it's not good to eat outside normal mealtimes

deshuesa *etc ver* **desosar, deshuesar**

deshuesadero *nm Méx* scrapyard

deshuesar *vt (carne)* to bone; *(fruto) Br* to stone, *US* to pit

deshuevarse *vpr Esp muy Fam* to piss oneself laughing, to split a gut; **todos se deshuevaban de mí cuando decía esto** they all pissed themselves laughing when I said that

deshumanización *nf* dehumanization

deshumanizar [14] **1** *vt* to dehumanize
2 **deshumanizarse** *vpr (relaciones, trabajo)* to become dehumanized; *(persona)* to lose one's humanity

desideologización *nf* **quieren la d. del debate** they want to remove the ideological element from the debate; **la d. de la clase obrera** the depoliticization of the working class

desideologizado, -a *adj* **una clase obrera desideologizada** a depoliticized working class

desideologizar *vt* **quieren d. el debate** they want to remove the ideological element from the debate; **la prosperidad ha desideologizado a la clase obrera** prosperity has depoliticized the working class

desiderativo, -a *adj Gram* desiderative

desiderátum *nm inv* greatest wish, desideratum

desidia *nf* (**a**) *(descuido) (en el trabajo)* carelessness; *(en el aspecto)* slovenliness; **hace las cosas con d.** she does things very carelessly; **cosas que pasan por d.** things that happen through carelessness (**b**) *(desgana)* listlessness; **me entró la d.** I was overcome by a feeling of listlessness

desidioso, -a *adj (en el trabajo)* careless; *(en el aspecto)* slovenly

desierto, -a 1 *adj* (**a**) *(vacío)* deserted, empty; **una isla desierta** a desert island; **la ciudad se queda desierta en agosto** the city is deserted in August; **las gradas se quedaron desiertas** the stands were deserted *o* empty
(**b**) *(vacante)* **la plaza quedó desierta** the post was left unfilled; **el premio quedó d.** the prize was not awarded; **declararon el concurso d.** the competition was declared void
2 *nm* desert; **un d. de arena** a sandy desert; EXPR **predicar *o* clamar en el d.** to be a voice crying in the wilderness ▸▸ ***el d. de Atacama*** the Atacama Desert; ***el d. de Gobi*** the Gobi Desert; ***el d. del Sáhara*** the Sahara Desert

designación *nf* (**a**) *(nombre)* designation (**b**) *(nombramiento)* appointment; **parlamentarios de *o* por d. real** members of parliament appointed by the monarch

designar *vt* (**a**) *(nombrar)* to appoint; **han designado a Gómez para el cargo** Gómez has been appointed to the post; **fue designada mujer del año por la revista "Time"** "Time" magazine named her woman of the year; **ha sido designada capital europea de la cultura** it has been designated the European capital of culture
(**b**) *(fijar, determinar)* to name, to fix; **d. medidas contra la corrupción** to draw up measures against corruption; **falta por d. una fecha y un lugar** a date and place have yet to be set *o* decided
(**c**) *(denominar)* to refer to; **el símbolo # lo designamos con el nombre de "almohadilla"** we refer to the # symbol as the "hash"; **este logotipo designa el empleo de papel reciclado** this logo denotes the use of recycled paper

designio *nm* intention, plan; **de acuerdo con los designios de su padre** in accordance with his father's plans; **los designios del Señor son inescrutables** the Lord works in mysterious ways; **pensaba que aquello había ocurrido por d. divino** she thought that God had planned it to happen

desigual *adj* (**a**) *(diferente)* different; **recibieron un trato d.** they weren't treated the same, they were treated differently; **un triángulo de lados desiguales** a triangle with unequal sides
(**b**) *(irregular) (terreno, superficie)* uneven; *(alumno, actuación)* inconsistent, erratic; **su filmografía es de d. calidad** his movies *o Br* films are of varying quality; **ha publicado varias novelas con d. fortuna** he has published several novels, with mixed results
(**c**) *(poco equilibrado) (lucha, competición)* unequal; *(fuerzas, rivales)* unevenly matched
(**d**) *(variable) (tiempo)* changeable; *(temperaturas)* variable; *(persona, humor)* changeable

desigualar 1 *vt* to make unequal
2 **desigualarse** *vpr* to get ahead

desigualdad *nf* (**a**) *(diferencia)* difference; **trataba a sus hijos con d.** he didn't treat all his children in the same way (**b**) *(de carácter)* changeability; *(de actuación, rendimiento)* inconsistency, erratic nature; *(del terreno)* unevenness (**c**) *(económica, social, racial)* inequality; **acabar con las desigualdades regionales** to put an end to inequalities between the regions (**d**) *Mat* inequality

desilusión *nf* (**a**) *(estado de ánimo)* disillusionment; **caer en la d.** to become disillusioned (**b**) *(decepción)* disappointment; **llevarse *o* sufrir una d. (con algo)** to be disappointed (with sth); **¡qué d.!** what a disappointment!

desilusionado, -a *adj* (**a**) *(sin ilusiones)* disillusioned (**b**) *(decepcionado)* disappointed; **estar d. con algo** to be disappointed with sth; **estoy muy d. contigo** I'm very disappointed with *o* in you; **está muy d. con la política** he's very disillusioned with politics

desilusionar 1 *vt* (**a**) *(decepcionar)* to disappoint, to disillusion; **su conferencia me desilusionó** I was disappointed by his talk; **desilusionaron al electorado** they let the voters down (**b**) *(desengañar)* to reveal the truth to; **no lo quiero d., se lo ve tan contento** I don't want to spoil things for him by telling him the truth, he looks so happy

2 **desilusionarse** *vpr* (**a**) *(decepcionarse)* to be disappointed *o* disillusioned; **me he desilusionado con la política** I've become disillusioned with politics (**b**) *(desengañarse)* to realize the truth; **desilusiónate, no te va a llamar** don't get your hopes up, he's not going to call you

desimantación *nf* demagnetization

desimantar *vt* to demagnetize

desincentivador, -ora *adj* **una medida desincentivadora (de)** a disincentive (to)

desincentivar *vt* to discourage

desincrustar *vt (tuberías)* to descale

desindustrialización *nf* deindustrialization

desinencia *nf* ending

desinfección *nf* disinfection

desinfectante 1 *adj (para objetos)* disinfectant; *(para heridas)* antiseptic

2 *nm (para objetos)* disinfectant; *(para heridas)* antiseptic

desinfectar *vt* to disinfect

desinflación *nf Econ* disinflation

desinflado, -a *adj (globo, pelota)* deflated; *(neumático)* flat

desinflamar 1 *vt* to reduce the inflammation in

2 **desinflamarse** *vpr* to become less inflamed

desinflar 1 *vt* (**a**) *(globo, pelota)* to deflate; *(rueda)* to let down, to deflate (**b**) *(quitar importancia a)* to play down (**c**) *(desanimar)* to depress

2 **desinflarse** *vpr* (**a**) *(perder aire) (balón)* to go down; *(neumático)* to go flat (**b**) *(desanimarse)* to get depressed (**c**) *(achicarse)* to become discouraged, to lose heart; **en el interrogatorio se terminó desinflando** he lost his confidence under questioning; **el equipo se desinfló en el último cuarto del partido** the team ran out of steam in the last quarter

desinformación *nf* misinformation

desinformar *vt* to misinform

desinhibición *nf* lack of inhibition; **se comporta con d.** he behaves with complete lack of inhibition

desinhibidamente *adv* uninhibitedly, without inhibitions

desinhibido, -a *adj* uninhibited

desinhibir 1 *vt* to free from inhibitions

2 **desinhibirse** *vpr* to lose one's inhibitions

desinsectación *nf (de casa)* fumigation

desinsectar *vt (casa)* to fumigate

desinstalar *vt Informát* to uninstall

desintegración *nf* (**a**) *(de objeto, materia)* disintegration; **la d. del átomo** the splitting of the atom (**b**) *(de grupo, organización)* break-up; **la d. de la Unión Soviética** the break-up of the Soviet Union; **la d. de la familia** the break-up of the family (**c**) *Fís* decay ►► ***d. nuclear*** nuclear decay

desintegrar 1 *vt* (**a**) *(objeto, materia)* to break into pieces; *(átomo)* to split; **el rayo desintegró la nave espacial** the ray disintegrated the spaceship (**b**) *(grupo, organización, familia)* to break up

2 **desintegrarse** *vpr* (**a**) *(objeto)* to disintegrate (**b**) *(grupo, organización, familia)* to break up

desinteligencia *nf Am* (**a**) *(malentendido)* misunderstanding (**b**) *(estupidez)* lack of intelligence

desinterés (*pl* **desintereses**) *nm* (**a**) *(indiferencia)* disinterest, lack of interest (**por** in); **mostró gran d. por nuestro trabajo** he showed very little interest in our work (**b**) *(generosidad)* unselfishness; **actúa con d.** she acts unselfishly

desinteresadamente *adv* unselfishly; **ayudar a alguien d.** to help sb with no thought of personal gain

desinteresado, -a *adj* (**a**) *(indiferente)* uninterested (**por** in) (**b**) *(generoso)* unselfish; **colabora de forma desinteresada** he's taking part with no thought of personal gain

desinteresarse *vpr* to lose interest (**de** in)

desintoxicación *nf* detoxification; **centro de d.** *(para toxicómanos)* detoxification centre; **clínica de d.** *(para alcohólicos)* drying-out clinic

desintoxicar [60] 1 *vt (persona intoxicada)* to detoxify; *(alcohólico)* to dry out; **la finalidad del programa es d. a los pacientes** the purpose of the scheme is to get the patients off drugs

2 **desintoxicarse** *vpr (dejar de beber)* to dry out; *(dejar de drogarse)* to come off drugs, to break one's drug habit; **se fue al campo para desintoxicarse de la ciudad** he went to the country to get the city out of his system

desinversión *nf Econ* disinvestment, divestment

desinvertir *vt Econ* to disinvest

desistimiento *nm Der (de demanda)* abandonment; *(de recurso)* withdrawal; *(de derechos)* waiving

desistir *vi* (**a**) **d. de (hacer) algo** to give up *o* stop (doing) sth; **al final desistieron de la idea** in the end they gave up the idea; **han desistido de comprarse una casa** they've given up the idea of buying a house; **¡nada me hará d.!** nothing will make me give up!

(**b**) *Der* **d. de una demanda** to abandon a lawsuit; **d. de un recurso** to withdraw an appeal; **d. de un derecho** to waive a right

deslavazado, -a *adj (discurso, relato)* disjointed, rambling; *(argumentación)* incoherent

deslave *nm Am* landslide, *Br* landslip *(caused by flooding or rain)*

desleal *adj (persona, acto)* disloyal (**a** *o* **con** to); **su amigo le fue d.** his friend was disloyal to him; **fue d. a sus principios** he didn't remain true to his principles, he betrayed his principles

deslealmente *adv* disloyally

deslealtad *nf* disloyalty; **un acto de d.** an act of disloyalty, a disloyal act

desleír [56] *vt (diluir)* to thin; *(disolver)* to dissolve; **deslíe la yema con un poco de agua** thin the egg yolk with a little water; **la temperatura del agua desleyó el hielo rápidamente** the heat of the water quickly melted the ice

deslenguado, -a 1 *adj* foul-mouthed

2 *nm,f* foul-mouthed person; **eres un d.** you've got a really foul mouth

deslía *etc ver* **desleír**

desliar [32] *vt* to unwrap

deslíe *etc ver* **desleír**

desligar [38] 1 *vt* (**a**) *(desatar)* to untie (**b**) *(separar)* to separate (**de** from); **en política conviene d. lo privado de lo público** in politics it's advisable to keep one's private and public lives separate

2 **desligarse** *vpr* (**a**) *(desatarse)* to untie oneself (**b**) *(separarse)* to become separated (**de** from); *(distanciarse)* to distance oneself (**de** from); **factores que no se pueden d.** factors that cannot be treated separately; **se desligó de la política en 1998** he left politics in 1998; **se ha ido desligando de su familia** she has gradually distanced herself from her family

deslindar *vt* (**a**) *(limitar)* to mark out (the boundaries of) (**b**) *(separar)* to define

deslinde *nm* (**a**) *(delimitación)* delimitation, demarcation (**b**) *(aclaración)* clarification, elucidation

deslió *etc ver* **desleír**

deslío *etc ver* **desleír**

desliz *nm* (**a**) *(error)* slip, error; **tener** *o* **cometer un d.** to slip up; **tuvo algunos deslices en el examen** she made a few slips in the exam; **deslices de juventud** youthful indiscretions (**b**) *(infidelidad conyugal)* lapse; **tener** *o* **cometer un d. (con alguien)** to have an adventure *o* a fling (with sb)

deslizable *adj* (**a**) *(resbaladizo)* slippery (**b**) *(corredero)* sliding

deslizamiento *nm* slide, sliding ►► ***d. de tierra*** landslide

deslizante *adj* (**a**) *(resbaladizo)* slippery (**b**) *(corredero)* sliding

deslizar [14] 1 *vt* (**a**) *(mano, objeto)* **d. algo en** to slip sth into; **le deslizó las llaves en el bolsillo** she slipped the keys into his pocket; **d. algo por algo** to slide sth along sth; **deslizó la mano por la barandilla** he ran his hand down the banister; **deslizó el trapo sobre la mesa** he ran the cloth over the table

(**b**) *(indirecta, comentario)* to slip in; **deslizó un comentario sarcástico** she slipped in a sarcastic comment

2 **deslizarse** *vpr* (**a**) *(resbalar)* to slide; **deslizarse por** to slide along; **el barco se deslizaba por la superficie** the boat glided along the surface; **los esquiadores se deslizaban por la nieve** the skiers slid across the snow; **los niños se deslizaron por el tobogán** the children slid down the chute; **las lágrimas se deslizaban por sus mejillas** tears ran down his cheeks; **el agua se desliza mansamente río abajo** the water flows gently downriver

(**b**) *(escabullirse)* to slip; **una lagartija se deslizó entre las rocas** a lizard slipped in between the rocks; **para entrar/salir tuvo que deslizarse sin que lo viera el portero** to get in/out he had to slip past the porter without being seen
(**c**) *(sujeto: error)* **deslizarse en** to creep into
(**d**) *(sujeto: tiempo, vida)* to slip away *o* by

deslomar 1 *vt (a golpes)* to thrash; *Fam* **¡como me vuelvas a gritar, te deslomo a palos!** if you shout at me again, I'm going to kick your head in!
2 **deslomarse** *vpr Fam* to break one's back, to wear oneself out; **me deslomé a estudiar, pero no aprobé** I did my head in studying, but I didn't pass

deslucido, -a *adj* (**a**) *(sin brillo) (color, tapicería, pintura)* faded; *(plata)* tarnished (**b**) *(sin gracia) (acto, ceremonia)* dull; *(actuación)* lacklustre, uninspired

deslucir [39] *vt* to spoil; **la lluvia deslució el desfile** the rain spoiled the parade; **las acusaciones deslucieron su victoria** the accusations took the shine off his victory

deslumbrador, -ora *adj* (**a**) *(luz)* dazzling (**b**) *(belleza)* dazzling, stunning; *(indumentaria, persona)* stunning

deslumbramiento *nm* (**a**) *(ceguera)* dazzling, dazzle; **sufrí un d. al mirar al sol** I was dazzled when I looked at the sun (**b**) *(confusión)* bewilderment

deslumbrante *adj* (**a**) *(luz)* dazzling (**b**) *(belleza)* dazzling, stunning; *(indumentaria)* stunning; *(concierto)* sensational; *(película, actuación)* sensational, stunning; **María estaba d.** Maria looked stunning; **poseía una voz d.** he had a sensational *o* an amazing voice

deslumbrar *vt* (**a**) *(sujeto: luz)* to dazzle (**b**) *(sujeto: belleza, persona, concierto)* to dazzle

deslustrado, -a *adj* (**a**) *(zapatos)* unpolished (**b**) *(ropa)* dingy (**c**) *(metal)* tarnished; **la madera quedó deslustrada** the wood lost its shine

deslustrar *vt* (**a**) *(zapatos)* to take the shine off (**b**) *(metal)* to tarnish; *(madera)* to take the shine off (**c**) *(victoria)* to tarnish, to take the shine off

desluzco *etc ver* **deslucir**

desmadejado, -a *adj (débil, flojo)* weak, worn out

desmadejar *vt* to wear *o* tire out

desmadrado, -a *adj Esp Fam* wild; **estar d.** to be wild *o* out of control; **una fiesta desmadrada** a really wild party

desmadrar *Fam* 1 *vt Méx* to break, to bust
2 *vi Méx* to break down
3 **desmadrarse** *vpr Esp* to go wild

desmadre *nm Fam* (**a**) *(caos)* chaos, utter confusion; **esta organización es el d. total** this organization is totally chaotic (**b**) *(desenfreno)* rave-up; **la fiesta fue un d.** the party was really wild

desmadroso, -a *adj Méx Fam* wild

desmagnetización *nf Informát* degaussing

desmalezar [14] *vt Am* to clear of undergrowth

desmán *nm* (**a**) *(exceso)* excess; **con sus desmanes ahuyenta a mis amigos** his outrageous behaviour scares off my friends; **cometer desmanes** *(gamberradas)* to behave violently; *(saqueos)* to commit excesses
(**b**) *(abuso de poder)* abuse (of power); **han denunciado los desmanes de los gobernantes** they have condemned the rulers' abuses of power
(**c**) *(animal)* Russian desman ►► ***d. del Pirineo o de los Pirineos*** Pyrenean desman

desmanchar 1 *vt Am* to remove the stains from
2 **desmancharse** *vpr Andes, PRico (apartarse)* to withdraw

desmandado, -a *adj (desobediente)* unruly

desmandarse *vpr (descontrolarse)* to get out of control; **enseguida se le desmanda la clase** he immediately loses control of the class; **se le desmandaron algunas ovejas** a few of his sheep went astray

desmano: a desmano *loc adv (fuera de alcance)* out of reach; *(fuera del camino seguido)* out of the way; **su pueblo me pilla a d.** his town is out of my way; **su casa cae muy a d.** his house is really off the beaten track

desmantelado, -a *adj* dismantled

desmantelamiento *nm* (**a**) *(de casa, fábrica)* clearing out, stripping; *(de organización)* disbanding; *(de arsenal, instalaciones)* dismantling; *(de puesto, quiosco, andamios)* taking down; **el d. de todas las bases americanas** the closing of all American bases (**b**) *(de barco)* unrigging

desmantelar *vt* (**a**) *(casa, fábrica)* to clear out, to strip; *(organización criminal)* to break up; *(arsenal, instalaciones)* to dismantle; *(quiosco, andamios)* to take down (**b**) *(barco)* to dismast, to strip of masts

desmañado, -a *adj* clumsy, awkward

desmaquillador, -ora 1 *adj* **crema/loción desmaquilladora** make-up remover
2 *nm* make-up remover

desmaquillar 1 *vt* to remove the make-up from
2 **desmaquillarse** *vpr* to take one's make-up off

desmarcado, -a *adj (en deporte)* unmarked; **quedarse d.** to lose one's marker

desmarcar [60] 1 *vt (en deporte)* to draw the marker away from
2 **desmarcarse** *vpr* (**a**) *(en deporte)* to lose one's marker (**b**) *(apartarse)* **desmarcarse de algo/alguien** to distance oneself from sth/sb

desmarque *nm* (**a**) *(en deporte)* **Rodríguez realizó un buen d.** Rodríguez lost his marker well; **buscar el d.** to try and shake off *o* lose one's marker (**b**) *(alejamiento)* **su d. de la política del gobierno ha sorprendido a todos** his disavowal of government policy has surprised everyone

desmayado, -a *adj* (**a**) *(inconsciente)* unconscious; **caer d.** to faint (**b**) *(hambriento)* **estar d. (de hambre)** to be faint with hunger (**c**) *(desvaído) (color)* pale; *(voz)* faint, weak

desmayar 1 *vi* to lose heart; **¡no desmayes!** don't lose heart!, don't be discouraged!
2 **desmayarse** *vpr* to faint

desmayo *nm* (**a**) *(físico)* fainting fit; **le dio un d.** she fainted; **sufrir un d.** to faint (**b**) *(moral)* loss of heart; **sin d.** unfalteringly; **luchar sin d.** to fight tirelessly

desmechado, -a *adj Am Fam (pelo)* untidy, tangled

desmedido, -a *adj* excessive, disproportionate

desmedirse [47] *vpr* to go too far, to go over the top

desmedrar 1 *vt (deteriorar)* to impair, to damage
2 *vi (decaer)* to decline, to deteriorate

desmedro *nm* decline, deterioration

desmejorado, -a *adj* poorly, unwell; **le encuentro un poco d.** he's not looking too well

desmejorar 1 *vt* to spoil; **ese peinado la desmejora mucho** that hairstyle does absolutely nothing for her
2 *vi* (**a**) *(enfermar)* to deteriorate, to get worse; **empezó a d. en el verano** his health began to deteriorate over the summer (**b**) *(perder cualidades, atractivo)* to go downhill, to deteriorate; **desmejoró mucho con la edad** he really went downhill as he got older
3 **desmejorarse** *vpr* (**a**) *(enfermar)* to deteriorate, to get worse (**b**) *(perder cualidades, atractivo)* to go downhill, to deteriorate

desmelenado, -a *adj* (**a**) *Fam (persona)* wild; **últimamente está d.** he's been a bit wild recently; **el equipo salió d. a por la victoria** the team went all out to win (**b**) *(cabello)* tousled, dishevelled

desmelenar 1 *vt (cabello)* to dishevel
2 **desmelenarse** *vpr* (**a**) *(sujeto: cabello)* to get into a mess, to get messed up (**b**) *Fam (desmadrarse)* to go wild (**c**) *Fam (enojarse)* to blow one's top

desmembración *nf*, **desmembramiento** *nm* (**a**) *(de cuerpo)* dismemberment; *(de miembro, extremidad)* loss (**b**) *(de partido, imperio, estado)* break-up

desmembrar [3] 1 *vt* (**a**) *(cercenar) (cuerpo)* to dismember; *(miembro, extremidad)* to cut off (**b**) *(disgregar)* to break up
2 **desmembrarse** *vpr* to break up, to fall apart; **el Estado se está desmembrando** the State is breaking up *o* falling apart

desmemoriado, -a 1 *adj* forgetful
2 *nm,f* forgetful person; **ser un d.** to be very forgetful

desmentido *nm* denial; **dar un d., hacer público un d.** to issue a denial

desmentir [63] *vt* (**a**) *(negar)* to deny; **desmintió la noticia** he denied the report; **el primer ministro desmintió a su portavoz** the prime minister contradicted his spokesperson (**b**) *(desmerecer)* to be unworthy of

desmenuzar [14] 1 *vt* (**a**) *(trocear) (pan, pastel, roca)* to crumble; *(carne)* to chop up, to cut up; *(papel)* to tear up into little pieces; **el pescado hay que dárselo desmenuzado** you have to take his fish off the bone for him (**b**) *(examinar, analizar)* to scrutinize
2 **desmenuzarse** *vpr (pan, pastel, roca)* to crumble

desmerecedor, -ora *adj* unworthy, undeserving

desmerecer [46], *Cuba* **desmeritar** 1 *vt* not to deserve, to be unworthy of
2 *vi* (**a**) *(perder mérito)* to lose value; **las hermosas flores**

desmerecían en aquel lóbrego salón the beautiful flowers didn't look their best in that gloomy room; **ganó el equipo visitante, pero el Betis no desmereció** the visiting team won, but Betis gave a good account of themselves

(**b**) *(ser inferior)* **d. (en algo) de algo/alguien** to compare unfavourably with sth/sb (in sth); **este vino no desmerece en nada de otros más conocidos** this wine easily bears comparison with other better-known ones

desmerezco *etc ver* **desmerecer**

desmeritar = **desmerecer**

desmesura *nf* lack of moderation; **comer con d.** to gorge oneself

desmesuradamente *adv* (**a**) *(excesivamente)* excessively, extremely (**b**) *(enormemente)* uncommonly, extremely

desmesurado, -a *adj* (**a**) *(excesivo)* excessive, disproportionate; **estás dando una importancia desmesurada al asunto** you're giving the issue more importance than it deserves (**b**) *(enorme)* enormous

desmidiera *etc ver* **desmedirse**

desmido *etc ver* **desmedirse**

desmiembro *etc ver* **desmembrar**

desmiento *etc ver* **desmentir**

desmigajar 1 *vt* to crumble

2 **desmigajarse** *vpr* to crumble

desmigar *vt* (**a**) *(desmigajar)* to crumble (**b**) *(quitar la miga a)* **d. una barra de pan** to remove the crumb from the centre of a baguette

desmilitarización *nf* demilitarization

desmilitarizar [14] *vt* to demilitarize

desmineralización *nf Med* demineralization

desmintiera *etc ver* **desmentir**

desmitificación *nf* **la d. de la democracia helénica** the demythologizing of ancient Greek democracy; **la d. del mundo del espectáculo** the shattering of people's illusions about show business; **la d. del presidente** the removal of the aura surrounding the president

desmitificador, -ora *adj* **revelaciones desmitificadoras de la figura de Gandhi** revelations which shatter the Gandhi myth

desmitificar [60] *vt* **el libro desmitifica la democracia helénica** the book demythologizes ancient Greek democracy; **hay que d. el mundo del espectáculo** we have to dispel people's illusions about show business; **el escándalo desmitificó al presidente** the scandal showed the president had feet of clay

desmochado, -a *adj (árbol)* polled

desmochar *vt (árbol)* to poll, to pollard

desmoche *nm (de árboles)* polling, pollarding

desmoldar *vt* to remove from its mould

desmonetización *nf Fin* demonetization, demonetarization

desmonetizar [14] *vt Fin* to demonetize, to demonetarize

desmontable *adj* (**a**) *(mueble)* that can be dismantled *o* taken apart; *(aparato, mecanismo)* that can be taken apart; **este aparato no es d.** this appliance cannot be disassembled *o* taken apart; **una estantería d.** a self-assembly bookcase; **una tienda de campaña fácilmente d.** a tent that is easy to take down (**b**) *(pieza, parte)* removable, detachable

desmontaje *nm* (**a**) *(desarme)* dismantling, disassembly (**b**) *(demolición)* demolition (**c**) *(de arma de fuego)* uncocking

desmontar 1 *vt* (**a**) *(desarmar) (máquina, mecanismo)* to take apart *o* to pieces, *Espec* to disassemble; *(mueble, librería, mesa)* to dismantle, to take to pieces; *(motor)* to strip down; *(piezas, partes)* to remove, to detach; *(rueda)* to remove, to take off; *(andamio, tablado, tienda de campaña)* to take down

(**b**) *(teoría, argumentación)* to demolish, to pull to pieces

(**c**) *(arma)* to uncock

(**d**) *(persona) (de caballo, moto, bicicleta)* to unseat; **el caballo desmontó al jinete** the horse threw its rider; **desmontó al niño de la bicicleta** he took the boy off the bicycle

(**e**) *Informát* to unmount

(**f**) *(terreno)* to level; *(área, bosque)* to clear

2 *vi* **d. de** *(caballo)* to dismount from; *(moto, bicicleta)* to get off; *(coche)* to get out of

3 **desmontarse** *vpr* **desmontarse de** *(caballo)* to dismount from; *(moto, bicicleta)* to get off; *(coche)* to get out of

desmonte *nm* (**a**) *(terreno allanado)* **un d.** an area of levelled ground (**b**) *(allanamiento)* levelling (**c**) *(de bosque)* clearing

desmoralización *nf* demoralization; **cundió la d. entre los familiares** dismay spread amongst the relatives

desmoralizado, -a *adj* demoralized

desmoralizador, -ora, desmoralizante *adj* demoralizing

desmoralizar [14] 1 *vt* to demoralize

2 **desmoralizarse** *vpr* to become demoralized, to lose heart; **ino te desmoralices, hombre!** come on, don't lose heart!

desmoronamiento *nm* (**a**) *(de edificio, roca)* crumbling, falling to pieces (**b**) *(de ideales)* crumbling; *(de persona)* going to pieces (**c**) *(de imperio, estado)* fall, collapse

desmoronar 1 *vt (edificio, roca)* to cause to crumble

2 **desmoronarse** *vpr* (**a**) *(edificio, roca)* to crumble, to fall to pieces (**b**) *(ideales)* to crumble, to fall to pieces; *(persona)* to go to pieces; **se desmoronaba mentalmente** she was going to pieces mentally; **se desmoronó a 100 metros de la llegada** he collapsed 100 metres from the finishing line (**c**) *(imperio, estado)* to collapse, to fall apart

desmotivado, -a *adj* lacking in motivation

desmotivar 1 *vt* to demotivate

2 **desmotivarse** *vpr* to get *o* become discouraged

desmovilización *nf* demobilization

desmovilizar [14] *vt* to demobilize

desnacionalización *nf* denationalization, privatization

desnacionalizar [14] *vt* to denationalize, to privatize

desnarizarse *vpr Méx Fam* **d. por hacer algo** to fall over oneself to do sth

desnatado, -a *adj (leche)* skimmed; *(yogur)* low-fat, made with skimmed milk

desnatar *vt* to skim

desnaturalización *nf* (**a**) *(de ciudadano)* denaturalization (**b**) *(de carácter)* perversion, corruption (**c**) *(de texto)* distortion (**d**) *(de sustancia)* adulteration

desnaturalizado, -a *adj* (**a**) *(sustancia)* adulterated; *(alcohol)* denatured (**b**) *(padre, madre, hijo)* unnatural, heartless

desnaturalizar [14] *vt* (**a**) *(ciudadano)* to deprive of citizenship (**b**) *(sustancia)* to adulterate; *(alcohol)* to denature

desnivel *nm* (**a**) *(cultural, social)* inequality; **ha aumentado el d. entre ricos y pobres** the gap between rich and poor has widened (**b**) *(de terreno, superficie)* **había un d. de 500 metros** there was a drop of 500 metres; **una cuesta con un d. del 15 por ciento** a gradient of 15 percent; **este sendero tiene muchos desniveles** this path goes up and down a lot

desnivelado, -a *adj (terreno, piso)* uneven; **la mesa está desnivelada** this table isn't level

desnivelar 1 *vt (terreno)* to make uneven; *(situación)* to upset the balance of; *(encuentro)* to make unequal; *(balanza)* to tip; **los votos que desnivelaron la balanza a favor de los socialistas** the votes which tipped the balance in favour of the socialists

2 **desnivelarse** *vpr* **el encuentro se desniveló con la expulsión de Ramírez** the game became a very unequal affair when Ramírez was sent off

desnucar [60] 1 *vt* to break the neck of

2 **desnucarse** *vpr* to break one's neck

desnuclearización *nf (de armas nucleares)* nuclear disarmament; *(de centrales nucleares)* = getting rid of nuclear power

desnuclearizado, -a *adj* nuclear-free

desnuclearizar [14] *vt* to make nuclear-free

desnudar 1 *vt* (**a**) *(persona)* to undress; EXPR **d. a un santo para vestir a otro** to rob Peter to pay Paul (**b**) *(cosa)* to strip (**de** of); **desnudó su discurso de toda floritura** he avoided all ornament in his speech (**c**) *Fam (quitar el dinero a)* to clean out

2 **desnudarse** *vpr* (**a**) *(quitarse la ropa)* to undress, to get undressed; **tuvo que desnudarse de cintura para arriba** he had to strip to the waist (**b**) *(despojarse)* **los árboles se desnudan de hojas en invierno** the trees lose *o* shed their leaves in autumn

desnudez *nf* (**a**) *(de persona)* nakedness, nudity (**b**) *(de cosa)* bareness; **la vasta d. de la Pampa** the vast bare expanse of the Pampas

desnudismo *nm* nudism

desnudista 1 *adj* nudist

2 *nmf* nudist

desnudo, -a 1 *adj* (**a**) *(persona, cuerpo)* naked; **nadar d.** to swim in the nude; **posó d. para "Mate"** he posed in the nude for "Mate"; **me siento d. sin mis gafas** I feel naked without my glasses; **d. de cintura para arriba/abajo** naked from the waist up/down; *Fam Fig* **necesito ir de compras porque ando d.** I need to go shopping because I haven't got a thing to wear

(**b**) *(brazo, hombro)* bare

(**c**) *(salón, pared, árbol, ramas)* bare; *(paisaje)* bare, barren; *(verdad)* plain, unvarnished

2 *nm* (**a**) *(pintura, imagen)* nude; **pintar un d.** to paint a nude; **un d.**

femenino/masculino a female/male nude; **el d. en el cine** nudity in the movies; **d. frontal** full-frontal nude; **contiene desnudos integrales** it has scenes of full-frontal nudity

(**b**) **al d.** *(a la vista)* for all to see; **el reportaje deja al d. las intrigas en el seno del partido** the article takes the lid off party in-fighting; **ésta es la verdad al d.** this is the plain, unadorned truth

desnutrición *nf* malnutrition

desnutrido, -a *adj* undernourished

desnutrirse *vpr* to become malnourished

desobedecer [46] *vt* to disobey

desobediencia *nf* disobedience ▸▸ ***d. civil*** civil disobedience; ***d. pacífica*** civil disobedience

desobediente 1 *adj* disobedient

2 *nmf* disobedient person; **es un d.** he's terribly disobedient

desocupación *nf* (**a**) *(desempleo)* unemployment (**b**) *(ociosidad)* idleness (**c**) *(desalojo)* vacation

desocupado, -a *adj* (**a**) *(persona) (sin empleo)* unemployed (**b**) *(persona) (ocioso)* free, unoccupied; **yo te llamo cuando esté más d.** I'll call you when I'm not so busy (**c**) *(asiento)* vacant, unoccupied; *(edificio, casa, apartamento)* empty; **¿está desocupada esta silla?** is this seat free? (**d**) *(tiempo)* free

desocupar 1 *vt* (**a**) *(vaciar de personas) (evacuar)* to evacuate; *(por la fuerza)* to clear (**b**) *(vaciar de cosas)* to clear, to empty; **d. un cajón/armario** to empty a drawer/wardrobe (**c**) *(abandonar) (habitación, mesa)* to leave; *(asiento)* to get out of; **desocupó su silla para cedérsela a la anciana** he gave up his seat for the old lady

2 **desocuparse** *vpr (casa, apartamento)* to become vacant; *(habitación, mesa, asiento)* to become free; **en cuanto me desocupé, salí en su busca** as soon as I was free I went out to find her; **el baño ya se ha desocupado** the bathroom is free now

desodorante 1 *adj* deodorant, deodorizing

2 *nm* deodorant; **darse** *o* **echarse** *o* **ponerse d.** to put some deodorant on; *Fam Hum* **le ha abandonado el d.** a bit of deodorant wouldn't do him any harm ▸▸ *CSur* ***d. ambiental*** air freshener; *CSur* ***d. de ambientes*** air freshener; ***d. de barra*** deodorant stick; ***d. de spray*** deodorant spray

desodorizar [14] *vt* to deodorize

desoír [44] *vt* not to listen to, to take no notice of; **d. los consejos de alguien** to ignore sb's advice

desolación *nf* (**a**) *(destrucción)* devastation (**b**) *(desconsuelo)* distress, grief; **sumir en la d. a alguien** to devastate sb

desolado, -a *adj* (**a**) *(paraje) (destruido)* devastated; *(sin vegetación)* desolate (**b**) *(persona)* devastated; **estar d. por algo** to be devastated by sth

desolador, -ora *adj* (**a**) *(devastador) (terremoto, guerra)* devastating (**b**) *(deprimente) (imagen, espectáculo)* heart-rending; *(noticia)* devastating; **ante un panorama tan d., nadie sabía cómo reaccionar** faced with such a bleak prospect, nobody knew how to react

desolar [64] 1 *vt* (**a**) *(destruir)* to devastate, to lay waste (**b**) *(afligir)* to cause anguish to; **la muerte del padre desoló a la familia** the father's death devastated the family

2 **desolarse** *vpr* to be devastated

desolladero *nm* skinning room

desollador *nm (ave)* butcherbird

desolladura *nf (arañazo)* graze

desollar [64] *vt* 1 (**a**) *(despellejar)* to skin; **si lo pillo, lo desuello (vivo)** if I catch him, I'll skin him alive (**b**) *(criticar)* to flay, to criticize

2 **desollarse** *vpr (rodillas, espalda, pies)* to graze, to take the skin off; **se desolló las manos sujetando la cuerda** holding on to the rope took the skin off his hands

desorbitado, -a *adj* (**a**) *(exagerado) (críticas, protestas, quejas)* excessive, disproportionate; *(precio)* exorbitant; **le han dado una importancia desorbitada a este asunto** they've given this matter much more importance than it merits (**b**) *(fuera de las órbitas)* **con los ojos desorbitados** pop-eyed, with one's eyes popping out of one's head

desorbitar 1 *vt* (**a**) *(descontrolar)* to send out of control; **la inflación ha desorbitado los precios** inflation has sent prices sky-high (**b**) *(exagerar)* to exaggerate, to blow out of proportion; **no desorbitemos las cosas** let's keep things in proportion

2 **desorbitarse** *vpr* to go out of control; **la inflación se ha desorbitado** inflation has gone out of control *o* through the roof

desorden *nm* (**a**) *(confusión)* disorder, chaos; *(falta de orden)* mess; **esto es un completo d.** this is absolute chaos, this is a complete mess; **no sé cómo puedes encontrar nada en medio de este d.** I don't know how you can find anything in this mess; **disculpa todo este d.** please excuse all this mess; **tu dormitorio está en d.** your bedroom is in a mess; **en esa casa reina el d.** it's chaos in this house

(**b**) *(vida desenfrenada)* excess

(**c**) **desórdenes** *(disturbios)* disturbance; **se han producido desórdenes por toda la ciudad** there have been disturbances throughout the city; **desórdenes callejeros** street disturbances

(**d**) *(alteración física)* disorder; **sufre desórdenes nerviosos/estomacales** he has a nervous/stomach complaint

desordenadamente *adv* (**a**) *(sin orden)* in a disorderly fashion; **lo guardó todo d. en la maleta** she put everything in the suitcase in a jumble (**b**) *(confusamente)* confusedly; **expuso sus ideas d.** he put forward his ideas in a very confusing way

desordenado, -a 1 *adj* (**a**) *(habitación, casa, mesa)* untidy, messy; *(persona)* untidy, messy; *(documentos, fichas)* jumbled (up); **lo tiene todo muy d.** it's all in a complete mess; **una secuencia de números desordenada** a jumbled sequence of numbers (**b**) *(vida)* disorganized; *(comportamiento)* disorderly

2 *nm,f* untidy *o* messy person; **es una desordenada** she's very untidy *o* messy

desordenar 1 *vt (habitación, casa, despacho)* to mess up, to make untidy; *(cajón, mesa)* to mess up; *(documentos, fichas)* to jumble up; *(pelo)* to mess up, to ruffle; **me han desordenado los ficheros** they've got my files out of order; **no me desordenes la ropa del armario** don't mess up the clothes in the wardrobe

2 **desordenarse** *vpr (habitación, cajón)* to get into a mess; *(documentos, fichas)* to get mixed up *o* out of order

desorejado, -a *adj* (**a**) *Andes, Pan (que tiene mal oído)* tone-deaf (**b**) *Cuba (derrochador)* wasteful (**c**) *Urug Fam (descuidado)* slapdash

desorganización *nf* disorganization

desorganizado, -a *adj* disorganized

desorganizar [14] 1 *vt* to disrupt, to disorganize; **le desorganizaron el archivo** they got her files out of order

2 **desorganizarse** *vpr* to get out of order, to get mixed up

desorientación *nf* (**a**) *(en el espacio)* disorientation (**b**) *(en la mente)* confusion

desorientado, -a *adj* (**a**) *(en el espacio)* lost; **anda completamente d.** he's totally lost (**b**) *(confuso)* confused; **tiene noventa y ocho años y anda ya algo d.** he's ninety-eight and he's a bit confused

desorientar 1 *vt* (**a**) *(en el espacio)* to disorientate, to mislead; **sus indicaciones me desorientaron aún más** his directions got me even more confused; **consiguió d. a sus perseguidores** he managed to throw his pursuers off the scent *o* trail (**b**) *(confundir)* to confuse

2 **desorientarse** *vpr* (**a**) *(en el espacio)* to lose one's way *o* bearings (**b**) *(confundirse)* to get confused

desosar [23] *vt (carne)* to bone; *(fruta) Br* to stone, *US* to pit

desovar *vi (peces, anfibios)* to spawn; *(insectos)* to lay eggs

desove *nm (de peces, anfibios)* spawning; *(de insectos)* egg-laying

desovillar 1 *vt (ovillo)* to unwind

2 **desovillarse** *vpr* to uncurl

desoxidante 1 *adj* (**a**) *Quím* deoxidizing (**b**) *(producto, agente)* rust-removing

2 *nm* (**a**) *Quím* deoxidizer, deoxidant (**b**) *(para metales)* rust remover

desoxidar *vt* (**a**) *Quím* to deoxidize (**b**) *(metales)* to remove the rust from (**c**) *(conocimientos)* to brush up

desoxirribonucleico *adj Quím* **ácido d.** deoxyribonucleic acid

despabilado, -a = **espabilado**

despabilar = **espabilar**

despachante *nm RP* ***d. de aduanas*** customs agent

despachar 1 *vt* (**a**) *(enviar) (mercancía)* to dispatch; *(paquete, envío postal)* to send; **le despacharemos el pedido por mensajero** we'll send your order by courier

(**b**) *(en tienda) (atender)* to serve; *(vender)* to sell; **¿lo despachan?** are you being served?; **despacha a esta señora** serve this lady; **no se despachan bebidas alcohólicas a menores de 18 años** *(en letrero)* alcohol is not for sale to persons under the age of 18

(**c**) *(tratar) (asunto, negocio)* to deal with; **despachó los asuntos del día con su secretario** she dealt with the day's business with her secretary

(**d**) *Fam (terminar) (trabajo, discurso)* to finish off; *(comida)* to polish off; **en media hora (se) despachó varias cervezas** he polished off *o* got through several beers in half an hour

(**e**) *Fam (despedir)* **d. a alguien (de)** *(del trabajo)* to dismiss *o* sack sb (from); **fuimos a pedir un crédito y nos despacharon con buenas palabras** we went to ask for a loan and they very politely told us where to go (**f**) *Fam (matar)* to bump off, to get rid of; **lo despacharon de un navajazo** they killed him with a knife

(**g**) *Am (facturar)* to check in

2 *vi* (**a**) *(sobre un asunto)* **d. con alguien (sobre algo)** to have a meeting with sb (about sth); **la reina despacha semanalmente con el primer ministro** the queen has a weekly meeting with the prime minister

(**b**) *(en una tienda)* to serve; **¿hasta qué hora despachan?** what time are you open till?

3 despacharse *vpr* (**a**) *(hablar francamente)* **despacharse con alguien** to give sb a piece of one's mind; **en su discurso se despachó a gusto contra el alcalde** he really let fly at the mayor in his speech

(**b**) *RP Fam (comer)* to polish off, to get through

despacho *nm* (**a**) *(oficina) (fuera de casa)* office; *(en casa)* study; **muebles y material de d.** office furniture and stationery; **trabaja en un d. de abogados** he works in a law firm *o US* office

(**b**) *(muebles)* set of office furniture

(**c**) *(establecimiento) Esp* ***d. de billetes*** ticket office; ***d. de localidades*** box office; ***d. de lotería*** lottery kiosk; ***d. de pan*** bakery, baker's (shop)

(**d**) *Com* ***d. aduanero*** customs clearance; ***d. de aduana(s)*** customs clearance

(**e**) *(venta)* sale; **los lunes no hay d. de localidades** the box office is not open on Mondays

(**f**) *(envío)* dispatch, sending

(**g**) *(comunicado) (oficial)* dispatch; *(de prensa)* communiqué; **un d. de (una) agencia** a news agency report

(**h**) *Am Formal (en carta)* **su d.** = formulaic phrase which appears immediately below name of addressee at head of formal letter

despachurramiento = **espachurramiento**

despachurrar = **espachurrar**

despacio 1 *adv* (**a**) *(lentamente)* slowly; **¿podría hablar más d., por favor?** could you speak more slowly, please?; **vamos muy d. con las reformas en la casa** the alterations to the house are going very slowly

(**b**) *esp Am (en voz baja)* in a low voice, quietly; *(sin hacer ruido)* quietly; **hablen d., que hay gente durmiendo** keep your voices down, there are people sleeping; **abrió la puerta con cuidado y salió d.** she opened the door carefully and quietly crept out

2 *interj* take it easy!; **¡d., que lo rompes!** take it easy! *o* steady on! *o* gently! you'll break it!

despaciosamente *adv Am* slowly

despacioso, -a *adj Am* slow

despacito *adv* slowly; EXPR **d. y buena letra** slowly and carefully

despampanante *adj* stunning; **una rubia d.** a stunning blonde

despanzurrar 1 *vt Fam* to cause to burst open

2 despanzurrarse *vpr* to burst (open); **se ha despanzurrado el sofá** the stuffing is coming out of the sofa

despapaye *nm Méx Fam* chaos, utter confusion

desparasitar *vt (de piojos)* to delouse

desparejado, -a *adj (calcetín, guante)* odd

desparejar *vt* to mix up

desparejo, -a *adj* uneven, variable; **la calidad es muy despareja** the quality varies a lot

desparpajo *nm Fam* (**a**) *(desenvoltura)* self-assurance; **tiene mucho d.** she's very self-assured; **con d.** with assurance, confidently (**b**) *(frescura)* cheek; **¡vaya d. que tiene este diablillo!** well, he's a cheeky little devil! (**c**) *CAm (desorden)* chaos, confusion

desparramado, -a *adj (líquido)* spilt; *(objetos, personas)* scattered; **las fotocopias quedaron desparramadas por todo el suelo** the photocopies ended up scattered *o* strewn all over the floor

desparramar 1 *vt* (**a**) *(líquido)* to spill; *(objetos, papeles)* to scatter (**b**) *(dinero)* to squander

2 *vi Esp Fam (desmadrarse)* to have a wild time

3 desparramarse *vpr (líquido)* to spill; *(objetos, papeles, personas)* to scatter, to spread out

desparrame *nm Esp Fam (caos, desmadre)* chaos, utter confusion; **la fiesta fue un verdadero d.** the party was really wild

desparramo *nm* (**a**) *(esparcimiento) (de líquido)* spillage; *(de objetos, papeles)* scattering (**b**) *Fam (desbarajuste)* **la fiesta fue un verdadero d.** the party was really wild; **¿qué es todo este d. en la cocina?** what's all this mess in the kitchen?

despatarrado, -a, espatarrado, -a *adj Fam* sprawled; **pisó mal y cayó d. en medio del arroyo** he missed his footing and fell sprawling into the middle of the stream

despatarrarse, espatarrarse *vpr Fam* to sprawl *(with one's legs wide open)*; **resbaló y se despatarró** she slipped and went sprawling; **se despatarró en el sofá y se quedó dormido** he sprawled out on the sofa and fell asleep; **la silla se despatarró con el peso** the chair's legs gave way under the weight

despavorido, -a *adj* terrified; **salir d.** to rush out in terror

despechado, -a *adj* resentful, spiteful

despecharse *vpr* to get angry

despecho 1 *nm (rencor)* spite; *(desengaño)* bitterness; **(hacer algo) por d.** (to do sth) out of spite

2 a despecho de *loc prep* in spite of, despite

despechugado, -a *adj Fam* (**a**) *(con el pecho al aire) (hombre)* barechested; *(mujer)* bare-breasted, topless (**b**) *(muy escotado) (hombre)* showing a lot of chest, with one's shirt open; *(mujer)* with a very low neckline, showing a lot of cleavage; **no salgas tan d., que te vas a congelar** don't go out with your shirt open like that or you'll freeze

despechugarse [38] *vpr Fam (hombre)* to bare one's chest, to go barechested; *(mujer)* to bare one's breasts, to go topless

despectivamente *adv* scornfully, contemptuously

despectivo, -a *adj* (**a**) *(despreciativo)* scornful, contemptuous; **hablar de algo/alguien en tono d.** to speak scornfully *o* contemptuously about sth/sb (**b**) *Ling (palabra, sufijo)* pejorative

despedazamiento *nm* (**a**) *(rotura)* breaking *o* tearing to pieces (**b**) *(ruina)* shattering

despedazar [14] *vt* **1** (**a**) *(físicamente) (objeto)* to tear apart; *(cadáver, presa, víctima)* to dismember (**b**) *(moralmente)* to shatter (**c**) *(criticar)* to tear *o* pull to pieces

2 despedazarse *vpr (objeto)* to come to pieces, to fall apart

despedida *nf* (**a**) *(adiós)* goodbye, farewell; *(en cartas, mensajes)* closing phrase; **odio las despedidas** I hate goodbyes; **como** *o* **por toda d. dijo "adiós"** he said "goodbye", and that was all the farewell we got; **dar la d. a alguien** to see sb off; **fórmulas de d.** *(para cartas)* closing phrases ►► ***d. y cierre*** *(en TV)* closedown

(**b**) *(fiesta)* farewell party; **una cena de d.** a farewell dinner; **hacer** *u* **organizar una (fiesta de) d. para alguien** to organize a farewell (party) for sb ►► ***d. de soltera*** hen party *o* night; ***d. de soltero*** stag party *o* night, *US* bachelor party

despedido, -a *adj (trabajador) (por cierre, reducción de plantilla)* redundant; *(por razones disciplinarias)* dismissed, sacked; **está** *o* **queda usted d.** consider yourself dismissed

despedir [47] **1** *vt* (**a**) *(decir adiós a)* to say goodbye to; **fuimos a despedirle a la estación** we went to see him off at the station; **nos despidió con la mano** he waved goodbye to us; **despídeme de tus padres** say goodbye to your parents for me; **despedimos así nuestra serie de documentales sobre la India** this will be the last in our series of documentaries on India; **muchos acudieron a d. el féretro al paso del cortejo fúnebre** many came to see the coffin off as the funeral procession passed; **¡vaya manera de d. el año!** what a way to see the New Year in!

(**b**) *(de un empleo) (por cierre, reducción de plantilla)* to make redundant, to lay off; *(por razones disciplinarias)* to sack, to fire

(**c**) *(lanzar, arrojar)* to fling; **la manguera despedía un chorro enorme** the hose sent out *o* shot out a huge jet of water; **el volcán dejó de d. lava** the volcano stopped spewing out lava; **salir despedido de/por/hacia algo** to fly out of/through/towards sth; **el copiloto salió despedido** the copilot shot out of his seat

(**d**) *(desprender)* to give off; **despide un olor insoportable** it gives off an unbearable smell

2 despedirse *vpr* (**a**) *(decir adiós)* to say goodbye (**de** to); **ven, despídete del abuelo** come and say goodbye to grandpa; **se despidieron emocionadamente** they had an emotional leave-taking; **los enamorados se despidieron con un beso** the lovers kissed each other goodbye; **se despide atentamente** *(en carta)* Yours sincerely/faithfully

(**b**) *(olvidar)* **si no apruebas, ya puedes despedirte de la moto** if you don't pass, you can kiss the motorbike goodbye

(**c**) *(de un empleo)* to leave one's job

despegable *adj* detachable

despegado, -a *adj (frío)* cold, indifferent (**con** towards)

despegar [38] **1** *vt* (**a**) *(pieza, etiqueta)* to remove (**de** from); **¿puedes despegarme la tirita?** can you take this *Br* plaster *o US* Band-Aid® off?; **despegue la etiqueta del envase** take the label off the container; EXPR **no despegó los labios** she didn't utter a word

(**b**) *CAm, Méx (caballos)* to unhitch

2 *vi* (**a**) *(avión)* to take off; *(cohete)* to take off, to blast off; **(estamos) listos para d.** (we're) ready for take-off

(**b**) *(empresa, equipo)* to take off; **la compañía no acaba de d.** the company hasn't really been able to take off

3 despegarse *vpr* **(a)** *(etiqueta, pegatina, sello)* to come unstuck (**de** from), to peel off; **se me despegó la venda** my bandage came undone

(b) *(persona)* **despegarse de alguien** to break away from sb; **no se despegó de su novia ni un minuto** he didn't leave his girlfriend's side for a minute; **no pudo despegarse de aquel pesado** she couldn't get rid of *o* away from that bore; **los ciclistas no consiguen despegarse del pelotón** the cyclists can't break away from the pack

despego *nm* detachment, indifference; **siento d. por mi familia** I feel detached from *o* indifferent to my family

despegue *nm* **(a)** *(de aeronave)* take-off; **(estamos) listos para el d.** (we're) ready for take-off ►► ***d. vertical*** vertical take-off **(b)** *(de empresa, proyecto)* take-off; **se produjo un d. económico en el país** the country's economy took off

despeinado, -a *adj* **(a)** *(por el viento)* windswept **(b)** *(descuidado) (pelo)* dishevelled, uncombed; **no vayas así, tan d.** don't go like that, with your hair in such a mess

despeinar 1 *vt (pelo)* to ruffle, to mess up; **d. a alguien** to mess up sb's hair; **el viento la había despeinado** the wind had ruffled *o* messed up her hair

2 despeinarse *vpr* to get one's hair messed up; EXPR *Fam* **sin despeinarse** *(sin esfuerzo)* without getting a hair out of place, easily

despejado, -a *adj* **(a)** *(tiempo, día)* clear; **tiempo seco y cielo d.** dry with clear skies

(b) *(sin sueño)* wide awake; **no estaba aún d.** he still wasn't properly awake

(c) *(lúcido)* clear-headed; **tener la mente despejada** to have a clear head; **cuando está d. es encantador, pero cuando bebe...** he's charming when he's sober, but when he drinks...

(d) *(espacioso)* spacious; **tener una frente despejada** to have a wide *o* broad forehead

(e) *(sin estorbos)* clear, uncluttered; **tener la nariz despejada** to have an unblocked nose; **seguiremos cuando el camino esté d. de nieve** we'll go on when the road is clear of snow

despejar 1 *vt* **(a)** *(habitación, camino, carretera)* to clear; *(nariz)* to unblock; *(mente)* to clear; **¡despejen la sala!** clear the room!

(b) *(pelota)* to clear; **el portero despejó la pelota a córner** the goalkeeper cleared the ball for a corner; **d. el balón de cabeza/de puños** to head/punch the ball away

(c) *(misterio, incógnita)* to clear up, to put an end to; **su respuesta no despejó mis dudas** her answer didn't clear up the things I wasn't sure about

(d) *Mat (incógnita)* to find

(e) *(persona) (de desmayo)* to bring round; **el aire fresco lo despejó** *(de aturdimiento, borrachera)* the fresh air cleared his head; **el paseo le despejó las ideas** the walk helped him get his ideas in order

2 *vi* **(a)** *(en fútbol, rugby, hockey)* to clear; **el defensa despejó a córner** the defender cleared the ball for a corner; **d. de cabeza/de puños** to head/punch the ball away

(b) *(apartarse)* **¡despejen, por favor!** move along there, please!

3 *v impersonal (aclarar el tiempo)* to clear up; *(aclarar el cielo)* to clear

4 despejarse *vpr* **(a)** *(persona)* **se fue despejando poco a poco** *(de desmayo)* he gradually came round; **se despejó con el aire fresco** *(de aturdimiento, borrachera)* the fresh air cleared his head

(b) *(misterio, incógnita)* to be cleared up

despeje *nm (en deporte)* clearance; **hacer un d.** to clear the ball, to make a clearance; **hacer un d. de cabeza/puños** to head/punch the ball clear

despellejar 1 *vt* **(a)** *(animal)* to skin; *Fam* **¡como te agarre, te despellejo vivo!** if I catch you, I'll skin you alive! **(b)** *(criticar)* to pull to pieces

2 despellejarse *vpr* to peel; **se te está despellejando la nariz** your nose is peeling

despelotado, -a *RP Fam* **1** *adj* **(a)** *(desprolijo)* messy, untidy **(b)** *(informal)* disorganized

2 *nm,f* **(a)** *(desprolijo)* untidy person **(b)** *(informal)* disorganized person

despelotar 1 *vt RP Fam* to mess up; **tratá de no d. mucho la casa** try not to leave the house in a mess

2 despelotarse *vpr Fam* **(a)** *esp Esp (desnudarse)* to strip off **(b)** *Esp (mondarse)* **despelotarse (de risa)** to laugh one's head off; **sus chistes son para despelotarse (de risa)** his jokes are hysterical *o* side-splitting **(c)** *RP (abandonarse)* to let oneself go; **en los últimos años se ha despelotado mucho** in the last few years she's really let herself go

despelote *nm Fam* **(a)** *Esp (desnudo)* **hay mucho d. en la playa** there are a lot of people *Br* starkers *o US* buck naked on the beach **(b)** *Am (caos)* chaos; **se armó un d.** there was complete chaos; **ser un d.** *(proyecto, reunión)* to be chaotic; **¡vaya d. de oficina!** this office is so chaotic! **(c)** *(cachondeo)* **tu primo es un d.** your cousin is hysterical *o* a scream; **esa película es un d.** that film is a scream

despeluchado, -a *adj* threadbare

despeluchar 1 *vt (quitar el pelo a)* **d. algo** to wear sth threadbare

2 despelucharse *vpr (pelarse)* to wear threadbare; **la alfombra se ha despeluchado por el uso** the carpet has worn threadbare with use

despeluzar *vt Cuba (dejar sin dinero)* to fleece

despenalización *nf* decriminalization

despenalizar [14] *vt* to decriminalize; **d. las drogas blandas** to decriminalize soft drugs

despenar *vt Chile (desesperanzar)* to deprive of hope

despendolado, -a *adj Esp Fam* wild

despendolarse *vpr Esp Fam* to go wild

despendole *nm* loss of control; **la fiesta fue un d.** the party was a rave-up

despensa *nf* **(a)** *(lugar) (en casa)* larder, pantry; *(en barco)* storeroom **(b)** *(provisiones)* provisions, supplies

despeñadero *nm* precipice

despeñar 1 *vt* to throw over a cliff

2 despeñarse *vpr* to fall over a cliff; **se despeñó por un acantilado** he fell off a cliff

despepitar *vt* **d. un fruto** to take the pips out of a fruit

despepitarse *vpr* **(a)** *(gritar)* to rant **(b)** *Fam (reír mucho)* **d. (de risa)** to split one's sides (laughing)

desperdiciado, -a *adj* wasted, squandered

desperdiciador, -ora 1 *adj* wasteful

2 *nm,f* spendthrift scoundrel, rogue

desperdiciar *vt (tiempo, energía, comida)* to waste; *(dinero)* to waste, to squander; *(ocasión, oportunidad)* to waste, to throw away

desperdicio *nm* **(a)** *(acción)* waste; **¡qué d. de comida!** what a waste of food!; **esto es un d. de tiempo y de dinero** this is a waste of time and money; EXPR **no tener d.: este libro no tiene d.** this book is excellent from start to finish; **el cerdo no tiene d.** no part of the pig goes to waste; **sus declaraciones no tienen d.** what he says is always worth listening to; **¡vaya cuerpo! este chico no tiene d.** what a body! that guy is a real hunk; *Irónico* **tus vecinos no tienen d., además de ser ruidosos no limpian la escalera** your neighbours don't go in for half measures, not only are they noisy, but they don't clean the stairs

(b) *(residuo)* **desperdicios** scraps

desperdigado, -a *adj* scattered (**por** over)

desperdigar [38] **1** *vt* to scatter, to disperse (**por** over)

2 desperdigarse *vpr* to scatter (**por** over)

desperezarse [14] *vpr* to stretch

desperezo *nm (estirón)* stretch, stretching

desperfecto *nm* **(a)** *(deterioro)* damage; **el paquete llegó con desperfectos** the package was damaged when it arrived; **causar** *u* **ocasionar** *o* **producir desperfectos** to cause damage; **pagar los desperfectos ocasionados** to pay for the damage caused; **sufrir desperfectos** to get damaged **(b)** *(defecto)* flaw, imperfection

despersonalizar [14] **1** *vt* to depersonalize

2 despersonalizarse *vpr* to become depersonalized

despertador *nm* **(a)** *(aparato)* alarm clock; **apagar/poner el d.** to turn off/set the alarm clock ►► ***d. telefónico*** alarm call service **(b)** *Arg (en carretera)* speed bump, *Br* sleeping policeman

despertar[1] [3] **1** *vt* **(a)** *(persona, animal)* to wake (up); **despiértame a las seis, por favor** could you wake me (up) at six, please?

(b) *(producir) (sentimientos)* to arouse; *(recuerdos)* to bring back, to revive; *(expectación)* to create, to arouse; *(debate, polémica)* to give rise to; **d. odio/pasión** to arouse hatred/passion; **el ejercicio me despierta el apetito** exercise gives me an appetite; **d. a alguien las ganas de hacer algo** to make sb want to do sth; **esta canción despierta en mí buenos recuerdos** this song brings back happy memories for me

2 *vi* **(a)** *(dejar de dormir)* to wake (up); **¡despierta, que ya hemos llegado!** wake up! we've arrived!; **despertó de repente de su sueño** she suddenly woke from her dream

(b) *(espabilar)* to wake *o* wise up

3 despertarse *vpr* to wake (up); **¡despiértate, que ya es la hora!** wake up! it's time!; **despertarse de la siesta** to wake from one's afternoon nap; **aún no me he despertado** I'm not really awake yet

despertar² *nm* (**a**) *(de sueño)* awakening; **tiene muy mal d.** he's always grumpy after he's just woken up (**b**) *(comienzo)* rise, emergence; **el d. de la civilización** the dawn of civilization

despezuñarse *vpr Andes, Hond, PRico* (**a**) *(caminar deprisa)* to go very quickly (**b**) *(esforzarse)* to exert oneself, to make an effort

despiadadamente *adv* pitilessly, mercilessly

despiadado, -a *adj (persona)* merciless; *(trato)* inhuman, pitiless; *(ataque)* savage, merciless

despidiera *etc ver* **despedir**

despido 1 *ver* **despedir**

2 *nm* (**a**) *(expulsión)* dismissal; **su falta de disciplina precipitó su d.** his lack of discipline led to his dismissal *o* sacking; **la reestructuración de la empresa significó docenas de despidos** the restructuring of the company meant dozens of redundancies ►► ***d. colectivo*** mass redundancy; ***d. forzoso*** compulsory redundancy; ***d. improcedente*** *(por incumplimiento de contrato)* wrongful dismissal; *(por ir contra el derecho laboral)* unfair dismissal; ***d. inmediato*** summary dismissal; ***d. libre*** dismissal without compensation; ***d. voluntario*** voluntary redundancy

(**b**) *(indemnización)* redundancy money *o* payment

despiece *nm (de res)* quartering; *(de carne)* cutting up; *(de aparato, motor)* dismantling

despierto, -a 1 *ver* **despertar**

2 *adj* (**a**) *(sin dormir)* awake; **¿estás d.?** are you awake? (**b**) *(espabilado, listo)* bright, sharp

despiezar *vt (res)* to quarter; *(carne)* to cut up; *(aparato, motor)* to dismantle

despilfarrador, -ora 1 *adj* wasteful, spendthrift

2 *nm,f* spendthrift, squanderer

despilfarrar *vt (dinero)* to squander, to waste; *(energía, agua, recursos)* to waste

despilfarro *nm (de dinero)* squandering, waste; *(de energía, agua, recursos)* waste; **sería un d. comprar esa lámpara** buying that lamp would be a waste of money; **¡menudo d.!** what a waste!

despintar 1 *vt (pared, puerta)* to take the paint off; *(uñas)* to take the varnish *o* polish off

2 **despintarse** *vpr (pared, puerta)* **se ha despintado** the paint has come off; **cada noche se despinta las uñas** every night she takes her nail varnish off

despiojar *vt* to delouse

despiolado, -a *RP Fam* **1** *adj* (**a**) *(desprolijo)* messy, untidy (**b**) *(informal)* feckless

2 *nm,f* (**a**) *(desprolijo)* untidy person (**b**) *(informal)* feckless person

despiolar *vt RP Fam* to mess up, to make a mess of; **si prometés que no la despiolás, te presto la casa un par de semanas** if you promise not to mess it up, I'll let you use the house for a couple of weeks

despiole *nm RP Fam* rumpus, shindy

despiporre *nm Fam* **armar un d.** to kick up a rumpus; **fue el d.** it was something else, it was really something

despistado, -a 1 *adj* (**a**) *(por naturaleza)* absent-minded; **soy muy d. para los cumpleaños** I'm hopeless at remembering birthdays

(**b**) *(momentáneamente)* distracted; **en ese momento estaba d. y no la vi** I was distracted at the time and didn't see her

(**c**) *(confuso)* muddled, mixed up; **aún se le ve d.** he still looks a bit lost *o* as if he doesn't quite know what he's doing; **nos tenías despistados a todos** you had us all fooled

2 *nm,f* **es una despistada** she's very absent-minded; **hacerse el d.** to act as if one hasn't noticed/heard/understood/*etc*; **no te hagas el d., te hablo a ti** stop acting as if you haven't heard, I'm talking to you

despistar 1 *vt* (**a**) *(dar esquinazo a)* to throw off the scent; **despistaron a sus perseguidores** they shook off their pursuers; **d. a los perros** to throw the dogs off the scent; **d. a las fans** to lose the fans (**b**) *(confundir)* to mislead; **nos despistó con sus indicaciones** he sent us the wrong way with his directions (**c**) *(distraer)* to distract; **el ruido me despista** the noise is distracting me

2 **despistarse** *vpr* (**a**) *(confundirse)* to get mixed up *o* confused; **me despisté pensando que hoy era jueves** I got mixed up *o* confused, thinking today was Thursday (**b**) *(distraerse)* to get *o* be distracted

despiste *nm* (**a**) *(distracción)* absent-mindedness, forgetfulness; **¡vaya d. que tiene!** she's so absent-minded *o* forgetful!; **¡qué d.! ¡creía que la reunión era mañana!** how forgetful of me! I thought the meeting was tomorrow!; **entraron en el edificio en un d. del vigilante** they got into the building when the nightwatchman wasn't looking; **en un momento de d. se me coló todo el mundo** everyone *Br* jumped the queue *o US* cut in line in front of me when I wasn't looking

(**b**) *(error)* mistake, slip; **el accidente se debió a un d. del conductor** the accident was caused by a mistake on the part of the driver; **tener un d.** to make a mistake, to slip up

(**c**) *(persona)* **Marta es un d.** Marta is very absent-minded *o* forgetful

despistolización *nf Méx* disarming; **campaña de d.** = government campaign to encourage people to hand in unlicensed firearms

despistolizar *vt Méx* to disarm; **quieren d. la ciudad** they want to withdraw illegal firearms from circulation in the city

desplantador *nm* trowel

desplantar *vt* to uproot, to pull up

desplante *nm* (**a**) *(grosería) (dicho)* insolent remark; *(gesto)* arrogant gesture; **hacer un d. a alguien** *(con palabras)* to be insolent to sb; *(con gesto)* to make an arrogant gesture towards sb; **le hizo el d. de no acudir a su boda** she was so rude as not to attend his wedding (**b**) *Taurom* = proud gesture made by bullfighter after a series of passes (**c**) *Chile (desenvoltura)* ease, self-confidence

desplayado *nm Arg* clearing

desplazado, -a 1 *adj* (**a**) *(desambientado)* out of place; **allí me sentía d.** I felt out of place there (**b**) *(emigrado forzoso)* displaced

2 *nm,f* displaced person; **los desplazados** displaced persons

desplazamiento *nm* (**a**) *(viaje)* journey; **los desplazamientos por carretera** road journeys, journeys by road; **gastos de d.** travelling expenses (**b**) *(traslado)* movement; **el d. de tropas a la zona** the movement of troops to the area ►► *Fís* ***d. Doppler*** Doppler shift; *Fís* ***d. hacia el rojo*** redshift (**c**) *(sustitución)* replacement (**d**) *Náut* displacement

desplazar [14] **1** *vt* (**a**) *(trasladar)* to move (**a** to); **desplazaron la sede de la empresa a otro edificio** they moved the firm's headquarters to another building; **d. algo/a alguien de** to remove sth/sb from; **el impacto lo desplazó por el aire unos metros** the impact tossed him several metres through the air

(**b**) *(tomar el lugar de)* to take the place of; **fue desplazado de su puesto por alguien más joven** he was pushed out of his job by a younger person; **la cerveza ha desplazado al vino como bebida más consumida** beer has replaced wine as the most popular drink; **el correo electrónico está desplazando al correo convencional** electronic mail is taking over from conventional mail

(**c**) *Fís* to displace

(**d**) *Náut* to displace

2 **desplazarse** *vpr* (**a**) *(viajar)* to travel; **se desplazó hasta el lugar del accidente en helicóptero** he travelled to the site of the accident by helicopter; **para desplazarse por Londres, lo mejor es el metro** the best way to get around London is on the underground

(**b**) *(moverse)* to move

desplegable 1 *adj* (**a**) *(mapa)* folded; *(libro)* pop-up (**b**) *Informát (menú)* pop-up

2 *nm (en revista)* fold-out page

desplegado *nm Méx* announcement in the press

desplegar [43] **1** *vt* (**a**) *(desdoblar) (tela, periódico, mapa)* to unfold; *(alas)* to spread, to open; *(vela, bandera)* to unfurl

(**b**) *(poner en práctica) (cualidades, conocimientos)* to use, to put to use; *(campaña)* to mount; *(estrategia)* to deploy, to use; *(actividad)* to carry out; **el gobierno desplegará todos los medios a su alcance** the government will deploy *o* use all the means at its disposal; **desplegó toda su sabiduría para encandilar al público** he used every way he knew to captivate the audience

(**c**) *(ejército, misiles)* to deploy

2 **desplegarse** *vpr* (**a**) *(desdoblarse)* to unfold, to spread out

(**b**) *(ejército)* to fan out; **el pelotón se desplegó** the platoon fanned out

despliegue *nm* (**a**) *(puesta en práctica) (de cualidades, conocimientos)* display; *(de recursos, estrategias)* use; **llevaron a cabo la campaña electoral con un gran d. de medios** they used a vast range of resources in their election campaign; **el impresionante d. técnico para retransmitir los campeonatos** the impressive range of technical wizardry used to broadcast the championships

(**b**) *(de ejército)* deployment ►► ***d. de misiles*** missile deployment

desplomar 1 *vt Ven (regañar)* to scold, to reprimand

2 **desplomarse** *vpr* (**a**) *(caer) (persona, edificio, andamio)* to collapse; *(techo)* to fall *o* cave in; **se desplomó agotado en el sillón** he collapsed exhausted into the chair (**b**) *(hundirse) (divisa, bolsa, precios)* to plummet; *(gobierno)* to collapse, to fall; *(imperio, sistema)* to collapse

desplome *nm* (**a**) *(caída) (de persona, edificio, andamio)* collapse; **el d. del techo los pilló desprevenidos** they weren't prepared for the roof caving in (**b**) *(hundimiento) (de divisa)* slump in value; *(de* *cotización, precios)* slump; *(de gobierno)* collapse, fall; *(de imperio, sistema)* collapse; **el d. de las bolsas asiáticas** the crash of *o* slump in the Asian stock markets (**c**) *(saledizo)* overhang

desplumar *vt* (**a**) *(ave)* to pluck (**b**) *Fam (dejar sin dinero) (en el juego)* to clean out; **un ladrón me desplumó** a thief took all my money

despoblación *nf* depopulation

despoblado, -a 1 *adj* unpopulated, deserted; **el centro de la ciudad se queda d. por la noche** the city centre is deserted at night
2 *nm* deserted spot

despoblar 1 *vt* (**a**) *(de gente)* to depopulate (**b**) *(de vegetación)* to clear
2 **despoblarse** *vpr* to become depopulated

despojar 1 *vt* **d. a alguien de algo** to strip sb of sth; **la despojaron de su cargo** she was removed from her post; **los árboles despojados de sus hojas** the trees stripped of their leaves; **la despojaron de todas las joyas** they robbed her of all her jewellery; **fue despojado de todos sus derechos** he was stripped of all his rights
2 **despojarse** *vpr* **despojarse de algo** *(bienes, alimentos)* to give sth up; *(ropa, adornos)* to take sth off; *(prejuicios)* to rid oneself of sth

despojo *nm* (**a**) *(acción)* stripping, plundering (**b**) **despojos** *(de animales)* = head, feet, intestines and other rarely eaten parts (**c**) **despojos** *(de comida)* leftovers (**d**) **despojos** *(cadáver)* remains (**e**) *(escoria)* **es un d. humano** he's a (physical/mental) wreck (**f**) *Literario (víctima)* prey, victim; **la juventud es d. del tiempo** youth eventually falls prey to time

despolitizar [14] *vt* to depoliticize

desportillado, -a *adj* chipped

desportilladura *nf* chip

desportillar 1 *vt* to chip
2 **desportillarse** *vpr* to get chipped

desposado, -a *nm,f Formal (hombre)* groom; *(mujer)* bride; **los desposados** the newlyweds

desposar *Formal* 1 *vt* (**a**) *(sujeto: cura)* to marry (**b**) *(sujeto: contrayente)* to marry
2 **desposarse** *vpr* to get married, to marry

desposeer [37] 1 *vt* **d. a alguien de algo** to dispossess sb of sth; **la federación de boxeo lo desposeyó de su título** the boxing federation stripped him of his title; **fue desposeído de sus derechos** he was stripped of his rights; **un hombre desposeído de todos sus bienes** a man deprived of all his possessions
2 **desposeerse** *vpr* **desposeerse de** to renounce, to give up

desposeído, -a 1 *adj* (**a**) *(pobre)* poor, dispossessed (**b**) **d. de** *(carente)* lacking (in)
2 *nm,f* **los desposeídos** the have-nots, the wretched, the dispossessed

desposeyera *etc ver* **desposeer**

desposorios *nmpl Formal* (**a**) *(compromiso)* betrothal (**b**) *(matrimonio)* marriage, wedding

despostar *vt Andes, RP (res)* to carve up, to quarter

déspota *nmf* (**a**) *(gobernante)* despot (**b**) *(persona autoritaria)* tyrant; **es un d. con sus hijos** he's a tyrant with his children

despóticamente *adv* despotically

despótico, -a *adj* despotic

despotismo *nm* despotism ▸▸ *Hist* ***d. ilustrado*** enlightened despotism

despotricar [60] *vi* to rant on (**contra** *o* **de** about); **se puso a d. contra el gobierno** he launched into a tirade against the government, he started ranting on about the government; **deja de d. del jefe** stop ranting on about the boss

despreciable 1 *adj* (**a**) *(indigno)* despicable, contemptible (**b**) *(de poca importancia)* negligible; **nada d.** considerable, significant; **la nada d. suma de $1.000** the not inconsiderable *o* insignificant sum of $1,000
2 *nmf* despicable *o* contemptible person, wretch

despreciar *vt* (**a**) *(desdeñar)* to look down on, to scorn; **lo desprecian por su egoísmo** they look down on him because of his selfishness; **no sabes cómo te desprecio** you can't imagine how much I despise you
(**b**) *(rechazar)* to spurn; **ha despreciado muchas ofertas** he has rejected many offers; **tómeselo, no me lo desprecie** take it, don't turn it down
(**c**) *(ignorar)* to scorn, to disregard; **despreció el mal tiempo y se fue a esquiar** scorning *o* disregarding the poor weather, he went skiing

despreciativamente *adv* scornfully, contemptuously

despreciativo, -a *adj (tono, mirada, actitud)* scornful, contemptuous

desprecintar *vt* to unseal; **sin d.** *(televisor, vídeo)* still in its box, unused

desprecio *nm* (**a**) *(desdén)* scorn, contempt; **siente un d. especial por los grandes estudios cinematográficos** he feels particular contempt for the big movie studios; **con d.** scornfully, contemptuously; **habla con d. de todo el mundo** she speaks contemptuously *o* scornfully of everyone, she speaks of everyone with contempt; **una mirada/un gesto de d.** a scornful *o* contemptuous look/gesture
(**b**) *(acto despreciativo)* snub; **hacer un d. a alguien** to snub sb
(**c**) *(desinterés)* disregard; **muestran un d. olímpico por los derechos humanos** they show complete disregard for human rights

desprender 1 *vt* (**a**) *(lo que estaba fijo)* to remove, to detach; **desprenda la pegatina y envíenosla** remove the sticker and send it to us; **el viento ha desprendido esta contraventana** the wind has pulled this shutter off; **desprendió los alfileres del vestido** she took the pins out of the dress
(**b**) *(olor, luz, calor)* to give off
(**c**) *RP (desabrochar)* to undo
2 **desprenderse** *vpr* (**a**) *(soltarse)* to come *o* fall off; **la etiqueta se desprendió del vestido** the label came *o* fell off the dress; **se te ha desprendido un botón** you've lost a button; **se está desprendiendo la pintura del techo** the paint is coming off the ceiling
(**b**) *(librarse)* **desprenderse de** to get rid of; **despréndete de todas esas ideas anticuadas** get rid of *o* forget all those old-fashioned ideas
(**c**) *(renunciar)* **desprenderse de** to part with, to give up; **no nos queremos d. de la mesa** we don't want to part with the table
(**d**) *(apartarse)* **jamás se desprende de su amuleto** he is never without his lucky charm; **no se desprendía de su madre** she wouldn't leave her mother's side
(**e**) *(deducirse)* **¿qué conclusiones se desprenden de esta decisión?** what conclusions can be drawn from this decision?; **de sus palabras se desprende que...** from his words it is clear *o* it can be seen that...

desprendido, -a *adj (generoso)* generous

desprendimiento *nm* (**a**) *(separación)* detachment ▸▸ ***d. de matriz*** prolapsed uterus, prolapse of the uterus; ***d. de retina*** detached retina, retinal detachment; ***d. de tierras*** landslide (**b**) *(de humos, gases)* giving off, emission (**c**) *(generosidad)* generosity

despreocupación *nf* (**a**) *(tranquilidad)* carefree state of mind, lack of worry; **con d.** in a carefree manner; **vive con total d.** she leads a completely carefree life, she's totally laid-back (**b**) *(negligencia)* lack of concern, unconcern; **con d.** in an offhand way

despreocupadamente *adv* in a carefree manner

despreocupado, -a *adj* (**a**) *(libre de preocupaciones)* carefree; **vive d.** he's very happy-go-lucky *o* laid-back; **es demasiado d.** he doesn't take things seriously enough, he's too laid-back (**b**) *(negligente)* unconcerned

despreocuparse *vpr (dejar de preocuparse)* to stop worrying; **tú despreocúpate, que yo me encargo** stop worrying *o* don't you worry, I'll take care of it; **d. de** *(dejar de preocuparse por)* to stop worrying about; *(desatender)* not to bother about; **se despreocupaban de los alumnos** they didn't bother about *o* pay proper attention to the pupils

despresado, -a *adj Andes* jointed

despresar *vt Andes* to joint

desprestigiado, -a *adj* discredited

desprestigiar 1 *vt* to discredit; **aquello lo desprestigió ante la opinión pública** that discredited him in the eyes of the public
2 **desprestigiarse** *vpr* **se ha desprestigiado como médico** he has damaged his reputation as a doctor

desprestigio *nm* (**a**) *(pérdida de prestigio)* discredit; **es un d. verse envuelto en este asunto** it's damaging to our reputation *o* good name to be involved in this business; **la acusación de fraude supone un d. para la empresa** the accusation of fraud will damage the company's reputation *o* good name
(**b**) *(falta de prestigio)* **el d. de esta empresa crece cada día** this company's reputation gets worse every day

despresurización *nf* depressurization; **en caso de d. de la cabina** *(en avión)* if there is a sudden fall in cabin pressure

despresurizar 1 *vt* to depressurize
2 **despresurizarse** *vpr* to depressurize

desprevenido, -a *adj* unprepared; **pillar** *o Esp* **coger d. a alguien** to catch sb unawares, to take sb by surprise; **el golpe lo pilló d.** the blow caught him off guard; **una decisión que pilló a todo el mundo d.** a decision which took everyone by surprise

desprogramar *vt* (**a**) *(vídeo)* to cancel the timer settings on (**b**) *(persona)* to deprogramme

desprolijidad *nf RP* untidiness, sloppiness; **siempre me llaman la atención por mi d.** they're always telling me off for being so untidy *o* sloppy; *Fam* **las cosas se han hecho con mucha d.** things have been done really sloppily

desprolijo, -a *adj RP (casa)* messy, untidy; *(cuaderno)* untidy; *(persona)* unkempt, dishevelled

desproporción *nf* disproportion

desproporcionado, -a *adj* disproportionate; **el jardín está d. en relación con la casa** the garden is the wrong size for the house; **la figurita del niño está desproporcionada con respecto a las de San José y la Virgen** the figure of the child is out of proportion to those of St Joseph and the Virgin; **una condena desproporcionada para el delito cometido** a sentence disproportionate *o* out of proportion to the crime committed; **recibió críticas de una dureza desproporcionada** he was criticized with unwarranted severity

desproporcionar *vt* to disproportion

despropósito *nm* (**a**) *(comentario absurdo)* stupid thing to say; **fue un d.** it was a stupid thing to say; **decir despropósitos** to say stupid things, to talk nonsense (**b**) *(acción absurda)* stupid thing to do; **sería un d. invertir en bolsa ahora** it would be stupid to invest on the stock market now

desproteger *vt Informát (programa)* to hack into

desprotegido, -a *adj* unprotected; **dejar el marco d.** *(en deportes)* to leave the goal undefended

desprovisto, -a *adj* **d. de** lacking in, devoid of; **un hombre totalmente d. de modales** a man with absolutely no manners; **animales desprovistos de dientes** animals that lack teeth, animals with no teeth; **la casa está desprovista de comodidades** the house lacks modern conveniences

despuebla *etc ver* **despoblar**

DESPUÉS 1 *adv* (**a**) *(en el tiempo) (más tarde)* afterwards, later; *(entonces)* then; *(justo lo siguiente)* next; **poco d.** soon after; **mucho d.** much later; **un año d.** a year later; **años d.** years later; **d. de Cristo** AD; **ellos llegaron d.** they arrived later; **llamé primero y d. entré** I knocked first and then I went in; **primero vienen los elefantes, luego los malabaristas y d. los payasos** first come the elephants, then the jugglers and then *o* after them the clowns; **yo voy d.** it's my turn next; **nos veremos d.** see you later; **ahora todo son risitas, d. vendrán los lloros** you may be giggling now, but you'll be crying later; **d. de** after; **llegó d. de ti** she arrived after you; **d. de él, nadie lo ha conseguido** no one else has done it since he did; **d. de hacer algo** after doing sth; **d. de hervir la pasta, añada la salsa** once the pasta is cooked, add the sauce; **d. de desayunar** after breakfast; **iqué pena que no ganaran, d. de lo bien que lo hicieron!** what a shame they lost after playing so well!; **d. de que** after; **d. de que amanezca** after dawn; **d. de que te fueras a la cama** after you went to bed; **d. de que lo hice** after I did it, after doing it; **d. de todo lo que han hecho por ti, ¿cómo puedes tratarlos tan mal?** how can you treat them so badly, after everything they've done for you?; **llegó d. que yo** she arrived after I did *o* after me

(**b**) *(en el espacio)* next, after; **¿qué viene d.?** what comes next *o* after?; **hay una farmacia y d. está mi casa** there's a chemist's and then there's my house; **varios bloques d.** several blocks further on; **está 2 kilómetros d. del pueblo** it's 2 kilometres past the village; **nos bajaremos cinco paradas d.** we get off five stops later; **d. de usted** *(al dejar pasar)* after you

(**c**) *(en una lista, jerarquía)* further down; **d. de** after; **d. de él, soy el primero de la clase** after him, I'm the best in the class; **d. del vino, la cerveza es la bebida más popular** after wine, beer is the most popular drink; **quedó d. del atleta ruso** he finished behind the Russian athlete; **primero viene el deber, y d. el placer** business before pleasure

2 **después de todo** *loc adv* after all; **d. de todo, no nos podemos quejar** we can't complain, after all

---

despuntar 1 *vt* (**a**) *(romper la punta de)* to break the point off (**b**) *(desgastar la punta de)* to blunt

2 *vi* (**a**) *(brotar) (flor, capullo)* to bud; *(planta)* to sprout (**b**) *(destacar)* to excel, to stand out; **despunta en francés** she excels in French; **despunta por su inteligencia** his intelligence makes him stand out (**c**) *(comenzar) (alba)* to break; *(día)* to dawn; **al d. el alba/día** at dawn/daybreak; **saldremos de viaje apenas despunte el día** we'll set off at the crack of dawn

3 **despuntarse** *vpr (tijeras, cuchillo)* to go blunt; *(lápiz)* to go blunt, to lose its point

despunte *nm Arg, Chile (leña menuda)* twigs

desquiciado, -a *adj (persona)* demented, unhinged; **nos tiene desquiciados con sus ruidos** he's driving us up the wall with the noises he makes; **el cansancio y el estrés lo tienen d.** tiredness and stress have got him at the end of his tether; **tengo los nervios desquiciados** my nerves are in shreds *o* tatters

desquiciante *adj* maddening

desquiciar 1 *vt* (**a**) *(puerta, ventana)* to unhinge (**b**) *(persona)* to drive mad; **ese ruido me desquicia los nervios** that noise is driving me up the wall

2 **desquiciarse** *vpr* (**a**) *(puerta, ventana)* to come off its hinges (**b**) *(persona)* to go mad; **se desquicia con cualquier cosa** the least thing sets him off

desquicio *nm Am* chaos, bedlam; **esta oficina es un d.** this office is absolute chaos *o* bedlam

desquitar 1 *vt (descontar)* to deduct

2 **desquitarse** *vpr (vengarse)* to get one's own back (**de algo/alguien** for sth/on sb); **dijo que volvería para desquitarse** he said he would come back to get even; **con este triunfo el equipo se desquita de las últimas derrotas** with this win the team has made up for its recent defeats

desquite *nm* revenge; **dame el d.** give me a chance to get even (with you); **tomarse el d.** to get one's own back

desratización *nf* rodent extermination

desratizar [14] *vt* to clear of rodents

desregulación *nf* deregulation

desregular *vt* to deregulate

desrielar *vi Andes, CAm, Ven (descarrilar)* to derail

desriñonar *Fam* 1 *vt (cansar)* to do in; **la sesión de gimnasio lo dejó desriñonado** he'd had it *o Br* he was completely knackered after the session in the gym

2 **desriñonarse** *vpr (cansarse)* **se desriñona trabajando** she breaks her back working; **no muevas el armario tú solo, que te vas a d.** don't try and move the wardrobe on your own or you'll do yourself an injury

destacable *adj* notable, worthy of comment; **lo más d. de la película fue...** the most notable thing about the movie was...; **un resumen con lo más d. de la jornada futbolística** a summary with today's soccer highlights

destacado, -a *adj* (**a**) *(persona)* distinguished, prominent; *(acto)* outstanding; **era uno de nuestros alumnos más destacados** he was one of our most outstanding pupils; **tuvo una destacada actuación** her performance was outstanding

(**b**) *(tropas)* stationed; *(corresponsales)* assigned, sent; **las tropas destacadas en Bosnia** the troops stationed in Bosnia; **conectamos con nuestra unidad móvil destacada en la zona** we're going over to our mobile unit in the area itself

destacamento *nm* (**a**) *(de tropas)* detachment (**b**) *Am* ***d. de policía*** *(comisaría)* police station

destacar [60] 1 *vt* (**a**) *(poner de relieve)* to emphasize, to highlight; **debo d. lo importante que es la operación** I must stress *o* emphasize how important the operation is; **cabe d. que...** it is important to point out that...; **hay que d. el trabajo de los actores** the acting deserves special mention (**b**) *(tropas)* to station; *(corresponsales)* to assign, to send

2 *vi (sobresalir)* to stand out; **tiene afán por d.** she is keen to excel; **destacó como concertista de piano** he was an outstanding concert pianist; **hay una alumna que destaca de los demás/entre todos** there is one student who stands out from the others/from all the others; **destaca en sus estudios** she is an outstanding student; **destaca entre sus otras novelas por su humor** it stands out from her other novels for *o* because of its humour; **destaca mucho por su imponente físico** he really stands out because of his impressive physique; **un pueblo que no destaca por nada en particular** a town that is not remarkable for anything in particular, a rather unremarkable town

3 **destacarse** *vpr* (**a**) *(sobresalir)* to stand out (**de/por** from/because of); **el actor se destacó por sus dotes de cómico** the actor was outstanding in comic roles (**b**) *(aventajarse)* to draw ahead (**de** of) (**c**) *(objeto)* to stand out

destajar *vt Ecuad, Méx (res)* to quarter

destajo *nm* piecework; **trabajar a d.** *(por trabajo hecho)* to do piecework; *(mucho)* to work flat out

destapado, -a *adj* (**a**) *(caja)* open, with the lid off; *(olla)* uncovered, with the lid off; *(botella)* open, with the top off (**b**) *(descubierto)* uncovered; **no dejes la comida destapada** don't leave food uncovered; **en verano duermo d.** I sleep without any covers on in summer

destapador *nm Am* bottle opener

destapar 1 *vt* (**a**) *(caja, botella)* to open; *(olla)* to take the lid off
(**b**) *(descubrir)* to uncover, to take the cover off
(**c**) *(en la cama)* to pull the covers *o* bedclothes off; **cada vez que te das la vuelta me destapas** every time you turn over you pull the bedclothes off me
(**d**) *(trama)* to uncover
(**e**) *(oídos)* to unblock
2 *vi Méx (caballo)* to bolt
3 **destaparse** *vpr* (**a**) *(desabrigarse)* to lose the covers; **el bebé se destapa por las noches** the baby kicks the blankets off at night
(**b**) *(oídos)* to become unblocked
(**c**) *(dar la sorpresa)* **se destapó como un gran cocinero** he revealed himself to be a great cook
(**d**) *(revelarse)* to open up; **al final se destapó el escándalo** in the end the scandal came to light
(**e**) *(desnudarse)* to take one's clothes off

destape *nm* (**a**) *(en revistas)* nude photos; *(en películas, teatro)* nudity; **película de d.** erotic movie *o Br* film; **revista de d.** nudie magazine (**b**) *Méx Fam* = public announcement of a party's official election candidate

destaponar *vt* (**a**) *(botella)* to uncork (**b**) *(oídos, nariz)* to unblock (**c**) *(atasco, taponamiento)* to unblock

destartalado, -a *adj* (**a**) *(viejo, deteriorado)* dilapidated (**b**) *(desordenado)* untidy

desta *nf Méx Fam* thingmajig

deste, -a *Méx Fam* 1 *nm,f (persona)* what's-his-name, *f* what's-her-name; **la desta me mandó una carta el otro día** what's-her-name sent me a letter the other day
2 *nm* (**a**) *(objeto)* thingmajig; **pásame el d.** pass me that thingmajig (**b**) *(como muletilla)* well, er, um; **d., ¿qué te estaba diciendo?** er, what was I saying?

destejer *vt* (**a**) *(tejido)* to undo, to unravel (**b**) *(cosido)* to unstitch

destellar *vi (diamante, ojos)* to sparkle; *(metal)* to glint; *(estrella)* to twinkle; **una luz/el faro destellaba a lo lejos** a light/the lighthouse was flashing in the distance

destello *nm* (**a**) *(de diamante)* sparkle; *(de metal)* glint; *(de estrella)* twinkle; **el diamante lanzaba destellos** the diamond sparkled (**b**) *(manifestación momentánea)* **un d. de esperanza** a glimmer of hope; **un partido con destellos de buen fútbol** a match with the odd moment of good football; **un d. de ironía** a hint of irony

destemplado, -a *adj* (**a**) *(persona)* **me siento un poco d.** I'm feeling out of sorts *o* under the weather (**b**) *(instrumento)* out of tune (**c**) *(tiempo, clima)* unpleasant (**d**) *(carácter, actitud)* irritable (**e**) *(voz, tono)* harsh, jarring

destemplanza *nf* (**a**) *(malestar)* indisposition; **tener d.** to feel out of sorts *o* under the weather (**b**) *(del tiempo, clima)* unpleasantness (**c**) *(del pulso)* irregularity, unevenness (**d**) *(en el tono, las palabras)* harshness

destemplar 1 *vt* (**a**) *(instrumento)* to put out of tune (**b**) *(causar malestar a)* **este tiempo me destempla** this weather makes me feel out of sorts (**c**) *(alterar)* to disturb the order *o* harmony of
2 **destemplarse** *vpr* (**a**) *(sentir malestar)* to feel out of sorts *o* under the weather (**b**) *(irritarse)* to get upset (**c**) *(instrumento musical)* to get out of tune (**d**) *(cuchillo, espada)* to lose its edge (**e**) *Andes, Guat, Méx (sentir dentera)* to have one's teeth on edge

destemple *nm* (**a**) *(de instrumento)* dissonance (**b**) *(de cuchillo, espada)* lack of edge, dullness (**c**) *(indisposición)* indisposition

destender [66] *vt* (**a**) *(ropa)* to take off the line (**b**) *Am (cama)* to strip; *(mesa)* to take the cloth off

destensar 1 *vt (músculo)* to relax; *(cuerda, cable)* to slacken
2 **destensarse** *vpr (cuerda, cable)* to slacken, to sag

desteñido, -a *adj (descolorido)* faded; *(manchado)* discoloured

desteñir [47] 1 *vt (decolorar)* to fade, to bleach; *(manchar)* to discolour
2 *vi* to run; **estos pantalones destiñen** the colour in these trousers runs
3 **desteñirse** *vpr* to fade; **se me destiñó la falda** the colour in my skirt has run

desternillante *adj* hysterically funny

desternillarse *vpr* **d. de risa** to split one's sides laughing *o* with laughter

desterrado, -a *nm,f* exile

desterrar [3] *vt* (**a**) *(persona)* to banish, to exile (**b**) *(idea)* to dismiss; *(dudas, recelos)* to banish (**c**) *(costumbre, hábito)* to do away with; *(prejuicios)* to root out

destetar 1 *vt (niño, cría, cachorro)* to wean
2 **destetarse** *vpr* (**a**) *(niño, cría, cachorro)* to be weaned (**b**) *Hum (independizarse)* to learn to fend for oneself; **no se destetó hasta los veinticinco años** he didn't leave the family nest till he was twenty-five (**c**) *Fam (enseñar el pecho)* to bare one's breasts; *(en la playa)* to go topless

destete *nm (de niño, cría, cachorro)* weaning

destiempo: a destiempo *loc adv* (**a**) *(en mal momento)* at the wrong time; **hacer un comentario a d.** to say something at the wrong time (**b**) *(sin sincronía)* out of time; **desfilaban a d.** they were marching out of step; **golpear la bola a d.** to mistime one's stroke; **entró al delantero a d. y cometió penalti** he mistimed his tackle on the forward and conceded a penalty

destierro 1 *ver* **desterrar**
2 *nm* (**a**) *(exilio) (fuera del país)* exile; *(dentro del país)* internal exile; **fue condenado al d.** he was sentenced to exile; **emprender el d.** to go into exile; **en el d.** in exile; **marchar al d.** to go into exile (**b**) *(de costumbres, tradiciones)* elimination

destilación *nf* distillation ►► *Quím* ***d. fraccionada*** fractional distillation

destilado *nm* distillate

destilador *nm* distiller

destilar 1 *vt* (**a**) *(agua, alcohol)* to distil (**b**) *(sangre, pus)* to ooze (**c**) *(cualidad, sentimiento)* to exude, to ooze; **sus comentarios destilan ironía** her remarks are steeped in *o* suffused with irony
2 *vi (gotear)* to trickle, to drip

destilería *nf* distillery

destinado, -a *adj* (**a**) *(predestinado)* **(estar) d. a algo/hacer algo** (to be) destined for sth/to do sth; **es una tradición destinada a morir** it is a tradition that is on its way out *o* dying out; **un pueblo d. a luchar** a people destined to fight; **estar d. al éxito/fracaso** to be destined to succeed/fail
(**b**) *(dirigido)* **d. a** *(cantidad, edificio)* allocated to, set aside for; *(medidas, programa)* aimed at; **fondos destinados a la lucha contra el cáncer** funds allocated to the fight against cancer; **un estadio d. a albergar los próximos Juegos Olímpicos** a stadium intended to host the next Olympic Games; **una reforma destinada a fomentar la inversión** a reform designed to encourage *o* aimed at encouraging investment
(**c**) *(enviado)* **d. a** *(carta, paquete)* addressed to; *(mercancía)* bound for
(**d**) *(con cierto puesto) (funcionario, embajador, militar)* **está d. en Colombia** he's been posted *o* sent to Colombia

destinar *vt* (**a**) *(dirigir, consagrar)* **d. algo a** *o* **para** *(cantidad, edificio)* to set sth aside for; *(medidas, programa, publicación)* to aim sth at; **han destinado el salón a oficina** they're using the lounge as an office; **el dinero recogido se destinará a comprar medicinas** the money collected will go to buy medicine; **¿no podría el ayuntamiento d. este edificio a mejor fin?** couldn't the council find a better use for this building?; **el gobierno destinará una importante partida presupuestaria para Sanidad** the government will allocate a significant proportion of the budget to the Department of Health
(**b**) *(enviar)* **d. algo a** *(carta, paquete)* to address sth to; *(mercancía)* to send sth to
(**c**) *(conceder puesto a)* **d. a alguien a** *(plaza, lugar)* to post *o* send sb to; **fue destinado como cónsul a Liverpool** he was posted to Liverpool as consul

destinatario, -a *nm,f* (**a**) *(de carta, paquete, mercancía)* addressee; **d. desconocido** *(en carta)* not known at this address (**b**) *(de giro o transferencia bancarios)* payee (**c**) *(de halagos)* object; *(de obsequios)* recipient; *(de insultos)* butt, target

destino *nm* (**a**) *(sino)* destiny, fate; **su d. era convertirse en estrella de cine** she was destined to become a movie *o Br* film star; **sigue tocando, tu d. está en la música** keep playing, your future lies in music; **nunca se sabe lo que el d. te puede deparar** you never know what fate might have in store for you; **el d. quiso que se conocieran** it came about that they met each other
(**b**) *(finalidad)* use, function; **la oposición pidió explicaciones sobre el d. del dinero recaudado** the opposition asked for an explanation of what the money raised was going to be used for; **productos con d. al consumo humano** products for human consumption
(**c**) *(rumbo)* **(ir) con d. a** (to be) bound for *o* going to; **un vuelo con d. a...** a flight to...; **el tren con d. a La Paz** the train for La Paz, the La Paz train; **pasajeros con d. a Chicago, embarquen por puerta 6** passengers flying to Chicago, please board at gate 6
(**d**) *(lugar de llegada)* destination; **llegamos tarde a nuestro d.** we arrived late at our destination; **uno de los destinos preferidos del**

turista europeo a favourite tourist destination for Europeans
(**e**) *(empleo, plaza)* posting; **un d. en el frente de guerra** a posting at the front; **le han dado un d. en las Canarias** he's been posted to the Canaries; **estar en expectativa de d.** to be awaiting a posting

destitución *nf (de alto ejecutivo, entrenador)* dismissal; *(cargo público)* removal from office

> **Falso amigo**: El sustantivo inglés **destitution** no es la traducción del español **destitución**. En inglés, **destitution** significa "indigencia".

destituir [34] *vt (alto ejecutivo, entrenador)* to dismiss; *(cargo público)* to remove from office; **lo destituyeron del puesto de tesorero** he was dismissed from his post as treasurer; **fue destituido de su cargo (de** *o* **como ministro)** he was relieved of his post (as minister), he was removed from office

destornillado, -a *adj Fam* crazy, harebrained

destornillador *nm* (**a**) *(herramienta)* screwdriver (**b**) *Fam (bebida)* screwdriver

destornillar 1 *vt* to unscrew
2 destornillarse *vpr* to become unscrewed *o* loose

destrabar *vt* (**a**) *(desatar)* to untie (**b**) *(apartar)* to separate, to disconnect

destrenzar [14] *vt (cabello)* to unplait, to unbraid; *(cuerda)* to unpick

destreza *nf* skill, dexterity; **tiene d. para la costura** he's very good at sewing; **hacer algo con d.** to do sth skilfully

destripador, -ora *nm,f* butcher, brutal murderer; **Jack el D.** Jack the Ripper

destripar *vt* (**a**) *(sacar las tripas a) (ave, res, conejo)* to disembowel; *(pescado)* to gut; **el asesino destripaba a sus víctimas** the murderer disembowelled his victims (**b**) *(colchón, muñeca)* to rip open; *(radio, juguete, aparato)* to take apart (**c**) *(película, historia, chiste)* to ruin, to spoil

destripaterrones *nmf inv Fam Pey* (**a**) *(campesino)* yokel, *US* hick (**b**) *(inculto, ignorante)* clodhopper, ignoramus

destronamiento *nm* (**a**) *(del rey)* dethronement (**b**) *(de líder político)* overthrow, toppling; *(de campeón)* unseating, toppling

destronar *vt* (**a**) *(rey)* to dethrone, to depose (**b**) *(líder político)* to overthrow, to topple; *(campeón)* to unseat, to topple

destronque *nm Chile, Méx (de planta)* uprooting

destrozado, -a *adj* (**a**) *(vestido, zapatos)* ruined; *(jarrón, cámara)* smashed; **esta estantería está destrozada** these shelves are falling apart; **la lavadora está destrozada** the washing machine is only fit for the scrapheap; **el gato tiene los sillones destrozados** the cat has clawed the chairs to shreds; **me devolvió el libro d.** the book was falling to bits when he gave it back to me; **tengo las manos destrozadas de tanto fregar** all that washing up has left my hands in a terrible state; **huyó dejándole el corazón d.** she ran off leaving him heartbroken; **el autobús quedó d.** the bus was wrecked
(**b**) *(persona) (emocionalmente)* shattered, devastated; *(físicamente)* shattered; **la noticia lo dejó d.** he was devastated by the news

destrozar [14] **1** *vt* (**a**) *(físicamente) (romper)* to smash; *(estropear)* to ruin; **el terremoto destrozó la ciudad** the earthquake destroyed the city; **vas a d.** *o* **destrozarte los zapatos de tanto usarlos** you'll ruin your shoes, wearing them so much
(**b**) *(emocionalmente) (persona)* to shatter, to devastate; *(matrimonio, relación)* to wreck; *(pareja)* to break up; *(vida)* to ruin; *(corazón)* to break; **el divorcio la ha destrozado** she was devastated by the divorce; **ese ruido le destroza los nervios a cualquiera** that noise is enough to drive anyone up the wall; **destrozó a su oponente en el debate** he destroyed his opponent in the debate
2 destrozarse *vpr (objeto)* to smash, to break into pieces

destrozo *nm* damage; **alguien tendrá que pagar los destrozos** someone will have to pay for the damage; **causar** *u* **ocasionar** *o* **provocar grandes destrozos** to cause a lot of damage; **el perro y el gato hicieron un d. en el jardín** the dog and the cat caused havoc in the garden; **¡vaya d. que te has hecho en la rodilla!** you've made a real mess of your knee!

destrozón, -ona *Fam* **1** *adj* **ese niño es muy d.** that child is always breaking things; **ser d. con la ropa** to be very hard on one's clothes
2 *nm,f* **ese niño es un d.** that child is always breaking things

destrucción *nf* destruction; **causar d.** to cause destruction; **causar la d. de algo** to destroy sth

destructivamente *adj* destructively

destructivo, -a *adj* destructive

destructor, -ora 1 *adj* destructive
2 *nm (barco de guerra)* destroyer

destructora *nf* **d. de papel** document shredder

destruido, -a *adj RP Fam* (**a**) *(físicamente)* shattered; **me costó reconocerlo, está d.** I could hardly recognize him, he's such a complete wreck (**b**) *(anímicamente)* shattered, devastated; **desde que perdió a la familia anda destruida** since she lost her family she's gone totally to pieces

destruir [34] **1** *vt* (**a**) *(destrozar)* to destroy (**b**) *(desbaratar) (argumento)* to demolish; *(proyecto)* to ruin, to wreck; *(ilusión, esperanzas)* to dash; *(reputación)* to ruin; *(matrimonio, relación)* to wreck; *(pareja)* to break up (**c**) *(hacienda, fortuna)* to squander
2 destruirse *vpr Mat* to cancel (each other) out

desubicación *nf Andes, RP* disorientation, confusion; **tiene la d. típica de su edad** she's a bit mixed-up, like most people her age

desubicado, -a *Andes, RP* **1** *adj* (**a**) **estar d.** *(perdido)* to feel lost (**b**) **ser d.** *(ridículo)* to have no idea of how to behave
2 *nm,f* **es un d.** he has no idea of how to behave

desubicar *Andes, RP* **1** *vt* to confuse; **este plano, en vez de ayudarme, me desubica** instead of helping me, this map just confuses me; **cada comentario suyo me desubica más** every new thing she says makes me even more confused
2 desubicarse *vpr* **a Pepe no lo invitamos más porque siempre se desubica** we don't invite Pepe any more because he can't behave properly

desubique *nm Andes, RP Fam* (**a**) *(desubicación)* **anda con un d. considerable** he doesn't seem to know what planet he's on (**b**) *(salida)* **no aguanto más tus desubiques** I've had it with the way you carry on

desuello[1] *etc ver* **desollar**

desuello[2] *nm (de animales)* skinning

desunión *nf* (**a**) *(separación)* separation (**b**) *(división, discordia)* disunity; **había mucha d. entre los trabajadores** there was a lot of division *o* disunity among the workers; **en el sindicato reina la d.** the union is very disunited

desunir *vt* **1** (**a**) *(separar)* to separate (**b**) *(enemistar) (grupos)* to divide, to cause a rift between
2 desunirse *vpr* to separate, to break apart

desusado, -a *adj* (**a**) *(pasado de moda)* old-fashioned, obsolete; **un término d.** an obsolete term, a term which is no longer in common use; **costumbres desusadas** customs that are no longer observed (**b**) *(desacostumbrado)* unusual; **actuó con una violencia desusada en él** he was unusually *o* uncharacteristically violent

desuso *nm* disuse; **un término en d.** a term which is no longer in common use; **una ley vigente, pero en d.** a law which is still on the statute books, but no longer enforced; **caer en d.** to become obsolete, to fall into disuse; **el sombrero fue cayendo en d.** people gradually stopped wearing hats

desvaído, -a *adj* (**a**) *(color, tono)* pale, washed-out; *(tela)* faded (**b**) *(forma, contorno)* blurred; *(mirada)* vague

desvalido, -a 1 *adj* needy, destitute
2 *nm,f* needy *o* destitute person; **los desvalidos** the needy, the destitute

desvalijador, -ora *nm,f (de casas)* burglar

desvalijamiento *nm (de casa, persona, tienda)* robbery; *(de banco)* raid, robbery

desvalijar *vt (casa)* to burgle; *(persona, tienda)* to rob; *(banco)* to raid, to rob; *Fig* **mis nietos me han desvalijado la nevera** my grandchildren have cleaned out my fridge

desvalimiento *nm Formal* destitution

desvalorización *nf (de propiedades, acciones)* fall in value; *(de moneda, divisa)* devaluation

desvalorizar [14] **1** *vt (propiedades, acciones)* to reduce the value of; *(moneda, divisa)* to devalue
2 desvalorizarse *vpr (propiedades)* to decrease in value; *(moneda, divisa)* to become devalued; *(acciones)* to fall in value

desván *nm* attic, loft

desvanecer [46] **1** *vt* (**a**) *(humo, nubes)* to disperse; *(perfil, figura)* to blur; *(colores)* to (cause to) fade
(**b**) *(sospechas, temores, dudas)* to dispel
2 desvanecerse *vpr* (**a**) *(desmayarse)* to faint; **caer desvanecido** to fall in a faint, to faint; **yacía desvanecido en el pavimento** he lay unconscious in the road
(**b**) *(humo, nubes)* to clear, to disappear; *(perfil, figura)* to become blurred; *(colores)* to fade; *(sonido, olor)* to fade away; **su imagen se desvanece y en la pantalla vemos un paisaje** her image fades out and we see a country scene

(**c**) *(sospechas, temores)* to be dispelled; *(esperanzas)* to be dashed; *(recuerdos)* to fade; **aquello hizo que se desvanecieran todas nuestras dudas** that dispelled all our doubts

desvanecimiento *nm* (**a**) *(desmayo)* fainting fit; **sufrir** *o* **tener un d.** to faint (**b**) *(desaparición)* vanishing, disappearance (**c**) *(de perfil, figura)* blurring; *(de colores)* fading

desvarar *vt CSur Fam* to patch up

desvariar [32] *vi* (**a**) *(delirar)* to be delirious (**b**) *(decir tonterías)* to talk nonsense; **¡no desvaríes!** don't talk nonsense!

desvarío *nm* (**a**) *(disparate)* **tu decisión me parece un d.** I think what you've decided is absolutely crazy; **¡no digas desvaríos!** don't talk nonsense! (**b**) *(delirio)* delirium

desvelar 1 *vt* (**a**) *(quitar el sueño a)* to keep awake; **el tictac del reloj me desveló** the ticking of the clock kept me awake; **pasé la noche desvelado** I had a sleepless night; **como estaba desvelado, me puse a leer** as I couldn't sleep, I read a book

(**b**) *(noticia, secreto)* to reveal, to tell; *(enigma)* to solve

2 desvelarse *vpr* (**a**) *(perder el sueño)* **me desvelo con el ruido del tráfico** the noise of the traffic keeps me awake; **te oí llegar y ya me desvelé** I heard you coming in and I couldn't get back to sleep

(**b**) *(volcarse)* **desvelarse por alguien** to do everything one can for sb; **se desvelaban por sus clientes** they did everything they could to keep their customers happy; **desvelarse por hacer algo** to make every effort *o* do everything one can to do sth

(**c**) *CAm, Méx (quedarse despierto)* to stay up *o* awake

desvelo *nm* (**a**) *(insomnio)* sleeplessness, insomnia; **una noche de d.** a sleepless night (**b**) *(esfuerzo, cuidado)* **cuida su hijo con d.** he takes great pains over looking after his son; **a pesar de nuestros desvelos...** despite all our care and effort...

desvencijado, -a *adj (mesa, armario)* rickety; *(puerta, vehículo)* battered; *(estructura)* ramshackle, tumbledown

desvencijar 1 *vt (romper)* to break; *(desencajar)* to cause to come apart

2 desvencijarse *vpr (romperse)* to break, to come apart; *(desencajarse)* to fall to pieces

desvendar *vt* to unbandage

desventaja *nf* disadvantage; **afrontan el encuentro de vuelta con una d. de quince puntos** they go into the return match trailing by fifteen points *o* fifteen points behind; **compite con d.** he's competing at a disadvantage; **estar en d.** to be at a disadvantage

desventajoso, -a *adj* disadvantageous, unfavourable

desventura *nf* misfortune; **el libro narra las aventuras y desventuras de...** the book tells the adventures and misadventures of...

desventurado, -a 1 *adj (persona)* unfortunate; *(día, momento)* fateful; *(suceso)* unfortunate

2 *nm,f* poor wretch

desvergonzado, -a 1 *adj (sin pudor, sin escrúpulos)* shameless; *(maleducado)* insolent

2 *nm,f* shameless person; **eres un d.** you're absolutely shameless; **¡habráse visto el d.!** what a bad-mannered lout!

desvergüenza *nf* (**a**) *(atrevimiento, frescura)* shamelessness; **¡después de lo que ocurrió, tiene la d. de llamarla!** after what happened, he still has the gall to phone her!; **su conducta es de una d. increíble** his behaviour is absolutely disgraceful *o* shameful (**b**) *(dicho)* shameless remark; *(hecho)* shameless act

desvestir [47] **1** *vt* to undress

2 desvestirse *vpr* to undress (oneself); **desvístase y túmbese en esta camilla** get undressed and lie on this trolley; **tuvo que desvestirse de cintura para arriba** he had to strip to the waist

desviación *nf* (**a**) *(reorientación) (en dirección)* change; *(en rumbo, de brújula)* deviation; *(de río, tráfico)* diversion; **fetichismos y otras desviaciones de la conducta** fetishism and other deviant behaviour; **aquello suponía una notable d. de sus promesas electorales** that constituted quite a departure from their electoral promises; **no toleran desviaciones de la línea oficial** they don't tolerate any deviation from the party line

(**b**) *(desvío) (en la carretera) Br* diversion, *US* detour; **tomar una d.** to make a detour; **toma la segunda d. a la derecha** take the second turn-off on the right

(**c**) *(en estadística)* deviation ▸▸ ***d. estándar*** standard deviation; ***d. media*** mean deviation; ***d. típica*** standard deviation

(**d**) *Med* ***d. de columna*** curvature of the spine

(**e**) *Der* ***d. de fondos públicos*** diversion of public funds

(**f**) *Econ* ***d. presupuestaria*** budgetary variance

desviacionismo *nm* deviationism

desviacionista *adj* deviationist

desviado, -a *adj (ojo)* squinty

desviar [32] **1** *vt* (**a**) *(tráfico, automóviles)* to divert; *(río, cauce)* to divert; *(dirección, rumbo)* to change; **aquello desvió al "Mayflower" de su rumbo** that caused the "Mayflower" to change course; **los vuelos fueron desviados al aeropuerto de Luton** flights were diverted to Luton airport

(**b**) *(fondos)* to divert (**a** into)

(**c**) *(golpe)* to parry; *(pelota, disparo)* to deflect; **Sanz desvió el balón a córner** Sanz deflected the ball for a corner

(**d**) *(pregunta)* to evade; *(conversación)* to change the direction of; **no desvíes la conversación** don't get us off the subject

(**e**) *(mirada, ojos)* to avert; **desvió la mirada avergonzado** he looked away in shame

(**f**) *(apartar)* to dissuade, to turn aside (**de** from); **aquel imprevisto lo desvió de sus planes** that unforeseen circumstance caused him to depart from his plans

2 desviarse *vpr* (**a**) *(cambiar de dirección) (conductor)* to make a detour; *(vehículo)* to go off course; **la carretera se desvía a la derecha** the road goes off to the right; **desvíate en la próxima a la derecha** take the next right turn

(**b**) *(apartarse)* **desviarse de** *(camino, senda)* to stray off; *(tema)* to get off; *(conversación)* to get off the subject of, to go off at a tangent from; *(propósito, idea)* to lose sight of; **nadie se desviaba de la línea del partido** no one departed from the party line

desvincular 1 *vt* (**a**) *(deshacer vínculo con)* to dissociate (**de** from); **la declaración del testigo lo desvinculaba del crimen** the witness's statement cleared him of any involvement in the crime (**b**) *Der (bienes, propiedades)* to disentail

2 desvincularse *vpr* to dissociate oneself (**de** from); **me he desvinculado por completo del fútbol** I no longer have any involvement in football; **se desvinculó de sus amigos al acabar la universidad** he lost touch with his friends after he left university

desvío *nm* (**a**) *(en carretera) (por obras, accidente) Br* diversion, *US* detour; *(salida)* turn-off; **un d. provisional** a temporary *Br* diversion *o US* detour; **toma el primer d. a la derecha** take the first turn-off to the right; **al llegar al cruce toma el d. de** *o* **a Guadalajara** when you get to the crossroads take the turning for *o* road to Guadalajara; **d. por obras** *(en letrero)* diversion, men at work

(**b**) *(de itinerario)* detour

(**c**) *(de pelota)* deflection

(**d**) *Tel* ***d. de llamada*** call transfer

desvirgar [38] *vt* to deflower

desvirtuar [4] *vt* (**a**) *(estropear)* to spoil; **el comercialismo desvirtúa la producción literaria** commercialism has a detrimental effect on literary writing; **su victoria quedó totalmente desvirtuada** his victory was rendered meaningless; **esta actuación desvirtúa el espíritu del acuerdo** this action violates the spirit of the agreement

(**b**) *(distorsionar)* to distort; **la prensa ha desvirtuado mis palabras** the press have twisted my words; **desvirtuó los hechos en su declaración al juez** he distorted the facts in his statement to the judge

desvistiera *etc ver* **desvestir**

desvisto *etc ver* **desvestir**

desvivirse *vpr (desvelarse)* to do everything one can (**por** for); **se desvive por su familia** he'd do anything for his family; **d. por hacer algo** to bend over backwards to do sth

desyerbar *vt* to weed

detal: al detal *loc adv* retail

detalladamente *adv* in (great) detail

detallado, -a *adj* (**a**) *(análisis, descripción, estudio)* detailed (**b**) *(factura, cuenta)* itemized

detallar 1 *vt* (**a**) *(historia, hechos)* to detail, to give a rundown of (**b**) *(factura, cuenta, gastos)* to itemize

2 *vi* to go into detail; **no hace falta que detalles tanto** you don't have to go into so much detail

detalle 1 *nm* (**a**) *(pormenor, dato)* detail; **nos dieron todo tipo de detalles** they gave us all sorts of details; **con d.** in detail; **con todo d., con todo lujo de detalles** in great detail, with a wealth of detail; **dar detalles** to give details; **entrar en detalles** to go into detail(s); **todo estaba organizado hasta el menor d.** everything was organized down to the smallest *o* last detail; **no perdieron d. de lo que se dijo** they didn't miss a thing that was said; **para más detalles, llame al teléfono...** for more information, call...

(**b**) *(elemento, rasgo)* detail; **un partido con detalles de buen fútbol** a match with the odd moment of good football; **un vestido de algodón con detalles en seda bordada** a cotton dress with embroidered silk detail; **observen los detalles decorativos alrededor del friso** notice the decorative detail around the frieze (**c**) *(obsequio)* gift; **te he traído un d.** I've brought you a little present *o* a little something

(**d**) *(atención)* nice gesture *o* thought; **iqué d. lo de acompañarnos a casa!** how kind of him *o* what a nice gesture to bring us home!; **ipero qué d. ha tenido!** what a nice gesture!, how thoughtful of him/her!; **tener un d. (con alguien)** to be considerate (to sb); **tener el d. de hacer algo** to be kind enough to do sth; **es todo un d.** how courteous *o* considerate; EXPR *Fam* **marcarse un d.** to do something nice *o* kind

(**e**) *(fragmento) (de cuadro, foto)* detail; **lámina 6: d. del "Guernica" de Picasso** plate 6: Picasso *Guernica* (detail)

2 **al detalle** *loc adv Com* retail; **en este almacén no se vende al d.** we don't sell retail in this warehouse

detallista 1 *adj* (**a**) *(meticuloso)* meticulous, thorough; **es muy d. en su trabajo** she is very meticulous *o* thorough in her work, she's a perfectionist in her work (**b**) *(atento)* considerate, thoughtful; **iya podías ser un poquito más d.!** you could have been a bit more considerate!

2 *nmf Com* retailer

detección *nf* detection

detectable *adj* detectable

detectar *vt* (**a**) *(descubrir)* to detect, to discover; **han detectado la presencia de toxinas en la carne** the meat has been found to contain toxins; **le han detectado un cálculo renal** they've discovered that he has a kidney stone; **la policía no tardó en d. el origen del dinero** it didn't take the police long to discover where the money came from

(**b**) *(percibir) (sujeto: persona)* to detect, to notice; *(sujeto: aparato)* to detect; **detecté cierta ironía en lo que dijo** I detected a hint of irony in what he said

detective *nmf* detective ►► ***d. privado*** private detective

detectivesco, -a *adj* **labor detectivesca** detective work; **novela detectivesca** detective novel

detector, -ora 1 *adj* **un aparato d.** a detector

2 *nm* detector ►► ***d. de explosivos*** explosives detector; ***d. de humo(s)*** smoke detector; ***d. de incendios*** smoke detector; ***d. de mentiras*** lie detector; ***d. de metales*** metal detector; ***d. de minas*** mine detector

detención *nf* (**a**) *(parada)* stopping, holding-up; **por favor, no se levanten de sus asientos hasta la d. total del aparato** please do not get out of your seats until the plane has come to a complete stop

(**b**) *(arresto)* arrest; **llevar a cabo la d. de alguien** to arrest sb; **una orden de d.** an arrest warrant ►► ***d. cautelar*** preventive detention; ***d. ilegal*** wrongful arrest; ***d. preventiva*** preventive detention

detener [67] 1 *vt* (**a**) *(parar)* to stop; **detenga el vehículo y estacione** stop the vehicle and park; **d. el avance enemigo** to halt the enemy advance; **d. la propagación de la epidemia** to stop the spread of the epidemic; **los bomberos lograron d. el fuego** firefighters managed to hold the fire in check *o* stop the fire spreading; **consiguieron d. la hemorragia** they managed to stop the bleeding; **estaba decidido, nada podía detenerlo** he had made up his mind, nothing could stop him; **iadelante, hazlo! ¿qué te detiene?** go on, do it! what's stopping you?

(**b**) *(arrestar)* to arrest

(**c**) *(entretener)* to keep, to delay; **¿qué fue lo que te detuvo?** what kept you?, what held you up?

2 **detenerse** *vpr* (**a**) *(pararse)* to stop; **no te detengas, sigue** don't stop, carry on; **no se levanten hasta que el avión se haya detenido** do not get up until the plane has come to a stop; **detenerse en seco** to stop dead; **detenerse a hacer algo** to stop to do sth; **se detuvo un momento a pensar** she stopped to think for a moment; **se detuvo a hablar con una amiga y llegó tarde** she stopped to talk to a friend and was late

(**b**) *(demorarse)* to hang about, to linger; **no te detengas tanto con la presentación y ve al grano** don't spend so much time on the presentation and get to the point

detenidamente *adv* carefully, thoroughly; **me miró d.** he looked at me intently

detenido, -a 1 *adj* (**a**) *(detallado) (análisis, estudio)* careful, detailed; **un examen d.** a careful *o* detailed *o* thorough examination

(**b**) *(paralizado)* **estar d.** to be at a standstill; **el tráfico se halla d. en la N-6 debido a un accidente** traffic on the N-6 is at a standstill due to an accident

(**c**) *(arrestado)* **(estar) d.** (to be) under arrest; **iqueda usted d.!** you're under arrest!; **lleva varios días d.** he has been in (police) custody for several days; **¿cuánto tiempo lo van a tener d.?** how long is he going to be detained *o* in (police) custody?

2 *nm,f* prisoner, person under arrest; **los detenidos pasaron a disposición judicial** the people who had been arrested were taken before a judge

detenimiento *nm* **con d.** carefully, thoroughly; **me miró con d.** he looked at me intently

detentar *vt* (**a**) *(ilegalmente)* to hold unlawfully; **los militares que detentan el poder en...** the military in power in... (**b**) *(considerado incorrecto) (título, puesto)* to hold

detergente *nm* detergent; **d. para la ropa** washing powder; *Am* **d. para la vajilla** *Br* washing-up liquid, *US* dish liquid ►► ***d. de*** *o* ***con acción biológica*** biological washing powder; ***d. líquido*** liquid detergent; ***d. en pastillas*** detergent in tablet form; ***d. en polvo*** soap powder

deteriorado, -a *adj (estropeado)* damaged, spoilt; *(por los elementos naturales)* damaged; *(edificio)* dilapidated; **el género llegó muy d.** the goods arrived in poor condition; **el famoso cuadro se halla muy d.** the famous painting is in very poor condition; **las relaciones entre ambos países están muy deterioradas** relations between the two countries have greatly deteriorated

deteriorar 1 *vt* (**a**) *(estropear)* to damage, to spoil; **el paso del tiempo ha ido deteriorando la fachada** the facade has deteriorated with the passage of time (**b**) *(empeorar)* to worsen; **d. las relaciones entre dos países** to worsen relations between two countries; **la enfermedad ha deteriorado mucho su salud** the illness has caused his health to deteriorate a lot

2 **deteriorarse** *vpr* (**a**) *(estropearse)* to deteriorate; **para que no se deteriore la pintura** to prevent the paint from deteriorating (**b**) *(empeorar)* to deteriorate, to get worse; **la situación se fue deteriorando** the situation gradually deteriorated *o* got gradually worse

deterioro *nm* (**a**) *(daño)* damage; **sufrir d.** to be damaged; **la mercancía no sufrió d. alguno** the goods were not damaged at all

(**b**) *(empeoramiento)* deterioration; **las relaciones entre ambos países han experimentado un serio d.** relations between the two countries have deteriorated considerably; **el d. de la situación** the worsening of *o* deterioration in the situation; **el progresivo d. de los servicios públicos** the progressive deterioration in public services; **el d. medioambiental** the deterioration of the environment

determinación *nf* (**a**) *(de precio, fecha)* fixing, setting (**b**) *(resolución)* determination, resolution; **se lanzó a rescatarlo con d.** she set off determinedly to rescue him; **lleno de d.** full of determination (**c**) *(decisión)* **tomar una d.** to make *o* take a decision

determinado, -a *adj* (**a**) *(cierto, alguno)* certain; **en determinadas fechas es mejor no viajar** it is better not to travel on certain dates; **hay determinados lugares donde la delincuencia es mayor** there are certain places where the crime rate is higher; **ante determinados síntomas es mejor acudir al médico** with some symptoms it is better to see your doctor

(**b**) *(preciso, concreto)* specific, particular; **en un momento d. no sabía qué hacer** there was a point where I just didn't know what to do

(**c**) *(resuelto)* determined; **estar d. a hacer algo** to be determined to do sth

(**d**) *Gram* definite; **artículo d.** definite article

determinante 1 *adj* decisive, determining; **ser un factor d.** to be a decisive *o* deciding factor; **él fue d. en la victoria de su equipo** he played a decisive role in his team's victory

2 *nm* (**a**) *Gram* determiner (**b**) *Mat* determinant

determinar 1 *vt* (**a**) *(fijar) (fecha, precio)* to settle on, to fix; *(lugar)* to decide; **se casarán en fecha aún sin** *o* **por d.** they will marry on a date that has yet to be decided *o* fixed; **reuniones para d. los términos del acuerdo** meetings to settle the terms of the agreement; **según determina la ley,...** as stipulated by law,...; **la normativa de tráfico determina que...** traffic regulations state that...

(**b**) *(averiguar)* to establish, to determine; **d. las causas de la muerte** to determine *o* establish the cause of death; **el lugar exacto del accidente es difícil de d.** it is difficult to determine *o* establish the exact spot where the accident occurred; **determinaron que el accidente se debió a un error humano** they established that the accident was the result of human error

(**c**) *(motivar)* to cause, to bring about; **protestas generalizadas determinaron su dimisión** widespread protests caused him to resign; **aquello determinó su decisión** that led to his decision

(**d**) *(decidir)* to decide; **d. hacer algo** to decide to do sth; **la tormenta lo determinó a salir antes** the storm made him decide to leave early

(**e**) *(distinguir)* to distinguish, to discern; **no pude d. quién era** I couldn't make out who he was

(**f**) *Der* to settle, to decide; **el juez determinó su ingreso en prisión** the judge ordered that he be sent to prison

2 **determinarse** *vpr* **determinarse a hacer algo** to make up one's mind to do sth

determinativo, -a *adj* determinative

determinismo *nm* determinism

determinista 1 *adj* deterministic
2 *nmf* determinist

detersión *nf Formal* cleansing

detestable *adj (persona, actitud)* hateful, detestable; *(comportamiento, trato)* despicable; *(comida)* revolting; *(alojamiento, calidad)* terrible, appalling

detestar *vt* to detest; **detesto trabajar los sábados** I hate working on Saturdays; **te detesto** I despise *o* hate you

detiene *etc ver* **detener**

detonación *nf* **(a)** *(acción)* detonation **(b)** *(sonido)* explosion

detonador *nm* detonator

detonante 1 *adj* explosive
2 *nm* **(a)** *(explosivo)* explosive **(b)** *(catalizador)* trigger; **la subida de los precios del pan fue el d. de la revuelta** the rise in bread prices was what sparked off *o* triggered the rebellion

detonar *vi* to detonate, to explode; **hicieron d. el explosivo** they detonated the explosive

detractor, -ora 1 *adj* disparaging (**de** about)
2 *nm,f* detractor

DETRÁS *adv* **(a)** *(en el espacio)* behind; **tus amigos vienen d.** your friends are coming on behind; **el interruptor está d.** the switch is at the back; **que se pongan d. los más altos** the tallest people at the back, please; **la calle de d. (de nuestra casa)** the street at the back (of our house), the street behind (our house); **d. de** behind; **d. de mí/ti** behind me/you; **la policía marchaba d. de la manifestación** the police were following on behind the demonstrators; **deja un espacio d. de la coma** leave a space after the comma; **ignoramos qué hay d. de su extraño comportamiento** we don't know the reasons behind her strange behaviour; **por d.** at the back; **entró por d. para que no la viera nadie** she came in the back way so nobody would see her; **sobresale un poco por d.** it sticks out a bit at the back; **miró el sobre por d.** he looked at the back of the envelope; *también Fig* **por d. de alguien** behind sb's back; **por d. no hacen más que tomarle el pelo** behind his back they just make fun of him; **por d. de la casa está el mar** behind the house is the sea; **andar** *o* **ir d. de algo** to be after sth, to be looking for sth; **andar** *o* **ir d. de alguien** to be after sb; **hablar de alguien por d.** to talk about sb behind his/her back
(b) *(en el orden)* then, afterwards; **Portugal y d. Puerto Rico** Portugal and then Puerto Rico; **fuimos pasando uno d. de otro** we went in one after another

detrasito *adv Méx, Ven* just *o* right behind

detrimento *nm* damage; **en d. de** to the detriment of; **la producción aumenta en d. de la calidad** output increases at the expense of quality; **ir en d. de** to be detrimental to; **eso iría en d. de tus intereses** that would be against your interests

detrito *nm,* **detritus** *nm inv* **(a)** *Biol* detritus **(b)** *Geol* detritus **(c)** *(residuo)* **detritos** waste ►► ***d. radioactivo*** radioactive waste

detuviera *etc ver* **detener**

deuce [djus] *nm inv (en tenis)* deuce

deuda *nf* **(a)** *(financiera)* debt; **tiene deudas pendientes con un proveedor** he owes money to a supplier; **contraer una d.** to get into debt; **contrajo deudas (por valor) de varios millones** he ran up debts (to the tune) of several million; **está lleno de deudas** he's heavily *o* deep in debt; **pagar** *o* **saldar una d.** to pay off *o* settle a debt ►► *Econ* ***d. amortizable*** repayable debt; *Econ* ***d. consolidada*** funded *o* long-term debt; *Econ* ***d. a corto plazo*** short-term debt; *Econ* ***d. exterior*** foreign debt; ***d. externa*** foreign debt; *Cont* ***deudas incobrables*** bad debt; *Econ* ***d. interior*** internal debt; ***d. interna*** internal debt; ***deudas de juego*** gambling debts; *Econ* ***d. a largo plazo*** long-term debt; *Econ* ***d. pública*** *Br* national debt, *US* public debt; **invertir en d. pública** to buy government bonds; *Econ* ***d. tributaria*** tax payable *o* due
(b) *(moral)* debt; **mi d. con ella es enorme** I am enormously indebted to her; **estar en d. con alguien** to be indebted to sb
(c) *(pecado)* **perdónanos nuestras deudas** forgive us our trespasses

deudo, -a *nm,f Formal* relative, relation

deudor, -ora 1 *adj* debtor; **un socio d.** a member in arrears with his/her subscription; **la compañía deudora** the debtor company; **la parte deudora se declaró insolvente** the debtor declared himself insolvent
2 *nm,f* debtor ►► *Fin* ***d. hipotecario*** mortgagor

deuterio *nm Quím* deuterium

deutóxido *nm Quím* dioxide

devaluación *nf* devaluation

devaluado, -a *adj (moneda)* devalued; **con la ausencia de Italia el torneo quedó bastante d.** Italy's absence greatly diminished the tournament

devaluar [4] 1 *vt* to devalue; **devaluaron el euro un 3 por ciento** the euro was devalued by 3 percent
2 **devaluarse** *vpr (moneda)* to fall (in value); *(precios)* to fall; *(bienes, terrenos)* to go down in value, to depreciate

devanadera *nf (bobina)* reel, spool

devanado *nm* **(a)** *Elec* winding ►► ***d. de campo*** field winding; ***d. de inductor*** field winding **(b)** *(de hilo)* reeling

devanador *nm,* **devanadora** *nf Am* winder, reel

devanar 1 *vt* to wind
2 **devanarse** *vpr* EXPR *Fam* **devanarse los sesos** to cudgel *o* rack one's brains; **no te devanes mucho los sesos con este problema** don't spend too much time racking your brains over this problem

devaneo *nm* **(a)** *(distracción)* idle pursuit **(b)** *(amorío)* affair; **tener un d. con alguien** to have an affair with sb; **tuvo un d. de fin de semana con alguien** he had a weekend fling with sb; **en su juventud tuvo sus devaneos con la ultraderecha** he flirted with the far right when he was young

devastación *nf* devastation

devastado, -a *adj* devastated

devastador, -ora *adj* devastating

devastar *vt* to devastate

develamiento *nm Am* **(a)** *(revelación)* revelation, disclosure **(b)** *(inauguración)* unveiling

develar *vt Am* **(a)** *(revelar)* to reveal, to disclose **(b)** *(inaugurar)* to unveil

devengar [38] *vt (intereses, dividendos)* to yield; *(sueldo)* to earn; **un depósito a plazo que devenga altos intereses** a fixed-term deposit that yields *o* pays a high rate of interest; **ingresos devengados durante el ejercicio** income earned *o* accrued during the *Br* financial *o US* fiscal year

devengo 1 *ver* **devengar**
2 *ver* **devenir**
3 *nm (cantidad adeudada)* amount due; *(intereses por cobrar)* interest payable; *(sueldo por cobrar)* wages/salary due

devenir [71] 1 *nm* **(a)** *(evolución)* transformation; **el d. de la historia** the course of history; **la vida es un continuo d.** life is a continual process of change **(b)** *Filosofía* becoming
2 *vi (convertirse)* **d. en** to become, to turn into; **la discusión devino en reyerta con navajas** the argument developed into a knife fight

devoción *nf* **(a)** *(veneración)* devotion; **con d.** devotedly **(b)** *(afición)* affection, attachment; **tener d. por algo/alguien** to be devoted to sth/sb; **tener d. por algo** to have a passion for sth; **es d. lo que tiene por el fútbol** he is passionate about football; **tener por d. hacer algo** to be in the habit of doing sth

devocionario *nm Rel* prayer book

devolución *nf* **(a)** *(de compra)* return; *(de dinero)* refund; *(de préstamo)* repayment; **declaraciones de la renta con derecho a d.** = income tax returns with entitlement to a rebate; **el plazo de d. del préstamo es de doce años** the loan is repayable over (a period of) twelve years; **no se admiten devoluciones** *(en letrero)* no refunds (given); **d. de monedas** *(en letrero de máquinas expendedoras)* refund, coin return ►► *Fin* ***d. fiscal*** tax rebate *o* refund
(b) *(de visita)* return
(c) *(de pelota)* return
(d) *(en lotería)* = prize which gives the winner their money back

devolutivo, -a *adj Der* returnable, restorable

devolver [41] 1 *vt* **(a)** *(restituir) (lo entregado o prestado) (automóvil, dinero, llaves)* to give back (**a** to); *(lo alquilado) (automóvil, televisor, videocinta)* to take back, to return (**a** to); *(producto defectuoso)* to return (**a** to); *(préstamo, crédito)* to repay (**a** to); **si no queda satisfecho, le devolvemos el dinero** if you're not satisfied, we'll refund you *o* give you back the money; **me devolvieron el dinero** they gave me a refund, they gave me my money back; **¿qué plazo tienes para d. los libros?** when do you have to take the books back (by)?; **es un regalo para mi sobrino... si ya lo tiene, ¿lo puedo d.?** it's a present for my nephew... if he already has it, can I bring it back?; **precio exacto: esta máquina no devuelve cambio** *(en letrero)* please insert the exact amount: no change given; **el Senado devolvió el proyecto de ley al Congreso con muchas enmiendas** the Senate sent the bill back to the Congress with lots of amendments; **me devolvieron la carta por un error en las señas** the letter was returned to me because it was not properly addressed (**b**) *(volver a dar)* to give back, to restore; **le devolvió la alegría** it made him feel happy again; **el triunfo devolvió la confianza al equipo** the victory gave the team back its confidence; **este aparato le devuelve la audición en un 70 por ciento** this device will give you back 70 percent of your hearing

(**c**) *(restablecer, volver a colocar)* **d. algo a** to return sth to; **devuelve los discos a su sitio** put the disks back (where they belong); **devolvieron a los refugiados a su país de origen** they sent the refugees back to their country of origin

(**d**) *(corresponder a) (favor, visita)* to return; **d. un agravio a alguien** to pay sb back for an insult; **d. los insultos a alguien** to insult sb back; **le devolví el favor que me había hecho** I returned the favour he had done me; **me dio un bofetón, pero yo se lo devolví** he slapped me, but I slapped him back; **aún no me ha devuelto carta** he still hasn't written back to me; **nunca me devuelves las llamadas** you never call me back; **habrá que devolverle la invitación** we'll have to return the invitation *o* invite him in return

(**e**) *(pelota)* to pass back; **Jones devolvió la pelota a su portero** Jones passed the ball back to the goalkeeper; **le devolvió la pelota no invitándole a su fiesta** she returned the compliment by not inviting him to her party

(**f**) *(vomitar)* to bring *o* throw up

2 *vi* to throw up; **tener ganas de d.** to feel like throwing up

3 devolverse *vpr Andes, CAm, Carib, Méx* to come back

> **Falso amigo**: El verbo inglés **to devolve** no es la traducción del español **devolver**. En inglés **to devolve** significa "transferir, traspasar" o "recaer".

devónico, -a *Geol* **1** *adj* Devonian
2 *nm* **el d.** the Devonian

devorador, -ora 1 *adj* (**a**) *(persona, animal)* **un murciélago d. de insectos** an insect-eating bat; **un adolescente d. de novelas de aventuras** a young boy who devours adventure stories

(**b**) *(pasión, celos, deseo)* all-consuming; **tener unas ansias de triunfo devoradoras** to have a burning desire for victory; **hambre devoradora** ravenous hunger; **me lanzó una mirada devoradora** he devoured me with his eyes; **un incendio d. arrasó el bosque** the forest was destroyed by an all-consuming blaze

2 *nm,f* devourer; *Fam Hum* **una devoradora de hombres** a man-eater

devorar *vt* (**a**) *(alimentos)* to devour; **el lobo devoró tres ovejas** the wolf ate three sheep; *Fam* **este niño devora los libros de aventuras** that child devours story books; *Fam* **devoraba a las chicas con la mirada** he ogled the girls

(**b**) *(destruir)* to destroy, to demolish; **el ciclón devoraba edificios y viviendas** the cyclone destroyed buildings and houses; **las llamas devoraron el palacio en dos horas** the fire destroyed the palace in two hours

(**c**) *(sujeto: sentimiento)* to devour; **lo devoraban los celos** he was consumed by jealousy; **esta pasión que me devora por dentro** this passion which consumes me *o* which is eating away inside me

devotamente *adv* piously

devoto, -a 1 *adj* (**a**) *(piadoso)* devout; **ser d. de** to have a devotion for (**b**) *(admirador)* devoted (**de** to) (**c**) *(imagen, templo, lugar)* devotional

2 *nm,f* (**a**) *(beato)* devout person; **es un d. de San Antonio** he has a special devotion to St Anthony; **los devotos** the faithful (**b**) *(admirador)* devotee (**de** of); **buenas noticias para los devotos del cine de ciencia ficción** good news for fans of science fiction movies *o Br* films

devuelta *nf Carib, Col* change

devueltismo *nm RP Fam* blasé *o* seen-it-all-before attitude

devuelto, -a 1 *participio ver* **devolver**
2 *nm Fam (vómito)* sick, puke

devuelvo *etc ver* **devolver**

dextrina *nf Quím* dextrin, dextrine

dextrógiro, -a *adj Quím* dextrogyre

dextrosa *nf Quím* dextrose

deyección *nf* (**a**) *Geol (de montaña)* debris *(singular)*; *(de volcán)* ejecta *(plural)* (**b**) *Med (expulsión de excremento)* excretion; **deyecciones** *(excrementos)* stools, faeces

> **Falso amigo**: El sustantivo inglés **dejection** no es la traducción del español **deyección**. En inglés **dejection** significa "abatimiento".

DF *nm (abrev de* **Distrito Federal**) *(en México)* = Mexico City; *(en Venezuela)* = Caracas

dg *(abrev de* **decigramo**) dg

DGI *nf RP (abrev de* **Dirección General Impositiva**) *Br* ≃ Inland Revenue, *US* ≃ IRS

DGT *nf (abrev de* **Dirección General de Tráfico**) = Spanish government department in charge of road transport

di (**a**) *ver* **dar** (**b**) *ver* **decir**

DÍA *nm* (**a**) *(periodo de tiempo)* day; **un d. de campo** a day out in the countryside; **todos los días** every day; **tres veces al d.** three times a day; **iremos unos días a la playa** we're going to the seaside for a few days; **el referéndum se celebrará el d. 25 de abril** the referendum will take place on 25 April; **un d. martes** one Tuesday; **me voy el d. 8** I'm going on the 8th; **me pagan el d. primero de cada mes** I get paid on the first of each month; **¿a qué d. estamos?** what day is it today?; **al d. siguiente** (on) the following day; **a los pocos días** a few days later; **al otro d.** the next day, the day after; **el otro d.** the other day; **un d. sí y otro no** every other day; *Fam Hum* **un d. sí y (el) otro también** every blessed day; *Am* **d. por medio** every other day; **un d. entre semana** a weekday; **algún d. me lo agradecerás** you'll thank me some day; **tienes que venir por casa algún d.** you should come round some time *o* one day; **¡buenos días!**, *RP* **¡buen d.!** good morning!; **un buen d. me voy a enfadar** one of these days I'm going to get angry; **cualquier** *o* **un d. de éstos** one of these days; **el d. de hoy** today; **el d. de mañana** in the future; **el d. menos pensado...** when you least expect it...; **el d. que se entere, nos mata** when he finds out, he'll kill us; **de d. en d., d. a d.** from day to day, day by day; **se recuperó de un d. a** *o* **para otro** he recovered overnight *o* from one day to the next; **d. tras d.**, *Méx* **d. con d.** day after day; *Méx Fam* **estar en sus días** to be having one's period; **este pan está seco, no es del d.** this bread's stale, it's not fresh; **ha sido la noticia del d.** it was the news of the day; **en su d.: en su d. te lo explicaré** I'll explain it to you in due course; **en su d. les advertí que esa inversión sería imposible** I told them at the time that the investment would be impossible; **la pintura abstracta no fue valorada en su d.** in its day abstract art wasn't highly thought of; **hoy (en) d.** these days, nowadays; **hoy no es mi d., todo me sale mal** it isn't my day today, I seem to be doing everything wrong; **mañana será otro d.** tomorrow's another day; **tener un buen/mal d.** to have a good/bad day; *Fam* **tener mis/tus/sus/***etc.* **días: ¿qué tal es tu compañero de casa? – tiene sus días** what's your flatmate like? – he has his moments; **has estado todo el (santo) d. protestando** you've been complaining all day (long), you've spent the whole day complaining; **no ha parado de llover en todo el (santo) d.** it hasn't stopped raining all day; EXPR *Fam* **un d. es un d.** this is a special occasion; EXPR **vivir al d.** to live from hand to mouth ►► ***d. de Año Nuevo*** New Year's Day; *RP Fam* ***el d. del arquero*** when pigs learn to fly; ***d. de asueto*** day off; ***d. de ayuno*** holy day; *Ferroc* ***d. azul*** = cheap day for rail travel in Spain; *Esp* ***d. de la banderita*** Red Cross Day; *RP* ***d. del canillita*** = day on which newspaper sellers do not work; ***d. de colegio*** school day; ***d. de descanso*** *(en competición deportiva)* rest day; *Com* ***d. de deuda*** pay-by date; *Esp* ***D. de Difuntos*** All Souls' Day; ***d. de los enamorados*** (St) Valentine's Day; ***d. del espectador*** = day when some cinemas sell tickets at a discount; ***d. festivo*** (public) holiday; ***d. de fiesta*** holiday; *RP Fam* ***d. del golero*** when pigs learn to fly; *Com* ***días de gracia*** days of grace; ***d. de guardar*** holy day; ***d. hábil*** working day; ***D. de la Hispanidad*** = day celebrating Columbus's landing in America *(12 October)*, *US* ≃ Columbus Day; ***d. de huelga*** day of action; ***D. de los Inocentes*** 28 December, ≃ April Fools' Day; ***el d. del Juicio:*** EXPR *Fam* **hasta el d. del Juicio** until doomsday; ***el D. del Juicio Final*** Judgement Day; ***d. laborable*** working day; ***d. lectivo*** school *o* teaching day; ***d. libre*** day off; ***d. de la madre*** Mother's Day; *Am* ***D. de los Muertos*** All Souls' Day; ***d. del padre*** Father's Day; ***d. de pago*** payday; *Am* ***d. patrio*** national holiday *(commemorating important historical event)*; *Am* ***D. de la Raza*** = day commemorating Columbus's landing in America *(12 October)*, *US* ≃ Columbus Day; ***D. de Reyes*** Epiphany *(6 January, day on which children receive presents)*; *Ferroc* ***d. rojo*** = day on which rail travel is more expensive in Spain; ***D. de San Valentín*** (St) Valentine's Day; *RP* ***d. sándwich*** = day between a public holiday and a weekend, which is also taken as a holiday; ***d. señalado*** red-letter day; ***el D. del Señor*** Corpus Christi; ***D. de Todos los Santos*** All Saints' Day; ***d. del trabajador*** Labour Day; ***d. de trabajo*** working day; **me pagan por d. de trabajo** I get paid for each day's work; ***d. útil*** working day; ***d. de vigilia*** day of abstinence

(**b**) *(luz diurna)* daytime, day; **los días son más cortos en invierno** the days are shorter in winter; **al caer el d.** at dusk; **al despuntar** *o* **romper el d.** at daybreak *o* dawn; **de d.** in the daytime, during the day; **es de d.** it's daytime; **despierta, ya es de d.** wake up, it's morning *o* it's already light; **hacer algo de d.** to do sth in the daytime *o* during the day; **d. y noche** day and night; **en pleno d., a plena luz del d.** in broad daylight; EXPR **como el d. a la noche: son tan**

parecidos como el d. a la noche they are as like as chalk and cheese (**c**) *(tiempo atmosférico)* day; **un d. lluvioso** a rainy day; **hacía un d. caluroso/invernal** it was a hot/wintry day; **hace un d. estupendo para pasear** it's a lovely day for a walk, it's lovely weather for walking; **hace buen/mal d.** it's a lovely/dismal day; **mañana hará un mal d.** tomorrow the weather will be bad; **¿qué tal d. hace?** what's the weather like today?

(**d**) **días** *(tiempo, vida)* days; **desde entonces hasta nuestros días** from that time until the present; **en los días de la República** in the days of the Republic; **en mis días** in my day; **en aquellos días no había televisión** in those days we didn't have television; **en aquellos días de felicidad** in those happy times; **terminó sus días en la pobreza** he ended his days in poverty; EXPR **no pasar los días por** *o* **para alguien: los días no pasan por** *o* **para ella** she doesn't look her age; EXPR **tener los días contados: el régimen/tigre de Bengala tiene los días contados** the regime's/Bengal tiger's days are numbered

(**e**) *(tanto, corriente)* **estar al d.** to be up to date; **está al d. de todo lo que ocurre en la región** she's up to date with everything that's going on in the region; **estamos al d. de todos nuestros pagos** we're up to date with all our payments; **poner algo/a alguien al d.** to update sth/sb; **ya me han puesto al d. sobre la situación de la empresa** they've already updated me *o* filled me in on the company's situation; **tenemos que poner este informe al d.** we have to update this report *o* bring this report up to date; **se ha puesto al d. de los últimos acontecimientos** he's caught up with the latest developments

---

diabetes *nf inv Med* diabetes *(singular)* ►► ***d. insípida*** diabetes insipidus; ***d. mellitus*** diabetes mellitus

diabético, -a *Med* **1** *adj* diabetic
2 *nm,f* diabetic

diabla *nf* (**a**) *Fam (diablo hembra)* she-devil (**b**) *Teatro* footlights

diablesa *nf Fam* she-devil

diablillo *nm Fam (persona traviesa)* little devil

diablo 1 *nm* (**a**) *(demonio)* devil; PROV **cuando el d. no tiene que hacer, mata moscas con el rabo** the devil makes work for idle hands; PROV **más sabe el d. por viejo que por d.** = experience is what really counts ►► *Andes, CAm* ***diablos azules*** delirium tremens; ***d. marino*** scorpion fish; ***d. de Tasmania*** Tasmanian Devil

(**b**) *(persona astuta, maliciosa)* devil; **el extremo argentino es un auténtico d.** the Argentinian winger is a real wizard; **este niño es un d.** that child is a little devil; **el muy d. tenía engañada a su mujer** the old devil was cheating on his wife; **pobre d.** poor devil; **no era más que un pobre d.** he was just a sad case

(**c**) *Fam (uso enfático)* **¿dónde/cómo/***etc* **diablos...?** where/how/*etc* the hell *o* devil...?; **¿y usted quién diablos es?** and who the devil are YOU?

(**d**) *Chile (vehículo)* ox-cart, dray

(**e**) EXPR **a diablos: esta comida huele/sabe a diablos** this food smells/tastes disgusting; **aquella música sonaba a diablos** that music sounded dreadful; **¡al d. con...!** to hell with...!; **¡al d. con los deberes!** to hell with the homework!; **como un d.** *(mucho)* like mad, like the devil; **el corte me escocía como un d.** the cut was stinging like mad; **del d., de mil diablos, de todos los diablos: hacía un frío del d.** it was colder than blue blazes; **hoy tiene un humor de mil diablos** he's in an absolutely foul mood today; **esta máquina hace un ruido de todos los diablos** this machine makes an infernal *o* incredible racket; *Andes, RP* **donde el d. perdió el poncho** in the middle of nowhere, in the back of beyond; **irse al d.: ¡vete al d.!** go to blazes!; **se fue al d. toda la operación** the whole thing went to pot; *Fam* **mandar algo al d.** to chuck sth in; **mandé al d. los estudios y me puse a trabajar** I chucked in university and got a job; *Fam* **mandar a alguien al d.** to tell sb to get lost

2 *interj Fam* **¡diablos!** *(¡maldita sea!)* damn it!

diablura *nf* prank; **hacer diabluras** to get up to mischief

diabólicamente *adv* diabolically

diabólico, -a *adj* (**a**) *(del diablo)* diabolic (**b**) *(muy malo)* evil, diabolical; **tiene una mente diabólica** she has an evil mind (**c**) *(difícil)* fiendishly difficult

diábolo *nm* diabolo

diacetilmorfina *nf Farm* diamorphine

diaconado *nm Rel* diaconate, deaconship

diaconisa *nf Rel* deaconess

diácono *nm Rel* deacon

diacrítico, -a *adj* (**a**) *Gram (signo)* diacritical (**b**) *Med (síntoma)* diagnostic

diacronía *nf* diachrony

diacrónico, -a *adj* diachronic

diadema *nf* (**a**) *(joya)* tiara (**b**) *(para el pelo)* hairband

diafanidad *nf* (**a**) *(tranparencia) (de cristal)* transparency; *(de tela)* transparency, gauziness (**b**) *(claridad)* clarity

diáfano, -a *adj* (**a**) *(casi transparente) (cristal)* (almost) transparent; *(tela)* diaphanous (**b**) *(claro) (luz, cielo, ojos)* clear; *(agua)* crystal-clear (**c**) *(sin tapujos) (respuesta, explicación)* crystal-clear (**d**) *Esp Constr* open-plan; **una oficina diáfana** an open-plan office

diafragma *nm* (**a**) *(músculo)* diaphragm (**b**) *Fot* diaphragm ►► ***d. de apertura*** aperture stop, aperture diaphragm (**c**) *(anticonceptivo)* diaphragm (**d**) *Tec* diaphragm

diagnosis *nf inv* diagnosis

diagnosticar [60] *vt* to diagnose; **le fue diagnosticada una angina de pecho** she was diagnosed with angina; **le diagnosticaron cáncer** he was diagnosed with *o* as having cancer

diagnóstico, -a 1 *adj* diagnostic
2 *nm* (**a**) *(médico)* diagnosis *(singular)*; **dar un d. a alguien** to diagnose sb; **realizar un d.** to make a diagnosis (**b**) *(de situación)* diagnosis

diagonal 1 *adj* diagonal
2 *nf* diagonal (line); **trazar la d. entre A y B** to draw the diagonal between A and B; **en d.** diagonally

diagonalmente *adv* diagonally

diagrama *nm* diagram; **hacer un d. (de algo)** to draw a diagram (of sth) ►► ***d. en árbol*** tree diagram; ***d. arbóreo*** tree diagram; ***d. de barras*** bar chart; ***d. circular*** pie chart; ***d. de dispersión*** scatter diagram *o* plot; ***d. de flujo*** flow diagram *o* chart; ***d. de sectores*** pie chart; *Mat* ***d. de Venn*** Venn diagram

día-hombre (*pl* **días-hombre**) *nm Econ* man-day

dial *nm* (**a**) *(de radio)* dial; **sintonízanos en el 108.8 de tu d.** tune in to 108.8 (**b**) *(de teléfono)* dial

dialectal *adj* dialectal; **expresión/variante d.** dialect expression/variant

dialectalismo *nm* dialect word/expression

dialéctica *nf* (**a**) *Filosofía* dialectics *(singular)* (**b**) *(capacidad de argumentación)* dialectical skill

dialéctico, -a *adj* dialectic(al)

dialecto *nm* dialect

dialectología *nf* dialectology

dialectólogo, -a *nm,f* dialectologist

diálisis *nf inv* dialysis; **se hace una d. todas las semanas** he has dialysis once a week

dialogadamente *adv* by means of dialogue

dialogado, -a *adj (obra)* written in dialogue

dialogante *adj* **ser una persona d.** to be open to dialogue

dialogar [38] **1** *vi* (**a**) *(hablar)* to have a conversation (**con/sobre** with/about), to talk (**con/sobre** to/about); **dialogaban tranquilamente en la barra** they were having a quiet conversation at the bar; **lo que más le gusta es d. con la gente** the thing she enjoys most is exchanging opinions with people

(**b**) *(negociar)* to hold a dialogue *o* talks (**con** with); **las dos partes siguen dialogando** talks between the two sides are continuing; **la patronal se ha negado a d. con los sindicatos** the employers have refused to talk to the unions

2 *vt (obra)* to write in dialogue

diálogo *nm* (**a**) *(conversación)* conversation; *Lit* dialogue; **tuvimos un d.** we had a conversation; **los diálogos** *(en película, serie)* the dialogue ►► *Fam* ***d. de besugos:*** **fue un d. de besugos** we/they were talking at odds with one another

(**b**) *(negociación)* dialogue; **se ha producido un intento de d. entre las partes** there has been an attempt at dialogue between the two sides; **hemos abierto un proceso de d. con la patronal** we have entered into talks with the employers; **fue un d. de sordos** no one listened to anyone else, it was a dialogue of the deaf

diamante 1 *nm* (**a**) *(gema)* diamond; **una sortija de diamantes** a diamond ring ►► ***d. en bruto*** uncut diamond; EXPR **ser un d. en bruto** to have a lot of potential; ***d. falso*** false diamond; ***d. de imitación*** imitation diamond; ***d. industrial*** industrial diamond (**b**) *(en béisbol)* diamond (**c**) *(naipe)* diamond

2 diamantes *nmpl (palo de baraja)* diamonds

diamantífero, -a *adj* diamond-bearing, *Espec* diamondiferous

diamantino, -a *adj* (**a**) *(de diamante)* diamond-like, diamantine (**b**) *Literario (duro)* adamantine

diametral *adj* diametric, diametrical; **existe una oposición d. entre ambos partidos** the two parties have diametrically opposing views

diametralmente *adv* (**a**) *(en geometría)* diametrically (**b**) *(en enfrentamientos, oposiciones)* diametrically; **d. opuesto a** diametrically opposed to

diámetro *nm* diameter; **mide 3 metros de d.** it's 3 metres in diameter

Diana *n Mitol* Diana

diana *nf* (**a**) *(blanco) (de dardos)* dartboard; *(de tiro con arco, arma)* target (**b**) *(centro del blanco)* bull's-eye; **hacer d., dar en la d.** to hit the bull's-eye; EXPR **¡has dado en la d.!** you've hit the nail on the head! (**c**) *(toque de corneta)* reveille; **tocar d.** to sound the reveille; *Fam* **en mi casa se toca d. a las siete** we all get up at seven in my house
(**d**) *(gol)* goal

diantre *interj Euf* dash it!; **¡d. de chiquillo!** dratted child!

diapasón *nm Mús* (**a**) *(para afinar)* tuning fork (**b**) *(en instrumento de cuerda)* fingerboard

diapositiva *nf* slide, transparency

diariamente *adv* daily, every day; **el museo abre d. de lunes a sábado** the museum is open daily from Monday to Saturday; **yo hago ejercicio d.** I take exercise every day

diariero, -a *nm,f Andes, RP* newspaper seller

diario, -a 1 *adj* (**a**) *(de todos los días, habitual)* daily; **la rutina diaria** the daily routine; **la vida diaria** daily life; **el funcionamiento d. del negocio** the day-to-day running of the business
(**b**) *(cada día)* daily; **hacen un entrenamiento d. de una hora** they have a daily one-hour training session; **tenemos una hora diaria de inglés** we do an hour of English every day; **hay dos trenes diarios a la capital** there are two trains a day to the capital; **ganaba $100 diarios** she earned $100 a day
2 *nm* (**a**) *(periódico)* newspaper, daily ►► ***d. hablado*** radio news (bulletin); ***d. de la mañana*** morning newspaper; ***d. matinal*** morning newspaper; ***d. de la noche*** evening newspaper; ***d. televisado*** television news (bulletin); ***d. vespertino*** evening newspaper
(**b**) *(relación día a día)* diary ►► ***d. de a bordo*** logbook; ***d. íntimo*** (personal) diary; ***d. de navegación*** logbook; ***d. de sesiones*** parliamentary report; ***d. de vuelo*** log, logbook
(**c**) *(gasto)* daily expenses
(**d**) *Com* journal, day book
3 a diario *loc adv* every day, daily; **viene por aquí a d.** she drops in here every day; **el complejo vitamínico ha de consumirse a d.** the vitamin complex must be taken daily
4 de diario *loc adj* everyday; **ropa de d.** everyday clothes

diarrea *nf* diarrhoea; **estar con** *o* **tener d.** to have diarrhoea; EXPR *Fam* **tener una d. mental** to have a brainstorm

diáspora *nf* diaspora; **la d. veraniega hacia la costa** the summer exodus to the coast

diástole *nf Fisiol* diastole

diatomea *nf* diatom

diatónico, -a *adj* diatonic

diatópico, -a *adj Ling (variación)* regional, diatopic

diatriba *nf* diatribe; **en su discurso lanzó diatribas contra el gobierno** he attacked *o* severely criticized the government in his speech

diazepán *nm Farm* diazepam

dibujante *nmf (artista)* drawer, sketcher; *(de dibujos animados, tebeos)* cartoonist; *(de dibujo técnico)* draughtsman, *f* draughtswoman

dibujar 1 *vt* (**a**) *(trazar a lápiz, bolígrafo)* to draw
(**b**) *(describir)* **dibujó un oscuro panorama para la economía** she painted a bleak future for the economy; **la novela dibuja el Londres victoriano** the novel portrays Victorian London
2 *vi* to draw
3 dibujarse *vpr* (**a**) *(mostrarse, verse)* to be outlined; **la montaña se dibujaba en el horizonte** the mountain was outlined on the horizon; **una mueca de disgusto se dibujó en su rostro** he scowled in annoyance; **una sonrisa inocente se dibujó en su rostro** a smile of innocent amusement played across his lips; **todavía no se dibuja el final de la crisis** the end of the crisis is still not in sight
(**b**) *(revelarse)* **Fuster se está dibujando como un futuro campeón** Fuster is beginning to look like a future champion

dibujo *nm* (**a**) *(técnica, obra)* drawing; **no se le da bien el d.** he's no good at drawing; **el profesor de d.** the drawing teacher; EXPR *Esp Fam* **meterse en dibujos** to complicate things unnecessarily ►► ***d. anatómico*** anatomical drawing; ***dibujos animados*** cartoons; **una película de dibujos animados** a cartoon film, a feature-length cartoon; **fue una jugada de dibujos animados** *(en fútbol)* it was a piece of wizardry; ***d. artístico*** drawing *(as school subject)*; ***d. al carboncillo*** charcoal drawing; ***d. a lápiz*** pencil drawing; ***d. lineal*** *(asignatura)* = drawing of geometrical figures; ***d. a mano alzada*** freehand drawing; ***d. técnico*** technical drawing
(**b**) *(en tela, prenda)* pattern; **un d. a cuadros/de círculos** a check/circle pattern

dic. (*abrev de* **diciembre**) Dec., December

dicción *nf* (**a**) *(pronunciación)* enunciation, pronunciation (**b**) *(manera de hablar)* diction

diccionario *nm* dictionary; **un d. jurídico** a law *o* legal dictionary; **un d. de informática** a dictionary of computing; **buscar** *o* **mirar algo en un d.** to look sth up in a dictionary ►► ***d. bilingüe*** bilingual dictionary; ***d. enciclopédico*** encyclopedic dictionary; ***d. etimológico*** etymological dictionary; ***d. ideológico*** = dictionary in which entries are organized according to themes rather than alphabetically; ***d. monolingüe*** monolingual dictionary; ***d. de sinónimos*** thesaurus; ***d. técnico*** technical dictionary; ***d. de uso*** dictionary of usage

dice *etc ver* **decir**

dicha *nf* (**a**) *(felicidad)* joy; **la noticia la colmó de d.** the news filled her with joy; **es una d. contar con tu presencia** it's marvellous to have you here (**b**) *(suerte)* good fortune; **esta asociación, a la que tengo la d. de pertenecer...** this association, to which I have the good fortune to belong...

dicharachero, -a *adj Fam* (**a**) *(hablador)* talkative (**b**) *(gracioso)* witty

DIÁLOGO

In literary works, the Spanish convention is to introduce direct speech with a long dash (—) or, less frequently, a short dash (-).

> **—Buenos días, jefe. —¿Qué tal, Mortadelo?**
> *"Good morning, boss." "How are things, Mortadelo?"*

There is no space between the dash and the first word. If there is a comment from the narrator, a dash is again used to introduce it:

> **—Buenos días, jefe —dijo. —¿Qué tal, Mortadelo? —respondió Filemón.**
> *"Good morning, boss," he said. "How are things, Mortadelo?" replied Filemón.*

If the end of the narrator's remark coincides with the end of the paragraph, there is no need for a closing dash, but one is needed if the direct speech continues, with no space being left between the remark and the two dashes:

> **—Buenos días, jefe —dijo. —¿Qué tal, Mortadelo? —respondió Filemón—. ¡Qué disfraz más original lleva!**
> *"Good morning, boss," he said. "How are things, Mortadelo?" replied Filemón. "What an original disguise you're wearing!"*

When what one person says extends over several paragraphs, "Spanish" closing inverted commas (») are placed at the start of each new paragraph to indicate the same speaker, and also at the end of the last paragraph, to show the speaker has finished. Quotations within direct speech are indicated by using "Spanish" inverted commas:

> **—El jefe me dijo ayer «tómese un mes de vacaciones».**
> *"My boss said to me yesterday, 'Take a month's holiday'."*

dicho, -a 1 *participio ver* **decir**
2 *adj* said, aforementioned; **dichos individuos...** the said *o* aforesaid individuals...; **recibió un paquete, d. paquete contenía...** she received a parcel, and this parcel contained...; **lo d. no significa que...** having said this, it does not mean (that)...; **de lo d. se desprende que...** from what has been said one gathers that...; **o mejor d.** or rather; **d. y hecho** no sooner said than done; **dejar d.** to leave word; **dejé d. que no me molestaran** I left word that I was not to be disturbed; *RP* **¿quiere dejarle algo d.?** *(al teléfono)* can I take a message?; **lo d.: lo d., no voy a ir** like I said, I'm not going to go; **lo d., os veré en el cine** ok then, I'll see you at the cinema
3 *nm* saying; **como dice** *o* **reza el d.,...** as the saying goes,...; PROV **del d. al hecho hay mucho** *o* **un gran trecho** there's many a slip 'twixt cup and lip

dichoso, -a *adj* (a) *(feliz)* happy; **hacer d. a alguien** to make sb happy; EXPR **¡dichosos los ojos (que te ven)!** how lovely to see you again!
(b) *Fam (para enfatizar)* blessed, confounded; **¡siempre está con la dichosa tele puesta!** he always has that blasted TV on!; **no vamos a resolver nunca este d. asunto** we'll never get to the bottom of this blessed business; **¡d. niño, no para de llorar!** the blessed child does nothing but cry!

diciembre *nm* December; *ver también* **septiembre**

dicotiledónea *Bot* 1 *nf* dicotyledon, member of the *Dicotyledonae* family
2 **dicotiledóneas** *nfpl (familia) Dicotyledonae*; **de la familia de las dicotiledóneas** of the *Dicotyledonae* family

dicotiledóneo, -a *adj Bot* of the Dicotyledonae family

dicotomía *nf* dichotomy

dicromático, -a *adj* dichromatic

dictablanda *nf Fam* semi-dictatorship, soft dictatorship

dictado *nm* (a) *(lectura de texto)* dictation; **escribir al d.** to take dictation; **hacer un d. a alguien** to give sb dictation (b) *(orden)* **dictados** dictates; **seguir los dictados del corazón/de la conciencia** to follow the dictates of one's heart/of conscience; **actuar al d. de alguien** to follow sb's dictates; **obedecer al d. de** to follow the dictates of

dictador, -ora *nm,f* dictator; **su padre era un auténtico d.** her father was a real tyrant

dictadura *nf* dictatorship; **la d. de la moda** the dictatorship of fashion ►► ***d. militar*** military dictatorship; ***d. del proletariado*** dictatorship of the proletariat

dictáfono *nm* Dictaphone®

dictamen *nm* (a) *(opinión)* opinion, judgement; **el d. del juez sobre la custodia de los niños** the judge's decision on the custody of the children; **dar** *o* **emitir un d.** to deliver an opinion ►► ***d. jurídico*** legal opinion; ***d. médico*** diagnosis *(singular)*; ***d. pericial*** expert opinion (b) *(informe)* report

dictaminar 1 *vt* **los expertos dictaminaron que no había peligro** the experts stated that there was no danger; **todavía no se han dictaminado las causas de la enfermedad** the cause of the illness has still not been found *o* determined
2 *vi* to express an opinion

dictar *vt* (a) *(texto, carta)* to dictate
(b) *(conferencia)* to give; *Am (clase)* to teach, to give
(c) *(emitir) (sentencia, fallo)* to pronounce, to pass; *(ley)* to enact; *(decreto)* to issue; **el gobierno dictará medidas contra la violencia doméstica** the government will enact measures to curb domestic violence; **d. auto de procesamiento contra alguien** to issue an indictment against sb
(d) *(inspirar, aconsejar)* **las modas que dictan lo que se ha de llevar cada temporada** the fashions that dictate *o* decree what people are supposed to wear each season; **haz lo que te dicte la conciencia** do as your conscience tells you

dictatorial *adj* dictatorial

dictatorialmente *adv* dictatorially

dicterio *nm Formal* insult

didáctica *nf* didactics *(singular)*

didácticamente *adv* didactically

didáctico, -a *adj (juego, juguete)* educational; *(enfoque, profesor)* didactic; **es una serie infantil muy didáctica** it's a very educational children's programme; **material d.** teaching materials; **método d.** teaching method

diecinueve *núm* nineteen; *ver también* **tres**

diecinueveavo, -a *núm (fracción)* nineteenth; **la diecinueveava parte** a nineteenth

dieciochesco, -a *adj* eighteenth-century

dieciocho *núm* eighteen; *ver también* **tres**

dieciochoavo, -a *núm (fracción)* eighteenth; **la dieciochoava parte** an eighteenth

dieciséis *núm* sixteen; *ver también* **tres**

dieciseisavo, -a 1 *núm (fracción)* sixteenth; **la dieciseisava parte** a sixteenth
2 *nm Dep* ***los dieciseisavos de final*** the last thirty-two

diecisiete *núm* seventeen; *ver también* **tres**

diecisieteavo, -a *núm (fracción)* seventeenth; **la diecisieteava parte** a seventeenth

dieléctrico, -a *Elec* 1 *adj* dielectric
2 *nm* dielectric

diente *nm* (a) *(pieza bucal)* tooth; **se le ha caído un d.** she has lost a tooth; **echar los dientes** *(niño)* to cut one's teeth; **me hace rechinar los dientes** it sets my teeth on edge; **le está saliendo un d.** he's got a tooth coming through; **tener un d. picado** to have a bad tooth; EXPR **iba armado hasta los dientes** he was armed to the teeth; EXPR *Fam* **daba d. con d.** her teeth were chattering; EXPR **enseñar los dientes** to bare one's teeth; **el pastor alemán nos enseñó los dientes** the Alsatian bared its teeth at us; **la guerrilla ha enseñado los dientes** the guerrillas have shown they mean business; EXPR **entre dientes: decir algo entre dientes** to mutter sth; **hablar entre dientes** to mumble, to mutter; EXPR *Fam* **hincar el d. a algo** *(a comida)* to sink one's teeth into sth; *(a trabajo, proyecto)* to tackle sth, to get one's teeth into sth; EXPR *Fam* **ponerle a alguien los dientes largos** to turn sb green with envy ►► ***d. canino*** canine (tooth); ***d. incisivo*** incisor; ***d. de leche*** milk *o* baby tooth; ***d. molar*** molar
(b) *(de rueda, engranaje, serrucho)* tooth; *(de tridente)* prong; *(de tenedor)* prong, tine; *(de peine)* tooth
(c) ***d. de ajo*** clove of garlic
(d) ***d. de león*** *(planta)* dandelion; ***d. de perro*** *(planta)* dogtooth violet

dientudo, -a *Am Fam* 1 *adj* toothy
2 *nm,f* toothy person

diera *etc ver* **dar**

diéresis *nf inv* (a) *(signo)* diaeresis (b) *(pronunciación)* diaeresis

dieron *ver* **dar**

diesel, diésel 1 *adj* diesel
2 *nm* (a) *(automóvil)* diesel (b) *(combustible)* diesel (fuel) (c) *(motor)* diesel (engine)

diestra *nf* right hand; **a la d.** on the right *o* right-hand side; **se sentó a la d. del anfitrión** he sat on the right of the host *o* on the host's right

diestramente *adv* skilfully

diestro, -a 1 *adj* (a) *(mano)* right; EXPR *Esp* **a d. y siniestro,** *Am* **a diestra y siniestra** left, right and centre, all over the place (b) *(persona)* right-handed; *(futbolista)* right-footed (c) *(hábil)* skilful (**en** at); **es muy d. con los pinceles** he's a talented painter; **es muy d. reparando averías en la casa** he's very good at mending things around the house
2 *nm* (a) *(persona)* right-handed person; *(futbolista)* right-footed player; **los diestros** the right-handed, right-handed people (b) *Taurom* matador

dieta *nf* (a) *(régimen)* diet; **una d. baja en calorías** a low-calorie diet; **una d. a base de líquidos** a liquid diet; **estar a d.** to be on a diet; **poner a alguien a d.** to put sb on a diet; **ponerse a d.** to go on a diet (b) *(alimentación diaria)* diet ►► ***la d. mediterránea*** the Mediterranean diet (c) *Com* **dietas** *(dinero para gastos)* expense *o* subsistence allowance (d) *Hist (asamblea)* diet

dietario *nm* (a) *(agenda)* diary (b) *(para contabilidad)* journal, day book

dietética *nf* dietetics *(singular)*

dietético, -a *adj* dietetic, dietary; **productos dietéticos** diet foods

dietista *nmf Am* dietician

diez 1 *núm* ten; *Fam* **una chica d.** a stunning woman, a ten; EXPR *muy Fam* **¡me cago en d.!** *Br* bleeding hell!, *US* goddamn it!; *ver también* **tres**
2 *nm (nota)* A, top marks

diezmar *vt* to decimate

diezmo *nm Hist* tithe

difamación *nf (verbal)* slander; *(escrita)* libel; **querellarse contra alguien por d.** to sue sb for libel

difamador, -ora 1 *adj (de palabra)* defamatory, slanderous; *(por escrito)* defamatory, libellous
2 *nm,f (de palabra)* slanderer; *(por escrito)* libeller

difamar *vt (de palabra)* to slander; *(por escrito)* to libel

difamatorio, -a *adj (de palabra)* defamatory, slanderous; *(por escrito)* defamatory, libellous

diferencia *nf* **(a)** *(disimilitud)* difference (**con/entre** from/between); **el problema de esa pareja es la d. de edad** that couple's problem is the difference in their ages; **la d. está en que tú eres hombre** the difference is that you're a man; **a d. de** unlike; **con d.** by far; **establecer** *o* **hacer una d. entre** to make a distinction between

(b) *(desacuerdo)* difference; **tuvieron sus diferencias** they had their differences; **limar diferencias** to settle one's differences

(c) *(en suma, resta)* difference (**entre** between); **tendremos que pagar la d.** we'll have to pay the difference ►► ***d. horaria*** time difference; *Elec* ***d. de potencial*** potential difference; ***d. salarial*** wage *o* pay differential

diferenciación *nf* differentiation

diferenciado, -a *adj (distinto)* differentiated; **existen tres sectores económicos bien diferenciados** there are three clearly differentiated economic sectors

diferencial 1 *adj* **(a)** *(rasgo, carácter)* distinguishing **(b)** *Mat* differential

2 *nm* **(a)** *Aut* differential **(b)** *Fin* differential; **el d. de inflación** the inflation differential

3 *nf Mat* differential

diferenciar 1 *vt* **(a)** *(distinguir)* to distinguish (**de/entre** from/between); **hay que d. el tai-chi de las artes marciales** you have to distinguish tai chi from the martial arts; **no sabe d. entre las setas venenosas y las comestibles** he can't tell the difference between poisonous mushrooms and edible ones

(b) *Mat* to differentiate

2 *vi* to distinguish, to differentiate

3 diferenciarse *vpr* **(a)** *(diferir)* to differ, to be different (**de/en** from/in); **se diferencia del hermano en que es más tímido** he's different from his brother in that he's shyer; **¿en qué se diferencia un roble de un olmo?** in what way does an oak differ from an elm?; **sólo se diferencian en el tamaño** the only difference between them is the size

(b) *(descollar)* **diferenciarse de** to stand out from; **se diferenciaba de los demás por su valentía** he stood out from the others for his bravery

diferendo *nm Andes, RP (desacuerdo)* dispute

diferente 1 *adj* **(a)** *(distinto)* different (**de** *o* **a** from *o* to); **una casa d. de** *o* **a la mía** a house different from mine; **yo soy muy d. de** *o* **a él** I'm very different from him; **fue una experiencia d.** it was something different

(b) diferentes *(varios)* various; **se oyeron diferentes opiniones al respecto** various opinions were voiced on the subject; **por diferentes razones** for a variety of reasons, for various reasons; **ocurre en diferentes lugares del planeta** it happens in various different places around the world

2 *adv* differently; **se comportan muy d. el uno del otro** they behave very differently (from one another)

diferentemente *adv* differently

diferido *nm* (pre-)recorded broadcast; **en d.** *(retransmisión, concierto)* (pre-)recorded; **el canal 2 retransmitirá el partido en d.** channel 2 will show a recording of the game later

diferir [63] **1** *vt (posponer)* to postpone, to put off; **el plazo de inscripción se difiere hasta el 5 de mayo** the deadline for enrolment has been extended to 5 May

2 *vi* **(a)** *(diferenciarse)* to differ, to be different; **d. de algo/alguien (en algo)** to differ from sth/sb (in sth); **difería de su padre casi en todo** he was different from his father in almost every way; **difiere bastante de lo que entendemos por teatro** it's rather different from what we understand by theatre

(b) *(discrepar)* to disagree, to differ; **d. de alguien en algo** to disagree with *o* differ from sb on sth; **difiero de ti en ese asunto** I disagree with you on that issue; **difiero de tu punto de vista** I don't share your point of view

difícil *adj* **(a)** *(complicado)* difficult; **va a ser d. encontrar un sitio abierto a estas horas** it's going to be difficult *o* hard to find anywhere that's open at this time; **son tiempos difíciles** these are difficult times; **pasaron por una situación d.** they went through a difficult period; **no es d. imaginar lo que pasó** it's not difficult *o* hard to imagine what happened; **es una pregunta d. de responder** it's a difficult question to answer; **hacerse d.: se hace d. entender por qué lo hizo** it's difficult to understand why she did it; **se me hace d. acostumbrarme a madrugar** I can't get used to getting up early; **ponérselo d. a alguien** to make things difficult for sb; **no me lo pongas d.** don't make things difficult *o* hard for me; **serle d. a alguien: le va a ser muy d. encontrar trabajo** it's going to be very difficult for him to find a job, he's going to find it very difficult to get a job; **tener d. algo: tiene muy d. encontrar trabajo** it's very difficult *o* hard for him to find work

(b) *(improbable)* unlikely; **puede ser, aunque me parece d.** maybe, but I think it's unlikely; **es d. que ganen** they're unlikely to win; **no es d. que ocurra** it could easily happen

(c) *(rebelde)* difficult, awkward; **es un niño muy d.** he's a very awkward *o* difficult child; **tener un carácter d.** to be an awkward person, to be difficult to get on with

difícilmente *adv* **(a)** *(con dificultad)* with difficulty; **algo d. imaginable** something difficult to imagine **(b)** *(improbablemente)* **si no me cuentas lo que te pasa, d. te podré ayudar** if you don't tell me what's wrong, I can hardly help you; **d. van a venir con el chaparrón que está cayendo** they're not likely to come in this downpour

dificultad *nf* **(a)** *(cualidad de difícil)* difficulty; **caminaba con d.** she walked with difficulty; **el grado** *o* **nivel de d. de los exámenes** the degree *o* level of difficulty of the exams; **un ejercicio de gran d.** a very difficult exercise

(b) *(obstáculo)* problem; **todo son dificultades con ella** she sees everything as a problem; **la d. está en hacerlo sin mojarse los pies** the difficult thing is to do it without getting your feet wet; **encontrar dificultades** to run into trouble *o* problems; **poner dificultades** to raise objections; **nos puso muchas dificultades para entrevistarlo** he put no end of obstacles in our way when we wanted to interview him; **superar** *o* **vencer las dificultades** to overcome the difficulties; **¿tuviste alguna d. para dar con la calle?** did you have any difficulty finding the street?

(c) *(penalidad)* **pasar por dificultades** to suffer hardship

dificultar *vt (estorbar)* to hinder; *(obstruir)* to obstruct; **la gran cantidad de transeúntes dificultaba el rodaje** the large number of passers-by made filming more difficult; **unas zanjas dificultaban el paso** some ditches made progress difficult; **el viento dificultaba la navegación** the wind made sailing difficult

dificultoso, -a *adj* hard, fraught with difficulties

difiero *etc ver* **diferir**

difiriera *etc ver* **diferir**

difracción *nf Fís* diffraction

difteria *nf Med* diphtheria

diftérico, -a *adj* **el bacilo d.** the diphtheria bacillus

difuminado, -a *adj* **(a)** *Arte* stumped **(b)** *Fot* soft-focus; **en d.** in soft focus **(c)** *(poco claro)* blurred

difuminar 1 *vt* **(a)** *(quitar nitidez a)* to blur **(b)** *Arte* = to soften with a stump, *Espec* to stump

2 difuminarse *vpr* to grow *o* become blurred

difumino *nm Arte* stump, = roll of paper used for blurring chalk or charcoal drawings

difundir 1 *vt* **(a)** *(divulgar) (noticia, pánico, religión)* to spread; *(comunicado, informe)* to publish; *(cultura, costumbres)* to spread, to diffuse

(b) *(sujeto: emisora radiofónica, canal televisivo)* to broadcast; **una cadena argentina difundió las imágenes** an Argentinian channel broadcast the pictures

(c) *(extender) (epidemia, olor)* to spread; *(sonido, ondas)* to diffuse, to propagate; **la estufa difunde muy bien el calor** the stove heats the place up well

2 difundirse *vpr* **(a)** *(noticia, pánico, religión)* to spread; *(cultura, costumbres)* to spread, to be diffused

(b) *(epidemia, olor, calor)* to spread; *(sonido, ondas)* to be diffused *o* spread

difunto, -a 1 *adj* deceased, dead; **el d. Sr. Pérez** the late Mr Pérez

2 *nm,f* **el d.** the deceased

difusión *nf* **(a)** *(de noticia, rumor)* spreading; *(de religión, ideología)* spread, dissemination; *(de cultura, costumbres)* spreading, diffusion; **el evento tuvo enorme d. en la prensa escrita** the event received extensive press coverage **(b)** *(por radio, televisión)* broadcasting; **los medios de d.** the media **(c)** *(de epidemia, olor, calor)* spread; *(de sonido, ondas)* diffusion, spread

difuso, -a *adj* **(a)** *(luz)* diffuse; *(imagen)* blurry **(b)** *(estilo, explicación)* wordy; *(ideas, conocimientos)* vague; **el contenido de su discurso fue más bien d.** the content of her speech was fairly vague

difusor, -ora 1 *adj* **(a)** *(medio, agencia)* broadcasting **(b)** *(divulgador)* **una institución difusora de la lengua española** an institution whose mission is to spread the Spanish language

2 *nm,f (divulgador)* **los difusores de la religión católica** those who spread the Catholic religion; **el principal d. de noticias en el país** the main source of news in the country

3 *nm (utensilio)* diffuser

diga *etc ver* **decir**

digerible *adj* digestible

digerir [63] *vt* (**a**) *(comida)* to digest (**b**) *(hechos, noticia)* to assimilate, to take in

digestible *adj* digestible

digestión *nf* digestion; **no te metas en el agua hasta que no hagas la d.** don't go into the water so soon after eating

digestivo, -a **1** *adj* digestive; **los helados son digestivos** ice cream helps your digestion
2 *nm* digestive (drink)

digiero *etc ver* **digerir**

digiriera *etc ver* **digerir**

digitación *nf Mús (en partitura)* fingering; *(ejercicio)* finger exercise

digitado, -a *adj RP Fam* rigged; **los resultados de la encuesta vienen muy digitados** the results of the survey have been heavily doctored

digitador, -ora *nm,f Am* keyboarder

digital **1** *adj* (**a**) *(del dedo)* **huellas digitales** fingerprints (**b**) *(reloj, televisión, tecnología)* digital
2 *nf (planta)* foxglove

digitalina *nf Farm* digitalin

digitalización *nf Informát* digitizing

digitalizador *nm Informát* digitizer

digitalizar *vt Informát* to digitize

digitar *vt* (**a**) *Am (teclear)* to key, to type (**b**) *RP Fam (manipular)* to rig

dígito *nm* digit ►► ***d. binario*** binary digit

digitopuntura *nf* acupressure

diglosia *nf Ling* diglossia

dignamente *adv* with dignity, in a dignified manner

dignarse *vpr* **d. (a) hacer algo** to deign to do sth; **no se dignó (a) contestarme** he didn't deign to reply; *Irónico* **¡por fin te dignas (a) aparecer por aquí!** so you've finally decided to honour us with your presence!; *Formal* **dígnese acudir con la documentación consignada** please ensure that you bring the required documents

dignatario, -a *nm,f* dignitary

dignidad *nf* (**a**) *(cualidad)* dignity; **lleva su enfermedad con mucha d.** he bears his illness with great dignity; **nunca aceptó limosnas por una cuestión de d.** she never accepted charity out of a sense of dignity (**b**) *(cargo)* office; *(título)* rank (**c**) *(personalidad)* dignitary

dignificar [60] *vt* to dignify; **una mujer que dignificó la profesión de enfermera** a woman who enhanced *o* improved the status of the nursing profession; **la sinceridad con que habla lo dignifica** the sincerity of his words lends him dignity

digno, -a *adj* (**a**) *(honroso) (actitud, respuesta)* dignified; *(persona)* honourable, noble; **tomó la postura más digna en estos casos: dimitir** she did the most honourable thing in the circumstances: she resigned; **son un pueblo d. y orgulloso** they are a proud and noble people
(**b**) *(decente) (sueldo, vivienda)* decent, good; *(actuación)* decent, good; **terminó el torneo en un muy d. cuarto puesto** she finished a very creditable fourth in the tournament; **una vida digna** a decent life
(**c**) *(merecedor)* **d. de** worthy of; **la labor de la Cruz Roja es digna de admiración** the work of the Red Cross is worthy of admiration; **no me siento d. de tantos elogios** I don't feel I deserve so much praise; **no eres d. de ella** you're not good enough for her; **d. de confianza** trustworthy; **d. de elogio** praiseworthy; **d. de mención/de ver** worth mentioning/seeing
(**d**) *(adecuado)* worthy; **recibió una digna recompensa por su trabajo** she received a fair reward for her work; **fue un d. sucesor del ex campeón del mundo** he was a worthy successor to the former world champion; **lo recibieron con honores dignos de un rey** they gave him a welcome fit for a king; **un guión d. de un verdadero genio** a script worthy of a true genius

digo *etc ver* **decir**

dígrafo *nm Ling* digraph

digresión *nf* digression; **hacer digresiones** to digress

dije[1] *adj Chile* nice, pleasant

dije[2] *nm (en cadena o pulsera)* charm

dijera *etc ver* **decir**

dilacerar *vt* to tear

dilación *nf* delay; **sin d.** without delay, at once; **sin más** *o* **mayor d.** without further delay

dilapidación *nf* waste, squandering

dilapidar *vt* to squander, to waste

dilatable *adj* expandable

dilatación *nf* (**a**) *(de sólido, gas)* expansion (**b**) *(de pupila, cuello del útero)* dilation, dilatation

dilatado, -a *adj* (**a**) *(pupila, cuello del útero)* dilated (**b**) *(extenso)* extensive; **tiene una dilatada experiencia como cirujano** he has extensive experience as a surgeon; **tras una dilatada estancia en Mallorca,...** after a lengthy stay in Majorca,...; **un d. historial de delitos** an extensive *o* a lengthy criminal record; **una dilatada trayectoria radiofónica** many years' experience in radio

dilatador, -ora **1** *adj* expanding
2 *nm Med* dilator

dilatar **1** *vt* (**a**) *(sólido, gas)* to expand; **el calor dilata los cuerpos** heat causes bodies to expand (**b**) *(pupila, cuello del útero)* to dilate (**c**) *(prolongar)* to prolong (**d**) *(demorar)* to delay
2 *vi* (**a**) *(antes del parto)* to dilate (**b**) *Méx (tardar)* to take; **la encomienda dilató dos semanas en llegar** the parcel took two weeks to arrive (**c**) *Méx Fam (durar)* to last; **ese curso dilata un mes** the course lasts one month
3 dilatarse *vpr* (**a**) *(extenderse)* to expand; **los cuerpos se dilatan con el calor** bodies expand when heated
(**b**) *(pupila, cuello del útero)* to dilate
(**c**) *(prolongarse)* to be prolonged, to go on; **la reunión se dilató hasta el amanecer** the meeting went on until dawn
(**d**) *(aplazarse)* to be delayed; **la reunión se dilató tres días** the meeting was put off for three days
(**e**) *Méx (tardar)* to be late; **espérame, no me dilato** wait for me, I won't be long; **el avión se dilató tres horas** the plane was three hours late

dilatoria *nf* delay; **andar con dilatorias** to waste time, to use delaying tactics

dilatorio, -a *adj* (**a**) *Formal (para retrasar)* delaying; **utilizan tácticas dilatorias** they use delaying tactics (**b**) *Der* dilatory

dilecto, -a *adj Formal* beloved, much-loved; **mi d. colega** my dear colleague

dilema *nm* dilemma; **estar en un d.** to be in a dilemma; **tener un d.** to be faced with a dilemma

diletante **1** *adj* dilettantish, dilettante
2 *nmf* dilettante

diletantismo *nm* dilettantism

diligencia *nf* (**a**) *(prontitud y esmero)* **actuar con d.** to act expeditiously; **este trabajo requiere d.** this work has to be done quickly and carefully
(**b**) *(trámite, gestión)* **diligencias** formalities, official paperwork; **hacer unas diligencias** to take care of some business; **la embajada está haciendo diligencias para poder repatriarlos** the embassy is taking the necessary steps to have them repatriated
(**c**) *Am (recado)* **hacer unas diligencias** to do some errands
(**d**) *Der* **diligencias** proceedings; **instruir diligencias** to start proceedings ►► ***diligencias judiciales*** legal proceedings; ***diligencias policiales*** police inquiry *o* investigation; ***diligencias previas*** preliminary investigation; ***diligencias procesales*** criminal proceedings
(**e**) *(vehículo)* stagecoach

diligenciar *vt* **estoy diligenciando la renovación de la licencia** I'm in the process of having my licence renewed; **la policía diligencia la expedición de pasaportes** the police are in charge of issuing passports

diligente *adj* (**a**) *(persona)* **un trabajador d.** a quick and careful worker (**b**) *(respuesta)* expeditious

diligentemente *adv* (**a**) *(con esmero, cuidado)* diligently (**b**) *(con prontitud)* speedily, quickly

dilucidación *nf* elucidation, explanation

dilucidar *vt (asunto, problema)* to clarify; **tratan de d. qué pasó** they are trying to clarify what happened

dilución *nf* (**a**) *(de zumo, aceite)* dilution; *(de pintura)* thinning (**b**) *(de polvos, azúcar, pastilla)* dissolving

diluido, -a *adj (zumo, aceite)* diluted, dilute; *(pintura)* thinned

diluir [34] **1** *vt* (**a**) *(zumo, aceite)* to dilute; *(pintura)* to thin; **diluya el puré con un poco de agua** dilute the purée with a little water (**b**) *(polvos, azúcar, pastilla)* to dissolve (**en** in); **una pastilla diluida en agua** one tablet dissolved in water
2 diluirse *vpr* (**a**) *(zumo, aceite)* to become diluted; *(pintura)* to become thinner (**b**) *(polvos, azúcar, pastilla)* to dissolve

diluvial *adj Geol* diluvial

diluviar *v impersonal* to pour with rain; **está diluviando** it's pouring with rain

diluvio *nm* (**a**) *(lluvia torrencial)* deluge; **caía un auténtico d. sobre la ciudad** torrential rain fell on the city ►► ***el D. Universal*** the Flood (**b**) *(abundancia)* flood; **hubo un d. de quejas** there was a flood *o* storm of complaints, complaints flooded in

diluyente *nm* thinner

diluyera *etc ver* **diluir**

diluyo *etc ver* **diluir**

dimanar *vi* **d. de** *(alegría)* to emanate from; *(medidas, consecuencias, situación)* to arise from; **el poder político dimana de las urnas** political power comes from the ballot box

dimensión *nf* (**a**) *(tamaño)* dimension; **las dimensiones del armario son...** the dimensions of the cupboard are...; **una habitación de grandes dimensiones** a large room; **una caja de pequeñas dimensiones** a small box
(**b**) *(en el espacio)* dimension; **una película en tres dimensiones** a 3-D film
(**c**) *(importancia, magnitud)* scale; **las dimensiones de la tragedia** the extent *o* scale of the tragedy; **la d. del problema es tal que...** the scale of the problem is such that...
(**d**) *(faceta, aspecto)* dimension; **la d. humana del entrevistado** the human side of the interviewee
(**e**) *Fís* ***la cuarta d.*** the fourth dimension

dimensional *adj* dimensional

dimes *nmpl Fam* **el anuncio provocó d. y diretes** the announcement set people talking; **andan todo el día con d. y diretes** they spend the whole day chattering *o* gossiping

diminutivo 1 *adj* diminutive
2 *nm* diminutive

diminuto, -a *adj* tiny, minute

dimisión *nf* resignation; **aceptar la d. de alguien** to accept sb's resignation; **presentar la d.** to hand in one's resignation; **la oposición ha solicitado su d.** the opposition has called for her resignation

dimisionario, -a 1 *adj* resigning
2 *nm,f* person resigning

dimitente *adj, nmf* = **dimisionario**

dimitir *vi* to resign (**de** from); **dimitió de su cargo como secretario** he resigned from his post as secretary

dimorfismo *nm* dimorphism

dimos *ver* **dar**

dina *nf Fís* dyne

Dinamarca *n* Denmark

dinamarqués, -esa 1 *adj* Danish
2 *nm,f* Dane

dinámica *nf* (**a**) *(situación, proceso)* dynamics *(singular)*; **la d. de nuestra empresa** the dynamics of our company; **entramos en una d. de desarrollo económico** we are beginning a process of economic development; **el conflicto ha entrado en una d. peligrosa** the dispute has taken a dangerous turn ►► ***d. de grupo*** group dynamics
(**b**) *Fís* dynamics *(singular)* ►► ***d. de fluidos*** fluid dynamics
(**c**) *Econ* ***d. de poblaciones*** population dynamics

dinámico, -a *adj* (**a**) *(del movimiento, la dinámica)* dynamic (**b**) *(activo)* dynamic; **necesitamos ejecutivos dinámicos y emprendedores** we need dynamic and enterprising executives

dinamismo *nm (de persona)* dynamism, drive; *(de mercado, sector)* dynamism; *(de estilo, obra)* dynamism, verve

dinamita *nf* dynamite; **volar algo con d.** to blow sth up with dynamite, to dynamite sth; EXPR *Fam* **ese cóctel/jugador es pura d.** that cocktail/player is pure dynamite

dinamitar *vt* (**a**) *(construcción, puente, edificio)* to dynamite (**b**) *(reunión, asamblea, proyecto)* to wreck; **trató de d. la representación** he tried to wreck the performance

dinamitero, -a *nm,f* dynamiter

dinamizar [14] *vt (economía, vida cultural)* to enliven, to stimulate; **el gobierno quiere d. el sector industrial** the government wants to stimulate the industrial sector

dinamo, dínamo *nf Esp* dynamo

dinamo, dínamo *nm Am* dynamo

dinamómetro *nm* dynamometer

dinar *nm* dinar

diñar *vt Esp Fam* **diñarla** to snuff it

dinastía *nf* (**a**) *(de monarcas)* dynasty (**b**) *(de artistas, profesionales)* **una conocida d. de actores de teatro/músicos** a well-known theatrical/musical family *o* dynasty

dinástico, -a *adj* dynastic

dineral *nm Fam* fortune

dinerario, -a *adj* monetary

dinero *nm* money; **llevaba algo de d. encima** she had some money on her; **¿pagará con d. o con tarjeta?** will you be paying in cash or by credit card?; **una familia de d.** a family of means; **se junta con gente de d.** she mixes with wealthy people; **andar bien/mal de d.** to be well

DIMINUTIVO

Spanish has a range of diminutive suffixes which are used to create new nouns and adjectives. The commonest are: **-ito**, **-illo**, **-ín**, but others include: **-iño**, **-ico**, **-uco**, **-ete**, **-eto**, **-uelo.** These suffixes indicate smaller size, but they often add an affectionate, informal overtone:

vamos a tomar una cervecita *let's go and have a beer*
fuimos muy despacito *we went nice and slow*
mis amiguetes y yo *me and my pals*

On other occasions the diminutive has a pejorative tone:

un tiranuelo *a petty tyrant*

The diminutive can also be used to minimize the importance of a critical remark:

son cosillas sin importancia *they're matters of no importance*
es un poco revoltosillo *he's a bit of a troublemaker*

In other cases it simply indicates smaller size:

dale un beso a tu hermanito *give your little brother a kiss*
¡qué chiquitillo! *how tiny!*
mira qué perrito *look, what a little dog*
sólo un poquitín *only a tiny bit*
me quedé un ratillo *I stayed for a little bit*

Many diminutives created in this way have evolved into new words with distinct sense:

maleta (*suitcase*)	**maletín** (*briefcase*)
mesa (*table*)	**mesilla** (*bedside table*)
palo (*stick*)	**palillo** (*toothpick*)
teléfono (*telephone*)	**telefonillo** (*entryphone*)
tesis (*doctoral thesis*)	**tesina** (*undergraduate dissertation*)

off for/short of money; **hacer d.** to make money; **hacer algo por d.** to do sth for money; **tirar el d.** to waste money; EXPR **(el) d. llama a(l) d.** money goes where money is ▸▸ *Econ* ***d. en circulación*** money in circulation; ***d. circulante*** money in circulation; ***d. contante (y sonante)*** hard cash; ***d. de curso legal*** legal tender; ***d. en efectivo*** cash; *Informát* ***d. electrónico*** e-cash; ***d. fácil*** easy money; ***d. falso*** counterfeit money; ***d. en metálico*** cash; ***d. negro*** undeclared income/payment; ***d. sucio*** dirty money; ***d. suelto*** loose change; *Fin* ***d. a la vista*** call money

dingo *nm* dingo

dinosaurio *nm* dinosaur

dintel *nm* lintel

dio *ver* **dar**

diocesano, -a *adj* diocesan

diócesis *nf inv* diocese

diodo *nm Elec* diode

dionea *nf* Venus flytrap

dionisíaco, -a, dionisiaco, -a *adj* **(a)** *(de Dionisio)* Dionysian, Dionysiac **(b)** *Literario (excesivo)* Dionysian, Dionysiac

Dionisio *n pr* Dionysus

dioptría *nf* dioptre; **¿cuántas dioptrías tienes?** what's your prescription?; **tengo sólo una d. de miopía en el ojo derecho** I have only one dioptre of myopia in my right eye

diorama *nm* diorama

DIOS, -OSA 1 *nm,f* god, *f* goddess; **Baco es el d. del vino** Bacchus is the god of wine; **la diosa del amor** the goddess of love; **los dioses del Olimpo** the gods of (Mount) Olympus ▸▸ ***d. griego*** Greek god; ***d. romano*** Roman god

2 *nm* **(a) D.** *(ser sobrenatural)* God; **el D. de los cristianos** the Christian God; EXPR *Fam* **a la buena de D.** any old how; **hace las cosas a la buena de D.** he does things any old how; **no sabía cocinar, e hizo el guiso a la buena de D.** he didn't know how to cook, so he trusted to luck when making the stew; EXPR *Fam* **se armó la de D. (es Cristo)** all hell broke loose; EXPR *Fam* **como D.: lo pasamos como D.** we had a high old time; **en esta oficina vivimos como D.** we've got it made in this office; **tu vecina está como D.** your neighbour's gorgeous; **la paella estaba como D.** the paella was sublime; EXPR *Fam* **como D. manda** *(apropiado)* proper; *(apropiadamente)* properly; **una novela como D. manda** a proper novel; **hacer algo como D. manda** to do sth properly; EXPR *Fam* **como D. me/te/***etc.* **trajo al mundo** in my/your/*etc* birthday suit, without a stitch on; EXPR **costar D. y ayuda: nos costó D. y ayuda subir el piano hasta el quinto piso** we had a heck *o* hell of a job getting the piano up to the fifth floor; EXPR **dejado de la mano de D.** godforsaken; EXPR **jurar algo por D.: ¡te lo juro por D.!** I swear to God!; **me juró por D. que no había sido él** he swore to God that he hadn't done it; EXPR *Fam* **ni D.: no vino ni D.** not a soul came; **esto no lo arregla ni D.** no way will anyone ever fix this; **tu letra es muy mala, no hay (ni) D. que la entienda** your handwriting's terrible, you can't expect anyone to be able to read it; EXPR **poner a D. por testigo: ¡pongo a D. por testigo que yo no lo hice!** may God be my witness, I didn't do it!; EXPR **sin encomendarse (ni) a D. ni al diablo** throwing caution to the winds; EXPR *Fam* **todo D.** all the world and his wife; **vino todo D.** the world and his wife were there; **a todo D. le encantó la comida** absolutely everybody loved the food; EXPR **a D. rogando y con el mazo dando** God helps those who help themselves; PROV **D. aprieta pero no ahoga** God tempers the wind to the shorn lamb; PROV **D. los cría y ellos se juntan** birds of a feather flock together

(b) *(en exclamaciones, invocaciones)* **¡a D. gracias!** thank heavens!; **¡a D. gracias no pasó nada!** nothing happened, thank heavens!; **¡alabado sea D.!** *(al rezar)* praise be (to God)!; *(indica fastidio, sorpresa, alivio)* thank God!; **¡alabado sea D.!, ¡otra factura!** heavens above, another bill!; **¡alabado sea D.!, ¡por fin ha llegado el pedido!** thank heavens, the order has finally arrived!; **¡anda con D.!** God be with you!; **¡bendito sea D.!** *(al rezar)* praise be (to God)!; **¡bendito sea D.!, ¡otra carrera en la media!** heavens above, another ladder in my tights!; **¡bendito sea D.!, ¡no les ha pasado nada!** thank heavens, they're all right!; *Vulg* **¡me cago en D.!** for fuck's sake!; **D. dirá** it's in the lap of the gods; **¡gracias a D.!** thank heavens!; **¡gracias a D. que has venido!** thank heavens you've come!; **¡D. lo quiera!** let's hope so!; **D. mediante** God willing; **¡D. mío!** good God!, (oh) my God!; **¡D. no lo quiera!** heaven forbid!; **D. sabe** God (alone) knows; **sabe D.** God (alone) knows; **¡D. santo!** (oh) my God!; **¡D. santo!, ¿qué vamos a hacer ahora?** oh my God! what are we going to do now?; **¡santo D.!** (oh) my God!; **¡santo D.!, ¿qué vamos a hacer ahora?** oh my God! what are we going to do now?; **si D. quiere** God willing; **¡por D.!** for God's sake!; **¡(que) D. me/nos/***etc.* **ampare!** heaven help me/us/*etc*! **(que) D. le/te bendiga** God bless you; *Esp* **¡(que) D. nos coja confesados!** heaven help us!; **¡(que) D. le/te oiga!** let's hope so!; **(que) D. se/te lo pague** God bless you; **(que) D. me perdone: (que) D. me perdone, pero es una mala persona** forgive me for saying this, but he's not a very nice person; **(que) D. me perdone, pero es un cabrón** pardon my French, but he's a bastard; **que sea lo que D. quiera** what will be will be; **¡válgame D.!** good heavens!; **¡vaya con D.!** may God be with you; **¡vaya por D.!** for heaven's sake!, honestly!; **¡ve con D.!** God be with you!

3 *interj Fam* God!; **¡D.!, ¡qué aburrimiento!** God, how boring!; **¡D.!, ¡qué hambre tengo!** God, I'm hungry!

Diosito *nm Am Fam* God

diostedé *nm* Ariel toucan

dióxido *nm* dioxide ▸▸ ***d. de azufre*** sulphur dioxide; ***d. de carbono*** carbon dioxide; ***d. de nitrógeno*** nitrogen dioxide

dioxina *nf Quím* dioxin

diplodocus *nm inv,* **diplodoco** *nm* diplodocus

diploide *adj Biol* diploid

diploma *nm* diploma; **sacarse** *u* **obtener un d.** to get *o* obtain a diploma

diplomacia *nf* **(a)** *(disciplina, carrera)* diplomacy **(b)** *(cuerpo diplomático)* diplomatic service; **la d. española en Bruselas** Spanish diplomats in Brussels **(c)** *(tacto)* diplomacy; **le informó de la decisión con mucha d.** she told him about the decision very tactfully ▸▸ ***la d. de los cañones*** gunboat diplomacy

diplomado, -a 1 *adj* qualified; **enfermero d.** qualified nurse

2 *nm,f* holder of a diploma; **diplomados en enfermería** qualified nurses

diplomar 1 *vt* to grant a diploma to

2 **diplomarse** *vpr* to graduate, to get a diploma; **se diplomó en enfermería** he got a diploma in nursing, he qualified as a nurse

diplomáticamente *adv* diplomatically, tactfully

diplomático, -a 1 *adj* **(a)** *(de la diplomacia)* diplomatic **(b)** *(sagaz, sutil)* diplomatic

2 *nm,f* diplomat; **un d. de carrera** a career diplomat

diplomatura *nf Educ* diploma *(qualification obtained after three years of university study)*

dipolo *nm* dipole

dipsomanía *nf* dipsomania

dipsómano, -a, dipsomaníaco, -a 1 *adj* dipsomaniac

2 *nm,f* dipsomaniac

díptero, -a *Zool* 1 *adj* dipterous, dipteran

2 *nm (insecto)* dipteran, member of the order *Diptera*

3 **dípteros** *nmpl (orden) Diptera*; **del orden de los dípteros** of the order *Diptera*

díptico *nm* **(a)** *Arte* diptych **(b)** *(folleto)* leaflet

diptongo *nm* diphthong

diputación *nf* **(a)** *(comisión)* committee ▸▸ ***d. permanente*** standing committee **(b)** *(delegación)* delegation, deputation **(c)** *Esp (de comunidad autónoma)* = government and administrative body in certain autonomous regions ▸▸ ***d. provincial*** = governing body of a province in Spain, *Br* ≃ county council

diputado, -a *nm,f Br* ≃ Member of Parliament, MP, *US* ≃ representative; **d. por Cádiz** *Br* ≃ MP for Cadiz, *US* ≃ representative for Cadiz

diputar *vt (delegar)* to delegate

dique *nm* **(a)** *(en río)* dyke ▸▸ ***d. de contención*** dam **(b)** *(en puerto)* dock ▸▸ ***d. flotante*** floating dock; ***d. seco*** dry dock; EXPR **estar en el d. seco** *(persona)* to be out of action **(c)** *Geol* dyke **(d)** EXPR *RP Fam* **darse d.** to show off

diquelar *vt Esp Fam* **(a)** *(entender, enterarse de)* to get **(b)** *(calar) (persona)* to see through, *Br* to suss

Dir. **(a)** *(abrev de* **director/directora***) (de película, empresa)* Dir; *(de hotel, hospital, banco)* Mgr; *(de periódico)* Ed **(b)** *(abrev de* **dirección***) (de empresa, hotel)* Mgt

dirá *etc ver* **decir**

dirección *nf* **(a)** *(sentido)* direction; **se halla interrumpido el tráfico en ambas direcciones** the road is closed in both directions; **cambiar de d.** to change direction; **en d. contraria** in the opposite direction; **calle de d. única** one-way street; **una señal de d. obligatoria** = sign indicating that traffic must turn left or right or go ahead; **d. prohibida** *(en letrero)* no entry; **no gires por la siguiente, que es d. prohibida** don't take the next turning, it's no entry; **circular en d. prohibida** to drive the wrong way up a one-way street

(b) *(rumbo)* direction; **con d. a, en d. a** towards, in the direction of; **los trenes con** *o* **en d. a Málaga** trains to Malaga; **¿en qué d. ibas?** which way were you going?; **íbamos en d. a mi casa** we were heading for my place; **se fue en d. (al) sur** he went south; **el buque avanzaba en la d. del viento** the ship had the wind behind it; **los acontecimientos han tomado una d. inesperada** events have taken an unexpected turn

(c) *(domicilio)* address; **déme su nombre y d., por favor** could you tell me your name and address, please?

(d) *Informát* address ►► ***d. de correo electrónico*** e-mail address; ***d. electrónica*** *(de correo)* e-mail address; *(de página)* web page address; ***d. IP*** IP address; ***d. de memoria*** memory address; ***d. web*** web address

(e) *(mando, gestión) (de empresa, hospital)* management; *(de partido)* leadership; *(de colegio)* headship; *(de periódico)* editorship; *(de película)* direction; *(de obra de teatro)* production; *(de orquesta)* conducting; **estudia d. de cine** he's studying film directing

(f) *(oficina) (de empresa, hospital)* manager's office; *(de colegio) Br* headmaster's/headmistress's *o US* principal's office; *(de periódico)* editor's office

(g) *(junta directiva) (de empresa, hospital)* management; *(de partido)* leadership; *(de colegio)* management team; *(de periódico)* editorial board; **la d. de este periódico no se hace responsable de la opinión de sus colaboradores** the editors of this newspaper are not responsible for opinions expressed by contributors ►► ***d. comercial*** commercial department; ***d. general*** head office; *RP* ***D. General Impositiva*** *Br* ≃ Inland Revenue, *US* ≃ IRS; ***D. General de Tráfico*** = government department in charge of road transport

(h) *(de vehículo)* steering ►► *Esp* ***d. asistida*** power steering; *Am* ***d. hidráulica*** power steering

(i) *Geol* strike

direccionable *adj Informát* addressable

direccionador *nm Informát* router

direccional 1 *adj* directional

2 *nm o nf Col, Ecuad, Méx* indicator

direccionamiento *nm Informát* addressing

direccionar *vt Informát* to address

directa *nf (en automóvil)* top gear; **poner** *o* **meter la d.** *(en automóvil)* to go into top gear; *(apresurarse)* to really get a move on

directamente *adv* (a) *(sin paradas)* straight; **¿hay vuelos que vayan d. a Buenos Aires?** are there direct flights to Buenos Aires? (b) *(derecho)* straight; **me voy d. a casa** I'm going straight home (c) *(sin intermediarios)* directly; **para eso lo mejor es que hable d. con el encargado** the best thing would be to talk about it directly to the manager

directiva *nf* (a) *(junta)* board (of directors); *(de partido político)* executive committee; *(de club deportivo)* board (of directors) (b) *(ley de la UE)* directive ►► ***d. comunitaria*** community directive

directivo, -a 1 *adj* managerial; **la junta directiva del club** the management team of the club; **un cargo d.** a management post

2 *nm,f (jefe)* manager

directo, -a 1 *adj* (a) *(en línea recta)* direct; **éste es el camino más d. para llegar al pueblo** this is the most direct way to get to the village; **es descendiente d. de los Stroganoff** he's a direct descendant of the Stroganoffs; **su jefe d. es el comandante de la nave** he reports directly to the ship's captain

(b) *(sin detención, sin obstáculos)* direct; **no hay tren d. de Barcelona a Roma** there isn't a direct train from Barcelona to Rome; **tiene línea directa con la Casa Blanca** he has a direct line to the White House; **acceso d. a información privilegiada** direct access to inside *o* privileged information; **le gusta el trato d. con el cliente** he enjoys the direct contact with customers

(c) *(persona, pregunta)* direct; **su lenguaje era d., sin rodeos** her words were direct, she didn't beat about the bush; **contestaba con respuestas directas y sinceras** her answers were direct and sincere

2 *nm* (a) *(en boxeo)* jab ►► ***d. de derecha*** right jab; ***d. de izquierda*** left jab

(b) *(tren)* through train

(c) *(en televisión)* live broadcast; **no le tengo ningún miedo al d.** I'm not scared of doing live broadcasts; **en d.** *(retransmisión, concierto)* live; **la televisión retransmite el debate en d.** the debate is being broadcast live on television

3 *adv* straight; **d. a** straight to

director, -ora *nm,f* (a) *(de empresa)* director; *(de hotel, hospital, banco)* manager, *f* manageress; *(de periódico)* editor; *(de colegio) Br* headmaster, *f* headmistress, *US* principal; *(de cárcel) Br* governor, *US* warden ►► ***d. adjunto*** associate *o* deputy director; ***d. comercial*** marketing manager; ***d. ejecutivo*** executive director; ***d. espiritual*** spiritual director; ***d. financiero*** finance *o* financial director, *US* chief financial officer; ***d. general*** general manager, *Br* managing director, *US* chief executive officer; ***d. gerente*** managing director, chief executive; ***d. técnico*** *(en fútbol)* director of football; ***d. de tesis*** supervisor; ***d. de ventas*** sales director *o* manager

(b) *(de obra artística)* director ►► ***d. artístico*** artistic director; ***d. de banda musical*** bandmaster; ***d. de cine*** movie *o Br* film director; ***d. de circo*** ringmaster; ***d. de escena*** producer, stage manager; ***d. de fotografía*** director of photography; ***d. musical*** musical director; ***d. de orquesta*** conductor

directorio *nm* (a) *(lista de direcciones)* directory (b) *(junta)* directorate, governing body; *(de empresa)* board (c) *Andes, CAm, Carib, Méx (de teléfonos)* directory (d) *Informát* directory ►► ***d. raíz*** root directory

directriz *nf* (a) **directrices** *(normas)* guidelines; **seguir las directrices marcadas** to follow the established guidelines (b) *Mat* directrix

dirham *nm* dirham

diría *etc ver* **decir**

dirigencia *nf Am* leadership

dirigente 1 *adj (en partido)* leading; *(en empresa)* management; **la clase d.** the ruling class

2 *nmf (de partido político)* leader; *(de empresa)* manager; **el máximo d. del partido** the leader of the party

dirigible *nm* airship

dirigido, -a *adj* (a) *(carta, paquete)* **d. a** addressed to (b) **d. por** *(empresa)* managed by; *(colegio, cárcel, periódico)* run by; *(película)* directed by; *(orquesta)* conducted by

---

DIRIGIR [24] 1 *vt* (a) *(conducir) (coche, barco)* to steer; *(avión)* to pilot; **el canal dirige el agua hacia el interior de la región** the canal channels the water towards the interior of the region

(b) *(estar al cargo de) (empresa, hotel, hospital)* to manage; *(colegio, cárcel, periódico)* to run; *(partido, revuelta)* to lead; *(expedición)* to head, to lead; *(investigación)* to supervise; **dirige mi tesis, me dirige la tesis** he's supervising my thesis, he's my PhD supervisor

(c) *(película, obra de teatro)* to direct; *(orquesta)* to conduct

(d) *(apuntar)* **dirigió la mirada hacia la puerta** he looked towards the door; **dirige el telescopio al norte** point the telescope towards the north; **dirigió sus acusaciones a las autoridades** her accusations were aimed at the authorities

(e) *(dedicar, encaminar)* **nos dirigían miradas de lástima** they were giving us pitying looks, they were looking at us pityingly; **d. unas palabras a alguien** to speak to sb, to address sb; **dirige sus esfuerzos a incrementar los beneficios** she is directing her efforts towards increasing profits, her efforts are aimed at increasing profits; **dirigen su iniciativa a conseguir la liberación del secuestrado** the aim of their initiative is to secure the release of the prisoner; **dirigió sus pasos hacia la casa** he headed towards the house; **no me dirigen la palabra** they don't speak to me; **un programa dirigido a los amantes de la música clásica** a programme (intended) for lovers of classical music; **consejos dirigidos a los jóvenes** advice aimed at the young

(f) *(carta, paquete)* to address

(g) *(guiar) (persona)* to guide

2 **dirigirse** *vpr* (a) *(encaminarse)* **dirigirse a** *o* **hacia** to head for; **se dirigió al centro de la ciudad por un atajo** she took a shortcut to the city centre; **pasajeros con destino a Miami: por favor, diríjanse a la puerta 5** would passengers flying to Miami please proceed to gate 5; **¿hacia dónde te diriges?** where are you heading for?; **nos dirigimos hacia el río** we made our way towards the river

(b) **dirigirse a** *(hablar con)* to address, to speak to; *(escribir a)* to write to; **se dirigió a mí en un tono amenazador** she addressed me threateningly, she spoke to me in a threatening tone of voice; **se dirigió a varias empresas por escrito para pedir ayuda financiera** he wrote to several firms asking for financial assistance; **el monarca se dirigió a la nación por televisión** the monarch addressed the nation on television, the monarch gave a television address to the nation; **me estoy dirigiendo tí, así que escúchame** I'm talking to you, so listen; **me dirijo a usted para solicitarle...** I'm writing to you to request...; **diríjase al apartado de correos 42** write to PO Box 42

---

dirigismo *nm* state control

dirimir *vt* (a) *(resolver)* to resolve (b) *Formal (disolver)* to annul, to dissolve

discado *nm Andes, RP* dialling

discal *adj* **hernia d.** slipped disc, *Espec* herniated disc

discante *nm Perú (patochada)* folly, craziness

discapacidad *nf* disability, handicap; **d. física/psíquica** physical/mental disability *o* handicap; **las personas con discapacidades** people with disabilities, the disabled

discapacitado, -a 1 *adj* disabled, handicapped
2 *nm,f* disabled *o* handicapped person; **los discapacitados** the disabled, the handicapped, disabled *o* handicapped people; **un d. físico/psíquico** a physically/mentally handicapped *o* disabled person

discar [60] *vt Andes, RP* to dial

discernible *adj* discernible

discernimiento *nm* discernment; **actuar con d.** to act wisely

discernir [25] 1 *vt* to discern, to distinguish; **d. algo de algo** to distinguish sth from sth; **no sabía d. lo superfluo de lo imprescindible** she was incapable of distinguishing what was superfluous from what was essential; **con aquel ruido no lograba d. qué decían en la tele** with all that noise she couldn't hear what they were saying on the television
2 *vi* to discern, to distinguish (**entre** between)

disciplina *nf* (**a**) *(normas)* discipline; **guardar** *o* **mantener la d.** to maintain discipline; **los soldados tienen que guardar la d.** the soldiers have to remain disciplined ►► *Pol* ***d. de partido*** party discipline; *Pol* ***d. de voto*** party discipline *(in voting)*; **romper la d. de voto del partido** to vote against the party line, *Br* to break the whip
(**b**) *(actitud)* discipline; **tiene mucha d.** he's very (self-)disciplined
(**c**) *(materia, asignatura)* discipline
(**d**) *(modalidad deportiva)* discipline
(**e**) ***d. de monja*** knotweed

disciplinado, -a *adj* disciplined; **es muy d. con** *o* **en los estudios** he's very self-disciplined about his studies

disciplinar[1] *vt* to discipline

disciplinar[2] *adj (disciplinario)* disciplinary

disciplinario, -a *adj* disciplinary

discípulo, -a *nm,f* (**a**) *(alumno)* pupil; *(de Jesús)* disciple; *(de filósofo)* disciple, pupil (**b**) *(seguidor)* follower, disciple; **un d. de Hemingway** a follower of Hemingway

disc-jockey [dis'jokei] *nmf* disc jockey

disco[1] 1 *nm* (**a**) *(de música)* record; **un d. de boleros/de música de cámara** an album of boleros/chamber music; **van a grabar otro d.** they're going to record another album; **pasamos la tarde poniendo discos** we spent the afternoon listening to records; EXPR *Fam* **ser como** *o* **parecer un d. rayado** to go on like a cracked record; EXPR *Fam* **¡cambia de d., que ya aburres!** give it a rest for heaven's sake, you're going on like a cracked record! ►► ***d. compacto*** compact disc; ***d. de larga duración*** LP, long-playing record; ***d. de oro*** gold disc; ***d. de platino*** platinum disc; ***d. recopilatorio*** compilation album; ***d. sencillo*** single
(**b**) *Informát* disk ►► ***d. de alta densidad*** high-density disk; ***d. de arranque*** start-up disk; ***d. compacto*** compact disc; ***d. compacto interactivo*** interactive compact disc; ***d. de demostración*** demo disk; ***d. de destino*** destination disk; ***d. de doble densidad*** double-density disk; ***d. duro*** hard disk; ***d. duro externo*** external hard disk; ***d. duro extraíble*** removable hard disk; ***d. flexible*** floppy disk; ***d. maestro*** master disk; ***d. magnético*** magnetic disk; ***d. óptico*** optical disk; ***d. RAM*** RAM disk; ***d. removible*** removable disk; ***d. rígido*** hard disk; ***d. del sistema*** system disk; ***d. virtual*** virtual disk
(**c**) *(semáforo)* (traffic) light; **el d. se puso en rojo/verde** the lights turned to red/green; **saltarse un d. en rojo** to jump a red light
(**d**) *(de teléfono)* dial
(**e**) *(prueba atlética, objeto que se lanza)* discus; **lanzamiento de d.** (throwing) the discus; **el campeón de (lanzamiento de) d.** the discus champion
(**f**) *(en hockey sobre hielo)* puck
(**g**) *Anat* disc; **una hernia de d.** a slipped disc, *Espec* a herniated disc
(**h**) *Astron* disc; **el d. solar/lunar** solar/lunar disc
(**i**) *Geom* disc
2 *nf Fam (discoteca)* club

disco[2] *adj inv Fam Mús (de discoteca)* disco; **la música d.** disco (music); **el sonido d. de los setenta** the seventies disco sound

discobar *nm* = bar with music, where one can dance

discóbolo *nm* discus thrower

discografía *nf* discography; **tiene una d. muy extensa** he has recorded lots of albums; **tengo toda la d. de los Beatles** I have all the Beatles' records

discográfica *nf Esp* record company

discográfico, -a *adj* record; **casa discográfica** record company; **la industria discográfica** the record *o* music industry; **el acontecimiento d. del año** the year's most eagerly awaited release

díscolo, -a *adj* disobedient, rebellious

disconforme *adj* in disagreement; **estar d. con** to disagree with; **se mostró muy d. con la decisión** he made his disagreement with the decision very clear

disconformidad *nf* (**a**) *(desacuerdo)* disagreement (**con** with); **el público mostró su d. lanzando objetos** the audience showed its dissatisfaction by throwing things; **dejaron clara su d. con el acuerdo alcanzado** they made it clear that they did not accept the agreement that had been reached (**b**) *Formal (falta de correspondencia)* disagreement (**con/entre** with/between)

discontinuar [4] *vt* to discontinue, to interrupt

discontinuidad *nf* (**a**) *(falta de continuidad)* lack of continuity; **una d. en el crecimiento** a change in the rate of growth (**b**) *Mat* discontinuity

discontinuo, -a *adj (intermitente)* intermittent; **línea discontinua** broken *o* dotted line

discopub *nm* = bar with music, where one can dance

discordancia *nf* (**a**) *(de sonidos)* discord; *(de colores)* clash (**b**) *(de opiniones)* clash, conflict; **una d. entre los planes y el resultado final** a discrepancy between the plans and the final result

discordante *adj* (**a**) *(sonidos)* discordant; *(colores)* clashing (**b**) *(opiniones, declaraciones, versiones)* conflicting; **él era la única voz d. en la reunión** he was the only one at the meeting to strike a discordant note

discordar [64] *vi* (**a**) *(colores)* to clash; *(instrumentos)* to be out of tune (**b**) *(opiniones, declaraciones, versiones)* to conflict (**c**) *(persona)* **d. de alguien (en)** to disagree with sb (on *o* about)

discorde *adj* (**a**) *(sonidos)* discordant; *(colores)* clashing (**b**) *(opiniones, declaraciones, versiones)* conflicting

discordia *nf* discord; **sembrar la d.** to sow discord

discoteca *nf* (**a**) *(local)* nightclub; **ir de d.** to go clubbing (**b**) *(colección)* record collection

discotequero, -a 1 *adj* disco; **música discotequera** disco music
2 *nm,f* nightclubber

discreción 1 *nf (reserva)* discretion; **miró a la otra mesa con d.** she glanced discreetly at the other table; **actuó con mucha d.** he was very discreet; **confiamos en tu d.** we trust in your discretion; **te ruego d.** please be discreet; **tuvo la d. de no mencionarlo** he had the tact not to mention it
2 **a discreción** *loc adv (a voluntad)* as much as one wants, freely; **pueden servirse del bufé a d.** you may have as much as you want from the buffet; **lo dejo a tu d.** I leave it to your discretion; **el descuento queda a d. del vendedor** the level of discount is at the salesman's discretion; **¡fuego a d.!** fire at will!

discrecional *adj (cantidad)* according to taste; *(poderes)* discretionary; **parada d.** *(en autobús)* request stop

discrepancia *nf* (**a**) *(desacuerdo)* disagreement; **expresó su d. con el comité** she made clear her disagreement with the committee; **había serias discrepancias entre ellos** there were serious disagreements between them; **tenemos nuestras discrepancias** we have our differences
(**b**) *(diferencia)* difference, discrepancy; **grandes discrepancias entre la ley y su aplicación práctica** serious discrepancies between the letter of the law and the way it is applied in practice

discrepante *adj* (**a**) *(en desacuerdo)* dissenting (**b**) *(diferente)* divergent, differing

discrepar *vi* (**a**) *(disentir)* to disagree (**de/en** with/on); **discrepamos en casi todo** we disagree on almost everything; **discrepa del pensamiento marxista** she disagrees with Marxist thinking (**b**) *(diferenciarse)* to differ (**de** from)

discretamente *adv* discreetly; **miró d. a la muchacha** he took a discreet look at the girl; **vestía muy d.** he was soberly dressed

discreto, -a *adj* (**a**) *(prudente, reservado)* discreet; **por favor, sé d.** please be discreet; **una mirada discreta** a discreet look
(**b**) *(no llamativo) (color, decoración)* sober, restrained; *(vestido)* simple, sober; *(maquillaje)* discreet; **ropa discreta** simple *o* modest attire; **su discreta labor a la sombra del gran científico** his quiet work in the shadow of the great scientist
(**c**) *(moderado, normal) (cantidad, sueldo)* moderate, modest; *(actuación, resultados)* fair, reasonable
(**d**) *Mat* discrete

discriminación *nf* discrimination ►► ***d. positiva*** positive discrimination; ***d. racial*** racial discrimination; ***d. sexual*** sex *o* sexual discrimination

discriminador *nm Elec* discriminator

discriminante *nm Mat* discriminant

discriminar *vt* (**a**) *(marginar)* to discriminate against; **d. a alguien por algo** to discriminate against sb because of sth; **sentirse discriminado** to feel discriminated against (**b**) *(distinguir)* to discriminate; **d. algo de** to discriminate *o* distinguish sth from

discriminatorio, -a *adj* discriminatory

discuerdo *etc ver* **discordar**

disculpa *nf* (**a**) *(excusa, perdón)* apology; **le debo una d. por lo de ayer** I owe you an apology for what happened yesterday; **pedir disculpas a alguien (por)** to apologize to sb (for); **les pido disculpas por el retraso** I apologize for the delay; **acércate y pídeles disculpas** come and apologize to them (**b**) *(pretexto)* excuse; **dar disculpas** to make excuses; **no hay d. que valga** there's no excuse, there can be no excuse; **su conducta no admite** *o* **tiene d.** her behaviour is inexcusable

disculpar 1 *vt* to excuse; **disculpen la tardanza** I'm sorry for being late; **disculpen este desorden** please forgive the mess; **d. a alguien (por algo)** *(perdonar)* to forgive sb (for sth); **discúlpame por haber olvidado tu cumpleaños** please forgive me for forgetting your birthday; **discúlpame por lo que te dije** please forgive me for what I said to you; **d. algo a alguien** *(excusar)* to forgive sb (for) sth; **su madre se lo disculpa todo** her mother forgives her everything; **no pretendo disculparlo, pero la culpa no es sólo suya** I'm not trying to make excuses for him, but he's not the only one to blame

2 *vi (en imperativo)* (**a**) *Formal (para llamar a alguien)* **disculpe, ¿tiene hora?** excuse me, have you got the time? (**b**) *(perdonar)* **disculpa, no era mi intención ofenderte** I'm sorry, I didn't mean to offend you

3 **disculparse** *vpr* to apologize (**con/por** to/for); **no te disculpes, hombre, son cosas que pasan** don't go apologizing, these things happen; **después de su mala actuación, se disculpó con el público** after his bad performance he apologized to the audience

discurrir 1 *vi* (**a**) *(transcurrir) (tiempo, vida)* to go by, to pass; *(acto, reunión)* to pass off; **las horas discurrían lentamente** the hours passed slowly; **la manifestación discurrió sin incidentes** the demonstration passed off without incident

(**b**) *(pasar) (personas)* to wander (**por** through); *(procesión, camino)* to pass (**por** through); *(río, tráfico)* to flow (**por** through); **el tráfico discurre con normalidad por la M-50** traffic is flowing normally on the M-50; **miles de turistas discurren por las calles de Barcelona** thousands of tourists wander through the streets of Barcelona

(**c**) *(pensar)* to think, to reflect

2 *vt* to come up with

discursear *vi Irónico* to hold forth (**sobre** on)

discursivo, -a *adj* discursive

discurso *nm* (**a**) *(exposición oral)* speech; **dar** *o* **pronunciar un d. (sobre)** to give *o* deliver a speech (on); **d. de apertura/clausura** opening/closing speech; **d. de bienvenida/despedida** welcome/farewell speech; **d. de agradecimiento** speech of thanks

(**b**) *Pey (sermón)* lecture; **me soltó uno de sus discursos** she gave me one of her lectures

(**c**) *(manera de expresarse)* **se dirigió a nosotros con su lento d.** he addressed us in his unhurried manner

(**d**) *(ideario)* discourse, ideology; **la oposición se ha quedado sin d.** the opposition now has nothing to offer; **el partido en el gobierno le ha robado el d. a la oposición** the government has stolen the opposition's clothes

(**e**) *(transcurso)* **el d. del tiempo** the passage of time; **con el d. de los años** with the passing years

(**f**) *Ling* discourse

discusión *nf* (**a**) *(conversación, debate)* discussion; **tuvimos una d. sobre política** we had a discussion about politics; **en d.** under discussion; **eso no admite d.** that's indisputable, there can be no doubt about that; **es, sin d., el mejor** it is, without question, the best (**b**) *(pelea)* argument; **tuvieron una d.** they had an argument

discutible *adj* debatable; **lo que dices es muy d.** what you say is highly debatable; **una decisión más que d.** a highly questionable decision; **su d. reputación como abogado** his questionable reputation as a lawyer

discutido, -a *adj (polémico)* controversial, contentious

discutidor, -ora 1 *adj* argumentative

2 *nm,f* argumentative person

discutir 1 *vi* (**a**) *(hablar)* to discuss; **d. de** *o* **sobre algo** to discuss sth, to talk about sth; **se pasan el día discutiendo de** *o* **sobre fútbol** they spend the whole day talking about *o* discussing football

(**b**) *(pelear)* to argue (**con/por** with/about); **ya han vuelto a d.** they've had another of their arguments; **ha discutido con su hermano** she's had an argument with her brother; **discuten por cualquier tontería** they argue about the least little thing

2 *vt* (**a**) *(hablar sobre)* to discuss; *(debatir)* to discuss, to debate; **eso mejor que lo discutas con tu padre** you'd be better discussing that with your father; **el asunto será discutido en el parlamento** the matter will be discussed in parliament

(**b**) *(contradecir)* to dispute; **no te discuto que tengas razón** I don't dispute that you're right; **es un buen tipo, sí, eso nadie te lo discute** he's a nice guy, sure, no one disputes that; **no me discutas lo que te mando y obedece** don't question what I tell you to do, just do it

disecación *nf* (**a**) *(de animal)* stuffing (**b**) *(de planta)* drying

disecado, -a *adj* (**a**) *(animal)* stuffed (**b**) *(planta)* dried

disecar [60] *vt* (**a**) *(animal)* to stuff (**b**) *(planta)* to dry

disección *nf* (**a**) *(de cadáver, animal)* dissection; **hacer la d. de un cuerpo** to dissect a body (**b**) *(análisis)* dissection, detailed analysis; **hacer una d. de algo** to dissect *o* analyse sth

diseccionar *vt* (**a**) *(cadáver, animal)* to dissect (**b**) *(analizar)* to dissect, to analyse in detail

diseminación *nf* (**a**) *(de semillas)* spreading, dissemination (**b**) *(de ideas, cultura, religión)* spreading, dissemination

diseminado, -a *adj* scattered; **los caseríos se hallan diseminados por el valle** the farmsteads are scattered along the valley

diseminar 1 *vt* (**a**) *(semillas)* to scatter (**b**) *(ideas, cultura, religión)* to spread, to disseminate (**c**) *(objetos, personas)* to spread, to disperse; **diseminaron tropas por todo el territorio** they spread *o* dispersed their troops throughout the territory

2 **diseminarse** *vpr* (**a**) *(semillas)* to be scattered (**b**) *(ideas, cultura, religión)* to spread (**c**) *(personas)* to disperse; **policías de paisano se diseminaron entre el gentío** plain-clothes police officers mingled with the crowds

disensión *nf* disagreement, dissension; **había graves disensiones en el seno del partido** there were serious internal disagreements within the party; **el régimen reprime cualquier d.** the regime quashes any dissent

disentería *nf* dysentery

disentimiento *nm* dissent, disagreement

disentir [63] *vi* to disagree (**de/en** with/on); **disentía de él en muchas cosas** she disagreed with him on many issues; **disiento de la forma en que se está llevando este asunto** I don't agree with the way this matter is being handled

diseñador, -ora *nm,f* designer ►► ***d. gráfico*** graphic designer; ***d. industrial*** industrial designer; ***d. de interiores*** interior designer; ***d. de modas*** fashion designer

diseñar *vt* (**a**) *(crear)* to design; **un estadio diseñado para albergar competiciones atléticas** a stadium designed to host athletic events; **diseñaron una estrategia para hacerse con el mercado** they designed a strategy to capture the market (**b**) *(dibujar)* to draw, to sketch (**c**) *(con palabras)* to outline

diseño *nm* (**a**) *(creación)* design; **se dedica al d.** she works in design; **la cocina tiene un d. muy original** the kitchen has a very original design; **el d. de la falda es de Borgia** the skirt is designed by Borgia; **bar de d.** trendy bar; **drogas de d.** designer drugs; **ropa de d.** designer clothes ►► *Informát* ***d. asistido por ordenador*** computer-aided design; *Educ* ***d. curricular*** curriculum design; ***d. gráfico*** graphic design; ***d. industrial*** industrial design; ***d. de interiores*** interior design; ***d. de modas*** fashion design

(**b**) *(dibujo)* drawing, sketch

(**c**) *(con palabras)* outline

disertación *nf (oral)* lecture; *(escrita)* dissertation; **hacer una d. sobre algo** to give a lecture on sth

disertante *nmf* lecturer

disertar *vi* to speak, to lecture (**sobre** on)

disfraz *nm* (**a**) *(traje)* disguise; *(para baile, fiesta)* fancy dress costume; **pasó los controles con un** *o* **bajo un d. de soldado** he got past the checkpoints disguised as a soldier; **llevar un d.** *(para camuflarse)* to wear a disguise; *(para baile, fiesta)* to wear fancy dress; **un d. de bruja/gorila** a witch/gorilla costume; **un baile/una fiesta de disfraces** a fancy dress ball/party (**b**) *(disimulo)* front, facade

disfrazar [14] 1 *vt* (**a**) *(para baile, fiesta)* to dress up; *(para engañar)* to disguise; **d. a alguien de** to dress sb up as; **disfrazaron a la niña de hada madrina** they dressed the little girl up as a fairy godmother (**b**) *(disimular) (intenciones)* to disguise; *(sentimientos, nervios)* to hide; *(verdad, hechos)* to disguise; **disfrazaba sus verdaderos deseos** he kept what he really wanted a secret; **disfrazó la voz para que no lo reconociera** he disguised his voice so she wouldn't recognize him

2 **disfrazarse** *vpr (para baile, fiesta)* to wear fancy dress; *(para engañar)* to disguise oneself; **fueron a la fiesta disfrazados** they went to the party in fancy dress; **a los niños les encanta disfrazarse** children love dressing up; **disfrazarse de princesa** to dress up as a princess; **¿tú de qué te vas a d.?** what are you going to dress up as?; **se disfrazó de policía para burlar la vigilancia** he disguised himself as a policeman to get past the guards

disfrutar 1 *vi* (**a**) *(sentir placer)* to enjoy oneself; **aquí hemos venido a d.** we've come here to enjoy ourselves; **¡disfruta, ahora que puedes!** enjoy yourselves while you can!; **los niños disfrutan en el circo** children enjoy themselves at the circus; **d. de lo lindo** to enjoy oneself very much, to have a great time; **d. con algo** to enjoy sth; **disfruté mucho con el concierto** I enjoyed the concert a lot; **d. de algo** to enjoy sth; **espero que disfruten del espectáculo** I hope you enjoy the show; **d. haciendo algo** to enjoy doing sth; **disfruto escuchándoles reír** I enjoy hearing them laugh

(**b**) *(disponer de)* **d. de algo** to enjoy sth; **disfruta de muy buena salud** he enjoys excellent health; **disfruta de una pensión vitalicia por invalidez** she has a disability pension for life; **afortunadamente, pudimos d. de su colaboración** we were fortunate enough to have her working with us; **disfruta de muchos amigos** he has lots of friends; **allá disfrutan de un clima excelente** they have *o* enjoy an excellent climate there

2 *vt* to enjoy; **¡que lo disfrutes con salud!** I hope you enjoy it!

disfrute *nm* (**a**) *(placer)* enjoyment (**b**) *(provecho)* benefit, use

disfuerzo *nm Perú* affectation

disfunción *nf* malfunction ►► *Med* ***d. eréctil*** erectile dysfunction

disgregación *nf* (**a**) *(de multitud, manifestación)* dispersal, breaking up; *(de familia, grupo, conjunto musical)* break-up, splitting up (**b**) *(de roca)* disintegration; *(de átomo)* splitting (**c**) *(de imperio, estado)* breaking up

disgregar [38] 1 *vt* (**a**) *(multitud, manifestación)* to disperse, to break up; *(familia, grupo, conjunto musical)* to break up (**b**) *(roca)* to break up; *(átomo)* to split (**c**) *(imperio, estado)* to break up

2 **disgregarse** *vpr* (**a**) *(multitud, manifestación)* to disperse, to break up; *(familia, grupo, conjunto musical)* to break up, to split up (**b**) *(roca)* to disintegrate; *(átomo)* to split (**c**) *(imperio, estado)* to break up

disgustado, -a *adj* (**a**) *(enojado)* annoyed, displeased; **estar d. con alguien/por algo** to be annoyed with sb/because of sth; **está muy disgustada con nosotros por nuestro comportamiento** she's very annoyed with us because of our behaviour

(**b**) *(consternado)* upset; **estar d. por algo** to be upset about *o* by sth; **está muy d. por haber suspendido el examen** he's very upset about failing the exam; **se le veía muy d. por la noticia** he seemed very upset by the news

disgustar 1 *vt* (**a**) *(desagradar)* **la propuesta disgustó al comité** the committee did not like the proposal; **ese sombrero no me disgusta** that hat's not bad; **me disgusta sobre manera tener que decirle esto** I really don't like to have to say this to you

(**b**) *(consternar)* to upset; **le disgustó que olvidáramos su cumpleaños** he was upset that we forgot his birthday

2 **disgustarse** *vpr* (**a**) *(enojarse)* to get annoyed; *(enemistarse)* to fall out; **disgustarse con alguien/por algo** *(enojarse)* to get annoyed with sb/about sth; *(enemistarse)* to fall out with sb/over sth; **no te disgustes conmigo, yo no tengo la culpa** don't get annoyed with me, it's not my fault; **se disgustó con su hermano por una tontería** she fell out with her brother over nothing

(**b**) *(consternarse)* to get upset; **disgustarse con** *o* **por algo** to get upset about sth

> **Falso amigo**: El verbo inglés **to disgust** no es la traducción del español **disgustar**. En inglés **to disgust** significa "repugnar".

disgusto 1 *nm* (**a**) *(enojo)* annoyance; **tenían cara de d.** they looked annoyed; **para d. de todos, el concierto se suspendió** to everyone's disappointment the concert was cancelled

(**b**) *(consternación)* **causar d. a alguien** to upset sb; **le producía d. tener que hablar de la separación** it pained her to have to talk about the separation

(**c**) *(motivo de consternación)* disappointment; **fue un gran d. para ella no aprobar el examen** it was a great disappointment for her not to pass the exam; **dar un d. a alguien** to upset sb; **¡menudo d. nos dio!** you can imagine how upset we were!; **¡este niño no nos da más que disgustos!** that child just gives us one headache after another!; **llevarse un d.** to be upset; **¡qué d. me llevé cuando lo supe!** I was so upset when I found out!; **tiene un d. enorme** she's terribly upset; EXPR **matar a alguien a disgustos** to worry sb to death; **¡me vas a matar a disgustos!** you'll be the death of me yet!; EXPR **no ganar para disgustos con alguien: con este niño no ganamos para disgustos** that child gives us nothing but trouble

(**d**) *(desgracia)* **desde que llegué aquí voy de d. en d.** it's been one disaster after another ever since I arrived; **tener un d.: si sigues trabajando sin casco vas a tener un d.** if you go on working without a helmet you'll have an accident; **o dejas de fumar, o tendrás un d.** quit smoking now, or you'll live to regret it; **casi nos da un d.** we almost had a tragedy on our hands

(**e**) *(pelea)* **tener un d. con alguien** to have a quarrel with sb; **como sigas así, tú y yo vamos a tener un d.** if you carry on like this, you and I are going to fall out

2 **a disgusto** *loc adv (sin ganas)* unwillingly; **hacer algo a d.** to do sth unwillingly *o* reluctantly; **para venir a d., es mejor que no vengas** if you really don't want to come, it'd be better if you didn't

3 **a disgusto** *loc adj (incómodo) (físicamente)* uncomfortable; *(psicológicamente)* uncomfortable, ill at ease; **estar a d.** to feel uncomfortable *o* uneasy; **en esta silla vas a estar a d.** you'll be uncomfortable in that chair; **se sentía muy a d. con sus compañeros de clase** he felt very uncomfortable with his classmates

> **Falso amigo**: El sustantivo inglés **disgust** no es la traducción del español **disgusto**. En inglés **disgust** significa "asco, repugnancia".

disidencia *nf* (**a**) *(política, religiosa)* dissent (**b**) *(desacuerdo)* disagreement; **las disidencias en la cúpula del sindicato** the disagreements within the union leadership; **manifestaron su d. con la resolución** they voiced their dissent from *o* disagreement with the resolution

disidente 1 *adj (en política)* dissident; *(en religión)* dissenting

2 *nmf (político)* dissident; *(religioso)* dissenter; **un d. soviético** a Soviet dissident

disidir *vi* to dissent

disiento *etc ver* **disentir**

disímbolo, -a *adj Méx* dissimilar

disímil *adj* dissimilar

disimilitud *nf* dissimilarity

disimuladamente *adv* quietly, discreetly; **agarró la maleta d. y se la llevó** without drawing attention to herself, she picked up the suitcase and walked off with it; **la miró d.** he stole a glance at her; **se marchó d.** she left quietly

disimulado, -a 1 *adj* (**a**) *(oculto)* concealed; **un enfado mal d.** barely concealed anger; **arrugas mal disimuladas con maquillaje** wrinkles barely concealed by make-up (**b**) *(discreto)* discreet; **no eres nada d.** you're so obvious; **lo dejó caer en la conversación de forma disimulada** she casually dropped it into the conversation

2 *nm,f* **hacerse el d.** to pretend not to notice; **lo saludé, pero se hizo el d.** I said hello, but he pretended he hadn't heard; **¡vamos, no te hagas el d. y dime qué ha ocurrido!** come on, stop pretending you don't know and tell me what happened!

disimular 1 *vt (ocultar)* to hide, to conceal; **lo disimulas muy mal** you're not very good at hiding it; **no podía d. la risa** she couldn't hide her laughter; **disimulaba los rotos del pantalón con parches** she covered up the tears in her trousers with patches

2 *vi* to pretend; **no disimules, que te he visto** don't try to pretend, I saw you; **¡qué mal disimulas!** you're so obvious!, you're so bad at pretending!; **disimula y sigue caminando** just act natural and keep walking

disimulo *nm* pretence, concealment; **con d.** furtively; **tiró el papel al suelo con d.** she surreptitiously dropped the piece of paper on the floor; **la miró con d.** he sneaked a look at her; **con mucho d. le pasó la nota** she surreptitiously passed the note to him; **salió con d. por la puerta de atrás** she sneaked out by the back door; **atracan a la gente en la calle sin ningún d.** they mug people in the street quite openly

disintiera *etc ver* **disentir**

disipación *nf* (**a**) *(libertinaje)* dissipation; **una vida de d.** a life of dissipation (**b**) *(de dudas, sospechas, temores)* dispelling; *(de ilusiones)* shattering (**c**) *(de fortuna, herencia)* squandering, wasting (**d**) *(de niebla, humo, vapor)* dispersion

disipado, -a *adj (libertino) (vida, conducta, persona)* dissipated, dissolute

disipador, -ora 1 *nm,f (de fortunas)* spendthrift

2 *nm Informát* ***d. térmico*** heat sink

disipar 1 *vt* (a) *(dudas, sospechas, temores)* to dispel; *(ilusiones)* to shatter (b) *(fortuna, herencia)* to squander, to throw away (c) *(niebla, humo, vapor)* to drive *o* blow away, to disperse; **las lluvias disiparon la contaminación** the rains washed away the pollution
2 **disiparse** *vpr* (a) *(dudas, sospechas, temores)* to be dispelled; *(ilusiones)* to be shattered (b) *(niebla, humo, vapor)* to disperse; **un frente cálido hará que se disipe la borrasca** a warm front will cause the low pressure to dissipate

diskette [dis'kete, dis'ket] *nm Informát* diskette, floppy disk

dislalia *nf Med* dyslalia

dislate *nm* piece of nonsense *o* absurdity; **su plan es un d.** her plan is absurd; **insinuar que la casa está encantada es un puro d.** suggesting that the house is haunted is pure nonsense; **un texto lleno de dislates** a text full of absurdities

dislexia *nf* dyslexia

disléxico, -a 1 *adj* dyslexic
2 *nm,f* dyslexic

dislocación *nf* dislocation

dislocado, -a *adj (tobillo)* dislocated

dislocar [60] 1 *vt* to dislocate
2 **dislocarse** *vpr* (a) *(tobillo, articulación)* **se me ha dislocado un codo** I've dislocated my elbow (b) *Esp Fam (desmadrarse)* to go wild

disloque *nm Fam* **ser el d.** to be the last straw; **se emborrachó, empezó a quitarse la ropa y aquello fue el d.** he got drunk, started to take his clothes off, and that was just IT

dismenorrea *nf Med* dysmenorrhoea

disminución *nf (de cantidad, velocidad, intensidad)* decrease, decline (**de** in); *(de precios, temperaturas)* fall (**de** in); *(de interés)* decline, waning (**de** of); **la d. del desempleo/de la contaminación** the decrease in unemployment/pollution; **una d. salarial** a decrease *o* drop in wages; **ir en d.** to be on the decrease

disminuido, -a 1 *adj* handicapped
2 *nm,f* handicapped person; **un d. físico/psíquico** a physically/mentally handicapped person; **los disminuidos** the handicapped

disminuir [34] 1 *vt* to reduce, to decrease; **disminuye la velocidad al entrar en la curva** reduce speed as you go into the curve; **pastillas que disminuyen el sueño** tablets that prevent drowsiness; **la lesión no ha disminuido su habilidad con el balón** the injury hasn't affected his skill with the ball
2 *vi (cantidad, velocidad, intensidad, contaminación)* to decrease, to decline; *(desempleo, inflación)* to decrease, to fall; *(precios, temperatura)* to fall, to go down; *(vista, memoria)* to fail; *(interés)* to decline, to wane; **disminuye el número de matriculaciones en la universidad** university enrolments are down; **medidas para que disminuyan los costes** cost-cutting measures; **no disminuye la euforia inversora** investor enthusiasm continues unabated

disnea *nf* difficulty in breathing, *Espec* dyspnoea

disociación *nf* dissociation

disociar 1 *vt* to dissociate (**de** from)
2 **disociarse** *vpr* (a) *(desentenderse)* to dissociate oneself (**de** from) (b) *Quím* to dissociate

disoluble *adj* soluble

disolución *nf* (a) *(acción)* dissolving (b) *(de familia, manifestación)* breaking up; *(de empresa, partido)* dissolution, winding up; *(de parlamento, matrimonio)* dissolution, dissolving; *(de contrato)* rescinding (c) *(mezcla)* solution ▸▸ ***d. acuosa*** solution in water; ***d. saturada*** saturated solution

disoluto, -a 1 *adj* dissolute
2 *nm,f* dissolute person

disolvente 1 *adj* solvent
2 *nm* solvent

disolver [41] 1 *vt* (a) *(en líquido)* to dissolve; **d. en leche agitando constantemente** dissolve it in milk, stirring continuously; **d. un caramelo en la boca** to suck a sweet (b) *(familia, manifestación)* to break up; *(empresa, partido)* to dissolve, to wind up; *(parlamento, matrimonio)* to dissolve; *(contrato)* to rescind
2 **disolverse** *vpr* (a) *(en líquido)* to dissolve; **dejar que la pastilla se disuelva en la boca** *(en prospecto)* allow the tablet to dissolve in your mouth (b) *(reunión, manifestación)* to break up (c) *(sociedad, partido)* to be dissolved; *(parlamento)* to dissolve; *(familia)* to break up; *(matrimonio)* to be dissolved; *(contrato)* to be rescinded

disonancia *nf* (a) *(de sonidos, ritmos, voces)* dissonance (b) *(de colores, estilos, decoración)* clash

disonante *adj* (a) *(sonidos, ritmos, voces)* dissonant, discordant (b) *(colores, estilos)* clashing; **ese sofá queda de lo más d.** that sofa simply screams it doesn't belong there

dispar *adj* disparate, dissimilar; **mantienen opiniones muy dispares al respecto** they have very different opinions on the matter; **el equipo ha conseguido resultados muy dispares esta temporada** the team has obtained very uneven results this season; **la calidad es muy d.** the quality varies a lot

disparada *nf* (a) *Am (huida)* flight (b) *CSur* **a la d.** in a tearing hurry

disparadero *nm* **poner a alguien en el d.** to push sb too far

disparado, -a *adj* **salir/entrar d.** to shoot out/in; **todos los días sale d. de casa** he leaves the house in a rush every day

disparador *nm* (a) *(de armas)* trigger (b) *(de cámara fotográfica)* shutter release ▸▸ ***d. automático*** automatic shutter release

disparar 1 *vt* (a) *(arma, persona)* to shoot; *(tiro)* to fire; **¿sabes d. un arma?** do you know how to fire a gun?; **disparaban tiros al aire** they fired (shots) into the air; **nos disparaban flechas** they were shooting arrows at us; **¡no me dispares!** don't shoot!
(b) *(fotografía)* to take
(c) *(penalti, falta, golpe de castigo)* to take; **d. un libre directo** to take a direct free kick
(d) *Méx Fam (pagar)* **ven, te disparo un tequila** go on, have a tequila on me
2 *vi* (a) *(con arma)* to shoot, to fire; **d. al aire** to shoot in the air; **d. a matar** to shoot to kill; **d. contra** *o* **sobre alguien** to shoot *o* fire at sb; **d. contra el enemigo** to shoot *o* fire at the enemy; **disparaban sobre la población civil** they were shooting at civilians; **¡no dispares!** don't shoot!; **tengo varias preguntas para ti – ¡dispara!** I have several questions for you – fire away! *o* shoot!
(b) *(con cámara)* to shoot, to take a photograph; **los fotógrafos no paraban de d.** the photographers kept on clicking their cameras
(c) *(futbolista)* to shoot; **d. a puerta** to shoot at goal
(d) *RP Fam (huir)* to shoot off
3 **dispararse** *vpr* (a) *(arma, alarma, flash)* to go off; **se le disparó el arma** his gun went off
(b) *(precios, inflación)* to shoot up
(c) *(precipitarse) (persona)* to rush off; *(caballo)* to bolt

disparatado, -a *adj* absurd, crazy; **precios disparatados** ridiculous *o* crazy prices; **una disparatada comedia de Brooks** a screwball comedy by Brooks

disparatar *vi (decir tonterías)* to talk nonsense; *(hacer tonterías)* to behave foolishly

disparate *nm* (a) *(comentario, acción)* silly thing; *(idea)* crazy idea; **cometer** *o* **hacer un d.** to do something crazy; **cometió** *o* **hizo el d. de invertirlo todo** she made the crazy mistake of investing it all; **¿no irás a cometer** *o* **hacer algún d.?** you're not going to go and do something stupid, are you?; **¡no digas disparates!** don't talk nonsense!; **¿casarme yo? ¡qué d.!** me, get married? don't be ridiculous!; **es un d. salir sin paraguas en un día como hoy** it's madness to go out without an umbrella on a day like this; **vivir tan aislado me parece un d.** it seems crazy to me to go and live in such an isolated place
(b) *Fam (cantidad exorbitante)* **gastar/costar un d.** to spend/cost a ridiculous amount; **¡estos precios son un d.!** these prices are ridiculous!

disparatero, -a *Am* 1 *adj* absurd, foolish
2 *nm,f (que dice disparates)* person who talks nonsense; *(que hace disparates)* person who acts foolishly

disparejo, -a *adj esp Am* uneven, variable; **la calidad es muy dispareja** the quality is very uneven

disparidad *nf* difference, disparity; **hay d. de criterios sobre este asunto** there are different opinions about *o* on this issue; **las estadísticas arrojan gran d. de resultados** the statistics reveal big differences in the results

disparo *nm* (a) *(de arma)* shot; **hubo disparos al aire** shots were fired in the air ▸▸ ***d. de advertencia*** warning shot; ***d. de aviso*** warning shot (b) *(de deportista)* shot; **el d. rozó el larguero** the shot grazed the crossbar (c) *(de mecanismo)* release, trip

dispendio *nm* extravagance, spending on luxuries; **no nos podemos permitir estos dispendios** we can't afford these luxuries

dispendioso, -a *adj* costly, expensive

dispensa *nf* (a) *(de examen)* exemption (b) *(para casarse)* dispensation

dispensable *adj* pardonable, excusable

dispensador, -ora 1 *adj* dispensing
2 *nm,f* dispenser

dispensar **1** *vt* (**a**) *Formal (dar) (honores)* to confer (**a** upon); *(bienvenida, ayuda)* to give (**a** to); *(medicamentos)* to dispense; *(alimentos)* to distribute; **el público le dispensó una calurosa acogida** the audience gave her a warm welcome; **le fue dispensado el honor de ser el abanderado olímpico** he was given the honour of being the standard bearer at the Olympics

(**b**) *Formal (disculpar)* to excuse, to forgive; **les ruego me dispensen por el retraso** please forgive the delay

(**c**) *(eximir)* to excuse, to exempt (**de** from); **le dispensamos de asistir a clase** he is excused from coming to class; **lo dispensaron de hacer el servicio militar/el examen** he was exempted from military service/ taking the exam

2 *vi Formal* **¡dispense!** excuse me!, pardon me!, I beg your pardon!

dispensario *nm* dispensary

dispepsia *nf* dyspepsia

dispéptico, -a **1** *adj* dyspeptic

2 *nm,f* dyspeptic

dispersar **1** *vt* (**a**) *(objetos)* to scatter; *(luz, sonido, ondas)* to scatter, to disperse; *(niebla, humo)* to disperse (**b**) *(gentío)* to disperse; *(manifestación)* to break up, to disperse; *(tropas enemigas, manada)* to disperse, to scatter (**c**) *(esfuerzos)* to dissipate

2 dispersarse *vpr* (**a**) *(objetos)* to scatter; *(luz, sonido, ondas)* to scatter, to be dispersed; *(niebla, humo)* to disperse (**b**) *(gentío)* to disperse; *(manifestación)* to break up, to disperse; *(tropas enemigas, manada)* to disperse, to scatter (**c**) *(distraerse)* to let one's attention wander

dispersión *nf* (**a**) *(de objetos)* scattering; *(de luz, sonido, ondas)* scattering, dispersal

(**b**) *(de gentío)* dispersal; *(de manifestación)* breaking up, dispersal; *(de un pueblo)* scattering

(**c**) *(de persona)* lack of concentration; **debemos evitar la d. de esfuerzos** we mustn't squander our efforts; **debes centrarte en algo, tu problema es la d.** you need to focus on something, you spread yourself too widely

(**d**) *Fís* dispersion

disperso, -a *adj* (**a**) *(esparcido) (objetos, personas, familia)* scattered; **un pueblo que está d. por todo el mundo** a people scattered *o* dispersed throughout the world; **chubascos dispersos** scattered showers (**b**) *(sin concentración) (mente, atención)* unfocussed; **ser d.** to be absent-minded; **es un alumno bastante d.** he finds it difficult to pay attention in class

display [dis'plei] *nm Informát* display

displicencia *nf* (**a**) *(desagrado)* offhandedness; **nos trató con d.** he treated us in an offhand manner (**b**) *(negligencia)* carelessness; *(desgana)* lack of enthusiasm

displicente *adj* (**a**) *(desagradable)* offhand (**b**) *(negligente)* careless; *(desganado)* unenthusiastic

disponer [50] **1** *vt* (**a**) *(colocar)* to arrange; **dispuso los libros por orden alfabético** she arranged the books in alphabetical order

(**b**) *(arreglar, preparar)* to arrange; **dispuso todo para el viaje** he made all the arrangements for the journey; **dispuso el salón para recibir a sus invitados** she got the living room ready for the guests

(**c**) *(cena, comida)* to lay on

(**d**) *(determinar) (sujeto: persona)* to decide; *(sujeto: ley, cláusula)* to stipulate; **el juez dispuso que se cerrara el local** the judge ordered that the premises be closed; **en su testamento dispuso que...** she stated in her will that...; **el consejo de administración dispuso ampliar el capital de la empresa** the board of directors decided to increase the company's capital; **el gobierno dispuso que se hiciera así** it was the government's decision that it should be done that way; **según lo dispuesto en el artículo 8,...** according to the provisions of Article 8,...; **la ley dispone que no haya pena de cárcel para mayores de setenta y cinco años** the law stipulates *o* lays down that people over the age of seventy-five cannot be sent to prison

2 *vi* (**a**) **d. de** *(poseer)* to have; **dispongo de todo el tiempo del mundo** I have all the time in the world; **el hotel dispone de piscina y cancha de tenis** the hotel has a swimming pool and a tennis court; **el personal de que disponemos no es suficiente** the number of staff we have at the moment is insufficient

(**b**) **d. de** *(usar)* to make use of; **dispón de mi casa siempre que quieras** you're welcome in my house whenever you like; **puede d. de mí para lo que quiera** I'm entirely at your disposal if ever you need anything

3 disponerse *vpr* **disponerse a hacer algo** to prepare *o* get ready to do sth; **me disponía a salir cuando...** I was getting ready to go out when...; **un nuevo país se dispone a entrar en la Unión Europea** a new country is preparing to join the European Union

disponibilidad *nf* (**a**) *(de plazas, producto, servicio)* availability; **¿qué d. tiene?** *(en entrevista de empleo)* how many hours would you be able to work?; **d. inmediata** *(en oferta de empleo)* must be able to start immediately (**b**) *(a ayudar)* readiness to help (**c**) **disponibilidades** *(medios)* financial resources

disponible *adj* available; **d. en versiones para Mac o PC** available for Mac or PC; **no tenemos habitaciones/plazas disponibles** we don't have any rooms/places available; **no tengo mucho tiempo d.** I don't have much free *o* spare time; **el director no está d. en estos momentos** the manager is not available at the moment; **si hay que ayudar, yo estoy d.** if you need any help, I'm available *o* free

disposición *nf* (**a**) *(colocación)* arrangement, layout; **la d. de las habitaciones** the layout of the rooms; **alteró la d. de los cuadros** she rearranged the paintings

(**b**) *(estado)* **estar** *o* **hallarse en d. de hacer algo** to be prepared *o* ready to do sth; **no está en d. de volver a los terrenos de juego** he's not fit to return to the game; **no estoy en d. de hablar con nadie** I'm not in the mood to talk to anybody ▸▸ ***d. de ánimo*** state of mind

(**c**) *(voluntad)* willingness; **se le veía d. a ayudar** she seemed willing to help

(**d**) *(aptitud)* talent; **no tiene d. para los deportes** he has no talent for sport; **tiene buena d. para la pintura** he has a natural gift for painting

(**e**) *(orden)* order; *(norma)* regulation; *(medida)* measure, step; *(de ley)* provision; **disposiciones administrativas** administrative orders/ regulations; **tomaremos las disposiciones necesarias para evitar el fraude** we shall take the necessary measures to prevent fraud; **el medicamento cumple con las disposiciones legales** the drug complies with the legal requirements ▸▸ *Der* ***d. adicional*** additional provision; *Der* ***disposiciones testamentarias*** provisions of a will; *Der* ***d. transitoria*** temporary provision

(**f**) *(uso)* **a d. de** at the disposal of; **estoy a tu d.** I am at your disposal; **teníamos a nuestra d. toda clase de medios** we had all kinds of means at our disposal; **me tienes a tu d. para lo que necesites** if I can be of any help, just let me know; *Formal* **quedo a su entera d. para cualquier información adicional** I will be pleased to provide any further information you may require; **poner algo a d. de alguien** to put sth at sb's disposal; **pusieron a mi d. su banco de datos** they made their database available to me, they put their database at my disposal; **debería poner su cargo a d. del partido** she should offer her resignation to the party; **los detenidos fueron puestos a d. del juez** the prisoners were brought before the judge

dispositivo *nm* (**a**) *(mecanismo)* device ▸▸ *Informát* ***d. de almacenamiento*** storage device; *Informát* ***d. de entrada*** input device; ***d. intrauterino*** intrauterine device, IUD; *Informát* ***d. periférico*** peripheral device; *Informát* ***d. de salida*** output device; ***d. de seguimiento*** tracking device; ***d. de seguridad*** safety device

(**b**) *(grupo de personas)* **un fuerte d. policial** a large contingent of police; **un impresionante d. de seguridad** impressive security arrangements; **se desplegó un d. militar a lo largo de la frontera** troops were deployed along the border

disprosio *nm Quím* dysprosium

dispuesto, -a **1** *participio ver* **disponer**

2 *adj* (**a**) *(preparado, organizado)* ready; **todo está d. para que comience la semifinal** everything is ready for the semifinal to start; **la mesa ya está dispuesta** the table has been laid

(**b**) *(decidido, con plena voluntad)* **d. a algo: parecían dispuestos al acuerdo** they seemed to be willing to reach an agreement; **está d. a todo con tal de conseguir lo que quiere** he's prepared to do anything as long as he gets what he wants; **estar d. a hacer algo** to be prepared to do sth; **siempre estuvo d. a cooperar** he was always willing to cooperate; **no estoy d. a tolerarlo más** I'm not prepared to tolerate it any longer

(**c**) *(capaz)* capable; *(a ayudar)* ready to help; **es un chico muy d.** he's a very obliging *o* willing lad

dispusiera *etc ver* **disponer**

disputa *nf* (**a**) *(discusión)* dispute, argument

(**b**) *(competición)* contest; **la d. por el título de liga** the battle for the league title; **entrar en la d. por algo** to enter the contest for sth; **hay mucha d. para conseguir el puesto** there's a lot of competition for the post

(**c**) *(polémica)* dispute; **mediar** *o* **terciar en la d.** to intervene in the dispute; **es, sin d., el más lujoso** it is indisputably *o* unquestionably the most luxurious

disputable *adj* disputable, debatable

disputar **1** *vt* (**a**) *(cuestión, tema)* to argue about; **d. algo a alguien** to dispute sth with sb; **algunos le disputan que él fuera el creador del mambo** his claim to be the creator of the mambo is disputed by some;

eso no te lo disputo I don't dispute that, I'll grant you that
(**b**) *(trofeo, puesto)* to compete for; *(partido)* to play; *(liga)* to play in; *(carrera, torneo, olimpiadas)* to compete in, to take part in; **disputarán el partido de ida en Madrid** the first leg will be played in Madrid; **mañana se disputará la final** the final takes place tomorrow
2 *vi (discutir)* to argue, to quarrel; **d. con alguien por** *o* **sobre algo** to argue with sb about *o* over sth
3 disputarse *vpr (competir por)* to contend *o* compete for; **varios candidatos se disputan el premio** several candidates are competing for the prize; **se disputan el liderazgo del partido en las primarias** they are contending for the leadership of the party in the primaries

disquera *nf Am* record company

disquería *nf RP* record *o* music shop

disquero, -a *adj Am* record; **sello d.** record label; **la industria disquera** the record *o* music industry

disquete *nm Informát* diskette, floppy disk

disquetera *nf Informát* disk drive

disquisición *nf* (**a**) *(análisis)* disquisition (**sobre** on) (**b**) *(digresión)* **disquisiciones** digressions; **entrar** *o* **meterse en disquisiciones** to digress; **perderse en disquisiciones** to lose track of the subject

distancia *nf* (**a**) *(espacio)* distance; **recorrer la d. entre dos pueblos** to cover the distance between two towns; **¿a qué d. está el próximo pueblo?** how far is the next town?; **¿cuál es la d.** *o* **qué d. hay entre Asunción y Montevideo?** what is the distance between Asunción and Montevideo?; **estábamos a bastante d. del incendio** we were quite a distance from the fire; **los viandantes observaban el incidente a cierta d.** the passers-by watched the incident from a distance; **a tanta d. no puedo decirte quién es** I can't say who it is from this distance; **mantenerse a una d. prudencial de** to keep at a safe distance from; **está a varios kilómetros de d.** it is several kilometres away; **a d.** from a distance; **estudiar a d.** to study by distance learning; **mantener algo/a alguien a d.** to keep sth/sb at a distance; **mantenerse a d. (de)** to keep one's distance (from); **en la d.** in the distance ►► ***d. focal*** focal distance, focal length; ***d. de frenado*** braking distance; ***d. de seguridad*** safe distance *(from the vehicle in front)*; **mantenga la d. de seguridad** *(en letrero de tráfico)* keep your distance
(**b**) *(en el tiempo)* gap, space; **está a dos minutos de d. del ciclista francés** he's two minutes away from the French cyclist; **hay varios años de d. entre estas dos fotografías** the two photographs were taken several years apart; **con la d. que da el tiempo, desde la d.** looking back, in retrospect; **ahora, desde la d., creo que nos equivocamos** now, in retrospect, I think we were wrong
(**c**) *(diferencia)* difference; **hay** *o* **media una gran d. entre ambas teorías** there is a great difference between the two theories; EXPR **salvando las distancias** allowing for the obvious differences
(**d**) *(entre personas)* distance; **la lucha por la herencia aumentó la d. entre los hermanos** the dispute over the inheritance drove the brothers further apart; **guardar** *o* **mantener las distancias (con alguien)** to keep one's distance (from sb); EXPR **acortar (las) distancias** to come closer (to an agreement)

distanciamiento *nm* (**a**) *(afectivo)* distance, coldness; **con los años, se produjo un d. entre ellos** as the years passed, they grew apart; **ver un asunto con cierto d.** to consider an issue with a certain detachment (**b**) *(de opiniones, posturas)* distancing; **se ha dado un claro d. de posturas entre ambos bandos** the two sides have adopted more clearly opposing positions

distanciar 1 *vt* (**a**) *(afectivamente)* to drive apart; **aquello los distanció bastante** that drove them apart; **¿qué fue lo que te distanció de tu marido?** what was it that estranged you from your husband?
(**b**) *(en el espacio o tiempo)* to move further apart; **distanciaron las fechas de los partidos** the dates of the games were moved further apart
(**c**) *(rival)* to forge ahead of
2 distanciarse *vpr* (**a**) *(afectivamente)* to grow apart; **con el tiempo se fueron distanciando** they grew *o* drifted apart as time went on
(**b**) *(físicamente)* to move away; **el barco se distanció de la costa** the ship drew away from the coast; **no se distancien del grupo** don't become separated from the group; **el corredor no consiguió distanciarse del pelotón** the runner couldn't pull away from the pack

distante *adj* (**a**) *(en el espacio)* far away (**de** from) (**b**) *(en el trato) (persona, comportamiento)* distant, aloof; **estaba d., con la mirada perdida** he was distant, staring into space

distar *vi* (**a**) *(hallarse lejos)* **ese sitio dista varios kilómetros de aquí** that place is several kilometres away from here (**b**) *(ser diferente)* **eso dista mucho de la verdad** *o* **de ser verdad** that is very far from the truth *o* from being true; **este libro dista mucho de ser bueno** this book is far from good

diste *ver* **dar**

distender [66] **1** *vt* (**a**) *(situación, relaciones)* to ease; *(ambiente)* to ease, to relax (**b**) *(cuerda, arco)* to slacken (**c**) *Med (músculo, tendón, ligamento)* to strain
2 distenderse *vpr* (**a**) *(situación, relaciones)* to ease; *(ambiente)* to become more relaxed (**b**) *(cuerda)* to become loose *o* slack (**c**) *Med (músculo, ligamento)* to become strained

distendidamente *adv* in a relaxed manner

distendido, -a *adj (relaciones, ambiente, diálogo)* relaxed

distensión *nf* (**a**) *(entre países)* détente; *(entre personas)* easing of tension; **la conferencia de paz favoreció la d.** the peace conference served to ease tensions; **la entrevista se produjo en un ambiente de d.** the interview was conducted in a relaxed atmosphere (**b**) *(de cuerda, arco)* slackening (**c**) *Med (muscular, de ligamentos)* strain

dístico *nm Lit* distich

disticoso, -a *adj Perú Fam* fussy, choosy

distiendo *etc ver* **distender**

distinción *nf* (**a**) *(diferencia)* distinction; **a d. de** in contrast to, unlike; **hacer** *o* **establecer una d. entre** to make *o* draw a distinction between; **hizo la d. entre estrella y asteroide** he drew a distinction between stars and asteroids; **hacer distinciones en el trato** to treat people differently; **no me gusta hacer distinciones con nadie** I don't like to give preferential treatment to anyone; **obsequió a todos sin d.** he gave presents to everyone alike; **sin d. de sexo, raza o religión** without distinction of sex, race or religion
(**b**) *(privilegio)* privilege; *(condecoración)* award; **le fue otorgada la d. de caballero del reino** he was honoured with a knighthood
(**c**) *(modales, elegancia)* refinement, elegance; **viste con d.** he dresses elegantly

distingo 1 *ver* **distinguir**
2 *nm esp CSur* reservation; **no hacer distingos (con** *o* **entre)** to make no distinctions (between); **este reglamento se aplica sin distingos** this rule applies to everyone without exception; **queremos la felicidad para todos, sin distingos** we want everyone to be happy, without exception

distinguible *adj* discernible

distinguido, -a *adj* (**a**) *(notable)* distinguished; **distinguidas personalidades del mundo de la política** distinguished figures from the world of politics; **d. público...** ladies and gentlemen... (**b**) *(elegante) (persona)* refined, distinguished; *(modales, vestimenta)* refined, elegant; **es un tipo d. en el vestir** he's someone who dresses very elegantly

distinguir [26] **1** *vt* (**a**) *(diferenciar)* to distinguish, to tell the difference between; **¿tú distingues estas dos camisas?** can you tell the difference between these two shirts?; **me es imposible distinguirlos** I can't tell them apart; **Kant distingue varios tipos de "razón"** Kant distinguishes between several kinds of "reason"; **d. algo de algo** to tell sth from sth; **por teléfono no distingo tu voz de la de tu madre** I can't tell your voice from your mother's on the telephone; **no distinguen el verde del azul** they can't tell green from blue
(**b**) *(caracterizar)* to distinguish, to characterize; **d. algo/a alguien de** to distinguish sth/sb from, to set sth/sb apart from; **esto lo distingue del resto de los mamíferos** this distinguishes it from other mammals; **¿qué es lo que distingue a un gorila?** what are the main characteristics of a gorilla?; **el grado de adherencia distingue los diversos tipos de neumático** the different types of tyre are distinguished by their road-holding capacity; **su amabilidad la distingue de las demás** her kindness sets her apart from the rest
(**c**) *(premiar)* to honour; **ha sido distinguido con numerosos premios** he has been honoured with numerous prizes; **hoy nos distingue con su presencia Don...** today we are honoured to have with us Mr...
(**d**) *(vislumbrar, escuchar)* to make out; **¿distingues algo?** *(al mirar)* can you see anything?, can you make anything out?; **desde aquí no distingo si es ella o no** I can't see if it's her or not from here; **podía d. su voz** I could make out her voice
2 *vi* to differentiate, to know the difference (**entre** between); **el público distingue entre un buen y un mal tenor** the audience can tell *o* knows the difference between a good and a bad tenor; **estudiando mucho uno aprende a d.** after a lot of study one learns how to discriminate
3 distinguirse *vpr* (**a**) *(destacarse)* to stand out; **distinguirse por algo** to be noted for sth, to stand out for sth; **un automóvil que se distingue del resto por su reducido tamaño** a car that stands out from the rest because of its small size; **una ciudad que se distingue por su limpieza** a city that is noted for its cleanness
(**b**) *(caracterizarse)* to be characterized (**por** by); **las amapolas se distinguen por su color rojo** poppies are characterized by their red colour

(c) *(vislumbrarse)* to be visible; *(escucharse)* to be audible; **desde tan lejos no se distingue nada** you can't see/hear a thing from so far away

distintivamente *adv* distinctly, clearly

distintivo, -a 1 *adj (elemento, rasgo, característica)* distinctive; *(señal)* distinguishing
2 *nm* (a) *(señal)* badge (b) *(marca)* distinguishing mark *o* characteristic

distinto, -a 1 *adj* (a) *(diferente)* different (**de** *o* **a** from *o* to); **su versión de los hechos era muy distinta** her version of events was very different; **es d. venir de vacaciones a vivir aquí** coming on *Br* holiday *o US* vacation is different to *o* from living here
(b) *(claro)* clear; **su voz se oía distinta entre las demás** her voice could be clearly heard among the others; **claro y d.** perfectly clear
(c) **distintos** *(varios)* various; **hay distintos libros sobre el tema** there are various books on the subject; **hay distintas maneras de preparar este plato** there are various different ways of making this dish
2 *adv* differently; **en este país hacen las cosas d.** they do things differently in this country

distorsión *nf* (a) *(de imágenes, sonidos)* distortion ▸▸ ***d. acústica*** acoustic distortion; ***d. óptica*** optical distortion (b) *(de palabras)* twisting; *(de hechos, realidad)* distortion, misrepresentation; **en su relato había una clara d. de los hechos** his account seriously distorted *o* misrepresented the facts

distorsionado, -a *adj* (a) *(sonido, imagen)* distorted (b) *(relato, interpretación, versión)* distorted, twisted

distorsionador, -ora *adj* (a) *(efecto)* distorting (b) *(análisis, enfoque, interpretación)* misleading; **una versión distorsionadora de lo que ocurrió en realidad** a misleading version of what actually happened

distorsionar *vt* (a) *(imágenes, sonidos)* to distort (b) *(palabras)* to twist; *(hechos, realidad)* to distort, to misrepresent; **la prensa distorsionó los hechos** the press distorted *o* misrepresented the facts

distracción *nf* (a) *(entretenimiento)* entertainment; *(pasatiempo)* hobby, pastime; **faltan distracciones para los niños** there isn't enough to keep the children entertained; **¿cuál es tu d. favorita?** what's your favourite pastime?; **la costura/hacer crucigramas le servía de d.** sewing/doing crosswords kept him entertained
(b) *(despiste)* slip; *(falta de atención)* absent-mindedness; **tener una d.** to let one's concentration slip, to be distracted; **la d. del piloto provocó el accidente** the pilot's lapse in concentration caused the accident
(c) *(malversación)* embezzlement, misappropriation

distraer [68] 1 *vt* (a) *(divertir)* to amuse, to entertain; **lo que más me distrae es el bricolaje** my favourite pastime is do-it-yourself; **les contaba cuentos para distraerlos** he told them stories to keep them entertained
(b) *(despistar)* to distract; **¡no me distraigas, que estoy trabajando!** don't distract me, I'm working!; **tú lo distraes para que yo pueda entrar** you distract his attention so I can get in; **algo distrajo su atención** something distracted her
(c) *(malversar)* to embezzle, to misappropriate
2 *vi (entretener)* to be entertaining; **la lectura distrae mucho** reading is fun
3 **distraerse** *vpr* (a) *(divertirse)* to enjoy oneself; *(pasar el tiempo)* to pass the time; **¿qué hacen en este pueblo para distraerse?** what do they do in this town for entertainment?; **se distraían jugando al billar** they kept themselves amused by playing pool; **trata de distraerte** try to take your mind off things; **necesita distraerse y trabajar menos** he needs to have some fun and work less
(b) *(despistarse)* to let one's mind wander; **no te distraigas y haz los deberes** don't get distracted and do your homework; **en este trabajo no puedes distraerte ni un momento** in this job you can't take your mind off what you're doing for a second; **este niño se distrae con una mosca** this child can't concentrate for two seconds

distraídamente *adv* absent-mindedly

distraído, -a 1 *adj* (a) *(entretenido) (libro)* readable; *(programa de TV, película)* watchable; *(persona)* amusing, entertaining; **una tarde/conversación distraída** quite a nice afternoon/conversation; **pasamos un rato muy d. jugando a las cartas** we had a good time playing cards; **los niños estaban muy distraídos con los dibujos animados** the children were very involved in the cartoons
(b) *(despistado)* **ser d.** to be absent-minded; **es un tipo muy d.** he's a very absent-minded guy; **estar d.** to be distracted; **estaba d. y me quitaron la maleta** I wasn't paying attention *o* I let my attention wander and I had my suitcase stolen; **lo siento, estaba d., ¿qué decías?** sorry, I was miles away; what were you saying?; **siempre va d.** he always has his head in the clouds
(c) *Chile, Méx (desaliñado)* ragged, shabby
2 *nm,f* **ser un d.** to have one's head in the clouds

distraigo *etc ver* **distraer**

distribución *nf* (a) *(reparto, división)* distribution; **una d. bastante desigual de los beneficios** a rather uneven distribution of the profits ▸▸ ***d. ecológica*** ecological distribution; ***d. de premios*** prizegiving; ***d. de la riqueza*** distribution of wealth; ***d. de tareas*** assignment of duties; ***d. del trabajo*** division of labour
(b) *(de mercancías, películas)* distribution; **d. comercial** commercial distribution
(c) *(de casa, habitaciones, mobiliario)* layout
(d) *(en estadística)* distribution ▸▸ ***d. binomial*** binomial distribution; ***d. normal*** normal distribution
(e) *Tec* timing gears

distribucionalismo *nm Ling* distributional analysis, distributionalism

distribucionalista *Ling* 1 *adj* distributional
2 *nmf* distributionist

distribuidor, -ora 1 *adj (entidad)* wholesale; **una red distribuidora** a distribution network
2 *nm,f* (a) *(repartidor)* deliveryman, *f* deliverywoman (b) *(firma)* wholesaler, supplier; *(de películas)* distributor
3 *nm* (a) *(máquina de tabaco, bebidas)* vending machine; *(cajero automático)* cash dispenser *o* machine (b) *(habitación)* = lobby *o* small room leading to other rooms (c) *Aut* distributor

distribuidora *nf (firma)* wholesaler, supplier; *(de películas)* distributor

distribuir [34] 1 *vt* (a) *(repartir) (dinero, alimentos, medicamentos)* to distribute, to hand out; *(carga, trabajo)* to spread; *(pastel, ganancias)* to divide up; *(correo)* to deliver; **distribuyen comida entre los pobres** they give out food to the poor, they distribute food among the poor; **d. propaganda por los buzones** to deliver advertising leaflets through *Br* letter boxes *o US* mailboxes; **d. la riqueza más justamente** to share out *o* distribute wealth more justly; **d. el trabajo/las tareas** to divide up *o* share out the work/the tasks; **trata de d. bien tu tiempo** try to manage your time carefully
(b) *Com (mercancías, productos, películas)* to distribute; **una empresa que distribuye material de papelería** a firm distributing stationery materials
(c) *(disponer)* **una casa muy bien distribuida** a house with a very nice layout; **nos distribuyeron en grupos de cinco** they divided *o* split us into groups of five; **distribuyó los libros por temas** she arranged the books by topic
2 **distribuirse** *vpr* (a) *(repartirse)* **nos distribuimos las tareas domésticas** we share the household chores; **las ganancias se distribuirán entre los accionistas** the profits will be divided up *o* shared out among the shareholders
(b) *(colocarse)* to spread out; **los policías se distribuyeron alrededor del edificio** the police surrounded *o* ringed the building; **los alumnos se distribuyeron en pequeños grupos** the pupils divided up into small groups

distributivo, -a *adj* (a) *(que distribuye)* distributive (b) *Mat* distributive (c) *Gram* distributive

distribuyo *etc ver* **distribuir**

distrital *adj Am* district; **las autoridades distritales** the district authorities

distrito *nm* district; **el fiscal del d.** *US* district attorney, *Br* public prosecutor ▸▸ ***d. electoral*** electoral district; ***D. Federal*** *(en México)* Federal District *(= Mexico City)*; *(en Venezuela)* Federal District *(= Caracas)*; ***d. municipal*** *Br* borough, *US* ward; ***d. postal*** *(número)* postal code

distrofia *nf* dystrophy ▸▸ *Med* ***d. muscular*** muscular dystrophy

disturbio *nm (altercado)* disturbance; *(violento)* riot; **se produjeron disturbios aislados** there were isolated outbreaks of violence; **disturbios callejeros** street disturbances, rioting; **d. racial** race riot

disuadir *vt* to dissuade, to deter (**de** from); **lograron disuadirle de la idea** they managed to dissuade her from the idea; **no pudimos disuadirle de que fuera** we couldn't dissuade him from going, we couldn't talk him out of going; **hablando con ella la disuadieron de seguir bebiendo** they managed to talk her out of having any more to drink

disuasión *nf* deterrence; **tiene gran capacidad de d.** he's very good at talking people out of things; **política de d.** policy of deterrence

disuasivo, -a, disuasorio, -a *adj* deterrent; **empleó un tono d. con ellos** she employed a discouraging tone with them; **armas disuasivas** *o* **disuasorias** deterrent weapons; **elemento d.** deterring factor; **tomar medidas disuasivas** *o* **disuasorias** to take measures meant to act as a deterrent

disuelto, -a *participio ver* **disolver**

disuelva *etc ver* **disolver**

disulfuro *nm Quím* disulphide

disyunción *nf* disjunction

disyuntiva *nf* straight choice; **verse en** *o* **estar ante la d. de hacer una cosa u otra** to be faced with a straight choice between doing one thing or another

disyuntivo, -a *adj Gram* disjunctive

disyuntor *nm Elec* circuit breaker

dita *nf CAm, Chile (deuda)* debt

ditirambo *nm* (**a**) *Lit* dithyramb (**b**) *Formal (elogio exagerado)* panegyric, eulogy

DIU [diu] *nm* (*abrev de* **dispositivo intrauterino**) IUD, coil

diuca *nf* diuca finch

diuresis *nf inv Med* diuresis

diurético, -a 1 *adj* diuretic

2 *nm* diuretic

diurno, -a *adj (de día)* daytime; *(planta, animal)* diurnal; **horas diurnas** daytime *o* daylight hours; **un tren d.** a daytime train

divagación *nf* digression

divagar [38] *vi* to ramble; **deja ya de d. y ve al grano** stop rambling and get to the point; **cuando se pone a d. no hay quien lo aguante** he's unbearable when he starts to ramble on

diván *nm (sofá)* divan; *(de psiquiatra)* couch

díver *adj Esp Fam (divertido)* great, *Br* fab

divergencia *nf* (**a**) *(de líneas)* divergence (**b**) *(de opinión)* difference of opinion; **surgieron divergencias en la jefatura del partido** differences of opinion emerged among the party leadership; **tenemos nuestras divergencias** we have our differences (of opinion)

divergente *adj* (**a**) *(líneas, rayos, calles)* divergent, diverging; **sus vidas siguieron caminos divergentes** their lives took separate paths (**b**) *(opiniones, posturas, gustos)* different, differing

divergir [24] *vi* (**a**) *(líneas, rayos, calles)* to diverge (**b**) *(opiniones, posturas, gustos)* to differ (**en** on); **sus posturas divergían bastante** their views differed considerably

diversidad *nf* diversity; **hay gran d. cultural en la sociedad americana** there is great cultural diversity in American society; **le ofrecemos una enorme d. de productos** we offer an enormous variety *o* range of products; **d. de opiniones** variety of opinions ►► ***d. biológica*** biological diversity

diversificación *nf* diversification

diversificar [60] **1** *vt* to diversify; **debemos d. la producción/nuestros servicios** we should diversify production/our services

2 diversificarse *vpr* to diversify

diversión *nf* (**a**) *(pasatiempo)* entertainment, amusement; **mi d. favorita es el cine** my favourite pastime is going to the movies; **la ciudad ofrece gran variedad de diversiones** the city offers a great variety of entertainment

(**b**) *(hecho de divertirse)* enjoyment; **hacer algo por d.** to do sth for enjoyment *o* fun; **tuvimos un rato de d.** we had a bit of fun; **un poco de d. no nos vendría mal** we could do with a bit of fun

diverso, -a *adj* (**a**) *(diferente)* different; **una producción literaria muy diversa** an extremely varied literary output; **el zoo cuenta con especies de lo más d.** the zoo has all sorts of species (**b**) **diversos** *(varios)* several, various; **no pude asistir por diversas razones** I couldn't attend for a number of reasons

divertido, -a *adj* (**a**) *(entretenido) (película, libro)* entertaining; *(fiesta)* enjoyable; **la fiesta fue de lo más d.** it was such an enjoyable party (**b**) *(gracioso) (persona, chiste)* funny, amusing; **es un chico muy d.** he's a very funny *o* amusing boy; **encontraba d. aquel entusiasmo pueril** I found this childish enthusiasm amusing (**c**) *Andes, Arg, Guat (achispado)* tipsy

divertimento *nm* (**a**) *(novela, película)* entertainment, divertissement (**b**) *Mús* divertimento

divertimiento *nm* entertainment, amusement

divertir [63] **1** *vt (entretener)* to entertain, to amuse; **divertía a sus invitados contando chistes** she entertained her guests by telling jokes; **leer es lo único que me divierte** reading is my only distraction; **nos divertía bastante su carácter gruñón** his grumpiness amused us a lot

2 divertirse *vpr* to enjoy oneself; **se divierte con cualquier cosa** she's easily amused; **me divierto mucho contigo** I enjoy being with you, I have a good time when I'm with you; **se divirtieron muchísimo en la excursión** they had a great time on the trip, they really enjoyed the trip; **hacer el vándalo es su manera de divertirse** being a vandal is his way of amusing himself *o* his idea of fun; **¡que te diviertas!** have a nice time!, enjoy yourself!

dividendo *nm* (**a**) *Mat* dividend (**b**) *Fin* dividend; **cobrar/repartir dividendos** to be paid/distribute dividends; **dar/obtener dividendos** to pay/receive dividends ►► ***d. en acciones*** dividends in shares *o* stocks; ***d. acumulado*** accumulated dividends; ***d. complementario*** final dividend; ***d. a cuenta*** interim dividend

dividido, -a *adj* divided

dividir 1 *vt* (**a**) *(separar)* to divide (**en** into); *(átomo)* to split (**en** into); **dividió la hoja en tres partes** she divided the page into three parts; **dividió a los alumnos en grupos de cinco** he split *o* divided the pupils into groups of five; **el río divide en dos la ciudad** the river divides *o* splits the city in two

(**b**) *(repartir)* to share out (**entre** among); **el resto de los beneficios fue dividido entre los empleados** the rest of the profits were shared out *o* divided among the employees; **dividimos las tareas domésticas entre todos** we shared the household chores between all of us

(**c**) *(desunir)* to divide; **un asunto que tiene dividida a la comunidad científica** an issue that has divided the scientific community; **el testamento dividió a los hermanos** the will set the brothers against one another

(**d**) *(en matemáticas)* to divide; **d. 12 entre 3** divide 12 by 3; **15 dividido entre** *o* **por 3 igual a 5** 15 divided by 3 is 5

2 *vi (en matemáticas)* to divide; EXPR **divide y vencerás** divide and rule

3 dividirse *vpr* (**a**) *(separarse)* to divide, to split (**en** into); *(átomo)* to split; **al llegar aquí el sendero se divide en dos** when you get here the path splits into two; **se dividieron en dos grupos** they split into two groups

(**b**) *(constituirse, estar integrado)* **el oído se divide en tres partes** the ear is made up of three parts; **su obra pictórica se divide en varias épocas** his painting falls into several periods

(**c**) *(repartirse)* to split (up), to divide (up); **nos dividimos el botín** we split *o* divided (up) the loot between us

divierto *etc ver* **divertir**

divieso *nm Med* boil

divinamente *adv Fam (estupendamente)* **en esta terraza se está d.** it's heavenly on this terrace; **jugó d.** he played like a dream

divinidad *nf* (**a**) *(dios)* divinity, god; **una d. griega** a Greek god/goddess (**b**) *(naturaleza divina)* divinity

divinizar *vt* (**a**) *(hacer dios)* to deify (**b**) *(idealizar)* to deify

divino, -a *adj* (**a**) *(de Dios, de los dioses)* divine; EXPR **habló de lo d. y lo humano** he talked about everything under the sun (**b**) *Fam (estupendo)* divine, heavenly; **una casita divina** a darling little house

divirtiera *etc ver* **divertir**

divisa *nf* (**a**) *(moneda)* foreign currency; **la principal fuente de divisas** the main source of foreign currency; **fuga de divisas** flight of capital; **una d. fuerte** a strong currency; **una d. débil** a soft *o* weak currency ►► ***d. convertible*** convertible currency; ***d. de reserva*** reserve currency

(**b**) *(distintivo)* emblem

(**c**) *(lema)* motto

(**d**) *Taurom* = ribbons which identify the farm from which a bull comes

divisar *vt* to spy, to make out; **divisó un barco en la lejanía** he could make out a ship in the distance; **el Everest se divisaba en la distancia** Everest could be made out in the distance

divisibilidad *nf* divisibility

divisible *adj* divisible (**por** by)

división *nf* (**a**) *(repartición)* division; *(partición)* splitting up; *(de átomo)* splitting; **hablaron sobre la d. de la herencia** they talked about how the inheritance was to be divided ►► ***d. de poderes*** separation of powers; ***d. del trabajo*** division of labour

(**b**) *(diversidad)* **hubo d. de opiniones** opinion was divided; **aquí hay d. de gustos musicales** people have different tastes in music here

(**c**) *(desunión)* division; **hay mucha d. en el partido** the party is very divided, there's a lot of division in the party

(**d**) *(departamento)* division, department; **la d. comercial de la empresa** the firm's commercial department *o* division

(**e**) *(matemática)* division

(**f**) *(militar)* division ►► ***d. acorazada*** armoured division (**g**) *(deportiva)* division; **primera/segunda d.** first/second division; **bajar a segunda d.** to be demoted to the second division ▸▸ ***la d. de honor*** the first division, *Br* ≃ the Premier League

divisional *adj* divisional

divisionismo *nm Arte* divisionism

divismo *nm Pey* **están hartos de su d.** they're sick of the way she acts like a prima donna

divisor *nm Mat* divisor

divisoria *nf (línea)* dividing line; *(de terreno de juego)* halfway line ▸▸ ***d. de aguas*** watershed

divisorio, -a *adj* dividing; **línea divisoria** dividing line

divo, -a *nm,f* (**a**) *Mús (mujer)* diva, prima donna; *(hombre)* opera singer (**b**) *(celebridad)* star; *Fam* **ir de d.** to give oneself airs

divorciado, -a **1** *adj* (**a**) *(persona, pareja)* divorced; **soy** *o* **estoy d.** I'm divorced (**b**) *(desligado)* **d. de** divorced from; **políticas divorciadas de la realidad del país** policies divorced from the reality of the country

2 *nm,f* divorcé, *f* divorcée

divorciar **1** *vt* (**a**) *(persona, pareja)* to divorce (**b**) *(desligar)* to divorce

2 divorciarse *vpr* to get divorced (**de** from); **decidí divorciarme de él** I decided to get divorced from him, I decided to divorce him; **sus padres se han divorciado hace poco** his parents (got) divorced recently

divorcio *nm* (**a**) *(separación)* divorce; **una demanda de d.** a divorce petition; **conceder el d. a alguien** *(juez)* to grant sb a divorce; *(pareja)* to give sb a divorce; **emprender los trámites de d.** to start divorce proceedings; **pedir el d. a alguien** to ask sb for a divorce

(**b**) *(diferencia)* divergence; **el d. entre las ideologías de los dos partidos** the divergence between the ideologies of the two parties; **el d. entre patronal y sindicatos es total** there's an unbridgeable gulf between management and unions; **el d. existente entre la ley y su aplicación práctica** the gulf which exists between the letter of the law and the way it is applied in practice

(**c**) *Col (cárcel)* women's jail

divulgación *nf* (**a**) *(de noticia, rumor)* spread, spreading (**b**) *(de cultura, ciencia, doctrina)* popularization; **ha escrito varias obras de d.** she has written several books aimed at the educated layperson; **una obra de d. científica** a work of popular science

divulgador, -ora **1** *adj* informative, popularizing; **el poder d. de la televisión** the informative power of television; **una serie de carácter d.** an informative TV series

2 *nm,f* **fue el mayor d. de la ópera francesa** he was the leading figure in French opera; **el d. más importante de las ideas monetaristas** the person who has done most to make monetarist ideas more widely known

divulgar [38] **1** *vt* (**a**) *(noticia, rumor)* to spread, to circulate; **la radio divulgó la noticia** the radio announced *o* broke the news (**b**) *(cultura, ciencia, doctrina)* to popularize

2 divulgarse *vpr* (**a**) *(noticia, rumor)* to spread, to circulate; **la noticia se divulgó con rapidez** the news spread *o* circulated quickly (**b**) *(cultura, ciencia, doctrina)* to spread; **sus ideas se divulgaron por todo el mundo** their ideas spread throughout the world

divulgativo, -a *adj* informative, popularizing; **obras/programas de carácter d.** informative works/programmes

dizque *adv Andes, Carib, Méx Fam* (**a**) *(aparentemente)* apparently; **d. se lo encontró** apparently she found it; **d. van a poner un hospital aquí** apparently they're going to put a hospital here

(**b**) *Irónico (supuestamente)* supposedly; **la Armada d. Invencible** the supposedly invincible Spanish Armada; **se fueron d. para no molestarnos** they left so as not to bother us, according to them

DJ ['dijei] *nmf Fam* (*abrev de* **disc jockey**) DJ

d. J.C. (*abrev de* **después de Jesucristo**) AD

dl (*abrev de* **decilitro**) dl

Dls, dls *Am* (*abrev de* **dólares**) dols

dm (*abrev de* **decímetro**) dm

DNA *nm* (*abrev de* **ácido desoxirribonucleico**) DNA

DNI *nm* (*abrev de* **documento nacional de identidad**) ID card

Dniéper *nm* **el D.** the Dnieper

Dña. (*abrev de* **doña**) *(con nombre)* **D. María Rey** *o* **D. María** *(casada)* Mrs Rey, Mrs Maria Rey; *(soltera)* Miss Rey; *(sin especificar)* Ms Rey

DO (*abrev de* **Denominación de Origen**) = certification that a product (e.g. wine) comes from a particular region and conforms to certain quality standards

do[1] *nm (nota musical)* C; *(en solfeo)* doh; **en do mayor/menor** in C major/minor; **do bemol/sostenido** C flat/sharp; **do de pecho** high *o* top C; EXPR *Fam* **dar el do de pecho** to pull out all the stops, to go for broke; **tendrás que dar el do de pecho para aprobar** you'll need to pull out all the stops to pass

do[2] *adv Arcaico* where

dóberman *nm* Doberman (pinscher)

dobladillo *nm (de traje, vestido)* hem; *(de pantalón) Br* turn-up, *US* cuff; **subir/bajar el d. de un vestido** to take up/lower the hem on a dress

doblado, -a *adj* (**a**) *(papel, camisa)* folded (**b**) *(voz, película)* dubbed

doblador, -ora **1** *nm,f (de película)* dubber

2 *nm Guat (de tabaco)* = maize husk for rolling tobacco

dobladura *nf* fold, crease

doblaje *nm* dubbing

doblar **1** *vt* (**a**) *(duplicar)* to double; **dobló la apuesta** he doubled the bet; **su padre le dobla la edad** *o* **en edad** his father is twice his age

(**b**) *(plegar)* to fold; **dobla bien tu ropa** fold your clothes carefully; **dobla los bajos del pantalón hacia dentro** fold the hems of your *Br* trousers *o US* pants up inside

(**c**) *(torcer)* to bend; **doble el brazo, por favor** bend your arm, please; EXPR **d. el espinazo** *(someterse)* to bend the knee

(**d**) *(esquina)* to turn, to go round; **al d. la esquina** when you turn the corner

(**e**) *(actor) (con la voz)* to dub; *(en escena)* to stand in for; **d. una película al español** to dub a film into Spanish

(**f**) *(corredor)* to lap

2 *vi* (**a**) *(girar)* to turn; **dobla en la primera a la derecha** take the first right

(**b**) *(campanas)* to toll

(**c**) *(toro)* to collapse *(after receiving the bullfighter's sword thrust)*

3 doblarse *vpr* (**a**) *(duplicarse)* to double

(**b**) *(someterse)* **doblarse a** to give in to

(**c**) *(plegarse)* to fold

(**d**) *(torcerse)* to bend

(**e**) *(de dolor, risa)* to double up

(**f**) *(en dominó)* to put down a double

doble **1** *adj* double; **tiene d. número de habitantes** it has double *o* twice the number of inhabitants; **un café d.** a large coffee; **un whisky d.** a double whisky; **la blanca/el seis d.** *(en dominó)* double blank/six; **es d. de ancho** it's twice as wide; **una frase de d. sentido** a phrase with a double meaning; **una calle de d. sentido** a two-way street; EXPR **jugar un d. juego** to play a double game ▸▸ *Esp* ***d. acristalamiento*** double glazing; ***d. falta*** *(en tenis)* double fault; ***d. fondo*** false bottom; ***d. hélice*** double helix; ***d. moral*** double standards; ***d. nacionalidad*** dual nationality; ***d. negación*** double negative; ***d. pareja*** *(en póquer)* two pairs; ***d. personalidad*** split personality; ***d. sentido*** double meaning; ***d. techo*** *(de tienda de campaña)* flysheet; ***d. ventana*** secondary glazing

2 *nmf (persona parecida)* double; *(en cine)* stand-in; **buscan a un d. de Groucho Marx** they're looking for a Groucho Marx lookalike; **esa chica es tu d.** that girl is your double

3 *nm* (**a**) *(duplo)* **el d.** twice as much/many; **8 es el d. de 4** 8 is twice 4; **es el d. de alto que su hijo** he's twice as tall as his son; **gana el d. que yo** she earns twice as much as I do; **ponme el d. de tónica que de ginebra** give me twice as much tonic as gin; **la gasolina subió el d. en un año** the price of *Br* petrol *o US* gas doubled in a year; **el d. de gente** twice as many people; **d. o nada** double or quits

(**b**) *(en tenis) (pareja)* doubles pair; **el d. formado por Evert y Williams** the Evert and Williams doubles pair; **dobles** *(modalidad)* doubles ▸▸ ***dobles femeninos*** women's doubles; ***dobles masculinos*** men's doubles; ***dobles mixtos*** mixed doubles

(**c**) *(en baloncesto)* **dobles** double dribble; **hacer dobles** to double-dribble

(**d**) *Fam (de cerveza)* = tall glass of beer

4 *adv* double; **trabajar d.** to work twice as hard; EXPR *Fam* **ver d.** to see double

doblegar [38] **1** *vt (someter)* to bend, to cause to give in; **era imposible d. a todo un pueblo** it was impossible to crush a whole people; **no lograron d. su voluntad** they failed to break his will

2 doblegarse *vpr (someterse)* to give in, to yield (**ante** to); **no se doblegaba ante nada** she wouldn't give in to anything

doblemente *adv (dos veces, por dos razones)* doubly; **estamos d. contentos** we're doubly content

doblete *nm* (**a**) *Dep* double; **hacer el d.** to do the double (**b**) *Teatro* **hacer d.** *(actor)* to play two roles *o* parts (**c**) *Ling* doublet

doblez 1 *nm (pliegue)* fold, crease; **hacer un d. a algo** to fold sth; **hazle un d. por la mitad** fold it in half

2 *nm o nf (falsedad)* deceit, duplicity; **actúa siempre con d.** he's always deceitful

doblón *nm* doubloon

doc. (*abrev de* **documento**) doc.

doce *núm* twelve; **las d. del mediodía** noon, twelve o'clock midday; **las d. de la noche** midnight, twelve o'clock at night; **las d. campanadas** the bells *(at New Year)*; *ver también* **tres**

doceavo, -a *núm (fracción)* twelfth; **un d., la doceava parte** a twelfth

docena *nf* dozen; **a docenas** by the dozen; **media d. de niños** half a dozen children; **una d. de huevos** a dozen eggs

docencia *nf* teaching; **se dedica a la d.** *(es profesor)* he's a teacher

docente 1 *adj* teaching; **la carrera d. está muy desprestigiada** a teaching career no longer has the status it once had; **centro d.** educational institution; **personal d.** teaching staff

2 *nmf* teacher

dócil *adj* (**a**) *(animal, niño)* obedient; *(persona)* docile, tractable; **es un caballo muy d.** he's a very docile *o* gentle horse; **no deberías ser tan d.** you shouldn't be so submissive *o* compliant (**b**) *(cabello)* manageable

docilidad *nf* obedience

dócilmente *adv* obediently

doctamente *adv* learnedly

docto, -a *adj* (**a**) *(persona)* learned; **ser d. en algo** to be well-versed in sth; **necesitas la opinión de alguien d. en la materia** you need the opinion of an expert on the subject (**b**) *(conferencia, ensayo, revista)* learned

doctor, -ora 1 *nm,f* (**a**) *(de universidad)* doctor (**en** of); **d. en derecho/psicología (por la Universidad de...)** doctor of law/psychology (from the University of...); EXPR **doctores tiene la Iglesia** there are others more qualified to give an opinion than I am ►► ***d. honoris causa*** honorary doctor; **ser d. honoris causa (por la Universidad de...)** to have an honorary doctorate (from the University of...)

(**b**) *(médico)* doctor; **¿es grave, d.?** is it serious, doctor?; **la doctora Piñán le atenderá enseguida** Dr Piñán will see you directly

2 *nm Am* sir; **¿qué se va a servir, d.?** how can I help you, sir?

doctorado *nm* doctorate; **alumno/curso de d.** doctoral student/course; **hacer/sacarse el d.** to do/get one's PhD *o* doctorate

doctoral *adj* (**a**) *(de doctor universitario)* doctoral (**b**) *Pey (tono, lenguaje)* pompous, pedantic

doctorando, -a *nm,f Formal* doctoral candidate

doctorar 1 *vt* to confer a doctorate on

2 **doctorarse** *vpr* to obtain one's doctorate (**en** in)

doctrina *nf* doctrine

doctrinal *adj* doctrinal

doctrinario, -a 1 *adj* doctrinaire

2 *nm,f* doctrinaire

docudrama *nm* docudrama

documentación *nf* (**a**) *(identificación) (de persona)* papers, identification; *(de vehículo, cargamento, mercancías)* documents; **muéstreme su d., por favor** could you show me your identification, please?

(**b**) *(documentos, información)* information; *(manuales de uso)* documentation

(**c**) *(técnica, disciplina)* library research skills, documentation; **equipo de d.** *(de programa de TV)* research team

documentado, -a *adj* (**a**) *(informado) (informe, estudio)* researched; *(persona)* well-informed; **un periodista muy d.** a very well-informed journalist; **estar bien/mal d. sobre algo** to be well-informed/ill-informed about sth (**b**) *(con papeles encima)* having identification; **no pudo entrar porque no iba d.** he couldn't get in because he had no identification with him

documental 1 *adj* (**a**) *(programa, película)* documentary (**b**) *(prueba, demostración)* documentary

2 *nm* documentary

documentalista *nmf* (**a**) *(en archivo)* archivist (**b**) *Cine & TV* documentary filmmaker

documentar 1 *vt (trabajo, ensayo, ponencia)* to document; *(teoría, hipótesis, afirmación)* to document, to provide evidence for; *(defensa, acusación, argumentos)* to provide evidence for, to back up; **hay abundantes testimonios que documentan este hecho** this fact is supported by abundant documentary evidence

2 **documentarse** *vpr* to do research; **hizo la entrevista sin haberse documentado sobre el personaje** she conducted the interview without having done any research on the person; **se documentó antes de escribir el artículo** he read up on the subject before writing the article

documento *nm* (**a**) *(escrito)* document ►► ***d. nacional de identidad*** identity card; *Der* ***d. privado*** private document; *Der* ***d. público*** public record *o* document; *Der* ***d. de venta*** bill of sale

(**b**) *(testimonio)* record; **uno de los primeros documentos sonoros que existen** one of the first sound recordings in existence; **estas fotos son un d. gráfico de incalculable valor** these photos are a visual record of incalculable value

(**c**) *Informát* document; **guárdalo en Mis documentos** save it in My documents

dodecaedro *nm* dodecahedron

dodecafonía *nf Mús* twelve-tone system, dodecaphony

dodecafónico, -a *adj Mús* twelve-tone

dodecafonismo *nm Mús* twelve-tone system, dodecaphony

dodecágono, -a 1 *adj* dodecagonal

2 *nm* dodecagon

dodecasílabo, -a 1 *adj* twelve-syllable, dodecasyllabic

2 *nm* twelve-syllable line, dodecasyllable

dodotis® *nm inv* disposable *Br* nappy *o US* diaper

dogal *nm (para ahorcar)* noose

dogma *nm* (**a**) *Rel* dogma ►► ***d. de fe*** article of faith (**b**) *(principio cierto)* dogma; **uno de los dogmas del capitalismo** one of the dogmas of capitalism

dogmáticamente *adv* dogmatically

dogmático, -a *adj* (**a**) *(persona, ideas, postura)* dogmatic (**b**) *Rel* dogmatic

dogmatismo *nm* dogmatism

dogmatizante *adj* dogmatic

dogmatizar *vi* to express oneself dogmatically, to pontificate

dogo *nm* bull mastiff

dólar *nm* dollar; EXPR *Esp Fam* **estar montado en el d.** *(ser rico)* to be rolling in it; EXPR *Esp Fam* **montarse en el d.** *(hacerse rico)* to make a pile

dolarización *nf* dollarization

dolarizar *vt* to dollarize

dolby® *nm inv* Dolby®; **grabado con d.** recorded with Dolby®

dolencia *nf* complaint, ailment; **sufre una grave d.** he's suffering from a serious illness; **una d. cardíaca/renal** a heart/kidney complaint; **una d. crónica** a chronic illness

doler [41] 1 *vi* (**a**) *(físicamente)* to hurt; **me duele la pierna** my leg hurts; **me duele la garganta** I have a sore throat; **me duele la cabeza/el estómago** I have a headache/a stomachache; **me duele todo el cuerpo** I ache all over; **aún me duele el pinchazo que me dieron** I'm still sore from the injection they gave me; **¿te sigue doliendo la herida?** does the wound still hurt?; **¿te duele?** does it hurt?; **no te preocupes, no te va a d.** don't worry, it won't hurt; EXPR *Fam* **¡ahí le duele!** that has really got to him!; **lo que necesitan es mano dura – ¡ahí le duele!** what they need is a firm hand – you've put your finger on it!

(**b**) *(moralmente)* to hurt, to pain; **lo que más me duele es su indiferencia** what hurts *o* pains me most is her indifference; **me duele ver tanta injusticia** it pains *o* saddens me to see so much injustice; **me duele tener que decirte esto, pero...** I'm very sorry *o* I hate to have to tell you this, but...; **le dolió en el alma** it upset her terribly; EXPR **no d. prendas a alguien: no me duelen prendas en reconocer que me he equivocado** I don't mind admitting I was wrong

2 **dolerse** *vpr* (**a**) *(físicamente)* **se dolía de un oído** she had earache; **estuve todo el verano doliéndome de la rodilla** my knee was hurting me all summer

(**b**) *(moralmente)* **dolerse de** *o* **por algo** *(quejarse)* to complain about sth; *(arrepentirse)* to be sorry about sth; **se duele de que nadie se acordara de él** he feels hurt that no one remembered him; **no te duelas por lo que pasó, no es culpa tuya** don't be upset *o* feel sorry about what happened, it's not your fault

dolido, -a *adj* hurt, upset; **estar/sentirse d. (por algo)** to be/feel hurt (by sth), to be/feel upset (about sth); **¿aún sigues d. por lo que pasó?** are you still upset about what happened?

doliente 1 *adj* (**a**) *(enfermo)* ill; *(dolorido)* suffering (**b**) *(afligido)* sorrowful; **su d. viuda** his grieving widow

2 *nmf (pariente del difunto)* bereaved relative; **los dolientes** the bereaved relatives, the family of the deceased

dolmen *nm* dolmen

dolo *nm Der* (**a**) *(fraude)* fraud (**b**) *(intención deliberada)* premeditation; **hacer algo con d.** to do sth with premeditation *o* wittingly

dolomita *nf Geol* dolomite

dolor *nm* (**a**) *(físico)* pain; **un d. sordo** a dull pain; **¿dónde tienes el d.?** where does it hurt?; **me dio un d. tremendo en los riñones** I felt a terrible pain in my lower back; **siento un d. en el costado** I have a pain in my side; **hizo un gesto de d.** she winced with pain; **tengo d. de huesos/dolores musculares** my bones/muscles ache ►► ***d. de barriga*** bellyache; ***d. de cabeza*** headache; **tener d. de cabeza** to have a headache; **¡este niño no nos da más que dolores de cabeza!** that child does nothing but make trouble for us!; ***d. de estómago*** stomachache; ***d. de garganta*** sore throat; **tener d. de garganta** to have a sore throat; ***dolores menstruales*** period pains; ***d. de muelas*** toothache; ***d. de oídos*** earache; **tener d. de oídos** to have earache; ***dolores del parto*** labour pains
(**b**) *(moral)* sorrow; **sentir d. por algo** to feel sorrow at sth; **separarse de su hijo les causó gran d.** being separated from their son was very painful for them; **le comunicó la noticia con gran d.** she told him the news with great sorrow; **lloraba de d. por su desgracia** she wept with sadness at her misfortune; **su fallecimiento nos llena de d.** his death fills us with sorrow; EXPR **con todo el d. de mi corazón: la castigué con todo el d. de mi corazón** it broke my heart to punish her; **tuve que irme de aquella ciudad con todo el d. de mi corazón** it was heartbreaking for me to have to leave that city

dolorido, -a *adj* (**a**) *(físicamente)* sore; **la caída lo dejó muy d.** the fall left him in great pain; **tengo todo el cuerpo d.** I'm aching all over; **tener la pierna/espalda dolorida** to have a sore leg/back (**b**) *(moralmente)* grieving, sorrowing; **estar d.** to be grieving *o* sorrowing

dolorosa *nf Fam Hum (cuenta) Br* bill, *US* check; **la d., por favor** what's the damage?

dolorosamente *adv* painfully

doloroso, -a *adj* (**a**) *(físicamente)* painful; **tuvo un parto muy d.** she had a very painful labour (**b**) *(moralmente)* distressing; **fue una decisión muy dolorosa para mí** it was a very painful decision for me; **tengo un recuerdo d. de aquella época** I have painful memories of that period; **resulta d. verlo en ese estado** it's distressing to see him in that state

doloso, -a *adj Der* fraudulent

dom. (*abrev de* **domingo**) Sun

doma *nf (de animales salvajes)* taming; **d. de caballos** breaking-in of horses; **concurso de d.** *(en equitación)* dressage competition

domable *adj (animal salvaje)* tameable; *(caballo)* breakable

domador, -ora *nm,f (de animales salvajes)* tamer; **d. de caballos** *Br* horsebreaker, *US* broncobuster; **d. de leones** lion tamer

domadura *nf (de animales salvajes)* taming; *(de caballos)* breaking

domar *vt* (**a**) *(animal salvaje)* to tame; *(caballo)* to break in (**b**) *(calzado)* to break in (**c**) *(personas, pasiones)* to control; **es un niño muy difícil de d.** he's a very difficult child to control

domeñar *vt Formal (persona, pueblo)* to subdue, to bring under control; *(deseos, sentimientos)* to restrain, to (keep under) control

domesticable *adj* **animales domesticables** animals which can be tamed *o* domesticated

domesticación *nf* domestication

domesticado, -a *adj* (**a**) *(animal)* tame, domesticated (**b**) *Hum (persona)* domesticated, house-trained

domesticar [60] *vt* (**a**) *(animal)* to tame, to domesticate (**b**) *Hum (persona)* to domesticate, to house-train; **su mujer se encargó de domesticarlo** his wife took on the job of domesticating *o* house-training him

domesticidad *nf* domesticity

doméstico, -a 1 *adj* (**a**) *(tarea, vida, problema)* domestic; **las tareas domésticas** housework, (the) domestic chores; **la economía doméstica** housekeeping; **el servicio d.** domestic service; **aparatos/productos de uso d.** appliances/products for domestic *o* household use (**b**) *(animal)* domestic
2 *nm,f (en ciclismo)* domestique

domiciliación *nf Esp* direct debiting; **hizo la d. del sueldo en su cuenta corriente** he had his salary paid directly into his current account; **pagar mediante d. (bancaria)** *(una cantidad fija)* to pay by standing *o* banker's order; *(una cantidad variable)* to pay by direct debit

domiciliado, -a *adj Esp* **tengo el pago del teléfono d.** I pay the phone bill by direct debit; **tengo el sueldo d. en mi cuenta** I have my salary paid directly into my account

domiciliar 1 *vt* (**a**) *Esp (pago) (de una cantidad fija)* to pay by standing *o* banker's order; *(de una cantidad variable)* to pay by direct debit; **d. la nómina** *o* **el sueldo** to have one's salary paid into a bank account (**b**) *Méx (carta)* to address
2 **domiciliarse** *vpr (persona)* to establish residence

domiciliario, -a *adj Der* **arresto d.** house arrest; **asistente d.** home help; **visita domiciliaria** *(de médico)* house call

domicilio *nm* (**a**) *(vivienda)* residence, home; **uno de nuestros encuestadores visitará su d.** one of our survey interviewers will call on you at your home; *Dep* **a d.** *(en campo contrario)* away; **reparto a d.** home delivery; **vender a d.** to sell door-to-door; **la segunda victoria a d. del Atlético** Atlético's second away win ►► ***d. conyugal*** matrimonial home; ***d. particular*** private residence
(**b**) *(dirección)* address; **cambio de d.** change of address ►► ***d. fijo*** permanent address; **sin d. fijo** of no fixed abode; ***d. fiscal*** registered office; ***d. habitual*** usual residence; ***d. social*** registered office
(**c**) *(localidad)* residence

dominación *nf* rule, dominion; **territorios bajo la d. otomana** territories under Ottoman control

dominador, -ora *adj* dominating

dominancia *nf Biol* dominance

dominante 1 *adj* (**a**) *(predominante) (nación, tendencia, característica)* dominant; *(vientos)* prevailing; **el color d. era el azul** the predominant colour was blue; **la empresa tiene una posición d. en el sector** the company holds a commanding position in the sector; **lo más d. en su personalidad es el optimismo** his most striking characteristic is his optimism
(**b**) *(persona)* domineering
(**c**) *Biol (gen)* dominant
(**d**) *Mús* dominant
2 *nf* (**a**) *(característica)* predominant feature
(**b**) *Mús* dominant

dominar 1 *vt* (**a**) *(controlar) (país, territorio, pueblo)* to dominate, to rule (over); *(persona, caballo)* to control; *(emociones, nervios)* to control, to keep under control; *(situación)* to be in control of; *(incendio, epidemia)* to bring under control; *(rebelión)* to put down; *(partido)* to dominate; **la guerrilla domina toda esta zona** guerrillas control this entire area; **la policía logró d. a los alborotadores** the police managed to bring the troublemakers under control; **tiene al marido dominado** she has her husband under her thumb; **era imposible d. el vehículo** it was impossible to maintain control of the vehicle; **no supo d. sus nervios** she couldn't control her nervousness; **el equipo local dominó el partido en todo momento** the local team dominated the game from the beginning
(**b**) *(sujeto: pasión, nervios, emociones)* to overcome; **lo dominaba el deseo irrefrenable de besarla** he was overcome by an irresistible desire to kiss her
(**c**) *(ser experto en) (técnica, tema)* to master; *(lengua)* to be fluent in; **domina a la perfección los temas de contabilidad** he has a perfect mastery of accounting; **domina varias lenguas** she speaks various languages fluently; **ha conseguido d. el inglés en pocos meses** he managed to acquire a good command of English in a few months; **¡cómo domina el balón!** what great ball control!
(**d**) *(divisar)* to overlook; **desde aquí se domina todo Bilbao** you can see the whole of Bilbao from here
(**e**) *(destacar por encima de)* to dominate; **el castillo domina el pueblo** the castle dominates the town
2 *vi (predominar)* to predominate; **una zona donde domina el voto socialista** an area with a predominantly socialist vote
3 **dominarse** *vpr* to control oneself

dómine *nm Hist* Latin teacher

domingas *nfpl muy Fam* boobs, knockers

domingo *nm* Sunday; **ponerse la ropa de d.** to put on one's Sunday best ►► ***D. de Pascua*** Easter Sunday; ***D. de Pentecostés*** Whit Sunday; ***D. de Ramos*** Palm Sunday; ***D. de Resurrección*** Easter Sunday; *ver también* **sábado**

dominguero, -a *Fam Pey* 1 *adj* **excursionistas domingueros** Sunday trippers
2 *nm,f (conductor)* Sunday driver; **el pueblo se llena de domingueros** the town gets packed with clueless day-trippers

Dominica *n* Dominica

dominical 1 *adj* Sunday; **excursión/suplemento d.** Sunday outing/supplement
2 *nm (suplemento)* Sunday supplement

dominicano, -a 1 *adj* Dominican
2 *nm,f* Dominican

dominico, -a *Rel* **1** *adj* Dominican
2 *nm,f* Dominican

dominio *nm* **(a)** *(dominación)* control (**sobre** over); **la guerrilla tiene el d. sobre esta zona** this area is under guerrilla control; **territorios bajo d. romano** territory under Roman rule; **tenía al partido bajo su absoluto d.** he had the party under his absolute control; **el d. del partido correspondió al equipo visitante** the visiting team had the best of the match; **en ningún momento perdió el d. de la situación** at no time did he lose control of the situation; **trata de mantener el d. de ti mismo** try to keep control of yourself
(b) *(territorio)* domain; **un antiguo d. portugués** a former Portuguese territory *o* colony; **la caza estaba prohibida en sus dominios** hunting was forbidden on his land *o* domain
(c) *(ámbito)* realm, field; **temas que pertenecen al d. de la cibernética** topics relating to the field of cybernetics; **entramos en los dominios de la ciencia ficción** we are entering the realms of science fiction
(d) *(conocimiento) (de arte, técnica)* mastery; *(de idiomas)* command; **su d. del tema** his mastery of the subject; **tiene un buen d. del pincel** she has a good command of the brush; **para el puesto requerimos d. de al menos dos lenguas** the post requires mastery of at least two languages; **tiene un gran d. del balón** he has great ball control; EXPR **ser de d. público** to be public knowledge; **era de d. público que vivían separados** it was common *o* public knowledge that they were living apart
(e) *Informát* domain ▸▸ ***d. público*** public domain
(f) *Der (propiedad)* ownership, domain

dominó *nm* **(a)** *(juego)* dominoes *(singular)*; **jugar al d.** to play dominoes **(b)** *(fichas)* set of dominoes

domo *nm (cúpula)* dome, cupola

domótica *nf* home automation

dompedro *nm (flor)* morning glory

Don *nm* **el D.** the Don

don[1] *nm* **(a)** *(tratamiento)* Mr; **d. Andrés Iturbe** Mr Andrés Iturbe; *(en cartas)* Mr Andrés Iturbe, Andrés Iturbe Esquire; **d. Andrés** Mr Iturbe
(b) *Irónico (para calificar)* Mr; **eres d. preocupaciones, olvídate ya** you're a professional worrier, aren't you? just forget about it; **d. perfecto** Mr Perfect, God's gift; EXPR *Fam* **ser un d. nadie** to be a nobody
(c) *Am (sin nombre)* **¿qué va a llevar hoy, d.?** what will you have today, *Br* guv *o US* pal?

don[2] *nm* **(a)** *(habilidad)* gift; **tiene un d. especial con los niños** he has a special gift for dealing with children; **tiene un d. para los idiomas** she has a flair *o* gift for languages; **tener el d. de la palabra** *(cualidad humana)* to have the gift of speech; *(de orador)* to be a gifted speaker; *Irónico* **tienes el d. de la oportunidad** you have a gift for putting your foot in it ▸▸ ***d. de gentes*** ability to get on well with people; **necesitamos una persona con d. de gentes** we need someone who is good with people; **tener d. de gentes** to have a way with people; ***d. de mando*** leadership qualities
(b) *Literario (regalo)* gift

dona *nf CAm, Méx* doughnut

donación *nf* donation; **d. de sangre/órganos** blood/organ donation; **hacer d. de algo a alguien** to donate sth to sb; **hizo d. de varios de sus cuadros al museo** he donated several of his paintings to the museum

donador, -ora *nm,f (de sangre, órgano)* donor; *Der & Econ (de bienes, capital)* donator, donor

donaire *nm Literario* **(a)** *(al expresarse)* wit; **contestó con mucho d.** he replied wittily **(b)** *(al andar, moverse)* grace; **bailaban con gran d.** they danced very gracefully

donante *nmf* **(a)** *(que dona)* donor ▸▸ ***d. de órganos*** organ donor; ***d. de sangre*** blood donor **(b)** *Arte* donor

donar *vt (bienes, capital)* to donate, to gift; *(órganos)* to donate; **d. sangre** to give blood

donatario, -a *nm,f Der (de bienes, capital)* donee, *US* donatee

donativo *nm* donation; **dar** *o* **hacer un d. a alguien** to give *o* make a donation to sb

doncel *nm* **(a)** *Hist (joven noble)* page **(b)** *Literario (muchacho)* youth **(c)** *(pez)* goldsinny

doncella **1** *nf* **(a)** *(sirvienta)* maid **(b)** *Literario (chica joven)* maiden, damsel **(c)** *Arcaico (muchacha virgen)* maiden, maid **(d)** *(pez)* rainbow wrasse
2 *adj Literario (virgen)* **quería conservarse d.** she wished to remain a virgin

doncellez *nf Arcaico* virginity

DONDE

> **donde** combines with the preposition **a** to form **adonde** when following a noun, pronoun or adverb expressing location (e.g. **el sitio adonde vamos** the place where we're going; **es allí adonde iban** that's where they were going).

1 *adv* where; **la casa d. nací** the house where I was born; **el bolso está d. lo dejaste** the bag is where you left it; **allí d. va, causa problemas** he causes trouble wherever he goes; **vayan d. vayan, siempre tienen éxito** wherever they go, they're always successful; **puedes ir d. quieras** you can go wherever you want; **de d.** *(de lo cual)* from which; **de d. se deduce que estás equivocado** from which it can be concluded that you're wrong; **la ciudad de d. viene** the town (where) she comes from, the town from which she comes; **desde d. estábamos no se veía el escenario** you couldn't see the stage from where we were; **el hotel en d. nos alojamos** the hotel where we're staying, the hotel at which we're staying; **el pueblo hacia d. nos dirigíamos** the town we were heading for, the town for which we were heading; **tienes que correr hasta d. está la valla** you have to run as far as the fence, you have to run up to where the fence is; **llegaré hasta d. pueda** I'll get as far as I can; **iré por d. me manden** I'll go wherever they send me; **la puerta por d. entró** the door she came in through, the door through which she came in
2 *prep* **(a)** *(al lugar de)* **ve d. la tienda y espérame allí** go and wait for me at the shop; **ve d. papá y dile que nos vamos** *(al lugar en que está, a su casa)* go over to dad's and tell him that we're going
(b) *(en el lugar de)* **está d. mi madre** she's at my mother's; **eso está d. la fábrica de harina** it's by the flour mill

DÓNDE

> **dónde** can combine with the preposition **a** to form **adónde** (e.g. **¿adónde vamos?** where are we going?).

1 *adv* where; **¿d. está el niño?** where's the child?; **no sé d. se habrá metido** I don't know where she can be; **dime d. lo has escondido** tell me where you've hidden it; **¿d. me llevas?** where are you taking me (to)?; **¿adónde vas?** where are you going?; **¿de d. eres?** where are you from?; **¿de d. has sacado esa corbata?** where on earth *o* wherever did you get that tie?; **¿desde d. se ve mejor?** where do you get the best view from?; **¿en d. cenas normalmente?** where do you normally go for dinner?; **¿hacia d. vas?** where are you heading?; **¿por d.?** whereabouts?; **¿por d. se va al teatro?** how do you get to the theatre from here?; **¿por d. has entrado?** where did you come in?; EXPR **mira por d.: mira por d., hemos estado discutiendo sobre el tema recientemente** you'll never believe it, but we were discussing the subject only recently; **mira por d., este regalo me hacía mucha falta** funnily enough, this present is just what I needed
2 *nm* **quiero saber el d. y el cuándo** I want to know the time and the place

> In conversational English a preposition is frequently placed at the end of a sentence beginning with an interrogative pronoun. In Spanish the preposition must always come at the beginning of the sentence before the interrogative pronoun:
> **¿de dónde eres?**
> *where are you from?*
> The same contrast is found in the use of relative pronouns in the two languages:
> **el punto hasta donde llegaron**
> *the point (where) they got to*

dondequiera *adv* **d. que** wherever; **d. que se esconda, lo encontrarán** wherever *o* no matter where he hides, they will find him

dondiego *nm (planta)* **d. (de noche)** marvel of Peru, four-o'clock

donjuán, don Juan *nm Fam* Casanova, Don Juan

donjuanesco, -a *adj Fam* womanizing

donosamente *adv Literario* **(a)** *(expresarse)* wittily **(b)** *(moverse, caminar)* gracefully

donoso, -a *adj Literario* **(a)** *(al expresarse)* witty **(b)** *(al moverse, caminar)* elegant, poised

donostiarra *Esp* **1** *adj* of/from San Sebastián *(Spain)*
2 *nmf* person from San Sebastián *(Spain)*

donosura *nf Literario (porte)* poise

dónut® *(pl* **dónuts***) nm* doughnut

doña *nf* **(a)** *(con nombre)* **d. María** *o* **d. María Rey** *(casada)* Mrs Rey; *(soltera)* Miss Rey; *(sin especificar)* Ms Rey **(b)** *Irónico (para calificar)* Miss; **eres d. preocupaciones, olvídate ya** you're Miss Worrier, just forget about it; **d. perfecta** little Miss Perfect (c) *Am (sin nombre)* madam; **¿qué va a llevar hoy, d.?** what would you like today, *Br* love *o US* lady?

dopa *nf Bioquím* dopa

dopado, -a *adj* **sancionaron a los deportistas dopados** those athletes who had taken drugs were punished

dopaje *nm (de deportistas)* doping, using performance-enhancing drugs; **el control de d.** the drug test

dopamina *nf Bioquím* dopamine

dopar 1 *vt (deportista)* to dope, to give performance-enhancing drugs to

2 doparse *vpr (deportista)* to take performance-enhancing drugs

doping ['dopin] *(pl* **dopings***) nm (de deportistas)* doping, using performance-enhancing drugs; **tres dopings positivos** three positive drug tests

doquier *adv* **por d.** everywhere

dorada *nf (pez)* gilt-head

dorado, -a 1 *adj* (a) *(de color de oro)* golden (b) *(de esplendor)* golden; **la edad dorada de la ópera italiana** the golden age of Italian opera

2 *nm* (a) *(parte dorada)* gilt; **limpiar los dorados** to clean the brass fittings (b) *Mitol* **el Dorado** El Dorado

dorador, -ora *nm,f* gilder

dorar 1 *vt* (a) *(cubrir con oro)* to gild; EXPR *Fam* **d. la píldora (a alguien)** to sweeten *o* sugar the pill (for sb); **no hace falta que me dores la píldora, dime cuál es el problema** you needn't sweeten the pill for me, just tell me what the problem is (b) *(comida)* to brown (c) *(piel)* to turn golden brown

2 dorarse *vpr* (a) *(comida)* to brown; **dejar que se dore la cebolla a fuego lento** leave the onion on a low heat until it turns golden brown (b) *(piel)* to tan

dórico, -a 1 *adj* Doric

2 *nm* Doric

dorio, -a 1 *adj* Dorian

2 *nm,f* Dorian

dormida *nf Am* **¿cómo estuvo la d. en la casa nueva?** what was it like sleeping in the new house?; **la d. es complicada con tanta gente** the sleeping arrangements are complicated with so many people

dormidera *nf Carib (sensitiva)* sensitive plant

dormido, -a *adj* (a) *(persona) (durmiendo)* asleep; **estar/quedarse d.** to be/fall asleep; **me quedé d. y llegué tarde a clase** I overslept and arrived late for class (b) *(persona) (despistado)* half asleep; **¿estás d. o qué?** are you asleep or what? (c) *(brazo, pierna)* **tengo el pie d.** my foot has gone to sleep

dormilón, -ona *Fam* **1** *adj* **es muy d.** he's a real sleepyhead, he likes his bed

2 *nm,f* sleepyhead

dormilona *nf Ven (prenda)* nightshirt, nightdress

dormir [27] **1** *vt* (a) *(bebé, niño, persona)* to get off to sleep; **lo durmió acunándolo en los brazos** she rocked him to sleep in her arms; **el rumor de la fuente terminó durmiéndolo** the murmur of the fountain eventually sent him to sleep; **el fútbol me duerme** soccer sends me to sleep

(b) *(pasar en sueños)* **d. la siesta** to have an afternoon nap; **durmió la borrachera en un banco del parque** he slept off the binge on a park bench; EXPR *Fam* **dormirla, d. la mona** to sleep it off

(c) *(anestesiar)* to anaesthetize; **me durmieron y no me enteré de nada** they put me to sleep and I didn't feel a thing; **el dentista me durmió la boca** the dentist made my mouth numb

2 *vi* (a) *(reposar)* to sleep; **baja la voz, que están durmiendo** keep your voice down, they're asleep; **¿duermes?** are you asleep?; **no puedo d.** I can't sleep *o* get to sleep; **intenta d. un poco** try to get some sleep; **¡a d.!, ¡es hora de d.!** off to bed!, it's time for bed!; **el ruido no me deja d.** I can't sleep for the noise; **d. bien/mal** to sleep well/badly; **irse a d.** to go to bed; **¿a qué hora sueles irte a d.?** what time do you usually go to bed?; **d. de un tirón** to sleep right through, to sleep without waking up; EXPR *Fam* **d. a pierna suelta** *o* **como un lirón** *o* **como un tronco** to sleep like a log

(b) *(pernoctar)* to spend the night; **dormimos en el autobús** we spent the night on the bus; **ayer no durmió en casa** he didn't sleep at home last night

(c) *Fam (tener relaciones sexuales)* **d. con alguien** to sleep with sb; **duermen juntos** they're sleeping together

(d) *(estar olvidado)* to languish; **su guión dormía en el cajón de algún productor** his script was languishing in some producer's desk drawer

3 dormirse *vpr* (a) *(persona) (empezar a soñar)* to fall asleep; **no puedo dormirme** I can't get (off) to sleep; **terminó durmiéndose al amanecer** he eventually fell asleep at dawn; **yo con el fútbol/la ópera me duermo** soccer/opera sends me to sleep

(b) *(persona) (no despertarse)* to oversleep, to sleep in; **se durmió y llegó tarde** she overslept and arrived late

(c) *(brazo, mano)* to go to sleep; **se me ha dormido la pierna** my leg has gone to sleep

(d) *(despistarse)* **si te duermes, te quedarás sin entradas** if you don't get a move on, you'll be left without tickets; **¡no te duermas y haz algo!** don't just stand there, do something!

dormitar *vi* to doze

dormitorio *nm* (a) *(de casa)* bedroom (b) *(de colegio)* dormitory (c) *(muebles)* bedroom suite

dorsal 1 *adj* (a) *(aleta, región)* dorsal (b) *Ling (consonante)* dorsal

2 *nm* (a) *Dep (número)* number *(on player's back)*; **con el d. número 7 Raúl** Raúl, wearing number 7 *o* the number 7 shirt (b) *Anat (músculo)* latissimus dorsi

3 *nf Geol* ridge ►► ***d. oceánica*** oceanic ridge

dorso *nm* back; **al d., en el d.** on the back; **escribió algo al d.** *o* **en el d.** she wrote something on the back; **véase al d.** see overleaf; **el d. de la mano** the back of the hand

DOS [dos] *nm Informát (abrev de* **disk operating system***)* DOS

dos *núm* two; **los d. vivimos aquí** we both live here; **es un regalo para los d.** it's a present for both *o* the two of you; **de d. en d.** in twos, two by two; **d. veces** twice; EXPR **cada d. por tres** every five minutes; **cada d. por tres aparecen por casa** they're always turning up at the house; **la lavadora se estropea cada d. por tres** the washing machine is always breaking down; EXPR **como d. y d. son cuatro** as sure as night follows day; EXPR **en un d. por tres** in no time at all; EXPR **no hay d. sin tres** everything comes in threes; EXPR **ya somos d.** that makes two of us; **no me gustó la película – ya somos d.** I didn't like the film – that makes two of us ►► ***d. caballos*** *(automóvil)* (Citroën) 2CV; ***d. contra uno*** *(en baloncesto)* double team; ***un d. piezas*** *(traje)* a two-piece suit; *(bañador)* a two-piece swimsuit; ***d. puntos*** *(signo de puntuación)* colon; *ver también* **tres**

dosaje *nm* (a) *Am (medicamento)* dosage (b) *Arg, Perú (prueba)* Breathalyser® test, breath test

doscientos, -as *núm* two hundred; *ver también* **treinta**

dosel *nm (sobre cama)* canopy; *(sobre trono, altar)* baldachin

doselera *nf* valance

dosificación *nf* dosage

dosificador *nm* dispenser

dosificar [60] *vt* (a) *(fármaco)* to measure out (b) *(fuerzas, alimentos)* to use sparingly

dosis *nf inv* (a) *(de medicamento, droga)* dose; **d. recomendada para niños** recommended dosage for children; **una d. de heroína** a dose of heroin ►► ***d. letal*** lethal dose (b) *(de paciencia, cariño)* amount; **hay grandes d. de humor en su última película** there is a good deal of humour in his latest film; **me encantan los niños, pero en pequeñas d.** I love children, but in small doses

dossier [do'sjer] *(pl* **dossiers***) nm* (a) *(informe)* dossier, file (b) *Prensa (reportaje)* report

dotación *nf* (a) *(de dinero, armas, medios)* amount granted; **la d. del premio era de 2 millones** there was a prize of 2 million; **una beca con una d. de 5.000 euros** a scholarship worth 5,000 euros; **la fábrica necesita mayor d. de maquinaria** the factory needs to be better equipped with machinery

(b) *(personal)* staff, personnel; *(tripulantes)* crew; *(patrulla)* squad; **un hotel con poca d.** an understaffed hotel

dotado, -a *adj* (a) *(persona)* gifted; **es un escritor muy d.** he's a very gifted writer; **estar d. para algo** to have a gift for sth; **está d. para el jazz** he has a talent for jazz; **d. de** blessed with; **un hombre d. de un gran sentido del humor/de una increíble paciencia** a man who's blessed with a fine sense of humour/incredible patience; **necesitamos gente dotada de experiencia** we need people who have experience; *Hum* **un hombre bien d.** a well-endowed *o* well-hung man; *Hum* **está muy bien dotada** she's very well-endowed

(b) *(premio)* **un premio d. con 5 millones de pesos** a prize worth 5 million pesos

(c) *(edificio, instalación, aparato)* **d. de** *o* **con** equipped with; **tejidos dotados de gran elasticidad** fabrics which have great elasticity

dotar *vt* (a) *(proveer) (con medios, dinero)* to provide; **d. (a) algo de** *o* **con** to provide sth with; **actos benéficos para d. de fondos (a) una organización humanitaria** charity events to raise funds for a humanitarian organization; **dotaron (a) todas las sucursales con sistemas**

de alarma they equipped all the branches with alarm systems
(**b**) *(con tripulación)* to man, to crew; *(con personal)* to staff; **d. algo de** *(barco, avión)* to man *o* crew sth with; *(hotel, tienda)* to staff sth with; **deben d. los vuelos internacionales de más personal** they should provide a larger crew for international flights
(**c**) *(asignar dinero a)* **han dotado el cargo con 40.000 euros** they've fixed the salary for the post at 40,000 euros; **la beca está dotada con $15.000** the scholarship is worth $15,000; **el premio fue dotado con 100.000 pesos** the prize was set at 100,000 pesos
(**d**) *(conferir)* **d. a algo/alguien de** to endow sth/sb with; **la naturaleza lo dotó de una gran inteligencia** nature endowed him with great intelligence
(**e**) *(dar una dote a)* to provide with a dowry; **su padre la dotó con una gran mansión** her father gave a large mansion for *o* as her dowry

dote *nf* (**a**) *(en boda)* dowry
(**b**) **dotes** *(aptitud)* qualities; **un pintor con muchas dotes** a painter of considerable talent; **personas con dotes para el baile** people with a talent for dancing; **tener dotes de** *o* **para algo** to have a talent for sth; **se le ve que tiene dotes de futbolista** he's clearly got the makings of a footballer; **tiene unas dotes excelentes para la música** he has real musical talent ▸▸ ***dotes de mando*** leadership qualities

dovela *nf* voussoir

doy *ver* **dar**

DP *nf* (*abrev de* **Democracia Popular**) = Ecuadoran political party

dpi *Informát* (*abrev de* **dots per inch**) dpi

dpto. (*abrev de* **departamento**) dept; **d. de personal** personnel dept

Dr. (*abrev de* **doctor**) Dr

Dra. (*abrev de* **doctora**) Dr

dracma *nm o nf Antes* drachma

draconiano, -a *adj (severo, cruel)* draconian

Drácula *n Mitol* **(el conde) D.** (Count) Dracula

DRAE ['drae] *nm* (*abrev de* **Diccionario de la Real Academia Española**) = dictionary of the Spanish Royal Academy

draga *nf* (**a**) *(máquina)* dredge (**b**) *(barco)* dredger

dragado *nm* dredging

dragaminas *nm inv* minesweeper

dragar [38] *vt* to dredge

drago *nm* dragon tree

dragón *nm* (**a**) *(monstruo)* dragon (**b**) *(reptil)* flying dragon (**c**) *(planta)* snapdragon (**d**) *(soldado)* dragoon (**e**) *(pez)* dragonet (**f**) *Dep (en vela)* Dragon Class yacht (**g**) *Urug Fam (pretendiente)* suitor, young man

dragona *nf Méx (capa)* man's cape

dragoncillo *nm (pez)* common dragonet

dragonear **1** *vt Urug Fam* to court
2 *vi Am* (**a**) **d. de** *(hacerse pasar por)* to pass oneself off as, to pose as (**b**) *(alardear)* to boast

draipen (*pl* **draipenes**), **drypen** ['draipen] (*pl* **drypenes**) *nm RP* fiber tip pen

dralon®, dralón *nm* Dralon®

DRAM [de'rram] *nf Informát* (*abrev de* **Dynamic Random Access Memory**) DRAM

drama *nm* (**a**) *(obra de teatro)* play (**b**) *(género literario)* drama (**c**) *(obra trágica)* drama (**d**) *(desgracia)* drama; **en la guerra se viven dramas a diario** dramatic events are an everyday occurrence in war; *Fam* **hacer un d. (de algo)** to make a drama (out of sth); **de cualquier cosa hace un d.** he makes a big deal out of everything, he turns everything into a drama

dramáticamente *adv* dramatically

dramático, -a *adj* (**a**) *(de teatro)* dramatic; **un autor d.** a dramatist *o* playwright; **estudia arte d.** she's studying drama
(**b**) *(muy grave)* dramatic; **se vivieron momentos dramáticos** there were dramatic moments
(**c**) *(exagerado, teatral)* theatrical, histrionic; **ponerse d.** to become theatrical, to over-dramatize; **no te pongas d., que no fue para tanto** don't make a big production out of it, it wasn't such a big deal

dramatismo *nm* dramatic nature, drama; **el d. del reencuentro hizo llorar a todos** the drama of the reunion brought tears to everybody's eyes; **con d.** dramatically

dramatización *nf* dramatization

dramatizar [14] **1** *vt* (**a**) *(hechos, problemas)* to dramatize (**b**) *(novela)* to dramatize
2 *vi* to overdramatize; **¡no hay que d.!** we shouldn't overdramatize the situation!

dramaturgia *nf* (**a**) *(género teatral)* dramatic art; **una obra maestra de la d. universal** a masterpiece of world theatre (**b**) *(obras de teatro)* plays, theatre; **la d. de Lope de Vega** the plays *o* theatre of Lope de Vega

dramaturgo, -a *nm,f* playwright, dramatist

dramón *nm Fam* (**a**) *(obra de teatro, película)* melodrama, tearjerker (**b**) *(vida, suceso)* sob-story

drapeado, -a **1** *adj (con pliegues)* pleated
2 *nm (pliegues)* drape

drásticamente *adv* drastically

drástico, -a *adj* drastic

drenaje *nm* (**a**) *(de terreno)* drainage (**b**) *Med* drainage

drenar *vt* (**a**) *(terreno)* to drain (**b**) *Med* to drain

Dresde *n* Dresden

dríada *nf* (**a**) *Mitol* dryad (**b**) *Bot* mountain avens

driblar *Dep* **1** *vt* **d. a un contrario** to dribble past an opponent
2 *vi* to dribble

drible *nm Dep (habilidad)* dribbling; *(regate)* dribble; **hacer un d.** to dribble

dribling ['driβlin] (*pl* **driblings**) *nm Dep (habilidad)* dribbling; *(regate)* dribble

dril *nm (tejido)* drill

driomio *nm* forest dormouse

drive [draif] *nm* (**a**) *(en tenis)* forehand (**b**) *(en golf)* drive (**c**) *Informát* drive

driver ['draiβer] (*pl* **drivers**) *nm* (**a**) *Informát* driver (**b**) *(en golf)* driver

droga *nf* (**a**) *(sustancia)* drug; **la d.** drugs; **el problema de la d.** the drug problem; **engancharse a/dejar la d.** to get hooked on/to come off drugs ▸▸ ***d. blanda*** soft drug; ***d. de diseño*** designer drug; ***d. dura*** hard drug; ***d. sintética*** designer drug
(**b**) *(afición)* **su d. son los toros** bullfighting is his passion, he's hooked on bullfighting
(**c**) *Chile, Méx, Perú (deuda)* bad debt
(**d**) EXPR *CAm, Cuba Fam* **mandar a alguien a la d.** to tell sb to get lost

drogadicción *nf* drug addiction

drogadicto, -a **1** *adj* addicted to drugs; **su padre es d.** his father is a drug addict
2 *nm,f* drug addict

drogado, -a *adj* drugged

drogar [38] **1** *vt* to drug; **lo drogaron y lo secuestraron** they drugged and then kidnapped him
2 drogarse *vpr* to take drugs; **se drogan con pegamento** they sniff glue

drogata, drogota *Fam* **1** *adj* junkie
2 *nmf* junkie

drogodependencia *nf* drug addiction *o* dependence

drogodependiente **1** *adj* drug-addicted, drug-dependent; **su hijo es d.** their son is addicted to drugs
2 *nmf* drug addict

drogota = **drogata**

droguería *nf* (**a**) *Esp (tienda)* = shop selling paint, cleaning materials etc (**b**) *Col (farmacia)* pharmacy, *Br* chemist's (shop), *US* drugstore (**c**) *Andes, CAm, RP (distribuidora)* drugs wholesaler (**d**) *RP (yuyería)* herbalist's

droguero, -a *nm,f* (**a**) *Esp (dependiente)* = shopkeeper in a "droguería" (**b**) *Chile, Méx, Perú (moroso)* defaulter, bad debtor

dromedario *nm* dromedary

drop *nm* (**a**) *(en golf)* drop (**b**) *(en rugby)* drop-kick

dropar *vt (en golf)* to drop

drosera *nf (planta)* common sundew

drugstore ['druɣstor] *nm* = establishment comprising late-night shop and bar

druida *nm* druid

druidesa *nf* druidess

drupa *nf* drupe

druso, -a **1** *adj* Druze, Druse
2 *nm,f* Druze, Druse

drypen = **draipen**

dto. (*abrev de* **descuento**) discount

Dtor. (*abrev de* **director**) Dir.

Dtora. (*abrev de* **directora**) Dir.

DTP *nm Informát* (*abrev de* **desktop publishing**) DTP

dual 1 *adj* (a) *(doble, binario)* dual (b) *Gram* dual
2 *nm Gram (número)* dual

dualidad *nf* duality

dualismo *nm* dualism

dualista *adj* dualist

dubitativamente *adv* doubtfully

dubitativo, -a *adj* doubtful; **me miró con gesto d.** she looked at me doubtfully

dubles *nmpl Fam* **hacer d.** *(saltando a la comba)* to do double unders

Dublín *n* Dublin

dublinés, -esa 1 *adj* of/from Dublin
2 *nm,f* Dubliner

ducado *nm* (a) *(tierras)* duchy (b) *(título)* dukedom (c) *(moneda)* ducat

ducal *adj* ducal

ducha *nf* (a) *(chorro)* shower; **tomar** *o* **darse una d.** to have *o* take a shower; *Fam Fig* **una d. de agua fría** a bucket of cold water (b) *(dispositivo)* shower; **un gorro de d.** a shower cap ►► ***d. de teléfono*** = shower with hand-held shower head (c) *(habitáculo)* shower (*Br* stall *o US* cabinet); **las duchas** *(de gimnasio, polideportivo)* the showers

duchar 1 *vt* (a) *(dar una ducha a)* to shower (b) *Fam (mojar)* to soak; **¡me has duchado entero con tu gaseosa!** you've soaked me with your lemonade!
2 **ducharse** *vpr* to have *o* take a shower

ducho, -a *adj* **ser** *o* **estar d. en** *(entendido)* to know a lot about; *(diestro)* to be skilled at; *(experimentado)* to be experienced in; **no estoy muy d. en química** I don't know a lot about chemistry; **es un jugador muy d. en torneos de Gran Slam** he's a very experienced player in Grand Slam tournaments

dúctil *adj* (a) *(metal)* ductile (b) *(material)* malleable (c) *(persona)* adaptable

ductilidad *nf* (a) *(de metal)* ductility (b) *(de material)* malleability, ductility (c) *(de persona)* adaptability

ducto *nm* (a) *CAm, Méx (gasoducto)* gas pipe line (b) *RP (pozo de aire)* ventilation shaft

---

DUDA *nf* (a) *(inseguridad, indecisión)* doubt; **la d. se apoderó de él** he was filled with doubt; **ante la d.,...** if in doubt,...; **sacar a alguien de la d.** to remove sb's doubts

(b) *(cuestión, problema)* **¿alguien tiene alguna d.?** does anyone have any questions?, is there anything anyone's not clear about?; **resolveré vuestras dudas al final de la clase** I'll answer your questions *o* I'll go over anything you're not sure about at the end of the class; **todavía me queda una d., ¿por qué lo hizo?** there's still one thing I don't understand, why did she do it?; **me asalta una d., ¿habré hecho bien en dejar a los niños solos?** I can't help wondering whether I was right to leave the children on their own; **queda la d. de qué habría pasado si...** the doubt remains about what would have happened if...; EXPR **salir de dudas** to clear up doubts; **pregúntale y así salimos de dudas** ask him and that will settle the matter; **con su detallada explicación salimos finalmente de dudas** her detailed explanation finally cleared up our doubts

(c) *(desconfianza, sospecha)* doubt; **expresó sus dudas sobre la oportunidad de celebrar un referéndum** he expressed some doubt about whether it was a good idea to have a referendum; **existen dudas sobre la autoría del atentado** there is some doubt surrounding who was responsible for the attack; **tengo mis dudas** I have my doubts; **nunca tuve la menor d. de que era inocente** I never for one moment doubted that she was innocent, I never had the slightest doubt that she was innocent; **estar fuera de toda d.** to be beyond the slightest doubt; **su inocencia está fuera de toda d.** her innocence is not in question, there is no question that she is innocent; **no cabe (la menor) d.** there is (absolutely) no doubt about it; **no cabe d. de que el tabaco es perjudicial para la salud** there's no doubt that smoking is bad for your health; **no te quepa (la menor) d.** don't doubt it, make no mistake about it; **no dejar lugar a dudas** to leave no room for doubt; **poner algo en d.** to put sth in doubt; **dice que ha resuelto el problema – lo pongo en d.** she says she has solved the problem – I would doubt that *o* I rather doubt that; **pongo en d. que pueda hacerlo en una semana** I doubt he can do it in a week, I would question whether he can do it in a week; **sin d.** without (a) doubt; **el avión es, sin d., el medio de transporte más cómodo** the plane is undoubtedly *o* without doubt the most comfortable form of transport; **es, sin d., la mejor lasaña que he probado nunca** it is beyond a doubt *o* definitely the best lasagne I've ever had; **¿vendrás a la fiesta? – ¡sin d.!** are you coming to the party? – of course!; **sin d. alguna, sin alguna d.** without (a) doubt; **sin la menor d.** without the slightest doubt; **sin sombra de d.** beyond the shadow of a doubt; EXPR **¡la d. ofende!: ¿te molestaría que invitáramos a mi madre? – la d. ofende** would you mind if we invited my mother? – of course you can, there's no need to ask; **no creía que fueras a acabar – ¡la d. ofende!** I never thought you'd finish – well thank you very much!

---

dudar 1 *vi* (a) *(desconfiar)* **d. de algo/alguien** to have one's doubts about sth/sb; **dudo de sus intenciones** I question his intentions; **no dudo de su buena voluntad** I don't doubt his goodwill; **sé que dudan de mí, pero yo soy inocente** I know they have their doubts about me, but I'm innocent; **¿acaso dudas de mí?** don't you trust me then?
(b) *(no estar seguro)* **d. sobre algo** to be unsure about sth
(c) *(vacilar)* to hesitate; **d. entre hacer una cosa u otra** to be unsure whether to do one thing or another; **no dudes en venir a preguntarme** don't hesitate to come and ask me
2 *vt* to doubt; **¿vas a venir? – lo dudo** are you going to come? – I doubt it, I don't think so; **lo dudo mucho** I very much doubt it; **después de dudarlo bastante se decidió a ir** after being in some doubt he decided to go; **¿que eres sincero? permíteme que lo dude** so you're telling the truth, are you? I think I'll reserve judgement on that, if I may; **yo no lo hice – no lo dudo, pero...** I didn't do it – I'm sure you didn't, but...; **no lo dude, ha hecho lo que debía** you can rest assured you've done the right thing; **dudo que venga** I doubt (whether) he'll come; **no dudo que lo hiciera con muy buena intención** no doubt he did it with the best of intentions

dudoso, -a *adj* (a) *(improbable)* doubtful; **una palabra de origen d.** a word of doubtful origin; **lo veo d.** I doubt it; **ser d. (que)** to be doubtful (whether), to be unlikely (that); **es d. que asista a la reunión** it's unlikely (that) he'll attend the meeting, it's doubtful whether he'll attend the meeting
(b) *(vacilante)* hesitant, indecisive; **estaba d. sobre qué hacer** she was unsure about what to do
(c) *(sospechoso)* questionable, suspect; **un individuo de dudosa reputación** an individual of doubtful reputation; **una broma de gusto d.** a joke in questionable taste; **un penalti d.** a dubious penalty

DUE *nmf Esp* (*abrev de* **diplomado universitario en enfermería**) qualified nurse

duela *nf* (a) *(gusano)* fluke (b) *(de barril)* stave (c) *Méx (de suelo)* floorboard

duelista *nm* duellist

duelo[1] *ver* **doler**

duelo[2] *nm* (a) *(combate por desafío)* duel; **un d. con pistola** a duel with pistols; **un d. a muerte** a duel to the death; **batirse en d.** to fight a duel; **desafiar** *o* **retar a alguien a (un) d.** to challenge sb to a duel
(b) *(enfrentamiento)* struggle, battle; **un d. dialéctico** a verbal duel, a bout of verbal sparring; **el d. entre los dos equipos por ganar la liga** the struggle between the two teams to win the league
(c) *(aflicción)* grief, sorrow; **en señal de d. (por la muerte de)** as a sign of mourning (for the death of)

duende *nm* (a) *(personaje)* imp, goblin (b) *(espíritu)* spirit; **una casa habitada por duendes** a house haunted by spirits (c) *(encanto)* charm, magical quality; **toca muy bien pero le falta d.** he plays very well but he lacks that indefinable something; **un bailaor con mucho d.** a dancer with a magical quality; **Granada tiene mucho d.** Granada is a truly magical place

dueño, -a *nm,f (propietario)* owner; *(de casa alquilada)* landlord, *f* landlady; **cambiar de d.** to change hands; **hacerse d. de algo** *(hacerse propietario de)* to take possession of sth, to acquire sth; *(dominar)* to take control of sth; **al morir el padre se hizo d. de la tienda** when his father died he took over the shop; **rápidamente se hizo d. de la situación** he quickly took control of the situation; **ser d. de** *(ser propietario de)* to own, to be the owner of; *(tener dominio de)* to have control over; **¿tú eres (el) d. de esta bici?** are you the owner of this bike?; **no era d. de sus actos cuando te agredió** he wasn't responsible for his actions when he attacked you; EXPR **(el) d. y señor de algo** (the) lord and master of sth; **Napoleón se convirtió en (el) d. y señor de Europa** Napoleon became the undisputed ruler of Europe; **parecía el d. y señor del negocio** he looked as if he owned the place; EXPR **ser d. de sí mismo** to be self-possessed; EXPR **ser (muy) d. de hacer algo** to be (completely) free to do sth; **eres muy d. de venir a la hora que te plazca** you are completely free to come and go as you please ►► *Am* ***d. de casa*** host

duermevela *nm o nf* snooze; **en d.** snoozing

duermo *etc ver* **dormir**

Duero *n* **el D.** the Douro

duetista *nmf* duettist

dueto *nm* duet

dulcamara *nf Bot* woody nightshade, bittersweet

dulce 1 *adj* (**a**) *(sabor)* sweet; **ha quedado demasiado d.** it's too sweet; **este café está muy d.** this coffee's very sweet; **le gusta todo lo d.** she loves anything sweet; **esta infusión se toma d.** you drink this tea with sugar
(**b**) *(agua)* fresh; **la pesca en agua d.** freshwater fishing
(**c**) *(persona, carácter)* sweet, gentle, mild
(**d**) *(mirada, sonrisa)* tender, sweet; *(voz, sonido, música)* mellow, sweet; *(recuerdo)* sweet; **sus años dulces** his golden years; EXPR **estar en un momento d.** to be on *o* riding the crest of a wave; **el actor se halla en un momento d. de su carrera** the actor is at a high point in his career; EXPR *Am* **la d. espera** pregnancy; **cuando estaba en la d. espera** when she was pregnant
2 *nm* (**a**) *(caramelo, postre)* sweet; *(pastel)* cake, pastry; *RP (mermelada)* jam; **me encanta el d.** *(todo lo dulce)* I love sweet things; EXPR *Fam* **a nadie le amarga un d.** everyone enjoys a treat; EXPR **de d.** *(muy bien)* marvellously; **su madre cocina de d.** her mother cooks like a dream ►► *Col, RP* ***d. de leche*** = toffee pudding made with caramelized milk; ***d. de membrillo*** quince jelly
(**b**) *CAm (pan de azúcar)* brown sugar
(**c**) *RP Fam (encanto)* dear
3 *adv (dulcemente)* sweetly

dulcemente *adv* sweetly

dulcera *nf RP* preserve dish

dulcero, -a *adj* (**a**) *Am (del dulce)* sweet; **opera en el ramo d.** he works in the confectionery sector (**b**) *Fam (goloso)* **ser d.** to have a sweet tooth

dulcificar [60] 1 *vt* (**a**) *(endulzar)* to sweeten (**b**) *(suavizar) (carácter, persona)* to mellow; *(actitud, comentarios)* to soften
2 **dulcificarse** *vpr (carácter, persona)* to mellow; *(actitud, comentarios)* to soften

dulzaina *nf* = musical instrument similar to a clarinet, but smaller and higher-pitched, used in folk music

dulzainero, -a *nm,f* "dulzaina" player

dulzarrón, -ona, dulzón, -ona *adj Fam* (**a**) *(sabor, comida, bebida)* sickly sweet (**b**) *(música, poesía, novela)* syrupy

dulzor *nm* sweetness

dulzura *nf* (**a**) *(de sabor)* sweetness (**b**) *(suavidad) (de persona, carácter)* sweetness, gentleness; *(de mirada, sonrisa)* tenderness, sweetness; *(de voz, sonido, música)* mellowness, sweetness; **habla a los niños con d.** she talks sweetly to the children; **intenta tratar al niño con más d.** try to be gentler with the boy (**c**) *Fam (apelativo)* **ven aquí, d.** come here, darling *o* sweetheart

dumping ['dumpin] *nm Econ* dumping; **hacer d.** to practise dumping

duna *nf* dune

dunlopillo® *nm Am* dunlopillo

dúo *nm* (**a**) *Mús (composición)* duet; *(dos músicos, cantantes)* duo; **un d. de guitarristas** a guitar duo, a pair of guitarists; **tocar (algo) a d.** to play (sth) as a duo (**b**) *(pareja)* duo; **hacer algo a d.** to do sth together; **levantaron la piedra a d.** they lifted the stone together; **contestaron a d.** they answered as one

duodécimo, -a *núm* twelfth; *ver también* **octavo**

duodenal *adj Anat* duodenal

duodeno *nm Anat* duodenum; **una úlcera de d.** a duodenal ulcer

duopolio *nm Com* duopoly

dupla *nf CSur* pair, couple; **¡qué d. forman esos dos!** what a pair they make!

dúplex 1 *adj (circuito)* duplex
2 *nm inv* (**a**) *(vivienda)* duplex (**b**) *Elec* linkup (**c**) *Informát* duplex (**d**) *muy Fam (sexo lesbiano)* girl-on-girl action; *(sexo entre tres)* threesome

duplicación *nf* (**a**) *(de cantidad, número)* doubling (**b**) *(de documento)* duplication

duplicado, -a 1 *adj* **lo tengo d.** *(libro, revista)* I have two copies; **por d.** in duplicate; **las instancias deberán presentarse por d.** two copies of the applications should be handed in
2 *nm* duplicate, copy

duplicar [60] 1 *vt* (**a**) *(cantidad, número)* to double (**b**) *(documento)* to duplicate
2 **duplicarse** *vpr* to double

duplicidad *nf* (**a**) *(repetición)* duplication (**b**) *(falsedad)* duplicity

duplo, -a 1 *adj* double
2 *nm* double

duque, -esa *nm,f* duke, *f* duchess

durabilidad *nf* durability

durable *adj* durable, lasting

duración *nf* length; **la d. del curso es de tres meses** the course lasts three months; **¿cuál es la d. de la obra?** how long does the play last?; **de corta** *o* **poca d.** short-lived; **de larga d.** *(pila, bombilla)* long-life; *(disco)* long-playing

duradero, -a *adj* (**a**) *(que permanece)* lasting; **es una vacuna de efecto d.** it is a long-acting vaccine (**b**) *(ropa, zapatos)* hard-wearing

duralex® *nm* = heat-resistant glass

duraluminio® *nm* ≃ Dural®, Duralumin®

duramadre, duramáter *nf Anat* dura mater

duramen *nm Bot* heartwood

duramente *adv* (**a**) *(con fuerza)* hard (**b**) *(con agresividad)* severely, harshly; **fue d. criticado** he was severely criticized

duranguense 1 *adj* of/from Durango *(Mexico)*
2 *nmf* person from Durango *(Mexico)*

durante *prep (en momentos a lo largo de)* during; *(en todo el periodo de tiempo de)* for; **d. un año se produjeron tres seísmos en la zona** there were three earthquakes in the area in the space of a year; **estuvo sin beber d. un año** he went (for) a year without drinking; **por favor, desconecten sus teléfonos móviles d. la proyección** please ensure mobile phones are switched off during the film; **d. su estancia en Londres visitó varios museos** he visited several museums while he was in London; **d. el verano mejoró su situación económica** his financial situation improved over the summer; **d. las vacaciones** during the *Br* holidays *o US* vacation; **d. una hora** for an hour; **d. toda la semana** all week; **llovió varias veces d. la semana** it rained several times during the week; **llovió d. toda la semana** it rained all week; **d. el mes de febrero** in February; **d. todo el mes de febrero** for the whole of February, throughout the month of February

durar *vi* (**a**) *(prolongarse)* to last; **¿cuánto dura la obra?** how long is the play?; **el viaje/la película dura tres horas** the journey/the film lasts three hours; **aún dura la fiesta** the party's still going on; **aún le dura el enfado** she's still angry; **les duró poco la felicidad** their happiness was short-lived; **estuvo bien mientras duró** it was good while it lasted
(**b**) *(permanecer, aguantar)* to last; **no durará mucho en ese puesto** he won't stay *o* last long in that job; **la leche fresca sólo dura unos pocos días** fresh milk only lasts a few days
(**c**) *(ropa, calzado, pilas)* to last; **cómprate ropa/calzado que dure** buy clothes/footwear that will last; **aquellas botas me duraron tres años** those boots lasted me three years; **los juguetes no le duran nada** his toys don't last long; **pilas que duran más** batteries which last longer

durativo, -a *adj Ling* durative

duraznero *nm Am* peach tree

duraznillo *nm* red shank, *US* lady's-thumb ►► ***d. fragante*** lady of the night; ***d. negro*** willow-leaved jessamine

durazno *nm Am* peach ►► ***d. en almíbar*** peaches in syrup

Durex® *nm Méx Br* Sellotape®, *US* Scotch® tape

dureza *nf* (**a**) *(de objeto, material, superficie, colchón, cama, sofá)* hardness; *(de carne)* toughness; *(de pan)* staleness
(**b**) *Geol (de roca, mineral, metal)* hardness
(**c**) *(de agua)* hardness
(**d**) *(de clima, invierno)* harshness, severity
(**e**) *(severidad, aspereza) (de persona)* harshness; *(de críticas, acciones)* harshness, severity; *(de juego, partido)* roughness; **la criticó/reprendió con d.** he criticized/reprimanded her harshly; **la d. de la entrada le cortó la respiración** the tackle was so hard it left him gasping for breath; **la violencia racista debe ser castigada con d.** racist violence must be severely punished; **el árbitro permitió demasiada d. en el juego** the referee allowed the game to get too rough
(**f**) *(fortaleza, resistencia)* strength
(**g**) *(callosidad)* callus, patch of hard skin; **tener durezas en las manos/los pies** to have calluses on the hands/feet

> **Falso amigo**: El sustantivo inglés **duress** no es la traducción del español **dureza**. En inglés, **duress** significa "coacción".

durian *nm (árbol)* durian

durillo *nm (arbusto)* laurustinus

durmiente 1 *adj* sleeping; **la Bella D.** Sleeping Beauty
2 *nm (traviesa) Br* sleeper, *US* tie

durmiera *etc ver* **dormir**

duro, -a 1 *adj* (**a**) *(objeto, material, superficie, roca, mineral, metal, colchón, cama, sofá)* hard; *(carne)* tough; *(pan)* stale; **estas peras están todavía muy duras** these pears are still hard *o* not ripe; EXPR **estar d. como una piedra** to be rock-hard; EXPR **más dura será la**

caída: cuanto más famosos se hagan, más dura será la caída the more famous they get, the worse it is when they fall from popularity; EXPR *Fam* **ser d. de mollera** *(estúpido)* to be thick in the head; *(testarudo)* to be pigheaded; EXPR *Fam* **ser d. de oído** to be hard of hearing; EXPR *Vulg* **ponérsele dura a alguien: se me puso dura** I got a hard-on

(**b**) *(cerradura, grifo, mecanismo)* stiff; **los cajones van un poco duros** the drawers are a bit stiff

(**c**) *(agua)* hard

(**d**) *(penoso, inclemente) (clima, invierno)* harsh, severe; *(etapa, experiencia, vida)* hard, tough; **fue un golpe muy d. para todos** it was a heavy blow for everybody; **son** *o* **corren tiempos muy duros** these are hard times; EXPR *Fam* **estar a las duras y a las maduras** *(sin rendirse)* to be there through thick and thin; *(sin quejarse)* to take the rough with the smooth

(**e**) *(severo, áspero) (persona, palabras, críticas)* harsh, severe; *(acciones, medidas, condena)* harsh; *(postura, sector)* hard-line; *(juego, partido)* rough; **estuvo muy d. con él** he was very hard on him; **el ala dura del partido** the hard-line faction of the party; **una entrada muy dura** *(de futbolista)* a very hard tackle

(**f**) *(fuerte, resistente)* tough; **un tipo d.** a tough guy; EXPR *Fam* **ser d. de pelar** to be a hard nut to crack

2 *nm* (**a**) *(persona)* tough guy; *(en partido político)* hardliner; **hacerse el d.** to act tough

(**b**) *Esp Antes (moneda)* 5-peseta coin; **me debes 1.000 duros** you owe me 5,000 pesetas; **5 duros** *(moneda)* 25-peseta coin; EXPR **estar sin un d.** to be flat broke; EXPR *Fam* **¡lo que faltaba para el d.!** that really is all we needed!; EXPR *Fam* **que le/te/***etc* **den dos duros** to hell with him/you/*etc*

3 *adv* (**a**) *(mucho)* hard; **trabajar d.** to work hard

(**b**) *Col, Ven Fam (alto)* loudly; **hablar d.** to talk loudly; **reír d.** to laugh noisily

(**c**) *Col, Ven Fam (rápido)* quickly, fast; **nadan muy d., es imposible alcanzarlos** they're very strong swimmers, it's impossible to catch them

(**d**) *Col, Ven Fam (fuerte)* hard; **pégale d.** hit him hard

duty free ['djuti'fri] (*pl* **duty frees**) *nm* duty-free shop

dux *nm inv Hist* doge

d/v (*abrev de* **días vista**) **15 d.** within 15 days

DVD *nm* (*abrev de* **Disco Versátil Digital**) DVD

DYA [dia] *nf* (*abrev de* **Detente y Ayuda**) = voluntary organization which operates ambulances on Spanish highways

E, e

E, e [e] *nf (letra)* E, e
E¹ *(abrev de* **este***)* E
E² *RP (abrev de* **estacionamiento***)* P
e *conj* and

> **e** is used instead of **y** in front of words beginning with "i" or "hi" (e.g. **apoyo e interés** support and interest; **corazón e hígado** heart and liver).

ea *interj* come on!, come along!
eagle ['iγel] *nm (en golf)* eagle; **hacer e. en un hoyo** to eagle a hole
EAU *nmpl (abrev de* **Emiratos Árabes Unidos***)* UAE
ebanista *nmf* cabinet-maker
ebanistería *nf* **(a)** *(oficio)* cabinet-making **(b)** *(taller)* cabinet-maker's
ébano *nm* ebony
ébola *nm (enfermedad)* Ebola; **el virus del é.** the Ebola virus
ebonita *nf* ebonite, vulcanite
ebriedad *nf Formal* inebriation; **hallarse en estado de e.** to be inebriated
ebrio, -a *adj Formal* **(a)** *(borracho)* inebriated; *Esp* **conducir** *o Am* **manejar e.** to drive under the influence **(b)** *(ofuscado)* **e. de** blind with; **estar e. de amor (por alguien)** to be besotted (with sb); **e. de ira** blind with rage; **e. de éxito** drunk with success
Ebro *nm* **el E.** the Ebro
ebullición *nf* **(a)** *(de líquido)* **en e.** boiling; **entrar en e.** to come to the boil, to begin to boil; **punto de e.** boiling point
(b) *(agitación)* ferment, turmoil; **se viven días de gran e. política** these are days of great political turmoil; **en e.** *(en apogeo)* at its height; *(en agitación)* in turmoil; **la revolución industrial estaba entonces en plena e.** the Industrial Revolution was then in full ferment
ebúrneo, -a *adj Literario* ivory
eccehomo, ecce homo *nm* **(a)** *Rel* ecce homo **(b)** *(persona maltrecha)* pitiful wretch; EXPR **estar hecho un e.** to be in a sorry state, to cut a sorry figure
eccema, eczema *nm Med* eczema; **le ha salido un e. en la espalda** she's got eczema on her back
ECG *nm (abrev de* **electrocardiograma***)* ECG
echada *nf Méx (fanfarronada)* boast
echado, -a *adj* **(a)** *(acostado)* lying down; **no se puede poner, está e.** he can't come to the phone, he's lying down; **estaba e. en la cama** he was lying in bed **(b)** *Esp Fam* **e. pa'lante** *(decidido, espabilado)* go-getting; *(valiente)* gutsy; **era un tío e. pa'lante** *(valiente)* he was a gutsy guy
echador, -ora *Cuba, Méx* **1** *adj (fanfarrón)* boastful, bragging
2 *nm (fanfarrón)* braggart, boaster

ECHAR **1** *vt* **(a)** *(tirar)* to throw; *(red)* to cast; **e. anclas, e. el ancla** to drop anchor; **échame el balón** throw me the ball; **e. algo a la basura** to throw sth in the bin; **e. una moneda al aire** to toss a coin; **échalo en la cesta de la ropa sucia** put it in the dirty-clothes basket; **e. una piedra por la ventana** to throw a stone through the window; **e. abajo** *(edificio)* to pull down, to demolish; *(puerta)* to break down; *(gobierno)* to bring down; *(proyecto)* to ruin
(b) *(meter, poner)* to put; **echa suficiente ropa en la maleta** make sure you pack enough clothes in your suitcase; **échalo en el asiento de atrás** put it on the back seat; **echa esta camisa a la lavadora** put that shirt in the washing machine; **echa una firma en esta postal** sign *o* put your name on this postcard; **no eches más leña al fuego** *(de hoguera, chimenea)* don't put any more wood on the fire; EXPR **e. leña al fuego** to add fuel to the fire; EXPR *Fam* **e. el resto: queda sólo una semana, ahora hay que e. el resto** there's only a week to go, so from now on we really have to give it our all
(c) *(carta, postal)* to post, *US* to mail; **¿(me) podrías e. esta carta?** could you post *o US* mail this letter (for me)?; **echó la carta al buzón y siguió caminando** he put the letter in the postbox *o US* mailbox and walked on; **e. algo al correo** to put sth in the post, to post sth, *US* to mail sth
(d) *(trago, sorbo)* to take, to have; *(cigarrillo)* to have
(e) *(vistazo)* to take, to have; **le he echado una mirada, pero no me parece interesante** I've had a look at it, but I don't think it's very interesting
(f) *(mover) (parte del cuerpo)* **echa la pierna a un lado** move your leg aside; **echó la cabeza hacia atrás** she threw her head back; **echa los hombros para atrás y saca el pecho** put your shoulders back and stick your chest out
(g) *(añadir) (vino, agua)* to pour (**a** *o* **en** into); *(sal, azúcar)* to add (**a** *o* **en** to); **échame más zumo, por favor** could you pour me some more juice, please?; **no me eches tanta azúcar en el café** don't put so much sugar in my coffee
(h) *(dar) (comida, bebida)* to give; **echa alpiste al canario** give the canary some birdseed; **hay que e. agua a las plantas** we need to water the plants; *Fam* **Alberto come lo que le echen** Alberto will eat whatever you put in front of him; *Fam* **es un hombre muy paciente, aguanta lo que le eches** he's a very patient man, he puts up with anything you can throw at him
(i) *(decir) (discurso, sermón)* to give; *(reprimenda)* to dish out; *(piropo, cumplido)* to pay; **e. una maldición a alguien** to put a curse on sb; *Fam* **le echaron una bronca por llegar tarde** they told her off for arriving late; **me echó en cara que no le hubiera ayudado** she reproached me for not helping her
(j) *(humo, vapor, chispas)* to give off, to emit; **la fábrica echa mucho humo a la atmósfera** the factory pours out a lot of smoke into the atmosphere; EXPR *Fam* **está que echa humo** she's fuming; EXPR *Fam* **e. pestes** *o Méx* **madres: volvió de vacaciones echando pestes** *o Méx* **madres del lugar** she came back from her *Br* holiday *o US* vacation cursing the place where she had stayed
(k) *(hojas, flores)* to sprout, to shoot; *(raíces, pelo, barba)* to begin to grow; *(diente)* to cut; **los almendros están echando flores** the almond trees are beginning to flower; **está empezando a e. los dientes** she's beginning to cut her teeth; *Fam* **en los últimos meses ha echado mucha barriga** he's developed quite a paunch over the past few months
(l) *(expulsar)* **e. a alguien (de)** to throw sb out (of); **le han echado del partido** he's been expelled from the party; **le echaron de clase por hablar con un compañero** he was thrown *o* sent out of the class for talking to a friend
(m) *(despedir)* **e. a alguien (de)** to sack sb (from); **¡que lo echen!** sack him!, kick him out!
(n) *(accionar)* **e. la llave/el cerrojo** to lock/bolt the door; **e. el freno** to brake, to put the brakes on; *Fam* **¡echa el freno! ¿estás seguro de que podemos pagarlo?** hold your horses, are you sure we can afford it?
(o) *(acostar)* to lie (down); **¿has echado al bebé?** have you put the baby to bed?
(p) *(tiempo)* **le he echado dos semanas a este proyecto** I've taken two weeks over this project, I've spent two weeks on this project; **echaron dos horas en llegar a Bogotá** it took them two hours to get to Bogotá
(q) *(calcular)* **¿cuántos años le echas?** how old do you reckon he is?; **siempre me echan años de menos** people always think I'm younger than I really am; **échale que de aquí a Málaga haya 600 kilómetros** let's say it's about 600 kilometres from here to Malaga
(r) *(naipe, partida)* to play; **te echo una carrera** I'll race you; **¿echamos un dominó?** shall we have a game of dominoes?
(s) *(buenaventura)* to tell; **e. las cartas a alguien** to read sb's fortune *(from the cards)*
(t) *(emplear)* **le echó muchas ganas al asunto** he went about it with a will; **le echan mucha ilusión a todo lo que hacen** they put a lot of enthusiasm into everything they do; **échale más brío al pedaleo** put

a bit more energy into the pedalling; **los ladrones le echaron mucho ingenio** the thieves showed a lot of ingenuity

(**u**) *Fam (sentencia)* **le echaron diez años** he got ten years

(**v**) *Fam (documento)* **tengo que ir a e. una instancia al Ministerio** I've got to go and hand in a form at the ministry

(**w**) *Esp Fam (en televisión, cine, teatro)* to show; **¿qué echan esta noche en la tele?** what's on telly tonight?; **¿qué echan en el Rialto?** what's on *o* showing at the Rialto?; **echan una película de acción** they're showing an action movie

(**x**) *Am (animales)* to urge on

(**y**) *(otras contrucciones)* **e. a perder algo** *(vestido, alimentos, plan)* to ruin sth; *(ocasión)* to waste sth; **no puedes e. todo a perder, después de tanto esfuerzo** you can't just throw it all away after all that effort; **e. algo a cara o cruz** to toss (a coin) for sth; **e. algo a suertes** to draw lots for sth; **e. de menos** to miss; **le echa mucho de menos** he misses her a lot; **echo de menos mi casa** I miss my house; *Chile* **echarlas** to run away; **e. algo por tierra** to put paid to sth, to ruin sth; **eso echa por tierra todas nuestras esperanzas** that dashes all our hopes

2 *vi* (**a**) *(encaminarse)* **e. por la calle arriba** to go *o* head up the street; **e. por la derecha** to go (to the) right

(**b**) *(empezar)* **e. a andar** to set off; **e. a correr** to break into a run; **e. a llorar** to burst into tears; **e. a reír** to burst out laughing; **e. a volar** to fly off

3 echarse *vpr* (**a**) *(lanzarse)* **echarse al agua** to dive *o* jump into the water; **echarse al suelo** to throw oneself to the ground; **se echó a sus brazos** she threw herself into his arms; **se echaron encima del enemigo** they fell upon the enemy; **el tren se les echó encima antes de que pudieran reaccionar** the train was upon them before they had time to react; **la noche se nos echó encima antes de llegar al refugio** night fell before we reached the shelter

(**b**) *(acostarse)* to lie down; **échate aquí** lie down here; **me voy a e. un rato** I'm going to have a nap; **se echó en el sofá** she lay down on the sofa; **echarse a dormir** *(acostarse)* to go to bed; *Fig* **no nos podemos e. a dormir** we can't afford to be complacent; **echarse una siesta** to have a nap

(**c**) *(empezar)* **echarse a hacer algo** to start to do sth, to start doing sth; **se echó a cantar/reír** he burst into song/laughter, he started singing/laughing; **se echó a correr** she broke into a run, she started running; **se echó a volar** it flew off

(**d**) *(ponerse)* **se echó encima todo el frasco de colonia** she put the whole bottle of cologne on; **échate un abrigo o pasarás frío** put a coat on or you'll be cold

(**e**) *(apartarse)* **echarse a un lado** to move aside; **se echó a la derecha para dejarle pasar** he moved to the right to allow her to pass; EXPR **echarse atrás: se echó atrás en el último momento** he backed out at the last moment; **ya es muy tarde para echarse atrás** it's a bit late to turn back now

(**f**) *(obtener)* **echarse (un) novio** to get oneself a boyfriend

(**g**) *Fam (expulsar)* **se echó un pedo en mitad de la película** he farted in the middle of the film; **se echó un eructo** he let out a belch

(**h**) *(tomarse)* **echarse un cigarrillo** to have a cigarette

(**i**) EXPR **echarse a perder** *(comida)* to go off, to spoil; *(plan)* to fall through; *(país, persona)* to go to the dogs; *Fam* **se las echa de entendido en arte** he makes out he's an expert on art

---

echarpe *nm* shawl

echón, -ona *Ven* **1** *adj (fanfarrón)* bigheaded

2 *nm (fanfarrón)* braggart, bighead

echonería *nf Ven Fam* bigheadedness

eclair [e'kler] (*pl* **eclairs**) *nm Chile* **(cierre) e.** zip fastener

eclecticismo *nm* eclecticism

ecléctico, -a 1 *adj* eclectic

2 *nm,f* eclectic

eclesial *adj Am* ecclesiastical, church; **actividades eclesiales** church activities

eclesiástico, -a 1 *adj* ecclesiastical, church; **la jerarquía eclesiástica** the ecclesiastical *o* church hierarchy

2 *nm* clergyman

eclipsar 1 *vt* (**a**) *(astro)* to eclipse (**b**) *(persona)* to eclipse

2 eclipsarse *vpr* (**a**) *(astro)* to go into eclipse (**b**) *(persona)* to drop out of the limelight

eclipse *nm* (**a**) *(de astro)* eclipse ▸▸ ***e. de luna*** eclipse of the moon; ***e. parcial*** partial eclipse; ***e. de sol*** eclipse of the sun, solar eclipse; ***e. solar*** solar eclipse, eclipse of the sun; ***e. total*** total eclipse (**b**) *(de persona)* eclipse

eclíptica *nf Astron* ecliptic

eclosión *nf* (**a**) *(de huevo)* hatching, *Espec* eclosion (**b**) *(aparición)* rise

eco[1] **1** *nm* (**a**) *(de sonido)* echo; **en este patio hay e.** there's an echo in this courtyard; **oímos el e. de sus voces** we heard the echo of their voices; EXPR **hacerse e. de algo** *(dar noticia)* to report sth; *(repetir)* to echo sth; **todos los periódicos se hicieron e. de lo ocurrido** all the newspapers reported what happened; EXPR **tener e.** to arouse interest; **su última novela tuvo poco e.** her latest novel failed to arouse much interest; **el suceso tuvo e. entre la prensa internacional** the incident aroused interest in the international press

(**b**) *(rumor)* rumour; **el e. lejano de los tambores** the distant sound of the drums; **aún resuenan los ecos del escándalo** the scandal still hasn't quite died down ▸▸ ***ecos de sociedad*** society column

(**c**) *Informát* echo

2 *nf Fam (ecografía)* (ultrasound) scan

eco[2] *interj Am Fam* exactly, absolutely; **¿entonces lo llamo a las once? – e.** I'll phone you at eleven then? – fine; **¿me pasan a buscar por casa? – e.** will you pick me up at home? – sure

ecoauditoría *nf* environmental audit

ecoetiqueta *nf* eco-label

Ecofin [eko'fin] *nm UE* (*abrev de* **Consejo de Ministros de Economía y Finanzas**) Ecofin

ecografía *nf (técnica)* ultrasound scanning; *(imagen)* ultrasound (image); **hacerse una e.** to have a scan

ecógrafo *nm* ultrasound scanner

ecoindustria *nf* **la e.** eco-industry, = sector of industry devoted to environmentally-friendly activities, such as recycling, alternative energy production etc

école, ecolecuá *interj Am Fam* that's it!

ecología *nf* (**a**) *(ciencia)* ecology (**b**) *(medio ambiente)* ecology

ecológicamente *adv* ecologically

ecológico, -a *adj* (**a**) *(medioambiental)* ecological; **preocupa mucho el tema e.** the subject of the environment is really worrying; **un desastre e.** an ecological disaster; **el deterioro/equilibrio e.** environmental deterioration/balance (**b**) *(alimentos)* organic; *(detergente, producto)* environmentally-friendly

ecologismo *nm* environmentalism

ecologista 1 *adj* environmental, ecological; **el movimiento e.** the ecology *o* green movement

2 *nmf* environmentalist, ecologist

ecólogo, -a *nm,f* environmentalist, ecologist

economato *nm* company cooperative shop

econometría *nf Econ* econometrics *(singular)*

economía *nf* (**a**) *(actividad productiva)* economy; **la e. mundial** the global *o* world economy ▸▸ ***e. capitalista*** capitalist economy; ***e. dirigida*** command economy; ***e. doméstica*** housekeeping; *Am* ***e. informal*** black economy; ***e. de libre mercado*** free-market economy; ***e. de mercado*** market economy; ***e. mixta*** mixed economy; ***e. planificada*** planned economy; ***e. social de mercado*** social market economy; ***e. socialista*** socialist economy; ***e. de subsistencia*** subsistence economy; ***e. sumergida*** black economy

(**b**) *(ciencia, estudio)* economics *(singular)* ▸▸ ***e. aplicada*** applied economics; ***e. de empresas*** business economics; ***e. familiar*** home economics; ***e. política*** political economy

(**c**) *(situación económica) (de persona, familia)* finances

(**d**) *(ahorro)* saving; **por e. de espacio** to save space; **hacer algo con gran e. de medios** to do sth with the optimum use of resources; **hacer economías** to economize *o* make economies ▸▸ ***e. de escala*** economy of scale

económicamente *adv* (**a**) *(en recursos económicos)* economically; **e., mis padres no tienen problemas** my parents have no problems financially; **un país e. pobre** an economically backward country (**b**) *(con ahorro)* cheaply, inexpensively

economicismo *nm Econ* economism

economicista *adj Econ* economicist

económico, -a *adj* (**a**) *(asunto, doctrina, crisis)* economic; **la política económica del gobierno** the government's economic policy; **una familia con problemas económicos** a family with financial problems; **mi situación económica es desesperante** my financial situation is desperate

(**b**) *(barato)* cheap, low-cost; **pagándolo al contado te sale más e.** it works out cheaper if you pay in cash

(**c**) *(que gasta poco) (motor, aparato)* economical; *(persona)* thrifty

economista *nmf* economist

economizar [14] 1 *vt* to save
2 *vi (ahorrar dinero)* to save, to economize
ecopunto *nm* recycling bank
ecosfera *nf* biosphere, ecosphere
ecosistema *nm* ecosystem
ecosonda *nf* sonar
ecotasa *nf (impuesto)* ecotax, green tax
ecoturismo *nm* ecotourism
ecoturista *nmf* ecotourist
ecovirus *nm inv Med* echo virus
ectodermo *nm Biol* ectoderm
ectoparásito, -a *Biol* 1 *adj* ectoparasitic
2 *nm* ectoparasite
ectópico, -a *adj Med* **embarazo e.** ectopic pregnancy
ectoplasma *nm* (a) *Biol* ectoplasm (b) *(en parapsicología)* ectoplasm
ecu ['eku] *nm Antes* (*abrev de* **unidad de cuenta europea**) ECU, ecu
ecuación *nf* (a) *Mat* equation; **resolver una e.** to solve an equation; **un sistema de ecuaciones** a set of equations ►► ***e. algebraica*** algebraic equation; ***e. diferencial*** differential equation; ***e. lineal*** linear equation; ***e. de primer grado*** simple equation; ***e. de segundo grado*** quadratic equation (b) *Quím* equation
Ecuador *n* Ecuador
ecuador *nm* (a) *(paralelo)* equator; **el E.** the Equator ►► ***e. magnético*** magnetic equator (b) *(punto medio)* half-way point; **nos hallamos en el e. del partido/torneo** we are at the half-way point of the game/tournament
ecualizador *nm* equalizer ►► ***e. gráfico*** graphic equalizer
ecuánime *adj* (a) *(en el ánimo)* level-headed (b) *(en el juicio)* impartial, fair
ecuanimidad *nf* (a) *(del ánimo)* equanimity, composure (b) *(del juicio)* impartiality, fairness
ecuatoguineano, -a 1 *adj* of/relating to Equatorial Guinea
2 *nm,f* native/inhabitant of Equatorial Guinea
ecuatorial *adj* equatorial
ecuatoriano, -a 1 *adj* Ecuadorian, Ecuadoran
2 *nm,f* Ecuadorian, Ecuadoran
ecuestre *adj* equestrian; **una estatua e.** an equestrian statue; **una exhibición e.** an equestrian exhibition
ecuménico, -a *adj Rel* ecumenic(al)
ecumenismo *nm Rel* ecumenism
eczema = **eccema**
ed. (a) (*abrev de* **editor**) ed. (b) (*abrev de* **edición**) edit. (c) (*abrev de* **editorial**) ed. (d) (*abrev de* **edificio**) bldg
edad *nf* (a) *(de persona, objeto)* age; **¿qué e. tienes?** how old are you?; **tiene veinticinco años de e.** she's twenty-five years old; **un joven de veinte años de e.** a young man of twenty; **él aparenta más e. que ella** he looks older than she does; **tiene el doble de e. que él** she's twice his age; **la e. media de los participantes es de treinta años** the average age of the participants is thirty; **a/desde temprana e.** at/from an early age; **a** *o* **con la tierna e. de tres años** at the tender age of three; **se casó a la e. de veintidós años** he got married at (the age of) twenty-two; **a mi e. uno se cansa con facilidad** one gets tired easily at my age; **a tu e. yo ya trabajaba** I already had a job at your age; **mujeres entre los treinta y cuarenta años de e.** women aged between thirty and forty; **una persona de e.** an elderly person; **una persona de avanzada e.** *o* **de e. avanzada** an elderly person; **una señora de cierta e.** a lady of a certain age; **un niño de corta e.** a young child; **una persona de mediana e.** a middle-aged person; **¡son cosas de la e.!** it's (just) his/her/their age!; **ya estás en e. de salir con chicos** you're old enough now to be going out with boys; **estar en e. de merecer** to be of marriageable age; **estar en e. de trabajar** to be of working age; **por e. le correspondería estar en un curso más avanzado** by age he should be in a higher year; **distribuir/ordenar un grupo por edades** to divide/organize a group by age ►► ***e. adulta*** adulthood, adult age; ***e. escolar*** school age; **estar en e. escolar** to be of school age; ***e. de jubilación*** retirement age; ***e. del juicio*** age of reason; ***e. madura*** middle age; ***e. mental*** mental age; *Fam* ***e. del pavo:*** **está en la e. del pavo** she's at that awkward age; *Méx Fam* ***e. de la punzada:*** **está en la e. de la punzada** she's at that awkward age; ***e. de la razón*** age of reason
(b) *(periodo)* age ►► ***la e. antigua*** ancient times; ***la E. de*** *o* ***del Bronce*** the Bronze Age; ***la E. Contemporánea*** the modern age *(since the French revolution)*; ***la E. de*** *o* ***del Hierro*** the Iron Age; ***la E. Media*** the Middle Ages; ***la e. de los metales*** = period comprising the Copper, Bronze and Iron Ages (c. 4000-500 BC); ***la E. Moderna*** = period between 1492 and the French Revolution; ***la e. de oro*** the golden age; **la e. de oro de la pintura holandesa** the golden age of Dutch painting; ***la E. de Piedra*** the Stone Age
edáfico, -a *adj Geol* pedological
edafología *nf Geol* soil science, pedology
edafólogo, -a *nm,f Geol* soil scientist, pedologist
edecán 1 *nm Mil* aide-de-camp
2 *nmf Méx* (a) *(en congreso)* conference usher (b) *(acompañante)* escort
edelweiss [eðel'bais] *nm inv Bot* edelweiss
edema *nm Med* oedema; **un e. pulmonar** (a) pulmonary oedema
edén *nm* (a) *Rel* Eden (b) *(lugar o situación paradisíacos)* paradise
edición *nf* (a) *(acción de publicar)* publication; **Ediciones Herrero** Herrero Publications; **e. (a cargo) de Jorge Urrutia** *(en libro)* edited by Jorge Urrutia
(b) *(ejemplares publicados)* edition; **una e. de dos mil ejemplares** an edition of two thousand copies; **nueva e. revisada y ampliada** new edition revised and enlarged ►► ***e. abreviada*** abridged edition; ***e. anotada*** annotated edition; ***e. de bolsillo*** pocket edition; ***e. crítica*** critical edition; ***e. electrónica*** electronic publishing; ***e. extraordinaria*** special edition; ***e. facsímil*** facsimile edition; ***e. limitada*** limited edition; ***e. de lujo*** deluxe edition; ***e. pirata*** pirate edition; ***e. príncipe*** first edition
(c) *Informát* editing
(d) *(de programa)* **la primera/segunda e. del telediario** ≃ the first/second news bulletin
(e) *(celebración periódica)* **la e. de los Oscars/del Mundial de 2002** the 2002 Oscars/World Cup; **la décima e. del festival** the tenth festival; **los cursos de verano cumplen su vigésima e.** the summer courses are now in their twentieth year
edicto *nm* edict; **un e. judicial/municipal** a judicial/municipal edict
edificabilidad *nf* suitability for building
edificable *adj* suitable for building; **lo declararon e.** it was classified as suitable for development, *US* it was zoned for building
edificación *nf* (a) *(edificio)* building; **una e. de piedra** a stone building (b) *(acción de construir)* construction; **solares reservados para la e. de oficinas** *Br* plots *o US* lots for the construction of office buildings
edificante *adj (conducta)* exemplary; *(libro, discurso)* edifying
edificar [60] 1 *vt* (a) *(construir)* to build (b) *(aleccionar)* to edify
2 *vi (construir)* to build
edificio *nm* building; **un e. de oficinas** an office building ►► ***e. inteligente*** intelligent *o* smart building
edil *nm* (a) *(concejal)* (town) councillor (b) *Hist* aedile
edila *nf* (town) councillor
edilicio, -a *adj* civic, municipal
Edimburgo *n* Edinburgh
edípico, -a *adj* Oedipal
Edipo *n Mitol* Oedipus
editar *vt* (a) *(publicar) (libro, periódico, revista)* to publish; *(disco, vídeo)* to release (b) *(modificar) (texto, programa, grabación)* to edit (c) *Informát* to edit
editor, -ora 1 *adj* publishing; **empresa editora** publishing company
2 *nm,f* (a) *(que publica) (libro, periódico, revista)* publisher (b) *(que modifica) (texto, programa, grabación)* editor
3 *nm Informát* editor ►► ***e. de textos*** text editor
editora *nf (empresa)* publisher, publishing house *o* company
editorial 1 *adj* publishing; **empresa e.** publishing house *o* company; **el proceso e.** the publishing process; **proyecto e.** publishing project; **el sector e.** the publishing sector
2 *nm (en periódico)* editorial, leader
3 *nf* publisher, publishing house *o* company
editorialista *nmf Prensa* leader writer
editorializar [14] *vi* to publish an editorial, *US* to editorialize (**sobre** on); **"El País" editorializa sobre la sequía** "El Pais" has an editorial on the drought, *US* "El Pais" editorializes on the drought
Edo. *Méx, Ven* (*abrev de* **Estado**) State
EdoMex [eðo'meks] *nm Méx* (*abrev de* **Estado de México**) Mexico State, the State of Mexico
edredón *nm* eiderdown, *Br* duvet
Eduardo *n pr* **E. I/II** Edward I/II
educación *nf* (a) *(enseñanza)* education; **quieren e. de calidad para sus hijos** they want high-quality education for their children; **el Ministerio de E.** the Ministry of Education ►► ***e. de adultos*** adult

education; ***e. ambiental*** environmental education; ***e. a distancia*** distance education; ***e. escolar*** schooling; ***e. especial*** special education; **escuela de e. especial** special school; ***e. física*** physical education; *Antes* ***e. general básica*** = stage of Spanish education system for pupils aged 6-14; ***e. infantil*** infant education; ***e. obligatoria*** compulsory education; ***e. preescolar*** preschool education; ***e. primaria*** primary education; ***e. secundaria*** secondary education; ***E. Secundaria Obligatoria*** = mainstream secondary education in Spain for pupils aged 12-16; ***e. sexual*** sex education; ***e. vial*** road safety education

(**b**) *(crianza)* upbringing, rearing

(**c**) *(modales)* good manners; **no tienes ninguna e.** you have no manners; **iqué poca e.!** how rude!; **iun poco de e.!** do you mind!; **mala e.** bad manners; **es una falta de e., es de mala e.** it's bad manners; **meterse el dedo en la nariz es una falta de e.** *o* **es de mala e.** picking your nose is bad manners

educacional *adj* educational

educadamente *adv* nicely, politely

educado, -a *adj (cortés)* polite, well-mannered; **bien e.** well-bred, well-mannered; **mal e.** rude, ill-mannered

educador, -ora *nm,f* teacher ▸▸ ***e. medioambiental*** environmental educator

educando, -a *nm,f Formal* pupil, student

educar [60] **1** *vt* (**a**) *(enseñar)* to educate (**b**) *(criar)* to bring up; **consejos sobre cómo e. a los hijos** advice about how to bring up children (**c**) *(cuerpo, voz, oído)* to train (**d**) *(animal doméstico)* to train; **hay que e. al perro para que no haga sus necesidades en la alfombra** you have to house-train the dog so it doesn't do its business on the carpet

2 educarse *vpr* to be educated, to receive one's education; **me eduqué en** *o* **con los jesuitas** I went to a Jesuit school

educativo, -a *adj* (**a**) *(que educa)* educational; **juegos educativos** educational games (**b**) *(de la educación)* educational; **un centro e.** an educational establishment; **sistema e.** education system

edulcorante 1 *adj* **sustancia e.** sweetener

2 *nm* sweetener

edulcorar *vt* to sweeten

EEB *nf (abrev de* **encefalopatía espongiforme bovina**) BSE

EEE *nm (abrev de* **espacio económico europeo**) EEA

EEG *nm Med (abrev de* **electroencefalograma**) EEG

EE.UU. *nmpl (abrev de* **Estados Unidos**) USA

efebo *nm* Adonis

efectismo *nm* striving for effect; **un guión lleno de e.** a script that's constantly striving for effect

efectista *adj* designed for effect, dramatic; **recursos efectistas** dramatic effects

efectivamente *adv (sí, eso es)* precisely, exactly; **¿o sea que te casas? – e.** in other words you're getting married – precisely; **¿es usted el dueño del vehículo? – e., yo soy** are you the owner of the vehicle? – I am, yes; **tendrá unos cuarenta años – e., tiene cuarenta y dos** he'll be about forty – correct, he's forty-two; **e., tal y como dijo el hombre del tiempo, llovió todo el día** sure enough, just as the weatherman said, it rained all day; **negó haber estado allí y, e., era cierto** she denied having been there, and this was in fact true

efectividad *nf* (**a**) *(eficacia)* effectiveness (**b**) *(validez)* **la ordenanza municipal tendrá e. desde el próximo lunes** the by-law will take effect as from next Monday

efectivo, -a 1 *adj* (**a**) *(eficaz, útil)* effective; **hacer e.** *(realizar)* to carry out; *(promesa)* to keep; *(dinero, crédito)* to pay; **hacer e. un cheque** to cash a cheque; **hacer e. un ingreso en una cuenta bancaria** to make a deposit in a bank account; **hacer e. un pago** to make a payment; **el técnico holandés hizo e. el cambio en el descanso** the Dutch manager made the substitution at half time

(**b**) *(real)* actual, true; **su nombramiento no será e. hasta mañana** her appointment will not take effect until tomorrow

2 *nm* (**a**) *(dinero)* cash; **en e.** in cash; **pagos/premios en e.** cash payments/prizes; **pagar/cobrar en e.** to pay/be paid in cash; **¿pagará con tarjeta o en e.?** would you like to pay by credit card or in cash? ▸▸ ***e. en caja*** *Br* cash in hand, *US* cash on hand; ***e. disponible*** available funds

(**b**) **efectivos** *(personal)* forces; **efectivos militares** troops; **habían llegado efectivos policiales** a number of policemen had arrived

EFECTO **1** *nm* (**a**) *(consecuencia, resultado)* effect; **los efectos del terremoto fueron devastadores** the effects of the earthquake were devastating; **sus declaraciones causaron el e. que él esperaba** his statements had the desired effect; **el analfabetismo es un e. de la falta de escuelas** illiteracy is a result of the lack of schools; **la decisión de bajar los tipos de interés tuvo un e. explosivo** the decision to lower interest rates had an explosive impact; **un medicamento de e. inmediato** a fast-acting medicine; **un mecanismo de e. retardado** a delayed-action mechanism; *Esp* **conducía** *o Am* **manejaba bajo los efectos del alcohol** she was driving under the influence (of alcohol); **hacer e.** to take effect; **todavía no me ha hecho e. la aspirina** the aspirin still hasn't taken effect; **llevar algo a e.** to put sth into effect, to implement sth; **el desalojo de las viviendas se llevará a e. mañana** the evacuation of the homes will be carried out tomorrow; **llevaron a e. sus promesas/amenazas** they made good *o* carried out their promises/threats; **surtir e.** to have an effect, to be effective; **las medidas contra el desempleo no han surtido e.** the measures against unemployment haven't had any effect *o* haven't been effective; **por e. de** as a result of; **el incendio se declaró por e. de las altas temperaturas** the fire broke out as a result of the high temperatures ▸▸ *Informát* ***el e. 2000*** the millennium bug; ***e. bumerán*** boomerang effect; ***e. dominó*** domino effect; *Fís* ***e. Doppler*** Doppler effect; ***e. fotoeléctrico*** photoelectric effect; ***e. invernadero*** greenhouse effect; ***e. mariposa*** butterfly effect; ***e. óptico*** optical illusion; ***e. placebo*** placebo effect; ***efectos secundarios*** side effects; *Fís* ***e. túnel*** tunnel effect

(**b**) *(finalidad)* aim, purpose; **al e., a dicho e., a tal e.** to that end; **rogamos contacte con nosotros, a tal e. le adjuntamos...** you are requested to contact us, and to that end please find attached...; **un andamio levantado al e.** scaffolding erected for the purpose; **las medidas propuestas a dicho e.** the measures proposed to this end; **a estos efectos, se te suministrará el material necesario** you will be provided with the necessary materials for this purpose; **a efectos** *o* **para los efectos de algo** as far as sth is concerned; **a efectos fiscales, estos ingresos no cuentan** this income is not counted for tax purposes, this income is not taxable; **a efectos legales, esta empresa ya no existe** as far as the law is concerned *o* in the eyes of the law, this company no longer exists; **a todos los efectos el propietario es usted** for all practical purposes you are the owner

(**c**) *(impresión)* impression; **sus declaraciones causaron gran e.** his statements made a great impression; **nos hizo mucho e. la noticia** the news came as quite a shock to us; **producir buen/mal e.** to make a good/bad impression

(**d**) *(vigencia)* effect; **con e. desde** with effect from; **con e. retroactivo** retroactively; **con e. inmediato** with immediate effect; **un juez ha declarado sin e. esta norma municipal** a judge has declared this by-law null and void; **tener e.** *(vigencia)* to come into *o* take effect; **¿desde cuándo tiene e. esa norma?** how long has that law been in force?

(**e**) *(de balón, bola)* spin; **lanzó la falta con mucho e.** he put a lot of bend on the free kick; **dar e. a la pelota, golpear la pelota con e.** *(en tenis)* to put spin on the ball, to spin the ball; *(en fútbol)* to put bend on the ball, to bend the ball; **dar a la bola e. de la derecha/izquierda** *(en billar)* to put right-hand/left-hand side on the ball; **dar a la bola e. alto** *(en billar)* to put topspin on the ball

(**f**) *Com (documento)* bill ▸▸ ***e. bancario*** bank bill; ***efectos a cobrar*** bills receivable; ***e. de comercio*** commercial paper; ***efectos del estado*** government securities; ***e. de favor*** accommodation bill; ***e. interbancario*** bank draft; ***efectos a pagar*** bills payable; ***efectos públicos*** government securities

2 efectos *nmpl* (**a**) *Cine & TV* ***efectos especiales*** special effects; ***efectos sonoros*** sound effects; ***efectos visuales*** visual effects

(**b**) *(posesiones)* ***efectos personales*** personal possessions *o* effects

(**c**) *(mercancías)* goods ▸▸ ***efectos de consumo*** consumer goods

3 en efecto *loc adv* indeed; **y, en e., fuimos a visitar la ciudad** and we did indeed visit the city; **¿lo hiciste tú? – en e.** did you do it? – I did indeed *o* indeed I did

efectuar [4] **1** *vt (realizar) (operación, maniobra, órdenes)* to carry out; *(compra, pago, viaje)* to make; **la policía efectuó varias detenciones/varios disparos** the police made a number of arrests/fired a number of shots; **deben efectuarse reparaciones en los conductos de gas** repairs should be carried out on the gas pipes; **el tren efectuará su salida a las ocho** the train will depart at eight; **el Papa efectuará una visita oficial a la zona** the Pope will make an official visit to the area

2 efectuarse *vpr (ocurrir)* to take place

efedrina *nf Farm* ephedrine

efeméride *nf (suceso)* major event; *(conmemoración)* anniversary; *Prensa* **efemérides** = list of the day's anniversaries published in a newspaper

eferente *adj Anat & Fisiol* efferent

efervescencia *nf* (**a**) *(de líquido)* effervescence; *(de bebida)* fizziness (**b**) *(agitación, inquietud)* unrest; **estar en plena e.** to be buzzing *o* humming with activity; **el país está en plena e. política** the country is in a state of political ferment

efervescente *adj (bebida)* fizzy; *(aspirina, comprimido)* effervescent

Éfeso *n* Ephesus

eficacia *nf* (**a**) *(de persona)* efficiency (**b**) *(de medicamento, medida, gestión)* effectiveness

eficaz *adj* (**a**) *(persona)* efficient (**b**) *(medicamento, medida, gestión)* effective; **un remedio e. contra el acné** an effective treatment *o* remedy for acne

eficazmente *adv* effectively

eficiencia *nf* efficiency

eficiente *adj* efficient

eficientemente *adv* efficiently

efigie *nf* (**a**) *(imagen)* effigy; *(en monedas)* image, picture; **medallas con la e. de la reina** medals bearing the likeness of the queen (**b**) *Formal (personificación)* personification, embodiment; **la e. de la belleza** beauty personified

efímera *nf (insecto)* mayfly

efímero, -a *adj* ephemeral

eflorescencia *nf* (**a**) *Quím* efflorescence (**b**) *Med* efflorescence

eflorescente *adj Quím* efflorescent

efluente *nm Geog* effluent

efluvio *nm* (**a**) *(emanación)* vapour; *(aroma)* scent; **los efluvios de su perfume** the smell of her perfume; *Fam Hum* **¡menudos efluvios salen de tus zapatos!** your shoes are smelling very fragrant! (**b**) *(de alegría, simpatía)* aura

EFTA ['efta] *nf* (*abrev de* **European Free Trade Association**) EFTA

efusión *nf* (**a**) *(cordialidad)* effusiveness, warmth (**b**) *Formal (de sangre)* effusion

efusivamente *adv* effusively

efusividad *nf* effusiveness

efusivo, -a *adj* effusive, demonstrative; **es efusiva y cariñosa** she's warm and affectionate; **no estuvo muy e. con su familia** he wasn't very demonstrative towards his family; **un abrazo e.** a warm embrace, a big hug

EGA *nm Informát* (*abrev de* **enhanced graphics adaptor**) EGA

EGB *nf Antes* (*abrev de* **educación general básica**) = stage of Spanish education system for pupils aged 6-14

Egeo *nm* **el (mar) E.** the Aegean (Sea)

égida *nf* aegis, protection; **bajo la é. de** under the aegis *o* auspices of

egipcio, -a 1 *adj* Egyptian
2 *nm,f* Egyptian

Egipto *n* Egypt

egiptología *nf* Egyptology

egiptólogo, -a *nm,f* Egyptologist

eglantina *nf Bot* eglantine, sweetbrier

égloga *nf* eclogue

ego *nm* (**a**) *Psi* ego (**b**) *(egolatría)* ego; **tiene un e. como una casa (de grande)** he's got an ego the size of a house

egocéntrico, -a 1 *adj* egocentric, self-centred
2 *nm,f* egocentric *o* self-centred person

egocentrismo *nm* egocentricity

egoísmo *nm* selfishness, egoism

egoísta 1 *adj* selfish, egoistic; **¡mira que eres e.!** you're so selfish!; **era muy e. con sus hermanos** he was very selfish towards his brothers and sisters
2 *nmf* selfish person, egotist; **ser un e.** to be very selfish, to be an egotist

egoístamente *adv* egoistically

ególatra 1 *adj* egotistical
2 *nmf* egotist

egolatría *nf* egotism

egotismo *nm Psi* egotism

egotista *Psi* 1 *adj* egotistic, egotistical
2 *nmf* egotist

egregio, -a *adj Formal* illustrious

> **Falso amigo**: El adjetivo inglés **egregious** no es la traducción del español **egregio**. En inglés **egregious** significa "atroz".

egresado, -a *nm,f Am* (**a**) *(de escuela)* = student who has completed their studies, *US* graduate (**b**) *(de universidad)* graduate

egresar *vi Am* (**a**) *(de escuela)* to leave school after completing one's studies, *US* to graduate (**b**) *(de universidad)* to graduate

egreso *nm* (**a**) *Am (de universidad)* graduation (**b**) *Méx (retirada)* withdrawal

eh *interj* (**a**) *(para llamar la atención)* hey!; **¡eh, oiga! se le ha caído la cartera** hey! you've dropped your wallet; **¡eh, tú, mira por dónde vas!** hey, you, look where you're going! (**b**) *(para preguntar)* **¿eh?, ¿y por qué?** really? why's that?; **estaba rico, ¿eh?** it was delicious, wasn't it?; **¿estás dormido? - ...¿eh?** are you asleep? - ...eh? *o* what?

EIA *n* (*abrev de* **evaluación de impacto ambiental**) EIA, environmental impact assessment

éider *nm* eider

eidético, -a *adj Psi* eidetic

einstenio *nm Quím* einsteinium

Eire *n Hist* Eire

ej. (*abrev de* **ejemplo**) example, ex.; **p. ej., por ej.** e.g.

eje *nm* (**a**) *(de rueda)* axle; *(de máquina)* shaft ▸▸ *Aut* ***e. delantero*** front axle; ***e. de transmisión*** drive shaft; *Aut* ***e. trasero*** rear axle
(**b**) *Geom, Astron & Fís* axis; **la Tierra gira sobre su propio e.** the Earth rotates on its own axis ▸▸ ***e. de abscisas*** x-axis; ***e. de ordenadas*** y-axis; ***e. de rotación*** axis of revolution; ***e. de simetría*** axis of symmetry
(**c**) *(cosa central) (de obra)* central theme; *(de doctrina, teoría)* central idea; **es el e. de la compañía** she holds the company together; **el e. argumental de la novela** the central strand of the novel's plot ▸▸ *Am* ***e. vial*** main road
(**d**) *Hist* **el E.** the Axis

ejecución *nf* (**a**) *(realización) (de trabajo, orden)* carrying out; *(de plan, proyecto)* implementation; *(de penalti, lanzamiento)* taking; *(de ejercicio, acrobacia)* performance; **tuvimos problemas durante la e. de la tarea** we had problems while carrying out the task; **la e. del golpe fue brillante** it was a brilliantly struck shot
(**b**) *(ajusticiamiento)* execution
(**c**) *(de pieza musical)* performance, rendition
(**d**) *Der (de desahucio)* carrying out, enforcement
(**e**) *Informát (de programa)* execution, running

ejecutable 1 *adj* (**a**) *(realizable)* feasible, practicable (**b**) *Informát* executable
2 *nm Informát* exe file

ejecutante *nmf (de pieza musical)* performer

ejecutar *vt* (**a**) *(realizar) (trabajo, tarea)* to carry out; *(plan, proyecto)* to implement, to carry out; *(penalti, lanzamiento, disparo)* to take; *(ejercicio, acrobacia)* to perform; **e. las órdenes de alguien** to carry out sb's orders; **e. la sentencia de un juez** to enforce a judge's sentence
(**b**) *(condenado)* to execute
(**c**) *(pieza musical)* to perform
(**d**) *Der (desahucio)* to carry out, to enforce
(**e**) *Informát (programa)* to execute, to run

ejecutiva *nf (junta)* executive; **la e. del partido socialista** the executive of the socialist party

ejecutivo, -a 1 *adj* executive
2 *nm,f (persona)* executive; **e. agresivo** thrusting executive; **un alto e. de la compañía** a top executive of the company ▸▸ ***e. de cuentas*** account executive; ***e. de ventas*** sales executive
3 *nm Pol* **el e.** *o* **E.** the government; **fuentes del e.** government sources

ejecutor, -ora *nm,f* (**a**) *Der* executor (**b**) *(verdugo)* executioner

ejecutoria *nf* (**a**) *(de título nobiliar)* letters patent of nobility (**b**) *(historial)* record of accomplishment (**c**) *Der (sentencia)* final judgement; *(despacho)* writ of execution

ejecutorio, -a *adj Der* final

ejem *interj* hum!, ahem!

ejemplar 1 *adj* (**a**) *(modélico)* exemplary; **tuvo un comportamiento e.** his behaviour was exemplary; **fue un marido e.** he was a model husband (**b**) *(aleccionador)* exemplary; **castigo e.** exemplary punishment
2 *nm* (**a**) *(de libro, diario)* copy; *(de revista)* issue, number; *(de moneda, sello)* example; **una tirada de diez mil ejemplares** a print run of ten thousand copies; **ejemplares atrasados del "New Yorker"** back issues of the "New Yorker" ▸▸ ***e. de muestra*** specimen copy; ***e. de regalo*** *(libro)* complimentary copy
(**b**) *(de especie, raza)* specimen; **pescó un e. de 200 kilos** he caught one weighing 200 kilos; **quedan pocos ejemplares de panda gigante**

there are few giant pandas left; **un magnífico e. de secuoya gigante** a magnificent specimen of the giant sequoia *o* redwood; *Fam* **¡menudo e.!** he's/she's a sly one!

ejemplaridad *nf* exemplary nature

ejemplarizante, *Andes* **ejemplarizador, ora** *adj* exemplary

ejemplarizar *vi (dar ejemplo)* to set an example

ejemplarmente *adv* in an exemplary manner

ejemplificación *nf* exemplification, illustration

ejemplificar [60] *vt* to exemplify

ejemplo 1 *nm* (a) *(caso ilustrativo)* example; **un e. más de mala gestión empresarial** another example of bad business management; **déjenme que les dé un e.** allow me to give you an example; **poner un e.** to give an example; **póngame un e.** give me an example

(b) *(modelo)* **nuestros vecinos son un e. de amabilidad** our neighbours are very kind; **es el vivo e. del optimismo** he's optimism personified; **dar e.** to set an example; **no des mal e. a los niños** don't set the children a bad example; **poner a alguien de e.** to give sb as an example; **servir de e. (a alguien)** to be an example (to sb); **toma e. de tu hermano** follow your brother's example

2 por ejemplo *loc adv* (a) *(para ilustrar)* for example, for instance; **grandes ciudades, por e. Nueva York o Londres** big cities, for example New York or London

(b) *(en respuestas)* **este trabajo tiene sus ventajas – ¿por e.?** this job has its advantages – such as?; *Irónico* **podría prestarme el dinero un amigo, ¿no? – ¡por e.!** I could get a friend to lend me the money, don't you think? – dream on!

ejercer [40] **1** *vt* (a) *(profesión)* to practise; *(cargo)* to hold; **ejerce la medicina** he's in practice as a doctor; **no tiene permiso para e. su profesión** she is not authorized to practise her profession; **ejerció la presidencia de la empresa durante años** he was *Br* chairman *o US* president of the company for years; **no es capaz de e. las funciones de ministro** she's not up to the demands of a ministerial post; **¿qué actividad ejerce usted?** what is your occupation?

(b) *(poder, derecho)* to exercise; **e. el derecho al voto** to exercise one's right to vote

(c) *(influencia, dominio)* to exert; **e. presión sobre** to put pressure on; **e. influencia (en** *o* **sobre)** to have an effect *o* influence (on); **ejercen una enorme atracción sobre los adolescentes** they hold a tremendous attraction for teenagers

(d) *Bolsa (opción)* to exercise

2 *vi* to practise (one's profession); **estudió enfermería, pero no ejerce** she studied as a nurse, but is not working in the profession; **e. de** *o* **como** to practise *o* work as; **ejerce como abogada** she practises as a lawyer, she's a practising lawyer; **ejercía de juez y alcalde a la vez** he held the office of judge and mayor at the same time; **ejerce mucho de jefe** he acts like he's the boss

ejercicio *nm* (a) *(deporte)* exercise; **hacer e.** to exercise, to do exercise ►► ***ejercicios de calentamiento*** warm-up exercises; ***e. físico*** physical exercise; ***ejercicios de mantenimiento*** keep-fit exercises

(b) *(tarea)* exercise; **ejercicios de inglés/guitarra** English/guitar exercises ►► *Rel* ***ejercicios espirituales*** retreat; ***ejercicios de tiro*** target practice

(c) *(examen)* test, *US* quiz; **el profesor nos puso un e. escrito/oral** the teacher gave us a written/an oral *Br* test *o US* quiz

(d) *Mil* exercise

(e) *(de profesión)* practising; *(de cargo, funciones)* carrying out; **se le acusa de negligencia en el e. de sus funciones** he has been accused of negligence in carrying out *o* in the performance of his duties; **(estar) en e.** (to be) in practice; **ya no está en e.** he no longer practises; **un médico en e.** a practising doctor

(f) *(de poder, derecho)* exercising; **el e. del voto** the use of one's vote

(g) *Econ* financial year ►► ***e. económico*** financial year; ***e. fiscal*** tax year

ejercitación *nf* (a) *(de derecho)* exercising, exercise (b) *(de idioma)* practising, practice (c) *(de la memoria, músculos, brazos)* exercising

ejercitar 1 *vt* (a) *(derecho)* to exercise; *(profesión)* to practise; **e. el derecho al voto** to exercise one's right to vote (b) *(idioma)* to practise (c) *(entrenar) (conocimientos)* to use, to put to use; *(memoria, músculos, brazos)* to exercise; *(atletas)* to train; *(soldados)* to drill, to train; *(alumnos)* to coach; **ejercitaron a la tropa en el reconocimiento de minas** they trained the troops in mine detection

2 ejercitarse *vpr* to train (**en** in)

ejército *nm* (a) *(fuerzas armadas)* army; **alistarse en el e.** to join the army, to enlist (in the army) ►► ***E. del Aire*** Air Force; ***e. profesional*** professional army; ***e. regular*** regular army; *Hist* ***el E. Rojo*** *(en Rusia)* the Red Army; ***el E. de Salvación*** the Salvation Army; ***E. de Tierra*** army *(as opposed to navy and air force)*; ***E. Zapatista de Liberación Nacional*** Zapatista Army of National Liberation

(b) *(grupo numeroso)* army; **un e. de admiradoras** an army *o* a host of admirers

ejidal *adj Méx* co-operatively owned

ejidatario, -a *nm,f Méx* = person who has been granted joint-title to an "ejido"

ejido *nm* (a) *Hist* common land (b) *Méx (institución)* = system of co-operative land tenure (c) *Méx (terreno)* = piece of land farmed by a cooperative (d) *Méx (sociedad)* = farming cooperative

ejote *nm CAm, Méx* green bean

EL (*f* **la**, *mpl* **los**, *fpl* **las**) *art determinado*

> **el** is used instead of **la** before feminine nouns which are stressed on the first syllable and begin with "a" or "ha" (e.g. **el agua, el hacha**). Note that **el** combines with the prepositions **a** and **de** to produce the contracted forms **al** and **del**.

(a) *(con valor especificador)* the; **el coche** the car; **la casa** the house; **los niños** the children; **el agua/hacha/águila** the water/axe/eagle; **fui a recoger a los niños** I went to pick up the children

(b) *(con sustantivo abstracto, valor genérico)* **el amor** love; **la vida** life; **el hombre** Man, human beings; **los derechos de la mujer** women's rights; **los niños imitan a los adultos** children copy adults; **el pan es un alimento básico** bread is a basic food; **la mayoría de la gente no la conoce** most people don't know her; **vuelve el biquini** bikinis are back

(c) *(indica posesión, pertenencia)* **se partió la pierna** he broke his leg; **se quitó los zapatos** she took her shoes off; **tiene el pelo oscuro** he has dark hair; **me han robado la maleta** my suitcase has been stolen; **se dieron la mano** they shook hands

(d) *(con días de la semana, fechas, horas)* **vuelven el sábado** they're coming back on Saturday; **los domingos vamos al cine** we go to the movies (on) Sundays; **llegaré el 1 de mayo** *(escrito)* I'll arrive on 1 May; *(hablado)* I'll arrive on the first of May; **son las siete** it's seven o'clock; **el año pasado/que viene** last/next year

(e) *(con nombres propios geográficos)* **el Sena** the (River) Seine; **el Everest** (Mount) Everest; **la India** India; **La Haya** The Hague; **E. Cairo** Cairo; **la España de la posguerra** post-war Spain

(f) *(con apellido)* **la señora Márquez** Mrs Márquez; **el señor/el doctor Juárez** Mr/Doctor Juárez; **los Amaya** *(matrimonio)* Mr and Mrs Amaya, the Amayas; *(familia completa)* the Amayas, the Amaya family; **los Austrias** the Hapsburgs; **el Hitler español** the Spanish Hitler

(g) *Fam (con nombre propio de persona)* **llama a la María** call Maria

(h) *(con numerales, porcentajes, fracciones)* **el siete es mi número de la suerte** seven's my lucky number; **llegó el tercero** he came third; **el tercer piso** the third floor; **un aumento del 30 por ciento** a 30 percent increase; **la quinta parte (de)** a fifth (of); **el 20 por ciento (de)** 20 percent (of)

(i) *(en proporciones, precios)* **100 pesos el kilo** 100 pesos a *o* per kilo

(j) *(con complemento especificativo)* **el/la del sombrero** the one with the hat; **los/las de azul** *(cosas)* the blue ones; *(personas)* the ones in blue; **he perdido el tren, cogeré el de las nueve** I've missed the train, I'll get the nine o'clock one; **el de aquí** this one here; **¿los del parque son amigos tuyos?** were those people in the park friends of yours?; **prefiero las del escaparate** I prefer the ones in the window; **los del fondo no se callan** the people at the back won't shut up

(k) *(con complemento posesivo)* **mi hermano y el de Juan** my brother and Juan's; **el mío** mine; **la tuya** yours; **los suyos** theirs

(l) *(con adjetivo)* **prefiero el rojo al azul** I prefer the red one to the blue one; **el/la mejor** the best; **es la mejor de la clase** she's the best in the class, she's top of the class; **los seleccionados realizarán un examen** those chosen will sit an exam; **el tonto de Ignacio se equivocó** that idiot Ignacio got it wrong

(m) *(con infinitivo)* **el beber tanto acabó con él** all that drinking is what finished him off; **es amante del buen comer** she loves good food; **me sienta mal el tener que decírtelo** I don't like to have to tell you

(n) *(con frases subordinadas)* **el/la que** *(cosa)* whichever; *(persona)* whoever; **los/las que** *(cosas)* whichever; *(personas)* whoever; **coge el/los que quieras** take whichever you like; **el que más corra** whoever runs fastest, the one who runs the fastest; **las que quieran venir que levanten la mano** those who want to come *o* anyone who wants to come should put their hand up; **el que no te guste no quiere decir que sea malo** the fact that you don't like him doesn't make him a bad person

(o) *(con valor enfático)* **¡la pena que me dio verlo en ese estado!** I felt so sorry for him when I saw him in that state!

ÉL, ELLA *pron personal* (**a**) *(sujeto) (persona)* he, *f* she; *(animal, cosa)* it; **él no sabe nada** he doesn't know anything; **¿quién lo dijo? – él** who said so? – he did *o* him; **nosotros estamos invitados, ella no** we're invited, but she's not *o* but not her; **ella misma lo organizó todo** she organized it (all by) herself; **he aprobado – él también** I passed – so did he; **ella se llama Clara** she's called Clara, her name is Clara

(**b**) *(predicado) (persona)* he, *f* she; *(animal, cosa)* it; **es él/ella, abre la puerta** it's him/her, open the door; **mi hermana es ella** she's my sister

(**c**) *(complemento con preposición o conjunción)* him, *f* her; **de él** his; **de ella** hers; **esta casa es de él/elia** this house is his/hers; **eres tan alto como él** you're as tall as him *o* as he is; **voy a ir de vacaciones con ella** I'm going on holiday with her; **díselo a ella** tell it to her, tell her it; **este regalo es para él** this present is for him; **excepto/incluso él** except/including him; **por él no hay problema** there's no problem as far as he's concerned

> Because Spanish verbs are inflected, subject pronouns such as **él** and **ella** are largely redundant. In fact, they are normally omitted, with no loss in clarity about who is being referred to:
> **¿dónde está Pedro? – creo que no va a venir**
> *where's Pedro? – I don't think he's going to come*
> The personal subject pronouns are used in cases where an explicit contrast is needed:
> **creo que él no va a venir, pero su esposa sí**
> *I don't think he's coming, but his wife is*

elaboración *nf* (**a**) *(de producto)* manufacture; *(de plato, alimento)* preparation; *(de bebida)* making, production; *(de sustancia orgánica, hormona)* production; **pasteles de e. propia** cakes made on the premises; **de e. casera** home-made; **un artefacto explosivo de e. casera** a home-made explosive device; **proceso de e.** *(industrial)* manufacturing process

(**b**) *(de idea, teoría)* working out, development; *(de plan, proyecto)* drawing up; *(de estudio, informe)* preparation

elaborado, -a *adj (trabajado)* **un plan muy e.** an elaborate plan; **el guión está muy e.** it's a very well-crafted script; **un plato e.** an elaborate dish

elaborar *vt* (**a**) *(producto)* to make, to manufacture; *(plato, alimento)* to prepare; *(bebida)* to make, to produce; *(sustancia orgánica, hormona)* to produce (**b**) *(idea, teoría)* to work out, to develop; *(plan, proyecto)* to draw up; *(estudio, informe)* to prepare

elanio *nm* ***e. azul*** black-winged kite

elasmobranquio *Zool* **1** *adj (pez)* elasmobranch

2 *nm (pez)* elasmobranch, member of the subclass *Elasmobranchii*

3 elasmobranquios *nmpl (subclase)* Elasmobranchii; **de la subclase de los elasmobranquios** of the subclass *Elasmobranchii*

elástica *nf (camiseta)* vest

elasticidad *nf* (**a**) *(de material, cuerpo)* elasticity (**b**) *(de horario)* flexibility (**c**) *(de interpretación)* flexibility

elástico, -a 1 *adj* (**a**) *(material, cuerpo)* elastic (**b**) *(horario)* flexible (**c**) *(interpretación)* flexible; **lo de que todos los hombres son iguales es muy e.** the idea that all men are equal is very debatable

2 *nm (cinta)* elastic; *(goma elástica)* rubber band; *(de pantalón, falda)* elasticated waistband

elastina *nf Bioquím* elastin

elastizado, -a *adj RP Br* elasticated, *US* elasticized

Elba *nm* **el E.** the Elbe

ELE, E/LE ['ele] *(abrev de* **español como lengua extranjera***)* Spanish as a foreign language

elección 1 *nf* (**a**) *(opción de escoger)* choice; **no tenemos e.** we have no choice; **el color lo dejo a tu e.** I'll leave the (choice of) colour up to you; **un regalo de su e.** a gift of his own choosing (**b**) *(por nombramiento)* appointment; *(por votación)* election; **su e. como ministro** his appointment as minister; **la e. del árbitro no llevó mucho tiempo** it didn't take long to choose the referee

2 elecciones *nfpl (votación)* election; **convocar elecciones** to call an election; **las elecciones se celebrarán en octubre** the elections will be held in October; **presentarse a las elecciones** to stand in the election ▸▸ ***elecciones anticipadas*** an early election; **convocar elecciones anticipadas** to call an early election; ***elecciones autonómicas*** elections to the regional parliament; ***elecciones generales*** elections to the national parliament, *Br* ≃ general election, *US* ≃ congressional elections; ***elecciones legislativas*** elections to the national parliament, *Br* ≃ general election, *US* ≃ congressional elections; ***elecciones municipales*** local elections; ***e. parcial*** by-election; ***elecciones presidenciales*** presidential election; ***elecciones primarias*** primary election

eleccionario, -a *adj Am* electoral

electivo, -a *adj* elective

electo, -a *adj* elect; **el presidente e.** the president elect

elector, -ora *nm,f* voter, elector

electorado *nm* electorate

electoral *adj (sistema, distrito, reforma)* electoral; *(campaña, resultado, propaganda)* election

electoralismo *nm* electioneering

EL

> **Omission of the article in Spanish**
> In general, the article is used more frequently in Spanish than in English. However, there are certain phrases where it is omitted in Spanish, but retained in English:
>
> **en manos de** *in the hands of*
> **a nombre de** *in the name of*
> **a corto/largo plazo** *in the short/long term*
>
> The definite article is also omitted before ordinals accompanying the names of monarchs and popes, in speech as in writing, as well as for dates when preceded by **ser**:
>
> **Juan Pablo Segundo** *John Paul the Second*
> **Juan Carlos Primero** *Juan Carlos the First*
> **hoy es tres de marzo** *today is the third of March*
>
> In compound nouns linked by **de**, the article is omitted before the second noun unless reference is made to a specific instance:
>
> **una mesa de cocina** *a kitchen table* but **la mesa de la cocina** *the kitchen table*
> **una silla de niño** *a child's chair* but **la silla del niño** *the child's chair*
>
> In many cases the article is omitted in Spanish as in English. For example, articles are not normally used with proper names or with months and dates, and they are omitted before days of the week after **ser** and always after **hay/había:**
>
> **viajar a Marte** *to travel to Mars*
> **nunca he estado en Guadalajara** *I've never been to Guadalajara*
> **nació en abril** *she was born in April*
> **hoy es martes** *today is Tuesday*
> **no hay pan** *there's no bread*

electoralista *adj* electioneering; **una medida e.** a vote-catching measure
eléctrica *nf* electricity company
electricidad *nf* (**a**) *(energía)* electricity ►► ***e. estática*** static electricity (**b**) *(suministro eléctrico)* electricity; **se ha cortado la e.** there's been a power cut
electricista 1 *adj* electrical
2 *nmf* electrician
eléctrico, -a *adj (corriente, luz, motor)* electric; *(energía)* electric, electrical; *(aparato, instalación)* electrical; **el sector e.** the electricity industry
electrificación *nf* electrification
electrificar [60] *vt* to electrify
electrizante *adj (discurso, actuación, ambiente)* electrifying
electrizar [14] *vt* (**a**) *(producir electricidad en)* to electrify (**b**) *(exaltar)* to electrify
electro *nm Fam* ECG
electroacústica *nf* electroacoustics *(singular)*
electrocardiografía *nf Med* electrocardiography
electrocardiógrafo *nm Med* electrocardiograph
electrocardiograma *nm* electrocardiogram, ECG
electrochoque *nm (terapia)* electric shock therapy
electrocución *nf* electrocution
electrocutar 1 *vt* to electrocute
2 electrocutarse *vpr* to electrocute oneself
electrodeposición *nf* electrodeposition
electrodiálisis *nf inv* electrodialysis
electrodinámica *nf* electrodynamics *(singular)*
electrodo *nm* electrode
electrodoméstico *nm* electrical (household) appliance; **tienda de electrodomésticos** electrical appliance shop
electroencefalógrafo *nm* electroencephalograph
electroencefalograma *nm* electroencephalogram
electrógeno, -a 1 *adj* **grupo e.** generator
2 *nm* generator
electroimán *nm* electromagnet
electrola *nf Perú* gramophone
electrólisis, electrolisis *nf inv* electrolysis
electrolítico, -a *adj* electrolytic
electrólito, electrolito *nm* electrolyte
electromagnético, -a *adj* electromagnetic
electromagnetismo *nm* electromagnetism
electromecánica *nf* electromechanics *(singular)*
electromecánico, -a *adj* electromechanical
electromotor, -ora *o* **-triz 1** *adj* electromotive
2 *nm* electromotor
electrón *nm* electron
electrónica *nf* electronics *(singular)*
electrónico, -a *adj* electronic; **microscopio e.** electron microscope
electroquímica *nf* electrochemistry
electroscopio *nm* electroscope
electroshock [elektro'ʃok] (*pl* **electroshocks**) *nm (terapia)* electric shock therapy
electrostática *nf* electrostatics *(singular)*
electrostático, -a *adj* electrostatic
electrotecnia *nf* electrical engineering
electroterapia *nf* electrotherapy
electrotrén *nm* electric railcar, *Br* sprinter
eledé *nm Am* LP (record)
elefante, -a 1 *nm,f* elephant ►► ***e. africano*** African elephant; ***e. asiático*** Asian *o* Indian elephant
2 *nm* ***e. marino*** elephant seal
elefantiasis *nf inv* elephantiasis
elegancia *nf* (**a**) *(en vestimenta) (de persona)* elegance, smartness; *(de ropa, calzado)* smartness (**b**) *(lujo) (de barrio, hotel, fiesta)* smartness, chicness (**c**) *(en garbo, porte)* gracefulness, elegance (**d**) *(en actitud, comportamiento)* graciousness; **la e. de respuesta** the graciousness of his reply (**e**) *(de estilo, frase)* elegance
elegante *adj* (**a**) *(en vestimenta) (persona)* elegant, smart; *(ropa, calzado)* smart, elegant; **estás muy e. con ese vestido** you look really smart in that dress; **ir e.** to be dressed smartly; **¡qué e. vas!** you look smart!; **ponte e., vamos a una boda** make yourself smart, we're going to a wedding; **es e. en el vestir** he dresses elegantly *o* smartly
(**b**) *(lujoso) (barrio, hotel, fiesta)* smart, chic; **los elegantes bulevares parisinos** the elegant boulevards of Paris
(**c**) *(en garbo, porte)* graceful, elegant
(**d**) *(en actitud, comportamiento)* gracious; **fue un gesto poco e. por su parte** it wasn't a very gracious gesture on his part
(**e**) *(estilo, frase)* elegant
elegantemente *adv* (**a**) *(vestir)* smartly, elegantly; *(decorar)* elegantly (**b**) *(moverse, caminar)* gracefully, elegantly (**c**) *(comportarse)* graciously; *(responder)* with grace, graciously
elegantoso, -a *adj Am Fam* smart, *Br* posh
elegía *nf* elegy (**a** to)
elegiaco, -a, elegíaco, -a *adj* elegiac
elegibilidad *nf* eligibility
elegible *adj* eligible
elegido, -a 1 *adj* (**a**) *(escogido)* selected, chosen (**b**) *(por votación)* elected
2 *nm,f* person chosen/elected; **los elegidos** the chosen few; **sólo unos cuantos elegidos podrán asistir al acto** only a select few will be able to attend the ceremony
elegir [55] **1** *vt* (**a**) *(escoger)* to choose, to select; **siempre elige a los más guapos** she always chooses the best-looking ones; **entre todos los candidatos te han elegido a ti** out of all the candidates you have been selected; **eligió la carrera de actor** he chose a career in acting; **tiene dos colores a e.** you have two colours to choose from; **rojo o verde, ¿cuál eliges?** red or green, which one do you want?
(**b**) *(por votación)* to elect; **fue elegido por unanimidad** he was elected unanimously; **ha sido elegida mejor película del año** it was voted best film of the year
2 *vi (escoger)* to choose; **tú eliges** YOU choose; **dar a alguien a e. entre varias cosas** to give sb a choice between several things; **si me das a e., prefiero el rojo** given the choice, I prefer the red; **hay mucho donde e.** there's a lot to choose from
elemental *adj* (**a**) *(básico) (conocimientos, característica, requisito)* basic; *(curso, nivel)* elementary; *(norma, ley, principio)* fundamental; **un derecho e. de todos los ciudadanos** a basic right of all citizens (**b**) *(sencillo)* simple; **e., querido Watson** elementary, my dear Watson
elemento[1] 1 *nm* (**a**) *(sustancia)* element; **e. (químico)** (chemical) element; **los cuatro elementos** the four elements
(**b**) *(medio natural)* element; **el agua es el e. de estos animales** water is these animals' natural element; EXPR **estar (uno) en su e.** to be in one's element; **entre niños está en su e.** he's in his element when he's with children; **le quitaron el puesto de bibliotecario y lo sacaron de su e.** he was removed from his post as librarian and taken out of his element
(**c**) *(parte, componente)* element; **el e. clave en el proceso de fabricación es la materia prima** the key element in the manufacturing process is the raw material; **cada e. del motor debe estar bien ajustado** every part of the engine must be fitted tightly
(**d**) *(factor)* factor; **un e. decisivo en el triunfo electoral** a decisive factor in the election victory; **un e. de distensión en las negociaciones** a certain easing of tension in the negotiations; **el e. sorpresa** the element of surprise
(**e**) *(persona)* **tiene muy buenos elementos trabajando para él** he has very good people working for him; **elementos incontrolados provocaron graves destrozos** unruly elements caused serious damage
2 elementos *nmpl* (**a**) *(fuerzas atmosféricas)* elements; **se desataron los elementos** the force of the elements was unleashed; EXPR **luchar contra los elementos** to struggle against the elements
(**b**) *(nociones básicas)* rudiments, basics
(**c**) *(medios, recursos)* resources, means; **carece de los elementos mínimos indispensables para la tarea** he lacks the minimum resources necessary for the task; **no tenemos elementos de juicio para pronunciarnos** we don't have sufficient information to give an opinion
elemento[2], -a *nm,f* (**a**) *Esp Fam Pey (persona)* **un e. de cuidado** a bad lot; **¡vaya e. que está hecho!** he's a prize specimen!, he's a real piece of work! (**b**) *Chile, Perú, PRico (torpe)* dimwit, blockhead
elenco *nm* (**a**) *(reparto)* cast (**b**) *(conjunto)* panoply, array (**c**) *Formal (catálogo)* list, index
elepé *nm* LP (record)
elevación *nf* (**a**) *(de pesos, objetos)* lifting (**b**) *(de nivel, altura, precios)* rise (**c**) *(de terreno)* elevation, rise (**d**) *(de cargo)* promotion (**a** to) (**e**) *(nobleza)* loftiness (**f**) *(de queja, recurso)* lodging, presentation; *(de propuesta)* submission, presentation

elevado, -a *adj* (**a**) *(alto) (monte, terreno, precio, inflación)* high; **un e. edificio** a tall building; **era de elevada estatura** he was tall in stature; **una persona de elevada estatura** a person tall in stature; **un e. número de accidentes** a large *o* high number of accidents; **consiguieron elevados beneficios** they made a large profit; **ocupa un e. cargo en la empresa** she has a high-ranking position in the company
(**b**) *(noble)* lofty, noble; **elevados ideales** lofty *o* noble ideals
(**c**) *(estilo, tono, lenguaje)* elevated, sophisticated; **emplea un vocabulario muy e.** she uses very sophisticated vocabulary

elevador *nm* (**a**) *(montacargas)* hoist (**b**) *Elec* booster (**c**) *Méx (ascensor) Br* lift, *US* elevator

elevadorista *nmf Méx (ascensorista) Br* lift operator, *US* elevator operator

elevalunas *nm inv* window winder ►► ***e. eléctrico*** electric window

elevar 1 *vt* (**a**) *(levantar) (peso, objeto)* to lift; **elevaron los muebles con poleas** they lifted the furniture with pulleys; **e. la moral de los jugadores** to boost the players' morale
(**b**) *(aumentar) (precio, nivel)* to raise; *(cantidad)* to increase; **e. las ventas/ganancias** to increase sales/profits; **e. el tono de voz** to raise one's voice; **elevaron a dos meses el plazo de matriculación** they extended the enrolment period to two months
(**c**) *Mat* to raise; **e. x al cuadrado/al cubo** to square/cube x; **diez elevado a quince** ten to the fifteenth (power)
(**d**) *(encumbrar)* to elevate (**a** to); **fue elevado al cargo de director** he was promoted to the post of director; **lo elevaron a la categoría de héroe** they made him into a hero
(**e**) *(presentar) (queja, recurso)* to lodge, to present; *(propuesta)* to submit, to present; **elevaremos un escrito de protesta al concejal** we shall present a formal protest to *o* lodge a formal protest with the councillor; **e. un recurso de apelación al Supremo** to lodge an appeal with *o* to present an appeal to the Supreme Court; **elevó una instancia al ministerio** he lodged an appeal with the Ministry
2 elevarse *vpr* (**a**) *(subir)* to rise; **el globo se elevó por los aires** the balloon rose into the air; **el avión comenzó a elevarse** the plane began to climb; **elevarse a** *(altura)* to reach
(**b**) *(edificio, montaña)* to rise up
(**c**) *(aumentar) (precio, temperatura)* to increase, to go up; **el peso se ha elevado con respecto al dólar** the peso has risen against the dollar; **elevarse a** *(gastos, daños)* to amount *o* come to; **el número de muertos se eleva ya a treinta** the number of dead has now risen to thirty

elfo *nm* elf

Elías *n pr* Elijah

elidir *vt* to elide

eligió *ver* **elegir**

elijo *etc ver* **elegir**

eliminación *nf* (**a**) *(en juego, deporte, concurso)* elimination (**b**) *(de contaminación, grasas, toxinas)* elimination; *(de residuos)* disposal; *(de fronteras, obstáculos)* removal, elimination ►► ***e. de residuos*** waste disposal (**c**) *Mat (de incógnita)* elimination; *Fig* **hallar algo por e.** to work sth out by a process of elimination (**d**) *Euf (de persona)* elimination

eliminar *vt* (**a**) *(en juego, deporte, concurso)* to eliminate (**de** from); **el que menos puntos consiga queda eliminado** the person who scores the lowest number of points is eliminated; **lo eliminaron en la segunda ronda** he was eliminated *o* knocked out in the second round
(**b**) *(acabar con) (contaminación)* to eliminate; *(grasas, toxinas)* to eliminate, to get rid of; *(residuos)* to dispose of; *(manchas)* to remove, to get rid of; *(fronteras, obstáculos)* to remove, to eliminate; **eliminó algunos trozos de su discurso** he cut out some parts of his speech
(**c**) *Mat (incógnita)* to eliminate
(**d**) *Euf (matar)* to eliminate, to get rid of

eliminatoria *nf (fase, ronda)* qualifying round; *(partido)* tie; *(en atletismo)* heat; **van cinco a dos a favor del Barcelona en el total de la e.** Barcelona are winning five-two on aggregate

eliminatorio, -a *adj* qualifying; **prueba eliminatoria** *(examen)* selection test; *(en deporte)* qualifying heat; **ronda eliminatoria** qualifying round

elipse *nf Geom* ellipse

elipsis *nf inv* (**a**) *Gram* ellipsis (**b**) *Cine & Lit* jump in time; **es muy dado a las e.** he favours elliptical narrative

elipsoidal *adj Geom* ellipsoidal

elipsoide *nm Geom* ellipsoid

elíptico, -a *adj* (**a**) *Gram* elliptic, elliptical (**b**) *Geom* elliptic, elliptical (**c**) *Cine & Lit* elliptical

élite, elite *nf* elite; **soldados de é.** elite *o* crack troops; **un deportista de é.** a top-class sportsman

elitismo *nm* elitism

elitista 1 *adj* elitist
2 *nmf* elitist

élitro *nm Zool* wing case

elixir, elíxir *nm* (**a**) *(medicamento)* **e. (bucal)** mouthwash (**b**) *(remedio milagroso)* elixir; **el e. de la eterna juventud** the elixir of eternal youth

ella *ver* **él**

ellas *ver* **ellos**

ello[1] *pron personal (neutro)* **no nos llevamos bien, pero e. no nos impide formar un buen equipo** we don't get on very well, but it *o* that doesn't stop us making a good team; **no quiero hablar de e.** I don't want to talk about it; **por e.** for that reason; **todo e. me hace pensar que...** it all makes me think that...

ello[2] *nm Psi* id

ELLOS, ELLAS *pron personal*

(**a**) *(sujeto)* they; **e. no saben nada** they don't know anything; **¿quién lo dijo? – e.** who said so? – they did *o* them; **nosotros estamos invitados, e. no** we're invited, but they're not *o* but not them; **ellas mismas lo organizaron todo** they organized it (all by) themselves; **hemos aprobado – e. también** we passed – so did they; **algunos de e.** some of them; **todos e.** all of them
(**b**) *(predicado)* they; **son e., abre la puerta** it's them, open the door; **los invitados son e.** they are the guests
(**c**) *(complemento con preposición o conjunción)* them; **de e.** theirs; **esta casa es de e.** this house is theirs; **me fui después que e.** I left after they did *o* after them; **me voy al bar con ellas** I'm going to the bar with them; **díselo a e.** tell it to them, tell THEM; **este regalo es para e.** this present is for them; **excepto/incluso e.** except/including them; **por e., no hay problema** there's no problem as far as they're concerned

> Because Spanish verbs are inflected, subject pronouns such as **ellos** and **ellas** are largely redundant. In fact, they are normally omitted, with no loss in clarity about who is being referred to:
> **¿dónde están Pedro y María? – creo que no van a venir**
> *where are Pedro and Maria? – I don't think they're going to come*
> The personal subject pronouns are used in cases where an explicit contrast is needed:
> **creo que ellos no van a venir, pero sus esposas sí**
> *I don't think they're coming, but their wives are*

ELN *nm (abrev de* **Ejército de Liberación Nacional**) Army of National Liberation, = Colombian guerrilla group

elocución *nf* elocution

elocuencia *nf* (**a**) *(de persona, discurso, declaraciones)* eloquence; **hablar con e.** to speak eloquently (**b**) *(de sonrisa, mirada, gesto)* eloquence, meaningfulness; *(de silencio, hechos, imágenes)* eloquence

elocuente *adj* (**a**) *(persona, discurso, declaraciones)* eloquent (**b**) *(sonrisa, gesto)* eloquent, meaningful; *(hechos, imágenes, datos)* eloquent; **se hizo un silencio e.** there was an eloquent *o* a meaningful silence; **una mirada e.** an eloquent *o* a meaningful look; **los datos son elocuentes** the facts speak for themselves

elocuentemente *adv* eloquently

elodea *nf Bot* Canadian pondweed *o* waterweed

elogiable *adj* praiseworthy

elogiar *vt* to praise; **e. a alguien por algo** to praise sb for sth

elogio *nm* praise; **la crítica sólo tuvo elogios para el director** the critics had nothing but praise for the director; **la colmaron de elogios, se deshicieron en elogios con ella** they heaped praise on her, they showered her with praise; **digno de e.** praiseworthy; **hizo un apasionado e. de los australianos** he paid the Australians a glowing tribute; **recibió el e. unánime de todos los partidos** he was praised by all the parties without exception

elogioso, -a *adj* (**a**) *(palabras, crítica, discurso)* appreciative, eulogistic; **sus declaraciones fueron elogiosas con el equipo rival** he spoke very highly *o* favourably of the opposing team (**b**) *(conducta, acto, actitud)* praiseworthy

elongación *nf* elongation

elote *nm CAm, Méx* (**a**) *(mazorca)* corncob, ear of maize *o US* corn (**b**) *(granos)* sweetcorn, *US* corn; **crema de e.** creamed sweetcorn *o US* corn; **torta de e.** corn cake

elucidación *nf Formal* elucidation

elucidar *vt Formal* to elucidate, to shed *o* throw light upon

elucubración, lucubración *nf* (**a**) *(reflexión)* deliberation, reflection (**b**) *(divagación, suposición)* **eso no son más que elucubraciones suyas** it's all just a lot of crazy ideas he's dreamed up; **pasaba el día haciendo elucubraciones sobre el futuro del negocio** he spent the day speculating on the future of the business

elucubrar, lucubrar 1 *vi* (**a**) *(reflexionar)* to deliberate (**sobre** on) (**b**) *(divagar)* to ramble

2 *vt* (**a**) *(idear) (teorías)* to come up with (**b**) *(imaginar) (fantasías)* to dream up

eludible *adj* avoidable

eludir *vt* (**a**) *(evitar) (compromiso, responsabilidad)* to avoid, to evade; *(problema, dificultad, tema)* to avoid; *(pregunta)* to evade, to avoid, to dodge; **e. el pago de una deuda** to avoid paying a debt; **e. al fisco** to avoid paying taxes; **e. el servicio militar** to avoid *o* get out of doing military service; **eludió hacer declaraciones** he avoided making any statement; **eludió su mirada** she avoided his eyes

(**b**) *(perseguidores)* **e. a** to avoid, to evade; **consiguió e. a la policía** he managed to avoid the police; *Der* **e. la acción de la justicia** to escape justice

elusión *nf* ***e. fiscal*** tax avoidance

elusivo, -a *adj* evasive

e.m. (*abrev de* **en mano**) by hand

e-mail ['imeil] (*pl* **e-mails**) *nm* e-mail

emanación *nf* emanation, emission; **emanaciones de gas** gas emissions ►► ***e. radiactiva*** radioactive emission

emanante *adj* emanating

emanar 1 *vt* (**a**) *(olor, humo, gas)* to give off, to exude (**b**) *(hostilidad)* to emanate; *(alegría, confianza)* to exude, to radiate; **emanaba tristeza** there was a tangible air of sadness about her

2 *vi* (**a**) *(olor, humo, gas)* to emanate (**de** from) (**b**) *(derecho, poder)* to derive (**de** from)

emancipación *nf (de esclavos)* emancipation; *(de menores de edad)* coming of age; *(de país)* liberation; **la e. de la mujer** the emancipation of women

emancipado, -a *adj (mujer)* emancipated; *(esclavo)* freed, emancipated; *(joven)* independent, self-supporting; *(país)* liberated

emancipador, -ora 1 *adj* emancipating

2 *nm,f* emancipator

emancipar 1 *vt (liberar) (esclavo, pueblo)* to free, to emancipate; *(país)* to liberate

2 **emanciparse** *vpr (país)* to become independent, to gain independence; *(mujer)* to become emancipated; **se emancipó (de su familia) a los diecisiete años** she became independent from her family at seventeen

emasculación *nf* emasculation

emascular *vt* to emasculate

embadurnado, -a *adj* smeared (**de** with)

embadurnar 1 *vt* to smear (**de** with); **embadurnó la bandeja de mantequilla** she greased the tray with butter

2 **embadurnarse** *vpr* to smear oneself (**de** with); **se embadurnó la cara de betún** he smeared his face with shoe polish

embajada *nf* (**a**) *(edificio)* embassy (**b**) *(cargo)* ambassadorship (**c**) *(empleados)* embassy staff

embajador, -ora *nm,f* (**a**) *(diplomático)* ambassador ►► ***e. itinerante*** roving ambassador (**b**) *(abanderado)* ambassador; **es el mejor e. del cine español en Estados Unidos** he is the best ambassador for Spanish cinema in the United States

embalado, -a *adj* (**a**) *(empaquetado)* packed, wrapped; **el paquete venía muy bien e.** the parcel was very well wrapped (**b**) *Fam (rápido)* **el tren pasó e. sin detenerse** the train sped *o* hurtled past without stopping; **corrió e. a avisar al médico** he rushed to tell the doctor (**c**) *RP Fam (entusiasmado)* excited; **está muy embalada con el casamiento** she's very excited about the wedding

embalador, -ora *nm,f Am (persona)* packer; *(máquina)* packing machine, packer

embaladura *nf Chile, Perú* packing

embalaje *nm* (**a**) *(acción)* packing (**b**) *(material)* packaging

embalar 1 *vt* (**a**) *(empaquetar)* to pack, to wrap up

(**b**) *RP Fam (entusiasmar)* **e. a alguien** to get sb excited; **no lo embales en proyectos irrealizables** don't get him all worked up *o* excited about plans that will never come to anything

2 **embalarse** *vpr Fam* (**a**) *(tomar velocidad) (corredor)* to race *o* speed off; *(vehículo)* to pick up speed; **no te embales, que vamos a tener un accidente** don't go so fast or we'll have an accident

(**b**) *(entusiasmarse)* to get carried away; **no te embales y piénsalo** don't get carried away, think about it; **cuando se embala a hablar no hay quien lo pare** once he gets into his stride you can't shut him up

embaldosado *nm* (**a**) *(acción)* tiling (**b**) *(pavimento)* tiled floor

embaldosar *vt (piso)* to tile

embalsamado, -a *adj* embalmed

embalsamador, -ora *nm,f* embalmer

embalsamamiento *nm* embalming

embalsamar *vt* to embalm

embalsar 1 *vt* to dam (up); **han aumentado los niveles de agua embalsada en la provincia** water levels have risen in the province's dams

2 **embalsarse** *vpr* to collect, to form puddles

embalse *nm* (**a**) *(pantano)* reservoir (**b**) *(recogida de agua)* collection, accumulation

embancarse *vpr* (**a**) *(barco)* to run aground (**b**) *Chile, Ecuad (río, lago)* to silt up

embanquetar *vt Méx* to pave

embarazada *nf* pregnant woman; **ropa para embarazadas** maternity wear

> **Falso amigo**: El adjetivo inglés **embarrassed** no es la traducción del español **embarazada**. En inglés **embarrassed** significa "avergonzado" o "azorado, violento".

embarazado, -a *adj* pregnant; **estar embarazada de ocho meses** to be eight months pregnant; **está embarazada de su tercer hijo** she is expecting her third child; **dejar embarazada a alguien** to get sb pregnant; **quedarse embarazada** to get pregnant; *Hum* **estamos embarazados** we're pregnant, we're going to have a baby

embarazar [14] 1 *vt* (**a**) *(preñar)* to get pregnant (**b**) *(avergonzar)* to inhibit (**c**) *(impedir)* to restrict

2 **embarazarse** *vpr (avergonzarse)* to get embarrassed

embarazo *nm* (**a**) *(preñez)* pregnancy ►► *Med* ***e. ectópico*** ectopic pregnancy; *Med* ***e. extrauterino*** ectopic pregnancy; ***e. no deseado*** unwanted pregnancy; ***e. psicológico*** phantom pregnancy (**b**) *(timidez)* embarrassment (**c**) *(impedimento)* obstacle

embarazoso, -a *adj* awkward, embarrassing

embarcación *nf* boat, vessel ►► ***e. deportiva*** sailing boat, *US* sailboat; ***e. de recreo*** pleasure boat

> **Falso amigo**: El sustantivo inglés **embarkation** no es la traducción del español **embarcación**. En inglés **embarkation** significa "embarque".

embarcadero *nm* jetty

embarcar [60] 1 *vt* (**a**) *(personas)* to board; *(mercancías)* to load; *(equipaje)* to load, to put on board

(**b**) *(involucrar)* **e. a alguien en algo** to get sb involved in sth; **me embarcaron en su negocio** they got me involved in their business

(**c**) *Ven Fam (plantar)* to let down, to leave in the lurch; **ya es la segunda vez que me embarca** that's the second time he's let me down *o* left me in the lurch

(**d**) *Ven Fam (embaucar)* to put one over on; **deja ya de intentar embarcarme** stop trying to put one over on me

2 *vi* to board; **pasajeros del vuelo 606, por favor embarquen por la puerta C** passengers on flight 606, please board the plane at gate C *o* proceed through gate C

3 **embarcarse** *vpr* (**a**) *(para viajar)* to board, to embark; **se embarcó en un mercante rumbo a Australia** he boarded a merchant ship *o* he embarked on a merchant ship bound for Australia

(**b**) *(aventurarse)* **embarcarse en algo** to get oneself involved in sth

embargable *adj* subject to embargo

embargado, -a *adj* **e. por la pena/la alegría** overcome with grief/joy

embargar [38] *vt* (**a**) *Der (bienes, casa)* to seize, *Espec* to distrain; *(vehículo)* to impound; *(cuenta bancaria)* to freeze; **le han embargado todos sus bienes** all his property has been seized (**b**) *(sujeto: emoción, pena, alegría)* **la emoción nos embargaba** we were overcome with emotion

embargo 1 *nm* (**a**) *Der (de bienes, casa)* seizure; *(de vehículo)* impounding; *(de cuenta bancaria)* freezing; **sobre su casa pesa un e. judicial** the house is the subject of a seizure order *o* *Espec* distrainment order

(**b**) *Pol (económico)* embargo; **el e. a Cuba de Estados Unidos** the United States' embargo against Cuba; **e. de armamento** arms embargo

2 **sin embargo** *loc conj* (**a**) *(no obstante)* however, nevertheless; **es, sin e., uno de los mejores jugadores del equipo** nevertheless, he's one of the best players in the team; **te engaña y, sin e., te quiere** she cheats on you, and yet she still loves you; **sin e., es un buen chico** he's a good lad though

(**b**) *(por el contrario)* on the other hand; **los ingresos han aumentado y, sin e., los gastos se han mantenido al mismo nivel** income has increased, while on the other hand expenses have remained largely the same

embarque *nm* (**a**) *(de personas)* boarding; *(de mercancías)* loading; **el e. se realizará por la puerta G** the flight will board at gate G (**b**) *Ven Fam (chasco)* let-down

embarrada *nf Andes, RP Fam Br* clanger, *US* boner; **¡qué e.!** talk about putting your foot in it!, how embarrassing!

embarrado, -a *adj (ropa, calzado, terreno)* muddy

embarrancamiento *nm* running aground

embarrancar [60] 1 *vi* (**a**) *(barco)* to run aground (**b**) *(en dificultad)* to get bogged down

2 **embarrancarse** *vpr (barco)* to run aground; *(coche)* to get stuck

embarrar 1 *vt* (**a**) *(con barro)* to cover with mud (**b**) *Méx (untar)* **e. el pan con mantequilla** to spread butter on the bread (**c**) *Am (calumniar, desacreditar)* to smear (**d**) *CAm, Méx, RP* **e. a alguien en algo** *(en asunto turbio)* to get sb mixed up in sth (**e**) *Méx Fam* **e. la mano a alguien** to grease sb's palm (**f**) *Andes, RP Fam* **embarrarla** *(meter la pata)* to put one's foot in it

2 **embarrarse** *vpr* to get covered in mud

embarullar *Fam* 1 *vt* (**a**) *(mezclar)* to mix up; **lo embarullaste todo** you got everything mixed up (**b**) *(confundir)* to mix up; **me has embarullado y he terminado equivocándome** you got me mixed up and I ended up making a mistake

2 **embarullarse** *vpr* (**a**) *(mezclarse)* to get mixed up (**b**) *(confundirse)* to get mixed up, to get into a muddle

embasado, -a *adj Am (jugador)* on base

embate *nm* (**a**) *(de mar)* pounding; **el e. de las olas** the pounding of the waves (**b**) *(de ejército, enemigo)* onslaught, offensive (**c**) *(de ira, celos)* fit

embaucador, -ora 1 *adj* deceitful

2 *nm,f* swindler, confidence trickster

embaucamiento *nm* deception, swindling

embaucar [60] *vt* to deceive, to take in; **no te dejes e.** don't (let yourself) be taken in; **e. a alguien para hacer algo** to trick sb into doing sth

embeber *vt* 1 (**a**) *(absorber)* to soak up (**b**) *(empapar)* to soak

2 **embeberse** *vpr* (**a**) *(ensimismarse)* to become absorbed (**en** in); **se embebió en sus fantasías** he lost himself in his dream world (**b**) *(asimilar)* **embeberse de algo** to immerse oneself in sth; **me embebí de la poesía de Lorca** I immersed myself in Lorca's poetry

embeleco *nm esp Am* deceit, fraud

embelesado, -a *adj* spellbound, entranced; **todos la miraban embelesados** everyone watched her spellbound *o* entranced; **su actuación lo dejó e.** he was entranced by her performance; **quedarse e. (con algo)** to be entranced (by *o* with sth)

embelesamiento *nm* enchantment

embelesar 1 *vt* to captivate; **su belleza lo embelesó** he was enchanted *o* captivated by her beauty

2 **embelesarse** *vpr* to be enchanted *o* captivated (**con** by)

embeleso *nm* (**a**) *(encanto)* enchantment; **ella lo miraba con e.** she watched him entranced *o* spellbound (**b**) *Cuba (planta)* leadwort

embellecedor, -ora 1 *adj* beauty; **tratamiento e.** beauty treatment

2 *nm* (**a**) *(moldura)* **embellecedores** *(de automóvil)* exterior trim; *(en mueble, puerta)* decorative fittings (**b**) *(tapacubos)* hubcap

embellecer [46] 1 *vt* (**a**) *(persona)* to make beautiful (**b**) *(pueblo, edificio)* to make more attractive, to smarten up

2 **embellecerse** *vpr (persona)* to beautify oneself, to make oneself beautiful; **se embellece con los años** she grows more beautiful with the years

embellecimiento *nm* (**a**) *(de persona)* beautification (**b**) *(de pueblo, edificio)* smartening up, beautification

embestida *nf (ataque)* attack; *(de toro)* charge; **la valla cedió ante las embestidas de la multitud** the barrier gave way under the onslaught of the crowd; **derribó la puerta de una e.** he broke down the door with a single charge

embestir [47] 1 *vt* (**a**) *(lanzarse contra) (sujeto: toro, antidisturbios)* to charge; *(sujeto: multitud)* to rush (at) (**b**) *(chocar contra) (sujeto: vehículo, embarcación)* to crash *o* run into; **el coche embistió al árbol** the car crashed *o* smashed into the tree

2 *vi (toro, antidisturbios, multitud)* to charge; **e. contra algo/alguien** *(toro, antidisturbios)* to charge sth/sb; *(multitud)* to rush (at) sth/sb

embetunar *vt (calzado)* to polish, to black

embicharse *vpr Méx Fam* to strip off, *Br* to get one's kit off

embijar *vt CAm, Méx (ensuciar)* to soil, to dirty

embisto *etc ver* **embestir**

emblanquecer [46] *vt* to whiten

emblema *nm* (**a**) *(divisa, distintivo)* emblem, badge (**b**) *(símbolo)* symbol

emblemático, -a *adj* symbolic, emblematic; **una figura emblemática del Renacimiento** a representative figure of the Renaissance

embobamiento *nm* stupefaction

embobar 1 *vt* to fascinate; **miraba embobado la televisión** he was watching television, fascinated; **esa mujer lo tiene embobado** he's crazy *o* potty about that woman

2 **embobarse** *vpr* to be captivated *o* fascinated (**con** by)

embocadura *nf* (**a**) *(de río, puerto)* mouth (**b**) *(de instrumento)* mouthpiece (**c**) *(de vino)* taste

embocar [60] *vt* (**a**) *(encajar)* to enter *(a narrow space)*, to squeeze into; **e. la pelota** *(en golf)* to get the ball in the hole (**b**) *RP Fam (acertar)* **le emboqué a todas las preguntas** I got all his questions right

embochinchar = **bochinchear**

embolado, -a *Fam* 1 *adj RP* (**a**) *(aburrido)* bored, fed up (**b**) *(ofendido) Br* narked, *US* pissed

2 *nm Esp* (**a**) *(lío)* mess, jam; **en menudo e. me he metido** this is a fine mess I've got myself into (**b**) *(mentira)* fib

embolador *nm Col* bootblack, shoeshine boy

embolante *adj RP Fam* boring

embolar 1 *vt* (**a**) **e. un toro** to tip the horns of a bull with wooden balls (**b**) *RP Fam (aburrir)* to bore; **esas películas me embolan** those movies bore me (**c**) *RP Fam (fastidiar)* to annoy; **les embola que les repitas veinte veces lo mismo** the way you say the same thing twenty times gets them *Br* narked *o US* pissed (**d**) *Col (lustrar)* to polish

2 **embolarse** *vpr RP Fam (aburrirse)* to get bored

embolatado, -a *adj Col Fam* in a muddle, mixed-up

embolatar *vt Col Fam* (**a**) *(timar)* to con (**b**) *(enredar)* to mess up, to mix up; **siempre me embolata todos mis papeles** she always messes up all my papers

embole *nm RP Fam* (**a**) *(aburrimiento)* bore; **ese libro que me recomendaste es un e. total** that book you recommended is really boring *o* a real bore

(**b**) *(fastidio)* pain; **¡qué e.!, cancelaron la proyección de la película** what a pain!, they cancelled the showing of the film

(**c**) *(complicación)* drag; **es un e. llegar hasta allá, hay que tomar dos trenes** it's a real drag getting over there, you have to catch two trains

embolia *nf* embolism; **e. cerebral/pulmonar** cerebral/pulmonary embolism

embolinar *vt Chile Fam* to bamboozle; EXPR **embolinarle la perdiz a alguien** to bamboozle sb

embolismar *vt Chile Fam (alborotar)* to stir up

émbolo *nm* (**a**) *Aut* piston (**b**) *(de jeringa, fumigador)* plunger

embolsado *nm* **se encargan del e. de la fruta** they put the fruit in bags

embolsar 1 *vt (meter en bolsas)* to bag, to put in bags; EXPR *Ven Fam Fig* **e. el violín** to be crushed *o* humiliated

2 **embolsarse** *vpr (ganar)* to make, to earn

embonar *vt Andes, Cuba, Méx Fam* (**a**) *(ajustar)* to suit (**b**) *(abonar)* to manure (**c**) *(ensamblar)* to join

emboque *nm Chile (juguete)* cup and ball

emboquillado, -a *adj* filter-tipped

emborrachar 1 *vt* (**a**) *(sujeto: persona)* to get drunk; *(sujeto: bebida)* to make *o* get drunk; **lo emborracharon con champán** they got him drunk on champagne

(**b**) *(pastel)* to soak; **emborrachó el bizcocho en jerez** he soaked the sponge cake in sherry

(**c**) *(sujeto: emoción, aplausos)* **e. a alguien** to go to sb's head; **la alegría lo emborrachaba** he was drunk with joy; **tiene que evitar que el éxito la emborrache** you should make sure success doesn't go to her head

2 **emborracharse** *vpr* (**a**) *(bebiendo)* to get drunk (**de** on); **se**

emborrachó de vino she got drunk on wine
(**b**) *(de emoción, éxito, aplausos)* **emborracharse de algo** to get drunk with sth; **se emborracha de balón** he hogs the ball

emborrascarse [60] *vpr* to cloud over, to turn black

emborronar *vt* (**a**) *(con garabatos)* to scribble on (**b**) *(con borrones)* to smudge (**c**) *(escribir sin cuidado)* to scribble

emboscada *nf* (**a**) *(militar)* ambush; **caer en una e.** to walk into an ambush; **tender una e. (a alguien)** to lay an ambush (for sb) (**b**) *(política, legal)* trap; **caer en una e.** to walk into a trap; **tender una e. (a alguien)** to set a trap (for sb)

emboscar [60] **1** *vt* to ambush
2 emboscarse *vpr* to lie in ambush

embotado, -a *adj (sentidos)* dulled; *(cabeza)* muzzy; **tenía la mente embotada de tanto estudiar** his mind had been dulled by so much studying; **me siento completamente e.** I feel as if my brain won't work any more

embotamiento *nm (de sentidos, mente)* dullness; *(de cabeza)* muzziness

embotar **1** *vt (sentidos, mente)* to dull; *(cabeza)* to make muzzy
2 embotarse *vpr (por ruido)* to get confused

embotellado, -a **1** *adj* (**a**) *(bebida, líquido)* bottled (**b**) *(carretera, calle)* jammed *o* blocked with traffic
2 *nm* bottling

embotelladora *nf* (**a**) *(aparato)* bottling machine (**b**) *(fábrica)* bottling plant

embotellamiento *nm* (**a**) *(de tráfico)* traffic jam (**b**) *(de líquidos)* bottling

embotellar *vt* (**a**) *(líquido)* to bottle (**b**) *(carretera, calle)* to jam, to block; *(tráfico)* to block (**c**) *Fam (equipo contrario)* **embotellaron al rival en su campo** they pinned the other team back in their own half

embozar [14] **1** *vt (rostro)* to cover (up) (**con** with)
2 embozarse *vpr (persona)* to cover one's face (**en** with)

embozo *nm* (**a**) *(de sábana)* turnover (**b**) *(de capa)* shoulder cape

embragar [38] *vi* to engage the clutch

embrague *nm* clutch; **pisar/soltar el e.** to depress/let out the clutch

embravecer [46] **1** *vt* to enrage
2 embravecerse *vpr* (**a**) *(animal, persona)* to become enraged (**b**) *(mar)* to become rough

embravecido, -a *adj (mar, aguas)* rough, stormy

embravecimiento *nm* fury, rage

embrear *vt* to cover with tar

embriagado, -a *adj Formal (borracho)* intoxicated

embriagador, -ora, embriagante *adj* (**a**) *(bebida)* intoxicating (**b**) *(olor, perfume, emoción)* intoxicating, heady; **alcanzó un éxito/poder e.** he reached the dizzy heights of success/power

embriagar [38] **1** *vt* (**a**) *Formal (sujeto: alcohol, bebida)* to inebriate, to intoxicate (**b**) *(sujeto: perfume, aroma, olor)* to intoxicate (**c**) *(sujeto: éxito, poder)* **tanto poder lo había embriagado** having so much power had gone to his head; **la ira la embriagó** she was overcome with anger
2 embriagarse *vpr* (**a**) *Formal (emborracharse)* to become inebriated *o* intoxicated (**con** on *o* with) (**b**) *(extasiarse)* to become intoxicated (**de** with)

embriaguez *nf* (**a**) *Formal (borrachera)* inebriation, intoxication; **conducir en estado de e.** to drive under the influence of alcohol; **lo detuvieron por conducir en estado de e.** he was arrested for drunk-driving (**b**) *(éxtasis)* intoxication

embridar *vt* to put a bridle on, to bridle

embriología *nf* embryology

embrión *nm* (**a**) *Biol* embryo (**b**) *(origen)* **contiene el e. de su teoría** it contains his theory in embryo

embrionario, -a *adj* (**a**) *Biol* embryonic (**b**) *(en desarrollo)* embryonic

embrocar *vi Méx (vestirse)* to put a garment on over one's head

embrollado, -a *adj (asunto, situación)* complicated, confused; *(historia, explicación)* involved, complicated; *(teoría)* complicated

embrollar **1** *vt* (**a**) *(asunto, situación)* to complicate, to confuse; *(historia, explicación)* to make confusing *o* involved; *(persona)* to confuse, to mix up (**b**) *(hilo, ovillo, cuerda)* to tangle up
2 embrollarse *vpr* (**a**) *(asunto, situación)* to get complicated *o* confused; *(historia, explicación)* to get confusing *o* involved; *(teoría)* to get confusing; *(persona)* to get mixed up *o* confused (**b**) *(hilo, ovillo, cuerda)* to get tangled (up)

embrollo *nm* (**a**) *(lío)* mess; **meterse en un e.** to get into a mess; **en menudo e. nos hemos metido** this is a fine mess we've got ourselves into; **la trama de la obra es un verdadero e.** the plot of the play is really complicated *o* confusing (**b**) *(mentira)* lie (**c**) *(de hilos, cuerdas, cables)* tangle

embromado, -a *adj Andes, Carib, RP Fam* (**a**) *(complicado)* tricky; **cuidado con esta máquina, es bastante embromada** careful with that machine, it's quite tricky to get the hang of
(**b**) *(mal)* **¿cómo andas de salud? – sigo bastante e.** how are you? – I'm still feeling pretty rough; **hace años que tiene la espalda embromada** she's had a bad back for years, she's been having problems with her back for years; **la situación económica de todo el mundo está muy embromada** financially, everyone is in a very bad way; **quedó muy e. después de la muerte de su padre** he was in a really bad way after his father died

embromar *Fam* **1** *vt* (**a**) *(tomar el pelo a)* to make fun of, *Br* to take the mickey out of; **la embroman por sus distracciones** they make fun of her *o Br* take the mickey out of her because she's so absent-minded
(**b**) *(fastidiar)* to annoy; **deja de e. a tu hermano** stop annoying your brother
(**c**) *Andes, Carib, RP (engañar)* to rip off, to cheat; **ahí siempre embroman a los clientes** they always rip the customers off there
(**d**) *Andes, Carib, RP (estropear)* to ruin; **la computadora le embromó la vista** the computer ruined his eyesight
(**e**) *Andes, Carib, RP (para expresar sorpresa)* **se ganó la lotería – ¡no me embromes!** he won the lottery – you're kidding!
2 *vi Andes, Carib, RP* (**a**) *(fastidiar)* **¡pará de e.!** stop being such a pest *o* pain!; **parás de llorar ya mismo, ¡qué e.!** stop crying this minute, I'm not having this!
(**b**) *(para expresar sorpresa)* **nos divorciamos – ¡no embromes!** we're getting divorced – you're kidding!
3 embromarse *vpr Andes, Carib, RP* (**a**) *(fastidiarse)* **si no le gusta, que se embrome** if she doesn't like it she can lump it
(**b**) *(estropearse)* **se embromó la espalda cargando peso** he put his back out carrying heavy weights; **la licuadora se embromó hace días** the blender packed up a few days ago

embrujado, -a *adj (persona)* bewitched, under a spell; *(castillo, pueblo)* haunted

embrujamiento *nm* spell; **practicar embrujamientos** to cast spells

embrujar *vt* (**a**) *(hechizar)* to bewitch (**b**) *(atraer, cautivar)* to bewitch

embrujo *nm* (**a**) *(hechizo)* curse, spell (**b**) *(atractivo)* magic, charm

embrutecedor, -ora *adj* stultifying

embrutecer [46] **1** *vt* to stultify, to make dull; **la televisión embrutece a los niños** television stunts children's mental development
2 embrutecerse *vpr* to become stultified

embrutecimiento *nm (acción)* stultification

embuchado, -a **1** *adj* **carne embuchada** cold cured meat
2 *nm (carne)* cold cured meat

embuchar *vt* (**a**) *(embutir) (carne)* to process into sausages; *(tripa)* to stuff with minced meat (**b**) *Culin (ave)* to feed up (**c**) *Fam (engullir)* to wolf down, to gobble up

embudo *nm* (**a**) *(para líquidos)* funnel (**b**) *(en vía, conducto)* blockage; *(en actividad, operación)* bottleneck; *(en líneas telefónicas, Internet)* overload, excess of traffic; **hay un e. en la entrada a la ciudad** there is a bottleneck in the approach to the city

embullado, -a *adj Carib Fam* excited, worked up; **están muy embullados con el viaje a la China** they're really excited about the trip to China

embullar *Carib Fam* **1** *vt (animar)* to get excited *o* worked up
2 embullarse *vpr* to get excited

emburujar *vt Carib (confundir)* to bewilder, to confuse

embuste *nm* lie, fib

embustero, -a **1** *adj (mentiroso)* lying; **¡mira que eres e.!** you lying hound!
2 *nm,f* liar, fibber

embute *nm Méx Fam* bribe, *Br* backhander

embutido *nm* (**a**) *(comida)* cold cured meat (**b**) *(acción)* sausage-making, stuffing (**c**) *Am (entredós)* panel of lace

embutir **1** *vt* (**a**) *(rellenar) (cojín, funda, colchón)* to stuff (**de** with) (**b**) *(meter) (lana, gomaespuma, carne)* to stuff (**en** into) (**c**) *(incrustar)* to inlay; **marfil embutido en madera** wood inlaid with ivory
2 embutirse *vpr Fam* (**a**) *(meterse)* **se embutió en unos pantalones de cuero** he squeezed himself into a pair of leather trousers; **iba embutido en una estrecha cazadora** he was squeezed into a tight

jacket (**b**) *RP Fam (hartarse)* to stuff oneself; **no te embutas, que después te sentís mal** don't stuff yourself with food, you'll only feel ill afterwards

eme *nf Fam Euf* **lo mandé a la e.** I told him where to go; **vete a la e.** *Br* take a running jump, *US* take a hike

emental *nm* Emmental

emergencia *nf* (**a**) *(urgencia)* emergency; **en caso de e.** in case of emergency (**b**) *(brote)* emergence

emergente *adj* emerging

emerger [52] *vi* (**a**) *(salir del agua)* to emerge; **el submarino emergió a la superficie** the submarine surfaced (**b**) *(aparecer)* to appear; **cineastas que emergen con fuerza en el panorama independiente** filmmakers who are making their presence felt on the independent scene

emeritense 1 *adj* of/from Mérida *(Spain)*
2 *nmf* person from Mérida *(Spain)*

emérito, -a 1 *adj* emeritus; **profesor e.** professor emeritus, emeritus professor
2 *nm,f* professor emeritus, emeritus professor

emerjo *etc ver* **emerger**

emerretista 1 *adj* MRTA, = relating to the Tupac Amaru Revolutionary Movement in Peru
2 *nmf* = member or supporter of the MRTA (Tupac Amaru Revolutionary Movement) guerrilla movement in Peru

emético, -a *Farm* 1 *adj* emetic
2 *nm* emetic

emigración *nf* (**a**) *(de animales)* migration (**b**) *(de personas)* emigration ►► *Méx* ***e. golondrina*** temporary labour migration (**c**) *(grupo de personas)* emigrant community

emigrado, -a *nm,f* emigrant

emigrante 1 *adj* emigrant
2 *nmf* emigrant; **emigrantes ilegales** illegal emigrants

emigrar *vi* (**a**) *(persona)* to emigrate (**a** to) (**b**) *(animal)* to migrate (**a** to)

emilio *nm Fam Informát* e-mail (message); **mandar un e. a alguien** to send sb an e-mail (message)

eminencia *nf* (**a**) *(persona eminente)* eminent figure, leading light; **es una e. en neurocirugía** he is an eminent neurosurgeon ►► ***e. gris*** éminence grise (**b**) *(excelencia)* excellence; **la e. de su obra** the outstanding nature of his work (**c**) *(tratamiento)* **Su E.** His Eminence

eminente *adj (excelente)* eminent

eminentemente *adv (principalmente)* predominantly, mainly; **una obra e. divertida** a largely enjoyable play

emir *nm* emir

emirato *nm* (**a**) *(reino)* emirate (**b**) **los Emiratos Árabes Unidos** the United Arab Emirates

emisario, -a 1 *nm,f (legado)* emissary
2 *nm (canal)* outlet

emisión *nf* (**a**) *(de rayos, gas)* emission; *(de energía)* output; **emisiones tóxicas** toxic emissions
(**b**) *(de monedas, sellos, acciones)* issue ►► *Bolsa* ***e. de acciones liberadas*** scrip issue; *Fin* ***e. convertible*** conversion issue; *Bolsa* ***e. con derecho preferente de suscripción*** rights issue; *Bolsa* ***e. gratuita de acciones*** bonus issue; *Fin* ***e. de obligaciones*** debentures issue
(**c**) *(radiotelevisiva) (transmisión)* broadcasting; *(programa)* programme, broadcast; **interrumpimos la e. para comunicarles que...** we interrupt this programme *o* broadcast to inform you that...

emisor, -ora 1 *adj* (**a**) *(de programas de radio o TV)* broadcasting; **nuestro centro e. en Bilbao** our broadcasting centre *o* studios in Bilbao (**b**) *(de energía, rayos, gas)* **una fuente emisora de calor/radiación** a heat/radiation source (**c**) *(de dinero, bonos, acciones)* issuing; **la entidad emisora** the issuing body
2 *nm* (**a**) *Elec (transmisor)* transmitter (**b**) *(fuente) (de partículas, ondas)* source; **un e. de ondas de radio** a source of radio waves (**c**) *Ling (del mensaje)* sender

emisora *nf (de radio)* radio station; **cambiar de e.** to change stations ►► ***e. pirata*** pirate radio station

emitir 1 *vt* (**a**) *(rayos, calor, sonido)* to emit; *(gases, humos, dioxinas)* to emit, to give off (**b**) *(monedas, sellos, acciones)* to issue (**c**) *(programa de radio o TV)* to broadcast (**d**) *(juicio, opinión)* to express; *(veredicto)* to return, to give; *(sentencia)* to pronounce; *(comunicado, manifiesto)* to issue; *(voto)* to cast; **el fallo emitido por el jurado** the jury's decision
2 *vi* to broadcast

emoción *nf* (**a**) *(conmoción, sentimiento)* emotion; **la e. le impedía hablar** he was so emotional he could hardly speak; **temblaba de e.** he was trembling with emotion; **lloraba de e.** he was moved to tears (**b**) *(expectación)* excitement; **¡qué e.!** how exciting!; **seguían el partido con e.** they followed the game with excitement

emocionadamente *adv* emotionally

emocionado, -a *adj* (**a**) *(conmocionado)* moved (**b**) *(expectante)* excited; **estaba e. con el viaje** he was excited about the trip

emocional *adj* emotional

emocionalmente *adv* emotionally

emocionante *adj* (**a**) *(conmovedor)* moving, touching (**b**) *(apasionante)* exciting, thrilling

emocionar 1 *vt* (**a**) *(conmover)* to move (**b**) *(excitar, apasionar)* to thrill, to excite
2 **emocionarse** *vpr* (**a**) *(conmoverse)* to be moved (**con** by) (**b**) *(excitarse, apasionarse)* to get excited

emoliente 1 *adj* emollient
2 *nm* emollient

emolumento *nm Formal* emolument

emoticón, emoticono *nm Informát* smiley

emotivamente *adv* emotionally

emotividad *nf* **no pudo controlar su e.** he couldn't control his emotions *o* feelings; **unas imágenes de gran e.** very moving images; **un reencuentro lleno de e.** a very emotional reunion

emotivo, -a *adj* (**a**) *(persona, reencuentro)* emotional (**b**) *(escena, palabras, imágenes)* moving

empacadora *nf* (**a**) *Agr (máquina)* baler, baling machine (**b**) *Ecuad, Méx (fábrica) (para tarros)* bottling plant; *(para latas)* cannery

empacar [60] 1 *vt* (**a**) *(empaquetar)* to pack (**b**) *Agr* to bale (**c**) *Méx (envasar) (en tarros)* to bottle; *(en latas)* to can, to tin
2 *vi Am* to pack (one's bags)
3 **empacarse** *vpr Fam* (**a**) *Andes, RP (con enojo)* to refuse to budge (**b**) *Méx (engullir)* to scoff

empachado, -a *adj* (**a**) *(indigesto)* **estar e.** to have indigestion (**b**) *Fam (harto)* **estar e. de algo** to be fed up with sth, to be sick and tired of sth (**c**) *(avergonzado)* embarrassed

empachar 1 *vt* (**a**) *(indigestar)* **e. a alguien** to give sb indigestion (**b**) *Fam (hartar)* to make fed up; **la familia siempre termina empachándome** I always end up getting fed up with *o* feeling I've had enough of my family
2 *vi (producir indigestión)* **un alimento que empacha** a food that is hard on the digestion
3 **empacharse** *vpr* (**a**) *(comer demasiado)* to stuff oneself (**de** with); *(sufrir indigestión)* to get indigestion (**b**) *Fam (hartarse)* **empacharse de algo** to have had too much of sth, to overdose on sth; **me he empachado de televisión** I've overdosed on television

empacho *nm* (**a**) *(indigestión)* indigestion; **se agarró un e. de pasteles** she gave herself indigestion eating too many cakes
(**b**) *Fam (hartura)* **tener (un) e. de** to have had one's fill *o* enough of; **tengo e. de tanta fiesta** I've had enough of all these parties, I'm partied out; **se dio un e. de televisión** he overdosed on television
(**c**) *(vergüenza)* embarrassment; **se dirigió a los asistentes sin ningún e.** he addressed the audience without the least embarrassment; **no tuvo e. en contárselo todo a la prensa** he had no qualms about telling everything to the press

empacón, -ona *nm,f Andes, RP Fam* **ser un e.** *(persona)* to be as stubborn as a mule

empadronamiento *nm (por cuestiones administrativas)* registration of residence; *(para votar)* registration on the electoral roll

empadronar 1 *vt* (**a**) *(persona) (por cuestiones administrativas)* to register as a resident; *(para votar)* to register to vote, to enter on the electoral roll (**b**) *Urug (terreno)* to register (**c**) *Chile, Urug (auto)* to license
2 **empadronarse** *vpr (por cuestiones administrativas)* to register as a resident; *(para votar)* to register to vote; **me he empadronado en Madrid** I'm registered to vote in Madrid

empajar 1 *vt Chile (arcilla)* to mix with straw
2 **empajarse** *vpr PRico, Ven (hartarse)* to eat one's fill

empalagar [38] 1 *vt* (**a**) *(sujeto: pastel, dulce, licor)* **los bombones me empalagan** I find chocolates sickly; **este vino me empalaga** this wine is far too sweet for me (**b**) *(sujeto: persona)* to weary, to tire; **me empalaga con tanta cortesía** I find his excessive politeness rather cloying
2 *vi* (**a**) *(pastel, dulces, licor)* to be sickly sweet (**b**) *(persona, estilo, actitud)* to be rather cloying
3 **empalagarse** *vpr* (**a**) *(hartarse)* **empalagarse de** *o* **con** to get sick of (**b**) *(cansarse)* to be weary, to be tired

empalago *nm* (**a**) *(por pastel, dulce, licor)* **me produce e.** I find it sickly sweet; **dulce hasta el e.** so sweet as to be sickly (**b**) *(por persona, actitud, afectación)* **esas películas me producen e.** I find films like that rather sickly

empalagoso, -a *adj* (**a**) *(pastel, dulce, licor)* sickly sweet (**b**) *(persona, estilo, actitud)* cloying; *(obra, película, discurso)* syrupy, saccharine

empalamiento *nm* impalement, impaling

empalar 1 *vt* to impale
 2 **empalarse** *vpr Chile (entumecerse)* to become numb *o* stiff

empalizada *nf (cerca)* fence; *(defensiva)* stockade

empalmar 1 *vt* (**a**) *(tubos, cables, cuerdas)* to connect, to join
 (**b**) *(película, foto)* to splice
 (**c**) *(planes, ideas, temas)* to link (up); **empalmamos la juerga del sábado con el desayuno del domingo** the night out on Saturday went on into breakfast on Sunday; **empalmaré las vacaciones con el puente de mayo** I'll take my *Br* holiday *o US* vacation so it combines with the long weekend in May; **el equipo ha empalmado cinco derrotas seguidas** the team has had five consecutive defeats
 (**d**) *(en fútbol)* to volley; **empalmó de cabeza el pase** he got his head to the pass
 2 *vi* (**a**) *(autocares, trenes)* to connect (**con** with)
 (**b**) *(carreteras)* to link *o* join (up) (**con** with)
 (**c**) *(sucederse)* to follow on (**con** from)
 (**d**) *Esp Fam (trasnochar)* **anoche salimos de juerga y hemos empalmado** we went out on the town last night and we carried on till this morning
 3 **empalmarse** *vpr Esp Vulg (persona)* to get a hard-on; **se le empalmó** he got a hard-on

empalme *nm* (**a**) *(entre tubos, cables)* connection; **hacer un e. entre dos tubos/cables** to connect two pipes/cables (**b**) *(de líneas férreas, carreteras)* junction (**c**) *(de película)* splice, splicing

empanada *nf (individual)* pasty; *(grande)* pie; **e. de atún** tuna pasty/pie; EXPR *Esp Fam* **tener una e. mental** to be in a real muddle, not to be able to think straight ►► ***e. gallega*** = pie typical of Galicia, with a seafood or meat filling

empanadilla *nf* small pasty

empanado, -a *adj* breaded, covered in breadcrumbs

empanar, *Méx* **empanizar** *vt Culin* to coat in egg and breadcrumbs

empanizado, -a *adj Méx* breaded, covered in breadcrumbs

empanizar = **empanar**

empantanado, -a *adj* (**a**) *(inundado)* flooded (**b**) *(atascado)* bogged down; **estoy e. con la tesis** I'm stuck *o* I can't see the way forward with my thesis; **las obras del hospital han quedado empantanadas** building work at the hospital has got held up

empantanar 1 *vt* to flood
 2 **empantanarse** *vpr* (**a**) *(inundarse)* to be flooded *o* waterlogged (**b**) *(atascarse)* to get bogged down

empañado, -a *adj* (**a**) *(cristal, ventana, espejo)* misted up, steamed up; *(metal)* tarnished; **tenía los ojos empañados por las lágrimas** his eyes were misted over with tears (**b**) *(reputación, imagen, historial)* tarnished

empañamiento *nm* (**a**) *(de cristal, ventana, espejo)* misting up, steaming up (**b**) *(de reputación, imagen, historial)* tarnishing

empañar 1 *vt* (**a**) *(cristal, ventana, espejo)* to mist up, to steam up; **las lágrimas empañaban sus ojos** his eyes misted over with tears (**b**) *(reputación, imagen, historial)* to tarnish; *(felicidad)* to spoil, to cloud
 2 **empañarse** *vpr* (**a**) *(cristal, ventana, espejo)* to mist up, to steam up (**b**) *(reputación, imagen, historial)* to become tarnished; *(felicidad)* to be spoiled

empapado, -a *adj* soaked, drenched; **iba e. en sudor** he was soaked *o* drenched in sweat

empapar 1 *vt* (**a**) *(humedecer)* to soak; **empapa la bayeta bien de** *o* **en agua** soak the cloth in plenty of water
 (**b**) *(absorber)* to soak up
 (**c**) *(calar)* to saturate, to drench; **la lluvia me empapó** I got soaked *o* drenched in the rain; **el sudor le empapaba la frente** his forehead was drenched in sweat
 2 **empaparse** *vpr* (**a**) *(mojarse mucho) (persona)* to get soaked *o* drenched; *(objeto, lugar, prenda)* to get soaked *o* soaking wet; **me he empapado los zapatos** I've got my shoes soaked
 (**b**) *(absorber)* **empaparse de algo** to soak sth up; **deje que el pescado se empape bien de la salsa** let the fish soak up the sauce thoroughly
 (**c**) *(enterarse bien)* **empaparse de** *o* **en** to become steeped in; **se empapó de ideas nacionalistas** he became steeped in nationalist ideas; **se empapó del tema antes de dar la conferencia** he immersed himself in *o* got to know all about the subject before giving the talk; EXPR *Fam* **¡para que te empapes!** so there!, stick that in your pipe and smoke it!

empapelado *nm* (**a**) *(acción)* papering (**b**) *(papel)* wallpaper

empapelador, -ora *nm,f* paperhanger

empapelar *vt* (**a**) *(pared, cuarto)* to paper, to wallpaper (**b**) *Esp Fam (delincuente, infractor) Br* to do, *US* to bust; **lo empapelaron por evadir impuestos** he was *Br* had up *o Br* done *o US* busted for tax evasion

empaque *nm* (**a**) *(seriedad, solemnidad) (de ocasión)* solemnity; *(de persona)* presence (**b**) *Andes, Carib, Méx (descaro)* nerve, cheek (**c**) *Méx (envase)* packaging (**d**) *RP (en tienda)* collection counter (**e**) *Méx Tec (arandela)* seal; *(de llave)* washer

empaquetado *nm* packaging

empaquetador, -ora *nm,f* packer

empaquetar 1 *vt* (**a**) *(envolver)* to pack, to package (**b**) *RP Fam (engañar)* to rip off; **eso no cuesta más de £100, te empaquetaron** that doesn't cost more than £100, you were ripped off
 2 **empaquetarse** *vpr RP* to dress up; **acá la gente se empaqueta mucho para ir al teatro** people here get all dressed up to go to the theatre

emparamado, -a *adj Col, Ven Fam* soaked, drenched

emparamar *Col, Ven Fam* 1 *vt* to soak, to drench
 2 **emparamarse** *vpr* to get soaked *o* drenched

emparchado, -a *adj Am Fam* patched up; **no quiero éste todo e., me voy a comprar uno nuevo** I don't want that patched up old thing, I'm going to buy a new one

emparchar *Am Fam* 1 *vt (ropa, vela)* to patch; **ella trata de e. la situación, pero se nota que no se llevan bien** she's trying to patch things up, but you can see they don't get on
 2 *vi* **no empecemos a e., es mejor comprar uno nuevo** don't let's start trying to patch it up, it's better to buy a new one

empardar *vt RP (igualar)* to match up to; **ninguno de sus otros libros emparda a este** none of her other books matches up to this one

emparedado, -a 1 *adj* walled up
 2 *nm* sandwich

emparedamiento *nm* walling up

emparedar *vt* to wall up

emparejamiento *nm* pairing

emparejar 1 *vt* (**a**) *(juntar en pareja) (personas)* to pair off; *(zapatos, calcetines)* to match (up)
 (**b**) *(nivelar)* to make level; **hay que e. los bajos del pantalón** the *Br* turn-ups *o US* cuffs on the trousers have to be made the same length
 2 *vi* to be a match
 3 **emparejarse** *vpr* (**a**) *(personas)* to find a partner; **están en edad de emparejarse** they're old enough to go out with boys/girls; **los invitados se emparejaron para el baile** the guests paired off for the dance
 (**b**) *(nivelarse)* to catch up, to draw level; **se emparejó con el corredor británico a la salida de la curva** he drew level with the British runner coming out of the bend
 (**c**) *Méx* **emparejarse con algo** *(conseguir)* to get hold of sth

emparentado, -a *adj* (**a**) *(persona)* related (**con** to); **está emparentada con una prima mía** she's related to a cousin of mine (**b**) *(asunto, problema)* related (**con** to)

emparentar [3] *vi (al casarse)* to become related; **e. con** *(una familia, clase social)* to marry into; *(una persona)* to become related to

emparrado *nm* = vines trained on an overhead frame to provide shade in a garden

emparrar *vt* to train

empastado, -a *adj Chile, Méx* turfed

empastar 1 *vt (diente)* to fill
 2 **empastarse** *vpr Chile* to become overgrown with weeds

empaste *nm (de diente)* filling; **hacerle un e. a alguien** to put a filling in sb's tooth

empatado, -a *adj* (**a**) *(partido)* drawn; *(equipos)* level; **los dos equipos van empatados en primer lugar** the two are tying for first place; **van empatados a uno en el descanso** at half-time the score is one all (**b**) *(en elecciones, votación)* equally placed, tied

empatar 1 *vi* (**a**) *(en competición)* to tie; *(en partido)* to draw; **González empató en el minuto treinta** González equalized in the thirtieth minute; **e. a cero** to draw nil-nil; **e. a dos/tres (goles)** to draw two/three all; **e. en un hoyo** *(en golf)* to half a hole (**b**) *(en elecciones, votación)* to tie, to get the same number of votes (**c**) *Andes, Ven (enlazar, empalmar)* to join, to link

2 *vt (partido, eliminatoria) (como resultado final)* to draw; **empataron el partido a dos minutos del final** they levelled the scores *o* equalized two minutes from the end

3 **empatarse** *vpr Ven Fam* to get together; **mira bien con quién te empatas** be careful who you go out with

empate *nm* (**a**) *(en competición)* tie; *(en partido)* draw; **un e. a cero/dos** a goalless/two-two draw; **el gol del e.** the equalizer; **el encuentro terminó con e.** the match ended in a draw; **un gol en el último minuto deshizo el e.** a goal in the last minute broke the stalemate

(**b**) *(en elecciones)* tie; **los sondeos arrojan un e. técnico entre ambos candidatos** polls are indicating a dead heat between the two candidates

(**c**) *Andes, Ven (de cables)* connection

(**d**) *Ven Fam* relationship; **cuando llevaban dos años de e. decidieron casarse** when they'd been going out for two years they decided to get married

(**e**) *Ven Fam* boyfriend, *f* girlfriend

empatía *nf* empathy

empático, -a *adj* empathetic

empatizar [14] *vi* **e. con alguien** to empathize with sb

empavar 1 *vt* (**a**) *Perú (burlarse de)* to tease (**b**) *Ecuad (irritar)* to annoy, to irritate (**c**) *Ven Fam (dar mala suerte a)* to jinx, to bring bad luck to; **no digas eso, me vas a e.** don't say that, you'll bring me bad luck

2 **empavarse** *vpr* (**a**) *Perú (avergonzarse)* to become embarrassed (**b**) *Ecuad (irritarse)* to get annoyed *o* irritated

empavonar 1 *vt Col, PRico (superficie)* to grease

2 **empavonarse** *vpr CAm* to dress up

empecinado, -a *adj* (**a**) *(tozudo)* stubborn (**b**) *(empeñado)* **estar e. en hacer algo** to be determined to do sth, to be set on doing sth

empecinamiento *nm* (**a**) *(tozudez)* stubbornness (**b**) *(empeño)* determination

empecinarse *vpr (obstinarse)* to dig one's heels in; **e. en hacer algo** to stubbornly insist on (doing) sth; **se empecinó en que tenía que viajar en tren** he was quite insistent that he had to go by train

empedar *Méx, RP muy Fam* 1 *vt* to get plastered *o Br* pissed

2 **empedarse** *vpr* to get plastered *o Br* pissed

empedernido, -a *adj (bebedor, fumador)* heavy; *(criminal, jugador)* hardened; *(solterón, solterona)* confirmed; **un lector e. de novelas de terror** a compulsive reader of horror stories

empedrado *nm* paving

empedrar [3] *vt* to pave

empegostado, -a *adj Ven Fam* sticky; **¿por qué siempre te dan los vasos empegostados?** why do they always give you glasses with sticky fingerprints all over them?

empegostar *Ven Fam* 1 *vt* to get all sticky

2 **empegostarse** *vpr* to get in a sticky mess

empeine *nm (de pie, zapato)* instep

empellón *nm* shove; **abrirse paso a empellones** to get through by pushing and shoving; **echar a alguien a empellones** to remove sb by force

empelotarse *vpr Andes, Cuba, Méx muy Fam (desnudarse)* to strip off

empeñado, -a *adj* (**a**) *(en prenda)* in pawn

(**b**) *(endeudado)* in debt; EXPR **estar e. hasta las cejas** to be up to one's eyes in debt

(**c**) *(obstinado)* determined; **estar e. en algo** to be set on sth; **estaba empeñada en una bici nueva** she had her heart set on a new bike; **estar e. en hacer algo** to be determined to do sth; **el gobierno está e. en acabar con el desempleo** the government is determined to eliminate unemployment; **estaba e. en que viéramos su casa** he was determined that we should see his house

empeñar 1 *vt* (**a**) *(joyas, bienes)* to pawn

(**b**) *(palabra)* to give; **empeñó su palabra en lograr un consenso** he gave his word that he would reach an agreement

2 **empeñarse** *vpr* (**a**) *(obstinarse)* to insist; **si te empeñas, te contaré la verdad** if you insist, I'll tell you the truth; **empeñarse en (hacer) algo** *(estar decidido a)* to be set on (doing) sth; *(persistir)* to insist on (doing) sth; **cuando se empeña en una cosa** when she is set on something; **se empeñó en que nos quedáramos** he insisted that we stay; **no sé por qué te empeñas en hablar de ello** I don't know why you insist on talking about it

(**b**) *(endeudarse)* to get into debt; EXPR **se empeñaron hasta las cejas** they got themselves up to their eyes in debt

empeño *nm* (**a**) *(de joyas, bienes)* pawning; **casa de empeño(s)** pawnshop

(**b**) *(obstinación)* determination; **no entiendo ese e. tuyo por justificarlo todo** I don't understand this insistence of yours on justifying everything; **con e.** persistently, tenaciously; **todo su e. es poder viajar** the one thing she wants is to be able to travel; **tener e. en hacer algo** to be determined to do sth

(**c**) *(afán, esfuerzo)* effort(s); **en su e. por ayudar, lo que hacía era estorbar** in his efforts to help, all he did was get in the way; **no cejaremos en nuestro e. (de...)** we will not flag in our efforts (to...); **puso gran e. en sus estudios** she put a lot of effort into her studies; **poner e. en hacer algo** to make a great effort to do sth, to take pains to do sth; **debes poner más e. en aprobar** you should make more of an effort to pass

(**d**) *(intento)* **morir en el e.** to die in the attempt

empeñoso, -a *adj Andes, RP* persevering, tenacious

empeoramiento *nm (de tiempo)* deterioration; *(de conflicto)* worsening; **el enfermo sufrió un e.** the patient's condition deteriorated

empeorar 1 *vi (enfermo, tiempo, conflicto)* to get worse, to deteriorate

2 *vt* to make worse; **sólo consiguió e. las cosas** she only managed to make things worse

empequeñecer [46] 1 *vt (quitar importancia a)* to diminish; *(en una comparación)* to overshadow, to dwarf; **el alto nivel de abstención empequeñece un tanto su victoria** the high level of abstention rather detracts from his achievement in winning

2 **empequeñecerse** *vpr* (**a**) *(sentirse inferior)* **empequeñecerse (ante)** to feel small *o* insignificant (beside) (**b**) *(ser inferior)* **ante líder como él los demás parecen empequeñecerse** beside such a leader the others seem smaller

empequeñecimiento *nm* (**a**) *(de tamaño)* diminishing, reduction (**b**) *(de importancia)* overshadowing

emperador *nm* (**a**) *(título)* emperor (**b**) *(pez espada)* swordfish (**c**) *Urug (sandwich)* toasted cheese and ham sandwich

emperatriz *nf* empress

emperejilar *Fam* 1 *vt* to doll *o* tart up

2 **emperejilarse** *vpr* to doll *o* tart oneself up

emperifollado, -a *adj Fam* dolled up, done up to the nines

emperifollar *Fam* 1 *vt* to doll *o* tart up

2 **emperifollarse** *vpr* to doll *o* tart oneself up

empero *adv Formal (sin embargo)* nevertheless, nonetheless; **yo, e., sigo teniendo fe en él** I nevertheless *o* nonetheless continue to have faith in him

emperramiento *nm Fam* (**a**) *(obstinación)* stubbornness (**b**) *(rabia)* rage, anger

emperrarse *vpr Fam* **e. con** *o* **en algo** to be dead set on sth; **e. en hacer algo** to be dead set on doing sth; **se emperró en que tenía que ir él mismo** he wouldn't have it any other way but that he had to go himself

empertigar [38] *vt Chile* to yoke

EMPEZAR [17] 1 *vt* to begin, to start; **empezó la conferencia dando la bienvenida a los asistentes** she began *o* started her speech by welcoming everyone there; **todavía no hemos empezado el colegio** we still haven't started school; **empecé el libro, pero no lo conseguí acabar** I started (reading) the book, but didn't manage to finish it; **hemos empezado la tarta** we've started the cake; **empezaron otra botella de vino** they started *o* opened another bottle of wine

2 *vi* to begin, to start **(a/por** to/by); **la clase empieza a las diez** the class begins *o* starts at ten o'clock; **¿a qué hora empieza el partido?** what time does the game start?; **el concierto empezó tarde** the concert started late; **la película empieza con una escena muy violenta** the film begins with a very violent scene; **tuvieron que e. de nuevo** they had to start again; **el aprender a nadar, todo es e.** with swimming, getting started is half the battle; **¡no empieces!, ¡ya hemos discutido este tema lo suficiente!** don't you start, we've spent long enough on this subject already!; **¡ya empezamos con el vecino y su música!** here we go again with our neighbour and his music!; **al e. la reunión** when the meeting started *o* began; **al e. resulta un poco difícil** it's quite hard at first *o* to begin with; **en noviembre empezó a hacer frío** it started getting colder in November; **empezó pidiendo disculpas por su retraso** she started *o* began by apologizing for being late; **e. por: empieza por el salón, yo haré la cocina** you start on the living room, I'll do the kitchen; **empieza por aflojar los tornillos** first, loosen the screws, start *o* begin by loosening the screws; **empieza por portarte bien, y ya hablaremos** first you start behaving well, then we'll talk; **para e.: para e., sopa** I'd like soup for starters *o* to start

with; **para e., habrá que comprar los billetes** first of all *o* to start with, we'll have to buy the tickets; **no me gusta, para e., es demasiado pequeño** I don't like it, it's too small to start with

empicharse *vpr Ven Fam* to go bad, *Br* to go off

empiece 1 *ver* **empezar**
2 *nm Fam* beginning, start

empiedro *etc ver* **empedrar**

empiezo *etc ver* **empezar**

empilchar *RP Fam* 1 *vi (vestir bien)* to dress smartly, to dress to kill
2 **empilcharse** *vpr (emperifollarse)* to doll *o* tart oneself up

empinado, -a *adj (calle, cuesta)* steep

empinar 1 *vt* (**a**) *(inclinar)* to tip up (**b**) *(levantar)* to raise; EXPR *Fam* **e. el codo** to bend the elbow
2 *vi Fam (beber alcohol)* to booze, to have a few drinks
3 **empinarse** *vpr* (**a**) *(animal)* to stand up on its hind legs (**b**) *(persona)* to stand on tiptoe (**c**) *(calle, cuesta)* to get steeper (**d**) *muy Fam (pene)* **se le empinó** he got a hard-on

empingorotado, -a *adj Fam Pey* stuck-up, posh

empipada *nf Chile, Ecuad, PRico* blow-out

empíricamente *adv* empirically

empírico, -a 1 *adj* empirical
2 *nm,f* empiricist

empirismo *nm* empiricism

empistolado, -a *nm Méx* gunman, *f* gunwoman

emplasto *nm* (**a**) *Med* poultice (**b**) *Fam (pegote, masa)* sticky *o* gooey mess

emplazamiento *nm* (**a**) *(ubicación)* location ►► ***e. arqueológico*** archaeological site (**b**) *Der* summons *(singular)*

emplazar [14] *vt* (**a**) *(situar)* to locate; *(armamento)* to position; *(misiles)* to site; *(tropas)* to post, to station; **la basílica está emplazada en el casco viejo** the basilica is located *o* situated in the old part of town
(**b**) *(citar)* to summon; *Der* to summons; **me emplazó a una reunión** he summoned *o* called me to a meeting; **fue emplazado para declarar ante el tribunal** he was summonsed to give evidence in court

empleado, -a *nm,f (asalariado)* employee; *(de banco, oficina)* clerk; **está de e. en una tienda/fábrica de ropa** he works in a clothes shop/ clothing factory; **consultaron la propuesta con los empleados** they discussed the proposal with the staff; **sólo empleados y personal autorizado** *(en letrero)* staff and authorized personnel only ►► ***e. de banca*** bank clerk; ***e. del estado*** civil servant; ***empleada de hogar*** maid; *Méx* ***e. de planta*** permanent employee; ***e. público*** public employee

empleador, -ora *nm,f* employer

emplear 1 *vt* (**a**) *(usar) (objeto, inteligencia, energía)* to use; *(medios, recursos, términos)* to use, to employ; *(tiempo, dinero)* to spend; **emplea unos métodos poco ortodoxos** he uses *o* employs rather unorthodox methods; **ahí el subjuntivo está mal empleado** the subjunctive is used incorrectly there; **empleó mucho tiempo en leer el libro** he took a long time to read the book; EXPR **dar algo por bien empleado: dio por bien empleado el esfuerzo** he thought it had been well worth the effort; **si lo consigo, daré por bien empleado el tiempo** if I manage to do it, I'll regard it as time well spent; EXPR *Esp* **lo tiene** *o* **le está bien empleado** he deserves it, it serves him right
(**b**) *(contratar) (sujeto: empresario, empresa)* to employ
2 **emplearse** *vpr* (**a**) *(colocarse)* to find a job; **se empleó de camarero** he found a job as a waiter
(**b**) *(usarse)* to be used; **una herramienta que se emplea en minería** a tool used in mining
(**c**) *(esforzarse)* **emplearse a fondo** to do one's utmost

empleo *nm* (**a**) *(uso)* use; **modo de e.** instructions for use
(**b**) *(trabajo)* employment; **la precariedad del e.** job insecurity ►► ***e. comunitario*** community service; ***e. juvenil*** youth employment, ***e. temporal*** temporary employment (**c**) *(puesto)* job; **un e. de oficinista** an office job; **estar sin e.** to be out of work; **estar suspendido de e. y sueldo** to be suspended without pay (**d**) *Mil* rank

emplomado, -a 1 *adj* leaded
2 *nm (de ventana)* leading

emplomadura *nf RP (de diente)* filling

emplomar *vt* (**a**) *(cubrir con plomo)* to lead (**b**) *RP (diente)* to fill

emplumar 1 *vt* (**a**) *(como adorno)* to adorn with feathers (**b**) *(como castigo)* to tar and feather (**c**) *Esp Fam (delincuente, infractor) Br* to do (**d**) *Col Fam* **emplumarlas** *(huir)* to make oneself scarce
2 *vi Andes, PRico (huir)* to flee, to take flight

empobrecer [46] 1 *vt* (**a**) *(en recursos, riqueza, patrimonio)* to impoverish (**b**) *(en calidad, valor, importancia)* to impoverish, to devalue
2 **empobrecerse** *vpr* to get poorer

empobrecido, -a *adj* (**a**) *(en recursos, riqueza, patrimonio)* impoverished (**b**) *(en calidad, valor, importancia)* impoverished, devalued

empobrecimiento *nm* (**a**) *(en recursos, riqueza, patrimonio)* impoverishment (**b**) *(en calidad, valor, importancia)* impoverishment, devaluation; **un e. de los contenidos televisivos** a reduction in quality of programme content on television

empollado, -a *adj Esp Fam* **está muy empollada en jardinería** she knows a lot about gardening

empollar 1 *vt* (**a**) *(huevo)* to incubate (**b**) *Esp Fam (estudiar)* to bone up on, *Br* to swot up (on)
2 *vi Fam Br* to swot, *US* to grind
3 **empollarse** *vpr Fam* to bone up (on), *Br* to swot up (on)

empollón, -ona *Esp Fam* 1 *adj* **ser e.** to be *Br* swotty *o US* a grind
2 *nm,f Br* swot, *US* grind

empolvado, -a *adj* (**a**) *(muebles, libros)* dusty, covered in dust (**b**) *(rostro)* powdered

empolvar 1 *vt (rostro, peluca)* to powder
2 **empolvarse** *vpr* (**a**) *(muebles, libros)* to get dusty (**b**) *(rostro)* to powder one's face; **voy a empolvarme la nariz** I'm going to powder my nose

emponchado, -a *adj Andes, RP (con poncho)* wearing a poncho

emponchar 1 *vt* to wrap in a poncho
2 **emponcharse** *vpr Andes, RP* to wrap oneself in a poncho

emponzoñar *vt* (**a**) *(aguas, persona)* to poison (**b**) *(relación, ambiente)* to poison

emporcar [69] 1 *vt* to soil, to dirty
2 **emporcarse** *vpr* to become soiled *o* dirty

emporio *nm* (**a**) *Hist (centro comercial)* centre of commerce (**b**) *(centro)* centre; **Detroit era el e. de la música negra** Detroit was the centre for black music; **es un importante e. cultural** it's an important cultural centre; **creó un auténtico e. financiero** he built a veritable financial empire

emporrado, -a *adj Esp Fam* stoned *(on cannabis)*

emporrarse *vpr Esp Fam* to get stoned *(on cannabis)*

empotrado, -a *adj (armario, mueble)* fitted, built-in

empotrar 1 *vt* (**a**) *(armario, mueble)* to build in; **empotraron el armario en la pared** they built the wardrobe into the wall (**b**) *(vehículo)* to smash; **empotró la moto en un árbol** he smashed the motorbike into a tree
2 **empotrarse** *vpr (vehículo)* **la moto se empotró contra** *o* **en la pared** the motorbike smashed into the wall

empozado, -a *adj Andes, RP, Ven (agua)* stagnant

empozarse *vpr Andes, RP, Ven* to accumulate in pools; **el problema es que aquí se empoza el agua** the problem is that the water gathers *o* accumulates here

emprendedor, -ora *adj* enterprising; **se necesita ejecutivo dinámico y e.** *(en anuncio de trabajo)* dynamic and enterprising executive required

emprender *vt (trabajo, tarea, proyecto)* to undertake; *(viaje)* to set off on; *(ataque, ofensiva)* to launch; **e. acciones judiciales contra alguien** to initiate legal proceedings against sb; **la prensa emprendió una campaña contra él** the press launched a campaign against him; **e. el vuelo** to fly off; **¿a qué hora emprenderás la marcha?** what time are you setting off?; **al oír la sirena emprendieron la huida** when they heard the siren they took flight; **el Papa emprendió viaje a Oriente Medio** the Pope left on a trip to the Middle East; EXPR **emprenderla con alguien: la emprendió con él sin provocación alguna** she started laying into him without any provocation; **la emprendió a puñetazos con su hermano** he started punching his brother

emprendimiento *nm CSur* undertaking, initiative

empresa *nf* (**a**) *(sociedad)* company; **pequeña y mediana e.** small and medium-sized business; **prohibido fijar carteles: responsable la e. anunciadora** *(en letrero)* stick no bills: advertisers will be held liable ►► ***e. común*** joint venture; ***e. conjunta*** joint venture; ***e. filial*** subsidiary; ***e. funeraria*** undertaker's; ***e. júnior*** junior enterprise, = firm set up and run by business studies students; ***e. libre, libre e.*** free enterprise; ***e. matriz*** parent company; ***e. mixta*** mixed company; ***e. privada*** private company; ***e. pública*** public sector firm; ***e. punto com*** dot.com (company); ***e. de seguridad*** security firm; ***e. de servicio público*** public utility, *US* public service corporation; ***e. de servicios*** service company; ***e. de trabajo temporal*** temping agency; ***e. de transportes*** haulage firm; *Urug* ***e. unipersonal*** small

business *(with no more than 2 or 3 employees)*
(b) *(dirección)* management; **las negociaciones con la e.** the negotiations with management
(c) *(acción)* enterprise, undertaking; **se embarcó en una peligrosa e.** he embarked on a risky enterprise *o* undertaking

empresariado *nm* employers

empresarial 1 *adj (estructura, crisis, líder)* business; **estudios empresariales** management *o* business studies; **organización e.** employers' organization
2 **empresariales** *nfpl Esp* business studies

empresario, -a *nm,f* (a) *(patrono)* employer; *(hombre, mujer de negocios)* businessman, *f* businesswoman; **las organizaciones de empresarios** employers' organizations; **los pequeños empresarios** owners of small businesses, small businesspeople ►► ***e. individual*** sole *Br* trader *o US* proprietor (b) *(de teatro)* impresario

empréstito *nm Fin* debenture loan

empuerca *etc ver* **emporcar**

empuerque *etc ver* **emporcar**

empujar 1 *vt* (a) *(puerta)* to push (open); *(persona, vehículo, objeto)* to push; *(palanca)* to push (down on); **empújame un poquito** give me a little push, push me a bit; **las olas empujaron el cuerpo hasta la orilla** the waves carried the body to the shore
(b) *(presionar)* to push; *(estimular)* to push, to encourage; **ella me empujó a mentir** she pushed me into lying; **a ese niño habría que empujarlo un poco** that child needs to be pushed a bit; **¿qué le empujaría a hacer una cosa así?** what would drive him to do a thing like that?; **verse empujado a hacer algo** to find oneself forced *o* having to do sth
2 *vi* to push; **¡eh, sin e.!** hey, stop pushing!; **e.** *(en letrero)* push; **las nuevas generaciones de abogados vienen empujando con fuerza** the new generation of lawyers is making its presence felt

empuje *nm* (a) *(presión)* pressure (b) *(energía)* energy, drive (c) *Fís (impulso)* thrust (d) *Arquit* thrust

empujón *nm* (a) *(empellón)* shove, push; **cerró la puerta de un e.** he pushed the door shut; **dar un e. a alguien** to give sb a shove *o* push; **a empujones: abrirse paso a empujones** to shove *o* push one's way through; **bajaban del tren a empujones** they were pushing and shoving their way off the train; **sus captores los trataban a empujones** their captors pushed them around
(b) *(avance)* **hay que darle un buen e. al trabajo** we need to get well ahead with the work; **dar un último e. a algo** to make one last effort with sth

empujoncito *nm* prod; **dar un e. a alguien** to give sb a prod; **hay que darle un e.** he needs a bit of prodding

empuntar 1 *vt* (a) *Col (encaminar, encarrilar)* to give directions to (b) *Col Fam* **empuntárselas** *(irse)* to scram
2 **empuntarse** *vpr Ven* to dig one's heels in

empuñadura *nf (de paraguas, bastón)* handle; *(de espada, puñal)* hilt; *(de hacha)* handle, haft; *(de látigo)* handle; *(de raqueta)* handle, grip

empuñar 1 *vt (bastón, paraguas)* to take hold of, to grasp; *(espada, hacha, látigo)* to take up; *(raqueta)* to hold, to grip; **avanzaba empuñando la espada** he advanced, sword in hand
2 *vi Chile (mano)* to make a fist

emputecer *vt esp RP muy Fam (fastidiar, hastiar)* to piss off

emputecido, -a *adj esp RP muy Fam* **estar e.** to have turned really nasty

emú *nm* emu

emulación *nf* (a) *(imitación)* emulation (b) *Informát* emulation ►► ***e. de terminal*** terminal emulation

emulador *nm Informát* emulator

emular *vt* (a) *(imitar)* to emulate (b) *Informát* to emulate

emulgente *nm* emulsifier

émulo, -a *nm,f Formal* imitator; **tiene ya un é. en su propio hijo** her own son now wants to follow in her footsteps

emulsificante *nm* emulsifier

emulsión *nf* emulsion ►► ***e. fotográfica*** photographic emulsion

emulsionante *nm* emulsifier

emulsionar *vt* to emulsify

EN *nm (abrev de* **Encuentro Nacional**) = Paraguayan political party

---

EN *prep* (a) *(lugar) (en el interior de)* in; *(sobre la superficie de)* on; *(en un punto concreto de)* at; **viven en la capital** they live in the capital; **tiene el dinero en el banco** he keeps his money in the bank; **en la mesa/el plato** on the table/plate; **en casa/el trabajo** at home/work; **en la pared** on the wall; **en el primer piso** on the first floor; **tenemos una casa en el campo** we have a house in the country; **en el primer capítulo** in the first chapter; **viven en el número 40** they live at number 40
(b) *(dirección)* into; **el avión cayó en el mar** the plane fell into the sea; **entraron en la habitación** they came/went into the room; **la llave no entra en la cerradura** the key won't fit in *o* into the lock
(c) *(tiempo) (mes, año)* in; *(día)* on; **nació en 1953/marzo** she was born in 1953/March; **en el año 36** in 1936; **en Nochebuena** on Christmas Eve; **en Navidades** at Christmas; **en aquella época** at that time, in those days; **en mis tiempos** in my day; **en esta ocasión** on this occasion; **en un par de días** in a couple of days; **en primavera/otoño** in (the) spring/autumn; *Am* **en la mañana/tarde** in the morning/afternoon; *Am* **en la noche** at night; *Am* **ayer salimos en la noche** we went out last night; **no he descansado en toda la noche** I didn't sleep all night; **lo leí en tres horas** I read it in three hours
(d) *(medio de transporte)* by; **ir en tren/coche/avión/barco** to go by train/car/plane/boat; **dimos un paseo en el coche de Eva** we went for a ride in Eva's car
(e) *(modo)* in; **en voz baja** in a low voice; **una televisión en blanco y negro** a black-and-white television; **lo dijo en inglés** she said it in English; **pagar en libras** to pay in pounds; **todo se lo gasta en ropa** he spends everything on clothes; **salió a abrir en pijama** he came to the door in his pyjamas; **vive en la miseria** she lives in poverty; **está en buenas condiciones** it's in good condition; **en la oscuridad no se ve nada** you can't see anything in the dark; **un edificio en construcción** a building under construction
(f) *(precio, cantidad)* in; **las ganancias se calculan en millones** profits are calculated in millions; **te lo dejo en 5.000** I'll let you have it for 5,000; **la inflación aumentó en un 10 por ciento** inflation increased by 10 percent; **las reservas de agua disminuyeron en una tercera parte** water reserves fell by a third
(g) *(tema)* **es un experto en la materia** he's an expert on the subject; **es doctor en medicina** he's a doctor of medicine
(h) *(causa)* from; **lo detecté en su forma de hablar** I could tell from the way he was speaking; **se lo noté en su mirada** I could see it in her eyes
(i) *(finalidad, objetivo)* **un concierto en ayuda de...** a concert in aid of...; **intervenir en favor de los necesitados** to take measures to help the poor
(j) *(materia)* in, made of; **en seda** in silk
(k) *(cualidad)* in terms of; **lo supera en inteligencia** she is more intelligent than he is

---

enagua *nf*, **enaguas** *nfpl* petticoat

enajenable *adj Der* transferable, alienable

enajenación *nf*, **enajenamiento** *nm* (a) *(locura)* **e. (mental)** mental derangement, insanity (b) *(éxtasis)* rapture (c) *Der (de propiedad, bienes)* transfer of ownership, alienation

enajenante *adj* alienating

enajenar 1 *vt* (a) *(volver loco)* to drive mad (b) *(extasiar)* to enrapture (c) *Der (propiedad, bienes)* to transfer ownership of, to alienate
2 **enajenarse** *vpr* (a) *(apartarse)* to become estranged (b) *(extasiarse)* to get carried away

enaltecedor, -ora *adj (elogioso)* praising; **palabras enaltecedoras** words of praise

enaltecer [46] *vt* (a) *(elogiar)* to praise, to extol (b) *(engrandecer)* to ennoble

enaltecimiento *nm (elogio)* praise

enamoradamente *adv* (a) *(con amor)* lovingly (b) *(con pasión)* passionately

enamoradizo, -a 1 *adj* **es muy e.** he falls in love very easily
2 *nm,f* person who falls in love easily; **es una enamoradiza** she falls in love very easily

enamorado, -a 1 *adj* in love (**de** with); **se los ve muy enamorados** they look very much in love with each other; **estaba muy e. de su mujer** he was very much in love with his wife; **está e. de su moto** he's in love with his motorbike
2 *nm,f* (a) *(amante)* lover; **son cosas de enamorados** that's lovers *o* sweethearts for you; **el día de los enamorados** St Valentine's Day (b) *(aficionado)* lover; **es un e. de la ópera** he's an opera lover; **es un e. de su trabajo** he's in love with his work (c) *Bol, Perú (novio)* boyfriend, *f* girlfriend

enamoramiento *nm* falling in love; **un e. pasajero** a brief infatuation

enamorar 1 *vt* to win the heart of; **la enamoró** she fell in love with him; **¿qué te enamoró de ella?** what made you fall in love with her?
2 **enamorarse** *vpr* (a) *(sentir amor)* to fall in love (**de** with); **se**

enamoró perdidamente de ella he fell madly in love with her (**b**) *(sentir entusiasmo)* to fall in love (**de** with); **me enamoré de la casa nada más verla** I fell in love with the house the moment I saw it

enamoriscarse [60], **enamoricarse** [60] *vpr* to be attracted; **e. de** to take a fancy to

enancarse [60] *vpr* (**a**) *Andes, Arg, Perú (montar)* to mount behind (**b**) *Méx (encabritarse)* to rear up

enana *nf* (**a**) *Astron* ***e. blanca*** white dwarf; ***e. roja*** red dwarf (**b**) *ver también* **enano**

enanismo *nm Med* dwarfism

enano, -a 1 *adj* (**a**) *(menor de lo normal)* dwarf; **un arbusto e.** a dwarf shrub (**b**) *Fam (pequeñísimo)* tiny

2 *nm,f* (**a**) *(persona pequeña, en cuentos)* dwarf; *Pey (como insulto)* midget; EXPR *Fam* **como un e.: disfruté como un e.** I had a whale of a time; **me lo pasé como un e.** I got a real kick out of it; **trabajar como un e.** to slog one's guts out; EXPR *Fam* **crecerle los enanos a alguien: siempre le crecen los enanos** his bread always falls butter side down

(**b**) *Fam (niño)* kid

enarbolar *vt (bandera)* to raise, to hoist; *(pancarta)* to hold up; *(arma, bastón)* to brandish

enarcar [60] *vt (cejas)* to raise, to arch

enardecedor, -ora *adj (discurso)* rousing, inflammatory; *(cántico, música)* rousing

enardecer [46] 1 *vt (multitud, público)* to inflame, to whip up into a frenzy; **sus comentarios enardecieron los ánimos** his comments aroused people's passions; **enardecía a la hinchada con sus jugadas** the fans went wild at the way he played

2 **enardecerse** *vpr* **los ánimos se enardecieron tras la intervención del presidente** people were whipped up by the president's speech; **la gente se enardecía al oírlo hablar** people were roused when they heard him speak

enarenar *vt* to cover with sand

enartrosis *nf inv Anat* ball-and-socket joint

encabalgamiento *nm Lit* enjambment

encabestrar *vt (poner cabestro a)* to put a halter on, to halter

encabezado *nm Chile, Méx (en periódico)* headline

encabezamiento *nm* (**a**) *(de carta)* opening; *(de escrito, lista, apartado)* heading; *(en periódico)* headline (**b**) *(preámbulo)* foreword

encabezar [14] *vt* (**a**) *(marcha, manifestación, carrera)* to lead; **e. la competición** to be in first place *o* in the lead in the competition; **el Real encabeza la clasificación** Real is at the top of the league

(**b**) *(revuelta, movimiento, campaña)* to lead; *(comisión, delegación, misión)* to head

(**c**) *(carta)* to begin, to open; *(escrito, lista, apartado)* to head; *(artículo de periódico)* to headline

(**d**) *(libro)* to write the foreword for

(**e**) *(vino)* to fortify

encabritarse *vpr* (**a**) *(caballo)* to rear up (**b**) *(moto)* to rear up (**c**) *Fam (persona)* to get shirty

encabronar *Vulg* 1 *vt Esp* to piss off

2 **encabronarse** *vpr Esp, Méx* to get pissed off

encachado, -a *adj Chile Fam* nice

encadenado, -a 1 *adj (verso)* linked

2 *nm* (**a**) *Cine* fade, dissolve (**b**) *Constr* buttress

encadenamiento *nm* (**a**) *(con cadenas)* chaining (**b**) *(sucesión)* **un e. de circunstancias** a chain of events

encadenar 1 *vt* (**a**) *(atar)* to chain (up) (**a** to) (**b**) *(enlazar)* to link (together)

2 **encadenarse** *vpr* (**a**) *(personas)* to chain oneself (**a** to); **se encadenaron a la entrada de la fábrica** they chained themselves to the factory gates (**b**) *(sucesos, acontecimientos, desgracias)* to happen in succession *o* one after another (**c**) *Cine (escenas, secuencias)* to fade into each other

encajar 1 *vt* (**a**) *(meter ajustando)* to fit (**en** into); *(hueso dislocado)* to set; **encajaron el cristal en el marco de la ventana** they fitted the glass into the window frame

(**b**) *(meter con fuerza)* to push (**en** into); **hay que e. el ropero en ese hueco** the wardrobe has to be squeezed into that space

(**c**) *(recibir) (golpe, críticas, noticia)* to take; *(goles, canastas)* to concede; **encajaron muy mal el cierre de la fábrica** they took the factory closure very badly; **encajaron pocas canastas triples** they didn't let them get many three-pointers; **ha encajado quince goles esta liga** he's let in fifteen goals this season; **e. una derrota** to be defeated

(**d**) *Fam (soltar) (insultos)* to hurl; **e. un golpe a alguien** to land sb a blow, to land a blow on sb; **nos encajó un sermón de dos horas** he treated us to a two-hour lecture

(**e**) *Fam (endosar)* to land, to dump (**a** on); **me ha encajado a su bebé porque se va al cine** she dumped her baby on me because she's going to the cinema

(**f**) *Fam (dar, engañar con)* to palm off; **le encajaron un billete falso** they palmed off a counterfeit note on him

2 *vi* (**a**) *(piezas, muebles)* to fit (**en** into); **esta puerta no encaja bien** this door doesn't fit the frame properly

(**b**) *(concordar) (hechos, declaraciones, datos)* to tally; **ahora todo encaja** it all falls into place now; **e. con algo** to tally with sth, to match sth

(**c**) *(ser oportuno, adecuado)* **ese mueble no encaja ahí** that piece of furniture doesn't go there *o* look right there; **¿crees que encajará bien en el grupo?** do you think she'll fit into the group all right?; **su ropa no encaja con la seriedad del acto** her clothes aren't in keeping with the seriousness of the occasion

3 **encajarse** *vpr* (**a**) *(pieza, objeto)* to get stuck (**b**) *Méx Fam (aprovecharse)* to take advantage; **si puede se encaja y me pide algo de dinero** whenever he gets the chance he takes advantage and asks me for money

encaje *nm* (**a**) *(ajuste)* insertion, fitting in (**b**) *(tejido)* lace; **pañuelo/bragas de e.** lace handkerchief/knickers; **un camisón de e.** a lacy nightdress ►► ***e. de bolillos*** bobbin lace; EXPR **habrá que hacer e. de bolillos para ajustarse al presupuesto** we'll have to perform a minor miracle to keep within the budget

encajonar 1 *vt* (**a**) *(en cajas, cajones) (mercancía)* to box, to put into boxes (**b**) *(en sitio estrecho)* to squeeze (**en** into); **encajonaron al corredor ruso** the Russian runner was boxed in; **tengo el coche encajonado y no puedo salir** my car's boxed in and I can't get out (**c**) *Taurom (toro)* to pen (up)

2 **encajonarse** *vpr (río)* to run through a narrow place

encalado, -a 1 *adj* whitewashed

2 *nm* whitewash

encalar *vt* to whitewash

encalatarse *vpr Perú Fam* to strip off, *Br* to get one's kit off

encaletarse *vpr Ven* **se lo encaletó** she kept it for herself

encalladero *nm* shoal, sandbank

encallado, -a *adj* stranded

encallar *vi* (**a**) *(barco)* to run aground (**b**) *(proceso, proyecto)* to founder

encallecer [46] 1 *vt* (**a**) *(manos, piel)* to harden (**b**) *(persona)* to harden, to make callous

2 **encallecerse** *vpr* (**a**) *(manos, piel)* to become calloused *o* hard (**b**) *(persona)* to become callous *o* hard

encallecido, -a *adj (manos)* calloused; *(piel)* hardened, calloused

encalomar *vt Esp Fam (endosar)* **e. algo a alguien** to lumber *o* land sb with sth; **siempre me encaloman los peores trabajos** I always get lumbered *o* landed with the worst jobs

encamarse *vpr* (**a**) *(enfermo)* to take to one's bed (**b**) *muy Fam* **e. con alguien** *(acostarse)* to go to bed with sb

encamellado, -a *adj Col Fam* **estar e.** to be up to one's eyes in work

encaminar 1 *vt* (**a**) *(dirigir) (persona)* to direct, to guide; *(esfuerzos, intereses, estudios)* to direct, to channel; **encaminaron sus pasos hacia el castillo** they made for the castle; **por esa senda vas mal encaminado** you're going the wrong way if you take that path; **sigue preguntando, que vas bien encaminado** keep asking, you're on the right track; **encaminó todos sus esfuerzos a lograr la paz** he directed *o* channelled all his efforts towards achieving peace; **han encaminado muy bien las negociaciones** the negotiations have been well-conducted; **supo e. su carrera deportiva** she made the right choices in her sporting career; **la tesis va bien/mal encaminada** the thesis is going well/badly

(**b**) *(medidas, leyes, actividades)* to aim; **estar encaminado a hacer algo** *(medidas, actividades)* to be aimed at doing sth; **esta emisora está encaminada a un público más joven** this radio station is aimed at a younger audience; **investigaciones encaminadas a esclarecer los hechos** investigations aimed at clarifying the facts

2 **encaminarse** *vpr* (**a**) *(hacia un lugar)* **encaminarse a/hacia** to set off for/towards; **se encaminó al jardín** she headed for the garden; **ahora nos encaminamos hacia la sala de Rubens** we are now making our way to the Rubens room (**b**) *(destinarse)* **encaminarse a** to be directed towards, to be aimed at

encamotado, -a *adj Andes, CAm Fam* in love

encamotarse *vpr Andes, CAm Fam* to fall in love

encampanar *vt* (**a**) *Col, PRico, Ven (elevar)* to raise, to lift (**b**) *Méx (dejar solo)* to leave in the lurch

encanar *vt Andes, Cuba, RP Fam* to put away, *Br* to bang up

encandelillar *vt* (**a**) *Am (deslumbrar)* to dazzle (**b**) *Andes, Arg (sobrehilar)* to overstitch

encandilado, -a *adj* dazzled, fascinated

encandilar 1 *vt* (**a**) *(fascinar)* to dazzle, to fascinate; **encandila a los niños con sus cuentos** he delights the children with his stories, the children are fascinated by his stories (**b**) *(enamorar)* to bewitch (**c**) *(avivar)* to stir, to poke

2 encandilarse *vpr* (**a**) *(quedarse fascinado)* to be dazzled, to be fascinated (**con** by) (**b**) *(enamorarse)* to be bewitched

encanecer [46] **1** *vi* to go grey

2 encanecerse *vpr* to go grey

encantado, -a *adj* (**a**) *(contento)* delighted (**con** with); **su profesor está e. con él** his teacher is really pleased *o* delighted with him; **está encantada con su nuevo trabajo** she loves her new job; **está e. de la vida** he's absolutely fine; **estar e. de haber hecho algo** to be really glad to have done sth; **estoy e. de haber ido** I'm really glad I went; **e. de poder ayudar** glad to be able to help; **no es ninguna molestia, te llevaré e.** it's no trouble, I'd be glad to take you; **¿quedamos para cenar? – por mí, e.** shall we stay to dinner? – that's fine by me

(**b**) *(como saludo)* **te presento a mi padre – e.** this my father – pleased to meet you, how do you do; **e. de conocerle** pleased to meet you

(**c**) *(hechizado) (bosque, castillo)* enchanted; *(persona)* bewitched

encantador, -ora 1 *adj* delightful, charming; **es un tipo e.** he's charming, he's a lovely guy

2 *nm,f* ***e. de serpientes*** snake charmer

encantadoramente *adv* charmingly

encantamiento *nm* enchantment

encantar *vt* (**a**) *(gustar)* **me encanta el chocolate** I love chocolate; **le encanta ir al cine** he loves going to the cinema; **¡me encanta!** I love it/him/her!; **me encantaría asistir, pero tengo otros compromisos** I'd love to go, but I've got other things on (**b**) *(embrujar)* to bewitch, to cast a spell on

encanto *nm* (**a**) *(atractivo)* charm; **una ciudad llena de e.** a charming *o* lovely town; **hoteles con e.** hotels with that special something; **esta película ha perdido su e. con los años** time hasn't been kind to this film; **no me pude resistir a sus encantos** I couldn't resist her charms; **una camiseta que realza sus encantos** a T-shirt that shows off her assets

(**b**) *(persona encantadora)* charming *o* lovely person; **ser un e.** to be a treasure *o* delight; **es un e. de mujer** she's a charming *o* lovely woman; **¡qué e. de nietos tiene!** what lovely grandchildren she has!

(**c**) *(apelativo cariñoso)* darling; **ven aquí, e.** come here, darling

(**d**) *(hechizo)* spell; **como por e.** as if by magic; **romper el e.** to break the spell

encañonar *vt* to point a gun at; **lo encañonó con un rifle** he pointed a rifle at him; **tenía encañonados a los rehenes** she had the hostages covered

encapotado, -a *adj* overcast

encapotarse *vpr* to cloud over

encaprichamiento *nm* whim, fancy

encapricharse *vpr* (**a**) *(obstinarse)* **e. con algo/hacer algo** to set one's mind on sth/doing sth (**b**) *(sentirse atraído)* **e. con** *o Esp* **de alguien** to become infatuated with sb; **e. con** *o Esp* **de algo** to take a real liking to sth

encapuchado, -a 1 *adj* hooded

2 *nm,f* hooded person; **unos encapuchados asaltaron el banco** some hooded men robbed the bank

encapuchar 1 *vt* to put a hood on

2 encapucharse *vpr* to put one's hood on

encaramar 1 *vt* (**a**) *(subir)* to lift up (**b**) *Am (abochornar)* to make blush

2 encaramarse *vpr* (**a**) *(trepar)* to climb (up) (**a** *o* **en** onto); **me encaramé a la silla** I climbed (up) onto the chair; **se encaramó a una farola** she climbed up a lamppost (**b**) *(subir puestos)* **e. a** to go to, to get to; **se encaramaron al primer puesto de la clasificación** they went *o* got to the top of the league (**c**) *Am (abochornarse)* to blush

encarar 1 *vt* (**a**) *(hacer frente a)* to confront, to face up to; **hay que e. la situación con valentía** you have to put a brave face on things; **¿usted cómo encararía este asunto?** how would you deal with *o* approach this? (**b**) *(poner frente a frente)* to bring face to face

2 encararse *vpr (enfrentarse)* **encararse a** *o* **con** to confront, to square up to; **se encaró con el policía** he confronted the policeman

encarcelación *nf*, **encarcelamiento** *nm* imprisonment

encarcelar *vt* to imprison, to jail; **fue encarcelado por homicidio** he was jailed for murder

encarecer [46] **1** *vt* (**a**) *(productos)* to make more expensive; **la subida del petróleo encarecerá los precios** the rise in oil prices will make things more expensive (**b**) *Formal (rogar)* to beg, to implore; **me encareció que la ayudara** she begged *o* implored me to help her; **encareció al ministro que se retractara** he urged the minister to withdraw his statement (**c**) *Formal (alabar)* to praise

2 encarecerse *vpr (producto)* to become more expensive; **los precios de la vivienda se han encarecido** house prices have increased

encarecidamente *adv Formal* **le ruego e. que guarde el secreto** I would urge you most earnestly to keep this secret; **me pidió e. que colaborara con él** he begged *o* implored me to help him

encarecimiento *nm* (**a**) *(de producto)* increase in price; *(de coste)* increase; **el e. de la vida** the rise in the cost of living (**b**) *Formal (empeño)* insistence; **con e.** insistently (**c**) *Formal (alabanza)* praise

encarezco *etc ver* **encarecer**

encargado, -a 1 *adj* responsible (**de** for), in charge (**de** of); **está e. de cerrar la oficina** he's responsible for locking up the office, it's his job to lock up the office

2 *nm,f (responsable) (de tarea, trabajo)* person in charge; *(de tienda, negocio)* manager, *f* manageress; **él es el e. de hacer las camas** he's responsible for making the beds, it's his job to make the beds; **póngame con el e.** can I speak to the person in charge, please? ▸▸ ***e. de negocios*** chargé d'affaires

---

ENCARGAR [38] **1** *vt* (**a**) *(poner al cargo de)* **e. a alguien de algo, e. algo a alguien** to put sb in charge of sth; **le han encargado la investigación del caso** they've put him in charge of the investigation, they've charged him with investigating the case; **e. a alguien que haga algo** to tell sb to do sth; **me encargó que vigilara la puerta** he told me to keep an eye on the door; **me han encargado que organice la fiesta** they've asked me to organize the party

(**b**) *(pedir)* to order; **encargó unas botas de montaña** she ordered some mountaineering boots; **compré unos discos que me había encargado mi hermano** I bought some records that my brother had asked me to get; **me encargó que le trajera un bumerán** he asked me to bring him back a boomerang; **si no lo tienen, encárgalo** if they haven't got it, order it; **he dejado encargada la comida para las dos** I've booked lunch for two o'clock; **el gobierno ha encargado un informe sobre la situación en las prisiones** the government has commissioned a report on the state of the prisons; **encargó su retrato a Goya** he commissioned Goya to paint his portrait; *Euf* **han encargado un bebé** they have a baby on the way; *Euf* **¿cuándo van a e. un niño?** when are they going to start a family?

2 encargarse *vpr (ocuparse)* **encargarse de algo** *(tener el control de)* to be in charge of sth; *(tomar el control de)* to take charge of sth; **él se encargaba de la tienda** he looked after the shop, he was in charge of the shop; **se encarga de la informática en la empresa** she is responsible for computing within the company; **yo me encargaré de eso** I'll take care of *o* see to that; **encargarse de alguien** to look after sb, to see to sb; **tú encárgate de los niños** you look after *o* see to the children; **si pone problemas, yo me encargaré de él** if he causes any problems, I'll deal with him; **encargarse de hacer algo** to undertake to do sth; **tú te encargarás de limpiar el baño** it'll be your job to clean the bathroom; **me encargo de abrir la puerta todas las mañanas** I see to it that the door is opened every morning; **ya habrá quien se encargue de contárselo a mis padres** no doubt someone will make it their business to tell my parents; **encargarse de que...** to see to it that..., to make sure that...; **encárgate de que nadie pase por aquí** see to it *o* make sure (that) no one comes through here; **yo me encargaré de que nadie se pierda** I'll make sure no one gets lost; **la lluvia se encargó de arruinar el espectáculo** the rain made sure the show was ruined, the rain ruined the show

---

encargo, *RP* **encargue** *nm* (**a**) *(pedido)* order; **hacer un e. a alguien** to order sth from sb; **les hicimos un e. de una mesa la semana pasada** we ordered a table from them last week; *Esp* **(hecho) de e.** tailor-made; *Esp* **mobiliario (hecho) de e.** furniture made to order; **se hacen paellas por e.** paella can be made to order; **el artista trabaja por e.** the artist does commission work; EXPR **ser más tonto que hecho de e.: es más tonta que hecha de e.** she couldn't be more stupid if she tried

(**b**) *(recado)* errand; **me han hecho un e. para que se lo compre en Londres** they've asked me to buy something for them in London

(**c**) *(tarea)* task, assignment; **viajó a Seattle con el e. de cerrar el trato** he went to Seattle charged with closing the deal

(**d**) *Am Fam (embarazo)* **estar de e.** to be expecting

encariñarse *vpr* **e. con algo/alguien** to become very attached to sth/sb, to grow fond of sth/sb; **se había encariñado con el viejo baúl** he'd become very attached to the old chest

encarnaceno, -a 1 *adj* of/from Encarnación *(Paraguay)*
2 *nm,f* person from Encarnación *(Paraguay)*

encarnación *nf* (a) *(personificación) (cosa)* embodiment; *(persona)* personification (b) *Rel* **la E.** the Incarnation

encarnado, -a 1 *adj* (a) *(color)* red (b) *(personificado)* incarnate; **era el demonio e.** he was the devil incarnate; **es la elegancia encarnada** he's the epitome of elegance (c) *(uña)* ingrown, ingrowing
2 *nm (color)* red

encarnar 1 *vt* (a) *(ideal, doctrina, cualidad)* to represent, to embody; **una organización que encarna el fanatismo religioso** an organization which is the very embodiment of religious fanaticism; **el búho encarna la prudencia y la sabiduría** the owl represents wisdom and knowledge (b) *(personaje, papel)* to play
2 **encarnarse** *vpr* (a) *Rel* to become incarnate, to be made flesh (**en** in) (b) *(uña)* to become ingrown

encarnizadamente *adv* fiercely, bitterly

encarnizado, -a *adj* bloody, bitter

encarnizamiento *nm (crueldad)* bloodthirstiness

encarnizar [14] 1 *vt* to blood
2 **encarnizarse** *vpr* **encarnizarse con** *(presa)* to tear to pieces; *(prisionero, enemigo)* to treat savagely

encarpetar *vt* to file away

encarrilar 1 *vt* (a) *(tren)* to put back on the rails (b) *(negocio, actividad)* to put on the right track; **por fin lograron e. el proyecto** at last they managed to get the project on the right track; **no ha sabido e. su vida** she hasn't been able to give her life a sense of direction (c) *(persona)* to guide *o* point in the right direction
2 **encarrilarse** *vpr* (a) *(negocio, proyecto)* to get on the right track (b) *(persona)* to find out what one wants to do in life (c) *Méx Fam (comprometerse)* to commit oneself; **no me quise e. con la compra de esa casa** I didn't want to commit myself to buying the house

encartar 1 *vt (naipes)* to lead
2 **encartarse** *vpr* (a) *(en naipes)* to have to follow suit (b) *Col Fam (complicarse)* **encartarse con algo/alguien** to take on sth/sb, to land oneself with sth/sb

encarte *nm* (a) *(en naipes)* lead (b) *(folleto)* insert (c) *Col Fam (complicación)* **qué e., ¿para qué trajiste esa maleta?** what a pain, why did you bring that case?

encasillamiento *nm* pigeonholing

encasillar *vt* (a) *(clasificar)* to classify, to pigeonhole (**como** as); **lo encasillaron como un provocador** he was marked down *o* branded as an agitator (b) *(actor, actriz)* to typecast; **fue encasillada en papeles de mala** she was typecast as a villain (c) *(poner en casillas)* to put in a box, to enter into a grid

encasquetar 1 *vt* (a) *(gorro, sombrero)* to pull on (b) *Fam (meter)* **e. algo a alguien** *(idea, teoría)* to drum sth into sb; **nos encasquetó un sermón de dos horas** he treated us to a two-hour lecture (c) *Fam (endilgar)* **e. algo a alguien** to lumber *o* land sb with sth; **me encasquetaron la mochila más pesada** I got lumbered *o* landed with the heaviest rucksack
2 **encasquetarse** *vpr (gorro, sombrero)* to pull on

encasquillador *nm Am* farrier

encasquillar 1 *vt* (a) *(atascar)* to jam (b) *Am (herrar)* to shoe
2 **encasquillarse** *vpr* (a) *(atascarse)* to get jammed (b) *Cuba Fam (acobardarse)* to get scared

encastillarse *vpr (empeñarse)* to insist, to be set (**en** on)

encastrar *vt (mueble, lavabo, electrodoméstico)* to fit, to install

encatrinarse *vpr CAm, Méx Fam* to doll *o* tart oneself up

encausado, -a *nm,f Der* defendant

encausar *vt Der* to prosecute

encauzar [14] 1 *vt* (a) *(agua)* to channel (b) *(orientar)* to direct; **encauzan todos sus esfuerzos hacia la obtención de un empleo** they direct *o* channel all their efforts into finding a job
2 **encauzarse** *vpr (arreglarse)* to get on the right track; **sus negocios se han encauzado bien** his business affairs are going well

encebollado, -a *Culin* 1 *adj* cooked with onions
2 *nm* = stew of fish or meat and onions

encebollar *vt Culin* to add onions to

encefálico, -a *adj Anat* brain, *Espec* encephalic; **masa encefálica** brain mass

encefalitis *nf inv Med* encephalitis

encéfalo *nm Anat* brain

encefalografía *nf Med* encephalograph, encephalogram

encefalograma *nm Med* electroencephalogram ▸▸ ***e. plano*** *(de muerto)* flat line; *Fam Fig* **tener un e. plano** *(persona)* to have no brains

encefalomielitis *nf inv Med* encephalomyelitis ▸▸ ***e. miálgica*** myalgic encephalomyelitis

encefalopatía *nf Med* **e. espongiforme bovina** bovine spongiform encephalopathy

enceguecer *vt Am* to blind; **la pasión lo enceguečió** he was blinded by passion; **estaba enceguecida de rabia** she was in a blind rage

encelar 1 *vt* to make jealous
2 **encelarse** *vpr (sentir celos)* to become jealous

encenagado, -a *adj (con cieno)* muddy

encendedor *nm* lighter

encender [66] 1 *vt* (a) *(vela, cigarro, chimenea)* to light; **e. una cerilla** to light *o* strike a match; **e. una hoguera** to light a bonfire
(b) *(aparato)* to switch on; *(motor)* to start up; **enciende la luz, que no veo** switch the light on, I can't see
(c) *(entusiasmo, ira)* to arouse; *(pasión)* to arouse, to inflame; **sus acusaciones encendieron los ánimos** his accusations aroused people's anger; **me enciende con esas cosas que dice** he makes me mad with those things he says
(d) *(guerra, contienda)* to spark off
2 **encenderse** *vpr* (a) *(fuego, gas)* to ignite; *(luz, bombilla, estufa)* to come on; *(llama, piloto)* to light; **se encendió en ella la llama de la venganza** the desire for revenge was kindled within her
(b) *(persona, rostro)* to go red, to blush; *(ojos)* to light up; *(de ira)* to flare up; **cuando oigo estas cosas me enciendo** I get really mad when I hear things like that
(c) *(guerra, contienda)* to break out

encendidamente *adv* passionately

encendido, -a 1 *adj* (a) *(luz, colilla)* burning; **la luz está encendida** the light is on; **te has dejado la estufa encendida** you've left the heater on (b) *(deseos, mirada, palabras)* passionate, ardent (c) *(mejillas)* red, flushed
2 *nm* (a) *(acción)* lighting (b) *Aut* ignition ▸▸ ***e. electrónico*** electronic ignition

encerado, -a 1 *adj* waxed, polished
2 *nm* (a) *(acción)* waxing, polishing (b) *(pizarra) Br* blackboard, *US* chalkboard; **salir al e.** to come/go out to the *Br* blackboard *o US* chalkboard

enceradora *nf (aparato)* floor polisher

encerar *vt* (a) *(suelo, mueble)* to wax, to polish (b) *Méx (iglesia)* to furnish *o* provide with candles

encerrado, -a *adj* **se quedaron encerrados en el ascensor** they were trapped in the lift; **se quedó e. en el desván** he got locked in the attic; **se pasó el día e. en su habitación** he spent the day shut away in his room; **llevo todo el día e.** I've been stuck inside all day; **decenas de obreros permanecen encerrados en la fábrica** dozens of workers remain locked in inside the factory

encerrar [3] 1 *vt* (a) *(recluir)* to shut up *o* in; *(con llave)* to lock up *o* in; *(en la cárcel)* to lock away *o* up; *(ganado, rebaño)* to pen (up); *(gallinas)* to shut up; *(en carreras)* to box in; **lo encerraron en un psiquiátrico** they shut him away *o* up in a mental hospital; **me encerraron en la curva y no pude esprintar** they boxed me in on the bend and I couldn't put on a sprint; EXPR *Fam* **estar para que lo/la/** *etc.* **encierren** to be off one's head
(b) *(contener)* to contain; **el espectáculo encierra grandes sorpresas** the show has some big surprises; **sus palabras encerraban una amenaza** there was a threat in his words
(c) *(en ajedrez)* to checkmate
(d) *(con signos de puntuación)* to enclose (**entre** in); **encerró el comentario entre paréntesis** she enclosed the comment in brackets
2 **encerrarse** *vpr (recluirse)* to shut oneself away; *(con llave)* to lock oneself away; **se encerró en su casa para acabar la novela** she shut herself away in her house to finish the novel; **se ha encerrado en sí misma y no quiere hablar con nadie** she's withdrawn into her shell and doesn't want to talk to anyone; **los estudiantes se encerraron en la biblioteca** the students occupied the library

encerrona *nf* (a) *(trampa)* trap; **preparar** *o* **tender una e. a alguien** to lay *o* set a trap for sb (b) *(protesta)* sit-in (c) *Taurom* = private bullfight, usually on bull-breeder's farm

encestador, -ora *nm,f (en baloncesto)* scorer; **el máximo e. del equipo** the team's top scorer

encestar 1 *vt (en baloncesto)* to score
2 *vi (en baloncesto)* to score; **e. de tres (puntos)** to score a three-pointer

enceste *nm Dep* basket; **¡e. de Johnson!** Johnson scores!

enchalecar *vt Am* to put a curb on

enchapado, *Am* **enchape** *nm* veneer

enchapar *RP* 1 *vt* to plate
2 *vi* to plate

enchapopotar *vt Méx* to tar

encharcado, -a *adj (calle, calzada)* covered in puddles; *(campo de juego, terreno)* waterlogged

encharcamiento *nm* flooding, swamping

encharcar [60] 1 *vt* to waterlog
2 **encharcarse** *vpr* **(a)** *(calle, calzada)* to get covered in puddles; *(campo de juego, terreno)* to become waterlogged **(b)** *(pulmones)* to become flooded

enchastrado, -a *adj RP Fam* **(a)** *(sucio)* dirty **(b)** *(desprestigiado)* **como político está muy e.** he has a really bad name as a politician

enchastrar *RP Fam* 1 *vt* **(a)** *(ensuciar)* to make dirty **(b)** *(desprestigiar)* to blacken
2 **enchastrarse** *vpr* to get dirty; **siempre me enchastro de barro cuando trabajo en el jardín** I always get covered in mud when I work in the garden; **se enchastró todo con el helado** he got ice cream all over himself

enchastre *nm RP Fam* mess; **cada vez que entra a la cocina deja un e.** every time she comes into the kitchen she leaves everything in a complete mess; **hay que limpiar este e.** this mess has to be cleaned up

enchicharse *vpr Andes, CAm, Méx (emborracharse)* to get drunk

enchilada *nf CAm, Méx* = filled tortilla baked in chilli sauce

enchilado, -a 1 *adj Méx* **(a)** *(alimento)* with chilli **(b)** *Fam (persona)* **está e.** that chilli has really got to him *o* has brought tears to his eyes
2 *nm Cuba, Méx* = shellfish stew with chilli, tomatoes and onions

enchilar 1 *vt* **(a)** *CAm, Méx (alimento)* to season with chilli **(b)** *Méx (persona)* to irritate, to annoy
2 *vi CAm, Méx* to be hot *o* spicy
3 **enchilarse** *vpr Méx* **(a)** *(con comida)* to overdose on chilli; **cuidado con el picante, no te vayas a e.** watch out for that bit of chilli, you don't want to set yourself on fire! **(b)** *Fam (enojarse)* to get angry

enchinar *Méx* 1 *vt* to curl
2 **enchinarse** *vpr Fam* **se le enchinó la piel** he got goose pimples *o US* bumps

enchinchar 1 *vt* **(a)** *CAm, Méx (dar largas)* to put off; **lo enchincharon durante meses** they put it off for months **(b)** *CAm, Méx* **e. el tiempo** *(hacer tiempo)* to kill time **(c)** *Andes, CAm, Méx Fam (enojar)* to bug
2 **enchincharse** *vpr RP Fam (enojarse)* to get mad; **no te enchinches, estaba bromeando** don't get mad, I was only joking

enchinchorrarse *vpr Ven Fam* **(a)** *(acostarse)* to get into one's hammock **(b)** *(vagar)* to laze around

enchiquerar *vt Taurom* to shut in the bullpen

enchironar *vt Esp Fam* to put away, *Br* to bang up

enchivarse *vpr Col, Ecuad, PRico (enfurecerse)* to fly into a rage

enchompado, -a *adj Perú Fam* wrapped up

enchompar *Perú Fam* 1 *vt* to wrap up
2 **enchomparse** *vpr* to wrap up

enchuecado, -a *adj Andes, Méx (planta)* twisted; *(mesa)* warped

enchuecar [60] *Andes, Méx* 1 *vt* to twist
2 **enchuecarse** *vpr* to grow twisted

enchufado, -a *Fam* 1 *adj* **(a)** **estar e.** *(en un puesto)* = to have got one's job through connections; **está e., la profesora siempre le pone buenas notas** he's well in with the teacher, she always gives him good marks
(b) *RP Fam (ocupado)* **ahora está muy e. con la lingüística** he's really into linguistics now; **se acaba de comprar una filmadora y está e.** he's just bought himself a cine camera and he's like a kid with a new toy
2 *nm,f* = person who has got where they are through connections; **el puesto se lo darán a algún e.** they'll give the job to someone with the right connections; **es el e. del director** he got the job because he knows the manager

enchufar 1 *vt* **(a)** *(aparato) (conectar)* to plug in; *Fam (encender)* to turn *o* put on
(b) *(acoplar) (a un tubo, boca de riego)* to connect
(c) *Fam (colocar en un trabajo)* **su padre lo enchufó en la compañía** his father got him a job in the company by pulling strings
(d) *Fam (dirigir) (manguera, reflector)* to point; **no me enchufes la linterna** don't shine that *Br* torch *o US* flashlight at me
(e) *RP Fam (endosar)* to land, to dump **(a** on); **me enchufó al bebé porque se va al cine** she dumped her baby on me because she's going to the cinema
(f) *RP Fam (dar, engañar con)* to palm off; **le enchufaron un billete falso** they palmed off a counterfeit note on him
2 *vi Informát* **e. y usar** plug and play
3 **enchufarse** *vpr RP Fam* **enchufarse algo** to stick sth on; **si hace frío, te enchufás unas medias bien gruesas** if it's cold, just stick some really thick socks on

enchufe *nm* **(a)** *Elec (macho)* plug; *(hembra)* socket ►► ***e. de clavija*** jack plug **(b)** *Fam (recomendación)* connections; **tener e.** to have connections; **obtener algo por e.** to get sth by pulling strings *o* through one's connections

enchufismo *nm Esp Fam* string-pulling

encía *nf* gum

encíclica *nf Rel* encyclical ►► ***e. papal*** papal encyclical

enciclopedia *nf* encyclopedia; *Hum* **es una e. viviente** *o* **ambulante** he's a walking encyclopedia

enciclopédico, -a *adj* encyclopedic

enciclopedista 1 *adj* encyclopedist
2 *nmf* encyclopedist

enciendo *etc ver* **encender**

encierro 1 *ver* **encerrar**
2 *nm* **(a)** *(protesta)* sit-in **(b)** *(retiro)* retreat **(c)** *Taurom* running of the bulls

ENCIMA 1 *adv* **(a)** *(arriba)* on top; *(en el piso de arriba)* upstairs; **un pastel con una guinda e.** a cake with a cherry on top; **pásame el de e.** pass me the top one *o* the one on top; **yo vivo e.** I live upstairs; **el vecino de e.** the upstairs neighbour; **tienes e. un mosquito** you've got a mosquito on you; *Am* **de e.** in addition, besides; **le cayó e. la responsabilidad de dirigir el partido** the responsibility of leading the party was thrust upon her; **el autobús se le echó e. antes de que pudiera reaccionar** the bus was upon him before he had time to react; **tiene a su jefe e. todo el día** his boss is on at him *o* on his back all day long
(b) *(en tiempo)* **las elecciones ya están e.** the elections are already upon us; **se nos echó la noche e.** night fell, night descended upon us
(c) *(además)* on top of that; **está lejos y e. no hay transporte público** it's a long way away and on top of that *o* what is more, there's no public transport; **voy a consolarlo y e. me grita** I go to comfort him and all he does is shout at me
(d) *(sobre sí)* **lleva un abrigo e.** she has a coat on; **ponte algo e., vas a tener frío** put something on, you'll be cold; **¿llevas dinero e.?** have you got any money on you?; **le quitaron todo lo que llevaba e.** they took everything he had with him
2 **encima de** *loc prep* **(a)** *(sobre, en)* on (top of); **el pan está e. de la nevera** the bread is on (top of) the fridge
(b) *(en lugar más alto que)* above; **e. de la montaña el cielo se encapotó** the sky above the mountain clouded over; **vivo e. de tu casa** I live upstairs from you; EXPR **estar e. de alguien** *(controlar, vigilar)* to be on sb's back; **mi madre está e. de mí todo el día** my mother's on at me *o* on my back all day long
(c) *(además de)* as well as; **e. de (ser) tonto, es feo** as well as being stupid, he's also ugly; **e. de no hacerlo bien...** not only did he not do it well...
3 **por encima** *loc adv* **(a)** *(sobre la parte superior)* on top; **por e. lleva una capa de chocolate** it has a layer of chocolate on top; **había ropa por e. de la cama** there were clothes on the bed
(b) *(por arriba)* **la ciudad tenía una capa de contaminación por e.** the city was covered with a layer of pollution; **por e. de** over; **volaron por e. de los Alpes** they flew over the Alps; **el sol asomaba por e. de las montañas** the sun was peeping over the mountains
(c) *(en nivel superior)* **sólo tiene a dos personas por e.** there are only two people above her; **por e. de** over, above; **un precio muy por e. de lo que habíamos presupuestado** a price well over *o* above what we had budgeted for; **una calidad muy por e. de lo habitual** a much higher quality than usual; **la salud de sus hijos está por e. de todo lo demás** their childrens' health comes before everything else; **está muy por e. de los otros alumnos** he's far better than the other students; **vive por e. de sus posibilidades** he lives beyond his means; EXPR **por e. de todo: por e. de todo, hazlo con mucho cuidado** above all *o* first and foremost, be very careful; **por e. de todo, lo que más me preocupa...** what worries me more than anything else...; **por e. de todo, no se lo digas a nadie** whatever else you do, don't tell anyone; **ponemos la seguridad por e. de todo** we place safety first *o* before everything else

(**d**) *(superficialmente)* **lo conozco por e.** I only know it roughly; **sólo lo he leído por e.** I've only skimmed through it; **ordené la casa por e. y me marché** I gave the house a quick tidy up and left

encimar 1 *vt* (**a**) *Chile (alcanzar la cima de)* to reach the top of (**b**) *Méx (apilar)* to put *o* pile one on top of the other, to put in a pile
2 *vi* to reach the top *o* summit
3 encimarse *vpr Méx, RP* **no puedo cursar más de dos materias, si no se me enciman los horarios** I can't study more than two subjects, otherwise the timetables clash

encimera *nf Esp* (**a**) *(de cocina)* worktop (**b**) *(sábana)* top sheet

encimero, -a *adj* top

encimoso, -a *adj Méx Fam* **es tan e.** he's such a pain

encina *nf* holm oak

encinar *nm* oak forest/grove

encinta *adj inv* pregnant; **estar e. de ocho meses** to be eight months pregnant; **está e. de su tercer hijo** she is expecting her third child; **dejar e. a alguien** to get sb pregnant; **quedarse e.** to get pregnant

enclaustrado, -a *adj* cloistered

enclaustrar 1 *vt (en convento)* to shut up in a convent
2 enclaustrarse *vpr* (**a**) *(en convento)* to shut oneself up in a convent (**b**) *(encerrarse)* to lock oneself away

enclavado, -a *adj* set, situated

enclave *nm* enclave

enclavijar *vt (instrumento)* to peg

enclenque *adj* sickly, frail

enclítico, -a *adj Ling* enclitic

encocorar *vt Fam* to bug, to get to

encofrado *nm* (**a**) *Constr* formwork, *Br* shuttering (**b**) *Min* plank lining, timbering

encofrador, -ora *nm,f* = building worker who puts up formwork *o Br* shuttering

encofrar *vt* (**a**) *Arquit* to put up formwork *o Br* shuttering for (**b**) *Min* to timber

encoger [52] **1** *vi (tejido, filete)* to shrink; **el algodón encoge al lavarlo** cotton shrinks when you wash it; **prendas que no encogen** non-shrink clothes
2 *vt* (**a**) *(ropa, tejido)* to shrink (**b**) *(miembro, músculo)* to contract; *(pierna, brazo)* to tuck in; **encoja las piernas** tuck your legs in (**c**) *(apocar)* **sus duras palabras me encogieron** her harsh words took my breath away; **e. el ánimo a alguien** to discourage sb
3 encogerse *vpr* (**a**) *(ropa, tejido, filete)* to shrink; **se me encoge el corazón de oírla llorar** it makes my heart bleed to hear her cry
(**b**) *(contraerse) (miembro, músculo)* to contract; **no te encojas al andar** don't slouch when you walk; **encogerse de hombros** to shrug one's shoulders
(**c**) *(apocarse)* to cringe; **es muy tímido y se encoge ante sus superiores** he's very timid and he clams up in the presence of his superiors

encogido, -a *adj (tímido)* shy; *(pusilánime)* fearful, faint-hearted

encogimiento *nm* (**a**) *(reducción)* shrinkage; **con un e. de hombros** with a shrug of the shoulders (**b**) *(timidez)* shyness; *(cobardía)* faint-heartedness

encolado 1 *adj Chile, Méx* foppish
2 *nm* (**a**) *(de material, objeto)* glueing; *(de papel pintado)* pasting (**b**) *(del vino)* fining

encolar *vt* (**a**) *(material, objeto)* to glue; *(papel pintado)* to paste (**b**) *(vino)* to clarify

encolerizado, -a *adj* furious, enraged

encolerizar [14] **1** *vt* to infuriate, to enrage
2 encolerizarse *vpr* to get angry

encomendar [3] **1** *vt* to entrust; **les fue encomendada la tarea de redactar la constitución** they were entrusted with the task of writing the constitution; **me han encomendado el cuidado de su perro** they've asked me to look after their dog; **encomendó su alma a Dios** he commended his soul to God
2 encomendarse *vpr* **encomendarse a** *(persona)* to entrust oneself to; *(Dios, santos)* to put one's trust in; EXPR *Fam* **(hacer algo) sin encomendarse a Dios ni al diablo** (to do sth) entirely off one's own bat

encomendero *nm* (**a**) *Hist* = Spanish colonist in charge of an "encomienda" (**b**) *Cuba (carnicero)* wholesale meat supplier (**c**) *Perú (tendero)* grocer

encomiable *adj* laudable, praiseworthy

encomiar *vt Formal* to praise, to extol

encomiástico, -a *adj Formal* laudatory, eulogistic

encomienda *nf* (**a**) *(encargo)* assignment, mission (**b**) *Hist* = area of land and its native inhabitants given to a conquistador (**c**) *Am (paquete)* package, parcel

encomiendo *etc ver* **encomendar**

encomio *nm Formal* praise; **digno de e.** praiseworthy

encomioso, -a *adj Am* laudatory, eulogistic

enconado, -a *adj* (**a**) *(lucha, pelea, conflicto)* bitter; *(discusión, debate)* heated; *(partidario)* passionate, ardent (**b**) *(herida)* inflamed

enconamiento *nm* (**a**) *(rencor)* rancour, animosity (**b**) *(de herida)* inflammation

enconar 1 *vt* (**a**) *(lucha, pelea, conflicto)* to intensify, to make more bitter; *(discusión, debate)* to make more heated (**b**) *(herida)* to inflame
2 enconarse *vpr* (**a**) *(persona)* to get angry (**b**) *(lucha, pelea, conflicto)* to intensify, to become more bitter; *(discusión, debate)* to become heated (**c**) *(herida)* to become inflamed

encono *nm (rencor)* rancour, animosity

encontradizo, -a *adj* **hacerse el e. (con alguien)** to contrive a meeting (with sb)

encontrado, -a *adj (intereses)* conflicting; *(opiniones)* opposing; **tener sentimientos encontrados** to have mixed feelings

ENCONTRAR [64] **1** *vt* (**a**) *(buscando, por casualidad)* to find; **he encontrado el paraguas** I've found my umbrella; **encontré el libro que buscaba** I found the book I was looking for; **le han encontrado un cáncer** they've diagnosed her as having cancer; **encontré la mesa puesta** I found the table already set; **lo encontré durmiendo** I found him sleeping; **no encuentro palabras para expresar mi gratitud** I can't find the words to express my gratitude; EXPR *CSur Fam* **e. la vuelta a algo** to get to grips with sth
(**b**) *(dificultades)* to encounter; **no encontraron ninguna oposición al proyecto** they encountered no opposition to the project
(**c**) *(juzgar, considerar)* to find; **encontré muy positivos tus comentarios** I found your comments very positive; **encuentro infantil tu actitud** I find your attitude childish; **encuentro la ciudad/a tu hermana muy cambiada** the city/your sister has changed a lot, I find the city/your sister much changed; **no lo encuentro tan divertido como dice la gente** I don't find it *o* think it is as funny as people say; **no sé qué le encuentran a ese pintor** I don't know what they see in that painter
2 encontrarse *vpr* (**a**) *(estar)* to be; **se encuentra en París** she's in Paris; **¿dónde se encuentra la Oficina de Turismo?** where's the Tourist Information Office?; *Méx* **el Sr. López no se encuentra** Mr López isn't in; **entre los supervivientes se encuentran dos bebés** two babies are amongst the survivors; **varias ciudades, entre las que se encuentra Buenos Aires** several cities, including Buenos Aires
(**b**) *(de ánimo, salud)* to feel; **¿qué tal te encuentras?** how are you feeling?; **no se encuentra muy bien** she isn't very well; **no me encuentro con ganas de salir** I don't feel like going out; **el médico ha dicho que se encuentra fuera de peligro** the doctor said she's out of danger
(**c**) *(descubrir)* to find; **me he encontrado un reloj** I've found a watch; **encontrarse con que: fui a visitarle y me encontré con que ya no vivía allí** I went to visit him only to discover that he no longer lived there; **nos encontramos con que no quedaba comida** we found that there was no food left
(**d**) *(coincidir)* **encontrarse (con alguien)** to meet (sb); **me encontré con Juan** I ran into *o* met Juan
(**e**) *(reunirse)* to meet; **¿dónde nos encontraremos?** where shall we meet?; **quedaron en encontrarse a la salida del cine** they arranged to meet outside the cinema
(**f**) *(chocar)* to collide; **los dos trenes se encontraron con violencia** the two trains were involved in a violent collision

encontronazo *nm* (**a**) *(golpe) (entre vehículos)* collision, crash; *(entre personas)* collision, clash; **tuvo un e. con un defensa y quedó lesionado** he clashed with a defender and was injured (**b**) *(discusión)* row, set-to; **tuvo un e. con su jefe** she had a set-to with the boss

encoñado, -a *adj Esp Vulg* (**a**) *(enamorado)* **estar e. con alguien** to have the hots for sb (**b**) *(encaprichado)* **estar e. con algo** to be crazy *o* nuts about sth

encoñarse *vpr Esp Vulg* (**a**) *(enamorarse)* **e. con alguien** to get the hots for sb (**b**) *(encapricharse)* **e. con algo** to go crazy *o* nuts about sth

encopetado, -a *adj Pey (de clase alta)* posh, swanky; *(presuntuoso)* snooty, snobby

encorajinarse *vpr* to get angry, to lose one's temper
encorbatarse *vpr Fam* to wear a tie
encordado *nm CSur* strings
encordar [64] **1** *vt* (**a**) *(instrumento, raqueta)* to string (**b**) *(atar con cuerda)* to bind with a cord
2 encordarse *vpr (montañeros)* to rope up
encorsetar *vt* (**a**) *(poner corsé a)* to corset (**b**) *(poner límites a)* to straitjacket
encorvado, -a *adj* hunched; **anda** *o* **camina e.** he slouches
encorvadura *nf*, **encorvamiento** *nm* bending, curving
encorvar *vt* **1** to bend
2 encorvarse *vpr* to bend down *o* over
encostalar *vt Méx* to bag
encrespar 1 *vt* (**a**) *(pelo)* to curl (**b**) *(mar)* to make choppy *o* rough (**c**) *(irritar) (persona)* to irritate; *(ambiente)* to inflame; **sus comentarios encresparon los ánimos** her remarks raised people's hackles
2 encresparse *vpr* (**a**) *(pelo) (rizarse)* to curl; *(erizarse)* to stand on end (**b**) *(mar)* to get rough (**c**) *(persona)* to get irritated; **los ánimos se encresparon** people's hackles rose
encriptación *nf Informát* encryption
encriptar *vt Informát* to encrypt
encrucijada *nf* (**a**) *(cruce)* **una e. (de caminos)** a crossroads; **su narrativa es una e. de varios estilos** her writing brings together several different styles (**b**) *(situación difícil)* **estoy** *o* **me hallo en una e.** I'm in a quandary; **el proceso de paz se encuentra en una e.** the peace process has reached a crossroads
encuadernación *nf* (**a**) *(técnica)* binding; *(tapas)* covers ▸▸ ***e. en canutillo*** (plastic) comb binding; ***e. en cuero*** leather binding; ***e. en rústica*** paperback binding; ***e. en tela*** cloth binding (**b**) *(taller)* binder's, bookbinder's; **Encuadernaciones Olarte** *(empresa)* Olarte the Bookbinders
encuadernador, -ora *nm,f* bookbinder
encuadernar *vt* to bind
encuadrar 1 *vt* (**a**) *(clasificar)* to categorize, to classify (**como** as); **es un texto difícil de e. en los géneros habituales** it's a text which is hard to classify according to conventional genres; **la selección mexicana ha quedado encuadrada en el grupo A** the Mexican team has been drawn in group A (**b**) *Cine, Fot & TV (imagen)* to frame (**c**) *(enmarcar) (lienzo, fotografía, dibujo)* to frame
2 encuadrarse *vpr* **esta ley se encuadra en la nueva política económica del gobierno** this law forms part of the government's new economic policy; **su obra se encuadra en el modernismo** her work can be classed *o* categorized as modernist
encuadre *nm Fot* composition
encubierto, -a 1 *participio ver* **encubrir**
2 *adj* (**a**) *(intento)* covert (**b**) *(insulto, significado)* hidden
encubridor, -ora 1 *adj* concealing; **no es más que una maniobra encubridora** it's just an attempt to conceal things
2 *nm,f (de delito)* accessory (**de** to)
encubrimiento *nm* **está acusado de e.** he is accused of being an accessory
encubrir *vt* (**a**) *(delito)* to conceal, to cover up (**b**) *(delincuente)* to cover up for (**c**) *(hechos, sentimientos, intenciones)* to conceal, to hide
encuentro 1 *ver* **encontrar**
2 *nm* (**a**) *(acción)* meeting, encounter; **tuvieron un e. fortuito** they had a chance encounter *o* meeting; **fijemos un lugar** *o* **sitio de e.** let's decide on a place to meet; **ir** *o* **salir al e. de alguien** *(para recibir)* to go to meet sb; *(para atacar)* to confront sb; **una dependienta fue a su e.** a sales assistant came over to her; **unos matones salieron a su e.** some thugs made towards him
(**b**) *(reunión)* meeting; **tener un e. con alguien** to have a meeting with sb
(**c**) *(congreso)* conference
(**d**) *(deportivo)* game, match
(**e**) *Mil* skirmish
encuerado, -a *adj Cuba, Méx Fam* naked, *Br* starkers, *US* buck naked
encuerar *Cuba, Méx Fam* **1** *vt* (**a**) *(desnudar)* to strip (**b**) *(en el juego)* to skin, to clear out
2 encuerarse *vpr (desnudarse)* to strip
encuerdo *etc ver* **encordar**
encuesta *nf* (**a**) *(sondeo)* survey, opinion poll; **hacer** *o* **realizar una e.** to carry out *o* conduct a survey; **me hicieron una e. en la calle** I was asked to answer a survey in the street ▸▸ ***e. de opinión*** opinion poll; ***e. a pie de urna*** exit poll; ***e. de población activa*** = survey of the economically active population (**b**) *(investigación)* investigation, inquiry
encuestado, -a *nm,f* person polled; **los encuestados** those polled, the respondents
encuestador, -ora *nm,f* pollster
encuestar *vt* to poll
encular 1 *vt Vulg (realizar sexo anal con)* to ass-fuck
2 encularse *vpr Arg muy Fam* to go into a huff, to take the huff
encumbrado, -a *adj* exalted, distinguished
encumbramiento *nm* (**a**) *(acción)* rise (**b**) *(posición)* distinguished *o* exalted position
encumbrar 1 *vt* (**a**) *(subir de categoría)* to bring to prominence; **la novela que lo encumbró (a la fama)** the novel which brought him fame (**b**) *(ensalzar, elogiar)* to extol; **fue encumbrado por la crítica** it was extolled by the critics
2 encumbrarse *vpr* to rise to a higher position; **se encumbró a** *o* **hasta la élite del atletismo mundial** he propelled himself into the ranks of the world's top athletes
encurtidos *nmpl* pickles
encurtir *vt* to pickle
ende: por ende *loc adv Formal* hence, therefore
endeble *adj* (**a**) *(persona)* weak, feeble (**b**) *(objeto, estructura, material)* fragile (**c**) *(argumento, pretexto, disculpa)* weak, feeble
endeblez *nf* (**a**) *(de persona)* weakness, feebleness (**b**) *(de objeto, estructura, material)* fragility (**c**) *(de argumento, pretexto, disculpa)* weakness, feebleness
endecágono *nm Geom* hendecagon
endecasílabo, -a 1 *adj* hendecasyllabic
2 *nm* hendecasyllabic verse
endecha *nf Lit* lament
endemia *nf Med* endemic disease
endémico, -a *adj* (**a**) *Med* endemic (**b**) *Biol* endemic (**c**) *(permanente)* endemic; **el hambre es e. en la región** hunger is endemic in the region; **uno de los males endémicos de nuestra economía** one of the endemic ills of our economy
endemismo *nm* endemic species
endemoniadamente *adv (difícil, complicado)* fiendishly
endemoniado, -a 1 *adj* (**a**) *(poseído)* possessed (by the devil) (**b**) *(maldito) (niño, aparato)* confounded, blasted (**c**) *(difícil) (trabajo, crucigrama, examen)* fiendishly difficult (**d**) *(desagradable) (olor, sabor, genio)* foul, vile; *(tiempo, clima, día)* foul, filthy
2 *nm,f* person possessed by the devil
endenantes *adv Am Fam* before
enderezamiento *nm* (**a**) *(acción de poner derecho)* straightening (**b**) *(acción de poner vertical)* putting upright
enderezar [14] **1** *vt* (**a**) *(poner derecho)* to straighten (**b**) *(poner vertical)* to put upright (**c**) *(corregir)* to set right, to straighten out; **el barco enderezó su rumbo** the ship steadied its course; **quiere e. su vida** she wants to get her life in order; **el gobierno trata de e. la economía** the government is trying to put the economy right *o* in order
2 *vi (en un vehículo)* to straighten up; **pude e. a tiempo** I managed to straighten up in time
3 enderezarse *vpr* (**a**) *(sentado)* to sit up straight; *(de pie)* to stand up straight (**b**) *(corregirse) (persona)* to straighten oneself out; *(economía, situación)* to right itself, to sort itself out
endeudado, -a *adj* indebted, in debt
endeudamiento *nm (de persona, país)* indebtedness
endeudarse *vpr* to get into debt
endiabladamente *adv (difícil, complicado)* fiendishly
endiablado, -a *adj* (**a**) *(maldito)* confounded, blasted; **el e. teléfono no paraba de sonar** the blasted phone wouldn't stop ringing; **¡esos niños endiablados me van a volver loco!** those little devils are going to drive me mad!
(**b**) *(difícil) (problema, crucigrama, examen)* fiendishly difficult
(**c**) *(desagradable) (olor, sabor, genio)* foul, vile; *(tiempo, clima, día)* foul, filthy; **soplaba un viento e.** there was a terrible wind blowing
(**d**) *(velocidad)* breakneck
endibia *nf* endive
endilgar [38] *vt Fam* **e. algo a alguien** *(bulto, tarea)* to lumber sb with sth; *(sermón, discurso)* to dish sth out to sb; **me han endilgado la limpieza de la casa** they've lumbered me with (the job of) cleaning

the house; **les endilgó una conferencia de dos horas** she subjected them to a two-hour lecture; **me endilgaron a los niños el sábado por la noche** they dumped their kids on me on Saturday evening

endiñar *vt Esp Fam* **(a)** *(golpe)* **le endiñó un puñetazo/una patada** she landed a punch/kick on him, she gave him a punch/kick; **le endiñó un bofetón** she gave him a slap in the face **(b)** *(trabajo, tarea)* **e. algo a alguien** to lumber sb with sth; **le endiñaron la tarea de llevar a los niños al cine** he was lumbered with taking the kids to the cinema

endiosamiento *nm* self-importance, conceit

endiosar 1 *vt* to deify
2 **endiosarse** *vpr* to become conceited *o* full of oneself

endivia *nf* endive

endocardio *nm Anat* endocardium

endocarditis *nf inv Med* endocarditis

endocarpio *nm Bot* endocarp

endocrino, -a *Med* 1 *adj* endocrine; **glándula endocrina** endocrine gland
2 *nm,f* endocrinologist

endocrinología *nf Med* endocrinology

endocrinólogo, -a *nm,f Med* endocrinologist

endodoncia *nf* **(a)** *(tratamiento)* root canal treatment; **hacer una e. a alguien** to give sb root canal treatment **(b)** *(especialidad)* endodontics *(singular)*

endoesqueleto *nm Zool* endoskeleton

endogamia *nf* **(a)** *(práctica cultural)* endogamy **(b)** *(en familia real, especies animales)* inbreeding **(c)** *Pey (en instituciones)* = tendency to favour internal candidates for appointments

endogámico, -a *adj* endogamous

endógeno, -a *adj* endogenous

endometrio *nm Anat* endometrium

endometriosis *nf inv Med* endometriosis

endometritis *nf inv Med* endometritis

endomingado, -a *adj Fam* dressed-up, dolled-up; **iba todo e.** he was all dressed up in his Sunday best, he was dressed (up) to the nines

endomingar [38] *Fam* 1 *vt* to dress up, to doll up
2 **endomingarse** *vpr* to get dressed *o* dolled up in one's best clothes

endomorfo, -a *nm,f* endomorph

endorfina *nf* endorphin

endorreico, -a *adj Geol* endorheic

endosante *nmf Com* endorser

endosar *vt* **(a)** *Com* to endorse **(b)** *Fam (bulto, tarea)* **e. algo a alguien** to lumber sb with sth; **le endosaron a los niños** they landed her with the children

endosatario, -a *nm,f Com* endorsee

endoscopia *nf Med* endoscopy

endoscopio *nm Med* endoscope

endosfera *nf Geol* core

endoso *nm Com* endorsement

endospermo *nm Bot* endosperm

endotelio *nm Anat* endothelium

endotérmico, -a *adj Chem* endothermic

endovenoso, -a *adj Med* intravenous

endrina *nf* sloe

endrino *nm* blackthorn, sloe

endrogado, -a *adj CAm, Méx* **estar e.** to be in debt

endrogarse [38] *vpr Chile, Méx, Perú (endeudarse)* to get into debt

endulzante *nm* sweetener

endulzar [14] *vt* **(a)** *(con azúcar)* to sweeten **(b)** *(con dulzura)* to ease, to make more bearable

endurecedor *nm* hardener

endurecer [46] 1 *vt* **(a)** *(hacer más duro) (pasta, mezcla, alimento)* to harden
(b) *(fortalecer) (persona)* to toughen, to strengthen; *(músculo)* to strengthen
(c) *(insensibilizar)* to harden; **el sufrimiento endureció su corazón** suffering hardened his heart
(d) *(hacer más severo) (ley, pena, requisitos)* to toughen; *(actitud, posturas)* to harden
2 **endurecerse** *vpr* **(a)** *(ponerse duro) (pasta, mezcla, alimento)* to harden, to become hard; *(cemento)* to set, to harden **(b)** *(fortalecerse) (persona)* to become tough *o* hardy; *(músculo)* to become stronger
(c) *(insensibilizarse) (persona)* to become hardened; *(corazón, carácter)* to grow hard **(d)** *(hacerse más severo) (ley, pena, requisitos)* to become tougher; *(actitud, posturas)* to harden

endurecimiento *nm* **(a)** *(de pasta, mezcla, alimento)* hardening **(b)** *(de músculo)* strengthening **(c)** *(de penas, requisitos)* toughening; *(de posturas)* hardening **(d)** *(insensibilización)* hardening

endurezco *etc ver* **endurecer**

ene. *(abrev de* **enero**) Jan., January

enea *nf Br* bulrush, *US* cattail; **silla de e.** chair with a wickerwork seat

eneágono *nm Geom* nonagon

Eneas *n Mitol* Aeneas

enebrina *nf* juniper berry

enebro *nm* juniper

eneldo *nm* dill

enema *nm* enema; **poner un e. a alguien** to give sb an enema

enemigo, -a 1 *adj* **(a)** *(rival)* enemy; **los ejércitos enemigos** the enemy armies **(b)** *(no partidario)* **ser e. de (hacer) algo** to be opposed to *o* against (doing) sth; **es e. de una educación muy estricta** he is not in favour of bringing children up strictly; **soy e. de tener animales en casa** I don't hold with keeping pets at home
2 *nm,f (rival)* enemy; **va haciéndose enemigos por todas partes** he makes enemies wherever he goes; **los enemigos de la patria** the enemies of the nation; EXPR **no hay e. pequeño** *(en general)* don't underestimate your opponent; *(en fútbol)* there are no easy games ▸▸ *Fam* ***el e. malo*** the Devil; ***el e. público número uno*** public enemy number one
3 *nm (ejército rival)* enemy; **pasarse al e.** to go over to the enemy; EXPR *Hum* **al e., ni agua** there'll be no quarter given

enemistad *nf* enmity; **su e. duraba ya años** they had been enemies for years; **una e. entre familias** a family feud; **siento una profunda e. hacia ellos** I feel intense hatred for them

enemistado, -a *adj* **dos países enemistados por...** two countries who are enemies because of...; **está e. con sus vecinos** he has fallen out with his neighbours

enemistar 1 *vt* to make enemies of; **el testamento enemistó a los hermanos** the will set the brothers against each other
2 **enemistarse** *vpr* to fall out **(con/por** with/over); **si Francia se enemistara con Alemania...** if France were to fall out with Germany...

energética *nf* energetics *(singular)*

energético, -a *adj* **(a)** *(de energía)* energy; **el consumo e.** energy consumption; **las legumbres proporcionan un alto aporte e.** pulses provide lots of energy **(b)** *(producto, alimento)* energy-giving

energía *nf* **(a)** *(para máquina, sistema)* power, energy; *(para el cuerpo, organismo)* energy; **fuentes de e.** sources of energy; **el aporte necesario de e. para el organismo** the body's energy needs ▸▸ ***energías alternativas*** alternative energy sources; ***e. atómica*** nuclear power *o* energy; ***e. calórica*** heat energy; *Fís* ***e. cinética*** kinetic energy; ***e. eléctrica*** electric energy; ***e. eólica*** wind energy *o* power; ***e. geotérmica*** geothermal energy *o* power; ***e. hidráulica*** water power; ***e. hidroeléctrica*** hydroelectric power; ***e. limpia*** clean energy; ***e. mareomotriz*** tidal *o* wave energy; ***e. nuclear*** nuclear power *o* energy; ***e. de las olas*** *o* ***del oleaje*** tidal *o* wave energy; *Fís* ***e. potencial*** potential energy; ***e. radiante*** radiant energy; ***energías renovables*** renewable forms of energy; ***e. solar*** solar energy *o* power; ***e. térmica*** thermal energy *o* power
(b) *(vigor físico)* energy; **su trabajo le resta energías** his work doesn't leave him much energy; **hay que empujar con e.** you have to push hard
(c) *(actitud)* vigour, forcefulness; **defendió su postura con e.** she energetically defended her position; **respondió con e.** he responded emphatically

enérgicamente *adv (vigorosamente)* vigorously

enérgico, -a *adj* **(a)** *(físicamente) (persona, salto)* energetic; *(golpe)* vigorous, powerful; *(gesto, movimiento)* vigorous, energetic **(b)** *(decidido, firme) (persona, carácter)* forceful; *(medida)* firm; *(defensa, protesta)* vigorous, energetic; *(respuesta)* emphatic

energúmeno, -a *nm,f* lunatic; **se puso hecho un e.** he went berserk *o* crazy; **gritaba como un e.** he was screaming like one possessed; **tuve que trabajar como un e.** I had to work like crazy; **bebían como energúmenos** they were drinking like crazy *o* like there was no tomorrow

enero *nm* January; *ver también* **septiembre**

enervante *adj* **(a)** *(debilitador)* draining **(b)** *Fam (exasperante)* irritating

enervar *vt* (a) *(debilitar)* to sap, to weaken (b) *Fam (poner nervioso)* to irritate

enésimo, -a *adj* (a) *Mat* nth; **X elevado a la enésima potencia** X (raised) to the nth power (b) *(para indicar repetición)* umpteenth; **por enésima vez** for the umpteenth time

enfadadizo, -a *adj* touchy, irritable

enfadado, -a *adj esp Esp (irritado)* angry; *(molesto)* annoyed; **estar e. con alguien** to be angry/annoyed with sb; **está e. con sus padres** he's angry/annoyed with his parents; **estoy muy e. contigo** I'm very angry/annoyed with you; **estar e. por algo** to be angry/annoyed about sth; **están enfadados desde hace años** they've been on bad terms with one another for years

enfadar *esp Esp* **1** *vt (irritar)* to anger; *(molestar)* to annoy; **consiguió e. a todo el mundo con sus impertinencias** she managed to annoy everybody with her cheeky remarks

2 enfadarse *vpr* (a) *(irritarse)* to get angry (**con** with); *(molestarse)* to get annoyed (**con** with); **vas a conseguir que me enfade** you're going to make me angry; **no te enfades, pero creo que te equivocas** don't get annoyed, but I think you're wrong; **no te enfades con quien no tiene la culpa** don't get angry with someone who's not to blame

(b) *(pelearse)* to fall out; **se enfadaron por una bobada** they fell out over a silly little thing

enfado *nm esp Esp* (a) *(por irritarse)* anger; *(por molestarse)* annoyance; **puso cara de e.** she scowled (in annoyance); **agarrarse un e.** to get angry/annoyed; **¿se te pasó ya el e.?** have you calmed down yet? (b) *(enemistad)* **su e.** the rift *o* hostility between them; **su e. dura ya años** *(entre ellos)* they fell out years ago, they've been on bad terms with one another for years

enfadoso, -a *adj esp Esp* annoying, irritating

enfangar [38] **1** *vt* to cover in mud

2 enfangarse *vpr* (a) *(con fango)* to get covered in mud (b) *Fam (involucrarse)* to get mixed up (**en** in); **enfangarse en un asunto sucio** to get mixed up in shady business

enfardar *vt* to pack, to wrap

énfasis *nm inv* (a) *(en la entonación)* stress, emphasis (b) *(relieve, importancia)* emphasis; **poner é. en algo** to emphasize sth (c) *(afectación)* exaggerated emphasis

enfáticamente *adv* emphatically

enfático, -a *adj* emphatic

enfatizar [14] *vt* to emphasize, to stress

enfermante *adj CSur* exasperating, infuriating

enfermar 1 *vt* (a) *(causar enfermedad a)* to make ill (b) *Fam (irritar)* to drive up the wall; **me enferma esa actitud** that kind of attitude really gets to me

2 *vi* to fall ill; **e. del corazón/pecho** to develop a heart condition/chest complaint

3 enfermarse *vpr* (a) *(de enfermedad)* to fall ill (b) *CSur Fam (menstruar)* to have one's period

enfermedad *nf* (a) *(física)* illness; **contraer una e.** to catch a disease *o* illness; **padecer** *o* **sufrir una e.** to suffer from an illness; **enfermedades pulmonares** lung *o Espec* pulmonary diseases; **enfermedades del corazón/de la piel** heart/skin diseases ►► ***e. de Alzheimer*** Alzheimer's disease; ***e. autoinmune*** autoimmune disease; ***e. congénita*** congenital disease; ***e. contagiosa*** contagious disease; ***e. de Chagas*** Chagas' disease; ***e. de Creutzfeld(t)-Jakob*** Creutzfeldt-Jakob disease; ***e. degenerativa*** progressive disease; ***e. hereditaria*** hereditary disease; ***e. incurable*** incurable disease; ***e. infecciosa*** infectious disease; ***e. inflamatoria pélvica*** pelvic inflammatory disease; ***e. laboral*** occupational disease; ***e. mental*** mental illness; ***e. notificable*** notifiable disease; ***e. obsesivo compulsiva*** obsessive compulsive disorder; ***e. de los olmos*** Dutch elm disease; ***e. de Parkinson*** Parkinson's disease; ***e. profesional*** occupational disease; ***e. del sueño*** sleeping sickness; ***e. de transmisión sexual*** sexually transmitted disease; *Fam* ***e. de las vacas locas*** mad cow disease; ***e. vascular*** vascular disease; ***e. venérea*** venereal disease

(b) *(problema)* ill; **una de las enfermedades de nuestra sociedad** one of the ills of our society

enfermera *nf* nurse ►► ***e. jefe*** charge nurse

enfermería *nf* (a) *(lugar)* sick bay (b) *(oficio, estudios)* nursing

enfermero *nm* male nurse ►► ***e. jefe*** charge nurse

enfermizo, -a *adj* (a) *(persona)* sickly (b) *(interés, pasión, curiosidad)* unhealthy

enfermo, -a 1 *adj* ill, sick; **cuidaba de gente enferma** he looked after sick people *o* people who were ill; **está enferma con paperas** she's ill with mumps; **caer e.** to fall ill; *Esp* **ponerse e.** to fall ill, to get sick; *Esp* **se puso e. del estómago** he got a stomach complaint; EXPR **poner e. a alguien** *(enojar)* to drive sb up the wall; **su actitud me pone e.** his attitude really gets to me

2 *nm,f (en general)* sick person; *(bajo tratamiento)* patient; **los enfermos** the sick; **los enfermos de este hospital** the patients in this hospital; **los enfermos de Parkinson** Parkinson's sufferers, people with *o* suffering from Parkinson's (disease); **un e. del hígado** a person with a liver complaint ►► ***e. mental*** *(en general)* mentally ill person; *(bajo tratamiento)* mental patient; ***e. terminal*** terminally ill person/patient; **los enfermos terminales** the terminally ill

enfervorizadamente *adv* with wild enthusiasm

enfervorizado, -a *adj* frenzied

enfervorizar [14] **1** *vt (entusiasmar)* to thrill, to enthuse; *(exaltar)* to inflame, to whip up

2 enfervorizarse *vpr (entusiasmarse)* to be thrilled, to go into ecstasies; *(exaltarse)* to get whipped up

enfiestarse *vpr Am* to live it up

enfilado, -a *adj Esp Fam* **tener a alguien e.** to have it in for sb

enfilar 1 *vt* (a) *(camino)* to go *o* head straight along; **el autobús enfiló la avenida hacia la plaza** the bus went down the avenue towards the square; **los atletas enfilaron la recta final** the runners headed into *o* entered the home stretch

(b) *(arma)* to aim (**a** *o* **hacia** at)

(c) *(protestas, acciones)* to aim, to direct; **enfiló la conversación hacia temas políticos** she steered the conversation towards political subjects

(d) *(enhebrar)* to thread, to string

2 *vi* **e. hacia/por** to go *o* head straight towards/for; **la embarcación enfiló hacia el norte** the boat headed north

enfisema *nm* emphysema ►► ***e. pulmonar*** pulmonary emphysema

enflaquecer [46] **1** *vt* to make thin

2 *vi* to grow thin, to lose weight

enflaquecimiento *nm* (a) *(adelgazamiento)* losing weight, slimming (b) *(debilitación)* weakening, debilitation

enflautar *vt Col, Guat, Méx Fam (encasquetar)* to foist, to unload

enflusarse *vpr Ven Fam* to get dressed up in a suit

enfocado *adj (imagen)* in focus

enfocar [60] **1** *vt* (a) *(para dar nitidez) (imagen)* to get in focus; *(objetivo, aparato)* to focus; **enfócanos bien** make sure you get us in focus; **enfocó su cámara y disparó** she focused her camera and took the shot

(b) *(dirigir la cámara hacia)* to focus on

(c) *(iluminar) (sujeto: luz, foco)* to shine on; *(sujeto: persona)* to shine a light on; **me enfocó con una linterna** he shone a *Br* torch *o US* flashlight at me; **enfocaron el avión con los reflectores** they caught the plane in the searchlights

(d) *(tema, asunto)* to approach, to look at; **lo enfocaré de otro modo** I'll approach it from a different angle

2 *vi* to focus; **e. hacia algo/alguien** *(sujeto: cámara)* to focus on sth/sb; *(sujeto: luz)* to shine on sth/sb

enfoque *nm* (a) *(de imagen) (acción)* focusing; *(resultado)* focus ►► ***e. automático*** automatic focusing; ***e. manual*** manual focusing

(b) *(de tema, asunto)* approach (**de** to), angle (**de** on); **le dio un e. muy original a su discurso** she took an original approach in her talk; **habría que darle otro e. al asunto** the issue should be approached from a different angle, we should look at the issue in a different way

enfrascado, -a *adj* **estar e. en** *(lectura, conversación, tarea)* to be totally absorbed *o* engrossed in; *(riña, pelea)* to be embroiled in

enfrascamiento *nm* total involvement

enfrascar [60] **1** *vt (en frascos)* to bottle

2 enfrascarse *vpr* **enfrascarse en** *(lectura, conversación, tarea)* to become absorbed *o* engrossed in; *(riña, pelea)* to get embroiled in

enfrentamiento *nm* confrontation; **hubo enfrentamientos con la policía** there were confrontations with the police; **un e. entre las dos alas del partido** a confrontation between the two wings of the party ►► ***e. armado*** armed confrontation *o* clash

enfrentado, -a *adj* **mantienen posturas enfrentadas** they hold conflicting views

enfrentar 1 *vt* (a) *(enemistar)* to bring into conflict (b) *(poner frente a frente)* to bring face to face (**con** with); **un partido que enfrentará al actual campeón con sus antiguos rivales** a game that will pit the current champions against their old rivals (c) *(hacer frente a)* to confront, to face; **enfrentan el futuro con inquietud** they face the future with unease

2 enfrentarse *vpr* (a) *(afrontar)* **enfrentarse a algo** to confront sth, to face sth; **nos enfrentamos a una grave crisis** we are facing a serious crisis; **enfrentarse a los hechos** to face the facts; **se enfrentó a su**

enfermedad con valor she faced up to her illness bravely
(**b**) *(en contienda) (dos bandos)* to meet, to clash; **los dos equipos se enfrentarán por el campeonato** the two teams will play each other for the championship; **enfrentarse a** *o* **con alguien** to confront sb; **nos enfrentamos al enemigo** we confronted the enemy; **los manifestantes se enfrentaron con la policía** the demonstrators clashed with the police; **a Brasil le toca enfrentarse con Suecia** Brazil has been drawn against Sweden
(**c**) *(discutir)* to clash

enfrente *adv* (**a**) *(al otro lado)* opposite; **vive e.** he lives opposite; **la tienda de e.** the shop across the road; **e. de algo** opposite *o* facing sth; **hay un hotel e. de la estación** there's a hotel opposite *o* facing the station; **e. de alguien** opposite *o* facing sb; **yo me senté e. de ella** I sat opposite *o* facing her; **lo tenía e. de mí y no me daba ni cuenta** he was right in front of me and I didn't even notice
(**b**) *(en contra)* **tiene a todos e.** everyone's against her; **tuvimos e. a un gran equipo** we were playing against a great team

enfriamiento *nm* (**a**) *(catarro)* chill (**b**) *(de motor, atmósfera)* cooling (**c**) *(de situación, relación, sentimiento)* cooling; **el e. de las relaciones entre Francia y Estados Unidos** the cooling of relations between France and the United States

enfriar [32] **1** *vt* (**a**) *(sopa, motor, atmósfera)* to cool (down); *(bebida fría)* to chill (**b**) *(situación, sentimiento)* to cool; **aquello enfrió su relación** that made their relationship more distant, their friendship cooled as a result
2 *vi* **esta nevera no enfría** this fridge doesn't work properly; **espera hasta que la sopa enfríe** wait for the soup to cool down; **mete las cervezas a e. en el refrigerador** put the beers in the fridge to get cold
3 *v impersonal* to get colder
4 enfriarse *vpr* (**a**) *(líquido) (quedarse suficientemente frío)* to cool down; **deja que se enfríe un poco el café** let the coffee cool down a bit
(**b**) *(líquido) (quedarse demasiado frío)* to go cold; **se te va a e. la sopa** your soup is going to get cold
(**c**) *(situación, relación, sentimiento)* to cool down
(**d**) *(coger frío)* to get cold; *(resfriarse)* to catch a chill; **enseguida se me enfrían las manos** my hands get cold straight away

enfundar 1 *vt (espada)* to sheathe; *(pistola)* to put in its holster, to reholster; *(paraguas)* to put the cover on; *(taco de billar)* to put in its case
2 enfundarse *vpr* **enfundarse algo** to wrap oneself up in sth

enfurecer [46] **1** *vt* to infuriate, to madden
2 enfurecerse *vpr* (**a**) *(persona)* to get furious (**b**) *(mar)* to become rough

enfurecido, -a *adj* (**a**) *(persona)* furious; **estaba e. con ella** I was furious with her (**b**) *(mar)* raging

enfurecimiento *nm* anger, fury

enfurezco *etc ver* **enfurecer**

enfurruñado, -a *adj Fam* sulky, in a huff; **estar e.** to be sulking

enfurruñamiento *nm Fam* sulking

enfurruñarse *vpr Fam* to sulk, to go in a huff

engalanado, -a *adj* (**a**) *(persona)* dressed up (**b**) *(ciudad, coche)* decked out (**con** *o* **de** with)

engalanar 1 *vt* to decorate
2 engalanarse *vpr* (**a**) *(persona)* to dress up (**b**) *(ciudad)* to be decked out (**con** with)

engalletamiento *nm Ven Fam* gridlock

engalletar *Ven Fam* **1** *vt* to entangle, to get into a jam
2 engalletarse *vpr* to become gridlocked

enganchada *nf Fam* dust-up, set-to; **tener una e. con alguien** to have a set-to *o* run-in with sb

enganchado, -a 1 *adj* (**a**) *(prendido)* **la falda se me quedó enganchada a la puerta** I caught my skirt on the door (**b**) *Fam (adicto)* hooked (**a** on)
2 *nm,f Andes, CAm, Méx* contract labourer

enganchador, -ora *nm,f Andes, CAm, Méx* = person who recruits labourers for a contractor

enganchar 1 *vt* (**a**) *(acoplar) (vagones, trenes)* to couple; *(remolque, caballos)* to hitch up
(**b**) *(colgar)* to hang (up); **había un jamón enganchado de un garfio** there was a ham hanging from a hook; **enganchó las riendas a una rama** she tied the reins to a branch; **me enganchó del brazo** he linked arms with me; **me enganchó del cuello** he put an arm round my neck
(**c**) *(pescar con anzuelo)* to hook
(**d**) *Fam (engatusar)* to cajole; **e. a alguien para que haga algo** to rope sb into doing sth
(**e**) *Fam (pillar) (empleo, marido)* to land (oneself); *(gripe, resfriado)* to catch; **¡como te enganche, te enteras!** if I catch you, you'll know all about it!
(**f**) *Taurom* to toss
(**g**) *Andes, CAm, Méx (reclutar)* to hire, to contract
2 *vi Fam (hacer adicto)* to be addictive; **un videojuego de los que enganchan** an addictive video game
3 engancharse *vpr* (**a**) *(prenderse)* **engancharse algo con** *o* **en** to catch sth on; **se le enganchó la falda en las zarzas** she caught her skirt on the brambles; **te has enganchado las medias** you've caught *o* snagged your tights on something
(**b**) *(alistarse)* to enlist, to join up
(**c**) *Fam (hacerse adicto)* to get hooked (**a** on)
(**d**) *Andes, CAm, Méx (para trabajo)* to sign up
(**e**) *RP Fam (enamorarse)* **engancharse con alguien** to hitch *o* hook up with sb

enganche *nm* (**a**) *(de vagones, trenes)* coupling; *(de remolque, caballos)* hitching up (**b**) *(gancho)* hook (**c**) *(reclutamiento)* enlistment (**d**) *Fam (afición)* **tener (un) e. con algo** to be hooked on sth (**e**) *Méx (depósito)* deposit (**f**) *RP (en prenda)* snag

enganchón *nm (de ropa, tela)* snag

engañabobos *Fam* **1** *nm inv (cosa)* con (trick); **esa promoción es un e.** that special offer is a con
2 *nmf inv (persona)* con man, con artist

engañadizo, -a *adj* gullible, credulous

engañapichanga *nf RP Fam* con (trick); **esa propuesta es e.** that scheme is a con

engañar 1 *vt* (**a**) *(mentir)* to deceive; **engañó a su padre haciéndole ver que había aprobado** she deceived her father into believing that she had passed; **es difícil engañarla** she is not easily deceived, she's hard to fool; **logró e. al portero** he managed to outsmart the goalkeeper; **me engañó lo bien que vestía y que hablaba** she was so well dressed and so well spoken that I was taken in; **¿a quién te crees que vas a e.?** who are you trying to fool *o* kid?; **a mí no me engañas, sé que tienes cincuenta años** you can't fool me, I know you're fifty
(**b**) *(ser infiel a)* to deceive, to cheat on; **engaña a su marido** she cheats on her husband; **me engañó con mi mejor amiga** he cheated on me with my best friend
(**c**) *(estafar)* to cheat, to swindle; **te engañaron vendiéndote esto tan caro** they cheated you if they sold that to you for such a high price; EXPR **e. a alguien como a un chino** *o* **a un niño** to take sb for a ride
(**d**) *(hacer más llevadero)* to appease; **e. el hambre** to take the edge off one's hunger
2 *vi* to be deceptive *o* misleading; **engaña mucho, no es tan tonto como parece** you can easily get the wrong impression, he's not as stupid as he seems; EXPR **las apariencias engañan** appearances can be deceptive
3 engañarse *vpr* (**a**) *(hacerse ilusiones)* to delude oneself; **se engaña si cree esto** she's deluding herself if she thinks so; **no te engañes, ya no lo volverás a ver** don't kid yourself, you'll never see it again now
(**b**) *(equivocarse)* to be wrong; **si no me engaño...** if I'm not mistaken...

engañifa *nf Fam (estafa)* swindle

engaño *nm* (**a**) *(mentira)* deception, deceit; **se ganó su confianza con algún e.** she gained his trust through a deception; **lo obtuvo mediante e.** she obtained it by deception; **todo fue un e.** it was all a deception; EXPR **llamarse a e.** *(lamentarse)* to claim to have been misled; *(engañarse)* to delude oneself; **para que luego no te llames a e.** so you can't claim to have been misled afterwards; **no nos llamemos a e., el programa se puede mejorar** let's not delude ourselves, the program could be improved; **que nadie se llame a e., la economía no va bien** let no one have any illusions about it, the economy isn't doing well
(**b**) *(estafa)* swindle; **ha sido víctima de un e. en la compra del terreno** he was swindled over the sale of the land
(**c**) *(ardid)* ploy, trick; **de nada van a servirte tus engaños** your ploys will get you nowhere; **las rebajas son un e. para que la gente compre lo que no necesita** sales are a ploy to make people buy things they don't need
(**d**) *Taurom* bullfighter's cape
(**e**) *(para pescar)* lure

engañosamente *adv (deshonestamente)* deceitfully

engañoso, -a *adj* (**a**) *(aspecto, apariencia, impresión)* deceptive (**b**) *(persona, palabras)* deceitful

engarabitarse *vpr Fam (subir)* to climb, to go up

engarce *nm* setting

engargolado, -a *adj Méx (metálico)* spiral binding; *(plástico)* comb binding

engarzar [14] *vt* (a) *(encadenar) (abalorios)* to thread; *(perlas)* to string (b) *(diamante, piedra preciosa)* to set; **un rubí engarzado en oro** a ruby set in gold (c) *(palabras, ideas, historias)* to string together

engastar *vt* to set, to mount

engaste *nm (en joyería) (acción)* setting, mounting; *(montura)* mount

engatillarse *vpr* to jam

engatusador, -ora *Fam* 1 *adj* coaxing, cajoling
2 *nm,f* coaxer

engatusamiento *nm Fam* coaxing, cajoling

engatusar *vt Fam* to sweet-talk; **se dejó e. por un timador** he let himself be taken in by a con artist; **no trates de engatusarme** don't try to get round me; **logré engatusarlo para que viniera** I managed to coax him into coming

engavetar *vt Ven* (a) *(guardar)* to put away in a drawer (b) *(esconder)* to move to the bottom of the pile

engendrar *vt* (a) *(hijo, cría)* to conceive (b) *(proyecto, idea)* to conceive (of) (c) *(sentimiento, sensación, duda)* to give rise to, to engender; *(situación, conflicto, problema)* to give rise to, to cause; **la falta de cariño engendra inseguridad** lack of affection gives rise to insecurity; **engendró un clima de miedo y desconfianza** it gave rise to *o* engendered an atmosphere of fear and distrust

engendro *nm* (a) *(ser deforme)* freak, deformed creature; *(niño)* malformed child (b) *(obra fea o mala)* monstrosity

englobar *vt* to include

engolado, -a *adj (presuntuoso)* presumptuous, arrogant; *(pomposo)* pompous, bombastic

engolar *vt* **e. la voz** to put on a pompous voice

engolosinarse *vpr* **e. con algo** to develop a taste for sth

engomado *nm (papel)* gummed paper

engomar *vt* to put glue on, to gum

engominado, -a *adj (pelo)* slicked-back

engominar 1 *vt* to put hair cream on
2 **engominarse** *vpr* to put on hair cream

engorda *nf Chile, Méx* (a) *(ceba)* fattening (up) (b) *(ganado)* cattle fattened for slaughter

engordar 1 *vt* (a) *(animal)* to fatten (up) (b) *(cifras, estadísticas)* to pad; *(cuenta bancaria)* to fatten
2 *vi* (a) *(persona)* to put on weight; *(animal)* to grow fat, to fatten; **he engordado 6 kilos** I've put on 6 kilos (b) *(comida, bebida)* to be fattening; **sólo como cosas que no engorden** I only eat non-fattening foods

engorde *nm* fattening (up)

engorro *nm* nuisance

engorroso, -a *adj (molesto)* bothersome; *(físicamente)* cumbersome; **la engorrosa tarea de hacer la compra** the tedious job of doing the shopping; **un problema muy e.** a very awkward problem; **el e. cinturón de seguridad** the irksome seat belt

engrampadora *nf RP* stapler

engrampar *vt RP* to staple

engranaje *nm* (a) *(acción)* gearing (b) *(mecanismo) (de reloj, piñón)* cogs; *(de automóvil)* gears ▸▸ ***e. cónico*** bevel gear; ***e. helicoidal*** helical gear; ***e. de tornillo sin fin*** worm gear (c) *(conjunto de dientes)* gear teeth (d) *(enlace) (de ideas)* chain, sequence (e) *(aparato) (político, burocrático)* machinery; **el lento e. de la administración de justicia** the slow grinding of the wheels of justice

engranar 1 *vt* (a) *(piezas)* to engage (b) *(ideas)* to link, to connect (c) *Am (marchas)* to engage
2 *vi RP Fam* to fly off the handle, to flare up; **ojo con él, que enseguida engrana** watch what you say to him, he flies off the handle at the least thing

engrandecer [46] *vt* (a) *(ennoblecer)* **su gesto lo engrandece** his gesture does him every credit *o* redounds to his credit (b) *(aumentar)* to increase, to enlarge

engrandecimiento *nm* (a) *(ensalzamiento)* enhancement (b) *(aumento)* increase

engrane *nm Méx* cog, cogwheel, gearwheel

engrapadora *nf Am* stapler

engrapar *vt Am (grapar)* to staple

engrasado *nm (acción)* lubrication

engrasador *nm* grease gun

engrasar *vt* (a) *(motor)* to lubricate; *(bisagra, mecanismo)* to oil; *(eje)* to grease; EXPR *Ven* **engrasarle la mano a alguien** to grease sb's palm (b) *Culin (molde, bandeja)* to grease, to oil

engrase *nm (de motor)* lubrication; *(de mecanismo)* oiling

engreído, -a 1 *adj* (a) *(creído)* conceited, full of one's own importance (b) *Perú (mimado)* spoiled
2 *nm,f* (a) *(creído)* conceited person; **ser un e.** to be very conceited (b) *Perú (mimado)* **ser un e.** to be spoiled

engreimiento *nm* conceit, self-importance

engreír [56] 1 *vt* (a) *(envanecer)* to make vain *o* conceited (b) *Perú (mimar)* to spoil, to pamper
2 **engreírse** *vpr* (a) *(envanecerse)* to become vain *o* conceited (b) *Ven (encariñarse)* **engreírse con alguien** to take a shine to sb

engrescar [60] *vt* to egg on, to incite

engría *etc ver* **engreír**

engriera *etc ver* **engreír**

engrifarse *vpr Fam (persona)* to get high

engrillarse *vpr PRico, Ven (caballo)* to lower its head

engringarse [38] *vpr Am Fam* to adopt American ways

engrió *etc ver* **engreír**

engripado, -a *adj CSur* **estar e.** to have (the) flu

engriparse *vpr CSur* to come down with (the) flu

engrosar [64] 1 *vt (aumentar)* to swell; **la herencia pasó a e. la fortuna familiar** the inheritance went to swell the family fortune; **diez mil personas pasaron a e. la lista de desempleados** a further ten thousand people swelled the ranks of the unemployed
2 *vi (engordar)* to put on weight

engrudo *nm* paste

engruesa *etc ver* **engrosar**

engrupido, -a *RP Fam* 1 *adj* stuck-up, bigheaded; **desde el éxito de sus discos anda muy engrupida** since her records started to be successful she's been very bigheaded
2 *nm,f* bighead; **no lo aguanto más, es un e.** I can't stand him any more, he's such a bighead

engrupir *RP Fam* 1 *vt* to con, to lead up the garden path; **para mí que te engrupieron** I reckon you were done
2 **engrupirse** *vpr* to get bigheaded, to get above oneself; **espero que no te engrupas con toda la plata que estás ganando** I hope all this money you're making doesn't go to your head

enguachinar *vt* (a) *(inundar)* to flood (b) *(aguar)* to water (down)

engualichado, -a *adj Andes, RP Fam* jinxed; **esta casa está engualichada** this house is jinxed; **ha andado más enfermo que sano este año, para mí que está e.** he's been ill more often than not this year, I reckon he must be jinxed

engualichar *vt Andes, RP Fam* to jinx, to put a jinx on; **le sale todo mal, para mí que lo engualicharon** nothing seems to go right for him, I reckon he must be jinxed

enguantado, -a *adj (persona)* wearing gloves; *(mano)* gloved

enguantarse *vpr* to put one's gloves on

enguatado, -a *adj (colcha, chaqueta)* padded

enguatar *vt Esp (colcha, chaqueta)* to pad

enguayabado, -a *adj Ven Fam* homesick

engullir 1 *vt* to gobble up, to wolf down; **mastica bien y no engullas la comida** chew properly and don't wolf your food down; **las olas engulleron a la barca** the waves swamped the boat
2 **engullirse** *vpr* to gobble up, to wolf down

enharinar *vt* to flour

enhebrar *vt* (a) *(aguja)* to thread; *(perlas)* to string (b) *(palabras, ideas, historias)* to string together

enhiesto, -a *adj Literario (figura)* upright, erect; *(árbol)* towering

enhorabuena 1 *nf* congratulations; **dar la e. a alguien por algo** to congratulate sb on sth; **estar de e.** to be in luck
2 *interj* **¡e. (por...)!** congratulations (on...)!

enigma *nm* enigma

enigmático, -a *adj* enigmatic

enjabonada *nf Ven Fam* dusting down

enjabonado, -a 1 *adj* (a) *(con jabón)* soapy (b) *Cuba (caballo)* piebald
2 *nm* soaping

enjabonar 1 *vt* (a) *(con jabón)* to soap (b) *Fam (dar coba a)* to soft-soap
2 **enjabonarse** *vpr* to soap oneself

enjaezar [14] *vt* to harness *(with decorative harness)*

enjalbegado *nm* whitewashing

enjalbegar *vt* to whitewash

enjambre *nm* (**a**) *(de abejas)* swarm (**b**) *(de admiradores, periodistas)* swarm

enjaretar *vt* (**a**) *(cinta, cordón)* to thread through a hem (**b**) *Fam (hacer de prisa)* to rush through, to do in a rush (**c**) *Fam (decir sin cuidado)* to reel *o* rattle off (**d**) *Fam (endilgar)* to palm *o* foist off (**e**) *Fam (intercalar)* to insert

enjaulado, -a *adj* caged; **como un perro e.** like a caged animal

enjaular *vt* (**a**) *(en jaula)* to cage (**b**) *Fam (en prisión)* to jail, to lock up

enjoyar 1 *vt* to adorn with jewels; **iban todos muy enjoyados** they were all covered in jewellery
2 **enjoyarse** *vpr* to put on (one's) jewels

enjuagada *nf RP Fam* quick wash

enjuagar [38] 1 *vt (platos, vasos)* to rinse; *(recipiente, ropa)* to rinse (out)
2 **enjuagarse** *vpr* **enjuagarse (la boca)** to rinse one's mouth (out); **enjuagarse (las manos)** to rinse one's hands; **enjuagarse el pelo** to rinse one's hair

enjuague *nm* (**a**) *(con agua)* rinse ►► ***e. bucal*** *(acción)* rinsing of the mouth; *(líquido)* mouthwash (**b**) *Fam (chanchullo)* **no me gustan los enjuages en que anda metido** I don't like the dodgy things he's involved in; **los enjuages de los políticos** politicians' wheeling and dealing (**c**) *Am (de pelo)* conditioning rinse

enjugador *nm Fot* photographic plate dryer

enjugar [38] 1 *vt* (**a**) *(secar)* to dry, to wipe away; **enjugó sus lágrimas** he dried his tears (**b**) *(pagar) (deuda)* to pay off; *(déficit)* to cancel out
2 **enjugarse** *vpr (secarse)* to wipe, to dry; **se enjugó el sudor de la frente** he wiped *o* mopped the sweat from his brow

enjuiciable *adj Der* indictable, liable to prosecution

enjuiciado, -a *nm,f Der* defendant

enjuiciamiento *nm* (**a**) *Der* trial ►► ***e. criminal*** criminal prosecution (**b**) *(opinión)* judgment

enjuiciar *vt* (**a**) *Der* to try; **lo enjuiciaron por estafa** he was tried for fraud (**b**) *(opinar)* to judge

enjundia *nf (sustancia)* substance; **su último libro tiene mucha e.** there's a lot in her last book; **un ensayo con mucha e.** a very substantial *o* meaty essay

enjundioso, -a *adj* (**a**) *(sustancioso)* substantial, meaty (**b**) *(grasiento)* fatty

enjuto, -a *adj (rostro, cuerpo, persona)* lean

enlace *nm* (**a**) *(conexión)* link; **el e. ferroviario/aéreo entre París y Madrid** the rail/air link between Paris and Madrid; **un e. vía satélite** a satellite link *o* hook-up
(**b**) *Informát (de hipertexto)* link
(**c**) *(persona)* go-between; **sirvió de e. en las negociaciones** he acted as mediator in the negotiations ►► *Esp* ***e. sindical*** shop steward
(**d**) *Ferroc (empalme)* connection; **estación de e.** junction; **vía de e.** crossover
(**e**) *Quím* bond ►► ***e. covalente*** covalent bond; ***e. de hidrógeno*** hydrogen bond; ***e. iónico*** ionic bond; ***e. químico*** chemical bond
(**f**) *Formal (boda)* **e. (matrimonial)** marriage

enladrillado *nm* brick paving

enladrillar *vt* to pave with bricks

enlatado, -a 1 *adj* (**a**) *(en lata)* canned, tinned (**b**) *TV (programa, música)* pre-recorded; *(risa)* canned
2 *nm* canning
3 **enlatados** *nmpl Am (comestibles)* groceries

enlatar *vt* (**a**) *(alimento)* to can, to tin (**b**) *CAm (techo)* to roof with tin

enlazar [14] 1 *vt* (**a**) *(relacionar) (lugares, ideas)* to link, to connect; **e. algo con** to link *o* connect sth with; **enlazó el tema con una crítica a la sociedad de consumo** he linked the issue with a criticism of consumer society; **la autopista que enlaza una ciudad con otra** the motorway that links the two cities (**b**) *(atar)* **e. algo a** to tie sth up to (**c**) *(con lazos)* to lace (**d**) *Am (animal)* to lasso
2 *vi (trenes)* to connect (**en** at); *(carreteras)* to join (up) (**con** with); **esta carretera enlaza con la autopista** this road joins up with the motorway; **en la terminal C enlaza usted con su vuelo a Lima** your connecting flight to Lima leaves from Terminal C
3 **enlazarse** *vpr* (**a**) *(unirse)* to become linked (**b**) *Formal (casarse)* to marry, to get married (**c**) *(emparentarse)* to become related by marriage

enlistar *Méx* 1 *vt* to list
2 **enlistarse** *vpr* to enlist

enlistado *nm Méx* list

enlodar *vt* to cover in mud

enloquecedor, -ora *adj (ruido, tarea)* maddening; *(dolor)* excruciating

enloquecer [46] 1 *vt* (**a**) *(volver loco)* to drive mad (**b**) *(gustar mucho a)* to drive wild *o* crazy; **le enloquece el esquí** she's mad *o* crazy about skiing
2 *vi* to go mad; **enloquecía de angustia/dolor** he was half-crazy with worry/pain

enloquecidamente *adv* madly

enloquecido, -a *adj* mad, crazed

enloquecimiento *nm* madness

enlosado *nm (con losas)* paving; *(con baldosas)* tiling, tiles

enlosar *vt (con losas)* to pave; *(con baldosas)* to tile

enlozado, -a *adj Am* enamelling

enlozar [14] *vt Am* to enamel

enlucido *nm* plaster

enlucir [39] *vt* (**a**) *(blanquear)* to whitewash (**b**) *(enyesar)* to plaster (**c**) *(metales)* to polish

enlutado, -a *adj* in mourning

enlutar 1 *vt* (**a**) *(poner de luto) (persona)* to dress in mourning; *(casa)* to drape in mourning; **un desastre que ha enlutado al país** a disaster which has plunged the country into mourning (**b**) *(entristecer)* to cast a shadow over
2 **enlutarse** *vpr (persona, ciudad, país)* to go into mourning; *(casa)* to be draped in mourning

enluzco *etc ver* **enlucir**

enmaderar *vt (pared)* to panel; *(suelo)* to lay the floorboards of

enmadrado, -a *adj Esp* **estar e.** *(niño, hombre)* to be a mother's boy

enmalecerse [46] *vpr (con maleza)* to become covered with undergrowth, to get overgrown

enmantequillar, *RP, Ven* **enmantecar** *vt* to grease, to butter

enmarañado, -a *adj* (**a**) *(pelo)* tangled; *(ovillo, manguera, cable)* tangled (**b**) *(asunto, situación)* complicated, confused; *(argumento, narración)* involved, convoluted

enmarañamiento *nm* (**a**) *(de pelo, ovillo, manguera)* tangle (**b**) *(de asunto, situación)* confusion

enmarañar 1 *vt* (**a**) *(enredar)* to tangle (up) (**b**) *(complicar)* to complicate, to confuse
2 **enmarañarse** *vpr* (**a**) *(enredarse)* to become tangled (**b**) *(complicarse) (asunto, situación)* to become confused *o* complicated; *(argumento, narración)* to become involved *o* convoluted

enmarcar [60] 1 *vt* (**a**) *(cuadro)* to frame (**b**) *(dar un contexto a)* **enmarcan su política energética dentro del respeto al medio ambiente** their energy policy is placed within a framework of respect for the environment; **enmarcan su obra artística dentro del vanguardismo** they regard his work as forming part of the avant-garde
2 **enmarcarse** *vpr* **las medidas se enmarcan dentro de la nueva política conciliadora** the measures form part of the new policy of reconciliation; **esta actuación se enmarca dentro de la convención de Viena** this action falls within the provisions of the Vienna convention; **el nuevo grupo se enmarca en el ala izquierda del partido** the new group is situated on the left of the party

enmascarado, -a 1 *adj* masked
2 *nm,f* masked man, *f* masked woman

enmascarar 1 *vt* (**a**) *(rostro)* to mask (**b**) *(encubrir) (sentimientos, intenciones, problema)* to disguise, to hide
2 **enmascararse** *vpr (persona)* to put on a mask

enmasillar *vt* to putty

enmendable *adj* (**a**) *(error)* correctable (**b**) *(ley)* amendable

enmendación *nf* (**a**) *(de error)* correction (**b**) *(de ley)* amendment

enmendar [3] 1 *vt* (**a**) *(error)* to correct; *(texto)* to correct, to emend; **el portero enmendó su error despejando la pelota** the goalkeeper made up for his mistake by clearing the ball (**b**) *(ley, dictamen)* to amend (**c**) *(comportamiento, actitud)* to mend, to improve (**d**) *(daño, perjuicio)* to redress
2 **enmendarse** *vpr* to mend one's ways

enmicado, -a *adj Méx* laminated

enmicar *vt Méx* to laminate

enmienda *nf* (**a**) *(acción)* **hacer propósito de e.** to promise to mend one's ways (**b**) *(en un texto)* correction (**c**) *(de ley, contrato)* amendment; **presentar una e. a un proyecto de ley** to propose an amendment to a bill

enmiendo *etc ver* **enmendar**

enmohecer [46] **1** *vt* (**a**) *(con moho)* to turn mouldy (**b**) *(metal)* to rust
2 enmohecerse *vpr* (**a**) *(con moho)* to grow mouldy (**b**) *(metal)* to go *o* get rusty (**c**) *(conocimientos, memoria)* to get rusty

enmohecido, -a *adj* (**a**) *(con moho)* mouldy (**b**) *(metal)* rusty (**c**) *(conocimientos, memoria)* rusty; **tengo los músculos enmohecidos** my muscles aren't used to much exercise

enmohecimiento *nm* (**a**) *(con moho)* mould (**b**) *(de metal)* rust (**c**) *(de conocimientos, memoria)* rustiness

enmontarse *vpr Col, Ven (campo)* to turn into a wilderness

enmoquetado, -a 1 *adj* carpeted; **un apartamento totalmente e.** a fully carpeted apartment
2 *nm* carpeting

enmoquetar *vt Esp, RP* to carpet

enmudecer [46] **1** *vt* to silence
2 *vi* (**a**) *(callarse)* to fall silent, to go quiet; *(dejar de sonar)* to fall silent; **todos enmudecieron de asombro** everyone stopped talking in astonishment; **las sirenas enmudecieron** the sirens fell silent (**b**) *(perder el habla)* to be struck dumb

enmudecimiento *nm* silence

enmugrecer [46], *Am* **enmugrar 1** *vt (ensuciar)* to soil, to dirty
2 enmugrecerse, *Am* **enmugrarse** *vpr (ensuciarse)* to become soiled *o* dirty

enmuinarse *vpr Méx Fam* to fly off the handle, *Br* to lose one's rag

ennegrecer [46] **1** *vt* (**a**) *(poner negro)* to blacken (**b**) *(oscurecer)* to darken
2 *vi* to darken
3 ennegrecerse *vpr* (**a**) *(ponerse negro)* to become blackened (**b**) *(oscurecerse)* to darken, to grow dark; **el cielo se ennegreció de repente** the sky suddenly darkened *o* grew dark

ennegrecimiento *nm* (**a**) *(acción)* blackening, turning black (**b**) *(oscurecimiento)* darkening

ennoblecer [46] *vt* (**a**) *(persona)* to ennoble, to dignify; **estas acciones lo ennoblecen** these actions do him credit; **tratan de e. la profesión de artista de circo** they seek to dignify the profession of circus performer (**b**) *(lugar)* **las alfombras persas ennoblecen la estancia** the Persian carpets give the room a grand air

ennoblecimiento *nm (de persona)* ennoblement

enojada *nm Méx* fit of anger; **se pegó terrible e. con él** she got terribly angry with him

enojadizo, -a *adj esp Am* irritable, touchy

enojado, -a *adj esp Am (irritado)* angry; *(molesto)* annoyed; **estar e. con alguien** to be angry/annoyed with sb; **está enojada con sus padres** she's angry/annoyed with her parents; **estoy muy e. contigo** I'm very angry/annoyed with you; **estar e. por algo** to be angry/annoyed about sth; **están enojados desde hace años** they've been on bad terms with one another for years

enojar *esp Am* **1** *vt (irritar)* to anger; *(molestar)* to annoy; **consiguió e. a todo el mundo con sus impertinencias** she managed to annoy everybody with her cheeky remarks
2 enojarse *vpr* (**a**) *(irritarse)* to get angry (**con** with); *(molestarse)* to get annoyed (**con** with); **vas a conseguir que me enoje** you're going to make me angry; **no te enojes, pero creo que te equivocas** don't get annoyed, but I think you're wrong; **no te enojes con quien no tiene la culpa** don't be angry with someone who's not to blame
(**b**) *(pelearse)* to fall out; **se enojaron por una bobada** they fell out over a silly little thing

enojo *nm esp Am (por irritarse)* anger; *(por molestarse)* annoyance; **puso cara de e.** she scowled (in annoyance); **¿ya se te pasó el e.?** have you calmed down yet?

enojón, ona *adj Méx Fam* cranky, testy

enojoso, -a *adj esp Am (delicado, espinoso)* awkward; **la situación era de lo más enojosa** it was an extremely awkward situation; **pongamos fin a este e. asunto** let's put an end to this unpleasant business

enología *nf* oenology, study of wine

enólogo, -a *nm,f* oenologist, wine expert

enorgullecer [46] **1** *vt* to fill with pride; **nada me enorgullecería más que tenerte por yerno** nothing would make me prouder than to have you as my son-in-law; **no me enorgullece ser de su mismo partido** it gives me no pride to belong to the same party as him
2 enorgullecerse *vpr* to be proud (**de** of); **un país que se enorgullece de su pasado** a country that is proud of its history; **hacen el gamberro y encima se enorgullecen de ello** they act like hooligans and what's more they're proud of it; **me enorgullezco de pertenecer a esta familia** I am proud to be a member of this family

enorme *adj* (**a**) *(muy grande) (objeto, persona, cantidad)* huge, enormous; *(defecto, error)* huge; **estos animales tienen una e. capacidad para reproducirse** these creatures have an enormous reproductive capacity; **una torre de e. altura** an enormously tall tower; **tu hijo está ya e.** your son's really huge; **le invadía una e. tristeza** he was overcome by a great sadness
(**b**) *Fam (excelente)* great, fantastic

enormemente *adv* enormously; **disfrutamos e.** we enjoyed ourselves enormously *o* hugely; **me satisface e. su decisión** I am extremely pleased about her decision; **un ejercicio e. complicado** an enormously *o* hugely complicated exercise

enormidad *nf* (**a**) *(de tamaño)* enormity, hugeness; **me gustó una e.** I liked it enormously *o* hugely; **ha debido de costarte una e. (de dinero)** it must have cost you a vast amount (of money) (**b**) *(despropósito)* **¡lo que dijo/hizo fue una e.!** what she said/did was crazy!; **las enormidades perpetradas por el ejército invasor** the enormities perpetrated by the invading army

enotecnia *nf* (art of) wine-making

enquistado, -a *adj (odio, costumbre)* deep-rooted, deeply entrenched

enquistamiento *nm Med* encystment

enquistarse *vpr* (**a**) *Med* to develop into a cyst (**b**) *(odio, costumbre)* to take root, to become entrenched; *(proceso)* to become bogged down

enrabietarse *vpr* to throw a tantrum

enraizado, -a *adj (costumbre, odio, prejuicio)* deep-rooted

enraizar [14] **1** *vi* (**a**) *(planta, árbol)* to take root, to put down roots (**b**) *(persona)* to put down roots (**c**) *(costumbre, odio, prejuicio)* to take root, to become entrenched
2 enraizarse *vpr* (**a**) *(planta, árbol)* to take root, to put down roots (**b**) *(persona)* to put down roots (**c**) *(costumbre, odio, prejuicio)* to take root, to become entrenched

enramada *nf* (**a**) *(espesura)* branches, canopy (**b**) *(cobertizo)* bower

enramar *vt (adornar)* to decorate with branches

enrarecer [46] **1** *vt* (**a**) *(situación, ambiente, relaciones)* to make strained *o* tense (**b**) *(aire, gas)* to rarefy
2 enrarecerse *vpr* (**a**) *(situación, ambiente, relaciones)* to become strained *o* tense (**b**) *(aire, gas)* to become rarefied

enrarecido, -a *adj* (**a**) *(situación, ambiente, relaciones)* strained, tense (**b**) *(aire, gas)* rarefied

enrarecimiento *nm* (**a**) *(de situación, ambiente, relaciones)* deterioration (**b**) *(de aire, gas)* rarefying

enrarezco *etc ver* **enrarecer**

enratonado, -a *adj Ven Fam* hung-over

enratonarse *vpr Ven Fam* to get a hang-over

enredadera *nf* creeper

enredado, -a *adj* (**a**) *(cuerdas, madeja, pelo)* tangled (**b**) *(asunto, situación)* complicated, involved (**c**) *(persona) (implicado)* **estar e. en algo** to be mixed up *o* involved in sth; **se vio e. en un asunto de tráfico de drogas** he found himself caught up in a case of drug-trafficking

enredador, -ora 1 *adj* (**a**) *(travieso)* naughty, mischievous (**b**) *(chismoso)* gossiping
2 *nm,f* (**a**) *(travieso)* mischief-maker (**b**) *(chismoso)* gossip

enredar 1 *vt* (**a**) *(cuerdas, madeja, pelo)* to tangle (up) (**b**) *(situación, asunto)* to complicate; **será mejor no e. más las cosas** it's best not to make matters more complicated (**c**) *(implicar)* **e. a alguien en** to get sb involved in, to embroil sb in; **me enredaron en sus sucios negocios** they got me mixed up in their dirty dealings (**d**) *(entretener)* to bother, to annoy
2 *vi Fam* (**a**) *(hacer travesuras)* to get up to mischief (**b**) *(juguetear)* **e. con algo** to fiddle with *o* mess about with sth
3 enredarse *vpr* (**a**) *(plantas)* to climb; *(cuerdas, madeja, pelo)* to get tangled up; **la hiedra se enredaba en las columnas** the ivy wound its way up the columns; **la cola de la cometa se enredó en unas ramas** the tail of the kite got tangled in some branches
(**b**) *(situación, asunto)* to become complicated *o* involved; **las cosas se enredaron mucho** things got very complicated *o* involved
(**c**) *(implicarse)* **enredarse en un asunto** to get mixed up *o* involved in something
(**d**) *Fam (embarullarse)* to get into a muddle, to get mixed up
(**e**) *Fam (entretenerse)* to get caught up; **me enredé ordenando unos papeles y llegué tarde** I got sidetracked putting some papers in order and I arrived late
(**f**) *Fam (sentimentalmente)* **enredarse con alguien** to get involved *o* have an affair with sb

enredo *nm* (**a**) *(en cuerdas, madeja, pelo)* tangle
(**b**) *(de una situación)* mess, complicated affair; **¡en menudo e. me he metido!** this is a fine mess I've got myself into!
(**c**) *(en la mente, al expresarse)* muddle; **tengo un e. tremendo de fechas** *o* **con las fechas** I've got into a terrific muddle over the dates
(**d**) *(asunto ilícito)* shady affair
(**e**) *(amoroso)* (love) affair, entanglement; **tener un e. con alguien** to have an affair with sb, to be involved with sb
(**f**) *(mentira, intriga)* mischief-making
(**g**) *Lit* plot

enredoso, -a *adj Chile, Méx* (**a**) *(intrigante)* troublemaking, mischievous (**b**) *(chismoso)* gossipy

enrejado *nm* (**a**) *(barrotes) (de balcón, verja)* railings; *(de jaula, celda, ventana)* bars (**b**) *(de cañas)* trellis

enrejar *vt (ventanas)* to bar

enrevesado, -a *adj* complex, complicated

enrielar *vt Chile, Méx (encarrilar)* to set *o* put on the right track

enripiar *vt Constr* to fill with rubble

Enrique *n pr* **E. I/II** Henry I/II

enriquecedor, -ora *adj* enriching

enriquecer [46] **1** *vt* (**a**) *(hacer rico) (persona, clase social, región)* to make rich, to enrich (**b**) *(alimento, sustancia)* to enrich (**c**) *(moralmente, espiritualmente, en valor artístico)* to enrich; **los viajes enriquecen la personalidad** travelling makes you richer as a person
2 enriquecerse *vpr (persona, pueblo, región)* to get rich; **la región se ha enriquecido con el turismo** tourism has made the region rich, the region has prospered through tourism

enriquecido, -a *adj* enriched; **yogures enriquecidos con vitamina C** yoghurts enriched with vitamin C

enriquecimiento *nm* (**a**) *(de persona, clase social, región)* enrichment (**b**) *(moral, espiritual, cultural)* enrichment

enriquezco *etc ver* **enriquecer**

enristrar *vt* (**a**) *(ajos, cebollas)* to string (**b**) *(lanza)* to couch

enrocar [60] **1** *vt (en ajedrez)* to castle
2 *vi (en ajedrez)* to castle
3 enrocarse *vpr (en ajedrez)* to castle

enrojecer [46] **1** *vt* (**a**) *(volver rojo)* to redden, to turn red; *(por turbación)* to cause to blush (**b**) *(con fuego)* to make red-hot
2 *vi (por calor, sofoco)* to flush; *(por turbación)* to blush; **enrojeció de vergüenza** he blushed with shame
3 enrojecerse *vpr* (**a**) *(volverse rojo)* to redden, to turn red; *(por calor, sofoco)* to flush; *(por turbación)* to blush; **cuando bebe mucho se le enrojece la nariz** when she drinks a lot her nose turns red (**b**) *(por fuego)* to turn red-hot

enrojecimiento *nm* (**a**) *(de piel)* redness, red mark (**b**) *(de cielo, hierro)* reddening

enrojezco *etc ver* **enrojecer**

enrolar **1** *vt* to enlist
2 enrolarse *vpr (en ejército)* to enlist (**en** in); *(en expedición, viaje)* to sign up (**en** for); **enrolarse en el ejército** to enlist in *o* join the army; **enrolarse en un barco** to join a ship's crew, to sign on board a ship

enrollado, -a *adj* (**a**) *(en forma de rollo) (papel, alfombra)* rolled up; *(manguera, cuerda)* coiled (up); **estar e. en algo** to be wound round sth; **un pastel e. de verduras** a vegetable roulade
(**b**) *Esp Fam (interesante, animado) (bar, música, película)* cool, great; **es un tío muy e.** he's a really great guy; **es un bar muy e.** it's a really cool *o* great bar
(**c**) *Fam (enfrascado)* **estar e. con algo: están muy enrollados con el parapente** they're into paragliding in a big way; **no puedo ir, estoy muy e. haciendo bricolaje en casa** I can't go, I'm getting stuck into some DIY at home; **estábamos muy enrollados hablando de música** we were having a great time talking about music
(**d**) *Fam (en relaciones amorosas)* **están enrollados desde hace tres años** they've been an item for the last three years; **¿pero están enrollados o no?** have they got something going or not?; **está e. con una sueca** he's got a thing going with a Swedish woman

enrollar **1** *vt* (**a**) *(arrollar) (papel, alfombra)* to roll up; *(manguera, cuerda)* to coil (up); **enrolló el hilo en su bobina** he wound the thread on to the bobbin
(**b**) *Fam (enredar, confundir)* to bamboozle; **me enrollaron para que lo comprara** they bamboozled me into buying it
(**c**) *Fam (gustar)* **me enrolla mucho** I love it, I think it's great; **me enrolla mucho ir de camping** I really get a kick out of going camping
2 enrollarse *vpr* (**a**) *(arrollarse) (papel)* to roll up; *(manguera, cuerda)* to coil up; **enrollarse alrededor de algo** to coil round sth
(**b**) *Fam (al hablar, escribir)* to go on (and on); **por teléfono se enrolla una barbaridad** whenever she calls she just goes on and on; **me enrollé a hablar con una vecina y se me olvidó** I got chatting to a neighbour and forgot about it; **no te enrolles y dime qué quieres** just get to the point and tell me what you want; **me enrollé demasiado en la tercera pregunta** I spent too much time on the third question; EXPR *Esp* **enrollarse como una persiana** *o* **como las persianas** *o* **de mala manera: se enrolla como una persiana** he could talk the hind legs off a donkey; EXPR *Esp Hum* **¡no te enrolles, Charles Boyer!** do us a favour and put a sock in it!
(**c**) *Fam (enfrascarse)* **me enrollé a hacer cosas en casa y se me pasó la tarde** I got really involved in doing things around the house and that was the afternoon gone; **se enrolló con lo de la pintura hace unos años** she got into painting and all that a few years ago
(**d**) *Esp Fam (sexualmente) (hacer el amor) Br* to have it away, *US* get it on; *(besarse, abrazarse)* to neck, *Br* to snog, *US* to make out; *(empezar a salir)* to hook up; **se enrolló con su jefa** he had an affair with his boss; **os enrollasteis, ¿no?** you did it, right?
(**e**) *Esp Fam (portarse bien)* **anda, enróllate y limpia la cocina** come on, do me a favour and clean the kitchen, will you?; **¡qué bien/mal se enrollan en este bar!** the people in that bar are really cool/unfriendly!; **se enrolla muy bien con los clientes** he gets on very well with the customers
(**f**) *Ven Fam (confundirse)* to get into a muddle

> **Falso amigo**: El verbo inglés **to enrol** no es la traducción del español **enrollar**. En inglés, **to enrol** significa "inscribir".

enronquecer [46] **1** *vt* to make hoarse
2 enronquecerse *vpr* to become hoarse

enroque *nm (en ajedrez)* castling ▸▸ ***e. corto*** short castling; ***e. largo*** long castling

enroscado, -a *adj (pelo)* curly

enroscadura *nf* (**a**) *(acción)* coiling (**b**) *(rosca)* coil

enroscar [60] **1** *vt* (**a**) *(tornillo)* to screw in; *(tuerca, tapa, tapón)* to screw on (**b**) *(enrollar) (manguera, cuerda)* to coil up; *(cuerpo, cola)* to curl up; **e. algo en algo** to wind sth round sth
2 enroscarse *vpr* (**a**) *(persona, animal)* to curl up; *(serpiente)* to coil up (**b**) *RP Fam (en conversación)* to go on (and on); *(en estudio)* to go deeply into; **nos enroscamos a hablar de autos** we got into a long discussion about cars; **se enroscaron con el tema del fútbol** they went on and on about football

enrostrar *vt Am Fam* **e. a alguien algo** to throw sth in sb's face

enrueca *etc ver* **enrocar**

enrulado, -a *adj CSur* curly

enrular *CSur* **1** *vt* to curl
2 enrularse *vpr* to curl

enrumbar *vi Andes* to head; **enrumbaron hacia la casa de la abuela** they headed for their grandmother's house

ensabanarse *vpr Ven* to rise up, to rebel

ensaimada *nf* = bun made of sweet coiled pastry

ensalada *nf* (**a**) *(de lechuga)* salad; **una e. de atún/arroz** a tuna/rice salad ▸▸ ***e. campera*** = salad of boiled potatoes, tomato, pepper, onion and hard-boiled egg, in vinaigrette; ***e. de frutas*** fruit salad; ***e. mixta*** mixed salad; ***e. rusa*** Russian salad, = salad of boiled, diced potatoes and carrots or peas, in mayonnaise; ***e. verde*** green salad
(**b**) *Fam (lío)* mishmash; **una e. de cifras** a jumble of figures; **la película acaba con una e. de tiros** the movie ends in a blaze of gunfire; *RP* **se hizo flor de e.** she got in a muddle
(**c**) *Cuba (refresco)* = mint-flavoured citrus drink

ensaladera *nf (fuente)* salad bowl ▸▸ ***e. de plata*** *(en tenis)* silver plate

ensaladilla *nf Esp* **e. (rusa)** Russian salad, = salad of boiled, diced potatoes and carrots or peas, in mayonnaise

ensalmo *nm* incantation, spell; **como por e.** as if by magic

ensalzador, -ora *adj* praising

ensalzamiento *nm* praise

ensalzar [14] *vt* (**a**) *(alabar)* to praise (**b**) *(enaltecer)* to exalt, to glorify

ensamblado, -a **1** *adj (mueble, piezas)* assembled
2 *nm* assembly

ensamblador, -ora **1** *nm,f (persona)* assembly-line worker
2 *nm Informát* assembler

ensambladura *nf*, **ensamblaje** *nm* (**a**) *(acción)* assembly (**b**) *(junta, unión)* joint

ensamblar *vt* (**a**) *(piezas)* to assemble; *(madera)* to join (**b**) *Informát* to assemble

ensamble = **ensambladura**

ensanchamiento *nm* (**a**) *(de orificio, calle)* widening; *(de ciudad)* expansion (**b**) *(de ropa)* letting out

ensanchar 1 *vt* (**a**) *(orificio, calle)* to widen; *(ciudad)* to expand (**b**) *(ropa)* to let out (**c**) *(horizontes, perspectivas)* to broaden
2 *vi Hum (engordar)* to fill out, to put on weight
3 **ensancharse** *vpr* (**a**) *(orificio, calle)* to widen, to open out (**b**) *(ropa) (a lo largo)* to stretch; *(a lo ancho)* to become baggy

ensanche *nm* (**a**) *(de calle)* widening (**b**) *(en ciudad)* new suburb

ensangrentado, -a *adj (persona, rostro, ropa)* bloodstained, covered in blood

ensangrentar [3] 1 *vt* to cover with blood
2 **ensangrentarse** *vpr* to become bloodstained

ensañamiento *nm* viciousness, savagery; **lo golpearon con e.** he was viciously *o* savagely beaten

ensañarse *vpr* **e. con alguien** to torment sb, to treat sb cruelly; **se ensañó con el pobre animal** she really laid into the poor creature; **la prensa amarilla se ensañó con ella** the gutter press tore her apart

ensartado, -a *adj (perlas)* strung; **trozos de carne ensartados en un pincho** pieces of meat threaded on a skewer

ensartar 1 *vt* (**a**) *(con hilo) (perlas)* to string; *(aguja)* to thread (**b**) *(con algo puntiagudo) (comida)* to skewer; *(torero)* to gore; **ensartó las verduras en pinchos** he threaded the vegetables on skewers; **le ensartó el puñal en la espalda** she plunged the dagger into his back (**c**) *(cosas inconexas)* to reel *o* rattle off; **e. mentiras** to tell one lie after another (**d**) *Am Fam (engañar)* to rip off; **me ensartaron con estos CDs** these CDs were a rip-off
2 **ensartarse** *vpr Am Fam (ser engañado)* to be ripped off

ensayar 1 *vt* (**a**) *(experimentar)* to test (**b**) *(obra de teatro, concierto, baile)* to rehearse (**c**) *(metales preciosos)* to assay
2 *vi* (**a**) *(en teatro)* to rehearse (**b**) *(en rugby)* to convert a try

ensayismo *nm* **el e.** the essay (genre); **un maestro del e.** a masterly essayist

ensayista *nmf* essayist

ensayístico, -a *adj (estilo)* essayistic; **su obra ensayística** her essays

ensayo *nm* (**a**) *(en teatro, música, danza)* rehearsal; **hoy tenemos e.** we've got a rehearsal today; **hacer un e. (de algo)** to rehearse (sth) ▸▸ ***e. general*** dress rehearsal
(**b**) *(prueba)* test; **el nuevo prototipo será sometido a e.** the new prototype will undergo testing; **le salió al primer e.** he got it at the first attempt; **hacer un e. de algo** to test sth ▸▸ *Farm* ***e. clínico*** clinical trial
(**c**) *(escrito)* essay; **el e.** *(género literario)* the essay
(**d**) *(en rugby)* try
(**e**) *(de metales preciosos)* assay

enseguida *adv (inmediatamente)* immediately, at once; *(pronto)* very soon; **lo haré e., antes de que se me olvide** I'll do it straight away before I forget; **llegará e.** he'll be here any minute now; **vino a las seis, pero se fue e.** he came at six, but he left soon after; **e. lo atiendo** I'll be with you in a minute *o* directly; **e. vuelvo** I'll be right back; **cruza el puente y e. verás la casa a la derecha** cross the bridge and you'll see the house on your right; *Am* **e. de comer no se debe hacer ejercicio** you should not exercise immediately after a meal

ensenada *nf* (**a**) *(en costa)* cove, inlet (**b**) *Arg (potrero)* paddock

enseña *nf* ensign

enseñado, -a *adj* (**a**) *(persona)* **bien/mal e.** well/badly brought-up (**b**) *(perro)* housebroken

enseñante *nmf* teacher

enseñanza *nf* (**a**) *(educación)* education; *(actividad docente)* teaching; **la calidad de la e. en este país** the quality of education in this country; **se dedica a la e.** he works as a teacher; **un centro de e.** an educational institution ▸▸ ***e. a distancia*** distance education; ***e. estatal*** state education; ***e. de idiomas*** language teaching; ***e. media*** secondary education; ***e. personalizada*** personal *o* individual tutoring; ***e. primaria*** primary education; ***e. privada*** private (sector) education; ***e. pública*** state education; ***e. secundaria*** secondary education; ***e. superior*** higher education; ***e. universitaria*** university education
(**b**) *(lección)* lesson; **de cualquier error puede extraerse** *o* **sacarse una e.** there's a lesson to be learned from every mistake you make; **aquello me sirvió de e.** that was a lesson to me; **enseñanzas** *(de filósofo, profeta)* teachings

enseñar 1 *vt* (**a**) *(instruir)* to teach; **enseña inglés en una academia de idiomas** he teaches English in a language school; **e. a alguien a hacer algo** to teach sb to do sth; **está enseñando a su hijo a** *Esp* **conducir** *o* *Am* **manejar** she's teaching her son to drive; **mi padre me enseñó a hacerlo** *o* **cómo hacerlo** my father taught me how to do it
(**b**) *(aleccionar)* to teach; **e. a alguien a hacer algo** to teach sb to do sth; **la derrota les enseñó a ser más humildes** the defeat taught them some humility
(**c**) *(mostrar)* to show; **enséñame tu vestido nuevo** show me your new dress; **enséñanos lo que has aprendido** show us what you've learned; **al estirarse, enseñaba el ombligo** when he stretched you could see his belly button; **va enseñando los hombros provocativamente** her shoulders are provocatively uncovered
2 **enseñarse** *vpr Méx Fam* **enseñarse a comer alimentos saludables** to get into the habit of eating healthy foods

enseñorearse *vpr* to take possession (**de** of)

enseres *nmpl* (**a**) *(efectos personales)* belongings (**b**) *(muebles, accesorios)* furnishings; *(herramientas, utensilios)* implements; **trajo consigo todos sus e. de trabajo** he brought with him all the tools of his trade ▸▸ ***e. de cocina*** kitchen utensils; ***e. domésticos*** household goods; ***e. de oficina*** office equipment; ***e. de pescar*** fishing tackle

enseriarse *vpr Carib, Perú* to become serious

ensillado, -a *adj (caballo)* saddled

ensillar *vt (caballo)* to saddle up

ensimismado, -a *adj* (**a**) *(enfrascado)* absorbed, engrossed (**en** in); **estaba e. oyendo música/en la lectura** he was engrossed in the music he was listening to/in what he was reading (**b**) *(pensativo)* lost in thought

ensimismamiento *nm* self-absorption

ensimismarse *vpr* (**a**) *(enfrascarse)* to become absorbed *o* engrossed (**en** in); **tanto se ensimismaba oyendo música/en la lectura que...** she became so engrossed in the music he was listening to/in what he was reading that... (**b**) *(abstraerse)* to lose oneself in thought, to become lost in thought

ensoberbecer [46] 1 *vt* to fill with pride
2 **ensoberbecerse** *vpr* to become puffed up with pride

ensombrecer [46] 1 *vt* (**a**) *(dar sombra a, oscurecer)* to cast a shadow over (**b**) *(dar aire triste a)* to cast a shadow over; **la noticia ensombreció el acto** the news cast a shadow over the proceedings; **una repentina sospecha ensombreció su rostro** a sudden suspicion caused his face to darken
2 **ensombrecerse** *vpr* (**a**) *(oscurecerse)* to darken (**b**) *(entristecerse) (expresión, rostro)* to become sad *o* gloomy; **se ensombreció** his mood darkened

ensoñación *nf* dream, daydream; **ni por e.** not even in one's wildest dreams; **tener ensoñaciones** to have daydreams

ensoñador, -ora 1 *adj* dreamy
2 *nm,f* dreamer

ensopar *Andes, RP, Ven Fam* 1 *vt* to soak, to drench
2 **ensoparse** *vpr* to get soaked *o* drenched

ensordecedor, -ora *adj* deafening

ensordecer [46] 1 *vt* (**a**) *(causar sordera a)* to cause to go deaf (**b**) *(no dejar oír)* to deafen (**c**) *(amortiguar)* to muffle, to deaden
2 *vi (quedarse sordo)* to go deaf

ensordecimiento *nm* deafness

ensordezco *etc ver* **ensordecer**

ensortijado, -a *adj (pelo)* in ringlets

ensortijamiento *nm* (**a**) *(acción)* curling (**b**) *(rizos)* curls

ensortijar 1 *vt (pelo)* to curl
2 **ensortijarse** *vpr (pelo)* to curl

ensuciar 1 *vt* (**a**) *(manchar)* to (make) dirty; **me ensuciaron los pantalones de grasa** they got my trousers covered in grease; **excursionistas que ensucian el campo** hikers who litter the countryside (**b**) *(desprestigiar)* to sully, to tarnish; **e. el nombre de alguien** to sully sb's name *o* reputation
2 **ensuciarse** *vpr* (**a**) *(mancharse) (persona, objeto, superficie)* to get dirty; **procura no ensuciarte el vestido** try not to get your dress dirty; **se me ensuciaron los pantalones** my trousers got dirty; **la alfombra se ha ensuciado de pintura** the carpet has got paint on it; **se ensució las manos de** *o* **con grasa** he got his hands covered in grease
(**b**) *Euf (evacuar)* to soil *o* dirty oneself

ensueño 1 *nm (ensoñación)* dream, daydream
2 **de ensueño** *loc adj* dream, ideal; **tienen una casa de e.** they have a dream house
3 **de ensueño** *loc adv* **baila de e.** he dances like a dream; **lo pasamos de e.** we had the most wonderful time

entablado *nm* (**a**) *(armazón)* wooden platform (**b**) *(suelo)* floorboards

entablamento *nm Arquit* entablature

entablar *vt* (**a**) *(suelo)* to put down floorboards on
(**b**) *(iniciar) (conversación, amistad)* to strike up; *(negociaciones)* to enter into, to open; *(relaciones)* to establish; **e. juicio contra alguien** to start court proceedings against sb; **los manifestantes entablaron batalla con la policía** the demonstrators joined battle with the police; **entablaron una acalorada discusión** they fell into a heated argument
(**c**) *(entablillar)* to put in a splint
(**d**) *(en juegos de tablero)* to set up
(**e**) *Am (empatar)* to tie, to draw

entablillar *vt* to put in a splint

entalegar [38] *vt* (**a**) *(meter en talegos)* to put into sacks (**b**) *(dinero)* to hoard (**c**) *Esp Fam (encarcelar)* to put away, *Br* to bang up

entallado, -a *adj (vestido, chaqueta)* tailored

entalpía *nf Quím* enthalpy

entapar *vt Chile* to bind

entarimado *nm* (**a**) *(plataforma)* wooden platform (**b**) *(suelo)* floorboards

entarimar *vt (suelo)* to put down floorboards on

ente *nm* (**a**) *(ser)* being ►► ***e. de ficción*** fictional character; ***e. jurídico*** legal entity; ***e. de razón*** imaginary being (**b**) *(corporación)* body, organization; **e. público** *(institución)* = state-owned body *o* institution; **el E. público** = the Spanish state broadcasting corporation (**c**) *Fam (personaje)* odd bod

entechar *vt Chile* to roof

enteco, -a *adj (flaco)* scrawny; *(enfermizo)* sickly

ENTEL [en'tel] *nf* (*abrev de* **Empresa Nacional de Telecomunicaciones**) = the Chilean national telephone company

entelequia *nf* (**a**) *(fantasía)* pipe dream (**b**) *Filosofía* entelechy

entelerido, -a *adj CAm, Ven (flaco)* weak, sickly

entenado, -a *nm,f Méx* stepson, *f* stepdaughter

entendederas *nfpl Fam* EXPR **ser corto de e., tener malas e.** to be a bit dim; **tener buenas e.** to be bright

entendedor *nm* PROV **a buen e., pocas palabras bastan** a word to the wise is sufficient

ENTENDER [66] **1** *vt* (**a**) *(comprender)* to understand; **ahora entiendo lo que quieres decir** now I understand *o* know what you mean; **entiendo perfectamente tu reacción** I completely understand your reaction; **¿es que no lo entiendes?** don't you understand?; **entiéndelo, lo hago por tu bien** try to understand, it's for your own good; **no te entiendo, habla más despacio** I don't understand you, could you speak more slowly?; **no entiendo los aparatos modernos** I don't understand modern technology; **no entiendo el chiste** I don't get the joke; **no entendí nada de lo que dijo** I didn't understand a word of what he said; **no entiendo nada, ¿no deberían haber llegado ya?** I just can't understand it, surely they were supposed to have arrived by now; **no entiendo la letra de mi médico** I can't read my doctor's handwriting; **e. mal algo** to misunderstand sth; **no entiendo cómo puede gustarte Arturo** I don't know what you see in Arturo; **no hay quien entienda a tu novio** no one knows what to make of your boyfriend; **¡no hay quien te entienda!** you're impossible!; **sabe e. a las personas mayores** she understands older people; **¿tú qué entiendes por "amistad"?** what do you understand by "friendship"?; **¿debo e. que no estás de acuerdo?** am I to understand that you disagree?; **¿cómo le puedo hacer e. que eso no se hace?** how can I make her understand *o* get it through to her that that sort of behaviour is out?; **hasta que no llegue no podemos empezar, ¿entiendes?** we can't start until she gets here, all right?; **¿entiendes?, si no se lo decimos se va a enfadar** look, if we don't tell him, he's going to get angry; **podríamos hacernos los despistados, ya me entiendes** we could make out we didn't really realize what was going on, you know what I mean; **dar a e. algo (a alguien): dio a e. que no le interesaba** she implied (that) she wasn't interested; **nos dio a e. que no estaba de acuerdo** she gave us to understand that she disagreed; **hacerse e.** to make oneself understood; **se hizo e. a base de signos** he made himself understood by using sign language; EXPR *Fam* **no entiendo ni jota** *o RP* **un pito** I can't understand a word (of it)
(**b**) *(juzgar, opinar)* to think; **yo no lo entiendo así** I don't see it that way; **entiendo que sería mejor no decir nada** I think it would be better not to say anything; **entendemos que deberías disculparte** we feel you ought to apologize
2 *vi* (**a**) *(saber)* **e. de algo** to know about sth; **e. poco/algo de** to know very little/a little about; **entiende un montón de jardinería** she knows loads about gardening; **no entiendo nada de informática** I don't know anything about computing; **tú que entiendes de estas cosas, ¿qué es el "rafting"?** you know about these things, what is "rafting"?
(**b**) *(ocuparse)* **e. de** *o* **en** *(en general)* to deal with; *(sujeto: juez)* to be in charge of; **el magistrado que entiende de casos de terrorismo** the magistrate responsible for *o* in charge of cases involving terrorism
(**c**) *Fam (ser homosexual)* to be gay; **¿entiendes?** are you gay? *(as a discreet enquiry)*
3 entenderse *vpr* (**a**) *(comprenderse) (uno mismo)* to know what one means; *(dos personas)* to understand each other; **yo ya me entiendo** I know what I'm doing; **el ilion, para entendernos, un hueso de la pelvis** the ilium, in other words *o* that is, one of the bones of the pelvis; **se entienden en inglés** they communicate with each other in English; **los sordomudos se entienden por señas** deaf-mutes communicate (with each other) using sign language
(**b**) *(llevarse bien)* to get on; **me entiendo muy bien con mis compañeros de trabajo** I get on very well with my workmates
(**c**) *(sentimentalmente)* to have an affair (**con** with); **se entendía con una vecina** he was having an affair with a neighbour
(**d**) *(ponerse de acuerdo)* to reach an agreement; **te vas a tener que e. con los organizadores** you're going to have to come to *o* reach an agreement with the organizers
(**e**) *Fam (apañarse)* **allá te las entiendas tú con la lavadora** the washing machine's your problem
4 *nm* **a mi e...., según mi e....** the way I see it...; **a** *o* **según mi modesto e., la culpa es del gobierno** in my humble opinion, it's the government's fault; **a tu e. ¿cuáles son las razones de la derrota?** in your view, what are the reasons for this defeat?

entendido, -a 1 *adj* (**a**) *(comprendido)* understood; **dar algo por e.: daba por e. que nos apoyarían** I understood that they would support us; **eso se da por e.** that goes without saying; **que quede bien e. que...** I want it clearly understood that...; **tener e.: tengo e. que te casas, ¿es verdad?** I understand *o* I've heard you're getting married, is that right?; **tenía e. que te mudabas de ciudad** I understood you were moving to another town; **según tenía e., era una casa grande** from what I'd understood, it was a large house
(**b**) *(en preguntas, respuestas)* **¿e.?** (is that) understood?; **si lo vuelves a hacer te castigaré, ¿e.?** if you do it again, you'll be punished, is that clear *o* understood?; **¡e.!** all right!, okay!
(**c**) *(versado)* expert (**en** in); **un político e. en relaciones internacionales** a politician well-versed in international relations
2 *nm,f* expert (**en** on); **según los entendidos en la materia...** according to the experts...

entendimiento *nm* (**a**) *(acuerdo)* understanding; **han llegado a un e.** they've reached an understanding (**b**) *(juicio)* judgement; *(inteligencia)* mind, intellect; **fenómenos que van más allá del e. humano** phenomena that are beyond human understanding (**c**) *(comprensión)* understanding

entenebrecer [19] *vt* to darken

entente *nf* (**a**) *Pol* ***e. cordial*** entente cordiale (**b**) *Com* agreement

enteradillo, -a *nm,f Fam Irónico* know-all

enterado, -a 1 *adj* (**a**) *Esp (ducho, versado)* well-informed (**en** about)
(**b**) *(informado)* **estar e. de algo** to be aware of sth, to know about sth; **el jefe estaba e. de todo** the boss knew all about it; **¿estás e. de lo que pasó ayer?** do you know about what happened yesterday?; EXPR **darse por e.** to take the hint; **ya me doy por e.** I get the idea; **no darse por e.** to turn a deaf ear
(**c**) *Chile (engreído)* conceited
2 *nm,f Fam Irónico* know-all; **va de e. por la vida** he acts as if he knows everything

enteramente *adv* completely, entirely

enterar 1 *vt* (**a**) *(informar)* **e. a alguien de algo** to inform sb about sth (**b**) *CAm, Chile, Col, Méx (pagar)* to pay (**c**) *Chile (completar)* to make up
2 enterarse *vpr* (**a**) *(descubrir, saber)* to find out (**de** about); **como se entere, me mata** if she finds out, she'll kill me; **nos acabamos de e.** we've just heard; **¿tú crees que se enterarán?** do you think they'll find out?; **no lo sabía, ahora me entero** I didn't know, this is the first I've heard of it; **se enterarán de tu pasado y lo publicarán** they'll find out about your past and make it public; **entérate bien de los horarios de los trenes** make sure you find out about the train times; **¿te has enterado de la noticia?** have you heard the news?; **¿te has enterado del accidente de Ana?** did you hear about Ana's accident?; **me enteré por mi prima** I heard about it from my cousin; **me enteré por la prensa** I read about it in the papers; EXPR **¡para que te enteres!** I'll have you know!, as a matter of fact!; EXPR **¡se va a e. de quién soy yo!** he's going to find out what sort of stuff I'm made of!; EXPR **¡te vas a e.!** you'll know all about it!, you'll catch it!; EXPR *Fam* **¡te vas a e. de lo que vale un peine!** I'll show you what's what!
(**b**) *(darse cuenta)* **enterarse (de algo)** to notice (sth); **tu mujer te**

está engañando y tú ni te enteras your wife is cheating on you and you haven't even noticed; **no se enteró del golpe** she didn't notice the impact; **es una operación muy sencilla, no te vas ni a e.** it's a very straightforward operation, you won't feel a thing

(c) *Fam (comprender)* to understand; **cuando habla tan rápido no me entero** when she talks so fast, I don't understand a word; **no quiero ir, ¿te enteras?** I don't want to go, have you got that clear?; **¡entérate de una vez! ¡yo no soy tu criado!** get this straight, I'm not your servant!; **no me enteré de lo que dijo en clase** I didn't understand what she said in class; **no te enteras de nada** you haven't got a clue, have you?

entereza *nf* (a) *(serenidad)* composure, self-possession; **aceptó su muerte con e.** he accepted his death with great dignity (b) *(honradez)* integrity (c) *(firmeza)* firmness

entérico, -a *adj Anat* enteric

enteritis *nf inv* enteritis

enterito *nm CSur (ropa) (de peto) Br* dungarees, *US* overalls; *(para bebé)* rompers

enterizo, -a *adj* (a) *(entero)* entire, whole (b) *(de una pieza)* in one piece

enternecedor, -ora *adj* touching, moving

enternecer [46] 1 *vt* to move, to touch

2 **enternecerse** *vpr* to be moved

enternecimiento *nm* **el desamparo de los refugiados consiguió su e.** he softened when he saw how helpless the refugees were

entero, -a 1 *adj* (a) *(completo)* whole; **vi la película entera** I watched the whole film; **pasó la noche entera en vela** I was awake all night; **¿quiere la pieza entera o se la hago trozos?** do you want it in one piece or shall I cut it up?; **es de mi entera confianza** she has my complete confidence; **por e.** entirely, completely

(b) *(sin desperfecto)* in one piece; **la vajilla llegó toda entera** the dinner service arrived in one piece; **este cristal está e.** this pane hasn't been broken

(c) *(en buen estado físico)* **acabó la maratón muy e.** he finished the marathon in good shape

(d) *(sereno)* composed; **se mostró muy e. en el juicio** he was very composed at the trial

(e) *(honrado)* upright, honest

(f) *Mat (número)* whole

(g) *(fruta)* hard

(h) *Guat, Perú Fam (idéntico)* identical

2 *nm* (a) *Bolsa* point; **Prunosa sube dos enteros** Prunosa gained two points (b) *Mat* integer, whole number (c) *CSur (ropa) (con mangas) Br* overalls, *US* coveralls; *(de peto) Br* dungarees, *US* overalls; *(para bebé)* rompers (d) *Andes, RP (lotería)* = complete lottery ticket (usually sold in one-tenth shares)

enterradero *nm RP* hide-out

enterrador, -ora *nm,f* gravedigger

enterramiento *nm* (a) *(acción)* burial (b) *(ceremonia)* burial (c) *(lugar)* burial site

enterrar [3] 1 *vt* (a) *(cadáver)* to bury (b) *(objeto, tesoro)* to bury; EXPR **e. el hacha de guerra** to bury the hatchet (c) *(clavar)* to sink *o* drive in; **le enterró el puñal en el vientre** he plunged the dagger into his belly (d) *(olvidar)* to forget about (e) *(sobrevivir)* **enterró a todos sus hermanos** he survived all his brothers

2 **enterrarse** *vpr* **enterrarse en vida** to hide oneself away

entibar *vt Min (apuntalar)* to shore

entibiar 1 *vt* (a) *(enfriar)* to cool (b) *(templar)* to warm

2 **entibiarse** *vpr* (a) *(líquido) (enfriarse)* to cool (down); *(templarse)* to warm (up) (b) *(sentimiento)* to cool, to become lukewarm; **sus relaciones se entibiaron** *(de pareja)* their relationship lost its passion; *(diplomáticas, de amistad)* relations between them became more distant

entidad *nf* (a) *(organismo)* body; *(empresa)* firm, company; **las entidades públicas** public bodies ►► ***e. aseguradora*** insurance company; ***e. bancaria*** bank; ***e. benéfica*** charitable organization; ***e. de crédito*** lending institution; ***e. deportiva*** sporting body; ***e. financiera*** financial institution

(b) *(ente)* entity; **no existe como e. política** it does not exist as a political entity

(c) *Filosofía* entity

(d) *(importancia)* importance; **de e.** of importance; **su lesión es de poca e.** his injury isn't serious; **autores de gran e.** authors of the first rank

entiendo *etc ver* **entender**

entierro 1 *ver* **enterrar**

2 *nm* (a) *(acción)* burial (b) *(ceremonia)* funeral; **el e. recorrió el centro de la ciudad** the funeral procession passed through the city centre; **ir de e., ir a un e.** to attend a funeral ►► ***el e. de la sardina*** the burial of the sardine, = mock burial of a sardine on Ash Wednesday, to mark the beginning of Lent

entintar *vt* (a) *Imprenta* to ink (b) *(teñir)* to dye, to tint

entlo. *(abrev de* **entresuelo**) mezzanine

entoldado, -a 1 *adj* (a) *(terraza)* with an awning; *(calle)* with awnings (b) *(tarde)* overcast

2 *nm (toldo)* awning; *(para fiesta, baile)* marquee

entoldar 1 *vt (con toldo)* to put an awning over

2 **entoldarse** *vpr (cielo)* to cloud over

entomófilo, -a *adj Bot (planta, fecundación)* entomophilous

entomología *nf* entomology

entomológico, -a *adj* entomological

entomólogo, -a *nm,f* entomologist

entonación *nf (al hablar, al cantar)* intonation; **darle a algo la e. adecuada** to give sth the appropriate intonation ►► ***e. ascendente*** rising intonation; ***e. descendente*** falling intonation

entonado, -a *adj* (a) *(canto)* in tune; *(instrumento)* tuned (b) *(en buena forma)* **estar e.** to be in good shape (c) *Fam (bebido)* merry; **después de dos cervezas ya se pone e.** after a couple of beers he's pretty merry

entonar 1 *vt* (a) *(cantar) (canción, himno)* to sing; *(nota musical)* to give; *(plegaria)* to sing, to sound; **e. el mea culpa** to admit one's responsibility, to cry mea culpa (b) *(tonificar) (persona)* to perk up; *(músculos)* to tone up; **esta sopa te entonará** this soup will perk you up

2 *vi* (a) *(al cantar)* to sing in tune (b) *(armonizar)* **e. (con algo)** to match (sth)

3 **entonarse** *vpr Fam* (a) *(al beber)* to perk up; **se entonaba con una copa de oporto** he would take a glass of port as a pick-me-up *o* to perk himself up; **yo con dos copas ya me entono** after two glasses I start to feel merry (b) *(recuperarse)* to rally, to bounce back

ENTONCES *adv* (a) *(en ese instante)* then; **e. abrí la puerta y salí corriendo** then I opened the door and ran out; **esperaremos a que se apaguen las luces y e. salimos** we'll wait until the lights go out and then (we'll) leave

(b) *(en esa época)* then; **e. yo vivía en Manchester** I was living in Manchester at the time; **el e. primer ministro** the then prime minister; **de e.** of the time, at that time; **los periódicos de e.** the newspapers at that time *o* in those days; **desde e.** since then; **desde e. vengo teniendo pesadillas** ever since then I've had nightmares; **desde e. son enemigos** they have been enemies ever since; **en aquel e.** at that time; **en aquel e. nos conocimos** we met at that time; **hasta e.** until then; **hasta e., devolvemos la conexión** until then, it's back to the studio; **para e.** by then; **esperan que para e. las obras estén finalizadas** they hope the roadworks will be finished by then; **por (aquel) e.** at that time; **por (aquel) e. estaba soltera** she was single at the time

(c) *(después)* then; **¿una bici?, primero aprueba el curso y e. hablamos** a bike? first pass the course and then we'll talk

(d) *(introduciendo conclusión)* then; **e. ella es la culpable** so she's to blame, then; **si no ha llegado, e. tiene que estar en la oficina** if he hasn't arrived yet, then he must still be at the office; **si no te gusta, e. no vayas** if you don't like it, then don't go; **e., ¿vienes o no?** are you coming or not, then?; **pero e., ¿quién lo hizo?** well, who did it, then?

entontecer [46] *vt* **e. a alguien** to dull sb's brain; **programas que entontecen a la audiencia** programmes which rot the audience's brains *o* minds

entorchado *nm* (a) *(bordado)* = silk braided with gold or silver (b) *Dep* title

entornado, -a *adj (puerta, ventana)* ajar; *(ojos)* half-closed

entornar *vt (puerta)* to half-close, to leave ajar; *(ventana)* to half-close, to leave half-open; *(ojos)* to half-close; **la luz del sol le hizo e. los ojos** the sunlight made her squint

entorno *nm* (a) *(ambiente)* environment, surroundings; **el e. familiar/social** the home/social environment; **fuentes bien informadas del e. del presidente** well-informed sources close to the president; **España y los países de su e.** Spain and her European neighbours (b) *(medio ambiente)* environment (c) *Informát* environment

entorpecedor, -ora *adj* obstructive

entorpecer [46] *vt* (a) *(dificultar) (proceso, movimientos, negociaciones)* to hinder; *(tráfico)* to slow down; **problemas de última hora entorpecen la firma del tratado** last-minute problems are holding up *o* delaying the signing of the treaty; **el viento entorpecía el ritmo de**

los ciclistas the wind slowed the cyclists down; **¡estás entorpeciendo el paso!** you're getting in the way!
(**b**) *(debilitar) (miembros)* to numb; *(mente)* to cloud

entorpecimiento *nm* (**a**) *(dificultad) (de proceso, movimientos, negociaciones)* hindrance, delay; **aquello provocó un e. de las negociaciones** that was a hindrance to *o* that hindered the negotiations; **el accidente provocó un e. del tráfico** the accident slowed down the traffic (**b**) *(debilitamiento) (físico)* numbness; *(mental)* haziness

ENTRADA *nf* (**a**) *(acción)* entry; **prohibida la e.** *(en letrero)* no entry; **hizo una e. espectacular** she made a spectacular entrance; **la e. del equipo en el campo fue recibida con aplausos** applause broke out when the team came out on to the pitch; **la e. de nuevos países a la organización** the entry of new countries into the organization; **están en contra de su e. en la organización** they're opposed to him joining the organization; **su e. en escena fue triunfal** he made a triumphant entrance; **celebraron su e. a** *o* **en la sociedad** they celebrated her admission into the society; **se ha aplazado la e. en funcionamiento de la nueva línea férrea** the opening of the new railway line has been postponed; **dar e. a** to let in, to admit ►► ***e. en vigor:*** **hoy se cumple un año de la e. en vigor de la ley** it is a year today since the act came into force
(**b**) *(lugar)* entrance; *(puerta)* doorway; *(recibidor)* entrance hall; *Min* adit; **la e. al teatro estaba llena de admiradores** the theatre entrance was packed with admirers; **se quedó esperando en la e.** she waited at the entrance; **te espero a la e. del cine** I'll meet you outside the cinema; **e.** *(en letrero)* entrance, way in ►► ***e. principal*** main entrance; ***e. de servicio*** service entrance
(**c**) *Tec* inlet, intake; **conducto/válvula de e.** intake pipe/valve ►► ***e. de aire*** air intake
(**d**) *(en espectáculos) (billete)* ticket; *(recaudación)* receipts, takings; **sacar una e. (a** *o* **para alguien)** to buy a ticket (for sb); **los mayores de 65 años no pagan e.** people over the age of 65 don't have to pay to get in; **no hay entradas** *(en letrero)* sold out; **e. libre** *o* **gratuita** *(en letrero)* admission free
(**e**) *(público)* audience; *(en estadio)* attendance; **el campo registró menos de media e.** the stadium was less than half full
(**f**) *Esp (pago inicial)* down payment, deposit; **hay que pagar un millón de e.** you have to put down a million as a deposit; **dimos una e. de dos millones** we paid a deposit of two million
(**g**) *(en contabilidad)* income
(**h**) *(en un menú)* starter
(**i**) *(en la frente)* **tener entradas** to have a receding hairline
(**j**) *(en un diccionario)* entry
(**k**) *(principio)* beginning, start; **la e. del año** the beginning of the year; **de e.: de e. no me gustó, pero...** at first I didn't like it, but...; **de e. me insultó y luego me explicó sus motivos** first she insulted me, then she explained why; **me di cuenta de e. de que algo andaba mal** I realized from the start *o* from the word go that something was wrong; **de e. lo reconocí** I recognized him right from the start
(**l**) *(en fútbol)* tackle; **hacer una e. a alguien** to tackle sb; **e. dura** *o* **violenta** heavy challenge; **e. en plancha** sliding tackle
(**m**) *(en béisbol)* inning
(**n**) *Informát* input ►► ***e. de datos*** data entry, data input; ***e.-salida*** input-output, I/O
(**o**) *Mús* **la e. de los violines es espectacular** violins come in very dramatically
(**p**) *Cuba, Méx (paliza)* beating
(**q**) EXPR *Méx, RP Fam* **dar e. a alguien** *(flirtear)* to flirt with sb; *Méx* **de e. por salida** *(tiempo)* for a moment; *(persona)* paid by the hour

entradilla *nf (en periódico)* lead

entrado, -a *adj* (**a**) *(periodo de tiempo)* **e. el otoño** once we're into autumn; **entrada la noche** once night has set in; **no volvieron hasta bien e. mayo** they didn't return until well into May (**b**) *(persona)* **e. en años** elderly; **e. en carnes** portly, rather large

entrador, -ora *adj* (**a**) *Méx, Perú, Ven (animoso)* spirited, energetic (**b**) *CRica, RP (agradable)* likeable, charming (**c**) *Chile, Perú (entrometido)* meddling, meddlesome

entramado *nm* (**a**) *(de hierro, madera)* framework (**b**) *(estructura)* framework, structure; **el e. financiero del país** the financial structure of the country (**c**) *(red)* network; **la prensa destapó un e. de corrupción en la policía** the press uncovered a web of corruption in the police force

entramar *vt Am* (**a**) *(hilos)* to interweave (**b**) *(articular)* to shape, to form

entrambos, -as *Formal* **1** *adj pl* both
2 *pron pl* both

entrampado, -a *adj Fam (endeudado)* **estar e.** to be up to one's neck in debt

entrampar 1 *vt* (**a**) *Fam (endeudar)* to burden with debts (**b**) *(animal)* to trap, to snare (**c**) *(engañar)* to deceive, to trick (**d**) *Fam (enredar)* to make a mess of
2 entramparse *vpr Fam (endeudarse)* to get into debt

entrante 1 *adj* (**a**) *(año, mes, semana)* coming; *Méx (día)* next; **el año/mes e.** next year/month (**b**) *(presidente, gobierno)* incoming; **el presidente/gobierno e.** the incoming president/government
2 *nm* (**a**) *Esp (plato)* starter; **¿qué tienen de entrantes?** what starters do you have? (**b**) *(hueco)* recess (**c**) *(en tierra, mar)* inlet

entraña *nf RP* skirt; **churrasco de e.** grilled skirt steak

entrañable *adj* (**a**) *(querido) (persona)* dear; *(amigo)* very dear; **es un anciano e.** he's a dear *o* lovely old man (**b**) *(cariño, amistad)* warm; *(recuerdo)* fond; **tengo un e. recuerdo de aquel país** I have very fond memories of that country; **recibió un e. homenaje de sus compañeros de trabajo** he received a warm tribute from his workmates

entrañar *vt* to involve

entrañas *nfpl* (**a**) *(vísceras)* entrails, insides; EXPR **arrancar a alguien las e.** to break sb's heart; EXPR *Fam* **echar (hasta) las e.** *(vomitar)* to puke *o* throw one's guts up; EXPR **no tener e.** to be heartless; **¿es que no tienes e.?** do you have no feelings?, are you made of stone? (**b**) *(centro)* heart; **en las e. de la cueva/selva** in the depths of the cave/forest; **las e. de la Tierra** the bowels of the earth

ENTRAR 1 *vi* (**a**) *(introducirse) (viniendo)* to enter, to come in; *(yendo)* to enter, to go in; **déjame e.** let me in; **e. en algo** to enter sth, to come/go into sth; **acababa de e. en casa cuando...** she had just got back home *o* got into the house when...; **lo vi e. en el restaurante** I saw him go into the restaurant; **entré por la ventana** I got in through the window; **no tiene edad para e. en discotecas** she's not old enough to go to discos; **entró a toda velocidad** he rushed in; **entra al campo Rubio en sustitución de un compañero** Rubio is coming on for his teammate
(**b**) *(penetrar)* to go in; **cierra la puerta, entra mucho viento** close the door, you're letting the wind in; **este disquete no entra en la disquetera** this disk won't go into the disk drive
(**c**) *(caber)* to fit (**en** in); **esta llave no entra en la cerradura** this key won't fit in the lock; **en esta habitación entran dos alfombras** there's room for two rugs in this room; **este anillo no me entra** I can't get this ring on my finger; **el pie no me entra en el zapato** I can't get this shoe on
(**d**) *(incorporarse)* **e. (en algo)** *(colegio, empresa)* to start (at sth); *(club, partido político)* to join (sth); **entró en la universidad a los dieciocho años** he went to university when he was eighteen; **e. en la Unión Europea** to join the European Union; **entró a trabajar de ayudante** he started off as an assistant
(**e**) *(empezar)* **entramos a las nueve** we start at nine o'clock; **e. a hacer algo** to start doing sth; **entró a trabajar hace un mes** she started work a month ago; *RP Fam* **cuando me lo dijo, entré a atar cabos** when he told me, I started putting two and two together; *RP Fam* **cuando entró a pensar en el asunto, ya era demasiado tarde** by the time he began thinking about the matter, it was already too late
(**f**) *(participar)* to join in; **e. en** *(discusión, polémica)* to join in; *(negocio)* to get in on; **no entremos en cuestiones morales** let's not get involved in moral issues; **no tuvo tiempo de e. en juego** she didn't have time to get into the game; **yo ahí ni entro ni salgo** it has nothing to do with me; **yo no entro en temas políticos porque no entiendo** I don't discuss politics because I don't understand it
(**g**) *(estar incluido)* **e. en, e. dentro de** to be included in; **la cena entra en el precio** dinner is included in the price; **¿cuántos entran en un kilo?** how many do you get to the kilo?; **¿esto entra en** *o* **para el examen?** does this come into the exam?
(**h**) *(figurar)* **entro en el grupo de los disconformes** I number among the dissidents; **este retraso no entraba en nuestros planes** this delay did not form part of our plans
(**i**) *(estado físico, de ánimo)* **le entraron ganas de hablar** he suddenly felt like talking; **me entran ganas de ponerme a cantar** I've got an urge to start singing; **me está entrando frío/sueño** I'm getting cold/sleepy; **me entró mucha pena** I was filled with pity; **entró en calor rápidamente** she soon warmed up *o* got warm; **me entran sudores sólo de pensarlo** it makes me break out in a cold sweat just thinking about it; **me entró la risa** I got the giggles
(**j**) *(periodo de tiempo)* to start; **el verano entra el 21 de junio** summer starts on 21 June; **e. en** *(edad, vejez)* to reach; *(año nuevo)* to start; **entramos en una nueva era de cooperación** we are entering a new era of cooperation
(**k**) *(concepto, asignatura)* **no le entra la geometría** he can't get the hang of geometry; **no le entra en la cabeza que eso no se hace** he

can't seem to get it into his head that that sort of behaviour is out

(l) *Aut* to engage; **no entra la tercera** it won't go into third gear

(m) *Mús* to come in; **ahora entra la sección de viento** now the wind section comes in

(n) *Taurom* to charge; **e. al engaño** to charge the cape

(o) *Fam (comida, bebida)* to go down; **iqué bien entra este vino!** this wine goes down a treat!; **no, gracias, no me entra más** no thanks, I couldn't take any more

2 *vt* **(a)** *(introducir) (trayendo)* to bring in; *(llevando)* to take in; **entra la ropa antes de que se moje** take *o* bring the washing in before it gets wet; **entra las herramientas en el cobertizo y vamos a pasear** put the tools in the shed and we'll go for a walk; **¿por dónde entraremos el piano?** where are we going to get the piano in?; **entran tabaco de contrabando** they bring in contraband tobacco, they smuggle tobacco

(b) *(acometer)* to approach; **a ése no hay por donde entrarle** it's impossible to know how to approach him; **hay un chico que le gusta, pero no sabe cómo entrarle** there's a boy she fancies, but she doesn't know how to get talking to him

(c) *(en fútbol)* to tackle; **entró al contrario con violencia** he made a heavy challenge on his opponent; **e. en falta a alguien** to commit a foul on sb

---

ENTRE **1** *prep* **(a)** *(en medio de dos)* between; **está e. mi casa y la suya** it's between my house and hers, it's on the way from my house to hers; **e. las diez y las once** between ten and eleven o'clock; **e. 1939 y 1945** between 1939 and 1945, from 1939 to 1945; **e. paréntesis** in brackets; **no abre e. semana** it doesn't open during the week; **no hay punto de comparación e. la ciudad y el campo** there's no comparison between the city and the countryside; **la diferencia entre tú y yo es que...** the difference between you and me is that...; **era un color e. verde y azul** the colour was somewhere between green and blue; **su estado de ánimo estaba e. la alegría y la emoción** his state of mind was somewhere between *o* was a mixture of joy and excitement; **se encuentra e. la vida y la muerte** she is fighting for her life; **e. nosotros** *(en confianza)* between you and me, between ourselves; **que quede esto e. tú y yo** this is between you and me; **dudo e. ir o quedarme** I don't know *o* can't decide whether to go or to stay; **e. una(s) cosa(s) y otra(s)...** what with one thing and another...; **no tuve tiempo de llamarte e. unas cosas y otras** between one thing and another I didn't have time to phone you

(b) *(en medio de muchos)* among, amongst; **estaba e. los asistentes** she was among those present; **e. los celtas se solía...** the Celts used to...; **e. los médicos se considera que...** most doctors believe that...; **lo hicieron e. tres amigos** the three friends did it between them; **e. todos estoy seguro de que lo conseguiremos** I'm sure we'll manage to do it between us; **es el favorito e. los expertos** the experts have him as the favourite; **estuvo e. los mejores** he was one of *o* amongst the best; **no temas, estás e. amigos** don't be afraid, you're amongst friends; **desapareció e. la multitud** she disappeared into the crowd; **apareció de e. el humo** it emerged from the smoke; **e. hombres y mujeres somos más de cien** there are over a hundred of us, men and women together; **me regaló, e. otras cosas, una botella de whisky** she gave me several things, including a bottle of whisky; **tu principal defecto, e. otros, es que...** your main defect, amongst others, is that...; **lo encontré e. mis papeles** I found it amongst my papers; **e. sí** amongst themselves; **discutían e. sí** they were arguing with each other

(c) *(en divisiones)* **divide veinte e. cuatro** divide twenty by four; **ocho e. dos cuatro** eight divided by two is four

2 entre que *loc conj Fam (mientras)* **e. que se levanta y se arregla, se le va media mañana** it takes her half the morning just to get up and get ready

3 entre tanto *loc adv (mientras tanto)* meanwhile; **haz las camas, e. tanto, yo lavo los platos** you make the beds, in the meantime, I'll do the washing up

4 entre más *loc adv Andes, CAm, Méx (cuanto más)* the more; **e. más duerme, más cansado se siente** the more she sleeps, the more tired she feels

---

entreabierto, -a **1** *participio ver* **entreabrir**

2 *adj (puerta)* half-open, ajar; *(ventana, ojos, boca)* half-open; **dejó la puerta entreabierta** he left the door half-open *o* ajar

entreabrir *vt (puerta)* to half-open, to leave ajar; *(ventana, ojos, boca)* to half-open

entreacto *nm* interval; **en el e.** during the interval

entrecano, -a *adj (cabello, barba, persona) Br* greying, *US* graying

entrecasa *nf Am* **estar de e.** to be casually dressed; **un batón de e.** a housecoat; **amo los guisos de e.** I love home cooking

entrecejo *nm* = space between the eyebrows; **arrugar** *o* **fruncir el e.** to frown

entrecerrado, -a *adj (puerta, ventana)* half-shut; *(ojos)* half-shut

entrecerrar [3] *vt (puerta)* to half-close, to leave ajar; *(ventana)* to half-close; **e. los ojos** to squint

entrechocar [60] **1** *vt (espadas)* to clash; *(vasos)* to clink

2 *vi (dientes)* to chatter

3 entrechocarse *vpr (dientes)* to chatter

entrecomillado, -a **1** *adj* in quotation marks

2 *nm* text in quotation marks

entrecomillar *vt* to put in quotation marks

entrecoro *nm* chancel

entrecortadamente *adv (hablar)* falteringly; *(respirar)* with difficulty; *(escucharse, recibirse)* intermittently

entrecortado, -a *adj (voz, habla)* faltering; *(respiración)* laboured; *(señal, sonido, comunicación)* intermittent; **se oía su llanto e.** you could hear her choking sobs

entrecortar *vt* **1** **(a)** *(cortar)* to cut into, to cut partially **(b)** *(interrumpir)* to interrupt, to cut off

2 entrecortarse *vpr (voz)* to falter; *(respiración)* to become laboured; *(señal, sonido, comunicación)* to become intermittent; **se le entrecortaba la voz de la emoción** her voice was choked with emotion

entrecot (*pl* **entrecots** *o* **entrecotes**) *nm* entrecôte

entrecruzado, -a *adj* interwoven; **varias historias entrecruzadas** several interconnected stories

entrecruzar [14] **1** *vt (líneas, trazos, hilos)* to interweave

2 entrecruzarse *vpr (líneas, carreteras, destinos)* to interweave

entrecubiertas *nfpl Náut* between-decks

entredicho *nm* **(a)** *(duda)* **estar** *o* **quedar en e.** to be in doubt; **la credibilidad del gobierno está/ha quedado en e.** the credibility of the government is in/has been brought into doubt; **poner en e.** to question, to call into question; **puso en e. la calidad de mi trabajo** he called into question the quality of my work

(b) *Rel* interdict

(c) *CSur (conflicto)* argument; **tuvieron un e. hace diez años y nunca más se hablaron** they fell out ten years ago and haven't spoken since

entredoble *adj (tejido)* of medium thickness

entredós (*pl* **entredoses**) *nm* **(a)** *(en costura)* insert, panel **(b)** *(armario)* dresser

entreforro *nm* interlining

entrega *nf* **(a)** *(acto de entregar)* handing over, handover; *(de pedido, paquete)* delivery; *(de premios)* presentation; **la e. de rehenes/de un rescate** the handover of hostages/ransom money; **el acto de e. de los Premios Nobel** the Nobel Prize award ceremony; **no acudió a la e. de premios** he didn't attend the prizegiving ceremony; **hacer e. de algo a alguien** to hand sth over to sb; **se le hizo e. de una placa conmemorativa** she was presented with a commemorative plaque; **hará e. de las medallas el presidente del COI** the president of the IOC will hand out *o* present the medals; **pagadero a la e.** payable on delivery ▸▸ *Com* ***e. contrarreembolso*** cash on delivery; ***e. a domicilio*** home delivery; **servicio de e. a domicilio** delivery service; ***e. de llaves:*** **el resto a pagar con la e. de llaves** the balance to be paid when the keys are handed over; ***e. urgente*** express delivery

(b) *(dedicación)* devotion (**a** to); **médicos que trabajan con gran e.** doctors who work with great dedication

(c) *(fascículo)* instalment; **por entregas** in instalments; **publicar por entregas** to serialize

(d) *(capítulo de serial, teleserie)* episode; **en nuestra anterior e....** in our previous episode...

(e) *(envío, partida)* delivery; **nos enviaron el pedido en dos entregas** they sent us the order in two deliveries *o* shipments

(f) *Dep* pass

(g) **e. inicial** *(pago inicial)* down payment, deposit

entregado, -a *adj* **(a)** *(dedicado)* dedicated (**a** to); **vive e. a su trabajo** he lives for his work; **gentes entregadas al vicio y a la depravación** people given over to vice and depravity; **toda una carrera entregada a la investigación médica** a lifetime's work devoted to medical research

(b) *(entusiasmado)* enthusiastic; **la estrella actuó ante un público e.** the star performed in front of an enthusiastic audience

(c) *RP (resignado)* resigned; **durante un tiempo trató de cambiar la situación, pero ahora ya está e.** for a while he tried to change the situation, but now he's given up

ENTREGAR [38] **1** *vt* **(a)** *(dar)* to hand over, to give; *(premio, medalla, diploma)* to present, to hand out; **exigen que se les entregue un rescate** they demand that a ransom be handed over; **me entregó las llaves de la habitación y se fue** she gave me the keys to the room and left; **me entregaron un libro para que se lo diera a mi hermano** they gave me a book for my brother; **le entregaron las llaves de la ciudad** they handed over the keys to the city to him; **el presidente entregó los premios a los ganadores** the president handed out *o* presented the prizes to the winners; **al final del curso te entregan un diploma** you're given a diploma at the end of the course

(b) *(pedido, paquete, correspondencia)* to deliver; *(examen, informe, solicitud)* to hand in; **una carta certificada hay que entregarla en mano** a registered letter must be delivered to the addressee in person

(c) *(ceder) (ciudad, posesiones)* to surrender; *(armas)* to hand over, to surrender; **entregó el poder a su hermano** he handed over power to his brother; **con cinco goles en contra, entregaron el partido** five goals down, they threw in the towel; EXPR *Ven Fam* **e. los papeles** *(rendirse)* to throw in the towel; *(morir)* to kick the bucket

(d) *(persona)* to turn over; **entregó al ladrón a la policía** she turned the thief over to the police; **no entregarán a los rehenes hasta que no reciban el rescate** they won't turn over *o* release the hostages until they receive the ransom

(e) *(dedicar)* to devote; **ha entregado su vida a la lucha por el desarme** she has devoted her life to fighting for disarmament

(f) *RP Fam (crimen)* **ese asalto lo entregó algún empleado del banco** that robbery was an inside job; **desvalijaron el apartamento de arriba, para mí que lo entregó el portero** they cleaned out the apartment above, I think the *Br* caretaker *o US* superintendent was in on it

2 entregarse *vpr* **(a)** *(rendirse)* to give oneself up; **el secuestrador se entregó sin oponer resistencia** the hijacker gave himself up without a struggle; **se fue a e. a la policía** he turned himself in (to the police)

(b) entregarse a *(persona, trabajo)* to devote oneself to; *(vicio, pasión)* to give oneself over to; **se entrega por completo a su trabajo** she's totally devoted to her work; **se ha entregado a la bebida** he's given himself over to drink

entreguerras: de entreguerras *loc adj* **periodo/literatura de e.** time/literature between the wars

entreguismo *nm* defeatism; **una oposición sin entreguismos al liberalismo económico** an uncompromising opposition to economic liberalism

entreguista *adj* defeatist

entrejuntar *vt (en carpintería)* to assemble, to joint

entrelazamiento *nm Informát* interleaving

entrelazar [14] **1** *vt (dedos)* to interlace; *(líneas, trazos)* to intertwine; *(hilos, cintas)* to interweave; *(historias, destinos, vidas)* to intertwine, to weave together; **entrelazaron sus manos** they joined hands

2 entrelazarse *vpr (líneas, trazos)* to be intertwined; *(hilos, cintas)* to be interwoven; *(historias, destinos, vidas)* to intersect, to be intertwined

entrelínea *nf Imprenta* leading, space between lines

entremedias, entremedio *adv* **(a)** *(en el espacio)* in between; **yo estaba sentado e. (de los dos)** I was sitting in between (the two of them); **había un barullo de gente, y e. había policías** there was a confused mass of people and some police in among them **(b)** *(en el tiempo)* in between; **e. nos tomamos un café** we had a coffee in between

entremés *(pl* **entremeses***)* *nm* **(a)** *(plato frío)* **entremeses** hors d'oeuvres **(b)** *(pieza teatral)* = short, amusing one-act play

entremeter 1 *vt* to insert, to put in

2 entremeterse *vpr (inmiscuirse)* to interfere, to meddle (**en** in)

entremetido, -a 1 *adj* interfering

2 *nm,f* meddler

entremezclar 1 *vt* to mix up

2 entremezclarse *vpr* to mix

entrenador, -ora *nm,f* **(a)** *(deportivo) (preparador)* coach; *(director técnico)* manager **(b)** *(de animales, pilotos)* trainer

entrenamiento *nm* **(a)** *(adiestramiento, preparación)* training, coaching; **el campo de e.** the training ground **(b)** *(sesión de ejercicios)* training session

entrenar 1 *vt* **(a)** *(deportistas)* to train **(b)** *(animales, soldados)* to train

2 *vi* **(a)** *(deportistas)* to train **(b)** *(soldados)* to train

3 entrenarse *vpr* **(a)** *(deportistas)* to train (**para** for) **(b)** *(soldados)* to train (**para** for)

entreno *nm Dep* training

entreoír [44] *vt* to half-hear

entrepaño *nm* **(a)** *Arquit* bay **(b)** *(estante)* shelf **(c)** *(de puerta)* panel

entrepierna *nf* **(a)** *(zona) (del cuerpo humano)* crotch; *(del pantalón)* inside leg; EXPR *muy Fam* **pasarse algo por la e.** to piss on sth from a great height **(b)** *Chile (traje de baño)* bathing *o* swimming trunks

entrepiso *nm Arquit* mezzanine

entrépito, -a *adj Ven Fam* meddling, interfering

entreplanta *nf* mezzanine

entresacar [60] *vt* **(a)** *(escoger)* to pick out **(b)** *(en peluquería)* to thin out

entresijo *nm* **1** *Anat* mesentery

2 entresijos *nmpl (detalles)* ins and outs; **tener muchos entresijos** *(dificultades)* to be very complicated; *(persona)* to be a dark horse

entresuelo *nm* **(a)** *(en edificio)* mezzanine **(b)** *(en cine)* balcony; *(en teatro)* dress circle

entretanto 1 *adv* meanwhile; **e., yo lavo los platos** in the meantime, I'll do the washing up

2 *nm* **en el e.** in the meantime

entretecho *nm Arg, Chile, Col, Méx* loft, attic

entretejer *vt* **(a)** *(hilos)* to interweave **(b)** *(enlazar)* to interlace **(c)** *(incluir)* to insert, to put in; **e. citas con el texto** to insert quotations throughout the text

entretela *nf* **(a)** *(de ropa)* inner lining **(b)** *(de persona)* **Granada de mis entretelas** my beloved Granada; **se me rompen las entretelas de sólo pensarlo** just thinking about it breaks my heart

entretención *nf Chile* entertainment

entretener [67] **1** *vt* **(a)** *(despistar)* to distract; **no me entretengas** don't distract me

(b) *(retrasar)* to hold up, to keep; **no te entretengo más** I won't keep you any longer

(c) *(divertir)* to entertain; **el libro lo entretuvo toda la mañana** the book kept him amused all morning; **escuchar la radio es lo que más me entretiene** listening to the radio is what I most enjoy doing

(d) *(hacer llevadero)* to while away; **entretuvo la espera leyendo una revista** while waiting she whiled away the time reading a magazine

(e) *(mantener)* to keep alive, to sustain

2 entretenerse *vpr* **(a)** *(despistarse)* to get distracted

(b) *(retrasarse)* to be held up; **no te entretengas y vuelve rápido** don't get held up on the way and come back quickly; **me entretuve hablando** *o* **en hablar con ella y perdí el tren** I got held up talking to her and I missed the train

(c) *(divertirse)* to amuse oneself; **se entretiene con cualquier cosa** he can keep himself amused with almost anything; **es mayor y ya se entretiene solo** he's older and he can keep himself amused now; **me entretenía viendo la tele** I passed the time watching TV

entretenida *nf Anticuado (amante)* mistress

entretenido, -a *adj* **(a)** *(ameno) (película, juego, actividad)* entertaining, enjoyable; *(persona)* entertaining, amusing **(b)** *(distraído, ocupado)* busy; **estar e. con algo/haciendo algo** to be busy with sth/doing sth; **necesita estar e. con algo** she needs to be occupied with sth **(c)** *(laborioso)* time-consuming; **pelar guisantes es muy e.** shelling peas is very time-consuming

entretenimiento *nm* **(a)** *(acción)* entertainment; **lo hace por e.** he does it for fun **(b)** *(pasatiempo)* pastime; **¿cuál es su e. preferido?** what is your favourite hobby; **coleccionar sellos le sirve de e.** stamp collecting keeps him amused **(c)** *(conservación, mantenimiento)* maintenance, upkeep

entretiempo 1 *nm CSur* half-time

2 de entretiempo *loc adj* **ropa de e.** spring/autumn clothes; **una chaqueta de e.** a light jacket

entretuviera *etc ver* **entretener**

entrever [72] **1** *vt* **(a)** *(vislumbrar)* to barely make out; *(por un instante)* to glimpse; **entrevimos unas luces a lo lejos** we glimpsed some lights in the distance; **sólo pude e. su rostro** I could barely make out his face

(b) *(adivinar)* to see signs of; **he podido e. cierta ironía en sus palabras** I could detect a certain irony in his words; **dejar e. algo** *(sujeto: persona)* to hint at sth; *(sujeto: hecho)* to suggest *o* indicate sth; **dejó e. que se volvería a presentar a las elecciones** he hinted that he would stand again as a candidate; **sus gestos dejan e. que**

está arrepentido his gestures suggest that he is sorry

2 **entreverse** *vpr* (**a**) *(vislumbrarse)* to be barely visible; **el faro se entreveía en el horizonte** the lighthouse could be glimpsed *o* could just be made out on the horizon

(**b**) *(adivinarse)* **se entrevé que las negociaciones serán largas** there are signs that the negotiations will take a long time; **no se entrevé una solución** there is no sign of a solution, there is no solution in sight

entreverado 1 *adj* (**a**) *CSur (mezclado)* mixed up; **guardan toda la ropa entreverada** they keep all the clothes mixed up together (**b**) *CSur (confuso)* muddled; **su planteo es muy e.** his proposal is very muddled (**c**) **tocino e.** streaky bacon

2 *nm Ven* = roast lamb with salt and vinegar

entreverar *CSur* 1 *vt* to mix

2 **entreverarse** *vpr* to get tangled

entrevero *nm CSur* (**a**) *(lío)* tangle, mess (**b**) *(pelea)* brawl

entreviera *etc ver* **entrever**

entrevía *nf* gauge

entrevista *nf* (**a**) *(de periodista)* interview; *(de trabajo)* interview; **hacer una e. a alguien** to interview sb; **le hicieron una e. en la tele** they interviewed him on TV ►► ***e. de trabajo*** job interview (**b**) *(cita)* meeting; **celebrar** *o* **mantener una e. con alguien** to hold a meeting with sb

entrevistado, -a *nm,f* interviewee; **uno de cada tres entrevistados...** *(en encuesta)* one in three people interviewed...

entrevistador, -ora *nm,f* interviewer

entrevistar 1 *vt (para un medio de comunicación)* to interview; *(para un empleo)* to interview

2 **entrevistarse** *vpr (reunirse)* to have a meeting (**con** with)

entrevisto *participio ver* **entrever**

entripado *nm RP Fam* awkward *o* nagging problem; **hablá con ella y sacate de encima ese e.** talk to her and get the problem off your shoulders

entristecer [46] 1 *vt* to sadden, to make sad; **su muerte entristeció a todos** her death saddened everyone; **no sabes lo que me entristece oírte decir eso** you don't know how sad it makes me to hear you say that

2 **entristecerse** *vpr* to become sad; **se entristeció por el resultado de las elecciones** he was saddened by the election result

entristecimiento *nm* sadness

entrometerse *vpr* to interfere, to meddle (**en** in); **tú no te entrometas, yo arreglaré esto** don't you go interfering, I'll sort this out myself; **no te entrometas donde no debes** don't interfere where you shouldn't; **no hacía más que e. en mis asuntos** she did nothing but interfere *o* meddle in my affairs

entrometidamente *adv* intrusively

entrometido, -a 1 *adj* interfering

2 *nm,f* meddler

entrometimiento *nm* meddling

entromparse *vpr* (**a**) *Fam (emborracharse)* to get legless (**b**) *Am (enfadarse)* to get angry

entrón, -ona *adj Méx Fam* gutsy; **es más entrona que muchos hombres** she's got more guts than a lot of men; **tiene un carácter e. y habla sin tapujos** he's gutsy by nature and doesn't mince his words

entroncamiento *nm (parentesco)* relationship, connection

entroncar [60] *vi* (**a**) *(emparentarse)* to become related (**con** to) (**b**) *(trenes)* to connect (**c**) *(relacionarse)* to be related (**con** to) (**d**) *Méx (caballos)* to mate

entronización *nf* (**a**) *(de monarca)* enthronement (**b**) *(ensalzamiento)* exaltation; **sus películas son la e. del mal gusto** his films revel in their bad taste

entronizar [14] *vt* (**a**) *(monarca)* to enthrone (**b**) *(ensalzar)* to exalt, to praise to the skies

entronque *nm* (**a**) *(parentesco)* blood relationship (**b**) *(de vías, carreteras)* junction

entropía *nf Fís* entropy

entubación *nf*, **entubamiento** *nm* tubing

entubado, -a *adj Med* **tener a alguien e.** to have tubes going into sb

entubar *vt* (**a**) *(río, aguas)* to pipe (**b**) *Med (enfermo)* to put tubes/a tube into

entuerto *nm* wrong, injustice; **deshacer entuertos** to right wrongs; **le tocó a él deshacer el e.** it fell to him to resolve the situation

entumecer [46] 1 *vt* to numb

2 **entumecerse** *vpr* to become numb

entumecido, -a *adj* numb

entumecimiento *nm* numbness

enturbiar 1 *vt* (**a**) *(líquido)* to cloud; *(aire)* to make murky (**b**) *(acto, relación, situación)* to cloud, to mar

2 **enturbiarse** *vpr* (**a**) *(líquido)* to become cloudy; *(aire)* to become murky (**b**) *(acto, relación, situación)* to be marred

entusiasmado, -a *adj* excited; **estamos entusiasmados con la nueva casa** we're really excited about the new house; **aplaudieron entusiasmados** they clapped enthusiastically

entusiasmar 1 *vt* (**a**) *(animar)* to fill with enthusiasm; **entusiasmaron al público con su actuación** their performance fired the public with enthusiasm (**b**) *(gustar)* **le entusiasma la música** he loves music; **la idea no le entusiasmó demasiado** he wasn't overly enthusiastic about the idea

2 **entusiasmarse** *vpr* to get excited (**con** about); **con cualquier cosa se entusiasma** he gets excited about the slightest thing; **no te entusiasmes demasiado, que no hay nada seguro aún** don't get too excited, there's nothing settled yet

entusiasmo *nm* enthusiasm; **aplaudieron con e.** they clapped enthusiastically; **despertar e. (en alguien)** to arouse (sb's) enthusiasm; **la noticia despertó un enorme e.** the news aroused great excitement; **pone mucho e. en todo lo que hace** she puts a lot of enthusiasm into everything she does

entusiasta 1 *adj* enthusiastic

2 *nmf* enthusiast; **es un e. de la jardinería** he's a keen gardener

entusiastamente *adv* enthusiastically

entusiástico, -a *adj* enthusiastic

enumeración *nf* enumeration, listing

enumerar *vt* to enumerate, to list

enunciación *nf* formulation, statement

enunciado *nm* (**a**) *(de problema, pregunta, idea)* formulation, statement (**b**) *Ling* utterance

enunciar *vt* to formulate, to state

enunciativo, -a *adj Ling (oración)* declarative

enuresis *nf inv Med* enuresis ►► ***e. nocturna*** bed-wetting, *Espec* nocturnal enuresis

envainar *vt* (**a**) *(enfundar)* to sheathe (**b**) *Ven muy Fam (fastidiar)* to shaft; **los envainaron con un contrato falso** they shafted them with a dodgy contract; **¿de verdad te ha dicho eso?, ¡no envaines!** did he really say that to you? you can't be serious!

envalentonamiento *nm* boldness

envalentonar 1 *vt* to urge on, to fill with courage

2 **envalentonarse** *vpr* to become daring

envanecer [46] 1 *vt* to make vain

2 **envanecerse** *vpr* to become vain

envanecimiento *nm* vanity

envarado, -a 1 *adj* stiff, formal

2 *nm,f* stiff *o* formal person

envasado *nm (en cajas)* packing; *(en paquetes)* packaging, packing; *(en bolsas)* bagging; *(en latas)* canning; *(en botellas)* bottling ►► ***e. al vacío*** vacuum packaging

envasador, -ora *nm,f (empaquetador)* packer; *(enlatador)* canner; *(embotellador)* bottler

envasadora *nf* (**a**) *(máquina) (para paquetes)* packaging machine; *(para latas)* canning machine; *(para botellas)* bottling machine (**b**) *(empresa) (de paquetes)* packaging plant; *(de latas)* canning plant; *(de botellas)* bottling plant

envasar *vt (en cajas)* to pack; *(en paquetes)* to package, to pack; *(en bolsas)* to bag, to put in bags; *(en latas)* to can; *(en botellas)* to bottle; **e. al vacío** to vacuum-pack

envase *nm* (**a**) *(envasado) (en cajas)* packing; *(en paquetes)* packaging, packing; *(en bolsas)* bagging; *(en latas)* canning; *(en botellas)* bottling

(**b**) *(recipiente)* container; *(botella)* bottle; **envases de plástico/cartón** plastic/cardboard containers ►► ***e. desechable*** disposable container; ***e. no retornable*** non-returnable bottle; ***e. retornable*** returnable bottle; ***e. sin retorno*** non-returnable bottle

envejecer [46] 1 *vi* (**a**) *(persona) (hacerse viejo)* to grow old; *(parecer viejo)* to age; **los disgustos le hicieron e.** his misfortunes aged him (**b**) *(vino, licor)* to age, to mature (**c**) *(libro, novela, película)* to show its age

2 *vt* (**a**) *(persona)* to age; **la muerte de su madre lo envejeció mucho** his mother's death aged him a lot; **la ropa que te pones te envejece** the clothes you wear make you look old (**b**) *(vino, licor)* to age, to mature (**c**) *(madera, mueble)* to distress

3 **envejecerse** *vpr (hacerse viejo)* to grow old; *(parecer viejo)* to age

envejecido, -a *adj* (**a**) *(persona) (de edad)* old; *(de aspecto)* aged; **está muy e.** he looks very old (**b**) *(vino, licor)* aged, matured; **vino e. en barrica de roble** wine aged *o* matured in oak casks (**c**) *(madera, mueble)* distressed

envejecimiento *nm* (**a**) *(de persona)* ageing (**b**) *(de piel)* ageing (**c**) *(de vino, licor)* ageing (**d**) *(de madera, mueble)* distressing

envejezco *etc ver* **envejecer**

envenenado, -a *adj* (**a**) *(bebida, alimento)* poisoned; **murió e.** he died from poisoning (**b**) *(comentario, mirada, lengua)* venomous

envenenador, -ora 1 *adj* poisonous, venomous
2 *nm,f* poisoner

envenenamiento *nm* (**a**) *(de persona)* poisoning (**b**) *(de relación, situación, amistad)* poisoning

envenenar 1 *vt* (**a**) *(persona, alimento, flecha)* to poison (**b**) *(relación, situación, amistad)* to poison
2 envenenarse *vpr* (**a**) *(tomar veneno) (a propósito)* to poison oneself; *(por accidente)* to be poisoned; **se envenenaron con setas** they ate poisonous mushrooms (**b**) *(relación)* to become bitter

envergadura *nf* (**a**) *(importancia)* size, extent; *(complejidad)* complexity; **para un negocio de esta e. se necesita mucho dinero** a business of this size needs a lot of money; **una reforma de gran e.** a large-scale reform; **políticos de poca e.** minor politicians; **el accidente fue de tal e. que hubo que cerrar el aeropuerto** the accident was so serious that the airport had to be shut down
(**b**) *(de ave, avión)* wingspan
(**c**) *(de brazos)* span
(**d**) *(de vela)* breadth

envés (*pl* **enveses**) *nm* (**a**) *(de hoja)* reverse (side), back (**b**) *(de tela)* wrong side

enviado, -a *nm,f* (**a**) *(diplomático)* envoy; **un e. de la ONU** a UN envoy ►► ***e. extraordinario*** special envoy (**b**) *(corresponsal)* correspondent ►► ***e. especial*** special correspondent

enviar [32] *vt* (**a**) *(mandar, remitir)* to send; *(por barco)* to ship; *(por fax)* to fax; **envían la mercancía por avión** they send the goods by air; **te enviaré la información por correo electrónico** I'll e-mail the information to you, I'll send you the information by e-mail; **envíale mis saludos a tu madre** give my regards to your mother; **envió el balón al fondo de la red** he sent the ball into the back of the net
(**b**) *(persona)* to send; **lo enviaron de embajador** they sent him as an ambassador; **lo enviaron (a) por agua** they sent him for water; **e. a alguien a hacer algo** to send sb to do sth; **me enviaron a negociar con vosotros** they sent me to negotiate with you

enviciar 1 *vt* to addict, to get hooked
2 enviciarse *vpr* to become addicted (**con** to)

envidia *nf* envy, jealousy; **¿pretendes darme e.?** are you trying to make me jealous?; **iqué e. me das al verte tan feliz con tu hijo!** it makes me really envious seeing you so happy with your son!; **tener e. de algo** to envy sth; **tenía e. de nuestro éxito** she was envious of our success; **tener e. de** *o* **a alguien** to be envious *o* jealous of sb; **tiene e. de su hermano, le tiene e. a su hermano** he's jealous of his brother; **siento una e. sana por él** I'm envious but I feel very happy for him; **eres la e. de todas las chicas** you're the envy of all the girls; *Fam* **se lo comía la e. al ver el éxito de sus rivales** he was consumed with jealousy *o* envy when he saw his rivals' success; *Fam* **morirse de e.** to be green with envy

envidiable *adj* enviable

envidiablemente *adv* enviably

envidiar *vt* to envy; **envidio su valor** I envy him his courage; **le envidian porque tiene dinero** they're jealous of him because he has money; **será muy rico pero yo no lo envidio** he may be very rich but I don't envy him; **mi casa poco tiene que e. a la tuya** my house is just as good as yours; **un joven golfista que en nada tiene que e. a los grandes campeones** a young golfer who is every bit as good as the great champions

envidioso, -a 1 *adj* envious, jealous; **no seas e., que tú tienes uno igual** don't be jealous, you've got one just like it
2 *nm,f* envious person; **ser un e.** to be very envious

> **Falso amigo**: El adjetivo inglés **invidious** no es la traducción del español **envidioso**. En inglés, **invidious** significa "odioso" o "ingrato".

envilecedor, -ora *adj* debasing

envilecer [46] **1** *vt* to debase
2 *vi* to become debased
3 envilecerse *vpr* to become debased

envilecimiento *nm* debasement

envinagrar *vt* to add vinegar to

envío *nm* (**a**) *Com* dispatch; *(de correo)* delivery; *(de víveres, mercancías)* consignment; *(de dinero)* remittance; **en el albarán figura la fecha y la hora de e.** the date and time of delivery is stated on the delivery note; **el precio no incluye gastos de e.** the price does not include postage and *Br* packing *o US* handling; **se hacen envíos a domicilio** *(en letrero)* we deliver (**b**) *(paquete)* package

envión *nm RP Fam* (**a**) *(empujón)* shove (**b**) *(impulso) (de vehículo)* jolt; **aprovecharon el e. del gol** they made good use of the boost given to them by the goal; **dar un e. a algo** to give sth a boost

envite *nm* (**a**) *(en el juego)* raise (**b**) *(ofrecimiento)* offer (**c**) *(empujón)* push, shove; EXPR **al primer e.** *(de buenas a primeras)* right away, from the outset

enviudar *vi* to be widowed

envoltorio *nm* (**a**) *(de producto)* packaging; *(de regalo)* wrapping; *(de caramelo)* wrapper (**b**) *(lío, atado)* bundle

envoltura *nf* (**a**) *(capa exterior)* covering; *(de semilla, reactor nuclear)* casing (**b**) *(de producto)* packaging; *(de regalo)* wrapping; *(de caramelo)* wrapper

envolvente *adj* (**a**) *(que envuelve) (niebla, atmósfera, sonido)* enveloping (**b**) *Mil (maniobra)* encircling

envolver [41] **1** *vt* (**a**) *(embalar)* to wrap (up); **envuélvamelo para regalo, por favor** could you giftwrap it, please?; **¿quiere que se lo envuelva?** would you like it wrapped?; **envolvió el paquete con** *o* **en papel de embalar** she wrapped the parcel in brown paper; **envuelve al niño con** *o* **en la manta** wrap the child in the blanket
(**b**) *(cubrir, rodear)* to envelop, to cover; **la niebla envolvía el valle** the valley was deep in mist; **la membrana que envuelve al feto** the membrane which envelops *o* covers the foetus; **una sensación de melancolía la envolvía** a feeling of melancholy enveloped him
(**c**) *(enrollar)* to wind; **e. hilo en un carrete** to wind thread onto a spool
(**d**) *(involucrar)* **e. a alguien en algo** to involve sb in sth
(**e**) *(conllevar)* to imply; **lo que dijo no envuelve crítica alguna** what he said doesn't imply any criticism whatsoever
(**f**) *Mil (enemigo)* to encircle, to surround
2 envolverse *vpr* (**a**) *(cubrirse)* **envolverse en** *o* **con algo** to wrap oneself in sth; **se envolvió el pelo con** *o* **en una toalla** she wrapped her hair in a towel (**b**) *(involucrarse)* **envolverse en algo** to get involved with sth; **se ha envuelto en un asunto de drogas** he has got involved in something to do with drugs

envuelto, -a 1 *participio ver* **envolver**
2 *adj* (**a**) *(embalado)* wrapped; **e. para regalo** giftwrapped (**b**) *(rodeado)* **un edificio e. en llamas** a building enveloped in flames; **el asesinato sigue e. en un gran misterio** the murder is still shrouded in mystery (**c**) *(involucrado)* **e. en algo** involved *o* implicated in sth; **se ha visto e. en un escándalo de corrupción** he's been involved *o* implicated in a corruption scandal
3 *nm Am (tortilla)* wrap

envuelvo *etc ver* **envolver**

enyesado, -a 1 *adj* plastered
2 *nm* plastering

enyesar *vt* (**a**) *(brazo, pierna)* to put in plaster (**b**) *(pared)* to plaster

enyetar *vt RP Fam* to jinx

enzarzar [14] **1** *vt* to entangle, to embroil
2 enzarzarse *vpr* **enzarzarse en** to get entangled *o* embroiled in; **se enzarzaron en un acalorado debate** they got embroiled in a heated debate; **nos enzarzamos en una pelea a puñetazos** we got involved in a punch-up

enzima *nm o nf* enzyme

enzimático, -a *adj* enzymatic

eoceno, -a *Geol* **1** *adj* Eocene
2 *nm* **el e.** the Eocene

eólico, -a *adj* wind; **energía eólica** wind energy

eón *nm* eon

EPA ['epa] *nf* (*abrev de* **encuesta de población activa**) = Spanish survey of economically active population

epa *interj Fam* (**a**) *CAm, Méx, Ven (¡hola!)* hi!, hello! (**b**) *(ante un imprevisto)* oops! (**c**) *Andes (¡ea!)* come on!

épale *interj Méx Fam* look out!

epatar *vt* to shock

epazote *nm* foetid goosefoot

e.p.d. (*abrev de* **en paz descanse**) RIP

epéntesis *nf inv Ling* epenthesis

eperlano *nm* smelt, sparling

épica *nf (género)* epic

epiceno, -a *adj Gram* **nombre/sustantivo e.** epicene name/noun

epicentro *nm* epicentre

épico, -a *adj* (**a**) *Lit* epic (**b**) *(hazaña, victoria, esfuerzo)* epic; **fue un partido é.** the game was an epic

epicureísmo *nm* Epicureanism

epicúreo, -a 1 *adj* Epicurean
 2 *nm,f* Epicurean

epidemia *nf* (**a**) *(de enfermedad)* epidemic; **una e. de gripe** a flu epidemic (**b**) *(de problema)* epidemic; **este problema se está convirtiendo en una verdadera e.** the problem is reaching epidemic proportions

epidémico, -a *adj* epidemic

epidemiología *nf Med* epidemiology

epidemiológico, -a *adj Med* epidemiological

epidemiólogo, -a *nm,f Med* epidemiologist

epidérmico, -a *adj Anat* epidermic

epidermis *nf inv Anat* epidermis

epidural *Med* **1** *adj* epidural; **anestesia e.** epidural (anaesthetic)
 2 *nf* epidural

Epifanía *nf Rel* Epiphany

epifenómeno *nm* epiphenomenon

epífisis *nf inv Anat (glándula)* pineal gland

epifito, -a *adj Bot* epiphyte

epigastrio *nm Anat* epigastrium

epiglotis *nf inv Anat* epiglottis

epígono *nm* epigone

epígrafe *nm* (**a**) *(texto)* epigraph (**b**) *(de apartado, capítulo)* heading (**c**) *(en piedra, metal)* inscription

epigrafía *nf* epigraphy

epigrama *nm* epigram

epigramático, -a *adj* epigrammatic

epilepsia *nf* epilepsy; **le dio un ataque de e.** he had an epileptic fit

epiléptico, -a 1 *adj* epileptic
 2 *nm,f* epileptic

epilogar [38] *vt (resumir)* to summarize, to sum up

epílogo *nm* (**a**) *(de libro)* epilogue (**b**) *(de acto, conferencia, acontecimiento)* conclusion

episcopado *nm* (**a**) *(dignidad)* episcopate (**b**) *(territorio)* diocese, bishopric (**c**) *(mandato)* episcopate, episcopacy (**d**) *(conjunto de obispos)* episcopate

episcopal *adj* episcopal

episcopalismo *nm Rel* Episcopalianism

episcopalista *Rel* **1** *adj* episcopalian
 2 *nmf* episcopalian

episiotomía *nf Med* episiotomy

episódico, -a *adj* episodic, episodical

episodio *nm* (**a**) *(de serie, libro)* episode; **un serial radiofónico de diez episodios** a radio series in ten episodes
 (**b**) *(suceso)* event; **otro e. más de su accidentada vida** one more chapter in his eventful life
 (**c**) *Med (ataque)* episode; **un nuevo e. de embolia pulmonar** another episode of pulmonary embolism
 (**d**) *Fam (odisea)* palaver; **¡no te puedes imaginar qué e. para salir de allí!** you can't imagine what a palaver it was to get out of there!

epistemología *nf* epistemology

epístola *nf* (**a**) *Formal (carta)* epistle (**b**) *Rel* Epistle

epistolar *adj Formal* epistolary

epistolario *nm* collected letters

epitafio *nm* epitaph

epitelial *adj Anat* epithelial

epitelio *nm Anat* epithelium

epíteto *nm* (**a**) *Gram* = adjective preceding the noun and usually denoting a conventional characteristic rather than a distinguishing feature (**b**) *(calificativo)* epithet; **la prensa le dedicó halagadores epítetos** the press referred to him in glowing terms

epítome *nm* summary, synopsis

EPL 1 *nf* (*abrev de* **Esperanza Paz Libertad**) = Colombian political party
 2 *nm* (*abrev de* **Ejército Popular de Liberación**) = Colombian guerrilla group

e.p.m. (*abrev de* **en propia mano**) by hand

época *nf* (**a**) *(periodo histórico)* epoch, era; **la é. victoriana** the Victorian era; **en la é. de Zapata** at the time of Zapata; **en aquella é. los dinosaurios poblaban la Tierra** at that time dinosaurs roamed the Earth; **coche de é.** vintage car; **muebles de é.** period furniture; **vestido de é.** period dress; EXPR **hacer é.** to become a symbol of its time; **una película/victoria de las que hacen é.** a movie/victory that will go down in history
 (**b**) *(periodo de la vida)* period; **prefiere no recordar esa é. de su vida** he prefers not to recall that period in his life; **un Dalí de su é. joven** an early Dali; **en aquella é. vivíamos en Manchester** at that time we lived in Manchester; **lleva una é. larga sin trabajar** he's been out of work for a long period; **la empresa ha pasado por una mala é.** the company has been through a bad spell
 (**c**) *(estación)* season; **la é. de las lluvias** the rainy season; **la é. del apareamiento** the mating season
 (**d**) *Geol* age

epónimo, -a 1 *adj* eponymous
 2 *nm* eponym

epopeya *nf* (**a**) *(poema)* epic (**b**) *(género)* epic (**c**) *(hazaña)* epic feat; **la ascensión de la montaña fue una auténtica e.** the ascent of the mountain was an epic feat

EPS *nm Informát* (*abrev de* **encapsulated PostScript**) EPS

épsilon *nf* epsilon

equidad *nf* fairness

equidistancia *nf* equidistance

equidistante *adj* equidistant

equidistar *vi* to be equidistant (**de** from)

equidna *nm* spiny anteater

équido, -a 1 *adj* equine
 2 *nm* = member of the horse family

equilátero, -a *adj Geom* equilateral

equilibrado, -a 1 *adj* (**a**) *(dieta)* balanced; **el partido/combate fue** *o* **estuvo muy e.** the teams/fighters were very evenly matched (**b**) *(persona)* sensible, well-balanced
 2 *nm (de ruedas)* balancing

equilibrar 1 *vt* (**a**) *(carga, ruedas, fuerza)* to balance; **e. el marcador** *(en partido)* to level the score, to equalize; EXPR **e. la balanza** *(al pesar algo)* to balance the scales; *(para igualar fuerzas)* to achieve a balance (**b**) *(en finanzas)* **e. las cuentas/el presupuesto** to balance the accounts/budget
 2 equilibrarse *vpr* (**a**) *(piezas, ruedas, mecanismo)* to balance; *(enfrentamiento, partido)* to even up; **con la llegada del nuevo jugador se equilibraron las fuerzas** the arrival of the new player evened things up; **el marcador se equilibró en la segunda parte** the score was levelled in the second half (**b**) *(cuentas, presupuesto)* to be balanced

equilibrio *nm* (**a**) *(estabilidad)* balance; *Fís* equilibrium; **la balanza permanecía en e.** the scales were evenly balanced; **hay e. de fuerzas en el parlamento** the forces are evenly balanced in the parliament; **el gobierno busca el e. presupuestario** the government is seeking a balanced budget; **mantener algo en e.** to balance sth; **mantuvo el balón en e. sobre un dedo** he balanced the ball on his finger; **mantener/perder el e.** to keep/lose one's balance; EXPR **hacer equilibrios** to perform a balancing act; **hacíamos verdaderos equilibrios para llegar a fin de mes** we performed balancing acts to reach the end of the month ►► *Fís* ***e. dinámico*** dynamic equilibrium; ***e. ecológico*** ecological balance; *Fís* ***e. inestable*** unstable equilibrium; ***e. de poder*** balance of power; ***e. político*** balance of power; ***e. químico*** chemical equilibrium
 (**b**) *(contrapeso)* counterbalance, counterpoise
 (**c**) *(sensatez)* composure, poise ►► ***e. mental*** mental equilibrium

equilibrismo *nm (en trapecio)* trapeze; *(en cuerda)* tightrope walking

equilibrista *nmf (trapecista)* trapeze artist; *(en cuerda)* tightrope walker

equilicuá *interj Fam* that's it!

equino, -a 1 *adj* equine
 2 *nm (caballo)* horse

equinodermo *Zool* **1** *adj* echinoderm
 2 *nm (animal)* echinoderm
 3 equinodermos *nmpl (orden)* echinodermata

equinoccial *adj* equinoctial

equinoccio *nm* equinox ►► ***e. de otoño*** autumnal equinox; ***e. de primavera*** vernal equinox

equipaje *nm (maletas) Br* luggage, *US* baggage; **hacer el e.** to pack ►► ***e. de mano*** hand luggage

equipal *nm Méx* = barrel-shaped wicker chair with leather seat and back

equipamiento *nm* (**a**) *(acción)* equipping (**b**) *(sanitario, industrial, militar)* equipment; *(de oficina, cocina, cuarto de baño)* furniture and fittings (**c**) *(de automóvil)* features, fittings ►► ***e. opcional*** optional extras; ***e. de serie*** standard features

equipar 1 *vt* (**a**) *(persona)* **e. a alguien (de** *o* **con)** *(instrumentos, herramientas)* to equip sb (with); *(ropa, uniforme, calzado)* to kit sb out (with); **un ejército bien equipado** a well-equipped army

(**b**) *(edificio, institución)* to equip, to provide; *(barco)* to fit out; *(vivienda)* to furnish; *(local, cocina, cuarto de baño)* to fit out; **el gimnasio está equipado con aparatos de última generación** the gymnasium is equipped with the latest apparatus; **un automóvil lujosamente equipado** a luxuriously fitted-out car

2 equiparse *vpr* to equip oneself (**de** *o* **con** with); **se equiparon bien para la expedición** they equipped themselves well for the expedition

equiparable *adj* comparable (**a** *o* **con** to)

equiparación *nf* (**a**) *(comparación)* comparison (**b**) *(igualación)* **quieren lograr la e. de su sueldo con el de los hombres** they want their pay to be on a par with men's, they want equal pay with men

equiparar 1 *vt* (**a**) *(igualar)* to make equal, to put on a par (**a** *o* **con** to *o* with); **la nueva ley nos equipara a** *o* **con los funcionarios** the new law puts us on a par with *o* makes us equal with government employees (**b**) *(comparar)* to compare (**a** *o* **con** to *o* with)

2 equipararse *vpr (compararse)* to be compared (**a** *o* **con** to *o* with)

equiparidad *nf Chile, Perú* equality

equipo *nm* (**a**) *(de trabajadores, profesionales, voluntarios)* team; **un e. de extinción de incendios** a fire-fighting team; **trabajar en e.** to work as a team; **trabajo en e.** teamwork ►► ***e. de rescate*** rescue team; ***e. de salvamento*** rescue team

(**b**) *(de jugadores, atletas)* team; **un e. de rugby** a rugby team; **deportes de e.** team sports ►► ***e. local*** local team; ***e. visitante*** visiting team

(**c**) *(equipamiento)* equipment; **un e. de submarinismo** scuba diving equipment; **ya tiene listo el e. de esquí** he has got his skiing gear ready now; EXPR *Fam* **caerse** *o* **estrellarse con todo el e.** to get it in the neck ►► ***e. de oficina*** office equipment; ***e. de primeros auxilios*** first-aid kit; ***e. quirúrgico*** surgical instruments

(**d**) *(indumentaria) (de novia)* trousseau; *(de soldado)* kit; *(de colegial)* uniform; *(de deportista)* strip ►► *Arg* ***e. buzo*** tracksuit

(**e**) *(de música)* system ►► ***e. de alta fidelidad*** hi-fi system; ***e. de música*** music *o* sound system; ***e. de sonido*** sound system

equis 1 *adj* X; **un número e. de personas** x number of people

2 *nf inv* (**a**) *(letra)* **la (letra) e.** (the letter) x; EXPR *CAm, Col, Ecuad Fam* **estar en la e.** *(estar flaco)* to be as thin as a rake (**b**) *Esp (en quinielas)* draw

equiseto *nm Bot* horsetail, *Espec* equisetum

equitación *nf* (**a**) *(deporte)* horse *o US* horseback riding, *Espec* equestrianism; **una escuela de e.** a riding school; **consiguió el oro en e.** he got a gold medal in equestrianism (**b**) *(como arte)* horsemanship, equestrianism

equitativamente *adv* fairly

equitativo, -a *adj* fair, even-handed

equivalencia *nf* equivalence; **cuadro** *o* **tabla de equivalencias (de medidas)** a conversion table (for measurements)

equivalente *adj* equivalent (**a** to)

equivaler [70] *vi* (**a**) *(ser igual)* to be equivalent (**a** to); **300 pies equivalen a unos 90 metros** 300 feet are equivalent to 90 metres; **un dólar equivale a 100 centavos** there are 100 cents in a dollar

(**b**) *(significar)* to amount, to be equivalent (**a** to); **aquello equivaldría a una rendición incondicional** that would amount to an unconditional surrender; **eso equivale a decir que todos los hombres son machistas** that's tantamout to saying that all men are male chauvinists

equivocación *nf (error)* mistake; **cometer una e.** to make a mistake; **ha debido de ser una e.** there must have been a mistake; **por e.** by mistake

> **Falso amigo**: El sustantivo inglés **equivocation** no es la traducción del español **equivocación**. En inglés, **equivocation** significa "evasivas, ambigüedades".

equivocadamente *adv* mistakenly, by mistake; **ellos pensaban e. que...** they mistakenly believed that...

equivocado, -a *adj* (**a**) *(erróneo)* wrong; **tomó la dirección equivocada** he went in the wrong direction (**b**) *(persona)* mistaken; **estás completamente e.** you're completely mistaken; **si crees que aquí se acaba todo, estás pero que muy e.** if you think that's the end of it, you are very much mistaken

equívocamente *adv* ambiguously, equivocally

equivocar [60] **1** *vt* (**a**) *(cosa)* **e. algo con algo** to mistake sth for sth; **e. el camino** to take the wrong road; **equivoqué la fecha** I got the date wrong (**b**) *(persona)* **no me preguntes, que me equivocas** don't ask me questions, you'll make me go wrong

2 equivocarse *vpr (estar en un error)* to be wrong; *(cometer un error)* to make a mistake; **yo creo que te equivocas** I think you're mistaken; **te equivocas si crees que me voy a asustar** you're mistaken if you think you're going to frighten me; **se equivocó al girar** she took the wrong turning; **te equivocas con tu profesor, no es tan mala persona** you're wrong about your teacher, he's not such a bad person; **se equivocó de nombre/puerta** he got the wrong name/door; **equivocarse de fecha/día** to get the date/day wrong; **te equivocaste de profesión, deberías haber sido actor** you're in the wrong profession, you should have been an actor; **equivocarse en algo** to make a mistake in sth; **¿en qué nos equivocamos con él?** where did we go wrong with him?; **se equivocó en la suma** she got the total wrong

equívoco, -a 1 *adj* (**a**) *(ambiguo)* ambiguous, equivocal (**b**) *(sospechoso)* suspicious

2 *nm* misunderstanding; **dar lugar a equívocos** to give rise to misunderstandings; **deshacer un e.** to clear up a misunderstanding

era[1] *ver* **ser**

era[2] *nf (periodo)* era; **la e. postindustrial** the postindustrial era *o* age; **vivimos en la e. de la informática** we are living in the computer age; **en el año 500 de nuestra e.** in 500 AD ►► ***e. atómica*** atomic age; ***e. cristiana*** Christian era; ***e. espacial*** space age; ***e. geológica*** geological era; ***e. glacial*** ice age

era[3] *nf (para trillar)* threshing floor

erario *nm* funds ►► ***e. público*** exchequer

Erasmo *n pr* Erasmus

Erasmus [e'rasmus] *nm inv* (*abrev de* **European Action Scheme for the Mobility of University Students**) Erasmus

erbio *nm Quím* erbium

erección *nf* (**a**) *(de órgano)* erection (**b**) *(de edificio, monumento)* construction, erection

eréctil *adj* erectile

erecto, -a *adj* erect

erector, -ora *adj* erecting

eremita *nmf* hermit

eremítico, -a *adj* hermitical, eremitic

eres *ver* **ser**

Ereván *n* Yerevan

ergativo, -a *adj Gram* ergative

ergio *nm Fís (unidad)* erg

ergo *conj Formal* ergo

ergonomía *nf* ergonomics *(singular)*

ergonómico, -a *adj* ergonomic

ergotina *nf* ergot

ergotismo *nm Med* ergotism

erguido, -a *adj* erect, upright; **se sentaba muy e.** she sat bolt upright

erguir [28] **1** *vt (cabeza)* to raise; *(cuerpo, espalda)* to straighten

2 erguirse *vpr* (**a**) *(persona)* to rise up (**b**) *(edificio, montañas)* to rise; **el castillo se yergue sobre el pueblo** the castle rises above the town; **un enorme obelisco se yergue en el centro de la plaza** a huge obelisk stands in the middle of the square

erial *nm* uncultivated land

eriazo, -a *adj Andes, Méx* waste, uncultivated

erigir [24] **1** *vt* (**a**) *(construir)* to erect, to build (**b**) *(nombrar)* to name; **fue erigido rey de Dinamarca** he was named king of Denmark

2 erigirse *vpr* **erigirse en** *(deliberadamente)* to set oneself up as; **se erigió en el máximo defensor del medio ambiente** he set himself up as the great champion of the environment; **con sus hazañas se erigió en héroe nacional** his exploits turned him into a national hero

erísimo *nm* hedge mustard

erisipela *nf Med* erysipelas

eritema *nm Med* skin rash, *Espec* erythema ►► ***e. solar*** severe sunburn, *Espec* solar erythema

Eritrea *n* Eritrea

eritrocito *nm* erythrocyte

erizado, -a *adj* (**a**) *(levantado)* **se me puso el vello e.** *(por excitación)* the hairs on the back of my neck stood on end; *(por miedo)* my hair stood on end; *(por frío)* I got goosepimples (**b**) *(con púas, espinas)* spiky (**c**) *(lleno)* **e. de** bristling with; **una ascensión erizada de obstáculos** an ascent bristling with obstacles

erizar [14] **1** *vt* (**a**) *(levantar)* **eso me erizó el vello** *(por excitación)* that made the hairs on the back of my neck stand on end; *(por miedo)* that made my hair stand on end; *(por frío)* that gave me goosepimples (**b**) *Am (irritar)* **ese chirrido me eriza** that screeching sets my teeth on edge

2 erizarse *vpr* (**a**) *(levantarse)* **se me erizó el vello** *(por excitación)* the hairs on the back of my neck stood on end; *(por miedo)* my hair stood on end; *(por frío)* I got goosepimples (**b**) *(alarmarse) (persona)* to stiffen

erizo *nm* (**a**) *(mamífero)* hedgehog (**b**) *(pez)* globefish ►► ***e. de mar*** sea urchin (**c**) EXPR *Méx Fam* **quedar e.: después de pagar las cuentas, quedé e.** after paying the bills I was cleaned out

ermita *nf* (**a**) *(capilla en el campo)* country chapel (**b**) *(morada del ermitaño)* hermitage

> **Falso amigo**: El sustantivo inglés **hermit** no es la traducción del español **ermita**. En inglés **hermit** significa "ermitaño".

ermitaño, -a **1** *nm,f (religioso)* hermit; **llevar una vida de e.** to live like a hermit

2 *nm (cangrejo)* hermit crab

erogación *nf* (**a**) *Der (distribución)* distribution (**b**) *Am Formal (gasto)* expenditure (**c**) *Chile (donativo)* contribution

erogar [38] *vt* (**a**) *Der (distribuir)* to distribute (**b**) *Am Formal (gastar)* to spend (**c**) *Chile (donar)* to contribute

erógeno, -a *adj* erogenous; **zona erógena** erogenous zone

Eros *n Mitol* Eros

eros *nm inv* eros

erosión *nf* (**a**) *(de piedra, superficie, suelo)* erosion (**b**) *(de prestigio, derechos, relación)* erosion; *(de persona, institución)* weakening (**c**) *(herida)* abrasion, graze

erosionar **1** *vt* (**a**) *(piedra, superficie, suelo)* to erode (**b**) *(prestigio, derechos, relación)* to erode; *(persona, institución)* to weaken

2 erosionarse *vpr* (**a**) *(piedra, superficie, suelo)* to erode (**b**) *(prestigio, derechos, relación)* to be eroded; *(persona, institución)* to be weakened

erosivo, -a *adj* erosive

erótica *nf* **la e. del poder** the thrill of power

erótico, -a *adj* erotic

erotismo *nm* eroticism

erotizar *vt* to eroticize

erotomanía *nf* erotomania

errabundo, -a *adj* wandering, roving

erradamente *adv* mistakenly

erradicación *nf* eradication

erradicar [60] *vt* to eradicate

errado, -a *adj* (**a**) *(tiro, golpe)* missed (**b**) *(persona, razonamiento)* mistaken; *(vocación, camino, rumbo)* wrong; *(cálculo, respuesta)* incorrect

errante *adj* wandering; **una estrella e.** a wandering star

errar [29] **1** *vt* (**a**) *(tiro, golpe)* to miss (**b**) *(no acertar en)* **e. el cálculo/la respuesta** to get the figures/answer wrong; **e. el rumbo** to choose the wrong course; **e. la vocación** to mistake one's vocation; *RP* **le erraron con el diagnóstico** he was misdiagnosed; EXPR *RP Fam* **e. el biscochazo** to be wide of the mark

2 *vi* (**a**) *(vagar) (persona, imaginación, mirada)* to wander; **erró de pueblo en pueblo** she wandered from town to town

(**b**) *(equivocarse)* to make a mistake; **erró en la elección de carrera** he chose the wrong course; *RP* **errarle** to make a mistake; **le erré en las cuentas** I made a mistake in the accounts; **le erró, no le tendría que haber dicho nada** he made a mistake, he shouldn't have told him anything

(**c**) *(al tirar)* to miss

errata *nf (de imprenta)* misprint; *(en manuscrito)* error

erráticamente *adv* erratically

errático, -a *adj* (**a**) *(conducta, política, decisiones)* erratic (**b**) *(errante) (rumbo)* erratic; *(vida)* itinerant (**c**) *Geol* **roca errática** erratic

erre *nf* EXPR **e. que e.: le dije que no y él, e. que e., seguía insistiendo** I said no, and he just went on and on insisting; **ella sigue e. que e., que no piensa venir** she still absolutely insists that she's not going to come

erróneamente *adv* erroneously, mistakenly

erróneo, -a *adj (juicio, afirmación, decisión)* mistaken, erroneous; *(cálculo, datos)* incorrect, wrong; **sería e. claudicar ahora** it would be a mistake to give in now

error *nm* (**a**) *(falta, equivocación)* mistake, error; **fue un e. invitarla a la fiesta** it was a mistake to invite her to the party; **debe de haber un e.** there must be a mistake; **cometer un e.** to make a mistake; **estar en un e.** to be mistaken; **por e.** by mistake; **me enviaron la carta por e.** they sent me the letter by mistake; **sacar a alguien del e.** *o* **de su e.** to put sb right; **salvo e. u omisión** errors and omissions excepted ►► ***e. absoluto*** absolute error; ***e. de bulto*** huge *o* big mistake; ***e. de cálculo*** miscalculation; ***e. de copia*** clerical error; ***e. no forzado*** *(en tenis)* unforced error; ***e. humano*** human error; ***e. de imprenta*** misprint; ***e. judicial*** miscarriage of justice; ***e. mecanográfico*** typing error; ***e. de muestreo*** sampling error; ***e. relativo*** relative error; *Informát* ***e. de sintaxis*** syntax error; ***e. típico*** standard error; ***e. tipográfico*** typo, typographical error; ***e. de traducción*** translation error

(**b**) *Informát (en un programa)* bug

ertzaina [er'tʃaina] *nmf Esp* = member of Basque regional police force

Ertzaintza [er'tʃaintʃa] *nf Esp* = Basque regional police force

eructar *vi* to belch

eructo *nm* belch; **soltar un e.** to let out a belch

erudición *nf* erudition

eruditamente *adv* eruditely

erudito, -a **1** *adj* erudite

2 *nm,f* scholar; **un e. en la materia** an expert on the subject

erupción *nf* (**a**) *(de volcán)* eruption; **en e.** erupting; **entrar en e.** to erupt (**b**) *Med* **e. (cutánea)** rash; **le salió una e.** she came out in a rash

eruptivo, -a *adj (roca)* volcanic; *(volcán)* active

E/S *Informát (abrev de* **entrada/salida**) I/O

es *ver* **ser**

ESA ['esa] *nf (abrev de* **European Space Agency**) ESA

esa *ver* **ese**

ésa *ver* **ése**

esbeltez *nf* slenderness, slimness

esbelto, -a *adj* (**a**) *(persona, figura)* slender, slim (**b**) *Literario (columna, torre, árbol)* slender

esbirro *nm (matón)* henchman, thug

esbozar [14] *vt* (**a**) *(dibujo, plano)* to sketch, to outline (**b**) *(directrices, tema, plan)* to outline (**c**) *(gesto)* **e. una sonrisa** to give a hint of a smile

esbozo *nm* (**a**) *(de dibujo, plano)* sketch, outline (**b**) *(de directrices, tema, plan)* outline (**c**) *(de gesto, sonrisa)* hint

escabechado, -a *Culin* **1** *adj* pickled *(in oil, vinegar and bay leaves)*

2 *nm* = pickling liquid made of oil and vinegar, flavoured with bay leaves

escabechar *vt* (**a**) *Culin* to pickle *(in oil, vinegar and bay leaves)* (**b**) *Fam (matar)* to bump off (**c**) *Esp Fam (suspender)* to fail, *US* to flunk

escabeche *nm Culin* = pickling liquid made of oil and vinegar, flavoured with bay leaves

escabechina *nf Fam* (**a**) *(matanza)* massacre, slaughter; **el asalto de la policía al avión fue una e. total** when the police stormed the plane it ended in a complete bloodbath; **me hice una e. afeitándome** I really hacked myself about when I was shaving (**b**) *Esp (en examen)* **el examen final fue una e.** a lot of people came to grief in the final exam

escabel *nm* (**a**) *(para pies)* footstool (**b**) *(asiento)* stool

escabro *nm Bot* scaly bark

escabrosamente *adv* luridly

escabrosidad *nf* (**a**) *(de terreno, superficie)* roughness, ruggedness (**b**) *(de tema)* unpleasantness; *(de detalles)* luridness (**c**) *(de algo difícil)* awkwardness

escabroso, -a *adj* (**a**) *(abrupto)* rough (**b**) *(por obsceno) (tema)* unpleasant; *(detalles)* lurid; **contiene imágenes bastante escabrosas** it contains some fairly crude images (**c**) *(difícil)* awkward, thorny

escabullirse *vpr* (**a**) *(con disimulo)* to slip off *o* away; **siempre que hay trabajo se escabulle** he always slips off *o* away when there's work to be done; **se escabulleron de la sala** they slipped out of the hall (**b**) *(escaparse)* **el atracador consiguió e.** the mugger managed to make his getaway; **se me escabulló** he slipped out of my hands

escacharrado, -a *adj Esp Fam* bust, *Br* knackered

escacharrar *Esp Fam* **1** *vt* to bust, *Br* to knacker
2 escacharrarse *vpr Br* to get knackered, *US* to bust

escachar *vt Fam* to squash

escafandra *nf* diving suit ►► ***e. espacial*** space suit

escafandrista *nmf* diver

escafoides *Anat* **1** *adj* scaphoid
2 *nm inv* scaphoid bone

escala *nf* (**a**) *(para medir, ordenar)* scale; *(de colores)* range; *(de cargos militares)* scale of ranks; **subió varios puestos en la e. social** he climbed several rungs of the social ladder ►► ***e. Celsius*** Celsius (temperature) scale; ***e. centígrada*** Celsius scale; ***e. Fahrenheit*** Fahrenheit scale; *Informát* ***e. de grises*** grayscale; ***e. Kelvin*** Kelvin scale; *Mat* ***e. logarítmica*** logarithmic scale; ***e. de popularidad*** popularity stakes; ***e. de Richter*** Richter scale; ***e. salarial*** salary scale; ***e. de valores*** set of values
(**b**) *(de dibujo, mapa)* scale; **un mapa a e. 1/3000** a 1/3000 scale map; **una reproducción a e.** a scale model; **un dibujo a e. natural** a life-size drawing
(**c**) *(de trabajo, plan, idea)* scale; **pretenden crear una casa de discos a e. reducida** they aim to set up a small-scale record company; **a e. nacional/mundial** on a national/worldwide scale; **una ofensiva a gran e.** a full-scale offensive
(**d**) *Mús* scale; **la e. musical** the musical scale ►► ***e. cromática*** chromatic scale; ***e. diatónica*** diatonic scale
(**e**) *(en un vuelo)* stopover; *(en un crucero)* port of call; **un vuelo a Estambul con e. en Roma** a flight to Istanbul with a stopover in Rome; **hacer e. (en)** to stop over (in); **sin e.** non-stop; **un vuelo sin escalas** a non-stop flight ►► ***e. de repostaje*** refuelling stop; ***e. técnica*** refuelling stop; **haremos e. técnica en Londres** we will make a refuelling stop in London
(**f**) *(escalera)* ladder ►► *Náut* ***e. de cuerda*** rope ladder; *Náut* ***e. de viento*** rope ladder

escalabrar = **descalabrar**

escalada *nf* (**a**) *(a montaña)* climb; **la difícil e. al Aconcagua** the difficult ascent of Aconcagua ►► ***e. artificial*** artificial climbing; ***e. libre*** free climbing; ***e. en roca*** rock climbing (**b**) *(de violencia, precios)* escalation, rise (**de** in); **se produjo una e. de violencia/precios** there was an escalation in violence/prices

escalador, -ora **1** *nm,f* (**a**) *(montañero)* climber (**b**) *(ciclista)* climber
2 *nm* ***e. mecánico*** step machine

> **Falso amigo**: El sustantivo inglés **escalator** no es la traducción del español **escalador**. En inglés, **escalator** significa "escalera mecánica".

escalafón *nm* scale, ladder; **ascendió rápidamente en el e.** she gained promotion quickly; **ascendió dos puestos en el e. de la empresa** he rose two places on the company promotion ladder

escálamo *nm Náut* tholepin

escalar **1** *vt* (**a**) *(montaña, pared)* to climb (**b**) *(en jerarquía, lista, ranking)* to climb; **ha escalado varios puestos en el ranking de la ATP** he has risen several places in the ATP ranking
2 *vi* (**a**) *(por montaña, pared)* to climb (**b**) *(en jerarquía, lista, ranking)* to rise

escaldado, -a *adj* (**a**) *Culin* scalded (**b**) *Fam (receloso)* wary

escaldadura *nf* (**a**) *(quemadura)* scald (**b**) *(acción)* scalding

escaldar **1** *vt* (**a**) *(sujeto: agua, vapor)* to scald (**b**) *Culin* to scald (**c**) *(abrasar)* to turn red-hot
2 escaldarse *vpr (con agua, vapor)* to scald oneself

escaleno *adj Geom* scalene

escalera *nf* (**a**) *(en edificio)* stairs, staircase; **e. (de mano)** ladder; **me crucé con ellos en la e.** I passed them on the stairs; **se cayó por el hueco de la e.** she fell down the stairwell; **salió corriendo escaleras abajo/arriba** he rushed down/up the stairs; **antes que eso prefiero estar por ahí limpiando escaleras** I'd sooner clean stairs than do that ►► ***e. automática*** escalator; ***e. de caracol*** spiral staircase; ***e. de emergencia*** emergency stairs; ***e. de incendios*** fire escape; ***e. mecánica*** escalator, moving staircase; ***e. de servicio*** service stairs; ***e. de tijera*** stepladder
(**b**) *(en naipes)* run ►► ***e. de color*** straight flush; ***e. real*** royal flush

escalerilla *nf* (**a**) *(de avión)* stairs (**b**) *(de barco)* gangway

escaléxtric *nm Fam* spaghetti junction

escalfado, -a *adj (huevo)* poached

escalfar *vt* to poach

escalinata *nf* staircase

escalofriante *adj* spine-chilling

escalofrío *nm* shiver; **dar escalofríos a alguien** to give sb the shivers; **cuando lo pienso, me dan escalofríos** it gives me the shivers when I think about it; **tener escalofríos** to be shivering; **me entraron escalofríos** I started shivering

escalón *nm* (**a**) *(de escalera) (peldaño)* step; *(barra, travesaño)* rung (**b**) *(en el terreno)* terrace (**c**) *(categoría, nivel)* grade; **ha ascendido varios escalones** he has risen several places up the ladder

escalona *nf* shallot

escalonadamente *adv* in stages

escalonado, -a *adj* (**a**) *(en el tiempo)* staggered, phased; **una retirada escalonada de las tropas de ocupación** a staggered *o* phased withdrawal of the occupying troops (**b**) *(terreno)* terraced; *(pirámide)* stepped

escalonar *vt* (**a**) *(en el tiempo)* to stagger, to phase (**b**) *(terreno)* to terrace

escalope, *Am* **escalopa** *nm* escalope; **e. de ternera** veal escalope

escalpelo *nm* scalpel

escama *nf* (**a**) *(de peces, reptiles)* scale (**b**) *(de piel)* flake (**c**) *(de jabón)* flake

escamado, -a *adj Fam* suspicious, wary

escamar **1** *vt* (**a**) *(pescado)* to scale (**b**) *Fam (causar recelo a)* to make suspicious
2 escamarse *vpr Fam* to smell a rat, to get suspicious

escamoso, -a *adj* (**a**) *(pez, reptil)* scaly (**b**) *(piel)* flaky, scaly

escamotear *vt* (**a**) *(ocultar)* to keep secret; **la prensa escamoteó información a la opinión pública** the press concealed information from the public; **el gobierno ha escamoteado los resultados de la encuesta** the government has suppressed the results of the survey
(**b**) *Fam (hurtar)* **e. algo a alguien** to rob sb of sth; **mi hermano me escamoteó la calculadora** my brother swiped my calculator
(**c**) *(hacer desaparecer)* to (cause to) vanish

escamoteo *nm* (**a**) *(ocultación)* concealment; **el e. de un informe** the suppression of a report (**b**) *Fam (hurto)* stealing (**c**) *(destreza)* sleight of hand

escampada *nf Fam* break (in the rain)

escampar *v impersonal* to clear up, to stop raining; **saldremos cuando escampe** we'll go out when it clears up

escanciador, -ora *nm,f (de sidra)* = person who serves cider, pouring it from a great height; *(de vino)* wine waiter

escanciar *vt* to serve, to pour out

escandalizar [14] **1** *vt* to scandalize, to shock; **logra e. a todos con las cosas que dice** he manages to shock everyone with the things he says; **casos de corrupción que escandalizan a la opinión pública** cases of corruption which scandalize *o* shock public opinion
2 *vi (alborotar)* to make a fuss
3 escandalizarse *vpr* to be shocked (**de** *o* **por** at *o* by); **se escandaliza por cualquier cosa** she is easily shocked; **no sé de qué se escandalizan tanto** I don't know what it is they find so shocking; **la gente se escandaliza al ver cómo suben los precios** people are shocked when they see how prices are rising

escandallar *vt Náut* to sound

escandallo *nm Náut* sounding lead

escándalo **1** *nm* (**a**) *(hecho inmoral)* scandal; *(indignación)* outrage; **un e. de corrupción política** a political corruption scandal; **hubo e. generalizado entre la opinión pública** there was widespread indignation among public opinion; **¡esto es un e.!, quiero que me devuelvan el dinero** this is outrageous! I want my money back; **los sueldos de los políticos son un e.** *o* **de e.** politicians' salaries are a scandal *o* a disgrace; **sus declaraciones causaron e.** her statements caused a great scandal ►► *Der* ***e. público*** public indecency; ***e. sexual*** sex scandal
(**b**) *(alboroto)* uproar, racket; **¡dejen ya de armar tanto e.!** stop making such a racket!; **armar un e.** to kick up a fuss; **menudo e. armó al enterarse** she made quite a scene when she found out
2 de escándalo *loc adj Fam* (**a**) *(enorme)* enormous; **una goleada de e.** a real hammering (**b**) *(asombroso)* astonishing; **precios de auténtico e.** really amazing prices

escandalosa *nf* (**a**) *Náut* topsail, gaff (**b**) *ver también* **escandaloso**

escandalosamente *adv* (**a**) *(actuar, vestir)* outrageously, scandalously; *(vestir)* outrageously (**b**) *(gritar, hablar)* noisily; *(reír)* uproariously

escandaloso, -a 1 *adj* (**a**) *(inmoral)* outrageous, shocking; **se vio envuelto en un asunto e.** he got caught up in a scandalous business (**b**) *(ruidoso)* very noisy; **¡mira que eres e.!** what a racket you make!
2 *nm,f* very noisy *o* loud person; **son unos escandalosos** they're terribly noisy people

Escandinavia *n* Scandinavia

escandinavo, -a 1 *adj* Scandinavian
2 *nm,f* Scandinavian

escandio *nm Quím* scandium

escanear *vt* (**a**) *Informát* to scan (**b**) *Med* to scan

escáner (*pl* **escáneres**) *nm* (**a**) *Informát* scanner ►► ***e. plano*** flatbed scanner; ***e. de sobremesa*** flatbed scanner; ***e. de tambor*** drum scanner (**b**) *Med* scanner; **hacer un e. a alguien** to give sb a scan

escaño *nm* (**a**) *(parlamentario) (asiento, cargo)* seat; **los escaños de la oposición** the opposition benches (**b**) *(banco)* bench

escapada *nf* (**a**) *(huida)* escape, flight (**b**) *(viaje)* quick trip; **hicimos una e. a la montaña el fin de semana** we made a quick trip to the mountains at the weekend; **iré a comprar el periódico en una e.** I'll pop out to get a newspaper (**c**) *(en ciclismo)* breakaway; **meterse en una e.** to join a breakaway

> **Falso amigo**: El sustantivo inglés **escapade** no es la traducción del español **escapada**. En inglés **escapade** significa "aventura, correría".

escapado, -a 1 *adj (en ciclismo)* breakaway
2 *nm,f* **el pelotón dio caza al e.** the pack gave chase to the breakaway rider; **los escapados llevan tres minutos de ventaja** the breakaway group have a three-minute lead

escapar 1 *vi* (**a**) *(huir)* to get away, to escape (**de** from); **escapó de la cárcel** he escaped from jail; **escapó por la salida de emergencia** he got out through the emergency exit; **nadie escapó con vida del incendio** nobody got out of the fire alive; **escaparon por los pelos de una muerte segura** they narrowly escaped certain death; **quieren e. de la monotonía de sus vidas** they want to get away from the monotony of their lives; **dejar e.** *(animal, persona)* to set free; *(carcajada, grito, suspiro)* to let out; *(ocasión)* to pass up, to let pass; **dejó e. un grito** he let out a scream; **no quiero dejar e. esta oportunidad para agradecer...** I don't want to let this opportunity pass by without thanking...
(**b**) *(quedar fuera del alcance)* **e. a: son temas que escapan a mi comprensión** these subjects are beyond my understanding; **ese asunto escapa a mis competencias** that matter is outside my sphere of responsibility; **tampoco los adultos escapan a la influencia de los videojuegos** nor are adults immune from the influence of video games
(**c**) *(en carrera)* to break away; **e. del pelotón** to break away from the pack
2 **escaparse** *vpr* (**a**) *(huir)* to get away, to escape (**de** from); **se escaparon de la cárcel** they escaped from prison; **escaparse de casa** to run away from home; **se me escaparon las cabras** the goats got away from me; **no te escapes, que quiero hablar contigo** don't run off, I want to talk to you
(**b**) *(librarse)* **me escapé de milagro** *(de accidente)* I escaped by a miracle; **siempre se escapa de hacer las camas** he always gets out of making the beds; *Fam* **¡de esta no te escaparás!** you're not going to get out of this one!
(**c**) *(en carrera)* to break away; **Herrera se escapó en solitario** Herrera broke away on his own
(**d**) *(sujeto: gas, agua)* to leak; **el aire se escapa por un agujero** the air is leaking out through a hole
(**e**) *(sin querer)* **se me escapó la risa/una palabrota** I let out a laugh/an expletive; *Fam* **se me ha escapado un pedo** I've just farted; **¡era un secreto! – lo siento, se me escapó** it was a secret! - I'm sorry, it just slipped out
(**f**) *(irse)* **se me escapó el tren** I missed the train; **se me escapó la ocasión** the opportunity slipped by
(**g**) *(quedar fuera del alcance)* to escape, to elude; **los motivos de su comportamiento se me escapan** the reasons for her behaviour are beyond me
(**h**) *(pasar inadvertido)* **a tu madre no se le escapa nada** your mother doesn't miss a thing; **se me escapó lo que dijo** I missed what he said
(**i**) *(sujeto: punto de tejido)* to drop; **se te han escapado unos puntos** you've dropped a couple of stitches

escaparate *nm* (**a**) *(de tienda)* (shop) window; **ir de escaparates** to go window-shopping; **la Exposición Universal será un e. para el país** the Universal Exposition will be a showcase for the country (**b**) *Col, Cuba, Ven (ropero)* wardrobe

escaparatismo *nm* window dressing

escaparatista *nmf* window dresser

escapatoria *nf* (**a**) *(fuga)* escape; **no tener e.** to have no way out (**b**) *Fam (evasiva)* way (of getting) out

escape *nm* (**a**) *(de gas, agua)* leak; EXPR *Esp Fam* **a e.** *(a toda prisa)* in a great hurry; **salir a e.** to leave in a rush, to rush off (**b**) *(de vehículo)* exhaust (**c**) *(en reloj, piano)* escapement (**d**) *Informát* **tecla de e.** escape key

escapero, -a *nm,f Andes Fam* bag snatcher

escapismo *nm* (**a**) *(magia)* escapology (**b**) *(de problemas, realidad)* escapism

escapista 1 *adj* escapist
2 *nmf* (**a**) *(mago)* escapologist (**b**) *(de problemas, realidad)* escapist

escápula *nf Anat* scapula

escapulario *nm Rel* scapular

escaque *nm (en ajedrez)* (chess) square

escaquearse *vpr Esp Fam* to duck out, *Br* to skive (off); **en el trabajo no para de e.** at work he's always ducking out *o Br* skiving off; **e. de (hacer) algo** to worm one's way out of (doing) sth; **nos escaqueamos de fregar los platos** we got out of washing the dishes

escaqueo *nm Esp Fam* shirking

escara *nf (costra)* eschar, scab

escarabajo *nm* (**a**) *(animal)* beetle ►► ***e. de agua*** water beetle; ***e. de la patata*** Colorado beetle; ***e. pelotero*** dung-beetle (**b**) *Fam (automóvil)* Beetle

escaramujo *nm* (**a**) *(rosal)* wild rose (**b**) *(fruto)* hip (**c**) *(percebe)* goose barnacle

escaramuza *nf* (**a**) *(combate)* skirmish (**b**) *(riña)* skirmish

escarapela *nf* rosette, cockade

escarapelar 1 *vt* (**a**) *Col (manosear)* to rumple (**b**) *Col, CRica, Ven (descascarar)* to peel
2 **escarapelarse** *vpr Perú* to get goose flesh *o* pimples

escarbadientes *nm inv* toothpick

escarbar 1 *vt* (**a**) *(suelo) (por encima)* to scratch; *(haciendo hoyo)* to dig (**b**) *(dientes)* to pick (**c**) *(fuego)* to rake, to poke (**d**) *(investigar)* to investigate
2 *vi* (**a**) *(en suelo) (por encima)* to scratch around; *(haciendo hoyo)* to dig (**b**) *(investigar)* to delve; **si uno escarba un poco más** if you dig *o* delve a bit deeper; **anduvieron escarbando en la vida del actor** they were delving into the actor's life
3 **escarbarse** *vpr* **escarbarse los dientes/la nariz** to pick one's teeth/nose

escarcela *nf (de cazador)* game bag

escarceo *nm* (**a**) *(incursión)* foray; **sus escarceos con** *o* **en la música pop** his ventures into pop music (**b**) *(aventura)* **e. (amoroso)** fling; **tuvo algún que otro e. en las vacaciones** she had the odd fling on holiday (**c**) **escarceos** *(en equitación)* caracoles

escarcha *nf* frost

escarchado, -a *adj* (**a**) *(fruta)* crystallized, candied (**b**) *(cubierto de escarcha)* frosty

escarchar 1 *v impersonal* to freeze (over)
2 *vt (fruta)* to crystallize

escarda *nf Agr* (**a**) *(azada)* weeding hoe (**b**) *(acción)* weeding

escardador *nm Tex* breaker

escardar *vt* to weed; EXPR *Fam* **mandar a alguien a e. cebollinos** to send sb packing

escariar *vt* to ream

escarificar [60] *vt* (**a**) *Agr* to scarify (**b**) *Med* to scarify

escarlata 1 *adj* scarlet
2 *nm* scarlet

escarlatina *nf* scarlet fever

escarmentado, -a *adj* **estar/quedar e.** to have learnt one's lesson; **salió e. de la experiencia** he emerged from the experience a wiser man

escarmentar [3] 1 *vt* to teach a lesson to
2 *vi* to learn (one's lesson); **con eso escarmentará para toda su vida** that's taught him a lesson he'll never forget; **este niño nunca escarmienta** this child never learns his lesson; EXPR **e. en cabeza ajena** to learn from sb else's mistakes

escarmiento *nm* lesson; **dar un e. a alguien** to teach sb a lesson; **servir de e. (a alguien)** to serve as a lesson (to sb)

escarnecer [46] *vt* to mock, to ridicule

escarnecimiento *nm* mockery, ridicule

escarnio *nm* mockery, ridicule; **ser motivo de e.** to be the object of ridicule

escarola *nf* (curly) endive

escarpa, escarpadura *nf* (a) *(en terreno)* slope (b) *(en fortificación)* escarpment

escarpado, -a *adj* (a) *(inclinado)* steep (b) *(abrupto)* craggy

escarpadura = **escarpa**

escarpia *nf* = L-shaped hook for hanging pictures etc

escarpín *nm* (a) *Hist (zapato)* pointed shoe (b) *(calcetín)* outer sock, woollen slipper (c) *Am (de bebé)* bootee (d) *(de neopreno)* shoe

escasamente *adv* (a) *(apenas)* scarcely, barely (b) *(con dificultad)* with difficulty

escasear *vi* to be scarce, to be in short supply; **empezaba a e. el agua** water was beginning to run short; **escasean los expertos en informática** computer experts are in short supply; **escaseaba la comida entre los refugiados** the refugees didn't have much food

escasez *nf* (a) *(insuficiencia)* shortage; **hay e. de agua en esa región** there a shortage of water in that region; **la e. de población es un problema en la zona** the dearth of population is a problem in the area; **montan espectáculos con gran e. de medios** they put on shows with very slender resources (b) *(pobreza)* poverty; **en tiempos de e.** in times of hardship

escaso, -a *adj* (a) *(insuficiente) (conocimientos, recursos, medios)* limited, scant; *(víveres, trabajo)* scarce; *(cantidad, número, temperaturas)* low; *(visibilidad, luz)* poor, low; **e. público se dio cita para ver el partido** a poor crowd turned out to see the match; **sus posibilidades son más bien escasas** her chances are rather slim; **vino tanta gente que la comida se quedó escasa** so many people came that there wasn't enough food; **joyas de e. valor** jewellery of scant *o* little value; **la obra tuvo e. éxito** the play had little success; **debido al e. tiempo con el que contaban** due to the little time they had, since time was short

(b) *(falto)* **andar** *o* **estar e. de** to be short of; **ando e. de dinero** I don't have much money; **el hotel está e. de personal** the hotel is short-staffed; **la comida está un poco escasa de sal** the food is in need of a bit more salt

(c) *(casi completo)* **un metro e.** barely a metre; **dura dos horas escasas** it lasts barely two hours; **a un mes e. de las elecciones** with barely a month to go to the elections; **pesó dos kilos escasos al nacer** she weighed barely two kilos at birth

escatimar *vt (comida, dinero, medios)* to skimp on; **no e. esfuerzos/gastos** to spare no effort/expense; **la prensa no escatimó elogios hacia ella** the press was unstinting in its praise for *o* of her

escatología *nf* (a) *Rel* eschatology (b) *(sobre excrementos)* scatology

escatológico, -a *adj* (a) *Rel* eschatological (b) *(de excrementos)* scatological

escay *nm* Leatherette®

escayola *nf* (a) *(material)* plaster of Paris; **techo de e.** plaster ceiling (b) *(vendaje)* plaster, plaster cast; **le pusieron una e. en la pierna** they put his leg in plaster, they put a plaster cast on his leg (c) *(figura, escultura)* (plaster) cast

escayolado, -a *adj (brazo, pierna)* in plaster; **lleva el brazo e.** her arm is in plaster, she has a (plaster) cast on her arm

escayolar *vt* to put in plaster

escayolista *nmf* decorative plasterer

escena *nf* (a) *(escenario)* stage; **el director de e.** the stage manager; **llevar a la e.** to dramatize; **poner en e.** to stage; **puesta en e.** staging; **salir a e.** to go on stage; **desaparecer de e.** *(actor)* to leave the stage; *(cualquier persona)* to disappear from the scene; **entrar en e.** *(actor)* to come on stage; *(cualquier persona)* to come *o* appear on the scene

(b) *(fragmento) (de obra de teatro, película)* scene; **rodar una e.** to film a scene; **acto primero, e. tercera** act one, scene three ►► ***e. de cama*** bedroom *o* sex scene; ***e. retrospectiva*** flashback

(c) *(arte dramático)* **la e.** the stage, the theatre; **Olivier, un monstruo de la e.** Olivier, a giant of the stage *o* theatre; **lleva años en el mundo de la e.** she's worked in theatre for years

(d) *(hecho real)* scene; **la e. del reencuentro fue conmovedora** their reunion was a moving scene

(e) *(lugar)* scene; **la policía se presentó en la e. del crimen** the police arrived at the scene of the crime

(f) *(ambiente, circunstancias)* scene; **la e. política está muy animada** the political scene is very lively

(g) *Fam (escándalo)* scene, fuss; **hacer** *o* **montar una e.** to make a scene *o* fuss; **no me hagas una e.** don't make such a fuss

escenario *nm* (a) *(tablas, escena)* stage; **el autor subió al e. a saludar** the author went up on stage to take a bow

(b) *(ambientación)* setting; **la película tiene como e. el Berlín de los años treinta** the movie *o Br* film is set in thirties Berlin

(c) *(de suceso, hecho, acto)* scene; **una ambulancia acudió al e. del suceso** an ambulance went to the scene of the incident; **el e. del crimen** the scene of the crime, the crime scene; **la cumbre tuvo por e. la capital mexicana** the summit took place in the Mexican capital

> **Falso amigo**: El sustantivo inglés **scenery** no es la traducción de la palabra española **escenario**. En inglés **scenery** significa "decorado" o "paisaje". Por otra parte, en el contexto de cine o teatro el sustantivo inglés **scenario** significa "argumento".

escénico, -a *adj* scenic

escenificación *nf (de novela)* dramatization; *(de obra de teatro)* staging

escenificar [60] *vt (novela)* to dramatize; *(obra de teatro)* to stage

escenografía *nf* (a) *(actividad)* set design (b) *(decorados)* sets, scenery

escenógrafo, -a *nm,f* set designer

escépticamente *adv* sceptically

escepticismo *nm* scepticism

escéptico, -a 1 *adj* (a) *(filósofo)* sceptic (b) *(incrédulo)* sceptical
2 *nm,f* sceptic

escindir 1 *vt* (a) *(grupo)* to split (**en** into) (b) *(átomo)* to split (**en** into)
2 **escindirse** *vpr* (a) *(dividirse)* to split (**en** into); **la organización se escindió en varios grupúsculos** the organization split into several splinter groups (b) *(desgajarse)* to split off, to break away (**de** from); **la rama política se escindió de la militar** the political wing split off *o* broke away from the military wing

escisión *nf* (a) *(del átomo)* splitting (b) *(de partido político)* split

esclarecedor, -ora *adj* illuminating

esclarecer [46] *vt* to clear up, to shed light on; **e. los hechos** to establish the facts

esclarecido, -a *adj Formal* distinguished

esclarecimiento *nm* clearing up, elucidation

esclarezco *etc ver* **esclarecer**

esclava *nf* (a) *(pulsera)* = metal identity bracelet (b) *ver también* **esclavo**

esclavina *nf* short cape

esclavismo *nm* (system of) slavery

esclavista 1 *adj* pro-slavery
2 *nmf* supporter of slavery

esclavitud *nf también Fig* slavery

esclavizar [14] *vt también Fig* to enslave; **sus hijos la esclavizan** her children treat her like a servant; **estaba esclavizada por las labores domésticas** she was a slave to housework

esclavo, -a 1 *adj* enslaved
2 *nm,f también Fig* slave; **el comercio de esclavos** the slave trade; **es una esclava del trabajo** she's a slave to her work; **es un e. del tabaco** he's addicted to tobacco

esclerosis *nf inv Med* sclerosis ►► ***e. múltiple*** multiple sclerosis

esclerótica *nf Anat* sclera, sclerotic

esclerótico, -a *adj Anat* sclerotic

esclusa *nf* (a) *(recinto de canal)* lock (b) *(compuerta)* floodgate

escoba *nf* (a) *(para barrer)* broom; **pasar la e.** to sweep (up); **¿has pasado la e. por la cocina?** have you swept the kitchen?; EXPR *Fam* **no vender una e.** to get nowhere; EXPR **e. nueva barre bien** a new broom sweeps clean (b) *(juego de cartas)* = type of card game (c) *(arbusto)* broom

escobada *nf (barrido)* sweep

escobar *vt (barrer)* to sweep

escobazo *nm* blow with a broom; EXPR **echar a alguien a escobazos** to kick sb out

escobilla *nf* (a) *(escoba pequeña)* brush; **la e. del retrete** the toilet brush (b) *(de limpiaparabrisas)* blade (c) *Mús (de batería)* brush (d) *Tec (en máquina eléctrica)* (dynamo) brush (e) *Chile* **e. (de dientes)** toothbrush

escobillar *vt Am (cepillar)* to brush

escobillón *nm Am* (sweeping) brush

escobón *nm* broom

escoch = **Scotch®**

escocedura *nf* stinging, smarting

escocer [15] **1** *vi* (**a**) *(herida, piel)* to sting, to smart; **me escuecen los ojos** my eyes are stinging *o* smarting; **dime si te escuece mucho** tell me if it stings *o* smarts too much (**b**) *(ofender)* to hurt; **la derrota escoció mucho al equipo** the defeat left the team smarting
2 escocerse *vpr* (**a**) *(herida, piel)* to sting, to smart (**b**) *(ofenderse)* **escocerse de algo** to be hurt by sth

escocés, -esa 1 *adj* (**a**) *(de Escocia)* Scottish; **whisky e.** Scotch whisky (**b**) *(de cuadros de colores)* tartan; **una falda escocesa** a kilt; **tela escocesa** tartan
2 *nm,f (persona) (hombre)* Scot, Scotsman; *(mujer)* Scot, Scotswoman
3 *nm (lengua)* (Scottish) Gaelic

Escocia *n* Scotland

escofina *nf* coarse file, rasp

escogencia *nf Col, Ecuad, Ven* choice

escoger [52] **1** *vt* to choose; **escoge una carta** pick a card; **de (entre) cien candidatos lo escogieron a él** out of a hundred candidates they chose *o* selected him; **escogemos la mejor fruta para nuestros clientes** we select the best fruit for our customers; **tiene dos sabores a e.** there are two flavours to choose from; **tener mucho donde e.** to have plenty of choice, *Br* to be spoilt for choice; **tenemos poco donde e.** we don't have much to choose from
2 *vi* to choose (**entre** between); **te toca e.** it's your turn to choose; **tenemos que e. entre tres candidatos** we have to choose between three candidates

escogido, -a *adj* (**a**) *(elegido)* selected, chosen (**b**) *(selecto)* choice, select; **fruta escogida** selected fruit; **un e. grupo de periodistas** a select group of journalists (**c**) *Méx Fam (descartado)* **a estas horas la fruta ya está muy escogida** all the best fruit has gone by now

escolanía *nf* choirboys

escolapio, -a *nm,f Rel* = member of the religious teaching order of the Escuelas Pías

escolar 1 *adj* school; **edad e.** school age
2 *nmf (niño)* pupil, schoolboy; *(niña)* pupil, schoolgirl

escolaridad *nf* schooling

escolarización *nf* schooling

escolarizar [14] *vt (niño)* to provide schooling for; **muchos niños están sin e.** many children receive no schooling

escolástica *nf Filosofía* scholasticism, Scholasticism

escolasticismo *nm* (**a**) *Filosofía* scholasticism (**b**) *(formalismo)* scholasticism

escolástico, -a *adj* scholastic

escoleta *nf Méx* (**a**) *(banda)* band *(of amateur musicians)* (**b**) *(ensayo)* rehearsal, practice

escoliosis *nf inv* scoliosis

escollar *vi* (**a**) *(barco)* to run aground on a reef (**b**) *Arg, Chile (propósito)* to fail, to come to nothing

escollera *nf* breakwater

escollo *nm* (**a**) *(en el mar)* reef (**b**) *(obstáculo)* stumbling block; **salvar** *o* **superar un e.** to overcome an obstacle

escolopendra *nf* centipede, *Espec* scolopendrid

escolta 1 *nf (acompañamiento)* escort; **lleva e. veinticuatro horas al día** he has a twenty-four-hour escort ▸▸ ***e. policial*** police escort
2 *nmf* (**a**) *(persona)* bodyguard (**b**) *(en baloncesto)* shooting guard

escoltar *vt* (**a**) *(proteger)* to escort (**b**) *(acompañar)* to accompany; **miles de ciudadanos escoltaron el féretro** thousands of citizens accompanied the coffin

escombrera *nf (vertedero)* tip

escombro *nm,* **escombros** *nmpl* (**a**) *(de obra)* rubble, debris *(singular)*; *(de mina, cantera)* debris, *Tec* spoil; **la comisaría quedó reducida a escombros** the police station was reduced to rubble; **siguen apareciendo cadáveres entre los escombros** bodies are still being found among the rubble (**b**) *RP Fam* **armar** *o* **hacer e.** to kick up a fuss

escón *nm CSur* scone

esconder 1 *vt* to hide, to conceal; **me esconden el tabaco** they hide my cigarettes
2 esconderse *vpr* (**a**) *(ocultarse) (sujeto: persona)* to hide (**de** from); *(sujeto: el sol)* to disappear, to hide; **¡rápido, escóndete!** quick, hide!; **no te escondas de mí** don't hide from me (**b**) *(subyacer)* to lie hidden; **detrás de su seriedad se esconde un gran sentido del humor** his seriousness conceals a lively sense of humour

escondidas 1 *nfpl RP* **las e.** hide-and-seek; **jugar a las e.** to play hide-and-seek
2 a escondidas *loc adv* in secret; **transportaban la mercancía de noche y a e.** they transported the goods secretly at *o* by night; **fumábamos a e.** we smoked in secret; **salían juntos a e. de sus padres** they went out together behind their parents' backs

escondido, -a 1 *adj (lugar)* secluded, remote; **una casa escondida entre las montañas** a house hidden *o* tucked away in the mountains; **el bar está en un sitio muy e.** the bar is in a very out-of-the-way place
2 *nm Ven* **el e.** *(juego)* hide-and-seek; **jugar al e.** to play hide-and-seek

escondite *nm* (**a**) *(lugar)* hiding place (**b**) **el e.** *(juego)* hide-and-seek; **jugar al e.** to play hide-and-seek

escondrijo *nm* hiding place

escoñar *Esp muy Fam* **1** *vt* to bust, *Br* to knacker; **escoñó la televisión de un golpe** he bust *o Br* knackered the TV with one blow
2 escoñarse *vpr* (**a**) *(objeto)* to get bust *o Br* knackered (**b**) *(persona)* **por poco me escoño** I nearly did myself an injury *o Br* did myself in; **se escoñó la muñeca jugando a tenis** he crocked *o Br* knackered his wrist playing tennis

escopeta *nf* shotgun ▸▸ ***e. de aire comprimido*** airgun; ***e. de cañones recortados*** *Br* sawn-off shotgun, *US* sawed-off shotgun; ***e. de dos cañones*** double-barrelled shotgun; ***e. recortada*** *Br* sawn-off shotgun, *US* sawed-off shotgun

escopetado, -a, escopeteado, -a *adj Esp Fam* **salir e.** to shoot off; **volví e. para casa** I rushed home; **fue escopetada a ayudar** she rushed to help

escopetazo *nm* (**a**) *(disparo)* shotgun blast (**b**) *(herida)* shotgun wound

escopeteado, -a = **escopetado**

escopetero *nm (insecto)* bombardier beetle

escoplo *nm* chisel

escora *nf Náut* (**a**) *(inclinación)* list (**b**) *(madero)* prop

escorar 1 *vi Náut* to list
2 escorarse *vpr* (**a**) *Náut* to list (**b**) *(jugador)* to swerve; **escorarse a la derecha/izquierda** *(partido político)* to veer to the right/left; *(jugador)* to swerve to the right/left (**c**) *Cuba, Hond (esconderse)* to hide oneself from view, to take cover

escorbuto *nm* scurvy

escorchar *RP* **1** *vt Fam* **no me escorches** don't be such a pain; **no (me) escorches la paciencia** don't try pushing it; EXPR *muy Fam* **e. las pelotas** *o* **las bolas** *o* **los huevos a alguien** *Br* to get on sb's tits, *US* to bust sb's balls; **dejá de e. las pelotas** *o* **las bolas** *o* **los huevos** stop being a pain in the *Br* arse *o US* ass
2 *vi Fam* to be a pain; **¡no escorches!** don't be such a pain!

escoria *nf* (**a**) *(desecho)* dregs, scum; **la e. de la sociedad** the dregs of society (**b**) *(metal)* slag

escoriación = **excoriación**

escoriar = **excoriar**

escorial *nm (vertedero)* slagheap

escorpiano, -a *Am* **1** *adj* Scorpio; **ser e.** to be (a) Scorpio
2 *nm,f* Scorpio; **los e. son...** Scorpios are...

escorpio 1 *adj inv Esp* Scorpio; **ser e.** to be (a) Scorpio
2 *nm (signo)* Scorpio; **los de E. son...** Scorpios are...
3 *nmf inv Esp (persona)* Scorpio; **los e. son...** Scorpios are...

escorpión *nm* (**a**) *(animal)* scorpion (**b**) *(signo)* Scorpio

escorrentía *nf* run-off

escorzo *nm* foreshortening; **en e.** foreshortened

escota *nf Náut* sheet ▸▸ ***e. mayor*** mainsheet

escotado, -a *adj (vestido)* low-cut, low-necked; **e. por detrás** with a low-cut back; **no salgas tan e., que hace frío** don't go out with an open neck like that, it's cold

escotadura *nf* low neckline

escotar *vt* to lower the neckline of

escote 1 *nm* (**a**) *(de prendas)* neckline; **un vestido con mucho/poco e.** a dress with a very low-cut/a fairly high neckline; **un e. generoso** a plunging *o* revealing neckline ▸▸ ***e. cuadrado*** square neck; ***e. de pico*** V-neck; ***e. redondo*** round neck; ***e. en V*** V-neck (**b**) *(de persona)* cleavage
2 a escote *loc adv Esp* **pagar a e.** to go Dutch; **lo compramos a e.** we went halves on it

escotera *nf Náut* clam cleat

escotilla *nf* hatch, hatchway

escotillón *nm* (a) *(trampilla)* trapdoor (b) *Náut* scuttle

escozor *nm* (a) *(sensación)* stinging (b) *(resentimiento)* resentment; *(desaprobación)* disapproval

escrachado, -a *adj RP Fam* (a) *(destrozado)* wrecked; **el auto quedó e.** the car was a write-off (b) *(puesto en evidencia)* **el actor y su amante salieron escrachados en todos los diarios** the actor and his lover were splashed across all the newspapers

escrachar *RP Fam* **1** *vt* **si no me hacés ese favor, te escracho con el jefe** if you don't do me that favour, I'll tell the boss what you've been up to; **van a empezar a e. a los torturadores** they're going to start showing the torturers up in public

2 escracharse *vpr* to have a smash-up; **se escracharon camino a la playa** they had a smash-up on the way to the seaside

escrache *nm RP Fam* (a) *(puesta en evidencia)* **salir en una foto con él es un e.** being photographed with him is a real embarrassment (b) *(forma de protesta)* = public protest aimed at humiliating a human rights violator

escracho *nm RP Fam* **es un e.** she's no oil painting

escrapie *nm (enfermedad lanar)* scrapie

escriba *nm* scribe

escribanía *nf* (a) *(mueble)* writing desk (b) *(útiles de escribir)* inkstand (c) *Andes, CRica, RP (notaría)* = notary public's position and duties (d) *Andes, CRica, RP (carrera)* **estudiar e.** to study to become a notary public

escribano, -a **1** *nm* (a) *Hist* scrivener (b) *(ave)* bunting ►► ***e. cerillo*** yellowhammer; ***e. nival*** snow bunting; ***e. palustre*** reed bunting (c) *(insecto)* **e. de agua** whirligig beetle

2 *nm,f Andes, CRica, RP (notario)* notary (public)

escribiente *nmf* clerk

escribir **1** *vt* (a) *(carta, novela, canción)* to write; **le escribí una carta** I wrote him a letter, I wrote a letter to him; **escribió unas notas a lápiz** she wrote some notes in pencil; **escriba las instrucciones en un papel** write the instructions on a piece of paper; **se ha escrito mucho sobre este tema** much has been written on this subject; **ha escrito una página brillante en la historia del ciclismo** he has added a glorious page to cycling history

(b) *(a persona, institución)* to write; **hace mucho que no me escribe** she hasn't written to me for a long time; **nos han escrito muchos oyentes protestando** many listeners have written in complaining; **¡escríbenos cuando llegues!** write to us when you get there!; **e. a casa** to write home

2 *vi* to write; **todavía no ha aprendido a e.** he still hasn't learnt (how) to write; **escribe muy mal y no se le entiende nada** he has terrible handwriting and you can't understand a word of it; **e. a lápiz** to write in pencil; **e. a mano** to write by hand; **e. a máquina** to type; **¡no te olvides de e.!** don't forget to write!

3 escribirse *vpr* (a) *(personas)* **llevamos años escribiéndonos** we've been writing to each other for years; **se escribe con un amigo alemán** he corresponds with a German friend (b) *(palabras)* **¿cómo se escribe?** how do you spell it?, how is it spelled?; **se escribe con "h"** it is spelled with an "h"; **se escribe con acento** it has an accent, it's written with an accent

escrito, -a **1** *participio ver* **escribir**

2 *adj* written; **por e.** in writing; EXPR **estar e.: estaba e. que acabaría mal** it was fated *o* destined to end badly; **estaba e. que nos conoceríamos** we were fated *o* destined to meet

3 *nm* (a) *(texto, composición)* text; *(documento)* document; *(obra literaria)* writing, work; **envió un e. de protesta al ayuntamiento** he sent a letter of protest to the council; **una antología de sus escritos periodísticos** a collection of his journalism; EXPR *Fam* **lo que no está en los escritos: trabajé lo que no está en los escritos** *Br* I slogged my guts out, *US* I worked my butt off; **aquello pesaba lo que no está en los escritos** it weighed a ton

(b) *Der* brief

escritor, -ora *nm,f* writer; **e. de cuentos** short-story writer

escritorio *nm* (a) *(mueble)* desk, bureau (b) *esp Am (oficina)* office (c) *esp Am (en casa)* study (d) *Informát* desktop

escritura *nf* (a) *(técnica)* writing

(b) *(sistema de signos)* script; **e. jeroglífica** hieroglyphic writing, hieroglyphics

(c) *(caligrafía)* handwriting

(d) *Der* deed; **firmar una e.** to sign a deed ►► ***e. de compraventa*** bill of sale; ***e. de hipoteca*** mortgage deed; ***e. hipotecaria*** mortgage deed; ***e. de propiedad*** title deed; **la e. de propiedad de la casa** the title deeds of *o* to the house; ***e. pública*** public instrument

(e) **(Sagradas) Escrituras** Holy Scripture

escrituración *nf Arg, PRico Der* notarizing, notarization

escriturar *vt Der (compraventa, préstamo hipotecario)* to execute (by deed); **escrituramos la casa a mi nombre** we registered the house in my name; **la propiedad está escriturada por 50.000 euros** the official purchase price for the property was 50,000 euros

escrofularia *nf (planta)* French figwort

escroto *nm* scrotum

escruchante *nmf RP Fam* picklock

escruche *nm RP Fam* = burglary carried out by an "escruchante"

escrúpulo *nm* (a) *(duda, recelo)* scruple; **sin escrúpulos** unscrupulous; **no tuvo ningún e. en reconocerlo** he had no scruples *o* qualms about admitting it (b) *(aprensión)* qualm; **le da e.** he has qualms about it (c) *(minuciosidad)* scrupulousness, great care

escrupulosamente *adv* scrupulously

escrupulosidad *nf* scrupulousness

escrupuloso, -a *adj* (a) *(minucioso)* scrupulous; **en su trabajo es muy e.** he is very scrupulous in his work; **el respeto e. de las leyes** strict observance of the law (b) *(aprensivo)* particular, fussy; **no seas tan e. con la comida** don't be such a fussy eater (c) *(honrado)* scrupulous; **no es nada e.** he has no scruples

escrutador, -ora **1** *adj (mirada)* searching

2 *nm,f Br* scrutineer, *US* electoral inspector

escrutar *vt* (a) *(con la mirada)* to scrutinize, to examine; **desde el balcón escrutaba el horizonte** from the balcony he surveyed *o* scanned the horizon (b) *(votos)* to count

escrutinio *nm* (a) *(de votos)* count; **efectuar el e. de los votos** to count the votes (b) *(inspección)* scrutiny (c) *(de quinielas)* results

escuadra *nf* (a) *(regla, plantilla)* set square *(with two angles of 45° and one of 90°)* ►► ***e. de agrimensor*** cross staff, surveyor's cross; ***e. falsa*** *(en carpintería)* bevel square, carpenter's square (b) *(para estantería, armario)* bracket (c) *(de portería)* **el disparo entró por la e.** the shot went into the top corner of the net (d) *(de buques)* squadron (e) *(de soldados)* squad

escuadrar *vt* to square

escuadrilla *nf* (a) *(de buques)* squadron (b) *(de aviones)* squadron

escuadrón *nm* (a) *(de aviones)* squadron (b) *(de caballería)* squadron ►► ***e. de la muerte*** death squad

escualidez *nf (delgadez)* emaciation

escuálido, -a *adj* emaciated

escualo *nm (tiburón)* shark

escuamaria *nf* toothwort

escucha **1** *nf (acción)* listening in, monitoring; **estar** *o* **permanecer a la e.** to listen in; **para mayor información permanezcan a la e.** stay tuned for more information ►► ***escuchas telefónicas*** telephone tapping

2 *nm (centinela)* night scout

3 *nmf Am (oyente)* listener

escuchar **1** *vt* (a) *(oír con atención) (sonido, radio, persona)* to listen to (b) *(hacer caso a) (consejo, aviso)* to listen to, to heed; *(persona)* to listen to; **nunca escucha mis consejos** he never listens to my advice; **tú nunca me escuchas** you never listen to me; **escúchame, eso que tú quieres es imposible** listen, what you want is impossible

2 *vi* to listen

3 escucharse *vpr* **parece que se escucha cuando habla** he likes the sound of his own voice

escuchimizado, -a *Esp Fam* **1** *adj* skinny, thin as a rake

2 *nm,f* skinny person

escudar **1** *vt* to shield

2 escudarse *vpr* **escudarse en algo** to hide behind sth, to use sth as an excuse; **el gobierno se escuda en la falta de estadísticas** the government is using the lack of statistics as an excuse

escudería *nf* (a) *(en automovilismo)* (motor racing) team (b) *Urug (compra cooperativa)* = communal savings scheme *(usually for buying cars)*

escudero *nm* squire

escudilla *nf* deep bowl

escudo *nm* (a) *(arma)* shield (b) *(emblema)* **e. (de armas)** coat of arms (c) *(de club, asociación, institución)* badge (d) *(protección)* shield; **utilizaron a civiles como escudos humanos** they used civilians as human shields (e) *Antes (moneda)* escudo

escudriñar *vt* (a) *(examinar)* to scrutinize, to examine (b) *(otear)* to search; **e. el horizonte** to scan *o* survey the horizon

escuece *etc ver* **escocer**

escuela *nf* (a) *(establecimiento)* school; **ir a la e.** to go to school; **no pudo ir a la e.** she was unable to go to school; **aprendió en la e. de la vida** she's a graduate of the university *o* school of life ►► ***e. de arte*** school of art, art school; ***e. de arte dramático*** drama school; ***e. de artes y oficios*** = college for the study of arts and crafts; ***e. de bellas artes*** art school; *Am* ***e. de choferes*** driving school; ***e. de comercio*** business school; *CSur* ***e. diferencial*** school for children with special needs, special school; *Cuba* ***e. elemental*** *Br* primary school, *US* elementary school; ***e. de equitación*** riding school; ***e. hípica*** (horse) riding school; ***e. de hostelería*** catering school; ***e. de magisterio*** *Br* teacher training college, *US* teacher's college; *Am* ***e. de manejo*** driving school; ***e. normal*** teacher training college; ***E. Oficial de Idiomas*** = Spanish State language-teaching institute; ***e. de párvulos*** kindergarten; ***e. primaria*** *Br* primary school, *US* elementary school; ***e. privada*** *Br* private school, public school; ***e. pública*** state school; ***e. de secretariado*** secretarial college; ***e. secundaria*** *Br* secondary school, *US* high school; ***e. taurina*** bullfighting school; ***e. de turismo*** school of tourism; ***e. universitaria*** = section of a university which awards diplomas in a vocational discipline (e.g. engineering, business) after three years of study; ***e. de verano*** summer school

(b) *(enseñanza, conocimientos)* training; **tiene talento, pero le falta e.** he's talented, but he still has a lot to learn

(c) *(de artista, doctrina)* school; **la e. cervantina** the school of Cervantes; **hacer e.** to have a following; **su forma de jugar al fútbol hizo e.** his style of football gained quite a following; **ser de la vieja e.** to be of the old school ►► ***e. de pensamiento*** school of thought

escuetamente *adv* concisely

escueto, -a *adj (sucinto)* concise; *(sobrio)* plain, unadorned; **fue** *o* **estuvo muy e. en la rueda de prensa** he was rather unforthcoming at the press conference

escueza *etc ver* **escocer**

escuincle, -a, escuintle, -a *Méx Fam* **1** *adj* young; **todavía es muy e. para casarse** he's far too young to get married yet

2 *nm,f* nipper, kid

esculcar [60] *vt Méx* to search

esculpir *vt (estatua)* to sculpt, to carve; *(inscripción)* to carve; **una estatua esculpida en granito** a statue carved out of *o* sculpted in granite

esculque *nm Méx* (police) search; **en el e. se encontraron varias armas** the search located several weapons; **dijo que no podían hacer el e. sin una orden oficial** he said they couldn't make a search without a warrant

escultismo *nm* scouting, scout movement

escultista *nmf* (boy) scout, *f* girl guide

escultor, -ora *nm,f* sculptor, *f* sculptress

escultórico, -a *adj* sculptural; **un grupo e.** a sculptural group; **la obra escultórica de Picasso** Picasso's sculptures

escultura *nf* sculpture; **una e. en mármol** a marble sculpture; **una e. en madera** *(pequeña)* a wood carving; *(grande)* a wooden sculpture

escultural *adj* (a) *(en arte)* sculptural (b) *(persona, figura)* statuesque

escupida *nf RP Fam* gob of spit; **como e.** like a shot

escupidera *nf* (a) *(para escupir)* spittoon (b) *Andes, RP (orinal)* chamberpot

escupidor *nm Andes, PRico* spittoon

escupir **1** *vi* to spit; EXPR *Am* **e. para arriba** to foul one's own nest

2 *vt* (a) *(sujeto: persona, animal)* to spit out; **¡escúpelo!** spit it out!; **e. sangre** to spit blood; **e. a alguien** to spit at sb; **le escupió en la cara** she spat in his face (b) *(sujeto: volcán)* to spew out; *(sujeto: chimenea)* to belch out; **las ametralladoras escupían fuego** the machine guns were blazing away

escupitajo *nm Fam* gob of spit; **echar un e.** to spit (on the ground/floor etc)

escurreplatos *nm inv* (a) *(bandeja)* dish *o* plate rack (b) *(mueble)* = cupboard with built-in dish rack above sink

escurridero *nm Br* draining board, *US* drainboard

escurridizo, -a *adj* (a) *(animal, material, suelo)* slippery (b) *(persona)* slippery, evasive; **hacerse el e.** *(desaparecer)* to make oneself scarce

escurrido, -a *adj* (a) *(ropa) (en lavadora)* spun-dry; *(estrujando)* wrung-out (b) *(verdura)* drained (c) *(persona)* thin, skinny

escurridor *nm* (a) *(colador)* colander (b) *(escurreplatos) (bandeja)* dish *o* plate rack; *(mueble)* = cupboard with built-in dish rack above sink

escurrir **1** *vt* (a) *(platos)* to drain; *(verdura, pasta)* to drain; *(huevos fritos, pescado)* to drain the fat off; *(ropa)* to wring out; **escúrrele el líquido a la lata de atún** drain the liquid from the can of tuna; EXPR *Fam* **e. el bulto** *(trabajo)* to get out of it; *(cuestión)* to evade the issue (b) *(botella)* to empty (out)

2 *vi* (a) *(soltar líquido)* to drain; *(gotear)* to drip; **deja los platos a e.** leave the dishes to drain; **deja aquí el paraguas para que vaya escurriendo** leave the umbrella here so it can dry off (b) *(resbalar)* to slide; **una lágrima escurrió por su mejilla** a tear slid down her cheek (c) *(estar resbaladizo)* to be slippery

3 escurrirse *vpr* (a) *(sujeto: líquido)* to drain off, to drain away; **pon la pasta aquí para que se le escurra el agua** put the pasta here for the water to drain off

(b) *(resbalarse)* to slip; **me escurrí en el hielo** I slipped on the ice; **se me escurrió de las manos** it slipped through my fingers

(c) *Fam (escabullirse)* to get away, to escape; **si puedo me escurriré de la reunión** I'll slip out of the meeting if I can

escusado = **excusado**

escúter *(pl* **escúteres***) nm o nf* (motor) scooter

esdrújula *nf* word stressed on the third-last syllable

esdrújulo, -a *adj* stressed on the third-last syllable

ese[1] *nf (figura)* zigzag; **hacer eses** *(en carretera)* to zigzag; *(al andar)* to stagger about

ESE[2], -A *(pl* **esos, -as***) adj demostrativo* (a) *(en general) (singular)* that; *(plural)* those; **esa corbata** that tie; **e. regalo** that present (b) *Fam Pey (singular)* that; *(plural)* those; **el hombre e. no me inspira confianza** I don't trust that man

ÉSE, -A *(pl* **ésos, -as***) pron demostrativo*

> Note that **ése** and its various forms can be written without an accent when there is no risk of confusion with the adjective.

(a) *(en general) (singular)* that one; *(plural)* those (ones); **ponte otro vestido, e. no te queda bien** put on another dress, that one doesn't suit you; **estos pasteles están muy buenos, pero ésos me gustan más** these cakes are very good but I like those (ones) better; **¡a e.!** stop that man!

(b) *Fam (despectivo)* **e. fue el que me pegó** that's the one who hit me; **ésa es una bocazas** she's a bigmouth, she is

(c) EXPR **¿conque ésas tenemos?** so that's the deal, is it?; **ahora no me vengas con ésas** don't give me that nonsense now!; **ni por ésas: ni por ésas aceptó el cargo** even then he didn't accept the job; **no me lo vendió ni por ésas** even then he wouldn't sell it to me

esencia *nf* (a) *(lo principal, lo básico)* essence; **en e.** in essence, essentially; **en e. sus opiniones apenas difieren** at bottom there's little difference between their views (b) *(extracto, concentrado)* essence; **e. de lavanda** lavender water; **e. de café/vainilla** coffee/vanilla essence ►► ***e. mineral*** mineral oil; ***e. de trementina*** oil of turpentine

esencial *adj* (a) *(básico)* essential; **su participación fue e. en el proyecto** her participation was essential to the project; **lo e.** the essential *o* main thing; **lo e. es una buena preparación física** the essential *o* main thing is to have trained properly beforehand; **en lo e. coincidimos** we agree on the basic points *o* the essentials; **no e.** non-essential, inessential (b) *(aceite)* essential

esencialmente *adv* essentially, in essence; **sus opiniones son e. las mismas** their views are essentially *o* basically the same

esfenoides *Anat* **1** *adj* sphenoid

2 *nm inv* sphenoid bone

esfera *nf* (a) *(figura)* sphere ►► ***e. armilar*** armillary sphere; ***e. celeste*** celestial sphere; ***e. terrestre*** (terrestrial) globe (b) *(de reloj)* face (c) *(círculo social)* circle; **las altas esferas de la política** high political circles; **es muy conocido en la e. teatral** he is very well-known in theatrical circles ►► ***e. de influencia*** sphere of influence

esférico, -a **1** *adj* spherical

2 *nm (balón)* ball

esfero, esferográfico *nm Col, Ecuad* ballpoint pen

esferoidal *adj* spheroidal

esferoide *nm* spheroid

esfinge *nf* (a) *Mitol* sphinx; EXPR **ser** *o* **parecer una e.** to be inscrutable (b) *(mariposa)* hawk moth

esfínter *(pl* **esfínteres***) nm* sphincter

esforzadamente *adv* (a) *(con valentía)* bravely, courageously (b) *(con ánimo)* spiritedly

esforzar [31] **1** *vt (voz, vista)* to strain; **tuve que e. la voz** I had to strain my voice
2 esforzarse *vpr* to make an effort; **tienes que esforzarte más si quieres aprobar** you'll have to make more of an effort if you want to pass; **nos esforzamos, pero fue imposible ganarlos** we tried very hard, but they were impossible to beat; **no te esfuerces, no puede oírte** don't bother (shouting), she can't hear you; **se esforzaron enormemente en la tarea** they put a huge amount of effort into the task; **esforzarse en** *o* **por hacer algo** to make an effort to do sth; **me esforcé por ayudarlos** I made a real effort *o* did my best to help them; **nos hemos esforzado mucho por ti** we've made a real effort for you, we've really put ourselves out for you; **se esforzó en contener las lágrimas** she tried hard to hold back the tears

esfuerzo *nm (físico, intelectual)* effort; **cualquier movimiento cuesta** *o* **supone un terrible e.** any movement requires a huge effort; **no hagas ningún e., que el médico ha recomendado reposo** don't exert yourself, the doctor has recommended rest; **hacer esfuerzos, hacer un e.** to make an effort, to try hard; **estoy haciendo esfuerzos por no llorar** I'm trying hard not to cry; **hizo un e. por agradar** he made an effort to be pleasant; **haz un último e., ya verás como ahora lo consigues** make one last attempt, you'll do it this time!; **sin e.** effortlessly

esfumar **1** *vt Arte (trazo)* to shade (off); *(contorno, figura)* to soften, to blur; *(color)* to tone down, to soften
2 esfumarse *vpr* **(a)** *(esperanzas, posibilidades)* to fade away; *(dudas, sospechas)* to be dispelled **(b)** *Fam (persona)* to vanish, to disappear; **¡esfúmate!** beat it!, get lost!

esfumino *nm Arte* stump, = roll of paper used for blurring chalk or charcoal drawings

esgrima *nf* fencing

esgrimidor, -ora *nm,f Dep* fencer

esgrimir *vt* **(a)** *(arma)* to brandish, to wield **(b)** *(argumento)* to use, to put forward; *(excusa)* to give; *(datos)* to use; *(pruebas)* to present, to produce

esguince *nm* sprain; **hacerse un e. en el tobillo** to sprain one's ankle; **tiene e. de tobillo** she has a sprained ankle

eslabón *nm* **(a)** *(de cadena)* link **(b)** *(de sucesión, serie)* link; **el e. perdido** the missing link **(c)** *(para pedernal)* steel

eslabonar *vt también Fig* to link together

eslalon (*pl* **eslalons**) *nm Dep* slalom ►► ***e. especial*** special slalom; ***e. gigante*** giant slalom

eslavo, -a **1** *adj* Slav, Slavonic
2 *nm,f (persona)* Slav
3 *nm (lengua)* Slavonic

eslip (*pl* **eslips**) *nm* briefs

eslogan (*pl* **eslóganes**) *nm* slogan

eslora *nf Náut* length; **un yate con 20 metros de e.** a 20-metre yacht

eslovaco, -a **1** *adj* Slovak, Slovakian
2 *nm,f (persona)* Slovak, Slovakian
3 *nm (lengua)* Slovak

Eslovaquia *n* Slovakia

Eslovenia *n* Slovenia

esloveno, -a **1** *adj* Slovene
2 *nm,f (persona)* Slovene
3 *nm (lengua)* Slovene

esmachar *vt (pelota) (en tenis)* to smash; *(en baloncesto)* to dunk

esmaltado, -a **1** *adj* enamelled
2 *nm* enamelling

esmaltar *vt* to enamel

esmalte *nm* **(a)** *(sustancia)* enamel; **e. (de uñas)** nail varnish *o* polish ►► ***e. vítreo*** vitreous enamel **(b)** *(dental)* enamel **(c)** *(objeto, joya)* enamel

esmeradamente *adv* painstakingly, with extreme care

esmerado, -a *adj (persona)* painstaking, careful; *(trabajo)* carefully done, polished

esmeralda **1** *nf (piedra preciosa)* emerald
2 *adj* emerald; **verde e.** emerald green
3 *nm inv (color)* emerald

esmeraldino, -a *adj* emerald, emerald-coloured

esmerarse *vpr (esforzarse)* to take great pains; **tendrás que esmerarte más si quieres aprobar** you'll have to make much more of an effort if you want to pass; **los maquilladores se esmeraron con ella** the make-up artists took especial pains with her; **se esmera mucho en su trabajo** she's very painstaking in her work; **se esmeró en hacerlo bien** she took great pains to do it well; **se esmeró por quedar bien delante de sus padres** he made a great effort to impress her parents

esmerejón *nm (ave)* merlin

esmeril *nm* emery

esmerilado, -a **1** *adj (translúcido)* frosted
2 *nm* **(a)** *(de vidrio)* polishing **(b)** *(de metal)* grinding

esmerilar *vt* **(a)** *(vidrio) (pulir)* to polish with emery; *(deslustrar)* to frost **(b)** *(metal)* to grind

esmero *nm* great care; **puso mucho e. en la tarea** he took great pains over the task; **hizo la comida con gran e.** she took great pains over the meal

esmirriado, -a *adj Fam (persona)* scrawny, weedy; *(planta)* spindly; *(animal)* scrawny

esmoquin (*pl* **esmóquines**) *nm Br* dinner jacket, *US* tuxedo

esnifada *nf Fam (de cola)* sniff; *(de cocaína)* snort

esnifar *vt Fam (cola)* to sniff; *(cocaína)* to snort

esnob (*pl* **esnobs**) **1** *adj* **es muy e.** he's always trying to look trendy and sophisticated
2 *nmf* = person who wants to appear trendy and sophisticated

esnobismo *nm* **sólo lo hace por e.** he's just doing that because he thinks it's trendy and sophisticated

ESO ['eso] *nf (abrev de* **Educación Secundaria Obligatoria**) = mainstream secondary education in Spain for pupils aged 12-16

ESO *pron demostrativo* **(a)** *(neutro)* that; **e. es la Torre Eiffel** that's the Eiffel Tower; **e. es lo que yo pienso** that's just what I think; **e. que propones es irrealizable** what you're proposing is impossible; **e. de vivir solo no me gusta** I don't like the idea of living on my own; **¿qué es e. de que no piensas acabarte la comida?** what's this about you not wanting to finish your dinner?; **¡y para e. me llamas!** you're ringing me up for THAT?; **para e. es mejor no ir** if that's all it is, you might as well not go; **por e. vine** that's why I came
(b) *(en frases)* **a e. de** *(aproximadamente)* (at) around *o* about; **a e. del mediodía** (at) around *o* about midday; **en e.** *(entonces)* just then, at that very moment; **en e. sonó el teléfono** just then *o* at that moment the telephone rang; **¿cómo es e.?** *(¿por qué?)* how come?; **¿no te han pagado?, ¿cómo es e.?** you haven't been paid? how come?; **¡e. es!** *(en efecto)* that's it!; **¿dices que te casas? – ¡e. es!** you say you're getting married? - that's right!; **¡e., e.!** *(sí)* that's right!, yes!; **¿os compro un helado? – ¡e., e.!** do you want me to get you an ice cream? – yes! *o* you bet!; *Irónico* **¡e., e.! tú sigue bebiendo y verás mañana qué bien te sientes** go on, you carry on drinking and see how good you feel tomorrow; **¿y e.?** *(¿por qué?)* how come?; **¿no te han pagado?, ¿y e.?** you haven't been paid? how come?; **y e. que: no me sale bien, y e. que lo intento** try as I might, I can't get it right; **sabe tocar el violín, y e. que sólo tiene cinco años** she can play the violin even though she's only five years old

---

esófago *nm* oesophagus

esos, -as *ver* **ese**

ésos, -as *ver* **ése**

esotérico, -a *adj* esoteric

esoterismo *nm* **(a)** *(impenetrabilidad)* esoteric nature **(b)** *(ciencias ocultas)* esotericism

esp. (*abrev de* **especialmente**) esp

espabilado, -a, despabilado, -a **1** *adj* **(a)** *(despierto)* awake
(b) *(avispado)* sharp, smart, on the ball; **para este trabajo hace falta gente espabilada** for this job you need people who are on the ball; **es muy e. para los negocios** he has a good eye for business; **Yáñez estuvo e. y se escapó** Yáñez had his wits about him and managed to get away; **para la poca edad que tiene está muy e.** he's very sharp *o* smart for someone so young; **este chico es muy poco e.** the boy is rather slow
2 *nm,f Fam Pey (listillo)* smart alec; **tú lo que eres es un e.** you're a smart alec, you are

espabilar, despabilar **1** *vt* **(a)** *(despertar)* to wake up; **una ducha te espabilará** a shower will wake you up **(b)** *(avispar)* **e. a alguien** to wise sb up; **en el ejército lo espabilaron** being in the army wised him up *o* made him buck his ideas up; **el hambre espabila la mente** hunger sharpens one's wits
2 *vi* **(a)** *(despertarse)* to wake up
(b) *(darse prisa)* to get a move on; **espabila o vamos a perder el tren** get a move on or we'll miss the train
(c) *(avisparse)* to wise up; **la vida en la calle lo hizo e. pronto** life on the streets soon wised him up; **¡espabila, que nos quedamos sin**

asiento! look sharp or we won't get a seat!; **si no espabilamos, la competencia se llevará todos los clientes** if we don't buck our ideas up the competition will get all our customers

3 espabilarse *vpr* **(a)** *(despertarse)* to wake up, to brighten up; **espabílate, que ya es la hora** wake up, it's time to get up

(b) *(darse prisa)* to get a move on; **como no te espabiles llegaremos tarde** if you don't get a move on we'll be late

(c) *(avisparse)* to wise up; **los niños se espabilan pronto yendo al colegio** children soon wise up when they start going to school

(d) *Cuba Fam (marcharse)* to clear off

espachurramiento, despachurramiento *nm Fam* squashing

espachurrar, despachurrar *Fam* **1** *vt* to squash

2 espachurrarse *vpr* to get squashed

espaciado, -a 1 *adj* **(a)** *(en el tiempo)* spaced out; **sus apariciones son ahora más espaciadas** his public appearances are now less frequent; **sus cartas llegaban cada vez más espaciadas** there were longer and longer intervals between her letters, her letters became less and less frequent

(b) *(en el espacio)* spaced out; **haz los renglones menos espaciados** reduce the space between the lines, make the lines closer together

2 *nm Informát* spacing

espaciador *nm* space bar

espacial *adj* **(a)** *(vuelo, lanzadera, estación)* space; **cohete e.** space rocket **(b)** *(dimensión, distribución)* spatial; **coordenadas espaciales** spatial coordinates

espaciar *vt* **(a)** *(en el tiempo)* to space out; **fue espaciando sus visitas** he visited less frequently, the intervals between his visits became longer **(b)** *(en el espacio)* to space out; **debes e. más los rosales** you should space the rosebushes out more, you should leave more space between the rosebushes **(c)** *Informát* to space

espacio *nm* **(a)** *(extensión física)* space; **la relación entre el e. y el tiempo** the relationship between space and time ►► *Fís* ***e.-tiempo*** space-time; *Mat* ***e. vectorial*** vector space

(b) *(hueco libre)* space, room; **hay e. de sobra para construir una piscina** there's plenty of space *o* room to build a swimming pool; **no queda e. en mi maleta** there's no room (left) in my suitcase; **deja más e. entre las plantas** leave more space *o* room between the plants ►► ***e. aéreo*** airspace; ***e. vital*** living space; **me falta e. vital** I need more space; *Informát* ***e. Web*** Web space

(c) *(lugar)* space; **no soporto los espacios cerrados** I can't bear enclosed spaces ►► ***e. verde*** *(grande)* park; *(pequeño)* lawn, green

(d) *(en texto)* space; **a dos espacios, a doble e.** double-spaced; **cuatro folios a un e.** four single-spaced sheets ►► ***e. en blanco*** blank; **rellene los espacios en blanco** fill in the blanks; *Informát* ***e. indivisible*** hard space

(e) *(más allá de la Tierra)* **el e.** (outer) space; **la conquista del e. es todavía un sueño** the conquest of (outer) space is still a dream ►► ***e. exterior*** outer space; ***e. interplanetario*** deep space; ***e. sideral*** outer space

(f) *(radiofónico, televisivo) (programa independiente)* programme; *(dentro de otro programa)* slot; **espacios informativos** news programmes; **tiene un e. en el programa de los sábados** he has a slot on the Saturday programme ►► ***e. electoral*** party political broadcast; ***e. publicitario*** advertising slot, commercial

(g) *(duración)* **cortaron el agua por e. de dos horas** the water was cut off for two hours; **en un corto e. de tiempo** in a short space of time; **en el e. de tiempo que se tarda en escribir una postal** in the time it takes to write a postcard

espacioso, -a *adj (vivienda, habitación, vehículo)* spacious, roomy; *(instalaciones, jardín, patio)* spacious

espada 1 *nf* **(a)** *(arma)* sword; **ceñirse la e.** to put *o Literario* gird on one's sword; **desenvainar la e.** to unsheathe one's sword; EXPR **estar entre la e. y la pared** to be between the devil and the deep blue sea, to be caught between a rock and a hard place; EXPR **ser un e. de dos filos** *o* **de doble filo** to be a double-edged *o* two-edged sword ►► ***la e. de Damocles*** the sword of Damocles; **el pago de la hipoteca era una e. de Damocles para la familia** the family always had the mortgage payments hanging over them

(b) *(naipe)* = any card in the "espadas" suit

(c) espadas *(palo)* = suit in Spanish deck of cards, with the symbol of a sword

2 *nm Taurom* matador

3 *nm o nf (espadachín)* swordsman

> **Falso amigo:** El sustantivo inglés **spade** no es la traducción del español **espada**. En inglés **spade** significa "pala" o "pica".

espadachín *nm* swordsman

espadaña *nf* **(a)** *(planta)* bullrush **(b)** *(campanario)* bell gable

espadilla *nf (en naipes)* = ace of the "swords" suit in a Spanish deck of cards

espadín *nm (pez)* sprat

espagueti *nm* piece of spaghetti; **espaguetis** spaghetti *(singular)*; EXPR *Fam* **estar como** *o* **hecho un e.** to be as thin as a *Br* rake *o US* rail ►► *Cine* ***e. western*** spaghetti western

espalda *nf* **(a)** *(de persona)* back; **dolor de e.** backache; **ancho de espaldas** broad-shouldered; **cargado de espaldas** round-shouldered; **caer** *o* **dar de espaldas** to fall flat on one's back; *Fig* **casi me caigo de espaldas cuando me dieron la noticia** you could have knocked me down with a feather when they told me; **dar la e. a alguien: perdone, le estoy dando la e.** I'm sorry, I've got my back to you; **su familia le dio la e.** his family turned their backs on him; *Am* **irse de espaldas** to fall flat on one's back; **túmbese de espaldas** lie (flat) on your back; **vuélvase de e.** turn onto your back; **lo vi de espaldas** I saw him from behind; **de espaldas a alguien** with one's back turned on sb; **e. con e.** back to back; **por la e.** from behind; *Fig* behind one's back; **le dispararon por la e.** he was shot in the back *o* from behind; **un atleta con varias olimpiadas a sus espaldas** an athlete with several Olympics behind him *o* under his belt; EXPR **cubrirse las espaldas** to cover oneself *o* one's back; EXPR **dar la e. a algo** to ignore sth, to close one's eyes to sth; **no podemos dar la e. a los hechos** we can't ignore the facts; EXPR *Euf Hum* **donde la e. pierde su (casto** *u* **honesto** *o* **santo) nombre: le dio una patada donde la e. pierde su casto nombre** she kicked him in his derriere *o* rear end; EXPR **echarse algo a** *o* **sobre las espaldas** to take sth on; **se echó a las espaldas toda la responsabilidad** she took on all the responsibility; EXPR **guardarse las espaldas** to cover oneself; EXPR **hacer algo a espaldas de alguien** to do sth behind sb's back; **hablaban de ella a sus espaldas** they talked about her behind her back; EXPR **tirar** *o* **tumbar de espaldas** to be amazing *o* stunning; **en la habitación había un tufo que tiraba de espaldas** there was a smell in the room that would have knocked you over; EXPR **volver la e. a alguien** to turn one's back on sb ►► ***e. mojada*** wetback

(b) *(de prenda de vestir)* back

(c) *(de lugar, edificio)* back; **a la e.** *o* **a espaldas de la casa hay una carretera** there is a road at the back of *o* behind the house

(d) *(en natación)* backstroke; **los 200 metros e.** the 200 metres backstroke; **nadar a e.** to do the backstroke

espaldar *nm Am* **(a)** *(de gimnasio)* wall bars **(b)** *(de silla)* back

espaldarazo *nm* **(a)** *(reconocimiento)* recognition; **eso le dio el e. (definitivo)** that finally gained her widespread recognition **(b)** *Hist (para armar caballero)* tap on the shoulder *(with a sword)*

espaldear *vt Chile (proteger)* to guard the back of

espalderas *nfpl* wall bars

espaldilla *nf* shoulder *(of lamb etc)*

espaldero *nm Ven* bodyguard

espaldista *nmf Dep* backstroker

espaldón *nm CRica, Ecuad Br* hard shoulder, *US* shoulder

espantada *nf* **(a)** *(caballo)* **dar** *o* **pegar una e.** to bolt **(b)** *Fam (de persona)* **dar la e.** to split, *Br* to leg it

espantadizo, -a *adj* nervous, easily frightened

espantado, -a *adj* **(a)** *(asustado)* frightened, scared; **huyó e.** he fled in fright **(b)** *(pasmado)* appalled, shocked; **sus malos modales me tenían e.** I was appalled at his bad manners

espantajo *nm* **(a)** *(espantapájaros)* scarecrow **(b)** *(persona mal vestida)* scarecrow; *(persona fea)* fright, sight

espantapájaros *nm inv* scarecrow

espantar 1 *vt* **(a)** *(ahuyentar)* to frighten *o* scare away; **espanta a las moscas con el rabo** it keeps the flies off with its tail; EXPR *RDom Fam* **e. la mula** to split

(b) *(asustar)* to frighten, to scare; *Fam* **el loco de mi hermano me espanta a todos los novios** my crazy brother frightens off *o* scares away all my boyfriends

(c) *(pasmar)* to appal, to shock; **sus costumbres espantarían a cualquier occidental** their customs would appal any Westerner

(d) *(apartar de la mente)* **espanta sus penas bebiendo** he drowns his sorrows in drink; **no conseguía e. el fantasma de los celos** she couldn't rid herself of the jealousy she felt

2 *vi* **(a)** *(asustar)* to be frightening; **esa casa espanta sólo de verla** that house is frightening just to look at **(b)** *Méx, Ven (haber apariciones)* **en esa casa espantan** that house is haunted

3 espantarse *vpr* **(a)** *(ser ahuyentado)* to get frightened away *o* off, to be scared off **(b)** *(asustarse)* to get frightened *o* scared **(con** by**)** **(c)** *(pasmarse)* to be appalled *o* shocked; **me espanté al ver lo caro que era todo** I got a shock when I saw how expensive everything was

espantasuegras *nm inv Méx* party blower

espanto *nm* **(a)** *(miedo)* fright; **le tiene e. a las arañas** he's frightened *o* scared of spiders

(b) *(pasmo)* **la noticia causó e. entre la gente** people were appalled at the news; **¡qué e.!** how terrible!; **hacía un calor de e.** the heat was appalling

(c) *Fam (persona o cosa fea)* **estos zapatos son un e.** those shoes are hideous; **tiene un novio que es un e.** she's got a boyfriend who's a real fright; **¡qué e. de traje!** what a hideous *o* frightful suit!

(d) *Am (fantasma)* ghost

espantosamente *adv* **(a)** *(pavorosamente)* terrifyingly, frighteningly; **un cuerpo e. mutilado** a horribly mutilated body **(b)** *(pasmosamente)* appallingly, shockingly; **jugamos e. mal** we played appallingly *o* shockingly badly

espantoso, -a *adj* **(a)** *(pavoroso)* horrific

(b) *(enorme)* terrible; **allí dentro hacía un calor e.** it was roasting *o* boiling *o* terribly hot in there; **tengo un frío e.** I'm freezing to death; **teníamos un hambre espantosa** we were famished *o* starving

(c) *(feísimo)* hideous, frightful; **llevaba un vestido e.** she was wearing a hideous *o* frightful dress

(d) *(pasmoso)* appalling, shocking; **el servicio postal era e.** the postal service was appalling; **su capacidad para mentir es espantosa** he's an appalling liar

España *n* Spain

español, -ola 1 *adj* Spanish

2 *nm,f (persona)* Spaniard; **los españoles** the Spanish, Spaniards

3 *nm (lengua)* Spanish ►► ***e. peninsular*** peninsular Spanish

españolada *nf Pey* **la película es una e.** the movie plays on all the old Spanish clichés

españolismo *nm* **(a)** *(apego, afecto)* affinity for things Spanish **(b)** *(carácter, naturaleza)* Spanishness, Spanish character **(c)** *(nacionalismo)* Spanish nationalism

españolista 1 *adj* **(a)** *(amante de lo español)* **es muy e.** she loves everything to do with Spain, she's a real Hispanophile **(b)** *(nacionalista)* Spanish nationalist, with Spanish nationalist sympathies

2 *nmf* **(a)** *(amante de lo español)* lover of all things Spanish, Hispanophile **(b)** *(nacionalista)* Spanish nationalist, person with Spanish nationalist sympathies

españolizar [14] **1** *vt* to make Spanish, to hispanicize

2 españolizarse *vpr* to adopt Spanish ways

esparadrapo *nm Br* (sticking-)plaster, *US* Band-aid®

esparaván *nm (ave)* sparrowhawk

esparavel *nm (red)* casting net

esparcido, -a *adj (semillas, papeles, objetos)* scattered

esparcimiento *nm* **(a)** *(diseminación)* scattering **(b)** *(ocio)* relaxation, time off

esparcir [74] **1** *vt* **(a)** *(diseminar) (semillas, papeles, objetos)* to scatter; *(sal, azúcar)* to sprinkle; **hay que e. las lentejas en la mesa** you need to spread the lentils out on the table **(b)** *(noticia, rumor)* to spread **(c)** *(entretener)* to amuse, to entertain

2 esparcirse *vpr* **(a)** *(diseminarse) (semillas, papeles, objetos)* to be scattered; *(líquido)* to spread (out); *(sal, azúcar)* to scatter; **el azúcar se esparció por toda la mesa** the sugar scattered all over the table **(b)** *(noticia, rumor)* to spread **(c)** *(entretenerse)* to amuse oneself; *(relajarse)* to relax

espárrago *nm* stalk of asparagus; **espárragos** asparagus; EXPR *Fam* **estar como** *o* **hecho un e.** to be a beanpole; EXPR *Fam* **irse a freír espárragos: ¡vete a freír espárragos!** get lost!; **me mandó a freír espárragos** he told me to get lost, he told me where to go ►► ***espárragos trigueros*** wild asparagus

esparraguera *nf* asparagus (plant)

Esparta *n Hist* Sparta

espartano, -a 1 *adj* **(a)** *(de Esparta)* Spartan **(b)** *(sobrio)* spartan

2 *nm,f* Spartan

esparto *nm* esparto (grass)

espasmo *nm* spasm; **le daban espasmos** he had spasms

espasmódico, -a *adj* spasmodic

espástico, -a *adj* spastic

espatarrado, -a = **despatarrado**

espatarrarse = **despatarrarse**

espato *nm Geol* spar ►► ***e. de Islandia*** Iceland spar

espátula *nf* **(a)** *(de albañil)* bricklayer's trowel; *(de empapelador)* scraper, stripping knife **(b)** *Arte* palette knife **(c)** *Culin* spatula **(d)** *Med* spatula **(e)** *(ave)* spoonbill

especia *nf* spice; **un plato con muchas especias** a very spicy dish

especiado, -a *adj* spicy, spiced

especial 1 *adj* **(a)** *(adecuado)* special; **e. para** especially for; **lejía e. para lavadoras** bleach especially for washing machines; **una oferta e. para nuestros clientes** a special offer for our customers

(b) *(particular, excepcional)* special; **hoy es un día e., celebramos nuestro aniversario** today's a special day, we're celebrating our anniversary; **tienen e. interés en conocerte** they're especially interested in meeting you; **recibe un trato e. por ser discapacitado** he receives special treatment because he is disabled

(c) *(peculiar)* peculiar, strange; **esa forma tan e. que tiene de mirar** that peculiar *o* strange way he has of looking at you

(d) *(quisquilloso)* fussy; **es muy e. con la comida** he's very fussy about his food, he's a very fussy eater

2 *nm* **(a)** *(programa)* special; **un e. informativo** a news special **(b)** *Chile (perrito caliente)* = hot dog with mayonnaise **(c)** *RP (sándwich) Br* baguette, *US* sub; **un e. de pavita** *Br* a turkey baguette, *US* a turkey sub

3 en especial *loc adv* especially, particularly; **me gusta la pasta, en e. los macarrones** I like pasta, especially macaroni; **¿alguno en e.?** any one in particular?

especialidad *nf* **(a)** *(culinaria) (en restaurante, de región)* speciality, *US* specialty ►► ***e. de la casa*** speciality *o US* specialty of the house

(b) *(en estudios) US* major, = main subject of degree; **estudia la e. de derecho canónico** she's specializing in canon law; **este tema no es de mi e.** this subject doesn't come into my specialist field; **son cinco años de carrera y tres de e.** there are five years of university study and three years of specialization

(c) *(en actividad)* speciality; *Hum* **meter la pata es su e.** she's an expert *o* a past master at putting her foot in it

especialista 1 *adj* specializing **(en** in**)**; **médico e.** specialist

2 *nmf* **(a)** *(experto)* specialist, expert **(en** in**)**; **los especialistas en materia financiera prevén otra subida** financial experts anticipate another rise; **un e. en balística** a specialist in ballistics, a ballistics expert; *Hum* **es e. en hacer la vida imposible a los demás** he's an expert *o* a past master at making life difficult for others ►► ***e. universitario*** = postgraduate university qualification below that of master's

(b) *(médico)* specialist; **mi médico me mandó al e.** my doctor referred me to the specialist; **el e. de riñón** the kidney specialist

(c) *Cine* stuntman, *f* stuntwoman

especialización *nf* specialization

especializado, -a *adj* specialized **(en** in**)**; **un abogado e. en casos de divorcio** a lawyer specializing in divorce cases; **un restaurante e. en carnes a la brasa** a restaurant whose speciality is barbecued meats; **mano de obra especializada** skilled labour; **obrero e.** skilled worker; **no e.** *(mano de obra)* unskilled

especializar [14] **1** *vt* to specialize

2 especializarse *vpr* to specialize **(en** in**)**

especialmente *adv* **(a)** *(con fin específico)* especially, specially **(b)** *(en especial)* especially, particularly; **me gusta la pasta, e. los macarrones** I like pasta, especially macaroni; **¿prefieres alguno e.?** do you want one in particular?

especie *nf* **(a)** *(biológica)* species *(singular)*; **el origen de las especies** the origin of species; **e. endémica** endemic species; **e. protegida** protected species; **e. en vías de extinción** endangered species

(b) *(clase)* kind, sort; **llevaba una e. de abrigo** she was wearing some sort of overcoat; **toda esta gente es de la misma e.** all these people are the same

(c) *(productos, servicios)* **en e.** in kind; **pagar en e.** to pay in kind; *Fin* **rendimientos** *o* **retribuciones en e.** *(de empresa)* benefits in kind

(d) *Formal (rumor)* rumour

(e) *Rel* **especies sacramentales** species

especiería *nf* spice shop

especiero *nm (mueble)* spice rack

especificación *nf* specification

específicamente *adv* specifically

especificar [60] *vt* to specify; **la guía no especifica nada sobre el tema** the guide doesn't say anything specific on the subject; **no especificó las razones de su dimisión** she didn't specify her reasons for resigning; **¿podría usted e. un poco más?** could you be a little more specific?; **por favor, especifique claramente el modo de pago** please state clearly the method of payment

especificativo, -a *adj* (**a**) *(aclarativo)* specifying (**b**) *Gram (oración)* defining

especificidad *nf* specificity

específico, -a 1 *adj* specific
2 *nm (medicamento)* specific

espécimen (*pl* **especímenes**) *nm* specimen

especioso, -a *adj Formal (engañoso)* specious

espectacular *adj* spectacular

espectacularidad *nf* spectacular nature; **todos se asustaron por la e. del accidente** it was such a spectacular accident it shocked everyone rigid

espectacularmente *adv (en sentido positivo)* spectacularly; *(en sentido negativo)* dramatically

espectáculo *nm* (**a**) *(diversión)* entertainment; **el público pide e.** the public wants entertainment; **tocan bien y además les gusta dar e.** they play well and they like to give a good show too
(**b**) *(función)* show, performance; **el e. comenzará a las ocho** the show *o* performance starts at eight; **un e. infantil/circense** a children's/circus show; **espectáculos** *(sección periodística)* entertainment section; **el mundo del e.** (the world of) show business ►► ***e. pirotécnico*** firework display; ***e. de variedades*** variety show
(**c**) *(suceso, escena)* sight; **desde el mirador, el paisaje es un verdadero e.** the view of the landscape from the lookout point is quite spectacular; **ver cómo le pegaban fue un penoso e.** seeing them hit him was a terrible sight; EXPR *Fam* **dar el e.** to cause a scene

espectador, -ora *nm,f* (**a**) *(de televisión)* viewer; *(de cine, teatro)* member of the audience; *(de espectáculo deportivo)* spectator; **los espectadores** *(de televisión)* the viewers; *(de cine, teatro)* the audience; *(de espectáculo deportivo)* the spectators, the crowd (**b**) *(de suceso, discusión)* onlooker; **yo fui un mero e.** I was just an onlooker

espectral *adj* (**a**) *(misterioso, lúgubre)* ghostly (**b**) *Fís* spectral; **análisis e.** spectral *o* spectrum analysis

espectro *nm* (**a**) *Fís* spectrum ►► ***e. luminoso*** light spectrum; ***e. solar*** solar spectrum; ***e. visible*** visible spectrum (**b**) *(gama, abanico)* spectrum; **el e. político** the political spectrum; **un antibiótico de amplio e.** a broad-spectrum antibiotic (**c**) *(fantasma)* spectre, ghost (**d**) *(de hambre, guerra)* spectre

espectrógrafo *nm Fís* spectrograph ►► ***e. de masas*** mass spectrograph

espectrómetro *nm Fís* ***e. de masas*** mass spectrometer

espectroscopia *nf* spectroscopy

espectroscopio *nm* spectroscope

especulación *nf* (**a**) *(económica, financiera)* speculation; **e. bursátil** stock market speculation, speculation on the stock exchange; **la e. inmobiliaria** property speculation (**b**) *(conjetura)* speculation

especulador, -ora *nm,f* speculator

especular *vi* (**a**) *(reflexionar, conjeturar)* to speculate (**sobre** on/about) (**b**) *(comerciar)* **e. con/en algo** to speculate in sth; **e. con terrenos/la propiedad** to speculate in land/property; **e. en bolsa** to speculate on the stock market *o* exchange

especulativo, -a *adj* (**a**) *(comercio, economía, actividad)* speculative (**b**) *(conocimiento)* speculative, theoretical

espéculo *nm Med* speculum

espejear *vi* to shine, to gleam

espejismo *nm* (**a**) *(ilusión óptica)* mirage (**b**) *(apariencia)* mirage, illusion

espejo *nm* (**a**) *(para mirarse)* mirror; **mirarse al** *o* **en el e.** to look at oneself in the mirror; **los padres se miran en los hijos como en un e.** parents see themselves in their children; EXPR **como un e.** *(muy limpio)* spotless; **dejó la mesa como un e.** he left the table spotless ►► ***e. de cuerpo entero*** full-length mirror; ***e. lateral*** *(de automóvil)* wing mirror; ***e. de mano*** hand mirror; ***e. retrovisor*** rear-view mirror
(**b**) *(imagen, reflejo)* mirror; **su teatro es el e. de la sociedad de la época** his plays mirror *o* reflect the society of his time; **la cara es el e. del alma** the face is the mirror of the soul
(**c**) *(modelo)* model, example; **es el e. en que se miran muchas jóvenes** many young people take her as a role model; **es un e. de virtud** he's a paragon of virtue
(**d**) ***e. de los Incas*** *(mineral)* obsidian
(**e**) ***e. de Venus*** *(planta)* Venus's looking glass

espejuelos *nmpl Cuba* glasses, spectacles

espeleología *nf* caving, pot-holing, *US* spelunking, *Espec* speleology

espeleólogo, -a *nm,f* caver, pot-holer, *US* spelunker, *Espec* speleologist

espeluznante *adj (escena, suceso)* horrific, horrifying; *(relato)* hair-raising; *(grito)* bloodcurdling; *(sonido)* terrifying

espeluznar *vt* **1** *(asustar)* to terrify
2 espeluznarse *vpr (asustarse)* to be terrified

espera *nf* (**a**) *(acción)* wait; **la larga e. había merecido la pena** the long wait had been worth it; **tras una e. de seis horas...** after a six-hour wait..., after waiting (for) six hours...; **después de una e. prudencial, partimos sin él** after waiting for a reasonable amount of time, we left without him; **la e. se nos hizo interminable** the waiting seemed endless; **en e. de, a la e. de** waiting for, awaiting; **seguimos a la e. de su respuesta** *(en cartas)* we await your reply; **en e. de lo que decida el jurado** while awaiting the jury's decision
(**b**) *Der (plazo)* period of grace

esperado, -a *adj* (**a**) *(anhelado)* long-awaited, eagerly awaited; **por fin llegó la fecha del e. concierto** at last the day of the long-awaited concert arrived; **su e. regreso a los escenarios** her long-awaited return to the stage
(**b**) *(previsto)* expected; **fue el resultado e.** it was the result they expected; **tuvo una reacción no por esperada menos violenta** he reacted in a way that was none the less violent for being expected

esperanto *nm* Esperanto

esperanza *nf* (**a**) *(confianza)* hope; **la reunión ha suscitado nuevas esperanzas de una solución** the meeting has given rise to new hopes of a solution; **aún hay e.** *o* **esperanzas, aún quedan esperanzas** there is still hope; **tengo e. de que todo se arregle** I have hopes that everything will be sorted out; **mantengo la e. de volver a verla** I still hope to see her again; **él es nuestra única e.** he's our only hope; **te queda la e. de que nadie se haya enterado** you can only hope that *o* your only hope is that no one has found out; **se dirigió a él con la e. de que le firmara un autógrafo** she approached him hoping that he would give her his autograph; **dar esperanzas a alguien** to give sb hope; **le dio esperanzas y él pensó que podría ser su novio** she raised his hopes and he thought he could be her boyfriend; **los médicos no nos han querido dar esperanzas** the doctors haven't wanted to build up our hopes; **no quiero darles falsas esperanzas** I don't want to build your hopes up for nothing, I don't want to give you false hope(s); **perder la e.** to lose hope; **habíamos perdido toda e.** we had lost all hope; **perdimos la e. de llegar a ser rescatados** we lost hope of ever being rescued; **tener e.** *o* **esperanzas de hacer algo** to hope to be able to do sth; **aún tengo esperanzas de volver algún día** I still hope to go back one day; PROV **la e. es lo último que se pierde** where there's life there's hope ►► ***e. de vida*** life expectancy; ***e. de vida al nacimiento*** life expectancy at birth
(**b**) *Rel* hope

esperanzadamente *adv* hopefully

esperanzado, -a *adj* hopeful

esperanzador, -ora *adj* encouraging, hopeful; **es una señal esperanzadora** it's an encouraging *o* hopeful sign; **la actuación del equipo ha sido esperanzadora** the team's performance was encouraging *o* promising

esperanzar [14] **1** *vt* to give hope to; **no nos esperanzaron mucho** they didn't give us much hope, they weren't very encouraging
2 esperanzarse *vpr* to be encouraged; **se esperanzaron al oír las noticias** they were encouraged when they heard the news; **no conviene esperanzarse demasiado** we shouldn't build our hopes up too much

ESPERAR 1 *vt* (**a**) *(aguardar)* to wait for; **e. el autobús** to wait for the bus; **te esperaremos en el aeropuerto** we'll meet you at the airport, we'll be waiting for you at the airport; **espéranos un minuto** wait for us a minute; **¡espérame, que voy contigo!** wait for me, I'm coming with you!; **¿a qué estás esperando?** what are you waiting for?; **e. a que alguien haga algo** to wait for sb to do sth; **esperaré a que vuelva** I'll wait till she gets back
(**b**) *(tener esperanza de)* **todos esperamos la victoria** we all hope for victory; **esperamos salir al campo el domingo** we are hoping to go on a trip to the countryside on Sunday; **espero poder ayudar** I hope I can be of some help; **e. que...** to hope that...; **espero que sí/no** I hope so/not; **espero que no te hayas ofendido** I hope you didn't take offence; **esperamos que no sea nada** let's hope it's nothing serious; **ser de e.: es de e. que no ocurra ninguna desgracia** let's hope nothing terrible happens; **era de e. que ocurriría esto** you could have predicted this would happen; **como era de e.** as was to be expected; **como era de e., llovió mucho** as was to be expected *o* as you might expect, there was a lot of rain
(**c**) *(tener confianza en)* to expect; **no esperábamos esta reacción** we didn't expect this reaction; **espero que venga esta noche** I expect (that) she'll come tonight; **e. algo de alguien** to expect sth from sb,

to hope for sth from sb; **espero discreción de usted** I expect discretion from you, I expect you to be discreet; **¿y qué esperabas (de alguien así)?** what did you expect (from someone like that)?; **no esperaba menos de él** I expected no less of him

(**d**) *(ser inminente para)* to await, to be in store for; **nos esperan un buen baño y una cama** there's a nice warm bath and a bed waiting for us; **le esperan dificultades** he's in for some problems, there are problems in store for him; *Fam* **¡me espera una buena en casa!** I'm in for it when I get home!; *Fam* **¡no sabes la** *o* **lo que te espera!** you don't know what you're in for!

2 *vi* (**a**) *(aguardar)* to wait; **espera en este despacho** wait in this office; **espera, que ya voy** wait a minute, I'm coming; **espera un instante** *o* **momento, ¿no es el famoso Pedro Valverde?** hang on *o* wait a minute, isn't that the famous Pedro Valverde?; **no creo que puedas hacerlo – espera y verás** I don't think you'll be able to do it – just (you) wait and see; **su enfado no se hizo e.** it didn't take long for her anger to surface; *Fam* **si crees que te voy a dejar dinero, puedes e. sentado** if you think I'm going to lend you some money, you've got another think coming; **hacer e. a alguien** to keep sb waiting, to make sb wait; **me hiciste e. una hora** you kept me waiting (for) an hour; PROV **quien espera desespera** a watched pot never boils

(**b**) *(estar embarazada)* to be expecting; **está esperando desde hace cuatro meses** she's four months pregnant

3 esperarse *vpr* (**a**) *(imaginarse, figurarse)* to expect; **ya me esperaba yo esta contestación** I expected that answer; **se esperaban lo peor** they expected *o* feared the worst; **esto no me lo esperaba** I wasn't expecting this; **ya me lo esperaba** I expected as much; **¿qué te esperabas?** what did you expect?; **esperarse algo de alguien** to expect sth of sb; **no me esperaba eso de ti** I didn't expect that of you, I never thought you'd do that

(**b**) *(aguardar)* to wait; **espérate un momento** wait a minute; **esperarse a que alguien haga algo** to wait for sb to do sth; **no te esperes a que nadie resuelva tus problemas** don't wait for other people to solve your problems

(**c**) *(uso impersonal)* to be expected; **se esperan lluvias en toda la región** rain is expected *o* there will be rain across the whole region; **se espera que acudan varios miles de personas** several thousand people are expected to attend; **se esperaba que hiciera unas declaraciones** he was expected to make a statement

---

esperma *nm o nf* sperm ▸▸ ***e. de ballena*** *(grasa)* sperm oil; *(producto)* spermaceti

espermaceti *nm (grasa)* sperm oil; *(producto)* spermaceti

espermaticida 1 *adj* spermicidal
2 *nm* spermicide

espermatozoide *nm* sperm, *Espec* spermatozoon

espermatozoo *nm* spermatozoon

espermicida 1 *adj* spermicidal
2 *nm* spermicide

esperpéntico, -a *adj* grotesque

esperpento *nm* (**a**) *(persona)* grotesque sight; **vestido así pareces un e.** you look a sight dressed like that (**b**) *(cosa)* absurdity, piece of nonsense (**c**) *Lit (género)* = style of writing created by the Spanish dramatist and novelist Ramón María del Valle-Inclán (1866-1936), which consists of deforming reality to intensify its grotesque and absurd characteristics

espesante *nm* thickening, thickener

espesar 1 *vt* to thicken
2 *vi (líquido, salsa)* to thicken
3 espesarse *vpr (bosque, vegetación)* to become more dense; *(niebla, humo)* to get thicker; *(líquido, salsa)* to thicken

espeso, -a *adj* (**a**) *(líquido, pintura, salsa)* thick (**b**) *(cabello, barba)* thick, bushy; *(bosque, vegetación)* dense; *(seto)* thick; *(niebla)* dense, thick; *(humo)* thick; *(nieve)* deep; *(muro)* thick (**c**) *(complicado)* dense, difficult (**d**) *Fam (torpe)* dense, slow; **hoy estás un poco e.** you're being a bit dense today, you're a bit slow today (**e**) *Perú, Ven Fam (pesado)* **¡no seas e.!** don't be a pain!

espesor *nm* (**a**) *(grosor)* thickness; **tiene 2 metros de e.** it's 2 metres thick (**b**) *(densidad) (de bosque, vegetación)* denseness; *(de seto)* thickness; *(de niebla)* denseness, thickness; *(de nieve)* depth

espesura *nf* (**a**) *(vegetación)* thicket; **se abrió camino entre la e.** he made his way through the undergrowth (**b**) *(grosor)* thickness (**c**) *(densidad)* density

espetar *vt* (**a**) *Fam (decir)* to snap; **de pronto me espetó que me callara** he suddenly snapped at me to be quiet; **"¡he dicho que no!", espetó ella** "I said no!" she snapped (**b**) *(carne)* to skewer

espetón *nm* (**a**) *(pincho)* skewer, spit (**b**) *(pez)* needlefish, pipefish

espía[1] **1** *adj* **avión/satélite e.** spy plane/satellite
2 *nmf (persona)* spy ▸▸ ***e. doble*** double agent

espía[2] *nf Náut (cabo)* warp

espiar[1] [32] **1** *vt* to spy on, to keep a watch on; **un detective espiaba sus movimientos** a detective was keeping a watch on his movements
2 *vi (en secreto)* to spy

espiar[2] [32] *vi Náut* to warp

espichado, -a *adj Ven Fam* down, deflated

espichar *vt* (**a**) *Chile, Perú (vasija, cuba)* to put a *Br* tap *o US* faucet on (**b**) *Ven Fam (desinflar)* to let down (**c**) *Fam* **espicharla** *(morir)* to kick the bucket

espídico, -a *adj Esp Fam* (**a**) *(nervioso)* on edge, uptight (**b**) *(lleno de energía)* hyper (**c**) *(drogado)* **estar e.** to be speeding

espiga *nf* (**a**) *(de cereal)* ear; *Bot (de flores)* spike (**b**) *(en telas)* herringbone (**c**) *(pieza) (de madera)* peg; *(de hierro)* pin (**d**) *(de espada)* tang (**e**) *Náut* masthead

espigado, -a *adj* (**a**) *(persona)* tall and slim (**b**) *(cereal)* ripe

espigar [38] **1** *vt (información)* to glean
2 espigarse *vpr* (**a**) *Fam (persona)* to shoot up (**b**) *(planta)* to go to seed

espigón *nm* breakwater

espiguilla *nf (en telas)* herringbone (pattern)

espín *nm Fís* spin

espina *nf* (**a**) *(astilla)* splinter; **se me ha clavado una e.** I've got a splinter
(**b**) *(de pez)* (fish) bone; **limpiar un pescado de espinas** to bone a fish; **se atragantó con una e.** she choked on a fish bone
(**c**) *(de planta)* thorn; *(de cactus)* spine; **una rosa con espinas** a thorny rose
(**d**) *Anat* spine ▸▸ *Med* ***e. bífida*** spina bifida; ***e. dorsal*** *(de vertebrado)* backbone, spine; *(de equipo, organización)* backbone
(**e**) *(pena, pesar)* grief, sorrow; **sacarse una e.** *(desquitarse)* to settle an old score; *(desahogarse)* to relieve a long-standing frustration; **queremos sacarnos la e. de la derrota del año pasado** we want to lay the ghost of last year's defeat; **todavía tengo clavada la e. de no haber ido a la universidad** I still feel bad about not having gone to university; EXPR *Fam* **darle mala e. a alguien** to make sb uneasy; **este sitio me da mala e.** I've got a bad feeling about this place, this place makes me uneasy
(**f**) ***e. blanca*** *(planta)* cotton thistle

espinaca *nf*, **espinacas** *nfpl* spinach

espinal *adj* spinal

espinazo *nm* spine, backbone; EXPR *Fam* **doblar el e.** *(humillarse)* to kowtow; *(trabajar duro)* to put one's back into it

espineta *nf* spinet

espinilla *nf* (**a**) *(hueso)* shin, shinbone (**b**) *(grano)* blackhead

espinillera *nf* shin pad *o* guard

espinillo *nm* (**a**) *RP (árbol)* nandubay (**b**) *Carib (arbusto)* = variety of mimosa

espino *nm* (**a**) *(planta)* hawthorn ▸▸ ***e. amarillo*** common sea-buckthorn; ***e. cerval*** purging buckthorn; ***e. falso*** common sea-buckthorn; ***e. negro*** buckthorn, blackthorn (**b**) *(alambre)* barbed wire

espinoso, -a 1 *adj* (**a**) *(planta, tallo)* thorny; *(cactus)* prickly (**b**) *(asunto, problema, tema)* thorny
2 *nm (pez)* three-spined stickleback

espionaje *nm* espionage, spying; **una red de e.** a spy ring; **hacía e. para los rusos** he spied for the Russians ▸▸ ***e. industrial*** industrial espionage

espira *nf* (**a**) *Mat* spiral, helix (**b**) *Zool (de concha) (espiral)* spire; *(cada vuelta)* whorl (**c**) *Arquit* surbase

espiración *nf* exhalation, breathing out

espirador, -ora *adj Anat* expiratory; **músculo e.** expiratory muscle

espiral *nf* (**a**) *(línea curva)* spiral; **un cuaderno de e.** a spiral-bound notebook; **en e.** *(escalera, forma)* spiral; **el avión descendió en e.** the plane spiralled downwards (**b**) *(escalada)* spiral ▸▸ *Econ* ***e. inflacionaria*** inflationary spiral; ***e. de violencia*** spiral of violence (**c**) *(anticonceptivo)* coil (**d**) *(de reloj)* balance spring, hairspring

espirar 1 *vt* to exhale, to breathe out
2 *vi* to exhale, to breathe out

espiritismo *nm* spiritualism; **hacer e.** to practise spiritualism; **sesión de e.** seance

espiritista *adj* spiritualist

espiritoso, -a, espirituoso, -a *adj (bebida)* alcoholic

espíritu *nm* (**a**) *(mente, alma)* spirit; *Rel* soul ►► ***e. maligno*** evil spirit; ***E. Santo*** Holy Spirit *o* Ghost
(**b**) *(fantasma)* ghost; **se nos apareció el e. del conde** the ghost of the Count appeared to us; **una casa poblada por espíritus** a haunted house
(**c**) *(actitud)* spirit; **fue un hombre de e. aventurero** he was a man with an adventurous spirit; EXPR **ser el e. de la contradicción, tener e. de contradicción** to be contrary ►► ***e. deportivo*** sporting spirit; ***e. de equipo*** team spirit; ***e. de lucha*** fighting spirit; ***e. de sacrificio*** spirit of sacrifice; ***e. de venganza*** desire for vengeance; **tener e. de venganza** to be vengeful
(**d**) *(carácter)* spirit; **siempre tuvo un e. juvenil** she was always young at heart, she always had a youthful spirit; **el e. de la época** the spirit of the age; **el e. de la ley** the spirit of the law
(**e**) *(ánimo)* **¡cómo quieres aprobar con ese e.!** how do you expect to pass if you feel like that!; **levantar el e.** to cheer up; **levantar el e. a alguien** to lift *o* raise sb's spirits
(**f**) *Quím* spirit; **e. de sal/de vino** spirits of salt/of wine

espiritual 1 *adj* spiritual
2 *nm (canto)* spiritual

espiritualidad *nf* spirituality

espirituoso, -a = **espiritoso**

espirómetro *nm* spirometer

espita *nf* spigot, *Br* tap, *US* faucet

espléndidamente *adv* (**a**) *(maravillosamente)* splendidly (**b**) *(con ostentación)* magnificently (**c**) *(con abundancia)* generously, lavishly

esplendidez *nf* (**a**) *(generosidad)* generosity (**b**) *(magnificencia)* splendour

espléndido, -a *adj* (**a**) *(maravilloso)* splendid, magnificent; **hace un día e.** it's a beautiful *o* glorious day; **hace un tiempo e.** the weather is beautiful *o* glorious; **me parece un tipo e.** I think he's a wonderful guy; **desperdició una oportunidad espléndida** he wasted a golden *o* wonderful opportunity; **este arroz está e.** this rice is wonderful; **estás espléndida con ese vestido** you look magnificent in that dress
(**b**) *(generoso) (persona)* generous; *(obsequio)* generous, lavish
(**c**) *(lujoso)* magnificent, lavish; **espléndidos decorados** magnificent *o* lavish sets

esplendor *nm* (**a**) *(magnificencia)* splendour (**b**) *(apogeo)* greatness; **la primavera se hallaba en todo su e.** spring was in its fullest glory; **la empresa atravesaba por su momento de máximo e.** the company was at its most successful

esplendoroso, -a *adj* magnificent

esplenio *nm Anat* splenius

espliego *nm* lavender

esplín *nm Literario* melancholy, depression

espolear *vt* (**a**) *(caballo)* to spur on (**b**) *(persona)* to spur on

espoleta *nf* (**a**) *(de proyectil)* fuse (**b**) *Zool (hueso)* wishbone

espolón *nm* (**a**) *(de ave)* spur (**b**) *(de caballo)* fetlock (**c**) *(de sierra, montaña)* spur (**d**) *Arquit* buttress (**e**) *(muro de contención) (de mar)* sea wall, dike; *(de río) Br* embankment, *US* levee (**f**) *Náut (de proa)* ram

espolvorear *vt (azúcar, queso)* to sprinkle (**de** with); *(harina, polvos)* to dust (**de** with); **espolvoree chocolate rallado sobre la tarta** sprinkle grated chocolate over the cake; **finalmente, e. los macarrones de** *o* **con parmesano** finally, sprinkle the macaroni with parmesan

espondeo *nm Lit* spondee

espongiario *Zool* 1 *adj* spongiform, spongelike
2 *nm (animal)* sponge
3 **espongiarios** *nmpl* sponges *(Porifera)*

esponja *nf* (**a**) *Zool* sponge (**b**) *(para aseo, limpieza)* sponge; **beber como una e.** to drink like a fish ►► ***e. vaginal*** contraceptive sponge; ***e. vegetal*** loofah, vegetable sponge (**c**) *Fam (borrachín)* lush, old soak (**d**) *Fam (persona capaz de asimilar)* sponge; **los niños son esponjas y todo lo aprenden con facilidad** children are like sponges, they learn everything so easily

esponjar 1 *vt* to fluff up
2 **esponjarse** *vpr* (**a**) *(bizcocho, masa)* to rise (**b**) *(toalla, jersey)* to go *o* become fluffy

esponjosidad *nf* (**a**) *(de toalla, jersey, tejido)* fluffiness (**b**) *(de bizcocho, masa)* lightness, fluffiness; *(de pan)* softness

esponjoso, -a *adj* (**a**) *(toalla, jersey, tejido)* fluffy (**b**) *(bizcocho, masa)* light, fluffy; *(pan)* soft

esponsales *nmpl Formal* betrothal

espónsor *nm* sponsor

esponsorizar *vt* to sponsor

espontáneamente *adv* spontaneously

espontaneidad *nf* spontaneity; **actúa con e.** he acts spontaneously

espontáneo, -a 1 *adj* spontaneous; **son hierbas que crecen de forma espontánea** they're plants that grow in the wild
2 *nm,f* = spectator who tries to join in an event (e.g. by jumping into the bullring or climbing on stage at a concert)

espora *nf* spore; **reproducción por esporas** reproduction by means of spores

esporádicamente *adv* sporadically

esporádico, -a *adj* sporadic; **habrá chubascos esporádicos** there will be intermittent showers

esport [es'port]: **de esport** *loc adj* **chaqueta de e.** sports jacket; **ropa de e.** casual clothes

esposa *nf* (**a**) *Am (anillo)* episcopal ring (**b**) *ver también* **esposo**

esposado, -a *adj* handcuffed; **se lo llevaron e.** he was taken away in handcuffs

esposar *vt* to handcuff

esposas *nfpl (objeto)* handcuffs; **ponerle las e. a alguien** to handcuff sb

esposo, -a *nm,f (persona)* husband, *f* wife; **los esposos salieron de la iglesia** the couple *o* the newlyweds left the church ►► ***esposa de hecho*** common-law wife; ***e. de hecho*** common-law husband

espot [es'pot] (*pl* **espots**) *nm* (TV) advert; **un e. publicitario** a (television) commercial

espray (*pl* **esprays**) *nm* (**a**) *(líquido)* spray; **desodorante/pintura en e.** deodorant spray/spray paint; **pintadas hechas con e.** spray-painted graffiti (**b**) *(envase)* spray, spray can

esprint (*pl* **esprints**) *nm* sprint; **la carrera se decidió al e.** it was a sprint finish ►► ***e. especial*** *(en ciclismo)* hot spot sprint

esprintar *vi* to sprint

esprínter (*pl* **esprínters**) *nmf* sprinter

espuela *nf* (**a**) *(en el talón)* spur; **picar al caballo con las espuelas** to use spurs on one's horse (**b**) *Fam (última copa)* **tomar la e.** to have one for the road (**c**) ***e. de caballero*** *(planta)* larkspur (**d**) *Arg, Chile (hueso)* wishbone

espuerta *nf (recipiente)* basket; EXPR *Fam* **a espuertas** by the sackful *o* bucket; **ganaron dinero a espuertas** they made pots of money

espulgar [38] 1 *vt (de pulgas, piojos)* to delouse
2 **espulgarse** *vpr (uso reflexivo)* to pick the fleas off itself, to groom itself; *(uso recíproco)* to pick the fleas off each other, to groom each other

espulgo *nm (de pulgas, piojos)* delousing

espuma *nf* (**a**) *(burbujas)* foam; *(de cerveza)* head; *(de jabón)* lather; *(de caldo)* scum; *(de olas)* surf; *(de cascada)* spray; *(de río)* foam; **al descorchar el champán brotó un montón de e.** the champagne fizzed all over the place when it was uncorked; **póngame una cerveza con mucha e.** give me a beer with a good head on it; **se te ha quedado e. en la barba** you've got some froth on your beard; **un baño de e.** a foam *o* bubble bath; **este gel hace mucha e.** this gel makes a lot of lather *o* lathers up really well; **al caldo quítale la e. que suelte** remove the scum that forms on the stock; *también Fig* **echar e. por la boca** to foam at the mouth; EXPR **como la e.: la bolsa subió como la e.** the share index shot up; **el negocio crecía como la e.** the business went from strength to strength; **su fortuna creció como la e.** his wealth increased dramatically
(**b**) *(cosmético, limpiador) (para pelo)* (styling) mousse; *(para alfombras, tapicerías)* shampoo ►► ***e. de afeitar*** shaving foam
(**c**) *(gomaespuma)* foam rubber; **un colchón de e.** a foam-rubber mattress ►► *Urug* ***e. de plast*** polyurethane foam; ***e. de poliuretano*** polyurethane foam
(**d**) *(tejido)* stretch nylon; **medias de e.** stretch tights
(**e**) ***e. de mar*** meerschaum

espumadera *nf* skimmer

espumante *adj* foaming, frothing

espumar 1 *vt (caldo)* to skim
2 *vi* to foam

espumarajo *nm* froth, foam; *también Fig* **echar espumarajos (por la boca)** to foam at the mouth; **el mar estaba lleno de espumarajos** there was lots of dirty foam on the sea

espumilla *nf CAm, Ecuad (merengue)* meringue

espumillón *nm* tinsel

espumoso, -a 1 *adj* (**a**) *(baño)* foamy, bubbly; *(cerveza)* frothy, foaming; *(jabón)* lathery (**b**) *(vino)* sparkling
2 *nm (vino)* sparkling wine

espundia *nf Bol, Perú, Ven Med* elephantiasis

espúreo, -a, espurio, -a *adj Formal* (**a**) *(bastardo)* illegitimate (**b**) *(falso)* spurious, false

espurrear *vt Esp (café, papilla)* to spit out

esputar *vi* to cough up *o* spit phlegm

esputo *nm (flema)* spittle; *Med* sputum

esqueje *nm (para injertar en planta)* scion; *(para plantar en tierra)* cutting

esquela *nf* (**a**) *Esp* funeral notice *(in newspaper)* (**b**) *Am (carta)* note

esquelético, -a *adj* (**a**) *Anat* skeletal (**b**) *Fam (muy delgado)* skinny; **estar e.** to be extremely *o* painfully thin

esqueleto *nm* (**a**) *(de persona, animal)* skeleton; EXPR *Fam* **menear** *o* **mover el e.** to boogie (on down) (**b**) *(armazón) (de edificio)* framework; *(de vehículo)* frame; *(de novela)* framework, outline; *(de argumento)* outline (**c**) *Fam (persona muy delgada)* skeleton; EXPR **estar como un** *o* **hecho un e.** to be like a skeleton, to be skin and bones (**d**) *CAm, Col, Méx (formulario)* form (**e**) *Col (camiseta) Br* vest, *US* undershirt

esquema *nm* (**a**) *(gráfico)* diagram; **hazme un e. de la ruta hasta tu casa** draw me a map of the route to your house
(**b**) *(resumen)* outline; **hacerse un e.** to draw up an outline
(**c**) *(estructura)* **los esquemas mentales de un niño** a child's view of the world; **los esquemas de comportamiento del enfermo anoréxico** the behaviour patterns of anorexics; EXPR **romper los esquemas a alguien: sus ideas sobre las drogas me rompieron los esquemas** his ideas on drugs really challenged my preconceptions; **ya tenía el itinerario preparado pero su respuesta me rompió los esquemas** I had already worked out the itinerary but her answer threw all my plans up in the air

esquemáticamente *adv* schematically

esquemático, -a *adj (dibujo, plano)* schematic; **un resumen e.** an outline; **explicó de manera esquemática su programa electoral** he set out the main points of his election programme; **un resumen muy/demasiado e.** a very simplified/an oversimplified summary

esquematismo *nm* schematism

esquematizar [14] *vt* (**a**) *(en forma de gráfico)* to draw a diagram of (**b**) *(resumir)* to outline

esquí *(pl* **esquíes** *o* **esquís***) nm* (**a**) *(tabla)* ski (**b**) *(deporte)* skiing; **una pista de e.** a ski slope *o* run; **saltos de e.** ski-jumping; **hacer e.** to go skiing, to ski ►► ***e. acuático*** water-skiing; ***e. alpino*** downhill skiing; ***e. de baches*** moguls; ***e. de fondo*** cross-country skiing; ***e. náutico*** water-skiing; ***e. nórdico*** cross-country skiing; ***e. de saltos*** ski jumping; ***e. de travesía*** cross-country skiing

esquiador, -ora *nm,f* skier

esquiar [32] *vi* to ski; **van a e. a los Alpes** they're going skiing in the Alps

esquife *nm* (**a**) *Hist* longboat (**b**) *Dep (en remo)* (single) kayak

esquijama *nm* thick winter pyjamas

esquila[1] *nf* (**a**) *(cencerro)* cowbell (**b**) *(campanilla)* small bell

esquila[2] *nf (acción de esquilar)* shearing

esquilador, -ora *nm,f (persona)* (sheep) shearer

esquiladora *nf (máquina)* (sheep)shearing machine

esquilar *vt* to shear

esquilmar *vt* (**a**) *(terreno, campo de cultivo)* to exhaust, overcultivate; *(recursos, riqueza natural)* to overexploit; *(bancos de pescado)* to deplete (**b**) *(fortuna, herencia)* to squander (**c**) *(persona)* **e. a alguien** to milk *o* bleed sb dry

esquimal 1 *adj* Eskimo
2 *nmf (persona)* Eskimo
3 *nm (lengua)* Eskimo

esquina *nf* (**a**) *(en calle)* corner; *también Fig* **a la vuelta de la e.** (just) round the corner; **el examen/la farmacia está a la vuelta de la e.** the exam/the chemist's is just around the corner; **doblar la e.** to turn the corner; **en la e.** on the corner; **hacer e. (con)** to be on the corner (of); **el banco hace e. con la calle principal** the bank is on the corner of *Br* the high street *o US* main street
(**b**) *(de objeto, habitación, página)* corner; **me di un golpe con la e. de la mesa** I bumped into the corner of the table
(**c**) *(en fútbol)* corner; **saque de e.** corner (kick); **sacar de e.** to take a corner (kick)

esquinado, -a *adj* (**a**) *(en la esquina)* on the corner; **un balcón e.** a corner balcony (**b**) *(de trato difícil)* prickly, awkward

esquinar 1 *vt (poner en esquina)* to put in a corner
2 *vi* to form a corner (**con** with)

esquinazo *nm* (**a**) *(esquina)* corner; EXPR *Esp* **dar (el) e. a alguien: consiguió dar e. a sus perseguidores** he managed to give his pursuers the slip *o* shake off his pursuers; **intenta dar e. a su ex novio** she tries to avoid her ex-boyfriend (**b**) *Chile (serenata)* serenade

esquinera *nf* (**a**) *(mueble)* cornerpiece, corner cupboard (**b**) *Fam (prostituta)* tart, *US* hooker (**c**) *Ven (sábana ajustable)* fitted sheet

esquirla *nf (de loza, hueso, cristal)* splinter

esquirol, -ola *nm,f* scab, *Br* blackleg

esquisto *nm Geol* schist

esquites *nmpl CAm, Méx* = cooked kernels of sweetcorn/maize used in soups

esquivar *vt* (**a**) *(golpe)* to dodge; *(valla, obstáculo)* to clear; **trató de e. al perro para no atropellarlo** he tried to avoid the dog so as not to knock it down (**b**) *(persona, discusión, tema)* to avoid; *(pregunta)* to evade, to dodge; *(compromiso, responsabilidad)* to evade, to get out of; *(problema, inconveniente)* to avoid, to get round

esquivez *nf* shyness

esquivo, -a *adj* uncommunicative, unsociable; **es algo e.** he's not very communicative *o* sociable; **está muy e. con todos nosotros** he's very unsociable towards us all; **estuvo e. con la prensa** he didn't give much away to the press

esquizofrenia *nf* schizophrenia

esquizofrénico, -a 1 *adj* schizophrenic
2 *nm,f* schizophrenic

esquizoide *adj* schizoid

esta *ver* **este**

ésta *ver* **éste**

estabilidad *nf* stability; **continuará la e. atmosférica** the settled weather will continue; **e. económica/emocional** economic/emotional stability; **e. en el empleo** job security ►► ***e. de precios*** price stability

estabilización *nf* stabilization

estabilizador, -ora 1 *adj* stabilizing
2 *nm (de avión, barco)* stabilizer

estabilizante *nm (aditivo)* stabilizer

estabilizar [14] 1 *vt* (**a**) *(vehículo, nave)* to stabilize (**b**) *(precios, economía, relación)* to stabilize
2 **estabilizarse** *vpr* (**a**) *(vehículo, nave)* to stabilize, to become stable (**b**) *(precios, economía, relación)* to stabilize, to become (more) stable; **el índice de la bolsa se ha estabilizado en el 1.100** the share index has stabilized at 1,100

estable *adj* (**a**) *(firme)* stable (**b**) *(permanente, fijo) (situación, relación, empleo)* stable; *(cliente)* regular; **el tiempo permanecerá e.** the weather will remain settled (**c**) *Quím* stable

establecer [46] 1 *vt* (**a**) *(instalar) (colonia, poblado)* to establish; *(campamento, negocio, sucursal)* to set up; **e. residencia en** to take up residence in
(**b**) *(fijar, emprender) (régimen, relaciones, comunicación)* to establish; *(costumbre)* to introduce; *(moda)* to start; *(récord)* to set; **no lograba e. contacto con la torre de control** he couldn't make *o* establish contact with the control tower
(**c**) *(expresar) (principios, criterios)* to establish, to lay down; *(teoría, hipótesis)* to formulate; **estableció las bases de la física moderna** he laid the foundations of modern physics
(**d**) *(estipular)* to state, to stipulate; **las normas del club establecen que...** the club rules state that...; **según establece la ley...** as stipulated by law...
(**e**) *(averiguar)* to establish, to determine; **la policía no ha podido e. la causa de su muerte** the police have been unable to establish *o* determine the cause of death
2 **establecerse** *vpr* (**a**) *(instalarse)* to settle; **se establecieron en Madrid** they settled in Madrid, they set up home in Madrid (**b**) *(poner un negocio)* to set up a business; **voy a establecerme por mi cuenta** I'm going to set up on my own *o* set up my own business

establecido, -a *adj (convencional)* established

establecimiento *nm* (**a**) *(tienda)* establishment ►► ***e. comercial*** commercial establishment (**b**) *(institución, centro)* institution ►► ***e. de enseñanza*** educational institution; ***e. penitenciario*** penal institution (**c**) *(de normas, hechos)* establishment; *(de récord)* setting (**d**) *(de negocio, colonia)* setting up (**e**) *(de emigrantes, colonos)* settlement

establezco *etc ver* **establecer**

establo *nm (para caballos)* stable; *(para vacas)* cowshed; **¡arregla este cuarto, que parece un e.!** tidy this room up, it looks like a pigsty!

estabulación *nf (de ganado)* stabling

estaca *nf* (**a**) *(para clavar, delimitar)* stake; *(de tienda de campaña)* peg; **le clavó una e. en el corazón** she drove a stake through his heart (**b**) *(garrote)* cudgel (**c**) *(de planta)* cutting

estacada *nf* stockade; EXPR **dejar a alguien en la e.** to leave sb in the lurch; EXPR **quedarse en la e.** to be left in the lurch

estacar 1 *vt Andes, CAm, Ven (sujetar)* to fasten down with stakes
2 estacarse *vpr CAm, Carib, Col (clavarse una astilla)* to get a splinter

estacazo *nm (golpe)* blow with a stake

estación *nf* (**a**) *(edificio) (de tren, metro, autobús)* station; **iré a esperarte a la e.** I'll meet you at the station; **te has pasado dos estaciones** you've gone two stations past your stop ►► ***e. de autobuses*** *o* ***autocares*** bus *o* coach station; *Andes, Méx* ***e. de bomberos*** fire station; ***e. climatológica*** weather station, *Spec* climatological station; ***e. emisora*** broadcasting station; ***e. espacial*** space station; ***la E. Espacial Internacional*** the International Space Station; ***e. de esquí*** ski resort; ***e. de ferrocarril*** railway station; ***e. invernal*** ski resort; ***e. de invierno*** ski resort; ***e. de lanzamiento*** launch site; ***e. meteorológica*** weather station; ***e. de metro*** *Br* underground station, *US* subway station; ***e. orbital*** space station; *Andes, CAm, Méx* ***e. de policía*** police station; ***e. de seguimiento*** tracking station; ***e. de servicio*** service station; ***e. de tren*** railway station
(**b**) *(del año, temporada)* season; **las cuatro estaciones** the four seasons; **la e. húmeda/seca** the rainy/dry season
(**c**) *Informát* ***e. de trabajo*** workstation
(**d**) *Rel* **estaciones (de la cruz)** Stations of the Cross
(**e**) *Am (de radio)* (radio) station

estacional *adj (del año, de temporada)* seasonal; **trabajo/empleo e.** seasonal work/employment

estacionamiento *nm* (**a**) *(acción)* parking ►► ***e. en batería*** *(en letrero)* = sign indicating one must park at an angle to the *Br* kerb *o US* curb; ***e. indebido*** illegal parking; ***e. en línea*** *(en letrero)* = sign indicating one must park parallel to the *Br* kerb *o US* curb
(**b**) *Am (para muchos vehículos) Br* car park, *US* parking lot ►► ***e. subterráneo*** underground car park; ***e. vigilado*** attended parking
(**c**) *Am (hueco)* parking place; **tardamos una hora en encontrar e.** it took us an hour to find a parking place *o* somewhere to park
(**d**) *(estabilización)* stabilization

estacionar 1 *vt* to park
2 *vi* to park; **prohibido e.** *(en letrero)* no parking
3 estacionarse *vpr* (**a**) *Am (en vehículo)* to park (**b**) *(estabilizarse)* to stabilize; **el crecimiento del empleo se estacionó en el último trimestre** employment growth stabilized in the last quarter

estacionario, -a *adj* (**a**) *(inmóvil)* stationary (**b**) *(sin cambio) (economía)* stagnant; *(déficit)* constant; *(estado de salud)* stable; *(tiempo)* settled; *(temperaturas)* stable

estacionómetro *nm CRica, Méx* parking meter

estadía, estada *nf Am* (**a**) *(estancia)* stay; **planeó una e. de tres días en Lima** he planned a three-day stop in Lima (**b**) *Com* lay day

estadio *nm* (**a**) *(deportivo)* stadium; **e. olímpico** Olympic stadium (**b**) *(fase)* stage

estadista *nmf* statesman, *f* stateswoman

estadística *nf* (**a**) *(ciencia)* statistics *(singular)* (**b**) *(dato)* statistic

estadísticamente *adv* statistically

estadístico, -a 1 *adj* statistical
2 *nm,f* statistician

estado *nm* (**a**) *(situación, condición)* state; **su e. es grave** his condition is serious; **me lo encontré en un e. penoso** I found him in a pitiful state; **el e. de su cuenta arroja un saldo positivo** your account is in credit; **estar en buen/mal e.** *(vehículo, terreno, edificio)* to be in good/bad condition; *(alimento, bebida)* to be fresh/off; **la moqueta se halla en muy mal e.** the carpet is in very bad condition; **en e. de alerta** on (the) alert; **en e. de guerra** at war; EXPR **estar en e. (de buena esperanza)** to be expecting, to be in the family way; **quedarse en e.** to become pregnant; EXPR **estar en e. de merecer** to be marriageable ►► ***e. de ánimo*** state of mind; ***e. de bienestar*** welfare state; ***e. civil*** marital status; ***e. de coma:*** **en e. de coma** in a coma; ***e. de cuentas*** statement of accounts; ***e. de emergencia*** state of emergency; ***e. de equilibrio*** state of equilibrium; ***e. estacionario*** *(de enfermo)* stable condition; ***e. de excepción*** state of emergency; ***e. de gracia*** *(de santo)* state of grace; **estar en e. de gracia** *(deportista)* to be on excellent form; ***e. de reposo:*** **en e. de reposo** at rest; ***e. de salud*** (state of) health; ***e. de sitio*** state of siege; ***e. vegetativo*** vegetative state; ***e. vegetativo permanente*** persistent vegetative state
(**b**) *Fís* state; **un cuerpo en e. sólido/líquido/gaseoso** a body in a solid/liquid/gaseous state ►► ***e. cristalino*** crystalline state
(**c**) *(gobierno)* state; **temas de e.** affairs of state; **un hombre de e.** a statesman; **el E.** *(el gobierno, la administración)* the State; **asuntos que atañen a la seguridad del E.** matters relating to state security; **el E. de las Autonomías** = the organization of the Spanish state into autonomous regions with varying degrees of devolved power
(**d**) *(país, división territorial)* state; **un e. independiente** an independent state; **un e. de derecho** a state which is subject to the rule of law ►► ***e.-nación*** nation state; ***e. policial*** police state; ***Estados Unidos (de América)*** United States (of America); ***Estados Unidos Mexicanos*** United Mexican States
(**e**) *Mil* ***E. Mayor*** general staff
(**f**) *Hist (estamento)* estate ►► *Hist* ***los Estados Generales*** the Estates General; ***el e. llano*** the third estate, the common people

estadounidense, *Méx* **estadunidense 1** *adj* American; **la política e.** American *o* US politics
2 *nmf* American; **los estadounidenses no necesitan visado** Americans *o* US citizens don't need a visa

estafa *nf* (**a**) *(timo, robo)* swindle; *(a empresa, organización)* fraud; **fue condenado por el delito de e.** he was convicted of fraud; **hicieron una e. a la empresa de varios millones** they swindled several million out of the company, they defrauded the company of several million (**b**) *Fam (precio abusivo)* rip-off

estafador, -ora *nm,f (timador)* swindler; *(de empresa, organización)* fraudster

estafar *vt* (**a**) *(timar, robar)* to swindle; *(a empresa, organización)* to defraud; **estafó millones a la empresa** he defrauded the company of millions (**b**) *Fam (cobrar abusivamente)* to rip off; **¿10.000 por esta camisa? a ti te han estafado** 10,000 for that shirt? you've been ripped off *o* had

estafeta *nf* sub-post office

estajanovismo *nm* Stakhanovism

estajanovista 1 *adj* Stakhanovite
2 *nmf* Stakhanovite

estafilococo *nm* staphylococcus

estalactita *nf* stalactite

estalagmita *nf* stalagmite

estalinismo *nm* Stalinism

estalinista 1 *adj* Stalinist
2 *nmf* Stalinist

estallar *vi* (**a**) *(reventar) (bomba)* to explode, to go off; *(misil)* to explode; *(petardo)* to go off; *(neumático, globo)* to burst; *(volcán)* to erupt; *(cristal)* to shatter; *(olas)* to break, to crash; *(botón)* to fly off; *(cremallera, costura)* to burst; *(vestido, falda, pantalón)* to split; **hacer e. un artefacto explosivo** to detonate an explosive device; **si sigo comiendo voy a e.** if I eat any more I'll burst
(**b**) *(sonar) (ovación)* to break out; *(látigo)* to crack; *(trueno)* to crash
(**c**) *(desencadenarse) (guerra, revolución, disturbios, epidemia)* to break out; *(tormenta)* to break; **ha estallado un nuevo escándalo de corrupción** a new corruption scandal has erupted
(**d**) *(expresarse bruscamente)* to blow up, to blow one's top; **se metieron tanto conmigo que al final estallé** they went on at me so much I eventually blew up *o* blew my top; **e. en aplausos** to burst into applause; **e. en una carcajada** to burst out laughing; **e. en llanto** *o* **sollozos** to burst into tears; **¡voy a e. de nervios!** I'm so nervous!

estallido *nm* (**a**) *(de bomba, misil, petardo)* explosion; *(de olas)* breaking, crashing; *(de trueno)* crash; *(de látigo)* crack; **se oyó el e. de un neumático/globo** we heard a tyre/balloon burst; **el motor pegó un e.** the engine went bang; **hubo un e. de aplausos** there was a burst of applause
(**b**) *(de guerra, revolución, disturbios, epidemia)* outbreak; **el e. de la tormenta se produjo a las cinco** the storm broke at five o'clock; **el e. del escándalo provocó su dimisión** he resigned when the scandal broke

estambre *nm* (**a**) *(de planta)* stamen (**b**) *(tejido)* worsted; *(hilo)* worsted yarn

Estambul *n* Istanbul

estamental *adj (relaciones, privilegios)* class; **una sociedad e.** a stratified society

estamento *nm* (**a**) *(clase social)* stratum, class; **los estamentos sociales** the strata *o* classes of society; **el e. eclesiástico** the clergy (**b**) *(sector)* **el e. intelectual** the intelligentsia; **el e. arbitral** the referees; **el presidente pidió calma a todos los estamentos del club** the president called for calm from everyone connected with the club

estameña *nf* worsted

estampa *nf* (**a**) *(ilustración)* illustration, picture; *(tarjeta)* print; **estampas de santos** pictures *o* images of saints
(**b**) *(aspecto)* appearance; **un pura sangre con una bella e.** a magnificent thoroughbred; **un caballero de fina e.** a fine-looking gentleman
(**c**) *(reflejo, ejemplo)* image; **su rostro era la viva e.** *o* **la e. misma del dolor** her face was a picture of misery; **¡es la viva e. de su madre!** he's the (spitting) image of his mother!; **¡maldita sea su e.!** damn *o* curse him!

> **Falso amigo**: El sustantivo inglés **stamp** no es la traducción del español **estampa**. En inglés el sentido básico de **stamp** es "sello".

estampación *nf (en tela, papel)* printing; *(en metal)* stamping

estampado, -a 1 *adj* printed
2 *nm* (**a**) *(acción) (en tela, papel)* printing; *(en metal)* stamping (**b**) *(dibujo)* pattern; **e. de flores/en azul** floral/blue pattern (**c**) *(tela)* (cotton) print; **e. de flores/en azul** floral/blue print

estampador, -ora *nm,f Informát* ***e. de CD-ROM*** CD-ROM writer

estampar *vt* **1** (**a**) *(imprimir) (en tela, papel)* to print; *(metal)* to stamp
(**b**) *(escribir)* **e. la firma** to sign one's name
(**c**) *(dejar huella de)* to leave a mark of; **e. el pie en la arena** to make a mark in the sand with one's foot
(**d**) *(arrojar)* **e. algo/a alguien contra** to fling sth/sb against, to hurl sth/sb against; **lo estampó contra la puerta de un puñetazo** he punched him, flinging *o* hurling him against the door
(**e**) *(dar) (beso)* to plant; *(bofetada)* to land
2 estamparse *vpr (lanzarse, golpearse)* **se estampó contra el muro** he crashed into the wall

estampida *nf* stampede; **de e.** suddenly, in a rush; **la gente salió de e.** people stampeded *o* rushed out

estampido *nm (de bomba)* bang; *(de pistola)* bang, report; *(de cañón)* boom ►► *Av* ***e. sónico*** sonic boom

estampilla *nf* (**a**) *(para marcar)* rubber stamp (**b**) *Am (de correos)* stamp

estampillado *nm Am* stamps; **sólo el e. costó veinte pesos** it cost twenty pesos just for the stamps

estampilladora *nf Am* franking machine

estampillar *vt (sellar)* to stamp; *(documentos)* to rubber-stamp

estancado, -a *adj* (**a**) *(agua)* stagnant (**b**) *(economía)* stagnant; *(situación)* at an impasse, in (a) deadlock; *(negociación)* in (a) deadlock, at a standstill; *(proyecto)* at a standstill (**c**) *(persona)* **me he quedado e. y no sé cómo seguir** I'm stuck and I don't know how to go on; **en este trabajo estoy e.** I'm in a rut in this job

estancamiento *nm* (**a**) *(de agua)* stagnation (**b**) *(de economía)* stagnation; *(de negociaciones)* deadlock; **temen el e. del proyecto** they're afraid the project will come to a standstill

estancar [60] **1** *vt* (**a**) *(aguas)* to dam up, to stem (**b**) *(progreso, negocio)* to bring to a standstill; *(negociación)* to deadlock (**c**) *Com* to monopolize, to convert into a monopoly
2 estancarse *vpr* (**a**) *(aguas)* to stagnate, to become stagnant (**b**) *(economía)* to stagnate; *(progreso, negocio, proyecto)* to come to a standstill; *(negociaciones)* to reach deadlock, to come to a standstill (**c**) *(persona)* to get stuck; **con ese problema nos estancamos** we've got stuck *o* we're not getting anywhere with this problem (**d**) *Com* to be converted into a monopoly

estancia *nf* (**a**) *Esp, Méx (tiempo)* stay; **durante su e. en Marruecos** during her stay in Morocco; **no quiso prolongar más su e.** he didn't want to prolong his stay any further (**b**) *Formal (habitación)* room (**c**) *CSur (hacienda)* cattle ranch

estanciera *nf RP Br* estate car, *US* station wagon

estanciero, -a *nm,f CSur* ranch owner, rancher

estanco, -a 1 *adj* watertight; **compartimento e.** watertight compartment
2 *nm* (**a**) *Esp (de tabaco)* tobacconist's *(also selling stamps)* (**b**) *Andes (de licores) Br* off-licence, *US* liquor store

estándar (*pl* **estándares**) **1** *adj* standard
2 *nm* standard ►► ***e. de vida*** standard of living

estandarización *nf* standardization

estandarizado, -a *adj (normalizado)* standardized

estandarizar [14] *vt* to standardize

estandarte *nm* (**a**) *(insignia, bandera)* standard, banner (**b**) *(símbolo)* standard bearer; **él fue el e. del movimiento estudiantil en los sesenta** he was the standard bearer of the student movement in the sixties

estanflación *nf Econ* stagflation

estanque *nm* (**a**) *(en parque, jardín)* pond; *(para riego)* reservoir (**b**) *Chile (depósito)* tank *(of petrol)*

estanquero, -a *nm,f* tobacconist

estanquillo *nm Méx* corner shop

estante *nm* (**a**) *(tabla)* shelf (**b**) *CAm (estaca)* post, pillar

estantería *nf (en general)* shelves, shelving; *(para libros)* bookcase

estañar *vt (cubrir con estaño)* to tin-plate; *(soldar con estaño)* to solder

estaño *nm Quím* tin

estaquear *vt RP* to stretch with stakes

estaquilla *nf (espiga)* wooden peg

ESTAR[1] [30] **1** *vi* (**a**) *(hallarse)* to be; **¿dónde está la llave?** where is the key?; **¿está María? – no, no está** is Maria there? – no, she's not here
(**b**) *(con fechas)* **¿a qué estamos hoy?** what's the date today?; **hoy estamos a martes/a 15 de julio** today is Tuesday/15 July; **estábamos en octubre** it was October; **estamos en invierno** it's winter
(**c**) *(quedarse)* to stay, to be; **estaré un par de horas y me iré** I'll stay a couple of hours and then I'll go; **¿cuánto tiempo piensas e.?** how long do you plan on staying?; **estuvimos una semana en su casa** we stayed with her for a week, we spent a week at her place
(**d**) *(antes de "a") (expresa valores, grados)* **estamos a 20 grados** it's 20 degrees here; **el dólar está a 10 pesos** the dollar is at 10 pesos; **están a dos euros el kilo** they're two euros a kilo
(**e**) *(hallarse listo)* to be ready; **¿aún no está ese trabajo?** is that piece of work still not ready?; **¿ya estás? pues, vámonos** are you ready? let's go then
(**f**) *(servir)* **e. para** to be (there) for; **para eso están los amigos** that's what friends are for; **para eso estoy** that's what I'm here for; **la vida está para vivirla** life is for living; **no tires eso al suelo, que las papeleras están para algo** don't throw that on the floor, the wastepaper bins are there for a reason
(**g**) *(antes de gerundio) (expresa duración)* to be; **están golpeando la puerta** they're banging on the door
(**h**) *(antes de "sin" + infinitivo) (expresa negación)* **estoy sin dormir desde ayer** I haven't slept since yesterday; **está sin acabar** it's not finished; **estuve sin voz dos días** I had no voice *o* I lost my voice for two days
(**i**) *(faltar)* **eso está aún por escribir** that has yet to be written; **eso está por ver** that remains to be seen; **todavía está por hacer** it hasn't been done yet
(**j**) *(consistir)* **e. en** to be, to lie in; **el problema está en la fecha** the problem is the date; **el truco está en no mirar nunca al suelo** the trick *o* secret is not to look at the ground
(**k**) *(hallarse a punto de)* **e. al llegar** *o* **caer** *(persona)* to be about to arrive; *(acontecimiento)* to be about to happen; **e. por hacer algo** to be on the verge of doing sth; **estuve por pegarle** I was on the verge of hitting him; **estoy por no ir** I'm not so sure I want to go; **estuve por llamarte** I was about to phone you, I was just going to phone you
(**l**) *(expresa disposición)* **e. para algo** to be in the mood for sth; **no estoy para bromas** I'm not in the mood for jokes; **el enfermo no está para ver a nadie** the patient is in no condition to see anyone
(**m**) *(ser favorable)* **e. por** to be in favour of; **estoy por la libertad de expresión** I'm in favour of *o* for freedom of speech
(**n**) *(hallarse embarazada)* **está de cinco meses** she's five months pregnant
(**o**) *RP (ir)* **estuve a verlo en el hospital** I went to see him in hospital; **estuvieron a visitarlo** they went to visit him
2 *v copulativo* (**a**) *(antes de adj) (expresa cualidad, estado)* to be; **los pasteles están ricos** the cakes are delicious; **esta calle está sucia** this street is dirty; **¡qué alta estás!** you've really grown!; **estoy cansado/enfadado** I'm tired/angry; **¿qué tal estás?** how are you?; **está muy irritable últimamente** she's been very irritable lately; **está divorciado** he's divorced; **estoy enfermo/mareado** I am ill/I feel sick; *Andes* **cuando estaba chiquito** when I was little
(**b**) *(antes de "con" o "sin" + sustantivo) (expresa estado)* to be; **estamos sin agua** we have no water, we're without water; *Fam* **estoy sin blanca** I'm broke, *Br* I'm skint
(**c**) *(expresa situación, acción)* **e. de vacaciones** to be on holiday; **e. de viaje** to be on a trip; **e. de mudanza** to be (in the process of) moving; **estamos de suerte** we're in luck; **e. de mal humor** to be in a (bad) mood; **¿has cambiado la rueda? – estoy en ello** have you changed the tyre? – I'm working on it *o* I'm doing it right now; **¡ya está bien!** that's enough (of that)!
(**d**) *(expresa permanencia)* **e. en uso** to be in use; **e. en guardia** to be on guard
(**e**) *(expresa apoyo, predilección)* **estoy contigo** I'm on your side

(f) *(expresa ocupación)* **e. como** *o* **de** to be; **está como** *o* **de cajera** she's a checkout girl; **yo he estado de portero toda la primera parte** I've been in goal all of the first half

(g) *Esp (ropa)* **este traje te está bien** this suit looks good on you; **esa falda te está corta** that skirt's too short for you; **¿cómo me está?** how does this look?

(h) *(antes de "que" + verbo) (expresa actitud)* **está que muerde porque ha suspendido** he's furious because he failed

3 *v aux* **(a)** *(antes de gerundio)* to be; **estuvo nevando** it was snowing; **se está peinando** she's brushing her hair; **estuvieron discutiendo durante toda la reunión** they spent the whole meeting arguing, they were arguing throughout the whole meeting; **mañana a estas horas estaré bañándome en la playa** this time tomorrow I'll be swimming at the beach

(b) *(antes de participio)* **está terminado** it's finished; **está organizado por el ayuntamiento** it's organized by the town council

4 estarse *vpr* **(a)** *(permanecer)* to stay; **te puedes e. con nosotros unos días** you can stay *o* spend a few days with us; **¡estáte quieto!** keep still!; **estáte ahí, ahora mismo vengo** stay *o* wait there, I'll be right with you **(b)** *RP (ir)* to be; **estáte en el cine a las seis** be at the cinema at six

---

estar[2] *nm Am* living room

estarcido *nm Tec* stencil printing

estarcir *vt Tec* to stencil

estárter *(pl* **estárters**) *nm* choke; **abrir/cerrar el e.** to pull the choke out/push the choke in

estasis *nf inv Med* stasis

estatal *adj* **(a)** *(público)* state; **una escuela e.** a state school; **una empresa e.** a state-owned company; **la política e.** government policy **(b)** *(del estado)* state; **una universidad e.** a state university

estatalizar [14] *vt* to nationalize

estática *nf Fís* statics *(singular)*

estático, -a *adj* **(a)** *(inmóvil)* stock-still; **se quedó e.** he stood stock-still; **los centrocampistas están demasiado estáticos** the mid-fielders are not moving around enough **(b)** *Fís* static

estatificar [60] *vt* to nationalize

estatismo[1] *nm (inmovilidad)* stillness

estatismo[2] *nm Pol* statism, state interventionism

estatización *nf Am* nationalization

estatizar 1 *vt* to nationalize

2 *vi* to become nationalized

estatua *nf* statue; **¿qué hace Pedro ahí parado como una e.?** what's Pedro doing just standing there?

estatuaria *nf* statuary, sculptures

estatuario, -a *adj* statuary

estatuilla *nf* statuette

estatuir [34] *vt* **(a)** *(establecer)* to establish; **según queda estatuido en la ley...** as established *o* stipulated by law... **(b)** *(demostrar)* to demonstrate, to prove; **e. una teoría** to demonstrate a theory

estatura *nf* **(a)** *(altura)* height, stature; **tiene** *o* **mide 1,80 de e.** he's 1.8 m tall; **de baja e.** short; **de mediana e.** of medium *o* average height **(b)** *(categoría)* stature; **un personaje de gran e. moral** a person of great moral stature

estatus *nm inv* status

estatutario, -a *adj* statutory

estatuto *nm (de asociación, organismo)* constitution, statutes; *(de club)* constitution, rules; *(de empresa)* articles of association ►► ***e. de autonomía*** statute of autonomy, = legislation devolving powers to an autonomous Spanish region; ***e. de los trabajadores*** labour code, = Spanish law governing labour relations and workers' rights

estatuyo *etc ver* **estatuir**

estay *(pl* **estayes**) *nm Náut* stay ►► ***e. mayor*** mainstay; ***e. de proa*** forestay

este[1] **1** *adj inv (posición, parte)* east, eastern; *(dirección)* easterly; *(viento)* east, easterly; **la cara e. del pico** the east face of the mountain; **la costa e.** the east coast; **tiempo soleado en la mitad e. del país** sunny weather in the eastern half of the country; **partieron con rumbo e.** they set off in an easterly direction; **un frente frío que se desplaza en dirección e.** a cold front moving eastwards

2 *nm* **(a)** *(zona)* east; **está al e. de Madrid** it's (to the) east of Madrid; **la fachada da al e.** the front of the building faces east; **viento del e.** east *o* easterly wind; **habrá lluvias en el e. (del país)** there will be rain in the east (of the country); **ir hacia el e.** to go east(wards)

(b) *(punto cardinal)* east; **el sol sale por el E.** the sun rises in the east

(c) *(bloque geopolítico)* **el E.** the East; **los países del E.** the countries of Eastern Europe

(d) *(viento)* easterly, east wind

ESTE[2]**, -A** *(pl* **estos, -as**) *adj demostrativo* **(a)** *(en general)* this; *(plural)* these; **esta camisa** this shirt; **e. año** this year; **esta mañana** this morning; **esta noche** tonight

(b) *Fam Pey (singular)* that; *(plural)* those; **no soporto a la niña esta** I can't stand that girl; **el teléfono e. no funciona** this telephone's not working

(c) *Méx, RP (como muletilla)* well, er, um; **y entonces, e., le propuse...** and then, um, I suggested...; **es un, e., cómo se dice, un lexicógrafo** he's a, oh, what do you call it, a lexicographer; **e., ¿me prestás plata?** er, can you lend me some money?

ÉSTE, -A *(pl* **éstos, -as**) *pron demostrativo*

> Note that **éste** and its various forms can be written without an accent when there is no risk of confusion with the adjective.

(a) *(en general)* this one; *(plural)* these (ones); **dame otro boli, e. no funciona** give me another pen, this one doesn't work; **aquellos cuadros no están mal, aunque éstos me gustan más** those paintings aren't bad, but I like these (ones) better; **ésta ha sido la semana más feliz de mi vida** this has been the happiest week of my life; **cualquier día de éstos** one of these days; **en éstas** just then; **en éstas sonó el teléfono** just then *o* at that very moment, the phone rang; **en una de éstas** one of these days; **en una de éstas te pillará la policía** one of these days the police will catch you; EXPR *Fam* **ésta es la mía/tuya/***etc.* this is the chance I've/you've/*etc* been waiting for, this is my/your/*etc* big chance; EXPR *Fam* **por éstas** *(lo juro)* I swear, honest to God; **¿seguro que no me estás mintiendo? – ¡por éstas!** are you sure you're not lying to me? – I swear *o* honest to God

(b) *(recién mencionado)* the latter; **entraron Juan y Pedro, e. con un abrigo verde** Juan and Pedro came in, the latter wearing a green coat

(c) *Fam (despectivo)* **e. es el que me pegó** this is the one who hit me; **éstos son los culpables de todo lo ocurrido** it's this lot who are to blame for everything

(d) *Formal (en correspondencia)* **espero que al recibo de ésta te encuentres bien** I hope this letter finds you well

---

esteatita *nf Geol* steatite, soapstone

estegosaurio *nm* stegosaurus

estela[1] *nf* **(a)** *(de barco)* wake; *(de avión, cohete)* vapour trail; *(de humo, olor, estrella fugaz)* trail; **por donde pasaba iba dejando una e. de perfume** she left a trail of perfume in her wake wherever she went **(b)** *(impresión)* **su visita dejó una e. imborrable** his visit left an indelible impression

estela[2] *nf Arquit* stele

estelar *adj* **(a)** *Astron* stellar **(b)** *Cine & Teatro* star; **una figura e.** a star; **un reparto e.** a star-studded cast; **con la actuación** *o* **participación e. de...** guest starring...

estelaridad *nf Andes, CAm, Carib, Méx* stardom

estelarizar *vt Méx* to star in

estenografía *nf* shorthand

estenógrafo, -a *nm,f* stenographer, shorthand writer

estenordeste, estenoreste *nm* east-north-east

estenotipia *nf* **(a)** *(arte)* stenotypy **(b)** *(máquina)* Stenotype®

estenotipista *nmf* stenotypist

estenotipo *nm* Stenotype®

estentóreo, -a *adj Formal* stentorian

estepa *nf* steppe

estepario, -a *adj* steppe; **clima e.** steppe climate

éster *nm Quím* ester

estera *nf* **(a)** *(tejido)* matting **(b)** *(alfombrilla)* mat; EXPR *Fam* **recibió** *o* **se llevó más (palos) que una e.** he was beaten black and blue

esterar *vt* to cover with mats

estercolar *vt (terreno)* to manure, to fertilize (with manure)

estercolero *nm* **(a)** *(para estiércol)* dunghill, dungheap **(b)** *(lugar sucio)* pigsty

estéreo 1 *adj inv* stereo

2 *nm* **(a)** *(estereofonía)* stereo; **una grabación/emisión en e.** a stereo recording/broadcast **(b)** *(equipo)* stereo

estereofonía *nf* stereo

estereofónico, -a *adj* stereophonic, stereo; **sonido e.** stereo sound

estereografía *nf* stereography

estereoscopia *nf* stereoscopy

estereoscopio, estereóscopo *nm* stereoscope

estereotipado, -a *adj* stereotyped, stereotypical; **una imagen estereotipada de México** a stereotyped image of Mexico; **personajes de ficción estereotipados** stereotypical *o* clichéd fictional characters

estereotipar *vt* (**a**) *(convertir en cliché)* to stereotype (**b**) *Imprenta* to stereotype

estereotipia *nf* (**a**) *(procedimiento)* stereotypy (**b**) *(máquina)* stereotype (**c**) *Med (comportamiento estereotipado)* stereotypy

estereotípico, -a *adj* stereotypical, stereotypic

estereotipo *nm* (**a**) *(idea, modelo)* stereotype (**b**) *Imprenta* stereotype

estéril *adj* (**a**) *(hombre, animal)* sterile, infertile; *(mujer)* infertile, barren, sterile; *(terreno)* barren, infertile; *(pensamiento, imaginación)* sterile (**b**) *(gasa, instrumental)* sterilized, sterile (**c**) *(inútil)* futile, fruitless

esterilete *nm* coil, IUD

esterilidad *nf* (**a**) *(de mujer, hombre, animal)* infertility, sterility; *(de terreno)* barrenness, infertility; *(de pensamiento, imaginación)* sterility (**b**) *(de gasa, instrumental)* sterility (**c**) *(inutilidad)* futility

esterilización *nf* (**a**) *(de persona, animal)* sterilization (**b**) *(de instrumental, biberón)* sterilization

esterilizado, -a *adj* (**a**) *(persona, animal)* sterilized (**b**) *(instrumental, biberón)* sterilized, sterile

esterilizador, -ora 1 *adj* sterilizing
2 *nm (aparato)* sterilizer

esterilizar [14] *vt* (**a**) *(persona, animal)* to sterilize (**b**) *(instrumental, biberón)* to sterilize

esterilla *nf* (**a**) *(para la playa)* beach mat; *(en casa)* mat (**b**) *Am (rejilla)* canework

estérilmente *adv* sterilely

esterlina *adj* **libra e.** pound sterling

esternocleidomastoideo *nm Anat* sternocleidomastoid (muscle)

esternón *nm* breastbone, sternum

estero *nm* (**a**) *Geog (zona costera) US* tideland, = land between high and low tide levels (**b**) *Am (pantano)* marsh, swamp (**c**) *Ven (charca)* puddle, pool (**d**) *Chile (arroyo)* stream

esteroide *nm* steroid ►► ***e. anabolizante*** anabolic steroid

estertor *nm* death rattle; **estar en los últimos estertores** to be in one's death throes

estesudeste, estesureste *nm* east-south-east

esteta *nmf* aesthete

estética *nf* (**a**) *Filosofía* aesthetics *(singular)* (**b**) *(belleza)* beauty (**c**) *(estilo)* style; **la e. de los años setenta** the style of the seventies

estéticamente *adv* aesthetically

esteticién *nmf* beautician

esteticismo *nm* aestheticism

esteticista *nmf* beautician

estético, -a *adj* aesthetic; **ese edificio resulta poco e. en el casco viejo** that building is something of an eyesore in the old part of town; **cirugía estética** cosmetic surgery

estetoscopio *nm* stethoscope

estevado, -a *adj* bow-legged, bandy-legged

esthéticienne [esteti'θjen] *nf* beautician

estiaje *nm* (**a**) *(nivel de río)* low water (**b**) *(periodo)* period of low water

estiba *nf Náut* stowage

estibador, -ora *nm,f* stevedore

estibar *vt* to stow

estiércol *nm (excrementos)* dung; *(abono)* manure

estigma *nm* (**a**) *(marca)* mark, scar (**b**) *Rel* **estigmas** stigmata (**c**) *(deshonra)* stigma (**d**) *Bot* stigma

estigmatización *nf* (**a**) *(marca)* branding (**b**) *(deshonra)* stigmatization

estigmatizar [14] *vt* (**a**) *(marcar)* to scar; *(con hierro candente)* to brand (**b**) *(deshonrar)* to stigmatize

estilarse *vpr Fam* to be in (fashion); **ahora se estilan las mujeres delgadas** it's the in thing now for women to be thin; **ya no se estila la minifalda** the miniskirt has gone out of fashion; **aún se estila ir a tomar el aperitivo antes de comer** it's still the custom to go and have an aperitif before eating

estilete *nm* (**a**) *(daga)* stiletto (**b**) *(punzón)* stylus, style (**c**) *Med* stylet

estilismo *nm* styling

estilista *nmf* (**a**) *(escritor)* stylist (**b**) *(de moda, accesorios)* stylist (**c**) *(peluquero)* (hair)stylist

estilística *nf Ling* stylistics *(singular)*

estilísticamente *adv* stylistically

estilístico, -a *adj* stylistic

estilización *nf* stylization

estilizado, -a *adj (figura, cuerpo)* slim and elegant

estilizar [14] **1** *vt* (**a**) *(hacer delgado)* **ese abrigo lo estilizaba** that coat made him look slim (**b**) *(hacer convencional)* to stylize
2 estilizarse *vpr (adelgazar)* to get slimmer

estilo *nm* (**a**) *(artístico, literario)* style; **esta iglesia es de e. gótico** this church was built in the Gothic style; **al e. de** in the style of; **al e. de Mozart** in the style of Mozart ►► ***e. imperio*** Empire style
(**b**) *(manera, carácter)* style; **cada uno tiene un e. de hacer las cosas** we all have our own way of doing things; **este vestido no es de su e.** that dress isn't her style; **mentiría, pero no es mi e.** I would tell a lie, but that's not my style *o* that's not me; **el e. de juego brasileño** the Brazilian style of play; **un e. de hablar pausado** a slow and deliberate way of speaking; **un peinado e. años veinte** a twenties-style hairdo; **al e. de: se visten al e. de los años sesenta** they wear sixties-style clothes; **al e. de lo que se hacía antes en los pueblos** in the way things used to be done in villages; EXPR **por el e.: dijo algo por el e.** she said something of the sort; **se apellida Garcés o algo por el e.** his surname's Garcés or something like that; **nos llevará tres horas o algo por el e.** it'll take us something like three hours; **ser por el e.** to be similar; **todos los bares son por el e.** all the bars are similar *o* like that ►► ***e. de vida*** lifestyle
(**c**) *(clase, elegancia)* style; **esa chica tiene mucho e.** that girl has a lot of style
(**d**) *(en natación)* stroke; **estilos** medley; **los 400 metros estilos** the 400 metres medley ►► ***e. libre*** freestyle
(**e**) *Gram* ***e. directo*** direct speech; ***e. indirecto*** indirect speech
(**f**) *Bot* style
(**g**) *(punzón)* stylus, style
(**h**) *(de reloj de sol)* gnomon

estilográfica *nf* fountain pen

estima *nf* (**a**) *(aprecio)* esteem, respect; **se ganó la e. del público** he earned the public's respect; **tiene una gran e. por su padre** he has great respect for his father; **no te tienen mucha e. por aquí** people don't have a very high opinion of you round here; **tener a alguien en gran** *o* **alta e.** to hold sb in high esteem; **en su trabajo lo tienen en gran e.** he is highly respected at his work
(**b**) *Náut* dead reckoning

estimable *adj* (**a**) *(cantidad, número)* considerable (**b**) *(digno de estimación)* worthy of appreciation (**c**) *(valorable)* **daños estimables en millones de dólares** damage that could run to millions of dollars

estimación *nf* (**a**) *(aprecio)* esteem, respect (**b**) *(valoración)* valuation; *(cálculo aproximado)* estimate; **hacer e. (de algo)** to estimate (sth) (**c**) *(en impuestos)* assessment

estimado, -a *adj* (**a**) *(querido)* esteemed, respected; **e. Señor** *(en carta)* Dear Sir (**b**) *(aproximado)* estimated

estimador, -ora *nm,f (en obra)* quantity surveyor

estimar 1 *vt* (**a**) *(apreciar) (persona)* to think highly of, to respect; *(cosa)* to value; **estima mucho a sus amigos** he values his friends highly; **te estimo mucho, pero esto no te lo puedo permitir** I have great respect for you, but I can't allow you to do this; **estimamos enormemente su colaboración** we value her help enormously, her help means a great deal to us; **estima su vida en bien poco** he has little regard for his own life; **un fruto muy estimado en la cocina oriental** a fruit that is highly prized in oriental cooking
(**b**) *(evaluar)* to value; **e. el valor de algo** to estimate the value of sth; **han estimado que las pérdidas superan los cien millones** the losses are estimated to be over a hundred million
(**c**) *Formal (creer)* to consider, to deem; **no estimó necesario realizar declaraciones** she didn't consider *o* deem it necessary to make any statement
2 estimarse *vpr (tener dignidad)* to have self-respect

estimativo, -a *adj (cálculo, cantidad)* approximate, rough; **un juicio e. (sobre** *o* **de)** an evaluation (of)

estimulación *nf* stimulation

estimulador, -ora *adj* encouraging

estimulante 1 *adj* (**a**) *(que anima)* encouraging (**b**) *(que excita)* stimulating
2 *nm* stimulant

estimular *vt* (**a**) *(animar)* to encourage; **el orgullo le estimula a seguir** his pride spurs him to go on (**b**) *(incitar)* to encourage, to urge on; **la muchedumbre lo estimuló con gritos** the crowd shouted him on (**c**) *(excitar sexualmente)* to stimulate (**d**) *(activar) (apetito)* to stimulate, to whet; *(circulación, economía)* to stimulate; *(ventas, inversión)* to stimulate, to encourage

estímulo *nm* (**a**) *(aliciente)* incentive; *(ánimo)* encouragement; **servir de e.** to act *o* serve as an incentive; **medidas de e. a la creación de empleo** measures to encourage job creation (**b**) *Fisiol* stimulus

estío *nm Literario* summer

estipendio *nm* remuneration

estíptico, -a *adj* (**a**) *(astringente)* styptic (**b**) *(estreñido)* constipated

estiptiquez *nf Am* constipation

estípula *nf Bot* stipule

estipulación *nf* (**a**) *(acuerdo)* agreement (**b**) *Der* stipulation

estipular *vt* to stipulate; **según lo estipulado en** *o* **por el artículo doce...** as stipulated in article twelve...

estirada *nf (en fútbol)* flying save

estirado, -a 1 *adj* (**a**) *(persona) (altanero)* haughty; *(adusto)* uptight (**b**) *(brazos, piernas)* outstretched (**c**) *(jersey)* baggy, shapeless
 2 *nm* stretching

estiramiento *nm* (**a**) *(de músculos)* stretching; **hacer estiramientos** *o* **ejercicios de e.** to do stretching exercises (**b**) *(de piel)* **e. (facial)** face-lift; **se ha hecho un e.** she's had a face-lift

estirar 1 *vt* (**a**) *(alargar, tensar)* to stretch; **hay que e. más la soga** the rope needs to be pulled tighter; **estire bien los brazos** really stretch your arms (out); **e. el cuello** to crane one's neck; **estira un poco el cuello, a ver si ves algo** crane your neck a bit and see if you can see anything; **e. las piernas** to stretch one's legs; *Méx* **estira y afloja** hard bargaining; EXPR *Hum* **e. la pata** to kick the bucket
 (**b**) *(desarrugar, alisar)* to straighten; **estira bien las sábanas** straighten the sheets properly, pull the sheets straight; **deja el vestido estirado sobre la cama** lay the dress out on the bed
 (**c**) *(dinero)* to make last; *(medios, recursos)* to make go further, to eke out; *(discurso, tema)* to spin out; **he de e. el sueldo para llegar a fin de mes** it's an effort to make my salary last till the end of the month
 2 *vi* (**a**) *(tirar)* **e. (de)** to pull (**b**) *(agrandarse)* **el jersey ha estirado al lavarlo** the jersey has gone baggy in the wash (**c**) *(crecer)* **el niño ha vuelto a e.** the boy has shot up again
 3 estirarse *vpr* (**a**) *(para desperezarse, para alcanzar)* to stretch; *(para ver)* to crane
 (**b**) *(tumbarse)* to stretch out
 (**c**) *(crecer)* to shoot up; **tu hijo se ha estirado mucho en el último año** your son has shot up over the past year
 (**d**) *(agrandarse)* **el jersey se ha estirado al lavarlo** the jersey has gone baggy in the wash
 (**e**) *Fam (ser generoso)* to splash out; **se estiró y nos invitó a cenar** he splashed out and treated us to dinner; **¡estírate un poco, hombre!** go on, splash out, why don't you! *o Br* push the boat out!

estirón *nm* (**a**) *(acción)* tug, pull (**b**) *(al crecer)* **dar** *o* **pegar un e.** to shoot up suddenly

estirpe *nf* stock, lineage

estivación *nf (adaptación al calor)* aestivation

estival *adj* summer; **la época e.** the summer period; **vacaciones estivales** summer *Br* holidays *o US* vacation

ESTO 1 *pron demostrativo* (**a**) *(en general) (neutro)* this thing; **e. es tu regalo de cumpleaños** this is your birthday present; **e. es lo que me dijo** this is what she said to me; **e. que acabas de decir no tiene sentido** what you've just said doesn't make sense; **e. de aquí es una probeta** this thing here is a test tube; **¿cuánto dura e. de la campaña electoral?** how long does this election campaign last?; **e. de trabajar de noche no me gusta** I don't like this business of working at night; **¿para e. me has hecho venir?** you got me to come here for THIS?; **por e. lo hice** that's why I did it
 (**b**) *Esp (como muletilla)* well, er, um; **y entonces, e., le dije...** and then, um, I told her...; **es un, e., cómo se llama, un taxidermista** he's a, oh, what do you call it, a taxidermist
 2 a todo esto *loc adv (por cierto)* by the way; **a todo e., ¿a qué hora sale el tren?** by the way, what time does the train leave?
 3 en esto *loc adv (entonces)* just then; **en e. se fue la luz** just then *o* at that very moment, the lights went out; **en e. que entró mi padre** just then *o* at that very moment my father came in
 4 esto es *loc adv (es decir)* that is (to say); **empezará el próximo mes, e. es, en marzo** it will begin next month, that is (to say) in March

estocada *nf* (**a**) *(en esgrima)* stab (**b**) *Taurom* (sword) thrust

Estocolmo *n* Stockholm

estofa *nf Pey* **de baja e.** lower-class; **son gente de baja e.** they're from the lower orders

estofado *nm* stew

estofar *vt* to stew

estoicamente *adv* stoically

estoicismo *nm* (**a**) *Filosofía* Stoicism (**b**) *(entereza)* stoicism

estoico, -a 1 *adj* (**a**) *Filosofía* Stoic (**b**) *(austero)* stoic, stoical
 2 *nm* (**a**) *Filosofía* Stoic (**b**) *(austero)* stoic

estola *nf* (**a**) *(de mujer)* stole (**b**) *(de sacerdote)* stole

estólido, -a *adj Formal* slow-witted

estolón *nm Bot* runner, *Espec* stolon

estoma *nm Bot* stoma

estomacal 1 *adj (del estómago)* stomach; *(bebida)* digestive; **afección e.** stomach complaint
 2 *nm (bebida)* digestive

estomagante *adj Fam* repellent, *Br* sick-making

estomagar [38] *vt Fam* **me estomaga** it makes me want to puke *o* hurl

estómago *nm* stomach; **¿te duele el e.?** have you got a stomach-ache *o* a sore stomach?; **me revuelve el e. ver imágenes de guerra** it turns my stomach to see pictures of war; **con el e. vacío** on an empty stomach; EXPR **tener (buen** *o* **mucho) e.** to be tough, to be able to stand a lot; **hay que tener e. para salir con un tipo así** you have to be hard *o* able to put up with a lot to go out with a guy like that

estomatitis *nf inv Med* stomatitis

estomatología *nf* stomatology

estomatólogo, -a *nm,f* stomatologist

Estonia *n* Estonia

estonio, -a 1 *adj* Estonian
 2 *nm,f (persona)* Estonian
 3 *nm (lengua)* Estonian

estopa *nf (fibra)* tow; *(tela)* burlap; EXPR *Fam* **dar e. a alguien** to give sb a thrashing, to lay into sb; EXPR *Fam* **repartir e.** to lay about oneself

estoperol *nm Col (tachuela)* stud

estoque *nm* (**a**) *(en esgrima)* rapier (**b**) *Taurom* sword *(for killing the bull)*

estoquear *vt* to stab

estor *nm* (Roman) blind

estorbar 1 *vt* (**a**) *(obstaculizar)* to hinder; **esta mesa estorba el paso** this table is in people's way (**b**) *(molestar)* to bother; **le estorba el flequillo para jugar al tenis** his fringe bothers him when he plays tennis; **el abrigo me estorba con tanto calor** I find wearing my coat uncomfortable in this heat
 2 *vi (estar en medio)* to be in the way; **no hace más que e.** all he does is get in the way; **no quites el aire acondicionado, que no estorba** don't turn the air conditioning off, it's not bothering me

estorbo *nm* (**a**) *(obstáculo)* hindrance; **quite cualquier objeto que pueda suponer un e.** remove any object that could get in people's way (**b**) *(molestia)* nuisance; **eres un e.** you're a nuisance

estornino *nm* (**a**) *(ave)* starling ►► ***e. pinto*** starling (**b**) *(pez)* Spanish *o* chub mackerel

estornudar *vi* to sneeze

estornudo *nm* sneeze; **soltar un e.** to sneeze

estos, -as *ver* **este**

éstos, -as *ver* **éste**

estoy *ver* **estar**

estrábico, -a 1 *adj* squint-eyed
 2 *nm,f* person with a squint

estrabismo *nm* squint

estrado *nm* (**a**) *(tarima) (de orador, personalidades)* platform, rostrum; *(para testigos)* witness *Br* box *o US* stand; **subir al e.** *(orador)* to go up onto the platform; *(testigo) Br* to enter the witness box, *US* to take the stand (**b**) *Der* **estrados** *(salas)* courtrooms

estrafalariamente *adv* (**a**) *(con extravagancia)* outlandishly, eccentrically (**b**) *(de forma desaliñada)* slovenly, sloppily

estrafalario, -a *adj* (**a**) *(extravagante) (persona, ropa, ideas)* outlandish, eccentric (**b**) *(desaliñado)* slovenly, sloppy

estragado, -a *adj (estropeado)* ravaged

estragar *vt (destruir)* to ravage

estragón *nm* tarragon

estragos *nmpl* **los e. de las heladas arruinaron la cosecha** frost damage ruined the harvest; **causar** *o* **hacer e. (en algo)** *(destruir)* to wreak havoc (on sth), to devastate (sth); **la epidemia de cólera sigue causando** *o* **haciendo e.** the cholera epidemic continues to cause devastation; **el huracán causó** *o* **hizo e. en la costa** the hurricane wreaked havoc on the coast; EXPR **hacer e.** *(triunfar)* to have devastating results; **el cantante hace e. entre las niñas** the singer drives young girls wild

estrambótico, -a *adj* outlandish, eccentric

estramonio *nm* thorn apple

estrangis = **extranjis**

estrangulación *nf* **(a)** *(de persona)* strangulation **(b)** *(de vena, conducto)* strangulation

estrangulado, -a *adj* **(a)** *(ahogado)* strangled **(b)** *(vena, conducto)* strangulated

estrangulador, -ora 1 *nm,f (persona)* strangler; **el e. de Boston** the Boston strangler

2 *nm (de automóvil)* choke

estrangulamiento *nm* **(a)** *(de persona)* strangulation **(b)** *(de vena, conducto)* strangulation

estrangular 1 *vt* **(a)** *(ahogar)* to strangle **(b)** *(vena, conducto)* to strangulate **(c)** *(proyecto)* to stifle, to nip in the bud

2 estrangularse *vpr* **(a)** *(ahogarse)* to strangle oneself **(b)** *(obstruirse)* to be *o* become blocked

estraperlista *nmf* black marketeer

estraperlo *nm* black market; **productos de e.** black market goods

Estrasburgo *n* Strasbourg

estratagema *nf* **(a)** *Mil* stratagem **(b)** *(astucia)* artifice, trick

estratega *nmf* strategist

estrategia *nf* strategy; **cambiar de e.** to change strategy ▸▸ *Mktg* ***e. de márketing*** marketing strategy

estratégicamente *adv* strategically

estratégico, -a *adj* strategic

estratificación *nf* stratification

estratificado, -a *adj* stratified

estratificar [60] **1** *vt* to stratify

2 estratificarse *vpr* **(a)** *Geol* to form strata **(b)** *(sociedad)* to become stratified

estratigrafía *nf Geol* stratigraphy

estratigráfico, -a *adj Geol* stratigraphic

estrato *nm* **(a)** *Geol* stratum **(b)** *Meteo* stratum **(c)** *(clase social)* stratum; **los estratos sociales** the social strata

estratocúmulo *nm Meteo* stratocumulus

estratosfera *nf* stratosphere

estratosférico, -a *adj* **(a)** *(de la estratosfera)* stratospheric **(b)** *Fam (precio)* astronomical, sky-high

estraza *nf* **papel de e.** brown paper

estrechamente *adv* **(a)** *(íntimamente)* closely; **e. relacionados** closely related **(b)** *(apretadamente)* tightly

estrechamiento *nm* **(a)** *(de calle, tubo)* narrowing; **atención: e. provisional de la calzada** *(en letrero)* road narrows ▸▸ *Med* ***e. del túnel carpiano*** carpal tunnel syndrome **(b)** *(de relaciones) (entre países)* rapprochement; **producir el e. de relaciones entre dos personas** to bring two people closer together

estrechar 1 *vt* **(a)** *(hacer estrecho)* to narrow; *(ropa)* to take in **(b)** *(amistad, relaciones)* to make closer; *(lazos)* to reinforce, to strengthen; **ambos países estrecharon sus vínculos de amistad** the two countries strengthened their ties of friendship **(c)** *(apretar)* to squeeze, to hug; **e. la mano a alguien** to shake sb's hand; **la estrechó entre sus brazos** he hugged *o* embraced her

2 estrecharse *vpr* **(a)** *(hacerse estrecho)* to narrow **(b)** *(amistad, relaciones)* to become *o* grow closer; *(lazos)* to grow stronger **(c)** *(apretarse)* to squeeze up; **se estrecharon en un fuerte abrazo** they hugged one another tightly; **se estrecharon la mano** they shook hands

> **Falso amigo**: El verbo inglés **to stretch** no es la traducción del español **estrechar**. En inglés el sentido básico de **to stretch** es "estirar" o "extender".

estrechez *nf* **(a)** *(falta de anchura)* narrowness; *(falta de espacio)* lack of space; *(de ropa)* tightness ▸▸ ***e. de miras*** narrow-mindedness **(b)** *(falta de dinero)* hardship; **vivir en la e.** to live on slender means; **pasar estrecheces** to be hard up; **vivir sin estrecheces** to live comfortably **(c)** *(intimidad)* closeness

estrecho, -a 1 *adj* **(a)** *(de poca anchura)* narrow; *(ropa)* tight; **es e. de caderas** he is narrow-hipped; **desde que he engordado toda la ropa me está estrecha** since I put on weight, all my clothes have been too tight for me; **aquí se está muy e.** it's very cramped in here; **íbamos muy estrechos en el autobús** our bus was packed

(b) *(íntimo)* close; **tengo una estrecha relación con él** I have a close relationship with him; **el asunto tiene una estrecha relación con los juicios a la mafia** the affair is closely tied up with the mafia trials; **ambos países mantienen estrechos lazos de amistad** the two countries have close ties of friendship

(c) *(tacaño)* miserly, mean

(d) *(rígido)* strict; **serán sometidos a estrecha vigilancia** they will be kept under close *o* strict surveillance; **e. de miras** narrow-minded

(e) *Fam Pey (reprimido)* prudish, hung-up

2 *nm,f Fam Pey (reprimido)* prude

3 *nm (entre dos mares)* strait(s) ▸▸ ***el Estrecho de Bering*** the Bering Strait(s); ***el Estrecho de Gibraltar*** the Strait(s) of Gibraltar; ***el Estrecho de Magallanes*** the Strait(s) of Magellan

estrechura *nf* **(a)** *(falta de anchura)* narrowness **(b)** *(aprieto, dificultad)* difficulty

estregar [43] *vt* to rub

estrella 1 *adj inv* star; **producto e.** star *o* flagship product; **el deporte e. de las Olimpiadas** the star event of the Olympics; **la pieza e. de la colección** the jewel of the collection

2 *nf* **(a)** *(astro)* star; **en forma de e.** star-shaped; EXPR **ver las estrellas** to see stars ▸▸ ***e. binaria*** binary star; ***e. doble*** binary star; ***e. enana*** dwarf star; ***e. enana blanca*** white dwarf star; ***e. enana roja*** red dwarf star; ***e. fugaz*** shooting star; ***e. gigante*** red giant; ***e. nova*** nova; ***E. polar*** Pole Star; ***e. supernova*** supernova

(b) *(suerte, destino)* fate; **su e. quiso que la conociera** fate willed that he should meet her; **nacer con e.** to be born lucky; **tener buena/mala e.** to be lucky/unlucky

(c) *(artista, deportista)* star; **es la e. del equipo** he's the star of the team ▸▸ ***e. de cine*** *Br* film star, *US* movie star; ***e. invitada*** guest star

(d) *(símbolo)* star; **un hotel de cuatro estrellas** a four-star hotel ▸▸ ***e. de David*** Star of David

(e) ***e. de mar*** starfish

estrellado, -a *adj* **(a)** *(con estrellas)* starry **(b)** *(por la forma)* star-shaped **(c)** *(que ha chocado)* smashed; EXPR **nacer e.** to be born unlucky

estrellar 1 *vt* **(a)** *(arrojar)* to smash; **estrelló el vaso contra el suelo** she smashed the glass on the floor; **estrelló el balón en el poste** he smashed the ball into the post **(b)** *(huevo)* to fry

2 estrellarse *vpr* **(a)** *(chocar) (objeto)* to smash (**contra** against); *(avión, vehículo)* to crash (**contra** into); **nos estrellamos con la moto** we crashed the motorbike; **se estrelló contra la oposición de su jefe** he ran smack into his boss's opposition

(b) *(fracasar)* to fail; **se estrelló con su última película** his last film was a disaster *o* a total flop

(c) *(cubrirse de estrellas)* to fill with stars

estrellato *nm* stardom; **alcanzó el e. con su quinta película** she achieved stardom with her fifth film; **lanzar a alguien al e.** to propel sb to stardom, to make sb a star

estrellón *nm Méx (choque)* crash

estremecedor, -ora *adj (ruido, grito)* horrifying, ghastly; *(crimen, imágenes, historia)* horrifying, appalling

estremecer [46] **1** *vt* to shake; **cualquier ruidito me estremecía** the slightest sound jangled my nerves; **un fuerte seísmo estremeció la ciudad** a violent earthquake shook the city; **el asesinato estremeció a todo el país** the assassination shook the whole country

2 *vi* **la explosión hizo e. los cimientos del edificio** the explosion shook the foundations of the building; **la sola idea me hace e.** just the thought of it makes me shudder

3 estremecerse *vpr (de horror, miedo)* to tremble *o* shudder (**de** with); *(de frío)* to shiver (**de** with); **me estremezco sólo de pensarlo** I get the shivers just thinking about it

estremecimiento *nm (de miedo)* shudder; *(de frío)* shiver; **el suceso causó e. entre la población** the crime horrified people

estrenar 1 *vt* **(a)** *(objeto)* to use for the first time; *(ropa)* to wear for the first time; *(casa)* to move into; **¿estrenas zapatos, eh?** new shoes, huh?; **aún no has estrenado el balón que te regalé** you still haven't used the football I gave you; **los que hoy han estrenado la nueva línea de metro dicen que...** those who have used the new underground line on its first day say that...; **el mes que viene estrenamos despacho** next month we'll be moving to a new office; **se vende bicicleta, a e.** *(en anuncio)* bike for sale, unused

(b) *(película)* to release, to show for the first time; *(obra de teatro)* to premiere; **su montaje de "Macbeth" se acaba de e. en el Olimpia** her production of "Macbeth" has just had its premiere at the Olympia

2 estrenarse *vpr (persona)* to make one's debut, to start; **se estrenó como jugador de rugby ayer** he made his debut as a rugby player yesterday; **se estrena mañana en su nuevo empleo** tomorrow is her first day in her new job

estreno *nm* **(a)** *(de cosa)* first use; **me puse de e. para el baile** I wore a new outfit to the dance; **unos zapatos de e.** a brand-new pair of shoes **(b)** *(de espectáculo, película)* premiere, first night; **la noche del e.** the opening night; **cine de e.** first-run cinema **(c)** *(de casa, exposición)* opening **(d)** *(primera actuación)* debut

estreñido, -a *adj* constipated

estreñimiento *nm* constipation

estreñir [47] **1** *vt* to constipate

2 *vi* to be binding; **los huevos estriñen** eggs are binding *o* cause constipation

3 estreñirse *vpr* to get constipated

estrépito *nm* **(a)** *(ruido)* racket, din; **se oyó un e. de platos rotos en la cocina** from the kitchen there came the crash of breaking crockery; **la estantería se cayó con gran e.** the shelves collapsed with a great crash **(b)** *(ostentación)* fanfare

estrepitosamente *adv* **(a)** *(ruidosamente)* noisily **(b)** *(fracasar, hundirse, caer derrotado)* spectacularly

estrepitoso, -a *adj* **(a)** *(ruidoso) (risa, carcajada)* noisy; *(explosión, aplausos)* deafening; *(ruido)* deafening, thundering **(b)** *(derrota)* resounding; *(fracaso, hundimiento)* spectacular

estreptococo *nm Biol* streptococcus

estreptomicina *nf Med* streptomycin

estrés *nm inv* stress

estresado, -a *adj* stressed, suffering from stress; **estar e.** to be stressed

estresante *adj* stressful

estresar *vt* to cause stress to; **ese ruido me está estresando** that noise is getting on my nerves

estresor *nm* source of stress

estría *nf* **(a)** *(surco)* groove **(b)** *(en piel)* stretch mark **(c)** *(en columna)* **estrías** fluting

estriado, -a *adj* **(a)** *(piel)* stretch-marked **(b)** *(columna)* fluted

estriar [32] **1** *vt* to groove

2 estriarse *vpr (sujeto: piel)* to become stretch-marked

estribaciones *nfpl* foothills; **en las estribaciones del Himalaya** in the foothills of the Himalayas

estribar *vi* **(a)** *Formal (fundamentarse)* **e. en** to lie in, to consist in; **la subida de tipos estriba en el repunte de la inflación** the interest rate rise is prompted by the resurgence of inflation; **su mayor problema estriba en la falta de dinero** her main problem is her lack of money **(b)** *Arquit (asentarse)* **e. en** to rest on

estribera *nf RP (correa)* stirrup strap

estribillo *nm* **(a)** *Mús* chorus **(b)** *Lit* refrain **(c)** *Fam (coletilla)* pet word *o* phrase

estribo *nm* **(a)** *(de montura)* stirrup; EXPR **estar con un pie en el e.** to be halfway out of the door, to have one's hand on the doorknob; EXPR *Fam* **perder los estribos** to fly off the handle **(b)** *(de tren, tranvía)* step; *(de automóvil)* running board; *(de moto)* footrest **(c)** *Anat* stirrup (bone), *Espec* stapes *(singular)* **(d)** *Arquit (contrafuerte)* buttress; *(de arco)* abutment

estribor *nm* starboard; **virar a e.** to turn to starboard; **¡barco a e.!** ship to starboard!

estricnina *nf* strychnine

estrictamente *adv* strictly; **desde un punto de vista e. jurídico...** from a strictly legal point of view...; **hay que aplicar e. el reglamento** the rules must be strictly enforced

estrictez *nf Am* strictness

estricto, -a *adj* strict; **no seas tan e. con él** don't be so strict with him; **la estricta aplicación del reglamento** strict enforcement of the rules

estridencia *nf* **(a)** *(de ruido, risa, voz)* stridency, shrillness **(b)** *(de colores)* loudness **(c)** *(de persona, comportamiento, quejas)* loudness

estridente *adj* **(a)** *(ruido, risa, voz)* strident, shrill **(b)** *(color)* garish, loud **(c)** *(persona, comportamiento, quejas)* loud

estriega *etc ver* **estregar**

estrilda *nf* ***e. ondulada*** waxbill

estro *nm* **(a)** *Zool (celo)* oestrus **(b)** *Literario (inspiración)* inspiration

estroboscopio *nm* stroboscope

estrofa *nf* stanza, verse

estrógeno *nm* oestrogen

estroncio *nm Quím* strontium

estropajo *nm* scourer; **e. de aluminio** metal scouring pad, brillo pad®

estropajoso, -a *adj* **(a)** *(pelo)* coarse; *(textura)* fibrous; *(carne)* dry and chewy **(b)** *(lengua, boca)* dry and pasty

estropeado, -a *adj* **(a)** *(averiado)* broken **(b)** *(dañado)* damaged **(c)** *(echado a perder)* ruined, spoiled **(d)** *(envejecido)* aged; **la vi muy estropeada** I thought she had aged a lot

estropear 1 *vt* **(a)** *(averiar)* to break

(b) *(dañar)* to damage; **no juegues al fútbol con esos zapatos, que los estropearás** don't play football in those shoes, you'll ruin them; **la lejía estropea la ropa** bleach damages clothes; **el exceso de sol estropea la piel** too much sun is bad for the skin

(c) *(echar a perder)* to ruin, to spoil; **la lluvia estropeó nuestros planes** the rain ruined *o* spoiled our plans; **siempre tienes que estropearlo todo** you always have to ruin everything

(d) *(envejecer)* to age

2 estropearse *vpr* **(a)** *(máquina)* to break down; *(ropa)* to be ruined; **se ha vuelto a e. el ascensor** the lift has broken down again; **se me ha estropeado el despertador** my alarm clock is broken; **se ha estropeado el día** the day has turned out badly

(b) *(comida)* to go off, to spoil; **no dejes la fruta fuera de la nevera, que se estropea** don't leave the fruit out of the fridge or it'll go off *o* spoil

(c) *(persona)* **María se ha estropeado mucho con los años** the years haven't been kind to María

(d) *(plan)* to fall through; **se me estropeó el plan** my plan turned out badly

estropicio *nm Fam* **hacer** *o* **causar un e.** *(desorden)* to cause mayhem; **¡menudo e. me has hecho en el pelo!** you've made a real mess of my hair!

estroquear 1 *vt (en béisbol)* **estroqueó la pelota** he was struck out

2 *vi (en béisbol)* to be struck out

estructura *nf* **(a)** *(de sustancia, cuerpo, de organización)* structure; **la e. del átomo** the structure of the atom; **la e. social en la India** the structure of Indian society **(b)** *(de edificio, mueble, nave)* frame, framework **(c)** *Ling (de oración, texto)* structure ▸▸ ***e. profunda*** deep structure; ***e. superficial*** surface structure

estructuración *nf* structuring, organization

estructural *adj* structural; **el puente tiene fallos estructurales** the bridge has structural faults *o* is structurally unsound; **desempleo de carácter e.** structural unemployment

estructuralismo *nm* structuralism; **el e. lingüístico** linguistic structuralism

estructuralista 1 *adj* structuralist

2 *nmf* structuralist

estructuralmente *adv* structurally

estructurar *vt* to structure, to organize

estruendo *nm* **(a)** *(ruido)* din, roar; *(de trueno)* crash; *(de explosión)* roar, boom; **las obras producían gran e.** the building work was causing a huge din **(b)** *(alboroto)* uproar, tumult

estruendoso, -a *adj* clamorous, noisy; **una estruendosa ovación** a thunderous ovation

estrujar 1 *vt* **(a)** *(limón, naranja)* to squeeze; *(trapo, ropa)* to wring (out); *(esponja)* to squeeze out **(b)** *(papel)* to screw up; *(caja)* to crush **(c)** *(persona, mano)* to squeeze; **me estrujó un pie** he squashed my foot; **¡no me estrujes!** don't squash *o* crush me! **(d)** *(aprovecharse de)* to bleed dry

2 estrujarse *vpr (apretujarse)* to huddle together; **íbamos todos estrujados en el asiento de atrás** we were all squashed together in the back seat; EXPR *Fam* **estrujarse la cabeza** *o* **el cerebro** to rack one's brains

estrujón *nm* **(a)** *(abrazo)* bear hug **(b)** *(apretujón)* **hubo muchos estrujones** there was a lot of pushing and shoving

Estuardo *n pr* **los E.** the Stuarts

estuario *nm* estuary

estucado *nm* stucco, stucco work

estucar [60] *vt* to stucco

estuchante *nmf Andes Fam* picklock

estuche *nm (de instrumento, gafas, pendientes, reloj)* case; *(de cubertería)* case, canteen; *(de joyas)* box; *(de lápices) (dura)* box; *(blanda)* case

estuco *nm* stucco

estudiado, -a *adj* studied

estudiantado *nm* students; **la mayoría del e.** the majority of the students

estudiante *nmf (de universidad, secundaria)* student; *(de primaria)* schoolchild, pupil; **una e. de Medicina** a medical student; **un bar de estudiantes** a student bar

estudiantil *adj* student; **protestas estudiantiles** student protests; **un bar con ambiente e.** a studenty bar

estudiantina *nf* = traditional musical ensemble formed by university students

estudiar 1 *vt* (**a**) *(carrera, asignatura, lección)* to study; **estudia biológicas** he's studying biology; **tengo que e. más inglés** I've got to work at my English; **¿qué estudiaste en la universidad?** what did you study at university?

(**b**) *(asunto)* to study; *(oferta, propuesta)* to study, to consider; **después de e. tu propuesta he decidido no aceptarla** having considered your proposal, I've decided not to accept it; **lo estudiaré y mañana te doy una respuesta** I'll consider it and get back to you tomorrow; **el gobierno estudia la posibilidad de subir las pensiones** the government is studying the possibility of raising pensions

(**c**) *(observar)* to observe; **estuvo estudiándonos durante un rato** he stayed watching us for a while; **desde allí podía e. todos los movimientos del animal** from there I could observe all the animal's movements

2 *vi* to study; **estudia todas las tardes** he spends every afternoon studying; **no puede salir, tiene que e.** she can't come out, she's got to study; **hay que e. más, González** you'll have to work harder, González; **estudió con el Presidente** he went to school/university with the President; **dejó de e. a los quince años** he left school at fifteen; **estudié en los jesuitas** I went to a Jesuit school; **estudia en la Universidad Centroamericana** he's a student *o* he's studying at the University of Central America; **e. para médico** to be studying to be a doctor; **¿estudias o trabajas?** do you work or are you still at school?; *Esp Hum* ≃ do you come here often?

3 **estudiarse** *vpr* (**a**) *(lección, tema, asignatura)* to study; **tengo que estudiarme cinco temas antes del viernes** I have to study five topics by Friday; **se estudió su papel en la obra** she learnt her part in the play (**b**) *(observarse)* **las dos fieras se estudiaron antes de atacar** the two animals studied *o* watched each other before attacking

estudio *nm* (**a**) *(actividad)* study; **ha dedicado muchos años al e. del tema** she has studied the subject for many years; **estar en e.** to be under consideration ▸▸ ***e. de mercado*** *(técnica)* market research; *(investigación)* market survey

(**b**) *(investigación)* study; **ha publicado un e. sobre el tema** she's published a study on the subject; **hacer un e. de algo** to survey sth; **le hicieron un e. de la flora intestinal** they investigated the composition of her intestinal flora ▸▸ ***e. de campo*** field study; ***e. geológico*** geological survey; ***e. de impacto ambiental*** environmental impact study; ***e. de viabilidad*** feasibility study

(**c**) **estudios** *(educación)* studies; **el niño va muy bien en los estudios** the boy is doing very well at school; **al terminar sus estudios en Viena, viajó a París** on completing his studies in Vienna he travelled to Paris; **dar estudios a alguien** to pay for *o* finance sb's education; **dejó los estudios a los quince años** he left school at fifteen; **tener estudios** to be educated ▸▸ ***estudios de posgrado*** postgraduate studies *o* education; ***estudios primarios*** primary education; ***estudios secundarios*** secondary education; ***estudios superiores*** higher education

(**d**) *(despacho)* study; *(de fotógrafo, pintor, arquitecto)* studio; *RP (de abogado)* practice

(**e**) *(apartamento)* studio *Br* flat *o US* apartment

(**f**) *Cine, Rad & TV* studio; **los estudios de la Metro** the Metro studios ▸▸ ***e. de grabación*** recording studio

(**g**) *Arte* study

(**h**) *Mús* étude, study; **e. para piano** piano study

estudioso, -a 1 *adj* studious

2 *nm,f (especialista)* expert, scholar; **un e. de la cultura persa** a scholar of Persian culture; **un e. de la naturaleza humana** a student of human nature

estufa *nf* (**a**) *(calefacción)* heater, *Br* fire ▸▸ ***e. eléctrica*** electric heater; ***e. de gas*** gas heater (**b**) *Méx (cocina)* stove

estulticia *nf Formal* stupidity, obtuseness

estupa *muy Fam* 1 *nm (persona)* drug squad detective, *US* narc; **los estupas** the drug squad, *US* the narcs

2 *nf (brigada)* **la e.** the drug squad, *US* the narcs

estupefacción *nf* astonishment

estupefaciente 1 *adj* narcotic

2 *nm* narcotic, drug; **brigada de estupefacientes** drugs squad

estupefacto, -a *adj* astonished, astounded; **dejar a alguien e.** to astonish *o* astound sb; **quedarse e.** to be astonished *o* astounded

estupendamente *adv* wonderfully; **estoy e.** I feel wonderful; **los niños lo pasaron e. en el parque** the children had a wonderful time in the park; **unas vacaciones te vendrían e.** a holiday would do you a world of good; **¿cómo te encuentras? – ¡e.!** how are you feeling? – great *o* fantastic!

estupendo, -a *adj* wonderful, marvellous; **estás estupenda** you look wonderful; **hace un día e.** it's a beautiful *o* wonderful day; **es una persona estupenda** she's a great person; **¡e.!** wonderful!, marvellous!; **¿vamos mañana a la playa? – ¡e.!** shall we go to the beach tomorrow? – good idea!

estúpidamente *adv* stupidly

estupidez *nf* stupidity; **decir/hacer una e.** to say/do something stupid; **no dice más que estupideces** all she ever talks is nonsense; **hizo la e. de preguntarle al portero** he made the foolish mistake of asking the caretaker; **sería un e. negarlo** it would be foolish to deny it; **¿y por eso se enfada? ¡pues vaya una e.!** she got annoyed about that? how stupid can you get!

estúpido, -a 1 *adj* stupid; **¡qué e. soy! me he vuelto a olvidar** what an idiot I am! I've gone and forgotten again; **sería e. no reconocerlo** it would be foolish not to admit it

2 *nm,f* idiot; **el e. de mi vecino** my idiot of a neighbour

estupor *nm* (**a**) *(asombro)* astonishment; **causar e.** to cause astonishment; **con e.** in astonishment (**b**) *Med* stupor

estupro *nm Der* = use of deception or misuse of authority by an adult to engage in sex with a minor

esturión *nm* sturgeon

estuve *etc ver* **estar**

estuviera *etc ver* **estar**

esvástica *nf* swastika

ETA ['eta] *nf* (*abrev de* **Euskadi Ta Askatasuna**) ETA, = terrorist Basque separatist organization

etano *nm* ethane

etanol *nm* ethanol

etapa *nf* (**a**) *(trayecto, fase)* stage; **está pasando una mala e.** he's going through a bad patch; **por etapas** in stages; **la reforma educativa será implantada por etapas** the educational reforms will be introduced in stages

(**b**) *Dep* stage; **una vuelta ciclista por etapas** a staged cycle race ▸▸ ***e. ciclista*** stage *(of cycle race)*; ***e. contrarreloj*** *(en ciclismo)* time trial; ***e. de montaña*** *(en ciclismo)* mountain stage; ***e. prólogo*** *(en ciclismo)* prologue

etarra 1 *adj* ETA; **el terrorismo e.** ETA terrorism

2 *nmf* member of ETA

etc. (*abrev de* **etcétera**) etc

etcétera 1 *adv* etcetera

2 *nm* **y un largo e. de...** and a long list of...

éter *nm* (**a**) *(gas)* ether (**b**) *Formal (cielo)* **el é.** the ether, the heavens

etéreo, -a *adj* ethereal

eternamente *adv* eternally; **te estaré e. agradecido** I will be eternally grateful to you

eternidad *nf* (**a**) *(existencia eterna)* eternity (**b**) *Fam (mucho tiempo)* **llevo esperando una e.** I've been waiting an eternity *o* for ages; **hace una e. que no la veo** it's ages since I last saw her

eternit® (*pl* **eternits** *o* **enternites**) *nm Andes, RP* = corrugated fibre cement sheeting

eternizar [14] 1 *vt* **e. algo** to make sth last forever

2 **eternizarse** *vpr* **eternizarse (haciendo algo)** to spend absolutely ages (doing sth); **no te eternices haciendo las camas** don't take forever making the beds; **la reunión se eternizó** the meeting went on and on

eterno, -a *adj* (**a**) *(perpetuo)* eternal; **se juraron amor e.** they swore eternal *o* undying love (**b**) *Fam (larguísimo)* never-ending, interminable; **la eterna canción** the same old story; **el e. problema** the eternal problem; **hacerse e.** to go on forever; **la obra se me hizo eterna** the play seemed to go on forever

Ethernet® [eθer'net] *nf Informát* Ethernet®

ética *nf* (**a**) *(en filosofía)* ethics *(singular)* (**b**) *(moralidad)* ethics; **gente que carece de é.** people who have no ethics ►► ***é. profesional*** (professional) ethics

éticamente *adv* ethically

ético, -a *adj* ethical

etilenglicol *nm Quím* ethylene glycol

etileno *nm Quím* ethylene, ethene

etílico, -a *adj Quím* ethyl; **alcohol e.** ethyl alcohol; **intoxicación etílica** alcohol poisoning

etilismo *nm* intoxication

etilo *nm* ethyl

etimología *nf* etymology

etimológicamente *adv* etymologically

etimológico, -a *adj* etymological

etimólogo, -a *nm,f* etymologist

etiología *nf Med* etiology

etíope 1 *adj* Ethiopian
2 *nmf (persona)* Ethiopian
3 *nm (lengua)* Ethiopian

Etiopía *n* Ethiopia

etiqueta *nf* (**a**) *(en envase, producto, prenda) (pegada o cosida)* label; *(colgada o atada)* tag, label; **la e. del precio** the price tag; **ponga una e. con su nombre a la maleta** put a label/tag with your name on it on the suitcase; **cada sobre lleva una e. con la dirección** each envelope has an address label on it
(**b**) *(calificativo)* label; **colgarle** *o* **ponerle a alguien la e. de...** to label sb as...; **no me gusta poner etiquetas a la gente** I don't like to label people
(**c**) *(ceremonial)* etiquette; **de e.** formal; **una cena de e.** a formal dinner; **vestirse de e.** to wear formal dress
(**d**) *Informát* label

etiquetado *nm* labelling

etiquetadora *nf* pricing gun

etiquetaje *nm* labelling

etiquetar *vt* (**a**) *(objeto)* to label (**b**) *(persona)* to label; **e. a alguien de algo** to label sb sth; **la etiquetaron de rebelde** she was labelled (as) a rebel

etiquetero, -a *adj* ceremonious, formal

etmoides *nm inv Anat* ethmoid bone

Etna *nm* **el E.** (Mount) Etna

etnia *nf* ethnic group; **una persona de e. oriental** a person of Asian extraction

étnico, -a *adj* ethnic

etnocéntrico, -a *adj* ethnocentric

etnocentrismo *nm* ethnocentrism

etnocidio *nm* genocide

etnografía *nf* ethnography

etnográfico, -a *adj* ethnographic

etnógrafo, -a *nm,f* ethnographer

etnología *nf* ethnology

etnológico, -a *adj* ethnologic, ethnological

etnólogo, -a *nm,f* ethnologist

etología *nf* ethology

etrusco, -a 1 *adj* Etruscan
2 *nm,f* Etruscan

ETT *nf* (*abrev de* **Empresa de Trabajo Temporal**) temping agency

EUA *nmpl* (*abrev de* **Estados Unidos de América**) USA

eucalipto *nm* eucalyptus; **caramelos de e.** eucalyptus sweets

eucarionte *nm*, **eucariota** *nf Biol* eucaryote, eukaryote

eucaristía *nf* **la e.** the Eucharist

eucarístico, -a *adj* Eucharistic

Euclides *n pr* Euclid

euclidiano, -a *adj* Euclidean

eufemismo *nm* euphemism

eufemísticamente *adv* euphemistically

eufemístico, -a *adj* euphemistic

eufonía *nf* euphony

eufónico, -a *adj* euphonic, euphonious

euforia *nf* euphoria, elation; **daban gritos de e.** they were shouting euphorically; **sentía una gran e.** he felt very elated

eufóricamente *adv* euphorically

eufórico, -a *adj* euphoric, elated; **los aficionados saltaban eufóricos** the fans were leaping up and down in excitement; **me sentía e.** I felt elated

Éufrates *nm* **el É.** the Euphrates

eugenesia *nf* eugenics *(singular)*

eugenésico, -a *adj* eugenic

eunuco *nm* eunuch

Eurasia *n* Eurasia

eurasiático, -a 1 *adj* Eurasian
2 *nm,f* Eurasian

EURATOM [eura'tom] *nf* (*abrev de* **Comunidad Europea de la Energía Atómica**) EURATOM

eureka *interj* eureka!

Euribor [euri'βor] *nm Fin* (*abrev de* **Euro InterBank Offered Rate**) EURIBOR

Eurípides *n pr* Euripides

euritmia *nf Med* regular heartbeat

euro *nm* (**a**) *(moneda)* euro; **la zona** *o* **el territorio (del) e.** the euro zone (**b**) *Literario (viento)* east wind

euro- *pref* Euro-; **euroeconomía** euro-economy

euroafricano, -a *adj* Afro-European

euroasiático, -a 1 *adj* Eurasian
2 *nm,f* Eurasian

eurobarómetro *nm UE* Eurobarometer

eurobono *nm* Eurobond

eurocámara *nf* European Parliament

eurocéntrico, -a *adj* Eurocentric

eurocheque *nm* Eurocheque

eurocomisario, -a *nm,f* EU commissioner

eurocomunismo *nm* Eurocommunism

eurocomunista 1 *adj* Eurocommunist
2 *nmf* Eurocommunist

euroconector *nm TV* SCART

eurócrata 1 *adj* Eurocrat
2 *nmf* Eurocrat

eurodiputado, -a *nm,f* Euro-MP, MEP

eurodivisa *nf Fin* eurocurrency

eurodólar *nm Fin* Eurodollar

euroejército *nm* Euro army

euroescéptico, -a 1 *adj* Eurosceptic
2 *nm,f* Eurosceptic

euroesceptismo *nm* Euroscepticism

Eurolandia *n* Euroland

euroliga *nf (de fútbol)* European super league

euromercado *nm Fin* Euromarket

Europa (**a**) *n* Europe ►► ***E. Central*** Central Europe; ***E. del Este*** Eastern Europe; ***E. Occidental*** Western Europe; ***E. Oriental*** Eastern Europe (**b**) *Mitol* Europa

europarlamentario, -a *nm,f* member of the European Parliament, Euro-MP

europeidad *nf* Europeanness

europeísmo *nm* Europeanism

europeísta 1 *adj* pro-European
2 *nmf* pro-European

europeización *nf* Europeanization

europeizante *adj* Europeanizing

europeizar [14] **1** *vt* to Europeanize
2 europeizarse *vpr* to become Europeanized

europeo, -a 1 *adj* European
2 *nm,f* European

europio *nm Quím* europium

Europol [euro'pol] *nf* (*abrev de* **European Police**) Europol

eurotúnel *nm* **el e.** the Channel tunnel, the Eurotunnel

eurovisión *nf* Eurovision; **el torneo será retransmitido por e.** the tournament will be broadcast by Eurovision

euscaldún, euscalduna 1 *adj* Basque-speaking
2 *nmf* Basque speaker

Euskadi *n* the Basque Country

euskaldún, euskalduna 1 *adj* Basque-speaking
2 *nmf* Basque speaker

euskera, eusquera *nm* Basque

eutanasia *nf* euthanasia; **practicar la e. a alguien** to practise euthanasia on sb ▸▸ ***e. pasiva*** passive euthanasia, = withholding of life-prolonging treatment from a terminally ill person

eutrofización *nf Biol* eutrophication

Eva *n pr* Eve

evacuación *nf* (**a**) *(de zona, edificio, personas)* evacuation (**b**) *Formal (de vientre)* evacuation, bowel movement

evacuado, -a 1 *adj* evacuated
2 *nm,f* evacuee

evacuar 1 *vt* (**a**) *(edificio, zona, personas)* to evacuate (**b**) *Formal (vientre)* **e. el vientre** to have a bowel movement (**c**) *(trámite)* to carry out, to transact
2 *vi Formal (defecar)* to have a bowel movement

evadido, -a 1 *adj* (**a**) *(persona)* escaped (**b**) *(divisas, impuestos)* evaded
2 *nm,f* escapee, fugitive; **un e. de la justicia** a fugitive from justice

evadir 1 *vt* (**a**) *(problema, peligro, tema)* to avoid; *(compromiso, responsabilidad)* to avoid, to evade (**b**) *(divisas, impuestos)* to evade
2 **evadirse** *vpr* (**a**) *(fugarse)* to escape (**de** from) (**b**) *(distraerse)* to escape (**de** from); **evadirse de la realidad** to escape from reality; **pasear en bici es su forma de evadirse** going for a bike ride is his way of taking his mind off things

evaluable *adj* calculable

evaluación *nf* (**a**) *(valoración)* evaluation, assessment; *(de daños, pérdidas, riesgos)* assessment; **una primera e. de las estadísticas confirma que...** a first assessment of the statistics confirms that...; **realizaron una e. de los daños** they assessed the damage; **hacen evaluaciones periódicas del rendimiento de los trabajadores** employees are given regular performance evaluations *o* appraisals; **hizo una e. positiva de la situación** he gave a positive assessment of the situation ▸▸ *Com* ***e. comparativa*** benchmarking; ***e. de impacto ambiental*** environmental impact assessment; ***e. de riesgos*** risk assessment
(**b**) *Educ (acción)* assessment; *(examen)* exam, test; *(periodo)* = division of school year, of which there may be three to five in total ▸▸ ***e. continua*** continuous assessment

evaluador, -ora *adj* evaluating, evaluative

evaluar [4] *vt* (**a**) *(valorar)* to evaluate, to assess; *(daños, pérdidas, riesgos)* to assess (**b**) *Educ (alumno)* to assess, to test; *(examen) Br* to mark, *US* to grade

evanescencia *nf Formal* evanescence

evanescente *adj Formal* evanescent

evangélico, -a 1 *adj* evangelical
2 *nm,f* evangelical

evangelio *nm* (**a**) *(de la Biblia)* gospel; **el e. según San Marcos** the Gospel according to St Mark; **predicar el e. a alguien** to preach the gospel to sb ▸▸ ***los evangelios apócrifos*** the apocryphal Gospels (**b**) *Fam (dogma)* **su opinión es el e.** whatever he says goes, his word is law

evangelismo *nm* evangelism

evangelista 1 *nm Rel* Evangelist; **los cuatro evangelistas** the four Evangelists; **San Juan E.** St John the Evangelist
2 *nmf Méx (escribano)* public letter-writer

evangelización *nf* evangelization, evangelizing

evangelizador, -ora 1 *adj* evangelizing
2 *nm,f* evangelist

evangelizar [14] *vt* to evangelize

evanol® *nm Arg* = an analgesic for period pain

evaporable *adj* evaporable

evaporación *nf* evaporation

evaporar 1 *vt* to evaporate
2 **evaporarse** *vpr* (**a**) *(líquido)* to evaporate (**b**) *Fam (persona)* to vanish *o* disappear (into thin air); *(fondos, fortuna)* to disappear, to vanish; *(posibilidad, esperanzas, ilusiones)* to evaporate, to vanish

evasión *nf* (**a**) *(huida)* escape (**b**) *(de dinero)* ***e. de capitales*** capital flight; ***e. de divisas*** capital flight; ***e. fiscal*** tax evasion; ***e. de impuestos*** tax evasion (**c**) *(entretenimiento)* amusement, recreation; *(escapismo)* escapism; **pasear, montar en bici y otras formas de e.** walking, cycling and other forms of relaxation; **literatura de e.** escapist literature

evasiva *nf* evasive answer; **contestar** *o* **responder con evasivas** to give evasive answers, to be evasive; **no me vengas con evasivas** don't beat about the bush, give me a straight answer

evasivo, -a *adj* evasive

evasor, -ora 1 *adj* guilty of evasion
2 *nm,f* (**a**) *(de la cárcel)* jailbreaker (**b**) *(de dinero)* ***e. de capitales*** *o* ***divisas*** = person who sends money abroad illegally; ***e. fiscal*** tax evader; ***e. de impuestos*** tax evader

evento *nm* event

eventual 1 *adj* (**a**) *(no fijo) (trabajador, empleo)* casual, temporary; *(cargo)* temporary; *(gastos, ingresos)* incidental; **un contrato de trabajo e.** a temporary (employment) contract (**b**) *(posible)* possible; **ante una e. reanudación de las hostilidades** in the event of a renewal of hostilities; **en el caso e. de que...** in the event that...
2 *nmf (trabajador)* casual *o* temporary worker

> **Falso amigo**: El adjetivo inglés **eventual** no es la traducción del español **eventual**. En inglés **eventual** significa "final".

eventualidad *nf* (**a**) *(temporalidad)* temporariness (**b**) *(hecho incierto)* eventuality; *(posibilidad)* possibility; **estamos preparados para cualquier e.** we are prepared for every eventuality; **en la e. de que viniera, lo recibiríamos** in the event of his coming, we would receive him

eventualmente *adv* (**a**) *(por casualidad)* by chance (**b**) *(posiblemente)* possibly

> **Falso amigo**: El adverbio inglés **eventually** no es la traducción del español **eventualmente**. En inglés **eventually** significa "finalmente, al final".

Everest *nm* **el E.** (Mount) Everest

evidencia *nf* (**a**) *(claridad)* obviousness; **ante la e. de las pruebas, tuvo que admitir su culpa** in the face of such undeniable evidence, he had to admit his guilt; **poner algo en e.** to demonstrate sth; **poner a alguien en e.** to show sb up; **quedar en e.** to be shown up; **me hiciste quedar en e. delante de todo el mundo** you showed me up in front of everyone
(**b**) *(prueba)* evidence, proof; **no hay evidencias de culpabilidad** there is no evidence of guilt

evidenciar 1 *vt* to show, to demonstrate; **estos hechos evidencian la falta de interés del gobierno** these facts demonstrate the government's lack of interest; **los candidatos evidenciaron falta de preparación** the candidates showed a lack of preparation
2 **evidenciarse** *vpr* to be obvious *o* evident; **tal y como se evidencia en su discurso** as is evident from her speech

evidente *adj* evident, obvious; **es e. que no les caemos bien** it's obvious they don't like us; **su enfado era e.** she was clearly *o* visibly angry; **¿te gustaría ganar más? – ¡e.!** would you like to earn more? – of course!

evidentemente *adv* evidently, obviously

evitable *adj* avoidable

evitar 1 *vt* (**a**) *(impedir) (desastre, accidente)* to avoid, to prevent; **¿podría haberse evitado esta catástrofe ecológica?** could this environmental disaster have been avoided *o* prevented?; **e. que alguien haga algo** to stop *o* prevent sb from doing sth; **no pude e. que se pelearan** I couldn't stop *o* prevent them from having a fight; **hemos de e. que se extienda el incendio** we have to stop the fire spreading
(**b**) *(eludir) (problema, cuestión, persona)* to avoid; **siempre me está evitando** she's always trying to avoid me; **Javier siempre evita encontrarse conmigo** Javier always avoids meeting me; **yo evité hablar del tema** I kept *o* steered clear of the subject; **no puede evitarlo** he can't help it; **no puedo e. ser como soy** I can't help (being) the way I am
(**c**) *(ahorrar)* to save; **esta máquina nos evitaría mucho trabajo** this machine would save us a lot of work; **esto me evita tener que ir** this gets me out of going, this saves me (from) having to go
2 **evitarse** *vpr (ahorrarse)* to save oneself; **si sigues mis consejos te evitarás muchos problemas** if you follow my advice, you'll save yourself a lot of problems

evocación *nf* recollection, evocation

evocador, -ora *adj* evocative; **un título e. de tiempos legendarios** a title that evokes legendary times

evocar [60] *vt* (**a**) *(recordar)* to recall; **la decoración evoca tiempos pasados** the decor recalls *o* evokes a bygone era; **evocó lo ocurrido en aquel último encuentro** she recalled what happened during that last meeting; **estas imágenes me hacen e. mi infancia** these pictures remind me of my childhood (**b**) *(espíritu)* to invoke, to call up

evocativo, -a *adj* evocative

evolución *nf* (**a**) *(progreso) (de sociedad, situación, negociaciones)* development, progress; *(de enfermo)* progress; **me preocupa la e. económica del país** I'm worried by the economic developments in

this country; **la e. tecnológica** technological development *o* progress; **una sociedad en plena e.** a rapidly developing society
(**b**) *(cambio)* change
(**c**) *(de especies)* evolution; **la e. de las especies marinas** the evolution of marine life
(**d**) *(movimiento)* **contemplaban las evoluciones del jugador en la banda** they watched the player warming up on the sidelines; **me gusta ver las evoluciones de los aviones en el aeropuerto** I like watching planes taking off and landing at the airport
(**e**) *Mil* manoeuvre

evolucionar *vi* (**a**) *(progresar) (sociedad, situación, negociaciones)* to develop, to progress; *(enfermo)* to make progress; **una sociedad muy evolucionada** a highly developed society; **esta tecnología ha evolucionado mucho** the technology has developed a great deal; **después de la operación evoluciona favorablemente** his progress since the operation has been satisfactory; **el paciente no evoluciona** the patient isn't making any progress
(**b**) *(cambiar)* to change; **mis padres han evolucionado con los años** my parents have changed with the years
(**c**) *(especies)* to evolve
(**d**) *(moverse)* **el jugador evolucionaba en la banda** the player was warming up on the sidelines; **el avión evolucionaba sobre la ciudad** the plane was flying over the city
(**e**) *Mil* to carry out manoeuvres

evolucionismo *nm* evolutionism

evolucionista 1 *adj* evolutionary
2 *nmf* evolutionist

evolutivamente *adv* in evolutionary terms

evolutivo, -a *adj* evolutionary

ex 1 *nmf Fam (cónyuge, pareja)* ex
2 *pref* ex-, former; **el ex presidente** the ex-president, the former president; **un ex alumno de la escuela** a former pupil of the school

exabrupto *nm* sharp word *o* remark

exacción *nf (de impuestos, multas)* exaction, collection

exacerbación *nf* exacerbation, aggravation

exacerbado, -a *adj* **los ánimos estaban exacerbados** people were furious, tempers were running high

exacerbar 1 *vt* (**a**) *(agudizar)* to exacerbate, to aggravate (**b**) *(irritar)* to irritate, to annoy; **su discurso exacerbó los ánimos** her speech worked people up even more
2 **exacerbarse** *vpr* (**a**) *(agudizarse)* to get worse (**b**) *(irritarse)* to get *o* become infuriated

exactamente *adv* exactly, precisely; **son e. iguales** they are exactly the same; **¿qué te dijo e.?** what exactly did she say to you?; **el problema es que nadie se atreve a protestar – e.** the problem is that nobody dares to complain – exactly

exactas *nfpl* mathematics *(singular)*

exactitud *nf* (**a**) *(precisión)* accuracy, precision; **describa con e. lo ocurrido** describe exactly what happened; **no lo sé con e.** I don't know exactly (**b**) *(rigor)* rigorousness

exacto, -a 1 *adj* (**a**) *(justo)* exact; **3 metros exactos** exactly 3 metres; **una hora exacta** exactly an hour
(**b**) *(preciso)* accurate, precise; *(correcto)* correct, right; **dio una descripción exacta del lugar** she gave an exact description of the place; **no sé la fecha exacta de la boda** I don't know the exact date of the wedding; **¿llevas la hora exacta?** have you got the right time?; **para ser exactos** to be precise
(**c**) *(idéntico)* identical (**a** to); **es e. a su padre** he looks just like his father; **una copia exacta del original** an exact copy of the original
2 *adv* exactly, precisely; **¡e.!, eso es lo que está pasando** exactly! that's what is happening

ex aequo *loc adv* **conceder un premio e.** to award a prize jointly to two people

exageración *nf* exaggeration; **decir que son amigos sería una e.** to say they were friends would be to go too far; **este precio es una e.** that's a ridiculous price; **su reacción me pareció una e.** I thought his reaction was a bit extreme; **en su casa tiene una e. de libros** she's got stacks of books at home

exageradamente *adv* excessively; **reaccionar e.** to overreact; **e. simplista** oversimplistic, excessively simplistic; **es e. rico** he's enormously rich; **los actores que gesticulan e.** actors who gesture exaggeratedly

exagerado, -a *adj* (**a**) *(persona)* **es muy e.** *(en sus cálculos, valoraciones)* he exaggerates a lot; *(en sus acciones)* he really goes too far, he really overdoes it; *(en sus reacciones)* he overreacts a lot; **¡qué e. eres! no había tanta gente** you're always exaggerating! there weren't as many people as that
(**b**) *(cifra, reacción, gesto)* exaggerated; *(precio)* exorbitant; **había una cantidad exagerada de comida** there was an enormous amount of food; **muestran exagerada cautela** they are excessively cautious

exagerar 1 *vt* to exaggerate; **la oposición exagera la trascendencia de este asunto** the opposition has blown this issue out of proportion
2 *vi* (**a**) *(al describir, calificar)* to exaggerate; **yo creo que exageras** I think you're exaggerating; **no exageremos, no fue para tanto** let's not exaggerate, it wasn't that bad (**b**) *(al actuar)* to go too far, to overdo it (**con** with); **tantas precauciones, ¿no estás exagerando un poco?** aren't you going a bit too far with *o* overdoing it with all these precautions?

exaltación *nf* (**a**) *(júbilo)* elation, intense excitement (**b**) *(acaloramiento)* overexcitement (**c**) *(ensalzamiento)* exaltation; **la obra es una e. romántica de la belleza** the work is a romantic paean to beauty

exaltado, -a 1 *adj* (**a**) *(acalorado) (persona)* worked up; *(discusión)* heated; *(discurso, defensa)* fervent; **no te pongas tan e.** don't get so worked up; **los ánimos están muy exaltados en la zona** tempers are running high in the area (**b**) *(excitable)* hotheaded (**c**) *(jubiloso)* elated
2 *nm,f (fanático)* hothead; **unos exaltados invadieron el campo** a few hotheads ran onto the pitch

exaltar 1 *vt* (**a**) *(excitar)* **el orador exaltó a las masas** the speaker whipped up the crowds; **la decisión exaltó la cólera de los aficionados** the decision enraged the fans (**b**) *(ensalzar)* to praise, to exalt; **exaltó la cocina argentina** he praised Argentinian cuisine to the skies
2 **exaltarse** *vpr* to get worked up *o* excited (**por** about)

examen *nm* (**a**) *(ejercicio)* exam, examination; **e. de inglés** English exam; **aprobar** *o Am* **pasar un e.** to pass an exam; *Esp* **suspender** *o Am* **reprobar un e.** to fail an exam; **hacer un e.** to do *o* take an exam; **poner un e. a alguien** to set *o* give sb an exam; **presentarse a un e.** to sit an exam ►► *Esp* ***e. de conducir*** driving test; ***e. escrito*** written exam; ***e. final*** final (exam); ***e. de ingreso*** entrance exam; *Am* ***e. de manejar*** driving test; ***e. oral*** oral (exam); ***e. parcial*** end-of-term exam
(**b**) *(indagación)* consideration, examination; **después de un detallado e., la policía descubrió la verdad** after careful consideration of the facts, the police found out the truth; **someter a e.** to examine; **hacer e. de conciencia** to take a good look at oneself; **libre e.** personal interpretation ►► ***e. médico*** medical examination *o* check-up

examinador, -ora 1 *adj* examining
2 *nm,f* examiner

examinando, -a *nm,f* examinee, candidate

examinar 1 *vt* (**a**) *(alumno)* to examine (**b**) *(analizar)* to examine; **examinó detenidamente el arma** he examined the weapon carefully; **examinaremos su caso** we shall examine her case; **tienes que ir al médico a que te examine** you must go and get the doctor to examine you
2 **examinarse** *vpr Esp* to sit *o* take an exam; **mañana me examino de matemáticas** I've got my maths exam tomorrow

exangüe *adj Formal* (**a**) *(agotado)* exhausted (**b**) *(muerto)* lifeless

exánime *adj Formal* (**a**) *(muerto)* lifeless (**b**) *(desmayado)* motionless, inert (**c**) *(agotado)* exhausted, worn-out

exantema *nm Med* exanthem, exanthema

exasperación *nf* exasperation

exasperante *adj* exasperating, infuriating

exasperantemente *adv* exasperatingly, infuriatingly

exasperar 1 *vt* to exasperate, to infuriate; **¿qué es lo que más te exaspera de él?** what is it you find most exasperating *o* infuriating about him?; **la actitud del equipo exasperó a los aficionados** the team's attitude exasperated *o* infuriated the fans
2 **exasperarse** *vpr* to get exasperated

Exc. (*abrev de* **Excelencia**) Excellency

excarcelación *nf* release (from prison)

excarcelar *vt* to release (from prison)

ex cátedra, ex cathedra *loc adv (en tono magistral)* ex cathedra

excavación *nf* (**a**) *(acción)* excavation (**b**) *(lugar)* dig, excavation; **e. arqueológica** archaeological dig

excavador, -ora 1 *adj* excavating, digging
2 *nm,f (persona)* excavator, digger

excavadora *nf (máquina)* digger

excavar *vt* (a) *(cavar)* to dig; **e. el terreno** to dig; **el perro excavó un hoyo** the dog dug a hole (b) *(en arqueología)* to excavate

excedencia *nf Esp (de funcionario, empleado)* leave (of absence); *(de profesor)* sabbatical; **un año de e.** *(de funcionario, empleado)* a year's leave of absence; *(de profesor)* a year's sabbatical; **estar de e.** *(funcionario, empleado)* to be on leave (of absence); *(profesor)* to be on sabbatical

excedentario, -a *adj* surplus; **la balanza de pagos ha sido excedentaria** the balance of payments has been in surplus

excedente 1 *adj* (a) *(producción)* surplus (b) *(funcionario)* on leave; *(profesor)* on sabbatical
2 *nmf Esp (persona)* person on leave ►► ***e. de cupo*** = person excused from military service because there are already enough new recruits
3 *nm Com* surplus; **excedentes agrícolas** agricultural surpluses

exceder 1 *vt* to exceed, to surpass; **e. el límite de velocidad** to exceed *o* go over the speed limit; **excede en dos kilos el peso permitido** it is two kilos over the weight limit; **una cifra que excede con mucho la deuda externa del país** a figure well in excess of the country's foreign debt; **esto excede mis atribuciones** that is beyond my authority
2 *vi* to be greater; **e. a** *o* **de** to exceed; **su fortuna excede de los cien millones** her fortune exceeds one hundred million
3 **excederse** *vpr* (a) *(propasarse)* to go too far, to overstep the mark (**en** in) (b) *(rebasar el límite)* **se excede en el peso** it's too heavy

excelencia 1 *nf (cualidad)* excellence; **elogió las excelencias de la cocina vasca** he praised the distinctive qualities of Basque cuisine; **por e.** par excellence; **Sartre, el existencialista por e.** Sartre, the existentialist par excellence
2 *nmf* **Su E.** His Excellency, *f* Her Excellency; **Su E. el presidente del gobierno** His Excellency, the President; **es para mí un honor, E.** I shall count it an honour, Your Excellency

excelente *adj* excellent

excelentísimo, -a *adj* most excellent; **el e. ayuntamiento de Málaga** Malaga city council; **el e. embajador de...** His Excellency the ambassador of...

excelso, -a *adj Formal* sublime; **una excelsa figura del teatro británico** a truly outstanding figure in British theatre

excéntricamente *adv* eccentrically

excentricidad *nf* (a) *(extravagancia)* eccentricity (b) *Geom* eccentricity

excéntrico, -a 1 *adj* (a) *(extravagante)* eccentric (b) *Geom* eccentric
2 *nm,f* eccentric

excepción *nf* exception; **a** *o* **con e. de** with the exception of, except for; **a e. de él, todos vinieron** they all came except for him *o* apart from him; **de e.** exceptional; **fue un ciclista de e.** he was an exceptional cyclist; **e. hecha de Pérez** Pérez excepted; **hacer una e.** to make an exception; **¿no podrías hacer una e. con ella?** couldn't you make an exception for her?; **sin e.** without exception; **todos sin e. deberán presentarse a las nueve** everyone without exception must be there at nine; EXPR **la e. confirma la regla** the exception proves the rule

excepcional *adj* (a) *(ocasional)* exceptional; **sólo en circunstancias excepcionales** only in exceptional circumstances (b) *(extraordinario)* exceptional; **alcanzar el segundo puesto es un logro e.** reaching second place is an exceptional achievement

excepcionalmente *adv* (a) *(como excepción)* exceptionally; **para viajes a Europa y, e., a África** for journeys to Europe and, exceptionally *o* in exceptional cases, to Africa (b) *(extraordinariamente)* exceptionally; **un verano e. caluroso** an exceptionally hot summer

excepto *adv* except (for); **vinieron todos, e. él** they all came except (for) him *o* apart from him; **todas cuestan lo mismo, e. estas dos** they all cost the same, except for these two; **todos e. tú** everyone except you; **me gusta hablar de todo e. de política** I like talking about any subject except politics; **abierto e. domingos y festivos** *(en letrero)* closed on Sundays and holidays

exceptuar [4] *vt (excluir)* to exclude (**de** from); *(eximir)* to exempt (**de** from); **lloverá en todo el país exceptuando el sur** it will rain throughout the country except in the south; **exceptuando a...** excluding...; **se exceptúa a los menores de dieciséis años** children under the age of sixteen are exempt; **todos fueron castigados, sin e. a ninguno** everyone was punished, without a single exception

excesivamente *adv* excessively

excesivo, -a *adj* excessive; **se pagan precios excesivos** people pay inflated prices, *Br* people pay over the odds; **protegen al niño de un modo e.** they are overprotective of the boy; **no tuvo excesiva suerte en semifinales** she didn't do too well in the semifinals

exceso *nm* (a) *(demasía)* excess; **el e. de sol puede provocar graves quemaduras** too much sun can cause serious sunburn; **en e.** *(fumar, beber, comer)* excessively, to excess; **trabaja en e.** he works too hard; **es meticuloso en e.** he is far too meticulous; **más vale pecar por e. que por defecto** too much is better than not enough ►► ***e. de confianza*** overconfidence; ***e. de equipaje*** excess baggage; ***e. de peso*** *(obesidad)* excess weight; ***e. de velocidad*** speeding
(b) *(abuso)* excess; **denunciaron los excesos de los invasores** they condemned the invaders' excesses *o* atrocities; **cometer un e.** to go too far; **cometer un e. en la bebida/comida** to drink/eat to excess; **los excesos se pagan** we pay for our overindulgence

excipiente *nm* excipient

excisión *nf Med* excision

excitabilidad *nf* excitability

excitable *adj* excitable

excitación *nf* (a) *(nerviosismo)* agitation; *(por enfado, sexo)* arousal (b) *Biol* excitation (c) *Elec* excitation

excitado, -a *adj* (a) *(nervioso)* agitated; *(por enfado, sexo)* aroused (b) *Biol* excited (c) *Elec* excited

excitador *nm Elec* exciter

excitante 1 *adj* (a) *(sustancia)* stimulant; **el café es e.** coffee is a stimulant, coffee gets you worked up (b) *(sexualmente)* arousing (c) *(emocionante)* exciting
2 *nm* stimulant

excitar 1 *vt* (a) *(agitar) (enfermo, niño)* to get worked up *o* over-excited; **el café me excita demasiado** coffee gets me too worked up (b) *(sexualmente)* to arouse (c) *(estimular) (sentidos)* to stimulate; *(apetito)* to whet; *(curiosidad, interés)* to excite; *(ira, pasión)* to arouse
2 **excitarse** *vpr* (a) *(alterarse)* to get worked up *o* over-excited (**por** about); **no te excites** don't get worked up *o* over-excited (b) *(sexualmente)* to become aroused

exclamación *nf* (a) *(interjección)* exclamation; *(grito)* cry (b) *(signo ortográfico)* exclamation mark

exclamar 1 *vt* to exclaim
2 *vi* to exclaim

exclamativo, -a *adj* exclamatory

excluir [34] *vt* (a) *(dejar fuera)* to exclude (**de** from); *(hipótesis, opción)* to rule out, to exclude; **fue excluido del equipo** he was excluded from the team, he was left out of the team; **no excluimos ninguna posibilidad** we are not ruling out *o* excluding any possibility; **excluyendo obras menores, toda su producción está aquí** excluding minor works, her entire output is here
(b) *(hacer imposible)* to rule out, to preclude; **esa postura excluye cualquier posibilidad de acuerdo** that stance rules out *o* precludes any possibility of an agreement

exclusión *nf* exclusion; **todos sin e.** all of them without exception

exclusiva 1 *nf* (a) *(periodística)* exclusive; **conceder una e. a una revista** to grant an exclusive interview to a magazine (b) *(comercial)* exclusive *o* sole right; **la e. del producto nos costará un diez por ciento más este año** the exclusive rights to the product will cost us ten percent more this year
2 **en exclusiva** *loc adv* **tenemos la distribución en España en e.** we are the sole distributor in Spain

exclusivamente *adv* exclusively

exclusive *adv* exclusive; **ambos e.** not inclusive; **los nacidos entre 1970 y 1980 (ambos e.)** those born between 1970 and 1980 (not inclusive)

exclusividad *nf* (a) *(de club, ambiente, producto)* exclusiveness (b) *Com (privilegio)* exclusive *o* sole right

exclusivismo *nm* exclusivism

exclusivista 1 *adj* exclusivist
2 *nmf* exclusivist

exclusivo, -a *adj* (a) *(club, ambiente)* exclusive (b) *(derecho, privilegio)* exclusive; **la política exterior es competencia e. del gobierno central** foreign policy is entirely within the jurisdiction of central government (c) *(producto)* exclusive; *(distribución, distribuidor)* sole

excluyente *adj* which excludes; **dos posibilidades que no son excluyentes** two possibilities that do not exclude one another *o* that are not mutually exclusive

excluyera *etc ver* **excluir**

excluyo *etc ver* **excluir**

Excmo., -a. (*abrev de* **Excelentísimo, -a**) **el E. Ayto. de Málaga** Malaga City Council

excombatiente *nmf Br* ex-serviceman, *f* ex-servicewoman, *US* war veteran

excomulgar [38] *vt* to excommunicate
excomunión *nf* excommunication
excoriación, escoriación *nf Med* excoriation
excoriar, escoriar *vt Med* to excoriate
excrecencia *nf* growth
excreción *nf* excretion
excremento *nm* excrement; **un e. de perro** a piece of dog dirt; **excrementos** *(de ave, conejo, oveja)* droppings; *(de persona)* excrement
excretar 1 *vt (soltar)* to secrete
2 *vi (evacuar)* to excrete
excretorio, -a *adj* excretory
exculpación *nf* exoneration; *Der* acquittal
exculpar 1 *vt* to exonerate; *Der* to acquit
2 **exculparse** *vpr* to declare oneself innocent (**de** of)
exculpatorio, -a *adj* exonerative
excursión *nf (viaje)* excursion, trip; **una e. a pie** *(de poca duración)* walk; *(de larga duración)* hike; **una e. de un día a Versalles** a day trip to Versailles; **una e. de una semana por los Alpes** a week-long excursion in the Alps; **hicimos una e. a Toledo** we went on an outing *o* a trip to Toledo; **ir de e.** to go on an outing *o* a trip; **ir de e. al campo** to go on a trip to the countryside ►► ***e. campestre*** picnic; ***e. con guía*** guided tour
excursionismo *nm (en el campo)* rambling; *(de montaña)* hiking
excursionista 1 *adj* **centro e.** hillwalking club
2 *nmf (en el campo)* rambler; *(en la montaña)* hiker; *(en ciudad)* tripper, visitor
excusa *nf* (**a**) *(pretexto, motivo)* excuse; **eso no es e. para que se peleen** that's no excuse for them to start fighting; **que mintieras a tu hermano no tiene e.** there's no excuse for you lying to your brother; **no busques más excusas** don't keep trying to find excuses; **¡nada de excusas!** no excuses!
(**b**) *(petición de perdón)* apology; **presentó sus excusas** *(en persona)* he apologized; *(a distancia)* he sent his apologies
excusable *adj* (**a**) *(perdonable)* excusable (**b**) *(evitable)* avoidable
excusado[1], -a, escusado, -a *adj* (**a**) *(disculpado)* excused (**b**) *(inútil)* unnecessary, superfluous; **e. (es) decir que...** needless to say...
excusado[2], escusado *nm Euf* **el e.** *(retrete)* the bathroom, *Br* the smallest room
excusar 1 *vt* (**a**) *(disculpar)* to excuse; *(disculparse por)* to apologize for; **eso no excusa tu falta de puntualidad** that is no excuse for your being late; **les ruego excusen mi ignorancia, pero...** forgive my ignorance, but...; **no trates de excusarla** don't make excuses for her
(**b**) *(eximir)* **e. a alguien de (hacer) algo** to excuse sb from (doing) sth; **quedas excusado de asistir** you are excused from attendance
(**c**) *Esp Formal (evitar)* to avoid; **excuso decir que todos están invitados** there's no need for me to say that you're all invited
2 **excusarse** *vpr* to apologize, to excuse oneself; **se excusaron por no venir a la cena** they apologized for not coming to the meal
exe *nm Informát* exe
execrable *adj* abominable, execrable
execrar *vt Formal* to abhor
exégesis *nf inv* exegesis, explanation
exegeta, exégeta *nmf* (**a**) *(de la Biblia)* exegete (**b**) *(de texto literario)* explicator
exención *nf* exemption ►► ***e. fiscal*** tax exemption
exento, -a *adj* exempt; **e. de** *(sin)* free from, without; *(eximido de)* exempt from; **una obra totalmente exenta de interés** a play entirely devoid of interest *o* of no interest whatsoever; **un final no e. de emoción** a final that had its moments of excitement; **quedan exentos de presentarse al examen** they are exempt *o* exempted from taking the exam
exequias *nfpl* funeral, funeral rites
exfoliación *nf* exfoliation
exfoliador *nm Andes, Méx (cuaderno)* loose-leaf notebook
exfoliante 1 *adj* exfoliating; **crema e.** exfoliating cream
2 *nm* = exfoliating cream/lotion etc
exfoliar 1 *vt* to exfoliate
2 **exfoliarse** *vpr* to flake off, *Espec* to exfoliate
ex gratia *adj* ex gratia
exhalación *nf* (**a**) *(emanación)* exhalation, vapour (**b**) *(suspiro)* breath; EXPR *Fam* **como una e.** as quick as a flash; **entró/salió como una e.** he rushed in/out, he shot in/out
exhalar *vt* (**a**) *(aire)* to exhale, to breathe out; *(suspiros)* to heave; **e. el último suspiro** to breathe one's last (breath) (**b**) *(olor, vapor)* to give off
exhaustivamente *adv* exhaustively
exhaustividad *nf* exhaustiveness; **investigaron el caso con e.** the case was exhaustively investigated
exhaustivo, -a *adj* exhaustive
exhausto, -a *adj* exhausted
exhibición *nf* (**a**) *(demostración)* show, display; **hicieron una e. de fuerza** they gave a show of strength; **el equipo dio una auténtica e.** the team put on a magnificent performance (**b**) *(artística)* exhibition; **una e. de objetos precolombinos** an exhibition of pre-Columbian artefacts (**c**) *(deportiva)* exhibition; **una e. de billar artístico** an exhibition of artistic billiards (**d**) *(de películas)* showing
exhibicionismo *nm* exhibitionism
exhibicionista *nmf* (**a**) *(que gusta de llamar la atención)* exhibitionist (**b**) *(pervertido sexual)* exhibitionist, flasher
exhibir 1 *vt* (**a**) *(exponer) (cuadros, fotografías)* to exhibit; *(modelos)* to show; *(productos)* to display; **exhibirá su colección primavera-verano en París** she will present her spring-summer collection in Paris
(**b**) *(alardear de) (joyas, trofeos)* to show off
(**c**) *(mostrar) (cualidades)* **exhibió sus dotes de cantante** she showed how good a singer she was; **exhibió su fuerza ante el público** he demonstrated his strength in front of the audience
(**d**) *(película)* to show, to screen
(**e**) *Méx (pagar)* to pay
2 **exhibirse** *vpr (alardear)* to show off
exhortación *nf Formal* exhortation
exhortar *vt Formal* **e. a alguien a hacer algo, e. a alguien a que haga algo** to exhort *o* urge sb to do sth; **ella me exhortó a no abandonar** she exhorted *o* urged me not to give up
exhorto *nm Der* letter rogatory
exhosto *nm Col* exhaust (pipe)
exhumación *nf* exhumation, disinterment
exhumar *vt* to exhume, to disinter
exigencia *nf* (**a**) *(requisito)* demand, requirement; **tuvo que desnudarse por exigencias del guión** she had to take her clothes off because the script required it (**b**) *(petición)* demand; **venirle a alguien con exigencias** to make demands on sb; **¡no me vengas con exigencias!** don't start demanding things from me!
exigente 1 *adj* demanding; **ser e. con alguien** to be demanding of sb; **no seas tan e. con el chico** don't ask so much from the lad; **últimamente está bastante e.** he's been pretty demanding recently
2 *nmf* demanding person; **ser un e.** to be very demanding
exigible *adj* payable on demand
exigir [24] 1 *vt* (**a**) *(pedir)* to demand; **exigimos nuestros derechos** we demand our rights; **exigen una licenciatura** you need to have a degree; **exijo saber la respuesta** I demand to know the answer; **¡exijo que venga el encargado!** I demand to see the manager!; **exigió que estuviera presente su abogado** she demanded that her lawyer be present; **e. algo de** *o* **a alguien** to demand sth from sb; **de tí se exigirá una conducta ejemplar** you will be expected to show exemplary behaviour; **no le exijas tanto, que acaba de empezar** you shouldn't demand so much of him, he's only just started
(**b**) *(requerir, necesitar)* to call for, to require; **este trabajo exige mucha concentración** this work calls for a lot of concentration; **si el guión lo exige** if the script requires it
2 *vi* to be demanding
exigüidad *nf* meagreness, paltriness
exiguo, -a *adj (ración, sueldo)* meagre; *(espacio)* tiny; **un presupuesto cada vez más e.** a dwindling budget; **una exigua mayoría** a wafer-thin majority
exiliado, -a, *Am* **exilado, -a** 1 *adj* exiled, in exile; **aún permanece e. en Italia** he is still living in exile in Italy
2 *nm,f* exile ►► ***e. político*** political exile
exiliar 1 *vt* to exile
2 **exiliarse** *vpr* to go into exile; **se exiliaron en Francia** they went into exile in France
exilio *nm* exile; **en el e.** in exile; **estar/vivir en el e.** to be/live in exile
eximente *Der* 1 *adj* absolutory, absolving; **una circunstancia e. de culpabilidad** a circumstance which frees one from blame
2 *nf* case for acquittal
eximio, -a *adj Formal* eminent, illustrious

eximir 1 *vt* to exempt (**de** from); **han sido eximidos de pagar el IVA** they've been exempted from paying VAT; **me eximieron de las tareas domésticas** I was exempted from housework; **su condición no le exime de cumplir las leyes** her condition does not exempt her from obeying the law
2 **eximirse** *vpr Am* to obtain an exemption, to be exempted; **se eximió de gimnasia por problemas de salud** he obtained an exemption from gym for health reasons

existencia *nf* (**a**) *(circunstancia de existir)* existence; **se ha confirmado la e. de varios manuscritos inéditos** it has been confirmed that there are several unpublished manuscripts
(**b**) *(vida)* life; **este niño me está amargando la e.** that child is making my life a misery
(**c**) *Com* **existencias** stock, inventory; **quedan muy pocas existencias en el almacén** there's isn't much stock in the warehouse; **en existencias** in stock; **hasta agotar existencias** *(en letrero)* while stocks last; **quedarse sin existencias (de algo)** to run out (of sth); **reponer (las) existencias** to restock

existencial *adj* existential

existencialismo *nm* existentialism

existencialista 1 *adj* existentialist
2 *nmf* existentialist

existencialmente *adv* existentially

existente *adj* existing, existent; **los programas informáticos existentes en el mercado** the software currently available on the market; **la falta de entendimiento e. entre ambos líderes** the lack of understanding between the two leaders; **los problemas existentes entonces aún no se han solucionado** the problems that existed then have still not been resolved

existir *vi* (**a**) *(ser real)* to exist; **los gnomos no existen** gnomes don't exist; **aquel año dejó de e. la Unión Soviética** that year the Soviet Union ceased to exist; **pienso, luego existo** I think, therefore I am
(**b**) *(haber)* to exist; **existen zonas sin explorar** there are some unexplored areas; **existe el riesgo de...** there is the risk that...
(**c**) *(vivir)* **mientras yo exista no tienes que preocuparte** you don't have to worry while I'm still here; *Euf* **dejar de e.** to pass away *o* on

exitazo *nm Fam (logro, fama)* great success; *(canción, película)* huge hit

éxito *nm* (**a**) *(logro, fama)* success; **é. clamoroso** *o* **rotundo** resounding success; **la fiesta fue un é.** the party was a success; **su é. se debe a su esfuerzo** she has achieved success through her own efforts; **con é.** successfully; **superó con é. sus exámenes** she passed her exams successfully; **tener é.** to be successful; **el experimento no tuvo é.** the experiment was unsuccessful *o* was not a success; **la obra tuvo poco é.** the play was not a success; **tuvimos mucho é. en América** we had great success *o* were very successful in America
(**b**) *(canción, película)* hit; *(producto, operación, experimento)* success; **é. (editorial)** bestseller; **la lista de éxitos** *(de libros)* the bestseller list; *(de canciones)* the charts; **un disco de grandes éxitos** a greatest hits album; **de é.** *(libro)* bestselling; *(canción)* hit; **ser un é. (de ventas)** *(libro)* to be a bestseller; *(canción)* to be a hit ▸▸ ***é. de taquilla*** box-office hit

> **Falso amigo**: El sustantivo inglés **exit** no es la traducción del español **éxito**. En inglés, **exit** significa "salida".

exitoso, -a *adj* successful

ex libris *nm inv* ex libris

éxodo *nm* (**a**) *(desplazamiento)* exodus; **el é. estival desde el centro del país a la playa** the summer exodus from the centre of the country to the coast (**b**) *Rel* **el É.** Exodus

exoesqueleto *nm Zool* exoskeleton

exogamia *nf Biol* exogamy

exogámico, -a *adj Biol* exogamous

exógeno, -a *adj* exogenous

exoneración *nf* (**a**) *(liberación) (de carga, obligación, tarea)* exemption (**de** from); **piden su e. de ambos cargos** they demand that he be cleared on both charges (**b**) *(despido)* removal (**de** from)

exonerar *vt* (**a**) *(liberar)* **e. a alguien de** *(carga, obligación, tarea)* to exempt sb from; *(responsabilidad)* to absolve sb from; **lo exoneraron de toda culpa** he was completely exonerated (**b**) *(despedir)* **e. a alguien de un cargo** to relieve sb of a post

exorbitante *adj* exorbitant

exorcismo *nm* exorcism

exorcista *nmf* exorcist

exorcizar [14] *vt* to exorcize

exordio *nm Formal* exordium

exotérmico, -a *adj Quím* exothermic

exótico, -a *adj* exotic

exotismo *nm* exoticism

expandible *adj Informát* expandible

expandir 1 *vt* (**a**) *(cuerpo, gas)* to expand; *(incendio)* to spread, to cause to spread (**b**) *(empresa, mercado, ciudad)* to expand; *(fronteras)* to extend (**c**) *(rumor, noticia)* to spread (**d**) *Informát* to expand
2 **expandirse** *vpr* (**a**) *(cuerpo, gas)* to expand; *(incendio)* to spread (**b**) *(empresa, mercado, territorio)* to expand, to grow (**c**) *(rumor, noticia)* to spread

expansión *nf* (**a**) *(de cuerpo, gas)* expansion; *(de incendio)* spread
(**b**) *(de empresa, mercado, territorio)* expansion, growth; **un periodo de e. económica** a period of economic expansion *o* growth; **en e.** expanding; **un sector económico en franca e.** a fast-growing *o* rapidly-growing sector of the economy
(**c**) *(de rumor, noticia)* spread, spreading
(**d**) *(relajación)* relaxation; *(diversión)* recreation

expansionar 1 *vt* to expand
2 **expansionarse** *vpr* (**a**) *(desarrollarse) (empresa, mercado, territorio)* to expand, to grow (**b**) *(relajarse)* to relax, to unwind; *(divertirse)* to have some fun *o* recreation (**c**) *(desahogarse)* to open up (**con** to)

expansionismo *nm* expansionism

expansionista *adj* expansionist

expansivo, -a *adj* (**a**) *(gases, vapores)* expansive (**b**) *(persona, modo de ser)* open, frank

expatriación *nf (emigración)* expatriation; *(exilio)* exile

expatriado, -a 1 *adj* **los españoles expatriados** *(emigrantes)* expatriate Spaniards; *(exiliados)* Spanish exiles
2 *nm,f (emigrante)* expatriate; *(exiliado)* exile

expatriar [32] 1 *vt (expulsar)* to exile
2 **expatriarse** *vpr (emigrar)* to leave one's country, to emigrate; *(exiliarse)* to go into exile

expectación *nf* (**a**) *(interés)* interest; **el juicio ha despertado una e. inusitada** the trial has aroused an unusual degree of interest (**b**) *(espera)* expectation

expectante *adj* expectant; **permaneció e. en su escondrijo** she waited expectantly in her hiding place

expectativa *nf* (**a**) *(esperanza)* hope; **no tiene muchas expectativas de encontrar trabajo** he doesn't have much hope of finding work
(**b**) *(perspectiva)* prospect; **las expectativas de una solución al conflicto son mínimas** the prospects for an end to the conflict are remote; **contra toda e.** against all expectations; **estar a la e.** to wait and see; **estar a la e. de** *(atento)* to be on the lookout for; *(a la espera)* to be hoping for ▸▸ ***e. de vida*** life expectancy

expectoración *nf Med* (**a**) *(acción)* expectoration (**b**) *(esputo)* sputum

expectorante *Med* 1 *adj* expectorant
2 *nm* expectorant

expectorar *Med* 1 *vi* to expectorate
2 *vt* to expectorate

expedición *nf* (**a**) *(viaje)* expedition; *(grupo)* expedition; **hicieron una e. al Aconcagua** they went on an expedition to Aconcagua; **una e. de cinco montañeros** an expedition of five climbers ▸▸ ***e. de salvamento*** *(viaje)* rescue mission; *(grupo)* rescue party
(**b**) *(de documento, decreto)* issue, issuing; **la e. del pasaporte tarda cinco días** it takes five days for the passport to be issued; **fecha de e.** date of issue
(**c**) *(envío)* shipment, sending

expedicionario, -a 1 *adj* expeditionary
2 *nm,f (en viaje, grupo)* member of an expedition

expedido, -a *adj (documento)* issued; **e. en Bogotá el 15 de diciembre de 1999** issued in Bogota on 15 December 1999

expedidor, -ora *nm,f* sender, dispatcher

expedientar *vt (castigar)* to take disciplinary action against; *(llevar a juicio)* to start proceedings against; **fue expedientado por no asistir al entrenamiento** he was disciplined for missing the training session

expediente *nm* (**a**) *(documentación)* documents; *(ficha)* file
(**b**) *(historial)* record; **el e. del paciente** the patient's record; EXPR *Fam* **cubrir el e.** to do the bare minimum; **hacer algo por cubrir el e.** to do sth for the sake of appearances ▸▸ ***e. académico*** academic record, *US* transcript
(**c**) *(investigación)* inquiry; **se ha abierto un e. para aclarar lo ocurrido** an inquiry has opened to find out what happened; **abrir e. a alguien** *(castigar)* to take disciplinary action against sb; *(llevar a*

juicio) to start proceedings against sb; **formar** *o* **instruir e. a un funcionario** to impeach a public official

(**d**) *Esp Econ* ***e. de crisis*** = statement of the economic difficulties of a company, presented to the authorities to justify redundancies; ***e. de regulación de empleo*** redundancy plan, workforce adjustment plan

expedir [47] 1 *vt* (**a**) *(carta, pedido, mercancías)* to send, to dispatch (**b**) *(pasaporte, certificado, decreto)* to issue; *(contrato, documento)* to draw up; **le fue expedido un visado** she was issued with a visa

2 **expedirse** *vprAm* to deliver an opinion; **la comisión todavía no se expidió sobre ese tema** the committee has not yet delivered an opinion on the subject

> **Falso amigo**: El verbo inglés **to expedite** no es la traducción del español **expedir**. En inglés, **to expedite** significa "acelerar, apresurar".

expeditivo, -a *adj* expeditious; **utilizar métodos expeditivos** to adopt harsh measures

expedito, -a *adj* clear, free; *también Fig* **tener el paso** *o* **camino e.** to have one's way clear

expeler *vt* to emit

expendedor, -ora 1 *adj* **máquina expendedora** vending machine; **una máquina expendedora de bebidas** a drinks machine

2 *nm,f (de mercancía)* dealer, retailer; *(de lotería)* seller, vendor

expendeduría *nf (de tabaco)* tobacconist's *(also selling stamps)*

expender *vt* to sell, to retail

expendio *nm Am* (**a**) *(tienda)* shop (**b**) *(venta)* sale; **e. de refrescos** *(en letrero)* cold drinks for sale; *Arg* **e. bajo receta** (available) by *o* on prescription only

expensar *vt Chile* to defray the costs of

expensas 1 *nfpl* (**a**) *Der (procesales)* costs, expenses (**b**) *Arg (de vivienda)* service charge

2 **a expensas de** *loc prep* at the expense of; **vive a e. de sus abuelos** his grandparents support him financially; **no le gusta vivir a e. de nadie** he doesn't want to live at anybody else's expense

experiencia *nf* (**a**) *(veteranía)* experience; **tiene mucha e. en la reparación de lavadoras** he has a lot of experience at repairing washing machines; **se necesita jefe de mantenimiento con amplia e.** *(en anuncio)* wanted: maintenance foreman with extensive experience; **¿qué e. tiene como jardinero?** what experience do you have as a gardener?; PROV **la e. es la madre de la ciencia** experience is the mother of wisdom ►► ***e. laboral*** work experience

(**b**) *(vivencia)* experience; **viví una e. única** I had a unique experience; **sé por (propia) e. que este trabajo implica sacrificio** I know from my own experience that this job involves a lot of sacrifices

(**c**) *(experimento)* experiment

experimentación *nf* experimentation; **e. con animales vivos** experiments on live animals; **en fase de e.** at the experimental stage

experimentado, -a *adj* (**a**) *(persona)* experienced (**b**) *(método)* tried and tested

experimentador, -ora 1 *adj* experimenting

2 *nm,f* experimenter

experimental *adj* experimental; **en fase e.** at the experimental stage

experimentalmente *adv* experimentally

experimentar 1 *vt* (**a**) *(sensación, sentimiento, efecto)* to experience; **e. frío/calor** to feel cold/hot; **experimenté una gran tristeza** I felt a great sadness

(**b**) *(derrota, pérdidas)* to suffer; *(cambios, empeoramiento)* to undergo, to suffer; *(mejoría)* to undergo, to experience; **las temperaturas experimentarán un leve ascenso/descenso** we will see a slight rise/fall in temperatures

(**c**) *(probar)* to test; *(hacer experimentos con)* to experiment with *o* on

2 *vi* **e. con** to experiment with *o* on

experimento *nm* experiment; **e. de laboratorio** laboratory experiment; **hacer un e.** to try an experiment

experticia *nf Ven* expertise, skill

experto, -a 1 *adj* expert; **es experta en temas medioambientales** she's an expert on environmental matters; **es e. en hacer diabluras** he's an expert at getting up to mischief

2 *nm,f* expert; **un e. en electrónica** an electronics expert; **déjese aconsejar por un e.** seek expert advice; **un comité** *o* **una comisión de expertos** a committee of experts; **¿poner pañales? ¡soy todo un e.!** changing nappies? I'm quite the expert *o Br* a dab hand!

expiación *nf* atonement, expiation

expiar [32] *vt* to atone for, to expiate

expiatorio, -a *adj* expiatory

expidiera *etc ver* **expedir**

expido *etc ver* **expedir**

expiración *nf* expiry

expirar *vi* (**a**) *(tener vencimiento)* to expire (**b**) *Formal (morir)* to expire

explanación *nf* (**a**) *(allanamiento)* levelling (**b**) *Formal (explicación)* explanation, explication

explanada *nf* area of flat *o* level ground

explanar *vt (terreno)* to level

explayarse *vpr* (**a**) *(hablar mucho)* to talk at length; **se explayó sobre su tema favorito** he went off on his hobbyhorse (**b**) *(desahogarse)* **me hacía falta e.** I needed to get it all off my chest; **e. con alguien** to open up to sb (**c**) *(divertirse)* to amuse oneself, to enjoy oneself

expletivo, -a *adj Gram* expletive

explicable *adj* explicable

explicación *nf* explanation; **les daré una breve e. de cómo funciona** I'll give you a brief explanation of how it works; **dar/pedir explicaciones** to give/demand an explanation; **no tengo que darte explicaciones de lo que hago** I don't have to explain my actions to you; **¡exijo una e.!** I demand an explanation!; **creo que te debo una e.** I think I owe you an explanation; **el fenómeno no tiene e.** there is no explanation for the phenomenon

explicar [60] 1 *vt* (**a**) *(exponer, contar)* to explain; *(teoría)* to expound; **explícame cómo funciona** tell me how it works; **¿te importaría explicarme qué pasa?** would you mind telling me *o* explaining what's going on?; **es una sensación rara, no lo puedo e.** it's a strange feeling, I can't explain it (**b**) *(enseñar)* to teach, to lecture in

2 **explicarse** *vpr* (**a**) *(comprender)* to understand; **todavía no se explican cómo pudo suceder** they still can't understand how it could have happened; **no me lo explico** I can't understand it

(**b**) *(dar explicaciones)* to explain; **a ver, explícate, ¿qué quieres decir con eso?** come on, explain, what do you mean by that?; **no sé si me explico** do you know what I mean?; **¿me explico?** do you see what I mean?; *(como advertencia)* is that clear?; **espero haberme explicado con la suficiente claridad** I hope I have made myself sufficiently clear

(**c**) *(expresarse)* to make oneself understood; **¡qué bien se explica!** she expresses herself so well!, she's so articulate!

explicativo, -a *adj* explanatory

explícitamente *adv* explicitly

explícito, -a *adj* explicit; **las razones están explícitas en su carta de dimisión** the reasons are clearly set out in her letter of resignation

exploración *nf* (**a**) *(de territorio)* exploration ►► ***e. submarina*** *(investigación)* underwater exploration; *(deporte)* skin diving (**b**) *Mil* reconnaissance (**c**) *Med (interna)* exploration; *(externa)* examination

explorador, -ora 1 *nm,f* (**a**) *(viajero)* explorer (**b**) *(scout)* boy scout, *f* girl guide (**c**) *Mil* scout

2 *nm Informát* browser

explorar *vt* (**a**) *(averiguar, reconocer)* to explore; **zonas aún por e.** as yet unexplored areas; **exploraremos todas las posibilidades** we will explore every option (**b**) *Mil* to scout (**c**) *Med (internamente)* to explore; *(externamente)* to examine (**d**) *Informát* to browse; **e. Internet** to browse the Internet

exploratorio, -a *adj* (**a**) *(instrumento, técnica)* exploratory (**b**) *(conversaciones)* preliminary (**c**) *Mil (misión)* scouting

explosión *nf* (**a**) *(de bomba, explosivo, caldera)* explosion; **una e. de gas** a gas explosion; **el gol provocó una e. de júbilo** there was an outburst of joy at the goal; **hacer e.** *(bomba, explosivo, petardo)* to explode, to go off; *(caldera)* to explode, to burst ►► ***e. atómica*** atomic explosion; ***e. controlada*** controlled explosion; ***e. nuclear*** atomic explosion

(**b**) *(desarrollo rápido)* explosion ►► ***e. demográfica*** population explosion; ***e. urbanística*** rapid urban expansion

explosionar 1 *vt* to explode, to blow up

2 *vi* to explode, to blow up

explosivo, -a 1 *adj* (**a**) *(sustancia, artefacto, paquete)* explosive; **material e.** explosive (**b**) *Gram* plosive (**c**) *(tema, discurso, situación)* explosive; **hizo unas explosivas declaraciones a la prensa** she made some explosive statements to the press; **una rubia explosiva** a blond bombshell

2 *nm* explosive ►► ***e. detonante*** high explosive; ***e. plástico*** plastic explosive; ***e. de gran potencia*** high explosive

explotable *adj* exploitable

explotación *nf* (**a**) *(acción) (de recursos)* exploitation; *(de fábrica, negocio)* running, operation; *(de yacimiento)* mining; *(agrícola)* farming; *(de petróleo)* drilling; **tiene el negocio en régimen de e.** he has the business on lease; **e. forestal** forestry
(**b**) *(de niños, trabajadores)* exploitation; **campaña contra la e. infantil** campaign against child labour
(**c**) *(instalaciones)* ***e. agrícola*** farm; ***e. agropecuaria*** arable and livestock farm; ***e. ganadera*** livestock farm; ***e. minera*** mine; ***e. petrolífera*** oilfield

explotador, -ora 1 *adj* (**a**) *(de niños, trabajadores)* exploiting (**b**) *(operador)* operating; **la sociedad explotadora del casino** the company that operates the casino
2 *nm,f* (**a**) *(de niños, trabajadores)* exploiter (**b**) *(operador)* operator

explotar[1] *vt* (**a**) *(niños, trabajadores)* to exploit; **en esta empresa explotan a los trabajadores** this firm exploits its workers (**b**) *(recursos naturales)* to exploit; *(fábrica, negocio)* to run, to operate; *(terreno)* to farm; *(mina)* to work (**c**) *(tema, asunto, situación)* to exploit

explotar[2] *vi* (**a**) *(bomba, explosivo, petardo)* to explode, to go off; *(globo, neumático, caldera)* to explode, to burst (**b**) *(persona)* to explode (with rage)

expo *nf (exposición universal)* expo

expoliación *nf* pillaging, plundering

expoliador, -ora 1 *adj* pillaging, plundering
2 *nm,f* pillager, plunderer

expoliar *vt* to pillage, to plunder

expolio *nm* (**a**) *(saqueo)* pillaging, plundering (**b**) *Esp Fam (alboroto)* fuss; **montaron un e.** they kicked up a fuss

exponencial 1 *adj* exponential; **crecer a ritmo e.** to increase exponentially
2 *nf* exponential

exponencialmente *adv* exponentially

exponente *nm* (**a**) *Mat* exponent (**b**) *(representante) (persona)* exponent; *(cosa)* example; **esta película es un buen e. del cine francés actual** this movie is a good example of current French cinema

exponer [50] 1 *vt* (**a**) *(de palabra) (teoría)* to expound; *(tema)* to present; *(ideas, propuesta)* to set out, to explain; *(argumentos, razones)* to set out, to state; **he expuesto los hechos tal y como ocurrieron** I have related *o* set out the events exactly as they occurred
(**b**) *(a la vista) (cuadro, obra)* to exhibit; *(objetos en vitrinas)* to display
(**c**) *(vida, prestigio, carrera)* to risk, to put at risk
(**d**) *(a agentes físicos) (objeto, parte del cuerpo)* to expose (**a** to); **no e. al sol o a temperaturas elevadas** *(en letrero)* do not expose to direct sunlight or high temperatures
2 *vi (en una galería, museo)* to exhibit
3 **exponerse** *vpr* (**a**) *(a riesgo)* to run the risk (**a** of); *(a ataque, crítica)* to expose oneself (**a** to); **ya sabes a lo que te expones** you know what you're letting yourself in for; **si salimos ahora nos exponemos a que nos caiga un chaparrón** if we go out now we run the risk of getting caught in a downpour
(**b**) *(a sol, radiaciones)* **exponerse a algo** to expose oneself to sth; **no se expongan al sol sin la debida protección** do not expose yourself to *o* go out in the sun without proper protection

exportable *adj* exportable

exportación *nf* (**a**) *(acción)* export; **una empresa de e. de cerámica** a ceramics export company; **productos de e.** export goods (**b**) *(mercancías)* exports ►► *Com* ***exportaciones invisibles*** invisible exports

exportador, -ora 1 *adj* exporting; **país e.** exporting country, exporter; **una compañía exportadora de objetos de artesanía** a company exporting handicrafts
2 *nm,f* exporter

exportar *vt* (**a**) *Com* to export (**a** to) (**b**) *Informát* to export (**c**) *(ideas, costumbres)* to export

exposición *nf* (**a**) *(de arte)* exhibition; *(de objetos en vitrina)* display; *(de máquinas, aparatos, herramientas)* show, fair; **una e. de flores** a flower show; **una e. canina** a dog show ►► ***e. universal*** international exposition *o* exhibition, *US* world's fair
(**b**) *(de teoría)* exposition; *(de tema)* presentation; *(de ideas, propuesta)* setting out, explanation; *(de argumentos, razones)* setting out, statement; **ofreció una detallada e. de los hechos** she gave a detailed account of the events
(**c**) *(al sol, calor, radiaciones)* exposure
(**d**) *Fot* exposure
(**e**) *Mús* exposition

exposímetro *nm* exposure meter

expositivo, -a *adj* explanatory

expósito, -a *Anticuado* 1 *adj* **niño e.** foundling
2 *nm,f* foundling

expositor, -ora 1 *adj* exponent
2 *nm,f* (**a**) *(en feria, galería)* exhibitor (**b**) *(de teoría)* exponent (**c**) *Andes, RP (conferenciante)* speaker
3 *nm (para productos, folletos, postales)* display stand; **un e. giratorio de libros** a revolving book display *o* stand

exprés 1 *adj inv* (**a**) *(café)* expresso (**b**) *(carta, correo)* ≃ first-class; *(servicio)* express
2 *nm inv (compañía de transportes)* courier company

expresado, -a *adj (mencionado)* above-mentioned

expresamente *adv* (**a**) *(a propósito)* expressly; **he venido e. para verte** I've come specially to see you; **una sociedad creada e. para fomentar las artes** a body specifically set up to foster the arts
(**b**) *(explícitamente)* explicitly, specifically; **pidió e. que su nombre no figurara en el contrato** she specifically asked that her name not be mentioned in the contract; **no se dirigió e. a nadie** he wasn't talking to anyone in particular

expresar 1 *vt* (**a**) *(manifestar)* to express; **quisiera expresarles mi más sincero agradecimiento** I would like to thank you most sincerely; **es una sensación rara, no sé cómo expresarlo** it is an odd feeling, I don't know how to express it; **exprésalo de una manera más formal** put it more formally; **tal y como queda expresado en los apartados dos y tres** as stated in sections two and three
(**b**) *(mostrar)* to show; **hechos que expresan por sí solos la hospitalidad de este pueblo** incidents that speak for themselves about this people's hospitality
2 **expresarse** *vpr* to express oneself; **no consigo expresarme con fluidez** I can't express myself well; **creo que me he expresado con suficiente claridad** I think I have made myself clear enough

expresión *nf* (**a**) *(en el rostro)* expression (**b**) *(de sentimientos, palabras)* expression; **tiene facilidad de e.** she is very articulate; **tómenlo como e. de nuestro agradecimiento** please accept it as a token of our gratitude ►► ***e. corporal*** self-expression through movement; ***e. escrita*** writing skills; ***e. oral*** oral skills (**c**) *(palabra, locución)* expression (**d**) *Mat* expression

expresionismo *nm* expressionism ►► ***e. abstracto*** abstract expressionism

expresionista 1 *adj* expressionist
2 *nmf* expressionist

expresivamente *adv* (**a**) *(con viveza)* expressively (**b**) *(afectuosamente)* affectionately

expresividad *nf* expressiveness

expresivo, -a *adj* (**a**) *(lleno de expresividad) (persona, rostro, lenguaje)* expressive; **hizo un gesto de enojo muy e.** she expressed her annoyance with an eloquent gesture (**b**) *(cariñoso)* affectionate

expreso, -a 1 *adj* (**a**) *(explícito)* specific; **las condiciones expresas en el presente contrato** the conditions set out in this agreement; **por deseo e. de los familiares** at the express wish of the family
(**b**) *(deliberado)* express; **con la expresa intención de hacer daño** with the express intention of causing harm
(**c**) *(claro)* clear; **por orden expresa del alcalde** by express order of the mayor
(**d**) *(tren)* express
(**e**) *(café)* espresso
2 *nm* (**a**) *(tren)* express train (**b**) *(café)* espresso (**c**) *(correo)* express mail
3 *adv* on purpose, expressly

exprimelimones *nm inv* lemon squeezer

exprimidor *nm* squeezer; **un e. eléctrico** an electric juicer

exprimir *vt* (**a**) *(fruta)* to squeeze; *(zumo)* to squeeze out (**b**) *(explotar)* to exploit; **aquí te exprimen al máximo** they get as much out of you as they can here, they really get their pound of flesh out of you here

ex profeso *adv* intentionally, expressly

expropiación *nf* expropriation

expropiar *vt* to expropriate

expuesto, -a 1 *participio ver* **exponer**
2 *adj* (**a**) *(desprotegido)* exposed (**a** to); **estar e. a** *(lluvia, ataques)* to be exposed to (**b**) *(arriesgado)* dangerous, risky (**c**) *(dicho)* stated, expressed; **a lo e. cabe añadir que...** to what has already been stated we should add that... (**d**) *(exhibido)* on display

expugnar *vt Formal* to (take by) storm

expulsar *vt* (**a**) *(de local)* to throw out; *(de clase)* to send out; *(de colegio, país, territorio)* to expel; *(de organización, club)* to expel, to throw out (**b**) *Dep* to send off (**c**) *(emitir) (humo)* to emit, to give off;

(lava, objeto, sustancia) to expel; *(disquete)* to eject; **contenga la respiración y expulse el aire** hold your breath, then breathe out; **e. la placenta** to expel the placenta

expulsión *nf* (**a**) *(de clase, organización, país)* expulsion (**b**) *Dep* sending-off (**c**) *(de humo, fuego, lava)* discharge, expulsion; *(de objeto, sustancia)* expulsion

expulsor *nm (en arma de fuego)* ejector

expurgar [38] *vt (texto)* to expurgate

expusiera *etc ver* **exponer**

exquisitamente *adv* exquisitely

exquisitez *nf* (**a**) *(cualidad)* exquisiteness; **se comporta con e.** he behaves impeccably (**b**) *(cosa)* exquisite thing; *(comida)* delicacy

exquisito, -a *adj* (**a**) *(refinado) (objeto, vestimenta, modales)* exquisite; *(persona)* exquisite; **es muy e. vistiendo** he dresses exquisitely (**b**) *(comida)* delicious, exquisite; **el asado está e.** the roast is delicious

ext. (*abrev de* **extensión**) *(de línea telefónica)* ext

extasiado, -a *adj* enthralled, enraptured; **quedarse e.** to be enthralled *o* enraptured

extasiarse [32] *vpr* **e. ante** *o* **con algo** to be enthralled o enraptured by sth

éxtasis *nm inv* (**a**) *(estado)* ecstasy (**b**) *(droga)* ecstasy

extemporáneo, -a *adj* (**a**) *(clima)* unseasonable (**b**) *(comentario, pregunta)* inopportune, untimely

> **Falso amigo**: El adjetivo inglés **extemporaneous** no es la traducción del español **extemporáneo**. En inglés, **extemporaneous** significa "improvisado".

extender [66] **1** *vt* (**a**) *(tela, plano, periódico)* to spread (out); *(brazos, piernas)* to stretch out; *(alas)* to spread (out); **extendió el mantel sobre la hierba** he spread the blanket (out) on the grass; **me extendió la mano** she held out her hand to me

(**b**) *(mantequilla, pegamento, barniz)* to spread; *(objetos)* to spread out

(**c**) *(ampliar)* to extend, to widen; **extendieron el castigo a todos los alumnos** the punishment was extended to include all the pupils

(**d**) *(documento)* to draw up; *(cheque)* to make out, to write (out); *(certificado)* to issue; *(factura)* to make out; *(receta)* to write (out); **le extenderé un cheque** I'll write you (out) a cheque, I'll make out a cheque to you

(**e**) *(prolongar)* to prolong, to extend

(**f**) *(propagar)* to spread; **e. una creencia** to spread a belief

2 extenderse *vpr* (**a**) *(ocupar)* **extenderse hasta** to go as far as; **extenderse por** to stretch *o* extend across; **sus tierras se extienden hasta la carretera/por todo el valle** his property extends as far as the main road/all the way along the valley

(**b**) *(durar)* to extend, to last; **su etapa de gobierno se extiende desde 1986 a 1994** her period of office extended *o* lasted from 1986 to 1994

(**c**) *(difundirse)* to spread (**por** across); **el incendio se extendió por el bosque** the fire spread through the forest; **el virus se extendió rápidamente por Internet** the virus spread quickly over the Internet; **pon servilletas para que no se extienda la mancha** put some paper napkins down so the stain doesn't spread; **la costumbre se ha extendido a otras zonas del país** the custom has spread to other parts of the country

(**d**) *(hablar mucho)* to enlarge, to expand (**en** on); **no quisiera extenderme más** I prefer not to say any more than that

(**e**) *(tenderse)* to stretch out

extendido, -a *adj* (**a**) *(esparcido)* spread out; **tiene el cáncer muy e.** his cancer has spread very extensively

(**b**) *(abierto)* outstretched, open; **con las piernas extendidas** with legs outstretched

(**c**) *(diseminado)* widespread, prevalent; **es un prejuicio muy e.** it is a very widespread prejudice; **el correo electrónico está muy e. en las empresas** electronic mail is very widely used in business

extensamente *adv* extensively; **disertó e. sobre temas políticos** he spoke at length on political matters

extensible *adj* extensible, extendible

extensión *nf* (**a**) *(superficie)* area, expanse; **solares con una e. de 500 metros cuadrados** plots with an area of 500m^2; **grandes extensiones de terreno desértico** large desert areas

(**b**) *(amplitud) (de país)* size; *(de conocimientos)* extent; **la novela tiene una e. de 600 páginas** the novel is 600 pages long

(**c**) *(duración)* duration, length; **debido a la e. de la película habrá un descanso** due to the length of the film there will be an interval

(**d**) *(ampliación)* extension; **se concedió una e. del plazo** an extension was granted

(**e**) *(sentido)* range of meaning; **en toda la e. de la palabra** in every sense of the word; **por e.** by extension

(**f**) *Informát* extension

(**g**) *(de línea telefónica)* extension

extensivo, -a *adj* (**a**) *(aplicable)* **ser e. a** to extend to; **esta norma es extensiva a todos los alumnos** this rule extends to all pupils; **hacer algo e. a** to extend sth to; **la medida se hará extensiva al resto del país** the measure will be extended to the rest of the country; **desearía hacer e. mi agradecimiento a...** I would like to extend my thanks to...

(**b**) *Agr* extensive

extenso, -a *adj* (**a**) *(terreno, solar)* large, extensive; *(país, región, desierto)* vast (**b**) *(duración, periodo, libro, película)* long; *(informe, discurso)* long, lengthy (**c**) *(conocimientos, vocabulario)* extensive

extensor, -ora 1 *adj (músculo)* extensor

2 *nm (aparato)* chest expander

extenuación *nf* severe exhaustion

extenuado, -a *adj* completely exhausted, drained

extenuante *adj* completely exhausting, draining

extenuar [4] **1** *vt* to exhaust completely, to drain

2 extenuarse *vpr* to exhaust oneself, to tire oneself out

exterior 1 *adj* (**a**) *(de fuera)* outside; *(capa)* outer, exterior; **no se observan desperfectos en la parte e. del vehículo** there are no signs of damage to the outside of the vehicle; **Ferreras adelanta a todos por la calle e.** Ferreras is overtaking them all in the outside lane

(**b**) *(visible)* outward; **su aspecto e. es de calma** she is outwardly calm

(**c**) *(extranjero) (asuntos, comercio)* foreign; **una empresa de comercio e.** an import-export company

(**d**) *(que da a la calle)* **apartamento/habitación e.** flat/room that looks onto the street

2 *nm* (**a**) *(superficie, zona)* outside; **el e. del edificio se halla acordonado** the area outside the building is cordoned off; **pintaremos el e. de la casa** we will paint the outside of the house; **desde el e. no se ve nada** there's no sign of anything from outside; **todas las habitaciones/ventanas dan al e.** all the rooms/windows look onto the outside *o* have exterior views

(**b**) *Cine* **exteriores** exteriors; **rodar los exteriores** to film the exteriors; **rodar en exteriores** to film on location

exterioridad *nf* outward appearance

exteriorización *nf* outward demonstration, manifestation

exteriorizar [14] *vt* to show, to reveal

exteriormente *adv* outwardly, externally

exterminación *nf* extermination

exterminador, -ora *adj* exterminating

exterminar *vt* to exterminate

exterminio *nm* extermination

externalización *nm Com* outsourcing

externalizar [14] *vt Com* to outsource

externamente *adv* externally, outwardly

externar *vt Méx (emoción, opinión)* to express

externo, -a 1 *adj* (**a**) *(de fuera)* external; *(capa, superficie)* outer; *(influencia)* outside; *(signo, aspecto)* outward; **pinta la parte externa del cajón** paint the outside of the box; **no había signos externos de violencia** there were no outward signs of violence (**b**) *(alumno)* **los alumnos externos** the day pupils (**c**) *Mat (ángulo)* exterior

2 *nm,f (alumno)* day pupil

extiendo *etc ver* **extender**

extinción *nf* (**a**) *(de especie)* extinction; **en peligro de e.** in danger of extinction (**b**) *(de fuego, incendio)* putting out, extinguishing (**c**) *(de esperanzas)* loss (**d**) *(de plazo, obligaciones)* termination, end

extinguidor *nm Am* fire extinguisher

extinguir [26] **1** *vt* (**a**) *(fuego, incendio)* to put out, to extinguish (**b**) *(animal, raza)* to wipe out (**c**) *(afecto, entusiasmo, esperanzas)* to put an end to

2 extinguirse *vpr* (**a**) *(fuego, incendio, luz)* to go out; *(volcán)* to become extinct (**b**) *(animal, raza)* to become extinct, to die out (**c**) *(ruido)* to die away (**d**) *(afecto, entusiasmo, esperanzas)* to die (**e**) *(plazo)* to expire

extinto, -a 1 *adj (especie, volcán, civilización)* extinct; *(organización)* defunct; **el e. Pedro Bustamante** the late Pedro Bustamante; **la ya extinta Agrupación Popular Democrática** the now defunct People's Democratic Grouping

2 *nm,f Am* **el e./la extinta** the deceased

extintor *nm Esp* fire extinguisher

extirpación *nf* (**a**) *(quirúrgica) (de órgano, tumor, quiste)* removal, *Espec* extirpation; *(de muela)* extraction (**b**) *(erradicación)* eradication, stamping out

extirpar *vt* (**a**) *(quirúrgicamente) (órgano, tumor, quiste)* to remove, *Espec* to extirpate; *(muela)* to extract (**b**) *(erradicar)* to eradicate, to stamp out

extornar *vt Com* to rebate

extorno *nm Com* rebate

extorsión *nf Der* extortion

extorsionar *vt Der* to extort money from

extorsionista *nmf Der* extortionist

extra 1 *adj* (**a**) *(adicional)* extra; **horas extras** overtime (**b**) *(de gran calidad)* top quality, superior; **chocolate e.** superior quality chocolate

2 *nmf (en película)* extra; **hizo de e. en una del oeste** he was an extra in a western

3 *nm (gasto)* extra

4 *nf* (**a**) *Fam (paga)* = additional payment of a month's salary or wages in June and December (**b**) *Am (gasolina) Br* 4-star petrol, *US* premium gas

5 *interj* extra; **ie., e.!, dimite el presidente** extra! extra! President resigns!

extra- *pref* extra-

extraacadémico, -a *adj* extracurricular

extracción *nf* (**a**) *(de astilla, bala)* removal, extraction; *(de diente)* extraction; **realizar una e. de sangre** *(para análisis)* to take a blood sample; *(para donación)* to take a blood donation (**b**) *(de carbón, mineral)* mining; *(de petróleo)* extraction (**c**) *(de humos)* extraction (**d**) *(en sorteos)* drawing (**e**) *(origen)* **de baja e.** of humble origins, from a humble background ►► ***e. social*** social extraction

extraconyugal *adj* extramarital

extractar *vt* to summarize, to shorten

extracto *nm* (**a**) *(resumen)* summary, résumé ►► ***e. de cuenta*** bank statement (**b**) *(concentrado)* extract ►► ***e. de carne*** meat extract; ***e. de malta*** malt extract

extractor *nm (de humos)* extractor fan

extracurricular *adj Educ* extracurricular

extradición *nf* extradition; **pedir/conceder la e. de alguien** to call for/grant sb's extradition

extraditable *adj* extraditable

extraditar *vt* to extradite

extraer [68] *vt* (**a**) *(sacar) (astilla, bala)* to extract, to take out (**de** from); *(diente, sangre, humo)* to extract (**de** from); **extraiga una de las bolas que hay en esta bolsa** take out one ball from this bag

(**b**) *(obtener) (datos, cita)* to extract (**de** from); *(conclusiones)* to draw (**de** from); **trató de extraernos información** she tried to extract information from us; **¿qué enseñanza podemos e. de todo esto?** what lesson can we learn from all this?

(**c**) *(carbón, mineral)* to mine (**de** from); *(petróleo)* to extract (**de** from) (**d**) *Mat* to extract

extraescolar *adj* extracurricular

extrafino, -a *adj* top quality, de luxe; **chocolate e.** premium chocolate

extrahumano, -a *adj* nonhuman

extraigo *etc ver* **extraer**

extrajera *etc ver* **extraer**

extrajudicial *adj* extrajudicial; **un acuerdo e.** an out-of-court settlement

extralegal *adj* extralegal

extralimitación *nf* abuse *(of power, authority)*

extralimitarse *vpr* to go too far; **se extralimitó en el ejercicio de su cargo** she exceeded her authority

extramatrimonial, extramarital *adj* extramarital

extramuros *adv* outside the city *o* town

extranet *nf* extranet

extranjería *nf* foreign status; **ley de e.** immigration law

extranjerismo *nm* foreign word

extranjerizar [14] *vt* to introduce foreign customs to

extranjero, -a 1 *adj* foreign

2 *nm,f (persona)* foreigner

3 *nm (territorio)* **me gusta viajar por el e.** I like travelling abroad; **del e.** from abroad; **en** *o* **por el e.** abroad; **está de viaje en** *o* **por el e.** she's away on a trip abroad; **ir al e.** to go abroad

extranjis, estrangis: de extranjis, de estrangis *loc adv Esp Fam* on the quiet; **salí de la casa de e.** I sneaked out of the house; **trajeron de e. un televisor** they sneaked in a television; **se encuentra con ella de e.** he meets her in secret

extrañamente *adv* strangely

extrañamiento *nm* banishment

extrañar 1 *vt* (**a**) *(sorprender)* to surprise; **me extraña (que digas esto)** I'm surprised (that you should say that); **no me extraña nada que no haya venido** I'm not in the least surprised he hasn't come; **se enfadó, y no me extraña** she was annoyed, and I'm not surprised; **no es de e. que pasen estas cosas** it's not surprising these things happen

(**b**) *(echar de menos)* to miss; **extraña mucho a sus amigos** she misses her friends a lot; **¿qué es lo que más extrañas de tu país?** what is the thing you miss most about your country?

(**c**) *(encontrar extraño)* to find strange, not to be used to; **he dormido mal porque extraño la cama** I slept badly because I'm not used to the bed

(**d**) *(desterrar)* to banish

2 *vi RP* to be *o* feel homesick; **a pesar de haber estado afuera años, todavía extraña mucho** although he's been abroad for years, he still feels really homesick

3 **extrañarse** *vpr (sorprenderse)* to be surprised (**de** at); **no sé de qué te extrañas, siempre han sido así** I don't know why you're so surprised, they've always been like that; **se extrañaba de que nadie le hubiera avisado** he was surprised that nobody had told him

extrañeza *nf* (**a**) *(sorpresa)* surprise; **nos miró con e.** he looked at us in surprise; **la decisión causó e. entre sus amigos** the decision surprised her friends (**b**) *(rareza)* strangeness

extraño, -a 1 *adj* (**a**) *(raro)* strange, odd; **es e. que no hayan llegado ya** it's strange *o* odd they haven't arrived yet; **¡qué e.!** how strange *o* odd!; **me resulta e. oírte hablar así** I find it strange *o* odd to hear you talk like that (**b**) *(ajeno)* detached, uninvolved (**c**) *Med* foreign

2 *nm,f* stranger; **no hables con extraños** don't talk to strangers

3 *nm (movimiento brusco)* **el vehículo hizo un e.** the vehicle went out of control for a second

extraoficial *adj* unofficial

extraoficialmente *adv* unofficially

extraordinaria *nf Esp (paga)* = additional payment of a month's salary or wages in June and December

extraordinariamente *adv* extraordinarily

extraordinario, -a 1 *adj* (**a**) *(insólito)* extraordinary (**b**) *(excelente)* extraordinary (**c**) *(especial) (edición, suplemento)* special; *(congreso, asamblea, junta)* extraordinary; **hacer gastos extraordinarios** to have extra expenses

2 *nm* (**a**) *Prensa* special edition (**b**) *(correo)* special delivery

extraparlamentario, -a *adj* non-parliamentary

extraplano, -a *adj (reloj)* super-slim, ultra-thin; *(calculadora)* ultra-thin; *(pantalla)* super flat, ultra-thin; *(compresa)* ultra-slim

extrapolación *nf* extrapolation

extrapolar *vt* to extrapolate; **a partir de los datos hemos extrapolado algunas conclusiones** based on the data, we have extrapolated some conclusions

extrarradio *nm* outskirts *(often with connotations of poverty)*; **en el e.** on the outskirts

extrasensorial *adj* extrasensory

extraterrestre 1 *adj* extraterrestrial

2 *nmf* extraterrestrial

extraterritorial *adj* extraterritorial

extraterritorialidad *nf* extraterritorial rights

extravagancia *nf* (**a**) *(excentricidad)* eccentricity (**b**) *(rareza)* outlandishness

extravagante *adj* (**a**) *(excéntrico)* eccentric (**b**) *(raro)* outlandish

extravasarse *vpr* to flow out

extraversión *nf* extroversion

extravertido, -a 1 *adj* extrovert

2 *nm,f* extrovert

extraviado, -a *adj* (**a**) *(perdido) (persona, objeto)* lost, missing; *(animal)* stray, lost; **tenía la mirada extraviada** she was staring into space (**b**) *Fig (descarriado)* debauched

extraviar [32] 1 *vt* (**a**) *(objeto)* to lose, to mislay (**b**) *(excursionista)* to mislead, to cause to lose one's way (**c**) *(mirada, vista)* to allow to wander

2 **extraviarse** *vpr (persona)* to get lost; *(objeto)* to be mislaid, to go missing; *(animal)* to get lost, to go astray

extravío *nm* (**a**) *(pérdida)* loss, mislaying (**b**) *(desenfreno)* excess

extremadamente *adv* extremely

extremado, -a *adj* extreme
Extremadura *n* Extremadura
extremar 1 *vt (precaución, vigilancia)* to maximize; **han extremado las medidas de seguridad** security measures have been stepped up to the maximum
2 extremarse *vpr* to take great pains *o* care
extremaunción *nf Rel* the last rites, *Espec* extreme unction; **dar la e. a alguien** to give sb the last rites
extremeño, -a 1 *adj* of/from Extremadura *(Spain)*
2 *nm,f* person from Extremadura *(Spain)*
extremidad *nf (extremo)* end; **extremidades** *(del cuerpo)* extremities
extremis *ver* **in extremis**
extremismo *nm* extremism
extremista 1 *adj* extremist; **¡no seas e.!, no es para tanto** don't exaggerate! it's not that bad
2 *nmf* extremist
extremo, -a 1 *adj* **(a)** *(sumo)* extreme; **con e. cuidado** with extreme care **(b)** *(al límite)* extreme; **una situación de pobreza extrema** a situation of extreme poverty; **las condiciones climáticas de ese lugar son extremas** the climate here is extreme; **la extrema izquierda/derecha** the far left/right **(c)** *(lejano)* far, furthest
2 *nm* **(a)** *(punta)* end; **agárralo por este e.** hold it by this end; **al otro e. de la calle** at the other end of the street; **mientras, en el otro e. del país...** meanwhile, at the other end of the country...; EXPR **los extremos se tocan** extremes meet
(b) *(límite)* extreme; **llegar a extremos ridículos/peligrosos** to reach ridiculous/dangerous extremes; **no desearía llegar a ese e.** I wouldn't want to go to those lengths; **llegamos al e. de pegarnos** we actually ended up coming to blows; **en e.: le mimas en e.** you spoil him far too much; **es meticuloso en e.** he is extremely meticulous *o* meticulous to a fault; **una decisión en e. sorprendente** an extremely surprising decision; **en último e.** as a last resort; **ir** *o* **pasar de un e. al otro** to go from one extreme to the other
(c) *(en fútbol)* winger ►► ***e. derecho*** *(en fútbol)* outside right; *(en rugby)* right wing; ***e. izquierdo*** *(en fútbol)* outside left; *(en rugby)* left wing
(d) *(punto, asunto)* issue, question; **...e. que ha sido rechazado por...** ...a claim which has been denied by...; **este e. está aún por confirmar** that remains to be confirmed
extremosidad *nf (efusividad)* effusiveness
extremoso, -a *adj (efusivo)* effusive, gushing
extrínseco, -a *adj* extrinsic
extroversión *nf* extroversion
extrovertido, -a 1 *adj* extrovert
2 *nm,f* extrovert
extrusión *nf Tec* extrusion
exuberancia *nf* **(a)** *(de jardín, selva, vegetación)* lushness **(b)** *(de persona)* exuberance **(c)** *(de colores, aromas)* richness
exuberante *adj* **(a)** *(jardín, selva, vegetación)* lush **(b)** *(persona)* exuberant; **una rubia e.** a curvaceous blond **(c)** *(colores, aromas)* rich, luscious
exudación *nf Med* exudation
exudado *nm Med* exudate
exudar *vt* to exude, to ooze
exultación *nf Formal* jubilation, exultation
exultante *adj Formal* jubilant, exultant; **estaban exultantes (de alegría) con la noticia** they were jubilant at the news
exultar *vi Formal* to rejoice, to exult (**de** with)
exvoto *nm* votive offering, ex voto
ey *interj Am Fam* hey, oi
eyaculación *nf* ejaculation ►► ***e. precoz*** premature ejaculation
eyacular *vi* to ejaculate
eyección *nf* ejection, expulsion
eyectar *vt* to eject, to expel
eyector *nm (de armas)* ejector; *(de aire, gases)* extractor
Ezequiel *n pr* Ezekiel
EZLN *nm Méx (abrev de* **Ejército Zapatista de Liberación Nacional***)* Zapatista Army of National Liberation

F, f

F, f ['efe] *nf (letra)* F, f; **el 23 F** 23rd February, = day of the failed coup d'état in Spain in 1981

f. (**a**) (*abrev de* **factura**) inv. (**b**) (*abrev de* **folio**) f

FA *nm* (*abrev de* **Frente Amplio**) = left-wing party in Uruguay

fa *nm (nota musical)* F; *(en solfeo)* fa; *ver también* **do**

F.A.B. *Com* (*abrev de* **franco a bordo**) f.o.b.

fabada *nf* = Asturian stew made of beans, pork sausage and bacon

fábrica *nf* (**a**) *(establecimiento industrial)* factory; **viene instalado de f.** it's pre-installed; **tiene un defecto de f.** it has a manufacturing defect; **es así de f.** it's like that when you buy it ►► ***f. de cerveza*** brewery; ***f. de conservas*** canning plant, cannery; ***F. Nacional de Moneda y Timbre*** = Spanish national mint; ***f. de papel*** paper mill; ***f. siderúrgica*** iron and steelworks *(singular)*
(**b**) *(construcción) (ladrillo)* brickwork; *(piedra)* stonework; **un muro de f.** *(de ladrillo)* a brick wall; *(de piedra)* a stone wall

> **Falso amigo**: El sustantivo inglés **fabric** no es la traducción de la palabra española **fábrica**. En inglés **fabric** significa "tejido" o "estructura".

fabricación *nf* manufacture; **un automóvil de f. nacional** a domestically produced car; **una bomba de f. casera** a home-made bomb ►► ***f. asistida por*** *Am* ***computadora*** *o Esp* ***ordenador*** computer-aided *o* computer-assisted manufacture; ***f. limpia*** *(ecológica)* environmentally friendly manufacturing; ***f. en serie*** mass production

fabricador, -ora 1 *adj (que inventa)* fabricating
2 *nm,f (inventor)* fabricator; **es un f. de mentiras** he's a liar

fabricante 1 *adj* manufacturing; **la empresa f.** the manufacturer
2 *nmf* manufacturer

fabricar [60] *vt* (**a**) *(producir)* to manufacture, to make; **f. en serie** to mass-produce; **fabricado en China** *(en etiqueta)* made in China (**b**) *(construir)* to build, to construct (**c**) *(inventar)* to fabricate, to make up

fabril *adj* industrial

fábula *nf* (**a**) *(relato)* fable; *(leyenda)* legend, myth (**b**) *(rumor)* piece of gossip; *(mentira)* story, invention; **sus hazañas no son más que fábulas** those exploits of his are all imaginary (**c**) **de f.** *(estupendo)* fabulous, fantastic; **la paella me salió de f.** my paella turned out wonderfully, my paella was superb; **lo pasamos de f.** we had a fabulous *o* fantastic time

fabulación *nf* invention, fantasy

fabular *vi* to make things up

fabulista *nmf* author of fables

fabulosamente *adv* (**a**) *(mucho)* fabulously, fantastically (**b**) *(estupendamente)* **lo pasamos f.** we had a fabulous *o* fantastic time

fabuloso, -a *adj* (**a**) *(muy bueno)* fabulous, fantastic (**b**) *(ficticio)* mythical

faca *nf* = type of large knife with curved blade

facción *nf* (**a**) *(bando)* faction (**b**) **facciones** *(rasgos)* features

faccioso, -a 1 *adj* factious, rebellious
2 *nm,f* rebel

faceta *nf* (**a**) *(aspecto)* aspect, facet (**b**) *(de piedra preciosa)* facet

facha[1] *nf* (**a**) *Fam (aspecto)* look; **con esta f. no puedo ir a ninguna parte** I can't go anywhere looking like this; **tener buena f.** *(situación)* to look good *o* promising; *(persona)* to look good *o* attractive; **tener mala f.** *(situación)* to look bad; *(persona)* to look unpleasant (**b**) *Fam (mamarracho)* mess; **vas hecho una f.** you look a mess (**c**) *Chile (presunción)* arrogance, presumption (**d**) *ver también* **facho**

facha[2] *Esp Fam Pey* 1 *adj (fascista)* fascist
2 *nmf (fascista)* fascist

fachada *nf* (**a**) *(de edificio)* facade; **con f. a** facing; **hacer f. con** *o* **a** to be opposite, to face (**b**) *(apariencia)* outward appearance; **bajo esa f. de tranquilidad se esconde una persona aventurera** behind that calm outward appearance of his there's a person who loves adventure; **es pura f.** it's just a show

fachenda *nf Fam (jactancia)* **tiene mucha f.** she's a real bighead

fachendoso, -a *Fam* 1 *adj (vanidoso)* bigheaded
2 *nm,f (vanidoso)* bighead

fachento, -a *adj Méx Fam* scruffy; **andar f.** to be *o* look scruffy

facho, -a *Am Fam Pey* 1 *adj* fascist
2 *nm,f* fascist

fachoso, -a *adj Fam* (**a**) *(desastrado)* scruffy; **ir f.** to be *o* look scruffy (**b**) *Pey (fascista)* fascist (**c**) *Andes, Méx, Ven (fachendoso)* bigheaded

fachudo, -a *adj Urug Fam* scruffy; **andar f.** to be *o* look scruffy

facial *adj* facial; **rasgos faciales** (facial) features

fácil 1 *adj* (**a**) *(sencillo)* easy; **f. de hacer/decir** easy to do/say; **dinero f.** easy money
(**b**) *(tratable)* easy-going; **me ha tocado una clase f.** I've got a really nice class; **es de carácter f.** he's an easy-going sort of person
(**c**) *(probable)* probable, likely; **es f. que no venga** it's likely she won't come, she probably won't come; **es f. que lo tenga que ayudar** it's likely that I'll have to help
(**d**) *(chiste)* obvious
(**e**) *(que se deja seducir)* easy; **tiene fama de f.** she has a reputation for being easy
2 *adv Fam* easily; **eso se dice f.** that's easy to say; **eso se arregla f.** that's easily fixed

facilidad *nf* (**a**) *(simplicidad)* ease, easiness; **destaca por su f. de uso** it is particularly user-friendly; **con f.** easily; **se cansa con mucha f.** she gets tired easily, she tires easily
(**b**) *(aptitud)* aptitude; **tener f. para algo** to have a gift for sth; **tiene f. de palabra** he has a way with words
(**c**) *(propensión)* **tiene mucha f. para el lloro/para enfadarse** he cries/gets angry very easily
(**d**) *(condiciones especiales)* **nos dieron todo tipo de facilidades para realizar el estudio** they gave us all sorts of help so we could carry out the study; **me dan muchas facilidades para pagar la casa** they're giving me very favourable financial terms to pay for the house ►► ***f. de crédito*** credit facilities; ***facilidades de pago*** easy (payment) terms

facilitación *nf* (**a**) *(acción)* facilitation (**b**) *(provisión)* provision

facilitador, -ora *adj* facilitating

facilitar *vt* (**a**) *(simplificar)* to facilitate, to make easy; *(posibilitar)* to make possible; **esta máquina nos facilita mucho la tarea** this machine makes the job a lot easier (for us); **la cooperación internacional facilitó el rescate** the rescue was made possible thanks to international cooperation; **su radicalismo no facilitó las negociaciones** her inflexibility did not make the negotiations any easier
(**b**) *(proporcionar)* to provide; **nos facilitaron toda la información que necesitábamos** they provided us with all the information we needed; **la nota de prensa facilitada por el portavoz del gobierno** the press release made available by the government spokesman

fácilmente *adv* (**a**) *(con facilidad)* easily; **esto se arregla f.** this can be easily fixed (**b**) *Fam (probablemente)* easily; **tardará f. tres meses** it'll easily take three months

facilón, -ona, *Andes, RP* **facilongo, -a** *adj Fam* (**a**) *(fácil)* dead easy (**b**) *(demasiado fácil)* simplistic

facineroso, -a 1 *adj* criminal
2 *nm,f* miscreant, criminal

facistol 1 *nm (atril)* lectern
2 *adj Carib, Méx (vanidoso)* vain, conceited
3 *nmf Carib, Méx (vanidoso)* vain *o* conceited person

facón *nm RP* sheath knife; **pelar el f.** to unsheathe one's knife

facóquero *nm* warthog

facsímil, facsímile 1 *adj* facsimile; **edición f.** facsimile edition
2 *nm* (a) *(copia)* facsimile (b) *(fax)* facsimile, fax

facsimilar *adj* facsimile

facsímile = **facsímil**

factible *adj* feasible

fáctico, -a *adj* de facto; **los poderes fácticos** the centres of power in society

factitivo, -a *adj Gram* factitive

facto: de facto *loc adv* de facto

factor[1] *nm* (a) *(elemento)* factor; **el precio del petróleo es el f. clave** the price of oil is the key factor; **sin olvidar el f. tiempo** without forgetting the time factor; **f. (de protección) 8** *(de crema solar)* factor 8 (protection) ►► *Dep* ***f. campo:*** **tienen la ventaja del f. campo** they have home advantage; ***f. humano*** human factor; *Econ* ***factores de producción*** factors of production, factor inputs; ***f. Rh*** Rh factor; ***f. riesgo*** risk factor
(b) *Mat* factor ►► ***f. común*** common factor

factor[2]**, -ora** *nm,f* (a) *Com* agent, *Espec* factor (b) *Ferroc* luggage clerk

factoría *nf* (a) *(fábrica)* factory (b) *Hist* trading post

factorial *nm Mat* factorial

factoring ['factorin] *nm Econ* factoring

factótum (*pl* **factótums**) *nmf* factotum

factual *adj* factual

factura *nf* (a) *(por mercancías, trabajo realizado)* invoice; *(de compra, luz, teléfono)* bill; **extender una f.** to issue an invoice; **pasar** *o* **presentar una f.** to send an invoice; EXPR **pasar f.** *(los excesos, años)* to take its/their toll; **ya verás cómo te pasa f. por el favor que te hizo** just you wait, he'll be wanting something back for the favour he did you ►► ***f. detallada*** itemized bill; *Com* ***f. pro forma*** *o* ***proforma*** pro forma invoice
(b) *(hechura)* **de buena/mala f.** well/badly made; **un mueble de muy bella f.** a beautifully made piece of furniture
(c) *Arg (repostería)* cakes and pastries

facturación *nf* (a) *(de equipaje) (en aeropuerto)* checking-in; *(en estación)* registration; **mostrador de f.** check-in desk (b) *(ventas)* turnover; **una f. anual de 1.000 millones** an annual turnover of 1,000 million (c) *(cobro)* invoicing

facturar *vt* (a) *(equipaje) (en aeropuerto)* to check in; *(en estación)* to register (b) *(vender)* to turn over; **facturaron 4.000 millones en 1999** they had a turnover of 4,000 million in 1999 (c) *(cobrar)* **facturarle a alguien algo** to invoice *o* bill sb for sth

facu *nf Fam (facultad)* **tengo que ir a la f.** I've got to go in to college *o Br* the uni

facultad *nf* (a) *(capacidad)* faculty; **facultades (mentales)** (mental) faculties; **está en pleno uso de sus facultades mentales** she is in full possession of her mental faculties; **está empezando a perder facultades** his mind is beginning to go; **un corredor con portentosas facultades físicas** a runner with remarkable physical attributes; **tiene grandes facultades para la pintura** he's a very talented painter
(b) *(centro universitario)* faculty; **fue compañera mía de f.** she was at university *o esp US* college with me; *Am* **llegué a las nueve de f.** I got back from the university at nine o'clock ►► ***F. de Derecho*** Law Faculty, Faculty of Law; ***F. de Filosofía y Letras*** Arts Faculty, Faculty of Arts; ***F. de Humanidades*** Arts Faculty, Faculty of Arts; ***F. de Medicina*** Medical Faculty, Faculty of Medicine
(c) *Am (enseñanza superior)* college; **mi hermano está en f.** my brother goes to college
(d) *(poder)* power, right; **su cargo no le da f. para autorizar compras** his position doesn't allow him to authorize purchases
(e) *(propiedad)* property; **tiene la f. de ablandar la madera** it has the property of softening wood

facultar *vt* to authorize; **este título lo faculta para ejercer en Francia** this qualification allows him to practise in France

facultativo, -a 1 *adj* (a) *(voluntario)* optional (b) *(médico)* medical; **un parte f.** a medical report; **por prescripción facultativa** on medical advice, on doctor's orders
2 *nm,f* doctor

facundia *nf* (a) *(elocuencia)* eloquence (b) *Fam (verbosidad)* gift of the gab

facundo, -a *adj* (a) *(elocuente)* eloquent (b) *Fam (parlanchín)* talkative

FAD [fað] *nmpl* (*abrev de* **Fondos de Ayuda al Desarrollo**) = Spanish development aid fund

fado *nm* fado, = melancholy Portuguese folk song

faena *nf* (a) *(tarea)* task, work; **hoy no puedo salir que tengo mucha f.** I can't go out today, I've got too much (work) to do; **estar en plena f.** to be hard at work; **meterse en f.** to get down to work, to start working ►► ***faenas agrícolas*** farm work, agricultural work; ***faenas del campo*** farm work, agricultural work; ***faenas domésticas*** housework, household chores
(b) *Fam (fastidio)* **me han hecho una f. cancelando el vuelo** they've really left me in it by cancelling the flight; **no me olvidaré de la f. que me hizo** I won't forget the dirty trick he played on me; **¡qué f.!** what a pain!
(c) *Taurom* = bullfighter's performance with the cape; **el torero ejecutó una f. brillante** the bullfighter did a series of brilliant passes with the cape
(d) *Cuba, Guat, Méx (en hacienda)* overtime
(e) *Chile (cuadrilla de obreros)* group of labourers
(f) *Ecuad (trabajo matinal)* morning work
(g) *RP (matanza)* slaughtering *(of cattle)*

faenador, -ora *RP* 1 *adj* **planta faenadora de reses** slaughterhouse, abattoir
2 *nm,f* slaughterhouse *o* abattoir worker

faenamiento *nm Chile* slaughtering *(of cattle)*

faenar 1 *vi* (a) *(pescar)* to fish (b) *(en el campo)* to work (c) *(trabajar)* to work
2 *vt RP (ganado)* to slaughter

faenero *nm (barco)* fishing boat

faetón *nm* phaeton

fagácea *Bot* 1 *nf (planta)* = member of the *Fagaceae* family of trees
2 **fagáceas** *nfpl (familia) Fagaceae*

fagáceo, -a *adj Bot* fagaceous

fagocitar *vt* (a) *Biol* to engulf (b) *(engullir)* to engulf, to swallow up

fagocito *nm Biol* phagocyte

fagocitosis *nf inv Biol* phagocytosis

fagot 1 *nm (instrumento)* bassoon
2 *nmf (músico)* bassoonist

fagotista *nmf* bassoonist

Fahrenheit [faren'χait] *adj* Fahrenheit

fainá *nf Urug (plato)* = baked dough made from chickpea flour, served with pizza

fair play ['ferplei] *nm* fair play

faisán *nm* pheasant ►► ***f. dorado*** golden pheasant

faja *nf* (a) *(prenda de mujer)* girdle; *(terapéutica)* (surgical) corset ►► ***f. pantalón*** panty girdle
(b) *(de esmoquin)* cummerbund; *(de campesino)* sash *(wrapped round waist)*; *(de presidente, general)* sash
(c) *(de terreno) (pequeña)* strip; *(grande)* belt; **la f. costera del este** the eastern coastal strip
(d) *(de periódico)* (newspaper) wrapper
(e) *(de libro)* band *(around new book)*
(f) *Arquit* fascia
(g) *(en heráldica)* fesse

fajada *nf Carib (acometida)* attack, assault

fajador, -ora *nm,f Dep* **es un f.** he can take a lot of punishment

fajar 1 *vt* (a) *(periódico)* to put a wrapper on; *(libro)* to put a band on
(b) *(niño)* to swaddle
(c) *Am Fam (acometer)* to attack, to assault
(d) *RP Fam (timar)* to rip off; **en ese restaurante te fajan** that restaurant's a rip-off; **qué camisa tan linda, ¿cuánto te fajaron?** what a lovely shirt, how much did they sting you for that?; **¿te costó 500? ¡te fajaron!** it cost you 500? you were ripped off!
(e) *Carib Fam (dinero)* **f. algo a alguien** to touch sb for sth
2 **fajarse** *vpr* (a) *(luchar)* **el delantero se pasó el partido fajándose con los defensas** there was a lot of needle between the forward and the defenders throughout the match (b) *Am Fam (pegarse)* **se fajaron** they had a scrap; **se fajaron a piñazos** they had a punch-up

fajín *nm* sash

fajina *nf* (a) *Cuba (trabajo extra)* overtime (b) EXPR *RP* **estar de f.** to be in one's work clothes

fajo *nm* (a) *(de billetes, papel)* wad; *(de leña, cañas)* bundle (b) *Méx (cinturón)* leather belt

fakir *nm* fakir

falacia *nf* (a) *(mentira)* lie, untruth; **eso es una f.** that's a lie, that's not true (b) *(concepción errónea)* fallacy

falange *nf* (**a**) *Anat* phalanx (**b**) *Mil* phalanx (**c**) *Pol* **la F. (Española)** the Falange, = Spanish fascist movement founded in 1933 which became the official party of the Franco regime

falangero *nm* phalanger

falangeta *nf Anat* third phalanx

falangina *nf Anat* second phalanx

falangismo *nm Pol (movimiento)* Falangist movement; *(ideología)* Falangist ideology

falangista *Pol* **1** *adj* Falangist
2 *nmf* Falangist, member of the "Falange"

falaz *adj* false

falca *nf* (**a**) *Méx, Ven (canoa)* = canoe with a roof (**b**) *Col (barcaza)* ferryboat *(at river crossing)*

falda 1 *nf* (**a**) *(prenda)* skirt; EXPR *Fam* **estar pegado** *o* **cosido a las faldas de su madre** to be tied to his/her mother's apron strings ►► ***f. acampanada*** skirt cut on the bias; ***f. escocesa*** kilt; ***f. fruncida*** gathered skirt; ***f. pantalón*** culottes, divided skirt; ***f. plisada*** pleated skirt *(with accordion pleats)*; ***f. portafolio*** wrapover skirt; ***f. recta*** straight skirt; ***f. tableada*** pleated skirt *(with knife pleats)*; ***f. de tubo*** pencil skirt; ***f. de volantes*** ruffled skirt; ***f. de vuelo*** full skirt
(**b**) *(de montaña)* lower slope; **las faldas de la montaña** the lower slopes of the mountain
(**c**) *(regazo)* lap; **se sentó en las faldas de su madre** she sat on her mother's lap
(**d**) **faldas** *(de mesa camilla)* tablecloth
(**e**) *(de carne)* flank, *Br* skirt
2 faldas *nfpl Fam (mujeres)* **está metido en un asunto de faldas, tiene un lío de faldas** he's got something going with some *Br* bird *o US* broad

faldeo *nm Andes, RP* lower slope

faldero, -a *adj* (**a**) *(dócil)* **perro f.** lapdog (**b**) *Fam (mujeriego)* **es muy f.** he's a real ladies' man

faldeta *nf PRico Fam (camisa)* shirt-tail

faldón *nm* (**a**) *(de chaqueta, camisa)* tail; *(de cortina, mesa camilla)* folds (**b**) *(de tejado)* gable

falencia *nf* (**a**) *Am Com (bancarrota)* bankruptcy (**b**) *CSur (error)* shortcoming

falibilidad *nf* fallibility

falible *adj* fallible

fálico, -a *adj* phallic

falla *nf* (**a**) *(defecto)* fault, defect; **este cajón tiene una f.** there's something wrong with this drawer; **está rebajado porque tiene una f.** it's reduced because it's imperfect
(**b**) *Am (error)* mistake; **un trabajo lleno de fallas** a piece of work full of mistakes; **una f. humana** a human error; **una f. técnica** a technical fault
(**c**) *Geol* fault
(**d**) *(figura de cartón)* = giant papier-mâché figure burnt during las Fallas in Valencia
(**e**) **las Fallas** *(fiesta)* = festival in Valencia during which giant papier-mâché figures are burnt
(**f**) *Méx (gorro)* baby bonnet

fallado, -a *adj RP* (**a**) *(defectuoso) (máquina)* faulty; *(argumento)* flawed (**b**) *Fam (loco)* crazy

fallar 1 *vt* (**a**) *(equivocar) (respuesta)* to get wrong; *(tiro)* to miss (**b**) *(sentenciar)* to pass sentence on; *(premio)* to award
2 *vi* (**a**) *(equivocarse)* to get it wrong; *(no acertar)* to miss; **sin f.** without fail; **este truco nunca falla** this trick never fails; **¡no falla, en cuanto salimos se pone a llover!** it never fails, whenever we go out, it starts raining!; **si la memoria no me falla** if my memory serves me correctly; EXPR *Fam Hum* **f. más que una escopeta de feria: esta impresora falla más que una escopeta de feria** this printer is a heap of junk
(**b**) *(fracasar, flaquear)* to fail; *(no funcionar)* to stop working; *(plan)* to go wrong; **me fallaron los frenos** my brakes didn't work; **falló el suministro eléctrico** there was a power cut; **nos fallaron las previsiones** our forecasts were out
(**c**) *(decepcionar)* **fallarle a alguien** to let sb down; **contigo somos cuatro, no nos falles** there'll be four of us if you come, don't let us down
(**d**) *(quebrarse, ceder)* to give way; **el cable falló** the cable broke *o* snapped
(**e**) *(sentenciar)* **f. a favor/en contra de alguien** to find in favour of/against sb
(**f**) *(en juegos de cartas)* to trump

falleba *nf* latch

fallecer [46] *vi* to pass away, to die; **un joven que falleció en accidente de circulación** a young man who died in a car accident

fallecido, -a 1 *adj* deceased
2 *nm,f* deceased; **los fallecidos en el accidente** those who died in the accident

fallecimiento *nm* decease, death; **el f. se produjo a las 5:50** death occurred at 5:50 a.m.

fallero, -a 1 *adj* = of/relating to the "las Fallas" celebrations in Valencia during which giant papier-mâché figures are burnt
2 *nm,f* = person who helps to make the giant papier-mâché figures burnt during "las Fallas" ►► ***fallera mayor*** = young woman picked to be festival queen during "las Fallas"

fallezco *etc ver* **fallecer**

fallido, -a *adj (esfuerzo, intento)* unsuccessful, failed; *(esperanza)* vain; *(disparo)* missed

fallo[1] *nm* (**a**) *Esp (error)* mistake; **tuve dos fallos en el examen** I made two mistakes in the exam; **tu ejercicio no ha tenido ningún f.** there were no mistakes in your exercise; **cometieron dos fallos desde el punto de penalti** they missed two penalties; **fue un f. no llevar el abrelatas** it was silly *o* stupid not to bring the tin opener; **un f. técnico** a technical fault; **un f. humano** a human error
(**b**) *Esp (defecto)* fault; **tener muchos fallos** to have lots of faults; **tener fallos de memoria** to have memory lapses
(**c**) *(veredicto)* verdict; *(en concurso)* decision; **el f. del jurado** the jury's verdict ►► ***f. absolutorio*** acquittal

fallo[2]**, -a** *adj Chile Agr* failed

falluca = **fayuca**

falluquear = **fayuquear**

falluquero, -a = **fayuquero, -a**

fallutería *nf RP Fam* hypocrisy

falluto, -a *RP Fam* **1** *adj* phoney, hypocritical
2 *nm,f* hypocrite

falo *nm* phallus

falocracia *nf* male chauvinism

falócrata *nm* male chauvinist

falopa *nf Fam* (**a**) *(cocaína)* coke, snow (**b**) *RP (droga)* dope

falopear *RP Fam* **1** *vt (drogar)* to drug
2 falopearse *vpr* to take drugs

falopero, -a *RP Fam* **1** *adj* **es muy f.** he's a real junkie
2 *nm,f* junkie

falsa *nf Méx (falsilla)* guide sheet *(for writing paper)*

falsamente *adv* falsely

falsario, -a 1 *adj (persona)* untruthful
2 *nm,f* liar

falseable *adj* forgeable; **un billete difícilmente f.** a note that is hard to forge

falseador, -ora *adj* falsifying

falseamiento *nm (falsificación)* falsifying, falsification

falsear *vt (hechos, historia, datos)* to falsify, to distort; *(dinero, firma)* to forge; *(pruebas, facturas)* to fake; **falseó su testimonio** he gave false evidence

falsedad *nf* (**a**) *(falta de verdad, autenticidad)* falseness (**b**) *(mentira)* falsehood, lie

falseo *nm (falsificación)* forgery

falsete *nm* (**a**) *Mús* falsetto; **voz de f.** falsetto voice (**b**) *Anticuado (puerta)* communicating door

falsificación *nf* (**a**) *(acción)* forging, forgery (**b**) *(pasaporte)* forgery, fake; *(firma, billete)* forgery

falsificado, -a *adj (firma, pasaporte)* forged; *(billete)* counterfeit, forged

falsificador, -ora *nm,f* forger

falsificar [60] *vt (firma, pasaporte)* to forge; *(billete)* to forge, to counterfeit

falsilla *nf* guide sheet *(for writing paper)*

falso, -a 1 *adj* (**a**) *(afirmación, información, rumor)* false, untrue; **eso que dices es f.** what you are saying is not true; **en f.** *(falsamente)* falsely; *(sin firmeza)* unsoundly; **si haces un movimiento en f., disparo** one false move and I'll shoot; **dio un paso en f. y se cayó** he missed his footing and fell; **jurar en f.** to commit perjury ►► ***falsa alarma*** false alarm; ***f. testimonio*** *(en juicio)* perjury, false evidence; **dar f. testimonio** to give false evidence
(**b**) *(dinero, firma, cuadro)* forged; *(pasaporte)* forged, false; *(joyas)* fake; **un diamante f.** an imitation diamond
(**c**) *(hipócrita)* deceitful; **no soporto a los falsos amigos que te**

critican a la espalda I can't stand false friends who criticize you behind your back; **basta ya de falsa simpatía** that's enough of you pretending to be nice; EXPR *Fam Hum* **es más f. que Judas** he's a real snake in the grass ►► *Ling* ***f. amigo*** false friend; ***falsa modestia*** false modesty

(**d**) *(simulado)* false ►► ***falsa costilla*** false rib; ***f. estuco*** *(en bricolaje)* stick-on plasterwork; ***f. muro*** false wall; ***f. techo*** false ceiling

2 *nm,f (hipócrita)* hypocrite

FALTA *nf* (**a**) *(ausencia)* absence; *(carencia)* lack; *(escasez)* shortage; **nadie notó su f.** nobody noticed his/its absence; **estos animales tienen f. de cariño** these animals suffer from a lack of affection; **en estos momentos hay f. de trabajo** there's a shortage of work at the moment; **la f. de agua impide el desarrollo de la región** water is in short supply in the region, something which is holding back its development; **estoy cometiendo muchos errores, es la f. de costumbre** I'm making a lot of mistakes, I'm out of practice; **fue absuelto por f. de pruebas** he was acquitted for lack of evidence; **ha sido una f. de delicadeza decirle eso** it was tactless of you to say that to him; **es una f. de educación** it's bad manners; **es una f. de respeto** it shows a lack of respect; **¡qué** *o* **vaya f. de seriedad!** it's disgraceful!; **a f. de** in the absence of; **a f. de un sitio mejor, podríamos ir a la playa** in the absence of anywhere better, we could always go to the beach; **echar en f. algo/a alguien** *(notar la ausencia de)* to notice that sth/sb is missing; *(echar de menos)* to miss sth/sb; **no fuimos de vacaciones por f. de dinero** we didn't go on holiday because we didn't have enough money; **si no voy contigo no es por f. de ganas** if I don't go with you, it isn't because I don't want to; **sin f.** without fail; **hemos de entregar este proyecto el lunes sin f.** this project has to be handed in on Monday without fail; EXPR **a f. de pan, buenas son tortas: no es ideal, pero a f. de pan, buenas son tortas** it's not ideal, but it will have to do for want of anything better

(**b**) **hacer f.** *(ser necesario)* to be necessary; **me hace f. suerte** I need some luck; **me haces mucha f.** I really need you; **si hiciera f., llámanos** if necessary, call us; **¡hace f. ser caradura!, ¡volver a pedirme dinero!** what a nerve, asking me for money again!; **espero que lo traten con disciplina, que buena f. le hace** I hope they are strict with him, he certainly needs it *o* it's high time someone was; **no va a venir, ni f. que hace** she isn't coming, not that anyone cares

(**c**) *(no asistencia)* absence; **me han puesto dos faltas este mes** I was marked absent twice this month ►► ***f. de asistencia*** absence

(**d**) *(imperfección)* fault; *(defecto de fábrica)* defect, flaw; **sacarle faltas a algo/alguien** to find fault with sth/sb

(**e**) *(infracción)* misdemeanour, offence; *(incumplimiento)* breach; *(error)* mistake; **una f. contra la disciplina** a breach of discipline; **f. grave/leve** serious/minor misdemeanour *o* offence; **he tenido tres faltas en el dictado** I made three mistakes in my dictation ►► ***f. de ortografía*** spelling mistake; *Com* ***f. de pago*** non-payment

(**f**) *Dep (infracción)* foul; *(en tenis)* fault; **cometer** *o* **hacer una f.** to commit a foul; **cometer** *o* **hacer una f. a alguien** to foul sb; **señalar una f.** to give *o* award a free kick ►► ***f. antideportiva*** *(en baloncesto)* unsportsmanlike foul; ***f. libre directa*** direct free kick offence; ***f. libre indirecta*** indirect free kick offence; ***f. personal*** *(en baloncesto)* personal foul; ***f. de pie*** *(en tenis)* foot fault; ***f. de saque*** *(en tenis)* service fault; ***f. técnica*** *(en baloncesto)* technical foul

(**g**) *Dep (tiro libre)* free kick; **marcar de f.** to score from a free kick; **lanzar** *o* **sacar una f.** to take a free kick ►► ***f. libre directa*** direct free kick; ***f. libre indirecta*** indirect free kick

(**h**) *(en la menstruación)* missed period; **ha tenido ya dos faltas** she has missed two periods

faltante *Am* **1** *adj* missing

2 *nm* deficit

FALTAR *vi* (**a**) *(no haber)* to be lacking, to be needed; **falta aire** there's not enough air; **le falta sal** it needs a bit of salt; **faltó comida** there wasn't enough food; **a esta casa no le falta nada** this house lacks nothing *o* has everything; **después del robo faltaban dos cuadros** after the robbery, two paintings were missing; **abrí la cartera y me faltaban varios documentos** I opened my briefcase and several documents were missing

(**b**) *(estar ausente)* to be absent *o* missing; **falta Elena** Elena is missing; **el día que yo falte** when I have passed on; **falta de su domicilio desde hace tres semanas** she has been missing (from home) for three weeks

(**c**) *(no acudir)* **sólo faltaron mis padres** only my parents weren't there *o* failed to turn up; **f. a una cita** not to turn up at an appointment; **¡no faltes (a la cita)!** don't miss it!, be there!; **ha faltado a clase tres veces esta semana** she has been absent *o* off three days this week; **últimamente ha faltado mucho al trabajo** he's been off work a lot recently, he's had a lot of time off work recently

(**d**) *(no cumplir)* **faltó a su palabra** she went back on her word, she broke *o* didn't keep her word; **faltó a su obligación** he neglected his duty; **faltó a la verdad** she wasn't being truthful, she wasn't telling the truth

(**e**) *(ofender)* **f. a alguien en algo** to offend sb in sth; **f. a alguien al respeto** to be disrespectful to sb; **¡a mí no me faltes!, ¡sin f.!** don't you speak to me like that!

(**f**) *(no tener)* **le faltan las fuerzas** he lacks *o* doesn't have the strength; **le falta experiencia** she lacks experience; **le falta una mano** he has got only one hand; **al equipo le faltan buenos defensas** the team is short of good defenders; **le falta una pata a la mesa** the table is missing a leg; **me faltan palabras para expresar mi agradecimiento** I can't find the words to express my gratitude

(**g**) *(hacer falta)* **me falta tiempo** I need time; **nos va a f. cerveza** we're going to run out of beer, we're not going to have enough beer; **para que su felicidad fuera completa sólo faltaba que viniera su hijo** all it needed to make her happiness complete was for her son to arrive; **ganas no nos faltan, pero no vamos a poder ir** it isn't because we don't want to, but we won't be able to go; **sólo le faltó ponerse a llorar** he did everything but burst into tears; **¡lo que me faltaba!** that's all I needed!; **¡lo que faltaba, otro pinchazo!** that's all I needed, another flat tyre!

(**h**) *(quedar)* **falta mucho por hacer** there is still a lot to be done; **falta poco para llenar del todo el camión** the lorry is almost completely full now; **sólo te falta firmar** all you have to do is sign; **falta un mes para las vacaciones** there's a month to go till the holidays; **¿falta mucho para el final?** is there long to go?; **falta poco para las once** it's nearly eleven o'clock; **falta poco para que llegue** it won't be long till he arrives, he'll soon be here; **¿cuánto falta para Bogotá?** how much further is it to Bogota?; **aún faltan 10 kilómetros** there are still 10 kilometres to go; **faltó poco para que lo matase** I very nearly killed him; **¿lo mató? – poco faltó** did she kill him? – very nearly

(**i**) *Euf (morir)* to pass away

(**j**) *(en frases)* **¡no faltaba** *o* **faltaría más!** *(asentimiento)* of course!; *(rechazo)* that tops it all!, that's a bit much!; **claro que puedes usar mi teléfono, ¡no faltaba** *o* **faltaría más!** of course you can use my telephone, there's no need for you to ask; **por supuesto que no te dejo ir, ¡faltaría más!** of course I'm not letting you go, what can you be thinking of!

falto, -a *adj* **f. de** lacking in, short of; **f. de escrúpulos** lacking scruples; **en estos momentos estamos faltos de recursos** we are short of resources at the moment; **f. de imaginación** unimaginative; **en su infancia estuvo f. de cariño** she was starved of affection in her childhood

faltón, -ona *Fam* **1** *adj* (**a**) *(irrespetuoso)* **¡no seas f.!** don't be so damn rude! (**b**) *(no fiable)* **es muy f.** he's dead unreliable

2 *nm,f (irrespetuoso)* **ese chico es un f.** that young man's damn rude

faltriquera *nf (bolso) Br* small handbag, *US* small purse

falúa, faluca *nf (embarcación)* launch

falucho *nm (embarcación)* felucca

fama *nf* (**a**) *(renombre)* fame; **un escritor/restaurante de f.** a well-known *o* famous writer/restaurant; **alcanzar la f.** to achieve fame, to become famous; **tener f.** to be famous *o* well-known; **salir en ese programa le ha dado mucha f.** being on that programme has made her very well-known

(**b**) *(reputación)* reputation; **buena/mala f.** good/bad reputation; **tener f. de tacaño/generoso** to have a reputation *o* name for being mean/generous; **su f. de excéntrico atrae a mucha gente** his reputation for eccentricity attracts a lot of people; PROV **cría f. y échate a dormir** build yourself a good reputation, then you can rest on your laurels

(**c**) *Literario* **es f. que...** *(se dice que)* it is said that...

famélico, -a *adj* (**a**) *(hambriento)* starving, famished (**b**) *(delgado)* emaciated

familia *nf* (**a**) *(grupo de personas)* family; **un asunto de f.** a family matter; **el director es f. mía** the director is a relative of mine; **ser como de la f.** to be like one of the family; **venir de f.** to run in the family; **en f.** *(con la familia)* with one's family; **pasamos el fin de año en f.** we spent New Year with the family; **estábamos en f.** *(casi solos)* there were only a few of us; **no te dé vergüenza, que estamos en f.** don't be shy – you're among friends ►► ***f. adoptiva*** adoptive family; ***f. desestructurada*** dysfunctional family; ***f. monoparental*** single parent family; ***f. nuclear*** nuclear family; ***f. numerosa*** large family; ***la f. política*** the in-laws

(**b**) *(hijos)* **no tuvieron f.** they never had children

(**c**) *(linaje)* family; **de buena f.** from a good family
(**d**) *(de plantas, animales)* family; **una f. de plantas** a family of plants
(**e**) *Ling* family; **una f. de lenguas** a family of languages

familiar 1 *adj* (**a**) *(de familia)* family; **reunión f.** family gathering (**b**) *(en el trato) (agradable)* friendly; *(en demasía)* overly familiar (**c**) *(lenguaje, estilo)* informal, colloquial; **una expresión f.** an informal *o* colloquial expression (**d**) *(conocido)* familiar; **su cara me es** *o* **me resulta f.** her face looks familiar; **su voz me es f.** I recognize her voice, her voice sounds familiar (**e**) *(tamaño)* family-sized; **un envase f.** a family pack; **un vehículo f.** a family car
2 *nmf* relative, relation

familiaridad *nf* (**a**) *(en el trato)* familiarity; **nos trató desde el principio con mucha f.** from the outset he dealt with us very informally (**b**) **familiaridades** *(exceso de confianza)* **tomarse muchas familiaridades** to be overly familiar

familiarizado, -a *adj* familiar, conversant (**con** with); **estar f. con algo** to be familiar *o* conversant with sth

familiarizar [14] 1 *vt* to familiarize (**con** with)
2 **familiarizarse** *vpr* **familiarizarse con** *(estudiar)* to familiarize oneself with; *(acostumbrarse a)* to get used to; **en pocos días se familiarizó con los nombres de todos los alumnos** within a few days she had learnt the names of all her pupils

familiarmente *adv* familiarly; **f. conocido como...** familiarly known as...

famoso, -a 1 *adj (actor, pintor, monumento)* famous; **se hizo f. por sus murales** his murals made him famous; **es famosa por su belleza** she is famous for her beauty; *Fam* **volvieron a debatir el f. artículo 14** they debated the famous clause 14 again
2 *nm,f* famous person, celebrity

fámulo, -a *nm,f Anticuado* servant

fan *nmf* fan

fanal *nm* (**a**) *(en puerto)* (harbour) beacon; *(en barco)* lantern (**b**) *(para pescar)* = lantern on fishing boat used for attracting the fish (**c**) *(campana)* bell jar; *(de lámpara)* chimney (**d**) *Méx (faro)* headlight, headlamp

fanaticada *nf Andes* fans

fanáticamente *adv* fanatically

fanático, -a 1 *adj* fanatical
2 *nm,f* (**a**) *(exaltado)* fanatic; *Dep* fanatical supporter (**b**) *(aficionado)* **es una fanática del cine** she's mad about the cinema; **es un f. de la comida italiana** he adores Italian food

fanatismo *nm* fanaticism; **con f.** fanatically

fanatizar [14] *vt* to arouse fanaticism in

fandango *nm* (**a**) *(baile)* fandango (**b**) *Fam (jaleo, bullicio)* racket; **montar un f.** to make a racket (**c**) *Andes Fam (fiesta)* party, bash

fandanguillo *nm* = type of fandango

fané *adj RP* **estar f.** *(cansado)* to be worn out; *(desgastado)* to be past it

faneca *nf* pout, bib

fanega *nf* (**a**) *(medida de capacidad)* = grain measure which varies from region to region (**b**) *(medida de superficie)* = unit of area equivalent to 1.59 acres or 0.66 hectares

fanerógama 1 *nf (planta)* seed-producing plant, *Espec* phanerogam
2 **fanerógamas** *nfpl (familia) Phanerogamae*

fanerógamo, -a *Bot adj* seed-producing, *Espec* phanerogamic

fanesca *nf* = fish stew made with milk and vegetables, typical Ecuadorian Easter dish

fanfarria *nf* (**a**) *(música)* fanfare (**b**) *(banda)* brass band (**c**) *Fam (ostentación)* show, razz(a)matazz; *(jactancia)* bragging

fanfarrón, -ona *Fam* 1 *adj (bravucón, arrogante)* bigheaded; *(ostentoso)* flashy
2 *nm,f (bravucón, arrogante)* bighead; *(ostentoso)* show-off

fanfarronada *nf Fam* brag; **decir** *o* **echar fanfarronadas** to brag; **estamos cansados de sus fanfarronadas** we're tired of his showing off

fanfarronear *vi Fam* to brag (**de** about); **fanfarronea de tener un BMW** she's always bragging about owning a BMW

fanfarronería *nf Fam (bravuconería, arrogancia)* bigheadedness; *(ostentación)* showing off; **no soporto sus fanfarronerías** I can't stand the way he shows off all the time

fangal *nm* quagmire

fangar *nm* quagmire

fangar[2] [38] *vt Esp Fam* to pinch, *Br* to nick; **f. algo a alguien** to pinch *o Br* nick sth off sb

fango *nm* (**a**) *(barro)* mud (**b**) *(deshonra)* **el escándalo cubrió de f. al presidente** the scandal sullied the president's reputation

fangoso, -a *adj* muddy

fangote *nm RP Fam* **un f.** heaps *o* loads (of money); **me salió un f.** it cost me a fortune

fantasear 1 *vi* to fantasize (**sobre** about)
2 *vt* to imagine, to fantasize about

fantasía 1 *nf* (**a**) *(imaginación)* imagination; **la realidad y la f.** reality and fantasy; **vive en un mundo de f.** she lives in a world of her own, she lives in a fantasy world (**b**) *(cosa imaginada)* fantasy ►► ***f. sexual*** sexual fantasy (**c**) *Mús* fantasia (**d**) *RP (joya)* piece of costume jewellery
2 **de fantasía** *loc adj* **bisutería de f.** costume jewellery; **ropa de f.** fancy clothes

fantasioso, -a *adj* imaginative

fantasma 1 *adj* (**a**) *(deshabitado)* **pueblo/barco f.** ghost town/ship (**b**) *(que no existe)* **una noticia f.** a false report; **una empresa f.** a bogus company; **el informe f. sobre la recuperación económica** the mythical report on the economic turnaround (**c**) *Esp Fam* **es muy f.** *(fanfarrón)* he's a real show-off (**d**) *RP Fam* **es muy f.** *(atontado)* she's absolutely crazy
2 *nm* (**a**) *(espectro)* ghost, phantom; **se le apareció el f. de un pirata** the ghost of a pirate appeared to him ►► ***el F. de la Ópera*** the Phantom of the Opera (**b**) *(amenaza)* spectre; **el f. de la guerra civil/del desempleo** the spectre of civil war/unemployment (**c**) *Am TV* ghost
3 *nmf* (**a**) *Esp Fam (fanfarrón)* show-off (**b**) *RP Fam (atontado)* loony

fantasmada *nf Fam* (**a**) *Esp (fanfarronería)* brag (**b**) *RP (tontería)* **decir/hacer una f.** to say/do something stupid

fantasmagoría *nf* phantasmagoria

fantasmagórico, -a *adj* phantasmagoric

fantasmal *adj* ghostly

fantasmón, -ona *nm,f Esp Fam* show-off

fantásticamente *adv* **lo pasamos f.** we had a fantastic time

fantástico, -a 1 *adj* (**a**) *(imaginario)* fantastic, imaginary (**b**) *Fam (estupendo)* fantastic, wonderful; **¿vamos a la ópera? – f.** shall we go to the opera? – yes, that would be terrific
2 *adv (muy bien)* **lo pasamos f.** we had a fantastic *o* wonderful time

fantochada *nf* (**a**) *(cosa grotesca)* **eso es una f.** that's ridiculous *o* absurd (**b**) *(fanfarronada)* brag

fantoche *nm* (**a**) *(títere)* puppet (**b**) *Fam (persona grotesca)* sight; **iba hecho un f.** she looked a real *o* complete sight (**c**) *Fam (presumido, vanidoso)* bighead

fanzine [fan'θine, fan'sin] *nm* fanzine

FAO [fao] *nf (abrev de* **Food and Agriculture Organization**) FAO

faquir *nm* fakir

faradio *nm* farad

farallón *nm (roca)* giant rock

farándula *nf* **la f.** the theatre, the stage

farandulero, -a *adj RP, Ven Fam (fanfarrón)* boastful, bragging

faraón *nm* pharaoh

faraónico, -a *adj* (**a**) *(del faraón)* pharaonic (**b**) *(fastuoso)* lavish, magnificent; **viven rodeados de un lujo f.** they live like kings (**c**) *(gigantesco)* enormous, huge; **un proyecto f.** a project on a monumental scale; **una tarea faraónica** a mammoth task

FARC [fark] *nfpl (abrev de* **Fuerzas Armadas Revolucionarias de Colombia**) Revolutionary Armed Forces of Colombia *(guerrilla group)*

fardada *nf Esp Fam* **se ha comprado una f. de casa** she's bought herself a really flashy house

fardar *vi Esp Fam* **¡cómo farda esa moto!** that bike will really get you noticed!, that bike's really cool!; **con esas botas se farda mucho** those boots are bound to get you noticed, those boots are really cool; **le gusta f. de tener padres ricos** she likes to brag about her rich parents

fardel *nm (talega)* knapsack

fardo *nm* bundle

fardón, -ona *Esp Fam* 1 *adj* (**a**) *(fanfarrón)* **es muy f.** he's a real show-off (**b**) *(vistoso)* **¡qué gafas más fardonas!** those glasses will really get you noticed!
2 *nm,f* show-off

farero, -a *nm,f* lighthouse keeper

fárfara *nf* coltsfoot

farfolla *nf* (**a**) *(de mazorca)* husk (**b**) *Pey (de texto, discurso)* waffle, padding
farfullar 1 *vt (deprisa)* to gabble; *(con enfado)* to splutter; *(en voz baja)* to mutter, to mumble
2 *vi (deprisa)* to gabble; *(con enfado)* to splutter; *(en voz baja)* to mutter, to mumble
faria *nm o nf Esp* = cheap Spanish cigar
farináceo, -a *adj* farinaceous
faringe *nf* pharynx
faríngeo, -a *adj* pharyngeal
faringitis *nf inv* sore throat, *Espec* pharyngitis
fariña *nf Andes, RP* coarse manioc *o* cassava flour
fario *nm Fam* **mal f.** bad luck
farisaico, -a *adj* (**a**) *Hist* Pharisaic, Pharisaical (**b**) *(hipócrita)* hypocritical
fariseísmo *nm* hypocrisy
fariseo, -a *nm,f* (**a**) *Hist* Pharisee (**b**) *(hipócrita)* hypocrite
farlopa *nf Fam (cocaína)* coke, snow
farmaceuta *nmf Col, Ven* pharmacist, *Br* chemist, *US* druggist
farmacéutico, -a 1 *adj* pharmaceutical; **la industria farmacéutica** the pharmaceutical industry
2 *nm,f* pharmacist, *Br* chemist, *US* druggist
farmacia *nf* (**a**) *(ciencia)* pharmacy (**b**) *(establecimiento)* pharmacy, *Br* chemist's (shop), *US* drugstore ►► ***f. de guardia*** duty chemist's; ***f. de turno*** duty chemist's
fármaco *nm* medicine, drug
farmacodependencia *nf* drug dependency *o* addiction
farmacodependiente 1 *adj* **ser f.** to be a drug addict
2 *nmf* drug addict
farmacología *nf* pharmacology
farmacológico, -a *adj* pharmacological
farmacólogo, -a *nm,f* pharmacologist
farmacopea *nf* pharmacopoeia
farmacoterapia *nf* = treatment using course of drugs
faro *nm* (**a**) *(para barcos)* lighthouse (**b**) *(de coche)* headlight, headlamp ►► ***f. antiniebla*** fog lamp *o* light; ***f. halógeno*** halogen lamp; ***f. trasero*** rear light, *US* tail-light
farol *nm* (**a**) *(farola)* street lamp *o* light; *(linterna)* lantern, lamp; EXPR *Fam* **¡adelante con los faroles!** go on, keep going! (**b**) *(en el juego)* bluff; **ir de f.** to be bluffing (**c**) *Fam (exageración)* brag; **no me lo creo, eso es un f.** I don't believe him, he's just bragging; EXPR *Esp* **marcarse** *o* **tirarse un f.** to brag
farola *nf* (**a**) *(farol)* street lamp *o* light (**b**) *(poste)* lamppost (**c**) **la F.** *(revista)* = magazine sold by the homeless in Spain, *Br* ≃ The Big Issue (**d**) *Col (de coche)* headlight, headlamp
farolear *vi Fam* to brag
farolero, -a 1 *adj Fam* bragging
2 *nm,f* (**a**) *(oficio)* lamplighter (**b**) *Fam (fanfarrón)* braggart
farolillo *nm* (**a**) *(de papel)* paper *o* Chinese lantern (**b**) *(planta)* Canterbury bell (**c**) *Dep* ***f. rojo*** *(en clasificación)* = competitor or team last in a table; **ser el f. rojo** to be propping up the bottom of the table
farra *nf* (**a**) *Fam (juerga)* binge, spree; **ir de f.** to go out on the town (**b**) EXPR *Andes, RP* **tomar a alguien para la f.** *(burlarse)* to make fun of sb
fárrago *nm* hotchpotch
farragoso, -a *adj (estilo, informe)* confused, rambling; *(legislación, normativa)* confused
farrear *vi Andes, RP Fam (ir de juerga)* to go out on the town
farrero, -a *Andes, RP Fam* 1 *adj* **es muy f.** he's a real party animal
2 *nm,f* party animal
farrista *adj, nmf* = **farrero**
farruco, -a *adj (valiente)* cocky; **ponerse f.** to get cocky
farsa *nf* (**a**) *(obra teatral)* farce (**b**) *(engaño)* farce; **la investigación fue una f.** the investigation was a complete farce
farsante 1 *adj* deceitful; **¡qué farsantes son!** they're such frauds!
2 *nmf* fraud; **es un f.** he's a fraud
farsear *vi Chile Fam* to fool around
FAS *nm inv* (**a**) (*abrev de* **Fondo de Asistencia Social**) = Spanish social welfare fund (**b**) *Com* (*abrev de* **free alongside ship**) f.a.s., FAS
fas: por fas o por nefas *loc adv Esp Fam* for one reason or another
fascículo *nm* (**a**) *(de publicación)* part, instalment *(of publication)*; **por fascículos (semanales/mensuales)** in (weekly/monthly) parts *o* instalments (**b**) *Anat* fasciculus
fascinación *nf* fascination; **sentir f. por algo** to be fascinated by sth; **ejercer una gran f.** to be truly fascinating
fascinante *adj* fascinating
fascinar *vt* to fascinate; **me fascina Klee** I love *o* adore Klee; **me fascina con su belleza** I find her stunningly beautiful; **su conferencia me fascinó** I found her lecture fascinating
fascismo *nm* fascism
fascista 1 *adj* fascist
2 *nmf* fascist
fascistizante *adj* **una dictadura f.** a dictatorship with fascist tendencies
fascistoide 1 *adj* fascist
2 *nmf* fascist
fase *nf* (**a**) *(etapa)* phase; **estamos pasando una f. difícil** we're going through a difficult phase; **el proyecto está en f. de estudio** the project is still being researched; **la primera f. de la competición** the first round of the competition; **la f. final del campeonato** the final stage of the championship ►► ***f. REM*** *(de los sueños)* REM stage
(**b**) *(de la luna)* phase
(**c**) *(de cohete)* stage
(**d**) *Elec* phase
(**e**) *Fís & Quím* phase
faso *nm RP Fam (cigarrillo)* smoke, *Br* fag
fastidiado, -a *adj Fam* (**a**) *Esp (de salud)* **ando f.** I'm feeling a bit rough; **ando f. del estómago** I've got an upset stomach, *Br* my stomach's feeling rather dodgy; **tengo la espalda fastidiada** I've done my back in
(**b**) *Esp (emocionalmente)* cut up; **la noticia de su despido lo dejó muy f.** he was very cut up when he heard that he had been laid off
(**c**) *Esp (estropeado)* **la máquina de café está fastidiada** *(no funciona)* the coffee machine is bust; *(funciona mal)* the coffee machine isn't working properly
(**d**) *Am (enojado, molesto)* upset
fastidiar 1 *vt* (**a**) *Esp (estropear) (máquina, objeto)* to break; *(fiesta, vacaciones)* to spoil, to ruin; EXPR **¡la hemos fastidiado!** that's really done it!
(**b**) *(molestar)* to annoy, to bother; **me fastidia tener que darle la razón** it annoys me having to admit that he's right; **fastidia que siempre lo sepa todo** it's annoying the way he always knows everything; EXPR *Esp* **¿no te fastidia?** *(¿qué te parece?)* would you believe it?
2 *vi Esp* **¡no fastidies!** you're having me on!; **¡no fastidies que se lo ha dicho a ella!** don't tell me he went and told her!
3 **fastidiarse** *vpr* (**a**) *Esp (estropearse) (máquina)* to break down; *(fiesta, vacaciones)* to be ruined; **se me ha fastidiado la impresora** the printer's broken down on me
(**b**) *Esp (aguantarse)* to put up with it; **si no le gusta, que se fastidie** if he doesn't like it he can lump it; EXPR **¡hay que fastidiarse!** that's really done it!
(**c**) *Esp (lesionar)* to injure, to hurt; **me fastidié la espalda levantando unas cajas** I hurt my back lifting some boxes
(**d**) *Am (molestarse)* to get annoyed; **se fastidió porque no la esperamos** she got annoyed because we didn't wait for her
fastidio *nm* (**a**) *(molestia)* nuisance, bother; **¡qué f.!** what a nuisance! (**b**) *(enfado)* annoyance (**c**) *(aburrimiento)* bore
fastidioso, -a *adj* (**a**) *(molesto)* annoying, irritating; **es un niño muy f.** he's a very annoying *o* irritating child; **es un dolor muy f.** it's a very annoying *o* irritating pain (**b**) *(aburrido)* boring, tedious

> **Falso amigo**: El adjetivo inglés **fastidious** no es la traducción del español **fastidioso**. En inglés, **fastidious** significa "meticuloso, puntilloso" o "quisquilloso".

fasto *nm* (**a**) *(lujo)* lavishness, sumptuousness; *(ostentación)* show, ostentation; **la ceremonia se celebró con gran f.** the ceremony was carried out with great pomp (**b**) *(acto)* **los fastos del quinto centenario** the five-hundredth anniversary celebrations (**c**) **fastos** *(anales)* annals
fastuosamente *adv (lujosamente)* lavishly, sumptuously; *(ostentosamente)* ostentatiously
fastuosidad *nf (lujo)* lavishness, sumptuousness; *(ostentación)* ostentation
fastuoso, -a *adj (lujoso)* lavish, sumptuous; *(ostentoso)* ostentatious
fatal 1 *adj* (**a**) *(mortal)* fatal; **el accidente fue f.** it was a fatal accident
(**b**) *(inevitable)* inevitable
(**c**) *(seductor)* **mujer f.** femme fatale
(**d**) *Esp Fam (muy malo)* terrible, awful; **una novela f.** a terrible *o* an

awful novel; **eso que has hecho está f.** what you've done is terrible *o* awful

(**e**) *Esp Fam (enfermo)* **me encuentro f.** I feel terrible *o* awful; **está f., igual se muere** he's in a very bad way and may well die

2 *adv Esp Fam* **pasarlo f.** to have a terrible *o* an awful time; **sentirse f.** to feel terrible *o* awful; **ese vestido te sienta f.** that dress looks terrible *o* awful on you; **me cae f. su novio** I can't stand her boyfriend

fatalidad *nf* (**a**) *(destino)* fate, destiny (**b**) *(desgracia)* misfortune (**c**) *(inevitabilidad)* fatality

> **Falso amigo**: Salvo en la acepción de "cualidad de fatal", el sustantivo **fatality** no es la traducción del español **fatalidad**. El sentido más frecuente del inglés **fatality** es "víctima mortal".

fatalismo *nm* fatalism

fatalista 1 *adj* fatalistic

2 *nmf* fatalist

fatalmente *adv* (**a**) *(desdichadamente)* unfortunately, unhappily (**b**) *(inevitablemente)* inevitably (**c**) *Esp Fam (muy mal)* terribly, awfully

fático, -a *adj Ling* phatic

fatídicamente *adv* fatefully

fatídico, -a *adj* fateful

fatiga *nf* (**a**) *(cansancio)* tiredness, fatigue; **siento una gran f.** I feel extremely tired ►► ***f. crónica*** chronic fatigue; ***f. del metal*** metal fatigue; ***f. muscular*** muscle fatigue; ***f. nerviosa*** strain, stress; ***f. visual*** eyestrain

(**b**) *(ahogo)* shortness of breath, breathlessness

(**c**) *(reparo)* **me dio f. decírselo** I felt bad about telling him

(**d**) **fatigas** *(penas)* troubles, hardships; **pasó muchas fatigas en su juventud** she endured many hardships in her youth; **mis compañeros de fatigas** my fellow sufferers

fatigado, -a *adj* tired, weary (**de** from)

fatigante *adj* tiring

fatigar [38] **1** *vt* to tire, to weary; **el abuelo fatiga a todos con sus historias** grandad tires us all with his stories; **la televisión me fatiga mucho la vista** my eyes get very tired watching television

2 fatigarse *vpr* (**a**) *(cansarse)* to get tired (**b**) *(ahogarse)* to get breathless *o* out of breath; **se fatiga al subir una cuesta** she gets breathless *o* out of breath going uphill

fatigosamente *adv* wearily; **respiraba f.** he was breathing with difficulty, his breathing was laboured

fatigoso, -a *adj* tiring, fatiguing

fato *nm RP Fam (lío)* **esos dos tienen un f.** those two have got a thing going; **¿tenés algún f.?** are you seeing anybody?

fatuidad *nf* (**a**) *(necedad)* fatuousness, foolishness (**b**) *(vanidad)* conceit

fatuo, -a *adj* (**a**) *(necio)* fatuous, foolish (**b**) *(engreído)* conceited

fauces *nfpl* jaws

faul [faul] *nf Am* foul

faulear *Am* **1** *vt* to foul

2 *vi* to commit a foul

faulero, -a *Am Fam* **1** *adj* **es muy f.** he's a really dirty player

2 *nm,f* dirty player

fauna *nf* (**a**) *(animales)* fauna (**b**) *Fam (grupo de gente)* **punks, cabezas rapadas y otras faunas urbanas** punks, skinheads and other urban tribes; **en ese bar se reúne una f. muy rica** you find all sorts of people in that bar

fauno *nm* faun

Fausto *n pr* Faust

fausto, -a *adj* happy, fortunate

fauvismo [fo'βismo] *nm* fauvism

fauvista [fo'βista] **1** *adj* fauvist

2 *nmf* fauvist, fauve

favela *nf* = Brazilian shanty town

favor *nm* (**a**) *(servicio)* favour; **pedir un f. a alguien** to ask sb a favour; **hacerle un f. a alguien** *(ayudar a)* to do sb a favour; **hágame el f. de cerrar la puerta** would you mind shutting the door, please?; **se ruega a los señores viajeros que hagan el f. de esperar sentados** passengers are requested to remain seated; *Am* **f. de pasar por la puerta B** please proceed through gate B; **¡haz el f. de no golpear la puerta!** would you kindly stop slamming that door?; **¿abro la ventana? – si haces el f....** shall I open the window? – please, if you don't mind...; **con esa actitud hace un flaco f. a la democracia** he's not doing anything for democracy with an attitude like that; *Fam* **tu amiga está como para hacerle un f., a tu amiga le hacía yo un f.** I wouldn't mind doing your friend a favour

(**b**) *Anticuado o Hum* **favores** *(de una mujer)* favours; **la dama le concedió sus favores** the lady graced him with her favours

(**c**) *(apoyo)* **tener a** *o* **en su f. a alguien** to enjoy sb's support; **tenía a todo el pueblo a su f.** he had the people on his side; **los políticos tienen el f. de sus votantes** the politicians enjoy the support of the voters; **goza del f. del público** he has public support

(**d**) **de f.** *(gratuito)* complimentary, free

(**e**) *(en frases)* **un viento/una corriente a f.** a favourable wind/current; **¿tú estás a f. o en contra de la nueva ley?** are you for or against the new law?; **tienen diez goles a f. y once en contra** they've scored ten goals and conceded eleven; **99-89 a f. de los Nets** 99-89 to the Nets; **el juez falló a su f.** the judge found in his favour; **a f. de** in favour of; **estar a f. de** to be in favour of; **extendió un cheque a f. de Henar y Cía.** she made out a cheque to Henar & Co; **en f. de** to the benefit of; **si ahora no contesta, más a mi f.** if he doesn't reply now, that proves I'm right all the more; **por f.** *(al pedir algo)* please; *(expresa indignación, sorpresa)* for heaven's sake!; **las cosas se piden por f.** you say "please" when you ask for something; **nos pidió por f. que la acompañáramos** she asked if we could please go with her

favorable *adj* (**a**) *(beneficioso)* favourable; **tiempo f.** good weather; **el sondeo le es f.** the poll puts him ahead (**b**) *(partidario)* **ser f. a algo** to be in favour of sth; **es f. a intervenir** she's in favour of intervening

favorablemente *adv* favourably; **el paciente evoluciona f.** the patient is making good progress

favorecedor, -ora *adj* flattering, becoming

favorecer [46] *vt* (**a**) *(beneficiar)* to favour; *(ayudar)* to help, to assist; **esta política favorece a los más pobres** this policy works in favour of the poorest; **el árbitro favoreció al equipo visitante** the referee was biased in favour of the visitors; **a pesar de ser peores, les favoreció la suerte y ganaron el partido** despite being worse players, luck was on their side and they won the game

(**b**) *(sentar bien)* to suit; **ese corte de pelo te favorece** that haircut suits you

favorecido, -a 1 *adj* (**a**) *(en foto)* **has salido muy favorecida** you've come out really well (**b**) *Am (en sorteo)* **resultó f. con cinco millones** he won five million

2 *nm,f Am* winner, prizewinner

favoritismo *nm* favouritism

favorito, -a 1 *adj* favourite

2 *nm,f* favourite

fax *nm* (**a**) *(aparato)* fax (machine); **mandar algo por f.** to fax sth (**b**) *(documento)* fax; **mandar un f.** to send a fax

faxear *vt Fam* to fax

fayuca, falluca *nf Méx Fam* contraband

fayuquear, falluquear *vi Méx Fam* to sell contraband

fayuquero, -a, falluquero, -a *nm,f Méx Fam* dealer in contraband

faz *nf* (**a**) *Formal (cara)* countenance, face (**b**) *(del mundo, de la tierra)* face; **fueron barridos de la f. de la tierra** they were swept off *o* from the face of the earth; **el desarrollo de la industria ha transformado la f. de la región** industrial development has transformed the appearance of the region (**c**) *(de tejido)* (right) side

FBI *nm (abrev de* **Federal Bureau of Investigation**) FBI

F.C. *nm* (**a**) *(abrev de* **ferrocarril**) railway, Ry (**b**) *Dep (abrev de* **Fútbol Club**) FC

Fdez. *(abrev de* **Fernández**) = written abbreviation of the surname Fernández

FDN *nm Antes (abrev de* **Frente Democrático Nacional**) National Democratic Front, = left-wing Mexican party, now renamed the PRD

FDNG *nm (abrev de* **Frente Democrático Nueva Guatemala**) = left-wing Guatemalan political party

fdo. *(abrev de* **firmado**) signed

fe *nf* (**a**) *(creencia)* faith; EXPR **la fe mueve montañas** faith can move mountains; EXPR **la fe obra milagros** faith can work miracles ►► ***la fe del carbonero*** blind *o* unquestioning faith; ***fe ciega*** blind faith; **tiene una fe ciega en ese medicamento** he has absolute faith in that medicine

(**b**) *(religión)* faith; **la fe católica/islámica** the Catholic/Islamic faith

(**c**) *(confianza)* faith, confidence; **ser digno de fe** to be credible; **tener fe en** to have faith in, to believe in; **hay que tener fe en el médico** one must have confidence in one's doctor

(**d**) *(documento)* certificate ►► ***fe de bautismo*** baptismal certificate; ***fe de erratas*** errata *(plural)*; ***fe de vida*** = certificate testifying that owner is still alive

(e) *(palabra de honor)* **dar fe de que** *(sujeto: notario)* to certify that; **doy fe de que ocurrió así** I confirm that this is how it happened; *Anticuado* **a fe mía** on my word (of honour)

(f) *(intención)* **buena/mala fe** good/bad faith; **hacer algo de buena/mala fe** to do sth in good/bad faith; **no pongo en duda su buena fe** I don't doubt her good intentions

fealdad *nf* (a) *(de rostro, paisaje, edificio)* ugliness (b) *(de conducta)* unworthiness

feb. *(abrev de* **febrero***)* Feb

febrero *nm* February; *ver también* **septiembre**

febrícula *nf* slight fever

febrífugo, -a *adj Farm* **tiene propiedades febrífugas** it reduces fever

febril *adj* (a) *(con fiebre)* feverish (b) *(actividad)* hectic

febrilmente *adv* hectically

fecal *adj* faecal; **aguas fecales** sewage

fecha *nf (día)* date; *(momento actual)* current date; **una f. señalada** an important date; **pon la f. en la carta** put the date on the letter, date the letter; **en f. próxima** in the next few days; **a f. de hoy todavía no se conocen los resultados** at the moment the results are still not known; **su lanzamiento todavía no tiene f.** a date has still not been set for its launch; **el 28 es la f. de su cumpleaños** the 28th is his birthday; **fijar la f. de algo** to set a date for sth; **a partir de esta f.** from this date; **hasta la f.** to date, so far; **ocurrió por estas fechas** it happened around this time of year ►► ***f. de caducidad*** *(de alimentos)* use-by date; *(de medicamento)* use before date; *Cont* ***f. de cierre*** closing date; ***f. de consumo*** use-by date; ***f. de entrega*** delivery date; ***f. de expedición*** date of issue; ***f. límite*** deadline, closing date; ***f. límite de venta*** sell-by date; ***f. de nacimiento*** date of birth; *Am* ***f. patria*** national holiday *(commemorating important historical event)*; ***f. tope*** deadline; *Fin* ***f. vencimiento*** due date

fechador *nm* postmark

fechar *vt* (a) *(carta)* to date (b) *(por arqueólogos)* to date

fechoría *nf* bad deed, misdemeanour; **cometer una f.** to do sth wicked; **los niños han vuelto a hacer más fechorías** the kids have been up to mischief again

fécula *nf* starch *(in food)*

feculento, -a *adj (harinoso)* starchy

fecundación *nf* fertilization ►► ***f. artificial*** artificial insemination; ***f. asistida*** artificial insemination; ***f. in vitro*** in vitro fertilization

fecundante *adj* fertilizing; **un espermatozoide f.** a fertilizing sperm

fecundar *vt* (a) *(fertilizar)* to fertilize (b) *(hacer productivo)* to make fertile; **la lluvia fecunda la tierra** the rain makes the soil fertile

fecundidad *nf* (a) *(fertilidad)* fertility (b) *(productividad)* fertility

fecundizar [14] *vt* (a) *(hembra)* to fertilize (b) *(tierra)* to make fertile

fecundo, -a *adj* (a) *(mujer)* fertile (b) *(tierra)* fertile (c) *(artista)* prolific

FED [feð] *nm UE (abrev* **Fondo Europeo de Desarrollo***)* EDF

fedatario, -a *nm,f* commissioner for oaths, = civil servant authorized to attest commercial documents

FE de las JONS *Hist (abrev de* **Falange Española de las Juntas de Ofensiva Nacional-Sindicalistas***)* the Falange, = Spanish fascist movement founded in 1933 which became the official party of the Franco regime

FEDER ['feðer] *nm UE (abrev de* **Fondo Europeo de Desarrollo Regional***)* ERDF

federación *nf* federation ►► ***f. deportiva*** sports federation; ***la F. Rusa*** the Russian Federation

federado, -a *adj (deportista)* **un corredor f.** a runner who is a member of a federation

federal 1 *adj* federal

2 *nmf* federal

federalismo *nm* federalism ►► ***f. asimétrico*** = form of federalism where the degree of autonomy allowed to each region is relative to its economic or cultural weight

federalista 1 *adj* federalist

2 *nmf* federalist

federar 1 *vt* to federate

2 **federarse** *vpr* (a) *(formar federación)* to become *o* form a federation (b) *(ingresar en federación)* to join a federation

federativo, -a 1 *adj* federative

2 *nm,f* member of a federation

Federico *n pr* **F. el Grande** Frederick the Great

feedback ['fiðβak] *(pl* **feedbacks***) nm* feedback

feérico, -a *adj Literario* fairy

féferes *nmpl Andes, Carib, Méx (trastos)* things, bits and pieces

fehaciente *adj* irrefutable

fehacientemente *adv* **no se ha comprobado f. su existencia** its existence has not been conclusively proved; **se sabe f. que es perjudicial para la salud** it is definitely known to be bad for your health

felación, felatio *nf* fellatio; **hacer una f. a alguien** to perform fellatio on sb

feldespato *nm* feldspar

feliciano *nm Esp Fam Hum (coito)* **echar un f.** to have a roll in the hay, *Br* to have a bonk

felicidad *nf* happiness; **es una f. volver a verla** it's a pleasure to see her again; **su mayor f. sería ser abuela** being a grandmother would give her the greatest happiness

felicidades *interj (enhorabuena)* congratulations!; *(en cumpleaños)* happy birthday!; **¡f. por tu premio!** congratulations on your prize!

felicitación *nf* (a) *(acción)* **felicitaciones** congratulations; **sus felicitaciones no fueron sinceras** his congratulations were not sincere; **recibe mi más sincera f.** my warmest congratulations

(b) *(tarjeta)* greetings card; **no pude asistir a su boda, pero les envié una f.** I couldn't be at the wedding but I sent them a card ►► ***f. de cumpleaños*** birthday card; ***f. de Navidad*** Christmas card

felicitaciones *interj Am (enhorabuena)* congratulations; **¡f. por el trabajo!** congratulations on your new job!

felicitar 1 *vt* to congratulate (**por** on); **¡te felicito!** congratulations!; **felicita a Juan, es su cumpleaños** wish Juan well, it's his birthday; **los vecinos vinieron a felicitarnos las navidades** the neighbours came round to wish us a happy Christmas

2 **felicitarse** *vpr* to be pleased *o* glad; **se felicitaron por su éxito** they were pleased about their success; **me felicito de que no haya pasado nada** I am glad that nothing has happened

félido, -a *Zool* 1 *adj* feline

2 *nm* feline, cat

3 **félidos** *nmpl (familia) Felidae*; **de la familia de los félidos** of the *Felidae* family

feligrés, -esa *nm,f* parishioner; **cuando los feligreses salen de la iglesia** when the congregation comes out of church

feligresía *nf* (a) *(feligreses)* parishioners (b) *(parroquia)* parish

felino, -a 1 *adj* (a) *(del gato)* feline (b) *(mirada)* catlike (c) *Zool (félido)* feline

2 *nm* feline, cat

3 **felinos** *nmpl (familia) Felidae*; **de la familia de los felinos** of the *Felidae* family

Felipe *n pr* **F. I/II** Philip I/II

felipista *nmf Esp Pol* = supporter of Felipe González

feliz *adj* (a) *(dichoso, alegre)* happy; **el f. acontecimiento** the happy event; **el anuncio de su boda me ha hecho muy f.** the announcement of their wedding has made me very happy; **no me hace muy f. que pierdas el tiempo de esa manera** I'm not very happy that you are wasting your time like that; **un final f.** a happy ending; **te deseo unas felices vacaciones** have a good holiday *o US* vacation!; **¡f. cumpleaños!** happy birthday!; **¡f. viaje!** have a good trip; **¡f. Navidad!** happy Christmas!; **¡f. Año Nuevo!** happy New Year!; **¡felices pascuas!** happy Easter!; EXPR **...y fueron felices y comieron perdices** ...and they all lived happily ever after

(b) *(afortunado)* lucky; **el f. ganador se llevará tres millones** the lucky winner will get three million

(c) *(bueno)* **el tenista chileno tuvo una actuación muy poco f.** the Chilean tennis player performed poorly

(d) *(oportuno)* timely; **tuvo la f. ocurrencia de llamarnos** fortunately, he thought to phone us

felizmente *adv* (a) *(alegremente)* happily; **todo acabó f.** it all *o* everything ended happily; **está f. casada con cuatro niños** she's happily married with four children (b) *(afortunadamente)* fortunately, luckily; **f., una ambulancia pasaba por el lugar de los hechos** fortunately, an ambulance was just passing the scene

felonía *nf Formal* (a) *(traición)* treachery, betrayal (b) *(infamia)* vile deed

felpa *nf (de seda)* plush; *(de algodón)* towelling

felpudo *nm* (a) *(alfombra)* doormat (b) *Esp muy Fam (vello púbico)* bush

femenino, -a 1 *adj* (a) *(de mujer)* women's; **baloncesto f.** women's basketball; **un programa dirigido al público f.** a programme aimed at women; **la asistencia femenina al fútbol** the number of women going to football matches; **un toque f.** a woman's touch; **el sexo f.** the female sex

(b) *(de la feminidad)* feminine

(**c**) *Bot & Zool* female; **los órganos sexuales femeninos** the female sex organs
(**d**) *Gram* feminine
2 *nm Gram* feminine

fémina *nf* woman, female

feminidad, femineidad *nf* femininity

feminismo *nm* feminism

feminista 1 *adj* feminist
2 *nmf* feminist

feminización *nf* feminization

feminizar [14] *vt* to make feminine

femoral 1 *adj* femoral
2 *nf* femoral artery

fémur (*pl* **fémures**) *nm* femur, thighbone

fenec (*pl* **fenecs**) *nm* fennec

fenecer [46] *vi Formal* (**a**) *(fallecer)* to pass away (**b**) *(desaparecer)* to die out

fenecimiento *nm Formal* (**a**) *(fallecemiento)* passing away, death (**b**) *(desaparición)* passing

Fenicia *n Hist* Phoenicia

fenicio, -a 1 *adj* Phoenician
2 *nm,f (persona)* Phoenician
3 *nm (lengua)* Phoenician

fénico, -a *adj Quím* carbolic

fenilo *nm Quím* phenyl

fénix *nm inv (ave)* phoenix; **volvió como el ave f.** he rose like a phoenix from the ashes ►► ***el F. de los Ingenios*** *(Lope de Vega)* = name used to refer to the Spanish Golden Age dramatist Lope de Vega

fenobarbital *nm Farm* phenobarbital, phenobarbitone

fenol *nm Quím* phenol

fenoma *nm Biol* phenome

fenomenal *Fam* 1 *adj* (**a**) *(magnífico)* great, fantastic; **eres un amigo f.** you're a great *o* wonderful friend; **este helado está f.** this ice cream is great *o* fantastic (**b**) *(enorme)* phenomenal; **una f. cantidad de dinero** a phenomenal sum of money; **se dio un golpe f.** she banged herself really hard
2 *adv* **lo pasamos f.** we had a great *o* fantastic time; **me siento f.** I feel great *o* fantastic
3 *interj* great!, terrific!

fenomenalmente *adv Fam* **lo pasamos f.** we had a great *o* fantastic time; **me siento f.** I feel great *o* fantastic

fenoménico, -a *adj* phenomenal

fenómeno, -a 1 *adj Fam* great, fantastic; **estás fenómena con esas gafas** you look great in those glasses; **es un f. en la cocina** he's a fantastic cook, he works wonders in the kitchen
2 *nm* (**a**) *(suceso)* phenomenon; **no se trata de un f. aislado** this is not an isolated phenomenon ►► ***f. atmosférico*** atmospheric phenomenon; ***f. metereológico*** meteorological phenomenon; ***f. natural*** natural phenomenon; ***f. paranormal*** paranormal phenomenon (**b**) *(monstruo)* freak (**c**) *Fam (genio)* **es un f. jugando al tenis** he's an amazing tennis player
3 *adv Fam* **pasarlo f.** to have a great *o* fantastic time; **me siento f.** I feel great *o* fantastic
4 *interj* great!, terrific!

fenomenología *nf* phenomenology

fenotipo *nm* phenotype

feo, -a 1 *adj* (**a**) *(persona, animal, traje)* ugly; **es un pueblo muy f.** it's a very ugly town; **es fea con ganas** she's as ugly as sin; EXPR **ser más f. que Picio** to be as ugly as sin; EXPR *Fam* **ser más f. que pegarle a un padre** to be as ugly as sin
(**b**) *(aspecto, herida)* nasty; *(tiempo)* foul, horrible; *(color)* unpleasant; **está metido en un asunto muy f.** he's mixed up in some really nasty business; **ponerse f.** *(situación, tiempo)* to turn nasty; **la cosa está fea** things are looking bad
(**c**) *(desagradable)* unpleasant; *(ofensivo)* rude; **es** *o* **está f. escupir** it's rude to spit; **cuando me vio me hizo un gesto f.** when she saw me she made a rude gesture; **lo que hiciste quedó f.** that wasn't a very nice thing to do
(**d**) *Am (olor, sabor)* unpleasant
2 *nm,f (persona)* ugly person; EXPR *Fam* **le tocó bailar con la más fea** he drew the short straw
3 *nm (desaire)* **hacer un f. a alguien** to offend *o* slight sb; **le hizo el f. de no saludarla** he snubbed her by not saying hello
4 *adv Am (oler, saber)* bad; **tus zapatos huelen muy f.** your shoes smell awful

FEOGA [fe'oga] *nm UE* (*abrev de* **Fondo Europeo de Orientación y de Garantía Agrícola**) EAGGF, European Agriculture Guidance and Guarantee Fund

feracidad *nf Literario (del campo)* fertility, fecundity

feraz *adj Literario* fertile, fecund

féretro *nm* coffin

feria *nf* (**a**) *(exhibición)* fair; *Méx Fam* **en ese negocio le fue como en f.** that deal turned out really badly for him; *Méx Fam* **al equipo le ha ido como en f.** the team has done terribly badly ►► ***f. de artesanía*** craft(s) fair; ***f. del automóvil*** car *o* motor show; ***f. de ganado*** cattle fair; ***f. del libro*** book fair; ***f. de muestras*** *(actividad)* trade fair; *(instalaciones)* = permanent site for trade fairs
(**b**) *(fiesta popular)* festival ►► ***F. de Abril*** = annual fair in Seville
(**c**) *(de atracciones)* funfair
(**d**) *Taurom* = series of bullfights during a fiesta
(**e**) *Andes, RP (mercado)* open-air market
(**f**) *Méx Fam (cambio)* small change; **¿me cambia diez pesos por f.?** could you give me change of ten pesos, please?; **ese pasaje costó doscientas libras y f.** the ticket cost a bit over two hundred pounds
(**g**) *CAm (propina)* tip
(**h**) *RP* ***f. judicial*** holiday *(when the courts are closed)*

feriado, -a *Am* 1 *adj* **día f.** (public) holiday
2 *nm* (public) holiday; **abierto domingos y feriados** open on Sundays and public holidays

ferial 1 *adj* fair; **recinto f.** showground, exhibition area
2 *nm* showground, exhibition area

feriante *nmf* (**a**) *(en feria de muestras)* exhibitor (**b**) *RP (en mercado)* stallholder, trader

fermentación *nf* fermentation

fermentado, -a *adj* fermented

fermentar 1 *vt* to ferment
2 *vi* (**a**) *(con fermento)* to ferment (**b**) *(sentimiento)* **el odio fermentó en su corazón** hatred simmered in her heart

fermento *nm* (**a**) *(sustancia)* ferment (**b**) *(de sentimiento)* cause; **la tensión racial fue el f. de los disturbios** the riots came about as a result of racial tension

fermio *nm Quím* fermium

Fernando *n pr* **F. el Católico** Ferdinand the Catholic

ferocidad *nf* ferocity, fierceness

ferodo® *nm* = material used for brake lining

Feroe *nfpl* **las (Islas) F.** the Faeroes, the Faeroe Islands

feromona *nf* pheromone

feroz *adj* (**a**) *(animal, bestia)* fierce, ferocious
(**b**) *(criminal, asesino)* cruel, savage
(**c**) *(intenso) (tempestad)* fierce, violent; *(dolor, angustia)* terrible; **tenía un hambre f.** I was ravenous *o* starving; **la competencia es f.** the competition is fierce; **lanzó un ataque f. contra la propuesta del gobierno** he launched a fierce attack against the government's proposal
(**d**) *Fam (enorme)* massive; **agarraron una f. borrachera** they got terribly *o* incredibly drunk

ferozmente *adv* ferociously, fiercely

férreo, -a *adj* (**a**) *(de hierro)* iron; **una estructura férrea** an iron structure; **la vía férrea** *Br* the railway line, *US* the railroad track (**b**) *(firme) (disciplina, voluntad)* iron; **ejercen un f. control sobre sus hijos** they are very strict with their children; **la sometieron a un f. marcaje** they marked her very tightly

ferretería *nf Br* ironmonger's (shop), *US* hardware store

ferretero, -a *nm,f Br* ironmonger, *US* hardware dealer

férrico, -a *adj* ferric

ferrita *nf* ferrite

ferrobús *nm* = small passenger train with an engine at both ends

ferrocarril *nm* (**a**) *(sistema, medio)* railway, *US* railroad; **ese pueblo no tiene f.** that town isn't on a railway line *o US* a railroad; **por f.** by train ►► ***f. de cremallera*** rack railway; ***f. elevado*** elevated railway; ***f. funicular*** funicular (railway); ***f. subterráneo*** underground railway; ***f. de vía estrecha*** narrow-gauge railway (**b**) *(tren)* train (**c**) *Urug Fam (en examen)* crib

ferrocarrilero, -a = **ferroviario**

ferroso, -a *adj* ferrous

ferroviario, -a, *Méx* **ferrocarrilero, -a** 1 *adj* **línea ferroviaria** railway *o US* railroad line; **red ferroviaria** rail(way) *o US* railroad network; **accidente f.** rail *o* train crash
2 *nm,f* railway *o US* railroad worker

ferruginoso, -a *adj* containing iron

ferry ['ferri] (*pl* **ferrys** *o* **ferries**) *nm* ferry

fértil *adj* (**a**) *(mujer)* fertile (**b**) *(tierra)* fertile (**c**) *(imaginación)* fertile

fertilidad *nf* (**a**) *(de mujer)* fertility (**b**) *(de tierra)* fertility (**c**) *(de imaginación)* fertility

fertilización *nf* (**a**) *(de mujer, óvulo)* fertilization ►► ***f. in vitro*** in vitro fertilization (**b**) *(de tierra)* fertilization, fertilizing

fertilizador, -ora *adj* fertilizing

fertilizante 1 *adj* fertilizing

2 *nm* fertilizer ►► ***f. orgánico*** organic fertilizer

fertilizar [14] *vt* (**a**) *(mujer, óvulo)* to fertilize (**b**) *(tierra)* to fertilize, to put fertilizer on

férula *nf* (**a**) *Med* splint (**b**) *(vara)* cane, ferule; EXPR **estar bajo la f. de alguien** to be under sb's thumb

ferviente, fervoroso, -a *adj (admirador, apoyo)* fervent, ardent; *(seguidor, defensor)* passionate, ardent

fervientemente, fervorosamente *adv (admirar, apoyar)* fervently, ardently; *(seguir, defender)* passionately, ardently

fervor *nm* (**a**) *(religioso)* fervour; **rezaba a la virgen con f.** she prayed fervently to the Virgin (**b**) *(entusiasmo)* eagerness, keenness; **trabajaba con f.** he worked away keenly *o* eagerly

fervoroso, -a = **ferviente**

fervorosamente = **fervientemente**

festejado, -a *nm,f CSur (en despedida)* guest of honour; *(en fiesta de cumpleaños)* birthday boy, *f* birthday girl; **los festejados** *(en casamiento)* the happy couple

festejante *nmf Anticuado* suitor

festejar 1 *vt* (**a**) *(celebrar)* to celebrate; **festejó su cumpleaños con los amigos** she celebrated her birthday with her friends (**b**) *(agasajar)* to fête; **la ciudad festejó a los campeones** the champions were fêted by the town (**c**) *Anticuado (cortejar)* to court (**d**) *Méx Fam (golpear)* to beat, to thrash

2 **festejarse** *vpr (celebrarse)* to be celebrated

festejo *nm* (**a**) *(fiesta)* party (**b**) **festejos** *(celebraciones)* public festivities ►► ***festejos taurinos*** bullfights (**c**) *(agasajo)* entertaining

festero, -a *nm,f Fam* party animal

festichola *nf RP Fam* party, bash

festín *nm* banquet, feast; **darse un f.** to have a feast

festinación *nf Andes, Méx, Ven (rapidez)* haste, speed

festinar *vt Andes, Méx, Ven (apresurar)* to hasten, to hurry up

festival *nm* festival; *Fam* **un f. de colores** a riot of colour ►► ***f. benéfico*** charity festival; ***f. de cine*** film festival; ***el F. de Eurovisión*** the Eurovision Song Contest

festivamente *adv* festively

festividad *nf* festivity

festivo, -a *adj* (**a**) *(de fiesta)* festive; **día f.** (public) holiday (**b**) *(alegre)* cheerful, jolly; *(chistoso)* funny, witty

festón *nm (en costura)* scallop; **adornar algo con un f.** to decorate sth with a scalloped edge, to scallop sth

festonear *vt (en costura)* to scallop

feta *nf RP* slice

fetal *adj* foetal

fetén 1 *adj inv* (**a**) *Esp Fam (genial)* great, *Br* brilliant; **esa moto es f.** that bike's great *o Br* brilliant; **tu hermana está f.** your sister looks great *o* fantastic; (**b**) *(auténtico)* real, genuine; **es un Rolex f.** it's a real *o* genuine Rolex

2 *nf* **la f.** the God's honest truth; **te digo la f.** I'm telling you the God's honest truth

3 *adv* **lo pasaron f.** they had a great *o Br* brilliant time

fetiche *nm* (**a**) *(ídolo, objeto)* fetish (**b**) *Psi* fetish

fetichismo *nm* (**a**) *(culto)* fetishism (**b**) *Psi* fetishism

fetichista 1 *adj* fetishistic

2 *nmf* (**a**) *(que adora fetiches)* fetishist (**b**) *Psi* fetishist

feticidio *nm* foeticide

fétidamente *adv* **olía f.** it smelt foul

fetidez *nf* fetidness, foul smell

fétido, -a *adj* fetid, foul-smelling

feto *nm* (**a**) *(embrión)* foetus (**b**) *Fam (persona fea)* ugly mug, face-ache ►► *Esp* ***f. malayo:*** **es un f. malayo** he's got a face like the back end of a bus, he's as ugly as sin

fetuchini, fettuccini [fetu'tʃini] *nmpl* fettuccine

feúcho, -a *adj Fam* plain, *US* homely

feudal *adj* feudal

feudalismo *nm* feudalism

feudo *nm* (**a**) *Hist* fief (**b**) *(dominio)* domain, area of influence; **el norte es uno de los feudos del partido en el gobierno** the north is one of the governing party's strongholds (**c**) *Dep (terreno)* home ground; **en su f. son invencibles** they are unbeatable at home

FEVE ['feβe] *nm* (*abrev de* **Ferrocarriles de Vía Estrecha**) = Spanish narrow-gauge railways

fez *nm* fez

FF. AA. *nfpl* (*abrev de* **Fuerzas Armadas**) = armed forces

FF. CC. *nmpl* (*abrev de* **Ferrocarriles**) railways

FGD *nm Fin* (*abrev de* **fondo de garantía de depósitos**) Deposit Guarantee Fund

FIA [fia] *nf Dep* (*abrev de* **Federación Internacional de Automovilismo**) FIA

fiabilidad *nf* reliability

fiable *adj* (**a**) *(máquina)* reliable (**b**) *(persona) (informal)* reliable; **ese electricista no es muy f.** that electrician is rather unreliable

fiaca *Fam* 1 *adj RP* lazy, idle; **es muy f.** she's a real lazybones *o* layabout

2 *nf* (**a**) *Méx, CSur (pereza)* **levantarme esta mañana, ¡me dio una f.!** I had to prise myself out of bed this morning!; **¡qué f. tener que ponerme a planchar!** what a pain *o Br* fag having to do the ironing!; **hacer f.** to loaf *o* laze around (**b**) *Urug (hambre)* hunger; **¡qué f. tengo!** I'm starving!

3 *nmf RP* lazybones, layabout

fiado, -a 1 *adj* trusting

2 *nm* **dar f.** to give credit; **no venden f. a nadie** they don't give credit to anyone

3 **al fiado** *loc adv* on credit

fiador, -ora 1 *nm,f* guarantor, surety; **salir f. por alguien** to stand surety for sb

2 *nm* (**a**) *(de escopeta)* safety (catch) (**b**) *Andes (de sombrero)* chinstrap

fiambre *nm* (**a**) *(alimento) Br* cold meat, *US* cold cut (**b**) *Fam (cadáver)* stiff; **dejar f. a alguien** to bump sb off; **estar f.** to have kicked the bucket

fiambrera *nf* (**a**) *(tartera)* lunch *o* sandwich box (**b**) *RP (fresquera)* meat safe

fiambrería *nf RP* delicatessen

FIAMM [fi'am] *nmpl Fin* (*abrev de* **Fondos de Inversión en Activos del Mercado Monetario**) = *Br* unit trusts *o US* mutual funds restricted to the currency market

fianza *nf* (**a**) *(depósito)* deposit; **piden medio millón de f.** they require a deposit of half a million (**b**) *Der* bail; **bajo f.** on bail; **salió en libertad bajo f.** she was released on bail

fiar [32] 1 *vt Com* to sell on credit

2 *vi* (**a**) *Com* to sell on credit; **en la carnicería me fían** they let me have credit at the butcher's; **en esta tienda no se fía** *(en letrero)* no credit (given here)

(**b**) **ser de f.** to be trustworthy; **los productos de esta marca son de f.** you can trust this brand; **no te dé reparo contarle el problema a él, que es de f.** you needn't have any qualms about telling him your problem, he's someone you can trust

3 **fiarse** *vpr* **¡no te fíes!** don't be too sure (about it)!; **fiarse de algo/alguien** to trust sth/sb; **yo no me fío de nadie** I don't trust anyone; **no me fío de sus palabras** I don't trust what he says; **no me fío de que vaya a ayudarnos** I don't really believe he's going to help us ►► *Esp Fam* **fíate de la Virgen y no corras: me dijo que me ayudaría – sí, fíate de la Virgen y no corras** she said she'd help me – if I were you I'd rely on yourself rather than on other people

fiasco *nm* fiasco

FIBA ['fiβa] *nf Dep* (*abrev de* **Federación Internacional de Baloncesto Amateur**) FIBA

fibra *nf* (**a**) *(de tela)* fibre; *(de madera)* grain; EXPR **tocar la f. sensible: ha sabido tocar la f. sensible del público juvenil** he's managed to strike a chord among young people ►► ***f. artificial*** artificial fibre, man-made fibre; ***f. de carbono*** carbon fibre; ***f. óptica*** optical fibre; ***f. sintética*** synthetic fibre; ***f. de vidrio*** fibreglass, glass fibre

(**b**) *(alimenticia)* fibre; **alimentos ricos en f.** foods rich in fibre ►► ***f. alimenticia*** dietary fibre

(**c**) *Anat* fibre; **el acróbata era pura f.** the acrobat was all muscle ►► ***f. muscular*** muscle fibre

(**d**) *Arg (marcador)* fibre-tip pen

fibrilación *nf Med* fibrillation

fibrilado, -a *adj* fibrillose, fibrillar

fibrilar 1 *adj* fibrillose, fibrillar
2 *vi Med* to fibrillate

fibrina *nf* fibrin

fibroma *nm Med* fibroma ►► ***f. uterino*** fibroid

fibrosis *nf inv Med* fibrosis ►► ***f. cística*** cystic fibrosis; ***f. pulmonar*** pulmonary fibrosis; ***f. quística*** cystic fibrosis

fibroso, -a *adj* (**a**) *(carne)* chewy, tough (**b**) *(persona)* lean (**c**) *Anat (tejido)* fibrous

ficción *nf* (**a**) *(invención)* fiction (**b**) *(simulación)* pretence, make-believe (**c**) *(género literario)* fiction; **literatura de f.** fiction

ficcional *adj* fictional

ficha *nf* (**a**) *(tarjeta)* (index) card; *(con detalles personales)* file, record card; **rellene esta f. con sus datos** fill in your details on this card ►► ***f. policial*** police record; ***f. técnica*** *(de producto)* (technical) specifications; *(de película)* credits
(**b**) *(de guardarropa, aparcamiento)* token
(**c**) *(de teléfono)* token
(**d**) *(de juego)* counter; *(de dominó)* domino; *(de ajedrez, damas)* piece; *(de ruleta)* chip
(**e**) *Dep (contrato)* contract ►► ***f. de traspaso*** transfer fee
(**f**) *Informát* card ►► ***f. perforada*** perforated card
(**g**) EXPR *Am Fam* **ser buena f.** to be a nasty piece of work

fichaje *nm* (**a**) *Dep (contratación)* signing (up) (**b**) *(jugador)* signing (**c**) *(importe)* transfer fee

fichar 1 *vt* (**a**) *(archivar)* to note down on an index card, to file (**b**) *(sujeto: policía)* to put on police files *o* records; *Fam* **a ese alumno ya lo tenemos fichado** we've got that pupil's number already (**c**) *(jugador, experto)* to sign up; **lo fichó el Deportivo** he was signed (up) by Deportivo
2 *vi* (**a**) *(en el trabajo) (al entrar)* to clock in, *US* to punch in; *(al salir)* to clock out *o* off, *US* to punch out (**b**) **f. por** *(equipo)* to sign up for; *(empresa)* to join; **fichó por una compañía suiza** she joined a Swiss company

fichera *nf Méx, Ven Fam (copera)* (nightclub) hostess, *US* B-girl

fichero *nm* (**a**) *(conjunto de fichas)* file (**b**) *(mueble)* filing cabinet; *(cajón)* filing cabinet drawer; *(caja)* card index box (**c**) *Informát* file ►► ***f. por lotes*** batch file

ficología *nf* phycology

ficólogo, -a *nm,f* phycologist

ficticio, -a *adj* (**a**) *(imaginario)* fictitious (**b**) *(convencional)* imaginary

ficus *nm inv* rubber plant

fidedigno, -a *adj* reliable

fideicomisario, -a *nm,f Der* trustee

fideicomiso *nm Der* trust

fidelidad *nf* (**a**) *(lealtad)* loyalty; *(de cónyuge, perro)* faithfulness; **su marido siempre le guardó f.** her husband always remained faithful to her; **destaca por su f. a la empresa** she has shown outstanding loyalty to the firm ►► ***f. del cliente*** customer loyalty
(**b**) *(precisión)* accuracy; **reprodujeron el original con gran f.** the original was very accurately *o* faithfully reproduced; **alta f.** high fidelity

fidelización *nf Com* building of customer loyalty

fidelizar *vt Com* **f. a los clientes** to build customer loyalty

fideo *nm* (**a**) **fideos** *(para sopa)* vermicelli (**b**) *RP* **fideos** *(pasta)* pasta (**c**) *Fam (persona delgada)* beanpole; EXPR **estar** *o* **quedarse como un f.** to be as thin as a rake

fideuá *nf Esp* = Catalan seafood stew with vermicelli

fidjiano, -a = **fijiano**

fiduciario, -a 1 *adj* (**a**) *Econ* fiduciary (**b**) *Der* fiduciary
2 *nm,f Der* fiduciary

fiebre *nf* (**a**) *(corporal)* fever; **tener f.** to have a temperature ►► ***f. aftosa*** foot and mouth disease; ***f. amarilla*** yellow fever; ***f. del heno*** hay fever; ***f. de Malta*** brucellosis; ***f. mediterránea*** brucellosis; ***f. palúdica*** malaria; ***f. puerperal*** puerperal fever; ***f. reumática*** rheumatic fever; ***f. tifoidea*** typhoid (fever)
(**b**) *(agitación, interés)* fever, mania; **una f. inversora** investment fever *o* mania; **ese año llegó la f. de los yoyós** that was the year the yoyo craze started ►► ***f. del oro*** gold fever

fiel 1 *adj* (**a**) *(leal) (amigo, seguidor)* loyal; *(cónyuge, perro)* faithful; **es muy f. a su dueño** he's very faithful to his master; **fue siempre f. a sus ideas** she always remained faithful to her ideas (**b**) *(preciso)* accurate; **esta novela ofrece un f. reflejo de la realidad** this novel gives a very accurate picture of reality
2 *nm* (**a**) *(de balanza)* needle, pointer (**b**) *Rel* **los fieles** the faithful; **el sacerdote y sus fieles** the priest and his flock

fielmente *adv* faithfully

fieltro *nm* (**a**) *(material)* felt (**b**) *(sombrero)* felt hat

fiera 1 *nf* (**a**) *(animal)* wild animal (**b**) *(persona) (cruel)* brute; **estar/ponerse hecho una f.** to be/go wild with anger
2 *nmf Esp Fam (genial)* demon; **es una fiera para la química** she's brilliant *o* a real star at chemistry

fieramente *adv* savagely, ferociously

fiereza *nf (crueldad)* savagery, ferocity; **con f.** savagely, ferociously

fiero, -a *adj* (**a**) *(feroz)* savage, ferocious (**b**) *RP Fam (feo) (persona, edificio)* hideous; *(situación)* horrendous; **no vayas a su casa que está fiera la cosa** don't go round to his place because things are pretty heavy

fierrero, -a *nm,f Am Fam* weightlifter

fierro *nm Am* (**a**) *(hierro)* iron; **hacer fierros** *(hacer pesas)* to pump iron; EXPR *RP Fam* **meter f.** to put one's foot down, *US* to step on the gas (**b**) *(marca para ganado)* brand (**c**) *Fam (arma)* shooter, *US* piece

fiesta *nf* (**a**) *(reunión)* party; **dar una f. en honor de alguien** to give a party in sb's honour; *Fam* **ise acabó la f., todo el mundo a trabajar!** the party's over, back to work everyone!; EXPR *Fam* **aguar la f. a alguien** to spoil sb's fun; EXPR *Fam* **no estar para fiestas** to be in no mood for joking; EXPR *Fam* **no sabe de qué va la f.** he hasn't got a clue; EXPR *Fam* **tengamos la f. en paz** let's have no more arguments ►► ***f. benéfica*** fête; ***f. de cumpleaños*** birthday party; ***f. de disfraces*** fancy dress party; ***f. de fin de año*** New Year *o* Year's party; *Urug* ***f. lluvia*** potluck party; ***la f. nacional*** *(de país)* national holiday; *Esp (los toros)* bullfighting; *Am* ***f. patria*** national holiday *(commemorating important historical event)*; ***f. sorpresa*** surprise party; ***la f. de los toros*** bullfighting
(**b**) **fiestas** *(de pueblo, barrio)* (local) festivities; **el pueblo está en fiestas** the town is holding its annual fair *o* festival ►► ***fiesta(s) mayor(es)*** = local celebrations for the festival of a town's patron saint; ***fiesta(s) patronal(es)*** = celebrations for the feast day of a town's patron saint
(**c**) *(día)* public holiday; **ser f.** to be a public holiday; **hacer f.** to be on holiday; **mañana tenemos f. en la oficina** it's an office holiday tomorrow; **fiestas** *(vacaciones) Br* holidays, *US* vacation; **ifelices fiestas!** *(en Navidad)* Merry Christmas!, *US* happy holidays! ►► *Rel* ***f. de guardar*** holiday of obligation; *Rel* ***f. movible*** moveable feast; *Rel* ***f. de prefecto*** holiday of obligation

fiestero, -a *nm,f Fam* party animal

FIFA ['fifa] *nf (abrev de* **Federación Internacional de Fútbol Asociación**) **la F.** FIFA

fifar *RP muy Fam* **1** *vi* to screw, *Br* to shag
2 *vt* to screw, *Br* to shag

fifí (*pl* **fifíes**) *nm RP Fam* wimp

fig. (*abrev de* **figura**) fig

figle *nm* ophicleide

figón *nm* cheap restaurant

figura 1 *nf* (**a**) *(objeto)* figure; **una f. de porcelana** a china *o* porcelain figure; **una f. geométrica** a geometrical figure *o* shape; *Fam* **f. decorativa** *(persona)* figurehead
(**b**) *(forma)* shape; **un objeto con f. de ave** an object shaped like a bird; **vislumbré una f. de mujer** I was able to make out the shape of a woman
(**c**) *(de persona)* figure; **hace ejercicio para mantener la f.** she exercises to stay in shape; **tener buena f.** to have a good figure
(**d**) *(en naipes)* picture card
(**e**) *(personaje literario, de ficción)* character
(**f**) *(personaje destacado)* (well-known) figure; **es una f. de las letras** she's a well-known figure in the literary world; **acudieron numerosas figuras del mundo del deporte** many well-known figures from the sporting world were in attendance
(**g**) *(del lenguaje)* **f. (retórica** *o* **del lenguaje)** figure of speech
(**h**) *(en baile, patinaje)* figure
(**i**) *Mús* note *(written)*
(**j**) *(de ajedrez)* piece
(**k**) *Der* **f. (jurídica)** legal concept
2 *nmf Esp Fam* **es todo un f.** he's really something

figuración *nf* (**a**) *(representación)* representation (**b**) *(invención)* invention; **figuraciones** imaginings; **son figuraciones tuyas** it's all in your imagination (**c**) *Cine* extras (**d**) EXPR *RP* **estar para la f.** to be all show

figuradamente *adv* figuratively

figurado, -a *adj* figurative; **en sentido f.** in a figurative sense

figurante, -a *nm,f* extra

figurar 1 *vi* (**a**) *(aparecer)* to appear, to figure (**en** in); **su nombre figura al final de la lista** her name appears at the end of the list; **figura entre los artistas más destacados de su época** he was one of the most outstanding artists of his day; **figura en los títulos de crédito como productor** he appears *o* is listed in the credits as the producer

(**b**) *Fam (destacar, sobresalir)* **le encanta f.** she likes to seem important; **acude a todas las fiestas por un afán de f.** she goes to all the parties because she wants to be seen

2 *vt* (**a**) *(representar)* to represent; **una imagen que figura una divinidad** an image representing a god (**b**) *(simular)* to feign, to simulate; **figuró estar satisfecho** he pretended to be satisfied

3 figurarse *vpr (imaginarse)* to imagine; **me figuro que vendrá en tren** I imagine she'll come by train; **ya me lo figuraba yo** I thought as much; **figúrate si había contaminación que se morían los pajaritos** imagine how polluted it must have been when birds were dying; **¿le gustó? – figúrate, fue a verla otra vez al día siguiente** did he like it? – what do you think? he went to see it again the next day; **¿se rió? – figúrate** did she laugh? – and how!

figurativismo *nm Arte* figurative *o* representational art

figurativo, -a *adj Arte* figurative

figurín *nm* (**a**) *(dibujo)* fashion sketch; EXPR **ir** *o* **estar hecho un f.** to be dressed up to the nines (**b**) *Anticuado (revista)* fashion magazine (**c**) *Cine & Teatro* costume design

> **Falso amigo**: El sustantivo inglés **figurine** no es la traducción del español **figurín**. En inglés, **figurine** significa "figurilla, estatuilla".

figurinista *nmf* costume designer

figurita *nf RP* picture card

figurón *nm Fam* (**a**) *(presumido)* show-off, poser (**b**) ***f. de proa*** figurehead

fija *RP Fam* **1** *nf* tip

2 *adv* **f. que lo sabe** he's bound *o* sure to know

fijación *nf* (**a**) *(sujección)* fixing; *(de cartel)* sticking up, posting (**b**) *(de horario, salario, precios)* fixing (**c**) *Fot* fixing (**d**) *(obsesión)* fixation; **tiene una f. con esa actriz** he's obsessed with that actress (**e**) **fijaciones** *(en esquí)* bindings; *(en ciclismo)* clipless pedals (**f**) *Gram* fixation

fijado *nm Fot* fixing, fixation

fijador *nm* (**a**) *Fot* fixer ▸▸ ***f. fotográfico*** fixer (**b**) *(cosmético)* **f. de pelo** *(crema)* Brylcreem®; *(gomina)* hair gel; *(espray)* hairspray

fijamente *adv* (**a**) *(con atención)* fixedly, attentively (**b**) *(con seguridad)* firmly, assuredly (**c**) *(con intensidad)* intensely, attentively; **mírame f. a los ojos** look me straight in the eye

fijar 1 *vt* (**a**) *(asegurar, sujetar)* to fix (**a** *o* **en** onto); *(cartel)* to stick up; *(sello)* to stick on; **fijaron las patas al suelo con clavos** they nailed the legs to the floor; **prohibido f. carteles** *(en letrero)* stick *o* post no bills

(**b**) *(establecer)* to fix; **se fijaron como objetivo acabar el año con beneficios** they set themselves the target of ending the year in profit; **f. la mirada/la atención en** to fix one's gaze/attention on

(**c**) *(fecha, precio)* to set, to fix

(**d**) *(significado)* to establish; **f. el domicilio** to take up residence

2 fijarse *vpr* (**a**) *(prestar atención)* to pay attention; **fijarse en algo** to pay attention to sth; **¡fíjate!** just imagine!; **¡fíjate en lo que te digo!** mark my words!

(**b**) *(notar algo)* **fijarse en algo** to notice sth; **¿no te has fijado en la expresión de su cara?** didn't you notice the expression on her face?; **qué atento eres, te fijas en todo** you're so alert, you notice everything; **fíjate qué mala suerte, llegué dos minutos tarde a la estación** can you believe my bad luck? I got to the station two minutes late; **¿te hizo ilusión? – fíjate, llevaba meses esperándolo** were you excited about it? – too right I was, I'd been waiting months for it

(**c**) *RP (consultar)* **fijarse en un diccionario** to consult a dictionary; **fíjate en aquel libro** have a look in that book

fijasellos *nm inv* stamp hinge

fijativo *nm* (**a**) *Fot* fixer (**b**) *Arte* fixative

fijeza *nf* **la miraba con f.** he stared at her intently

fijiano, -a, fidjiano, -a [fi'jiano, -a] **1** *adj* Fijian

2 *nm,f* Fijian

fijo, -a 1 *adj* (**a**) *(sujeto)* firmly attached; **un mueble f.** a fixed piece of furniture

(**b**) *(inmóvil)* fixed; **tiene residencia fija en Lima** he is domiciled in Lima, his permanent home is in Lima

(**c**) *(mirada, vista)* fixed; **tenía los ojos fijos en él** she didn't take her eyes off him, she had her eyes fixed on him

(**d**) *(seguro, definitivo)* definite; *(empleado, trabajo)* permanent; *(cliente)* regular; **estoy f. en la empresa** I've got a permanent job in the company; **no tienen fecha fija para la boda** they haven't set a date for the wedding; **el reglamento todavía no es f.** the rules haven't been fixed yet

2 *adv Fam* definitely; **f. que viene** he's definitely coming; **en que llegue a casa te llamo, f.** I promise I'll phone you as soon as I get home

3 de fijo *loc adv Fam* definitely

fila *nf* (**a**) *(hilera)* line; **en f., en f. india** in line, in single file; **marchaban en f. de a dos** they were marching two abreast; **ponerse en f.** to line up; **estacionar en doble f.** to double-park

(**b**) *(de asientos)* row

(**c**) *(de letras, números)* row

(**d**) *Mil* **filas** ranks; **en filas** doing military service; **entrar en filas** to start one's military service; **llamar a filas a alguien** to call sb up; **romper filas** to fall out; **¡rompan filas!** fall out!; EXPR **cerrar filas (en torno a alguien)** to close ranks (around sb)

(**e**) **filas** *(de partido)* ranks; **militaba en las filas socialistas** she was an active member of the socialist party; **milita en las filas del Águilas** he plays for Águilas

Filadelfia *n* Philadelphia

filamento *nm* filament

filandro *nm* four-eyed opossum

filantropía *nf* philanthropy

filantrópico, -a *adj* philanthropic

filantropismo *nm* philanthropy

filántropo, -a *nm,f* philanthropist

filarmónica *nf* philharmonic (orchestra)

filarmónico, -a *adj* philharmonic

filatelia *nf* stamp collecting, philately

filatélico, -a 1 *adj* **colección filatélica** stamp collection; **exposición filatélica** stamp exhibition; **congreso f.** stamp collectors' congress

2 *nm,f* stamp collector, philatelist

filatelista *nmf* stamp collector, philatelist

fildeador, -ora *nm,f Am (en béisbol)* fielder

fildear *Am* **1** *vt (en béisbol)* to field

2 *vi (en béisbol)* to field

fildeo *nm Am (en béisbol)* fielding

filet [fi'le(t)] *nm RP (grueso)* (fillet) steak; *(delgado)* fillet; *(solomillo)* sirloin ▸▸ ***f. de lomo*** rump steak; ***f. de pescado*** fillet of fish, fish fillet

filete *nm* (**a**) *(grueso)* (fillet) steak; *(delgado)* fillet; *(solomillo)* sirloin ▸▸ ***f. de lomo*** rump steak; ***f. de pescado*** fillet of fish, fish fillet (**b**) *(de tornillo)* thread (**c**) *(franja)* (decorative) border (**d**) *Imprenta (línea)* rule (**e**) *Esp Fam* EXPR **darse el f. (con)** to neck (with), *Br* to snog

filetear *vt* (**a**) *(hacer filetes)* to cut into fillets (**b**) *(adornar)* to fillet, to decorate with fillets

filfa *nf Fam* **¡menuda f.!** *(mentira)* what a whopper!; *(engaño)* what a swizz!; **eso que me has contado es pura f.** what you've told me is nothing but lies

filia *nf* **tener f. por algo** to like sth; **filias y fobias** likes and dislikes

filiación *nf* (**a**) *(datos personales)* personal details (**b**) *Pol* affiliation; **un ministro de f. ecologista** a minister with ecological sympathies (**c**) *(parentesco)* relationship (**d**) *(origen)* origin

filial 1 *adj* (**a**) *(de hijo)* filial (**b**) *(de empresa)* subsidiary; **una empresa f.** a subsidiary (company) (**c**) *Dep* **el equipo f.** the reserves

2 *nm* **el f.** the reserves

3 *nf* subsidiary

filiar *vt* to take down a description of

filibustero *nm* buccaneer, pirate *(in 17th century Caribbean)*

filiforme *adj* thread-like

filigrana *nf* (**a**) *(en orfebrería)* filigree (**b**) *(en billetes)* watermark (**c**) *(habilidad)* **hace filigranas con el balón** he performs all sorts of trickery with the ball; **tuve que hacer filigranas para dejar a todos contentos** it took some fancy footwork on my part to keep everyone happy (**d**) *Cuba (planta)* = variety of lantana

filípica *nf* **echar** *o* **soltar una f. a alguien** to give sb a dressing down

Filipinas *nfpl* **(las) F.** the Philippines *(singular)*

filipino, -a 1 *adj* Filipino

2 *nm,f (persona)* Filipino

3 *nm (lengua)* Filipino

filisteo, -a 1 *adj* Philistine

2 *nm,f* Philistine

film (*pl* **films**) *nm* movie, *Br* film

filmación *nf* filming, shooting

filmadora *nf* (**a**) *(cámara)* cine camera (**b**) *Informát* imagesetter, photosetter

filmar *vt* to film, to shoot

filme *nm* movie, *Br* film

fílmico, -a *adj* movie, *Br* film; **la industria fílmica** the movie *o Br* film industry

filmina *nf* slide

filmografía *nf* filmography

filmoteca *nf* (**a**) *(archivo)* film library (**b**) *(sala de cine)* film institute

filo[1] **1** *nm* (**a**) *(borde)* (cutting) edge; EXPR **ser un arma de doble f.** *o* **de dos filos** to be a two-edged *o* double-edged sword; EXPR **en el f. de la navaja** on a knife edge; **sacar f. a algo** to sharpen sth (**b**) *RP Fam (novio)* main squeeze

2 al filo de *loc prep (en el tiempo)* just before; **al f. de la medianoche** at the stroke of midnight; **al f. de la desesperación** on the verge of despair; **se quedaron al f. de la mayoría absoluta** they were just short of an absolute majority

filo[2] *pref* pro-; **filonacionalista** pro-nationalist

filocomunista 1 *adj* pro-communist

2 *nmf* pro-communist, communist sympathizer

filogénesis *nf inv*, **filogenia** *nf Biol* phylogeny

filogenético *adj* phylogenetic

filogenia = **filogenesis**

filología *nf* (**a**) *(ciencia)* philology; **f. clásica/comparada** classical/comparative philology (**b**) *(carrera)* language and literature; **estudié f. inglesa** I studied English

filológico, -a *adj* philological

filólogo, -a *nm,f* philologist

filón *nm* (**a**) *(de carbón, oro)* seam, vein (**b**) *Fam (cosa provechosa)* gold mine

filoso, -a *adj Am* sharp

filosofal *adj* **piedra f.** philosopher's stone

filosofar *vi* to philosophize

filosofía *nf* (**a**) *(estudio)* philosophy ▸▸ ***f. del lenguaje*** philosophy of language; ***F. y Letras*** humanities; ***f. moral*** moral philosophy; ***f. natural*** natural philosophy

(**b**) *(ideas)* philosophy; **no entiendo la f. de estos cambios** I don't understand the thinking behind these changes; **tiene una f. del trabajo muy distinta a la mía** she has a very different attitude to work to me

(**c**) *(resignación)* **tomarse algo con f.** to be philosophical about sth

filosóficamente *adv* philosophically

filosófico, -a *adj* philosophical

filósofo, -a *nm,f* philosopher

filoxera *nf* phylloxera

filtración *nf* (**a**) *(proceso)* filtration, filtering (**b**) *(gotera)* leak (**c**) *(de información, noticia)* leak; **fue responsable de la f. de la noticia** he was responsible for leaking the news

filtrante *adj* filtering

filtrar 1 *vt* (**a**) *(tamizar)* to filter (**b**) *(información, noticia)* to leak (**c**) *(llamadas)* to screen

2 filtrarse *vpr* (**a**) *(penetrar)* to filter, to seep (**por** through); **la luz se filtra por una rendija** the light filters in through a crack; **la humedad se filtra por la pared** the damp seeps through the wall (**b**) *(información, noticia)* to be leaked

filtro *nm* (**a**) *(de café, aparato, cámara)* filter ▸▸ ***f. acústico*** acoustic filter; ***f. de agua*** water filter; ***f. del aire*** air filter; *Fot* ***f. de color*** colour filter; *Fot* ***f. polarizador*** polarizing filter; ***f. solar*** sun filter

(**b**) *(de cigarrillo)* filter; **un cigarrillo con f.** a filter-tipped cigarette; **un cigarrillo sin f.** an unfiltered cigarette

(**c**) *Elec* filter

(**d**) *Informát (para monitor)* filter ▸▸ ***f. de pantalla*** glare filter *o* screen

(**e**) *Informát (software)* filter

(**f**) *(de llamadas)* screening; **es un f. para eliminar a los peores candidatos** it filters out *o* screens out the poorer candidates

(**g**) *(pócima)* love potion, philtre ▸▸ ***f. de amor*** love potion

filudo, -a *adj Andes* sharp

filum *nm Biol & Zool* phylum

FIM [fim] *nmpl Fin* (*abrev de* **Fondos de Inversión Mobiliaria**) *Br* unit trust, *US* mutual fund

fimosis *nf inv Med* phimosis, = condition in which the foreskin is too tight to be retracted

---

FIN *nm* (**a**) *(final)* end; **el f. del invierno** the end of winter; **F.** *(en película)* The End; **dar** *o* **poner f. a algo** to put an end to sth; **un infarto puso f. a su vida** she died from a heart attack; **tocar a su f.** to come to a close; **a fines de** at the end of; **a f.** *o* **fines de mes** at the end of the month; **al** *o* **por f.** at last, finally; **¡al** *o* **por f. hemos llegado!** we've arrived, at last!; **en f., lo volveremos a intentar** well *o* anyway, we can try again; **en f., que si no te interesa, no lo compres** well, if you don't want it, don't buy it; **en f., para resumir...** anyway, to summarize...; **sin f.** endless; **diversión sin f.** no end of fun, endless fun; **recibió un sin f. de regalos** she got hundreds of presents; EXPR **a f. de cuentas, al f. y al cabo, al f. y a la postre** after all ▸▸ ***f. de año*** *(Nochevieja)* New Year's Eve; **voy a pasar el f. de año con la familia** I'm going to stay with my family over New Year; **nuestros resultados de f. de año** our year end results; ***f. de curso*** *(en colegio)* end of the school year; *(en universidad)* end of the academic year; ***f. de fiesta*** grand finale; ***el f. del mundo*** the end of the world; **anímate, no es el f. del mundo** cheer up, it isn't the end of the world; **al f. del mundo** to the end of the earth (and back); ***f. de semana*** weekend

(**b**) *(objetivo)* aim, goal; **el f. último** the ultimate goal; **con este f.** with this aim, to this end; **una organización con fines benéficos** a charity, a charitable organization; **un concierto con fines benéficos** a charity concert; **con fines lucrativos** profit-making; **esfuérzate a f. de aprobar** make an effort (in order) to try and pass; **han subido los intereses a f. de contener la inflación** they have raised interest rates (in order) to keep inflation down; **compórtate bien a f. de que no te puedan reprochar nada** behave well so (that) they can't reproach you for anything; **el f. justifica los medios** the end justifies the means

---

finado, -a *nm,f* **el f.** the deceased

final 1 *adj* (**a**) *(último)* final, end; **sus palabras finales fueron muy aplaudidas** her closing words were loudly applauded; **punto f.** end point (**b**) *Gram* final

2 *nm* (**a**) *(terminación)* end; **el f. del libro es sorprendente** the book has a surprise ending; **a finales de** at the end of; **al f.** *(en conclusión)* in the end; **la cocina está al f. del pasillo** the kitchen is at the end of the corridor; **responderé preguntas al f. de la charla** I will answer questions at the end of the talk; **al f. siempre tengo que ayudarles** I always have to help them in the end; **ya verás como al f. acepta** she'll agree in the end, you'll see ▸▸ ***f. feliz*** happy ending

(**b**) *(examen)* final (exam)

3 *nf* final; **cuartos de f.** quarter finals ▸▸ ***f. de consolación*** 3rd/4th place play-off; ***f. de la copa*** cup final; ***f. a cuatro*** *(en baloncesto)* final four

finalidad *nf* aim, purpose; **sin ninguna f.** aimlessly; **¿con qué f. nos hicieron venir?** what was the purpose of getting us to come?, why did they get us to come?

> **Falso amigo**: El sustantivo inglés **finality** no es la traducción del español **finalidad**. En inglés, **finality** significa "rotundidad, irrevocabilidad".

finalísima *nf Dep* grand final

finalista 1 *adj* **los equipos finalistas** *(en final)* the teams in the final, the finalists; **los atletas finalistas** the athletes competing in the final

2 *nmf* finalist

finalización *nf (terminación)* end; *(de contrato)* completion

finalizar [14] **1** *vt (terminar)* to finish, to complete; *(contrato)* to complete

2 *vi* to end, to finish (**con** in); **el plazo de inscripciones ya finalizó** the deadline for registration has passed; **la ceremonia finalizó con un desfile** the ceremony ended with a parade

finalmente *adv* finally; **si f. cambias de opinión, dímelo** if in the end you change your mind, let me know; **f. no se llegó a ninguna conclusión** in the end no conclusion was reached; **f., me gustaría agradecer a...** finally, I should like to thank...

finamente *adv* (**a**) *(con cuidado)* finely (**b**) *(con cortesía)* courteously, politely (**c**) *(en trozos finos)* **picar f. la cebolla** chop the onion finely

financiación *nf*, *Am* **financiamiento** *nm* financing; **la f. de los partidos políticos** the funding of political parties ▸▸ *Fin* ***f. mediante déficit*** deficit financing

financiador, -ora *nm,f* financial backer

financiamiento = **financiación**

financiar *vt* (**a**) *(proyecto, organismo)* to fund, to finance (**b**) *(compra)* to offer credit facilities for; **la compra del televisor se la financiamos hasta en 10 veces** we allow you to pay for your television in up to 10 instalments

financiera *nf (firma)* finance company

financiero, -a 1 *adj* financial
2 *nm,f (persona)* financier

financista *nmf Am* financier

finanzas *nfpl (disciplina)* finance; **el ministro de f.** the finance minister; **las f. de la empresa** the company's finances

finar *vi Formal* to pass away

finasangre *Chile* **1** *adj inv* thoroughbred
2 *nmf inv* thoroughbred

finca *nf* (**a**) *(bien inmueble)* property ►► ***f. rústica*** property *(in the country)*; ***f. urbana*** property *(in the city)* (**b**) *(casa de campo)* country house (**c**) *Am (plantación)* plantation (**d**) *Col* ***f. raíz*** real estate

fincar *vt Méx* to build; **fincaron su casa en la capital** they built their house in the capital

finde *nm Esp Fam* weekend

finés, -esa (*pl* **fineses**) **1** *adj* Finnish
2 *nm,f (persona)* Finn
3 *nm (lengua)* Finnish

fineza *nf* (**a**) *(finura)* **trabaja con una f. excepcional** his workmanship is exceptionally fine; **una pieza hecha con mucha f.** a very finely-crafted piece (**b**) *(cortesía)* courtesy; **siempre va diciendo finezas a las mujeres** he is always paying compliments to the ladies

finger (*pl* **fingers**) *nm* jetty *(for boarding aircraft)*

fingidamente *adv* feignedly, falsely

fingido, -a *adj* feigned, apparent

fingimiento *nm* pretence; **su enfado es puro f.** he's only pretending to be angry

fingir [24] **1** *vt* to feign; **fingió alegría para no desilusionarme** he pretended to be happy so as not to disappoint me; **fingió no saber nada** he pretended not to know anything
2 *vi* to pretend
3 fingirse *vpr* **se fingió enfermo/cansado** he pretended to be ill/tired

finiquitar *vt* (**a**) *(deuda)* to settle; *(trabajador)* to pay off (**b**) *(concluir)* to end; **f. la transición democrática** to complete the transition to democracy

finiquito *nm Fin (de deuda)* settlement; *(por despido)* redundancy settlement; **dar f.** *(saldar cuenta)* to close *o* settle; *(concluir)* to finish, to wind up

finisecular *adj* turn-of-the-century, fin-de-siècle; **la Europa f.** turn-of-the-century Europe, Europe at the turn of the century

finito, -a *adj* finite

finjo *ver* **fingir**

finlandés, -esa 1 *adj* Finnish
2 *nm,f (persona)* Finn
3 *nm (lengua)* Finnish

Finlandia *n* Finland

finlandización *nf Pol* Finlandization

finn [fin] (*pl* **finns**) *nm Náut* finn

fino, -a 1 *adj* (**a**) *(de calidad) (tela, alimentos)* fine, high-quality
(**b**) *(delgado) (capa, filete)* thin; *(lluvia)* fine
(**c**) *(cintura, cuerpo)* slim
(**d**) *(delicado) (manos)* delicate; *(piel)* smooth; *(pelo)* fine; **es de facciones finas** she has fine features
(**e**) *(cortés)* refined; **es una persona de finos modales** she has impeccable *o* exquisite manners
(**f**) *(oído, olfato)* sharp, keen; *(gusto)* refined
(**g**) *(humor, ironía)* refined
2 *nm* dry sherry

finolis *Fam* **1** *adj inv* affected, fussy; **es muy f. con la comida** he's very fussy about his food
2 *nmf inv* affected *o* fussy person; **es un f.** he's terribly affected *o* fussy

finta *nf (en esgrima, boxeo)* feint; **hacer una f.** *(en fútbol, baloncesto)* to dummy

fintar 1 *vt* **f. a alguien** *(en esgrima, boxeo)* to feint at sb; *(en fútbol, baloncesto)* to sell sb a dummy
2 *vi* (**a**) *(en esgrima, boxeo)* to feint; *(en fútbol, baloncesto)* to dummy (**b**) *Méx (fingir)* to bluff

finura *nf* (**a**) *(buena calidad)* fineness, high quality (**b**) *(delgadez) (de lluvia)* thinness (**c**) *(delicadeza) (de manos)* delicacy; *(de piel)* smoothness; *(de pelo)* fineness (**d**) *(cortesía)* refinement (**e**) *(de oído, olfato)* sharpness, keenness; *(de gusto)* refinement (**f**) *(de humor, ironía)* refinement

fiordo *nm* fjord

fique *nm Am* sisal

firma *nf* (**a**) *(rúbrica)* signature; **estampó su f.** he signed (his name), he wrote his signature; **echa aquí una f.** put your signature here, sign here ►► *Informát* ***f. digital*** digital signature; *Informát* ***f. electrónica*** digital signature
(**b**) *(acción)* signing; **la f. de un acuerdo** the signing of an agreement
(**c**) *(escritor)* name; **una de las grandes firmas que escribe en el diario** one of the big names who writes for the newspaper
(**d**) *(estilo propio)* hallmark; **este robo lleva la f. de la banda de Martínez** the robbery has all the hallmarks of Martínez's gang
(**e**) *(empresa)* firm

firmamento *nm* firmament

firmante 1 *adj* **los países firmantes del acuerdo** the countries that have signed the agreement; **las partes firmantes de un acuerdo** the signatories to an agreement
2 *nmf* signatory; **el abajo f.** the undersigned

firmar 1 *vt* to sign; EXPR **f. algo en blanco** to rubber-stamp sth; *Fam* **ahora mismo firmaría porque nos dieran la mitad de lo que prometieron** I'd settle right now for half of what they promised
2 *vi* to sign

firme 1 *adj* (**a**) *(fuerte, sólido)* firm; *(andamio, construcción)* stable; *(pulso)* steady; *(paso)* resolute; **tiene unos principios muy firmes** she has very firm principles, she's extremely principled; **tiene la f. intención de resolver el problema** she fully intends to solve the problem, she has every intention of solving the problem; **llovió de f. durante varias horas** it rained hard for several hours
(**b**) *(argumento, base)* solid; **trabaja de f. en el nuevo proyecto** she's working full-time on the new project; **una respuesta en f.** a definite answer; **quedamos en f. para el miércoles** we are definitely agreed on Wednesday; **tenemos un acuerdo en f. para intercambiar información** we have a firm agreement to exchange information
(**c**) *(carácter, actitud)* resolute; **hay que mostrarse f. con los empleados** you have to be firm with the workers; EXPR *Fam* **poner f. a alguien** to bring sb into line
(**d**) *Mil* **¡firmes!** attention!; **en la posición de firmes** standing to attention
2 *nm* road surface; **f. en mal estado** *(en letrero)* uneven road surface
3 *adv* hard; **mantenerse f. en** to hold fast to; **se mantuvo f. en su actitud** he refused to give way, he stood his ground

firmemente *adv* firmly; **me aseguró f. que vendría** he assured me he would definitely be coming

firmeza *nf* (**a**) *(fortaleza, solidez)* firmness; *(de construcción)* stability (**b**) *(de argumento)* solidity (**c**) *(de carácter, actitud)* firmness; **defendió con f. su postura** he firmly defended his stance

firmware ['firmwer] *nm Informát* firmware

firulete *nm Andes, RP (en vestido)* frill, fancy trimming; *(en carta)* adornment

fiscal 1 *adj* (**a**) *(del fisco)* fiscal, tax; **año/asesor/fraude f.** tax year/adviser/evasion (**b**) *Der* **el ministerio f.** *Br* ≃ Office of the Director of Public Prosecutions, *US* ≃ Attorney General's Office
2 *nmf* (**a**) *Der Br* ≃ public prosecutor, *US* ≃ district attorney ►► ***F. General del Estado*** *Br* ≃ Director of Public Prosecutions, *US* ≃ Attorney General (**b**) *Andes (ayuda de párroco)* churchwarden (**c**) *Ven* ***f. de tránsito*** traffic policeman

fiscalía *nf Der* (**a**) *(cargo) Br* ≃ post of public prosecutor, *US* ≃ post of district attorney
(**b**) *(oficina) Br* ≃ public prosecutor's office, *US* ≃ district attorney's office; ***F. General del Estado*** *Br* ≃ Office of the Director of Public Prosecutions, *US* ≃ Attorney General's Office

fiscalidad *nf (impuestos)* tax burden; **países con distintos regímenes de f.** countries with different tax regimes

fiscalización *nf* (**a**) *(de acciones, persona)* investigation (**b**) *(de cuentas)* inspection; *(de empresa)* tax investigation

fiscalizador, -ora *adj Formal* investigating, auditing; **órgano f.** auditing body; **función fiscalizadora** auditing function

fiscalizar [14] *vt* (**a**) *(acciones)* to inquire into, to investigate; *(persona)* to inquire into *o* investigate the affairs of (**b**) *(cuentas)* to inspect for tax purposes; *(empresa)* to investigate for tax purposes

fiscalmente *adv* **una inversión que es más rentable f.** a more tax-efficient investment; **una empresa domiciliada f. en las Bahamas** a company that has its registered office in the Bahamas for tax purposes

fisco *nm* **el f.** the Treasury, *Br* ≃ the Exchequer; **defraudar al f.** to evade tax; **pagar al f.** to pay *Br* the Inland Revenue *o US* the IRS

fisga *nf Guat, Méx Taurom* banderilla, = barbed dart thrust into bull's back

fisgar [38] *vi Fam* to pry, to nose around; **¿quién ha estado fisgando en mis papeles?** who's been nosing around (in) my papers?

fisgón, -ona *Fam* 1 *adj* nosy, prying
2 *nm,f* busybody, nosy parker

fisgonear *vi Fam* to pry, to nose around; **estaba fisgoneando por el ojo de la cerradura** he was spying through the keyhole

fisgoneo *nm Fam* prying, nosing around; **en esta casa todo el mundo se dedica al f.** everyone in this house pokes their nose into everyone else's business

fisible *adj* fissile

física *nf* (**a**) *(ciencia)* physics *(singular)*; **un licenciado en física(s)** a physics graduate ▸▸ ***f. aplicada*** applied physics; ***f. cuántica*** quantum physics; ***f. nuclear*** nuclear physics; ***f. de partículas*** particle physics (**b**) *ver también* **físico**

físicamente *adv* physically; **me resulta f. imposible estar allí a las seis** it's physically impossible for me to be there at six

físico, -a 1 *adj* (**a**) *(de la física)* physical (**b**) *(geografía, mapa)* physical (**c**) *(del cuerpo)* physical (**d**) *Cuba, Méx Fam (melindroso)* finicky
2 *nm,f (persona)* physicist
3 *nm (complexión) (de hombre, atleta)* physique; *(de mujer)* figure; **una modelo con un f. impresionante** a model with a stunning figure; **tiene un f. atlético** he has an athletic physique

fisicoquímica *nf* physical chemistry

fisicoquímico, -a 1 *adj* physicochemical
2 *nm,f* physical chemist

fisiocracia *nf Hist* physiocracy

fisioculturismo *nm* body building

fisioculturista *nmf* body builder

fisiología *nf* physiology

fisiológico, -a *adj* physiological

fisiólogo, -a *nm,f* physiologist

fisión *nf Fís* fission ▸▸ ***f. nuclear*** nuclear fission

fisionable *adj* fissionable

fisionomía = **fisonomía**

fisionomista = **fisonomista**

fisioterapeuta *nmf Med* physiotherapist

fisioterapia *nf Med* physiotherapy

fisonomía, fisionomía *nf* (**a**) *(de persona)* features, physiognomy (**b**) *(de ciudad, paisaje)* appearance

fisonómico, -a *adj* physiognomic(al); **rasgos fisonómicos** facial features

fisonomista, fisionomista *nmf* **ser un buen/mal f.** to be good/bad at remembering faces

fistol *nm Méx* tie pin

fístula *nf Med* fistula

fisura *nf* (**a**) *(grieta)* fissure, crack (**b**) *Med (en ano)* fissure (**c**) *Med (en hueso)* crack (**d**) *(quiebra, ruptura)* crack, split; **aparecieron las primeras fisuras en la coalición** the first cracks in the coalition appeared

fitipaldi *nm Esp Fam (conductor)* **es un f.** he drives like a maniac

fitness ['fitnes] *nm* fitness training

fitófago, -a *Bot* 1 *adj* plant-eating, *Espec* phytophagous
2 *nm,f* plant-eater, *Espec* phytophagous

fitología *nf* botany

fitopatología *nf* phytopathology, plant pathology

fitoplancton *nm* phytoplankton

fitosanitario, -a *adj* plant health; **control f.** plant health measure

fitoterapéutico, -a *adj (remedio)* herbal; *(tratamiento, producto)* herbal medicine

fitoterapia *nf* herbal medicine

fixture ['fikstur, fiks'ture] *nm RP* fixture list

Fiyi *n* Fiji

fiyiano, -a 1 *adj* Fijian
2 *nm,f* Fijian

flacidez, flaccidez *nf* flabbiness

flácido, -a, fláccido, -a *adj* flaccid, flabby

flaco, -a 1 *adj* (**a**) *(delgado)* thin; *(esquelético)* skinny (**b**) *(frágil)* weak; **su punto f. es la ortografía** his weak point is spelling (**c**) *(pobre)* **le haces un f. servicio** *o* **favor mimándolo tanto** you're not doing him any favours by spoiling him like that
2 *nm,f Am Fam (como apelativo)* **¿cómo estás, flaca?** hey, how are you doing?; **¿qué auto tiene el f.?** what kind of car has the guy got?

flacucho, -a, *Am* **flacón, -ona** *adj* skinny

flag [flaɣ] (*pl* **flags**) *nm Informát* flag

flagelación *nf* flagellation

flagelado, -a *Biol* 1 *adj* flagellate(d)
2 *nm* flagellate

flagelante *nmf (penitente)* flagellant

flagelar 1 *vt* to flagellate
2 **flagelarse** *vpr* to flagellate oneself

flagelo *nm* (**a**) *(látigo)* whip (**b**) *(calamidad)* catastrophe, scourge (**c**) *Biol* flagellum

flagrancia *nf* flagrancy

flagrante *adj* (**a**) *(evidente) (injusticia)* flagrant; *(verdad, prueba)* glaringly obvious; *(mentira)* blatant (**b**) *Der* **en f. delito** in flagrante delicto

flama *nf Méx* flame

flamable *adj Méx* flammable, inflammable

flamante *adj* (**a**) *(vistoso)* resplendent; **nos enseñó fotos de su f. yate** he showed us photos of his magnificent yacht (**b**) *(nuevo)* brand-new; **el f. campeón del mundo** the new world champion

flambear *vt Culin* to flambé

flameante *adj (bandera)* fluttering; *(vela)* flapping

flamear 1 *vt (ave)* to singe
2 *vi* (**a**) *(fuego)* to blaze, to flare up (**b**) *(bandera)* to flutter; *(vela)* to flap

flamenco, -a 1 *adj* (**a**) *(música, baile)* flamenco; **cante/espectáculo f.** flamenco singing/show (**b**) *(de Flandes)* Flemish (**c**) *Esp Fam (robusto, saludable)* **está muy flamenca** she's bursting with health and vitality (**d**) *Esp Fam (chulo)* cocky; **ponerse f. (con alguien)** to get cocky (with sb) (**e**) *Carib, Méx (flaco)* skinny
2 *nm,f (persona)* Fleming; **los flamencos** the Flemish
3 *nm* (**a**) *(ave)* flamingo (**b**) *(lengua)* Flemish (**c**) *(música, baile)* flamenco

flamencología *nf* study of flamenco

flamencólogo, -a *nm,f* expert in flamenco

flamígero, -a *adj* (**a**) *Literario (que arde)* blazing, flaming; **dragón f.** fire-breathing dragon (**b**) *Arte (en forma de llama)* flamboyant

flámula *nf* streamer

flan *nm* (**a**) *(dulce)* crème caramel; **f. de huevo/vainilla** = crème caramel made with egg/vanilla; EXPR *Fam* **estar hecho un f., estar como un f.** to be shaking like a jelly, to be a bundle of nerves (**b**) *(salado)* mould; **f. de verduras** vegetable mould, timbale of vegetables

> **Falso amigo**: El sustantivo inglés **flan** no es la traducción del español **flan**. En inglés **flan** significa "tarta".

flanco *nm* (**a**) *(de formación militar)* flank; *(de barco)* side (**b**) *(de cuerpo) (de persona)* side; *(de animal)* flank

Flandes *n* Flanders

flanera *nf* crème caramel mould

flanqueado, -a *adj* flanked (**de** *o* **por** by)

flanquear *vt* to flank; **dos guardaespaldas flanqueaban al presidente** the president was flanked by two bodyguards

flanqueo *nm* flanking

flap (*pl* **flaps**) *nm Av* flap

flaquear *vi* (**a**) *(disminuir) (entusiasmo, equipo)* to flag; **al final del día le flaqueaban las fuerzas** at the end of the day he was beginning to flag; **le flaquea la vista** her eyesight is getting worse (**b**) *(flojear)* to lose heart (**c**) *(mostrarse débil)* to be weak *o* poor; **flaquea especialmente en latín** he's particularly weak in *o* poor at Latin

flaqueza *nf* (**a**) *(física)* weakness (**b**) *(de carácter)* weakness; **le dijo que sí en un momento de f.** she said yes to him in a moment of weakness (**c**) *(acción)* weakness; **la compra de ese abrigo fue una f.** buying that coat was a weakness on my part

flas, flash [flas] (*pl* **flashes**) *nm* (**a**) *Fot* flash ▸▸ ***f. de relleno*** fill-in flash (**b**) *Rad & TV* **f. (informativo)** newsflash (**c**) *Fam (imagen mental)* flash of inspiration (**d**) *Esp Fam (impresión)* shock; **¡me llevé un f.!** I got a bit of a shock! (**e**) *Fam (por drogas)* rush

flashback ['flasβak] (*pl* **flashbacks**) *nm Cine* flashback

flato *nm* (**a**) *Esp (dolor abdominal)* **tener f.** to have a stitch; **me dio** *o* **entró f.** I got a stitch (**b**) *Am (tristeza)* sadness, melancholy

flatulencia *nf* flatulence, wind

flatulento, -a *adj* flatulent

flauta 1 *nf* (**a**) *(instrumento)* **f. (dulce)** recorder; **f. (travesera)** flute; EXPR **sonar la f. (por casualidad): compró un décimo por si sonaba la f.** I bought a tenth of a lottery ticket on the off-chance I might get lucky; **me sonó la f. y acerté todas las preguntas** by a sheer fluke I answered all the questions right ►► ***f. de pico*** recorder
(**b**) *Fam (pan)* baguette
(**c**) *Esp Fam (bocadillo) Br* filled baguette, *US* submarine (sandwich)
(**d**) *CSur Fam* **de la gran f.: hace un frío de la gran f.** it's *Br* flipping *o US* goddamn freezing; **tiene una casa de la gran f.** he's got one hell of a house; **¡(la gran) f.!** good grief!, good heavens!
2 *nmf* flautist

flautín *nm* piccolo

flautista *nmf* flautist ►► ***el f. de Hamelín*** the Pied Piper of Hamelin

flebitis *nf inv Med* phlebitis

flebólogo, -a *nm,f* = doctor specializing in circulatory disorders

flebotomía *nf Med* blood letting

flecha 1 *nf* (**a**) *(arma)* arrow; EXPR **como una f.** like a shot; EXPR **salir como una f.** to shoot *o* fly out (**b**) *(indicando dirección)* arrow; *RP, Ven (en calle)* one-way sign; **siga la f.** follow the arrow ►► *Informát* ***f. de desplazamiento*** scroll arrow (**c**) *Arquit* spire (**d**) *Geom* sagitta (**e**) *PRico (eje)* axle
2 *adj Ven (calle)* one-way

flechado, -a *adj Fam* **salió f.** he shot *o* flew out

flechar *vt Fam* **lo flechó en cuanto se conocieron** he fell for her as soon as they met

flechazo *nm* (**a**) *(con saeta)* arrow shot; *(herida)* arrow wound (**b**) *Fam (amoroso)* **fue un f.** it was love at first sight

fleco *nm* (**a**) *(adorno)* fringe; **con flecos** fringed (**b**) *(de tela gastada)* frayed edge (**c**) *(asunto pendiente)* unresolved issue; **discutieron los flecos que quedaban por cerrar** they discussed the points that still had to be settled *o* the loose ends that needed tying up (**d**) *Méx (flequillo)* fringe

fleje *nm* (**a**) *(cinta adhesiva)* packing tape (**b**) *(aro)* barrel hoop

flema *nf* (**a**) *(en los bronquios)* phlegm (**b**) *(calma)* composure, phlegm; **la f. británica** British phlegm *o* sangfroid

flemáticamente *adv* phlegmatically

flemático, -a *adj (tranquilo)* phlegmatic

flemón *nm* gumboil, abscess; **le ha salido un f.** he's got an abscess in his gum

fleo *nm* timothy (grass)

flequillo *nm Br* fringe, *US* bangs

fletador, -ora *nm,f, Am* **fletante** *nmf* (**a**) *(que alquila)* charterer (**b**) *(que embarca)* transport hirer

fletamiento, fletamento *nm* charter, chartering

fletán *nm* halibut ►► ***f. negro*** Greenland halibut

fletante = **fletador**

fletar 1 *vt* (**a**) *(buque, avión)* to charter (**b**) *Andes (insultos)* to hurl (**c**) *CSur Fam (enviar)* to dispatch, to pack off
2 fletarse *vpr Am Fam (marcharse)* to scram, to split

flete *nm* (**a**) *(precio)* freightage (**b**) *(carga)* cargo, freight (**c**) *RP (caballo)* spirited horse

fletera *nf Cuba (prostituta)* prostitute

fletero, -a *Am* **1** *adj (que se alquila)* for hire
2 *nm* (**a**) *(de barco)* boatman, ferryman (**b**) *(de carro) (propietario, conductor)* haulier

flexibilidad *nf* (**a**) *(de material)* flexibility; *(de cuerpo)* suppleness; **un atleta con gran f.** a very supple athlete (**b**) *(de actitud)* flexibility; **aplican la normativa con f.** there is some flexibility in how the rules are applied (**c**) ***f. de horarios*** *(de trabajador)* flexibility about working hours

flexibilización *nf (de normas)* relaxation; *(del mercado de trabajo)* liberalization

flexibilizar [14] *vt (normas)* to make more flexible; *(mercado de trabajo)* to liberalize

flexible *adj* (**a**) *(material)* flexible; *(cuerpo)* supple (**b**) *(actitud)* flexible (**c**) *(horario)* flexible

flexión *nf* (**a**) *(de brazo, pierna)* ***flexiones abdominales*** sit-ups; ***flexiones de brazo*** push-ups, *Br* press-ups (**b**) *Gram* inflection ►► ***f. nominal*** noun inflection; ***f. verbal*** verb inflection

flexionar *vt* to bend

flexivo, -a *adj Gram* inflected

flexo *nm Esp* adjustable table lamp *o* light, Anglepoise® lamp

flexor, -ora *Anat* **1** *adj* flexional
2 *nm* flexor

flipado, -a *adj Esp Fam* (**a**) *(asombrado)* flabbergasted, *Br* gobsmacked; **está f. con su nuevo ordenador** he's crazy *o Br* mad about his new computer; **me quedé f. de verla tan simpática** I was flabbergasted *o Br* gobsmacked to see her being so nice (**b**) *(drogado)* stoned, high

flipante *adj Esp Fam* cool, wild

flipar *Esp Fam* **1** *vi* (**a**) *(asombrarse)* to be flabbergasted *o Br* gobsmacked; **yo flipo con las tonterías que dice** I just can't believe the rubbish *o US* garbage he talks; EXPR **f. en colores** to be absolutely flabbergasted *o Br* gobsmacked (**b**) *(con una droga)* to be stoned *o* high
2 *vt (gustar)* **me flipan los videojuegos** I'm wild about video games
3 fliparse *vpr* (**a**) *(disfrutar)* to go wild (**con** about) (**b**) *(drogarse)* to get stoned *o* high

flipe *nm Esp Fam* (**a**) *(asombro)* **tiene un f. de moto** he's got an amazing *o* fantastic motorbike; **¡qué f.!** what a gas! (**b**) *(por drogas)* **coger un f.** to get stoned *o* high

flíper (*pl* **flípers**), **flipper** (*pl* **flippers**) *nm* pinball machine

flirt [flirt] (*pl* **flirts**) *nm* (**a**) *(relación)* fling; **tener un f. con alguien** to have a fling with sb (**b**) *(persona)* boyfriend, *f* girlfriend

flirtear *vi (con persona)* to flirt; **flirteó con la idea de presentarse candidato** she flirted with the idea of running as a candidate

flirteo *nm (acción)* flirting; *(relación)* fling; **tuvo un breve f. con Raúl** she had a fling with Raúl

flit® *nm Am* insecticide

FLN *nm* (*abrev de* **Frente de Liberación Nacional**) FLN

flojear *vi* (**a**) *(piernas, fuerzas)* to weaken; *(película, libro)* to flag; *(calor, trabajo)* to ease off; *(ventas)* to fall off; **me flojeaban las fuerzas** I was feeling weak; **le flojea la memoria** his memory is going *o* failing; **flojea especialmente en literatura** she is especially weak in literature
(**b**) *Andes Fam (holgazanear)* to laze about *o* around; **pasamos el domingo entero flojeando** we just lazed about *o* around all Sunday

flojedad *nf* weakness

flojera *nf Fam* **tengo f. en los brazos** my arms feel weak

flojo, -a 1 *adj* (**a**) *(suelto)* loose; **esta falda me queda floja** this skirt is too loose for me
(**b**) *(débil) (persona)* weak; *(sonido)* faint; *(salud)* poor; *(viento)* light; *(bebida)* weak
(**c**) *(sin calidad, aptitudes)* poor; **una obra muy floja** a very poorly written play; **estar f. en algo** to be poor *o* weak at sth; **el pianista ha estado un poco f. hoy** the pianist was a bit off form today; **tuvo una floja actuación** he gave a poor performance; **tus notas son muy flojas** your *Br* marks *o US* grades are very poor
(**d**) *(mercado, negocio)* slack; **las ventas están muy flojas** sales are very slack
(**e**) EXPR *muy Fam* **me la trae floja** *Br* I couldn't give a toss, *US* I couldn't give a rat's ass
2 *nm,f Andes Fam (holgazán)* layabout, lazybones

floppy ['flopi] (*pl* **floppys**) *nm Informát* **f. (disk)** floppy disk

flor[1] *nf* (**a**) *(en planta)* flower; **en f.** in flower, in bloom; **una camisa de flores** a flowery shirt; EXPR **echar flores a alguien** to pay sb compliments; EXPR **echarse flores** to praise oneself, to blow one's own trumpet; EXPR **ir de f. en f.** to flit from one relationship to another; EXPR **ser f. de un día** to be a flash in the pan; EXPR **ser la f. de la canela** to be the crème de la crème *o* the cream; EXPR *RP* **tirarse con flores** to be at one another's throats ►► ***f. de azahar*** orange blossom; ***f. de cerezo*** cherry blossom; ***f. de lis*** fleur-de-lis; ***f. de nieve*** edelweiss; ***f. del Paraíso*** bird of paradise flower; ***f. de Pascua*** poinsettia, Christmas flower
(**b**) *(lo mejor)* **la f. (y nata)** the crème de la crème, the cream; **en la f. de la edad** *o* **de la vida** in the prime of life
(**c**) *(superficie)* **a f. de agua/tierra** at water/ground level; **tiene una sensibilidad a f. de piel** she's extremely sensitive; **tengo los nervios a f. de piel** my nerves are really on edge
(**d**) *Chile (en uñas)* white spot *(on fingernails)*
(**e**) EXPR *Esp Fam (idea)* **no tener ni flores (de)** not to have a clue (about); **¿cuál es la capital de Mali? – ni flores** what's the capital of Mali? – no idea *o* I haven't a clue

flor² *CSur Fam* **1** *adj inv (muy bueno)* great, fantastic; **un espectáculo f.** a great *o* fantastic show
2 flor de *loc adv* **hicimos f. de paseo** we had a lovely outing; **tenía f. de gripe** she had a really bad dose of the flu

flora *nf* (**a**) *(en planta)* flora, plant life (**b**) *Biol* ***f. bacteriana*** intestinal flora; ***f. intestinal*** intestinal flora

floración *nf* (**a**) *(acción)* flowering, blossoming (**b**) *(época)* flowering season

floral *adj* floral

floreado, -a *adj (con flores)* flowery

florear 1 *vt RP (adornar)* to embellish
2 *vi* (**a**) *CAm, Méx (florecer)* to flower (**b**) *Méx (halagar)* to compliment

florecer [46] **1** *vi* (**a**) *(dar flor)* to flower (**b**) *(prosperar)* to flourish; **el sector de la telefonía móvil está floreciendo** the mobile phone industry is flourishing
2 florecerse *vpr* (**a**) *(enmohecerse)* to go mouldy (**b**) *RP (el pelo)* **se me florecen las puntas muy rápido** I get split ends very easily

florecido, -a *adj RP (pelo)* **tendrías que cortarte el pelo, lo tenés todo f.** you should get your hair cut, you've got a lot of split ends

floreciente *adj (próspero)* flourishing

florecimiento *nm* (**a**) *(de planta)* flowering (**b**) *(prosperidad)* flourishing; **el f. del imperio inca** the flowering of the Inca empire

Florencia *n* Florence

florentino, -a 1 *adj* Florentine
2 *nm,f* Florentine

floreo *nm* (**a**) *(a la guitarra)* arpeggio (**b**) *(en danza)* flourish

florería *nf* florist's (shop)

florero *nm* vase; EXPR *Fam Hum* **estar de f.: esa secretaria joven está de f.** that young secretary is there purely for decorative purposes

florescencia *nf* (**a**) *Bot* florescence (**b**) *Quím* efflorescence

floresta *nf (terreno)* wood

floretazo *nm (golpe)* foil thrust

florete *nm* fencing foil

floretista *nmf* foilist

florezca *etc ver* **florecer**

floricultor, -ora *nm,f* flower grower

floricultura *nf* flower growing

floridez *nf (de lenguaje, estilo)* floridity, floweriness

florido, -a *adj* (**a**) *(con flores)* flowery (**b**) *(estilo, lenguaje)* florid, flowery (**c**) **lo más f. de** *(lo más selecto de)* the cream of

florilegio *nm* anthology

florín *nm* (**a**) *Antes (moneda holandesa)* guilder (**b**) *(moneda húngara)* forint (**c**) *Hist* florin

floripón *nm Col, RP* (**a**) *Fam (adorno)* great big flower (**b**) *(arbusto)* datura (**c**) *Fam Pey (homosexual) Br* poof, *US* fag

floripondio *nm* (**a**) *Fam (adorno)* great big flower (**b**) *(arbusto)* datura (**c**) *Andes Fam Pey (homosexual) Br* poof, *US* fag

florista *nmf* florist

floristería *nf* florist's (shop)

florístico, -a *adj* floral

floritura *nf* (**a**) *(adorno)* flourish (**b**) *Fam (cosa innecesaria)* **que se deje de florituras y se dedique a marcar goles** he should quit showboating and concentrate on scoring some goals; **ese texto necesita más contenido y menos florituras** this text needs less flowery language and more content

florón *nm Arte* rosette, *Espec* fleurón

flota *nf* (**a**) *(de barcos)* fleet ►► ***f. de guerra*** battle fleet; ***f. mercante*** merchant fleet; ***f. pesquera*** fishing fleet (**b**) *(de vehículos)* fleet (**c**) *Col Fam (fanfarronada)* brag, boast (**d**) *Bol, Col (bus interurbano) Br* coach, *US* bus

flotabilidad *nf* (**a**) *(en el agua)* buoyancy (**b**) *Econ* floatability

flotación *nf* (**a**) *(en el agua)* flotation (**b**) *Econ* flotation

flotador *nm* (**a**) *(para nadar)* rubber ring (**b**) *(de caña de pescar)* float (**c**) *(de cisternas)* ballcock (**d**) *RP Fam (grasa)* spare tyre

flotante *adj* (**a**) *(en el agua)* floating (**b**) *Econ* floating (**c**) *(población)* floating (**d**) *Col Fam (fanfarrón)* bragging, boastful

flotar 1 *vt Econ* to float
2 *vi* (**a**) *(en líquido)* to float; **el aceite flota en el agua** oil floats on water (**b**) *(en el aire)* to float (**c**) *(desconfianza, tensión)* to hang, to hover (**d**) *Econ* to float; **hacer f. una divisa** to float a currency

flote: a flote *loc adv* afloat; **mantenerse a f.** to stay afloat; **sacaron a f. el pesquero hundido** they refloated the sunken fishing boat; EXPR **sacar algo a f.** to get sth back on its feet; EXPR **salir a f.** to get back on one's feet

flotilla *nf* flotilla

fluctuación *nf* (**a**) *(variación)* fluctuation ►► ***f. del mercado*** market fluctuation (**b**) *(vacilación)* wavering

fluctuante *adj* fluctuating

fluctuar [4] *vi* (**a**) *(variar)* to fluctuate (**b**) *(vacilar)* to waver

fluidez *nf* (**a**) *(de sustancia, líquido)* fluidity (**b**) *(del tráfico)* free flow (**c**) *(de relaciones)* smoothness (**d**) *(en el lenguaje)* fluency; **hablar un idioma con f.** to speak a language fluently

fluidificar [60] *vt* to fluidize

fluido, -a 1 *adj* (**a**) *(sustancia, líquido)* fluid (**b**) *(tráfico)* free-flowing (**c**) *(relaciones)* smooth (**d**) *(lenguaje)* fluent
2 *nm* (**a**) *(sustancia, líquido)* fluid (**b**) *(corriente)* current; **les cortaron el f.** their electricity was cut off; EXPR ***f. eléctrico*** electric current *o* power

fluir [34] *vi* (**a**) *(líquido, gas)* to flow (**b**) *(tráfico)* to flow (**c**) *(palabras, pensamientos)* to flow

flujo *nm* (**a**) *(movimiento)* flow ►► *Com* ***f. de caja*** cash flow; *Com* ***f. de fondos*** cash flow; ***f. migratorio*** flow of immigrants; ***f. sanguíneo*** bloodstream; *Com* ***f. de tesorería*** cash flow (**b**) *(secreción)* ***f. menstrual*** menstrual flow; ***f. vaginal*** vaginal discharge (**c**) *(marea)* **el f. de la marea** the rising *o* incoming tide; **f. y reflujo** ebb and flow

fluminense 1 *adj* of/from Río de Janeiro
2 *nm,f* person from the state of Río de Janeiro

flúor *nm Quím* fluorine

fluoración *nf* fluoridation

fluorado, -a *adj* fluoridized, fluoridated

fluorescencia *nf* fluorescence

fluorescente 1 *adj* fluorescent; **rotulador f.** highlighter (pen)
2 *nm (lámpara)* strip light; *(tubo individual)* fluorescent tube

fluorina, fluorita *nf Geol* fluorite

fluorización *nf* fluoridation

fluoruro *nm Quím* fluoride

fluvial *adj* river; **cuenca f.** river basin

fluviómetro *nm* fluviometer, fluviograph

flux *nm inv* (**a**) *(en naipes)* flush (**b**) *Carib, Col, Méx (traje)* suit

fluya *etc ver* **fluir**

fluyera *etc ver* **fluir**

FM *nf* (*abrev de* **frecuencia modulada**) FM

FMI *nm* (*abrev de* **Fondo Monetario Internacional**) IMF

FMLN *nm* (*abrev de* **Movimiento** *o* **Frente Farabundo Martí de Liberación Nacional**) FMLN

F.O.B. *Com* (*abrev de* **free on board**) f.o.b.

fobia *nf* phobia; **le tiene f. a los perros** he's terrified of dogs; *Fam* **el profesor me tiene f.** the teacher can't stand me

foca *nf* (**a**) *(animal)* seal; EXPR *Fam* **está como una f.** *(está gorda)* she's a fat cow ►► ***f. gris*** grey seal; ***f. monje*** monk seal (**b**) *Fam (persona)* fat cow

focal *adj* focal

focalizar [14] *vt* to focus

focha *nf* coot ►► ***f. americana*** American coot

foco *nm* (**a**) *(centro)* centre, focal point; *(de epidemia)* source, breeding ground; **un f. de miseria** a severely deprived area; **un f. de infecciones** a source of infection; **un f. cultural** a cultural centre; **el f. de atención** the centre of attention
(**b**) *(lámpara) (para un punto)* spotlight; *(para una zona)* floodlight
(**c**) *Geom* focus
(**d**) *Fot (enfoque)* focus; **fuera de f.** *(desenfocado)* out of focus; **tiene el f. estropeado** the focus doesn't work
(**e**) *Andes, Méx (bombilla)* light bulb
(**f**) *Am (farola)* street light
(**g**) *Am Aut* (car) headlight

fodongo, -a *Méx Fam* **1** *adj* scruffy
2 *nm,f* slovenly person

fofo, -a *adj* flabby

fogaje *nm* (**a**) *Cuba, Méx (erupción)* rash (**b**) *Ecuad (llamarada)* blaze (**c**) *Carib (sofoco)* stifling heat

fogata *nf* bonfire, fire

fogón *nm* (**a**) *(para cocinar)* stove (**b**) *(de máquina de vapor)* firebox (**c**) *CRica, CSur (fogata)* bonfire; EXPR *CSur* **arrimate** *o* **acercate al f.** come and join us

fogonazo *nm* flash

fogonero, -a *nm,f* stoker

fogosamente *adv* passionately

fogosidad *nf (de persona)* passion; *(de caballo)* spirit

fogoso, -a *adj (persona)* passionate, intense; *(caballo)* spirited, lively

fogueado, -a *adj (experimentado)* experienced

foguear 1 *vt* (**a**) *(arma, escopeta)* to scale (**b**) *(soldado, caballo)* to accustom to gunfire (**c**) *(dar experiencia)* **f. a alguien en algo** to give sb experience of sth

2 foguearse *vpr* to gain experience; **foguearse en algo** to gain experience in sth

fogueo *nm* **de f.** blank

foie-gras [fwa'ɣras] *nm inv* (pâté de) foie gras

foja *nf Am Der (hoja)* folio; **a fojas 8** on page 8; EXPR **volver a fojas cero** to go back to square one, to start again from scratch ▸▸ ***f. de servicios*** record (of service), track record

fol. *(abrev de* **folio***)* f.

folclore, folclor *nm* folklore

folclórico, -a, folklórico, -a 1 *adj* traditional, popular

2 *nm,f Esp* = singer of traditional Spanish songs

folclorismo, folklorismo *nm* folklore

fólder *nm Andes, CAm, Méx (carpeta)* folder

folía *nf* = folk song and dance from the Canary Islands

foliáceo, -a *adj* (**a**) *Bot* leaf-like, *Espec* foliaceous (**b**) *Geol* foliaceous

foliación *nf* (**a**) *Bot* foliation (**b**) *Imprenta* pagination, *Espec* foliation

foliar 1 *adj Bot* foliate

2 *vt Imprenta* to foliate, to number the pages of

folicular *adj* follicular

folículo *nm* (**a**) *Bot* follicle (**b**) *Anat* follicle ▸▸ ***f. piloso*** hair follicle

folio *nm* (**a**) *(hoja de papel)* leaf, sheet *(approximately A4 size)*; **tamaño f.** ≃ A4-sized *(approximately)* (**b**) *(hoja de libro, cuaderno)* page (**c**) *Imprenta* header, page heading

folíolo, foliolo *nm Bot* leaflet, *Espec* foliole

folk *nm* folk (music)

folklore *nm* folklore

folklórico = **folclórico**

folklorismo = **folclorismo**

folk-rock *nm* folk rock (music)

folla *nf Esp muy Fam* **tener mala f.** *(mala intención)* to be a mean *o* complete bastard

follado, -a *adj Esp muy Fam* (**a**) *(con prisa)* **no me puedo detener, voy f.** I can't stop, I'm rushed off my *Br* bloody *o US* goddamn feet (**b**) *(agotado)* bushed, *Br* shagged out

follaje *nm* foliage

follar *Esp muy Fam* **1** *vt* to shag; EXPR **¡que te folle un pez!** piss off!

2 *vi* to shag

3 follarse *vpr* (**a**) *(hacer el amor)* **follarse a alguien** to shag sb (**b**) *(suspender)* **se me han follado en inglés** I screwed up in English

folletín *nm (melodrama)* melodrama; **de f.** *(vida, incidente)* melodramatic

folletinesco, -a *adj* melodramatic

folleto *nm (librito)* brochure; *(hoja suelta)* leaflet ▸▸ ***f. informativo*** (information) leaflet

follón *nm Esp Fam* (**a**) *(discusión)* row; **se armó un f.** there was an almighty row; **me montó un f. tremendo porque faltaba dinero** he kicked up an almighty fuss *o* row because there was some money missing

(**b**) *(lío)* mess; **¡vaya f.!** what a mess!; **tengo un f. de libros encima de la mesa** I've got piles of books scattered all over my desk; **¡dejad de armar f.!** stop making such a row!; **me hice un f. con las listas** I got into a real muddle *o* mess with the lists; **está metido en un f. de dinero** he's got into some money trouble; **esta tarde tengo mucho f., mañana sería mejor** I won't have a minute this afternoon, so tomorrow would be better

follonero, -a *Esp Fam* **1** *adj* **es muy f.** he's a real troublemaker

2 *nm,f* troublemaker

follones *nmpl Ecuad (braga)* panties, *Br* knickers

fome *adj Chile Fam* boring

fomentar *vt* (**a**) *(favorecer)* to encourage, to promote; **medidas para f. el ahorro** measures to encourage saving; **una campaña para f. la lectura** a campaign to encourage *o* promote reading (**b**) *Carib, Méx (organizar)* to open, to set up

fomento *nm* (**a**) *(de cultura, comercio, turismo)* encouragement, promotion; **Ministerio de F.** Ministry of Public Works (**b**) *Med* poultice

fon *nm Fís* phon

fonación *nf* phonation

fonador, -ora *adj* **el aparato f.** the speech apparatus; **los órganos fonadores** the speech organs

FONASA [fo'nasa] *nm (abrev de* **Fondo Nacional de Salud***)* = Chilean national health service

fonazo *nm Méx Fam* phone, call; **echar un f. a alguien** to give sb a buzz *o Br* bell

fonda *nf* (**a**) *(pensión)* boarding house (**b**) *(restaurante)* cheap restaurant

fondant *nm* (**a**) *(para glasear)* fondant icing (**b**) *(chocolate)* **(chocolate) f.** cooking chocolate

fondeadero *nm* anchorage

fondeado, -a *adj* (**a**) *(barco)* anchored (**b**) *Am (acaudalado)* rich, wealthy

fondear 1 *vi* to anchor

2 *vt* (**a**) *(barco)* to anchor (**b**) *CSur (presos políticos)* = to throw from a plane over the sea

3 fondearse *vpr Am* to get rich

fondeo *nm* (**a**) *(de barco)* anchoring (**b**) *CSur (de presos políticos)* = drowning of political prisoners by throwing them from a plane over the sea

fondillos *nmpl* seat *(of trousers)*

fondista *nmf* (**a**) *Dep (corredor)* long-distance runner; *(nadador)* long-distance swimmer; *(esquiador)* cross-country skier (**b**) *(propietario de fonda)* landlord, *f* landlady

FONDO *nm* (**a**) *(parte inferior)* bottom; **el f. del mar** the bottom of the sea; **fondos** *(de embarcación)* bottom; **dar f.** *(embarcación)* to drop anchor; **echar a f.** *(embarcación)* to sink; **irse a f.** *(embarcación)* to sink, to founder; **sin f.** bottomless; EXPR *RP Fam* **¡f. blanco!** bottoms up!; EXPR **tocar f.** *(embarcación)* to hit the bottom (of the sea/river); *(crisis)* to bottom out; **su popularidad ha tocado f.** their popularity has reached an all-time low *o* rock bottom; **mi paciencia ha tocado f.** my patience has reached its limit

(**b**) *(de habitación, escenario)* back; **al f. de** *(calle, pasillo)* at the end of; *(sala)* at the back of; **el f. de la pista** the back of the court; **los baños están al f. del pasillo, a la derecha** the toilets are at the end of the corridor, on the right

(**c**) *(dimensión)* depth; **un río de poco f.** a shallow river; **tener un metro de f.** to be one metre deep

(**d**) *(de cuadro, foto, tela)* background; **quiero una tela de flores sobre f. negro** I'd like some material with a pattern of flowers on a black background; **al f.** in the background

(**e**) *(de alcachofa)* heart

(**f**) *(de asunto, problema)* heart, bottom; **el problema de f.** the underlying problem; **la cuestión de f.** the fundamental issue; **llegar al f. de** to get to the heart *o* bottom of; **el gobierno quiere llegar al f. de la cuestión** the government wants to get to the bottom of the matter; **en el f.** *(en lo más íntimo)* deep down; *(en lo esencial)* basically; **en el f. está enamorada de él** deep down, she loves him; **en el f., no es mala persona** deep down, she's not a bad person; **en el f. tus problemas son los mismos** basically, you have the same problems

(**g**) *(de una persona)* **tener buen f.** to have a good heart; **tener mal f.** to be a nasty piece of work

(**h**) *(de obra literaria)* substance

(**i**) *(de dinero)* fund; **a f. perdido** *(préstamo)* non-returnable; **no estamos dispuestos a invertir a f. perdido** we're not prepared to pour money down the drain; **fondos** *(capital)* funds; **nos hemos quedado sin fondos** our funds have run out; **un cheque sin fondos** a bad cheque; **estar mal de fondos** *(persona)* to be badly off; *(empresa)* to be short of funds; **recaudar fondos** to raise funds ▸▸ *Econ* ***f. de amortización*** sinking fund; ***fondos bloqueados*** frozen funds; ***f. de cohesión*** cohesion fund; *Fin* ***f. de comercio*** goodwill; ***f. de compensación interterritorial*** interterritorial compensation fund; ***f. común*** kitty; **poner un f. (común)** to set up a kitty; *Fin* ***f. de crédito permanente*** evergreen fund; ***f. de emergencia*** contingency fund; *UE* ***fondos estructurales*** structural funds; *Fin* ***f. ético*** ethical fund; *UE* ***F. Europeo de Desarrollo*** European Development Fund; *UE* ***F. Europeo de Desarrollo Regional*** European Regional Development Fund; ***f. de fideicomiso*** trust fund; *Fin* ***f. de garantía de***

depósitos deposit guarantee fund; *Fin* ***f. de inversión*** investment fund; *Fin* ***f. de inversión ético*** ethical investment fund; ***f. de inversión inmobiliaria*** real estate investment fund; ***f. de inversión mobiliaria*** *Br* trust fund, *US* mutual fund; ***F. Monetario Internacional*** International Monetary Fund; *Econ* ***f. de pensiones*** pension fund; ***fondos públicos*** public funds; *Fin* ***f. de renta fija*** non-equity fund, bond fund; *Fin* ***f. de renta variable*** equity fund; ***fondos reservados*** = contingency funds available to ministries, for which they do not have to account publicly; *Fin* ***f. rotativo*** revolving fund; *UE* ***F. Social Europeo*** European Social Fund; ***f. vitalicio*** life annuity

(**j**) *(fundamento)* reason, basis; **sus acciones tienen siempre un f. humanitario** everything she does is for humanitarian reasons

(**k**) **hacer algo a f.** *(en profundidad)* to do sth thoroughly; **hicimos una lectura a f.** we read it through carefully; **hacer una limpieza a f.** to have a thorough clean; **el juez ha ordenado una investigación a f.** the judge has ordered a full enquiry *o* an in-depth investigation; **emplearse a f.** to do one's utmost

(**l**) *(de biblioteca, archivo)* catalogue, collection ►► ***f. editorial*** backlist

(**m**) *Dep (resistencia física)* stamina

(**n**) *Dep (larga distancia)* long-distance running; **medio f.** middle-distance running; **carrera de f.** long-distance race; **esquí de f.** cross-country skiing; **de medio f.** middle-distance ►► ***f. en carretera*** *(ciclismo)* road racing

(**o**) *Dep (ejercicio)* push-up, press-up

(**p**) *Carib, Méx (prenda)* petticoat

(**q**) *Cuba (caldero)* cauldron

(**r**) *RP (patio)* back patio

---

fondón, -ona *adj Fam* **se ha puesto muy f.** he's got quite beefy *o* chunky

fondue [fon'du] *nf* (**a**) *(comida)* fondue ►► ***f. de queso*** cheese fondue (**b**) *(utensilios)* fondue set

fonema *nm* phoneme

fonémico, -a *adj* phonemic

fonendo, fonendoscopio *nm* stethoscope

fonética *nf* phonetics *(singular)*

fonéticamente *adv* phonetically

fonético, -a *adj* phonetic

fonetista *nmf* phonetician

foniatra *nmf* speech therapist

foniatría *nf* speech therapy

fónico, -a *adj* phonic

fono *nm Am Fam* phone

fonoaudiología *nf RP* speech therapy

fonoaudiólogo, -a *nm,f RP* speech therapist

fonográfico, -a *adj* phonographic

fonógrafo *nm* gramophone, *US* phonograph

fonología *nf* phonology

fonológico, -a *adj* phonological

fonólogo, -a *nm,f* phonologist

fonometría *nf* phonometry

fonómetro *nm* phonometer

fonoteca *nf* record library

fontana *nf Literario* spring, fount

fontanal *nm* spring

fontanela *nf Anat* fontanel, fontanelle

fontanería *nf* (**a**) *(oficio)* plumbing (**b**) *(instalaciones)* plumbing

fontanero, -a *nm,f* plumber

footing ['futin] *nm* jogging; **hacer f.** to go jogging

FOP *nfpl Esp* (*abrev* **Fuerzas de Orden Público**) security forces

foque *nm Náut* jib

forajido, -a *nm,f* outlaw

foral *adj* = relating to ancient regional laws still existing in some parts of Spain

foráneo, -a *adj* foreign

forastero, -a *nm,f* stranger

forcejear *vi* to struggle; **forcejeó con la cerradura** he struggled with the lock; **el preso forcejeó para liberarse** the prisoner struggled to free himself

forcejeo *nm* struggle

fórceps *nm inv* forceps

forense 1 *adj* forensic; **médico f.** forensic scientist, pathologist
2 *nmf* forensic scientist, pathologist

forestación *nf* forestation

forestal *adj* forest; **incendio f.** forest fire; **repoblación f.** reforestation

forestar *vt* to plant with trees

forfait [for'fait, for'fe] (*pl* **forfaits**) *nm* (**a**) *(para esquiar)* ski pass (**b**) *Dep* default (**c**) *(precio invariable)* fixed rate; **a f.** fixed price

forint, forinto *nm* forint

forja *nf* (**a**) *(taller)* forge (**b**) *(forjadura)* forging

forjado, -a 1 *adj (hierro)* wrought
2 *nm* forging

forjador, -ora *nm,f* (metal) forger

forjar 1 *vt* (**a**) *(metal)* to forge (**b**) *(persona, nación)* to create, to form; **las guerras forjan héroes** wars create heroes (**c**) *(mentira)* to invent; *(plan)* to form
2 **forjarse** *vpr* (**a**) *(labrarse)* to carve out for oneself; **se ha forjado una fama de duro** he has earned himself *o* built up a reputation as a hard man (**b**) *(ilusiones)* to build up; **forjarse demasiadas ilusiones** to build up false hopes (for oneself) (**c**) *(crearse, originarse)* to be forged; **la revolución se forjó en las minas de carbón** the revolution was forged in the coal mines

---

FORMA *nf* (**a**) *(figura)* shape, form; **¿qué f. tiene?** what shape is it?; **en f. de triángulo** in the shape of a triangle; **en f. de L** L-shaped; **el escultor dio f. al barro** the sculptor shaped the clay; **tener f. ovalada** *o* **de óvalo** to be oval (in shape); **el proyecto comienza a tomar f.** the project is starting to take shape

(**b**) *(manera)* way, manner; **tiene una f. de hablar muy divertida** she has a very funny way of talking; **no ha habido f. de localizarlo** it was impossible to find him; **se puede hacer de varias formas** it can be done in several different ways; **lo siento, es mi f. de ser** I'm sorry, that's just the way I am *o* that's just my way; **¡qué f. de llover!** it's absolutely pouring down!; **de cualquier f., de todas formas** anyway, in any case; **si lo hacemos de esta f., acabaremos antes** if we do it this way, we'll finish earlier; **viajaremos en segunda, de esta f. recortaremos gastos** we can travel second class, that way we'll keep the cost down; **han organizado las conferencias de f. que haya diez minutos de intervalo entre ellas** they've arranged the speeches in such a way that there's a ten minute break between each one; **llegaremos a las ocho, de f. que podamos comenzar temprano** we'll be there by eight so (that) we can start early; **dobla la camisa de f. que no se arruguen las mangas** fold the shirt so (that) the sleeves don't get creased ►► ***f. de pago*** method of payment

(**c**) *(manifestación)* form; **la fotografía es una f. de arte** photography is an art form

(**d**) *(condición física)* fitness; **estar en f.** to be fit; **estar en baja/plena f.** to be in poor/top shape; **vuelvo a estar en plena f.** I'm fully fit again; **mantenerse/ponerse en f.** to keep/get fit

(**e**) *(de equipo, artista)* form; **estar en f.** to be on form; **estar en baja/plena f.** to be off form/on top form

(**f**) **formas** *(silueta)* figure, curves; **un cuerpo de formas armoniosas** a curvaceous body

(**g**) **formas** *(modales)* manners, social conventions; **guardar las formas** to keep up appearances

(**h**) *(horma, molde)* mould

(**i**) *Rel* host; **la Sagrada F.** the Holy Host

(**j**) *Arte & Lit* form; **a este escritor le importa más la f. que el contenido** this writer is more interested in form than content

(**k**) *Ling* form; **en f. plural** in the plural

(**l**) *Méx (formulario)* form

---

formación *nf* (**a**) *(creación)* formation; **la f. de un gobierno** the formation of a government; *Ling* **la f. de palabras** word formation

(**b**) *(educación)* training; **la f. de los jóvenes es prioritaria para combatir el desempleo** it is extremely important to train young people in order to combat unemployment; **recibió una f. clásica** he received a traditional education; **sin f. académica** with little formal education ►► ***f. en alternancia*** sandwich courses; ***f. continua*** in-service training; ***f. de formadores*** training of trainers; ***f. ocupacional*** vocational *o* occupational training; ***f. pedagógica*** teacher training; ***f. profesional*** *(ocupacional)* = vocational *o* occupational training; *(ciclo educativo)* = vocationally orientated secondary education in Spain for pupils aged 14-18, currently being phased out

(**c**) *(equipo)* team; *(alineación)* line-up; **f. política** political party

(**d**) *Mil* formation; **marchar en f.** to march in formation

(e) *Geol* formation; **una f. rocosa** a rock formation; **esta zona presenta formaciones calcáreas** there are limestone formations in this area

formado, -a *adj* (a) *(hecho, modelado)* formed, shaped (b) *(desarrollado)* grown, developed

formador, -ora 1 *adj* forming, constituting
2 *nm,f* trainer

formal *adj* (a) *(de la forma)* formal; **en su aspecto f. la novela es excelente** the formal aspects of the novel are excellent
(b) *(legal)* formal; **un requisito f.** an official requirement
(c) *(que se porta bien)* well-behaved, good
(d) *(responsable, fiable)* reliable; **son muy poco formales** they're very unreliable
(e) *(serio)* serious, sober; **el lenguaje f.** formal language; **ser novios formales** to be engaged

formaldehído *nm Quím* formaldehyde

formalidad *nf* (a) *(requisito)* formality; **es una mera f.** it's just a formality (b) *(fiabilidad)* reliability; **este mecánico no tiene ninguna f.** this mechanic is totally unreliable; **¡qué poca f.!** you just can't rely on some people! (c) *(seriedad)* seriousness

formalina *nf Quím* formalin, formol

formalismo *nm* formalism

formalista 1 *adj* formal
2 *nmf* formalist

formalización *nf* formalization; **ayer tuvo lugar la f. del contrato** the contract was officially signed yesterday

formalizar [14] *vt* to formalize; **formalizaron su relación** they made their relationship official

formalmente *adv* formally

formar 1 *vt* (a) *(hacer)* to form; **f. una bola con algo** to make sth into a ball; **f. un equipo** to make up a team; **f. gobierno** to form a government; **formó una asociación cultural** he set up a cultural organization; **los manifestantes formaron una cadena** the demonstrators formed a human chain; **f. parte de** to form *o* be part of; **forma parte del equipo del colegio** she's a member of the school team
(b) *(educar)* to train, to educate
(c) *Mil* to form up
2 *vi Mil* to fall in; **¡a f.!** fall in!
3 **formarse** *vpr* (a) *(hacerse, crearse)* to form; **se formó un corro de gente en torno al accidentado** a circle of people formed around the injured person; **se formó espuma en la superficie** froth formed on the surface; **con esto ya me formo una idea de lo que pasó** that gives me a pretty good idea of what happened
(b) *(educarse)* to be trained *o* educated; **se formó en la Universidad de Harvard** she was educated at Harvard

formateado, -a *Informát* 1 *adj* formatted
2 *nm (proceso)* formatting

formatear *vt Informát* to format

formateo *nm Informát* formatting

formativo, -a *adj* formative

formato *nm* (a) *(de libro, fotografía, película)* format (b) *Informát* format ►► ***f. de archivo*** file format

formero *nm Arquit* supporting arch

formica®, fórmica® *nf* Formica®

fórmico, -a *adj Quím* formic

formidable 1 *adj* (a) *(enorme)* tremendous (b) *(extraordinario)* amazing, fantastic
2 *adv Fam* **lo pasaron f.** they had an amazing *o* a fantastic time

formol *nm* formalin

formón *nm* firmer chisel

Formosa *n* Formosa

fórmula *nf* (a) *(matemática)* formula
(b) *(química)* formula ►► *Farm* ***f. magistral*** = medicine made up by pharmacist to doctor's prescription; *Quím* ***f. molecular*** molecular formula; ***f. química*** chemical formula
(c) *(oral, escrita)* expression, formula; **una f. de despedida** an expression used to say goodbye ►► ***f. de cortesía*** polite expression
(d) *(en automovilismo)* formula ►► ***F. uno*** formula one
(e) *(solución)* formula; **tengo la f. para convencerlo** I know the way to persuade him; **llegaron a una f. de compromiso** they reached a compromise solution; **no existe una f. mágica** there's no magic formula
(f) *Col (receta)* prescription
(g) *RP Pol (electoral)* ticket; **la f. Batlle-Hierro** the Batlle-Hierro ticket

formulación *nf* formulation

formular 1 *vt* (a) *(solicitud)* to make; *(reclamación)* to make, to lodge; **f. una pregunta** to ask a question; **f. un deseo** to express a wish; **formuló cuidadosamente su respuesta** she phrased her reply carefully; **f. graves cargos contra alguien** to bring serious charges against sb; **los que formulan la política del gobierno** the government's policy makers
(b) *(con números)* to formulate
(c) *Col (receta)* to prescribe
2 *vi* to write formulae

formulario¹, -a *adj (lenguaje)* formalaic; **una visita formularia** a courtesy visit

formulario² *nm* form; **rellenar un f.** to fill in *o* out a form

formulismo *nm (apego) (a las formas)* formalism; *(a las normas)* sticking to the rules

formulista 1 *adj* formulistic
2 *nmf* formulist

fornicación *nf Formal* fornication

fornicar [60] *vi Formal* to fornicate

fornido, -a *adj* well-built

foro *nm* (a) *(lugar de discusión)* forum ►► ***f. de debate*** forum for debate; *Informát* ***f. de discusión*** discussion group (b) *Teatro* back of the stage; EXPR **desaparecer por el f.** to slip away unnoticed (c) *Hist (en Roma)* forum (d) *(tribunal)* court (of law)

forofo, -a *Esp Fam* 1 *adj* **es muy f.** he's really fanatical
2 *nm,f Fam* fan; **es un f. de la escalada** he's crazy *o Br* mad about climbing

forrado, -a *adj* (a) *(libro)* covered; *(ropa)* lined (**de** with); *(asiento)* upholstered (b) *Fam (rico)* **estar f.** to be rolling in it

forraje *nm* fodder, forage

forrajear *vt* to forage for

forrajero, -a *adj (planta)* for fodder

forrar 1 *vt* (a) *(cubrir) (libro)* to cover; *(ropa)* to line (**de** with); *(asiento)* to upholster (b) *Fam (pegar)* **lo forraron a puñetazos** they beat the hell out of him; EXPR *Esp Vulg* **f. a alguien a hostias** to beat the shit out of sb
2 **forrarse** *vpr* (a) *Fam* **forrarse (de dinero** *o Chile* **en billetes)** *(enriquecerse)* to make a packet (b) *Am Fam (de comida)* to stoke up on food

forro *nm* (a) *(cubierta) (de libro)* cover; *(de ropa)* lining; *(de asiento)* upholstery; **tela de f.** lining material; EXPR *Vulg* **pasarse algo por el f. de** *Esp* **los cojones** *o RP* **las bolas** to shit on sth from a great height; EXPR *Fam* **¡ni por el f.!: no se le parece ni por el f.** he doesn't look anything like him ►► ***f. polar*** fleece (jacket)
(b) *Cuba (trampa)* trick
(c) *RP Fam (preservativo)* rubber, *Br* johnny
(d) *Méx Fam (persona)* babe

fortachón, -ona *adj Fam* strapping

fortalecer [46] 1 *vt* to strengthen; **el acuerdo fortalecerá las relaciones entre los dos países** the agreement will strengthen relations between the two countries
2 **fortalecerse** *vpr (físicamente)* to become stronger

fortalecimiento *nm* strengthening

fortaleza *nf* (a) *(fuerza) (física)* strength; *(moral, mental)* strength, fortitude; **tiene mucha f. en los brazos** he has really strong arms (b) *(recinto)* fortress (c) *Chile (hedor)* stench, stink

fortalezco *etc ver* **fortalecer**

forte *Mús* 1 *nm* forte
2 *adv* forte

fortificación *nf* (a) *(recinto)* fortification (b) *(acción)* fortification

fortificante *adj* fortifying

fortificar [60] *vt* (a) *(dar fuerza)* to fortify, to strengthen (b) *(lugar)* to fortify

fortín *nm* small fort

fortísimo, -a *superlativo ver* **fuerte**

FORTRAN, Fortran *nm Informát* FORTRAN, Fortran

fortuitamente *adv* fortuitously, by chance

fortuito, -a *adj* chance; **encuentro f.** chance encounter

fortuna *nf* (a) *(suerte)* (good) luck; **por f.** fortunately, luckily; **probar f.** to try one's luck; **quiere probar f. en América** he's going to America to seek his fortune; **he tenido la f. de encontrar un buen trabajo** I've had the good fortune *o* I've been lucky enough to find a good job; **tuvo la mala f. de caerse** he had the misfortune *o* bad luck to fall; **tuvo muy poca f. en la vida** he was very unlucky in life
(b) *(destino)* fortune, fate; **quiso la f. que...** as fate would have it...

(**c**) *(riqueza)* fortune; **amasar una f.** to amass a fortune; **hacer f.** to make one's fortune; **se gasta una f. en ropa** he spends a fortune on clothes

(**d**) *(éxito, aceptación)* **este libro tendrá f. entre los jóvenes** this book will be very popular with young people; **sus ideas no tuvieron mucha f.** his ideas did not become widely accepted

fórum (*pl* **fórums** *o* **fórum**) *nm* (**a**) *(lugar de discusión)* forum (**b**) *Informát* forum

forúnculo *nm* boil

forzadamente *adv* by force, forcibly

forzado, -a *adj (sonrisa, amabilidad)* forced; **trabajos forzados** hard labour; **verse f. a hacer algo** to find oneself forced to do sth

forzar [31] *vt* (**a**) *(obligar, empujar)* to force; **f. a alguien a hacer algo** to force sb to do sth; **yo no forzaría la situación** I wouldn't force the situation (**b**) *(cerradura, mecanismo)* to force; **no fuerces el motor** don't overtax the engine; **f. la vista** to strain one's eyes; *Informát* **f. la salida** *(de programa)* to force quit (**c**) *(violar)* to rape

forzosamente *adv (necesariamente)* **el ladrón tuvo que entrar f. por esta ventana** the thief MUST have come in through this window; **esto no quiere decir, f., que haya que abandonar todas las esperanzas** this doesn't necessarily mean that we have to give up all hope

forzoso, -a *adj* (**a**) *(obligatorio)* obligatory, compulsory (**b**) *(inevitable)* inevitable (**c**) *(necesario)* necessary (**d**) *(de emergencia)* **aterrizaje f.** emergency landing

forzudo, -a 1 *adj* strong

2 *nm,f* strong man, *f* strong woman

fosa *nf* (**a**) *(sepultura)* grave ►► ***f. común*** common grave (**b**) *Anat* cavity; **fosas nasales** nostrils (**c**) *(hoyo)* pit ►► ***f. abisal*** oceanic trench; ***f. marina*** oceanic trench; ***f. séptica*** septic tank; *Geol* ***f. tectónica*** fault trough, *Espec* graben (**d**) *RP (en taller)* pit

fosfatar *vt (fertilizar)* to fertilize with phosphates

fosfatina *nf Fam* EXPR **estar hecho f.** to be wrecked *o Br* knackered; **hacer f.** to destroy, to smash up

fosfato *nm* phosphate ►► ***f. de cal*** calcium phosphate; ***f. cálcico*** calcium phosphate

fosforecer = **fosforescer**

fosforera *nf (fábrica)* match factory

fosforero, -a 1 *adj* **la industria fosforera** the match-making industry

2 *nm,f* match seller

fosforescencia *nf* phosphorescence

fosforescente *adj* (**a**) *Fís* phosphorescent (**b**) *(color, chaleco)* fluorescent

fosforescer, fosforecer [46] *vi* to phosphoresce

fosfórico, -a *adj Quím* phosphoric

fosforito, -a 1 *adj Fam* (**a**) *Esp (color, rotulador)* fluorescent (**b**) *Ven (impaciente)* **ser f.** to have a short fuse

2 *nm Ven (petardo)* firecracker, *Br* banger

fósforo *nm* (**a**) *Quím* phosphorus (**b**) *Andes, Carib, RP (cerilla)* match

fosforoso, -a *adj Quím* phosphorous

fosgeno *nm* phosgene

fósil 1 *adj* fossil; **combustible f.** fossil fuel

2 *nm* (**a**) *(resto)* fossil (**b**) *Fam (viejo)* old fossil

fosilización *nf* fossilization

fosilizado, -a *adj* fossilized

fosilizarse [14] *vpr* (**a**) *(animal, hueso)* to fossilize (**b**) *Fam (persona)* to turn into an old fossil

foso *nm* (**a**) *(hoyo)* ditch (**b**) *(de castillo)* moat (**c**) *(de garaje)* pit (**d**) *(de teatro)* pit (**e**) *Dep (en salto de longitud)* pit; *(en campo de fútbol)* moat ►► ***f. olímpico*** *(en tiro)* Olympic trench clay-pigeon shooting

foto *nf* photo, picture; **le saqué** *o* **tomé** *o* **tiré una f.** I took a photo *o* picture of him ►► ***f. de familia*** family photo; **los presidentes se hicieron una f. de familia** the presidents had a group photo taken; ***f. fija*** still

fotocélula *nf* photocell, photoelectric cell

fotocomponedora *nf Imprenta* typesetter, typesetting machine

fotocomponer *vt Imprenta* to typeset

fotocomposición *nf Imprenta* typesetting, photocomposition

fotocopia *nf* (**a**) *(objeto)* photocopy; **hacer una f. de** to make *o* take a photocopy of (**b**) *(procedimiento)* photocopying

fotocopiadora *nf* (**a**) *(máquina)* photocopier (**b**) *(tienda)* copy shop

fotocopiar *vt* to photocopy

fotodegradable *adj* photodegradable

fotoelectricidad *nf* photoelectricity

fotoeléctrico, -a *adj* photoelectric

foto-finish [foto'finis], **fotofinis** *nf inv Dep* photo finish

fotofobia *nf* photophobia

fotogenia *nf* photogenic qualities

fotogénico, -a *adj* photogenic

fotograbado *nm* photogravure

fotograbar *vt* to photoengrave

fotografía *nf* (**a**) *(arte)* photography ►► ***f. aérea*** aerial photography; ***f. digital*** digital photography; ***f. infrarroja*** infrared photography; ***f. publicitaria*** commercial photography

(**b**) *(objeto)* photograph; **hacer** *o* **sacar una f. a alguien** to take a picture *o* photograph of sb ►► ***f. aérea*** aerial photograph; ***f. de (tamaño) carné*** passport-sized photograph; ***f. instantánea*** snapshot

fotografiar [32] *vt* to photograph, to take a photograph of

fotográfico, -a *adj* photographic

fotógrafo, -a *nm,f* photographer ►► ***f. de prensa*** press photographer

fotograma *nm* still

fotolisis, fotólisis *nf inv Quím* photolysis

fotolito *nm Imprenta* piece of film; **ya han llegado los fotolitos** the film has arrived

fotolitografía *nf* (**a**) *(arte)* photolithography (**b**) *(objeto)* photolithograph

fotomatón *nm* passport photo machine

fotomecánica *nf* (**a**) *(técnica)* printing (**b**) *(lugar)* printer's

fotometría *nf* photometry

fotómetro *nm* (**a**) *(en fotografía)* light *o* exposure meter (**b**) *Fís* photometer

fotomodelo *nmf* photographic model

fotomontaje *nm* photomontage

fotón *nm Fís* photon

fotonoticia *nf* picture story *(in newspaper)*

fotonovela *nf* photo romance

fotoperiodismo *nm* photojournalism

fotoprotector, -ora 1 *adj* **factor f.** sun protection factor

2 *nm* sun cream, sunblock

fotoquímica *nf* photochemistry

fotoquímico, -a *adj* photochemical

fotorrealismo *nm Informát* photorealism

fotorrealista *adj Informát* photorealistic

fotosensible *adj* photosensitive

fotosfera *nf* photosphere

fotosíntesis *nf inv* photosynthesis

fotosintético, -a *adj* photosynthetic

fototeca *nf* photograph library

fototipia *nf* (**a**) *(arte)* collotype (**b**) *(objeto)* collotype

fototropismo *nm* phototropism

fotovoltaico, -a *adj* photovoltaic

fotuto *nm* (**a**) *Cuba (bocina)* horn (**b**) *Ven (trompeta)* = indigenous wind instrument made from gourd or conch shell

foul [faul, ful] (*pl* **fouls**) *nm Am* foul

foulard [fu'lar] (*pl* **foulards**) *nm* headscarf *(of fine material)*

foulear [faule'ar] *vt Am Fam* to foul

foulero, -a [fau'lero, -a] *Am Fam* **1** *adj* **es muy f.** he's a really dirty player

2 *nm,f* dirty player

fovismo *nm* fauvism

foxterrier [fokste'rrjer, foks'terrjer] (*pl* **foxterriers**) *nm* fox terrier

foxtrot *nm* foxtrot

foyeque *nm Perú Fam* heap, banger

foyer [fua'je] (*pl* **foyers**) *nm RP* foyer

FP *nf* (*abrev de* **formación profesional**) = vocationally oriented education in Spain for pupils aged 14 and upwards

FPLP *nf* (*abrev de* **Frente Popular de Liberación de Palestina**) PFLP

FPU *nf Informát* (*abrev de* **floating-point unit**) FPU

fra. (*abrev de* **factura**) inv

frac (*pl* **fracs**) *nm* tails, dress coat

fracasado, -a 1 *adj* failed

2 *nm,f* failure

fracasar *vi* (**a**) *(intento)* to fail; *(producto)* to be a failure; **el modelo fracasó en Europa** the model was a failure in Europe (**b**) *(persona)* to fail; **fracasó en su intento de obtener un acuerdo** he failed in his attempt to get an agreement; **fracasó como cantante** she was a failure as a singer

fracaso *nm* (**a**) *(falta de éxito)* failure; **ha sufrido varios fracasos amorosos** he has had a number of failed relationships; **todo fue un f.** it was a complete failure; **la película fue un f. comercial** the movie *o Br* film was a commercial failure *o* flop ►► ***f. escolar*** school failure; **el entorno familiar contribuye al f. escolar** the family environment is a contributory factor to educational failure
(**b**) *(persona)* failure; **como profesor es un f.** as a teacher he's a failure, he's useless as a teacher

> **Falso amigo**: El sustantivo inglés **fracas** no es la traducción del español **fracaso**. En inglés, **fracas** significa "gresca, refriega".

fracción *nf* (**a**) *(parte)* fraction; **todos recibieron su f. de la herencia** everyone received their part *o* share of the legacy; **f. de segundo** split second (**b**) *(quebrado)* fraction ►► ***f. decimal*** decimal fraction; ***f. impropia*** improper fraction; ***f. mixta*** compound fraction; ***f. propia*** proper fraction (**c**) *Pol* faction

fraccionador, -ora *nm,f Méx Br* estate agent, *US* real estate agent

fraccionadora *nf Méx Br* estate agents, *US* real estate agents

fraccionamiento *nm* (**a**) *(división)* division, breaking up (**b**) *Méx (urbanización)* housing estate

fraccionar *vt* (**a**) *(dividir)* to divide, to break up (**b**) *(pago)* to split up into instalments (**c**) *Am (parcelar)* to split up into plots, to divide out into plots

fraccionario, -a *adj* fractional; **moneda fraccionaria** small change

fractal *nm* fractal

fractura *nf* (**a**) *(de hueso)* fracture; **presenta f. craneal** he has a fractured skull ►► ***f. abierta*** compound *o* open fracture; ***f. expuesta*** compound *o* open fracture; ***f. impactada*** impacted fracture; ***f. ósea*** (bone) fracture; *Fig* ***f. social*** breakdown of the fabric of society (**b**) *Geol* fault

fracturar 1 *vt* to fracture
2 **fracturarse** *vpr* to fracture; **fracturarse un brazo/una pierna** to fracture one's arm/leg

fragancia *nf* fragrance

fragante *adj* fragrant

fraganti *ver* **in fraganti**

fragata *nf* (**a**) *(nave)* frigate ►► ***f. ligera*** corvette (**b**) *(ave)* frigate bird

frágil *adj* (**a**) *(objeto)* fragile; **f.** *(en letrero)* fragile (**b**) *(persona)* frail; *(salud, situación)* delicate

fragilidad *nf* (**a**) *(de objeto)* fragility (**b**) *(de persona)* frailty; *(de situación)* delicacy; **la f. de su salud** his delicate health

fragmentación *nf* (**a**) *(rotura)* fragmentation (**b**) *(división)* division; *Informát (de disco duro)* fragmentation

fragmentado, -a *adj* (**a**) *(roto)* fragmented (**b**) *(dividido)* divided; *Informát (disco duro)* fragmented

fragmentar 1 *vt* (**a**) *(romper)* to break up (**b**) *(dividir)* to divide (**c**) *Informát (disco duro)* to fragment
2 **fragmentarse** *vpr* (**a**) *(romperse)* to break up (**b**) *(dividirse)* to break up (**c**) *Informát (disco duro)* to become fragmented

fragmentario, -a *adj (incompleto)* fragmentary

fragmento *nm* (**a**) *(pedazo)* fragment, piece (**b**) *(de película)* excerpt, clip; *(de novela)* excerpt, passage; *(de ópera, sinfonía)* passage

fragor *nm (de batalla)* clamour; *(de trueno)* crash; *(de tormenta)* roar, raging

fragoroso, -a *adj* roaring, thunderous

fragosidad *nf* (**a**) *(de terreno)* ruggedness (**b**) *(de monte)* ruggedness; *(de bosque)* denseness

fragoso, -a *adj* (**a**) *(terreno)* rough, rugged (**b**) *(monte)* rugged; *(bosque)* dense (**c**) *(ruidoso)* roaring, thunderous

fragua *nf* (**a**) *(fogón)* forge, furnace (**b**) *(taller)* forge

fraguado *nm* (**a**) *(en fragua)* forging (**b**) *Constr* setting, hardening

fraguar [11] 1 *vt* (**a**) *(forjar)* to forge (**b**) *(idear)* to think up
2 *vi* (**a**) *(cemento)* to set, to harden (**b**) *(idea, plan)* to be successful; **su proyecto no llegó a f.** their project never came to anything
3 **fraguarse** *vpr (tramarse)* to be in the offing; *(crearse, originarse)* to be hatched; **durante aquellos años se fraguó la revolución** it was during those years that the groundwork was laid for the revolution

fraile *nm* (**a**) *(sacerdote)* friar (**b**) *(pez)* (freshwater) blenny

frailecillo *nm* puffin

frailejón *nm* frailejon

frambesia *nf* yaws *(singular)*

frambuesa *nf* raspberry

frambueso *nm* raspberry cane

francachela *nf Fam* (**a**) *(juerga)* **se gastaron el premio en una f.** they blew the prize on a party; **estuvieron toda la noche de f.** they were out partying all night (**b**) *(comilona)* spread

francamente *adv* (**a**) *(con sinceridad)* frankly; **f., no sé por qué te enfadas** frankly *o* to be honest, I don't know why you're angry (**b**) *(verdaderamente)* really; **es f. divertido** it's really funny

francés, -esa 1 *adj* French
2 *nm,f (persona)* Frenchman, *f* Frenchwoman; **los franceses** the French; EXPR **marcharse** *o* **despedirse a la francesa** to leave without even saying goodbye
3 *nm* (**a**) *(lengua)* French (**b**) *muy Fam (felación)* blowjob

francesada *nf Fam Pey (costumbre)* Frenchified habit; **¡es una f.!** *(película, libro)* it's typical French *Br* rubbish *o US* trash!

francesilla *nf* turban *o* Persian buttercup

Fráncfort *n* **F. (del Meno)** Frankfurt (am Main)

franchute, -a *Fam* 1 *adj* Froggy, = frequently pejorative term meaning "French"
2 *nm,f (persona)* Frog, = frequently pejorative term referring to a French person
3 *nm (lengua)* Frog

Francia *n* France

francio *nm Quím* francium

franciscano, -a 1 *adj* Franciscan
2 *nm,f* Franciscan

Francisco *n pr* **San F. de Asís** St Francis of Assisi

francmasón *nm* Freemason

francmasonería *nf* Freemasonry

francmasónico, -a *adj* masonic

franco, -a 1 *adj* (**a**) *(sincero)* frank, open; *(directo)* frank; **si quieres que te sea f....** to tell you the truth..., to be honest with you...; **sé f. y admite que te equivocaste** be honest and admit you were wrong
(**b**) *(sin obstáculos)* free; **golpe f.** *(en fútbol)* free kick; *Esp* **piso f.** safe house; **el camino estaba f. de obstáculos** the road was clear
(**c**) *(sin impuestos)* free; **puerto f.** free port; **f. de porte** *(carta)* postpaid; *(pedido)* carriage-paid; **f. a bordo** free on board
(**d**) *(manifiesto)* clear, marked; **el paciente ha experimentado una franca mejoría** the patient is markedly better *o* has clearly improved; **la economía ha sufrido un f. deterioro** there has been a clear *o* marked downturn in the economy
(**e**) *Hist* Frankish
(**f**) **estar f. de servicio** *(de permiso)* to be off duty; *CSur, Méx* **me dieron el día f.** they gave me the day off
2 *nm,f Hist (persona)* Frank
3 *nm* (**a**) *(moneda)* franc ►► *Antes* ***f. belga*** Belgian franc; *Antes* ***f. francés*** French franc; ***f. suizo*** Swiss franc (**b**) *(lengua)* Frankish (**c**) *CSur, Méx (permiso)* **esta semana tengo f.** I'm off work this week; **ayer tuvimos f.** we had the day off yesterday

franco- *pref* Franco-; **f.-español** Franco-Spanish

francocanadiense 1 *adj* French Canadian
2 *nmf* French Canadian

francófilo, -a 1 *adj* francophile, pro-French
2 *nm,f* francophile

francófobo, -a 1 *adj* francophobe, anti-French
2 *nm,f* francophobe

francófono, -a 1 *adj* francophone
2 *nm,f* Francophone

francotirador, -ora *nm,f* (**a**) *Mil* sniper (**b**) *(rebelde)* maverick

franela *nf* (**a**) *(tejido)* flannel (**b**) *Bol, Col, Ven (camiseta) (interior) Br* vest, *US* undershirt; *(exterior)* T-shirt (**c**) *Bol, Col, Ven (sudadera)* sweatshirt (**d**) *RP (trapo)* dust cloth, *Br* duster

franfrúter = **frankfúrter**

frangollo *nm Carib (dulce)* = dessert made from mashed bananas

franja *nf (banda, tira)* strip; *(en bandera, uniforme)* stripe ►► ***la F. de Gaza*** the Gaza Strip; ***f. horaria*** *(en televisión)* time slot; *(huso horario)* time zone

frankfúrter, franfrúter *nm Urug* hotdog

franqueadora *nf* franking machine

franquear 1 *vt* (a) *(dejar libre)* to clear; **el guardia nos franqueó el paso** the guard let us pass
(b) *(atravesar) (río)* to negotiate, to cross; *(puerta)* to go through; *(frontera)* to cross; *también Fig* **f. el umbral** to cross the threshold
(c) *(correo)* to attach postage to; *(con máquina)* to frank; **enviar un sobre franqueado** send a stamped (addressed) envelope; **a f. en destino** *(en sobre)* postage paid, post-paid, *Br* ≃ Freepost
2 **franquearse** *vpr* **franquearse (con alguien)** to open one's heart to sb

franqueo *nm* postage; **f. pagado** postage paid, post-paid, *Br* ≃ Freepost

franqueza *nf (sinceridad)* frankness, openness; **con toda f.** to be perfectly frank *o* honest

franquicia *nf* (a) *(tienda)* franchise (b) *(exención)* exemption ►► ***f. aduanera*** duty-free allowance; ***f. postal*** exemption from postage, free postage (c) *(en seguro)* excess (d) *Urug* **franquicias** *(en club)* free membership; **este verano: franquicias** this summer: free membership

franquiciado *nm Com* franchisee, franchise-holder

franquiciador, -ora *nm,f Com* franchiser

franquiciar *vt Com* to franchise

franquismo *nm* **el f.** *(régimen)* the Franco regime; *(doctrina)* Francoism; **durante el f.** under Franco, when Franco was in power

franquista 1 *adj* pro-Franco, Francoist; **el régimen f.** the Franco regime
2 *nmf* supporter of Franco, Francoist

frasca *nf* carafe

frasco *nm* bottle; EXPR *Esp Fam Hum* **¡toma del f. (Carrasco)!** (it) serves you right!

frase *nf* (a) *(oración)* sentence (b) *(locución)* expression ►► ***f. hecha*** *(modismo)* set phrase; *(tópico)* cliché; ***f. lapidaria*** memorable phrase; ***f. proverbial*** proverbial expression (c) *Mús* **f. (musical** *o* **melódica)** (musical) phrase

frasear *vt* to phrase

fraseo *nm Mús* phrasing

fraseología *nf* (a) *(estilo)* phraseology (b) *(palabrería)* verbiage

fraternal *adj* brotherly, fraternal

fraternidad *nf* brotherhood, fraternity

fraternizar [14] *vi* to fraternize (**con** with)

fraterno, -a *adj* brotherly, fraternal

fratricida 1 *adj* fratricidal
2 *nmf* fratricide

fratricidio *nm* fratricide

fraude *nm* fraud ►► ***f. electoral*** election *o* electoral fraud; ***f. fiscal*** tax evasion; ***f. informático*** computer fraud

fraudulencia *nf* fraudulence

fraudulentamente *adv* fraudulently, by fraudulent means

fraudulento, -a *adj* fraudulent; **consiguió la victoria de forma fraudulenta** he won by fraudulent means *o* by cheating

fray *nm* brother; **F. Esteban** Brother Esteban

frazada *nf Am* blanket ►► ***f. eléctrica*** electric blanket

freático, -a *adj Geol* **capa freática** aquifer; **manto f.** aquifer; **nivel f.** water table, groundwater level

frecuencia *nf* (a) *(asiduidad)* frequency; **el tren pasa con una f. de dos horas** there's a train every two hours; **con f.** often; **¿con qué f.?** how often? (b) *Fís* frequency; **alta f.** high frequency; **baja f.** low frequency ►► ***f. muy alta*** very high frequency; ***f. modulada*** frequency modulation; ***f. natural*** natural frequency

frecuentación *nf* frequenting

frecuentado, -a *adj* **una plaza muy frecuentada** a very busy square; **un lugar muy f. por estudiantes** a place which is very popular with students; **un sitio f. por carteristas** a place frequented by pickpockets

frecuentar *vt* (a) *(lugar)* to frequent; **frecuenta unos ambientes poco recomendables** he has some rather dubious haunts (b) *(persona)* to see, to visit; **fuera del trabajo, no frecuenta a sus compañeros** she doesn't socialize with *o* see her colleagues outside work

frecuentativo, -a *adj* frequentative

frecuente *adj (reiterado)* frequent; *(habitual)* common

frecuentemente *adv* frequently

Fredemo [fre'ðemo] *nm* (*abrev de* **Frente Democrático**) = coalition of right wing Peruvian parties

freelance, free lance ['frilans] 1 *adj inv* freelance
2 *nmf inv* freelance; **colabora como f. en varias revistas** he freelances for several magazines

free shop ['friʃop] (*pl* **free shops**) *nm RP* duty-free shop

Freetown ['fritaun] *n* Freetown

freeware ['friwer] *nm Informát* freeware

freezer ['friser] (*pl* **freezers**) *nm Am* freezer

fregada *nf* (a) *(limpiada)* scrub, scrubbing
(b) EXPR *Méx Fam* **mandar a alguien a la f.** to tell sb to get lost; **está que se lo lleva la f.** he's at his wits' end; **irse algo a la f.** to go to pot; **...y la fregada: me dijo que yo era egoísta, egocéntrica, mezquina y la f.** he called me selfish, egocentric, mean and everything else you can think of; **cuando se van de vacaciones cargan con todo, la tostadora, el televisor, la cafetera, la licuadora y la f.** whenever they go on holidays they take everything but the kitchen sink: the toaster, the telly, the coffee machine, the blender

fregadera *nf Andes, CAm, Carib, Méx Fam* pain, drag; **ir al supermercado es una f.** going to the supermarket is such a pain *o* drag; **tener que estudiar, ¡qué f.!** what a pain *o* drag it is, having to study!

fregadero *nm* (kitchen) sink

fregado, -a 1 *adj Andes, Méx, Ven Fam* (a) *(persona) (ser)* annoying; **mi vecino es muy f.** my neighbour's a real pain (b) *(persona) (estar)* **perdí las llaves, ¡estoy fregada!** I've lost my keys, I've had it! (c) *(situación)* tricky; **este problema es muy f.** this problem is really tricky *o* a real stinker (d) *(objeto)* bust; **ese reloj está f.** that watch has had it
2 *nm* (a) *(lavado) (de platos, suelo)* wash; *(frotando)* scrub (b) *Fam (lío)* mess; **meterse en un f.** to get into a mess (c) *Fam (discusión)* row, rumpus
3 *nm,f Andes, Méx, Ven Fam (persona)* pain, awkward customer; **tu hermano es un f.** your brother's an awkward little beggar

fregador, -ora *nm,f Cuba* dishwasher

fregar [43] 1 *vt* (a) *(limpiar)* to wash; *(frotar)* to scrub; **f. los platos** to wash the dishes, *Br* to do the washing-up; **f. el suelo** to mop the floor
(b) *Andes, Méx, Ven Fam (molestar)* to bother, to pester; **no friegues al perro** don't annoy the dog; **me está fregando la paciencia** he's driving me up the wall
(c) *Andes, Méx, Ven Fam (estropear)* **vas a f. el televisor** you're going to bust the television; **la lluvia nos fregó el fin de semana** the rain messed up our weekend
(d) *Andes, Méx, Ven Fam (fastidiar)* **me fregó con su decisión de quedarse en mi casa** it was a pain, him deciding to stay in my house
2 *vi* (a) *(limpiar)* to clean; *(frotar)* to scrub; *(limpiar los platos)* to wash the dishes, *Br* to do the washing-up (b) *Andes, Méx, Ven Fam (molestar)* to be a pain; **¡deja de f.!** stop being such a pain!; **lo hace por f.** he just does it to be a pain (c) *Andes, Méx, Ven Fam* **¡no friegues!** *(expresando sorpresa)* you're kidding!, you can't be serious!
3 **fregarse** *vpr* (a) *Andes, Méx, Ven Fam (estropearse)* **se nos han fregado las vacaciones** that's gone and messed our holidays up (b) *Andes, Méx, Ven Fam (fastidiarse)* **si no está de acuerdo, que se friegue** if she doesn't like it, she can lump it

fregón[1] *nm RP* scourer

fregón[2]**, -ona** *Fam* 1 *adj* (a) *Col, Ecuad, Méx (molesto)* annoying; **¡es más fregona!** she's such a pain! (b) *Méx (sobresaliente)* wicked; **es bien f. para la física** he's really hot *o Br* ace at physics; **tiene una moto fregona** she's got this wicked *o Br* ace motorbike
2 *nm,f Col, Ecuad, Méx* pain

fregona *nf* (a) *Esp (utensilio)* mop; **pasar la f.** to mop (b) *Fam Pey (criada)* skivvy

fregotear *vt Fam* to give a good wash to; **f. el suelo** to give the floor a good mop

freidora *nf* deep fat fryer

freiduría *nf* = shop where fried food, especially fish, is cooked and served

freír [56] 1 *vt* (a) *(alimento)* to fry; *(con mucho aceite)* to deep fry (b) *Fam (molestar)* **f. a alguien a preguntas** to pester sb with questions; **me están friendo con tantas peticiones** they've got me at my wits' end with all these requests (c) *Fam (matar)* **f. a alguien (a tiros)** to gun sb down
2 **freírse** *vpr* to fry; *Fam* **me estoy friendo (de calor)** I'm boiling *o* roasting

frejol, fréjol *nm Andes, CAm, Méx* bean

frenada *nf Am (frenazo)* **dar una f.** to brake hard; **el cinturón protege en caso de f.** the seat belt protects you if the driver brakes suddenly

frenado *nm* braking

frenar 1 *vt* (a) *(en vehículo)* to brake (b) *(contener)* to check; *(disminuir)* to curb, to slow down; **medidas para f. el desempleo** measures to curb unemployment; **nadie pudo f. a la estrella brasileña** no one could stop the Brazilian star; **los altos tipos de interés frenan a los**

inversores the high interest rates are holding investors back
2 *vi (en vehículo)* to brake
3 **frenarse** *vpr* (**a**) *(detenerse)* to slow down (**b**) *(contenerse)* to restrain oneself

frenazo *nm* (**a**) *(en vehículo)* **dar un f.** to brake hard; **el cinturón protege en caso de f.** the seat belt protects you if the driver brakes suddenly (**b**) *(parón)* sudden stop; **el f. del crecimiento económico** the sharp slowdown in economic growth

frenesí (*pl* **frenesíes**) *nm* frenzy; **trabajaba con f.** she was working frenetically; **se besaban con f.** they were kissing passionately

frenéticamente *adv* frenziedly, frantically

frenético, -a *adj* (**a**) *(colérico)* furious, mad; **su hermana lo pone f.** his sister drives him mad (**b**) *(enloquecido)* frenzied, frantic

frenillo *nm* (**a**) *(membrana)* frenum, frenulum (**b**) *(defecto del habla)* = speech impediment caused by defect in frenum (**c**) *CAm, Carib (de cometa)* kite strings

freno 1 *nm* (**a**) *(en automóvil)* brake; **pisar el f.** to step on the brakes; EXPR *Fam* **¡echa el f.!** *(detente, cállate)* put a sock in it!, that's enough of that!; *(no te pases)* hold your horses! ►► ***frenos ABS*** ABS brakes; ***f. automático*** automatic brake; ***frenos de disco*** disc brakes; ***f. hidráulico*** hydraulic brake; ***f. de mano*** *Br* handbrake, *US* emergency brake; ***f. neumático*** air brake; ***f. de pie*** foot brake; ***f. de tambor*** drum brake; ***f. de vacío*** vacuum brake
(**b**) *(de caballerías)* bit; **morder** *o* **tascar el f.** to champ at the bit
(**c**) *(contención)* check; **la inflación es un f. al crecimiento** inflation holds back growth; **una lucha sin f.** an all-out struggle; **su deseo de poder no tiene f.** his lust for power is insatiable; **poner f. a** to put a stop to
2 *nmf* **frenos** *Méx (en ortodoncia)* braces, *Br* brace

frenología *nf* phrenology

frenólogo, -a *nm,f* phrenologist

frenopatía *nf* psychiatry

frenopático, -a 1 *adj* psychiatric
2 *nm Fam (manicomio)* loony bin

frentazo *nm* (**a**) *Méx (decepción)* blow, disappointment (**b**) *RP (golpe) (con la frente)* head butt; *(en la frente)* bump on the head; **se dio un f. con** *o* **contra la lámpara** he bumped his head on the lamp (**c**) *Dep* header

FRENTE 1 *nf* forehead; **arrugar la f.** to knit one's brow, to frown; **f. a f.** face to face; EXPR **ir con la f. muy alta** to hold one's head high
2 *nm* (**a**) *(parte delantera)* front; **el f. de la casa está pintado de amarillo** the front of the house is painted yellow; **que den un paso al f. los voluntarios** could the volunteers please step forward?; **su hermano está al f. de la compañía** her brother is in charge of the company; **marchaba al f. de los manifestantes** she was marching at the front of *o* leading the demonstration; **el Académico sigue al f. de la liga** Académico are still top of the league; *Am* **pasar al f.** *(en clase)* to come to the front of the class *(to recite a lesson)*; **de f.** *(hacia delante)* forwards; *(uno contra otro)* head on; **chocaron de f.** they collided head on, they were involved in a head-on collision; **me encontré de f. con él** I found myself face to face with him; **abordar un problema de f.** to tackle a problem head on; *Am* **de f. a** facing; **se puso de f. a la casa** he stood facing the house; **hay una panadería en f.** there's a baker's opposite; **en f. de mi casa** opposite my house; **f. a** *(enfrente de)* opposite; **se encuentra f. a él** she's opposite him
(**b**) *Mil* front; **murió en el f.** he died on the front; **hacer** *o* **formar f. común** to make common cause ►► ***f. de batalla*** battlefront
(**c**) *Meteo* front ►► ***f. cálido*** warm front; ***f. frío*** cold front
(**d**) *(grupo, organización)* front ►► ***F. Amplio*** = coalition of left-wing Uruguayan political parties; ***f. popular*** popular front; ***F. Sandinista (de Liberación Nacional)*** Sandinista (National Liberation) Front
(**e**) **hacer f. a algo** *(enfrentar algo)* to face up to sth, to tackle sth; **hicieron f. a la situación** they faced up to the situation; **hacer f. a un problema** to tackle a problem
3 *prep* **f. a la injusticia es necesario actuar** we must act to combat injustice; **estamos f. a una revolución científica** we are facing a scientific revolution; **f. al cielo nublado de ayer, hoy tendremos sol** unlike yesterday, when it was cloudy, today it will be sunny; **f. a las duras críticas de la oposición...** in the face of harsh criticism from the opposition...; **f. a los habitantes de la costa, los del interior...** compared to people who live on the coast, those who live inland...

frenteamplismo *nm Pol* = ideology of the Uruguayan "Frente Amplio" coalition

frentista, frenteamplista *Pol* 1 *adj* = of/relating to the Uruguayan "Frente Amplio" coalition
2 *nmf* = member of the "Frente Amplio" coalition

Frepaso [fre'paso] *nm Pol* (*abrev de* **Frente País Solidario**) = Argentinian centre-left political party

fresa 1 *nf* (**a**) *Esp, CAm, Carib, Méx (fruto)* strawberry (**b**) *Esp, CAm, Carib, Méx (planta)* strawberry plant (**c**) *(de dentista)* drill (**d**) *(de orfebre)* milling cutter
2 *adj Méx Fam* (**a**) *(esnob)* posh (**b**) *(conservador)* square
3 *nmf Méx Fam (esnob)* posh person

fresador, -ora *nm,f (persona)* milling machine operator

fresadora *nf (máquina)* milling machine

fresar *vt* to mill

fresca *nf* (**a**) *(frescor)* **salir a tomar la f.** to go out for a breath of fresh air; **saldremos por la mañana, con la f.** we'll leave early in the morning when it's cool (**b**) *Fam (insolencia)* EXPR **soltarle una f.** *o* **cuatro frescas a alguien** to tell sb a few home truths (**c**) *Pey (mujer)* loose woman (**d**) *Méx (cubalibre)* tequila and coke

frescales *nmf inv Esp Fam* brazen *o* cheeky person

fresco, -a 1 *adj* (**a**) *(temperatura, aire)* cool; **corría un viento f.** there was a cool breeze; **tómate algo f.** have a cold drink
(**b**) *(ropa)* **un vestido f.** a cool dress
(**c**) *(alimento) (reciente)* fresh
(**d**) *(alimento) (no congelado)* fresh
(**e**) *(pintura, tinta)* wet
(**f**) *(lozano)* fresh; **ha pasado la noche en vela y está tan f.** he was up all night but he's still fresh as a daisy; EXPR *Fam* **estar f. como una rosa** to be as fresh as a daisy
(**g**) *(despreocupado)* **no ha estudiado y sigue tan f.** he hasn't studied but he's not in the least bothered; EXPR *Fam* **quedarse tan f.** not to bat an eyelid; **dijo una tontería enorme y se quedó tan f.** he made an incredibly stupid remark and just carried on as if nothing was wrong; **no sé cómo te puedes quedar tan f. después de lo que ha pasado** I don't know how you can be so laid-back after what happened
(**h**) *(espontáneo)* fresh; **este escritor tiene un estilo f.** this writer has a refreshing style
(**i**) *(reciente)* fresh; **noticias frescas** fresh news
(**j**) *(caradura)* cheeky, forward, *US* fresh; **¡qué f.!** what a nerve *o* cheek!
(**k**) *Pey (mujer)* loose
2 *nm,f (caradura)* cheeky *o* forward person; **es un f.** he's really cheeky *o* forward
3 *nm* (**a**) *(frescor)* coolness; **al f.** in a cool place; **hace f.** it's chilly; **tomar el f.** to get a breath of fresh air (**b**) *Arte* fresco; **al f.** in fresco (**c**) *Andes, CAm, Méx (refresco)* soft drink (**d**) EXPR *Fam* **me trae al f. lo que digan los demás** I don't give two hoots what people say

frescor *nm* coolness, freshness

frescura *nf* (**a**) *(de fruta, verdura)* freshness (**b**) *(espontaneidad)* freshness (**c**) *(descaro)* cheek, nerve; **¡qué f.!** what a cheek *o* nerve!

fresno *nm* ash (tree)

fresón *nm* large strawberry

fresquera *nf* food cabinet

fresquería *nf Am* refreshment stand

fresquilla *nf (fruta)* = type of peach

freudiano, -a [froi'ðjano, -a] *adj* Freudian

freza *nf* (**a**) *(desove)* spawning (**b**) *(huevos)* spawn

frezar [14] *vi (desovar)* to spawn

FRG *nm* (*abrev de* **Frente Republicano Guatemalteco**) = Guatemalan right-wing political party

fría *nf Col, Ven Fam* cold beer

friable *adj* friable

frialdad *nf* (**a**) *(baja temperatura)* coldness (**b**) *(indiferencia)* **la f. de su mirada** the coldness of her look; **lo recibieron con f.** he was given a rather cool reception; **me trata con mucha f.** he's very cold towards me, he treats me very coldly (**c**) *(serenidad)* **examinar las cosas con f.** to look at things calmly *o* coolly

fríamente *adv* (**a**) *(con indiferencia)* coldly, coolly; **me miró f.** he looked at me coldly, he gave me a cold look; **la recibieron muy f.** she got a very cool *o* chilly reception (**b**) *(con serenidad)* calmly, coolly; **debemos abordar el problema f.** we must tackle the problem calmly

fricación *nf Ling* friction

fricasé *nm* fricassee

fricativa *nf Ling* fricative

fricativo, -a *adj Ling* fricative

fricción *nf* (**a**) *(rozamiento)* friction (**b**) *(tensión)* friction; **hubo fricciones entre los negociadores** there was some friction between the negotiators (**c**) *(friega)* rub, massage; **dar fricciones** to give a rub-down *o* massage

friccionar *vt* to rub, to massage

fríe *ver* **freír**

friega *nf* (**a**) *(masaje)* massage, rub; **dar friegas de alcohol a alguien** to give sb an alcohol rub (**b**) *Andes, Méx Fam (molestia)* pain, drag (**c**) *Andes, Méx Fam (zurra)* thrashing, hiding; **dar una f. a alguien** to give sb a thrashing *o* hiding

friegaplatos 1 *nm inv (máquina)* dishwasher
2 *nmf inv (persona)* dishwasher

friego *etc ver* **fregar**

friera *etc ver* **freír**

Frigia *n Hist* Phrygia

frigider, friyider *nm Andes* refrigerator, *Br* fridge, *US* icebox

frigidez *nf* (**a**) *(sexual)* frigidity (**b**) *(de acogida, respuesta)* coldness, frostiness

frígido, -a *adj* (**a**) *(persona)* frigid (**b**) *(acogida, respuesta)* cold, frosty

frigio, -a *Hist* 1 *adj* Phrygian
2 *nm,f* Phrygian

frigoría *nf Fís* negative kilo-calorie

frigorífico, -a 1 *adj (que produce frío)* **cámara frigorífica** cold store; **camión f.** refrigerated *Br* lorry *o US* truck; *RP* **planta frigorífica** meat processing plant
2 *nm* (**a**) *Esp (nevera)* refrigerator, *Br* fridge, *US* icebox (**b**) *RP (matadero)* meat processing plant

frigorista *nmf* refrigeration engineer

frijol, fríjol *nm Andes, CAm, Carib, Méx* bean

frijolar *nm* beanfield

frió *ver* **freír**

frío, -a 1 *ver* **freír**
2 *adj* (**a**) *(a baja temperatura)* cold; **una bebida fría** a cold drink; **hoy está el día f.** it's cold today; **tengo las manos frías** my hands are cold; **me he quedado f. esperándote** I've got cold waiting for you; **me quedé f. cuando me lo contaron** I was stunned when they told me; EXPR **dejar a alguien f.** to leave sb cold; **el fútbol me deja f.** football leaves me cold
(**b**) *(que no abriga)* not very warm; **esta camisa es muy fría** this shirt isn't very warm
(**c**) *(tono, color)* cold; **es una habitación muy fría** it's a very cold *o* unwelcoming room
(**d**) *(indiferente)* cold; **es demasiado fría y calculadora** she's too cold and calculating; **un recibimiento muy f.** a cold *o* frosty reception; **me dirigió una fría mirada** he gave me a cold look, he looked at me coldly; **estuvo muy f. conmigo** he was very cold towards me
(**e**) *(sereno)* cool, calm; **mantener la cabeza fría** to keep a cool head
(**f**) *Fam (al buscar algo)* (you're) cold!
3 *nm* (**a**) *(baja temperatura)* cold; **¡qué f. (hace)!** it's freezing!; *Fam* **¡hace un f. que pela!** it's freezing cold!; **los montañeros se murieron de f.** they mountaineers froze to death; *Fam* **¡me muero de f.!** I'm freezing (to death)!
(**b**) *(sensación)* **tener f.** to be *o* feel cold; **tengo f. en la orejas** my ears are cold; *Esp* **coger** *o Am* **tomar f.** to catch a chill; EXPR **no me da ni f. ni calor** I can take it or leave it
4 **en frío** *loc adv* **el aceite hay que cambiarlo en f.** the engine has to be cold when you change the oil; **mañana, en f., lo analizarás mejor** tomorrow, in the cold light of day, you'll look at it more clearly; **sorprendido en f., no supe qué decir** they caught me cold and I didn't know what to say; EXPR *Esp Fam* **coger a alguien en f.** to catch sb on the hop

friolento, -a *adj Am* 1 *adj* sensitive to the cold
2 *nm,f* **es un f.** he really feels the cold

friolera *nf Fam* **costó la f. de 20.000 pesos** it cost a cool 20,000 pesos

friolero, -a *Esp* 1 *adj* sensitive to the cold
2 *nm,f* **es un f.** he really feels the cold

friqui *nm (en fútbol)* free kick

frisa *nf* (**a**) *(tela)* frieze (**b**) *CSur (de felpa)* nap

frisar 1 *vt* **frisa los cuarenta** she's getting on for forty, she's pushing forty
2 *vi* **su edad frisa en los sesenta** he's getting on for sixty, he's pushing sixty

frisbee® ['frisβi:] *nm* frisbee®

friso *nm* (**a**) *Arquit* frieze (**b**) *(zócalo)* skirting board

frisón, -ona 1 *adj* Frisian
2 *nm,f* Frisian

fritada *nf* fry-up, dish of fried food

fritanga *nf Fam* (**a**) *Esp (comida frita)* fry-up; **olor a f.** smell of fried food (**b**) *Am Pey (comida grasienta)* greasy food

fritanguería *nf Am Fam* = cheap restaurant or stall selling fried snacks

fritar *vt Am* to fry

frito, -a 1 *participio ver* **freír**
2 *adj* (**a**) *(alimento)* fried
(**b**) *Fam (harto)* fed up (to the back teeth); **me tienen f. con tantas quejas** I'm sick (and tired) of all their complaining; **estos niños me tienen frita** I'm fed up with these children
(**c**) *Fam (exhausto)* fit to drop, shattered
(**d**) *Fam (dormido)* flaked out, asleep; **me estoy quedando f.** I'm nodding off; **todas las noches se queda f. en el sofá** in the evenings, he flakes out on the sofa
(**e**) *Esp Fam (muerto)* dead, stiff; **lo dejaron f. delante de su casa** they did him in *o* bumped him off right outside his house
(**f**) *RP Fam (perdido)* **si no cobramos hoy, estamos fritos** if we don't get paid today, we've had it
3 **fritos** *nmpl* fried food

fritura *nf* fry-up, dish of fried food

frívolamente *adv* frivolously

frivolidad *nf* frivolity; **con f.** frivolously

frivolité *nm* tatting

frívolo, -a *adj* (**a**) *(superficial)* frivolous (**b**) *(despreocupado)* flippant

friyider = **frigider**

fronda *nf* (**a**) *(follaje)* foliage, leaves (**b**) *(hoja)* frond

frondosidad *nf* leafiness

frondoso, -a *adj (planta, árbol)* leafy; *(bosque)* dense

frontal 1 *adj* (**a**) *(ataque)* frontal; *(colisión)* head-on; **la parte f.** the front, the front part; **cuenta con mi oposición f.** I am totally opposed to it (**b**) *Anat* frontal
2 *nm* (**a**) *Anat (hueso)* frontal bone (**b**) *Anat (músculo)* frontal muscle (**c**) *(de automóvil)* front

frontalmente *adv* head-on; **chocaron f.** they collided head-on, they had a head-on collision; **se opuso f. a la iniciativa** he was totally opposed to the initiative

frontenis *nm inv Dep* = ball game played on pelota court with rackets and balls similar to those used in tennis, *US* ≃ racquetball

frontera *nf* (**a**) *(división administrativa)* border
(**b**) *(límite)* bounds; **dice que no está clara la f. entre amor y odio** he says there is no clear dividing line between love and hate; **una película en la f. del mal gusto** a movie *o Br* film bordering on bad taste; **su ambición no tiene fronteras** her ambition is limitless *o* knows no bounds; **alcanzó el éxito ya en la f. de la vejez** he achieved success just as he was reaching old age

fronterizo^1, -a *adj* border; **Perú es f. con Brasil** Peru shares a border with Brazil; **ciudad fronteriza** border town; **conflicto f.** border dispute

fronterizo^2, -a *Urug* 1 *adj* of/from the border region with Brazil
2 *nm,f* person from the border region with Brazil
3 *nm* = border variety of Spanish influenced by Brazilian Portuguese

frontero, -a *adj* facing, opposite

frontil *nm Am (para caballos)* browband

frontis *nm inv* facade

frontispicio *nm* (**a**) *(de edificio) (fachada)* facade (**b**) *(de edificio) (remate)* pediment (**c**) *(de libro)* frontispiece

frontón *nm* (**a**) *(deporte)* pelota (**b**) *(cancha)* pelota court (**c**) *Arquit* pediment

frotación *nf*, **frotamiento** *nm* rubbing

frotar 1 *vt (rozar, masajear)* to rub; *(al fregar)* to scrub
2 *vi (rozar, masajear)* to rub; *(al fregar)* to scrub
3 **frotarse** *vpr* **frotarse las manos** *(por frío, entumecimiento)* to rub one's hands (together); *(regocijarse)* to rub one's hands (with glee)

frote *nm* rub, rubbing; **darle un buen f. a algo** to give sth a good rub

frotis *nm inv* smear ►► ***f. cervical*** cervical smear; ***f. de exudado nasal*** nasal swab *o* smear

fructífero, -a *adj* fruitful

fructificación *nf* fructification

fructificar [60] *vi* (**a**) *(sujeto: árbol)* to bear *o* produce fruit (**b**) *(dar resultados)* to bear fruit

fructosa *nf* fructose

fructuoso, -a *adj* fruitful

frufrú *nm* swish

frugal *adj* frugal

frugalidad *nf* frugality

frugalmente *adv* frugally

frugívoro, -a *adj Zool* fruit-eating

fruición *nf* gusto, delight; **comió con f.** she ate with relish *o* gusto; **devoró la novela con f.** she gleefully devoured the novel

frunce *nm (en tela)* gathering

fruncido, -a 1 *adj* (**a**) *(tela)* gathered (**b**) **entró con el ceño f.** he was frowning as he came in (**c**) *(persona)* grumpy; **no me cae nada bien, está siempre f.** I don't like him much, he's always so grumpy
2 *nm (en tela)* gathering

fruncir [74] *vt* (**a**) *(tela)* to gather (**b**) *(labios)* to purse; **f. el ceño** to frown

fruslería *nf* triviality, trifle

frustración *nf* frustration

frustrado, -a *adj* (**a**) *(persona)* frustrated; **se quedó muy f. cuando se enteró del suspenso** he was very frustrated when he found out he'd failed (**b**) *(plan)* failed; **un golpe de Estado f.** a failed coup; **un intento f. de mandar una nave tripulada a Marte** an unsuccessful attempt to send a manned spacecraft to Mars

frustrante *adj* frustrating

frustrar 1 *vt* (**a**) *(persona)* to frustrate (**b**) *(posibilidades, ilusiones)* to thwart, to put paid to; *(plan, robo)* to thwart; **el mal tiempo frustró nuestras vacaciones** the bad weather ruined our holiday
2 frustrarse *vpr* (**a**) *(persona)* to get frustrated (**b**) *(ilusiones)* to be thwarted; *(proyecto)* to fail

fruta *nf* fruit ►► *Cuba* ***f. bomba*** papaya; ***f. confitada*** candied *o* crystallized fruit; ***f. escarchada*** candied *o* crystallized fruit; *RP* ***f. de estación*** seasonal fruit, fruit in season; ***f. de la pasión*** passion fruit; ***la fruta prohibida*** the forbidden fruit; *Esp* ***f. de sartén*** fritter; ***f. del tiempo*** seasonal fruit, fruit in season

frutal 1 *adj* fruit; **árbol f.** fruit tree
2 *nm* fruit tree

frutera *nf* (**a**) *CSur (recipiente)* fruit bowl (**b**) *ver también* **frutero**

frutería *nf* fruit shop

frutero, -a 1 *nm,f (persona)* fruit seller, *Br* fruiterer
2 *nm (recipiente)* fruit bowl

frutícola *adj* **la producción f.** fruit production; **una región f.** a fruit-growing region

fruticultor, -ora *nm,f* fruit grower *o* farmer

fruticultura *nf* fruit farming

frutilla *nf Bol, CSur, Ecuad* strawberry

frutillado, -a *adj Am* **leche frutillada** strawberry-flavoured milk drink

fruto *nm* (**a**) *(naranja, plátano)* fruit; *(nuez, avellana)* nut ►► ***f. prohibido*** forbidden fruit; **esos lujos son, para mí, f. prohibido** I can't permit myself such luxuries; ***frutos secos*** dried fruit and nuts
(**b**) *(resultado)* fruit; **fue f. de su empeño** it was the fruit *o* result of her efforts; **no es más que el f. de su imaginación** it's just a figment of his imagination; **dar f.** to bear fruit; **sacar f. a** *o* **de algo** to profit from sth; **los frutos de la tierra** the fruits of the earth

FSE *nm UE* (*abrev de* **Fondo Social Europeo**) ESF

FSLN *nm* (*abrev de* **Frente Sandinista de Liberación Nacional**) FSLN, Sandinista National Liberation Front

FTP *Informát* (*abrev de* **file transfer protocol**) FTP; **hacer F.** to do FTP ►► ***F. anónimo*** anonymous FTP

fu: ni fu ni fa *loc adv Fam* so-so; **¿te gustó? – ni fu ni fa** did you like it? – it was so-so; **¿te gustaría ir? – ni fu ni fa** would you like to go? – I'm not that bothered (either way); **a mí la natación ni fu ni fa** as far as swimming's concerned, I can take it or leave it

fuchi *interj Méx Fam* ugh!, yuck!

fuco *nm* wrack

fucsia 1 *nf (planta)* fuchsia
2 *adj inv (color)* fuchsia
3 *nm inv (color)* fuchsia

fucú *nm Col Fam* bad luck

FUCVAM [fuk'bam] *nf* (*abrev de* **Federación Uruguaya de Cooperativas de Viviendas por Ayuda Mutua**) = umbrella organization for Uruguayan housing cooperatives

fue (**a**) *ver* **ir** (**b**) *ver* **ser**

fuego 1 *nm* (**a**) *(incandescencia)* fire; **pegar f. a algo** to set sth on fire, to set fire to sth; EXPR **echar f. por los ojos** to look daggers; EXPR **jugar con f.** to play with fire ►► ***fuegos artificiales*** fireworks; ***fuegos de artificio*** fireworks; ***f. fatuo*** will-o'-the-wisp; ***f. de San Telmo*** St Elmo's fire
(**b**) *(hoguera)* fire; **atizar el f.** to poke the fire; **hacer un f.** to make a fire
(**c**) *(incendio)* fire; **los bomberos no pudieron controlar el f.** the firemen couldn't control the fire *o* blaze
(**d**) *(para cigarrillo)* **pedir/dar f.** to ask for/give a light; **¿tiene f.?** have you got a light?
(**e**) *(de cocina, fogón)* ring, burner; *(eléctrico)* ring; *(de vitrocerámica)* ring; **una cocina de cuatro fuegos** a cooker with four rings; **poner el agua al f. hasta que empiece a hervir** heat the water until it starts to boil; **a f. lento/vivo** *(cocinar)* over a low/high heat; **apagar/bajar el f.** to turn off/lower the heat
(**f**) *(disparos)* fire; **abrir** *o* **hacer f.** to fire, to open fire; **romper el f.** to open fire; EXPR **estar entre dos fuegos** to be between the devil and the deep blue sea ►► ***f. cruzado*** crossfire
(**g**) *(apasionamiento)* passion, ardour; **la distancia avivó el f. de su pasión** distance rekindled the fires of his passion; **tenía f. en la mirada** his eyes blazed (with passion/anger)
(**h**) *(sensación de ardor)* heat, burning
2 *interj* fire!

fueguino, -a 1 *adj* of/from Tierra del Fuego *(Argentina and Chile)*
2 *nm,f* person from Tierra del Fuego *(Argentina and Chile)*

fuel *nm* fuel oil

fuelle *nm* (**a**) *(para soplar)* bellows (**b**) *(de maletín, bolso)* accordion pleats (**c**) *(de cámara fotográfica)* bellows (**d**) *(entre vagones)* connecting corridor, concertina vestibule

fuel-oil, fuelóleo *nm* fuel oil

fuente *nf* (**a**) *(para beber)* fountain ►► ***f. de agua potable*** drinking fountain; *Chile, Carib, Col, Méx* ***f. de soda*** *(cafetería)* = cafe or counter selling ice cream, soft drinks etc, *US* soda fountain
(**b**) *(bandeja)* (serving) dish
(**c**) *(de información)* **no quiso revelar su f. de información** he didn't want to reveal the source of his information; **fuentes oficiosas/oficiales** unofficial/official sources; **según fuentes del ministerio de Educación...** according to Ministry of Education sources...; **ha manejado gran número de fuentes para escribir su tesis** she has made use of many sources to write her thesis
(**d**) *(origen)* source; **la Biblia es la f. de muchas obras medievales** the Bible provides the source material for many medieval works ►► ***f. de energía*** energy source; **f. de energía ecológica/limpia/renovable** environmentally-friendly/clean/renewable source of energy; ***f. de ingresos*** source of income; ***f. de riqueza*** source of wealth
(**e**) *(causa)* cause, source; **f. de problemas** a source of problems *o* trouble; **la falta de higiene es f. de infecciones** lack of hygiene is a cause of infection
(**f**) *(manantial)* spring ►► ***f. termal*** thermal spring
(**g**) ***f. de alimentación*** *Elec* feed source; *Informát* power supply
(**h**) *Imprenta* font

fuentón *nm RP* = large washing-up bowl

fuer: a fuer de *loc adv Anticuado* as a, like a; **a f. de hombre de bien** as a good man

FUERA 1 (**a**) *ver* **ir**
(**b**) *ver* **ser**
2 *adv* (**a**) *(en el exterior)* outside; **hace frío f.** it's cold outside; **lo echó f.** she threw him out; **salen mucho a comer f.** they eat out a lot; **f. de la casa** outside the house; **el ruido viene de f.** the noise is coming from outside; **hacia f.** outwards; **sólo vimos la catedral por f.** we only saw the cathedral from the outside; **llevas la camisa por f.** your shirt isn't tucked in properly; **por f. es de color amarillo** it's yellow on the outside
(**b**) *(en otro lugar)* away; *(en el extranjero)* abroad; **de f.** *(extranjero)* from abroad; **Marta está f.** *(de viaje)* Marta is away; *(ha salido)* Marta is out; **a los de f. les sorprenden mucho las costumbres locales** people who aren't from round here *o* strangers find the local customs very strange
(**c**) **f. de** *(alcance, peligro)* out of; *(cálculos, competencia)* outside; **estar f. de sí** to be beside oneself (with rage); **ese comentario está f. de lugar** that remark is out of place; **f. de plazo** after the closing date; **f. de la ley** illegal; **f. de control** out of control; **presentó su película f.**

de concurso his film was shown, but not judged as part of the competition

(**d**) *Dep (de límites)* **la pelota salió f.** the ball went out (of play) ►► ***f. de banda*** out of play; ***f. de combate*** knocked out; *Fig* out of action; ***f. de juego*** offside; **estar en f. de juego** to be offside; EXPR *Esp* **pillar a alguien en f. de juego** to catch sb out; *Am* ***f. de lugar*** offside; *Am* **estar en f. de lugar** to be offside

(**e**) *Dep (en campo ajeno)* away; **jugar f.** to play away (from home); **el equipo de f.** the away team

(**f**) **f. de** *(excepto)* except for, apart from; **f. de eso, he cumplido todos tus caprichos** apart from that, I've done everything you wanted me to; **f. de bromas, ¿has fijado ya una fecha para la boda?** seriously though *o* joking apart, have you set a date for the wedding yet?; **f. de serie** exceptional, out of the ordinary; EXPR **ser un f. de serie** to be one of a kind

3 *interj (de habitación, lugar)* get out!; *(en el teatro)* get off!; **¡f., f., f.!** *(cántico)* off!, off!, off!; **¡f. los políticos corruptos!** out with all corrupt politicians!; **¡f. de aquí!** get out of my sight!

---

fueraborda 1 *adj inv* outboard; **motor (de) f.** outboard motor *o* engine; **lancha f.** outboard, boat with outboard motor
2 *nm inv (motor)* outboard motor *o* engine
3 *nf inv (lancha)* outboard, boat with outboard motor

fuerce *ver* **forzar**

fuereño, -a *nm,f Méx Fam* stranger; **es un f.** he's not from round here

fuero *nm* (**a**) *(ley local)* = ancient regional law still existing in some parts of Spain (**b**) *(jurisdicción)* code of laws (**c**) EXPR **en su f. interno** in her heart of hearts, deep down; **el equipo ha vuelto por sus fueros** the team has recovered its form

fuerte 1 *adj* (**a**) *(persona) (físicamente)* strong; EXPR **estar f. como un roble** to be as strong as an ox
(**b**) *(persona) (psicológicamente)* strong; **tiene un carácter muy f.** she has a strong character
(**c**) **hacerse f. en** *Mil* to make one's stronghold in; *Fig* **el equipo se hizo f. en su área** the team fell back into their own half
(**d**) *(material)* strong; **necesito un tejido f.** I need a strong material
(**e**) *(viento)* strong; *(lluvia)* heavy
(**f**) *(intenso) (frío, dolor, color)* intense; *(golpe, pelea)* hard
(**g**) *(medicamento)* powerful
(**h**) *(influyente, sólido)* strong; **es una empresa f. en el sector** the company's strong in this sector; **una moneda f.** a strong currency; **fuertes razones** powerful reasons
(**i**) *(violento, impactante)* powerful, shocking; **lenguaje f.** strong language; **un chiste f.** a crude joke; **algunas de las escenas son muy fuertes** some of the scenes are very shocking
(**j**) *(grande)* large, considerable; **una f. cantidad de dinero** a large *o* considerable amount of money; **una f. presencia de artistas caribeños** a large contingent of Caribbean artists
(**k**) *(comida) (pesado)* heavy; *(picante)* hot
(**l**) *(nudo)* tight
(**m**) *(sílaba)* accented, stressed
(**n**) *(vocal)* strong
(**o**) *(versado)* **estoy f. en idiomas** I'm good at languages
(**p**) *(alto) (sonido)* loud; **la televisión está demasiado f.** the television is on too loud
(**q**) *Fam (increíble)* astonishing, amazing; **¡qué f.!** *(fabuloso)* wow!, amazing!; *(terrible)* how awful!, oh no!; **...y después me insultó – ¡qué f.!** ...and then he insulted me - that's awful *o* terrible!
2 *adv* (**a**) *(intensamente)* hard; *(abrazar, agarrar)* tight; **está nevando f.** it's snowing hard *o* heavily; **lo ató bien f.** she tied it tight; **chuta f.** he has a powerful kick (**b**) *(abundantemente)* a lot; **en España se suele almorzar f.** in Spain, people usually have a big meal at lunchtime (**c**) *(en voz alta)* loudly; **¿podría hablar más f.?** could you speak louder?
3 *nm* (**a**) *(fortificación)* fort (**b**) *(especialidad)* strong point, forte; **su f. son las matemáticas** mathematics is his forte

fuertemente *adv* (**a**) *(con fuerza)* hard; **me apretó f.** he squeezed me hard (**b**) *(vehementemente)* vehemently, intensely

---

FUERZA 1 *ver* **forzar**
2 *nf* (**a**) *(fortaleza)* strength; **el animal tiene mucha f.** the animal is very strong; **no me siento con fuerzas para caminar** I don't feel strong enough to walk, I don't feel up to walking; **su amor fue cobrando f. con el tiempo** her love grew stronger with time; **recuperar fuerzas** to recover one's strength, to get one's strength back; **tener fuerzas para** to have the strength to; EXPR *Fam* **se le va la f. por la boca** he's all talk and no action; EXPR **sacar fuerzas de flaqueza** to screw up one's courage ►► ***la f. de la costumbre*** force of habit; ***la f. del destino*** the power of destiny; ***f. física*** strength; **se necesita mucha f. física para hacer eso** you need to be very strong to do that; *Der* ***f. mayor*** force majeure; *(en seguros)* act of God; **no llegué por un caso de f. mayor** I didn't make it due to circumstances beyond my control; ***f. de voluntad*** willpower
(**b**) *(resistencia) (de material)* strength
(**c**) *(intensidad) (de sonido)* loudness; *(de dolor)* intensity; **aprieta con f.** press hard; **llueve con f.** it's raining hard; **un viento de f. 8** a force 8 wind
(**d**) *(violencia)* force; **ceder a la f.** to give in to force; **emplear la f.** to use force; **por la f.** by force; **recurrir a la f.** to resort to force ►► ***f. bruta*** brute force
(**e**) *Mil* force ►► ***f. aérea*** air force; ***fuerzas armadas*** armed forces; ***fuerzas de choque*** shock troops, storm troopers; ***f. disuasoria*** deterrent; ***f. de intervención*** troops, forces; ***f. de intervención rápida*** rapid reaction force; ***fuerzas del orden (público)*** security forces; ***fuerzas de pacificación*** peacekeeping force; ***fuerzas de seguridad*** security forces
(**f**) **fuerzas** *(grupo)* forces; **las diferentes fuerzas sociales** the different forces in society; **todas las fuerzas políticas se han puesto de acuerdo** all the political groups have reached an agreement; **las fuerzas vivas de la ciudad** the most influential people in the city
(**g**) *Fís* force ►► ***f. centrífuga*** centrifugal force; ***f. centrípeta*** centripetal force; ***f. electromotriz*** electromotive force; ***f. de la gravedad*** force of gravity; ***f. hidráulica*** water power; ***f. motriz*** *(que causa movimiento)* driving force; *Fig (impulso)* prime mover; *Fís* ***f. nuclear débil*** weak nuclear force; *Fís* ***f. nuclear fuerte*** strong nuclear force
(**h**) *Elec* power; **han cortado la f.** the power has been cut
3 **a la fuerza** *loc adv* (**a**) *(contra la voluntad)* by force, forcibly; **firmaron a la f.** they were forced to sign; **tuvo que llevarlo al colegio a la f.** she had to drag him to school by force, she had to forcibly drag him to school
(**b**) *(forzosamente)* inevitably; **a la f. tenía que saber la noticia** she must have known the news; **a la f. tenía que ocurrir un accidente** there was bound to be an accident, an accident was inevitable
4 **a fuerza de** *loc prep (a base de)* by dint of; **a f. de gritar mucho, conseguimos que nos oyera** after a lot of shouting, we eventually managed to make him hear us; **he aprendido la lección a f. de mucho estudiar** I learnt the lesson by studying hard
5 **por fuerza** *loc adv (forzosamente)* inevitably; **tenía que ocurrir un desastre por f.** a disaster was inevitable; **esta noche tengo que salir por f. para atender a un paciente** I absolutely have to go out tonight to see a patient

---

fuerzo *etc ver* **forzar**

fuese (**a**) *ver* **ir** (**b**) *ver* **ser**

fuet *nm* = type of cured pork sausage typical of Catalonia

fuetazo *nm Andes, CAm, Carib, Méx* lash

fuete *nm Andes, CAm, Carib, Méx* whip

fuga *nf* (**a**) *(huida)* escape; **darse a la f.** to take flight; **poner a alguien en f.** to rout sb, to put sb to flight ►► ***f. de capitales*** capital flight; ***f. de cerebros*** brain drain; ***f. de divisas*** capital flight (**b**) *(de gas, líquido)* leak (**c**) *Mús* fugue

fugacidad *nf* fleeting nature

fugarse [38] *vpr* (**a**) *(persona)* to escape; **se fugaron de la prisión** they escaped from prison; **f. de casa** to run away from home; **f. con alguien** to run off with sb; **se fugó con el dinero** he ran off with the money (**b**) *(gas, líquido)* to leak, to escape

fugaz *adj* fleeting; **su alegría fue f.** her happiness was short-lived; **una visita f.** a flying visit

fugazmente *adv* briefly; **la película pasó f. por las pantallas de la ciudad** the movie *o Br* film made a brief appearance on the city's cinema screens

fugitivo, -a 1 *adj* (**a**) *(en fuga)* fleeing (**b**) *(fugaz)* fleeting
2 *nm,f* fugitive; **un f. de la justicia** a fugitive from justice

führer ['firer] (*pl* **führers**) *nm* führer

fui (**a**) *ver* **ir** (**b**) *ver* **ser**

Fujiyama *nm* **el F.** Fujiyama, Mount Fuji

ful 1 *adj Esp Fam* (**a**) *(malo)* terrible (**b**) *(falso)* bogus
2 *nm (en póquer)* full house

fula *nf Cuba Fam (dólar)* buck

fulana *nf (prostituta)* tart, whore

fulano, -a 1 *nm,f (hombre)* so-and-so, what's-his-name; *(mujer)* so-and-so, what's-her-name; **siempre se queja, que si f. no le habla, que si mengano le molesta...** she's always complaining, either it's someone who won't talk to her, or someone's bothering her...; **(don) f. de tal** *Br* Joe Bloggs, *US* John Doe
2 *nm Br* bloke, *US* guy; **vino un f. preguntando por ti** there was a *Br* bloke *o US* guy looking for you

fular *nm* headscarf *(of fine material)*

fulbito *nm* **(a)** *Andes (fútbol sala)* indoor five-a-side football **(b)** *Perú (fútbol callejero)* kickabout ►► ***f. de mano*** table football; ***f. de mesa*** table football

fulcro *nm* fulcrum

fulero, -a *Fam* **1** *adj* **(a)** *(chapucero)* shoddy **(b)** *(malo)* cheap (and nasty); **un reloj f.** a cheap watch **(c)** *(tramposo)* **es muy f.** he's a cheating so-and-so **(d)** *(mentiroso)* **es muy f.** he's a lying so-and-so **(e)** *RP (feo)* ugly **(f)** *RP (complicado)* tricky; **la situación está fulera** it's a tricky situation

2 *nm,f* **(a)** *(tramposo)* cheating so-and-so **(b)** *(mentiroso)* lying so-and-so

fulgente, fúlgido,-a *adj Formal* brilliant, radiant

fulgor *nm (resplandor)* shining; *(de disparo)* flash

fulguración *nf Astron* ***f. cromosférica*** solar flare

fulgurante, fulguroso, -a *adj* **(a)** *(resplandeciente)* flashing **(b)** *(rápido)* rapid; **un ascenso/éxito f.** a lightning rise/success

fulgurar *vi (resplandecer)* to gleam; *(intermitentemente)* to flash

full [ful] **1** (*pl* **fulls**) *nm (en póquer)* full house

2 a full *loc adj RP, Ven Fam* packed; **el restaurante estaba a f.** the restaurant was packed; **hoy no puedo ir, estoy a f.** I can't go today, I'm really busy

3 a full *loc adv RP, Ven Fam* flat out; **trabajar a f.** to work flat out

fullería *nf Fam* **(a)** *(trampa)* cheating **(b)** *(astucia)* craftiness

fullero, -a *Fam* **1** *adj* **(a)** *(tramposo)* **es muy f.** he's a cheating so-and-so **(b)** *(mentiroso)* **es muy f.** he's a lying so-and-so

2 *nm,f* **(a)** *(tramposo)* cheating so-and-so **(b)** *(mentiroso)* lying so-and-so

fulmar *nm* fulmar ►► ***f. boreal*** northern fulmar

fulminante **1** *adj* **(a)** *(despido, muerte)* sudden; *(mirada)* withering **(b)** *(enfermedad)* devastating, *Espec* fulminant **(c)** *(explosivo)* fulminating

2 *nm* initiating explosive

fulminar *vt (sujeto: enfermedad)* to strike down; **un rayo la fulminó** she was struck by lightning; **f. a alguien con la mirada** to look daggers at sb

fulo, -a *adj RP Fam* mad, fuming

fumadero *nm* ***f. de opio*** opium den

fumador, -ora *nm,f* smoker; **no f.** nonsmoker; **¿quiere f. o no f.?** would you like smoking or non-smoking?; **la zona de no fumadores** the no-smoking area ►► ***f. empedernido*** chain-smoker; ***f. pasivo*** passive smoker

fumar **1** *vt* to smoke

2 *vi* to smoke; **f. en pipa** to smoke a pipe; **prohibido f., se prohibe f.** *(en cartel)* no smoking; EXPR **f. como un carretero** to smoke like a chimney

3 fumarse *vpr* **(a)** *(cigarillo)* to smoke **(b)** *Esp Fam* **fumarse una clase** *(en colegio)* to skip a class; *(en universidad)* to skip a lecture **(c)** *Esp Fam (fortuna, ahorros)* to blow **(d)** *RP Fam (a alguien, una situación)* to put up with; **se la fumó hasta la madrugada** she had to put up with her until the small hours; **otra espera como esta no me fumo** I won't put up with another wait like this

> **Falso amigo**: El verbo inglés **to fume** no es la traducción del español **fumar**. En inglés **to fume** significa "despedir gases" o "echar humo".

fumarada *nf* **(a)** *(de humo)* puff **(b)** *(de tabaco)* pipeful

fumarel *nm* black tern

fumaria *nf* fumitory

fumarola *nf* fumarole

fumata *nf* ***f. blanca*** white smoke *(as signal of election of a new Pope)*

fumeta *nmf Fam* pothead, dopehead

fumigación *nf* **(a)** *(de cosechas)* dusting, spraying; **f. de cosechas** crop-dusting, crop-spraying **(b)** *(de habitación)* fumigation

fumigador *nm* fumigator

fumigante *nm* fumigant

fumigar [38] *vt* **(a)** *(cosechas)* to fumigate **(b)** *(habitación)* to fumigate

fumo *nm RP Fam* pot, dope

fumón, -ona *nm,f Ven Fam* pothead, dopehead

funambulesco, -a *adj (extravagante)* grotesque, ridiculous

funámbulo, -a *nm,f*, **funambulista** *nmf* tightrope walker

funcar *vi RP Fam* **esta radio no funca** this radio is bust; **sus planes no funcaron** his plans fell through *o* didn't work out

función **1** *nf* **(a)** *(actividad, objetivo)* function; *(trabajo)* duty; **la f. de estas columnas es sólo decorativa** these columns have a purely decorative function; **esta pieza desempeña una f. clave** this part has a crucial function *o* role; **la f. del coordinador es hacer que todo discurra sin contratiempos** the coordinator's job *o* function is to make sure everything goes smoothly; **desempeña las funciones de portavoz** he acts as spokesperson; **director en funciones** acting director; **entrar en funciones** *(en empresa, organización)* to take up one's post; *(ministro)* to take up office ►► *Biol* ***f. clorofílica*** photosynthesis

(b) *(en teatro, cine)* show ►► ***f. benéfica*** charity performance, benefit; ***f. continua*** continuous performance; *RP* ***f. continuada*** continuous performance; ***f. de noche*** evening performance; ***f. de tarde*** matinée

(c) *Ling* function; **en f. de sujeto** functioning as a subject

(d) *Mat* function ►► ***f. periódica*** periodic function

2 en función de *loc prep* depending on; **estar** *o* **ir en f. de** to depend on, to be dependent on; **las ayudas se conceden en f. de los ingresos familiares** the amount of benefit given depends *o* is dependent on family income, the benefits are means-tested

funcional *adj* **(a)** *(práctico)* functional **(b)** *Mat* functional

funcionalidad *nf* functional qualities; **este mueble no tiene mucha f.** this piece of furniture is not very practical; **su reducido tamaño añade f.** its smaller size makes it more practical

funcionalismo *nm* functionalism

funcionalmente *adv* functionally; **este edificio es f. inadecuado** this building is badly designed (for its purpose)

funcionamiento *nm* operation, functioning; **el f. de esta impresora es perfecto** this printer works perfectly; **me explicó el f. de la empresa** she explained to me how the company works; **entrar/estar en f.** to come into/be in operation; **la máquina lleva ya dos horas en f.** the machine has been running for two hours; **poner algo en f.** to start sth (working); **la puesta en f. de una central nuclear** the commissioning *o* bringing on-line of a nuclear power station

funcionar *vi* to work; **el sistema funciona de maravilla** the system works superbly; **funciona con gasolina** it runs on *Br* petrol *o US* gasoline; **funciona a** *o* **con pilas** it uses *o* runs off batteries, it's battery-powered; **no funciona** *(en letrero)* out of order; **su matrimonio no está funcionando** their marriage isn't working (out); **conmigo los lloros no funcionan** you won't get anywhere with me by crying

funcionariado *nm* **(a)** *(del Estado) (de la Administración central)* civil service; *(profesor, bombero, enfermero)* public sector workers **(b)** *(de organismo internacional)* staff

funcionario, -a *nm,f* **(a)** *(del Estado) (de la Administración central)* civil servant; *(profesor, bombero, enfermero)* public sector worker; **un f. público** *(de la Administración central)* a civil servant; *(del Estado)* a public sector worker; **los funcionarios de Correos** *Br* Post Office workers, *US* mail service workers; **alto f.** senior civil servant ►► ***f. de aduanas*** customs official *o* officer; ***f. de prisiones*** prison officer

(b) *(de organismo internacional)* employee, staff member

(c) *RP (de empresa)* employee, worker

funda *nf* **(a)** *(de sofá)* cover; **f. de almohada** pillowcase **(b)** *(de máquina de escribir, guitarra, raqueta)* cover; *(de gafas)* pouch **(c)** *(de disco)* sleeve **(d)** *(de diente)* cap

fundación *nf* **(a)** *(creación, establecimiento)* foundation **(b)** *(organización)* foundation; **una f. benéfica** a charitable foundation

fundado, -a *adj* **(a)** *(argumento, idea)* well-founded; **sus temores no son fundados** his fears are groundless **(b)** *(creado, establecido)* founded

fundador, -ora **1** *adj* founding

2 *nm,f* founder

fundamentación *nf* foundation, basis

fundamental *adj* fundamental; **lo f. es que hallemos una solución** the most important thing is that we find a solution; **es f. que no nos pongamos nerviosos** it's essential that we don't get nervous

fundamentalismo *nm* fundamentalism

fundamentalista **1** *adj* fundamentalist

2 *nmf* fundamentalist

fundamentalmente *adv* **(a)** *(primordialmente)* mainly; **afecta f. a las personas mayores** it mainly affects older people **(b)** *(en esencia)* fundamentally, basically; **es f. un cómico** he's basically a comedian, in essence, he's a comedian

fundamentar **1** *vt* **(a)** *(basar)* to base; **fundamentó sólidamente su tesis** she underpinned her theory with sound arguments; **fundamentó su defensa en la falta de pruebas** he based his defence on the lack of evidence **(b)** *(afianzar)* **el nuevo acuerdo fundamenta sus relaciones**

the new agreement puts their relations on a firm footing (**c**) *Constr* to lay the foundations of
2 **fundamentarse** *vpr (basarse)* to be based *o* founded (**en** on)

fundamento *nm* (**a**) *(base)* foundation, basis (**b**) *(razón)* reason, grounds; **sin f.** unfounded, groundless (**c**) *(seriedad)* reliability, responsibility (**d**) **fundamentos** *(principios)* basic principles (**e**) **fundamentos** *(cimientos)* foundations

fundamentoso, -a *adj Ven Fam* responsible, reliable

fundar 1 *vt* (**a**) *(crear, establecer)* to found (**b**) *(basar)* to base; **f. algo en algo** to base sth on sth
2 **fundarse** *vpr* (**a**) *(basarse)* to be based (**en** on); **¿en qué te fundas para decir eso?** what grounds do you have for saying that?; **su conclusión se funda en los resultados de su investigación** her conclusion is based on the results of her research
(**b**) *(crearse, establecerse)* to be founded; **en esa reunión se fundaron las bases del mercado común** at that meeting the foundations were laid for the common market

> **Falso amigo**: El verbo inglés **to fund** no es la traducción del español **fundar**. En inglés **to fund** significa "financiar".

fundición *nf* (**a**) *(taller)* foundry ►► ***f. de acero*** steelworks *(singular)*, steel mill (**b**) *(fusión)* smelting (**c**) *(aleación)* cast iron

fundido, -a 1 *adj* (**a**) *(derretido) (mantequilla, hielo)* melted; *(roca, hierro, plomo)* molten (**b**) *Am Fam (arruinado)* broke; **la mitad de los productores se fundieron** half of the producers went bust (**c**) *RP Fam (agotado)* shattered, *Br* knackered; **quedé f.** I was shattered *o Br* knackered (**d**) *Perú Fam (fastidioso)* **tu vecino es bien f.** your neighbour is a real pain
2 *nm Cine (apareciendo)* fade-in; *(desapareciendo)* fade-out ►► ***f. encadenado*** dissolve; ***f. en negro*** fade-out (to black)

fundidor, -ora 1 *adj RP Fam* shattering, exhausting
2 *nm,f* foundry worker

fundidora *nf Méx* foundry

fundillo *nm Col, Ven Fam* behind, *Br* bum

fundillos *nmpl* (**a**) *Am (de pantalón)* seat (**b**) *Chile (calzoncillos) Br* underpants, *US* shorts

fundir 1 *vt* (**a**) *(derretir) (mantequilla, hielo)* to melt; *(roca, hierro, plomo)* to smelt
(**b**) *(estatua)* to cast; *(oro)* to melt down; **f. oro en lingotes** to melt down gold into ingots
(**c**) *Com* to merge
(**d**) *Cine* to fade; **f. un plano con otro** to fade one scene into another
(**e**) *(fusible, bombilla)* to blow
(**f**) *Esp Fam (gastar)* to blow
(**g**) *Am (motor)* **f. el motor** to make the engine seize up
(**h**) *Am (arruinar)* to bankrupt, to ruin
(**i**) *Fam (derrotar)* **con ese comentario fundió a su oponente** he floored his opponent with this remark
2 *vi Perú Fam (molestar)* to be a pest; **los vecinos están siempre fundiendo** our neighbours are a real pest
3 **fundirse** *vpr* (**a**) *(derretirse) (mantequilla, hielo, plomo, roca, hierro)* to melt; EXPR **se fundieron en un abrazo** they fell into one another's arms
(**b**) *(fusible, bombilla)* to blow; **se han fundido los plomos** the fuses have gone; **se ha fundido la bombilla de la cocina** the light in the kitchen has gone
(**c**) *Com* to merge
(**d**) *Am (motor)* to seize up
(**e**) *Esp Fam (gastar)* to blow; **se fundió el sueldo en una tarde** he blew his wages in one afternoon
(**f**) *Am Fam (arruinarse) (persona, negocio)* to go bust; **Rodolfo se fundió** Rodolfo went bust

fundo *nm Der* rural property

fúnebre *adj* (**a**) *(de funeral)* funeral; **coche f.** hearse; **misa f.** funeral mass (**b**) *(triste) (paisaje, rostro)* gloomy; *(música)* funereal; *(ropa)* sombre; **¿por qué están todos tan fúnebres?** what are they all looking so gloomy for?

funeral *nm* (**a**) *(misa)* funeral (service *o* mass); **los funerales del presidente** the president's funeral ►► ***f. de córpore insepulto*** funeral mass *(before the body is buried or cremated)* (**b**) *(entierro, cremación)* funeral

funerala *nf* **a la f.** *(ojo)* black

funeraria *nf* undertaker's, *US* mortician's, funeral home *o US* parlor

funerario, -a *adj* funeral; **rito f.** funeral *o* funerary rite

funesto, -a *adj* fateful, disastrous; **tuvo la funesta idea de dejar solos a los niños** he had the fateful *o* disastrous idea of leaving the children on their own

fungible *adj* disposable; **bienes fungibles** perishables

fungicida 1 *adj* fungicidal
2 *nm* fungicide

fungiforme *adj* mushroom-shaped

fungir [24] *vi Méx, Perú* to act, to serve (**de** *o* **como** as)

fungoso, -a *adj* fungous

funicular 1 *adj* funicular
2 *nm* (**a**) *(por tierra)* funicular (**b**) *(por aire)* cable car

funk [funk], **funky** ['funki] 1 *adj* **música f.** funk
2 *nm* funk

fuñido, a *adj Ven Fam* (**a**) *(persona)* annoying, difficult; **mi vecino es muy f.** my neighbour's a real pain (**b**) *(situación)* tricky, tough; **la economía está fuñida** the economic situation is pretty tricky at the moment

fuñir *Ven Fam* 1 *vt* (**a**) *(fastidiar)* to mess things up for; **siempre termina fuñendo a quien lo ayuda** he always ends up causing hassle for anyone who tries to help him (**b**) *(molestar)* to mess around
2 *vi (molestar)* **llamarme a estas horas, son ganas de f.** calling me at this time is just messing me around *o* about

furcia *nf Esp Pey* slag, whore

furgón *nm* (**a**) *(furgoneta)* van ►► ***f. policial*** *Br* police van, *US* patrol wagon
(**b**) *(de tren)* wagon, van ►► ***f. de cola*** = rear wagon of a train; **el país ocupa el f. de cola en lo que se refiere a inversión en educación en Europa** this country brings up the rear in terms of investment in education in Europe; **la cultura continúa siendo el f. de cola de la política europea** culture is still the poor relation in terms of EU policy; ***f. de equipajes*** *Br* guard's van, *US* caboose

furgoneta *nf* van ►► ***f. de reparto*** delivery van

furia *nf* (**a**) *(enfado)* fury, rage; **ponerse hecho una f.** to fly into a rage (**b**) *(violencia)* fury; **la f. de los elementos** the fury of the elements (**c**) *(ímpetu, entusiasmo)* **atacaron con furia durante la segunda parte** they attacked relentlessly throughout the second half; **atacaron con f. la posición enemiga** they launched a fierce *o* furious attack on the enemy position

furibundo, -a *adj* (**a**) *(enfadado)* furious; **me lanzó una mirada furibunda** he shot me a furious look (**b**) *(ímpetuoso, entusiasmado)* fanatical; **un f. seguidor del equipo** a fanatical supporter of the team

fúrico, -a *adj Méx Fam* mad; **ponerse f.** to go ballistic; **estaba f.** he was foaming at the mouth

furiosamente *adv* (**a**) *(con enfado, irritación)* furiously (**b**) *(violentamente)* furiously; **las olas golpeaban f. la costa** the waves beat furiously against the shore (**c**) *(con ímpetu, entusiasmo)* **atacaron f. durante toda la segunda parte** they attacked relentlessly throughout the second half

furioso, -a *adj* (**a**) *(enfadado)* furious; **ponerse f.** to get mad (**b**) *(violento)* furious; **nos atrapó una furiosa tempestad** we were caught in a raging *o* violent storm

furor *nm* (**a**) *(enfado)* fury, rage (**b**) *(violencia)* fury, raging; **el f. del viento** the fury of the wind (**c**) *(ímpetu, entusiasmo)* **trabajaban con f.** they worked furiously; **siente f. por la música country** he has a passion for country music; EXPR **causar** *o* **hacer f.** to be all the rage ►► ***f. uterino*** nymphomania

furriel *nm Mil* quartermaster

furruco *nm Ven* (**a**) *(tambor)* = traditional instrument consisting of a waxed stick passing through a drumhead, played by pulling the stick up and down (**b**) *Fam (ruido)* racket (**c**) *Fam (conversación)* tedious chatter (**d**) *Fam (vehículo)* boneshaker, jalopy

furruqueado, -a *adj Ven Fam (silla, mesa)* battered, *Br* knackered; *(camión, coche)* beat up, *Br* clapped-out

furtivamente *adv* (**a**) *(mirar, sonreír)* furtively; **sonrío f.** he smiled to himself; **la miró f.** he sneaked a look at her (**b**) *(ilegalmente)* **cazar/pescar f.** to poach

furtivo, -a 1 *adj* (**a**) *(mirada, sonrisa)* furtive; *Literario* **una lágrima furtiva recorrió su rostro** a silent tear slid down her cheek (**b**) *(ilegal)* **cazador/pescador f.** poacher; **la caza/pesca furtiva** poaching
2 *nm,f (cazador, pescador)* poacher

furúnculo *nm* boil

fusa *nf Mús* demisemiquaver

fusca *nf Esp Fam (pistola)* rod, piece; *(escopeta) Br* sawn-off shotgun, *US* sawed-off shotgun

fusco *nm Esp Fam (revólver)* rod, piece

fuseaux [fu'so] *nm inv* ski pants

fuselaje *nm* fuselage

fusible 1 *adj* fusible
2 *nm* fuse

fusil *nm* rifle ►► ***f. ametrallador*** (light) machine-gun; ***f. de asalto*** assault rifle; ***f. automático*** automatic rifle

fusilamiento *nm* (**a**) *(ejecución)* execution by firing squad; **pelotón de f.** firing squad (**b**) *Fam (plagio)* plagiarism

fusilar *vt* (**a**) *(ejecutar)* to execute by firing squad, to shoot (**b**) *Fam (plagiar)* to plagiarize

fusilería *nf* (**a**) *(fusiles)* rifles; **una descarga de f.** a salvo of rifle shots *o* fire (**b**) *(salva)* rifle shots *o* fire

fusilero *nm* fusilier, rifleman ►► *Am* ***f. naval*** marine

fusión *nf* (**a**) *(unión) (de empresas, bancos)* merger; *(de partidos)* merger, amalgamation (**b**) *Informát* merge ►► ***f. de archivos*** file merging (**c**) *(de metal, hielo)* melting (**d**) *(nuclear)* fusion ►► ***f. fría, f. en frío*** cold fusion; ***f. nuclear*** nuclear fusion; ***f. termonuclear*** thermonuclear fusion (**e**) *(estilo musical)* fusion

fusionar 1 *vt* (**a**) *(empresas, bancos)* to merge; *(de partidos)* to merge, to amalgamate (**b**) *Informát* to merge
2 **fusionarse** *vpr* to merge

fusta *nf* riding crop

fustán *nm Am* petticoat

fuste *nm* (**a**) *Arquit* shaft (**b**) *(categoría, importancia)* standing, importance; **una persona/empresa de mucho f.** a person/company of considerable standing (**c**) *Am (enagua)* petticoat

fustigar [38] *vt* (**a**) *(azotar)* to whip (**b**) *(censurar)* to criticize harshly

futbito *nm Bol, Esp* five-a-side

fútbol, *Méx* **futbol** *nm* soccer, *Br* football ►► ***f. americano*** American football, *US* football; *Esp* ***f. sala*** indoor five-a-side; *Urug* ***f. de salón*** indoor five-a-side

futbolero, -a *Fam* 1 *adj* **es muy f.** he is soccer *o Br* football crazy
2 *nm,f* soccer *o Br* football fan

futbolín *nm Esp* (**a**) *(juego) Br* table football, *US* foosball (**b**) **f., futbolines** *(local)* amusement arcade

futbolista *nmf* soccer *o Br* football player, *Br* footballer

futbolístico, -a *adj* soccer, *Br* football; **campeonato f.** soccer *o Br* football championship

futbolito *nm* (**a**) *Chile, Ven (fútbol sala)* indoor five-a-side (**b**) *Méx, Urug (futbolín) Br* table football, *US* foosball

futesa *nf* (mere) trifle

fútil *adj* trivial

futileza *nf CSur* triviality

futilidad *nf* triviality

futón *nm* futon

futre *Fam* 1 *adj* (**a**) *Chile (presumido)* big-headed, full of oneself (**b**) *Bol, Perú (endomingado)* dolled-up, *Br* tarted-up; **ponerse f.** to doll *o Br* tart oneself up
2 *nm,f* (**a**) *Chile (rico)* toff, posh person (**b**) *Bol, Perú (endomingado)* fancy dresser; **andan por ahí hechos unos futres** they go around all dolled *o Br* tarted up
3 *nm* dandy

futurible *adj* potential

futurismo *nm* futurism

futurista 1 *adj* (**a**) *Arte* futurist (**b**) *(diseño, ropa)* futuristic
2 *nmf Arte* futurist

futuro, -a 1 *adj* (**a**) *(venidero)* future; **el f. sucesor del rey** the king's heir; **su futura esposa** his wife-to-be; **no cree que haya una vida futura** he doesn't believe in an afterlife; **mi futura cuñada** my future sister-in-law; **generaciones futuras** future generations (**b**) *Gram* future
2 *nm* (**a**) *(tiempo)* future; **en el f....** in future...; **en un f. cercano** in the near future; **sin f.** with no future, without prospects; **ese negocio no tiene f.** there's no future in that business (**b**) *Gram* future; **en f.** in the future (tense) ►► ***f. imperfecto*** future (tense); ***f. perfecto*** future perfect (**c**) *Fin* **futuros** futures
3 *nm,f Fam (novio)* intended; **¿cuándo me vas a presentar a tu futura?** when are you going to introduce me to your intended?
4 **a futuro** *loc adv CSur, Méx* in the future; **eso lo veremos a f.** we'll see about that in the future *o* at some future date

futurología *nf* futurology

futurólogo, -a *nm,f* futurologist

G, g

G, g [χe] *nf (letra)* G, g
g *(abrev de* **gramo**) g
G7 *nm (abrev de* **Grupo de los Siete**) G7
G8 *nm (abrev de* **Grupo de los Ocho**) G8
Gª *(abrev de* **García**) = written abbreviation of the surname García
gabacho, -a *Fam* **1** *adj* **(a)** *Esp (francés)* Froggy **(b)** *Méx (estadounidense)* Yankee, Gringo **(c)** *Méx (rubio)* blond(e)
2 *nm,f* **(a)** *Esp (francés)* Frog **(b)** *Méx (estadounidense)* Yank, Gringo **(c)** *Méx (rubio)* blondie
gabán *nm* **(a)** *(prenda)* overcoat **(b)** *(ave)* wood stork *o* ibis
gabardina *nf* **(a)** *(prenda)* raincoat, mac **(b)** *(tela)* gabardine
gabarra *nf* barge, lighter
gabato, -a *nm,f* **(a)** *(ciervo)* faun **(b)** *(liebre)* leveret
gabela *nf* **(a)** *Hist (impuesto)* tax, duty **(b)** *(carga)* burden **(c)** *Carib, Col, Ecuad (ventaja)* advantage
gabinete *nm* **(a)** *(gobierno)* cabinet; **el g. ministerial** the cabinet; **un g. de crisis** a crisis cabinet
(b) *(despacho)* office; **g. de abogados** law practice *o* firm; **g. de arquitectos** firm of architects ▸▸ ***g. de estudios*** research department; ***g. jurídico*** legal department; ***g. de prensa*** press office; ***g. psicopedagógico*** educational psychology service
(c) *(sala)* study
(d) *Méx, RP (cubículo)* cubicle, stall
(e) *Méx (en restaurante)* private room
(f) *Méx (mueble)* cabinet, cupboard
(g) *Col (balcón)* enclosed balcony
gablete *nm Arquit* gable *(above arch)*
Gabón *n* Gabon
gabonés, -esa 1 *adj* Gabonese
2 *nm,f* Gabonese
gacela *nf* gazelle
gaceta *nf* **(a)** *(publicación)* gazette **(b)** *Fam (persona)* gossip-monger; **esa mujer es la g. del barrio** that woman is the local news service
gacetilla *nf (noticia breve)* short news item
gacetillero, -a *nm,f* **(a)** *(redactor de breves)* reporter *(responsible for writing short news items)* **(b)** *Fam Anticuado (periodista)* hack
gacha *nf Col, Ven (cuenco)* bowl
gachas *nfpl* (corn) porridge
gachí *nf Fam* chick, *Br* bird
gacho, -a *adj* **(a)** *(caído)* drooping; **caminaba con la cabeza gacha** he was walking along with his head bowed *o* hanging his head **(b)** *Méx Fam (persona)* nasty, rotten; **cómprame un helado, no seas g.** don't be rotten, buy me an ice cream **(c)** *Méx Fam (objeto)* awful, ghastly; **siempre lleva ropa muy gacha** he always dresses in awful *o* ghastly clothes **(d)** *Méx Fam (feo)* ugly as sin
gachó *nm Fam* guy, *Br* bloke
gachupín, -ina *nm,f CAm, Méx Pey* Spaniard *(living in the Americas)*
gaditano, -a 1 *adj* of/from Cadiz *(Spain)*
2 *nm,f* person from Cadiz *(Spain)*
gadolinio *nm Quím* gadolinium
gaélico, -a 1 *adj* Gaelic
2 *nm (lengua)* Gaelic
gafado, -a *adj Esp Fam* **estar g.** to be jinxed
gafar *vt Esp Fam* to jinx, to bring bad luck to
gafas *nfpl* glasses; *(protectoras, para nadar)* goggles; *(para submarinismo)* diving mask; **unas g.** a pair of glasses; **llevar g.** to wear glasses ▸▸ ***g. bifocales*** bifocal spectacles, bifocals; ***g. de cerca*** reading glasses; ***g. de esquí*** skiing goggles; ***g. graduadas*** prescription glasses; ***g. oscuras*** dark glasses; ***g. de sol*** sunglasses; ***g. submarinas*** *(para submarinismo)* diving mask; *(para nadar)* goggles
gafe *Esp Fam* **1** *adj* jinxed; **ser g.** to be jinxed
2 *nmf* jinxed person; **es un g.** he's jinxed, he's got a jinx on him
3 *nm* **tener (el) g.** to be jinxed

> **Falso amigo**: El sustantivo inglés **gaffe** no es la traducción del español **gafe**. En inglés **gaffe** significa "desliz, metedura de pata".

gafera, gafería *nf Ven Fam* **está hoy con la g.** he's in a really silly mood today
gafete *nm Méx* badge
gaffe ['gafe] *nm RP* gaffe
gafo, -a *Ven Fam* **1** *adj* **(a)** *(tonto)* dumb, dim-witted **(b)** *(ingenuo)* innocent, naive **(c)** *(torpe)* oafish, clumsy
2 *nm,f* **(a)** *(tonto)* dummy, dim-wit **(b)** *(ingenuo)* innocent **(c)** *(torpe)* clumsy oaf
gafotas *nmf inv Esp Fam* four-eyes, *Br* speccy
gag *nm (broma)* gag
gagá *adj Fam* **(a)** *(decrépito)* gaga **(b)** *Perú (elegante)* posh
gago, -a *Andes, Carib Fam* **1** *adj* stammering, stuttering; **ser g.** to have a stammer *o* stutter, to stammer, to stutter
2 *nm,f* stammerer, stutterer
gaguear *vi Andes, Carib Fam* to stammer, to stutter
gagueo *nm Andes, Carib Fam* stammer, stutter
gaguera *nf Andes, Carib Fam* stammer, stutter
gai 1 *adj* gay
2 *nm* gay
gaita[1] **1** *nf* **(a)** *(instrumento con bolsa)* bagpipes ▸▸ ***g. escocesa*** (Scottish) bagpipes; ***g. gallega*** Galician bagpipes
(b) *(flauta)* = flute similar to a flageolet
(c) *Esp Fam (molestia)* drag, pain; **es una g. tener que ir en tren** it's a pain *o* drag having to go on the train; **¡qué g.! me he vuelto a olvidar** what a pain *o* nuisance! I've forgotten again
(d) *Esp Fam (historia)* **¡déjate de gaitas!** stop your nonsense!; **¿qué lluvia ni qué gaitas! iremos aunque nieve** rain? never mind the rain! we're going even if it snows
2 *nmf RP Fam (español)* = sometimes pejorative term used to refer to a Spaniard, especially an immigrant
gaita[2] *nm Ven (canto)* = Christmas folksong
gaitero, -a *nm,f* **(a)** *(de gaita gallega)* piper, bagpiper **(b)** *(flautista)* = player of "gaita" flute
gaje *nm* **son gajes del oficio** it's all part of the job, it's an occupational hazard
gajo *nm* **(a)** *(de naranja, limón)* segment **(b)** *(racimo)* bunch **(c)** *(rama)* broken-off branch **(d)** *RP (de planta)* cutting
GAL [gal] *nm o nmpl (abrev de* **Grupos Antiterroristas de Liberación**) = former Spanish terrorist group that directed its attacks against ETA
gal *nmf (terrorista)* = member of GAL
gala *nf* **(a)** *(fiesta)* gala; **cena de g.** black tie dinner, formal dinner; **recepción de g.** gala reception; **traje de g.** formal dress; **uniforme de g.** dress uniform; **iba vestido de g.** he was in full formal dress; EXPR **hacer g. de algo** *(preciarse de)* to be proud of sth; *(exhibir)* to demonstrate sth; EXPR **tener a g. algo** to be proud of sth ▸▸ ***g. benéfica*** benefit gala
(b) **galas** *(ropa)* finery; **se puso sus mejores galas** she put on all her finery
(c) *Esp (actuación)* gala show *o* performance
(d) *ver también* **galo**
galáctico, -a *adj* galactic
galactita *nf*, **galactites** *nf inv Geol* galactite
galaico, -a *adj Formal* Galician

galaicoportugués, -esa 1 *adj* **tradiciones galaicoportuguesas** = traditions common to Portugal and Galicia
2 *nm* = language spoken in Galicia and the north of Portugal in medieval times

galán *nm* (**a**) *(hombre atractivo)* heartthrob (**b**) *Teatro* leading man, lead (**c**) ***g. de noche*** *(planta)* lady of the night; *(percha)* = bedroom stand for man's suit

galano, -a *adj* (**a**) *(en el vestir)* spruce, smart (**b**) *(estilo, discurso)* elegant (**c**) *CAm, Cuba, Méx (res)* mottled

galante *adj* gallant

galanteador, -ora 1 *adj* flirtatious
2 *nm,f* flirt

galantear *vt* to court, to woo

galantemente *adv* gallantly

galanteo *nm* courting, wooing

galantería *nf* (**a**) *(cualidad)* politeness (**b**) *(acción)* gallantry, compliment

galantina *nf* galantine; **g. de pollo** galantine of chicken

galápago *nm* (**a**) *(tortuga)* terrapin (**b**) *Hond, Perú, Ven (silla de montar)* sidesaddle (**c**) *Col (sillín)* saddle

Galápagos *nfpl* **las (islas) G.** the Galapagos Islands

galapagueño, -a *adj* of/from the Galapagos Islands

galardón *nm* award, prize

galardonado, -a 1 *adj* award-winning, prize-winning; **el g. director** the award-winning director
2 *nm,f* award winner, prizewinner

galardonar *vt* to award a prize to; **fue galardonada con un Óscar** she won an Oscar

gálata *Hist* 1 *adj* Galatian
2 *nmf* Galatian

galaxia *nf* (**a**) *(en el firmamento)* galaxy; *Fam* **es un deportista de otra g.** as a sportsman he's in a different class *o* league ►► ***g. elíptica*** elliptical galaxy; ***g. espiral*** spiral galaxy (**b**) *(mundo)* world

galbana *nf Fam* laziness, sloth

galega *nf* goat's rue, French lilac

galena *nf* galena, lead sulphide

galeno *nm Anticuado o Hum* doctor

galeón *nm* galleon

galeote *nm* galley slave

galera *nf* (**a**) *(embarcación)* galley; **condenar a galeras** to send to the galleys (**b**) *(marisco)* mantis shrimp, squilla (**c**) *CSur (sombrero)* top hat; EXPR *Fam* **sacar algo de la g.** *(improvisar)* to make sth up on the spur of the moment; *(idear)* to come up with sth (**d**) *CAm, Méx (cobertizo)* shed

galerada *nf* galley proof

galería *nf* (**a**) *(pasillo, en mina)* gallery; *(corredor descubierto)* verandah ►► ***g. subterránea*** underground passage(way) (**b**) *(establecimiento)* gallery ►► ***g. de arte*** art gallery; ***g. comercial*** shopping arcade; ***g. de tiro*** shooting gallery *(for target practice)* (**c**) *(para cortinas)* curtain rail (**d**) *(vulgo)* masses; EXPR **hacer algo para la g.** to play to the gallery

galerista *nmf* gallery owner

galerna *nf* strong north-west wind

galerón *nm* (**a**) *Col, Ven (canción, baile)* = popular song and dance (**b**) *CAm (cobertizo)* shed

Gales *n* **(el país de) G.** Wales

galés, -esa 1 *adj* Welsh
2 *nm,f (persona)* Welshman, *f* Welshwoman; **los galeses** the Welsh
3 *nm (lengua)* Welsh

galga *nf* (**a**) *Med* rash (**b**) *(piedra)* boulder (**c**) *(freno)* wagon hub brake (**d**) *(de molino)* millstone (**e**) *(para calibrar)* gauge (**f**) *CRica (hormiga)* = fast-moving yellow ant

galgo *nm* greyhound; **carreras de galgos** greyhound races; EXPR **correr como un g.** to run like the wind; EXPR **¡échale un g.!** *(cualquiera lo alcanza)* you'll never catch him now!; *(olvídate de ello)* you can forget it!; EXPR *Fam* **que no se lo salta un g.: tengo un hambre que no se lo salta un g.** I'm absolutely ravenous; **me comí un filete que no se la salta un g.** I had an absolutely huge steak ►► ***g. afgano*** Afghan hound; ***g. inglés*** greyhound

galguear *vi RP Fam (no tener plata)* to be broke *o Br* skint; **vive galgueando** he lives from hand to mouth

Galia *nf Hist* **la G.** Gaul

gálibo *nm Tec* gauge

Galicia *n* Galicia

galicismo *nm* gallicism

Galilea *n* Galilee

galileo, -a 1 *adj* Galilean
2 *nm,f* Galilean

galimatías *nm inv Fam* **las instrucciones de esta lavadora son un g.** the instructions for this washing machine are complete gibberish; **su explicación fue un g.** his explanation was in double Dutch; **el debate acabó en un auténtico g.** the debate ended up in a free-for-all

galio *nm Quím* gallium

gallada *nf Andes Fam* (**a**) *(bravuconería)* act of bravado; **hacer eso fue una g.** what he did was an act of pure bravado (**b**) *(grupo de gente)* gang; **no podemos cosechar porque falta g.** we can't bring in the harvest because we just haven't got enough bodies

gallardete *nm* pennant

gallardía *nf* (**a**) *(valentía)* bravery (**b**) *(apostura)* noble bearing

gallardo, -a *adj* (**a**) *(valiente)* brave, dashing (**b**) *(bien parecido)* fine-looking, striking

gallareta *nf* coot

gallear *vi* to strut about, to show off

gallegada *nf CSur, Cuba Fam* (**a**) *(gente española)* crowd *o* mob of Spaniards (**b**) *(españolada)* **la película es una g.** the movie plays on all the old Spanish clichés (**c**) *Pey (tontería)* silly *o* stupid thing; **deja de hacer gallegadas** stop messing about *o* playing the fool

gallego, -a 1 *adj* (**a**) *(de Galicia)* Galician (**b**) *CSur, Cuba Fam* = sometimes pejorative term used to refer to a Spanish person
2 *nm,f* (**a**) *(de Galicia)* Galician (**b**) *CSur, Cuba Fam* = sometimes pejorative term used to refer to a Spaniard, especially an immigrant
3 *nm (lengua)* Galician

galleguismo *nm* (**a**) *(palabra, expresión)* = word or expression of Galician origin (**b**) *(nacionalismo)* Galician nationalism

gallera *nf* (**a**) *(lugar de pelea)* cockpit (**b**) *(gallinero)* gamecock coop

gallería *nf Am (de gallos)* cockpit

gallero, -a *nm,f* (**a**) *(criador)* breeder of gamecocks (**b**) *(aficionado)* cockfighting enthusiast

galleta *nf* (**a**) *(para comer) Br* biscuit, *US* cookie ►► *RP* ***g. de campaña*** = type of round crusty bread; ***g. maría*** *Br* = type of tea biscuit, similar to Rich Tea, *US* = plain sweet cookie; ***g. salada*** cracker; *Andes, CAm, Méx, Ven* ***g. de soda*** cracker
(**b**) *Esp Fam (cachete)* slap, smack; **dar una g. a alguien** to give sb a slap *o* smack
(**c**) *Esp Fam (golpe)* **se dieron una g.** *(en automóvil)* they crashed the car; **me di una g. en la rodilla bajando las escaleras** I banged myself on the knee coming down the stairs
(**d**) *Méx Fam (fuerza)* **tiene mucha g.** he's dead strong
(**e**) *Chile (pan)* coarse bread
(**f**) *Ven Fam (desorden)* chaos; **se armó una g.** all hell broke loose
(**g**) *Ven Fam (atasco)* jam, bottleneck
(**h**) EXPR *Arg Fam* **colgar** *o* **dar la g. a alguien** *(despedir)* to fire sb, to give sb the sack; *(novio)* to dump sb, to jilt sb

galletero, -a 1 *adj Am Fam (adulador)* fawning
2 *nm,f Br* biscuit maker, *US* cookie maker
3 *nm Br* biscuit tin, *US* cookie tin

galliforme 1 *adj* gallinaceous
2 *nmf (animal)* bird of the *Galliformes* order
3 **galliformes** *nfpl (orden) Galliformes*

gallina 1 *adj Fam (persona)* chicken, wimp; **es muy g.** he's such a chicken *o* wimp
2 *nf* hen; **cría gallinas** *(gallinas, pollos y gallos)* he keeps chickens; EXPR *Fam* **acostarse con las gallinas** to go to bed early; EXPR *Fam* **levantarse con las gallinas** to get up at cock-crow, to be up with the lark; EXPR *Fam* **como g. en corral ajeno** like a fish out of water ►► ***g. de agua*** coot; *Fam* ***la g. ciega*** blind man's buff; ***g. clueca*** broody hen; ***g. de Guinea*** guinea fowl; ***la g. de los huevos de oro*** the golden goose, the goose that lays the golden eggs; EXPR *Fam* **matar la g. de los huevos de oro** to kill the goose that lays the golden eggs; ***g. pintada*** guinea fowl
3 *nmf Fam (persona)* chicken, coward

gallináceo, -a *Zool* 1 *adj* gallinaceous
2 *nm,f (animal)* bird of the *Galliformes* order
3 **gallináceas** *nfpl (grupo) Galliformes*

gallinazo *nm Am* turkey buzzard *o* vulture

gallinero *nm* (**a**) *(corral)* henhouse (**b**) *Fam Teatro* gods *(singular)* (**c**) *Fam (lugar alborotado)* madhouse

gallineta *nf* (**a**) *(pez)* blackbelly rosefish (**b**) *Am (ave)* guinea fowl

gallito, -a 1 *adj Fam (bravucón)* cocky; **ponerse g.** to get all cocky
2 *nm* (**a**) *Fam (bravucón)* **es un g.** he's cocky (**b**) *(ave)* northern jacana (**c**) *Col (dardo)* dart

gallo, -a 1 *adj Fam (bravucón)* cocky, full of oneself
2 *nm* (**a**) *(ave)* cock, cockerel; EXPR *Méx Fam* **ser g. duro de pelar** to be a tough nut to crack; EXPR *Fam* **en menos (de lo) que canta un g.** in no time at all; EXPR **al canto del g.** at daybreak; EXPR **otro g. cantaría, otro g. me/te/***etc.* **cantaría** it would be a different story; EXPR *Méx Fam* **se le durmió el g.** he let the chance go by; EXPR *Méx Fam* **haber comido g.** to have got out of bed on the wrong side; EXPR *Col, Ven Fam* **mamar g. a alguien** to pull sb's leg; EXPR *Méx Fam* **matarle el g. a alguien** to shut sb up; EXPR *Méx Fam* **pelar g.** to kick the bucket ▸▸ ***g. lira*** black grouse; ***g. de pelea*** fighting cock; *Carib, Nic* ***g. pinto*** rice and beans; *Andes, RP* ***g. de riña*** fighting cock
(**b**) *(al cantar)* false note; *(al hablar)* squeak; **está cambiando la voz y le salen gallos de vez en cuando** his voice is breaking so it goes squeaky sometimes
(**c**) *(pez)* John Dory
(**d**) *(bravucón)* **es un g.** he's cocky; EXPR **bajar el g. a alguien** to take sb down a peg or two; EXPR **alzar** *o* **levantar el g.** to strut about, to put on airs
(**e**) *(en boxeo)* bantamweight; **peso g.** bantamweight
(**f**) *Chile (de bomberos)* fire engine
(**g**) *Méx (serenata)* serenade; **esta noche le va a llevar g.** he's going to serenade her tonight
(**h**) *Méx, RP Fam (flema)* gob, spit
(**i**) EXPR *RP* **entre gallos y medianoche** on the fly

galludo *nm* longnose spurdog

galo, -a 1 *adj* (**a**) *Hist* Gallic (**b**) *(francés)* French
2 *nm,f* (**a**) *Hist* Gaul (**b**) *(francés)* Frenchman, *f* Frenchwoman

galocha *nf* patten

galón *nm* (**a**) *(adorno)* braid (**b**) *(de militar)* stripe (**c**) *(medida)* gallon

galopada *nf* gallop

galopante *adj (inflación, ritmo, enfermedad)* galloping

galopar *vi* to gallop

galope *nm* gallop; **al g.** at a gallop; *también Fig* **a g. tendido** at full gallop

galopín *nm* (**a**) *(pilluelo)* urchin, ragamuffin (**b**) *(pícaro)* rascal, rogue

galpón *nm Andes, Carib, RP* shed

galvánico, -a *adj* galvanic

galvanismo *nm* galvanism

galvanización *nf* galvanization

galvanizado, -a 1 *adj* galvanized
2 *nm* galvanization

galvanizar [14] *vt* (**a**) *(metal)* to galvanize (**b**) *(estimular)* to galvanize; **su llegada galvanizó a los compañeros de equipo** his arrival galvanized his teammates

galvanómetro *nm* galvanometer

galvanoplastia *nf* electroplating

gama *nf* (**a**) *(conjunto)* range; **de g. alta** top of the range; **de g. media** middle of the range; **un modelo de g. baja** an economy *o* budget model; **una computadora de g. baja** an entry-level computer (**b**) *(de colores, modelos)* range (**c**) *Mús* scale

gamada *adj* **cruz g.** swastika

gamba *nf* (**a**) *(animal) (grande)* prawn, *US* shrimp; *(pequeño)* shrimp; **cóctel de gambas** prawn cocktail ▸▸ ***gambas a la*** *o* ***con gabardina*** scampi (**b**) *Fam (pierna)* leg; EXPR **meter la g.** to put one's foot in it (**c**) *Esp Fam Antes (moneda)* = 100 peseta coin

gambado, -a *adj Carib* bowlegged

gamberrada *nf Esp (acto violento)* act of hooliganism; *(travesura)* loutish act; **¡deja de hacer gamberradas!** stop wrecking the place!

gamberrismo *nm Esp* hooliganism

gamberro, -a *Esp* 1 *adj* loutish; **es muy g.** he's a real lout *o Br* yob
2 *nm,f (persona)* hooligan, lout, *Br* yob; **hacer el g.** to behave loutishly, to cause trouble

gambeta *nf* (**a**) *(al bailar)* caper, prance (**b**) *(de caballo)* curvet

Gambia *n* The Gambia

gambiense 1 *adj* Gambian
2 *nmf* Gambian

gambito *nm (en ajedrez)* gambit

gambusia *nf (pez)* gambusia

gamelote *nm (planta)* guinea grass

gameto *nm* gamete

gamín, -ina *nm,f Col* street urchin

gamma *nf* gamma

gammaglobulina *nf* gamma globulin

gamo *nm* fallow deer

gamón *nm* onion-leaved asphodel

gamonal *nm Andes, CAm, Ven* (**a**) *(cacique)* village chief (**b**) *(caudillo)* cacique, local political boss

gamonalismo *nm Andes, CAm, Ven* caciquism

gamulán *nm RP* (**a**) *(cuero)* sheepskin (**b**) *(abrigo)* sheepskin coat

gamuza *nf* (**a**) *(tejido)* chamois (leather) (**b**) *(trapo)* duster (**c**) *(animal)* chamois

---

GANA *nf* (**a**) *(afán, deseo)* desire, wish (**de** to); **de buena/mala g.: lo hizo de buena/mala g.** she did it willingly/unwillingly; **de buena g. lo dejaría todo y me iría lejos** I'd quite happily drop everything and go off somewhere far away; **no es nada trabajador, todo lo hace de mala g.** he's not very hardworking, he always drags his feet when he has to do something; **comía con mucha g.** he ate with great relish *o* gusto; **hace el trabajo con ganas** she goes about her work with relish *o* enthusiastically; **¡con qué ganas la mandaría a paseo!** I'd just love to tell her to get lost!; **me dan ganas de llorar** I feel like crying; **me entraron ganas de marcharme** I felt like walking out; **le entraron ganas de llorar** he felt like crying; **hacer algo sin ganas** to do sth without any great enthusiasm; **morirse de ganas de hacer algo** to be dying to do sth; **me quedé con las ganas de contestarle** I would have loved to answer her back; **se me han quitado las ganas de volver al cine** it's made me feel like never going to the cinema again; **tener** *o* **sentir ganas de (hacer) algo** to feel like (doing) sth; **ya tengo ganas de que vuelvas** I'm really looking forward to you coming back; **tengo ganas de comerme un pastel** I feel like (eating) a cake; **no tengo ganas de que me pongan una multa** I don't fancy getting a fine; **tengo ganas de ir al baño** I need to go to the toilet; **¡qué ganas tengo de empezar las vacaciones!** I can't wait for the holidays to start!; **¡qué ganas tienes de buscarte problemas!** you just can't resist looking for trouble!; **¿por qué habrá dicho eso? – son ganas de fastidiar** why would he say a thing like that? – he's just being nasty; EXPR *Fam* **con ganas: tu amigo es tonto con ganas** *Br* your friend isn't half stupid, *US* your friend sure is stupid; **es un libro malo con ganas** it's a terrible book; EXPR *Fam* **dar la g.: no me da la g.** I don't feel like it; EXPR *Fam* **no le dio la real g. de ayudar** she couldn't be bothered to help; **porque me da la (real) g.** because I (jolly well) feel like it; EXPR *Fam* **tenerle ganas a alguien** *(odiarlo)* to have it in for sb; *Andes, RP Fam (desearlo)* to be after sb, to have one's eye on sb; EXPR **venirle en g. a alguien: hace/come todo lo que le viene en g.** she does/eats whatever she pleases
(**b**) *(apetito)* appetite; **comer sin ganas** to eat without appetite, to pick at one's food; **no tengo g.** I've got no appetite; **el paciente ha perdido la g.** the patient has lost his appetite

---

ganadería *nf* (**a**) *(actividad)* livestock farming (**b**) *(ganado)* livestock (**c**) *Taurom* **un toro de la g. de Pedro Jiménez** a bull from the ranch of Pedro Jiménez

ganadero, -a 1 *adj* livestock-farming; **región ganadera** livestock-farming region; **la exportación de productos ganaderos** livestock exports
2 *nm,f (propietario)* livestock farmer; *(criador)* stockbreeder; *(empleado)* stockman

ganado *nm* (**a**) *(animales)* livestock ▸▸ ***g. bovino*** cattle; ***g. caballar*** horses; ***g. cabrío*** goats; ***g. de cerda*** pigs; ***g. equino*** horses; ***g. lanar*** sheep and goats; ***g. mayor*** = cattle, horses and mules; ***g. menor*** = sheep, goats and pigs; ***g. ovino*** sheep; *Am* ***g. en pie*** livestock (on the hoof); ***g. porcino*** pigs; ***g. vacuno*** cattle
(**b**) *Fam (personas)* crowd; **en esa discoteca hay muy buen g.** you get some nice chicks *o Br* birds in that disco

ganador, -ora 1 *adj* winning; **el escritor g. del Nobel** the Nobel prize-winning writer
2 *nm,f* winner

ganancia *nf* (**a**) *(rendimiento)* profit; *(ingreso)* earnings; **ganancias y pérdidas** profit and loss; EXPR *Fam* **no te arriendo la g.** *(no te envidio)* I wouldn't like to be in your shoes, I don't envy you ▸▸ ***g. bruta*** gross profit *o* earnings; ***ganancias de capital*** capital gains; ***g. inesperada*** windfall profit; ***ganancias invisibles*** invisible earnings; ***g. líquida*** net profit *o* earnings; ***g. neta*** net profit *o* earnings; ***ganancias sobre el papel*** paper profits; ***g. total*** gross profit *o* earnings
(**b**) *Elec* gain
(**c**) *Chile, Guat, Méx (propina)* extra, bonus

ganancial *adj* **bienes gananciales** shared possessions

ganapán *nm* odd-job man

GANAR 1 *vt* (**a**) *(premio, competición)* to win; **ganaron las elecciones** they won the elections; **ganó un millón en la lotería** he won a million on the lottery
(**b**) *(obtener) (sueldo, dinero)* to earn; **gana dos millones al año** she earns *o* she's on two million a year; **¿cuánto ganas?** how much do you earn?
(**c**) *(obtener) (peso, tiempo)* to gain; **g. fama** to achieve fame; **g. importancia** to grow in importance; **g. terreno** *(avanzar)* to gain ground; **en tren ganas una hora** you save an hour by taking the train; **ganaron nuevos adeptos para la causa** they won over new converts to the cause
(**d**) *(conseguir)* **¿qué gano yo con eso?** what's in it for me?, what do I stand to gain from that?; **llorando no ganas nada** it's no use crying, crying won't change anything
(**e**) *(derrotar)* to beat; **te voy a g.** I'm going to beat you; EXPR *RP Fam* **g. de mano a alguien** to beat sb to it
(**f**) *(aventajar)* **me gana en velocidad** he's faster than me; **me gana en hermosura pero no en inteligencia** she's prettier than me, but not as intelligent; *Fam* **a tonto no hay quien le gane** he's as thick as they come
(**g**) *(alcanzar)* to reach, to make it to; **ganó la orilla a nado** she made it to *o* gained the shore
(**h**) *(conquistar)* to take, to capture; **los aliados ganaron la playa tras una dura batalla** the Allies took *o* captured the beach after a hard battle
(**i**) *(recuperar)* **han ganado terreno al desierto** they have reclaimed land from the desert
2 *vi* (**a**) *(vencer)* to win; **ganaron por tres a uno** they won three one; **ganaron por penalties** they won on penalties; **ganan de cuatro puntos** they're winning by four points, they're four points ahead; **no es justo, te has dejado g.** it's not fair, you let me beat you *o* you lost on purpose; **que gane el mejor** may the best man win
(**b**) *(lograr dinero)* to earn money; *Am* **g. bien** to be well paid; **g. mal** not to earn very much, to be badly paid; **sólo gana para subsistir** she earns only enough to live on; EXPR *Fam* **no gano para disgustos** *o* **sustos** I've more than enough worries *o* troubles
(**c**) *(mejorar)* to benefit (**con** from); **gana mucho con la barba** he looks a lot better with a beard; **ha ganado con el cambio de trabajo** he has benefited from changing jobs; **g. en algo** to gain in sth; **ha ganado en amplitud** *(parece mayor)* it looks bigger; **hemos salido ganando con el cambio** we've benefited from the change
(**d**) *Urug Fam (con hombre, mujer)* **¿viste como te mira? estás ganando** have you seen her looking at you? she fancies you *o* you're well in there
3 ganarse *vpr* (**a**) *(conquistar) (simpatía, respeto)* to earn; *(persona)* to win over; **se ganó el aprecio de sus alumnos** she earned the respect of her pupils; **se ganó el odio de sus compañeros** his colleagues came to hate him
(**b**) *(obtener)* **se gana la vida de barrendero** he earns his living as a street sweeper
(**c**) *(merecer)* to deserve; **nos hemos ganado unas vacaciones** we've earned *o* we deserve a holiday; **te vas a g. una bofetada** you'll end up getting a smack; EXPR **ganarse algo a pulso: se ha ganado a pulso su reputación de mujeriego** he has certainly earned his reputation as a ladies' man, he has a well-deserved reputation as a ladies' man; EXPR *Esp Fam* **ganársela: como no te estés quieto, te la vas a g.** if you don't stay still, you'll catch it

ganchete *nm* **ir del g.** to walk arm-in-arm

ganchillo *nm* (**a**) *(aguja)* crochet hook (**b**) *(labor)* crochet; **hacer g.** to crochet; **colcha de g.** crocheted bedspread

ganchito *nm* (**a**) *Esp (aperitivo)* = cheese-flavoured snack made from maize, *Br* ≃ Wotsit®, *US* ≃ Cheeto® (**b**) *RP (grapa)* staple (**c**) *RP (broche)* hook and eye

gancho *nm* (**a**) *(garfio)* hook; *(de percha)* peg; EXPR *Esp Fam* **echar el g. a alguien: como le eche el g. al que me ha robado la bici...** just wait till I get my hands on whoever stole my bike...
(**b**) *(cómplice) (de timador)* decoy
(**c**) *Fam (atractivo)* **esa chica tiene mucho g.** that girl is quite something *o* can really turn heads; **tiene g. como relaciones públicas** she has a real gift for public relations; **uno de los ganchos del proyecto es su bajo coste** one of the big plusses of the project is its low cost
(**d**) *(en baloncesto)* hook
(**e**) *(en boxeo)* hook; **g. de izquierda/derecha** left/right hook
(**f**) *Andes, CAm, Méx, Ven (percha)* hanger
(**g**) *Col, Ven (pinza) Br* (clothes) peg, *US* clothespin
(**h**) *Andes, CAm, Méx (horquilla)* hairpin
(**i**) *Bol, Col (imperdible)* safety pin
(**j**) *Ecuad (silla)* sidesaddle
(**k**) *Méx (labor)* crochet
(**l**) *RP (para papeles)* staple
(**m**) *RP Fam (contacto)* **hacerle g. a alguien con alguien** to fix sb up with sb; **si te gusta mi prima, te hago g.** if you fancy my cousin, I'll try to fix you up with her; **las madres les hicieron g.** their mothers tried to get them together

ganchudo, -a *adj* hooked

gandalla *nmf Méx Fam* (**a**) *(sinvergüenza)* swine (**b**) *(deshonesto)* crook

gandido, -a *adj CAm, Carib, Méx Fam* **ser g.** to be a greedy pig

gandinga *nf Carib (guisado)* liver stew

gandola *nf Ven Br* articulated lorry, *US* semitrailer

gandolero, -a *nm,f Ven* truck *o Br* lorry driver

gandul, -ula *Fam* **1** *adj* lazy
2 *nm,f* lazybones, layabout

gandulear *vi Fam* to loaf *o* bum around

gandulería *nf Fam* idleness

ganga *nf* (**a**) *(bicoca)* snip, bargain; **se lo dejo a precio de g.** I'll let you have it for a knockdown price (**b**) *(de mineral)* slag (**c**) *(ave)* pin-tailed sandgrouse

Ganges *nm* **el G.** the Ganges

ganglio *nm Anat* (**a**) **g. (linfático)** *(en vaso)* lymph node *o* gland (**b**) **g. (nervioso)** *(en nervio)* ganglion

gangoso, -a **1** *adj (voz)* nasal *(caused by cleft palate)*
2 *nm,f* = person with a nasal voice caused by a cleft palate

gangrena *nf* gangrene

gangrenado, -a *adj* gangrenous

gangrenarse *vpr* to become gangrenous; **se le gangrenó la herida** his wound became gangrenous

gangrenoso, -a *adj* gangrenous

gángster ['ganster], **gánster** (*pl* **gángsters, gángsteres**) *nm* gangster

gangsterismo [ganste'rismo], **gansterismo** *nm* gangsterism

ganguear *vi* to speak nasally, to speak through one's nose

gansada *nf Fam (acto, dicho)* **hacer gansadas** to clown around; **no digas gansadas** don't talk nonsense

gansear *vi Fam (hacer tonterías)* to clown around; *(decir tonterías)* to talk nonsense

ganso, -a **1** *adj Fam* (**a**) *(alto)* tall (**b**) *(grande)* huge, enormous; *Esp* **me costó una pasta gansa** it cost me a fortune *o* an arm and a leg (**c**) *Esp (genial)* great, terrific
2 *nm,f* (**a**) *(ave) (hembra)* goose; *(macho)* gander ▸▸ ***g. de las nieves*** snow goose; ***g. del Nilo*** Egyptian goose (**b**) *Fam (tonto)* idiot, fool; **hacer el g.** to clown around (**c**) *Fam (perezoso)* lazy so-and-so
3 *nm Ven* rump (steak)

gánster = **gángster**

gansterismo = **gangsterismo**

ganzúa *nf* picklock

gañán *nm* (**a**) *(hombre rudo)* lout, boor (**b**) *(bracero)* farm labourer

gañido *nm* yelp

gañir *vi* (**a**) *(perro)* to yelp (**b**) *(ave)* to croak, to caw (**c**) *(persona)* to wheeze

gañote *nm Fam* gullet

garabatear, garrapatear **1** *vt* (**a**) *(escribir)* to scribble (**b**) *(dibujar) (como un bebé)* to scribble; *(más artísticamente)* to doodle
2 *vi* (**a**) *(escribir)* to scribble (**b**) *(dibujar) (como un bebé)* to scribble; *(más artísticamente)* to doodle

garabato, garrapato *nm* (**a**) *(escribir)* scribble; **hacer garabatos** to scribble (**b**) *(dibujo) (de bebé)* scribble; *(más artístico)* doodle (**c**) *(gancho)* hook

garaje, *Am* **garage** *nm* (**a**) *(estacionamiento)* garage (**b**) *(taller)* garage

garajista, *Am* **garagista** *nmf* garage attendant

garambaina *nf* (**a**) *(adorno)* trinket (**b**) *Fam (tontería)* **¡déjate de garambainas!** stop that nonsense!, stop messing about!

garambullo *nm* myrtillocactus

garante *nmf (de productos)* warrantor; *(de créditos)* guarantor; **salir g.** to act as guarantor

garantía **1** *nf* (**a**) *(seguro, promesa)* guarantee; **me ha dado su g. de que lo hará** she guaranteed that she'd do it; **no tenemos ninguna g. de que vaya a lucir el sol** there's no guarantee that it will be sunny; **ser g. de algo** to guarantee sth; **su diseño futurista es g. de éxito** its futuristic design means its success is assured ►► *Pol* ***garantías constitucionales*** constitutional rights; *Fin* ***g. prendaria*** collateral security

(**b**) *(de producto)* guarantee, warranty; **viene con una g. de tres años, tiene tres años de g.** it comes with a three-year guarantee *o* warranty, it has a three-year guarantee *o* warranty; **estar en g.** to be under guarantee ►► ***g. de por vida*** lifetime guarantee

(**c**) *(fianza)* surety; **dejó su reloj como g.** he left his watch as security

2 de garantía *loc adj* reliable, dependable

garantizado, -a *adj* guaranteed

garantizar [14] *vt* (**a**) *(asegurar)* to guarantee; **te garantizo que te lo devolveré el viernes** I guarantee *o* I assure you I'll give it back to you on Friday; **la central garantiza el suministro eléctrico a la ciudad** the power station ensures the city's supply of electricity

(**b**) *(contra riesgo, deterioro)* to guarantee; **les garantizaron el televisor por un año** they guaranteed the television for a year, they gave them a year's guarantee for the television

(**c**) *(avalar)* to vouch for

garañón *nm (caballo)* stud horse

garapiña *nf Cuba, Méx (bebida)* = drink made with pineapple skin and sugar

garbancero, -a *adj* chickpea; **zona garbancera** chickpea-growing area

garbanzo *nm* chickpea; EXPR *Fam* **ganarse** *o* **buscarse los garbanzos** to earn one's living *o* one's daily bread; EXPR *Fam* **ser el g. negro (de la familia)** to be the black sheep of the family

garbeo *nm Esp Fam* **dar un g.** *(caminando)* to go for *o* take a stroll; *(en vehículo)* to go for a spin

garbo *nm* (**a**) *(de persona)* grace; **se mueve con mucho g.** he moves very gracefully (**b**) *(de escritura)* stylishness, style

garbosamente *adv (con gracia)* gracefully

garboso, -a *adj* (**a**) *(persona)* graceful (**b**) *(escritura)* stylish

garceta *nf* little egret

garchar *RP Vulg* **1** *vt* to screw, to fuck

2 *vi* to screw, to fuck

garcilla *nf* ►► ***g. bueyera*** cattle egret; ***g. cangrejera*** squacco heron

garçon: a lo garçon *loc adv* in a bob, very short; **llevaba el pelo cortado a lo g.** she had her hair in a bob

garçonniere [garso'njer] *nm RP* bachelor pad

gardenia *nf* gardenia

garduña *nf* beech *o* stone marten

garete *nm* EXPR *Fam* **ir** *o* **irse al g.** *(fracasar)* to go down the drain, to go to pot

garfio *nm* hook

gargajear *vi* to spit

gargajo *nm Fam* gob of phlegm; **el suelo estaba lleno de gargajos** the floor was covered in phlegm; **escupió un g. en el suelo** he spat a gob of phlegm on the floor

garganta *nf* (**a**) *(conducto interno)* throat; **me duele la g.** I've got a sore throat; EXPR *Fam* **lo tengo atravesado en la g.** he/it sticks in my gullet *o* throat (**b**) *(cuello)* neck (**c**) *(voz)* (singing) voice; **tiene buena g.** he has a good (singing) voice (**d**) *(desfiladero)* gorge

gargantilla *nf* choker

gargantúa *nmf* big eater, glutton

gárgara *nf Col, Chile, Méx (elixir)* gargle

gárgaras *nfpl* gargling; **hacer g.** to gargle; *Fam* **nuestros planes se fueron a hacer gárgaras** our plans went out the window; EXPR *Fam* **mandar a alguien a hacer g.** to send sb packing; EXPR *Fam* **¡vete a hacer g.!** get lost!

gargarismo *nm* (**a**) *(líquido)* gargle (**b**) *(acción)* gargle, gargling

gárgola *nf* gargoyle

garguero, gargüero *nm Fam* windpipe

garita *nf* (**a**) *(de centinela)* sentry box (**b**) *(de conserje)* lodge

garito *nm* (**a**) *(casa de juego)* gambling den (**b**) *Fam (establecimiento)* **vamos a un g. a tomar algo** let's go someplace for a drink; **un g. de mala muerte** a dive

garlar *vi Fam* to chatter

garlito *nm Fam (trampa)* trap, snare; EXPR **caer en el g.** to fall for it

garlopa *nf* trying plane, jointing plane

garnacha *nf (uva)* grenache, = very sweet purplish grape

garpar *RP Fam* **1** *vt* to fork out for

2 *vi* to cough up

garra *nf* (**a**) *(de mamífero)* claw; *(de ave)* talon, claw

(**b**) *(de persona)* paw, hand; **¡quítame las garras de encima!** get your paws *o* dirty hands off me!; **caer en las garras de alguien** to fall into sb's clutches; EXPR *Fam* **echar la g. a alguien** to get *o* lay hold of sb; **quedó atrapado en las garras de la droga** he was trapped in the clutches of drug addiction

(**c**) *Fam (atractivo)* **tener g.** *(persona)* to have charisma; *(novela)* to be gripping; *(canción)* to be catchy

(**d**) *(coraje)* gutsiness, fighting spirit; **un ciclista con mucha g.** a very gutsy cyclist ►► *RP* ***la g. charrúa*** Uruguayan fighting spirit *(inherited from the Charrúa, a nomadic indigenous people)*

(**e**) *RP Fam (objeto malo)* **esta computadora es una g.** this computer is *Br* rubbish *o US* garbage

garrafa *nf* (**a**) *(botella)* carafe; *Fam* **de g.** *(bebida alcohólica)* cheap and nasty (**b**) *RP (bombona)* gas cylinder *o* bottle

garrafal *adj* monumental, enormous

garrafón *nm* (**a**) *(damajuana)* demijohn (**b**) *Méx (botella grande)* = large glass bottle for purified water

garrapata *nf* tick

garrapatear = **garabatear**

garrapato = **garabato**

garrapiñado, -a *adj* caramel-coated

garrapiñar *vt (fruta)* to candy; *(almendras)* to coat with caramelized sugar

garrido, -a *adj* elegant, smart

garriga *nf* uncultivated scrubland

garrobo *nm CAm* iguana

garrocha *nf* (**a**) *(lanza)* pike, lance (**b**) *Am (pértiga)* (vaulting) pole; **salto con g.** pole vault

garrochista *nm Am* pole vaulter

garrón *nm* (**a**) *(de animal)* = hoof by which dead animals are hung

(**b**) *RP Fam (decepción)* let-down; **la película fue un g.** the movie *o Br* film was a real let-down

(**c**) *RP Fam (contratiempo)* drag; **dos horas de cola, ¡qué g.!** two hours *Br* queuing *o US* standing in line, what a drag!

(**d**) EXPR *RP Fam* **de g.** *(sin pagar)* (for) free; *(de pura suerte)* by sheer luck; **siempre fuma de g.** he's always scrounging *o* cadging cigarettes; **nos salvamos de g.** it was sheer luck that we escaped

garronear *RP Fam* **1** *vt* (**a**) *(pedir)* to scrounge, to cadge; **siempre está garroneando cigarros** she's always scrounging *o* cadging cigarettes (**b**) *(ser tacaño con)* to be stingy with, to skimp on; **vamos a cenar a un restaurante, que en su casa siempre te garronea (la comida)** let's go to a restaurant for dinner, he's always really stingy with the food at his place

2 *vi* to scrounge, to sponge; **mi vecino vive garroneando** my neighbour's always scrounging, my neighbour's always sponging off people

garronero, -a *RP Fam* **1** *adj* **ser g.** to be a scrounger *o* sponger

2 *nm,f* scrounger, sponger

garrota *nf* (**a**) *(garrote)* club, stick (**b**) *(bastón)* (walking) stick

garrotazo *nm* blow with a club *o* stick; **dar un g. a alguien** to club sb

garrote *nm* (**a**) *(palo)* club, stick (**b**) *(instrumento de ejecución)* **g. (vil)** garrotte; **dar g. (vil) a alguien** to garotte sb (**c**) *Méx (freno)* brake

garrotero, -a *nm,f Méx Ferroc* brakeman, *f* brakewoman

garrotillo *nm Med* croup

garrucha *nf* pulley

garrudo, -a *adj Méx (forzudo)* muscular, brawny

garrulería *nf Fam Pey* **garrulerías** *(de garrulo)* uncouth *o* loutish behaviour

garrulo, -a *Fam Pey* **1** *adj* coarse, uncouth

2 *nm,f* country bumpkin, yokel, *US* hick

gárrulo, -a *adj* (**a**) *(hablador)* garrulous, talkative (**b**) *(ave)* noisy

garúa *nf Andes, RP, Ven* drizzle; **caía una suave g.** it was drizzling gently

garuar *v impersonal Andes, RP, Ven (lloviznar)* to drizzle

garufa *nm RP* **es un g.** he likes living it up, he's a fun-loving sort of person; **irse de g.** to go out on the town

garza *nf* heron ►► ***g. imperial*** purple heron; ***g. real*** grey heron

garzo, -a *adj Literario* azure

garzón, -ona *nm,f Chile* waiter, *f* waitress

gas *nm* (**a**) *(fluido)* gas; **un horno de g.** a gas oven; **calefacción de g.** gas heating; **acaban de instalarnos el g.** they've just connected the gas; **con g.** *(agua, bebida)* sparkling; *Aut* **dale g.** step on the accelerator ►► ***g. butano*** butane (gas); *CSur* ***g. de cañería*** town gas; ***g. de carbón*** coal gas; *Esp* ***g. ciudad*** town gas; ***g. hilarante*** laughing gas;

g. de hulla coal gas; ***g. ideal*** ideal gas; ***gas inerte*** inert gas; ***g. lacrimógeno*** tear gas; ***g. licuado*** liquefied gas; *Méx* ***g. LP*** LPG, liquefied petroleum gas; ***g. mostaza*** mustard gas; ***g. natural*** natural gas; ***g. noble*** noble gas; ***g. de los pantanos*** marsh gas; ***g. perfecto*** ideal gas; ***g. propano*** propane gas; ***g. sarín*** sarin gas; ***g. tóxico*** poison gas

(**b**) **gases** *(en el estómago)* wind; **las legumbres dan muchos gases** pulses give you a lot of wind *o US* gas

(**c**) *Esp Fam (fuerza)* **aun jugando a medio g. ganaron** they won even though they weren't really trying; **quedarse sin g.** to run out of steam

(**d**) *Esp Fam (velocidad)* **corrió a todo g.** he ran flat out *o* at top speed; **leí el periódico a todo g.** I read the newspaper as fast as I could

gasa *nf* gauze

gasear *vt* to gas

gaseoducto *nm* gas pipeline

gaseosa *nf* (**a**) *Esp, Arg (bebida transparente)* pop, *Br* lemonade (**b**) *CAm, RP (refresco con gas)* fizzy drink, *US* soda

gaseoso, -a *adj* (**a**) *(estado)* gaseous (**b**) *(bebida)* fizzy

gásfiter *nmf Chile, Perú* plumber

gasfitería *nf Chile, Perú* plumber's (shop)

gasfitero, -a *nm,f Ecuad* plumber

gasificación *nf* gasification

gasificar [60] *vt* (**a**) *(convertir en gas)* to gasify (**b**) *(bebida)* to carbonate

gasoducto *nm* gas pipeline

gasofa *nf Esp Fam (fuel)* juice

gasóleo, gasoil *nm* (**a**) *(para vehículos)* diesel (oil) (**b**) *(para calderas)* oil, gas-oil

gasolero, -a *RP* **1** *adj* (**a**) *(vehículo)* diesel-powered, diesel-engined (**b**) *Fam (persona)* thrifty

2 *nm (vehículo)* diesel, diesel-engined *o* diesel-powered vehicle

3 *nm,f Fam (persona)* thrifty person

gasolina *nf Br* petrol, *US* gas, *US* gasoline; **echar** *o* **poner g.** to put some *Br* petrol *o US* gas in ►► ***g. normal*** *Br* three-star petrol, *US* regular gasoline; ***g. con plomo*** leaded *Br* petrol *o US* gasoline; ***g. sin plomo*** unleaded *Br* petrol *o US* gasoline; ***g. súper*** *Br* four-star petrol, *US* premium-grade gasoline

gasolinera *nf* (**a**) *(establecimiento) Br* petrol station, *US* gas station (**b**) *(lancha)* motorboat

gasolinería *nf Méx Br* petrol station, *US* gas station

gasómetro *nm* gasometer

Gaspar *n pr* Caspar

gastado, -a *adj (objeto)* worn out; *(frase, tema)* hackneyed; *(persona)* broken, burnt out; *(pila)* dead; *(batería)* flat

gastador, -ora 1 *adj* spendthrift

2 *nm,f* spendthrift

gastar 1 *vt* (**a**) *(dinero)* to spend; **g. algo en algo** to spend sth on sth; **gastó una fortuna en decorar la casa** she spent a fortune (on) decorating the house

(**b**) *(consumir) (tiempo)* to spend; *(gasolina, electricidad)* to use; **esta lámpara gasta mucha electricidad** this lamp uses a lot of electricity; **esta moto gasta muy poco** this motorbike uses very little *Br* petrol *o US* gas; **mi coche gasta 7 litros a los cien** ≃ my car does 41 miles to the gallon

(**c**) *(malgastar) (dinero, energía)* to waste

(**d**) *(desgastar) (ropa, zapatos)* to wear out

(**e**) *Esp (tener, usar) (ropa)* to wear; **gasta sombrero** he wears a hat; **gasto el 42** I take a size 42, I'm a size 42

(**f**) *Esp (hacer)* **g. una broma (a alguien)** to play a joke (on sb)

(**g**) *Esp (genio)* **g. mal genio** to have a bad temper; *Esp* **gastarlas** to carry on, to behave; **¡no sabes cómo se las gastan allí!** you can't imagine how they carry on there!

(**h**) *RP Fam (burlarse de)* to make fun of

2 *vi* to spend (money)

3 gastarse *vpr* (**a**) *(deteriorarse, desgastarse)* to wear out (**b**) *(consumirse)* to run out; **se nos ha gastado el aceite** we've run out of oil; **se gastó toda el agua que teníamos** we've used up all the water we had; **se han gastado las pilas** the batteries have run out *o* gone dead (**c**) *(dinero)* to spend; **nos gastamos veinte pesos en comida** we spent twenty pesos on food

gasto *nm (dinero gastado)* spending; *(costo)* expense; **el g. de energía** energy consumption; **el g. educativo/militar** *(de país)* spending on education/defence; **los gastos de la casa** household expenses; **mis padres me dan dinero para mis gastos** my parents give me pocket money; **correr con los gastos (de algo)** to meet *o* bear the cost (of sth), to pay (for sth); **cubrir gastos** to cover costs, to break even; **no reparar en gastos** to spare no expense ►► *Fin* ***g. amortizable*** capitalized expense; *CSur* ***gastos comunes*** service charge; ***gastos de comunidad*** service charge; *Com* ***gastos corrientes*** running costs; *Fin* ***g. deducible*** tax-deductible expense; ***gastos de desplazamiento*** relocation expenses, settling-in allowance; *Com* ***gastos diversos*** sundries; ***gastos de envío*** postage and packing; *Com* ***gastos de explotación*** operating costs; *Com* ***gastos fijos*** fixed charges *o* costs; *(en una casa)* overheads; ***gastos financieros*** financing charges; *Com* ***gastos generales*** overheads; *Fin* ***gastos de gestión*** handling charges; ***gastos de mantenimiento*** maintenance costs; ***gastos de personal*** personnel expenses, staffing costs; ***g. público*** public expenditure; ***gastos de representación*** entertainment allowance; *Fin* ***gastos de tramitación*** handling charges; ***gastos de transporte*** freight charges, transport costs; ***gastos de viaje*** travelling expenses

gástrico, -a *adj* gastric

gastritis *nf inv Med* gastritis

gastroenteritis *nf inv* gastroenteritis

gastroenterología *nf* gastroenterology

gastrointestinal *adj* gastrointestinal

gastronomía *nf* gastronomy

gastronómico, -a *adj* gastronomic

gastrónomo, -a *nm,f* gourmet, gastronome

gata *nf* (**a**) *Chile, Perú Aut* jack (**b**) *ver también* **gato**

gatas: a gatas *loc adv* (**a**) *Fam (a cuatro patas)* on all fours; **andar** *o* **ir a g.** to crawl

(**b**) *RP (apenas)* barely; **estoy cansadísima, a g. llegué aquí** I'm shattered, I barely managed to make it here; **¿sabes la lección? – a g.** do you know your lesson? – sort of; **¿le pedimos que nos regale un auto? – a g. va a poder comprarnos una bicicleta** shall we ask him to give us a car? – he can barely afford to buy us a bicycle

gatear *vi* to crawl

gatera *nf* (**a**) *(puerta)* cat flap *o* door (**b**) *Andes (persona)* market stallholder

gatillazo *nm Fam* **dio** *o* **pegó (el) g.** he couldn't get it up

gatillero, -a *nm,f Méx* hired gunman *o* killer

gatillo *nm* trigger

gatito, -a *nm,f* kitten

gato, -a 1 *nm,f* (**a**) *(animal)* cat; EXPR *Fam* **dar g. por liebre a alguien** to swindle *o* cheat sb; EXPR *Fam* **aquí hay g. encerrado** there's something fishy going on here; EXPR *Fam* **llevarse el g. al agua** to pull it off; EXPR *Fam* **cuatro gatos,** *RP* **cuatro gatos locos: sólo había cuatro gatos** there was hardly a soul there; *Esp* **nos apuntamos cuatro gatos** hardly anyone signed up for it; EXPR *Fam* **defenderse/resistir como g. panza arriba** to defend oneself/resist tooth and nail; EXPR *Fam* **tener más vidas que un g.** to have nine lives; PROV *Fam* **cuando el g. duerme, bailan los ratones** when the cat's away the mice will play; PROV **g. escaldado (del agua fría huye)** once bitten twice shy ►► ***g. de algalia*** civet; ***g. de Angora*** Angora cat; ***el g. con botas*** Puss in Boots; ***g. montés*** wildcat; ***g. persa*** Persian cat; ***g. siamés*** Siamese cat

(**b**) *Esp Fam (madrileño)* = person from Madrid

(**c**) *Méx Fam Pey (sirviente)* flunkey

2 *nm* (**a**) *Aut* jack (**b**) *(danza)* = Argentine folk dance (**c**) *Méx (tres en raya) Br* noughts and crosses, *US* tick-tack-toe

GATT [gat] *nm (abrev de* **General Agreement on Tariffs and Trade***)* GATT

gatuno, -a *adj* catlike, feline

gatuña *nf* restharrow

gauchada *nf CSur* favour; **hacerle una g. a alguien** to do sb a favour

gauchesco, -a *adj* gaucho; **literatura gauchesca** = literature about gauchos and their life

gauchismo *nm* = literary movement focused on gaucho life

gaucho, -a 1 *adj RP Fam (servicial)* helpful, obliging

2 *nm,f* gaucho

gaullismo [go'lismo] *nm Pol* Gaullism

gaullista [go'lista] *Pol* **1** *adj* Gaullist

2 *nmf* Gaullist

gavera *nf Ven* (**a**) *(para botellas)* crate (**b**) *(para hielo)* ice tray

gaveta *nf* drawer

gavia *nf* (**a**) *(vela)* topsail (**b**) *(gaviota)* seagull

gavial *nm* gavial

gavilán *nm* sparrowhawk

gavilla *nf* **(a)** *(haz)* sheaf **(b)** *RP (banda)* gang

gavillero *nm Am (persona)* thug

gavión *nm (armazón)* gabion

gaviota *nf* seagull ►► ***g. argéntea*** herring gull; ***g. cabecinegra*** Mediterranean gull; ***g. cana*** gull; ***g. enana*** little gull; ***g. reidora*** black-headed gull; ***g. sombría*** lesser black-backed gull; ***g. tridáctila*** kittiwake

gay [gai, gei] **1** *adj inv* gay
2 *nm* gay

gayal *nm* gayal

gayo, -a *adj Literario (alegre)* gay ►► ***gaya ciencia*** *(la poesía)* art of poetry

gayola *nf RP Fam* slammer, clink; **en g.** in the slammer *o* clink

gayomba *nf* Spanish broom

gayumbos *nmpl Esp Fam (calzoncillos)* pants, *US* shorts

gazapera *nf (madriguera)* burrow, rabbit hole

gazapo *nm* **(a)** *(animal)* young rabbit **(b)** *(error) (en texto)* misprint; *(al hablar)* slip of the tongue; *(en película)* goof

gazmoñería *nf* sanctimoniousness

gazmoño, -a **1** *adj* sanctimonious, priggish
2 *nm,f* prig

gaznápiro, -a *Fam* **1** *adj* simple-minded, dull-witted
2 *nm,f* numbskull, dunce

gaznatada *nf CAm, Carib (bofetada)* slap

gaznate *nm Fam* gullet; **se echó un trago de ron al g.** he took a swig of rum; EXPR **remojar el g.** to wet one's whistle, to have a drink

gazpacho *nm* gazpacho, = Andalusian soup made from tomatoes, peppers, cucumbers and bread, served chilled

gazpachuelo *nm* = hot gazpacho with poached eggs

gazuza *nf Fam (hambre)* **tener g.** to be famished *o* ravenous

gazuzo, -a *adj Fam* famished, ravenous

GB *nf* **(a)** *(abrev de* **Gran Bretaña**) GB **(b)** *Informát (abrev de* **gigabyte**) GB

géiser, géyser *nm* geyser

geisha ['geisa] *nf* geisha

gel *nm* gel ►► ***g. de baño*** shower gel; ***g. moldeador*** styling gel; ***g. de sílice*** silica gel

gelatina *nf* **(a)** *(de carne)* gelatine **(b)** *(en jamón)* jelly **(c)** *(de fruta) Br* jelly, *US* Jell-O®

gelatinoso, -a *adj* gelatinous

gélido, -a *adj* gelid, icy

gelificar **1** *vt* to gel
2 *vi* to gel

gelifracción = **gelivación**

gelignita *nf* gelignite

gelivación, gelifracción *nf Geol* gelifraction

gema *nf* gem

gemación *nf Bot* gemmation

gemelo, -a **1** *adj* **hermano g.** twin brother, twin; **ser el alma gemela de alguien** to be sb's soulmate
2 *nm,f (persona)* (identical) twin ►► ***g. monocigótico*** identical twin; ***g. univitelino*** identical twin
3 *nm* **(a)** *(músculo)* calf muscle **(b)** **gemelos** *(de camisa)* cuff links
4 **gemelos** *nmpl (prismáticos)* binoculars; *(para teatro)* opera glasses; **unos gemelos** a pair of binoculars/opera glasses

gemido *nm* **(a)** *(de persona)* moan, groan; **dar gemidos** to groan **(b)** *(de animal)* whine **(c)** *(de viento)* moan; **los gemidos del viento** the moaning of the wind

geminación *nf Ling* gemination

geminado, -a *adj* geminate

geminiano, -a *Am* **1** *adj* Gemini; **ser g.** to be (a) Gemini
2 *nm,f* Gemini; **los g. son...** Geminis are...

Géminis **1** *adj inv* Gemini; *Esp* **ser G.** to be (a) Gemini
2 *nm (signo)* Gemini; *Am* **los de G. son...** Geminis are...
3 *nmf inv (persona)* Gemini; *Esp* **los G. son...** Geminis are...

gemir [47] *vi* **(a)** *(persona)* to moan, to groan; **g. de placer** to moan *o* groan with pleasure **(b)** *(animal)* to whine **(c)** *(viento)* to moan

gemología *nf* gemology

gemólogo, -a *nm,f* gemologist

gen *nm Biol* gene ►► ***g. dominante*** dominant gene

genciana *nf* gentian

gendarme *nmf* gendarme

gendarmería *nf* gendarmerie

genealogía *nf* genealogy

genealógico, -a *adj* genealogical

genealogista *nmf* genealogist

generación *nf* **(a)** *(conjunto de personas)* generation
(b) *(de artistas, intelectuales)* generation
(c) *(de máquinas, tecnología)* generation; **los monitores de la última g. son más ligeros** the latest generation of monitors are lighter
(d) *(acción)* generation; **la g. de puestos de trabajo** job creation; **la g. de basuras es un grave problema** waste production is a serious problem ►► ***g. espontánea*** spontaneous generation

generacional *adj* generational; **conflicto g.** conflict between the generations, generation gap

generador, -ora **1** *adj* generating
2 *nm Elec* generator ►► ***g. eléctrico*** electric generator; ***g. eólico*** wind turbine

general **1** *adj* **(a)** *(común)* general; **sólo tengo unas nociones muy generales de griego** I only have a very general knowledge of Greek; **esa es la opinión g. de los que no leen los periódicos** that's what people who don't read the papers usually think; **mi valoración g. es negativa** my overall opinion of it is negative
(b) *(en frases)* **por lo g., en g.** in general, generally; **los candidatos, en g., estaban muy cualificados** the candidates were generally very well qualified, in general, the candidates were very well qualified; **en g. el clima es seco** on the whole, the climate is dry, the climate is generally dry; **¿qué tal te va la vida? – en g., no me puedo quejar** how's life treating you? – I can't complain, on the whole; **por lo g., suelo ir en tren** I generally go by train, in general I go by train
2 *nm Mil* general ►► ***g. de brigada*** *Br* brigadier, *US* brigadier general; ***g. de división*** major general
3 *nf Dep (clasificación)* overall standings; **con su victoria se ha puesto segunda en la g.** her victory has moved her up to second place in the overall standings

generala *nf* **(a)** *Mil (toque)* call to arms; **tocar a g.** to sound the call to arms **(b)** *Fam (mujer del general)* general's wife

generalato *nm* **(a)** *(grado)* rank of general **(b)** *(conjunto)* generals

Generalidad *nf* **la G.** = the autonomous government of the regions of Catalonia or Valencia or the Balearic Islands

generalidad *nf* **(a)** *(mayoría)* majority **(b)** *(vaguedad)* generalization **(c)** **generalidades** *(principios básicos)* basic principles

generalísimo *nm* supreme commander, generalissimo; *Hist* **el G.** = title given to Franco

generalista **1** *adj* generalist; **un enfoque g.** a generalist approach; **médico g.** general practitioner
2 *nmf* general practitioner

Generalitat [jenerali'tat] *nf* **la G.** = the autonomous government of the regions of Catalonia or Valencia or the Balearic Islands

generalizable *adj* **un análisis g. al mundo capitalista** an analysis that can also be applied to the capitalist world; **esta técnica está lejos de ser g.** this technique can by no means be applied in all cases

generalización *nf* **(a)** *(comentario)* generalization **(b)** *(extensión) (de conflicto)* spread, widening; *(de prácticas, enseñanza)* spread; **apoyan la g. del uso de la bicicleta** they are in favour of more widespread use of the bicycle

generalizado, -a *adj* widespread

generalizar [14] **1** *vt* to spread, to make widespread
2 *vi* to generalize; **no generalices** don't generalize, don't make generalizations
3 **generalizarse** *vpr* to become widespread; **una costumbre que se ha generalizado** a custom that has become widespread

generalmente *adv* generally

generar *vt* **(a)** *(originar, causar)* to generate; **la decisión generó odios** the decision caused much resentment **(b)** *(crear) (energía)* to generate; *(empleo)* to create; **g. algo por ordenador** to generate sth by computer; **generado por ordenador** computer-generated

generativo, -a *adj* generative

generatriz *Geom* **1** *adj* generational
2 *nf* generatrix

genéricamente *adv* generically

genérico, -a **1** *adj (común)* generic
2 *nm (medicamento)* generic drug

género *nm* **(a)** *(clase)* kind, type; **es el mejor de su g.** it's the best of its kind; **sin ningún g. de dudas** absolutely without a doubt; **el g. humano** the human race
(b) *(literario, cinematográfico)* genre ►► ***el g. chico*** = type of short,

often musical farce, popular in Spain at the turn of the 20th century; ***g. lírico*** opera

(**c**) *Gram* gender; **de g. ambiguo** = that may be either masculine or feminine ►► ***g. femenino*** feminine gender; ***g. masculino*** masculine gender; ***g. neutro*** neuter gender

(**d**) *Biol* genus

(**e**) *(productos)* merchandise, goods

(**f**) *(tejido)* cloth, material ►► *Esp* ***géneros de punto*** knitwear

generosamente *adv* generously

generosidad *nf* generosity; **con g.** generously

generoso, -a *adj* (**a**) *(dadivoso)* generous; **fue muy g. con sus hermanos** he was very generous to his brothers and sisters; **ha sido muy g. de tu parte** it was very generous of you; *Irónico* **¡gracias, g.!** you're too kind!

(**b**) *(grande)* generous; **una ración generosa** a generous helping; **una mujer de formas generosas** a woman with an ample figure, an amply-proportioned woman

(**c**) *(vino)* generous, full-bodied

génesis 1 *nf inv* genesis

2 *nm inv Rel* **el G.** Genesis

genética *nf* genetics *(singular)*

genéticamente *adv* genetically

geneticista *nmf* geneticist

genético, -a *adj* genetic

genetista *nmf* geneticist

Gengis Kan *n pr* Genghis Khan

genial 1 *adj* (**a**) *(artista, escritor)* **un escritor g.** an author who was a genius, an author of genius; **Dalí fue un artista g.** Dalí was an artistic genius (**b**) *Fam (estupendo)* great, *Br* brilliant; **me parece g.** it sounds like a great idea to me; **estuviste g.** you were brilliant *o* great; *Irónico* **¡g., tendré que empezar otra vez!** great *o Br* brilliant! now I'll have to start all over again!

2 *adv Fam* brilliantly; **canta g.** she's a great *o Br* brilliant singer

> **Falso amigo**: El adjetivo inglés **genial** no es la traducción del español **genial**. En inglés **genial** significa "cordial, amable".

genialidad *nf* (**a**) *(capacidad)* genius (**b**) *(acción)* stroke of genius

> **Falso amigo**: El sustantivo inglés **geniality** no es la traducción del español **genialidad**. En inglés **geniality** significa "cordialidad, amabilidad".

genialmente *adv (con talento)* brilliantly

> **Falso amigo**: El adverbio inglés **genially** no es la traducción del español **genialmente**. En inglés **genially** significa "cordialmente, amablemente".

génico, -a *adj Biol* gene; **terapia génica** gene therapy

geniecillo *nm* elf

genio *nm* (**a**) *(talento)* genius; EXPR **g. y figura (hasta la sepultura)** a true genius

(**b**) *(persona)* genius; **un g. del arte moderno** one of the geniuses of modern art

(**c**) *(carácter)* nature, disposition; **corto de g.** timid

(**d**) *(personalidad fuerte)* spirit; **tiene mucho g.** she's very feisty

(**e**) *(mal carácter)* bad temper; **estar de mal g.** to be in a mood; **tener mal** *o* **mucho g.** to be bad-tempered

(**f**) *(ser fantástico)* genie

(**g**) *Mitol* genie

genioso, -a *adj Méx Fam* bad tempered, moody

genista *nf* broom *(plant)*

genital 1 *adj* genital

2 genitales *nmpl* genitals

genitivo *nm Gram* genitive ►► ***g. sajón*** = English form of the possessive formed with 's or just '

genitourinario, -a *adj* genitourinary, urogenital

genocidio *nm* genocide

genoma *nm* genome

genómico, -a *adj* genomic

genoteca *nf* gene bank

genotipo *nm* genotype

Génova *n* Genoa

genovés, -esa 1 *adj* Genoese

2 *nm,f* Genoese

gente[1] *adj inv Am (amable)* decent; **son muy g.** they're very decent folk

gente[2] *nf* (**a**) *(personas)* people; **acudió muy poca g.** very few people went; **toda la g.** everyone, everybody; **son buena g.** they're good people; **David es buena g.** David is a good guy; EXPR *CSur Fam* **como la g.: hacer algo como la g.** to do sth properly; **una comida como la g.** a decent meal ►► ***g. bien*** well-to-do people; **el barrio donde vive la g. bien** the part of town where the well-to-do *o Br* posh people live; ***g. de bien*** decent folk; *Méx* ***g. bonita*** beautiful people; ***g. de la calle*** ordinary people; *Esp* ***g. guapa*** beautiful people; *Andes, RP Fam* ***g. linda*** beautiful people; ***g. menuda*** kids

(**b**) *Fam (grupo de amigos)* crowd; **ahora se ve con otra g.** she goes around with a different crowd now

(**c**) *Fam (familia)* folks

(**d**) **gentes** *(habitantes)* people; **las gentes del lugar** the local people, the locals

gentil 1 *adj* (**a**) *(amable)* kind, nice (**con** to); *(cortés)* courteous, polite (**con** to) (**b**) *Rel* gentile

2 *nmf Rel* gentile

> **Falso amigo**: El adjetivo inglés **genteel** no es la traducción del español **gentil**. En inglés **genteel** significa "fino, afectado" o "respetable".

gentileza *nf (amabilidad)* kindness; *(cortesía)* courtesy, politeness; **¿tendría la g. de decirme...?** would you be so kind as to tell me...?; **tuvo la g. de invitarme** he was kind enough to invite me; **por g. de** by courtesy of; **esta ronda es g. de la casa** this round is on the house

gentilhombre *nm Hist* gentleman *(in the royal court)*

gentilicio *nm* = term referring to the natives or inhabitants of a particular place

gentilmente *adv (con amabilidad)* kindly; *(con cortesía)* courteously

gentío *nm* crowd; **se perdió entre el g.** he disappeared into the crowd

gentuza *nf Pey* riffraff, rabble

genuflexión *nf Rel* genuflection; **hacer una g.** to genuflect

genuflexo, -a *adj* **estaba g. delante del altar** he was kneeling *o* on his knees in front of the altar

genuinamente *adv* genuinely

genuino, -a *adj* genuine; **es un Picasso g.** it's a genuine Picasso; **hizo un g. esfuerzo por agradar** he made a genuine *o* real effort to please

GEO [χeo] *nm o nmpl* (*abrev de* **Grupo Especial de Operaciones**) = specially trained Spanish police force, *Br* ≃ SAS, *US* ≃ SWAT

geo *nmf* = member of the "GEO"

geoambiental *adj* geo-environmental

geobotánica *nf* plant geography, geobotany

geocéntrico, -a *adj* geocentric

geoda *nf Geol* geode

geodemografía *nf Com* geodemographics

geodesia *nf* geodesy

geodésico, -a *adj* geodesic

geodinámica *nf* geodynamics *(singular)*

geoestacionario, -a *adj (órbita, satélite)* geostationary

geofísica *nf (ciencia)* geophysics *(singular)*

geofísico, -a 1 *adj* geophysical

2 *nm,f (persona)* geophysicist

geografía *nf* (**a**) *(ciencia)* geography ►► ***g. física*** physical geography; ***g. humana*** human geography; ***g. lingüística*** linguistic geography; ***g. política*** political geography (**b**) *(territorio)* **conozco muy bien la g. de la región** I know the region very well; **por toda la g. nacional** throughout *o* all over the country; **la g. de la zona es muy accidentada** the area's terrain is very rugged

geográfico, -a *adj* geographical

geógrafo, -a *nm,f* geographer

geolingüística *nf* geolinguistics *(singular)*

geología *nf* geology

geológico, -a *adj* geological

geólogo, -a *nm,f* geologist

geomagnético, -a *adj* geomagnetic

geomagnetismo *nm* geomagnetism

geomancia *nf* geomancy

geómetra *nmf* geometrician

geometría *nf* geometry ►► ***g. analítica*** analytical geometry; ***g. fractal*** fractal geometry

geométricamente *adv* geometrically

geométrico, -a *adj* geometric; **progresión geométrica** geometric progression

geomorfología *nf* geomorphology

geopolítica *nf* geopolitics *(singular)*

geopolítico, -a *adj* geopolitical

geoquímica *nf* geochemistry

geoquímico, -a *adj* geochemical

Georgetown ['jortʃtaun] *n* Georgetown

Georgia *n* Georgia

georgiano, -a 1 *adj* **(a)** *(de Georgia)* Georgian **(b)** *(estilo)* Georgian
2 *nm,f (persona)* Georgian
3 *nm (lengua)* Georgian

geosinclinal *nm Geol* geosyncline

geotermia *nf* geothermics *(singular)*

geranio *nm* geranium

gerbo *nm* jerboa

gerencia *nf* **(a)** *(dirección)* management **(b)** *(cargo)* post of manager **(c)** *(oficina)* manager's office **(d)** *(periodo)* time as management

gerencial *adj* managerial, management; **a nivel g.** at management level

gerenciar *vt Am* to manage

gerente *nmf* manager ▸▸ ***g. de banco*** bank manager; ***g. general*** general manager; *Com* ***g. de línea*** line manager

geriatra *nmf* geriatrician

geriatría *nf* geriatrics *(singular)*

geriátrico, -a 1 *adj* geriatric
2 *nm* **(a)** *(hospital)* geriatric hospital **(b)** *(residencia)* old folks' home

gerifalte *nm* **(a)** *(ave)* gerfalcon **(b)** *Fam (persona)* bigwig

germanía *nf Hist* thieves' slang

germánico, -a 1 *adj (tribus, carácter)* Germanic, Teutonic
2 *nm (lengua)* Germanic

germanio *nm Quím* germanium

germanismo *nm* Germanism

germanista *nmf* German scholar

germanización *nf* germanization

germanizar [14] *vt* to germanize

germano, -a 1 *adj* **(a)** *(alemán)* German **(b)** *(tribus, carácter)* Germanic, Teutonic
2 *nm,f* **(a)** *(alemán)* German **(b)** *Hist* Teuton

germanófilo, -a 1 *adj* Germanophile
2 *nm,f* Germanophile

germanófobo, -a 1 *adj* Germanophobic
2 *nm,f* Germanophobe

germanooccidental *adj Antes* West German

germanooriental *adj Antes* East German

germen *nm* **(a)** *(microbio)* germ ▸▸ ***g. patógeno*** pathogen **(b)** *(origen)* origin; **esa asociación fue el g. del partido comunista** that association was the origin of the communist party **(c)** *(de planta)* shoot ▸▸ ***g. de trigo*** wheat germ

germicida 1 *adj* germicidal
2 *nm* germicide

germinación *nf* germination

germinal *adj* germinal

germinar *vi* **(a)** *(planta)* to germinate **(b)** *(idea)* to germinate; *(movimiento)* to come into being; **la idea germinó en su mente** the idea took shape in his mind

germinativo, -a *adj Bot* germinative

gerontocracia *nf* gerontocracy

gerontología *nf Med* gerontology

gerontólogo, -a *nm,f Med* gerontologist

gerundense 1 *adj* of/from Gerona *(Spain)*
2 *nmf* person from Gerona *(Spain)*

gerundio *nm* gerund; EXPR *Esp Fam Hum* **¡andando** *o* **arreando** *o* **marchando, que es g.!** let's get a move on!, let's get going!

gesta *nf* exploit, feat

gestación *nf* **(a)** *(embarazo)* pregnancy, *Espec* gestation **(b)** *(de idea, proyecto)* gestation

gestalt *nf Psi* gestalt

gestáltico, -a *adj Psi* gestalt; **una estructura g.** a gestalt structure

gestante 1 *adj* pregnant, expectant
2 *nf* expectant mother, pregnant woman

gestar 1 *vi* to gestate
2 **gestarse** *vpr* **se estaba gestando una nueva era** the seeds of a new era had been sown; **se está gestando un golpe de estado** they're plotting a coup, there's a coup in the offing

gesticulación *nf (de manos, brazos)* gesticulation; *(de cara)* face-pulling

gesticular *vi (con manos, brazos)* to gesticulate; *(con la cara)* to pull faces

gesticulero, -a *adj* **es muy g.** he gesticulates a lot

gestión *nf* **(a)** *(diligencia)* **tengo que hacer unas gestiones en el ayuntamiento** I have a few things to do at the town hall; **las gestiones para obtener un visado** the formalities involved in getting a visa; **sus gestiones para obtener la beca no dieron fruto** his efforts to get a grant were unsuccessful; **las gestiones del negociador fracasaron** the negotiator's efforts came to nothing; **voy a intentar hacer unas gestiones a ver si puedo conseguirlo** I'll try and speak to a few people to see if I can manage it; EXPR *RP* **no hay peor g. que la que no se hace** there's no harm in trying
(b) *(administración)* management ▸▸ ***g. de calidad*** quality control; *Fin* ***g. de cartera*** portfolio management; *Com* ***g. de cobro*** = collection of outstanding payments; ***g. de crisis*** crisis management; ***g. de empresas*** business management; ***g. financiera*** financial management; *Com* ***g. de línea*** line management; *Com* ***g. de personal*** personnel management; ***g. política*** *(de gobierno, ministro)* conduct in

GENTILICIO

Spanish forms adjectives from place names with much greater facility than does English. These **gentilicios**, as they are called, exist for most cities in the Spanish-speaking world, and further afield. They also serve as nouns for natives of the place in question. **Gentilicios** are most frequently formed by adding one of these ending onto the place name:

-ano(a):	**sevillano** (Seville, Spain)
-ense:	**bonaerense** (Buenos Aires, Argentina)
-eño(a):	**acapulqueño** (Acapulco, Mexico)
-és(esa):	**vigués** (Vigo, Spain)
-ino(a):	**alicantino** (Alicante, Spain)

The adjectives can often be translated by use of the English place name itself, either before the noun or in a possessive structure:

la niebla londinense *London fog*
la noche neoyorquina *New York nightlife*
los barrios bajos madrileños *the rougher parts of Madrid*

Note that some **gentilicios** can be quite opaque in derivation:

donostiarra (San Sebastián, Spain – from Basque)
gaditano(a) (Cádiz, Spain)
pacense (Badajoz, Spain)
tapatío(a) (Guadalajara, Mexico)

government; ***g. de recursos*** resource management; ***g. de riesgos*** risk management; *Fin* ***g. de stocks*** stock control
(c) *Informát* ***g. de ficheros*** file management; ***g. de memoria*** memory management
(d) *(gobierno)* administration; **tres años de g. del gobierno socialista** three years under the socialist administration

gestionar *vt* (a) *(tramitar)* to arrange; **g. un préstamo** to arrange a loan; **g. un visado** to arrange *o* to get a visa; **g. una beca** to try to get a grant; **están gestionando el traspaso del jugador** they're arranging the transfer of the player (b) *(administrar)* to manage; **gestiona la empresa con eficacia** she manages *o* runs the business well

gesto *nm* (a) *(ademán)* gesture; **hacer un g.** *(con las manos)* to gesture, to make a gesture; **nos hizo un g. con la mano para que paráramos** he flagged us down, he signalled us to stop; **hacer un g. de asentimiento** *(con la cabeza)* to nod
(b) *(mueca)* face, grimace; **llegó con el g. descompuesto** he arrived looking very upset; EXPR **torcer el g.** to pull a face *(expressing displeasure)*
(c) *(acción)* gesture; **un g. de buena voluntad** a gesture of goodwill; **ha sido un g. muy bonito ir a visitarla** visiting her was a very nice gesture

gestor, -ora 1 *adj* **el equipo g. del proyecto** the project management team; **el órgano g. de las ayudas** the body responsible for the administration of the grants
2 *nm,f* = person who carries out dealings with public bodies on behalf of private customers or companies, combining the roles of solicitor and accountant ▸▸ *Fin* ***g. de fondos*** fund manager
3 *nm Informát* ***g. de archivos*** file manager; ***g. de correo*** mail manager; ***g. de memoria*** memory manager

gestoría *nf* = office of a "gestor"

gestual *adj* using gestures; **lenguaje g.** sign language

géyser = **géiser**

Ghana *n* Ghana

ghanés, -esa 1 *adj* Ghanaian
2 *nm,f* Ghanaian

ghetto ['geto] *nm* ghetto

giba *nf (de camello)* hump; *(de persona)* hunchback, hump

gibar *vt Esp Fam (molestar)* to annoy, to bother

gibón *nm (simio)* gibbon

giboso, -a 1 *adj* hunchbacked
2 *nm,f* hunchback

Gibraltar *n* Gibraltar

gibraltareño, -a 1 *adj* Gibraltarian
2 *nm,f* Gibraltarian

GIF [gif] *nm Informát* (*abrev de* **graphics interchange format**) GIF

giga- *pref* giga-

gigabyte [χiɣa'βait] *nm Informát* gigabyte

gigahercio *nm* gigahertz

giganta *nf* giantess

gigante[1] *adj* gigantic

gigante[2] *nm* (a) *(personaje fantástico)* giant (b) *(persona alta)* giant (c) *(en fiestas)* = giant papier-mâché carnival figure; **gigantes y cabezudos** = giant and giant-headed carnival figures (d) *(personalidad)* giant; **un g. de la música latina** a giant of Latin music

gigantesco, -a *adj* gigantic

gigantismo *nm Med* gigantism

gigantón, -ona *nm,f (en fiestas)* = giant papier-mâché carnival figure

gigoló [jiɣo'lo] *nm* gigolo

gil, -ila *CSur Fam* 1 *adj* stupid
2 *nm,f* jerk, *Br* twit

gilada *nf CSur Fam* **hacer una g.** to do something stupid; **hacer giladas** to do silly *o* stupid things; **decir una g.** to say something stupid; **decir giladas** to talk nonsense

gilí *Fam* 1 *adj* stupid
2 *nmf* jerk, *Br* twit

gilipollada, jilipollada *nf Esp muy Fam* **hacer una g.** to do something *Br* bloody *o US* goddamn stupid; **deja de hacer gilipolladas** stop being so *Br* bloody *o US* goddamn stupid; **decir una g.** to say something *Br* bloody *o US* goddamn stupid; **decir gilipolladas** to talk *Br* rubbish *o US* garbage

gilipollas, jilipollas *Esp muy Fam* 1 *adj inv* **ser g.** to be a *Br* prat *o Br* pillock *o US* dork
2 *nmf inv Br* prat, *Br* pillock, *US* dork

gilipollez, jilipollez *nf Esp muy Fam* (a) *(acto)* **hacer una g.** to do something *Br* bloody *o US* goddamn stupid; **deja de hacer gilipolladas** stop being so *Br* bloody *o US* goddamn stupid; **decir una g.** to say something *Br* bloody *o US* goddamn stupid; **decir gilipolleces** to talk *Br* rubbish *o US* garbage
(b) *(cosa insignificante)* silly *o* stupid little thing; **se pelearon por una g.** they fell out over some silly *o* stupid little thing; **le compré una g.** I bought her some silly *o* stupid little present

gilipuertas, jilipuertas *Esp Fam Euf* 1 *adj inv* daft, *US* dumb
2 *nmf inv* dumbo, *Br* twit

gillete® [ji'let] *nf* razor blade

gimiera *etc ver* **gemir**

gimnasia *nf* gymnastics *(singular)*; **hacer g.** *(ejercicios)* to do gymnastics, to do exercises; EXPR *Hum* **estás confundiendo la g. con la magnesia** you're mixing up two completely different things ▸▸ ***g. artística*** gymnastics; ***g. correctiva*** physiotherapy exercises; ***g. deportiva*** gymnastics; ***g. de mantenimiento*** keep-fit; ***g. médica*** physiotherapy exercises; ***g. mental*** mental exercise; ***g. terapéutica*** physiotherapy exercises; ***g. rítmica*** rhythmic gymnastics; ***g. sueca*** Swedish gymnastics

gimnasio *nm* gymnasium, gym

gimnasta *nmf* gymnast

gimnástico, -a *adj* gymnastic

gimnosperma *nf Bot* gymnosperm

gimnoto *nm* banded knifefish

gimo *etc ver* **gemir**

gimotear *vi* to whine, to whimper

gimoteo *nm* whining, whimpering

gincana *nf (carrera de obstáculos)* gymkhana; *(de automóviles)* rally

Ginebra *n* Geneva

ginebra *nf* gin

gineceo *nm* (a) *Hist* gynaeceum (b) *Bot* gynoecium, gynaeceum

ginecología *nf* gynaecology

ginecológico, -a *adj* gynaecological

ginecólogo, -a *nm,f* gynaecologist

ginesta *nf Bot* broom

gineta *nf* genet

ginger ale [jinje'reil] *nm inv* ginger ale

gingival *adj* gum; **una afección g.** a gum infection

gingivitis *nf inv Med* gingivitis

gingo, ginkgo *nm* ginkgo, maidenhair tree

ginseng [jin'sen] *nm* ginseng

gintonic, gin-tonic [jin'tonik] (*pl* **gintonics, gin-tonics**) *nm* gin and tonic

giñar = **jiñar**

gira *nf* (a) *(recorrido)* tour; **una g. turística por Escandinavia** a tour of Scandinavia; **la g. del rey por Sudamérica** the king's tour of South America (b) *(de artista)* tour; **estar de g.** to be on tour; **salir de g.** to go on tour

giradiscos *nm inv (de tocadiscos)* turntable

girador, -ora *nm,f Com* drawer

giralda *nf* (a) *(veleta)* weather vane (b) **la G.** *(de Sevilla)* = the 12th century cathedral tower in Seville

girándula *nf (de cohete)* pinwheel

girar 1 *vi* (a) *(doblar)* to turn; **el camino gira a la derecha** the road turns to the right; **el conductor giró a la izquierda** the driver turned left *o* made a left turn
(b) *(dar vueltas)* to turn; *(rápidamente)* to spin; **la Luna gira alrededor de la Tierra** the Moon revolves *o* goes around the Earth; **este coche gira muy bien** this car has a tight turning circle
(c) *(darse la vuelta)* to turn (round); **giré para verla mejor** I turned round to see her better
(d) *(tratar)* **g. en torno a** *o* **alrededor de** to be centred around, to centre on; **el coloquio giró en torno a la pena de muerte** the discussion dealt with the topic of the death penalty
(e) *Com* to remit payment; **g. en descubierto** to write a check without sufficient funds
2 *vt* (a) *(hacer dar vueltas a)* to turn; **giró la llave en la cerradura** she turned the key in the lock; **g. la cabeza** to turn one's head (b) *Com* to draw (c) *(dinero)* to transfer, to remit
3 **girarse** *vpr* to turn round; **me giré para ver mejor** I turned round to see better

girasol *nm* sunflower

giratorio, -a *adj (puerta)* revolving; *(silla)* swivel
giro *nm* (**a**) *(rotación)* rotation
(**b**) *(de vehículo)* turn; **el camión dio un g. repentino** the truck *o Br* lorry turned suddenly; **el avión dio un g. completo** the plane turned right round; *también Fig* **un g. de 180 grados** a U-turn
(**c**) *(cambio de dirección)* turn; **el partido ha dado un g. a la derecha** the party has veered to the right; **los acontecimientos dieron un g. inesperado** events took an unexpected turn; **la conversación tomó otro g.** the conversation took a different turn ►► ***un g. copernicano*** a complete change
(**d**) *(rotación)* rotation
(**e**) *(postal, telegráfico)* money order; **poner un g.** to send a money order; **enviar algo por g.** to send sth by money order; **le envió 100 euros por giro** she sent him a money order for 100 euros ►► ***g. bancario*** banker's draft; ***g. postal*** postal order; ***g. telegráfico:*** **poner un g. telegráfico a alguien** to wire money to sb; *Fin* ***g. a la vista*** sight draft
(**f**) *(de letras, órdenes de pago)* draft
(**g**) *(expresión)* turn of phrase
(**h**) *Am (ramo)* industry; **el g. de la carne** the meat industry
girocompás *(pl* **girocompases***)* *nm* gyrocompass
girola *nf Arquit* ambulatory
girómetro *nm* gyrometer
giróscopo, giroscopio *nm* gyroscope, gyro
GIS [χis] *nm inv Informát* (*abrev de* **geographical information system**) GIS
gis *nm Méx* chalk
gitanada *nf Pey (costumbre)* **eso es una g.** that's typical of the sort of things gypsies do
gitanería *nf* (**a**) *Pey (gitanada)* **eso es una g.** that's typical of the sort of things gypsies do (**b**) *(gitanos)* gypsies
gitanismo *nm* (**a**) *(forma de vida)* gypsy way of life (**b**) *(palabra, expresión)* = gypsy word or expression
gitano, -a 1 *adj* (**a**) *(raza, persona)* gypsy (**b**) *Fam (artero)* **ser g.** to be a crafty devil (**c**) *Fam (con gracia)* **es muy g.** he knows how to get round people
2 *nm,f* gypsy; EXPR *Esp Fam* **que no se lo salta un g.: tengo un hambre que no se la salta un g.** I'm absolutely ravenous; **me comí un filete que no se lo salta un galgo** I had an absolutely huge steak
glaceado, -a *adj Urug* glacé
glaciación *nf* (**a**) *(periodo)* ice age (**b**) *(proceso)* glaciation
glacial *adj* (**a**) *(época)* glacial (**b**) *(viento)* icy (**c**) *(silencio)* stony
glaciar 1 *adj* glacial
2 *nm* glacier
glaciología *nf* glaciology
gladiador *nm* gladiator
gladiola *nf Méx, Ven* gladiolus
gladiolo, gladíolo *nm* gladiolus
glamoroso, -a *adj Fam* glamorous, ritzy
glamour [gla'mur] *nm* glamour
glamouroso, -a [glamu'roso, -a], **glamuroso, -a** *adj Fam* glamorous, ritzy
glande *nm* (**a**) *Anat* glans (penis) (**b**) *Bot* glans, acorn
glándula *nf Anat* gland ►► ***g. adrenal*** adrenal gland; ***g. endocrina*** endocrine gland; ***g. mamaria*** mammary gland; ***g. pineal*** pineal gland; ***g. pituitaria*** pituitary gland; ***g. salivar** o **salival*** salivary gland; ***g. sebácea*** sebaceous gland; ***g. sudorípara*** sweat gland; ***g. suprarrenal*** adrenal gland
glandular *adj* glandular
glasé 1 *adj* glacé
2 *nm* glacé silk
glaseado, -a 1 *adj* glacé
2 *nm* (**a**) *(de postre)* icing (**b**) *(de superficie, tela)* glaze
glasear *vt* (**a**) *(postre)* to ice (**b**) *(superficie, tela)* to glaze
glásnost *nf* glasnost
glaucio *nm* yellow horned poppy
glauco, -a *adj Literario (ojos)* green
glaucoma *nm* glaucoma
gleba *nf* (**a**) *(terrón)* clod (**b**) *Hist* feudal land
glicerina *nf* glycerine
glicerol *nm* glycerol
glicina, glicinia *nf (planta)* wisteria
glifo *nm* (**a**) *(maya)* glyph (**b**) *Arquit* glyph
glíptica *nf* glyptics
global *adj* (**a**) *(acuerdo)* general; *(solución, enfoque)* global; *(análisis)* comprehensive; *(aumento)* overall; *(precio)* total; *Informát* **una búsqueda g.** a global search; **lo compraron por un importe g. de 10 millones** they bought it for a total sum of 10 milllion (**b**) *(mundial)* global, worldwide; **una economía g.** a global economy
globalidad *nf* (**a**) *(totalidad)* whole; **hay que defender el medio ambiente en su g.** it is necessary to protect the environment as a whole (**b**) *(carácter mundial)* global nature
globalización *nf* globalization
globalizar [14] *vt* (**a**) *(generalizar)* to give an overall view of (**b**) *(internacionalizar)* to globalize
globalmente *adv* globally, overall
globo *nm* (**a**) *(Tierra)* globe, earth ►► ***g. terráqueo*** globe; ***g. terrestre*** globe
(**b**) *(aeróstato)* balloon; EXPR *Col* **echar globos** to ponder ►► ***g. aerostático*** hot-air balloon; ***g. sonda*** weather balloon; *Fig* **lanzar un g. sonda** to fly a kite
(**c**) *(juguete)* balloon
(**d**) *Dep (disparo) (en tenis, fútbol)* lob; *(en rugby)* up-and-under
(**e**) *(lámpara)* round glass lampshade
(**f**) *(en cómic)* speech bubble, balloon ►► *Informát* ***globos de ayuda*** balloon help
(**g**) *Anat* ***g. ocular*** eyeball
(**h**) *(de chicle)* bubble; **hacer globos** to blow bubbles
(**i**) *Esp Fam (preservativo)* rubber, *Br* johnny
(**j**) *Esp Fam* **globos** *(pechos)* melons
(**k**) *Esp Fam (borrachera)* **agarrar un g.** to get smashed
(**l**) *Esp Fam (por drogas)* high; **coger un g.** to get high
(**m**) *Esp Fam (enfado)* **coger un g.** to go ballistic
globular *adj* globular
globulina *nf* globulin
glóbulo *nm* blood cell, corpuscle ►► ***g. blanco*** white blood cell, white corpuscle; ***g. rojo*** red blood cell, red corpuscle
gloria 1 *nf* (**a**) *(en religión)* glory; **ganar** *o* **alcanzar la g.** to go to heaven; **que en g. esté** God rest his/her soul
(**b**) *(celebridad)* celebrity, star; **alcanzar la g.** to achieve fame
(**c**) *(grandeza, esplendor)* glory; **la g. de un país** the glory of a country
(**d**) *Fam (placer)* **da g. verlo comer** it's a treat to watch him eat; **estar en la g.** to be in seventh heaven; **saber a g.** to taste divine *o* heavenly; **este vino es una g.** this wine is divine *o* heavenly; **en esta playa se está en la g.** this beach is absolute heaven *o* bliss
(**e**) *(persona)* **es una vieja g. del ciclismo** he's one of the former greats of cycling; **las viejas glorias del toreo** the great names in the history of bullfighting
2 *nm (oración)* Gloria
gloriarse *vpr* (**a**) *(preciarse)* to boast, to brag; **g. de algo** to boast *o* brag about sth (**b**) *(complacerse)* to glory
glorieta *nf* (**a**) *(de jardín)* arbour (**b**) *(plazoleta)* square; *(circular)* circus (**c**) *Esp (rotonda) Br* roundabout, *US* traffic circle
glorificación *nf* glorification
glorificar [60] *vt* to glorify
gloriosamente *adv* gloriously
glorioso, -a *adj* (**a**) *(hazaña)* glorious; *(personaje)* great (**b**) *(del cielo)* blessed
glosa *nf* marginal note
glosador, -ora *nm,f* commentator *(on text)*
glosar *vt* (**a**) *(anotar)* to annotate (**b**) *(comentar)* to comment on
glosario *nm* glossary
glosopeda *nf* foot-and-mouth disease
glotal *adj Ling* glottal
glótico, -a *adj Anat* glottal
glotis *nf inv Anat* glottis
glotón, -ona 1 *adj* gluttonous, greedy
2 *nm,f (persona)* glutton
3 *nm (animal)* wolverine, glutton
glotonear *vi* to eat greedily
glotonería *nf* gluttony, greed
gloxínea *nf* gloxinia
glucemia *nf Med* glycaemia
glúcido *nm* carbohydrate
glucógeno *nm* glycogen
glucosa *nf* glucose

gluglú *nm* glug-glug
glutamato *nm* glutamate ▸▸ ***g. monosódico*** monosodium glutamate
gluten *nm* gluten
glúteo, -a 1 *adj* gluteal
2 *nm* gluteus ▸▸ ***g. mayor*** gluteus maximus
glutinoso, -a *adj* glutinous
gneis [neis] *nm inv* gneiss
gnómico, -a ['nomiko, -a] *adj Lit* gnomic
gnomo ['nomo] *nm* gnome
gnosis ['nosis] *nf inv* gnosis
gnosticismo [nosti'θismo] *nm* gnosticism
gnóstico, -a ['nostiko, -a] **1** *adj* gnostic
2 *nm,f* gnostic
gobelino *nm (tapiz)* Gobelin (tapestry)
gobernabilidad *nf* governability
gobernable *adj* governable
gobernación *nf* **(a)** *(gestión)* governing **(b)** *Méx* **G.** *(ministerio del interior) Br* ≃ the Home Office, *US* ≃ the Department of the Interior **(c)** *Col (de provincia)* provincial government
gobernador, -ora 1 *adj* governing
2 *nm,f* governor ▸▸ *Esp Antes* ***g. civil*** = person representing the central government in each province; ***g. general*** governor general
gobernanta *nf* **(a)** *(en hotel)* cleaning and laundry staff manageress **(b)** *(en casa, institución)* governess
gobernante 1 *adj* ruling; **partido g.** governing party
2 *nmf* ruler, leader
gobernanza *nf* governance
gobernar [3] **1** *vt* **(a)** *(regir, dirigir)* to govern, to rule; *(casa, negocio)* to run, to manage; **no tiene carácter, se deja g. por su marido** she has no character of her own, she allows herself to be ruled by her husband; **sus sentimientos gobiernan sus acciones** his feelings govern his actions **(b)** *(barco)* to steer; *(avión)* to fly
2 *vi* **(a)** *(político, partido)* to govern, to be in power **(b)** *(barco)* to steer
Gobi *nm* **el desierto de G.** the Gobi Desert
gobiernismo *nm Andes, Méx (actitud)* pro-government position; *(conjunto de personas)* government supporters
gobiernista *Andes, Méx* **1** *adj* pro-government
2 *nmf* government supporter
gobierno 1 *ver* **gobernar**
2 *nm* **(a)** *(organismo)* government; **el g. en pleno asistió al acto** all the members of the government attended ▸▸ ***g. autónomo*** autonomous government; ***g. central*** central government; *Esp Antes* ***g. civil*** = body representing the central government in each province; ***g. de coalición*** coalition government; ***g. de concentración*** government of national unity; ***g. directo*** direct rule; ***g. mayoritario*** majority rule; *Esp* ***g. militar*** = body representing the army in each province; ***g. títere*** puppet government; ***g. de transición*** caretaker *o* interim government
(b) *(edificio)* government buildings
(c) *(administración, gestión)* running, management; **g. de la casa** housekeeping
(d) *(de barco)* steering
gobio *nm (pez)* gudgeon
goce *nm* **(a)** *(placer)* pleasure; **es un g. verlos bailar** it's a pleasure to watch them dance **(b)** *(uso, provecho)* **en pleno g. de sus facultades** in full possession of her faculties; **la enfermedad no le permitió el g. de su herencia** the illness didn't allow him to enjoy his inheritance
godo, -a 1 *adj* **(a)** *Hist* Gothic **(b)** *Fam (en Canarias)* (Peninsular) Spanish **(c)** *Col, Ven Fam (conservador)* conservative
2 *nm,f* **(a)** *Hist* Goth **(b)** *Fam (en Canarias)* (Peninsular) Spaniard **(c)** *Col, Ven Fam (conservador)* conservative
gofio *nm* **(a)** *Andes, Carib, RP (harina)* roasted maize *o US* corn meal **(b)** *CAm, Ven (pastel)* = sweet cake made with maize *o US* corn meal
gofrado, -a 1 *adj* corrugated
2 *nm* goffering
gofrar *vt Imprenta* to goffer
gofre *nm Esp* waffle
gofrera *nf Esp* waffle iron
gogó 1 *nf* go-go dancer
2 a gogó *loc adv Esp Fam* **hubo comida/bebida a g.** there was loads of food/drink
gol *(pl* **goles***) nm* **(a)** *(tanto)* goal; **marcar** *o* **meter un g.** to score a goal; **ganaron por tres goles a cero** they won three-nil; EXPR *Fam* **meter un g. a alguien** *(con ingenio)* to put one over on sb; *(con engaño)* to con sb ▸▸ ***g. average*** goal difference; ***un g. cantado*** an open goal; *RP* ***g. en contra*** own goal; ***g. del empate*** equalizer; ***un g. fantasma*** *(no concedido)* a clear goal that wasn't given by the referee; *(concedido)* a goal that should never have been allowed; ***g. del honor*** consolation goal; ***g. de oro*** golden goal; ***g. de penalty*** penalty goal; ***g. en propia meta*** *o* ***puerta*** own goal
(b) *(graderío)* stand *(behind either goal)*
gola *nf* **(a)** *(garganta)* gullet, throat **(b)** *(adorno)* ruff **(c)** *(de fortificación)* gorge **(d)** *Arquit* ogee **(e)** *(canal)* channel, narrows
golaveraje, golaverage [golaβe'raχe] *nm* goal difference
golazo *nm Fam* amazing goal
goleada *nf* **el equipo local ganó por g.** the home team scored a heavy victory
goleado, -a *adj* **el portero más g. del campeonato** the goalkeeper who conceded the most goals in the championship
goleador, -ora 1 *adj* goal-scoring; **un centrocampista g.** a midfielder who scores a lot of goals
2 *nm,f* (goal) scorer; **el máximo g.** the top scorer
golear *vt* to thrash; **el Atlético goleó al Fluminense** Atlético thrashed Fluminense
golero, -a *nm,f RP* goalkeeper
goleta *nf* schooner
golf *nm* golf
golfa *nf Esp Fam (mujer promiscua)* tart, slag
golfante *Fam* **1** *adj* **¡qué g. eres!** you little rascal!
2 *nmf* scoundrel, rascal
golfear *vi Fam (hacer el golfo)* to hang out
golfería *nf Fam* **(a)** *(golfos)* layabouts, good-for-nothings **(b)** *(actitud, comportamiento)* loutish *o Br* yobbish behaviour
golfillo *nm* urchin
golfista *nmf* golfer
golfístico, -a *adj* golf; **un torneo g.** a golf tournament
golfito *nm Am* mini-golf
golfo, -a 1 *adj (gamberro)* loutish, *Br* yobbish; *(pillo)* roguish
2 *nm* **(a)** *(gamberro)* lout, *Br* yob; *(pillo)* rogue, wide boy
(b) *Geog* gulf, bay ▸▸ ***el g. de Bengala*** the Bay of Bengal; ***el g. de California*** the Gulf of California; ***el g. de Guinea*** the Gulf of Guinea; ***el g. de León*** the Gulf of Leon; ***el g. de México*** the Gulf of Mexico; ***el g. de Omán*** the Gulf of Oman; ***el g. de Panamá*** the Gulf of Panama; ***el g. Pérsico*** the Persian Gulf; ***el g. de Tonkín*** the Gulf of Tonkin; ***el g. de Venezuela*** the Gulf of Venezuela; ***el g. de Vizcaya*** the Bay of Biscay
Gólgota *nm* **el G.** Golgotha
Goliat *n pr* Goliath
golilla *nf* **(a)** *(adorno)* ruff **(b)** *RP (pañuelo)* neckerchief **(c)** *Ven Fam (cosa fácil)* cinch, piece of cake
golletazo *nm Taurom* = sword thrust in the neck
gollete *nm* neck; EXPR *RP Fam* **no tener g.** to be absurd
golletear *vt Col* to collar, to grab by the neck
golondrina *nf* **(a)** *(ave)* swallow; PROV **una g. no hace verano** one swallow doesn't make a summer ▸▸ ***g. de mar*** tern **(b)** *CAm, Méx (planta)* spurge **(c)** *Chile (camioneta)* moving van, *Br* removal van
golondrino *nm* **(a)** *(polluelo)* swallow chick **(b)** *Med* boil in the armpit
golosina *nf* **(a)** *(dulce)* sweet; **los niños están comiendo todo el día caramelos y golosinas** the children do nothing but eat *Br* sweets *o US* candy all day **(b)** *(exquisitez)* titbit, delicacy
goloso, -a 1 *adj* sweet-toothed; **ser muy g.** to have a very sweet tooth
2 *nm,f* sweet-toothed person; **es un g.** he has a sweet tooth

GOLPE 1 *nm* **(a)** *(impacto)* blow; *(en puerta)* knock; *(entre coches)* bump; **se oyó un g. en el piso de arriba** something went bump upstairs; **no le des tantos golpes a la fotocopiadora** stop hitting *o* banging the photocopier like that; **me di un g. en la rodilla** I banged my knee; **la ventana estaba dando golpes** the window was banging; **el g. me lo dieron cuando estaba detenido en un semáforo** they hit me *o* bumped into me when I was stopped at a traffic light; **el niño daba golpes en la pared** the child was banging on the wall; **darse golpes de pecho** to beat one's breast; **cerrar la puerta de g.** to slam the door; **devolver un g.** to strike back; **errar** *o* **fallar el g.** to miss the mark; **g. seco** thud; EXPR *Fam* **dar el g.** to cause a sensation, to be a hit; **con ese**

vestido seguro que das el g. en la fiesta in that dress, you're bound to be a hit at the party; EXPR *Fam* **no dio** *o* **pegó g.** he didn't lift a finger, he didn't do a stroke of work; EXPR **de g.** suddenly; EXPR *Fam* **de g. y porrazo** without warning, just like that; EXPR **de un g.** at one fell swoop, all at once ►► ***g. de efecto:*** **hacer algo para dar un g. de efecto** to do sth for effect; ***g. de fortuna*** stroke of luck; ***g. de gracia*** coup de grâce; ***g. maestro*** masterstroke; ***g. de mar*** huge wave; ***g. de suerte*** stroke of luck; *Fig* ***g. de timón*** change of course; ***g. de tos*** coughing fit; ***g. de viento*** gust of wind; ***g. de vista*** glance; **al primer g. de vista** at a glance

(**b**) *(bofetada)* smack; *(puñetazo, en boxeo)* punch; **a golpes** by force; *Fig* in fits and starts; **moler a alguien a golpes** to beat sb up ►► ***g. bajo*** blow below the belt; **fue un g. bajo** that was a bit below the belt

(**c**) *(de corazón)* beat; **los golpes de su corazón** her heartbeat

(**d**) *(efecto)* **mira qué g. tengo en el brazo** look, I banged my arm; **el coche tiene un g. en la puerta** the car door has a dent in it

(**e**) *(en tenis, golf)* shot; **dos golpes por encima/debajo** two shots ahead/behind; **dos golpes bajo par** two under par ►► ***g. de castigo*** *(en rugby)* penalty; ***g. franco*** free kick; ***g. liftado*** *(en tenis)* topspin drive; ***g. de penalización*** *(en golf)* penalty stroke; ***g. de salida*** *(en golf)* tee shot, drive; ***g. de talón*** back heel

(**f**) *(disgusto)* blow; **la muerte de su madre fue un g. muy duro para ella** her mother's death hit her very hard

(**g**) *(atraco)* raid, job, *US* heist; **dar un g.** to do a job

(**h**) *Pol* **g. (de Estado)** coup (d'état) ►► ***g. de mano*** surprise attack; ***g. de palacio*** palace coup

(**i**) *(ocurrencia)* witticism; **¡tienes unos golpes buenísimos!** you really come out with some witty remarks!

(**j**) *(pestillo)* spring lock

(**k**) *Méx (mazo)* sledgehammer

2 a golpe de *loc prep (a base de)* through, by dint of; **aprenderá a g. de fracasos** he'll learn from his mistakes; **no se puede crear un equipo a g. de talonario** you can't build a team just by throwing money at it; **salió de la cárcel a g. de talonario** he used his wealth to buy his way out of prison

3 al golpe *loc adv Cuba* instantly

---

golpeador *nm Chile, Col, Guat* door knocker

golpear 1 *vt* (**a**) *(impactar)* to hit; *(puerta)* to bang; **las olas golpeaban el rompeolas** the waves beat against the breakwater; **no golpees la impresora** stop hitting *o* banging the printer

(**b**) *(pegar)* to hit; *(con puño)* to punch; **lo golpearon hasta dejarlo inconsciente** they beat him unconscious

(**c**) *(afectar, sacudir)* **la crisis económica ha golpeado a toda la zona** the economic crisis has hit *o* affected the whole region; **la vida lo ha golpeado duramente** life has dealt him some harsh blows

2 *vi* (**a**) *(impactar)* **g. contra algo** to beat against sth (**b**) *Andes, RP (llamar)* to knock at the door; **están golpeando** someone's knocking at the door

3 golpearse *vpr* (**a**) *(darse un golpe)* to give oneself a bump *o* bang; **se golpeó en la cabeza** he bumped *o* banged his head (**b**) *Am (sujeto: puerta)* to bang

golpetazo *nm* thump; **dar un g. a alguien** to thump sb; **dio un g. sobre la mesa con el puño** he thumped the table with his fist; **se dio un g. con la moto** she had a crash on her bike

golpetear 1 *vt* to drum on *o* against; **golpeteaba la mesa con los dedos** he was drumming his fingers on the table

2 *vi (dedos, lluvia)* to drum; *(puerta, persiana)* to bang; **la lluvia golpeteaba contra la ventana** the rain was drumming on *o* against the window

golpeteo *nm* (**a**) *(de dedos, lluvia)* drumming (**b**) *(de puerta, persiana)* banging (**c**) *(de máquina)* hammering

golpismo *nm* **militares propensos al g.** military officers prone to staging coups; **el g. sigue siendo un riesgo en este país** there is still a danger that there could be a coup in this country

golpista 1 *adj (militares)* involved in a military coup; **la amenaza g.** the threat of a military coup; **una intentona g.** an attempted coup

2 *nmf* = person involved in a military coup; **el presidente anunció su apoyo a los golpistas** the president announced his support for those who staged the coup

golpiza *nf Am* beating; **dar una g. a alguien** to beat sb up, to give sb a beating

goma *nf* (**a**) *(sustancia viscosa)* gum ►► ***g. 2*** *(explosivo)* plastic explosive; ***g. laca*** shellac; ***g. de mascar*** chewing gum

(**b**) *(pegamento)* glue, gum ►► ***g. arábiga*** gum arabic

(**c**) *(caucho)* rubber; **botas de g.** rubber boots, *Br* wellingtons; EXPR *Fam* **de g.: esa gimnasta parece de g.** that gymnast's so supple, it's as if she were made of rubber ►► ***g. de borrar*** eraser, *Br* rubber; ***g. espuma*** foam rubber

(**d**) *(tira elástica)* **g. (elástica)** rubber band, *Br* elastic band; **una g. para el pelo** a hair elastic

(**e**) *Cuba, CSur (neumático)* tyre; *Cuba* **g. de repuesto** spare wheel

(**f**) *Méx (en béisbol)* home plate

(**g**) *Fam (preservativo)* rubber

(**h**) *Esp Fam (hachís)* good quality hash *o* pot

(**i**) *CAm, Méx Fam (resaca)* hangover

(**j**) *RP muy Fam (pecho)* tit

gomaespuma *nf* foam rubber

gomería *nf CSur* tyre centre

gomero, -a 1 *adj* (**a**) *(de la Gomera)* of/from la Gomera *(Canary Islands)* (**b**) *RP Fam (aficionado a los autos)* car-mad

2 *nm,f* (**a**) *(de la Gomera)* person from la Gomera *(Canary Islands)* (**b**) *Andes (en plantación)* rubber plantation worker (**c**) *CSur (en gomería)* tyre centre attendant

3 *nm CSur (planta)* rubber plant

gomina *nf* hair gel

gominola *nf Esp Br* fruit jelly, *US* soft fruit candy

gomorresina *nf* gum resin

gomoso[1], -a *adj* gummy

gomoso[2] *nm Anticuado* dandy, popinjay

gónada *nf Anat* gonad

góndola *nf* (**a**) *(embarcación)* gondola (**b**) *(de dirigible)* gondola (**c**) *Perú (autobús interurbano)* (inter-city) bus (**d**) *Bol (autobús urbano)* city bus (**e**) *(en supermercado)* gondola

gondolero *nm* gondolier

gong (*pl* **gongs**) *nm* gong

gongorino, -a *Lit* **1** *adj* Gongoristic

2 *nm,f* Gongorist

gongorismo *nm Lit* Gongorism

goniómetro *nm Tec* goniometer

gonococo *nm Med* gonococcus

gonorrea *nf* gonorrhoea

gordal *adj* **aceituna g.** queen olive, = type of large olive used for marinating

gordinflón, -ona *Fam* **1** *adj* chubby, tubby

2 *nm,f* fatty; **es un g.** he's quite chubby

gordo, -a 1 *adj* (**a**) *(persona)* fat; **está más g. que antes** he's put on weight; EXPR *Fam* **me cae g.** I can't stand him; **el G. y el Flaco** Laurel and Hardy

(**b**) *(grueso)* thick; *Esp* **sal gorda** cooking salt

(**c**) *(grande)* big; **dedo g.** *(de la mano)* thumb; *(del pie)* big toe; **cayó una tormenta gorda** there was a big *o* terrible storm

(**d**) *Fam (problema, asunto)* major; **cometió un error muy g.** he made a major mistake; **tuve una discusión muy gorda con él** I had one hell of an argument with him

(**e**) *Fam* EXPR **armar la gorda** to kick up a row *o* stink; **cuando llegó la policía se armó la gorda** when the police arrived all hell broke loose; **ni gorda: no vi/no entendí ni gorda** *(nada)* I couldn't see/I didn't understand a thing

2 *nm,f* (**a**) *(persona obesa)* fat man, *f* fat woman; **los gordos** fat people (**b**) *Am Fam (como apelativo)* **¿cómo estás, g.?** how's it going, big man?

3 *nm* (**a**) *(en lotería)* first prize, jackpot; **le tocó el g.** *(en lotería)* he won first prize, he won the jackpot; **le tocó el g. con ese trabajo** *(tuvo buena suerte)* he hit the jackpot with that job; **con esa hermana que tiene le ha tocado el g.** *(tuvo mala suerte)* you've got to feel sorry for him having a sister like that (**b**) *(grasa)* fat

gordolobo *nm* mullein

gordura *nf* (**a**) *(obesidad)* fatness, obesity (**b**) *(en carne)* fat

gore 1 *adj inv* **el género g.** slasher movies

2 *nm* slasher movies

goretex® *nm* Goretex®

gorgojo *nm (insecto)* weevil

gorgonzola *nm* gorgonzola

gorgoritear *vi* to warble, to trill

gorgorito *nm* warble; *Fam* **hacer gorgoritos** *(cantar)* to warble

górgoro *nm Chile, Méx* bubbles

gorgotear *vi* to gurgle

gorgoteo *nm* gurgle, gurgling

gorguera *nf* (**a**) *(adorno)* ruff (**b**) *(en armadura)* gorget

gorigori *nm Fam* dirge, funeral chant

gorila[1] *nm* (**a**) *(animal)* gorilla (**b**) *Fam (guardaespaldas)* bodyguard (**c**) *Esp Fam (en discoteca, pub)* bouncer

gorila[2] *CSur Fam* 1 *adj (fascista)* fascist, reactionary
2 *nm (fascista)* fascist, reactionary

gorjear *vi* (**a**) *(ave)* to chirp (**b**) *(niño)* to gurgle

gorjeo *nm* (**a**) *(de ave)* chirping (**b**) *(de niño)* gurgling

gorra *nf* (peaked) cap; *Esp, Méx Fam* **de g.** for free; *Esp, Méx Fam* **vivir de g.** to sponge, to scrounge; EXPR *Esp Fam* **con la g.** easily, no problem ▸▸ *Am* ***g. de baño*** *(para piscina)* swimming cap, bathing cap; *(para ducha)* shower cap; ***g. de plato*** peaked cap *(of officer)*; ***g. de visera*** baseball cap

gorrear *Fam* 1 *vt* to sponge, to scrounge
2 *vi* to sponge, to scrounge

gorrero, -a *nm,f Fam* sponger, scrounger

gorrinada, gorrinería *nf* (**a**) *(acción sucia)* **no hagas gorrinadas con la comida** stop being so disgusting when you're eating; **hacer eso es una g.** that's a disgusting thing to do (**b**) *(lugar sucio)* pigsty (**c**) *(indecencia)* **una revista llena de gorrinadas** a magazine full of filth; **una pareja haciendo gorrinadas en un banco** a couple being gross on a park bench (**d**) *(jugarreta)* dirty trick

gorrino, -a *nm,f* (**a**) *(animal)* pig (**b**) *(persona sucia)* pig (**c**) *(persona malintencionada)* swine

gorrión *nm* (house) sparrow ▸▸ ***g. chillón*** rock sparrow; ***g. molinero*** tree sparrow

gorro *nm* (**a**) *(para la cabeza)* cap; EXPR *Fam* **estar hasta el g. (de)** to be fed up (with); EXPR *Méx Fam* **me vale g.** I couldn't care less ▸▸ ***g. de baño*** *(para piscina)* swimming cap, bathing cap; *(para ducha)* shower cap; ***g. de dormir*** nightcap; ***g. de ducha*** shower cap; ***g. frigio*** Phrygian cap; ***g. de piscina*** swimming cap, bathing cap
(**b**) *Fam (en baloncesto)* block; **poner** *o* **hacer un g.** to block a shot

gorrón, -ona *Esp, Méx Fam* 1 *adj* sponging, scrounging; **es muy g.** he's always sponging *o* scrounging, he's always on the scrounge
2 *nm,f* sponger, scrounger

gorronear *Esp, Méx Fam* 1 *vt* to sponge, to scrounge; **siempre me gorronea cigarros** she's always scrounging cigarettes off me
2 *vi* to sponge, to scrounge; **siempre está gorroneando** he's always sponging *o* scrounging, he's always on the scrounge

gorronería *nf Esp Fam* sponging, scrounging

góspel *nm Mús* gospel (music)

gota *nf* (**a**) *(de líquido)* drop; *(de sudor)* bead; **no probé una g. de alcohol** I didn't drink a drop of alcohol; EXPR **caer cuatro gotas** to spit (with rain); EXPR **ni g.: ni g. de sentido común** not an ounce of common sense; **no entiendo ni g. de alemán** I don't understand a word of German; **no queda ni una g. de azúcar** we're completely out of sugar; **no se veía ni g.** you couldn't see a thing; **no corre ni una g. de brisa** there isn't a breath of wind; EXPR **fue la g. que colma el vaso, fue la última g.** it was the last straw; EXPR **como dos gotas de agua** like two peas in a pod ▸▸ ***g. a g.*** intravenous drip; **me va entregando el dinero de la deuda g. a g.** he's paying off his debt to me a little at a time
(**b**) *(medicamento)* **gotas (para los ojos)** eye drops; **gotas (para los oídos)** ear drops
(**c**) *Meteo* **g. fría** = cold front that brings torrential rain
(**d**) *(enfermedad)* gout

gotear 1 *vi (líquido)* to drip; *(techo, depósito)* to leak; *Fig* to trickle through; **el grifo gotea** the tap is dripping
2 *v impersonal (chispear)* to spit, to drizzle

gotelé *nm* **pintado al g.** ≃ decorated with Artex

goteo *nm* (**a**) *(de líquido)* dripping (**b**) *(de gente, información)* trickle

gotera *nf* (**a**) *(filtración)* leak; **tener goteras** to leak (**b**) *(mancha)* stain *(left by leaking water)* (**c**) *Andes* **goteras** *(afueras)* outskirts

gotero *nm* (**a**) *(gota a gota)* (intravenous) drip; **le pusieron un g.** they put him on a drip (**b**) *Am (cuentagotas)* dropper

goterón *nm (gota)* big raindrop; **están cayendo goterones** it's raining big raindrops

gótico, -a 1 *adj* (**a**) *(arte)* Gothic (**b**) *(letra)* Gothic (**c**) *(de los Godos)* Gothic
2 *nm* (**a**) *(estilo)* Gothic ▸▸ ***G. flamígero*** flamboyant Gothic; ***G. florido*** flamboyant Gothic (**b**) *(lengua)* Gothic

gotoso, -a 1 *adj* **un hombre g.** a man with gout
2 *nm,f* person with gout, gout sufferer

gouache [guaʃ] *nm Arte* gouache

gouda ['guda] *nm* Gouda

gourde *nm* gourde *(unit of currency of Haiti)*

gourmet [gur'met] (*pl* **gourmets**) *nmf* gourmet

goya *nm* = annual award by Spanish Academy of Cinema, ≃ Oscar

goyesco, -a *adj* = relating to or like Goya's paintings

gozada, *Ven* **gozadera** *nf Fam* **la fiesta fue una g.** the party was great fun; **¡qué g. de coche/película!** what a wonderful car/film!

gozar [14] 1 *vi* to enjoy oneself; **g. de algo** to enjoy sth; **g. de buena salud** to be in good health; **goza de la confianza del presidente** he is trusted by the president; **goza de una buena posición social** he has *o* enjoys good social standing; **g. con** to (take) delight in; **goza haciendo sufrir a los demás** she delights *o* takes delight in making others suffer
2 *vt* (**a**) *Literario (sexualmente)* to take, to have (**b**) EXPR *Fam* **gozarla: realmente la gozamos en la fiesta** we had a great *o* fantastic time at the party; *RP* **cuando pierde Peñarol, la goza** he loves it when Peñarol lose

gozne *nm* hinge

gozo 1 *nm (alegría)* joy, pleasure; **sentí mucho g. al verla tan feliz** it was lovely to see her so happy; **canta que es un g.** she sings beautifully, it's a joy *o* pleasure to hear her sing; EXPR **no caber en sí de g.** to be beside oneself with joy; EXPR *Fam* **mi g. en un pozo** that's just my (bad) luck
2 **gozos** *nmpl Rel* = verses written in honour of the Virgin Mary or the saints

gozoso, -a *adj* (**a**) *(que siente gozo)* joyful, delighted (**b**) *(que produce gozo)* joyous, delightful

g/p, g.p. (*abrev de* **giro postal**) p.o.

GP *nm* (*abrev de* **gran premio**) GP

GPS *nm* (*abrev de* **Global Positioning System**) GPS

gr. (*abrev de* **gramo**) g, gr

grabación *nf* (**a**) *(acción)* recording ▸▸ ***g. en cinta*** tape recording; ***g. digital*** digital recording; ***g. en vídeo*** video recording (**b**) *(cinta, disco)* recording

grabado *nm* (**a**) *(técnica)* engraving ▸▸ ***g. al aguafuerte*** etching; ***g. sobre madera*** woodcut (**b**) *(lámina)* engraving

grabador, -ora *nm,f (artista)* engraver

grabadora *nf* (**a**) *(magnetófono)* tape recorder (**b**) *Informát* ***g. de CD-ROM*** CD-ROM recorder *o* burner

grabar 1 *vt* (**a**) *(en metal)* to engrave; *(en madera)* to carve; **grabó su nombre en un tronco** she carved her name on a tree
(**b**) *(sonido)* to record; *(imagen)* to record; *(en cinta)* to record, to tape; **han grabado un nuevo disco** they've recorded a new album
(**c**) *(fijar)* **grabado en su memoria** imprinted *o* engraved on his memory; **¡que te quede bien grabado!** don't you forget it!
(**d**) *Informát (documento)* to save; *(CD-ROM)* to record, to burn
2 **grabarse** *vpr* (**a**) *(registrarse, reproducirse)* to be recorded (**b**) *(fijarse)* **grabársele a alguien en la memoria** to become imprinted *o* engraved on sb's mind

gracejo, -a 1 *nm (gracia)* **tener mucho g.** to be a good talker; **contar una historia con g.** to tell a story in an amusing way
2 *nm,f Méx (payaso)* clown, joker

GRACIA 1 *nf* (**a**) *(humor, comicidad)* **¡qué g.!** how funny!; **su voz me hace mucha g.** *(me divierte)* I think he's got a really funny voice, his voice makes me laugh; **me hizo g. verlo con traje y corbata** it was funny seeing him in a suit and tie; **mi sombrero le hizo g. a Ana** *(le gustó)* Ana liked my hat; **no me hizo g.** I didn't find it funny; **yo no le veo la g.** I don't see what's so funny about it; **tener g.** *(ser divertido, curioso)* to be funny
(**b**) *(arte, habilidad)* skill, natural ability; **tiene una g. especial** she has a special talent; *Esp* **todavía no le he pillado** *o* **cogido la g. a esta cámara** I still haven't got the hang of using this camera
(**c**) *(encanto)* grace, elegance; **baila con mucha g.** she's a very graceful dancer; **no consigo verle la g. a este cuadro** I just don't know what people see in this painting; **la g. del plato está en la salsa** the secret of the dish is (in) the sauce; **tiene mucha g. contando chistes** she's really good at telling jokes
(**d**) *(ocurrencia)* **estuvo toda la tarde soltando gracias** he spent all afternoon making funny remarks; **no le rías las gracias al niño** don't laugh when the child does/says something silly
(**e**) *(incordio)* nuisance; **vaya g. tener que salir a mitad de la noche** it's a real nuisance having to go out in the middle of the night; *Fam* **¡maldita la g. que me hace tener que volverlo a hacer!** it's a real pain having to do it all over again!
(**f**) *(favor)* favour; **procura caer en g. al director para que te dé el puesto** try and get in the manager's good books so he gives you the job; **por la g. de Dios** by the grace of God
(**g**) *(indulto)* pardon; **esperan una medida de g. del gobierno** they are hoping to be pardoned by the government
(**h**) *Rel* grace; **en estado de g.** in a state of grace

(i) *Mitol* **las tres gracias** the three Graces
2 gracias *nfpl* **dar las gracias a alguien (por)** to thank sb (for); **se marchó sin ni siquiera dar las gracias** she left without even saying thank you; *Fam* **a ese amigo tuyo yo no le doy ni las gracias** I've no time at all for that friend of yours; **lo he conseguido gracias a ti** I managed it thanks to you; **pudimos ir gracias a que no llovió** we were able to go thanks to the fact that it didn't rain; **salvó la vida gracias a que llevaba casco** the fact that he was wearing a crash helmet saved his life; **gracias a Dios ya estamos en casa** thank God we're home
3 *interj* **gracias** thank you, thanks; **muchas gracias** thank you very much, thanks very much; **mil gracias por tu ayuda** thank you so much for your help, *esp Br* thanks ever so much for your help; **te pagarán el viaje, y gracias** you should be thankful *o* you're lucky they're paying your travel expenses

---

grácil *adj* **(a)** *(armonioso)* graceful **(b)** *(delicado)* delicate

gracilidad *nf* **(a)** *(armonía)* gracefulness **(b)** *(delicadeza)* delicacy

gracioso, -a 1 *adj* **(a)** *(divertido)* funny, amusing; **se cree muy g.** he thinks he's so funny; *Irónico* **sería g. que ahora me echaran la culpa a mí** it would be a bit rich if they blamed me now
(b) *(curioso)* funny; **es g. que...** it's funny how...; **¡qué g., los dos se llaman Vicente González!** how funny, they're both called Vicente González!; **lo g. es que no es la primera vez que me pasa** the funny thing is, it's not the first time it's happened to me
(c) *(bonito, atractivo)* pretty; **ese sombrero le queda muy g.** that hat looks very pretty *o* nice on her
(d) su Graciosa Majestad her Gracious Majesty
2 *nm,f* **(a)** *(persona divertida)* funny *o* amusing person; **es un g.** he's really funny **(b)** *(persona molesta)* smart alec, comedian; **¿quién ha sido el g. que ha apagado la luz?** who's the smart alec *o* joker who turned the light out?
3 *nm Teatro* fool, clown

grada *nf* **(a)** *(peldaño)* step **(b)** *Teatro* row **(c) gradas** *(en estadio)* terraces

gradación *nf* **(a)** *(en retórica)* climax **(b)** *(escalonamiento)* scale

gradería *nm* **(a)** *Teatro* rows **(b)** *Am (en estadio)* terraces **(c)** *Am (público)* crowd

graderío *nm Esp* **(a)** *Teatro* rows **(b)** *(en estadio)* terraces **(c)** *(público)* crowd

gradiente 1 *nm Fís* gradient
2 *nf CSur, Ecuad (pendiente)* gradient, slope

grado *nm* **(a)** *(de temperatura)* degree ►► ***g. Celsius*** degree Celsius; ***g. centígrado*** degree centigrade; ***g. Fahrenheit*** degree Fahrenheit; ***g. Kelvin*** Kelvin
(b) *(de alcohol)* **¿cuántos grados tiene ese whisky?** how strong is that whisky?; **alcohol de 90 grados** 90 degree proof alcohol
(c) *(índice, nivel)* degree; **el candidato mostró un alto g. de preparación** the candidate was very well prepared; **un fenómeno que afecta en menor g. a las ciudades** a phenomenon that affects cities to a lesser extent *o* degree; **eso depende del g. de intransigencia de la gente** that depends on how prepared people are to compromise; **están examinando su g. de ceguera** they're checking to see how blind she is; **la situación empeoró en tal** *o Am* **a tal g. que...** the situation deteriorated to such a degree *o* to such an extent that...; **en g. sumo** greatly
(d) *(en escala)* degree; **quemaduras de primer g.** first-degree burns; **asesinato en segundo g.** second-degree murder
(e) *(rango)* grade; **es primo mío en segundo g.** he's my second cousin
(f) *Mil* rank
(g) *Educ (año)* year, class, *US* grade
(h) *Educ (título)* degree; **obtuvo el g. de doctor** he obtained his doctorate
(i) *Ling* degree ►► ***g. comparativo*** comparative degree; ***g. superlativo*** superlative degree
(j) *Mat (de ángulo)* degree
(k) *Mat (de ecuación)* **una ecuación de segundo g.** a quadratic equation
(l) *(voluntad)* **hacer algo de buen/mal g.** to do sth willingly/unwillingly; **te lo prestaré de buen g.** I'd be happy to lend it to you

graduable *adj* adjustable

graduación *nf* **(a)** *(acción)* grading **(b)** *(de la vista)* eye-test **(c)** *(de gafas)* strength **(d)** *Educ (obtención de título)* graduation; *(ceremonia)* graduation (ceremony) **(e)** *(de bebidas)* **g. (alcohólica)** strength; **¿cuál es la g. de ese whisky?** how strong is that whisky?; **bebidas de alta g.** spirits **(f)** *Mil* rank

graduado, -a 1 *adj* **(a)** *(termómetro)* graduated; **gafas graduadas** prescription glasses; **recipiente g.** *(jarra)* measuring jug **(b)** *(universitario)* graduate
2 *nm,f (persona)* graduate ►► ***g. social*** graduate in social work
3 *nm Esp Educ* ***g. escolar*** *(título)* = certificate of primary education

gradual *adj* gradual; **se ha producido un empeoramiento g. de la situación** the situation has gradually got worse

gradualmente *adv* gradually

graduar [4] **1** *vt* **(a)** *(medir)* to gauge, to measure
(b) *(regular)* to regulate; **la temperatura se gradúa con este botón** this button regulates *o* controls the temperature
(c) *(vista)* to test; **me graduaron mal las gafas** they gave me the wrong prescription for my glasses
(d) *(escalonar)* to stagger; **graduó su esfuerzo para llegar hasta el final** she paced herself to make sure she finished
(e) *Educ* to confer a degree on
(f) *Mil* to confer a rank on, to commission
2 graduarse *vpr* **(a)** *(titularse)* to graduate **(en** in) **(b)** *Esp (la vista)* **tengo que ir a graduarme la vista** I have to (go and) get my eyes tested

grafema *nm Ling* grapheme

graffiti [gra'fiti] *nm* piece of graffiti; **la pared estaba llena de graffitis** the wall was covered in graffiti

grafía *nf* spelling; **tienen la misma g., pero se pronuncian de forma diferente** they are spelt the same but are pronounced differently

gráfica *nf (figura)* graph, chart; *(dibujo)* diagram

gráficamente *adv* graphically

gráfico, -a 1 *adj* **(a)** *(de la imprenta)* graphic; **artes gráficas** graphic arts
(b) *(con signos, dibujos)* graphic; **una representación gráfica** a graph; **diseño g.** graphic design
(c) *(con imágenes)* graphic; **un reportaje g.** a photo story, an illustrated feature; **un reportero g.** a press photographer
(d) *(expresivo, claro)* graphic; **hizo un gesto muy g.** he made a very expressive gesture; **lo explicó de una manera muy gráfica** she explained it very graphically
2 *nm (figura)* graph, chart; *(dibujo)* diagram ►► ***g. de barras*** bar chart; ***g. circular*** pie chart; *Am* ***gráficos de computadora*** computer graphics; *Esp* ***gráficos de ordenador*** computer graphics; ***gráficos para presentaciones*** presentation *o* business graphics; ***g. de sectores*** pie chart; ***g. de tarta*** pie chart; ***gráficos vectoriales*** vector graphics
3 *nm,f RP* printer

grafila, gráfila *nf* milling, reeding

grafiosis *nf inv* Dutch elm disease

grafismo *nm (diseño)* graphics

grafista *nmf* graphic artist *o* designer

grafito *nm* graphite

grafología *nf* graphology

grafológico, -a *adj* graphological

grafólogo, -a *nm,f* graphologist, handwriting expert

gragea *nf* **(a)** *(píldora)* pill, tablet **(b)** *(confite)* sugar-coated sweet

graifrú, greifrú *nm CAm, Ven* grapefruit

grajilla *nf* jackdaw

grajo[1], -a *nm,f (ave)* rook

grajo[2] *nm Andes, Carib Fam (olor)* BO, body odour

gral. (*abrev de* **general**) gen.

grama *nf* **(a)** *(planta)* Bermuda grass ►► ***g. del norte*** couch grass; ***g. de olor*** vernal grass **(b)** *Am (césped)* lawn

gramaje *nm Imprenta* weight

gramática *nf* **(a)** *(disciplina)* grammar; EXPR *Fam* **tener g. parda** to be streetwise *o* worldly-wise ►► ***g. comparada*** comparative grammar; ***g. descriptiva*** descriptive grammar; ***g. estructural*** structural grammar; ***g. funcional*** functional grammar; ***g. general*** general grammar; ***g. generativa*** generative grammar; ***g. genérico-contrastiva*** contrastive grammar; ***g. normativa*** prescriptive grammar; ***g. prescriptiva*** prescriptive grammar; ***g. tradicional*** traditional grammar; ***g. transformacional*** transformational grammar; ***g. transformativa*** transformational grammar
(b) *(libro)* grammar
(c) *ver también* **gramático**

gramatical *adj* grammatical

gramaticalidad *nf* grammatical correctness

gramaticalmente *adv* grammatically

gramático, -a 1 *adj* grammatical
2 *nm,f (persona)* grammarian

gramilla *nf CSur (césped)* grass, lawn

gramínea *Bot* 1 *nf* grass, *Espec* gramineous plant
2 **gramíneas** *nfpl (familia)* grasses, *Espec* gramineae

gramíneo, -a *adj Bot* **una planta g.** a grass, *Espec* a gramineous plant

gramo *nm* gram; *Fig* **no tiene ni un g. de cordura** he hasn't an ounce of good sense

gramófono *nm* gramophone

gramola *nf* gramophone

grampa *nf RP* staple

GRAN [gran] *nm (abrev de* **Grupo Andino**) = Andean organization for trade and economic cooperation, formed by Bolivia, Peru, Colombia, Ecuador and Venezuela

gran *ver* **grande**

grana *nf* (**a**) *(color)* scarlet (**b**) *(cochinilla)* cochineal (**c**) ***g. del Paraíso*** cardamom

Granada *n* (**a**) *(en España)* Granada (**b**) *(en las Antillas)* Grenada

granada *nf* (**a**) *(fruta)* pomegranate (**b**) *(bomba de mano)* grenade ►► ***g. de mano*** hand grenade (**c**) *(proyectil)* shell ►► ***g. de mortero*** mortar shell

granadero *nm Mil* grenadier

granadilla *nf* (**a**) *(planta)* passion flower (**b**) *(fruto)* passion fruit

granadillo *nm* granadilla, cocuswood

granadina *nf* (**a**) *(bebida)* grenadine (**b**) *(cante)* = type of flamenco from Granada

granadino, -a 1 *adj* (**a**) *(en España)* of/from Granada (**b**) *(en las Antillas)* Grenadian
2 *nm,f* (**a**) *(en España)* person from Granada (**b**) *(en las Antillas)* Grenadian

granado, -a 1 *adj (notable)* prominent; **acudió lo más g. de la localidad** the cream of local society attended; **la exposición reúne lo más g. del artista** the exhibition brings together all the artist's major works
2 *nm* pomegranate tree

granar *vi* to seed

granate 1 *nm* (**a**) *(gema)* garnet (**b**) *(color)* maroon
2 *adj inv* maroon

granazón *nm* seeding; **estar en g.** to be seeding

GRANDE

gran is used instead of **grande** before singular nouns (e.g. **gran hombre** great man).

1 *adj* (**a**) *(de tamaño)* big, large; **este traje me está** *o* **me queda g.** this suit is too big for me; **el gran Buenos Aires/Santiago** greater Buenos Aires/Santiago, the metropolitan area of Buenos Aires/Santiago; *Fig* **el cargo le viene g.** he's not up to the job; *Fam* **pagó con un billete de los grandes** he paid with a large note ►► ***grandes almacenes*** department store; *Fot* ***gran angular*** wide-angle lens; ***la Gran Barrera de Coral*** the Great Barrier Reef; ***Gran Bretaña*** Great Britain; ***el Gran Cañón (del Colorado)*** the Grand Canyon; ***gran danés*** Great Dane; *Hist* ***la Gran Depresión*** the Great Depression; ***gran ducado*** grand duchy; ***la Gran Explosión*** the Big Bang; ***la Gran Guerra*** the Great War; ***los Grandes Lagos*** the Great Lakes; ***gran maestro*** *(en ajedrez)* grand master; ***la Gran Muralla (China)*** the Great Wall (of China); *Dep* ***Gran Premio*** Grand Prix; ***gran simio antropoide*** great ape; ***gran slam*** *(en tenis)* grand slam; *Esp Com* ***gran superficie*** hypermarket
(**b**) *(de altura)* tall; **¡qué g. está tu hermano!** your brother's really grown!
(**c**) *(en importancia)* great; **una gran mujer** a great woman; **los grandes bancos** the major banks; **la gran mayoría está a favor del proyecto** the great *o* overwhelming majority are in favour of the project; **el éxito se debe en gran parte a su esfuerzo** the success is largely due to her efforts, the success is in no small measure due to her efforts
(**d**) *(en intensidad)* great; **es un gran mentiroso** he's a real liar; **¡qué alegría más g.!** what joy!
(**e**) *Fam (adulto)* **cuando sea g. quiere ser doctora** she wants to be a doctor when she grows up; **me dijeron que todavía no soy g. como para salir solo** they told me I'm not big enough to go out on my own yet
(**f**) *Méx, RP (de edad)* **cuando se casó ya era g.** she was already quite old when she got married; **siempre se llevó bien con gente más g.** he always got on well with older people
(**g**) *RP Fam (fantástico)* fantastic, *Br* brilliant
(**h**) *RP Irónico (genial)* great; **ayer le hice un favor y hoy me vuelve la espalda, ¡g.!** great! I did him a favour and now he doesn't want to know!
(**i**) EXPR *Fam* **hacer algo a lo g.** to do sth in a big way *o* in style; **vivir a lo g.** to live in style; **pasarlo en g.** to have a great time
2 *nm* (**a**) *(noble)* grandee ►► ***G. de España*** = one of highest-ranking members of Spanish nobility
(**b**) *(persona, entidad importante)* **uno de los grandes del sector** one of the major players in the sector; **los tres grandes de la liga** the big three in the league; **uno de los grandes de la literatura mexicana** one of the big names in Mexican literature
(**c**) *Fam* **grandes** *(adultos)* grown-ups
3 *nf RP (en lotería)* first prize, jackpot; **sacarse la g.** *(en lotería)* to win first prize *o* the jackpot; **se sacó la g. con ese trabajo** *(tuvo buena suerte)* she hit the jackpot with that job; **con esa nuera que tiene le tocó la g.** *(tuvo mala suerte)* you've got to feel sorry for her having a daughter-in-law like that
4 *interj RP Fam (fantástico)* great!

---

grandemente *adv (en extremo)* extremely, greatly

grandeza *nf* (**a**) *(de tamaño)* (great) size (**b**) *(esplendor)* magnificence, grandeur; **en toda su g.** in all its splendour *o* grandeur (**c**) *(de sentimientos)* generosity, graciousness; **aceptó su derrota con g.** he accepted defeat graciously, he was gracious in defeat; **g. de espíritu** generosity of spirit, magnanimity (**d**) *Esp (dignidad)* rank of grandee (**e**) *Esp (nobles)* **la g.** the Spanish grandees

grandilocuencia *nf* grandiloquence

grandilocuente *adj* grandiloquent

grandiosidad *nf* grandeur

grandioso, -a *adj* grand, splendid

grandullón, -ona, *CSur, Ven* **grandulón, -ona** *Fam* 1 *adj* overgrown
2 *nm,f* big boy, *f* big girl

granel: a granel *loc adv* (**a**) *(sin envase)* loose; *(en gran cantidad)* in bulk; **vender/comprar vino a g.** to sell/buy wine from the barrel (**b**) *(en abundancia)* in abundance; **habrá bebida a g.** there will be loads of drink; **hubo quejas a g.** there was a barrage of complaints

granelero, -a *adj* **barco g.** bulk carrier

granero *nm* (**a**) *(edificio)* granary (**b**) *(zona rica)* breadbasket

granítico, -a *adj* (**a**) *(de granito)* granitic, granite; **roca granítica** granite (**b**) *(apoyo)* rock solid

granito *nm* (**a**) *(roca)* granite (**b**) *(en la piel)* spot, pimple (**c**) EXPR **aportar** *o* **poner uno su g. de arena** to do one's bit

granívoro, -a *adj* granivorous

granizada *nf* (**a**) *Meteo* hailstorm (**b**) *(abundancia)* hail, shower

granizado, -a 1 *adj RP (helado)* **helado g.** chocolate chip ice cream
2 *nm* = drink of flavoured crushed ice; **g. de café** = coffee-flavoured crushed ice; **g. de limón** = lemon-flavoured crushed ice

granizar [14] *v impersonal* to hail; **está granizando** it's hailing

granizo *nm* hail

granja *nf* (**a**) *(en el campo)* farm ►► ***g. agropecuaria*** agricultural and livestock farm; ***g. avícola*** poultry farm; ***g. escuela*** = farm which schoolchildren visit or stay at to learn about farming life and animals; ***g. marina*** marine farm (**b**) *Urug (tienda)* = shop selling farm produce

granjear 1 *vt* (**a**) *(conquistar)* to earn; **su generosidad le ha granjeado la admiración de todos** his generosity has earned him everyone's admiration (**b**) *Chile (estafar)* to swindle
2 **granjearse** *vpr* to gain, to earn; **con su actitud se ha granjeado el respeto de todos los alumnos** her attitude has earned *o* won her the respect of all her pupils; **con esa decisión se granjeó el odio de sus compañeros** that decision made his colleagues hate him

granjero, -a *nm,f* farmer

grano *nm* (**a**) *(de cereal, arena)* grain; **un g. de uva** a grape; EXPR **aportar** *o* **poner uno su g. de arena** to do one's bit; EXPR **ir al g.** to get to the point ►► ***g. de café*** coffee bean; ***g. de pimienta*** peppercorn (**b**) *(cereal)* grain; EXPR **apartar** *o* **separar el g. de la paja** to separate the wheat from the chaff (**c**) *(partícula)* grain (**d**) *(en la piel)* spot, pimple (**e**) *Fot* grain

granola *nf Am* granola

granuja *nmf* (**a**) *(pillo)* rogue, scoundrel (**b**) *(canalla)* trickster, swindler

granujada *nf* dirty trick

granulado, -a 1 *adj* granulated
2 *nm* granules

granular 1 *adj (granuloso)* granular, grainy
2 *vt* to granulate

gránulo *nm* (**a**) *(grano)* granule (**b**) *(píldora)* small pill

granuloso, -a *adj* bumpy

granza *nf* (**a**) *Min* coal *(in pieces measuring between 15 and 25 cm)* (**b**) *(del trigo)* chaff (**c**) *(del hierro)* dross

grao *nm* beach, shore *(where boats can land)*

grapa *nf* (**a**) *(para papeles)* staple; **sujetar con grapas** to staple (**b**) *(para heridas)* stitch, (wire) suture (**c**) *CSur (bebida)* grappa

grapadora *nf* stapler ►► ***g. industrial*** staple gun

grapar *vt* to staple

grapia *nf (árbol)* grapia, garapa

GRAPO ['grapo] *nmpl (abrev de* **Grupos de Resistencia Antifascista Primero de Octubre**) = left-wing Spanish terrorist group mainly active in the 70s and early 80s

grapo *nmf (terrorista)* member of "GRAPO"

grasa[1] *nf* (**a**) *(en comestibles)* fat; *(de cerdo)* lard; **la comida de la región tiene mucha g.** the food of the region is very greasy; **necesitas eliminar grasas** you need to get rid of some fat ►► ***g. de ballena*** blubber; ***g. saturada*** saturated fat; ***g. vegetal*** vegetable fat
(**b**) *(lubricante)* grease, oil
(**c**) *(suciedad)* grease; **esta camisa está llena de g.** this shirt is covered in grease *o* is all greasy
(**d**) *Méx (betún)* shoe polish; **dar g. a algo** to polish sth

grasa[2] *RP Fam* 1 *adj* common
2 *nmf* **sos un g.** you're so common

grasiento, -a, *esp Am* **grasoso, -a** *adj* (**a**) *(mantecoso)* greasy (**b**) *(cabello)* greasy; *(piel)* oily (**c**) *(sucio)* greasy

grasilla *nf* butterwort

grasitud *nf RP* grease

graso, -a *adj* (**a**) *(mantecoso)* greasy; *(con alto contenido en grasas)* fatty (**b**) *(cabello)* greasy; *(piel)* oily

grasoso, -a = **grasiento**

gratamente *adv* (**a**) *(agradablemente)* pleasingly; **estoy g. impresionado** I am pleasantly surprised, I am favourably impressed (**b**) *(con agrado)* with pleasure

gratarola, graterola *RP Fam* 1 *adj* free; **ser g.** to be free
2 *adv* (for) free, for nothing; **me salió g. el viaje** the journey didn't cost me anything

gratén *nm Culin* gratin; **al g.** au gratin

gratificación *nf* (**a**) *(moral)* reward (**b**) *(monetaria) (por un trabajo)* bonus; *(por hallar algo)* reward

> **Falso amigo**: El sustantivo inglés **gratification** no es la traducción del español **gratificación**. En inglés, **gratification** significa "satisfacción".

gratificador, -ora, gratificante *adj* rewarding

gratificar [60] *vt* (**a**) *(complacer)* to reward (**b**) *(retribuir)* to give a bonus to; *(dar propina a)* to tip; **se gratificará** *(en letrero)* reward

gratinado, -a 1 *adj* au gratin
2 *nm* **g. de langostinos** king prawns au gratin

gratinador *nm* grill

gratinar *vt* to cook au gratin

gratis 1 *adj inv* free; **ser g.** to be free; **entrada g.** *(en letrero)* entrance free
2 *adv* (for) free, for nothing; **entré g. al concierto** I got into the concert (for) free *o* for nothing; **me salió g. el viaje** the journey didn't cost me anything

gratitud *nf* gratitude

grato, -a *adj* (**a**) *(agradable)* pleasant; **nos es g. comunicarle que...** we are pleased to inform you that... (**b**) *Bol, Chile (agradecido)* grateful

gratuidad *nf* (**a**) *(de servicio)* **mantener la g. de la enseñanza** to keep education free; **el gobierno ha prometido la g. de los libros de texto** the government has promised free textbooks for all children (**b**) *(de comentario)* gratuitousness

gratuitamente *adv* (**a**) *(gratis)* free (of charge) (**b**) *(sin fundamento)* gratuitously

gratuito, -a *adj* (**a**) *(gratis)* free (**b**) *(arbitrario)* gratuitous; *(infundado)* unfair, uncalled for; **violencia gratuita** gratuitous violence

grava *nf* gravel

gravamen *nm* (**a**) *(impuesto)* tax; **libre de g.** unencumbered, free from encumbrances (**b**) *(obligación moral)* burden

gravar *vt (con impuestos)* to tax; **el local está gravado con una fuerte hipoteca** the premises are heavily mortgaged

grave 1 *adj* (**a**) *(enfermedad)* serious; **estar g.** to be seriously ill; **presenta heridas graves** he is seriously injured
(**b**) *(situación)* serious; **cometió un g. error** he made a serious mistake
(**c**) *(serio)* serious; **su semblante g. impone respeto** her serious features inspire respect
(**d**) *(estilo)* formal
(**e**) *(sonido, voz)* low, deep
(**f**) *Gram (palabra)* stressed on the second-last syllable, *Espec* paroxytone
(**g**) *Gram (tilde)* grave
2 *nm* **graves** *(sonidos)* bass; **el control de los graves** the bass control
3 *nf Gram* word stressed on the second-last syllable, *Espec* paroxytone

gravedad *nf* (**a**) *(de lesiones, enfermedad)* seriousness; **resultó herido de g. en el accidente** he was seriously injured in the accident (**b**) *(de situación)* seriousness (**c**) *(solemnidad)* seriousness; **con g.** seriously, gravely (**d**) *Fís* gravity; **en la nave espacial no había g.** there was zero gravity within the spaceship ►► ***g. cero*** zero gravity

gravemente *adv* seriously; **está g. enfermo** he is seriously ill; **"necesito hablarte", dijo g.** "I must speak to you," he said seriously *o* gravely

gravidez *nf Formal* pregnancy, *Espec* gravidity

grávido, -a *adj Formal* (**a**) *(mujer)* pregnant, *Espec* gravid (**b**) *(lleno)* full; **estaba g. de dudas** he was weighed down *o* oppressed by doubts

gravilla *nf* gravel

gravitación *nf* (**a**) *Fís* gravitation ►► ***g. universal*** universal gravitation (**b**) *CSur (influencia)* influence; **la g. de la economía en la vida de un país** the economy's influence on people's lives

gravitacional = **gravitatorio**

gravitar *vi* (**a**) *Fís* to gravitate
(**b**) *(centrarse)* to centre, to be centred; **su novela gravita en torno al problema colonial** his novel centres *o* is centred around the colonial problem
(**c**) **g. sobre** *(recaer)* to rest on; **la bóveda gravita sobre los arbotantes** the vault rests on *o* is supported by the flying buttresses; **sobre mí gravita toda la responsabilidad** all the responsibility rests on my shoulders
(**d**) **g. sobre** *(pender)* to hang *o* loom over; **la desgracia gravita sobre el pueblo** disaster is looming for the town

gravitatorio, -a, gravitacional *adj* gravitational

gravoso, -a *adj* (**a**) *(molesto)* burdensome (**b**) *(costoso)* expensive, costly

graznar *vi* (**a**) *(cuervo)* to caw; *(ganso)* to honk; *(pato)* to quack (**b**) *(persona)* to squawk

graznido *nm* (**a**) *(de cuervo)* caw, cawing; *(de ganso)* honk, honking; *(de pato)* quack, quacking; **el pato dio un g.** the duck gave a quack (**b**) *(de personas)* squawk, squawking

greca *nf* (**a**) *Arquit* fret (**b**) *Col, Ven (cafetera)* filter coffee maker

Grecia *n* Greece

grecochipriota 1 *adj* Greek Cypriot
2 *nm,f* Greek Cypriot

grecolatino, -a *adj* Graeco-Latin

grecorromano, -a *adj* Graeco-Roman

greda *nf* fuller's earth, clay

green [grin] *(pl* **greens**) *nm (en golf)* green

gregario, -a 1 *adj* (**a**) *(animal)* gregarious (**b**) *(persona)* **no seas tan g.** stop always following the herd
2 *nm (en ciclismo)* domestique

gregarismo *nm* (**a**) *(de animal)* gregariousness (**b**) *(de persona)* tendency to follow the herd

gregoriano, -a *adj* Gregorian

Gregorio *n pr* **San G.** St Gregory

greifrú = **graifrú**

grela *nf RP Fam* filth

grelo *nm* turnip leaf

gremial 1 *adj* (**a**) *Hist* guild; **ordenanzas gremiales** guild statutes (**b**) *Am (sindical) Br* trade-union, *US* labor-union; **dirigente g.** union leader; **organización g.** *Br* trade-union *o US* labor-union organization
2 *nf Am Br* trade union, *US* labor union

gremialismo *nm* (**a**) *Pey (corporativismo)* = self-interested behaviour, especially of professional groups (**b**) *Am (sindicalismo)* unionism, *Br* trade unionism

gremialista *nmf Am* union member, *Br* trade unionist

gremio *nm* (**a**) *Hist* guild (**b**) *(conjunto de profesionales)* profession, trade; **el g. del textil/de la construcción** the textiles/building trade (**c**) *Fam (grupo)* club; **soy del g. de los fumadores** I'm a fully paid up member of the smokers' club (**d**) *Am (sindicato) Br* trade union, *US* labor union; *(de estudiantes)* student's union

greña *nf* (**a**) *(mechón)* tangle of hair; **greñas** matted *o* tangled hair; EXPR *Fam* **andar a la g. (con alguien)** to be at loggerheads (with sb); EXPR *Am Fam* **acabaron agarrándose de las greñas** they ended up at each other's throats (**b**) *Méx* **en g.** *(trigo)* unthreshed; *(droga)* unrefined

greñudo, -a *adj Pey* with matted *o* tangled hair

gres *nm* stoneware

gresca *nf* (**a**) *(alboroto)* row; **se armó una g.** there was a fuss *o* row (**b**) *(pelea)* fight; **resultó herido en una g.** he was injured in a fight

grey (*pl* **greyes**) *nf* (**a**) *Literario (de ovejas)* flock; *(de vacas)* herd (**b**) *(fieles)* flock, congregation (**c**) *(conjunto de individuos)* **la g. estudiantil** the students; **dirigió su discurso a la g. nacionalista** he aimed his speech at the nationalist constituency

Grial *nm* **el (Santo) G.** the (Holy) Grail

griego, -a 1 *adj* Greek
2 *nm,f (persona)* Greek; **los antiguos griegos** the ancient Greeks
3 *nm (lengua)* Greek

grieta *nf (ranura)* crack; *(entre montañas)* crevice; *(en glaciar)* crevasse; *(que deja pasar luz)* chink

grifa *nf Fam* dope, marijuana

grifería *nf* taps

grifero, -a *nm,f Perú Br* petrol pump attendant, *US* gas pump attendant

grifo[1] *nm* (**a**) *Esp (llave) Br* tap, *US* faucet; **agua del g.** *Br* tap water, *US* water from the faucet; EXPR **cerrar el g.: la banca internacional ha amenazado con cerrar el g. de las ayudas** the international banks have threatened to cut the aid ▸▸ ***g. monomando*** mixer tap
(**b**) *Mitol* griffin
(**c**) *Perú (gasolinera) Br* petrol station, *US* gas station
(**d**) *Chile (toma de agua)* (fire) hydrant, *US* fireplug
(**e**) *Col Fam (presuntuoso)* **ser un g.** to be conceited

grifo[2]**, -a** *Méx Fam* 1 *adj* **andar g.** *(drogado)* to be stoned *o* high; *(loco)* to be off one's head; **andas g. mano, ¿cómo se te ocurren esas cosas?** are you off your head, pal? where do you get these ideas from?
2 *nm,f* drunk, wino

grifón *nm (perro)* griffon

grill [gril] (*pl* **grills**) *nm* (**a**) *(electrodoméstico)* grill (**b**) *(restaurante)* grillroom

grilla *nf* (**a**) *Andes (molestia)* annoyance, bother (**b**) *Col (riña)* struggle, scuffle

grillado, -a *adj Esp Fam* crazy, loopy; **estar g.** to be crazy *o* loopy

grillarse *vpr Esp Fam* to go crazy

grillete *nm* shackle; **ponerle grilletes a alguien** to shackle sb

grillo *nm* (**a**) *(insecto)* cricket ▸▸ ***g. cebollero*** mole cricket; ***g. real*** mole cricket; ***g. topo*** mole cricket (**b**) **grillos** *(grilletes)* shackles

grima *nf* (**a**) *(disgusto)* **me da g. que malgasten el dinero** I hate to see money being wasted, it really annoys me to see money being wasted (**b**) *(dentera)* **me da g.** it sets my teeth on edge

grimillón *nm Chile Fam (multitud, gran cantidad)* **un g. de** loads of, masses of

grímpola *nf Náut* pennant

gringada *nf Am* **la película es una g.** the movie is the usual Hollywood nonsense

gringo, -a *Fam* 1 *adj* (**a**) *(estadounidense)* gringo, Yankee (**b**) *Am (extranjero)* gringo, foreign
2 *nm,f* (**a**) *(estadounidense)* gringo, Yank (**b**) *Am (extranjero)* gringo, foreigner *(from a non-Spanish speaking country)*

gringolandia *nf Am Fam Hum* Yankeeland

griñón *nm* wimple

gripa *nf Col, Méx* flu

gripaje *nm* **para evitar gripajes** to prevent the engine (from) seizing up

gripal *adj* flu-like; **síntomas gripales** flu(-like) symptoms

griparse *vpr* to seize up

gripe *nf* flu; **estar con (la) g.** to have (the) flu; **tener g.** to have (the) flu

griposo, -a *adj* fluey; **estar g.** to have the flu

gris (*pl* **grises**) 1 *adj* (**a**) *(de color)* grey (**b**) *(triste)* gloomy, miserable (**c**) *(insignificante)* dull, characterless
2 *nm* (**a**) *(color)* grey ▸▸ ***g. marengo*** dark grey; ***g. perla*** pearl-grey (**b**) *Esp Fam Antes* **los grises** *(la policía)* the cops *(who formerly wore grey uniforms)*

grisáceo, -a *adj* greyish

grisalla *nf Méx* scrap metal

grisear *vi* to become grey

grisín *nm RP* breadstick

grisma *nf Chile* bit, strand

grisú (*pl* **grisúes**) *nm* firedamp

gritadera *nf Andes Fam* screaming, shouting

gritar 1 *vi* (**a**) *(hablar alto)* to shout; **no grites tanto, habla más bajo** don't shout so much, lower your voice a bit (**b**) *(chillar)* to scream, to yell; **gritó de dolor** he cried in pain; **gritó de alegría** he shouted for joy
2 *vt* (**a**) *(en voz alta)* **g. algo a alguien** to shout sth at sb; **"¡no cruces!", me gritó** "don't cross!" he shouted at me (**b**) *(reñir)* to shout *o* yell at; **¡no me grites, que no fue culpa mía!** don't shout *o* yell at me, it wasn't my fault!; **no me gusta que me griten** I don't like being shouted at

griterío *nm* screaming, shouting

grito *nm (chillido)* shout; *(de dolor, miedo)* cry, scream; *(de sorpresa, de animal)* cry; **se escuchaban los gritos de los manifestantes** you could hear the demonstrators chanting; **los gritos de ánimo le ayudaron a finalizar la carrera** the shouts of encouragement helped him to finish the race; **dar** *o* **pegar un g.** to shout *o* scream (out); EXPR *CSur Fam* **estar en un g.** to be in agony; **hablar a gritos** to shout, to talk at the top of one's voice; EXPR **pedir algo a gritos** to be crying out for sth; **este niño está pidiendo a gritos que le den unos azotes** this boy is asking to get slapped; EXPR *Fam* **poner el g. en el cielo** to hit the roof; EXPR **ser el último g.** to be the latest fashion *o* craze, to be the in thing ▸▸ ***g. de guerra*** war o battle cry

gritón, -ona *adj Fam* loudmouthed

groenlandés, -esa (*pl* **groenlandeses**), **groelandés, -esa** (*pl* **groelandeses**) 1 *adj* Greenlandic
2 *nm,f* Greenlander

Groenlandia *n* Greenland

grog (*pl* **grogs**) *nm* grog

grogui *adj Fam* (**a**) *(en boxeo)* groggy (**b**) *(adormilado)* **esa pastilla me dejó g.** that pill made me feel groggy; **se quedó g. delante del televisor** he crashed out in front of the television

grojo *nm* common juniper

gronchada *nf RP Fam* (**a**) **la g.** *(personas)* the unhip *o* uncool (**b**) *(acción)* **llevar botas turquesa es una g.** wearing turquoise boots is so uncool *o Br* naff

groncho, -a *RP Fam* 1 *adj* uncool, *Br* naff
2 *nm,f* **es un g.** he's so uncool *o Br* naff

grosella *nf* **g. (roja)** redcurrant ▸▸ ***g. espinosa*** gooseberry; ***g. negra*** blackcurrant

grosellero *nm* currant bush ▸▸ ***g. silvestre*** gooseberry bush

groseramente *adv* rudely

grosería *nf* (**a**) *(cualidad)* rudeness (**b**) *(acción)* rude thing; **ese comentario fue una g.** that was a terribly rude thing to say (**c**) *(palabrota)* swear word; **siempre anda soltando groserías** she goes around swearing all the time

grosero, -a 1 *adj* (**a**) *(maleducado)* rude, crude (**b**) *(tosco)* coarse, rough (**c**) *(malhablado)* foul-mouthed
2 *nm,f* rude person; **es un g.** he's terribly rude

grosor *nm* thickness; **una tabla de 3 cm de g.** a board 3 cm thick

grosso: grosso modo *loc adv* roughly, in broad terms; **firmaron el documento, g. modo, 5.000 personas** roughly *o* around 5,000 people signed the document; **su proyecto coincide, g. modo, con el mío** his project is broadly speaking *o* roughly the same as mine

grotesco, -a *adj (personaje)* grotesque; *(traje)* hideous; *(declaración)* absurd

groupie ['grupi] *nf Fam* groupie

grúa *nf* (**a**) *(máquina)* crane ▸▸ *Chile* ***g. horquilla*** fork-lift truck (**b**) *(vehículo) (para averías) Br* breakdown van *o* truck, *US* tow truck; **la g. (municipal)** = tow truck which removes illegally parked cars; **se me llevó el coche la g.** my car's been towed away; **se avisa g.** *(en letrero)* cars parked here will be towed away (**c**) *Cine & TV* crane

gruero, -a *nm,f Ven* crane operator

grueso, -a 1 *adj* (a) *(espeso)* thick (b) *(corpulento)* thickset; *(obeso)* fat (c) *(en grano)* coarse; **sal gruesa** coarse salt (d) *Meteo* **mar gruesa** = rough sea with waves under 6 metres (e) *Méx Fam* **¡está g.!** *(¡está difícil!)* it's a tough one!
2 *nm* (a) *(grosor)* thickness (b) *(parte mayor)* **el g. de** the bulk of; **el g. del público ya se ha marchado** most of the crowd has already left; **el g. del ejército está cerca de la frontera** the bulk of the army is near the border

grulla *nf (ave)* crane ►► ***g. canadiense*** sandhill crane; ***g. cantora*** whooping crane

grullo, -a *adj* (a) *Guat, Méx (gris)* dark grey (b) *Méx Fam (gorrón)* sponging

grumete *nm* cabin boy

grumo *nm (en líquido)* lump

grumoso, -a *adj* lumpy

grunge [gruntʃ] *nm* grunge

gruñido *nm* (a) *(de perro)* growl (b) *(de cerdo)* grunt (c) *(de persona)* grumble; **dar gruñidos** to grumble; **dijo con un g. que no quería ir** he grumbled that he didn't want to go

gruñir *vi* (a) *(perro)* to growl (b) *(cerdo)* to grunt (c) *(persona)* to grumble

gruñón, -ona *Fam* 1 *adj* grumpy
2 *nm,f* old grump

grupa *nf* hindquarters; **montar a la g.** to ride pillion

grupaje *nm* groupage

grupal *adj* group; **terapia g.** group therapy

grupo *nm* (a) *(conjunto)* group; *(de árboles)* cluster; **g. (de empresas)** (corporate) group; **en g.** in a group; **el g. de cabeza** *(en carrera)* the leading group ►► *Pol* ***g. de contacto*** contact group; *Econ* ***g. de control*** control group; *Informát* ***g. de discusión*** discussion group; ***g. ecologista*** environmental group; ***g. de edad*** age group; ***g. empresarial*** (business) group *o* combine; ***g. de estudio*** study group; *Pol* ***g. mixto*** = independent MPs and MPs from minor parties in Spanish parliament; *Informát* ***g. de noticias*** newsgroup; ***el g. de los ocho (grandes)*** the G8 countries; ***g. parlamentario*** parliamentary group; *Pol* ***g. de presión*** pressure group, lobby; ***g. de riesgo*** group at risk; *UE* ***G. de Sabios*** Committee of Wise Men; ***g. sanguíneo*** blood group; ***el g. de los siete (grandes)*** the G7 countries; *Informát* ***g. de usuarios*** user group
(b) *(de músicos)* group, band
(c) *Tec* unit, set ►► *Elec* ***g. electrógeno*** generator
(d) *Quím* group
(e) *Ling* ***g. consonántico*** consonant cluster; ***g. fónico*** phonic group; ***g. nominal*** noun phrase; ***g. de palabras*** word group; ***g. vocálico*** vowel cluster

grupúsculo *nm* minor group

gruta *nf* (a) *(natural)* cave (b) *(artificial)* grotto

gruyere [gru'jer], **gruyer** 1 *adj* **queso g.** Gruyère
2 *nm* Gruyère

gta. *abrev de* **glorieta**

gua *interj Perú, Ven Fam* wow!

guaba *nf CAm, Ecuad, PRico (fruta)* guama

guabina *nf* blind corvina

guabinear *vi Ven Fam* to dodge the issue

guaca *nf* (a) *Am (sepultura)* = pre-Columbian Indian tomb (b) *Am (tesoro)* hidden treasure (c) *CRica, Cuba (hucha)* moneybox (d) *CRica, Cuba (hoyo)* = pit for ripening fruit (e) *ver también* **guaco**

guacal *nm* (a) *CAm, Méx (calabaza)* gourd (b) *Carib, Col, Méx (jaula)* cage

guácala, guácatelas *interj Méx Fam (¡qué asco!)* ugh!, yuck!

guacamayo, -a *nm,f (ave)* macaw

guacamol, guacamole *nm* guacamole, avocado dip

guacarnaco, -a *adj Col, Cuba, Ecuad (tonto)* foolish, silly

guácatelas = **guácala**

guachada *nf Andes, RP Fam* mean trick

guachafita *nf Col, Ven Fam* racket, uproar

guáchara *nf CRica (maraca)* maraca

guácharo *nm* oilbird

guache *nm* (a) *Arte* gouache (b) *Col, Ven (canalla)* thug (c) *Col (maraca)* maraca

guachimán *nm Am* night watchman

guachinango *nm Méx (pez)* red snapper

guacho, -a, huacho, -a *Andes, RP* 1 *adj* (a) *(calcetín)* odd (b) *Fam (persona)* single; **la veo medio triste, debe ser porque anda guacha** she seems rather sad, it must be because she's not going out with anyone at the moment
2 *nm,f* (a) *(animal huérfano)* orphan (b) *muy Fam (persona huérfana)* orphan (c) *Fam (sinvergüenza)* bastard, swine

guaco, -a 1 *adj* (a) *Andes (con el labio leporino)* harelipped (b) *Méx (mellizo)* twin
2 *nm* (a) *Carib, Méx (planta)* guaco (b) *(ave gallinácea)* currasow (c) *CAm (ave falcónida)* caracara (d) *Am (cerámica)* = pottery object found in pre-Columbian Indian tomb

guadal *nm Am* sandy bog

guadalajareño, -a, guadalajarense 1 *adj* of/from Guadalajara *(Spain and Mexico)*
2 *nm,f* person from Guadalajara *(Spain and Mexico)*

Guadalupe *n (país)* Guadeloupe

guadalupeño, -a 1 *adj* of/from Guadeloupe
2 *nm,f* person from Guadeloupe

guadaña *nf* scythe

guadañar *vt* to scythe

guadaño *nm Cuba, Méx* = small harbour boat

guadarnés *nm* (a) *(lugar)* harness room (b) *(mozo)* stable boy

Guadiana *nm* EXPR *Esp* **ser como el G.** to pop up every now and again

guagua *nf* (a) *Andes (niño)* baby (b) *Cuba, PRico, RDom (autobús)* bus

guaina *Andes, Arg* 1 *adj* young
2 *nmf (chico)* lad, young man; *(chica)* girl, young woman

guaira *nf* (a) *Andes (horno)* = earthenware smelting furnace (b) *Am (vela)* triangular sail (c) *CAm (flauta)* = Indian panpipe

guajira *nf* = Cuban popular song about country life

guajiro, -a 1 *adj* (a) *(de Guajira)* of/from Guajira *(Colombia, Venezuela)* (b) *Cuba Fam (tímido)* shy
2 *nm,f* (a) *Cuba Fam (campesino)* peasant (b) *Cuba Fam (del interior)* out-of-towner (c) *(de Guajira)* person from Guajira *(Colombia, Venezuela)*

guajolote *CAm, Méx* 1 *adj (tonto)* silly, foolish
2 *nm* (a) *(pavo)* turkey (b) *(tonto)* fool, idiot

gualda *nf Bot* dyer's rocket

gualdo, -a *adj* yellow

gualdrapa *nf (adorno)* caparison; *(manto sencillo)* horse blanket

gualicho *nm Andes, RP (hechizo)* evil spell; **hacer un g. a alguien** to give sb the evil eye

guama *nf CAm, Col, Ven* (a) *(fruto)* guama fruit (b) *(mentira)* lie

guamazo *nm Col, Méx, Ven Fam* punch

guamo *nm CAm, Col, Ven* guama

guampa *nf Bol, CSur* horn

guampudo, -a *Bol, CSur* 1 *adj* (a) *(animal)* horned (b) *Fam (persona)* cuckolded
2 *nm,f Fam* cuckold

guamúchil, huamúchil *nm* camachile

guanábana *nf Am* soursop

guanábano *nm Am* soursop tree

guanacaste *nm* ear pod tree

guanaco 1 *adj Am Fam (bobalicón)* nitwit
2 *nm* (a) *(animal)* guanaco, wild llama (b) *Chile Fam (camión)* water cannon

guanajo *nm Carib* turkey

guanajuatense 1 *adj* of/from Guanajuato *(Mexico)*
2 *nm,f* person from Guanajuato *(Mexico)*

guanche *nmf* guanche, = original inhabitant of the Canary Islands

guando *nm Andes* stretcher

guandú *nm CAm, Carib, Col (arbusto)* guandu, pigeon pea

guanera *nf Am* guano deposit

guango, -a *adj Méx (holgado)* loose-fitting, baggy; **me queda g.** it's too loose *o* baggy; EXPR *Fam* **me viene** *o* **queda g.** I couldn't care less

guangoche *nm* sacking

guano *nm* (a) *(abono)* guano (b) *Cuba (hojas)* palm leaves *(used as roofing)*

guantada = **guantazo**

guantanamero, -a 1 *adj* of/from Guantanamo *(Cuba)*
2 *nm,f* person from Guantanamo *(Cuba)*

guantazo, guantada *nm Fam* slap; **dar un g. a alguien** to give sb a slap (on the face)

guante *nm* glove; EXPR **arrojar** *o* **tirar el g.** to throw down the gauntlet; EXPR **colgar los guantes** *(boxeador)* to hang up one's gloves; EXPR **de g. blanco** gentlemanly; **un partido de g. blanco** a match played in a good spirit; EXPR *Fam* **echarle el g. a algo/alguien** to get hold of sth/sb, to get one's hands on sth/sb; EXPR **estar más suave que un g.** to be as meek as a lamb; EXPR **recoger el g.** to take up the challenge *o* gauntlet; EXPR **sentar como un g.** *(ropa)* to fit like a glove; EXPR **tratar a alguien con g. de seda** *o CSur* **g. blanco** to handle sb with kid gloves ▸▸ ***guantes de boxeo*** boxing gloves; ***guantes de cirujano*** surgeon's gloves; ***guantes de golf*** golf(ing) gloves; ***guantes de portero*** goalkeeper's gloves

guantear *vt Méx Fam (agarrar)* to collar

guantelete *nm* gauntlet

guantera *nf* glove compartment

guantería *nf* **(a)** *(fábrica)* glove factory **(b)** *(tienda)* glove shop

guantón *nm Col, Perú Fam* slap

guapamente *adv Esp Fam* **todo salió g.** it all went dead well; **¿vendrás? – ¡g.!** are you coming? – sure thing! *o* you bet!

guapango = **huapango**

guapear *vi Perú, RP, Ven Fam* to act the tough guy

guaperas *Esp Fam* **1** *adj inv* **es muy g.** *(hombre)* he's a typical smooth good-looker; *(mujer)* she's the Barbie-doll type
2 *nm inv (hombre)* typical smooth good-looker; *(mujer)* Barbie-doll type

guapetón, -ona *adj Fam* **(a)** *Esp (guapo)* **es guapetona** she's not bad-looking; **estás muy g. con ese traje** you look really good in that suit **(b)** *Esp (ostentoso)* flashy

guapeza *nf Am Fam* **(a)** *(valentía)* guts **(b)** *(bravuconería)* **no me vengas con guapezas** stop your macho posing

guapo, -a 1 *adj* **(a)** *esp Esp (atractivo) (hombre)* handsome, good-looking; *(mujer)* pretty, good-looking; **¡guapa!** *(piropo)* hello, gorgeous!
(b) *esp Esp (elegante)* smart; **¡qué guapa te has puesto!** you look really nice!; **dame diez minutos para ponerme g.** give me ten minutes to get ready
(c) *Esp Fam (muy bueno)* cool, ace; **se ha comprado un piso muy g.** he's bought himself a really cool *o* ace apartment
(d) *Am (valiente)* gutsy; **ser g.** to have guts
2 *nm,f* **(a)** *(valiente)* **a ver quién es el g. que...** let's see who's brave enough to... **(b)** *Esp Fam (apelativo)* pal, *Br* sunshine; **oye, g., devuélveme mi bolígrafo** listen pal *o Br* sunshine, I want my pen back

guapura *nf (de hombre)* handsomeness; *(de mujer)* prettiness

guaquear = **huaquear**

guaqueo = **huaqueo**

guaquero = **huaquero**

guaraca *nf Andes* sling

guaracha *nf Carib (baile, música)* = popular song and dance

guarachar, guarachear *vi Carib Fam* to party, to live it up

guarache = **huarache**

guarachear = **guarachar**

guaragua *nf* **(a)** *Andes (contoneo)* swing, turn **(b)** *Andes (rodeo)* evasion, indirectness **(c)** *Guat, Hond (mentira)* lie

guarangada *nf Bol, CSur* rude remark

guaraní (*pl* **guaraníes**) **1** *adj* Guarani
2 *nmf (persona)* Guarani
3 *nm* **(a)** *(lengua)* Guarani **(b)** *(moneda)* guarani

guaranismo *nm* = Guarani word or expression

guarao *nmf* person from the Orinoco delta

guarapeta *nf Méx Fam* **agarrar una g.** to get plastered

guarapita *nf Ven* = drink made from rum, juice of a citrus fruit and sugar

guarapo *nm* **(a)** *Am (licor)* = cane liquor **(b)** *Ven (café)* = very weak filtered coffee

guarapón *nm Andes* broad-brimmed hat

guarda 1 *nmf* **(a)** *(vigilante)* guard, keeper ▸▸ ***g. forestal*** gamekeeper, forest ranger; ***g. jurado*** security guard; ***g. de seguridad*** security guard **(b)** *Urug (cobrador)* conductor
2 *nf* **(a)** *(tutela)* guardianship **(b)** *(de libros)* flyleaf **(c)** *(de cerradura)* ward **(d)** *Andes, RP (ribete)* ribbing, trimming

guardabarrera *nmf Ferroc Br* level crossing keeper, *US* grade crossing keeper

guardabarros *nm inv Esp, Bol, RP (de automóvil, bicicleta) Br* mudguard, *US* fender

guardabosque *nmf* forest ranger

guardacoches *nmf inv* parking attendant

guardacostas 1 *nm inv (barco)* coastguard boat
2 *nmf inv (persona)* coastguard

guardador, -ora *nm,f* keeper

guardaespaldas *nmf inv* bodyguard

guardafango *nm Andes, CAm, Carib (de automóvil, bicicleta) Br* mudguard, *US* fender

guardafaro *nm CSur* lighthouse keeper

guardafrenos *nmf inv Ferroc* brakeman, *f* brakewoman

guardagujas *nmf inv Ferroc Br* pointsman, *f* pointswoman, *US* switchman, *f* switchwoman

guardameta *nmf* goalkeeper

guardamuebles *nm inv* furniture warehouse *(for storage)*

guardapelo *nm* locket

guardapolvo *nm* **(a)** *(bata)* overalls; *(delantal)* pinafore **(b)** *(para mueble)* dust sheet, dust cover

---

GUARDAR 1 *vt* **(a)** *(conservar)* to keep; **guarda el vestido en el armario** she keeps the dress in the wardrobe; **esta caja guarda documentos muy antiguos** this box contains some very old documents; **guardo muy buenos recuerdos de mi infancia** I have very good memories of my childhood
(b) *(poner en su sitio)* to put away; **¡guarda los juguetes!** put your toys away!
(c) *(vigilar)* to keep watch over; *(proteger)* to guard; **guarda un rebaño de ovejas** he tends a flock of sheep; **el perro guarda la casa** the dog guards the house; **guarda a tu hijo del peligro** keep your child away from danger; **¡Dios guarde al rey!** God save the King!
(d) *(secreto, promesa)* to keep; **guardó su palabra** she kept her word
(e) *(reservar, ahorrar)* to save (**a** *o* **para alguien** for sb); **¿me guardas un sitio?** will you save a place for me?; **guarda un poco de pastel para tu hermano** leave *o* save a bit of cake for your brother; **he guardado parte de la paga para las vacaciones** I've put by *o* saved part of my wages for my *Br* holidays *o US* vacation; **el carnicero siempre me guarda la mejor carne** the butcher always saves *o* keeps the best meat for me
(f) *(observar) (ley, norma, fiesta)* to observe; **g. cama** to stay in bed; **g. silencio** to keep quiet; **g. las apariencias** to keep up appearances; *también Fig* **g. las distancias** to keep one's distance
(g) *Informát* to save; **g. cambios** to save changes
2 guardarse *vpr* **(a)** *(colocar)* **se guardó la pluma en el bolsillo** she put the pen in her pocket
(b) *(quedarse con)* **guárdate tu ironía para otro momento** save *o* keep your irony for someone else
(c) guardarse de hacer algo *(evitar)* to avoid doing sth; *(abstenerse de)* to be careful not to do sth; **me guardaré de criticarle** I'll be careful not to criticize him; **guárdate de gente como él** be on your guard against *o* be careful of people like him
(d) *Fam* **ésta te la guardo** I'll get you for that, I won't forget that

---

guardarraya *nf Méx* = boundary line between plots of farmland

guardarredes *nm inv* goalkeeper

guardarropa 1 *nm* **(a)** *(armario)* wardrobe **(b)** *(de cine, discoteca)* cloakroom **(c)** *(ropa)* wardrobe
2 *nmf (persona)* cloakroom attendant

guardarropía *nf Teatro* wardrobe

guardavallas *nmf inv Am* goalkeeper

guardavía *nm* signalman

guardavida *nmf RP (salvavidas)* lifeguard

guardería *nf (establecimiento)* nursery; *(en aeropuerto, supermercado)* crèche ▸▸ ***g. infantil*** nursery, day care centre

guardés, -esa *nm,f* caretaker

guardia 1 *nf* **(a)** *(conjunto de personas)* guard; **la vieja g.** the old guard; **el cambio de g.** the changing of the guard ▸▸ ***G. Civil*** Civil Guard, = armed Spanish police force who patrol rural areas and highways, guard public buildings in cities and police borders and coasts; ***g. costera*** coastguard service; ***g. fronteriza*** border guard; ***g. de honor*** guard of honour; ***la g. municipal*** the local police; ***G. Nacional*** National Guard; ***g. pretoriana*** *Hist* Praetorian Guard; *Fig* phalanx of bodyguards; ***g. real*** royal guard; ***la G. Suiza*** the Swiss guard; ***la g. urbana*** the local police
(b) *(vigilancia)* watch, guard; *también Fig* **aflojar** *o* **bajar la g.** to lower *o* drop one's guard; **de g.** on guard; **me quedé de g. toda la**

noche I stayed up watching all night; **¡en g.!** en garde!; **hacer g.** to stand guard; **montar (la) g.** to mount guard; **poner a alguien en g.** to put sb on their guard; **ponerse en g.** *(en boxeo)* to raise one's guard
(c) *(turno)* shift; **este mes hice cinco guardias** *(médico)* I've done five shifts this month; *(soldado)* I've done five turns at guard duty this month; **le atenderá el médico de g.** the doctor on duty *o* duty doctor will see you; **estar de g.** *(médico)* to be on duty *o* call; *(farmacia)* to be open 24 hours *(on a given day)*
2 *nmf* (a) *(agente)* policeman, *f* policewoman ►► ***g. civil*** civil guard; ***g. municipal*** (local) policeman, *f* (local) policewoman; ***g. de tráfico*** traffic policeman, *f* traffic policewoman; ***g. urbano*** (local) policeman, *f* (local) policewoman (b) *(centinela)* guard ►► ***g. jurado*** security guard; ***g. de seguridad*** security guard

guardiamarina *nmf* = sea cadet in final two years of training

guardián, -ana 1 *adj* **ángel g.** guardian angel
2 *nm,f (de persona)* guardian; *(de cosa)* watchman, keeper; **los guardianes de la fe** the keepers of the faith

guarecer [46] 1 *vt* to protect, to shelter (**de** from)
2 **guarecerse** *vpr* to shelter (**de** from)

guarida *nf* (a) *(de animal)* lair (b) *(escondite)* hideout

guarismo *nm* figure, number

guarnecer [46] *vt* (a) *(adornar)* to decorate; *(ropa)* to trim; **guarneció la habitación de cortinas verdes** she finished the room off with green curtains (b) *(plato)* to garnish (c) *Mil (vigilar)* to garrison

guarnición *nf* (a) *(adorno)* decoration; *(de ropa)* trimming (b) *(de plato)* garnish (c) *Mil* garrison (d) **guarniciones** *(arreos)* tack (e) *(de espada)* guard

guarnicionero, -a *nm,f* (a) *(de objetos de cuero)* leather worker (b) *(de arreos)* saddler

guaro *nm* (a) *(loro)* = small parrot (b) *CAm (aguardiente)* cane liquor

guarrada, guarrería *nf Esp Fam* (a) *(cosa sucia)* filthy thing; **es una g.** it's filthy; **hacer guarradas** *(porquerías)* to be disgusting (b) *(grosería)* dirty word; **decir guarradas** to use foul language; **hacer guarradas** *(sexuales)* to be naughty; **esa revista es una g.** that magazine is disgusting *o* filthy (c) *(mala jugada)* dirty trick; **hacer una g. a alguien** to play a dirty trick on sb

guarrazo *nm Esp Fam* **me di un g. con la puerta** I banged myself on the door; **se dieron un g. con la moto** they had a crash on their motorbike

guarrear *vt Esp Fam* **g. algo** to get sth all dirty, to mess sth up

guarrería = **guarrada**

guarro, -a *Esp* 1 *adj Fam* (a) *(sucio)* filthy (b) *(malintencionado)* mean (c) *(obsceno)* dirty
2 *nm,f* (a) *(animal)* pig, *f* sow (b) *Fam (persona sucia)* dirty *o* filthy pig (c) *Fam (persona malintencionada)* pig, swine

guarura[1] *nm Méx Fam* bodyguard

guarura[2] *nm Ven (caracol)* conch (shell)

guasa *nf* (a) *Fam (burla, broma)* **lo dijo con g.** he was joking; **estar de g.** to be joking; **parece que has venido con ganas de g.** it looks like you're in the mood for having a laugh; **tomarse algo a g.** to treat sth as a joke (b) *Cuba, Méx, Ven (pez)* jewfish

guasacaca *nf Ven* = chilli or red pepper-based sauce with avocado and onion

guasada *nf RP* rude word

guasca *nf Andes* whip

guascazo *nm Andes* lash

guasearse *vpr Fam* to take the mickey (**de** out of)

guasería *nf Chile* coarseness, crudeness

guasipungo = **huasipungo**

guaso, -a 1 *adj Andes, RP (grosero)* crude, coarse; *(maleducado)* rude
2 *nm,f* (a) *Chile (campesino)* farmer, peasant (b) *Andes, RP* **ser un g.** *(grosero)* to be crude *o* coarse; *(maleducado)* to be rude

guasón, -ona 1 *adj (comentario, risa)* joking, teasing; **¡qué g. eres!** you're such a joker *o* tease!; **hoy estás muy g.** you're in the mood for jokes today
2 *nm,f* joker, tease

guata *nf* (a) *(de algodón)* cotton padding *o* wadding (b) *Andes Fam (barriga)* belly

guate *nm CAm* = maize *o US* corn grown for cattle fodder

guateado, -a *adj* padded

guatear *vt* to pad

Guatemala *n* (a) *(país)* Guatemala (b) *(ciudad)* Guatemala City (c) EXPR *Fam Hum* **de G. a Guatepeor** out of the frying pan, into the fire

guatemalteco, -a, guatemaltense 1 *adj* Guatemalan
2 *nm,f* Guatemalan

guateque *nm Esp, Cuba, Méx (fiesta)* party

guatero *nm Chile* hot water bottle

guatitas *nfpl Chile (tripas)* tripe

guato = **huato**

guatón, -ona *adj Andes Fam* potbellied

guau 1 *nm* **un g. g.** *(lenguaje infantil)* a bow-wow
2 *interj* (a) *(ladrido)* woof! (b) *(de admiración)* wow!; **¡g.!, ¡qué moto te has comprado!** wow! that's some motorbike you've bought yourself!

guay *Esp Fam* 1 *adj* cool, *US* neat; **una fiesta tope g.** a dead cool party; EXPR *Hum* **es g. del Paraguay** it's dead cool
2 *adv* **pasarlo g.** to have a great time
3 *interj (genial)* cool!

guaya *nf Col, Ven* steel cable

guayaba *nf* (a) *(fruta)* guava (b) *Andes, CAm, Cuba Fam (mentira)* fib

guayabate *nm CAm, Méx* guava paste

guayabear *vi Andes, CAm, Cuba Fam* to tell stories

guayabera *nf CAm, Carib, Col* = lightweight man's shirt with pockets and sometimes tucks or embroidery, worn outside trousers

guayabo *nm* (a) *(árbol)* guava tree (b) *Andes Fam (resaca)* hangover (c) *Ven Fam (nostalgia)* homesickness; **tengo g. de mis amigos** I really miss my friends

guayacán *nm* lignum vitae

guayaco *nm* guaiacum

Guayana *n* ***G. francesa*** French Guiana; *Hist* ***G. holandesa*** Dutch Guiana; *Hist* ***G. Inglesa*** British Guiana

guayanés, -esa 1 *adj* Guyanese
2 *nm,f* Guyanese

guayaquileño, -a 1 *adj* of/from Guayaquil *(Ecuador)*
2 *nm,f* person from Guayaquil *(Ecuador)*

guayar 1 *vt Carib (rallar)* to grate; *(raspar)* to scrape
2 **guayarse** *vpr* (a) *PRico (emborracharse)* to get drunk (b) *Carib (fatigarse)* to get tired

guayo *nm* (a) *Carib (rallo)* grater (b) *(borrachera)* drunkenness (c) *(música mala)* poor-quality music, caterwauling

guayoyo *nm Ven (café)* = very weak filtered coffee

guayuco *nm Col, Ven* loincloth *(made of an old pair of trousers, cut down)*

guayule *nm* guayule

gubernamental *adj* government; **política g.** government policy; **organización no g.** non-governmental organization

gubernativo, -a *adj* government; **orden gubernativa** government decree

gubernatura *nf Méx* (a) *(puesto)* governorship (b) *(gestión)* governorship

gubia *nf* gouge

güemul = **huemul**

guepardo *nm* cheetah

güero, -a *Méx Fam* 1 *adj (rubio)* blond, *f* blonde, fair-haired
2 *nm,f* (a) *(rubio)* blond, *f* blonde; **se casó con un g.** she got married to a blond guy (b) *(como apelativo)* **¿cómo estás g.?** how are you, blondie?

guerra *nf (conflicto)* war; *(referido al tipo de conflicto)* warfare; *(pugna)* struggle, conflict; *(de intereses, ideas)* conflict; **la marina de g.** the navy; **nombre de g.** nom de guerre; **declarar la g.** to declare war; *Fig* **le tiene declarada la g. a García** he's at daggers drawn with García, he really has it in for García; EXPR **dar g.** to be a pain, to be annoying; **los niños han estado todo el día dando g.** the children have been misbehaving all day; EXPR *Fam* **de antes de la g.** ancient, prehistoric; **en g.** at war; **ir a la g.** to go to war; EXPR **buscar** *o* **pedir g.** *(problemas)* to look for trouble; *Fam (sexualmente)* to be looking to get laid, *Br* to be up for it ►► ***g. abierta*** open warfare; ***g. atómica*** nuclear war; ***g. bacteriológica*** germ warfare; ***la G. de los Cien Años*** the Hundred Years War; ***g. de cifras*** war of numbers; ***g. civil*** civil war; ***la G. Civil*** *(en España)* the Spanish Civil War; ***g. comercial*** trade war; ***g. convencional*** conventional warfare; ***la G. de Crimea*** the Crimean War; ***g. sin cuartel*** all-out war; ***g. espacial*** star wars; ***g. fría*** cold war; ***g. de las galaxias*** star wars; ***la g. del Golfo*** the Gulf War; ***g. de guerrillas*** guerrilla warfare; ***la G. de la Independencia*** *(en España)* the Peninsular War; ***las guerras médicas*** the Persian Wars; ***g. mundial*** world war; ***g. de nervios*** war of nerves; ***g. nuclear*** nuclear war; ***g. de precios*** price war; ***g. psicológica*** psychological warfare;

las guerras púnicas the Punic Wars; ***g. química*** chemical warfare; ***g. relámpago*** blitzkrieg; ***g. santa*** Holy War; ***la G. de Secesión*** the American Civil War; ***la G. de los Seis Días*** the Six Day War; ***la G. de Sucesión*** the War of (the) Spanish Succession; ***g. sucia*** dirty war; ***la G. de los Treinta Años*** the Thirty Years War; ***la G. de Troya*** the Trojan War; ***la G. de Vietnam*** the Vietnam War

guerrear *vi* to wage war (**contra** on *o* against)

guerrera *nf* (**a**) *(prenda)* (military) jacket (**b**) *ver también* **guerrero**

guerrerense 1 *adj* of/from Guerrero *(Mexico)*
2 *nmf* person from Guerrero *(Mexico)*

guerrero, -a 1 *adj (belicoso)* warlike; *(peleón)* argumentative, quarrelsome
2 *nm,f* warrior

guerrilla *nf (grupo)* guerrilla group

guerrillero, -a 1 *adj* guerrilla; **ataque g.** guerrilla attack
2 *nm,f* guerrilla

gueto *nm* ghetto

guevarismo *nm Pol* = political ideas of Che Guevara

guevarista *Pol* 1 *adj* of Che Guevara
2 *nmf* supporter of Che Guevara

güevo = **huevo**

güevón = **huevón**

güey 1 *nm Méx muy Fam (tonto)* jerk, *Br* plonker
2 *interj* **iay g.!** *(expresión de asombro) Br* bloody hell!, *US* goddamn!

guía 1 *nmf (persona)* guide ►► ***g. espiritual*** *(persona, libro)* spiritual guide; ***g. de montaña*** mountain guide; ***g. turístico*** tourist guide
2 *nf* (**a**) *(indicación)* guidance; **te dejaré una copia para que te sirva de g.** I'll leave you a copy for your guidance *o* as a guide
(**b**) *(libro)* guide (book) ►► ***g. de campo*** field guide; ***g. de carreteras*** road atlas; ***g. de conversación*** phrase book; ***g. de espectáculos*** entertainment guide, what's on guide; ***g. de ferrocarriles*** train timetable; ***g. del ocio*** entertainment guide, what's on guide; *Esp, RP* ***g. telefónica*** telephone book *o* directory; *Esp, RP* ***g. de teléfonos*** telephone book *o* directory; ***g. turística*** tourist guide
(**c**) *(de bicicleta)* handlebars
(**d**) *(para cortinas)* rail

guiar [32] 1 *vt* (**a**) *(indicar dirección)* to guide, to lead; **la estrella les guió al pesebre** the star guided *o* led them to the manger; **no les guía ningún afán de lucro** they are not motivated by profit (**b**) *(aconsejar)* to guide, to direct; **no te dejes g. por sus consejos** don't be guided by his advice (**c**) *(coche)* to drive; *(barco)* to steer (**d**) *(plantas, ramas)* to train
2 **guiarse** *vpr* **guiarse por algo** to be guided by *o* to follow sth; **se guiaban por la posición de los astros** they were guided by the position of the stars; **se guía por el instinto** he's guided by instinct

guija *nf* (**a**) *(guijarro)* pebble (**b**) *(almorta)* chickling vetch

guijarral *nm* stony ground

guijarro *nm* pebble

guijarroso, -a *adj* pebbly

guillado, -a *adj Esp Fam* crazy

guillar 1 *Fam vt Ven (vigilar)* to spy on
2 **guillarse** *vpr Esp* (**a**) *(chiflarse)* to go crazy (**b**) *(irse)* to run off

Guillermo *n pr* **G. I/II** William I/II; **G. Tell** William Tell

guillo *Ven Fam* 1 *nm* (**a**) *(cuidado)* care; **con g.** carefully
2 *adv (con cuidado)* carefully; **andar g. con alguien** to watch out with sb
3 *interj* (**a**) *(cuidado)* careful!, watch out! (**b**) *(ante mal agüero)* God *o* Heaven forbid!

guillotina *nf* (**a**) *(para ejecutar)* guillotine (**b**) *(para papel)* guillotine

guillotinar *vt* (**a**) *(decapitar)* to guillotine (**b**) *(papel)* to guillotine

güincha = **huincha**

guinche, güinche *nm Am* winch, hoist

guinda *nf* (**a**) *(fruta)* morello cherry (**b**) **la g.** *(el remate)* the finishing touch, the icing on the cake

guindar *Fam* 1 *vt* (**a**) *Esp (robar)* to pinch, *Br* to nick; **g. algo a alguien** to pinch *o Br* nick sth off sb (**b**) *CAm, Méx, Ven (colgar)* to hang up; *(hamacas)* to hang
2 **guindarse** *vpr* (**a**) *CAm, Méx, Ven (colgarse)* to hang (**b**) *Ven (pelearse)* to have a scrap; **guindarse con alguien** to get into a scrap with sb

guindilla 1 *nf* (**a**) *(fruto)* chilli (pepper) (**b**) *Esp Fam Anticuado* **la g.** *(la policía) Br* the peelers, *US* the cops
2 *nm Esp Fam Anticuado (policía) Br* peeler, *US* cop

guindo *nm* morello cherry tree; EXPR *Esp Fam* **caerse de un g.: ¿te crees que me he caído de un g.?** I wasn't born yesterday, you know!

Guinea *n* Guinea ►► ***G. Ecuatorial*** Equatorial Guinea

guinea *nf* guinea

Guinea-Bissau *n* Guinea-Bissau

guineano, -a 1 *adj* Guinean
2 *nm,f* Guinean

guineo *nm Andes, CAm* banana

guiñada *nf (pestañeo)* wink

guiñador *nm Bol Br* indicator, *US* turn signal

guiñapo *nm* (**a**) *(andrajo)* rag (**b**) *Fam* EXPR **estar hecho un g.** to be a wreck; **la enfermedad lo dejó hecho un g.** the illness left him completely washed out; **poner a alguien como un g.** to lay into sb, to tear sb to pieces

guiñar 1 *vt* to wink; **guiñarle un ojo a alguien** to wink at sb
2 **guiñarse** *vpr* to wink at each other

guiño *nm* wink; **me hizo un g.** she winked at me

guiñol *nm* puppet theatre

guiñolesco, -a *adj* farcical

guiñote *nm* = card game similar to whist

guión, guion *nm* (**a**) *(resumen)* framework, outline (**b**) *Cine & TV* script, screenplay; *Fig* **eso no estaba en el g.** that wasn't in the script, that wasn't meant to happen (**c**) *(corto)* hyphen; *(más largo)* dash (**d**) ►► ***g. de codornices*** corncrake

guionista *nmf* scriptwriter

güipil = **huipil**

guipuzcoano, -a 1 *adj* of/from Guipúzcoa *(Spain)*
2 *nm,f* person from Guipúzcoa *(Spain)*

güira *nf Carib, Méx (fruto, árbol)* calabash

guiri *Esp Fam* 1 *adj* foreign
2 *nmf* foreigner

guirigay *nm Esp Fam* (**a**) *(jaleo)* racket (**b**) *(lenguaje ininteligible)* gibberish

guirlache *nm* almond brittle

guirnalda *nf* garland

güiro *nm* (**a**) *Am (planta)* gourd, calabash (**b**) *Carib (instrumento)* guiro, = musical instrument made from a gourd (**c**) *Andes (tallo de maíz)* green maize *o US* corn stalk (**d**) EXPR *Ven Fam* **coger el g. a algo** to get the hang *o* knack of sth

guisa *nf* way, manner; **a g. de** by way of, as; **utilizaba una bolsa de plástico a g. de impermeable** she used a plastic bag as a raincoat; **de esta g.** in this way; **con declaraciones de esa g. no se fomenta el diálogo** that sort of statement does not encourage dialogue

guisado *nm* stew

guisante *nm Esp* pea ►► ***g. de olor*** sweet pea

guisar *esp Esp* 1 *vt (cocinar)* to cook; *(en salsa)* to stew
2 *vi* to cook
3 **guisarse** *vpr Fam (ocurrir, planearse)* to be cooking, to be going on; **se está guisando algún asunto turbio** there's some shady business going on; EXPR *Fam* **él se lo guisa, él se lo come: le ofrecí ayuda pero me dijo que prefería hacerlo solo – sí, él se lo guisa, él se lo come** I offered to help him but he said he'd rather do it on his own – yes, he prefers to do everything by himself

güiscola *nm RP Fam* whisky and coke

guiso *nm* (**a**) *(plato)* stew (**b**) *Col (salsa)* = lightly fried onions, garlic, and usually also pepper, used as a base for sauces, stews etc

güisqui *nm* whisky

guita *nf* (**a**) *Esp, RP Fam (dinero)* dough, *Br* dosh; **estoy sin g.** I'm broke; EXPR *RP* **tener la g. loca** to be rolling in it (**b**) *(cuerda)* twine, string

guitarra 1 *nf* (**a**) *(instrumento)* guitar ►► ***g. acústica*** acoustic guitar; ***g. eléctrica*** electric guitar; ***g. española*** Spanish guitar; ***g. solista*** solo guitar; **a la g. solista** on lead guitar (**b**) *(pez)* guitar fish
2 *nmf* guitarist

guitarreada *nf CSur* singalong *(to guitars)*

guitarreo *nm* strumming (of a guitar)

guitarrero, -a *nm,f* guitar maker

guitarrillo *nm* = small four-string guitar

guitarrista *nmf* guitarist

guitarro *nm* = small four-string guitar

guitarrón *nm* = large, low-pitched guitar typical of the Mexican mariachi

güito *nm Br* stone, *US* pit

gula *nf* gluttony

gulag (*pl* **gulags**) *nm* gulag

gulasch [gu'las] *nm inv* goulash

gurí, -isa *RP* **1** *adj* young

2 *nm,f (niño)* kid, child; *(chico)* lad, boy; *(chica)* lass, girl

guripa *nm Esp Fam* **(a)** *(policía)* cop **(b)** *(soldado)* soldier, *Br* squaddie

gurrumina *nf* **(a)** *CAm, Cuba, Méx (fruslería)* trifle **(b)** *Ecuad, Guat, Méx (molestia)* annoyance, bother

gurrumino, -a 1 *adj* **(a)** *(enclenque)* sickly, frail **(b)** *Andes (cobarde)* cowardly

2 *nm,f* **(a)** *Méx (niño)* child **(b)** *Hond (persona astuta)* shrewd person

gurruño *nm Esp Fam* **estar hecho un g.** *(ropa)* to be all wrinkled; *(papel)* to be crumpled up; **hizo un g. con la carta y la tiró a la papelera** she screwed *o* crumpled up the letter and threw it in the bin

gurú, guru *nm* guru

gusa *nf Esp Fam (hambre)* **tener g.** to be starving; **tener un poco de g.** to be peckish

gusanillo *nm Fam* **el g. de la conciencia** conscience; **le entró el g. del viaje** he was bitten by the travel bug; EXPR **matar el g.** *(bebiendo)* he was a drink on an empty stomach; *(comiendo)* to have a snack between meals; EXPR **sentir un g. en el estómago** to have butterflies (in one's stomach)

gusano *nm* **(a)** *(animal)* worm **(b)** *(larva)* grub; *(de mariposa)* caterpillar; *(de mosca)* maggot ►► ***g. de luz*** glow-worm; ***g. de (la) seda*** silkworm **(c)** *Informát* worm **(d)** *Fam (persona despreciable)* worm **(e)** *Fam Pey (exiliado cubano)* = anti-Castro Cuban living in exile

gusarapo, -a *nm,f* creepy-crawly

GUSTAR **1** *vi* **(a)** *(agradar)* **me gusta esa chica** I like that girl; **me/te/le gustan las novelas** I like/you like/she likes novels; **las fresas me gustan con locura** I'm mad about strawberries, I adore strawberries; **¿te gustó la película?** did you like *o* enjoy the movie *o Br* film?; **no me gustó nada** I didn't like it at all; **no me gusta la playa** I don't like the seaside; **me gusta ir al cine** I like going to the cinema; **me gusta hacer las cosas bien** I like to do things properly; **me hubiera gustado ser famoso como él** I would have liked to be famous, like him; **me gusta como juega** I like the way he plays; **sus declaraciones no gustaron a los dirigentes del partido** her comments didn't go down too well with the party leaders; **el tipo de película que gusta al público** the sort of film that the audience likes; **la comedia no gustó** the comedy didn't go down well; **no nos gusta que pongas la música tan fuerte** we don't like you playing your music so loud; **así me gusta, has hecho un buen trabajo** that's what I like to see, you've done a fine job; **hazlo como más te guste** do it whichever way you see fit, do it however you like

(b) *(atraer)* **me gustas mucho** I like you a lot, I really like you; **Andrés y Lidia se gustan** Andrés and Lidia fancy each other *o* are pretty keen on each other

(c) *(en fórmulas de cortesía)* **como/cuando guste** as/whenever you wish; **para lo que usted guste mandar** at your service; **¿gustas?** *(¿quieres?)* would you like some?

(d) *Formal* **g. de hacer algo** to like *o* enjoy doing sth; **gusta de pasear por las mañanas** she likes *o* enjoys going for a walk in the mornings; **no gusta de bromas durante el horario laboral** he doesn't like people joking around during working hours; **gusta de recordar sus tiempos de embajador** he likes to reminisce about his time as ambassador

2 *vt* **(a)** *(saborear, probar)* to taste, to try; **gustó el vino y dio su aprobación** she tasted *o* tried the wine and said it was fine **(b)** *Am Formal (querer)* **¿gusta sentarse?** would you like to sit down?

gustativo, -a *adj* taste; **papila gustativa** taste bud

gustazo *nm Fam* **me di el g. de mandarlo a paseo** it gave me great pleasure to tell him to get lost

gustillo *nm* **(a)** *(de alimento)* aftertaste **(b)** *(impresión)* **su protesta me dejó un g. amargo** his objection left a nasty taste in my mouth

GUSTO **1** *nm* **(a)** *(sentido)* taste; **tiene atrofiado el sentido del g.** she has a poor sense of taste; **añada sal a g.** add salt to taste

(b) *(sabor)* taste, flavour; **este postre tiene un g. muy raro** this dessert tastes very odd; **tiene g. a chocolate** it tastes of chocolate; **tiene g. a plástico** it tastes like plastic; **una barra de helado de dos gustos** a block of ice cream with two flavours

(c) *(estilo)* taste; **el buen g. se forma desde la infancia** good taste is something you develop as a child; **es un cuadro de g. romántico** the painting is rather Romantic in style; **está decorado al g. de la época** it is decorated in the style of the period; **una casa decorada con (buen) g.** a tastefully decorated house; **de buen/mal g.** in good/bad taste; **fue una broma de mal g.** the joke was in bad *o* poor taste; **tener buen/mal g.** to have good/bad taste; **tiene muy buen g. para la ropa** she has very good taste in clothes; PROV **sobre gustos no hay nada escrito** there's no accounting for taste, each to his own

(d) *(preferencia)* taste; **tenemos gustos distintos sobre ropa** we have different tastes in clothes; **no comparto su g. por la violencia** I don't share his liking for violence; **su g. por el mar es bien conocido** he is well known for liking the sea

(e) *(placer)* pleasure; **ponte a g.** make yourself comfortable; **contigo estoy muy a g.** I feel really comfortable *o* at ease with you; **a g. del consumidor** in line with the customer's wishes; **siempre quieres que haga las cosas a tu g.** you always want me to do things your way; **con mucho g.** gladly, with pleasure; **iría con (mucho) g., pero no puedo** I'd love to go but I can't; **lo haré con g.** I'll be pleased to do it, I'll do it with pleasure; **da g. estar aquí** it's really nice here; **lo hago por darte g.** I'm doing it for you *o* to make you happy; **me di el g. de contestarle** I allowed myself the satisfaction of answering him back; **date el g., cómpratelo** go on, treat yourself and buy it; **encontrarse** *o* **estar** *o* **sentirse a g.** to feel comfortable *o* at ease; **está a g. consigo mismo** he's at ease with himself; **hacer algo a g.** *(de buena gana)* to do sth willingly *o* gladly; *(cómodamente)* to do sth comfortably; **tomar** *o Esp* **coger g. a algo** to take a liking to sth; EXPR *Fam* **que da g.: canta que da g.** it's a pleasure to hear her sing; **esta cerveza entra que da g.** this beer goes down a treat

(f) *(en fórmula de cortesía)* **mucho** *o* **tanto g. – el g. es mío** pleased to meet you – the pleasure's mine; **¿me podrías despertar a las 7? – con mucho g.** can you wake me at 7? – of course *o* with pleasure; **tener el g. de hacer algo** to have the pleasure of doing sth; **no tengo el g. (de conocerla)** I don't think I've had the pleasure

2 de gusto, por gusto *loc adv Perú, RP (adrede)* on purpose; **hacer algo de** *o* **por g.** to do sth on purpose *o* deliberately; **es por g. que se queda** she's only staying to annoy us

gustosamente *adv (con placer)* gladly; **lo haré g.** I will do it gladly; **g. te acompañaría, pero no voy a poder** I'd be more than happy to go with you, but I won't be able to; **accedió g. a enseñarles la casa** he willingly agreed to show them around the house

gustoso, -a *adj* **(a)** *(con placer)* **hacer algo g.** to do sth gladly *o* willingly; **lo habría hecho g., pero no pude** I'd gladly have done it, but I wasn't able to; **acepto g. su invitación** I'm pleased to accept your invitation **(b)** *(sabroso)* tasty

gutapercha *nf* **(a)** *Bot* gutta-percha **(b)** *(tela)* = cloth treated with gutta-percha

gutural *adj* guttural

Guyana *nf* Guyana

guyanés, -esa 1 *adj* Guyanese

2 *nm,f* Guyanese

gymkhana [jin'kana] *nf (carrera de obstáculos)* gymkhana; *(de automóviles)* rally

Gzlez. (*abrev de* **González**) = written abbreviation of the surname González

H, h

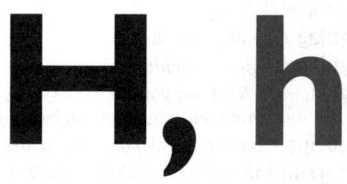

H, h ['atʃe] *nf (letra)* H, h; EXPR *Fam* **por h o por b** for one reason or another

H¹ (*abrev de* **Hermano**) Br.

H² (**a**) (*abrev de* **Hombre**) M (**b**) (*abrev de* **Hembra**) F

h, h. (*abrev de* **hora**) hr, h.

ha 1 *ver* **haber**
2 *nf* (*abrev de* **hectárea**) ha
3 *interj* ah!, oh!

haba *nf*

Takes the masculine articles **el** and **un**.

(planta) broad bean; *(semilla)* broad bean; EXPR *Fam* **en todas partes (se) cuecen habas** it's the same the world over; EXPR *Fam* **ser habas contadas: mi sueldo son habas contadas** I earn peanuts; **o aceptas o te vas, son habas contadas** either you agree to it or you leave, that's all there is to it *o* it's as simple as that

habanera *nf Mús* habanera

habanero, -a 1 *adj* of/from Havana
2 *nm,f* person from Havana

habanitos *nmpl RP* = chocolate finger biscuits

habano *nm* Havana cigar

habeas corpus *nm inv* habeas corpus

HABER¹ [1] **1** *v aux* (**a**) *(en tiempos compuestos)* to have; **lo he/había hecho** I have/had done it; **los niños ya han comido** the children have already eaten; **no he estado en la India** I haven't been to India; **en el estreno ha habido mucha gente** there were a lot of people at the première

(**b**) *(expresa reproche)* **h. venido antes** you could have come a bit earlier; **¡haberlo dicho!** why didn't you say so?; **haberme escuchado** I told you (so), you should have listened to me; **de haberlo sabido...** if only I'd known...

(**c**) *(expresa obligación)* **h. de hacer algo** to have to do sth; **has de estudiar más** you have to study more; **he de llamarle** I ought to call him; **ha de llegar un día en el que todo se arregle** there's bound to come a time when everything gets sorted out; **siempre has de ser tú el que se queje** you always have to be the one to complain

2 *v impersonal* (**a**) *(existir, estar)* **hay** there is/are; **hay un regalo para ti** there's a present for you; **hay dos árboles en la plaza** there are two trees on the square; **hay mucha gente en la calle** there are a lot of people in the street; **había/hubo muchos problemas** there were a lot of problems; **no hubo tal penalty** it wasn't a penalty; **habrá dos mil** *(expresa futuro)* there will be two thousand; *(expresa hipótesis)* there must be two thousand; **los hay de distintas tallas** they come in different sizes; **¿cuánto hay de aquí a Santiago?** how far is it from here to Santiago?; **hay quien opina que...** there are those who think that...; **es un caballero como hay pocos** he's a real gentleman; **es un artista donde los haya** he's as good an artist as you'll find; **algo habrá cuando todo el mundo habla de ello** if everyone's talking about it there must be something in it; **(todo) lo habido y por h.** everything under the sun; **gracias – no hay de qué** thank you – don't mention it; **no hay día (en) que no haya algún accidente** a day doesn't go by without there being some kind of accident; **no hay más que apretar el botón** simply press the button; **no hay nada como una buena comida** there's nothing like a good meal; **no hay nadie como ella** there's no one like her; **no hay quien lo entienda** there's no understanding him; **no hay más que hablar** there is no more to be said; **¡hay que ver!** well I never!; **no hay más que ver lo feliz que está** you just have to see how happy she is; **¡eres de lo que no hay!** you're unbelievable!

(**b**) *(expresa obligación)* **hay que hacer más ejercicio** one *o* you should do more exercise; **hay que comer para vivir** we must eat in order to live; **hay que esforzarse más, Luis** you need to try harder, Luis; **no hay que apretar tanto** there's no need to press so hard; **creo que habría que contárselo** I think we ought to tell him; **¡aquello había que verlo!** you should have seen it!; **habrá que soportar su mal humor** we'll have to put up with his bad mood

(**c**) *Fam (en preguntas)* **¿qué hay?** *(saludo)* how are you doing?; *CSur (¿qué importa?)* so (what)?, big deal!; **¿qué hay de nuevo?** what's new?; *CSur* **está lloviendo – ¿y qué hay?, estamos en auto** it's raining – so what? we're in the car; *CAm, Col, Méx, Ven* **¿qué hubo?** *(saludo)* how are you doing?

(**d**) *Literario (hacer)* **tres meses ha que marchó** it is three months since she left

3 *vt Formal (tener)* **el abuelo, que Dios haya en su gloria...** grandfather, God rest his soul...; **los hijos habidos en el matrimonio** the children from the marriage

4 haberse *vpr* **habérselas con alguien** to face *o* confront sb; **allá se las haya** that's his/her problem; **¡habráse visto cosa igual!** have you ever seen such a thing *o* the likes of it!

haber² *nm* (**a**) *(bienes)* assets; **confiscaron sus haberes** they confiscated his assets (**b**) *(en cuentas, contabilidad)* credit (side) (**c**) **haberes** *(sueldo)* remuneration; **todavía no han cobrado sus haberes del mes pasado** they still haven't been paid last month's wages (**d**) *(mérito)* **tiene en su h. su capacidad de trabajo** in his favour is the fact that he's a good worker

habichuela *nf Esp, Carib, Col* bean

habido, -a *adj* occurred; **los accidentes habidos este verano** the number of accidents this summer

hábil *adj* (**a**) *(diestro)* skilful; **estuvo muy h. en el debate** she argued very skilfully in the debate; **es muy h. con las manos** he's very good with his hands; *Irónico* **se me ha quemado la comida – ¡qué h.!** I've burned the dinner – that was clever (of you)! *o Br* nice one!

(**b**) *(inteligente)* clever; **utilizó una h. estrategia para convencernos** he used a clever strategy to persuade us

(**c**) *(utilizable) (lugar)* suitable, fit; **días hábiles** working days

habilidad *nf* (**a**) *(destreza)* skill; **una de sus muchas habilidades es la música** music is just one of his many skills; **tener h. para algo** to be good at sth (**b**) *(inteligencia)* cleverness; **salió del compromiso con h.** she cleverly extricated herself from the situation (**c**) *Ling* performance

habilidoso, -a *adj* (**a**) *(diestro)* handy, good with one's hands; **es muy h.** he's very handy, he's very good with his hands (**b**) *(inteligente)* skilled, clever

habilitación *nf* (**a**) *(acondicionamiento)* fitting out; **la h. de un almacén para oficinas** the fitting out of a warehouse as offices (**b**) *Der (autorización)* authorization, right (**c**) *(financiación)* **h. de fondos** provision of funds

habilitado, -a 1 *adj Der* authorized
2 *nm,f* paymaster

habilitar *vt* (**a**) *(acondicionar)* to fit out, to equip; **habilitó el desván para cuarto de huéspedes** he fitted out the attic as a guest bedroom

(**b**) *Der (autorizar)* to authorize; **no está habilitado para ejercer en el país** he's not authorized to practise in this country

(**c**) *(financiar)* to finance; **el gobierno ha habilitado créditos para la reconstrucción de la zona** the government has made funds available for the reconstruction of the area

hábilmente *adv* skilfully

habiloso, -a *adj Chile* shrewd, astute

habitabilidad *nf* habitability; **estar/no estar en condiciones de h.** to be fit/unfit for human habitation

habitable *adj* habitable, inhabitable

habitación *nf (cuarto)* room; *(dormitorio)* bedroom; **quisiera una h. con baño** I'd like a room with a bath *o* an en-suite room ►► ***h. doble*** *(con cama de matrimonio)* double room; *(con dos camas)* twin room; ***h. individual*** single room; ***h. de invitados*** spare room; ***h. sencilla*** single room; ***h. simple*** single room

habitacional *adj CSur, Méx* housing; **problemas habitacionales** housing problems; **un complejo h.** a housing development

habitáculo *nm* (**a**) *(casa)* dwelling (**b**) *(habitación)* room (**c**) *(de vehículo)* cabin

habitado, -a *adj (región, casa)* inhabited (**por** by)

habitante *nm (de ciudad, país)* inhabitant; *(de barrio)* resident; **una ciudad de doce millones de habitantes** a city with a population of twelve million; **un insecto h. habitual de las zonas pantanosas** an insect commonly found in marshy areas

habitar 1 *vi* to live; **una región sin h.** an unpopulated area
2 *vt* to live in, to inhabit; **una especie que habita las zonas montañosas** a species found in mountainous areas

hábitat (*pl* **hábitats**) *nm* (**a**) *Biol* habitat ►► ***h. marino*** marine habitat (**b**) *Geog* environment ►► ***h. rural*** rural environment; ***h. urbano*** urban environment (**c**) *(vivienda)* housing conditions

hábito *nm* (**a**) *(costumbre)* habit; **tener el h. de hacer algo** to be in the habit of doing sth; **adquirió malos hábitos** she picked up bad habits
(**b**) *(adicción)* **crear h.** to be addictive
(**c**) *(de monje, monja)* habit; EXPR **colgar los hábitos** *(monja)* to renounce one's vows; *(sacerdote)* to leave the priesthood; **el senador decidió colgar los hábitos** the senator decided to leave politics; EXPR **tomar el h.** *o* **los hábitos** *(monja)* to take the veil; *(sacerdote)* to take holy orders; PROV **el h. no hace al monje** clothes maketh not the man

habituación *nf* (**a**) *(a situación)* **la h. al nuevo trabajo fue difícil** getting used to the new job was difficult (**b**) *(a drogas)* addiction

habitual *adj (costumbre, respuesta)* habitual; *(cliente, lector)* regular; **es h.** it's not uncommon, it's normal; **el mal humor es h. en él** he's more often than not in a bad mood; **lo h. es dejar propina** it is usual *o* customary to leave a tip; **lo h. en un caso así es llamar a la policía** in a case like this you would normally call the police

habitualmente *adv* usually, normally

habituar [4] **1** *vt* **h. a alguien a** to accustom sb to
2 habituarse *vpr* **habituarse a** *(acostumbrarse)* to get used *o* accustomed to; *(drogas)* to become addicted to

habitué *RP Fam* **1** *adj* regular
2 *nm,f* regular

habla *nf*

> Takes the masculine articles **el** and **un**.

(**a**) *(idioma)* language; *(dialecto)* dialect; **el h. popular** everyday speech; **el h. de los abogados** legal parlance, the language used by lawyers; **de h. española** Spanish-speaking; **los países de h. inglesa** English-speaking countries
(**b**) *(facultad)* speech; **no saben si recuperará el h.** they don't know if she will ever speak again; **quedarse sin h.** to be left speechless
(**c**) *Ling* parole
(**d**) *(al teléfono)* **estar al h. con alguien** to be on the line to sb; **¿el Sr. Pastor? – al h.** Mr Pastor? – speaking!

hablado, -a *adj* spoken; **bien h.** well-spoken; **mal h.** foul-mouthed

hablador, -ora 1 *adj* (**a**) *(parlanchín)* talkative; **es demasiado h.** he talks too much (**b**) *(chismoso)* gossipy; **es muy h.** he's a real gossip (**c**) *Méx, RDom (mentiroso)* liar
2 *nm,f* (**a**) *(parlanchín)* **ser un h.** to be talkative (**b**) *(chismoso)* gossip (**c**) *Méx, RDom (mentiroso)* liar

habladurías *nfpl (rumores)* rumours; *(chismes)* gossip; **no son más que h.** it's all just idle gossip

hablante 1 *adj* speaking
2 *nmf* speaker; **h. nativo** native speaker

hablantina *nf Col, Ven (charla)* idle talk, chatter

HABLAR 1 *vi* (**a**) *(emitir palabras)* to speak; **h. en voz alta/baja** to speak loudly/softly; **el bebé ya habla** the baby is talking already
(**b**) *(expresarse, comunicarse)* to speak; **h. claro** to speak clearly; **h. en español/inglés** to speak Spanish/English; **h. por señas** to use sign language; **dejar h. a alguien** to let sb speak; **déjame h. a mí** *(como representante)* let me do the talking; *(en discusión)* let me get a word in; **hacer h. a alguien** *(a tímido)* to get sb talking; *(en interrogatorio)* to get sb to talk; **h. solo** to talk to oneself; **estos detalles hablan mucho del tipo de persona que es** these small points say a lot about the sort of person she is; **estaba hablando en broma** I was only joking; **sus actos hablan por sí solos** his actions speak for themselves; **¡así se habla!** hear, hear!; **¡qué bien habla este político!** this politician's a really good speaker; **h. por h.** to talk for the sake of talking; EXPR **¡mira quién habla** *o* **quién fue a h.!** look who's talking!
(**c**) *(conversar)* to talk (**con** *o Am* **a** to), to speak (**con** *o Am* **a** to); **estaba hablando en broma** I was only joking; **¿podemos h. un momento?** could I have a word with you?; **estuvimos toda la noche hablando** we talked all night, we spent all night talking; **no debes h. en clase** you mustn't talk in class; **necesito h. contigo** I need to talk *o* speak to you, we need to talk; **hablé con ella ayer por la noche** I spoke to her last night; **¿has hablado con él alguna vez?** have you ever talked *o* spoken to him?; **hablé con él por teléfono** I spoke to him on the phone; **está hablando por teléfono** he's on the phone; **¡(de eso) ni h.!** no way!; EXPR **hablando se entiende la gente** it's good to talk
(**d**) *(tratar)* **h. de algo/alguien** to talk *o* speak about sth/sb; **h. sobre** *o* **acerca de algo** to talk *o* speak about sth; **h. bien/mal de** to speak well/badly of; **háblame de ti** tell me about yourself; **me han hablado muy bien de este restaurante** I've heard a lot of good things about this restaurant, I've heard people speak very highly of this restaurant; **mi hermano me ha hablado mucho de ti** my brother's told me a lot about you; **es mejor no h. del tema** it would be best if we didn't mention that subject; **tenemos muy buenos tenistas, y no hablemos de futbolistas...** we have very good tennis players, and as for footballers...
(**e**) *(murmurar)* to talk; **h. mal de alguien** to criticize sb, to run sb down; **siempre va hablando de los demás** she's always going around saying things about *o* talking about other people; **dar que h.** to make people talk
(**f**) *(pronunciar un discurso)* to speak; **el presidente habló a las masas** the president spoke to *o* addressed the masses
(**g**) *(confesar)* to talk; **lo torturaron y al final habló** they tortured him and in the end he talked
(**h**) *(dar un tratamiento)* **me puedes h. de tú** you can address me as "tú"; **¡a mí no me hables así!** don't you speak to me like that!
2 *vt* (**a**) *(idioma)* to speak; **habla danés y sueco** she can speak *o* she speaks Danish and Swedish; **habla muy bien el portugués** he speaks very good Portuguese
(**b**) *(asunto)* to discuss (**con** with); **es mejor que lo hables con el jefe** it would be better if you talked to the boss about it; **vamos a ir, y no hay nada más que h.** we're going, and that's that
3 hablarse *vpr* (**a**) *(comunicarse)* to speak (to each other); **no se hablan** they aren't speaking, they aren't on speaking terms; **no se hablan desde que tuvieron la discusión** they haven't been speaking since they had the row; **no se habla con nadie en la oficina** she isn't speaking to *o* on speaking terms with anyone in the office
(**b**) *(uso impersonal)* **se habla de una subida de precios** there is talk of a price rise, a price rise is rumoured; **se habla inglés** *(en letrero)* English spoken; **¡no se hable más! me voy** I'm going, and there's an end to it *o* and that's that!

---

habón *mn (roncha)* lump *(on skin)*

habrá *ver* **haber**

Habsburgo *n pr* **los H.** the Hapsburgs

hacedero, -a *adj* feasible, practicable

hacedor, -ora *nm,f* (**a**) *(creador)* maker; **el H.** the Maker (**b**) *Perú (de licor)* = person who makes or sells corn liquor

hacendado, -a 1 *adj* landowning; **una familia hacendada** a family of landowners
2 *nm,f* (**a**) *(terrateniente)* landowner (**b**) *CSur (ganadero)* rancher

hacendista *nmf* public finance expert

hacendoso, -a *adj* hard-working around the house; **tiene un hijo muy h.** she has a son who does a lot *o* is very hard-working around the house

---

HACER [33] **1** *vt* (**a**) *(elaborar, crear, cocinar)* to make; **h. un vestido/planes** to make a dress/plans; **h. una fiesta** to have a party; **h. un poema/una sinfonía** to write a poem/symphony; **h. un nudo** to tie a knot; **los cristianos creen que Dios hizo al hombre** Christians believe that God created mankind; **haz un poco más la carne** cook the meat a bit longer; *Fam* **tu hermano ha hecho una de las suyas** your brother has been up to his usual tricks; EXPR *Fam* **¡buena la has hecho!** you've really gone and done it now!
(**b**) *(construir)* to build; **han hecho un edificio nuevo** they've put up a new building
(**c**) *(generar)* to produce; **el árbol hace sombra** the tree gives shade; **la carretera hace una curva** there's a bend in the road
(**d**) *(movimientos, sonidos, gestos)* to make; **le hice señas** I signalled to her; **hizo un gesto de aprobación con la cabeza** she nodded her approval; **el gato hace "miau"** cats go "miaow"; **el reloj hace tic-tac** the clock goes tick-tock; **h. ruido** to make a noise
(**e**) *(obtener) (fotocopia)* to make; *(retrato)* to paint; *(fotografía)* to take
(**f**) *(realizar) (trabajo, estudios)* to do; *(viaje)* to make; *(comunión)* to take; *(sacrificio)* to make; *(promesa, oferta)* to make; *(milagro)* to

perform; *(experimento)* to do, to perform; *(favor)* to do; *(pregunta)* to ask; *(declaración)* to make; *(crucigrama)* to do; **h. una entrevista** to do an interview; **h. una entrevista a alguien** to interview sb; **tengo mucho que h.** I have a lot to do; **hoy hace guardia** she's on duty today; **estoy haciendo segundo** I'm in my second year; **hago ingeniería** I'm doing *o* studying engineering

(g) *(obrar, realizar una acción)* to do; **¿qué habré hecho con las llaves?** what have I done with the keys?; *CSur Fam* **y mis llaves, ¿qué las hice?** and my keys, now what did I do with them?; **¡mira que le he dicho veces que eso no se hace!** I've told him time and again that it's wrong to do that!; *Fam* **haz lo que te dé la gana** do whatever you want; **¿qué haces? vas a romper la bicicleta** what are you doing *o* what do you think you're doing, you're going to break the bicycle!; **¡qué le vamos a h.!** never mind!

(h) *(practicar) (en general)* to do; *(tenis, fútbol)* to play; **debes h. deporte** you should start doing some sport

(i) *(arreglar) (casa, colada)* to do; *(cama)* to make; *(maleta)* to pack; *(uñas)* to do; *(barba)* to trim

(j) *(dar aspecto a)* to cause to look *o* seem; **este espejo te hace gordo** this mirror makes you look fat

(k) *(transformar en)* **h. a alguien feliz** to make sb happy; **la guerra no lo hizo un hombre** the war didn't make him (into) a man; **hizo pedazos el papel** he tore the paper to pieces; **h. de algo/alguien algo** to make sth/sb into sth; **hizo de ella una buena cantante** he made a good singer of her

(l) *(comportarse como)* **h. el tonto** to act the fool; **h. el vándalo** to act like a hooligan; **h. el ridículo** to make a fool of oneself

(m) *(causar)* **h. daño a alguien** to hurt sb; **me hizo gracia** I thought it was funny; **un poco de aire fresco le hará bien** a bit of fresh air will do her good; *Am* **esos ñoquis me hicieron mal** those gnocchi disagreed with me

(n) *Cine & Teatro (papel)* to play; *(obra)* to do, to perform; **hace el papel de la hija del rey** she plays (the part of) the king's daughter; **hoy hacen una obra de Brecht** today they're putting on *o* doing one of Brecht's plays

(o) *(suponer)* to think, to reckon; **a estas horas yo te hacía en París** I thought *o* reckoned you'd be in Paris by now; **te hacía más joven** I thought you were younger, I'd have said you were younger

(p) *(ser causa de)* **h. que alguien haga algo** to make sb do sth; **me hizo reír** it made me laugh; **has hecho que se enfadara** you've made him angry; **haces que me avergüence** you make me ashamed; **la tormenta hizo que se cancelara el concierto** the storm caused the concert to be called off

(q) *(mandar)* **h. que se haga algo** to have sth done; **voy a h. teñir este vestido** I'm going to have this dress dyed; **la hizo callarse** he made her shut up

(r) *(acostumbrar)* **la prisión lo hizo a la soledad** prison made *o* got him used to being alone

(s) *(cumplir)* **hizo los cincuenta la semana pasada** he was fifty last week, he celebrated his fiftieth birthday last week

(t) *(completar)* to make; **tres y dos hacen cinco** three and two make five; **y este huevo hace la docena** and this egg makes (it) a dozen; **hago el número seis en la lista** I'm number six on the list

(u) *(conseguir)* to make; **hizo una gran fortuna** he made a large fortune; **hizo muchas amistades en Australia** she made a lot of friends in Australia

(v) *(recorrer)* to do; **¿cuántos kilómetros hiciste ayer?** how many kilometres did you do yesterday?; **hago dos kilómetros a pie todos los días** I walk two kilometres every day

(w) *(referido a necesidades fisiológicas)* to do; *Euf* **tengo que h. mis necesidades** I have to answer a call of nature; *Fam* **los niños quieren h. pipí** the children want to have a pee

(x) *(sustituyendo a otro verbo)* to do; **se negó a ir y yo hice lo mismo** she refused to go and I did likewise; **ya no puedo leer como solía hacerlo** I can't read as well as I used to

2 *vi* **(a)** *(intervenir, actuar)* **déjame h. (a mí)** let me do it; EXPR **ser el que hace y deshace** to call the shots; **en la empresa, él es el que hace y deshace** he's the one who calls the shots in the company

(b) h. de *(trabajar)* to work as; *(servir)* to serve as, to act as; *Cine & Teatro (actuar)* to play; **hace de electricista** he's an electrician, he works as an electrician; **este tronco hará de asiento** this tree trunk will do for somewhere to sit; **hace de don Quijote** he's playing don Quixote

(c) *(aparentar)* **h. como si** to act as if; **haz como que no te importa** act as if you don't care

(d) *(procurar, intentar)* **h. por h. algo** to try to do sth; **haré por verle esta noche** I'll try to see him tonight

(e) *(proceder)* **haces mal en callarte** it's wrong of you not to say anything; **hizo bien dimitiendo** she was right to resign; **¿cómo hay que h. para abrir esta caja?** how do you open this box?, what do you have to do to open this box?

(f) *Esp Fam (apetecer)* **¿hace un vaso de vino?** do you fancy a glass of wine?

(g) *Am (necesidades fisiológicas)* **¿hiciste?** have you done anything?; **preciso un baño, no hice antes de salir** I need to find a bathroom, I didn't go before I came out

(h) *Méx Fam* **hacer(la) buena:** *(ojalá)* **dicen que te sacaste la lotería – ¡házmela buena!** they say you've won the lottery – if only!; **me ofreció empleo don Paco, voy a ver si me la hace buena** Don Paco offered me a job, I'll see if he comes through for me

(i) *Méx Fam* **hacerle a** *(profesión)* to do; **por las mañanas estudia y en la tarde le hace a la peluquería** she studies in the morning and in the afternoon she does hairdressing

(j) *Méx Fam* **hacerle a** *(droga)* to do; **ese tipo le hace a la cocaína** that guy does coke

(k) *Méx Fam* **hacerle a** *(aparentar)* to pretend to be; **le hace al tonto, pero bien que sabe** he pretends to be clueless but he knows perfectly well; **dile que no le haga al cuento** tell him to stop *Br* spinning me a line *o US* jerking me around

(l) *Méx Fam* **no le hagas** *(exclamación)* come off it!, *Br* do me a favour!, *US* give me a break!; **perdí mi libro – ¡no le hagas!** I lost my book – pull the other one! *o* sure you did!

(m) *Méx, RP* **no le hace** *(no importa)* it doesn't matter; **no sé si voy a poder ir – no le hace** I don't know if I'll be able to go – it doesn't matter; **¿qué le hace?** so what?, big deal!

3 *v impersonal* **(a)** *(tiempo meteorológico)* **hace frío/sol/viento** it's cold/sunny/windy; **hace un día precioso** it's a beautiful day; **mañana hará mal tiempo** the weather will be bad tomorrow

(b) *(tiempo transcurrido)* **hace diez años** ten years ago; **hace mucho** a long time ago; **hace poco** not long ago; **hace un rato** a short while ago; **hace un mes que llegué** it's a month since I arrived; **no la veo desde hace un año** I haven't seen her for a year; **¿cuánto hace de eso?** how long ago was that?

4 hacerse *vpr* **(a)** *Literario (formarse)* **se hizo la noche** night fell; **y se hizo la luz** *(cita bíblica)* and there was light

(b) *(convertirse en)* **hacerse viejo** to grow old; **se hizo hombre** he became a man

(c) *(guisarse, cocerse)* to cook; **el pavo se está haciendo** the turkey's in the oven

(d) *(fabricar)* to make oneself; **me hice un vestido** *(yo misma)* I made myself a dress; *(la modista)* I had a dress made; **se han hecho una casa al lado del mar** they've built (themselves) a house by the sea

(e) *(arreglarse)* **hacerse las uñas** to do one's nails

(f) *(convertirse en)* to become; **hacerse musulmán** to become a Muslim; **hacerse del Universitario** to sign for *o* join Universitario

(g) *(resultar)* to get; **se hace muy pesado** it gets very tedious; **se me ha hecho muy corto el viaje** the journey seemed very short; **la clase se me ha hecho eterna** the class seemed to go on forever

(h) *(crearse en la mente)* **hacerse ilusiones** to get one's hopes up; **con lo que me has dicho ya me hago una idea de cómo es la escuela** from what you've told me I've got a pretty good idea of what the school is like; **no me hago una idea de cómo debió ser** I can't imagine what it must have been like

(i) *(mostrarse)* **se hace el gracioso/simpático** he acts the comedian/nice guy; **hacerse el distraído** to pretend to be miles away; **¿eres tonto o te lo haces?** are you stupid or are you just pretending to be?

(j) *(conseguir)* **se hizo con la medalla de oro** she won the gold medal; **se hizo con el control de la empresa** he took control of the company

(k) *(acostumbrarse)* **no consiguió hacerse a la comida británica** she couldn't get used to British food; **no me hago a su forma de trabajar** I can't get used to the way they work; **hacerse a una idea** to get used to an idea; **hazte a la idea de que no vamos a poder ir de vacaciones** you'd better start getting used to the idea that we won't be able to go on holiday

(l) *(causarse)* **me he hecho daño en el brazo** I've hurt my arm; **se hizo un corte en la mano** she cut her hand

(m) *(moverse)* **el policía se hizo a un lado** the policeman moved aside; **el camión se hizo a un lado para dejarnos adelantar** the truck *o Br* lorry pulled over to let us past

(n) *(referido a necesidades fisiológicas)* **el bebé se ha hecho encima** *(orina)* the baby has wet himself; *(excremento)* the baby has dirtied his *Br* nappy *o US* diaper; *Fam* **el bebé se ha hecho pipí** the baby's wet himself

(o) *Esp muy Fam* **hacérselo con alguien** *(tener relaciones sexuales)* to do it with sb, *Br* to have it off with sb

(p) *Am Fam* **hacerse de** *(obtener)* to get hold of; **tengo que hacerme de unas llaves para poder entrar** I need to get hold of some keys to get in; **se hizo de un diploma y salió a buscarse la vida** she got herself a qualification and set out to make her fortune; **nos hicimos de algo de comida y pasamos el día en el campo** we got some food together and spent the day in the country

(**q**) *Am Fam* **¿qué se habrá hecho mi vestido?** *(¿dónde estará?)* what's happened to my dress?; **¿y tu prima? ¿qué se hizo?** *(corto plazo)* where has your cousin got to?; *(largo plazo)* whatever happened to that cousin of yours?

(**r**) *Am Fam (salir bien)* **precisaba una beca y por suerte se le hizo** she needed a scholarship and luckily she got one; **después de años, se me hizo, gané la grande** after waiting for years, at last it happened for me, I got the big one

(**s**) *Méx, RP Fam (creer)* **¿llegará Pedro? – se me hace que no** do you think Pedro will come? – I don't think so

hacha *nf*

Takes the masculine articles **el** and **un**.

axe; EXPR *RP Fam* **bajar el h. a alguien** to run sb down; EXPR **desenterrar el h. de guerra** to sharpen one's sword; EXPR **enterrar el h. de guerra** to bury the hatchet; EXPR *Fam* **ser un h. (en algo)** to be a whizz *o* an ace (at sth)

hachazo *nm* (**a**) *(con hacha)* blow of an axe, hack; **lo partió de un h.** he split it with a single blow of the axe (**b**) *Dep Fam (patada)* scything tackle (**c**) *Taurom* = glancing blow from a sideways thrust from the bull's horn (**d**) *Col (de caballo)* start

hache *nf* = the letter "h"; EXPR *Fam* **por h. o por be** for one reason or another; EXPR *Fam* **llamémosle h., llámale h.** call it what you like

hachear 1 *vt* to hew

2 *vi* to hew with an axe

hachemita, hachemí 1 *adj* Hashemite

2 *nmf* Hashemite

hachís [χa'tʃis] *nm* hashish

HACIA *prep* (**a**) *(dirección)* towards; **h. aquí/allí** this/that way; **h. abajo** downwards; **h. arriba** upwards; **h. adelante** forwards; **h. atrás** backwards; **h. la izquierda/derecha** to the left/right; **viajar h. el norte** to travel north; **h. el norte del país** towards the north of the country; **miró h. el otro lado** she looked the other way; **muévete h. un lado** move to one side

(**b**) *(tiempo)* around, about; **h. las diez** around *o* about ten o'clock; **empezó a perder la vista h. los sesenta años** he started to lose his sight at around the age of sixty; **h. finales de año** towards the end of the year

(**c**) *(sentimiento)* towards; **siente hostilidad h. las reformas** he is hostile towards the reforms; **su actitud h. el trabajo es muy seria** she has a very serious attitude towards her work, she takes her work very seriously

(**d**) *(tendencia)* towards; **este año se marcha h. una cosecha excepcional** we are heading for a bumper crop this year; **un paso más h. la guerra civil** a further step towards civil war

hacienda *nf* (**a**) *(finca)* country estate *o* property

(**b**) *(bienes)* property; **repartió su h. entre sus hijos** she divided her property among her children

(**c**) *(del Estado)* **(el Ministerio de) H.** *Br* ≃ the Treasury, *US* ≃ the Department of the Treasury; **declarar algo a H.** to declare sth (to the *Br* Inland Revenue *o US* IRS); **pagar a H.** to pay *Br* the Inland Revenue *o US* the IRS ►► ***h. pública:*** **un delito contra la h. pública** a case of tax evasion; **las deudas de la empresa con la h. pública** the company's debts to the State

(**d**) *RP (ganadería)* livestock

hacina *nf (montón)* pile, heap

hacinamiento *nm (de personas)* overcrowding; *(de objetos)* heaping, piling

hacinar 1 *vt* to pile *o* heap (up)

2 hacinarse *vpr (gente)* to be crowded together; *(cosas)* to be piled *o* heaped (up)

hacker ['χaker] (*pl* **hackers**) *nmf Informát* hacker

hada *nf* fairy ►► ***h. madrina*** fairy godmother

Takes the masculine articles **el** and **un**.

Hades *n Mitol* Hades

hado *nm* fate, destiny

hadrón *nm Fís* hadron

hafnio *nm Quím* hafnium

hagiografía *nf* (**a**) *Rel* hagiography (**b**) *Pey (biografía exagerada)* hagiography

hagiográfico,-a *adj* (**a**) *Rel* hagiographic (**b**) *Pey (acrítico)* hagiography

hago *etc ver* **hacer**

hahnio *nm Quím* hahnium

haiga *nm Esp Anticuado Fam* big, flashy car

Haití *n* Haiti

haitiano, -a 1 *adj* Haitian

2 *nm,f* Haitian

hala *interj Esp* (**a**) *(para dar ánimo, prisa)* come on! (**b**) *(para expresar incredulidad)* no!, you're joking! (**c**) *(para expresar admiración, sorpresa)* wow! (**d**) *(como coletilla)* **si tú no vas yo tampoco, ih.!** if you're not going, neither am I, so there!

halagador, -ora 1 *adj* (**a**) *(alabador)* **palabras halagadoras** words of praise (**b**) *(adulador)* flattering

2 *nm,f (adulador)* flatterer

halagar [38] *vt* (**a**) *(alabar)* to praise; **me halaga que diga eso** I'm flattered that you say that (**b**) *(adular)* to flatter

halago *nm* (**a**) *(alabanza)* praise; **la cubrió de halagos** he showered her with praise (**b**) *(adulación)* flattery; **lo colmó de halagos** she showered him with flattery

halagüeño, -a *adj* (**a**) *(halagador)* flattering (**b**) *(prometedor)* promising, encouraging; **un futuro poco h.** a rather unpromising future

halar = **jalar**[1]

halcón *nm* (**a**) *(ave)* falcon, hawk ►► ***h. abejero*** honey buzzard; ***h. gerifalte*** gyrfalcon; ***h. peregrino*** peregrine (falcon) (**b**) *Pol* hawk

halconería *nf* falconry

halconero *nm* falconer, hawker

hale *interj Esp* come on!; **iy h. hop!** *(¡y ya está!)* and there you are!

halibut *nm* halibut

halita *nf Geol* halite

hálito *nm* (**a**) *(aliento)* breath (**b**) *Literario (brisa)* zephyr

halitosis *nf inv* bad breath, *Espec* halitosis

hall [χol] (*pl* **halls**) *nm (en casa)* hall; *(de cine, hotel)* foyer; *(de edificio)* entrance hall

hallaca, hayaca *nf Col, Ven* = traditional Christmas dish consisting of cornmeal dough stuffed with a variety of meats and vegetables and wrapped in banana leaves and then steamed

hallar 1 *vt* (**a**) *(encontrar)* to find; **hallaron el cadáver en el fondo del río** they found the body on the river bed; **h. errores en un texto** to spot errors in a text; **no hallo palabras para expresar mi agradecimiento** I can't find the words to express my gratitude; **por fin he hallado la felicidad** I've finally found happiness; **cuando llegué hallé que ya no había nadie** when I arrived, I found there was nobody there any more; **halló la muerte en un safari** he met his death on a safari

(**b**) *(averiguar)* to find out; **no hallo la solución al problema** I can't find the solution to the problem

(**c**) *(notar)* **hallé rencor en sus palabras** I detected some resentment in her words; **hallé muy rejuvenecida a su mujer** I thought his wife seemed totally rejuvenated

2 hallarse *vpr* (**a**) *(en un lugar) (persona)* to be, to find oneself; *(cosa, edificio)* to be (situated); **se hallaba sentado en el sofá** he was sitting on the sofa; **cuando despertó se halló en el medio del desierto** when she woke up she found herself in the middle of the desert; **la capital se halla en la costa** the capital is (situated) on the coast

(**b**) *(en una situación)* to be; **hallarse enfermo** to be ill; **el equipo se halla en un buen momento** the team is doing well; **se halla en lo mejor de la vida** she's in the prime of life; **se halla entre los mejores del mundo en su especialidad** he's among the best in the world in his field

(**c**) **no hallarse** *(no estar a gusto)* **no se halla en su nuevo trabajo** she doesn't feel at home in her new job

hallazgo *nm* (**a**) *(descubrimiento)* discovery; **comunicaron el h. del cuerpo a las autoridades** they informed the authorities that the body had been discovered *o* found; **publicó sus hallazgos en una revista científica** he published his findings in a scientific journal

(**b**) *(objeto)* find; **un h. arqueológico** an archaeological find; **ese restaurante fue todo un h.** that restaurant was a real find

hallulla *nf Chile* = type of round, slightly leavened bread

halo *nm* (**a**) *(de santos)* halo (**b**) *(de objetos, personas)* aura; **un h. de misterio** an aura *o* air of mystery (**c**) *Astron* halo, corona ►► ***h. lunar*** lunar halo

halógeno, -a 1 *adj* halogenous; **faros halógenos** halogen headlights; **lámpara halógena** halogen lamp
2 *nm Quím* halogen

haloideo, -a *adj Quím* haloid

halón *nm Andes, CAm, Carib, Méx* pull, tug; **dar un h. de orejas a alguien** *(tirón)* to tweak sb's ear; *(reprimenda)* to give sb a telling-off *o Br* ticking-off

haltera *nf Dep* dumbbell

halterofilia *nf* weightlifting

halterófilo,-a *Dep* 1 *adj* weightlifting; **competición halterófila** weightlifting competition
2 *nm,f* weightlifter

haluro *nm Quím* haloid acid

hamaca *nf* (**a**) *(para colgar)* hammock ▸▸ *RP* ***h. paraguaya*** hammock (**b**) *Esp (tumbona) (silla)* deck chair; *(canapé)* sunlounger (**c**) *RP (columpio)* swing (**d**) *RP (mecedora)* rocking chair

hamacar [60] *RP* 1 *vt (en columpio)* to swing; *(en cuna)* to rock
2 **hamacarse** *vpr (en columpio)* to swing; *(en cuna)* to rock

hambre *nf*

Takes the masculine articles **el** and **un**.

(**a**) *(apetito)* hunger; *(inanición)* starvation; **tener h.** to be hungry; **me ha entrado h.** I'm starting to feel hungry, I'm getting hungry; **prepara una buena cena, que venimos con h.** make sure there's plenty for dinner because we'll be hungry when we arrive; **me voy a tomar un yogur para entretener** *o* **engañar el h.** I'm going to have a yoghurt to keep me going (until my next meal); **matar el h.** to satisfy one's hunger; *Fig* **nos mataban de h.** they had us on a starvation diet; **morir** *o* **morirse de h.** *(literalmente)* to be starving, to be dying of hunger; *(tener mucha hambre)* to be starving; **pasar h.** to starve; **durante la posguerra, la población pasó mucha h.** in the years after the war, people often went hungry; **me he quedado con h.** I'm still hungry; EXPR **se juntan el h. con las ganas de comer** it's one thing on top of another; EXPR **ser más listo que el h.** to be nobody's fool; PROV **a buen h. no hay pan duro,** *RP* **cuando hay h. no hay pan duro** *(de comida)* hunger is the best sauce; *(de mujeres, placeres)* beggars can't be choosers ▸▸ ***h. canina*** ravenous hunger
(**b**) *(problema)* famine; **el problema del h. en la región** the problem of famine in the area; **una campaña contra el h.** a campaign against hunger
(**c**) *(deseo)* **h. de** hunger *o* thirst for; **se destaca por su h. de justicia** his hunger for justice sets him apart; **su h. de poder es insaciable** his hunger *o* thirst for power is insatiable

hambreado, -a *adj Am* starving

hambreador, -ora *Andes, RP* 1 *adj* oppressive; **¡abajo este gobierno h.!** down with this government that's got us starving!
2 *nm,f* exploiter

hambrear *vt Andes, RP* (**a**) *(explotar)* to exploit (**b**) *(hacer pasar hambre)* to starve

hambriento, -a 1 *adj* starving
2 *nm,f* starving person; **los hambrientos** the hungry

hambrón, -ona *Esp Fam* 1 *adj* **es h.** he's always hungry
2 *nm,f* **es un h.** he's always hungry

hambruna *nf (catástrofe)* famine

Hamburgo *n* Hamburg

hamburgués, -esa 1 *adj* of/from Hamburg
2 *nm,f* person from Hamburg

hamburguesa *nf* (**a**) *(filete)* (ham)burger, *Br* beefburger (**b**) *(bocadillo)* (ham)burger; **h. con queso** cheeseburger

hamburguesería *nf* hamburger joint

hampa *nf* **el h.** the underworld

Takes the masculine articles **el** and **un**.

hampón *nm* thug

hámster ['χamster] (*pl* **hámsters**) *nm* hamster

handball ['χanβol] *nm Am* handball

hándicap ['χandikap] (*pl* **hándicaps**) *nm* (**a**) *(dificultad)* handicap (**b**) *(en equitación)* handicap (**c**) *(en golf)* handicap

handling ['χandlin] *nm* baggage handling

hangar *nm* hangar

Hanoi *n* Hanoi

hanseático, -a *adj Hist* Hanseatic

haploide *adj Biol* haploid

haragán, -ana 1 *adj* lazy, idle
2 *nm,f* layabout, idler
3 *nm Ven (lampazo)* squeegee

haraganear *vi* to laze about, to lounge around

haraganería *nf* laziness, idleness

harakiri = **haraquiri**

harapiento, -a *adj* ragged, tattered

harapo *nm* rag, tatter

haraposo, -a *adj* ragged, tattered

haraquiri, harakiri *nm* hara-kiri; **hacerse el h.** to commit hara-kiri

Harare *n* Harare

haras *nm inv Andes, RP, Ven* stud farm

hardcore ['χarkor] *nm* (**a**) *(música)* hardcore (**b**) *(pornografía)* hardcore pornography

hardware ['χarwer] *nm Informát* hardware

haré *etc ver* **hacer**

harekrishna [χare'krisna] *nmf inv* Hare Krishna

harén *nm* harem

harina *nf* flour; EXPR *Fam* **estar metido en h. con algo: no me interrumpas, estoy metido en h.** don't interrupt me, I'm right in the middle of something; EXPR *Fam* **ser h. de otro costal** to be a different kettle of fish ▸▸ ***h. de avena*** oatmeal; ***h. en flor*** extra fine flour; ***h. integral*** whole wheat flour; ***h. lacteada*** = baby food containing wheat flour and dried milk; *RP* ***h. leudante*** *Br* self-raising flour, *US* self-rising flour; *Esp* ***h. con levadura*** *Br* self-raising flour, *US* self-rising flour; ***h. de maíz*** corn meal; ***h. de pescado*** fish meal; *Am* ***h. con polvos de hornear*** *Br* self-raising flour, *US* self-rising flour

harinoso, -a *adj (consistencia, textura, manzana)* floury

harmonía = **armonía**

harmonizar = **armonizar**

harnero *nm* sieve

harpía *nf* harpy eagle

harpillera = **arpillera**

hartada *nf*, **hartazgo** *nm* fill; **darse una h. (de)** to have one's fill (of); **nos dimos una h. de moras** we stuffed ourselves with blackberries; **se dieron una h. de ver la televisión** we did nothing but watch television

hartar 1 *vt* (**a**) *(atiborrar)* to stuff (full); **hartaron de regalos a sus nietos** they showered gifts on their grandchildren; **sus detractores lo hartaron a insultos** his critics showered him with insults; **los atacantes los hartaron a golpes** they were very badly beaten up by the attackers
(**b**) *(fastidiar, cansar)* **h. a alguien** to annoy sb, to get on sb's nerves; **me estás hartando con tantas exigencias** I'm getting fed up with all your demands
2 *vi* **esta comida harta mucho** you can't eat a lot of this food; **esta telenovela ya está empezando a h.** this soap is beginning to get tedious
3 **hartarse** *vpr* (**a**) *(atiborrarse)* to stuff *o* gorge oneself (**de** with); **se hartó de beber cerveza** she drank her fill of beer; **comió pasteles hasta hartarse** she ate cakes until she was sick of them
(**b**) *(cansarse)* to get fed up; **hartarse de algo** to get fed up with sth; **hartarse de hacer algo** to get fed up of doing sth
(**c**) *(no parar)* **hartarse de hacer algo** to do sth non-stop; **nos hartamos de reír** we laughed ourselves silly; **se harta de trabajar** he works himself into the ground; **en las últimas vacaciones me harté de tomar el sol** I did nothing but sunbathe on our last holidays

hartazgo = **hartada**

harto, -a 1 *adj* (**a**) *(de comida)* full; **estoy h. de dulces** I've had enough sweet things; EXPR *Esp Fam* **ni h. de vino: ése no ayuda a nadie ni h. de vino** he wouldn't help you if you were drowning; **no le dejaría mi coche ni h. de vino** I wouldn't lend him my car in a million years
(**b**) *(cansado)* tired (**de** of), fed up (**de** with); **estoy h. de mi jefe** I'm sick of my boss; **estoy h. de repetirte que cierres la puerta** I'm sick and tired of telling you to shut the door; **me tiene h. con el piano** I'm fed up of her and her piano; **empiezo a estar un poco h. de sus quejas** I'm starting to get rather tired of *o* fed up with his complaints
(**c**) *Andes, CAm, Carib, Méx (mucho)* a lot of, lots of; **tiene h. dinero** she has a lot of *o* lots of money; **de este aeropuerto salen hartos aviones** a lot of *o* lots of planes fly from this airport
2 *adv* (**a**) *Esp Formal (muy)* extremely; **es h. frecuente** it's extremely common; **el examen fue h. difícil** the exam was extremely difficult (**b**) *Andes, CAm, Carib, Méx (muy)* very, really; *(mucho)* a lot, very much; **es h. grande** it's very *o* really big; **nos cansamos h.** we got really tired; **te quiero h.** I love you very much

3 *pron Andes, CAm, Carib, Méx (mucho)* **¿tiene muchos muebles? – hartos** does she have a lot of furniture? – yes, she's got loads; **sabes h. que te quiero** you know perfectly well that I love you

hartón, -ona 1 *adj Méx, Ven Fam (glotón)* greedy-guts
2 *nm Esp (hartazgo)* fill; **darse un h. (de)** to have one's fill (of); **nos dimos un h. de moras** we stuffed ourselves with blackberries; **se dieron un h. de ver la televisión** they watched so much television that they got bored with it

hash [χaʃ, χas] *nm inv Fam* hash

HASTA 1 *prep* **(a)** *(en el espacio)* as far as, up to; **desde aquí h. allí** from here to there; **llegaré h. allí en diez minutos** I'll get there in ten minutes; **¿h. dónde va este tren?** where does this train go?; **¿h. dónde viajas?** where are you travelling to?, how far are you going?; **voy h. la próxima estación** I'm going as far as the next station
(b) *(en el tiempo)* until, till; **quedan dos semanas h. Navidad** there are two weeks to go until *o* till Christmas; **h. el final** right up until the end; **no vi el mar h. los diez años** I never saw the sea until I was ten years old; **no parará h. lograr su objetivo** she won't stop until she gets what she wants; **nos reímos h. no poder más** we laughed ourselves silly; **h. ahora** *(por ahora)* (up) until now, so far; *(como despedida)* see you later *o* in a minute; **Carolina Méndez, la h. ahora portavoz del gobierno** Carolina Méndez, who until now has been the government's spokesperson; **h. que** until, till; **esperaré h. que llegues** I'll wait until *o* till you arrive; **no me detendré h. que descubra la verdad** I won't stop until *o* till I find out the truth; **falta mucho h. que esté acabado** there's still a long way to go until *o* till *o* before it's finished
(c) *(en saludos)* **h. luego** *o* **pronto** *o* **la vista** see you (later); **h. mañana** see you tomorrow; **h. más ver** I'll be seeing you; **h. nunca** I hope I never see you again; **h. otra** I'll see you when I see you, see you again sometime; **h. la próxima** see you next time; **h. siempre** farewell; **h. la vuelta** I'll see you when you get back
(d) *CAm, Col, Ecuad, Méx (no antes de)* **pintaremos la casa h. fin de mes** we won't start painting the house until the end of the month; **¿llevas diez días aquí y h. ahora me llamas?** you've been here ten days and it's taken you that long to phone me?
(e) *(con cantidades)* up to; **puedes ganar h. un millón** you can earn up to a million; **un interés de h. el 7 por ciento** interest rates of up to 7 percent; **leí h. la página 30** I read as far as *o* up to page 30
2 *adv (incluso)* even; **h. en verano hace frío** it's even cold in summer; **h. cuando descansa está pensando en el trabajo** even when he's resting he's (still) thinking about work; **h. ellos querían venir** even they wanted to come

hastial *nm Constr* gable

hastiar [32] **1** *vt* **(a)** *(aburrir)* to bore **(b)** *(asquear)* to sicken, to disgust
2 hastiarse *vpr* **hastiarse de** to tire of, to get fed up with; **me hastié rápidamente de la fiesta** I quickly got bored with the party; **se hastió de esperar y se fue** she tired of waiting and left, she got fed up with waiting and left

hastío *nm* **(a)** *(tedio)* boredom; **se lo repetí hasta el h.** I've lost count of the number of times I told him; **sus clases me producen h.** I find his classes boring **(b)** *(repugnancia)* disgust

hatajo *nm* **(a)** *(de ganado)* herd; *(de ovejas)* flock **(b)** *Esp Pey (panda)* **¡h. de cobardes/ladrones!** you bunch of cowards/thieves!; **dijo un h. de disparates** he talked a load of nonsense

hatillo *nm* bundle of clothes; EXPR *Fam* **tomar el h.** *(marcharse)* to up sticks

hato *nm* **(a)** *(de ganado)* herd; *(de ovejas)* flock **(b)** *(de ropa)* bundle **(c)** *Carib, Col Fam (hacienda)* cattle ranch

Havre *n* **el H.** Le Havre

Hawai [χa'wai] *n* Hawaii

hawaiana [χawai'ana] *nf CSur, Perú (sandalia)* flip-flop, *US* thong

hawaiano, -a [χawai'ano] **1** *adj* Hawaiian
2 *nm,f* Hawaiian

hay *ver* **haber**

haya 1 *ver* **haber**
2 *nf* **(a)** *(árbol)* beech (tree) **(b)** *(madera)* beech (wood)

Takes the masculine articles **el** and **un**.

hayaca = **hallaca**

hayal, hayedo *nm* beech wood

hayuco *nm* beechnut

haz 1 *ver* **hacer**
2 *nm* **(a)** *(de leña)* bundle; *(de cereales)* sheaf **(b)** *(de luz, electrones)* beam **(c)** *Bot* face

haza *nf* = plot of arable land

Takes the masculine articles **el** and **un**.

hazaña *nf* feat, exploit; **fue toda una h.** it was quite a feat *o* an achievement; *Irónico* **¡vaya h., engañar a un niño!** congratulations, that's some feat, tricking a child like that!

hazmerreír *nm* laughing stock; **se convirtió en el h. de la política nacional** he became the laughing stock of national politics

HB *nf (abrev de* **Herri Batasuna***)* = former name of the political wing of ETA

HD *Informát* **(a)** *(abrev de* **alta densidad***)* HD **(b)** *(abrev de* **hard drive***)* HD

Hdez. *(abrev de* **Hernández***)* = written abbreviation of the surname Hernández

he[1] *ver* **haber**

he[2] *adv Formal* **he aquí el libro que te prometí** here's the book I promised you; **he aquí los resultados** here are the results; **mujer, he aquí a tu Hijo** *(lenguaje bíblico)* woman, behold thy Son; **te dije que vendría, y heme aquí** I told you I'd come and here I am

heavy ['χeβi] *(pl* **heavys** *o* **heavies***)* **1** *adj* **(a)** *(música, concierto)* **un concierto h.** a heavy metal concert; **música h.** heavy metal **(b)** *Fam (increíble)* awesome; **es una película h. total** it's an awesome movie **(c)** *Fam (fuerte)* **es muy h. que ahora venga y me pida ayuda** it's a bit much of her to come and ask me for help now; **se ha rapado el pelo al cero – ¡qué h.!** he's had a skinhead – way out!
2 *nmf Fam (persona)* heavy metal fan
3 *nm Mús* heavy metal ►► ***h. metal*** heavy metal

hebdomadario, -a 1 *adj* weekly
2 *nm* weekly

hebilla *nf* **(a)** *(de cinturón, zapato)* buckle **(b)** *Arg (para pelo) Br* slide, *US* barrette

hebra *nf* **(a)** *(de hilo)* thread **(b)** *(fibra)* fibre **(c)** *(de judías, puerros)* string; *(de tabaco)* strand **(d)** *(de discurso)* **no cojo la h. de lo que dice** I can't follow what she's saying; **he perdido la h. de su explicación** I've lost the thread of his explanation; EXPR *Esp Fam* **pegar la h.** to start chatting **(e)** EXPR *Chile* **de una h.** all at once, in one breath

hebraico, -a *adj* Hebraic

hebraísta *nmf* Hebrew scholar, hebraist

hebreo, -a 1 *adj* Hebrew
2 *nm,f (persona)* Hebrew
3 *nm (lengua)* Hebrew

Hébridas *nfpl* **las H.** the Hebrides

hebroso, -a *adj (material, planta)* fibrous; *(judías, puerros)* stringy

hecatombe *nf* **(a)** *(desastre)* disaster **(b)** *(partido, examen)* massacre; **la inundación causó una h.** the flood caused great loss of life **(c)** *Hist (sacrificio)* hecatomb

hechicería *nf* **(a)** *(arte)* witchcraft, sorcery **(b)** *(maleficio)* spell

hechicero, -a 1 *adj (personalidad, ojos, sonrisa)* enchanting, bewitching
2 *nm,f (hombre)* wizard, sorcerer; *(mujer)* witch, sorceress

hechizado, -a *adj* spellbound

hechizante *adj* bewitching

hechizar [14] *vt* **(a)** *(echar un maleficio)* to cast a spell on **(b)** *(encantar)* to bewitch, to captivate; **hechizó al público con su voz** she bewitched *o* captivated the audience with her wonderful voice

hechizo 1 *adj Chile, Méx* home-made
2 *nm* **(a)** *(maleficio)* spell **(b)** *(encanto)* magic, charm; **se rindió al h. de sus palabras** she surrendered to the magic of his words

HECHO, -A 1 *participio ver* **hacer**
2 *adj* **(a)** *(llevado a cabo)* **h. a mano** handmade; **h. a máquina** machine-made; **una película bien hecha** a well-made film; **¡eso está h.!** it's a deal!, you're on!; **¡bien h.!** well done!; **¡mal h., me tenías que haber avisado!** you were wrong not to tell me!; **¿me podrás conseguir entradas? – ¡eso está h.!** will you be able to get me tickets? – it's as good as done!; EXPR **lo h., h. está** what is done is done; EXPR *Fam* **a lo h., pecho: no me gusta, pero a lo h., pecho** I don't like it, but what's done is done; **tú lo hiciste, así que a lo h., pecho** you did it, so you'll have to take what's coming
(b) *(acabado)* mature; **una mujer hecha y derecha** a fully-grown woman; **estás h. un artista** you've become quite an artist
(c) *(carne, pasta)* done; **quiero el filete muy h./poco h.** I'd like my steak well done/rare
(d) *(acostumbrado)* **estar h. a algo/a hacer algo** to be used to sth/to doing sth; **está hecha a la dureza del clima** she's used to the harsh

climate; **no estoy h. a levantarme tan temprano** I'm not used to getting up so early

(**e**) *Andes, RP Fam* **estar h.** *(en condiciones)* to have it all; **con la compra de estos zapatos creo que estoy h.** after buying these shoes I think I've got everything I need; **me faltan dos materias de la carrera y estoy hecha** I need to do two more subjects in my degree and that's me done

3 *nm* (**a**) *(suceso)* event; **los hechos tuvieron lugar de madrugada** the events took place in the early morning; **el cuerpo de la víctima fue retirado del lugar de los hechos** the victim's body was removed from the scene of the crime ▸▸ ***h. consumado*** fait accompli

(**b**) *(realidad, dato)* fact; **el h. de que seas el jefe no te da derecho a comportarte así** just because you're the boss doesn't mean you have the right to behave like that; **es un h. indiscutido que...** it is an indisputable fact that...; **el h. es que...** the fact is that...; **h. ineludible** fact of life

(**c**) *(obra)* action, deed; **sus hechos hablan por él** his actions speak for him; **queremos hechos, y no promesas** we want action, not promises ▸▸ ***los Hechos de los Apóstoles*** the Acts of the Apostles; *Mil* ***h. de armas*** feat of arms

(**d**) **de h.** *(en realidad)* in fact, actually; **claro que lo conozco, de h., fuimos juntos al colegio** of course I know him, indeed *o* in fact we actually went to school together

(**e**) *(en la práctica)* de facto; **es el presidente de h.** he's the de facto president

4 *interj* it's a deal!, you're on!; **te lo vendo por un millón – ¡h.!** I'll sell it to you for a million – done! *o* it's a deal!

---

hechor, -ora *nm,f Andes* wrongdoer

hechura *nf* (**a**) *(de traje)* cut (**b**) *(forma)* shape; **un cuerpo de h. robusta** a sturdy frame (**c**) *(confección)* craftmanship; **un disco de h. brillante** a brilliantly crafted record

hectárea *nf* hectare

hectogramo *nm* hectogram

hectolitro *nm* hectolitre

hectómetro *nm* hectometre

heder [66] *vi* (**a**) *(apestar)* to stink, to reek (**b**) *Formal (fastidiar)* to be annoying *o* irritating

hediondez *nf* stench, stink

hediondo, -a *adj* (**a**) *(pestilente)* stinking, foul-smelling (**b**) *Formal (insoportable)* unbearable

hedonismo *nm* hedonism

hedonista **1** *adj* hedonistic

2 *nmf* hedonist

hedor *nm* stink, stench

hegemonía *nf (dominación)* dominance; *Pol* hegemony

hegemónico, -a *adj (dominante)* dominant; *(clase, partido)* ruling

hégira, héjira *nf* hegira

helada *nf* frost; **anoche cayó una h.** there was frost last night

heladera *nf CSur* (**a**) *(nevera)* fridge (**b**) *(portátil)* cool box (**c**) *ver también* **heladero**

heladería *nf (tienda)* ice cream parlour; *(puesto)* ice cream stall

heladero, -a *nm,f* ice cream seller

helado, -a **1** *adj* (**a**) *(hecho hielo) (agua)* frozen; *(lago)* frozen over

(**b**) *(muy frío) (manos, agua)* freezing; **esta sopa está helada** this soup is stone-cold; **llegó h. de frío y mojado** he arrived frozen stiff and wet through; **me quedé h. esperándola bajo la lluvia** I nearly froze to death waiting for her in the rain

(**c**) *Andes, RP (bebida)* ice-cold, well chilled; **sírvase bien h.** serve well chilled

(**d**) *(atónito)* dumbfounded, speechless; **¡me dejas h.!** I don't know what to say!; **me dejó h. cuando me contó lo que le había pasado** she left me speechless when she told me what had happened to her

2 *nm* ice cream ▸▸ *CSur* ***h. de agua*** *Br* ice lolly, *US* Popsicle®; *RP* ***h. palito*** *Br* ice lolly, *US* Popsicle®

helador, -ora *adj* freezing; **hace un frío h.** it's freezing; *Fig* **se escuchó un grito h.** we heard a spine-chilling cry

heladora *nf* ice cream machine

helar [3] **1** *vt* (**a**) *(líquido)* to freeze (**b**) *(planta)* **el frío heló las plantas** the plants were caught by the frost (**c**) *(dejar atónito)* to dumbfound

2 *v impersonal* **anoche heló** there was a frost last night

3 helarse *vpr* (**a**) *(líquido)* to freeze; **el lago se ha helado** the lake has frozen over (**b**) *(plantas)* **las plantas se helaron** the plants were caught by the frost (**c**) *(persona)* to freeze; **me hielo de frío** I'm freezing; **se me están helando los pies** my feet are freezing

helecho *nm* fern; **helechos** ferns, bracken

helénico, -a *adj* Hellenic, Greek

helenio *nm* elecampane

helenismo *nm* (**a**) *Hist* Hellenism (**b**) *Ling* = Greek word or expression

helenista *nmf* Hellenist

helenístico, -a *adj* Hellenistic

helenización *nf* Hellenization

helenizar [14] *vt* to Hellenize

heleno, -a **1** *adj* (**a**) *(de Grecia antigua)* Hellenic, (Ancient) Greek (**b**) *(de Grecia moderna)* Greek

2 *nm,f* (**a**) *(de Grecia antigua)* (Ancient) Greek (**b**) *(de Grecia moderna)* Greek

helero *nm* patch of snow *(left on mountain after thaw)*

heliantemo *nm* rock rose

hélice *nf* (**a**) *(de barco, avión)* propeller (**b**) *(espiral)* spiral, helix (**c**) *Anat* helix

helicoidal *adj* helicoid, spiral

helicóptero *nm* helicopter ▸▸ ***h. de guerra*** helicopter gunship

helio *nm Quím* helium

heliocéntrico, -a *adj* heliocentric

heliocentrismo *nm* heliocentrism

heliogábalo *nm Literario* glutton

heliograbado *nm* (**a**) *(técnica)* photogravure (**b**) *(grabado)* photogravure

heliografía *nf* (**a**) *(grabado)* photogravure (**b**) *Astron (fotografía)* photograph of the Sun

heliógrafo *nm* heliograph

helioterapia *nf* heliotherapy

heliotropismo *nm* heliotropism

heliotropo *nm (planta)* heliotrope

helipuerto *nm* heliport

helitransportar *vt* to take by helicopter

hélix *nm Anat* helix

Helsinki *n* Helsinki

Helvecia *n Hist* Helvetia

helvético, -a **1** *adj* (**a**) *Hist* Helvetian (**b**) *(suizo)* Swiss

2 *nm,f* (**a**) *Hist* Helvetian (**b**) *(suizo)* Swiss

hemático, -a *adj* hematic

hematíe *nm* red blood cell

hematites *nf inv Geol* haematite

hematófago, -a *adj Biol* haematophagous

hematología *nf* haematology

hematológico, -a *adj* haematological

hematólogo, -a *nm,f* haematologist

hematoma *nm* bruise

hematuria *nf Med* haematuria

hembra **1** *adj* female; **un búho h.** a female owl

2 *nf* (**a**) *(animal, planta)* female (**b**) *(mujer)* woman; *(niña)* girl; *muy Fam* **una h. muy atractiva** a very attractive bit of skirt (**c**) *(del enchufe)* socket

hembraje *nm Andes, RP Agr* female livestock

hembrilla *nf (de corchete)* eye

hemeroteca *nf* newspaper and periodicals library *o* archive

hemiciclo *nm* (**a**) *(semicírculo)* semicircle (**b**) *(en el parlamento) (cámara)* chamber; *(espacio central)* floor

hemiono, hemión *nm* wild ass, onager

hemiplejia, hemiplejía *nf* hemiplegia

hemipléjico, -a **1** *adj* hemiplegic

2 *nm,f* hemiplegic

hemisférico, -a *adj* hemispheric

hemisferio *nm* (**a**) *(terrestre)* hemisphere ▸▸ ***h. austral*** southern hemisphere; ***h. boreal*** northern hemisphere; ***h. norte*** northern hemisphere; ***el h. occidental*** the western hemisphere; ***h. oriental*** eastern hemisphere; ***h. sur*** southern hemisphere (**b**) *Anat* hemisphere

hemoderivado, -a *adj* derived from blood

hemodiálisis *nf inv* kidney dialysis

hemofilia *nf* haemophilia

hemofílico, -a **1** *adj* haemophiliac

2 *nm,f* haemophiliac

hemoglobina *nf* haemoglobin

hemograma *nm* blood test results

hemopatía *nf* blood disease *o* disorder

hemorragia *nf* haemorrhage; **se puso un torniquete para detener la h.** he put on a tourniquet to stop the bleeding ▸▸ ***h. cerebral*** brain haemorrhage; ***h. nasal*** nosebleed

hemorrágico, -a *adj* haemorrhagic

hemorroides *nfpl* haemorrhoids, piles

hemos *ver* **haber**

hemostático, -a *adj* haemostatic

henchido, -a *adj* bloated; **h. de orgullo** bursting with pride

henchir [47] **1** *vt* to fill (up)

2 henchirse *vpr* **(a)** *(hartarse)* to stuff oneself **(b)** *(llenarse)* to be full (**de** of)

hender [66], **hendir** *vt (carne, piel)* to carve open, to cleave; *(piedra, madera)* to crack open; *(aire, agua)* to cut *o* slice through

hendido, -a *adj* split (open)

hendidura *nf (en carne, piel)* cut, split; *(en piedra, madera)* crack

hendija *nf Am* crack, gap

hendir [64] = **hender**

henequén *nm* sisal, henequen

henna ['χena] *nf* henna

heno *nm* hay

hepática *nf* liverwort ▸▸ ***h. blanca*** grass of parnassus; ***h. dorada*** golden saxifrage

hepático, -a *adj* liver; **afección hepática** liver complaint; **insuficiencia hepática** liver failure

hepatitis *nf inv* hepatitis

heptagonal *adj* heptagonal

heptágono *nm* heptagon

heptámetro *nm* heptameter

heptasílabo, -a **1** *adj* heptasyllabic

2 *nm* heptasyllabic verse

heptatleta *nmf* heptathlete

heptatlón *nm* heptathlon

Heracles *n Mitol* Heracles

heráldica *nf* heraldry

heráldico, -a *adj* heraldic

heraldista *nmf* heraldist

heraldo *nm* herald

herbácea *nf Bot* herbaceous plant

herbáceo, -a *adj* herbaceous

herbaje *nm (pasto)* pasture, herbage

herbario *nm (colección)* herbarium

herbicida *nm* weedkiller, herbicide

herbívoro, -a **1** *adj* herbivorous

2 *nm,f* herbivore

herbolario, -a **1** *nm,f (persona)* herbalist

2 *nm (tienda)* herbalist's (shop)

herboristería *nf* herbalist's (shop)

herboso, -a *adj* grassy

herciniano, -a *adj Geol* Hercynian

hercio *nm* hertz

hercúleo, -a *adj* very powerful, incredibly strong; **un esfuerzo h.** a Herculean effort

Hércules *n* Hercules; **las Columnas de H.** *(el estrecho de Gibraltar)* the Pillars of Hercules; **los trabajos de H.** the labours of Hercules

hércules *nm inv* **es un h.** he's as strong as an ox

heredad *nf* country estate *o* property

heredar *vt* **(a)** *(recibir) (dinero)* to inherit (**de** from); **heredó el título de su padre** he inherited the title from his father

(b) *(recibir) (rasgos)* to inherit (**de** from); **ha heredado la nariz de su padre** he has his father's nose; PROV *Am* **lo que se hereda no se roba** like father, like son

(c) *(recibir) (objetos, ropa)* to inherit (**de** from); **heredó el abrigo de su hermano** she inherited the coat from her brother; **es un problema heredado del gobierno anterior** it's a problem we have inherited from the previous government

(d) *Méx (legar) (dinero)* to bequeath; *(rasgos)* **su padre le ha heredado la nariz** he has his father's nose

heredero, -a *nm,f* heir, *f* heiress; **el príncipe h.** the crown prince; **el h. al trono** the heir to the throne; **el h. del título** the heir to the title; **instituir h.** *o* **por h. a** to name as one's heir, to name in one's will; **es el h. de la generosidad de su madre** he has his mother's generosity; **un estilo h. de los grandes clásicos** a style in the tradition of the classics ▸▸ *Der* ***h. forzoso*** heir apparent; *Der* ***h. legal*** heir (at law); *Der* ***h. universal*** residuary legatee

hereditariamente *adv* **la enfermedad se transmite h.** it is a hereditary disease

hereditario, -a *adj* **(a)** *(bienes, rasgos)* hereditary **(b)** *(enfermedad)* hereditary

hereje[1] *adj Ven Fam* **pasaron un hambre h.** they were dead hungry, they were starving

hereje[2] *nmf* **(a)** *(renegado)* heretic **(b)** *(irreverente)* iconoclast

herejía *nf* **(a)** *(heterodoxia)* heresy **(b)** *(insulto)* insult; *(disparate)* outrage

herencia *nf* **(a)** *(de bienes)* inheritance; **dejar algo en h. a alguien** to bequeath sth to sb; **recibir una h.** to receive an inheritance; **la casa le corresponde por h.** the house has been left *o* bequeathed to him; **el conflicto es h. de su pasado colonial** the conflict is a legacy of their colonial past; **la h. cultural de un país** a country's cultural heritage ▸▸ ***h. yacente*** unclaimed estate, estate in abeyance

(b) *(de rasgos)* heredity; **los ojos azules son h. de su madre** she gets her blue eyes from her mother ▸▸ ***h. genética*** genetic inheritance

herético, -a *adj* heretical

herida *nf* **(a)** *(lesión)* injury; *(en lucha, atentado)* wound; **me hice una h. con un cuchillo** I cut myself on a knife; **sufrió heridas leves/graves** she suffered minor/serious injuries; **me golpeé con el techo y me hice una h. en la cabeza** I hurt my head when I banged it on the ceiling ▸▸ ***h. abierta*** open wound; **los crímenes de la dictadura siguen siendo una h. abierta** the crimes of the dictatorship are a wound that still hasn't healed; ***h. de bala*** bullet *o* gunshot wound; ***heridas múltiples*** multiple injuries; ***h. punzante*** stab wound; ***h. superficial*** flesh wound

(b) *(ofensa)* injury, offence; EXPR **escarbar** *o* **hurgar** *o* **tocar en la herida: no quería escarbar** *o* **hurgar** *o* **tocar en la h., pero ¿cómo le va a tu ex esposa?** I know it's a sore point, but how's your ex-wife?; EXPR **renovar la h.** to reopen an old wound

(c) *(pena)* wound; **su desaparición es una h. que tardará en cicatrizar** her disappearance is a wound that will take a long time to heal

herido, -a **1** *adj* **(a)** *(físicamente) (en accidente)* injured; *(en lucha, atentado)* wounded; **resultaron heridos once civiles** eleven civilians were wounded; **resultó h. leve/de gravedad** he suffered minor/serious injuries; **había dos personas heridas en el suelo** there were two people lying injured/wounded on the ground

(b) *(sentimentalmente)* hurt, wounded; **está herida por tus comentarios** she was hurt *o* wounded by your remarks; **se sintió h. en su amor propio** his pride was hurt

2 *nm,f (persona) (en accidente)* injured person; *(en lucha, atentado)* wounded person; **no hubo heridos** there were no casualties; **los heridos** *(en accidente)* the injured; *(en lucha, atentado)* the wounded; **hubo dos heridos graves/leves en el accidente** two people were seriously/slightly injured in the accident

herir [64] *vt* **(a)** *(físicamente) (en accidente)* to injure; *(en lucha, atentado)* to wound; **lo hirieron en el hombro** he was wounded in the shoulder, he suffered a shoulder wound; **la hirieron de muerte** she was fatally wounded

(b) *(vista)* to hurt; *(oído)* to pierce; **el nuevo edificio hiere la vista** the new building is an eyesore

(c) *(sentimentalmente)* to hurt; **me hiere que desconfíes de mí** I feel hurt that you don't trust me; **lo que dijiste lo hirió profundamente** what you said hurt *o* wounded him deeply; **lo hirió en su amor propio** it hurt his pride; **estas imágenes pueden h. la sensibilidad del espectador** some viewers may find these images disturbing

(d) *Literario (golpear)* to pound against; **el granizo hería las ventanas** the hail pounded *o* lashed against the windows

hermafrodita **1** *adj* hermaphrodite

2 *nmf* hermaphrodite

hermanado, -a *adj* **(a)** *(unido, ligado)* united, joined (**con** to) **(b)** *(ciudades)* twinned (**con** with); **dos ciudades hermanadas** two twin towns, *US* two sister cities

hermanamiento *nm* **(a)** *(unión)* union **(b)** *(de ciudades)* twinning

hermanar **1** *vt* **(a)** *(esfuerzos, personas)* to unite **(b)** *(ciudades)* to twin **(c)** *(compatibilizar)* to combine; **el director hermana la tragedia y la comedia** the director combines *o* blends tragedy with comedy;

hermana la inteligencia con la sencillez she combines intelligence with unaffectedness

2 **hermanarse** *vpr (ciudades)* to be twinned

hermanastro, -a *nm,f* (**a**) *(medio hermano)* half brother, *f* half sister (**b**) *(hijo del padrastro o de la madrastra)* stepbrother, *f* stepsister

hermandad *nf* (**a**) *(parentesco) (de hombres)* brotherhood; *(de mujeres)* sisterhood (**b**) *(asociación)* association (**c**) *Rel (cofradía) (de hombres)* brotherhood; *(de mujeres)* sisterhood (**d**) *(amistad)* intimacy, close friendship

hermanita *nf Rel* sister ►► ***h. de la Caridad*** Little Sister of Charity

hermano, -a 1 *adj* **ciudades hermanas** twin towns, *US* sister cities; **la amistad entre dos pueblos hermanos como México y España** the friendship between two countries with close ties, such as Mexico and Spain

2 *nm,f* (**a**) *(pariente)* brother, *f* sister; **todos los hermanos se parecen mucho entre sí** all the brothers and sisters look very much alike; **son medio hermanas** they're half sisters; **los dos son como hermanos** the two of them are like brothers ►► ***hermanos gemelos*** twin brothers; ***h. de leche*** foster brother; ***hermana de leche*** foster sister; ***h. de madre*** half brother *(on mother's side)*; ***hermana de madre*** half sister *(on mother's side)*; ***h. mayor*** older *o* big brother; ***hermana mayor*** older *o* big sister; ***hermanos mellizos*** twin brothers; ***hermanas mellizas*** twin sisters; ***h. menor*** younger *o* little brother; ***hermana menor*** younger *o* little sister; ***h. de padre*** half brother *(on father's side)*; ***hermana de padre*** half sister *(on father's side)*; *Fig* ***h. pobre*** poor relation; ***h. político*** brother-in-law; ***hermana política*** sister-in-law; ***h. de sangre*** blood brother; ***hermana de sangre*** blood sister; ***hermanos siameses*** Siamese twins

(**b**) *Rel* brother, *f* sister; **la hermana Teresa** Sister Teresa ►► ***hermana de la Caridad*** Sister of Charity

(**c**) *Fam (como apelativo)* my friend; **¡cómo te han engañado, h.!** you've been cheated, my friend!

hermenéutica *nf* hermeneutics *(singular)*

hermenéutico, -a *adj* hermeneutic

Hermes *n Mitol* Hermes

herméticamente *adv* hermetically; **h. cerrado** hermetically sealed

hermeticidad *nf (al aire)* airtightness; *(al agua)* watertightness

hermético, -a *adj* (**a**) *(al aire)* airtight, hermetic; *(al agua)* watertight, hermetic (**b**) *(persona)* uncommunicative; *(texto, comentario)* impenetrable

hermetismo *nm* (**a**) *(al aire)* airtightness; *(al agua)* watertightness (**b**) *(de persona)* uncommunicativeness; *(de texto, comentario)* impenetrability

hermosear *vt* to beautify, to make beautiful

hermosilla *nf* trachelium

hermosillense 1 *adj* of/from Hermosillo *(Mexico)*

2 *nmf* person from Hermosillo *(Mexico)*

hermoso, -a *adj* (**a**) *(bello) (paisaje, paseo, mujer)* beautiful, lovely; *(hombre)* handsome; **¡qué atardecer más h.!** what a beautiful *o* lovely sunset!

(**b**) *(grande)* **la casa tiene un salón muy h.** the house has a nice big living room; **cazaron un h. ejemplar** they caught a really big one; **¡qué melones más hermosos!** what lovely big melons!

(**c**) *(noble)* kind; **fue un gesto muy h.** it was a very kind gesture

(**d**) *Fam (sano, fuerte)* strapping; *(gordo, grande)* plump; **el bebé está muy h.** he's a real bouncing baby; **con lo que come no me extraña que esté tan h.** it doesn't surprise me that he's so plump, considering how much he eats

hermosura *nf* (**a**) *(belleza)* beauty; *(de hombre)* handsomeness (**b**) *(persona, cosa)* **su hija es una h.** her daughter is really beautiful; **¡qué h. de lago!** what a beautiful lake!

hernia *nf* hernia, rupture ►► ***h. discal*** slipped disc, *Espec* herniated disc; ***h. estrangulada*** strangulated hernia; ***h. de hiato*** hiatus hernia; ***h. inguinal*** inguinal hernia

herniado, -a 1 *adj* ruptured

2 *nm,f* person suffering from a hernia

herniarse *vpr* (**a**) *(sufrir hernia)* to rupture oneself (**b**) *Fam Irónico* **¡cuidado, no te vayas a herniar!** careful! you don't want to strain yourself!

Herodes *n pr* Herod; EXPR *Fam Hum* **de H. a Pilatos** out of the frying pan, into the fire

héroe *nm* hero

heroicamente *adv* heroically

heroicidad *nf* (**a**) *(cualidad)* heroism (**b**) *(hecho)* heroic deed; **atreverse a cuestionar al profesor fue una h.** it was heroic of her to question what the teacher said

heroico, -a *adj* heroic

heroína *nf* (**a**) *(mujer)* heroine (**b**) *(droga)* heroin

heroinomanía *nf* heroin addiction

heroinómano, -a *nm,f* heroin addict

heroísmo *nm* heroism

herpes *nm inv* herpes ►► ***h. genital*** genital herpes; ***h. simple*** herpes simplex; ***h. zóster*** herpes zoster

herpesvirus *nm inv Med* herpes virus

herpético, -a *adj Med* herpetic

herrador, -ora *nm,f* blacksmith

herradura *nf* horseshoe

herraje *nm* iron fittings, ironwork

herramienta *nf* tool ►► *Informát* ***h. de autor*** authoring tool

herrar [3] *vt* (**a**) *(caballo)* to shoe (**b**) *(ganado)* to brand

herrería *nf* (**a**) *(taller)* smithy, forge (**b**) *(oficio)* smithery, blacksmith's trade

herrerillo *nm* blue tit ►► ***h. capuchino*** crested tit

herrerismo *nm Pol* = philosophy/supporters of former Uruguayan president Luis Alberto de Herrera

herrerista *Pol* 1 *adj* = of/relating to the philosophy of former Uruguayan president Luis Alberto de Herrera

2 *nm,f* = supporter of former Uruguayan president Luis Alberto de Herrera

herrero *nm* (**a**) *(herrador)* blacksmith, smith (**b**) *Am (de caballos)* horseshoer

herrete *nm* tag, metal tip *(of shoelace, etc)*

herrumbrarse *vpr* to rust, to go rusty

herrumbre *nf* (**a**) *(óxido)* rust (**b**) *(sabor)* **sabe a h.** it tastes of rusty metal

herrumbroso, -a *adj* rusty

hertz [χerts] (*pl* **hertzs**), **hertzio** ['χertsjo] *nm* hertz

hertziano, -a [χert'sjano, -a] *adj* hertz

hervidero *nm* (**a**) *(de pasiones, intrigas)* hotbed; **el mercado bursátil es un h. de rumores** the stock market is currently alive with rumours (**b**) *(de gente) (muchedumbre)* swarm, throng; **la sala era un h. de periodistas** the hall was swarming with journalists; **durante el verano la ciudad se convierte en un h. de gente** during the summer, crowds throng the streets of the city

hervido, -a 1 *adj* boiled

2 *nm Ven* = soup made with fish, chicken or beef and vegetables, usually served as a main course

hervidor *nm (para agua)* kettle; *(para leche)* milk pan

hervir [74] 1 *vt* to boil

2 *vi* (**a**) *(líquido)* to boil; **h. a fuego lento** to simmer; **h. a borbotones** to be at a rolling boil; **cuando empiece a h.** when it comes to the boil; EXPR **le hervía la sangre** his blood was boiling

(**b**) *(estar caliente)* to be boiling (hot); **esa sopa está hirviendo** that soup is boiling (hot)

(**c**) *(lugar)* **h. de** to swarm with; **la ciudad hierve de turistas** the city is swarming with tourists

(**d**) *(persona)* **h. de emoción** to be buzzing with excitement; **hervía de cólera** she was boiling with rage; **hiervo en deseos de decirle lo que pienso** I'm dying to tell him what I think

hervor *nm* (**a**) *(acción de hervir)* **dar un h. a algo** to bring sth to the boil; **añadir las hierbas durante el h.** add the herbs while it's boiling (**b**) *(fogosidad)* fervour; **calentó hasta el h. a su público** she whipped the audience up into a frenzy

herzegovino, -a 1 *adj* Herzegovinan

2 *nm,f* Herzegovinan

hetaira *nf* high-class prostitute

heterocigótico, -a *adj Biol* heterozygous

heteróclito, -a *adj (heterogéneo)* heterogeneous

heterodoxia *nf* (**a**) *Rel* heterodoxy (**b**) *(de método, ideas)* unorthodox nature

heterodoxo, -a 1 *adj* (**a**) *Rel* heterodox (**b**) *(método, ideas)* unorthodox

2 *nm,f* (**a**) *Rel* = person holding heterodox beliefs (**b**) *(en método, ideas)* unorthodox person; **es un h.** he is unorthodox

heterogeneidad *nf* heterogeneity

heterogéneo, -a *adj* heterogeneous; **un montón de objetos heterogéneos** a huge amount of all sorts of different things
heteromorfo, -a *adj* heteromorphous
heteronimia *nf* heteronymy
heterónimo *nm* heteronym
heterosexual 1 *adj* heterosexual
2 *nmf* heterosexual
heterosexualidad *nf* heterosexuality
heterótrofo, -a *adj Biol* heterotrophic
heurística *nf* heuristics *(singular)*
heurístico, -a *adj* heuristic
hevea *nm* hevea
hexadecimal *adj Informát* hexadecimal
hexaedro *nm* hexahedron, cube
hexagonal *adj* hexagonal
hexágono *nm* hexagon
hexámetro *nm* hexameter
hexasílabo, -a 1 *adj* hexasyllabic
2 *nm* hexasyllabic verse
hez *nf* (**a**) *(excremento)* dregs; **heces** faeces, excrement ►► ***heces fecales*** faecal matter (**b**) **heces** *(del vino)* lees
Hezbolá *n* Hezbollah, Hizbollah
hg *(abrev de* **hectogramo**) hg
hiato *nm* (**a**) *Gram* hiatus (**b**) *Anat* hiatus
hibernación *nf* (**a**) *(de animales)* hibernation (**b**) *(de personas)* cryogenic freezing
hibernar 1 *vi* to hibernate
2 *vt* to freeze cryogenically
hibisco *nm*, **hibiscus** *nm inv* hibiscus
hibridación *nf* hybridization
hibridar *vt* to hybridize
híbrido, -a 1 *adj* (**a**) *(animal, planta)* hybrid (**b**) *(estilo)* hybrid
2 *nm* (**a**) *(animal, planta)* hybrid (**b**) *(mezcla)* cross
hice *etc ver* **hacer**
hiciera *etc ver* **hacer**
hico *nm Carib, Col, Pan* = cord for suspending a hammock
hicotea *nf* hicatee
hidalgo, -a 1 *adj* (**a**) *(noble)* noble (**b**) *(caballeroso)* courteous, gentlemanly
2 *nm,f* nobleman, *f* noblewoman *(from the lower ranks of the nobility)*
hidalguense 1 *adj* of/from Hidalgo *(Mexico)*
2 *nmf* person from Hidalgo *(Mexico)*
hidalguía *nf* (**a**) *(aristocracia)* lower ranks of the nobility (**b**) *(caballerosidad)* courtesy, chivalry
hidra *nf* (**a**) *(animal)* hydra (**b**) *Mitol* Hydra
hidrácido *nm Quím* hydrazide
hidrante *nm CAm, Carib* hydrant
hidratación *nf* (**a**) *(de la piel)* moisturizing; *(de persona)* rehydration (**b**) *Quím* hydration
hidratado, -a *adj* (**a**) *(piel)* moist (**b**) *Quím* hydrated
hidratante 1 *adj* moisturizing
2 *nm (crema, loción)* moisturizer
hidratar *vt* (**a**) *(piel)* to moisturize (**b**) *Quím* to hydrate
hidrato *nm* hydrate ►► ***h. de calcio*** calcium hydrate; ***h. de carbono*** carbohydrate
hidráulica *nf* hydraulics *(singular)*
hidráulico, -a *adj* hydraulic
hídrico, -a *adj* **los recursos hídricos de una región** the water resources of a region; **la legislación en materia hídrica** the legislation governing rivers and lakes
hidroala *nm* hydrofoil
hidroavión *nm* seaplane, *US* hydroplane
hidrocálido, -a 1 *adj* of/from Aguascalientes *(Mexico)*
2 *nm,f* person from Aguascalientes *(Mexico)*
hidrocarburo *nm* hydrocarbon
hidrocefalia *nf Med* water on the brain, *Espec* hydrocephalus
hidrocéfalico, -a *adj Med* hydrocephalic
hidrocéfalo, -a *adj Med* hydrocephalic
hidrocortisona *nf* hydrocortisone
hidrocultivo *nm Agr* hydroponics *(singular)*, aquiculture
hidrodinámica *nf* hydrodynamics *(singular)*
hidrodinámico, -a *adj* hydrodynamic
hidroelectricidad *nf* hydroelectricity
hidroeléctrico, -a *adj* hydroelectric; **central hidroeléctrica** hydroelectric power station
hidrófilo, -a *adj* (**a**) *(sustancia)* absorbent; **algodón h.** *Br* cotton wool, *US* cotton (**b**) *Bot* hydrophilous
hidrofobia *nf* rabies *(singular)*, hydrophobia
hidrófobo, -a *adj* rabid, hydrophobic
hidrofoil (*pl* **hidrofoils**) *nm* hydrofoil
hidrófugo, -a *adj (contra filtraciones)* waterproof; *(contra humedad)* damp-proof
hidrogenación *nf Quím* hydrogenation
hidrogenar *vt Quím* to hydrogenate
hidrógeno *nm Quím* hydrogen
hidrografía *nf* hydrography
hidrográfico, -a *adj* hydrographic(al)
hidrólisis *nf inv Quím* hydrolysis
hidrólito *nm Quím* hydrolyte
hidrolizado, -a *adj Quím* hydrolyzed
hidrolizar [14] *vt Quím* to hydrolyze
hidrología *nf* hydrology
hidrológico, -a *adj* hydrologic, hydrological; **un plan h.** a water management plan
hidromasaje *nm* whirlpool bath, Jacuzzi®; **bañera de h.** whirlpool bath, Jacuzzi®
hidromecánico, -a *adj* hydrodynamic, water-powered
hidrometría *nf* hydrometry
hidrómetro *nm Fís* hydrometer
hidropesía *nf Med* dropsy
hidrópico, -a *adj* (**a**) *Med* dropsical (**b**) *Formal (sediento)* extremely thirsty
hidroplano *nm* (**a**) *(barco)* hydrofoil (**b**) *(avión)* seaplane
hidroponía *nf* hydroponics *(singular)*
hidropónico, -a *adj* **cultivo h.** hydroponics, aquiculture
hidrosfera *nf* hydrosphere
hidrosoluble *adj* water-soluble
hidrostática *nf* hydrostatics *(singular)*
hidrostático, -a *adj* hydrostatic
hidroterapia *nf* hydrotherapy
hidrotermal *adj* hydrothermal
hidrovía *nf Am* waterway
hidróxido *nm Quím* hydroxide ►► ***h. de calcio*** calcium hydroxide
hidroxilo *nm Quím* hydroxyl
hidruro *nm Quím* hydride
hiedo *etc ver* **heder**
hiedra *nf* ivy
hiel *nf* (**a**) *(bilis)* bile; EXPR **echar** *o* **sudar la h.** to sweat blood (**b**) *(mala intención)* spleen, bitterness; **sus palabras destilaban h.** his words were dripping with venom (**c**) **hieles** *(sufrimientos)* trials; **las hieles de la derrota** the bitter taste of defeat
hielera *nf CSur, Méx* cool box, cooler
hielo 1 *ver* **helar**
2 *nm* (**a**) *(agua congelada)* ice; **un whisky con h.** a whisky on the rocks; **me lanzó una mirada de h.** she gave me a frosty *o* icy look; EXPR **quedarse de h.** to be stunned *o* speechless; EXPR **romper el h.** to break the ice ►► ***h. seco*** dry ice (**b**) *(helada)* frost
hiena *nf* hyena ►► ***h. manchada*** laughing hyena
hiendo *etc ver* **hender**
hierático, -a *adj* (**a**) *(expresión, actitud)* impassive (**b**) *(en arte)* hieratic
hieratismo *nm* (**a**) *(de expresión)* impassiveness (**b**) *(en arte)* hieratic style
hierba *nf* (**a**) *(planta)* plant; **mala h.** weed; EXPR *Fam* **ser mala h.** to be a nasty piece of work; EXPR *Fam* **y otras hierbas** and so on; PROV *Hum* **mala h. nunca muere** ill weeds grow apace ►► ***h. limonera*** lemon grass; ***h. de las pampas*** pampas grass; ***h. de los pordioseros*** traveller's joy
(**b**) *(medicinal)* herb ►► ***hierbas medicinales*** medicinal herbs
(**c**) *(para condimentar)* herb; **a las finas hierbas** with herbs, aux fines herbes ►► ***hierbas aromáticas*** aromatic herbs

(**d**) *(césped)* grass; **hockey sobre h.** *Br* hockey, *US* field hockey ►► ***h. artificial*** artificial turf *o* surface, Astroturf®

(**e**) *Fam (marihuana)* grass

hierbabuena *nf* mint

hierbal *nm Chile* grassland, pasture

hierbaluisa *nf* lemon verbena

hiero *etc ver* **herir**

hierro **1** *ver* **herrar**

2 *nm* (**a**) *(metal)* iron; **una valla de h.** iron railings; **se enganchó en un h.** he got himself caught on a piece of metal; EXPR **tener una salud de h.** to have an iron constitution; EXPR **quitarle h. a algo** to play sth down ►► ***h. colado*** cast iron; ***h. dulce*** mild steel; ***h. forjado*** wrought iron; ***h. fundido*** cast iron; ***h. laminado*** sheet metal

(**b**) *(de puñal)* blade; *(de flecha)* point; PROV **quien a h. mata a h. muere** he who lives by the sword dies by the sword

(**c**) *(palo de golf)* iron; **un h. del 5** a 5 iron; **un h. corto/largo** a short/long iron

(**d**) *(para marcar animales)* branding iron

(**e**) *Fam (arma)* shooter, *US* piece

hiervo *etc ver* **hervir**

hi-fi ['ifi] *nf* (*abrev de* **high fidelity**) hi-fi

higa *nf Fam* **¡me importa una h.!** I couldn't care less!

higadillo, higadito *nm* ***higadillos de pollo*** chicken livers

hígado *nm* liver; EXPR *Fam* **echar los hígados** to nearly kill oneself (with the effort); EXPR *Fam* **patear el h.: ese estofado me pateó el h.** that stew nearly did for me; *CSur Fam* **me patea el h. que me mienta** it makes me sick when he lies to me like that; EXPR *Esp Fam* **me pone del h. que...** it makes me sick that..; EXPR *Fam* **tener hígados** to have guts

higiene *nf* hygiene; **seguridad e h.** *(en el trabajo)* health and safety ►► ***h. bucal*** oral hygiene; ***h. dental*** dental hygiene; ***h. íntima*** personal hygiene; ***h. mental*** mental health; ***h. personal*** personal hygiene

higiénico, -a *adj* (**a**) *(limpio)* hygienic (**b**) **papel h.** toilet paper; *Am* **toalla higiénica** sanitary towel

higienista *nmf* hygienist ►► ***h. dental*** dental hygienist

higienización *nf* sterilization

higienizar [14] **1** *vt* (**a**) *(acondicionar)* to improve hygiene in (**b**) *(limpiar)* to sanitize

2 higienizarse *vpr RP Formal* to wash

higo *nm* fig; EXPR *Fam* **de higos a brevas** once in a blue moon; EXPR *Fam* **estar hecho un h.** *(persona)* to be wrecked; *(cosa)* to be falling apart; *(ropa)* to be all wrinkled ►► ***h. chumbo*** prickly pear; ***higos secos*** dried figs

higrometría *nf* hygrometry

higrómetro *nm* hygrometer

higroscópico, -a *adj* hygroscopic

higuera *nf* fig tree; EXPR *Fam* **estar en la h.** to have one's head in the clouds ►► ***h. chumba*** prickly pear

higueruela *nf* pitch trefoil

hijastro, -a *nm,f* stepson, *f* stepdaughter; **sus hijastros** her stepchildren

hijear *vi CAm, Méx* to shoot

HIJO, -A **1** *nm,f* (**a**) *(descendiente)* son, *f* daughter; **Alfonso Sánchez, h.** Alfonso Sánchez Junior; **estar esperando un h.** to be expecting (a baby); EXPR *Fam* **hacerle un h. a alguien** to get sb pregnant; EXPR *Fam* **cualquier** *o* **todo h. de vecino: nos gusta salir por la noche, como a cualquier** *o* **todo h. de vecino** like most people, we like going out in the evening; **cualquier** *o* **todo h. de vecino tiene derecho a trabajar** everyone, no matter who they are, has a right to work; EXPR *Fam Hum* **ser h. de cristalero** *o RP* **vidriero: échate a un lado, que no eres h. de cristalero** *o RP* **vidriero** move over a bit, I can't see through you! ►► ***h. adoptivo*** adopted son; ***hija adoptiva*** adopted daughter; ***h. bastardo*** bastard son; ***hija bastarda*** bastard daughter; ***h. biológico*** biological son; ***hija biológica*** biological daughter; *Méx Vulg* ***h. de la chingada*** fucking bastard, motherfucker; *Méx Vulg* ***hija de la chingada*** fucking bitch; ***H. de Dios*** Son of God; *Méx Fam* ***h. de la guayaba*** pest; ***H. del Hombre*** Son of Man; ***h. ilegítimo*** illegitimate son; ***hija ilegítima*** illegitimate daughter; ***h. legítimo*** legitimate son; ***hija legítima*** legitimate daughter; *Fam Euf* ***h. de su madre*** *Br* beggar, *US* s.o.b.; ***h. natural*** illegitimate son; ***hija natural*** illegitimate daughter; *Fam Pey* ***h. de papá*****: es un h. de papá** daddy does everything for him; **este bar está lleno de hijos de papá** this bar is full of rich kids; *Vulg* ***h. de perra*** bastard; *Vulg* ***hija de perra*** bitch; ***h. político*** son-in-law; ***hija política*** daughter-in-law; ***h. pródigo*** prodigal son; *Vulg* ***h. de puta*** fucking bastard, motherfucker; *Vulg* ***hija de puta*** fucking bitch; *Vulg* **¡será h. de puta!** he's a right fucking bastard!; *Méx Vulg* ***h. de la tiznada*** fucking bastard, motherfucker; *Méx Vulg* ***hija de la tiznada*** fucking bitch; ***h. único*** only son; ***hija única*** only daughter

(**b**) *(natural)* native ►► ***h. predilecto*** = honorary title given by a city to a famous person born there or whose family comes from there

(**c**) *(como forma de dirigirse a alguien)* **¡h., no te pongas así!** don't be like that!; **¡pues h., podrías haber avisado!** you could at least have told me, couldn't you?; **¡h., te lo he explicado ya veinte veces!** for heaven's sake, I must have explained it to you at least twenty times!; **¡hija mía, qué bruta eres!** God, you're stupid!; **¡h. mío, haz caso a los consejos de los mayores!** you should listen to the advice of your elders, son; **¡h., eres el colmo!** you really are the limit!

(**d**) *(resultado)* child; **los errores son hijos de la precipitación** mistakes are what comes of being too hasty

2 *nm (hijo o hija)* child; **hijos** children; **no han tenido ningún h.** they don't have any children ►► ***h. adoptivo*** adopted child; ***h. bastardo*** bastard child; ***h. biológico*** biological child; ***h. ilegítimo*** illegitimate child; ***h. legítimo*** legitimate child; ***h. natural*** illegitimate child; ***h. no deseado*** unwanted child; ***h. único*** only child

3 *interj Méx Fam* **¡hijos!** wow!

híjole, híjoles *interj Méx* wow!

hijoputa *nmf Vulg* fucking bastard, motherfucker

hijuela *nf Andes, CRica (división territorial)* = plot forming a subdivision of an estate

hijuna *interj RP muy Fam (admiración)* son of a gun!; *(maldición) US* godammit!, *Br* bloody hell!

hilacha *nf* loose thread; EXPR *RP Fam* **mostrar la h.** to show one's true colours

hilachiento, -a, hilachento, -a *CSur* **1** *adj* (**a**) *(prenda)* frayed (**b**) *(persona)* ragged

2 *nm,f* ragged person; **un h.** a man dressed in rags

hilada *nf* row

hilado *nm* (**a**) *(actividad)* spinning (**b**) *(fibra)* yarn, thread

hilador, -ora *nm,f* spinner

hiladora *nf* spinning machine

hilandería *nf* (**a**) *(arte)* spinning (**b**) *(taller)* (spinning) mill

hilandero, -a *nm,f* spinner

hilar **1** *vt* (**a**) *(hilo)* to spin; **la araña hiló una telaraña** the spider spun a web (**b**) *(ideas, planes)* to think up

2 *vi* EXPR **h. delgado** *o* **muy fino: eso es h. delgado** *o* **muy fino** that's splitting hairs; **voy a tener que h. muy delgado** *o* **fino para que no rechace mi propuesta** I'm going to have to tread very carefully so he doesn't reject my proposal

hilarante *adj* hilarious; **gas h.** laughing gas

hilaridad *nf* hilarity; **la caída provocó la h. de los asistentes** the fall gave rise to much hilarity among those present

hilatura *nf* (**a**) *(actividad)* spinning (**b**) *(fábrica)* spinning mill

hilera *nf* (**a**) *(fila)* row, line; **en h.** in a row (**b**) *Tec* drawplate

hilio *nm Anat* hilum, hilus

hilo *nm* (**a**) *(fibra, hebra)* thread; EXPR *Am* **al h.** in a row; *Am* **me leí cinco libros al h.** I read five books one after the other *o* in a row; EXPR **colgar** *o* **pender de un h.** to be hanging by a thread; EXPR **mover los hilos** to pull some strings; **es él quien mueve los hilos de la empresa** he's the person who really runs the firm ►► ***h. de bramante*** twine; ***h. dental*** *(para la boca)* dental floss; *Am (bañador)* G-string

(**b**) *(tejido)* linen; **un mantel de h.** a linen tablecloth

(**c**) *(cable)* wire; **sin hilos** wireless; EXPR **tener h. directo con alguien** to have direct access to sb

(**d**) *(de agua, sangre)* trickle; **entraba un h. de luz por la ventana** a thin shaft of light came in through the window; **apenas le salía un h. de voz** he was barely able to speak

(**e**) *Mús* ***h. musical*** piped music

(**f**) *(de pensamiento)* train; *(de discurso, conversación)* thread; **perder el h.** to lose the thread; **seguir el h.** to follow (the thread); **tomar** *o* **retomar el h. (de la conversación)** to pick up the thread (of the conversation); **el h. conductor del argumento de la película** the central strand of the film's plot; **al h. de** *(a propósito de)* following on from; **esto viene al h. de lo que dijimos ayer** this relates to what we were saying yesterday

hilván *nm* (**a**) *(costura) Br* tacking, *US* basting (**b**) *(hilo) Br* tacking stitch, *US* basting stitch (**c**) *Ven (dobladillo) (de traje, vestido)* hem; *(de pantalón) Br* turn-up, *US* cuff

hilvanado *nm Br* tacking, *US* basting

hilvanar *vt* (**a**) *(ropa) Br* to tack, *US* to baste (**b**) *(coordinar)* to piece together; **hilvanó sus argumentos en un discurso perfecto** he wove his arguments into a perfect speech (**c**) *(improvisar)* to throw together; **tuvieron que h. una propuesta en el último minuto** they had to throw together a proposal at the last minute

Himalaya *nm* **el H.** the Himalayas

himen (*pl* **hímenes**) *nm* hymen

himeneo *nm Literario* wedding

himnario *nm* hymn book

himno *nm* (**a**) *(religioso)* hymn (**b**) *(en honor de algo)* anthem, hymn; **entonaron el h. del colegio** they sang the school song ▸▸ ***h. nacional*** national anthem

hincada *nf Am* genuflection

hincapié *nm* **hacer h. en** *(insistir)* to insist on; *(subrayar)* to emphasize, to stress; **hizo mucho h. en ese punto** he laid stress *o* emphasis on that point

hincar [60] **1** *vt* (**a**) *(introducir)* **h. algo en algo** to stick sth into sth; **hincó los postes en el suelo** he drove the posts into the ground; EXPR *Fam* **h. el diente a algo** *(a comida)* to sink one's teeth into sth; *(a trabajo, proyecto)* to tackle sth, to get one's teeth into sth

(**b**) *(apoyar)* to set (firmly); EXPR *Fam* **h. los codos** *(estudiar)* to study hard; **si quieres aprobar, vas a tener que h. los codos** if you want to pass you're going to have to roll up your sleeves and do some serious studying

2 hincarse *vpr* **se hincó ante el altar** he knelt before the altar; **hincarse de rodillas** to fall to one's knees

hincha 1 *adj RP Fam (fastidioso, pesado)* boring

2 *nmf* (**a**) *(seguidor)* fan (**b**) *RP Fam (fastidioso, pesado)* pain, bore

3 *nf Esp (rabia)* **tener h. a alguien** to have it in for sb

hinchable *adj* inflatable

hinchabolas, hinchahuevos, hinchapelotas *RP muy Fam* **1** *adj inv (fastidioso, pesado)* **no seas h., ya te dije que no** stop being such a pain in the *Br* arse *o US* ass, I've already said no

2 *nmf inv (pesado)* pain in the *Br* arse *o US* ass

hinchada *nf* (**a**) *(afición)* fans (**b**) *Am (genuflexión)* genuflection (**c**) *Ven (pinchazo)* prick

hinchado, -a *adj* (**a**) *(rueda, globo)* inflated (**b**) *(cara, tobillo)* swollen (**c**) *(engreído) (persona)* bigheaded, conceited; *(lenguaje, estilo)* bombastic

hinchahuevos = **hinchabolas**

hinchapelotas = **hinchabolas**

hinchar 1 *vt* (**a**) *(soplando)* to blow up, to inflate; *(con bomba)* to pump up; *Esp Fam* **lo hincharon a palos** they beat him till he was black and blue; EXPR *Esp Fam* **ya me está hinchando las narices** he's beginning to get up my nose

(**b**) *(exagerar)* to blow up, to exaggerate

(**c**) *RP Fam (fastidiar)* **no me hinches** stop bugging me; **no (me) hinches la paciencia** don't push your luck; EXPR *muy Fam* **h. las pelotas** *o* **las bolas** *o* **los huevos a alguien** *Br* to get on sb's tits, *US* to bust sb's balls; **dejá de h. las pelotas** *o* **las bolas** *o* **los huevos** stop being such a pain in the *Br* arse *o US* ass

2 *vi* (**a**) *CSur Fam* **h. por** *(ser fan de)* to support (**b**) *RP Fam (molestar)* to be a pest; **¡no hinches!** stop being a pest!

3 hincharse *vpr* (**a**) *(de aire)* to inflate; **el globo se hinchó en pocas horas** the balloon was inflated in a few hours

(**b**) *(pierna, mano)* to swell (up); **se me ha hinchado el brazo** my arm has swollen (up)

(**c**) *(persona)* to get puffed up; **siempre que habla de sus títulos se hincha** she gets all puffed up whenever she talks about her qualifications

(**d**) *(hartarse)* **se hinchó a comer** she stuffed herself; **nos hinchamos de paella** we stuffed ourselves with paella; **nos hinchamos de reír** we laughed ourselves silly

hinchazón *nf* swelling; **ya está bajando la h.** the swelling is already going down

hinchiera *etc ver* **henchir**

hincho *etc ver* **henchir**

hindi *nm* Hindi

hindú (*pl* **hindúes**) **1** *adj* (**a**) *(de la India)* Indian (**b**) *Rel* Hindu

2 *nmf* (**a**) *(de la India)* Indian (**b**) *Rel* Hindu

hinduismo *nm* Hinduism

hinduista 1 *adj* Hindu

2 *nmf* Hindu

hiniesta *nf* broom *(plant)*

hinojo *nm* fennel

hinojos: de hinojos *loc adv Literario* on bended knee; **hincarse de h.** to fall to one's knees

hip *interj* (**a**) *(hipido)* hic! (**b**) **ih.! ih.! ihurra!** *(vítores)* hip, hip, hooray!

hipar *vi* to hiccup

híper (*pl* **híper** *o* **hípers**) *nm inv Fam* hypermarket

hiper- *pref Fam (muy)* mega-; **me ha salido hipercaro** it was mega-expensive; **¡es hiperguapo!** he's a real dish!

hiperactividad *nf* hyperactivity

hiperactivo, -a *adj* hyperactive

hipérbaton (*pl* **hipérbatos** *o* **hiperbatones**) *nm Lit* hyperbaton

hipérbola *nf Mat* hyperbola

hipérbole *nf* hyperbole

hiperbólico, -a *adj* (**a**) *Mat* hyperbolic (**b**) *Lit* hyperbolic

hipercolesterolemia *nf Med* **tener h.** to have excessive cholesterol

hipercorrección *nf* hypercorrection

hipercrítico, -a 1 *adj* hypercritical

2 *nm,f* hypercritical person; **es un h.** he is hypercritical

hiperenlace *nm Informát* hyperlink

hiperespacio *nm Informát* hyperspace

hiperestesia *nf Med* hyperaesthesia

hiperfunción *nf Med* = increase in normal rate of functioning

hiperglicemia *nf Am Med* hyperglycaemia

hiperglicémico, -a *adj Am Med* hyperglycaemic

hiperglucemia *nf Med* hyperglycaemia

hiperglucémico, -a *adj Med* hyperglycaemic

hipérico *nm* St John's wort

hiperinflación *nf Econ* hyperinflation

hipermedia *nf Informát* hypermedia

hipermercado *nm* hypermarket

hipermétrope 1 *adj* long-sighted

2 *nmf* long-sighted person; **es un h.** he's long-sighted

hipermetropía *nf* long-sightedness, *Espec* hypermetropia, *US* hypertropia

hiperón *nm Fís* hyperon

hiperplasia *nf Med* hyperplasia

hiperrealismo *nm Arte* hyperrealism

hiperrealista *Arte* **1** *adj* hyperrealist

2 *nmf* hyperrealist

hipersensibilidad *nf* hypersensitivity (**a** to)

hipersensible *adj* hypersensitive (**a** to)

hipersónico, -a *adj* hypersonic

hipertensión *nf* **h. (arterial)** high blood pressure, *Espec* hypertension

hipertenso, -a 1 *adj* with high blood pressure, *Espec* hypertensive

2 *nm,f* person with high blood pressure, *Espec* hypertensive

hipertermia *nf Med* hyperthermia

hipertexto *nm Informát* hypertext

hipertextual *adj Informát* **enlace h.** hypertext link

hipertiroidismo *nm Med* hyperthyroidism

hipertrofia *nf* (**a**) *Med* hypertrophy (**b**) *(de empresa)* overexpansion

hipertrofiar 1 *vt Med* to over-develop

2 hipertrofiarse *vpr* (**a**) *Med* to become over-developed, *Espec* to hypertrophy (**b**) *(empresa)* to grow too big

hiperventilación *nf Med* hyperventilation

hiperventilar *vi Med* to hyperventilate

hipervitaminosis *nf inv Med* hypervitaminosis

hip-hop ['χipχop] *nm* hip-hop

hípica *nf* (**a**) *(carreras)* horseracing (**b**) *(concursos de saltos)* show jumping

hípico, -a *adj* (**a**) *(de las carreras)* **carrera hípica** horserace; **el mundo h.** the horseracing world (**b**) *(de los concursos de saltos)* show jumping; **concurso h.** show jumping event

hipido *nm* hiccup, hiccough

hipismo *nm* horseracing

hipnosis *nf inv* hypnosis

hipnoterapia *nf* hypnotherapy

hipnótico, -a 1 *adj* hypnotic

2 *nm* hypnotic, narcotic

hipnotismo *nm* hypnotism

hipnotización *nf* hypnotizing

hipnotizador, -ora 1 *adj* (**a**) *(de la hipnosis)* hypnotic (**b**) *(fascinante)* spellbinding, mesmerizing
2 *nm,f* hypnotist

hipnotizar [14] *vt* (**a**) *(dormir)* to hypnotize (**b**) *(fascinar)* to mesmerize

hipo *nm* hiccups; **tener h.** to have (the) hiccups; EXPR *Fam* **quitar el h.: el volumen de trabajo que tenemos es como para quitar el h.** we're really snowed under with work; **se ha comprado una casa que quita el h.** she's bought an awesome new house

hipo- *pref* hypo-

hipoacusia *nf Med* hearing loss, *Espec* hypoacousis

hipoacúsico, -a *Med* 1 *adj* **ser h.** to suffer from hearing loss
2 *nm,f* **ser un h.** to suffer from hearing loss

hipoacústico, -a *adj (aparato, teléfono)* for the hard of hearing

hipoalergénico, -a, hipoalérgico, -a *adj* hypoallergenic

hipocalórico, -a *adj (alimento, dieta)* low-calorie

hipocampo *nm (caballito de mar)* seahorse

hipocentro *nm* hypocentre, focus

hipocondría *nf* hypochondria

hipocondriaco, -a 1 *adj* hypochondriac
2 *nm,f* hypochondriac

hipocorístico *nm Ling* hypocorism

Hipócrates *n pr* Hippocrates

hipocrático, -a *adj* **juramento h.** Hippocratic oath

hipocresía *nf* hypocrisy

hipócrita 1 *adj* hypocritical; **es muy h.** she's a real hypocrite, she's really hypocritical
2 *nmf* hypocrite

hipócritamente *adv* hypocritically

hipodérmico, -a *adj* hypodermic

hipódromo *nm* racecourse, racetrack

hipófisis *nf inv Anat* pituitary gland, *Espec* hypophysis

hipofunción *nf Med* = decrease in normal rate of functioning

hipogeo *nm (sepultura)* underground tomb

hipoglicemia *nf Am Med* hypoglycaemia

hipoglicémico, -a *adj Am Med* hypoglycaemic

hipoglucemia *nf Med* hypoglycaemia

hipoglucémico, -a *adj Med* hypoglycaemic

hipología *nf* study of horses

hipónimo *nm Ling* hyponym

hipopótamo *nm* hippopotamus

hipóstasis *nf inv* hypostasis

hipotálamo *nm Anat* hypothalamus

hipotaxis *nf inv Gram* hypotaxis

hipoteca *nf* mortgage; **levantar una h.** to pay off a mortgage; **sobre su casa pesa una h.** they took out a mortgage to buy the house ►► ***h. a interés fijo*** fixed-rate mortgage; ***h. a interés variable*** variable-rate mortgage

hipotecable *adj* mortgageable

hipotecar [60] *vt* (**a**) *(bienes)* to mortgage (**b**) *(poner en peligro)* **hipotecó su futuro con esa decisión** he mortgaged his future with that decision; **está hipotecando su salud con tantos excesos** all his excesses are putting his health at risk

hipotecario, -a *adj* mortgage; **crédito h.** mortgage (loan)

hipotensión *nf* low blood pressure

hipotenso, -a 1 *adj* with low blood pressure, *Espec* hypotensive
2 *nm,f* person with low blood pressure, *Espec* hypotensive

hipotensor *nm* hypotensive drug

hipotenusa *nf Geom* hypotenuse

hipotermia *nf Med* hypothermia

hipótesis *nf inv* hypothesis ►► ***h. de trabajo*** working hypothesis

hipotéticamente *adv* hypothetically

hipotético, -a *adj* hypothetic, hypothetical; **en el caso h. de que se produjera una inundación** in the hypothetical case of there being a flood

hipotiroidismo *nm Med* hypothyroidism

hipotonía *nf Med* hypotonia

hippy, hippie ['χipi] (*pl* **hippies**) 1 *adj* hippy
2 *nmf* hippy

hiriente *adj (palabras)* hurtful, cutting

hiriera *etc ver* **herir**

Hiroshima [iro'ʃima] *n* Hiroshima

hirsutismo *nm Med* hirsutism

hirsuto, -a *adj* (**a**) *(cabello)* wiry; *(brazo, pecho)* hairy (**b**) *(persona)* gruff, surly

hirviente *adj* boiling

hirviera *etc ver* **hervir**

hisopo *nm* (**a**) *Rel* aspergillum, sprinkler (**b**) *(planta)* hyssop (**c**) *Chile (brocha de afeitar)* shaving brush

hispalense 1 *adj* Sevillian
2 *nmf* Sevillian

Hispania *n Hist* Hispania

hispánico, -a *adj* (**a**) *(de España)* Hispanic (**b**) *Hist (de Hispania)* Hispanic (**c**) *(hispanohablante)* Spanish-speaking; **el mundo h.** the Spanish-speaking world

hispanidad *nf* (**a**) *(cultura)* Spanishness (**b**) **la h.** *(pueblos)* the Spanish-speaking world

hispanismo *nm* (**a**) *(palabra, expresión)* Hispanicism (**b**) *(afición)* = interest in or love of Spain

hispanista *nmf* Hispanist, student of Hispanic culture

hispanizar 1 *vt* to hispanize
2 **hispanizarse** *vpr* to become hispanized

hispano[1], -a 1 *adj* (**a**) *(español)* Spanish (**b**) *(hispanoamericano)* Spanish-American; *(en Estados Unidos)* Hispanic
2 *nm,f* (**a**) *(español)* Spaniard (**b**) *(hispanoamericano)* Spanish American; *(estadounidense)* Hispanic

hispano-[2] *pref* Hispano-, Spanish-; **h.-francés** Franco-Spanish, Spanish-French

Hispanoamérica *n* Spanish America

hispanoamericano, -a 1 *adj* Spanish-American
2 *nm,f* Spanish American

hispanoárabe 1 *adj* Hispano-Arabic
2 *nmf* Spanish Arab

hispanofilia *nf* Hispanophilia

hispanófilo, -a 1 *adj* Hispanophile
2 *nm,f* Hispanophile

hispanofobia *nf* Hispanophobia

hispanófobo, -a 1 *adj* Hispanophobic
2 *nm,f* Hispanophobe

hispanohablante 1 *adj* Spanish-speaking
2 *nmf* Spanish speaker

hispanojudío, -a 1 *adj* Spanish-Jewish
2 *nm,f* Spanish Jew

hispanoparlante 1 *adj* Spanish-speaking
2 *nmf* Spanish speaker

hispanorromano, -a *adj* Hispano-Roman

histamina *nf Bioquím* histamine

histerectomía *nf Med* hysterectomy

histeria *nf* hysteria; **le dio** *o* **sufrió un ataque de h.** he had (an attack of) hysterics; **h. colectiva** mass hysteria

histérico, -a 1 *adj* (**a**) *Psi* hysterical (**b**) *Fam (nervioso)* **estar h.** to be a bag *o* bundle of nerves; **ponerse h.** to get in a flap; **ese ruido me pone h.** that noise really gets on my nerves
2 *nm,f* (**a**) *Psi* hysteric (**b**) *Fam (nervioso)* **es una histérica** she's always getting in a flap

histerismo *nm* hysteria

histerotomía *nf Med* hysterotomy

histocompatibilidad *nf Med* histocompatibility

histograma *nm* histogram

histología *nf* histology

histológico, -a *adj* histological

histólogo, -a *nm,f* histologist

histopatología *nf Med* histopathology

histopatológico, -a *adj Med* histopathological

HISTORIA *nf* (**a**) *(ciencia)* history; **un profesor/libro de h.** a history teacher/book; **h. de la ciencia/literatura** history of science/literature; **he comprado una h. de Grecia** I've bought a history of Greece; **ha sido la mayor catástrofe de la h.** it was the worst disaster in history; EXPR **hacer h.** to make history; EXPR **pasar a la h.: una victoria que pasará a la h.** a victory that will go down in history; **el cine mudo ya pasó a la h.** silent movies are now a thing of the past ►► ***h. antigua*** ancient history; ***h. del arte*** art history; ***h. contemporánea*** = modern history since the French Revolution; ***h. económica***

economic history; ***h. medieval*** medieval history; ***h. moderna*** = history of the period between 1492 and the French Revolution; ***h. natural*** natural history; ***h. oral*** oral history; ***h. política*** political history; ***h. sagrada*** biblical history; ***h. universal*** world history

(**b**) *(narración)* story; **una h. de amor/fantasmas** a love/ghost story; **una h. real** a true story; **nos contó varias historias de su viaje a Rusia** she told us several stories about her trip to Russia; **es siempre la misma h.** it's the same old story; **es una h. larga de contar** it's a long story

(**c**) *Fam (excusa, enredo)* story; **idéjate de historias!** that's enough of that!; **no me vengas ahora con historias** don't give me that!, you don't expect me to believe that, do you?; **es siempre la misma h.** it's always the same old story

(**d**) *Fam (asunto)* **a mí no me enredes en tus historias** don't drag me into your problems; **está metido en una h. muy turbia** he's involved in a very shady business; **está metido en una h. de drogas** he's mixed up in something to do with drugs

(**e**) *Fam (amorosa)* fling; **tener una h. con alguien** to have a fling with sb

(**f**) ***h. clínica*** medical *o* case history

historiado, -a *adj* gaudy

historiador, -ora *nm,f* historian

historial *nm* (**a**) *(ficha)* record ►► ***h. clínico*** medical *o* case history; ***h. médico*** medical *o* case history (**b**) *(historia)* history; **tiene un h. de fracasos** she has a history of failure

historiar *vt (relatar)* to tell the story of, to narrate

históricamente *adv* historically

historicidad *nf* historicity, historical authenticity

historicismo *nm* historicism

historicista *adj* historicist

histórico, -a *adj* (**a**) *(de la historia)* historical; **una novela histórica** a historical novel; **el legado h. de los romanos** the historical legacy of the Romans; **el centro h. de una ciudad** the historic centre of a city; **el dólar alcanzó ayer su máximo h.** the dollar climbed to an all-time high yesterday

(**b**) *(importante)* historic; **un acuerdo h.** an historic agreement

(**c**) *(veterano)* veteran; **uno de los líderes históricos del partido** one of the party's veteran leaders

historieta *nf* (**a**) *(tira cómica)* comic strip (**b**) *(chiste)* funny story, anecdote

historiografía *nf* historiography

historiógrafo, -a *nm,f* historiographer

histrión *nm* (**a**) *(actor)* actor (**b**) *(persona afectada)* play-actor

histriónico, -a *adj* histrionic

histrionismo *nm* histrionics

hit [χit] *(pl* **hits**) *nm* (**a**) *(musical)* hit ►► ***h. parade*** hit parade (**b**) *(en béisbol)* hit

hitita 1 *adj* Hittite

2 *nmf* Hittite

hitleriano, -a [χitle'rjano, -a] **1** *adj* Hitlerian, Hitler; **el régimen h.** the Hitler regime; **la Alemania hitleriana** Hitler's Germany

2 *nm,f* Hitlerite

hito *nm* (**a**) *(poste)* milestone; EXPR **mirar a alguien de h. en h.** to stare at sb (**b**) *(suceso)* milestone; **un descubrimiento que marcará un h. en la lucha contra el cáncer** a landmark discovery in the fight against cancer

hizo *ver* **hacer**

hl *(abrev de* **hectolitro**) hl

hm *(abrev de* **hectómetro**) hm

hnos. *(abrev de* **hermanos**) bros

hoatzín *nm* hoatzin

hobby ['χoβi] *(pl* **hobbys** *o* **hobbies**) *nm* hobby

hocicar 1 *vt (cerdo)* to root among

2 *vi* (**a**) *(cerdo)* to root around (**b**) *Hum (persona)* to fall flat on one's face

hocico *nm* (**a**) *(de perro, zorro)* muzzle; *(de gato, ratón)* nose; *(de cerdo)* snout

(**b**) *Fam (de personas) (boca)* rubber lips; *(cara)* mug; EXPR **caer de hocicos** to fall flat on one's face; EXPR **meter los hocicos en algo: siempre está metiendo los hocicos donde lo llaman** he's always sticking his nose into other people's business; EXPR **partir el h.: como no te calles te voy a partir el h.** if you don't shut up I'm going to smash your face in; EXPR **torcer el h.** to pull a face

hocicón, -ona 1 *adj* (**a**) *(animal)* big-snouted (**b**) *Méx Fam (hablador)* **ser h.** to have a big mouth

2 *nm,f Méx Fam (hablador)* bigmouth

hocicudo, -a *adj (animal)* big-snouted

hociquera *nf Perú* muzzle

hockey ['χokei] *nm* hockey ►► *Am* ***h. sobre césped*** *Br* hockey, *US* field hockey; ***h. sobre hielo*** *Br* ice hockey, *US* hockey; ***h. sobre hierba*** *Br* hockey, *US* field hockey; ***h. sobre patines*** roller hockey

hoco *nm* great curassow

hogaño *adv Literario (este año)* this year; *(actualmente)* nowadays

hogar *nm* (**a**) *(de chimenea)* fireplace; *(de horno, cocina)* grate; **pasaron la tarde al calor del h.** they spent the whole afternoon in front of the hearth

(**b**) *(domicilio)* home; **las tareas del h.** the housework; **trabajaba como empleada del h.** she worked as a maid; **su marido trabaja fuera y ella se ocupa del h.** her husband goes out to work and she's a housewife; **en más de la mitad de los hogares del país** in more than half of the households in the country; **el consumo medio por h. subió un 3 por ciento** average consumption per household *o* family rose by 3 percent; **aquí me siento como en mi propio h.** I feel at home here; **el problema de los jóvenes sin h.** the problem of young homeless people; EXPR **h. dulce h.** home sweet home ►► ***h. del jubilado*** *o* ***pensionista*** = social centre for elderly people

(**c**) *(familia)* family; **quiere casarse y formar un h.** she wants to get married and start a family

(**d**) *(asignatura)* home economics *(singular)*

hogareño, -a *adj* (**a**) *(persona)* **es una persona hogareña** she enjoys family life (**b**) *(tarea, economía)* domestic; *(ambiente)* family; **ambiente h.** family atmosphere; **la paz hogareña** domestic bliss

hogaza *nf* large round loaf

hoguera *nf* bonfire; **morir en la h.** to be burned at the stake

hoja *nf* (**a**) *(de planta)* leaf; *(de hierba)* blade ►► ***h. caduca*** deciduous leaf; **árbol de h. caduca** deciduous tree; ***h. de coca*** coca leaf; ***h. dentada*** dentate leaf; ***h. de parra*** vine leaf; *(en arte)* fig leaf; ***h. perenne*** perennial leaf; **árbol de h. perenne** evergreen (tree)

(**b**) *(de papel)* sheet (of paper); *(de libro)* page; **¿tienes una h. suelta?** do you have a sheet of paper?; **volver la h.** to turn the page; *(cambiar de tema)* to change the subject ►► ***h. informativa*** *(de gobierno, asociación)* fact sheet; *(entregada en la calle)* flyer; *(boletín)* newsletter; ***h. parroquial*** parish newsletter; *Com* ***h. de pedido*** order form; ***h. de reclamación*** complaint form; ***h. de ruta*** waybill; ***h. de servicios*** record (of service), track record; *Col* ***h. de vida*** curriculum vitae, *US* résumé

(**c**) *(de cuchillo)* blade ►► ***h. de afeitar*** razor blade

(**d**) *(de puertas, ventanas)* leaf

(**e**) *Informát* ***h. de cálculo*** spreadsheet; ***h. de estilos*** style sheet

(**f**) *(lámina)* sheet, foil ►► ***h. de lata*** tin plate

hojalata *nf* tin plate

hojalatería *nf* (**a**) *(tienda artesana)* tinsmith's (**b**) *Méx (chapistería) (lugar)* body shop; *(actividad)* panel beating

hojalatero, -a *nm,f* (**a**) *(artesano)* tinsmith (**b**) *Méx (chapista)* panel beater

hojaldrado, -a *adj* puff; **masa hojaldrada** puff pastry

hojaldre *nm* puff pastry

hojarasca *nf* (**a**) *(hojas secas)* (dead) leaves; *(frondosidad)* tangle of leaves (**b**) *(palabrería)* waffle

hojear *vt* to leaf through

hojilla *nf Ven* (razor) blade

hojuela *nf* (**a**) *(masa frita)* pancake (**b**) *Cuba, Guat (hojaldre)* puff pastry

hola *interj* (**a**) *(saludo)* hello! (**b**) *(expresión de sorpresa, admiración)* **ih., menudo coche!** hey, that's some car! (**c**) *RP (al teléfono)* hello?

holá *interj RP (al teléfono)* hello?

Holanda *n* Holland

holandés, -esa 1 *adj* Dutch

2 *nm,f (persona)* Dutchman, *f* Dutchwoman; **los holandeses** the Dutch ►► *Mitol* **el h. errante** the Flying Dutchman

3 *nm (lengua)* Dutch

holandesa *nf (hoja de papel)* = piece of paper measuring 22 x 28cm

holding ['χoldin] *(pl* **holdings**) *nm Com* holding company

holgadamente *adv* (**a**) *(ampliamente)* **cabemos todos h.** we can all fit in easily; **triunfaron h.** they won easily; **cumplió h. lo que prometió** he more than fulfilled his promise, he did what he had promised and more; **la abstención sobrepasó h. el 60 por ciento** well over 60 percent abstained

(**b**) *(con bienestar)* comfortably, easily; **viven h.** they live comfortably, they are comfortably off

holgado, -a *adj* (**a**) *(ropa)* baggy, loose-fitting; **los pantalones me están muy holgados** the trousers are very loose on me
(**b**) *(habitación, espacio)* roomy; **en los asientos de atrás cabemos cuatro holgados** there's (more than enough) room for four of us in the back seat
(**c**) *(victoria, situación)* comfortable; **gobernará con una holgada mayoría** he will govern with an ample *o* comfortable majority; **vamos holgados de tiempo** we're fine for time, we've got plenty of time
(**d**) *(económicamente)* comfortable; **están en una posición muy h.** they're very comfortably off

holganza *nf* idleness

holgar [16] *vi* (**a**) *(estar ocioso)* to be idle, to be taking one's ease; **pasamos las horas holgando** we spend the time lazing around (**b**) *(sobrar)* to be unnecessary; **en cuanto a su comportamiento, huelgan los comentarios** as far as his behaviour is concerned, what can I say?; **huelga decir que...** needless to say...

holgazán, -ana 1 *adj* idle, lazy
2 *nm,f* layabout, lazybones

holgazanear *vi* to laze about

holgazanería *nf* idleness, laziness

holgura *nf* (**a**) *(de ropa)* bagginess, looseness (**b**) *(entre piezas)* play, give (**c**) *(comodidad)* **vencieron con h.** they won easily (**d**) *(bienestar)* **vivir con h.** to be comfortably off; **ahora que tenemos dos sueldos viviremos con más h.** we'll be able to live more comfortably now we've got two salaries coming in

holístico, -a *adj* holistic

hollado, -a *adj* trodden

hollar [64] *vt* to tread (on); **la primera persona en h. la superficie de la Luna** the first person to walk on the surface of the moon

hollejo *nm* skin *(of grape, olive)*

hollín *nm* soot

hollinar *vt Chile* to cover with soot

hollywoodiense [χoliβu'ðjense] *adj* Hollywood; **la vida h.** life in Hollywood, the Hollywood scene

holmio *nm Quím* holmium

holocausto *nm* (**a**) *(sacrificio)* burnt offering (**b**) *(desastre)* holocaust; **un h. nuclear** a nuclear holocaust (**c**) *Hist* **el H.** the Holocaust

holoceno, -a *Geol* 1 *adj* Holocene
2 *nm* **el h.** the Holocene (period)

holografía *nf* holography

holográfico, -a *adj* holographic

hológrafo, -a 1 *adj* holographical
2 *nm* holograph

holograma *nm* hologram

holoturia *nf* sea cucumber

hombrada *nf* **hicieron la h. de subir el piano entre los dos** they heroically carried the piano up between the two of them

HOMBRE 1 *nm* (**a**) *(varón adulto)* man; **ropa de h.** menswear; **el h. blanco** white men; **paseaba del brazo de su h.** she walked along arm in arm with her man; **un pobre h.** a nobody; **¡pobre h.!** poor guy!; **¡h. al agua!** man overboard!; **de h. a h.** man to man; **el h. es un lobo para el h.** man is a wolf to man; EXPR **como un solo h.: los trabajadores defendieron a su compañera como un solo h.** the workers defended their colleague as one; EXPR **hacer un h. a alguien: el ejército no lo hizo un h.** the army failed to make a man of him; EXPR **ser h.: da la cara si eres h.** show your face if you're a man; EXPR **ser h. muerto: si me descubren, soy h. muerto** if they find me out, I'm a dead man; **¡arroja el arma o eres h. muerto!** throw down your weapon or you're a dead man!; EXPR **ser muy h.** to be a (real) man; **te crees muy h., ¿no?** you think you're a big man, don't you?; EXPR *Fam* **ser un h. de pelo en pecho** to be a real man, to be every inch a man; EXPR **ser todo un h.** to be a real man, to be every inch a man; PROV **el h. y el oso, cuanto más feos más hermosos** people often prefer brawn to classical good looks; PROV **h. precavido** *o* **prevenido vale por dos** forewarned is forearmed; PROV **el h. propone y Dios dispone** Man proposes and God disposes ►► ***h. de acción*** man of action; ***h. anuncio*** sandwich-board man; ***h. de bien*** honourable man; ***el h. de la calle*** the man in the street; ***el h. de las cavernas*** cavemen; ***h. de ciencias*** man of science; ***h. de confianza*** right-hand man; ***h. de Estado*** statesman; ***h. de familia*** family man; ***h. fuerte*** strongman; **el h. fuerte del régimen** the strongman of the regime; ***h. de iglesia*** man of the cloth; ***el h. invisible*** the invisible man; ***h. de letras*** man of letters; ***h. lobo*** werewolf; ***h. de mar*** seaman, sailor; ***h. de mundo*** man of the world; ***h. de Neanderthal*** Neanderthal man; ***h. de negocios*** businessman; ***el h. de las nieves*** the abominable snowman; ***h. objeto:*** **me tratan como a un h. objeto** they treat me as a sex object; ***h. orquesta*** one-man band; ***h. de paja*** front (man), *US* straw man; ***h. de palabra:*** **es un h. de palabra** he's a man of his word; ***el h. de a pie*** the man in the street; ***h. público*** public figure; ***h. rana*** frogman; *Fam* ***el h. del saco*** the bogeyman; ***h. del tiempo*** weatherman
(**b**) **el h.** *(la humanidad)* man, mankind; **la evolución del h.** the evolution of mankind
2 *interj* (**a**) *Esp (como apelativo)* **¡h.! ¡qué alegría verte!** (hey,) how nice to see you!; **¿te acuerdas de Marisol?, ¡sí, h., nuestra compañera de clase!** do you remember Marisol? you know, she was at school with us!; **¿me acercas a casa? – sí, h.** can you give me a *Br* lift *o US* ride home? – sure; **¡sí, h., que ya voy!** all right, all right, I'm coming!; **h., ¡qué pena!** oh, what a shame!; **pero h., no te pongas así** oh, don't be like that!; **h., no es exactamente mi plato favorito, pero...** well, it's not exactly my favourite dish, but...; **¡h. Pepe, tú por aquí!** hey, Pepe, fancy seeing you here!
(**b**) *Méx Fam* **n'h.** *(uso enfático)* **¿cómo les fue? – n'h., nos la pasamos súper-bien** how did it go? – man, we had a blast!; **n'h., no vayas a ver esa película, es aburridísima** god no, don't go to that movie *o Br* film, it's unbelievably boring

hombrear *vi Méx* to act the man

hombrera *nf* (**a**) *(de traje, vestido)* shoulder pad (**b**) *(de uniforme)* epaulette

hombrerío *nm Am* crowd *o* bunch of men

hombría *nf* manliness

hombrillo *nm Ven (arcén) (de autopista) Br* hard shoulder, *US* shoulder; *(de carretera)* verge

hombro *nm* shoulder; **al h.** across one's shoulder; **llevaba la caja al h.** he carried the box on his shoulder; **a hombros** over one's shoulders; **sacaron al torero a hombros** they carried the bullfighter out shoulder-high; **una camiseta sin hombros** a strapless top; **la chaqueta me queda ancha de hombros** this jacket is too wide in the shoulder, the shoulders are too wide on this jacket; **encogerse de hombros** to shrug one's shoulders; EXPR **arrimar el h.** to lend a hand; EXPR **hacer algo h. con h.** to do sth together; EXPR **mirar por encima del h. a alguien** to look down one's nose at sb

hombruno, -a *adj (mujer)* masculine-looking, mannish; *(rasgo, voz)* masculine

homeless ['χomles] *nm inv* homeless person

homenaje *nm* (**a**) *(tributo) (en honor de alguien)* tribute; *(al soberano)* homage; **en h. de** *o* **a** in honour of, as a tribute to; **rendir h. a** to pay tribute to (**b**) *(acto)* ceremony, celebration; **dedicaron un h. al poeta galardonado** they held a ceremony *o* organized a celebration in honour of the award-winning poet; **partido (de) h.** testimonial (match)

homenajeado, -a 1 *adj* honoured
2 *nm,f* guest of honour

homenajear *vt* to pay tribute to, to honour

homeópata *nmf* homeopath

homeopatía *nf* homeopathy

homeopático, -a *adj* homeopathic

homeostasis *nf inv Biol* homeostasis

homeotermo, -a, homotermo,-a *adj Biol* warm-blooded, *Espec* homeothermic

homérico, -a *adj* (**a**) *Lit* Homeric (**b**) *Am (enorme)* epic

Homero *n pr* Homer

homicida 1 *adj (agresión, mirada, intención)* murderous; **arma h.** murder weapon
2 *nmf* murderer

homicidio *nm* homicide, murder ►► ***h. involuntario*** manslaughter

homilía *nf Rel* homily, sermon

homínido *nm* hominid

Homo, homo *nm* Homo ►► ***H. erectus*** Homo erectus; ***H. hábilis*** Homo habilis; ***H. sapiens*** Homo sapiens

homocigótico, -a *adj Biol* **gemelos homocigóticos** identical twins, *Espec* homozygotic twins

homoeroticismo *nm* homoeroticism

homoerótico, -a *adj* homoerotic

homofilia *nf* homophilia

homofobia *nf* homophobia

homofóbico, -a *adj* homophobic

homófobo, -a 1 *adj* homophobic
2 *nm,f* homophobe

homofonía *nf Ling* homophony

homófono, -a *Ling* **1** *adj* homophonic
2 *nm* homophone

homogeneidad *nf* homogeneity

homogeneización *nf* homogenization

homogeneizador, -ora, homogeneizante *adj* homogenizing

homogeneizar [14] *vt* to homogenize

homogéneo, -a *adj* homogenous; **mezclarlo hasta obtener una masa homogénea** mix it until it is of uniform consistency

homografía *nf Ling* homography

homógrafo, -a *Ling* **1** *adj* homographic
2 *nm* homograph

homologable *adj (equiparable)* equivalent (**a** to); *(comparable)* comparable (**a** to *o* with)

homologación *nf* (**a**) *(equiparación)* bringing into line; **reivindican la h. salarial de todos los docentes** they are demanding that all teachers should be on a uniform salary scale (**b**) *(de un producto)* official authorization (**c**) *(de un récord)* official confirmation (**d**) *(de un título)* = certification of equivalence to an officially recognized qualification

homologado, -a *adj (producto)* officially approved; **un juguete h. por la Unión Europea** a toy that meets European Union standards

homologar [38] *vt* (**a**) *(equiparar)* to bring into line, to make comparable (**con** with); **reivindican que se homologuen sus salarios con los del resto de los funcionarios** they are demanding that their wages be brought into line with those of other public sector workers
(**b**) *(producto)* to authorize officially
(**c**) *(récord)* to confirm officially
(**d**) *(título)* = to certify as equivalent to an officially recognized qualification

homólogo, -a **1** *adj (semejante)* equivalent
2 *nm,f* counterpart

homonimia *nf* homonymy

homónimo, -a **1** *adj* homonymous
2 *nm,f (tocayo)* namesake
3 *nm Ling* homonym

homosexual **1** *adj* homosexual
2 *nmf* homosexual

homosexualidad *nf* homosexuality

homotermo, -a = **homeotermo**

honda *nf* (**a**) *(de cuero)* sling (**b**) *RP (tirachinas) Br* catapult, *US* slingshot

hondamente *adv* deeply

hondo, -a **1** *adj* (**a**) *(profundo) (lago, herida, plato)* deep; **lo h.** the depths; **en lo más h. de** in the depths of; **en lo más h. de su corazón sabía que no era cierto** in his heart of hearts he knew this wasn't true (**b**) *(intenso)* deep; **me causa honda alegría** it makes me very happy; **dio un h. suspiro** she gave a deep sigh
2 *adv* **respire h.** breathe deeply

hondonada *nf* hollow

hondura *nf* depth; EXPR **meterse en honduras** to get bogged down

Honduras *n* Honduras

hondureño, -a **1** *adj* Honduran
2 *nm,f* Honduran

honestamente *adv* (**a**) *(con honradez)* honestly (**b**) *(con sinceridad)* honestly; **si quieres que te diga lo que h. pienso...** if you want me to tell you what I honestly *o* really think..., if you want me to tell you my honest opinion...

honestidad *nf* (**a**) *(honradez)* honesty (**b**) *(sinceridad)* honesty; **dime con h., ¿qué te parece?** tell me honestly, what do you think? (**c**) *(decencia)* modesty, decency

honesto, -a *adj* (**a**) *(honrado)* honest (**b**) *(sincero)* honest; **sé honesta y dime lo que piensas** be honest and tell me what you think (**c**) *(decente)* modest, decent

hongkonés,-esa [χonko'nes, -esa] **1** *adj* of/from Hong Kong
2 *nm,f* person from Hong Kong

Hong Kong [χon'kon] *n* Hong Kong

hongo *nm* (**a**) *Biol* fungus
(**b**) *esp Am (comestible)* mushroom; *(no comestible)* toadstool; EXPR *Am Fam* **aburrirse como un h.** to be bored stiff; EXPR *Am* **como hongos: los celulares están proliferando como hongos** it's like those cellphones are breeding like rabbits ▸▸ ***h. atómico*** mushroom cloud; ***h. venenoso*** poisonous mushroom
(**c**) *(enfermedad)* fungus; **tiene hongos en la piel** he has a fungal infection
(**d**) **(sombrero) h.** *Br* bowler (hat), *US* derby

Honolulú [χonolu'lu] *n* Honolulu

honor *nm* (**a**) *(cualidad)* honour; **un hombre de h.** a man of honour, an honourable man; **luchó por defender su h.** he fought to defend his honour; **hacer h. a** to live up to; **hizo h. a su fama de generoso, y nos invitó a todos a cenar** he lived up to his reputation for being generous and bought us all a meal; **una cena en h. del poeta** a dinner in honour of the poet *o* in the poet's honour; **gol** *o* **tanto del h.** consolation goal; EXPR **en h. a la verdad** to be (quite) honest
(**b**) *(orgullo, satisfacción)* honour; **es un h. para mí presentarles a...** it's an honour for me to present to you...; **nos hizo el h. de invitarnos** he did us the honour of inviting us; **tener el h. de** to have the honour of
(**c**) **honores** *(ceremonial)* honours; **lo recibieron con honores de jefe de Estado** he was welcomed with all the ceremony befitting a head of state; **rendir honores a alguien** to salute sb; **hacer los honores a** to pay one's respects to; **hizo los honores al excelente vino servido** he commended the excellent wine; **hacer los honores de la casa** to do the honours, to look after the guests
(**d**) *Anticuado (de mujer)* honour, virtue

honorabilidad *nf* honour

honorable *adj* honourable

honorar *vt* to honour

honorario, -a **1** *adj* honorary
2 **honorarios** *nmpl* fees

honorífico, -a *adj* honorific

honoris causa *adj inv* honoris causa; **doctor h.** doctor honoris causa

honra *nf* (**a**) *(dignidad)* honour; **ser la h. de** to be the pride of; **es la h. de su país** she's the pride *o* toast of her country; **tener algo a mucha h.** to be proud of sth; EXPR **¡y a mucha h.!** and proud of it! ▸▸ ***honras fúnebres*** funeral (**b**) *Anticuado (virginidad)* honour, virtue

honradamente *adv* honestly, honourably

honradez *nf* (**a**) *(honestidad)* honesty (**b**) *(decencia)* decency

honrado, -a *adj* (**a**) *(honesto)* honest, honourable (**b**) *(decente)* decent, respectable

honrar **1** *vt* to honour; **su sinceridad lo honra** his sincerity does him credit; **nos honró con su presencia** she honoured us with her presence; **honrarás a tu padre y tu madre** *(lenguaje bíblico)* thou shalt honour thy father and thy mother
2 **honrarse** *vpr* to be honoured; **me honro con su amistad** I am honoured to have him as a friend; **me honro de ser su hermano** it is an honour to be his brother

honrilla *nf Fam* pride, face

honrosamente *adv* honourably

honroso, -a *adj (acto, gesto)* honourable

hontanar *nm* spring

hooligan ['χuliγan] (*pl* **hooligans**) *nmf* (soccer) hooligan

hop [χop] *interj* hup!

hopa *interj* oops!

HORA *nf* (**a**) *(del día)* hour; **una h. y media** an hour and a half; **se marchó hace una h. y media** she left an hour and a half ago; **media h.** half an hour; **a primera h.** first thing in the morning; **a altas horas de la noche** in the small hours; **(pagar) por horas** (to pay) by the hour; **cobra 80 euros por h.** she charges 80 euros an hour; **el tren circulaba a 100 kilómetros por h.** the train was travelling at 100 kilometres an hour; **comer entre horas** to eat between meals; **se pasa las horas jugando** he spends his time playing; **el enfermo tiene las horas contadas** the patient hasn't got long to live; **se rumorea que el ministro tiene las horas contadas** it is rumoured that the minister's days are numbered; **a última h.** *(al final del día)* at the end of the day; *(en el último momento)* at the last moment; **hasta última h. no nos dimos cuenta del error** we didn't notice the mistake until the last moment; **órdenes/preparativos de última h.** last-minute orders/preparations; **y nos llega una noticia de última h.** *(en telediario)* and here's some news just in; **última h.: atentado en Madrid** *(titular)* stop press: terrorist attack in Madrid ▸▸ ***horas extra(s)*** *o* ***extraordinarias*** overtime; **hacer horas extra(s)** to do *o* work overtime; ***horas libres*** free time; **tengo una h. libre entre latín y griego** I've got an hour free between my Latin and Greek; ***horas de oficina*** office hours; *RP* ***h. puente*** = free period between classes; ***h. de salida*** departure time; *RP* ***h. sándwich*** = free period between classes; ***horas de trabajo*** working hours; ***horas de visita*** visiting hours; ***horas de***

vuelo flying hours; *Fig* **tiene muchas horas de vuelo** he's an old hand (**b**) *(momento determinado)* time; **¿qué h. es?,** *Am* **¿qué horas son?** what time is it?; **¿tiene h., por favor?** have you got the time, please?; **¿a qué h. sale?** what time *o* when does it leave?; **el desfile comenzará a las 14 horas** the procession will begin at 14.00 hours *o* at 2 p.m.; **a esa h. no me va bien** that's not a good time for me; **es h. de irse** it's time to go; **es h. de cenar** it's time for dinner; **se ha hecho la h. de irse a dormir** it's time for bed; **ha llegado la h. de marcharnos** the time has come for us to leave; **el equipo pasa por horas bajas** the team's going through a bad patch; **a estas horas deben estar aterrizando en Managua** they should be landing in Managua around now; **estaré ahí a la h.** I'll be there on time, I'll be punctual; **hay que tener cuidado a la h. de aplicar la pintura** care should be taken when applying the paint; **a la h. de cenar** at dinnertime; **a la h. de ir de vacaciones, prefiero la playa** when it comes to holidays, I prefer the seaside; **a su h.** when the time comes, at the appropriate time; **el vuelo no llegó a su** *o RP* **en h.** the flight didn't arrive on time; **a todas horas** *(constantemente)* all the time; **el tren llegó antes de h.** the train arrived early; **cada h.** hourly; **dar la h.** *(reloj)* to strike the hour; **me dio la h.** she told me the time; **poner el reloj en h.** to set one's watch *o* clock; **¡ya era h.!** and about time too!; **ya es** *o* **ya iba siendo h. de que te fueses a casa** it's about time you went home; EXPR *Fam* **¡a buenas horas!** that's a lot of good now!; **¡a buenas horas me avisas!** now's a fine time to tell me!; EXPR *Fam Hum* **¡a buenas horas mangas verdes!** that's a fat lot of good now!; EXPR *Fam* **no dar ni la h.: ese tío no te dará ni la h.** that guy's as stingy *o* tight as they come; EXPR *Esp, Andes, Carib, RP* **la h. de la verdad,** *CAm, Méx* **la h. de la h.** the moment of truth; *Esp, Andes, Carib, RP* **a la h. de la verdad,** *CAm, Méx* **a la h. de la h.** when it comes to the crunch; EXPR **en mala h. le conté el secreto** I wish I'd never told him the secret; **en mala h. salimos de excursión** we couldn't have chosen a worse time to go on a trip; EXPR **no veo la h. de hacerlo** I can't wait to do it ►► ***la h. del bocadillo*** *(en fábrica)* = break for refreshment during morning's work, *Br* ≃ morning tea break; ***h. cero*** zero hour; ***la h. de cerrar*** *o* ***de cierre*** closing time; ***la h. de dormir*** bedtime; ***h. de Greenwich*** Greenwich Mean Time, GMT; ***h. H*** zero hour; ***h. legal*** standard time; ***h. local*** local time; ***h. muerta*** free hour; *Educ* free period; ***h. oficial*** official time; *Esp* ***h. peninsular*** = local time in mainland Spain as opposed to the Canaries, which are an hour behind; *Am* ***h. pico*** *(de mucho tráfico)* rush hour; *(de agua, electricidad)* peak times; *Esp* ***h. punta*** *(de mucho tráfico)* rush hour; *(de agua, electricidad)* peak times; ***h. del té*** teatime; ***h. valle*** off-peak times

(**c**) *(cita)* appointment; **pedir/dar h.** to make/give an appointment; **tengo h. en la peluquería** I've got an appointment at the hairdresser's; **tengo h. con el dentista** I've got a dental appointment

(**d**) *(muerte)* **llegó su h.** her time has come

(**e**) *Rel* **horas** *(libro)* book of hours; **horas canónicas** canonical hours

---

horadar *vt (perforar)* to pierce; *(con máquina)* to bore through

hora-hombre (*pl* **horas-hombre**) *nf Econ* man-hour

horario, -a 1 *adj* **cambio h.** *(bianual)* = putting clocks back or forward one hour; **huso h.** time zone

2 *nm* (**a**) *(de actividad) Br* timetable, *US* schedule; **se limitan a cumplir el h.** they just work the hours they are supposed to do; *Tel* **una llamada hecha en h. diurno/nocturno** a daytime/evening call ►► ***h. de atención al público*** *(en oficina)* opening *o* office hours; **h. de atención: de 9 a 6** *(al teléfono)* lines open between 9 and 6; ***h. comercial*** opening hours; *Esp* ***h. continuo*** = working day with no lunch break, and an earlier finishing time; *Am* ***h. corrido*** = working day with no lunch break, and an earlier finishing time; ***h. escolar*** school *Br* timetable *o US* schedule; ***h. flexible*** flexitime; ***h. intensivo*** = working day with no lunch break, and an earlier finishing time; ***h. laboral*** working hours; ***h. lectivo*** *Br* lesson *o US* class time; ***h. de oficina*** office hours; ***h. partido*** = working day with long (2-3 hour) lunch break, ending at 7-8 p.m.; ***h. previsto*** scheduled time; ***h. de trabajo*** working hours; ***h. de verano*** summer opening hours; ***h. de visitas*** visiting hours

(**b**) *(de reloj)* hour hand

horca *nf* (**a**) *(patíbulo)* gallows; **condenar a alguien a la h.** to sentence sb to be hanged (**b**) *(herramienta)* pitchfork

horcajadas: a horcajadas *loc adv* astride; **se sentó a h. en la silla** she sat astride the chair

horcajo *nm (de ríos)* fork

horcar *vt Méx* to hang

horchata *nf* (**a**) *(de chufa)* = cold drink made from ground tiger nuts, water and sugar (**b**) *(de arroz)* = Mexican cold drink made from rice, flavoured with sugar and cinnamon

horchatería *nf* = milk bar where "horchata de chufa" is served

horcón *nm Am (para vigas)* = wooden column supporting ceiling beams

horda *nf* (**a**) *(tribu)* horde (**b**) *(masa descontrolada)* horde, gang; **hordas de gamberros destrozaron varias tiendas** hordes *o* gangs of hooligans smashed up several shops (**c**) *CSur, Méx (multitud)* horde; **hordas de niños se apiñan para ver el espectáculo** hordes of children crowd round to see the show

hordiate *nm* barley water

horero *nm Am* hour hand

horizontal 1 *adj* (**a**) *Geom* horizontal (**b**) *(posición)* horizontal; **poner en posición h.** to place horizontally (**c**) *(en crucigrama)* across; **3 h.** 3 across (**d**) *Informát (orientación)* landscape

2 *nf Geom* horizontal

horizontalidad *nf* flatness

horizontalmente *adv* horizontally

horizonte *nm* (**a**) *(línea)* horizon; **la línea del h.** the horizon; **la barca se perdió por el h.** the boat disappeared over the horizon ►► ***h. artificial*** artificial horizon

(**b**) *(perspectivas)* **un h. poco prometedor** an unpromising outlook; **este proyecto amplía nuestros horizontes** this project represents a widening of our horizons; **no hay perspectivas de mejora en el h. más cercano** there is no prospect of improvement in the immediate future

horma *nf* (**a**) *(molde)* mould, pattern; *(de zapatos)* shoe tree; *(de sombrero)* hat block; EXPR **encontrar** *o* **hallar alguien la h. de su zapato** to meet one's match (**b**) *RP* **una h. de queso** a (whole) cheese

hormiga *nf* (**a**) *(insecto)* ant; EXPR *RP muy Fam* **tener hormigas en el culo** *(moverse)* to have ants in one's pants; *(cambiar de vida)* to have itchy feet ►► ***h. blanca*** termite, white ant; ***h. león*** antlion (fly); ***h. obrera*** worker ant; ***h. reina*** queen ant (**b**) *Fam (persona)* **ser una h.** to be hard-working and thrifty

hormigón *nm* concrete ►► ***h. armado*** reinforced concrete

hormigonar *vt* to construct with concrete

hormigonera *nf* concrete mixer

hormiguear *vi* (**a**) *(dar sensación de hormigueo)* **me hormiguean las piernas** I've got pins and needles in my legs (**b**) *(moverse, bullir)* to swarm; **los asistentes hormigueaban en el vestíbulo del teatro** the foyer was thronged *o* seething with theatregoers

hormigueo *nm* (**a**) *(sensación)* pins and needles; **siento un h. en las piernas** I've got pins and needles in my legs; **sentía un h. de placer en la nuca** she felt a pleasant tingling at the back of her neck (**b**) *(movimiento)* bustle

hormiguero 1 *adj* **oso h.** anteater

2 *nm* (**a**) *(de hormigas) (agujero)* ants' nest; *(promontorio)* ant hill (**b**) *(lugar bullicioso)* **Tokio es un h. humano** Tokyo is swarming *o* teeming with people

hormiguita *nf Fam* **ser una h.** to be hard-working and thrifty

hormona *nf* hormone ►► ***h. del crecimiento*** growth hormone

hormonal *adj* hormonal; **sufre un desarreglo h.** she is suffering from a hormonal imbalance

hornacina *nf* (vaulted) niche

hornada *nf* (**a**) *(de pan, cerámica)* batch (**b**) *Fam (de personas)* crop; **la última h. de jóvenes actores** the latest crop of young actors

hornalla *nf RP (de cocina, fogón)* ring, burner

hornear *vt* to bake

hornero *nm (ave)* ovenbird

hornilla *nf Andes, Esp, Méx* ring, burner

hornillo *nm* (**a**) *Esp (de cocina, fogón)* ring, burner (**b**) *(para cocinar)* **un h. (de gas)** a camping *o* portable stove

horno *nm* (**a**) *(de cocina)* oven; **pescado al h.** baked fish; EXPR *Fam* **no está el h. para bollos** the time is not right ►► ***h. de convección*** fan oven; ***h. eléctrico*** electric oven; ***h. de gas*** gas oven; ***h. microondas*** microwave (oven)

(**b**) *Tec* furnace; *(de cerámica, ladrillos)* kiln ►► ***h. crematorio*** crematorium; ***h. industrial*** industrial oven

(**c**) *Fam (lugar caluroso)* oven, furnace; **esta oficina es un h. en verano** this office is like an oven *o* furnace in summer

(**d**) **h. (de pan)** *(panadería)* (baker's) oven

horóscopo *nm* (**a**) *(signo zodiacal)* star sign; **¿qué h. eres?** what sign are you? (**b**) *(predicción)* horoscope

horqueta *nf Am* (**a**) *(de camino)* fork (**b**) *(de río)* bend

horquetilla *nf Ven* hairpin, *Br* hairgrip

horquilla *nf* (**a**) *(para el pelo)* hairpin, *Br* hairgrip (**b**) *(de bicicleta)* fork (**c**) *(herramienta)* pitchfork (**d**) *(entre valores)* range; **sitúan su mayoría en una h. entre el 51 y el 53 por ciento** they put their majority at somewhere between 51 and 53 percent

horrendo = **horroroso**

hórreo *nm* = raised granary typical of Asturias and Galicia

horrible *adj* (**a**) *(terrorífico)* horrific, terrifying; **un accidente h.** a horrific accident
(**b**) *Fam (muy malo)* appalling, awful; **nos hizo un tiempo h.** we had terrible *o* awful weather
(**c**) *Fam (muy feo)* horrible, hideous; **tiene un novio h.** she's got a horrible-looking *o* hideous boyfriend; **ese vestido le queda h.** that dress looks horrible *o* hideous on her
(**d**) *Fam (muy grande)* **tengo un frío h.** I'm absolutely freezing; **¡qué frío más h.!** it's absolutely freezing!; **tengo un hambre h.** I'm ravenous *o* starving

horripilante *adj* (**a**) *(terrorífico)* horrifying, spine-chilling (**b**) *Fam (muy malo)* appalling (**c**) *Fam (muy feo)* hideous

horripilar *vt* (**a**) *(dar terror)* to terrify, to scare to death; **me horripilan las arañas** I'm terrified of spiders (**b**) *(repugnar)* to horrify

horro, -a *adj Literario* (**a**) *(animal)* sterile (**b**) *(esclavo)* emancipated

horror **1** *nm* (**a**) *(miedo)* terror, horror; **me da h. pensarlo** just thinking about it gives me the shivers; **se quedó paralizado de h.** he was paralysed with fear; **¡qué h.!** how awful!; **¡qué h. de día!** what an awful day!
(**b**) *(atrocidad)* atrocity; **los horrores de la guerra** the horrors of war
(**c**) *Fam* **un h.** *(mucho)* an awful lot; **me gusta un h.** I absolutely love it; **la quiero un h.** I love her to bits, I really love her; **nos costó un h. convencerle** it was an incredible job to convince him
2 *adv Fam* **horrores** terribly, an awful lot; **me gusta horrores** I absolutely love it; **la quiero horrores** I love her to bits, I really love her

horrorizado, -a *adj* terrified, horrified

horrorizar [14] **1** *vt* to horrify; **me horroriza viajar en barco** I'm terrified of travelling by boat
2 horrorizarse *vpr* to be horrified; **me horroricé cuando me dieron la noticia** I was horrified when they told me the news

horrorosamente *adv* horribly; **sufrieron h.** they suffered terribly; **viste h.** she has terrible dress sense

horroroso, -a, horrendo, -a *adj* (**a**) *(terrorífico)* horrific, horrifying, terrifying; **un accidente h.** a horrific accident
(**b**) *Fam (muy malo)* appalling, awful; **nos hizo un tiempo h.** we had appalling *o* awful weather
(**c**) *Fam (muy feo)* hideous; **tiene un novio h.** she's got a hideous boyfriend; **ese vestido le queda h.** that dress looks hideous on her
(**d**) *Fam (muy grande)* **tengo un frío h.** I'm absolutely freezing; **¡qué frío más h.!** it's absolutely freezing!; **tengo un hambre horrorosa** I'm ravenous *o* starving; **tengo unas ganas horrorosas de leerlo** I'm dying to read it

horst [χorst] (*pl* **horsts**) *nm Geol* horst

hortaliza *nf* (garden) vegetable

hortelano, -a *nm,f Br* market gardener, *US* truck farmer

hortensia *nf* hydrangea

hortera *Esp Fam* **1** *adj* (**a**) *(decoración, ropa, canción)* tacky, *Br* naff (**b**) *(persona)* **es muy h.** he has really tacky *o Br* naff taste
2 *nmf* **es un h.** he has really tacky *o Br* naff taste

horterada *nf Esp Fam* **una h. de zapatos** an incredibly tacky *o Br* naff pair of shoes; **esa canción es una h.** that song is really tacky *o Br* naff; **la ceremonia fue una h.** the ceremony was really tacky *o Br* naff

hortícola *adj* horticultural

horticultor, -ora *nm,f* horticulturalist

horticultura *nf* horticulture

hortofrutícola *adj* **el sector h.** the fruit and vegetable growing sector

hortofruticultura *nf* fruit and vegetable growing

hosanna **1** *nm* hosanna
2 *interj* hosanna; **ih. el Señor!** praise the Lord!

hosco, -a *adj* (**a**) *(persona)* sullen, gruff (**b**) *(lugar)* grim, gloomy

hospedaje *nm* (**a**) *(alojamiento)* accommodation, lodgings, *US* accommodations; **dieron h. al peregrino** they gave lodging to the pilgrim (**b**) *(dinero)* (cost of) board and lodging (**c**) *Informát (de páginas web)* hosting

hospedar **1** *vt* to put up
2 hospedarse *vpr* to stay (**en** at *o* in)

hospedería *nf* (**a**) *(lugar de alojamiento)* guest house (**b**) *(de convento)* hospice

hospedero, -a *nm,f* innkeeper

hospiciano, -a *nm,f* = resident of an orphanage

hospicio *nm* (**a**) *(para niños)* orphanage, children's home (**b**) *(para pobres)* poorhouse

hospital *nm* hospital; **la ingresaron en el h.** she was admitted to hospital; **tengo que ir al h. a visitar a un tío** I have to go to the hospital to visit an uncle ►► ***h. de campaña*** field hospital; ***h. clínico*** teaching hospital; ***h. infantil*** children's hospital; ***h. psiquiátrico*** mental hospital; ***h. universitario*** teaching hospital

hospitalariamente *adv* hospitably

hospitalario, -a *adj* (**a**) *(acogedor)* hospitable (**b**) *(de hospital)* hospital; **atención hospitalaria** hospital care

hospitalidad *nf* hospitality

hospitalización *nf* hospitalization

hospitalizar [14] **1** *vt* to hospitalize, to take *o* send to hospital
2 hospitalizarse *vpr Am Br* to go into hospital, *US* to go into the hospital

hosquedad *nf* sullenness, gruffness

host [χost] (*pl* **hosts**) *nm Informát* host

hostal *nm* guesthouse, cheap hotel ►► ***h. residencia*** boarding house

hostelería *nf (sector hostelero)* hotel and catering industry

hostelero, -a **1** *adj* **sector h.** hotel and catering industry
2 *nm,f* landlord, *f* landlady

hostería *nf* (**a**) *(pensión)* guesthouse (**b**) *CSur (hotel)* country hotel

hostia

> Although always considered rude, it is not uncommon to hear this word used in public by respected politicians and businessmen.

1 *nf* (**a**) *Rel* host; EXPR *Esp Vulg* **ime cago en la h.!** fucking hell!
(**b**) *Esp Vulg (golpe)* **dar** *o* **pegar una h. a alguien** to belt *o* clobber sb; **inflar a alguien a hostias** to beat the shit out of sb; **nos dimos** *o* **pegamos una h. con el coche** we smashed up the car
(**c**) *Esp Vulg (para intensificar)* **¿para qué hostias...?** why the hell...?; **¿dónde hostias habré puesto las llaves?** where the hell did I put my keys?; **había la h. de gente** the place was heaving; **estoy harto de este ordenador de la h.** I'm sick of this *Br* bloody *o US* goddamn computer; **hace un frío de la h.** it's *Br* bloody *o US* goddamn freezing out there!; **tiene una casa de la h.** she's got a house you just wouldn't believe; **con el viaje y toda la h. me he quedado sin dinero** what with that *Br* bloody *o US* goddamn trip and everything, I'm out of cash; **ser la h.** *(de bueno)* to be *Br* bloody *o US* goddamn amazing; *(de malo)* to be *Br* bloody *o US* goddamn awful; **tus amigos son la h., me encanta salir con ellos** your friends are *Br* bloody *o US* goddamn brilliant, I love going out with them; **tío, eres la h., ¿cómo se te ocurre pegar a tu hermana?** you're fucking unbelievable! how could you hit your own sister?
(**d**) *Esp Vulg (velocidad)* **a toda h.** at full pelt *o* flat out; EXPR **ir cagando hostias** to run like fuck *o Br* buggery
(**e**) *Esp Vulg (humor)* **tener mala h.** to be a mean bastard; **hoy está de una mala h. tremenda** he's in a really filthy mood today
(**f**) *Esp Vulg (excusas)* **idéjate de hostias y cuéntame lo que pasó!** cut the crap *o Br* stop pissing around and tell me what happened!
2 *interj Esp Vulg* **ih.!, ihostias!** *Br* bloody hell!, *US* goddamn it!; **ih., no me había dado cuenta!** Christ *o Br* bloody hell!, I didn't realize!; **ih., cómo has crecido!** Christ, haven't you grown!; EXPR **ihostias en vinagre!** *Br* Christ on a bike!, *US* Jesus H. Christ!

hostiar [32] *vt Vulg* to bash

hostiario *nm* (**a**) *Rel* wafer box (**b**) *(molde)* wafer mould

hostigamiento *nm* harassment

hostigar [38] *vt* (**a**) *(acosar)* to pester, to bother (**b**) *(golpear)* to whip (**c**) *Mil* to harass (**d**) *Andes, CAm, Méx (sujeto: dulces)* **los bombones me hostigan** I find chocolates sickly

hostigoso, -a *adj Andes, CAm, Méx* cloying, sickening

hostil *adj (persona, medio, actitud)* hostile; **fue muy h. conmigo** he was very unfriendly *o* hostile towards me; **se mostraron h. a la idea** their reaction to the idea was hostile

hostilidad *nf* (**a**) *(sentimiento)* hostility; **me trató con mucha h.** she was very unfriendly *o* hostile towards me (**b**) *Mil* **hostilidades** hostilities; **romper las hostilidades** to start hostilities

hostilizar [14] *vt* to harass

hostión *nm Esp Vulg (golpe)* **dar** *o* **pegar un h. a alguien** to belt *o* clobber sb; **nos dimos** *o* **pegamos un h. con el coche** we smashed up the car

hot dog ['χotdoɣ] (*pl* **hot dogs**) *nm* hot dog

hotel *nm* hotel ►► *CSur* ***h. alojamiento*** = hotel where rooms are let by the hour; *Esp* ***h. apartamento*** apartment hotel

hotelería *nf Andes, RP* hotel and catering industry

hotelero, -a 1 *adj* hotel; **hay escasez de plazas hoteleras** there is a shortage of hotel accommodation
2 *nm,f (hombre)* hotelier, hotel manager; *(mujer)* hotelier, hotel manageress

hotentote 1 *adj* Hottentot
2 *nmf* Hottentot

hotline ['χotlain] *nf* hot line

house [χaus] *nm (estilo musical)* house

hovercraft [oβer'kraf] (*pl* **hovercrafts**) *nm* hovercraft

hoy 1 *adv* (**a**) *(en este día)* today; **h. es martes** today is Tuesday, it's Tuesday today; **¿a qué estamos h.?** what's today's date?; **h. hace cuatro meses de su muerte** it's four months today since she died; **en un día como h.** on a day like today; **de h. en adelante,** *RP* **de h. en más** as from today; **de h. no pasa, tengo que ordenar esta mesa** it can't wait any longer, I have to tidy this table today; **de h. para mañana** as soon *o* quickly as possible; **lo necesito para h.** I need it for today; **la reforma entra en vigor a partir de h. mismo** the reform comes in to force as of today *o* from today; **por h. ya hemos terminado** we've finished for today; EXPR **h. por ti y mañana por mí** you can do the same for me some time
(**b**) *(en la actualidad)* nowadays, today; **h. es más fácil viajar** travelling is much easier nowadays, travel today is much easier; **h. (en) día** these days, nowadays; **la mujer de h. en día** women today, modern women; **h. por h.** at the present moment, as things are at the moment; **en aquel tiempo el h. presidente era un abogado laboralista** at that time the man who is now president was a labour lawyer
2 *nm* **el h.** the here and now; **aprende a disfrutar el h.** learn to enjoy the moment *o* the here and now

hoya *nf* (**a**) *(llanura)* plain *(surrounded by mountains)* (**b**) *Am (cuenca de río)* river basin

hoyanco *nm Méx* pothole

hoyar *vt Cuba, Chile, PRico* to dig holes in

hoyito *nm Am* dimple

hoyo *nm* (**a**) *(agujero)* hole; *(artificial)* pit; **la carretera estaba llena de hoyos** the road was full of potholes (**b**) *(de golf)* hole; **un campo de nueve hoyos** a nine-hole course; **h. en uno** hole in one (**c**) *Fam (sepultura)* grave (**d**) *Méx Astron* ***h. negro*** black hole

hoyuelo *nm* dimple

hoz *nf* (**a**) *(herramienta)* sickle; **la h. y el martillo** *(símbolo)* the hammer and sickle (**b**) *(barranco)* gorge, ravine

HR (*abrev de* **Hostal Residencia**) boarding house

HTML *nm Informát* (*abrev de* **hypertext markup language**) HTML

HTTP *nm Informát* (*abrev de* **hypertext transfer protocol**) HTTP

huaca *nf* (**a**) *Am (sepultura)* = pre-Columbian Indian tomb (**b**) *Am (tesoro)* hidden treasure

huacal *nm CAm, Col, Méx* (**a**) *(jaula)* cage (**b**) *(cajón)* drawer

huacarear = **guacarear**

huachafería *nf Perú Fam* (**a**) *(hecho)* tacky thing (**b**) *(dicho)* naff comment

huachinango *nm Méx (pez)* red snapper

huacho = **guacho**

huaco *nm Am (cerámica)* = pottery object found in pre-Columbian Indian tomb

huaico = **huayco**

huaino, huayno *nm* = traditional Peruvian song and dance

huamúchil = **guamúchil**

huancaíno, -a 1 *adj* of/from Huancayo *(Peru)*
2 *nm,f* person from Huancayo *(Peru)*

huapango, guapango *nm* = lively popular song and dance from the Huasteca region of Eastern Mexico

huapanguero, -a *nm,f Méx* "huapango" singer

huaquear, guaquear *vi Am* to rob graves

huaqueo, guaqueo *nm Am* grave robbing

huaquero, -a, guaquero, -a *Am nm,f* grave robber

huarache, guarache *nm Méx* (**a**) *(sandalia)* = crude sandal with a sole made from a tyre (**b**) *(parche)* patch *(on tyre)*

huasca *nf Andes* whip

huasipungo, guasipungo *nm Andes* = small plot of land given by landowner to Indians in exchange for their labour

huaso, -a *nm,f Chile Fam* farmer, peasant

huasteco, -a *Méx* 1 *adj* Huasteca, Huastecan
2 *nm,f (persona)* Huasteca, = Indian of Mayan stock, from Eastern Mexico
3 *nm (lengua)* Huasteca

huata *nf Arg, Chile Fam (barriga)* belly

huato, guato *nm Bol* lace

huayco, huaico *nm Perú* landslide

huayna *Andes, Arg* 1 *adj* young
2 *nmf (chico)* lad, young man; *(chica)* girl, young woman

huayno = **huaino**

hubara *nf* houbara bustard

hubiera *etc ver* **haber**

hucha *nf Esp (alcancía)* moneybox; *(en forma de cerdo)* piggy bank

hueco, -a 1 *adj* (**a**) *(vacío)* hollow
(**b**) *(sonido)* resonant, hollow
(**c**) *(sin ideas)* empty; **su discurso fue h.** there was no substance to his speech; **eso no son más que palabras huecas** those are just empty words; *Fam* **es una cabeza hueca** she's an airhead
(**d**) *(mullido, esponjoso) (bizcocho)* light and fluffy; **lleva el pelo muy h.** she has a very bouffant hairstyle
(**e**) *Esp (orgulloso)* proud; **se puso muy h. cuando anunciaron su triunfo** he swelled with pride when they announced his victory
2 *nm* (**a**) *(cavidad)* hole; *(en pared)* recess; **suena a h.** it sounds hollow
(**b**) *(espacio libre)* space, gap; *(de ascensor)* shaft; **el h. de la escalera** the stairwell; **no había ni un h. en el teatro** there wasn't an empty seat in the theatre; **hazme un h. en el sofá** make a bit of room for me on the sofa; **deja un h. para poder insertar los gráficos** leave a space for the graphs; **estoy buscando un h. para aparcar** I'm looking for a parking space; **la marcha de los hijos dejó un h. en sus vidas** the children leaving left a gap in their lives; **deja un h. que será difícil de llenar** she leaves a gap that will be hard to fill; **se abrió h. entre la masa de curiosos** he made his way through the crowd of onlookers; **un producto que se ha abierto un h. en el mercado** a product that has carved out a niche in the market
(**c**) *(rato libre)* spare moment; **tengo un h. a la hora del almuerzo** I've got a moment at lunchtime; **te puedo hacer un h. esta tarde** I can fit *o* squeeze you in this afternoon
(**d**) *(vacante)* vacancy; **ha quedado un h. vacante en la cúpula del partido** there's a vacancy in the party leadership

huecograbado *nm* photogravure

huecú (*pl* **huecúes**) *nm Chile* bog, swamp

huela *etc ver* **oler**

huelga 1 *ver* **holgar**
2 *nf* strike; **estar en h.** to be on strike; **declararse en h.** to go on strike; **hacer h.** to strike; **ir a la h.** to go on strike; **los trabajadores en h.** the strikers ►► ***h. de apoyo*** sympathy strike; ***h. de brazos caídos*** sit-down (strike); ***h. de celo*** *Br* work-to-rule, *US* job action; ***h. general*** general strike; ***h. de hambre*** hunger strike; ***h. indefinida*** indefinite strike; ***h. patronal*** lockout; ***h. salvaje*** wildcat strike; ***h. de solidaridad*** sympathy strike

huelgo *etc ver* **holgar**

huelguista *nmf* striker

huelguístico, -a *adj* strike; **convocatoria huelguística** strike call

huella 1 *ver* **hollar**
2 *nf* (**a**) *(de persona)* footprint; *(de animal, rueda)* track; EXPR **seguir las huellas de alguien** to follow in sb's footsteps ►► ***h. dactilar*** fingerprint; ***h. digital*** fingerprint; ***h. genética*** genetic fingerprint
(**b**) *(vestigio)* trace; **todavía no han desaparecido las huellas de las inundaciones** you can still see the signs of the flooding
(**c**) *(impresión profunda)* mark; **su rostro reflejaba las huellas del esfuerzo** her face showed signs of the effort she was putting in; EXPR **dejar h.: desaparecieron sin dejar h.** they vanished without trace; **un estilo de componer que ha dejado h.** a style of composing that has been very influential; **sus enseñanzas dejaron h. en sus discípulos** her teachings influenced her followers
(**d**) *(de escalón)* tread

huemul, güemul *nm* huemul, = species of deer found in Southern Andes, national symbol of Chile

huérfano, -a 1 *adj* (**a**) *(persona)* orphan; **se quedó h. muy joven** he was orphaned at a very young age; **es h. de madre** his mother died, he lost his mother (**b**) **h. de** *(carente de)* devoid of; **el partido está h. de un líder** the party is without a leader
2 *nm,f* orphan
3 *nm Imprenta* orphan

huero, -a *adj Literario (vacío)* hollow; *(palabras)* empty

huerta *nf* (**a**) *(huerto) Br* market garden, *US* truck farm (**b**) *(tierra de regadío)* = irrigated crop-growing region

huertano, -a *nm,f Esp* (**a**) *(murciano)* = person from Murcia (**b**) *(valenciano)* Valencian

huertero, -a *nm,f Br* market gardener, *US* truck farmer

huerto *nm (de hortalizas)* vegetable garden; *(de frutales)* orchard; EXPR *Fam* **llevarse a alguien al h.** *(engañar)* to con sb; *(acostarse con)* to have one's way with sb

huesa *nf* grave

huesero, -a *nm,f Andes, RP Fam* bone doctor

huesillo *nm Andes* dried peach

hueso *nm* (**a**) *(del cuerpo)* bone; *Fam* **nos calamos hasta los huesos** we got soaked to the skin; **de color h.** ivory (coloured); EXPR *Fam* **acabar** *o* **dar con sus huesos en** to end up in; *Fam* **tropezó y dio con sus huesos en el suelo** she tripped and tumbled to the ground; *Fam* **la descubrieron y acabó con sus huesos en la cárcel** she was caught out and ended up in jail; EXPR *Fam* **estar en los huesos** to be all skin and bones; EXPR *Fam* **no puedo con mis huesos** I'm ready to drop, I'm exhausted; EXPR *Fam* **ser un h. duro de roer** to be a hard nut to crack ►► ***h. del cráneo*** skull bone; ***h. maxilar*** jawbone, *Espec* mandible; ***h. de santo*** *(pastel)* = small roll of marzipan filled with sweetened egg yolk
(**b**) *(de fruto) Br* stone, *US* pit; **aceitunas sin h.** pitted olives
(**c**) *Fam (persona)* very strict person; **el profe de inglés es un h.** our English teacher is dead strict
(**d**) *Fam (asignatura)* difficult subject
(**e**) **huesos** *(restos)* bones; **el cementerio en el que descansan sus huesos** the cemetery where her bones were laid to rest
(**f**) *Fam* **la sin h.** *(la lengua)* the tongue; **soltar la sin h.** to shoot one's mouth off
(**g**) *Méx Fam (enchufe)* contacts, influence; *(trabajo fácil)* cushy job

huésped, -eda 1 *nm,f* guest
2 *nm Biol (de parásito)* host

huestes *nfpl* (**a**) *(ejército)* army (**b**) *(seguidores)* followers (**c**) *(masa)* hordes, army

huesudo, -a *adj* bony

hueva *nf* (**a**) *(de pescado)* roe; **huevas de bacalao** cod roe (**b**) *Méx Fam (aburrimiento)* **iqué h.!** what a pain *o* drag!

huevada *nf Andes, RP muy Fam (dicho)* crap; **lo que dijiste es una h.** what you said is a load of crap; **no digas huevadas** don't talk crap

huevazos *nm inv muy Fam* **es un h.** he's pussy-whipped

huevear, huevonear *vi Andes Fam* to muck about

huevera *nf* (**a**) *(para servir)* egg cup (**b**) *(para guardar)* egg box (**c**) *ver también* **huevero**

huevería *nf* = shop selling eggs

huevero, -a *nm,f* egg seller

huevo *nm* (**a**) *(de animales)* egg; EXPR *Fam* **es el h. de Colón** it's so blindingly obvious that no one had thought of it ►► *Andes* ***h. a la copa*** soft-boiled egg; ***h. duro*** hard-boiled egg; ***h. escalfado*** poached egg; *Méx* ***h. estrellado*** fried egg; ***h. frito*** fried egg; ***h. de granja*** free-range egg; *Andes* ***h. pasado*** soft-boiled egg; ***h. pasado por agua*** soft-boiled egg; ***h. de Pascua*** *(de chocolate)* Easter egg; *Col* ***huevos pericos*** scrambled eggs; ***huevos al plato*** = eggs cooked in the oven in an earthenware dish; *RP* ***h. poché*** poached egg; *Méx* ***huevos rancheros*** ranch-style eggs, = tortilla topped with fried eggs, tomato sauce and chilli; ***huevos revueltos*** scrambled eggs; *Ven* ***h. sancochado*** hard-boiled egg; *Méx* ***h. tibio*** soft-boiled egg
(**b**) *(cigoto)* zygote, egg
(**c**) *muy Fam* **huevos** *(testículos)* balls, nuts; **iestoy hasta los huevos!** I'm *Br* bloody *o US* goddamn sick of it!; **tu comentario le sentó como una patada en los huevos** *Br* what you said really pissed him off, *US* he was really pissed about what you said
(**d**) *muy Fam (valor)* **tener huevos** to have balls; **itiene huevos la cosa!** it's a *Br* bloody *o US* goddamn disgrace!; **iqué huevos tiene, insultarme delante de todos!** what a *Br* bloody *o US* goddamn nerve, insulting me in front of everyone!; **le echó huevos al asunto, y le confesó la verdad** he showed he had balls by telling her the truth
(**e**) *muy Fam (mucho)* **me duele un h.** it hurts like hell, *Br* it's bloody painful; **costar un h.** to cost a heck of a lot, *Br* to be bloody expensive; **sabe un h. de informática** he knows *Br* bloody *o US* goddamn loads about computers
(**f**) EXPR *Fam* **me viene a h.** it's just what I need, it's just the right thing; *Fam* **le puso el gol a h.** he laid on an absolute sitter for him; *Méx muy Fam* **lo hicimos a h.** we did it because we *Br* bloody *o US* goddamn had to; *muy Fam* **me importa un h. lo que piense** I couldn't give a *Br* toss *o US* good goddamn what she thinks; *muy Fam* **manda huevos que estando enfermo tenga que hacerlo yo** *Br* bloody *o US* goddamn great *o* can you *Br* bloody *o US* goddamn believe it, I'm the one who has to do it even though I'm ill!; *muy Fam* **no me sale de los huevos** I can't be *Br* bloody *o US* goddamn bothered; *muy Fam* **se ha pasado todo el día tocándose los huevos** *Br* he's done bugger-all all day, *US* he hasn't done a shit all day; *Fam* **cuando se enteró de su embarazo se le pusieron los huevos de corbata** he really freaked out when he found out she was pregnant; *muy Fam* **ino me toques los huevos, y déjame en paz!** why can't you just damn well *o Br* bloody well leave me alone!; *muy Fam* **iy un h.!** *Br* my arse!, *US* my ass!

huevón, -ona, güevón, -ona *muy Fam* 1 *adj* (**a**) *Cuba, Méx (vago)* **es muy h.** *Br* he's a lazy sod *o* git, *US* he's so goddamn lazy (**b**) *Andes, Arg, Ven (tonto, torpe)* **es muy h.** *Br* he's a prat *o* pillock, *US* he's a jerk; **me dio una respuesta huevona** she gave me a really *Br* prattish *o US* jerky answer
2 *nm,f* (**a**) *Cuba, Méx (vago)* **es un h.** *Br* he's a lazy sod *o* git, *US* he's so goddamn lazy (**b**) *Andes, Arg, Ven (tonto, torpe) Br* prat, *Br* pillock, *US* jerk; **son una tropa de huevones** *Br* they're a bunch of prats *o* pillocks, *US* they're a bunch of jerks; **hacer el h.** *Br* to prat around, *US* to act like a jerk

huevonada *nf Ven muy Fam (acto) Br* bloody *o US* goddamn stupid thing to do; *(dicho) Br* bloody *o US* goddamn stupid thing to say; **hacer una h.** to do something *Br* bloody *o US* goddamn stupid; **decir una h.** to say something *Br* bloody *o US* goddamn stupid

huevonear = **huevear**

hugonote, -a 1 *adj* Huguenot
2 *nm,f* Huguenot

huida *nf* escape, flight; **el ladrón abandonó la moto y continuó su h. a pie** the thief abandoned the motorbike and continued to flee on foot; **los refugiados tuvieron que abandonar todo en su h. del país** the refugees had to leave everything behind when they fled the country; **emprender la h.** to take flight; **la ley es una h. hacia delante** the law is an attempt to stay one step ahead of events; **h. de capitales** capital flight; **la h. a Egipto** *(en Biblia)* the flight to Egypt

huidizo, -a *adj (esquivo)* shy, elusive

huido, -a *adj* (**a**) *(fugitivo)* **se busca a dos presos huidos** two escaped prisoners are being hunted; **están huidos de la justicia** they are on the run (from the law); **la joven se encuentra huida de su domicilio desde el lunes** the young woman ran away from home last Monday (**b**) *(reservado)* withdrawn

huincha, güincha *nf* (**a**) *Andes (cinta)* ribbon ►► ***h. aisladora*** insulating tape (**b**) *Andes (para pelo)* hairband (**c**) *Chile (metro)* tape measure

huifa *nf* EXPR *Chile Fam* **esto está hecho como la h.** this is lousy quality; **se viste como la h.** she has lousy dress sense

huipil, güipil *nm CAm, Méx* = colourful embroidered dress or blouse traditionally worn by Indian women

huir [34] 1 *vi* (**a**) *(escapar) (de enemigo, peligro)* to flee (**de** from); **h. del país** to flee the country; **huyó a Francia** she fled to France; **los jóvenes que huyen de sus hogares** young people who run away from home; **los aldeanos huían del incendio** the villagers were fleeing from the fire; **el tesorero huyó con varios millones** the treasurer ran off with several million; **se metieron en un taxi huyendo de los periodistas** they got into a taxi in an attempt to get away from the journalists
(**b**) *(evadirse) (de cárcel)* to escape (**de** from)
(**c**) **h. de algo** *(evitar)* to avoid sth, to keep away from sth; **siempre huyo de las grandes masas de gente** I always try to avoid *o* stay away from large crowds of people; **huye de la polémica** she steers clear of controversy
(**d**) *(tiempo)* to fly by
2 *vt* to avoid; **me está huyendo últimamente** he's been avoiding me lately

huiro *nm Chile, Perú* seaweed

huisache = **huizache**

huitlacoche *nm CAm, Méx* corn smut, = edible fungus which grows on maize

huizache, huisache *nm CAm, Méx* sweet acacia, perfume acacia

hula-hoop [χula'χop] (*pl* **hula-hoops**) *nm* hula-hoop®

hule *nm* (**a**) *(tela)* oilskin (**b**) *(mantel)* oilcloth (**c**) *CAm, Méx (caucho)* rubber ►► ***h. espuma*** foam rubber

hulero, -a *nm,f CAm, Méx* rubber tapper

hulla *nf* soft coal ►► ***h. blanca*** water power, white coal

hullero, -a *adj* soft coal; **producción hullera** soft coal production

humanamente *adv* (a) *(posible, imposible)* **hicimos todo lo h. posible** we did everything humanly possible; **es h. imposible acabarlo antes del lunes** it isn't humanly possible to finish it before Monday (b) *(con humanidad)* humanely

humanidad *nf* (a) *(género humano)* humanity; **el progreso de la h.** the progress of the human race *o* of humankind; *Fam* **aquí huele a h.** it's humming in here
(b) *(sentimiento)* humanity; **los trataron con h.** they were treated humanely
(c) *Educ* **humanidades** humanities; **la Facultad de Humanidades** the Faculty of Humanities
(d) *Fam (cuerpo, corpulencia)* bulk; **tropezó y dio con toda su h. en el suelo** he tripped and his enormous bulk came crashing to the ground

humanismo *nm* humanism

humanista 1 *adj* humanist, humanistic
2 *nmf* humanist

humanístico, -a *adj* humanistic

humanitario, -a *adj* (a) *(ayuda, organización)* humanitarian (b) *(persona)* kind-hearted

humanitarismo *nm* humanitarianism

humanización *nf* humanization; **la h. de las condiciones laborales** making working conditions more humane

humanizar [14] 1 *vt* to humanize, to make more human
2 **humanizarse** *vpr* to become more human

humano, -a 1 *adj* (a) *(del hombre)* human (b) *(compasivo)* humane
2 *nm* human being; **los humanos** mankind

humanoide 1 *adj* humanoid
2 *nmf* humanoid

humarada, humareda *nf* cloud of smoke; **¡qué h.!** what a lot of smoke!, it's so smoky!

humazo *nm* cloud of smoke

humeante *adj* (a) *(que echa humo)* smoking; **las ruinas de las viviendas aún estaban humeantes** the ruins of the houses were still smouldering (b) *(que echa vapor)* steaming; **una h. taza de café** a steaming *o* piping hot cup of coffee

humear 1 *vi* (a) *(salir humo)* to smoke; **los restos del avión todavía humeaban** the wreckage of the plane was still smouldering (b) *(salir vapor)* to steam
2 *vt Am (fumigar)* to fumigate

humectador, -ora *Fot* 1 *adj* humectant
2 *nm* humectant

humectante *adj Fot* humectant

húmeda *nf Fam Hum* **irse de la h.** to let the cat out of the bag

humedad *nf* (a) *(de suelo, tierra)* dampness; *(de pared, techo)* damp; **hay mucha h. en la casa** the house is very damp; **hay manchas de h. en el techo** there are damp patches on the ceiling; **huele a h.** it smells of damp
(b) *(de labios, ojos)* moistness
(c) *(de atmósfera)* humidity; **con una h. superior al 90 por ciento** with over 90 percent humidity ►► ***h. absoluta*** absolute humidity; ***h. relativa*** relative humidity

humedal *nm* wetland

humedecer [46] 1 *vt* to moisten; **humedézcalo con un paño antes de pegarlo** moisten with a damp cloth before sticking it on
2 **humedecerse** *vpr* to become moist; **humedecerse los labios** to moisten one's lips

humedecimiento *nm* moistening

húmedo, -a *adj* (a) *(suelo, tierra, casa)* damp; **mantenga la planta húmeda** keep the plant well-watered, keep the soil moist (b) *(labios, ojos)* moist (c) *(ropa, pelo)* damp (d) *(clima) (frío)* damp; *(cálido)* humid (e) *(aire, atmósfera)* humid

húmero *nm Anat* humerus

humidificación *nf* humidification

humidificador *nm* humidifier

humidificar [60] *vt* to humidify

humildad *nf* (a) *(cualidad)* humility; **con h.** humbly (b) *(de origen social)* humbleness; **la h. de sus orígenes** the humbleness of his background

humilde *adj* (a) *(actitud, comportamiento)* humble (b) *(pobre)* humble; **bienvenido a mi h. morada** welcome to my humble abode

humildemente *adv* humbly

humillación *nf* humiliation; **sufrieron una h.** they were humiliated

humillado, -a *adj* humiliated

humillante *adj* humiliating

humillar 1 *vt* to humiliate; **lo humillaron delante de todos** he was humiliated in front of everyone
2 **humillarse** *vpr* to humble oneself; **se humilló ante su jefe** he grovelled to his boss; **humillarse a hacer algo** *(rebajarse)* to lower oneself to do sth, to stoop to doing sth

humita *nf* (a) *Chile (pajarita)* bow tie (b) *Andes, Arg (pasta de maíz)* = paste made of mashed *Br* maize *o US* corn kernels mixed with cheese, chilli, onion and other ingredients, wrapped in a maize *o US* corn husk and steamed

humo *nm* (a) *(producto de combustión)* smoke; *(de vehículo)* fumes; EXPR **convertirse en h.: su fortuna se convirtió en h. en pocos meses** his fortune went up in smoke within a few months; EXPR *Fam* **echar h.** to be fuming, to have smoke coming out of one's ears; *Fam* **estoy que echo h.** I'm fuming; EXPR *Fam* **se hizo h.** *(desapareció)* he made himself scarce
(b) *(vapor)* steam
(c) *(soberbia)* **humos: este profesor tiene demasiados humos** this teacher is too full of himself; EXPR *Fam* **bajarle a alguien los humos** to take sb down a peg or two; *Fam* **con esa derrota se les han bajado los humos** that defeat has brought them back down to earth; EXPR *Fam* **se le subieron los humos a la cabeza** it went to his head; EXPR *Fam* **darse humos** to give oneself airs

humor *nm* (a) *(estado de ánimo)* mood; *(carácter)* temperament; **estar de buen/mal h.** to be in a good/bad mood; EXPR *Fam* **estar de un h. de perros** to be in a filthy mood
(b) *(gracia)* humour; **un programa de h.** a comedy programme; **no tiene sentido del h.** she doesn't have a sense of humour; **en vez de enfadarme, me lo tomé con h.** rather than get upset, I just laughed it off ►► ***h. negro*** black humour
(c) *(ganas)* mood; **no estoy de h.** I'm not in the mood; **no está de h. para ponerse a cocinar** she doesn't feel like cooking
(d) *Anat* humour ►► ***h. ácueo*** aqueous humour; ***h. acuoso*** aqueous humour; ***h. vítreo*** vitreous humour

humorada *nf (chiste)* joke

humorado, -a *adj* **bien h.** good-humoured; **mal h.** ill-humoured

humoral *adj Fisiol* humoral

humorismo *nm* (a) *(carácter burlón)* humour (b) *(en televisión, teatro)* comedy

humorista *nmf* (a) *(persona burlona)* humorist (b) *(en televisión, teatro)* comedian, *f* comedienne ►► ***h. gráfico*** cartoonist

humorísticamente *adv* humorously

humorístico, -a *adj* humorous; **un programa h.** a comedy programme

humoso, -a *adj* smoky

humus *nm inv* (a) *(suelo)* hummus, humus (b) *(comida)* humus

hundido, -a *adj* (a) *(desmoralizado)* devastated (b) *(ojos)* sunken, deep-set (c) *(mejillas)* hollow, sunken

hundimiento *nm* (a) *(de barco)* sinking (b) *(de terreno)* subsidence (c) *(de empresa)* collapse

hundir 1 *vt* (a) *(sumergir)* to sink; **el peso de los espectadores hundió el estrado** the platform collapsed under the weight of the spectators
(b) *(introducir)* to bury; **le hundió el cuchillo en la espalda** she buried the knife in his back; **hundió los dedos en su cabello** he ran his fingers through her hair
(c) *(afligir)* to devastate; **el anuncio de su fallecimiento hundió a todos sus familiares** his family was devastated by the news of his death
(d) *(hacer fracasar)* to ruin; **la tormenta hundió el espectáculo** the storm ruined the show
(e) *(abollar)* to dent
2 **hundirse** *vpr* (a) *(sumergirse)* to sink; *(intencionadamente)* to dive
(b) *(derrumbarse)* to collapse; *(techo)* to cave in; *(suelo)* to subside; *Fig* **el estadio se hundió tras el tercer gol del equipo** the stadium went wild after the team scored its third goal
(c) *(deformarse) (carrocería)* to get dented; **se le hundieron las mejillas** he became hollow-cheeked
(d) *(afligirse)* to be devastated; **se hundió tras conocer su despido** he was devastated when he found out that he was being made redundant
(e) *(fracasar)* to be ruined

húngaro, -a 1 *adj* Hungarian
2 *nm,f (persona)* Hungarian
3 *nm (lengua)* Hungarian

Hungría *n* Hungary

huno, -a 1 *adj* Hunnish
2 *nm,f* Hun

huracán *nm* hurricane

huracanado, -a *adj (viento)* hurricane-force

huraño, -a *adj* unsociable

hurgar [38] **1** *vi (rebuscar)* to rummage around (**en** in); *(con dedo, palo)* to poke around (**en** in)
2 hurgarse *vpr* **hurgarse la nariz** to pick one's nose; **hurgarse los bolsillos** to rummage around in one's pockets

hurgón *nm* poker

hurgonear *vt* to poke

hurguetear *Am* **1** *vt* to poke *o* rummage around in
2 *vi (rebuscar)* to rummage around (**en** in)
3 hurguetearse *vpr* **hurguetearse la nariz** to pick one's nose

hurí (*pl* **huríes**) *nf* houri

Hurón *nm* **lago H.** Lake Huron

hurón, -ona 1 *adj* (**a**) *(huraño)* unsociable (**b**) *Fam (curioso)* nosy
2 *nm* (**a**) *(animal)* ferret (**b**) *Hist (indio)* Huron (**c**) *Fam (persona curiosa)* nosy parker

huronear *vi* (**a**) *(cazar)* to ferret (**b**) *Fam (curiosear)* to nose around

huronera *nf (madriguera)* ferret hole

huroniano, -a *adj Geol* Huronian

hurra *interj* hurray!

hurtadillas: a hurtadillas *loc adv* on the sly, stealthily; **la miraba a h.** he was casting furtive glances at her

hurtar 1 *vt (robar)* to steal
2 hurtarse *vpr* **hurtarse a** *o* **de alguien** to conceal oneself *o* hide from sb

hurto *nm* (**a**) *(robo)* theft (**b**) *(botín)* stolen goods

húsar *nm Mil* hussar

husillo *nm (tornillo)* screw

husky ['χaski] (*pl* **huskies** *o* **huskys**) *nm* husky

husmeador, -ora *adj* (**a**) *(perro)* sniffer (**b**) *Fam (persona)* nosy

husmear 1 *vt (olfatear)* to sniff out, to scent
2 *vi Fam (curiosear)* to nose around

husmeo *nm* (**a**) *(olfateo)* sniffing (**b**) *Fam (curioseo)* nosing around

huso *nm* (**a**) *(para hilar)* spindle; *(en máquina)* bobbin (**b**) ***h. horario*** time zone

hutu 1 *adj* Hutu
2 *nmf* Hutu

huy *interj* (**a**) *(expresa dolor)* ouch! (**b**) *(expresa sorpresa)* gosh! (**c**) *(expresa alivio)* phew!; **¡h. que bien, no trabajamos mañana!** phew, what a relief, we don't have to work tomorrow!

huyera *etc ver* **huir**

huyo *etc ver* **huir**

Hz (*abrev de* **hertz**) Hz

I, i

I, i [i] *nf (letra)* I, i ►► ***i griega*** = name of the letter "y"; ***i latina*** = name of the letter "i"

IAE *nm* (*abrev de* **Impuesto sobre Actividades Económicas**) = Spanish tax paid by professionals and shop owners

IB *Esp Antes* (*abrev de* **Instituto de Bachillerato**) = state secondary school for 14-18-year-olds, *US* ≃ Senior High School

ib. (*abrev de* **ibídem**) ibid

iba *etc ver* **ir**

Iberia *n Hist* Iberia

ibérico, -a 1 *adj* Iberian
2 *nm,f* Iberian

íbero, -a, ibero, -a 1 *adj* Iberian
2 *nm,f (persona)* Iberian
3 *nm (lengua)* Iberian

Iberoamérica *n* Latin America

iberoamericano, -a 1 *adj* Latin American
2 *nm,f* Latin American

íbice *nm* ibex

ibicenco, -a 1 *adj* of/from Ibiza *(Spain)*
2 *nm,f* person from Ibiza *(Spain)*

ibíd. (*abrev de* **ibídem**) ibid

ibídem, ibidem *adv* ibidem, ibid

ibis *nm inv* ibis ►► ***i. sagrado*** sacred ibis

IBM® *nf Perú* calculator

ibón *nm Esp* = small Pyrenean lake

ibopé *nm* mesquite

ICAIC [i'kaik] *nm* (*abrev de* **Instituto Cubano del Arte e Industria Cinematográficos**) = Cuban national film institute

Ícaro *n Mitol* Icarus

ice *etc ver* **izar**

iceberg [iθe'βer] (*pl* **icebergs**) *nm* iceberg

ICEX ['iθeks] *nm* (*abrev de* **Instituto de Comercio Exterior**) Spanish Department of Foreign Trade

ICI ['iθi] *nm* (*abrev de* **Instituto de Cooperación Ibero-americana**) Institute for Latin American cooperation

Icona [i'kona] *nm Antes* (*abrev de* **Instituto Nacional para la Conservación de la Naturaleza**) = Spanish national institute for conservation, *Br* ≃ NCC

icónico, -a *adj* iconic

icono, *Am* **ícono** *nm* (**a**) *Arte* icon (**b**) *Informát* icon (**c**) *Literario (símbolo)* icon

iconoclasia *nf* iconoclasm

iconoclasta 1 *adj* iconoclastic
2 *nmf* iconoclast

iconoclastia *nf* iconoclasm

iconografía *nf* iconography

iconográfico, -a *adj* iconographical

iconología *nf* iconology

icosaedro *nm Geom* icosahedron

ICRT *nm* (*abrev de* **Instituto Cubano de Radio y Televisión**) = Cuban state broadcasting company

ictericia *nf* jaundice

ictiología *nf* ichthyology

ictiólogo, -a *nm,f* ichthyologist

ictiosaurio *nm* ichthyosaur

ictus *nm inv* stroke

ID *nf* (*abrev de* **Izquierda Democrática**) = left-wing Ecuadoran political party

I+D ['imas'de] *nf* (*abrev de* **investigación y desarrollo**) R & D

id *ver* **ir**

id. (*abrev de* **ídem**) id., idem

ida *nf* outward journey; **el viaje de i. lo haremos de noche** we'll travel out there overnight; **a la i. fuimos en tren** we went out there by train; **(billete de) i. y vuelta** *Br* return (ticket), *US* round-trip (ticket); **partido de i.** first leg; **tras muchas idas y venidas conseguí localizarla** I managed to find her after a lot of running backwards and forwards; **la policía vigila sus idas y venidas** the police are monitoring his comings and goings

---

IDEA *nf* (**a**) *(concepto)* idea; **la i. del bien y del mal** the concept of good and evil; **yo tenía otra i. de Estados Unidos** I had a different image of the United States; **tiene una i. peculiar de lo que es la honradez** he has a funny idea of (what's meant by) honesty; **hazte a la i. de que no va a venir** you'd better start accepting that she isn't going to come; **no conseguía hacerme a la i. de vivir sin ella** I couldn't get used to the idea of living without her; **con lo que me has dicho ya me hago una i. de cómo es la escuela** from what you've told me I've got a pretty good idea of what the school is like; **no me hago una i. de cómo debió ser** I can't imagine what it must have been like ►► ***i. fija*** obsession; **ser una persona de ideas fijas** to be a person of fixed ideas

(**b**) *(ocurrencia)* idea; **una buena/mala i.** a good/bad idea; **ha sido muy buena i. escoger este restaurante** it was a very good idea to choose this restaurant; **se le ve falto de ideas en su última novela** he seems short of ideas in his latest novel; **lo que contaste me dio la i. para el guión** what you said to me gave me the idea for the script; **se me ocurre una i., podríamos...** I know what, we could...; **¿a quién se le habrá ocurrido la i. de apagar las luces?** can you believe it, somebody's gone and turned the lights out!; **¡más vale que te quites esa i. de la cabeza!** you can forget that idea!; **una i. brillante** *o* **luminosa** a brilliant idea, a brainwave; **cuando se le mete una i. en la cabeza...** when he gets an idea into his head...; EXPR *Esp* **tener ideas de bombero** to have wild *o* crazy ideas

(**c**) *(conocimiento, nociones)* idea; **la policía no tenía ni i. de quién pudo haber cometido el crimen** the police had no idea who could have committed the crime; **no tengo ni i.** I haven't got a clue; **no tengo ni i. de física** I don't know the first thing about physics; **no tengo (ni) la menor** *o* **la más remota i.** I haven't the slightest idea; *Esp muy Fam* **no tengo ni pajolera i.** I haven't the faintest *Br* bloody *o US* goddamn idea; *Vulg* **no tengo ni puta i.** I haven't got a fucking clue; *Fam* **¡ni i.!** *(como respuesta)* search me!, I haven't got a clue!; **tener i. de cómo hacer algo** to know how to do sth; **tener una ligera i.** to have a vague idea; **por la forma en que maneja las herramientas se ve que tiene i.** from the way she's handling the tools, you can tell she knows what she's doing; **¡no tienes i.** *o* **no puedes hacerte una i. de lo duro que fue!** you have no idea *o* you can't imagine how hard it was!

(**d**) *(propósito)* intention; **nuestra i. es volver pronto** we intend to *o* our intention is to return early; **con la i. de** with the idea *o* intention of; **tener i. de hacer algo** to intend to do sth; **a mala i.** maliciously; **tener mala i.** *(ser malintencionado)* to be a nasty piece of work; **¡mira que tienes mala i.!** that's really nasty of you!

(**e**) *(opinión)* opinion; **mi i. de ella era totalmente errónea** I had completely the wrong impression of her; **no tengo una i. formada sobre el tema** I don't have a clear opinion on the subject; **cambiar de i.** to change one's mind; **yo soy de la i. de que mujeres y hombres deben tener los mismos derechos** I'm of the opinion that men and women should have equal rights; **somos de la misma i.** we agree, we're of the same opinion

(**f**) **ideas** *(ideología)* ideas; **mi padre es de ideas progresistas** my father is a progressive *o* has progressive attitudes; **fue perseguido por sus ideas** he was persecuted for his beliefs *o* ideas

(**g**) *CSur (manía)* **le tengo i. a su hermana** I can't stand her sister; **le tengo i. a eso** that drives me nuts; **si te vas a poner el vestido con i., mejor ponete otra cosa** if you're not sure about the dress, you'd do better to wear something else

---

ideal 1 *adj* ideal; **el hombre i.** the ideal man; **un mundo i.** an ideal world; **lo i. sería hacerlo mañana** ideally, we would do it tomorrow; **sería i. que lo enviaras por correo electrónico** it would be best if you could send it by e-mail
2 *nm* (**a**) *(prototipo)* ideal; **el i. de belleza de los griegos** the Greek ideal of beauty (**b**) *(aspiración)* ideal, dream; **su i. es ayudar a los demás** her ideal *o* dream would be to help others (**c**) **ideales** *(ideología)* ideals; **ese tipo de actuación va en contra de mis ideales** that type of behaviour is against my principles
3 *adv* **el domingo me vendría i.** Sunday would be perfect

idealismo *nm* idealism

idealista 1 *adj* idealistic
2 *nmf* idealist

idealización *nf* idealization

idealizar [14] *vt* to idealize

idealmente *adv* ideally

idear *vt* (**a**) *(planear)* to think up, to devise; **hemos ideado un plan para salir del aprieto** we've devised *o* come up with a plan to get out of trouble (**b**) *(inventar)* to invent

ideario *nm* ideology

ideático, -a *adj Am (caprichoso)* whimsical, capricious

ídem *pron* ditto; EXPR **í. de í.** *(lo mismo)* exactly the same; *(yo también)* same here; **el golf me aburre y el tenis, í. de í.** I find golf boring and the same goes for tennis; **a mí me cayó muy bien y a ella, í. de í.** I liked him a lot and so did she; **creo que al final lo invitaré, y a su mujer í. de í.** I think I'll invite him and his wife after all

idéntico, -a *adj* identical (**a** to); **un edificio i. al Capitolio** a building just like *o* identical to the Capitol; **es i. a su abuelo** *(físicamente)* he's the image of his grandfather; *(en carácter)* he's exactly the same as *o* just like his grandfather

identidad *nf* (**a**) *(de persona, pueblo)* identity; **todavía no se ha podido descubrir la i. de las víctimas** the victims have not yet been identified; **la i. nacional de los griegos** Greek national identity; **la i. corporativa de la empresa** the company's corporate identity (**b**) *(igualdad)* identical nature (**c**) *Mat* identity

identificable *adj* identifiable

identificación *nf* (**a**) *(acción)* identification (**b**) *(documentos)* papers, ID; **la i., por favor** may I see your papers, please?

identificado, -a *adj* identified; **no i.** unidentified

identificador, -ora 1 *adj* identifying
2 *nm Informát* identifier

identificar [60] 1 *vt* (**a**) *(establecer la identidad de)* to identify; **han identificado al autor del robo** the person who carried out the robbery has been identified; **la identificaron como responsable del crimen** she was identified as the person who committed the crime; **descubrieron varios cuerpos sin i.** a number of unidentified bodies were found
(**b**) *(equiparar)* **i. algo con algo** to identify sth with sth
2 **identificarse** *vpr* (**a**) **identificarse con** *(persona, ideas)* to identify with; **la revista no se identifica con las opiniones de sus colaboradores** the opinions expressed by contributors are not necessarily those of the editor
(**b**) *(mostrar documentos)* to show one's ID; **se identificó ante el guardia de seguridad** she showed the security guard her ID; **se identificó como trabajador de la empresa** he identified himself as a company employee; **¡identifíquese!** *(diga quién es)* identify yourself!; *(muestre una identificación)* show me some ID!

identikit *nm RP* Identikit® (picture)

ideografía *nf* ideography

ideográfico, -a *adj* ideographic

ideograma *nm* ideogram, ideograph

ideología *nf* ideology

ideológicamente *adv* ideologically

ideológico, -a *adj* ideological

ideologizado, -a *adj* **un debate i.** a debate which has become ideological

ideólogo, -a *nm,f* ideologist; *Pey* ideologue

ideoso, -a *adj Méx (caprichoso)* whimsical, capricious

idílico, -a *adj* idyllic

idilio *nm* (**a**) *(amoroso)* romance; **vivieron un i. apasionado** they had a passionate romance; **la crisis puso fin al i. entre los dos países** the crisis put an end to the love affair between the two countries (**b**) *Lit* idyll

idiolecto *nm Ling* idiolect

idioma *nm* language

idiomático, -a *adj* idiomatic

idiosincrasia *nf (de persona, pueblo)* character; **conoce muy bien la i. europea** he is well acquainted with the ways of the Europeans

idiosincrático, -a *adj* characteristic

idiota 1 *adj* (**a**) *(tonto)* stupid (**b**) *(enfermo)* mentally deficient
2 *nmf* (**a**) *(tonto)* idiot (**b**) *(enfermo)* idiot

idiotez *nf* (**a**) *(acto, dicho)* stupid thing; **decir/hacer una i.** to say/do something stupid; **no dice más que idioteces** he talks nothing but nonsense; **¿y por eso se enfada? ¡vaya (una) i.!** and she got angry about that? how stupid! (**b**) *(enfermedad)* mental deficiency

idiotismo *nm Ling* idiom, idiomatic expression

idiotizar [14] 1 *vt* to turn into a zombie; **la televisión idiotiza a los jóvenes** television turns young people into zombies
2 **idiotizarse** *vpr* to turn into a zombie; **se ha idiotizado de tanto ver la televisión** she's turned into a zombie from watching so much television

ido, -a *adj Fam* (**a**) *(loco)* mad, touched (**b**) *(despistado)* distracted; **caminaba con un aire un poco i.** she was walking along rather distractedly; **estar i.** to be miles away

idólatra 1 *adj* idolatrous
2 *nmf* (**a**) *(pagano)* idolater, *f* idolatress (**b**) *(fanático)* idolizer

idolatrar *vt* (**a**) *(dios)* to worship (**b**) *(amar ciegamente a)* to idolize

idolatría *nf* (**a**) *(culto)* idolatry (**b**) *(admiración ciega)* worship, idolization

ídolo *nm* (**a**) *(religioso)* idol (**b**) *(persona)* idol

idoneidad *nf* suitability

idóneo, -a *adj (adecuado)* suitable (**para** for); *(ideal)* ideal (**para** for); **no es un candidato i. para el puesto** he's not the most suitable candidate for the job; **es el lugar i. para construir la escuela** it's the ideal place to build the school; **no es el momento i.** it's not the best time

i.e. (*abrev de* **id est**) i.e.

IES *nm Esp Antes* (*abrev de* **Instituto de Educación Secundaria**) HS

iglesia *nf* (**a**) *(edificio)* church; **ir a la i.** to go to church; **una i. católica/protestante** a Catholic/Protestant church
(**b**) *(institución)* church; **un hombre de i.** a man of the cloth; **casarse por la i.** *o Andes, RP* **por i.** to have a church wedding ►► ***la i. adventista*** the Adventist church; ***la i. anglicana*** *Br* the Church of England, *US* the Anglican Church; ***la i. católica (romana)*** the (Roman) Catholic church; ***las iglesias evangélicas*** the evangelical churches; ***la i. luterana*** the Lutheran church; ***la i. metodista*** the Methodist church; ***la i. ortodoxa*** the Orthodox church; ***la i. presbiteriana*** the Presbyterian church; ***las iglesias protestantes*** the Protestant churches; ***I. de la Unificación*** Unification Church

iglú (*pl* **iglúes**) *nm* (**a**) *(esquimal)* igloo (**b**) *Esp (contenedor)* bottle bank *(shaped like an igloo)*

Ignacio *n pr* **San I. de Loyola** St Ignatius of Loyola

ígneo, -a *adj* igneous

ignición *nf (de motor)* ignition; **la chispa provocó la i. del combustible** the spark ignited the fuel

ignífugo, -a *adj* fireproof, flameproof

ignominia *nf* (**a**) *(deshonor)* ignominy (**b**) *(acción)* outrage

ignominiosamente *adv* ignominiously

ignominioso, -a *adj* ignominious

ignorancia *nf* (**a**) *(desconocimiento)* ignorance; **la i. de la ley no exime de su cumplimiento** ignorance of the law is not a valid defence; **i. supina** blind ignorance (**b**) *(falta de cultura)* ignorance; **por i.** out of ignorance; **mi i. sobre el tema es completa** I know nothing whatsoever about the subject

ignorante 1 *adj* (**a**) *(sin conocimiento)* ignorant; **i. de lo que ocurría...** unaware of what was happening... (**b**) *(con falta de cultura)* ignorant
2 *nmf* ignoramus

ignorar *vt* (**a**) *(desconocer)* not to know; **ignoro su dirección** I don't know her address; **ignoro por qué lo hizo** I don't know why he did it; **lo ignoro por completo** I have absolutely no idea; **se ignoran las causas del accidente** the cause of the accident is unknown; **no ignoro que es una empresa arriesgada** I'm not unaware of the fact that it's a risky venture
(**b**) *(hacer caso omiso de)* to ignore; **lleva tiempo ignorándome** she's been ignoring me for some time

ignoto, -a *adj* unknown, undiscovered

IGUAL 1 *adj* (**a**) *(idéntico)* the same (**que** *o* **a** as); **llevan jerseys iguales** they're wearing the same sweater; **son iguales** they're the same; **¿has visto qué casa?, me gustaría tener una i.** have you seen that house? I wouldn't mind having one like it; **tengo una bicicleta i.**

que la tuya I've got a bicycle just like yours; **lo hirieron con un cuchillo i. a éste** he was wounded with a knife just like this one; **su estadio es i. de grande que el nuestro** their stadium is as big as *o* the same size as ours; **todos los chicos eran i. de guapos** all the boys were equally good-looking, all the boys were just as good-looking as each other; **sigue siendo i. de presumido** he's (just) as vain as ever; **todos los hombres sois iguales** you men are all the same; **todos somos iguales ante la ley** we are all equal in the eyes of the law

(**b**) *(parecido)* similar (**que** to); **son dos atletas muy iguales en su forma de correr** they are two athletes who have a very similar style of running; **este niño, de cara, es i. que su padre** this child looks just like his father; **físicamente no se parecen, pero de carácter son iguales** they don't look anything like each other, but they have very similar characters

(**c**) *(tal, semejante)* **no había visto cosa i. en toda mi vida** I'd never seen the like of it; **¿has oído alguna vez mentira i.?** have you ever heard such a lie?

(**d**) *(equivalente)* equal (**a** to); **su brillantez era i. a su ambición** his brilliance was matched by his ambition

(**e**) *(llano)* even; *(sin asperezas)* smooth

(**f**) *(constante) (velocidad, aceleración)* constant; *(clima, temperatura)* even

(**g**) *Mat* **A más B es i. a C** A plus B equals C

2 *nmf* equal; **sólo se relacionaba con sus iguales** she only mixed with her equals; **de i. a i.** as an equal; **te hablo de i. a i.** I am speaking to you as an equal; **llevan una relación de i. a i.** they treat each other as equals; **no tener i.** to have no equal, to be unrivalled; **sin i.** without equal, unrivalled; **el actor principal tiene un talento sin i.** the leading man is unrivalled in his ability; **es un espectáculo sin i.** it is a sight without equal

3 *nm (signo)* equal *o* equals sign

4 iguales *nmpl Antes (de la ONCE)* = tickets for the Spanish National Association for the Blind lottery

5 *adv* (**a**) *(de la misma manera)* the same; **yo pienso i.** I think the same, I think so too; **¡qué curioso!, a mí me pasó i.** how odd, the same thing happened to me!; **el café estaba frío y el té i.** the coffee was cold and so was the tea; **al i. que: es muy alto, al i. que su padre** he's very tall, just like his father; **el limón, al i. que la naranja, tiene mucha vitamina C** lemons, like oranges, contain a lot of vitamin C; **baila i. que la Pavlova** she dances just like Pavlova; **por i.** equally; **nos trataron a todos por i.** they treated us all the same *o* equally

(**b**) *Esp (posiblemente)* **i. llueve** it could well rain; **con suerte, i. llego mañana** with a bit of luck I may arrive tomorrow; **i. dejo este trabajo y me busco otra cosa** I may well give up this job and look for something different

(**c**) *Dep* **van iguales** the scores are level; **treinta iguales** *(en tenis)* thirty all; **cuarenta iguales, iguales a cuarenta** *(en tenis)* deuce

(**d**) **dar i.: me da i. lo que piense la gente** *(no me importa)* I don't care what people think; **¿quieres salir o prefieres quedarte? – me es i.** do you want to go out, or would you rather stay in? – it's all the same to me *o* I don't mind; **lo siento, no voy a poder ayudar – da** *o* **es i., no te preocupes** I'm sorry but I won't be able to help – it doesn't matter, don't worry; **¿vamos o nos quedamos? – da** *o* **es i.** should we go or should we stay? – it doesn't make any difference; **es i., si no tienen vino tomaré otra cosa** never mind, if you haven't got any wine I'll have something else

(**e**) *Andes, RP (aún así)* all the same; **estaba nublado pero i. fuimos a la playa** it was cloudy but we went to the beach all the same

---

iguala *nf* retainer *(esp for medical services)*

igualación *nf* (**a**) *(de terreno)* levelling; *(de superficie)* smoothing (**b**) *(de cantidades)* equalizing; **piden la i. de salarios** they are asking for salaries to be made the same

igualada *nf (empate)* **la i. se mantuvo hasta el final del partido** the scores remained level until the end of the match; **el tanto de la i.** the equalizer

igualado, -a *adj* (**a**) *(terreno)* levelled, level (**b**) *Dep* **de momento van igualados** *(empatados)* the scores are level at the moment; **acabaron el encuentro igualados** they drew (**c**) *(parejo)* evenly matched; **un partido muy i.** a very evenly balanced match; **son dos equipos muy igualados** they are two very evenly matched teams

igualamiento *nm* equalization

igualar 1 *vt* (**a**) *(hacer igual)* to make equal, to equalize; **les han igualado los sueldos** they've brought their salaries into line with each other, they've started paying them the same salary; **i. algo a** *o* **con** to equate sth with; **esa acción lo iguala a sus enemigos** that act takes him down to his enemies' level; **intentan i. sus productos a los de la competencia** they are trying to match their products to those of their competitors; **todavía no han conseguido i. su récord** her record still hasn't been equalled

(**b**) *(persona)* to be equal to; **nadie la iguala en generosidad** her generosity is unrivalled

(**c**) *(terreno)* to level; *(superficie)* to smooth

(**d**) *(hierba, cabello)* to trim

(**e**) *Dep* **igualaron el marcador en el último minuto** they equalized in the last minute

2 *vi Dep* to equalize; **igualaron en el último minuto** they equalized in the last minute; **igualaron a cero** they drew nil-nil

3 igualarse *vpr* (**a**) *(cosas diferentes)* to become equal; **igualarse a** *o* **con** *(otra persona, equipo)* to become equal with, to match (**b**) *(compararse)* **su problema no puede igualarse con el nuestro** her problem cannot be compared *o* likened to ours

igualdad *nf* (**a**) *(equivalencia)* equality; **la i. ante la ley** equality before the law; **piden un trato de i.** they are asking for equal treatment; **en i. de condiciones** on equal terms; **para garantizar la i. de condiciones** in order to ensure a level playing field; **en pie de i.** on an equal footing ▸▸ ***i. de derechos*** equal rights; ***i. de oportunidades*** equal opportunities; ***i. de retribuciones*** equal pay; ***i. de sexos*** sexual equality

(**b**) *(identidad)* sameness (**c**) *Mat* equation

igualitario, -a *adj* egalitarian

igualitarismo *nm* egalitarianism

igualmente *adv* (**a**) *(de manera igual)* equally; **la riqueza no está repartida i.** wealth is not distributed equally; **dos proyectos i. importantes** two equally important projects

(**b**) *(también)* also, likewise; **ofreció i. dar asilo a los refugiados** he also *o* likewise offered to grant the refugees asylum; **i., querría recordar a nuestro querido maestro** I would also like us to remember our beloved former teacher

(**c**) *(fórmula de cortesía)* **que pases un buen fin de semana – i.** have a good weekend – you too; **que aproveche – i.** enjoy your meal – you too; **¡Feliz Navidad! – i.** Merry Christmas! – same to you!; **encantado de conocerlo – i.** pleased to meet you – likewise; **recuerdos a tu madre – gracias, i.** give my regards to your mother – thanks, give mine to yours too

iguana *nf* iguana

iguanodonte *nm* iguanodon

Iguazú *n* **el I.** the Iguaçú

IGV *nm Perú* (*abrev de* **impuesto general a las ventas**) *Br* ≃ VAT, *US* ≃ sales tax

IICA *nm* (*abrev de* **Instituto Interamericano de Cooperación para la Agricultura**) IICA, Inter-American Institute for Co-operation on Agriculture

ijada *nf*, **ijar** *nm* flank, side

ikastola *nf* = primary school in the Basque country where classes are given entirely in Basque

ikurriña *nf* = Basque national flag

ilación *nf* cohesion

ilativo, -a *adj* illative

ilegal 1 *adj* illegal; **de forma i.** illegally

2 *nmf (inmigrante)* illegal immigrant, *US* illegal; *(trabajador)* illegal worker, *US* illegal

ilegalidad *nf* (**a**) *(acción)* unlawful act (**b**) *(cualidad)* illegality; **estar en la i.** to be illegal *o* outside the law; **un inmigrante en situación de i.** an illegal immigrant; **la i. de las ayudas económicas recibidas por el partido** the illegal nature of the payments received by the party

ilegalización *nf* banning

ilegalizar *vt* to ban

ilegalmente *adv* illegally

ilegibilidad *nf* illegibility

ilegible *adj* illegible

ilegítimamente *adv* illegitimately

ilegitimar *vt (logro)* to invalidate; **su pasado lo ilegitima para ser alcalde** his past makes him unfit to be mayor; **sus infidelidades ilegitiman sus celos** her infidelities deny her the right to be jealous

ilegitimidad *nf* illegitimacy

ilegítimo, -a *adj* illegitimate; **hijo i.** illegitimate child

íleon *nm Anat (en intestino)* ileum

ilerdense 1 *adj* of/from Lerida *(Spain)*

2 *nmf* person from Lerida *(Spain)*

ileso, -a *adj* unhurt, unharmed; **salir** *o* **resultar i.** to escape unharmed; **salió i. del accidente** he was not injured in the accident

iletrado, -a 1 *adj* illiterate
2 *nm,f* illiterate

iliaco, -a, ilíaco, -a *adj Anat* ileac, ileal

Ilíada *nf* **la I.** the Iliad

ilícito, -a 1 *adj* illicit
2 *nm,f Am* crime

ilicitud *nf* illegality

ilimitado, -a *adj* unlimited, limitless; **poder i.** absolute power

ilion *nm Anat* ilium

ilmo., -a. (*abrev de* **ilustrísimo, -a**) *adj* **el I. Ayuntamiento de Madrid** the City Council of Madrid; **el I. señor juez don Lucas Hernández** Judge Lucas Hernández

ilocalizable *adj* **se encuentra i.** he cannot be found

ilógico, -a *adj* illogical

ilomba *nf* false nutmeg

iluminación *nf* (**a**) *(luces)* lighting; **lo mejor del concierto fue la i.** the best part of the concert was the light show; **en esta sala hay muy poca i.** this room is very poorly lit; **trabaje con buena i.** make sure you have plenty of light when you are working (**b**) *(acción)* illumination; **de la i. me encargo yo** I'll take care of the lighting (**c**) *Rel* enlightenment

iluminado, -a 1 *adj* (**a**) *(con luz)* lit (up); **el lugar estaba mal i. y no pude verle la cara** the place was poorly lit and I couldn't see his face (**b**) *Rel* enlightened (**c**) *Pey (político, terrorista)* **un político i.** a politician who thinks he's on a mission from above
2 *nm,f* (**a**) *Rel* enlightened person (**b**) *Pey (político, terrorista)* **son unos iluminados** they think they're on a mission from above

iluminador, -ora 1 *adj* illuminating
2 *nm,f* lighting technician

iluminar 1 *vt* (**a**) *(dar luz a)* to illuminate, to light; **la antorcha iluminaba la cueva** the torch lit up the cave; **los focos que iluminan la iglesia** the floodlights which light up the church
(**b**) *(adornar con luces)* to light up; **en Navidad iluminan el centro de la ciudad con luces** at Christmas they light up the city centre; **iluminan el castillo por la noche** the castle is lit up at night
(**c**) *(grabado, códice)* to illuminate
(**d**) *Rel* to enlighten
2 *vi* to give light; **la lámpara ilumina muy poco** the lamp doesn't give much light
3 **iluminarse** *vpr* (**a**) *(con luz)* to light up; **el baño se ilumina por una pequeña ventana** a small window provides the bathroom with light; **el cielo se iluminó con la bengala** the flare lit up the sky (**b**) *(de alegría)* **se le iluminó el rostro** his face lit up (**c**) *Rel* to become enlightened

ilusión *nf* (**a**) *(esperanza)* hope; **con i.** hopefully, optimistically; **la i. de su vida es ir al espacio** his life's dream is to travel into space; **hacerse** *o* **forjarse ilusiones** to build up one's hopes; **no te hagas demasiadas ilusiones** don't get your hopes up too much; **no me hago muchas ilusiones de que me vayan a dar la beca** I'm not too optimistic about getting the grant
(**b**) *(infundada)* delusion, illusion; **vive de ilusiones** he's completely deluded
(**c**) *esp Esp (emoción)* **han trabajado con mucha i.** they have worked with real enthusiasm; **¡qué i.!** how exciting!; **¡qué i. verte otra vez!** it's great to see you again!; **me hace mucha i.** I'm really looking forward to it; **me hace mucha i. que vengas** I'm really delighted *o* thrilled that you're coming; **la novia lleva los preparativos de la boda con i.** the bride is very excited about the preparations for the wedding
(**d**) *(espejismo)* illusion ▸▸ ***i. óptica*** optical illusion

ilusionar 1 *vt* (**a**) *(esperanzar)* **i. a alguien (con algo)** to build up sb's hopes (about sth) (**b**) *(emocionar)* to excite, to thrill; **les ilusiona la llegada del nuevo bebé** they are thrilled about the new baby
2 **ilusionarse** *vpr* (**a**) *(esperanzarse)* to get one's hopes up (**con** about); **se ha ilusionado mucho con el concurso** he's really got his hopes up about winning the competition (**b**) *(emocionarse)* to get excited (**con** about)

ilusionismo *nm* conjuring, magic

ilusionista *nmf* conjurer, magician

iluso, -a 1 *adj* naive; **¡no seas i.!** don't be so naive!
2 *nm,f* naive person, dreamer; **piensa que le van a subir el sueldo, ¡i.!** he's so naive, he thinks he's going to get a pay rise!; **eres un i. si crees que vas a conseguir algo así** you're dreaming *o* kidding yourself if you think you can achieve anything like that

ilusorio, -a *adj (imaginario)* illusory; *(promesa)* empty

ilustración *nf* (**a**) *(estampa, dibujo)* illustration (**b**) *(ejemplo)* illustration; **sirvan de i. los siguientes datos...** the following facts and figures illustrate my point... (**c**) *(cultura)* learning; **no tiene mucha i.** he's not very educated (**d**) *Hist* **la I.** the Enlightenment

ilustrado, -a 1 *adj* (**a**) *(publicación)* illustrated (**b**) *(persona)* learned (**c**) *Hist* **un filósofo/monarca i.** a philosopher/monarch influenced by the Enlightenment
2 *nm,f Hist* person influenced by the Enlightenment

ilustrador, -ora 1 *adj* illustrative
2 *nm,f* illustrator

ilustrar 1 *vt* (**a**) *(explicar)* to illustrate, to explain; **ilústrame sobre la situación actual** explain the current situation to me, fill me in on the current situation; **i. algo con un ejemplo** to illustrate sth with an example (**b**) *(publicación)* to illustrate (**c**) *(educar)* to enlighten
2 **ilustrarse** *vpr* to educate oneself

ilustrativo, -a *adj* illustrative

ilustre *adj* (**a**) *(distinguido)* illustrious, distinguished (**b**) *(título)* **el i. señor alcalde** his Worship, the Mayor

Ilustrísima *nf* **Su I.** Your/His Grace, Your/His Worship

ilustrísimo, -a *adj* **el I. Ayuntamiento de Madrid** the City Council of Madrid; **el I. señor juez don Lucas Hernández** Judge Lucas Hernández

imagen *nf* (**a**) *(figura)* image; **su i. se reflejaba en el agua** she could see her reflection in the water; **contemplaba su i. en el espejo** he was looking at his reflection in the mirror; **su rostro era la pura i. del sufrimiento** her face was a picture of suffering; **eran la i. de la felicidad** they were a picture of happiness; EXPR **ser la viva i. de alguien** to be the spitting image of sb; EXPR **a i. y semejanza: Dios creó al hombre a su i. y semejanza** God created man in his own image; **reconstruyeron el museo a i. y semejanza del original** they rebuilt the museum so that it looked just like the old one
(**b**) *(en física)* image; *(televisiva)* picture; **las imágenes en movimiento** the moving image; **imágenes del partido/de la catástrofe** pictures of the game/the disaster; EXPR **una i. vale más que mil palabras** one picture is worth a thousand words ▸▸ ***imágenes de archivo*** library pictures; ***i. virtual*** virtual image
(**c**) *(aspecto)* image; **necesitas un cambio de i.** you need a change of *o* a new image; **tiene una i. de intolerante** she has the image of being an intolerant person; **quieren proyectar una i. positiva** they want to project a positive image; **tener buena/mala i.** to have a good/bad image; **los casos de corrupción han deteriorado la i. del gobierno** the corruption scandals have tainted the image of the government ▸▸ ***i. corporativa*** corporate identity; ***i. de empresa*** corporate image; ***i. de marca*** brand image; ***i. pública*** public image
(**d**) *(recuerdo)* picture, image; **guardo una i. muy borrosa de mis abuelos** I only have a very vague memory of my grandparents; **tenía una i. diferente del lugar** I had a different picture *o* image of the place, I had pictured the place differently ▸▸ ***i. mental*** mental image
(**e**) *(estatua)* statue
(**f**) *(literaria)* image; **utiliza unas imágenes muy ricas** she uses very rich imagery

imaginable *adj* imaginable, conceivable

imaginación *nf* (**a**) *(facultad)* imagination; **un niño con mucha i.** a child with a very vivid imagination, a very imaginative child; **pasar por la i. de alguien** to occur to sb, to cross sb's mind; **no me pasó por la i.** it never occurred to me *o* crossed my mind; **se deja llevar por la i.** he lets his imagination run away with him; EXPR **dar rienda suelta a la i.** to let one's imagination run wild
(**b**) *(idea falsa)* **imaginaciones** delusions, imaginings; **son imaginaciones tuyas** you're just imagining things, it's all in your mind

imaginar 1 *vt* (**a**) *(suponer)* to imagine; **imagino que te has enterado de la noticia** I imagine *o* suppose you've heard the news; **imagina por un momento que eres millonario** imagine for a moment that you are a millionaire; **no puedes i. cuánto me enfadé** you can't imagine how angry I was; **imagina que llega y no estamos preparados** imagine what would happen if she arrived and we weren't ready
(**b**) *(visualizar)* to imagine, to picture; **imagina un mundo más justo** imagine a fairer world
(**c**) *(idear)* to think up, to invent
2 **imaginarse** *vpr* (**a**) *(suponer)* to imagine; **no te llamé porque me imaginé que estabas muy ocupada** I didn't call you because I thought you'd be very busy; **me imagino que estarás cansado** I imagine *o* suppose you must be tired; **no te imaginas cómo me alegré** you can't imagine how pleased I was; **¡imagínate!** just think *o* imagine!; **me imagino que sí** I suppose so; **se puso muy contenta – me lo imagino** she was very happy – I can well believe it; *Fam* **¿te imaginas que viene?** what if he were to come?

(**b**) *(visualizar)* to imagine, to picture; **no me lo imagino vestido de indio** I can't imagine *o* picture him dressed as an Indian; **no me lo imaginaba así** I hadn't imagined *o* pictured it like this

imaginaria *nf (guardia)* reserve guard, nightguard; **estar de i.** to be on nightguard duty

imaginario, -a 1 *adj* imaginary
2 *nm (conjunto de imágenes)* imagery; **el i. colectivo** the collective consciousness

imaginativo, -a *adj* imaginative

imaginería *nf* (**a**) *Arte* religious image-making (**b**) *Lit* imagery

imaginero, -a *nm,f* = painter or sculptor of religious images

imam *nm (entre musulmanes)* imam

imán *nm* (**a**) *(para atraer)* magnet (**b**) *(persona, lugar)* magnet (**c**) *(entre musulmanes)* imam

imanación, imantación *nf* magnetization

imanar, imantar *vt* to magnetize

Imax® *nm* IMAX®

imbancable *adj RP Fam (insoportable)* unbearable

imbaque *nm Ven* (**a**) *(recipiente)* earthenware container (**b**) *Fam (persona)* barrel, *Br* gutbucket

imbatibilidad *nf* **la derrota puso fin a su i.** this defeat ended their unbeaten run

imbatible *adj* unbeatable

imbatido, -a *adj* unbeaten

imbebible *adj* undrinkable

imbécil 1 *adj* (**a**) *(tonto)* stupid (**b**) *(enfermo)* imbecile
2 *nmf* (**a**) *(tonto)* idiot (**b**) *(enfermo)* imbecile

imbecilidad *nf (acto, dicho)* stupid thing; **decir/hacer una i.** to say/do something stupid; **no dice más que imbecilidades** he talks nothing but nonsense; **¿y por eso se enfada? ¡vaya (una) i.!** and she got angry about that? how stupid!

imberbe 1 *adj* beardless
2 *nm* **todavía es un i.** he hasn't started shaving yet

imbombera *nf Ven Fam* jaundice

imbornal *nm* scupper

imborrable *adj* (**a**) *(tinta)* indelible (**b**) *(recuerdo)* unforgettable

imbricación *nf* overlap

imbricado, -a *adj* (**a**) *(láminas, escamas)* overlapping (**b**) *(temas)* interwoven

imbricar [60] *vt* (**a**) *(láminas, escamas)* **imbricó las láminas** he arranged the sheets so they overlapped (**b**) *(temas)* to interweave

imbuir [34] 1 *vt* to imbue (**de** with); **los imbuyen de valores patrióticos** they are imbued with patriotic values, they have patriotic values instilled in them
2 **imbuirse** *vpr* **se imbuyó de ideas revolucionarias** he filled his head with revolutionary ideas

imbunchar *vt Chile* (**a**) *(embrujar)* to bewitch, to cast a spell over (**b**) *(estafar)* to swindle

imbunche *nm Chile* (**a**) *(ser mitológico)* = deformed evil spirit who helps witches (**b**) *(maleficio)* curse (**c**) *Fam (barullo)* mess

IME ['ime] *nm UE* (*abrev de* **Instituto Monetario Europeo**) EMI

imitación *nf* (**a**) *(copia)* imitation; **una i. burda de algo** a crude imitation of sth; **a i. de** in imitation of; **piel de i.** imitation leather; **joyas de i.** imitation jewellery (**b**) *(de humorista)* impression, impersonation; **hacer una i. de alguien** to do an impression of sb, to impersonate sb

imitador, -ora *nm,f* (**a**) *(que copia)* imitator (**b**) *(humorista)* impressionist, impersonator

imitamonas, imitamonos *nmf inv Fam* copycat

imitar *vt* (**a**) *(copiar)* to imitate, to copy; **intentaron i. mi firma** they tried to forge my signature; **se marchó del bar y nosotros la imitamos** she left the bar and we followed suit
(**b**) *(producto, material)* to simulate; **un material que imita al cuero** a material which looks like leather
(**c**) *(a personajes famosos)* to do an impression of, to impersonate; **imitó al presidente** he did an impression of *o* impersonated *o* took off the president

imitativo, -a *adj* imitative

impaciencia *nf* impatience; **con i.** impatiently

impacientar 1 *vt* to make impatient, to exasperate; **su impuntualidad me impacienta** I find his lack of punctuality exasperating
2 **impacientarse** *vpr* to grow impatient; **comenzábamos a impacientarnos** we were beginning to get impatient; **me impaciento con sus tonterías** I'm getting fed up with him clowning around

impaciente *adj* impatient; **no seas i.** be patient, don't be so impatient; **i. por hacer algo** impatient *o* anxious to do sth; **estoy i. por que llegue Jaime** I can't wait for Jaime to get here

impacientemente *adv* impatiently

impactado, -a *adj Am* shocked

impactante *adj (imágenes)* hard-hitting; *(belleza)* striking, stunning

impactar 1 *vt* (**a**) *(impresionar)* to have an impact on; **me impactó oírle hablar de esa manera** it made a real impression on me to hear him talk like that; **la noticia de su asesinato nos impactó a todos** the news of her murder shocked us all (**b**) *(golpear)* **le impactó un ladrillo en la cara** he was struck in the face by a brick
2 *vi (bala)* to hit

impacto *nm* (**a**) *(choque)* impact; **recibió varios impactos de bala** he was shot several times
(**b**) *(señal)* (impact) mark ►► ***i. de bala*** bullet hole
(**c**) *(impresión)* impact, impression; **causar un gran i. en alguien** to have a big impact *o* make a big impression on sb; **el accidente le causó un gran i.** the accident made a big impression on him *o* affected him very severely; **el i. político del cierre de una fábrica** the political impact *o* fallout of the closure of a factory ►► ***i. ambiental*** environmental impact

impagable *adj* invaluable; **me hizo un favor i.** I'll never be able to repay the favour she did me

impagado, -a 1 *adj* unpaid
2 *nm* unpaid bill

impago, -a 1 *adj Am (no pagado)* unpaid; **los salarios impagos** the unpaid wages; **los obreros impagos** the workers who haven't been paid; **factura impaga** unpaid *o* outstanding invoice
2 *nm* non-payment; **el i. de una multa** non-payment of a fine

impala *nm* impala

impalpable *adj* impalpable

impar 1 *adj* (**a**) *(número)* odd (**b**) *(sin igual)* unequalled
2 *nm* odd number

imparable *adj* unstoppable

imparablemente *adv* unstoppably

imparcial *adj* impartial

imparcialidad *nf* impartiality

imparcialmente *adv* impartially

impartir *vt* to give; **i. clases** to teach; **el obispo impartió la bendición** the bishop gave his blessing; **los tribunales imparten justicia** the courts dispense justice

impase = **impasse**

impasibilidad *nf* impassivity

impasible *adj* impassive; **su rostro permaneció i.** his face showed *o* betrayed no emotion; **escuchó i. el veredicto** she listened impassively as the verdict was read out

impasiblemente *adv* impassively

impasse, impase [im'pas] *nm* impasse; **encontrarse** *o* **estar en un i.** to have reached an impasse

impavidez *nf* (**a**) *(valor)* fearlessness, courage (**b**) *(impasibilidad)* impassivity

impávido, -a *adj* (**a**) *(valeroso)* fearless, courageous (**b**) *(impasible)* impassive

impecable *adj* impeccable

impecablemente *adv* impeccably

impedancia *nf* impedance

impedido, -a 1 *adj* disabled; **estar i. de un brazo** to have the use of only one arm
2 *nm,f* disabled person; **los impedidos** the disabled

impedimento *nm* (**a**) *(obstáculo)* obstacle; **no hay ningún i. para hacerlo** there's no reason why we shouldn't do it; **no nos puso ningún i. para la celebración de la fiesta** he didn't put any obstacles in the way of our having the party, he in no way tried to stop us having the party; **si no surge ningún i. llegaremos a las ocho** all being well, we'll be there at eight o'clock
(**b**) *(para el matrimonio)* impediment

impedir [47] *vt* (**a**) *(imposibilitar)* to prevent; **i. a alguien hacer algo** to prevent sb from doing sth; **la lesión le impedía correr** the injury stopped *o* prevented her from running; **impedirle el paso a alguien** to

bar sb's way; **este camión impide el paso a la calle** this truck *o Br* lorry is blocking the street; **la nieve impidió la celebración del partido** the snow prevented the match from taking place; **nada te impide hacerlo** there's nothing to stop you doing it; **si nada lo impide saldremos por la mañana** all being well we'll leave in the morning
(**b**) *(dificultar)* to hinder, to obstruct

impeler *vt Formal* (**a**) *(hacer avanzar)* to propel (**b**) *(incitar)* **i. a alguien a algo/hacer algo** to drive sb to sth/to do sth

impenetrabilidad *nf* (**a**) *(de bosque, barrera)* impenetrability (**b**) *(de estilo, misterio)* impenetrability; *(de sonrisa)* inscrutability

impenetrable *adj* (**a**) *(bosque, barrera)* impenetrable (**b**) *(estilo, misterio)* impenetrable; *(sonrisa)* inscrutable

impenitencia *nf* impenitence

impenitente *adj* (**a**) *(que no se arrepiente)* unrepentant, impenitent (**b**) *(incorregible)* inveterate

impensable *adj* unthinkable

impensado, -a *adj* (**a**) *(inesperado)* unexpected (**b**) *(sin pensar)* **dio una respuesta impensada** she answered without thinking

impepinable *adj Esp Fam Hum* **sus argumentos son impepinables** you can't deny her arguments; **lo que has dicho es una verdad i.** there's no denying what you said; **¡eso es i.!** that's for sure!

imperante *adj* (**a**) *(estilo, tendencia, corrupción)* prevailing (**b**) *(régimen)* ruling

imperar *vi* (**a**) *(predominar) (estilo, tendencia)* to prevail; **la corrupción que impera en la administración** the corruption which prevails throughout the administration (**b**) *(dominar) (político, general)* to rule

imperativamente *adv* as a matter of utmost urgency

imperativo, -a 1 *adj* (**a**) *Gram* imperative (**b**) *(autoritario)* imperious
2 *nm* (**a**) *Gram* imperative (**b**) *(circunstancias, mandato)* **para él ayudar a los necesitados sigue siendo un i. moral** helping the poor remains a moral imperative for him; **imperativos económicos** economic considerations; **por i. legal** for legal reasons ▸▸ *Filosofía* ***el i. categórico*** the categorical imperative

imperatoria *nf* masterwort

imperceptible *adj* imperceptible

imperceptiblemente *adv* imperceptibly

imperdible *nm* safety pin

imperdonable *adj* unforgivable; **fue i. que te olvidaras de su cumpleaños** it was unforgivable of you to forget her birthday

imperdonablemente *adv* unforgivably

imperecedero, -a *adj* (**a**) *(producto)* non-perishable (**b**) *(eterno)* immortal, eternal

imperfección *nf* (**a**) *(cualidad)* imperfection (**b**) *(defecto)* flaw, defect

imperfecto, -a 1 *adj* (**a**) *(no perfecto)* imperfect (**b**) *(defectuoso)* faulty, defective (**c**) *Gram* **futuro i.** future (tense); **pretérito i.** (past) imperfect
2 *nm Gram* imperfect

imperial *adj* imperial

imperialismo *nm* imperialism

imperialista 1 *adj* imperialist
2 *nmf* imperialist

impericia *nf* (**a**) *(torpeza)* lack of skill (**b**) *(inexperiencia)* inexperience

imperio 1 *adj (estilo, moda)* Empire
2 *nm* (**a**) *(territorio)* empire; EXPR **valer un i.** to be worth a fortune ▸▸ ***el I. Romano*** the Roman Empire (**b**) *(mandato)* emperorship; **durante el i. de Carlos V** during the reign of the emperor Charles V (**c**) *(dominio)* rule; **el i. de la ley** the rule of law

imperiosamente *adv* (**a**) *(con autoridad)* imperiously (**b**) *(con apremio)* urgently

imperiosidad *nf* (**a**) *(autoritarismo)* imperiousness (**b**) *(apremio)* urgency

imperioso, -a *adj* (**a**) *(autoritario)* imperious (**b**) *(apremiante)* urgent, pressing

impermeabilidad *nf* impermeability

impermeabilización *nf* waterproofing

impermeabilizante *adj* waterproofing

impermeabilizar [14] *vt* to (make) waterproof

impermeable 1 *adj* (**a**) *(al líquido)* waterproof; **es i. al agua** it's waterproof (**b**) *(insensible)* impervious; **es i. a las críticas** he's impervious to criticism; **permaneció i. a las presiones políticas** she remained impervious to political pressure
2 *nm* (**a**) *(prenda)* raincoat, *Br* mac (**b**) *Esp Fam Hum (preservativo)* rubber

impersonal *adj* (**a**) *(trato, decoración)* impersonal (**b**) *(verbo)* impersonal

impersonalidad *nf (de trato)* impersonality; *(de decoración)* impersonal nature

impersonalmente *adv* impersonally

impertérrito, -a *adj (impávido)* unperturbed, unmoved; *(ante peligros)* fearless

impertinencia *nf* (**a**) *(cualidad)* impertinence (**b**) *(comentario)* impertinent remark; **estoy cansado de sus impertinencias** I'm tired of his impertinent remarks *o* his impertinence

impertinente 1 *adj* (**a**) *(insolente)* impertinent; **no te pongas i. con tu madre** don't be rude *o* impertinent to your mother; **hoy estás muy i.** you're being very impertinent today (**b**) *(inoportuno)* inappropriate
2 *nmf (persona)* impertinent person; **es un i.** he's very rude *o* impertinent
3 **impertinentes** *nmpl (anteojos)* lorgnette

impertinentemente *adv* impertinently

imperturbabilidad *nf* imperturbability

imperturbable *adj* (**a**) *(persona)* imperturbable; **escuchó i. las acusaciones** he listened impassively to the accusations (**b**) *(sonrisa)* impassive

impétigo *nm Med* impetigo

ímpetu *nm* (**a**) *(brusquedad)* force; **el í. del tornado arrasó el pueblecito** the force of the tornado flattened the village (**b**) *(energía)* energy; **empezó la carrera con gran í.** he started the race very energetically; **perder í.** to lose momentum (**c**) *Fís* momentum

impetuosamente *adv* impetuously

impetuosidad *nf* (**a**) *(de olas, viento, ataque)* force (**b**) *(de persona)* impetuosity, impetuousness

impetuoso, -a 1 *adj* (**a**) *(olas, viento)* raging; *(ataque)* furious (**b**) *(persona)* impulsive, impetuous
2 *nm,f* impulsive person; **es un i.** he's very impulsive

impidiera *etc ver* **impedir**

impido *etc ver* **impedir**

impiedad *nf* (**a**) *(falta de religión)* godlessness, impiety (**b**) *(falta de piedad)* mercilessness

impío, -a *adj* (**a**) *(sin religión)* godless, impious (**b**) *(sin piedad)* merciless

implacable *adj* (**a**) *(odio, ira)* implacable; *(sol)* relentless; *(clima)* harsh; **el i. avance del desierto** the relentless *o* inexorable advance of the desert (**b**) *(persona)* inflexible, firm; **es i. con sus alumnos** she's very hard on her pupils (**c**) *(incontestable)* unassailable; **un argumento de una lógica i.** an argument of unassailable logic

implacablemente *adv* relentlessly

implantación *nf* (**a**) *(establecimiento)* introduction; **la i. de la pena de muerte** the introduction of the death penalty; **la i. de la democracia** the establishment of democracy; **durante el periodo de i. del euro** when the euro is introduced; **una empresa con fuerte i. en este país** a company which is well-established in this country; **una tradición sin i. en la región** a tradition which never took hold in the region; **un medio de pago de creciente i.** an increasingly widely-used method of payment
(**b**) *Biol* implantation (**c**) *Med (de nuevo)* insertion

implantar 1 *vt* (**a**) *(establecer)* to introduce; **han implantado el toque de queda** they have imposed a curfew; **implantaron un racionamiento de los alimentos** food rationing was introduced *o* was brought in; **una moda implantada desde el exterior** a fashion introduced *o* imported from abroad (**b**) *Med (huevo)* to insert
2 **implantarse** *vpr* (**a**) *(establecerse)* to be introduced; **una costumbre que se está implantando** a practice which is becoming more common; **la moda no llegó a implantarse** the fashion didn't catch on (**b**) *Biol* to become implanted

implante *nm* implant ▸▸ ***i. dental*** (dental) implant

implementación *nf* implementation

implementar *vt* to implement

implemento *nm* implement; *Am* **implementos deportivos** sports equipment

implicación *nf* (**a**) *(participación)* involvement (**b**) **implicaciones** *(consecuencias)* implications

implicancia *nf CSur* implication

implicar [60] 1 *vt* (a) *(conllevar)* to involve (en in); **la protección del medio ambiente implica sacrificios** protecting the environment involves *o* means making sacrifices
(b) *Der (involucrar)* to implicate (en in); **lo implicaron en el asesinato** he was implicated in the murder
(c) *(significar, suponer)* to mean, to imply; **dije que sí, lo que no implica que vaya a participar** I said yes, but that doesn't necessarily mean I'll take part
2 **implicarse** *vpr* (a) *Der* to incriminate oneself (b) *(comprometerse)* **implicarse en** to become involved in

implícito, -a *adj* implicit

imploración *nf* entreaty, plea

implorante *adj* imploring; **una mirada i.** an imploring look

implorar *vt* to implore; **te lo imploro, déjales marchar** let them go, I implore *o* beg you; **le imploró clemencia** she begged (him) for mercy

implosión *nf* implosion

implosivo, -a *adj* implosive

impoluto, -a *adj* (a) *(puro, limpio)* unpolluted, pure (b) *(sin mácula)* unblemished, untarnished

imponderabilidad *nf* imponderability

imponderable 1 *adj* (a) *(incalculable)* invaluable (b) *(imprevisible)* imponderable
2 *nm* imponderable

imponencia *nf Am* grandeur; **nos impresionó la i. del Aconcagua** we were impressed by Aconcagua in all its imposing grandeur

imponente 1 *adj* (a) *(impresionante)* imposing, impressive; **un perro i. guardaba la entrada** an imposing-looking *o* a formidable dog guarded the entrance (b) *Fam (estupendo)* sensational, terrific (c) *Fam (guapo)* stunning; **estaba i. con esa falda** she looked stunning in that skirt; **¡la profesora está i.!** the teacher is a stunner!
2 *nmf Esp* depositor

IMPONER [50] 1 *vt* (a) *(forzar a aceptar)* **i. algo (a alguien)** to impose sth (on sb); **a nadie le gusta que le impongan obligaciones** no one likes to have responsibilities forced upon them; **desde el principio el campeón impuso un fuerte ritmo de carrera** the champion set a healthy pace right from the start of the race; **el profesor impuso silencio en la clase** the teacher silenced the class; **una política impuesta por el Banco Mundial** a policy imposed by the World Bank
(b) *(aplicar)* **i. una multa/un castigo a alguien** to impose a fine/a punishment on sb; **el juez le impuso una pena de dos años de cárcel** the judge sentenced him to two years' imprisonment; **le impusieron la difícil tarea de sanear las finanzas de la empresa** he was charged with the difficult task of straightening out the company's finances; **impusieron la obligatoriedad de llevar casco** they made it compulsory to wear a helmet
(c) *(inspirar) (miedo, admiración)* to inspire (a in); **i. respeto (a alguien)** to command respect (from sb)
(d) *(establecer) (moda)* to set; *(costumbre)* to introduce
(e) *(asignar) (nombre)* to give; *(medalla, condecoración, título)* to award; **a la isla se le impuso el nombre de su descubridor** the island was named after the person who discovered it; **le fue impuesto el título de doctor honoris causa por la Universidad de México** he received an honorary doctorate from the University of Mexico
(f) *(tributos, cargas fiscales)* to impose (a on)
(g) *(en banca)* to deposit
2 *vi* to be imposing; **el edificio impone por sus grandes dimensiones** the size of the building makes it very imposing; **imponía con su presencia** he had an imposing presence
3 **imponerse** *vpr* (a) *(hacerse respetar)* to command respect, to show authority; **trató de imponerse ante sus alumnos** she tried to assert her authority over her pupils
(b) *(ponerse) (obligación, tarea)* to take on; **me he impuesto una dieta muy estricta** I've imposed a very strict diet on myself, I've put myself on a very strict diet; **me impuse un fuerte ritmo de trabajo** I set myself a good pace for my work
(c) *(predominar)* to prevail; **esta primavera se impondrán los colores vivos y los vestidos cortos** this spring the fashion will be for bright colours and short dresses
(d) *(ser necesario)* to be necessary; **se impone una rápida solución al problema** a rapid solution to the problem must be found; **se impone tomar medidas urgentes** urgent measures are necessary
(e) *(vencer)* to win; **Francia se impuso por dos goles a uno** France won by two goals to one; **se impuso al resto de los corredores** she beat the other runners; **se impuso al esprint** he won the sprint for the line; **al final se impuso la sensatez y dejaron de insultarse** common sense finally prevailed and they stopped insulting each other

imponible *adj Fin* **base i.** taxable income

impopular *adj* unpopular

impopularidad *nf* unpopularity

importación *nf* (a) *(acción)* importing, importation; **la i. de alimentos** the importing *o* importation of foodstuffs (b) *(artículo)* import; **un aumento de las importaciones** an increase in imports; **de i.** imported

importado, -a *adj* imported

importador, -ora 1 *adj* importing; **empresa importadora** importer, importing company
2 *nm,f* importer

importancia *nf* importance; **de i.** important, of importance; **un tratamiento médico reservado a los casos de i.** a treatment reserved for serious cases; **un arquitecto de i.** an important architect; **recibió un golpe de cierta i.** he took a fairly heavy knock; **adquirir** *o* **cobrar i.** to become important, to take on significance; **dar i. a algo** to attach importance to sth; **darse i.** to give oneself airs; **no tiene i.** *(no es importante)* it's not important; *(no pasa nada)* it doesn't matter; **sin i.** unimportant; **ha sido un rasguño sin i.** it's only a little scratch; **quitar** *o* **restar i. a algo** to play sth down

importante *adj* (a) *(destacado, significativo)* important; **el descontento está adquiriendo proporciones importantes** dissatisfaction is becoming widespread; **ocupa un cargo i. en el ministerio** he has an important job at the ministry; **ella es muy i. para mí** she's very important to me; **lo i. es hacerlo despacio** the important thing is to do it slowly; **no te preocupes, lo i. es que tengas buena salud** don't worry, the most important thing is for you to be healthy; EXPR **dárselas de i., hacerse el/la i.** to give oneself airs, to act all important
(b) *(cantidad)* considerable; *(lesión)* serious; **una cantidad i. de dinero** a significant *o* considerable amount of money; **el tren llegó con un retraso i.** the train was very late

IMPORTAR 1 *vt* (a) *(productos, materias primas, costumbres)* to import (de from) (b) *Informát* to import (c) *Formal (sujeto: factura, coste)* to amount to, to come to; **la factura importa 5.000 pesos** the bill comes to 5,000 pesos
2 *vi* (a) *(preocupar, tener interés)* to matter; **no importa el precio, cómpralo de todas formas** the price doesn't matter, buy it anyway; **no me importa lo que piense la gente** I don't care what people think; **ya no te importo – al contrario, sí que me importas** you don't care about me any more – on the contrary, you do matter to me; **lo que importa es que todos salieron ilesos del accidente** what matters *o* the important thing is that nobody was hurt in the accident; **lo que me importa es saber quién lo hizo** the important thing for me is to know who did it
(b) *(incumbir, afectar)* **esto es algo entre tú y yo, y a nadie más le importa** this is between you and me and hasn't got anything to do with anyone else; **¡no te importa!** it's none of your business!; **¿a mí qué me importa?** what's that to me?, what do I care?; **¿y a ti qué te importa?** what's it got to do with you?; **¿adónde vas? – ¿te importa?** *(con enfado)* where are you going? – what's it to you!; *Fam* **siempre está metiéndose en lo que no le importa** she's always sticking her nose into other people's business; EXPR *Fam* **me importa un bledo** *o* **comino** *o* **pito** *o Chile* **pucho** *o* **rábano** I don't give a damn, I couldn't care less; EXPR *Esp Vulg* **me importa un cojón** *o* **tres cojones** I couldn't give a shit *o Br* toss
(c) *(molestar)* to mind; **no me importa tener que tomar el tren todos los días** I don't mind having to catch the train every day; **no me importa que venga tu familia** I don't mind if your family comes; **preferiría no salir, si no te importa** I'd rather not go out, if you don't mind *o* if it's all the same to you; **¿le importa que me siente?** do you mind if I sit down?; **¿te importaría acompañarme?** would you mind coming with me?
3 *v impersonal* to matter; **no importa** it doesn't matter; **si no vienes, no importa, ya nos arreglaremos** it doesn't matter *o* never mind if you can't come, we'll manage; **¡qué importa que llueva!** so what if it's raining?

importe *nm (precio)* price, cost; *(de factura)* total; **i. total** total cost; **pagué el i. de la consumición** I paid for what I'd had; **devolvió el i. íntegro del préstamo** he repaid the loan in full; **ayudas por un i. cercano a los 5.000 millones** aid to the tune of almost 5,000 million; **un cheque por un i. de dos millones** a cheque for two million; **una inversión por un i. máximo de 100 millones** a maximum investment of 100 million

importunar 1 *vt* to bother, to pester; **no me importunes con preguntas** don't bother *o* pester me with questions
2 *vi* to be tiresome *o* a nuisance

importuno, -a *adj* (**a**) *(en mal momento)* inopportune, untimely (**b**) *(molesto)* inconvenient (**c**) *(inadecuado)* inappropriate

imposibilidad *nf* impossibility; **su i. para contestar la pregunta** his inability to answer the question; **reconoció la i. de controlar la violencia** she acknowledged that it was impossible to control the violence; **i. física** physical impossibility

imposibilitado, -a *adj* (**a**) *(paralítico)* paralysed; *(discapacitado)* disabled; **se quedó i. de las piernas tras el accidente** he lost the use of both legs in the accident (**b**) *(incapaz)* **estar i. para hacer algo** to be unable to do sth; **se vio i. de seguir caminando debido a la herida** he was unable to carry on walking because of his injury

imposibilitar *vt* **i. a alguien (para) hacer algo** to make it impossible for sb to do sth, to prevent sb from doing sth; **las nuevas normas imposibilitan el fraude** the new regulations make fraud impossible; **el atentado imposibilitó el acuerdo** the attack made it impossible to reach an agreement; **la lesión lo imposibilita para moverse** he's unable to move because of the injury, the injury makes it impossible for him to move

imposible 1 *adj* (**a**) *(irrealizable)* impossible; **nos fue i. asistir** we were unable to be there; **es i. de arreglar** it's impossible to fix, it can't be fixed; **es i. que no se haya enterado** he must have found out; **es i. que se lo haya dicho** he can't possibly have told her; **hacer lo i.** to do everything possible and more

(**b**) *Fam (insoportable)* impossible; **estos niños son imposibles** these kids are impossible; **el tráfico en el centro estaba i.** the traffic in the centre was impossible *o* a nightmare

2 *nm* **me estás pidiendo un i.** you're asking the impossible of me; **pedir imposibles** to ask for the impossible

imposición *nf* (**a**) *(obligación)* imposition; **fue una i. de su jefe** it was imposed *o* forced on them by their boss

(**b**) *(de impuesto)* imposition; *(de condecoración)* awarding; **tras la i. de una pena de diez años** after he had been sentenced to ten years' prison

(**c**) *(impuesto)* taxation; **doble i.** double taxation ►► ***i. directa*** direct taxation; ***i. indirecta*** indirect taxation

(**d**) *Com* deposit; **hacer** *o* **efectuar una i.** to make a deposit ►► ***i. a plazo*** fixed-term deposit

(**e**) *Rel* ***i. de manos*** laying on of hands

Impositiva *nf Br* ≃ the Inland Revenue, *US* ≃ the IRS; **declarar algo a I.** to declare sth (to *Br* the Inland Revenue *o US* the IRS); **pagar a I.** to pay *Br* the Inland Revenue *o US* the IRS

impositivo, -a *adj* tax; **política impositiva** tax *o* taxation policy; **la carga impositiva de las empresas** the tax burden on companies

impositor, -ora *nm,f Esp* depositor

imposta *nf Arquit* impost

impostar *vt (la voz)* to make resonate

impostergable *adj* extremely urgent, impossible to postpone; **tengo una reunión i.** I have an extremely urgent meeting; **el debate es i.** the debate cannot be postponed

impostor, -ora 1 *adj (suplantador)* fraudulent

2 *nm,f (suplantador)* impostor

impostura *nf* (**a**) *(suplantación)* fraud (**b**) *(calumnia)* slander

impotencia *nf* (**a**) *(falta de fuerza, poder)* powerlessness, impotence (**b**) *(sexual)* impotence

impotente 1 *adj* (**a**) *(sin fuerza, poder)* powerless, impotent (**b**) *(sexual)* impotent

2 *nm* impotent man

impracticable *adj* (**a**) *(irrealizable)* impracticable (**b**) *(intransitable)* impassable

imprecación *nf Formal* imprecation, curse

imprecar [60] *vt Formal* to curse

imprecatorio, -a *adj Formal* imprecatory; **expresiones imprecatorias** imprecations, curses

imprecisión *nf* imprecision, vagueness; **contestó con imprecisiones** he gave vague answers

impreciso, -a *adj* imprecise, vague

impredecible *adj* (**a**) *(inesperado)* unforeseeable (**b**) *(imprevisible)* unpredictable

impregnación *nf* impregnation

impregnar 1 *vt* (**a**) *(empapar)* to soak (**de** in), to impregnate (**de** with); **impregna el paño en aceite** soak the cloth in oil (**b**) *(sujeto: olor)* to fill (**c**) *(sujeto: idea)* to pervade

2 **impregnarse** *vpr* (**a**) *(con líquido)* to get soaked (**de** in), to become impregnated (**de** with) (**b**) *(de olor)* to become filled (**de** with)

impremeditación *nf* lack of premeditation

impremeditado, -a *adj* unpremeditated

imprenta *nf* (**a**) *(máquina)* (printing) press (**b**) *(establecimiento)* printing house, printer's

imprentar *vt Chile (planchar)* to iron

imprescindible *adj* indispensable, essential; **mete sólo lo i.** only pack absolute essentials; **sé lo i. de informática** I know the basics of computing; **es i. subir los salarios** a pay rise is essential; **es i. que vengas** it is essential that you come; **i.: dominio de UNIX** *(en anuncio)* familiarity with UNIX essential

imprescriptible *adj (derecho)* imprescriptible

impresentable 1 *adj* unpresentable; **con esos pelos estás i.** you can't go anywhere with your hair like that

2 *nmf* **es un i.** he's a disgrace

impresión *nf* (**a**) *(efecto)* impression; **causar (una) buena/mala i.** to make a good/bad impression; **dar la i. de** to give the impression of; **me dio la i. de que estaban enfadados** I got the impression they were annoyed; **le dio mucha i. ver el cadáver** seeing the body was a real shock to him; **me causó mucha i. esa película** that film had a great effect on me ►► *Dep* ***i. artística*** artistic impression

(**b**) *(opinión)* **me gustaría conocer tu i. del tema** I'd like to know what your thoughts are on the issue; **tener la i. de que** to have the impression that; **cambiar impresiones** to compare notes, to exchange views

(**c**) *Esp Fam* **de i.** *(como intensificador)* incredible; **me di un susto de i.** I got a hell of a fright; **tiene una casa de i.** he has an incredible *o* amazing house

(**d**) *(huella)* imprint ►► ***i. dactilar*** fingerprint; ***i. digital*** fingerprint

(**e**) *Imprenta (acción)* printing; *(edición)* edition; **una i. de lujo** a deluxe edition; **i. en color** colour printing; **i. a una/dos caras** one-/two-sided printing ►► *Informát* ***i. subordinada*** background printing

impresionable *adj* impressionable

impresionante *adj* (**a**) *(asombroso, extraordinario)* amazing, astonishing; **tuvo un éxito i.** it was amazingly successful (**b**) *(conmovedor)* moving; **era i. verlos sufrir** it was terrible to watch them suffer (**c**) *(maravilloso)* impressive; **una puesta de sol i.** an impressive *o* spectacular sunset (**d**) *(grande)* enormous; **hace un frío i.** it's absolutely freezing

impresionar 1 *vt* (**a**) *(asombrar)* to amaze, to astonish

(**b**) *(emocionar)* to move; *(conmocionar, horrorizar)* to shock; **me impresiona mucho ver sangre** the sight of blood horrifies me; **le impresionó mucho ver el cadáver** seeing the body was a real shock to him

(**c**) *(maravillar)* to impress

(**d**) *Fot* to expose

(**e**) *RP (causar impresión)* **me impresionó muy bien/mal** he made a very good/bad impression on me

2 *vi* (**a**) *(asombrar)* to be amazing *o* astonishing (**b**) *(emocionar)* to be moving; *(conmocionar, horrorizar)* to be shocking (**c**) *(maravillar)* to make an impression (**d**) *(fanfarronear)* **lo dice sólo para i.** he's just saying that to show off *o* impress

3 **impresionarse** *vpr (maravillarse)* to be impressed; *(emocionarse)* to be moved; *(conmocionarse, horrorizarse)* to be shocked

impresionismo *nm* impressionism

impresionista 1 *adj* impressionist

2 *nmf* impressionist

impreso, -a 1 *participio ver* **imprimir**

2 *adj* printed

3 *nm* (**a**) *(texto)* printed sheet, printed matter; **impresos** *(en sobre)* printed matter (**b**) *(formulario)* form; **rellenar un i.** to fill in *o* out a form ►► ***i. de solicitud*** application form

impresor, -ora *nm,f (persona)* printer

impresora *nf Informát* printer ►► ***i. de agujas*** dot matrix printer; ***i. de chorro de tinta*** inkjet printer; ***i. de inyección*** bubble-jet (printer); ***i. láser*** laser printer; ***i. matricial*** dot matrix printer; ***i. térmica*** thermal printer

imprevisibilidad *nf* unpredictability

imprevisible *adj* unpredictable; **el tiempo aquí es muy i.** the weather here is very unpredictable; **una persona i.** an unpredictable person; **lograron un triunfo i.** they achieved an unexpected victory

imprevisión *nf* lack of foresight

imprevisor, -ora 1 *adj* lacking foresight

2 *nm,f* **es un i.** he doesn't think ahead

imprevisto, -a 1 *adj* unexpected

2 *nm* (**a**) *(hecho)* unforeseen circumstance; **surgió un i.** something unexpected happened; **salvo imprevistos** barring accidents (**b**) **imprevistos** *(gastos)* unforeseen expenses

imprimación *nf* (**a**) *(acción)* priming (**b**) *(sustancia)* primer

imprimátur *nm inv* imprimatur

imprimir 1 *vt* (**a**) *(libro, documento)* to print; **i. algo a todo color** to print sth in full colour; **impreso en México** printed in Mexico
(**b**) *(huella, paso)* to leave, to make; **imprimió sus pisadas en la alfombra** she left footprints on the carpet
(**c**) *(dar) (movimiento)* **i. velocidad a algo** to speed sth up; **el atleta mexicano imprimió un ritmo endiablado a la carrera** the Mexican athlete set a fiendish pace in the race
(**d**) *(dar) (carácter)* **imprimió a su novela un carácter revolucionario** she imbued her work with a revolutionary spirit; **imprimió a su gobierno un toque progresista** he brought a progressive touch to his government; **imprimieron al acuerdo un carácter conciliador** they made the agreement conciliatory in tone; **sus dibujos imprimen carácter al libro** her illustrations lend character to the book; **su voz imprime un sello propio al grupo** his voice gives the group its own distinctive quality
2 *vi* to print

improbabilidad *nf* improbability, unlikelihood

improbable *adj* improbable, unlikely; **es i. que lo consigamos** we are unlikely to get it, it's unlikely that we'll get it

ímprobo, -a *adj Formal (trabajo)* Herculean, enormous; *(esfuerzo)* enormous

improcedencia *nf* (**a**) *(desacierto)* inappropriateness (**b**) *Der* inadmissibility

improcedente *adj* (**a**) *(inoportuno)* inappropriate (**b**) *Der (pruebas)* inadmissible; **despido i.** wrongful dismissal

improductividad *nf* unproductiveness

improductivo, -a *adj* unproductive

impromptu *nm Mús* impromptu

impronta *nf* mark, impression; **llevar la i. de** to have the hallmarks of

impronunciable *adj* unpronounceable

improperio *nm* insult; **lanzar improperios** to sling insults

impropiedad *nf* (**a**) *(cualidad)* inappropriateness (**b**) *(dicho, hecho)* **eso es una i.** that's inaccurate

impropio, -a *adj* (**a**) *(no adecuado)* improper (**de** for), unbecoming (**de** to); **es un comportamiento i. de un cargo público** it is improper behaviour for someone in public office; **llevaba una camiseta impropia para la ocasión** she was wearing a T-shirt that was inappropriate for the occasion
(**b**) *(no habitual)* **es i. en ella** it's not what you expect from her; **tiene una madurez impropia de su edad** he's unusually mature for his age

improrrogable *adj (plazo)* unextendable; **durante seis días improrrogables** for six days only; **la fecha es i.** the deadline is final

improvisación *nf* improvisation

improvisadamente *adv* **comimos una tortilla preparada i.** we ate an omelette that we had thrown together; **se reunieron i. en el aparcamiento** they had an impromptu meeting in the car park

improvisado, -a *adj (comida, plan, actuación artística)* improvised; *(discurso)* impromptu; *(comentario)* ad-lib; *(cama, refugio)* makeshift

improvisador, -ora *adj* improviser

improvisar 1 *vt (discurso, plan, actuación artística)* to improvise; *(comida)* to rustle up, to improvise; **i. una cama** to make (up) a makeshift bed; **improvisaron un campamento para albergar a los refugiados** a makeshift camp was set up to provide shelter for the refugees
2 *vi (músico, orador, actor)* to improvise; *(al olvidar el diálogo)* to ad-lib

improviso: de improviso *loc adv* **llegó de i.** she arrived unexpectedly; **todo sucedió de i.** it all happened very suddenly; **se desató una tormenta de i.** a storm came out of the blue; *Esp* **coger a alguien de i.** to catch sb unawares

imprudencia *nf* (**a**) *(falta de prudencia) (en los actos)* carelessness, recklessness; *(en los comentarios)* indiscretion; **actuó con i.** she acted recklessly; **fue una i. conducir bebido** it was reckless of him to drive while he was drunk ►► *Der* ***i. concurrente*** contributory negligence; *Der* ***i. temeraria*** criminal negligence
(**b**) *(acción)* careless *o* reckless act, indiscretion; *(dicho indiscreto)* tactless remark, indiscretion; *(dicho desacertado)* foolish *o* reckless remark; **confiar en él fue una i.** it was unwise to trust him; **cometió una i. y atropelló a un peatón** she knocked over a pedestrian as a result of a reckless piece of driving

imprudente 1 *adj (en los actos)* careless, rash; *(en los comentarios)* indiscreet; **es muy i. al conducir** he's a reckless driver
2 *nmf* (**a**) *(en los actos)* reckless person; **es un auténtico i.** he's very reckless (**b**) *(en los comentarios)* indiscreet person; **es un i.** he's very indiscreet

impúber 1 *adj* pre-pubescent
2 *nmf* pre-pubescent child

impublicable *adj* unpublishable

impudicia *nf* immodesty; **viste con i.** she dresses rather immodestly

impúdico, -a *adj* immodest, indecent

> **Falso amigo**: El adjetivo inglés **impudent** no es la traducción del español **impúdico**. En inglés, **impudent** significa "desvergonzado, insolente".

impudor *nm* immodesty

impuesto, -a 1 *participio ver* **imponer**
2 *nm* tax; **pagar impuestos** to pay tax *o* taxes; **ganamos cinco millones antes de impuestos** we earned five million before tax; **beneficios antes de impuestos** pre-tax profits; **libre de impuestos** *(alcohol, cigarrillos)* tax-free, duty-free ►► ***i. sobre actividades económicas*** = Spanish tax paid by professionals and shop owners; ***i. adicional*** surtax; ***i. sobre el capital*** capital tax; ***i. de circulación*** road tax; ***i. complementario*** surtax; ***i. al consumo*** tax on consumption; ***i. directo*** direct tax; ***i. ecológico*** ecotax, green tax; ***i. indirecto*** indirect tax; ***i. de lujo*** luxury tax; ***i. de matriculación*** = tax paid on a new car; ***i. municipal*** local tax; ***i. sobre el patrimonio*** wealth tax; ***i. sobre plusvalías*** capital gains tax; ***i. progresivo*** progressive tax; ***i. sobre la propiedad inmobiliaria*** property tax; *Fig* ***i. de protección*** protection money; ***i. sobre la renta (de las personas físicas)*** income tax; *Fig* ***i. revolucionario*** revolutionary tax, = protection money paid by businessmen to terrorists; ***i. de sociedades*** corporation tax; ***i. de sucesión*** inheritance tax; ***i. sobre sucesiones*** inheritance tax; *Am* ***i. sobre el valor agregado*** value-added tax; *Esp* ***i. sobre el valor añadido*** value-added tax

impugnable *adj* contestable

impugnación *nf* contestation, challenge

impugnar *vt* to contest, to challenge

impulsar *vt* (**a**) *(empujar)* to propel, to drive (**b**) *(incitar)* **i. a alguien (a algo)** to drive sb (to sth); **¿qué te impulsó a marcharte?** what drove you to leave? (**c**) *(promocionar) (economía)* to stimulate; *(amistad)* to foster; **debemos i. las relaciones Norte-Sur** we should promote North-South relations; **las claves que impulsan el sector** the key drivers for the industry

impulsivamente *adv* impulsively

impulsividad *nf* impulsiveness

impulsivo, -a 1 *adj* impulsive
2 *nm,f* impulsive person, hothead

impulso *nm* (**a**) *Fís* impulse
(**b**) *(empuje)* momentum; **llevaba tanto i. que no pudo detenerse** he was going so fast that he couldn't stop; **tomar i.** *(tomar carrerilla)* to take a run-up; **esta nueva tendencia está tomando mucho i.** this new tendency is gaining momentum
(**c**) *(estímulo)* stimulus, boost; **la medida supondrá un i. al consumo** the measure will boost consumption; **dar i. a una iniciativa** to encourage *o* promote an initiative
(**d**) *(deseo, reacción)* impulse, urge; **un i. me hizo gritar** a sudden impulse made me shout; **mi primer i. fue marcharme** my first instinct was to leave; **sentir el i. de hacer algo** to feel the urge to do sth; **se deja llevar por sus impulsos** he acts on impulse

impulsor, -ora 1 *adj* driving; **fuerza impulsora** driving force
2 *nm,f* dynamic force; **él fue el i. del proyecto** he was the driving force behind the project

impune *adj* unpunished; **quedar i.** to go unpunished

impunemente *adv* with impunity

impunidad *nf* impunity; **las armas químicas se utilizaron con total i.** chemical weapons were used with total impunity

impuntual *adj* unpunctual

impuntualidad *nf* unpunctuality

impureza *nf* (**a**) *(elemento extraño)* impurity (**b**) *(del agua)* impurity (**c**) *(falta de decencia)* impurity

impuro, -a *adj* (**a**) *(aire, agua)* impure (**b**) *(inmoral)* impure

impusiera *etc ver* **imponer**

imputabilidad *nf* imputability

imputable *adj* attributable; **un accidente i. a un fallo técnico** an accident caused by a technical fault; **un error i. al director** a mistake for which the manager was responsible

imputación *nf* accusation

imputar *vt* (**a**) *(atribuir)* **i. algo a alguien** *(delito)* to accuse sb of sth; *(fracaso, error)* to attribute sth to sb; **i. algo a algo** *(error, accidente)* to attribute sth to sth, to put sth down to sth; **negó los cargos que se le imputaban** he denied the charges made against him (**b**) *Com* to allocate, to assign

IMSERSO [im'serso] *nm* (*abrev de* **Instituto de Migraciones y Servicios Sociales**) = Spanish government agency responsible for social services for the elderly and disabled, and for citizens living, or recently returned from, abroad

IMSS *nm* (*abrev de* **Instituto Mexicano del Seguro Social**) *Br* ≃ NHS, *US* ≃ Medicaid

in *adj Fam* in; **una de las zonas más in de la ciudad** one of the most in places to go in town; **está in hablar de agricultura ecológica** it's very in *o* trendy to talk about organic farming

inabarcable *adj* **un concepto i.** a concept which is too vast to grasp; **es una ciudad i.** it's such a big city that it's impossible to take it all in; **posee una cultura i.** he is immensely cultured

inabordable *adj* (**a**) *(persona)* unapproachable (**b**) *(tema)* **un asunto i. para los políticos** a subject which politicians do not want to broach

inacabable *adj* interminable, endless

inacabado, -a *adj* unfinished

inaccesibilidad *nf* inaccessibility

inaccesible *adj* (**a**) *(lugar, montaña)* inaccessible (**b**) *(persona) (por carácter)* unapproachable; *(difícil de contactar)* inaccessible (**c**) *(tema, idea)* inaccessible

inacción *nf* inaction, inactivity

inacentuado, -a *adj (vocal)* unaccented; *(sílaba)* unstressed

inaceptable *adj* unacceptable

inactivación *nf* inactivation

inactivar *vt Quím (gen, proteína)* to deactivate, to switch off

inactividad *nf* (**a**) *(de persona)* inactivity (**b**) *(de mercado)* sluggishness

inactivo, -a *adj* (**a**) *(persona)* inactive (**b**) *(mercado)* sluggish, flat (**c**) *(volcán)* inactive, dormant

inadaptable *adj* unadaptable

inadaptación *nf (psicológica)* maladjustment; **los inmigrantes sufren problemas de i. social** immigrants have difficulty fitting into society

inadaptado, -a 1 *adj* maladjusted
2 *nm,f* misfit; **es un i. social** he is a social misfit

inadecuación *nf* mismatch (**entre** between); **la i. del producto a las necesidades del mercado** the fact the product fails to meet the needs of the market

inadecuado, -a *adj (conducta, comportamiento)* inappropriate; *(iluminación)* inadequate; *(traje)* unsuitable; **muchos niños reciben una alimentación inadecuada** many children do not have a proper diet; **este es un lugar i. para discutir del tema** I don't think this is the best *o* right place to discuss the matter

inadmisible *adj* inadmissible

inadvertencia *nf* **el accidente se produjo por una i. del conductor** the accident was caused by a mistake by the driver; **una corrección que se me pasó por i.** a correction which I inadvertently missed

inadvertidamente *adv* inadvertently

inadvertido, -a *adj* unnoticed; **pasar i.** to go unnoticed

inagotable *adj* (**a**) *(fuente de energía)* inexhaustible; *(paciencia)* infinite; **sus conocimientos de informática son inagotables** she's infinitely knowledgeable about computers; **su conducta era una fuente i. de chistes** her behaviour was an endless *o* inexhaustible source of jokes (**b**) *Fam (persona)* **este niño es i.** this child never stops

inaguantable *adj (dolor, persona)* unbearable; **los alumnos están hoy inaguantables** the pupils are being unbearable today

INAH ['ina] *nm* (*abrev de* **Instituto Nacional de Antropología e Historia**) = Spanish state body responsible for museums and sites of archaeological interest

inalámbrico, -a 1 *adj* cordless
2 *nm (teléfono)* cordless phone; *(micrófono)* wireless

in albis *loc adv* in the dark; **quedarse i.** to be left none the wiser

inalcanzable *adj* unattainable

inalienable *adj* inalienable

inalterabilidad *nf* immutability

inalterable *adj* (**a**) *(salud)* stable; *(amistad)* undying; *(principios)* unshakeable; *(decisión)* final; **permanecer i.** to remain unchanged (**b**) *(color)* fast (**c**) *(rostro, carácter)* impassive (**d**) *Dep Fam* **el marcador permanece i.** the score remains unchanged

inalterado, -a *adj* unaltered, unchanged

inamovible *adj* immovable, fixed

inane *adj Formal* futile

inanición *nf* starvation; **morir de i.** to die of starvation, to starve to death

inanidad *nf Formal* futility

inanimado, -a *adj* inanimate

inánime *adj Formal* lifeless

inapagable *adj* (**a**) *(llamas)* inextinguishable (**b**) *(deseo, sed)* unquenchable

inapelable *adj* (**a**) *Der* not open to appeal; **el fallo será i.** there will be no right of appeal against the ruling (**b**) *(inevitable)* inevitable

inapetencia *nf* lack of appetite

inapetente *adj* lacking in appetite; **estar i.** to have no appetite

inaplazable *adj* (**a**) *(reunión, sesión)* **el debate es i.** the debate cannot be postponed *o* put off (**b**) *(necesidad)* urgent, pressing

inaplicable *adj* inapplicable, not applicable

inapreciable *adj* (**a**) *(incalculable)* invaluable, inestimable (**b**) *(insignificante)* imperceptible

inapropiado, -a *adj* inappropriate, unsuitable

inarrugable *adj* crease-resistant

inarticulado, -a *adj* inarticulate

in articulo mortis *loc adv Formal* in articulo mortis

inasequible *adj* (**a**) *(por el precio)* prohibitive; **en este momento una casa me resulta i.** I can't afford to buy a house at the moment (**b**) *(meta, ambición)* unattainable (**c**) *(persona)* unapproachable

inasistencia *nf* absence (**a** from)

inastillable *adj* shatterproof

inatacable *adj* (**a**) *(fortaleza, país)* unassailable (**b**) *(argumento)* irrefutable

inatención *nf* inattention

inatento, -a *adj* inattentive

inaudible *adj* inaudible

inaudito, -a *adj* unprecedented, unheard-of; **¡esto es i.!** *(expresa indignación)* this is outrageous *o* unheard-of!

inauguración *nf* (**a**) *(acto) (de edificio, puente, Juegos Olímpicos)* opening (ceremony); *(de congreso)* opening session; **ceremonia de i.** opening ceremony (**b**) *(entrada en funcionamiento) (de carretera, pantano)* opening; **la i. de la central nuclear** the commissioning of the nuclear power station

inaugural *adj* opening, inaugural

inaugurar *vt (edificio, congreso)* to (officially) open; *(año académico, época)* to mark the beginning of, to inaugurate; *(estatua)* to unveil; **el delantero inauguró el marcador en el minuto 5** the forward opened the scoring in the fifth minute

INB *Esp Antes* (*abrev de* **Instituto Nacional de Bachillerato**) = state secondary school for 14-18-year-olds, *US* ≃ Senior High School

inca 1 *adj* Inca
2 *nmf* Inca

incaico, -a *adj* Inca

incalculable *adj* (**a**) *(que no se puede calcular)* incalculable (**b**) *(grande)* **de i. valor** *(cuadro, casa)* priceless; *(ayuda)* invaluable

incalificable *adj* unspeakable, indescribable; **su comportamiento fue i.** her behaviour was unspeakable, she behaved unspeakably

incanato *nm* Inca empire

incandescencia *nf* incandescence

incandescente *adj* incandescent

incansable *adj* untiring, tireless

incansablemente *adv* untiringly, tirelessly

incapacidad *nf* (**a**) *(imposibilidad)* inability
(**b**) *(falta de aptitud)* **su i. para organizar fiestas es manifiesta** he's clearly no good at *o* useless at organizing parties; **tengo i. para los idiomas** I'm no good at *o* useless at languages
(**c**) *Der* incapacity ▸▸ ***i. laboral*** industrial disability *o Br* disablement; ***i. laboral transitoria*** temporary disability; ***i. legal*** legal incapacity; ***i. permanente*** invalidity; ***i. temporal*** temporary disability

incapacitación *nf* (**a**) *(física, psicológica)* incapacitation (**b**) *Der (para ejercer cargos, votar)* disqualification; *(para testar, testificar)* incapacity

incapacitado, -a 1 *adj* (**a**) *(físicamente, psicológicamente)* unfit; **está i. para conducir vehículos** he is unfit to drive; **quedó i. tras un accidente** he was disabled in an accident (**b**) *Der (para ejercer cargos, votar)* disqualified (**para** from); *(para testar, testificar)* incapacitated
2 *nm,f* (**a**) *(físico)* disabled person; *(psicológico)* mentally handicapped person (**b**) *Der* disqualified person, person declared unfit

incapacitar *vt* (**a**) *(sujeto: circunstancias) (para trabajar)* to render unfit (**para** for); **su lesión en la columna lo incapacita para el deporte de competición** his spinal injury makes him unable to participate in competitive sport
(**b**) *Der (sujeto: circunstancias) (para ejercer cargos, votar)* to disqualify (**para** from); *(sujeto: juez) (para ejercer cargos, votar)* to disqualify, to declare disqualified (**para** from); *(para trabajar)* to declare unfit (**para** for *o* to)

incapaz 1 *adj* (**a**) *(no capaz)* incapable (**de** of); **fuimos incapaces de coronar la cumbre** we weren't able to *o* didn't manage to reach the top; **es i. de hacer daño a nadie** he would never harm anyone; **es i. de matar una mosca** he wouldn't hurt a fly; **es i. de pedir perdón** she would never say she's sorry; **me siento i. de seguir** I don't feel able to continue; **es i. de hacer una suma sin equivocarse** he can't do the simplest sum without making a mistake
(**b**) *(sin talento)* **i. para** no good at, useless at; **soy i. para las sumas** I'm no good at *o* useless at sums
(**c**) *Der* **declarar i. a alguien** to declare sb incapable *o* unfit
2 *nmf* incompetent, incompetent person

incario *nm* Inca Empire

incásico, -a *adj* Inca

incautación *nf* seizure, confiscation

incautamente *adv* incautiously, unwarily

incautarse *vpr* (**a**) *Der* **i. de** to seize, to confiscate; **la policía se incautó de un alijo de heroína** the police seized a consignment of heroin (**b**) *(apoderarse)* **i. de** to grab

incauto, -a 1 *adj* gullible, naive
2 *nm,f* gullible *o* naive person; **es un i.** he's very gullible *o* naive

incendiar 1 *vt* to set fire to; **los guerrilleros incendiaron varios casas** the guerrillas set fire to *o* torched several houses
2 incendiarse *vpr* to catch fire; **se ha incendiado el bosque** the forest has caught fire *o* is on fire

incendiario, -a 1 *adj* (**a**) *(bomba)* incendiary (**b**) *(artículo, libro)* inflammatory
2 *nm,f* arsonist, fire-raiser

incendio *nm* fire; **peligro de i.** *(en letrero)* fire hazard ►► ***i. forestal*** forest fire; ***i. provocado:*** **fue un i. provocado** it was a case of arson

incensario *nm* censer

incentivación *nf* **el plan pretende la i. de la pequeña empresa** the plan seeks to provide incentives for small businesses; **una campaña de i. al voto** a campaign to encourage people to vote; **programa de i.** incentive scheme

incentivador, -ora *adj* **medidas incentivadoras de las exportaciones** measures that provide an incentive to encourage exports

incentivar *vt* to encourage; **incentivan la compra de vehículos con rebajas fiscales** they are using tax cuts as an incentive to encourage people to buy vehicles

incentivo *nm* incentive; **un i. para la compra de viviendas** an incentive for people to buy their own home ►► ***i. fiscal*** tax incentive

incertidumbre *nf* uncertainty

incesante *adj* incessant, ceaseless

incesantemente *adv* incessantly, ceaselessly

incesto *nm* incest

incestuoso, -a *adj* incestuous

incidencia *nf* (**a**) *(repercusión)* impact, effect; **tener i. sobre algo** to have an impact *o* effect on sth
(**b**) *(suceso)* event; **me contó las incidencias de la reunión** she told me what had happened at the meeting; **el viaje transcurrió sin incidencias** the journey passed without incident; **siguen las incidencias del conflicto con interés** they are following developments in the conflict with interest
(**c**) *Geom* incidence

incidental *adj* incidental

incidentalmente *adv* (**a**) *(por casualidad)* by chance; **i. pasaba por ahí** I happened to be passing (**b**) *(a propósito)* incidentally

incidente 1 *adj (luz, rayo)* incident
2 *nm* incident; **el viaje transcurrió sin incidentes** the journey passed without incident; **tuve un pequeño i. con mi jefe** I had a minor altercation with my boss; **los hinchas ingleses protagonizaron graves incidentes** there were some serious incidents involving English fans

incidir *vi* (**a**) **i. en** *(incurrir en)* to fall into, to lapse into; **volví a i. en los mismos errores** I made the same mistakes again
(**b**) **i. en** *(insistir en)* to emphasize; **el conferenciante incidió en la importancia de una alimentación sana** the lecturer emphasized the importance of a healthy diet
(**c**) **i. en** *(influir en)* to have an impact on, to affect; **el frío incide en el consumo energético** cold weather affects energy consumption
(**d**) **i. en** *o* **sobre** *(luz, ondas, proyectil)* to hit, to fall on

incienso *nm* incense; **oro, i. y mirra** gold, frankincense and myrrh

incierto, -a *adj* (**a**) *(dudoso)* uncertain; **les espera un futuro i.** their future is uncertain (**b**) *(falso)* untrue

incinerable *adj* incinerable

incineración *nf* (**a**) *(de cadáver)* cremation (**b**) *(de basura)* incineration

incineradora *nf*, **incinerador** *nm (de basura)* incinerator ►► ***i. de residuos*** waste incinerator

incinerar *vt* (**a**) *(cadáver)* to cremate (**b**) *(basura)* to incinerate

incipiente *adj* (**a**) *(calvicie)* incipient; **lucía una barba i.** *(de joven)* he was starting to get a beard; *(sin afeitar)* his chin was covered in stubble (**b**) *(inicial)* incipient; *(democracia)* fledgling; *(amistad, talento)* budding

incircunciso, -a *adj* uncircumcised

incisión *nf* incision

incisivo, -a 1 *adj* (**a**) *(instrumento)* sharp, cutting (**b**) *(diente)* **diente i.** incisor (**c**) *(mordaz)* incisive
2 *nm (diente)* incisor

inciso *nm* (**a**) *(corto)* comment, passing remark; *(más largo)* digression; **me gustaría hacer un i.** I'd like to digress for a moment (**b**) *Urug Der (párrafo)* paragraph

incitación *nf* incitement; **sus declaraciones fueron una i. a la violencia** her statements constituted an incitement to violence

incitador, -ora 1 *adj* inciting
2 *nm,f* inciter

incitante *adj* (**a**) *(insinuante)* provocative (**b**) *(interesante)* enticing

incitar *vt* to incite; **un discurso que incita a la violencia** a speech inciting people to violence; **el hambre lo incitó a robar** hunger made him steal; **¿qué le incitó a hacerlo?** what made him do it?; **i. a alguien a la fuga/venganza** to urge sb to flee/avenge himself

incivil, incívico, -a *adj* antisocial

incivilizado, -a *adj* uncivilized

incl. (*abrev de* **inclusive**) incl.

inclasificable *adj* unclassifiable

inclemencia *nf* harshness, inclemency; **las inclemencias del tiempo** the inclemency of the weather

inclemente *adj* harsh, inclement

inclinación *nf* (**a**) *(de terreno, tejado)* slope; **una i. del 15 por ciento** *(en carretera)* a gradient of 15 percent; **preocupa la i. del edificio** the angle at which the building is leaning is cause for concern ►► *Fís* ***i. magnética*** magnetic inclination *o* dip
(**b**) *(afición)* penchant *o* propensity (**a** *o* **por** for); **preocupa la i. a la violencia de los seguidores del equipo** the team's fans' penchant for violence is worrying; **tiene una i. natural por la música** she has a natural bent for music; **tiene i. a utilizar colores vivos** he favours bright colours; **siento i. por el golf** I'm keen on golf ►► ***i. sexual*** sexual orientation
(**c**) *(cariño)* **i. hacia** *o* **por alguien** fondness towards sb
(**d**) *(saludo)* bow; **hizo una i. cuando pasaba el obispo** he bowed as the bishop went past; **nos saludó con una i. de cabeza** he greeted us with a nod

inclinado, -a *adj* (**a**) *(edificio, torre)* leaning, slanting; *(terreno)* sloping (**b**) *(cabeza)* bowed (**c**) *(objeto)* sloping, at *o* on a slant; **ese cuadro está i.** that picture isn't straight (**d**) *(tendente)* **una persona muy inclinada a la depresión** a person who is very prone to depression; **no estoy i. a aceptar sus argumentos** I'm not inclined to accept their arguments

inclinar 1 *vt* (**a**) *(doblar)* to bend; *(ladear)* to tilt; *Fig* **i. la balanza a favor de** to tip the balance in favour of (**b**) *(cabeza)* to bow; **inclinó la cabeza hacia un lado** she tilted her head to one side (**c**) *(influir)* **i. a alguien a hacer algo** to make sb inclined to do sth; **el anuncio me**

inclinó a no invertir the advertisement made me inclined not to invest

2 **inclinarse** *vpr* (a) *(doblarse)* to lean; **la grúa se está inclinando peligrosamente** the crane is leaning *o* tilting dangerously; **inclínate hacia adelante** lean forward; *Fig* **la balanza se inclinó a nuestro favor** the balance tipped in our favour

(b) *(para saludar)* to bow (**ante** before)

(c) *(tender)* to be *o* feel inclined (**a** to); **me inclino a pensar que no** I'm rather inclined to think not; **me inclino a aceptar** I feel *o* I am inclined to accept

(d) *(preferir)* **inclinarse por** to favour, to lean towards

ínclito, -a *adj Formal* illustrious

incluir [34] *vt* (a) *(comprender)* to include; **el precio incluye desayuno y cena en el hotel** the price includes breakfast and evening meals at the hotel (b) *(adjuntar)* to enclose (c) *(contener)* to contain (d) *(poner)* **te he incluido en la lista de participantes** I've included *o* put you on the list of participants; **a mí no me incluyas** count me out

inclusa *nf* foundling hospital, orphanage

inclusero, -a *nm,f* = person (who has been) brought up in an orphanage

inclusión *nf* inclusion

inclusive *adv* inclusive; **las solicitudes se pueden pedir hasta el día 15 i.** application forms may be requested up to and including the 15th; **del primero al tercero, ambos i.** from the first to the third inclusive

incluso 1 *adv* even; **me gustó i. a mí** even I liked it; **la comida de ayer estaba buena, la de hoy, mejor i.** yesterday's meal was good, and today's was even better

2 *prep* even; **todos, i. tú, debemos ayudar** we must all help, even you

incluyera *etc ver* **incluir**

incluyo *etc ver* **incluir**

incoación *nf* commencement, inception

incoar *vt* to commence, to initiate

incoativo, -a *adj Gram* inchoative

incobrable *adj* irrecoverable

incoercible *adj* incoercible

incógnita *nf* (a) *Mat* unknown (quantity) (b) *(misterio)* mystery; **el contenido del libro sigue siendo una i.** the book's contents remain a mystery; **esta tarde se despejará la i.** the mystery will be cleared up this evening; **todavía queda la i. de saber cuántos vendrán** we still don't know how many people will come

incógnito, -a 1 *adj* unknown

2 **de incógnito** *loc adv* **viajar/estar de i.** to travel/be incognito

incognoscible *adj* unknowable

incoherencia *nf* (a) *(inconexión)* incoherence (b) *(inconsecuencia)* inconsistency (c) *(comentario absurdo)* nonsensical remark; **no dice más que incoherencias** nothing he says makes sense, he's just talking nonsense (d) *(hecho)* **comprar ese abrigo de pieles fue una i.** buying that fur coat was inconsistent with her principles

incoherente *adj* (a) *(inconexo)* incoherent (b) *(inconsecuente)* inconsistent

incoloro, -a *adj* (a) *(líquido, mineral)* colourless (b) *(persona)* colourless

incólume *adj Formal* unscathed; **salió i. del accidente** he emerged unscathed from the accident

incombustible *adj* (a) *(resistente al fuego)* fire-resistant (b) *(person)* **es i.** he's still going strong; **el i. líder del partido se vuelve a presentar a las elecciones** the party leader, who is still going strong after all these years, is standing for election once more

incomestible, incomible *adj* inedible

incómodamente *adv* uncomfortably

incomodar 1 *vt* (a) *(causar molestia)* to bother, to inconvenience; *(violentar)* to embarrass, to make uncomfortable; **su presencia me incomoda** her presence makes me feel uncomfortable *o* uneasy; **me incomoda su impuntualidad** his lack of punctuality is a nuisance for me; **¿te incomoda que fume?** would it bother you if I smoked?, do you mind if I smoke?; **¿te incomoda que te pregunte por tu vida privada?** do you mind if I ask you about your private life?

(b) *(enfadar)* to annoy

2 **incomodarse** *vpr* (a) *(violentarse)* to get embarrassed *o* uncomfortable; **se incomodó mucho cuando le pregunté por su edad** she was very embarrasssed when I asked how old she was (b) *(enfadarse)* to get annoyed (**por** about)

incomodidad *nf* (a) *(de silla)* uncomfortableness (b) *(de situación, persona)* awkwardness, discomfort; **su pregunta me produjo i.** her question made me feel awkward *o* uncomfortable; **es una i. vivir tan lejos del centro** it's inconvenient living so far from the centre

incomodo *nm* **te acompaño, no es ningún i.** I'll go with you, it's no trouble

incómodo, -a *adj* (a) *(silla, postura)* uncomfortable; **ya sabes lo i. que es viajar en autobús** you know how uncomfortable travelling by bus is

(b) *(situación)* awkward, uncomfortable; **una pregunta incómoda** an awkward question; **me resulta i. hablar con ella de estos temas** I find it embarrassing *o* I feel uncomfortable talking to her about these matters; **sentirse i.** to feel awkward *o* uncomfortable

(c) *(persona)* bothersome; **ese es un político i.** that politician is an awkward customer

incomparable *adj* incomparable

incomparablemente *adv* incomparably

incomparecencia *nf* failure to appear; **el juicio se suspendió por i. de una de las partes** the trial was suspended because one of the parties failed to appear in court; **el equipo perdió tres puntos por i.** the team was deducted three points for failing to turn up

incompatibilidad *nf* (a) *(de medicamento, soluciones)* incompatibility; **hay i. entre los dos sistemas informáticos** the two computer systems are incompatible ►► *Der* ***i. de caracteres*** incompatibility; **entre ellos hay i. de caracteres** their personalities really clash

(b) *(de funcionario)* conflict of interests; **defiende que no hay i. entre su cargo de ministro y el de directivo de la empresa** he maintains that there is no conflict of interests between his ministerial post and his position as director of the company; **ley de incompatibilidades** = act regulating which other positions may be held by people holding public office

incompatible *adj* (a) *(medicamento, personalidad)* incompatible (**con** with); **el perdón es i. con el rencor** forgiveness and resentment are incompatible; **un programa i. con versiones anteriores del sistema operativo** a program which is incompatible with previous versions of the operating system

(b) *(cargo)* **estos dos puestos son incompatibles** the two posts cannot be held by the same person at the same time

incompetencia *nf* incompetence

incompetente *adj* incompetent

incompleto, -a *adj* (a) *(falto de una parte)* incomplete (b) *(inacabado)* unfinished

incomprendido, -a 1 *adj* misunderstood

2 *nm,f* misunderstood person; **fue siempre un i.** no one ever understood him

incomprensibilidad *nf* incomprehensibility

incomprensible *adj* incomprehensible; **su discurso me resultó i.** I couldn't understand his speech; **me parece i. que ahora quiera marcharse** I find it incomprehensible that she wants to leave now, I cannot understand why she wants to leave now

incomprensiblemente *adv* incomprehensibly

incomprensión *nf* lack of understanding

incomprensivo, -a *adj* unsympathetic

incomunicación *nf* (a) *(falta de comunicación)* lack of communication (b) *(de una localidad)* isolation (c) *(de preso)* solitary confinement; **protestaron por la i. de los detenidos** they complained about the fact that the detainees had been held incommunicado

incomunicado, -a *adj* (a) **estar i.** *(sin líneas de comunicación)* to be isolated; *(por la nieve)* to be cut off (b) **estar i.** *(preso)* to be in solitary confinement; *(detenido)* to be held incommunicado

incomunicar [60] *vt* (a) *(dejar sin líneas de comunicación)* to keep isolated; *(sujeto: la nieve)* to cut off (b) *(preso)* to place in solitary confinement; *(detenido)* to hold incommunicado

inconcebible *adj* inconceivable; **es i. que no te guste** it's inconceivable that you won't like it; **resulta i. que no se dé cuenta del daño que causa** it's unbelievable *o* it seems inconceivable that he doesn't realize the damage he's causing

inconcebiblemente *adv* inconceivably

inconciliable *adj* irreconcilable

inconcluso, -a *adj* unfinished

inconcreto, -a *adj* vague, imprecise

inconcuso, -a *adj Formal* indisputable

incondicional 1 *adj* (a) *(rendición, perdón)* unconditional; *(ayuda)* wholehearted (b) *(seguidor)* staunch

2 *nmf* staunch supporter

inconficionalmente *adv* unconditionally

inconducta *nf RP* misbehaviour

inconexo, -a *adj* (**a**) *(parte)* unconnected (**b**) *(pensamiento, texto)* disjointed

inconfesable *adj* shameful, unmentionable

inconfeso, -a *adj* **murió i.** he died without confessing

inconforme 1 *adj* **mostrarse i. con algo** not to be in agreement with sth, to disagree with sth; **una persona de carácter i.** a nonconformist
2 *nmf* nonconformist

inconformismo *nm* nonconformism

inconformista 1 *adj* nonconformist
2 *nmf* nonconformist

inconfundible *adj* unmistakable

inconfundiblemente *adv* unmistakably

incongruencia *nf* (**a**) *(cualidad)* inconsistency (**b**) **hacer/decir una i.** *(algo fuera de lugar)* to do/say sth incongruous; *(algo absurdo)* to do/say sth crazy *o* illogical; **lleno de incongruencias** *(relato, libro)* full of inconsistencies

incongruente *adj (fuera de lugar)* incongruous; *(desarticulado)* inconsistent; *(absurdo)* crazy, illogical

inconmensurabilidad *nf (de espacio)* vastness

inconmensurable *adj* (**a**) *(sentimiento)* unmeasurable (**b**) *(espacio)* vast

inconmovible *adj* (**a**) *(seguro, firme)* firm, solid (**b**) *(inalterable)* unshakeable, unyielding

inconmutable *adj* immutable

inconquistable *adj* unassailable, impregnable

inconsciencia *nf* (**a**) *(aturdimiento, desmayo)* unconsciousness; **el accidentado estaba en estado de i.** the accident victim was unconscious (**b**) *(falta de juicio)* thoughtlessness

inconsciente 1 *adj* (**a**) *(sin conocimiento)* unconscious; **estar i.** to be unconscious (**b**) *(reflejo)* unconscious; **un acto i.** an unconscious action (**c**) *(irreflexivo)* thoughtless, reckless; **i. de lo que hacía, se fue metiendo en la jungla** without realizing what she was doing, she went deeper and deeper into the jungle
2 *nmf* thoughtless *o* reckless person; **es un i.** he's very thoughtless *o* reckless
3 *nm Psi* **el i.** the unconscious; **el i. colectivo** the collective unconscious

inconscientemente *adv (sin darse cuenta)* unconsciously, unwittingly

inconsecuencia *nf* inconsistency

inconsecuente 1 *adj* inconsistent; **ser i. con algo** to be inconsistent with sth
2 *nmf* inconsistent person; **es un i.** he's very inconsistent

inconsistencia *nf* flimsiness

inconsistente *adj* flimsy, insubstantial

inconsolable *adj* disconsolate

inconsolablemente *adv* inconsolably

inconstancia *nf* (**a**) *(en el trabajo, la conducta)* unreliability (**b**) *(de opinión, ideas)* changeability

inconstante *adj* (**a**) *(en el trabajo, escuela)* **es muy i.** he never sticks at anything (**b**) *(de opinión, ideas)* changeable, fickle

inconstitucional *adj* unconstitutional

inconstitucionalidad *nf* unconstitutionality

incontable *adj* (**a**) *(innumerable)* countless, innumerable (**b**) *Gram* uncountable

incontaminado, -a *adj* uncontaminated, unpolluted

incontenible *adj (alegría)* unbounded; *(llanto)* uncontrollable; **me entró un deseo i. de comerme una ensalada** I had an uncontrollable urge to eat a salad

incontestable *adj* (**a**) *(argumento, razones)* indisputable; **ganaron al equipo visitante por un i. 6-0** they thrashed the visitors 6-0 (**b**) *(campeón, líder)* undisputed

incontestado, -a *adj (argumentos)* uncontested, unquestioned; **el líder i. de los socialistas** the undisputed leader of the socialists

incontinencia *nf* (**a**) *(vicio)* lack of restraint (**b**) *Med* incontinence

incontinente *adj* (**a**) *(insaciable)* lacking all restraint (**b**) *Med* incontinent

incontrolable *adj* uncontrollable

incontrolado, -a 1 *adj* (**a**) *(velocidad)* furious; *(vehículo)* out of control; *(situación)* out of hand; *(aumento de precios)* spiralling; **la explotación incontrolada de los recursos naturales** the uncontrolled exploitation of natural resources; **un vertedero i.** an unauthorized rubbish tip
(**b**) *(comando)* maverick, not controlled by the leadership; **aficionados incontrolados se enfrentaron a la policía** wild fans clashed with police
2 *nm* **un grupo de incontrolados asaltó la redacción del periódico** a wild mob attacked the paper's editorial staff

incontrovertible *adj* incontrovertible, indisputable

inconveniencia *nf* (**a**) *(inoportunidad)* inappropriateness (**b**) *(comentario)* tactless remark; *(acto)* faux pas, mistake

inconveniente 1 *adj* (**a**) *(inoportuno)* inappropriate (**b**) *(descortés)* rude
2 *nm* (**a**) *(dificultad)* obstacle, problem; **si no tienes (ningún) i., me voy a marchar** if you don't mind *o* if it's all right by you, I'll leave; **han puesto inconvenientes a su nombramiento** they have raised objections to his appointment; **no tener i. en hacer algo** to have no objection to doing sth; **no tengo i. en que venga ella también** I have no problem with *o* I have no objection to her coming too; **¿tienes algún i.?** is that all right with you?, do you have any objections?
(**b**) *(desventaja)* disadvantage, drawback; **las ventajas y los inconvenientes de una propuesta** the advantages and disadvantages of a proposal; **tiene el i. de que es muy caro** it suffers from the disadvantage *o* drawback of being very expensive; **tu plan presenta** *o* **reúne algunos inconvenientes** your plan has some drawbacks

incordiar *Esp Fam* **1** *vt* to bother, to pester
2 *vi* to be a pest; **¡deja ya de i.!** stop being such a pest!

incordio *nm Esp Fam* pain; **este coche es un i.** this car is a real pain; **nuestros vecinos son un i.** our neighbours are a pain (in the neck); **es un i. tener que madrugar tanto** it's a pain having to get up so early

incorporación *nf (unión, adición)* incorporation (**a** into); **la escasa i. de la mujer al mercado laboral** the low number of women in the labour market; **su i. tendrá lugar el día 31** *(a un puesto)* she starts work on the 31st; **la i. a filas de los nuevos reclutas tendrá lugar la próxima semana** the new recruits will start their military service next week

incorporado, -a *adj* built-in; **con DVD i.** with built-in DVD; **llevar** *o* **tener algo i.** to have sth built in

incorporar 1 *vt* (**a**) *(añadir)* to incorporate (**a** into); **i. el azúcar a la nata** to mix the sugar into the cream; **incorporaron los territorios al imperio** the territories became part of the empire; **incorporaron las propuestas de los verdes en su programa electoral** they incorporated the Greens' proposals into their election manifesto
(**b**) *(levantar)* **i. a alguien** to sit sb up
(**c**) *(incluir)* to include, to incorporate; **el modelo incorpora la última tecnología digital** the model incorporates the latest digital technology
2 **incorporarse** *vpr* (**a**) *(unirse) (a equipo)* to join; *(a trabajo)* to start; **incorporarse a filas** *(empezar el servicio militar)* to start one's military service (**b**) *(levantarse)* to sit up

incorpóreo, -a *adj* incorporeal, intangible

incorrección *nf* (**a**) *(falta de corrección)* incorrectness; *(error gramatical)* mistake (**b**) *(descortesía)* **no invitarla fue una i.** it was rude not to invite her

incorrectamente *adv* (**a**) *(con errores)* incorrectly (**b**) *(con descortesía)* rudely

incorrecto, -a *adj* (**a**) *(equivocado)* incorrect, wrong (**b**) *(descortés)* rude

incorregible *adj* (**a**) *(defecto, problema)* **tiene un defecto del habla i.** he has an incurable speech defect; **este es un problema i.** this is a problem which can't be solved (**b**) *(persona)* incorrigible

incorruptible *adj* (**a**) *(substancia)* imperishable (**b**) *(persona)* incorruptible

incorrupto, -a *adj (cadáver)* **encontraron el cuerpo i. del montañero** they found the mountaineer's body which had still not decomposed

incredibilidad *nf* incredibleness

incredulidad *nf* incredulity

incrédulo, -a 1 *adj* (**a**) *(que no cree)* sceptical, incredulous (**b**) *(que no tiene fe)* unbelieving
2 *nm,f* unbeliever

increíble *adj* (**a**) *(inconcebible)* unbelievable; **es i. que pasen cosas así** it's hard to believe that such things can happen; **me parece i. que no te haya llamado** I think it's unbelievable that she hasn't called you (**b**) *(extraordinario)* incredible; **hace un calor i.** it's incredibly hot; **tuvimos una suerte i.** we were incredibly lucky

increíblemente *adv* incredibly, unbelievably

incrementar 1 *vt* to increase
2 **incrementarse** *vpr* to increase

incremento *nm (de precios, salario)* increase, rise; *(de actividad)* increase; *(de temperatura)* rise ►► ***i. porcentual*** percentage increase

increpación *nf* severe rebuke *o* reproach

increpar *vt* (**a**) *(reprender)* to reprimand (**b**) *(insultar)* to abuse, to insult; **los manifestantes increparon a la policía** the demonstrators hurled abuse at the police

incriminación *nf* accusation

incriminar *vt* to accuse; **lo han incriminado de un delito de evasión fiscal** he has been accused of tax evasion

incriminatorio, -a *adj* incriminating; **no se han hallado pruebas incriminatorias** no incriminating evidence has been found

incruento, -a *adj* bloodless

incrustación *nf* (**a**) *(acción)* embedding; *(de joya)* inlaying (**b**) *(objeto, cuerpo)* inlay; **un marco con incrustaciones de oro** a frame with a gold inlay *o* inlaid with gold; **un collar con incrustraciones de diamantes** a diamond-studded necklace (**c**) *(en tuberías, calderas)* scale, sinter (**d**) *Andes, RP (corona)* crown

incrustado, -a *adj* **i. en** *(encajado)* embedded in; **tiene un diamante i. en un diente** he has a diamond (set) in one of his teeth; **con rubíes incrustados** inlaid with rubies

incrustar 1 *vt* (**a**) *(introducir, empotrar)* to embed; **i. nácar en la madera** to inlay the wood with mother of pearl; **incrustó la espada en la roca** he plunged the sword deep into the rock; *Fam* **me incrustó un codo en el costado** he jabbed his elbow into my ribs (**b**) *Informát* to embed
2 **incrustarse** *vpr (introducirse, empotrarse)* **la bala se incrustó en el hueso/muro** the bullet embedded itself in the bone/wall; *Fam* **el coche se incrustó en el muro** the car ploughed into the wall; **la cal se había incrustado en las tuberías** the pipes had become furred up

incubación *nf* (**a**) *(de huevos)* incubation ►► ***i. artificial*** artificial incubation (**b**) *(de enfermedad)* incubation; **periodo de i.** incubation period

incubadora *nf* incubator

incubar 1 *vt* (**a**) *(huevo)* to sit on, *Espec* to incubate (**b**) *(enfermedad)* **debo estar incubando una gripe** I must have a dose of flu coming on (**c**) *(plan, complot)* to hatch
2 **incubarse** *vpr* **se está incubando un golpe de estado** a coup is being plotted; **se está incubando un nuevo proyecto** a new project is being prepared *o* planned

íncubo *nm Literario* incubus

incuestionable *adj (teoría, razón)* irrefutable; *(deber)* bounden

inculcación *nf* inculcation

inculcar [60] *vt* **i. algo a alguien** to instil sth into sb; **desde pequeños les inculcan el respeto al medio ambiente** respect for the environment is instilled into them from an early age

inculpación *nf* charge

inculpado, -a 1 *adj* charged
2 *nm,f* **el i., la inculpada** the accused

inculpar *vt* to charge (**de** with); **todas las pruebas le inculpan** all the evidence points to him being guilty

incultivable *adj* uncultivable, unfit for cultivation

inculto, -a 1 *adj* (**a**) *(persona)* uneducated (**b**) *(tierra)* uncultivated
2 *nm,f* ignoramus

incultura *nf* lack of education

incumbencia *nf* **es/no es de nuestra i.** it is/isn't a matter for us, it falls/doesn't fall within our area of responsibility; **no es asunto de tu i.** it's none of your business

incumbir *vi* **i. a alguien** to be a matter for sb, to be within sb's area of responsibility; **esto no te incumbe** this is not a matter for you, this doesn't concern you

incumplido, -a *Col, Méx, Perú* 1 *adj* unreliable
2 *nm,f* unreliable person

incumplidor, -ora *CSur* 1 *adj* unreliable
2 *nm,f* unreliable person

incumplimiento *nm* **el i. de una orden/ley** failure to comply with an order/a law; **el i. de una promesa** failure to keep a promise; **el i. de una obligación** failure to fulfil an obligation ►► ***i. de contrato*** breach of contract

incumplir *vt (deber)* to fail to fulfil, to neglect; *(orden, ley)* to fail to comply with; *(promesa)* to break; *(contrato)* to breach

incunable 1 *adj* incunabular
2 *nm* incunabulum

incurabilidad *nf* incurability

incurable *adj* incurable; **un vicio i.** an incurable vice

incurrir *vi* (**a**) **i. en** *(delito, falta)* to commit; *(error)* to make (**b**) **i. en** *(desprecio, castigo)* to incur; **incurrió en el odio de sus compañeros** he incurred the hatred of his colleagues (**c**) **i. en** *(gasto)* to incur; **incurrimos en muchos gastos en nuestro viaje por Asia** we incurred a lot of expenses during our Asian trip

incursión *nf* incursion; **su breve i. en el mundo de la política** his brief incursion into the world of politics; *Fig* **hicieron una i. en la cocina** they raided the kitchen ►► ***i. aérea*** air raid

incursionar *vi* (**a**) *(en territorio)* to make an incursion (**en** into), to make a raid (**en** into); *(en ciudad)* to make a raid (**en** on); **los soldados incursionaron en el campamento** the soldiers raided the camp (**b**) *(en tema, asunto)* to dabble; **es veterinario pero ha incursionado en la literatura** he's a vet but he has also dabbled in literature

indagación *nf* investigation, inquiry; **hacer indagaciones acerca de algo** to investigate sth, to inquire into sth

indagar [38] 1 *vt* to investigate, to inquire into
2 *vi* to investigate, to inquire; **i. acerca de algo** to investigate sth, to inquire into sth

indagatoria *nf Der* statement

indagatorio, -a *adj* investigatory

indebidamente *adv* (**a**) *(ilegalmente)* illegally, unlawfully (**b**) *(inadecuadamente)* unduly, improperly

indebido, -a *adj* (**a**) *(ilegal)* unlawful, wrongful; **fue acusado de uso i. de fondos** he was accused of unlawful *o* improper use of funds (**b**) *(incorrecto)* improper; **el uso i. de medicamentos** the improper use of medicines

indecencia *nf* (**a**) *(cualidad)* indecency (**b**) **¡es una i.!** *(es impúdico)* it's not decent!; *(es indignante)* it's outrageous!

indecente *adj* (**a**) *(impúdico)* indecent (**b**) *(indigno)* miserable, wretched

indecentemente *adv* indecently

indecible *adj* indescribable, unspeakable; **sufrió lo i. para llegar a la meta** she suffered indescribable *o* unspeakable pain to reach the finishing line; **hice lo i. para convencerla** I did my utmost to persuade her

indecisión *nf* indecisiveness; **una i. del piloto causó el accidente** indecisiveness *o* indecision on the part of the pilot caused the accident; **me molesta su i.** her indecisiveness annoys me

indeciso, -a 1 *adj* (**a**) *(persona) (inseguro)* indecisive; *(que está dudoso)* undecided; **es una persona muy indecisa** she's a very indecisive person; **estar i. sobre algo** to be undecided about sth (**b**) *(pregunta, respuesta)* hesitant; *(resultado)* undecided
2 *nm* **es un i.** he's indecisive; **buscan el voto de los indecisos** they are after the votes of people who haven't yet made up their minds *o* haven't yet decided how to vote

indeclinable *adj* (**a**) *(ineludible)* **era una invitación i.** it was an invitation that we couldn't decline; **tengo varios compromisos indeclinables** I have several things arranged that I can't change; **nos hicieron una oferta i.** they made us an offer we couldn't refuse (**b**) *Gram* indeclinable

indecoroso, -a *adj* unseemly

indefectible *adj Formal (apoyo, lealtad)* unfailing; **llegó fumando su i. cigarro** he arrived smoking the inevitable cigar; **llegaron con su i. buen humor** they arrived in their usual good mood, they arrived in a good mood, as ever

indefectiblemente *adv Formal* unfailingly; **su recuperación pasa i. por que deje de fumar** his recovery is totally dependent on him giving up smoking; **fuimos al bar donde, i., se encontraba mi abuelo** we went to the bar where, without fail, my grandfather could always be found

indefendible *adj (comportamiento, actitud)* indefensible; *(teoría)* untenable

indefensión *nf* defencelessness; **estar en una situación de i.** to be defenceless

indefenso, -a *adj* defenceless

indefinible *adj* indefinable; **de edad i.** of indeterminate age

indefinición *nf* vagueness

indefinidamente *adv* indefinitely; **y así i.** and so on ad infinitum

indefinido, -a *adj* (**a**) *(ilimitado) (tiempo)* indefinite; *(contrato)* permanent (**b**) *(impreciso)* vague (**c**) *Gram* indefinite

indeformable *adj* that keeps its shape

indeleble *adj* indelible; **me llevé un recuerdo i. de su visita** I will never forget their visit

indelicadeza *nf* (**a**) *(cualidad)* lack of tact, indelicacy (**b**) *(comentario)* tactless *o* indelicate remark

indelicado, -a *adj* indelicate

indemallable = **indesmallable**

indemne *adj* unhurt, unharmed; **salir i.** to escape unhurt

indemnidad *nf Formal* indemnity

indemnización *nf (compensación) (por catástrofe)* compensation; **i. (por despido)** severance pay, redundancy money ▸▸ *Der* ***i. por daños y perjuicios*** damages

indemnizar [14] *vt* **i. a alguien (por)** to compensate sb (for); **le indemnizaron con varios millones** he was given several million in compensation; **la despidieron pero la indemnizaron** she was dismissed but received severance pay *o* redundancy money

indemostrable *adj* unprovable

independencia *nf* independence; **con i. de** irrespective *o* regardless of; **el ser soltero le da mucha i.** being single allows him to be very independent

independentismo *nm* independence movement

independentista 1 *adj* pro-independence
2 *nmf* pro-independence campaigner

independiente 1 *adj* (**a**) *(país, persona)* independent (**b**) *(aparte)* separate
2 *nmf (político)* independent

independientemente *adv* (**a**) *(con independencia)* independently; **i. de si...** regardless of *o* irrespective of whether...; **te lo dejo i. de que me lo puedas pagar o no** I'll let you have it (regardless of) whether you can pay me for it or not; **vive i. desde hace años** she has lived on her own for years
(**b**) *(separadamente)* separately; **las dos piezas funcionan i.** the two parts function independently of each other

independizar [14] 1 *vt* to grant independence to
2 **independizarse** *vpr* to become independent (**de** of); **un país que se independizó el siglo pasado** a country which became independent *o* gained its independence in the last century; **sus hijos ya se han independizado** her children are independent now

indescifrable *adj* (**a**) *(código)* unbreakable; *(letra)* indecipherable (**b**) *(misterio)* inexplicable, impenetrable

indescriptible *adj* indescribable

indescriptiblemente *adv* indescribably

indeseable 1 *adj* undesirable
2 *nmf* undesirable

indeseado, -a *adj* undesirable

indesmallable, *CSur* **indemallable** *adj* run-resistant, *Br* ladder-proof

indesmayable *adj* unwavering

indestructible *adj* indestructible

indeterminable *adj* indeterminable

indeterminación *nf (indecisión)* indecisiveness

indeterminado, -a *adj* (**a**) *(sin determinar)* indeterminate; **por tiempo i.** indefinitely (**b**) *(impreciso)* vague (**c**) *Gram* **artículo i.** indefinite article

indeterminismo *nm* indeterminacy

indexación *nf Econ & Informát* indexing

indexado, -a *adj Econ* index-linked

indexar *vt Econ & Informát* to index

India *nf* **(la) I.** India ▸▸ ***las Indias Occidentales*** the West Indies; ***las Indias Orientales*** the East Indies

indiada *nf* (**a**) *Am Pey (indios)* bunch of Indians (**b**) *RP Fam (travesura)* prank; **estos niños se pasan haciendo indiadas todo el día** these kids spend the whole day getting up to mischief

indiano, -a 1 *adj* (Latin American) Indian
2 *nm,f* (**a**) *(indígena)* (Latin American) Indian (**b**) *(emigrante)* = Spanish emigrant to Latin America who returned to Spain having made his/her fortune

indicación *nf* (**a**) *(señal, gesto)* sign, signal; **me hizo una i. para que me sentara** he motioned me to sit down
(**b**) *(instrucción)* instruction; **sigan las indicaciones de los agentes de tráfico** follow the directions of the traffic police; **pedir/dar indicaciones** *(para llegar a un sitio)* to ask for/give directions; **ha dejado de fumar por i. del médico** she's given up smoking on medical advice; **cerraron la puerta con llave por i. del presidente** the door was locked on the president's instructions
(**c**) *(nota, corrección)* note
(**d**) **indicaciones** *(de medicamento)* uses

indicado, -a *adj* (**a**) *(apropiado)* suitable, appropriate; **este jarabe está i. para la tos** this syrup is recommended for coughs; **un método i. únicamente para casos extremos** a method recommended *o* to be used only in extreme cases; **no es el juguete más i. para un niño de tres años** it's not the most suitable *o* appropiate toy for a three-year-old child; **este no es el momento i. para discutir ese asunto** this is not the right time to talk about this matter; **no eres el más i. para dar consejos** you're the last person who should be giving advice; **es el candidato más i. para el trabajo** he's the best man for the job
(**b**) *(marcado)* specified; **se entregará en la fecha indicada por el cliente** it will be delivered on the date specified by the client

indicador, -ora 1 *adj* indicating; **siga las flechas indicadoras** follow the arrows; **encontrarás un cartel i.** you'll find a sign showing the way
2 *nm* (**a**) *(signo)* indicator; **los principales indicadores bursátiles** the main stock market indicators; **ese fallo es un i. de la poca calidad del producto** that fault shows the poor quality of the product ▸▸ ***i. económico*** economic indicator
(**b**) **i. (de dirección)** *(intermitente) Br* indicator, *US* turn signal
(**c**) *Tec* gauge, meter ▸▸ ***i. de nivel de gasolina*** fuel gauge, *Br* petrol gauge; ***i. de velocidad*** speedometer

indicar [60] *vt* (**a**) *(señalar)* to indicate; **esa flecha indica a la derecha** that arrow points to the right; **esa luz indica que le falta agua al radiador** that light shows that the radiator is low on water; **todo parece i. que ganará el equipo visitante** everything seems to indicate that the visitors will win; **me indicó con un gesto que me sentara** she motioned to me to sit down; **el pronóstico del tiempo indica que va a llover** the weather forecast says it's going to rain; **su nerviosismo indica que no ha estudiado** his nervousness indicates *o* suggests that he hasn't studied; **un animal que, como su nombre indica, es salvaje** an animal which, as its name suggests, is wild
(**b**) *(explicar)* to tell, to explain to; **nos indicó el camino del aeropuerto** she told us the way to the airport; **¿me podría i. cómo llegar al centro?** could you tell me how to get to the town centre?; **yo te indicaré lo que tienes que hacer** I'll tell you *o* explain what you have to do
(**c**) *(prescribir)* **el médico me indicó que reposara** the doctor told *o* advised me to rest
(**d**) *(sugerir)* to give an idea of, to intimate; **sólo indicaremos los resultados generales** we will only give an idea of the overall results

indicativo, -a 1 *adj* indicative; **una señal indicativa de la crisis económica** a sign of the recession; **una reacción indicativa de su buen humor** a reaction indicative of her good mood
2 *nm* (**a**) *Gram* indicative; **presente de i.** present indicative (**b**) *Rad* call sign (**c**) *Tel Br* dialling code, *US* area code

índice *nm* (**a**) *(indicador)* index; *(proporción)* level, rate ▸▸ ***í. de audiencia*** audience ratings; ***í. bursátil*** stock market index; *Quím* ***í. de cetano*** cetane number; *Informát* ***í. de compresión*** compression ratio; ***í. del costo*** *o Esp* ***coste de la vida*** cost of living index; ***í. de desempleo*** unemployment rate; **el í. de desempleo ha caído** unemployment has fallen; *Bolsa* ***í. Dow Jones*** Dow-Jones index; ***í. económico*** economic indicator; ***í. de golpes*** *(en golf)* stroke index; ***í. de mortalidad*** mortality rate; ***í. de natalidad*** birth rate; *Bolsa* ***í. Nikkei*** Nikkei index; ***í. de popularidad*** popularity rating; ***í. de precios al consumo*** *Br* retail price index, *US* consumer price index; *Fís* ***í. de refracción*** refractive index
(**b**) *(señal, indicio)* sign, indicator; **el número de llamadas es í. del interés despertado** the number of calls is a sign of how much interest has been generated
(**c**) *(lista, catálogo)* catalogue; *(de libro)* index; **í. (de contenidos)** (table of) contents ▸▸ ***í. alfabético*** alphabetical index; ***í. de materias*** table of contents; ***í. onomástico*** index of proper names; ***í. temático*** subject index
(**d**) *Hist* **el Índice** the Index (Librorum Prohibitorum)
(**e**) **(dedo) í.** index finger
(**f**) *(letra)* index
(**g**) *Mat* index

indicio *nm* (**a**) *(señal)* sign; *(pista)* clue; **hay indicios de violencia** there are signs of violence; **la propuesta es un i. de su voluntad de negociar** the proposal is a sign of their willingness to negotiate (**b**) *(cantidad pequeña)* trace; **se encontraron indicios de veneno en su cuerpo** traces of poison were found in her body

Índico, -a 1 *adj* **el océano Í.** the Indian Ocean
2 *nm* **el Í.** the Indian Ocean

indiferencia *nf* indifference

indiferente *adj* (**a**) *(indistinto)* indifferent; **me es i.** *(me da igual)* I don't mind, it's all the same to me; **me es i. que vayas o no** it's all the same to me whether you go or not; **¿prefieres hacerlo hoy o mañana? – me es i.** would you rather do it today or tomorrow? – I don't mind (**b**) *(apático)* **siempre se muestra i.** he always seems so apathetic; **es i. a la miseria ajena** other people's suffering means nothing to him; **no puedo permanecer i. ante tanto sufrimiento** I cannot remain indifferent in the face of so much suffering; **su belleza me deja i.** her beauty leaves me cold *o* does nothing for me

indígena 1 *adj* indigenous, native
2 *nmf* native

indigencia *nf* destitution, poverty

indigenismo *nm* (**a**) *(cultural)* Indianism (**b**) *(político)* indigenism (**c**) *(palabra, frase)* indigenism, = word originating from an indigenous language

indigenista 1 *adj* (**a**) *(cultural)* Indianist (**b**) *(político)* indigenist
2 *nmf* (**a**) *(cultural)* Indianist (**b**) *(político)* indigenist

indigente 1 *adj* poor, destitute
2 *nmf* poor person; **los indigentes** the poor, the destitute

indigerible *adj* (**a**) *(comida)* indigestible (**b**) *Fam (novela)* stodgy; **la película fue i.** the movie was awful to watch

indigestarse *vpr* (**a**) *(sufrir indigestión)* to get indigestion (**b**) *(causar indigestión)* **se me ha indigestado el guiso** the stew gave me indigestion (**c**) *Fam (persona, asignatura)* **se me ha indigestado esa chica** I can't stomach that girl; **se me indigestó el latín de primero** I couldn't stand first year Latin

indigestión *nf* indigestion; **tener una i.** to have indigestion; **tuve una i. de pistachos** I got indigestion from eating pistachio nuts

indigesto, -a *adj* (**a**) *(comida)* hard to digest; **estar i.** *(persona)* to have indigestion (**b**) *Fam (novela)* stodgy; **la película fue i.** the movie was awful to watch

indignación *nf (enfado)* indignation; *(cólera)* outrage; **su liberación provocó la i. de las víctimas** his release caused outrage among his victims

indignado, -a *adj (enfadado)* indignant; *(colérico)* outraged; **están indignados por el asesinato del obispo** they are outraged by the bishop's murder

indignamente *adv* unworthily

indignante *adj* shocking, outrageous

indignar 1 *vt (enfadar)* to anger; *(encolerizar)* to outrage; **me indigna que los traten así de mal** it makes me really angry that they should be treated so badly
2 **indignarse** *vpr (enfadarse)* to get angry *o* indignant (**por** about); *(encolerizarse)* to be outraged (**por** about); **se indignó conmigo** she got angry with me

indignidad *nf* unworthiness

indigno, -a *adj* (**a**) *(impropio)* unworthy, not worthy (**de** of); **una reacción indigna de alguien en su posición** a reaction which was unworthy of somebody in her position (**b**) *(no merecedor)* unworthy, not worthy (**de** of); **soy i. de tal honor** I am not worthy of such an honour (**c**) *(degradante)* shameful, appalling

índigo *nm* indigo

indino, -a *CAm, Méx* 1 *adj* roguish
2 *nm,f* rogue

indio, -a 1 *adj* (**a**) *(nativo)* Indian (**b**) *(de India)* Indian
2 *nm,f* (**a**) *(nativo)* Indian; EXPR *Esp Fam* **hacer el i.** to play the fool; EXPR *CSur Fam* **se le subió el i., le salió el i.** he flew off the handle ►► ***i. americano*** Native American (**b**) *(de India)* Indian (**c**) *RP (niño travieso)* rascal (**d**) *Carib, Méx (gallo)* = dark red cockerel with a black chest
3 *nm Quím* indium

indirecta *nf* hint; **lanzar una i. a alguien** to drop sb a hint; **no ha debido cazar** *o Esp* **coger la i.** she can't have taken the hint; **siempre dice todo con indirectas** he always talks in such a roundabout way

indirectamente *adv* indirectly

indirecto, -a *adj* (**a**) *(intervención, causa)* indirect; **una ley que nos afecta de forma indirecta** a law which affects us indirectly; **la fábrica creará 500 empleos indirectos** the factory will create 500 indirect jobs
(**b**) *(impuesto, costo)* indirect
(**c**) *(iluminación)* indirect
(**d**) *Dep (falta)* indirect
(**e**) *Gram (objeto)* indirect; **estilo i.** indirect *o* reported speech, *US* indirect discourse

indiscernible *adj* **las diferencias entre un caso y el otro son indiscernibles** there are no discernible differences between the cases

indisciplina *nf* (**a**) *(de alumno, hijo)* indiscipline, lack of discipline (**b**) *(de soldado)* insubordination

indisciplinado, -a 1 *adj* (**a**) *(jugador)* undisciplined; *(alumno, hijo)* badly behaved (**b**) *(soldado)* insubordinate
2 *nm,f* **es un i.** *(jugador)* he's very undisciplined; *(alumno, hijo)* he's very badly behaved

indisciplinarse *vpr* (**a**) *(jugador)* to show a lack of discipline; *(alumno, hijo)* to behave badly (**b**) *(soldado)* to be insubordinate

indiscreción *nf* (**a**) *(cualidad)* indiscretion (**b**) *(comentario)* indiscreet remark; *(hecho)* indiscretion; **si no es i.** if you don't mind my asking; **fue una i. preguntarle su edad** it was a bit tactless *o* indiscreet to ask her her age; **quieren evitar que una i. descubra el resultado** they want to avoid the result being given away by an indiscreet *o* careless remark ►► ***i. amoroso*** romantic adventure

indiscreto, -a 1 *adj (persona, comentario, mirada)* indiscreet
2 *nm,f* indiscreet person; **tu hermano es un i.** your brother is very indiscreet

indiscriminadamente *adv* indiscriminately

indiscriminado, -a *adj* indiscriminate

indiscutible *adj* (**a**) *(argumento, razones, realidad)* indisputable (**b**) *(campeón, líder)* undisputed

indiscutiblemente *adv* indisputably

indisociable *adj* inseparable (**de** from)

indisolubilidad *nf* (**a**) *(de sustancia)* insolubility (**b**) *(de matrimonio)* indissolubility

indisoluble *adj* (**a**) *(sustancia)* insoluble (**b**) *(matrimonio)* indissoluble

indispensable *adj* indispensable, essential; **es i. que me llames** it's essential that you call me; **lo i.** the (bare) essentials

indisponer [50] 1 *vt* (**a**) *(enfermar)* to make ill; **la comida le indispuso el estómago** the food he ate upset his stomach (**b**) *(enemistar)* to set at odds; **i. a alguien con alguien** to turn sb against sb
2 **indisponerse** *vpr* (**a**) *(enfermar)* to fall *o* become ill (**b**) *(enemistarse)* to fall out (**con** with) (**c**) *CSur Euf (menstruar)* to start one's period

indisponibilidad *nf* unavailability

indisposición *nf* (**a**) *(malestar)* indisposition (**b**) *(reticencia)* unwillingness

indispuesto, -a 1 *participio ver* **indisponer**
2 *adj* (**a**) *(enfermo)* indisposed, unwell; **estar i.** to be unwell *o* indisposed (**b**) *CSur Euf (mujer)* **estoy indispuesta** it's my time of the month

indisputable *adj* (**a**) *(argumento, razones, realidad)* indisputable (**b**) *(campeón, líder)* undisputed

indistinguible *adj* indistinguishable (**de** from)

indistintamente *adv* (**a**) *(sin distinción)* equally, alike; **se refería a jóvenes y viejos i.** he was referring to young and old alike; **utilizan i. el español y el inglés** they use Spanish and English interchangeably; **permite enviar i. datos e imágenes** it allows you to send both data and images equally well (**b**) *(sin claridad)* indistinctly

indistinto, -a *adj* (**a**) *(indiferente)* **es i.** it doesn't matter, it makes no difference; **es i. que lo haga aquí o desde casa** it doesn't matter *o* it makes no difference whether she does it here or from home (**b**) *(cuenta, cartilla)* joint (**c**) *(perfil, figura)* indistinct, blurred

individual 1 *adj* (**a**) *(del individuo)* individual; **los derechos individuales** the rights of the individual (**b**) *(habitación, cama)* single; *(despacho)* personal (**c**) *(prueba, competición)* singles; **competición i.** singles competition
2 **individuales** *nmpl Dep* singles

individualidad *nf* individuality

individualismo *nm* individualism

individualista 1 *adj* individualistic
2 *nmf* individualist

individualización *nf* individualization

individualizado, -a *adj* individualized

individualizar [14] *vt* (**a**) *(personalizar)* to individualize; **i. un tratamiento médico** to tailor a course of treatment for individual patients (**b**) *(caracterizar)* **su imaginación lo individualiza** his imagination singles him out

individualmente *adv* individually, one by one

individuo, -a *nm,f* (**a**) *(ser individual)* person, individual; **los derechos del i.** the rights of the individual
(**b**) *(persona desconocida)* person, individual; **dos individuos atracaron un banco** two people *o* individuals robbed a bank
(**c**) *(mala persona)* individual; **no me gusta nada el i. con el que sales** I don't like that individual *o* character you're going out with at all
(**d**) *(de especie)* **quedan sólo 200 individuos de esta especie** only 200 individuals remain of this species; **algunos individuos de la especie** some members of the species; **cada i. ocupa un territorio** each animal occupies its own territory

indivisibilidad *nf* indivisibility

indivisible *adj* indivisible

indivisión *nf Der* joint ownership

indiviso, -a *adj* undivided

indización *nf* indexation

Indo *n* **el (río) I.** the Indus

Indochina *n Antes* Indochina

indochino, -a *Antes* **1** *adj* Indochinese
2 *nm,f* Indochinese

indocumentado, -a 1 *adj (sin documentación)* without identity papers; **estar i.** to have no (means of) identification
2 *nm,f Esp Fam (ignorante)* **es un i.** he's a complete ignoramus

indoeuropeo, -a 1 *adj* Indo-European
2 *nm,f (persona)* Indo-European
3 *nm (lengua)* Indo-European

índole *nf* (**a**) *(naturaleza)* nature; **un problema de í. cardiaca** a heart problem (**b**) *(tipo)* type, kind; **de toda í.** of every kind

indolencia *nf* indolence

indolente *adj* indolent

indoloro, -a *adj* painless

indomable *adj* (**a**) *(animal)* untameable (**b**) *(carácter)* rebellious; *(pueblo)* unruly

indomesticable *adj* untameable

indómito, -a *adj* (**a**) *(animal)* untameable (**b**) *(carácter)* rebellious; *(pueblo)* unruly

Indonesia *n* Indonesia

indonesio, -a 1 *adj* Indonesian
2 *nm,f (persona)* Indonesian
3 *nm (lengua)* Indonesian

Indostán *n* Hindustan

indostánico, -a 1 *adj* Hindustani
2 *nm (lengua)* Hindustani

indubitable *adj Formal* indubitable

inducción *nf* (**a**) *Fís* induction ►► ***i. electromagnética*** electromagnetic induction (**b**) *Filosofía* induction (**c**) *Med* induction (**d**) *Der* incitement (**a** to)

inducido *nm Elec* armature

inducir [18] *vt* (**a**) *(incitar)* **i. a alguien a algo/a hacer algo** to lead sb into sth/into doing sth; **ello les indujo a pensar que el asesino era el mayordomo** this led them to think that the butler was the murderer; **i. a error: esa frase puede i. a error** that sentence could be misleading; **sus instrucciones me indujeron a error** her instructions caused *o* led me to make a mistake
(**b**) *(deducir)* to infer
(**c**) *Fís* to induce

inductancia *nf Fís* inductance

inductivo, -a *adj* inductive

inductor, -ora 1 *adj* instigating
2 *nm* (**a**) *(de crimen)* instigator (**b**) *Elec* inductor

indudable *adj* undoubted; **tiene un atractivo i.** it is undoubtedly appealing, it has undoubted appeal; **un libro de i. interés** an undoubtedly *o* unquestionably interesting book; **es i. que...** there is no doubt that...

indudablemente *adv* undoubtedly

indujera *etc ver* **inducir**

indujo *etc ver* **inducir**

indulgencia *nf* (**a**) *(actitud) (tolerancia)* indulgence; *(a la hora de castigar)* leniency; **mostrar i. con alguien** to be indulgent/lenient towards *o* with sb (**b**) *Rel* indulgence ►► ***i. plenaria*** plenary indulgence

indulgente *adj (tolerante)* indulgent; *(a la hora de castigar)* lenient; **ser i. con alguien** to be indulgent/lenient with *o* towards sb

indultar *vt* to pardon

indulto *nm* pardon; **otorgar** *o* **conceder el i. a alguien** to grant sb a pardon

indumentaria *nf* attire; **iban vestidos con i. paramilitar** they were dressed in paramilitary attire; **lo recibieron dos mujeres ataviadas con la i. tradicional** he was received by two women in traditional dress *o* costume

industria *nf* (**a**) *(sector)* industry ►► ***la i. agroalimentaria*** the food and agriculture industry; ***i. armamentística*** arms industry; ***i. automotriz*** automobile industry; ***i. del automóvil*** automobile industry; ***i. automovilística*** automobile industry; ***i. del entretenimiento*** entertainment industry; ***i. en expansión*** growth industry; ***i. ligera*** light industry; ***i. del ocio*** leisure industry; ***i. pesada*** heavy industry; ***i. punta*** sunrise industry; ***i. textil*** textile industry; ***i. de transformación*** manufacturing industry; ***i. del turismo*** tourist industry; ***i. turística*** tourist industry
(**b**) *(fábrica)* factory
(**c**) *(habilidad)* industry, hard work

industrial 1 *adj* (**a**) *(de la industria)* industrial (**b**) *Fam (muy grande)* **fumaba cantidades industriales de habanos** he used to smoke vast quantities of cigars; **había cerveza en cantidades industriales** there were gallons of beer
2 *nmf* industrialist

industrialismo *nm* industrialism

industrialista *adj* = of/relating to industrialism

industrialización *nf* industrialization

industrializado, -a *adj* industrialized; **países industrializados** industrialized countries

industrializador, -ora *adj* **un proceso i.** a process of industrialization

industrializar [14] **1** *vt* to industrialize
2 industrializarse *vpr* to become industrialized

industrioso, -a *adj* industrious

induzco *etc ver* **inducir**

inecuación *nf Mat* inequality

inédito, -a *adj* (**a**) *(no publicado)* unpublished (**b**) *(nuevo)* new (**c**) *(sorprendente)* unheard-of, unprecedented

inefable *adj* indescribable

inefablemente *adv* ineffably

ineficacia *nf* (**a**) *(bajo rendimiento)* inefficiency (**b**) *(baja efectividad)* ineffectiveness

ineficaz *adj* (**a**) *(de bajo rendimiento)* inefficient (**b**) *(de baja efectividad)* ineffective

ineficiencia *nf* (**a**) *(bajo rendimiento)* inefficiency (**b**) *(baja efectividad)* ineffectiveness

ineficiente *adj* (**a**) *(de bajo rendimiento)* inefficient (**b**) *(de baja efectividad)* ineffective

inelegibilidad *nf* ineligibility

inelegible *adj* ineligible

ineluctable *adj Formal* inevitable, inescapable

ineludible *adj* unavoidable

ineludiblemente *adv* unavoidably

INEM [i'nem] *nm* (*abrev de* **Instituto Nacional de Empleo**) = Spanish department of employment; **oficina del I.** *Br* ≃ Jobcentre, *US* ≃ Job Center

inembargable *adj* not subject to seizure

inenarrable *adj* indescribable

inepcia *nf Formal (ineptitud)* ineptitude, incompetence

ineptitud *nf* incompetence, ineptitude

inepto, -a 1 *adj* incompetent, inept
2 *nm,f* incompetent *o* inept person

inequívoco, -a *adj (apoyo, resultado)* unequivocal; *(señal, voz)* unmistakable

inercia *nf* (**a**) *Fís* inertia (**b**) *(pereza)* inertia; **hacer algo por i.** to do sth out of inertia

inerme *adj* (**a**) *(sin armas)* unarmed (**b**) *(sin defensa)* defenceless

inerte *adj* (**a**) *(materia)* inert (**b**) *(cuerpo, cadáver)* lifeless

inescrutable *adj* (**a**) *(persona, rostro)* inscrutable (**b**) *(misterio, verdad)* impenetrable

inesperadamente *adv* unexpectedly

inesperado, -a *adj* unexpected; **hacer algo de forma inesperada** to do sth unexpectedly

inestabilidad *nf* (**a**) *(de construcción)* instability (**b**) *(de régimen, economía)* instability (**c**) *(de carácter)* instability (**d**) *(de tiempo)* changeability

inestable *adj* (**a**) *(construcción)* unstable (**b**) *(régimen, economía)* unstable (**c**) *(carácter)* unstable (**d**) *(tiempo)* changeable

inestimable *adj* inestimable, invaluable

inevitable *adj* inevitable; **apareció con su i. habano** he turned up smoking the inevitable cigar

inevitablemente *adv* inevitably

inexactitud *nf* inaccuracy

inexacto, -a *adj* (**a**) *(impreciso)* inaccurate (**b**) *(erróneo)* incorrect, wrong

inexcusable *adj* (**a**) *(imperdonable)* inexcusable (**b**) *(ineludible)* unavoidable

inexistencia *nf* nonexistence; **la i. de competencia ha favorecido su expansión** the absence of competition has made it easy for them to expand

inexistente *adj* nonexistent

inexorabilidad *nf* inexorability

inexorable *adj* (**a**) *(avance)* inexorable (**b**) *(persona)* pitiless, unforgiving

inexorablemente *adv* inexorably

inexperiencia *nf* inexperience

inexperto, -a 1 *adj* (**a**) *(falto de experiencia)* inexperienced (**b**) *(falto de habilidad)* unskilful, inexpert

2 *nm,f* (**a**) *(falto de experiencia)* inexperienced person (**b**) *(falto de habilidad)* **es un i.** he lacks the necessary skills

inexplicable *adj* inexplicable

inexplicablemente *adv* inexplicably

inexplicado, -a *adj* unexplained

inexplorado, -a *adj* unexplored

inexplotable *adj* unexploitable

inexpresable *adj* inexpressible

inexpresividad *nf (de rostro)* inexpressiveness, lack of expression; *(de persona, carácter)* undemonstrativeness

inexpresivo, -a *adj (rostro)* expressionless; *(persona, carácter)* undemonstrative

inexpugnable *adj* unassailable, impregnable

inextinguible *adj (fuego)* unextinguishable; *(sentimiento)* undying

inextirpable *adj* ineradicable

in extremis *loc adv* right at the very last moment

inextricable *adj* (**a**) *(problema, concepto)* intricate; *(misterio)* unfathomable (**b**) *(bosque)* impenetrable

infalibilidad *nf* infallibility

infalible *adj* (**a**) *(método, persona)* infallible; *(puntería)* unerring (**b**) *(inevitable)* inevitable; **es i., siempre que la invito está ocupada** it's the same every time without fail, whenever I invite her over she's busy

infalsificable *adj (pasaporte, dinero)* forgery-proof

infaltable *adj CSur* inevitable; **la torta es i. en una fiesta de cumpleaños** you can't have a proper birthday party without a cake

infamar *vt Formal* to defame

infamatorio, -a *adj Formal* defamatory

infame *adj* (**a**) *(persona)* vile, base (**b**) *Fam (libro, película)* dire, dreadful; **vivían en una casa i.** they lived in a dreadful house

infamia *nf* (**a**) *(deshonra)* infamy, disgrace; **padeció la i. de ser desterrado** he suffered the disgrace of being banished (**b**) *(mala acción)* vile *o* base act; **es una i. tratarlos así** treating them like that is despicable

infancia *nf* (**a**) *(periodo)* childhood; **tuvo una i. muy feliz** she had a very happy childhood; **se interesó por la música desde su más tierna i.** he was interested in music from early childhood; **se casó con un amigo de la i.** she married a childhood friend (**b**) *(todos los niños)* children; **la salud de la i.** children's health

infantado, infantazgo *nm (título)* = title of infante or infanta

infante, -a 1 *nm,f* (**a**) *(niño)* infant (**b**) *(hijo del rey) (niño)* infante, prince; *(niña)* infanta, princess

2 *nm (soldado)* infantryman ►► ***i. de marina*** marine

infantería *nf* infantry ►► ***i. ligera*** light infantry; ***i. de marina*** marines

infanticida 1 *adj* infanticidal

2 *nmf* infanticide, child-murderer

infanticidio *nm* infanticide

infantil 1 *adj* (**a**) *(para niños)* children's; **lenguaje i.** children's speech; **literatura i.** children's literature; **psicología i.** child psychology; **hospital i.** children's hospital (**b**) *(inmaduro)* childish, infantile; **es muy i.** she's very childish (**c**) *Dep* **equipo i.** ≃ youth team *(ages 12 to 13)*

2 *nmf Dep* **infantiles** ≃ youth team *(ages 12 to 13)*

infantilismo *nm* (**a**) *Med* infantilism (**b**) *(de comportamiento)* childishness

infantilización *nf* infantilization

infantiloide *adj* childlike

infanzón *nm Hist* = in the Middle Ages, member of the lesser nobility

infarto 1 *nm (ataque al corazón)* heart attack; **le dio un i.** he had a heart attack; *Fam Fig* **casi le dio un i.** she almost had a heart attack *o* a seizure ►► ***i. cerebral*** stroke; ***i. de miocardio*** heart attack

2 de infarto *loc adj Fam* heart-stopping; **el partido tuvo un final de i.** the end of the match was heart-stoppingly exciting

infatigable *adj* indefatigable, tireless

infatigablemente *adv* indefatigably, untiringly

infatuación *nf* vanity

infatuar [4] **1** *vt* to make conceited

2 infatuarse *vpr* to become *o* get conceited

infausto, -a *adj* very sad; **un día de i. recuerdo para todos nosotros** a day which is remembered with great sadness by all of us

infección *nf* infection

infeccioso, -a *adj* infectious

infectado, -a *adj* infected

infectar 1 *vt* to infect

2 infectarse *vpr* to become infected

infecto, -a *adj* (**a**) *(agua, carroña)* putrid (**b**) *(población, zona)* infected (**c**) *(repugnante)* foul

infectocontagioso, -a *adj* infectious

infecundidad *nf* infertility

infecundo, -a *adj* (**a**) *(tierra)* infertile, barren (**b**) *(mujer)* infertile

infelicidad *nf* unhappiness

infeliz 1 *adj* (**a**) *(desgraciado)* unhappy (**b**) *(ingenuo)* trusting (**c**) *(desafortunado) (comentario, decisión)* unfortunate; *(intento)* unsuccessful; *(coincidencia)* unhappy

2 *nmf (ingenuo)* **es un i.** he's a trusting soul; **un pobre i.** a poor wretch

inferencia *nf* inference

inferior 1 *adj* (**a**) *(de abajo)* bottom; **la parte i. (de algo)** the bottom (of sth); **la mitad i.** the bottom *o* lower half; **labio/mandíbula i.** lower lip/jaw

(**b**) *(menor)* lower (**a** than); **ser i. en número, ser numéricamente i.** to be fewer in number; **temperaturas inferiores a los 10 grados** temperatures below 10 degrees; **una cifra i. a 100** a figure under *o* below 100; **lo venden a un precio un 30 por ciento i. al del mercado** they are selling it for 30 percent less than the market price; **por un periodo no i. a tres años** for a period of not less than three years

(**c**) *(peor)* inferior (**a** to); **es i. a la media** it's below average; **un producto de calidad i.** an inferior *o* poor-quality product; **no me creo i. a nadie** I don't consider myself inferior to anybody

(**d**) *Geog* **curso i.** lower reaches

(**e**) *Geol* lower; **el Paleolítico i.** the Lower Paleolithic

2 *nm* inferior; **el jefe trata con desprecio a sus inferiores** the boss treats those beneath him with contempt

inferioridad *nf* inferiority; **complejo de i.** inferiority complex; **estar en i. de condiciones** to be at a disadvantage; **acabaron el partido en i. numérica** they ended the game with fewer players on the pitch than their opponents

inferiormente *adv* in an inferior way

inferir [63] *vt* (**a**) *(deducir)* to deduce, to infer (**de** from); **de sus declaraciones infiero que no está de acuerdo** I deduce *o* infer from her statements that she does not agree

(**b**) *(ocasionar) (herida)* to inflict; *(mal)* to cause; **el toro le infirió una grave cornada** he was badly gored by the bull

infernal *adj* (**a**) *(del infierno)* infernal (**b**) *(ruido, tiempo)* abominable; **hizo un calor i.** it was infernally hot

infértil *adj* (**a**) *(mujer)* infertile (**b**) *(campo)* barren, infertile

infertilidad *nf* (**a**) *(mujer)* infertility (**b**) *(campo)* barrenness, infertility

infestación *nf* infestation

infestado, -a *adj* **i. de algo** infested with sth; **un lugar i. de turistas** a place crawling with tourists

infestar *vt* to infest; **durante el verano, los turistas infestan la ciudad** in summer the city is overrun by tourists

infición *nf Méx* pollution

infidelidad *nf (conyugal)* infidelity; *(a la patria, un amigo)* unfaithfulness, disloyalty

infiel 1 *adj* **(a)** *(desleal) (cónyuge)* unfaithful; *(amigo)* disloyal; **su mujer le es i.** his wife is unfaithful to him; **fuiste i. a tu promesa** you broke your promise; **si la memoria no me es i....** if my memory serves me right... **(b)** *(inexacto)* inaccurate, unfaithful; **es una descripción i. de lo que ocurrió** it is an inaccurate description of what happened **(c)** *Rel* unbelieving

2 *nmf Rel* infidel

infiernillo *nm* portable stove

infierno *nm* **(a)** *(en religión)* hell; EXPR *Fam* **¡al i. con...!: ¡al i. con la fiesta!** to hell with the party!; EXPR *Fam* **el quinto i.: vive en el quinto i.** she lives in the back of beyond *o* in the middle of nowhere; **tuvimos que ir hasta el quinto i. para encontrar una farmacia** we had to go miles to find a *Br* chemist's *o US* drugstore; EXPR *Fam* **irse al i.** to go down the tubes *o Br* the pan; *Fam* **¡vete al i.!** go to hell!; EXPR *Fam* **mandar a alguien al i.** to tell sb to go to hell

(b) *(lugar de sufrimiento)* hell; **su vida con él era un i.** her life with him was hell; **está habitación es un i., hace un calor horrible** this room's an oven, it's baking hot

infiero *etc ver* **inferir**

infijo *nm Gram* infix

infiltración *nf* **(a)** *(de líquido)* seeping; **la i. de agua había corrompido la madera** seeping water had rotted the wood **(b)** *(de persona, ideas)* infiltration **(c)** *Med* infiltration

infiltrado, -a 1 *adj* infiltrated

2 *nm,f* infiltrator

infiltrar 1 *vt* **(a)** *(sujeto: espía)* to infiltrate; **infiltraron un agente en la organización** they infiltrated an agent into the organization **(b)** *(inyectar)* to inject; **lo infiltraron antes del partido** they gave him an injection before the game

2 infiltrarse *vpr* **(a) infiltrarse en algo** *(espía)* to infiltrate sth; **se infiltró en el grupo terrorista** he infiltrated the terrorist organization; **se infiltraron en la red de la CIA** they hacked into the CIA's computer network **(b)** *(líquido)* to seep; **la humedad se infiltró en la pared** the damp seeped through the wall **(c)** *(ideas)* **sus ideas se infiltraron en el país rápidamente** her ideas quickly spread through the country

ínfimo, -a *adj (calidad, categoría)* extremely low; *(precio)* giveaway; *(importancia)* minimal; **un producto de í. calidad** a very poor *o* low quality product; **sólo una ínfima minoría está en contra del proyecto** only a tiny minority are against the project

infinidad *nf* **i. de** countless, innumerable; **existen i. de formas de hacerlo** there are countless ways of doing it; **en un día sucedieron i. de cosas** in the course of one day thousands of things happened; **en i. de ocasiones** on countless occasions; **nos ofrecieron una i. de regalos** they showered us with gifts

infinitamente *adv* infinitely; **es i. mejor** it's infinitely better; **siento i. que no puedas ir** I'm extremely sorry that you can't go; **les estoy i. agradecido** I'm extremely grateful to them

infinitesimal *adj* infinitesimal

infinitivo *nm* infinitive; **en i.** in the infinitive

infinito, -a 1 *adj* **(a)** *(sin límites)* infinite; **tiene una infinita paciencia** she has infinite patience, she's infinitely patient; **siento por ella un cariño i.** I'm immensely fond of her **(b)** *(incontable)* countless; **infinitas veces** hundreds of times

2 *nm* **(a)** *Mat* infinity; **tender al i.** to tend to infinity **(b)** *(espacio)* infinity; **su figura se perdió en el i.** his figure disappeared into the distance **(c)** *Fot* infinity

3 *adv (mucho)* extremely, infinitely; **me alegro i.** I'm extremely pleased

infinitud *nf* infinity

infiriera *etc ver* **inferir**

infla *RP Fam Euf* **1** *adj* boring, tedious

2 *nmf* bore, pain; **es un i.** he's a pain

inflable *adj* inflatable

inflabolas, inflahuevos, inflapelotas *RP muy Fam* **1** *adj inv (fastidioso, pesado) Br* bloody *o US* goddamn boring

2 *nmf inv (pesado)* bore, pain; **es un i.** he bores the *Br* arse *o US* ass off you

inflación *nf Econ* inflation ►► ***i. interanual*** year-on-year inflation; ***i. subyaciente*** underlying inflation

inflacionario, -a, inflacionista *adj Econ* inflationary

inflacionismo *nm Econ* inflationism

inflado, -a *adj (balón, cifras)* inflated

inflador *nm RP* bicycle pump

inflahuevos = **inflabolas**

inflamabilidad *nf* inflammability, flammability

inflamable *adj* inflammable, flammable

inflamación *nf* **(a)** *(de herida) (por infección)* inflammation; *(por golpe)* swelling **(b)** *(de gas)* ignition

inflamado, -a *adj* **(a)** *(herida) (por infección)* inflamed; *(por golpe)* swollen **(b)** *(con fuego)* burning, in flames **(c)** *(con pasiones)* heated

inflamar 1 *vt* **(a)** *(con fuego)* to set alight **(b)** *(hinchar) (sujeto: infección, fiebre)* to inflame; **el golpe le inflamó el codo** the blow caused her elbow to swell up **(c)** *(con pasiones)* to inflame

2 inflamarse *vpr* **(a)** *(con fuego)* to catch fire, to burst into flames **(b)** *(hincharse) (por infección)* to become inflamed; *(por golpe)* to swell up; **se me ha inflamado la rodilla por el golpe** my knee has swollen up as a result of the blow **(c)** *(con pasiones)* to become inflamed; **se inflamó cuando escuchó las noticias** he became inflamed with anger when he heard the news

inflamatorio, -a *adj* inflammatory

inflapelotas = **inflabolas**

inflar 1 *vt* **(a)** *(soplando)* to blow up, to inflate; *(con bomba)* to pump up; *Esp Fam* **lo inflaron a golpes** they beat him up

(b) *(exagerar)* to blow up, to exaggerate

(c) *RP Fam (fastidiar)* **no me infles** stop bugging me!; **no (me) infles la paciencia** don't push your luck; *muy Fam* **i. las pelotas** *o* **las bolas** *o* **los huevos a alguien** *Br* to get on sb's tits, *US* to break sb's balls; *muy Fam* **dejá de i. las pelotas** *o* **las bolas** *o* **los huevos** stop being such a pain in the *Br* arse *o US* ass

2 *vi RP Fam (molestar)* to be a pain; **¡no infles!** don't be such a pain!

3 inflarse *vpr Fam (hartarse)* to stuff oneself (**de** with)

inflexibilidad *nf* **(a)** *(de material)* inflexibility **(b)** *(de persona)* inflexibility

inflexible *adj* **(a)** *(material)* inflexible **(b)** *(persona)* inflexible; **es i. con sus alumnos** he's very strict with his pupils

inflexiblemente *adv* inflexibly

inflexión *nf* **(a)** *Gram* inflection **(b)** *Geom* inflection **(c)** *(de voz)* inflection **(d)** *(cambio)* turnaround; **un punto de i. histórico** a historical turning point

infligir [24] *vt (pena)* to inflict; *(castigo)* to impose

inflorescencia *nf Bot* inflorescence

influencia *nf* **(a)** *(poder)* influence; **ejerce una gran i. sobre su marido** she has a lot of influence over her husband; **está creciendo su i. dentro del partido** her influence within the party is growing; **tuvo gran i. sobre el resultado de las elecciones** it had a considerable influence on the result of the election, it greatly influenced the result of the election; **un país dentro de la esfera de i. de Rusia** a country within Russia's sphere of influence; **bajo la i. de la anestesia** under (the influence of the) anaesthetic

(b) influencias *(contactos)* contacts, pull; **consiguió ese puesto por influencias** she got that job through knowing the right people

influenciable *adj* easily influenced

influenciar *vt* to influence, to have an influence on

influenza *nf* influenza ►► ***i. aviaria*** fowl pest

influir [34] **1** *vt* to influence

2 *vi* to have influence; **i. en** *o* **sobre** to influence, to have an influence on; **su muerte influyó mucho en él** her death made a great impression on him; **nuestra relación de parentesco no influyó para nada en mi decisión** the fact that we are related did not influence my decision in the slightest

influjo *nm* influence

influyente *adj* influential

infoadicto,-a *nm,f Informát* infoaddict

infografía *nf Informát* computer graphics *(singular)*

infografista *nmf Informát* computer graphics artist

infolio *nm* folio *(book)*

infopista *nf Informát* information highway

información *nf* **(a)** *(conocimiento)* information; **estoy buscando i. sobre este autor** I'm looking for information on this writer; **para tu i.** for your information; **para mayor i., visite nuestra página web** for more information visit our website; **i. confidencial** inside

information; **i. privilegiada** privileged information
(**b**) *(noticias)* news *(singular)*; *(noticia)* report, piece of news; **hemos recibido informaciones contradictorias sobre el accidente** we have received conflicting reports about the accident; **ciencias de la i.** media studies ►► ***i. deportiva*** sports news; ***i. meteorológica*** weather report *o* forecast
(**c**) *(oficina)* information office; **(el mostrador de) i.** the information desk; **Sr. López, acuda a i.** would Mr López please come to the information desk
(**d**) *(telefónica)* *Br* directory enquiries, *US* information ►► ***i. horaria*** speaking clock
(**e**) *Biol* ***i. genética*** genetic information
(**f**) *Informát (datos)* data

informado, -a *adj (sobre un tema, noticia)* informed; **no tengo una opinión informada del tema** I don't have an informed opinion on the subject, I don't know enough about the subject to give an opinion; **un periodista i.** a well-informed journalist; **muy i. (sobre)** well-informed (about); **estás muy mal i., no ocurrió así** you've been badly informed, it didn't happen like that; **según fuentes bien informadas...** according to well-informed sources...

informador, -ora 1 *adj* informing, reporting
2 *nm,f* (**a**) *(periodista)* reporter ►► ***i. gráfico*** press photographer (**b**) *(informante)* informer

informal 1 *adj* (**a**) *(desenfadado, no solemne)* informal; **una reunión i.** an informal meeting; **vestido de manera i.** casually dressed; **la lengua i.** informal language (**b**) *(irresponsable)* unreliable (**c**) *Am* **la economía i.** *(no regularizada)* the informal economy
2 *nmf* **es un i.** he's an unreliable person

informalidad *nf* (**a**) *(desenfado, falta de formalismo)* informality (**b**) *(irresponsabilidad)* unreliability

informalmente *adv* (**a**) *(desenfadadamente)* informally; **iba vestido i.** he was informally *o* casually dressed (**b**) *(irresponsablemente)* unreliably

informante 1 *adj* informing
2 *nmf* informant, informer

informar 1 *vt* (**a**) *(dar información a)* **i. a alguien (de)** to inform *o* tell sb (about); **le han informado mal** he has been misinformed; **me informan que el avión llega con retraso** I've been told that the flight is delayed; **se ha de i. a los detenidos de sus derechos** you have to read people who have been arrested their rights; **¿me podría i. de los horarios de trenes a Boston?** could you tell me the times of the trains to Boston?
(**b**) *Formal (impregnar)* to pervade, to inform; **la filosofía que informa sus novelas** the philosophy which informs her novels
2 *vi* (**a**) *(dar información a)* to inform; **en esa oficina informan sobre el Festival** you can get information about the Festival from that office (**b**) *(periódico)* to report; **según informa nuestro corresponsal,...** according to our correspondent,...
3 **informarse** *vpr* **me informaré y luego te llamo** I'll call you once I've found out the details; **informarse de** *o* **sobre** to find out about; **infórmate de dónde se puede encontrar alojamiento** find out where you can find somewhere to stay; **la próxima vez, infórmate mejor antes de acusar** next time get your facts straight before you make accusations

informática *nf* (**a**) *(tecnología)* computing, information technology; **el departamento de i. de una empresa** the IT department of a company; **la empresa va a invertir más en i.** the company is going to invest more in computers; **no sé nada de i.** I don't know anything about computers; **se requieren conocimientos de i.** candidates should be computer-literate ►► ***i. de gestión*** business computing
(**b**) *(asignatura)* computer science
(**c**) *ver también* **informático**

informáticamente *adv* by computer

informático, -a 1 *adj* computer; **red informática** computer network
2 *nm,f (experto)* computer expert; *(técnico)* computer technician

informativo, -a 1 *adj* (**a**) *(de la información)* **boletín i.** news bulletin; **folleto i.** information leaflet (**b**) *(útil)* informative; **es un folleto muy i.** it's a very informative leaflet
2 *nm* news (bulletin)

informatización *nf* computerization

informatizado, -a *adj* computerized

informatizar [14] 1 *vt* to computerize
2 **informatizarse** *vpr* to become computerized; **empresas que todavía no se han informatizado** companies which have yet to computerize their operations

informe[1] 1 *nm* (**a**) *(documento, estudio)* report (**sobre** on *o* about); **un i. policial** a police report; **han solicitado el i. de un técnico** they have asked for a report from an expert ►► ***i. anual*** annual report; *Com* ***i. de gestión*** management report (**b**) *Der* = oral summary of case given to the judge by counsel for defence or prosecution, ≃ closing speech
2 **informes** *nmpl (información)* information; *(sobre comportamiento)* report; *(para un empleo)* reference(s)

informe[2] *adj* shapeless

infortunado, -a 1 *adj (persona)* unfortunate, unlucky; *(encuentro, conversación)* ill-fated
2 *nm,f* unfortunate *o* unlucky person

infortunio *nm* (**a**) *(hecho desgraciado)* calamity, misfortune (**b**) *(mala suerte)* misfortune, bad luck; **tuvo el i. de contraer la enfermedad** he had the misfortune to catch the disease

infracción *nf (de reglamento)* infringement, violation; **una i. del reglamento** an infringement *o* a violation of the rules; **i. leve/grave** minor/serious offence; **cometió una i. contra las normas** she broke the rules; **i. de circulación** *o* **tráfico** driving offence, traffic violation

infraccionar *Am* 1 *vt (multar)* to fine
2 *vi (en deporte)* to commit a foul; *(contra la ley)* to offend, to break the law; *(contra reglamento)* to violate the rules

infractor, -ora 1 *adj* offending
2 *nm,f* offender

infradotado, -a 1 *adj* (**a**) *(sin financiación)* underfunded; *(sin recursos materiales)* under-resourced; *(sin personal)* understaffed (**b**) *RP Fam Pey (subnormal)* moronic
2 *nm,f RP Fam Pey* moron

infraestructura *nf* (**a**) *(de organización, país)* infrastructure (**b**) *(de construcción)* foundations

in fraganti *loc adv* in flagrante; **agarrar** *o Esp* **pillar a alguien i.** to catch sb red-handed *o* in the act

infrahumano, -a *adj* subhuman

infranqueable *adj* (**a**) *(río, abismo)* impassable (**b**) *(problema, dificultad)* insurmountable; *(diferencia)* irreconcilable

infrarrojo, -a *adj* infrared

infrascrito, -a *nm,f Formal* **el i.** the undersigned

infrasonido *nm* infrasound

infrautilización *nf* underuse

infrautilizar [14] *vt* to underuse

infravaloración *nf* underestimation

infravalorado, -a *adj* underrated

infravalorar 1 *vt* to undervalue, to underestimate
2 **infravalorarse** *vpr* to undervalue oneself

infravivienda *nf* **el problema de la i.** the problem of housing which is unfit for human habitation

infrecuente *adj* infrequent; **no es i.** it's not uncommon *o* unusual

infringir [24] *vt (quebrantar)* to infringe, to break

infructuosamente *adv* unfruitfully, fruitlessly

infructuoso, -a *adj* fruitless, unsuccessful

ínfulas *nfpl* pretensions; **darse** *o* **tener í.** to give oneself airs

infumable *adj* (**a**) *(cigarrillo)* unsmokable (**b**) *Esp, RP Fam (insoportable) (comportamiento)* unbearable, intolerable; *(libro, película)* awful, terrible

infundado, -a *adj* unfounded

infundio *nm Formal* untruth, lie

infundir *vt* **i. algo a alguien** to fill sb with sth, to inspire sth in sb; **i. miedo/respeto** to inspire fear/respect

infusión *nf* herbal tea, infusion ►► ***i. de manzanilla*** camomile tea

infuso, -a *adj* EXPR *Hum* **por ciencia infusa** through divine inspiration

ingeniar 1 *vt* to invent, to devise
2 **ingeniarse** *vpr Fam* **ingeniárselas** to manage, to pull it off; **no sé cómo se las ingenia, pero siempre gana él** I don't know how he does it, but he always wins; **ingeniárselas para hacer algo** to manage to do sth; **se las ingenió para no tener que lavar los platos** she managed to wangle her way out of doing the dishes

ingeniería *nf* engineering; *Fig* **una obra de i.** a major operation ►► ***i. civil*** civil engineering; ***i. financiera*** financial engineering; ***i. genética*** genetic engineering; ***i. industrial*** mechanical engineering; ***i. naval*** marine engineering; ***i. de sistemas*** system(s) engineering; ***i. social*** social engineering

ingeniero, -a 1 *nm,f* engineer ▸▸ ***i. aeronáutico*** aeronautical engineer; ***i. agrónomo*** agronomist; *Esp* ***i. de caminos, canales y puertos*** civil engineer; ***i. civil*** civil engineer; ***i. electrónico*** electrical *o* electronic engineer; ***i. de imagen*** *Br* vision mixer, *US* switcher; ***i. industrial*** industrial engineer; ***i. de minas*** mining engineer; ***i. de montes*** forester, forestry engineer; ***i. naval*** marine engineer; ***i. de programas*** software engineer; ***i. químico*** chemical engineer; *RP* ***i. sanitario*** drainage engineer; ***i. de sistemas*** systems engineer; ***i. de sonido*** sound engineer; ***i. superior*** = engineer who has done a full five-year university course; ***i. técnico*** = engineer who has done a three-year university course rather than a full five-year course; ***i. de telecomunicaciones*** telecommunications engineer; ***i. de vuelo*** flight engineer

2 *nm Andes, CAm, Carib, Méx* = title used to address businessmen and professionals (even if they are not actually qualified as an engineer)

ingenio *nm* (**a**) *(inteligencia)* ingenuity; EXPR **aguzar el i.** to sharpen one's wits (**b**) *(agudeza)* wit, wittiness (**c**) *(máquina)* device (**d**) *(azucarero)* sugar mill

ingeniosamente *adv* ingeniously

ingenioso, -a *adj* (**a**) *(inteligente)* ingenious, clever (**b**) *(agudo)* witty

ingente *adj* enormous, huge; **recibimos una i. cantidad de información** we received an enormous amount of information; **el terremoto causó un número i. de muertos** the earthquake caused a huge number of deaths; **realizan una i. labor de prevención del sida** they are making a huge effort to prevent the spread of AIDS

ingenuamente *adv* ingenuously, naively

ingenuidad *nf* ingenuousness, naivety

ingenuo, -a 1 *adj* naive, ingenuous; **¡no seas i.!** don't be so naive!

2 *nm,f* ingenuous *o* naive person; **es un i.** he's (very) naive; **hacerse el i.** to act the innocent

ingerir [63] *vt* to consume, to ingest

ingesta *nf* intake ▸▸ *Psi* ***i. compulsiva*** compulsive eating

ingestión *nf* consumption, ingestion; **en caso de i. accidental** if accidentally swallowed

ingiero *etc ver* **ingerir**

ingiriera *etc ver* **ingerir**

Inglaterra *n* England

ingle *nf* groin

inglés, -esa 1 *adj* (**a**) *(de Inglaterra)* English (**b**) *(británico)* British

2 *nm,f* (**a**) *(de Inglaterra)* Englishman, *f* Englishwoman; **los ingleses** the English (**b**) *(británico)* British person, Briton; **los ingleses** the British

3 *nm (lengua)* English

inglete *nm* mitre (joint)

ingletera *nf* mitre box

ingobernabilidad *nf* ungovernability

ingobernable *adj* (**a**) *(país)* ungovernable (**b**) *(niño)* uncontrollable, unmanageable

ingratitud *nf* ingratitude, ungratefulness

ingrato, -a 1 *adj* (**a**) *(persona)* ungrateful; **ser i. con alguien** to be ungrateful to sb (**b**) *(trabajo)* thankless

2 *nm,f* ungrateful person; **es un i.** he's so ungrateful

ingravidez *nf* weightlessness; **en estado de i.** in conditions of zero-gravity

ingrávido, -a *adj* weightless

ingrediente *nm* ingredient

ingresar 1 *vt* (**a**) *Esp (dinero) (meter)* to deposit, to pay in; **i. dinero en una cuenta** to deposit money in an account, to pay money into an account; **los pagos me los ingresan en mi cuenta** the money is paid into my account, the payments are credited to my account

(**b**) *(dinero) (ganar)* to make, to earn; **la empresa ingresa varios millones cada día** the company makes several million a day

(**c**) *(persona)* **lo ingresaron en el hospital** he was admitted to hospital

2 *vi* (**a**) **i. en** *(asociación, ejército)* to join; *(convento, universidad)* to enter; **la primera mujer que ingresa en la Academia** the first woman to become a member of the Academy

(**b**) **i. en** *(hospital)* to be admitted to; *Esp* **i. cadáver** to be dead on arrival

(**c**) **i. en** *(prisión)* to go to, to be sent to; **el terrorista ingresó ayer en prisión** the terrorist went *o* was sent to prison yesterday

(**d**) *Am* **i. a** *(lugar)* to get into; **un desconocido ingresó al palacio real** an unidentified intruder got into the royal palace

ingreso *nm* (**a**) *(entrada)* entry, entrance; *(en universidad)* admission; **examen de i.** entrance exam; **solicitud de i.** membership application; **todavía recuerdo la fecha de mi i. en el club** I still remember the day I joined the club; **han solicitado su i. en la organización** they have applied for membership of the organization, they have applied to join the organization

(**b**) *(en hospital)* admission; **se produjeron diez ingresos hospitalarios por salmonelosis** ten people were admitted to hospital with salmonella poisoning

(**c**) *(en prisión)* **el juez decretó el i. en prisión del banquero** the judge ordered that the banker be sent to prison

(**d**) *Am (acceso a lugar)* entry; **el i. a la sala de conciertos fue muy lento** it took a long time to get into the concert hall

(**e**) *Esp (de dinero)* deposit; **realizó un i.** she made a deposit

(**f**) **ingresos** *(sueldo)* income; *(recaudación)* revenue; **ingresos por publicidad** advertising revenue; **tienen unos ingresos anuales de 200 millones** they have an annual income of 200 million ▸▸ ***ingresos brutos*** gross income; ***ingresos netos*** net income

íngrimo, -a *adj CAm, Col, Méx, Ven* (**a**) *(persona)* **el asesinato del líder nos dejó íngrimos** our leader's murder left us all on our own (**b**) *(lugar)* adandoned, lonely

inguinal *adj* groin, *Espec* inguinal; **hernia i.** inguinal hernia

inhábil *adj* (**a**) *(torpe)* clumsy, unskilful; **ser i. para algo** to be unsuited to sth (**b**) *(incapacitado) (por defecto físico)* unfit; *(por la edad)* disqualified (**c**) *(día)* **el día 31 será i. a efectos bancarios** the banks will be closed on 31st

inhabilidad *nf* (**a**) *(falta de destreza)* lack of skill; **su i. para la música** his lack of musical ability (**b**) *(minusvalía)* disability, handicap (**c**) *(jurídica)* ineligibility

inhabilitación *nf (jurídica)* disqualification

inhabilitar *vt* (**a**) *(jurídicamente)* to disqualify (**para** from); **fue inhabilitado para ejercer cargos públicos** she was disqualified from holding public office (**b**) *(físicamente)* to put out of action; **la tormenta inhabilitó la red telefónica** the storm put the telephone system out of action; **la caída lo inhabilitó para el ciclismo** the fall put an end to his cycling

inhabitable *adj* uninhabitable

> **Falso amigo**: El adjetivo inglés **inhabitable** no es la traducción del español **inhabitable**. En inglés **inhabitable** significa "habitable".

inhabitado, -a *adj* uninhabited

> **Falso amigo**: El adjetivo inglés **inhabited** no es la traducción del español **inhabitado**. En inglés **inhabited** significa "habitado".

inhalación *nf* inhalation

inhalador *nm* inhaler

inhalar *vt* to inhale

inherente *adj* inherent; **ser i. a** to be inherent in *o* to, to be an inherent part of; **un problema i. a la infraestructura del país** a problem inherent to the country's infrastructure; **un derecho i. a los seres humanos** an inherent human right

inhibición *nf* (**a**) *(de tribunal, autoridad)* disqualification (**b**) *Fisiol* inhibition (**c**) *Psi* inhibition

inhibido, -a *adj* inhibited

inhibir 1 *vt* (**a**) *(cohibir)* to inhibit; **su agresividad me inhibe** I feel inhibited by his aggressiveness (**b**) *Psi* to inhibit (**c**) *Fisiol* to inhibit

2 **inhibirse** *vpr* (**a**) *(cohibirse)* to become inhibited *o* shy; **no te inhibas** don't be shy (**b**) *(mantenerse al margen)* **en esa discusión vuestra yo me inhibo** I'm keeping out of *o* I'm not going to get involved in your argument; **se inhibió de decir nada** he refrained from saying anything (**c**) *Der* to disqualify oneself; **el tribunal se inhibió en el caso** the court said it could not try the case

inhibitoria *nf Der* restraining order

inhospitalario, -a *adj* inhospitable

inhóspito, -a *adj* inhospitable

inhumación *nf* burial

inhumanamente *adv* (**a**) *(despiadadamente)* inhumanly (**b**) *(desconsideradamente)* inhumanely

inhumanidad *nf* inhumanity

inhumano, -a *adj* (**a**) *(despiadado)* inhuman (**b**) *(desconsiderado)* inhumane (**c**) *Chile (sucio)* filthy

inhumar *vt* to inter, to bury

INI ['ini] *nm* (**a**) *Antes* (*abrev de* **Instituto Nacional de Industria**) = Spanish governmental organization responsible for the promotion of industry (**b**) (*abrev de* **Instituto Nacional Indigenista**) = Mexican government organization responsible for matters concerning the indigenous peoples of the country

iniciación *nf* (**a**) *(introducción)* initiation; **i. a la carpintería** introduction to carpentry (**b**) *(a sociedad, secreto)* initiation; **ceremonia de i.** initiation ceremony (**c**) *(principio)* start, beginning

iniciado, -a 1 *adj* (**a**) *(empezado)* started (**b**) *(neófito)* initiated
2 *nm,f* initiate; **para los no iniciados...** for the uninitiated...

iniciador, -ora 1 *adj* initiating
2 *nm,f* initiator

inicial 1 *adj* initial
2 *nf* (**a**) *(letra)* initial (**b**) *Ven (pago)* down payment

inicialar *vt RP* to initial

inicialista *nmf Am (en béisbol)* first base

inicialización *nf Informát* initialization

inicializar [14] *vt Informát* to initialize

inicialmente *adv* initially

iniciar 1 *vt* (**a**) *(empezar)* to start, to initiate; *(debate, discusión)* to start off (**b**) *(en sociedad, secreto)* **i. a alguien en algo** to initiate sb into sth (**c**) *(en disciplina)* **i. a alguien en algo** to introduce sb to sth
2 iniciarse *vpr* (**a**) *(empezar)* to start, to commence (**b**) *(en sociedad, secreto)* **i. en algo** to be initiated into sth (**c**) *(en disciplina)* **iniciarse en el estudio de algo** to begin one's studies in sth; **se inició en el piano a los sesenta años** he took up the piano at sixty

iniciático, -a *adj* initiation; **rito i.** initiation rite

iniciativa *nf* (**a**) *(propuesta)* proposal, initiative ►► ***la i. privada*** private enterprise (**b**) *(cualidad, capacidad)* initiative; **tener i.** to have initiative; **tomar la i.** to take the initiative; **lo hice por i. propia** I did it on my own initiative

inicio *nm* start, beginning

inicuo, -a *adj* iniquitous

inidentificable *adj* unidentifiable

inigualable *adj (belleza)* unrivalled, matchless; *(oferta)* unbeatable; *(oportunidad)* unique

inigualado, -a *adj* unequalled

in illo tempore *loc adv Formal* in those days

inimaginable *adj* unimaginable

inimitable *adj* inimitable

ininteligible *adj* unintelligible

ininterrumpidamente *adv* uninterruptedly, continuously; **corrió durante siete horas i.** she ran without stopping for seven hours; **nevó i. durante una semana** it snowed non-stop *o* uninterruptedly for a week; **el servicio funciona i. 24 horas al día** the service operates continuously *o* non-stop, twenty-four hours a day

ininterrumpido, -a *adj* uninterrupted, continuous; **bailaron durante cinco horas ininterrumpidas** they danced for five hours non-stop; **lleva tres años ininterrumpidos viviendo en el país** she's been living in the country continuously for three years

iniquidad *nf Formal* iniquity

injerencia *nf* interference, meddling; **su i. en países vecinos** its interference in neighbouring countries

injerir [63] **1** *vt* to introduce, to insert
2 injerirse *vpr (entrometerse)* to interfere (**en** in), to meddle (**en** in)

injertar *vt* (**a**) *(en planta)* to graft (**b**) *(en ser humano)* to graft

injerto *nm* (**a**) *(acción)* grafting (**b**) *(rama)* graft (**c**) *(en ser humano)* graft; **i. de cabello** hair implants; **i. de piel** skin graft

injiero *etc ver* **injerir**

injiriera *etc ver* **injerir**

injuria *nf* (**a**) *(insulto)* insult; *(agravio)* offence (**b**) *Der* slander

injuriante = **injurioso**

injuriar *vt* (**a**) *(insultar)* to insult, to abuse; *(agraviar)* to offend (**b**) *Der* to slander

injurioso, -a, injuriante *adj* (**a**) *(insultante)* insulting, abusive (**b**) *Der* slanderous

injustamente *adv* unfairly, unjustly

injusticia *nf* (**a**) *(acto)* injustice; **¡es una i.!** *(quejándose)* it's not fair!; *(con indignación)* it's an outrage!; **es una i. que tenga que hacerlo yo todo** it's not fair that I have to do it all (**b**) *(cualidad)* unfairness, injustice; **la i. de una decisión** the unfairness *o* injustice of a decision

injustificable *adj* unjustifiable

injustificado, -a *adj* unjustified

injusto, -a *adj (persona)* unfair, unjust; *(castigo, ley)* unjust, unfair; **vivimos en un mundo i.** we live in an unjust world; **fue muy i. con nosotros** he was very unfair to us; **es i. que siempre me echen la culpa a mí** it's not fair that they always blame me

Inmaculada *nf* **la I.** the Virgin Mary; **la I. Concepción** the Immaculate Conception

inmaculado, -a *adj* (**a**) *(sin mancha)* spotless; **llevaba un i. traje blanco** he was wearing a spotless white suit (**b**) *(sin pecado)* unblemished; **el candidato tiene un pasado i.** the candidate has an unblemished past

inmadurez *nf* immaturity

inmaduro, -a *adj* (**a**) *(fruta)* unripe (**b**) *(persona)* immature

inmancable *adj Ven Fam* foolproof

inmanencia *nf Formal* immanence

inmanente *adj Formal* immanent, inherent

inmanentismo *nm Filosofía* immanentism

inmarcesible *adj Literario* unfading, imperishable

inmarchitable *adj* unfading, imperishable

inmaterial *adj* immaterial

inmediaciones *nfpl (de localidad)* surrounding area; *(de lugar, casa)* vicinity; **en las i. del accidente** in the immediate vicinity of the accident

inmediatamente *adv* (**a**) *(en el tiempo)* immediately, at once; **i. después del accidente** immediately after the accident; **¡ven aquí i.!** come here immediately *o* at once!; **i. de conocido el resultado, se marchó a su casa** as soon as she found out the result, she went home (**b**) *(en el espacio)* **estaba sentada i. a su lado** she was sitting right beside him; **mi casa está i. después del cruce** my house is immediately *o* just after the crossroads

inmediatez *nf* immediateness, immediacy

inmediato, -a *adj* (**a**) *(instantáneo)* immediate; **de i.** immediately, at once (**b**) *(contiguo)* next (**a** to); **está en un barrio i. al centro** it's in an area near the town centre

inmejorable *adj (momento, situación)* ideal; *(oferta, precio, calidad)* unbeatable

inmemorial *adj* immemorial; **desde tiempo(s) inmemorial(es)** from time immemorial

in memoriam *loc adv* in memoriam

inmensamente *adv* immensely

inmensidad *nf* (**a**) *(grandeza)* immensity (**b**) *(multitud)* huge amount

inmenso, -a *adj* (**a**) *(grande) (lago, continente)* immense, vast; *(camión, casa)* enormous, huge (**b**) *(profundo)* deep; **sintió una inmensa alegría** she felt deeply o tremendously happy (**c**) *Fam (fantástico)* marvellous, wonderful; **es un escritor i.** he's a marvellous writer; **el tenor estuvo i.** the tenor was wonderful

inmensurable *adj* immeasurable

inmerecidamente *adv* undeservedly

inmerecido, -a *adj* undeserved

inmersión *nf* (**a**) *(de submarino, submarinista)* dive (**b**) *(en situación, cultura)* immersion; **su total i. en la cultura árabe** his total immersion in Arab culture ►► ***i. lingüística*** immersion; **un curso de i. lingüística** an immersion course

inmerso, -a *adj* (**a**) *(en líquido)* immersed (**en** in) (**b**) *(en situación)* immersed (**en** in); **la empresa está inmersa en una grave crisis** the company has been plunged into a serious crisis; **estaba i. en sus pensamientos** he was absorbed in his thoughts

inmesurado, -a *adj Am* (**a**) *(excesivo)* excessive, disproportionate; **le están dando una importancia inmesurada** you're giving it too much importance, you're making it more important than it is (**b**) *(enorme)* enormous; **hubo protestas inmesuradas** there were massive protests

inmigración *nf* (**a**) *(movimiento de personas)* immigration (**b**) *(oficina)* Immigration

inmigrante 1 *adj* immigrant
2 *nmf* immigrant

inmigrar *vi* to immigrate

inmigratorio, -a *adj* **política inmigratoria** immigration policy; **una corriente inmigratoria** a flow of immigrants

inminencia *nf* imminence

inminente *adj* imminent, impending

inmiscuirse [34] *vpr* to interfere (**en** in); to meddle (**en** in); **siempre se inmiscuye en mis asuntos** he's always interfering *o* meddling in my affairs

inmisericorde *adj* pitiless, merciless

inmobiliaria *nf* (**a**) *(agencia) Br* estate agency *o* agent's, *US* real estate agency (**b**) *(constructora)* property developer

inmobiliario, -a *adj* property, *US* real estate; **agente i.** *Br* estate agent, *US* realtor; **propiedad inmobiliaria** real estate

inmoderación *nf* immoderation, excess

inmoderado, -a *adj* immoderate, excessive

inmodestia *nf* immodesty

inmodesto, -a *adj* immodest

inmolación *nf* immolation, sacrifice

inmolar 1 *vt* to sacrifice
2 **inmolarse** *vpr* to sacrifice oneself; **inmolarse por alguien** to sacrifice oneself for sb

inmoral *adj* immoral

inmoralidad *nf* (**a**) *(cualidad)* immorality (**b**) *(acción)* immoral action; **lo que hizo fue una i.** what he did was immoral

inmortal 1 *adj* (**a**) *(que no muere)* immortal (**b**) *(fama)* undying; *(artista)* immortal
2 *nmf* immortal

inmortalidad *nf* immortality

inmortalización *nf* immortalization

inmortalizar [14] 1 *vt* to immortalize
2 **inmortalizarse** *vpr* to achieve immortality

inmotivado, -a *adj (acción)* motiveless; *(temor)* groundless

inmovible *adj* immovable, fixed

inmóvil *adj (quieto)* motionless, still; *(coche, tren)* stationary; **quédate i.** stay still, don't move

inmovilidad *nf* immobility

inmovilismo *nm* resistance to change, conservatism

inmovilista 1 *adj* conservative
2 *nmf* conservative

inmovilización *nf* (**a**) *(física)* immobilization (**b**) *(de capital)* tying-up

inmovilizado, -a 1 *adj* immobilized
2 *nm Econ* fixed assets

inmovilizador *nm* immobilizer

inmovilizar [14] *vt* (**a**) *(físicamente)* to immobilize (**b**) *(capitales)* to tie up

inmueble 1 *adj* **bienes inmuebles** real estate
2 *nm (edificio)* building

inmundicia *nf* (**a**) *(suciedad)* filth, filthiness; *(basura) Br* rubbish, *US* garbage (**b**) *(inmoralidad)* **esa novela es una i.** that novel is utter filth

inmundo, -a *adj* (**a**) *(sucio)* filthy, dirty (**b**) *(inmoral)* filthy, disgusting

inmune *adj* (**a**) *(a enfermedad)* immune; **ser i. a algo** to be immune to sth (**b**) *(a insulto, tristeza)* immune; **ser i. a las críticas** to be immune to criticism (**c**) *(exento)* exempt; **una región i. a los efectos del turismo** a region untouched by the effects of tourism

inmunidad *nf* (**a**) *(contra enfermedad)* immunity (**b**) *(privilegio)* immunity ►► ***i. diplomática*** diplomatic immunity; ***i. parlamentaria*** parliamentary immunity

inmunitario, -a *adj* immune

inmunización *nf* immunization

inmunizado, -a *adj* (**a**) *(contra enfermedad)* immunized (**contra** against) (**b**) *(contra tristeza, críticas)* immune (**contra** to)

inmunizar [14] *vt* (**a**) *(contra enfermedad)* to immunize (**contra** against) (**b**) *(contra tristeza, críticas)* to make immune (**contra** to)

inmunodeficiencia *nf* immunodeficiency

inmunodeficiente *adj* immunodeficient

inmunodepresión *nf* immunodepression

inmunodepresor, -ora 1 *adj* immunodepressant
2 *nm* immunodepressant

inmunoensayo *nm Biol* immunoassay

inmunoglobulina *nf Fisiol* immunoglobulin

inmunología *nf* immunology

inmunológico, -a *adj* immune, immunological; **sistema i.** immune system

inmunólogo, -a *nm,f* immunologist

inmunosupresión *nf Med* immunosuppression

inmunosupresor, -ora *Med* 1 *adj* immunosuppressive, immunosuppressant
2 *nm* immunosuppressant

inmunoterapia *nf* immunotherapy

inmutabilidad *nf* immutability

inmutable *adj* (**a**) *(que no cambia)* immutable, unchangeable; **un principio i.** an unchanging principle (**b**) *(imperturbable)* impassive; **permaneció i. mientras leían la sentencia** he remained impassive while the sentence was read out

inmutar 1 *vt* to upset, to perturb
2 **inmutarse** *vpr* to get upset, to be perturbed; **ni se inmutó** he didn't bat an eyelid; **no se inmutó por las acusaciones que le dirigieron** he didn't allow the accusations made against him to upset him

innatismo *nm Filosofía* nativism

innato, -a *adj* innate; **tiene una simpatía innata** she's friendly by nature; **es i. en él** it comes naturally to him

innavegabilidad *nf* (**a**) *(de mar, río)* unnavigability (**b**) *(embarcación)* unseaworthiness

innavegable *adj* (**a**) *(mar, río)* unnavigable (**b**) *(embarcación)* unseaworthy

innecesariamente *adv* unnecessarily, needlessly

innecesario, -a *adj* unnecessary

innegable *adj* undeniable; **tiene un atractivo i.** it is undeniably attractive

innegablemente *adv* undeniably

innegociable *adj* unnegotiable, not negotiable

innoble *adj* ignoble

innombrable *adj* unmentionable

innovación *nf* innovation

innovador, -ora 1 *adj* innovative, innovatory
2 *nm,f* innovator

innovar 1 *vt (método, técnica)* to improve on
2 *vi* to innovate

innumerable *adj* countless, innumerable; **el terremoto provocó innumerables víctimas** the number of casualties in the earthquake was huge; **te he dicho innumerables veces que no te comas las uñas** I've told you countless times not to bite your nails

inobjetable *adj* indisputable

inobservancia *nf* non-observance; **la i. de una ley** failure to observe a law

inocencia *nf* (**a**) *(falta de malicia)* innocence (**b**) *(falta de culpabilidad)* innocence; **proclamó su i.** she proclaimed her innocence

inocentada *nf* practical joke, trick *(played on 28th December)*, ≃ April Fool's joke; **hacerle una i. a alguien** to play a practical joke *o* trick on sb

inocente 1 *adj* (**a**) *(no culpable)* innocent; **todo el mundo es i. hasta que no se demuestre lo contrario** everyone is innocent until proven guilty (**b**) *(ingenuo)* naive, innocent (**c**) *(sin maldad)* harmless
2 *nmf* (**a**) *(no culpable)* innocent person (**b**) *(sin maldad)* harmless person

inocentemente *adv* innocently

inocentón, -ona *Fam* 1 *adj* naive
2 *nm,f* **es un i.** he's so naive

inocuidad *nf* innocuousness, harmlessness

inoculación *nf* inoculation

inocular *vt* to inoculate

inocultable *adj* unconcealable

inocuo, -a *adj* innocuous, harmless

inodoro, -a 1 *adj* odourless
2 *nm* toilet (bowl)

inofensivo, -a *adj* inoffensive, harmless

inoficioso, -a *adj* (**a**) *Der* inofficious (**b**) *Am (inútil)* ineffective, useless

inolvidable *adj* unforgettable

inoperable *adj* (**a**) *(enfermo, tumor)* inoperable (**b**) *RP (aeropuerto)* closed

inoperancia *nf* ineffectiveness

inoperante *adj* ineffective; **las medidas resultaron inoperantes** the measures were ineffective

inopia *nf Fam* **estar en la i.** *(distraído)* to be miles away, to be daydreaming; **a mí no me preguntes, yo estoy en la i.** don't ask me, I haven't got a clue

inopinadamente *adv* unexpectedly

inopinado, -a *adj* unexpected

inoportunamente *adv* inopportunely

inoportunidad *nf* inopportuneness, untimeliness

inoportuno, -a *adj* (**a**) *(en mal momento)* inopportune, untimely (**b**) *(molesto)* inconvenient (**c**) *(inadecuado)* inappropriate

inorgánico, -a *adj* inorganic

inoxidable *adj (acero)* stainless

input ['imput] (*pl* **inputs**) *nm Informát* input

inquebrantable *adj (fe, amistad)* unshakeable; *(lealtad)* unswerving

inquiero *etc ver* **inquirir**

inquietante *adj* worrying

inquietar 1 *vt* to worry, to trouble
2 **inquietarse** *vpr* to worry, to get anxious; **inquietarse por algo** to worry about sth

inquieto, -a *adj* (**a**) *(preocupado)* worried, anxious (**por** about); **estoy i. por su ausencia** I'm worried that he's not here
(**b**) *(agitado, nervioso)* restless; **es un niño muy i.** he's a very restless *o* fidgety child; **el paciente está muy i.** the patient is very unsettled
(**c**) *(con afán de saber)* curious; **tiene una mente inquieta** he has an enquiring mind
(**d**) *CAm (predispuesto)* inclined, predisposed

inquietud *nf* (**a**) *(preocupación)* worry, anxiety; **esperan el resultado con i.** they are awaiting the result anxiously; **hay i. por el comportamiento de la inflación** people are worried *o* concerned about inflation
(**b**) *(afán de saber)* **desde pequeño mostró sus inquietudes musicales** she showed musical leanings from an early age; **tener inquietudes** to have an inquiring mind; **tiene inquietudes por la botánica** he's very interested in botany; **mis alumnos no tienen inquietudes de ningún tipo** my pupils aren't interested in anything

inquilinato *nm* (**a**) *(arriendo)* leasing (**b**) *(derecho)* tenancy (**c**) *RP (vivienda)* = communal dwelling where poor families each live in a single room and share a bathroom and kitchen with others

inquilino, -a 1 *nm,f* tenant; **el i. de 10 Downing Street** the current occupant of number 10 Downing Street
2 *nm Biol* inquiline

inquina *nf* antipathy, aversion; **tener i. a** to feel aversion towards, to be averse to; **el profesor me tiene i.** the teacher seems to have something against me

inquirir [5] *vt* (**a**) *(indagar)* to inquire into, to investigate (**b**) *(preguntar)* to inquire

inquisición *nf* (**a**) *(indagación)* inquiry, investigation (**b**) **la I.** *(tribunal)* the Inquisition

inquisidor, -ora 1 *adj* inquisitive, inquiring
2 *nm* inquisitor

inquisitivo, -a *adj* inquisitive

inquisitorial, inquisitorio, -a *adj* inquisitorial

INRI ['inrri] (*abrev de* **Iesus Nazarenus Rex Iudaeorum**) INRI

inri *nm* EXPR *Esp Fam* **para más i.** to add insult to injury, to crown it all

insaciabilidad *nf* insatiability

insaciable *adj (apetito, curiosidad)* insatiable; *(sed)* unquenchable

insalubre *adj* insalubrious, unhealthy

insalubridad *nf* insalubrity, unhealthiness

Insalud [in'salud] *nm Esp* (*abrev de* **Instituto Nacional de la Salud**) *Br* ≃ NHS, *US* ≃ Medicaid

insalvable *adj (obstáculo)* insuperable, insurmountable

insania *nf Literario* insanity

insano, -a *adj* (**a**) *(no saludable)* unhealthy (**b**) *(loco)* insane

insatisfacción *nf (disgusto, descontento)* dissatisfaction

insatisfactorio, -a *adj* unsatisfactory

insatisfecho, -a *adj* (**a**) *(descontento)* dissatisfied (**de** *o* **con** with); **quedó i. con la reparación** he was unhappy with *o* wasn't satisfied with the repair work (**b**) *(no saciado)* not full, unsatisfied; **un deseo i.** an unsatisfied desire; **quedarse i.** to be left unsatisfied, to be left (still) wanting more

inscribir 1 *vt* (**a**) *(grabar)* to engrave, to inscribe (**en** on); **inscribieron sus nombres en el tronco** they carved their names on the tree trunk; **inscribió su nombre en el historial del torneo** he ensured that his name would go down in the history of the tournament
(**b**) *(apuntar)* **i. algo/a alguien (en)** to register sth/sb (on); **te he inscrito en un curso de cocina** I've enrolled you on a cookery course
(**c**) *Geom* to inscribe
2 **inscribirse** *vpr* (**a**) *(apuntarse)* **inscribirse en** *(colegio)* to enrol in; *(curso)* to enrol on; *(asociación, partido)* to join; *(concurso)* to enter; **me inscribí en el censo electoral** I put my name on the electoral roll *o* register; **se inscribieron en la maratón** they entered (for) the marathon
(**b**) *(incluirse)* **esta medida se inscribe dentro de nuestra política de cooperación** this measure forms part of our policy of cooperation; **una guerra que se inscribe dentro del expansionismo romano** a war which was waged as part of the Roman policy of expansionism

inscripción *nf* (**a**) *(en colegio, curso)* registration, enrolment; *(en censo, registro)* registration; *(en concursos)* entry; **desde su i.** *(en asociación, partido)* since he joined; **abierto el plazo de i.** *(en letrero)* now enrolling, registration now open (**b**) *(de nacimiento, boda)* registration (**c**) *(escrito)* inscription

inscrito, -a, *RP* **inscripto, -a** *participio ver* **inscribir**

insecticida 1 *adj* insecticidal
2 *nm* insecticide

insectívoro, -a *Zool* **1** *adj* insectivorous
2 *nm* insectivore
3 **insectívoros** *nmpl (orden) Insectivora*

insecto *nm* insect ►► ***i. palo*** stick insect

inseguridad *nf* (**a**) *(falta de confianza)* insecurity (**b**) *(duda)* uncertainty (**c**) *(peligro)* lack of safety ►► ***i. ciudadana:*** **ha aumentado la i. ciudadana** there has been a rise in street crime

inseguro, -a *adj* (**a**) *(sin confianza)* insecure (**b**) *(dudoso)* uncertain (**de** about), unsure (**de** of *o* about) (**c**) *(no estable)* unsafe, unstable (**d**) *(peligroso)* unsafe

inseminación *nf* insemination ►► ***i. artificial*** artificial insemination

inseminar *vt* to inseminate

insensatez *nf* (**a**) *(cualidad)* foolishness, senselessness (**b**) *(acto, dicho)* **hacer una i.** to do something foolish; **decir una i.** to say something foolish

insensato, -a 1 *adj* foolish, senseless
2 *nm,f* foolish *o* senseless person, fool; **iqué has hecho, i.!** what have you done, you fool *o* idiot?

insensibilidad *nf* (**a**) *(emocional)* insensitivity (**b**) *(física)* numbness

insensibilización *nf* (**a**) *(emocional)* lack of sensitivity, insensitivity (**b**) *(física)* anaesthetization; **después de la i. de la encía** after the gum has been made numb

insensibilizar 1 *vt* (**a**) *(emocionalmente)* to harden, to desensitize (**a** to) (**b**) *(físicamente)* to numb
2 **insensibilizarse** *vpr (emocionalmente)* to become desensitized (**a** to)

insensible *adj* (**a**) *(indiferente)* insensitive (**a** to); **es i. a su sufrimiento** she's indifferent to his suffering (**b**) *(físicamente)* insensitive (**a** to); **es i. al calor** he doesn't feel the heat (**c**) *(imperceptible)* imperceptible

inseparable *adj* inseparable

inseparablemente *adv* inseparably

insepulto, -a *adj Formal* unburied

inserción *nf* (**a**) *(de pieza)* insertion (**b**) *(de texto, párrafo)* insertion (**c**) *(de anuncio)* insertion, placing (**d**) *(de preso)* integration; **la i. de los jóvenes en el mercado laboral** getting young people into work; **iniciativas de i. laboral** employment initiatives; **la i. social de los inmigrantes** the social inclusion of immigrants

INSERSO [in'serso] *nm Antes* (*abrev de* **Instituto Nacional de Servicios Sociales**) = Spanish government agency responsible for the elderly and disabled, and for citizens living, or recently returned from, abroad

insertar 1 *vt* (**a**) *(pieza)* to insert; **i. algo en algo** to insert sth into sth (**b**) *(texto, párrafo)* to insert (**c**) *(anuncio)* to insert, to place (**d**) *(preso)* to integrate; **i. a jóvenes en el mercado laboral** to get young people into work
2 **insertarse** *vpr* **insertarse en algo** *(enmarcarse)* to form part of sth; **un libro que se inserta en el debate sobre el totalitarismo** a book which forms part of the debate on totalitarianism

inservible *adj* useless; **guarda un montón de objetos inservibles** she keeps loads of useless stuff; **esta lavadora está i.** this washing machine doesn't work

insidia *nf* (**a**) *(trampa)* trap, snare (**b**) *(mala acción)* malicious act

insidiosamente *adv* maliciously

insidioso, -a *adj* malicious

insigne *adj* distinguished, illustrious

insignia *nf* (**a**) *(distintivo)* badge; *(militar)* insignia (**b**) *(bandera)* flag, banner

insignificancia *nf* (**a**) *(cualidad)* insignificance (**b**) *(cosa, hecho)* trifle, insignificant thing

insignificante *adj* insignificant

insinceridad *nf* insincerity

insincero, -a *adj* insincere

insinuación *nf* hint, insinuation; **insinuaciones** *(amorosas)* advances; **se pasó toda la fiesta haciéndole insinuaciones** she spent the the whole party coming on to him

insinuante *adj (mirada, ropa)* suggestive; *(comentarios)* full of innuendo

insinuar [4] **1** *vt* to hint at, to insinuate; **¿qué insinúas?** what are you suggesting *o* insinuating?; **insinuó que había sido culpa mía** she implied it had been my fault

2 insinuarse *vpr* (**a**) *(amorosamente)* to make advances (**a** to); **yo creo que se te está insinuando** I think he's coming on to you (**b**) *(notarse)* **empiezan a insinuarse problemas** it's beginning to look as if there might be problems; **insinuarse detrás de algo** *(asomar)* to peep out from behind sth; **empezaba a insinuarse el día** dawn was beginning to break

insípido, -a *adj* (**a**) *(comida)* insipid, tasteless (**b**) *(película, fiesta)* insipid, dull

insistencia *nf* insistence; **su i. en venir acabó por convencerme** his insistence on coming finally persuaded me; **grité con i. pero no me oyó** I shouted repeatedly but she didn't hear me; **ante la i. de mis padres, acabé por invitarla** my parents insisted so much *o* were so insistent that I ended up inviting her

insistente *adj (persona)* insistent; *(preguntas)* persistent; **la i. lluvia obligó a cancelar el concierto** the persistent rain meant that the concert had to be cancelled; **circulaban insistentes rumores sobre un golpe de estado** there were persistent rumours of a coup d'état

insistentemente *adv* insistently

insistir *vi* to insist (**en** on); **bueno, si insistes, tomaré uno** all right, if you insist, I'll have one; **tú insiste, que ya verás cómo al final abre la puerta** don't give up, she'll open the door eventually, you'll see; **insistió mucho sobre este punto** he laid great stress on this point; **no insistas, te he dicho que no** don't keep on about it, I've told you the answer is no; **no sé por qué insiste en llamarme** I don't know why he keeps on *o* persists in calling me; **insistió en la importancia del problema** he stressed the importance of the problem; **i. en que** to insist *o* maintain that; **la dirección insiste en que los empleados deben llevar corbata** the management insist on employees wearing a tie; **insistió en que él no era culpable** he insisted that he was not to blame

in situ **1** *adj* on-the-spot; *(garantía)* on-site

2 *adv* on the spot; *(reparar)* on site

insobornable *adj* incorruptible

insociabilidad *nf* unsociability

insociable *adj* unsociable

insolación *nf* (**a**) *(exposición al sol)* sunstroke; **le dio una i., agarró** *o Esp* **cogió una i.** he got sunstroke (**b**) *Meteo* sunshine

insolarse *vpr* to get sunstroke

insolencia *nf* (**a**) *(falta de respeto)* insolence; **respondió con i.** she replied insolently (**b**) *(dicho)* insolent remark; **ya estoy harto de sus insolencias** *(actos)* I'm fed up of her insolent behaviour; **ha hecho otra i.** he's been insolent again; **decir una i.** to make an insolent remark

insolentarse *vpr* to be insolent (**con** to)

insolente **1** *adj (descarado)* insolent; *(orgulloso)* haughty

2 *nmf* insolent person; **es un i.** he's very insolent

insolentemente *adv* insolently

insolidaridad *nf* **la i. de una política económica** the unfairness of an economic policy; **estamos hartos de la i. que muestra hacia los demás** we're fed up of the way she never supports anyone else

insolidario, -a **1** *adj* **se mostraron insolidarios con los huelguistas** they didn't support the strikers; **un sistema fiscal muy i.** an unfair tax system

2 *nm,f* **no seas un i. y apoya a tus compañeros** don't be so selfish and support your colleagues; **es una insolidaria, con ella no cuentes** you can't rely on her, she always looks after number one

insólito, -a *adj* very unusual

insolubilidad *nf* insolubility

insoluble *adj* (**a**) *(sustancia)* insoluble (**b**) *(problema)* insoluble, unsolvable

insolvencia *nf* insolvency

insolvente *adj* insolvent

insomne **1** *adj* insomniac

2 *nmf* insomniac

insomnio *nm* insomnia, sleeplessness

insondable *adj* (**a**) *(abismo, mar)* unfathomable, bottomless (**b**) *(misterio, sentimientos)* unfathomable

insonorización *nf* soundproofing

insonorizado, -a *adj* soundproof

insonorizar [14] *vt* to soundproof

insonoro, -a *adj* soundless

insoportable *adj* unbearable, intolerable; **en agosto hace un calor i.** it's unbearably hot in August

insoslayable *adj* inevitable, unavoidable

insospechable *adj* impossible to tell, unforeseeable

insospechado, -a *adj* unexpected, unforeseen

insostenible *adj* (**a**) *(situación)* untenable (**b**) *(afirmación, tesis)* untenable

inspección *nf* (**a**) *(examen)* inspection; *(policial)* search; **pasar una i.** to have *o* undergo an inspection ►► ***i. de calidad*** quality control inspection; ***i. ocular*** visual inspection *o* examination; *Esp* ***i. técnica de vehículos*** = annual technical inspection for motor vehicles with an age of five years or more, *Br* ≃ MOT (**b**) *(lugar)* inspectorate

inspeccionar *vt* to inspect; **la policía inspeccionó la zona** the police searched the area

inspector, -ora *nm,f* inspector ►► ***i. de aduanas*** customs officer; ***i. de Hacienda*** tax inspector; ***i. de policía*** police inspector; ***i. de sanidad*** public health inspector, sanitary inspector

inspectoría *nf Chile* police station

inspiración *nf* (**a**) *(artística)* inspiration; **me llegó la i. de repente** I had a sudden flash of inspiration; **un trabajo de i. modernista** a piece of work which draws its inspiration from modernism ►► ***i. divina*** divine inspiration (**b**) *(respiración)* inhalation, breath

inspirado, -a *adj* inspired (**en** by); **estar i.** to be inspired

inspirador, -ora **1** *adj* (**a**) *(que inspira)* inspiring (**b**) *(músculo)* inspiratory

2 *nm,f* inspirer

inspirar **1** *vt* (**a**) *(sentimientos, ideas)* to inspire; **me inspira mucha simpatía** I really like him; **me inspira terror** I find him frightening; **no me inspira mucha confianza** he doesn't inspire much confidence in me (**b**) *(artísticamente)* to inspire; **la belleza del paisaje lo inspiró a componer la sinfonía** the beauty of the landscape inspired him to compose the symphony (**c**) *(respirar)* to inhale, to breathe in

2 *vi (respirar)* to inhale, to breathe in

3 inspirarse *vpr* to be inspired (**en** by); **su trabajo se inspira en los clásicos** her work is inspired by the classics; **viajó al Caribe para inspirarse** he went to the Caribbean in search of inspiration

INSS (*abrev de* **Instituto Nacional de la Seguridad Social**) *Br* ≃ DWP, *US* ≃ Department of Health and Human Services

instalación *nf* (**a**) *(acción)* installation; *(de local, puesto)* setting up; **han anunciado la i. de un hipermercado en las afueras de la ciudad** they have announced that a hypermarket is to be built on the outskirts of town

(**b**) *(aparatos)* system ►► ***i. de aire acondicionado*** air-conditioning system; ***i. eléctrica*** wiring; ***i. del gas*** gas pipes; ***i. sanitaria*** plumbing

(**c**) *(lugar)* **el acto se celebró en las instalaciones de la empresa** the ceremony took place on company premises; **instalaciones deportivas** sports facilities; **instalaciones militares** military installations; **instalaciones portuarias** port facilities *o* installations; **instalaciones nucleares** nuclear installations *o* plants

instalador, -ora **1** *adj* installing, fitting; **una empresa instaladora de cable** a cable-laying company

2 *nm,f* fitter

3 *nm Informát* installer

instalar **1** *vt* (**a**) *(montar) (aparato)* to install, to fit; *(antena)* to install, to put up; *(computador)* to install; *(local, puesto)* to set up (**b**) *(situar) (objeto)* to place; *(tienda)* to pitch; *(gente)* to put; **instalaron a los refugiados en tiendas de campaña** they put the refugees up in tents (**c**) *Informát (programa)* to install (**d**) *Am (comisión)* to set up

2 instalarse *vpr (establecerse)* **instalarse en** to settle (down) in; *(nueva casa)* to move into; **a falta de dormitorios, se instalaron en el salón** as there were no bedrooms, they installed themselves in the living room; *Literario* **la tristeza se instaló en su corazón** his heart was filled with sadness

instancia *nf* (**a**) *(solicitud)* application (form)

(**b**) *(ruego)* request; **a instancias de** at the request *o* bidding of; **el abogado actuaba a instancias mías** the lawyer was acting on my instructions

(**c**) *(recurso)* **en última i.** as a last resort

(**d**) *(institución)* **se mueve entre las altas instancias del partido** he moves in the upper echelons of the party; **se goza del apoyo de las**

más altas instancias eclesiásticas he enjoys the support of the highest authorities of the Church

(e) *Am (momento)* **en (una) primera i., introduciremos los datos** first of all we'll input the data

instantánea *nf* snapshot, snap

instantáneamente *adv* instantaneously

instantáneo, -a *adj* (a) *(momentáneo)* momentary (b) *(rápido)* instantaneous; **provoca una reacción instantánea** it gets an immediate reaction; **el medicamento proporciona un alivio i.** the drug brings instant *o* immediate relief; **el impacto le produjo la muerte instantánea** he was killed instantly by the impact (c) *(café, sopa)* instant

instante *nm* moment, instant; **desde el i. en que te vi, supe que estabas enfadado** I knew you were angry the moment I saw you; **en un i.** in a second; **un i., por favor** one moment *o* just a moment, please; **a cada i.** all the time, constantly; **al i.** instantly, immediately; **por un i. pensé que me había equivocado** for a moment I thought I'd made a mistake; **la tensión crece por instantes** the tension is increasing by the minute

instar *vt* **i. a alguien a hacer algo** *o* **a que haga algo** to urge sb to do sth

instauración *nf* establishment

instaurador, -ora *adj* **el proceso i. de la democracia** the process of establishing democracy

instaurar *vt* to establish, to set up

insti *nm Esp Fam* (high) school

instigación *nf* **lo acusan de i. a la violencia** he is accused of inciting violence; **por i. de** at the instigation of

instigador, -ora 1 *adj* instigating

2 *nm,f* instigator

instigar [38] *vt* **i. a alguien (a hacer algo** *o* **a que haga algo)** to incite sb (to do sth); **i. a algo** to incite to sth

instilar *vt Formal (idea)* to instil; **i. algo a alguien** to instil sth in sb

instintivamente *adv* instinctively

instintivo, -a *adj* instinctive

instinto *nm* instinct; **tiene un i. para detectar el peligro** he senses danger instinctively; **por i.** instinctively ▸▸ ***i. de conservación*** survival instinct; ***i. maternal*** maternal instinct; ***i. de supervivencia*** survival instinct

institución *nf* (a) *(organización)* institution; **la i. monárquica** the institution of the monarchy; *Fig* **ser una i.** *(persona, establecimiento)* to be an institution ▸▸ ***i. benéfica*** charitable organization; ***i. pública*** public institution (b) *(de ley, sistema)* introduction; *(de organismo, premio)* establishment, setting up (c) **instituciones** *(del Estado)* institutions

institucional *adj* institutional

institucionalización *nf* institutionalization

institucionalizado, -a *adj* institutionalized

institucionalizar [14] *vt* to institutionalize

instituir [34] *vt* (a) *(fundar) (gobierno)* to establish; *(premio, sociedad)* to found, to establish; *(sistema, reglas)* to introduce (b) *(nombrar)* to appoint, to name

instituto *nm* (a) *(corporación)* institute ▸▸ ***I. Cervantes*** = organization that promotes Spain and its language in the rest of the world, *Br* ≃ British Council; ***I. Nacional de Meteorología*** = Spanish national weather forecasting agency, *Br* ≃ Met Office

(b) *Esp (militar)* **el i. de la Guardia Civil** the Civil Guard, = armed Spanish police force who patrol rural areas and highways, and guard public buildings in cities and police borders and coasts

(c) *Esp (colegio)* high school; *Antes* **I. (Nacional) de Bachillerato** *o* **Enseñanza Media** = state secondary school for 14-18-year-olds, *US* ≃ Senior High School ▸▸ ***I. de Formación Profesional*** technical college

(d) *(salón)* ***i. de belleza*** beauty salon; ***i. capilar*** hair clinic

institutor, -ora *nm,f Col* schoolteacher

institutriz *nf* governess

instrucción *nf* (a) *(conocimientos)* education; **una persona con gran i.** a very well-educated person

(b) *(docencia)* instruction

(c) *(militar)* **hacer i.** to drill, to go through one's drill ▸▸ ***i. militar*** military training

(d) **instrucciones** *(órdenes)* instructions; **recibí instrucciones de no abandonar mi puesto** I received instructions not to leave my post

(e) **instrucciones** *(explicación)* instructions; **sigue las instrucciones** follow the instructions; **instrucciones (de uso)** instructions (for use)

(f) *Informát* instruction

(g) *Der (investigación)* preliminary investigation; *(curso del proceso)* proceedings

instructivo, -a *adj (experiencia, narración)* instructive; *(juguete, película)* educational

instructor, -ora 1 *adj* training; **juez i.** examining magistrate

2 *nm,f* instructor ▸▸ ***i. de vuelo*** flying instructor

instruido, -a *adj* educated; **muy i.** well educated; **está i. en el arte de la diplomacia** he's well versed in the art of diplomacy

instruir [34] 1 *vt* (a) *(enseñar)* to instruct; **la instruyó en las artes marciales** he taught her martial arts (b) *Der* to prepare; **el juez que instruye el sumario** the examining magistrate

2 *vi* **los viajes instruyen mucho** travel really broadens the mind

3 **instruirse** *vpr* **instruirse en algo** to teach oneself sth; **se instruyó en un colegio bilingüe** she was educated in a bilingual school

instrumentación *nf* (a) *(en música)* orchestration, instrumentation (b) *(de plan, acuerdo)* implementation (c) *(de vehículo)* controls

instrumentador, -ora *nm,f* (a) *Am (instrumentalizador)* architect, prime mover (b) *Arg Med Br* theatre nurse, *US* OR nurse

instrumental 1 *adj* (a) *(composición musical)* instrumental (b) *(central)* **fue i. para la consecución de la paz** it was key to the achievement of peace

2 *nm* (a) *(equipamiento)* instruments ▸▸ ***i. médico*** surgical instruments (b) *(canción)* instrumental

instrumentalización *nf* exploitation

instrumentalizador, -ora *nm,f* architect, prime mover

instrumentalizar *vt* to use, to exploit

instrumentar *vt* (a) *(composición musical)* to orchestrate, to score (b) *(plan, acuerdo)* to implement

instrumentista *nmf* (a) *(músico)* instrumentalist (b) *Med Br* theatre nurse, *US* OR nurse

instrumento *nm* (a) *(musical)* instrument; **i. musical** *o* **de música** musical instrument ▸▸ *Méx* ***i. de aliento*** wind instrument; ***i. de cuerda*** stringed *o* string instrument; ***i. de percusión*** percussion instrument; ***i. de viento*** wind instrument

(b) *(herramienta)* tool, instrument ▸▸ ***i. de medida*** measuring instrument; ***i. óptico*** optical instrument; ***i. de precisión*** precision tool *o* instrument

(c) *(medio)* means, tool; **un i. para estimular la demanda** a means of stimulating demand; **ella fue el i. del gobierno** she was a tool of the government; **el canal televisivo es un i. de propaganda de la oposición** the television channel is a propaganda tool for the opposition

(d) *Der* instrument

(e) *Fam (pene)* tool

instruyera *etc ver* **instruir**

instruyo *etc ver* **instruir**

insubordinación *nf* insubordination

insubordinado, -a 1 *adj* insubordinate

2 *nm,f* insubordinate (person), rebel

insubordinar 1 *vt* to stir up, to incite to rebellion

2 **insubordinarse** *vpr* to rebel

insubstancial = **insustancial**

insubstituible = **insustituible**

insuceso *nm Col, Ecuad, Méx, RP* unfortunate incident

insuficiencia *nf* (a) *(escasez)* lack, shortage; **el proyecto fue abandonado por i. de medios** the project was dropped owing to a lack of resources; **fue producido por una i. vitamínica** it was caused by a vitamin deficiency; **las insuficiencias de un tratado** the deficiencies *o* weak points of a treaty (b) *Med* failure, insufficiency ▸▸ ***i. cardiaca*** heart failure; ***i. renal*** kidney failure; ***i. respiratoria*** respiratory failure

insuficiente 1 *adj* insufficient

2 *nm (nota)* fail

insuficientemente *adv* insufficiently

insuflar *vt* (a) *(gas, vapor)* to blow (**a** into) (b) *(ideas, sentimientos)* **los aficionados insuflaban ánimos a la selección** the supporters urged the team on; **me han insuflado ánimos para seguir adelante** they have given me the heart to carry on

insufrible *adj (carácter, persona)* insufferable, unbearable; *(dolor)* unbearable

ínsula *nf Literario* isle

insular 1 *adj* insular, island; **el clima i.** the island climate
2 *nmf* islander

insularidad *nf* insularity

insulina *nf* insulin

insulinodependiente 1 *adj* insulin-dependent
2 *nmf* insulin-dependent (person)

insulso, -a *adj* (a) *(comida)* bland, insipid (b) *(persona, libro)* insipid, dull

insultada *nf Andes, CAm, Méx* insult

insultante *adj* insulting, offensive

insultar *vt* to insult

insulto *nm* insult; **proferir insultos** to hurl insults; **sus declaraciones son un i. a la inteligencia** his statements are an insult to people's intelligence

insumergible *adj* unsinkable

insumir *vt RP* (a) *(demorar)* to take (b) *(costar)* to cost

insumisión *nf* (a) *Esp Mil* = refusal to do military service or a civilian equivalent (b) *(rebeldía)* rebelliousness

insumiso, -a 1 *adj* rebellious
2 *nm,f* (a) *Esp Mil* = person who refuses to do military service or a civilian equivalent (b) *(rebelde)* rebel

insumo *nm Am* (a) *Com* **insumos** *(bienes)* raw materials; **un producto fabricado a partir de insumos chilenos** a product manufactured using Chilean materials (b) *Com* **insumos** *(suministros)* supplies; **van a mejorar la dotación de insumos para los hospitales** the provision of supplies to hospitals is to be improved (c) *Ling* input

insuperable *adj* (a) *(inmejorable)* unsurpassable (b) *(sin solución)* insurmountable, insuperable

insurgente 1 *adj* insurgent
2 *nmf* insurgent

insurrección *nf* insurrection, revolt

insurreccionar 1 *vt* to incite to insurrection
2 **insurreccionarse** *vpr* to rebel, to revolt

insurrecto, -a 1 *adj* insurgent, rebel
2 *nm,f* insurgent, rebel

insustancial, insubstancial *adj* insubstantial

insustituible, insubstituible *adj* irreplaceable

intachable *adj* irreproachable

intacto, -a *adj* (a) *(que no ha sido tocado)* untouched (b) *(entero, íntegro)* intact; **el autobús quedó i. después del accidente** the bus survived the accident intact, the bus was undamaged as a result of the accident; **el partido conserva i. el apoyo de sus votantes** the support of the party's voters has been unaffected; **mantienen intactas sus esperanzas** their hopes are still alive

intangible *adj* intangible

integración *nf* (a) *(acción)* integration; **la i. de los refugiados en la sociedad** the integration of refugees into society ►► ***i. racial*** racial integration; ***i. vertical*** vertical integration (b) *Mat* integration

integrado, -a *adj* integrated

integrador, -ora *adj* **un proceso i.** a process of integration; **una iniciativa integradora** an initiative promoting integration

integral 1 *adj* (a) *(total)* total, complete; **una educación i.** an all-round education; **contiene desnudos integrales** there are scenes of total nudity; *Fam* **es un idiota i.** he's a total *o* complete idiot
(b) *(esencial)* integral; **la creación de empleo es parte i. del plan** job creation is an integral part of the plan
(c) *(sin refinar) (pan, harina, pasta) Br* wholemeal, *US* wholewheat; *(arroz)* brown
(d) *(constituyente)* integral; **ser parte i. de algo** to be an integral part of sth
(e) *Mat (cálculo)* integral
2 *nf Mat* integral

íntegramente *adv* wholly, entirely; **una casa í. de madera** a house built entirely of wood; **el partido será televisado í.** the whole game will be televised, the game will be televised in its entirety

integrante 1 *adj* integral, constituent; **estado i. de la UE** member state of the EU; **ser parte i. de algo** to be an integral part of sth
2 *nmf* member

integrar 1 *vt* (a) *(incluir)* to integrate; **han integrado un chip en el motor** the motor has a chip built into it; **integra fax y fotocopiadora en un solo aparato** it combines a fax and a photocopier in one machine; **su objetivo es i. a los inmigrantes en la comunidad** their aim is to integrate immigrants into the community
(b) *(componer)* to make up; **integran la comisión expertos en el tema** the committee is made up of *o* composed of experts on the subject; **una banda integrada por siete asaltantes robó el banco** a gang of seven robbed the bank
(c) *Mat* to integrate
(d) *CSur (pagar)* to pay
2 **integrarse** *vpr* (a) *(unirse)* to join; **integrarse en** to join; **se integraron en la ONU en 1972** they joined the UN in 1972 (b) *(adaptarse)* to integrate; **no llegó a integrarse con el resto de sus compañeros** he never integrated with *o* fitted in with the rest of his colleagues; **se integró rápidamente al nuevo equipo** she quickly fitted into the new team

integridad *nf* (a) *(moral)* integrity (b) *(física)* safety; **el estado del estadio ponía en peligro la i. física de los espectadores** the condition of the stadium posed a safety risk to spectators; **van a defender la i. territorial del país** they will defend the country's borders (c) *(totalidad)* wholeness; **leí la ley en su i.** I read the law in its enterity

integrismo *nm (religioso, económico)* fundamentalism; *(de terroristas no religiosos)* extremism; **el i. islámico** Islamic fundamentalism

integrista 1 *adj (en religión, economía)* fundamentalist; *(terroristas no religiosos)* extremist
2 *nmf (en religión, economía)* fundamentalist; *(terrorista no religioso)* extremist

íntegro, -a *adj* (a) *(completo)* whole, entire; **versión íntegra** *(de libro)* unabridged edition; *(de película)* uncut version (b) *(honrado)* upright, honourable

intelecto *nm* intellect

intelectual 1 *adj* intellectual
2 *nmf* intellectual

intelectualidad *nf* intelligentsia, intellectuals

intelectualizar [14] *vt* to intellectualize

intelectualmente *adv* intellectually

intelectualoide *nmf Fam* pseudo-intellectual, *Br* pseud

inteligencia *nf* (a) *(entendimiento)* intelligence ►► *Informát* ***i. artificial*** artificial intelligence (b) *(seres inteligentes)* intelligent life (c) *(espionaje)* intelligence; **servicio de i.** intelligence service (d) **la i.** *(la intelectualidad)* the intelligentsia

inteligente *adj* (a) *(que piensa)* intelligent (b) *(con mucha inteligencia)* intelligent (c) *Informát (sistema, edificio)* intelligent; *(tarjeta, bomba)* smart

inteligentemente *adv* intelligently

inteligibilidad *nf* intelligibility

inteligible *adj* intelligible

inteligiblemente *adv* intelligibly

intelligentsia [inteli'ɣensja] *nf* intelligentsia

intemperancia *nf* intemperance, immoderation

intemperie *nf* **no encontraron un sitio donde guarecerse de la i.** they couldn't find anywhere to shelter from the elements; **la lona protege la moto de la i.** the tarpaulin protects the motorbike from the effects of the weather; **a la i.** in the open air; **pasamos una noche a la i.** we spent a night out in the open; **el problema de los refugiados que viven a la i.** the problem of refugees sleeping rough; **el cadáver quedó expuesto a la i.** the body was exposed to the elements

intempestivamente *adv (visitar, proponer)* inopportunely

intempestivo, -a *adj (clima, comentario)* harsh; *(hora)* ungodly, unearthly; *(proposición, visita)* inopportune

intemporal *adj* timeless, independent of time

intemporalidad *nf* timelessness

intención *nf* intention; **su i. es volver a presentarse al concurso** she intends to enter the competition again; **ya veo cuáles son tus intenciones** I see what you're up to now; **el prólogo del acuerdo es una declaración de intenciones** the preface to the agreement is a declaration of intent; **se agradece la i.** it was a nice thought; **tener la i. de hacer algo** to intend to do sth; **no tengo i. alguna de ir** I have no intention of going; **con i.** *(intencionadamente)* intentionally; **lo hizo con i. de ayudar** he was trying to help; **los fans llegaron con i. de causar problemas** the fans came with the intention of causing trouble; **buena/mala i.** good/bad intentions; **tener buenas/malas intenciones** to have good/bad intentions; **lo hizo sin mala i.** he didn't mean any harm; **lo dije sin i. de ofender a nadie** it wasn't my intention to offend anyone, I didn't mean any offence; **lo dijo con segundas intenciones** he had an ulterior motive for saying it; EXPR **la i. es lo que cuenta** it's the thought that counts; PROV **de buenas intenciones está empedrado el camino del infierno** the road to hell is paved with good intentions ►► ***i. de voto*** voting intentions; **la encuesta le da el 20 por ciento de la i. de voto** 20 percent of those interviewed in the poll said they would vote for her

intencionadamente *adv* deliberately, intentionally, on purpose

intencionado, -a *adj* intentional, deliberate; **cometió una falta de forma intencionada** he committed a deliberate foul; **bien i.** *(acción)* well-meant; *(persona)* well-meaning; **mal i.** *(acción)* ill-meant, ill-intentioned; *(persona)* malevolent

intencional *adj* intentional, deliberate

intencionalidad *nf* intent

intencionalmente *adv* intentionally

intendencia *nf* **(a)** *(administración)* management, administration
(b) *(militar) Br* ≃ Royal Army Service Corps, *US* ≃ Quartermaster Corps
(c) *Chile (gobernación)* regional government
(d) *RP (corporación municipal)* town council, *US* city council
(e) *RP (edificio)* town hall, *US* city hall

intendente *nm* **(a)** *(militar)* quartermaster **(b)** *RP (alcalde)* mayor **(c)** *Chile (gobernador)* provincial governor

intensamente *adv (con intensidad)* intensely; *(llover)* heavily; *(iluminar)* brightly; *(amar)* passionately; *(trabajar)* intensively; **me duele i.** it really hurts; **lo odio i.** I detest him, I really hate him; **vive su vida muy i.** she really lives life to the full; **el viento soplaba i.** there was a very strong wind

intensidad *nf* **(a)** *(fuerza)* intensity; *(de dolor)* intensity, acuteness; *(de lluvia)* heaviness; *(de viento)* strength; *(de luz, color)* brightness; *(de amor, odio)* strength; *(de vivencia)* intensity; **de poca i.** *(luz)* dim, weak; **llovía con poca i.** light rain was falling ►► ***i. luminosa*** luminous intensity **(b)** *Elec* intensity

intensificación *nf* intensification

intensificador, -ora *adj* intensifying

intensificar [60] **1** *vt* to intensify
2 intensificarse *vpr* to intensify; **el viento se intensificó** the wind stiffened *o* got stronger

intensivamente *adv* intensively

intensivista *nmf* intensive care specialist

intensivo, -a *adj* intensive; **curso i.** intensive course

intenso, -a *adj (mirada, calor)* intense; *(dolor)* intense, acute; *(lluvia)* heavy; *(viento)* strong; *(luz, color)* bright; *(amor, odio)* passionate; *(vivencia)* intense, powerful; **poco i.** *(lluvia)* light; *(luz)* dim, weak

intentar *vt* **i. (hacer algo)** to try (to do sth); **¡inténtalo!** have a try *o* go!; **¡ni lo intentes!** *(advertencia)* don't even try it!; **intentarán finalizar el trabajo antes del fin de semana** they will try to finish the work before the weekend; **intenta ser más discreto** try to be more discreet; **la próxima vez, intenta que no se te caiga** try not to drop it next time; **intenté que cambiara de opinión pero no hubo manera** I tried to get her to change her mind but she wasn't having any of it; EXPR **no se pierde nada por intentarlo, por intentarlo que no quede** there's no harm in trying

intento *nm (tentativa)* attempt; *(intención)* intention; **aprobó el examen en el segundo i.** he passed the exam at the second attempt; **lo conseguiré aunque muera en el i.** I'll do it if it kills me; **i. de golpe de Estado** attempted coup; **i. de robo** attempted robbery; **i. de suicidio** suicide attempt

intentona *nf Pol* **i. (golpista)** attempted coup

inter- *pref* inter-

interacción *nf* interaction

interaccionar *vi* to interact

interactividad *nf* interactivity

interactivo, -a *adj* interactive

interactuar *vi* to interact

interamericano, -a *adj* inter-American

interandino, -a *adj* inter-Andean

interanual *adj* year-on-year

interbancario, -a *adj* interbank; **mercado i.** interbank market

intercalación *nf* insertion

intercalar *vt* to insert, to put in; **intercala los banderines rojos con los verdes** alternate red flags with green ones; **intercaló canciones de su nuevo disco con clásicos** she interpersed songs from her new album with old favourites; **intercaló varios chistes en el discurso** she interspersed her speech with a number of jokes; **intercaló la postal entre las demás** he inserted *o* put the postcard between the others

intercambiable *adj* interchangeable

intercambiador *nm* **(a)** *Esp (de transporte)* = station where passengers can change to various other means of transport **(b) i. (de calor)** heat exchanger

intercambiar *vt (objetos, ideas)* to exchange; *(lugares, posiciones)* to change, to swap; *(cromos)* to swap; **los dos presidentes intercambiaron saludos** the two presidents exchanged greetings *o* greeted each other; **los jugadores se intercambiaron las camisetas** the players swapped shirts

intercambio *nm (de objetos, ideas)* exchange; *(de cromos)* swap; **se ha producido un i. de lugares en la clasificación** the two teams have swapped places in the table; **la discusión acabó con un i. de puñetazos** the argument ended with them trading punches; **un alumno de i.** an exchange student; **hizo i. con una chica canadiense** she did an exchange with a Canadian girl ►► ***i. comercial*** trade; ***i. cultural*** cultural exchange; *Fin* ***i. de la deuda*** debt swap; ***i. de golpes*** *(en tenis)* rally; ***i. de ideas*** exchange of ideas; ***i. de parejas*** swinging

interceder *vi* **i. (por alguien)** to intercede (on sb's behalf); **mi hermano intercedió ante mi novia para que me perdonara** my brother talked to my girlfriend to try to persuade her to forgive me

intercelular *adj Biol* intercellular

intercentros *adj inv Ind* **comité i.** central works committee

interceptación *nf* **(a)** *(detención)* interception **(b)** *(de teléfono)* tapping **(c)** *(obstrucción)* blockage **(d)** *Dep (de pase)* interception

interceptar *vt* **(a)** *(detener)* to intercept; **el mensaje fue interceptado por el servicio secreto** the message was intercepted by the secret service; **la policía interceptó un alijo de cocaína** the police intercepted a shipment of cocaine **(b)** *(teléfono)* to tap **(c)** *(obstruir)* to block; **un tronco intercepta el camino** a fallen tree is blocking the road **(d)** *Dep (pase)* to intercept

interceptor, -ora 1 *adj* intercepting
2 *nm* interceptor

intercesión *nf* intercession

intercesor, -ora 1 *adj* interceding
2 *nm,f* interceder, intercessor

intercity *nm* intercity train

interclasista *adj* **un fenómeno i.** a phenomenon that crosses class boundaries

intercomunicación *nf* intercommunication

intercomunicador *nm* intercom

intercomunicar *vt* to link, to connect

interconexión *nf* interconnection

interconfesional *adj* interdenominational

intercontinental *adj* intercontinental

intercostal *adj* intercostal

intercultural *adj* intercultural

interdental *adj Ling* interdental

interdepartamental *adj* interdepartmental

interdependencia *nf* interdependence

interdependiente *adj* interdependent

interdicción *nf* interdiction

interdicto *nm Der* interdict

interdigital *adj (membrana)* interdigital

interdisciplinar, interdisciplinario, -a *adj* interdisciplinary

interés (*pl* **intereses**) *nm* **(a)** *(utilidad, valor)* interest; **de i.** interesting; **un descubrimiento de gran i. para los enfermos de sida** a discovery of great signifiance to people with AIDS; **una construcción de i. histórico** a building of historical interest
(b) *(curiosidad)* interest; **un tema de i. común** a subject of interest to everyone; **el hallazgo ha despertado el i. de los científicos** the discovery has aroused scientists' interest; **tener i. en** *o* **por** to be interested in; **tengo i. por recorrer el centro de la ciudad** I'm interested in doing a tour of the town centre; **sigo con i. la polémica** I'm following the debate with interest
(c) *(esfuerzo)* interest; **trabajó con mucho i. en el proyecto** she was an enthusiastic worker on the project; **poner i. en algo** to take a real interest in sth; **tienes que poner más i. en los estudios** you must show a bit more interest in your schoolwork
(d) *(conveniencia, provecho)* interest; **una obra de i. general** *o* **público** a construction project that is in everyone's *o* the public interest; **hacer algo por el i. de alguien, hacer algo en i. de alguien** to do sth in sb's interest; **tengo i. en que venga pronto** it's in my interest that he should come soon; **a todos nos mueve un i. común** we are all motivated by a common interest

(**e**) *(egoísmo)* self-interest, selfishness; **por i.** out of selfishness; **casarse por (el) i.** to marry for money ►► ***intereses creados*** vested interests

(**f**) **intereses** *(aficiones)* interests; **entre sus intereses se cuentan el golf y la vela** his interests include golf and sailing

(**g**) **intereses** *(económicos)* interests; **los intereses españoles en Latinoamérica** Spanish interests in Latin America; **tiene intereses en una empresa del sector** he has interests *o* a stake in a company in that sector; **su hermana administra sus intereses** her sister looks after her financial interests

(**h**) *Fin* interest; **un préstamo con un i. del 5 por ciento** a loan at 5 percent interest; **i. a corto/largo plazo** short-/long-term interest; **tipo** *o* **tasa de i.** interest rate ►► ***i. acumulable*** cumulative interest; ***i. compuesto*** compound interest; ***intereses de demora*** penalty interest *(for late payment)*; ***i. devengado*** accrued interest; ***i. interbancario*** interbank deposit rate; ***i. de mora*** penalty interest *(for late payment)*; ***i. preferencial*** preferential interest rate; ***i. simple*** simple interest; ***intereses vencidos*** interest due

interesadamente *adv* selfishly; **ofreció su ayuda i.** he offered to help because he knew there was something in it for him

interesado, -a 1 *adj* (**a**) *(preocupado, curioso)* interested (**en** *o* **por** in); **estoy muy i. en la evolución del conflicto** I am very interested in the development of the conflict; **está i. en comprar una casa** he's interested in buying a house; **estaría i. en recibir más información sobre el festival** I would be interested in receiving more information about the festival

(**b**) *(egoísta)* selfish, self-interested; **actuó de forma interesada** she acted selfishly *o* out of self-interest

(**c**) *(implicado)* **las partes interesadas** the interested parties; **deben presentar la firma de la persona interesada** the signature of the person concerned is required

2 *nm,f* (**a**) *(deseoso, curioso)* interested person; **los interesados** those interested; **una cita para los interesados en el cine** a date for movie fans; **yo soy el primer i. en que lleguemos a un acuerdo** I'm as keen as anyone for us to reach an agreement

(**b**) *(egoísta)* selfish *o* self-interested person; **es un i.** he's a very selfish person, he always acts out of self-interest

(**c**) *(involucrado)* person concerned; **los interesados** the parties concerned, those involved

interesante *adj* interesting; EXPR *Fam* **hacerse el/la i.** to try to draw attention to oneself

interesar 1 *vi* (**a**) *(atraer el interés)* to interest; **le interesa el arte** she's interested in art; **me interesaría conocerla** I'd like to meet her; **por si te interesa** in case you're interested; **este asunto nos interesa a todos** this matter concerns us all; **es un tema que no interesa** it's a subject of little interest; **a quien pueda i.** *(en carta)* to whom it may concern

(**b**) *(convenir)* **no les interesa que baje el precio** it wouldn't be to their advantage for the price to come down; **siempre hace lo que más le interesa** he always does whatever suits his interests best; **sólo le interesa acostarse con ella** all he's interested in is going to bed with her

2 *vt* (**a**) *(despertar interés)* to interest; **lo interesé en mi proyecto** I got him interested in my project (**b**) *Med* **la bala interesó el riñón** the bullet damaged his kidney

3 **interesarse** *vpr* to take an interest, to be interested (**en** *o* **por** in); **se interesó por ti/tu salud** she asked after you/your health; **se han interesado mucho por el prototipo** they have shown a lot of interest in the prototype

interestatal *adj* interstate

interestelar *adj* interstellar

interétnico, -a *adj* interethnic

interfaz, interface *nm o nf Informát* interface ►► ***i. común de pasarela*** common gateway interface; ***i. gráfico*** graphical interface; ***i. de usuario*** user interface

interfecto, -a *nm,f* (**a**) *(víctima)* murder victim (**b**) *Esp Hum (de quien se habla)* **hice un comentario pero el i. no se dio por aludido** I made a remark, but the person for whom it was intended didn't take the hint

interferencia *nf* (**a**) *Rad & Tel* interference; *(intencional)* jamming; **hay interferencias en la televisión** there's interference on the television (**b**) *(intromisión)* interference; **no voy a permitir interferencias políticas** I'm not going to allow any political interference (**c**) *Ling* interference

interferir [63] 1 *vt* (**a**) *Rad & Tel* to interfere with; *(intencionadamente)* to jam (**b**) *(interponerse a)* to interfere in (**c**) *(interceptar) (tráfico)* to obstruct; *(pase)* to intercept, to block

2 *vi* to interfere (**en** in); **no quiero i. en su vida privada** I don't want to interfere in his private life

interferón *nm Fisiol* interferon

interfijo *nm Gram* infix

interfono *nm* intercom

intergaláctico, -a *adj* intergalactic

interglacial, interglaciar *adj Geol* interglacial; **periodo i.** interglacial stage

intergubernamental *adj* intergovernmental

ínterin *nm inv Formal* interim; **en el í. ocupó la presidencia el secretario** the secretary took over the chair in the interim; **ella entró al museo y en el í. paseé por la ciudad** she went into the museum and in the meantime I went for a walk round the town

interinamente *adv* temporarily, provisionally

interinato *nm esp Am* (**a**) *(interinidad)* temporary nature; **el i. de su cargo no le permite tomar muchas decisiones** the temporary nature of her post doesn't allow her to make many decisions (**b**) *(empleo interino)* temporary post (**c**) *(periodo)* **durante su i. en la presidencia** during the time that he was acting chairman

interinidad *nf* (**a**) *(cualidad)* temporary nature (**b**) *(periodo)* **durante su i. en la presidencia** during the time that he was acting chairman

interino, -a 1 *adj (provisional)* temporary; *(presidente, director)* acting; *(gobierno)* interim; **un médico i.** a locum; **un juez i.** an interim judge

2 *nm,f (suplente)* stand-in, deputy; *(médico, juez)* locum; *(profesor) Br* supply teacher, *US* substitute teacher

interior 1 *adj* (**a**) *(de dentro)* inside, inner; *(patio, jardín)* interior, inside; *(habitación, vida)* inner; **ropa i., prendas interiores** underwear; **adelantó por la calle i.** he overtook on the inside

(**b**) *(nacional)* domestic; **comercio i.** domestic trade; **un asunto de política i.** it is a domestic (policy) issue

(**c**) *Geog* inland

2 *nm* (**a**) *(parte de dentro)* inside, interior; **desalojaron el i. del edificio** they evacuated the (inside of the) building; **pintaron el i. de la habitación** they painted the room; **en el i. del hotel se agolpaban las admiradoras** his admirers formed a crowd inside the hotel; **en el i. de la botella había un mensaje** there was a message inside the bottle

(**b**) *(de país)* interior, inland area

(**c**) *(de una persona)* inner self, heart; **en mi i.** deep down

(**d**) *Col, Ven (calzoncillos)* underpants

3 *nmf Dep (jugador)* central midfielder ►► ***i. izquierdo*** inside left; ***i. derecho*** inside right

interioridad *nf (carácter)* inner self; **interioridades** *(asuntos)* private affairs; **conoce todas las interioridades del ministerio** he knows everything that goes on inside the ministry

interiorismo *nm* interior design

interiorista *nmf* interior designer

interiorización *nf (de sentimientos, ideas)* internalization

interiorizado, -a *adj CSur* **estar i. de** *o* **sobre algo** to be au fait with sth, to know about sth

interiorizar [14] 1 *vt* (**a**) *(asumir, consolidar)* to internalize (**b**) *(no manifestar)* **interioriza sus emociones** he doesn't show his emotions; **su problema es que todo lo que le pasa lo interioriza** her problem is that she keeps everything bottled up inside (**c**) *CSur (informar)* to fill in; **i. a alguien de algo** to fill sb in on sth

2 **interiorizarse** *vpr CSur (informarse)* to familiarize oneself; **me interioricé de** *o* **sobre el tema** I familiarized myself with the subject

interiormente *adv* (**a**) *(en el interior)* inside; **la caja está revestida i.** the box is lined on the inside, the inside of the box is lined (**b**) *(en la mente, el corazón)* inwardly, inside; **i. sentía mucha rabia** inwardly she felt very angry, she felt very angry inside

interjección *nf* interjection

interjectivo, -a *adj Gram* interjectional, interjectory

interlengua *nf Ling* interlanguage

interletraje *nm Informát* kern, kerning

interlínea *nf Imprenta (interlineado)* line spacing

interlineado *nm* line spacing

interlineal *adj* interlinear

interlock [inter'lok] (*pl* **interlocks**) *nm* interlock

interlocución *nf* dialogue

interlocutor, -ora *nm,f (en negociación, debate)* participant; **su i.** the person she was speaking to; **un i. válido en las negociaciones de paz** an acceptable mediator in the peace negotiations ►► ***interlocutores sociales*** social partners

interludio *nm* (**a**) *(intermedio)* interlude (**b**) *Mús* interlude

intermediación *nf* (**a**) *(en conflicto)* intervention, mediation; **por i. de** through the intervention *o* mediation of (**b**) *Fin* intermediation

intermediar *vi* to mediate

intermediaria *nf Ven (en cine)* mid-evening showing; *(en teatro)* mid-evening performance

intermediario, -a 1 *adj* intermediary
2 *nm,f* intermediary, go-between ►► *Com* ***i. comercial*** middleman; *Fin* ***i. financiero*** credit broker

intermedio, -a 1 *adj* (**a**) *(etapa, nivel)* intermediate, halfway; *(calidad)* average; *(tamaño)* medium (**b**) *(tiempo)* intervening; *(espacio)* in between; **se halla en un punto i. entre la comedia y la tragedia** it's somewhere between a comedy and a tragedy; *Dep* **tiempo i.** split time
2 *nm* (**a**) *(en actividad)* interval; **vamos a hacer un i. de diez minutos** we'll have *o* take a ten-minute break (**b**) *(en teatro)* interval; *(en cine)* intermission; *(en televisión)* break
3 **por intermedio de** *loc prep* through; **la enfermedad se transmite por i. de animales** the disease is transmitted through *o* by animals; **se estuvieron insultando por i. de la prensa** they insulted each other through the press

interminable *adj* endless, interminable; **este viaje se me está haciendo i.** it feels like this journey's never going to end

interminablemente *adv* endlessly

interministerial *adj (entre ministerios)* interdepartmental; *(entre ministros)* interministerial; **comisión i.** interdepartmental committee

intermisión *nf* intermission

intermitencia *nf* intermittence, intermittency

intermitente 1 *adj* (**a**) *(lluvia, ruido)* intermittent; *(luz)* flashing (**b**) *(fenómeno)* sporadic
2 *nm Esp, Col Br* indicator, *US* turn signal; **poner el i.** to switch on one's *Br* indicator *o US* turn signal

intermitentemente *adv* intermittently

Intermón *n* = Spanish non-governmental development aid organization

internación *nf CSur* admission

internacional 1 *adj* (**a**) *(de las naciones)* international (**b**) *(aeropuerto, vuelo)* international (**c**) *(mercado, noticias)* international (**d**) *(deportista)* international; **fue diez veces i. por México** he was capped ten times for Mexico
2 *nmf (deportista)* international
3 *nf* (**a**) **la I.** *(himno)* the International (**b**) **la I.** *(organización)* the International; **la I/II I.** the First/Second International ►► ***la I. Socialista*** the Socialist International

internacionalidad *nf* internationality

internacionalismo *nm* internationalism

internacionalista 1 *adj* internationalist
2 *nmf* internationalist

internacionalización *nf* internationalization

internacionalizar [14] 1 *vt* to internationalize
2 **internacionalizarse** *vpr* to become international; **quieren evitar que el conflicto se internacionalice** they want to prevent the conflict from spreading internationally

internacionalmente *adv* internationally, worldwide

internada *nf Dep* run

internado, -a 1 *nm* (**a**) *(colegio)* boarding school (**b**) *(estancia) (en manicomio)* confinement; *(en colegio)* boarding (**c**) *Am (del médico)* internship
2 *nm,f RP* patient

internamente *adv* internally

internamiento *nm (en manicomio)* confinement; *(en colegio)* boarding; *(en campo de concentración)* internment

internar 1 *vt (en colegio)* to send to boarding school (**en** at); *(en manicomio)* to commit (**en** to); *(en campo de concentración)* to intern (**en** in); *RP (en hospital)* to admit (**en** to); **la internaron en un colegio muy prestigioso** they sent her to a very prestigious boarding school
2 **internarse** *vpr* (**a**) *(penetrar) (en lugar)* to go *o* penetrate deep (**en** into); **se internaron en el bosque** they went (deep) into the forest; **el delantero se internó por la banda** the forward made a run down the wing
(**b**) *(penetrar) (en tema)* **desde muy joven se internó en el mundo de los templarios** he had a deep interest in the world of the Templars from an early age
(**c**) *RP (en hospital)* **hoy se interna y mañana lo operan** he is being admitted (to hospital) today and they're operating tomorrow

internauta *nmf Informát* Net user

Internet *nf Informát* Internet; **está en I.** it's on the Internet

internista 1 *adj* internist
2 *nmf* internist

interno, -a 1 *adj* (**a**) *(de dentro)* internal; *(capa)* inner; **pinta la parte interna del cajón** paint the inside of the box; **escucha voces internas** she hears voices
(**b**) *(política)* domestic; **la política interna de un país** a country's domestic policy
(**c**) *(medicina)* internal
(**d**) *(hemorragia)* **ha sufrido una hemorragia interna** she has suffered internal bleeding
(**e**) *(alumno)* boarding; **estuvo i. en Suiza** he went to a boarding school in Switzerland
(**f**) **médico i.** *Br* house officer, *US* intern
2 *nm,f* (**a**) *(alumno)* boarder (**b**) *(preso)* prisoner, inmate (**c**) *(médico) Br* house officer, *US* intern
3 *nm RP (extensión)* (telephone) extension; **i. 28, por favor** extension 28, please

inter nos *loc adv* between ourselves, between you and me; **aquí, i., creo que no te puedes quejar** between you and me, I don't think you've got anything to complain about here

interoceánico, -a *adj* interoceanic

interóseo, -a *adj Anat* interosseous

interparlamentario, -a *adj* interparliamentary

interpelación *nf* formal question

interpelar *vt* to question

interpersonal *adj* interpersonal

interplanetario, -a *adj* interplanetary

Interpol [inter'pol] *nf* (*abrev de* **International Criminal Police Organization**) Interpol

interpolación *nf (en texto)* interpolation, insertion

interpolar *vt (texto)* to interpolate, to insert

interponer [50] 1 *vt* (**a**) *(entre dos cosas)* to put *o* place *(between two things)*, to interpose; **interpusieron un biombo entre nuestra mesa y la suya** they put a screen between our table and theirs (**b**) *Der* to lodge, to make; **interpuso un recurso contra la orden de arresto** he lodged *o* made an appeal against the arrest warrant, he appealed against the arrest warrant
2 **interponerse** *vpr* **interponerse entre** *(estar)* to be placed *o* situated between; *(ponerse)* to come *o* get between; **se interponía una barrera entre ellos** there was a barrier between them; **interponerse entre dos contendientes** to intervene between two opponents; **la enfermedad se interpuso en su carrera** the illness interrupted her career; **no piensa dejar que nadie se interponga en su camino** she's not going to let anyone get in her way

interposición *nf* (**a**) *(entre dos contendientes)* mediation; **la i. del panel evita que llegue el ruido** the panel serves as a barrier against noise (**b**) *Der* lodging *(of an appeal)*

interpretable *adj* interpretable

interpretación *nf* (**a**) *(de ideas, significado)* interpretation; **mala i.** misinterpretation; **i. judicial** legal interpretation; **i. literal/restrictiva** literal/limited interpretation
(**b**) *(artística)* performance, interpretation; *(de obra musical)* performance, rendition; **estudia i. teatral** she's studying acting; **su i. de la quinta sinfonía fue emocionante** their performance of the fifth symphony was thrilling
(**c**) *(traducción)* interpreting ►► ***i. consecutiva*** consecutive interpreting; ***i. simultánea*** simultaneous interpreting

interpretador, -ora 1 *adj* interpreting
2 *nm Informát* interpreter

interpretar 1 *vt* (**a**) *(entender, explicar)* to interpret; **i. mal** to misinterpret; **interpretamos sus palabras como una amenaza** we are interpreting *o* taking his words as a threat (**b**) *(artísticamente) (obra de teatro, sinfonía)* to perform; *(papel)* to play; *(canción)* to sing (**c**) *(traducir)* to interpret
2 *vi (traducir)* to interpret; **i. del español al inglés** to interpret from Spanish into English

interpretativo, -a *adj* (**a**) *(de la interpretación artística)* **tiene mucha capacidad interpretativa para los papeles cómicos** he's very good in comic roles; **el pianista tiene un gran estilo i.** he's a very stylish pianist (**b**) *(del significado)* interpretative

intérprete 1 *nmf* (**a**) *(traductor)* interpreter ►► ***i. jurado*** = interpreter qualified to work in court; ***i. simultáneo*** simultaneous interpreter (**b**) *(artista)* performer (**c**) *(comentarista)* commentator
2 *nm Informát* interpreter

interprofesional *adj* industry-wide; **una asociación i.** an industry-wide association; **el salario mínimo i.** the minimum wage

interpuesto, -a *participio ver* **interponer**

interracial *adj* interracial

Inter-Rail, Inter-Raíl *nm* Inter-Rail

interregno *nm Formal* interregnum

interrelación *nf* interrelation

interrelacionar 1 *vt* to interrelate
2 **interrelacionarse** *vpr* to be interrelated

interrogación *nf* (**a**) *(signo)* question mark (**b**) *(pregunta)* question (**c**) *(interrogatorio)* interrogation

interrogador, -ora 1 *adj* questioning
2 *nm,f (que interroga)* questioner; *(con amenazas)* interrogator

interrogante *nm o nf* (**a**) *(incógnita)* question (**b**) *(signo de interrogación)* question mark

interrogar [38] *vt (preguntar)* to question; *(con amenazas)* to interrogate

interrogativo, -a *adj* interrogative

interrogatorio *nm (preguntas)* questioning; *(con amenazas)* interrogation; **someter a alguien a un i.** *(con preguntas)* to question sb; *(con amenazas)* to interrogate sb

interrumpir 1 *vt* (**a**) *(conversación, frase)* to interrupt; **¿interrumpo algo importante?** am I interrupting anything important?
(**b**) *(servicio)* to suspend; **el servicio de metro quedó interrumpido durante dos horas** *Br* underground *o US* subway services were suspended for two hours
(**c**) *(acortar) (viaje, vacaciones)* to cut short; **interrumpió sus vacaciones el día 8** he ended his holiday early on the 8th
(**d**) *(circulación)* to block; **un árbol caído interrumpía el paso** a fallen tree was blocking the way
(**e**) *(embarazo)* to terminate
2 *vi* to interrupt; **espero no i.** I hope I'm not interrupting
3 **interrumpirse** *vpr* to be interrupted; *(tráfico)* to be blocked; **se interrumpió para beber agua** she paused to take a drink of water

interrupción *nf* (**a**) *(corte, parada)* interruption ►► ***i. (voluntaria) del embarazo*** termination of pregnancy (**b**) *(de discurso, trabajo)* breaking-off; *(de viaje, vacaciones)* cutting short (**c**) *(de circulación)* blocking

interruptor *nm* switch ►► ***i. de corriente*** power switch; *Elec* ***i. de cuchilla*** knife switch; ***i. general*** mains switch; ***i. de la luz*** light switch; ***i. de pie*** foot switch

intersecarse *vpr Geom* to intersect

intersección *nf* intersection; **la i. entre dos calles** the intersection of two streets; **gire a la izquierda en la próxima i.** turn left at the next junction *o US* intersection ►► *Mat* ***i. de conjuntos*** intersection of sets

intersideral *adj* interstellar

intersticio *nm Formal* crack, gap

intertanto *Am* 1 *adv* meanwhile, in the meantime
2 *nm* **en el i.** meanwhile, in the meantime

interurbano, -a *adj (autobús, llamada)* long-distance; *(tren)* intercity

intervalo *nm* (**a**) *(entre lugares)* interval; **distribuyeron las mesas a intervalos regulares** they spaced the tables at regular intervals
(**b**) *(en el tiempo)* interval; **a intervalos** at intervals; **en el i. de un mes** in the space of a month; **intervalos nubosos/soleados** cloudy/sunny intervals *o* spells
(**c**) *(entre números, valores)* range; **en este i. de temperatura** in this temperature range
(**d**) *Mús* interval
(**e**) *(en representación) Br* interval, *esp US* intermission

intervención *nf* (**a**) *(acción, participación)* intervention; **la pelea fue controlada gracias a la rápida i. de la policía** the fight was brought under control thanks to the rapid intervention of the police; **no i.** non-intervention; **i. televisiva** television appearance
(**b**) *(discurso)* speech; *(pregunta)* question; *(comentario)* remark, comment
(**c**) *(operación)* **i. (quirúrgica)** operation
(**d**) *Com (de cuentas)* auditing
(**e**) *(vigilancia) (de teléfono, línea)* tapping; **el juez ordenó la i. de su correspondencia** the judge ordered her correspondence to be opened (by the authorities)
(**f**) *(incautación)* seizure, confiscation

intervencionismo *nm* interventionism

intervencionista 1 *adj* interventionist
2 *nmf* interventionist

intervenir [71] 1 *vt* (**a**) *(operar)* **i. (quirúrgicamente)** to operate on (**b**) *Com (cuentas)* to audit (**c**) *(teléfono, línea)* to tap; *(correspondencia)* to open (**d**) *(incautarse de)* to seize (**e**) *Am (institución privada)* to put into administration
2 *vi* (**a**) *(participar)* to take part (**en** in); *(en pelea, discusión)* to get involved (**en** in); **intervino en varias películas cómicas** she appeared in several comedy films; **en la evolución de la economía intervienen muchos factores** several different factors play a part in the state of the economy; **después del presidente intervino el Sr. Ramírez** Mr Ramírez spoke after the president; **yo quisiera i. para decir que no estamos de acuerdo con la propuesta** I would just like to say something: we do not agree with the proposal; **¿alguien más quisiera i. sobre esta cuestión?** would anyone else like so say something on this issue?
(**b**) *(interferir, imponer el orden)* to intervene (**en** in); **la policía tuvo que i. para separar a las dos aficiones** the police had to intervene to separate the two groups of fans
(**c**) *(mediar)* to intervene, to intercede; **su padre intervino ante su madre para que lo dejara salir** his father spoke to his mother to persuade her to let him go out; **la ONU intervino para lograr un acuerdo** the UN intervened *o* interceded in order to get an agreement
(**d**) *(operar)* **i. (quirúrgicamente)** to operate

interventor, -ora *nm,f* (**a**) *Com (de cuentas)* auditor (**b**) *(de tren)* ticket collector (**c**) *(en elecciones)* scrutineer (**d**) *Am (administrador)* administrator *(appointed by the government)*

intervertebral *adj Anat* intervertebral

interviú (*pl* **interviús**) *nf* interview

intervocálico, -a *adj* intervocalic

intestado, -a *Der* 1 *adj* intestate; **morir i.** to die intestate
2 *nm,f* intestate

intestinal *adj* intestinal

intestino, -a 1 *adj* internecine
2 *nm* intestine ►► ***i. ciego*** caecum; ***i. delgado*** small intestine; ***i. grueso*** large intestine

inti *nm Antes* inti *(former unit of currency in Peru)*

intifada *nf* intifada

íntimamente *adv* (**a**) *(privadamente)* privately (**b**) *(a solas)* in private (**c**) *(a fondo)* intimately; **dos fenómenos í. relacionados** *o* **ligados** two phenomena which are intimately *o* closely connected (with each other)

intimar *vi* to get close (**con** to); **intimé con ella cuando íbamos a la universidad** I got close to her when we were at university; **no es fácil i. con él** it's not easy to get close to him

intimatorio, -a *adj Der* notifying

intimidación *nf* intimidation; **robo con i.** aggravated robbery

intimidad *nf* (**a**) *(vida privada)* private life; **en la i.** in private; **violar la i. de alguien** to invade sb's privacy (**b**) *(privacidad)* privacy; **en la i. de** in the privacy of (**c**) *(amistad)* intimacy (**d**) **intimidades** *(asuntos privados)* personal matters (**e**) *Fam Euf* **intimidades** *(partes pudendas)* privates, private parts

intimidante *adj* intimidating

intimidar *vt* to intimidate; **es tan serio que intimida** it's frightening how serious he is; **nos intimidó con un cuchillo** he threatened us with a knife

intimidatorio, -a *adj* intimidating, threatening

intimismo *nm* intimisme

intimista *adj* **pintor i.** painter of domestic scenes; **novela i.** novel of family life

íntimo, -a 1 *adj* (**a**) *(vida, fiesta, ceremonia)* private; *(ambiente, restaurante)* intimate; **una cena íntima** a romantic dinner for two; **la higiene íntima** personal hygiene
(**b**) *(relación)* close; **existe una íntima relación entre los dos crímenes** the two crimes are closely connected
(**c**) *(amistad)* close
(**d**) *(sentimiento)* **me contó sus pensamientos más íntimos** she told me her innermost thoughts; **en lo (más) í. de su corazón/alma** deep down in her heart/soul
2 *nm,f* close friend

intitular *vt Formal* to entitle

intocable 1 *adj* (**a**) *(persona, institución)* above criticism (**b**) *(tema)* taboo
2 **intocables** *nmfpl (en India)* untouchables

intolerable *adj* (**a**) *(inaceptable, indignante)* intolerable, unacceptable (**b**) *(dolor, ruido)* unbearable

intolerancia *nf* (**a**) *(intransigencia)* intolerance (**b**) *Med* intolerance; **tener i. a algo** to be allergic to sth

intolerante 1 *adj* intolerant
2 *nmf* intolerant person; **es un i.** he's very intolerant

intonso, -a *adj* (**a**) *Literario (persona)* unshorn (**b**) *Imprenta (libro)* untrimmed

intoxicación *nf* (**a**) *(médica)* poisoning; **sufrió una i. alimentaria** he had a bout of food poisoning; **una i. por monóxido de carbono** carbon monoxide poisoning ►► ***i. etílica*** alcohol poisoning (**b**) *(manipulación)* **la i. informativa orquestada por el régimen** the regime's manipulation of the media

intoxicar [60] 1 *vt* (**a**) *(médicamente)* to poison (**b**) *(manipular)* **nos intoxican con tanta publicidad** we are being manipulated by all this advertising; **intoxican a la opinión pública con sus informes** their reports manipulate public opinion
2 **intoxicarse** *vpr* to poison oneself

> **Falso amigo**: El verbo inglés **to intoxicate** no es la traducción del español **intoxicar**. En inglés **to intoxicate** significa "embriagar" o "emborrachar".

intra- *pref* intra-

intracomunitario, -a *adj* within the EU; **ventas intracomunitarias** internal EU sales, sales within the EU

intradós *nm Arquit* intrados

intraducible *adj* untranslatable

intragable *adj Fam (película, libro)* unbearable, awful

intramuros *adv* within the city walls

intramuscular *adj* intramuscular

intranet *nf Informát* intranet

intranquilidad *nf* (**a**) *(preocupación)* unease, anxiety (**b**) *(nerviosismo)* restlessness

intranquilizar [14] 1 *vt* to worry, to make uneasy
2 **intranquilizarse** *vpr* to get worried

intranquilo, -a *adj* (**a**) *(preocupado)* worried, uneasy; **me quedé muy i. por sus amenazas** his threats made me very uneasy *o* worried me (**b**) *(nervioso)* restless

intranscendencia = **intrascendencia**

intranscendente = **intrascendente**

intransferible *adj* non-transferable, untransferable

intransigencia *nf* intransigence

intransigente *adj* intransigent

intransitable *adj* impassable

intransitividad *nf* intransitivity

intransitivo, -a *adj* intransitive

intraocular *adj Anat* intraocular

intrascendencia, intranscendencia *nf* insignificance, unimportance

intrascendente, intranscendente *adj* insignificant, unimportant

intratable *adj* unsociable, difficult to get on with; **hoy estás i.** there's no talking to you today

intrauterino, -a *adj* intrauterine

intravenosamente *adv* intravenously

intravenoso, -a *adj* intravenous

intrepidez *nf* daring, bravery

intrépido, -a *adj* intrepid

intriga *nf* (**a**) *(suspense)* suspense; **película/novela de i.** thriller; **la i. se mantiene hasta el final** the suspense is maintained right to the end (**b**) *(curiosidad)* curiosity; **tengo i. por saber el resultado** I'm curious to know the result; **¡qué i.! ¿qué habrá pasado?** how intriguing! what can have happened? (**c**) *(maquinación)* intrigue; **intrigas palaciegas** court *o* palace intrigues (**d**) *(trama)* plot

intrigado, -a *adj* intrigued

intrigante 1 *adj* intriguing
2 *nmf (maquinador)* schemer; *(chismoso)* stirrer

intrigar [38] 1 *vt* to intrigue; **me intriga saber qué habrá pasado** I'm intrigued to know what has happened
2 *vi* to intrigue

intrincado, -a *adj* (**a**) *(bosque)* thick, dense (**b**) *(complejo) (problema)* intricate; **se perdió por las intrincadas callejuelas de la ciudad** she disappeared into the city's maze of sidestreets; **la intrincada orografía del país** the country's varied and difficult terrain

intrincar [60] *vt* to complicate, to confuse

intríngulis *nm inv Fam (dificultad)* snag, catch; *(quid)* nub, crux; **este juego tiene su i.** there's a knack to this game, this game is quite tricky

intrínsecamente *adv* intrinsically

intrínseco, -a *adj* intrinsic (**a** to)

intro *nm Informát* enter (key), return (key); **darle al i.** to press enter *o* return

introducción *nf* (**a**) *(presentación)* introduction (**a** to); **i. a la lingüística** *(título)* an introduction to linguistics; **un curso de i. a la informática** an introductory course in computing
(**b**) *(de libro)* introduction
(**c**) *(de composición musical)* introduction; *(en música pop)* intro
(**d**) *(inserción) (de objeto)* insertion; *Informát (de datos)* input, entering
(**e**) *(de novedad, medida, política, en mercado)* introduction; **precio especial de i.** special introductory price; **la i. de la moneda única** the introduction of the single currency; **a él se debe la i. de la patata en Europa** he was responsible for the introduction of the potato to Europe; **una banda que se dedica a la i. de tabaco de contrabando en Europa** a gang that smuggles tobacco into Europe

introducir [18] 1 *vt* (**a**) *(meter) (llave, carta)* to put in, to insert; *Informát (datos)* to input, to enter; **introdujo la moneda en la ranura** she put *o* inserted the coin in the slot; **introdujo la carta en el sobre** he put the letter in the envelope; **introduzca su número secreto** enter your PIN number
(**b**) *(conducir) (persona)* to show in; **introdujo a los visitantes en la sala de espera** she showed the visitors into the waiting room
(**c**) *(en película, novela)* to introduce; **en su última obra el autor introduce a dos nuevos personajes** in his latest work the author introduces two new characters
(**d**) *(medidas, ley)* to introduce, to bring in; **introdujeron un plan para combatir el desempleo** they introduced *o* brought in a scheme to combat unemployment; **piensan i. cambios en la ley** they are planning to make changes to the law
(**e**) *(mercancías)* to bring in, to introduce; **los españoles introdujeron los caballos en América** the Spanish introduced horses to America; **una banda que introduce droga en el país** a gang smuggling drugs into the country; **fue él quien introdujo las ideas revolucionarias en el país** it was he who introduced *o* brought revolutionary ideas to the country
(**f**) *(dar a conocer)* **i. a alguien en** to introduce sb to; **la introdujo en el mundo de la moda** he introduced her to the world of fashion; **nos introdujo en los principios básicos de la astronomía** he introduced us to the basic principles of astronomy
2 **introducirse** *vpr* **introducirse en** to get into; **los ladrones se introdujeron en la casa por la ventana** the burglars got into the house through the window; **el balón se introdujo lentamente en la portería** the ball trickled into the goal; **se ha introducido un mosquito en la habitación** a mosquito has got into the room; **se está introduciendo agua en la mochila** water is getting into the rucksack; **se introdujo en la organización a los veinte años** she joined the organization at twenty; **poco a poco se ha introducido en el mundo del teatro** she has gradually established a footing in the world of theatre; **una costumbre que se introdujo el siglo pasado** a custom introduced during the last century

introductor, -ora 1 *adj* introductory; **el país i. de esta moda** the country that brought in this fashion
2 *nm,f* introducer

introductorio, -a *adj* introductory

introdujera *etc ver* **introducir**

introduzco *etc ver* **introducir**

introito *nm* (**a**) *(introducción)* preliminary section, introduction (**b**) *Rel* introit

intromisión *nf* intrusion

introspección *nf* introspection

introspectivo, -a *adj* introspective

introversión *nf* introversion

introvertido, -a 1 *adj* introvert
2 *nm,f* introvert

intrusión *nf* (**a**) *(en lugar)* intrusion (**b**) *Geol* intrusion

intrusismo *nm* = illegal practice of a profession; **han denunciado el i. en el sector médico** the existence of unqualified medical practitioners has been condemned

intruso, -a *nm,f* intruder

intubar *vt* to intubate

intuición *nf* intuition; **la i. femenina** female intuition; **lo hice por i.** I did it instinctively; **tuvo la i. de que algo iba a salir mal** she had a feeling something was going to go wrong

intuir [34] *vt* **intuyo que es una buena inversión** my intuition *o* instinct tells me it's a good investment; **intuyo que no va a hacer buen tiempo** I've got a feeling the weather's not going to be very good

intuitivamente *adv* intuitively

intuitivo, -a *adj* intuitive

intuyera *etc ver* **intuir**

intuyo *etc ver* **intuir**

inuit (*pl* **inuits** *o* **inuit**) **1** *adj* Inuit
2 *nmf* Inuit

inundación *nf (acción)* flooding; *(resultado)* flood; **es la segunda i. que sufren este año** it's the second flood they've had this year; **las lluvias produjeron inundaciones** the rain caused floods *o* flooding; **los daños causados por las inundaciones** the damage caused by the floods *o* the flooding

inundar **1** *vt* **(a)** *(las aguas)* to flood; **las tormentas inundaron la región** the storms caused flooding in the area
(b) *(sujeto: gente)* to swamp; **los aficionados inundaban el centro de la ciudad** fans swamped the town centre; **los turistas inundaban las carreteras** the roads were jammed with tourists
(c) *(sujeto: sentimiento)* to overwhelm, to overcome; **la tristeza/la alegría me inunda** I am overwhelmed *o* overcome with sadness/joy
(d) *(con quejas, pedidos)* to inundate, to swamp; **inundaron el mercado con imitaciones baratas** they flooded the market with cheap imitations; **estoy inundado de trabajo** I'm inundated *o* swamped with work
2 inundarse *vpr* **(a)** *(con agua)* to flood; **se inundó el sótano** the basement flooded; **se le inundaron los ojos de lágrimas** her eyes flooded with tears
(b) *(con visitantes, turistas)* to be inundated *o* swamped; **la playa se inundó de gente** the beach was inundated *o* swamped with people
(c) inundarse de *(de quejas, pedidos)* to be inundated *o* swamped with; **el mercado se ha inundado de imitaciones** the market has been flooded with imitations

inusitado, -a *adj* uncommon, rare; **con una valentía inusitada** with uncommon valour

inusual *adj* unusual

inútil **1** *adj* **(a)** *(objeto)* useless; *(intento, esfuerzo)* unsuccessful, vain; **sus intentos resultaron inútiles** his attempts were unsuccessful *o* in vain; **es i., ya es demasiado tarde** there's no point, it's too late; **es i. que lo esperes, se ha ido para siempre** there's no point in waiting for him, he's gone for good
(b) *(inválido)* disabled; **le dieron la baja por i.** he was allowed to take disability leave; **quedó i. tras el accidente** she was disabled as a result of the accident
(c) *(no apto)* unfit; **fue declarado i. para el servicio militar** he was declared unfit for military service
2 *nmf* hopeless case, useless person; **es un i.** he's useless *o* hopeless

inutilidad *nf* **(a)** *(falta de utilidad)* uselessness; *(falta de eficacia)* ineffectiveness; *(falta de sentido)* pointlessness **(b)** *(invalidez)* disablement **(c)** *(persona)* **es una i.** he's useless *o* hopeless

inutilización *nf* **la humedad puede provocar la i. del mecanismo** damp can ruin the mechanism; **eran responsables de la i. de la alarma** they were responsible for putting the alarm out of action

inutilizado, -a *adj* unused; **tras el accidente, la máquina quedó inutilizada** after the accident the machine was useless

inutilizar [14] *vt (máquinas, dispositivos)* to disable, to put out of action; **esas cajas inutilizan la habitación de huéspedes** those boxes are stopping us from using the guest room

inútilmente *adv* in vain, to no avail; **no sueñes i., no podemos permitirnos hacer ese viaje** there's no point in dreaming about it, we can't afford that trip

invadir *vt* **(a)** *(ejércitos)* to invade; **el caza invadió el espacio aéreo ruso** the fighter plane encroached on Russian airspace; **una plaga de langostas invadió los campos** a plague of locusts invaded the fields
(b) *(turistas)* **los turistas invadieron el museo** the tourists poured *o* flooded into the museum; **la población invadió las calles** people poured onto the streets
(c) *(sentimiento)* to overcome, to overwhelm; **lo invadió la tristeza** he was overcome *o* overwhelmed by sadness; **nos invade la alegría** we are overcome *o* overwhelmed with joy; **me invadió una sensación repentina de cansancio** a sudden feeling of tiredness overcame me
(d) *(vehículo)* **el vehículo invadió el carril contrario** the vehicle went onto the wrong side of the road; **la moto invadió la acera y atropelló a dos peatones** the motorbike mounted the *Br* pavement *o US* sidewalk and hit two pedestrians
(e) *(sobrepasar límite)* **acusaron al ministro de i. las competencias de otro departamento** the minister was accused of encroaching upon another department's area of responsibility; **los fotógrafos invadieron la intimidad de la actriz** the photographers invaded the actress's privacy

invalidación *nf* invalidation

invalidar *vt (sujeto: circunstancias)* to invalidate; *(sujeto: juez)* to declare invalid; **les invalidaron dos goles** they had two goals disallowed

invalidez *nf* **(a)** *(física, psíquica)* disablement, disability ►► ***i. permanente*** permanent disability; ***i. temporal*** temporary disability **(b)** *Der* invalidity

inválido, -a **1** *adj* **(a)** *(física, psíquica)* disabled **(b)** *Der* invalid
2 *nm,f* invalid, disabled person; **los inválidos** the disabled

invalorable *adj CSur* invaluable

invariabilidad *nf* invariability

invariable *adj* **(a)** *(que no varía)* invariable **(b)** *Ling* invariable

invariablemente *adv* invariably

invasión *nf* **(a)** *(por ejércitos)* invasion
(b) *(por turistas)* invasion
(c) *(por vehículo)* **la i. por un camión del carril contrario provocó el accidente** the accident was caused by a truck *o Br* lorry going onto the wrong side of the road
(d) *(de competencias)* **acusó al juez de i. de competencias** he accused the judge of overreaching his powers
(e) *Col (barrio)* shantytown

invasor, -ora **1** *adj* invading; **el ejército i.** the invading army
2 *nm,f* invader

invectiva *nf Formal* diatribe; **lanzar una i. contra alguien** to launch into a diatribe against sb

invencible *adj* **(a)** *(ejército, enemigo)* invincible **(b)** *(timidez)* insurmountable, insuperable

invención *nf* **(a)** *(acción)* invention **(b)** *(objeto)* invention **(c)** *(mentira)* fabrication, invention; **eso es una i. suya** that's just something he's made up

invendible *adj* unsaleable

inventado, -a *adj* made-up

inventar **1** *vt* **(a)** *(máquina, sistema)* to invent **(b)** *(narración, falsedades)* to make up
2 inventarse *vpr* to make up; **una excusa que se ha inventado para no ir a clase** an excuse he has made up to get out of going to school

inventariar [32] *vt* to make an inventory of

inventario *nm* inventory; **hacer el i.** to do the stocktaking; **cerrado por i.** *(en letrero)* closed for stocktaking; **hizo el i. de los muebles de la casa** she made an inventory of the furniture in the house

inventiva *nf* inventiveness; **tener mucha i.** to be very inventive, to have a very inventive mind

inventivo, -a *adj* inventive

invento *nm* **(a)** *(invención)* invention ►► *Esp Fam* ***un i. del tebeo*** *Br* a Heath Robinson invention, *US* a Rube Goldberg invention **(b)** *(mentira)* lie, fib **(c)** EXPR *Esp Fam* **fastidiarse el i.: con esta lluvia se ha fastidiado el i., ya no podemos salir de excursión** this rain has really gone and messed things up, we can't go on that trip now

inventor, -ora *nm,f* inventor

invernada *nf* **(a)** *Andes, RP (pasto)* winter pasture **(b)** *Andes, RP (periodo)* winter season **(c)** *Ven (aguacero)* heavy downpour

invernadero *nm (para criar plantas)* greenhouse, glasshouse; *(en jardín botánico)* hothouse; **el efecto i.** the greenhouse effect

invernal *adj (de invierno)* winter; *(tiempo, paisaje)* wintry; **temporada i.** winter season

invernante **1** *adj* wintering
2 *nmf* winter visitor

invernar [3] *vi* **(a)** *(pasar el invierno)* to (spend the) winter **(b)** *(hibernar)* to hibernate

inverosímil *adj* improbable, implausible

inverosimilitud *nf* improbability, implausibility

inversamente *adv* **(a)** *(en proporción)* inversely; **i. proporcional a** inversely proportional to **(b)** *(a la inversa)* conversely

inversión *nf* (**a**) *(del orden)* inversion ►► *Meteo* ***i. térmica*** temperature inversion (**b**) *(de dinero)* investment ►► ***i. de capital*** capital investment; ***i. ética*** ethical investment; ***inversiones en paraísos fiscales*** offshore investments (**c**) *(de tiempo)* investment; **inversiones extranjeras** foreign investments

inversionista *nmf* investor

inverso, -a *adj* (**a**) *(contrario)* opposite; **en sentido i.** in the opposite direction; **en orden i.** in reverse *o* inverse order; **contar/escribir en orden i.** to count/write backwards; **a la inversa** the other way round (**b**) *(traducción)* **una traducción inversa** a translation out of one's own language, a prose translation (**c**) *Mat* inverse

inversor, -ora 1 *adj* **los países inversores en la región** the countries that have invested in the region; **ha habido un gran esfuerzo i. en el sector** there has been heavy investment in the sector

2 *nm,f* investor; **i. extranjero** foreign investor; **i. institucional** institutional investor

3 *nm Elec* inverter

invertebrado, -a 1 *adj* (**a**) *(animal)* invertebrate (**b**) *(incoherente)* disjointed

2 *nm (animal)* invertebrate

invertido, -a 1 *adj* (**a**) *(al revés)* reversed, inverted; *(sentido, dirección)* opposite; **i. de arriba a abajo** (turned) upside down; **en forma de pirámide invertida** in the shape of an inverted pyramid (**b**) *(dinero)* invested (**c**) *Anticuado (homosexual)* homosexual

2 *nm,f Anticuado* homosexual

invertir [63] 1 *vt* (**a**) *(orden)* to reverse; *(poner boca abajo)* to turn upside down, to invert; **si invertimos estos dos elementos** if we reverse the order of these two elements; **invirtió la dirección de la marcha** he put the vehicle into reverse; EXPR **i. los papeles** to swap roles (**b**) *(dinero)* to invest (**c**) *(tiempo, esfuerzo)* to invest (**d**) *(tardar) (tiempo)* to spend; **invirtieron dos horas en llegar a la cumbre** they took two hours getting to the summit

2 *vi (dinero)* to invest (**en** in); **i. en bolsa** to invest on the stock market

3 **invertirse** *vpr (tendencia)* to be reversed; EXPR **se han invertido los papeles** their roles have been reversed

investidura *nf* investiture; **la ceremonia de i. del presidente** the presidential inauguration ceremony

investigación *nf* (**a**) *(estudio)* research; **estoy haciendo una i. sobre los incas** I'm doing a research project *o* I'm doing some research on the Incas ►► ***i. científica*** scientific research; ***i. y desarrollo*** research and development; ***i. de mercado*** market research

(**b**) *(indagación)* investigation, inquiry; **la i. de un atentado** the investigation into an attack; **se ha abierto una i. sobre el incidente** an inquiry *o* an investigation into the incident has been opened; **comisión de i.** committee of inquiry ►► ***i. judicial*** judicial inquiry

investigador, -ora 1 *adj* (**a**) *(que estudia)* research; **un equipo i.** a research team; **capacidad investigadora** research capability (**b**) *(que indaga)* investigating; **comisión investigadora** committee of inquiry

2 *nm,f* (**a**) *(estudioso)* researcher (**b**) *(detective)* investigator ►► ***i. privado*** private investigator *o* detective

investigar [38] 1 *vt* (**a**) *(estudiar)* to research (**b**) *(indagar)* to investigate; **un equipo investiga las causas del accidente** a team is investigating the causes of the accident; **la policía investigó a varios sospechosos** the police investigated several suspects

2 *vi* (**a**) *(estudiar)* to do research (**sobre** into *o* on) (**b**) *(indagar)* to investigate

investir [47] *vt* **fue investido doctor honoris causa** he was awarded an honorary doctorate; **fue investido presidente de la nación** he was sworn in *o* inaugurated as president; **i. a alguien de** *o* **con algo** to invest sb with sth; **lo invistieron con el título de duque** he was granted the title of duke, he was made a duke

inveterado, -a *adj* **es un lector i. de novelas cortas** he is a great reader of novellas; **sigue con su inveterada costumbre de fumar** she smokes just as much as ever, she continues to be an inveterate smoker

inviabilidad *nf* impracticality

inviable *adj* impractical, unviable

invicto, -a *adj (ejército)* unconquered, undefeated; *(equipo)* unbeaten

invidencia *nf* blindness

invidente 1 *adj* blind, sightless

2 *nmf* blind person; **los invidentes** the blind

invierno *nm* (**a**) *(estación)* winter; **en i.** in winter, in wintertime; **cuando llegue el i.** when winter comes; **el último i.** last winter; **deporte de i.** winter sport; **ropa de i.** winter clothes; **estación de i.** ski resort ►► ***i. nuclear*** nuclear winter (**b**) *(estación lluviosa)* rainy season

invierto *etc ver* **invertir**

inviolabilidad *nf* inviolability ►► ***i. parlamentaria*** parliamentary immunity

inviolable *adj* inviolable; **una fortaleza i.** an impregnable fortress

invirtiera *etc ver* **invertir**

invisibilidad *nf* invisibility

invisible *adj* invisible

invitación *nf* (**a**) *(acción)* invitation; **hacer una i. a alguien** to invite sb; **sus palabras fueron una i. a la revolución** her words were an incitement to revolution (**b**) *(tarjeta)* invitation

invitado, -a 1 *adj* **estoy i. a la boda** I've been invited *o* I'm invited to the wedding; **estrella invitada** guest star

2 *nm,f* guest; **hoy no podemos salir, tenemos invitados** we can't go out today, we've got guests *o* we're having some people over ►► ***i. especial*** special guest

invitar 1 *vt* (**a**) *(convidar)* **i. a alguien (a algo/a hacer algo)** to invite sb (to sth/to do sth); **me han invitado a una fiesta** I've been invited to a party; **me invitó a la playa** she asked me to go the beach with her; **me invitó a entrar** she asked me in

(**b**) *(pedir)* to invite, to request; **la policía las invitó a desalojar la sala** the police invited *o* requested them to leave the room

(**c**) *(pagar)* **te invito** it's my treat, this one's on me; **i. a alguien a algo** to buy sb sth *(food, drink)*; **me invitó a una cerveza** he bought me a beer; **te invito a cenar fuera** I'll take you out for dinner

2 *vi* (**a**) *(pagar)* to pay; **invito yo** it's my treat, this one's on me; **invita la casa** it's on the house (**b**) **i. a algo** *(incitar)* to encourage sth; **este sol invita a salir** the sun makes you want to go out

in vitro 1 *adj inv* **fecundación i.** in vitro fertilization

2 *adv (fecundar)* in vitro

invocación *nf* (**a**) *(a dios, espíritu, diablo) (para pedir ayuda)* invocation; *(para pedir su presencia)* summoning (**b**) *(petición)* plea (**c**) *(a derecho, ley)* **insistió en la i. de la Constitución** he insisted on invoking the Constitution (**d**) *(de amistad)* appeal; **su i. de nuestra amistad no me conmovió** I was unmoved by her appeal to our friendship

invocar [60] *vt* (**a**) *(dios, espíritu, diablo) (para pedir ayuda)* to invoke; *(para pedir su presencia)* to summon up (**b**) *(pedir)* to plead for, to make a plea for; **invocó auxilio** he pleaded for help, he made a plea for help (**c**) *(derecho, ley)* to invoke (**d**) *(amistad)* to appeal to

involución *nf* regression, deterioration

involucionar *vi* to regress, to deteriorate

involucionismo *nm* reactionary nature; **las fuerzas del i.** the forces of reaction

involucionista 1 *adj* regressive, reactionary

2 *nmf* reactionary

involucración *nf* involvement

involucrado, -a *adj (en acciones, proyecto, accidente)* involved; *(en delito, escándalo)* implicated

involucrar 1 *vt* (**a**) *(comprometer)* **i. a alguien (en)** to involve sb (in); **no quiere i. a su familia** he doesn't want to involve his family (**b**) *Am (conllevar)* to involve; **esto involucra gastos que no había calculado** this involves expenses I hadn't reckoned with

2 **involucrarse** *vpr* to get involved (**en** in); **se involucró en un negocio de contrabando** he got involved in a smuggling racket

involuntariamente *adv* (**a**) *(espontáneamente)* involuntarily (**b**) *(sin querer)* unintentionally

involuntario, -a *adj* (**a**) *(espontáneo)* involuntary (**b**) *(sin querer)* unintentional

involutivo, -a *adj (fase)* reactionary; **sufre un proceso i. en su enfermedad** he has had a relapse

invulnerabilidad *nf* invulnerability

invulnerable *adj* (**a**) *(físicamente)* invulnerable (**a** to) (**b**) *(moralmente)* immune, invulnerable (**a** to)

inyección *nf* (**a**) *(con jeringa)* injection; **poner** *o RP* **dar una i. a alguien** to give sb an injection; **me tengo que poner la i. de insulina** I have to give myself my insulin injection ►► ***i. intramuscular*** intramuscular injection; ***i. intravenosa*** intravenous injection; ***i. subcutánea*** subcutaneous injection

(**b**) *Tec & Aut* injection; **motor de i.** fuel-injection engine ►► ***i. electrónica*** electronic fuel injection; ***i. de plástico*** injection moulding; ***la i. de tinta*** inkjet technology; **una impresora de i. de tinta** an inkjet printer

(**c**) *(de dinero)* injection; **una i. de capital extranjero** an injection of foreign capital; **una i. de 300 millones de dólares** an injection of 300 million dollars

(**d**) *(de humor, vitalidad)* injection; **sus palabras fueron una i. de**

moral para las tropas his words were a morale boost for the troops; **el gol supuso una i. de ánimo para el equipo** the goal gave the team new heart

inyectable 1 *adj* injectable
 2 *nm* injection

inyectado, -a *adj* flushed, red; **ojos inyectados en sangre** bloodshot eyes

inyectar 1 *vt* (**a**) *(con jeringa)* to inject; **le inyectaron insulina** they gave him an insulin injection; **le inyectaron un antídoto en la pierna** they injected an antidote into her leg (**b**) *(dinero)* to inject (**c**) *(humor, vitalidad)* to inject; **su presencia inyectó ánimos a los trabajadores** his presence gave the workers new heart
 2 **inyectarse** *vpr* **inyectarse (drogas)** to take drugs intravenously; **inyectarse algo** to inject oneself with sth, to take sth intravenously

inyector *nm* injector

iodo *nm* iodine

ion, ión *nm* ion ▸▸ ***i. hidrógeno*** hydrogen ion

iónico, -a *adj* ionic

ionización *nf* ionization

ionizador *nm* ionizer

ionizar [14] *vt* to ionize

ionosfera *nf* ionosphere

IP *nm Informát* (*abrev de* **Internet protocol**) IP

IPC *nm* (*abrev de* **índice de precios al consumo**) *Br* RPI, *US* CPI

IPCA *nm UE* (*abrev de* **índice de precios al consumo armonizado**) HICP

ipecacuana *nf* ipecacuanha, ipecac

iperita *nf* mustard gas, yperite

ipso facto *loc adv* immediately

iquiqueño, -a 1 *adj* of/from Iquique *(Chile)*
 2 *nm,f* person from Iquique *(Chile)*

iquiteño, -a 1 *adj* of/from Iquitos *(Peru)*
 2 *nm,f* person from Iquitos *(Peru)*

IR [35] 1 *vi* (**a**) *(desplazarse, dirigirse, acudir)* to go; **fuimos a caballo** we went on horseback, we rode there; **iremos andando** we'll go on foot, we'll walk there; **ir en autobús** to go by bus, to take the bus; **ir en automóvil** to go by car, to drive; **ir en taxi** to go by taxi, to catch *o* take a taxi; **ir en barco** to go by boat; **ir en avión** to go by plane, to fly; **ir por carretera/mar** to go by road/sea; **ir a casa/a la iglesia/al cine** to go home/to church/to the cinema; **ir a la escuela/al trabajo** to go to school/work; **los niños no tienen que ir a clase hoy** children don't have to go to school today; **me voy a clase, nos veremos luego** I'm going to my lecture, see you later; **ir de compras/de pesca** to go shopping/fishing; **ir de vacaciones** to go on *Br* holiday *o US* vacation; **ir hacia el sur/norte** to go south/north; **¿adónde va este autocar?** where's this coach going?; **este tren va a** *o* **para Guadalajara** this train is going to Guadalajara, this is the Guadalajara train; **todas las mañanas voy de la estación a** *o* **hasta la fábrica** every morning I go from the station to the factory; **¿para dónde vas?** where are you heading (for)?; **ahora mismo voy para allá** I'm on my way there right now; **¿por dónde** *o* **cómo se va a la playa?** how do you get to the beach from here?, could you tell me the way to the beach?; **no vayas por ahí que hay mucho barro** don't go that way, it's muddy; **¿eres alumno oficial? – no, sólo voy de oyente** are you an official student? – no, I'm just sitting in on classes; **fue a la zona como emisario de la ONU** he travelled to the area on behalf of the UN; **¡ahí** *o* **allá va!** *(al lanzar una cosa)* there you go; **ahí va el informe que me pediste** here's the report you asked for; **¡allá voy!** *(al lanzarse uno mismo)* here goes!, here we go!; *Anticuado* **¿quién va?** who goes there?; **¡Sergio, te llaman por teléfono! – ¡voy!** Sergio, there's a phone call for you! – (I'm) coming!; **¡ya voy!, ¡ya va!** *(cuando llaman a la puerta)* (I'm) coming!; **ir a alguien con algo** *(contar)* to go to sb with sth; **todos le van con sus problemas** everyone goes to her with their problems; **el autocar se salió de la calzada y fue a dar** *o* **a parar a un lago** the coach came off the road and ended up in a lake; **estuvimos de paseo y fuimos a dar a una bonita plaza** we were out walking when we came across a beautiful square; *Fam Fig* **¿dónde vais con tantos aperitivos? luego no podremos con la comida** steady on with the snacks or we won't be able to manage our dinner!; *Fam Fig* **les habrá costado unas 100.000 – ¡dónde vas! mucho menos, hombre** it must have cost them about 100,000 – what are you talking about, it was much less!; PROV **(allá) donde fueres haz lo que vieres** when in Rome, do as the Romans do

(**b**) *(conducir) (camino, calle, carretera)* to lead, to go; **esta es la calle que va al museo** this is the road (that leads *o* goes) to the museum; **esta calle va a dar al puerto** this road leads to the harbour; **el camino va desde el pueblo hasta la cima de la montaña** the path leads *o* goes from the village to the top of the mountain

(**c**) *(abarcar)* **la zona de fumadores va del asiento 24 al 28** the smoking area is between seats 24 and 28; **el examen de arte va desde el Barroco hasta el Romanticismo** the art exam will cover the Baroque period to the Romanticism period; **la mancha iba de un lado a otro del techo** the stain stretched from one side of the ceiling to the other; **las películas seleccionadas van desde la comedia urbana hasta el clásico western** the films that have been selected range from urban comedies to classic westerns

(**d**) *Esp (buscar)* **ir (a) por algo/alguien** to go and get sth/sb, to go and fetch sth/sb; **fui (a) por él al aeropuerto** I went to meet him at the airport, I went to pick him up from the airport; **ha ido (a) por leche a la tienda** she's gone to the shop to get *o* for some milk; **el perro fue a por él** the dog went for him; **tendrás que esconderte porque van a por ti** you'll have to hide because they're (coming) after you; **a eso voy/iba** *(al relatar)* I am/was just getting to that

(**e**) *(expresa estado, situación, posición)* **fue muy callada todo el camino** she was very quiet throughout the journey; **con esta bufanda irás calentito** this scarf will keep you warm; **el precio va impreso en la contraportada** the price is printed on the back cover; **la manivela va floja** the crank is loose; **iba tiritando de frío** she was shivering with cold; **ir a lo suyo** to look out for oneself, to look after number one; **iba en el tren pensando en sus cosas** she was travelling on the train lost in thought; **los niños iban armando jaleo en el asiento de atrás** the children were kicking up a row in the back seat; **ve con cuidado, es un barrio peligroso** be careful, it's a dangerous area; **tu caballo va tercero/en cabeza** your horse is third/in the lead

(**f**) *(expresa apoyo o rechazo)* **ir con** to support; **voy con el Real Madrid** I support Real Madrid; **ir contra algo, ir en contra de algo** to be opposed to *o* against sth; **ir en contra de la violencia** to be opposed to *o* against violence; **esta ley va contra la Constitución** this act goes against *o* contravenes the Constitution; **ir en beneficio de alguien** to be to sb's benefit, to be in sb's interest; **ir en perjuicio de alguien** to be detrimental to *o* against sb's interests

(**g**) *(vestir)* **ir con/en** to wear; **iba en camisa y corbata** he was wearing a shirt and tie; **aquí la gente va con** *o* **en bañador a todas partes** people here go around in their swimsuits; **ir de azul** to be dressed in blue; **ir de uniforme** to be in uniform; **iré (disfrazado) de Superman a la fiesta** I'm going to the party (dressed up) as Superman; **iba hecho un pordiosero** he looked like a beggar

(**h**) *(marchar, evolucionar)* to go; **le va bien en su nuevo trabajo** things are going well for him in his new job; **el niño va muy bien en la escuela** the child's doing very well at school; **¿cómo va el negocio?** how's business?; **su negocio va mal, el negocio le va mal** his business is going badly; **¿cómo te va?** how are you doing?; **¿cómo te va en la universidad?** how's university?, how are you getting on at university?; **¿cómo van?** *(en partido)* what's the score?; *(en carrera, juego)* who's winning?; **van empate a cero** it's zero-zero; **vamos perdiendo** we're losing; **¿qué tal te va con tus nuevos alumnos?** how are you getting on with your new pupils?; **¿qué tal va esa paella?** how's that paella coming along?; **¡hasta pronto! ¡que te vaya bien!** see you later, take care!; **¡que te vaya muy bien con el nuevo empleo!** I hope things go well for you in your new job!, the best of luck with your new job!

(**i**) *(cambiar, encaminarse)* **ir a mejor/peor** to get better/worse; **el partido fue a más en la segunda parte** the game improved *o* got better in the second half; **como sigamos así, vamos a la ruina** if we carry on like this we'll be heading for disaster; **voy para viejo** I'm getting old; **esta chica va para cantante** this girl has all the makings of a singer; **va para un mes que no llueve** it's getting on for *o* almost a month now since it last rained

(**j**) *(alcanzar)* **va por el cuarto vaso de vino** he's already on his fourth glass of wine; **vamos por la mitad de la asignatura** we've covered about half the subject; **¿por qué parte de la novela vas?** which bit in the novel are you at?; **aún voy por el primer capítulo** I'm still on the first chapter

(**k**) *(expresa cantidades, diferencias)* **con éste van cinco ministros destituidos por el escándalo** that makes five ministers who have now lost their job as a result of the scandal; **ya van dos veces que me tuerzo el tobillo** that's the second time I've twisted my ankle; **van varios días que no lo veo** it's several days since I (last) saw him; **en lo que va del** *o Esp* **de mes he ido tres veces al médico** so far this month I've been to the doctor three times, I've already been to the doctor three times this month; **de dos a cinco van tres** the difference between two and five is three; **va mucho de un apartamento a una casa** there's a big difference between *Br* a flat *o US* an apartment and a house

(**l**) *(corresponder)* to go; **estas tazas van con estos platos** these cups go with these saucers; **¿con qué clase de tornillos va esta tuerca?** what sort of screw does this nut take?

(**m**) *(colocarse)* to go, to belong; **esto no va ahí** that doesn't go *o* belong there; **¿en qué cajón van los calcetines?** which drawer do the socks go in?

(**n**) *(escribirse)* **"Edimburgo" va con "m"** "Edimburgo" is written *o* spelt with an "m"; **toda la oración va entre paréntesis** the whole sentence goes in brackets; **el "solo" adjetivo no va con acento** "solo" doesn't have an accent when used as an adjective

(**o**) *(sentar) (ropa)* **irle (bien) a alguien** to suit sb; **¡qué bien te van los abrigos largos!** long coats really suit you!; **ir con algo** to go with sth; **esta camisa no va con esos pantalones** this shirt doesn't go with those trousers

(**p**) *(sentar) (vacaciones, tratamiento)* **irle bien a alguien** to do sb good; **esa infusión me ha ido muy bien** that herbal tea did me a lot of good

(**q**) *(funcionar)* to work; **la televisión no va** the television isn't working; **una radio que va a** *o* **con pilas** a radio that uses batteries, a battery-powered radio; **estas impresoras antiguas van muy lentas** these old printers are very slow

(**r**) *(depender)* **en aquel negocio le iba su futuro como director de la empresa** his future as manager of the company depended on that deal; **todos corrieron como si les fuera la vida en ello** everyone ran as if their life depended on it; **esto de la ropa va en gustos** clothes are a matter of taste; *CSur* **¿es fácil aprobar? – va en el profesor** is it easy to pass? – it depends on the teacher

(**s**) *(comentario, indirecta)* **ir con** *o* **por alguien** to be meant for sb, to be aimed at sb; **y eso va por ti también** and that goes for you too; **hizo como si no fuera con él** he acted as if he didn't realize she was referring to him; **lo que digo va por todos** what I'm saying applies to *o* goes for all of you; **va** *o* **voy en serio, no me gustan estas bromas** I'm serious, I don't like this sort of joke

(**t**) *Esp Fam (gustar)* **no me va el pop** I'm not a big fan of pop music; **a mí lo que me va es la cocina** I'm really into cooking; **ni me va ni me viene** I don't care one way or the other

(**u**) *Fam (costar)* **ir a** to be, to cost; **¿a cómo** *o* **cuánto va el kilo de tomates?** how much is a kilo of tomatoes?

(**v**) *Esp Fam (tratar) (conferencia, película, novela)* **ir de** to be about; **¿de qué va "1984"?** what's "1984" about?

(**w**) *Fam Esp* **ir de,** *RP* **irla de** *(dárselas) (persona)* to think oneself; *Esp* **va de inteligente,** *RP* **la va de inteligente** he thinks he's clever; *Esp* **¿de qué vas?,** *RP* **¿de qué la vas?** just who do you think you are?

(**x**) *Fam (apostarse)* **¿va una cerveza a que llevo razón?** I bet you a beer I'm right

(**y**) *(en frases) Fam* **fue y dijo que...** he went and said that...; **y de repente va y se echa a reír** and suddenly she just goes and bursts out laughing; *Fam* **fue y se marchó sin mediar palabra** she upped and went without a word; *Fam* **¡ahí va! ¡qué paisaje tan bonito!** wow, what a beautiful landscape!; *Fam* **¡ahí va! me he dejado el paraguas en casa** oh no, I've left my umbrella at home!; **¡qué va!** *(por supuesto que no)* not in the least!, not at all!; *(me temo que no)* I'm afraid not; *(no digas tonterías)* don't be ridiculous!; **¡no va más!** *(en el casino)* no more bets!; EXPR *Esp* **ser el no va más** to be the ultimate; **este gimnasio es el no va más** this gym is the ultimate; EXPR *RP Fam* **desde el vamos** *(desde el principio)* from the word go; **me cayó mal desde el vamos** I didn't like him from the word go; EXPR *Fam* **¡dónde va a parar!** there's no comparison!; EXPR **sin ir más lejos: tu madre, sin ir más lejos** we need look no further than your mother; **sin ir más lejos, nos vimos ayer** we saw each other only yesterday

2 *v aux* (**a**) *(con gerundio) (expresa acción lenta o gradual)* **ir haciendo algo** to be (gradually) doing sth; **va anocheciendo** it's getting dark; **me voy haciendo viejo** I'm getting old; **voy mejorando mi estilo** I'm gradually improving my style; **su cine ha ido mejorando últimamente** her movies have been getting better recently; **fui metiendo las cajas en el almacén** I began putting the crates in the warehouse; **iremos aprendiendo de nuestros errores** we'll learn from our mistakes; **ve deshaciendo las maletas mientras preparo la cena** you can be unpacking the suitcases while I get dinner; **vete haciéndote a la idea** you'd better start getting used to the idea; **como iba diciendo...** as I was saying...

(**b**) *(con a + infinitivo) (expresa acción próxima, intención, situación futura)* **ir a hacer algo** to be going to do sth; **voy a hacerle una visita** *(ahora mismo)* I'm about to go and visit him; *(en un futuro próximo)* I'm going to visit him; **iré a echarte una mano en cuanto pueda** I'll come along and give you a hand as soon as I can; **¡vamos a comer, tengo hambre!** let's have lunch, I'm hungry!; **el tren con destino a Buenos Aires va a efectuar su salida en el andén 3** the train for Buenos Aires is about to depart from platform 3; **van a dar las dos** it is nearly two o'clock; **va a hacer una semana que se fue** it's coming up to *o* nearly a week since she left; **voy a decírselo a tu padre** I'm going to tell your father; **¿no irás a salir así a la calle?** surely you're not going to go out like that?; **he ido a comprar pero ya habían cerrado** I had intended to go shopping, but they were shut; **te voy a echar de menos** I'm going to miss you; **vas a hacerte daño como no tengas cuidado** you'll hurt yourself if you're not careful; **todo va a arreglarse, ya verás** it'll all sort itself out, you'll see; **¿qué van a pensar los vecinos?** what will the neighbours think?; **no le quise decir nada, no fuera a enfadarse conmigo** I didn't want to say anything in case she got angry with me

(**c**) *(con a + infinitivo) (en exclamaciones que expresan consecuencia lógica, negación)* **¿qué voy a pensar si llevas tres días fuera de casa?** what do you expect me to think if you don't come home for three days?; **¿la del sombrero es tu hermana? – ¿quién va a ser? ¡pues claro!** is the woman with the hat your sister? – of course she is, who else could she be?; **y ¿dónde fuiste? – ¿dónde iba a ir? ¡a la policía!** and where did you go? – where do you think? to the police, of course!; **¡cómo voy a concentrarme con tanto ruido!** how am I supposed to concentrate with all that noise?; **¡cómo voy a pagarte si estoy sin dinero!** how do you expect me to pay you if I haven't got any money?; **¡cómo no me voy a reír con las cosas que dices!** how can I fail to laugh *o* how can you expect me not to laugh when you say things like that!; **¿te ha gustado? – ¡qué me va a gustar!** did you like it? – like it? you must be joking!

3 *vt Méx* **irle a** to support; **le va al Nexaca** he supports Nexaca

4 irse *vpr* (**a**) *(marcharse)* to go, to leave; **me voy, que mañana tengo que madrugar** I'm off, I've got to get up early tomorrow; **tenemos que irnos o perderemos el tren** we have to be going or we'll miss the train; **irse a** to go to; **este verano nos vamos a la playa** we'll be going *o* off to the seaside this summer; **se ha ido a trabajar** she's gone to work; **se fueron a Venezuela a montar un negocio** they went (off) to Venezuela to start a business; **se fue de casa/del país** he left home/the country; **se me va uno de mis mejores empleados** I'm losing one of my best employees; **¡vete!** go away!; *Fam* **¡vete por ahí!** get lost!; **irse abajo** *(edificio)* to fall down; *(negocio)* to collapse; *(planes)* to fall through

(**b**) *(desaparecer)* to go; **se fue el mal tiempo** the bad weather went away; **se ha ido la luz** there's been a power cut; **estas manchas no se van tan fácilmente** these stains aren't easy to get out; **los granos se le irán con el tiempo** the spots will go *o* disappear in time; **no se me ha ido el dolor** the pain hasn't gone, the pain is still there

(**c**) *(gastarse)* to go; **se me fueron todos los ahorros en el viaje** all my savings went on the journey; **se me ha ido la mañana limpiando la casa** I've spent the whole morning cleaning the house; *Irónico* **el tiempo se va que es un gusto** I've no idea where all my time goes

(**d**) *(salirse, escaparse)* **ponle un corcho al champán para que no se le vaya la fuerza** put a cork in the champagne bottle so it doesn't go flat; **al motor se le va el aceite por alguna parte** the oil's leaking out of the engine somewhere, the engine's losing oil somewhere; **sin doble acristalamiento el calor se va por las rendijas** if you haven't got double glazing, the heat escapes through the gaps in the windows

(**e**) *(resbalar)* **se me fue el cuchillo y me corté un dedo** the knife slipped and I cut my finger; **se le fue un pie y se cayó** her foot slipped and she fell; **tomó la curva muy cerrada y todos nos fuimos para un lado** he took the bend very tight and we all slid to one side

(**f**) *(olvidarse)* **tenía varias ideas, pero se me han ido** I had several ideas, but they've all slipped my mind; **se me ha ido su nombre** her name escapes me

(**g**) *RP (en cartas, juegos)* **me voy** I'm out

(**h**) *RP* **irse a examen** *(en asignatura)* to have to do the exam *(if you fail to get an exemption)*

(**i**) *Euf (morirse)* **se nos fue hace un año** she passed away a year ago, we lost her a year ago

(**j**) *Fam Hum (ventosear)* to let off

(**k**) *muy Fam (tener un orgasmo)* to come

(**l**) EXPR **¡vete a saber!** who knows!

5 *nm* **el ir y venir de los albañiles con sus carretillas** the comings and goings of the builders with their wheelbarrows; **con tanto ir y venir toda la mañana tengo los pies destrozados** my feet are really sore after all that running around this morning

IRA ['ira] *nm (abrev de* **Irish Republican Army***)* IRA ►► ***el I. Provisional*** the Provisional IRA

ira *nf* anger, rage; **en un arrebato de i. la insultó** he insulted her in a fit of rage; **sus declaraciones provocaron la i. de la clase política** politicians were enraged at his statement, his statement incurred the wrath of politicians; **los exploradores tuvieron que hacer frente a la i. de los elementos** the explorers had to contend with the fury of the elements

iraca *nf Col* Panama-hat palm

iracundia *nf* (**a**) *(propensión)* irascibility (**b**) *(cólera)* ire, wrath

iracundo, -a *adj* (**a**) *(furioso)* angry, irate (**b**) *(irascible)* irascible

Irak = **Iraq**

irakí = **iraquí**

Irán *nm* **(el) I.** Iran

iraní (*pl* **iraníes**) **1** *adj* Iranian
2 *nmf (persona)* Iranian
3 *nm (lengua)* Iranian

Iraq, Irak *nm* **(el) I.** Iraq

iraquí (*pl* **iraquíes**), **irakí** (*pl* **irakíes**) **1** *adj* Iraqi
2 *nmf* Iraqi

irascibilidad *nf* irascibility

irascible *adj* irascible

irbis *nm inv* snow leopard

irgo *etc ver* **erguir**

irguiera *etc ver* **erguir**

iridio *nm Quím* iridium

iridiscencia *nf* iridescence

iridiscente *adj* iridescent

iridología *nf* iridology

iridólogo, -a *nm,f* iridologist

iris *nm inv (del ojo)* iris

irisación *nf* iridescence

irisado, -a *adj* iridescent

irisar *vi* to be iridescent

Irlanda *n* Ireland ▸▸ ***I. del Norte*** Northern Ireland

irlandés, -esa 1 *adj* Irish
2 *nm,f (persona)* Irishman, *f* Irishwoman; **los irlandeses** the Irish
3 *nm* (**a**) *(lengua)* Irish (**b**) *(café)* Irish coffee

ironía *nf* (**a**) *(cualidad)* irony; **¡qué i.!** how ironic!; **una i. del destino** an irony of fate; **lo dijo con mucha i.** she said it very ironically (**b**) *(comentario)* ironic remark; **soltó unas ironías** he made some ironic remarks

irónicamente *adv* ironically

irónico, -a *adj* ironic, ironical; **lo dije en tono i.** I was being ironic

ironizar [14] **1** *vt* to ridicule
2 *vi* to be ironical (**sobre** about)

iroqués, -esa (*pl* **iroqueses**) **1** *adj* Iroquois
2 *nm,f* Iroquois

IRPF *nm* (*abrev de* **Impuesto sobre la Renta de las Personas Físicas**) = Spanish personal income tax

irracional *adj* irrational

irracionalidad *nf* irrationality

irradiación *nf* (**a**) *(de luz, calor)* radiation (**b**) *(de cultura, ideas)* dissemination, spreading (**c**) *(de alimentos, enfermo, órgano)* irradiation

irradiar *vt* (**a**) *(luz, calor)* to radiate (**b**) *(cultura, ideas)* to disseminate (**c**) *(alimentos, enfermo órgano)* to irradiate (**d**) *(simpatía, felicidad)* to radiate (**e**) *RP (emitir)* to broadcast

irrazonable *adj* unreasonable

irreal *adj* (**a**) *(imaginario)* imaginary; **un mundo i.** a fantasy world; **aquel lugar tenía un aire i.** there was something unreal about that place (**b**) *(excesivo)* unrealistic

irrealidad *nf* unreality

irrealizable *adj (sueño, objetivo)* unattainable; *(plan)* impractical

irrebatible *adj* irrefutable, indisputable

irreconciliable *adj* irreconcilable

irreconocible *adj* unrecognizable; **con barba está i.** he's unrecognizable with a beard

irrecuperable *adj* irretrievable

irredentismo *nm Pol* irredentism

irredentista *Pol* **1** *adj* irredentist
2 *nmf* irredentist

irredento, -a *Pol adj* unredeemed

irredimible *adj* unredeemable

irreductible *adj* (**a**) *(fenómeno, fracción)* irreducible (**b**) *(país, pueblo)* unconquerable

irreemplazable *adj* irreplaceable

irreflexión *nf* rashness

irreflexivamente *adv* unthinkingly; **actuó i.** he acted unthinkingly *o* without thinking

irreflexivo, -a *adj* rash; **es muy i.** he's very rash

irreformable *adj* incorrigible

irrefrenable *adj* irrepressible, uncontainable

irrefutable *adj* irrefutable

irregular *adj* (**a**) *(comportamiento)* erratic; **su rendimiento en los estudios es i.** her marks are inconsistent; **el equipo tuvo una actuación muy i.** the team's performance was very patchy; **el comportamiento i. de la inflación** the erratic behaviour of inflation
(**b**) *(situación)* irregular; **un inmigrante en situación i.** an immigrant without the proper documentation, an immigrant who is not legally registered
(**c**) *(terreno, superficie)* uneven
(**d**) *(poco honesto)* irregular; **consiguió su fortuna de forma i.** the way he obtained his fortune was not entirely honest *o* was somewhat irregular; **la financiación i. de los partidos** the irregular funding of the parties
(**e**) *(verbo)* irregular
(**f**) *Geom* irregular

irregularidad *nf* (**a**) *(de comportamiento)* erratic nature; **la i. del viento** the changeability of the wind; **la i. de los discos de un artista** the erratic *o* inconsistent quality of an artist's records
(**b**) *(de situación)* irregularity
(**c**) *(de terreno, superficie)* unevenness
(**d**) *(de verbo)* irregularity
(**e**) *(delito, falta)* irregularity ▸▸ ***i. administrativa*** administrative *o* procedural irregularity

irregularmente *adv* irregularly

irrelevancia *nf* unimportance, insignificance

irrelevante *adj* unimportant, insignificant

irreligioso, -a 1 *adj* irreligious
2 *nm,f* irreligious person

irremediable *adj* (**a**) *(inevitable)* unavoidable; **una consecuencia i.** an inevitable *o* unavoidable consequence (**b**) *(irreparable)* irremediable, irreparable

irremediablemente *adv* inevitably; **la responsabilidad pesó i. sobre él** he was inevitably held responsible

irremisible *adj* (**a**) *(imperdonable)* **una condena i.** a sentence which cannot be revoked (**b**) *(irremediable)* inevitable

irremisiblemente *adv* inevitably; **una guerra que cambió i. el país** a war that changed the country for good

irremplazable *adj* irreplaceable

irrenunciable *adj* **para ellos la subida salarial es un objetivo i.** the pay rise is non-negotiable as far as they are concerned, obtaining the pay rise is an aim that they are not prepared to abandon

irreparable *adj* irreparable; **su muerte es una pérdida i.** her death is an irreparable loss; **el terremoto causó daños irreparables** the earthquake caused irreparable damage

irrepetible *adj* unique, unrepeatable

irreprimible *adj* irrepressible

irreprochable *adj* irreproachable

irresistible *adj* (**a**) *(dolor)* unbearable (**b**) *(persona, oferta)* irresistible

irresistiblemente *adv* irresistibly

irresoluble *adj* unsolvable

irresolución *nf* irresolution, indecisiveness

irresoluto, -a *Formal* **1** *adj* irresolute
2 *nm,f* irresolute person

irrespetar *vt Col, Ven (persona)* to be disrespectful to; *(cosa)* not to respect, to show no respect for

irrespetuoso, -a *adj* disrespectful

irrespirable *adj* (**a**) *(aire)* unbreathable (**b**) *Fig (ambiente)* oppressive; **la atmósfera en esta oficina es i.** the atmosphere in this office is really oppressive

irresponsabilidad *nf* irresponsibility

irresponsable 1 *adj* irresponsible
2 *nmf* irresponsible person; **es un i.** he's very irresponsible

irrestricto, -a *adj Am* unconditional, complete; **amnistía irrestricta** general amnesty; **apoyo i.** undconditional *o* complete support; **tengo confianza irrestricta en él** I have complete *o* the utmost confidence in him

irretroactividad *nf Der* nonretroactive nature

irreverencia *nf* (**a**) *(cualidad)* irreverence (**b**) *(dicho)* irreverent remark; **eso es una i.** *(acto)* that's irreverent, that's an irreverent thing to do

irreverente *adj* irreverent

irreversibilidad *nf* irreversibility

irreversible *adj* irreversible

irrevocable *adj* irrevocable; **presentó su dimisión i.** he handed in his resignation, saying that there was no prospect of him changing his mind

irrevocablemente *adv* irrevocably

irrigación *nf* (**a**) *(de campo)* irrigation (**b**) *Med (circulación)* circulation (**c**) *Med (con líquido)* irrigation ►► ***i. del colon*** colonic irrigation; ***i. rectal*** rectal irrigation; ***i. vaginal*** douche

irrigador *nm Med* irrigator

irrigar [38] *vt* (**a**) *(campo)* to irrigate (**b**) *Med (órgano)* to supply with blood (**c**) *Med (con líquido)* to irrigate

irrisión *nf (mofa)* ridicule, derision

irrisorio, -a *adj* (**a**) *(excusa, historia)* laughable, risible (**b**) *(muy pequeño)* derisory; **nos ofrecieron un precio i.** we were offered a derisory sum; **una cantidad irrisoria** a derisory amount

irritabilidad *nf* irritability

irritable *adj* irritable

irritación *nf* (**a**) *(enfado)* irritation, annoyance (**b**) *(de la piel)* irritation; *(de la garganta)* inflammation

irritado, -a *adj* (**a**) *(persona)* irritated, annoyed (**b**) *(garganta)* sore; **tengo la piel irritada** I've got a rash

irritante *adj* irritating, annoying

irritar 1 *vt* (**a**) *(enfadar)* to irritate, to annoy (**b**) *(piel, garganta)* to irritate; **me irritó la garganta/piel** it gave me a sore throat/a rash; **el humo me irrita los pulmones** smoke irritates my lungs

2 **irritarse** *vpr* (**a**) *(enfadarse)* to get annoyed; **se irrita con cualquier cosa** he gets annoyed at the slightest thing; **se irritó por mis comentarios** he was annoyed about what I said (**b**) *(sujeto: piel, garganta)* **se me irritó la garganta** I got a sore throat; **se me irritó la piel** I got a rash

irrogar [38] *vt Formal* to cause, to occasion

irrompible *adj* unbreakable

irrumpir *vi* **i. en** *(lugar, vida)* to burst into; *(escena política, pantalla)* to burst onto

irrupción *nf (en lugar)* **la i. de los alborotadores obligó a suspender la reunión** the meeting had to be stopped when troublemakers burst in; **tras su i. en la política** after she burst onto the political scene; **su i. en mi vida se produjo hace seis años** she burst into my life six years ago

IRTP *nm* (*abrev de* **Impuesto sobre el Rendimiento del Trabajo Personal**) payroll tax, ≃ *Br* PAYE

irupé *nm* giant *o* royal water lily

Isaac *n pr* Isaac

Isabel *n pr* **I. I/II** Elizabeth I/II; **I. la Católica** Isabella the Catholic

isabelino, -a *adj* (**a**) *(en España)* Isabelline (**b**) *(en Inglaterra)* Elizabethan

Isaías *n pr* Isaiah

isatis *nm inv* Arctic fox

ISBN *nm* (*abrev de* **International Standard Book Number**) ISBN

isla *nf* (**a**) *(en el agua)* island; **una i. desierta** a desert island ►► ***las islas Afortunadas*** *(las Canarias)* the Canary Islands, the Canaries; ***las islas Anglonormandas*** the Channel Islands; ***las islas Azores*** the Azores; ***las islas Baleares*** the Balearic Islands; ***las islas Británicas*** the British Isles; ***las islas Canarias*** the Canary Islands, the Canaries; ***las islas Carolinas*** the Caroline Islands; ***las islas Filipinas*** the Philippines; ***las islas Galápagos*** the Galapagos Islands; ***las islas Malvinas*** the Falkland Islands; ***la i. de Man*** the Isle of Man; ***la i. de Pascua*** Easter Island; ***la i. de la Reunión*** Réunion; ***las islas Salomón*** the Solomon Islands

(**b**) *Méx, RP (de árboles)* grove

(**c**) *Chile (terrero)* flood plain

(**d**) *Ven (mediana) Br* central reservation, *US* median (strip)

islam *nm* **el i.** Islam

Islamabad *n* Islamabad

islámico, -a *adj* Islamic

islamismo *nm* Islam

islamista 1 *adj* (**a**) *(estudioso del islam)* Islamist (**b**) *(integrista)* Islamic fundamentalist, Islamist

2 *nmf* (**a**) *(estudioso del islam)* Islamist, Islamic scholar (**b**) *(integrista)* Islamic fundamentalist, Islamist

islamizar [14] **1** *vt* to Islamize, to convert to Islam

2 **islamizarse** *vpr* to convert to Islam

islandés, -esa 1 *adj* Icelandic

2 *nm,f (persona)* Icelander

3 *nm (lengua)* Icelandic

Islandia *n* Iceland

isleño, -a 1 *adj* (**a**) *(de una isla)* island; **las costumbres isleñas** the island customs (**b**) *Ven (de Canarias)* of/from the Canary Islands

2 *nm,f* (**a**) *(de una isla)* islander (**b**) *Ven (de Canarias)* immigrant from the Canary Islands

isleta *nf (en calle)* traffic island

islote *nm* small island

ismo *nm* ism

ISO ['iso] *nf* (*abrev de* **International Standards Organization**) ISO

isobara, isóbara *nf* isobar

isobárico, -a *adj* isobaric

isoca *nf RP* = butterfly larva which damages crops

isocarro *nm* three-wheeled van

isoglosa *nf Ling* isogloss

isómero *nm Quím* isomer

isometría *nf* isometrics *(singular)*

isométrico, -a *adj* isometric

isomorfismo *nm* isomorphism

isomorfo, -a *Quím* **1** *adj* isomorphic

2 *nm* isomorph

isósceles *adj inv* isosceles

isoterma *nf* isotherm

isotérmico, -a, isotermo, -a *adj* isothermal; **camión i.** refrigerated truck *o Br* lorry; **un recipiente i.** a container that keeps the contents at a constant temperature

isotónico, -a *adj* isotonic

isótopo, -a 1 *adj* isotopic

2 *nm* isotope ►► ***i. radiactivo*** radioactive isotope

isquemia *nf Med* ischaemia

isquion *nm Anat* ischium

Israel *n* Israel

israelí (*pl* **israelíes**) **1** *adj* Israeli

2 *nmf* Israeli

israelita 1 *adj* Israelite

2 *nmf* Israelite

ISSSTE ['iste] *nm* (*abrev* **Instituto de Seguridad y Servicios Sociales de los Trabajadores del Estado**) = Mexican department that deals with healthcare and social security for public sector workers

istmo *nm* isthmus ►► ***i. de Panamá*** Isthmus of Panama

itacate *nm Méx* packed lunch

Italia *n* Italy

italianada *nf RP Fam (gente)* Italian crowd; EXPR **se le subió la i.** she flew off the handle

italianismo *nm* Italianism

italianizante *adj* Italianizing

italiano, -a 1 *adj* Italian

2 *nm,f (persona)* Italian

3 *nm (lengua)* Italian

itálico, -a 1 *adj* (**a**) *Hist* Italic (**b**) *(letra)* italic; **en i.** in italics

2 *nm,f* (**a**) *Hist* Italic (**b**) *(letra)* italic

ítalo, -a *Literario* **1** *adj* Italian

2 *nm,f* Italian

ítem (*pl* **ítems**) *nm* (**a**) *(elemento)* item (**b**) *(en test)* question

itemizar *vt Am* to itemize, to list

iteración *nf* repetition

iterar *vt* to repeat

iterativo, -a *adj* (**a**) *(canción, persona)* repetitive (**b**) *Ling* iterative

iterbio *nm Quím* ytterbium

itinerante *adj (vida)* itinerant; *(exposición)* travelling; *(embajador)* roving

itinerario *nm* route, itinerary

itrio *nm Quím* yttrium

ITV *nf Esp* (*abrev de* **inspección técnica de vehículos**) = annual technical inspection for motor vehicles with an age of five years or more, *Br* ≃ MOT

IU *nf* (*abrev de* **Izquierda Unida**) = Spanish left-wing coalition party

IVA ['iβa] *nm* (*abrev de* **impuesto sobre el valor añadido,** *Am* **impuesto al valor agregado**) *Br* VAT, *US* ≃ sales tax

Iván *n pr* **I. el Terrible** Ivan the Terrible

ixtle *nm Méx* istle, ixtle, = fibre, especially from the maguey plant

izar [14] *vt* to raise, to hoist

izda. (*abrev de* **izquierda**) L, l

izdo. (*abrev de* **izquierdo**) L, l

izote *nm* Spanish dagger

izqda. (*abrev de* **izquierda**) L, l

izqdo. (*abrev de* **izquierdo**) L, l

izquierda 1 *nf* (**a**) *(contrario de derecha)* left, left-hand side; **el de la i. es mi primo** the person on the left is my cousin; **a la i. (de)** on *o* to the left (of); **la primera bocacalle a la i.** the first turning on the left; **a mi/vuestra i.** on my/your left(-hand side); **a su i. el Ayuntamiento** on your left is the Town Hall; **girar a la i.** to turn left; **prohibido girar a la i.** no left turn; **de la i.** on the left; **por la i.** on the left
(**b**) *(en política)* left (wing); **la i.** the left; **un partido de** *Esp* **izquierdas** *o Am* **i.** a left-wing party; **ser de** *Esp* **izquierdas** *o Am* **i.** to be left-wing
(**c**) *(mano)* left hand; *(pierna)* left foot; **marcó con la i.** he scored with his left foot
(**d**) *(puerta)* **el segundo i.** *Br* the left-hand flat on the second floor, *US* the left-hand apartment on the third floor
2 *interj (orden militar)* left wheel!

izquierdismo *nm (de persona, partido)* left-wing views; **el i. del gobierno** the government's left-wing policies

izquierdista 1 *adj* left-wing
2 *nmf* left-winger

izquierdización *nf (en política)* move to the left

izquierdo, -a *adj* left; **mano/pierna izquierda** left hand/leg; **el margen i.** the left-hand margin; **a mano izquierda** on the left-hand side

izquierdoso, -a *adj Fam* leftish

J, j

J, j ['χota] *nf (letra)* J, j
J *(abrev de* **jueves***)* Th
ja *interj Fam* **(a)** *(expresando risa)* ha! **(b)** *(expresando desafío)* ha!; **ya verás como te gano – ¡ja!, que te lo has creído** I'll beat you, just you wait and see – ha, that's what you think!
jab [jaβ] *(pl* **jabs***) nm (en boxeo)* jab
jaba *nf* **(a)** *Andes (cajón)* crate **(b)** *Cuba (bolsa)* bag
jabado, -a *adj PRico (ave)* mottled
jabalí *(pl* **jabalíes***) nm* wild boar ►► ***j. verrugoso*** warthog
jabalina *nf* **(a)** *Dep* javelin **(b)** *(animal)* wild sow
jabato, -a 1 *adj Esp Fam (valiente)* brave
2 *nm* **(a)** *(animal)* young wild boar **(b)** *Esp Fam (valiente)* dare-devil; **estar hecho un j.** to be a dare-devil
jábega *nf* **(a)** *(red)* dragnet **(b)** *(barco)* small fishing boat
jabillo *nm* sandbox tree
jabón *nm* **(a)** *(para lavar)* soap; **una pastilla de j.** a bar of soap; EXPR *Fam* **dar j. a alguien** to soft-soap sb ►► ***j. de afeitar*** shaving soap; *Ven* ***j. en panela*** laundry soap; ***j. en polvo*** soap powder; ***j. de sastre*** soapstone, French chalk; ***j. de tocador*** toilet soap **(b)** *Méx, RP Fam* **dar un j. a alguien** *(asustar)* to freak sb; **¡me pegué un j.!** I freaked!
jabonada *nf* **(a)** *(con jabón)* **dar una j. a algo** to wash sth with soap **(b)** *Chile, Méx Fam (reprimenda)* telling-off, *Br* ticking-off
jabonar 1 *vt* to soap
2 jabonarse *vpr* to soap oneself
jaboncillo *nm* **(a)** *(de sastre)* tailor's chalk **(b)** *Chile (para afeitar)* shaving soap **(c)** *Bol (de tocador)* toilet soap
jabonera *nf* soap dish
jabonero, -a 1 *adj* soap; **la industria jabonera** the soap industry
2 *nm,f* soapmaker
jabonoso, -a *adj* soapy
jabuco *nm Cuba* large straw basket
jabugo *nm* = good quality Spanish cured ham from Jabugo, similar to Parma ham
jaca *nf* **(a)** *(caballo pequeño)* pony; *(yegua)* mare **(b)** *muy Fam (mujer) Br* stunner, *US* tomato **(c)** *Am (gallo)* gamecock, fighting cock
jacal *nm Méx* hut
jacalear *vi Méx Fam* to gossip
jacalerío *nm Méx* **(a)** *(en el campo)* group of huts **(b)** *(en la ciudad)* shanty town
jacalón *nm Méx* lean-to, shed
jacana *nf* jacana
jácara *nf Lit* = picaresque ballad
jacarandá *nm* jacaranda
jacarandoso, -a *adj Fam* merry, lively
jácena *nf Arquit* summer (beam)
jacinto *nm* **(a)** *(planta)* hyacinth **(b)** *(piedra)* hyacinth, jacinth
jack [jak] *(pl* **jacks***) nm* jack
jaco *nm* **(a)** *(caballo)* nag **(b)** *Fam (heroína)* junk, smack
Jacob *n pr* Jacob
jacobeo, -a *adj* of/relating to St James; **año j.** = year in which the feast of St James (25th July) falls on a Sunday, during which special religious celebrations are held; **la ruta jacobea** = pilgrims' route to Santiago de Compostela
jacobinismo *nm Hist* Jacobinism
jacobino, -a *Hist* **1** *adj* Jacobin
2 *nm,f* Jacobin
jacobita *Hist* **1** *adj* Jacobite
2 *nmf* Jacobite
Jacobo *n pr* **J. I/II** James I/II (of England)
jacolote *nm* ocote pine
jactancia *nf* boasting; **habla de sus hijos con j.** he speaks boastfully about his children
jactancioso, -a *adj* boastful
jactarse *vpr* to boast (**de** about *o* of), to brag (**de** about); **se jacta de tener un Mercedes** she brags *o* boasts about having a Mercedes
jaculatoria *nf* short prayer
jacuzzi® [ja'kusi] *nm* Jacuzzi®
jade *nm* jade
jadeante *adj* panting; **llegó a la cima j.** she was panting when she got to the top
jadear *vi* to pant; **jadeaba de emoción** she was gasping with excitement
jadeo *nm* panting
jaez *nm* **(a)** *(arreo)* harness **(b)** *Pey (carácter)* ilk, kind; **todos esos son del mismo j.** they are all of the same ilk
jagua *nf* **(a)** *(árbol)* genipa, marmalade box **(b)** *(fruta)* genipa fruit **(c)** *(tintura)* genipa dye
jaguar *nm* jaguar
jaguay *nm Perú* **(a)** *(aguada)* watering trough **(b)** *(charca)* pond
jagüel *nm Andes, RP, Ven* pond
jagüey *nm* **(a)** *(bejuco)* liana **(b)** *Andes, RP, Ven (charca)* pond
jai *nf Fam* **(a)** *Esp (mujer) Br* bird, *US* chick **(b)** *Am* **la j.** *(la alta sociedad)* high society
jai alai *nm* jai alai, pelota
jaiba 1 *nmf Carib, Méx Fam (persona)* sharp customer
2 *nf* **(a)** *Andes, CAm, Carib, Méx (cangrejo)* crayfish **(b)** *Méx Fam (policía)* **la j.** the cops
jaibol *nm Méx Br* whisky and soda, *US* highball
jaima *nf* = Bedouin tent
Jaime *n pr* **J. I/II** Jaime I/II
jaimitada *nf Esp Fam* **¡estoy harto de sus jaimitadas!** I'm sick of his antics!
jalabolas *nmf inv Ven muy Fam* crawler
jalada *nf* **(a)** *Méx (tirón)* pull; *(suave)* tug; **dar una j. a algo** to pull sth; *(suavemente)* to tug sth **(b)** *Méx Fam (reprimenda)* telling-off; **dar una j. a alguien** to tell sb off **(c)** *Ven Fam (adulancia)* soft soap; **con las jaladas al jefe, consiguió un aumento** all that soft-soaping the boss got him a raise; **dar una j. a alguien** to soft-soap sb **(d)** *Perú Fam (aventón) Br* lift, *US* ride; **pedir una j.** to ask for a *Br* lift *o US* ride; **dar una j. a alguien** to give sb a *Br* lift *o US* ride
jalado, -a *adj Fam* **(a)** *CAm, Méx, Ven (borracho)* smashed, plastered **(b)** *Ven (demacrado)* gaunt
jalador, -ora 1 *nm,f Fam* **(a)** *Méx (emprendedor)* **es un j.** he's always more than happy to help out **(b)** *Ven (adulador)* crawler
2 *nm Méx* squeegee
jalapa *nf (planta)* jalap
jalapeño, -a 1 *adj* of/from Jalapa *(Mexico)*
2 *nm,f* person from Jalapa *(Mexico)*
3 *nm (chile)* jalapeño chilli
jalar[1]**, halar** [χa'lar] **1** *vt* **(a)** *Andes, CAm, Carib, Méx (tirar de)* to pull; *(suavemente)* to tug; **j. la cadena** to pull the chain, to flush (the toilet); **j. un cajón** to pull out a drawer; **lo jaló de la manga** she pulled his sleeve; **j. el pelo a alguien** to pull sb's hair; *Méx, Ven* **jaló al niño hasta la escuela** she dragged the child to school; EXPR *Fam* **j. la lengua a alguien** to draw sb out; EXPR *Fam* **j. las orejas a alguien** to bawl sb out; EXPR *Ven Fam* **j. mecate (a alguien)** *(adular)* to crawl (to sb)
(b) *Méx (extender)* to stretch out; **jaló tanto el suéter que lo deformó** she stretched the sweater out of shape
(c) *Méx Fam (atraer)* **el deporte me jala mucho** I'm crazy about sport

o US sports, I'm really into sport *o US* sports

(d) *Méx Fam (convencer)* **lo jalaron para que participara en la campaña** they talked him into joining the campaign

(e) *Perú Fam (transportar)* to give a *Br* lift *o US* ride; **me jaló hasta la estación** she gave me a *Br* lift *o US* ride to the station

(f) *Perú Fam (suspender)* to fail, *US* to flunk

(g) *Perú Fam (cobrar)* to sting; **¿cuánto te jalaron por esos zapatos?** how much did they sting you for when you bought those shoes?

(h) *Ven Fam (succionar)* to suck up

(i) *Ven Fam (consumir) (energía, combustible)* to guzzle; *(dinero)* to eat up

2 *vi* (a) *Andes, CAm, Carib, Méx (tirar)* to pull; **jale** *(en letrero)* pull

(b) *Andes, CAm, Carib, Méx (irse)* to go; **jala a la derecha en la tercera calle** take the third street on the right; **jálale por la leche, que ya van a cerrar** go for some milk, the shop will be closing soon; **cada uno jaló por su lado** they all headed off their own way

(c) *Méx Fam (trabajar)* to work; **¿en qué jalas?** what are you working on?

(d) *Méx Fam (robar)* **jalaron con tres computadoras** they made off with *o Br* nicked three computers

(e) *Méx muy Fam (molestar)* to be a *Br* bloody *o US* goddamn pain; **deja de j.** stop being such a *Br* bloody *o US* goddamn pain

(f) *Méx Fam (funcionar)* to work; **este reloj es muy viejo pero todavía jala** this watch is very old, but it's still hanging on in there; **¿cómo van los estudios? – jalando** how are your studies going? – OK *o* not bad; **el negocio está jalando muy bien** the business is coming along nicely

(g) *Méx Fam (apresurarse)* to get a move on; **dejen de platicar y jálenle, que se hace tarde** stop gabbing and get a move on, it's late

(h) *Ven Fam (adular)* to crawl

(i) *Ven (chimenea)* to draw

(j) *Méx Fam* EXPR **j. parejo** *(compartir el gasto)* to go halves; **si queremos resolver el problema hay que j. parejo** if we want to solve the problem we'll all have to pull our weight; **no j. con alguien: éramos compañeras de primaria, pero nunca jalé con ella** we were at the same primary school, but we were never friends

(k) *Perú, RP Fam (inhalar)* to snort cocaine

3 **jalarse** *vpr* (a) *Ven Fam (emborracharse)* to get plastered (b) *Méx Vulg* **jalársela** *(masturbarse)* to jerk off, *Br* to have a wank (c) *Méx Fam* **jalársela** *(exagerar)* to put on an act (d) *Méx Fam* **jalarse las medias** *Br* to ladder one's tights, *US* to get a run in one's tights

jalar[2] *Esp Fam* 1 *vt* to eat, *Br* to scoff

2 *vi* to eat, *Br* to nosh

3 **jalarse** *vpr* to eat, *Br* to scoff; **se jaló dos manzanas** she ate *o Br* scoffed two apples

jale *nm Méx Fam* work; **acabo de perder el j.** I've just got the sack

jalea *nf* jelly ▸▸ ***j. de guayaba*** guava jelly; ***j. de membrillo*** quince jelly; ***j. real*** royal jelly

jalear *vt* (a) *(animar) (cantante, bailarín, equipo)* to cheer on (b) *Chile (molestar)* to pester, to bother

jaleo *nm Fam* (a) *(lío)* mess, confusion; **había un j. enorme a la entrada del estadio** it was utter chaos outside the stadium; **no encuentro el documento entre tanto j. de papeles** I can't find the document amongst such a muddle *o* jumble of papers; **tengo mucho j. en la oficina** things are pretty hectic for me at the office just now; **un j. de cifras** a jumble of figures; **en menudo j. te has metido** that's a real mess you've landed yourself in; **con este programa me armo mucho j.** this program is a nightmare

(b) *(alboroto)* row, rumpus; **armar j.** to kick up a row *o* fuss

(c) *(ruido)* racket, row; *(aplausos, gritos)* cheering; **armar j.** to make a racket

jalifa *nf Hist* = Spanish Moroccan governor

jalisciense 1 *adj* of/from Jalisco *(Mexico)*

2 *nmf* person from Jalisco *(Mexico)*

jalisco *nm Méx* straw hat

jalisquillo, -a *nm,f Méx* = pejorative term for a person from Guadalajara

jalón *nm* (a) *(vara)* marker pole

(b) *(hito)* landmark, milestone

(c) *Andes, CAm, Carib, Méx (tirón)* pull; *(suave)* tug; **dar un j. de orejas a alguien** *(tirón)* to tweak sb's ear; *(reprimenda)* to give someone a telling-off *o Br* ticking-off; EXPR **hacer algo de un j.** to do sth in one go

(d) *Bol, Méx, Ven (trecho)* stretch, distance; **todavía nos queda un buen j.** we've still got quite a way to go

(e) *Méx (trago)* swig

(f) *Méx Fam* **hazme (el) j. y acompáñame al centro, ¿sí?** be a love and come into town with me, will you?

jalonar *vt* (a) *(con varas)* to stake out, to mark out (b) *(señalar)* to mark; **un viaje jalonado de dificultades** a trip dogged by problems

jalonear *Méx* 1 *vt (tirar)* to pull; *(suavemente)* to tug

2 *vi (regatear)* to barter, to haggle

jaloneo *nm Méx* (a) *(tirón)* pulling; *(suave)* tugging (b) *(regateo)* barter, haggling

Jamaica *n* Jamaica

jamaica *nf* (a) *CAm, Méx (verbena)* street party (b) *(planta)* roselle (c) *Méx (bebida)* = non-alcoholic drink made from roselle flowers (d) *CAm, Méx (fiesta benéfica) Br* jumble sale, *US* rummage sale

jamaicano, -a, *Am* **jamaiquino, -a** 1 *adj* Jamaican

2 *nm,f* Jamaican

jamaquear *vt Ven Fam* (a) *(sacudir)* to shake (b) *(criticar)* to have a go at

jamar *Esp Fam* 1 *vt* **¿hay algo para j.?** is there any *Br* grub *o US* chow?

2 **jamarse** *vpr* to eat, *Br* to scoff; **se jamó dos bocadillos** she ate *o Br* scoffed two sandwiches; **en este restaurante se jama muy bien** the *Br* grub *o US* chow is very good at this restaurant

jamás *adv* never; **no lo he visto j.** I've never seen him; **la mejor novela que j. se haya escrito** the best novel ever written; **j. en la vida había visto algo así** never before had I seen such a thing, I'd never seen such a thing in all my life; **nunca j.** never ever; **por siempre j.** for evermore; EXPR *Fam* **¡j. de los jamases!** not in a million years!

jamba *nf* jamb, door post

jambar *vt CAm, Méx Fam* to wolf down, *Br* to scoff

jamelgo *nm Fam* nag

jamón *nm* (a) *(embutido)* ham; EXPR *Esp Fam* **¡y un j. (con chorreras)!** you've got to be joking!, not on your life!; EXPR *Esp Fam* **estar j.** to be dishy ▸▸ ***j. dulce*** (boiled) ham; ***j. ibérico*** = type of cured ham, similar to Parma ham; ***j. de pata negra*** = type of top-quality cured ham, similar to Parma ham; ***j. serrano*** = cured ham, similar to Parma ham; ***j. (de) York*** (boiled) ham (b) *Carib Fam (ganga)* snip, bargain

jamona *Fam* 1 *adj* well-stacked, buxom

2 *nf* buxom wench, well-stacked woman

jane® *nf Urug* bleach

jansenismo *nm Hist* Jansenism

jansenista *Hist* 1 *adj* Jansenist

2 *nmf* Jansenist

Januká *n* Chanukkah, Hanukkah

japo *nm Esp Fam* gob, spit

Japón *nm* **(el) J.** Japan

japonés, -esa 1 *adj* Japanese

2 *nm,f (persona)* Japanese; **los japoneses** the Japanese

3 *nm (lengua)* Japanese

japuta *nf* Ray's bream, Atlantic pomfret

jaque *nm* **j. (al rey)** check; **¡j.!** check!; EXPR **tener** *o* **traer en j. a alguien** to keep sb in a state of anxiety ▸▸ ***j. mate*** checkmate; **dar j. mate a alguien** to checkmate sb

jaqué [ja'ke], **jaquet** [ja'ket] (*pl* **jaquets**) *nm CSur* morning coat

jaquear *vt (en ajedrez)* to check

jaqueca *nf* migraine; **tener j.** to have a migraine; *Fam* **dar j. a alguien** to bother sb, to pester sb

jaquetón *nm (tiburón)* great white shark

jáquima *nf CAm Fam (borrachera)* drunkenness

jara *nf* (a) *(arbusto)* rockrose (b) *Carib, Méx Fam* **la j.** *(policía)* the cops

jarabe *nm* (a) *(bebida)* syrup ▸▸ ***j. de arce*** maple syrup; *Ven Fam* ***j. de lengua:*** **dar un j. de lengua a alguien** to bawl sb out; ***j. de maíz*** corn syrup; *Esp Fam* ***j. de palo:*** **el único lenguaje que entiende el niño es el j. de palo** the only language that child understands is a good thrashing; **¡te voy a dar j. de palo!** *(a un niño)* you're going to feel the back of my hand!; *(a un adulto)* I'm going to give you a sound thrashing!; *Fam* ***j. de pico*** smooth talk; **esas promesas son puro j. de pico** those promises are just so much hot air; *Fam* **tener mucho j. de pico** to have the gift of the gab, to be a smooth talker; ***j. para la tos*** cough mixture *o* syrup

(b) *Méx (canto, baile)* = traditional Mexican song and dance, derived from flamenco ▸▸ ***el j. tapatío*** the Mexican hat dance

jaramago *nm* hedge mustard

jarana *nf Fam* (a) *(juerga)* **estar de j.** to party; **irse de j.** to go out on the town (b) *(alboroto)* rumpus; **se organizó una gran j.** all hell broke loose (c) *Méx (guitarra)* small guitar (d) *Méx (baile)* = traditional dance of the Yucatan (e) *CAm (deuda)* debt

jaranear *Fam* 1 *vt Andes, CAm (estafar)* to swindle, to cheat
2 *vi* to go out on the town
jaranero, -a *Fam* 1 *adj* **es muy j.** he's a party animal
2 *nm,f* party animal
jarano *nm Méx* sombrero
jarapa *nf* = rug made from rags woven together
jarcia *nf* (**a**) *Náut* rigging (**b**) *CAm, Cuba, Méx (cordel)* rope
jardín *nm* (**a**) *(con plantas) Br* garden, *US* yard ►► ***j. botánico*** botanical garden; ***j. colgante*** hanging garden; ***j. del Edén*** Garden of Eden; ***j. floral*** flower garden; ***j. de infancia*** kindergarten, nursery school; *RP* ***j. de infantes*** kindergarten, nursery school; *Chile, Col* ***j. infantil*** kindergarten, nursery school; ***j. de invierno*** winter garden; ***j. de rocalla*** rock garden; ***j. zoológico*** zoo
(**b**) *Am* **los jardines** *(en béisbol)* the outfield ►► ***j. central*** centerfield; ***j. exterior*** outfield
jardinera *nf* (**a**) *(para plantas)* planter (**b**) **a la j.** *(carne)* garnished with vegetables (**c**) *Col (vestido)* pinafore dress (**d**) *Urug (jardín de infancia)* kindergarten, nursery school (**e**) *ver también* **jardinero**
jardinería *nf* gardening
jardinero, -a 1 *nm,f* (**a**) *(de plantas)* gardener (**b**) *Am (en béisbol)* outfielder ►► ***j. central*** centerfielder
2 *nm RP Br* dungarees, *US* overalls
jareta *nf (dobladillo)* hem
jaretón *nm* wide hem
jarina *nf RDom* (**a**) *(pizca)* pinch (**b**) *(llovizna)* drizzle
jaripeo *nm Méx* = rodeo including bull-riding, display of horse riding skills, music and dance
jarocho, -a 1 *adj* of/from Veracruz *(Mexico)*
2 *nm,f* native of Veracruz *(Mexico)*
jarra *nf* (**a**) *(para servir)* jug; *(para beber)* tankard (**b**) **en jarras, con los brazos en jarras** *(postura)* hands on hips, with arms akimbo
Jarrai *n* = radical Basque nationalist youth organization
jarrear *v impersonal Fam* **está jarreando** it's bucketing down, it's pouring
jarrete *nm* hock
jarretera *nf* (**a**) *(liga)* garter (**b**) *(orden militar)* Order of the Garter
jarro *nm* (**a**) *(vasija)* jug; EXPR **fue** *o* **sentó como un j. de agua fría** it was a bolt from the blue; EXPR *Fam* **llover a jarros** to be bucketing down (**b**) *CSur (taza alta)* mug; *(de cerveza)* mug, tankard
jarrón *nm* vase
jartarse *vpr Col Fam* to get fed up; **j. de algo** to get fed up with sth; **j. de hacer algo** to get fed up of doing sth
jarto, -a *adj Col Fam* tired (**de** of), fed up (**de** with); **estoy j. de mi jefe** I'm sick of my boss; **estoy j. de repetirte que cierres la puerta** I'm sick and tired of telling you to shut the door; **me tiene jarta con el piano** I'm fed up of her and her piano; **empiezo a estar un poco jarta de sus quejas** I'm starting to get rather tired of *o* fed up with his complaints
Jartum *n* Khartoum
Jasón *n Mitol* Jason
jaspe *nm (piedra)* jasper
jaspeado, -a 1 *adj (mármol)* veined; *(tela)* mottled
2 *nm* mottling
jaspear *vt* to mottle
jato *nm Perú Fam* bachelor pad
jauja *nf Fam* heaven on earth, paradise; **ser j.** to be heaven on earth *o* paradise; **¡esto es j.!** this is a cushy number!; **¿qué te has creído, que esto es j.?** do you think this is a holiday camp, or what?
jaula *nf* (**a**) *(para animales)* cage ►► *Fig* ***una j. de grillos*** a madhouse; **aquello era una j. de grillos** it was bedlam *o* a madhouse; *Fig* ***j. de oro*** gilded cage (**b**) *(en mina)* cage (**c**) *Fam (cárcel)* slammer (**d**) *Carib, Col, RP Fam (policial) Br* Black Maria, *US* paddy wagon
jauría *nf (de perros)* pack; **una j. de lobos** a wolf pack; **una j. de periodistas** a pack of journalists
Java[1] *n* Java
Java[2] *nm Informát* Java
javanés, -esa 1 *adj* Javanese
2 *nm,f* Javanese
jazmín *nm* jasmine ►► *Arg, Chile* ***j. del pago*** hardy fuchsia
jazz [jas] *nm inv* jazz
jazzista [ja'sista] *nmf* jazz musician
jazzístico, -a [ja'sistiko] *adj* jazz; **música con elementos jazzísticos** music with jazz elements
J.C. *(abrev de* **Jesucristo**) JC

je *interj* ha!
jean [jin] *(pl* **jeanes**) *nm Am* jeans; **un j.** a pair of jeans
jeans [jins] *nmpl* jeans; **unos j.** a pair of jeans
jeba = **jeva**
jebe *nm Andes* (**a**) *(planta)* rubber plant (**b**) *(caucho)* rubber (**c**) *(tira elástica)* rubber band, *Br* elastic band (**d**) *Fam (preservativo)* rubber, *Br* johnny
jebo = **jevo**
jedi *(forma verbal invertida de* **decir**) *RP Fam* **el que te j.** you-know-who
jeep [jip] *(pl* **jeeps**) *nm* jeep
jefatura *nf* (**a**) *(cargo)* leadership; **ocupa la j. de la organización** he is the head of the organization; **los candidatos a la j. del gobierno** the candidates for prime minister (**b**) *(organismo)* headquarters, head office ►► ***j. de policía*** police station; *Esp* ***j. de tráfico*** = traffic department, responsible for renewing driving licences, fines etc
jefazo, -a *nm,f Fam* big boss, *esp US* head honcho
jefe, -a *nm,f* (**a**) *(persona al mando)* boss; *(de empresa)* manager, *f* manageress; *(líder)* leader; *(de tribu, ejército)* chief; *(de departamento)* head; *Mil* **en j.** in-chief; EXPR *Méx Fam* **como j.: entró a la oficina como j.** he walked into the office as if he owned the place ►► ***j. de bomberos*** fire chief; ***j. de cocina*** chef; ***j. de compras*** purchasing manager; ***j. de estación*** stationmaster; ***j. de Estado*** head of state; ***j. del estado mayor*** chief of staff; ***j. de estudios*** director of studies; *Dep* ***j. de fila(s)*** team leader *(driver or cyclist)*; ***j. de gabinete*** chief of staff; ***j. de gobierno*** prime minister; **una reunión de jefes de gobierno** a meeting of heads of government; ***j. de policía*** police chief, chief of police, *Br* chief constable; ***j. de prensa*** press officer; ***j. de producción*** production manager; ***j. de producto*** product line manager; ***j. de protocolo*** chief of protocol; ***j. de proyecto*** project manager; ***j. de redacción*** editor-in-chief; ***j. de sección*** departmental head *o* chief; ***j. de ventas*** sales manager
(**b**) *Fam (como apelativo)* **pregúntale al j. qué se debe** ask the guy for the bill; **j., póngannos dos cervezas** give us two beers, *Br* guv *o US* mac
(**c**) *Méx Fam (padre, madre)* old man, *f* old girl
(**d**) *Esp Fam* **mis jefes** *(mis padres)* my folks
jefear *Ven Fam* 1 *vt* to boss around; **¡no nos jefees!** stop bossing us around!
2 *vi* **le gusta mucho j.** he loves bossing people around
Jehová *nm* Jehova
jején *nm Am* gnat
jemer *nm* ***los jemeres rojos*** the Khmer Rouge
jemiquear, jeremiquear *vi Andes, Carib, Chile* to whimper, to snivel
jengibre *nm* ginger
jeniquén *nm* henequen
jenízaro *nm (soldado)* janissary
jeque *nm* sheikh
jerarca *nm (de iglesia)* leader; **los jerarcas del partido** the party bosses
jerarquía *nf* (**a**) *(autoridades)* hierarchy; **la j. católica del país** the leaders of the Catholic church in the country; **las altas jerarquías de la nación** the nation's leaders (**b**) *(rango)* rank; **en esta oficina hay varias jerarquías** there is a clear hierarchy in this office
jerárquico, -a *adj* hierarchical
jerarquización *nf (efecto)* hierarchical structure; *(acción)* structuring into a hierarchy; **preocupa la j. de prioridades del gobierno** the way the government has ordered its priorities is a cause for concern
jerarquizar [14] *vt* to structure in a hierarchical manner; **la empresa está jerarquizada según la antigüedad de sus empleados** one's position in the company is dependent on seniority; **el poder jerarquiza la sociedad** power creates a hierarchy within society
jerbo *nm* jerboa
Jeremías *n pr* Jeremiah
jeremiquear = **jemiquear**
jerez *nm* sherry ►► ***j. fino*** dry sherry
jerga *nf* (**a**) *(habla)* jargon; **la j. juvenil** youth slang; **la j. periodística** journalese (**b**) *(galimatías)* gibberish (**c**) *Méx, RP (manta de caballo)* saddle blanket
jergal *adj* **el habla j.** jargon
jergón *nm* straw mattress
jeribeque *nm* (**a**) *(mueca)* grimace (**b**) *(guiño)* wink
Jericó *n* Jericho

jerifalte *nm* (**a**) *(ave)* gerfalcon (**b**) *Fam (persona)* bigwig

jerigonza *nf* (**a**) *(galimatías)* gibberish (**b**) *(jerga)* jargon

jeringa 1 *nf* syringe ►► ***j. hipodérmica*** hypodermic syringe
2 *nmf RP Fam* pain

jeringar, *Am* **jeringuear** *Fam* 1 *vt* (**a**) *(fastidiar)* to cheese off; **me jeringa que me hable así** it really cheeses me off when he talks to me like that (**b**) *(estropear)* to bust, *Br* to knacker
2 **jeringarse** *vpr* (**a**) *(fastidiarse)* **¡que se jeringue!** he can like it or lump it!; **si no estás de acuerdo, te jeringas** if you don't agree, tough! (**b**) *(estropearse)* to bust; **se ha jeringado la televisión** the television's bust *o Br* knackered

jeringón, -ona *adj RP, Ven Fam* **ser j.** to be a pain

jeringoso, -a 1 *adj RP, Ven Fam* **ser j.** to be a pain
2 *nm RP* = children's language in which each syllable is repeated with the same vowel preceded by a "p", e.g. "vamos" becomes "vapamospo"

jeringuear = **jeringar**

jeringuilla *nf* syringe ►► ***j. hipodérmica*** hypodermic syringe

jeroglífico, -a 1 *adj* hieroglyphic
2 *nm* (**a**) *(inscripción)* hieroglyphic (**b**) *(pasatiempo)* rebus (**c**) *(problema)* puzzle, mystery; **estas instrucciones son un j.** these instructions are indecipherable

Jerónimo *n pr* (**a**) *(jefe apache)* Geronimo (**b**) **san J.** St Jerome

jerónimo, -a *Rel* 1 *adj* Hieronymite
2 *nm,f* Hieronymite monk, *f* Hieronymite nun

jerosolimitano, -a 1 *adj* of/from Jerusalem
2 *nm,f* person from Jerusalem

jersey[1] *(pl* **jerseys** *o* **jerséis***)* *nm Esp* (**a**) *(de punto)* sweater, *Br* jumper ►► ***j. de cuello alto*** polo-neck (sweater); ***j. de cuello de pico*** V-neck (sweater) (**b**) *(en ciclismo)* jersey; **el j. amarillo** the yellow jersey

jersey[2] ['jersei] *nm Am (tejido)* jersey

Jerusalén *n* Jerusalem

Jesucristo *nm* Jesus Christ

jesuita 1 *adj* Jesuit
2 *nm* (**a**) *(sacerdote)* Jesuit; **estudió en los jesuitas** he went to a Jesuit school (**b**) *RP (aperitivo)* = small rectangular pastry snack filled with ham or cheese

jesuítico, -a *adj* (**a**) *(de la Compañía de Jesús)* Jesuit (**b**) *(ambiguo, disimulado)* jesuitical, devious

Jesús 1 *n pr* Jesus; **el niño J.** the baby Jesus
2 *interj (expresando sorpresa)* gosh!, good heavens!; *Esp (tras estornudo)* bless you!; EXPR *Fam* **¡J., María y José!** holy smoke *o* cow!; EXPR *Fam* **en un decir J.** in the blink of an eye; EXPR *Fam* **estuve con el J. en la boca** my heart was in my mouth

jet[1] [jet] *(pl* **jets***)* *nm* jet

jet[2] [jet] *nf Esp* **la j.** the jet set

jeta 1 *nf* (**a**) *Fam (cara)* mug, face; **no pongas esa j.** there's no need to pull a face *o* wrinkle your nose; **romperle la j. a alguien** to smash sb's face in; EXPR *Am* **estirar la j.** to pull a face
(**b**) *Esp Fam (descaro)* nerve, cheek; EXPR **entrar por la j.** to get in without paying; **tener (mucha) j.** to be a cheeky so-and-so *o* devil; **¡qué j.!** what a nerve *o* cheek!
(**c**) *(de cerdo, jabalí)* snout
(**d**) *Am Fam (boca)* kisser, *esp Br* gob
2 *nmf Esp Fam* cheeky so-and-so, cheeky devil; **tu hermana es una j.** your sister's got a nerve *o* cheek; **el muy j. se quedó el dinero** the cheeky so-and-so *o* devil kept the money; **¡qué j., ahora dice que fui yo!** what a nerve *o* cheek, now he's saying it was me!

jet-foil ['jet'foil] *(pl* **jet-foils***)* *nm* jetfoil, hovercraft

jet lag ['jet'laɣ] *nm* jet lag; **tener j.** to be jet-lagged

jetón, -ona *adj Fam* (**a**) *Am (de boca grande)* big-mouthed; *(de labios gruesos)* thick-lipped (**b**) *Méx (dormido)* **quedarse j.** to crash (**c**) *Méx (enojado)* cheesed off; **ponerse j.** to get cheesed off

jet-set ['jetset] *Esp nf, Am nm* jet set

jetudo, -a *adj* (**a**) *Esp Fam (caradura)* cheeky (**b**) *(de boca abultada)* thick-lipped

jeva, jeba *nf Carib Fam (mujer)* chick, *Br* bird

jevo, -a, jebo, -a *nm,f Ven Fam (novio)* man, boyfriend; *(novia)* woman, girlfriend

ji *interj* **¡ji, ji, ji!** hee-hee!

jíbaro, -a 1 *adj* (**a**) *(indio)* Jivaro; **las tribus jíbaras** the Jivaro tribes (**b**) *CAm, Carib, Méx (animal)* wild (**c**) *CAm, Carib, Méx Fam (huraño)* shy
2 *nm,f* (**a**) *(indio)* Jivaro (**b**) *Ven Fam (traficante)* pusher

jibia *nf (molusco)* cuttlefish

jibión *nm* cuttlebone

jícama *nf* jicama, yam bean

jícara *nf CAm, Méx, Ven* (**a**) *(calabaza)* calabash, gourd (**b**) *(taza)* mug

jicote *nm CAm, Méx* (**a**) *(insecto)* wasp (**b**) *(nido)* wasp's nest

jicotera *nf CAm, Méx* (**a**) *(nido)* wasp's nest (**b**) *(zumbido)* buzzing (**c**) *(bullicio)* commotion, row

jiennense 1 *adj* of/from Jaén *(Spain)*
2 *nmf* person from Jaén *(Spain)*

jijona *nf* **(turrón de) j.** = soft almond nougat from Jijona, Spain

jilguero *nm* goldfinch

jilipollada, jilipollas *etc* = **gilipollada, gilipollas** *etc*

jilote *nm CAm, Méx* = unripened ear of corn

jineta *nf* genet

jinete *nmf (civil)* horseman, *f* horsewoman; *(militar)* cavalryman; **el caballo derribó al j.** the horse threw its rider; **los cuatro Jinetes del Apocalipsis** the Four Horsemen of the Apocalypse

jineteada *nf Arg (doma)* = rural festival for the display of horse-riding skills

jinetear 1 *vt Méx Fam (deuda, pago)* = to delay paying in order to gain interest
2 *vi* to ride on horseback

jinetera *nf Cuba Fam* prostitute

jinetero *nm Cuba Fam* pimp

jingle ['jingel] *nm* jingle

jingoísmo *nm Pol* jingoism

jiña *nf* (**a**) *Chile (fruslería)* trifle (**b**) *Cuba (excremento)* (human) excrement

jiñar, giñar *Esp muy Fam* 1 *vi* to have a shit
2 **jiñarse** *vpr* to shit oneself; **jiñarse de miedo** to be scared shitless; **me he comprado una moto que te jiñas** I've bought a shit-hot new motorbike; **hace un frío que te jiñas** it's *Br* bloody *o US* goddamn freezing

jiote *nm Méx* rash

jipatearse *vpr Ven Fam* (**a**) *(empalidecer)* to turn white *o* pale (**b**) *(acobardarse)* to chicken out

jipato, -a *adj Méx, Ven Fam* pale

jipi 1 *adj* hippy
2 *nmf* hippy

jipiar *vt Esp Fam* **¡desde aquí no se jipia nada!** you can't see a damn thing from here!; **no hagas ninguna tontería, que te estoy jipiando** don't try and pull any tricks, I've got my eye on you

jipijapa *nm* (**a**) *(tira)* = strip of palm leaf (**b**) *(sombrero)* straw hat, Panama hat

jipío *nm* = cry given when singing flamenco

jipioso, -a *adj Fam (de estilo hippie)* hippy

jirafa *nf* (**a**) *(animal)* giraffe (**b**) *(para micrófono)* boom

jiribilla *nf Méx* spin; EXPR *Cuba Fam* **es una j.** he never sits still for five minutes

jirón *nm* (**a**) *(andrajo)* shred, rag; **hecho jirones** in tatters (**b**) *Perú (calle)* street

jitomate *nm Méx* tomato ►► ***j. bola*** beef tomato

jiu-jitsu [jiu'jitsu] *nm* ju-jitsu

JJ.OO. *nmpl* (*abrev de* **Juegos Olímpicos**) Olympic Games

jo *interj Esp Fam* (**a**) *(fastidio)* sugar!, shoot!; **¡jo, me he vuelto a olvidar las llaves!** sugar *o* shoot! I've forgotten my keys again!; **¡jo, mamá, yo quiero ir!** but mum, I want to go!; **¡jo, déjame en paz!** leave me alone, will you! (**b**) *(sorpresa)* gosh!, wow!; **me han dado la beca – ¡jo, qué suerte!** I got the grant – gosh *o* wow, you lucky thing!

Job *n pr* Job

job [joβ] *(pl* **jobs***)* *nm Informát* job

jobar *interj Esp Fam Euf* Jeez!, *Br* flipping heck!; **¡j., ya me han vuelto a suspender!** *Br* flipping heck *o US* shoot, I've failed again!; **¡j.!, ¿por qué no te callas?** why don't you *Br* flipping well *o US* dang well shut up?

jobo *nm* (**a**) *(árbol)* mombia *o* hog plum, yellow mombin (**b**) *(fruto)* mombia *o* hog plum ►► ***j. de la India*** ambarella

jocketta [jo'keta] *nf CSur* jockey

jockey ['jokei] (*pl* **jockeys**) *nm* jockey

jocoque *nm Méx* thick buttermilk

jocosamente *adv* jocularly, jokingly

jocosidad *nf* jocularity

jocoso, -a *adj* jocular; **se dirigió a mí en tono j.** he addressed me light-heartedly; **hoy estás muy j.** you're full of fun today

jocundo, -a *adj Formal* jovial, cheerful

joda *nf RP, Ven muy Fam* (**a**) *(fastidio)* pain in the *Br* arse *o US* ass; **este auto es una j., se rompe a cada rato** this car is a pain in the *Br* arse *o US* ass, it keeps breaking down
(**b**) *(broma)* piss-take; **¡no te enojes! lo dije/hice en j.** don't be angry, I was just pissing around; EXPR **no ser j.: hay una pobreza que no es j.** the poverty there's beyond a *Br* bloody *o US* goddamn joke; **hace un frío que no es j.** it's *Br* bloody *o US* goddamn freezing
(**c**) *(fiesta)* **los espero el sábado en casa, va a haber j.** I'll see you at my place on Saturday, we're having a bash

jodedera *nf Ven Vulg* pain in the *Br* arse *o US* ass

jodedor, -ora 1 *adj Ven Vulg (fastidioso)* **ser j.** to be a pain in the *Br* arse *o US* ass
2 *nm,f RP Fam (mala persona)* nasty piece of work

joder *Vulg*

This word is generally considered vulgar in Spain. However, some uses would not be shocking even in Spain, and in most of Latin America it is regarded as a relatively mild swearword.

1 *vt* (**a**) *(fastidiar)* **j. a alguien** to fuck sb about *o* around; **deja de j. al gato** stop being such a bastard to the cat; **le encanta j. al personal** he loves being a real bastard to people; **j. vivo a alguien** to well and truly fuck sb
(**b**) *(disgustar)* to piss off; **me jodió mucho que no vinieras** I was really pissed off *o US* pissed that you didn't come; **no sabes cómo me jode** *o* **lo que me jode tener que madrugar** you've no idea how much it pisses me off having to get up early
(**c**) *(estropear) (fiesta, planes, relación)* to screw (up), *Br* to bugger; **el desgraciado ha jodido la economía del país** the bastard has fucked up the country's economy *o* has made a fucking mess of the country's economy
(**d**) *(romper) (objeto, aparato)* to screw, *Br* to bugger; **¡ya has jodido la tele!** you've gone and fucked the TV now!
(**e**) *(lesionar) (espalda, pierna)* to screw, *Br* to bugger
(**f**) *(traumatizar)* to fuck up; **a mí donde me jodieron bien fue en el orfanato** they well and truly fucked me up at the orphanage
(**g**) *Esp (quitar, sisar)* **me jodieron 2 euros por entrar al museo** they really screwed me at the museum, it cost 2 euros to get in
(**h**) *Esp (copular con)* to fuck
(**i**) EXPR *Esp* **¡anda y que te/le/***etc.* **jodan!** fuck you/him/*etc*; *Esp* **joderla** to screw *o Br* bugger everything up; *Esp* **¡como nos pille, la hemos jodido!** if he catches us, we're in the shit *o* we're up shit creek (without a paddle)!; *Esp* **j. la marrana** to screw *o Br* bugger everything up; **¡no me jodas!** no shit!, *Br* well, bugger me!; **¿no me jodas que no te ha ayudado nadie?** shit *o Br* bloody hell, didn't anybody help you?; *Esp* **¡no te jode!, ahora nos viene con quejas** shit *o Br* bloody hell, and now she's got the nerve to complain!; *Esp* **claro que no me importaría ser millonario, ¡no te jode!** would I like to be a millionaire? no shit! *o Br* too bloody right I would!; *Esp Hum* **¡nos ha jodido mayo (con sus flores)!: dice que la empresa va bien, ¡nos ha jodido mayo con sus flores!** he says the company is doing fine, he really must think we're a bunch of *Br* bloody *o US* goddamn morons!
2 *vi* (**a**) *(fastidiar)* **¡deja ya de j. con el mando a distancia!** stop pissing around with the remote control!; **¡cómo jode!** it's a real bummer *o* bastard!; **¡cómo jode cuando te dicen esas cosas!** it really pisses me off when they say things like that!; **¡no jodas!** *(incredulidad, sorpresa)* no shit!, *Br* well, bugger me!; **¿no jodas que esto lo has hecho tú solo?** shit *o Br* bloody hell, did you really do this all by yourself?; **lo hizo por j.** he was just being a bastard; **son ganas de j.** he's just doing it to be a bastard
(**b**) *Esp (copular)* to fuck
(**c**) *Ven* **que jode** *(mucho)*: **¡esta gente tiene plata que jode!** those people are *Br* bloody *o US* goddamn loaded!
3 joderse *vpr* (**a**) *(aguantarse)* to fucking well put up with it; **no hay otra cosa, así que te jodes y te lo comes** it's all we've got, so tough shit, you'll just have to eat it *o* you'll just have to fucking well put up with it and eat it; **si no puedes venir, te jodes** if you can't come, tough shit *o* too fucking bad!; **¡hay que joderse!** can you fucking believe it?; **¡que se joda!** he can fuck off!; EXPR *Esp* **a joderse y a aguantarse** tough shit!, too fucking bad!; EXPR *Esp* **¡jódete y baila!** tough shit!; EXPR *Am* **joderse y tomar quina es la mejor medicina** too bad!, it can't be helped!
(**b**) *(estropearse)* **se nos han jodido las vacaciones** that's gone and fucked up our holidays; *Esp* **¡se jodió el invento!** that's really gone and fucked things up!
(**c**) *(romperse) (objeto, aparato)* **se ha jodido la tele** the TV's screwed *o Br* buggered
(**d**) *(lesionarse)* **me jodí la espalda haciendo pesas** I screwed *o Br* buggered my back lifting weights
4 *interj Esp (expresa dolor, enfado, sorpresa)* Christ!, Jesus!; **¡j., cómo escuece la herida** Jesus, this wound really stings!; **¡calla ya, j.!** for fuck's sake, shut up!, shut the fuck up!; **¡j. con el niño de los cojones!** I've had it up to here with that fucking brat!; **¡j. qué sitio más bonito!** shit *o Br* bloody hell, this place is really beautiful!; **¡j., qué caro!** Christ, that's expensive!; **¡j. qué frío hace!** Christ but it's freezing!

jodido, -a *Vulg*

This word is generally considered vulgar in Spain. However, some uses would not be shocking even in Spain, and in most of Latin America it is regarded as a relatively mild swearword.

1 *adj* (**a**) *(físicamente, anímicamente)* **tengo la rodilla jodida** I've screwed *o Br* buggered my knee; **el orfanato lo dejó j. de por vida** the orphanage really fucked him up for life
(**b**) *(estropeado)* **la radio está jodida** the *Br* bloody *o US* goddamn radio's bust *o Br* knackered
(**c**) *(difícil)* **es muy j. levantarse a las seis** getting up at six is a real bastard; **con ese profesor está muy j. aprobar** it's fucking difficult getting a pass off that teacher
(**d**) *(maldito)* **el muy j. me ha quitado la novia** the bastard's stolen my girlfriend; **ha ganado la lotería, la muy jodida** she's won the lottery, the lucky bitch
(**e**) *(persona)* **es un tipo muy j.** he's a really nasty piece of work
2 *nm,f* (**a**) *(maldito)* **el j. de tu hermano** that *Br* bloody *o US* goddamn brother of yours
(**b**) *RP (perjudicado)* screwed; **los jodidos son siempre los mismos** it's always the same people who end up getting screwed

jodienda *nf Esp Vulg* (**a**) *(cosa mala)* pain in the *Br* arse *o US* ass; **no tener vacaciones es una j.** it's a real bastard not having any holidays
(**b**) *(acto sexual)* **la j.** fucking

jodo, jopé, jope *interj Esp Fam Euf (expresando sorpresa, enfado)* Jeez!, *Br* flipping heck!; **¡j.!, ¡cómo ha crecido!** Jeez *o Br* flipping heck, she's grown!; **¡j.!, ¡me podías haber avisado!** you could have damn *o Br* flipping well told me!

jodón, -ona *nm,f* (**a**) *Am muy Fam (persona fastidiosa)* pain in the *Br* arse *o US* ass (**b**) *Méx Vulg (mala persona)* bastard (**c**) *RP muy Fam (bromista)* joker, live wire

jofaina *nf* washbasin

jogging ['joɣin] (*pl* **joggings**) *nm* (**a**) *(deporte)* jogging; **hacer j.** to go jogging (**b**) *RP (ropa)* tracksuit

Johannesburgo, Johanesburgo [joχanes'burɣo] *n* Johannesburg

jojoba *nf* jojoba

joker ['jokjer] (*pl* **jokers**) *nm* joker *(in cards)*

jol *nm Am (en casa)* hall; *(en hotel)* lobby

jolgorio *nm* merrymaking; **se organizó un gran j. en la oficina** everybody in the office started celebrating; **la hinchada celebró el triunfo con j.** the fans jubilantly celebrated the victory

jolín, jolines *interj Esp Fam Euf* (**a**) *(expresando fastidio)* **¡j., mamá, yo quiero ir!** oh *o* but mum, I want to go!; **¡j., déjame en paz!** Jeez, just leave me alone, can't you?, *Br* just blinking well leave me alone!
(**b**) *(expresando sorpresa)* wow!; **conseguí el trabajo – ¡j., qué bien!** I got the job – Jeez, that's great! *o Br* that's flipping brilliant!

Jonás *n pr* Jonah

jondo *adj* **cante j.** = traditional flamenco singing, characterized by the elaborate drawing out of the words being sung, and a melancholy tone

jónico, -a 1 *adj* (**a**) *Arquit* Ionic (**b**) *(mar)* **el (mar) J.** the Ionian Sea
2 *nm* **el J.** the Ionian Sea

jonrón *nm Am (en béisbol)* home run; **pegar un j.** to hit a home run

jonronear *vi Am (en béisbol)* to hit a home run

jonronero, -a *Am* **1** *adj* **campeón j.** home run champion
2 *nm,f (en béisbol)* home run hitter, power hitter

jopé, jope = **jodo**

jopo *nm* (**a**) *(rabo)* bushy tail (**b**) *RP (copete)* quiff

jora *nf Andes* = type of maize used to make "chicha"

Jordán *n* **el (río) J.** the (River) Jordan

Jordania *n* Jordan

jordano, -a 1 *adj* Jordanian
2 *nm,f* Jordanian

Jorge *n pr* **san J.** St George; **J. I/II** George I/II

jornada *nf* (**a**) *(día)* day; **una dura j. de trabajo** a hard day's work; **una j. de huelga** a day of strike action; **una j. de lucha** a day of protest ►► ***j. electoral*** election day, polling day; ***j. de puertas abiertas*** open day; ***j. de reflexión*** = day immediately before elections when campaigning is forbidden
(**b**) *(de viaje)* day's journey
(**c**) *(laboral)* working day; **media j.** half day ►► ***j. completa*** full working day; **un empleo a j. completa** a full-time job; ***j. continua*** = working day from early morning to mid-afternoon with only a short lunch break; ***j. intensiva*** = working day from early morning to mid-afternoon with only a short lunch break; ***j. laboral*** working day; **tenemos una j. laboral de ocho horas** we work an eight-hour day; **una j. laboral de 35 horas** a 35-hour week; ***j. partida*** = working day with lunch break of several hours, finishing in the evening
(**d**) *Dep* round of matches; **llevan seis jornadas sin perder** they have gone six games without losing
(**e**) **jornadas (sobre)** *(congreso)* conference (on)
(**f**) *Lit* act

jornal *nm* day's wage ►► ***j. mínimo*** minimum wage

> **Falso amigo**: El sustantivo inglés **journal** no es la traducción del español **jornal**. En inglés, **journal** significa "revista, boletín" o "diario".

jornalero, -a *nm,f* day labourer

joroba **1** *nf* hump
2 *interj Esp Fam Euf (expresando sorpresa, enfado)* Jeez!, *Br* flipping heck!

jorobado, -a **1** *adj* (**a**) *(con joroba)* hunchbacked (**b**) *Fam (estropeado)* bust, *Br* knackered; **tengo el estómago j.** my stomach's playing up *o Br* giving me gyp
2 *nm,f (con joroba)* hunchback

jorobar *Fam* **1** *vt* (**a**) *(molestar)* to bug; **ese ruido me está jorobando** that noise is really bugging me; **lo que más me joroba es que no haya pedido perdón** what really bugs me is that she didn't say sorry (**b**) *(estropear) (fiesta, planes)* to mess up; *(máquina, objeto)* to bust, *Br* to knacker; **me jorobó las vacaciones** it messed up my *Br* holiday *o US* vacation
2 *vi (molestar)* to be a pain; **¡deja ya de j.!** stop being such a pain!; **lo hizo por j.** he just did it to be difficult; **no jorobes y déjame estudiar** stop being such a pain and let me study; **¿sabías que se casó Claudia? – ¡no jorobes!** did you know that Claudia got married? – she never did! *o* you're kidding!
3 jorobarse *vpr* (**a**) *(fastidiarse, aguantarse)* **¡pues te jorobas!** you can like it or lump it!; **¿no te joroba?** it's makes you want to puke, doesn't it? (**b**) *(estropearse)* to bust; **se ha jorobado el televisor** the television's bust; **me he jorobado el tobillo** I've done my ankle in

jorobón, -ona *RP Fam* **1** *adj* **ser j.** to be a pain
2 *nm,f* (**a**) *(persona fastidiosa)* pain (**b**) *(bromista)* joker, wag

jorongo *nm Méx* (**a**) *(manta)* blanket (**b**) *(poncho)* poncho

joropo *nm* (**a**) *(danza)* = popular Colombian and Venezuelan folk dance (**b**) *Ven (fiesta)* party

José *n pr* **san J.** St Joseph

josefino, -a **1** *adj* of/from San José *(Costa Rica)*
2 *nm,f* person from San José *(Costa Rica)*

Josué *n pr* Joshua

jota *nf* (**a**) *(letra)* = name of the letter "j"; EXPR *Fam* **sin faltar una j.** without missing a thing, in minute detail
(**b**) *(baile)* = lively folk song and dance, originally from Aragon; EXPR *RP Fam* **bailar una j.** to jump for joy
(**c**) *(en cartas)* jack
(**d**) EXPR *Fam* **no entender ni j. (de)** *(no comprender)* not to understand a word (of); **no saber ni j. de algo** not to know the first thing about sth; **no ver ni j.** *(por mala vista)* to be as blind as a bat; *(por oscuridad)* not to be able to see a thing

jote *nm* (**a**) *Arg, Chile (ave)* turkey buzzard *o* vulture (**b**) *Chile (cometa)* kite

jotero, -a *nm,f (que baila)* jota dancer; *(que canta)* jota singer

joto *nm Méx Fam Pey Br* queer, *US* fag

jovato, -a *nm,f RP Fam* oldie, *Br* wrinkly

joven **1** *adj (en edad)* young; **moda j.** youth fashion; **de j.** as a young man/woman; **está muy j. para su edad** he looks very young for his age; **esa ropa te hace más j.** those clothes make you look younger; **la noche es j.** the night is young
2 *nmf* (**a**) *(persona joven)* young man, *f* young woman; **los jóvenes** young people (**b**) *(como apelativo)* **¡oiga, j., se le ha caído esto!** excuse me young man, you dropped this; *Am* **el j. Alfonso llegó ayer** young Alfonso arrived yesterday

jovencito, -a *nm,f* young man, *f* young lady

jovenzuelo, -a *nm,f* youngster

jovial *adj* jovial, cheerful

jovialidad *nf* joviality, cheerfulness

jovialmente *adv* jovially, cheerfully

joya *nf* (**a**) *(pieza de adorno)* jewel ►► ***las joyas de la corona*** the crown jewels; **esa empresa es la j. de la corona del sector público** that company is the jewel in the crown of the public sector; ***j. de familia*** family heirloom; ***joyas de fantasía*** costume jewellery (**b**) *(persona, cosa)* gem; **el nuevo empleado es una j.** the new worker is a real gem; **una de las joyas del arte barroco** one of the jewels of baroque art

joyería *nf* (**a**) *(tienda)* jeweller's (shop) (**b**) *(arte, comercio)* jewellery

joyero, -a **1** *nm,f (persona)* jeweller
2 *nm (caja)* jewellery box

joystick ['joistik] (*pl* **joysticks**) *nm* joystick

joyuyo *nm* wood duck

JPEG [χota'peχ] *nm Informát* (*abrev de* **Joint Photographic Experts Group**) JPEG

Jr. (*abrev de* **júnior**) Jr

juagado, -a *adj Col* soaked

juagar *vt Col* to rinse

Juan *n pr Fam* **don J.** lady-killer, Casanova, Don Juan; **san J. Bautista** (St) John the Baptist; *Ven Fam* **J. Bimba(s)** *o* **Bimbe** *Br* Joe Bloggs, *US* Joe Schmo; **san J. de la Cruz** St John of the Cross; **san J. Evangelista** (St) John the Evangelist; **J. Pablo I/II** (Pope) John Paul I/II; *Cuba, RP Fam* **J. de los Palotes** anybody (you like), whoever (you like); **J. sin Tierra** King John (of England)

Juana *n pr* **J. de Arco** Joan of Arc; **J. la Loca** Juana the Mad

juana, juanita *nf Méx Fam* pot, grass

juancarlista *nmf Esp* = supporter of King Juan Carlos of Spain

juanete *nm* (**a**) *(en el pie)* bunion (**b**) *Náut (vela)* topgallant

juanita = **juana**

jubilación *nf* (**a**) *(retiro)* retirement ►► ***j. anticipada*** early retirement; ***j. forzosa*** compulsory retirement; ***j. voluntaria*** voluntary retirement (**b**) *(pensión)* pension

jubilado, -a **1** *adj* retired
2 *nm,f Br* pensioner, *US* retiree; **club de jubilados** senior citizens' club

jubilar[1] **1** *vt* (**a**) *(persona)* **j. a alguien (de)** to pension sb off (from), to retire sb (from) (**b**) *Fam (objeto)* to get rid of; **van a j. los trenes más viejos** they're going to get rid of the oldest trains
2 jubilarse *vpr* (**a**) *(retirarse)* to retire (**b**) *Cuba, Méx (ganar experiencia)* to gain experience (**c**) *Ven Fam (ausentarse) (de clase, colegio) Br* to skive off, *US* to play hooky; *(del trabajo) Br* to skive off, *US* to goof off

jubilar[2] *adj Am Rel* jubilee

jubileo *nm Rel* jubilee

júbilo *nm* jubilation, joy

jubiloso, -a *adj* jubilant, joyous

jubón *nm* (**a**) *(vestidura)* jerkin, doublet (**b**) *(de mujer)* bodice

judaico, -a *adj* Judaic, Jewish

judaísmo *nm* Judaism

Judas *n pr* **J. (Iscariote)** Judas (Iscariot)

judas *nm inv Fam* Judas, traitor

Judea *n* Judaea

judeada = **judiada**

judeocristiano, -a *adj* Judaeo-Christian

judeoespañol, -ola **1** *adj* Sephardic
2 *nm,f (persona)* Sephardic Jew
3 *nm (lengua)* Sephardi

judeomasónico, -a *adj* Judaeo-Masonic

judería *nf Hist* Jewish ghetto *o* quarter

judía *nf* (**a**) *(planta)* bean ►► ***j. blanca*** haricot bean; ***j. negra*** black bean; ***j. pinta*** pinto bean; *Esp* ***j. verde*** green bean (**b**) *ver también* **judío**

judiada, *Urug* **judeada** *nf Fam* dirty trick; **despedirte sin aviso fue una j.** it stinks that they sacked you without notice

judicatura *nf* (**a**) *(cargo)* office of judge (**b**) *(institución)* judiciary

judicial *adj* judicial; **el poder j.** the judiciary; **recurrir a la vía j.** to go to *o* have recourse to law

judicialización *nf* **la j. de la política** the growing tendency to deal with political issues through the courts

judicializar 1 *vt* **el gobierno ha judicializado la vida política** the government now frequently deals with political matters through the courts

2 judicializarse *vpr* **la vida política se ha judicializado** political matters are increasingly dealt with through the courts

judicialmente *adv* judicially; **resolvieron sus conflictos j.** they settled their disputes through the courts

judío, -a 1 *adj* **(a)** *(hebreo)* Jewish **(b)** *Fam Pey (tacaño)* Jewish, tight

2 *nm,f* **(a)** *(hebreo)* Jew, *f* Jewess **(b)** *Fam Pey (tacaño)* Jew, skinflint

judión *nm* large bean

judo ['juðo] *nm* judo

judogui [ju'ðoɣi] *nm* judogi, judo outfit

judoka [ju'ðoka] *nmf* judo player, judoka

jue. *(abrev de* **jueves)** Thur

JUEGO 1 *ver* **jugar**

2 *nm* **(a)** *(entretenimiento, deporte)* game; **no es más que un j.** it's only a game; **terreno de j.** field, *esp Br* pitch; EXPR **ser un j. de niños** to be child's play ►► ***j. de azar*** game of chance; ***j. de cartas*** card game; *Am* ***j. de computadora*** computer game; ***juegos florales*** poetry competition; ***j. de ingenio*** guessing game; ***juegos malabares*** juggling; *Fig* balancing act; *Fig* **tuve que hacer juegos malabares para tener contentas a las dos partes** I had to perform a real balancing act to keep both sides happy; ***j. de mesa*** board game; ***j. de naipes*** card game; ***el j. de la oca*** *Br* ≃ snakes and ladders, *US* ≃ chutes and ladders; ***Juegos Olímpicos*** Olympic Games; ***Juegos Olímpicos de Invierno*** Winter Olympics, Winter Olympic Games; *Esp* ***j. de ordenador*** computer game; ***j. de palabras*** play on words, pun; **hacer juegos de palabras** to make puns; ***los Juegos Panamericanos*** the pan-American games; ***j. de prendas*** game of forfeit; ***j. de rol*** *(técnica terapéutica, de enseñanza)* role-play; *(juego de fantasía)* fantasy role-playing game; ***j. de salón*** parlour game; ***el j. de las sillas*** musical chairs

(b) *(acción de entretenerse o practicar deporte)* play, playing; **a los perros les encanta el j.** dogs love playing; **se vio buen j. en la primera parte** there was some good play in the first half; **su j. es más agresivo que el mío** she's a more aggressive player than I am, her game is more aggressive than mine; **es el encargado de crear j.** he's the playmaker; EXPR **dar j.: este traje me da mucho j.** this dress is very versatile; **mi horario de trabajo da bastante j.** my working hours give me a lot of freedom; EXPR **entrar en j.** *(factor)* to come into play; **no ha entrado en j. en todo el partido** he's found it difficult to get into the game; EXPR **estar en j.** to be at stake; EXPR **poner algo en j.** *(arriesgar)* to put sth at stake; *(utilizar)* to bring sth to bear ►► ***j. aéreo*** *(en fútbol)* aerial game; ***j. limpio*** fair play; ***j. peligroso*** dangerous play; ***j. subterráneo*** dirty play; ***j. sucio*** foul play

(c) *(en tenis, voleibol)* game ►► ***j. en blanco*** love game

(d) *Am Dep (partido)* game, *Br* match

(e) *Am (en feria)* fairground attraction

(f) *(con dinero)* gambling; **se arruinó con el j.** he lost all his money gambling; **¡hagan j.!** place your bets!

(g) *(truco)* trick; **voy a hacerte un j.** I'm going to show you a trick ►► ***j. de manos*** conjuring trick

(h) *(mano) (de cartas)* hand; **me salió un buen j.** I was dealt a good hand

(i) *(artimaña, estratagema)* game; **ya me conozco tu j.** I know your game; **descubrirle el j. a alguien** to see through sb; **hacerle el j. a alguien** to play along with sb; **jugar** *o* **tener un doble j.** to play a double game

(j) *(conjunto de objetos)* set; **un j. de llaves/sábanas** a set of keys/sheets; **un j. de herramientas** a tool kit; **un j. de té/café** a tea/coffee service; *Esp* **a j.** *(ropa)* matching; *Esp* **zapatos a j. con el bolso** shoes with matching *Br* handbag *o US* purse; **hacer j.** to match; **las cortinas hacen j. con la tapicería del sofá** the curtains match the couch ►► *Informát* ***j. de caracteres*** character set; *Teatro* ***j. de luces*** lighting effects

(k) *(articulación de piezas)* joint; *(movimiento de las piezas)* movement; **sufre una lesión en el j. de la muñeca** she's injured her wrist; **el j. de la rodilla me produce dolor** it hurts when I move my knee ►► ***j. de piernas*** footwork

---

juegue *etc ver* **jugar**

juepucha, jueputa *interj CSur muy Fam Euf* son of a gun!

juerga *nf Fam* **montar una j.** to party, *Br* to have a rave-up; **correrse una j., irse de j.** to go out on the town; **estar de j.** to be partying; **tomar algo a j.** to take sth as a joke; **¡qué j. nos pasamos anoche con su primo!** what a laugh we had with her cousin last night!

juerguista 1 *adj* **es muy j.** she's a party animal

2 *nmf* party animal

jueves *nm inv* Thursday; EXPR *Fam* **no es nada del otro j.** it's nothing out of this world; EXPR *Fam Hum* **está siempre en medio, como el j.** he's always under my feet, he's always in the way ►► *Rel* ***J. Santo*** Maundy Thursday; *ver también* **sábado**

juez *nmf,* **juez, -a** *nm,f*

> it is not unusual for the feminine form **jueza** to be used in sense **(a)**

(a) *Der* judge; EXPR **ser j. y parte: no puedes ser j. y parte** you can't judge objectively when you're involved ►► ***j. de alzado*** appeal court judge; ***j. de apelaciones*** appeal court judge; ***j. de instrucción*** examining magistrate; ***j. de paz*** Justice of the Peace; ***j. de primera instancia*** examining magistrate

(b) *Dep (árbitro)* referee; *(en atletismo)* official ►► ***j. árbitro*** referee; ***j. de línea*** *(en fútbol)* linesman; *(en rugby)* touch judge; ***j. de red*** net cord judge; ***j. de salida*** starter; ***j. de silla*** umpire

jugada *nf* **(a)** *Dep (en fútbol, baloncesto, rugby, ajedrez)* move; *(en billar)* shot; **una j. excelente del equipo visitante** an excellent move by the visitors; **¡maravillosa j. de Raúl!** what a great play by Raúl!; **las mejores jugadas del partido** the highlights of the game ►► ***j. a balón parado*** *(en fútbol)* set piece, dead ball situation; *RP* ***j. a pelota detenida*** *(en fútbol)* set piece, dead ball situation

(b) *Fam (treta)* dirty trick; **hacer una mala j. a alguien** to play a dirty trick on sb

(c) *(operación hábil)* move, operation

(d) *Méx (movimiento)* dodge

jugador, -ora 1 *adj* **(a)** *(en deporte)* playing **(b)** *(en casino, timba)* gambling

2 *nm,f* **(a)** *(en deporte)* player; **j. de fútbol** soccer player, *Br* footballer; **j. de baloncesto** basketball player **(b)** *(en casino, timba)* gambler

---

JUGAR [36] **1** *vi* **(a)** *(practicar un deporte, juego)* to play; **los niños juegan en el patio del colegio** the children are playing in the playground; **j. al ajedrez/a las cartas** to play chess/cards; **j. a la pelota/a las muñecas** to play ball/with one's dolls; **juegan a ser astronautas** they're playing at astronauts; **¿a qué juegas?** what are you playing?; *Fam* **¿tú a qué juegas, chaval?** *(en tono de enfado)* what do you think you're playing at, pal?; **les gusta j. con la arena** they like playing in the sand; **j. en un equipo** to play for a team; **te toca j.** it's your turn *o* go; **j. limpio/sucio** to play fair/dirty; EXPR **j. a dos bandas** to play a double game; EXPR **j. con fuego** to play with fire; EXPR **el que juega con fuego se quema** if you play with fire you'll get burned; EXPR *Fam* **o jugamos todos o se rompe la baraja** either we all do it or nobody does

(b) *(con dinero)* to gamble (**a** on); **jugó al bingo y perdió mucho dinero** she played bingo and lost a lot of money; **le gusta j. en los casinos** she likes gambling in casinos; **j. a la lotería** to play the lottery; **j. a las quinielas** to do the pools; **le gusta j. a los caballos** he likes a bet on the horses; **j. a** *o* **en la Bolsa** to speculate (on the Stock Exchange); *Bolsa* **j. al alza** to try to bull the market, to speculate on share prices rising; *Bolsa* **j. a la baja** to try to bull the market, to speculate on share prices falling; **j. fuerte** to bet a lot of money

(c) *(ser desconsiderado)* **j. con alguien** to play with sb; **j. con los sentimientos de alguien** to toy with sb's feelings

(d) *(influir)* **j. a favor de alguien** to work in sb's favour; **el tiempo juega en su contra** time is against her; **el tiempo juega a nuestro favor** time is on our side

2 *vt* **(a)** *(partido, juego, partida)* to play; *(ficha, pieza)* to move; *(carta)* to play; **¿jugamos un póquer?** shall we have a game of poker?; EXPR **jugó bien sus bazas** *o* **cartas** she played her cards well

(b) *(dinero)* to gamble (**a** on); **jugué 25 euros a mi número de la suerte** I gambled 25 euros on my lucky number

(c) *(desempeñar)* **j. un papel** *(considerado incorrecto)* to play a role; **la creatividad juega un importante papel en nuestro trabajo** creativity plays a very important part *o* role in our work

3 jugarse *vpr* **(a)** *(apostarse)* to bet; **se lo jugó todo al 17** she bet *o* staked everything on number 17; **me juego contigo una cena a que no ganas** I bet you a meal out you won't win; **me juego lo que quieras a que no vienen** I bet you anything they won't come; **¿qué te juegas a que miente?** how much do you want to bet that he's lying?; EXPR **jugárselo todo a una carta** to put all one's eggs in one basket; **el equipo se lo juega todo a una carta** it's do or die for the team; EXPR **jugarse el todo por el todo** to stake everything

(b) *(arriesgar)* to risk; **se juega su futuro con este proyecto** she's staking her entire future on this project; **el equipo se juega esta noche el pase a la final** tonight the team is playing for a place in the final; **jugarse la vida** to risk one's life; EXPR *Fam* **jugarse el pellejo** to risk one's neck

(**c**) EXPR **jugársela a alguien** to play a dirty trick on sb

---

jugarreta *nf Fam* dirty trick; **nos hizo una j.** she played a dirty trick on us

juglar, -esa *nm,f* minstrel

juglaresco, -a *adj* minstrel; **poesía juglaresca** troubadour poetry

juglaría *nf* (**a**) *(de trovadores)* minstrelsy (**b**) *(de bufones)* buffoonery

jugo *nm* (**a**) *(líquido)* juice; **el j. de la carne** the meat juices ►► ***jugos gástricos*** gastric juices; ***j. pancreático*** pancreatic juice (**b**) *Am (de fruta)* juice; **j. de naranja** orange juice (**c**) *(provecho, interés)* meat, substance; **este libro tiene mucho j.** this is a very meaty book, this book has a lot of substance; EXPR **sacar (el) j. a algo/alguien** *(aprovechar)* to get the most out of sth/sb

jugosidad *nf* juiciness

jugoso, -a *adj* (**a**) *(con jugo)* juicy (**b**) *(picante)* juicy; **traigo un cotilleo muy j.** I've got some juicy gossip (**c**) *(sustancioso)* meaty, substantial; *(rentable)* profitable

juguera *nf CSur* juicer

juguete *nm* (**a**) *(para niños)* toy; **una pistola/un carro de j.** a toy gun/car ►► ***juguetes bélicos*** war toys; ***j. educativo*** educational toy (**b**) *(persona, cosa)* **tratar a alguien como un j.** to treat sb as a plaything; **el presidente es un j. en manos de los militares** the president is a puppet of the military; **el barco era un j. de los elementos** the boat was at the mercy of the elements (**c**) *Teatro* sketch, skit

juguetear *vi* to play (around); **j. con algo** to toy with sth

juguetería *nf* (**a**) *(tienda)* toy shop (**b**) *(sector)* toy industry

juguetón, -ona *adj* playful

juguetonamente *adv* playfully

juicio *nm* (**a**) *Der* trial; **llevar a alguien a j.** to take sb to court; **tener un j. justo** to receive a fair trial ►► ***j. civil*** civil action; *Rel* ***el J. Final*** the Last Judgement; **el Día del J. Final** Judgement Day; ***j. nulo*** mistrial; ***j. oral*** hearing; ***j. sumario*** summary trial; ***j. sumarísimo*** summary trial

(**b**) *(sensatez)* (sound) judgement; *(cordura)* sanity, reason; **no está en su (sano) j.** he is not in his right mind; EXPR **perder el j.** to lose one's reason, to go mad

(**c**) *(opinión)* opinion; **a mi j.** in my opinion; **en el j. de Emilio** in Emilio's opinion; **no tengo un j. formado sobre su actuación** I haven't yet formed an opinion on their performance; **no tengo suficientes elementos de j. como para formarme una opinión** I don't have enough information to base an opinion on ►► ***j. de valor*** value judgement

juiciosamente *adv* sensibly, wisely

juicioso, -a *adj* sensible, wise

juil *nm* carp

Jujem [χu'χem] *nf* (*abrev de* **Junta de Jefes de Estado Mayor**) = joint chiefs of staff of the Spanish armed forces

juke-box ['jukboks] *nm inv* jukebox

jul. (*abrev de* **julio**) Jul

julai, julay, jula *nm Esp muy Fam* (**a**) *(homosexual) Br* poof, *US* fag (**b**) *(inocente)* mug, sucker (**c**) *(mala persona) Br* git, *US* jerk

julandrón *nm Esp muy Fam (homosexual) Br* poof, *US* fag

julay = **julai**

julepe *nm* (**a**) *(juego de naipes)* = type of card game (**b**) *Fam (esfuerzo)* slog; **me di un j. subiendo las cajas** I slogged my guts out carrying the boxes upstairs (**c**) *Fam (reprimenda)* telling-off, *Br* ticking-off; **nos metieron un j. por faltar a clase** they had a go at us for missing class (**d**) *PRico, RP Fam (susto)* scare, fright; **dar un j. a alguien** to give sb a scare (**e**) *(bebida)* julep

julepear **1** *vt* (**a**) *RP Fam (asustar)* to scare, to frighten (**b**) *Méx (fatigar)* to tire, to exhaust (**c**) *Col (urgir)* to hurry along

2 julepearse *vpr RP Fam (asustarse)* to get a fright

julia[1] *nf (pez)* rainbow wrasse

julia[2] *nf Méx Fam (policial) Br* Black Maria, *US* paddy wagon

juliana *nf (sopa)* = soup made with chopped vegetables and herbs; **cortar en j.** to cut into julienne strips

juliano, -a *adj* Julian

Julio *n pr* **J. César** Julius Caesar

julio *nm* (**a**) *(mes)* July; *ver también* **septiembre** (**b**) *Fís* joule

juma, jumera *nf Fam* drunkenness; **agarrar una j.** to get sloshed *o* plastered

jumado, -a *adj Fam* sloshed, plastered

jumar *Fam* **1** *vi Esp* to stink

2 jumarse *vpr* to get sloshed *o* plastered

jumbo ['jumbo] *nm* jumbo (jet)

jumento, -a *nm,f (asno)* ass, donkey

jumera = **juma**

jumil *nm* = type of edible Mexican insect

jumo, -a *adj CAm, Carib, Méx Fam* sloshed, plastered

jumper ['jamper] (*pl* **jumpers**) *nm* (**a**) *(prenda) CSur, Méx Br* pinafore (dress), *US* jumper (**b**) *Informát (puente)* jumper

jun. (*abrev de* **junio**) Jun

junar *vt Esp, RP Fam* to watch; **cuidado con lo que haces, que te estoy junando** watch what you get up to, I've got my eye on you

juncal *nm* bed of rushes

juncia *nf* sedge

junco[1] *nm (planta)* rush, reed ►► ***j. florido*** flowering rush; ***j. marinero*** alkali bulrush; ***j. oloroso*** jonquil

junco[2] *nm (embarcación)* junk

jungla *nf* jungle ►► ***j. de(l) asfalto*** concrete jungle

junio *nm* June; *ver también* **septiembre**

júnior ['junior] (*pl* **júniors**) **1** *adj* (**a**) *Dep* **equipo j.** ≃ youth team *(ages 18 to 21)* (**b**) *(hijo)* junior

2 *nmf Dep* **júniors** ≃ youth team *(ages 18 to 21)*

junípero *nm (planta)* juniper

Juno *n Mitol* Juno

junquera *nf* rush, bulrush

junquillo *nm* (**a**) *(flor)* jonquil (**b**) *(junco de Indias)* rattan (**c**) *Arquit* rounded moulding

junta *nf* (**a**) *(grupo, comité)* committee; *(de empresa, examinadores)* board ►► ***j. arbitral*** arbitration panel; *Urug* ***j. departamental*** provincial government; ***j. directiva*** board of directors; ***j. electoral*** electoral board; ***j. de gobierno*** *(de universidad)* senate, governing body; ***j. militar*** military junta; ***j. municipal*** town *o* local council

(**b**) *(reunión)* meeting ►► ***j. de accionistas*** shareholders' meeting; ***j. general de accionistas*** shareholders' meeting; ***j. general anual*** annual general meeting; ***j. general extraordinaria*** extraordinary general meeting; ***j. de portavoces*** = meeting of the party spokespersons in a parliament or council to discuss a particular issue; ***j. de vecinos*** residents' meeting

(**c**) *Esp (gobierno autónomo)* = government and administrative body in certain autonomous regions

(**d**) *(juntura)* joint ►► ***j. cardánica*** universal joint; ***j. de culata*** gasket; ***j. de dilatación*** expansion joint; ***j. esférica*** ball joint; ***j. de solape*** lap joint; ***j. universal*** universal joint

(**e**) *RP, Ven Fam (compañía)* **anda con malas juntas** she hangs out with a bad crowd

juntamente *adv* **j. con** together with

JUNTAR **1** *vt* (**a**) *(unir)* to put together; **junta los pies** put your feet together; **como no cabíamos todos, decidimos j. las mesas** as we didn't all fit, we decided to push the tables together; **junté los cables con cinta aislante** I tied the wires together with some insulating tape

(**b**) *(reunir)* to put together; *(cromos, sellos, monedas)* to collect; *(fondos)* to raise; *(personas)* to bring together; **poco a poco ha juntado una valiosa colección de cuadros** she has gradually put together a valuable collection of paintings; **he ido juntando dinero todo el año para las vacaciones** I've been saving up all year for my holidays; **juntaron todos los departamentos en un solo edificio** they brought all the departments together in a single building

2 juntarse *vpr* (**a**) *(ríos, caminos)* to meet; **aquí se junta la A-1 con la M-40** this is where the A-1 joins *o* meets the M-40

(**b**) *(reunirse)* to get together; **se juntó con el resto de la familia para cenar** she got together with the rest of the family for dinner

(**c**) *(arrimarse)* **tenemos que juntarnos un poco, que si no no cabemos** we have to squeeze up a bit, otherwise we won't all fit; **juntaos algo más, que no salís todos** move together a bit or you won't all be in the photo

(**d**) *(convivir)* **se ha juntado con una compañera de trabajo** he's moved in with a woman from work; **los jóvenes ya no se casan sino que se juntan** young people don't get married any more, they just live together

(**e**) *(coincidir)* to coincide (**con** with); **se junta su boda con nuestras vacaciones** her wedding clashes *o* coincides with our holidays; **¡caramba, se nos junta todo!** God, it never rains but it pours!; EXPR

se junta el hambre con las ganas de comer it's one thing on top of another
(**f**) *(copular)* to copulate, to mate

---

juntillas: a pies juntillas *loc adv* unquestioningly

JUNTO, -A 1 *adj* (**a**) *(unido)* together; **si seguimos juntos, no nos perderemos** if we stay together, we won't get lost; **saltaba con los pies juntos** she was jumping up and down with her feet together
(**b**) *(agrupado, reunido)* together; **con tu dinero y el mío juntos nos compraremos el barco** with your money and mine we can buy the boat between us; **nunca he visto tanto niño j.** I've never seen so many children all in one place; **hacer algo juntos** to do sth together; **¿comemos juntos el viernes?** shall we eat together on Friday?; **no se han casado pero viven juntos** they're not married, but they live together; EXPR *Fam* **juntos pero no revueltos: los dos partidos gobiernan juntos pero no revueltos** the two parties govern together but that doesn't mean they're the best of friends
(**c**) *(próximo, cercano)* close together; **las casas están muy juntas** the houses are too close together; **si los cables están demasiado juntos, sepáralos** if the cables are too close together, move them apart; **si no se ponen más juntos, no saldrán todos** if they don't all squeeze up a bit more I won't be able to get them all in the photo; **bailaban muy juntos** they were dancing very close
(**d**) *(al mismo tiempo)* **no puedo atender a tantos clientes juntos** I can't serve all these customers at the same time; **llegaron juntos a la meta** they crossed the line together
2 **junto a** *loc prep (al lado de)* next to; *(cerca de)* right by, near; **el listín de teléfonos está j. a la lámpara** the telephone directory is next to the lamp; **una casa j. al mar** a house by the sea
3 **junto con** *loc conj* together with; **nuestro objetivo, j. con la calidad, es la competitividad** our aim is not only to achieve quality, but also to be competitive
4 **todo junto** *loc adv (ocurrir, llegar)* all at the same time; **se escribe todo j.** it's written as one word; **¿se lo envuelvo todo j.?** shall I wrap everything up together for you?

---

juntura *nf* (**a**) *Tec* joint (**b**) *Anat* joint

Júpiter 1 *nm (planeta)* Jupiter
2 *n Mitol* Jupiter

jura *nf (promesa solemne)* oath; *(de un cargo)* swearing-in; **la ceremonia de j. del nuevo presidente** the inauguration *o* swearing-in of the new president ►► ***j. de bandera,*** *Am* ***j. a la bandera,*** *RP* ***j. de la bandera*** oath of allegiance to the flag

juraco *nm CAm, Carib* hole

jurado, -a 1 *adj (declaración)* sworn; **enemigo j.** sworn enemy
2 *nm* (**a**) *(en juicio)* jury (**b**) *(en concurso, competición)* (panel of) judges
3 *nm,f* (**a**) *(en juicio)* member of the jury (**b**) *(en concurso, competición)* judge

juramentado, -a *adj* sworn, under oath

juramentar 1 *vt* to swear in
2 **juramentarse** *vpr* to swear; **juramentarse para hacer algo** to swear to do sth

juramento *nm* (**a**) *(promesa solemne)* oath; **bajo j.** on *o* under oath; **hacer un j. a alguien (de que)...** to swear to sb (that)...; **prestar j.** to take the oath; **tomar j. a alguien** to swear sb in ►► ***j. falso*** perjury; ***j. hipocrático*** Hippocratic oath (**b**) *(blasfemia)* oath, curse; **soltar juramentos** to curse, to swear

jurar 1 *vt* (**a**) *(prometer solemnemente)* to swear; *(constitución, bandera)* to pledge *o* swear allegiance to; **j. un cargo** to be sworn in; **j. bandera,** *Am* **j. la bandera** to swear allegiance to the flag; **juró vengar la muerte de su padre** she swore to avenge her father's death; **j. que** to swear that; **j. por...** to swear by...; **te lo juro por mi madre** I swear to God; **te lo juro** I promise, I swear (it); *Irónico* **no sé mucho alemán – no hace falta que lo jures** I don't know much German – you don't say! *o* tell me something I don't know!; EXPR *Fam* **tenérsela jurada a alguien** to have it in for sb
(**b**) *(asegurar)* to swear; **te juro que no ha sido culpa mía** I swear that it wasn't my fault; **habría jurado que era tu hermana** I could have sworn it was your sister; **juraba y perjuraba que él no había sido** he swore blind that it wasn't him
2 *vi* to swear; **j. en falso** *o* **vano** *(mentir)* to tell an outright lie; *Der* to commit perjury; EXPR *Fam* **j. en hebreo** *o* **arameo** to swear like a trooper, *Br* to eff and blind
3 **jurarse** *vpr* **se juraron amor eterno** they pledged their eternal love for each other; **los conspiradores se juraron fidelidad** the plotters swore to be loyal to one another

jurásico, -a *Geol* 1 *adj* Jurassic
2 *nm* **el j.** the Jurassic (period)

jurel *nm* horse mackerel

jurgar *vi RP, Ven Fam* to be a pain

jurgo *nm Col Fam (gran cantidad)* **un j.** tons, loads; **habla un j. de lenguajes** she speaks tons *o* loads of languages

jurguillo *nm RP Fam* **es un j.** it's as if he had ants in his pants

jurídicamente *adv* legally

jurídico, -a *adj* legal; **asesor j.** legal adviser

jurisconsulto, -a *nm,f* jurist

jurisdicción *nf* (**a**) *(autoridad)* jurisdiction; **tener j. sobre algo** to have jurisdiction over sth (**b**) *(territorio)* jurisdiction

jurisdiccional *adj* jurisdictional; **aguas jurisdiccionales** territorial waters

jurispericia = **jurisprudencia**

jurisperito, -a *nm,f* legal expert, jurist

jurisprudencia, jurispericia *nf* (**a**) *(ciencia)* jurisprudence (**b**) *(casos previos)* case law, (legal) precedents; **no hay j. en casos parecidos** there is no legal precedent; **sentar j.** to set a legal precedent

jurista *nmf* legal expert, jurist

juro: a juro *loc adv Ven Fam* **se lo comió a j.** he was made to eat it; **se puso esos zapatos a j.** she wore those shoes because she was made to

jurungar *Ven Fam* 1 *vt (hurgar)* to rummage around in; **no jurungues mis papeles** stop rummaging through my papers
2 *vi (indagar)* to pry; EXPR **j. el avispero** to stir up a hornet's nest

justa *nf* (**a**) *Hist* joust (**b**) *(certamen)* competition

justamente *adv* (**a**) *(con justicia)* justly; **obró j.** she acted justly *o* fairly
(**b**) *(merecidamente)* deservedly; **fue j. recompensado por su labor** he received a fair reward for his work
(**c**) *(exactamente)* exactly, precisely; **j., eso es lo que estaba pensando** exactly, that's just what I was thinking; **j. ahora te iba a llamar** I was just about to call you this minute; **tuvo que retirarse j. cuando iba primero** he had to pull out, and just when he was in the lead, too; **te pedí j. lo contrario** I asked you for the exact opposite

justedad, justeza *nf* fairness

justicia *nf* (**a**) *(equidad)* fairness, justice; **en j.** in (all) fairness; **se le hizo j. entregándole el premio** she received the recognition she deserved when she was awarded the prize; **esa foto no le hace j.** that photo doesn't do him justice ►► ***j. social*** social justice
(**b**) *(derecho)* justice; **administrar j.** to administer justice; EXPR **ser de j.** to be only fair; **es de j. que la indemnicen** it is only right *o* fair that she should be compensated; EXPR **tomarse la j. por su mano** to take the law into one's own hands
(**c**) **la j.** *(sistema de leyes)* the law
(**d**) *(organización)* **la j. española** the Spanish legal system; **la persigue la j. británica** she is being sought by the British courts

justicialismo *nm Pol* = nationalistic Argentinian political movement founded by Juan Domingo Perón

justicialista *Pol* 1 *adj* = belonging or related to "justicialismo"
2 *nmf* = member or supporter of the "Partido Justicialista"

justiciero, -a *adj* righteous; **ángel j.** avenging angel

justificable *adj* justifiable

justificación *nf* (**a**) *(de comportamiento)* justification; **su actuación no tiene j.** there can be no justification for her actions (**b**) *Imprenta* justification ►► ***j. automática*** automatic justification; ***j. horizontal*** horizontal justification; ***j. vertical*** vertical justification

justificadamente *adv* justifiably; **se marchó de la sala, y j.** he left the room, and with good reason

justificado, -a *adj* justified

justificante *nm* written proof, documentary evidence; **como ayer no fui a clase hoy tengo que llevar un j. de mi madre** as I didn't go to school yesterday, I have to take a note from my mother today ►► ***j. de compra*** receipt; ***j. médico*** doctor's note, sick note

justificar [60] 1 *vt* (**a**) *(probar)* to justify; **justifiqué todos los gastos** I accounted for all the expenses
(**b**) *(hacer admisible)* to justify; **con sus treinta goles justificó el costo de su fichaje** his thirty goals justified *o* made up for the size of his transfer fee
(**c**) *(excusar)* **j. a alguien** to make excuses for sb; **que estuviera cansado no justifica su comportamiento** the fact that he was tired doesn't justify *o* excuse his behaviour
(**d**) *Imprenta* to justify
2 **justificarse** *vpr* (**a**) *(actitud, decisión)* to be justified (**b**) *(persona)*

to justify *o* excuse oneself; **justificarse por algo** to excuse oneself for sth; **justificarse con alguien** to make one's excuses to sb; **no intentes justificarte** I don't want to hear any excuses

justificativo, -a *adj* **un recibo j. de la compra** a receipt as proof of purchase

Justiniano *n pr* Justinian

justipreciar *vt* to value

justiprecio *nm* valuation

justo, -a 1 *adj* (a) *(equitativo)* fair; **luchó por una sociedad justa** she fought for social justice; **no es j. que tenga que hacerlo todo yo** it isn't fair that I should have to do it all myself

(b) *(merecido) (recompensa, victoria)* deserved; *(castigo)* just; **fue el j. campeón** he was the deserved champion

(c) *(lógico)* **es j. que él también quiera ir** it is only normal that he should want to go too

(d) *(exacto)* exact; **tengo el dinero j. para comprar el libro** I've got exactly the right amount of *o* just enough money to buy the book; **estamos los justos para jugar un partido de dobles** there's just enough of us for a game of doubles

(e) *(idóneo)* right; **no encuentro la palabra justa** I can't find the right word

(f) *(apretado, ceñido)* tight; **estar** *o* **venir j.** to be a tight fit; **cabemos cinco, pero un poco justos** there's room for five of us, but it's a bit of a squeeze

(g) *(escaso)* **vamos justos de tiempo** we've only just got enough time; **estamos justos de leche** we've barely *o* only just got enough milk; **ando j. de dinero** I haven't got much money at the moment; **viven con lo j.** they only just have enough to live on; **le quedan las fuerzas justitas** he has barely enough strength left; **la comida fue muy justa** there was barely enough food to go round

(h) *Rel* righteous

2 *nm Rel* **los justos** the righteous; EXPR **pagarán justos por pecadores** the innocent will suffer instead of the guilty

3 *adv* (a) *(exactamente)* just; **j. a tiempo** just in time, in the nick of time; **j. en medio** right in the middle; **¿al lado del puente? – j. ahí** by the bridge? – spot on *o* exactly (b) *(precisamente)* just; **j. ahora iba a llamarte** I was just about to ring you; **vaya, j. ahora que llego yo se va todo el mundo** honestly, everybody's leaving just as I get here

jutía *nf* hutia, hog-rat

juvenil 1 *adj* (a) *(aspecto)* youthful; *(desempleo, violencia)* youth; **delincuencia j.** juvenile delinquency; **moda j.** youth fashion; **en lenguaje j.** in young people's language (b) *Dep* **equipo j.** ≃ youth team *(ages 16 to 17)*

2 *nmf Dep* **juveniles** ≃ youth team *(ages 16 to 17)*

juventud *nf* (a) *(edad, época)* youth; **en su j.** when she was young, in her youth; EXPR **j., divino tesoro** oh, to be young again!

(b) *(los jóvenes)* young people *(plural)*; **la j. ha perdido el respeto por los ancianos** young people no longer respect the elderly; **cuenta con el apoyo de las juventudes del partido** he enjoys the support of the youth wing of the party ►► ***Juventudes Comunistas*** Young Communists; *Hist* ***Juventudes Hitlerianas*** Hitler Youth; ***Juventudes Socialistas*** Young Socialists

juzgado *nm* (a) *(tribunal)* court ►► ***j. de lo civil*** civil court; ***j. de guardia*** = court open during the night or at other times when ordinary courts are shut; EXPR *Fam* **ser de j. de guardia** to be criminal *o* a crime; ***j. de instrucción*** court of first instance, *Br* ≃ magistrates' court, *US* ≃ justice's court; ***j. de lo penal*** criminal court; ***j. de primera instancia*** court of first instance, *Br* ≃ magistrates' court, *US* ≃ justice's court; ***j. de lo social*** = civil court dealing with employment and social security matters, *Br* ≃ industrial tribunal

(b) *(jurisdicción)* jurisdiction

juzgar [38] 1 *vt* (a) *Der* to try (b) *(enjuiciar)* to judge; *(estimar, considerar)* to consider, to judge; **j. mal a alguien** to misjudge sb; **a j. por (cómo)** judging by (how); **no tienes derecho a juzgarme** you have no right to judge me; **enseguida juzga a la gente** she's very quick to judge

2 **juzgarse** *vpr* to consider oneself

juzgón, -ona *adj CAm, Méx Fam* overcritical; **es muy j.** nothing's good enough for him, he's a real nitpicker

K, k

K, k [ka] *nf (letra)* K, k
K *nm Informát* (*abrev de* **kilobyte**) K
Kabul *n* Kabul
kafkiano, -a *adj Fig* Kafkaesque
káiser (*pl* **káisers**) *nm* Kaiser
kaki = **caqui**
kala-azar *nm Med* kala-azar
Kalahari *nm* **el (desierto del) K.** the Kalahari Desert
kamikaze 1 *adj* (**a**) *Hist* kamikaze (**b**) *(atentado, táctica)* kamikaze
2 *nmf* (**a**) *Hist* kamikaze (**b**) *(terrorista)* kamikaze
Kampala *n* Kampala
Kampuchea *n Antes* Kampuchea
kan (*pl* **kans**) *nm Hist (de los tártaros)* khan
kantiano, -a 1 *adj* Kantian
2 *nm,f* Kantian
kaón *nm Fís* kaon
kaput, kaputt [ka'put] *adj inv Fam* kaput; **la radio está k.** the radio's kaput
karaoke *nm* (**a**) *(aparato)* karaoke (machine) (**b**) *(bar)* karaoke bar
kárate, karate *nm* karate
karateka, karateca *nmf* karate expert, karateka
kárdex® *nm Andes, Ven Br* card index, *US* card catalog
karma *nm* karma
karst *nm Geol* karst
kárstico, -a *adj Geol* karstic
kart (*pl* **karts**) *nm* go-kart, kart
karting ['kartin] *nm* go-kart racing, karting
kartódromo *nm* go-kart *o* karting track
KAS [kas] *nf* (*abrev de* **Koordinadora Abertzale Sozialista**) = Basque left-wing nationalist umbrella organization which includes the terrorist organization ETA
kasbah *nf* kasbah
kata *nm Dep* kata
katiusca, katiuska *nf Esp Br* wellington boot, *US* rubber boot
Katmandú *n* Kathmandu
katún *nm* = period of 20 360-day years in the Mayan calendar
kayac (*pl* **kayacs**), **kayak** (*pl* **kayaks**) *nm* kayak
kazaco, -a, kazako, -a, kazajo, -a 1 *adj* Kazak(h)
2 *nm,f* Kazak(h)
Kazajistán *n* Kazak(h)stan
kazajo, kazako = **kazaco**
Kb *nm Informát* (*abrev de* **kilobyte**) Kb
kbps *Informát* (*abrev de* **kilobytes por segundo**) kbps
kebab *nm* kebab
kefia, kufia *nf* keffiyeh
kéfir *nm* kefir
kelvin (*pl* **kelvins**) *nm* kelvin; **grados K.** degrees Kelvin
kendo *nm* kendo
Kenia *n* Kenya
keniano, -a, keniata 1 *adj* Kenyan
2 *nm,f* Kenyan
kentia *nf* kentia
kepis *nm inv* kepi
kermés, kermesse [ker'mes] *nf* fair, kermesse
kero *nm* = decorated Inca ceremonial vessel made of earthenware or wood
keroseno, *Am* **kerosén,** *Am* **kerosene** *nm* kerosene
ketchup ['ketʃup] (*pl* **ketchups**) *nm* ketchup, *US* catsup
keynesianismo *nm Econ* Keynesianism
keynesiano, -a *Econ* 1 *adj* Keynesian
2 *nm,f* Keynesian
kg (*abrev de* **kilogramo**) kg
KGB *nm o nf Antes* KGB
kHz (*abrev de* **kilohertz**) kHz
kibbutz, kibutz [ki'βuts] *nm inv* kibbutz
kichua *nm* Quechua, Quichua
Kiev *n* Kiev
kif *nm* kif
kifi *nm Esp Fam* pot
kiki = **quiqui**
kikirikí (*pl* **kikirikíes**) 1 *nm* crowing
2 *interj* cock-a-doodle-do!
kiko *nm (maíz tostado)* = toasted, salted maize kernel
kilim (*pl* **kilims**) *nm (alfombra)* kilim
Kilimanjaro *nm* **el K.** (Mount) Kilimanjaro
kilo *nm* (**a**) *(peso)* kilo, kilogram (**b**) *Esp Fam (millón de pesetas)* million (pesetas); **gana cinco kilos al año** she earns five million (pesetas) a year (**c**) *RP Fam (mucho)* **cuesta un k. de plata** it costs a fortune; **tengo kilos de cosas que hacer** I've got tons *o* loads of things to do
kilo- *pref* kilo-
kilobit (*pl* **kilobits**) *nm Informát* kilobit
kilobyte [kilo'βait] *nm Informát* kilobyte
kilocaloría *nf* kilocalorie
kilociclo *nm* kilocycle
kilogramo *nm* kilogram(me)
kilohercio, kilohertz *nm* kilohertz
kilojulio *nm* kilojoule
kilolitro *nm* kilolitre
kilometraje *nm* (**a**) *(de vehículo)* ≃ mileage; **sin límite de k.** *(vehículo alquilado)* unlimited mileage (**b**) *(de carretera)* distance in kilometres
kilometrar *vt* **k. una carretera** to put distance markers along a road
kilométrico, -a 1 *adj* (**a**) *(distancia)* kilometric (**b**) *Fam (largo)* dead long; **había una cola kilométrica** there was a massive *Br* queue *o US* line
2 *nm Esp* = ticket to travel a set distance
kilómetro *nm* kilometre ►► ***k. cero*** *(de carretera)* = point from which road distances are measured, usually in a country's capital; **desde el k. cero de la carrera salieron a por todas** they went flat out from the very start of the race; ***k. cuadrado*** square kilometre
kilopondio *nm Fís (unidad)* kilopond
kilotón *nm* kiloton
kilovatio *nm* kilowatt ►► ***k. hora*** kilowatt hour
kilovoltio *nm* kilovolt
kilt (*pl* **kilts**) *nm* kilt
kiludo, -a *adj Ven Fam* chubby
kimono *nm, Méx* **kimona** *nf* kimono
kindergarten, *Andes, Méx* **kínder** *nm* kindergarten, nursery school
kindergarterina *nf Ven* kindergarten *o* nursery school teacher
kinesioterapeuta, kinesiterapeuta *nmf* kinesitherapist
kinesioterapia, kinesiterapia *nf* kinesitherapy
kiosco *nm* (**a**) *(de periódico, revistas)* newspaper stand *o* kiosk; *(de refrescos)* kiosk; *(de helados)* ice-cream stand; *(de lotería)* = kiosk where lottery tickets are sold ►► ***k. de música*** bandstand (**b**) *RP (estanco)* tobacconist's (kiosk)

kiosquero, -a, quioskero, -a *nm,f* = person selling newspapers, drinks etc from a kiosk

Kioto *n* Kyoto

kipa, kipá *nf* yarmulke, yarmulka

Kirguizistán *n* Kirg(h)izia, Kirg(h)izstan

kirguizo, -a 1 *adj* Kirghiz
2 *nm,f* Kirghiz

kirial *nm Rel* plainsong book

Kiribati *n* Kiribati

kirie, kirieleisón *nm Rel* kyrie, kyrie eleison; EXPR *Fam* **cantar el k.** to plead for mercy

kirsch [kirs] *nm* kirsch

kit (*pl* **kits**) *nm* *(conjunto)* kit, set; *(para montar)* kit ▸▸ *Informát* ***k. de conexión*** connection kit

kitsch [kitʃ] *adj inv* kitsch, kitschy

kiwi *nm* (**a**) *(ave)* kiwi (**b**) *(fruto)* kiwi (fruit)

kleenex® ['klines, 'klineks], **klínex** *nm inv* tissue, paper handkerchief, Kleenex®

km (*abrev de* **kilómetro**) km

km/h (*abrev de* **kilómetros por hora**) km/h

knickers ['nikers] *nmpl Urug* knickerbockers, *US* knickers

knockout [no'kaut] (*pl* **knockouts**) *nm* knockout

know how ['nou'χau] *nm* know-how

K.O. *nm* (*abrev de* **knockout**) KO; **dejar K. a alguien** *(en boxeo)* to knock sb out; *Fig* to stun *o* floor sb; **ganar por K.** *(en boxeo)* to win by a knockout; *Fig* to win convincingly; **quedar K.** *(en boxeo)* to be knocked out; *Fig* to be stunned *o* floored ▸▸ ***K. técnico*** technical knockout

koala *nm* koala (bear)

koljós, koljoz *nm Hist* kolkhoz

kopek (*pl* **kopeks**) *nm* kopeck

kosher *nm* kosher food

kosovar 1 *adj* Kosovan; **la capital k.** the Kosovo *o* Kosovan capital
2 *nmf* Kosovan, Kosovar

Kosovo *n* Kosovo

Kremlin *nm* **el K.** the Kremlin

kril *nm* krill

kriptón *nm Quím* krypton

krugerrand *nm* Krugerrand

Kuala Lumpur *n* Kuala Lumpur

kufia = **kefia**

kung-fu *nm* kung fu

Kurdistán *nm* Kurdistan

kurdo, -a 1 *adj* Kurdish
2 *nm,f (persona)* Kurd
3 *nm (lengua)* Kurdish

Kuriles *nfpl* **las (islas) K.** the Kuriles, the Kuril(e) Islands

Kuwait [ku'βait] *n* Kuwait

kuwaití [kuβai'ti] (*pl* **kuwaitíes**) 1 *adj* Kuwaiti
2 *nmf* Kuwaiti

kW (*abrev de* **kilovatio**) kW

kWh (*abrev de* **kilovatio hora**) kWh

kV (*abrev de* **kilovoltio**) kV

L, l

L, l ['ele] *nf (letra)* L, l

L *(abrev de* **lunes***)* Mon

l *(abrev de* **litro***)* l

la[1] *nm (nota musical)* A; *(en solfeo)* lah; *ver también* **do**

la[2] **1** *art ver* **el**
2 *pron ver* **lo**[1]

laberíntico, -a *adj* (**a**) *(del laberinto)* labyrinthine (**b**) *(complejo)* labyrinthine

laberinto *nm* (**a**) *(mitológico)* labyrinth; *(en jardín)* maze; **un l. de calles** a labyrinth *o* maze of streets (**b**) *(cosa complicada)* labyrinth, maze

labia *nf Fam* smooth talk; **tener mucha l.** to have the gift of the gab

labiado, -a *adj Bot* labiate

labial 1 *adj* (**a**) *(de los labios)* lip, *Espec* labial; **protector l.** lip salve *o* balm (**b**) *Ling* labial
2 *nf Ling* labial

labialización *nf Ling* labialization

labializar [14] *vt Ling* to labialize

labiérnago *nm* mock privet

lábil *adj (sustancia, estructura)* unstable; *(persona, situación)* volatile

labilidad *nf (de sustancia, estructura)* instability; *(de persona, situación)* volatility, volatile nature

labio *nm* (**a**) *(de boca)* lip; **l. superior/inferior** upper/lower lip; **leer los labios** to lip-read; **leer los labios a alguien** to read sb's lips; EXPR **estar pendiente de los labios de alguien** to hang on sb's every word; EXPR **morderse los labios** to bite one's tongue; EXPR **no despegar los labios** not to utter a word ▸▸ ***l. leporino*** harelip
(**b**) *(de vulva)* labium ▸▸ ***labios mayores*** labia majora; ***labios menores*** labia minora
(**c**) *(borde)* edge

labiodental *Ling* **1** *adj* labiodental
2 *nf* labiodental

labioso, -a *adj CAm, Ecuad, Méx* glib

labor *nf* (**a**) *(trabajo)* work; *(tarea)* task; **hizo una buena l. al frente de la empresa** she did a good job at the helm of the company; **profesión: sus labores** occupation: housewife; **ser de profesión sus labores** to be a housewife; EXPR **no estar por la l.** not to have one's mind on the job; **quiero ir al concierto pero mis padres no están por la l. de dejarme** I want to go to the concert, but my parents won't let me go ▸▸ ***labores agrícolas*** farm work; ***labores domésticas*** household chores; ***l. de equipo*** teamwork; ***l. de mina*** mining
(**b**) *(de costura)* needlework ▸▸ ***l. de encaje*** lacemaking; ***l. de punto*** knitting
(**c**) *Agr* **casa de l.** farm; **tierra de l.** agricultural land, arable land

laborable 1 *adj* **día l.** *(hábil)* working day; *(de semana)* weekday
2 *nm (día hábil)* working day; *(día de la semana)* weekday

laboral *adj (semana, jornada, horario, condiciones)* working; *(derecho, costos, mercado)* labour; *(conflicto)* industrial; **accidente l.** industrial accident

laboralista 1 *adj* **abogado l.** labour lawyer
2 *nmf* labour lawyer

laboralmente *adv* **l. las cosas me van bien** things are going well on the work front; **la ley discrimina l. a los refugiados** the law discriminates against refugees in terms of employment

laborar *vt* (**a**) *(cultivar)* to cultivate (**b**) *(arar)* to plough

laboratorio *nm* laboratory ▸▸ ***l. espacial*** spacelab; ***l. farmacéutico*** pharmaceutical laboratory; ***l. fotográfico*** photographic laboratory; ***l. de idiomas*** language laboratory; ***l. de investigación*** research laboratory; ***l. de lenguas*** language laboratory

laborear *vt (trabajar)* to work; **l. la tierra** to work the land

laboreo *nm (del campo)* cultivation

laboriosamente *adv* laboriously, elaborately

laboriosidad *nf* (**a**) *(dedicación)* application, diligence (**b**) *(dificultad)* laboriousness

laborioso, -a *adj* (**a**) *(aplicado)* hard-working (**b**) *(difícil)* laborious, arduous

laborismo *nm* **el l.** *(ideología)* Labourism; *(movimiento)* the Labour Movement

laborista 1 *adj* Labour
2 *nmf* Labour Party supporter *o* member; **los laboristas** Labour

labrado, -a 1 *adj* (**a**) *(tela, género)* embroidered (**b**) *(metales)* wrought; *(madera, piedra)* carved (**c**) *(pieles)* tooled (**d**) *(tierra)* cultivated, tilled
2 *nm (de metales)* working; *(de madera, piedra)* carving

Labrador *n* Labrador

labrador, -ora *nm,f* (**a**) *(agricultor)* farmer; *(trabajador)* farm worker (**b**) *(perro)* Labrador

labrantío, -a *adj* arable

labranza *nf Agr* **casa de l.** farm; **tierra de l.** agricultural land, arable land

labrar 1 *vt* (**a**) *(campo) (arar)* to plough; *(cultivar)* to cultivate (**b**) *(piedra, metal)* to work (**c**) *(porvenir, fortuna)* to carve out
2 labrarse *vpr* **labrarse un porvenir** to carve out a future for oneself

labriego, -a *nm,f* farm worker

laburante *nmf RP Fam* worker

laburar *vi RP Fam* to work; **labura de vendedora** she works in a shop

laburo *nm RP Fam* job

laca *nf* (**a**) *(para muebles)* lacquer (**b**) *(para el pelo)* hairspray (**c**) *(objeto)* lacquered box (**d**) ***l. de uñas*** nail polish *o* varnish

lacado, -a 1 *adj* lacquered
2 *nm* lacquering

lacandón, -ona 1 *adj* Lacandon
2 *nm,f (persona)* Lacandon Indian
3 *nm (lengua)* Lacandon

lacar [60] *vt* to lacquer

lacayo *nm* (**a**) *(criado)* footman (**b**) *Pey (persona servil)* lackey

laceador, -ora *nm,f CSur* cowboy *(whose job it is to lasso cattle)*

lacear *vt CSur* to lasso

laceración *nf* laceration

lacerante *adj* (**a**) *(dolor)* excruciating, stabbing (**b**) *(palabras)* hurtful, cutting; *(grito)* piercing

lacerar 1 *vt* (**a**) *(herir)* to lacerate (**b**) *(apenar)* to wound
2 lacerarse *vpr* to injure oneself; **se laceró el brazo** she injured her arm

laceria *nf Literario* tribulation

lacería *nf Arte* = decorative designs of interlacing lines which form geometrical patterns, typical of Arab art

lacero *nm (de animales)* lassoer, roper; *(de perros)* dogcatcher

lacho, -a *Chile, Perú Fam* **1** *nm,f* lover
2 *nm* dandy

lacio, -a *adj* (**a**) *(cabello) (liso)* straight; *(sin fuerza)* lank (**b**) *(planta)* wilted (**c**) *(sin fuerza)* limp

lacón *nm* shoulder of pork

lacónicamente *adv* laconically

lacónico, -a *adj* (**a**) *(persona)* laconic (**b**) *(respuesta, estilo)* terse

laconismo *nm (de respuesta, estilo)* terseness

lacra *nf* (**a**) *(secuela)* **la enfermedad le dejó como l. una cojera** he was left lame by the illness (**b**) *(problema)* scourge; **la l. del terrorismo** the scourge of terrorism; **la droga se ha convertido en una l. social** drugs have become the scourge of our society (**c**) *(defecto)* blight (**d**) *Am (costra)* scab

lacrar *vt* to seal *(with sealing wax)*

lacre *nm* (**a**) *(para sellar)* sealing wax (**b**) *Cuba (de abeja)* propolis

lacrimal *adj* lachrymal, tear; **conducto l.** tear duct

lacrimógeno, -a *adj* (**a**) *(novela, película)* weepy, tear-jerking (**b**) **gas l.** tear gas

lacrimoso, -a *adj* (**a**) *(ojos)* tearful (**b**) *(historia)* weepy, tear-jerking

lactancia *nf* lactation ▸▸ ***l. artificial*** bottle-feeding; ***l. materna*** breastfeeding

lactante 1 *adj* (**a**) *(que amamanta)* **madre l.** breastfeeding mother (**b**) *(que mama)* **bebé l.** baby *(not yet eating solid food)*
2 *nmf (que mama)* baby *(not yet eating solid food)*
3 *nf (que amamanta)* breastfeeding mother

lactato *nm Bioquím* lactate

lacteado, -a *adj* **producto l.** = product ready-mixed with milk, usually for babies

lácteo, -a *adj* (**a**) *(industria, productos)* dairy (**b**) *(blanco)* milky; **de aspecto l.** milky

láctico, -a *adj* lactic

lactosa *nf Bioquím* lactose

lacustre *adj (animal, planta)* lake-dwelling, lacustrine; **hábitat l.** lake habitat

ladeado, -a *adj (torcido)* tilted, at an angle; **el cuadro está l.** the painting isn't straight; **mételo l.** put it in sideways

ladear 1 *vt* to tilt
2 **ladearse** *vpr* (**a**) *(cuadro)* to tilt; *(persona)* to turn sideways (**b**) *Chile Fam (enamorarse)* to fall in love

ladera *nf* (**a**) *(de montaña)* slope, mountainside (**b**) *Bol (chabola)* shanty town

ladero, -a *nm,f RP Fam* regular companion; **llegó con sus laderos** he arrived accompanied by the usual crowd

ladilla 1 *nf* (**a**) *(insecto)* crab (louse) (**b**) *Ven Vulg (fastidio) Br* bloody *o US* goddamn pain; **limpiar la casa es una l.** doing the housework is a *Br* bloody *o US* goddamn pain
2 *nmf RP, Ven muy Fam (fastidioso) Br* bloody *o US* goddamn pain

ladillado, -a *adj Ven muy Fam* **estar l. con algo** to be bored shitless with sth

ladillar *muy Fam* 1 *vi RP, Ven* to be a *Br* bloody *o US* goddamn pain; **¡deja de l.!** stop being such a *Br* bloody *o US* goddamn pain!
2 **ladillarse** *vpr Ven* to get bored shitless

ladilloso, -a *adj Ven muy Fam* **ser l.** to be a *Br* bloody *o US* goddamn pain

ladino, -a 1 *adj* (**a**) *(astuto)* crafty (**b**) *(judeoespañol)* Ladino (**c**) *CAm, Méx, Ven (no blanco)* non-white
2 *nm* (**a**) *(sefardí)* Ladino (**b**) *(lengua románica)* Ladino
3 *nm,f CAm, Méx, Ven (no blanco)* = non-white Spanish-speaking person

LADO *nm* (**a**) *(costado, cara, parte lateral)* side; **me duele el l. izquierdo** my left side is hurting; **el cine está a este l. de la calle** the cinema is on this side of the street; **el l. más áspero de la tela** the rougher side of the cloth; **un polígono con cuatro lados** a four-sided *o* quadrilateral polygon; **este cuadro se puede colgar en el l. de la chimenea** we can hang this painting on the wall behind the fireplace; **a ambos lados** on both sides; **al l.** *(cerca)* nearby; **yo vivo aquí al l.** I live just round the corner from here; **al l. de** *(junto a)* beside, next to; *(comparado con)* compared to; **la zapatería está al l. de la joyería** the shoe shop is next to the jeweller's; **Juan, al l. de su hermano, es muy alto** Juan is very tall compared to his brother; **al otro l. de** on the other side of; **la mesa de al l.** the next table; **la casa de al l.** the house next door; **los vecinos de al l.** the next-door neighbours; **no te vayas de su l.** do not leave her side; **en el l. de arriba/abajo** on the top/bottom; **de l.** *(torcido)* at an angle; **el cuadro está de l.** the painting isn't straight; **mételo de l.** put it in sideways; **dormir de l.** to sleep on one's side; **el viento sopla de l.** there's a crosswind; **atravesar algo de l. a l.** to cross sth from one side to the other; **echarse** *o* **hacerse a un l.** to move aside; **poner algo a un l.** to put sth aside *o* to one side
(**b**) *(lugar)* place; **por este l. no oímos nada** we can't hear anything over here; **debe de estar en otro l.** it must be somewhere else; **columpiarse de un l. para** *o* **a otro** to swing to and fro; **estuve todo el día corriendo de un l. para otro** I've been running around all day; **hacerle un l. a alguien** to make room for sb; **iremos cada uno por nuestro l. y nos reuniremos en el hotel** we will go our separate ways and meet up later at the hotel; **si cada cual va por su l., nunca sacaremos este proyecto adelante** if everyone does their own thing, we'll never make a success of this project; **por todos lados** everywhere, all around; **por todos lados se ven anuncios de este nuevo refresco** there are adverts for this new drink everywhere
(**c**) *(bando)* side; **y tú ¿de qué l. estás?** whose side are you on?; **estoy de su l.** I'm on her side; **ponerse del l. de alguien** to take sb's side
(**d**) *(línea de parentesco)* side; **por el l. paterno** on my/his/her/*etc* father's side
(**e**) *(aspecto)* side; **siempre ve el l. negativo de las cosas** she always sees the negative side of things; **la entrevista se centra en el l. humano del campeón** the interview focuses on the human side of the champion; **por un l.** *(en primer lugar)* on the one hand; *(en cierto modo)* in one sense; **por otro l.**, *Am* **de otro l.** *(en segundo lugar)* on the other hand; *(además)* in any case
(**f**) EXPR **dar de l. a alguien,** *Méx, RP* **dar a alguien por su l.** to cold-shoulder sb; **dejar algo de l.** *o* **a un l.** *(prescindir)* to leave sth to one side; *Méx, RP Fam* **estar del otro l.** to be over the worst; **mirar de l. a alguien** *(despreciar)* to look askance at sb; *RP, Ven Fam* **pasar al otro l.** to kick the bucket, to snuff it; *RP, Ven Fam* **pasar a alguien para el otro l.** to bump sb off; *CSur Fam* **ser** *o* **patear para el otro l.** to be one of them, to be queer

ladrador, -ora *adj* barking

ladrar *vi* (**a**) *(perro)* to bark (**b**) *(persona)* to bark; EXPR *Fam* **está que ladra** he's hopping mad, *US* he's fit to be tied; EXPR *Ven Fam* **estar ladrando** *(sin dinero)* to be broke, *Br* to be skint; *(con hambre)* to be starving

ladrido *nm (de perro)* bark; **dar** *o* **soltar un l.** to bark; **nos despertaron los ladridos de un perro** we were woken by the sound of a dog barking

ladrillar *nm* brick factory *o* works *(singular)*

ladrillazo *nm* **dar un l. a alguien** to throw a brick at sb; **me dieron un l. en la cabeza** I was hit on the head by a brick

ladrillo *nm* (**a**) *(para construir)* brick; **una casa de l.** a brick house ▸▸ ***l. crudo*** adobe (**b**) *Fam (pesadez)* drag, bore (**c**) **color l.** *(color)* brick red; **de color l.** brick red

ladrón, -ona 1 *adj* thieving; **en esa tienda son muy ladrones** they're real crooks in that shop
2 *nm,f (persona) (de coches)* thief; *(de bancos)* robber; *(de casas)* burglar; **ese tendero es un l.** that shopkeeper is a crook; PROV **cree** *o* **piensa el l. que todos son de su condición** evildoers expect the worst of everyone ▸▸ ***l. de guante blanco*** gentleman burglar *o* thief; *Am* ***l. y poli*** *(juego infantil)* cops and robbers
3 *nm (para enchufes)* adaptor

ladronera, ladronería *nf Andes Fam* (**a**) *(delincuencia)* crime, crookery; **por aquí no hay mucha l.** there isn't much crime round here; **su gobierno fue muy ineficiente y además, hubo tanta l....** her government was very inefficient and besides, it was appallingly corrupt (**b**) *(estafa)* **hace años que se dedica a la l.** he's been ripping people off for years

lagaña = **legaña**

lagar *nm (de vino)* winepress; *(de sidra)* cider press; *(de aceite)* oil press

lagarta *nf* (**a**) *Fam (mujer)* scheming woman (**b**) *(insecto)* gypsy moth (**c**) *ver también* **lagarto**

lagartear *vt Chile* to pinion, to hold by the arms

lagartija *nf* (small) lizard

lagarto, -a 1 *nm,f (reptil)* lizard
2 *nm* (**a**) *Méx (caimán)* alligator (**b**) *Méx Fam (persona)* crafty so-and-so (**c**) *Ven (de carne)* silverside
3 *interj Esp* **¡l., l.!** God *o* Heaven forbid!

lago *nm* lake ▸▸ ***el l. Constanza*** Lake Constance; ***el l. Tiberíades*** the Sea of Galilee; ***el l. Titicaca*** Lake Titicaca; ***el l. Victoria*** Lake Victoria

lagópodo *nm* ***l. alpino*** ptarmigan; ***l. escandinavo*** willow grouse; ***l. escocés*** (red) grouse

Lagos *n* Lagos

lágrima *nf* tear; **hacer saltar las lágrimas** to bring tears to the eyes; **beberse las lágrimas** to hold back one's tears; **nos costó muchas lágrimas** it caused us a lot of heartache; **deshacerse en lágrimas** to cry one's eyes out; **enjugarse** *o* **secarse las lágrimas** to wipe away *o* dry one's tears; **llorar a l. viva** to cry buckets ▸▸ ***lágrimas de cocodrilo*** crocodile tears

lagrimal 1 *adj* lachrymal, tear; **conducto l.** tear duct
2 *nm* (inner) corner of the eye

lagrimear *vi* (**a**) *(persona)* to weep (**b**) *(ojos)* to water

lagrimeo *nm* (**a**) *(acción)* weeping (**b**) *(en ojo)* watering

lagrimilla *nf Chile* unfermented grape juice

lagrimoso, -a *adj* (**a**) *(ojo)* watery (**b**) *(persona)* tearful

laguna *nf* (**a**) *(lago) (de agua salada)* lagoon; *(de agua dulce)* pool (**b**) *(en memoria)* gap; **tengo lagunas importantes en latín** I have some major gaps in my knowledge of Latin (**c**) *(en colección)* gap (**d**) *(en leyes, reglamento)* loophole

La Habana *n* Havana

La Haya *n* The Hague

laicalización = **laicización**

laicalizar [14] *vt Andes* to laicize

laicismo *nm* laicism

laicización, *Andes* **laicalización** *nf* secularization

laicizar *vt* to secularize

laico, -a 1 *adj* lay, secular

2 *nm,f* layman, *f* laywoman

laísmo *nm* = incorrect use of "la" instead of "le" as indirect object, characteristic of certain regions in Spain

laissez-faire [le'se'fer] *nm Econ* laissez-faire

laísta 1 *adj* prone to "laísmo"

2 *nmf* = person prone to "laísmo"

laja *nf* (**a**) *Hond (arena)* fine sand (**b**) *Ecuad (declive)* bank, slope

lama[1] *nf* (**a**) *Am (musgo)* moss (**b**) *Am (verdín)* slime (**c**) *Méx (moho)* mould

lama[2] *nm* lama

lambada *nf* lambada

lambeculo = **lameculos**

lamber *vt Fam* (**a**) *Am (lamer)* to lick (**b**) *Col, Méx (adular)* to suck up to

lambeta *RP Fam* **1** *adj* **ser l.** to be a greedy-guts

2 *nmf* greedy-guts

lambetear *vt Fam* (**a**) *Méx, RP (lamer)* to lick (**b**) *Méx (adular)* to suck up to

lambiscón, -ona, lambón, -ona *Méx Fam* **1** *adj* crawling, creeping

2 *nm,f* crawler, creep

lambisconear, lambisquear *vt Méx Fam* to suck up to

lambón = **lambiscón**

lambucio, -a *Ven Fam* **1** *adj* (**a**) *(glotón)* **ser l.** to be a greedy-guts (**b**) *(tacaño)* tight, stingy

2 *nm,f* (**a**) *(glotón)* greedy-guts (**b**) *(tacaño)* tightwad, miser

lamé *nm* lamé

lameculos, *Méx* **lambeculo** *nmf inv muy Fam* brown-nose, arse-licker

lamentable *adj* (**a**) *(conducta, accidente, confusión)* regrettable; **sería l. que no pudiera acudir** it would be a shame if she couldn't come (**b**) *(malo)* lamentable, deplorable; **llegó a casa con un aspecto l.** she looked terrible *o* she was in a pitiful state when she got home

lamentablemente *adv* unfortunately, sadly

lamentación *nf* moaning

lamentar 1 *vt* to regret, to be sorry about; **lo lamento** I'm (very) sorry; **lamento tener que tomar una decisión así** I regret having to take a decision like this, I'm sorry to have to take a decision like this; **no hubo que l. víctimas mortales** nobody was killed; **lamentamos comunicarle...** we regret to inform you...

2 lamentarse *vpr* to complain (**de** *o* **por** about); **ya es tarde para lamentarse** it's no use complaining now; **me lamenté de mi mala suerte** I cursed my bad luck

lamento *nm (por dolor)* moan, cry (of pain); *(por pena, disgusto)* groan, wail

lamer 1 *vt* (**a**) *(con lengua)* to lick; EXPR *muy Fam* **lamerle el culo a alguien** to brown-nose sb; EXPR *Méx Fam* **l. los pies** *o* **las patas a alguien** to lick sb's boots (**b**) *(acariciar, rozar)* **las olas lamían los costados del barco** the waves lapped against the sides of the boat; **las llamas lamían el techo** the flames licked (at) the roof; **la pelota lamió el larguero** the ball grazed the crossbar

2 lamerse *vpr* to lick oneself; EXPR **lamerse las heridas** to lick one's wounds

lametada *nf* lick

lametazo *nm* lick; **dar un l. a algo** to lick sth, to give sth a lick

lametear *vt* to lick

lametón *nm* lick

lamida *nf* lick; **dar una l. a algo** to lick sth, to give sth a lick; *RP Fam* **darse una l.** to freshen up

lamido, -a *adj* (**a**) *(delgado)* skinny (**b**) *(pulcro)* immaculate

lámina *nf* (**a**) *(plancha)* sheet; *(placa)* plate (**b**) *(rodaja)* slice (**c**) *(grabado)* engraving (**d**) *(dibujo)* plate (**e**) *Chile (cromo)* picture card

laminado, -a 1 *adj* (**a**) *(cubierto por láminas)* laminated (**b**) *(reducido a láminas)* rolled

2 *nm* (**a**) *(cubrir con láminas)* lamination (**b**) *(reducir a láminas)* rolling

laminador *nm*, **laminadora** *nf* rolling mill

laminar[1] *adj* laminar

laminar[2] *vt* (**a**) *(hacer láminas)* to roll (**b**) *(cubrir con láminas)* to laminate

lampa *nf Andes, RP (de agricultor)* hoe; *(de minero)* pick

lampalagua 1 *adj Chile (glotón)* gluttonous

2 *nf* (**a**) *Arg (serpiente)* boa constrictor (**b**) *Chile Mitol* = mythical snake that is said to drink the rivers dry

lampar *vi Esp Fam* to beg

lámpara *nf* (**a**) *(aparato)* lamp ►► ***l. de aceite*** oil lamp; ***la l. de Aladino*** Aladdin's lamp; ***l. de araña*** chandelier; ***l. de arco*** arc lamp; ***l. fluorescente*** fluorescent lamp; ***l. de gas*** gas lamp; ***l. halógena*** halogen lamp; ***l. de incandescencia*** incandescent lamp; ***l. de mesa*** table lamp; ***l. de neón*** neon light; ***l. de noche*** bedside lamp; ***l. de pie*** *Br* standard lamp, *US* floor lamp; ***l. de queroseno*** kerosene lamp; ***l. de rayos ultravioletas*** sun lamp; ***l. solar*** sun lamp; ***l. de soldar*** blowtorch

(**b**) *(bombilla)* bulb

(**c**) *Tec* valve

(**d**) *Fam (mancha)* stain *(of oil or grease)*

lamparazo *nm Col, Méx* long draught

lamparilla *nf* small lamp

lamparita *nf RP* light bulb; EXPR *Fam* **se le prendió la l.** she had a flash of inspiration

lamparón *nm* (**a**) *(mancha) Fam* stain *(of oil or grease)* (**b**) *Med* scrofula

lampazo *nm* (**a**) *Náut* swab (**b**) *RP (de goma)* squeegee (**c**) *Ven (fregona)* mop

lampear *vt Andes* to shovel

lampiño, -a *adj (sin barba)* beardless, smooth-cheeked; *(sin vello)* hairless

lampista *nmf* plumber

lamprea *nf* lamprey

lamprear *vt Culin* = to braise meat or fish and then cook it in wine or stock containing honey or sugar and spices

LAN [lan] *nf Informát (abrev de* **local area network***)* LAN

lana *nf* (**a**) *(de oveja)* wool; **de l.** woollen; PROV **ir a por l. y volver trasquilado** to be hoist with one's own petard ►► ***l. mineral*** rock wool; ***l. de vidrio*** glass wool; ***l. virgen*** virgin wool (**b**) *Andes, Méx Fam (dinero)* dough, cash; EXPR **ser de l.** to be rolling in it

lanar *adj* **industria l.** wool industry; **ganado l.** sheep and goats

lance *nm* (**a**) *(acontecimiento)* event ►► ***l. de fortuna*** stroke of luck

(**b**) *(jugada) (en deportes)* incident; *(en naipes)* play; **se lesionó en un l. fortuito** he was injured in a freak incident; EXPR *CSur Fam* **tirarse un l.** to try one's luck; EXPR *CSur Fam* **tirarse el l.: dale, tirate el l.** *(con mujer)* go on, ask her out

(**c**) *Taurom (de capa, muleta)* pass; **ejecutó el l. de banderillas a la perfección** he did a magnificent job with the banderillas

(**d**) *(situación crítica)* predicament; **me hallé en un l.** I found myself in a predicament; **no sabía cómo salir de ese l.** I didn't know how to get out of my predicament

(**e**) *(riña)* dispute ►► ***l. de honor*** duel

(**f**) *Chile (regate)* duck, dodge

(**g**) **de l.** *(rebajado)* discounted; **libros de l.** discounted books; **comprar algo de l.** *(de segunda mano)* to buy sth second-hand

> **Falso amigo**: El sustantivo inglés **lance** no es la traducción del español **lance**. En inglés **lance** significa "lanza".

lancear *vt* (**a**) *(herir)* to spear (**b**) *Perú, Ven muy Fam (robar)* to lift, *Br* to nick

lanceolado, -a *adj* lanceolate

lancero *nm* (**a**) *(soldado)* lancer (**b**) *Perú, Ven Fam (ladrón)* dip, pickpocket

lanceta *nf* (**a**) *Med* lancet (**b**) *Andes, Méx (aguijón)* sting

lancha[1] *nf (embarcación) (grande)* launch; *(pequeña)* boat ►► ***l. cañonera*** gunboat; ***l. de desembarco*** landing-craft; ***l. motora*** motor launch, motorboat; ***l. neumática*** rubber dinghy; ***l. patrullera*** patrol boat; ***l. salvavidas*** lifeboat; ***l. torpedera*** torpedo boat

lancha[2] *nf (piedra)* slab

lancha³ *nf Ecuad* **(a)** *(niebla)* fog **(b)** *(escarcha)* frost

lanchón *nm* lighter, barge

lancinante *adj Literario* lancing, stabbing

landa *nf* moor

landó *nm* landau

land rover® [lan'rroβer] (*pl* **land rovers**) *nm* four-wheel drive (vehicle), all-terrain vehicle

lanero, -a 1 *adj* wool; **la producción lanera** wool production
 2 *nm,f (persona)* wool dealer

langanazo *nm Ven Fam* **(a)** *(golpe)* thump, wallop *(with fist)* **(b)** *(bebida)* shot

langosta *nf* **(a)** *(crustáceo)* rock *o* spiny lobster **(b)** *(insecto)* locust

langostino *nm* king prawn

lánguidamente *adv* languidly

languidecer [46] *vi (persona)* to languish; *(conversación, entusiasmo)* to flag

languideciente *adj* languid, sluggish

languidez *nf (debilidad)* listlessness; *(falta de ánimo)* disinterest

lánguido, -a *adj (débil)* listless; *(falto de ánimo)* disinterested

langur *nm* langur

lanilla *nf* **(a)** *(pelillo)* nap **(b)** *(tejido)* flannel

lanolina *nf* lanolin

lanoso, -a *adj* woolly

lantánido *Quím* **1** *adj* lanthanide
 2 *nm* lanthanide

lantano *nm Quím* lanthanum

lanudo, -a *adj* **(a)** *(con lana, vello)* woolly **(b)** *Ven Fam (adinerado)* loaded

lanza 1 *nf* **(a)** *(arma) (arrojadiza)* spear; *(en justas, torneos)* lance; EXPR **estar con la l. en ristre** to be ready for action; EXPR **romper una l. por alguien** to stand up for sb; EXPR *Am Fam* **ser una (buena) l.** to be sharp, to be on the ball **(b)** *(de carruaje)* shaft
 2 *nmf Andes Fam* dip, pickpocket

lanzabombas *nm inv (de trinchera)* trench mortar; *(de avión)* bomb release

lanzacohetes *nm inv* rocket launcher

lanzadera *nf* **(a)** *(de telar)* shuttle **(b)** ***l. espacial*** space shuttle

lanzado, -a *adj Fam* **(a)** *(atrevido)* forward; *(valeroso)* fearless; **es muy l. con las chicas** he's not backward at coming forward with girls
 (b) *(impetuoso)* hot-headed; **es muy lanzada, no piensa las cosas dos veces** she's very hot-headed, she doesn't think twice before she acts
 (c) *(rápido)* **iba muy l. y no pudo frenar** he was bombing along and didn't have time to brake; **¿dónde vas tan lanzada?** where are you going in such a hurry?; **en cuanto me enteré salí l.** as soon as I found out I was off in a flash

lanzador, -ora *nm,f* **(a)** *(de objeto) (en béisbol)* pitcher; **es un excelente l. de faltas** he's an excellent free-kick taker ►► *Am* ***l. de bala*** shot-putter; ***l. de cuchillos*** knife thrower; ***l. de disco*** discus thrower; ***l. de martillo*** hammer thrower; ***l. de peso*** shot-putter **(b)** *(en ciclismo)* = cyclist who leads out a sprint

lanzagranadas *nm inv* grenade launcher

lanzallamas *nm inv* flamethrower

lanzamiento *nm* **(a)** *(de objeto)* throwing
 (b) *(de bomba)* dropping; *(de flecha, misil)* firing
 (c) *(de cohete, satélite)* launching
 (d) *(de ataque)* launching
 (e) *Dep (de pelota) (con la mano)* throw; *(con el pie)* kick; *(en béisbol)* pitch; **un l. de dos puntos** *(en baloncesto)* a two-pointer; **un l. de tres puntos** *(en baloncesto)* a three-pointer ►► *Am* ***l. de bala*** the shot put; ***l. de disco*** the discus; ***l. de jabalina*** the javelin; ***l. de lateral*** *(en rugby)* line-out; ***l. de martillo*** the hammer; ***l. de penalti*** penalty kick; **su l. del penalti fue perfecto** he took a perfect penalty; **perdieron en los lanzamientos de penalti** they lost on penalties, they lost in the penalty shoot-out; ***l. de peso*** the shot put
 (f) *(de producto, artista, periódico)* launch; *(de disco, película)* release
 (g) *CSur Der* **(orden de) l.** eviction order

lanzamisiles *nm inv* rocket launcher

lanzaplatos *nm inv Dep* clay-pigeon trap

LANZAR [14] **1** *vt* **(a)** *(tirar)* to throw; *(con fuerza)* to hurl, to fling; **l. a alguien al mar/río** to throw sb into the sea/river; **los alborotadores lanzaban palos y piedras a la policía** the rioters were hurling sticks and stones at the police
 (b) *(bomba)* to drop; *(flecha, misil)* to fire
 (c) *(cohete, satélite)* to launch
 (d) *(ataque)* to launch
 (e) *Dep (pelota) (con la mano)* to throw; *(con el pie)* to kick; *(en béisbol)* to pitch; **lanzó el balón a las gradas (de una patada)** he kicked *o* sent the ball into the stands; **l. el balón fuera** to put the ball out of play; **l. un penalty** to take a penalty; **l. peso** to put the shot
 (f) *(grito, gemido, aullido)* to let out; *(acusación)* to make; *(suspiro)* to heave; *(mirada, sonrisa)* to give; *(beso)* to blow; **l. insultos contra alguien** to insult sb; **el lobo lanzaba aullidos** the wolf was howling
 (g) *(producto, artista, periódico)* to launch; *(disco, película)* to release; **l. una campaña de descrédito contra alguien** to start a campaign to discredit sb
 (h) *Informát (programa)* to launch
 (i) *(en ciclismo)* to lead out
 (j) *(despojar)* to dispossess; *(desalojar)* to evict
 2 lanzarse *vpr* **(a)** *(tirarse)* to throw oneself; **lanzarse en paracaídas desde un avión** to parachute from a plane; **lanzarse a la piscina/al agua** to jump into the pool/water; **lanzarse de cabeza** to dive
 (b) *(abalanzarse)* **los atracadores se lanzaron sobre él** the robbers fell upon him; **los niños se lanzaron sobre la comida** the children fell upon the food; **el toro se lanzó contra** *o* **hacia ellos** the bull charged (at) them; **varios espectadores se lanzaron al campo** a number of spectators ran onto the pitch
 (c) *(empezar)* **era escritora y decidió lanzarse a la política** she was a writer who decided to enter the world of politics; **me lancé a correr calle abajo** I dashed off down the street; **hubo un grito y todos se lanzaron a disparar** there was a shout and everyone suddenly started shooting; **si se confirma la noticia los inversores se lanzarán a vender** if the news is confirmed, investors will not hesitate to start selling
 (d) *(atreverse)* **¿escribir novelas? es fácil, sólo es cuestión de lanzarse** writing novels? that's easy, it's just a question of giving it a go; **después de meses, se lanzó y la invitó a cenar** after several months, he plucked his courage up and asked her out to dinner

Lanzarote 1 *n Mitol* Lancelot
 2 *n (isla)* Lanzarote

lanzatorpedos *nm inv* torpedo tube

lanzazo *nm (golpe)* lance thrust; *(herida)* lance wound

Laos *n* Laos

laosiano, -a 1 *adj* Laotian
 2 *nm,f* Laotian

lapa *nf* **(a)** *(molusco)* limpet **(b)** *Fam (persona)* hanger-on, pest; EXPR **pegarse como una l.** to cling like a leech **(c)** *Col, Ven (roedor)* paca

laparoscopia *nf Med* laparoscopy

laparoscópico, -a *adj Med* laparoscopic

laparoscopio *nm Med* laparoscope

laparotomía *nf Med* laparotomy

La Paz *n* La Paz

lapicera *nf CSur* ballpoint (pen), Biro®; **l. fuente** fountain pen

lapicero *nm* **(a)** *Esp (lápiz)* pencil **(b)** *Chile (estilográfica)* fountain pen **(c)** *CAm, Perú (bolígrafo)* ballpoint (pen), Biro® **(d)** *Am (portaminas) Br* propelling pencil, *US* mechanical pencil

lápida *nf* memorial stone ►► ***l. mortuoria*** tombstone

lapidación *nf* stoning

lapidar *vt* to stone

lapidario, -a 1 *adj* **(a)** *(de lápida)* lapidary **(b)** *(conciso, preciso)* lapidary **(c)** *(de piedras preciosas)* gem-cutting
 2 *nm,f* **(a)** *(de lápidas)* tombstone engraver **(b)** *(de piedras preciosas)* gem-cutter, lapidary

lapilli *nmpl Geol* lapilli

lapislázuli *nm* lapis lazuli

lápiz *nm* pencil; **un dibujo a l.** a pencil drawing ►► *Arg* ***l. de cera*** wax crayon; ***lápices de colores*** coloured pencils, crayons; ***l. de labios*** lipstick; *Urug* ***l. mecánico*** *Br* propelling pencil, *US* mechanical pencil; ***l. de ojos*** eyeliner; *Informát* ***l. óptico*** light pen; *Chile* ***l. de pasta*** *(bolígrafo)* ballpoint pen

lapo, -a *Fam* 1 *adj Ven* (a) *(incauto)* **es muy l.** he's a real sucker *o Br* mug (b) *(provinciano)* **es muy l.** he's a real country bumpkin *o US* hick
2 *nm* (a) *Esp (escupitajo)* spit; **echar un l.** to spit (b) *Ven (incauto)* sucker, *Br* mug (c) *Ven (provinciano)* country bumpkin, *US* hick

lapón, -ona 1 *adj* Lapp
2 *nm,f (persona)* Lapp, Laplander
3 *nm (lengua)* Lapp

Laponia *n* Lapland

lapso *nm* space, interval; **en el l. de unas semanas** in the space of a few weeks ►► ***l. de tiempo*** space of time

lapsus *nm inv* lapse, slip; **tener un l.** to make a slip of the tongue ►► ***l. cálami*** slip of the pen; ***l. linguae*** slip of the tongue

laptop *nm Informát* laptop (computer)

laquear *vt* to lacquer

lar 1 *nm* (a) *(lumbre)* hearth (b) *Mitol* household god
2 **lares** *nmpl (hogar)* hearth and home; **¿qué haces tú por estos lares?** what are you doing in these parts?

larga 1 *nf* (a) **largas** *(luces) Br* full beam, *US* high beam; **dar** *o* **poner las largas** to put one's headlights on *Br* full *o US* high beam (b) *Taurom* = one-handed pass with the "muleta" (c) EXPR **dar largas a algo** to put sth off; **siempre me está dando largas** he's always putting me off
2 **a la larga** *loc adv* in the long run

largada *nf CSur* start *(of race)*; **dar la l.** to start the race, to give the starting signal

largamente *adv* (a) *(mucho tiempo)* for a long time, at length; **la propuesta fue l. debatida** the proposal was discussed at length; **la l. esperada aprobación llegó ayer** the long-awaited approval came through yesterday; **el público ovacionó l. al cantante** the audience gave the singer a lengthy ovation (b) *(cómodamente)* easily, comfortably (c) *(con generosidad)* generously, liberally

> **Falso amigo**: El adverbio inglés **largely** no es la traducción del español **largamente**. En inglés **largely** significa "en gran medida" o "principalmente".

largar [38] 1 *vt* (a) *Fam (dar)* to give; **le largué un bofetón** I smacked him, I gave him a smack; **me largó una patada** she kicked me, she gave me a kick
(b) *Fam (decir)* **nos largó un sermón** she gave us a lecture *o* talking-to; **me largó que no era asunto mío** he snapped that it was none of my business; **le preguntamos sobre la decisión final pero no quiso l. nada** we asked her if a final decision had been taken, but she wasn't giving anything away
(c) *(cuerda)* to pay out; **l. amarras** to cast off; **l. el ancla** to drop anchor
(d) *(soltar) (persona)* to release, to let go; **largaron a los prisioneros** they released the prisoners
(e) *(despedir)* to fire; **l. a un criado** to fire a servant
(f) *RP (olor)* to give off
2 *vi* (a) *Esp Fam (hablar)* to yack (away) (b) *CSur (dar la salida)* to start the race, to give the starting signal; **¡ya largaron!** and they're off!
3 **largarse** *vpr* (a) *Fam (marcharse)* to clear off; **lárgate antes de que lleguen mis padres** clear off *o* get out of here before my parents arrive; **¡me largo!** I'm off!; **se largó a la calle** he took off
(b) *CSur* **largarse a hacer algo** *(empezar a)* to begin to do sth, to start doing sth; **se largó a llorar** she began to cry, she started crying; **se largó a correr** he started running, he broke into a run; **el niño se largó a caminar al año** the baby started walking when he was one year old
(c) *CSur Fam (tirarse)* **se largó de cabeza al agua** she dived headfirst into the water; **se largó un pedo** he farted; **se largó un erupto** she burped

largavistas *nm inv Bol, CSur* binoculars

LARGO, -A 1 *adj* (a) *(en el espacio)* long; **lleva el pelo l.** she has long hair; **un misil de l. alcance** a long-range missile; **un vestido l.** a long dress; **unos pantalones largos** long trousers *o US* pants; **me está** *o* **queda l.** it's too long for me; **vestirse de l.** to wear evening dress
(b) *(en el tiempo)* long; **estuvo enfermo l. tiempo** he was ill for a long time; **los parados de larga duración** the long-term unemployed; **vivió allí largos años** she lived there for many years; **es l. de contar/explicar** it's a long story; **la película se me hizo muy larga** the movie seemed to drag on forever; **la espera fue muy larga** it was a very long wait
(c) *(sobrado)* **media hora larga** a good half hour; **debió de costar un millón l.** it must have cost a million and then some; **tiene setenta años largos** she's well into her seventies
(d) *Fam (alto)* tall; **¡qué tipo más l.!** that guy's really tall!
(e) **a lo l.** *(en espacio)* lengthways; **es más fácil si lo cortas a lo l.** it's easier if you cut it lengthways; **a lo l. de** *(en el tiempo)* throughout; **a lo l. de veinte años nunca había visto algo así** in twenty years I'd never seen such a thing; **recibimos varias llamadas a lo l. del día de ayer** we received several calls throughout yesterday; **el virus se extendió a lo l. y ancho del país** the virus spread throughout the country; **han construido numerosos hoteles a lo l. de la costa** they've built several hotels all along the coast
(f) EXPR *Fam* **ser más l. que un día sin pan** *(de duración)* to go on forever; *(de estatura)* to be a giant; *RP* **ser más l. que esperanza de pobre** to go on forever
(g) *Esp* ***larga duración*** long-life; *CSur, Ecuad* ***larga vida*** long-life
2 *adv* (a) *(largamente)* **un asunto sobre el que hemos hablado l.** a matter that we have discussed at length; **esta huelga va para l.** this strike looks like it's going to be with us for a while yet; EXPR **l. y tendido: habló l. y tendido sobre su último disco** she talked at great length about her latest record; **ha escrito l. y tendido sobre el asunto** he has written extensively on the matter
(b) *Mús* largo
3 *nm* (a) *(longitud)* length; **¿cuánto mide** *o* **tiene de l.?, ¿cómo es de l.?** how long is it?; **tiene dos metros de l.** it's two metres long
(b) *(de piscina)* length; **hacerse tres largos** to swim *o* do three lengths
(c) *Fam (largometraje)* feature
(d) *Mús* largo
4 *interj* go away!; **¡l. de aquí!** get out (of here)!

> **Falso amigo**: El adjetivo inglés **large** no es la traducción del español **largo**. En inglés **large** significa "grande".

largometraje *nm* feature film

larguero *nm* (a) *Constr* main beam (b) *Dep* crossbar

largueza *nf (generosidad)* generosity

larguirucho, -a *adj Fam* lanky

largura *nf* length

laringe *nf* larynx

laríngeo, -a *adj* laryngeal

laringitis *nf inv* laryngitis

laringología *nf Med* laryngology

laringólogo, -a *nm,f Med* laryngologist

laringoscopia *nf Med* laryngoscopy

laringotomía *nf Med* laryngotomy

La Rioja *n* La Rioja

larva *nf* larva

larvado, -a *adj* latent; **un conflicto l.** a latent conflict; **la tensión permanece larvada** the tension remains just under the surface

larval, larvario, -a *adj* larval

las 1 *art ver* **el**
2 *pron ver* **lo**[1]

lasaña *nf* lasagne, lasagna

lasca *nf (de piedra)* chip

lascivamente *adv (comportarse)* lasciviously, lewdly; *(gesticular)* lewdly; *(mirar)* lustfully, lecherously

lascivia *nf (de comportamiento)* lasciviousness, lewdness; *(de gesto)* lewdness; *(de persona, mirada)* lustfulness, lecherousness

lascivo, -a 1 *adj (comportamiento)* lascivious, lewd; *(gesto)* lewd; *(persona, mirada)* lustful, lecherous
2 *nm,f* lascivious *o* lewd person; **es un l.** he's a lecher

láser 1 *adj inv* laser; **rayo l.** laser beam
2 *nm inv* laser ►► ***l. disc*** laser disc

laserterapia *nf* laser therapy

lasitud *nf Literario* lassitude

laso, -a *adj Literario* (a) *(cansado)* weary (b) *(liso)* straight

lástex® *nm* Lastex®

lástima *nf* (a) *(compasión)* pity; **tener** *o* **sentir l. de** to feel sorry for
(b) *(pena)* shame, pity; **¡qué l.!** what a shame *o* pity!; **¿no podrás venir?, ¡l.!** you can't come? what a shame *o* pity!; **fue una l. que no te invitaran** it's a shame *o* pity they didn't invite you; **dar l. a alguien** to make sb feel sad; **da l. ver gente así** it's sad to see people in that state; *Fam* **es tan malo que da l.** he's painfully bad; **me da l. que no pueda venir** I'm sorry I can't come, it's a shame I can't come; **quedarse hecho una l.** to be a sorry *o* pitiful sight

lastimadura *nf Am* graze

lastimar 1 *vt* (**a**) *(físicamente)* to hurt (**b**) *(sentimentalmente)* to hurt, to wound; **ha acabado por l. nuestra relación** it's ended up damaging our relationship
2 **lastimarse** *vpr* to hurt oneself; **se lastimó el tobillo** she hurt her ankle; **se lastimó en una caída** she was hurt in a fall

lastimero, -a *adj* pitiful

lastimosamente *adv* pitifully

lastimoso, -a *adj* (**a**) *(que produce lástima)* pitiful, pathetic (**b**) *(en mal estado)* pitiful; **la casa estaba en un l. estado** the house was in a pitiful *o* terrible state

lastrar 1 *vt* (**a**) *(globo, barco)* to ballast (**b**) *(estorbar)* to hamper
2 *vi RP Fam* to pig out, to stuff one's face

lastre *nm* (**a**) *(peso)* ballast; **soltar l.** to discharge ballast (**b**) *(estorbo)* burden

lata *nf* (**a**) *(envase)* can, *esp Br* tin; *(de bebidas)* can; **una l. de sardinas** a can of sardines; **los garbanzos son de l.** the chickpeas are out of a can; **en l.** canned, *esp Br* tinned
(**b**) *(hojalata)* tin plate; **un juguete hecho de l.** a toy made of tin
(**c**) *Fam (fastidio)* drag; **una l. de libro** a dead boring book; **levantarse tan temprano es una l.** getting up so early is a real pain *o* drag; **¡qué l.!** what a pain *o* drag!; EXPR **dar la l. a alguien** to pester sb; **¡deja ya de dar la l.!** stop going on and on!, give it a rest!
(**d**) *Ven Fam (beso)* French kiss

latazo *nm Esp Fam* drag

latear *vt Andes Fam* to bore stiff

latencia *nf* latency; **período de l.** latent period

latente *adj* (**a**) *(calor, virus)* latent (**b**) *(sentimiento)* latent

lateral 1 *adj* (**a**) *(del lado)* lateral; *(puerta, pared)* side (**b**) *(indirecto)* indirect (**c**) *Ling* lateral
2 *nm* (**a**) *(lado)* side (**b**) *(calle)* side street (**c**) *(de escenario)* **los laterales** the wings (**d**) *Dep* ***l. derecho*** right back; ***l. izquierdo*** left back

lateralmente *adv* laterally, sideways

latero, -a 1 *adj Andes Fam* tiresome
2 *nm,f* (**a**) *Am (hojalatero)* tinsmith (**b**) *Andes Fam (pesado)* pain (in the neck)

látex *nm inv* latex

Latibex *nm Bolsa* Latibex index, = index of Latin American stocks traded in Spain

latido *nm* (**a**) *(del corazón)* beat; **oigo los latidos de su corazón** I can hear her heartbeat (**b**) *(en dedo, herida)* throbbing

latiente *adj (corazón)* beating

latifundio *nm* large rural estate

latifundismo *nm* = system of land tenure characterized by the "latifundio"

latifundista *nmf* large landowner

latigazo *nm* (**a**) *(golpe)* lash; **dar latigazos** to whip; **le dieron diez latigazos** he was given ten lashes (**b**) *(chasquido)* crack (of the whip) (**c**) *Esp Fam (trago)* swig; **darse** *o* **pegarse un l.** to have a swig (**d**) *(dolor)* shooting pain

látigo *nm* (**a**) *(fusta)* whip (**b**) *(en feria)* whip (**c**) *Ecuad, Hond (latigazo)* whiplash (**d**) *Chile (meta)* finishing post

latigueada *nf Hond* flogging, whipping

latiguear *vt Hond (azotar)* to flog, to whip

latiguillo *nm* (**a**) *(muletilla)* verbal tic (**b**) *(expresión manida)* catchphrase (**c**) *(tubo)* hose, tube

latín *nm* Latin; EXPR **saber (mucho) l.** to be sharp, to be on the ball ►► ***l. clásico*** Classical Latin; ***l. macarrónico*** dog Latin; ***l. vulgar*** Vulgar Latin

latinajo *nm Fam Pey* (**a**) *(expresión, término en latín)* **soltó un l.** he came out with some fancy term in Latin; **el l. de la flor es Iris germanica** the fancy Latin name for the flower is *Iris germanica* (**b**) *(latín macarrónico)* dog Latin

latinismo *nm* Latinism

latinista *nmf* Latinist

latinización *nf* Latinization

latinizar [14] *vt* to Latinize

latino, -a 1 *adj* (**a**) *(país, lengua, cultura)* Latin (**b**) *(latinoamericano)* Latin American; **América Latina** Latin America (**c**) *(en Estados Unidos)* Latino
2 *nm,f* (**a**) *(de España, Francia, Italia)* Latin (**b**) *(de Latinoamérica)* Latin American (**c**) *(en Estados Unidos)* Latino

Latinoamérica *n* Latin America

latinoamericano, -a 1 *adj* Latin American
2 *nm,f* Latin American

latir 1 *vi* (**a**) *(corazón)* to beat; *(arteria)* to pulse (**b**) *(percibirse)* to lurk; **en sus declaraciones late un cierto nerviosismo** there is a certain amount of nervousness lurking in his statements
2 *v impersonal Méx, Ven (parecer)* **¿vendrá? – me late que sí** will she come? – I have a feeling she will

latitud *nf* (**a**) *Geog* latitude; **a 10 grados de l. sur** at (a latitude of) 10 degrees south (**b**) *Astron* (celestial) latitude (**c**) **latitudes** *(parajes)* region, area; **por** *o* **en estas latitudes** in this part of the world

lato, -a *adj Formal* (**a**) *(discurso)* extensive, lengthy (**b**) *(sentido)* broad; **en sentido l.** in the broad sense

latón *nm* (**a**) *(material)* brass (**b**) *RP (palangana)* brass washtub

latonero, -a *nm,f Col, Ven* panel beater

latoso, -a *Fam* 1 *adj* tiresome, *US* pesky
2 *nm,f* pain (in the neck)

latrocinio *nm* larceny

laucha *nf CSur* (**a**) *(ratón)* baby *o* small mouse (**b**) *Fam (persona)* **es una l.** he's a tiny little thing

laúd *nm* lute

laudable *adj* praiseworthy

láudano *nm* laudanum

laudatorio, -a *adj* laudatory

laudo *nm Der* **l. (arbitral)** = binding judgement in arbitration

laureado, -a 1 *adj* prize-winning
2 *nm,f* winner, prize-winner

laurear *vt* to honour; **l. a alguien con algo** to honour sb with sth, to award sth to sb

laurel *nm* (**a**) *(planta)* laurel (**b**) *(condimento)* bay leaf; **añada unas hojas de l.** add some bay leaves (**c**) **laureles** *(honores)* laurels; EXPR **dormirse en los laureles** to rest on one's laurels

laurencio *nm Quím* lawrencium

lauro *nm Literario* **lauros** laurels

lava *nf* (**a**) *(volcán)* lava (**b**) *Ven Fam (fastidio)* pain

lavable *adj* washable

lavabo *nm* (**a**) *(objeto) Br* washbasin, *US* washbowl (**b**) *(habitación) Br* lavatory, *US* washroom; **ir al l.** to go to the toilet; **los lavabos** *Br* the toilets, *US* the rest rooms

lavacoches *nmf inv* car washer

lavada *nf* wash; **a esta mesa le hace falta una buena l.** this table needs a good wipe; **me doy una l. y voy** I'll have a quick wash and then I'll go

lavadero *nm* (**a**) *(habitación)* laundry room (**b**) *(público)* washing place (**c**) *(pila)* sink (**d**) *Min* washery (**e**) *RP (lavandería) (en hospital, hotel)* laundry; *(automática)* launderette, *US* Laundromat®

lavado, -a 1 *adj* (**a**) *(color)* faded (**b**) *RP (persona)* pale (**c**) *Ven Fam (descarado)* cheeky
2 *nm* (**a**) *(de manos, ropa)* wash; **dar un l. a algo** to give sth a wash, to wash sth; **un simple l. de manos puede prevenir el contagio** you can avoid infection simply by washing your hands; **yo me encargo del l. de los platos** I'll do the dishes, *Br* I'll do the washing-up; **con un buen l. quedará como nuevo** all it needs is a good wash and it'll be as good as new; **l. y engrase** *(en garaje)* car wash and lubrication; **l. y planchado** *(en tintorería)* washing and pressing ►► *Fig* ***l. de cara*** face-lift; ***l. de cerebro*** brainwashing; **hacer un l. de cerebro a alguien** to brainwash sb; ***l. de coches*** car wash; ***l. de estómago*** stomach pumping; **le hicieron un l. de estómago** she had her stomach pumped; ***l. de imagen*** makeover; ***l. en seco*** dry-cleaning
(**b**) *(de dinero, capitales)* laundering

lavador *nm Guat (lavabo) Br* washbasin, *US* washbowl

lavadora *nf* washing machine; **poner la l.** to do some washing (in the machine); **al volver del viaje puso tres lavadoras** when she came back from the trip she did three loads of washing ►► ***l. secadora*** washer-dryer

lavafrutas *nm inv* = bowl containing water for washing fruit at the table

La Valeta *n* Valletta

lavamanos *nm inv Br* washbasin, *US* washbowl

lavanda *nf* lavender

lavandera *nf* (**a**) *(mujer)* laundress (**b**) *(ave)* wagtail ►► ***l. boyera*** yellow wagtail; ***l. cascadeña*** grey wagtail

lavandería *nf (en hospital, hotel)* laundry; *(automática)* launderette, *US* Laundromat®

lavandero *nm* laundryman

lavandina *nf Arg (lejía)* bleach

lavándula *nf* lavender

lavaojos *nm inv Br* eyebath, *US* eye-cup

lavaplatos 1 *nm inv* (a) *(aparato)* dishwasher (b) *Chile, Col, Méx, Ven (fregadero)* (kitchen) sink (c) *CAm, Ven (detergente)* dishwasher detergent
2 *nmf inv (persona)* dishwasher, washer-up

lavar 1 *vt* (a) *(limpiar) (ropa, coche)* to wash; **l. los platos** to do the dishes, *Br* to do the washing-up; **l. a mano** to hand-wash, to wash by hand; **l. en seco** to dry-clean; **lavado a la piedra** *(vaquero)* stone-washed; *RP* **l. el mate** to spoil the maté *(by brewing it incorrectly)*; EXPR **lavarle el cerebro a alguien** to brainwash sb (b) *(dinero)* to launder (c) *(honor)* to clear; *(ofensa)* to make up for
2 *vi* (a) *(detergente)* to get things clean (b) *(hacer la colada)* to do the washing (c) *(tejido)* to wash; **esta chaqueta lava muy bien** this jacket washes very well (d) **l. y marcar** *(en peluquería)* to shampoo and set
3 **lavarse** *vpr* to wash; **espera un momento, que me estoy lavando** hold on a minute, I'm washing *o* I'm getting washed; **me lavo todas las mañanas** I wash every morning; **lavarse las manos/la cara** to wash one's hands/face; **lavarse los dientes** to brush *o* clean one's teeth; **lavarse una herida** to bathe one's wound

lavarropas *nm inv RP* washing machine

lavaseco *nm Andes* dry-cleaner's

lavativa *nf* (a) *Med* enema (b) *Ven Fam (problema)* pain

lavatorio *nm* (a) *(en misa)* lavabo (b) *(de Jueves Santo)* Maundy (c) *Andes, RP (lavabo) Br* washbasin, *US* washbowl

lavavajillas *nm inv* (a) *(aparato)* dishwasher (b) *(líquido) Br* washing-up liquid, *US* dish soap

laxante 1 *adj* laxative
2 *nm* laxative

laxar *vt (vientre)* to loosen

laxativo, -a 1 *adj* laxative
2 *nm* laxative

laxitud *nf* (a) *(de músculo, cable)* slackness (b) *(de moral)* laxity

laxo, -a *adj* (a) *(músculo, cable)* slack (b) *(moral)* lax

laya *nf Formal Pey* ilk; **gente de esa l.** people of that ilk

lazada *nf* (a) *(nudo)* bow (b) *CSur (al tejer)* slip stitch

lazar *vt* to lasso

lazareto *nm (leprosería)* leper hospital

lazarillo *nm* (a) *(persona)* blind person's guide (b) **(perro) l.** guide dog, *US* seeing-eye dog

Lázaro *n pr* Lazarus

lazo *nm* (a) *(atadura)* bow; **hacer un l.** to tie a bow; **hacerle el l. del zapato a alguien** to tie sb's shoelace ►► ***l. corredizo*** slipknot
(b) *(cinta)* ribbon
(c) *(bucle)* loop
(d) *(trampa)* snare; *(de vaquero)* lasso; **echar el l. a un animal** to lasso an animal; EXPR **echar el l. a alguien** to snare sb; EXPR *Méx Fam* **poner a alguien como l. de cochino** to have a go at sb
(e) **lazos** *(vínculos)* ties, bonds; **los lazos económicos entre los dos países** the economic ties *o* links between the two countries; **los unen fuertes lazos de amistad** they share a strong bond of friendship; **no hay lazos de parentesco entre las víctimas** the victims were not related to each other
(f) *(en arte)* tracery motif
(g) *Col (juego)* skipping; *(cuerda)* skipping rope, *US* jump rope **jugar** *o* **saltar al l.** to skip, *US* to jump rope
(h) *RP* ***l. de amor*** spider plant

LCD *(abrev de* **liquid crystal display**) LCD

LD *nm Am* (*abrev de* **eledé**) LP

Lda. (*abrev de* **licenciada**) graduate *(used as title)*

Ldo. (*abrev de* **licenciado**) graduate *(used as title)*

L-dopa *nf Farm* L-dopa

le *pron personal* (a) *(complemento indirecto) (hombre)* (to) him; *(mujer)* (to) her; *(cosa)* to it; *(usted)* to you; **le expliqué el motivo** I explained the reason to him/her; **le tengo miedo** I'm afraid of him/her; **ya le dije lo que pasaría** *(a usted)* I told you what would happen; **le pegó una patada a la silla** she kicked the chair; **le pegaron un empujón** they pushed him; **se le cayó** she dropped it; **no le agrada viajar en tren** he doesn't like travelling by train; **le será de gran ayuda** it will be very helpful to her; **a esta novela le falta más acción** this novel could do with some more action in it
(b) *Esp (complemento directo) (a él)* him; *(a usted)* you; **le conozco** I know him; **le visitaré mañana** I'll visit you tomorrow; **le atracaron en la calle** he was mugged in the street
(c) *(uso impersonal)* **a todo el mundo le gusta que lo halaguen** everyone likes to be flattered
(d) *ver* **se**

leal 1 *adj* loyal (a to); **se mantuvo l. a sus ideas** he remained true *o* faithful to his beliefs
2 *nmf* loyal supporter (a of)

lealmente *adv* loyally

lealtad *nf* loyalty (a to); **faltar a su l.** to be unfaithful

leandra *nf Esp Fam Anticuado* peseta

leasing ['lisin] (*pl* **leasings**) *nm Fin (sistema)* leasing; *(documento)* lease; **tener algo en l.** to lease sth

lebrato *nm* leveret

lebrel *nm* whippet ►► ***l. irlandés*** Irish wolfhound

lebrero *nm* courser

lección *nf* (a) *(clase)* lesson ►► ***l. magistral*** *Mús* master class; *Educ* = lecture given by eminent academic to mark a special occasion; ***l. de vuelo*** flying lesson
(b) *(en libro de texto)* lesson; **aprenderse la l.** to learn the lesson
(c) *(enseñanza)* lesson; **su humildad fue una l. para todos nosotros** her humility was a lesson to us all; EXPR **aprenderse la l.** to learn one's lesson; EXPR **dar lecciones de algo: ¿quién es él para dar lecciones de honradez?** who does he think he is, giving lectures about honesty?; EXPR **dar a alguien una l.** *(como castigo, advertencia)* to teach sb a lesson; *(como ejemplo)* to give sb a lesson; EXPR **servir de l.** to serve as a lesson; **¡que te sirva de l.!** let that be a lesson to you!

lechada *nf* (a) *(de paredes)* whitewash; *(de argamasa)* grout ►► ***l. de cal*** limewash (b) *(para papel)* pulp

lechal 1 *adj* suckling, sucking; **cordero l.** suckling lamb
2 *nm* suckling lamb

lechar *vt Andes (ordeñar)* to milk

lechazo *nm* (a) *(cordero)* suckling lamb (b) *Ven muy Fam (suerte)* **el examen fue un l.** I was dead lucky with the exam

leche *nf* (a) *(de mujer, hembra)* milk; **l. de cabra/vaca** goat's/cow's milk ►► ***l. condensada*** condensed milk; ***l. descremada*** skimmed milk; ***l. desnatada*** skimmed milk; ***l. entera*** full cream milk, whole milk; ***l. esterilizada*** sterilized milk; ***l. evaporada*** evaporated milk; ***l. frita*** = sweet made from milk and flour fried in batter and cut into cubes; ***l. homogeneizada*** homogenized milk; *Am* ***l. instantánea*** powdered milk; ***l. malteada*** malted milk; ***l. materna*** mother's milk; ***l. maternizada*** *Br* baby milk, *US* formula; ***l. merengada*** = drink made from milk, beaten egg whites, sugar and cinnamon; ***l. pasteurizada*** pasteurized milk; ***l. en polvo*** powdered milk; ***l. semidesnatada*** *Br* semi-skimmed milk, *US* two percent milk; ***l. de soja*** soya milk; ***l. UHT*** UHT milk; ***l. uperisada*** UHT milk
(b) *(de planta)* milk, milky sap ►► ***l. de almendras*** almond milk; ***l. de coco*** coconut milk
(c) *(loción)* ***l. bronceadora*** sun lotion; ***l. hidratante*** moisturizing lotion; ***l. limpiadora*** cleansing milk; ***l. de magnesia*** milk of magnesia
(d) *Esp muy Fam (golpe)* **darse** *o* **meterse una l.** to come a cropper; **se dio** *o* **metió una l. con el coche** he was in a car smash, *US* he was in a car wreck
(e) *Esp muy Fam (bofetada)* **dar** *o* **pegar una l. a alguien** to belt *o* clobber sb; **como no te calles te voy a dar una l.** if you don't shut up I'm going to sock you one; **nos liamos a leches** we beat the crap out of each other
(f) *muy Fam (semen)* come
(g) *muy Fam (humor)* **estar de mala l.** to be in a *Br* bloody *o US* goddamn awful mood; **tener mala l.** *(mala intención)* to be a mean *o* complete bastard
(h) *esp Am muy Fam (suerte)* luck; **tener buena l.** to be *Br* bloody *o US* goddamn lucky, *Br* to be a jammy bastard
(i) EXPR *Esp muy Fam* **echando leches** like a bat out of hell, flat out; **correr/trabajar a toda l.** *(muy rápido)* to run/work like hell; **¡esto es la l.!** *(el colmo)* this is the absolute *Br* bloody *o US* goddamn limit!; **eres la l., ¿por qué no me avisaste antes?** you're *Br* bloody *o US* goddamn unbelievable, why didn't you tell me before?; **su nuevo disco es la l.** *(muy bueno)* her new record is *Br* bloody *o US* goddamn brilliant; *(muy malo)* her new record sucks, *Br* her new record is crap; **¿cuándo/qué/por qué leches...?** when/what/why the hell...?; **¡una l.!** no way!; **¡me cago en la l.!** *Br* bloody hell!, *US* goddamn it!; **ya te he dicho que no, ¡l.!** *Br* Jesus bloody Christ, haven't I already said no?, *US* I've already said no, goddamn it!; **prepara unas paellas de la l.** *Br* she cooks a bloody mean paella, *US* she sure as hell cooks a mean paella; **hace un frío de la l.** it's *Br* bloody *o US* goddamn freezing

lechecillas *nfpl (mollejas)* sweetbreads

lechera *nf* (**a**) *(para transportar)* milk churn; *(para servir)* milk jug (**b**) *muy Fam (coche de policía)* cop car (**c**) *RP (vaca)* dairy cow (**d**) *ver también* **lechero**

lechería *nf* dairy

lechero, -a 1 *adj* (**a**) *(de la leche)* milk, dairy; **producción lechera** milk production; **vaca lechera** dairy cow; EXPR *Am* **parecer** *o* **ser un carro** *o* **tren l.** to stop at every station (**b**) *Bol, CAm, Méx, Perú muy Fam (afortunado) Br* bloody *o US* goddamn lucky (**c**) *Ven Fam (tacaño)* tight, stingy
2 *nm,f (persona)* milkman, *f* milkwoman

lechiguana *nf RP (avispa)* = small honey-producing wasp

lechina *nf Ven* chickenpox

lecho *nm* (**a**) *(cama)* bed; EXPR **ser un l. de rosas** to be a bed of roses ►► ***l. de muerte*** deathbed; **en su l. de muerte** on her deathbed (**b**) *(de río)* bed; *(de mar)* bed, floor (**c**) *(capa)* layer

lechón[1] *nm* (**a**) *(cerdo que mama)* suckling pig (**b**) *(cerdo macho)* boar

lechón[2]**, -ona** *adj Ecuad muy Fam Br* bloody *o US* goddamn lucky

lechona *nf Col (carne)* roast suckling pig

lechosa *nf Carib* papaya

lechoso, -a 1 *adj* (**a**) *(con leche)* milky (**b**) *Ven muy Fam (con suerte) Br* bloody *o US* goddamn lucky
2 *nm Carib* papaya tree

lechucear *vi Fam* (**a**) *RP (husmear)* to snoop around (**b**) *Perú (trabajar de noche)* to work nights (**c**) *Hond (trasnochar)* to stay up late

lechudo, -a *Bol, Ven muy Fam* 1 *adj Br* bloody *o US* goddamn lucky
2 *nm,f* lucky devil *o Br* jammy beggar

lechuga *nf (planta)* lettuce; EXPR *Fam* **estar tan fresco como una l.** *(lozano)* to be as fresh as a daisy; **a sus noventa años está tan fresco como una l.** at ninety he's as fit as a fiddle; EXPR *Fam* **ser más fresco que una l.** *(descarado)* to be a cheeky so-and-so ►► ***l. iceberg*** iceberg lettuce; ***l. de mar*** sea lettuce; ***l. repolluda*** iceberg lettuce; ***l. romana*** cos lettuce

lechuguilla *nf Col, Cuba, Méx* lechuguilla, shindagger

lechuguino *nm Fam* (**a**) *(muchacho)* callow youth (**b**) *(petimetre)* fancy dresser

lechuza *nf* barn owl ►► ***l. campestre*** short-eared owl; ***l. gavilana*** hawk owl

lechuzo *nm Fam (tonto)* idiot, fool

lecitina *nf* lecithin

leco *nm Ven Fam (grito)* shout; **pegar un l.** to shout

lectivo, -a *adj* school; **día l.** school *o* teaching day; **durante el horario l.** during school hours; **el curso se compone de sesenta horas lectivas** the course consists of sixty hours of classes

lector, -ora 1 *adj* reading; **el público l.** the reading public
2 *nm,f* (**a**) *(de libros)* reader; **los lectores de esta revista** our readers *o* readership (**b**) *Esp Educ* language assistant
3 *nm (aparato)* reader ►► *Informát* ***l. de CD-ROM*** CD-ROM drive; ***l. de código de barras*** bar-code scanner *o* reader; *Informát* ***l. de disco compacto*** compact disc player; ***l. de DVD*** DVD player; *Informát* ***l. de noticias*** news reader; *Informát* ***l. óptico*** optical scanner; *Informát* ***l. óptico de caracteres*** optical character reader

lectorado *nm Esp Educ* = post of language assistant; **hacer un l.** to work as a language assistant

lectura *nf* (**a**) *(de libro, texto)* reading; **dar l. a algo** to read sth out loud
(**b**) *Educ (de tesis) Br* viva (voce), *US* defense
(**c**) *(escrito)* reading (matter); **siempre voy de vacaciones con mucha l.** I always take plenty to read on *Br* holiday *o US* vacation
(**d**) *(interpretación)* reading, interpretation; **mi l. de la ley es completamente diferente** my reading *o* interpretation of the law is completely different; **hizo una l. de la novela en clave política** she gave a political reading *o* interpretation of the novel
(**e**) *(de contador)* reading
(**f**) *Informát* read-out; *(de datos)* scanning

LED *nm Elec (abrev de* **light-emitting diode***)* LED

leer [37] 1 *vt* (**a**) *(libro)* to read; **leo el francés, pero no lo hablo** I can read French, but I can't speak it; **l. el pensamiento a alguien** to read sb's mind; **l. la mano a alguien** to read sb's palm; **l. los labios a alguien** to read sb's lips; **todavía no sabe l. la hora** he still hasn't learned to tell the time (**b**) *(tesis)* **l. la tesis** *Br* ≃ to have one's viva, *US* ≃ to defend one's dissertation (**c**) *Informát* to read
2 *vi* to read; **l. en alto** to read aloud; **l. de corrido** to read fluently; EXPR **l. entre líneas** to read between the lines

lefa *nf Esp muy Fam* come

legación *nf* legation ►► ***l. diplomática*** legation

legado[1] *nm* (**a**) *(herencia)* legacy; **como l. le dejó un montón de deudas** all she left him was a mountain of debts; **una ciudad con un gran l. histórico** a city steeped in history (**b**) *(representante) (cargo)* legation; *(persona)* legate

legado[2] *nm* (**a**) *(persona)* legate ►► ***l. pontificio*** papal legate (**b**) *(cargo)* legation

legajador *nm Col* folder

legajar *vt Chile, Col, Hond* to file

legajo *nm* file

legal *adj* (**a**) *(conforme a la ley)* legal; **su actuación no tiene base l. alguna** his actions have no legal basis; **no cumple los requisitos legales** it doesn't meet the legal requirements; **una moneda de curso l.** a currency which is legal tender
(**b**) *(relativo a la ley)* legal; **asesoramiento l.** legal advice; **una batalla l.** a legal battle
(**c**) *(forense)* forensic; **medicina l.** legal medicine
(**d**) *Esp (terrorista, comando)* with no criminal record; **detuvieron a tres terroristas legales** they arrested three terrorists who had never previously been charged
(**e**) *Esp Fam (de confianza)* honest, decent; **es un tío muy l.** he's a great guy *o Br* bloke

legalidad *nf* (**a**) *(conjunto de leyes)* legislation, law; **según la l. vigente** according to current legislation, as the law stands at the moment; **dentro de la l.** within the law, legal (**b**) *(cualidad de legal)* legality, lawfulness; **la l. de una medida** the legality *o* lawfulness of a measure

legalismo *nm* fine legal point, legalism

legalista 1 *adj* legalistic
2 *nmf* legalist

legalización *nf* (**a**) *(de droga, partido, sindicato)* legalization (**b**) *(de documento)* (certificate of) authentication

legalizar [14] *vt* (**a**) *(droga, partido, sindicato)* to legalize (**b**) *(documento)* to authenticate

legalmente *adv* legally, lawfully

légamo *nm* (**a**) *(lodo)* ooze, slime (**b**) *(arcilla)* loam

legaña, *Col, RP, Ven* **lagaña** *nf* sleep *(in the eyes)*; **tienes legañas** you've got sleep in your eyes

legañoso, -a *adj (ojos)* full of sleep; **un niño sucio y l. pedía limosna** a dirty, bleary-eyed child was begging

legar [38] *vt* (**a**) *(dejar en herencia)* to bequeath; **un gusto por la ópera legado por sus padres** a liking of opera inherited from her parents (**b**) *(delegar)* to delegate; **l. algo en alguien** to delegate sth to sb

legatario, -a *nm,f Der* legatee ►► ***l. universal*** general legatee

legendario, -a *adj* (**a**) *(de la leyenda)* legendary (**b**) *(muy famoso)* legendary

leggings ['leɣins] *nm inv* leggings

legibilidad *nf* legibility

legible *adj* legible

legión *nf* (**a**) *(unidad militar)* legion ►► ***la l. extranjera*** the Foreign Legion; ***L. de Honor*** Legion of Honour (**b**) *(gran cantidad)* **tiene una l. de admiradores** she has legions of admirers; **sus detractores son l.** he has many detractors

legionario, -a 1 *adj* legionary
2 *nm* (**a**) *Hist (en Roma)* legionary (**b**) *(en la actualidad)* legionnaire

legionella [leχio'nela] *nf* (**a**) *(enfermedad)* Legionnaires' Disease (**b**) *(bacteria)* legionella bacterium

legionelosis *nf inv (enfermedad)* Legionnaires' Disease

legislación *nf* (**a**) *(leyes)* legislation; **l. antiterrorista** antiterrorism laws; **la l. española en la materia es confusa** Spanish law *o* legislation is unclear on the matter (**b**) *(ciencia)* law

legislador, -ora 1 *adj* legislative
2 *nm,f* legislator

legislar *vi* to legislate

legislativas *nfpl (elecciones)* parliamentary elections

legislativo, -a *adj* legislative

legislatura *nf* (**a**) *(período)* term of office (**b**) *Am (congreso)* legislative body

legista *nmf (jurista)* legist, specialist in law

legitimación *nf* (**a**) *(de comportamiento, gobierno)* legitimation (**b**) *(de documento, firma)* authentication (**c**) *(de hijo)* legitimization

legítimamente *adv* legitimately, rightfully

legitimar *vt* (**a**) *(comportamiento, gobierno)* to legitimize (**b**) *(documento, firma)* to authenticate (**c**) *(hijo)* to legitimize

legitimidad *nf* legitimacy

legitimismo *nm Pol* legitimism

legitimista *nmf Pol* legitimist

legítimo, -a *adj* (**a**) *(conforme a derecho)* lawful; *(hijo)* legitimate; *(esposo)* lawful; *(sucesor)* rightful (**b**) *(lícito, justificado)* legitimate; **actuar en legítima defensa** to act in self-defence (**c**) *(auténtico)* real, genuine

lego, -a 1 *adj* (**a**) *(profano, laico)* lay (**b**) *(ignorante)* ignorant; **ser l. en** to know nothing about

2 *nm,f* (**a**) *(laico)* layman, *f* laywoman (**b**) *(en convento)* lay brother, *f* lay sister (**c**) *(ignorante)* ignorant person; **es un l. en la materia** he knows nothing about the subject

legón *nm* small hoe

legra *nf Med (para matriz)* curette; *(para hueso)* raspatory

legrado *nm Med (de matriz)* curettage; *(de hueso)* scraping

legrar *vt Med (matriz)* to curette; *(hueso)* to scrape

legua *nf* league; EXPR *Fam* **verse a la l.** to stand out a mile; EXPR *Fam* **se nota a la l.** you can tell it a mile away ►► ***l. marina*** marine league

leguaje *nm CAm, Méx* distance in leagues

leguleyo, -a *nm,f Pey* bad lawyer

legumbre *nf* (**a**) *(garbanzo, lenteja)* pulse; **legumbres secas** (dried) pulses; **legumbres verdes** green vegetables (**b**) *(hortaliza)* vegetable

leguminosa 1 *nf* leguminous plant

2 leguminosas *nfpl (familia) Leguminosae*; **de la familia de las leguminosas** of the family *Leguminosae*

leguminoso, -a *adj* leguminous

lehendakari [lenda'kari] *nm* = president of the autonomous Basque government

leída *nf* read; **dar una l. a algo** to read sth

leído, -a *adj* (**a**) *(obra)* **muy/poco l.** much/little read (**b**) *(persona)* well-read

leísmo *nm Gram* = use of "le" as direct object instead of "lo", characteristic of certain regions in Spain, considered acceptable when referring to male persons, but not otherwise (see box)

leísta 1 *adj* prone to "leísmo"

2 *nmf* = person prone to "leísmo"

leitmotiv [leitmo'tif] (*pl* **leitmotivs**) *nm* leitmotif

lejanía *nf* (**a**) *(condición de lejano)* distance (**b**) *(lugar lejano)* **en la l.** in the distance

lejano, -a *adj* (**a**) *(en el espacio)* distant; **un país l.** a distant land *o* country ►► ***el Lejano Oeste*** the Far West; ***el Lejano Oriente*** the Far East (**b**) *(en el tiempo)* **su boda queda ya muy lejana** her wedding is still a long way off; **no está l. el día de su triunfo** her hour of glory is not far off (**c**) *(familiar)* distant

lejía *nf* bleach

LEJOS *adv* (**a**) *(en el espacio)* far (away); **¿está** *o* **queda l.?** is it far?; **eso queda muy l.** that's a long way away; **me hace falta un taxi porque voy bastante l.** I'll need to take a taxi because I'm going quite a long way; **vivo l. del centro de la ciudad** I live a long way from the city centre; **desde aquí l. no se le oye** you can't hear him from over here; **el castillo está allá l.** the castle is right over there; **no veo bien de l.** I'm short-sighted; **a lo l.** in the distance; **de** *o* **desde l.** from a distance; *Hum & Literario* **l. del mundanal ruido** far from the madding crowd

(**b**) *(en el pasado)* long ago; **eso queda ya l.** that happened a long time ago; **la pasión por el campo le viene de l.** her love of the countryside goes back a long way; **esta situación viene de l.** this situation has a history to it

(**c**) *(en el futuro)* **la fecha del estreno aún está** *o* **queda l.** the première is still a long way off, there's still a long while to go until the première

(**d**) *RP (con diferencia)* **ganaron l.** they won easily *o* by a mile; **es, l. , el más rápido** he's by far *o* easily the fastest

(**e**) EXPR **no andar l.: no acertó pero tampoco andaba l.** she didn't get it right, but she wasn't far off; **de l.** by far, easily; **es, de l., el más rápido** he's by far *o* easily the fastest; **ir demasiado l.** to go too far; **sin ir más l.: este año, sin ir más l., ha habido dos terremotos** this year alone there have been two earthquakes; **algo que sí sucede, sin ir más l., en India** something which does happen in India, to name but one example; **l. de** far from; **l. de mejorar...** far from getting better...; **l. estábamos de sospechar lo que estaba pasando** we didn't have the faintest suspicion of what was going on; **llegará l.** she'll go far; *Fam* **ni de l.: no es el mejor ni de l.** he's nowhere near *o* nothing like the best; **no se le parece ni de l.** she's nothing like her, she doesn't look anything like her; *RP* **por l.: es, por l., el más rápido** he's by far *o* easily the fastest; **¿cuál te gusta más? – el alto, por l.** which one do you like best? – the tall one, it's no contest

---

lelo, -a 1 *adj* stupid, slow

2 *nm,f* idiot

lema *nm* (**a**) *(norma)* motto (**b**) *(eslogan político, publicitario)* slogan (**c**) *(de diccionario)* headword (**d**) *Esp (pseudónimo)* pseudonym (**e**) *Urug Antes (partido político)* (political) party

Leman *nm* **el lago L.** Lake Geneva

lemario *nm Ling* headword list

LEÍSMO

According to the official canons of Spanish grammar, the personal pronoun **le** should be regarded as an indirect object pronoun (as in the examples given at **(a)** in the entry for **le**). However, the use of **le** as a direct object (eg **quiero a Carlos ► le quiero**) is typical of the Spanish spoken in central Spain, and as a consequence this usage is widely encountered in the Spanish media (see the examples given at **(b)**). This usage is referred to as **leísmo**.

The Spanish Academy considers that the use of **le** as a direct object pronoun is acceptable when it refers to a man or boy, but not to a female person (**quiero a mi madre ► le quiero**) or an inanimate masculine noun (**quiero un coche más grande ► le quiero más grande**). Examples of this last use are however common in the Spanish of Castile, where the tendency is for object pronouns to be marked for the gender of the nouns they stand for (**lo** for inanimate masculine nouns, **la** for inanimate feminine nouns and female persons, and **le** for male persons), rather than for their syntactic roles (ie whether they are direct or indirect objects).
The use of **le** as a direct object pronoun for male persons is also found in Latin America, particularly Mexico and the Southern Cone countries (Argentina, Uruguay and Chile), and especially when the subject of the clause is inanimate:

le asustó el ruido
the noise frightened him
but:
lo asusté al tocarle el hombro de espaldas
I gave him a fright when I touched him on the shoulder from behind

It should be noted that many would regard the **le** in the first of these examples as standing for an indirect object, and thus conforming to the general rule.

In addition, **le** is also often used when preceded by **se**:

un escritor al que se le quiere mucho en nuestro país
a writer who is much-loved in our country

últimamente se le ha visto con una modelo del brazo
recently he's been seen with a model on his arm

lemming ['lemin] (*pl* **lemmings**) *nm* lemming

lempira *nm* lempira

lémur *nm* lemur

lencería *nf* (**a**) *(ropa interior)* lingerie; **departamento de l.** lingerie department ▸▸ ***l. fina*** fine lingerie; ***l. íntima*** lingerie (**b**) *(tienda)* lingerie shop (**c**) *(ropa blanca)* linen

lendrera *nf* fine-tooth comb *(for removing lice)*

lengua *nf* (**a**) *(órgano)* tongue; **sacarle la l. a alguien** to stick one's tongue out at sb; **se le trabó la l.** she stumbled over her words; *también Fig* **morderse la l.** to bite one's tongue; EXPR *Fam* **darle a la l.** to chatter; EXPR *Fam* **irse de la l.**, *RP* **aflojar** *o* **soltar la l.** to let the cat out of the bag; EXPR *Fam* **ir/llegar con la l. fuera** to go along/arrive puffing and panting; EXPR *Fam* **ser largo de l., tener la l. muy larga** to be a gossip; **las malas lenguas dicen que...** according to the gossip...; EXPR **lo tengo en la punta de la l.** I've got it on the tip of my tongue; EXPR *Fam* **¿(se) te ha comido la l. el gato?**, *Am* **¿te comieron la l. los ratones?** has the cat got your tongue?; EXPR *Fam* **tirar a alguien de la l.** to draw sb out ▸▸ ***l. de buey*** *(planta)* bugloss; ***l. de ciervo*** *(planta)* hart's-tongue fern; ***l. de fuego*** tongue of flame; *Esp* ***l. de gato*** *(de chocolate)* chocolate finger, langue de chat; *Fig* ***l. de víbora*** malicious tongue; *Fig* ***l. viperina*** malicious tongue
(**b**) *(de tierra)* tongue ▸▸ *Geol* ***l. glaciar*** glacier tongue
(**c**) *(idioma, lenguaje)* language ▸▸ ***l. culta*** educated speech; ***l. de destino*** target language; ***l. escrita*** written language; ***l. estándar*** standard language; ***l. franca*** lingua franca; ***l. hablada*** spoken language; ***l. de llegada*** target language; ***l. materna*** mother tongue; **mi l. materna no es el español** I'm not a native speaker of Spanish; ***l. meta*** target language; ***lenguas modernas*** modern languages; ***l. muerta*** dead language; ***l. normativa*** standard language; ***l. de oc*** langue d'oc; ***l. de oíl*** langue d'oœl; ***l. romance*** Romance language; ***l. románica*** Romance language; ***l. viva*** living language; ***l. vulgar*** vulgar *o* coarse language
(**d**) *Esp (asignatura)* Spanish (language)

lenguado *nm* sole

lenguaje *nm* language; **sólo entienden el l. de la violencia** violence is the only language they understand ▸▸ *Informát* ***l. de alto nivel*** high-level language; *Informát* ***l. de autor*** authoring language; *Informát* ***l. de bajo nivel*** low-level language; ***l. cifrado*** code; ***l. coloquial*** colloquial language; *Informát* ***l. comando*** command language; *Informát* ***l. de comandos*** command language; ***l. comercial*** business language; ***l. corporal*** body language; *Informát* ***l. ensamblador*** assembly language; ***l. gestual*** gestures; *Informát* ***l. máquina*** machine language; *Informát* ***l. de programación*** programming language; ***l. de señas*** sign language; ***l. por signos*** sign language; ***l. de los sordomudos*** sign language

lenguaraz *adj* (**a**) *(malhablado)* foul-mouthed (**b**) *(charlatán)* talkative

lengüeta[1] *nf* (**a**) *(de instrumento musical)* tongue (**b**) *(de zapato)* tongue (**c**) *(de disquete)* sliding shield

lengüeta[2] *nmf RP Fam (charlatán)* chatterbox

lengüetazo *nm*, **lengüetada** *nf* lick; **dar un l. a algo** to lick sth

lengüetear *vi Carib, RP Fam (hablar)* to chatter

lengüetero, -a *adj Ven Fam* gossipy

lengüón, -ona *Andes, CAm, Méx Fam* **1** *adj* talkative
2 *nm,f* chatterbox

lenidad *nf Formal* leniency

lenificar *vt* to soothe, to alleviate

Leningrado *n Antes* Leningrad

leninismo *nm* Leninism

leninista **1** *adj* Leninist
2 *nmf* Leninist

lenitivo, -a **1** *adj* (**a**) *(físicamente)* soothing, lenitive (**b**) *(moralmente)* soothing
2 *nm* (**a**) *(físico)* lenitive (**b**) *(moral)* balm

lenocinio *nm Formal* procuring, pimping; **casa de l.** house of ill repute

lentamente *adv* slowly

lente **1** *nf* lens ▸▸ ***l. de aumento*** magnifying glass; ***lentes bifocales*** bifocals; *Esp* ***l. de contacto*** contact lens; *Esp* ***lentes de contacto blandas*** soft lenses; *Esp* ***lentes de contacto duras*** hard lenses; ***lentes progresivas*** varifocals
2 lentes *nmpl Am* glasses ▸▸ ***lentes de aumento*** prescription glasses; ***lentes bifocales*** bifocals; ***lentes de contacto*** contact lenses; ***lentes de contacto blandos*** soft lenses; ***lentes de contacto duros*** hard lenses; ***lentes negros*** dark glasses; ***lentes oscuros*** dark glasses; ***lentes de sol*** sunglasses

lenteja *nf* lentil; EXPR *Esp Fam* **son lentejas, si las quieres las tomas y si no, las dejas** if you don't like it you'll have to lump it

lentejuela *nf* sequin; **un vestido de lentejuelas** a sequined dress

lenticular *adj* lenticular; *Dep* **rueda l.** disc wheel

lentilla *nf Esp* contact lens; **lentillas** contact lenses, contacts ▸▸ ***lentillas blandas*** soft lenses; ***lentillas duras*** hard lenses

lentitud *nf* slowness; **con l.** slowly

lento, -a **1** *adj* (**a**) *(pausado)* slow; *(muerte, agonía)* lingering, long-drawn-out; **es muy l. trabajando** he's a very slow worker; **una película lenta** a slow film; **¡qué lentas pasan las horas!** time is passing so slowly!; **l., pero seguro** slow but sure; EXPR *Fam Hum* **ser más l. que un desfile de cojos** *o* **que el caballo del malo** to be a real *Br* slowcoach *o US* slowpoke
(**b**) *(con poca intensidad)* **cocer algo a fuego l.** to cook over a low heat
(**c**) *Mús* lento
2 *nm Mús* lento
3 *adv* (**a**) *(pausadamente)* slowly; **trabaja muy l.** he's a very slow worker; **l., pero seguro** slowly but surely (**b**) *Mús* lento

leña *nf* (**a**) *(madera)* firewood; **cortar l.** to chop firewood; **l. menuda** kindling; EXPR **añadir** *o* **echar l. al fuego** to add fuel to the flames *o* fire; EXPR **hacer l. del árbol caído** to turn somebody else's misfortune to one's advantage; EXPR **llevar l. al monte** to make a pointless effort, *Br* to carry coals to Newcastle
(**b**) *Fam (golpes)* **dar l. a alguien** to beat sb up; **es un futbolista que da mucha l.** he's a very dirty soccer player *o Br* footballer; **los gamberros repartieron l. por todas partes** the hooligans beat up anyone who crossed their path; **hubo mucha l. en la final** the final was really dirty

leñador, -ora *nm,f* woodcutter

leñazo *nm Fam* (**a**) *(bofetada)* whack; **dar un l. a alguien** to whack sb (**b**) *(golpe)* **se metió un l. contra una farola** *(en vehículo)* she smashed into a lamppost; *(caminando)* she walked smack into a lamppost; **me di un l. contra el techo** I banged my head on the ceiling (**c**) *RP, Ven Fam (no físico)* blow; **con la cuenta de la luz, nunca se sabe cuánto va a ser el l.** you never know how much they're going to hit you for with the electricity bill

leñe *interj Esp Fam Euf* for heaven's sake!; **ya te he dicho que no, ¡l.!** for heaven's sake, I've already said no!

leñera *nf* woodshed

leñero, -a *Fam Dep* **1** *adj* dirty
2 *nm,f* dirty player

leño *nm* (**a**) *(de madera)* log; EXPR *Fam* **dormir como un l.** to sleep like a log (**b**) *Fam (persona)* blockhead

leñoso, -a *adj* woody

Leo **1** *adj inv* Leo; *Esp* **ser L.** to be (a) Leo
2 *nmf inv (persona)* Leo; *Esp* **los L. son...** Leos are...
3 *nm (signo del zodiaco)* Leo; *Am* **los de L. son...** Leos are...

león, -ona *nm,f* (**a**) *(africano) (macho)* lion; *(hembra)* lioness; PROV **no es tan fiero el l. como lo pintan** he/it/*etc* is not as bad as he/it/*etc* is made out to be (**b**) *Am (puma)* puma (**c**) ***l. marino*** sea lion (**d**) *Fam (valiente)* fighter

leonado, -a *adj* tawny

leonera *nf* (**a**) *(jaula)* lion's cage (**b**) *Esp Fam (cuarto desordenado)* **este cuarto es una l.** this room is in a real state, *Br* this room is a tip

leonés, -esa **1** *adj* of/from León *(Spain)*
2 *nm,f* person from León *(Spain)*

leonino, -a **1** *adj* (**a**) *(rostro, aspecto)* leonine (**b**) *(contrato, condiciones)* one-sided, unfair (**c**) *Am (de Leo)* Leo; **ser l.** to be (a) Leo
2 *nm,f Am* Leo; **los leoninos son...** Leos are...

leontina *nf* watch chain

leopardo *nm* leopard

leotardos *nmpl* (**a**) *Esp (medias)* thick tights (**b**) *(de gimnasta)* leotard

Lepe *n pr* EXPR **saber más que L.** to be very clever *o* astute

leperada *nf CAm, Méx Fam* (**a**) *(expresión)* coarse *o* vulgar remark (**b**) *(acción)* coarse *o* vulgar thing to do

lépero, -a *Fam* **1** *adj* (**a**) *CAm, Méx (vulgar)* coarse, vulgar (**b**) *Cuba (ladino)* smart, crafty
2 *nm,f CAm, Méx (grosero)* oaf

lepidóptero *Zool* 1 *nm* lepidopteran
2 **lepidópteros** *nmpl (orden) Lepidoptera*; **del orden de los lepidópteros** of the order *Lepidoptera*

leporino *adj* **labio l.** harelip

lepra *nf* leprosy

leprosario *nm Am* leper colony

leprosería *nf* leper colony

leproso, -a 1 *adj* leprous
2 *nm,f* leper

leptón *nm Fís* lepton

lerdear *vi CAm* to lumber

lerdo, -a *Fam* 1 *adj* (a) *(idiota)* dim, slow-witted (b) *(torpe)* useless, hopeless
2 *nm,f* (a) *(idiota)* fool, idiot (b) *(torpe)* useless idiot

leridano, -a 1 *adj* of/from Lérida *(Spain)*
2 *nm,f* person from Lérida *(Spain)*

les *pron personal pl* (a) *(complemento indirecto) (ellos)* (to) them; *(ustedes)* (to) you; **l. expliqué el motivo** I explained the reason to them; **l. tengo miedo** *(a ellos)* I'm afraid of them; **ya l. dije lo que pasaría** *(a ustedes)* I told you what would happen; **se l. olvidó** they forgot; **l. será de gran ayuda** it will be a great help to them; **a estos niños l. falta salir más** these children could do with getting out more
(b) *Esp (complemento directo) (ellos)* them; *(ustedes)* you; **l. conozco** I know them; **l. visitaré mañana** I'll visit you tomorrow; **l. atracaron en la calle** they were mugged in the street
(c) *ver* **se**

lesbiana *nf* lesbian

lesbianismo *nm* lesbianism

lesbiano, -a, lésbico, -a *adj* lesbian

lesear *vi Chile Fam* (a) *(hacer tonterías)* to clown around (b) *(decir tonterías)* to talk nonsense *o Br* rubbish (c) *(perder el tiempo)* to fart around

leseras *nfpl Chile Fam (tonterías)* nonsense, *Br* rubbish

lesión *nf* (a) *(daño físico)* injury; **varios pasajeros sufrieron lesiones de diversa consideración** passengers suffered varying degrees of injury; **l. de columna/craneal** spinal/head injury; *Der* **lesiones graves** grievous bodily harm (b) *(perjuicio)* damage, harm

lesionado, -a 1 *adj* injured
2 *nm,f* injured person; **llegan a la final con varios lesionados** they will have a number of players out with injury for the final, a number of players will miss the final through injury

lesionar 1 *vt* (a) *(físicamente)* to injure (b) *(perjudicar)* to damage, to harm; **el acuerdo lesiona los intereses de la empresa** the agreement is harmful to the company's interests
2 **lesionarse** *vpr* to injure oneself; **se lesionó un hombro** she injured her shoulder

lesivo, -a *adj Formal* damaging, harmful; **una sustancia lesiva para la salud** a substance which can damage your health

leso, -a *adj* (a) *Formal* **crimen de lesa humanidad** crime against humanity; **crimen de lesa patria** high treason; **delito de lesa majestad** treason, lese-majesty (b) *Andes Fam (tonto)* stupid, dumb

Lesoto *n* Lesotho

let *(pl* **lets**) *nm (en tenis)* let

letal *adj* lethal

letalidad *nf* lethality, lethal nature

letanía *nf* (a) *Rel* litany (b) *(retahíla)* litany; **una l. de quejas** a litany of complaints

letárgico, -a *adj* (a) *Med* lethargic (b) *Zool* hibernating (c) *(aburrido)* lethargic

letargo *nm* (a) *Med* lethargy; **este medicamento produce l.** this medicine makes you feel lethargic (b) *(hibernación)* hibernation (c) *(inactividad)* lethargy; **el sector continúa en un estado de l.** the sector has remained sluggish

letón, -ona 1 *adj* Latvian
2 *nm,f (persona)* Latvian
3 *nm (lengua)* Latvian

Letonia *n* Latvia

letra *nf* (a) *(signo)* letter ►► ***l. doble*** double letter
(b) *(escritura, caligrafía)* handwriting; **escribe la carta con buena l.** write the letter in neat handwriting; **no entiendo su l.** I can't read her writing *o* handwriting; **mandar cuatro letras a alguien** to drop sb a line; PROV **la l. con sangre entra** spare the rod and spoil the child ►► *Am* ***l. chica*** small print; ***l. pequeña*** small print
(c) *(en imprenta)* type, typeface ►► ***l. bastardilla*** italic type, italics; ***l. capitular*** drop cap; ***l. cursiva*** italic type, italics; ***l. de imprenta*** *(impresa)* print; *(en formulario)* block capitals; **escriba en l. de imprenta** please write in block capitals; ***l. itálica*** italic type, italics; ***l. mayúscula*** capital letter, *Espec* upper-case letter; **en letra(s) mayúscula(s)** in capitals *o* capital letters, *Espec* in upper case; ***l. minúscula*** small letter, *Espec* lower-case letter; **en letra(s) minúscula(s)** in small letters, *Espec* in lower case; ***l. de molde*** *(impresa)* print; *(en formulario)* block capitals; ***l. muerta*** dead letter; ***l. negrita*** bold (face); ***l. redonda*** roman type; ***l. redondilla*** roman type; ***l. versalita*** small capital
(d) *(texto de canción)* lyrics
(e) *Com* **l. (de cambio)** bill of exchange; **girar una l.** to draw a bill of exchange; **protestar una l.** to protest a bill ►► ***l. avalada*** guaranteed bill of exchange; ***l. de cambio a la vista*** sight bill; ***l. del Tesoro*** treasury bill
(f) *(sentido)* literal meaning; **nos atuvimos a la l. del contrato** we abided by the contract word for word; **seguir instrucciones al pie de la l.** to follow instructions to the letter
(g) *Educ* **letras** arts; **soy de letras** I studied arts; **una asignatura de letras** an arts subject ►► ***letras mixtas*** = secondary school course comprising mainly arts subjects but including some science subjects; ***letras puras*** = secondary school course comprising arts subjects only

letrado, -a 1 *adj* (a) *(culto)* learned (b) *(del abogado)* **asistencia letrada** legal advice
2 *nm,f* lawyer ►► ***l. de oficio*** legal aid lawyer

letrero *nm* sign ►► ***l. luminoso*** illuminated sign; ***l. de neón*** neon sign

letrina *nf* latrine

letrista *nmf* lyricist

leu *nm* leu

leucemia *nf Med* leukaemia

leucocito *nm Anat Br* leucocyte, *US* leukocyte

leucoma *nm Med* leucoma

leucorrea *nf Med Br* leucorrhoea, *US* leukorrhea

leudar *vt* to leaven

lev *nm* lev

leva *nf* (a) *Mil* levy (b) *Náut* weighing anchor; **la l. de la flota** the departure of the fleet (c) *Tec* cam

levadizo, -a *adj* **puente l.** drawbridge

levadura *nf* yeast, leaven ►► ***l. de cerveza*** brewer's yeast; ***l. de panadero*** fresh *o* baker's yeast; *Esp* ***l. en polvo*** baking powder

levantacristales *nm inv Arg* electric window

levantada *nf Andes, RP Fam* **la l. siempre es difícil** it's always hard to drag yourself out of bed

levantado, -a *adj* up; **pasamos toda la noche levantados** we were up all night

levantador[1]**, -ora** *nm,f Dep* ***l. de pesas*** weightlifter

levantador[2]**, -ora** *Ven Fam* 1 *adj* (a) *(atractivo)* gorgeous (b) *(conquistador)* **ser l.** to be a womanizer; **ser levantadora** to be a man-eater
2 *nm,f (conquistador) (hombre)* womanizer; *(mujer)* man-eater

levantadora *nf Col* dressing gown

levantamiento *nm* (a) *(elevación)* raising; **el juez ordenó el l. del cadáver** the judge ordered the body to be removed ►► *Dep* ***l. de pesas*** weightlifting (b) *Geol* uplift, upheaval (c) *(sublevación)* uprising; **el l. de los militares contra el gobierno** the military uprising against the government (d) *(supresión)* lifting, removal; **el l. de un embargo** the lifting of an embargo (e) *(en topografía)* survey

LEVANTAR 1 *vt* (a) *(alzar, elevar)* to raise; *(objeto pesado, capó, trampilla)* to lift (up); *(persiana)* to pull up; **l. el telón** to raise the curtain; **el que quiera venir conmigo que levante la mano** anyone who wants to come with me should put their hand up; **levanta la tapa de la olla y verás qué bien huele** lift the lid off the pot and you'll see how good it smells; **l. algo del suelo** to pick sth up off the ground; **l. a alguien del suelo** to help sb up off the ground; **levantó al bebé en alto** she lifted the baby up in the air; **el juez ordenó l. el cadáver** the judge ordered the body to be removed; **los perros levantaron el zorro** the dogs flushed out the fox; **levantaba polvo al barrer** she was raising clouds of dust as she swept; **l. la vista** *o* **mirada** to look up; **l. la voz** to raise one's voice; EXPR **no ha conseguido l. cabeza** he's still not back to his old self
(b) *(de la cama)* **l. a alguien de la cama** to get sb out of bed; **¿no te habré levantado?** I hope I didn't wake *o* get you up
(c) *(enderezar)* **l. algo** to stand sth upright; **levanta la papelera, que se ha vuelto a caer** stand the wastepaper basket up, it's fallen over again

(**d**) *(construir) (edificio, muro)* to build, to construct; *(estatua, monumento)* to put up, to erect; **de la nada logró l. un inmenso imperio empresarial** she managed to build a huge business empire from nothing

(**e**) *(quitar) (pintura, venda, tapa)* to remove

(**f**) *(retirar) (campamento)* to strike; *(tienda de campaña, tenderete)* to take down; *(mantel)* to take off; EXPR *RP Fam* **l. (el) campamento** to hit the road, to make tracks

(**g**) *(causar) (protestas, polémica, rumores)* to give rise to; **me levanta dolor de cabeza** it makes my head ache; **esto levantó las sospechas de la policía** this aroused the suspicions of the police

(**h**) *(poner fin a) (embargo, prohibición)* to lift; *(asedio)* to raise; **l. el castigo a alguien** to let sb off; **levantaron el embargo a la isla** they lifted the embargo on the island; **el presidente levantó la sesión** *(terminarla)* the chairman brought the meeting to an end; *(aplazarla)* the chairman adjourned the meeting; **si no hay más preguntas, se levanta la sesión** *(en reunión)* if there are no more questions, that ends the meeting

(**i**) *(realizar) (atestado, plano, mapa)* to draw up; **el notario levantó acta del resultado del sorteo** the notary recorded the result of the draw; **l. las actas** *(de una reunión)* to take the minutes

(**j**) *(dar un empuje a) (equipo, público)* to lift; **el gol levantó al equipo** the goal lifted the team; **no ha conseguido l. la economía** he hasn't managed to get the economy back on its feet; **l. el ánimo** to cheer up; **l. la moral a alguien** to boost sb's morale

(**k**) *(sublevar)* **l. a alguien contra** to stir sb up against

(**l**) *Fam (robar)* to pinch, to swipe; **levantarle algo a alguien** to pinch *o* swipe sth off sb

(**m**) *RP, Ven Fam (ligar)* to pick up, *Br* to pull

2 *vi (niebla, nubes)* to lift; **saldremos cuando levante el día** we'll go out when it clears up

3 levantarse *vpr* (**a**) *(ponerse de pie)* to stand up; *(de la cama)* to get up; **levantarse de la silla** to get up from one's chair; **levantarse tarde** to sleep in, to get up late; EXPR **levantarse con el pie izquierdo** to get out of bed on the wrong side

(**b**) *(pintura, venda)* to come off

(**c**) *(viento, oleaje)* to get up; *(tormenta)* to gather; **con el viento se levantó una gran polvareda** the wind blew up a huge cloud of dust

(**d**) *(sobresalir)* **la cúpula de la catedral se levanta sobre la ciudad** the dome of the cathedral stands out against *o* rises up above the rest of the city

(**e**) *(sublevarse)* to rise up (**contra** against); **levantarse en armas** to rise up in arms

(**f**) *(elevarse) (sol)* to climb in the sky; *(niebla)* to lift

(**g**) *muy Fam (pene)* **no se le levanta** he can't get it up

(**h**) *RP, Ven Fam (ligar)* **se levantó una mina espectacular** he scored (with) *o Br* got off with a real babe

---

Levante *nm* Levant, = the coastal provinces of Spain between Catalonia and Andalusia: Castellón, Valencia, Alicante and Murcia

levante[1] *nm* (**a**) *(este)* east; *(región)* east coast (**b**) *(viento)* east wind

levante[2] *nm* (**a**) *CAm, PRico (calumnia)* slander (**b**) *Chile (tasa)* = fee paid by a woodcutter (**c**) *RP, Ven Fam (ligue)* **salimos de l.** we went out on the pull; **apareció con un l.** he turned up with some *Br* bird *o US* chick he'd just picked up

levantino, -a 1 *adj* of/from the Levant region of Spain

2 *nm,f* person from the Levant region of Spain

levantisco, -a *adj* restless, turbulent

levar *vt Náut* **l. anclas** to weigh anchor; *Fam (marcharse)* to sling one's hook

leve *adj* (**a**) *(de poco peso)* light

(**b**) *(poco importante) (pecado, falta, herida)* minor; *(enfermedad)* mild, slight; **resultó herido de carácter l.** he suffered minor injuries; **la inflación experimentó una l. subida** inflation rose slightly; **no tengo la más l. sospecha de que sea él** I don't suspect him in the slightest; **el paciente experimentó una l. mejoría** there was a slight improvement in the patient's condition

(**c**) *(poco intenso) (dolor)* slight; *(olor, sabor)* slight, faint; *(castigo)* mild; **soplaba una l. brisa** a gentle breeze was blowing; **se produjo un l. temblor de tierra** there was a minor earth tremor; **se detectaba un l. temblor en su voz** a faint tremor was noticeable in her voice; **nos ofreció una l. sonrisa** she gave us a faint smile

levedad *nf* (**a**) *(livianidad)* lightness (**b**) *(poca importancia) (de pecado, falta, herida)* minor nature; *(de enfermedad)* mildness (**c**) *(poca intensidad) (de dolor)* slightness; *(de olor, sabor)* faintness; *(castigo)* mildness

levemente *adv* (**a**) *(con poca importancia) (aumentar)* slightly; **pecar l.** to commit a minor sin (**b**) *(con poca intensidad) (doler)* slightly; *(oler, saber)* faintly; *(castigar)* mildly

leviatán *nm* leviathan

levita 1 *nmf* Levite

2 *nf* frock coat

levitación *nf* levitation

levitar *vi* to levitate

Levítico *nm Rel* **el L.** Leviticus

levodopa *nf Farm* levodopa

levógiro, -a *adj Quím* laevorotatory

lexema *nm Ling* lexeme

lexicalización *nf Ling* lexicalization

lexicalizar *Ling* **1** *vt* to lexicalize

2 lexicalizarse *vpr* to become lexicalized

léxico, -a 1 *adj* lexical

2 *nm* (**a**) *(vocabulario)* vocabulary; *Ling* lexis (**b**) *(diccionario)* lexicon

lexicografía *nf* lexicography

lexicográfico, -a *adj* lexicographic(al)

lexicógrafo, -a *nm,f* lexicographer

lexicología *nf* lexicology

lexicológico, -a *adj* lexicological

lexicólogo, -a *nm,f* lexicologist

lexicón *nm* lexicon

ley *nf* (**a**) *(norma)* law; *(parlamentaria)* act; EXPR **hecha la l., hecha la trampa** laws are made to be broken; **leyes** *(derecho)* law ►► ***l. de extranjería*** immigration law; ***l. de fugas*** = illegal execution of prisoner pretending that he was shot while trying to escape; ***l. fundamental*** basic law, constitutional law; ***l. de incompatibilidades*** = act regulating which other positions may be held by people holding public office; ***l. marcial*** martial law; *Pol* ***l. marco*** framework law; *Pol* ***l. orgánica*** organic law; *Hist* ***l. sálica*** Salic law; ***l. seca*** prohibition law; *Dep* ***l. de la ventaja*** advantage (law); **aplicar la l. de la ventaja** to play the advantage

(**b**) *(precepto religioso)* law ►► ***la l. coránica*** Koranic law; ***la l. judía*** Jewish law

(**c**) *(principio)* law ►► *Fam* ***l. del embudo*** one law for oneself and another for everyone else; ***la l. del más fuerte*** the survival of the fittest; ***la l. del mínimo esfuerzo:*** **seguir la l. del mínimo esfuerzo** to take the line of least resistance; ***l. natural*** law of nature; ***l. de la oferta y de la demanda*** law of supply and demand; ***la l. de la selva*** the law of the jungle; ***la l. del talión*** an eye for an eye and a tooth for a tooth; **no cree en la l. del talión** she doesn't believe in "an eye for an eye"; ***l. de vida:*** **es l. de vida** it's a fact of life

(**d**) **la l.** *(la justicia)* the law; **la igualdad ante la l.** equality before the law; EXPR *Fam* **con todas las de la l.: ganaron con todas las de la l.** they won fair and square; EXPR **ser de l.** *(situación)* to be right and proper; *(persona)* to be totally trustworthy

(**e**) *(de metal precioso)* **de l.** *(oro)* = containing the legal amount of gold; *(plata)* sterling; EXPR **de buena l.** reliable, sterling; EXPR **de mala l.** crooked, disreputable

leyenda *nf* (**a**) *(narración)* legend ►► ***la l. negra*** *Hist* = the negative picture traditionally given of Spain by many European historians, and especially of the Inquisition and the conquest of the Americas; *Fig* **sobre él pesa una l. negra** he has an appalling reputation (**b**) *(ídolo)* legend; **una l. del jazz** a jazz legend (**c**) *(inscripción) (en moneda, escudo, estandarte)* inscription, legend; *(en mapa)* legend

leyera *etc ver* **leer**

LFP *nf* (*abrev de* **Liga de Fútbol Profesional**) = association of Spanish first-division soccer teams

liado, -a *adj Fam* (**a**) *(ocupado)* tied up; **ahora ando muy l.** I'm pretty tied up at the moment; EXPR *Hum* **estar más l. que la pata de un romano** to have an awful lot on one's plate (**b**) *(involucrado)* involved; **está l. con una compañera de clase** he's got a thing going with a girl in his class

liana *nf* liana

liante *Esp Fam* **1** *adj* (**a**) *(persuasivo)* smooth-talking (**b**) *(enredador)* **¡no seas l.!** don't complicate things!

2 *nmf* (**a**) *(persuasivo)* smooth talker; **claro que me convenció, es un l.** of course he persuaded me, he could talk you into anything! (**b**) *(enredador)* stirrer, trouble-maker

liar [32] **1** *vt* (**a**) *(atar)* to tie up

(**b**) *(envolver)* **l. algo en** *(papel)* to wrap sth up in

(**c**) *(cigarrillo)* to roll

(**d**) *(involucrar)* to rope in; **l. a alguien en algo** to rope sb into sth; **me liaron para que fuera con ellos a la fiesta** they roped me into going to the party with them

(**e**) *(complicar)* to confuse; **¡ya me has liado!** now you've really got me confused!; **su declaración no hizo más que l. el tema** his statement only complicated *o* confused matters

(**f**) *Esp Fam* **liarla** *(meter la pata)* to mess things up; **¡ya la hemos liado!, ¿por qué la invitaste?** you've really gone and done it now, why did you invite her?

2 liarse *vpr* (**a**) *(complicarse)* to get complicated

(**b**) *(confundirse)* to get muddled (up) *o* confused; **me lié y tardé tres horas en terminar** I got muddled *o* confused and took three hours to finish

(**c**) *Esp (entretenerse)* to get caught up; **me lié hablando con los amigos y llegué tarde** I got caught up talking to some friends and arrived late

(**d**) *Esp (empezar)* to begin, to start; **liarse a hacer algo** to start *o* begin doing sth; **se liaron a puñetazos** they started hitting each other; **se liaron a insultarse** they started insulting each other

(**e**) *Esp Fam (sentimentalmente)* to get involved (**con** with); **se ha liado con una compañera de clase** he's got a thing going with a girl in his class

libación *nf* (**a**) *(de néctar)* **la l. de néctar** drinking the nectar of flowers (**b**) *Literario (de bebida)* libation (**c**) *(ceremonia)* libation

libanés, -esa 1 *adj* Lebanese
2 *nm,f* Lebanese

Líbano *nm* **el L.** the Lebanon

libar *vt* (**a**) *(néctar)* to drink (**b**) *Literario (bebida)* to imbibe

libelo *nm* lampoon

libélula *nf* dragonfly

liberación *nf* (**a**) *(de ciudad, país)* liberation; *(de rehén, prisionero)* freeing ►► ***l. femenina*** women's liberation; ***l. de la mujer*** women's liberation; ***l. sexual*** sexual liberation (**b**) *(de hipoteca)* redemption

liberado, -a 1 *adj* (**a**) *(ciudad, país)* liberated; *(rehén, prisionero)* freed (**b**) *(mujer)* liberated (**c**) *Esp (sindicalista)* full-time; **un terrorista l.** a full-time terrorist *(receiving financial support from his organization)* (**d**) *Fin (acciones)* paid-up
2 *nm,f Esp (sindicalista)* full-time union official; *(terrorista)* full--time member of a terrorist organization

liberador, -ora 1 *adj* liberating
2 *nm,f* liberator

liberal 1 *adj* (**a**) *(en política)* liberal (**b**) *(tolerante)* liberal (**c**) *(generoso)* liberal
2 *nmf* (**a**) *(en política)* liberal (**b**) *(tolerante)* liberal (**c**) *(generoso)* liberal

liberalidad *nf* (**a**) *(tolerancia)* liberality (**b**) *(generosidad)* liberality

liberalismo *nm* (**a**) *(en política)* liberalism (**b**) ***l. económico*** economic liberalism, free-market economics

liberalización *nf* (**a**) *(de régimen, leyes)* liberalization (**b**) *(de economía, sector)* deregulation; **la l. de precios** the abolition of price controls

liberalizar [14] *vt* (**a**) *(régimen, leyes)* to liberalize (**b**) *(economía, sector)* to deregulate; **l. los precios** to abolish price controls

liberalmente *adv* liberally

liberar 1 *vt* (**a**) *(ciudad, país)* to liberate; *(rehén, prisionero)* to free (**b**) *(de compromiso)* **l. a alguien de algo** to free sb from sth (**c**) *(emitir)* to release, to give off

2 liberarse *vpr* (**a**) *(librarse)* to free oneself (**de** from); **el prisionero se liberó de sus ataduras** the prisoner managed to untie himself; **me he liberado de la responsabilidad de cuidar de ellos** I have freed myself of the responsibility of looking after them (**b**) *(desinhibirse)* to become liberated, to lose one's inhibitions (**c**) *(emitirse)* to be released, to be given off

Liberia *n* Liberia

liberiano, -a 1 *adj* Liberian
2 *nm,f* Liberian

líbero *nm Dep* sweeper

libérrimo, -a *adj (superlativo)* entirely *o* absolutely free

libertad *nf* (**a**) *(para hacer algo)* freedom, liberty; **dejar** *o* **poner a alguien en l.** to set sb free, to release sb; **estar en l.** to be free; **quedas en l.** you are free to go; **tener l. para hacer algo** to be free to do sth; **l., igualdad y fraternidad** liberty, equality and fraternity ►► ***l. de cátedra*** academic freedom; *Econ* ***l. de circulación de capitales*** free movement of capital; ***l. de circulación de trabajadores*** free movement of workers; ***l. de conciencia*** freedom of conscience; *Der* ***l. condicional*** parole; ***l. de culto*** freedom of worship; ***l. de expresión*** freedom of speech; ***l. de horarios (comerciales):*** **las tiendas tienen l. de horarios** shops can open when they like; ***l. de imprenta*** freedom of the press; ***l. de movimientos*** freedom of movement; ***l. de pensamiento*** freedom of thought; ***l. de prensa*** freedom of the press; *Der* ***l. provisional*** bail; ***l. religiosa*** religious freedom; ***l. de reunión*** freedom of assembly

(**b**) **libertades** *(derechos)* rights; **las libertades civiles/individuales/ fundamentales** civil/individual/basic human rights

(**c**) *(confianza, familiaridad)* freedom; **puede entrar en mi casa con toda l.** she is entirely free to come into my house as she pleases; **tomarse la l. de hacer algo** to take the liberty of doing sth; **tomarse libertades (con)** to take liberties (with)

libertador, -ora 1 *adj* liberating
2 *nm,f* liberator; **el Libertador** *(en Latinoamérica)* the Liberator *(name given to certain leaders of the fight for independence from Spain)*

libertar *vt* to liberate

libertario, -a 1 *adj* libertarian
2 *nm,f* libertarian

libertinaje *nm* licentiousness

libertino, -a 1 *adj* licentious
2 *nm,f* libertine

liberto, -a *nm,f Hist* freedman, *f* freedwoman

Libia *n* Libya

libidinoso, -a *adj* libidinous, lewd

libido *nf* libido

libio, -a 1 *adj* Libyan
2 *nm,f* Libyan

libra[1] **1** *adj inv* Libra; **ser l.** to be (a) Libra
2 *nmf inv (persona)* Libran; **los l. son...** Librans *o* Libras are...
3 *nf (signo del zodiaco)* Libra; **los de L. son...** Librans *o* Libras are...

libra[2] *nf* (**a**) *(moneda)* pound ►► ***l. esterlina*** pound sterling (**b**) *(unidad de peso)* pound (**c**) *Esp Fam (cien pesetas)* = a hundred pesetas

libraco *nm* (**a**) *Pey (libro malo)* worthless book (**b**) *(libro grueso)* big book

librado, -a 1 *adj* **salir bien l.** to get off lightly; **salir mal l.** to come off badly
2 *nm,f Com* drawee

librador, -ora *nm,f Com* drawer

libramiento *nm* (**a**) *Com* order of payment (**b**) *Méx (circunvalación) Br* ring road, *US* beltway

librancista *nmf Com* bearer

librano, -a *Am* **1** *adj* Libra; **ser l.** to be (a) Libra
2 *nm,f* Libran; **los libranos son...** Librans *o* Libras are...

libranza *nf Com* order of payment

librar 1 *vt* (**a**) **l. a alguien de** *(eximir)* to free sb from; *(de pagos, impuestos)* to exempt sb from; *(de algo indeseable)* to rid sb of; **¡líbreme Dios!** God *o* Heaven forbid! (**b**) *(entablar) (pelea, lucha)* to engage in; **l. una batalla** to fight a battle; **los manifestantes libraron una batalla campal con la policía** the demonstrators fought a pitched battle with the police (**c**) *Com (entablar)* to draw (**d**) *Der (sentencia)* to hand down *(in writing)*

2 *vi Esp (no trabajar)* to be off work; **libro los lunes** I get Mondays off

3 librarse *vpr* (**a**) *(salvarse)* **librarse (de hacer algo)** to escape (from doing sth); **se libró del servicio militar** he got off having to do military service; **me libré de tener que ir a la fiesta** I got out of having to go to the party; EXPR **de buena te libraste** you had a lucky escape

(**b**) *(deshacerse)* **librarse de algo/alguien** to get rid of sth/sb; **el asesino consiguió librarse de sus perseguidores** the killer managed to shake off his pursuers; **no conseguimos librarnos de ese olor** we can't get rid of that smell

libre *adj* (**a**) *(sin limitaciones)* free; **el amor l.** free love; **ser l. de** *o* **para hacer algo** to be free to do sth; **eres l. de hacer lo que quieras** you are free to do as you wish; **es l. para casarse con quien quiera** she is free to marry whoever she pleases; **entrada l.** *(en letrero)* entry free ►► ***l. albedrío*** free will; *Econ* ***l. cambio*** free trade; *(de divisas)* floating exchange rates; *Econ* ***l. circulación de capitales*** free circulation of capital; ***l. circulación de mercancías*** free movement of goods; ***l. circulación de personas*** free movement of people; ***l. mercado*** free market

(**b**) *(no encarcelado)* free

(**c**) *(país)* free

(**d**) *(sin novio, pareja)* free, available

(**e**) *(sin obstáculos) (camino, carretera)* clear

(**f**) **l. de** *(exento)* exempt from; **l. de culpa** free from blame; **l. de**

franqueo post-free; **l. de impuestos** *(alcohol, cigarrillos)* tax-free, duty-free

(g) *(desocupado) (asiento)* free; *(retrete)* vacant; *(casa)* empty; **¿estarás l. mañana?** will you be free tomorrow?; **el puesto de tesorero ha quedado l.** the post of treasurer is now vacant; **un taxi l.** a free *o* empty taxi; **l.** *(en taxi)* for hire; **ahora no tengo las manos libres** my hands are full at the moment; **aparcamiento: l.** *(en letrero)* parking: spaces

(h) *(tiempo)* free, spare; **cuando tenga un rato l., te llamo** I'll call you when I've got a (spare) moment; **en mis ratos libres me gusta tocar el piano** in my spare *o* free time I like to play the piano; **mañana tengo el día l.** I've got the day off tomorrow; **tengo dos horas libres** I have two hours spare

(i) *(independiente)* independent; *(alumno)* external; **trabajar por l.** to work freelance; **estudiar por l.** to be an external student; *Esp* **ir por l.** to do things one's own way; *Esp* **cuando viajo me gusta ir por l. más que ir en grupo** I prefer travelling alone to travelling in a group

(j) *(estilo, traducción)* free; *Dep* **200 metros libres** 200 metres freestyle

librea *nf* livery; **un portero de l.** a liveried doorman

librecambio *nm* free trade

librecambismo *nm* free trade

librecambista 1 *adj* free-market
2 *nmf* free-marketeer

libremente *adv* freely

librepensador, -ora 1 *adj* freethinking
2 *nm,f* freethinker

librepensamiento *nm* freethinking

librería *nf* (a) *(tienda)* bookshop, *US* bookstore ►► ***l. de lance*** second-hand bookshop; ***l. de ocasión*** second-hand bookshop; ***l. de viejo*** antiquarian bookshop (b) *Esp (mueble)* bookcase (c) *Informát* library

> **Falso amigo**: Excepto en la acepción de informática, el sustantivo inglés **library** no es la traducción del español **librería**. En inglés **library** significa "biblioteca".

librero, -a 1 *nm,f (persona)* bookseller
2 *nm CAm, Col, Méx (mueble)* bookcase

> **Falso amigo**: El sustantivo inglés **librarian** no es la traducción del español **librero**. En inglés **librarian** significa "bibliotecario".

libresco, -a *adj* (a) *(del libro)* **el mercado l.** the book market (b) *(irreal)* **su conocimiento de la vida es puramente l.** he only knows about life from books

libreta *nf* (a) *(para escribir)* notebook ►► *Am* ***l. de calificaciones*** *Br* (school) report, *US* report card; *RP* ***l. de casamiento*** = document containing personal details of a married couple and, later, their children; *RP* ***l. de cheques*** chequebook; ***l. de direcciones*** address book; *Arg* ***l. de enrolamiento*** military service record book; *Urug* ***l. de manejar*** *Br* driving licence, *US* driver's license; *Andes* ***l. de matrimonio*** = document containing personal details of a married couple and, later, their children
(b) *(de banco)* **l. (de ahorros)** savings book

libretista *nmf* (a) *Mús* librettist (b) *Am (guionista)* screenwriter, scriptwriter

libreto *nm* (a) *Mús* libretto (b) *Am (guión)* script; *Fig* **eso estaba fuera del l.** that wasn't in the script, that wasn't meant to happen

Libreville [liβre'βil] *n* Libreville

libriano, -a *Am* 1 *adj* Libra; **ser l.** to be (a) Libra
2 *nm,f* Libran; **los librianos son...** Librans *o* Libras are...

librillo *nm* (a) *Zool* third stomach (b) *(de papel de fumar)* packet *(of cigarette papers)*

libro *nm* (a) *(impreso)* book; **un l. de aventuras** a book of adventure stories; EXPR **hablar como un l.** to express oneself very clearly; EXPR *Fam* **ser (como) un l. abierto** to be an open book ►► ***l. de bolsillo*** (pocket-sized) paperback; ***l. de cabecera*** bedside book; ***l. de canciones*** song book; ***l. de cocina*** cookery book, cookbook; ***l. de consulta*** reference book; ***l. de cuentos*** storybook; ***l. de ejercicios*** workbook; ***l. electrónico*** electronic book; ***l. de estilo*** style guide; ***l. de himnos*** hymn book; ***l. de instrucciones*** instruction book *o* manual; *Rel* ***l. sagrado*** Book *(in Bible)*; ***l. de texto*** textbook; ***l. de viajes*** travel book
(b) *Pol* paper ►► ***l. blanco*** white paper; ***l. verde*** green paper
(c) *(registro)* book; **llevar los libros** to keep the books ►► *Com* ***l. de caja*** cashbook; *Fin* ***l. de contabilidad*** accounts book; *Fin* ***l. diario*** *(para transacciones)* journal; *Educ* ***l. de escolaridad*** = book containing a complete record of a pupil's academic results throughout his or her time at school; ***l. de familia*** = document containing personal details of the members of a family; ***l. de oro*** visitors' book *(for important guests)*; ***l. de pedidos*** order book; ***l. de reclamaciones*** complaints book; ***l. de registro (de entradas)*** register; ***l. de visitas*** visitors' book

Lic. *(abrev de* **licenciado, -a***)* (a) *(de universidad)* graduate *(used as title)* (b) *Andes, CAm, Carib, Méx (forma de tratamiento)* = form of address used to indicate respect

licantropía *nf* lycanthropy

licántropo *nm* werewolf

licaón *nm* African painted hunting dog

liceal 1 *adj Am Br* secondary school, *US* high school; **las autoridades liceales** the *Br* secondary school *o US* high school authorities
2 *nmf Urug Br* secondary school *o US* high school pupil

liceano, -a *nm,f Chile Br* secondary school *o US* high school pupil

liceísta *nmf Ven Br* secondary school *o US* high school pupil

licencia *nf* (a) *(documento)* licence, permit; *(de software, vídeo)* licence agreement ►► ***l. de armas*** gun licence; ***l. artística*** artistic licence; ***l. de caza*** hunting licence *o* permit; *Carib, Chile, Ecuad* ***l. de conducir*** *Br* driving licence, *US* driver's license; *Méx* ***l. para conducir*** *Br* driving licence, *US* driver's license; *Méx* ***l. de conductor*** *Br* driving licence, *US* driver's license; ***l. de exportación*** export licence; ***l. fiscal*** = official authorization to practise a profession; ***l. de importación*** import licence; *Méx* ***l. de manejo*** *Br* driving licence, *US* driver's license; ***l. de obras*** planning permission; ***l. de pesca*** fishing permit
(b) *(eclesiástica) (para predicar)* licence; *(para publicar un texto)* imprimatur
(c) *(autorización)* permission; **dar l.** to give permission; *Méx* **con l.** *(con permiso)* if I may, if you'll excuse me; *Méx* **con l., ¿puedo pasar?** may I come in?
(d) *(en el ejército)* leave ►► ***l. absoluta*** discharge
(e) *Am (en el trabajo)* leave; **estar de l.** to be off work ►► *RP* ***l. por enfermedad*** sick leave; *RP* ***l. por maternidad*** maternity leave
(f) *(libertad)* liberty; **me he permitido la l. de venir sin llamar** I took the liberty of coming without calling first; **tomarse licencias con alguien** to take liberties with sb ►► *Lit* ***l. métrica*** metrical licence *o* freedom; *Lit* ***l. poética*** poetic licence

licenciado, -a 1 *adj (soldado)* discharged
2 *nm,f* (a) *(de universidad)* graduate; **l. en económicas/derecho** economics/law graduate; **l. en Filosofía y Letras** Bachelor of Arts; **es l. en Derecho por la Universidad de Córdoba** he has a law degree from the University of Córdoba (b) *(soldado)* discharged soldier (c) *Andes, CAm, Carib, Méx (forma de tratamiento)* = form of address used to indicate respect; **el l. Pérez** Mr Pérez; **¡por supuesto, l.!** of course, Mr Pérez, Sir

licenciamiento *nm (de soldado)* discharge

licenciar 1 *vt* (a) *(soldado)* to discharge (b) *Am (en universidad)* to confer a degree on
2 **licenciarse** *vpr* (a) *(soldado)* to be discharged (b) *(en universidad)* to graduate; **me licencié en Filosofía por la Universidad de Salamanca** I obtained a philosophy degree from the University of Salamanca

licenciatura *nf* degree; **l. en económicas/derecho** economics/law degree; **l. en Filosofía y Letras** Bachelor of Arts (degree)

licencioso, -a *adj* licentious

liceo *nm* (a) *(en Francia)* lycée (b) *(de recreo)* social club (c) *CSur, Ven (colegio) Br* secondary school, *US* high school; **durante mis años de l.** while I was at *Br* secondary school *o US* high school

lichi *nm* lychee

licitación *nf* tender; **estar en l.** to be out to tender; **salir a l.** to be put out to tender; **un proceso de l.** a call for tenders

licitador, -ora *nm,f* bidder

lícitamente *adv* lawfully

licitante 1 *adj* bidding
2 *nmf* bidder

licitar 1 *vt* (a) *(en subasta, concurso)* to bid (b) *(sacar a concurso)* to put out to tender
2 *vi (en subasta)* to bid

lícito, -a *adj* (a) *(legal)* lawful (b) *(correcto)* right (c) *(justo)* fair

licor *nm* (a) *(alcohol)* spirits, *US* liquor (b) *(bebida dulce)* liqueur ►► ***l. de menta*** crème de menthe

licorera *nf* (a) *(botella)* decanter (b) *(mueble)* cocktail cabinet

licorería *nf* (**a**) *(fábrica)* distillery (**b**) *(tienda) Br* off-licence, *US* liquor store

licra *nf Am* Lycra®

licuado *nm Am (con leche)* milkshake; *(con agua, jugo)* smoothy

licuadora *nf* (**a**) *Esp (para extraer zumo)* juice extractor, juicer (**b**) *Am (para batir)* blender, *Br* liquidizer

licuar [4] **1** *vt* (**a**) *Fís* to liquefy (**b**) *Culin* to liquidize

2 licuarse *vpr Fís* to liquefy

licuefacción *nf Fís* liquefaction

lid *nf* (**a**) *Literario (lucha)* fight; EXPR **en buena l.** in a fair contest; **ganó el combate en buena l.** he won the fight fair and square (**b**) *(asunto)* **un experto en estas lides** an old hand in these matters; **un veterano en lides amorosas** an expert in matters of the heart

líder 1 *adj* leading; **el equipo l.** the leading team; **la empresa es l. en el sector** it is the leading company in the industry

2 *nmf* (**a**) *(de partido político, país)* leader; **un l. sindical** a union boss *o* leader ▸▸ *Pol* ***el l. de la oposición*** the leader of the opposition (**b**) *(de clasificación, mercado)* leader; **el Deportivo es el l. de la liga** Deportivo are top of the league *o* are the current league leaders

liderar 1 *vt* (**a**) *(partido político)* to head, to lead (**b**) *(clasificación)* to be top of; **nuestra empresa lidera el sector** we are the leading company in the industry; **la empresa lidera el mercado** the company is the market leader

2 *vi (ir en cabeza)* **l. en** to be at the top of, to lead

liderazgo, liderato *nm* (**a**) *(de partido político, país)* leadership (**b**) *(primer puesto)* lead; *(en liga)* first place

lideresa *nf Méx* (woman) leader

liderizar *vt Ven* to lead

lidia *nf* (**a**) **la l.** *(arte)* bullfighting (**b**) *(corrida)* bullfight; **toro de l.** fighting bull (**c**) *Col, Ven Fam (trabajo)* **iqué l. dan estos gatos!** these cats are a real hassle!; **la tesis le está dando mucha l.** she's really got her hands full with her thesis

lidiador, -ora *nm,f Taurom* bullfighter

lidiar 1 *vi* **l. con** *(luchar)* to struggle with; *(hacer frente a)* to oppose, to face; *(soportar)* to put up with; **tengo que l. con 30 alumnos todos los días** I have to deal with *o* cope with 30 pupils every day

2 *vt Taurom* to fight

lidioso, -a *adj Ven Fam* (**a**) *(difícil)* **iqué l. eres!** you're an awkward so-and-so! (**b**) *(molesto)* **ser l.** to be a pain

liebre *nf* (**a**) *(animal)* hare; EXPR **correr como una l.** to run like a hare; EXPR **levantar la l.** to let the cat out of the bag; EXPR **donde menos se piensa, salta la l.** you never know what might happen ▸▸ ***l. patagónica*** Patagonian hare (**b**) *Dep* pacemaker

Liechtenstein ['liχtenstain] *n* Liechtenstein

Lieja *n* Liège

liencillo *nm Andes, Carib, RP* rough cotton cloth

liendre *nf* nit

lienza *nf Chile* (**a**) *(cordel)* cord (**b**) *(sedal)* (fishing) line

lienzo *nm* (**a**) *(tela)* (coarse) cloth; *(paño)* piece of cloth (**b**) *(para pintar)* canvas (**c**) *(cuadro)* painting (**d**) *Arquit (pared)* wall; *(trozo)* stretch of wall (**e**) *Méx (corral)* corral *(for rodeo)*

liftado, -a *adj Dep* topspin

liftar *vt Dep* to put topspin on

lifting ['liftin] *(pl* **liftings**) *nm* face-lift

liga *nf* (**a**) *(confederación, agrupación)* league ▸▸ *Pol* ***la L. Árabe*** the Arab League

(**b**) *(para medias) (elástico)* garter; *(colgante) Br* suspender, *US* garter

(**c**) *(goma elástica)* elastic band

(**d**) *(deportiva)* league ▸▸ ***la L. de Campeones*** the Champions League; *Esp* ***la L. Fantástica®*** = competition where players pick their own fantasy soccer teams, *Br* ≃ Fantasy Football League

(**e**) *(sustancia pegajosa)* bird-lime

ligado, -a 1 *adj (vinculado, unido)* linked, connected; **un fenómeno l. al cambio climático** a phenomenon linked to *o* connected with climate change; **está íntimamente ligada al partido conservador** she is closely linked to the Conservative Party; **estuvo sentimentalmente l. a varias actrices** he was (romantically) involved with several actresses; **me siento muy l. a mi familia** I have very close ties with my family

2 *nm Mús (de notas)* legato; *(modo de tocar)* slur

ligadura *nf* (**a**) *Med* ligature ▸▸ ***l. de trompas*** tubal ligation; **le hicieron una l. de trompas** she had her tubes tied (**b**) *(atadura)* bond; **el prisionero logró librarse de sus ligaduras** the prisoner managed to break free of his bonds *o* untie himself (**c**) *(compromiso)* tie; **rompió todas sus ligaduras familiares** she broke off all contact with her family (**d**) *Mús* ligature (**e**) *Imprenta* ligature

ligamento *nm* ligament; **rotura de ligamentos** torn ligaments

ligar [38] **1** *vt* (**a**) *(atar)* to tie (up); **liga bien los paquetes** tie the packages up tightly; **les ligaron las manos** they tied their hands

(**b**) *(unir)* to bind; **los ligan muchos lazos afectivos** they are bound together by a lot of emotional ties; **un contrato lo liga con la empresa** he is contractually bound to the company

(**c**) *(salsa)* to thicken

(**d**) *Med* to put a ligature on

(**e**) *Mús* to slur

(**f**) *(en naipes)* to get; **ligué un póquer de ases** I got four aces

(**g**) *(metales)* to alloy

(**h**) *Fam (droga)* to score, to get hold of

(**i**) *RP (conseguir)* to get; **siempre viene a ver si liga algo** he always comes along to see what he can get

(**j**) EXPR *Fam* **l. bronce** to catch some rays

(**k**) *Cuba (cosecha)* to contract in advance for

(**l**) *Ven Dep (béisbol)* to hit; **ligó un cuadrangular** he hit a home run

2 *vi* (**a**) *Fam (encontrar pareja)* to score, *Br* to pull; **en esta ciudad no se liga nada** it's a nightmare trying to score *o Br* pull in this town; **esta noche vamos a salir a l.** we're going out to score with someone tonight, *Br* we're going out on the pull tonight

(**b**) *(salsa)* to bind

(**c**) *RP, Ven Fam (tener suerte)* to be damn lucky, *Br* to be jammy

(**d**) *Carib, Guat, Perú (deseo)* to be fulfilled

(**e**) *Ven Dep (en béisbol)* to go into the wind-up

3 ligarse *vpr* (**a**) *(unirse)* to unite, to join together

(**b**) *Esp Fam (conseguir)* **ligarse a alguien** *Br* to get off with sb, *US* to make out with sb

(**c**) *RP Fam* **ligársela: como se entere nos la vamos a l.** we'll be in for it if she finds out; **si no te callas te la vas a l.** you're going to catch it if you don't shut up

(**d**) *Arg, Ven (línea telefónica)* **se ligan las comunicaciones** there's a crossed line

ligazón *nf* link, connection; **es un asesor sin ninguna l. con el partido** he's an adviser who has no links with the party

ligeramente *adv* (**a**) *(levemente)* lightly; *(aumentar, bajar, doler)* slightly; **está l. torcido** it's not quite straight; **estoy l. cansado** I'm a little tired (**b**) *(superficialmente)* lightly; **la pelota rozó l. el larguero** the ball just grazed the crossbar; **lo juzgaste muy l.** you were very quick to judge him; **estudiaron el asunto muy l.** they looked at the matter very superficially

ligereza *nf* (**a**) *(levedad)* lightness

(**b**) *(de dolor)* slightness

(**c**) *(agilidad)* agility; **se movía con gran l.** he was very nimble *o* agile

(**d**) *(rapidez)* speed

(**e**) *(superficialidad)* **abordaron el problema con mucha l.** they tackled the problem in a very superficial manner

(**f**) *(irreflexión)* rashness; **cometí la l. de contárselo todo** I very rashly told her everything; **fue una l. decir eso** it was rash *o* reckless to say that; **actuar con l.** to act flippantly

LIGERO, -A **1** *adj* (**a**) *(de poco peso)* light; **ir** *o* **viajar l. de equipaje** to travel light; **iba muy ligera de ropa** *(provocativa)* she was very scantily clad; *(poco abrigada)* she wasn't wearing enough clothes; EXPR **ser l. como una pluma** to be as light as a feather

(**b**) *(traje, tela)* thin

(**c**) *(comida)* light; **en casa hacemos cenas ligeras** we have a light meal in the evening at home

(**d**) *(armamento)* light

(**e**) *(leve) (roce, toque, golpe)* light; *(olor, rumor, sonido)* faint; *(sabor)* slight, mild; *(dolor, resfriado)* slight; *(herida, accidente, daño)* minor; *(descenso, diferencia, inconveniente)* slight; *(conocimientos, sospecha, idea)* vague; **sufrieron heridas de ligera consideración** they suffered minor injuries; **tengo la ligera impresión de que te equivocas** I have a vague feeling that you might be wrong; **tener el sueño l.** to be a light sleeper

(**f**) *(literatura, teatro)* light; **una comedia ligera** a light comedy; **quiero leer algo l. que no me haga pensar** I want to read something light that I don't have to think about too hard

(**g**) *(rápido)* quick, swift; **caminar a paso l.** to walk at a brisk pace; **tener una mente ligera** to be quick-thinking

(**h**) *(ágil)* agile, nimble

(**i**) *(irreflexivo)* flippant; **hacer algo a la ligera** to do sth without much thought; **juzgar (algo/a alguien) a la ligera** to be superficial in one's judgements (about sth/sb); **tomarse algo a la ligera** not to take sth seriously; EXPR **ser l. de cascos** *(irresponsable)* to be irresponsible; *(mujer)* to be flighty

2 *adv (rápidamente)* quickly; **l., que tengo mucha prisa** hurry up, I'm in a rush

---

light [lait] *adj inv* (**a**) *(comida)* low-calorie; *(refresco)* diet; *(cigarrillos)* light (**b**) *(suavizado)* toned down; **un chiste l.** a bland *o* inoffensive joke; **un marxismo l.** a watered-down Marxism; **la película es una versión l. de la vida del pintor** the movie is a sanitized version of the painter's life

lignito *nm* brown coal, lignite

ligón, -ona *Esp Fam* **1** *adj* **es muy l.** he's always getting off with somebody or other

2 *nm,f* womanizer, *f* flirt; **el l. de tu hermano** that womanizing brother of yours

ligoteo *nm Esp Fam* **salir de l.** to go out to score *o Br* on the pull; **el ambiente relajado de ese bar facilita mucho el l.** the bar's relaxed atmosphere makes it a happy hunting ground for singles

ligue *nm Esp Fam* (**a**) *(acción)* **salir de l.** to go out to score *o Br* on the pull; **domina el arte del l.** he's an expert at scoring with *Br* birds *o US* chicks (**b**) *(novio) Br* bloke, *US* squeeze; *(novia) Br* bird, *US* squeeze; **vino a la fiesta con su último l.** she came to the party with her new man (**c**) *(relación)* **tiene un l. con una compañera de trabajo** he's having a fling with a woman from work

liguero, -a 1 *adj Dep* league; **partido l.** league game *o* match

2 *nm Br* suspender belt, *US* garter belt

liguilla *nf Dep* mini-league; **quedaron primeros en la l. y pasaron a las semifinales** they finished top of their group and went through to the semifinals

lija 1 *adj* (**a**) *Méx (persona)* shrewd, sharp (**b**) *RP Fam* **vino l.** rough wine, *Br* plonk

2 *nf* (**a**) *(papel)* sandpaper (**b**) *(pez)* dogfish (**c**) EXPR *Carib Fam* **darse l.** to put on *o* give oneself airs

lijado *nm (de suelo)* sanding; **l. de pisos** floor sanding

lijadora *nf* sander

lijar *vt* to sand, to sand down

lijoso, -a *adj Carib Fam* **ser l.** to put on *o* give oneself airs

lila 1 *adj inv (color)* lilac

2 *nf (flor)* lilac

3 *nm (color)* lilac

liliácea *Bot* **1** *nf* liliaceous plant

2 **liliáceas** *nfpl (familia) Liliaceae*; **de la familia de las liliáceas** of the family *Liliaceae*

liliáceo, -a *adj Bot* liliaceous

Liliput *n* Lilliput

liliputiense 1 *adj* dwarfish

2 *nmf* midget

lilo *nm* common lilac

Lima *n* Lima

lima *nf* (**a**) *(herramienta)* file; EXPR **comer como una l.** to eat like a horse ►► ***l. de uñas*** nail file (**b**) *(fruto)* lime (**c**) *(árbol)* lime tree

limaco *nm* slug

limado *nm* (**a**) *(pulimento)* filing (**b**) *(perfeccionamiento)* polishing

limadora *nf* polisher

limadura *nf* filing ►► ***limaduras de hierro*** iron filings

limanda *nf* dab

limar *vt* (**a**) *(pulir)* to file down; EXPR **l. asperezas** to iron out one's differences (**b**) *(perfeccionar)* to polish, to add the finishing touches to

limatón *nm Am* roof beam

limbo *nm* (**a**) *Rel* limbo; EXPR *Fam* **estar en el l.** to be miles away (**b**) *Astron* limb (**c**) *Bot* limb (**d**) *(baile)* limbo

limeño, -a 1 *adj* of/from Lima *(Peru)*

2 *nm,f* person from Lima *(Peru)*

limero *nm* lime tree

limitación *nf* (**a**) *(restricción)* limitation, limit; **acuerdo de l. de armamento** arms limitation agreement; **poner limitaciones a** to place restrictions on; **sin l. de tiempo** with no time limit; **alquiler sin l. de kilometraje** unlimited mileage ►► ***l. de velocidad*** speed limit (**b**) *(de distrito)* boundaries (**c**) **limitaciones** *(carencias)* limitations; **reconozco mis limitaciones** I know my own limitations

limitado, -a *adj* (**a**) *(restringido)* limited; **disponemos de un espacio muy l.** we have very limited space; **tienen un acceso l. a los servicios sanitarios** they have limited access to healthcare services; **el problema no está l. a un solo país** the problem is not limited *o* restricted to just one country

(**b**) *(poco dotado)* of limited ability, not very gifted; **es un alumno muy l.** he's a pupil of limited ability; **como cantante es muy l.** he has limited ability as a singer

(**c**) *Com* **sociedad limitada** private limited company

limitador *nm Elec* limiter, clipper ►► ***l. de corriente*** current limiter

limitante *nf CSur* limitation; **esta localización tiene algunas limitantes** this position has certain limitations; **sé que tengo limitantes** I know that I have certain limitations

limitar 1 *vt* (**a**) *(restringir)* to limit, to restrict; **quieren l. el poder del presidente** they want to limit *o* restrict the president's power; **han limitado la velocidad máxima a cuarenta por hora** they've restricted the speed limit to forty kilometres an hour; **este sueldo tan bajo me limita mucho** I can't do very much on such a low salary (**b**) *(terreno)* to mark out; **limitaron el terreno con una cerca** they fenced off the area

2 *vi* to border (**con** on); **limita al norte con Venezuela** it borders on Venezuela to the north

3 **limitarse** *vpr* **limitarse a** to limit oneself to; **él se limitó a recordarnos nuestros derechos** he merely *o* just reminded us of our rights; **me limitaré a enumerar los puntos principales** I will restrict myself to a description of the main points; **limítate a ayudar** just concentrate on helping

límite *nm* (**a**) *(tope)* limit; **al l.** at the limit; **dentro de un l.** within limits; **tiene una amabilidad sin límites** his kindness knows no bounds; **su pasión no tiene l.** her passion knows no bounds; **está trabajando al l. de sus posibilidades** she's working at full stretch; **estoy al l. de mis fuerzas** I've reached the limit of my strength; **me dejan estar conectado a Internet sin l. de tiempo** I have unlimited access to the Internet; **mi paciencia tiene un l.** my patience has limits; **no hay l. de edad** there's no age limit ►► *Fin* ***l. de crédito*** credit limit; ***l. de velocidad*** speed limit

(**b**) *(confín)* boundary; **el l. norte de la finca** the northernmost boundary of the property

(**c**) *Mat* limit

(**d**) *(como adjetivo) (precio, velocidad, edad)* maximum; *(situación)* extreme; *(caso)* borderline; **fecha l. de entrega: 15 de junio** deadline for submissions: 15 June

limítrofe *adj (país, territorio)* bordering; *(terreno, finca)* neighbouring

limo *nm* (**a**) *(barro)* mud, slime (**b**) *Andes, CAm (árbol)* lime tree

limón *nm* (**a**) *(fruta amarilla)* lemon (**b**) *Méx (fruta verde)* lime ►► *Méx, Ven* ***l. francés*** lemon (**c**) *(bebida) (natural)* lemonade, = iced, sweetened lemon juice drink; *(refresco) Br* lemonade, *US* lemon soda

limonada *nf (natural)* lemonade, = iced, sweetened lemon juice drink; *(refresco) Br* lemonade, *US* lemon soda

limonar *nm* (**a**) *(plantación)* lemon grove (**b**) *Guat (árbol)* lemon tree

limonero *nm* (**a**) *(de limones)* lemon tree (**b**) *Méx (de limas)* lime tree

limonita *nf Geol* limonite

limosna *nf* (**a**) *Rel* alms (**b**) *(a mendigo)* **dar l.** to give money; **pedir l.** to beg; *Fig* to ask for charity; **una l., por el amor de Dios** can you spare me some change, please? (**c**) *Fam (poco dinero)* pittance; **cobró una l. por el trabajo que hizo** he earned peanuts *o* a pittance for the work he did

limosnear *vi* to beg

limosnero, -a *nm,f Méx* beggar

limpia *nmf Fam (limpiabotas)* shoeshine, *Br* bootblack

limpiabarros *nm inv* doormat

limpiabotas *nmf inv* shoeshine, *Br* bootblack

limpiabrisas *nm inv Col Br* windscreen wiper, *US* windshield wiper

limpiacabezales *nm inv* head cleaner

limpiachimeneas *nm inv* chimney-sweep

limpiacoches *nmf inv* squeegee *Br* merchant *o US* kid

limpiacristales, *Am* **limpiavidrios 1** *nm inv* window-cleaning fluid

2 *nmf* window cleaner

limpiador, -ora 1 *adj* cleaning, cleansing

2 *nm,f* cleaner

3 *nm* (**a**) *(producto)* cleaning product (**b**) *Méx (limpiaparabrisas) Br* windscreen wiper, *US* windshield wiper

limpiamente *adv* (**a**) *(con destreza)* cleanly; **le robaron la billetera l.** they stole his wallet without him even noticing (**b**) *(honradamente)* honestly; **ganaron l.** they won fair and square

limpiametales *nm inv* metal polish

limpiaparabrisas *nm inv Br* windscreen wiper, *US* windshield wiper

limpiapiés *nm inv Chile* doormat

limpiar 1 *vt* (a) *(quitar la suciedad)* to clean; *(con trapo)* to wipe; *(mancha)* to wipe away; *(zapatos)* to polish; **limpia la mesa de migas** clean *o* wipe the crumbs off the table; **limpia la superficie de grasa y polvo** wipe the grease and dust off *o* from the surface
(b) *(honor)* to restore
(c) *(pollo, pescado)* to clean
(d) *(desembarazar)* **l. algo de algo** to clear sth of sth; **la policía limpió la ciudad de delincuentes** the police cleared the city of criminals
(e) *Fam (en el juego)* to clean out
(f) *Fam (robar)* to swipe, to pinch; **los ladrones limpiaron el banco** the robbers cleaned out the bank
(g) *Méx (castigar)* to beat
(h) *RP, Ven Fam (matar)* to do in, *US* to whack
2 *vi* to clean; **este detergente no limpia** this detergent doesn't clean well
3 **limpiarse** *vpr* to clean *o* wipe oneself; **límpiate esa mancha** wipe that stain off yourself; **se limpió con una servilleta** she wiped herself with a napkin; **límpiate la nariz** wipe your nose

limpiavidrios = **limpiacristales**

limpidez *nf Formal* limpidity

límpido, -a *adj Formal* limpid

limpieza *nf* (a) *(cualidad)* cleanliness ▸▸ *Hist* ***l. de sangre*** racial purity
(b) *(acción)* cleaning; **hacer la l.** to do the cleaning; **esta oficina necesita una l. general** this office could do with a good spring-clean; **hacer l. general** to spring-clean ▸▸ ***l. de cutis*** facial; ***l. étnica*** ethnic cleansing; ***l. en seco*** dry-cleaning
(c) *(destreza)* skill, cleanness; **sobrepasó el listón con l.** she cleared the bar cleanly; **le quitó la pelota con l.** he took the ball off him cleanly
(d) *(honradez)* honesty; **ganaron con l.** they won fair and square

limpio, -a 1 *adj* (a) *(sin suciedad)* clean; *(cielo, imagen)* clear; **tiene la casa muy limpia y ordenada** her house is very neat and tidy; EXPR **l. de polvo y paja** all-in, including all charges
(b) *(pulcro, aseado)* clean and smart; **un joven muy l.** a very clean and smart young man
(c) *(no contaminante)* clean
(d) *(pollo, pescado)* cleaned
(e) *(fractura)* clean
(f) *(neto)* net; **gana cinco millones limpios al año** she earns five million a year net
(g) *(honrado)* honest; *(intenciones)* honourable; *(juego)* clean
(h) *(sin culpa)* **estar l.** to be in the clear; **l. de culpa/sospecha** free of blame/suspicion
(i) *Fam (sin dinero)* broke, *Br* skint
(j) *Fam (para enfatizar)* **a puñetazo l.** with bare fists, bareknuckle; **abrió la puerta a patada limpia** he bust down *o* booted in the door
2 *adv* cleanly, fair; *Fig* **jugar l.** to play fair; **pasar** *Esp* **a** *o Am* **en l., poner en l.** to make a fair copy of, to write out neatly; **sacar algo en l. de** to make sth out from

limpión *nm Carib, Col (paño)* cleaning rag

limusina *nf* limousine

linaje *nm* lineage; **de noble l.** of noble lineage

linaza *nf* linseed

lince *nm* (a) *(animal)* lynx ▸▸ ***l. ibérico*** Spanish lynx; ***l. rojo*** bobcat
(b) *(persona)* **ser un l.** to be very sharp; **es un l. para los negocios** he has a very sharp business sense; **no hace falta ser un l. para entenderlo** you don't have to be a genius to understand it

linchamiento *nm* lynching

linchar *vt* to lynch; **l. a alguien** to lynch sb

lindamente *adv (con belleza)* prettily; **iba l. vestida** she was prettily dressed

lindante *adj* (a) **l. (con)** *(espacio)* bordering (b) **l. (con)** *(conceptos, ideas)* bordering (on)

lindar *vi* (a) **l. con** *(terreno)* to adjoin, to be next to; **su finca linda con la mía** her land borders on mine (b) **l. con** *(conceptos, ideas)* to border on, to verge on; **un chiste que linda con lo grosero** a joke which borders *o* verges on being rude

linde *nm o nf* boundary

lindero, -a 1 *adj* **l. (con)** *(espacio)* bordering
2 *nm* boundary

lindeza *nf* (a) *(belleza)* prettiness (b) *Irónico* **lindezas** *(insultos)* insults; **le llamó "imbécil" y otras lindezas por el estilo** she called him an idiot and a few other choice names too

lindo, -a 1 *adj* (a) *esp Am (bonito)* pretty; *(agradable)* nice; **tu hermana es muy linda** your sister's very pretty; **hace un día muy l.** it's a lovely day; **es la ciudad más linda que vi** it's the most beautiful city I've ever seen (b) EXPR **de lo l.** a great deal; **nos reímos de lo l.** we laughed ourselves silly; **lloraba de lo l.** she was crying her eyes out; **sufrimos de lo l.** we suffered badly
2 *adv Am* very well, beautifully; **dibuja muy l.** he draws very well *o* beautifully; **baila muy l.** she's a lovely dancer

lindura *nf Am* prettiness; **me emociona la l. del paisaje** I'm moved by how pretty the landscape is

---

LÍNEA *nf* (a) *(raya, trazo, renglón, límite)* line; **una l. recta** a straight line; **una l. quebrada** a crooked line; **la l. del cielo** the skyline; **ir en l. recta** to go in a straight line; **leerle a alguien las líneas de la mano** to read (the lines on) sb's hand; **estar en l.** to be in (a) line; **poner/ponerse en l.** to line up; **estacionar en l.** to park end-to-end; **escribir** *o* **mandar unas líneas a alguien** to drop sb a line; EXPR **leer entre líneas** to read between the lines ▸▸ ***l. continua*** *(en carretera)* solid white line; *Com* ***l. de crédito*** credit limit; *Com* ***l. de descubierto*** overdraft limit; ***l. discontinua*** *(en carretera)* broken white line; ***l. divisoria*** dividing line; ***l. de flotación*** waterline; *Mil* ***l. de fuego*** firing line; *Imprenta* ***l.huérfana*** orphan; ***l. de mira*** line of fire; ***l. punteada*** dotted line; ***l. de puntos*** dotted line; ***l. de tiro*** line of fire; *Imprenta* ***l.viuda*** widow
(b) *(ruta)* line; **una nueva l. de autobús** a new bus route; **han añadido varias paradas a la l. 30** the number 30 bus has several new stops; **la l. circular del metro** the *Br* underground *o US* subway circle line ▸▸ ***l. férrea*** *Br* railway (line), *US* railroad track; ***l. de ferrocarril*** *Br* railway (line), *US* railroad track
(c) *(compañía aérea)* **una l. de vuelos charter** a charter airline ▸▸ ***l. aérea*** airline
(d) *(de telecomunicaciones)* line; **cortar la l. (telefónica)** to cut off the phone; **dar l. a alguien** to put in a line for sb; **no hay** *o* **no tenemos l.** the line's dead ▸▸ ***l. arrendada*** leased line; *Fam* ***l. caliente*** *(erótica)* chat line, telephone sex line; *(de atención al cliente)* hot line; ***l. directa*** direct line; *Fig* **tiene l. directa con el presidente** she has a direct line to the president's office; ***l. erótica*** telephone sex line; ***l. exterior*** outside line; ***l. privada*** private line; *Informát* ***l. RDSI*** ISDN line; *RP* ***líneas rotativas*** *(centralita)* switchboard
(e) *(en deportes)* line; **la l. defensiva/delantera** the back/front line, the defence/attack; **la l. medular** the midfield ▸▸ ***l. de banda*** sideline, touchline; ***l. de fondo*** *(en fútbol)* goal line *(at end of field)*; *(en baloncesto)* end line; ***l. de gol*** goal line *(between goalposts)*; ***l. de llegada*** finishing line; ***l. de marca*** *(en rugby)* try *o* goal line; ***l. de medio campo*** halfway line; ***l. de meta*** *(en fútbol)* goal line; *(en carreras)* finishing line; ***l. de salida*** starting line; ***l. de saque*** baseline, service line; ***l. de servicio*** service line; ***l. de seis veinticinco*** *(en baloncesto)* three-point line; ***l. de tiros libres*** *(en baloncesto)* free throw line
(f) *(en comercio)* line; **una nueva l. de productos** a new line of products ▸▸ ***l. blanca*** white goods; ***l. marrón*** brown goods
(g) *(silueta) (de persona)* figure; **guardar/mantener la l.** to watch/keep one's figure
(h) *(contorno)* **un coche de l. aerodinámica** a streamlined car
(i) *(estilo, tendencia)* style; **la l. del partido** the party line; **la l. dura del sindicato** the union's hard line; **la l. de pensamiento keynesiana** Keynesian thinking; **de l. clásica** classical; **eso está muy en su l.** that's just his style; **seguir la l. de alguien** to follow sb's style ▸▸ ***l. de conducta*** course of action; ***l. de investigación*** line of inquiry
(j) *(categoría)* class, category; **de primera l.** *(actor, pintor, producto)* first-rate; *(marca, empresa)* top
(k) *(de parentesco)* line; **está emparentada con ella por l. materna** she's related to her on her mother's side
(l) *Informát* line; **en l.** on-line; **fuera de l.** off-line ▸▸ ***l. de base*** baseline; ***l. de comando*** command line; ***l. dedicada*** dedicated line
(m) *(en el bingo)* line; **cantar l.** to call a line; **¡l.!** line!
(n) *Fam (de cocaína)* line
(o) EXPR **en líneas generales** in broad terms; **fueron derrotados en toda la l.** they were emphatically beaten

---

lineal *adj* (a) *(de la línea)* linear; **no l.** non-linear; **dibujo l.** = drawing of geometrical figures (b) *(hoja)* linear (c) *(aumento, descenso)* steady

lineamientos *nmpl Am* (a) *(generalidades)* outline; **sólo me comentaron los l. del proyecto** they only told me the general outline of the project (b) *(directrices)* guidelines

linfa *nf Fisiol* lymph

linfático, -a *adj* (**a**) *Anat* lymphatic (**b**) *(letárgico, apático)* lethargic

linfocito *nm Fisiol* lymphocyte ►► ***l. B*** B-cell, B-lymphocyte; ***l. T*** T-cell, T-lymphocyte

linfoma *nm Med* lymphoma

lingotazo *nm Esp Fam* swig; **un buen l. de whisky** a good swig of whisky

lingote *nm* ingot; **l. de oro** gold ingot

lingual *adj Anat* lingual

lingüista *nmf* linguist *(academic specialist)*

lingüística *nf* linguistics *(singular)* ►► ***l. aplicada*** applied linguistics; ***l. computacional*** computational linguistics; ***l. descriptiva*** descriptive linguistics; ***l. teórica*** theoretical linguistics

lingüístico, -a *adj* (**a**) *(de la lengua)* linguistic; **habilidades lingüísticas** language *o* linguistic abilities (**b**) *(de la lingüística)* linguistic

linier (*pl* **liniers**) *nm* linesman

linimento *nm* liniment

lino *nm* (**a**) *(planta)* flax (**b**) *(tejido)* linen

linóleo *nm* linoleum

linón *nm* lawn *(fabric)*

linotipia *nf* Linotype®

linotipista *nmf* linotypist

linotipo *nm* Linotype®

linterna *nf* (**a**) *(de pilas) Br* torch, *US* flashlight (**b**) *(farol)* lantern, lamp ►► ***l. mágica*** magic lantern (**c**) *Arquit* lantern (**d**) *Méx Fam (ojo)* eye

linudo, -a *adj Chile* woolly, fleecy

linuxero, -a *Informát* **1** *adj* Linux; **la comunidad linuxera** Linux users, the Linux community

2 *nm,f* Linux user

linyera *nmf RP (vagabundo)* tramp, *US* bum

lío *nm* (**a**) *Fam (enredo)* mess; **esto de la declaración de hacienda es un l.** filling in your tax return is a real pain *o Br* palaver; **hacerse un l.** to get muddled up; **son tantos hermanos que siempre me armo un l. con sus nombres** there are so many different brothers, I always get their names muddled up; **estoy hecho un l., no sé qué hacer** I'm all confused, I don't know what to do

(**b**) *Fam (problema)* **meterse en líos** to get into trouble; **me he metido en un l. del que no sé salir** I've got myself into a mess that I don't know how to get out of

(**c**) *Fam (jaleo)* racket, row; **armar un l.** to kick up a fuss

(**d**) *Fam (amorío)* affair; **está casado pero tiene un l. con alguien del trabajo** he's married, but he's having an affair with someone from work EXPR **tener un l. de faldas** to be having an affair

(**e**) *(paquete)* bundle

liofilización *nf* freeze-drying, *Espec* lyophilization

liofilizado, -a *adj* freeze-dried

liofilizar [14] *vt* to freeze-dry

lioso, -a *adj Fam* (**a**) *(complicado) (asunto)* complicated; *(explicación, historia)* convoluted, involved (**b**) *(persona)* **es muy l.** he's always messing us about *o* around

lipa *nf Ven Fam* gut, belly

lípido *nm Bioquím* lipid

lipoescultura *nf* liposculpture

lipón, -ona *adj Ven Fam* **ser l.** to have a potbelly

liposoluble *adj* soluble in fat

liposoma *nm Bioquím* liposome

liposucción *nf* liposuction

lipotimia *nf* fainting fit; **sufrió** *o* **le dio una l.** she fainted

liquen *nm* lichen

liquidación *nf* (**a**) *(pago)* settlement, payment; **hacer la l. de una cuenta** to settle an account ►► *Fin* ***l. de activos*** asset-stripping; *Com* ***l. de bienes*** liquidation of assets

(**b**) *(rebaja)* **l. (de existencias)** clearance sale; **estar de l.** to be having a clearance sale ►► ***l. por cese de negocio*** closing-down sale; ***l. por fin de temporada*** end-of-season sale; ***l. por reforma*** = sale before a shop is closed for renovation; ***l. por traspaso*** = sale before a business is sold to new management

(**c**) *(final)* liquidation

(**d**) *(finiquito)* redundancy settlement

(**e**) *Fam (eliminación)* liquidation

liquidador, -ora 1 *adj* liquidating

2 *nm,f* liquidator

liquidámbar *nm* liquidambar

liquidar 1 *vt* (**a**) *(pagar) (deuda)* to pay; *(cuenta)* to settle

(**b**) *(negocio, sociedad)* to wind up

(**c**) *(rebajar)* to sell off; **l. existencias** to have a stock clearance sale

(**d**) *Fam (malgastar)* to throw away; **liquidó la herencia en dos años** she frittered away *o* squandered her inheritance in two years

(**e**) *Fam (asunto)* to deal with, to see to; **y con esto hemos liquidado el tema segundo** that's the second subject seen to *o* dealt with; **no la invites, y asunto liquidado** just don't invite her and there's your problem solved

(**f**) *Fam (matar)* to liquidate

(**g**) *(gas, sólido)* to liquefy

2 liquidarse *vpr* (**a**) *(gas, sólido)* to liquefy (**b**) *Fam (acabar)* to polish off; **se liquidó la botella él solito** he polished off the bottle by himself; **nos liquidamos el premio en dos semanas** we blew the prize money in two weeks

liquidez *nf* liquidity

líquido, -a 1 *adj* (**a**) *(estado)* liquid; *Am* **crema líquida** single cream; **el l. elemento** water (**b**) *Econ (neto)* net (**c**) *Ling (sonido)* liquid

2 *nm* (**a**) *(sustancia)* liquid ►► ***l. de frenos*** brake fluid; ***l. refrigerante*** coolant (**b**) *Econ* liquid assets (**c**) *Med* fluid; ►► ***l. amniótico*** amniotic fluid; ***l. cefalorraquídeo*** cerebrospinal fluid; ***l. cerebroespinal*** cerebrospinal fluid; ***l. sinovial*** synovial fluid

liquiliqui, liquilique *nm Col, Ven* = linen suit with stand-up collar

lira *nf* (**a**) *Antes (moneda)* lira (**b**) *Mús* lyre

lírica *nf* lyric poetry

lírico, -a *adj* (**a**) *Lit* lyric, lyrical (**b**) *(musical)* musical

lirio *nm* iris ►► ***l. africano*** African lily; ***l. de agua*** yellow flag *o* iris; ***l. azul*** bearded lily; ***l. naranja*** tiger lily; ***l. de los valles*** lily of the valley

lirismo *nm* lyricism

lirón *nm* dormouse; EXPR **dormir como un l.** to sleep like a log ►► ***l. careto*** garden dormouse

lis *nf* **(flor de) l.** *(planta)* iris; *(en heráldica)* fleur-de-lis

lisa *nf* (**a**) *(pez)* striped mullet (**b**) *Ven (cerveza)* beer (**c**) *ver también* **liso**

Lisboa *n* Lisbon

lisboeta 1 *adj* of/from Lisbon *(Portugal)*

2 *nmf* person from Lisbon *(Portugal)*

lisbonense, -a, lisbonés, -esa *Literario* **1** *adj* of/from Lisbon *(Portugal)*

2 *nm,f* person from Lisbon *(Portugal)*

lisiado, -a 1 *adj* crippled

2 *nm,f* cripple

lisiar 1 *vt* to maim, to cripple

2 lisiarse *vpr* to be maimed *o* crippled

liso, -a 1 *adj* (**a**) *(llano)* flat; *(sin asperezas)* smooth; *Esp* **los 400 metros lisos** the 400 metres; **lisa y llanamente** quite simply; **hablando lisa y llanamente** to put it plainly (**b**) *(no estampado)* plain; **una tela lisa** a plain fabric (**c**) *(pelo)* straight (**d**) *(mujer)* flat-chested

2 *nm,f Andes, CAm, Ven* cheeky; **es un l.** he's so cheeky

lisonja *nf* flattering remark

lisonjeador, -ora 1 *adj* flattering

2 *nm,f* flatterer

lisonjear 1 *vt* to flatter

2 lisonjearse *vpr (mutuamente)* to flatter one another

lisonjero, -a *adj (persona, comentario)* flattering; *(perspectiva)* promising

lisp *nm Informát* LISP

lista *nf* (**a**) *(enumeración)* list; **hazme una l. de lo que quieres** write me a list of what you want; **pasar l.** to call the register ►► ***l. de boda*** wedding list; *Esp* ***l. de la compra*** shopping list; *Am* ***l. de las compras*** shopping list; *Informát* ***l. de correo*** mailing list; ***l. de correos*** *Br* poste restante, *US* general delivery; *Informát* ***l. de distribución*** mailing list; ***l. electoral*** = list of candidates put forward by a political party; *Av* ***l. de embarque*** passenger list; ***l. de espera*** waiting list; ***l. de éxitos*** *(musicales)* hit parade; ***l. negra*** blacklist; ***l. de precios*** price list

(**b**) *(de tela, madera)* strip; *(de papel)* slip

(**c**) *(en tela, de color)* stripe; **una camiseta a listas** a striped shirt

(**d**) *ver también* **listo**

listado¹, -a 1 *adj* striped

2 *nm* (**a**) *Informát* listing; **sacar un l.** to print a list, to do a listing (**b**) *(lista)* list

listado² *nm* skipjack tuna

listar *vt* (**a**) *Informát* to list (**b**) *Am (hacer una lista de)* to list

listeria *nf Med* listeria *(bacteria)*

listeriosis *nf Med* listeriosis, listeria *(illness)*

listero, -a *nm,f Informát Fam* list member

listillo, -a *nm,f Esp Fam Pey* smart alec(k)

listín *nm Esp* ***l. (de teléfonos)*** (telephone) directory

listo, -a 1 *adj* (**a**) *(inteligente, hábil)* clever, smart; EXPR **dársela de l.** to make oneself out to be clever; EXPR **pasarse de l.** to be too clever by half; **¡no te pases de l.!** don't be such a smart alec(k)!; EXPR **ser más l. que el hambre** to be nobody's fool

(**b**) *Fam (aprovechado)* **fue muy l. y se marchó sin pagar** he was really smart and left without paying

(**c**) *(preparado)* ready; **¿estás l.?** are you ready?; **¡l.!** (that's me) ready!, finished!; **lo pones cinco minutos al fuego, y l.** you heat it for five minutes and that's it; **preparados** *o RP* **prontos, listos, ¡ya!** ready, steady, go!, on your marks, get set, go!

(**d**) *Fam (apañado)* **estás** *o* **vas l. (si crees que...)** you've got another think coming (if you think that...); **¡estamos listos!** we're in real trouble!, we've had it!

2 *nm,f* **¿quién es el l. que ha apagado la luz?** who's the bright spark who switched the light off?; **hay mucho l. por ahí que se cree que esto es fácil** there are a lot of smart alec(k)s around who think this is easy; EXPR **hacerse el l.: no te hagas el l., que conozco tus intenciones** don't try and be clever, I know what you're up to

3 *interj Andes, RP* OK; **¿nos vemos a las ocho? – ¡l.!** shall we meet at eight? – OK! *o* sure!

listón *nm* (**a**) *(de madera)* lath (**b**) *Dep (en salto de altura)* bar; EXPR **poner** *o* **colocar el l. muy alto** to set very high standards (**c**) *Méx (de tela)* ribbon

lisura *nf* (**a**) *Andes, CAm, Ven (atrevimiento)* cheek (**b**) *Andes, CAm, Ven (dicho grosero)* rude remark (**c**) *Perú (donaire)* grace

litera *nf* (**a**) *(cama)* bunk (bed); *(de barco)* berth; *(de tren)* couchette (**b**) *(vehículo)* litter

literal *adj* (**a**) *(sentido, significado)* literal (**b**) *(traducción)* literal

literalmente *adv* (**a**) *(de manera literal)* literally (**b**) *(traducir)* literally, word for word

literariamente *adv* literarily

literario, -a *adj* literary

literato, -a *nm,f* writer, author

> **Falso amigo**: El adjetivo inglés **literate** no es la traducción del español **literato**. En inglés **literate** significa "que sabe leer y escribir" o "culto, instruido".

literatura *nf* (**a**) *(arte, obras)* literature ►► ***l. comparada*** comparative literature; ***l. fantástica*** fantasy (literature); ***l. de ficción*** fiction (**b**) *(bibliografía)* literature; **hay mucha l. sobre el periodo** there's a lot of literature on the period

litiasis *nf inv Med* lithiasis

litigación *nf* litigation

litigante 1 *adj* litigant

2 *nmf* litigant

litigar [38] *vi* to go to law

litigio *nm* (**a**) *Der* court case, lawsuit (**b**) *(disputa)* dispute; **en l.** in dispute; **entrar en l. con alguien** to enter into a dispute with sb

litigioso, -a *adj* litigious

litio *nm Quím* lithium

litografía *nf* (**a**) *(arte)* lithography (**b**) *(grabado)* lithograph (**c**) *(taller)* lithographer's (workshop)

litografiar [32] *vt* to lithograph

litográfico, -a *adj* lithographic

litología *nf* lithology

litoral 1 *adj* coastal

2 *nm* coast

litosfera *nf* lithosphere

lítote *nf*, **lítotes** *nf inv Ling* litotes

litro *nm* litre

litrona *nf Esp Fam* = litre bottle of beer

Lituania *n* Lithuania

lituano, -a 1 *adj* Lithuanian

2 *nm,f (persona)* Lithuanian

3 *nm (lengua)* Lithuanian

liturgia *nf* liturgy

litúrgico, -a *adj* liturgical

liudez *nf Chile* laxity

liviandad *nf* (**a**) *(levedad)* lightness (**b**) *(frivolidad)* flightiness, frivolousness

liviano, -a *adj* (**a**) *(de poco peso) (carga)* light (**b**) *(delgado) (blusa)* thin (**c**) *(alimento)* light (**d**) *(poco intenso)* **es un trabajo l.** it's not a very demanding job; **tengo el sueño muy l.** I'm a very light sleeper; **un dolor l.** a slight pain (**e**) *(frívolo)* frivolous

lividez *nf (palidez)* pallor

lívido, -a *adj* (**a**) *(pálido)* very pale, pallid (**b**) *(amoratado)* livid

living ['liβin] *(pl* **livings**) *nm* living-room; *CSur* **juego de l.** three-piece suite ►► *CSur* ***l. comedor*** living-cum-dining room

liza *nf (lucha)* battle; **en l.** in opposition; **los dos candidatos en l. intercambiaron acusaciones** the two opposing candidates exchanged accusations; **entrar en l.** to enter the arena

Ll, ll ['eʎe, 'eje] *nf (letra)* = double l character, traditionally considered a separate character in the Spanish alphabet

llaga *nf* (**a**) *(herida)* sore, ulcer (**b**) *(desgracia)* open wound

llagar [38] 1 *vt* to bring out in sores

2 **llagarse** *vpr* to become covered in sores; **se llagó los pies por caminar descalzo** his feet got cut and bruised from him walking around barefoot

llama *nf* (**a**) *(de fuego)* flame; **en llamas** ablaze (**b**) *(de pasión)* flame; **mantenían viva la l. de su amor** they kept the flame of their love alight (**c**) *(animal)* llama

llamada *nf* (**a**) *(para atraer atención)* call; *(a la puerta)* knock; *(con timbre)* ring ►► ***l. de atención*** warning; ***l. al orden*** call to order; ***l. de socorro*** call for help; *Av & Náut* distress call

(**b**) *(telefónica)* call; **hacer una l.** to make a phone call; **tienes dos llamadas en el contestador** you have two messages on your answering machine ►► ***l. a cobro revertido*** *o Am* ***l. por cobrar*** *o Ecuad, Urug* ***a cobrar*** *Br* reverse-charge call, *US* collect call; **hacer una l. a cobro revertido** *Br* to make a reverse-charge call, *US* to call collect; ***l. en espera*** call waiting; ***l. interurbana*** long-distance *o Br* national call; ***l. local*** local call; ***l. nacional*** national call; *Col* ***l. por pagar*** *Br* reverse-charge call, *US* collect call; ***l. telefónica*** telephone call, phone call; ***l. para tres*** three-way calling; ***l. urbana*** local call

(**c**) *(en un libro)* note, reference mark

(**d**) *Informát* call

llamado, -a 1 *adj* (**a**) *(con nombre)* **fueron descubiertas por un naturalista l. Marcelino** they were discovered by a naturalist called *o* named Marcelino; **el l. "efecto invernadero"** what is known as the "greenhouse effect"; **Roma, también llamada la Ciudad Eterna** Rome, also known as the Eternal City; **la ardilla gris, llamada así por el color de su piel** the grey squirrel, so called because of the colour of its fur

(**b**) *(destinado)* **un descubrimiento l. a revolucionar la vida moderna** a discovery destined to revolutionize modern life; **un joven l. a convertirse el líder del partido** a young man destined to become party leader

2 *nm Am* (**a**) *(en general)* call; *(a la puerta)* knock; *(con timbre)* ring ►► ***l. de atención*** warning; ***l. al orden*** call to order; ***l. de socorro*** distress signal

(**b**) *(telefónico)* call; **hacer un l.** to make a phone call; **tienes dos llamados en el contestador** you have two messages on your answering machine ►► ***l. a cobro revertido*** *Br* reverse-charge call, *US* collect call; **hacer un l. a cobro revertido** *Br* to make a reverse-charge call, *US* to call collect; ***l. interurbano*** long-distance *o Br* national call; ***l. local*** local call; ***l. nacional*** national call; ***l. telefónico*** telephone call, phone call; ***l. urbano*** local call

(**c**) *(apelación)* appeal, call; **hacer un l. a alguien para que haga algo** to call upon sb to do sth; **hacer un l. a la huelga** to call a strike

(**d**) *Mil* call-up; **un l. a filas** call-up

llamador *nm (aldaba)* door knocker; *(timbre)* bell

llamamiento *nm* (**a**) *(apelación)* appeal, call; **un l. a la calma** an appeal *o* call for calm; **hacer un l. a alguien para que haga algo** to call upon sb to do sth; **hacer un l. a la huelga** to call a strike (**b**) *Mil* call-up

LLAMAR 1 *vt* (**a**) *(dirigirse a, hacer venir)* to call; *(con gestos)* to beckon; **llamó por señas/con la mano al camarero** she beckoned to the waiter; **l. a alguien a voces** to shout to sb to come over; **l. al ascensor** to call the *Br* lift *o US* elevator; **l. (a) un taxi** *(en la calle)* to hail a cab; *(por teléfono)* to call for a taxi

(**b**) *(por teléfono)* to phone, to call, to ring; *(con el buscapersonas)* to page; **l. a los bomberos/al médico** to call the fire brigade/doctor; **te llamo mañana** I'll call *o* ring you tomorrow; **te ha llamado Luis** Luis phoned (for you), there was a call from Luis for you; **te han llamado de la oficina** there was a call from the office for you; **¿quién lo/la llama, por favor?** who's calling, please?

(**c**) *(dar nombre, apelativo, apodo)* to call; **¿ya sabes cómo vas a l. al perro?** have you decided what you're going to call the dog yet?; **me llamó mentiroso** she called me a liar; **fue lo que se dio en l. la Guerra de los Seis Días** it was what came to be known as the Six Day War; **¿a eso llamas tú un jardín?** do you call that a garden?; **eso es lo que yo llamo un buen negocio** that's what I call a good deal; **es un aparato para la humedad del aire, un humidificador, que lo llaman** it's a device for making the air more humid, a humidifier as they call it *o* as it is known

(**d**) *(convocar)* to summon, to call; **el jefe me llamó a su despacho** the boss summoned *o* called me to his office; **la han llamado para una entrevista de trabajo** she's got an interview for a job; **l. a alguien a filas** to call sb up; **l. a los trabajadores a la huelga** to call the workers out (on strike); **l. a alguien a juicio** to call sb to trial

(**e**) *(atraer)* to attract; **nunca me han llamado los deportes de invierno** I've never been attracted *o* drawn to winter sports

2 *vi* (**a**) *(a la puerta) (con golpes)* to knock; *(con timbre)* to ring; **l. a la puerta** *(con golpes)* to knock on the door; **están llamando** there's somebody at the door; **por favor, llamen antes de entrar** *(en letrero)* please knock/ring before entering

(**b**) *(por teléfono)* to phone

3 llamarse *vpr (tener por nombre, título)* to be called; **¿cómo te llamas?** what's your name?; **me llamo Patricia** my name's Patricia; **¿cómo se llama su última película?** what's her latest film called?; **¡tú vienes conmigo, como que me llamo Sara!** you're coming with me, or my name's not Sara!; **eso es lo que se llama buena suerte** that's what you call good luck; **no nos llamemos a engaño, el programa se puede mejorar y mucho** let's not kid ourselves, the programme could be a lot better; **que nadie se llame a engaño, la economía no va bien** let no one have any illusions about it, the economy isn't doing well

---

llamarada *nf* (**a**) *(de fuego)* blaze (**b**) *(de ira)* blaze; *(de rubor)* flush (**c**) *Informát* flame

llamativamente *adv (vestir)* showily, flamboyantly

llamativo, -a *adj (color)* bright, gaudy; *(ropa)* showy, flamboyant

llameante *adj* flaming, blazing

llamear *vi* to burn, to blaze

llana *nf* (**a**) *Gram* = word stressed on the last syllable (**b**) *(herramienta)* trowel

llanamente *adv* simply

llanear *vi* to roam the plains

llanero, -a 1 *adj* (**a**) *(del llano)* of the plainspeople (**b**) *Col, Ven (de los Llanos)* of/from the region of los Llanos *(Venezuela, Colombia)*

2 *nm,f* (**a**) *(del llano)* plainsman, *f* plainswoman ►► ***el L. Solitario*** the Lone Ranger (**b**) *Col, Ven (del campo) (dueño)* farmer; *(empleado)* farm labourer (**c**) *Col, Ven (de los Llanos)* person from the region of los Llanos *(Venezuela, Colombia)*

llaneza *nf* naturalness, straightforwardness

llanito, -a *Esp Fam* **1** *adj* Gibraltarian

2 *nm,f* Gibraltarian

llano, -a 1 *adj* (**a**) *(campo, superficie)* flat; **un plato l.** a (dinner) plate; *Am* **los 400 metros llanos** the 400 metres (**b**) *(trato, persona)* natural, straightforward (**c**) *(pueblo, clase)* ordinary (**d**) *(lenguaje, expresión)* simple, plain (**e**) *Gram* = stressed on the last syllable

2 *nm (llanura)* plain; *Col, Ven* **los Llanos** = name of vast region of tropical plains, mainly in Venezuela and Colombia

llanta *nf* (**a**) *Aut (aro metálico)* rim (**b**) *Am Aut (cubierta)* tyre; EXPR *RP* **estar en l.** to have a flat tyre ►► *Méx* ***l. de refacción*** spare wheel; *Col* ***l. de repuesto*** spare wheel (**c**) *Méx Fam (pliegue de grasa)* spare tyre

llantén *nm* (**a**) *(planta)* plantain (**b**) *Ven Fam (llanto)* crying fit

llantera, llantina *nf Fam* crying fit

llanto *nm* crying; **se escuchaba el l. de un bebé** we could hear a baby crying; **anegarse en l.** to burst into a flood of tears

llanura *nf* (**a**) *(terreno)* plain ►► ***l. aluvial*** flood plain (**b**) *(de superficie)* flatness

llave *nf* (**a**) *(de cerradura)* key; **una l. extra** *o* **adicional** a spare key; **bajo l.** under lock and key; **echar la l.**, *Am* **pasar l.**, **cerrar con l.** to lock up; **l. en mano** *(vivienda)* ready for immediate occupation; EXPR **bajo siete llaves** under lock and key; **guardaba el secreto bajo siete llaves** he didn't tell the secret to another soul ►► ***l. de contacto*** ignition key; *Informát* ***l. de hardware*** dongle; ***l. maestra*** master key

(**b**) *(grifo) Br* tap, *US* faucet ►► ***l. de paso*** stopcock; **cerrar la l. de paso** to turn the water/gas off at the mains

(**c**) *(interruptor)* ***l. de la luz*** light switch

(**d**) *(herramienta)* ***l. allen*** Allen key; ***l. inglesa*** monkey wrench, *Br* adjustable spanner; ***l. de torsión*** torque wrench; ***l. de tuerca*** spanner

(**e**) *(clave)* key

(**f**) *(de judo, lucha libre)* hold, lock

(**g**) *(signo ortográfico)* curly bracket

(**h**) *(de flauta)* key; *(de órgano)* stop; *(de trompeta)* valve

(**i**) *RP* **llaves** *(en compra inmobiliaria)* occupancy fee *(paid when keys are handed over)*

(**j**) *RP Dep (grupo)* group

(**k**) *Col, Ven muy Fam (amigo)* pal, *Br* mate, *US* buddy

llavero *nm* key ring

llavín *nm* latchkey

lleca *nf RP Fam* street *(in reverse slang)*

llegada *nf* (**a**) *(acción)* arrival; **a mi l.** on my arrival, when I arrived; **con la l. del invierno las aves migran** with the onset of winter the birds migrate; **llegadas nacionales/internacionales** *(en aeropuerto)* domestic/international arrivals (**b**) *Dep* finish

---

LLEGAR [38] **1** *vi* (**a**) *(persona, vehículo, medio de transporte)* to arrive (**de** from); **l. a un hotel/al aeropuerto** to arrive at a hotel/at the airport; **l. a una ciudad/a un país** to arrive in a city/in a country; **l. a casa** to get home; **l. a la meta** to cross the finishing line; **cuando llegué a esta empresa...** when I arrived at *o* first came to this company...; **llegaremos a la estación de Caracas a las dos** we will be arriving at Caracas station at two o'clock; **nosotros llegamos primero** *o* **los primeros** we arrived first; **el atleta cubano llegó primero** the Cuban athlete came first; **llegaban muy contentos** they were very happy when they arrived, they arrived very happy; **llegaré pronto** I'll be there early; **este avión llega tarde** this plane is late; **estar al l.: deben de estar al l.** they must be about to arrive, they're bound to arrive any minute now; **los Juegos Olímpicos están al l.** the Olympics are coming up soon; **¿falta mucho para l.** *o* **para que lleguemos?** is there far to go?; **así no llegarás a ninguna parte** you'll never get anywhere like that; *Fig* **llegará lejos** she'll go far

(**b**) *(carta, recado, mensaje)* to arrive; **llegarle a alguien: no me ha llegado aún el paquete** the parcel still hasn't arrived, I still haven't received the parcel; **ayer me llegó un mensaje suyo por correo electrónico** I got *o* received an e-mail from him yesterday; **hacer l. un mensaje** *o* **recado a alguien** to pass a message on to sb; **si llega a oídos de ella...** if she gets to hear about this...

(**c**) *(tiempo, noche, momento)* to come; **cuando llegue el momento te enterarás** you'll find out when the time comes; **ha llegado el invierno** winter has come *o* arrived

(**d**) *(alcanzar)* **l. a** to reach; **no llego al techo** I can't reach the ceiling; **el barro me llegaba a las rodillas** the mud came up to my knees, I was up to my knees in mud; **quiero una chaqueta que me llegue por debajo de la cintura** I want a jacket that comes down to below my waist; **l. a un acuerdo** to come to *o* reach an agreement; **llegamos a la conclusión de que era inútil seguir** we came to *o* reached the conclusion that it wasn't worth continuing; **l. hasta** to reach up to; **esta carretera sólo llega hasta Veracruz** this road only goes as far as Veracruz; **el ascensor no llega a** *o* **hasta la última planta** the *Br* lift *o US* elevator doesn't go up to the top floor

(**e**) *(ascender)* **el importe total de la reparación no llega a 5.000 pesos** the total cost of the repairs is less than *o* below 5,000 pesos; **los espectadores no llegaban ni siquiera a mil** there weren't even as many as a thousand spectators there

(**f**) *(ser suficiente)* to be enough (**para** for); **el dinero no me llega para comprarme una casa** the money isn't enough for me to buy a house

(**g**) *(lograr)* **l. a (ser) algo** to get to be sth, to become sth; **llegó a ser campeón de Europa** he became European champion; **l. a hacer algo** to manage to do sth; **pesaba mucho, pero al final llegué a levantarlo** it was very heavy, but I managed to lift it up in the end; **nunca llegó a (entrar en) las listas de éxitos** she never made it into the charts; **nunca llegué a conocerlo** I never actually met him; **si llego a saberlo...** *(en el futuro)* if I happen to find out...; *(en el pasado)* if I had known...

(**h**) *(al extremo de)* **llegó a decirme...** he went as far as to say to me...; **hemos llegado a pagar 4.000 euros** at times we've had to pay as much as 4,000 euros; **cuesta l. a creerlo** it's very hard to believe it; EXPR **¡hasta aquí** *o* **ahí podíamos l.!** this is beyond a joke *o* absolutely outrageous!

(**i**) *(causar impresión, interesar)* **tiene una imagen que no llega al electorado** she fails to project a strong image to the electorate; **son canciones sencillas que llegan a la gente** they are simple songs that mean something to people; **lo que dijo me llegó al alma** her words really struck home

(**j**) *(durar)* **l. a** *o* **hasta** to last until; **este año las rebajas llegarán hasta bien entrado febrero** the sales this year will last until well into

February; **está muy enferma, no creo que llegue a las Navidades** she's very ill, I doubt whether she'll make it to Christmas
(**k**) *Méx Fam* **voy a llegarle** *(ya me voy)* I'm off home; **illégale!** *(no hay problema)* no problem!, don't worry!
(**l**) *Méx Fam* **llegarle a alguien** *(pedirle salir)* to ask sb out
2 llegarse *vpr* **llegarse a** to go round to; **llégate donde el abuelo y que te preste las herramientas** go over *o* round to your grandfather's and ask if you can borrow his tools; **me llegué a casa para ver si habías vuelto** I went home to see if you were back yet

llegue *nm Méx Fam* bump

llenado *nm* filling

llenador, -ora 1 *adj* (**a**) *CSur (comida)* filling (**b**) *Urug Fam (persona)* **ser l.** to be a pain
2 *nm,f Urug Fam (persona)* pain

LLENAR 1 *vt* (**a**) *(ocupar) (vaso, hoyo, habitación)* to fill (**de** *o* **con** with); **llenó la casa de muebles usados** she filled the house with second-hand furniture; **l. el depósito** *(del coche)* to fill up the tank; **illénemelo!** *(el depósito)* fill her up, please; **llenan su tiempo libre leyendo y charlando** they spend their spare time reading and chatting
(**b**) *(cubrir) (pared, suelo)* to cover (**de** with); **llenó de adornos el árbol de Navidad** she covered the Christmas tree with decorations; **has llenado la pared de salpicaduras de aceite** you've spattered oil all over the wall
(**c**) *(colmar)* **l. a alguien de** *(alegría, tristeza)* to fill sb with; **este premio me llena de orgullo** this prize fills me with pride *o* makes me very proud; **llenaron de insultos al árbitro** they hurled abuse at the referee; **nos llenaron de obsequios** they showered gifts upon us
(**d**) *(rellenar) (impreso, solicitud, quiniela)* to fill in *o* out
(**e**) *(satisfacer)* **le llena su trabajo** he's fulfilled in his job; **no le llena la relación con su novio** she finds her relationship with her boyfriend unfulfilling
(**f**) *Fam (gustar)* **a mí el queso no me termina de l.** cheese isn't really my thing
(**g**) *RP Fam (fastidiar)* **ino me llenes!** stop bugging me!; **no (me) llenes la paciencia** don't push your luck; EXPR *muy Fam* **l. las pelotas** *o* **las bolas** *o* **los huevos a alguien** *Br* to get on sb's tits, *US* to bust sb's balls; **dejá de l. las pelotas** *o* **las bolas** *o* **los huevos** stop being a pain in the *Br* arse *o US* ass
2 *vi* (**a**) *(comida)* to be filling (**b**) *RP Fam (molestar)* to be a pest; **ino llenes!** stop being a pest!
3 llenarse *vpr* (**a**) *(ocuparse)* to fill up (**de** with); **la sala se llenó para ver al grupo** the venue was full for the band's performance; **la calle se llenó de gente** the street filled with people; **se le llenó de humo la cocina** the kitchen filled with smoke; **su mente se iba llenando de remordimientos** her mind was plagued by remorse
(**b**) *(cargar)* **se llenó el bolsillo de monedas** he filled his pocket with coins; **se llenó la mochila de comida para el viaje** she filled her backpack with food for the journey
(**c**) *(cubrirse)* **llenarse de** to get covered in; **el traje se me llenó de barro** my suit got covered in mud; **las manos se le llenaron de ampollas** his hands got covered in blisters
(**d**) *(saciarse)* **comieron hasta llenarse** they ate their fill; **me he llenado mucho con el arroz** this rice has really filled me up

llenazo *nm* full house

llenito, -a *adj Fam (regordete)* chubby

lleno, -a 1 *adj* (**a**) *(recipiente, habitación)* full (**de** of); *(suelo, mesa, pared)* covered (**de** in *o* with); **l., por favor** *(en gasolinera)* fill her up, please; **el estadio estaba l. hasta los topes** *o* **hasta la bandera** the stadium was packed to the rafters; **estaba l. de tristeza** I was full of sadness; **su discurso estaba l. de promesas** her speech was full of promises
(**b**) *(regordete)* plump
(**c**) *(satisfecho)* full (up); **no quiero postre, gracias, estoy l.** I don't want a dessert, thanks, I'm full (up)
(**d**) *(luna)* full
(**e**) *Urug Fam (harto)* fed up; **estoy l. de esta computadora** I'm fed up *o* I've had it up to here with this computer; **me tiene llena** I've had it with him; EXPR *muy Fam* **tengo las pelotas llenas** I'm *Br* bloody *o US* goddamn fed up!
2 *nm (en teatro, estadio)* full house; **se espera un l. total** a full house is expected
3 de lleno *loc adv* **le dio de l. en la cara** it hit him full in the face; **acertó de l.** he was bang on target

llevadero, -a *adj* bearable

LLEVAR 1 *vt* (**a**) *(de un lugar a otro)* to take; **le llevé unos bombones al hospital** I took her some chocolates at the hospital, I brought some chocolates for her to the hospital with me; **llevaré a los niños al zoo** I'll take the children to the zoo; **llevó una botella de vino a la fiesta** he brought a bottle of wine to the party; **nosotros llevamos la mercancía del almacén a las tiendas** we bring *o* transport the goods from the warehouse to the shops; **me llevó en coche** he drove me there; **¿vas al colegio? isube, que te llevo!** are you going to school? get in, I'll give you a *Br* lift *o US* ride; **¿para tomar aquí o para l.?** is it to eat in or *Br* to take away *o US* to go?; **pizzas para l.** *(en letrero) Br* takeaway pizzas, *US* pizzas to go
(**b**) *(acarrear)* to carry; **llevaba un saco a sus espaldas** she was carrying a sack on her back; **llevaban en hombros al entrenador** they were carrying the coach on their shoulders; **¿llevas rueda de recambio?** have you got a spare wheel?; **l. adelante algo** *(planes, proyecto)* to go ahead with sth; **l. consigo** *(implicar)* to lead to, to bring about; **está prohibido l. armas** carrying arms is prohibited
(**c**) *(encima) (ropa, objeto personal)* to wear; **llevo gafas** I wear glasses; **¿llevas reloj?** *(en este momento)* have you got a watch on?, are you wearing a watch?; *(habitualmente)* do you wear a watch?; **llevaba una falda azul** she was wearing a blue skirt; **no lleva nada puesto** she hasn't got anything *o* any clothes on; **no llevo dinero** I haven't got any money on me; **nunca llevo mucho dinero encima** I never carry a lot of money on me *o* around; **todavía lleva pañales** he's still in *Br* nappies *o US* diapers
(**d**) *(tener)* to have; **l. bigote** to have a moustache; **lleva el pelo largo** he has long hair; **me gusta l. el pelo recogido** I like to wear my hair up; **llevas las manos sucias** your hands are dirty; **los productos ecológicos llevan una etiqueta verde** environmentally friendly products carry a green label
(**e**) *(como ingrediente)* **esta tortilla lleva cebolla** this omelette has got onion in it; **¿qué lleva el daiquiri?** what do you make a daiquiri with?
(**f**) *(guiar, acompañar)* to take; **los llevé por otro camino** I took them another way; **lo llevaron a la comisaría** he was taken to the police station; **un guía nos llevó hasta la cima** a guide led us to the top; *Méx* **lléveme con el gerente** I want to see the manager
(**g**) *(dirigir)* to be in charge of; *(casa, negocio)* to look after, to run; **lleva la contabilidad** she keeps the books
(**h**) *(manejar, ocuparse de) (problema, persona)* to handle; *(asunto, caso, expediente)* to deal with; *(automóvil)* to drive; *(bicicleta, moto)* to ride; **este asunto lo lleva el departamento de contabilidad** this matter is being handled by the accounts department; **ella llevó las negociaciones personalmente** she handled the negotiations herself; **el inspector que lleva el caso** the inspector in charge of the case; **lleva muy bien sus estudios** he's doing very well in his studies; **sabe cómo l. a la gente** she's good with people
(**i**) *(mantener)* to keep; **el hotel lleva un registro de todos sus clientes** the hotel keeps a record of all its guests; **llevo la cuenta de todos tus fallos** I've been keeping count of all your mistakes; **l. el paso** to keep in step; **l. el ritmo** *o* **compás** to keep time; **llevan una vida muy tranquila** they lead a very quiet life
(**j**) *(soportar)* to deal *o* cope with; **l. algo bien/mal** to deal *o* cope with sth well/badly; **¿qué tal llevas** *o* **cómo llevas el régimen?** how are you getting on with the diet?; **llevo bien lo de ir en tren todos los días, pero lo de madrugar...** I can quite happily cope with catching the train every day, but as for getting up early...; *Fam* **¿cómo lo llevas con el nuevo jefe?** how are you getting on with your new boss?
(**k**) *(ir por)* **la dirección que lleva el vehículo** the direction in which the vehicle is heading; **lleva camino de ser famoso/rico** he's on the road to fame/riches; EXPR **l. las de ganar/perder: el equipo local lleva las de ganar/perder** the local team are favourites to win/lose; **en un juicio, llevamos las de ganar** if the matter goes to court, we can expect to win; **no te enfrentes con él, que llevas las de perder** don't mess with him, you can't hope to win
(**l**) *(conducir)* **l. a alguien a algo** to lead sb to sth; **aquella inversión le llevaría a la ruina** that investment was to bring about his ruin; **¿adónde nos lleva la ingeniería genética?** where is all this genetic engineering going to end?; **l. a alguien a hacer algo** to lead *o* cause sb to do sth; **esto me lleva a creer que miente** this makes me think she's lying; **¿qué pudo llevarle a cometer semejante crimen?** what could have led *o* caused him to commit such a crime?
(**m**) *(sobrepasar en)* **te llevo seis puntos** I'm six points ahead of you; **me lleva dos centímetros/dos años** he's two centimetres taller/two years older than me
(**n**) *(amputar)* **la motosierra casi le lleva una pierna** the power saw nearly took *o* cut his leg off
(**o**) *(costar) (tiempo, esfuerzo)* to take; **aprender a conducir** *o Am* **manejar lleva tiempo** it takes time to learn to drive; **me llevó un día**

hacer este guiso it took me a day to make this dish

(**p**) *(pasarse) (tiempo)* **lleva tres semanas sin venir** she hasn't come for three weeks now, it's three weeks since she was last here; **llevaba siglos sin ir al cine** I hadn't been to the cinema for ages, it was ages since I'd been to the cinema; **¿cuánto tiempo llevas aquí?** how long have you been here?; **llevo todo el día llamándote** I've been trying to get through to you on the phone all day; **l. mucho tiempo haciendo algo** to have been doing sth for a long time

(**q**) *Esp (cobrar)* to charge; **¿qué te llevaron por la revisión del coche?** how much *o* what did they charge you for servicing the car?

(**r**) *CSur (comprar)* to take; **llevaré la roja** I'll take *o* have the red one; **¿lo envuelvo o lo lleva puesto?** shall I wrap it up for you or do you want to keep it on?

2 *vi (conducir)* **l. a** to lead to; **esta carretera lleva al norte** this road leads north

3 *v aux (antes de participio)* **llevo leída media novela** I'm halfway through the novel; **llevo dicho esto mismo docenas de veces** I've said the same thing time and again; **llevaba anotados todos los gastos** she had noted down all the expenses

4 llevarse *vpr* (**a**) *(tomar consigo)* to take; **alguien se ha llevado mi sombrero** someone has taken my hat; **voy a llevarme esta falda** *(comprar)* I'll take *o* have this skirt; **¿se lo envuelvo o se lo lleva puesto?** shall I wrap it up for you or do you want to keep it on?

(**b**) *(trasladar, desplazar)* to take; **los agentes se lo llevaron detenido** the policemen took him away; **se llevó el cigarrillo a la boca** she brought *o* raised the cigarette to her lips; **llevarse algo por delante: la riada se llevó por delante casas y vehículos** the flood swept *o* washed away houses and vehicles; **un coche se lo llevó por delante** he was run over by a car

(**c**) *(conseguir)* to get; **se ha llevado el premio** she has carried off *o* won the prize

(**d**) *(recibir) (susto, sorpresa)* to get; *(reprimenda)* to receive; **como vuelvas a hacerlo te llevarás una bofetada** if you do it again you'll get a smack; **me llevé un disgusto/una desilusión** I was upset/disappointed; **llevarse una alegría** to have *o* get a pleasant surprise; **yo me llevo siempre las culpas** I always get the blame

(**e**) *(entenderse)* **llevarse bien/mal (con alguien)** to get on well/badly (with sb); **no me llevo muy bien con él** I don't get on very well with him; EXPR **se llevan a matar** they are mortal enemies

(**f**) *(estar de moda)* to be in (fashion); **este año se lleva el verde** green is in this year; **ahora se llevan mucho las despedidas de soltera** hen parties are really in at the moment

(**g**) *(recíproco) (diferencia de edad)* **mi hermana mayor y yo nos llevamos cinco años** there are five years between me and my older sister

(**h**) *(en operaciones matemáticas)* **me llevo una** carry (the) one

---

lloradera *nf Am Fam* (**a**) *(llanto)* crying fit (**b**) *(lamento)* wailing

llorado, -a *adj* late lamented

llorar 1 *vi* (**a**) *(con lágrimas)* to cry; **me entraron ganas de l.** I felt like crying; **l. por alguien** to mourn sb; **cuando se enteró rompió a l.** when she found out she burst into tears; **l. de rabia** to cry with anger *o* rage; **l. de risa** to cry with laughter; EXPR **l. a moco tendido, l. a lágrima viva** to cry one's eyes out, to sob one's heart out; EXPR *Fam* **l. como una Magdalena** to cry one's eyes out, to sob one's heart out; EXPR **para echarse a l.** dismal, depressingly bad; **su examen estaba para echarse a l.** his exam was dismal *o* depressingly bad

(**b**) *(ojos)* to water; **me lloran los ojos** my eyes are watering

(**c**) *Fam (quejarse)* to whinge; **consigue lo que quiere a fuerza de l.** she gets what she wants by whingeing until you give it to her

2 *vt* **l. la muerte de alguien** to mourn sb's death; **todos lloraron su desaparición** everybody lamented her disappearance

llorera *nf Fam* crying fit; **agarró una l.** she burst into tears; **le entró la l.** he burst into tears

llorica *Esp Fam Pey* **1** *adj* **ser l.** to be a crybaby

2 *nmf* crybaby

lloriqueadera, lloriquera *nf Ven Fam* whining, snivelling

lloriquear *vi* to whine, to snivel

lloriqueo *nm* whining, snivelling

lloriquera = **lloriqueadera**

lloro *nm* crying; **nos despertaron sus lloros** we were woken by the sound of him crying

llorón, -ona 1 *adj* (**a**) *(que llora)* **ser l.** to cry a lot; **no seas l.** don't be such a crybaby (**b**) *(quejica)* whining, *Br* whingeing

2 *nm,f* (**a**) *(que llora)* crybaby (**b**) *(quejica)* whiner, *Br* whinger

llorona *nf* (**a**) *Esp Fam* **coger la l.** *(por borrachera)* to get maudlin drunk (**b**) *RP (espuela)* spur

lloroso, -a *adj* tearful; **se acercó a la tumba y l. depositó una corona de flores** he approached the grave and tearfully laid a wreath of flowers on it; **tenía los ojos llorosos** she had tears in her eyes

llovedera *nf Col, Ven Fam* (**a**) *(lluvia)* **una l.** a downpour, torrential rain (**b**) *(estación)* rainy season

llover [41] **1** *v impersonal* to rain; **está lloviendo** it's raining; *CSur* **se largó a l.** it suddenly started raining; EXPR **está lloviendo a cántaros** *o* **a mares** *o Méx* **duro** it's pouring, *Br* it's bucketing down; EXPR **nunca llueve a gusto de todos** you can't please everyone; EXPR **llueve sobre mojado** it's just one thing after another; EXPR **él, como quien oye l.** he wasn't paying a blind bit of attention; EXPR **ha llovido mucho desde entonces** a lot of water has passed *o* gone under the bridge since then; EXPR **como llovido del cielo: el trabajo me cayó** *o* **llegó como llovido del cielo** the job fell into my lap; **la ayuda cayó** *o* **llegó como llovida del cielo** the help came just at the right moment, the help was a godsend; EXPR *Am Hum* **anda a la esquina a ver si llueve** go and play with the traffic

2 *vi* **le llueven las ofertas** offers are raining down on him; **las peticiones de indulto llovieron sobre el presidente** the president was inundated with pleas for pardon; **le llovieron las felicitaciones** everyone rushed to congratulate her; **sobre esa familia han llovido las desgracias** misfortune has rained down on that family, that family has suffered one misfortune after another

llovida *nf Andes, RP* shower; **el campo precisa una l.** the fields could do with some rain

llovido, -a *adj RP (pelo)* thin and lank

llovizna *nf* drizzle

lloviznar *v impersonal* to drizzle

lloviznoso, -a *adj Am Fam* rainy

llueva *etc ver* **llover**

lluvero *nm Urug* shower

lluvia *nf* (**a**) *(precipitación)* rain; **caía una l. torrencial** there was torrential rain; **la época de lluvias** the rainy season; **la falta de lluvias ha dañado la cosecha** the lack of rain *o* low rainfall has damaged the crops; **bajo la l.** in the rain ►► ***lluvias de abril*** April showers; ***l. ácida*** acid rain; ***l. artificial*** artificial rain; ***l. de cenizas*** shower of ash; ***l. de estrellas*** shower of shooting stars; ***l. de meteoritos*** meteor shower; ***l. radiactiva*** (nuclear) fallout

(**b**) *(de panfletos, regalos)* shower; *(de preguntas)* barrage

(**c**) *CAm, CSur (ducha)* shower

lluvioso, -a *adj* rainy

LO[1], -A (*mpl* **los**, *fpl* **las**) *pron personal (complemento directo)* (**a**) *(a él, a ella)* him, *f* her; *pl* them; **lo conocí en una fiesta** I met him at a party; **la han despedido** she's been sacked, they've sacked her; **¡si lo insultan a uno, habrá que contestar!** if people insult you, you have to answer back!

(**b**) *(a usted)* you; **¿la acerco a algún sitio?** can I give you a *Br* lift *o US* ride anywhere?

(**c**) *(ello, esa cosa)* it; *pl* them; **no lo he visto** I haven't seen it; **esta pared hay que pintarla** this wall needs painting

---

LO[2] **1** *pron personal* (**a**) *(neutro & predicado)* it; **lo pensaré** I'll think about it; **no lo sé** I don't know; **me gusta – ¡ya lo veo!** I like it – I can see that!; **su hermana es muy guapa pero él no lo es** his sister is very good-looking, but he isn't; **¿estás cansado? – sí que lo estoy** are you tired? – yes, I am; **es muy bueno aunque no lo parezca** it's very good, even if it doesn't look it

(**b**) *RP (lugar)* **vamos a lo de Claudio** let's go to Claudio's (place); **compré este vestido en lo de Vicky** I bought this dress at Vicky's (shop)

2 *art (neutro)* (**a**) *(antes de adjetivo, frase sustantiva o pronombre)* **lo antiguo me gusta más que lo moderno** I like old things better than modern things; **te olvidas de lo principal** you're forgetting the most important thing; **lo interesante viene ahora** now comes the interesting bit *o* part; **lo mejor/peor es que...** the best/worst part is (that)...; **quiere lo mejor para sus hijos** she wants the best for her children; **¿y lo de la fiesta?** what about the party, then?; **siento lo de ayer** I'm sorry about yesterday; **lo de abrir una tienda no me parece mala idea** opening a shop doesn't seem at all a bad idea to me; **lo de la huelga sigue sin resolverse** that strike business still hasn't been resolved; **lo mío/tuyo/suyo/***etc. (cosas personales)* my/your/his/*etc* things; **lo mío son los toros** *(lo que me va)* bullfighting's my thing, I'm a big bullfighting fan; **el ajedrez no es lo mío** *(mi punto fuerte)* chess isn't really my thing *o* game, I'm not very good at chess

(**b**) *(con valor enfático)* **¡mira que no gustarle el queso, con lo bueno que está!** how can she say she doesn't like cheese when it's so good?;

no me quiere ayudar, ¡con todo lo que yo he hecho por ella! she doesn't want to help me – and after all I've done for her!; **no te imaginas lo grande que era** you can't imagine how big it was; **¡lo que me pude reír con sus chistes!** I did laugh *o* I really laughed at his jokes!

(**c**) *(con frases de relativo)* **lo cual** which; **no quiso participar, lo cual no es de extrañar** she didn't want to take part, which is hardly surprising; **acepté lo que me ofrecieron** I accepted what they offered me; **gano menos de lo que te imaginas** I earn less than you think; **lo que ocurre es que...** the thing is (that)...; **puedes tomar lo que te apetezca** you can have whatever you want; **en lo que respecta a...** as far as... is concerned, with regard to...

3 a lo que *loc conj Andes, RP (en cuanto)* as soon as; **a lo que lo vio, salió corriendo** she ran away as soon as she saw him

---

loa *nf* (**a**) *(alabanza)* praise; **cantar l. a, hacer l. de** to sing the praises of (**b**) *Lit* eulogy (**c**) *Méx (regañina)* ticking-off

loable *adj* praiseworthy

loar *vt* to praise

lob *nm (en tenis)* lob

lobanillo *nm (tumor)* cyst, wen

lobato *nm* (**a**) *(animal)* wolf cub (**b**) *(niño)* Cub (Scout)

lobbista *nmf RP* lobbyist

lobby ['loβi] (*pl* **lobbies**) *nm* lobby

lobelia *nf* lobelia

lobezno *nm* wolf cub

lobizón *nm RP* werewolf

lobo, -a *adj* **1** *Col Fam (cursi)* tacky, *Br* naff

2 *nm,f* wolf; EXPR *Fam* **¡menos lobos!** tell me another one!, come off it! ►► ***el l. feroz*** the big bad wolf; ***l. de mar*** *(marinero)* sea dog; ***l. marino*** *(foca)* seal; ***l. de río*** *(pez)* stone loach; ***l. solitario*** lone wolf

lobotomía *nf* lobotomy ►► ***l. frontal*** frontal lobotomy

lóbrego, -a *adj* (**a**) *(oscuro, sombrío)* gloomy (**b**) *(triste, melancólico)* sombre, gloomy

lobreguez *nf* (**a**) *(oscuridad)* gloominess (**b**) *(tristeza)* gloominess

lobulado, -a *adj* lobulate

lóbulo *nm* (**a**) *(de la oreja)* lobe (**b**) *(de pulmón, hígado)* lobe ►► *Anat* ***l. frontal*** frontal lobe; *Anat* ***l. occipital*** occipital lobe; *Anat* ***l. temporal*** temporal lobe (**c**) *(de arco, planta)* lobe

lobuno, -a *adj* wolf-like

loca *nf* (**a**) *Fam (homosexual)* queen (**b**) *RP Fam (prostituta)* whore, *US* hooker (**c**) EXPR *RP Fam* **darle la l. a alguien: le dio la l. y se mandó mudar** he had a sudden brainstorm and decided to move house; **le dio la l. de irse al Tíbet** she took it into her head to head off for Tibet (**d**) *ver también* **loco**

locación *nf Méx* location

local 1 *adj* (**a**) *(de un lugar)* local; **el equipo l.** the home team (**b**) *(anestesia)* local

2 *nm (establecimiento)* premises ►► ***l. comercial*** business premises; ***l. de ensayo*** rehearsal space; **buscan un l. de ensayo** they're looking for somewhere to rehearse; ***l. nocturno*** night spot

localidad *nf* (**a**) *(población)* place, town (**b**) *(asiento)* seat; **el estadio sólo tiene localidades de asiento** it's an all-seater stadium (**c**) *(entrada)* ticket; **no hay localidades** *(en letrero)* sold out; **las localidades de asiento cuestan 2.000 pesos** seats cost 2,000 pesos

localismo *nm* (**a**) *(carácter local)* **el l. abunda en sus novelas** her novels are full of local colour (**b**) *(preferencia por lo local)* local patriotism (**c**) *Ling* localism

localista *adj* (**a**) *(del lugar)* local (**b**) *(que prefiere lo local)* **sentimientos localistas** feelings of local patriotism

localizable *adj* **en estos momentos no está l.** we can't get hold of him at the moment

localización *nf* (**a**) *(acción)* tracking down; **la l. de los montañeros extraviados fue difícil** it proved difficult to track down *o* find the mountaineers (**b**) *(emplazamiento)* **la l. del tumor hace difícil la intervención** the position of the tumour makes it a difficult operation; **buscan una l. para la central nuclear** they are searching for a site for the nuclear power station (**c**) *Informát (de software)* localization

localizado, -a *adj* located; **estar bien l.** *(casa)* to be conveniently located

localizador, -ora 1 *nm* (**a**) *Informát (de página Web)* URL (**b**) *Méx (buscapersonas)* pager

2 *nm,f Informát (de software)* localizer

localizar [14] **1** *vt* (**a**) *(encontrar)* to locate, to find; **l. una llamada** to trace a call; **no han localizado al excursionista extraviado** the missing hiker hasn't been found; **llevo horas intentando localizarlo** I've been trying to get hold of him for hours (**b**) *(circunscribir)* to localize; **han localizado la epidemia** the epidemic has been localized (**c**) *Informát (software)* to adapt for the local market, to localize

2 localizarse *vpr* **la infección se localiza en el hígado** the infection is localized in the liver

localmente *adv* locally

locamente *adv* madly; **está l. enamorada** she's madly *o* head over heels in love

locatario, -a *nm,f* tenant

locateli *CSur Fam* **1** *adj inv* nutty

2 *nmf* nutcase

locatis *Esp Fam* **1** *adj inv* nutty

2 *nmf inv* nutcase

locativo *nm* locative

loc. cit. (*abrev de* **loco citato**) loc. cit.

locha *nf Ven* = old coin formerly worth 25 cents; **estar en la lucha por la l.** to be struggling to make ends meet

loción *nf* lotion ►► ***l. bronceadora*** sun *o* suntan lotion; ***l. de calamina*** calamine lotion; ***l. capilar*** hair lotion; ***l. para después del afeitado*** aftershave (lotion); ***l. limpiadora*** cleansing lotion; ***l. para las manos*** hand lotion

locker [lo'ker] (*pl* **lockers**) *nm Am* locker

lock-out [lo'kaut] (*pl* **lock-outs**) *nm Ind* lockout

LOCO, -A **1** *adj* (**a**) *(demente)* mad, crazy; **volver l. a alguien** *(enajenar, aturdir)* to drive sb mad; **esos martillazos en la pared me van a volver l.** that hammering on the wall is driving me mad; **el dolor lo volvía l.** the pain was driving him mad; **volverse l.** to go mad; **este niño me trae l.** this child is driving me mad; EXPR **estar l. de atar** *o* **de remate** to be stark raving mad; EXPR **¡ni l.!** (absolutely) no way!; **¡no lo haría ni l.!** there's no way you'd get me doing that!

(**b**) *(insensato)* mad, crazy; **no seas loca, es muy peligroso** don't be (so) stupid, it's very dangerous; **está medio l. pero es muy simpático** he's a bit crazy, but he's very nice with it; **a lo l.** *(sin pensar)* hastily; *(temerariamente)* wildly; **conduce** *o Am* **maneja a lo l.** he drives like a madman

(**c**) *(apasionado, entusiasmado)* mad, crazy; **la abuela está loca con su nieto** the grandmother's mad *o* crazy about her grandson; **estar l. de contento/pasión** to be wild with joy/passion; **estar l. de amor** to be madly in love; **estar l. de celos** to be wildly *o* insanely jealous; **estar l. de ira** to be raging mad; **estar** *o CSur* **ser l. por algo/alguien** to be mad about sth/sb; **está** *o CSur* **es l. por ella** *(enamorado)* he's madly in love with her, he's crazy about her; **está loca por conocerte** she's dying to meet you; **está (como) l. por que lleguen los invitados** he's desperate for the guests to arrive, he can't wait for the guests to arrive; **le vuelve l. el fútbol** he's mad about soccer, he's soccer-crazy; **la vuelve loca la paella** she absolutely adores paella

(**d**) *(muy ajetreado)* mad, hectic; **llevamos una semana loca** it's been a mad week for us

(**e**) *(enorme)* **tengo unas ganas locas de conocer Italia** I'm absolutely dying to go to Italy; **tuvimos una suerte loca** we were extraordinarily *o* amazingly lucky; *RP Fam* **tener la guita loca** to be rolling in it

(**f**) *RP Fam (insignificante)* **sólo van a venir tres o cuatro invitados locos** only a handful of guests will show up; **no nos vamos a pelear por dos pesos locos** let's not quarrel over a few measly pesos

2 *nm,f* (**a**) *(enfermo) (hombre)* lunatic, madman; *(mujer)* lunatic, madwoman; **conduce** *o Am* **maneja como un l.** he drives like a madman; **corrimos como locos** we ran like mad *o* crazy; **el l. de tu marido se puso a chillar** that madman husband of yours started shouting; **ponerse como un l.** *(enfadarse)* to go mad; **sería de locos empezar de nuevo todo el trabajo** it would be crazy *o* madness to start the whole job over again; *Fam* **¡deja de hacer el l.!** stop messing around!; EXPR **cada l. con su tema: ya está otra vez Santi con lo del yoga, cada l. con su tema** Santi's going on about yoga again, the man's obsessed!; EXPR *Fam* **hacerse el l.** to play dumb, to pretend not to understand

(**b**) *RP, Ven Fam (como apelativo)* **este l. se encarga de todo** this guy's in charge of everything; **l., ven para acá** come over here, *Br* mate *o US* buddy

(**c**) *Chile (molusco comestible)* false abalone

---

locochón, -ona *nm,f Méx Fam* junkie

locomoción *nf* (**a**) *(movimiento)* locomotion; **órgano de l.** organ of locomotion *o* movement; **medio de l.** means of transport (**b**) *Am (transporte público)* public transport

locomotor, -ora *o* **-triz** *adj* locomotive

locomotora *nf* engine, locomotive; *Fig* **el turismo es la l. de la economía** tourism is the driving force behind the economy ▸▸ ***l. diesel*** diesel engine; ***l. eléctrica*** electric locomotive; ***l. de tracción*** traction engine; ***l. de vapor*** steam locomotive

locoto *nm Andes* chilli

locro *nm Andes, RP* = stew of meat, potatoes and sweetcorn

locuacidad *nf* loquacity, talkativeness

locuaz *adj* loquacious, talkative

locución *nf* phrase ▸▸ ***l. adjetiva*** adjectival phrase; ***l. adverbial*** adverbial phrase; ***l. conjuntiva*** conjunctional phrase; ***l. prepositiva*** prepositional phrase; ***l. verbal*** verb phrase

locuelo, -a 1 *adj* crazy, halfwitted
2 *nm,f* **es un l.** he's crazy *o* a halfwit

locura *nf* **(a)** *(demencia)* madness; **la mató en un arrebato de l.** he killed her in a fit of madness
(b) *(imprudencia)* **hacer locuras** to do stupid *o* crazy things; **decir locuras** to talk nonsense; **temía que hiciera una l.** I was afraid he might do something desperate; **sería una l. hacerlo** it would be folly *o* madness to do it
(c) *(exageración)* **estos precios son una l.** these prices are extortionate; **con l.** madly; **se quieren con l.** they're madly in love (with one another)
(d) una l. *(mucho)* a fortune, a ridiculous amount; **gastar una l.** to spend a fortune

locutor, -ora *nm,f (de noticias)* newsreader; *(de continuidad)* announcer; *(de programa de radio)* presenter

locutorio *nm* **(a)** *(para visitas)* visiting room **(b) l. (telefónico)** = establishment containing a number of telephone booths for public use **(c)** *(radiofónico)* studio

lodazal *nm* quagmire

loden *nm* loden coat

lodo *nm* mud; EXPR **arrastrar por el l.** to drag through the mud

loes *nm inv Geol* loess

logarítmico, -a *adj* logarithmic

logaritmo *nm* logarithm

logia *nf* **(a)** *(masónica)* lodge **(b)** *Arquit* loggia

lógica *nf* **(a)** *(ciencia)* logic ▸▸ *Informát* ***l. booleana*** Boolean logic; *Informát* ***l. borrosa*** fuzzy logic; *Informát* ***l. difusa*** fuzzy logic; ***l. matemática*** mathematical logic **(b)** *(coherencia)* logic; **por l.** obviously; **tener l.** to make sense; **eso no tiene l.** that doesn't make any sense **(c)** *ver también* **lógico**

lógicamente *adv* logically; **l., no volvió a acercarse por ahí** naturally *o* obviously, he didn't go near there again

lógico, -a 1 *adj* **(a)** *(del pensamiento)* logical **(b)** *(natural)* logical; **como es l., ellos también están invitados** naturally, they are also invited; **es l. que se enfade** it stands to reason that he should get angry; **es l. que tras la enfermedad se sienta débil** it's only natural that she should feel weak after the illness; **¿te gustaría acompañarnos? – ¡l.!** would you like to come with us? – of course I would!
2 *nm,f* logician

logística *nf* logistics *(singular o plural)*; **la l. desempeña un papel fundamental en nuestra empresa** logistics plays a vital role in our company; **la l. de la operación es bastante complicada** the logistics of the operation are quite complicated

logístico, -a *adj* logistic

logo *nm (logotipo)* logo

logopeda *nmf* speech therapist

logopedia *nf* speech therapy

logorrea *nf Med* logorrhoea

logos *nm inv Filosofía* logos

logotipo *nm* logo

logrado, -a *adj (bien hecho)* accomplished; **es una imitación muy lograda** it is a very authentic imitation

lograr *vt (objetivo)* to achieve; *(puesto, beca, divorcio)* to get, to obtain; *(resultado)* to obtain, to achieve; *(perfección)* to attain; *(victoria, premio)* to win; *(deseo, aspiración)* to fulfil; **¡lo logramos!** we did it!, we've done it!; **l. hacer algo** to manage to do sth; **l. que alguien haga algo** to manage to get sb to do sth; **no logro entender cómo lo hizo** I just can't see how he managed it

logro *nm* **(a)** *(consecución)* achievement; **su objetivo es el l. de la paz** her aim is to achieve peace **(b)** *(éxito)* achievement; **destacó los logros del gobierno** she highlighted the government's achievements

logroñés, -esa 1 *adj* of/from Logroño *(Spain)*
2 *nm,f* person from Logroño *(Spain)*

LOGSE ['loɣse] *nf (abrev de* **Ley Orgánica de Ordenación General del Sistema Educativo***)* = Spanish education act

Loira *nm* **el L.** the (river) Loire

loísmo *nm Gram* = incorrect use of "lo" as indirect object instead of "le"

loísta 1 *adj* prone to "loísmo"
2 *nmf* = person prone to "loísmo"

lola *RP Fam* **1** *nf* **(a)** *(teta)* tit **(b)** *ver también* **lolo**
2 *interj (lo lamento)* I'm sorry

lolerío *nm Chile Fam* kids; **a ese bar va todo el l.** that bar is where all the kids go

lolo, -a *nm,f Chile Fam* kid

loma *nf* hillock; EXPR *RP Fam* **la l. del diablo: vive en la l. del diablo** *o* **del quinoto** she lives in the middle of nowhere *o* the back of beyond

lomada *nf Perú, RP (loma)* hillock

lombarda *nf (verdura)* red cabbage

Lombardía *n* Lombardy

lombardo, -a 1 *adj* Lombard
2 *nm,f* Lombard

lombriz *nf* **(a)** *(gusano)* worm ▸▸ ***l. de tierra*** earthworm **(b) l. (intestinal)** tapeworm; **tener lombrices** to have worms

Lomé *n* Lomé

lomillo *nm Bol, Carib, RP (de montar)* saddle pad

lomito *nm Ven* sirloin steak

lomo *nm* **(a)** *(de animal)* back; **a lomos de un caballo/elefante** astride *o* riding a horse/elephant ▸▸ *RP* ***l. de burro*** *Br* sleeping policeman, *US* speed ramp
(b) *(de cerdo)* loin ▸▸ *Esp* ***l. embuchado*** cured pork loin sausage; *(de vaca)* tenderloin
(c) *(de libro)* spine
(d) *Fam (de persona)* loins, lower back
(e) *(de cuchillo)* blunt edge
(f) EXPR *Ven Fam* **me da l.** I couldn't give a hoot; *Am* **hacer l. a la carga** to take responsibility; *Am* **tener hecho el l. a la carga** to be battle-hardened; *Méx Fam* **sobarse el l.** to work one's socks off; *RP muy Fam* **tiene buen l.** she has an amazing body

lompa *nm RP Fam (pantalón)* trousers

lona *nf* **(a)** *(tela)* canvas; **una l.** a tarpaulin **(b)** *(en cuadrilátero)* canvas; *(en circo)* marquee; **besar la l.** to hit the canvas, to be knocked down; EXPR *RP, Ven Fam* **estar** *o* **quedar en la l.** *(cansado)* to be beat *o Br* knackered; *(empobrecido)* to be broke; *(deteriorado)* to have had it **(c)** *RP (para la playa)* canvas beach mat

lonch *nm Méx Fam* (packed) lunch

loncha *nf (de queso, jamón)* slice; *(de panceta)* rasher

lonchar *vi Méx* to have one's lunch

lonche *nm* **(a)** *Perú, Ven (merienda) (en escuela)* = snack eaten during break time; *(en casa)* (afternoon) tea **(b)** *Am (comida fría)* (packed) lunch **(c)** *Méx (torta)* filled roll

lonchera *nf Perú, Ven* lunchbox

lonchería *nf Méx, Ven* = small fast food restaurant selling snacks, sandwiches etc

lonchero, -a *nm,f Méx, Ven* = person who works in a "lonchería"

londinense 1 *adj* London; **las calles londinenses** the London streets, the streets of London
2 *nmf* Londoner

Londres *n* London

loneta *nf* sailcloth

longanimidad *nf Formal* magnanimity

longánimo, -a *adj Formal* magnanimous

longaniza *nf* = type of spicy cold pork sausage

longevidad *nf* longevity

longevo, -a *adj* long-lived

longitud *nf* **(a)** *(dimensión)* length; **tiene medio metro de l.** it's half a metre long; **tiene una l. de cinco metros** it's five metres long **(b)** *Astron & Geog* longitude **(c)** *Fam (distancia)* distance **(d)** ***l. de onda*** wavelength; EXPR **estar en la misma l. de onda** to be on the same wavelength

longitudinal *adj* longitudinal, lengthways

longitudinalmente *adv* lengthwise

long play ['lomplei] *(pl* **long plays***)* *nm* LP, album

longui, longuis *nmf* EXPR *Esp Fam* **hacerse el l.** to act dumb, to pretend not to understand

lonja *nf* (**a**) *(loncha)* slice (**b**) *Esp (de pescado)* fish market (**c**) *Hist (edificio)* (stock) exchange (**d**) *RP (tira)* thong, strap

lontananza *nf* background; **en l.** in the distance

look [luk] (*pl* **looks**) *nm Fam* look; **tiene un l. retro** it has an old-fashioned look about it; **¿qué te parece mi nuevo l.?** what do you think of my new look *o* image?

loor *nm Literario* **fue recibido en l. de multitudes** he was welcomed by enraptured crowds

loquear *vi Am Fam* to fool around

loquera *nf Fam* (**a**) *Am (acceso de locura)* fit of madness (**b**) *Am (acción)* **hacer loqueras** to act crazy *o* like a madman (**c**) *Col (alboroto)* commotion, uproar; **se armó una l.** there was a huge commotion; **su casa es una l.** her home is a madhouse (**d**) *ver también* **loquero**

loqueras *Fam* **1** *adj inv* loony
2 *nmf inv* loony, *Br* nutter

loquero, -a *Fam* **1** *nm,f* **se lo llevaron los loqueros** the men in white coats took him away
2 *nm* (**a**) *(manicomio)* loony-bin, madhouse (**b**) *Am (alboroto)* commotion, uproar; **se armó un l.** there was a huge commotion; **su casa es un l.** her home is a madhouse

lora *nf Andes, CAm (papagayo)* parrot

lord (*pl* **lores**) *nm* lord

lordosis *nf inv Med* lordosis

loriga *nf* (**a**) *(para soldado)* lamellar armour (**b**) *(para caballo)* armour

loro *nm* (**a**) *(animal)* parrot; EXPR *Fam* **hablar como un l.** to chatter; **enumeró la lista como un l.** she reeled off the list parrot-fashion ►► ***l. real*** yellow-headed *o* yellow-crowned amazon
(**b**) *Fam (charlatán)* chatterbox
(**c**) *Esp Fam (aparato de música)* = radio and/or cassette or CD player
(**d**) EXPR *Esp Fam* **estar al l.** *(alerta)* to keep a lookout *o* an eye open; *(enterado)* to be well up (on what's happening); **si no estamos al l., no conseguiremos entradas** if we're not quick off the mark we won't get tickets; **¿estás al l. de lo que le ha pasado a Claudia?** are you up on what happened to Claudia?; **¡al l.!, ¿a que no sabes a quien he visto?** listen! you'll never guess who I saw; **¡al l. con Luis, si puede te engañará!** be careful with Luis, he'll cheat you if he gets a chance!
(**e**) *Chile Fam (espía)* spy
(**f**) *Chile Fam (orinal)* bedpan

lorquiano, -a *adj* = of/relating to Federico García Lorca

los 1 *art ver* **el**
2 *pron ver* **lo**[1]

losa *nf* (**a**) *(piedra)* paving stone, flagstone ►► *RP* ***l. radiante*** *(calefacción)* underfloor heating (**b**) *(de tumba)* tombstone

loseta *nf* floor tile

lota *nf* threebeard rockling

lote *nm* (**a**) *(parte) (para vender, subastar)* share; **han hecho varios lotes con sus muebles** they've divided their furniture into several lots (**b**) *(conjunto)* batch, lot; **un l. de libros** a set of books (**c**) *Esp Fam* **darse** *o* **pegarse el l. (con)** to neck (with), *Br* to snog (**d**) *Am (solar)* plot (of land) (**e**) *CSur Fam (cantidad)* **acaba de comprarse un l. de cosas** she's just bought a whole load of stuff

loteamiento *nm Bol, Urug* parcelling out, division into plots

lotear *vt Andes, Méx, RP* to parcel out, to divide into plots

loteo *nm Andes, Méx, RP* parcelling out, division into plots

lotería *nf* (**a**) *(sorteo)* lottery; **jugar a la l.** to play the lottery; **le tocó la l.,** *Am* **se sacó la l.** she won the lottery; *también Irónico* **con esa novia que tiene le ha tocado** *o Am* **se sacó la l.** he's really hit the jackpot with that girlfriend of his; EXPR **es una l.** *(es aleatorio)* it's a lottery ►► ***L. Nacional*** = state-run lottery in which prizes are allocated to randomly chosen five-figure numbers; *Esp* ***l. primitiva*** weekly state-run lottery, *Br* ≃ National Lottery
(**b**) *(tienda)* = place selling lottery tickets
(**c**) *(juego de mesa)* lotto

lotero, -a *nm,f* lottery ticket seller

lotificación *nf CAm, Méx, Perú* parcelling out, division into plots

lotificar *vt CAm, Méx, Perú* to parcel out, to divide into plots

lotización *nf Ecuad, Perú* parcelling out, division into plots

lotizar *vt Ecuad, Perú* to parcel out, to divide into plots

loto 1 *nf Esp Fam* = weekly state-run lottery, *Br* ≃ National Lottery
2 *nm (planta)* lotus

loza *nf* (**a**) *(material)* earthenware; *(porcelana)* china (**b**) *(objetos)* crockery (**c**) *Ven (azulejo)* (glazed) tile

lozanía *nf* (**a**) *(de plantas)* luxuriance (**b**) *(de persona)* youthful vigour

lozano, -a *adj* (**a**) *(planta)* lush, luxuriant (**b**) *(persona)* full of youthful vigour

LP *nm (abrev de* **elepé**) LP

LSD *nm (abrev de* **lysergic acid diethylamide**) LSD

Luanda *n* Luanda

lubina *nf* sea bass

lubricación, lubrificación *nf* lubrication

lubricante, lubrificante 1 *adj* lubricating
2 *nm* lubricant

lubricar [60], **lubrificar** [60] *vt* to lubricate

lubricidad *nf* lewdness

lúbrico, -a *adj Formal* lewd, salacious

lubrificante, lubrificar *etc* = **lubricante, lubricar** *etc*

luca *nf Fam* (**a**) *Arg, Chile (mil pesos)* = 1,000 pesos; EXPR *Chile* **le importa una l.** he doesn't give a hoot *o* damn; EXPR *Chile* **ni l.: no me dio ni l.** she didn't give me a damn thing (**b**) *Perú (un nuevo sol)* = 1 (new) sol (**c**) *Col* **unas lucas** some cash *o* dough (**d**) *Urug (un nuevo peso)* = 1 (new) peso (**e**) *Ven (mil bolívares)* = 1,000 bolivars

Lucas *n pr* **san L.** St Luke

lucense 1 *adj* of/from Lugo *(Spain)*
2 *nmf* person from Lugo *(Spain)*

lucero 1 *nm* bright star; EXPR **como un l.** as bright as a new pin ►► ***l. del alba*** morning star; ***l. de la mañana*** morning star; ***l. de la tarde*** evening star; ***l. vespertino*** evening star
2 luceros *nmpl Literario (ojos)* eyes

lucha *nf* (**a**) *(combate físico)* fight ►► ***la l. armada*** the armed struggle
(**b**) *(enfrentamiento)* fight; **la l. contra el cáncer/el desempleo** the fight against cancer/unemployment; **hubo una l. muy dura por el liderato** the leadership was bitterly contested; **fracasó en su l. por cambiar la ley** she failed in her struggle *o* fight to change the law; **las luchas internas del partido** the in-fighting within the party ►► ***l. de clases*** class struggle
(**c**) *(esfuerzo)* struggle; **es una l. conseguir que se coman todo** it's a struggle to get them to eat it all up
(**d**) *(deporte)* wrestling ►► ***l. grecorromana*** Graeco-Roman wrestling; ***l. libre*** freestyle *o* all-in wrestling
(**e**) *(en baloncesto)* jump ball

luchador, -ora 1 *adj* **ser muy l.** to be a fighter *o* battler
2 *nm,f* (**a**) *(deportista)* wrestler (**b**) *(persona tenaz)* fighter, battler

luchar *vi* (**a**) *(combatir físicamente)* to fight; **l. contra** to fight (against) (**b**) *(enfrentarse)* to fight; **l. contra** to fight (against); **l. por** to fight for (**c**) *(esforzarse)* to struggle; **llevo todo el día luchando con esta traducción** I've been struggling *o* battling with this translation all day long; **tuvieron que l. mucho para sacar a su familia adelante** they had to struggle hard to provide for their family (**d**) *(en deporte)* to wrestle

luche *nm Chile* (**a**) *(alga)* = type of edible seaweed (**b**) *(tejo)* hopscotch

lúcidamente *adv* lucidly

lucidez *nf* lucidity

lucido, -a *adj* (**a**) *(vistoso, bello)* splendid; **una ceremonia lucida** a magnificent ceremony (**b**) *(saludable)* healthy-looking

lúcido, -a *adj (razonamiento, análisis)* lucid; *(decisión)* well-reasoned; **es una persona muy lúcida** he's a very clear-thinking person; **el enfermo está l.** the patient is lucid at the moment

luciérnaga *nf* glow-worm

Lucifer *n pr* Lucifer

lucimiento *nm* (**a**) *(brillo)* sparkle (**b**) *(de artista)* **una obra pensada para el l. de los actores** a work designed to allow the actors to shine

lucio *nm* pike

lución *nm* slowworm

lucir [39] **1** *vi* (**a**) *(brillar)* to shine; **la montaña lucía blanca tras la nevada** the mountain glistened white in the snow
(**b**) *(dar luz)* **esta lámpara luce muy poco** this lamp isn't very bright
(**c**) *(rendir)* **no me lucían tantas horas de trabajo** I didn't have much to show for all those hours of work; **dijo que estudió mucho para el examen – pues no le ha lucido** he said he studied very hard for the exam – well, it hasn't done him much good
(**d**) *(quedar bonito)* to look good; **ese sofá luce mucho en el salón** that couch looks really good in the lounge; **luce mucho decir que**

hablas cinco idiomas being able to say that you speak five languages looks really good

(**e**) *Am (parecer)* to look; **luces cansada** you seem *o* look tired; **luce muy joven** she looks very young

2 *vt (llevar)* to wear, to sport; *(exhibir)* to show off, to sport; **lucía un collar de perlas** she was wearing *o* sporting a pearl necklace

3 lucirse *vpr (destacar)* to shine (**en** at); **a la hora de cocinar, siempre se luce** he's a real star when he gets in the kitchen; *Irónico* **te has lucido** you've really excelled yourself!; *Irónico* **te luciste con tu pregunta** now that was a really bright question, wasn't it?

lucrar 1 *vt* to win, to obtain

2 lucrarse *vpr* to make money (for oneself)

lucrativo, -a *adj* lucrative; **no l.** non-profit-making

lucro *nm* profit, gain; **una asociación sin ánimo de l.** a non-profit-making organization, a not-for-profit organization

luctuoso, -a *adj* sorrowful, mournful

lucubración = **elucubración**

lucubrar = **elucubrar**

lúcuma *nf* egg-plum

lúcumo *nm* egg-plum tree

lúdico, -a *adj* **espacios lúdicos** play areas; **actividades lúdicas** leisure activities; **quieren fomentar el espíritu l. en los niños** they want to encourage children to play

ludista, ludita *adj también Fig* Luddite

ludo *nm RP* ludo

ludópata *nmf* pathological gambling addict

ludopatía *nf* pathological addiction to gambling

ludoteca *nf* toy library

luego 1 *adv* (**a**) *(a continuación)* **primero aquí y l. allí** first here and then there; **l. de** after; **l. de hablar con ella, me volví a casa** after talking to her I went home; **l. que** as soon as; **l. que se levantó me llamó** he called me as soon as he had got up

(**b**) *(más tarde)* later; **te veo l.** I'll see you later; **hazlo l.** do it later; **¡hasta l.!** see you (later)!; EXPR *CAm, Méx* **para l. es tarde** what are you waiting for?

(**c**) *(en el espacio)* then; **primero hay un parque y l. la plaza** first you come to a park and then the square

(**d**) *Chile, Méx, Ven (pronto)* soon; **acaba l., te estoy esperando** hurry up and finish, I'm waiting for you; *Méx Fam* **l. l., l. lueguito** immediately, straight away

(**e**) *Méx Fam (a veces)* from time to time

2 *conj (así que)* so, therefore; **estaba enfermo aquel día – l. no pudo ser él** he was ill that day – it can't have been him, then; EXPR **pienso, l. existo** I think, therefore I am

lueguito *adv Am Fam* later; **¡hasta l.!** see you (later)!

luengo, -a *adj Anticuado o Literario* long; **pasó luengos años en el anonimato** she spent many long years out of the public eye

lugano, lúgano *nm* siskin

LUGAR 1 *nm* (**a**) *(sitio)* place; *(del crimen, accidente)* scene; *(para acampar, merendar)* spot; **encontraron una pistola en el l. de los hechos** they found a gun at the crime scene *o* scene of the crime; **¿en qué l. habré metido las tijeras?** where can I have put the scissors?; **en algún l.** somewhere; **no lo veo por ningún l.** I can't see it anywhere; **vuelve a ponerlo todo en su l.** put everything back where it belongs; **he cambiado el televisor de l.** I've moved the television; **estoy buscando un l. donde pasar la noche** I'm looking for somewhere to spend the night; **éste no es (el) l. para discutir eso** this is not the place to discuss that matter ►► ***l. de anidación*** nesting site; ***l. de encuentro*** meeting place; ***l. de interés*** place of interest; ***l. de reunión*** meeting place; ***l. sagrado*** sanctum; ***l. de trabajo*** workplace

(**b**) *(localidad)* place, town; **las gentes del l.** the local people; **ni los más viejos del l. recuerdan algo semejante** not even the oldest people there can remember anything like it ►► ***l. de nacimiento*** *(en biografía)* birthplace; *(en formulario, impreso)* place of birth; ***l. de residencia*** *(en formulario, impreso)* place of residence; ***l. turístico*** holiday resort; ***l. de veraneo*** summer resort

(**c**) *(puesto)* position; **ocupa un l. importante en la empresa** she has an important position in the company, she is high up in the company; **¿puedes ir tú en mi l.?** can you go in my place?; **en primer/segundo l., quiero decir...** in the first/second place, I would like to say..., firstly/secondly, I would like to say...; **llegó en primer/segundo l.** she finished *o* came first/second; **en último l., quiero decir...** lastly *o* last, I would like to say...; **llegó en último l.** she came last; **ponte en mi l.** put yourself in my place; **yo en tu l.** if I were you

(**d**) *(espacio libre)* room, space; **esta mesa ocupa mucho l.** this table takes up a lot of room *o* space; **aquí ya no hay l. para más gente** there's no room for anyone else here; **hacerle l. a algo/alguien** to make room *o* some space for sth/sb

(**e**) ***l. común*** platitude, commonplace

(**f**) *(ocasión)* **dar l. a** *(rumores, comentarios, debate, disputa)* to give rise to; *(polémica)* to spark off, to give rise to; *(catástrofe)* to lead to, to cause; *(explosión, escape)* to cause; *Am* **a como dé l.** whatever the cost, whatever it takes; *Der* **no ha l.** objection overruled; **no hay l. a duda** there's no (room for) doubt; **sin l. a dudas** without doubt, undoubtedly

(**g**) **tener l.** to take place; **la recepción tendrá l. en los jardines del palacio** the reception will be held in the palace gardens

(**h**) EXPR **dejar en buen l.: el cantante mexicano dejó en buen l. a su país** the Mexican singer did his country proud; **dejar en mal l.: no nos dejes en mal l. y pórtate bien** be good and don't show us up; **estar fuera de l.** to be out of place; **poner a alguien en su l.** to put sb in his/her place; **poner las cosas en su l.** to set things straight

2 en lugar de *loc prep* instead of; **acudió en l. de mí** she came in my place *o* instead of me; **en l. de la sopa, tomaré pasta** I'll have the pasta instead of the soup; **en l. de mirar, podrías echarnos una mano** you could give us a hand rather than *o* instead of just standing/sitting there watching

lugareño, -a 1 *adj* village; **vino l.** local wine

2 *nm,f* villager

lugarteniente *nm* deputy

luge *nm Dep* luge

lugre *nm Náut* lugger

lúgubre *adj* (**a**) *(triste, melancólico) (semblante, expresión)* gloomy, mournful; *(pensamiento, tono)* gloomy, sombre (**b**) *(fúnebre) (idea, relato)* morbid; *(voz)* sepulchral

Luis *n pr* **L. I/II** Louis I/II

Luisiana *n* Louisiana

lujo *nm* (**a**) *(fastuosidad)* luxury; **a todo l.** with no expense spared; **de l.** luxury; **un hotel de l.** a luxury hotel; **hoy contamos con un invitado de l.** we have a really special guest today; **permitirse el l. de algo/de hacer algo** to be able to afford sth/to do sth; **no nos podemos permitir el l. de irnos un mes de vacaciones** we can't afford to go on holiday for a month; **se permitió el l. de criticar a su profesor** she had the gall to criticize her teacher; **l. asiático** undreamt-of opulence *o* luxury

(**b**) *(profusión)* profusion; **con todo l. de detalles** in great detail

lujosamente *adv* luxuriously

lujoso, -a *adj* luxurious

lujuria *nf* lust

> **Falso amigo**: El sustantivo inglés **luxury** no es la traducción del español **lujuria**. En inglés **luxury** significa "lujo".

lujuriante *adj* luxuriant, lush

lujurioso, -a 1 *adj* lecherous

2 *nm,f* lecher

lulú *nm* Pomeranian

lumbago *nm* lumbago

lumbalgia *nf Med* lumbago

lumbar *adj* lumbar

lumbre *nf* (**a**) *(en cocina)* **encender la l.** to put the stove on; **poner algo a la l.** to put sth on the stove (**b**) *(de leña)* fire; **conversaban a la luz de la l.** they were talking in the firelight (**c**) *(para cigarrillo)* **pedir l. a alguien** to ask sb for a light; **dar l. a alguien** to give sb a light (**d**) *(luz)* glow

lumbrera *nf* (**a**) *(sabio)* genius; **su hijo es una l. para la música** her son is a musical genius; **no es precisamente una l.** he's no genius *o* Einstein (**b**) *Tec* port ►► ***l. de admisión*** inlet port; ***l. de escape*** exhaust port

lumen *nm* lumen

luminaria *nf* (**a**) *(luz)* light (**b**) *(en iglesia)* altar lamp (**c**) *esp Am (sabio)* luminary (**d**) *Am (persona importante)* celebrity; **a la fiesta acudieron varias luminarias de la televisión** the party was attended by several television celebrities *o* stars

lumínico, -a *adj* light; **energía lumínica** light energy

luminiscencia *nf* luminescence

luminiscente *adj* luminescent

luminosidad *nf* (**a**) *(por luz)* brightness, luminosity (**b**) *(por alegría)* brightness, brilliance

luminoso, -a 1 *adj* (**a**) *(con mucha luz)* bright (**b**) *(que despide luz)* bright; **cuerpo l.** luminous body; **fuente luminosa** light source; **rótulo l.** illuminated *o* neon sign (**c**) *(idea)* brilliant (**d**) *(alegre)* bright
2 *nm* illuminated *o* neon sign

luminotecnia *nf* lighting

luminotécnico, -a 1 *adj* lighting; **equipo l.** lighting equipment
2 *nm,f* lighting specialist

lumpen 1 *adj* (**a**) *(marginado)* deprived (**b**) *(del lumpenproletariado)* lumpenproletariat
2 *nm* (**a**) *(sector marginado)* underclass (**b**) *(lumpenproletariado)* lumpenproletariat

lumpenproletariado *nm* lumpenproletariat

lun. *(abrev de* **lunes***)* Mon

luna *nf* (**a**) *(astro)* moon; **la L.** the Moon; **media l.** *(bandera islámica)* half moon; EXPR **estar en la l.** to be miles away; EXPR **pedir la l.** to ask the impossible; EXPR *Esp Fam* **se quedó a la l. de Valencia** his hopes were dashed ►► ***l. creciente*** crescent moon *(when waxing)*; ***l. llena*** full moon; ***l. menguante*** crescent moon *(when waning)*; ***l. nueva*** new moon
(**b**) *(cristal)* window (pane)
(**c**) *(espejo)* mirror
(**d**) ***l. de miel*** *(de novios)* honeymoon; **se fueron de l. de miel al Caribe** they went to the Caribbean for their honeymoon; **las relaciones entre los dos países atraviesan una l. de miel** relations between the two countries are going through a honeymoon period
(**e**) *RP Fam (mal humor)* **estar de l.** to be in a mood, *Br* to be in a strop

lunación *nf Astron* lunar month, *Espec* lunation

lunar 1 *adj* lunar
2 *nm* (**a**) *(en la piel humana)* mole, beauty spot (**b**) *(en la piel animal)* spot (**c**) *(en telas)* spot; **a lunares** spotted (**d**) *(defecto)* minor blemish

lunarejo, -a *adj Andes* spotted

lunático, -a 1 *adj* crazy
2 *nm,f* lunatic

lunch [lantʃ] *(pl* **lunches***)* *nm* buffet lunch

lunes *nm inv* Monday ►► ***L. de Pascua*** Easter Monday; *ver también* **sábado**

luneta *nf* (**a**) *(de vehículo)* *Br* windscreen, *Am* windshield ►► ***l. térmica*** *Br* demister, *US* defogger; ***l. trasera*** rear *Br* windscreen *o US* windshield (**b**) *RP* **lunetas** *(para nadar)* goggles

lunfardo *nm* = working-class Buenos Aires slang

lúnula *nf (de uñas)* half-moon

lupa *nf* magnifying glass; EXPR **mirar algo con l.** to examine sth in minute detail

lupanar *nm Formal* brothel

lúpulo *nm* hops

lupus *nm inv Med* lupus

Lusaka *n* Lusaka

Lusitania *n* (**a**) *Hist (región)* Lusitania (**b**) *(país)* Portugal

lusitanismo *nm* = Portuguese word or expression

lusitano, -a, luso, -a 1 *adj* (**a**) *Hist (de Lusitania)* Lusitanian (**b**) *(de Portugal)* Portuguese
2 *nm,f* (**a**) *Hist (de Lusitania)* Lusitanian (**b**) *(de Portugal)* Portuguese

lustrabotas *nmf inv Andes, RP* shoeshine, *Br* bootblack

lustrada *nf Andes, RP* polish; **cobra 10 pesos (por) la l.** he charges 10 pesos for polishing *o* shining your shoes; **a este suelo le hace falta una l.** this floor could do with a polish

lustrador, -ora *nm,f Andes, RP* shoeshine, *Br* bootblack

lustradora *nf* floor polisher

lustramuebles *nm inv CSur* furniture polish

lustrar 1 *vt (muebles, zapatos)* to polish
2 **lustrarse** *vpr* **se lustró los zapatos** he polished his shoes

lustre *nm* (**a**) *(brillo)* shine; **dar l. a** *(muebles, zapatos)* to polish (**b**) *(prestigio, esplendor)* glory; **su presencia dio l. a la ceremonia** her presence gave an extra sparkle to the ceremony

lustrín *nm* (**a**) *Chile (cajón)* shoeshine's box (**b**) *Arg (persona)* shoeshine, *Br* bootblack

lustro *nm* five-year period; *Fig* **desde hace lustros** for ages

lustroso, -a *adj (muebles, zapatos)* shiny

lutecio *nm Quím* lutetium

luteranismo *nm* Lutheranism

luterano, -a 1 *adj* Lutheran
2 *nm,f* Lutheran

luthier [luti'e] *(pl* **luthiers***)* *nmf* = maker or repairer of stringed instruments

luto *nm* mourning; **estar de l.** to be in mourning; **la ciudad está de l. por la muerte de su alcalde** the city is mourning the death of the mayor; **en los pueblos el l. puede durar varios años** in villages the period of mourning may last several years; **las banderas ondean a media asta en señal de l.** the flags are flying at half-mast as a sign of mourning; **vestirse** *o* **ir de l.** to wear black *(as a sign of mourning)* ►► ***l. oficial*** official mourning

lux *nm inv Fís* lux

luxación *nf Med* dislocation

luxar 1 *vt* to dislocate
2 **luxarse** *vpr* to dislocate

Luxemburgo *n* Luxembourg

luxemburgués, -esa 1 *adj* of/from Luxembourg; **un ciudadano l.** a citizen of Luxembourg, a Luxembourg citizen
2 *nm,f* Luxembourger

LUZ *nf* (**a**) *(foco, energía, luminosidad)* light; *(destello)* flash (of light); **se veía una l. a lo lejos** a light could be seen in the distance; **estas farolas dan poca l.** these streetlights don't shine very brightly *o* aren't very bright; **esta habitación tiene mucha l.** you get a lot of sunlight in this room; **ya no hay l. a esas horas** it's no longer light at that time of day, the light has gone by that time of day; **apagar la l.** to switch off the light; **encender** *o Esp* **dar** *o Am* **prender la l.** to switch on the light; **la habitación estaba a media l.** *(con luz natural)* it was almost dark in the room; *(con luz artificial)* the room was dimly lit; **ponlo a la l., que lo veamos mejor** hold it up to the light so we can see it better; **con las primeras luces** *(al amanecer)* at first light; **quitarle la l. a alguien** *(ponerse en medio)* to block sb's light; **leer a la l. de una vela** to read by the light of a candle; **una cena a la l. de las velas** a candlelit dinner; *Fig* **a la l. de** *(los hechos, los acontecimientos)* in the light of; **a plena l. del día** in the full light of day; **arrojar l. sobre** to shed light on; **a todas luces** whichever way you look at it; **dar a l. (un niño)** to give birth (to a child); EXPR **con l. y taquígrafos** with absolute transparency; EXPR **dar l. verde (a)** to give the green light *o* the go-ahead (to); EXPR **entre dos luces** *Literario (entre el día y la noche)* at twilight; *Literario (entre la noche y el día)* at first light; *Fam Fig (achispado)* tipsy; EXPR **sacar algo a la l.** *(revelar)* to bring sth to light; *(publicar)* to bring sth out, to publish sth; EXPR **salir a la l.** *(descubrirse)* to come to light; *(publicarse)* to come out; EXPR *RP Fam* **ser una l.** to be a bright spark; EXPR **ver la l.** *(publicación, informe)* to see the light of day; *(tras penalidades)* to see the light at the end of the tunnel ►► ***l. blanca*** white light; ***l. cenital*** light from above; ***l. del día*** daylight; ***l. de discoteca*** strobe light; ***l. eléctrica*** electric light; ***l. de luna*** moonlight; *RP* **l. mala** will-o'-the-wisp; ***l. natural*** *(del sol)* natural light; ***l. de neón*** neon light; ***l. del sol*** sunlight; ***l. solar*** sunlight
(**b**) *(electricidad)* electricity; **cortar la l. a alguien** to cut off sb's electricity supply; **se ha ido la l.** the lights have gone out; **pagar (el recibo de) la l.** to pay the electricity (bill)
(**c**) **luces** *(de automóvil)* lights; **darle las luces a alguien** to flash (one's lights) at sb; **dejarse las luces del coche puestas** to leave one's lights on ►► *Am* ***luces altas:*** **poner las luces altas** to put one's headlights on *Br* full *o US* high beam; *Am* ***luces bajas*** *Br* dipped headlights, *US* low beams; ***luces de carretera:*** **poner las luces de carretera** to put one's headlights on *Br* full *o US* high beam; ***luces cortas*** *Br* dipped headlights, *US* low beams; ***luces de cruce*** *Br* dipped headlights, *US* low beams; ***luces de emergencia*** *Br* hazard (warning) lights, *US* emergency lights; ***luces de frenado*** brake lights; ***luces de freno*** brake lights; ***luces de gálibo*** clearance lights; *Arg* ***l. de giro*** *Br* indicator, *US* turn signal; ***luces largas:*** **poner las luces largas** to put one's headlights on *Br* full *o US* high beam; ***l. de marcha atrás*** reversing light; ***luces de navegación*** navigation lights; ***luces de niebla*** fog lamps *o* lights; ***luces de posición*** sidelights; ***luces de señalización*** traffic lights; ***luces de situación*** sidelights; ***luces de tráfico*** traffic lights; ***luces traseras*** *Br* rear lights, *US* tail-lights
(**d**) **luces** *(inteligencia)* intelligence; **es de** *o* **tiene pocas luces** he's not very bright
(**e**) *Hist* **las Luces** the Enlightenment
(**f**) *(modelo, ejemplo)* **Alá es la l. que dirige nuestras vidas** Allah is our guiding light
(**g**) *Arquit (ventana)* window; *(ancho de ventana)* span

---

luzco *etc ver* **lucir**

lycra® *nf* Lycra®

M, m

M, m ['eme] *nf* **(a)** *(letra)* M, m **(b)** EXPR *Fam Euf* **lo mandé a la m** I told him where to go

M (*abrev de* **martes**) Tues

m **(a)** (*abrev de* **metro**) m **(b)** (*abrev de* **millón**) m

M-19 *nm* (*abrev de* **Movimiento 19 de Abril**) = Colombian political party founded by left-wing guerrillas

maca *nf* **(a)** *(de fruta)* bruise **(b)** *(de objetos)* flaw

macá *nf* pied-billed grebe

macabeo, -a *adj Fam* **un rollo m.** *(una mentira)* a ridiculous spiel; **ser un rollo m.** *(un aburrimiento)* to be a real bore *o* drag

macabí (*pl* **macabíes**) *nm Carib, Col* banana fish

macabro, -a *adj* macabre

macacada *nf Urug Fam* **hacer macacadas** to clown around

macaco, -a 1 *adj Chile, Cuba, Méx Fam (feo)* ugly, misshapen
2 *nm,f* **(a)** *(animal)* macaque **(b)** *Fam (niño) (insulto)* brat; *(apelativo cariñoso)* kid **(c)** *Urug Fam (diablillo)* little monkey

macadam (*pl* **macadams**), **macadán** (*pl* **macadanes**) *nm* macadam

macagua *nf* **(a)** *(ave)* laughing falcon **(b)** *(serpiente)* Columbian lance head **(c)** *Cuba (árbol)* breadfruit tree

macal, macale *nm Méx* cocoyam, yautia

macán *nm Ven Fam (alboroto)* fuss, uproar

macana *nf* **(a)** *Andes, Carib, Méx (garrote)* wooden *Br* truncheon *o US* billy club
(b) *Méx, Ven Hist (machete)* = wooden club used as weapon by Indians
(c) *CAm, Cuba (azada)* hoe
(d) *CSur, Perú, Ven Fam (disparate)* stupid thing; **siempre dice macanas** he's always talking nonsense *o Br* rubbish; **no hagas macanas** don't do anything crazy *o* hot-headed; **me temo que haga una m.** I'm afraid he might do something desperate
(e) *Andes, RP, Ven Fam (fastidio)* pain, drag; **iqué m., acaba de empezar a llover!** what a pain *o* drag, it's just started raining!
(f) *Andes, RP, Ven Fam (pena)* shame; **iqué m.!** what a shame!

macaneador, -ora *nm,f CSur Fam* **es un m.** he's always talking nonsense

macanear *Fam* **1** *vt CSur, Ven (hacer mal)* to botch, to do badly
2 *vi CSur (decir tonterías)* to talk nonsense; *(hacer tonterías)* to be stupid

macaneo *nm CSur Fam* **(a)** *(disparate)* stupid thing **(b)** *(broma)* joke

macanudo, -a *Fam* **1** *adj* **(a)** *Andes, RP (bueno)* great, terrific; **tu vecino nuevo es m.** your new neighbour is dead nice **(b)** *Ecuad, Ven (sobresaliente)* ace **(c)** *Andes, Ven (grande, fuerte)* **es un tipo m.** he's a great hulk of a man
2 *interj Andes, RP* great!, terrific!; **¿vamos al cine mañana? – ¡m.!** shall we go to the cinema tomorrow? – that's a great idea!

macao *nm Cuba* hermit crab

macaquear *vi CSur Fam* to clown around

macarra *Esp Fam* **1** *adj* **(a)** *(matón)* loutish, *Br* yobbish **(b)** *(vulgar)* flashy; **conduce un coche muy m.** he drives a really tasteless flashy car
2 *nm* **(a)** *(de prostitutas)* pimp **(b)** *(matón)* lout, *Br* yob **(c)** *(vulgar)* flash Harry

macarrón *nm* **(a)** **macarrones** *(pasta)* macaroni **(b)** *(dulce)* macaroon **(c)** *(tubo)* sheath *(of cable)*

macarrónico, -a *adj Fam* **tiene un inglés m.** his English is atrocious

macarse *vpr* to go bad

macartismo *nm* McCarthyism

Macedonia *n* **(a)** *Hist* Macedonia **(b)** *(país)* Macedonia; **Antigua República Yugoslava de M.** Former Yugoslavian Republic of Macedonia, FYROM

macedonia *nf* **(a)** *(de frutas)* fruit salad **(b)** *(de verduras)* mixed vegetables

macedonio, -a 1 *adj* **(a)** *Hist* Macedonian **(b)** *(del país)* Macedonian
2 *nm,f (persona)* **(a)** *Hist* Macedonian **(b)** *(del país)* Macedonian
3 *nm (lengua)* Macedonian

macegual, macehual *nm Méx* = Indian from the lowest social class at the time of the Spanish conquest

maceración *nf* **(a)** *(golpeando)* tenderizing **(b)** *(en líquido)* soaking, maceration

macerar *vt* **(a)** *(golpeando)* to tenderize **(b)** *(en líquido)* to soak, to macerate

macero *nm* mace-bearer

maceta *nf* **(a)** *(tiesto)* flowerpot **(b)** *(herramienta)* mallet **(c)** *Chile (ramo)* bouquet **(d)** *Méx Fam (cabeza)* nut

macetero *nm* flowerpot holder

macetudo, -a *adj RP Fam* **una mujer macetuda** a woman with fat ankles

mach *nm Fís* mach

macha *nf* Chilean wedge clam

machaca[1] *Esp Fam* **1** *adj (pesado)* boring, tedious; **música m.** really annoying music
2 *nmf* **(a)** *(pesado)* pain, bore **(b)** *(trabajador)* **es un m.** he's a real workhorse; **trabaja de m. en un almacén** he works as a general dogsbody in a warehouse

machaca[2], **machacado** *nm (plato)* = Mexican dish of ground dried beef, onion, tomato, chilli and egg

machacador, -ora *adj* crushing

machacadora *nf* crusher

machacante *nm Esp Fam* five pesetas

machacar [60] **1** *vt* **(a)** *(desmenuzar)* to crush
(b) *Fam (ganar)* to thrash
(c) *Fam (destrozar)* **estas gafas me están machacando la vista** these glasses are ruining *o Br* knackering my eyesight; **la caminata me ha machacado** I'm beat *o Br* knackered after that walk
(d) *Esp Fam (estudiar) Br* to swot up on, *US* to bone up on
(e) *Esp Fam (insistir sobre)* to go on and on about; **sigue machando las mismas ideas** she keeps on trotting out the same old ideas
(f) *(en baloncesto)* to dunk
2 *vi* **(a)** *Esp Fam (insistir)* to go on and on (**sobre** about) **(b)** *(en baloncesto)* to dunk
3 machacarse *vpr* **(a)** *(chafarse)* to crush; **se machacó el pie en el accidente** her foot got crushed in the accident; **me machaqué un dedo con el martillo** I banged my finger with the hammer
(b) *Fam (esforzarse)* to slog one's guts out; **me machaqué para preparar el examen** I slogged my guts out getting ready for the exam
(c) *muy Fam* **machacársela** *(masturbarse)* to beat one's meat; EXPR **por mí, como si se la machaca** I couldn't give a shit *o Br* toss (about him)

machacón, -ona *Fam* **1** *adj* tiresome
2 *nm,f* pain, bore

machaconamente *adv Fam* **me lo repitió m.** she kept on and on about it

machaconería *nf Fam* annoying insistence; **su m. me tiene harto** I'm fed up with the way she just won't let it drop

machada *nf Fam* act of bravado; **hizo la m. de subir todas las cajas él solito** he tried to show what a he-man he is by carrying all the boxes up himself

machamartillo: a machamartillo *loc adv* very firmly; **creer algo a m.** to be firm in one's belief of sth

machaque *nm (en baloncesto)* dunk

machaqueo *nm* (**a**) *(trituración)* crushing, pounding (**b**) *Fam (insistencia)* **estaba harto de tanto m. sobre el tema** I was sick of them going on and on *o Br* banging on about the subject
machazo, -a *adj RP Fam* **tuvo una enfermedad machaza** she was dead ill; **hace un calor m.** it's dead hot; **tiene una suerte machaza** he's dead lucky, *Br* he's a jammy sod
maché *adj* **papel m.** papier-mâché
machetazo *nm* (**a**) *(golpe)* machete blow (**b**) *(herida)* machete wound
machete[1] **1** *adj Ven Fam* (**a**) *(valiente)* **ser m.** to have guts (**b**) *(estupendo)* ace
2 *nm* (**a**) *(arma)* machete (**b**) *Ven Fam (valiente)* **ser un m.** to have guts (**c**) *Ven Fam (amigo) Br* mate, *US* buddy (**d**) *Arg Fam (chuleta)* crib note
machete[2]**, -a** *adj RP Fam* scrooge, stingy so-and-so
machetear 1 *vt* (**a**) *(cortar)* to cut (with a machete) (**b**) *RP Fam (escatimar)* to skimp on
2 *vi* (**a**) *Méx Fam (trabajar duro)* to slog away; **hay que m. mucho para salir adelante** it's a real slog just to get by (**b**) *Méx Fam (estudiar)* to study hard, *Br* to swot (**c**) *RP Fam (ser tacaño)* to be stingy
machetero, -a *nm,f* (**a**) *(cortador de caña)* cane-cutter (**b**) *Méx Anticuado (trabajador) (en el campo)* farm labourer; *(cargador)* porter; *(en puerto)* stevedore (**c**) *Méx Fam (estudiante)* swot
máchica *nf Perú* roasted cornmeal
machihembrado *nm* tongue and groove
machismo *nm* male chauvinism, machismo
machista 1 *adj* male chauvinist
2 *nmf* male chauvinist
machito *nm Méx (tapa)* = snack of fried offal
macho, -a 1 *adj* (**a**) *(del sexo masculino)* male; **un hipopótamo m.** a male hippopotamus (**b**) *Fam (hombre)* macho; **es muy m.** he's a real man (**c**) *RP, Ven Fam (valiente)* brave (**d**) *RP, Ven Fam (fuerte, resistente)* industrial-strength; **un galpón m.** an industrial-strength shed (**e**) *RP, Ven Fam (importante, de peso)* major, serious; **un problema m.** a major *o* serious problem
2 *nm* (**a**) *(animal, planta)* male ►► ***m. cabrío*** billy goat (**b**) *(mulo)* (male) mule (**c**) *Fam (hombre)* macho man, he-man (**d**) *(enchufe)* male plug, jack plug; *(pata de enchufe)* pin (**e**) EXPR *Fam* **atarse** *o* **apretarse los machos** to brace oneself
3 *interj Esp Fam* **¡oye, m.!** *Br* hey, mate, *US* hey, buddy!; **¡mira, m., cómo llueve!** Jesus, look at that rain!; **¡m., a ver si te callas!** just shut up will you *Br* mate *o US* buddy?
machón *nm Arquit* buttress
machona *RP Fam* **1** *adj* mannish
2 *nf (marimacho) (niña)* tomboy; *(mujer)* butch woman
machonga *nf Col* (**a**) *(de cobre)* copper pyrite (**b**) *(de hierro)* iron pyrite
machorra *adj (oveja)* sterile
machote, -a 1 *adj Fam* brave; **dárselas de m.** to act like a he-man
2 *nm,f Fam (niño)* big boy, *f* big girl
3 *nm CAm, Méx (modelo)* rough draft
machucadura *nf (en fruta)* bruise
machucar [60] *vt* (**a**) *(golpear)* to pound, to beat (**b**) *(magullar)* to bruise
macilento, -a *adj (rostro)* wan, pale; *(luz)* wan; *(piel)* pale
macillo *nm (de instrumento musical)* hammer
macis *nf inv* mace
macizo, -a 1 *adj* (**a**) *(sólido)* solid; **una pulsera de oro m.** a solid gold wristwatch (**b**) *Fam (atractivo)* **estar m.** *(hombre)* to be hunky; *(mujer)* to be gorgeous; **¡maciza!** *(piropo)* fwoar!, hello gorgeous!
2 *nm* (**a**) *(montañoso)* massif (**b**) *(de plantas)* flower-bed (**c**) *(en pared)* section
macla *nf Geol* macle
macón, -ona, macote *adj Col* huge, very big
macramé *nm* macramé
macro 1 *nm Fot* macro
2 *nf Informát* macro
macro- *pref* macro-
macró *nm Fam* pimp
macrobiótica *nf* macrobiotics *(singular)*
macrobiótico, -a *adj* macrobiotic
macrocárcel *nf* super-prison
macrocefalia *nf Med* macrocephaly
macrocéfalo, -a *adj* macrocephalic, macrocephalous
macroconcierto *nm* big concert
macrocosmo *nm*, **macrocosmos** *nm inv* macrocosm
macroeconomía *nf* macroeconomics *(singular)*
macroeconómico, -a *adj* macroeconomic
macroencuesta *nf* large-scale opinion poll
macrófago *nm Biol* macrophage
macrofestival *nm* = large open-air music festival
macrofotografía *nf* macrophotography
macroinstrucción *nf Informát* macro(instruction)
macromolécula *nf* macromolecule
macroproceso *nm* super-trial *(of important case with many defendants)*
macroscópico, -a *adj* macroscopic
macuarro *nm Méx Fam Pey* builder
macuco, -a, macucón, -ona *adj Chile Fam (astuto)* sly, crafty
mácula *nf* (**a**) *Formal (mancha)* blemish; **tiene un pasado sin m.** she has a spotless *o* unblemished past (**b**) *Astron* sunspot (**c**) *Anat* macula ►► ***m. lútea*** macula lutea
macuto *nm* backpack
Madagascar *n* Madagascar
madam, madama *nf* (**a**) *Fam (en prostíbulo)* madam (**b**) *Urug (comadrona)* midwife
Madeira *n* Madeira
madeira *nm (vino)* Madeira
madeja *nf* hank, skein; EXPR *Fam* **enredar** *o* **liar la m.** to complicate matters
madera *nf* (**a**) *(en árbol)* wood; *(en carpintería)* timber, *US* lumber; **m. de pino** pine; **m. de caoba** walnut; **de m.** wooden; EXPR *RP Fam* **ser de m.** to be slow on the uptake; EXPR *Fam* **tocar m.** *Br* to touch wood, *US* to knock on wood ►► ***m. contrachapada*** plywood; ***m. noble*** fine wood; ***m. policromada*** polychrome wood
(**b**) *(tabla)* piece of wood; **atrancaron la puerta con dos maderas** they barred the door with two planks of wood
(**c**) *(cualidades)* **tener m. de algo** to have the makings of sth; **tener m. para algo** to have what it takes for sth
(**d**) *(palo de golf)* wood; **una m. del 5** a 5 wood
(**e**) *(en orquesta)* **la m.** the woodwind instruments
(**f**) *Esp muy Fam (policía)* **la m.** the pigs
maderable *adj* timber-yielding, *US* lumber-yielding
maderaje, maderamen *nm Constr* timbers
maderería *nf* timberyard, *US* lumberyard
maderero, -a 1 *adj* timber, *US* lumber; **industria maderera** timber *o US* lumber industry
2 *nm,f* timber *o US* lumber merchant
madero *nm* (**a**) *(tabla)* (piece of) timber *o US* lumber (**b**) *Esp muy Fam (agente de policía)* pig
madona, madonna *nf* Madonna; EXPR *Arg* **¡a la m.!** *(sorpresa)* what a nice surprise!
madrás *nm inv (tejido)* madras
madrastra *nf* stepmother
madraza *nf Fam* = indulgent or doting mother
madrazo *nm Méx* hard blow; **se dio un m.** he banged himself; **un m. a los derechos humanos** a severe blow to human rights
madre *nf* (**a**) *(mujer)* mother; **es m. de tres niños** she's a mother of three; **Alicia va a ser m.** Alicia's going to have a baby; *Fam* **¡m. mía!, ¡mi m.!** Jesus!, Christ!; *Fam* **¡m. mía, cómo llueve!** Jesus *o* Christ, it's pouring down!; *Fam* **¡mi m.! ¿y ahora qué vamos a hacer?** oh my God, what are we going to do now? ►► ***m. adoptiva*** foster mother; ***m. de alquiler*** surrogate mother; ***m. biológica*** natural mother; ***la m. naturaleza*** Mother Nature; ***la m. patria*** the motherland; *Am (España)* Spain; ***m. política*** mother-in-law; ***m. soltera*** single mother; ***la m. tierra*** earth mother
(**b**) *(hembra)* mother; **la m. cuida de los cachorros** the mother looks after the pups
(**c**) *(religiosa)* mother; **la m. Teresa** Mother Teresa ►► ***m. superiora*** mother superior
(**d**) *(origen)* source; **la pobreza extrema es la m. de todos los males de la región** extreme poverty is the source of all the region's problems
(**e**) *(cauce)* bed; **salirse de m.** *(río)* to burst its banks; *(persona)* to go too far
(**f**) EXPR *Fam* **eran ciento y la m.** everybody and his dog *o* the world and his wife was there; *Fam* **ser la m. del cordero** to be at the very root of the problem; *Méx Fam* **dar a alguien en la m.** to kick sb's head in; *Méx Fam* **de a m.: estoy aburrido de a m.** I'm fed up to the back teeth; **su casa está sucia de a m.** her house is a tip *o* pigsty; **me cae de**

a m. I hate his guts; *Méx Fam* **echar madres** to swear, *Br* to eff and blind; *Méx muy Fam* **¡en la m.!** *Br* bloody hell!, *US* goddamn!; *Méx Fam* **estar hasta la m.** *(lleno)* to be jam-packed; *Méx Fam* **ir hecho m.** to bomb along; *Fam* **nombrar** *o* **mentar la m. a alguien** = to insult someone by referring to their mother; *Méx Fam* **ni m.: no oye ni m.** she can't hear a damn thing; *Méx Fam* **¡ni madres!** no way!; *Am muy Fam* **no tener m.** to be a shameless bastard; *muy Fam* **¡la m. que te parió!** you bastard!; *Esp Fam* **¡viva la m. que te parió!** *(en concierto, corrida de toros)* we love you!; *Méx Fam* **estar de poca m.** to be great *o* fantastic; *Méx Fam* **ser de poca m.** to be great *o* fantastic; *Méx Fam* **tener poca m.** to be a swine; *Méx Fam* **ser a toda m.** to be a really great *o* nice person; *Fam* **ser una m. para alguien** to be like a mother to sb; *Fam* **ser una m. haciendo algo** *Chile (bueno)* to be a whizz at sth; *RP (malo)* to be useless at sth; *Méx muy Fam* **me vale m.** I couldn't give a damn *o Br* a toss

madrear *vt Méx Fam* **(a)** *(golpear)* **m. a alguien** to knock the hell out of sb **(b)** *(estropear)* to bust, to jigger

madreperla *nf (ostra)* pearl oyster; *(nácar)* mother-of-pearl

madrépora *nf* **(a)** *(celentéreo)* madrepore **(b)** *(polípero)* coral reef

madreselva *nf* honeysuckle

Madrid *n* Madrid; EXPR *Esp Fam Hum* **pareces de M.** shut that door, will you?, were you born in a stable *o* barn?

madridismo *nm Dep (apoyo)* = support for Real Madrid Football Club; *(seguidores)* = Real Madrid Football Club supporters

madridista *adj Dep* = of/relating to Real Madrid Football Club

madrigal *nm* **(a)** *Lit* madrigal **(b)** *Mús* madrigal

madriguera *nf* **(a)** *(de animal)* den; *(de conejo)* burrow, rabbit hole **(b)** *(escondrijo)* den

madrileño, -a 1 *adj* of/from Madrid
2 *nm,f* person from Madrid

Madriles *nmpl Esp Fam* **los M.** Madrid

madrina *nf* **(a)** *(de bautizo)* godmother **(b)** *(de boda)* ≃ matron of honour **(c)** *(de confirmación)* sponsor **(d)** *(de barco)* = woman who launches a ship **(e)** *Am (animal)* tame older animal *(used when driving or breaking in younger animals)*; *(manada)* herd of tame older animals

madriza *nf Méx Vulg (paliza)* **le dieron una m.** they kicked the shit out of him

madroñal *nm* strawberry-tree grove

madroño *nm* **(a)** *(árbol)* strawberry tree **(b)** *(fruto)* strawberry-tree berry

madrugada *nf* **(a)** *(amanecer)* dawn; **de m.** at dawn **(b)** *(noche)* early morning; **las tres de la m.** three in the morning; **la fiesta duró hasta la m.** the party went on into the early hours of the morning; **la programación de m.** *(en televisión, radio)* the late-night programmes **(c)** *(acción)* **me tuve que dar una m. para llegar a tiempo** I had to get up early to get there on time

madrugador, -ora 1 *adj* early-rising; **es muy m.** he's a very early riser
2 *nm,f* early riser

madrugar [38] **1** *vi* **(a)** *(levantarse temprano)* to get up early; PROV **no por mucho m. amanece más temprano** time must take its course; PROV **al que madruga, Dios le ayuda** the early bird catches the worm **(b)** *(anticiparse)* to be quick off the mark **(c)** *(ocurrir pronto)* **los goles madrugaron** it wasn't long before the goals started flowing
2 *vt Am Fam* to beat to it; **nos madrugaste, te íbamos a hacer la misma sugerencia** you beat us to it, we were going to make the same suggestion to you

madrugón *nm Fam* early rise; **darse** *o* **pegarse un m.** to get up dead early

madrugonazo *nm Ven Fam* military coup

maduración *nf* **(a)** *(de fruta)* ripening **(b)** *(de persona)* maturing; **una experiencia que contribuye a la m. de la persona** an experience which helps a person attain maturity **(c)** *(de idea, proyecto)* **la m. del proyecto llevará tiempo** it will take time for the project to take proper shape

madurar 1 *vt* **(a)** *(fruto)* to ripen **(b)** *(persona)* to mature **(c)** *(idea, proyecto)* to think through
2 *vi* **(a)** *(fruto)* to ripen **(b)** *(persona)* to mature **(c)** *(idea, proyecto)* to take proper shape; **cuando haya madurado un poco más tomaremos una decisión** when it has developed a bit further we'll take a decision

madurez *nf* **(a)** *(de fruto)* ripeness **(b)** *(de persona) (sensatez, juicio)* maturity **(c)** *(edad adulta)* adulthood; **a los veinte años había alcanzado ya la m. artística** by the age of twenty she had already matured *o* grown up as an artist

maduro, -a *adj* **(a)** *(fruto)* ripe **(b)** *(persona) (sensata)* mature **(c)** *(persona) (adulta)* mature, older; **le gustan los hombres maduros** she likes mature *o* older men; **una mujer de edad madura** a middle-aged woman **(d)** *(idea, proyecto)* thought through; **este poema aún no está m. para ser publicado** this poem isn't ready for publication yet

maese *nm Anticuado* Master

maestranza *nf Mil* **(a)** *(talleres)* arsenal **(b)** *(obreros)* arsenal workers

maestrazgo *nm Hist* = office and territory of the master of a military order

maestre *nm Mil* master

maestresala *nmf* head waiter, maître d'hôtel

maestría *nf* **(a)** *(habilidad)* mastery, skill; **pinta con gran m.** she's a very skilful painter **(b)** *Am (título)* master's degree

maestrillo *nm* EXPR **cada m. tiene su librillo** everyone has their own way of doing things

maestro, -a 1 *adj* **(a)** *(excelente)* masterly; **una obra maestra de la literatura universal** one of the masterpieces of world literature **(b)** *(principal)* main; **llave maestra** passkey, master key; **viga maestra** main beam
2 *nm,f* **(a)** *(profesor)* teacher ►► ***m. de escuela*** schoolmaster, *f* schoolmistress; *Col, RP* ***maestra jardinera*** kindergarten *o* nursery school teacher
(b) *Méx (en universidad) Br* lecturer, *US* professor
(c) *(experto)* master; **un m. de la cocina francesa** a master of French cuisine
(d) *(en oficio)* master; **m. carpintero/albañil** master carpenter/builder
(e) *Mús* maestro
(f) *(director)* ***m. de ceremonias*** master of ceremonies; ***m. de obras*** foreman
(g) *Taurom* matador
3 *nm Am (apelativo) Br* mate, *US* buddy; **¿qué tal está, m.?** how's it going *Br* mate *o US* buddy?; **¿cuánto le debo, m.?** what do I owe you *Br* mate *o US* buddy?

mafia *nf* **(a) la M.** *(italiana)* the Mafia **(b)** *(de criminales)* mafia **(c)** *(de profesionales)* **una m. literaria** a literary mafia

mafioso, -a 1 *adj* mafia; **organización mafiosa** mafia organization
2 *nm,f* **(a)** *(italiano)* Mafioso **(b)** *(criminal)* crook

mafufada *nf Méx Fam* weird nonsense; **¿qué mafufadas dices?** what's that nonsense you're saying?

mafufo, -a *adj Méx Fam* weird; **está todo m.** he's in a really weird state

magacín = **magazine**

Magallanes *n pr* Magellan

magallánico, -a 1 *adj* of/from Magallanes *(Chile)*
2 *nm,f* person from Magallanes *(Chile)*

maganzón, -ona *adj Col, CRica Fam* lazy, idle

magazine, magacín *nm* **(a)** *(revista)* magazine **(b)** *(programa)* magazine programme

magdalena *nf* = small sponge cake; EXPR **llorar como una m.** to cry one's eyes out

magdaleniense 1 *adj* Magdalenian
2 *nm* **el M.** the Magdalenian

magenta 1 *adj inv* magenta
2 *nm* magenta

magia *nf* **(a)** *(sobrenatural)* magic ►► ***m. blanca*** white magic; ***m. negra*** black magic **(b)** *(trucos)* magic, conjuring; **hacer m.** to do conjuring *o* magic tricks; **un número de m.** a conjuring *o* magic trick **(c)** *(encanto)* magic; **la m. del cine** the magic of the silver screen

magiar 1 *adj* Magyar
2 *nmf (persona)* Magyar
3 *nm (lengua)* Magyar

mágicamente *adv* as if by magic

mágico, -a *adj* **(a)** *(de la magia)* magic **(b)** *(maravilloso)* magical; **fue un momento m.** it was a magical moment

magín *nm Esp Fam* imagination

magisterio *nm* **(a)** *(profesión)* teaching profession; **ejerció el m. durante cuarenta años** he was a teacher for forty years; **el m. español** Spanish teachers **(b)** *(estudios)* teaching degree; **estudiar m.** to do teacher training, to study to be a teacher **(c)** *(enseñanza)* teaching; **su m. dejó una huella profunda en varias generaciones de estudiantes** her teaching had a profound influence on several generations of students

magistrado, -a *nm,f (juez)* judge

magistral *adj* (**a**) *(de maestro)* magisterial (**b**) *(excelente)* masterly
magistralmente *adv* masterfully
magistratura *nf Der* (**a**) *(oficio)* judgeship; **ejerce la m. desde hace cinco años** he has been a judge for five years (**b**) *(periodo)* term of office as a judge (**c**) **la m.** *(jueces)* the magistrature (**d**) *(tribunal)* tribunal; **llevar a alguien a m.** to take sb to court ►► *Esp* ***m. de trabajo*** industrial tribunal
magma *nm* (**a**) *(rocas fundidas)* magma (**b**) *(sustancia informe)* shapeless mass (**c**) *(mezcla confusa)* muddle; **la ciudad es un m. de culturas** the city is a cultural melting-pot
magmático,-a *adj* volcanic, *Espec* magmatic
magnanimidad *nf* magnanimity
magnánimo, -a *adj* magnanimous
magnate *nm* magnate, tycoon ►► ***m. del petróleo*** oil baron; ***m. de la prensa*** press baron *o* magnate
magnavoz *nm Méx* (**a**) *(bocina)* megaphone (**b**) *(con micrófono) Br* loudhailer, *US* bullhorn
magnesia *nf Quím* magnesia, magnesium oxide
magnesio *nm Quím* magnesium
magnético, -a *adj* (**a**) *(del imán)* magnetic (**b**) *(atractivo)* magnetic
magnetismo *nm* (**a**) *(del imán)* magnetism ►► ***m. terrestre*** geomagnetism (**b**) *(atractivo)* magnetism ►► ***m. personal*** charisma
magnetita *nf Geol* magnetite
magnetización *nf* magnetization
magnetizar [14] *vt* (**a**) *Fís* to magnetize (**b**) *(fascinar)* to mesmerize
magneto *nm o nf* magneto
magnetofón = **magnetófono**
magnetofónico, -a *adj (cinta)* magnetic
magnetófono, magnetofón *nm* tape recorder
magneto-óptico, -a *adj Informát* magneto-optical
magnetoscopio *nm* video (cassette) recorder
magnetosfera *nf* magnetosphere
magnetrón *nm Elec* magnetron
magnicida *nmf* assassin
magnicidio *nm* assassination
magníficamente *adv* magnificently; **me parece m. que te vayas de vacaciones** I think it's a splendid idea for you to go on holiday
magnificar [60] *vt* (**a**) *(exagerar)* to exaggerate, to magnify (**b**) *(ensalzar)* to praise highly (**c**) *Am (aumentar)* to magnify
magníficat *nm* Magnificat
magnificencia *nf Literary* (**a**) *(grandiosidad)* magnificence (**b**) *(generosidad)* munificence
magnífico, -a *adj* (**a**) *(muy bueno) (idea, invento, oportunidad)* wonderful, magnificent; **una habitación con magníficas vistas al mar** a room with a magnificent view of the sea; **tus amigos son una gente magnífica** your friends are wonderful; **llegaré a las ocho – ¡m.!** I'll be there at eight – splendid!
(**b**) *(grandioso, espléndido)* great, fantastic; **¡con esa falda estás magnífica!** you look great *o* fantastic in that skirt!
(**c**) *(tratamiento)* Honourable; **el Rector M. de la Universidad** the Honourable Chancellor of the University
magnitud *nf* (**a**) *(tamaño, importancia)* magnitude; **la m. de la crisis forzó a dimitir al presidente** the magnitude *o* severity of the crisis forced the president to resign; **todavía no se conoce la m. de los daños** the extent *o* scale of the damage is still not known; **un problema de primera m.** a major problem (**b**) *Mat & Fís* magnitude (**c**) *Astron* magnitude; **una estrella de primera/segunda m.** a first/second magnitude star
magno, -a *adj Literario* great, major; **un m. acontecimiento** a major event
magnolia *nf* magnolia
magnolio *nm* magnolia (tree)
mágnum (*pl* **mágnums**) *nm* (*botella*) magnum
mago, -a *nm,f* (**a**) *(prestidigitador)* magician (**b**) *(en cuentos, leyendas)* wizard (**c**) *(persona habilidosa)* wizard; **un m. de las finanzas** a financial wizard
magra *nf* (**a**) *(lonja)* slice (**b**) *(magro)* lean pork
magrear *Esp muy Fam* **1** *vt* to touch up
2 magrearse *vpr Br* to snog, *US* to neck
Magreb *nm* **el M.** the Maghreb
magrebí (*pl* **magrebíes** *o* **magrebís**) **1** *adj* Maghrebi
2 *nmf* Maghrebi
magreo *nm Esp muy Fam* touching up
magro, -a 1 *adj* (**a**) *(carne)* lean (**b**) *Literario (persona)* lean
2 *nm Esp* lean pork
maguey, magüey *nm* maguey
magullado, -a *adj* bruised
magulladura *nf* bruise
magullar 1 *vt* (**a**) *(persona)* to bruise (**b**) *(fruta)* to bruise
2 magullarse *vpr* **me magullé la pierna** I bruised my leg
magullón *nm Am* bruise
maharajá [mara'χa] *nm* maharajah
maharaní [maχara'ni] (*pl* **maharaníes**) *nm* maharani
Mahoma *n pr* Mohammed
mahometano, -a 1 *adj* Muslim
2 *nm,f* Muslim
mahometismo *nm* Mohammedanism, Islam
mahón *nm (tela)* nankeen
mahonesa *nf* mayonnaise
mai *m Fam* joint
maiceado, -a *Ven Fam* **1** *adj Br* well-fed, *US* corn-fed
2 *nm,f* = well-fed person or animal
maicena *nf Br* cornflour, *US* cornstarch
maicería *nf Cuba, Méx Br* maize shop, *US* corn shop
maicero, -a 1 *adj* (**a**) *Am (animal) Br* maize-fed, *US* corn-fed (**b**) *Am (región, sector) Br* maize-growing, *US* corn-growing
2 *nm* oriole
3 *nm,f Am Br* maize grower, *US* corn grower
maicillo *nm* (**a**) *(planta)* = type of sorghum (**b**) *Chile (arena)* gravel
mail ['mail, 'meil] (*pl* **mails**) *nm Informát* e-mail (message); **enviar un m. a alguien** to e-mail sb
mailing ['meilin] (*pl* **mailings**) *nm Com* mailshot; **hacer un m.** to do a mailshot
maillot [ma'jot] (*pl* **maillots**) *nm* (**a**) *(prenda femenina)* leotard (**b**) *(en ciclismo)* jersey ►► ***el m. amarillo*** the yellow jersey; ***el m. de lunares*** the polka-dot jersey; ***el m. verde*** the green jersey
mainel *nm Arquit* mullion
maitines *nmpl Rel* matins
maître ['metre] *nm Br* head waiter, *US* maître d'
maíz *nm* (**a**) *(planta) Br* maize, *US* (Indian) corn (**b**) *(utilizado en cocina) Br* sweetcorn, *US* corn ►► ***m. dulce*** *Br* sweetcorn, *US* corn; *Col* ***m. pira*** popcorn; ***m. tostado*** = toasted, salted maize kernels
maizal *nm Br* maize field, *US* cornfield
maizena® *nf Br* cornflour, *US* cornstarch
maja *nf* (**a**) *(de mortero)* pestle (**b**) *ver también* **majo**
majá (*pl* **majáes**) *Cuba* **1** *adj Fam* sluggish, sluggardly
2 *nmf Fam Br* slowcoach, *US* slowpoke
3 *nm* Cuban boa
majada *nf* (**a**) *(redil)* sheepfold (**b**) *CSur (manada)* flock of sheep
majaderear *Carib, Col Fam* **1** *vt* to pester
2 *vi* to be a nuisance *o* a pest
majadería *nf* (**a**) *(cualidad)* idiocy (**b**) *(acción, dicho)* **hacer majaderías** to do stupid *o* crazy things; **decir majaderías** to talk nonsense; **eso que has dicho es una m.** what you said is nonsense
majadero, -a 1 *adj* (**a**) *(tonto)* stupid, idiotic (**b**) *CSur Fam (pesado) Br* tiresome, *US* pesky
2 *nm,f* (**a**) *(tonto)* idiot (**b**) *CSur Fam (pesado)* pest, nuisance
majado *nm* (**a**) *(cosa triturada)* mash, pulp (**b**) *Chile (guiso)* = dish of ground wheat soaked in hot water
majagua *nf Carib* (**a**) *(árbol)* mahoe, sea hibiscus (**b**) *(fibra)* = mahoe fibre, used for making cord
majamama *nf Chile Fam* tangle, jumble
majar *vt (machacar)* to crush; *(moler)* to grind
majareta, *Esp* **majara** *Fam* **1** *adj* nutty
2 *nmf* nutcase
majarete *nm Ven* = cornflour and coconut custard
maje *Méx Fam* **1** *adj* silly, *Br* daft, *US* dumb
2 *nmf* dope; **hacerse el m.** to act dumb; **hacer m. a alguien** to make a fool of sb, to dupe sb
majestad *nf* (**a**) *(grandiosidad)* majesty (**b**) **Su M.** *(tratamiento)* His/Her Majesty; **Sus Majestades los Reyes** their Majesties the King and Queen (**c**) *Arte* **Cristo en m.** Christ Enthroned, Christ in Majesty

majestuosamente *adv* majestically

majestuosidad *nf* majesty

majestuoso, -a *adj* majestic

majo, -a 1 *adj Esp Fam* (a) *(simpático)* nice; **tienen unos críos muy majos** they've got lovely kids (b) *(bonito)* pretty; **se compró una casa muy maja** she bought herself a beautiful *o* lovely house (c) *(apelativo)* **¡oye, m., déjame ya!** look, leave me alone, will you?; **¿maja, por qué no me ayudas?** come on, give me a hand; **¡bueno, majos, nos veremos mañana!** right guys, I'll see you tomorrow, then
2 *nm,f Arte & Hist* = lower-class native of 18th-19th century Madrid, characterized by colourful traditional dress and proud manner

majorette [majo'ret] *nf* majorette

majuela *nf* hawthorn fruit

majuelo *nm* hawthorn

majuga *nf Urug* (a) *(pescadito)* whitebait (b) *Fam (niños)* **la m.** the young 'uns, *Br* the tiddlers; **vino a la fiesta una m. increíble** a horde of kids came to the party

majunche *Ven Fam* 1 *adj* (a) *(persona)* dull, drab (b) *(cosa)* shoddy
2 *nmf* **ser un m.** to be a nobody

MAL 1 *adj ver* **malo**
2 *nm* (a) *(maldad)* **el m.** evil; *Literario* **las fuerzas del m.** the forces of darkness *o* evil
(b) *(daño)* harm, damage; **nadie sufrió ningún m.** no one was harmed, no one suffered any harm; **¿no le hará m. al bebé tanta agua?** all that water can't be good for the baby, can it?; **no te hará ningún m. salir un rato** it won't harm you *o* it won't do you any harm to go out for a while; **todas aquellas habladurías le hicieron mucho m.** all the gossip hurt her deeply ►► ***m. de ojo*** evil eye; **echarle** *o CSur* **hacerle (el) m. de ojo a alguien** to give sb the evil eye; *Arquit* ***el m. de la piedra*** = the problem of crumbling masonry caused by pollution etc
(c) *(enfermedad)* illness; *Fig* **esto te curará todos los males** this will make you feel better; **tener m. de amores** to be lovesick ►► ***m. de (las) altura(s)*** altitude sickness; ***m. de montaña*** mountain sickness; *Ven* ***m. de páramo*** altitude sickness; *Fam* ***el m. de las vacas locas*** mad cow disease
(d) *(problema, inconveniente)* bad thing; **el hambre y la pobreza son males que afectan al Tercer Mundo** hunger and poverty are problems *o* ills which affect the Third World; **entre las dos opciones, es el m. menor** it's the lesser of two evils; **un m. necesario** a necessary evil
(e) EXPR **del m., el menos** it's the lesser of two evils; **la crisis pasará, no hay m. que cien años dure** the recession will end sooner or later, these things never last forever; PROV **a grandes males, grandes remedios** drastic situations demand drastic action; PROV **m. de muchos, consuelo de todos** *o* **de tontos: he suspendido, pero también mis compañeros – m. de muchos, consuelo de tontos** *o* **de todos** I failed, but so did my classmates – it doesn't make it all right, just because they did too; **lo mismo pasa en otros países – m. de muchos, consuelo de tontos** *o* **de todos** the same thing happens in other countries – that doesn't make it any better, though; PROV **no hay m. que por bien no venga** every cloud has a silver lining
3 *adv* (a) *(incorrectamente)* wrong; **obrar m.** to do wrong; **portarse m.** to behave badly; **juzgar m. a alguien** to judge sb wrongly, to be wrong in one's judgement of sb; **está m. hecho** *(un informe, un trabajo)* it hasn't been done properly; *(un producto, un aparato)* it's badly made; **eso está m. hecho, no debían haberlo aceptado** it was wrong of them, they shouldn't have accepted it; **está m. eso que has hecho** what you've done is wrong; **hacer algo m.** to do sth wrong; **has escrito m. esta palabra** you've spelt that word wrong; **hiciste m. en decírselo** it was wrong of you to tell him; **está m. que yo lo diga, pero esta sopa esta buenísima** this soup is delicious, although I say so myself
(b) *(inadecuadamente, insuficientemente)* badly; **creo que me he explicado m.** I'm not sure I've explained myself clearly; **oigo/veo m.** I can't hear/see very well; **el niño come bastante m.** the boy isn't eating properly *o* very well; **calculé m. el tiempo** I miscalculated the time; **canta muy m.** she sings terribly, she's a terrible singer; **esta puerta cierra m.** this door doesn't shut properly; **andar m. de dinero** to be short of money; **andamos m. de azúcar** we're running out of sugar; **la empresa/el equipo va m.** the company/team isn't doing very well; **va m. en la universidad** she's not doing very well at university; **le fue m. en la entrevista** his interview didn't go very well; **el sueldo no está nada m.** the pay's pretty good, the pay isn't at all bad; **ese chico no está nada m.** that boy's not bad *o* pretty nice; **la reparación quedó m.** it wasn't repaired properly; **me quedó m. el retrato** my portrait didn't come out right; **la conferencia/reunión salió m.** the talk/meeting went badly; **la fiesta salió m.** the party was a failure
(c) *(desagradablemente, desfavorablemente)* **encontrarse m.** *(enfermo)* to feel ill; *(incómodo)* to feel uncomfortable; **estar m.** *(de salud)* to be *o* feel ill; *(de calidad)* to be bad; **hablar m. de alguien** to speak ill of sb; **oler m.** to smell bad; **¡qué m. huele!** what a smell!; *Fam Fig* **esto me huele m.** this smells fishy to me; **pasarlo m.** to have a bad time; **pensar m. de alguien** to think ill of sb; **saber m.** to taste bad; *Fig* **me supo m. que no vinieses a despedirme** I was a bit put out that you didn't come to see me off; **me sabe muy m. que hablen a mis espaldas** I don't like it that they talk behind my back; **sentar m. a alguien** *(ropa)* not to suit sb; *(comida)* to disagree with sb; *(comentario, actitud)* to upset sb
(d) *(difícilmente)* hardly; **m. puede saberlo si no se lo cuentas** he's hardly going to know it if you don't tell him, how's he supposed to know it if you don't tell him?
(e) EXPR **estar a m. con alguien** to have fallen out with sb; **ir de m. en peor** to go from bad to worse; **no estaría m. que...** it would be nice if...; **tomar algo a m.** to take sth the wrong way
4 **mal que** *loc conj* although, even though; **m. que te pese, las cosas están así** whether you like it or not, that's the way things are; **m. que bien** somehow or other

malabar *adj* **juegos malabares** juggling

malabarismo *nm Fig* juggling; **hacer malabarismos** to juggle; *Fig* **tuve que hacer malabarismos para tener contentas a las dos partes** I had to perform a real balancing act to keep both sides happy

malabarista *nmf* (a) *(artista)* juggler (b) *Chile (ladrón)* clever thief

Malabo *n* Malabo

malacate *nm CAm, Méx (huso)* spindle

malaconsejado, -a 1 *adj* ill-advised
2 *nm,f* ill-advised person

malacostumbrado, -a *adj* spoiled

malacostumbrar 1 *vt* to spoil
2 **malacostumbrarse** *vpr* to become spoiled

malacrianza *nm Ven* (a) *(grosería) (al hablar)* vulgarity; *(en conducta)* bad manners; **sería una m. rechazar su oferta** it would be bad manners *o* very rude to reject their offer (b) *(mala educación)* **es insoportable debido a la m. que le dio su madre** he's unbearable because of the spoiled upbringing his mother gave him

málaga *nm (vino)* Malaga (wine)

malagradecido, -a *adj* ungrateful, unappreciative

malagua *nf Perú* jellyfish

malagueño, -a 1 *adj* of/from Malaga *(Spain)*
2 *nm,f* person from Malaga *(Spain)*

malagueta *nf* grains of paradise, Guinea *o* melegueta pepper

Malaisia *n* Malaysia

malaisio, -a 1 *adj* Malaysian
2 *nm,f* Malaysian

malaje *nmf Esp Fam* (a) *(persona)* nasty piece of work (b) *(mala intención)* **tener m.** to be a nasty piece of work

malaleche *Esp muy Fam* 1 *adj* nasty, mean
2 *nmf Br* nasty git, *US* mean son of a bitch

malambo *nm RP (baile)* = folk dance for men, involving fast rhythmic stamping

malamente *adv Fam* (a) *(muy mal)* badly; **todo acabó m.** it all ended badly (b) *(difícilmente)* hardly; **m. te pudo llamar sin saber tu número** she could hardly have rung you if she didn't have your number

malandanza *nf Literario* misfortune, calamity

malandraje *nm Carib, RP Fam* crooks, hustlers, *US* punks

malandrín, -ina 1 *adj* wicked, evil
2 *nm,f* scoundrel

malandro, -a *nm,f Carib, RP Fam* (a) *(delincuente) Br* crook, hustler, *US* punk (b) *(mentiroso)* cheat

malanga 1 *adj Cuba Fam (torpe)* ineffectual, useless
2 *nf CAm, Carib, Méx* (a) *(planta)* dalo, elephant's ear (b) *(tubérculo)* taro, dasheen

malapata *nmf Esp Fam (persona)* clumsy oaf

malaquita *nf* malachite

malar *adj Anat* cheek, *Espec* malar; **el hueso/la región m.** the cheek *o Espec* malar bone/region

malaria *nf* malaria

malasangre *nmf (persona)* **ser un m.** to be malicious *o* spiteful

Malasia *n* Malaysia

malasio, -a 1 *adj* Malaysian
2 *nm,f* Malaysian

malasombra *nmf Esp Fam (persona)* pest

Malaui *n* Malawi

malaui 1 *adj* Malawian
2 *nmf* Malawian

malaventura *nf Literario* misfortune

malaventurado, -a *Literario* 1 *adj* ill-fated, unfortunate
2 *nm,f* unfortunate person; **es un m.** he's a poor soul

malaya *nf Chile* flank, *Br* skirt

malayo, -a 1 *adj* Malay, Malayan
2 *nm,f (persona)* Malay, Malayan
3 *nm (lengua)* Malay, Malayan

malbaratar *vt* (**a**) *(malvender)* to undersell (**b**) *(malgastar)* to squander

malcarado, -a *adj* grim-faced

malcasar 1 *vt* to mismatch
2 **malcasarse** *vpr* to make an unhappy *o* a bad marriage

malcomer *vi* to eat poorly

malcriadez, malcrianza *nf Am* bad manners, lack of breeding

malcriado, -a 1 *adj* spoiled
2 *nm,f* spoiled brat

malcrianza = **malcriadez**

malcriar [32] *vt* to spoil

maldad *nf* (**a**) *(cualidad)* evil (**b**) *(acción)* evil thing; **cometer maldades** to do evil *o* wrong

maldecir [51] 1 *vt* to curse; **maldigo el día en que te conocí** I curse the day I ever met you
2 *vi* to curse; **m. de** to speak ill of

maldiciente 1 *adj* slandering, defaming
2 *nmf* slanderer

maldición 1 *nf* curse; **echar una m. a alguien** to put a curse on sb; **una m. divina** God's curse
2 *interj* damn!

maldigo *etc ver* **maldecir**

maldijera *etc ver* **maldecir**

maldita *nf Carib* (**a**) *(llaga)* boil (**b**) *(picadura)* = infected insect bite

maldito, -a 1 *adj* (**a**) *(condenado)* cursed, damned (**b**) *(artista, poeta)* doomed, cursed (**c**) *Fam (para enfatizar)* damned; **¡apaga la maldita radio!** turn the damned radio off!; **malditas las ganas que tengo de madrugar** getting up early is the last thing I want to do; EXPR **¡maldita sea!** damn it!; **¡maldita (sea) la hora en que se me ocurrió invitarlos!** I wish it had never crossed my mind to invite them!
2 *nm* **el m.** the Devil, Satan

Maldivas *nfpl* **las (Islas) M.** the Maldives

maldivo, -a 1 *adj* Maldivian
2 *nm,f* Maldivian

maldoso, -a *adj Méx* nasty, mean

maleabilidad *nf* malleability

maleable *adj* (**a**) *(material)* malleable (**b**) *(persona)* malleable

maleante 1 *adj* wicked
2 *nmf* criminal

malear 1 *vt* to corrupt
2 **malearse** *vpr* to become corrupted

malecón *nm* (**a**) *(muelle)* jetty (**b**) *(rompeolas)* breakwater, mole (**c**) *CAm, Cuba (paseo marítimo)* seafront; *(de un lago)* lakefront

maledicencia *nf (difamación)* slander

maleducadamente *adv* rudely

maleducado, -a 1 *adj* rude, bad-mannered
2 *nm,f* rude *o* bad-mannered person; **es un m.** he's very rude *o* bad-mannered

maleficencia *nf* evil-doing

maleficio *nm* curse

maléfico, -a *adj* evil

malenseñado, -a *CSur* 1 *adj* rude, bad-mannered
2 *nm,f* rude *o* bad-mannered person; **es un m.** he's very rude *o* bad-mannered

malenseñar *vt CSur* to spoil

malentender *vt* to misunderstand, to misinterpret

malentendido *nm* misunderstanding; **ha debido haber un m.** there must have been some misunderstanding

malestar *nm* (**a**) *(indisposición)* upset, discomfort; **sentir m. (general)** to feel unwell; **siento un m. en el estómago** I've got an upset stomach (**b**) *(inquietud)* **su dimisión causó un profundo m. en el seno del partido** her resignation caused a lot of upset within the party; **su decisión creó mucho m.** her decision upset a lot of people

maleta 1 *nf* (**a**) *(de equipaje)* suitcase; **hacer** *o* **preparar la m.** to pack (one's bags); EXPR *Chile* **largar** *o* **soltar la m.** to kick the bucket (**b**) *Andes, Guat (fardo)* bundle (**c**) *Chile (alforja)* saddlebag (**d**) *Chile, Ven (maletero) Br* boot, *US* trunk
2 *nmf Esp, Méx Fam (inútil, malo)* **ser un m.** to be a waste of space

maletera *nf Andes Br* boot, *US* trunk

maletero *nm* (**a**) *Esp, Cuba (de automóvil) Br* boot, *US* trunk (**b**) *(persona)* porter (**c**) *Ven (trastero)* storeroom

maletilla *nmf Taurom* apprentice bullfighter

maletín *nm* (**a**) *(de mano)* briefcase (**b**) *(maleta pequeña)* small suitcase ▸▸ ***m. de médico*** doctor's bag

maletón *Col Fam* 1 *adj* hunchbacked
2 *nm* hunchback

maletudo, -a *Méx Fam* 1 *adj* hunchbacked
2 *nm* hunchback

malevaje *nm Bol, RP Anticuado* band of rogues

malevo *nm Bol, RP Anticuado* rogue

malevolencia *nf* malevolence, wickedness

malévolo, -a *adj* malevolent, wicked

maleza *nf (arbustos)* undergrowth; *(malas hierbas)* weeds

malformación *nf* malformation ▸▸ ***m. congénita*** congenital deformity

malgache 1 *adj* Madagascan, Malagasy
2 *nmf* Madagascan, Malagasy

malgastador, -ora 1 *adj* spendthrift
2 *nm,f* spendthrift

malgastar *vt (dinero, tiempo)* to waste

malgeniado, -a *adj Col, Perú* ill-tempered, irritable

malgenioso, -a *adj Chile, Méx* ill-tempered, irritable

malhablado, -a 1 *adj* foul-mouthed
2 *nm,f* foul-mouthed person; **es un m.** he's foul-mouthed

malhadado, -a *adj Formal* wretched, unfortunate

malhaya *interj Am Fam* **im. sea mi suerte!** curse my luck!

malhechor, -ora 1 *adj* criminal, delinquent
2 *nm,f* criminal, delinquent

malherir [63] *vt* to injure seriously

malhumor *nm* bad temper

malhumoradamente *adv* **"idéjame!", replicó m.** "leave me alone!" he replied bad-temperedly *o* crossly

malhumorado, -a *adj* (**a**) *(de mal carácter)* bad-tempered (**b**) *(enfadado)* in a bad mood

malhumorar *vt* to annoy, to irritate

Malí, Mali *n* Mali

malí 1 *adj* of/from Mali
2 *nmf* person from Mali

malicia *nf* (**a**) *(mala intención)* malice; **fue una decisión tomada con mucha m.** it was a thoroughly malicious decision (**b**) *(astucia, agudeza)* cunning, craftiness; **a este niño le falta m.** the boy needs to wise up

maliciar 1 *vt* (**a**) *(sospechar)* to suspect (**b**) *(malear)* to corrupt
2 **maliciarse** *vpr* (**a**) *(sospechar)* to suspect; **me maliciaba que eso era un timo** I suspected it was a con (**b**) *(malearse)* to go bad, to be corrupted

maliciosamente *adv* (**a**) *(con maldad)* maliciously (**b**) *(con astucia, agudeza)* cunningly, craftily

malicioso, -a *adj* (**a**) *(malintencionado)* malicious (**b**) *(astuto, agudo)* cunning, crafty

malignidad *nf* (**a**) *(maldad)* malign nature (**b**) *(de tumor)* malignancy

maligno, -a *adj* (**a**) *(con maldad)* evil, malign (**b**) *(tumor)* malignant

Malinche *n* = Mexican Indian who became Cortés' mistress

malinchismo *nm Méx* = preference for foreign goods, culture, values etc

malinchista *Méx* 1 *adj* = demonstrating "malinchismo"
2 *nmf* = person who displays "malinchismo"

malinformar *vt Am* to misinform

malintencionado, -a 1 *adj (acción)* ill-meant, ill-intentioned; *(persona)* malevolent
2 *nm,f* spiteful *o* malicious person; **es un m.** he is spiteful *o* malicious

malinterpretar *vt* to misinterpret, to misunderstand

malla *nf* (a) *(tejido)* mesh ►► ***m. de alambre*** wire mesh; ***m. cristalina*** crystal lattice; ***m. metálica*** wire mesh
(b) *(red)* net; **envió el balón al fondo de las mallas** he drove the ball into the back of the net
(c) *Ecuad, Perú, RP (traje de baño)* swimsuit
(d) *Esp* **mallas** *(de gimnasia)* leotard; *(de ballet)* tights
(e) *RP (de gimnasia)* leotard ►► ***m. amarilla*** *(en ciclismo)* yellow jersey
(f) *RP (de reloj)* metal wristband

mallku *nm Hist* = chief of an indigenous Peruvian or Bolivian community

mallo *nm (mazo)* mallet

Mallorca *n* Majorca

mallorquín, -ina 1 *adj* Majorcan
2 *nm,f (persona)* Majorcan
3 *nm (lengua)* Majorcan

malmeter *vt* **m. a la gente** to turn *o* set people against one another

malnacido, -a *nm,f* **ser un m.** to be a foul *o* nasty person

malnutrición *nf* malnutrition

malnutrido, -a *adj* undernourished

MALO, -A

Mal is used instead of **malo** before singular masculine nouns (e.g. **un mal ejemplo** a bad example). The comparative form of **malo** (= worse) is **peor**, the superlative forms (= the worst) are **el peor** (masculine) and **la peor** (feminine).

1 *adj* (a) *(perjudicial, grave)* bad; **traigo malas noticias** I have some bad news; **es m. para el hígado** it's bad for your liver; **¿es algo m., doctor?** is it serious, doctor?; **una mala caída** a nasty fall
(b) *(sin calidad, sin aptitudes)* poor, bad; **una mala novela/actriz** a bad novel/actress; **tiene muy malas notas** her marks are very poor *o* bad; **ser de mala calidad** to be poor quality; **este material/producto es muy m.** this material/product is very poor quality; **soy muy m. para la música** I'm no good at *o* very bad at music; EXPR *Hum* **es más m. que hecho de encargo** *(producto, jugador)* he's/it's truly awful *o* as bad as they come; PROV **más vale lo m. conocido que lo bueno por conocer** better the devil you know (than the devil you don't)
(c) *(inapropiado, adverso)* bad; **fue una mala decisión** it was a bad decision; **he dormido en mala postura** I slept in a funny position; **es mala señal** it's a bad sign; **lo m. es que...** the problem is (that)...; **disparó con la pierna mala y metió gol** he shot with his weaker foot and scored; **tener mala suerte** to be unlucky; **¡qué mala suerte!** how unlucky! ►► *Am* ***mala palabra*** swearword
(d) *(malvado)* wicked, evil; **es muy mala persona** she's a really nasty person; **tiene muy mala intención** he's very spiteful; **eso sólo lo haría un mal amigo** it's a poor friend who would do a thing like that; **¡mira que eres m., criticarla así!** it's not very nice of you to criticize her like that!; **anda, no seas m. y déjame que vaya** go on, don't be mean, let me go
(e) *(travieso)* naughty; **¡no seas m. y obedece!** be good and do as I say!; **el crío está muy m. últimamente** the child has been very naughty recently
(f) *(enfermo)* ill, sick; **estar/ponerse m.** to be/fall ill; **tiene a su padre m.** her father's ill; EXPR **poner m. a alguien** to drive sb mad; **me pongo mala cada vez que la veo** I get mad every time I see her
(g) *(desagradable)* bad; **esta herida tiene mal aspecto** this wound looks nasty; **mal tiempo** bad weather; **hace mal tiempo** the weather's bad; *Esp* **está muy m. el día** it's a horrible day
(h) *(podrido, pasado)* bad, off; **la fruta está/se ha puesto mala** the fruit is/has gone off
(i) *(uso enfático)* **ni un mal trozo de pan** not even a crust of bread; **no había ni un mal supermercado en el pueblo** there wasn't a single supermarket to be found in the village
(j) *(difícil)* **el asunto es m. de entender** the matter is hard *o* difficult to understand; **una lesión muy mala de curar** an injury that won't heal easily
(k) *Esp Fam Euf (con la menstruación)* **estar/ponerse mala** to be on/start one's period
2 *nm,f* **el m., la mala** *(en cine)* the villain, the baddy
3 *interj* **cuando nadie se queja, ¡m.!** it's a bad sign when nobody complains
4 **malas** *nfpl* **está** *o* **se ha puesto a malas con él** she's fallen out with him; **estar de malas** to be in a bad mood; **por las malas** *(a la fuerza)* by force; **lo vas a hacer, aunque tenga que ser por las malas** you're going to do it, whether you like it or not; **por las malas es de temer** she's a fearful sight when she's angry; EXPR *Am* **estar** *o* **andar de malas** to be having a hard time; EXPR *Andes, CSur* **en las malas** *(de mal humor)* in a bad mood; **los amigos no te abandonan en las malas** friends don't let you down when things get bad

---

maloca *nf Hist* communal hut

malogrado, -a *adj* (a) *(desaprovechado)* wasted; **un actor/deportista m.** *(muerto)* an actor/sportsman who died before fulfilling his promise (b) *(fracasado)* unsuccessful, failed (c) *(fallecido)* late, departed; **un concierto en homenaje a la malograda princesa** a concert in memory of the late princess (d) *Andes (averiado) (vehículo)* broken down; *(máquina)* broken, out of order

malograr 1 *vt* (a) *(desperdiciar)* to waste; **malograron dos penalties** they wasted two penalties (b) *Andes (estropear)* to make a mess of, to ruin (c) *Ven Fam (matar)* to do in, to waste
2 **malograrse** *vpr* (a) *(fracasar)* **la cosecha se malogró con la helada** the frost ruined the harvest; *Méx* **se le malogró el hijo** she had a miscarriage and lost the baby; **por la pobreza, su talento se malogró** because of poverty, his talent went to waste (b) *Andes (estropearse) (máquina)* to break down; *(alimento)* to go off, to spoil; **se malogró el día** the day turned nasty

maloja *nf*, **malojo** *nm Am Br* maize *o US* corn stalks and leaves

malojal *nm Am Br* maize field, *US* cornfield

malojo = **maloja**

maloliente *adj* smelly

malón *nm* (a) *CSur (ataque)* = surprise Indian attack (b) *CSur Fam (masa de gente)* crowd, gang (c) *Chile (fiesta)* surprise party

malora *adj Méx Fam* naughty, rascally; **ser m.** to be a scamp

malparado, -a *adj* **salir m. de algo** to come out of sth badly; **el gobierno salió m. del escándalo** the government came out of the scandal looking bad; **la moto salió malparada pero el piloto no sufrió ningún rasguño** the bike was badly damaged but the rider got away without a scratch

malparido, -a *nm,f muy Fam* **ser un m.** to be an utter swine

malpensado, -a 1 *adj* cynical, evil-minded; **no seas m., seguro que tienen una buena excusa** don't be such a cynic, I bet they've got a good excuse; **no seas m., que no estoy hablando de sexo** don't be dirty-minded, I'm not talking about sex
2 *nm,f* cynic, evil-minded person; **es un m.** he always thinks the worst of people

malqueda *nmf Esp Fam* **es un m.** you can never rely on him

malquerencia *nf* dislike

malquerer [53] *vt* to dislike

malquistarse *vpr* **m. con alguien** to fall out with sb

malsano, -a *adj* (a) *(para la salud)* unhealthy (b) *(enfermizo)* unhealthy, unwholesome; **un interés m. por controlar a la gente** an unhealthy desire to control people

malsonante *adj (palabra)* rude

Malta *n* Malta

malta *nm* (a) *(cereal)* malt (b) *(bebida)* = coffee substitute made from roasted malt

malteada *nf Am* milk shake

malteado, -a *adj* malted

maltear *vt* to malt

maltés, -esa 1 *adj* Maltese
2 *nm,f* Maltese

maltosa *nf* malt sugar, maltose

maltraer [68] *vt* **traer a m. a alguien** *(sujeto: persona)* to give sb a hard time; *(sujeto: problema)* to cause sb headaches

maltraído, -a *adj Andes* dishevelled

maltratado, -a *adj* (a) *(persona)* battered; **una asociación de mujeres maltratadas** an association for victims of domestic violence (b) *(objeto)* damaged

maltratar *vt* (a) *(pegar, insultar)* to ill-treat; **maltrató a su mujer durante cinco años** he mistreated his wife over a five-year period; **la novela fue maltratada por la crítica** the novel was mauled by the critics (b) *(estropear)* to damage

maltrato *nm* ill-treatment; **sufrió maltratos cuando era un niño** he was mistreated as a child

maltrecho, -a *adj* (**a**) *(física, moralmente)* battered; **sus maltrechas rodillas no aguantaron el ritmo** his battered knees couldn't withstand the pace; **el divorcio lo dejó m.** the divorce left him in a sorry state
(**b**) *(dañado)* damaged; **la maltrecha economía del país** the country's battered economy; **la posición del presidente ha quedado maltrecha tras el escándalo** the president has been left with a shakier hold on power after the scandal

maltusianismo *nm* Malthusianism

maltusiano, -a 1 *adj* Malthusian
2 *nm,f* Malthusian

maluco, -a *adj* (**a**) *Col (medio enfermo)* poorly (**b**) *RP Fam Hum (loco)* crazy, mad; **¡está m.!** he's off his head! (**c**) *Ven Fam (perverso) Br* toerag, *US* varmint

maluqueza *nf Ven Fam* (**a**) *(maldad)* nastiness (**b**) *(acción)* wicked act

malura *nf Chile* malaise, indisposition

malva 1 *adj inv* mauve
2 *nf* mallow; EXPR *Fam* **criar malvas** to push up daisies
3 *nm (color)* mauve

malvado, -a 1 *adj* evil, wicked
2 *nm,f* villain, evil person; **es un m.** he's evil *o* wicked

malvasía[1] *nf* (**a**) *(uva)* malvasia (**b**) *(vino)* malmsey

malvasía[2] *nmf (pato)* white-headed duck ►► ***m. canela*** ruddy duck

malvavisco *nm* marshmallow

malvender *vt* to sell off cheap

malversación *nf* **m. (de fondos)** embezzlement

malversador, -ora *nm,f* **m. (de fondos)** embezzler

malversar *vt* to embezzle

Malvinas *nfpl* **las (islas) M.** the Falkland Islands, the Falklands

malvinense 1 *adj* of/from the Falkland Islands
2 *nmf* Falkland Islander, Falklander

malviviente *nmf CSur* criminal

malvivir *vi* to live badly, to scrape together an existence; **malvivía de las limosnas** he scraped a living by begging; **malvive con un sueldo mísero** he scrapes by on starvation wages

malvón *nm Méx, RP (planta)* geranium

mama *nf* (**a**) *(de mujer)* breast; *(de animal)* udder (**b**) *Fam (madre)* mum, mummy

mamá *nf (utilizado por niño) Br* mummy, *US* mommy; *Am (utilizado por adulto) Br* mum, *US* mom ►► *Col, Méx Fam* ***m. grande*** grandma

mamacita *nf* (**a**) *CAm, Carib, Méx (mamá) Br* mummy, *US* mommy (**b**) *CAm, Carib, Méx Fam (piropo)* baby

mamada *nf* (**a**) *(de bebé)* (breast)feed, (breast)feeding (**b**) *Vulg (felación)* blow job; **hacerle una m. a alguien** to give sb a blow job (**c**) *Chile, Perú (ganga)* cinch, piece of cake (**d**) *Méx Fam (tontería) (acto)* silly *o* stupid thing; *(dicho)* silly *o* stupid remark; **¡no digas mamadas!** don't talk rubbish!

mamadera *nf* (**a**) *RP (biberón)* (baby's) bottle (**b**) *Carib (tetina)* rubber nipple (**c**) *Ven Fam* ***m. de gallo*** hoax, leg-pull

mamado, -a *adj* (**a**) *Esp, RP muy Fam (borracho)* shit-faced, plastered, *Br* pissed (**b**) *Esp muy Fam (fácil)* **estar m.** to be piss easy (**c**) *Col, Ven Fam (cansado)* beat, *Br* knackered

mamador, -ora *nm,f Ven Fam* **ser un m. de gallo** to be a joker *o* comedian

mamar 1 *vt* (**a**) *(leche)* to suckle (**b**) *(aprender)* to grow up with; **mamó las telenovelas desde pequeña** she was brought up on TV soaps (**c**) *Esp muy Fam (beber)* to knock back (**d**) *Vulg (pene)* to suck; **se la mamó** she gave him head *o* a blow job, she sucked him off
2 *vi* (**a**) *(bebé)* to suckle; **dar de m.** to breastfeed (**b**) *Esp muy Fam (beber) Br* to go on the piss, *US* to hit the sauce (**c**) *Méx Fam* **¡no mames!** *(no fastidies)* come off it!; *(no molestes)* cut it out!
3 **mamarse** *vpr* (**a**) *Esp, RP muy Fam (emborracharse)* to get plastered (**b**) *Vulg* **mamársela a alguien** *(hacer una felación)* to give sb head *o* a blow job, to suck sb off (**c**) *Andes Fam (matar)* **mamarse a alguien** to bump sb off, to do sb in (**d**) *Ven Fam (aguantar)* to put up with

mamario, -a *adj* mammary

mamarrachada *nf Fam* stupid *o* idiotic thing; **tu plan es una m.** your plan is crazy; **pintar la puerta de rosa me parece una m.** I think it's daft *o* crazy to paint the door pink

mamarracho, -a *nm,f Fam* (**a**) *(persona ridícula, despreciable)* **no seas m. y déjame entrar** don't be an idiot and let me in; **ir hecho un m.** to look a sight *o* mess (**b**) *(cosa ridícula)* sight, monstrosity; **tiene una colección de mamarrachos en las paredes de su casa** he's got a load of junk on his walls

mamba *nf* mamba

mambí, -isa *(pl* **mambises, mambisas***) nm,f Hist* = rebel soldier in the 19th century Cuban wars of independence

mambo *nm* (**a**) *(baile, música)* mambo (**b**) *RP Fam (confusión)* **¡qué m.!** what a madhouse!; **tengo un m.** *(estoy confundido)* my head is swimming

mameluco *nm* (**a**) *Hist* Mameluke (**b**) *Fam (torpe, necio)* idiot (**c**) *(ropa) Méx (con mangas) Br* overalls, *US* coveralls; *CSur (de peto) Br* dungarees, *US* overalls; *(para bebé)* rompers

mamerto, -a *nm,f RP Fam* drunk, lush

mamey *nm* (**a**) *(árbol)* mamey, mammee (**b**) *(fruto)* mamey, mammee (apple)

mami *nf Fam* (**a**) *(mamá)* mum, mummy (**b**) *Andes, Carib (apelativo)* love, honey

mamífero, -a 1 *adj* mammal
2 *nm* mammal

mamila[1] *nf Cuba, Méx, Ven (biberón)* baby's bottle

mamila[2] *nmf Méx, Ven muy Fam (idiota) Br* prat, *US* jerk

mamita *nf Am Fam Br* mummy, *US* mommy

mamografía *nf* (**a**) *(técnica)* breast scanning, mammography (**b**) *(imagen)* breast scan

mamón[1]**, -ona** 1 *adj* (**a**) *(que mama)* unweaned; **es un bebé muy m.** the baby's a real guzzler (**b**) *muy Fam (idiota)* **¡qué m. eres!** you bastard! (**c**) *Méx Fam (creído)* cocky, too big for his/her/*etc* boots
2 *nm,f* (**a**) *(que mama)* unweaned baby (**b**) *muy Fam (idiota) Br* prat, *US* jerk (**c**) *Méx Fam (creído)* bighead

mamón[2] *nm* (**a**) *Bol, RP (papaya)* papaya, papaw (**b**) *Col, Ven (árbol)* Spanish lime, genip (**c**) *Col, Ven (fruta)* genip fruit

mamotreto *nm* (**a**) *Fam (libro)* hefty volume (**b**) *(objeto grande)* unwieldy object; **ayúdame a mover ese m. de armario** help me move that massive great wardrobe

mampara *nf* screen

mamporro *nm Fam (golpe)* punch, clout; *(al caer)* bump; **acabaron liándose a mamporros** they ended up clobbering one another; **tropezó y se dio un m. en la rodilla** he tripped and bashed his knee

mamposta *nf (en mina)* prop

mampostería *nf* **muro de m.** dry-stone wall; **obra de m.** rubblework masonry

mampuesto *nm* (**a**) *(piedra)* rubble, rough stone (**b**) *(parapeto)* parapet, ledge (**c**) *Chile (de arma)* support, rest

mamúa *nf RP Fam* **andaba con una m.** he was sloshed; **agarrarse una m.** to get sloshed

mamut *(pl* **mamuts***) nm* mammoth

maná *nm inv* (**a**) *Rel* manna; EXPR **como m. caído del cielo** like manna from heaven (**b**) *Bol (dulce) Br* nut sweet, *US* nut candy

manada *nf* (**a**) *(rebaño)* herd; *(de lobos)* pack; *(de ovejas)* flock; *(de leones)* pride (**b**) *Fam (de gente)* crowd, mob; **acudieron en m.** they turned up *o* out in droves

mánager ['manajer] *(pl* **managers***) nmf* manager

Managua *n* Managua

managüense 1 *adj* Managuan
2 *nmf* person from Managua *(Nicaragua)*

manantial *nm* (**a**) *(de agua)* spring (**b**) *(de conocimiento, riqueza)* source

manar 1 *vi* (**a**) *(líquido)* to flow (**de** from) (**b**) *(abundar)* **su mente manaba en ideas** his mind teemed with ideas
2 *vt (agua)* **la fuente manaba agua** water was flowing from the fountain; **la herida manaba sangre** blood was flowing from the wound

manare *nm Ven* sieve

manatí *(pl* **manatíes** *o* **manatís***) nm* manatee

manazas *Fam* 1 *adj inv* clumsy
2 *nmf inv* clumsy person; **ser un m.** to be clumsy, to have two left hands

mancarse *vpr RP Fam* to get it wrong; **pensé que iba a llegar a tiempo, pero me manqué** I thought I was going to arrive in time but I miscalculated

manceba *nf* (**a**) *Literario (concubina)* concubine (**b**) *ver también* **mancebo**

mancebía *nf Formal (burdel)* house of ill repute, brothel

mancebo, -a 1 *nm,f (en farmacia)* assistant
2 *nm Literario o Hum (mozo)* swain

mancha *nf* (a) *(de suciedad)* stain, spot; *(de tinta)* blot; **me he echado una m. en la camisa** I've stained my shirt, I've got a stain on my shirt; **no consiguió que se fuera la m.** she couldn't get the stain out; **una m. de petróleo** *(en el mar)* an oil slick; **una m. de aceite** oil stain; EXPR **extenderse como una m. de aceite** to spread like wildfire
(b) *(de color)* spot, mark; **un caballo con manchas negras** a horse with black patches; EXPR *RP* **¿qué le hace una m. más al tigre?** what difference does one more make?, one more won't make any difference
(c) *(en la piel) (por reacción)* blotch; *(de la vejez)* liver spot; **le han salido unas manchas en la piel** he's come out in blotches ►► ***m. de nacimiento*** birthmark
(d) *Astron* ***m. solar*** sunspot
(e) *(deshonra)* blemish, blot; **este suspenso supondrá una m. en su expediente** this fail will be a blot on his academic record; **tiene un historial sin m.** she has a spotless record
(f) *Perú Fam (grupo de amigos)* gang
(g) *RP* **la m.** *(juego)* tag

manchado, -a *adj* (a) *(sucio)* dirty; *(con manchas)* stained; *(emborronado)* smudged; **el mantel está muy m. de aceite** the tablecloth has oil stains on it (b) *(piel) (por reacción)* blotchy; *(por vejez)* spotted

manchar 1 *vt* (a) *(ensuciar)* to make dirty (**de** *o* **con** with); *(con manchas)* to stain (**de** *o* **con** with); *(emborronar)* to smudge (**de** *o* **con** with) (b) *(deshonrar)* to tarnish; **manchó la reputación de la institución** he tarnished the reputation of the institution
2 *vi* to stain; **el vino blanco no mancha** white wine doesn't stain; **no toques la puerta, que la acaban de pintar y mancha** don't touch the door, it's just been painted and it's still wet
3 **mancharse** *vpr (ensuciarse)* to get dirty; **se ha manchado la pared** the wall has got dirty, there are stains on the wall; **me manché el vestido de grasa mientras cocinaba** I got grease stains on my dress while I was cooking; **el niño se ha manchado de barro los pantalones** the boy has got mud on his trousers

manchego, -a 1 *adj* of/from La Mancha *(Spain)*
2 *nm,f* person from La Mancha *(Spain)*
3 *nm (queso)* manchego, = hard yellow cheese made in La Mancha

mancheta *nf* (a) *(en periódico)* masthead (b) *Ven (nota, dibujo)* = short editorial or cartoon commenting on an important current event

manchón *nm Chile (de manos)* muff

mancilla *nf* stain, blemish

mancillar *vt Formal* to tarnish, to sully

manco, -a 1 *adj* (a) *(sin una mano)* one-handed; *(sin un brazo)* one-armed; **se quedó m. del brazo derecho** he lost his right arm; EXPR *Fam* **no ser m.: empezó insultando ella, pero él tampoco es m.** she started the insults, but he gave as good as he got; *Fam* **no ser m. para** *o* **en algo** to be pretty good *o Br* a dab hand at sth (b) *(incompleto)* imperfect, defective
2 *nm,f (sin una mano)* one-handed person; *(sin un brazo)* one-armed person ►► ***el m. de Lepanto*** = nickname given to Miguel de Cervantes

mancomunar 1 *vt* to pool (together)
2 **mancomunarse** *vpr* to join together, to unite

mancomunidad *nf* association

mancorna *nf CAm, Chile, Col, Méx, Ven* cufflink

mancuerna *nf* (a) *(pesa)* dumbbell (b) *CAm, Chile, Col, Méx, Ven (gemelo)* cufflink

manda *nf* (a) *(oferta)* offer, proposal (b) *(legado)* legacy, bequest

mandadero, -a *nm,f RP (recadero)* errand boy, *f* errand girl

mandado[1], -a *adj* (a) *Méx Fam (aprovechado)* **¡órale, no sea m., quieto con las manos!** hey, stop trying it on, keep your hands to yourself!; **lo invité, y el muy m. llegó con tres amigos** I invited him but the wise guy *o Br* chancer arrived with three friends
(b) EXPR *CSur* **ser (como) m. a hacer para algo: este niño es (como) m. a hacer para ser veterinario** this boy was born to be a vet; **este lugar es (como) m. a hacer para que vos vivas** this place is just perfect for you

mandado[2], -a 1 *nm,f* (a) *(subordinado)* underling; *Fam* **yo sólo soy un m.** I'm only doing what I was told (to do) (b) *Méx Fam (caradura)* shameless person, swine
2 *nm* (a) *(recado)* errand; **hacer un m.** to do *o* run an errand; **estuve toda la mañana haciendo mandados** I spent the whole morning running errands (b) *Méx (compra)* **comprar el m.** to do the shopping; EXPR **comerle a alguien el m.** to do the dirty on sb, to steal a march on sb

mandamás *(pl* **mandamases***) nmf Fam Br* big boss, *US* head honcho

mandamiento *nm* (a) *(orden)* order, command (b) *Der* writ ►► ***m. de arresto*** arrest warrant; ***m. de detención*** arrest warrant; ***m. judicial*** warrant (c) *Rel* commandment; **los diez mandamientos** the Ten Commandments

mandanga *nf Fam* (a) **mandangas** *(tonterías)* nonsense; **¡déjate de mandangas y ven a ayudar!** don't give me that rubbish and come and help! (b) *(marihuana)* dope

---

MANDAR 1 *vt* (a) *(ordenar)* to order; **el juez mandó la inmediata ejecución de la sentencia** the judge ordered the sentence to be carried out immediately; **la profesora nos ha mandado deberes/una redacción** the teacher has set *o* given us some homework/an essay; **m. a alguien hacer algo, m. a alguien que haga algo** to order sb to do sth; **le mandaron que se fuera** they ordered him to leave; **yo hago lo que me mandan** I do as I'm told; **m. hacer algo** to have sth done; **mandaron revisar todas las máquinas** they had all the machines checked; **mandó llamar a un electricista** she asked for an electrician to be sent; **el maestro mandó callar** the teacher called for silence, the teacher told the class to be silent; **la jefa le mandó venir a su despacho** the boss summoned him to her office; **¿quién te manda decirle nada?** who asked you to say anything to her?; **¿quién me mandará a mí meterme en estos líos?** why did I have to get involved in this mess?
(b) *(recetar)* **el médico le ha mandado estas pastillas** the doctor prescribed her these pills; **el médico me mandó nadar** the doctor told me I had to go swimming
(c) *(enviar)* to send; **m. algo a alguien** to send sb sth, to send sth to sb; **me mandó un correo electrónico** she sent me an e-mail, she e-mailed me; **me lo mandó por correo electrónico** he sent it to me by e-mail; **lo mandaron a un recado/una misión** he was sent on an errand/mission; **lo mandaron a la cárcel/la guerra** he was sent to prison/away to war; **m. a alguien a hacer algo** *o* **a que haga algo** to send sb to do sth; **m. a alguien (a) por algo** to send sb for sth; **lo mandaron de embajador a Irlanda** he was sent to Ireland as an ambassador; **me mandan de la central para recoger un paquete** I've been sent by our main office to pick up a package; EXPR *Vulg* **m. a alguien a la mierda** to tell sb to piss off; EXPR *Fam* **m. a alguien a paseo** to send sb packing; EXPR *Fam* **m. a alguien a la porra** to tell sb to go to hell; EXPR *Fam* **m. a alguien al demonio** to tell sb to go to the devil
(d) *(dirigir) (país)* to rule; **manda a un grupo de voluntarios** she is in charge of a group of voluntary workers; **el corredor que manda el grupo perseguidor** the runner leading the chasing pack
(e) *Fam (lanzar)* to send; **mandó la jabalina más allá de los 90 metros** he sent the javelin beyond the 90 metre mark; **mandó el balón fuera** *(por la banda)* he put the ball out of play; *(disparando)* he shot wide
(f) *Fam (propinar)* to give; **le mandé un bofetón** I gave him a slap, I slapped him
(g) *Am (encargar)* **mandó decir que llegaría tarde** he sent word that he'd arrive late; **lo mandaron llamar del hospital** the hospital sent for him
(h) EXPR *Esp Fam* **¡manda narices!** can you believe it!; *Esp muy Fam* **¡manda huevos!** can you *Br* bloody *o US* goddamn believe it!
2 *vi* (a) *(dirigir)* to be in charge; *(partido político, jefe de estado)* to rule; **aquí mando yo** I'm in charge here; *Méx* **¡mande!** *(a sus órdenes)* at your orders!; *Esp, Méx* **¿mande?** *(¿cómo?)* sorry?, pardon?; **a m., que para eso estamos** certainly, Sir/Madam!, at your orders!
(b) *Pey (dar órdenes)* to order people around
3 **mandarse** *vpr* (a) *RP, Ven Fam (desplazarse)* **se mandó para adentro de su casa** he rushed indoors; **se mandó por la escalera** he rushed down the stairs
(b) *RP, Ven Fam (comida, bebida)* to polish off; **se mandó 2 litros de jugo en un ratito** he downed 2 litres of juice in a flash
(c) *RP, Ven Fam (expresando asombro)* **se mandó una casa de novela** he built himself a dream house; **¡qué cena te mandaste!** what a dinner you managed to come up with!
(d) EXPR *RP Fam* **mandarse (a) mudar** to be off, to walk out; **¡mandate (a) mudar!** clear off!; **mandarse la parte** to exaggerate, to lay it on thick

---

mandarín *nm* (a) *(título)* mandarin (b) *(dialecto)* Mandarin

mandarina *nf* mandarin; EXPR *RP Fam* **chupate esa m.** *Br* get that!, *US* how do you like them apples?

mandarino *nm* mandarin tree

mandatario, -a *nm,f* (a) *Der* representative, agent (b) *(gobernante)* ruler, governor; **primer m.** *(jefe de Estado)* head of state

mandato *nm* (a) *(orden, precepto)* order, command; **fue detenido por m. del juez** he was arrested on the judge's instructions ►► *Der* ***m. judicial*** warrant

(**b**) *(poderes de representación)* mandate ►► ***m. electoral*** electoral mandate
(**c**) *(periodo)* term of office; **durante el m. del alcalde** during the mayor's term of office; **el candidato republicano aspira a un tercer m. consecutivo** the Republican candidate is seeking his third consecutive term

mandíbula *nf* jaw, *Espec* mandible

mandil *nm* (**a**) *(delantal)* apron (**b**) *Méx Fam (condescendiente)* henpecked husband; **ser un m.** to be *Br* henpecked *o US* whipped

mandilón *nm Méx Fam* henpecked husband; **ser un m.** to be *Br* henpecked *o US* whipped

Mandinga *n pr Am* the devil; **es cosa de M.** it's the devil's doing

mandioca *nf* (**a**) *(planta)* cassava (**b**) *(fécula)* tapioca, manioc

mando *nm* (**a**) *(poder)* command, authority; **entregar el m.** to hand over command; **estar al m. (de)** to be in charge; **el grupo de rescate está al m. de un capitán** the rescue group are under the command of a captain; **tomar el m.** to take command *o* control (of)
(**b**) *(jefe)* **el alto m.** the high command; **los mandos** *(militares)* the command; **los mandos policiales se reunieron para discutir la visita papal** senior police officers met to discuss the Pope's visit; **mandos intermedios** middle management
(**c**) *(dispositivo)* control; **tomó los mandos del avión** he took the controls of the plane; **tablero de mandos** *(de avión)* instrument panel; *(de coche)* dashboard ►► ***m. automático*** automatic control; ***m. a distancia*** remote control

mandoble *nm* (**a**) *(con la mano)* slap (**b**) *(con la espada)* two-handed blow

mandolina *nf* mandolin

mandón, -ona *Fam* **1** *adj* bossy; **es muy mandona** she's really bossy
2 *nm,f* (**a**) *(que manda)* bossy-boots (**b**) *Chile (de mina)* foreman

mandrágora *nf* mandrake

mandria *Esp Fam* **1** *adj* (**a**) *(cobarde)* cowardly (**b**) *(inútil)* useless, worthless
2 *nmf* (**a**) *(cobarde)* coward (**b**) *(inútil)* useless person; **es un m.** he's useless

mandril *nm* (**a**) *(animal)* mandrill (**b**) *(pieza)* mandrel

manduca *nf Esp Fam* grub

manducar *Fam* **1** *vt* to scoff
2 *vi* to scoff
3 manducarse *vpr* **se manducó dos chuletones** he scoffed two steaks

maneador *nm Méx, RP* = long strap used for hobbling animals

manecilla *nf* (**a**) *(del reloj)* hand ►► ***m. de las horas*** big hand, hour hand (**b**) *(cierre)* clasp

manejabilidad *nf (de vehículo)* manoeuvrability

manejable *adj* (**a**) *(cosa)* manageable; *(herramienta)* easy to use; *(vehículo)* manoeuvrable (**b**) *(persona)* easily led

manejador *nm Informát* handle ►► ***m. de dispositivos*** device (driver)

manejar 1 *vt* (**a**) *(máquina, mandos)* to operate; *(herramienta)* to use; *(arma)* to handle; *(caballo, bicicleta)* to ride
(**b**) *(datos)* to handle; *(conocimientos)* to use, to marshal; **maneja varios lenguajes de programación** she can use several programming languages; **manejan información de primera mano** they use primary sources
(**c**) *(negocio)* to manage, to run; *(gente)* to handle
(**d**) *(dominar)* to boss about; **maneja a su novio a su antojo** she can twist her fiancé round her little finger
(**e**) *Am (conducir)* to drive
2 *vi Am (conducir)* to drive
3 manejarse *vpr (desenvolverse)* to manage, to get by; **se maneja muy bien en la Bolsa** he knows his way round the stock exchange; **no se maneja nada bien con las computadoras** he doesn't have much of an idea of how to use computers

manejo *nm* (**a**) *(de máquina, mandos)* operation; *(de armas, herramientas)* use; *(de caballo, bicicleta)* handling; **me están explicando el m. del módem** they are telling me how to use the modem; **de fácil m.** user-friendly; **instrucciones de m.** user instructions
(**b**) *(de datos)* handling; *(de conocimientos)* marshalling; *(de idiomas)* command; **sus poemas destacan por el excelente m. de las metáforas** her poems are remarkable for their superb use of metaphor
(**c**) *(de negocio)* management, running
(**d**) *(intriga)* intrigue
(**e**) *Am (de automóvil)* driving

MANERA *nf* (**a**) *(forma)* way, manner; **m. de pensar** way of thinking; **tiene una m. de ser muy agradable** she has a very pleasant nature; **no me gusta su m. de ser** I don't like the way he is; **no encuentro la m. de dejar el tabaco** whatever I do, I just can't seem to give up smoking; **esa no es m. de decir las cosas** that's no way to speak; **¿has visto la m. en que** *o* **la m. como te mira?** have you seen how *o* the way he's looking at you?; **esta vez lo haremos a mi m.** this time we'll do it my way; **a la m. de** in the style of, after the fashion of; **a m. de** *(como)* as, by way of; **a mi m. de ver** the way I see it; **de alguna m.** somehow; **se le cayó el botón porque lo cosió de cualquier m.** the button fell off because he sewed it on carelessly *o* any old how; **hazlo de cualquier m.** do it however you like; **no te preocupes, de cualquier m. no pensaba ir** don't worry, I wasn't going to go anyway; **de esta/esa m.** this/that way; **trata a su hijo de mala m.** he treats his son badly; **lo dijo de mala m.** she said it very rudely; *Esp Fam* **estuvo lloviendo de mala m.** it was pouring *o Br* bucketing down; *Esp Fam* **se pusieron a beber de mala m.** they started a serious drinking session; *Esp Fam* **tu hermana se enrolla de mala m.** your sister goes on a bit; **de la misma m.** similarly, in the same way; **lo hice de la misma m. que ayer/tú** I did it the same way as yesterday/you; **lo organizaron de m. que acabara antes de las diez** they organized it so (that) it finished before ten; **¿de m. que no te gusta?** so, you don't like it (then)?; **de ninguna m.** *o* **en m. alguna deberíamos dejarle salir** under no circumstances should we let her out; **de ninguna m.** *o* **en m. alguna quise ofenderte** I in no way intended to offend you; **¿te he molestado? – de ninguna m.** *o* **en m. alguna** did I annoy you? – not at all *o* by no means; **¿quieres que lo invitemos? – ¡de ninguna m.!** shall we invite him? – no way *o* certainly not!; **de otra m....** *(si no)* otherwise...; **de tal m. (que)** *(tanto)* so much (that); **de todas maneras** anyway; **de todas maneras, ¿qué es eso que decías de un viaje?** anyway, what's that you were saying about going away?; **de una m. o de otra** one way or another; **en cierta m.** in a way; *Formal* **la ópera me aburre en gran m.** I find opera exceedingly tedious; **no hay m.** there is no way, it's impossible; **no hay m. de que haga los deberes** it's impossible to get him to do his homework; **¡contigo no hay m.!** you're impossible!; **¡qué m. de hacer las cosas!** that's no way to do things!; **¡qué m. de llover!** just look at that rain!; *Formal* **me place sobre m. que recurran a nuestros servicios** I'm exceedingly pleased that you should have decided to use our services
(**b**) **maneras** *(modales)* manners; **buenas/malas maneras** good/bad manners; **de muy buenas maneras nos dijo que saliéramos** she very politely asked us to leave; **atiende a los clientes de malas maneras** he's rude to the customers; EXPR *Esp* **de aquella m.: lo hicieron de aquella m.** they did it any old how; **¿crees en Dios? – de aquella m.** do you believe in God? – well, sort of

manflor, -ora *nm,f Carib, Méx* (**a**) *(hermafrodita)* hermaphrodite (**b**) *Fam Pey (homosexual) (hombre) Br* poof, *US* fag; *(mujer)* dyke

manga[1] *nf* (**a**) *(de prenda)* sleeve; **en mangas de camisa** in shirtsleeves; **un vestido sin mangas** a sleeveless dress; EXPR *Fam* **andar** *o* **ir m. por hombro** to be all higgledy-piggledy *o* topsy-turvy; EXPR **sacarse algo de la m.** *(improvisar)* to make sth up on the spur of the moment; *(idear)* to come up with sth; **eso de que es ilegal se lo ha sacado de la m.** he's just made up the bit about it being illegal; EXPR **ser de m. ancha, tener m. ancha** to be over-indulgent; EXPR **tener** *o* **guardar algo en la m.** to have sth up one's sleeve; EXPR *RP Fam* **tirarle la m. a alguien** to ask sb a favour/for money ►► ***m. corta*** short sleeve; ***m. de jamón*** leg-of-mutton sleeve; ***m. japonesa*** batwing sleeve; ***m. larga*** long sleeve; ***m. ranglan*** raglan sleeve; *Col* ***m. sisa:*** **una camisa con m. sisa** a sleeveless shirt
(**b**) *(manguera)* **m. (de riego)** hosepipe
(**c**) *(filtro)* muslin strainer
(**d**) *(medidor de viento)* windsock, wind cone
(**e**) *(de pastelería)* **m. (pastelera** *o* **de pastelero)** forcing *o* piping bag
(**f**) *Náut* beam
(**g**) *Dep (en competición)* stage, round; *(en tenis)* set
(**h**) *(en aeropuerto)* jetty *(for boarding aircraft)*
(**i**) *Am (mango)* = large, round mango
(**j**) *Méx, RP Fam Pey (grupo de gente)* **tus amigos son una m. de locos** your friends are a bunch of lunatics; **¡qué m. de idiotas!** what a bunch *o Br* shower of idiots!
(**k**) *Méx (capa)* waterproof cape
(**l**) *CAm (manta)* blanket
(**m**) *Am (para ganado)* cattle chute

manga[2] *nm* **el m.** manga (comics)

manganeso *nm Quím* manganese

mangante *Esp Fam* **1** *adj* (**a**) *(sinvergüenza)* good-for-nothing (**b**) *(ladrón)* thieving
2 *nmf* (**a**) *(sinvergüenza)* good-for-nothing, layabout (**b**) *(ladrón)* thief

manganzón, -ona *Andes, CAm, Ven Fam* **1** *adj* lazy, idle
2 *nm,f* layabout

mangar [38] **1** *vt* (**a**) *Esp Fam (robar)* to pinch, *Br* to nick; **m. algo a alguien** to pinch *o Br* nick sth off sb (**b**) *RP Fam (pedir)* to cadge, to scrounge; **siempre me manga cigarros** he's always cadging cigarettes off me
2 *vi RP Fam* to sponge, to scrounge; **siempre está mangando** he's always sponging *o* scrounging

mangazo *nm RP Fam* sponging; **vive del m.** he lives by sponging *o* scrounging

manglar *nf* mangrove swamp

mangle *nm* mangrove tree ►► ***m. blanco*** white mangrove; ***m. botoncillo*** buttonwood, button mangrove; ***m. colorado*** red mangrove; ***m. negro*** black mangrove

mango[1] *nm* (**a**) *(asa)* handle
(**b**) *muy Fam (pene)* cock
(**c**) *Méx, Ven Fam (persona)* stunner
(**d**) *RP Fam (dinero)* **en ese trabajo no gana un m.** you earn peanuts in that job; **no tengo un m.** I haven't got a bean, I'm broke; **¿cuánto te costó? – barato, tres mangos** how much did it cost? – dirt-cheap, almost nothing
(**e**) *RP Fam (peso)* peso
(**f**) EXPR *RP Fam* **ir al m.** to go flat out; **poner la radio al m.** to put the radio on full blast

mango[2] *nm* (**a**) *(árbol)* mango tree (**b**) *(fruta)* mango

mangonear *Fam* **1** *vi* (**a**) *(entrometerse)* to meddle; **siempre está mangoneando en nuestros asuntos** he's always poking his nose in our affairs (**b**) *(mandar)* to push people around, to be bossy
2 *vt (mandar)* to push *o* boss around

mangoneo *nm Fam (intromisión)* **ya estoy harto de su m.** I'm fed up with his meddling

mangosta *nf* mongoose

manguarear *vi Ven Fam* to laze about, *Br* to skive

manguareo *nm Ven Fam* idleness, *Br* skiving

manguear **1** *vt* (**a**) *CSur, Méx (ganado)* to drive into a gangway (**b**) *RP Fam (pedir)* to cadge, to scrounge; **siempre me manguea cigarros** he's always cadging cigarettes off me
2 *vi RP Fam* to sponge, to scrounge; **siempre está mangueando** he's always sponging *o* scrounging

manguera *nf* (**a**) *(para regar)* hosepipe; *(de bombero)* fire hose (**b**) *ver también* **manguero**

manguerear *vt CSur Fam (plants)* to water; *(car)* to hose down

manguero, -a *RP Fam* **1** *adj* scrounging
2 *nm,f* freeloader, cadger

mangui *Esp Fam* **1** *adj (no fiable)* sneaky
2 *nmf* (**a**) *(ladrón)* crook, thief (**b**) *(persona no fiable)* crook

manguito *nm* (**a**) *(para el frío)* muff (**b**) *(media manga)* protective sleeve, oversleeve (**c**) *Tec (tubo)* sleeve (**d**) *(para nadar)* armband

maní (*pl* **maníes**) *nm* (**a**) *Andes, Carib, RP (semilla)* peanut (**b**) *Ven Fam (problema)* tricky business; **¿cuál es el m.?** what's the problem?

manía *nf* (**a**) *(enfermedad)* mania ►► ***m. persecutoria*** persecution complex
(**b**) *(idea fija)* obsession
(**c**) *(mala costumbre)* bad habit; **tiene la m. de morderse las uñas** he's always biting his fingernails; **le ha dado la m. de tirar la ropa por el suelo** she has got into the bad habit of leaving her clothes scattered on the floor
(**d**) *(afición exagerada)* mania, craze
(**e**) *Fam (ojeriza)* dislike; **tomar** *o Esp* **coger m. a alguien** to take a dislike to sb; **tener m. a alguien: le tengo m. a su hermana** I can't stand her sister

maniaco, -a, maníaco, -a **1** *adj* manic
2 *nm,f* maniac ►► ***m. depresivo*** manic-depressive; ***m. sexual*** sex maniac

maniatar *vt* to tie the hands of

maniático, -a **1** *adj* fussy
2 *nm,f* fussy person; **es un m.** he's terribly fussy; **es un m. de los detalles** he's a stickler for detail; **es una maniática con la limpieza** she's a cleaning freak; **es un m. del fútbol** he's soccer-crazy

manicero, -a = **manisero**

manicomio *nm Br* mental *o* psychiatric hospital, *US* insane asylum; *Fam* **esta oficina es un m.** this office is a madhouse

manicura *nf (técnica)* manicure; **hacerle la m. a alguien** to give sb a manicure; **hacerse la m.** to have a manicure

manicuro, -a *nm,f, Am* **manicurista** *nmf* manicurist

manido, -a *adj* **un tema muy m.** a well-worn *o* much-discussed topic

manierismo *nm Arte* mannerism

manierista **1** *adj* mannerist
2 *nmf* mannerist

manifa *nf Esp Fam (manifestación)* demo

manifestación *nf* (**a**) *(de alegría, dolor)* show, display; *(indicio)* sign; **una m. artística** an art form (**b**) *(de opinión)* declaration, expression; **en sus manifestaciones a la prensa se declaró inocente** in his statements to the press he said he was innocent (**c**) *(por la calle)* demonstration; **hacer una m. a favor de/contra algo** to demonstrate *o* take part in a demonstration in favour of/against sth

manifestante *nmf* demonstrator

manifestar [3] **1** *vt* (**a**) *(alegría, dolor)* to show; **manifestó su enfado golpeando la mesa** he showed his annoyance by banging on the table (**b**) *(opinión)* to express; **manifestó su intención de presentarse como candidato** he announced his intention to put himself forward as a candidate; **manifestaron su agradecimiento por la ayuda recibida** they expressed their gratitude for the help received
2 manifestarse *vpr* (**a**) *(por la calle)* to demonstrate; **manifestarse a favor de/contra algo** to demonstrate for/against; **los sindicalistas se manifestaron por el centro de la ciudad** the union members demonstrated in the city centre
(**b**) *(hacerse evidente)* to become clear *o* apparent; **su odio se manifiesta en su mirada** you can see the hatred in her eyes
(**c**) *(expresarse)* **se manifestó contrario a la intervención militar** he spoke out against military intervention; **les dieron el proyecto para que se manifestaran sobre él** they gave them the plan so that they could give an opinion on it

manifiestamente *adv* clearly, evidently; **es un trabajo m. mejorable** there is obvious room for improvement in this piece of work; **el presupuesto era m. insuficiente** the budget was clearly inadequate

manifiesto, -a **1** *adj* clear, evident; **es un hecho m. que está insatisfecho** it's obvious he's not satisfied; **poner de m. algo** *(revelar)* to reveal sth; *(hacer patente)* to make sth clear; **ponerse de m.** *(descubrirse)* to become clear *o* obvious
2 *nm* (**a**) *(político)* manifesto ►► ***el Manifiesto comunista*** the Communist Manifesto (**b**) *Náut* manifest

manigua *nf*, **manigual** *nm Carib, Col (selva)* marshy tropical forest

manija *nf* (**a**) *esp Am (asa)* handle (**b**) *esp Am (manivela)* handle, crank; *(tirador)* handle (**c**) *RP Fam (cerveza) Br* pint, *US* brew (**d**) EXPR *RP Fam* **dar m.: ya está enojado, no le des más m.** he's already angry, don't wind him up more; **si no me hubieran dado m., no habría ido** if they hadn't egged me on I wouldn't have gone; *RP Fam* **tener la m.** to rule the roost; **¿quién tiene la m. acá?** who's boss round here?

manijear *vt RP Fam* to egg on

Manila *n* Manila

manilargo, -a *adj Fam* (**a**) *(generoso)* generous (**b**) *(ladrón)* light-fingered (**c**) *RP (con las mujeres)* free with one's hands

manilense **1** *adj* of/from Manila
2 *nmf* person from Manila

manilla *nf* (**a**) *(del reloj)* hand (**b**) *(tirador)* handle (**c**) *(grillete)* manacle (**d**) *esp Am (manivela)* crank

manillar *nm (de bicicleta)* handlebars ►► ***m. de cuerno de cabra*** drop handlebars; ***m. de triatlón*** time-trial bars

maniobra *nf* (**a**) *(con vehículo, máquina)* manoeuvre; **el accidente se produjo durante la m. de adelantamiento** the accident occurred while the vehicle was overtaking; **evitó la colisión con una brusca m.** with a prompt manoeuvre he managed to avoid a collision; **hacer maniobras** to manoeuvre; **tuvo que hacer varias maniobras para estacionar** she had to do a lot of manoeuvring to park; **la nueva ley nos deja muy poco margen de m.** the new law gives us very little room for manoeuvre ►► *Av* ***m. de aproximación*** approach; *Av* **hacer la m. de aproximación** to approach
(**b**) **maniobras** *(militares)* manoeuvres; **maniobras conjuntas** joint exercises *o* manoeuvres; **estar de maniobras** to be on manoeuvres
(**c**) *(treta)* trick; **el anuncio ha sido una hábil m. para distraer la atención** the announcement was a clever ploy to distract attention

maniobrabilidad *nf* manoeuvrability

maniobrable *adj* manoeuvrable

maniobrar *vi* (**a**) *(con vehículo)* to manoeuvre (**b**) *(ejércitos)* to carry out manoeuvres (**c**) *(tramar)* to manoeuvre, to scheme

manipulación *nf* (**a**) *(de objeto)* handling; **m. de alimentos** food handling; **la m. del aparato invalida la garantía** any interference with the device invalidates the guarantee ►► ***m. genética*** genetic manipulation (**b**) *(de persona, datos)* manipulation; **denunció la m. de sus declaraciones** he claimed his statements had been distorted

manipulador, -ora **1** *adj (dominador)* manipulative
2 *nm,f* (**a**) *(operario)* handler (**b**) *(dominador)* manipulator

manipular *vt* (**a**) *(manejar)* to handle; **manipuló el explosivo con mucho cuidado** he handled the explosives very carefully; **alguien había manipulado la cerradura** someone had tampered with the lock; **m. genéticamente** to genetically modify
(**b**) *(trastocar, dominar)* to manipulate; **le acusaron de m. las papeletas** they accused him of tampering with the ballot papers; **están manipulando a las masas** they are manipulating the masses

maniqueísmo *nm* (**a**) *(actitud)* black-and-white view of things; **el m. de su argumento** the black-and-white nature of his argument (**b**) *Rel* Manicheanism

maniqueo, -a **1** *adj* (**a**) *(simplista)* **una visión maniquea de la historia** a black-and-white view of history; **una tendencia maniquea** a tendency to see things in black and white (**b**) *Rel* Manichean
2 *nm,f* (**a**) *(simplista)* **es un m.** he sees everything in black and white (**b**) *Rel* Manichean, Manichee

maniquí (*pl* **maniquíes**) **1** *nm* dummy, mannequin
2 *nmf (modelo)* model

manirroto, -a **1** *adj* extravagant
2 *nm,f* spendthrift

manisero, -a, manicero, -a *nm,f Andes, CAm, Carib, RP* peanut vendor

manitas *Esp Fam* **1** *adj inv* handy; **ser muy m.** to be very good with one's hands
2 *nmf inv* (**a**) *(persona habilidosa)* handy person; EXPR **ser un m. de plata** to be (very) good with one's hands (**b**) EXPR **hacer m.** *(acariciarse)* to cuddle, to canoodle
3 *nfpl* **m. (de cerdo)** pig's trotters

manito *nm* (**a**) *Méx Fam (amigo)* pal, *Br* mate, *US* buddy (**b**) *RP Fam* **hacer m.** to cuddle, to canoodle

manivela *nf* crank

manizaleño, -a **1** *adj* of/from Manizales *(Colombia)*
2 *nm,f* person from Manizales *(Colombia)*

manjar *nm* (**a**) *(alimento exquisito)* **manjares** delicious food; **¡este queso es un m.!** this cheese is delicious!; EXPR **ser m. de dioses** to be a dish fit for the gods (**b**) *Chile (dulce de leche)* = toffee pudding made with caramelized milk

---

MANO[1] **1** *nf* (**a**) *(de persona)* hand; **dar** *o* **estrechar la m. a alguien** to shake hands with sb; **darse** *o* **estrecharse la m.** to shake hands; **le dije adiós con la m.** I waved goodbye to him; **bolso de m.** *Br* handbag, *US* purse; **equipaje de m.** hand luggage; **paseaban de la m.** they were walking along hand in hand; **ir de la m.** *(asuntos, problemas)* to go hand in hand; **de m. en m.: la foto fue** *o* **pasó de m. en m.** the photo was passed around; **entregar algo a alguien en m.** to deliver sth to sb in person; **frotarse las manos** *(por frío, entumecimiento)* to rub one's hands (together); *(regocijarse)* to rub one's hands (with glee); **hecho a m.** handmade; **lo tuve que hacer a m.** I had to do it by hand; **lavarse las manos** *(literalmente)* to wash one's hands; **¡yo me lavo las manos!** *(me desentiendo)* I wash my hands of it!; **leerle la m. a alguien** to read sb's palm; **¡manos arriba!, ¡arriba las manos!** hands up!; **¡manos a la obra!** let's get down to it!; **pedir la m. de una mujer** to ask for a woman's hand (in marriage); **robo a m. armada** armed robbery; **votación a m. alzada** show of hands ►► ***m. derecha*** *(persona)* right-hand man/woman; **ser la m. derecha de alguien** to be sb's right-hand man/woman; *Der* ***manos muertas*** mortmain
(**b**) *(de animal)* forefoot; *(de perro, gato)* (front) paw; *(de cerdo)* (front) trotter
(**c**) *(de pintura, barniz)* coat; **dar una m. de pintura a algo** to give sth a coat *o* lick of paint
(**d**) *(de mortero)* pestle
(**e**) *(de naipes) (partida)* game; *(ronda)* hand; **eres m.** it's your lead
(**f**) *(en deportes) (falta)* handball; **el árbitro pitó m.** the referee blew for handball
(**g**) *(deporte)* pelota *(played with hand rather than with hand-held basket)*
(**h**) *(serie, tanda)* series
(**i**) *(lado)* **a m. derecha/izquierda (de)** on the right/left (of); **gire a m. derecha** turn right
(**j**) *Andes, CAm, Méx (objetos)* = group of four or five objects
(**k**) *Am (de plátanos)* bunch
(**l**) *CAm, Chile, Méx (accidente)* mishap, accident
(**m**) *RP (dirección)* direction *(of traffic)*; **calle de una/doble m.** one-/two-way street
(**n**) *(influencia)* influence; **tener m. con alguien** to have influence with sb
(**o**) *(intervención)* hand; **la m. de la CIA está detrás de todo esto** you can see the hand of the CIA in this affair ►► ***m. negra*** hidden hand; ***m. oculta*** hidden hand
(**p**) *(habilidad)* **tener buena m. para algo** to have a knack for sth; **¡que m. tienes para las plantas!** you've really got *Br* green fingers *o* *US* a green thumb! ►► ***m. izquierda:*** **tener m. izquierda con algo/alguien** to know how to deal with sth/sb
(**q**) *(poder, posesión)* **a manos de** at the hands of; **de manos de alguien: recibió la medalla de manos del ministro** he received the medal from the minister himself; **cambiar de manos** to change hands; **en manos de: caer en manos de alguien** to fall into sb's hands; **dejar algo en manos de alguien** to leave sth in sb's hands; **estar en manos de alguien** to be in sb's hands; **estar en buenas manos** to be in good hands; **haré lo que esté en mi m.** I'll do everything within my power; **ponerse en manos de alguien** to put oneself in sb's hands; **de primera m.** *(vehículo)* brand new; *(noticias)* first-hand; **de segunda m.** second-hand
(**r**) **manos** *(ayudantes)* helpers; **nos van a hacer falta varias manos para mover el piano** we're going to need several people to help us move the piano
(**s**) EXPR **abrir la m.** to be more lenient; **alzar la m. contra alguien** to raise one's hand to sb; *CSur* **agarrar la m. a algo** to get the hang of sth; **bajo m.** secretly; **de manos a boca** suddenly, unexpectedly; **cargar la m.** to go over the top; *RP Fam* **con una m. en la cintura: esto lo hago con una m. en la cintura** I can do this with my hands tied behind my back; **con la m. en el corazón: te lo digo con la m. en el corazón** I'm being perfectly honest with you; *Fam* **con una m. delante y otra detrás: está en la ruina, con una m. delante y otra detrás** he hasn't got a penny to his name; **estar dejado de la m. de Dios** *(lugar)* to be godforsaken; *(persona)* to be a total failure; **echar m. a algo: echó m. al bolso y se marchó** she took her bag and left; **echar m. de algo** *(recurrir a)* to make use of sth, to resort to sth; **echar m. de alguien** *(recurrir a)* to turn to sb; **echar una m. a alguien** to give/offer sb one's hand; **ensuciarse las manos** to get one's hands dirty; **escaparse** *o* **irse de las manos: se me escapó** *o* **fue de las manos una oportunidad excelente** an excellent chance slipped through my hands; **este proyecto se nos ha escapado** *o* **ido de las manos** this project has got out of hand; **ganar por la m.** *o RP* **de m. a alguien** to beat sb to it; **írsele la m. a alguien: se le fue la m.** *(perdió el control)* she lost control; *(exageró)* she went too far; **se me fue la m. con la sal** I overdid the salt; **levantarle la m. a alguien** to raise one's hand to sb; **llegar a las manos (por algo)** to come to blows (over sth); **a manos llenas** generously; **llevarse las manos a la cabeza** *(gesticular)* to throw one's hands in the air (in horror); *(indignarse, horrorizarse)* to be horrified; **con m. dura** *o* **de hierro** with a firm hand; *Fam* **m. a m.: se bebieron la botella m. a m.** they drank the bottle between the two of them; **estar m. sobre m.** to be sitting around doing nothing; *Esp* **coger** *o Am* **agarrar a alguien con las manos en la masa** to catch sb red-handed *o* in the act; *Fam* **meter m. a alguien** *(investigar)* to get onto sb; *(sobar sin consentimiento)* to grope sb; *(sobar con consentimiento)* to pet sb; *Fam* **meter m. a algo** to tackle sth; **meter la m. en algo** *(intervenir)* to poke one's nose into sth, to meddle in sth; *RP Fam* **meter la m. en el tarro** *o* **la lata** to dip one's fingers in the till; **ponerle la m. encima a alguien: ¡como te ponga la m. encima...!** if I lay *o* get my hands on you...!; **¡no me pongas las manos encima!** don't you touch me *o* lay a finger on me!; **poner la m. en el fuego: creo que es así, pero no pondría la m. en el fuego** I think that's the case, but I couldn't vouch for it; *Fam* **ser m. de santo** to work wonders; **tender una m. a alguien** to give/offer sb one's hand; *Fam Hum* **tener manos de árbol** to be ham-fisted *o* ham-handed; **tengo las manos atadas** my hands are tied; **tener las manos muy largas** *(aficionado a pegar)* to be fond of a fight; *(aficionado a robar)* to be light-fingered; **tener manos libres para hacer algo** to have a free rein to do sth; **tengo las manos limpias** my hands are clean; **tener manos de mantequilla** to be butter-fingered; **traerse algo entre manos** to be up to sth; **untarle la m. a alguien** to grease sb's palm; **con las manos vacías** empty-handed ►► ***m. de obra*** *(trabajadores)* labour, workers; *(trabajo manual)* labour; **la m. de obra barata atrae a los inversores** investors are attracted by the cheap labour costs; ***m. de obra cualificada*** skilled labour *o* workers; ***m. de obra especializada*** skilled labour *o* workers; ***m. de obra semicualificada*** semi-skilled labour *o* workers

2 *nmf* EXPR *RP Fam* **ser un m. abierta** to be open-handed; **es un m. larga** *(toquetón)* he's always poking around where he shouldn't; *(con las mujeres)* he has wandering-hand trouble

3 **a mano** *loc adv* **(a)** *(cerca)* to hand, handy; **¿tienes el encendedor a m.?** have you got your lighter handy *o* to hand?; **el supermercado está** *o* **queda muy a m.** the supermarket is very close by; **mi casa es muy a m. de todo** my house is very handy for everything **(b)** *Am (en paz)* **estar** *o* **quedar a m.** to be quits *o* all square

4 **mano a mano** *nm* **un m. a m. entre los dos candidatos** a head-to-head between the two candidates

---

mano[2] *nm Andes, CAm, Carib, Méx Fam* pal, *Br* mate, *US* buddy

manojo *nm* **(a)** *(de hierbas)* bunch; EXPR **estar hecho** *o* **ser un m. de nervios** to be a bundle of nerves **(b)** *(de llaves)* bunch **(c)** *(gran cantidad)* loads; **tiene un m. de gatos** she's got loads of cats

manoletina *nf* **(a)** *Taurom* = pass with the cape **(b)** *(zapato)* = type of open, low-heeled shoe, often with a bow

manomanista *nmf Dep* pelota player *(who plays with hand rather than with hand-held basket)*

manómetro *nm* pressure gauge, manometer

manopla *nf* **(a)** *(guante)* mitten; *(para el aseo)* bath glove *o* mitten ►► ***manoplas de cocina*** oven gloves **(b)** *(de béisbol)* baseball glove *o* mitt

manosanta *nmf RP (curandero)* traditional healer

manoseado, -a *adj* **(a)** *(objeto)* shabby, worn **(b)** *(tema)* well-worn, hackneyed

manosear 1 *vt* **(a)** *(tocar)* to handle (roughly); *(papel, tela)* to rumple; **no manosees la fruta si no la vas a comprar** don't handle *o* touch the fruit if you're not going to buy it **(b)** *(persona)* to paw; *(sexualmente)* to grope

2 **manosearse** *vpr* **(a)** **manosearse el pelo/la falda** *(tocar)* to fiddle with one's hair/skirt **(b)** *(mutuamente)* to fondle one another

manoseo *nm* **(a)** *(de objeto)* handling, touching **(b)** *(de persona)* pawing, groping

manotazo *nm*, **manotada** *nf* slap; **mató la mosca de un m.** he killed the fly with a swipe of his hand; **dar un m. a alguien** to give sb a slap

manotear 1 *vt* **(a)** *(golpear)* to slap, to cuff **(b)** *RP Fam (quitar)* to grab

2 *vi* to gesticulate; **el niño manoteaba en la piscina** the boy was thrashing about in the pool

manoteo *nm* gesticulation

manotón *nm CSur* grab ►► ***m. de ahogado*** a last-ditch effort; **la decisión de unir fuerzas para la elección fue el típico m. de ahogado** the decision to join forces for the election was a classic case of clutching at straws

mansalva: a mansalva *loc adv (en abundancia)* **vinieron invitados a m.** loads of guests came; **lanzaron bombas a m.** they dropped tons of bombs

mansamente *adv (con mansedumbre)* calmly, gently

mansedumbre *nf* **(a)** *(tranquilidad)* calmness, gentleness **(b)** *(docilidad)* tameness

mansión *nf* mansion

manso, -a *adj* **(a)** *(animal) (dócil)* docile; *(domesticado)* tame **(b)** *(persona)* gentle, meek **(c)** *(aguas)* calm **(d)** *Chile Fam (extraordinario)* tremendous; **tiene la mansa casa** he has a gigantic *o* massive house

manta[1] *nf* **(a)** *(abrigo)* blanket; EXPR **liarse la m. a la cabeza** to take the plunge; EXPR **tirar de la m.** to let the cat out of the bag ►► ***m. eléctrica*** electric blanket

(b) *(pez)* manta ray

(c) *Méx (algodón)* = coarse cotton cloth ►► ***m. de cielo*** muslin

(d) *Méx (pancarta)* cloth banner

(e) *Ven (vestido)* = traditional Indian woman's dress

(f) *Esp Fam* **a m.** *(muchísimo)* in abundance; **llovía a m.** it was pouring down; **han cosechado éxitos a m.** they have had loads of hits

manta[2] *nmf Esp Fam (persona)* layabout; **ser un m.** to be a waste of space; **hacer el m.** *(vaguear)* to bum around

mantear *vt* to toss in a blanket

manteca 1 *nf* **(a)** *Esp (grasa animal)* fat; EXPR *Fam* **tener buenas mantecas** to be a tub of lard ►► ***m. de cerdo*** lard

(b) *(grasa vegetal)* vegetable fat ►► ***m. de cacahuete*** *o Méx* ***cacahuate*** peanut butter; ***m. de cacao*** cocoa butter; *Andes, CAm, RP, Ven* ***m. de maní*** peanut butter

(c) *RP, Ven (mantequilla)* butter; EXPR *RP Fam* **ser una m.** to be very tender; EXPR *RP Fam* **tener dedos de m.** to be a butterfingers; EXPR *RP Fam* **tirar m. al techo** *(despilfarrar)* to splash money around; *(ser millonario)* to be rolling in it

(d) *Esp Fam (dinero)* dough

2 *nmf* EXPR *RP Fam* **ser un m.** to be a wimp

mantecada *nf (magdalena)* = small rectangular sponge cake

mantecado *nm* **(a)** *Esp (dulce)* = very crumbly shortbread biscuit made with lard **(b)** *Esp (helado)* dairy ice cream **(c)** *RP (magdalena)* = small sponge cake

mantecoso, -a *adj* fatty, greasy

mantel *nm* tablecloth

> **Falso amigo**: El sustantivo inglés **mantle** no es la traducción del español **mantel**. En inglés **mantle** significa "manto", "manguito incandescente" o "capa".

mantelería *nf* set of table linen

manteleta *nf* shawl

mantención *nf CSur* **(a)** *(de persona)* support, maintenance **(b)** *(de máquina)* maintenance

mantenedor, -ora *nm,f* president *(of a jury)*

MANTENER [67] 1 *vt* **(a)** *(sustentar)* to support; *(mascota, animal)* to keep; **con su sueldo mantiene a toda la familia** he has to support *o* keep his whole family with his wages

(b) *(sostener)* to support; **un andamio mantiene el edificio en pie** a scaffold supports the building *o* keeps the building from falling down; **mantén los brazos en alto** keep your arms in the air; **mantén el cable ahí** hold the cable there

(c) *(conservar)* to keep; *(ritmo, niveles, presión)* to keep up; **m. las amistades** to keep up one's friendships; **m. algo en buen estado** to keep sth in good condition; **m. la calma** to stay calm; **m. el orden** to keep order; **m. la línea** to keep one's figure; **m. una promesa/la palabra** to keep a promise/one's word; **mantenga limpia su ciudad** *(en letrero)* keep your city tidy; **manténgase en un lugar seco** *(en etiqueta)* keep in a dry place; **manténgase fuera del alcance de los niños** *(en medicamento, producto tóxico)* keep out of the reach of children; **es incapaz de m. la boca cerrada** he can't keep his mouth shut

(d) *(tener) (conversación)* to have; *(negociaciones, diálogo)* to hold; **m. correspondencia con alguien** to correspond with sb; **m. relaciones con alguien** to have a relationship with sb; **m. contactos con alguien** to be in contact with sb

(e) *(defender) (convicción, idea)* to stick to; *(candidatura)* to refuse to withdraw; **mantiene su inocencia** she maintains that she is innocent; **mantiene que no la vio** he maintains that he didn't see her

2 **mantenerse** *vpr* **(a)** *(sustentarse económicamente)* to support oneself; *(alimentarse)* to live (**con** *o* **de** *o* **a base de** on); **nos mantenemos a duras penas con mi sueldo** my wages are barely enough for us to get by on

(b) *(permanecer, continuar)* to remain; *(edificio)* to remain standing; **¡manténte quieto!** keep still!; **¡por favor, manténganse alejados!** please keep clear!; **mantenerse aparte** *(en discusión)* to stay out of it; **mantenerse en contacto con alguien** to stay in touch with sb; **mantenerse joven/en forma** to stay *o* keep young/fit; **mantenerse en pie** to remain standing

(c) *(perseverar)* **se mantiene en su postura** he refuses to change his position; **me mantengo en mi intención de decírselo** I still intend to tell her; **me mantengo en lo dicho** I stick by what I said before

---

mantenido, -a 1 *adj* sustained

2 *nm,f (hombre)* gigolo; *(mujer)* kept woman

mantenimiento *nm* **(a)** *(de persona)* **se encarga del m. de sus hijos** he provides for *o* supports his children

(b) *(de máquina)* maintenance; *(de parque, edificio)* upkeep; **gastos de m.** maintenance costs; **manual de m.** service manual; **servicio de m.** maintenance service

(c) *(de situación)* preservation; *(de ley)* upholding; *(de promesa)* keeping; **las tropas se encargan del m. de la paz** the troops are in charge of peacekeeping; **protestan contra el m. del embargo** they are protesting against the continuation of the embargo

(d) *(gimnasia)* keep fit; **clases de m.** keep-fit classes; **ejercicios de m.** keep-fit exercises

manteo *nm (en manta, brazos)* = practice of tossing a person up in the air repeatedly and catching them either in a blanket or the linked arms of several people

mantequera *nf* butter dish

mantequería *nf* **(a)** *(fábrica)* dairy, butter factory **(b)** *(tienda)* grocer's (shop)

mantequilla *nf* (a) *(grasa)* butter ▸▸ ***m. de cacahuete*** peanut butter; ***m. salada*** salted butter (b) *Ven Fam (asunto)* **¡qué m.!** that was a piece of cake! (c) *Ven Fam (persona)* soft touch

mantequillera *nf* butter dish

mantequita *RP Fam* 1 *adj* **ser m.** to be a crybaby
2 *nmf* crybaby

mantiene *etc ver* **mantener**

mantilla *nf* (a) *(de mujer)* mantilla (b) *(de bebé)* shawl; EXPR *Fam* **estar en mantillas** *(persona)* to be wet behind the ears; *(plan)* to be in its infancy

mantillo *nm* (a) *(capa)* humus (b) *(abono)* compost

mantis *nf inv* mantis ▸▸ ***m. religiosa*** praying mantis

mantisa *nf Mat* mantissa

manto *nm* (a) *(indumentaria)* cloak (b) *(de nieve, barro)* mantle, layer; **un m. de nieve cubría los campos** the fields were blanketed in snow (c) *Geol (capa)* stratum, layer; **el m. terrestre** the earth's mantle ▸▸ ***m. freático*** aquifer (d) *Arg* ***m. negro*** Alsatian, German Shepherd

mantón *nm* shawl ▸▸ ***m. de Manila*** embroidered silk shawl

mantra *nm Rel* mantra

mantuano, -a *Ven Hist* 1 *adj* = relating to the Venezuelan ruling class
2 *nm,f* = member of the Venezuelan ruling class

mantuviera *etc ver* **mantener**

manual 1 *adj* manual; **tiene gran habilidad m.** she's very good with her hands
2 *nm* manual ▸▸ ***m. de instrucciones*** instruction manual; ***m. de uso*** instruction manual; ***m. del usuario*** user's manual

manualidades *nfpl* (a) *(objetos)* craftwork, handicrafts (b) *Educ (asignatura)* craft

manualmente *adv* manually, by hand

manubrio *nm* (a) *(manivela)* crank (b) *Am (manillar)* handlebars

manuela *nf Carib muy Fam* hand-job; **hacerse una** *o* **la m.** to jerk off

manufactura *nf* (a) *(actividad)* manufacture (b) *(producto)* product; **las importaciones de manufacturas** imports of manufactured goods (c) *(fábrica)* factory

manufacturado, -a *adj* manufactured; **productos manufacturados** manufactured goods

manufacturar *vt* to manufacture

manufacturero, -a *adj* manufacturing; **la industria manufacturera** manufacturing industry

manumisión *nf Formal (de esclavo)* liberation

manumiso, -a *adj Formal (esclavo)* freed, emancipated

manumitir *vt Formal (esclavo)* to emancipate

manuscrito, -a 1 *adj* handwritten
2 *nm* (a) *(escrito a mano)* manuscript ▸▸ ***los Manuscritos del Mar Muerto*** the Dead Sea Scrolls (b) *(original)* original manuscript, typescript

manutención *nf* (a) *(sustento)* support, maintenance (b) *(alimento)* food

manyar [man'ʒar] *RP Fam* 1 *vt* (a) *(comer)* to eat (b) *(entender)* to understand; **no manyo nada de inglés** I don't understand a word of English; EXPR **tener a alguien muy manyado** to have sb's number
2 *vi (comer)* to get a bite to eat

manzana *nf* (a) *(fruta)* apple; **m. asada** *o* **al horno** baked apple ▸▸ ***m. deliciosa*** Golden Delicious; *Fig* ***m. de la discordia*** bone of contention; *Fig* ***m. podrida*** rotten apple; ***m. reineta*** = type of apple with tart flavour used for cooking and eating (b) *(grupo de casas)* block (of houses); **dar la vuelta a la m.** to go round the block (c) ***m. de Adán*** *(nuez)* Adam's apple

manzanal *nm* (a) *(huerto)* apple orchard (b) *(árbol)* apple tree

manzanar *nm* apple orchard

manzanilla *nf* (a) *(planta)* camomile (b) *(infusión)* camomile tea (c) *(vino)* manzanilla (sherry) (d) *(aceituna)* manzanilla, = type of small olive

manzano *nm* apple tree

maña *nf* (a) *(destreza)* skill; **tener m. para** to have a knack for; PROV **más vale m. que fuerza** brain is better than brawn (b) *(astucia)* wits, guile; **darse m. para hacer algo** to contrive to do sth (c) *(engaño)* ruse, trick (d) *(mala costumbre)* bad habit; **tener la m. de hacer algo** to have the bad habit of doing sth (e) *Am Fam (capricho)* **ese niño tiene muchas mañas** that child is spoiled rotten (f) *ver también* **maño**

mañana 1 *nf* morning; **(muy) de m.** (very) early in the morning; **trabajo de m.** *o* **mañanas** I work mornings; **a la m. siguiente** the next morning; **a las dos de la m.** at two in the morning; *Esp* **por la m.**, *Am* **en la m.**, *Arg* **a la m.**, *Urug* **de m.** in the morning; **m./el sábado** *Esp* **por la m.** *o Am* **en la m.** *o Arg* **a la m.** *o Urug* **de m.** tomorrow/Saturday morning
2 *nm* **el m.** tomorrow, the future; **la tecnología del m.** the technology of tomorrow *o* the future; EXPR **m. será otro día** tomorrow is another day
3 *adv* tomorrow; **m. es martes** tomorrow is Tuesday, it's Tuesday tomorrow; **m. hará tres años de su muerte** it's three years tomorrow since she died; **a partir de m.** starting tomorrow, as of tomorrow; **de m. no pasa, tengo que llamarla** I have to ring her without fail tomorrow; **la ley entra en vigor a partir de m. mismo** the law comes into effect as of tomorrow; **¡hasta m.!** see you tomorrow!; **m. por la m.** tomorrow morning; **pasado m.** the day after tomorrow

mañanero, -a *adj* (a) *(madrugador)* **son una familia muy mañanera** they are a family of early risers (b) *(matutino)* morning; **paseo m.** morning walk

mañanita *nf (prenda)* bed-jacket

mañanitas *nfpl Méx* birthday song

mañero, -a *adj RP (persona, animal)* difficult; *(máquina)* temperamental

maño, -a *Esp Fam* 1 *adj* Aragonese
2 *nm,f* Aragonese

mañoco *nm Ven* tapioca

mañosear *vi Chile, Ven Fam* to play up

mañoso, -a *adj* (a) *Esp (hábil)* skilful (b) *Andes, RP (caprichoso)* difficult; **no quiero andar más en este caballo, es demasiado m.** I don't want to ride this horse again, it's too strong-willed; **nunca se queda a cuidar a sus nietos, dice que son muy mañosos** he never stays and looks after his grandchildren, he says they play up too much

maoísmo *nm* Maoism

maoísta 1 *adj* Maoist
2 *nmf* Maoist

maorí (*pl* **maoríes**) 1 *adj* Maori
2 *nmf* Maori

mapa *nm* map; EXPR *Fam* **borrar algo del m.** to wipe sth off the map; EXPR *Fam* **desaparecer del m.** to vanish into thin air ▸▸ *Informát* ***m. de bits*** bit map; *Informát* ***m. de caracteres*** character map; ***m. de carreteras*** road map; ***m. celeste*** celestial map; ***m. físico*** physical map; ***m. genético*** genetic map; *Informát* ***m. interactivo*** *(en página Web)* clickable image map; ***m. lingüístico*** linguistic map; ***m. mudo*** blank map *(without names of countries, cities, rivers etc)*; ***m. político*** political map; ***m. de relieve*** relief map; ***m. del tiempo*** weather map; ***m. topográfico*** contour map

mapache *nm* raccoon

mapamundi *nm* world map

mapresa® *nf Perú* Formica®

mapuche 1 *adj* Mapuche
2 *nmf (persona)* Mapuche (Indian)
3 *nm (lengua)* Mapuche

mapurite *nm Ven* skunk

Maputo *n* Maputo

maquero, -a *Informát* 1 *adj* Mac; **la comunidad maquera** Mac users, the Mac community
2 *nm,f* Mac user

maqueta *nf* (a) *(reproducción a escala)* (scale) model (b) *(de libro)* dummy (c) *(de disco)* demo (tape) (d) *ver también* **maqueto**

maquetación *nf Informát* page layout

maquetador, -ora *nm,f Informát* layout editor

maquetar *vt Informát* to do the layout of

maquetista *nmf* model maker

maqueto, -a *Esp Fam Pey* 1 *adj* = not born in the Basque Country
2 *nm,f* = term for a person living in the Basque country who was not born there

maqui 1 *nm* (a) *(guerrilla)* resistance movement (b) *Chile (árbol)* maqui
2 *nmf inv* resistance fighter

maquiavélico, -a *adj* Machiavellian

maquiavelismo *nm* Machiavellianism

maquila *nf CAm, Méx (de artículos electrónicos)* assembly; *(de ropa)* making-up

maquiladora *nf CAm, Méx* = bonded assembly plant set up by a foreign firm near the US border, *US* maquiladora

maquilar *vt CAm, Méx (artículos electrónicos)* to assemble; *(ropa)* to make up

maquillador, -ora *nm,f* make-up artist

maquillaje *nm* (a) *(producto)* make-up ▸▸ ***m. de cuerpo*** body paint (b) *(acción)* making-up

maquillar 1 *vt* (a) *(pintar)* to make up; **la maquillaron de vieja** she was made up like an old woman (b) *(disimular)* to cover up, to disguise; **intentaron m. las pérdidas** they tried to massage the figures to hide the losses

2 **maquillarse** *vpr* to make oneself up; **se maquilla demasiado** she wears *o* uses too much make-up

maquillista *nmf Méx* make-up artist

máquina *nf* (a) *(aparato)* machine; **coser a m.** to machine-sew; **escribir a m.** to type; **escrito a m.** typewritten; **hecho a m.** machine-made; **lavar a m.** to machine-wash; **pasar algo a m.** to type sth out *o* up; EXPR *Fam* **ser una m.** *(muy rápido, muy bueno)* to be a powerhouse ▸▸ ***m. de afeitar*** electric razor; ***m. de bebidas*** drinks machine; ***m. de café*** (espresso) coffee machine; ***m. de cambios*** change machine; ***m. de coser*** sewing-machine; ***m. de discos*** *(en bar)* jukebox; ***m. destructora de documentos*** document shredder; ***m. de escribir*** typewriter; ***m. expendedora*** vending machine; ***m. fotográfica*** camera; ***m. de fotos*** camera; ***m. herramienta*** machine tool; ***m. de oficina*** office machine; ***m. quitanieves*** snowplough; ***m. recreativa*** arcade machine; ***m. registradora*** cash register; ***m. de tabaco*** cigarette machine; ***m. del tiempo*** time machine; ***m. voladora*** flying machine

(b) *(para jugar)* **jugar a las máquinas** to play on the slot machines ▸▸ ***m. de azar*** slot machine, *Br* fruit machine; ***m. de marcianos*** Space Invaders® machine; *Am* ***m. tragamonedas*** slot machine, *Br* fruit machine; *Esp* ***m. tragaperras*** slot machine, *Br* fruit machine

(c) *(locomotora)* engine ▸▸ ***m. de vapor*** steam engine

(d) *(en buque)* engine; **sala de máquinas** engine room; *también Fig* **a toda m.** at full pelt; *Fig* **no fuerces la m.** don't overdo it

(e) *(de estado, partido)* machinery

(f) *Fam (vehículo) (moto)* (motor)bike; *(bicicleta)* bike; *(automóvil)* wheels, *Br* motor

(g) *Cuba (automóvil)* car

maquinación *nf* plot; **maquinaciones** machinations; **declaró ser víctima de maquinaciones** he claimed he was the victim of a plot

maquinador, -ora 1 *adj* plotting, scheming

2 *nm,f* plotter, schemer

maquinal *adj* mechanical

maquinalmente *adv* mechanically

maquinar *vt* to plot, to scheme; **estaban maquinando una conspiración contra el gobierno** they were plotting against the government

maquinaria *nf* (a) *(aparatos)* machinery ▸▸ ***m. agrícola*** agricultural *o* farming machinery; ***m. industrial*** industrial machinery; ***m. pesada*** heavy machinery (b) *(mecanismo) (de reloj, aparato)* mechanism (c) *(de Estado, partido)* machinery

maquinilla *nf* (a) *(de afeitar)* ***m. de afeitar*** razor; ***m. eléctrica*** electric razor (b) *Tec* ***m. de carga*** cargo winch

maquinismo *nm* mechanization

maquinista *nmf* (a) *(operador)* (machine) operator (b) *(de tren) Br* engine-driver, *US* engineer (c) *(de barco)* engineer

maquinizar [14] *vt* to mechanize

maquis 1 *nm* resistance movement

2 *nmf inv* resistance fighter

MAR *nm o nf*

Note that the feminine is used in literary language, by people such as fishermen with a close connection with the sea, and in some idiomatic expressions.

(a) *(océano, masa de agua)* sea; **al nivel del m.** at sea level; **se cayó al m.** she fell into the sea; **hacerse a la m.** to set sail, to put (out) to sea; **pasan meses en el m.** *(navegando)* they spend months at sea; **m. adentro** out to sea; **por m.** *(viajar, enviar)* by sea; **un viaje por m.** a sea voyage; *Literario* **surcar los mares** to ply the seas; EXPR **a mares: llover a mares** to rain cats and dogs; **lloraba a mares** she was crying her eyes out; **sudaba a mares** he was sweating buckets; EXPR *RP Fam* **la m. en coche** the whole shebang; EXPR *Esp muy Fam* **me cago en la m.** *Br* bloody hell!, *US* goddamn it!; EXPR *Esp Fam Euf* **mecachis en la m.** *Br* sugar!, *US* shoot! ▸▸ ***m. abierto*** open sea; ***el m. Adriático*** the Adriatic Sea; ***el m. Amarillo*** the Yellow Sea; ***el m. Arábigo*** the Arabian Sea; ***el m. de Aral*** the Aral Sea; ***m. arbolada*** = rough sea with waves between 6 and 9 metres in height; ***el m. Báltico*** the Baltic Sea; ***m. calma*** calm sea; ***el m. Cantábrico*** the Bay of Biscay; ***el m. Caribe*** the Caribbean (Sea); ***el m. Caspio*** the Caspian Sea; ***el m. de China*** the China Sea; ***el m. de(l) Coral*** the Coral Sea; ***el m. Egeo*** the Aegean Sea; *también Fig* ***m. de fondo*** groundswell; **el asunto ha creado mucha m. de fondo en la opinión pública** the affair has given rise to a groundswell of public opinion; ***m. gruesa*** = rough sea with waves under 6 metres; ***un m. interior*** an inland sea; ***el m. de Irlanda*** the Irish Sea; ***el m. Jónico*** the Ionian Sea; ***m. llana*** calm sea; ***el m. Mediterráneo*** the Mediterranean Sea; ***el m. Muerto*** the Dead Sea; ***el m. Negro*** the Black Sea; ***el m. del Norte*** the North Sea; ***m. picada*** very choppy sea; ***m. rizada*** choppy sea; ***el m. Rojo*** the Red Sea; ***el m. de los Sargazos*** the Sargasso Sea

(b) *(litoral)* seaside; **nos vamos a vivir al m.** we're going to live by the sea; **veranean en el m.** they spend their summer holidays at the seaside; **una casa en el m.** a house by the sea; **junto al m.** at the seaside

(c) *(gran abundancia)* **un m. de gente** a sea of people; **un m. de sangre** a river of blood; **estoy inmersa en un m. de dudas** I'm plagued with doubts; EXPR **estar hecho un m. de lágrimas** to be crying one's eyes out

(d) *Fam* **la m. de** *(muchos)* loads of; *(muy)* dead; **es la m. de inteligente** she's dead intelligent; **todo va la m. de lento** everything's going dead slowly; **está la m. de nerviosa** she's dead nervous; **tengo la m. de cosas que hacer** I've got loads of things to do

---

mar. (a) *(abrev de* **marzo***)* Mar (b) *(abrev de* **martes***)* Tues

mara *nf* Patagonian hare

marabino, -a = **maracaibero, -a**

marabú *(pl* **marabúes** *o* **marabús***)* *nm* marabou stork, marabou

marabunta *nf* (a) *(de hormigas)* plague of ants (b) *Fam (muchedumbre)* crowd, throng; **cuando llega la m. de turistas** when the hordes of tourists arrive

maraca *nf* (a) *(instrumento)* maraca (b) *Chile muy Fam (prostituta)* hooker

maracaibero, -a, marabino, -a 1 *adj* of/from Maracaibo *(Venezuela)*

2 *nm,f* person from Maracaibo *(Venezuela)*

maracayero, -a 1 *adj* of/from Maracay *(Venezuela)*

2 *nm,f* person from Maracay *(Venezuela)*

maracucho, -a *Fam* 1 *adj* of/from Maracaibo *(Venezuela)*

2 *nm,f* person from Maracaibo *(Venezuela)*

maracuyá *nf* passion fruit

maragota *nf* ballan wrasse

marajá *nm* maharajah; EXPR **vivir como un m.** to live in the lap of luxury

maraña *nf* (a) *(de cabellos, hilos)* tangle; **encontré el interruptor entre una m. de cables** I found the switch amid a tangle of electric cables

(b) *(maleza)* thicket; **la m. de arbustos no nos permitía avanzar** the dense undergrowth prevented us from going any further

(c) *(complicación)* tangle; **están intentando desenrollar la m. de normas que regulan el sector** they are trying to unravel the tangle of regulations that regulate the industry; **no hay quien se entienda con la m. de idiomas que se hablan allí** nobody can understand the jumble of languages they speak there; **le cuesta mucho encontrar lo que busca en la m. de Internet** he finds it difficult to find what he's looking for on-line, the Internet is such a maze

maraquear *vi Carib* to play the maracas

maraquero, -a *nm,f Carib* maraca player

marasmo *nm* (a) *Med* wasting, *Espec* marasmus (b) *(de ánimo)* apathy; *(de negocio)* stagnation; **la economía sigue sumida en el m.** the economy is continuing to stagnate

maratón *nm o nf* (a) *(carrera)* marathon ▸▸ ***m. popular*** marathon *(in which professional and amateur athletes participate)* (b) *Fam (actividad larga)* marathon; **un m. de 23 conciertos** a 23-concert marathon; **el acuerdo se logró tras un m. negociador** the agreement was reached after a marathon bout of negotiations ▸▸ ***m. televisivo*** telethon

maratoniano, -a *adj* marathon; **una reunión maratoniana** a marathon meeting

maratonista *nmf* marathon runner, marathoner

maravedí *(pl* **maravedíes***)* *nm Hist* maravedi *(old Spanish coin)*

maravilla *nf* (a) *(cosa maravillosa)* marvel, wonder; **una m. de niño/carretera** a wonderful *o* marvellous child/road; **¡qué m. de lugar!** what a wonderful place!; **las siete maravillas del mundo** the Seven Wonders of the World; **es una m.** it's wonderful; **canta que es una m.** she's a wonderful singer; **nos han contado maravillas sobre esa**

película we've heard wonderful things about that movie; **decir maravillas de algo/alguien** to praise sth/sb to the skies; **hacer maravillas** to do *o* work wonders; EXPR **a las mil maravillas, de m.: cocina a las mil maravillas** *o* **de m.** he's an absolutely wonderful cook; **la fiesta salió a las mil maravillas** *o* **de m.** the party went absolutely wonderfully; **se llevan de m.** they get on brilliantly; EXPR **venir de m.** to be just the thing *o* ticket; **esta sartén viene de m. para freír huevos** this pan is excellent for frying eggs; **su ayuda me vino de m.** her help was an absolute godsend

(**b**) *(admiración)* amazement; **su actuación causó m.** her performance was amazing

(**c**) *(planta compuesta)* calendula, pot marigold

(**d**) *(planta trepadora)* morning glory

(**e**) *Chile (girasol)* sunflower

maravillar 1 *vt* to amaze; **este juguete maravilla a los niños** children are amazed by this toy; **me maravilla que esté tan tranquilo** I'm amazed that he is so calm

2 maravillarse *vpr* to be amazed; **se maravilló de mi simpatía** he was amazed by my kindness

maravillosamente *adv* marvellously, wonderfully

maravilloso, -a *adj* (**a**) *(extraordinario)* marvellous, wonderful (**b**) *(milagroso)* miraculous; **la maravillosa intervención del portero evitó el gol** the goalkeeper's miraculous save prevented a goal

marbellí (*pl* **marbellíes** *o* **marbellís**) **1** *adj* of/from Marbella *(Spain)*

2 *nmf* person from Marbella *(Spain)*

marbete *nm* (**a**) *(etiqueta)* label, tag (**b**) *(orilla)* border, edge

marca *nf* (**a**) *(señal)* mark; *(de rueda, animal)* track; *(en ganado)* brand; *(en papel)* watermark; *(cicatriz)* mark, scar; **se le nota la m. del bañador** you can see her tan line, you can see where she's been wearing her swimsuit; **se quemó y le ha quedado una m.** she burned herself and has been left with a scar; *Dep* **en sus marcas, listos, ¡ya!** on your marks, get set, go! ▸▸ *Imprenta* ***m. de corte*** crop mark; *Informát* ***m. de párrafo*** paragraph mark; *Imprenta* ***m. de recorte*** crop mark

(**b**) *Com (de tabaco, café, perfume)* brand; *(de vehículo, computadora)* make; **sólo compro ropa de m.** I only buy designer clothes; **unos vaqueros de m.** a pair of designer jeans; *Fam* **de m. mayor** *(muy grande)* enormous; *(excelente)* outstanding ▸▸ ***m. blanca*** own-brand, own-label; ***m. comercial*** trademark; ***m. de fábrica*** trademark; ***m. registrada*** registered trademark

(**c**) *(etiqueta)* label

(**d**) *Dep (tiempo, distancia, altura)* performance; **la mejor m. mundial del año en los 100 metros** the fastest time in the world this year for the 100 metres; **su mejor m. del año** her personal best this year

(**e**) *Dep (marcaje)* marking; **se encarga de la m. del delantero más peligroso** he's marking the most dangerous forward

(**f**) *(en rugby)* **línea de m.** try *o* goal line; **zona de m.** in-goal area

marcación *nf* (**a**) *CSur Dep (marcaje)* marking (**b**) *Náut (orientación)* bearing

marcadamente *adv* markedly, noticeably

marcado, -a 1 *adj (pronunciado)* marked; **tiene un m. acento mexicano** he has a strong Mexican accent

2 *nm* (**a**) *(señalado)* marking (**b**) *(peinado)* set

marcador, -ora 1 *adj* marking; **siga las flechas marcadoras** follow the arrows

2 *nm* (**a**) *(tablero)* scoreboard ▸▸ ***m. electrónico*** electronic scoreboard; ***m. simultáneo*** scoreboard *(on which the results of other matches being played are shown)*

(**b**) *(resultado)* score; **¿cuál es el m.?** what's the score?; **el m. está empatado** the scores are level

(**c**) *(jugador) (defensor)* marker

(**d**) *(jugador) (goleador)* scorer

(**e**) *(para libros)* bookmark

(**f**) *Informát (de página web)* bookmark

(**g**) *Am (rotulador)* felt-tip pen; *Méx (fluorescente)* highlighter pen

marcaje *nm Dep* marking; **le hicieron un m. muy duro** he was very closely marked ▸▸ ***m. al hombre*** man-to-man marking; ***m. individual*** man-to-man marking

marcapáginas *nm inv* bookmark

marcapasos *nm inv* pacemaker

marcar [60] **1** *vt* (**a**) *(poner marca en)* to mark; *(nombre en una lista)* to tick off; *(poner precio a)* to price; **marcó el itinerario en el mapa** she marked the route on the map; **asegúrate de que marcas las maletas con tu nombre** make sure your suitcases are identified with your name; **marcó la ropa con mis iniciales** she put my initials on the clothes; **m. los naipes** to mark the cards

(**b**) *(indicar)* to mark, to indicate; **la cruz marca el lugar donde está enterrado el tesoro** the cross marks *o* indicates (the spot) where the treasure is buried

(**c**) *(dejar marca en)* to mark; **ese acontecimiento marcó su vida** her life was marked by that event

(**d**) *(significar)* to mark, to signal; **el tratado marcó un hito en las relaciones entre las dos potencias** the treaty was a landmark in relations between the two powers

(**e**) *(número de teléfono)* to dial

(**f**) *(sujeto: termómetro, contador)* to read; *(sujeto: reloj)* to say; **la balanza marca 3 kilos** the scales read 3 kilos; **¿qué precio marca la etiqueta?** what is the price on the label?; **cuando el reloj marque las seis** when the clock strikes six; **el euro ha marcado un nuevo mínimo frente al dólar** the euro has fallen to another all-time low against the dollar

(**g**) *(paso)* **m. el ritmo** to beat the rhythm; **el corredor más lento marcó el ritmo del resto del grupo** the slowest runner set the pace for the whole group

(**h**) *Dep (tanto)* to score

(**i**) *Dep (a un jugador)* to mark

(**j**) *Dep (tiempo)* to record; *(récord)* to set

(**k**) *(cabello)* to set

(**l**) EXPR *RP* **m. tarjeta** *(en el trabajo) (a la entrada)* to clock in; *(a la salida)* to clock out; *Fam* **tengo que m. tarjeta** *(en casa de la novia)* I have to see my girlfriend

2 *vi* (**a**) *(dejar secuelas)* to leave a mark (**b**) *(peinar)* to set, to style (**c**) *Dep (anotar un tanto)* to score; **m. en propia puerta** *o* **meta** to score an own goal

3 marcarse *vpr* (**a**) *Dep (defender)* to mark each other (**b**) *(notarse)* to show; **se le marca el sostén por debajo de la blusa** you can see the outline of her bra under her blouse (**c**) *Esp Fam* **¿nos marcamos un baile?** shall we have a dance?; EXPR **marcarse un detalle** to do something nice *o* kind; EXPR **marcarse un tanto** to earn a brownie point

marcasita *nf Min* marcasite

MARCHA *nf* (**a**) *(partida)* departure; **ha anunciado su m. de la empresa** she has announced that she will be leaving the company

(**b**) *(ritmo, velocidad)* speed; **acelerar la m.** to go faster; **reducir la m.** to slow down; **el tren detuvo su m.** the train stopped; **a esta m. terminaremos pronto** at this rate we'll soon be finished; *Esp* **a marchas forzadas** *(contrarreloj)* against the clock; *RP* **a media m.** slowly; **trabajar a media m.** to work at half speed; **a toda m.** at top speed; *Esp* **¡llevas una m. que no hay quien te siga!** you're going so fast, no one can keep up with you!; *Esp* **¡vaya m. que llevan los pasteles!** those cakes are disappearing at a rate of knots!

(**c**) *(funcionamiento)* **para la buena m. de su automóvil son necesarias revisiones periódicas** in order to make sure your car runs smoothly, it should be serviced regularly

(**d**) *(transcurso)* course; *(progreso)* progress; **un apagón interrumpió la m. del partido** a power cut interrupted the (course of the) game; **informó sobre la m. de la empresa** she gave a report on the company's progress; **se bajó en m. del tren** he jumped off the train while it was moving; **estar en m.** *(motor, máquina)* to be running; *(campaña)* to be under way; *(tren)* to be moving; **ya están en m. las nuevas medidas para combatir la inflación** the new measures to fight inflation have been introduced; **poner en m. un automóvil/motor/proyecto** to start a car/an engine/a project; **ponerse en m.** *(automóvil, tren, autocar)* to set off; *(proyecto, campaña)* to get under way; **hacer algo sobre la m.** to do sth as one goes along

(**e**) *(en automóvil)* gear; **cambiar de m.** to change gear; **no me entra la m. atrás** it won't go into reverse; **meter la cuarta m.** to go into fourth gear ▸▸ ***m. atrás*** *(en automóvil)* reverse; *Fam Hum (al hacer el amor)* coitus interruptus; **el proceso de paz no tiene m. atrás** the only way for the peace process is forwards; **dar m. atrás** *(en automóvil)* to reverse; *(arrepentirse, desistir)* to back out; *Fam Hum (al hacer el amor)* to withdraw (halfway through)

(**f**) *(de soldados, manifestantes)* march; *(de montañeros, senderistas)* hike; **abrir la m.** to head the procession; **cerrar la m.** to bring up the rear; **emprender la m.** to set out; **¡en m.!** *(dicho a soldados)* forward march!; *(dicho a niños, montañeros)* on we go!, let's get going!; **hacer una m.** *(soldados, manifestantes)* to go on a march; *(montañeros, senderistas)* to go on a hike; **ir de m.** *(montañeros, senderistas)* to go hiking; **ponerse en m.** *(persona)* to set off

(**g**) *(obra musical)* march ▸▸ ***m. fúnebre*** funeral march; ***m. militar*** military march; ***m. nupcial*** wedding march; ***la M. Real*** = the Spanish national anthem

(**h**) *Dep* **m. (atlética)** walk; **los 20 kilómetros m.** the 20 kilometres walk

(**i**) *Esp Fam (animación)* liveliness, life; **los lugares** *o* **sitios de m.** the places to go; **¿dónde está la m. en esta ciudad?** where's the action in this city?; **hay mucha m.** there's a great atmosphere; **ir de m.** to go out on the town; **estuvimos de m. hasta las siete** we were out on the town until seven in the morning; **este tío tiene mucha m.** this guy's a real live wire; **mis abuelos tienen mucha m.** my grandparents are dead cool; **esta ciudad tiene mucha m.** the atmosphere's great in this city; **¡qué poca m. tienes!** you're so boring!; **le va la m.** *(le gusta divertirse)* she likes to have a good time; *(le gusta sufrir)* she's a sucker for punishment; **parece que te vaya la m., mira que discutirle al jefe** have you got a death wish or something, questioning what the boss says like that?

---

marchador, -ora 1 *adj* (a) *Cuba (andarín)* fond of walking (b) *Chile, Cuba (animal)* ambling
2 *nm,f Dep* walker

marchamo *nm* (a) *(de aduana)* customs seal *o* stamp (b) *(marca distintiva)* seal (c) *Arg, Bol (impuesto)* = tax charged on each head of slaughtered cattle

marchand [mar'tʃan] *(pl* **marchands**) *nmf RP* (art) dealer

marchanta *nf* EXPR *RP Fam* **tirar algo a la m.** to throw sth away

marchante, -a *nm,f* (a) *(de arte)* (art) dealer (b) *CAm, Méx, Ven Fam (cliente)* customer, patron; **¿qué va a llevar hoy marchanta?** what would you like today, *Br* love *o US* ma'am? (c) *CAm, Méx, Ven Fam (vendedor)* = one's usual shop assistant or stallholder; **le preguntaré a mi m. cuándo llegan las peras nuevas** I'll ask the man on the stall I always go to when the new season's pears will be in

marchantería, marchantía *nf CAm, Méx, Ven Fam* clientele, customers

marchar 1 *vi* (a) *(caminar)* to walk
(b) *(soldados, manifestantes)* to march; **los agricultores marcharon sobre la capital** the farmers marched on the capital
(c) *(partir)* to leave, to go
(d) *(funcionar)* to work; **¿qué tal te marcha la moto?** how's your motorbike running?; **hay algo aquí que no marcha** something's not quite right here
(e) *(desarrollarse)* to progress; **el negocio marcha** business is going well; **¿cómo marchan las cosas con tu mujer?** how are things going with your wife?
(f) **¡marchando!** *(en bar)* coming up!; **¡marchando dos cafés con leche!** two white coffees, coming up!
(g) *Méx Fam* **¡no marches!** *(no te pases)* cool it!, take it easy!
2 **marcharse** *vpr* to leave, to go; **se marchó de aquí cuando era muy pequeño** he left here when he was very young; **me tengo que m.** I've got to go

marchista *nmf RP, Ven* marcher

marchitar 1 *vt* (a) *(planta)* to wither (b) *(persona)* to wither; **la vejez marchitó su belleza** her beauty faded with age
2 **marchitarse** *vpr* (a) *(planta)* to fade, to wither (b) *(persona)* to languish, to fade away

marchito, -a *adj* (a) *(planta)* faded (b) *(persona)* worn; **sus ilusiones quedaron marchitas** all his hopes faded away

marchoso, -a *Esp Fam* 1 *adj (bar)* lively; *(música)* groovy; **la parte más marchosa de la ciudad** the liveliest part of the city; **es una chica muy marchosa** she loves having a good time; **hoy estoy muy marchosa** I feel really up for it today
2 *nm,f* live wire

marcial *adj (ley)* martial; *(disciplina)* military

marcialidad *nf* military air

marcianitos *nmpl (juego)* Space Invaders®

marciano, -a 1 *adj* Martian
2 *nm,f* Martian

marco *nm* (a) *(de cuadro)* frame; *(de puerta)* doorframe; **m. de ventana** window frame
(b) *(ambiente, paisaje)* setting; **un m. incomparable** a perfect *o* an ideal setting
(c) *(ámbito)* framework; **su decisión se sitúa en el m. del creciente interés por el mercado latinoamericano** their decision should be seen in the context of the growing interest in the Latin American market; **darán un concierto en el m. del festival** they will give a concert as part of the festival; **el desarrollo económico en el m. del Mercosur** economic development within Mercosur; **actuó en el m. de la constitución** he acted within the framework of the constitution; **acuerdo m.** general *o* framework agreement
(d) *(moneda)* mark ▸▸ *Antes* ***m. alemán*** Deutschmark, German mark
(e) *Dep (portería)* goalmouth

Marcos *n pr* **San M.** St Mark

marea *nf* (a) *(del mar)* tide; **está subiendo/bajando la m.** the tide is coming in/going out ▸▸ ***m. alta*** high tide; ***m. baja*** low tide; ***m. negra*** oil slick; ***m. roja*** red tide; ***m. viva*** spring tide (b) *(multitud)* flood; **una m. de turistas invadió la ciudad** hordes of tourists invaded the city

mareado, -a *adj* (a) **estar m.** *(con náuseas)* to feel sick *o* queasy; *(en coche, avión)* to feel travel-sick; *(en barco)* to feel seasick (b) *(aturdido)* dizzy; **tantas cifras lo han dejado m.** all these figures have made his head spin (c) *Fam (fastidiado)* fed up, sick; **estoy m. con tanto niño de aquí para allá** I'm sick of kids running around all over the place

mareante *adj (cifra)* bewildering

marear 1 *vt* (a) *(provocar náuseas)* to make sick; *(en coche, avión)* to make travel-sick; *(en barco)* to make seasick; **los viajes en barco me marean** I get seasick when I travel by boat (b) *(aturdir)* to make dizzy; EXPR **m. la perdiz** to beat about the bush (c) *Fam (fastidiar)* to annoy; **me marea con sus quejas** she drives me up the wall with her complaining
2 *vi* (a) *(emborrachar)* **este vino marea** this wine goes to your head (b) *Fam (fastidiar)* to be a pain; **¡niño, deja de m.!** stop being such a pain!
3 **marearse** *vpr* (a) *(tener náuseas)* to get sick; *(en coche, avión)* to get travel-sick; *(en barco)* to get seasick (b) *(aturdirse)* to get dizzy (c) *(emborracharse)* to get tipsy

marejada *nf* (a) *(mar agitada)* heavy sea, swell (b) *(agitación)* wave of discontent

marejadilla *nf* slight swell

mare mágnum, maremagno *nm Fam* jumble; **su despacho es un m.** her office is a mess; **tengo un m. de ideas en la cabeza** my head is full of confused ideas; **un m. de gente protestaba delante de la embajada** there was a sea of protesters outside the embassy; **el congreso era un m. de nacionalidades** the conference was attended by a plethora of different nationalities

maremoto *nm* (a) *(ola)* tidal wave (b) *(seísmo)* seaquake

marengo *adj* **gris m.** dark grey

Mare Nostrum *n* **el M.** the Mediterranean

mareo *nm* (a) *(náuseas)* sickness; *(en coche, avión)* travel sickness; *(en barco)* seasickness (b) *(aturdimiento)* dizziness; **le dio un m.** he had a dizzy spell *o* turn, he felt dizzy; **tantas cifras me dan m.** all these figures are making my head spin (c) *Fam (fastidio)* drag, pain; **es un m. tener que ir de una oficina a otra** it's a drag *o* pain having to go from one office to another

marfil *nm* (a) *(material)* ivory ▸▸ ***m. vegetal*** ivory nut (b) *(color)* ivory; **de color m.** ivory-coloured, ivory

marfileño, -a *adj* ivory; **piel marfileña** ivory skin

marga *nf Geol* marl

margarina *nf* margarine

margarita 1 *nf* (a) *(flor)* daisy; EXPR *Fam* **es como echar margaritas a los cerdos** *o* **puercos** it's like casting pearls before swine; EXPR **deshojar la m.** to pull the petals off a daisy saying "she loves me, she loves me not" (b) *Imprenta* daisy-wheel
2 *nm o nf (cóctel)* margarita

margariteño, -a 1 *adj* of/from Margarita *(Venezuela)*
2 *nm,f* person from Margarita *(Venezuela)*

margen 1 *nm* (a) *(de camino)* side
(b) *(de página)* margin; **deja un m. más amplio** leave a wider margin; **ver nota al m.** see note in the margin
(c) *Com* margin; **este negocio deja mucho m.** this business is very profitable ▸▸ ***m. de beneficio(s)*** profit margin
(d) *(límite)* margin; **ganaron por un m. de 1.000 votos** they won by a margin of 1,000 votes; **tengo un m. de dos meses para acabar el trabajo** I have two months to finish the work; **dar a alguien m. de confianza** to allow sb to use his/her initiative ▸▸ ***m. de actuación*** room for manoeuvre; ***m. de error*** margin of error; ***m. de maniobra*** room for manoeuvre; ***m. de seguridad:* puedo decir, con un m. de seguridad del 99 por ciento, que...** I can say with a 99 percent degree of certainty that...
(e) *(ocasión)* **dar m. a alguien para hacer algo** to give sb the chance to do sth; **con su comportamiento dio m. a críticas** his behaviour exposed him to criticism
2 *nf (de río)* bank
3 **al margen** *loc adv* **lleva muchos años al m. del deporte** she has spent many years on the fringes of the sport; **al m. de eso, hay otros factores** over and above that, there are other factors; **al m. de la polémica, ha hecho un buen trabajo** irrespective of the controversy,

she has done a good job; **al m. de la ley** outside the law; **dejar al m.** to exclude; **estar al m. de algo** to have nothing to do with sth; **mantenerse al m. de algo** to keep out of sth

marginación *nf* exclusion; **los inmigrantes sufren m.** immigrants are excluded; **un colectivo que vive en la m.** a socially excluded group ►► ***m. social*** social exclusion

marginado, -a 1 *adj* excluded; **sentirse m.** to feel excluded; **un barrio m.** an area where there is a lot of social exclusion
2 *nm,f* socially excluded person; **los marginados** the socially excluded

marginal *adj* **(a)** *(de fuera de la sociedad) (persona, grupo social)* socially excluded; **una zona m. de la ciudad** a deprived area of the city **(b)** *(sin importancia)* minor; **un asunto m.** a matter of minor importance **(c)** *(en página)* marginal; **una nota m.** a marginal note **(d)** *Econ* marginal; **costo m.** marginal cost; **tipo m.** marginal rate

marginalidad *nf* **vivir en la m.** to live on the fringes of society; **todavía quedan en la ciudad algunos reductos de m.** there are still some areas in the city where social exclusion remains a problem

marginalizar *vt esp Am (discriminar)* to exclude; **sus compañeros lo marginalizan** his colleagues exclude him from the group, his colleagues give him the cold shoulder

marginar 1 *vt* **(a)** *(persona) (discriminar)* to exclude; **la nueva ley margina a los inmigrantes** the new law marginalizes immigrants; **sus compañeros lo marginan** his colleagues exclude him from the group, his colleagues give him the cold shoulder **(b)** *(asunto, diferencias)* to set aside, to set to one side **(c)** *(texto)* **margina un poco menos la página** leave a smaller margin on the page
2 marginarse *vpr* to exclude oneself

María *n pr* **(la virgen) M.** (the Virgin) Mary; **M. Magdalena** Mary Magdalene

maría *nf Fam* **(a)** *(mujer sencilla)* (typical) housewife **(b)** *Esp, Ven (marihuana)* grass **(c)** *Esp (asignatura)* Mickey-Mouse course, easy subject **(d)** *Méx* = poor, indigenous migrant from country to urban areas

mariachi[1] *nm* **(a)** *(música)* mariachi (music) **(b)** *(orquesta)* mariachi band **(c)** *(músico)* mariachi (musician)

mariachi[2] *adj Méx Fam* ham-fisted; **Celia es bien m. para cocinar** Celia is hopeless at cooking

marianista 1 *adj* = of/relating to the Company of Mary, a religious order founded in 19th century France
2 *nm* = member of the Company of Mary, a religious order founded in 19th century France

mariano, -a *adj* Marian

marica, *Ven* **marico** *nm Fam Br* poof, *US* fag

maricón, -ona *muy Fam* **1** *adj* **(a)** *(homosexual) Br* poofy, *US* faggy; **venga, subamos corriendo, ¡m. el último!** the last person to the top's a sissy! **(b)** *(como insulto) (cobarde)* wimpy **(c)** *(como insulto) (mala persona)* **iqué tío más m.!** what a bastard!
2 *nm,f* **(a)** *(como insulto) (cobarde)* wimp **(b)** *(como insulto) (mala persona)* bastard
3 *nm (homosexual) Br* poof, *US* fag ►► *muy Fam* ***m. de playa*** *(fanfarrón)* braggart, loud-mouth

mariconada *nf Fam* **(a)** *(dicho, hecho típico de homosexuales)* **eso es una m.** that's really *Br* poofy *o US* faggy; **se compró una m. de pantalones** he bought some really *Br* poofy *o US* faggy trousers
(b) *(mala jugada)* dirty trick; **es una m. que te hagan levantar a las seis** it's a bummer that they make you get up at six o'clock
(c) *(tontería)* **no dice más que mariconadas** he talks a load of old nonsense; **se pelearon por una m.** they fell out over something really stupid

mariconear *vi Fam* to camp it up

mariconera *nf Fam* (man's) clutch bag

mariconería *nf Fam* **(a)** *(dicho, hecho)* **eso es una m.** that's really *Br* poofy *o US* faggy **(b)** *(cualidad)* campness

maridaje *nm (unión)* union; **un perfecto m. entre música celta y ritmos africanos** a perfect fusion of Celtic music and African rhythms

maridar *vt (unir)* to join, to unite

marido *nm* husband

marielitos *nmpl Fam* = exiles who left Cuba from the port of El Mariel in 1980

marihuana, mariguana, marijuana *nf* marijuana

marihuanero, -a, mariguanero, -a, marijuanero, -a *Fam* **1** *adj* **es muy m.** he's a real pothead
2 *nm,f* pothead

marihuano, -a, mariguano, -a *Méx Fam* **1** *adj* **es muy m.** he's a real pothead
2 *nm,f* pothead

marimacho *nm Fam* **(a)** *(niña)* tomboy **(b)** *(mujer)* butch woman

marimandón, -ona *Esp Fam* **1** *adj* bossy
2 *nm,f* bossy-boots

marimba *nf* **(a)** *(xilofón)* marimba **(b)** *Andes Fam (marihuana)* grass

marimorena *nf Fam* row; EXPR **armar la m.** to kick up a row; **la insultó, y allí se armó la m.** he insulted her and then all hell broke loose

marina *nf* **(a)** *(flota)* navy ►► ***m. de guerra*** navy; ***m. mercante*** merchant navy **(b)** *(ciencia de navegar)* navigation; **un término de m.** a nautical term **(c)** *(cuadro)* seascape

marinar *vt* to marinate

marine *nm Mil* marine

marinera *nf* **(a)** *(blusa)* sailor top **(b)** *(baile)* marinera, = popular Andean dance

marinería *nf* **(a)** *(profesión)* sailoring **(b)** *(marineros)* crew, seamen

marinero, -a 1 *adj (de la marina, de los marineros)* sea; *(buque)* seaworthy; **un pueblo m.** *(nación)* a seafaring nation; *(población)* a fishing village; **vestido m.** sailor-suit
2 *nm* sailor ►► ***m. mercante*** merchant seaman; ***m. de primera*** able-bodied seaman
3 a la marinera *loc adj Culin* **almejas a la marinera** moules marinières; **arroz a la marinera** = dish similar to paella but in which the rice is cooked in a white wine and garlic sauce

marino, -a 1 *adj* sea, marine; **el fondo m.** the sea bed; **brisa marina** sea breeze; **azul m.** navy blue
2 *nm* sailor ►► ***m. mercante*** merchant seaman

marioneta *nf* **(a)** *(muñeco)* marionette, puppet; **marionetas** *(teatro)* puppet show **(b)** *(persona)* puppet; **es una m. del gobierno** he's a government puppet

marionetista *nmf* puppeteer

mariposa 1 *nf* **(a)** *(insecto)* butterfly ►► ***m. de la col*** cabbage white; ***m. monarca*** monarch butterfly; ***m. nocturna*** moth; ***m. tigre*** tiger moth
(b) *(tuerca)* wing nut
(c) *(candela, luz)* oil lamp
(d) *(en natación)* butterfly; **los 100 metros m.** the 100 metres butterfly; **nadar a m.,** *Méx* **nadar de m.** to do the butterfly
(e) ***m. cervical*** *(almohada)* Butterfly Pillow
(f) *(pájaro)* painted bunting
(g) *Cuba (planta)* butterfly jasmine
(h) EXPR *Fam Hum* **a otra cosa, m.** let's move on; **acabamos la carta, y a otra cosa, m.** let's finish the letter and move on to something else
2 *nm Fam (homosexual)* fairy

mariposear *vi Fam* **(a)** *(cambiar de trabajo, pareja)* to flit about; **le gusta m. con unas y otras** he never stays with the same woman for more than about five minutes **(b)** *(revolotear)* to hover; **los camareros mariposeaban en torno a la mesa** the waiters were flapping around the table **(c)** *(comportarse afeminadamente)* to act camp

mariposista *nmf Dep* butterfly specialist

mariposón *nm Fam* **(a)** *(afeminado)* fairy, pansy **(b)** *(ligón)* flirt

mariquera *nf Ven muy Fam* **déjate de mariqueras** stop being such a wimp

mariquita 1 *nf (insecto) Br* ladybird, *US* ladybug
2 *nm Fam (homosexual)* fairy

marisabidilla *nf Esp Fam* know-all

mariscada *nf* seafood meal

mariscador, -ora *nm,f* shellfish gatherer

mariscal *nm* **(a)** *(oficial)* marshal ►► ***m. de campo*** *Mil* field marshal; *Méx (en fútbol americano)* quarterback **(b)** *Chile (plato)* = dish of raw seafood with parsley, onion and lemon juice

mariscar [60] *vi* to gather shellfish

marisco *nm* seafood, shellfish; *Esp* **el m.** *o Am* **los mariscos de la región** the local seafood *o* shellfish

marisma *nf* marsh, salt marsh

marismeño, -a *adj* marshy

marisquería *nf* seafood restaurant

marista 1 *adj* Marist
2 *nm* Marist

marital *adj* marital; **la vida m.** married life

maritates *nfpl CAm (chucherías)* knick-knacks, trinkets

marítimo, -a *adj (del mar)* maritime; *(comunicaciones, comercio)* maritime; **transporte m.** sea transport; **pueblo m.** seaside town; **paseo m.** promenade

marjal *nm* marsh, bog

marketing, márketing ['marketin] *nm* marketing ▸▸ ***m. telefónico*** telesales, telemarketing

marlín *nm (pez)* marlin

marlo *nm RP* corncob

marmita *nf* cooking pot

marmitaco, marmitako *nm* = Basque stew containing tuna and potatoes

mármol *nm* (**a**) *(piedra)* marble; **suelo de m.** marble floor (**b**) *(escultura)* marble (**c**) *Urug (encimera)* worktop

marmolería *nf* (**a**) *(mármoles)* marbles, marblework (**b**) *(taller)* workshop, studio

marmolista *nmf* marble cutter

marmóreo, -a *adj Formal* marmoreal

marmosa *nf* yacca

marmota *nf* (**a**) *(animal)* marmot; EXPR *Fam* **dormir como una m.** to sleep like a log (**b**) *Fam (dormilón)* sleepyhead

maroma *nf* (**a**) *(cuerda)* rope (**b**) *Andes, CAm, Carib, Méx (acrobacia)* acrobatic stunt; EXPR *Méx Fam* **hacer maromas en un popote** to work miracles (**c**) *Andes, CAm, Carib, Méx Fam (cambio)* **hacer maromas** to lean one way then the other

maromear *vi Andes, CAm, Carib, Méx* (**a**) *(hacer acrobacias) (en el suelo)* to perform acrobatics; *(en la cuerda floja)* to walk the tightrope (**b**) *Fam (cambiar de idea)* to lean one way then the other

maromero, -a *nm,f Andes, CAm, Carib, Méx* (**a**) *(acróbata)* tightrope walker (**b**) *Fam (político)* political opportunist

maromo *nm Esp Fam* (**a**) *(hombre)* guy, *Br* bloke (**b**) *(novio)* man, other half

maronita 1 *adj* Maronite
 2 *nmf* Maronite

marote *nm RP Fam* nut, head

marplatense 1 *adj* of/from Mar del Plata *(Argentina)*
 2 *nmf* person from Mar del Plata *(Argentina)*

marqués, -esa *nm,f* marquis, *f* marchioness

marquesado *nm* marquisate

marquesina *nf (cubierta)* canopy; *(en parada de autobús, estación de tren)* shelter

marquetería *nf* marquetry

marrajo *nm (tiburón)* porbeagle

marramuncia *nf Ven Fam* dirty trick

marramunciero, -a *nm,f Ven Fam* swindler

marranada, marranería *nf Fam* (**a**) *(porquería)* filthy thing; **esa camisa es una m.** that shirt is filthy (**b**) *(obscenidad)* filthy thing; **estaban haciendo marranadas sentados en un banco** they were sitting on a bench doing filthy things (**c**) *(mala jugada)* dirty trick; **le hicieron la m. de no dejarle ir a la fiesta** they very nastily refused to let him go to the party

marrano, -a 1 *adj Fam* (**a**) *(sucio)* filthy (**b**) *(malintencionado)* mean
 2 *nm,f* (**a**) *(animal)* pig, *f* sow (**b**) *Fam (sucio)* dirty *o* filthy pig (**c**) *Fam (persona malintencionada)* pig, swine (**d**) *Hist* = Jewish convert to Christianity (**e**) EXPR *Esp Vulg* **joder la marrana** to fuck everything up

marrar 1 *vt (disparo)* to miss; **el delantero marró el gol** the forward failed to convert the chance
 2 *vi* (**a**) *(fallar)* to fail; *(disparo)* to miss (**b**) *(desviarse)* to go astray *o* wrong

marras: de marras *loc adj Fam* **el perrito de m.** that blasted dog; **el problema de m.** the same old problem; **negó ser el autor de la llamada de m.** he denied having made the famous call

marrasquino *nm (licor)* maraschino

marro, -a 1 *adj Méx Fam* tight-fisted
 2 *nm* (**a**) *(juego)* = children's game where two teams try to touch or catch each other (**b**) *Méx (mazo)* mallet *(with metal head)*; *(más grande)* sledgehammer (**c**) *Méx Fam (avaro)* tightwad

marrón 1 *adj* brown; **m. claro** light brown, tan
 2 *nm* (**a**) *(color)* brown; **el m. es mi color favorito** brown is my favourite colour
 (**b**) ***m. glacé*** marron glacé
 (**c**) *RP (mazo)* large club *(for killing animals)*
 (**d**) *Ven Fam (café)* = coffee with a dash of milk
 (**e**) *Esp Fam (situación desagradable)* **¡qué m.!** what a pain!; **me cayó el m. de acompañar a mi madre** I was the one who got stuck with having to go with my mother; **el profesor nos metió un m.** we got done by the teacher; EXPR **comerse el m.: me ha tocado a mí comerme el m. de limpiar la casa tras la fiesta** I got lumbered with having to clean the house after the party; EXPR **pillar a alguien de m.** to catch sb in the act

marroquí *(pl* **marroquíes***)* **1** *adj* Moroccan
 2 *nmf* Moroccan

marroquinería *nf* (**a**) *(arte)* leatherwork (**b**) *(artículos)* leather goods

marrubio *nm* common hoarhound

marrueco *nm Chile* fly, zipper

Marruecos *n* Morocco

marrullería *nf (trucos sucios)* underhand dealing; *(juego sucio)* dirty play

marrullero, -a 1 *adj (tramposo)* underhand; *(futbolista)* dirty
 2 *nm,f (tramposo)* cheat; *(futbolista)* dirty player

Marsella *n* Marseille, Marseilles

Marsellesa *nf* **la M.** the Marseillaise

marsopa *nf* porpoise

marsupial 1 *adj* marsupial
 2 *nm* marsupial

marta *nf* (pine) marten ▸▸ ***m. cebellina*** *o* ***cibelina*** sable

martajar *vt CAm, Méx (maíz)* to crush

Marte 1 *nm (planeta)* Mars
 2 *n Mitol* Mars

martes *nm inv* Tuesday; PROV **en m., ni te cases ni te embarques** = proverb recommending that it is best to avoid doing anything important on a Tuesday, traditionally seen as an unlucky day in Spain ▸▸ ***M. de Carnaval*** Shrove Tuesday; ***m. y trece*** ≃ Friday 13th; *ver también* **sábado**

martiano, -a *Am* **1** *adj* = of/relating to Jose Martí, Cuban nationalist hero (1853-95)
 2 *nm,f* = supporter of the ideas of Jose Martí

martillazo *nm* hammer blow; **dale otro m.** hit it again with the hammer; **me di un m. en el dedo** I hit my finger with a hammer; **tuvieron que abrir la hucha a martillazos** they had to smash the moneybox open with a hammer

martillear, martillar 1 *vt* (**a**) *(carpintero)* to hammer (**b**) *(lluvia, ruido)* to pound on; **las gotas le martilleaban la cara** the raindrops were lashing his face
 2 *vi* (**a**) *(con martillo)* to hammer (**b**) *(lluvia, ruido)* to pound; **la lluvia martilleaba en los cristales** the rain was pounding against the windowpanes

martilleo *nm* hammering; **el m. de la lluvia en la ventana** the pounding of the rain against the window

martillero *nm CSur* auctioneer

martillo *nm* (**a**) *(herramienta)* hammer ▸▸ ***m. neumático*** *Br* pneumatic drill, *US* jackhammer; ***m. de oreja*** claw hammer (**b**) *Anat* hammer, *Espec* malleus (**c**) *(en pistola)* hammer (**d**) *(en piano)* hammer (**e**) *Dep* hammer; **lanzamiento de m.** the hammer; **el campeón de (lanzamiento de) m.** the hammer champion

martinete *nm* (**a**) *(máquina)* pile-driver, maul (**b**) *(en piano)* hammer (**c**) *(ave)* night heron

martingala *nf* (**a**) *(artimaña)* trick, ploy (**b**) *RP (cinturón trasero)* back-belt

martini *nm (vermú)* martini; **m. (seco)** *(cóctel)* (dry) martini

Martinica *n* Martinique

martín pescador *nm* kingfisher

mártir *nmf* (**a**) *(persona que muere)* martyr; EXPR **hacerse el m.** to act the martyr (**b**) *(persona que sufre)* saint; **tu madre es una m., con el trabajo que le dais** your mother is a saint to put up with the work you all create for her

martirio *nm* (**a**) *(muerte)* martyrdom (**b**) *(sufrimiento)* trial, torment; **¡qué m. aguantar a este cantante!** it's torture having to listen to this singer!

martirizar [14] **1** *vt* (**a**) *(torturar)* to martyr (**b**) *(hacer sufrir)* to torment, to torture
 2 martirizarse *vpr* to torment *o* torture oneself

martirologio *nm* martyrology

maruca *nf* ling

maruja *nf Esp Fam* typical housewife; **mi hermana está hecha una m.** my sister has become a typical housewife

marujear *vi Esp Fam (hacer tareas domésticas)* to do housework; *(cotillear)* to gossip

marxismo *nm* Marxism

marxismo-leninismo *nm* Marxism-Leninism

marxista 1 *adj* Marxist
2 *nmf* Marxist

marxista-leninista 1 *adj* Marxist-Leninist
2 *nmf* Marxist-Leninist

marzo *nm* March; *ver también* **septiembre**

MAS [mas] *nm* (*abrev de* **Movimiento al Socialismo**) = left-wing political party in Argentina and Venezuela

mas *conj* but

MÁS 1 *adj inv* **(a)** *(comparativo)* more; **m. aire/manzanas** more air/apples; **tener m. hambre** to be hungrier *o* more hungry; **m.... que...** more... than...; **hace m. frío que ayer** it's colder than yesterday; **colócate a m. distancia** stand further away; **ellas eran m. y mejor preparadas** there were more of them and they were better prepared

(b) *(superlativo)* **es el alumno que m. preguntas hace** he's the pupil who asks (the) most questions; **la que m. nota sacó en el examen** the girl who did (the) best *o* got the best marks in the exam; **lo que m. tiempo llevó** the thing that took (the) longest; **lo m. que puede ocurrir/que te pueden decir es...** the worst thing that can happen/that they can say to you is...; **es lo m. que puedo hacer** it's all *o* the most I can do; **compré varios kilos de manzanas, pero las m. (de ellas) estaban malas** I bought several kilos of apples, but most of them were rotten

(c) *(en frases negativas)* any more; **no necesito m. trabajo/libros** I don't need any more work/books; **ya no hay m. leche/peras** there isn't any milk/aren't any pears left, there's no more milk/there are no more pears left; **no tengo m. especias que las que ves ahí** these are all the spices I have, the only spices I have are the ones you can see here; **no te lo diré m. veces** I'm not going to tell you again

(d) *(con pron interrogativos e indefinidos)* else; **¿qué/quién m.?** what/who else?; **¿cuándo/dónde m.?** when/where else?; **te voy a decir algo m.** I'm going to tell you something else; **¿algo m.?** *o* **¿alguna cosa m.? – nada m., gracias** would you like anything else? – no, that's everything, thank you; **todavía falta alguien m.** somebody else is still missing; **¿te vio alguien m.?** did anyone else see you?; **no hay nada/nadie m.,** *Am* **no hay m. nada/nadie** there's nothing/no one else; **¿no quieres nada m.?** don't you want anything else?; **¿nada m. que mil?** as little as a thousand?, only a thousand?; **no queda nadie m. en la sala** there's no one left in the room

(e) *(indica intensidad)* **¡tengo m. hambre!** I'm so *o* really hungry!; **¡me da m. miedo!** it really scares me!

(f) *Fam (mejor)* **éste es m. coche que el mío** this is a better car than mine; **es m. hombre que tú** he's more of a man than you are

2 *adv* **(a)** *(comparativo)* more; **Pepe es m. alto/ambicioso** Pepe is taller/more ambitious; **m. tarde** later; **m. adentro** further in; **m. arriba** higher up; **nos quedaremos un poco m.** we'll stay a bit longer; **ésta me gusta m.** I like this one better *o* more; **m. de** more than; **había m. de mil personas** there were more than *o* over a thousand people there; **eran m. de las diez** it was past *o* gone ten o'clock; **bebió m. de lo normal** he drank more than usual; **nos retrasamos m. de lo esperado** we took longer than expected; **es m. fácil de lo que parece** it's easier than it seems; **m. que** more than; **vas al cine m. que yo** you go to the cinema more (often) than I do; **el vino me gusta m. que la cerveza** I like wine better *o* more than beer; **la inflación subió m. que los salarios** inflation rose by more than salaries; **ésta me gusta m. que las demás** I like this one better *o* more than the others; **m.... que...** more... than...; **Juan es m. alto/ambicioso que tú** Juan is taller/more ambitious than you; **no hay persona m. preparada que él** no one is better qualified than he is; **yo soy liberal como el/la que m., pero...** I'm as liberal as the next man/woman, but...; **el que m. y el que menos** everyone; **el motivo del conflicto es ni m. ni menos que la religión** the cause of the conflict is actually religion; **la catedral se tardó en construir ni m. ni menos que tres siglos** the cathedral took no less than three centuries to build; **apareció ni m. ni menos que el presidente** who should appear but the president?

(b) *(superlativo)* **el/la/lo m.** the most; **el m. listo/ambicioso** the cleverest/most ambitious; **es la m. alta de todos/de la clase** she's the tallest of everyone/in the class; **lo m. bonito que vimos** the most beautiful thing we saw; **el que m. trabaja** the person *o* one who works (the) hardest; **lo que m. me molesta es...** what annoys me most is...; **¿dónde te duele m.?** where does it hurt (the) most?; **no es el m. indicado para criticar** he's hardly in a position to criticize; **a lo m.** *(como mucho)* at the most ►► ***el m. allá*** the great beyond

(c) *(en frases negativas)* **no hice m. que lo que me pediste** I only did what you asked me to; **no nos queda m. que esperar** all we can do is wait; **ya no lo haré m.** I won't do it again; **nunca m.** never again

(d) *(indica suma)* plus; **dos m. dos igual a cuatro** two plus two is four; **tome una pastilla con las comidas m. otra antes de acostarse** take one tablet with meals and another before going to bed

(e) *(indica intensidad)* **no lo aguanto, ¡es m. tonto!** I can't stand him, he's so stupid!; **¡qué día m. lindo!** what a lovely day!; **ser de lo m. divertido** to be incredibly funny; **hoy está de lo m. amable** she's being really nice today; **m. y m.** increasingly; **cada vez es m. y m. difícil** it gets harder and harder, it gets increasingly harder; **ir a m.** to improve

(f) *(indica preferencia)* **m. vale que nos vayamos a casa** it would be better for us to go home; **m. te vale que tengas razón** you'd better be right; **m. que cansado, estoy agotado** I don't feel so much tired as exhausted; **mejor no fumar, m. que nada por los niños** it would be better not to smoke, as much as anything for the sake of the children

(g) *(en frases)* **es m., m. aún** indeed, what is more; **lo que es m.** moreover; **¿qué m. da?** what difference does it make?; **sin m. (ni m.)** just like that; **gritaban/reían a m. y mejor** they were shouting/laughing their heads off

3 más o menos *loc adv (aproximadamente)* more or less; *(regular)* so-so; **deben de ser m. o menos las dos** it must be about two o'clock; **¿te gustó? – m. o menos** did you like it? – well, sort of; **¿qué tal te encuentras? – m. o menos** how are you feeling? – so-so

4 a más de *loc adv (además de)* in addition to, as well as

5 de más *loc adv (en exceso)* too much; *(de sobra)* spare; **me han cobrado 100 pesos de m.** they've charged me 100 pesos too much, they've overcharged me by 100 pesos; **tengo entradas de m. para el estreno** I've got some spare tickets for the première; **eso está de m.** that's not necessary; **sé cuando estoy de m. en un sitio** I know when I'm not wanted; **no estaría de m. llevar un paraguas** it wouldn't be a bad idea *o* it wouldn't harm to take an umbrella

6 más bien *loc adv* rather; **es m. bien caro** it's a bit *o* rather expensive; **m. bien parece que la culpa es de ella** it seems more like she is to blame

7 por más que *loc adv* however much; **por m. que lo intente no lo conseguirá** however much *o* hard she tries, she'll never manage it

8 *pron* any more; **no necesito m.** I don't need any more; **ya no hay m.** there isn't/aren't any left, there is/are no more left

9 *nm inv (signo)* plus (sign); EXPR **tiene sus m. y sus menos** *(pros y contras)* it has its good points and its bad points; **tuvieron sus m. y sus menos** *(diferencias)* they had their differences

masa *nf* **(a)** *(en general)* mass; **las grandes masas de agua de la Tierra** the major expanses of water on the Earth ►► *Meteo* ***m. de aire*** air mass; ***m. atómica*** atomic mass; ***m. crítica*** critical mass; ***m. molecular*** molecular mass; *Econ* ***m. monetaria*** money supply; ***m. salarial*** total wage bill

(b) *(mezcla, pasta)* mixture

(c) *(de pan, bizcocho)* dough

(d) *(multitud)* crowd; **al poco tiempo se formó una m. de curiosos** a crowd of onlookers quickly formed

(e) las masas *(el pueblo)* the masses

(f) en m. en masse; **fabricación** *o* **producción en m.** mass production; **los fusilamientos en m. de disidentes** the mass execution by firing squad of dissidents; **fuimos en m. a escuchar la conferencia** a large group of us went to listen to the lecture; **el pueblo acudió en m. a recibir a los héroes** the town turned out en masse to welcome the heroes

(g) *Fís* mass ►► ***m. específica*** specific mass

(h) *Elec (tierra) Br* earth, *US* ground; **hacer m.** to go to *Br* earth *o US* ground

(i) *RP (pastelito)* cake ►► ***m. seca*** = cookie served with tea or coffee

masacrar *vt* to massacre

masacre *nf* massacre

masai 1 *adj* Masai
2 *nmf* Masai

masaje *nm* massage; **dar un m. a alguien** to give sb a massage ►► ***m. cardíaco*** cardiac massage; ***m. terapéutico*** therapeutic massage

masajear *vt* to massage

masajista *nmf* masseur, *f* masseuse; *(de equipo deportivo)* physio

masato *nm* **(a)** *Andes, CAm, Ven (bebida)* = lightly fermented drink made of maize, rice or wheat flour, cane syrup, orange leaves and cloves **(b)** *Arg, Col (golosina)* = dessert made of coconut, maize and sugar

mascada *nf* **(a)** *CAm, Méx, Ven (de tabaco)* plug **(b)** *CSur (bocado)* mouthful **(c)** *Cuba, Méx (pañuelo)* neckerchief

mascadura *nf Hond (pan, bollo)* roll, bun

mascar [60] **1** *vt* to chew
2 mascarse *vpr Fam* **se masca un golpe de estado** all the signs are that a coup d'état is imminent; **se mascaba la crisis** you could tell that a crisis was imminent

máscara *nf* (**a**) *(en teatro)* mask
(**b**) *(protectora)* mask ▸▸ ***m. antigás*** gas mask; ***m. de oxígeno*** oxygen mask
(**c**) *(de belleza)* face pack
(**d**) *(persona enmascarada)* **vimos muchas máscaras en la fiesta** we saw a lot of people wearing masks at the party; **baile de máscaras** masked ball
(**e**) *(fachada)* mask; **bajo esa m. de felicidad se esconde un alma infeliz** behind that mask *o* outward show of happiness lies an unhappy person; **quitar la m. a alguien** to unmask sb; **quitarse la m.** to reveal oneself
(**f**) *Informát* mask

mascarada *nf* (**a**) *(fiesta)* masquerade (**b**) *(farsa)* farce

mascarilla *nf* (**a**) *(de protección)* mask (**b**) *(de oxígeno)* mask (**c**) *(cosmética)* face pack (**d**) *(vaciado)* = plaster cast of a person's face

mascarón *nm* (**a**) *Arquit* grotesque head (**b**) ***m. de proa*** figurehead

mascota *nf* (**a**) *(emblema)* mascot (**b**) *(animal doméstico)* pet (**c**) *(amuleto)* charm (**d**) *Ven Dep (en béisbol)* baseball glove *o* mitt

masculinidad *nf* masculinity

masculinizarse [14] *vpr* to become mannish

masculino, -a 1 *adj* (**a**) *(género, órgano, población)* male; **un programa dirigido al público m.** a programme aimed at male viewers; **los 100 metros masculinos** the men's 100 metres; **el sexo m.** the male sex (**b**) *(varonil)* manly (**c**) *Bot & Zool* male; **los órganos sexuales masculinos** the male sexual organs (**d**) *Gram* masculine
2 *nm Gram* masculine

mascullar *vt* to mutter

masetero *nm Anat* masseter

masía *nf* = traditional Catalan farmhouse

masificación *nf* overcrowding; **la m. de las universidades** excessive student numbers at universities

masificar [60] 1 *vt (con gente)* to cause overcrowding in; **los turistas masifican los museos** the museums are packed with tourists
2 **masificarse** *vpr (con gente)* to become overcrowded; **las playas se masifican en verano** in summer, the beaches are packed; **las universidades se han masificado** universities have become overcrowded

masilla *nf (para sujetar cristales)* putty; *(para tapar grietas)* filler

masita *nf RP* cake ▸▸ ***m. seca*** = cookie served with tea or coffee

masivo, -a *adj* (**a**) *(en gran cantidad)* mass; **despidos masivos** mass redundancies (**b**) *(con mucha gente)* massive; **una fiesta masiva** an enormous party; **la asistencia masiva a los campos de fútbol** the huge crowds at *US* soccer stadia *o Br* football grounds (**c**) *(dosis)* massive

masoca *Fam* 1 *adj* masochistic
2 *nmf* masochist

masón, -ona 1 *adj* Masonic
2 *nm,f* Mason, Freemason

masonería *nf* Masonry, Freemasonry

masónico, -a *adj* Masonic

masoquismo *nm* masochism

masoquista 1 *adj* masochistic
2 *nmf* masochist

mass media, mass-media ['mas'media] *nmpl* mass media

mastaba *nf Arte* mastaba

mastectomía *nf* mastectomy

mastelerillo *nm Náut* topgallant mast

mastelero *nm Náut* topmast

máster[1] (*pl* **masters**) 1 *nm (título)* Master's (degree); **un m. en lingüística** an MA in linguistics
2 *nmf (alumno)* **es m. en economía por la Universidad de Harvard** she has a Master's (degree) in economics from the University of Harvard

máster[2] (*pl* **masters**) 1 *adj inv* master; **copia m.** master copy
2 *nm (cinta)* master

masters *nm inv Dep* **el m.** the Masters

masticación *nf* chewing, *Espec* mastication

masticar [60] 1 *vt* (**a**) *(mascar)* to chew, *Espec* to masticate (**b**) *(pensar)* to chew over, to ponder (**c**) *(preparar)* **a él no le pongas problemas difíciles, dáselo todo masticado** don't give him any difficult problems, you need to spoon-feed him *o* make everything as easy as possible for him
2 *vi* to chew

mástil *nm* (**a**) *(de barco)* mast; *(de bandera, tienda de campaña)* pole (**b**) *(de guitarra)* neck

mastín *nm* mastiff ▸▸ ***m. del Pirineo*** Pyrenean Mastiff

mástique, mastique *nm Méx, Ven (para sujetar cristales)* putty; *(para tapar grietas)* filler

mastitis *nf inv Med* mastitis

mastodonte 1 *nm* mastodon
2 *nmf Fam* giant

mastodóntico, -a *adj Fam* mammoth, ginormous

mastoides *Anat* 1 *adj inv* mastoid
2 *nm inv* mastoid

mastranzo *nm* apple mint

mastuerzo 1 *adj Fam* oafish
2 *nm* (**a**) *Fam (idiota)* oaf (**b**) *(planta)* watercress

masturbación *nf* masturbation

masturbar 1 *vt* to masturbate
2 **masturbarse** *vpr* to masturbate

mata *nf* (**a**) *(arbusto)* bush, shrub; **matas** scrub (**b**) *(matojo) (de hierba)* tuft; **una m. de tomates** a bunch of tomatoes; **una m. de perejil** a sprig of parsley (**c**) **m. de pelo** mop (of hair)

mataburros *nm inv RP Fam Hum (diccionario)* dictionary

matacán *nm Ecuad (cervato)* fawn

matacandil *nm* London rocket

matachín *nm Fam* (**a**) *(matarife)* slaughterman (**b**) *(bravucón)* bully-boy

matadero *nm* abattoir, slaughterhouse

matado, -a *Fam* 1 *adj (agotado)* shattered
2 *nm,f Esp (desgraciado)* poor wretch

matador, -ora 1 *adj Fam* (**a**) *(cansado)* exhausting; **esta tarea es matadora** this job is a killer; **aguantar a su madre es m.** it's murder putting up with his mother (**b**) *(feo, de mal gusto)* awful, horrendous; **esos zapatos te quedan matadores** those shoes look awful on you
2 *nm Taurom* matador

matadura *nf (de animal)* sore, gall

matagigantes *nm inv Dep* giant killer

matalahúva *nf* anise

matalotaje *nm Náut* ship's stores

matambre *nm Andes, RP* (**a**) *(carne)* flank *o Br* skirt steak (**b**) *(plato)* = flank steak rolled with boiled egg, olives and red pepper, which is cooked, then sliced and served cold

matamoscas *nm inv* (**a**) *(pala)* flyswat (**b**) *(espray)* flyspray

matanza *nf* (**a**) *(masacre)* slaughter (**b**) *(de cerdo) (acción)* slaughtering (**c**) *Esp (de cerdo) (productos)* = pork products from a farm-slaughtered pig

mataperrada *nf Perú Fam* prank; **hacer mataperradas** to play pranks, to get up to mischief

mataperro, -a *nm,f Perú Fam (diablillo)* little rascal; *(niño de la calle)* street urchin

matapolillas *nm inv* moth killer

MATAR 1 *vt* (**a**) *(quitar la vida a)* to kill; *(animal) (para consumo)* to slaughter; **lo mató un rayo** he was struck by lightning and killed; **lo mató un tren** he died after being hit by a train; **lo mató de una puñalada/de un tiro en el corazón** she killed him with a single stab/shot to the heart; **en este comedor nos matan de hambre** the portions are terribly small in this canteen; **lo mataron a puñaladas** they stabbed him to death, he was stabbed to death; **lo mataron a tiros** they shot him (dead), he was shot (dead); **el alcohol la está matando** alcohol is killing her; *Fam Fig* **como descubra al responsable, lo mato** if I find out who's responsible I'll kill him; *Fam Fig* **si se entera me mata** she'll kill me if she finds out; *Fam Fig* **es para matarte que no sepas eso** you ought to be ashamed of yourself not knowing a thing like that; EXPR **m. dos pájaros de un tiro** to kill two birds with one stone; EXPR **estar** *o* **llevarse a m. (con alguien)** to be at daggers drawn (with sb); EXPR *Fam* **matarlas callando** *(tramar algo)* to be up to something on the quiet; *(obrar con hipocresía)* to be a wolf in sheep's clothing; EXPR *Fam* **que me maten si: que me maten si lo entiendo** I'm damned if I can understand it; **que me maten si no ocurrió así** I swear to God that's what happened
(**b**) *(hacer sufrir, molestar mucho)* **¡me vais a m. a disgustos!** you'll be the death of me!; **¡este calor/dolor me mata!** the heat/pain is killing me!; **¡estos zapatos me están matando!** these shoes are killing me!; **me matas con esas tonterías que dices** you're driving me mad with all the nonsense you talk!
(**c**) *(apagar, hacer pasar) (color)* to tone down; *(sed)* to quench; *(fuego)*

to put out; *(cal)* to slake; **mato las horas** *o* **el tiempo viendo la televisión** I kill time watching television; **tomaré unas galletas para m. el hambre** *o* **el gusanillo** I'll have some *Br* biscuits *o Am* cookies to keep me going

(**d**) *(redondear, limar)* to round (off)

(**e**) *(en juegos) (carta)* to beat, to top; *(ficha, pieza de ajedrez)* to take, to capture

(**f**) *Fam (destrozar, estropear)* to ruin; **no quisiera m. sus ilusiones** I don't want to dash your hopes; **el salón es bonito, pero ese cuadro lo mata** the living-room is nice, but that picture totally ruins it

2 *vi* to kill; **no matarás** *(mandamiento)* thou shalt not kill; EXPR **hay amores que matan** you can love somebody too much; EXPR **hay miradas que matan** if looks could kill; EXPR *RP Fam* **que mata: tiene un olor que mata** it smells disgusting; **con esa mini quedás que matás** you look drop-dead gorgeous in that miniskirt

3 matarse *vpr* (**a**) *(morir)* to die; **se mató en un accidente de coche** he was killed in a car accident; **por poco me mato bajando las escaleras** I nearly killed myself going down the stairs

(**b**) *(suicidarse)* to kill oneself

(**c**) *Fam (esforzarse)* **matarse trabajando,** *Esp* **matarse a trabajar** to work oneself to death; **no te mates estudiando,** *Esp* **no te mates a estudiar** don't wear yourself out studying; **matarse por hacer/conseguir algo** to kill oneself in order to do/get sth

(**d**) *Fam (desentonar)* to clash; **esos dos colores se matan** those two colours clash

---

matarife *nm* slaughterman

matarratas *nm inv* (**a**) *(veneno)* rat poison (**b**) *Fam (bebida)* rotgut

matasanos *nmf inv Fam Pey* quack

matasellado *nm* postmarking, franking

matasellar *vt* to postmark, to frank

matasellos *nm inv* (**a**) *(sello)* stamp *(for postmarking)* (**b**) *(marca)* postmark

matasuegras *nm inv* party blower

matazón *nf CAm, Col, Ven Fam* massacre

match [matʃ] *(pl* **matchs** *o* **matches**) *nm* match

match-ball ['matʃβol] *(pl* **match-balls**) *nm Dep* match point

match-play ['matʃplei] *(pl* **match-plays**) *nm Dep* match play

mate 1 *adj* matt

2 *nm* (**a**) *(en ajedrez)* mate, checkmate

(**b**) *(en baloncesto)* dunk

(**c**) *(en tenis)* smash

(**d**) *(planta)* yerba maté

(**e**) *Andes (té)* herbal tea, herbal infusion ►► ***m. de coca*** coca leaf tea; ***m. de manzanilla*** camomile tea; ***m. de menta*** peppermint tea

(**f**) *CSur (infusión)* maté; EXPR *Fam* **itomá m.!** *Br* get that!, *US* how do you like them apples? ►► ***m. cocido*** = maté drunk from a teacup

(**g**) *CSur (calabaza) (con semillas)* gourd *(used as ornament or type of maraca)*; *(para beber)* maté gourd

(**h**) *CSur Fam (cabeza)* nut; **estar (mal) del m.** to be nuts

mateada *nf CSur* maté drinking session

matear *vi CSur* to drink maté

matelassé [matela'se] *nm RP* = quilted fabric for making bedspreads

matemática *nf,* **matemáticas** *nfpl* mathematics *(singular)* ►► ***matemáticas aplicadas*** applied mathematics; ***matemáticas puras*** pure mathematics

matemáticamente *adv* mathematically

matemáticas = **matemática**

matemático, -a 1 *adj* (**a**) *(de la matemática)* mathematical (**b**) *(exacto)* mathematical (**c**) *Fam (infalible)* **es m.** it's like clockwork, it never fails

2 *nm,f (científico)* mathematician

Mateo *n pr* **San M.** St Matthew

matera *nf* (**a**) *(bolsa) Urug* = leather shoulder bag used to hold a maté gourd, maté and a vacuum flask (**b**) *ver también* **matero**

materia *nf* (**a**) *(sustancia)* matter ►► *Anat* ***m. gris*** grey matter; ***m. orgánica*** organic matter; *Astron* ***m. oscura*** dark matter

(**b**) *(asunto)* matter; **m. de reflexión** food for thought; **en m. de** on the subject of, concerning; **un especialista en m. de higiene** a hygiene expert; **han llegado a un acuerdo en m. de impuestos** they have come to an agreement on *o* concerning taxation; **la legislación en m. de medio ambiente** the legislation on the subject of *o* concerning the environment; EXPR **entrar en m.** to get down to business

(**c**) *(material)* material ►► ***m. prima*** raw material

(**d**) *(asignatura)* subject ►► *RP Univ* ***m. previa*** = module that has to be passed in order to do a more advanced module

material 1 *adj* (**a**) *(físico)* physical; *(consecuencias)* material; **los daños materiales fueron cuantiosos** the physical damage *o* damage to property was considerable; **el objeto robado no tenía ningún valor m.** the stolen object had no material *o* financial value

(**b**) *(real)* real, actual; **el autor m. del asesinato** the person actually responsible for carrying out the murder; **no hay tiempo m. para discutir el problema** there's simply no time to discuss the problem

2 *nm* (**a**) *(sustancia)* material ►► ***m. de desecho*** waste material; ***m. genético*** genetic material; ***m. refractario*** heat-resistant *o* fireproof material

(**b**) *(datos, información)* material; **no hay suficiente m. como para escribir una novela** there isn't enough material to write a novel

(**c**) *(instrumentos)* equipment ►► ***m. audiovisual*** audiovisual equipment and material; ***m. bélico*** military equipment; ***materiales de construcción*** building materials; ***m. deportivo*** sports equipment, ***m. didáctico*** teaching materials; ***m. escolar*** school materials; ***m. fotográfico*** photographic equipment; ***m. fungible*** *(desechable)* disposable materials; *Informát (cartuchos, disquetes)* consumables; ***m. de guerra*** war material; ***m. de laboratorio*** laboratory materials; ***m. de oficina*** office stationery

(**d**) *Esp Fam (droga)* gear, merchandise

(**e**) *RP* **de m.** *(de obra)* built of brick, brick-built; **una casa de m.** a house built of brick, a brick-built house

materialismo *nm* materialism ►► ***m. dialéctico*** dialectical materialism; ***m. histórico*** historical materialism

materialista[1] **1** *adj* materialistic

2 *nmf* materialist

materialista[2] *Méx, Ven* **1** *adj (de la construcción)* **camión m.** builder's truck *o Br* lorry

2 *nmf* (**a**) *(comerciante)* builder's merchant (**b**) *(camionero)* truck *o Br* lorry driver

3 *nm (camión)* builder's truck *o Br* lorry

materialización *nf (de proyecto, acuerdo)* implementation; **este viaje supone la m. de sus sueños** this journey is a dream come true for her

materializar [14] **1** *vt* (**a**) *(idea, proyecto)* to realize; **con ese proyecto materializó sus deseos** this project enabled him to fulfil his wishes (**b**) *(hacer aparecer)* to produce

2 materializarse *vpr* (**a**) *(idea, proyecto)* to materialize; **al final la propuesta no se materializó en un proyecto** in the end the proposal never made it to the project stage (**b**) *(aparecer)* to appear (**c**) *(volverse materialista)* to become materialistic

materialmente *adv* **el país quedó m. destrozado** the country was totally devastated; **nos será m. imposible llegar a tiempo** it will be physically impossible for us to get there in time; **m., vivíamos mucho mejor antes** from a material point of view, we used to live much better

maternal *adj* motherly, maternal

maternidad *nf* (**a**) *(cualidad)* motherhood ►► ***m. subrogada*** surrogate motherhood, surrogacy (**b**) *(hospital)* maternity hospital; *(sección)* maternity ward

maternizado, -a *adj* **leche maternizada** *Br* baby milk, *US* formula

materno, -a *adj* **leche materna** mother's milk; **apellido m.** = second surname; **lengua materna** mother tongue; **mi abuela por parte materna** my maternal grandmother, my grandmother on my mother's side

matero[1]**, -a** *CSur* **1** *adj* fond of maté

2 *nm,f* maté drinker

matero[2] *nm Ven (maceta)* flowerpot

mates *nfpl Fam Br* maths, *US* math

matete *nm RP Fam* muddle; **con tantos números me armo un m.** I get into a muddle with all these figures; **tengo un m. en la cabeza** my head's spinning

matico *nm* matico

matinal 1 *adj* morning; **sesión m.** *(de cine)* morning showing

2 *nf* morning showing

matinée, matiné *nf (por la mañana)* morning showing; *RP (por la tarde)* matinée

matiz *nm* (**a**) *(de color)* shade

(**b**) *(rasgo)* **una revolución con m. anarquista** a revolution with anarchist characteristics; **un conflicto que ha adquirido matices de guerra abierta** a conflict which is beginning to look like open warfare; **sus palabras tienen un m. irónico** his words are tinged with irony

(**c**) *(diferencia)* subtle difference; **se parecen en mucho, con algunos matices importantes** they are very similar, although they have a few important if subtle differences; **expresó su apoyo sin matices a la intervención militar** he expressed his unqualified *o* unconditional support for military intervention

matización *nf* (**a**) *(de colores)* blending (**b**) *(puntualización)* clarification, explanation; **me gustaría hacer una m.** I'd like to clarify something

matizar [14] *vt* (**a**) *(mezclar) (colores)* to blend
(**b**) *(teñir)* to tinge; **matizó de sarcasmo su discurso** his speech was tinged with sarcasm
(**c**) *(puntualizar)* to clarify, to explain; **quisiera m. unos aspectos de mi propuesta** I'd like to clarify a few points in my proposal, I'd like to explain a few points in my proposal in more detail; **matizó que no todo habían sido éxitos** he pointed out that it hadn't been an unqualified success story; **"acataré la ley," matizó, "aunque no esté de acuerdo con ella"** "I shall obey the law," he explained, "even though I don't agree with it"

mato *nm Ven* ameiva lizard, jungle runner

matojo *nm (mata)* tuft; *(arbusto)* bush, shrub

matón, -ona *nm,f Fam* (**a**) *(persona agresiva)* thug, bully (**b**) *(guardaespaldas)* heavy

matonismo *nm* bullying

matorral *nm* (**a**) *(conjunto de matas)* thicket (**b**) *(terreno)* scrubland, brush

matraca 1 *nf* (**a**) *(instrumento)* rattle; EXPR *Fam* **dar la m.** *(molestar)* to be a pain; **dar la m. con algo** to go on about sth; **¡deja ya de dar la m.!** stop being such a pain!; **nos da la m. con la guitarra todos los días** he plagues us with his guitar-playing every day (**b**) *Am Fam (metralleta)* machine-gun (**c**) *Ven Fam (soborno)* bribe, *Br* backhander (**d**) *Ven Fam (carro)* old crock, *Br* old banger
2 *nmf Fam (persona)* pain
3 matracas *nfpl Fam (matemáticas) Br* maths, *US* math

matraquear *vi Fam* (**a**) *(hacer ruido)* to rattle (**b**) *(molestar)* to be a pain; **¡deja de m., no te voy a prestar el dinero!** stop going on about it, I'm not going to lend you the money! (**c**) *Ven (recibir sobornos)* to receive bribes *o Br* backhanders

matraqueo *nm Ven Fam* **se dedica al m.** he accepts bribes

matraquero, -a *Ven Fam* **1** *adj* on the take, *Br* bent; **un policía m.** a bad *o Br* bent cop
2 *nm,f* **ser un m.** to be on the take *o Br* bent

matraz *nm* flask

matrero, -a *nm,f Andes, RP (fugitivo)* outlaw

matriarca *nf* matriarch

matriarcado *nm* matriarchy

matricaria *nf* feverfew

matriarcal *adj* matriarchal

matricial *adj* (**a**) *Informát (impresora)* dot matrix (**b**) *Mat* matrix, done with a matrix

matricida 1 *adj* matricidal
2 *nmf* matricide

matricidio *nm* matricide

matrícula *nf* (**a**) *(inscripción)* enrolment, registration; **el plazo de m. se abre la próxima semana** enrolment *o* registration starts next week; **tengo que hacer la m. para dos cursos** I have to enrol in *o* register for two courses
(**b**) *(importe)* enrolment *o* registration fee
(**c**) *(documento)* registration document
(**d**) *(personas matriculadas)* number of students, roll
(**e**) *Univ* ***m. de honor*** = distinction which exempts the student from the fees for a course in the following year
(**f**) *(de vehículo) Br* number plate, *US* license plate; **un vehículo con m. extranjera** a vehicle with a foreign *Br* number plate *o US* license plate
(**g**) *(de barco)* registration (document); **un barco con m. de Liberia** a ship registered in Liberia

matriculación *nf (inscripción)* registration

matricular 1 *vt* (**a**) *(alumno)* to register, to enrol (**b**) *(vehículo)* to register (**c**) *(barco)* to register
2 matricularse *vpr* to register, to enrol; **me he matriculado en cinco asignaturas** I've registered for five subjects

matrimonial *adj* marital; **vida m.** married life; **enlace m.** marriage

matrimoniar 1 *vi* to marry, to get married
2 matrimoniarse *vpr* to marry, to get married

matrimonio *nm* (**a**) *(institución)* marriage; **consumar el m.** to consummate one's marriage; **contraer m.** to get married; **fuera del m.** out of wedlock; **cama de m.** double bed ►► ***m. civil*** civil wedding; ***m. de conveniencia*** marriage of convenience; ***m. religioso*** church wedding (**b**) *(pareja)* married couple (**c**) *Andes, Carib (boda)* wedding

matrioska *nf* Russian doll

matriz 1 *nf* (**a**) *Anat* womb, *Espec* uterus (**b**) *(molde)* mould (**c**) *Imprenta (espacio)* character (**d**) *(de talonario)* (cheque) stub (**e**) *Informát* matrix ►► ***m. activa*** active matrix (**f**) *Mat* matrix (**g**) *(empresa)* parent company
2 *adj (empresa)* parent; **casa m.** head office

matrona *nf* (**a**) *(madre)* matron (**b**) *(comadrona)* midwife

matufia *nf RP Fam* shady deal

matungo *nm RP Fam* old nag

maturranguero, -a *adj Cuba* tricky, cajoling

Matusalén *n pr* Methuselah; EXPR **ser más viejo que M.** to be as old as Methuselah

matusalén *nm Fam* ancient person; **ser un m.** to be ancient

matute: de matute *Fam* **1** *loc adv (clandestinamente)* on the quiet; **viajó de m.** he travelled without paying
2 *loc adj (de contrabando)* smuggled, contraband; **tabaco de m.** contraband tobacco

matutino, -a *adj* morning; **paseo m.** morning walk

matzá *nm o nf* matzo(h)

maul [mol] (*pl* **mauls**) *nm (en rugby)* maul

maula *Fam* **1** *adj* (**a**) *(inútil)* useless (**b**) *RP (cobarde)* yellow, chicken
2 *nmf* (**a**) *(inútil)* good-for-nothing (**b**) *(estafador)* swindler
3 *nf (cosa inútil)* piece of junk, useless thing

maulear *vi Chile* to cheat

maullar *vi* to miaow

maullido *nm* miaow; **se oían los maullidos de un gato** a cat could be heard miaowing

Mauricio *n* Mauritius

Mauritania *n* Mauritania

mauritano, -a 1 *adj* Mauritanian
2 *nm,f* Mauritanian

máuser (*pl* **máuseres** *o* **máusers**) *nm* Mauser

mausoleo *nm* mausoleum

maxi- *pref* maxi-

maxifalda *nf* maxi, maxiskirt

maxilar 1 *adj* maxillary; **hueso m.** jawbone
2 *nm* jaw ►► ***m. inferior*** lower jaw, *Espec* mandible; ***m. superior*** upper jaw, *Espec* maxilla

maxilofacial *adj Med* facial, *Espec* maxillofacial

máxima *nf* (**a**) *(sentencia)* maxim (**b**) *(principio)* maxim (**c**) *(temperatura)* high, highest temperature; **una m. de veinte grados** a high of twenty degrees; **ayer se midieron veinte grados de m.** the highest temperature recorded yesterday was twenty degrees, there was a high of twenty degrees yesterday

maximalismo *nm* maximalism

maximalista 1 *adj* maximalist
2 *nmf* maximalist

máxime *adv* especially; **deberías visitarla, m. cuando sabes que está enferma** you should visit her, especially as you know she's ill; **hay que ahorrar, m. ahora que no ganamos mucho dinero** we have to save, especially now we're not earning much money

maximizar *vt* to maximize

máximo, -a 1 *superlativo ver* **grande**
2 *adj (capacidad, cantidad, temperatura)* maximum; *(honor, galardón)* highest; **la máxima puntuación** *(posible)* the maximum score; *(entre varias)* the highest score; **el m. goleador** the top scorer; **soy el m. responsable del proyecto** I am the most senior person on the project; **los máximos responsables políticos del partido** the party's senior politicians ►► *Mat* ***m. común denominador*** highest common denominator; *Mat* ***m. común divisor*** highest common factor
3 *nm* maximum; **trabajan un m. de 35 horas** they work a maximum of 35 hours; **al m.** to the utmost; **llegar al m.** to reach the limit; **pon la calefacción al m.** put the heating on maximum *o* as high as it will go; **están trabajando al m.** they're working flat out; **la libra alcanzó un m. histórico frente al dólar** the pound reached an all-time high against the dollar
4 como máximo *loc adv (a más tardar)* at the latest; *(como mucho)*

at the most; **llegaremos como m. a las seis** we'll be there by six at the latest; **podemos gastar como m. cinco millones** we can spend up to a maximum of five million

maxisingle [maksi'singel] (*pl* **maxisingles**) *nm* twelve-inch (single)

maxwell ['masɣwel] (*pl* **maxwells**) *nm Fís* maxwell

may. (*abrev de* **mayo**) May

maya 1 *adj* Mayan
2 *nmf (persona)* Maya, Mayan; **los mayas** the Maya, the Mayans
3 *nm (lengua)* Maya

mayate *nm* (**a**) *(escarabajo)* = black-winged beetle (**b**) *Méx Fam Pey (homosexual) Br* poof, *US* fag

mayativo, -a *adj Méx Fam* garish

mayestático, -a *adj* majestic; **el plural m.** the royal we

mayo 1 *nm* May ►► *Hist* ***el m. francés*** the Paris spring; *ver también* **septiembre**
2 *nf Méx, RP Fam (mayonesa)* mayo

mayólica *nf* majolica ware

mayonesa *nf* mayonnaise

MAYOR 1 *adj* (**a**) *(comparativo) (en tamaño)* bigger (**que** than); *(en edad)* older (**que** than); *(en importancia)* greater (**que** than); *(en número)* higher (**que** than); **este puente es m. que el otro** this bridge is bigger than the other one; **mi hermana m.** my older sister; **es ocho años m. que yo** she's eight years older than me; **un m. número de víctimas** a higher number of victims; **una m. tasa de inflación** a higher rate of inflation; **en m. o menor grado** to a greater or lesser extent; **no creo que tenga m. interés** I don't think it's particularly interesting; **no te preocupes, no tiene m. importancia** don't worry, it's not (all) that important; **apartamentos mayores de 100 metros cuadrados** *Br* flats *o US* apartments of over 100 square metres; **subsidios para parados mayores de cuarenta y cinco años** benefits for unemployed people (of) over forty-five; **la m. parte de** most of, the majority of; **la m. parte de los británicos piensa que...** most British people *o* the majority of British people think that...; *Mat* **m. que** greater than
(**b**) *(superlativo)* **el/la m....** *(en tamaño)* the biggest...; *(en edad)* the oldest...; *(en importancia)* the greatest...; *(en número)* the highest...; **la m. de las islas** the biggest island, the biggest of the islands; **la m. crisis que se recuerda** the biggest crisis in living memory; **el m. de todos nosotros/de la clase** the oldest of all of us/in the class; **el m. de los dos hermanos** the older of the two brothers; **vive en la m. de las pobrezas** he lives in the most abject poverty
(**c**) *(más)* further, more; **para m. información solicite nuestro catálogo** for further *o* more details, send for our catalogue
(**d**) *(adulto)* grown-up; **cuando sea m.** when I grow up; **hacerse m.** to grow up; **ser m. de edad** to be an adult
(**e**) *(no joven)* older; *(anciano)* elderly; **una mujer ya m.** an older woman; **ser muy m.** to be very old; **hay que escuchar a las personas mayores** you should listen to older people; **la gente m., las personas mayores** *(los ancianos)* the elderly
(**f**) *(principal)* major, main; **la plaza m.** the main square; **la calle m.** the main street; **el palo m.** the main mast
(**g**) *Mús* major; **en do m.** in C major
(**h**) *Com* **al por m.** wholesale; **un almacén de venta al por m.** a wholesaler's
2 *nmf* **el/la m.** *(hijo, hermano)* the eldest; **mayores** *(adultos)* grown-ups; *(antepasados)* ancestors, forefathers; **es una película/revista para mayores** it's an adult movie/magazine; **respeta a tus mayores** you should respect your elders; EXPR **llegar** *o* **pasar a mayores: la cosa no llegó** *o* **pasó a mayores** the matter didn't go any further
3 *nm Mil* major

mayoral *nm* (**a**) *(capataz)* foreman, overseer (**b**) *(pastor)* chief herdsman (**c**) *Hist (cochero)* coachman

mayorazgo *nm Hist* (**a**) *(institución)* primogeniture (**b**) *(bienes)* entailed estate (**c**) *(persona)* = heir to an entailed estate

mayordomo *nm* butler

mayoreo *nm Am* wholesale; **vender algo al m.** to sell sth wholesale; **venta al m.** wholesale

mayoría *nf* (**a**) *(mayor parte)* majority; **la m. de** most of, the majority of; **la m. de los españoles** most Spaniards, the majority of Spaniards; **la m. de las veces** usually, most often; **en su m.** in the main ►► ***m. absoluta*** absolute majority; ***m. cualificada*** qualified majority; ***m. relativa*** *Br* relative majority, *US* plurality; ***m. silenciosa*** silent majority; ***m. simple*** simple majority
(**b**) *(edad adulta)* ***m. de edad*** (age of) majority; **llegar a la m. de edad** to come of age; **la m. de edad democrática del país** the country's democratic coming of age

mayorista 1 *adj* wholesale
2 *nmf* wholesaler

mayoritariamente *adv* (**a**) *(con mayoría)* **se acordó m. declarar una huelga** a majority decision was taken to go on strike; **la reforma fue aprobada m.** the reform was approved by a majority (**b**) *(principalmente)* mainly; **un barrio m. residencial** a mainly residential area; **financiado con capital m. público** financed mainly with public funds

mayoritario, -a *adj* majority; **decisión mayoritaria** majority decision; **el partido m. formará gobierno** the party with a majority will form a government

mayormente *adv* (**a**) *(especialmente)* mainly; **lo que m. me molesta es su actitud** the main thing that annoys me is his attitude; **ritmos m. latinos** mainly Latin rhythms (**b**) *Fam (mucho)* particularly; **no me importa m.** I'm not (all) that bothered *o* particularly bothered

mayúscula *nf* capital letter, upper-case letter; **en mayúsculas** in capitals *o* capital letters, in upper case; **se escribe con m.** it's written with a capital letter ►► ***mayúsculas fijas*** *(en teclado)* caps lock

mayúsculo, -a *adj* (**a**) *(letra)* **letra mayúscula** capital letter, upper-case letter (**b**) *(grande)* terrible; **nos dieron un disgusto m.** they upset us terribly, they really upset us; **cometió un error m.** he made a terrible mistake; **mi sorpresa fue mayúscula al encontrarte allí** I was amazed to see you there

maza *nf* (**a**) *(arma)* mace (**b**) *(de bombo)* drumstick (**c**) *(en gimnasia)* club (**d**) *Chile (de rueda)* hub

mazacote *nm Fam* (**a**) *(plato)* **el arroz era un auténtico m.** the rice had stuck together (**b**) *(objeto, edificio)* eyesore; **están construyendo un m. de viviendas** they're building a housing development that's going to be a complete eyesore *o* a blot on the landscape

mazamorra *nf* (**a**) *Perú (gachas) Br* maize porridge, *US* cornmeal mush (**b**) *Carib (bebida)* = drink made from a maize mixture, sugar and spices (**c**) *RP (maíz blanco)* = maize mixture used in the preparation of stews

mazapán *nm* marzipan

mazazo *nm* (**a**) *(golpe con mazo)* blow *(with a mallet)*; **me di un m. en el dedo** I banged my finger with a mallet (**b**) *(golpe emocional)* real blow; **su muerte fue un m.** her death was a real blow

mazdeísmo *nm Hist* Mazdaism, Mazdeism

mazmorra *nf* dungeon

mazo 1 *nm* (**a**) *(martillo)* mallet (**b**) *(de mortero)* pestle (**c**) *(conjunto) (de cartas, papeles)* bundle; *(de billetes)* wad (**d**) *(de naipes)* pack; EXPR *RP Fam* **irse al m.** to pull out (**e**) *Esp Fam (mucho)* **mola un m.** it's dead cool; **tuve que leer a m.** I had to read piles of stuff
2 *adv Esp Fam* **mola m.** it's dead cool

mazorca *nf* cob; **m. de maíz** corncob, *Br* ear of maize

mazurca *nf Mús* mazurka

MB *Informát* (*abrev de* **megabyte**) MB

MBA *nm* (*abrev de* **Master of Business Administration**) MBA

mbar *nm (unidad)* mb

MBps *Informát* (*abrev de* **megabytes por segundo**) MBps

Mbps *Informát* (*abrev de* **megabits por segundo**) Mbps

mburucuyá *nm RP* blue *o* common passionflower

MCA *nm* (*abrev de* **Mercado Común Andino**) Andean Common Market

MCCA *nm* (*abrev de* **Mercado Común Centroamericano**) CACM, Central American Common Market

mdd *Méx* (*abrev de* **millones de dólares**) million dollars; **800 m.** 800 million dollars

ME *pron personal* (**a**) *(complemento directo)* me; **le gustaría verme** she'd like to see me; **me atracaron en plena calle** I was attacked in the middle of the street; **me han aprobado** I've passed
(**b**) *(complemento indirecto)* (to) me; **me lo dio** he gave it to me, he gave me it; **me tiene miedo** he's afraid of me; **me lo compró** *(yo se lo vendí)* she bought it from *o* off me; *(es para mí)* she bought it for me; **¿me sujetas esto?** will you hold this for me?; **me extrajeron sangre** they took some of my blood; **me han quitado el bolso** they've stolen my bag; **me mancharon el traje** they stained my suit; **me pegaron un empujón** someone pushed me, I was pushed; **se me cayó** I dropped it; **no me resulta agradable hacer esto** it's not very pleasant for me to have to do this; **me será de gran ayuda** it will be a great help to me
(**c**) *(reflexivo)* myself; **me visto** I get dressed; **me serví un whisky** I poured myself a whisky; **me puse la falda** I put my skirt on; **me acosté**

en el sofá I lay down on the sofa; **me rompí una pierna** I broke a leg; **me he arreglado estos pantalones** *(yo mismo)* I've mended these trousers; *(en modista, sastre)* I've had these trousers mended

(**d**) *(con valor intensivo o expresivo)* **ino me lo creo!** I can't believe it!; **me espero lo peor** I'm expecting the worst; **me lo comí todo** I ate the whole lot; **no te me eches a llorar ahora** don't start crying on me now; **se me ha estropeado la lavadora** the washing machine has gone and got broken; **yo sé lo que me digo** I know what I'm talking about

(**e**) *(para formar verbos pronominales)* **me refiero a ti** I'm referring to you; **yo me abstengo** I abstain

---

mea culpa *nm* mea culpa; **¿quién ha apagado la luz? – m.** who switched the light off? – mea culpa; **entono el m.** mea culpa, I acknowledge I have made a mistake

meada *nf Fam* (**a**) *(acción, orina)* piss, pee; **echar una m.** to have a piss *o* pee (**b**) *(mancha)* piss *o* pee stain

meadero *nm Fam Br* bog, *US* john

meado *nm Fam* piss, pee

meandro *nm* meander

meapilas *nmf inv Fam Pey* holy Joe

mear *Fam* **1** *vt* to piss, to pee

2 *vi* to piss

3 mearse *vpr* (**a**) *(orinar)* to piss oneself; **mearse en la cama** to wet one's bed; **el niño se ha meado encima** the child has wet himself; EXPR **estás meando fuera del tiesto** you've got hold of the wrong end of the stick; EXPR *RP muy Fam* **estás meando afuera del tarro** you've got hold of the wrong end of the *Br* bloody *o US* goddamn stick

(**b**) **mearse (de risa)** *(desternillarse)* to piss oneself laughing; **yo con tu hermano me meo** I think your brother's a scream; **la película fue de mearse** we nearly wet ourselves laughing in the movie

(**c**) *Dep* **se meó a varios contrarios** he weaved his way past several defenders

meato *nm Anat* meatus ▸▸ ***m. auditivo*** auditory meatus; ***m. urinario*** urinary meatus

MEC [mek] *nm (abrev de* **Ministerio de Educación y Ciencia**) = Spanish ministry of education and science

meca *nf* (**a**) *(centro)* mecca; **la m. del arte abstracto** the mecca for abstract art; **la m. del cine** Hollywood (**b**) **La M.** *(ciudad)* Mecca (**c**) *Chile Fam Euf (excremento)* dung

mecachis *interj Fam Euf (expresando enfado) Br* sugar!, *US* shoot!; *(expresando sorpresa)* my God!, wow!; EXPR *Esp* **im. en la mar!** *Br* sugar!, *US* shoot!

mecánica *nf* (**a**) *(ciencia)* mechanics *(singular)* ▸▸ ***m. cuántica*** quantum mechanics *(singular)* (**b**) *(mecanismo)* mechanics; **la m. del motor es muy sencilla** the mechanics of the engine are very simple (**c**) *Fam (funcionamiento)* mechanics; **conoce a fondo la m. de la oficina** he knows everything about how the office works (**d**) *ver también* **mecánico**

mecánicamente *adv* (**a**) *(automáticamente)* mechanically (**b**) *(con la mecánica)* mechanically

mecanicismo *nm* mechanism

mecanicista **1** *adj* mechanistic

2 *nmf* mechanist

mecánico, -a **1** *adj* (**a**) *(de la mecánica)* mechanical (**b**) *(automático)* mechanical; **un gesto m.** a mechanical gesture; **lo hace de forma mecánica** he does it mechanically

2 *nm,f (persona)* mechanic ▸▸ ***m. dentista*** dental technician; ***m. de vuelo*** flight engineer

mecanismo *nm* (**a**) *(estructura)* mechanism; **acordaron un m. automático de revisión salarial** they agreed on a procedure *o* system for automatic salary reviews ▸▸ *Psi* ***m. de defensa*** defence mechanism; *Fin* ***m. de los tipos de cambio*** exchange rate mechanism (**b**) *(funcionamiento)* way of working, modus operandi; **conoce muy bien el m. electoral** she's very familiar with the electoral procedure

mecanización *nf* mechanization

mecanizado, -a *adj* mechanized

mecanizar [14] *vt* to mechanize

mecano® *nm* Meccano®

mecanografía *nf* typing ▸▸ ***m. al tacto*** touch-typing

mecanografiar [32] *vt* to type

mecanógrafo, -a *nm,f* typist

mecanoterapia *nf Med* mechanotherapy

mecapal *nm CAm, Méx* = porter's leather harness

mecapalero, -a *nm,f CAm, Méx* porter *(who uses a leather carrying-harness)*

mecatazo *nm* (**a**) *CAm, Méx (latigazo)* whiplash (**b**) *CAm Fam (trago)* drink, slug

mecate *nm* (**a**) *CAm, Méx, Ven* rope (**b**) EXPR *Méx Fam* **a todo m.: se compró una casa a todo m.** she bought herself a really posh house; **organizó una recepción a todo m.** he organized a lavish reception

mecatero, -a *nm,f Ven Fam* toady, bootlicker

mecato *nm Col* packed lunch

mecedora *nf, Col, Ven* **mecedor** *nm* rocking chair

mecenas *nmf inv* patron

mecenazgo *nm* patronage

mecer [40] **1** *vt* to rock; **las olas mecían la barca** the waves gently rocked the boat

2 mecerse *vpr (en silla)* to rock; *(en columpio, hamaca)* to swing; *(árbol, rama)* to sway

mecha *nf* (**a**) *(de vela)* wick; *(de explosivos)* fuse; EXPR *Fam* **a toda m.: arréglate a toda mecha, que llegamos tarde** hurry up and get ready or we'll be late; **acabamos el trabajo a toda m.** we worked flat out to finish the job; **tenía la radio a toda m.** he had the radio on at full blast; EXPR *Fam* **aguantar m.** to grin and bear it

(**b**) *Culin (relleno)* = bacon used for larding or stuffing

(**c**) *Andes, RP (broca)* bit

(**d**) *Andes, Ven Fam (broma)* gag; **eso no es cosa de m.** that's no laughing matter

(**e**) *(mechón)* lock

(**f**) **mechas** *(en el pelo)* highlights

(**g**) *Am Fam* **mechas** *(pelo)* mop; **tengo que ir a cortarme estas mechas** I have to go and get my hair cut, it's a mess; **se agarraron de las mechas** they grabbed each other by the hair; EXPR *Fam* **venir tirado de las mechas** to have been thrown together at the last minute

mechar *vt Culin (carne)* to lard

mechero[1] *nm* (**a**) *Esp (encendedor)* (cigarette) lighter (**b**) *(en laboratorio)* burner ▸▸ ***m. Bunsen*** Bunsen burner; ***m. de gas*** gas burner

mechero[2]**, -a** *nm,f Esp Fam (ladrón)* shoplifter

mechón, -ona **1** *nm* (**a**) *(de pelo)* lock (**b**) *(de lana)* tuft

2 *nm,f Chile Fam (estudiante) Br* fresher, *US* freshman

mechudo, -a *Fam* **1** *adj Am (de pelo largo)* long-haired; *(despeinado)* dishevelled; **no vayas así, tan m.** don't go like that, with your hair in such a mess

2 *nm Méx* mop

3 *nm,f Am* long-haired man, *f* long-haired woman

meconio *nm* meconium

medalla **1** *nf* medal; EXPR *Fam* **ponerse** *o* **colgarse medallas** to show off; **no querría ponerme** *o* **colgarme medallas, pero...** I don't like to blow my own trumpet, but...; **se está poniendo** *o* **colgando medallas que no le corresponden** he's taking the credit for something he didn't do ▸▸ ***m. de bronce*** bronze medal; ***m. de oro*** gold medal; ***m. de plata*** silver medal

2 *nmf* medallist; **fue m. de oro en Barcelona** she was a gold medallist in Barcelona, she won a gold medal in Barcelona

medallero *nm* medals table

medallista *nmf* medallist

medallón *nm* (**a**) *(joya)* medallion (**b**) *(rodaja)* médaillon ▸▸ ***m. de pescado*** *(empanado)* fishcake

medanal *nm Chile (pantano)* marshy land

médano *nm* (**a**) *(duna)* (sand) dune (**b**) *(banco de arena)* sandbank

medellinense **1** *adj* of/from Medellín *(Colombia)*

2 *nm,f* person from Medellín *(Colombia)*

media **1** *nf* (**a**) **medias** *(prenda interior) (hasta la cintura) Br* tights, *US* pantyhose; *(hasta medio muslo)* stockings ▸▸ *RP* ***medias bombacha*** *o* ***cancán*** *Br* tights, *US* pantyhose; ***medias elásticas*** surgical stockings; *RP* ***medias largas*** *Br* tights, *US* pantyhose; *Col* ***m. pantalón*** *Br* tights, *US* pantyhose

(**b**) *(calcetín) (hasta la rodilla)* (knee-length) sock; *Am (de cualquier longitud)* sock; EXPR *CSur Fam* **chupar las medias a alguien** to lick sb's boots ▸▸ *Col* ***m. m.*** *(hasta la rodilla)* knee-length sock; *(calcetín corto)* ankle sock; *Col* ***medias rodilleras*** knee-length socks; *Col* ***medias tobilleras*** *(calcetines cortos)* ankle socks; *RP* ***medias tres cuartos*** knee-length socks

(**c**) *(promedio)* average, mean ▸▸ ***m. aritmética*** arithmetic mean; ***m. geométrica*** geometric mean; ***m. horaria*** hourly average; ***m. ponderada*** weighted mean; ***m. proporcional*** proportional mean

(**d**) *(hora)* **al dar la m.** on the half-hour

2 *nmpl (medios de comunicación)* media

3 a medias *loc adv* (**a**) *(sin completar)* **hacer algo a medias** to half-do *o* half-finish sth; **la central está funcionando sólo a medias** the power station is operating at only half its full capacity; **se ve**

perfectamente que este trabajo está hecho a medias it's perfectly obvious that this piece of work is only half-finished; **me contó la verdad a medias** he only told me half the truth

(**b**) *(por la mitad)* **dejaron la comida a medias** they left their food half-eaten

(**c**) *(a partes iguales)* **pagar a medias** to go halves, to share the cost; **el alquiler lo pagamos a medias** we split the rent; **¿por qué no compramos el libro a medias?** why don't we go halves on the book?

mediación *nf* mediation; **por m. de** through

mediado, -a *adj* (**a**) *(a media capacidad)* half-full, half-empty; **una botella mediada** a half-full *o* half-empty bottle (**b**) *(a media duración)* **mediada la película** halfway through the movie

mediados *nmpl* **a m. de abril/de año** in the middle of *o* halfway through April/the year

mediador, -ora 1 *adj* **los esfuerzos mediadores del presidente** the president's attempts at mediating

2 *nm,f* mediator

mediagua *nf* (**a**) *Andes, CAm (cabaña)* shack, hut (**b**) *Andes (casa)* = house with a roof that slopes one way only

medial *adj* (**a**) *Anat* medial (**b**) *Ling* medial

medialuna *nf* (**a**) *Am (bollo)* croissant (**b**) *(símbolo musulmán)* crescent (**c**) *(instrumento)* hamstringing *o* hacking knife

mediana *nf* (**a**) *(en autopista) Br* central reservation, *US* median (strip) (**b**) *Geom* median

medianamente *adv* acceptably, tolerably; **habla francés m. bien** he can get by in French; **sólo entendí m. lo que dijo** I only half understood what he said; **buscamos a alguien m. experimentado** we're looking for somebody with at least a reasonable amount of experience

medianería *nf (pared)* dividing *o* party wall

medianero, -a *adj (pared, muro)* dividing

medianía *nf* (**a**) *(mediocridad)* **como futbolista es una m.** he's a pretty mediocre footballer (**b**) *(parte media)* halfway point (**c**) *Andes (medianería)* dividing *o* party wall

mediano, -a *adj* (**a**) *(de tamaño)* medium; **una talla mediana** a medium size; **de estatura mediana** of average *o* medium height (**b**) *(de calidad)* average (**c**) *(mediocre)* average, ordinary

medianoche *nf* (**a**) *(hora)* midnight; **a m.** at midnight; **llegaremos hacia la m.** we'll be there around midnight (**b**) *Esp (pl* **mediasnoches***) (bollo)* = small bun used for sandwiches (**c**) *Méx (pan)* hot dog roll, finger roll

mediante *prep* (**a**) *(por medio de)* by means of; **lo levantaron m. una polea** it was lifted by means of a pulley system; **las obras se adjudicarán m. concurso público** the contract for the work will be put out to tender; **puede aplazar la compra m. 12 pagos mensuales** you can spread the purchase over 12 monthly payments; **la información se puede encontrar m. un motor de búsqueda** the information can be found using *o* with a search engine

(**b**) EXPR **Dios m.** God willing; **nos veremos el lunes, Dios m.** I'll see you Monday, hopefully

mediapunta *nm (en fútbol)* **jugar como m.** to play just in behind the strikers

mediar *vi* (**a**) *(llegar a la mitad)* to be halfway through; **mediaba julio** it was mid-July; **al m. la tarde** halfway through the afternoon

(**b**) *(haber en medio)* **m. entre** to be between; **media un jardín/un kilómetro entre las dos casas** there is a garden/one kilometre between the two houses; **la distancia que media entre las dos capitales** the distance between *o* that separates the two capitals; **media un abismo entre ambas posturas** the two positions are poles apart; **de ahí a decir que es el mejor media un abismo** there's a world of difference between that and saying he's the best; **medió una semana** a week passed by; **sin m. palabra** without saying a word

(**c**) *(intervenir)* to mediate; **medió en la disputa entre las dos partes** he mediated between the two sides in the dispute

(**d**) *(interceder)* to intercede, to intervene; **m. en favor de** *o* **por** to intercede *o* intervene on behalf of *o* for; **medió por su sobrino para que le dieran el trabajo** he interceded *o* intervened on behalf of his nephew in order to get him the job

(**e**) *(ocurrir)* to intervene, to happen; **íbamos a reunirnos el sábado, pero medió el accidente** we were going to meet on Saturday, but then the accident happened; **media la circunstancia de que...** it so happens that...

mediasnueves *nfpl inv Col* mid-morning snack, *Br* elevenses; **hoy hay de m. helado** there's ice cream for mid-morning snack *o Br* elevenses today

mediático,-a *adj* media

mediatización *nf* interference

mediatizar [14] *vt* to interfere in

mediatriz *nf Geom* perpendicular bisector

medicación *nf* medication

medicamento *nm* medicine ►► ***m. genérico*** generic drug

medicamentoso, -a *adj* medicinal

medicar [60] **1** *vt* to give medicine to

2 medicarse *vpr* to take medicine

medicatura *nf Ven* small clinic, community health centre

medicina *nf* (**a**) *(ciencia)* medicine; **estudiar m.** to study medicine; **ejercer la m.** to practise medicine ►► ***m. alternativa*** alternative medicine; ***m. deportiva*** sports medicine; ***m. forense*** forensic medicine; ***m. general*** general medicine; ***m. homeopática*** homeopathic medicine; ***m. intensiva*** intensive-care medicine; ***m. interna*** = branch of medicine which deals with problems of the internal organs, without surgery, *US* internal medicine; ***m. legal*** legal medicine; ***m. naturista*** naturopathy, natural medicine; ***m. nuclear*** nuclear medicine; ***m. ortomolecular*** orthomolecular medicine; ***m. preventiva*** preventive medicine; ***m. social*** community medicine; ***m. tropical*** tropical medicine; ***m. veterinaria*** veterinary medicine

(**b**) *(medicamento)* medicine

medicinal *adj* medicinal; **balón m.** medicine ball

medición *nf* (**a**) *(de temperatura, presión)* measurement; **un instrumento de m.** a measuring instrument (**b**) *(de un verso)* scansion

médico, -a 1 *adj* medical; **reconocimiento m.** medical examination *o* checkup; **realizó estudios médicos** he studied medicine

2 *nm,f* doctor; **ir al m., ir a la consulta del m.** to go to the doctor *o* doctor's ►► *Am* ***m. asimilado*** = doctor attached to the army; ***m. de cabecera*** family doctor, general practitioner; ***m. de cámara*** royal physician; ***m. de familia*** family doctor, general practitioner; ***m. forense*** specialist in forensic medicine; ***m. de guardia*** duty doctor; ***m. interno (residente)*** *Br* house officer, *US* intern; *Am* ***m. legista*** specialist in forensic medicine; ***m. militar*** army *o* military doctor

MEDIDA *nf* (**a**) *(dimensión, medición)* measurement; **¿qué medidas tiene el contenedor?** what are the measurements of the container?; **unidades de m.** units of measurement; **a (la) m.** *(mueble)* custom-built; *(ropa, calzado)* made-to-measure; **es una casa/un trabajo a tu m.** it's the ideal house/job for you, it's as if the house/job were made for you; **a (la) m. de mi deseo** just as I would have wanted it; **medidas** *(del cuerpo)* measurements; **tomar las medidas a alguien** to take sb's measurements; **tomar las medidas de algo** to measure sth; *Fig* **le tengo tomada la m. al jefe** I know what the boss is like; *Fig* **ya le voy tomando la m. al nuevo trabajo** I'm getting the hang of the new job ►► ***m. agraria*** unit of land measurement; ***m. de capacidad*** measure *(liquid or dry)*; ***m. de superficie*** unit of area; ***m. de volumen*** unit of volume

(**b**) *(cantidad específica)* measure; **el daiquiri lleva una m. de limón por cada tres de ron** a daiquiri is made with one part lemon to three parts rum

(**c**) *(disposición)* measure, step; **adoptar** *o* **tomar medidas** to take measures *o* steps; **yo ya he tomado mis medidas** I'm prepared, I've made my preparations; **tomar medidas disciplinarias (contra)** to take disciplinary action (against); **ejercer medidas de presión contra alguien** to lobby sb; **tomar medidas represivas (contra)** to clamp down (on) ►► ***medidas de choque*** emergency measures; ***medidas de seguridad*** security measures

(**d**) *(moderación)* moderation; **con/sin m.** in/without moderation

(**e**) *(grado)* extent; **¿en qué m. nos afecta?** to what extent does it affect us?; **en cierta/gran m.** to some/a large extent; **en mayor/menor m.** to a greater/lesser extent; **en la m. de lo posible** as far as possible; **a m. que iban entrando** as they were coming in; *Formal* **en la m. en que** insofar as

(**f**) *Lit (de verso)* measure

medido, -a *adj CSur* moderate, restrained; **es muy m. con los gastos** he is very careful with his money

medidor *nm Am (contador)* meter

mediería *nf RP* hosier's, hosiery shop

mediero, -a *nm,f Am* sharecropper

medieval *adj* medieval

medievalismo *nm* medievalism

medievalista *nmf* medievalist

medievo *nm* Middle Ages

medina *nf* medina

MEDIO, -A 1 *adj* (a) *(igual a la mitad)* half; **media docena** half a dozen; **media hora** half an hour; **m. litro** half a litre; **el estadio registra media entrada** the stadium is half full; **m. pueblo estaba allí** half the town was there; **m. Quito se quedó sin electricidad** half of Quito was left without electricity; **la bandera ondeaba a media asta** the flag was flying at half mast; **a m. camino** *(en viaje)* halfway there; *(en trabajo)* halfway through; **a media luz** in the half-light; **nos salimos a media película** we left halfway through the movie; **como algo a media mañana** I have something to eat halfway through the morning, I have a mid-morning snack; **docena y media** one and a half dozen; **un kilo y m.** one and a half kilos; **son las dos y media** it's half past two; **son y media** it's half past ►► *Andes, Méx, Ven* ***m. fondo*** waist petticoat *o* slip; ***la media luna*** the crescent; ***la Media Luna Roja*** the Red Crescent; *Fam Fig* ***media naranja:* mi/su/***etc.* **media naranja** my/your/*etc* other *o* better half; ***media pensión*** half board; *CSur* ***m. pupilo*** *(que va a dormir a casa)* day pupil; *(que va a casa el fin de semana)* boarder; ***media suela*** half-sole; ***media volea*** half volley

(b) *(intermedio) (estatura, tamaño)* medium; *(posición, punto)* middle; **de una calidad media** of average quality; **a m. plazo** in the medium term; **de clase media** middle-class; **a media distancia** in the middle distance ►► ***m. campo*** midfield; *Am* ***m. tiempo*** half-time

(c) *(de promedio) (temperatura, velocidad)* average; *Mat* mean; **el consumo m. de agua por habitante** the average water consumption per head of the population; **a una velocidad media de 50 km/h** at an average speed of 50 km/h

(d) *(corriente)* ordinary, average; **el ciudadano m.** the average person, ordinary people

2 *adv* half; **m. borracho** half drunk; **estaba m. muerto** he was half dead; **a m. hacer** half done; **han dejado la obra a m. hacer** they've left the building half finished; **aún estoy a m. arreglar** I'm only half ready; **pasé la noche m. en vela** I had a very restless night

3 *nm* (a) *(mitad)* half; **uno y m.** one and a half

(b) *(centro)* middle, centre; **íbamos por el carril del m.** *o* **de en m.** we were driving in the middle lane; **en m. (de)** in the middle (of); **estaba incómoda en m. de toda aquella gente** I felt uncomfortable among all those people; **está en m. de una profunda depresión** she's in the middle of a deep depression; **no se oía nada en m. de tanto ruido** you couldn't hear a thing with all that noise; **han puesto una valla en m.** they've put a fence in the way; **si te pones en m. no veo la tele** I can't see the TV if you're in the way; **quítate de en m.** get out of the way; **siempre tienes todas tus cosas por m.** your things are always lying around all over the place; **estar por (en) m.** *(estorbar)* to be in the way; **hay muchos intereses de por m.** there are a lot of interests involved; **meterse** *o* **ponerse (de) por m.** *(estorbar)* to get in the way; *Fig (entrometerse)* to interfere; EXPR **equivocarse de m. a m.** to be completely wrong; EXPR *Fam* **quitar de en m. a alguien** to get rid of sb; EXPR **quitarse de en m.** *(suicidarse)* to do away with oneself

(c) *(sistema, manera)* means *(singular or plural)*, method; **utilice cualquier m. a su alcance** use whatever means are available, use every means available; **encontró un m. para pagar menos impuestos** she found a way of paying less tax; **no hay m. de convencerla** she won't be persuaded; **por m. de** by means of, through; **ha encontrado trabajo por m. de un conocido** she got a job through an acquaintance; **por todos los medios** by all possible means; **intentaré conseguir ese trabajo por todos los medios** I'll do whatever it takes to get that job; **su m. de vida es la chatarra** he earns his living from scrap metal ►► ***los medios de comunicación*** the media; ***medios de comunicación electrónicos*** electronic media; ***los medios de comunicación de masas*** the mass media; ***los medios de difusión*** the media; ***m. de expresión*** medium; ***los medios de información*** the media; ***medios de producción*** means of production; ***m. de transporte*** means of transport

(d) **medios** *(recursos)* means, resources; **no cuenta con los medios económicos para realizarlo** she lacks the means *o* the (financial) resources to do it

(e) *(elemento físico)* environment; **animales que viven en el m. acuático** animals that live in an aquatic environment ►► ***m. ambiente*** environment; *Biol* ***m. de cultivo*** culture medium; ***m. físico*** physical environment

(f) *(ámbito)* **el m. rural/urbano** the countryside/city; **en medios financieros/políticos** in financial/political circles; **en medios bien informados** in well-informed circles

(g) *Dep (en fútbol, hockey)* midfielder; *(en rugby)* halfback ►► ***m. (de) apertura*** *(en rugby)* fly half, stand-off; ***m. (de) melé*** *(en rugby)* scrum half

(h) *Taurom* **los medios** = centre of bullring

(i) EXPR *CSur Fam* **ni m.: no oye ni m.** he's as deaf as a post; **no entiende ni m.** she hasn't got a clue; **por m.: nado día por m.** I swim every other day

---

medioambiental *adj* environmental

mediocampista *nmf Dep* midfielder

mediocre *adj* mediocre, average

mediocridad *nf* mediocrity

mediodía *nm* (a) *(hora)* midday, noon; **a m., al m.** at midday *o* noon (b) *(tiempo del día)* lunchtime; **a m. me suelo quedar en el trabajo** I usually stay at work over lunchtime (c) *(sur)* south

medioevo *nm* Middle Ages

mediofondista *nmf Dep* middle-distance runner

mediometraje *nm Cine* = film which lasts between thirty and sixty minutes

mediopensionista 1 *adj* = who has school dinners

2 *nmf* = child who has school dinners

medir [47] 1 *vt* (a) *(hacer mediciones)* to measure; EXPR **m. por el mismo rasero** to treat alike

(b) *(verso)* to scan

(c) *(sopesar)* to weigh up; **tenemos que m. las ventajas y desventajas de este sistema** we have to weigh up the advantages and disadvantages of this system

(d) *(palabras)* to weigh carefully; **mide bien tus palabras cuando hables con ellos** be careful what you say when you talk to them

(e) *(fuerzas)* **los dos equipos medirán sus fuerzas en la semifinal** the two sides will do battle in the semifinal

2 *vi (tener de medida)* **¿cuánto mides?** how tall are you?; **¿cuánto mide de largo?** how long *o* what length is it?; **mido 1,80** I'm 6 foot (tall); **mide diez metros** it's ten metres long; **el cuadro mide 30 por 90** the picture measures *o* is 30 by 90; **mide dos metros de ancho por cuatro de largo** it's two metres wide by four metres long; **mide 90-60-90** her vital statistics are 36-24-36; **este armario mide demasiado** this cupboard is too big

3 **medirse** *vpr* (a) *(tomarse medidas)* to measure oneself; **se midió la cintura** she measured her waist (b) *(moderarse)* to act with restraint (c) *(enfrentarse)* **medirse con** to meet, to take on; **Cuba se medirá en la final contra Estados Unidos** Cuba will meet *o* take on the United States in the final (d) *Méx (probarse)* to try on; **se midió el sombrero** he tried the hat on

meditabundo, -a *adj* thoughtful, pensive

meditación *nf* meditation ►► ***m. trascendental*** transcendental meditation

meditar 1 *vt* (a) *(considerar)* to consider, to ponder; **meditó cuidadosamente su respuesta** he considered *o* pondered his reply very carefully; **estamos meditando qué hacer** we are pondering over *o* considering what to do (b) *(planear)* to plan, to think through

2 *vi* to meditate (**sobre** on)

meditativo, -a *adj* pensive

mediterráneo, -a 1 *adj* Mediterranean; **el mar Mediterráneo** the Mediterranean Sea

2 *nm* **el Mediterráneo** the Mediterranean

médium *nmf inv* medium

medo, -a *Hist* 1 *adj* Median

2 *nm,f* Mede, Median

medrar *vi* (a) *(prosperar)* to prosper; *(enriquecerse)* to get rich; **no lo hizo por afán de m.** he didn't do it for personal gain *o* for what he could get out of it (b) *(crecer)* to grow; **los hierbajos medran por todas partes** there are weeds growing all over the place

medro *nm* (a) *(mejora)* improvement, progress; *(enriquecimiento)* prosperity (b) *(aumento)* increase, growth

medroso, -a *Literario* 1 *adj (miedoso)* fearful

2 *nm,f* coward

médula *nf* (a) *Anat* (bone) marrow ►► ***m. espinal*** spinal cord; ***m. oblongada*** medulla oblongata; ***m. ósea*** bone marrow

(b) *(esencia)* core; EXPR **hasta la m.: está metido hasta la m. en la organización del congreso** he's very heavily involved in the organization of the conference; **es cuidadoso hasta la m.** he's scrupulously careful; **un cocinero mediterráneo hasta la m.** a chef who is Mediterranean through and through; **tuvo una actuación profesional hasta la m.** she gave a thoroughly professional performance

(c) *Bot* pith

medular *adj* (a) *Anat* medullary, medullar (b) *Dep* **línea m.** midfield

medusa *nf* jellyfish, medusa

mefistofélico, -a *adj* diabolical

mega *nm Fam Informát* meg, megabyte

mega- *pref* (a) *(millón)* mega- (b) *Fam (grande)* **un megaproyecto** a huge project; **es megarrico** he's mega-rich

megabit (*pl* **megabits**) *nm Informát* megabit

megabyte [meɣa'βait] (*pl* **megabytes**) *nm Informát* megabyte

megaciclo *nm* megacycle

megafonía *nf* public-address *o* PA system; **llamar por m. a alguien** to page sb (over the PA system); **anunciar algo por m.** to announce sth over the public-address *o* PA system

megáfono *nm* megaphone

megahercio, megaherzio *nm* megahertz

megalítico, -a *adj* megalithic

megalito *nm* megalith

megalomanía *nf* megalomania

megalómano, -a 1 *adj* megalomaniac
2 *nm,f* megalomaniac

megalópolis *nf inv* megalopolis

megatón *nm* megaton

megavatio *nm* megawatt

meiga *nf* witch

meiosis *nf inv Biol* meiosis

mejicanismo *nm* Mexicanism

mejicano, -a 1 *adj* Mexican
2 *nm,f* Mexican

Méjico *n* Mexico

mejilla *nf* cheek; EXPR **ofrecer** *o* **poner la otra m.** to turn the other cheek

mejillón *nm* mussel

mejillonera *nf* mussel bed

MEJOR 1 *adj* (a) *(comparativo)* better (**que** than); **un mundo m.** a better world; **ella tiene una moto mucho m.** she has a much better motorbike; **una televisión de m. calidad** a better-quality television; **no hay nada m. que...** there's nothing better than...; **es m. que no vengas** it would be better if you didn't come; **será m. que te calles** you'd better shut up, I suggest you shut up; **sería m. que llamáramos a un médico** we ought to call a doctor; **un cambio a** *o* **para m.** a change for the better
(b) *(superlativo)* **el/la m....** the best...; **el m. vino de todos/del mundo** the best wine of all/in the world; **un producto de la m. calidad** a top-quality product, a product of the highest quality; **lo hice lo m. que pude** I did my best; **es lo m. que nos pudo ocurrir** it was the best thing that could have happened to us; **lo m. es que nos marchemos** it would be best if we left; **te deseo lo m.** I wish you all the best; **lo m. fue que...** the best thing was that...
2 *nmf* **el/la m. (de)** the best (in); **el m. de todos/del mundo** the best of all/in the world; **el m. de los dos** the better of the two; **en el m. de los casos** at best; **que gane el m.** may the best man win
3 *adv* (a) *(comparativo)* better (**que** than); **ahora veo m.** I can see better now; **el inglés se me da m. que el alemán** I'm better at English than I am at German; **lo haces cada vez m.** you're getting better and better at it; **¿qué tal las vacaciones? – m. imposible** how were your holidays? – they couldn't have been any better; **estar m.** *(no tan malo)* to feel better; *(recuperado)* to be better; **nos va m. con este gobierno** we're better off under this government; **me lo he pensado m.** I've thought better of it; **m. dicho** (or) rather; **m. para ti/él/***etc.* so much the better; **si tienen mucho dinero, m. para ellos** if they've got lots of money, so much the better; **me han invitado a la ceremonia – m. para ti** I've been invited to the ceremony – good for you; **m. que m., tanto m.** so much the better
(b) *(superlativo)* best; **el que la conoce m.** the one who knows her best; **esto es lo que se me da m.** this is what I'm best at; **los vinos m. elaborados** the finest wines; **el personal m. preparado** the best-qualified staff
(c) *(indicando preferencia)* **m. me quedo** I'd better stay; **m. no se lo digas** it'd be better if you didn't tell him; **m. quedamos mañana** it would be better if we met tomorrow
4 **a lo mejor** *loc adv* maybe, perhaps; **a lo m. voy** I may go

---

mejora *nf* (a) *(progreso)* improvement; **se nota una clara m.** you can see a clear improvement; **un factor que contribuye a la m. de la calidad de vida** a factor which contributes to a better quality of life (b) *(cambio)* improvement; **este trabajo necesita varias mejoras** several things about this piece of work need improving

mejorable *adj* **la calidad es m.** the quality could be improved (on) *o* could be better

mejorado, -a *adj* (a) *(mejor)* **el paciente está muy m.** the patient is much better; **está muy m. de la lesión de rodilla** she's made a good recovery from her knee injury (b) *(aumentado)* increased

mejoramiento *nm* improvement

mejorana *nf* marjoram

mejorar 1 *vt* (a) *(hacer mejor)* to improve; **mejoraron las condiciones de trabajo** working conditions were improved; **su principal objetivo es m. la economía** their main aim is to improve the economy's performance
(b) *(enfermo)* to make better; **estas pastillas lo mejorarán** these tablets will make him better
(c) *(superar)* to improve; **m. una oferta** to make a better offer; **mejoró el récord mundial** she beat the world record
2 *vi* (a) *(ponerse mejor)* to improve, to get better; **el paciente está mejorando** the patient's condition is improving, the patient is getting better; **necesita m. en matemáticas** he needs to improve *o* do better in mathematics
(b) *(tiempo, clima)* to improve, to get better; **tan pronto como mejore, salimos a dar un paseo** as soon as the weather improves *o* gets better we'll go out for a walk; **después de la lluvia el día mejoró** after the rain it cleared up
3 **mejorarse** *vpr* to improve, to get better; **¡que te mejores!** get well soon!

mejoría *nf* improvement; **el paciente ha experimentado una clara m.** the patient's condition has shown a clear improvement; **se prevé una ligera m. del tiempo** the weather is forecast to improve slightly

mejunje *nm Fam Pey* (a) *(bebida)* concoction (b) *(ungüento)* muck, *Br* gunge

melado *nm Am* thick cane syrup

melancolía *nf* melancholy

melancólico, -a 1 *adj (música)* melancholy, melancholic; *(paisaje)* gloomy; **está muy m.** he's very melancholy
2 *nm,f* melancholy *o* melancholic person

Melanesia *n* Melanesia

melanesio, -a 1 *adj* Melanesian
2 *nm,f* Melanesian

melanina *nf Fisiol* melanin

melanoma *nm Med* melanoma

melatonina *nf Fisiol* melatonin

melaza *nf* molasses ►► ***m. de caña*** golden syrup

Melchor *n pr* Melchior

melcocha *nf* = type of chewy toffee made by cooling hot honey

melcochudo, -a *adj CAm, Cuba* soft, flexible

melé *nf* (a) *Esp (en rugby)* scrum ►► ***m. espontánea*** ruck (b) *(aglomeración)* **se formó una m. de jugadores en el área** the players all massed together in the penalty area; **había una m. de papeles encima de la mesa** there was a jumble of papers on the desk

melena 1 *nf* (a) *(de persona)* long hair; EXPR *Fam* **soltarse la m.** to let one's hair down (b) *(de león)* mane (c) **melenas** *(pelo largo)* mop of hair; **a ver si te cortas esas melenas** why don't you cut that mop of yours?
2 **melenas** *nm inv Fam* long-haired guy

melenudo, -a *Fam* 1 *adj* long-haired
2 *nm* long-haired guy

meliáceo, -a *Bot* 1 *adj* meliaceous
2 **meliáceas** *nfpl (familia) Meliaceae*; **de la familia de las meliáceas** of the family *Meliaceae*

melifluo, -a *adj* honeyed, mellifluous

melillense 1 *adj* of/from Melilla *(Spain)*
2 *nmf* person from Melilla *(Spain)*

melindre *nm* (a) *(dulce)* = fried cake made from honey and sugar (b) **melindres** *(afectación)* affected scrupulousness; **no te andes con melindres** stop affecting scruples like that; **hace muchos melindres antes de sentarse en un banco público** he makes a big fuss of making sure it's clean before he sits on a public bench

melindroso, -a 1 *adj* affectedly scrupulous *o* fussy
2 *nm,f* affectedly scrupulous *o* fussy person

melisa *nf* lemon balm

melívora *nf* honey badger

mella *nf* (a) *(muesca) (en navaja)* nick; *(en porcelana)* chip; EXPR **hacer m.: el calor no le hace m.** the heat doesn't affect her at all; **sus críticas acabaron haciendo m. en él** their criticism of him eventually struck home; **tanto gasto está haciendo m. en la economía familiar** all this expense is having an effect on *o* making inroads into the family budget (b) *(en dentadura)* gap

mellado, -a *adj* (**a**) *(dañado) (navaja)* nicked; *(porcelana)* chipped (**b**) *(sin dientes)* gap-toothed

mellar *vt* (**a**) *(hacer mellas) (en navaja)* to nick; *(en porcelana)* to chip (**b**) *(menoscabar)* to damage

mellizo, -a 1 *adj* twin
2 *nm,f* twin

melocotón *nm esp Esp* peach ▸▸ ***melocotones en almíbar*** peaches in syrup

melocotonar *nm esp Esp* peach orchard

melocotonero *nm esp Esp* peach tree

melodía *nf* melody, tune

melódico, -a *adj* melodic

melodioso, -a *adj* melodious

melodrama *nm* (**a**) *(obra, película)* melodrama (**b**) *(suceso emocionante)* drama; **su despedida fue un m.** his dismissal was a real drama

melodramático, -a *adj* melodramatic

melolonta *nf* May beetle *o* bug

melomanía *nf* love of music

melómano, -a *nm,f* music lover

melón *nm* (**a**) *(fruta)* melon (**b**) *Fam (idiota)* lemon, idiot (**c**) *Fam (cabeza)* nut, *Br* bonce (**d**) *Esp muy Fam* **melones** *(pechos)* knockers, *Br* boobs

melonada *nf Fam* **hacer una m.** to do something stupid; **decir una m.** to say something stupid; **decir melonadas** to talk nonsense

melonar *nm* melon field *o* patch

meloncillo *nm* Egyptian mongoose

melopea *nf Esp Fam* **agarrar** *o* **coger una m.** to get plastered *o* wasted

melosidad *nf (dulzura)* sweetness; *(empalago)* sickliness

meloso, -a *adj* (**a**) *(fruta)* sweet (**b**) *(persona) (dulce)* sweet; *(empalagoso)* sickly

melva *nf* frigate mackerel

mema *nf* (**a**) *RP Fam* (baby's) bottle (**b**) *ver también* **memo**

membrana *nf* (**a**) *(tejido)* membrane ▸▸ ***m. mucosa*** mucous membrane (**b**) *(de tambor)* skin

membranoso, -a *adj* membranous

membresía *nf Am* membership

membretado, -a, membreteado, -a *adj Am* headed

membrete *nm* letterhead

membreteado = **membretado**

membrillero *nm* quince (tree)

membrillo *nm* (**a**) *(fruto)* quince (**b**) *(dulce)* quince jelly

memela *nf Méx* = thick corn tortilla, oval in shape ▸▸ ***m. con chile*** = tortilla filled with chilli; ***m. de queso*** = cheese-filled tortilla

memento *nm* (**a**) *Rel* memento (**b**) *(libreta)* memo book, notebook

memez *nf* (**a**) *(cualidad)* stupidity (**b**) **hacer una m.** to do something stupid; **decir una m.** to say something stupid; **decir memeces** to talk nonsense (**c**) *Fam (insignificancia)* trifle, silly little thing; **discutieron por una m.** they had an argument over nothing *o* over some silly little thing

memo, -a *Esp* 1 *adj* stupid
2 *nm,f* idiot, fool

memorable *adj* memorable

memorándum, memorando *(pl* **memorandos***)* *nm* (**a**) *(cuaderno)* notebook (**b**) *(nota diplomática)* memorandum

MEMORIA *nf* (**a**) *(capacidad de recordar)* memory; **tener buena/mala m., tener mucha/poca m.** to have a good/bad memory; **tengo mala m.** *o* **no tengo buena m. para las caras** I'm not very good at remembering faces; **borrar algo de la m.** to erase sth from one's memory; **de m.** *(aprender, saber)* by heart; **recita poemas de m.** she recites poems from memory; **falta de m.** forgetfulness; **ser flaco de m.** to be forgetful; **hacer m.** to try to remember; **se me fue de la m.** it slipped my mind; **perdió la m.** she lost her memory; **su nombre se me quedó grabado en la m.** his name remained etched on my memory; **refrescar la m. a alguien** to refresh sb's memory; **si la m. no me engaña** *o* **falla** if I remember correctly; **tener (una) m. fotográfica** to have a photographic memory; **me trae a la m. los tiempos de antes de la guerra** it calls to mind the years before the war; **esto me trae a la m. el colegio** this reminds me of when I was at school; **venir a la m.** to come to mind; **ahora no me viene a la m.** I can't think of it right now; EXPR **tener (una) m. de elefante** to have an excellent memory ▸▸ ***m. colectiva*** collective memory

(**b**) *Informát* memory ▸▸ ***m. de acceso aleatorio*** random access memory; ***m. alta*** high memory; ***m. de burbuja*** bubble memory; ***m. caché*** cache memory; ***m. convencional*** conventional memory; ***m. expandida*** expanded memory; ***m. extendida*** extended memory; ***m. intermedia*** buffer; ***m. principal*** main memory; ***m. programable*** programmable memory; ***m. RAM*** RAM; ***m. ROM*** ROM; ***m. de sólo lectura*** read-only memory; ***m. virtual*** virtual memory; ***m. volátil*** volatile memory

(**c**) *(recuerdo)* remembrance, remembering; **conservar la m. de algo/alguien** to remember sth/sb; **ser de feliz/ingrata m.** to be a happy/an unhappy memory; **un día de triste m.** a sad day (to remember); **digno de m.** memorable; **en m. de** in memory of; **un monumento en m. del héroe nacional** a memorial to the national hero; **aún queda m. de aquello** it is still remembered

(**d**) *(disertación)* (academic) paper (**sobre** on) ▸▸ ***m. de licenciatura*** dissertation

(**e**) *(informe)* **m. (anual)** (annual) report

(**f**) *(lista)* list, record

(**g**) **memorias** *(en literatura)* memoirs; **ha escrito unas** *o* **sus memorias** she has written her memoirs

---

memorial *nm* petition, request

memorión *Fam* 1 *adj* **ser m.** to have an amazing memory
2 *nm* (**a**) *(memoria)* amazing memory (**b**) *(persona)* **es un m.** he has an amazing memory

memorioso, -a 1 *adj* having a good memory
2 *nm,f* person with a good memory; **es un m.** he has a good memory

memorístico, -a *adj* memory; **ejercicio m.** memory exercise

memorización *nf* memorizing, memorization

memorizar [14] *vt* to memorize

mena *nf* ore

ménade *nf Literario (mujer furiosa)* hysterical woman; **parecía una m.** she was totally hysterical

ménage à trois [me'naʃa'trwa] *nm* threesome *(for sex)*

menaje *nm* household goods and furnishings ▸▸ ***m. de cocina*** kitchenware

menarquía, menarquia *nf Med* menarche

menchevique *Hist* 1 *adj* Menshevik
2 *nmf* Menshevik

mención *nf* (**a**) *(distinción)* mention; **hacer m. de** to mention; **ser digno de m.** to be worth mentioning ▸▸ ***m. honorífica*** honourable mention (**b**) *RP, Ven (especialidad)* **licenciatura en Historia, m. hispanoamericana** degree in history, specializing in Spanish American studies

mencionar *vt* to mention; **en el mencionado estudio se afirma que...** in the above-mentioned study it is stated that...

menda *Esp Fam* 1 *pron Hum (el que habla)* yours truly, *Br* muggins; **el m. tuvo que limpiar la casa solito** yours truly *o Br* muggins had to clean the house on his own; **mi m. se va a casa** I'm off home
2 *nmf (uno cualquiera)* guy, *Br* bloke, *f* girl; **vino un m. y...** this guy came along and...; **se enamoró de un m. que la engañó** she fell in love with some guy who cheated on her

mendacidad *nf Formal* mendacity, untruthfulness

mendaz *adj Formal* mendacious, untruthful

mendelevio *nm Quím* mendelevium

mendeliano, -a *adj* Mendelian

mendelismo *nm* Mendelism

mendicante 1 *adj* (**a**) *(que pide limosna)* begging (**b**) *(orden religiosa)* mendicant
2 *nmf* beggar

mendicidad *nf* begging

mendigar [38] 1 *vt* to beg for; **siempre está mendigando favores** she's always asking for favours
2 *vi* to beg

mendigo, -a *nm,f* beggar

méndigo, -a *adj Méx Fam* (**a**) *(tacaño)* stingy, tight-fisted (**b**) *(despreciable)* mean, nasty

mendocino, -a 1 *adj* of/from Mendoza *(Argentina)*
2 *nm,f* person from Mendoza *(Argentina)*

mendrugo *nm* (**a**) *(de pan)* crust (of bread) (**b**) *Esp Fam (idiota)* fathead, idiot

mene *nm Ven* = deposit of oil at surface level

menear 1 *vt* (**a**) *(mover)* to move; *(cabeza)* to shake; *(cola)* to wag; *(caderas)* to wiggle; **el viento meneaba las aguas** the wind ruffled the water; EXPR *Ven Fam* **m. la mata** to shake things up (**b**) *(activar)* to get moving; EXPR *Fam* **más vale no menearlo** *o* **meneallo: el tema**

ése, más vale no menearlo *o* **meneallo** it would be best not to mention that subject

2 menearse *vpr* **(a)** *(moverse)* to move (about); *(agitarse)* to shake; *(oscilar)* to sway; **siéntate ahí y ni te menees** sit there and don't move *o* budge

(b) *(darse prisa, espabilarse)* to get a move on

(c) *muy Fam* **meneársela** *(masturbarse) Br* to wank, *US* to jerk off; EXPR *Esp* **me la menea** I couldn't give a shit *o Br* toss

(d) EXPR *Esp Fam* **de no te menees: un susto de no te menees** a hell of a scare; **es un idiota de no te menees** he's a complete idiot; **cogí un resfriado de no te menees** I caught a stinking cold

meneo *nm* **(a)** *(movimiento)* movement; *(de cola)* wagging; *(de caderas)* wiggle; **nos saludó con un m. de la cabeza** he greeted us with a nod of his head; *Esp Fam* **dar un m. a algo** to shake sth **(b)** *Esp Fam (golpe)* knock, bang; **dar un m. a alguien** to give sb a hiding

menester *nm* **(a)** *(necesidad)* necessity; **haber m. de algo** to be in need of sth; **ser m. que alguien haga algo** to be necessary for sb to do sth; **es m. continuar con las reformas** it is necessary to continue with the reforms

(b) menesteres *(asuntos)* business, matters; **se ocupa de la limpieza y demás menesteres** he does the cleaning and other odd jobs; **un abogado sin experiencia en estos menesteres** a lawyer with no experience in these matters

(c) *Fam* **menesteres** *(herramientas)* things, tools

menesteroso, -a *Formal* **1** *adj* needy, poor

2 *nm,f* needy *o* poor person

menestra *nf* vegetable stew

menestral, -ala *nm,f* artisan, craftsman, *f* craftswoman

mengano, -a *nm,f (hombre)* so-and-so, what's-his-name; *(mujer)* so-and-so, what's-her-name

mengua *nf (reducción)* reduction; **la empresa ha experimentado una fuerte m. en los ingresos** the company has seen its income considerably reduced; **sin m. de** without detriment to; **esto no supone ninguna m. de su reputación** this in no way detracts from his reputation

menguado, -a 1 *adj* reduced, diminished

2 *nm* drop stitch *(in knitting)*

menguante *adj (luna)* waning; **en cuarto m.** on the wane

menguar [11] **1** *vi* **(a)** *(disminuir)* to decrease, to diminish; **su salud ha menguado mucho** her health has deteriorated a lot; **la diferencia entre los dos equipos menguó en los últimos minutos** the gap between the two teams narrowed in the closing minutes; **su fortuna ha menguado** his fortune has dwindled; **el caudal del río está menguando** the river level is going down *o* falling; **el calor, lejos de m., está aumentando** the heat, far from letting up, is increasing

(b) *(luna)* to wane

(c) *(en labor de punto)* to decrease

2 *vt* **(a)** *(disminuir)* to lessen, to diminish; **la enfermedad menguó su resistencia** the illness sapped his resistance; **esto no mengua en nada su fama** this in no way detracts from his reputation **(b)** *(en labor de punto)* to decrease

mengue *nm Fam* **(a)** *(diablo)* devil **(b)** *RP (duende)* imp, goblin

menhir *nm* menhir

meninge *nf Anat* meninx; **meninges** meninges; EXPR *Fam Hum* **estrujarse las meninges** to rack one's brains

meníngeo, -a *adj Anat* meningeal

meningitis *nf inv* meningitis

menisco *nm* **(a)** *Anat* meniscus **(b)** *Fís* meniscus

menopausia *nf* menopause ►► ***m. masculina*** male menopause

menopáusica *nf* menopausal woman

menopáusico, -a *adj* menopausal

MENOR 1 *adj* **(a)** *(comparativo) (en tamaño)* smaller (**que** than); *(en edad)* younger (**que** than); *(en importancia)* less, lesser (**que** than); *(en número)* lower (**que** than); **este apartamento es m. que el otro** this *Br* flat *o US* apartment is smaller than the other one; **mi hermana m.** my younger sister; **es ocho años m. que yo** he's eight years younger than me; **reciben m. formación que nosotros** they receive less training than us; **en m. grado** to a lesser extent; **un m. número de víctimas** a lower *o* smaller number of victims; **una m. tasa de inflación** a lower rate of inflation; **apartamentos menores de 100 metros cuadrados** *Br* flats *o US* apartments of less than *o* under 100 square metres; **ayudas para empresarios menores de veinticinco años** grants for businessmen (of) under twenty-five; **sólo la m. parte de los encuestados estaba en contra** only a minority of those interviewed were opposed; *Mat* **m. que** less than

(b) *(superlativo)* **el/la m....** *(en tamaño)* the smallest...; *(en edad)* the youngest...; *(en importancia)* the slightest...; *(en número)* the lowest...; **la m. de las islas** the smallest island, the smallest of the islands; **la m. de todos nosotros/de la clase** the youngest of all of us/in the class; **la m. de las dos hermanas** the younger of the two sisters; **el m. ruido le molesta** the slightest noise disturbs him; **no creo que tenga el m. interés** I don't think it's at all *o* the slightest bit interesting; **no te preocupes, no tiene la m. importancia** don't worry, it doesn't matter at all *o* in the least; **no tengo la m. idea** I haven't the slightest idea

(c) *(intrascendente, secundario)* minor; **un problema m.** a minor problem

(d) *(joven)* **aún es m. para salir solo** he's still a bit young to go out on his own; **ser m. de edad** *(para votar, conducir)* to be under age; *Der* to be a minor

(e) *Mús* minor; **en do m.** in C minor

(f) *Com* **al por m.** retail; **vender algo al por m.** to retail sth; **puntos de venta al por m.** retail outlets

2 *nmf* **(a)** *(superlativo)* **el/la m.** *(hijo, hermano)* the youngest **(b)** *Der (niño)* minor; **es una película no apta para menores** this film has been classified as unsuitable for children; **no apta para menores** *(en letrero)* = unsuitable for children ►► ***m. de edad*** minor

Menorca *n* Minorca

menorista = **minorista**

menorquín, -ina 1 *adj* Minorcan

2 *nm,f* Minorcan

menorragia *nf* menorrhagia

MENOS 1 *adj inv* **(a)** *(comparativo) (cantidad)* less; *(número)* fewer; **m. aire** less air; **m. manzanas** fewer apples; **m.... que...** less/fewer... than...; **tiene m. experiencia que tú** she has less experience than you; **vino m. gente que otras veces** there were fewer people there than on other occasions; **hace m. calor que ayer** it's not as hot as it was yesterday; **colócate a m. distancia** stand closer; **eran m. pero mejor preparadas** there were fewer of them, but they were better prepared

(b) *(superlativo) (cantidad)* the least; *(número)* the fewest; **el que compró m. acciones** the one who bought the fewest shares; **lo que m. tiempo llevó** the thing that took the least time; **la que m. nota sacó en el examen** the girl who did (the) worst *o* got the worst marks in the exam

(c) *Fam (peor)* **éste es m. coche que el mío** this car isn't as good as mine; **es m. hombre que tú** he's less of a man than you are

2 *adv* **(a)** *(comparativo)* less; **a mí échame un poco m.** give me a bit less; **ahora con el bebé salen m.** they go out less now they've got the baby; **últimamente trabajo m.** I haven't been working as *o* so much recently; **estás m. gordo** you're not as *o* so fat; **¿a cien? no, íbamos m. rápido** a hundred km/h? no, we weren't going as fast as that; **m. de/que** less than; **Pepe es m. alto (que tú)** Pepe isn't as tall (as you); **Pepe es m. ambicioso (que tú)** Pepe isn't as ambitious (as you), Pepe is less ambitious (than you); **este vino me gusta m. (que el otro)** I don't like this wine as much (as the other one), I like this wine less (than the other one); **son m. de las diez** it's not quite ten o'clock yet; **es difícil encontrar alquileres de** *o* **por m. de 50.000** it's hard to find a place to rent for less than *o* under 50,000; **tardamos m. de lo esperado** we took less time than expected, it didn't take us as long as we expected; **es m. complicado de lo que parece** it's not as complicated as it seems, it's less complicated than it seems

(b) *(superlativo)* **el/la/lo m.** the least; **ella es la m. adecuada para el cargo** she's the least suitable person for the job; **el m. preparado de todos/de la clase** the least well trained of everyone/in the class; **el m. preparado de los dos** the less well trained of the two; **la que m. trabaja** the person *o* one who works (the) least; **aquí es donde m. me duele** this is where it hurts (the) least; **él es el m. indicado para criticar** he's the last person who should be criticizing; **es lo m. que puedo hacer** it's the least I can do; **era lo m. que te podía pasar** it was the least you could expect; **debió de costar lo m. un millón** it must have cost at least a million; **había algunas manzanas podridas, pero eran las m.** some of the apples were rotten, but only a very few

(c) *(indica resta)* minus; **tres m. dos igual a uno** three minus two is one

(d) *Esp, RP (con las horas)* to; **son las dos m. diez** it's ten to two; **son m. diez** it's ten to

(e) *(otras frases hechas)* **ir a m.** *(fiebre, lluvia)* to die down; *(delincuencia)* to drop; **¡m. mal!** just as well!, thank God!; **m. mal que llevo rueda de repuesto/que no te pasó nada** thank God I've got a spare wheel/(that) nothing happened to you; **nada m. (que)** no less (than); **le recibió nada m. que el Papa** he was received by none other than the Pope; **no es para m.** not without (good) reason; **no pude por m.**

que reírme I had to laugh; **venir a m.** *(negocio)* to go downhill; *(persona)* to go down in the world; **no pienso montar y m. si conduces** *o* *Am* **manejas tú** I've no intention of getting in, much less so if you're driving; EXPR **hacer de m. a alguien** to snub sb

3 *pron* **había m. que el año pasado** there were fewer than the previous year; **ya queda m.** it's not so far to go now

4 *nm inv Mat* minus (sign)

5 *prep (excepto)* except (for); **todo m. eso** anything but that; **vinieron todos m. él** everyone came except (for) *o* but him; **m. el café, todo está incluido en el precio** everything except the coffee is included in the price

6 al menos *loc conj* at least; **costará al m. tres millones** it will cost at least three million; **dame al m. una hora para prepararme** give me at least an hour to get ready

7 a menos que *loc conj* unless; **no iré a m. que me acompañes** I won't go unless you come with me

8 de menos *loc adv* **hay dos libros de m.** there are two books missing; **me han dado 80 céntimos de m.** they've given me 80 cents too little, they've short-changed me by 80 cents; **eso es lo de m.** that's the least of it

9 por lo menos *loc adv* at least; **por lo m. pide perdón** you at least ought to apologize

---

menoscabar *vt (fama, honra)* to damage; *(derechos, intereses, salud)* to harm; *(belleza, perfección)* to diminish; **sus acciones han menoscabado la confianza que teníamos en él** what he did has diminished the trust we had in him

menoscabo *nm (de fama, honra)* damage; *(de derechos, intereses, salud)* harm; *(de belleza, perfección)* diminishing; **nuestros intereses no han sufrido m.** our interests have not been damaged; **(ir) en m. de** (to be) to the detriment of; **sin m. del papel de los profesores, se consultará también a los padres** without in any way wishing to devalue *o* diminish the role of teachers, parents will also be consulted; **defienden su lengua propia sin m. de las demás** they defend their own language without diminishing the importance of others

menospreciar *vt* **(a)** *(despreciar)* to scorn, to despise **(b)** *(infravalorar)* to undervalue

menosprecio *nm* scorn, contempt

mensáfono *nm* pager

mensaje *nm* **(a)** *(comunicación)* message; **te dejé un m. en el contestador** I left you a message on your answering machine ►► ***m. publicitario*** advertisement

(b) *(discurso)* message, address; **un m. del presidente a la nación** a message from the president to the nation, a presidential address to the nation

(c) *Ling* message

(d) *(idea profunda)* message; **¿cuál es el m. de la novela?** what is the novel's message?

(e) *Informát* message ►► ***m. de alerta*** alert message; ***m. en clave*** coded message; ***m. por correo electrónico*** e-mail message; ***m. de error*** error message

mensajería *nf* **(a)** *(de paquetes, cartas)* courier service **(b)** *Informát* messaging

mensajero, -a 1 *adj* **(a)** *(de mensajes)* message-carrying; **paloma mensajera** carrier *o* homing pigeon **(b)** *(de presagios)* announcing, presaging

2 *nm,f (portador)* messenger; *(de mensajería)* courier; EXPR **matar al m.** to shoot the messenger

menso, -a *Méx Fam* **1** *adj* foolish, stupid

2 *nm,f* fool

menstruación *nf* menstruation

menstrual *adj* menstrual

menstruar [4] *vi* to menstruate, to have one's period

menstruo *nm* menstruation

mensual *adj* **(a)** *(que sucede cada mes)* monthly; **una inspección m.** a monthly inspection; **5.000 pesos mensuales** 5,000 pesos a month **(b)** *(que dura un mes)* monthly; **un pase m.** a monthly pass

mensualidad *nf* **(a)** *(sueldo)* monthly salary **(b)** *(pago)* monthly payment *o* instalment; **lo puede pagar en seis mensualidades** you can pay for it in six monthly instalments

mensualmente *adv* monthly

ménsula *nf Arquit* corbel

mensurable *adj* measurable

mensurar *vt* to measure

menta *nf* **(a)** *(planta)* mint **(b)** *(licor)* crème de menthe **(c)** *(esencia)* mint, peppermint; **un caramelo de m.** a mint, a peppermint; **té de m.** peppermint tea

mentada *nf Andes, Méx, Ven Fam* **una m. (de madre)** *(un insulto)* = grave insult directed at sb's mother; **contestaron con mentadas (de madre)** they answered by insulting his mother

mentado, -a *adj* **(a)** *(mencionado)* above-mentioned, aforementioned **(b)** *(famoso)* famous

mental *adj* mental

mentalidad *nf* mentality; **m. abierta/cerrada** open/closed mind; **la m. del siglo pasado** the mentality of people in the last century

mentalización *nf* mental preparation; **una campaña de m. de la opinión pública** a campaign to raise public awareness

mentalizar [14] **1** *vt* **m. a alguien de un problema** to make sb aware of a problem; **m. a alguien para que haga algo** to get sb to see *o* realize that they should do sth; **están mentalizados de la importancia del partido** they are fully aware of the importance of the match

2 mentalizarse *vpr* **todavía no se ha mentalizado de que ya no es el jefe** he still hasn't come to terms with the fact that he's not the boss any more; **ya me he mentalizado de que tengo que dejar de fumar** I've come to accept the fact that I have to stop smoking; **mentalízate, va a ser muy difícil** you've got to realize that it's going to be very difficult; **nos tenemos que mentalizar de que éste es un problema que nos afecta a todos** we have to realize that this is a problem that affects us all

mentalmente *adv* **(a)** *(con la mente)* mentally **(b)** *(intelectualmente)* intellectually

mentar [3] *vt* to mention; EXPR *Fam* **le mentó la madre,** *Méx* **le mentó madres** he swore at him, insulting his mother; EXPR *Méx Fam* **mejor miéntamela** I'd rather you gave me a kick in the head

mente *nf* **(a)** *(intelecto)* mind; **tiene una m. analítica** she has an analytical mind

(b) *(pensamiento)* mind; **no consigo borrar de la m. el accidente** I can't get the accident out of my mind; **me quedé con la m. en blanco** my mind went blank; **tener en m. algo** to have sth in mind; **tener en m. hacer algo** to intend to do sth; **traer a la m.** to bring to mind; **me vienen a la m. una serie de soluciones** a number of possible solutions come to mind; **el nombre no me viene a la m.** I can't think of the name

(c) *(mentalidad)* mentality; **abierto de m.** open-minded; **cerrado de m.** set in one's ways *o* opinions; **tiene una m. muy abierta** she's very open-minded

mentecato, -a 1 *adj* silly

2 *nm,f* nitwit

mentidero *nm* **(a)** *(lugar)* **es el m. del pueblo** it's where you get all the good village gossip **(b)** *(círculo de personas)* **en los mentideros políticos/intelectuales** in political/intellectual circles

mentir [63] *vi* to lie; **no me mientas** don't lie to me; **miente más que habla** he's a born liar; **esas estadísticas mienten, porque no tienen en cuenta...** those statistics give a false picture *o* are misleading, because they don't take into account...; **llovía, miento, granizaba cuando nos preparábamos para salir** it was raining, I tell a lie, it was hailing as we were getting ready to leave

mentira *nf* **(a)** *(falsedad)* lie; **una m. como una casa** *o* **una catedral** a whopping great lie; **¡m. cochina!** that's a filthy lie!; **siempre soy yo el que tiene que lavar los platos – ¡m.!** I'm always the one who has to wash the dishes – that's not true! *o* that's a lie!; **es m.** it's a lie, it's not true; **decir mentiras** to tell lies; **de m.** pretend, false; EXPR **parecer m.: aunque parezca m.** strange as it may seem; **parece m. que lo hayamos conseguido** I can hardly believe we've done it; **parece m. que te creas una cosa así** how can you possibly believe a thing like that?; **¡parece m., las cinco y todavía no ha llegado!** can you believe it, it's five o'clock and she still hasn't arrived! ►► ***m. piadosa*** white lie

(b) *Fam (en la uña)* white mark

mentirijilla *nf Fam* fib; **de mentirijillas** *(en broma)* as a joke, in fun; *(falso)* pretend, make-believe

mentiroso, -a 1 *adj* lying; *(engañoso)* deceptive

2 *nm,f* liar

mentís *nm inv* denial; **dar un m. (a)** to issue a denial (of)

mentol *nm* menthol

mentolado, -a *adj* menthol, mentholated

mentón *nm* chin

mentor, -ora *nm,f* mentor

menú *nm* (**a**) *(lista)* menu; *(comida)* food; **el m. (del día)** the set meal ►► ***m. de degustación*** = set meal comprising small portions of various typical dishes (**b**) *Informát* menu ►► ***m. de ayuda*** help menu; ***m. desplegable*** pull-down menu; ***m. jerárquico*** hierarchical menu

menudear **1** *vi* (**a**) *(abundar)* **en el debate menudearon las acusaciones** accusations flew thick and fast in the debate; **por la calle menudeaban los turistas** tourists thronged the streets; **en septiembre menudearon las tormentas** there were a lot of storms in September (**b**) *Andes, Méx Com* to sell retail
2 *vt* (**a**) *(repetir)* **sus padres menudeaban las visitas** her parents visited her repeatedly (**b**) *Andes, Méx Com* to sell retail

menudencia *nf* (**a**) *(tontería)* trifle, insignificant thing; **se pelearon por una m.** they had a fight over nothing *o* over some stupid little thing (**b**) *Am* **menudencias** *(menudillos)* giblets

menudeo *nm Andes, Méx Com* retailing; **vender al m.** to sell retail; **venta al m.** retailing

menudillos *nmpl* giblets

menudo, -a **1** *adj* (**a**) *(pequeño)* small; **gente menuda** kids
(**b**) *(insignificante)* trifling, insignificant
(**c**) *(para enfatizar)* **¡m. lío/gol!** what a mess/goal!; **¡menuda resaca llevas!** that's some hangover you've got there!; **¡m. susto me diste!** you gave me a real fright!, you frightened the life out of me!; **¡m. frío hace aquí!** it's absolutely freezing here!; **¡menuda hambre tengo!** I'm absolutely starving!; **claro que no pidió perdón, ¡menuda es ella!** of course she didn't apologize, she's not one to do things like that!
(**d**) **menudos** *(vísceras) (de aves)* giblets; *(de otros animales)* offal
(**e**) *(plato)* = stew made with tripe
2 a menudo *loc adv* often

meñique *nm* **(dedo) m.** little finger, *US & Scot* pinkie

meódromo *nm Esp Fam Hum Br* bog, *US* john

meollo *nm* core, heart; **el m. de la cuestión** the nub of the question, the heart of the matter

meón, -ona *nm,f Fam* **es un m.** *(adulto)* he has a weak bladder; *(niño)* he's always wetting himself

mequetrefe *nmf Fam* good-for-nothing

meramente *adv* merely

merca *nf CSur Fam* snow

mercachifle *nmf Pey* (**a**) *(comerciante)* pedlar (**b**) *(usurero)* money-grabber, shark

mercadear **1** *vi (comerciar)* to trade, to do business
2 *vt Col (productos)* to sell, to market

mercadeo *nm* marketing

mercader *nmf* merchant, trader

mercadería *nf esp Am* merchandise, goods; **se me arruinó toda la m.** all my produce was ruined

mercadillo *nm* flea market

mercado *nm* (**a**) *(lugar)* market ►► *RP* ***m. de abasto*** wholesale market; ***m. de abastos*** wholesale market; ***m. al aire libre*** open-air market; ***m. de alimentación*** food market; ***m. de ganado*** cattle market; ***m. mayorista*** wholesale market; *Chile* ***m. persa*** flea market; EXPR *RP Fam* **ser un m. persa** to be a mess; *Méx* ***m. sobre ruedas*** street market
(**b**) *Com & Fin* ***m. alcista*** bull market; ***m. al alza*** bull market; ***m. a la baja*** bear market; ***m. bajista*** bear market; ***m. bursátil*** stock market; ***m. de capitales*** capital market; ***m. común*** Common Market; ***M. Común Centroamericano*** Central Amercian Common Market, = Central American economic community formed by Costa Rica, El Salvador, Guatemala, Honduras and Nicaragua; ***M. Común del Sur*** MERCOSUR, = South American economic community consisting of Argentina, Brazil, Paraguay and Uruguay; ***m. continuo*** continuous market; ***m. de divisas*** currency market, foreign exchange market; ***m. exterior*** foreign market; ***mercados financieros*** financial markets; ***m. de futuros*** futures market; ***m. inmobiliario*** housing market, property market; ***m. interbancario*** interbank market; ***m. interior*** domestic market; ***m. laboral*** labour market; ***m. libre*** free market; ***m. de materias primas*** commodity market; ***m. monetario*** money market; ***m. nacional*** domestic market; ***m. negro*** black market; *Am* ***m. paralelo*** parallel market; ***m. de trabajo*** labour *o* job market; *UE* ***m. único*** single market; ***m. de valores*** securities market

mercadotecnia *nf* marketing

mercadotécnico, -a *adj* marketing; **técnicas mercadotécnicas** marketing techniques

mercancía **1** *nf* (**a**) *(producto)* merchandise, goods; **mercancías perecederas** perishable goods, perishables; **mercancías peligrosas** hazardous products; **transporte de mercancías** freight transport (**b**) *Fam (droga)* merchandise
2 mercancías *nm inv Ferroc Br* goods train, *US* freight train

mercante **1** *adj* merchant
2 *nm (barco)* merchantman, merchant ship

mercantil *adj* mercantile, commercial

mercantilismo *nm* (**a**) *Econ* mercantilism (**b**) *Pey (actitud)* commercialism

mercantilista **1** *adj* (**a**) *(partidario)* mercantilist (**b**) *(abogado)* specializing in commercial law
2 *mf* (**a**) *(partidario)* mercantilist (**b**) *(abogado)* expert in commercial law

mercantilizar [14] *vt* to commercialize

mercar [60] *vt Fam* to buy

merced *nf* (**a**) *(favor)* favour; **conceder una m. a alguien** to grant sb a favour; **m. a** thanks to; **a m. de algo/alguien** at the mercy of sth/sb (**b**) *(fórmula de tratamiento)* **vuestra** *o* **su m.** Your Grace

mercenario, -a **1** *adj* (**a**) *(soldado)* mercenary (**b**) *Pey (vendido)* mercenary
2 *nm,f* (**a**) *(soldado)* mercenary (**b**) *Pey (persona vendida)* **ser un m.** to be mercenary

mercería *nf* (**a**) *(género) Br* haberdashery, *US* notions (**b**) *(tienda) Br* haberdasher's (shop), *US* notions store

mercero, -a *nm,f Br* haberdasher, *US* notions seller

merchandising [mertʃan'daisin] *nm* merchandising

merchero, -a *nm,f Esp Fam (ladrón)* shoplifter

Mercosur [merko'sur] *nm (abrev de* **Mercado Común del Sur***)* MERCOSUR, = South American economic community consisting of Argentina, Brazil, Paraguay and Uruguay

mercromina® *nf* mercurochrome®

mercurial *adj* (**a**) *(del metal)* mercurial (**b**) *(del dios, del planeta)* Mercurial

Mercurio *nm* Mercury

mercurio *nm* mercury

mercurocromo *nm* mercurochrome®

merecedor, -ora *adj* **no soy m. de tu amor** I am not worthy of your love; **el jurado lo consideró m. del premio** the jury thought he deserved to win the prize; **no es m. de un castigo tan duro** he doesn't deserve such a harsh punishment

merecer [46] **1** *vt* to deserve, to be worthy of; **la isla merece una visita** the island is worth a visit; **merece la pena detenernos un poco más en este punto** it's worth spending a bit more time on this point; **no merece la pena** it's not worth it; **no merece la pena que te enfades** it's not worth getting angry about, there's no point in getting angry about it; **merece ser ascendido** he deserves to be promoted
2 *vi* to be worthy; **en edad de m.** of marriageable age
3 merecerse *vpr* to deserve; **se merece algo mejor** she deserves better; **se merece ganar** she deserves to win; **se lo tiene bien merecido** it serves him right; **te mereces que te expulsen** you deserve to be expelled; **no se merece la mujer que tiene** he doesn't deserve a wife like that

merecidamente *adv* deservedly; **ganaron m.** they deserved to win; **recibió m. el premio al mejor actor** he deservedly won the award for best actor

merecido *nm* **darle a alguien su m.** to give sb his/her just deserts; **recibió su m.** he got his just deserts

merendar [3] **1** *vi* to have tea *(as a light afternoon meal)*
2 *vt* to have for tea *(as a light afternoon meal)*
3 merendarse *vpr Fam* (**a**) *(derrotar)* **merendarse a alguien** to thrash sb (**b**) *(terminar)* to polish off; **me merendé el libro en una semana** I polished the book off in a week

merendero *nm* (**a**) *(chiringuito)* = open-air café or bar in the country or on the beach (**b**) *(zona de picnic)* picnic area

merendola *nf Esp Fam* splendid spread, *Br* slap-up tea

merengue **1** *nm* (**a**) *(dulce)* meringue (**b**) *(música, baile)* merengue (**c**) *RP Fam (lío, desorden)* mess; **tengo un m. de papeles encima de la mesa** my desk is covered in a mess *o* a jumble of papers
2 *adj Esp Fam Dep* = relating to Real Madrid Football Club; **el equipo m.** Real Madrid

merequetén *nm Ven Fam* rumpus

meretriz *nf Formal* prostitute

merezco *etc ver* **merecer**

meridano, -a 1 *adj* of/from Mérida *(Mexico)*
2 *nm,f* person from Mérida *(Mexico)*

merideño, -a 1 *adj* of/from Mérida *(Spain or Venezuela)*
2 *nm,f* person from Mérida *(Spain or Venezuela)*

meridiana *nf (sofá)* chaise longue

meridiano, -a 1 *adj* (a) *(hora)* midday (b) *(claro)* crystal clear; **su razonamiento es de una claridad meridiana** her reasoning is crystal clear
2 *nm* (a) *Geog* meridian ▸▸ ***el m. celeste*** the celestial meridian; ***el m. cero*** the Greenwich meridian; ***el m. de Greenwich*** the Greenwich meridian (b) *Geom* meridian

meridional 1 *adj* southern
2 *nmf* southerner

merienda *nf* (a) *(por la tarde)* tea *(as a light afternoon meal)*; *(en el campo)* picnic; EXPR *Esp Fam* **fue una m. de negros** *(fue un caos)* it was total chaos; *(fue una masacre)* it was a massacre ▸▸ ***m. cena*** early evening meal (b) *Cuba, RP (para la escuela)* snack

meriendo *etc ver* **merendar**

merino, -a 1 *adj* merino
2 *nm (tela)* merino (wool)

mérito *nm* merit; **todo el m. es suyo** she deserves all the credit; **tiene mucho m.** it's no mean achievement; **tiene mucho m. que cuide él solo de sus padres** he deserves a lot of praise for looking after his parents on his own; **de m.: un dramaturgo de m.** an accomplished playwright; **un edificio de m.** a fine building; **no quiero quitar m. a lo que ha hecho** I don't want to take away from *o* detract from what she has done; EXPR **hacer méritos: está haciendo méritos para que lo elijan** he is doing everything he can to get elected; **no ha hecho méritos para merecer un aprobado** he hasn't done enough to deserve a pass; **se está esforzando por hacer méritos ante su jefe** she's trying to get into her boss's good books ▸▸ ***m. técnico*** *(en patinaje sobre hielo)* technical merit

meritocracia *nf* meritocracy

meritorio, -a 1 *adj* worthy, deserving; **no es m. de tal distinción** he is not worthy of such an honour, he does not deserve such an honour
2 *nm,f* unpaid trainee *o* apprentice

Merlín *n pr* **(el mago) M.** Merlin (the Magician)

merlón *nm* brown wrasse

merluza *nf* (a) *(pez, pescado)* hake (b) *Esp Fam (borrachera)* **agarrar una m.** to get sozzled

merluzo, -a *nm,f Esp Fam* dimwit

merma *nf (de caudal)* fall; *(de energía, vitalidad, dinamismo)* diminishing; *(de ingresos, productividad)* fall; *(de calidad)* deterioration; **se ha producido una m. en los ingresos** there has been a reduction *o* fall in income, income has fallen

mermar 1 *vi (caudal)* to go down, to fall; *(energía, vitalidad, dinamismo)* to diminish; *(ingresos, productividad)* to fall; *(calidad)* to deteriorate
2 *vt (energía, vitalidad, dinamismo)* to diminish; *(ingresos, productividad, calidad)* to reduce

mermelada *nf* jam ▸▸ ***m. de naranja*** marmalade

mero, -a 1 *adj* (a) *(simple)* mere; **una mera excusa** just an excuse; **eso no deja de ser una mera opinión** that's still only an opinion; **es una mera coincidencia** it's a mere coincidence, it's nothing more than a coincidence
(b) *CAm, Méx Fam (propio, mismo)* **¿es usted? – yo m.** is that you? – the very same *o* it sure is; **me lo contó a mí m.** he told me himself *o* in person; **las meras vacaciones ya pasaron** *Br* the holidays as such are over, *US* the vacation as such is over; **viven en el m. centro** they live right in the centre
(c) *CAm, Méx Fam (preciso)* **llegó a la mera hora** he arrived on the dot *o* right on time; **el disparo dio en el m. centro** the shot hit it right *o* bang in the centre
2 *adv CAm, Méx Fam* (a) *(exactamente)* sharp; **aquí m.** right here; **nos vemos en el cine, ahí m.** I'll see you there, at the cinema (b) *(casi)* nearly, almost; **m. me mato** I nearly *o* almost got killed (c) **ya m.** *(ahora mismo)* right now; **ya m. me voy** I'm on my way right now
3 *nm* (a) *(pez)* grouper (b) *Méx Fam* **el m. m.: ¿quién es el m. m. en esta oficina?** who calls the shots in this office?

merodeador, -ora *nm,f* prowler, snooper

merodear *vi* to snoop, to prowl (**por** about *o* around)

merodeo *nm* prowling, snooping

merolico, -a *nm,f Méx Fam* = street vendor of patent medicines and herbal remedies

mersa *RP Fam* 1 *adj (decoración, ropa, canción)* tacky, *Br* naff; **es muy m.** *(persona)* he has really tacky *o Br* naff taste
2 *nmf* **es un m.** he has really tacky *o Br* naff taste
3 *nf* **la m.** the plebs, the riff-raff

mersada *nf RP Fam* **la ceremonia fue una m.** the ceremony was really tacky; **esa canción es una m.** that song is incredibly corny

mes *nm* (a) *(del año)* month; **se va unos meses de vacaciones** she's going away on *Br* holiday *o US* vacation for a few months; **las elecciones se celebrarán en el m. de enero** the election will take place in January; **al m. siguiente** the following month; **a los pocos meses** only a few months later; **todos los meses** every month; **un m. sí y otro no** every other month; **no ha parado de llover en todo el (santo) m.** it hasn't stopped raining all month (long); **al** *o* **por m.** a month; **viajo a Lima tres veces al** *o* **por m.** I go to Lima three times a month
(b) *(salario)* monthly salary
(c) *Fam (menstruación)* **está con el m.** it's her time of the month

mesa *nf* (a) *(mueble)* table; *(de oficina, despacho)* desk; **de m.: vino de m.** table wine; **calendario de m.** desk calendar; **quería reservar una m.** I'd like to book a table; **bendecir la m.** to say grace; **poner** *o Am* **tender la m.** to set the table; **quitar la m.** to clear the table; **sentarse a la m.** to sit down at the table; **¡a la m.!** dinner/tea/lunch is ready!; EXPR **a m. puesta** with all one's needs provided for; EXPR *Ven Fam* **pasar algo por debajo de la m.** not to bother with sth ▸▸ ***m. de billar*** billiard table; ***m. camilla*** = small round table under which a heater is placed; ***m. de comedor*** dining table; ***m. de dibujo*** drawing board; ***m. de juego*** gambling *o* gaming table; *RP* ***m. de luz*** bedside table; ***m. de mezclas*** mixing desk, mixer; ***m. (de) nido*** = nest of tables; *RP* ***m. de noche*** bedside table; ***m. de operaciones*** operating table; ***m. plegable*** folding table; *CSur* ***m. ratona*** coffee table; *Hist* ***la M. Redonda*** the Round Table; ***m. de trabajo*** worktable
(b) *(comité)* board, committee; *(en un debate)* panel ▸▸ *Esp* ***m. del congreso*** parliamentary committee; ***m. directiva*** executive board *o* committee; ***m. electoral*** = group supervising the voting in each ballot box; *RP* ***m. de examen*** examining board; ***m. de negociación*** negotiating table; ***m. redonda*** *(coloquio)* round table
(c) *(comida)* food; **le gusta la buena m.** she likes good food

mesada *nf* (a) *Am (pago mensual)* monthly payment, monthly instalment (b) *RP (para adolescentes)* pocket money, *US* allowance (c) *RP (encimera)* worktop

mesana *nf* (a) *(mástil)* mizzenmast (b) *(vela)* mizzensail

mesar 1 *vt* to tear
2 **mesarse** *vpr* **mesarse los cabellos** to pull *o* tear at one's hair

mescalero, -a 1 *adj* Mescalero, = of/from an Apache tribe once living in the south east of New Mexico
2 *nm,f* Mescalero, = person from an Apache tribe once living in the south east of New Mexico

mescalina *nf* mescaline

mescolanza = **mezcolanza**

mesenterio *nm Anat* mesentery

mesero, -a *nm,f Col, Guat, Méx, Salv* waiter, *f* waitress

meseta *nf* (a) *(llanura)* plateau, tableland; **la M. (Central)** the Castilian plateau *o* tableland (b) *(de escalera)* landing

mesetario, -a *adj* of the plateau *o* tableland; **la vegetación mesetaria** the vegetation of the plateau *o* tableland, the plateau's *o* tableland's vegetation

mesiánico, -a *adj* (a) *Rel* Messianic (b) *Pey (líder, comportamiento)* messianic

mesianismo *nm* (a) *Rel* Messianism (b) *Pey (fe ciega)* righteous faith

mesías *nm inv* (a) *Rel* **el M.** the Messiah (b) *Pey (salvador)* saviour, Messiah

mesilla, *RP* **mesita** *nf* **m. (de noche)** bedside table

mesnada *nf* armed retinue

Mesoamérica *n* Mesoamerica, = the cultural and geographical area extending from northern Mexico to Panama

mesoamericano, -a *adj* Mesoamerican

mesocarpio *nm Bot* mesocarp

mesocéfalo, -a *adj Med* mesocephalic

mesocracia *nf* government by the middle classes

mesocrático, -a *adj (sociedad)* governed by the middle classes; *(partido)* supporting government by the middle classes

mesolítico, -a 1 *adj* Mesolithic
2 *nm* **el Mesolítico** the Mesolithic (period)

mesomorfo, -a *nm,f* mesomorph

mesón *nm* (**a**) *(posada)* inn (**b**) *(bar, restaurante)* = old, country-style restaurant and bar (**c**) *Fís* meson (**d**) *Chile (mostrador) (en bar)* bar; *(en tienda)* counter

mesonero, -a *nm,f* (**a**) *Esp (en mesón)* innkeeper (**b**) *Chile, Ven (camarero)* waiter, *f* waitress

Mesopotamia *n* (**a**) *(en Asia)* Mesopotamia (**b**) *(en Argentina)* = region between the Paraná and the Uruguay-Pepirí Guazú rivers

mesopotámico, -a *adj* Mesopotamian

mesosfera *nf Geog* mesosphere

mesozoico, -a *Geol* 1 *adj* Mesozoic

2 *nm* **el Mesozoico** the Mesozoic (era)

mesta *nf Hist* **la M.** = organization set up during the reign of Alfonso X of Spain to oversee seasonal movements of livestock

mester *nm Anticuado* trade, craft ►► *Lit* ***m. de clerecía*** = Spanish medieval poetry composed by clerics and learned people; *Lit* ***m. de juglaría*** = popular Spanish medieval poetry performed by minstrels

mestizaje *nm* (**a**) *(de razas)* mixed-race breeding, racial interbreeding (**b**) *(de animales)* crossbreeding, interbreeding; *(de plantas)* crossing (**c**) *(de culturas)* mixing, cross-fertilization

mestizo, -a 1 *adj* (**a**) *(persona)* of mixed race, half-caste (**b**) *(animal, planta)* cross-bred

2 *nm,f* person of mixed race, half-caste

mesura *nf* (**a**) *(moderación)* moderation, restraint; **con m.** in moderation (**b**) *(cortesía)* courtesy, politeness (**c**) *(gravedad)* dignity, seriousness

> **Falso amigo**: El sustantivo inglés **measure** no es la traducción del español **mesura**. En inglés **measure** significa "medida" o "indicador".

mesurado, -a *adj* moderate, restrained

mesurar 1 *vt* to measure

2 **mesurarse** *vpr* to restrain oneself

meta 1 *nf* (**a**) *Dep (llegada)* finishing line ►► ***m. volante*** *(en ciclismo)* hot spot sprint (**b**) *Dep (portería)* goal; **marcar en propia m.** to score an own goal (**c**) *(objetivo)* aim, goal; **fijarse una m.** to set oneself a target *o* goal

2 *nmf Dep (portero)* goalkeeper

metabólico, -a *adj* metabolic

metabolismo *nm* metabolism ►► *Fisiol* ***m. basal*** basal metabolism

metabolizar *vt* to metabolize

metacarpiano *nm Anat* metacarpal

metacarpo *nm Anat* metacarpus

metacrilato *nm* methacrylate (resin)

metadona *nf* methadone

metafísica *nf* metaphysics *(singular)*

metafísico, -a 1 *adj* metaphysical

2 *nm,f* metaphysician

metáfora *nf* metaphor

metafóricamente *adv* metaphorically

metafórico, -a *adj* metaphorical

metagoge *nf Ling* personification

metal *nm* (**a**) *(material)* metal; *Hum* **el vil m.** filthy lucre ►► ***m. blanco*** white metal; ***m. noble*** noble metal; ***m. pesado*** heavy metal; ***metales preciosos*** precious metals (**b**) *Mús* brass (**c**) *(de voz)* timbre (**d**) *(medalla)* medal

metalenguaje *nm* metalanguage

metálico, -a 1 *adj* (**a**) *(objeto)* metal (**b**) *(sonido)* metallic (**c**) *(color)* metallic

2 *nm* **pagar en m.** to pay (in) cash; **recibieron una compensación en m.** they received a cash payment as compensation

metalífero, -a *adj* metal-bearing, metalliferous

metalingüístico, -a *adj* metalinguistic

metalización *nf* metallization

metalizado, -a *adj (pintura)* metallic

metalizar [14] 1 *vt* to metallize

2 **metalizarse** *vpr* to become metallized

metalografía *nf* metallography

metaloide *nm* metalloid

metalurgia *nf* metallurgy

metalúrgico, -a 1 *adj* metallurgical

2 *nm,f* metallurgist

metamórfico, -a *adj* metamorphic

metamorfismo *nm* metamorphism

metamorfosear 1 *vt* to metamorphose

2 **metamorfosearse** *vpr* to be metamorphosed *o* transformed (**en** into)

metamorfosis *nf inv* (**a**) *(en animales)* metamorphosis (**b**) *(en personas, ciudades)* metamorphosis, transformation

metano *nm* methane

metanol *nm* methanol

metástasis *nf inv Med* metastasis

metatarsiano, -a *adj Anat* metatarsal

metatarso *nm Anat* metatarsus

metate *nm Guat, Méx* grinding stone

metátesis *nf inv Ling* metathesis

metazoo *Zool* 1 *nm* metazoan

2 **metazoos** *nmpl (reino) Metazoa*; **de la familia de los metazoos** of the family *Metazoa*

metedura *nf Fam* ***m. de pata*** blunder, *Br* clanger

metegol *nm Arg Br* table football, *US* foosball

metejón *nm RP Fam* **tener un m. con alguien** to be crazy about sb

metempsícosis, metempsicosis *nf inv* metempsychosis, transmigration of souls

meteórico, -a *adj* (**a**) *(de los meteoros)* meteoric (**b**) *(crecimiento, desarrollo)* extremely rapid; **un ascenso m.** a meteoric rise

meteorismo *nm Med* tympanites, meteorism

meteorito *nm* meteorite

meteorización *nf (de roca)* weathering

meteoro *nm* meteor

meteorología *nf* meteorology

meteorológico, -a *adj* meteorological

meteorólogo, -a *nm,f (científico)* meteorologist; *(en televisión)* weatherman, *f* weatherwoman

metepatas *Fam* 1 *adj* **iqué m. eres!** you're always putting your foot in it!

2 *nmf inv* **es un m.** he's always putting his foot in it

METER 1 *vt* (**a**) *(introducir)* to put in; **m. algo/a alguien en algo** to put sth/sb in sth; **metió las manos en los bolsillos** she put her hands in her pockets; **no puedo m. la llave en la cerradura** I can't get the key in the lock; **lo metieron en la cárcel** they put him in prison; **su padre lo metió de conserje en la empresa** his father got him a job in the company as a porter; **m. dinero en el banco** to put money in the bank; **he metido todos mis ahorros en este proyecto** I've put all my savings into this project; **¿podrás m. todo en un solo disquete?** will you be able to get *o* fit it all on one disk?; *Fam* **meterle ideas a alguien en la cabeza** to put ideas into sb's head; *Fam* **no consigo meterle en la cabeza (que...)** I can't get it into his head (that...); *Fam* **mete la tijera todo lo que quieras** cut off as much as you like

(**b**) *(hacer participar)* **m. a alguien en algo** to get sb into sth; **¡en buen lío nos has metido!** this is a fine mess you've got us into!

(**c**) *(obligar a)* **m. a alguien a hacer algo** to make sb start doing sth; **me dieron un trapo y me metieron a limpiar el polvo** they gave me a cloth and set me dusting

(**d**) *(causar)* **m. prisa/miedo a alguien** to rush/scare sb; **m. ruido** to make a noise

(**e**) *(en automóvil)* **m. la primera/la marcha atrás** to go into first gear/reverse; **m. el freno** to brake

(**f**) *(en deportes) (anotar)* to score; **nos metieron dos goles** they scored two goals against us

(**g**) *Fam (asestar)* to give; **le metió un puñetazo** she gave him a punch

(**h**) *Fam (echar, soltar)* to give; **m. una bronca a alguien** to tell sb off; **me metió un rollo sobre la disciplina militar** he gave me this routine about military discipline; **te han metido un billete falso** they've given you a forged banknote

(**i**) *(prenda, ropa)* to take in; **hay que m. los pantalones de cintura** the trousers need taking in at the waist; **m. el bajo de una falda** to take up a skirt

(**j**) *Fam (dedicar, destinar)* **sabe jugar muy bien al billar porque le ha metido muchas horas** he plays billiards really well because he's put the hours in *o* spent hours practising

(**k**) *Am Fam* **¡métele!** *(date prisa)* get a move on!, hurry up!; **¡métele, que empieza la película!** get a move on *o* hurry up, the movie's starting!

(**l**) *RP Fam (aprobar)* to pass

2 *vi* (**a**) *muy Fam (copular)* to do it, *Br* to get one's end away (**b**) EXPR *Fam* **a todo m.** at full pelt

3 **meterse** *vpr* (**a**) *(entrar)* **no pudimos meternos** we couldn't get in;

nos metimos a *o* **en un cine** we went into a cinema; **se metió debajo de un árbol para protegerse de la lluvia** she took refuge from the rain under a tree; **se metió dentro del bosque** she entered the forest; **meterse en** to get into; **meterse en la cama** to get into bed; **dos semanas más y nos metemos en marzo** another two weeks and we'll be into March already; **se me ha metido agua en los oídos** I've got water in my ears; **se metió las manos en los bolsillos** she put her hands in her pockets; **meterse el dedo en la nariz** to pick one's nose; *Fig* **meterse mucho en algo** *(un papel, un trabajo, una película)* to get very involved in sth; *Fam* **se le ha metido en la cabeza (que...)** he's got it into his head (that...); **muchos jóvenes se meten en sí mismos** a lot of young people go into their shell; EXPR *muy Fam* **imétetelo donde te quepa!** stick it where the sun don't shine!

(**b**) *(en frase interrogativa) (estar)* to get to; **¿dónde se ha metido ese chico?** where has that boy got to?

(**c**) *(dedicarse)* **meterse a algo** to become sth; **meterse a torero** to become a bullfighter; **se ha metido de dependiente en unos grandes almacenes** he's got a job as a shop assistant in a department store; **me metí a vender seguros** I became an insurance salesman, I got a job selling insurance

(**d**) *(involucrarse)* to get involved (**en** in); **meterse en problemas** *o* **líos (con alguien)** to get into trouble (with sb)

(**e**) *(entrometerse)* to meddle, to interfere; **no te metas donde no te llaman** *o* **en lo que no te importa** mind your own business; **se mete en todo** he's always sticking his nose into other people's business; **meterse por medio** to interfere

(**f**) *(empezar)* **meterse a hacer algo** to get started on doing sth

(**g**) *(atacar)* **se meten con él en colegio** they pick on him at school; **ino te metas con mi novia!** leave my girlfriend alone!

(**h**) *Fam (comer)* to wolf down, *Br* to scoff

(**i**) *Fam (drogas)* **meterse coca/pastillas** to do coke/pills

---

meterete = **metomentodo**

metete = **metomentodo**

metiche = **metomentodo**

metición, -ona *Fam* **1** *adj* **no seas m.** don't be such a busybody *o Br* nosey-parker

2 *nm,f* busybody, *Br* nosey-parker

meticulosamente *adv* meticulously

meticulosidad *nf* meticulousness

meticuloso, -a *adj* meticulous

metida *nf Am Fam* ***m. de pata*** blunder, *Br* clanger

metido, -a **1** *adj* (**a**) *(implicado)* involved; **andar** *o* **estar m. en** to be involved in; **está m. en un lío** he's in trouble; **lleva años m. en el mundo del teatro** he's been involved in theatre for years; **el actor estaba muy m. en su papel** the actor was very involved in his part *o* had really got into his part

(**b**) *(abundante)* **m. en años** elderly; **m. en carnes** plump

(**c**) *Am Fam (entrometido)* **no seas m.** don't be such a busybody *o Br* nosey-parker

(**d**) *RP Fam (enamorado)* **estar m. con alguien** to be crazy about sb

2 *nm,f Am Fam* busybody, *Br* nosey-parker

metilo *nm* methyl

metlapil *nm Méx* = roller for grinding corn

metódicamente *adv* methodically

metódico, -a *adj* methodical

metodismo *nm* Methodism

metodista **1** *adj* Methodist

2 *nmf* Methodist

metodizar [14] *vt* to methodize, to systematize

método *nm* (**a**) *(sistema)* method; **no estoy de acuerdo con sus métodos de hacer las cosas** I don't agree with her way of doing things *o* her methods ▸▸ ***m. anticonceptivo*** method of contraception; ***el m. (de) Ogino*** the rhythm method (**b**) *(modo ordenado)* method; **proceder con m.** to proceed methodically (**c**) *(educativo)* method; **un m. de mecanografía** a method of teaching typing

metodología *nf* methodology

metodológico, -a *adj* methodological

metomentodo, *Andes, CAm* **metete,** *RP* **meterete,** *Méx, Ven* **metiche** *Fam* **1** *adj* **no seas m.** don't be such a busybody *o Br* nosey-parker

2 *nmf* busybody, *Br* nosey-parker

metonimia *nf* metonymy

metopa *nf Arte* metope

metra *nf Ven* (**a**) *(canica)* marble (**b**) *Fam (cabeza)* nut, *Br* bonce

metraje *nm* (**a**) *(longitud)* length (in metres); *(de película)* length, running time (**b**) *esp RP (extensión)* area; **según el m. del jardín** depending on how many square metres the garden is

metralla *nf* shrapnel

metralleta *nf* submachine gun

métrica *nf Lit* metrics

métrico, -a *adj* (**a**) *(del metro)* metric (**b**) *Lit* metrical

metrificación *nf Lit* versification

metro[1] *nm* (**a**) *(unidad)* metre; **metros por segundo** metres per second ▸▸ ***m. cuadrado*** square metre; ***m. cúbico*** cubic metre (**b**) *(cinta métrica)* tape measure (**c**) *Lit* metre

metro[2] *nm (transporte) Br* underground, *US* subway; **en m.** *Br* on the *o* by underground, *US* on the *o* by subway

metrología *nf* metrology

metrónomo *nm* metronome

metrópoli *nf,* **metrópolis** *nf inv* (**a**) *(ciudad importante)* metropolis (**b**) *(de colonia) (nación)* mother country; *(ciudad)* metropolis

metropolitano, -a **1** *adj* metropolitan; **el cinturón m. de Barcelona** the metropolitan area of Barcelona, greater Barcelona; **ferrocarril m.** *Br* underground, *US* subway

2 *nm (metro) Br* underground, *US* subway

mexica [me'χika] **1** *adj* Mexica

2 *nmf* Mexica

mexicalense [meχika'lense] **1** *adj* of/from Mexicali *(Mexico)*

2 *nmf* person from Mexicali *(Mexico)*

mexicanismo [meχika'nismo] *nm* Mexicanism

mexicano, -a [meχi'kano, -a] **1** *adj* Mexican

2 *nm,f* Mexican

México ['meχiko] *n* (**a**) *(país)* Mexico (**b**) *(capital)* Mexico City ▸▸ ***M. Distrito Federal*** the Federal District of Mexico

mexiquense [meχi'kense] **1** *adj* of/from the state of Mexico

2 *nmf* person from the state of Mexico

mezanina, mezzanina *nf Ven* mezzanine

mezanine, mezzanine *nm CAm, Col, Méx* mezzanine

mezcal *nm* (**a**) *(planta)* mescal (**b**) *(bebida)* mescal

mezcalina *nf* mescaline

mezcla *nf* (**a**) *(de materiales, productos) (resultado)* mixture, combination; *(acción)* mixing; **una m. de tabacos/whiskys** a blend of tobaccos/whiskies; **el verde es resultado de la m. del azul y del amarillo** green is the result of mixing blue and yellow; **cuando hierva la leche, añádala a la m.** when the milk boils, add it to the mixture; **es una m. de comedia y tragedia** it's a mixture of comedy and tragedy

(**b**) *(de culturas, pueblos) (resultado)* mixture; *(acción)* mixing

(**c**) *(tejido)* mix

(**d**) *Mús & TV (resultado)* mix; *(acción)* mixing; **mesa de mezclas** mixing desk, mixer

(**e**) ***m. explosiva*** explosive mixture; *Fig* **la m. explosiva de alcohol y drogas** the explosive combination of alcohol and drugs

mezclador, -ora **1** *nm,f (persona)* mixer ▸▸ ***m. de imagen*** vision mixer; ***m. de sonido*** sound mixer

2 *nm (dispositivo)* mixer ▸▸ ***m. de imagen*** *Br* vision mixer, *US* switcher; ***m. de sonido*** mixer

mezcladora *nf (hormigonera)* cement mixer

mezclar **1** *vt* (**a**) *(combinar, unir)* to mix; *(tabaco, whisky)* to blend; **m. algo con algo** to mix sth with sth; **mezcló la pintura roja con la amarilla** she mixed the red and yellow paint together, she mixed the red paint with the yellow

(**b**) *(culturas, pueblos)* to mix

(**c**) *(confundir, desordenar)* to mix up; **no mezcles las piezas** don't mix the pieces up; **creo que estás mezclando los países** I think you're mixing up *o* muddling up the countries

(**d**) *(implicar)* **m. a alguien en algo** to involve sb in sth, to get sb mixed up in sth; **no me mezcles en tus asuntos** don't involve me in your affairs, don't get me mixed up in your affairs

2 mezclarse *vpr* (**a**) *(juntarse)* to mix (**con** with); **no me mezclo con gente como esa** I don't mix *o* associate with people like that

(**b**) *(culturas, pueblos)* to mix

(**c**) *(difuminarse)* **mezclarse entre** to disappear *o* blend into; **se mezcló entre la muchedumbre** she disappeared into the crowd

(**d**) *(implicarse)* **mezclarse en** to get involved in, to get mixed up in; **se mezcló en un asunto de contrabando** he got involved *o* mixed up in a smuggling racket

mezclilla *nf* (**a**) *(tela basta)* = cloth woven from mixed fibres (**b**) *Chile, Méx (tela vaquera)* denim; **pantalones de m.** jeans

mezco *etc ver* **mecer**

mezcolanza, mescolanza *nf Fam* mishmash, *Br* hotchpotch, *US* hodgepodge; **había una m. de cosas encima de su mesa** there was a jumble of things on her desk; **su música es una m. de estilos** his music is a *Br* hotchpotch *o US* hodgepodge of styles

mezquinar *vt Am Fam* to be mean *o* stingy with, to skimp on

mezquindad *nf* (**a**) *(avaricia)* meanness, stinginess (**b**) *(carácter miserable)* meanness, nastiness (**c**) *(acción avara)* **estoy harta de tus mezquindades** I'm fed up of you being so mean *o* stingy (**d**) *(acción miserable)* **estoy harta de tus mezquindades** I'm fed up of you being so mean *o* nasty

mezquino[1], -a 1 *adj* (**a**) *(avaro)* mean, stingy (**b**) *(miserable)* mean, nasty (**c**) *(diminuto)* miserable
2 *nm,f* (**a**) *(avaro)* miser; **eres un m.** you're so mean *o* stingy (**b**) *(miserable)* **eres un m.** you're so mean *o* nasty

mezquino[2] *nm Méx* wart

mezquita *nf* mosque

mezquite *nm* mesquite

mezzanina = **mezanina**

mezzanine = **mezanine**

mezzosoprano, mezzo-soprano [metsoso' prano] *nf* mezzo-soprano

mg (*abrev de* **miligramo**) mg

MHz (*abrev de* **megahercio**) MHz

mi[1] *nm (nota musical)* E; *(en solfeo)* mi; *ver también* **do**

mi[2] (*pl* **mis**) *adj posesivo* (**a**) *(en general)* my; **mi casa** my house; **mis libros** my books (**b**) *(en tratamiento militar)* **¡sí, mi teniente/capitán!** yes, sir!

mí *pron personal (después de prep)* (**a**) *(en general)* me; **este trabajo no es para mí** this job isn't for me; **no se fía de mí** he doesn't trust me
(**b**) *(reflexivo)* myself; **debo pensar más en mí (mismo)** I should think more about myself
(**c**) *(en frases)* **¡a mí qué!** so what?, why should I care?; **para mí** *(yo creo)* as far as I'm concerned, in my opinion; **por mí** as far as I'm concerned; **por mí, no hay inconveniente** it's fine by me

mía *ver* **mío**

miaja *nf Fam* (**a**) *(miga)* crumb (**b**) *(pizca)* tiny bit; **dame una m. de helado** give me a tiny bit of ice cream; **su casa está una m. lejos** her house is a tad far away

mialgia *nf Med* myalgia

miasma *nm* miasma

miau *nm* miaow

Mibor ['miβor] *nm Fin* (*abrev de* **Madrid InterBank Offered Rate**) Mibor

mica *nf* (**a**) *(mineral)* mica (**b**) *Méx (plástico)* plastic sheet

micado = **mikado**

micción *nf Med (acción)* urination

micénico, -a *adj* Mycenaean

miche *nm Ven* (**a**) *(aguardiente)* = cane spirit flavoured with herbs and spices (**b**) *Fam (bebida alcohólica)* booze

michelín *nm Fam* spare tyre

michero, -a *nm,f Ven Fam* boozer

michino, -a, micho, -a *nm,f Fam* kitty, pussy

michoacano, -a 1 *adj* of/from Michoacán *(Mexico)*
2 *nm,f* person from Michoacán *(Mexico)*

micifuz *nm Fam* kitty, puss

mico *nm* (**a**) *(animal)* (long-tailed) monkey; EXPR **ser el último m.** to be the lowest of the low; EXPR *Fam* **volverse m.: me volví m. para hacerlo** I had a hell of a job doing it; **se volvió m. para encontrar la salida** I nearly did my head in trying to find the way out (**b**) *Fam (pequeño)* **es un m.** he's a midget *o Br* titch (**c**) *Fam (feo)* **es un m.** he's an ugly devil

micología *nf* mycology

micólogo, -a *nm,f* mycologist

micosis *nf inv* mycosis

micra *nf* micron

micrero, -a *Chile* 1 *adj* bus; **la huelga micrera** the bus strike
2 *nm,f* bus driver

micro- *pref* micro-

micro 1 *nm* (**a**) *Fam (micrófono)* mike (**b**) *Fam (microbús)* minibus
2 *nm o nf Arg, Bol, Chile (autobús)* bus

microamperio *nm Fís* microampere

microbiano, -a *adj* microbial

microbicida *adj* germicidal

microbio *nm* (**a**) *(organismo unicelular)* germ, microbe (**b**) *Fam (niño)* ankle-biter (**c**) *Fam (enano)* shrimp

microbiología *nf* microbiology

microbiológico, -a *adj* microbiological

microbiólogo, -a *nm,f* microbiologist

microbús (*pl* **microbuses**) *nm* (**a**) *(autobús)* minibus (**b**) *Méx (taxi)* (collective) taxi

microcéfalo, -a *adj* microcephalic

microcentro *nm RP* business district *(in a city centre)*

microchip *nm* microchip

microcircuito *nm* microcircuit

microcirugía *nf* microsurgery

microclima *nm* microclimate

microcomputador *nm*, **microcomputadora** *nf esp Am* microcomputer

microcosmo *nm*, **microcosmos** *nm inv* microcosm

microcrédito *nm Econ* microcredit

microeconomía *nf* microeconomics *(singular)*

microeconómico, -a *adj* microeconomic

microelectrónica *nf* microelectronics *(singular)*

microelectrónico, -a *adj* microelectronic

microempresa *nf Com* very small company

microficha *nf* microfiche

microfilm (*pl* **microfilms**), **microfilme** *nm* microfilm

microfilmación *nf* microfilming

microfilmar *vt* to microfilm

microfilme = **microfilm**

micrófono *nm* microphone ▸▸ ***m. inalámbrico*** cordless microphone

microfotografía *nf* (**a**) *(actividad)* microphotography (**b**) *(fotografía)* microphotograph

microinformática *nf Informát* microcomputing

microlentilla *nf* contact lens

micrómetro *nm* micrometer

micrón *nm* micron

Micronesia *n* Micronesia

microonda *nf* microwave

microondas *nm inv* microwave (oven)

microordenador *nm Esp* microcomputer

microorganismo *nm* micro-organism

microporoso, -a *adj* microporous

microprocesador *nm Informát* microprocessor

microprogramación *nf Informát* microprogramming

microscopía *nf* microscopy

microscópico, -a *adj* (**a**) *(con microscopio)* microscopic (**b**) *(organismo)* microscopic (**c**) *Fam (diminuto)* microscopic

microscopio *nm* microscope ▸▸ ***m. electrónico*** electron microscope

microsegundo *nm* microsecond

microsurco *nm* (**a**) *(surco)* microgroove (**b**) *Anticuado (disco)* long-playing record, LP

microtomo, micrótomo *nm Tec* microtome

Midas *n Mitol* **el rey M.** King Midas

MIDI ['miði] *nm Informát* (*abrev de* **musical instrument digital interface**) MIDI

midiera *etc ver* **medir**

mido *etc ver* **medir**

miéchica *interj Andes Fam Euf Br* sugar!, *US* shoot!; **¿dónde m. estabas?** where the heck were you?

miedica *Esp Fam* 1 *adj* yellow, chicken
2 *nmf* scaredy-cat, coward

mieditis *nf inv Fam Hum* the jitters, the willies; **le tiene m. al dentista** the dentist gives him the willies; **le entró m.** he got the jitters *o* willies

miedo *nm* fear; **m. cerval** terrible fear, terror; **dar m.** to be frightening; **me da m. conducir** *o Am* **manejar** I'm afraid *o* frightened of driving; **me da m. que se entere** I'm frightened *o* scared she'll find out; **agarró** *o Am* **tomó** *o Esp* **cogió m. a volar** he developed a fear of flying; **meter m. a alguien** to frighten sb; **nos metió m. en el cuerpo** it put the fear of God into us; **por m. a** for fear of; **no le dije la verdad por m. a ofenderla** I didn't tell her the truth for fear of offending her; **temblar de m.** to tremble with fear; **tener m. a** *o* **de (hacer algo)** to be afraid of (doing sth); **le tiene m. a la oscuridad** he's scared *o* afraid of the dark; **tengo m. de que se estropee** I'm frightened it'll get damaged; **morirse de m.** to die of fright, to be terrified; EXPR *Esp Fam* **de m.: la película estuvo de m.** the movie was brilliant; **lo pasamos de m.** we had a fantastic time; **cogió una borrachera de m.** he got totally plastered; **cocina de m.** he's a fantastic *o* an amazing cook; EXPR *muy Fam* **cagarse de m.** to shit oneself; EXPR *muy Fam* **estar cagado de m.** to be shit-scared ▸▸ ***m. escénico*** stage fright

miedoso, -a 1 *adj* **¡no seas m.!** don't be so scared *o* frightened!; **es muy m.** he gets scared very easily

2 *nm,f* **es un m.** he gets scared easily

miel *nf* **(a)** *(sustancia)* honey; EXPR **ser pura m.** to be as sweet as honey; EXPR **m. sobre hojuelas** all the better; EXPR **no está hecha la m. para la boca del asno** it's like casting pearls before swine; EXPR **dejar a alguien/quedarse con la m. en los labios** to leave sb/to be left feeling frustrated ▸▸ ***m. líquida*** clear honey

(b) mieles *(satisfacción)* **saborear las mieles del éxito/de la victoria** to savour the sweet taste of success/victory

miela *etc ver* **melar**

mielga *nf* **(a)** *(pez)* spiny dogfish **(b)** *(alfalfa)* alfalfa

mielina *nf Fisiol* myelin

mieloma *nf Med* myeloma

miembro *nm* **(a)** *(integrante)* member; **los países miembros de la OTAN** NATO's member states ▸▸ ***m. fundador*** founder member; ***m. de pleno derecho*** full member **(b)** *(extremidad)* limb, member ▸▸ ***miembros inferiores*** lower limbs; ***miembros superiores*** upper limbs **(c)** *Euf (pene)* **m. (viril)** male member

mientes *nfpl* mind; **parar m. (en algo)** to consider (sth); **traer a las m.** to bring to mind

miento (a) *ver* **mentar (b)** *ver* **mentir**

mientras 1 *conj* **(a)** *(al tiempo que)* while; **leía m. comía** she was reading while she ate

(b) *(siempre que)* **m. viva** as long as I live; **m. pueda** as long as I can

(c) *(hasta que)* **m. no se pruebe lo contrario** until proved otherwise

(d) *(cuanto)* **m. más/menos** the more/less; **m. menos hables, mejor** the less you speak the better

(e) m. que *(con tal de que)* as long as; **m. que no hagas ruido, puedes quedarte** as long as you don't make any noise, you can stay

(f) m. (que) *(por el contrario)* whereas, whilst

2 *adv* **m. (tanto)** meanwhile, in the meantime

miér. *(abrev de* **miércoles***)* Wed

miércoles 1 *nm inv* Wednesday ▸▸ ***M. de Ceniza*** Ash Wednesday; *ver también* **sábado**

2 *interj Fam Euf Br* sugar, *US* shoot; *Am* **¡de m.!: ¡qué irresponsable de m.!** what an irresponsible so-and-so!; *Am* **¡hace un frío de m.!** *Br* it's blinking freezing!, *US* it's goddamn freezing!

mierda *muy Fam* **1** *nf* **(a)** *(excremento)* shit; **casi piso una m.** I almost trod in some shit

(b) *(suciedad)* crap; **tu mesa está llena de m.** your desk is covered in crap; **la casa está hecha una m.** the house is *Br* a bloody *o US* a goddamn tip

(c) *(cosa sin valor)* **una m. de guitarra** a crappy guitar; **es una m.** it's (a load of) crap; **fue una m. de actuación** it was a crap performance; *Hum* **es una m. pinchada en un palo** it's a heap of shite; **de m.** *(malo)* shitty, crappy; **es un imbécil de m.** he's a *Br* bloody *o US* goddamn idiot

(d) *Esp (borrachera)* **agarrar** *o* **coger una m.** to get shit-faced; **tener una m.** to be shit-faced

(e) *(hachís)* shit

(f) EXPR **¡a la m. con el examen!** screw the exam!; *Esp* **¡y una m.!** like hell (I/you/*etc* will)!; **cubrirse de m.** to make a complete *Br* arse *o US* ass of oneself; **estar hecho una m.** to be a complete wreck; **irse a la m.** *(proyecto)* to go down the tubes; **mandar a alguien a la m.** to tell sb to piss off; **mandó el proyecto a la m.** she said to hell with the project; **¡vete a la m.!** go to hell!, piss off!

2 *nmf* shithead

3 *interj* shit!; **¡m., ya me he olvidado!** shit, I've forgotten!

mierdoso, -a *muy Fam adj* **(a)** *(sucio)* disgusting, gross **(b)** *(despreciable) (persona)* shitty; *(cosa)* crappy

mies 1 *nf (cereal)* ripe corn

2 mieses *nfpl (campo)* cornfields

miga *nf* **(a)** *(de pan)* crumb **(b) migas** *(plato)* fried breadcrumbs **(c)** EXPR *Fam* **hacer buenas/malas migas** to get on well/badly; *Fam* **hacerse migas** *(cosa)* to be smashed to bits; *Fam* **estar hecho(a) migas** *(persona)* to be shattered; *Fam* **hacer migas a alguien** *(desmoralizar)* to shatter sb; *Fam* **tener m.** *(ser sustancioso)* to have a lot to it; *(ser complicado)* to have more to it than meets the eye

migaja *nf* **(a)** *(de alimento)* bit; *(de pan)* crumb **(b) migajas** *(restos)* leftovers; **los hijos se disputaron las migajas de la herencia** the children fought over what was left of their inheritance

migala, migale *nf (araña)* bird spider ▸▸ ***m. albañil*** trapdoor spider

migar [38] *vt* **(a)** *(pan)* to crumble **(b)** *(líquido)* to add crumbs to

migra *nf Méx Fam Pey* **la m.** = US police border patrol

migración *nf* migration

migraña *nf* migraine

migrar *vi* to migrate

migratorio, -a *adj* migratory

Miguel *n pr* **San M.** St Michael

miguelito *nm CSur* = three-headed nail spread on the road to puncture vehicles' tyres

mijo[1] *nm* millet

mijo[2]**, -a** *nm,f Am Fam* **(a)** *(a un hijo) Br* love, *US* honey; **¿por qué lloras, m.?** why are you crying, *Br* love *o US* honey? **(b)** *(a un adulto)* dear; **¿qué precisa, mija?** what is it you need, dear? **(c)** *(entre iguales)* pal, *Br* mate, *US* buddy; **¡mira, m., cállate la boca!** listen, pal *o Br* mate *o US* buddy, just shut your mouth!

mikado, micado *nm* mikado

mil *núm* thousand; **dos m.** two thousand; **m. pesos** a thousand pesos; **miles de dólares** thousands of dollars; **m. cien** one thousand one hundred; **miles (de)** *(gran cantidad)* thousands (of); **tengo m. cosas que hacer** I've got loads of things to do; EXPR *RP Fam* **a m.: estar a m.** to be rushed off one's feet; **ponerse a m.** to go flat out; EXPR **m. y una** *o* **uno** a thousand and one; *ver también* **treinta**

milagrero, -a *Fam* **1** *adj* **(a)** *(crédulo)* = who believes in miracles **(b)** *(milagroso)* miraculous, miracle-working

2 *nm,f* = person who believes in miracles

milagro *nm* **(a)** *(crédulo)* miracle; *Fig* **hacer milagros** to work wonders

(b) *(cosa sorprendente)* wonder, miracle; **fue un m. que nos encontráramos** it was a wonder *o* miracle we found each other; **se acordó de mi cumpleaños – ¡m.!** he remembered my birthday – wonders will never cease!; **de m.: cupieron todos de m.** it was a wonder *o* miracle that they all fitted in; **me acordé de su cumpleaños de m.** by some miracle or other *o* amazingly enough, I remembered his birthday

milagrosamente *adv* miraculously

milagroso, -a *adj* **(a)** *(aparición)* miraculous **(b)** *(solución)* **un remedio m.** a miracle cure **(c)** *(asombroso)* amazing; **es m. que el jarrón siga entero** it's a wonder *o* miracle the vase is still in one piece

Milán *n* Milan

milanés, -esa 1 *adj* of/from Milan *(Italy)*

2 *nm,f* person from Milan *(Italy)*

milanesa *nf (de ternera)* Wiener schnitzel, breaded veal escalope; **m. de pollo/pescado** chicken/fish fried in breadcrumbs; **m. de berenjena** *Br* aubergine *o US* eggplant fried in breadcrumbs; **a la m.** fried in breadcrumbs

milano *nm* kite ▸▸ ***m. negro*** black kite; ***m. real*** red kite

mildiú, mildíu *nm* mildew

milenario, -a 1 *adj (antiguo)* (very) ancient

2 *nm* **(a)** *(milenio)* millennium **(b)** *(aniversario)* millennium

milenarismo *nm (creencia)* millenarianism

milenarista 1 *adj* millenarianist

2 *nmf* millenarianist

milenio *nm* millennium

milenrama *nf* yarrow, milfoil

milésima *nf (fracción)* thousandth ▸▸ ***m. de segundo*** millisecond

milésimo, -a *núm* thousandth; **la milésima parte** a thousandth; *ver también* **octavo**

milhojas *nm inv (dulce)* millefeuille

mili *nf Esp Fam* military service; **hacer la m.** to do one's military service

miliamperio *nm Fís* milliampere

milibar *nm (unidad)* millibar

milicia *nf* **(a)** *(profesión)* military (profession) **(b)** *(grupo armado)* militia ▸▸ *Antes* ***milicias universitarias*** = in Spain, military service for students

miliciano, -a *nm,f* militiaman, *f* female soldier

milico *nm Andes, RP Fam Pey* **(a)** *(militar)* soldier; **los milicos tomaron el poder** the military took power **(b)** *(policía)* pig

miligramo *nm* milligram

mililitro *nm* millilitre

milimetrado *adj* **papel m.** graph paper

milimétrico, -a *adj (preciso)* very precise; **con una precisión milimétrica** with pinpoint accuracy

milímetro *nm* millimetre; EXPR **al m.: tengo calculada la duración al m.** I've calculated how long it will take down to the last second; **siento no poder ofrecer datos al m.** I'm sorry I can't give you exact figures

militancia *nf* militancy; **la m. activa del partido** the active membership of the party

militante 1 *adj* militant
2 *nmf* member; **un antiguo m. comunista** a former Communist Party member ►► ***m. de base*** grass roots *o* rank and file member

militar[1] 1 *adj* military
2 *nmf* soldier; **el general es el segundo m. que asesina el grupo en lo que va de año** the general is the second member of the military to be murdered by the group this year; **los militares** the military

militar[2] *vi* **(a)** *(en partido, sindicato)* to be a member **(en** of); **militó en la izquierda durante su juventud** he was an active left-winger in his youth **(b)** *(apoyar)* **son muchas circunstancias las que militan a** *o* **en su favor** there are many circumstances in his favour; **en** *o* **a su defensa milita que es menor de edad** in his defence is the fact that he is a minor

militarismo *nm* militarism

militarista 1 *adj* militarist
2 *nmf* militarist

militarización *nf* militarization

militarizar [14] *vt* to militarize

militarmente *adv* militarily

militroncho *nm Esp Fam Hum (soldado) Br* squaddie, *US* grunt

milivoltio *nm Elec* millivolt

milla *nf* **(a)** *(terrestre)* mile **(b)** *(marina)* mile ►► ***m. marina*** nautical mile ***m. náutica*** nautical mile

millar *nm* **(a)** *(mil unidades)* thousand; **un m. de personas** a thousand people **(b) millares** *(grandes cantidades)* thousands; **a millares** by the thousand

millardo *nm* billion, thousand million

millo *nm Esp Br* maize, *US* corn

millón *núm* **(a)** *(mil millares)* million; **dos millones** two million; **un m. de personas** a million people; **tengo un m. de cosas que hacer** I've got a million things to do; **un m. de gracias** thanks a million; EXPR *Ven Fam* **a m.: estar a m.** to be rushed off one's feet; **ponerse a m.** to go flat out **(b) millones** *(un dineral)* a fortune, millions; **su casa costó millones** their house cost a fortune

millonada *nf Fam* **una m.** a fortune, millions

millonario, -a 1 *adj* **un premio m.** a prize worth millions; **pérdidas millonarias** losses running into millions
2 *nm,f* millionaire, *f* millionairess

millonésima *nf* millionth

millonésimo, -a *núm* millionth; **la millonésima parte** a millionth

milonga *nf* **(a)** *(baile)* = popular dance from Argentina and Uruguay **(b)** *(canción)* = popular song from Argentina and Uruguay; EXPR *RP* **llorar la m.: anda siempre llorando la m.** he's always moaning about something; **¡no vengas a llorarme la m.!** don't come crying to me! **(c)** *RP Fam (juerga)* partying; **salieron de m.** they went out on the town

milonguear *vi RP* to sing/dance milongas

milonguero, -a *RP Fam* **1** *adj* **ser muy m.** to be a real party animal
2 *nm,f* party animal

milpa *nf CAm, Méx* cornfield

milpear *CAm, Méx* **1** *vt (labrar)* to till
2 *vi (brotar)* to sprout

milpero *nm CAm, Méx* cornfield hand

milpiés *nm inv* millipede

milrayas *nm inv* striped cloth

miltomate *nm CAm, Méx* = small, whitish wild tomato

mimado, -a 1 *adj* spoiled
2 *nm,f* **es un m.** he's very spoiled

mimar *vt* to spoil, to pamper

> **Falso amigo**: El verbo inglés **to mime** no es la traducción del español **mimar**. En inglés **to mime** significa "hacer mímica" o "representar con gestos".

mimbre *nm* **(a)** *(material)* wicker, wickerwork; **una cesta de m.** a wicker *o* wickerwork basket **(b)** *(arbusto)* osier

mimbrera *nf* **(a)** *(arbusto)* osier **(b)** *(plantación)* osier bed

mimbrería *nf RP (arte)* wickerwork

mimeografiar *vt* to mimeograph

mimeógrafo *nm* mimeograph

mímesis, mimesis *nf inv* mimesis

miméticamente *adv* **seguir algo m.** to follow sth exactly

mimético, -a *adj* **(a)** *(de la mímesis)* mimetic **(b)** *(que muestra mimetismo)* imitative

mimetismo *nm (de animal, planta)* mimicry, *Espec* mimesis

mimetizar [14] **1** *vt (imitar)* to copy, to imitate
2 mimetizarse *vpr (camaleón)* to change colour

mímica *nf* **(a)** *(mimo)* mime **(b)** *(lenguaje)* sign language

mímico, -a *adj* mime; **lenguaje m.** sign language

mimo 1 *nm* **(a)** *(zalamería)* pampering; **con tanto m. lo están malcriando** they're spoiling him by pampering him like that
(b) *(cariño)* **trata a sus nietos con mucho m.** she makes a real fuss of her grandchildren; **hacerle mimos a alguien** to kiss and cuddle sb
(c) *(cuidado, esmero)* loving care; **con m.** with loving care, lovingly; **trata su colección de discos con mucho m.** he looks after his record collection with loving care
(d) *(representación teatral)* mime; **hacer m.** to perform mime
2 *nmf (artista)* mime artist

mimosa *nf* mimosa

mimoso, -a *adj* affectionate; **el bebé está m.** the baby wants a cuddle

min *(abrev de* **minuto***)* min

mina[1] *nf* **(a)** *(de mineral)* mine; **m. de carbón/oro** coal/gold mine ►► ***m. a cielo abierto*** opencast mine
(b) *Mil* mine; *(en tierra)* mine, land mine ►► ***m. antipersona*** *o* ***antipersonal*** antipersonnel mine; ***m. antitanque*** antitank mine; ***m. magnética*** magnetic mine; ***m. terrestre*** land mine; ***m. submarina*** undersea mine
(c) *(de lápiz)* lead
(d) *(cosa, persona rentable)* gold mine; **este bar es una m.** this bar is a gold mine
(e) *(fuente)* mine; **la enciclopedia es una m. de información** the encyclopaedia is a mine of information

mina[2] *nf CSur Fam* **(a)** *(mujer) Br* bird, *US* chick; **esta noche salimos a buscar minas** we're going out to try and *Br* pull some birds *o US* score some chicks tonight **(b)** *(amante)* **tiene una m.** he has a bit on the side

minado, -a *adj* mined

minador, -ora *Mil* **1** *nm,f* sapper
2 *nm (buque)* mine layer

minar *vt* **(a)** *Mil* to mine **(b)** *(socavar)* to undermine; **están minando los intentos de alcanzar un acuerdo** they are undermining the efforts to reach an agreement; **el tabaco está minando su salud** cigarettes are damaging her health

minarete *nm* minaret

mineral 1 *adj* mineral
2 *nm* **(a)** *(sustancia)* mineral **(b)** *(mena)* ore; **m. de hierro** iron ore

mineralización *nf* mineralization

mineralizar [14] **1** *vt* to mineralize
2 mineralizarse *vpr* to become mineralized

mineralogía *nf* mineralogy

mineralogista *nmf* mineralogist

minería *nf* **(a)** *(técnica)* mining **(b)** *(sector)* mining industry

minero, -a 1 *adj* mining; *(producción, riqueza)* mineral; **industria minera** mining industry
2 *nm,f* miner

mineromedicinal *adj* **agua m.** mineral water

Minerva *n Mitol* Minerva

minestrone *nf*, **minestrón** *nm Am* minestrone

minga[1] *Fam* **1** *nf* **(a)** *Esp (pene) Br* willy, *US* peter **(b)** *RP (negación)* **hablé con él pero m. de conseguir lo que quería** I spoke to him but there was no way he was going to give me what I wanted; **no tiene m. de oído para la música** he's got absolutely no ear for music at all
2 *interj RP* **¿terminaste el trabajo? – im.! ¡es larguísimo!** have you finished the work? – you must be joking, it's taking ages!

minga[2] *nf*, **mingaco** *nm Andes* **(a)** *(trabajo)* = farm labour done on holidays in exchange for a meal **(b)** *(cooperación)* = traditional communal labour performed in Andean rural communities; EXPR **hacer algo en m.** to do sth as a group, to do sth as a joint effort

mingitorio, -a 1 *adj* urinary
2 *nm* urinal

mingo *nm Ven* (**a**) *(en béisbol)* = hard rubber centre of a baseball (**b**) *(en bolas criollas)* jack

mini- *pref* mini-; **una minicumbre presidencial** a presidential mini-summit

mini[1] *nf Fam (minifalda)* mini

mini[2] *nm Esp Fam* **un m. de cerveza** a litre (glass) of beer

mini®[3] *nm (coche)* Mini®

miniatura *nf* (**a**) *(reproducción)* miniature; **en m.** in miniature (**b**) *(objeto pequeño)* **el apartamento es una m.** the *Br* flat *o US* apartment is tiny (**c**) *Informát* thumbnail

miniaturista *nmf* miniaturist

miniaturización *nf* miniaturization

miniaturizar [14] *vt* to miniaturize

minibar *nm* minibar

minibásket *nm* minibasket

minibús (*pl* **minibuses**) *nm* minibus

minicadena *nf* midi system

minicine *nm* = cinema with several small screens

MiniDisc® *nm inv* MiniDisc®

minifalda *nf* mini skirt

minifaldera *nf* = girl in a miniskirt

minifaldero, -a *adj* **un vestido m.** a minidress; **una chica minifaldera** a girl in a miniskirt

minifundio *nm* smallholding

minifundismo *nm* = system of land tenure characterized by the minifundio

minifundista *nmf* smallholder

minigolf (*pl* **minigolfs**) *nm* (**a**) *(lugar)* crazy golf course (**b**) *(juego)* crazy golf

mínima *nf* (**a**) *(temperatura)* low, lowest temperature; **una m. de cinco grados** a low of five degrees; **ayer se midieron cinco grados de m.** the lowest temperature recorded yesterday was five degrees, there was a low of five degrees yesterday

(**b**) *(provocación)* **saltar a la m.** to blow up at the slightest thing; **tu jefe se enfada a la m.** your boss gets annoyed at the slightest thing

(**c**) *Dep* **ganar/perder por la m.** to win/lose by the narrowest of margins

minimalismo *nm* minimalism

minimalista *adj* minimalist

mínimamente *adv* minimally

minimizar [14] *vt* (**a**) *(gastos, pérdidas, riesgos)* to minimize (**b**) *(quitar importancia a)* to minimize, to play down

mínimo, -a **1** *superlativo ver* **pequeño**

2 *adj* (**a**) *(lo más bajo posible o necesario)* minimum; **la mínima puntuación para aprobar es el cinco** you need a minimum score of five to pass; **salario** *o* **sueldo m.** minimum wage; **lo m. que podría hacer es disculparse** the least she could do is apologize ▸▸ *Mat* ***m. común denominador*** lowest common denominator; *Mat* ***m. común múltiplo*** lowest common multiple

(**b**) *(muy pequeño) (efecto, importancia)* minimal, very small; *(protesta, ruido)* slightest; **no tengo la más mínima idea** I haven't the slightest idea; **sus hijos no le importan lo más m.** he couldn't care less about his children; **en este país no existe la más mínima libertad** there's absolutely no freedom at all in this country; **en lo más m.** in the slightest

3 *nm* minimum; **trabaja un m. de 10 horas** she works a minimum of 10 hours; **al m.** to a minimum; **pon la calefacción al m.** put the heating at minimum; **la libra alcanzó un m. histórico frente al dólar** the pound reached an all-time low against the dollar; **no tiene un m. de sentido común** he hasn't an ounce of common sense; **si tuviera un m. de decencia la llamaría** if he had an ounce of decency he'd call her; EXPR **estar bajo mínimos** *(de comida, gasolina)* to have almost run out; **la popularidad del presidente se encuentra bajo mínimos** the president's popularity is at rock bottom; **el equipo se presenta a la final bajo mínimos** the team is going into the final well below strength *o* with a severely depleted side

4 como mínimo *loc adv (como muy tarde)* at the latest; *(como poco)* at the very least; **llegaremos como m. a las cinco** we'll be there by five at the latest; **si te vas, como m. podrías avisar** if you're going to leave, you could at least let me know

minino, -a *nm,f Fam* pussy (cat)

minio *nm* red lead

miniordenador *nm Esp* minicomputer

minipímer® *nf* hand-held mixer *(for whipping cream, mayonnaise)*

miniserie *nf* miniseries

ministerial *adj (cargo, cumbre)* ministerial; **remodelación m.** cabinet reshuffle; **equipo m.** cabinet

ministerio *nm* (**a**) *(institución) Br* ministry, *US* department; *(periodo)* time as minister; **durante el m. de Sánchez** while Sánchez was minister ▸▸ ***M. de Agricultura*** Ministry of Agriculture, *Br* ≃ Department for Environment, Food and Rural Affairs, *US* ≃ Department of Agriculture; ***M. de Asuntos Exteriores*** Ministry of Foreign Affairs, *Br* ≃ Foreign Office, *US* ≃ State Department; ***M. de Comercio*** Ministry of Trade, *Br* ≃ Department of Trade and Industry, *US* ≃ Department of Commerce; ***M. de Defensa*** Ministry of Defence, *US* ≃ Defense Department; ***M. de Economía*** Ministry of Economic Affairs, *Br* ≃ Treasury, *US* ≃ Treasury Department; ***M. de Finanzas*** Ministry of Finance; ***M. de Fomento*** Ministry of Public Works; ***M. de Gobernación*** Ministry of the Interior, *Br* ≃ Home Office, *US* ≃ Department of the Interior; ***M. de Hacienda*** Ministry of Economic Affairs, *Br* ≃ Treasury, *US* ≃ Treasury Department; ***M. de Industria*** Ministry of Industry, *Br* ≃ Department of Trade and Industry; ***M. del Interior*** Ministry of the Interior, *Br* ≃ Home Office, *US* ≃ Department of the Interior; ***M. de Justicia*** Ministry of Justice, *Br* ≃ Office of the Attorney General, *US* ≃ Department of Justice; *Am* ***M. de Relaciones Exteriores*** Ministry of Foreign Affairs, *Br* ≃ Foreign Office, *US* ≃ State Department; ***M. de Sanidad*** Ministry of Health, *Br* ≃ Department of Health; ***M. de Trabajo*** Ministry of Employment, *Br* ≃ Department of Employment, *US* ≃ Department of Labor

(**b**) *Der* ***m. fiscal*** *(acusación)* public prosecutor; ***m. público*** *(acusación)* public prosecutor

(**c**) *Rel* ministry

ministrable *Pol* **1** *adj* likely to be appointed minister

2 *nmf* potential minister

ministro, -a *nm,f* (**a**) *Pol Br* minister, *US* secretary; **primer m.** prime minister ▸▸ ***M. de Agricultura*** Minister of Agriculture, *Br* ≃ Minister for the Environment, Food and Rural Affairs, *US* ≃ Secretary of Agriculture; ***M. de Asuntos Exteriores*** Foreign Minister, *Br* ≃ Foreign Secretary, *US* ≃ Secretary of State; ***m. sin cartera*** minister without portfolio; ***M. de Comercio*** Minister of Trade, *Br* ≃ Secretary of State for Trade and Industry, *US* ≃ Secretary of Commerce; ***M. de Defensa*** Defence Minister, *US* ≃ Defence Secretary; ***M. de Economía*** Minister for Economic Affairs, *Br* ≃ Chancellor of the Exchequer, *US* ≃ Secretary of the Treasury; ***M. de Finanzas*** Minister of Finance; ***M. de Fomento*** Minister of Public Works; ***M. de Gobernación*** Minister of the Interior, *Br* ≃ Home Secretary, *US* ≃ Secretary of the Interior; ***M. de Hacienda*** Minister for Economic Affairs, *Br* ≃ Chancellor of the Exchequer, *US* ≃ Secretary of the Treasury; ***M. de Industria*** Minister for Industry, *Br* ≃ Secretary of State for Trade and Industry; ***M. del Interior*** Minister of the Interior, *Br* ≃ Home Secretary, *US* ≃ Secretary of the Interior; ***M. de Justicia*** Minister of Justice, *Br* ≃ Attorney General, *US* ≃ Secretary of Justice; ***m. plenipotenciario*** envoy extraordinary and minister plenipotentiary; *Am* ***M. de Relaciones Exteriores*** Foreign Minister, *Br* ≃ Foreign Secretary, *US* ≃ Secretary of State; ***M. de Sanidad*** Minister of Health, *US* ≃ Secretary of Health; ***M. de Trabajo*** Minister of Employment, *Br* ≃ Secretary of State for Employment, *US* ≃ Secretary of Labor

(**b**) *Rel* minister ▸▸ ***m. de Dios*** minister of God

miniturismo *nm Arg* = short sightseeing trips in one's local area

mino *nm CSur Fam* (**a**) *(hombre)* hunk (**b**) *(amante)* man, boyfriend

minoico, -a *adj* Minoan

minorar *vt* to diminish, to reduce

minoría *nf* minority; **los que piensan así son una m.** people who think like that are in a minority; **estar en m.** to be in a minority ▸▸ ***m. de edad*** (legal) minority; ***minorías étnicas*** ethnic minorities; ***m. racial*** racial minority

minorista, *Chile, Méx* **menorista** **1** *adj* retail; **comercio m.** retail trade

2 *nmf* retailer

minoritario, -a *adj* minority; **son un grupo m.** they are a minority

Minotauro *n Mitol* **el M.** the Minotaur

mintiera *etc ver* **mentir**

minucia *nf* (**a**) *(cosa pequeña)* silly little thing; **se pelearon por una m.** they had a fight over nothing *o* some silly little thing (**b**) *(meticulosidad)* detail; *(detalle)* minor detail; **describió con m. lo ocurrido** she described what had happened in great detail

minuciosamente *adv (con meticulosidad)* meticulously; *(con detalle)* in great detail

minuciosidad *nf (meticulosidad)* meticulousness; *(detalle)* attention to detail

minucioso, -a *adj (meticuloso)* meticulous; *(detallado)* highly detailed

minué *nm* minuet

minuendo *nm Mat* minuend

minueto *nm* minuet

minúscula *nf* small letter; *Espec* lower-case letter; **en minúsculas** in small letters, in lower case; **se escribe con m.** it's written with a small letter

minúsculo, -a *adj* **(a)** *(tamaño)* tiny, minute **(b)** *(letra)* small; *Espec* lower-case

minusvalía *nf* **(a)** *(física, psíquica)* handicap **(b)** *Econ* depreciation

minusválido, -a 1 *adj (físico, psíquico)* handicapped
2 *nm,f (físico, psíquico)* handicapped person; **los minusválidos** the handicapped

minusvalorar *vt* to underestimate

minuta *nf* **(a)** *(factura)* fee **(b)** *(menú)* menu **(c)** *RP (comida rápida)* = single-course meal which usually consists of meat or fish accompanied by French fries and sometimes vegetables

minutero *nm* minute hand

minutisa *nf* sweet william

minuto *nm* **(a)** *(de hora)* minute; **al m.** *(al momento)* a moment later; **vuelvo en un m.** I'll be back in a minute; **no tardo un m.** I won't be a minute; **¿tienes un m.?** do you have a minute?; **vivo a cinco minutos de aquí** I live five minutes from here; **no tengo (ni) un m. libre** I don't have a minute free ►► ***minutos de la basura*** *(en baloncesto)* garbage time; ***un m. de silencio*** a minute's silence; **guardar un m. de silencio (por alguien)** to observe a minute's silence (in memory of sb)
(b) *(de grado sexagesimal)* minute

mío, -a 1 *adj posesivo* mine; **este libro es m.** this book is mine; **un amigo m.** a friend of mine; **no es asunto m.** it's none of my business
2 *pron posesivo* **el m.** mine; **el m. es rojo** mine is red; *Fam* **los míos** *(mi familia)* my folks; *(mi bando)* my lot, my side; EXPR **lo m.: lo m. es el teatro** *(lo que me va)* theatre is what I should be doing; *Fam* **me costó lo m.** *(mucho)* it wasn't easy for me; EXPR *Fam* **ésta es la mía** this is the chance I've been waiting for *o* my big chance

miocardio *nm Anat* myocardium; **infarto de m.** heart attack

mioceno, -a *Geol* **1** *adj* Miocene
2 *nm* **el m.** the Miocene (era)

mioma *nm Med* myoma

mionca *nm CSur Fam* truck, *Br* lorry

miope 1 *adj* **(a)** *(corto de vista)* short-sighted, *US* near-sighted, *Espec* myopic **(b)** *(poco perspicaz)* short-sighted; **una política m.** a short-sighted policy
2 *nmf* short-sighted *o US* near-sighted person, *Espec* myopic person; **es un m.** he's short-sighted *o US* near-sighted, *Espec* he's myopic

miopía *nf* **(a)** *(en la visión)* short-sightedness, *US* near-sightedness, *Espec* myopia **(b)** *(falta de perspicacia)* short-sightedness

miosotis *nm inv* forget-me-not, *Espec* myosotis

MIR[1] [mir] *Esp (abrev de* **médico interno residente) 1** *nm (examen)* = competitive national examination for placement in house officer's post
2 *nmf (médico) Br* house officer, *US* intern

MIR[2] [mir] *nm (abrev de* **Movimiento de Izquierda Revolucionaria)** = left-wing political party in Chile, Bolivia, Peru and Venezuela

mira *nf* **(a)** *(en instrumento, arma)* sight ►► ***m. telescópica*** telescopic sight
(b) *(intención, propósito)* intention; **con miras a** with a view to, with the intention of; **celebraron una reunión con miras a llegar a un acuerdo** they held a meeting with a view to reaching an agreement; **se están preparando con miras a los Juegos Olímpicos** they are training with a view to competing in the Olympic Games; **poner la m.** *o* **las miras en algo** to set one's sights on sth; EXPR **ser amplio de miras** to be enlightened; EXPR **ser corto de miras** to be short-sighted **(c)** *RP* **miras** *(posibilidades)* **no hay ni miras de que podamos mudarnos antes del verano** there's no chance whatsoever of us being able to move before the summer; **no tengo ni miras de que me aumenten el sueldo** I haven't the slightest chance *o* prospect of getting a pay rise

mirada *nf* **(a)** *(acción de mirar)* look; **fue el blanco de todas las miradas** all eyes were on her; **apartar la m.** to look away; **dirigir** *o* **lanzar la m. a** to glance at; **fulminar con la m. a alguien** to look daggers at sb; **levantar la m.** to look up; **siguió con la m. todos sus movimientos** his eyes followed her every movement; **sostener la m. de alguien** to hold sb's gaze; EXPR **si las miradas mataran** if looks could kill
(b) *(manera de mirar) (con cariño, placer, admiración)* gaze; **m. asesina** glare; **me dirigió una m. asesina** she looked daggers at me; **m. fija** stare; **caminaba con la m. fija en el suelo** he walked along staring at the ground; **m. furtiva** peek; **le lanzó una m. furtiva** he looked at her out of the corner of his eye; **le dirigió una m. lasciva** he leered at her; **m. perdida** distant look; **tenía la m. perdida** she was staring into space
(c) *(vistazo, ojeada)* look; **echar una m. (a algo)** to glance *o* to have a quick look (at sth); **¿le podrías echar una m. a esta carta que he escrito?** could you have a look at this letter I've written?; **echa una mirada a ver si está lloviendo** have a look and see if it's raining
(d) *(intención, propósito)* **tener puestas las miradas en algo** to have one's sights set on sth

mirado, -a *adj* **(a)** *(prudente)* careful; **es muy m. para el dinero** he's very careful with his money **(b) ser bien m.** *(bien considerado)* to be well regarded; **es mal m.** *(mal considerado)* he's not well regarded *o* thought of

mirador *nm* **(a)** *(para ver un paisaje)* viewpoint **(b)** *(balcón)* enclosed balcony

miramiento *nm* consideration; **no es del tipo de personas que se anda con miramientos** he's not one to stand on ceremony; **siempre se anda con muchos miramientos** he always treads very carefully; **sin miramientos** without the least consideration; **expresó su opinión sin ningún m.** he expressed his opinion with no thought for anyone else; **la prensa se cebó con él sin m. alguno** the press laid into him unceremoniously; **los rebeldes fueron ejecutados sin miramientos** the rebels were summarily executed

miranda: de miranda *loc adv Esp Fam* **estar de m.** to be loafing about *o* around

mirandino, -a 1 *adj* of/from Miranda *(Venezuela)*
2 *nm,f* person from Miranda *(Venezuela)*

MIRAR 1 *vt* **(a)** *(dirigir la vista a)* to look at; *(detenidamente, con atención)* to watch; *(fijamente)* to stare at; **m. algo de cerca/lejos** to look at sth closely/from a distance; **¡míralos!** look at them!; **mira lo que pone en ese cartel** look (at) what that sign says; **m. a la gente pasar** to watch people go by; **no paraba de mirarme** he kept staring at me; **pasaba horas mirando las estrellas** I would spend hours gazing at the stars; **m. algo/a alguien con disimulo** to glance furtively at sth/sb; **m. algo por encima** to glance over sth, to have a quick look at sth; **m. a alguien con ira** to look angrily at sb, to glare at sb; **m. a alguien de arriba abajo** to look sb up and down; EXPR **m. a alguien por encima del hombro** to look down on sb; EXPR *Fam* **ser de mírame y no me toques** to be very fragile
(b) *(fijarse en)* **primero mira cómo lo hago yo** first, watch *o* see how I do it; **mira que no falte nada en las maletas** check to see nothing's missing from the suitcases; **míralos bien y dime cuál te gusta más** have a good look at them and tell me which you like best
(c) *(examinar)* to check, to look through; **he mirado todo el periódico** I've looked through the whole newspaper; **miraremos tu expediente con mucha atención** we'll look at your file very carefully; **le miraron todas las maletas** they searched all her luggage; **eso te lo tiene que m. un médico** you should have that looked at by a doctor
(d) *(considerar)* **mira bien lo que haces** be careful about what you do; **míralo desde este ángulo...** look at it this way...; **bien mirado..., mirándolo bien...** if you think about it...; **aunque bien mirado, podemos ir los dos** on second thoughts, we could both go; **lo mires por donde lo mires** whichever way you look at it; **m. a alguien bien/mal** to approve/disapprove of sb; **en este país miran mucho la puntualidad** punctuality is very important to people in this country; **m. mucho el dinero** to be very careful with money
2 *vi* **(a)** *(dirigir la vista)* to look; *(detenidamente, con atención)* to watch; *(fijamente)* to stare; **mira bien antes de cruzar** look carefully before crossing the road; **miraban por la ventana** they were looking out of the window; **¡mira!** look (at that)!; **mira, yo creo que...** look, I think (that)...; *Esp* **mira por dónde** guess what?, would you believe it?; *también Irónico* **¡mira qué bien!** isn't that great!; **mira que te avisé** I told you so; **¡mira que eres pesado/tonto!** you're so annoying/silly!; **¡mira que salir sin paraguas con la que está cayendo!** fancy going out without an umbrella in this rain!; **¡mira si haría calor que no pude dormir!** it was so hot I couldn't sleep!; EXPR **¡mira quién fue a hablar!** look who's talking!; EXPR *Am Fam* **m. feo: siempre miraba feo a mis amigos** she always looked down her nose at my friends
(b) *(buscar)* to check, to look; **he mirado en todas partes** I've looked everywhere
(c) m. a *(orientarse hacia) (casa, fachada)* to face; *(habitación, terraza)* to look out onto; **la mezquita mira al este** the mosque faces east; **la habitación mira al mar** the room looks out onto the sea
(d) m. por *(cuidar de)* to look after; **m. por los demás** to look out for

other people; **sólo mira por sus intereses** she only looks after her own interests

(e) *Fam (averiguar, comprobar)* **m. a ver si** to see if *o* whether; **mira a ver si ha llegado la carta** (go and) see if the letter has arrived; **mira a ver si tienes algo de cambio para dejarme** (have a look and) see if you've got any change you could lend me

3 mirarse *vpr (uno mismo)* to look at oneself; *(uno al otro)* to look at each other; **mirarse al espejo** to look at oneself in the mirror; **mirarse en el agua** to look at one's reflection in the water; EXPR **si bien se mira** if you really think about it

---

mirasol *nm* sunflower

miríada *nf* myriad

miriápodo *nm Zool* myriapod

mirilla *nf* **(a)** *(en puerta)* spyhole **(b)** *(en arma)* sight

miriñaque *nm (de falda)* hoopskirt, crinoline

mirista 1 *adj* = of/relating to the MIR party in Chile, Bolivia, Peru or Venezuela

2 *nmf* = member *o* supporter of the MIR party in Chile, Bolivia, Peru or Venezuela

mirlo *nm* blackbird; EXPR **ser un m. blanco** to be one in a million ▸▸ ***m. acuático*** dipper

mirobolano *nm* cherry plum

mirón, -ona *Fam* **1** *adj (curioso)* nosey; *(con lascivia)* peeping

2 *nm,f* **(a)** *(espectador)* onlooker; *(curioso)* busybody, *Br* nosey parker; *(voyeur)* peeping Tom; **estar de m.** to just stand around watching *o* gawping; **no te quedes allí de m., echa una mano** don't just stand there gawping, lend a hand **(b)** *Informát (en fórum)* lurker

mironiano, -a *adj* = of/relating to the style of Joan Miró

mirra *nf* **(a)** *(resina)* myrrh **(b)** *Ven (migaja)* scrap, crumb

mirringa *nf Cuba Fam* tiny bit

mirruña *nf Méx Fam* tiny bit

mirtácea *Bot* **1** *adj* myrtaceous

2 mirtáceas *nfpl (familia) Myrtaceae*

mirto *nm* myrtle

misa *nf* mass; **cantar/decir/oír m.** to sing/say/hear mass; **ir a m.** to go to mass *o* church; *Fam Fig* **lo que yo digo va a m. y no quiero que nadie rechiste** what I say goes, I don't want to hear a word of protest from anyone; EXPR **como en m.** *(en silencio)* in total silence; EXPR *Fam* **por mí como si dice m.** I couldn't care less what he says; EXPR *Fam* **no saber de la m. la media** *o* **la mitad** not to know half the story ▸▸ ***m. de campaña*** open-air mass; ***m. cantada*** sung mass; ***m. concelebrada*** concelebrated mass; ***m. de cuerpo presente*** funeral mass *(before the body is buried or cremated)*; ***m. de difuntos*** requiem, mass for the dead; ***m. del gallo*** midnight mass *(on Christmas Eve)*; ***m. negra*** black mass; ***m. solemne*** High Mass

misal *nm* missal

misantropía *nf* misanthropy

misantrópico, -a *adj* misanthropic

misántropo, -a *nm,f* misanthrope, misanthropist

miscelánea *nf* **(a)** *(mezcla)* miscellany **(b)** *Méx (tienda)* = small general store

misceláneo, -a *adj* miscellaneous

miserable 1 *adj* **(a)** *(pobre)* poor; *(vivienda)* wretched, squalid **(b)** *(penoso, insuficiente)* miserable **(c)** *(vil)* contemptible, base **(d)** *(tacaño)* mean

2 *nmf* **(a)** *(persona vil)* wretch, vile person **(b)** *(tacaño)* mean person, miser

miserablemente, míseramente *adv (insuficientemente)* miserably

miserere *nm* miserere

miseria *nf* **(a)** *(pobreza)* poverty; **viven en la m.** they live in poverty

(b) *(desgracia)* **las miserias de la guerra** the hardships of war

(c) *(tacañería)* meanness

(d) *(vileza)* baseness, wretchedness

(e) *(poco dinero)* pittance; **le pagan una m.** he gets paid a pittance, they pay him next to nothing; *CSur Fam* **llorar m.** to plead poverty

(f) EXPR *RP Fam* **a la m.: es alérgica y está a la m.** she's allergic and she's in a really bad way; **después de tantos días sin agua, esa planta quedó a la m.** after so many days without water the plant was in a real state *o* half dead

> **Falso amigo**: El sustantivo inglés **misery** no es la traducción del español **miseria**. En inglés **misery** significa "tristeza, infelicidad".

misericordia *nf* compassion; **pedir m.** to beg for mercy; **para obras de m.** for charity

misericordioso, -a 1 *adj* compassionate, merciful

2 *nm,f* **los misericordiosos** the merciful

mísero, -a *adj* **(a)** *(pobre, desdichado)* wretched, miserable; **vive en una mísera choza** he lives in a miserable hovel; **no nos ofreció ni un m. vaso de vino** she didn't even offer us a measly *o* miserable glass of wine **(b)** *(tacaño)* mean, stingy

misia, misiá *nf CSur, Ven* Mistress, Miss

misil *nm* missile ▸▸ ***m. balístico*** ballistic missile; ***m. de crucero*** cruise missile; ***m. intercontinental*** intercontinental missile; ***m. teledirigido*** guided missile; ***m. tierra-aire*** ground-to-air missile

misio, -a *Perú Fam* **1** *adj* broke, *Br* skint

2 *nm,f* pauper

misión *nf* **(a)** *(delegación)* mission ▸▸ ***m. diplomática*** diplomatic delegation *o Br* mission **(b) misiones** *(religiosas)* (overseas) missions **(c)** *(cometido)* task, mission; **¡m. cumplida!** mission accomplished! ▸▸ ***m. suicida*** suicide mission **(d)** *(expedición científica)* expedition; **una m. de la NASA a Marte** a NASA mission to Mars

misionero, -a 1 *adj* **(a)** *(religioso)* missionary **(b)** *(de Misiones)* of/from Misiones *(Argentina)*

2 *nm,f* **(a)** *(religioso)* missionary **(b)** *(de Misiones)* person from Misiones *(Argentina)*

Misisipi, Misisipí *nm* **el M.** the Mississippi

misiva *nf* missive

mismamente *adv Fam* **(a)** *(precisamente)* exactly, precisely; **lo encontrarás m. dentro de la caja** you'll find it right inside the box **(b)** *(por ejemplo)* for example; **yo m. he estado allí varias veces** I myself have been there several times

mismísimo, -a 1 *adj (superlativo)* very; **en ese m. día** on that very day; **el m. presidente acudió a la ceremonia** the president himself attended the ceremony

2 mismísimos *nmpl* EXPR *Fam Euf* **estoy hasta los mismísimos (de)** I've just had it up to here (with)

MISMO, -A 1 *adj* **(a)** *(igual, idéntico)* same; **son del m. pueblo** they're from the same town/village; **vive en la misma calle que yo** she lives in the same street as me, she lives in my street; **del m. color/tipo que** the same colour/type as

(b) *(para enfatizar lugar, tiempo)* **en este m. sitio** in this very place; **en aquel m. momento** at that very moment; **delante de sus mismas narices** right in front of his nose; **eso m. digo yo** that's exactly what I say; **y por eso m. deberíamos ayudarles** and that is precisely why we should help them

(c) *(para reforzar pronombres)* **yo m.** I myself; **¿lo hiciste tú m.?** did you do it (by) yourself?; **él m. se construyó la casa** he built his house (by) himself, he built his own house; **me dije a mí m....** I said to myself...; **por mí/ti m.** by myself/yourself; *Fam* **¡tú m.!** it's up to you!, suit yourself!

2 *pron* **(a)** *(igual cosa o persona)* **el m./la misma** the same; **el pueblo ya no era el m.** the town was no longer the same; **la misma del otro día** the same one as the other day; **el m. que vi ayer** the same one I saw yesterday; *Fam* **¿ése es el presidente? – sí, el m. (que viste y calza)** is that the president? – yes, the very same *o* yes, that's him all right; *Méx* **enviamos un paquete a su oficina, m. que no ha llegado a destino** we sent a package to his office which didn't arrive *o* but it didn't arrive; EXPR **estar en las mismas** to be no further forward

(b) lo m. *(igual cosa, iguales cosas)* the same (thing); **¡qué aburrimiento, todos los días lo m.!** how boring, it's the same every day!; **póngamos otra de lo m.** (the) same again, please; *Fam* **lo m. se pone a hablar contigo que no te saluda** one day he might start chatting to you and the next he won't even say hello; **lo m. que** the same as; **me gusta lo m. que a él** I like the same things as him; **yo tengo mis manías, lo m. que todo el mundo** I've got my idiosyncrasies just like everyone else; **lloraba lo m. que un niño** she was crying like a child; **me da lo m.** it's all the same to me, I don't mind *o* care; **¿vamos o nos quedamos? – da lo m.** should we go *o* should we stay? – it doesn't make any difference; **me da lo m.** I don't care; **lo m. digo** *(como respuesta)* likewise, me too; **más de lo m.** more of the same; **o lo que es lo m.** *(en otras palabras)* or in other words; **por lo m.** for that (very) reason

(c) *(tal vez)* **lo m. llegamos y ya no hay entradas** it's quite possible that we might arrive there and find there are no tickets left; **lo m. está enfermo** maybe *o* perhaps he's ill, he may be ill; **lo m. te saluda que te ignora por completo** he's just as likely to say hello to you as to ignore you completely

(d) *(antes mencionado)* **hay una cripta y un túnel para acceder a la misma** there is a crypt and a tunnel leading to it

(e) *RP Fam* **lo m.** *(igualmente)* still; **le dije que se callara y lo m. siguió hablando** I told him to be quiet but he still carried on talking *o* he carried on talking all the same; **está nevando pero lo m. el avión va a salir** it's snowing but the plane is still going to take off

3 *adv* (a) *(para enfatizar)* **lo vi desde mi casa m.** I saw it from my own house; **ahora/aquí m.** right now/here; **ayer m.** only yesterday; **salimos hoy m.** we are leaving this very day; **llegarán mañana m.** they'll be arriving tomorrow, actually; **tiene que estar listo para mañana m.** it absolutely has to be ready by tomorrow; **por eso m.** precisely for that reason

(b) *(por ejemplo)* **escoge uno cualquiera, este m.** choose any one, this one, for instance; **¿y ahora quién me arregla a mí esto? – yo m.** who's going to fix this for me now? – I will *o* I'll do it (myself)

---

misoginia *nf* misogyny

misógino, -a 1 *adj* misogynistic
2 *nm,f* misogynist

misquito, -a 1 *adj* Misquito
2 *nm,f* Misquito

miss (*pl* **misses**) *nf* beauty queen ▸▸ ***M. Mundo*** Miss World; ***M. Universo*** Miss Universe

mistela *nf* = unfermented wine made from alcohol and grape must

míster (*pl* **místers**) *nm* (a) *Fam Dep* **el m.** *(el entrenador)* the boss, *Br* the gaffer (b) *(como apelativo)* sir

misterio *nm* (a) *(hecho inexplicable)* mystery; **la desaparición del empresario sigue siendo un m.** the disappearance of the businessman remains a mystery; *Fam* **yo no le veo el m.** I don't see what's so hard to understand about it

(b) *(secretismo)* secrecy; **están preparando la fiesta con mucho m.** they're being very secretive about the preparations for the party

(c) *(intriga)* mystery; **una novela de m.** a mystery

(d) *Rel (de la vida de Jesús)* mystery

(e) *Rel (verdad)* mystery; **el m. de la Santísima Trinidad** the mystery of the Holy Trinity

(f) *Rel (del rosario)* mystery

(g) *Teatro* mystery play

misteriosamente *adv* mysteriously

misterioso, -a *adj* mysterious

misti *nmf Perú Fam Pey* whitey

mística *nf* (a) *(en teología)* mysticism (b) **la m.** *(en literatura)* mystic literature (c) *ver también* **místico**

misticismo *nm* mysticism

místico, -a 1 *adj* mystical
2 *nm,f (persona)* mystic

mistificación *nf* falsification

mistificar [60] *vt* to falsify

mistral *nm (viento)* mistral

mita *nf Hist* = forced labour by Indians during the Spanish colonial era

mitad *nf* (a) *(parte)* half; **la m. de** half (of); **4 es la m. de 8** 4 is half of 8; **la primera/segunda m. del partido** the first/second half of the match; **la m. del tiempo no está** half the time she's not in; **gana la m. que yo** he earns half as much as I do; **me costó la m. que a él** it cost me half what he paid, it cost me half as much as it cost him; **a m. de precio** at half price; **m. y m.** half and half; **el centauro es m. hombre m. caballo** the centaur is half man half horse; **está m. esperanzado m. triste** he's half hopeful, half down-hearted

(b) *(centro)* middle; **a m. de camino** halfway there; **a la m. del viaje decidieron regresar** halfway through the journey they decided to turn back; **en m. de** in the middle of; **había un camión cruzado en m. de la calle** there was a truck *o Br* lorry across the middle of the road; **se marcharon en m. de la ceremonia** they left in the middle of *o* halfway through the ceremony; **a m. de película** halfway through the movie; **(cortar algo) por la m.** (to cut sth) in half

mitayo, -a *nm,f Hist* = Indian forced to work for the Spanish during the colonial era

mítico, -a *adj* mythical

mitificación *nf* mythologization

mitificar [60] *vt* to mythologize

mitigación *nf (de efecto)* mitigation; *(de miseria)* alleviation; *(de daño)* reduction; *(de ánimos)* calming; *(de sed)* quenching; *(de hambre)* lessening; *(de choque, golpe)* softening; *(de dudas, sospechas)* allaying

mitigar [38] *vt (aplacar) (efecto)* to mitigate; *(miseria)* to alleviate; *(daño)* to reduce; *(ánimos)* to calm; *(sed)* to quench, to slake; *(hambre)* to take the edge off; *(choque, golpe)* to soften; *(dudas, sospechas)* to allay

mitin (*pl* **mítines**), *Am* **mítin** (*pl* **mitines**) *nm* rally, political meeting; **celebrar un m.** to hold a rally

mito *nm* (a) *(leyenda)* myth (b) *(personaje)* legend; **es un m. de la canción** he is a legend in the world of song (c) *(invención)* myth; **lo de su boda es un m.** all that about them getting married is a myth

mitocondria *nf Biol* mitochondria

mitología *nf* mythology

mitológico, -a *adj* mythological

mitomanía *nf* mythomania

mitómano, -a 1 *adj* mythomaniac
2 *nm,f* mythomaniac

mitón *nm* (a) *(con dedos al aire)* (fingerless) mitten (b) *RP (manopla)* mitten

mitosis *nf Biol* mitosis

mitote *nm Méx Fam* (a) *(alboroto)* commotion; **se armó un gran m. al final de la manifestación** there was a big commotion *o* set-to at the end of the demonstration (b) *(fiesta)* house party (c) *(ceremonia)* = Aztec dance performed before sowing or harvesting of crops

mitotear *vi Méx Fam (hacer remilgos)* to fuss

mitotero, -a *Méx Fam* 1 *adj* (a) *(que alborota)* rowdy, boisterous (b) *(remilgado)* fussy, finicky
2 *nm,f* (a) *(alborotador)* rowdy *o* boisterous person; **es un m.** he's terribly rowdy *o* boisterous (b) *(remilgado)* finicky person

mitra *nf* (a) *(tocado)* mitre (b) *(cargo)* office of archbishop/bishop

mitrado, -a 1 *adj* mitred
2 *nm* (a) *(obispo)* bishop (b) *(arzobispo)* archbishop

mitral *adj Anat* **válvula m.** mitral valve

miura *nm Taurom* = Spanish breed of bull

mixomatosis *nf* myxomatosis

mixteco, -a 1 *adj* Mixtec
2 *nm,f (persona)* Mixtec
3 *nm (lengua)* Mixtec

mixtificar [60] *vt* to mystify

mixtilíneo, -a *adj Geom* mixtilineal, mixtilinear

mixto, -a 1 *adj* (a) *(con dos elementos)* mixed; **capital m.** mixed capital **comisión mixta** joint committee; **financiación mixta** public-private financing (b) *(con hombres y mujeres)* mixed; **un colegio m.** a mixed school; **los dobles mixtos** the mixed doubles (c) *(matrimonio)* mixed
2 *nm (sándwich)* cheese and ham sandwich

mixtura *nf* mixture

mízcalo *nm* saffron milk cap

ml (*abrev de* **mililitro**) ml

MLN *nm* (*abrev de* **Movimiento de Liberación Nacional**) = Guatemalan party of the far right founded in 1960

mm (*abrev de* **milímetro**) mm

MMM *nf Informát* (*abrev de* **Multimalla Mundial**) WWW

MN, m/n (*abrev de* **moneda nacional**) national currency

mnemónico, -a *adj* mnemonic

mnemotecnia, mnemotécnica *nf* mnemonics *(singular)*

mnemotécnico, -a *adj* mnemonic

MNR *nm* (*abrev de* **Movimiento Nacionalista Revolucionario**) = Bolivian centre-right political party

moai *nm* Easter Island statue

moaré *nm* moiré

mobiliario *nm* furniture ▸▸ ***m. de baño*** bathroom furniture; ***m. de cocina*** kitchen furniture; ***m. urbano*** street furniture *(litter bins, shelters, plant displays etc)*

moblaje *nm* furniture, furnishings

moca = **moka**

mocasín *nm* loafer; *(de indios)* moccasin

mocedad *nf* youth

mocetón, -ona *nm,f Fam* strapping lad, *f* strapping lass

mocha *nf* (a) *Cuba (machete)* = type of machete (b) *Ven (engranaje)* extra low gear (c) *ver también* **mocho**

mochales *adj inv Esp Fam* crazy, mad; **estar m.** to have a screw loose, to be a bit touched

mocharse *vpr Méx Fam* (a) *(compartir)* **tienes que mocharte conmigo** you have to go *Br* halves *o US* halfies with me (b) *(sobornar)* **tuve que mocharme con el policía** I had to give the policeman a bribe *o Br* backhander (c) *(cooperar)* to chip in; **móchate con algo para ir a comprar más cerveza** chip something in so we can go and buy some more beer

mochila *nf* (a) *(bolsa)* rucksack, backpack (b) *Informát* dongle

mochilero, -a *nm,f* (a) *(excursionista)* backpacker (b) *Ven Fam (basurero) Br* dustman, *US* garbageman

mocho, -a 1 *adj* (a) *(extremo, punta)* blunt; *(árbol)* lopped (b) *Méx Fam Pey (beato)* holier-than-thou (c) *Méx Fam Pey (mojigato)* prudish, straitlaced (d) *RP, Ven Fam (mutilado)* **tiene un brazo m.** he has lost an arm, he only has one arm; **la pata de la silla está mocha** the chair has a leg missing; **mi gato está m. de una oreja** my cat only has one ear (e) *RP, Ven Fam (corto)* too short
2 *nm (fregona)* mop
3 *nm,f Méx Fam Pey* (a) *(beato)* holy Joe (b) *(mojigato)* **las mochas de la oficina se asustaron con mi escote** the straitlaced old prudes at the office got a shock when they saw my neckline

mochuelo *nm (ave)* little owl; EXPR *Fam* **cargar con el m.** to be landed with it; EXPR *Fam* **cargar a alguien el m.** to lumber sb with it ►► ***m. chico*** little owl; ***m. duende*** elf owl

moción *nf* motion; **presentar una m.** to present *o* bring a motion; **apoyo la m.** I second the motion ►► ***m. de censura*** motion of censure; ***m. de confianza*** motion of confidence

mocionar *vt Am* **m. que se haga algo** to propose *o* move that sth be done; **mocionar una propuesta** to put forward *o* present a proposal

mocito, -a 1 *adj* very young
2 *nm,f* youngster, *f* young girl; **está hecha una mocita** she's quite a young lady now

moco *nm* (a) *(de la nariz)* snot; **un m.** a piece of snot, a bogey; **limpiarse los mocos** to wipe one's nose; **sonarse los mocos** to blow one's nose; **tener mocos** to have a runny nose; EXPR *Fam* **llorar a m. tendido** to cry one's eyes out
(b) *(mucosidad)* mucus ►► ***m. vaginal*** vaginal mucus
(c) ***m. de pavo*** *(cresta)* comb; *(planta)* love-lies-bleeding; EXPR *Fam* **no es m. de pavo** it's not to be sneezed at, it's no mean feat; *Fam* **conseguir un buen trabajo no es m. de pavo** getting a good job is no mean feat
(d) *Esp Fam (borrachera)* **pillarse un m.** to get plastered
(e) EXPR *Esp Fam* **tirarse el m.** to brag; **¡no te tires el m., no sabes ruso!** stop bragging *o* showing off, you can't speak Russian!

mocochinche *nm Bol* = drink made of peach juice with water, caramelized sugar, cloves, cinnamon and dried peach

mocoso, -a 1 *adj* runny-nosed
2 *nm,f Fam* **tú no puedes entrar, eres sólo un m.** you can't come in, you're just a kid; **unos mocosos rompieron el cristal** some little brats broke the window; **nos vinieron a visitar con sus dos mocosos** they came to see us with their two little brats

Moctezuma *n pr* Montezuma; *Fam* **la venganza de M.** Montezuma's revenge

mod 1 *adj* mod
2 *nmf* mod

moda *nf* fashion; **no estoy al tanto de las últimas modas** I'm not very well up on the latest fashions; **un traje a la m. actual** a fashionable dress; **fue una m. pasajera** it was a passing fad; **la m. de llevar el móvil a todas partes** the craze for taking your mobile phone everywhere; **estar de m.** to be fashionable *o* in fashion; **el escritor/restaurante de m.** the most fashionable writer/restaurant at the moment; **estar pasado de m.** to be unfashionable *o* out of fashion; **pasar de m.** to go out of fashion; **ir a la última m.** to wear the latest fashion; **ponerse de m.** to come into fashion; **un bar que se ha puesto muy de m.** a bar that has become very fashionable

modal 1 *adj* modal
2 **modales** *nmpl* manners; **tener buenos/malos modales** to have good/bad manners

modalidad *nf (tipo, estilo)* form, type; **participa en la m. de dobles** she's competing in the doubles; **es campeón en la m. de los 100 metros** he is the 100 metres champion ►► *Com* ***m. de pago*** method of payment

modelado *nm* modelling

modelador, -ora 1 *nm,f Arte* modeller
2 *nm RP* (a) *(corsé)* corset (b) *(para el pelo)* hair gel

modelaje *nm* (a) *(modelado)* modelling (b) *Am (carrera)* modelling; **escuela de m.** school of modelling

modelar 1 *vt* (a) *Arte* to model (b) *(dar forma, configurar)* to form, to shape; **su padre modeló su personalidad** her father shaped *o* moulded her character (c) *Am (ropa)* to model
2 *vi Arte* to model

modélico, -a *adj* model, exemplary; **los fans tuvieron un comportamiento m.** the fans' behaviour was exemplary, the fans were a model of good behaviour

modelismo *nm* modelling

modelista *nmf* (a) *(creador)* modeller, model maker (b) *(operario)* mould operator

modelito *nm Fam* **llevaba un m. muy sexy** she was wearing a sexy little number

modelo 1 *adj* model; **es un estudiante m.** he is a model student
2 *nmf* (a) *(de moda)* model; **desfile de modelos** fashion show *o* parade (b) *(de artista)* model
3 *nm* (a) *(diseño)* model; **tengo un m. anterior** I have an older model; **tengo una bicicleta último m.** I have the latest-model bicycle
(b) *(representación a escala)* model ►► ***m. a escala*** scale model; ***m. reducido*** scale model
(c) *(prenda de vestir)* outfit; **llevaba un m. de Versace** she was wearing a Versace outfit
(d) *(patrón, referencia)* model; **servir de m.** to serve as a model; **usaré tu carta como m.** I'll use your letter as a model
(e) *(teórico)* model ►► ***m. económico*** economic model; ***m. matemático*** mathematical model

módem (*pl* **modems**) *nm Informát* modem ►► ***m. fax*** fax modem

moderación *nf* (a) *(mesura)* moderation; **con m.** in moderation; **m. salarial** wage restraint (b) *(de debate)* chairing; **me han encargado la m. de un debate** I've been asked to chair *o* facilitate a debate

moderadamente *adv* moderately, in moderation

moderado, -a 1 *adj* (a) *(persona)* moderate; **es una persona moderada** he's not given to excesses (b) *(velocidad)* moderate; *(precio)* reasonable; **habrá lluvias moderadas en el norte** there will be some rain in the north (c) *(en política)* moderate
2 *nm,f* moderate

moderador, -ora 1 *adj* moderating; **un elemento m. de las temperaturas** a factor which keeps temperatures at a reasonable level
2 *nm,f* (a) *(de debate)* chair, facilitator (b) *Informát (de grupo de noticias)* moderator
3 *nm Fís* moderator

moderar 1 *vt* (a) *(templar, atenuar)* to moderate; **le pidieron que moderara su estilo agresivo** he was asked to tone down his aggressive style; **modere el consumo de alcohol** you should try to avoid drinking excessive amounts of alcohol
(b) *(velocidad)* to reduce; **modere su velocidad** *(en cartel)* reduce speed
(c) *(debate)* to chair, to facilitate
(d) *(contener)* to contain, to restrain; **m. las pasiones** to contain one's passions
2 **moderarse** *vpr* to restrain oneself; **moderarse en algo** to moderate sth; **moderarse en la bebida** to cut down on alcohol

modernamente *adv* (a) *(recientemente)* recently, lately (b) *(actualmente)* nowadays

modernidad *nf* (a) *(cualidad)* modernity, modernness; **la m. de un estilo** the modernness of a style; **una propuesta retrógrada maquillada de m.** a retrograde proposal masquerading as something modern (b) *(periodo)* **uno de los grandes poetas de la m.** one of the great poets of the modern era

modernismo *nm* (a) *Lit* modernism (b) *Arte* Art Nouveau

modernista 1 *adj* (a) *Lit* modernist (b) *Arte* Art Nouveau
2 *nmf* (a) *Lit* modernist (b) *Arte* Art Nouveau artist

modernización *nf* modernization

modernizador, -ora, modernizante *adj* modernizing; **un esfuerzo m.** an effort to modernize

modernizar [14] 1 *vt* to modernize
2 **modernizarse** *vpr* to modernize

moderno, -a 1 *adj* (a) *(de la actualidad)* modern; **la mujer moderna** the modern woman (b) *(innovador)* modern; **un diseño muy m.** a very modern design (c) *(historia, edad)* modern (d) *Fam (persona)* trendy
2 *nm,f Fam* trendy (person)

modess® *nm Arg, Ven Br* sanitary towel, *US* sanitary napkin

modestamente *adv* modestly

modestia *nf* (a) *(humildad)* modesty; EXPR **m. aparte** though I say so myself; **mi propuesta es la más innovadora, m. aparte** my proposal is the most innovative, though I say so myself; **m. aparte, creo que somos los mejores del grupo** modesty apart, I think we're the best in the group, I think we're the best in the group, though I say so myself
(b) *(sencillez)* modesty; **a pesar de su puesto vive con m.** he lives modestly, in spite of his position

modesto, -a 1 *adj* (a) *(humilde)* modest; **a mi m. entender...** in my humble opinion... (b) *(sencillo)* modest; **vive en una casa m.** she lives in a modest house (c) *(reducido, pequeño)* modest; **contamos con un m. presupuesto** we have a small *o* limited budget; **la producción creció un m. 1 por ciento** production increased by a modest 1 percent
2 *nm,f* modest person; **es un m.** he's very modest

módico, -a *adj (cantidad)* modest; *(precio)* reasonable; **a la venta por un m. precio de 1.000 pesos** available at the very reasonable price of 1,000 pesos

modificable *adj* modifiable

modificación *nf* (a) *(de diseño)* alteration, modification; *(de plan, ley)* change; *(de programa)* alteration; *(de presupuesto)* revision (b) *Gram* modification

modificado, -a *adj* modified; **m. genéticamente** genetically modified

modificador, -ora 1 *adj* modifying
2 *nm,f Gram* modifier; **m. del nombre/verbo** noun/verb modifier

modificar [60] *vt* (a) *(diseño)* to alter, to modify; *(plan, ley)* to change; *(programa)* to change, to alter; *(presupuesto)* to revise; **m. genéticamente** to genetically modify (b) *Gram* to modify

modillón *nm Arquit* modillion

modismo *nm* idiom

modista *nmf* (a) *(diseñador)* fashion designer (b) *(sastre)* tailor, *f* dressmaker

modistería *nf* dress shop

modisto *nm* (a) *(diseñador)* fashion designer (b) *(sastre)* tailor

---

MODO 1 *nm* (a) *(manera, forma)* way; **no encuentro el m. de dejar el tabaco** whatever I do, I just can't seem to give up smoking; **ése no es m. de comportarse** that's no way to behave; **¿has visto el m. en que** *o* **el m. como te mira?** have you seen how *o* the way he's looking at you?; **esta vez lo haremos a mi m.** this time we'll do it my way; **al m. de** in the style of, after the fashion of; **a m. de** as, by way of; **a mi m. de ver** the way I see it; **de algún m.** somehow; **se le cayó el botón porque lo cosió de cualquier m.** the button fell off because he sewed it on carelessly *o* any old how; **hazlo de cualquier m.** do it however you like; **no te preocupes, de cualquier m. no pensaba ir** don't worry, I wasn't going to go anyway; **de ese/este m.** that/this way; **del mismo m.** similarly, in the same way; **lo hice del mismo m. que ayer/tú** I did it the same way as yesterday/you; **lo organizaron de m. que acabara antes de las diez** they organized it so (that) it finished before ten; **¿de m. que no te gusta?** so, you don't like it (then)?; **de ningún m.** *o* **en m. alguno deberíamos dejarle salir** under no circumstances should we let her out; **de ningún m.** *o* **en m. alguno quise ofenderte** I in no way intended to offend you; **¿te he molestado? – de ningún m.** *o* **en m. alguno** did I annoy you? – not at all *o* by no means; **¿quieres que lo invitemos? – ¡de ningún m.!** shall we invite him? – no way *o* certainly not!; **de otro m.** *(si no)* otherwise; **de tal m. (que)** *(tanto)* so much (that); **de todos modos** in any case, anyway; **de todos modos seguiremos en contacto** in any case, we'll keep in touch; **de todos modos, ¿qué es eso que decías de un viaje?** anyway, what's that you were saying about going away?; **de un m. u otro** one way or another; **dicho de otro m.** in other words, put another way; **en cierto m.** in a way; **¡qué m. de hacer las cosas!** that's no way to do things! ►► *Ling* ***m. de articulación*** manner of articulation; ***m. de empleo*** instructions for use; ***m. de pensar*** way of thinking; **a mi m. de pensar** to my way of thinking; ***m. de ser:*** **tiene un m. de ser muy agradable** she has a very pleasant nature; **no me gusta su m. de ser** I don't like the way he is; ***m. de vida*** way of life, lifestyle
(b) **modos** *(modales)* manners; **buenos/malos modos** good/bad manners; **me contestó de buenos/malos modos** she answered politely/rudely
(c) *Gram* mood; **m. indicativo/subjuntivo** indicative/subjunctive mood; **en m. indicativo** in the indicative (mood)
(d) *Informát* mode ►► ***m. de edición*** edit mode; ***m. gráfico*** graphic mode; ***m. de inserción*** insert mode
(e) *Mús* mode
2 **ni modo** *loc adv Andes, CAm, Carib, Méx (de ninguna manera)* no way, not a chance; **¿llegaremos a tiempo? – ni m.** will we get there on time? – no way *o* not a chance; **ni m. pues** there's nothing we can do about it, then

---

modorra *nf Fam* drowsiness; **tener m.** to be *o* feel sleepy

modoso, -a *adj (recatado)* modest; *(formal)* well-behaved

modulación *nf* modulation ►► *Rad* ***m. de amplitud*** amplitude modulation; *Rad* ***m. de frecuencia*** frequency modulation

modulado, -a *adj* **frecuencia modulada** frequency modulation, FM

modulador, -ora 1 *adj* modulating
2 *nm* modulator

modular¹ *adj* modular

modular² 1 *vt* (a) *(voz, sonido)* to modulate (b) *Rad* to modulate
2 *vi Mús (entonar)* to modulate

modular³ *nm RP* (a) *(sofá)* modular sofa; *(pieza de sofá)* module, unit (b) *(estantería)* shelf unit

módulo *nm* (a) *(pieza, unidad)* module (b) *(de muebles)* unit ►► ***m. de cocina*** kitchen unit (c) *(en educación)* module (d) *(en cárcel)* unit (e) **m. (espacial)** (space) module ►► ***m. de alunizaje*** lunar module (f) *Fís* modulus (g) *Mat* modulus

modus operandi *nm inv* modus operandi

modus vivendi *nm inv* (a) *(acuerdo)* modus vivendi (b) *(manera de vivir)* way of life

mofa *nf* mockery; **hacer m. de algo/alguien** to mock sth/sb, to make fun of sth/sb; **su metedura de pata fue motivo de m.** everyone made fun of *o* laughed at his blunder

mofarse *vpr* to scoff; **m. de algo/alguien** to mock sth/sb, to make fun of sth/sb

mofeta *nf* skunk

mofle *nm CAm, Méx* silencer

moflete *nm* chubby cheek

mofletudo, -a *adj* chubby-cheeked

Mogadiscio *n* Mogadishu

mogol, -a 1 *adj* Mongolian
2 *nm,f (persona)* Mongol, Mongolian
3 *nm (lengua)* Mongol, Mongolian

mogollón *Esp Fam* 1 *nm* (a) **m. de** *(muchos)* tons of, loads of; **invitó a un m. de amigos** he invited loads of friends *o* a whole load of friends; **tiene (un) m. de dinero** she's got loads of money, she's loaded (b) *(lío)* row, commotion; **entraron/salieron a m.** everyone rushed in/out at once; **acudieron en m. a ver qué pasaba** everyone crowded over to see what was happening
2 *adv* **me gusta m.** I like it loads *o Br* heaps; **me divierto m. con ese cómico** that comedian really cracks me up

mogote *nm* hillock *(with a flat top)*

mogrebí (*pl* **mogrebíes** *o* **mogrebís**) 1 *adj* Maghrebi
2 *nmf* Maghrebi

mohair [mo'er] *nm* mohair

mohicano, -a *Hist* 1 *adj* Mohican
2 *nm,f* Mohican

mohín *nm* grimace, face; **hacer un m., hacer mohines** to grimace, to pull faces

mohíno, -a *adj* (a) *(triste)* sad, melancholy (b) *(enfadado)* sulky

moho *nm* (a) *(hongo)* mould; **criar m.** to go *o* get mouldy (b) *(herrumbre)* rust

mohoso, -a *adj* (a) *(con hongo)* mouldy (b) *(oxidado)* rusty

moiré [mwa're], **muaré** *nm* (a) *Imprenta & Fot* moiré (b) *(tela)* moiré

Moisés *n pr* Moses

moisés *nm inv (cuna)* Moses basket; *(portátil)* carrycot

moishe ['moiʃe] *RP Fam* 1 *adj* Jewish
2 *nmf* Jew

mojabobos *nm inv CAm, Méx* drizzle

mojado, -a 1 *adj (empapado)* wet; *(húmedo)* damp; **ten cuidado, el suelo está m.** be careful, the floor is wet; **llegué a casa completamente m.** I got home completely soaked; **tengo los zapatos mojados** my shoes are wet; **todavía tengo la ropa mojada** my clothes are still damp
2 *nm,f Méx Fam (inmigrante)* wetback; **irse de m.** to enter the United States as an illegal immigrant

mojama *nf* dried salted tuna

mojamé *nm Esp Fam* = term used to refer to Arabs, which is sometimes offensive

mojar 1 *vt* (a) *(con líquido)* to wet; *(humedecer)* to moisten; **la lluvia nos mojó de pies a cabeza** we got soaked through in the rain; **moje bien el trapo antes de limpiar la ventana** wet the cloth thoroughly before using it to clean the window; **moje la parte de atrás de la etiqueta con la lengua** moisten the back of the label with your tongue; **el niño ya no moja la cama** the boy doesn't wet his bed any more
(b) *(comida)* to dunk; **moja el pan en la salsa** dip your bread in the sauce
(c) *Fam (celebrar con bebida)* to celebrate with a drink; **esta victoria hay que mojarla** we'll have to celebrate this win with a drink
2 *vi muy Fam (copular)* to get one's rocks off
3 **mojarse** *vpr* (a) *(con líquido)* to get wet; *(humedecerse)* to get

damp; **me he mojado el pelo para no pasar calor** I've wet my hair so I don't get too hot; **se ha mojado la ropa** the clothes have got wet; **no dejes que se moje la cámara** don't let the camera get wet; **no llevaba paraguas y se me mojó el pelo** I didn't have an umbrella and my hair got wet; **con esas nubes seguro que nos vamos a m.** by the look of those clouds we're going to get wet

(**b**) *Fam (comprometerse)* **yo prefiero no mojarme** I don't want to get involved; **no se moja por nadie** he wouldn't stick his neck out for anyone; **me han pedido que me moje y colabore económicamente** they've asked me to put my money where my mouth is

mojarra *nf* common two-banded sea bream

mojicón *nm* (**a**) *(bizcocho)* = small cake with marzipan icing (**b**) *Fam (golpe)* slap in the face

mojiganga *nf (ridiculez)* farce

mojigatería *nf* (**a**) *(beatería)* prudery (**b**) *(falsa humildad)* sanctimoniousness

mojigato, -a 1 *adj* (**a**) *(beato)* prudish (**b**) *(falsamente humilde)* sanctimonious

2 *nm,f* (**a**) *(beato)* prude (**b**) *(persona falsamente humilde)* sanctimonious person

mojito *nm* (**a**) *(cóctel)* = cocktail containing rum, sugar, lemon juice and mint (**b**) *Ven (plato)* = dish of flaked fish with coconut milk and seasoning

mojo *nm (salsa)* = spicy Canarian sauce made with oil, garlic, chilli, cumin and vinegar

mojón *nm* (**a**) *(piedra)* milestone (**b**) *(poste)* milepost (**c**) *Fam (excremento)* turd (**d**) *Ven Fam (mentira)* fib (**e**) *Ven Vulg (como insulto)* shit

mojonear *vi Ven Fam* to tell fibs, to fib

mojonero, -a *adj Ven Fam* fibber

moka, moca *nf* mocha

mol *nm Quím* mole

mola *nf Col, Pan (camisa)* = decorative shirt

molacho, -a *adj Méx Fam* **anda m.** he has a tooth missing

molar[1] *adj Quím* molar

molar[2] **1** *adj* **diente m.** molar

2 *nm* molar

molar[3] *vi Esp Fam* **¡cómo me mola esa moto/ese chico!** that motorbike/that guy is really cool!; **me mola esquiar** I'm really into skiing; **¿te mola una birra?** fancy a beer?; **hacer surf mola cantidad** surfing is really cool; **ahora mola mucho ir en patinete** skateboarding is really in at the moment; **trabajar los fines de semana no mola** it's such a drag working at weekends; **¡mola!** cool!; EXPR **m. (un) mazo, m. un pegote: esas gafas molan mazo** *o* **un pegote** those glasses are mega-cool

molaridad *nf Quím* molarity

molasa *nf Geol* molasse

molcajete *nm Méx* mortar

molcajetear *Méx* **1** *vt* to grind (in a mortar)

2 *vi* to grind

molcajetero, -a *nm,f Méx* = person who makes mortars

molcas *nmf inv Méx Fam* a certain person; **supe que m. tiene una relación con su secretaria** I found out that a certain person is having an affair with his secretary

Moldavia *n* Moldavia

moldavo, -a 1 *adj* Moldavian

2 *nm,f* Moldavian

molde *nm* (**a**) *(objeto hueco)* mould; **un m. de yeso** a plaster cast

(**b**) *(para tartas)* baking tin; *(para flanes)* mould ►► ***m. de pastel*** cake tin

(**c**) *(norma)* tradition; EXPR **romper moldes: un estilo que rompe moldes** a style that breaks with tradition *o* breaks the mould; **una mujer acostumbrada a romper moldes en la política** a woman used to breaking with political tradition; EXPR *RP Fam* **quedarse en el** *o* **hacer m.** to behave

(**d**) *Imprenta* form

(**e**) *Am (para coser)* pattern

moldeable *adj (material)* mouldable, malleable; *(persona)* malleable

moldeado *nm* (**a**) *(con molde)* moulding (**b**) *Esp (del pelo)* soft perm

moldeador, -ora 1 *adj* moulding

2 *nm,f* moulder

3 *nm Esp (del pelo)* soft perm

moldear 1 *vt* (**a**) *(dar forma)* to mould (**b**) *(cabello)* to give a soft perm to

2 moldearse *vpr* to curl; **se moldea el cabello** she curls her hair

moldeo *nm Tec* moulding ►► ***m. por inyección*** injection moulding

moldura *nf* (**a**) *Arquit* moulding (**b**) *(marco)* frame

mole[1] *nf* **una m. de cemento** *(edificio)* a huge mass *o* block of concrete; **chocaron contra una gigantesca m. de hielo** they hit an enormous block of ice; **el toro, una m. de centenares de kilos, miraba amenazador** the bull, a huge hulk of a beast weighing hundreds of kilos, looked around threateningly; **está hecho una m.** *(está gordo)* he's enormous

mole[2] *nm Méx* (**a**) *(salsa)* = thick, cooked chilli sauce ►► ***m. poblano*** = rich, cooked chilli sauce, made with nuts, raisins and chocolate

(**b**) *(guiso)* = dish served in "mole" sauce ►► ***m. de olla*** = stew made with meat, vegetables, and chilli

(**c**) EXPR *Fam* **darle a alguien en su (mero) m.** to chat to somebody about their pet subject; **con hablar de los caballos le dieron en su mero m.** when they got talking about horses they had him in his element; *Fam* **ser algo el (mero) m. de alguien: la física es su m.** physics has always been her (pet) subject; **la pesca siempre ha sido mi mero m.** fishing has always been my thing

molécula *nf* molecule

molecular *adj* molecular

moledura *nf* (**a**) *(acción)* grinding; *(de aceitunas)* pressing; *(de trigo)* milling (**b**) *Esp Fam (cansancio)* **fue una m. tener que ir andando** it was dead tiring having to walk

molejón *nm Cuba (roca)* = rock near the water's surface

moler [41] *vt* (**a**) *(pulverizar)* to grind; *(aceitunas)* to press; *(trigo)* to mill (**b**) *(destrozar)* to beat; **lo molieron a palos** he was beaten to a pulp; **estas zapatillas me están moliendo los pies** these shoes are killing my feet (**c**) *Fam (cansar)* to wear out

MOLESTAR **1** *vt* (**a**) *(perturbar)* to bother; **el calor no me molesta** the heat doesn't bother me; **esa luz tan brillante me molesta** that bright light is hurting my eyes; **deja ya de m. al gato** leave the cat alone; **¡deja de molestarme!** stop annoying me!; **¿te están molestando los niños?** are the children bothering you?; **las moscas no paraban de molestarnos** the flies were a real nuisance; **¿le molesta que fume** *o* **si fumo?** do you mind if I smoke?; **¿te molesta la radio?** is the radio bothering you?; **¿te molesta si abro la ventana?** do you mind if I open the window?; **perdone que le moleste...** I'm sorry to bother you...

(**b**) *(doler)* **me molesta una pierna** my leg is giving me a bit of trouble; **me molesta un poco la herida** my wound is rather uncomfortable *o* a bit sore; **vuelva dentro de un mes si le sigue molestando** come back in a month's time if it's still troubling you

(**c**) *(ofender)* to upset; **me molestó que no me saludaras** I was rather upset that you didn't say hello to me; **... todo esto dicho sin ánimo de m. a nadie** I don't want to cause anyone offence but...

2 *vi* **vámonos, aquí no hacemos más que m.** let's go, we're in the way here; **deja ya de m. con tantas preguntas** stop being such a nuisance and asking all those questions; **¿molesto? – no, no, pasa** am I interrupting? – no, not at all, come in; **no querría m., pero necesito hablar contigo un momento** I don't want to interrupt, but I need to have a word with you; **puedes aparcar el camión allí, que no molesta** you can park the truck *o Br* lorry over there where it won't be in the way; **no m.** *(en letrero)* do not disturb

3 molestarse *vpr* (**a**) *(tomarse molestias)* to bother; **no te molestes, yo lo haré** don't bother, I'll do it; **molestarse en hacer algo** to bother to do sth; **se molestó en prepararnos una comida vegetariana** she went to the trouble of preparing a vegetarian meal for us; **te agradezco que te hayas molestado en llamar** thank you for taking the trouble to phone; **ni siquiera se molestó en acompañarme a la puerta** he didn't even bother to show me to the door; **molestarse por algo/alguien** to put oneself out for sth/sb; **por mí no te molestes, aquí estoy bien** don't worry about me, I'm fine here

(**b**) *(ofenderse)* **molestarse (con alguien por algo)** to get upset (with sb about sth); **espero que no se molestara por lo que le dije** I hope what I said didn't upset you

molestia *nf* (**a**) *(incomodidad)* nuisance; **este ruido es una m.** this noise is a real nuisance *o* is really annoying; **es una m. vivir lejos del trabajo** it's a real nuisance living a long way from work; **ahórrese molestias y pague con tarjeta** save yourself a lot of trouble and pay by credit card; **¿te llevo a la estación? – ahórrate la m., iré en taxi** shall I give you a *Br* lift *o US* ride to the station? – don't bother, I'll get a cab; **ocasionar** *o* **causar molestias a alguien** to cause sb trouble; **si no es demasiada m.** if it's not too much trouble; **no es ninguna m.** it's no trouble; **perdone la m., pero...** sorry to bother you, but...; **(les rogamos) disculpen las molestias (causadas)** we apologize for any inconvenience (caused); **tomarse la m. de hacer algo** to go to the trouble of doing sth, to take the trouble to do sth; **¡no tenías por qué tomarte tantas molestias!** you didn't have to go to such trouble!, you shouldn't have!

(**b**) *(malestar)* discomfort; **siento molestias en el estómago** my stomach doesn't feel too good; **se retiró porque sentía algunas molestias en la rodilla** he came off because his knee wasn't quite right

molesto, -a *adj* (**a**) **ser m.** *(incordiante) (costumbre, tos, ruido)* to be annoying; *(moscas)* to be a nuisance; *(calor, humo, sensación)* to be unpleasant; *(ropa, zapato)* to be uncomfortable; **es muy m. tener que mandar callar constantemente** it's very annoying to have to be constantly telling you to be quiet; **tengo un dolor m. en la espalda** I've got an ache in my back which is causing me some discomfort

(**b**) **ser m.** *(inoportuno) (visita, llamada)* to be inconvenient; *(pregunta)* to be awkward

(**c**) **ser m.** *(embarazoso)* to be embarrassing; **esta situación empieza a resultarme un poco molesta** this situation is beginning to make me feel a bit uncomfortable

(**d**) **estar m.** *(irritado)* to be rather upset; **está molesta porque no la invitamos a la fiesta** she's upset because we didn't invite her to the party; **están molestos por sus declaraciones** they are upset by what he has been saying

(**e**) **estar m.** *(con malestar, incomodidad) (por la fiebre, el dolor)* to be in some discomfort; **no tenía que haber comido tanto, ahora estoy m.** I shouldn't have eaten so much, now I don't feel too well; **¿no estás m. con tanta ropa?** aren't you uncomfortable in all those clothes?

molestoso, -a *Andes, CAm, Carib, Méx Fam* **1** *adj* annoying
2 *nm,f* nuisance

molibdeno *nm Quím* molybdenum

molicie *nf* (**a**) *(blandura)* softness (**b**) *(comodidad)* luxurious *o* easy living

molida *nf Chile Br* mince, *US* ground beef

molido, -a *adj* (**a**) *(pulverizado)* ground; *(trigo)* milled (**b**) *Fam (cansado)* shattered; **estoy m. de tanto caminar** I'm shattered after all that walking

molienda *nf* (**a**) *(acción de moler)* grinding; *(de trigo)* milling (**b**) *(cantidad)* batch *(of something to be ground or milled)* (**c**) *(temporada)* milling season

moliente *adj Fam* **corriente y m.** run-of-the-mill

molinero, -a *nm,f* miller

molinete *nm* (**a**) *(ventilador)* extractor fan (**b**) *(torniquete de entrada)* turnstile (**c**) *(juguete)* toy windmill (**d**) *(en gimnasia)* flair

molinillo *nm* (**a**) *(aparato)* grinder ▸▸ ***m. de café*** coffee mill *o* grinder; ***m. de pimienta*** pepper mill (**b**) *(juguete)* toy windmill

molino *nm* (**a**) *(aparato)* mill ▸▸ ***m. de aceite*** olive oil mill; ***m. de agua*** water mill; ***m. de viento*** *(para grano)* windmill; *(aerogenerador)* wind turbine (**b**) *(fábrica)* mill

molla *nf* (**a**) *(parte blanda)* flesh (**b**) *Esp Fam (gordura)* **con esos pantalones se le notan mucho las mollas** those trousers really show up her flab

mollar *adj* (**a**) *(blando)* soft, tender (**b**) *(carne)* lean and boneless

molleja *nf* (**a**) *(de ave)* gizzard (**b**) **mollejas** *(de ternera)* sweetbreads

mollera *nf Fam (cabeza)* nut, *Br* bonce; **se le ha metido en la m. que va a nevar** he's got it into his head that it's going to snow; **le he dado vueltas a la m. y no hallo una solución** I've been going over and over it in my head but I can't find a solution; EXPR **ser cerrado** *o* **duro de m.** *(estúpido)* to be thick in the head; *(testarudo)* to be pig-headed

molón, -ona *adj Fam* (**a**) *Esp (que gusta) Br* brilliant, *US* neat; **es un disco muy m.** it's a really *Br* brilliant *o US* neat album (**b**) *Esp (elegante)* smart; **iqué gafas más molonas!** those glasses are really smart! (**c**) *Méx (pesado)* **ser m.** to be a pain

molote *nm* (**a**) *Méx (tortilla)* filled tortilla (**b**) *CAm, Carib, Méx (alboroto)* uproar, riot (**c**) *Méx (moño)* bun *(of hair)*

molotera *nf CAm, Cuba* uproar, riot

molotov *adj inv* **cóctel m.** petrol bomb, Molotov cocktail

molturar *vt (moler)* to grind; *(trigo)* to mill

Molucas *nfpl* **las (islas) M.** the Moluccas

molusco *nm* mollusc

moma *nf* dogfish

momentáneamente *adv* (**a**) *(en un momento)* immediately, right now (**b**) *(de forma pasajera)* momentarily

momentáneo, -a *adj* (**a**) *(de un momento)* momentary; **tuvieron que improvisar una solución momentánea** they had to come up with a solution on the spur of the moment (**b**) *(pasajero)* temporary; **no te preocupes, es un efecto m.** don't worry, the effect is only temporary

MOMENTO *nm* (**a**) *(instante preciso)* moment; **a partir de este m.** from this moment (on); **desde el m. (en) que...** *(indica tiempo)* from the moment that...; *(indica causa)* seeing as...; **desde ese m.** from that moment on, since that moment; **hasta ese m.** until that moment, until then; **lo podemos hacer en cualquier m.** we can do it any time; **en cualquier m. se puede producir la dimisión del presidente** the president could resign at any moment; **llegará en cualquier m.** she'll be arriving any moment now; **justo en ese m. entró mi padre** at that very moment *o* right then, my father came in; **en ese m. vivía en Perú** I was living in Peru at that time; **en este m. está reunida** she's in a meeting at the moment; **en el m. menos pensado te puede ocurrir un accidente** accidents can happen when you least expect them; **en todo m.** at all times; **en/hasta el último m.** at/right up until the last moment; **nos permite calcular la temperatura en un m. dado** it enables us to calculate the temperature at any given moment; **si en un m. dado necesitas ayuda, llámame** if at any time you need my help, call me; **m. decisivo** turning point; **el m. de la verdad** the moment of truth; **la situación podría cambiar de un m. a otro** the situation could change at any moment; **era difícil predecir lo que iba a pasar de un m. a otro** it was hard to predict what was going to happen from one moment to the next

(**b**) *(rato corto)* moment, minute; **¿puedo hablar un m. contigo?** could I speak to you for a moment *o* minute?; **sólo será un m.** I'll only *o* I won't be a minute; **dentro de un m.** in a moment *o* minute; **le arreglamos sus zapatos en el m.** *(en letrero)* shoes mended while you wait; **estará preparado en un m.** it'll be ready in a moment *o* minute; *también Fig* **espera un m.** hold on a minute; **hace un m.** a moment ago; **momentos después** moments later; **sin dudarlo un m.** without a moment's hesitation; **¡un m.!** just a minute!

(**c**) *(periodo)* time; **llegó un m. en que...** there came a time when...; **estamos pasando un mal m.** we're going through a difficult patch at the moment; **está en un buen m. (de forma)** she's in good form at the moment; **las reformas fueron rechazadas por los políticos del m.** the reforms were rejected by the politicians of the day; **es el artista del m.** he's the artist of the moment; **en un primer m.** initially, at first; **la película tiene sus (buenos) momentos** the movie has its moments

(**d**) *(ocasión)* time; **cuando llegue el m.** when the time comes; **en algún m.** sometime; **si en algún m. te sientes solo** if you ever feel lonely, if at any time you should feel lonely; **has venido en buen/mal m.** you've come at a good/bad time; **en momentos así** at times like this; **en ningún m. pensé que lo haría** at no time did I think that she would do it, I never thought she would do it

(**e**) *Fís* moment ▸▸ ***m. angular*** angular momentum; ***m. de inercia*** moment of inertia; ***m. lineal*** momentum; ***m. de torsión*** torque

(**f**) *(en frases)* **a cada m.** all the time; **al m.** *(inmediatamente)* straightaway; *Am (hasta ahora)* at the moment, so far; **quiere todo lo que pide al m.** she expects to get whatever she asks for straightaway; *Am* **al m. se cuentan 38 muertos** at the moment the number of deaths stands at 38, the number of deaths so far stands at 38; **¿quieres café? – de m. no** do you want some coffee? – not just now *o* not at the moment; **te puedes quedar de m.** you can stay for now *o* for the time being; **de m. estoy de acuerdo contigo** for the moment, I'll agree with you; **por el m.** for the time being, for the moment; **por momentos** by the minute; **me estoy poniendo nerviosa por momentos** I'm getting more and more nervous by the minute

momia *nf* mummy

momificación *nf* mummification

momificar [60] **1** *vt* to mummify
2 momificarse *vpr* to mummify

momio, -a *adj Chile Fam (carcamal)* square, untrendy

mona *nf* (**a**) *Fam (borrachera)* **agarrar una m.** to get plastered; **dormir la m.** to sleep it off (**b**) *(pastel)* **m. (de Pascua)** = cake traditionally eaten at Easter especially in Catalonia (**c**) *Chile (maniquí)* mannequin (**d**) EXPR *CSur Fam* **como la m.** *(terrible)* terrible; **me siento como la m.** I feel terrible; **este libro está escrito como la m.** this book is atrociously written (**e**) *ver también* **mono**

monacal *adj* monastic

monacato *nm (de monjes)* monasticism, monastic life; *(de monjas)* convent life

Mónaco *n* Monaco

monada *nf Fam* (**a**) *(persona)* **tienen una m. de niña** they've got a lovely little girl; **¡qué m. de bebé!** what a lovely baby!; **su mujer es una m.** his wife's gorgeous; **¿bailas, m.?** hey gorgeous, do you fancy a dance?

(**b**) *(cosa)* **viven en una m. de apartamento** they live in a gorgeous

Br flat *o US* apartment; **ese sombrero es una m.** that's a lovely hat (**c**) *(gracia)* **el bebé estaba haciendo monadas** the baby was being all cute

mónada *nf Filosofía* monad

monaguillo *nm* altar boy

monarca *nm* monarch ►► ***m. absoluto*** absolute monarch

monarquía *nf* monarchy ►► ***m. absoluta*** absolute monarchy; ***m. constitucional*** constitutional monarchy; ***m. parlamentaria*** parliamentary monarchy

monárquico, -a **1** *adj* (**a**) *(régimen, poder)* monarchic (**b**) *(partido, ideas)* monarchist
2 *nm,f* monarchist

monasterio *nm (de monjes)* monastery; *(de monjas)* convent

monástico, -a *adj* monastic

Moncloa *nf* **La M.** = residence of the Spanish premier which by extension refers to the Spanish government

monda *nf* (**a**) *(piel)* peel (**b**) *(acción de pelar)* peeling (**c**) *Esp Fam* **ser la m.** *(extraordinario)* to be amazing; *(gracioso)* to be a scream; **baila que es la m.** she's one hell of a dancer; **eres la m., ¿cómo te has podido olvidar del regalo?** you're unbelievable, how could you forget the present?

mondadientes *nm inv* toothpick

mondadura *nf (piel)* peel

mondar **1** *vt* to peel
2 mondarse *vpr Esp Fam* **mondarse (de risa)** to laugh one's head off; **¡yo me mondo con ella!** I have a really good laugh with her!

mondo, -a *adj (pelado, limpio)* bare; *(huesos)* picked clean; EXPR *Fam* **m. y lirondo: dejaron el pollo m. y lirondo** they picked the chicken clean; **la verdad monda y lironda** the plain, unvarnished truth

mondongo *nm* (**a**) *(víscera)* guts (**b**) *RP, Ven (platillo)* tripe

moneda *nf* (**a**) *(pieza)* coin; **una m. de diez pesos** a ten peso coin; EXPR **pagar a alguien con** *o* **en la misma m.** to pay sb back in kind; EXPR *RP* **y monedas: costó 400 y monedas** it cost just over 400 ►► ***m. falsa*** counterfeit coin; ***m. fraccionaria*** small change
(**b**) *(divisa)* currency ►► ***m. convertible*** convertible currency; ***m. corriente*** legal tender; EXPR **ser m. corriente** to be commonplace; ***m. de curso legal*** legal tender; ***m. débil*** weak currency; ***m. extranjera*** foreign currency; ***m. fiduciaria*** fiat money; ***m. fraccionaria*** fractional money; ***m. fuerte*** strong currency; ***m. nacional*** national *o* local currency; *UE* ***m. única*** single currency
(**c**) **La M.** *(en Chile)* = Chile's presidential palace

monedero *nm* (**a**) *(bolsa)* purse ►► ***m. electrónico*** electronic purse (**b**) *Am (teléfono)* phone box

monegasco, -a **1** *adj* Monacan, Monegasque
2 *nm,f* Monacan, Monegasque

monei, moni *nm Fam (dinero)* dough

monema *nm Ling* moneme

monería *nf Fam* (**a**) *(cosa)* **tienen una m. de cocina** they have a gorgeous kitchen (**b**) *(persona)* **sus bebés son una m.** her babies are lovely (**c**) *(gracia)* **el bebé estaba haciendo monerías** the baby was being all cute (**d**) *(bobada)* **deja de hacer monerías** stop monkeying around

monero, -a *nm,f Méx* cartoonist

monetario, -a *adj* monetary

monetarismo *nm Econ* monetarism

monetarista *Econ* **1** *adj* monetarist
2 *nmf* monetarist

monetizar [14] *vt Econ* (**a**) *(cursar)* to make legal tender (**b**) *(convertir en moneda)* to mint, to coin

mongol, -ola **1** *adj* Mongolian
2 *nm,f (persona)* Mongol, Mongolian
3 *nm (lengua)* Mongol, Mongolian

Mongolia *n* Mongolia

mongólico, -a **1** *adj* (**a**) *(enfermo)* Down's syndrome; **niño m.** Down's syndrome child (**b**) *Fam (imbécil)* moronic (**c**) *(de Mongolia)* Mongolian
2 *nm,f* (**a**) *(enfermo)* person with Down's syndrome; **es un m.** he has Down's syndrome (**b**) *Fam (imbécil)* moron (**c**) *(de Mongolia)* Mongol, Mongolian

mongolismo *nm* Down's syndrome

mongoloide *nm* mongoloid

moni = **monei**

monicaco, -a *nm,f Fam* shrimp, squirt

monigote *nm* (**a**) *(muñeco)* rag *o* paper doll (**b**) *(dibujo)* **hacer monigotes** to doodle pictures (**c**) *(persona)* puppet; **es un m. del gobierno** he's a government puppet

monises *nmpl Fam (dinero)* dough

monitor, -ora **1** *nm,f (persona) (profesor)* instructor; *(en campamento infantil)* monitor; *Am (en universidad)* teaching assistant ►► ***m. de autoescuela*** driving instructor; ***m. de esquí*** skiing instructor; ***m. de tenis*** tennis coach
2 *nm Informát & Tec* monitor; **m. en color** colour monitor

monitorear *vt Am* to monitor

monitoreo *nm Am (control)* monitoring

monitorización *nf (control)* monitoring

monitorizar *vt* to monitor

monitos *nmpl Méx* cartoon

monja *nf* nun

monje *nm* monk

monjil *adj* (**a**) *(de monja)* nun's (**b**) *Pey (demasiado recatado)* extremely demure

monjita *nf (ave)* = small bird of the Pampas

mono- *pref* mono-; **una reunión monotemática** a meeting on a single subject

mono[1], -a *adj* (**a**) *Fam (bonito)* lovely, pretty; **es mona, pero muy sosa** she's pretty but really dull; **está muy mona con ese vestido** she looks really lovely in that dress; **viste siempre muy mona** she always wears really pretty clothes (**b**) *(sonido)* mono (**c**) *Col (rubio)* blond, *f* blonde (**d**) *Ven Fam (presumido)* conceited

mono[2], -a **1** *nm,f* (**a**) *(animal)* monkey; EXPR *Fam* **mandar a alguien a freír monas** *o Ven* **monos** to tell sb to get lost; EXPR *Ven Fam* **en lo que pestañea un m.** in the blink of an eye; EXPR *Fam* **tener monos en la cara: ¿qué miras? ¿tengo monos en la cara?** what are you looking at? have I got two heads or something?; EXPR *Fam* **ser el último m.** to be bottom of the heap; PROV **aunque la mona se vista de seda, mona se queda** you can't make a silk purse out of a sow's ear ►► ***m. araguato*** red howler monkey; ***m. araña*** spider monkey; ***m. aullador*** howler monkey; ***m. caparro*** common woolly monkey; ***m. capuchino*** capuchin monkey; ***m. marimonda*** white-bellied spider monkey; ***m. tití*** squirrel monkey (**b**) *Col (rubio)* blond, *f* blonde
2 *nm* (**a**) *(prenda) (con mangas) Br* overalls, *US* coveralls; *(de peto) Br* dungarees, *Br* boiler suit, *US* overalls; **un m. de esquiar** salopettes
(**b**) *Esp Fam (síndrome de abstinencia)* cold turkey; **estar con el m.** to have gone cold turkey
(**c**) *Esp Fam (ganas)* **tengo m. de playa** I'm dying to go to the beach
(**d**) *Méx (muñeco)* soft toy
(**e**) *RP, Ven (ropa de bebé)* romper suit, *Br* Babygro®
(**f**) *Ven (ropa deportiva)* tracksuit
(**g**) *Ven (comodín)* joker
(**h**) *Ven Fam (deuda)* bad debt
(**i**) *Andes, Méx (monigote)* cartoon figure ►► *Andes* ***m. animado*** cartoon
(**j**) *Chile (montón)* pile of produce
(**k**) EXPR *Col* **meterle a alguien los monos** to frighten sb

monoambiente *nm Arg Br* studio flat, *US* studio apartment

monoaural *adj* monaural

monobikini, monobiquini *nm* monokini

monobloc *adj* **grifo m.** mixer tap *(with single control)*

monobloque *nm Arg* tower block

monocarril **1** *adj* monorail
2 *nm* monorail

monocasco *nm Náut* monohull

monociclo *nm* unicycle, monocycle

monocolor *adj* monochrome

monocorde *adj* (**a**) *(monótono)* monotonous (**b**) *Mús* single-stringed

monocotiledónea *nf Bot* monocotyledon

monocotiledóneo, -a *adj Bot* monocotyledonous

monocromático, -a *adj* monochromatic

monocromo, -a *adj* monochrome

monóculo *nm* monocle

monocultivo *nm Agr* monoculture

monoespaciado *Informát* **1** *adj* monospaced
2 *nm* monospacing

monoesquí (*pl* **monoesquís**) *nm* monoski

monofásico, -a *adj Elec* single-phase

monogamia *nf* monogamy

monógamo, -a 1 *adj* monogamous
2 *nm,f* monogamous person

monografía *nf* monograph

monográfico, -a *adj* monographic

monograma *nm* monogram, initials

monokini, monoquini *nm* monokini

monolingüe *adj* monolingual

monolítico, -a *adj* monolithic

monolito *nm* monolith

monologar [38] *vi* to give a monologue

monólogo *nm* monologue; *Teatro* soliloquy

monomando 1 *adj* **grifo m.** mixer tap *(with single control)*
2 *nm* mixer tap *(with single control)*

monomanía *nf* obsession

monomaniaco, -a, monomaníaco, -a 1 *adj* obsessive
2 *nm,f* obsessive

monómero *nm Quím* monomer

monomio *nm Mat* monomial

monono, -a *adj CSur Fam* gorgeous

mononucleosis *nf inv* mononucleosis ►► ***m. infecciosa*** glandular fever, *US* mono

monoparental *adj* **familia m.** one-parent *o* single-parent family

monopartidismo *nm* single-party system

monopatín *nm* (**a**) *Esp (tabla)* skateboard (**b**) *RP (patinete)* scooter

monoplano, -a 1 *adj* monoplane
2 *nm* monoplane

monoplataforma *adj Informát* single-platform

monoplaza 1 *adj* single-seater; **avión m.** single-seater aeroplane
2 *nm (avión, coche)* single-seater; *(coche de carreras)* racing car

monopolio *nm* (**a**) *(de sector)* monopoly (**b**) *(empresa)* monopoly (**c**) *(privilegio)* monopoly; **la riqueza en el país es m. de unos pocos** the country's wealth is concentrated in the hands of a chosen few; **se cree que tiene el m. de la verdad** he thinks he has a monopoly on the truth

monopolista *adj* monopolist; **tienen una posición m.** they have a monopoly

monopolización *nf* monopolization

monopolizador, -ora 1 *adj* monopolistic
2 *nm,f* monopolist

monopolizar [14] *vt* (**a**) *(en economía)* to monopolize (**b**) *(atraer)* to monopolize; **la actriz monopolizó la atención** all eyes were on the actress; **el reciente escándalo monopolizó la rueda de prensa** the recent scandal dominated the press conference

monoprocesador *nm Informát* single-chip computer

monoquini = **monokini**

monorraíl, *Am* **monorriel** 1 *adj* monorail
2 *nm* monorail

monosabio *nm Taurom* = picador's assistant in a bullfight

monosacárido *nm Quím* monosaccharide

monosilábico, -a *adj* monosyllabic

monosílabo, -a 1 *adj* monosyllabic
2 *nm* monosyllable; **responder con monosílabos** to reply in monosyllables

monoteísmo *nm* monotheism

monoteísta 1 *adj* monotheistic
2 *nmf* monotheist

monotema *nm* **el sexo es su m.** all he ever talks about is sex

monotemático, -a *adj* **es m.** he always talks about the same thing; **sus películas son monotemáticas** all her films deal with the same theme

monotipia *nf*, **monotipo** *nm* monotype

monótonamente *adv* monotonously

monotonía *nf* (**a**) *(falta de variedad)* monotony (**b**) *(de voz)* monotone

monótono, -a *adj* monotonous

monousuario *adj* single-user

monovalente *adj Quím* monovalent, univalent

monovolumen *nm* people carrier

monóxido *nm* monoxide ►► ***m. de carbono*** carbon monoxide

monra *nf Andes Fam* breaking and entering

monrero, -a *nm,f Andes Fam* burglar *(who breaks his way into a house)*

Monrovia *n* Monrovia

monseñor *nm* (**a**) *(religioso)* Monsignor (**b**) *(aristócrata)* Monseigneur

monserga *nf Esp Fam* drivel; **no me vengas con monsergas** don't give me that rubbish; **nos soltó una m. sobre la santidad del matrimonio** he droned on at us about the sanctity of marriage

monstruo 1 *nm* (**a**) *(ser fantástico)* monster ►► ***el m. de Frankenstein*** Frankenstein's monster; ***el m. del Lago Ness*** the Loch Ness monster
(**b**) *(persona deforme)* **es un m.** he's terribly deformed
(**c**) *(persona cruel)* monster
(**d**) *(persona fea)* **es un m.** he's hideous
(**e**) *Fam (prodigio)* **uno de los monstruos del arte contemporáneo** one of the giants of contemporary art; **es un m. de la electrónica** he's a wizard at electronics; **es un m. esquiando** he's a brilliant skier ►► ***m. sagrado*** legend
2 *adj inv Fam* massive; **una concentración m.** a mass meeting

monstruosidad *nf* (**a**) *(anomalía)* freak (**b**) *(enormidad)* hugeness (**c**) *(crueldad)* monstrosity, atrocity (**d**) *(fealdad)* **han construido una m. de edificio** they've built a monstrosity of a building

monstruoso, -a *adj* (**a**) *(enorme)* huge, enormous (**b**) *(deforme)* terribly deformed (**c**) *(cruel)* monstrous; **un crimen m.** a monstrous crime (**d**) *(feo)* hideous

monta *nf* (**a**) *(suma)* total (**b**) *(importancia)* importance; EXPR **de poca m.** of little importance; **un ladrón de poca m.** a petty *o* small-time thief; **un problema de poca m.** a minor problem; **tendrá consecuencias de poca m.** the consequences will be of little importance (**c**) *(en caballo)* ride; **el arte de la m.** the art of riding; **un caballo de m.** a saddle horse

montacargas *nm inv Br* goods lift, *US* freight elevator

montado *nm Esp (bocadillo)* = small piece of bread with a savoury topping

montador, -ora *nm,f* (**a**) *(obrero)* fitter (**b**) *Cine* editor

montaje *nm* (**a**) *(de máquina, estructura)* assembly; **m. de andamios** putting up *o* erecting scaffolding (**b**) *Teatro* staging (**c**) *Fot, Arte* montage; **un m. fotográfico** a photomontage (**d**) *Cine* editing (**e**) *(farsa)* **el rescate fue un m. de la CIA** the rescue was staged by the CIA; **la enfermedad fue un m. para poder quedarse en casa** his illness was a ruse to enable him to stay at home

montallantas *nm inv Col* (**a**) *(persona)* = person who retreads tyres (**b**) *(taller)* = garage that retreads tyres

montante *nm* (**a**) *Arquit (de armazón)* upright; *(de ventana)* mullion; *(de puerta)* jamb (**b**) *(ventanuco)* fanlight (**c**) *(importe)* total

montaña *nf* (**a**) *(elevación)* mountain; **bicicleta de m.** mountain bike, **botas de m.** climbing boots; **tengo una m. de papeles sobre mi mesa** I've got a mountain of papers on my desk; EXPR **si la m. no va a Mahoma, Mahoma va a la m.** if the mountain won't come to Mohammed, Mohammed must go to the mountain; EXPR **hacer una m. de algo** to make a big thing of sth; EXPR **hacer una m. de un grano de arena** to make a mountain out of a molehill ►► ***las Montañas Rocosas*** *o Am* ***Rocallosas*** the Rocky Mountains; ***m. rusa*** rollercoaster
(**b**) *(región)* **la m.** the mountains; **pasaremos el verano en la m.** we'll spend summer in the mountains
(**c**) *Fam* **una m. de** *(un montón de)* piles of; **tengo una m. de cosas que hacer** I've got piles of things to do

montañero, -a 1 *adj* **la vida montañera** life in the mountains; **unos calcetines montañeros** hiking socks
2 *nm,f* mountaineer

montañés, -esa 1 *adj* (**a**) *(de la montaña)* **pueblo m.** mountain village; **mis padres son montañeses** my parents are from the mountains (**b**) *Esp (cántabro)* of/from Cantabria *(Spain)*
2 *nm,f* (**a**) *(de la montaña)* **los montañeses** people from the mountains (**b**) *Esp (cántabro)* person from Cantabria *(Spain)*

montañismo *nm* mountaineering

montañoso, -a *adj* mountainous; **una cadena montañosa** a mountain chain

montaplatos *nm inv* dumbwaiter

MONTAR 1 *vt* (**a**) *(ensamblar) (máquina, estantería, armario)* to assemble; *(tienda de campaña, tenderete, barricada)* to put up
(**b**) *Cine (película)* to cut, to edit
(**c**) *(encajar)* **m. algo en algo** to fit sth into sth; **m. una joya en un anillo** to set a jewel in a ring

(**d**) *(organizar) (negocio, empresa)* to set up; *(tienda)* to open; *(ataque, ofensiva)* to mount; *(exposición, congreso)* to organize; *(fiesta)* to throw; *(obra teatral)* to stage; **han montado un cibercafé cerca de mi casa** they've opened a cybercafe near my house; **m. la casa** to set up home

(**e**) *Esp Fam (organizar) (escándalo, jaleo)* to make; **m. ruido** to make a noise; **me montó una escena** *o* **escándalo** *o* **numerito** she made a scene in front of me

(**f**) *(cabalgar)* to ride

(**g**) *(poner encima)* **m. a alguien en algo** to lift sb onto sth

(**h**) *Esp (nata)* to whip; *(claras, yemas)* to beat, to whisk

(**i**) *(para criar) (yegua, vaca, cerda)* to mount

(**j**) *muy Fam (mujer)* to screw

(**k**) *(arma)* to cock

(**l**) *Informát (partición)* to mount

(**m**) *Ven Fam (alimentos)* to get, *US* to fix

2 *vi* (**a**) *(subir)* to get on; *(en automóvil)* to get in; *(en un animal)* to mount; **m. en** *(subir a)* to get onto; *(automóvil)* to get into; *(animal)* to mount

(**b**) *(ir cabalgando, conduciendo)* to ride; **¿sabes m.?** *(en caballo)* can you ride?; *(en bicicleta)* do you know how to ride a bike?; **m. en bicicleta/a caballo/en burro** to ride a bicycle/a horse/a donkey

(**c**) *Esp (sumar)* **m. a** to come to, to total; **¿a cuánto montan los ingresos?** what is the total income?; EXPR **tanto monta (monta tanto, Isabel como Fernando)** it's all the same

(**d**) **m. en cólera** to get angry, to fly into a temper *o* rage

3 montarse *vpr* (**a**) *(subirse)* to get on; *(en automóvil)* to get in; *(en animal)* to mount; **montarse en** *(subirse)* to get onto; *(automóvil)* to get into; *(animal)* to mount; **nos montamos en todas las atracciones** we had a go on all the rides

(**b**) *RP muy Fam (copular)* to screw; **montarse a alguien** to screw sb

(**c**) EXPR *Esp Fam* **montárselo: móntatelo para tenerlo acabado mañana** try and work it *o* to organize things so you have it finished by tomorrow; **móntatelo como quieras pero lo necesito para el lunes** I don't care how you do it, but I need it for Monday; **me lo monté para que me invitaran a cenar** I managed to get myself invited to dinner; **con nosotros siempre se lo ha montado bien** he's always been a good *Br* mate *o US* buddy to us; **se lo montan muy mal con la música en ese bar** the music's rubbish in that bar; *Fam* **¡qué bien te lo montas!** you've got it well worked out!; *muy Fam* **montárselo con alguien** *(sexualmente)* to screw sb, *Br* to have it off with sb

---

montaraz *adj* (**a**) *(del monte)* **un animal m.** a wild animal (**b**) *(tosco, rudo)* savage, wild

Mont Blanc *nm* **el M.** Mont Blanc

monte *nm* (**a**) *(elevación)* mountain ►► ***el M. Sinaí*** Mount Sinai

(**b**) *(terreno) (con arbustos)* scrubland; *(bosque)* woodland; **echarse** *o* **tirarse al m.** to take to the hills; *Fig* to go to extremes; PROV **no todo el m. es orégano** life's not a bowl of cherries ►► ***m. alto*** forest; *RP* ***m. artificial*** plantation; ***m. bajo*** scrub; *RP* ***m. natural*** natural woodland

(**c**) *Esp* ***m. de piedad*** *(casa de empeños)* state pawnbroker's; *(mutualidad)* mutual aid society

(**d**) ***m. de Venus*** mons veneris

(**e**) *Méx (pasto)* pasture

(**f**) *Ven (ensalada)* salad

(**g**) *Col, Ven Fam (marihuana)* grass

(**h**) EXPR *RP, Ven Fam* **tener a m. a alguien** to hassle sb

montear *vt* to give chase to

Montecarlo *n* Monte Carlo

montenegrino, -a 1 *adj* Montenegran

2 *nm,f* Montenegran

Montenegro *n* Montenegro

montepío *nm* (**a**) *(institución)* mutual aid society (**b**) *(fondo)* charitable fund *(for workers and their dependents)* (**c**) *(pensión)* pension *(from mutual aid society)*

montera *nf* bullfighter's hat

montería *nf* (**a**) *(caza mayor)* hunting *(of big game)* (**b**) *(cinegética)* hunting

montero *nm (ojeador)* beater

montés *(pl* **monteses***)* *adj* wild

montevideano, -a 1 *adj* of/from Montevideo

2 *nm,f* person from Montevideo

Montevideo *n* Montevideo

montgomery [mon'gomeri] *nm CSur* duffle coat

montículo *nm* (**a**) *(montaña)* hillock; **un m. de piedras** a heap of stones (**b**) *(en béisbol)* mound

montilla *nm* Montilla, = sherry-type wine from Montilla near Córdoba, Spain

monto *nm* total

montón *nm* (**a**) *(pila)* heap, pile; **roba dos cartas del m.** take two cards from the pile; *Fam* **del m.** ordinary, run-of-the-mill

(**b**) *Fam (cantidad)* **un m. de** loads of; **me gusta un m.** I'm mad about him; **me duele un m.** it hurts like mad; **pregúntale a él que sabe un m. de astronomía** ask him, he knows loads about astronomy; **a montones** by the bucketload; **tiene dinero a montones** she's got loads of money, she's loaded; **en verano vienen turistas a montones** in summer the place is crawling with tourists

montonera *nf* (**a**) *Am Hist (milicia)* militia (**b**) *RP Fam (cantidad)* **una m. de** loads of; **tengo una m. de cosas que hacer** I've got loads of things to do

montonero, -a 1 *adj* = of/relating to the Montoneros

2 *nm,f* (**a**) *(de los Montoneros)* = member of the Montoneros (**b**) *Am Hist (miliciano)* = member of a militia

Montoneros *nmpl* = Peronist urban guerrilla movement

montubio, -a *Andes* **1** *adj* rustic

2 *nm,f* = peasant living in a coastal area

montuno, -a 1 *adj* (**a**) *(del monte)* mountain; **la región montuna** the mountain region (**b**) *Carib (rudo)* rustic; *(brutal)* wild, savage (**c**) *Carib (huraño)* unsociable

2 *nm,f Cuba Fam (guajiro)* peasant

montura *nf* (**a**) *(cabalgadura)* mount (**b**) *(arreos)* harness; *(silla)* saddle (**c**) *(de gafas)* frame (**d**) *(de joyas)* mounting

monumental *adj* (**a**) *(ciudad, lugar)* **es una ciudad m.** it's a city with a lot of historic monuments; **la ciudad contiene un espléndido conjunto m. renacentista** the city has a wonderful collection of Renaissance buildings (**b**) *(fracaso, éxito)* monumental; **agarró un enfado m.** he flew into an almighty rage; **el concierto fue un aburrimiento m.** the concert was incredibly boring

monumento *nm* (**a**) *(construcción)* monument; *(estatua)* monument, statue; **un m. a los caídos (en la guerra)** a war memorial; **un m. a la constitución** a monument to the constitution; *Fam* **a tu madre habría que hacerle un m.** your mother deserves a medal ►► ***m. funerario*** burial monument; ***m. histórico*** historical monument; ***m. nacional*** national monument

(**b**) *(obra artística o científica)* classic; **un m. de la poesía del XIX** a classic of nineteenth-century poetry

(**c**) *(altar)* = decorated altar used during Holy Week

(**d**) *Fam (mujer atractiva)* babe

monzón *nm* monsoon

monzónico, -a *adj* monsoon; **lluvias monzónicas** monsoon rains

moña 1 *nf* (**a**) *(adorno)* ribbon (**b**) *Esp Fam (borrachera)* **agarrar una m.** to get smashed (**c**) *RP (lazo)* bow

2 *nm Esp muy Fam Br* poof, *US* fag

moñiga *nf Fam* cowpat

moñigo *nm Fam* cowpat

moñita *nf Urug* bow tie

moñito *nm Arg* bow tie

moño *nm* (**a**) *(de pelo)* bun *(of hair)*; **hacerse un m.** to put one's hair up in a bun; EXPR **agarrarse del m.** *(pegarse)* to pull each other's hair out; EXPR *Esp Fam* **estar hasta el m. (de)** to be sick to death (of) (**b**) *Am (lazo)* bow (**c**) *Méx (pajarita)* bow tie (**d**) EXPR *Méx Fam* **ponerse los moños** to give oneself airs

mopa *nf* = soft brush for polishing floors

moquear *vi* (**a**) *(nariz)* to have a runny nose (**b**) *RP, Ven Fam (llorar)* to snivel

moqueo *nm* runny nose; **tener m.** to have a runny nose

moquero *nm Fam* snot rag

moqueta *nf Esp* fitted carpet

moquete *nm RP Fam* slap in the face

moquetear *RP* **1** *vt* to carpet

2 *vi* to have a carpet fitted

moquette [mo'ket] *nf RP* fitted carpet

moquillo *nm (enfermedad)* distemper

mor: por mor de *loc adv Formal* on account of, for the sake of; **por m. de la verdad, debo decírselo** out of respect for the truth I have to tell him

mora *nf* (**a**) *(de la zarzamora)* blackberry (**b**) *(del moral)* (black) mulberry (**c**) *(de la morera)* (white) mulberry (**d**) *Fin* default (**e**) *ver también* **moro**

morada *nf Literario* dwelling, abode; **entren en mi humilde m.** welcome to my humble abode; **miles de personas lo acompañaron a su última m.** thousands of people accompanied him to his final resting place

morado, -a 1 *adj (color)* purple; EXPR *Esp Fam* **pasarlas moradas** to have a tough time of it; **las pasamos moradas para encontrar alojamiento** it was a nightmare finding somewhere to stay; EXPR *Esp Fam* **ponerse m.** *(de comida)* to stuff oneself; **nos pusimos morados de cerveza** we drank gallons of beer; **me puse m. de bailar** I did nothing but dance
2 *nm* (**a**) *(color)* purple (**b**) *(moratón)* bruise

morador, -ora *nm,f* inhabitant

moradura *nf* bruise

moral[1] 1 *adj* (**a**) *(espiritual)* moral; **tienen el apoyo m. de todos nosotros** they have our moral support; **presentó una demanda por daños morales** she made a claim for psychological damage
(**b**) *(ético)* moral; **tengo la obligación m. de ayudarlos** I am morally obliged to help them; **no tiene autoridad m. para exigir mi dimisión** she does not have the moral authority to demand my resignation
2 *nf* (**a**) *(ética)* morality; **es un ejemplo de la doble m. del presidente** it's an example of the president's double standards
(**b**) *(ánimo)* morale; **su victoria nos dio mucha m.** her win lifted our spirits *o* improved our morale; **estar bajo de m.** to be in poor spirits; **levantarle** *o* **subirle la m. a alguien** to lift sb's spirits, to cheer sb up; EXPR *Esp Fam Hum* **tiene más m. que el Alcoyano** she's not one to get downhearted easily

moral[2] *nm (árbol)* black mulberry tree

moraleja *nf* moral; **m.: lo importante es participar** the moral of the story is that the important thing is to take part

moralidad *nf* morality

moralina *nf Pey* moralizing; **una novela con m.** a moralistic novel

moralismo *nm* moralism

moralista 1 *adj* moralistic
2 *nmf* moralist

moralización *nf* **la m. de la vida pública** raising moral standards in public life

moralizador, -ora 1 *adj* moralizing
2 *nm,f* moralizer

moralizante *adj* moralistic

moralizar [14] 1 *vt* to raise the moral standards of
2 *vi* to moralize

moralmente *adv* morally

morapio *nm Esp Fam* cheap red wine, *Br* plonk

morar *vi Literario* to dwell (**en** in)

moratón, moretón *nm* bruise

moratoria *nf* moratorium

morbidez *nf* delicacy

mórbido, -a *adj* (**a**) *(de la enfermedad)* morbid (**b**) *(delicado)* delicate

morbilidad *nf Med* morbidity

morbo *nm* (**a**) *Fam (atractivo)* **el m. atrajo a la gente al lugar del accidente** people were attracted to the scene of the accident by a sense of morbid fascination; **los cementerios le dan mucho m.** he gets a morbid pleasure out of visiting cemeteries; **esa chica tiene mucho m.** there's something perversely attractive about that girl (**b**) *(enfermedad)* illness

morbosidad *nf* **la m. del accidente atrajo a los espectadores** the gruesomeness of the accident attracted the onlookers; **abordaron la información del accidente con mucha m.** they reported the accident rather morbidly

morboso, -a 1 *adj* (**a**) *(persona, interés)* morbid, ghoulish; *(escena, descripción)* gruesome (**b**) *(de la enfermedad)* morbid
2 *nm,f* ghoul

morcilla *nf Br* black pudding, *US* blood sausage; EXPR *Esp Fam* **¡que te den m.!** you can stick *o* shove it, then!; **si no quiere ayudar, ¡que le den m.!** if he doesn't want to help, he can stuff it!

morcillo *nm* foreknuckle

morcón *nm* = cured pork sausage

mordacidad *nf* sharpness, mordacity

mordaz *adj* caustic

mordaza *nf* (**a**) *(para la boca)* gag (**b**) *(herramienta)* clamp, jaw

mordedura *nf* bite

mordelón, -ona *adj Méx (corrupto)* open to bribery

morder [41] 1 *vt* (**a**) *(con los dientes)* to bite (**b**) *(apretar)* to grip (**c**) *(gastar)* to eat into (**d**) *Carib, Méx Fam (sobornar)* to buy off (**e**) *Carib, Méx (estafar)* to cheat (**f**) *Ven Fam (entender)* to get
2 *vi* (**a**) *(con los dientes)* to bite; *Fam* **salúdala, que no muerde** you can say hello to her, she doesn't bite; *Fam* **está que muerde** he's hopping mad (**b**) *Carib, Méx Fam (aceptar soborno)* to accept bribes *o Br* backhanders (**c**) *Ven Fam (entender)* to get it
3 **morderse** *vpr* **morderse las uñas** to bite one's nails; *también Fig* **morderse la lengua** to bite one's tongue

mordida *nf* (**a**) *(mordisco)* bite (**b**) *CAm, Méx Fam (soborno)* bribe, *Br* backhander; **cobrar m.** to receive a bribe *o Br* backhander; **dar m.** to offer a bribe *o Br* backhander (**c**) *CSur (bocado)* bite

mordiente 1 *adj* (**a**) *(que muerde)* biting (**b**) *(fijador)* mordant
2 *nm* caustic acid

mordisco *nm* (**a**) *(con los dientes)* bite; **dar** *o* **pegar un m. a algo** to take a bite of sth; **dio un m. a la manzana** he took a bite out of the apple; **¿me dejas darle un m.?** can I have a bite?; **los perros acabaron a mordiscos** the dogs ended up biting each other (**b**) *Fam (beneficio)* **obtuvieron un buen m. de la venta del terreno** they made a nice fat profit from the sale of the land

mordisquear *vt* to nibble (at)

morelense 1 *adj* of/from Morelos *(Mexico)*
2 *nmf* person from Morelos *(Mexico)*

moreliano, -a 1 *adj* of/from Morelia *(Mexico)*
2 *nm,f* person from Morelia *(Mexico)*

morena *nf* (**a**) *(pez)* moray eel (**b**) *ver también* **moreno**

morenez *nf (de pelo, piel)* darkness

moreno, -a 1 *adj* (**a**) *(pelo, piel)* dark; **ser m.** *(por el pelo)* to have dark hair; *(por la piel)* to have dark skin (**b**) *(por el sol)* tanned; **ponerse m.** to get a tan; **volvió muy m. de sus vacaciones** he came back from his holiday looking very tanned (**c**) *(pan, azúcar)* brown
2 *nm,f* (**a**) **ser un m.** *(por el pelo)* to have dark hair; *(por la piel)* to have dark skin (**b**) *Fam Euf (negro)* coloured person
3 *nm Esp (bronceado)* suntan, tan

morera *nf* white mulberry tree

morería *nf* Moorish quarter

moretón = **moratón**

morfa *nf Fam* morf

morfar *RP Fam* 1 *vt* to eat, *Br* to scoff
2 *vi* to eat, *Br* to nosh
3 **morfarse** *vpr* **m. algo** to eat *o Br* scoff sth

morfe, morfi *nm RP Fam* grub

morfema *nm Ling* morpheme

morfémico, -a *adj Ling* morphemic

Morfeo *n Mitol* Morpheus; EXPR **estar en brazos de M.** to be in the arms of Morpheus

morfi = **morfe**

morfina *nf* morphine

morfinomanía *nf* morphine addiction

morfinómano, -a 1 *adj* addicted to morphine
2 *nm,f* morphine addict

morfología *nf* morphology

morfológico, -a *adj* morphological

morfosintaxis *nf inv* morphosyntax

morganático, -a *adj* morganatic

morgue *nf* morgue

moribundo, -a 1 *adj* dying; **un paciente m.** a dying patient
2 *nm,f* dying man, *f* dying woman; **los moribundos** the dying

moridera *nf Ven Fam* (**a**) *(desmayo)* fainting fit (**b**) *(desánimo)* **anda con m.** he's on a downer

morigerado,-a *adj Formal* moderate

morillo *nm* firedog

MORIR [27] 1 *vi* (**a**) *(fallecer)* to die (**de** of); **murió apuñalado** he was stabbed to death; **murió asesinado** he was murdered; **murió ahogado** he drowned; **m. (de) joven** to die young; **m. de cáncer/de frío/de muerte natural** to die of cancer/of cold/of natural causes; **murió de (un) infarto** he died from a heart attack; **m. por la patria/por una causa** to die for one's country/for a cause; **¡muera el tirano!** death to the tyrant!; EXPR *Fam* **a m.: la quiero a m.** I love her to death; **aquella noche bebimos a m.** we had absolutely loads to drink that night
(**b**) *(terminar)* **este río muere en el lago** this river runs into the lake;

aquel camino muere en el bosque that path peters out in the forest
(**c**) *Literario (extinguirse) (fuego)* to die down; *(luz)* to go out; *(día)* to come to a close; *(tradición, costumbres, civilización)* to die out; **nuestra relación murió hace tiempo** our relationship died a long time ago
2 morirse *vpr* (**a**) *(fallecer)* to die (**de** of); **se está muriendo** she's dying; **se le ha muerto la madre** his mother has died; *Fam* **nadie se muere por hacer unas cuantas horas extras** a few hours of overtime never hurt anyone; *Fam* **¡muérete!** drop dead!; EXPR *Fam* **¡por mí como si se muere!** she could drop dead for all I care!
(**b**) *(sentir con fuerza)* **morirse de envidia/ira** to be burning with envy/rage; **morirse de miedo** to be scared to death; **casi me muero de risa/vergüenza** I nearly died laughing/of embarrassment; **me muero de ganas de ir a bailar/fumar un pitillo** I'm dying to go dancing/for a cigarette; **me muero de hambre/frío** I'm starving/freezing; **morirse por algo** to be dying for sth; **se mueren por tener un niño** they're desperate to have a child; **morirse por alguien** to be crazy about sb
(**c**) *Ven Fam (como exclamación)* **¡muérete! que conseguí trabajo** guess what, I've got a job!; **¡muérete! que se robaron tu carro** you won't believe it, but your car's been stolen

---

morisco, -a 1 *adj* = referring to Moors in Spain baptized after the Reconquest
2 *nm,f* baptized Moor

morisqueta *nf (mueca)* **hacer morisquetas** to make *o* pull faces

morito *nm* glossy ibis

morlaco *nm* (**a**) *(toro)* large fighting bull (**b**) *Am Fam (dinero)* dough; **¿me prestas unos morlacos?** can you lend me some dough?

mormado, -a *adj Méx* **tengo la nariz mormada** my nose is blocked

mormón, -ona 1 *adj* Mormon
2 *nm,f* Mormon

mormónico, -a *adj* Mormon

mormonismo *nm* Mormonism

moro, -a 1 *adj* (**a**) *Hist* Moorish (**b**) *Esp muy Fam (machista)* **ser muy m.** to be a sexist pig
2 *nm,f* (**a**) *Hist* Moor; EXPR *Fam* **no hay moros en la costa** the coast is clear; **ahora no te lo puedo contar, que hay moros en la costa** I can't tell you right now, I don't want to be overheard ►► ***moros y cristianos*** *(en España)* = traditional Spanish festival involving mock battle between Moors and Christians; *(en el Caribe)* rice and beans
(**b**) *Esp Fam Pey (árabe)* = term used to refer to Arabs, which is sometimes offensive
3 *nm Esp* (**a**) *muy Fam (machista)* sexist pig (**b**) *Fam* **el m.** *(Marruecos)* Morocco; EXPR **bajarse al m.** to go over to Morocco to score some hash

morocho, -a 1 *adj* (**a**) *Andes, RP (moreno)* dark-haired; **es m.** he's got dark hair (**b**) *Andes, RP Euf (negro)* coloured (**c**) *Ven (gemelo)* twin
2 *nm,f* (**a**) *Andes, RP (moreno)* dark-haired person (**b**) *Andes, RP Euf (negro)* coloured person (**c**) *Ven (gemelo)* twin

morondanga: de morondanga *loc adj RP Fam* lousy; **siempre trae esos brochecitos de m.** she always wears those cheap and nasty little brooches; **es un campito de m.** it's a lousy little field

moronga *nf CAm, Méx Br* black pudding, *US* blood sausage

morosidad *nf* (**a**) *Com* defaulting, failure to pay on time (**b**) *(lentitud)* slowness

moroso, -a *Com* **1** *adj* defaulting; **un cliente m.** a debtor who is behind with his payments
2 *nm,f* defaulter, bad debtor

> **Falso amigo**: El término inglés **morose** no es la traducción del español **moroso**. En inglés **morose** significa "hosco, huraño".

morral *nm (saco)* haversack; *(de cazador)* gamebag

morralla *nf* (**a**) *(personas)* scum (**b**) *(cosas)* junk (**c**) *(pescado)* small fry (**d**) *Méx (suelto)* loose change

morrazo *nf Fam* EXPR **se dio** *o* **pegó un m. contra un árbol** he went smack into a tree

morrear *Esp Fam* **1** *vi* to smooch
2 morrearse *vpr* to smooch

morrena *nf* moraine

morreo *nm Esp Fam* smooch; **se estaban dando un m.** they were having a smooch

morriña *nf Esp (por el país)* homesickness; *(por el pasado)* nostalgia; **tener** *o* **sentir m.** *(por el país)* to feel homesick

morrión *nm* (**a**) *(casco)* morion, helmet (**b**) *(gorro)* shako

morro[1] *nm* (**a**) *(hocico)* snout
(**b**) *Esp (de avión)* nose; *(de coche)* front
(**c**) *Esp Fam* **morros** *(labios)* lips; *(boca)* mouth; **límpiate los morros** give your chops a wipe; **beber a m.** to drink straight out of the bottle; EXPR **estar de morros** to be in a bad mood; EXPR **romperle los morros a alguien** to smash sb's face in
(**d**) *Esp Fam (caradura)* **¡qué m. tiene!** he's got a real nerve!; EXPR **echarle m.: tú échale m., ya verás como te dejan entrar** just go for it, they'll let you in, you'll see; **no se puede ir por ahí echándole tanto m. a la vida** you can't just go around behaving with such a cheek; EXPR *Hum* **¡tiene un m. que se lo pisa!** she's got one hell of a nerve!; EXPR **por (todo) el m.** *(gratis)* without paying, free; **me pidió que le diera clases así, por el m.** he had the nerve to ask if I would give him lessons for free; **se presentó allí por (todo) el m.** *(con caradura)* he had the nerve just to walk straight in there

morro[2]**, -a** *nm,f Méx Fam* (**a**) *(muchacho)* kid (**b**) *(novio)* squeeze

morrocotudo, -a *adj* (**a**) *Fam (enorme, tremendo)* tremendous (**b**) *Col (rico)* rich, well-off

morrocoy *nm Col, Ven* (**a**) *(animal) (sabanero)* red-footed tortoise; *(montañero)* yellow-footed tortoise (**b**) *Fam (persona) Br* slowcoach, *US* slowpoke

morrón 1 *adj* **pimiento m.** red pepper
2 *nm* (**a**) *Esp Fam (golpe)* **darse un m.** to give oneself a real thump (**b**) *CSur (pimiento)* red pepper

morroñoso, -a *adj* (**a**) *CAm (áspero)* rough (**b**) *Perú (débil)* weak, sickly

morrudo, -a *adj RP* strong

morsa *nf* walrus

morse *nm* Morse (code); **un mensaje en m.** a Morse code message

mortadela *nf* mortadella

mortaja *nf* (**a**) *(de muerto)* shroud (**b**) *Andes (papel de tabaco)* cigarette paper

mortal 1 *adj* (**a**) *(no inmortal)* mortal (**b**) *(herida, caída, picadura)* fatal; **tiene una enfermedad m.** she is terminally ill (**c**) *(aburrimiento, odio)* deadly; **me dio un susto m.** he gave me the fright of my life (**d**) *(enemigo)* mortal, deadly (**e**) *Fam (aburrido)* deadly boring; **es un libro m.** it's a deadly boring book
2 *nmf* mortal

mortalidad *nf* mortality ►► ***m. infantil*** infant mortality

mortalmente *adv* (**a**) *(de muerte) (enfermo, herido)* mortally, fatally (**b**) *(a muerte)* **se odian m.** they have a deadly hatred for each other

mortandad *nf* loss of life; **el terremoto causó una gran m.** the earthquake caused great loss of life

mortecino, -a *adj (luz, brillo)* faint; *(color, mirada)* dull

mortero *nm* (**a**) *(de cocina)* mortar (**b**) *(argamasa)* mortar (**c**) *(arma)* mortar

mortífero, -a *adj* deadly

mortificación *nf* (**a**) *(sufrimiento)* mortification (**b**) *(cosa)* torture; **era una m. verlos jugar** it was torture watching them play

mortificante *adj* mortifying

mortificar [60] **1** *vt* (**a**) *(el cuerpo)* to mortify (**b**) *(angustiar, molestar)* to torment; **el recuerdo del accidente lo mortifica** he is tormented by the memory of the accident
2 mortificarse *vpr (torturarse)* to torment oneself; **no te mortifiques, no fue culpa tuya** don't torment yourself, it wasn't your fault

mortuorio, -a *adj* death; **cámara mortuoria** funerary chamber

moruno, -a *adj* Moorish; *Esp* **pincho m.** = marinated pork cooked on a skewer

mosaico *nm* (**a**) *(artístico)* mosaic (**b**) *(mezcla)* patchwork; **un m. de colores/ideologías** a patchwork of colours/ideologies (**c**) *Am (baldosa)* tile; **un piso de m.** a tiled floor

mosca 1 *adj inv* (**a**) *(en boxeo)* **peso m.** flyweight
(**b**) *Esp Fam* **estar m.** *(con sospechas)* to smell a rat; **estoy m. con su oferta, no me inspira confianza** there's something fishy about his offer, I don't trust it
(**c**) *Esp Fam* **estar m.** *(enfadado)* to be in a mood; **está m. conmigo** she's in a mood with me; **está m. porque se ha vuelto a estropear el ordenador** he's in a mood because the computer's broken again
(**d**) *Ven Fam (alerta)* on the ball; **para ganar dinero hay que estar muy m.** if you want to make money you've got to be on the ball
2 *nmf (en boxeo)* flyweight
3 *nf* (**a**) *(insecto)* fly ►► ***m. escorpión*** scorpion fly; ***m. de la fruta*** fruit fly; *Fam Fig* ***m. muerta:*** **con lo m. muerta que parecía y el**

novio tan guapo que se ha buscado she's a dark horse, you'd never have thought she'd end up with a good-looking boyfriend like that; **parece una m. muerta** he looks very innocent; ***m. tse-tsé*** tsetse fly
(**b**) *(en pesca)* fly
(**c**) *RP Fam (dinero)* dough; **estoy sin m.** I'm flat broke, *Br* I'm skint
(**d**) EXPR **aflojar** *o* **soltar la m.** to cough up, to fork out; **cazar moscas** to twiddle one's thumbs; *Fam* **estar con** *o* **tener la m. detrás de la oreja** to be suspicious *o* distrustful; **no se oía ni una m.** you could have heard a pin drop; *Fam* **¿qué m. te ha picado?** what's up with you?, who's rattled your cage?; *Fam* **por si las moscas** just in case; *Méx Fam* **viajar de m.** = to ride for free on a bus by clinging to the outside of it
4 *interj Ven Fam* watch it!

moscada *adj* **nuez m.** nutmeg

moscarda *nf* bluebottle, blowfly

moscardón *nm* (**a**) *(insecto)* blowfly (**b**) *Fam (persona)* pest, creep

moscatel *nm* Muscatel, = dessert wine made from muscat grapes; **uvas de m.** muscat grapes

moscón *nm* (**a**) *(insecto)* meatfly, bluebottle (**b**) *Fam (persona)* pest, creep

mosconear **1** *vt Fam* to pester
2 *vi* (**a**) *(zumbar)* to buzz (**b**) *Fam (molestar)* **lleva toda la semana mosconeando a mi alrededor** he's been pestering me all week

moscoso *nm Esp Fam* = one of several days off that public sector workers can take to deal with personal matters and which are not deducted from their annual leave

moscovita **1** *adj* Muscovite
2 *nmf* Muscovite
3 *nf Geol* muscovite, mirror stone

Moscú *n* Moscow

mosén (*pl* **mosenes**) *nm Esp Rel* father, reverend

mosqueado, -a *adj Fam* (**a**) *(enfadado)* in a huff; **estar m. con alguien** to be in a huff with sb (**b**) *(con sospechas)* suspicious; **está m. porque no han llamado todavía** he's rather surprised that they haven't phoned yet

mosquear *Fam* **1** *vt* (**a**) *(enfadar)* **m. a alguien** *Br* to get up sb's nose, *US* to tick sb off (**b**) *(hacer sospechar)* **me mosquea que no haya llamado todavía** I'm a bit surprised he hasn't phoned yet; **su amabilidad me mosquea** I find his friendliness rather suspicious
2 mosquearse *vpr (enfadarse)* to get in a huff (**con** with); **no te mosquees, no lo ha hecho a propósito** there's no need to get in a huff, he didn't do it on purpose; **se mosqueó por una bobada** he got in a huff over nothing

mosqueo *nm Fam* (**a**) *(enfado)* **tengo un m., me acaban de decir que no me van a subir el sueldo** I'm really hacked off, they've just told me they aren't going to give me a pay rise; **tener un m. con alguien** to be in a huff with sb; **cuando se lo dije agarró un m. tremendo** when I told him he got in a real huff (**b**) *(sospechas)* **tener un m.** to be suspicious

mosquerío, mosquero *nm Am* swarm of flies

mosquete *nm* musket

mosquetero *nm* musketeer

mosquetón *nm* (**a**) *(para escalada)* karabiner (**b**) *(arma)* short carbine

mosquita *nf Fam* ***m. muerta:*** **con lo m. muerta que parecía y el novio tan guapo que se ha buscado** she's a dark horse, you'd never have thought she'd end up with a good-looking boyfriend like that; **parece una m. muerta** he looks very innocent

mosquitera *nf* mosquito net

mosquitero *nm* (**a**) *(mosquitera)* mosquito net (**b**) *(ave)* chiffchaff ►► ***m. musical*** willow warbler; ***m. silbador*** wood warbler

mosquito *nm* mosquito ►► ***m. anófeles*** anopheles mosquito

Mosso ['moso] *nm* ***M. d'Esquadra*** = member of the Catalan police force

mostacho *nm* moustache

mostacilla *nf* (**a**) *RP (plástico)* plastic bead *(for threading)* (**b**) *Ven (perla)* small pearl (**c**) *Ven Fam (dinero)* dough

mostajo *nm* common whitebeam

mostaza *nf* mustard; EXPR *Arg Fam* **se le subió la m.** he got really mad

mosto *nm* (**a**) *(zumo de uva)* grape juice (**b**) *(residuo)* must

mostrador *nm (en tienda)* counter; *(en bar)* bar; *(en aeropuerto)* desk; *RP (encimera)* worktop ►► ***m. de caja*** cash desk; ***m. de facturación*** check-in desk; ***m. de información*** information desk

mostrar [64] **1** *vt* (**a**) *(objeto)* to show; **me mostró su colección de sellos** he showed me his stamp collection; **el macho muestra su plumaje a la hembra** the male displays his plumage to the female
(**b**) *(sentimiento)* to show; **mostró su satisfacción por la concesión del premio** she expressed pleasure at having been awarded the prize
(**c**) *(demostrar)* to show; **muéstranos cómo se pone en marcha** show us how to start it; **te mostraré que lo que digo es verdad** I'll show you *o* prove to you that what I'm saying is true
2 mostrarse *vpr* **se mostró muy amable con los invitados** he was very nice to the guests; **se mostró muy interesado** he expressed great interest; **se mostró reacia a colaborar** she was reluctant to cooperate; **se mostró conforme con el plan** he agreed to the plan

mostrenco, -a **1** *adj* (**a**) *(sin dueño)* without an owner, unclaimed (**b**) *Fam (torpe)* thick, dense
2 *nm,f Fam* (**a**) *(torpe)* clot; **es un m.** he's a clot, he's thick *o* dense (**b**) *(gordo)* fatso

mota *nf* (**a**) *(de polvo)* speck (**b**) *(en una tela)* dot; **una camisa con motas azules** a shirt with blue dots (**c**) *Andes, RP* **motas** *(rulos)* tight curls (**d**) *Méx, RP, Ven (de algodón)* cotton ball (**e**) *Cuba, Méx (cosmética)* powder puff (**f**) *Andes (bolita)* burl (**g**) *CAm, Méx Fam (marihuana)* grass

mote *nm* (**a**) *(nombre)* nickname; **poner m. a alguien** to nickname sb, to give sb a nickname (**b**) *Andes (maíz)* stewed *Br* maize *o US* corn ►► ***m. con huesillos*** = drink made from *Br* maize *o US* corn and peaches

moteado, -a *adj* speckled

motear *vi Perú (comer maíz)* to eat stewed *Br* maize *o US* corn

motejar *vt (poner mote a)* to nickname; **m. a alguien de algo** to brand sb sth

motel *nm* (**a**) *(hotel)* motel (**b**) *CSur (para parejas)* = hotel where rooms are let by the hour

motero, -a *nm,f Fam* biker

motete *nm* (**a**) *Mús* motet (**b**) *CAm, PRico (lío)* bundle

motilón, -ona *nm,f* Motilon Indian

motín *nm (del pueblo)* uprising, riot; *(de las tropas, en barco)* mutiny; *(en cárcel)* riot

motivación *nf* (**a**) *(causa)* motive (**b**) *(estímulo)* motivation; **no tengo ninguna m. para estudiar** I have no motivation to study

motivado, -a *adj (persona)* motivated

motivador, -ora *adj* motivating

motivar **1** *vt* (**a**) *(causar)* to cause; **la tormenta motivó el aplazamiento del concierto** the storm caused the concert to be postponed (**b**) *(estimular)* to motivate; **un incentivo así no me motiva nada** I'm not at all motivated by an incentive like that; **la desesperada situación lo motivó a emigrar** the desperate situation caused him to emigrate
2 motivarse *vpr* to motivate oneself; **estos niños no se motivan con nada** nothing seems to motivate these children

motivo *nm* (**a**) *(causa)* reason (**de** for); *(de crimen)* motive (**de** for); **la situación económica se ha vuelto a convertir en m. de preocupación** the economy has once again become a cause for concern; **el éxito de la misión es m. de orgullo para todos nosotros** the success of the mission is a reason for all of us to be proud; **se retiró por motivos personales** she withdrew for personal reasons; **con m. de** *(por causa de)* because of; *(para celebrar)* on the occasion of; *(con el fin de)* in order to; **implantaron el toque de queda con m. de los desórdenes callejeros** a curfew was imposed because of the rioting; **las fiestas con m. del V centenario** the celebrations to mark the 500th anniversary *o* on the occasion of the 500th anniversary; **con mayor m.** even more so; **dar m. a** to give reason to; **no ser m. para** to be no reason to *o* for; **por m. de** because of; **tener motivos para** to have reason to; **tiene un buen m. para no acudir porque va a estar su ex mujer** he has good reason for not coming because his ex-wife is going to be there; **sin m.** for no reason
(**b**) *(melodía)* motif
(**c**) *(dibujo, figura)* motif; **un m. decorativo** *o* **ornamental** a decorative motif
(**d**) *Chile* **motivos** finickiness

moto[1] *nf* motorbike, bike; **montar en m.** to ride a motorbike; EXPR *Esp Fam* **estar como una m.** *(loco)* to be off one's head; *(nervioso)* to be hyper; *(excitado)* to be out of one's face; EXPR *Fam* **ir como una m.** to go full tilt ►► ***m. acuática*** jet ski; ***m. de carreras*** racing bike; ***m. náutica*** jet ski

moto[2]**, -a** *adj Bol Fam* (**a**) *(romo)* blunt (**b**) *(mutilado)* **tiene un dedo m.** she's lost a finger, she has a finger missing

motobomba *nf* motorized pump

motocarro *nm* three-wheeled van

motocicleta *nf* motorcycle, motorbike
motociclismo *nm* motorcycling
motociclista *nmf* motorcyclist
motociclo *nm* motorcycle
motocross [moto'kros] *nm* motocross
motocultivo *nm* mechanized farming
motocultor, motocultivador *nm* Rotavator®
motoesquí (*pl* **motoesquíes** *o* **motoesquís**) *nm* snowbike
motonáutica *nf* speedboat racing
motonáutico, -a *adj* speedboat; **competición motonáutica** speedboat race
motonave *nf* motorboat, motor vessel
motoneta *nf Am* (motor) scooter
motonetista *nmf Am* scooter rider
motor[1]**, -ora** *o* **-triz** *adj* (**a**) *Anat* motor; **habilidades motoras** motor skills (**b**) *(que produce desarrollo)* **el sector m. de la economía** the sector which is the driving force of the economy
motor[2] *nm* (**a**) *(máquina)* engine, motor ►► ***m. alternativo*** reciprocating engine; ***m. de arranque*** starter, starter motor; ***m. de cohete*** rocket engine; ***m. de combustión*** combustion engine; ***m. de combustión interna*** internal combustion engine; ***m. de cuatro tiempos*** four-stroke engine; ***m. diesel*** diesel engine; ***m. de dos tiempos*** two-stroke engine; ***m. eléctrico*** electric motor; ***m. de explosión*** internal combustion engine; ***m. (de) fueraborda*** outboard motor *o* engine; ***m. de inducción*** induction motor; ***m. de inyección*** fuel-injection engine; ***m. iónico*** ion engine; ***m. de reacción*** jet engine; ***m. rotativo*** rotary engine; ***m. de turbina*** turbine engine
(**b**) *(fuerza)* driving force; **el m. de la economía** the driving force in the economy; **el m. del equipo** *(en deporte)* the team dynamo
(**c**) *(causa)* instigator, cause
(**d**) *Informát* ***m. de búsqueda*** search engine
motora *nf* motorboat
motorismo *nm* motorcycling
motorista *nmf* (**a**) *Esp (motociclista)* motorcyclist (**b**) *CAm, Andes (automovilista)* driver, motorist
motorización *nf* (**a**) *(índice)* **la alta m. del país** the high level of car ownership in the country (**b**) *Esp (tipo de motor)* engine size
motorizado, -a 1 *adj* motorized; **infantería motorizada** motorized infantry; **un agente m.** a police motorcyclist; *Fam* **estar m.** *(tener vehículo)* to have wheels
2 *nm,f Ven* motorcyclist
motorizar [14] **1** *vt* to motorize
2 motorizarse *vpr Fam* to get oneself some wheels
motosierra *nf* power saw
motoso[1] *nm Col Fam* nap
motoso[2]**, -a, motudo, -a** *adj Fam* (**a**) *Andes, RP (pelo)* frizzy (**b**) *Col (lana)* pilled (**c**) *Perú (persona)* = who speaks Spanish with the accent of a native speaker of an indigenous Indian language
motovelero *nm* motorized sailing boat
motricidad *nf* motor function
motriz *ver* **motor**
motudo = **motoso**
motu propio, motu proprio *adv* **(de) m.** of one's own accord
mouse [maus] *nm inv Am Informát* mouse
moussaka [mu'saka] *nf* moussaka
mousse [mus] *nf, Esp nm* mousse; **m. de chocolate** chocolate mousse
mouton [mu'ton] *nm* sheepskin
movedizo, -a *adj* (**a**) *(movible)* movable, easily moved (**b**) *(inestable)* unsteady, unstable; **arenas movedizas** quicksand (**c**) *(inconstante)* changeable

MOVER [41] **1** *vt* (**a**) *(desplazar, trasladar)* to move (**de/a** from/to); *(mecánicamente)* to drive; **el viento mueve las palas** the wind drives *o* turns the blades; *Informát* **m. un fichero** to move a file; **m. una ficha** *(en juegos)* to move a counter; **el fútbol profesional mueve mucho dinero** a lot of money changes hands in the world of professional soccer; **ese cantante mueve masas** huge numbers of people go to see that singer wherever he performs; EXPR *Esp* **m. ficha: ahora le toca al gobierno m. ficha** it's the government's move, it's the government's turn to make the next move
(**b**) *(menear, agitar) (caja, sonajero)* to shake; *(bandera)* to wave; **movía las caderas** she was wiggling *o* swinging her hips; **la vaca movía la cola** the cow was swishing its tail; **el perro movía la cola** the dog was wagging its tail; **m. la cabeza** *(afirmativamente)* to nod; *(negativamente)* to shake one's head; **muévelo bien** *(removiéndolo con cucharilla)* stir it well; *(agitándolo con las manos)* shake it well
(**c**) *(impulsar)* **m. a alguien a hacer algo** to make sb do sth, to prompt sb to do sth; **¿qué te movió a hacerlo?** what made you do it?, what prompted you to do it?; **eso fue lo que nos movió a la huelga** that was what made us strike *o* prompted us to strike; **sólo la mueve la ambición** she is driven solely by ambition; **m. a alguien a compasión** to move sb to pity
(**d**) *(hacer trámites con)* to do something about; **hay muchos interesados en m. este asunto** there are several people who are interested in doing something about this issue
2 *vi* (**a**) *(en ajedrez, damas, juego de mesa)* to move; **tú mueves** it's your move (**b**) *(provocar)* **su triste mirada movía a compasión** her sad gaze made you feel pity for her
3 moverse *vpr* (**a**) *(desplazarse, trasladarse)* to move; *(en la cama)* to toss and turn; **no te muevas** don't move; **yo no me he movido de aquí** I've been here the whole time, I haven't left this spot; **si no dejas de moverte no te puedo vestir** if you don't stop moving about I won't be able to dress you; EXPR *Esp Fam* **el que se mueva, no sale en la foto** step out of line and you're out of the frame
(**b**) *(darse prisa)* to get a move on; **muévete, que es tarde** get a move on, it's late
(**c**) *Fam (hacer gestiones)* to get things going *o* moving; **me moví mucho para conseguir la subvención** I did everything I could to get the grant; **si te mueves puedes encontrar trabajo** if you make an effort *o* try you can get a job
(**d**) *(relacionarse)* **moverse en/entre** to move in/among; **se mueve con gente de la universidad** she mixes with people from the university

movible *adj* movable
Movicom® *nm RP* mobile phone, cellphone
movida *nf* (**a**) *Esp, RP Fam (lío, problema)* problem; **cuando llegó la policía se organizó una gran m.** there was a lot of aggro when the police arrived; **a mí no me metas en tus movidas** don't get me involved in any of your funny stuff; **mudarse es una m.** moving house is a real headache; **tener movidas** *o* **una m. con alguien** to have a spot of bother with sb
(**b**) *Esp, RP Fam (ambiente, actividad)* scene; **en esta ciudad hay mucha m.** there's a lot going on in this city; **estuvieron toda la noche de m.** they were out on the town all night; **han organizado una gran m. para pedir el cambio de la ley** a big campaign has been organized calling for the law to be changed; **no me va esa m.** it's not my scene ►► ***la m. madrileña*** = the Madrid cultural scene of the late 1970s and early 1980s
(**c**) *Méx, RP, Ven Fam (negocio)* shady deal
(**d**) *RP, Ven Fam (fiesta)* bash
(**e**) *Ven Fam (aventura)* fling
movido, -a *adj* (**a**) *(debate, torneo)* lively; *(jornada, viaje)* hectic (**b**) *(mar)* rough, choppy (**c**) *(fotografía)* blurred, fuzzy (**d**) *CAm Fam (enclenque, raquítico)* feeble (**e**) *Chile (huevo)* soft-shelled
móvil 1 *adj* **un blanco m.** a moving target; **teléfono m.** mobile phone; **unidad m.** mobile unit
2 *nm* (**a**) *(motivo)* motive; **se desconoce el m. del secuestro** the motive for the kidnapping is unknown (**b**) *(teléfono)* mobile (**c**) *(juguete)* mobile
movilidad *nf* (**a**) *(movimiento)* mobility; **tener coche me da mucha m.** owning a car makes me very mobile; **una indemnización por m. geográfica** a relocation allowance ►► ***m. social*** social mobility (**b**) *Bol (transporte)* bus
movilización *nf* (**a**) *(de tropas, policía)* mobilization (**b**) *(protesta)* protest, demonstration; **una m. estudiantil** a student protest *o* demonstration; **los camioneros han anunciado movilizaciones** the truck *o Br* lorry drivers have announced a series of protests (**c**) *Chile (transporte público)* public transport
movilizar [14] **1** *vt* (**a**) *(tropas, policía)* to mobilize (**b**) *(obreros, estudiantes)* to mobilize (**c**) *CSur (transportar)* to transport
2 movilizarse *vpr* (**a**) *(tropas, policía)* to mobilize (**b**) *(obreros, estudiantes)* to mobilize (**c**) *CSur (moverse)* to get around

MOVIMIENTO *nm* (**a**) *(desplazamiento, traslado)* movement; **hizo un m. con la mano** she made a movement with her hand; **asintió con un m. de la cabeza** he nodded in agreement; **seguía con la mirada todos mis movimientos** he was watching my every move; **¡no hagas ningún m.!** don't move!; **si haces un m. en falso, disparo** if you move, I'll shoot, one false move and I'll shoot; **la escayola entorpecía sus movimientos** the plaster cast meant she couldn't move freely; **hay**

pocos movimientos en la clasificación general there have been few changes in the overall standings ▸▸ ***m. migratorio*** migratory movement; *Med* ***movimientos oculares rápidos*** rapid eye movement; ***movimientos de población*** population shifts; ***m. sísmico*** earth tremor

(**b**) *(en física y mecánica)* motion; **en m.** moving, in motion; **se bajó del tren cuando todavía estaba en m.** she got off the train while it was still moving; **poner algo en m.** to set sth in motion; **ponerse en m.** to start moving ▸▸ *Fís* ***m. acelerado*** accelerated motion; *Fís* ***m. continuo*** perpetual motion; *Fís* ***m. ondulatorio*** wave motion; *Fís* ***m. oscilatorio*** oscillatory motion; *Fís* ***m. de rotación*** rotational motion; *Fís* ***m. de traslación*** orbital motion; *Fís* ***m. uniforme*** motion at a constant velocity

(**c**) *(corriente ideológica, artística)* movement; **el m. dadaísta** the Dadaist movement; **el m. obrero** the working-class movement; **el m. pacifista** the peace movement

(**d**) *Hist* **el M. (Nacional)** *(en España)* = organisation uniting all Fascist groups supporting Franco, founded on 19th April 1937, and which served as the official party of his regime until 1975

(**e**) **m. (militar)** *(sublevación)* (military) uprising

(**f**) *(actividad)* activity; *(de vehículos)* traffic; *(de personal, mercancías)* turnover; *(en cuenta bancaria)* transaction; *(en contabilidad)* operation; **últimos movimientos** *(opción en cajero automático)* print mini-statement ▸▸ ***m. de capital*** cash flow

(**g**) *Mús (parte de la obra)* movement

(**h**) *Mús (velocidad del compás)* tempo

(**i**) *(en ajedrez, damas, juego de mesa)* move

(**j**) *(alzamiento)* uprising

---

moviola *nf* (**a**) *(proyector)* editing projector (**b**) *(repetición de jugada)* action replay

moza *nf* (**a**) *(sirvienta)* girl, maid (**b**) *ver también* **mozo**

mozalbete *nm* young lad

Mozambique *n* Mozambique

mozambiqueño, -a 1 *adj* Mozambican

2 *nm,f* Mozambican

mozárabe 1 *adj* Mozarabic, = Christian in the time of Moorish Spain

2 *nmf (persona)* Mozarab, = Christian of Moorish Spain

3 *nm (lengua)* Mozarabic

mozo, -a 1 *adj* (**a**) *(joven)* young; **en mis años mozos...** when I was young... (**b**) *(soltero)* single, unmarried

2 *nm,f* (**a**) *(niño)* young boy, young lad; *(niña)* young girl

(**b**) *Andes, RP (camarero)* waiter, *f* waitress; *Esp, Andes, RP* **¡m., la cuenta!** the *Br* bill *o US* check please, waiter!

(**c**) *(trabajador)* ***m. de caballos*** groom; ***m. de cordel*** porter; ***m. de cuadra*** stable lad; ***m. de cuerda*** porter; ***m. de equipajes*** porter; ***m. de estación*** (station) porter; *Taurom* ***m. de estoques*** = bullfighter's assistant who looks after his equipment

(**d**) *Col (novio)* boyfriend; *(novia)* girlfriend

(**e**) EXPR **ser buen m.** to be good-looking

3 *nm Esp (recluta)* conscript

mozuelo, -a *nm,f* lad, *f* girl

mozzarella [motsa'rela, moθa'rela] *nm* mozzarella

MPM *nm (abrev de* **Movimiento Peronista Montonero**) = Peronist urban guerrilla movement

MRS *nm (abrev de* **Movimiento de Renovación Sandinista**) = breakaway Sandinista party

MRTA *nm (abrev de* **Movimiento Revolucionario Túpac Amaru**) = Peruvian Marxist guerrilla organization

ms *Informát (abrev de* **milisegundos**) ms

m.s. *(abrev de* **manuscrito**) ms., MS

MS-DOS *nm Informát (abrev de* **Microsoft Disk Operating System**) MS-DOS

MTA *nm (abrev de* **Movimiento de los Trabajadores Argentinos**) = radical trade union movement opposed to the main union federation

Mtro., -a *nm,f* (**a**) *(abrev de* **ministro, -a**) Min (**b**) *Méx (abrev de* **maestro, -a**) Prof

mu *nm (mugido)* moo; EXPR *Fam* **no decir ni mu** not to say a word

muá *interj* muah *(sound made when giving a kiss)*

muaré = **moiré**

mucamo, -a *nm,f Andes, RP* (**a**) *(en casa)* servant, *f* maid (**b**) *(en hotel)* chamberperson, *f* chambermaid

muceta *nf* cloak

muchacha *nf* (**a**) *(sirvienta)* maid; *Am* **m. de adentro** live-in maid (**b**) *ver también* **muchacho**

muchachada *nf* bunch of kids; **toda la m. del lugar** all the local kids

muchachera *nf,* **muchachero** *nm Ven Fam* bunch of kids

muchacho, -a *nm,f* (**a**) *(joven)* boy, *f* girl; **un grupo de muchachas esperaba al cantante** a group of girls was waiting for the singer; **es un buen m.** he's a good sort; **anda m., no seas tonto** come on son, don't be silly (**b**) *(recadero)* errand boy

muchachón *nm* (**a**) *RP (gamberro)* lout (**b**) *Ven (joven)* lad

muchedumbre *nf (de gente)* crowd, throng; *(de cosas)* great number, masses

---

MUCHO, -A 1 *adj* (**a**) *(gran cantidad de)* a lot of; **comemos m. pescado/mucha verdura** we eat a lot of fish/vegetables; **había mucha gente** there were a lot of people there; **producen muchos residuos** they produce a lot of waste; **tengo muchos más/menos amigos que tú** I've got a lot more/fewer friends than you; **no tengo m. tiempo** I haven't got much *o* a lot of time; **no nos quedan muchas entradas** we haven't got many *o* a lot of tickets left; **¿hay muchas cosas que hacer?** are there a lot of things to do?, is there much to do?; **no tengo muchas ganas de ir** I don't really *o* much feel like going; **tengo m. sueño** I'm very sleepy; **hoy hace m. calor** it's very hot today; **hace m. tiempo** a long time ago; **¡mucha suerte!** the best of luck!; **¡muchas gracias!** thank you very much!

(**b**) *(singular) (demasiado)* **hay m. niño aquí** there are rather a lot of kids here; **mucha sal me parece que le estás echando** I think you're overdoing the salt a bit, I think you're adding a bit too much salt; **ésta es mucha casa para mí** this house is much too big for me; *Fam* **es m. hombre** he's a real man; **es m. coche para un conductor novato** it's far too powerful a car for an inexperienced driver; *Fam* **m. lujo y m. camarero trajeado pero la comida es horrible** it's all very luxurious and full of smartly dressed waiters, but the food's terrible

2 *pron (singular)* a lot; *(plural)* many, a lot; **tengo m. que contarte** I have a lot to tell you; **¿queda dinero? – no m.** is there any money left? – not much *o* not a lot; **muchos de ellos** many *o* a lot of them; **somos muchos** there are a lot of us; **muchos piensan igual** a lot of *o* many people think the same; **realizaba experimentos, muchos sin resultado** he performed a lot of experiments, many of which failed

3 *adv* (**a**) *(gran cantidad)* a lot; **habla m.** he talks a lot; **trabajo/me esfuerzo m.** I work/try very hard; **llovía/nevaba m.** it was raining/snowing hard, it was raining/snowing heavily; **ayer llovió/nevó m.** it rained/snowed a lot yesterday, there was a lot of rain/snow yesterday; **me canso m.** I get really *o* very tired; **me gusta m.** I like it a lot *o* very much; **no me gusta m.** I don't like it much; **m. más/menos** much more/less, a lot more/less; **m. mayor/menor** much bigger/smaller, a lot bigger/smaller; **m. mejor/peor** much better/worse, a lot better/worse; **¿es caro? – sí, m.** is it expensive? – yes, very; **como m.** at the most; **con m.** by far, easily; **no es ni con m. tan divertida como su anterior novela** it's nowhere near as funny as her previous novel; **ni m. menos** far from it, by no means; **no está ni m. menos decidido** it is by no means decided; **por m. que** no matter how much, however much; **por m. que insistas** no matter how much you insist, however much you insist; EXPR *Fam* **ser m.** *(ser excepcional)* to be something else

(**b**) *(largo tiempo)* **hace m. que no te veo** I haven't seen you for a long time; **¿dura m. la obra?** is the play long?; **¿te queda m.?** *(para terminar)* have you got long to go?; **m. antes/después** long before/after; **(no) m. más tarde** (not) much later

(**c**) *(a menudo)* often; **¿vienes m. por aquí?** do you come here often?

(**d**) *Méx* **m. muy** *(para enfatizar)* very, very; **es m. muy grande** it's very, very big

---

mucílago *nm* mucilage

mucosa *nf* mucous membrane ▸▸ ***m. bucal*** buccal mucosa; ***m. nasal*** nasal mucus

mucosidad *nf* mucus

mucoso, -a *adj* mucous

múcura, mucura *nf* (**a**) *Andes, Ven (vasija)* earthenware pitcher (**b**) *Col Fam (tonto)* blockhead, dunce

mucus *nm inv* mucus

muda *nf* (**a**) *(de plumas)* moulting; *(de piel)* shedding (**b**) *(ropa interior)* change of underwear (**c**) *ver también* **mudo**

mudable *adj (persona)* changeable; *(carácter)* fickle

mudada *nf Andes, CAm* (**a**) *(de ropa)* change of clothing (**b**) *(de domicilio)* move, change of address

mudanza *nf* (**a**) *(de casa)* move; **estar de m.** to be moving; **un camión de mudanzas** *Br* a removal van, *US* a moving van; **una empresa de mudanzas** a furniture remover (**b**) *(cambio)* change; *(de carácter)* changeability, fickleness

mudar 1 *vt* (a) *(cambiar)* to change; **cuando mude la voz** when his voice breaks (b) *(piel, plumas)* **muda la piel en verano** it sheds its skin in summer; **m. las plumas** to moult (c) *Am (bebé)* to change; **ya es hora de mudarla** it's time to change her *o* change her nappy
2 *vi* (a) *(cambiar)* **m. de opinión/color** to change opinion/colour; **m. de domicilio** to move home; **está mudando de voz** his voice is breaking (b) *Méx (niño)* to lose one's milk teeth
3 **mudarse** *vpr* (a) *(trasladarse)* to move; **mudarse de casa** to move house; **se mudaron a una casa en el campo** they moved to a house in the country (b) *(cambiarse)* **mudarse (de ropa)** to change (clothes); **se mudó de camisa** he changed his shirt

mudéjar 1 *adj* Mudejar, = of/relating to Muslims in Christian-occupied Spain
2 *nmf* Mudejar, = Muslim in Christian-occupied Spain

mudez *nf* muteness, inability to speak

mudo, -a 1 *adj* (a) *(sin habla)* mute, dumb; **es m. de nacimiento** he was born mute (b) *(callado)* silent, mute; **fue m. testigo del asesinato** she was a silent witness to the murder; **se quedó m.** he was left speechless; **me quedé m. de terror** I was speechless *o* I was struck dumb with fright (c) *(sin sonido)* silent; **cine m.** silent films (d) *(letra)* silent
2 *nm,f* dumb person, mute

mueble 1 *nm* (a) *(objeto)* piece of furniture; **los muebles** the furniture ►► ***muebles de baño*** bathroom furniture; ***m. bar*** cocktail cabinet; ***m. cama*** foldaway bed; ***muebles de cocina*** kitchen furniture; ***muebles de época*** period furniture; ***muebles de jardín*** garden furniture; ***muebles de oficina*** office furniture (b) *RP Fam (hotel)* = cheap hotel where prostitutes take their clients
2 *adj Der* **bienes muebles** personal property

mueblería *nf* furniture shop

mueca *nf (gesto)* face, expression; **hacer una m.** to make *o* pull a face; **hizo una m. de dolor** she winced in pain, she grimaced with pain; **esbozó la m. de una sonrisa** he forced a smile; **los alumnos hacían muecas a espaldas del profesor** the children were making *o* pulling faces behind the teacher's back

muecín *nm* muezzin

muela *nf* (a) *(diente)* back tooth, molar; **dolor de muelas** toothache; **tiene varias muelas picadas** she has several teeth with tooth decay ►► ***m. del juicio*** wisdom tooth (b) *(de molino)* millstone (c) *(para afilar)* grindstone (d) *(cerro)* = flat-topped hill

muelle 1 *adj* (a) *(asiento)* comfortable (b) *(vida)* easy, comfortable
2 *nm* (a) *(resorte)* spring (b) *(en puerto)* dock, quay; *(en el río)* wharf (c) *(de carga y descarga)* loading bay

muelo *etc ver* **moler**

muérdago *nm* mistletoe

muerdo 1 *ver* **morder**
2 *nm Esp* (a) *Fam (mordisco)* bite; **¿me dejas darle un m. al bocadillo?** can I have a bite of your sandwich? (b) *Fam (beso)* **se estaban dando un m.** they were necking *o Br* snogging

muere *nm* EXPR *RP Fam* **irse al m.** *(proyecto)* to go down the tubes; *(planes)* to be ruined

muérgano, -a *Col, Ven Fam* 1 *adj (inútil)* useless, worthless
2 *nm,f (mala persona)* swine
3 *nm (objeto inútil)* useless *o* worthless object

muermo *nm Esp Fam* (a) *(aburrimiento)* **fue un m. de conferencia** it was a deadly boring lecture; **¡menudo m. de película!** what a deadly boring movie!; **me entró un m. terrible** I was overcome with boredom (b) *(persona)* **ser un m.** to be a bore

muero *etc ver* **morir**

muerte *nf* (a) *(fin de la vida)* death; **la malaria le produjo la m.** malaria was the cause of death; **ha sido herido de m.** he has been fatally wounded; **una lucha a m.** a fight to the death; **la odio a m.** I hate her with all my heart, I absolutely loathe her; **hasta que la m. nos separe** till death us do part; **tener una m. dulce** to die peacefully; EXPR *Am Fam* **cada m. de obispo** once in a blue moon; EXPR *Fam* **de m.: vas a agarrar un resfriado de m.** you're going to catch your death of cold; **me he llevado un susto de m.** I got the fright of my life; **hace un frío de m.** it's absolutely freezing; **esta sopa está de m.** this soup is yummy; EXPR *Fam* **de mala m.** *(cine, restaurante)* third-rate; **un bar de mala m.** a dive; **un pueblo/una casa de mala m.** a hole, a dump; EXPR *Ven Fam* **ser de m.** *(muy bueno)* to be fantastic; *(muy malo)* to be the pits ►► ***m. aparente*** suspended animation; ***m. cerebral*** brain death; *Der* ***m. civil*** civil death, attainder; ***m. natural:*** **morir de m. natural** to die of natural causes; **vivió en una residencia hasta su m. natural** she lived in a home until she died of old age; ***m. súbita*** *(del bebé)* sudden infant death; *(en tenis)* tie break; *(en golf)* play-off; ***m. violenta*** violent death; **morir de m. violenta** to die a violent death
(b) *(homicidio)* murder; **se le acusa de la m. de varias mujeres** he has been accused of murdering *o* of the murder of several women; **dar m. a alguien** to kill sb
(c) **la m.** *(ser imaginario)* death
(d) *(final, desaparición)* death, demise; **la m. de los regímenes comunistas** the demise of the Communist regimes

MUERTO, -A 1 *participio ver* **morir**
2 *adj* (a) *(sin vida)* dead; **caer m.** to drop dead; **dar por m. a alguien** to give sb up for dead; **varios transeúntes resultaron muertos** a number of passers-by were killed; **este sitio está m. en invierno** this place is dead in winter; **estar m. de frío** to be freezing to death; **estar m. de hambre** to be starving; **estar m. de miedo** to be scared to death; **estábamos muertos de risa** we nearly died laughing; EXPR *Fam* **estar m. de risa** *(objeto)* to be lying around doing nothing; EXPR **estar más m. que vivo de hambre/cansancio** to be half dead with hunger/exhaustion; EXPR *Am* **estar m. por alguien** *(enamorado)* to be head over heels in love with sb; EXPR **no tiene dónde caerse m.** he doesn't have a penny to his name; PROV **m. el perro, se acabó la rabia** the best way to solve a problem is to attack its root cause
(b) *Fam (muy cansado)* **estar m. (de cansancio), estar medio m.** to be dead beat; **estoy que me caigo m.** I'm fit to drop
(c) *Formal (matado)* **fue m. de un disparo** he was shot dead; **m. en combate** killed in action
(d) *(color)* dull
3 *nm,f* (a) *(fallecido)* dead person; *(cadáver)* corpse; **hubo dos muertos** two people died; **hacer el m.** *(sobre el agua)* to float on one's back; **hacerse el m.** to pretend to be dead, to play dead; **las campanas tocaban a m.** the bells were tolling the death knell; EXPR *Fam* **cargar con el m.** *(trabajo, tarea)* to be left holding the baby; *(culpa)* to get the blame; EXPR *Fam* **cargarle** *o* **echarle el m. a alguien** *(trabajo, tarea)* to leave the dirty work to sb; *(culpa)* to put the blame on sb; EXPR *Fam* **un m. de hambre: se casó con un m. de hambre** she married a man who didn't have a penny to his name; PROV **el m. al hoyo y el vivo al bollo** life goes on (in spite of everything)
(b) **los muertos** *(los fallecidos)* the dead; **el ejército derrotado enterraba a sus muertos** the defeated army was burying its dead; **resucitar de entre los muertos** to rise from the dead; EXPR *Vulg* **¡(me cago en) tus muertos!** you motherfucker!
4 *nm (en naipes)* dummy hand

muesca *nf* (a) *(marca, concavidad)* notch, groove (b) *(corte)* nick

muesli *nm* muesli

muestra *nf* (a) *(cantidad representativa)* sample; **una m. gratuita** *o* **de regalo** a free sample; EXPR **para m. (basta) un botón** one example is enough
(b) *(de sangre, orina)* sample
(c) *(en estadística)* sample ►► ***m. aleatoria*** random sample; ***m. piloto*** pilot sample; ***m. representativa*** cross-section
(d) *(señal)* sign, show; *(prueba)* proof; *(de cariño, aprecio)* token; **los recibieron con muestras de cariño** they gave them an affectionate welcome; **recibe este regalo como m. de aprecio** please accept this gift as a token of appreciation; **dio claras muestras de alegría/enfado** it was clear that she was happy/annoyed; **este contrato supone una clara m. de confianza en la empresa** this contract is a clear indication of confidence in the company; **existe nerviosismo, m. de ello son las declaraciones del delegado** there is some anxiety, as evidenced by the delegate's statements
(e) *(modelo)* model, pattern
(f) *(exposición)* show, exhibition

muestrario *nm* collection of samples

muestreo *nm* sampling ►► ***m. aleatorio*** random sampling

muestro *etc ver* **muestrar**

muevo *etc ver* **mover**

mufa *nf RP Fam* foul mood; **hoy tiene una m. impresionante** she's in a really foul mood today

mufado, -a *adj RP Fam* **andar m.** to be in a foul mood

mufarse *vpr RP Fam* to get in a huff

muflón *nm* mouflon

mugido *nm* (a) *(de vaca)* **un m.** a moo; **el m. de las vacas** the mooing of the cows (b) *(de toro)* **un m.** a bellow; **el m. de los toros** the bellowing of the bulls

mugir [24] *vi (vaca)* to moo; *(toro)* to bellow

mugre 1 *adj Méx (inútil)* useless
2 *nf* filth, muck; **este cuarto está lleno de m.** this room is filthy

mugriento, -a, *Méx* **mugroso, -a** *adj* filthy

mugrón *nm* (**a**) *(de vid)* layer (**b**) *(vástago)* shoot
mugroso, -a = **mugriento**
muguete, *RP* **muguet** *nm* lily of the valley
muino, -a *adj Méx Fam* **andar m.** to be in a foul mood
mujer 1 *nf* (**a**) *(hembra adulta)* woman; **ropa de m.** women's clothes; **los derechos de la m.** women's rights; **la m. española** Spanish women; **ya eres toda una m.** you're a grown-up woman now; **una m. hecha y derecha** a fully-grown woman; **de m. a m.** woman to woman ►► *RP* ***m. de la calle*** streetwalker; ***m. de su casa*** good housewife; ***m. fatal*** femme fatale; ***m. de la limpieza*** cleaning lady; ***m. de mala vida*** streetwalker; ***una m. de mundo*** a woman of the world; ***m. de negocios*** businesswoman; ***m. objeto*** woman treated as a sex object; ***m. piloto*** woman pilot; ***m. policía*** policewoman; ***m. pública*** prostitute; ***m. sacerdote*** woman priest; ***m. de vida alegre*** loose woman (**b**) *(cónyuge)* wife
2 *interj Esp* **¿te acuerdas de Marisol?, ¡sí, m., nuestra compañera de clase!** do you remember Marisol? you know, she was at school with us!; **¿me acercas a casa? – sí, m.** can you give me a *Br* lift *o US* ride home? – sure; **pero m., no te pongas así** oh, don't be like that!
mujerero *Ven Fam* 1 *adj* fond of the ladies; **es muy m.** he's a real womanizer
2 *nm* (**a**) *(grupo)* crowd of women (**b**) *(hombre)* womanizer, ladies' man
mujeriego, -a 1 *adj* fond of the ladies; **es muy m.** he's a real womanizer
2 *nm* womanizer, ladies' man
mujeril *adj* female
mujerío, *Am* **mujererío** *nm Fam* crowd of women
mujerzuela *nf Pey* loose woman
mújol *nm* striped mullet
mula *nf* (**a**) *(animal)* mule; EXPR **trabajar como una m.** to work like a dog
(**b**) *Fam (terco)* **ser una m.** to be as stubborn as a mule
(**c**) *Fam (estúpido)* thickhead
(**d**) *RP, Ven (traficante)* mule, courier
(**e**) *Méx (cojín)* shoulder pad
(**f**) *Méx (mercancía)* junk, unsaleable goods
(**g**) *RP Fam (mentira)* fib; **meterle una m. a alguien** to tell sb a fib
(**h**) *Méx (en dominó)* **m. de treses** double three
muladar *nm (lugar sucio)* tip, pigsty
mulato, -a 1 *adj* of mixed race, mulatto
2 *nm,f* person of mixed race, mulatto
mulero[1] *nm* muleteer
mulero[2]**, -a** *RP Fam* 1 *adj* **es muy m.** he's a real fibber
2 *nm,f* fibber
muleta *nf* (**a**) *(para andar)* crutch; **camina con muletas** he uses crutches, he walks on crutches (**b**) *(apoyo)* prop, support (**c**) *Taurom* muleta, = red cape hanging from a stick used to tease the bull
muletazo *nm Taurom* = pass made with the "muleta"
muletilla *nf (frase)* pet phrase; *(palabra)* pet word
muleto *nm Dep (coche reserva)* spare car
muletón *nm* flannelette
mulillas *nfpl Taurom* = team of mules which drag out the dead bull at the end of a fight
mulita *nf RP* armadillo
mullido, -a *adj (sofa, sillón)* soft, springy; *(cojín)* soft
mullir *vt* (**a**) *(almohada, lana)* to fluff up (**b**) *(tierra)* to turn over
mulo *nm* (**a**) *(animal)* mule (**b**) *Fam (persona fuerte)* **es un m.** he's as strong as a horse (**c**) *Fam (estúpido)* thickhead
multa *nf* fine; **una m. por exceso de velocidad** a speeding ticket; **poner una m. a alguien** to fine sb; **le pusieron cinco euros de m.** he was fined five euros
multar *vt* to fine
multicelular *adj* multicellular
multicentro *nm* large shopping mall
multicine *nm* multiplex (cinema)
multicolor *adj* multicoloured
multiconferencia *nf Tel* conference call
multicopista *nf Esp* duplicator, duplicating machine
multicultural *adj* multicultural
multidifusión *nf Informát & TV* multicast
multidisciplinario, -a, multidisciplinar *adj* multidisciplinary
multifamiliar *nm Méx Br* block of flats, *US* apartment block
multiforme *adj* multiform, differently shaped
multifrecuencia *nf Informát* multi-scanning
multigrado *adj* multigrade
multigrafiar *vt Ven* to mimeograph
multígrafo *nm Ven* mimeograph
multilateral *adj* multilateral
multilingüe *adj* (**a**) *(en varias lenguas)* multilingual (**b**) *(políglota)* multilingual
Multimalla *nf Informát* ***la M. Mundial*** the World Wide Web
multimedia *Informát* 1 *adj inv* multimedia
2 *nf* multimedia
multimillonario, -a 1 *adj* **es m.** he's a multimillionaire; **un negocio m.** a multimillion pound/dollar/*etc* business
2 *nm,f* multimillionaire
multinacional 1 *adj* (**a**) *(de varias naciones)* multinational (**b**) *(empresa)* multinational
2 *nf* multinational
multipartidario, -a *adj (pacto)* cross-party; **un gobierno m.** a coalition government; **negociaciones multipartidarias** negotiations between various parties
multipartidismo *nm* multiparty system
multipartidista *adj (pacto)*cross-party; *(sistema)* multiparty; **un gobierno m.** a coalition government; **negociaciones multipartidistas** negotiations between various parties
múltiple *adj* (**a**) *(variado)* multiple; **una colisión m.** a multiple collision, a pile-up (**b**) **múltiples** *(numerosos)* many, numerous
múltiplex *adj inv Informát* multiplex
multiplicable *adj* multipliable
multiplicación *nf* (**a**) *(operación matemática)* multiplication (**b**) *(incremento)* rapid increase; **la m. de los casos de gripe** the rapid increase in the number of flu cases
multiplicador, -ora 1 *adj* multiplying
2 *nm Mat* multiplier
multiplicando *nm Mat* multiplicand
multiplicar [60] 1 *vt* (**a**) *(en matemáticas)* to multiply; **m. 4 por 5** to multiply 4 by 5; **4 multiplicado por 3 igual a 12** 4 multiplied by 3 is 12, 4 times 3 is 12 (**b**) *(efecto)* to magnify; *(riesgo, probabilidad)* to increase
2 *vi* to multiply
3 **multiplicarse** *vpr* (**a**) *(reproducirse)* to multiply (**b**) *(incrementarse)* to increase rapidly; **se han multiplicado los robos en la zona** there has been a rapid rise in the number of burglaries in the area (**c**) *(desdoblarse)* to attend to lots of things at the same time; **se multiplicó para atender a todo el mundo** she ran around all over the place trying to attend to everyone
multiplicidad *nf* multiplicity
múltiplo *nm* multiple; **30 es m. de tres** 30 is a multiple of three
multiprocesador *Informát* 1 *adj* multiprocessor
2 *nm* multiprocessor
multiproceso *nm Informát* multiprocessing
multiprogramación *nf Informát* multiprogramming
multipropiedad *nf* time-sharing
multipuesto *adj inv Informát* multi-terminal; **red m.** multi-terminal network
multirracial *adj* multiracial
multirriesgo *adj (seguro)* all risks
multisalas *nm inv (cine)* multiscreen cinema
multitarea *Informát* 1 *adj inv* multitasking
2 *nf* multitasking
multitratamiento *nm Informát* multiprocessing
multitud *nf* (**a**) *(de personas)* crowd (**b**) **una m. de** *(gran cantidad)* a huge number of; **tengo una m. de cosas que hacer** I've got a huge number of things to do
multitudinario, -a *adj (concierto)* packed; *(fiesta)* huge; **un bautismo m.** a mass baptism; **un grupo m. se concentró ante la embajada** a large crowd gathered in front of the embassy; **una manifestación multitudinaria** a mass demonstration
multiuso *adj inv* multipurpose
multiusuario *adj Informát* multi-user
multivariable *adj (en estadística)* multivariate; **análisis m.** multivariate analysis
muna *nf Ven Fam* dough; **no tengo m.** I'm strapped for cash, I'm out of dough

mundanal *adj* worldly; **placeres mundanales** worldly pleasures

mundano, -a *adj* (a) *(del mundo)* worldly, of the world (b) *(de la vida social)* (high) society

> **Falso amigo**: El adjetivo inglés **mundane** no es la traducción del español **mundano**. En inglés **mundane** significa "prosaico" o "banal".

mundial 1 *adj (política, economía, guerra)* world; *(tratado, organización)* worldwide; **los líderes del sector a nivel m.** the world leaders in the sector; **un escritor de fama m.** a world-famous writer
2 *nm* World Championships; *(de fútbol, rugby)* World Cup; *(de Fórmula 1, motociclismo)* world championship ►► ***M. de Clubes*** *(de fútbol)* World Club Championship; ***m. de rallies*** world rally championship

mundialista *Dep* 1 *adj* **equipo m.** World Championship team; *(en fútbol)* World Cup squad
2 *nmf* = competitor in a World Cup or World Championship

mundialito *nm* World Club Championship

mundialización *nf* globalization

mundialmente *adv* **es m. conocido** he's known throughout the world; **es m. famoso** he's world-famous

mundillo *nm Fam* world; **el m. literario** the literary world, literary circles

MUNDO *nm* (a) **el m.** *(la Tierra, el universo)* the world; **el récord/campeón del m.** the world record/champion; **el mejor/mayor del m.** the best/biggest in the world; **es un actor conocido en todo el m.** he's a world-famous actor; **ha vendido miles de discos en todo el m.** she has sold thousands of records worldwide *o* all over the world; **seres de otro m.** creatures from another world; **el m. árabe/desarrollado** the Arab/developed world; **traer un niño al m.** to bring a child into the world; **venir al m.** to come into the world, to be born; EXPR **se le cayó el m. encima** his world fell apart; EXPR **no se va a caer** *o* **hundir el m. por eso** it's not the end of the world; EXPR **comerse el m.: vino a la ciudad a comerse el m.** when he came to the city he was ready to take on the world; EXPR **¡hay que ver cómo está el m.!** what is the world coming to!; EXPR **desde que el m. es m.** since the dawn of time; EXPR *Euf Anticuado* **echarse al m.** *(prostituirse)* to go on the streets; EXPR **el m. es un pañuelo** it's a small world; EXPR **el m. anda al revés** the world has been turned on its head; EXPR **hacer un m. de cualquier cosa** *o* **de algo sin importancia** to make a mountain out of a molehill; EXPR **todo se le hace un m.** she makes heavy weather out of everything; EXPR **el otro m.** the next world, the hereafter; EXPR **irse al otro m.** to pass away; EXPR **mandar a alguien al otro m.** to kill sb; EXPR **no es nada del otro m.** it's nothing special; EXPR *Fam* **se pone el m. por montera** she doesn't *o* couldn't give two hoots what people think; EXPR **por esos mundos de Dios: están de viaje por esos mundos de Dios** they're travelling around (all over the place); EXPR **como nada en el m.: querer a alguien como a nada en el m.** to love sb more than anything else in the world; EXPR **por nada del m.: no me lo perdería por nada del m.** I wouldn't miss it for (all) the world *o* for anything; EXPR **tenemos todo el tiempo del m.** we have all the time in the world; EXPR **se le vino el m. encima** his world fell apart; EXPR **vivir en otro m.** to live in a world of one's own
(b) *(la civilización)* world; **el m. precolombino** pre-Columbian civilizations ►► ***el M. Antiguo*** the Old World
(c) *(ámbito, actividad)* world; **el m. animal** the animal kingdom *o* world; **el m. rural** the countryside, the country; **el m. de los negocios/de las artes** the business/art world; **el m. del espectáculo** show business; **Lupe vive en su (propio) m.** *o* **en un m. aparte** Lupe lives in her own little world
(d) *(gente)* **medio m.** half the world, a lot of people; **todo el m.,** *Méx* **todo m.** everyone, everybody; **no vayas por ahí contándoselo a todo el m.** don't go around telling everyone; **pago mis impuestos como todo el m.** I pay my taxes the same as everyone else
(e) *(gran diferencia)* **hay un m. entre ellos** they're worlds apart
(f) *(experiencia)* **un hombre/una mujer de m.** a man/woman of the world; **correr m.** to see life; **tener (mucho) m.** to be worldly-wise, to know the ways of the world; **ver m.** to see life
(g) *(vida seglar)* **renunciar al m.** to renounce the world

mundología *nf* worldly wisdom, experience of life

Múnich *n* Munich

munición *nf* ammunition; **municiones** ammunition; *Fig* **el escándalo sirvió de m. para atacar al gobierno** the scandal gave them ammunition to attack the government

municipal 1 *adj (cementerio, polideportivo)* municipal; *(policía, elecciones)* local; *(instalaciones)* public; **trabajadores municipales** council workers; **las fiestas municipales** the local *o* town festival
2 *nmf Esp (guardia)* (local) policeman, *f* policewoman

municipales *nfpl (elecciones)* local elections

municipalidad *nf* (a) *(corporación)* local council (b) *(territorio)* town, municipality

municipalizar [14] *vt* to municipalize, to bring under municipal authority

municipio *nm* (a) *(corporación)* local council (b) *(edificio)* town hall, *US* city hall (c) *(territorio)* town, municipality (d) *(habitantes)* **asistió todo el m.** the whole town was there

munido, -a *adj RP* **m. de algo** equipped with sth; **acudieron al rescate munidos de todo lo necesario** they went to take part in the rescue operation equipped with everything they needed; **se ruega presentarse m. del pasaporte** you are requested to have your passport with you

munificencia *nf Formal* munificence

munificente *adj Formal* munificent

muniqués, -esa 1 *adj* of/from Munich *(Germany)*
2 *nm,f* person from Munich *(Germany)*

munir *RP* 1 *vi* **m. de algo a algo/alguien** to provide sth/sb with sth
2 **munirse** *vpr* **m. de algo** to equip oneself with sth

muñeca *nf* (a) *(del cuerpo)* wrist
(b) *(juguete)* doll ►► ***m. rusa*** Russian doll; ***m. de trapo*** rag doll
(c) *Fam (como apelativo)* darling, *US* doll; **¿cómo te llamas, m.?** what's your name, darling *o US* doll?
(d) *Andes, RP Fam* **tener m.** *(enchufe)* to have friends in high places; **llegó hasta ahí por m.** he got there by using his influence *o* by pulling strings
(e) *Andes, RP Fam* **tener m. (para hacer algo)** *(habilidad)* to have the knack (of doing sth)
(f) *Méx (mazorca)* baby sweetcorn

muñeco *nm* (a) *(juguete)* doll; *(marioneta, títere)* puppet; *(de ventrílocuo)* dummy; **m. (de peluche)** cuddly *o* soft toy; EXPR *Perú Fam* **estar con (todos) los muñecos** to be a bundle of nerves, to have the jitters ►► ***m. de nieve*** snowman; ***m. de trapo*** rag doll (b) *Fam (como apelativo)* sweetie, *US* honey

muñeira *nf* = popular Galician dance and music

muñequeado, -a *adj Perú Fam* **estar m.** to be a bundle of nerves, to have the jitters

muñequear *Fam* 1 *vt Andes, RP* to wangle; **le muñequearon un cargo** they pulled a few strings to get her a job, they wangled her a job
2 **muñequearse** *vpr Perú* to get all jumpy, to get the jitters

muñequera *nf* wristband

muñequilla *nf Chile* young ear of *Br* maize *o US* corn

muñequitos *nmpl Méx, Ven Fam* comic strip ►► ***m. animados*** cartoons

muñón *nm* stump

muón *nm Fís* muon

mural 1 *adj (pintura)* mural; *(mapa)* wall
2 *nm* mural

muralismo *nm* (a) *(arte)* mural painting (b) *(movimiento)* muralist movement

muralista 1 *adj* muralist
2 *nmf* muralist

muralla *nf* (a) *(muro)* wall; **la m. de la ciudad** the city walls ►► ***la M. China*** the Great Wall of China (b) *(barrera)* wall; **pasó la pelota por encima de la m. de jugadores** he sent the ball over the wall

murciano, -a 1 *adj* of/from Murcia *(Spain)*
2 *nm,f* person from Murcia *(Spain)*

murciélago *nm* bat ►► ***m. enano*** pipistrelle; ***m. frugívoro*** fruit bat

murga *nf* (a) *(charanga)* band of street musicians (b) *Esp Fam (pesadez)* drag, pain; **dar la m.** to be a pain (c) *Urug (comparsa)* = group of dancers in a carnival

muriera *etc ver* **morir**

murmullo *nm* **el m. del agua** the murmuring of the water; **se escuchó un m. de aprobación** there was a murmur of approval; **el m. de las hojas** the rustling of the leaves

murmuración *nf* backbiting, gossip; **no hagas mucho caso de las murmuraciones** don't pay too much attention to gossip

murmurador, -ora 1 *adj* gossiping; **ser m.** to be a gossip
2 *nm,f* gossip

murmurar 1 *vt* to mutter; **se murmura que engaña a su mujer** there are rumours that he cheats on his wife
2 *vi* (**a**) *(criticar)* to gossip (**de** about); **se pasan el tiempo murmurando del jefe** they do nothing but gossip about the boss (**b**) *(susurrar) (agua, viento)* to murmur, to gurgle; *(hojas)* to rustle (**c**) *(rezongar, quejarse)* to grumble

muro *nm* (**a**) *(construcción)* wall ►► ***el M. de Berlín*** the Berlin Wall; ***m. de contención*** retaining wall; ***el M. de*** *Esp* ***las Lamentaciones*** *o Am* ***los Lamentos*** the Wailing Wall (**b**) *Fig (barrera)* **nunca superó el m. de su timidez** she never overcame her shyness; **entre los dos hay un m. de silencio** there is a wall of silence between them

murria *nf Fam* the blues; **sentir m.** to feel blue, to have the blues

murrio, -a *adj Fam* blue, down

mus *nm inv* = Spanish card game played in pairs with bidding and in which players communicate by signs

musa *nf* (**a**) *Mitol* Muse (**b**) *(inspiración)* muse

musaka *nf* moussaka

musaraña *nf (animal)* shrew; EXPR *Fam* **mirar a las musarañas** to stare into space *o* thin air; EXPR *Fam* **pensar en las musarañas** to have one's head in the clouds

muscardino *nm* hazel dormouse, common dormouse

musculación *nf* body-building

muscular *adj* muscular

musculatura *nf* muscles

músculo *nm* muscle ►► ***m. cardíaco*** myocardium, cardiac muscle; ***m. estriado*** striated muscle; ***m. liso*** smooth muscle

musculosa *nf RP Br* vest, *US* undershirt *(sleeveless)*

musculoso, -a *adj* muscular

museístico, -a *adj* museum; **archivos museísticos** museum archives

muselina *nf* muslin

museo *nm (de ciencias, historia)* museum; *(de arte)* (art) gallery ►► ***m. arqueológico*** museum of archaeology; ***m. de arte moderno*** museum *o* gallery of modern art; ***m. de cera*** waxworks, wax museum; ***m. de la ciencia*** science museum; ***m. de ciencias naturales*** natural science museum

museología *nf* museology

museólogo, -a *nm,f* museologist

musgaño *nm* southern water shrew

musgo *nm* moss

musgoso, -a *adj* mossy, moss-covered

música[1] *adj Méx Fam* (**a**) **ser m.** *(inútil)* to be useless *o* hopeless; **soy muy m. para los idiomas** I'm useless *o* hopeless at languages (**b**) **ser m.** *(egoísta)* to be mean; **no seas m., déjame dar una vuelta en la moto** don't be so mean, let me have a go on the motorbike

música[2] *nf* (**a**) *(arte)* music; **pon un poco de m.** put some music on; **estudia m. en el conservatorio** she is studying music at the conservatoire; **es el autor de la m. y la letra** he wrote the music and the lyrics; EXPR **la m. amansa a las fieras** music has a really calming effect; EXPR *Fam* **irse con la m. a otra parte: nos fuimos con la m. a otra parte** we made ourselves scarce; **¡vete con la m. a otra parte!** clear off!, *US* take a hike! ►► ***m. de acompañamiento*** incidental music; ***m. ambiental*** piped music; ***m. antigua*** early music; ***m. de baile*** dance music; ***m. de cámara*** chamber music; ***m. celestial:*** **eso me suena a m. celestial** *(a falsa promesa)* that sounds like a lot of hot air; *(maravillosamente)* that's music to my ears; ***m. clásica*** classical music; ***m. en directo*** live music; ***m. disco*** disco music; ***m. electrónica*** electronic music; ***m. enlatada*** canned music; ***m. étnica*** world music; ***m. folk*** folk music; ***m. de fondo*** background music; *RP* ***m. funcional*** piped music; ***m. heavy*** heavy metal; ***m. instrumental*** instrumental music; ***m. ligera*** light music; ***m. militar*** military music; ***m. pop*** pop music; ***m. popular*** folk music; ***m. rock*** rock music; ***m. sinfónica*** orchestral music; ***m. tecno*** techno (music); ***m. tradicional*** traditional music; ***m. vocal*** vocal music (**b**) *ver también* **músico**

musical 1 *adj* musical
2 *nm* musical

musicalidad *nf* musicality

musicalmente *adv* musically

musicante *nmf Am Fam* **un m.** a musician of a sort

musicar [74] *vt* to set to music

musicasete *nf* cassette

music-hall ['musik'χol] (*pl* **music-halls**) *nm Br* music hall, *US* vaudeville

músico, -a 1 *adj* musical
2 *nm,f (persona)* musician ►► ***m. ambulante*** street musician, *Br* busker; ***m. callejero*** street musician, *Br* busker

musicología *nf* musicology

musicólogo, -a *nm,f* musicologist

musicoterapia *nf* music therapy

musiquilla *nf* (**a**) *(música)* tune (**b**) *(tono)* singsong tones *o* voice

musitar *vt* to mutter, to mumble

musiú, -iúa (*pl* **musiúes, -iúas**) *Ven Fam* 1 *adj* gringo
2 *nm,f* gringo *(especially of Anglo-German origin)*

muslamen *nm Esp Fam Hum* thighs

muslera *nf* thighband

muslo *nm* (**a**) *(de persona)* thigh (**b**) *(de pollo, pavo) (entero)* leg; *(parte inferior)* drumstick

mustela *nf* (**a**) *(comadreja)* weasel (**b**) *(pez)* dogfish

mustélido, -a 1 *adj* musteline
2 *nm* musteline
3 **mustélidos** *nmpl (familia) Mustelidae*

mustiar 1 *vt* to wither, to wilt
2 **mustiarse** *vpr* to wither, to wilt

mustio, -a *adj* (**a**) *(flor, planta)* withered, wilted (**b**) *(persona)* down, gloomy (**c**) *Méx Fam (hipócrita)* two-faced

musulmán, -ana 1 *adj* Muslim, Moslem
2 *nm,f* Muslim, Moslem

mutable *adj* changeable, mutable

mutación *nf* (**a**) *(cambio)* sudden change (**b**) *Biol* mutation

mutágeno, -a *adj* mutagenic

mutante 1 *adj* mutant
2 *nmf* mutant

mutar *vt* to mutate

mutilación *nf* mutilation ►► ***m. genital femenina*** female genital mutilation

mutilado, -a 1 *adj* mutilated
2 *nm,f* cripple ►► ***m. de guerra*** disabled war veteran

mutilar *vt* (**a**) *(persona)* to mutilate (**b**) *(texto)* to mutilate; *(estatua)* to vandalize

mutis *nm inv Teatro* exit; EXPR **hacer m. (por el foro)** *(en teatro)* to exit; *(marcharse)* to leave, to go away

mutismo *nm* (**a**) *(mudez)* muteness, dumbness (**b**) *(silencio)* silence

mutua *nf Br* friendly society, *US* mutual benefit society ►► ***m. de accidentes*** mutual accident insurance company; ***m. de seguros*** mutual insurance company

mutual *nf CSur, Perú Br* friendly society, *US* mutual benefit society

mutualidad *nf* (**a**) *(asociación) Br* friendly society, *US* mutual benefit society (**b**) *(reciprocidad)* mutuality

mutualismo *nm* (**a**) *(corporación) Br* friendly society, *US* mutual benefit society (**b**) *Biol* mutualism

mutualista 1 *nmf* member of a *Br* friendly society *o US* mutual benefit society
2 *nf Urug Br* friendly society, *US* mutual benefit society

mutuamente *adv* mutually; **se vigilaban m.** they were both watching each other

mutuo, -a *adj* mutual; **de m. acuerdo** by mutual *o* joint agreement; **el sentimiento es m.** the feeling is mutual; **se tienen una admiración mutua** they have a mutual admiration, they both admire each other; **tienen un amigo m.** they have a mutual friend; **los dos países se brindaron apoyo m.** the two countries offered each other mutual support

muy *adv* (**a**) *(en alto grado)* very; **m. bueno/cerca** very good/near; **estoy m. cansado** I'm very tired; **es m. hombre** he's very manly, he's a real man; **m. de mañana** very early in the morning; **¡m. bien!** *(vale)* OK!, all right!; *(qué bien)* very good!, well done!; **eso es m. de ella** that's just like her; **eso es m. de los americanos** that's typically American; **¡el m. fresco!** the cheeky devil!; **¡la m. tonta!** the silly idiot!; **me gusta m. mucho** I really, really like it; **te cuidarás m. mucho de hacerlo** just make absolutely sure you don't do it
(**b**) *(demasiado)* too; **no cabe ahí, es m. grande** it won't fit in there, it's too big; **ahora ya es m. tarde** it's too late now

muyahidín *nm inv* mujaheddin

muzzarella [musa'rela] *nm RP* mozzarella

Myanmar *n* Myanmar

N, n

N, n ['ene] *nf (letra)* N, n; **el 20 N** 20th November, = the date of Franco's death

N (**a**) (*abrev de* **norte**) N (**b**) *Esp* (*abrev de* **carretera nacional**) ≃ *Br* A road, *US* ≃ state highway (**c**) *Am* (*abrev de* **Nuevo nacional**) **N$100** 100 new pesos

n *(cantidad indeterminada)* n

n (*abrev de* **número**) No, no

naba *nf* turnip

nabo[1] *nm* (**a**) *(planta)* turnip ►► ***n. sueco*** *Br* swede, *US* rutabaga (**b**) *muy Fam (pene)* tool, *Br* knob

nabo[2], **-a** *RP Fam* 1 *adj* dumb

2 *nm,f* dope, *Br* twit

naborí, -ía *nm,f Hist* = Indian servant at the time of the Spanish conquest

nácar *nm* mother-of-pearl, nacre

nacarado, -a, nacarino, -a *adj* mother-of-pearl; **piel nacarada** pearly skin

nacatamal *nm CAm* = steamed maize dumpling with savoury filling, wrapped in a banana leaf

nacer [42] *vi* (**a**) *(niño, animal)* to be born; **al n.** at birth; **pesó al n. 3.700 g** he weighed 3.7 kg at birth; **¿dónde naciste? – nací en Brasil** where were you born? – I was born in Brazil; **n. de familia humilde** to be born into a poor family; **nació de padres italianos** she was born of Italian parents, her parents were Italian; **n. para algo** to be born for sth; **ha nacido cantante** she's a born singer; EXPR *Fam* **tú has nacido cansado** you were born lazy; EXPR **no he nacido ayer** I wasn't born yesterday; EXPR **nació con un pan debajo del brazo** the birth of the child was a blessing for the family; EXPR *Esp Fam* **nació** *o* **ha nacido con una flor en el culo** he has the luck of the devil; EXPR *Ven Fam* **n. parado** to be born lucky; EXPR *Fam Hum* **unos nacen con estrella y otros nacen estrellados** fortune smiles on some people and not on others; EXPR **volver a n.** to have a lucky escape; PROV *Méx Fam* **el que ha nacido en petate, siempre anda apestando a tule** you can't make a silk purse out of a sow's ear

(**b**) *(ave, reptil)* to hatch (out)

(**c**) *(planta)* to sprout, to begin to grow

(**d**) *(pelo)* to grow

(**e**) *(río)* to rise, to have its source

(**f**) *(sol, luna)* to rise

(**g**) *(originarse)* **la costumbre nació en Italia** this custom has its roots in Italy; **desde aquel momento, nació una gran amistad entre los dos** that moment was the beginning of a close friendship between them; **su nerviosismo nace de su inseguridad** his nervousness stems from his insecurity; **la revolución nació en el norte del país** the revolution started in the north of the country; **el Renacimiento nació en Italia** the Renaissance had its origins in Italy

nacho *nm* nacho

nacido, -a 1 *adj* born

2 *nm,f* **los nacidos hoy** people born today; **los no nacidos** people as yet unborn; **recién n.** newborn baby; EXPR **ser un mal n.** to be a wicked *o* vile person

naciente[1] 1 *adj* (**a**) *(día)* dawning; *(sol)* rising (**b**) *(gobierno, estado)* fledgling, new; *(interés, amistad)* budding; **la fragilidad de la n. democracia** the precarious nature of the fledgling democracy

2 *nm (este)* east

naciente[2] *nf,* **nacientes** *nfpl RP (nacimiento)* source

naciera *etc ver* **nacer**

nacimiento *nm* (**a**) *(de niño, animal)* birth; **de n.** from birth; **ser ciego de n.** to be born blind; **por n.** by birth (**b**) *(de ave, reptil)* hatching (**c**) *(de planta)* sprouting (**d**) *(de pelo)* hairline (**e**) *(de río)* source (**f**) *(origen) (de amistad)* start, beginning; *(de costumbre)* origin (**g**) *(belén)* Nativity scene

nación *nf (pueblo)* nation; *(territorio)* nation, country ►► *Econ* ***n. más favorecida*** most favoured nation; ***Naciones Unidas*** United Nations

nacional 1 *adj* (**a**) *(de la nación)* national; **el equipo n.** the national team; **la moneda n.** the national currency; **el ron es la bebida n.** rum is the national drink

(**b**) *(del Estado)* national; **monumento/biblioteca n.** national monument/library

(**c**) *(vuelo)* domestic

(**d**) *(mercado, noticias)* domestic, home; **una cadena de televisión de ámbito n.** a national television channel; **consuma productos nacionales** buy British/Spanish/*etc* products

(**e**) *Esp Hist* **las fuerzas nacionales** the Nationalist forces

2 **nacionales** *nmpl Esp Hist* **los nacionales** the Nationalists

nacionalidad *nf* (**a**) *(situación jurídica)* nationality; **tengo la n. española** I have Spanish nationality *o* citizenship; **un bailarín de n. rusa** a Russian dancer; **trabajadores de n. extranjera** foreign workers; **doble n.** dual nationality (**b**) *(nación)* people

nacionalismo *nm* nationalism

nacionalista 1 *adj* nationalist

2 *nmf* nationalist

nacionalización *nf* (**a**) *(de banca, bienes)* nationalization (**b**) *(de persona)* naturalization

nacionalizado, -a *adj* nationalized

nacionalizar [14] 1 *vt* (**a**) *(banca, bienes)* to nationalize (**b**) *(persona)* to naturalize

2 **nacionalizarse** *vpr* to become naturalized; **nacionalizarse español** to become a Spanish citizen, to acquire Spanish nationality

nacionalmente *adv* nationally

nacionalsindicalismo *nm Hist* National Syndicalism, = Falangist doctrine adopted by the Franco regime

nacionalsindicalista *adj Hist* National Syndicalist, = in favour of the Falangist doctrine adopted by the Franco regime

nacionalsocialismo *nm Hist* National Socialism

nacionalsocialista *Hist* 1 *adj* National Socialist

2 *mf* National Socialist

naco, -a 1 *adj CAm, Méx Fam* (**a**) *Pey (indio)* Indian (**b**) *(ordinario)* common

2 *nm* (**a**) *Am (de tabaco)* chew, plug (**b**) *Col (puré)* thick soup; EXPR *Fam* **quedar vuelto n.** to be smashed to pulp

3 *nm,f* (**a**) *CAm, Méx Fam Pey (indio)* Indian (**b**) *CAm, Méx Fam (ordinario)* common person, *Br* pleb

NADA 1 *pron* (**a**) *(ninguna cosa o cantidad)* nothing; *(en negativas)* anything; **no he leído n. de Lorca** I haven't read anything by Lorca; **no pasó n.** nothing happened; **a él n. parece satisfacerle** he never seems to be satisfied with anything; **de n. vale insistir** there's no point in insisting; **n. me gustaría más que poder ayudarte** there's nothing I'd like more than to be able to help you; **no hay n. como un buen libro** there's nothing (quite) like a good book; **tranquilos, no es n.** don't worry, it's nothing serious; **casi n.** almost nothing; **de n.,** *Am* **por n.** *(respuesta a "gracias")* you're welcome, don't mention it; **esto no es n.** that's nothing; **no queda n. de café** there's no coffee left; **no tengo n. de ganas de ir** I don't feel like going at all; **no dijo n. de n.** he didn't say anything at all; **no me ha gustado n. de n.** I didn't like it at all *o* one little bit; **n. de quejas ¿de acuerdo?** no complaining, right?, I don't want any complaints, right?; **n. más** nothing else, nothing more; **¿desean algo más? – n. más, gracias** do you want anything else? – no, that's everything *o* all, thank you; **no quiero n. más** I don't want anything else; **me dio de plazo dos días n. más** she only gave me two days to do it; **me ha costado n. más que 20 dólares** it only cost me 20 dollars; **¡tanto esfuerzo para n.!** all that effort for nothing!

(**b**) *(poco, muy poco)* **yo apenas sé n. de ese tema** I hardly know anything about that subject; **es muy frágil y con n. se parte** it's very fragile and is easily broken; **dentro de n.** any second now; **lo he visto salir hace n.** I saw him leave just a moment ago *o* just this minute; **no hace n. que salió** he left just a moment ago *o* just this minute; **por n. se enfada** she gets angry at the slightest thing, it doesn't take much for her to get angry; *CAm, Col, Ven Fam* **a cada n.** every five minutes, constantly; *Méx* **en n. estuvo que se casara** he very nearly got married

(**c**) *Esp (en tenis)* love; **treinta n.** thirty love

(**d**) *(expresando negación)* **¡n. de eso!** absolutely not!; **no pienso ir, ni llamar, ni n.** I won't go, or call, or anything; **no tenemos ni coche, ni moto, ni n. que se le parezca** we don't have a car or a motorbike, or anything of that sort

(**e**) EXPR **¡ahí es n.!** *o* **¡casi n.!: cuesta cinco millones, ¡ahí es n.!** *o* **¡casi n.!** it costs a cool five million!; **como si n.** as if nothing was the matter, as if nothing had happened; **(n. más y) n. menos que** *(cosa)* no less than; *(persona)* none other than; *Fam* **ni n.: ¡no es alta ni n. la chica!** she's tall all right!, you could say she's tall!; **no es por n.: no es por n. pero creo que estás equivocado** don't take this the wrong way, but I think you're mistaken; **no es por n. pero llevas la bragueta abierta** by the way, your fly's undone

2 *adv* (**a**) *(en absoluto)* at all; **la película no me ha gustado n.** I didn't like the movie at all; **no he dormido n.** I didn't get any sleep at all; **no es n. extraño** it's not at all strange; **la obra no es n. aburrida** the play isn't the slightest bit boring; **no está n. mal** it's not at all bad; **no nos llevamos n. bien** we don't get on at all well; *Fam* **¿te importa que me quede? – ¡para n.!** do you mind if I stay? – of course not! *o* not at all!

(**b**) *Fam (enfático)* **n., que no hay manera de convencerle** but no, he just won't be persuaded

3 *nf* (**a**) **la n.** nothingness, the void; *(el no ser)* **salir** *o* **surgir de la n.** to appear out of *o* from nowhere (**b**) *Méx, RP Fam (muy poco)* **le pedí plata y me dio una n.** I asked him for some money and he gave me next to nothing; **comí una n. de helado** I had a tiny bit of ice cream

4 **de nada** *loc adj* **te he traído un regalito de n.** I've brought you a little something; **es sólo un rasguño de n.** it's just a little scratch

5 **nada más** *loc adv* (**a**) *(al poco de)* **n. más salir de casa...** no sooner had I left the house than..., as soon as I left the house...; **nos iremos n. más cenar** we'll go as soon as we've had dinner, we'll go straight after dinner

(**b**) *Méx (solamente)* **n. más vine yo** I'm the only one who's come

(**c**) *Méx (sin más)* **de la fiesta regresaron a casa y n. más** they went straight home after the party

---

nadador, -ora *nm,f* swimmer

nadar *vi* (**a**) *(avanzar en el agua)* to swim; **no sé n.** I can't swim; *Esp* **n. a braza,** *Am* **n. pecho** to do the breaststroke; *Esp* **n. a espalda,** *Andes, CAm, Carib, RP* **n. espalda,** *Méx* **n. de dorso** to do the backstroke; *Esp* **n. a mariposa,** *Am* **n. mariposa** to do the butterfly; **n. contra corriente** to go against the tide; EXPR **n. en la abundancia** to be living in the lap of luxury; EXPR **nadan en deudas** they're up to their necks in debt; EXPR **n. entre dos aguas** to sit on the fence; EXPR **n. y guardar la ropa** to have one's cake and eat it

(**b**) *(flotar)* to float

nadería *nf* trifle, little thing; **se pelearon por una n.** they fell out over nothing; **hemos traído unas naderías para los abuelos** we've bought a few little things for grandma and grandpa

nadie 1 *pron* nobody, no one; **n. lo sabe** nobody *o* no one knows; **no se lo dije a n.** I didn't tell anybody *o* anyone; **no vi a n.** I didn't see anybody *o* anyone; **llamé a la puerta pero no había n.** I knocked on the door but there was nobody *o* no one in; **no ha llamado n.** nobody *o* no one phoned

2 *nm* **un don n.** a nobody

nadir *nm Astron* nadir

nado *nm Méx, RP, Ven (natación)* swimming; **cruzaron a n. el canal** they swam across the canal; **llegaron a n. hasta la orilla** they swam to the shore ►► ***n. sincronizado*** synchronized swimming

NAFTA ['nafta] *nm (abrev de* **North American Free Trade Agreement**) NAFTA

nafta *nf* (**a**) *Quím* naphtha (**b**) *RP (gasolina) Br* petrol, *US* gas, *US* gasoline; **cargar n.** to fill up (with *Br* petrol *o US* gas) ►► ***n. sin plomo*** unleaded *Br* petrol *o US* gasoline; ***n. súper*** *Br* four-star petrol, *US* premium-grade gasoline

naftaleno *nm* naphthalene

naftalina *nf* naphthalene; **bolas de n.** mothballs; **sus trajes olían a n.** his suits smelled of mothballs

nagua *nf,* **naguas** *nfpl CAm, Col* petticoat

nagual *CAm, Méx* 1 *nm* (**a**) *(hechicero)* sorcerer, wizard (**b**) *(animal)* pet

2 *nf* lie

naguas = **nagua**

nahua, náhuatl 1 *adj* Nahuatl

2 *nmf (persona)* Nahuatl Indian

3 *nm (lengua)* Nahuatl

nahuatlato, -a *adj* Nahuatl-speaking

naiboa *Ven* 1 *nf* = cassava bread sandwich containing brown sugar and cheese

2 *adv Fam* nothing, *US* diddly-squat; **¿y qué novedades? – n.** what's new? – nothing

naíf, naïf (*pl* **naifs, naïfs**) *adj Arte* naïve, primitivistic

nailon, náilon *nm* nylon

naipe *nm* (playing) card; **jugar a los naipes** to play cards

naira *nf* naira

Nairobi *n* Nairobi

naja *nf* EXPR *Esp Fam* **salir de n.** to beat it, *Br* to scarper

najarse *vpr Esp Fam* to beat it, *Br* to scarper

nalga *nf* (**a**) *(de persona)* buttock; **le dio un pellizco en las nalgas** she pinched his bottom (**b**) *RP (carne)* silverside

nalgada *nf Méx (palmada)* slap on the bottom

Namibia *n* Namibia

namibio, -a 1 *adj* Namibian

2 *nm,f* Namibian

nana *nf* (**a**) *(canción)* lullaby; EXPR *Fam* **el año de la n.** the year dot; EXPR *Fam* **del año de la n., más viejo que la n.** as old as the hills, ancient (**b**) *Fam (abuela)* grandma, nana (**c**) *Col, Méx (niñera)* nanny (**d**) *Col, Méx (nodriza)* wet nurse (**e**) *CSur (rasguño)* **el nene se cayó y se hizo n.** the little boy fell and hurt himself (**f**) *CSur (achaque)* **la abuela está llena de nanas** grandma has lots of aches and pains

nanay *interj Fam* no way!, not likely!

nandrolona *nf* nandrolone

nanosegundo *nm* nanosecond

nanotecnología *nf* nanotechnology

nao *nf Literario* vessel

napa *nf* leather

napalm *nm* napalm

napia *nf,* **napias** *nfpl Fam Br* conk, *US* schnozz

Napoleón *n pr* **N. (Bonaparte)** Napoleon (Bonaparte)

napoleónico, -a *adj* Napoleonic

Nápoles *n* Naples

napolitana *nf* = flat, rectangular cake filled with cream

napolitano, -a 1 *adj* Neapolitan

2 *nm,f* Neapolitan

naranja 1 *adj inv* orange

2 *nm (color)* orange; **el n. es mi color favorito** orange is my favourite colour

3 *nf (fruto)* orange; EXPR *Fam* **¡naranjas de la china!** no way!; EXPR *RP, Ven Fam* **no pasa n.: salí sin los documentos – no pasa n.** I left without my documents – no hassle; **este es un pueblo muy aburrido, acá no pasa n.** this is a really boring town, there's zilch going on here ►► ***n. agria*** Seville orange; ***n. navelina*** navel orange; ***n. sanguina*** blood orange

naranjada *nf* = orange juice drink

naranjal *nm* orange grove

naranjero, -a 1 *adj* **la industria naranjera** the orange industry; **una región naranjera** an orange-growing region

2 *nm,f* (**a**) *(vendedor)* orange seller (**b**) *(cultivador)* orange grower

naranjo *nm* (**a**) *(árbol)* orange tree (**b**) *(madera)* orange (wood)

narcisismo *nm* narcissism

narcisista 1 *adj* narcissistic

2 *nmf* narcissist

narciso *nm* (**a**) *(planta)* narcissus ►► ***n. de los prados*** daffodil (**b**) *(persona)* narcissist

narco 1 *adj Am Fam* drug; **dinero n.** drug money

2 *nmf Fam* (**a**) *(narcotraficante)* drug trafficker (**b**) *(narcotráfico)* drug trafficking

narcodependencia *nf* drug dependence, drug addiction

narcodinero *nm* drug money

narcodólares *nmpl* drug money

narcolepsia *nf Med* narcolepsy

narcomanía *nf* narcotism
narcosis *nf inv* narcosis
narcótico, -a 1 *adj* narcotic
2 *nm (somnífero)* narcotic; *(droga)* drug
narcotismo *nm* narcotism
narcotizante 1 *adj* narcotic
2 *nmf* narcotic
narcotizar [14] *vt* to drug
narcotraficante *nmf* drug trafficker
narcotráfico *nm* drug trafficking
nardo *nm (flor)* nard, spikenard
narguile *nm* hookah
narigón, -ona 1 *adj Fam* big-nosed
2 *nm,f* big-nosed person; **es un n.** he has a big nose
3 *nm Cuba (agujero)* hole
narigudo, -a 1 *adj* big-nosed
2 *nm,f* big-nosed person; **es un n.** he has a big nose

NARIZ 1 *nf* (a) *(órgano)* nose; **operarse (de) la n.** to have a nose job; **sangraba por la n.** her nose was bleeding; **sonarse la n.** to blow one's nose; **taparse la n.** to hold one's nose; **tengo la n. tapada** my nose is blocked; **tener la n. aguileña/griega** to have a Roman nose/Grecian profile; **tener la n. chata/respingona** to have a snub/turned-up nose
(b) *(olfato)* sense of smell
(c) EXPR **dar a alguien en las narices con algo** to rub sb's nose in sth; **me da en la n. que...** I've got a feeling that...; **darse de narices con** *o* **contra algo/alguien** to bump into sth/sb; **se dio de narices contra el semáforo** he went smack into the traffic lights; **delante de mis narices: me insultó delante de mis narices** he insulted me to my face; **me han robado el bolso delante de mis narices** they stole my *Br* handbag *o US* purse from right under my nose; *Esp Fam* **de las narices: ¡otra vez el teléfono de las narices!** that damn telephone's ringing again!; *Fam* **de narices** *(estupendo)* great, brilliant; **he agarrado un resfriado de narices** I've got a really nasty cold; **llueve de narices** it's raining like mad, it's chucking it down; **lo pasamos de narices** we had a great time; *Fam* **echarle narices: le eché narices y le pedí salir** I plucked up my courage and asked her out; **a esto de las carreras de coches hay que echarle narices** you've got to be really brave to be a racing driver; **en mis propias narices: me lo dijo/se reía de mí en mis propias narices** she said it/she was laughing at me to my face; **me lo robaron en mis propias narices** they stole it from right under my nose; *Fam* **estar hasta las narices (de algo/alguien)** to be fed up to the back teeth (with sth/sb); *Esp Fam* **me estás hinchando las narices** you're beginning to get up my nose; *Fam* **meter las narices en algo** to poke *o* stick one's nose into sth; *Fam* **no hay más narices que hacerlo** there's nothing for it but to do it; **no ve más allá de sus narices** she can't see past the end of her nose; *RP Fam* **ser un n. para arriba** to be stuck-up *o* snooty; *Esp Fam* **por narices: tenemos que ir por narices** we have to go whether we like it or not; **tuve que hacerlo por narices** I had no choice but to do it; **restregar algo a alguien en** *o* **por las narices** to rub sb's nose in sth; *Fam* **romper las narices a alguien** to smash sb's face in; **romperse las narices** to fall flat on one's face; *Fam* **porque me sale/no me sale de las narices** because I damn well feel like it/damn well can't be bothered; *Esp Fam* **¡tiene narices (la cosa)!** it's an absolute scandal!; *Fam* **tocarle las narices a alguien** *(fastidiar)* to get up sb's nose; *Fam* **tocarse las narices** *(holgazanear)* to sit around doing nothing
2 **narices** *interj Esp Fam (ni hablar)* no way!

narizotas *nmf inv Fam* big-nose
narración *nf* (a) *(cuento, relato)* narrative, story (b) *(acción)* narration
narrador, -ora *nm,f* narrator
narrar *vt (contar)* to recount, to tell; **la película narra la caída del imperio romano** the movie tells the story of the fall of the Roman empire
narrativa *nf* narrative; **la n. española contemporánea** contemporary Spanish fiction
narrativo, -a *adj* narrative
narval *nm* narwhal
NASA ['nasa] *nf* (*abrev de* **National Aeronautics and Space Administration**) **la N.** NASA
nasa *nf* creel, lobster pot
nasal 1 *adj* (a) *(orificio)* nasal; **fosa n.** nostril (b) *Ling* nasal
2 *nm Anat* nasal bone
3 *nf Ling* nasal
nasalidad *nf Ling* nasality
nasalización *nf Ling* nasalization
nasalizar [14] *vt* to nasalize
nasciturus *nm inv Der* unborn child
násico *nm* proboscis monkey
naso *nm RP Fam Br* conk, *US* schnozz
Nassau *n* Nassau
nata *nf* (a) *Esp (crema de leche)* cream; **n. (batida)** whipped cream ►► ***n. agria*** sour cream; ***n. líquida*** single cream; ***n. montada*** whipped cream; ***n. para montar*** whipping cream (b) *(en leche hervida)* skin (c) *Méx (escoria)* slag
natación *nf* swimming ►► ***n. sincronizada*** synchronized swimming
natal 1 *adj (país, ciudad)* native; *(pueblo)* home; **la casa n. de Goya** the house where Goya was born
2 *nmf Méx (nativo)* native; **un n. de Chiapas** a native of Chiapas
natalicio *nm Formal* birthday
natalidad *nf* **(tasa** *o* **índice de) n.** birth rate
natatorio, -a *adj* swimming
natilla *nf Andes, RP (dulce sólido)* custard-flavoured sweet
natillas *nfpl Esp (dulce cremoso)* custard
natividad *nf* nativity; **la N.** Christmas
nativo, -a 1 *adj* (a) *(persona, costumbre)* native; **profesor n.** native-speaker teacher (b) *(mineral)* native
2 *nm,f* (a) *(natural)* native (b) *(hablante)* native (speaker)
nato, -a *adj (de nacimiento)* born; **un criminal n.** a born criminal
natura *nf* nature; **una alianza contra n.** an unholy alliance
natural 1 *adj* (a) *(de la naturaleza) (recursos, frontera)* natural; **un fenómeno n.** a natural phenomenon
(b) *(sin aditivos) (yogur)* natural; *(zumo)* fresh; **al n.** *(fruta)* in its own juice; *(en persona)* in the flesh; **es más guapa al n. que en la fotografía** she's prettier in real life *o* in the flesh than in the photograph
(c) *(fresco) (flores, fruta, leche)* fresh
(d) *(lógico, normal)* natural, normal; **ser n. en alguien** to be in sb's nature; **es lo más n. del mundo** it's the most natural thing in the world, it's perfectly natural; **es n. que se enfade** it's natural that he should be angry
(e) *(nativo)* native; **ser n. de** to come from
(f) *(ilegítimo)* illegitimate; **hijo n.** illegitimate child
(g) *(hábil y no hábil)* **año/mes n.** calendar year/month; **30 días naturales de vacaciones** 30 working days' holiday *o US* vacation
(h) *RP (del tiempo)* unchilled, at room temperature; **un agua n.** a glass of unchilled water
(i) *Mús* natural
2 *nmf (nativo)* native
3 *nm* (a) *(talante)* nature, disposition (b) *Arte* **un dibujo del n.** a life drawing (c) *Taurom* = left-handed pass without the sword
naturaleza *nf* (a) **la n.** *(seres del universo)* nature; **aman a la n.** they love nature, they are nature lovers; **por n.** by nature; **la madre n.** Mother Nature ►► ***n. muerta*** still life
(b) *(características)* nature; **se desconoce la n. de la enfermedad** the nature of the illness is unknown
(c) *(complexión)* constitution
(d) *(carácter)* nature; **la n. humana** human nature; **una persona de n. nerviosa** a person of a nervous disposition, a person who is nervous by nature
(e) *(tipo, clase)* nature; **prefiero no meterme en negocios de esa n.** I prefer not to get involved in deals of that nature *o* in that kind of deal
naturalidad *nf* naturalness; **la n. con la que anunció su divorcio sorprendió a todos** the natural way she announced her divorce surprised everybody; **con n.** naturally
naturalismo *nm* naturalism
naturalista 1 *adj* naturalistic
2 *nmf* naturalist
naturalización *nf* naturalization
naturalizar [14] 1 *vt* to naturalize
2 **naturalizarse** *vpr* to become naturalized; **naturalizarse español** to become a Spanish citizen, to acquire Spanish nationality
naturalmente *adv* (a) *(por naturaleza)* naturally; **una persona n. calmada** a naturally calm person, a person who is calm by nature (b) *(por supuesto)* of course; **¿me podrías ayudar? – ¡n.!** could you help me? – of course!; **¿te gusta? – n. que sí** do you like it? – of course I do!
naturismo *nm* nudism
naturista 1 *adj* naturist, nudist
2 *nmf* naturist, nudist

naturópata *nmf* naturopath

naturopatía *nf* naturopathy

naufragar [38] *vi* (**a**) *(barco)* to sink, to be wrecked; *(persona)* to be shipwrecked (**b**) *(fracasar)* to fail, to collapse

naufragio *nm* (**a**) *(de barco)* shipwreck (**b**) *(fracaso)* failure, collapse

náufrago, -a 1 *adj* shipwrecked
2 *nm,f* shipwrecked person, castaway

náusea *nf* (**a**) *(vómitos)* nausea, sickness; **me da náuseas** it makes me feel sick; **sentir** *o* **tener náuseas** to feel sick *o* nauseous (**b**) *(repugnancia)* **me da náuseas** it makes me sick

nauseabundo, -a *adj* nauseating, sickening

náutica *nf* navigation, seamanship; **la n. deportiva** sailing

náutico, -a 1 *adj (de la navegación)* nautical; **deportes náuticos** water sports; **club n.** yacht club
2 **náuticos** *nmpl (zapatos)* = lightweight lace-up shoes, made of coloured leather

nautilo *nm* nautilus

nauyaca *nf* fer-de-lance, lancehead

nava *nf* valley

navaja *nf* (**a**) *(cuchillo) (pequeño)* penknife; *(más grande)* jackknife ▸▸ ***n. de afeitar*** razor; ***n. automática*** flick knife, switchblade; ***n. barbera*** razor; ***n. multiusos*** Swiss army knife (**b**) *(molusco)* razor-shell, razor clam

navajazo *nm* stab, slash; **le dieron un n. en el estómago** he was stabbed in the stomach

navajero, -a *nm,f* = thug who carries a knife

navajo 1 *adj* Navajo
2 *nmf* Navajo

naval *adj* naval

Navarra *n* Navarre

navarro, -a 1 *adj* Navarrese
2 *nm,f* Navarrese

nave *nf* (**a**) *(barco)* ship; EXPR **quemar las naves** to burn one's boats *o* bridges
(**b**) *(vehículo)* craft ▸▸ ***n. espacial*** spaceship, spacecraft
(**c**) *(de fábrica)* shop, plant; *(almacén)* warehouse ▸▸ ***n. industrial*** = large building for industrial or commercial use
(**d**) *(de iglesia)* ***n. central*** nave; ***n. del crucero*** transepts and crossing; ***n. lateral*** side aisle; ***la n. de San Pedro*** the Roman Catholic Church
(**e**) *Ven Fam (automóvil)* wheels

navegabilidad *nf* (**a**) *(de río)* navigability (**b**) *(de barco)* seaworthiness

navegable *adj* navigable

navegación *nf* (**a**) *(en río, mar, aire)* navigation ▸▸ ***n. aérea*** air navigation; ***n. de altura*** ocean navigation; ***n. de cabotaje*** coastal navigation; ***n. deportiva*** sailing; ***n. fluvial*** river navigation; ***n. marítima*** sea navigation; ***n. por satélite*** satellite navigation; ***n. a vela*** sailing
(**b**) *Informát (en página web)* navigation; **una página de fácil n.** a page that is easy to navigate; **un programa de n. por Internet** an Internet browser

navegador *nm Informát* browser

navegante 1 *adj (pueblo)* seafaring
2 *nmf* (**a**) *(marino)* navigator (**b**) *(piloto)* navigator (**c**) *(de Internet)* Internet user

navegar [38] *vi* (**a**) *(barco)* to sail (**b**) *(avión)* to fly (**c**) *Informát* to browse; **n. por Internet** to surf *o* browse the Net; **lleva toda la mañana navegando** he's been surfing the Net all morning, he's been on the Internet all morning

naveta *nf (recipiente)* censer

Navidad *nf* (**a**) *(día)* Christmas (Day) (**b**) *(periodo)* **Navidad(es)** Christmas (time); **en N.** at Christmas; **feliz N., felices Navidades** Merry Christmas; **Navidades blancas** white Christmas

navideño, -a *adj* Christmas; **adornos navideños** Christmas decorations

naviera *nf (compañía)* shipping company

naviero, -a 1 *adj* shipping
2 *nm (armador)* shipowner

navío *nm* large ship; **n. de guerra** warship; **n. mercante** merchant ship

náyade *nf Mitol* naiad

nayarita, nayaritense 1 *adj* of/from Nayarit *(Mexico)*
2 *nmf* person from Nayarit *(Mexico)*

nazareno, -a 1 *adj* Nazarene
2 *nm,f* Nazarene
3 *nm* = penitent in Holy Week processions; **el Nazareno** Jesus of Nazareth, the Nazarene

Nazaret *n* Nazareth

nazarí (*pl* **nazaríes**), **nazarita** *adj Hist* Nazarite, = of/relating to the Arab dynasty that ruled in Granada between the 13th and 15th centuries

nazco *etc ver* **nacer**

nazi 1 *adj* Nazi
2 *nmf* Nazi

nazismo *nm* Nazism

NB (*abrev de* **nota bene**) NB

NBA *nf* (*abrev de* **National Basketball Association**) NBA

N. del T. (*abrev de* **nota del traductor**) translator's note

NE (*abrev de* **Nordeste**) NE

neandertal, neanderthal *nm* neanderthal

nébeda *nf* catmint, catnip

neblina *nf* mist

neblinear *v impersonal Chile* to drizzle

neblinoso, -a *adj* misty

nebulizador *nm* atomizer, spray

nebulosa *nf* nebula

nebulosidad *nf (de nubes)* cloudiness; *(de niebla)* fogginess

nebuloso, -a *adj* (**a**) *(con nubes)* cloudy; *(de niebla)* foggy (**b**) *(poco claro)* vague, nebulous

necedad *nf* (**a**) *(estupidez)* stupidity, foolishness (**b**) *(dicho, hecho)* stupid *o* foolish thing; **decir necedades** to talk nonsense; **fue una n. dejarle salir solo** it was stupid to let him go out on his own

necesariamente *adv* necessarily; **tuvo que ser él n.** it must have been him; **tiene que estar n. en esta habitación** it has to *o* it's got to be in this room, it must be in this room

necesario, -a *adj* (**a**) *(que hace falta)* necessary; **me llevé la ropa necesaria para una semana** I took enough clothes for a week; **me eres muy necesaria** I really need you; **es n. hacerlo** it needs to be done; **es n. descansar regularmente** you need to rest regularly; **hacer n. algo** to make sth necessary; **no es n. que lo hagas** you don't need to do it; **si es n.** if need be, if necessary
(**b**) *(inevitable)* inevitable; **el desempleo es consecuencia necesaria de la desindustrialización** unemployment is an inevitable consequence of deindustrialization

neceser *nm (bolsa)* toilet bag; *(maleta pequeña)* vanity case

necesidad *nf* (**a**) *(en general)* need; **discutieron la n. de detener la violencia** they discussed the need to stop the violence; **en esta oficina tenemos una urgente n. de espacio** we are in urgent need of more space in this office; **no veo la n. de darle un premio** I don't see any reason to give him a prize; **nos recordaron la n. de ser discretos** they reminded us of the need for discretion; **tener n. de algo** to need sth; **no hay n. de que se lo digas** there's no need for you to tell her; **obedecer a la n. (de)** to arise from the need (to); **n. perentoria** urgent need; **puedes hablarme, sin n. de gritar** there's no need to shout; **se puede comer sin n. de calentarlo previamente** can be eaten cold, needs no preheating; **de (primera) n.** essential; **un artículo de primera n.** a basic commodity
(**b**) *(obligación)* necessity; **por n.** out of necessity; **una herida mortal de n.** a fatal wound
(**c**) *(hambre)* hunger; *(pobreza)* poverty, need; **pasar necesidades** to suffer hardship; **la n. la obligó a mendigar** poverty forced her to beg
(**d**) *Euf* **tengo que hacer mis necesidades** I have to answer a call of nature; **ya estoy harto de que los perros de los vecinos se hagan sus necesidades en la escalera** I'm fed up of neighbours' dogs doing their business on the stairs

necesitado, -a 1 *adj* needy; **están muy necesitados de ayuda humanitaria** they are urgently in need of humanitarian aid; **este cuarto está n. de una capa de pintura** this room needs a coat of paint, this room could do with a coat of paint
2 *nm,f* needy *o* poor person; **los necesitados** the poor

necesitar 1 *vt* to need; **necesito llamarla cuanto antes** I need to call her as soon as possible; **necesito que me lo digas** I need you to tell me; **esta planta necesita que la rieguen** this plant needs watering; **se necesita camarero** *(en letrero)* waiter wanted; **se necesita ser ignorante para no saber eso** you'd have to be an ignoramus not to know that
2 *vi* **n. de** to need, to have need of; **necesitamos de tu ayuda** we need your help

necio, -a 1 *adj* (**a**) *(tonto)* stupid, foolish (**b**) *Am (terco)* stubborn, pigheaded (**c**) *Méx (susceptible)* touchy
2 *nm,f* (**a**) *(tonto)* idiot, fool (**b**) *Am (terco)* stubborn *o* pigheaded person; **es un n.** he's really stubborn o pigheaded (**c**) *Méx (susceptible)* touchy person; **es un n.** he's really touchy

nécora *nf* = small edible crab

necrófago, -a *adj* carrion-eating, *Espec* necrophagous

necrofilia *nf* necrophilia

necrófilo, -a 1 *adj* necrophiliac, necrophile
2 *nm,f* necrophiliac, necrophile

necrofobia *nf* necrophobia

necrología *nf (noticia)* obituary; *(lista de fallecidos)* obituaries, obituary column

necrológica *nf (noticia)* obituary; **necrológicas** *(sección de periódico)* obituaries, obituary column

necrológico, -a *adj* **nota necrológica** obituary

necromancia *nf* necromancy

necrópolis *nf inv* (**a**) *(restos)* necropolis (**b**) *(cementerio)* cemetery

necropsia *nf* autopsy

necrosis *nf inv* necrosis

néctar *nm* (**a**) *(en flor)* nectar (**b**) *(licor)* nectar; **n. de albaricoque** apricot nectar

nectarina *nf* nectarine

nectario *nm Bot* nectary

neerlandés, -esa 1 *adj* Dutch
2 *nm,f* Dutchman, *f* Dutchwoman
3 *nm (idioma)* Dutch

nefando, -a *adj* abominable, odious

nefasto, -a *adj (funesto)* ill-fated; *(dañino)* bad, harmful; *(pésimo)* terrible, awful

nefregar *vt Arg Fam* **me nefrega** I don't give a damn

nefrítico, -a *adj* renal, nephritic; **cólico n.** renal colic

nefritis *nf inv* nephritis

nefrología *nf* nephrology

nefrólogo, -a *nm,f* nephrologist

nefrón *nm Astron* nephron

negación *nf* (**a**) *(desmentido)* denial (**b**) *(negativa)* refusal (**c**) **la n.** *(lo contrario)* the antithesis, the complete opposite; **es la n. de la amabilidad** she's the antithesis of kindness (**d**) *Gram* negative (**e**) *(persona)* useless person; **ser una n. para algo** to be useless *o* no good at sth

negado, -a 1 *adj* useless, inept; **ser n. para algo** to be useless *o* no good at sth
2 *nm,f* useless person; **ser un n. para algo** to be useless *o* no good at sth

negar [43] **1** *vt* (**a**) *(rechazar)* to deny; **niega que existan los ovnis** he denies the existence of UFOs; **niega haber tenido nada que ver con el robo** he denies having had anything to do with the robbery; **no voy a n. que la idea me atrae** I won't deny that the idea appeals to me
(**b**) *(denegar)* to refuse, to deny; **le negaron el permiso de trabajo** they refused *o* denied him a work permit; **nos negaron la entrada a la fiesta** they refused to let us into the party, they wouldn't let us into the party; **no le puedo n. ese favor** I can't refuse *o* deny her that favour; **me niega el saludo** she won't say hello to me
2 *vi* **n. con la cabeza** to shake one's head
3 negarse *vpr* to refuse (**a** to); **se negó a ayudarme** she refused to help me; **me niego a creer que fuera él** I refuse to believe it was him; **se negó en redondo a escucharnos** she refused point-blank to listen to us

negativa *nf* (**a**) *(rechazo)* refusal; **han condenado la n. de los empresarios a negociar** they have condemned employers' refusal to negotiate (**b**) *(desmentido)* denial

negativamente *adv* negatively; **reaccionar n.** to react negatively; **responder n.** to reply in the negative, to say no

negativo, -a 1 *adj* (**a**) *(respuesta, oración)* negative (**b**) *(perjudicial)* negative (**c**) *(resultado)* negative; **el análisis ha dado n.** the test results were negative, the test came back negative (**d**) *(pesimista)* negative; **no seas tan n.** don't be so negative (**e**) *Mat* minus, negative; **signo n.** minus sign (**f**) *(carga eléctrica)* negative
2 *nm (fotográfico)* negative

negligé [neɣli'je] *nm* negligée

negligencia *nf* negligence

negligente *adj* negligent

negociabilidad *nf* negotiability

negociable *adj* negotiable

negociación *nf* (**a**) *(para obtener acuerdo)* **el primer ministro participó en la n. del acuerdo** the prime minister was involved in negotiating the agreement; **negociaciones** negotiations ►► ***n. colectiva*** collective bargaining; **negociaciones colectivas** round of collective bargaining; ***negociaciones de paz*** peace talks; ***n. salarial*** pay bargaining; **negociaciones salariales** wage negotiations, pay talks
(**b**) *(de compra, venta)* negotiation
(**c**) *Méx (empresa)* business

negociado *nm* (**a**) *(departamento)* department, section (**b**) *Andes, RP (chanchullo)* shady deal

negociador, -ora 1 *adj* negotiating; **una comisión negociadora** a negotiating committee
2 *nm,f* negotiator

negociante *nmf* (**a**) *(comerciante)* businessman, *f* businesswoman; **un n. de diamantes** a diamond merchant (**b**) *Fam Pey (interesado)* sharp customer

negociar 1 *vi* (**a**) *(comerciar)* to do business; **n. con** to deal *o* trade with (**b**) *(discutir)* to negotiate
2 *vt* to negotiate; **n. un acuerdo** to negotiate an agreement

negocio *nm* (**a**) *(empresa)* business; **tiene un n. de electrodomésticos** he has an electrical appliance business; **¿cómo va el n.?** how's business? ►► ***n. familiar*** family business
(**b**) **negocios** *(actividad)* business; **el mundo de los negocios** the business world; **un viaje de negocios** a business trip; **se dedica a los negocios** he's in business; **hacer negocios con** to do business with; **estoy aquí por cuestiones de negocios** I'm here on business
(**c**) *(transacción)* deal, (business) transaction; **hacer n.** to do well; **con esta compra hicimos (buen) n.** this was a good buy; **n. redondo** great bargain, excellent deal
(**d**) *(ocupación)* business; **¡ocúpate de tus negocios!** mind your own business!; **¿en qué negocios andas metido?** what are you involved in now?; EXPR **¡mal n.!** that's a nasty business!; **n. sucio** shady deal, dirty business
(**e**) *RP (tienda)* store

negra *nf* (**a**) *Mús Br* crotchet, *US* quarter note (**b**) *(en ajedrez, damas)* black (piece); **las negras tienen ventaja** black is winning (**c**) EXPR **tener la n.** to have bad luck; **vérselas negras: se las va a ver negras para llegar a fin de mes** he'll have a hard job to get to the end of the month
(**c**) *ver también* **negro**

negrada *nf* (**a**) *Urug, Ven Fam Pey (negros)* crowd of blacks (**b**) *Urug Fam Pey (pobres)* low-class people

negrear 1 *vt* (**a**) *Fam Pey (explotar)* to treat like a slave (**b**) *RP Fam (no declarar)* to conceal, to keep quiet about; **las empresas suelen n. parte de sus ingresos, para no pagar tantos impuestos** companies usually conceal part of their income in order to pay less tax (**c**) *Ven (excluir)* to leave out
2 *vi* (**a**) *(ponerse negro)* to turn black; **la noche negreaba** night was falling (**b**) *RP Fam (evadir impuestos)* to avoid paying tax

negrero, -a 1 *adj (explotador)* tyrannical
2 *nm,f* (**a**) *Hist* slave trader (**b**) *(explotador)* slave driver

negrilla 1 *adj* **letra n.** bold (type), boldface
2 *nf* bold (type), boldface; **en n.** in bold, in boldface

negrita 1 *adj* **letra n.** bold (type), boldface
2 *nf* bold (type), boldface; **en n.** in bold, in boldface

negritud *nf* negritude

negro, -a 1 *adj* (**a**) *(color)* black; **estos pantalones están negros** these *Br* trousers *o US* pants are filthy *o* absolutely black; EXPR **n. como el azabache** jet black; EXPR **n. como el carbón** as black as coal
(**b**) *(bronceado)* tanned; **estar n.** to have a deep tan
(**c**) *(pan)* brown
(**d**) *(tabaco)* black, dark
(**e**) *(raza)* black
(**f**) *(suerte)* awful, rotten; *(porvenir)* black, gloomy; **llevo una tarde negra** I'm having a terrible afternoon; **ver(lo) todo n.** to be pessimistic; EXPR **pasarlas negras** to have a hard time
(**g**) *Fam (furioso)* furious, fuming; **me pone n. que nunca me avisen de nada** it makes me mad that they never tell me anything
(**h**) *(ilegal) (trabajo)* illegal, in the black economy; *(mercado)* black; *(dinero)* dirty
(**i**) *Cine* **cine n.** film noir
2 *nm,f* (**a**) *(de raza negra)* black man, *f* black woman; EXPR **trabajar como un n.** to work like a slave (**b**) *Fam (escritor)* ghost writer
3 *nm* (**a**) *(color)* black; **el n. es mi color favorito** black is my favourite colour (**b**) *(tabaco)* black *o* dark tobacco (**c**) *Ven Fam (café)* black coffee

negroide *adj* negroid

negrón *nm* common scoter ►► ***n. especulado*** velvet scoter
negrura *nf* blackness
negruzco, -a *adj* blackish
negundo *nm* box elder
neis *nm inv* gneiss
nel *adv Méx Fam* no; **dijeron que llamarían, pero n., hasta ahora nada** they said they'd call, but I haven't heard anything yet; **n. carnal, yo no quiero ir contigo** no pal *o Br* mate, I don't want to go with you; **ya te dije que n., no te voy a prestar mi moto** I already told you no, I'm not going to lend you my motorbike
némesis *nf inv* nemesis
nemónico, -a *adj* mnemonic
nemorosa *nf* wood anemone
nemotecnia, nemotécnica *nf* mnemonics *(singular)*
nemotécnico, -a *adj* mnemonic
nena *nf Fam* (**a**) *(chica)* chick, *Br* bird (**b**) *(como apelativo)* darling; **¿bailas, n.?** do you want to dance, darling?
nene, -a *nm,f Fam (niño)* little boy; *(niña)* little girl; **los nenes** the kids
nené *nmf Ven Fam (niño)* little boy; *(niña)* little girl
nenúfar *nm* water lily
neo- *pref* neo-
neocapitalismo *nm* neocapitalism
neocapitalista 1 *adj* neocapitalist
2 *nm* neocapitalist
neocelandés, -esa = **neozelandés**
neoclasicismo *nm* neoclassicism
neoclásico, -a 1 *adj* neoclassical
2 *nm,f* neoclassicist
neocolonial *adj* neocolonial
neocolonialismo *nm* neocolonialism
neocórtex *nm Anat* neocortex
neodimio *nm Quím* neodymium
neofascismo *nm* neofascism
neofascista 1 *adj* neofascist
2 *nmf* neofascist
neófito, -a *nm,f* (**a**) *Rel* neophyte (**b**) *(aprendiz)* novice
neofobia *nf* fear of change
neogótico, -a *adj* neo-Gothic
neoimpresionismo *nm* neo-impressionism
neolatino, -a *adj (lengua)* Romance
neoleonés, -esa 1 *adj* of/from Nuevo León *(Mexico)*
2 *nm,f* person from Nuevo León *(Mexico)*
neoliberal 1 *adj* neoliberal
2 *nmf* neoliberal
neoliberalismo *nm* neoliberalism
neolítico, -a 1 *adj* Neolithic
2 *nm* **el Neolítico** the Neolithic (period)
neologismo *nm* neologism
neón *nm* (**a**) *Quím* neon (**b**) **(luz de) n.** neon light
neonatal *adj* neonatal
neonato, -a *nm,f* newborn baby; *Biol & Med* neonate
neonazi 1 *adj* neo-Nazi
2 *nmf* neo-Nazi
neoplasia *nf* tumour
neoplatónico, -a *adj* neo-Platonic
neopreno *nm* neoprene; **traje de n.** wet suit
neorrealismo *nm* neorealism
neoyorquino, -a 1 *adj* New York, of/from New York; **las calles neoyorquinas** the New York streets, the streets of New York
2 *nm,f* New Yorker
neozapatismo *nm Pol* = Zapatista movement that originated in Chiapas, Mexico in 1994
neozapatista *Pol* 1 *adj* neo-Zapatista, = of/relating to the Zapatista movement that originated in Chiapas, Mexico in 1994
2 *nmf* neo-Zapatista, = supporter of the Zapatista movement that originated in Chiapas, Mexico in 1994
neozelandés, -esa, neocelandés, -esa 1 *adj* New Zealand, of/from New Zealand; **un producto n.** a New Zealand product
2 *nm,f* New Zealander
Nepal *n* Nepal
nepalés, -esa, nepalí (*pl* **nepalíes**) 1 *adj* Nepalese
2 *nm,f (persona)* Nepalese
3 *nm (lengua)* Nepalese
nepotismo *nm* nepotism
neptuniano, -a, neptúnico, -a *adj (del planeta)* Neptunian
neptunio *nm Quím* neptunium
Neptuno *n Mitol* Neptune
nerd *nmf RP Fam* nerd
nereida *nf* Nereid
Nerón *n pr* Nero
nerudiano, -a *adj* = typical of the style of the poet Pablo Neruda (1904-1973)
nervadura *nf* (**a**) *(de bóveda)* rib (**b**) *(de insecto)* nervure (**c**) *(de hoja)* vein
nervio *nm* (**a**) *(de persona)* nerve ►► ***n. auditivo*** auditory nerve; ***n. ciático*** sciatic nerve; ***n. craneal*** cranial nerve; ***n. cubital*** cubital nerve; ***n. femoral*** femoral nerve; ***n. lumbar*** lumbar nerve; ***n. mediano*** median nerve; ***n. óptico*** optic nerve; ***n. radial*** radial nerve; ***n. sacro*** sacral nerve; ***n. vestibular*** vestibular nerve
(**b**) *(en filete, carne)* sinew
(**c**) *(de insecto)* vein
(**d**) *(de hoja)* vein, rib; *(de libro, bóveda)* rib
(**e**) **nervios** *(estado mental)* nerves; **me entraron los nervios** I got nervous; **tener nervios** to be nervous; EXPR **me ataca** *o* **crispa los nervios** it gets on my nerves; EXPR **estar de los nervios** to be in a nervous state; EXPR **perder los nervios** to lose one's cool *o* temper; EXPR **poner los nervios de punta a alguien** to get on sb's nerves; EXPR **tener nervios de acero** to have nerves of steel; EXPR **tener los nervios de punta** to be on edge
(**f**) *(vigor)* energy, vigour; **es buen jugador pero le falta n.** he's a good player, but he lacks steel; EXPR *Fam* **ser puro n.: estos niños son puro n.** these children never sit still for five minutes
nerviosamente *adv* nervously
nerviosismo *nm* **el n. de los inversores** the nervousness of investors; **una atmósfera de n.** a nervous atmosphere; **tras la quinta vuelta comenzó a mostrar n.** his nerves began to show after the fifth lap; **cantó con mucho n.** she sang very nervously
nervioso, -a *adj* (**a**) *(sistema, enfermedad)* nervous; **centro/tejido n.** nerve centre/tissue
(**b**) *(inquieto, agitado)* nervous; **está muy n.** he's very nervous; **está muy n. por la operación de su padre** he's very anxious about his father's operation; **quise hablar con ella pero me puse muy n.** I wanted to talk to her but I got all nervous; **todavía no me han dicho el resultado y me estoy poniendo n.** they still haven't told me the result and I'm getting nervous *o* a bit jumpy; **ese ruidito me está poniendo n.** that noise is getting on my nerves
(**c**) *(muy activo) Br* highly strung, *US* high-strung; **es muy n.** he's very *Br* highly strung *o US* high-strung
nescafé® *nm* instant coffee, Nescafé®
net (*pl* **nets**) *nm (en tenis)* let
neta *nf Méx Fam* **la n.** *(la verdad)* the truth; **¿cómo estás? – ¿la n.? ¡muy mal!** how are you? – if you really want to know, terrible!; **la n. que estábamos enamorados** the truth is, we were in love
netamente *adv* clearly, distinctly
netiqueta *nf Informát* netiquette
neto, -a *adj* (**a**) *(sueldo, ingresos)* net (**b**) *(peso, contenido)* net (**c**) *(claro) (perfil, recuerdo)* clear
neumático, -a 1 *adj* pneumatic
2 *nm* tyre ►► ***n. de repuesto*** *o* ***de recambio*** spare tyre
neumococo *nm Biol* pneumococcus
neumología *nf* pneumology
neumonía *nf* pneumonia
neumopatía *nf Med* pneumopathy
neumotórax *nm* pneumothorax
neura *Fam* 1 *adj* neurotic; **no seas tan n.** don't be so neurotic
2 *nmf* neurotic; **es un n.** he's a complete neurotic, he's really neurotic
3 *nf* (**a**) *(manía)* bug, mania; **le dio la n. de las maquetas** he caught the model-making bug; **le dio la n. y se fue al Nepal** she took it into her head to go to Nepal (**b**) *(neurastenia)* **estar con la n.** to be really down
neural *adj* neural
neuralgia *nf* neuralgia

neurálgico, -a *adj* (**a**) *(de la neuralgia)* neuralgic (**b**) *(importante)* critical; **un punto n. de la red ferroviaria** one of the key interchanges in the rail network

neurastenia *nf Med* nervous exhaustion, *Espec* neurasthenia

neurasténico, -a *Med* **1** *adj* suffering from nervous exhaustion, *Espec* neurasthenic

2 *nm,f* person suffering from nervous exhaustion, *Espec* neurasthenic person

neuritis *nf inv* neuritis

neuroanatomía *nf* neuroanatomy

neurobiología *nf* neurobiology

neurociencia *nf* neuroscience

neurocirugía *nf* neurosurgery

neurocirujano, -a *nm,f* neurosurgeon

neurofisiología *nf* neurophysiology

neurolingüística *nf* neurolinguistics *(singular)*

neurología *nf* neurology

neurológico, -a *adj* neurological

neurólogo, -a *nm,f* neurologist

neurona *nf* neuron(e), nerve cell

neuronal *adj* neural

neurópata *nmf* neuropath

neuropatía *nf* nervous disorder, *Espec* neuropathy

neuropatología *nf* neuropathology

neuropsicología *nf* neuropsychology

neuropsiquiatra *nmf* neuropsychiatrist

neuropsiquiatría *nf* neuropsychiatry

neurosis *nf inv* neurosis

neurótico, -a **1** *adj* neurotic

2 *nm,f* neurotic

neurotismo *nm* neuroticism

neurotizante *adj* **tiene un efecto n.** it makes people neurotic

neurotizar *vt* **n. a alguien** to make sb neurotic

neurotoxina *nf* neurotoxin

neurotransmisor *nm* neurotransmitter

neutral **1** *adj* neutral

2 *nmf* neutral

neutralidad *nf* neutrality

neutralismo *nm* neutralism

neutralista **1** *adj* neutralistic

2 *nmf* neutralist

neutralizable *adj (efecto, consecuencia)* remediable

neutralización *nf (de efecto)* neutralization

neutralizador, -ora *adj* neutralizing

neutralizante **1** *adj* neutralizing

2 *nmf* neutralizer

neutralizar [14] **1** *vt* (**a**) *(efecto)* to neutralize (**b**) *Dep (carrera)* to neutralize

2 neutralizarse *vpr (mutuamente)* to neutralize each other

neutrino *nm Fís* neutrino

neutro, -a **1** *adj* (**a**) *(color, voz)* neutral (**b**) *(actitud)* neutral (**c**) *Biol* neuter (**d**) *Elec* neutral (**e**) *Gram* neuter

2 *nm* (**a**) *Gram* neuter (**b**) *Am (marcha)* neutral

neutrón *nm* neutron

nevada *nf* snowfall; **anoche cayó una n.** it snowed last night

nevado, -a **1** *adj (tejado)* snow-covered; *(cumbre)* snowcapped, snow-covered

2 *nm Andes, RP* snowcapped mountain

nevar [3] *v impersonal* to snow; **está nevando** it's snowing

nevasca *nf* (**a**) *(nevada)* snowfall (**b**) *(ventisca)* snowstorm, blizzard

nevazón *nf Arg, Chile* blizzard, snowstorm

nevera *nf* (**a**) *(electrodoméstico)* refrigerator, *Br* fridge, *US* icebox (**b**) *(de cámping)* **n. (portátil)** cool box (**c**) *Fam (lugar frío)* fridge, icebox; **este apartamento es una n.** this apartment is like a fridge *o* an icebox

nevería *nf Carib, Méx* ice cream parlour

nevero *nm* snowfield

nevisca *nf* snow flurry

neviscar [60] *v impersonal* to snow lightly

nevoso, -a *adj* snowy

news [nius] *nfpl Informát* newsgroups

newton ['niuton] (*pl* **newtons**) *nm Fís* newton

newtoniano, -a [niuto'njano, -a] *adj* Newtonian

nexo *nm* (**a**) *(enlace)* link, connection (**b**) *Ling* linking word, *Espec* connective

ni **1** *conj* **ni... ni...** neither... nor...; **ni mañana ni pasado** neither tomorrow nor the day after; **ni mi padre ni mi madre vendrá** neither my father nor my mother is coming; **no... ni...** neither... nor..., not... or... (either); **no es alto ni bajo** he's neither tall nor short, he's not tall or short (either); **no es rojo ni verde ni azul** it's neither red nor green nor blue; **ni un/una...** not a single...; **no me quedaré ni un minuto más** I'm not staying a minute longer; **ni uno/una** not a single one; **no he aprobado ni una** I haven't passed a single one; **ni que** as if; **¡ni que yo fuera tonto!** as if I were that stupid!; **¡ni que nos sobrara el dinero!** it's not as if we have money to burn!, anyone would think we had money to burn!; **ni que decir tiene** it goes without saying; **¡no es listo ni nada!** he isn't half clever!; **te queda que ni hecho a medida** it couldn't look better on you if it had been tailor-made; **¡ni hablar!** certainly not!, it's out of the question!

2 *adv* not even; **ni siquiera** not even; **ni (siquiera) me saludó** she didn't even say hello; **anda tan atareado que ni tiene tiempo para comer** he's so busy he doesn't even have time to eat

niacina *nf* niacin

Niágara *n* **las cataratas del N.** the Niagara Falls

Niamey *n* Niamey

nibelungo, -a *nm,f* Nibelung

nica *Am Fam* **1** *adj* Nicaraguan

2 *nmf* Nicaraguan

Nicaragua *n* Nicaragua

nicaragüense **1** *adj* Nicaraguan

2 *nmf* Nicaraguan

niche *Ven Fam Pey* **1** *adj* (**a**) *(persona)* common, plebby (**b**) *(objeto)* tacky, *Br* naff

2 *nmf* (**a**) *(negro)* darkie (**b**) *(hortera)* pleb

nicho *nm* (**a**) *(hueco)* niche ►► ***n. de mercado*** niche (market) (**b**) *(en cementerio)* niche *(for coffin)* (**c**) ***n. biológico*** biological niche, niche; ***n. ecológico*** ecological niche

Nicolás *n pr* **San N.** St Nicholas

Nicosia *n* Nicosia

nicotina *nf* nicotine

nicotinismo *nm* nicotine poisoning, *Espec* nicotinism

nidada *nf* (**a**) *(pollitos)* brood (**b**) *(huevos)* clutch

nidal *nm* nest

nidificar [60] *vi* to (build a) nest

nido *nm* (**a**) *(refugio de animal)* nest; EXPR **caerse de un n.: ¿te crees que me he caído de un n.?** I wasn't born yesterday, you know

(**b**) *(en hospital)* baby unit; *(en guardería)* babies' room

(**c**) *(lugar de reunión)* **un n. de vicio/ladrones** a den of vice/thieves; **esa zona es un n. de prostitución** that area is crawling with prostitutes; **ese cuartel es un n. de conspiradores** that barracks is crawling with conspirators; EXPR **ser un n. de víboras** to be a nest of vipers

(**d**) *(hogar)* nest; **los niños ya han salido del n.** the children have already left *o* flown the nest; **n. de amor** love nest

(**e**) *(origen)* breeding ground; **esa mesa es un n. de polvo** that table seems to attract the dust

(**f**) ***n. de abeja*** *(punto)* smocking

(**g**) ***n. de ametralladoras*** *(emplazamiento)* machine-gun nest

niebla *nf* (**a**) *(densa)* fog; *(neblina)* mist; **hay n.** it's foggy/misty; **hay n. densa** it's very foggy, there is thick *o* dense fog; **la n. obligó a cerrar el aeropuerto** the airport had to be closed because of the fog ►► ***n. tóxica*** smog

(**b**) *(confusión)* **sus vidas están rodeadas de n.** their lives are shrouded in mystery; **una espesa n. rodeaba la designación del nuevo presidente** the naming of the new president was a murky business

niego *etc ver* **negar**

niegue *etc ver* **negar**

nieto, -a *nm,f* grandson, *f* granddaughter

nieva *etc ver* **nevar**

nieve *nf* (**a**) *(precipitación)* snow ►► ***n. carbónica*** dry ice; ***nieves perpetuas*** permanent snow; ***n. en polvo*** powder (snow) (**b**) **nieves** *(nevada)* snows, snowfall (**c**) *Fam (cocaína)* snow (**d**) *Carib, Méx (dulce)* sorbet

NIF [nif] *nm Esp* (*abrev de* **número de identificación fiscal**) = identification number for tax purposes, *Br* tax reference number, *US* TIN

Níger *n* Niger

Nigeria *n* Nigeria

nigeriano, -a 1 *adj* Nigerian
2 *nm,f* Nigerian

nigerino, -a 1 *adj* Nigerien
2 *nm,f* Nigerien

nigromancia *nf* necromancy

nigromante *nmf* necromancer

nigua *nf* (**a**) *(insecto)* jigger; EXPR *Chile, Perú, PRico Fam* **pegarse como n.** to stick like glue; EXPR *Ven Fam* **comer más que una n.** to eat like a horse (**b**) *Guat (cobarde)* coward

niguas *adv Méx Fam* no way; **n., tú no vuelves a usar mi carro** no way are you going to use my car again

nihilismo *nm* nihilism

nihilista 1 *adj* nihilistic
2 *nmf* nihilist

Nilo *nm* **el N.** the (river) Nile

nilón *nm* nylon

nimbo *nm* (**a**) *Meteo (nube)* nimbus (**b**) *(de astro, santo)* halo, nimbus

nimboestrato *nm Meteo (nube)* nimbostratus

nimiedad *nf* (**a**) *(cualidad)* insignificance, triviality (**b**) *(dicho, hecho)* trifle; **se enfadaron por una n.** they fell out over nothing

nimio, -a *adj* insignificant, trivial

ninfa *nf* (**a**) *Mitol* nymph (**b**) *(mariposa)* ***n. de los bosques*** white admiral

ninfómana 1 *adj f* nymphomaniac
2 *nf* nymphomaniac

ninfomanía *nf* nymphomania

ningún = **ninguno**

ningunear *vt (menospreciar)* to look down one's nose at; *(tratar con frialdad)* to cold-shoulder; **es arriesgado n. a los candidatos antes de conocerlos** it's a bit risky to write off candidates as no good before you've even seen them

ninguneo *nm* **me fastidian mucho su ambición y su n.** I find his ambition and his dismissive attitude towards people very annoying; **fuimos víctimas del n.** we were cold-shouldered

NINGUNO, -A

Ningún is used instead of **ninguno** before singular masculine nouns (e.g. **ningún hombre** no man).

1 *adj* (**a**) *(antes de sustantivo)* no; **no se dio ninguna respuesta** no answer was given; **no tengo ningún interés en hacerlo** I've no interest in doing it, I'm not at all interested in doing it; **no tengo ningún hijo/ninguna buena idea** I don't have any children/any good ideas; **no lo veo por ninguna parte** I can't see it anywhere; **no tiene ninguna gracia** it's not funny; **en ningún momento** at no time; **yo no soy ningún mendigo ¿sabe usted?** I'm not a beggar, you know; **¿tijeras? yo no veo ningunas tijeras** scissors? I can't see any scissors; **no tengo ningunas ganas de ir** I don't feel like going at all
(**b**) *(después de sustantivo) (enfático)* **no es molestia ninguna** it's no trouble
2 *pron (cosa)* none, not any; *(persona)* nobody, no one; **n. funciona** none of them works; **no hay n.** there aren't any, there are none; **n. lo sabrá** no one *o* nobody will know; **n. de** none of; **n. de ellos/nosotros** none of them/us; **n. de los dos** neither of them *o* of the two; **no me gusta n. de los dos** I don't like either of them

---

ninja *nm* ninja

niña *nf* (**a**) *(del ojo)* pupil; EXPR **ser la n. de los ojos de alguien** to be the apple of sb's eye (**b**) *ver también* **niño**

niñada = **niñería**

niñato, -a *nm,f Fam Pey* (**a**) *(arrogante)* spoiled brat (**b**) *(inexperto)* amateur, novice

niñera *nf* nanny

niñería, niñada *nf* (**a**) *(cualidad)* childishness (**b**) *(tontería)* silly *o* childish thing

niñez *nf (infancia)* childhood

niño, -a 1 *adj* (**a**) *(pequeño, joven)* young (**b**) *Pey (infantil, inmaduro)* childish
2 *nm,f* (**a**) *(crío) (varón)* child, boy; *(hembra)* child, girl; *(bebé)* baby; **los niños** the children; **¿es n. o niña?** is it a boy or a girl?; **de n. era muy gordo** he was very fat as a child; **desde n.** from childhood; EXPR **estar como un n. con zapatos nuevos** to be as pleased as punch; EXPR *Fam* **ni qué n. muerto: es culpa de la crisis – ¡qué crisis ni qué n. muerto!** it's the fault of the recession – don't give me that recession stuff!; EXPR **ser el n. bonito de alguien** to be sb's pet *o* blue-eyed boy ▸▸ *Pey* ***n. bien*** rich kid; ***niños envueltos*** *(plato)* beef olives; ***el n. Jesús*** the Baby Jesus; ***n. mimado*** spoilt child; ***n. de pecho*** tiny baby; ***n. probeta*** test-tube baby; ***n. prodigio*** child prodigy; ***n. de teta*** tiny baby
(**b**) *(hijo)* son; *(hija)* daughter; **tuvo dos niñas con su primera mujer** he had two daughters by his first wife
(**c**) *(joven)* young boy, *f* young girl ▸▸ *RP* ***niños cantores*** = children who sing the results of the state lottery
(**d**) *Meteo* **el Niño** el Niño; **la Niña** la Niña
(**e**) *Andes, CAm, Carib, Méx (amo)* master, *f* mistress; **hay que planchar la ropa de la niña Ana** Miss Anna's clothes need ironing
(**f**) *Col* ***niña del servicio*** maid, servant girl
(**g**) *Cuba (como apelativo)* dear; **¡n.!, ¿por dónde se va a la estación de tren?** which way is it to the railway station, dear?

niobio *nm Quím* niobium

niple *nm* (**a**) *Carib, CSur (unión)* nipple (**b**) *Carib (explosivo)* pipe bomb

nipón, -ona 1 *adj* Japanese
2 *nm,f* Japanese

níquel *nm* (**a**) *(metal)* nickel (**b**) *Carib (moneda)* coin; **níqueles** money

niquelado, -a 1 *adj (con níquel)* nickel-plated
2 *nm* nickel plating

niquelar *vt* to nickel-plate

niqui *nm Esp* polo shirt

nirvana *nm* nirvana

níscalo *nm* saffron milk cap

níspero *nm* (**a**) *(árbol)* medlar tree (**b**) *(fruta)* medlar

NIT [nit] *nm Col* (*abrev de* **número de identificación tributaria**) = identification number for tax purposes, *Br* tax reference number, *US* TIN

nitidez *nf (claridad)* clarity; *(de imagen, color)* sharpness

nítido, -a *adj (claro)* clear; *(imagen, color)* sharp

nitrato *nm* nitrate ▸▸ ***n. de Chile*** sodium nitrate; ***n. de plata*** silver nitrate

nítrico, -a *adj* nitric

nitrito *nm* nitrite

nitro *nm* nitre, potassium nitrate

nitrobenceno *nm* nitrobenzene

nitrocelulosa *nf* nitrocellulose

nitrogenado, -a *adj* nitrogenous

nitrógeno *nm* nitrogen

nitroglicerina *nf* nitroglycerine

nitroso, -a *adj* nitrous

nitruro *nm* nitride

nivel *nm* (**a**) *(altura)* level, height; **al n. de** level with; **al n. del mar** at sea level; **la capital está a 250 metros sobre el n. del mar** the capital is 250 metres above sea level
(**b**) *(piso, capa)* level ▸▸ *Geol* ***n. freático*** groundwater level *o* table
(**c**) *(grado)* level, standard; **a n. europeo** at a European level; **son los líderes a n. mundial** they are the world leaders; **una campaña realizada a n. mundial** a worldwide campaign; **un problema que hay que abordar a n. mundial** a problem that has to be tackled internationally *o* globally; **tiene un buen n. de inglés** she speaks good English; **en esa universidad tienen un n. altísimo** the standard at that university is very high; **una reunión al más alto n.** a meeting at the highest level, a top-level meeting; **al mismo n. (que)** on a level *o* par (with) ▸▸ *Informát* ***n. de acceso*** access level; ***n. de colesterol*** cholesterol level; *Informát* ***niveles de gris*** grey(scale) levels; ***n. mental*** level of intelligence; ***n. de vida*** standard of living
(**d**) *(instrumento)* **n. (de burbuja)** spirit level
(**e**) **a n. de** *(considerado incorrecto)* as regards, as for; **a n. de salarios** as regards *o* as for salaries; **a n. personal estoy contento** on a personal level I'm happy

nivelación *nf* (**a**) *(de superficie)* levelling (**b**) *(de diferencias)* evening out; **están pidiendo la n. de salarios con el resto del sector** they are calling for their salaries to be brought into line with the rest of the sector

nivelador, -ora *adj* levelling

niveladora *nf* bulldozer

nivelar *vt* (**a**) *(superficie)* to level (**b**) *(objetos)* **nivela las dos mesas** push the two tables together so they're flush (**c**) *(diferencias)* to even out; *(salarios)* to bring into line with each other (**d**) *(presupuesto)* to balance

níveo, -a *adj Literario* snow-white

nixtamal *nm CAm, Méx* tortilla dough

Niza *n* Nice

NO *(abrev de* **Noroeste**) NW

NO *(pl* **noes**) 1 *adv* (**a**) *(para construir frases negativas)* not; **no sé** I don't know; **no es fácil** it's not easy, it isn't easy; **no tiene dinero** he has no money, he hasn't got any money; **no veo nada** I can't see anything; **no vino nadie** nobody came; **no me lo dijiste nunca** you never told me; **todavía no** not yet; **no pasar** *(en letrero)* no entry; **no a la central nuclear** *(en letrero)* no to the nuclear power station; EXPR *Am* **nunca tuve ni un sí ni un no con él** I never had a cross word with him

(**b**) *(en respuestas)* no; **¿vienes? – no** are you coming? – no; **¿has oído las noticias? – no** have you heard the news? – no *o* no, I haven't; **¿aprobó? – no** did she pass? – no *o* no, she didn't; **¿comen juntos? – no siempre** do they go for lunch together? – not always; **¿ganaremos? – no (lo) creo** will we win? – I don't think so

(**c**) *(para sustituir a frases negativas)* **pídeme lo que quieras, pero eso no** ask me for anything, but not that; **¿vendrá tu familia a verte? – preferiría que no** will your family come to visit you? – I'd rather they didn't; **¿tú vas a ir? yo creo que no** are you going? I don't think I will; **me parece que no** I don't think so; **¡(he dicho) que no!** I said no!

(**d**) *(con sustantivos)* non-; **no fumadores** non-smokers; **la zona de no fumadores** the no-smoking area

(**e**) *(con adjetivos)* **un embarazo no deseado** an unwanted pregnancy; **fuentes de información no identificadas** unidentified information sources; **los países no alineados** non-aligned countries

(**f**) *(indica duda, extrañeza)* **¿no irás a venir?** you're not coming, are you?; **¿no te sobrará algo de dinero?** you wouldn't have any spare cash, would you?; **es un transexual – ¡no!** he's a transsexual – no!; *Méx* **¿no que no querías sopa?** you didn't want any soup, did you?

(**g**) *(muletilla para pedir confirmación)* **estamos de acuerdo, ¿no?** we're agreed then, are we?; **es español, ¿no?** he's Spanish, isn't he?; **usted vive en Lima, ¿no?** you live in Lima, don't you?; **mejor no le echamos sal, ¿no?** we'd better not put any salt in it, don't you think?

(**h**) *(redundante sin significado negativo)* **es mejor que sobre que no que falte** it's better to have too much than too little; **no me voy hasta que no me lo digas** I won't go until you tell me to; **me da miedo no se vaya a romper** I'm scared it might get broken

(**i**) *(en frases)* **a no ser que llueva** unless it rains; **¡a que no lo haces!** I bet you don't do it!; **¡cómo no!** of course!; **no ya... sino que...** not only... but (also)...; *Fam* **¡no es listo/guapo ni nada!** is he clever/good-looking or what?; **pues no** certainly not

2 *nm* no; **nos dio un no por respuesta** his answer was no

Nobel *nm* (**a**) *(premio)* Nobel Prize; **el N. de literatura/medicina** the Nobel Prize for literature/medicine (**b**) *(galardonado)* Nobel Prize winner, Nobel laureate; **el N. de literatura/medicina** the winner of the Nobel Prize for literature/medicine

nobelio *nm* nobelium

nobiliario, -a *adj* noble

noble 1 *adj* (**a**) *(de la nobleza)* noble (**b**) *(sentimiento, causa)* noble; **fue un gesto muy n.** it was a very noble gesture (**c**) *(animal)* noble (**d**) *(metal)* noble; *(madera)* fine (**e**) *(gas)* noble

2 *nmf* noble; **los nobles** the nobility

nobleza *nf* nobility; EXPR **n. obliga** noblesse oblige

nobuk *nm* nubuck

nocaut *(pl* **nocauts**) *Am* 1 *adj* **quedé n.** I was knocked unconscious

2 *nm* knockout

NOCHE *nf* (**a**) *(en oposición al día)* night; *(atardecer)* evening; **una n. cerrada** a dark night; **una n. de perros** a foul night; **el turno de n.** the night shift; **un lugar clásico de la n. neoyorquina** a classic New York nightspot; **a las diez de la n.** at ten o'clock at night; **a estas horas de la n.** at this time of night; **ayer (por la) n.** last night; **bien entrada la n.** late at night; **de n.** at night; **trabaja de n.** she works nights; **esta n.** tonight; **de n.,** *Esp* **por la n.,** *Am* **en la n.,** *Arg* **a la n.** at night; **mañana/el sábado** *Esp* **por la n.** *o Am* **en la n.** *o Arg* **a la n.** tomorrow/Saturday night; **salir de n.** *o Esp* **por la n.** *o Am* **en la n.** *o Arg* **a la n.** to go out in the evening; **toda la n.** all night; **vemos la tele todas las noches** we watch the TV every night; **mi manzanilla de todas las noches** my nightly cup of camomile tea; **buenas noches** *(saludo)* good evening; *(despedida)* good night; **de la n. a la mañana** overnight; **hicimos n. en Puebla** we spent the night in Puebla; **n. y día** *(constantemente)* day and night; EXPR **pasar la n. en claro** *o* **vela** *(sin poder dormir)* to have a sleepless night; *(trabajando, cuidando de alguien)* to be up all night; EXPR **ser (como)** *o* **parecerse como la n. y el día** to be as different as night and day; EXPR *Esp Fam* **pasar una n. toledana** to have a sleepless night, not to sleep a wink ►► ***n. de bodas*** wedding night; ***la n. del estreno*** the first *o* opening night; ***n. temática*** *(en televisión)* themed evening

(**b**) *(oscuridad)* **al caer** *o* **cuando cae la n.** at nightfall; **antes de que caiga la n.** before nightfall, before it gets dark; **hacerse de n.** to get dark; **a las cinco ya es de n.** it's already dark by five o'clock; *Literario* **en la n. de los tiempos** in the mists of time

Nochebuena *nf* Christmas Eve

nochecita *nf CSur* dusk; **saldremos de n.** we'll go out at dusk *o* early in the evening

nochero *nm* (**a**) *CSur (vigilante)* night watchman (**b**) *Col (mesilla de noche)* bedside table

Nochevieja *nf* New Year's Eve

noción *nf* (**a**) *(concepto)* notion; **tener n. (de)** to have an idea (of); **perdió la n. del tiempo** he lost all track of time (**b**) **nociones** *(conocimiento básico)* a basic knowledge; **se busca guía con nociones de japonés** we are looking for a guide with a basic knowledge of Japanese; **tener nociones de francés** to have a smattering of French

nocividad *nf (cualidad de dañino)* harmfulness; *(de gas)* noxiousness

nocivo, -a *adj (dañino)* harmful; *(gas)* noxious; **el tabaco es n. para la salud** smoking damages your health; **su abuelo ha ejercido una influencia nociva en él** his grandfather has been a bad influence on him

noctámbulo, -a 1 *adj* **es muy n.** he's a real night owl; **animal n.** nocturnal animal

2 *nm,f (persona)* night owl

nóctulo *nm* noctule bat

nocturnidad *nf Der* **con n.** under cover of darkness

nocturno, -a 1 *adj* (**a**) *(de la noche)* night; *(de la tarde)* evening; **tren/vuelo n.** night train/flight (**b**) *(animales, plantas)* nocturnal

2 *nm* (**a**) *Mús* nocturne (**b**) *Educ* = classes held in the evening

nodo *nm* (**a**) *Astron* node (**b**) *Fís* node (**c**) *Informát* node

nodriza *nf* (**a**) *(mujer)* wet nurse (**b**) **buque/avión n.** refuelling ship/plane

nódulo *nm* nodule

Noé *n pr* Noah

nogal *nm,* **noguera** *nf* walnut (tree)

nogalina *nf* walnut stain

noguera = **nogal**

nogueral *nm* walnut grove

nómada, *CSur* **nómade** 1 *adj* nomadic

2 *nmf* nomad

nomadismo *nm* nomadism

nomás *adv* (**a**) *Am (solamente)* just; **estaba aquí n. descansando** I was just having a rest here; **hasta allí n.** that far and no further; **n. lo hizo por molestar** she only did it to be difficult

(**b**) *Am (mismo)* **así n.** just like that; **déjelo ahí n.** just leave it there

(**c**) *Am (como muletilla)* **¡pase n.!** come right in!; **¿me presta su teléfono? – llame n.** can I borrow your phone? – be my guest; **¿hay algo de comer? – sírvase n.** is there anything to eat? – go ahead and help yourself

(**d**) *Méx* **n. que** *(tan pronto como)* as soon as; **n. que acabe te llamaré** I'll call you as soon as I finish

nombradía *nf* renown, fame

nombrado, -a *adj* (**a**) *(citado)* mentioned (**b**) *(famoso)* famous, well-known

nombramiento *nm* appointment

nombrar *vt* (**a**) *(citar)* to mention (**b**) *(designar)* to appoint

NOMBRE *nm* (**a**) *(apelativo)* name; **un vecino, de quien no diré el n., avisó a la policía** a neighbour, who shall remain nameless, told the police; **a n. de** *(carta, sobre, paquete)* addressed to; *(cheque)* made out to; *(cuenta bancaria)* in the name of; *(propiedades)* belonging to; **el apartamento está a su n.** the *Br* flat *o US* apartment is in his name; **quiero abrir una cuenta a n. de mi hijo** I'd like to open an account for my son; **se le conoce con el n. de laparoscopia** it is known as a laparoscopy; **de n. Juan** called Juan; **en n. de** *(representando a)* on behalf of; **en (el) n. de Dios/de la democracia** in the name of God/democracy; **en el n. del Padre...** *(al rezar)* in the name of the Father...; **llamar a alguien por el n.** to call sb by his/her first name; **lleva** *o* **tiene por n....** it is known as..., it is called...; **¿qué n. le vas a poner al perro?** what are you going to call the dog?; **le pusieron el n. de su abuelo** they named him *Br* after *o US* for his grandfather; **santificado sea tu n.** *(en padrenuestro)* hallowed be thy name; *Hum* **esto de jardín sólo tiene el n.** you call this a garden?; **como su propio n. indica...** as its name indicates *o* suggests...; EXPR **llamar a las cosas por su n.** to call a spade a spade; EXPR **no tener n.** *(ser indignante)* to be outrageous ►► ***n. y apellidos*** full name; ***n. artístico*** stage name; *Am* ***n. de batalla*** nom de guerre; ***n. científico*** *(de planta, animal)* scientific name; ***n. comercial*** trade name; ***n. completo*** full name; ***n. compuesto*** = two-part Christian name; ***n. común*** *(de planta, animal)* common name; *Informát* ***n. de dominio*** domain name; ***n. de guerra*** nom de guerre; ***n. de lugar*** place name; ***n. de pila*** first *o* Christian name; ***n. de soltera*** maiden name; *Informát* ***n. de usuario*** user name

(**b**) *(fama)* reputation; **hacerse un n. (como)** to make a name for oneself (as); **manchar el buen n. de alguien/algo** to tarnish sb's/sth's good name; **tener buen/mal n.** to have a good/bad name; **tener mucho n.** to be renowned *o* famous

(**c**) *Gram* noun ►► ***n. abstracto*** abstract noun; ***n. colectivo*** collective noun; ***n. común*** common noun; ***n. propio*** proper noun

---

nombrete *nm Urug* nickname; **le pusieron el n. de "el Adusto"** he was nicknamed "el Adusto"

nomenclatura *nf* nomenclature

nomeolvides *nm inv* (**a**) *(flor)* forget-me-not (**b**) *(pulsera)* identity bracelet

nómina *nf* (**a**) *(lista de empleados)* payroll; **estar en n.** to be on the payroll *o* staff (**b**) *(pago)* wage packet, wages (**c**) *(hoja de salario)* pay slip (**d**) *(lista de nombres)* list

nominación *nf* nomination

nominado, -a *adj* nominated

nominal 1 *adj* nominal

2 *nm Econ* face *o* nominal value

nominalmente *adv* nominally

nominar *vt* to nominate

nominativo, -a 1 *adj* **cheque n.** = cheque made out to a specific person; **un cheque n. a favor de Carla Gimeno** a cheque made out to Carla Gimeno

2 *nm Gram* nominative

nomo *nm* gnome

non 1 *adj* odd, uneven

2 *nm* odd number

nonada *nf* trifle

nonagenario, -a 1 *adj* ninety-year old

2 *nm,f* person in his/her nineties

nonagésimo, -a *núm* ninetieth; *ver también* **octavo**

nonato, -a 1 *adj* (**a**) *(bebé)* born by Caesarian section (**b**) *(inexistente)* nonexistent

2 *nm CSur* (**a**) *(carne)* lamb *(from unborn animal)* (**b**) *(cuero)* lambskin *(from unborn animal)*

nones *adv Fam* no way; **dijo que n., que no me dejaba la moto** he said there was no way he was going to lend me the motorbike

nono[1], **-a** *núm Formal* ninth; *ver también* **octavo**

nono[2], **-a** *nm,f RP, Ven Fam* grandpa, *f* grandma

non plus ultra *nm* **ser el n.** to be the best ever; **ese disco es el n. de la música caribeña** that's the best ever Caribbean music record

nopal *nm* prickly pear

noquear *vt* (**a**) *(en boxeo)* to knock out (**b**) *Am (derrotar)* to thrash

noray *(pl* **norays**) *nm Náut* bollard

norcoreano, -a 1 *adj* North Korean

2 *nm,f* North Korean

nordeste = **noreste**

nórdico, -a 1 *adj* (**a**) *(del norte)* northern, northerly (**b**) *(escandinavo)* Nordic

2 *nm,f* Nordic person

nordista *Hist* 1 *adj* Yankee *(in US Civil War)*

2 *nmf* Yankee *(in US Civil War)*

noreste, nordeste 1 *adj (posición, parte)* northeast, northeastern; *(dirección, viento)* northeasterly

2 *nm* north-east

noria *nf* (**a**) *(para agua)* water wheel (**b**) *Esp (de feria) Br* big wheel, *US* Ferris wheel

norirlandés, -esa 1 *adj* Northern Irish

2 *nm,f* person from Northern Ireland; **los norirlandeses** the people of Northern Ireland

norma *nf* (**a**) *(patrón, modelo)* standard; *(regla)* rule; **las normas de circulación** *o* **de tráfico** the traffic regulations, *Br* the Highway Code; **este producto no cumple la n. europea** this product does not meet European standards; **normas de conducta** *(principios)* standards (of behaviour); *(pautas)* patterns of behaviour; **la n. es que llueva al final de la tarde** it usually *o* normally rains towards the end of the afternoon; **es la n. hacerlo así** it's usual to do it this way; **por n. (general)** as a rule; **tener por n. hacer algo** to make it a rule to do sth

(**b**) *Ling* norm

normal 1 *adj* (**a**) *(natural, regular)* normal; **lleva una vida n.** she leads a fairly normal *o* ordinary life; **el paciente tiene una temperatura/un pulso n.** the patient's temperature/pulse is normal; **cuando se lo dije se enfadó mucho – ¡n.!** he was really cross when I told him – that's hardly surprising!; **este hermano tuyo no es n.** there must be something wrong with that brother of yours; **es n. que estés cansado** it's hardly surprising that you're tired; **no es n. que llore por una tontería así** it's not normal for him to cry over a silly thing like that; **n. y corriente** ordinary; **contiene todo lo que un usuario n. y corriente necesita** it contains everything the average user needs; **es una persona n. y corriente** he's a perfectly ordinary person

(**b**) *(gasolina) Br* three-star, *US* regular

(**c**) *Mat* perpendicular

2 *nf (gasolina) Br* three-star petrol, *US* regular gasoline

3 *adv Fam* normally; **me cuesta mucho caminar n.** I find it really hard to walk normally

normalidad *nf* (**a**) *(cualidad)* normality; **volver a la n.** to return to normal; **la jornada electoral transcurrió con n.** election day passed off without incident (**b**) *Quím* normality

normalista *nmf Bol, Méx* (**a**) *(estudiante)* student teacher (**b**) *(profesor)* teaching graduate

normalización *nf* (**a**) *(vuelta a la normalidad)* return to normal, normalization (**b**) *(regularización)* standardization ►► *Esp* ***n. lingüística*** = regulation by legal means of the use of the different languages spoken in a multilingual region

normalizar [14] 1 *vt* (**a**) *(volver normal)* to return to normal, to normalize (**b**) *(estandarizar)* to standardize

2 **normalizarse** *vpr* to return to normal

normalmente *adv* usually, normally; **n. se reúnen a primera hora de la mañana** they usually *o* normally meet first thing in the morning

Normandía *n* Normandy

normando, -a 1 *adj* (**a**) *(de Normandía)* of/from Normandy *(France)*; **el paisaje n.** the Normandy countryside (**b**) *Hist (nórdico)* Norse; *(de Normandía)* Norman

2 *nm,f* (**a**) *(habitante de Normandía)* person from Normandy *(France)* (**b**) *Hist (nórdico)* Norseman, *f* Norsewoman; *(de Normandía)* Norman

normar *vt Am* (**a**) *(regir)* to govern (**b**) *(dotar de norma)* to regulate

normativa *nf* regulations; **según la n. vigente** under current rules *o* regulations

normativo, -a *adj* normative

nornordeste *nm* north-northeast

nornoroeste *nm* north-northwest

noroeste 1 *adj (posición, parte)* northwest, northwestern; *(dirección, viento)* northwesterly

2 *nm* northwest

norte 1 *adj inv (posición, parte)* north, northern; **viento n.** north wind; **la cara n. de la montaña** the north face of the mountain; **la costa n.** the north coast; **habrá tiempo soleado en la mitad n. del país** it will be sunny in the northern half of the country; **partieron con rumbo n.** they set off northwards; **un frente frío que se desplaza en dirección n.** a cold front moving north *o* northwards

2 *nm* (**a**) *(zona)* north; **está al n. de Santiago** it's (to the) north of Santiago; **la fachada da al n.** the front of the building faces north; **viento del n.** north wind; **habrá lluvias en el n. (del país)** there will be rain in the north (of the country); **ir hacia el n.** to go north(wards); **el N. de África** North Africa ►► ***n. geográfico*** true north; ***el n. magnético*** magnetic north

(**b**) *Pol* **el N.** *(mundo desarrollado)* the North

(**c**) *Am* **el N.** *(Estados Unidos)* the United States

(**d**) *(punto cardinal)* north

(**e**) *(viento)* north wind

(**f**) *(objetivo)* goal, objective; EXPR **perder el n.** to lose one's bearings *o* way

(**g**) *PRico (llovizna)* drizzle

norteafricano, -a 1 *adj* North African
2 *nm,f* North African

Norteamérica *n* (**a**) *(América del Norte)* North America (**b**) *(Estados Unidos)* the United States, America

norteamericano, -a 1 *adj* (**a**) *(de América del Norte)* North American (**b**) *(de Estados Unidos)* American
2 *nm,f* (**a**) *(de América del Norte)* North American (**b**) *(de Estados Unidos)* American

norteño, -a 1 *adj* northern
2 *nm,f* northerner

nortino, -a *Andes* 1 *adj* northern
2 *nm,f* northener

Noruega *n* Norway

noruego, -a 1 *adj* Norwegian
2 *nm,f (persona)* Norwegian
3 *nm (lengua)* Norwegian

norvietnamita 1 *adj* North Vietnamese
2 *nmf* North Vietnamese

NOS *pron personal* (**a**) *(complemento directo)* us; **le gustaría vernos** she'd like to see us; **n. atracaron en plena calle** we were attacked in the middle of the street; **n. aprobaron a todos** we all passed, they passed us all

(**b**) *(complemento indirecto)* (to) us; **n. lo dio** he gave it to us, he gave us it; **n. tiene miedo** he's afraid of us; **n. lo ha comprado** *(nosotros se lo vendimos)* she bought it from *o* off us; *(es para nosotros)* she bought it for us; **n. extrajeron sangre** they took some of our blood; **n. han quitado una maleta** they've stolen one of our suitcases; **n. hicieron quitarnos la ropa** they made us take off our clothes; **n. pegaron un empujón** someone pushed us, we were pushed; **se n. olvidó** we forgot; **n. será de gran ayuda** it will be a great help to us

(**c**) *(reflexivo)* ourselves; **n. servimos un whisky** we poured ourselves a whisky; **n. vestimos** we get dressed; **n. hacíamos llamar "los cinco magníficos"** we called ourselves "the magnificent five"; **n. pusimos los abrigos y salimos** we put our coats on and left; **n. acostamos en la cama** we lay down on the bed

(**d**) *(recíproco)* each other; **n. enamoramos** we fell in love (with each other); **n. concedimos una segunda oportunidad** we gave ourselves a second chance

(**e**) *(con valor intensivo o expresivo)* **n. tememos lo peor** we fear the worst; **n. lo comimos todo** we ate the whole lot; **no te n. eches a llorar ahora** don't start crying on us now; *Fam* **tú descuida, que nosotros sabemos lo que n. hacemos** don't you worry, we know what we're doing here

(**f**) *(para formar verbos pronominales)* **n. pusimos cómodos** we made ourselves comfortable

(**g**) *(plural mayestático)* we; **n. estamos de acuerdo** we agree

nosocomio *nm Am* hospital

NOSOTROS, -AS *pron personal* (**a**) *(sujeto)* we; **n. somos los mejores** we're the best; **¿quién va primero? – n.** who's first? – we are; **n. los americanos** we Americans; **ellos están invitados, n. no** they're invited, but we're not *o* but not us; **algunos de n./todos n. pensamos que deberías ir** some of us/all of us think you should go; **n. mismos lo organizamos todo** we organized it all ourselves; **he aprobado – n. también** I passed – so did we

(**b**) *(predicado)* **somos n.** it's us; **sus hermanos somos n.** we are her brothers

(**c**) *(complemento con preposición o conjunción)* us; **juegan mejor que n.** they play better than we do *o* than us; **trabaja tanto como n.** she works as hard as we do *o* as us; **excepto/según n.** apart from/according to us; **nos lo dijo a nosotras** she said it to us; **vente a comer con n.** come and eat with us; **de n.** *(nuestro)* ours; **todo esto es de n.** all this is ours; **lo arreglaremos entre n.** we'll sort it out among ourselves; **entre n.** *(en confidencia)* between you and me, just between the two of us; **por n. no hay problema** there's no problem as far as we're concerned

> Because Spanish verbs are inflected, subject pronouns such as **nosotros** are largely redundant. In fact, they are normally omitted, with no loss in clarity about who is being referred to:
> **vamos a la playa mañana**
> *we're going to the beach tomorrow*
> The personal subject pronouns are used in cases where an explicit contrast is needed:
> **nosotros tendremos que hacer la prueba, pero ellos no**
> *we'll have to do the test, but they won't*

nostalgia *nf (del pasado)* nostalgia; *(de país, amigos)* homesickness; **tengo n. de mi infancia** I miss my childhood days; **siente n. por su país** he's homesick for his country

nostálgico, -a 1 *adj (del pasado)* nostalgic; *(de país, amigos)* homesick
2 *nm,f* nostalgic person; **es un n.** he's very nostalgic

nosticismo *nm* gnosticism

nóstico, -a 1 *adj* gnostic
2 *nm,f* gnostic

nota[1] *nf* (**a**) *(apunte)* note; **déjale una n. encima de la mesa** leave her a note on the table; **tomar n. de algo** *(apuntar)* to note sth down; *(fijarse)* to take note of sth; **tomamos n. de sus comentarios** we note your comments; EXPR **tomar buena n. de algo** to take careful note of sth

(**b**) *(acotación)* note ►► ***n. aclaratoria*** explanatory note; ***n. bene*** nota bene, N.B.; ***n. al margen*** marginal note; ***n. a pie de página*** footnote

(**c**) *(noticia breve)* ***n. necrológica*** obituary; ***n. de prensa*** press release; *Méx* ***n. roja*** police reports (section); ***notas de sociedad*** society column

(**d**) *(cuenta)* bill; *(en restaurante)* *Br* bill, *US* check ►► *Méx* ***n. de consumo*** expenses claim; ***n. de gastos*** expenses claim; *Méx* ***n. de remisión*** delivery note

(**e**) *(calificación)* *Br* mark, *US* grade; **mañana nos dan las notas** we get our marks *o US* grades tomorrow; **sacar** *o* **tener buenas notas** to get good marks; EXPR *Esp Fam* **ir para n.** to go for top marks ►► ***n. de corte*** = minimum marks for entry into university; ***n. media*** average mark

(**f**) *(toque, rasgo)* touch; **una n. de distinción/de color** a touch of elegance/colour

(**g**) *(reputación)* **de mala n.** of ill repute

(**h**) *(musical)* note ►► ***n. discordante*** discordant note; **la n. discordante la puso el discurso agresivo del presidente ruso** the Russian president's aggressive speech was out of key with the tone of the occasion; ***n. dominante*** dominant note; **la tensión fue la n. dominante de la reunión** an atmosphere of tension predominated at the meeting; **la n. dominante de su estilo es la ironía** the predominant feature of his style is irony; ***n. falsa*** false note; ***n. tónica*** keynote

(**i**) EXPR *Fam* **dar la n.: allá donde vamos, siempre da la n.** she always has to draw attention to herself wherever we go; **con estos pantalones das la n.** nobody could miss you in those trousers; *Fam* **forzar la n.,** *Ven* **pasarse de n.** to go too far

nota[2] *nm Esp Fam* (**a**) *(individuo)* guy, *Br* bloke (**b**) *Pey (que llama la atención)* poser

notabilidad *nf* notability

notable 1 *adj* remarkable, outstanding; **hay una n. diferencia entre las dos propuestas** there's a significant *o* clear difference between the two proposals; **es un violinista n.** he's an outstanding violinist
2 *nm* (**a**) *(nota)* = mark between 7 and 8.9 out of 10, ≃ (pass with) credit, ≃ B (**b**) *(persona)* dignitary

notablemente *adv (visiblemente)* clearly, evidently; *(notoriamente)* considerably, markedly

notación *nf* notation

notar 1 *vt (advertir)* to notice; *(sentir)* to feel; **noté que alguien me miraba** I sensed that someone was watching me; **¿notas una corriente de aire?** can you feel a draught?; **noto frío en los pies** my feet feel cold; **te noto cansado** you look tired; **lo noto raro** he's acting strangely; **la noté muy cambiada** she'd changed a lot; **la crisis económica se está dejando n.** the recession is really making itself felt; **hacer n. algo** to point sth out; **nótese que el acusado estaba bebido** note *o* observe that the accused was drunk

2 **notarse** *vpr (advertirse)* to be apparent; *(sentirse)* to feel; **me noto agotado** I feel exhausted; **ya no se nota la herida** you can't see where the wound was any more; **se nota que le gusta** you can tell she likes it; **se nota a la legua que no se ha preparado el discurso** it's blindingly obvious that he hasn't prepared his speech; **se le nota en la cara que no ha dormido nada** you can tell from her face that she didn't get any sleep; **no has descansado, ¿verdad? – ¿se me nota?** you didn't sleep well, did you? – can you tell? *o* is it that obvious?; *Fam* **¡pues no se nota!** you could have fooled me!; **¡cómo se nota que no es tu casa!** do you always behave like this in other people's houses?

notaría *nf Esp, CAm, Carib, Méx* (**a**) *(profesión)* profession of notary (**b**) *(oficina)* notary's office

notariado *nm* (**a**) *(profesión)* profession of notary (**b**) *(colectividad)* notaries

notarial *adj* notarial

notario, -a *nm,f Esp, CAm, Carib, Méx* notary (public); **en sorteo celebrado ante n.** in a draw which took place in the presence of a notary

noticia *nf* (a) *(información, hecho)* news *(singular)*; **una n.** a piece of news; **tengo una buena/mala n.** I've got some good/bad news; **me enteré de la n. ayer** I heard the news yesterday; **su hijo le dio la n.** his son broke the news to him; **noticias de última hora** the latest news ►► *Fam* ***n. bomba*** bombshell; **in. bomba!: ¡nos van a subir el sueldo!** shock! horror! we're getting a pay rise!
(b) **las noticias** *(en televisión)* the news
(c) *(conocimiento)* **¿tienes noticias suyas?** have you heard from him?; **no tengo n. de que se haya cambiado la fecha** I haven't heard anything about the date being changed

> **Falso amigo**: El sustantivo inglés **notice** no es la traducción del español **noticia**. En inglés **notice** significa "aviso", "cartel" o "atención".

noticiario, *Am* **noticiero** *nm* (a) *Cine* newsreel (b) *Rad & TV* television news

notición *nm Fam* bombshell; **in.!: ¡nos van a subir el sueldo!** shock! horror! we're getting a pay rise!

noticioso *nm Andes, RP* television news

notificación *nf* notification

notificar [60] *vt* to notify, to inform

notoriedad *nf* (a) *(fama)* fame (b) *(evidencia)* obviousness

notorio, -a *adj* (a) *(conocido)* widely-known; **un n. pianista** a famous pianist (b) *(evidente)* obvious; **es notoria la antipatía que siente por ella** it's obvious he doesn't like her; **hay un malestar n. entre los empleados** there is obvious *o* manifest discontent among the staff

> **Falso amigo**: El adjetivo español **notorio** se traduce al inglés como **notorious** únicamente si las connotaciones de aquél son negativas, ya que en inglés **notorious** significa "famoso por algo negativo, infame".

nov. (*abrev de* **noviembre**) Nov

nova *nf Astron* nova

novatada *nf* (a) *(broma)* practical joke *(on newcomer)*; **las novatadas** *Br* ragging, *US* hazing; **gastar una n. a alguien** *Br* to rag sb, *US* to haze sb (b) *(error)* beginner's mistake; EXPR **pagar la n.** to learn the hard way; **pagué la n. de irme de vacaciones durante la estación de los huracanes** I learned the hard way that you shouldn't go on holiday during the hurricane season

novato, -a 1 *adj* inexperienced
2 *nm,f* novice, beginner

novecientos, -as *núm* nine hundred; *ver también* **treinta**

novedad *nf* (a) *(cosa nueva)* new thing; *(innovación)* innovation; **el nuevo sistema operativo incluye muchas novedades** the new operating system incorporates many new features; **es igual que el model anterior con la n. de que utiliza energía solar** it is the same as the previous model except that it now uses solar power
(b) **novedades** *(discos)* new releases; *(libros)* new publications; *(moda)* latest fashions; *(en página web)* what's new
(c) *(cualidad) (de nuevo)* newness; *(de novedoso)* novelty
(d) *(cambio)* change; **el enfermo evoluciona sin n.** there has been no change in the patient's condition; **desde que te fuiste ha habido muchas novedades en la oficina** there have been a lot of changes in the office since you left
(e) *(noticia)* news *(singular)*; **sin n.** *(sin contratiempo)* without incident; *Mil* all quiet; EXPR *Hum* **sin n. en el frente** there's nothing to report

novedoso, -a *adj* novel, new; **una iniciativa novedosa para combatir el desempleo** a novel initiative to combat unemployment; **lo n. del producto es que no funciona con electricidad** the original thing about the product is that it doesn't use electricity

novel *adj* **un escritor n.** a new writer; **un futbolista n.** an inexperienced player

novela 1 *nf* novel; **la n. contemporánea** the contemporary novel ►► ***n. de caballería(s)*** tale of chivalry; ***n. por entregas*** serial; ***n. de intriga*** mystery story; ***n. negra*** crime novel; ***n. policíaca*** detective story; ***n. rosa*** romance, romantic novel
2 **de novela** *loc adj RP Fam (muy bueno)* amazing; **se compró una estancia de n.** he bought this amazing ranch
3 **de novela** *loc adv RP Fam (muy bien)* fantastically; **cocina de n.** he's a fantastic *o* an amazing cook

novelar *vt* to fictionalize, to make into a novel

novelería *nf* (a) *(ficciones)* fantasies (b) *Am* **novelerías** *(cosas novedosas)* novelties

novelero, -a 1 *adj* (a) *(fantasioso)* over-imaginative (b) *(aficionado a las novelas)* **es muy n.** he's a great reader of novels (c) *(aficionado a lo novedoso)* **es muy n.** he always has to have the latest thing
2 *nm,f* (a) *(fantasioso)* **es un n.** he has an overactive imagination, he tends to exaggerate (b) *(aficionado a las novelas)* **es un n.** he's a great reader of novels (c) *(aficionado a lo novedoso)* **es un n.** he always has to have the latest thing

novelesco, -a *adj* (a) *(de la novela)* fictional (b) *(fantástico)* fantastic, extraordinary

novelista *nmf* novelist

novelística *nf* (a) *(estudio)* study of the novel (b) *(literatura)* novels, fiction; **la n. hispanoamericana** Spanish American novels *o* fiction

novelístico, -a *adj* novelistic

novelón *nm (novela)* huge great novel

novena *nf Rel* novena

noveno, -a *núm* ninth; *ver también* **octavo**

noventa *núm* ninety; **los (años) n.** the nineties; *ver también* **treinta**

noventavo, -a *núm* ninetieth; *ver también* **octavo**

noventón, -ona *nm,f* nonagenarian

noviar *vi CSur, Méx Fam* **n. con alguien** to go out with sb, *US* to date sb; **están noviando** they're going out together, *US* they're dating; **novian hace tiempo** they've been going out together *o US* dating for a while

noviazgo *nm* engagement; **se casaron después de dos meses de n.** they marrried after a two-month engagement *o* after being engaged for two months

noviciado *nm* (a) *Rel* novitiate (b) *(aprendizaje)* apprenticeship

novicio, -a *nm,f* (a) *Rel* novice (b) *(aprendiz)* novice

noviembre *nm* November; *ver también* **septiembre**

noviero, -a *adj* **desde chiquito fue muy n.** he was never shy of the girls, even as a child

novillada *nf Taurom* = bullfight with young bulls

novillero, -a *nm,f Taurom* apprentice bullfighter

novillo, -a *nm,f* (a) *(animal)* young bull, *f* young cow (b) EXPR *Esp Fam* **hacer novillos** to play *Br* truant *o US* hookey

novilunio *nm* new moon

novio, -a *nm,f* (a) *(compañero)* boyfriend, *f* girlfriend; *(prometido)* fiancé, *f* fiancée (b) *(el día de la boda)* bridegroom, *f* bride; **los novios** *(antes de la boda)* the bride and groom; *(después de la boda)* the newly-weds; **¡vivan los novios!** to the bride and groom!

novísimo, -a *adj* brand-new, up-to-the-minute

novocaína® *nf* Novocaine®

npi *adv Esp Fam Euf* (*abrev de* **ni puta idea**) no idea

NS/NC (*abrev de* **no sabe, no contesta**) *(en encuesta)* don't know, no reply given

NT (*abrev de* **Nuevo Testamento**) NT

Ntra. Sra. (*abrev de* **Nuestra Señora**) Our Lady

nubarrón *nm* storm cloud

nube *nf* (a) *(de lluvia)* cloud; EXPR **como caído de las nubes** out of the blue; EXPR *Fam* **estar en las nubes** to have one's head in the clouds; EXPR *Fam* **poner algo/a alguien por las nubes** to praise sth/sb to the skies; EXPR *Fam* **estar por las nubes** *(caro)* to be terribly expensive ►► ***n. de tormenta*** thundercloud; ***n. de verano*** summer shower; **¿se enfadó mucho? – no, sólo fue una n. de verano** was she very angry? – no, it soon blew over
(b) *(de humo)* cloud ►► ***n. de polvo*** dust cloud
(c) *(de personas, moscas)* swarm; **una n. de periodistas rodeó al ministro** a swarm of reporters surrounded the minister
(d) *(en ojo)* film

núbil *adj Literario* nubile

nubilidad *nf Literario* nubility

nubio, -a 1 *adj* Nubian
2 *nm,f* Nubian

nublado, -a 1 *adj* (a) *(cielo)* cloudy, overcast; **está n.** it's cloudy *o* overcast (b) *(vista, entendimiento)* clouded
2 *nm (nube)* storm cloud

nublar 1 *vt* (a) *(cielo)* to cloud; *(sol)* to hide (b) *(vista, entendimiento)* to cloud
2 **nublarse** *vpr* (a) *(cielo)* to cloud over; **se está nublando** it's clouding over (b) *(vista)* to cloud over; *(entendimiento)* to become clouded

nublazón *nf Am* storm cloud

nubloso, -a *adj* cloudy

nubosidad *nf* **la n. aumentará por la tarde** the cloud will increase in the afternoon, it will become cloudier in the afternoon; **n. parcial** partial cloud cover; **n. total** total cloud cover; **n. variable** variable cloud cover

nuboso, -a *adj* cloudy

nuca *nf* nape, back of the neck; EXPR *RP Fam* **estar de la n.** to be off one's head

nuclear[1] **1** *adj* nuclear
2 *nf* nuclear power station

nuclear[2] *Am* **1** *vt* to bring together; **el foro nuclea a la intelectualidad del lugar** the forum brings together local intellectuals
2 nuclearse *vpr* to congregate; **en ese barrio se nuclean los artistas de la región** the region's artists are congregated in this part of town

nuclearización *nf* **(a)** *(con energía nuclear)* introduction of nuclear power **(b)** *(con armas nucleares)* acquisition of nuclear weapons

nuclearizar [14] *vt* **(a)** *(con energía nuclear)* to introduce nuclear power into **(b)** *(con armas nucleares)* to acquire nuclear weapons for

nucleico, -a *adj Bioquím* nucleic

núcleo *nm* **(a)** *(de la Tierra)* core
(b) *(centro)* nucleus ►► ***n. duro*** *(en economía, política)* hard core
(c) *(foco)* **un n. de pobreza** an area with an extremely high level of poverty, an area where poverty is concentrated; **forman el n. intelectual del partido** they are the party's brains
(d) *(grupo)* core; **un pequeño n. de rebeldes** a small core of rebels
(e) *(lugar habitado)* centre ►► ***n. de población*** population centre
(f) *Astron* nucleus ►► ***n. de la galaxia*** galaxy's core
(g) *Biol* nucleus ►► ***n. celular*** cell nucleus
(h) *Fís* nucleus ►► ***n. atómico*** atomic nucleus
(i) *Ling* nucleus

nucléolo *nm Biol* nucleolus, nucleole

nucleón *nm* nucleon

nudillo *nm* knuckle; **llamar con los nudillos** *(a la puerta)* to knock (on *o* at the door)

nudismo *nm* nudism

nudista 1 *adj* nudist
2 *nmf* nudist

nudo *nm* **(a)** *(lazo)* knot; **hacer un n.** to tie a knot; **se le hizo un n. en la garganta** she got a lump in her throat ►► ***n. corredizo*** slipknot; ***n. gordiano*** Gordian knot; ***n. marinero*** reef knot
(b) *(cruce)* junction; **un n. de autopistas** a motorway interchange ►► ***n. de comunicaciones*** communications centre
(c) *(en madera)* knot
(d) *(en planta)* node
(e) *(vínculo)* tie, bond
(f) *(punto principal)* crux, nub
(g) *(unidad de velocidad)* knot
(h) *Teatro* crisis point, climax

nudoso, -a *adj* **(a)** *(mano)* knotted, gnarled **(b)** *(tallo)* knotty, gnarled

nuera *nf* daughter-in-law

nuestro, -a 1 *adj posesivo* our; **n. coche** our car; **este libro es n.** this book is ours, this is our book; **un amigo n.** a friend of ours; **no es asunto n.** it's none of our business; **lo n. es el teatro** *(lo que nos va)* theatre is what we should be doing; *Fam Fig* **nos costó lo n.** *(mucho)* it wasn't easy for us
2 *pron posesivo* **el n.** ours; **el n. es rojo** ours is red; *Fam* **ésta es la nuestra** this is the chance we've been waiting for *o* our big chance; *Fam* **los nuestros** *(nuestra familia)* our folks; *(nuestro bando)* our lot, our side

nueva *nf* **(a)** *Literario* (piece of) news; **la buena n.** *(el evangelio)* the good news; *Fam* **¿te has enterado de la buena n.?** have you heard the good news?; EXPR *Esp* **me coge de nuevas** that's news to me **(b)** *ver también* **nuevo**

nuevamente *adv (de nuevo)* again, once more

nueve *núm* nine; EXPR *Col* **tomar las medias nueves** to have a mid-morning snack, *Br* to have elevenses; *ver también* **tres**

nuevo, -a 1 *adj* **(a)** *(reciente)* new; **tengo una casa nueva** I've got a new house; **es el n. director** he's the new manager ►► ***Nueva Caledonia*** New Caledonia; ***el n. continente*** *(América)* the New World; ***Nueva Delhi*** New Delhi; ***Nueva Guinea*** New Guinea; ***Nueva Inglaterra*** New England; ***Nueva Jersey*** New Jersey; ***N. México*** New Mexico; ***el N. Mundo*** the New World; ***la nueva ola*** the New Wave; ***el n. orden mundial*** the new world order; ***Nueva Orleans*** New Orleans; ***n. rico*** nouveau riche; ***n. sol*** *(moneda)* new sol; ***nuevas tecnologías*** new technology; ***el N. Testamento*** the New Testament; ***Nueva York*** New York; ***Nueva Zelanda*** New Zealand
(b) *(poco usado)* new; **este abrigo está n.** this coat is new; **un poco de betún y quedarán como nuevos** with a bit of polish they'll be as good as new; **después del baño me quedé como n.** I felt like a new person after my bath
(c) *(inédito)* new; **esto es n. para mí, no lo sabía** that's news to me, I didn't know
(d) *(sin experiencia)* new; **soy n. en esta clase** I'm new in this class; **es n. en la profesión** he's new to the profession
(e) *(hortaliza)* new, fresh; *(vino)* young
(f) *(repetido)* renewed, **de n.** again; **se han producido nuevos enfrentamientos** there have been renewed clashes
2 *nm,f* newcomer

nuevoleonés, -esa 1 *adj* of/from Nuevo León *(Mexico)*
2 *nm,f* person from Nuevo León *(Mexico)*

nuez *nf* **(a)** *(de nogal)* walnut ►► *Méx* ***n. de Castilla*** walnut; *Méx* ***n. encarcelada*** pecan; *Méx* ***n. de la India*** cashew nut; ***n. moscada*** nutmeg **(b)** *Anat* Adam's apple

nulidad *nf* **(a)** *(no validez)* nullity **(b)** *(ineptitud)* incompetence **(c)** *Fam (persona)* **ser una n.** to be useless; **es una n. para la física** he's useless *o* hopeless at physics

nulo, -a *adj* **(a)** *(sin validez)* null and void, invalid; **n. y sin valor** null and void **(b)** *Fam (inútil)* useless (**para** at) **(c)** *Fam (inexistente)* **mis conocimientos sobre la materia son nulos** I know absolutely zilch about the subject; **mi fe en ellos es nula** I have absolutely no faith in them

núm. (*abrev de* **número**) No, no

numantino, -a *adj* heroic

numbat (*pl* **numbats**) *nm* numbat, marsupial *o* banded anteater

numen *nm* **(a)** *(deidad)* numen **(b)** *Formal (inspiración)* inspiration, muse

numeración *nf* **(a)** *(acción)* numbering **(b)** *(sistema)* numerals, numbers ►► ***n. arábiga*** Arabic numerals; ***n. binaria*** binary numbers; ***n. decimal*** Arabic numerals; ***n. romana*** Roman numerals

numerador *nm Mat* numerator

numeral *adj* numeral

numerar 1 *vt* to number
2 numerarse *vpr (personas)* to number off

numerario, -a 1 *adj (profesor, catedrático)* tenured, permanent; *(miembro)* full
2 *nm (dinero)* cash
3 *nm,f Rel* = member of Opus Dei who lives in one of their institutions and is celibate

numéricamente *adv* numerically

numérico, -a *adj* numerical

numerito *nm* EXPR *Esp Fam* **montar el n.** to make *o* cause a scene

número *nm* **(a)** *(signo)* number; **mi n. de la suerte** my lucky number; **en números rojos** in the red; **hacer números** to reckon up; **ser el n. uno** to be number one; *(en lista de éxitos)* to top the charts; **fue el n. uno de su promoción** he was the best in his year; **el n. dos del partido republicano** the number two *o* second in command of the Republican Party; **sin n.** *(muchos)* countless, innumerable; **un sin n. de modelos diferentes** countless *o* innumerable different models ►► ***n. atómico*** atomic number; ***n. binario*** binary number; ***n. cardinal*** cardinal number; ***n. complejo*** complex number; ***n. complementario*** *(en lotería)* = complementary number, *Br* ≃ bonus ball; ***n. de cuenta*** account number; ***n. entero*** whole number, integer; *Fot* ***n. f*** f number; ***n. de fax*** fax number; ***n. fraccionario*** fraction; ***n. de identificación personal*** PIN (number); ***n. impar*** odd number; *Informát* ***n. IP*** IP number; ***n. irracional*** irrational number; ***n. de matrícula*** *(de vehículo) Br* registration number, *US* license number; *(de alumno)* matriculation number; ***n. natural*** natural number; ***n. ordinal*** ordinal number; ***n. par*** even number; ***n. primo*** prime number; ***n. quebrado*** fraction; ***n. racional*** rational number; ***n. redondo*** round number; ***n. de referencia*** reference number; *Informát* ***n. de registro*** registration number; ***n. romano*** Roman numeral; ***n. de serie*** serial number; ***n. de sucursal*** *(de banco)* sort code; ***n. de teléfono*** telephone number
(b) *(tamaño, talla)* size; **¿qué n. calzas?** what size shoe are you?, what size shoe do you take?
(c) *(de publicación)* issue, number ►► ***n. atrasado*** back number; ***n. extraordinario*** special edition *o* issue
(d) *(de lotería)* ticket
(e) *Gram* number
(f) *(de espectáculo)* turn, number; EXPR *Esp Fam* **montar el n.** to make *o* cause a scene
(g) *Esp (de policía)* officer
(h) *Rel* **Números** Numbers

In Spanish, thousands are marked using a full stop, rather than a comma:
3.234 euros *3,234 euros*
1.200.000 dólares *$1,200,000*
On the other hand, decimal fractions begin with a comma, rather than a full stop, as in English:
5,3 segundos *5.3 seconds*

numerología *nf* numerology

numeroso, -a *adj* (**a**) *(con muchos elementos)* numerous; **un grupo n.** a large group (**b**) **numerosos** *(muchos)* many, several; **sufrieron numerosas bajas** they suffered many *o* several casualties

numerus clausus *nm inv Educ* = restriction on number of students in university course

numismática *nf (estudio)* numismatics *(singular)*

numismático, -a 1 *adj* numismatic
2 *nm,f* numismatist

nunca *adv (en frases afirmativas)* never; *(en frases negativas)* ever; **no me cuentan n. nada** they never tell me anything; **casi n. viene** he almost never comes, he hardly ever comes; **¿n. la has visto?** have you never seen her?, haven't you ever seen her?; **como n.** like never before; **más que n.** more than ever; **n. jamás** *o* **más** never more *o* again; **in. vi nada parecido!** I never saw anything like it!; PROV **n. es tarde si la dicha es buena** better late than never

nunciatura *nf Rel* (**a**) *(cargo)* nunciature (**b**) *(edificio)* nuncio's residence

nuncio *nm Rel* nuncio ►► ***n. apostólico*** papal nuncio

nupcial *adj* wedding; **ceremonia n.** wedding *o* marriage ceremony; **lecho n.** marriage bed

nupcias *nfpl* wedding; **contraer n. con alguien** to marry sb; **nunca contrajo segundas nupcias** he never remarried; **contrajo segundas n. con Carolina, se casó en segundas n. con Carolina** he got married for the second time, to Carolina

nurse ['nurse] *nf* nurse, nanny

nursery [nurse'ri] *nf Urug* baby unit

nutria *nf* (**a**) *(animal)* otter ►► ***n. de mar*** sea otter (**b**) *(piel)* otter (skin)

nutrición *nf* nutrition

nutricional *adj* nutritional

nutricionista *nmf* nutritionist

nutrido, -a *adj* (**a**) *(alimentado)* nourished, fed; **bien n.** well-fed; **mal n.** undernourished (**b**) *(numeroso)* large; **un grupo n. de manifestantes** a large group of demonstrators; **una nutrida lista de peticiones** a long list of requests

nutriente *nm* nutrient

nutrir 1 *vt* (**a**) *(alimentar)* to nourish, to feed (**con** *o* **de** with) (**b**) *(fomentar)* to feed, to nurture (**c**) *(suministrar)* to supply (**de** with)
2 nutrirse *vpr* (**a**) *(alimentarse)* **nutrirse de** *o* **con** to feed on (**b**) *(utilizar)* **la programación televisiva se nutre de los ingresos publicitarios** TV programmes are financed by advertising revenue; **sus novelas se nutren de leyendas tradicionales** his novels draw on folk legends

nutritivo, -a *adj* nutritious

nylon ['nailon] (*pl* **nylons**) *nm* nylon

Ñ, ñ

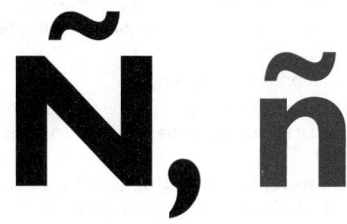

Ñ, ñ ['eɲe] *nf (letra)* Ñ, ñ, = 15th letter of the Spanish alphabet

ña *nf Am Fam* Mrs, = contraction of "doña"

ñac = **ñácate**

ñacañaca *nm Esp Fam Hum* **hacer ñ.** *Br* to have a bit of rumpy-pumpy, *US* to make out

ñácate, ñac *interj RP Fam* **iba caminando y, iñ.!, tropecé** I was walking along and all of a sudden, bang, I tripped up!; **cuando la película se empezaba a poner interesante, iñ.!, corte de luz** the movie was just starting to get interesting when, bang, there was a power cut!

ñacundá *nm* nacunda nighthawk

ñame *nm CAm, Carib, Col* yam

ñandú (*pl* **ñandúes**) *nm* rhea

ñandubay *nm* = type of mesquite

ñandutí *nm Par* fine lace

ñángara *Carib Fam Pey* **1** *adj* commie, red
2 *nmf* commie, red

ñango, -a *adj Méx Fam (persona)* weedy; *(animal)* scrawny

ñaño, -a 1 *adj* (**a**) *Col, Pan (consentido)* spoiled, pampered (**b**) *Andes (muy amigo)* close, intimate
2 *nm* (**a**) *Chile (hermano)* older brother (**b**) *Perú (niño)* child

ñapa *Ven Fam* **1** *nf* bonus, extra
2 de ñapa *loc adv* to cap *o* crown it all; **llovía y de ñ. se pinchó una rueda** it was raining and, to cap *o* crown it all, we got a puncture; EXPR **ni de ñ.** no way

ñata *nf Fam* (**a**) *Am (nariz)* nose, *Br* conk, *US* schnozz (**b**) *Andes, RP (nariz chata)* snub nose

ñato, -a *Andes, RP* **1** *adj* snub-nosed; **ser ñ.** to have a snub nose
2 *nm,f* snub-nosed person

ñemita *nf Ven* = sweet made from egg yolk and sugar

ñeque 1 *adj CAm, Andes* strong, vigorous
2 *nm* (**a**) *CAm, Andes (fuerza)* strength, vigour (**b**) *CAm, Méx (bofetada)* slap, blow (**c**) *Chile Fam (tesón)* **tener mucho ñ.** to have a lot of grit *o* guts; **si queremos que este proyecto resulte, tenemos que ponerle ñ.** if we want this project to amount to anything we'll have to give it all we've got

ñero, -a 1 *adj Ven* **ser ñ.** to be a mug *o* sucker
2 *nm,f Fam* (**a**) *Méx (hombre)* pal, *Br* mate, *US* buddy; *(mujer)* pal (**b**) *Ven (tipo)* guy, *Br* bloke; *(mujer)* woman; *(mujer joven)* girl

ñinga *nf Ven Fam (cantidad pequeña)* bit; *(de agua)* drop; *(de humor)* hint

ñisca *nf* (**a**) *CAm (excremento)* excrement (**b**) *Andes (pizca)* bit, small amount

ño, ñor *nm Am Fam* Mr, = contraction of "señor"

ñongo, -a *adj Ven Fam* (**a**) *(difícil)* tricky, awkward (**b**) *(remilgado)* fussy

ñoña *nf Andes, Ven muy Fam* (**a**) *(excremento)* crap, shit (**b**) *(cosa mala)* piece of crap; **esta ñ. de bicicleta otra vez está sin frenos** the brakes have gone on this lousy bike again; **hoy todo me fue para la ñ.** I've had a lousy day today

ñoñería, ñoñez *nf* inanity

ñoño, -a *adj* (**a**) *(remilgado)* squeamish; *(quejica)* whining (**b**) *(soso)* dull, insipid (**c**) *Bol Fam (gordo)* porky (**d**) *Bol Fam (viejo)* gaga

ñoqui *nm* (**a**) *(plato)* gnocchi (**b**) *Arg Fam (persona)* = someone who receives a salary but does not turn up for work (**c**) *RP Fam (puñetazo)* punch; **le dio un ñ.** he socked him one

ñor = **ño**

ñorbo *nm Andes* passion flower

ñu *nm* gnu

ñudo: al ñudo *loc adv RP Fam* in vain

O, o

O, o [o] *nf (letra)* O, o; EXPR *Fam* **no saber hacer la o con un canuto** to be as thick as two short planks

O (*abrev de* **oeste**) W

o *conj*

> **u** is used instead of **o** in front of words beginning with "o" or "ho" (e.g. **mujer u hombre** woman or man). Note that **ó** (with acute accent) is used between figures (e.g. **25 ó 26 invitados** 25 or 26 guests).

(a) *(disyuntiva)* or; **¿vienes o no vienes?** are you coming or not?; **cansado o no, tendrás que ayudar** (whether you're) tired or not, you'll have to help; **o sea (que)...** in other words...
(b) *(equivalencia)* or; **la propiedad de magnetizarse, o paramagnetismo, es propia de algunos metales** some metals exhibit the ability to magnetize themselves, or paramagnetism
(c) *(en correlación)* **o.... o....** either... or...; **o te comportas, o te quedarás sin cenar** either you behave yourself or you're not getting any dinner, unless you behave yourself, you won't get any dinner; **o lo tomas o lo dejas, no hay más opciones** take it or leave it, there are no other alternatives

o/ (*abrev de* **orden**) order

oasis *nm inv* (**a**) *(en el desierto)* oasis (**b**) *(circunstancia agradable)* oasis; **un o. de paz/tranquilidad** an oasis *o* island of peace/tranquillity

oaxaqueño, -a 1 *adj* of/from Oaxaca *(Mexico)*
2 *nm,f* person from Oaxaca *(Mexico)*

obcecación *nf* blindness, stubbornness

obcecado, -a *adj* (**a**) *(tozudo)* stubborn (**b**) *(cegado)* **o. por** blinded by (**c**) *(obsesionado)* obsessed; **están obcecados con vivir en la costa** they're obsessed with the idea of living on the coast

obcecar [60] **1** *vt* to blind; **me obcecaba la envidia** I was blinded by jealousy
2 obcecarse *vpr* to become stubborn; **obcecarse en hacer algo** to stubbornly insist on doing sth; **se ha obcecado y no quiere escuchar a nadie** she has dug her heels in and refuses to listen to anyone; **se ha obcecado con la idea** she has become obsessed with the idea

ob. cit. (*abrev de* **obra citada**) op cit

obedecer [46] **1** *vt* to obey; **o. a alguien** to obey sb; **obedece a tu madre** obey your mother, do as *o* what your mother tells you; **o. las normas** to obey the rules
2 *vi* (**a**) *(acatar)* to obey, to do as one is told; **procura o.** try to do as you're told; **hacerse o.** to command obedience
(**b**) *(estar motivado)* **o. a algo** to be due to sth; **una actitud que sólo obedece al miedo** an attitude which is due entirely to fear; **los malos resultados obedecen a fallos en el sistema** the poor results are due to faults in the system
(**c**) *(responder)* to respond; **las piernas no me obedecían** my legs wouldn't do what I wanted them to; **los mandos no me obedecían** the controls wouldn't respond

obediencia *nf* obedience; **o. ciega** blind obedience; **se comporta con o.** he's obedient

obediente *adj* obedient; **tienes que ser o.** you must be obedient, you must do as you're told

obedientemente *adv* obediently

obelisco *nm* obelisk

obenque, obenquillo *nm Náut* shroud

obertura *nf* overture

obesidad *nf* obesity

obeso, -a 1 *adj* obese
2 *nm,f* obese person

óbice *nm Formal* **no ser ó. para: eso no es ó. para que cumplan los objetivos** that does not prevent them from meeting the objectives, that is no reason why they should not meet the objectives

obispado *nm* (**a**) *(cargo)* bishopric (**b**) *(territorio)* bishopric, diocese

obispal *adj* episcopal

obispo *nm* bishop ▸▸ ***o. auxiliar*** auxiliary bishop

óbito *nm Formal* decease, demise

obituario *nm* (**a**) *(en la administración)* parish register of deaths (**b**) *(en periódico)* obituary

objeción *nf* objection; **poner objeciones a** to raise objections to; **tener objeciones** to have objections; **o. denegada** *(en juicio)* objection overruled ▸▸ ***o. de conciencia*** conscientious objection; **se negó a practicar abortos por razones de o. de conciencia** he refused to carry out abortions on moral grounds

objetable *adj* objectionable

objetar 1 *vt* to object to; **no tengo nada que o.** I have no objection; **¿tienes algo que o. a su propuesta?** do you have any objection to her proposal?; **¿algo que o.?** any objections?; **objetó que era demasiado caro** he objected that it was too expensive
2 *vi Esp* to register as a conscientious objector

objetivamente *adv* objectively

objetivar *vt* **intenta o. la situación/los problemas** try to look at the situation/the problems objectively

objetividad *nf* objectivity; **analizó la situación con o.** he analysed the situation objectively

objetivismo *nm Filosofía* objectivism

objetivo, -a 1 *adj* objective
2 *nm* (**a**) *(finalidad)* objective, aim; **hemos logrado cumplir con nuestro o.** we have succeeded in achieving our objective *o* aim; **plantearse un o.** to set oneself an objective; **la medida tiene como o. facilitar la comunicación** the aim of the measure is to make communication easier, the measure is aimed at making communication easier ▸▸ *Com* ***o. de producción*** production target; *Com* ***o. de ventas*** sales target
(**b**) *Mil* target
(**c**) *Fot* lens

objeto *nm* (**a**) *(cosa)* object ▸▸ ***objetos perdidos*** lost property, *US* lost and found; ***objetos personales*** personal effects; ***objetos de valor*** valuables; ***o. volador no identificado*** unidentified flying object
(**b**) *(propósito)* purpose, object; **el o. de la visita** the purpose *o* object of the visit; **¿cuál es el o. de estos cambios?** what is the purpose of these changes? **tener por o.** *(sujeto: persona)* to have as one's aim; *(sujeto: plan)* to be aimed at; **el ministro tiene por o. reducir las importaciones** the minister is aiming to reduce imports; **con (el) o. de** *(para)* in order to, with the aim of; **¿con qué o.?** to what end?; **sin o.** *(inútilmente)* to no purpose, pointlessly
(**c**) *(blanco)* **ser o. de** to be the object of; **el artículo ha sido o. de duras críticas** the article has come in for some harsh criticism; **fue o. de las burlas de sus compañeros** he was the butt of his classmates' jokes; **de niño fue o. de malos tratos** he was beaten as a child
(**d**) *Gram* object ▸▸ ***o. directo*** direct object; ***o. indirecto*** indirect object

objetor, -ora *nm,f* objector ▸▸ ***o. de conciencia*** conscientious objector

oblación *nf Rel* oblation

oblada *nf (pez)* sea bream

oblar *vt RP Der* to pay

oblea *nf* wafer

oblicuamente *adv* at a slant

oblicuo, -a 1 *adj* (**a**) *(inclinado)* oblique, slanting (**b**) *(mirada)* sidelong (**c**) *Mat* oblique
2 *nm Anat* oblique (muscle) ▸▸ ***o. mayor*** *(del ojo)* superior oblique; *(del abdomen)* external (abdominal) oblique; ***o. menor*** *(del ojo)* inferior oblique; *(del abdomen)* internal (abdominal) oblique

obligación *nf* (**a**) *(deber, imposición)* obligation, duty; **me sentí** *o* **vi en la o. de ayudarlos** I felt obliged to help them; **tu o. es estudiar** what you have to do is study; **no lo hagas, no tienes ninguna o.** don't do it, you're not under any obligation; **me he puesto por o. levantarme pronto** I've decided I must get up early; **todos los días hace ejercicio, se lo toma como una o.** he makes it a rule to exercise every day; **faltó a sus obligaciones** she failed in her duty; **cumple con tus obligaciones** fulfil your obligations *o* duties; **lo hice por o.** I did it out of a sense of duty

(**b**) *Fin* bond, security ▸▸ ***o. convertible*** convertible bond; ***o. del Estado*** Treasury bond, *Br* gilt; ***o. del Tesoro*** Treasury bond, *Br* gilt

obligacionista *nmf Fin* bondholder

obligado, -a *adj* **es de obligada lectura** it's essential reading; **una norma de o. cumplimiento** a compulsory regulation; **las obligadas preguntas de cortesía** the obligatory polite questions; **fueron a la fiesta obligados** they were obliged to go to the party

obligar [38] **1** *vt* (**a**) *(sujeto: persona)* **o. a alguien (a hacer algo)** to force sb to do sth, to make sb do sth; **yo no quería hacerlo, me obligaron** I didn't want to do it, they forced me to *o* they made me; **no lo compres, nadie te obliga** don't buy it, nobody is forcing you; **la obligué a descansar** I made her have a rest; **a los jefes de departamento se les obliga a presentar un informe al mes** the heads of department are required to hand in a monthly report; **o. a alguien a que haga algo** to force sb to do sth, to make sb do sth; **la obligué a que me contestase** I forced her to answer me, I made her answer me

(**b**) *(sujeto: ley, norma)* **la ley obliga a todos los ciudadanos a declarar sus ingresos** all citizens are required by law to declare their income; **esta norma obliga a los mayores de dieciocho años** this rule applies to people over eighteen

2 obligarse *vpr* (**a**) *(comprometerse)* **obligarse a hacer algo** to undertake to do sth; **con este acuerdo se han obligado a dar marcha atrás al plan** under this agreement they have undertaken to withdraw the plan; **se obligó a ser más organizado con el dinero** he undertook to be more organised where money was concerned

(**b**) *(forzarse)* **obligarse a hacer algo** to force oneself to do sth; **se obliga a estudiar cada día** she forces herself to study every day

obligatoriedad *nf* **la ley establece la o. de ponerse el cinturón de seguridad en la ciudad** the law makes it compulsory to wear a seatbelt in the city

obligatorio, -a *adj* compulsory, obligatory; **un requisito o.** an essential requirement; **no es o. llevar corbata al trabajo** you don't have to wear a tie to work

obliteración *nf Med* obliteration

obliterar *vt* **1** (**a**) *Formal (borrar, anular)* to obliterate, to wipe out; **el tiempo obliteró todos sus recuerdos** time erased all his memories (**b**) *Med* to obliterate

2 obliterarse *vpr Med* to be obliterated

oblongo, -a *adj* oblong

obnubilación *nf* (mental) confusion

obnubilar 1 *vt* (**a**) *Formal (ofuscar)* to overwhelm, to confuse; **la ira obnubiló su juicio** anger clouded his judgement (**b**) *Formal (visión)* to blind, to dazzle (**c**) *Fam (fascinar)* to hold spellbound; **ese chico la ha obnubilado** that boy has her spellbound; **dejar obnubilado(a) a alguien** to bowl sb over; **quedar obnubilado(a)** to be bowled over, to be awestruck

2 obnubilarse *vpr* (**a**) *Formal (ofuscarse)* to be overwhelmed, to become confused (**b**) *Fam (quedar fascinado)* to be all agog; **este hombre en cuanto ve una moto se obnubila** whenever this man sees a motorbike he's all agog

oboe 1 *nm (instrumento)* oboe

2 *nmf (persona)* oboist

oboísta *nmf* oboist, oboe player

óbolo *nm* small contribution

OBRA *nf* (**a**) *(trabajo, acción)* **hacer** *o* **realizar una buena o.** to do a good deed; **ya he hecho la buena o. del día** I've done my good deed for the day; **poner algo en o.** to put sth into effect; **por o. (y gracia) de** thanks to; **por sus obras los conoceréis** by their works will you know them; **es o. suya** it's his doing; **la ruina de las cosechas es o. de la sequía** the crops have been ruined as a result of the drought; PROV **obras son amores y no buenas razones** actions speak louder than words ▸▸ ***o. benéfica*** *o* ***de beneficencia*** *o* ***de caridad*** *(institución)* charity; *(acción, trabajo)* charitable deed; *Anticuado* ***o. pía*** charitable institution; *Arg* ***o. social*** benevolent fund; ***obras sociales*** community work

(**b**) *(creación artística)* work; *(de teatro)* play; *(de música)* work, opus; **la o. pictórica de Miguel Ángel** Michelangelo's paintings; **una o. de artesanía** a piece of craftsmanship ▸▸ ***o. de arte*** work of art; ***obras completas*** complete works; ***o. de consulta*** reference work; ***o. dramática*** *(pieza)* play, drama; *(conjunto)* plays, dramatic works; ***o. maestra*** masterpiece; ***o. menor*** minor work

(**c**) *(trabajo de construcción)* work; *(reforma doméstica, en local)* alteration; **el ayuntamiento va a empezar una o. en el descampado** the council is going to start building on the wasteground; **vamos a hacer o.** *o* **obras en la cocina** we're going to make some alterations to our kitchen; **toda la calle está en obras** there are roadworks all along the road; **el edificio lleva en obras más de dos meses** the work on the building has been going on for over two months; **cortada por obras** *(letrero en calle)* road closed for repairs; **cerrado por obras** *(letrero en restaurante, edificio)* closed for refurbishment; **obras** *(en carretera)* roadworks; EXPR **parece (más largo que) la o. del Escorial** it seems like it's been going on for ever ▸▸ *Náut* ***o. muerta*** freeboard; ***obras públicas*** public works

(**d**) *(solar en construcción)* building site; **encontró trabajo en una o.** he found work on a building site

(**e**) *(trabajo de albañilería)* **un horno de o.** a brick oven

(**f**) **la O.** the Opus Dei, = traditionalist Roman Catholic organization, whose members include many professional people and public figures

---

obrador *nm (de pastelería)* bakery

obraje *nm RP* mill, factory ▸▸ ***o. maderero*** timber operation

obrar 1 *vi* (**a**) *(actuar)* to act; **el gobierno obró bajo una tremenda presión popular** the government acted under immense public pressure; **yo obré con toda inocencia** I acted in all innocence

(**b**) *(causar efecto)* to work, to take effect; **el remedio obró como se esperaba** the remedy took effect *o* worked as anticipated

(**c**) *(estar en poder)* **o. en manos de** *o* **en poder de** to be in the possession of

2 *vt* (**a**) *(producir)* to bring about; *(milagro)* to work; **esta experiencia obró un cambio profundo en su persona** this experience brought about a profound change in him (**b**) *(trabajar)* to work; **o. la madera** to work wood

obrera *nf* (**a**) *Zool* worker (**b**) *ver también* **obrero**

obrerismo *nm (movimiento)* labour movement

obrero, -a 1 *adj* (**a**) *(trabajador)* **clase obrera** working class; **movimiento o.** labour movement (**b**) *Zool* worker; **las abejas obreras** worker bees

2 *nm,f (en fábrica)* worker; *(en obra)* workman, labourer ▸▸ ***o.*** *Esp* ***cualificado*** *o Am* ***calificado*** skilled worker

obscenidad *nf* obscenity

obsceno, -a *adj* obscene

obscurantismo = **oscurantismo**

obscurantista = **oscurantista**

obscurecer, obscuridad *etc* = **oscurecer, oscuridad** *etc*

obsedido, -a *adj Ven* obsessed

obsequiar *vt Esp* **o. a alguien con algo,** *Am* **o. a alguien algo** to present sb with sth; *Esp* **le obsequiaron con un reloj como recuerdo,** *Am* **le obsequiaron un reloj como recuerdo** they presented him with a watch as a keepsake; **nos obsequiaron con todo tipo de atenciones** they lavished all kinds of attention on us; **finalizó obsequiando a su público su mayor éxito** he ended the concert by rewarding his fans with his greatest hit

obsequio *nm* gift, present; **el vino es o. de la casa** the wine is on the house; **en obsequio a su gran labor** in recognition of her valuable work ▸▸ ***o. de empresa*** corporate gift

> **Falso amigo**: El sustantivo inglés **obsequies** no es la traducción del español **obsequio**. En inglés **obsequies** significa "exequias".

obsequiosamente *adv* ingratiatingly

obsequiosidad *nf* eagerness to please

obsequioso, -a *adj* ingratiating; **sus obsequiosas atenciones (para) con nosotros** their eagerness to please us

observable *adj* observable

observación *nf* (**a**) *(examen, contemplación)* observation; **el paciente está en** *o* **bajo o.** the patient is under observation; **tengo buenas dotes de o.** I have strong powers of observation

(**b**) *(comentario)* comment, remark; **hacer una o.** to make a comment *o* remark; **si se me permite una o.** if I might make an observation

(**c**) *(nota)* note; **el autor ha añadido una o. en este punto** the author has added a note at this point (**d**) *(cumplimiento)* observance; **Sanidad recomienda la o. de estas normas** the Department of Health recommends following these guidelines

observador, -ora 1 *adj* observant
2 *nm,f* observer

observancia *nf* observance

observar *vt* (**a**) *(contemplar)* to observe, to watch; **observaban todos sus movimientos mediante unos prismáticos** they observed *o* followed all his movements through binoculars; **pasó años observando el comportamiento de estos animales** he spent years observing the behaviour of these animals
(**b**) *(advertir)* to notice, to observe; **observé que sus zapatos tenían barro** I noticed that his shoes were muddy; **no se observaron anomalías** no anomalies have been observed
(**c**) *(acatar) (ley, normas)* to observe, to respect; *(conducta, costumbre)* to follow
(**d**) *(comentar, señalar)* to remark, to observe; **"eso no es totalmente cierto", observó** "that's not entirely true," he remarked *o* pointed out

observatorio *nm* observatory ►► ***o. astronómico*** (astronomical) observatory; ***o. meteorológico*** weather station

obsesión *nf* obsession; **tiene la o. de que va a suceder de nuevo** he's obsessed with the idea that it's going to happen again

obsesionar 1 *vt* to obsess; **le obsesiona la muerte** he's obsessed with death; **está obsesionado con** *o* **por el dinero** he's obsessed with money
2 **obsesionarse** *vpr* to become obsessed

obsesivo, -a 1 *adj* obsessive
2 *nm,f* obsessive (person)

obseso, -a 1 *adj* obsessed
2 *nm,f* obsessive (person); **es un o. de la salud** he's a health freak *o* fanatic ►► ***o. sexual*** sex maniac

obsidiana *nf* obsidian

obsolescencia *nf* obsolescence

obsoleto, -a *adj* obsolete; **este uso ha quedado o.** this usage has become obsolete

obstaculizar [14] *vt (proceso, relación)* to block, to put obstacles in the way of; *(salida)* to block, to obstruct; *(tráfico)* to hold up, to obstruct; **o. el paso** to block the way

obstáculo *nm* (**a**) *(impedimento)* obstacle (**para** to); **poner obstáculos a algo/alguien** to put obstacles in the way of sth/sb (**b**) *(en una carrera)* hurdle

obstante: no obstante *loc adv* (**a**) *(sin embargo)* nevertheless, however; **no me parece el sitio indicado, no o., lo consideraré** I don't think it's the most suitable place; nevertheless *o* all the same, I'll consider it (**b**) *(a pesar de)* in spite of, despite; **no o. mis recelos, decidí hacer lo que sugería** in spite of *o* despite my reservations, I decided to do as he suggested

obstar *vi Formal* **eso no obsta para que vengan si así quieren** that is no reason for them not to come if they so wish

obstetra *nmf esp Am* obstetrician

obstetricia *nf* obstetrics *(singular)*

obstétrico, -a *adj* obstetric, obstetrical

obstinación *nf* (**a**) *(terquedad)* obstinacy, stubbornness (**b**) *(tenacidad)* tenacity (**c**) *Ven Fam (molestia)* pain (in the neck) (**d**) *Ven Fam (aburrimiento)* drag

obstinadamente *adv* (**a**) *(con terquedad)* obstinately, stubbornly (**b**) *(con tenacidad)* tenaciously

obstinado, -a *adj* (**a**) *(terco)* obstinate, stubborn (**b**) *(tenaz)* tenacious (**c**) *Ven Fam (hastiado)* fed up

obstinante *adj Ven Fam* (**a**) *(irritante)* aggravating, exasperating (**b**) *(aburrido)* deadly, deadly dull

obstinar 1 *vt Ven Fam* to aggravate, to exasperate; **para ya de gritar, estás obstinando a los invitados** stop shouting, you're getting on the guests' nerves
2 **obstinarse** *vpr* (**a**) *(insistir)* to refuse to give way; **o. en** to insist on; **se obstina en seguir adelante con el proyecto** he insists on going ahead with the project; **se ha obstinado en conseguirlo** he is determined to achieve it
(**b**) *Ven Fam (exasperarse)* to get fed up; **tanto me molestan que termino obstinándome** they disturb me so much that in the end I get really fed up

obstrucción *nf* (**a**) *(taponamiento)* obstruction; **hay una o. en la cañería** there's a blockage in the pipe (**b**) *(impedimento)* obstruction; **les acusaron de o. al proceso democrático** they accused him of obstructing the democratic process; **o. a la justicia** obstructing justice (**c**) *Dep* obstruction (**d**) *Med* obstruction; **o. intestinal** intestinal obstruction

obstruccionismo *nm* obstructionism

obstruccionista 1 *adj* obstructionist
2 *nmf* obstructionist

obstructor, -ora 1 *adj* obstructing
2 *nm,f* obstructor

obstruido, -a *adj* (**a**) *(bloqueado)* blocked (**b**) *(obstaculizado)* obstructed

obstruir [34] 1 *vt* (**a**) *(tubería, salida, camino)* to block, to obstruct; **o. el paso** to block the way; **o. el tráfico** to hold up *o* obstruct the traffic (**b**) *(desarrollo, proceso)* to obstruct, to impede; **la oposición no deja de o. el proceso** the opposition is constantly obstructing the process; **o. el progreso de la cultura** to hinder cultural progress (**c**) *Dep* to block
2 **obstruirse** *vpr* to get blocked (up)

obtención *nf* obtaining; **los requisitos para la o. de la beca** the requirements to obtain the grant

obtener [67] *vt (beca, cargo, puntos, información)* to get, to obtain; *(resultado)* to obtain, to achieve; *(premio, victoria)* to win; *(ganancias)* to make; *(satisfacción, ventaja)* to gain, to obtain; **obtuvieron dos millones de beneficio de la venta de su casa** they made a profit of two million from the sale of their house; **la sidra se obtiene de las manzanas** cider is obtained *o* made from apples

obturación *nf* blockage, obstruction

obturador *nm* (**a**) *Fot* shutter (**b**) *Aut* choke

obturar *vt* to block

obtuso, -a 1 *adj* (**a**) *(sin punta)* blunt (**b**) *(ángulo)* obtuse (**c**) *(torpe)* obtuse
2 *nm,f (torpe)* **es un o.** he's obtuse

obtuviera *etc ver* **obtener**

obús (*pl* **obuses**) *nm* (**a**) *(cañón)* howitzer (**b**) *(proyectil)* shell (**c**) *Aut (de neumático)* cap

obviamente *adv* obviously; **o. se trata de un error** it's obviously a mistake

obviar *vt* to avoid; **obviaré en mi exposición los detalles técnicos** I shall avoid technical details in my presentation

obvio, -a *adj* obvious; **como es o., me equivoqué** needless to say *o* obviously, I was wrong

oca *nf* (**a**) *(animal)* goose (**b**) *(juego)* **la o.** = board game in which players move counters along a series of squares arranged in a spiral

ocarina *nf* ocarina

ocasión *nf* (**a**) *(oportunidad)* opportunity, chance; **una o. de oro** a golden opportunity; **una o. irrepetible** an unrepeatable opportunity; **aprovechar una o.** to take advantage of an opportunity; **estaba esperando una buena o. para preguntarle** I was waiting for a suitable opportunity to ask him; **en** *o* **a la primera o.** at the first opportunity; **tener o. de hacer algo** to have the chance to do sth; **apenas tuve o. de hablar con ella** I scarcely had the chance to speak to her; **no tuvimos o. de vernos** we didn't have the chance to meet up; EXPR *Fam* **la o. la pintan calva** this is my/your/*etc* big chance; **tenía ganas de ir a París y al tener unos días de vacaciones pensé, la o. la pintan calva** I was keen to go to Paris and since I had a few days off I thought it's now or never; EXPR *Esp Fam* **coger la o. por los pelos** to seize the opportunity (by the scruff of the neck); PROV **quien quita la o. quita el peligro** opportunity makes the thief
(**b**) *(momento)* moment, time; *(vez)* occasion; **en dos ocasiones** on two occasions; **en alguna o.** sometimes; **en cierta o.** once; **en ocasiones** sometimes, at times; **en otra o.** some other time
(**c**) *(motivo)* **con o. de** on the occasion of; **dar o. para algo/para hacer algo** to give cause for sth/to do sth; **no le des o. para regañarte** don't give him cause to tell you off
(**d**) *(ganga)* bargain; **artículos de o.** bargains; **automóviles de o.** secondhand *o* used cars

ocasional *adj* (**a**) *(lluvias, visitantes, sucesos)* occasional; **un trabajo o.** a casual job (**b**) *(accidental)* **un encuentro o.** a chance meeting

ocasionalmente *adv* (**a**) *(de vez en cuando)* occasionally (**b**) *(accidentalmente)* by chance, accidentally

ocasionar *vt* to cause; **los rumores ocasionaron su dimisión** the rumours brought about his resignation; **no quiero o. molestias** I don't want to put you to any trouble

ocaso *nm* (**a**) *(puesta del sol)* sunset (**b**) *(de civilización, vida, era)* decline

occidental 1 *adj (zona, área)* western; *(economía, cultura, sociedad)* Western
2 *nmf* westerner

occidentalismo *nm* (a) *(caracter)* western nature (b) *(ideología)* occidentalism, westernism

occidentalista 1 *adj* occidentalist, westernist
2 *nmf* occidentalist, westernist

occidentalización *nf* westernization

occidentalizar [14] 1 *vt* to westernize
2 **occidentalizarse** *vpr* to become westernized

occidente *nm* west; **(el) O.** *(bloque de países)* the West

occipital *Anat* 1 *adj* occipital
2 *nm* occipital (bone)

occipucio *nm Anat* occiput

occiso, -a *Formal* 1 *adj* murdered, killed
2 *nm,f* murder victim

OCDE *nf (abrev de* **Organización para la Cooperación y el Desarrollo Económico**) OECD

Oceanía *n* Oceania *(including Australia and New Zealand)*

oceánico, -a *adj (del océano)* oceanic

océano *nm* (a) *(mar)* ocean ▸▸ ***o. Atlántico*** Atlantic Ocean; ***o. Antártico*** Antarctic Ocean; ***o. Ártico*** Arctic Ocean; ***o. Glacial Antártico*** Antarctic Ocean; ***o. Glacial Ártico*** Arctic Ocean; ***o. Índico*** Indian Ocean; ***o. Pacífico*** Pacific Ocean (b) *(inmensidad)* sea, host; **afrontamos un o. de problemas** we face a host of problems

oceanografía *nf* oceanography

oceanográfico, -a *adj* oceanographic(al)

oceanógrafo, -a *nm,f* oceanographer

oceanología *nf* oceanology

ocelo *nm Zool* (a) *(ojo)* ocellus (b) *(dibujo)* ocellus, eyelet

ocelote *nm* ocelot

ochava *nf* (a) *Arquit* chamfer (b) *RP (esquina)* corner

ochavo *nm* = former Spanish copper coin of little value; EXPR *Fam* **no valer un o.** to be worthless; EXPR *Fam* **no tener un o.** to be penniless

ochavón, -ona *adj Cuba* octoroon

ochenta *núm* eighty; **los (años) o.** the eighties; *ver también* **treinta**

ochentavo, -a *núm* eightieth; *ver también* **octavo**

ochentón, -ona *Fam* 1 *adj* eighty-year-old
2 *nm,f* person in their eighties; **es un o.** he's in his eighties

ocho 1 *núm* eight; **de aquí en o. días** *(en una semana)* a week today; *Fam* **¡qué fiesta ni qué o. cuartos!** it wasn't what I'd call a party!; EXPR *Fam* **dar igual o. que ochenta** to make no difference; *ver también* **tres**
2 *nm (en remo)* eight ▸▸ ***o. con timonel*** coxed eight

ochocientos, -as *núm* eight hundred; *ver también* **treinta**

ochomil *nm (montaña)* = mountain over eight thousand metres high

ocio *nm (tiempo libre)* leisure; *(inactividad)* idleness; **en sus ratos de o. se dedica a leer** he spends his spare time reading

ociosidad *nf* idleness; PROV **la o. es la madre de todos los vicios** the devil finds work for idle hands (to do)

ocioso, -a 1 *adj* (a) *(inactivo)* idle (b) *(inútil)* pointless; **un comentario o.** a pointless *o* an idle remark; **volver a analizar las razones resultaba un ejercicio o.** analysing the reasons again was a pointless exercise; **es o. repetirlo** there's no point in repeating it
2 *nm,f* idler

ocluir [34] 1 *vt* to occlude
2 **ocluirse** *vpr* to become occluded

oclusión *nf* (a) *(cierre)* blockage (b) *Meteo* occlusion (c) *Ling* occlusion

oclusiva *nf Ling* occlusive

oclusivo, -a *adj Ling* occlusive

ocluyo *etc ver* **ocluir**

ocote *nm* ocote pine

ocozol *nm* ***o. americano*** witch hazel

OCR *nm Informát (abrev de* **optical character recognition**) OCR

ocráceo, -a *adj* ochreous

ocre 1 *nm* ochre
2 *adj inv* ochre; **fachadas ocres** ochre-coloured facades

oct. *(abrev de* **octubre**) Oct.

octaédrico, -a *adj* octahedral

octaedro *nm* octahedron

octagonal *adj* octagonal

octágono *nm* octagon

octanaje *nm* octane number *o* rating

octano *nm* octane; **es de más octanos** it has a higher octane number

octava *nf Mús* octave

octavilla *nf* (a) *(de propaganda)* pamphlet, leaflet (b) *(tamaño)* octavo

octavo, -a 1 *núm* (a) *(ordinal)* eighth; **el o. día** the eighth day; **el o. aniversario** the eighth anniversary; **en o. lugar, en octava posición** eighth, in eighth place; **quedó o. en la carrera** he was eighth in the race; **Enrique O.** *(escrito Enrique VIII)* Henry the Eighth *(written Henry VIII)*; **el capítulo o.** chapter eight; **el o. centenario** the eight hundredth anniversary (b) *(partitivo)* **le tocó la octava parte** he got an eighth
2 *nm,f* **el o., la octava** the eighth (one); **llegó el o.** *(en carrera)* he came eighth; **quedar el o.** *(en carrera)* to come eighth; *(en examen)* to be eighth; **fue el o. en venir** he was the eighth person *o* one to come
3 *nm* (a) *(parte)* eighth (b) *Dep* ***los octavos de final*** the last sixteen; **llegar a octavos de final** to reach the last sixteen (c) *(piso)* eighth floor; **el o. izquierda** the left-hand *Br* flat *o US* apartment on the eighth floor

octeto *nm* (a) *Mús* octet (b) *Informát* byte

octogenario, -a 1 *adj* octogenarian
2 *nm,f* octogenarian

octogésimo, -a *núm* eightieth; *ver también* **octavo**

octogonal *adj* octagonal

octógono *nm* octagon

octosílabo, -a 1 *adj* octosyllabic
2 *nm* octosyllabic line

octubre *nm* October; *ver también* **septiembre**

óctuplo, -a *adj* octuple, eightfold

ocular 1 *adj* eye; **globo o.** eyeball; **testigo o.** eye-witness
2 *nm* eye-piece

oculista *nmf* ophthalmologist

ocultación *nf* concealment, hiding ▸▸ *Der* ***o. de pruebas*** concealment, non-disclosure

ocultar 1 *vt* (a) *(esconder)* to conceal, to hide; **o. algo a alguien** to conceal *o* hide sth from sb (b) *(información, noticia)* to conceal, to hide; **o. algo a alguien** to conceal *o* hide sth from sb; **le ocultaron la verdad** they concealed the truth from him (c) *(sorpresa, irritación)* to conceal, to hide; **oculté mis verdaderos sentimientos** I concealed my true feelings (d) *(delito)* to cover up
2 **ocultarse** *vpr* to hide

ocultismo *nm* occultism

ocultista *nmf* occultist

oculto, -a *adj* (a) *(escondido)* hidden (b) *(que se desconoce)* secret, hidden; **su objetivo o.** his secret goal (c) *(sobrenatural)* occult; **las ciencias ocultas** the occult sciences, the occult; **lo o.** the occult

ocumo *nm Ven* cocoyam

ocupa = **okupa**

ocupación *nf* (a) *(de territorio, edificio)* occupation; **la o. de la embajada por parte de los manifestantes** the occupation of the embassy by the demonstrators; **o. ilegal de viviendas** squatting; **los hoteles registraron una o. del 80 por ciento** the hotels reported occupancy rates of 80 percent
(b) *(empleo)* job, occupation
(c) *(actividad)* activity; **una de mis ocupaciones favoritas** one of my favourite activities

ocupacional *adj* occupational

ocupado, -a *adj* (a) *(atareado)* busy; **tengo toda la tarde ocupada** I'm busy all afternoon (b) *(teléfono) Br* engaged, *US* busy; *(plaza, asiento)* taken; *(lavabo)* engaged; *Méx, RP* **dar o.** *(teléfono)* to be *Br* engaged *o US* busy (c) *(territorio)* occupied; **casa ocupada** *(ilegalmente)* squat

ocupante 1 *adj* occupying
2 *nmf* occupant; **o. ilegal de viviendas** squatter

OCUPAR 1 *vt* (a) *(invadir) (territorio, edificio)* to occupy; **han ocupado la casa** *(ilegalmente)* squatters have moved into the house
(b) *(llenar) (mente)* to occupy; **¿en qué ocupas tu tiempo libre?** how do you spend your spare time?; **ocupa su tiempo en estudiar** she spends her time studying; **los niños me ocupan mucho tiempo** the children take up a lot of my time; **este trabajo sólo te ocupará unas horas** this task will only take you a few hours
(c) *(abarcar, utilizar) (superficie, espacio)* to take up; *(habitación, piso)* to live in; *(mesa)* to sit at; *(sillón)* to sit in; **ocupamos los despachos que hay al final del pasillo** our offices are at the end of the

corridor; **¿cuándo ocupas la casa?** when do you move into the house *o* move in?; **los embajadores siempre ocupan las primeras filas** the ambassadors always occupy the first few rows

(**d**) *(cargo, puesto, cátedra)* to hold; **ocupa el primer puesto en las listas de éxitos** she's top of the charts; **¿qué lugar ocupa el Flamingo en la clasificación?** where are Flamingo in the league?

(**e**) *(dar trabajo a)* to find *o* provide work for; **el sector turístico ocupa a la mayoría de la población del litoral** most of the people who live on the coast are employed in the tourist industry; **ha ido ocupando a toda su familia** he's found work for all of his family

(**f**) *Esp Der (confiscar)* **o. algo a alguien** to seize *o* confiscate sth from sb

(**g**) *CAm, Méx (usar, emplear)* to use; **¿qué palabra ocuparías tú en esta oración?** what word would you use in this sentence?; **en esa oficina ocupan veinte computadoras** twenty computers are used in that office

2 **ocuparse** *vpr (encargarse)* **ocúpate tú, yo no puedo** you do it, I can't; **ocuparse de algo/alguien** *(encargarse de)* to deal with sth/sb; **ocuparse de alguien** *(cuidar, atender)* to look after sb; **¿quién se ocupa de la compra/de cocinar en tu casa?** who does the shopping/cooking in your house?; **un contable se ocupa de las cuentas de la empresa** an accountant deals with *o* looks after the company's accounts; **él se ocupa de llevar a los niños al colegio** he takes the children to school; **en este capítulo nos ocuparemos de la poesía medieval** this chapter will look at medieval poetry; **¡tú ocúpate de lo tuyo!** mind your own business!; **se ocupa mucho de su madre** he takes good care of his mother

---

ocurrencia *nf* (**a**) *(idea)* bright idea; **¡vaya o.!** the very idea!, what an idea!; **su o. nos metió en un buen lío** his bright idea got us into a real mess (**b**) *(dicho gracioso)* witty remark (**c**) *Ling* frequency of use

> **Falso amigo**: El sustantivo inglés **occurrence** no es la traducción del español **ocurrencia**. En inglés **occurrence** significa "suceso" o "incidencia".

ocurrente *adj* witty

ocurrido, -a *adj* (**a**) *(que ha sucedido)* **lo o. demuestra que estábamos en lo cierto** what happened proved that we were right (**b**) *Ecuad, Perú (ocurrente)* witty

ocurrir 1 *vi* (**a**) *(suceder)* to happen; **ocurre muy frecuentemente** it happens very often; **nadie sabe lo que ocurrió** nobody knows what happened; **ha ocurrido un accidente** there's been an accident; **lo que ocurre es que...** the thing is...; **¿qué le ocurre a Juan?** what's up with Juan?; **¿qué ocurre?** what's the matter?; **¿te ocurre algo?** is anything the matter?

(**b**) *Méx (ir)* to go; **ocurrí a la central camionera** I went to the central bus station

2 **ocurrirse** *vpr (venir a la cabeza)* **se me ha ocurrido una idea** I've got an idea; **no se me ocurre ninguna solución** I can't think of a solution; **dije lo primero que se me ocurrió** I said the first thing that came into my head; **se me ocurre que...** it occurs to me that...; **¡ni se te ocurra!** don't you dare!; **como se te ocurra desobedecerme te la vas a ganar** if you even think of disobeying me, you're in for it; **después del accidente no se le ocurrió nada mejor que comprarse una moto** what did he do after the accident but buy a motorbike!; **¡se te ocurre cada cosa!** you do come out with some funny things!; **¿cómo se le ocurrió hacer semejante barbaridad?** whatever made him do such a frightful thing?; **sólo a tí se te podía o. algo así** only you could come up with something like this; **pero, ¡a quién se le ocurre salir con esta lluvia!** it's madness to go out in this rain!

oda *nf* ode

odalisca *nf* odalisque

ODECA *nf* (*abrev de* **Organización de los Estados Centroamericanos**) OCAS

odeón *nm* odeon

odiar *vt* to hate; **o. a muerte a alguien** to loathe sb; **odio las aceitunas** I hate *o* can't stand olives; **odio levantarme pronto** I hate getting up early

odio *nm* hatred; **tener o. a algo/alguien** to hate sth/sb; *Esp* **cogerle** *o Am* **tomarle o. a algo/alguien** to develop a hatred for *o* of sth/sb

odioso, -a *adj (persona, actitud, acción)* hateful, horrible; **tiene la odiosa manía de interrumpir a todo el mundo** she has the annoying *o* irritating habit of interrupting everyone

odisea *nf* (**a**) *(viaje)* odyssey; **llegar hasta la frontera fue una o.** it was a real trek to get to the border (**b**) *(aventura)* **conseguir las entradas fue toda una o.** it was a real job to get the tickets (**c**) **la O.** the Odyssey

odontología *nf* dentistry

odontológico, -a *adj* dental

odontólogo, -a *nm,f* dentist, dental surgeon

odorífero, -a *adj* odoriferous

odre *nm (de vino)* wineskin

OEA *nf* (*abrev de* **Organización de Estados Americanos**) OAS

oesnoroeste, oesnorueste *nm* west-northwest

oeste 1 *adj inv (posición, parte)* west, western; *(dirección, viento)* west, westerly; **la cara o. del pico** the west face of the mountain; **la costa o.** the west coast; **tiempo nuboso en la mitad o. de la región** overcast in the western half of the region; **partieron con rumbo o.** they set off westward(s); **un frente frío que se desplaza en dirección o.** a cold front moving westward(s)

2 *nm* (**a**) *(zona)* west; **está al o. de Madrid** it's (to the) west of Madrid; **la fachada da al o.** the facade faces west; **viento del o.** west wind; **habrá lluvias en el o. (del país)** there will be rain in the west (of the country); **ir hacia el o.** to go west(wards)

(**b**) *(punto cardinal)* West; **el sol se pone por el O.** the sun sets in the West

(**c**) *(viento)* westerly

(**d**) *(de Estados Unidos)* West; **el lejano O.** the Wild West; **una película del O.** a Western

oesudoeste, oesudueste *nm* west-southwest

ofender 1 *vt* (**a**) *(injuriar, molestar)* to offend; **tus palabras me ofenden** your words offend me; **disculpa si te he ofendido en algo** I'm sorry if I've offended you in some way (**b**) *(a la vista, al oído)* to offend; **una monstruosidad arquitectónica que ofende la vista** an architectural monstrosity that offends the eye

2 *vi* to cause offence

3 **ofenderse** *vpr* to take offence (**por** at); **se ofende por nada** she takes offence at the slightest thing; **no te ofendas, pero creo que te equivocas** don't be offended but I think you're wrong

ofendido, -a 1 *adj* offended

2 *nm,f* offended party

ofensa *nf* (**a**) *(acción)* offence, insult; **una o. a la dignidad humana** an offence *o* insult to human dignity; **una o. a la buena educación** an affront to good manners (**b**) *(injuria)* slight, insult; **no lo tomes como una o. personal** don't take it as a personal insult *o* offence

ofensiva *nf* offensive; **pasar a la o.** to go on the offensive; **tomar la o.** to take the offensive; **una o. política** a political offensive

ofensivo, -a *adj* (**a**) *(conducta, palabra)* offensive, rude (**b**) *(arma, táctica)* offensive

ofensor, -ora 1 *nm,f* offender

2 *adj* attacking

oferta *nf* (**a**) *(propuesta, ofrecimiento)* offer; **ofertas de empleo** *o* **trabajo** *(en anuncio)* situations vacant, job opportunities; **me han hecho una o. de empleo** *o* **de trabajo** they've offered me a job; **o. en firme** firm offer; **la ciudad cuenta con una enorme o. teatral** the city offers a very wide choice of theatrical entertainment

(**b**) *Econ (suministro)* supply; **la o. y la demanda** supply and demand ►► ***o. monetaria*** money supply

(**c**) *(rebaja)* bargain, special offer; **o. especial** special offer; **artículos de o.** sale goods, goods on offer; **estar de** *o* **en o.** to be on offer; **han puesto muchas ofertas en el supermercado** there are a lot of special offers at the supermarket ►► ***o. de lanzamiento*** introductory offer

(**d**) *Fin (proposición)* bid, tender ►► ***o. pública de adquisición*** takeover bid; ***o. pública hostil*** hostile takeover bid

ofertante 1 *adj* bidding

2 *nm,f* bidder

ofertar 1 *vt (plaza, puesto)* to offer; *(producto, servicio)* to offer for sale; *(a un precio reducido)* to put on special (offer)

2 *vi (en una subasta)* to bid (**por** for)

ofertorio *nm Rel* offertory

off 1 **en off** *loc adj* **voz en o.** *Cine* voice-over; *Teatro* voice offstage

2 **en off** *loc adv* **se oyó en o. una voz** *Teatro* a voice was heard offstage; *Cine* a voice-over was heard, a voice was heard offscreen

3 **off the record** *loc adv* off the record

4 **off line** *loc adv Informát* off line

office ['ofis] *nm inv* scullery

offset (*pl* **offsets**) *nm Imprenta* offset

offside [of'saið] *nm (en fútbol)* offside; **estar en o.** to be offside; EXPR **pillar** *o Am* **pescar a alguien en o.** to catch sb out

oficial[1] 1 *adj* official

2 *nmf* (**a**) *Mil* officer ►► ***o. de guardia*** officer of the watch; ***o. al mando*** commanding officer; ***o. de reserva*** reserve officer (**b**) *(de policía)* police officer (**c**) *(funcionario)* clerk

oficial², -**ala** *nm,f* skilled worker, journeyman; **o. montador** journeyman fitter; **o. electricista** skilled electrician

oficialía *nf* (**a**) *(en el ejército)* officer rank (**b**) *(en la administración)* clerkship

oficialidad *nf* (**a**) *(carácter oficial)* official nature (**b**) *Mil* officer corps, officers

oficialismo *nm Am* (**a**) **el o.** *(gobierno)* the government (**b**) **el o.** *(partidarios del gobierno)* government supporters

oficialista *Am* **1** *adj* pro-government
2 *nm,f* government supporter

oficializar [14] *vt* to make official

oficialmente *adv* officially

oficiante 1 *nmf Rel* officiant
2 *adj* officiating

oficiar 1 *vt (misa)* to celebrate; *(ceremonia)* to officiate at
2 *vi* (**a**) *(sacerdote)* to officiate (**b**) **o. de** *(actuar de)* to act as

oficina *nf* (**a**) *(despacho)* office; **puedes llamarlo a su o.** you can phone him at the office ►► ***o. de cambio*** bureau de change; ***o. de clasificación de correo*** sorting office; ***o. de colocación*** employment agency; ***o. de correos*** post office; ***o. de empleo*** *Br* Jobcentre; ***o. de información*** information office; ***o. inteligente*** intelligent office; ***o. de objetos perdidos*** *Br* lost property, *US* lost-and-found office; ***o. de prensa*** press office; ***o. pública*** public office; ***o. de reclamaciones*** *o Am* ***reclamos*** complaints office; ***o. de turismo*** tourist office
(**b**) *Ven (en hacienda)* = buildings where coffee or cocoa beans are processed and stored

oficinista *nmf* office worker

oficio *nm* (**a**) *(profesión manual)* trade; **de o.** by trade
(**b**) *(trabajo)* job; EXPR *Fam* **no tener o. ni beneficio** to have no trade; EXPR **ser del o.** *Fam Euf* to be a working girl, *Br* to be on the game ►► *Euf* ***el o. más viejo del mundo*** the oldest profession (in the world)
(**c**) *Der* **de o.** *(abogado)* court-appointed, legal aid; *(diligencia)* judicial proceedings
(**d**) *(documento)* official minute
(**e**) *(experiencia)* **tener mucho o.** to be very experienced; **se llegó a un acuerdo gracias a los buenos oficios del ministro** an agreement was reached thanks to the good offices of the minister
(**f**) *Rel (ceremonia)* service ►► ***o. de difuntos*** funeral service
(**g**) *(función)* function, role
(**h**) *(comunicación)* communiqué, official notice
(**i**) *Col, Ven Fam (tarea doméstica)* household chore; **hacer oficios** to do housework

oficiosamente *adv (no oficialmente)* unofficially

oficiosidad *nf* unofficial nature

oficioso, -**a** *adj* unofficial

> **Falso amigo**: El adjetivo inglés **officious** no es la traducción del español **oficioso**. En inglés **officious** significa "excesivamente celoso" o "entrometido".

ofidio *nm (serpiente)* snake, *Espec* ophidian

ofimática *nf* (**a**) *(técnicas informáticas)* office IT, office automation (**b**) *(material de oficina)* office computer equipment

ofimático, -**a** *adj* **material o.** office computer equipment; **gestión ofimática integrada** integrated office automation

OFRECER [46] **1** *vt (proporcionar, dar)* to offer; **ofrecerle algo a alguien** to offer sb sth; **me han ofrecido el puesto de director** they've offered me the job of manager; **¿puedo ofrecerle algo de beber?** may I offer you something to drink?; **ofrecen una recompensa por él** they are offering a reward for his capture; **le ofrecieron una cena homenaje** they held a dinner in his honour; **¿cuánto te ofrecen por la casa?** how much are they offering you for the house?; **me ofrece la oportunidad** *o* **la ocasión de conocer la ciudad** it gives me the chance to get to know the city
(**b**) *(en subastas)* to bid; **¿qué ofrecen por esta mesa?** what am I bid for this table?
(**c**) *(tener, presentar)* to present; **la cocina ofrece un aspecto lamentable** the kitchen is in a real mess; **esta tarea ofrece algunas dificultades** this task poses *o* presents a number of problems; **aquel negocio ofrecía inmejorables perspectivas** that business had excellent prospects
(**d**) *(oraciones, sacrificio)* to offer up; **o. una misa por alguien** to have a mass said for sb
2 ofrecerse *vpr* (**a**) *(presentarse)* to offer, to volunteer; **varios se ofrecieron voluntarios** several people volunteered; **ofrecerse a** *o* **para hacer algo** to offer to do sth; **me ofrecí de guía para enseñarles la ciudad** I volunteered *o* offered to act as a guide and show them round the city; **se ofrece diseñadora con mucha experiencia** *(en letrero, anuncio)* highly experienced designer seeks employment
(**b**) *(aparecer)* **se nos ofrece una oportunidad de oro para hacer dinero** this is a golden opportunity for us to make some money; **un hermoso paisaje se ofrecía ante sus ojos** a beautiful landscape greeted her eyes
(**c**) *Formal (desear)* **¿qué se le ofrece?** what can I do for you?; **estamos aquí para lo que se le ofrezca** we are here to be of service to you

ofrecimiento *nm* offer

ofrenda *nf* offering

ofrendar *vt* to offer up

ofrezco *etc ver* **ofrecer**

oftalmía, oftalmia *nf* ophthalmia

oftalmología *nf* ophthalmology

oftalmológico, -**a** *adj* ophthalmological

oftalmólogo, -**a** *nm,f* ophthalmologist

oftalmoscopia *nf* ophthalmoscopy

oftalmoscopio *nm* ophthalmoscope

ofuscación *nf,* **ofuscamiento** *nm* (**a**) *(deslumbramiento)* blindness (**b**) *(turbación)* **el odio ha provocado su o.** he was so full of hatred he couldn't think clearly; **los mató en un momento de o.** he killed them in a moment of madness *o* blind rage

ofuscar [60] **1** *vt* (**a**) *(deslumbrar)* to dazzle, to blind (**b**) *(turbar)* to blind; **la envidia la ofuscó** she was blinded with envy
2 ofuscarse *vpr* (**a**) *(deslumbrarse)* to be dazzled *o* blinded (**con** *o* **por** by) (**b**) *(turbarse)* to become confused; **después de equivocarse, se ofuscó y no sabía como seguir** after making the mistake he got flustered and couldn't go on (**c**) *(obsesionarse)* **se ha ofuscado con la idea** the idea has blinded him to everything else

ogro *nm también Fig* ogre

oh *interj* oh!

ohmio *nm* ohm

oídas: de oídas *loc adv* by hearsay; **lo conozco de o.** I know of him, I've heard of him; **sabemos la noticia sólo de o.** the news is only hearsay

oído *nm* (**a**) *(órgano)* ear; **se me han tapado los oídos** my ears are blocked; **le dolían los oídos** he had earache; **me zumban los oídos** my ears are ringing *o* buzzing; *(porque alguien habla de ti)* my ears are burning; **decir algo al o. a alguien** to whisper sth in sb's ear; **si llega a oídos de ella...** if she gets to hear about this...; EXPR **abrir el o.** *o* **los oídos** to pay close attention; EXPR **dar** *o* **prestar oídos a algo** to pay attention to sth; EXPR **entrar por un o. y salir por el otro** to go in one ear and out the other; EXPR **hacer oídos sordos** to turn a deaf ear; EXPR **lastimar los oídos** to offend one's ears; EXPR *Fam* **¡o. al parche!** listen!, *US* listen up!; EXPR **regalarle el o. a alguien** to flatter sb; EXPR **ser todo oídos** to be all ears ►► ***o. externo*** outer ear; ***o. interno*** inner ear; ***o. medio*** middle ear
(**b**) *(sentido)* (sense of) hearing; **aguzar el o.** to prick up one's ears; **ser duro de o.** to be hard of hearing; **tener o., tener buen o.** to have a good ear; **tocar de o.** to play by ear

OIEA *nm (abrev de* **Organismo Internacional para la Energía Atómica**) IAEA

oigo *ver* **oír**

OÍR [44] **1** *vt* (**a**) *(percibir el sonido de)* to hear; **la oí salir** I heard her leaving; **los oí hablando** *o* **hablar** *o* **que hablaban** I heard them talking; **he oído muchas cosas buenas de ti** I've heard a lot of good things about you; **ahora lo oigo** I can hear it now; **¿me oyes?** *(al teléfono, a distancia)* can you hear me?; *(¿entendido?)* do you hear (me)?; **¡no se oye!** *(en público, auditorio)* I can't hear!; **hacerse o.** to make oneself heard; **¡lo que hay que o.!, ¡se oye cada cosa!** whatever next!; **o. algo de labios de alguien** to hear sth from sb; **lo oí de sus propios labios** I heard it from the horse's mouth; **o. a alguien decir algo** to hear sb say *o* saying sth; **he oído hablar de él/ello** I've heard of him/about it; **¡no quiero ni o. hablar de él/ello!** don't mention him/it to me!; **se ha teñido el pelo de rubio, así, como lo oyes** he's dyed his hair blond, believe it or not; **se ha divorciado – ¿de verdad? – como lo oyes** she's got divorced – really? – that's what I said; **como quien oye llover** without paying the least attention; *Fam* **¡me va a o.!** I'm going to give him a piece of my mind!
(**b**) *(escuchar, atender)* to listen to; **voy a o. las noticias** I'm going to listen to the news; **¿has oído alguna vez algo de Bartok?** have you ever heard any Bartok?; **¿tú crees que oirán nuestras demandas?** do you think they'll listen to our demands?; **oye bien lo que te digo**

listen carefully to what I'm going to tell you; **¿estás oyendo lo que te digo?** are you listening to me?; **o. a alguien en confesión** to hear sb's confession

(**c**) *(saber, enterarse de)* to hear; **¿has oído algo de mi hermano?** have you heard from my brother?; **he oído lo de tu padre** I heard about your father; **he oído (decir) que te marchas** I hear *o* I've heard you're leaving

(**d**) *Der (sujeto: juez)* to hear

(**e**) **o. misa** to hear mass

2 *vi* to hear; **de este oído no oigo bien** I don't hear very well with this ear; **¡oiga, por favor!** excuse me!; *Fam* **oye...** *(mira)* listen...; **oye, te tengo que dejar** listen *o* look, I have to go; *Fam* **¡oye!** *(¡eh!)* hey!; **¡oye, no te pases!** hey, steady on!; PROV **o., ver y callar** hear no evil, see no evil, speak no evil

OIRT *nf (abrev de* **Organisation Internationale de Radiodiffusion et Télévision**) OIRT

OIT *nf (abrev de* **Organización Internacional del Trabajo**) ILO

ojal *nm* buttonhole

ojalá *interj* I hope so!; **¿saldrá el sol? – ¡o.!** will the sun come out? – I hope so!; **¡o. lo haga!** I hope she does it!; **¡o. fuera viernes!** I wish it was Friday!; **¡o. que salga bien!** I hope it goes well!

OJD *nf (abrev de* **Oficina de Justificación de la Difusión**) = Spanish audience measurement organization, ≃ Audit Bureau of Circulations (ABC)

ojeada *nf* glance, look; **echar una o. a algo/alguien** to take a quick glance *o* look at sth/sb; **darle una o. a algo** to have a quick look at sth; **le he dado una o. al informe** I've glanced through the report

ojeador *nm* (**a**) *(en caza)* beater (**b**) *Dep* scout

ojear *vt* to have a look at

ojeras *nfpl* bags *o* rings under the eyes; **llegó al trabajo con o. de tres días** he arrived at work looking haggard

ojeriza *nf* dislike; **tener o. a alguien** to have it in for sb

ojeroso, -a *adj* with bags *o* rings under the eyes, haggard

ojete, -a 1 *adj Méx Vulg* **ser o.** to be an *Br* arsehole *o US* asshole

2 *nm* (**a**) *(bordado)* eyelet (**b**) *muy Fam (ano)* arsehole, ring (**c**) *RP muy Fam (buena suerte)* the luck of the devil; **¡qué o. tiene, se ganó la lotería!** what a lucky bastard, he's won the lottery!

3 *nm,f Méx Vulg* shit, arsehole

ojetillo *nm Am* eyelet

ojímetro: a ojímetro *loc adv Fam* at a rough guess; **a o. serán unos tres metros** at a rough guess it's about three metres; **lo medí a o.** I made a rough guess of the measurements

ojiva *nf* (**a**) *Arquit* ogive (**b**) *Mil* warhead

ojival *adj* ogival, pointed

OJO 1 *nm* (**a**) *(órgano)* eye; **una chica de ojos azules** a girl with blue eyes; **lleva un parche en el o.** he has an eyepatch; **guiñar** *o Col* **picar el o. a alguien** to wink at sb; **mírame a los ojos cuando te hablo** look at me when I'm speaking to you; **no me atrevía a mirarla a los ojos** I didn't dare look her in the eye; **me pican los ojos** my eyes are stinging; **a los ojos de la ley/de la sociedad** in the eyes of the law/of society; *también Fig* **poner los ojos en blanco** to roll one's eyes; **lo vi con mis propios ojos** I saw it with my own eyes; **abrir (bien) los ojos** *(estar atento)* to keep one's eyes open; **habrá que tener los ojos bien abiertos** we'll have to keep our eyes open; *Fig* **abrirle los ojos a alguien** to open sb's eyes; **cerré los ojos y me decidí a comprar una casa** I decided to ignore the consequences and buy a house anyway; **cerrar los ojos ante algo** *(ignorar)* to close one's eyes to sth; **con los ojos cerrados** *(sin dudarlo)* blindly, with one's eyes closed; **sabría ir allí con los ojos cerrados** *o* **vendados** I could find my way there blindfolded *o* with my eyes closed; *Fam* **mirar algo/a alguien con los ojos como platos** to stare at sth/sb wide-eyed; EXPR **cuatro ojos ven más que dos** four eyes are better than two; EXPR *Fam* **¡dichosos los ojos que te ven!** long time no see!; EXPR **en un abrir y cerrar de ojos** in the twinkling of an eye; EXPR *Am* **meter el o.** to pry, to snoop; EXPR **no pegar o.** not to get a wink of sleep; EXPR *CAm, Méx, Ven* **pelar los ojos** to keep one's eyes peeled; EXPR **ser el o. derecho de alguien** to be the apple of sb's eye; EXPR **¿es que no tienes ojos en la cara?** are you blind?; EXPR **tener entre ojos a alguien** to detest sb; EXPR **tener ojos de lince** to have eyes like a hawk; EXPR *RP* **tener ojos en la nuca** *(profesor)* to have eyes in the back of one's head; *(la izquierda)* to be stuck in the past, to be always looking backwards; EXPR **sólo tiene ojos para él** she only has eyes for him; EXPR **valer** *o* **costar un o. de la cara** to cost an arm and a leg; PROV **o. por o., diente por diente** an eye for an eye, a tooth for a tooth; PROV **ojos que no ven, corazón que no siente** what the eye doesn't see, the heart doesn't grieve over ▸▸ *RP* ***o. en compota*** *(ojo morado)* black eye; *Esp* ***o. de cristal*** glass eye; *Esp Fam* ***o. a la funerala*** shiner; **ponerle a alguien un o. a la funerala** to give sb a shiner; ***o. morado*** black eye; **ponerle a alguien un o. morado** to give sb a black eye; ***ojos rasgados*** almond eyes; ***ojos saltones:*** **tiene los ojos saltones** he's pop-eyed *o US* bug-eyed; **una niña de ojos saltones** a girl with bulging eyes; *Am* ***o. de vidrio*** glass eye; *Fam* ***o. a la virulé*** shiner; *Fam* **ponerle a alguien un o. a la virulé** to give sb a shiner

(**b**) *(mirada, vista)* **los ojos expertos del relojero enseguida detectaron el problema** the watchmaker's expert eye spotted the problem immediately; **alzar** *o* **levantar los ojos** to look up, to raise one's eyes; **bajar los ojos** to lower one's eyes *o* gaze, to look down; **los ojos se le iban detrás del muchacho/de la tarta** she couldn't keep her eyes off the boy/the cake; **come más con los ojos que con la boca** his eyes are bigger than his stomach; **mirar a alguien con ojos tiernos** to look fondly at sb; **poner los ojos en alguien** to set one's sights on sb; EXPR **a o. (de buen cubero)** roughly, approximately; **echo los ingredientes a o.** I just add roughly the right amount of each ingredient without measuring them all out; **a ojos vistas** visibly; EXPR *Fam* **comerse a alguien con los ojos** to drool over sb; EXPR **echar el o. a algo/alguien: le he echado un o. a una compañera de clase** I've got my eye on a girl in my class; **le tenía el o. echado a aquella moto** I had my eye on that motorbike; EXPR **echar un o. a algo** to keep an eye on sth; EXPR **entrar por los ojos: esos pasteles entran por los ojos** those cakes look really mouthwatering; EXPR **mirar** *o* **ver algo/a alguien con buenos ojos** to approve of sth/sb; EXPR **mirar** *o* **ver algo/a alguien con malos ojos** to disapprove of sth/sb; EXPR **mirar algo/a alguien con otros ojos** to look differently at sth/sb; EXPR **no quitarle o. a algo/alguien, no quitar los ojos de encima a algo/alguien** not to take one's eyes off sth/sb; EXPR **donde pone el o., pone la bala** he's a dead shot; EXPR **ojos de carnero** *o* **cordero (degollado)** pleading eyes; **puso ojos de cordero degollado** she looked at me with pleading eyes

(**c**) *(cuidado)* **(ten) mucho o. con lo que haces/al cruzar la calle** be very careful what you do/when crossing the road; **hay que andar(se) con (mucho) o.** you need to be (very) careful; EXPR **hay que andar(se) con cien ojos** you really have to keep your eyes open *o* be on your guard; EXPR **estar o. avizor** to be on the lookout

(**d**) *(habilidad, perspicacia)* **es un tipo con mucho o.** *o* **con buen o. para los negocios** he has an eye for a good deal, he has great business acumen; **tener (un) o. clínico para algo** to be a good judge of sth

(**e**) *(agujero, hueco) (de aguja)* eye; *(de puente)* span; *(de arco)* archway; **el o. de la cerradura** the keyhole; **el o. de la escalera** the stairwell; **el o. del huracán** the eye of the hurricane; *Fig* **el ministro está en el o. del huracán** the minister is at the centre of the controversy ▸▸ ***o. de buey*** *(ventana)* porthole; *Vulg* ***el o. del culo*** *Br* arsehole, *US* asshole; *Am* ***o. mágico*** peephole

(**f**) *Med* ***o. de gallo*** *(callo)* corn

(**g**) *Fot* ***o. de pez*** fish-eye lens

(**h**) *Méx, Ven* ***o. de agua*** spring

(**i**) *Ven* ***o. de gato*** cat's eye

2 *interj* be careful!, watch out!

ojón, -ona *adj Andes, Carib* big-eyed

ojota *nf* (**a**) *Andes (zapatilla)* sandal (**b**) *RP (chancleta) Br* flip-flop, *US, Austr* thong

OK, okey [o'kei] *interj* OK

okapi *nm* okapi

okey *interj Am* OK

okupa, ocupa *nmf Esp Fam* squatter; **están de okupas en una vieja escuela** they're squatting in a disused school

okupar *vt Esp Fam* to squat

ola *nf* wave; **una o. de atentados terroristas** a wave *o* spate of terrorist attacks; **una o. de visitantes** a flood of visitors ▸▸ ***o. de calor*** heatwave; ***o. de frío*** cold spell; ***la o. mexicana*** the Mexican wave; **hacer la o. (mexicana)** to do the Mexican wave

OLADE *nf (abrev de* **Organización Latinoamericana de Energía**) OLADE, Latin American Energy Organization

olán *nm Méx* frill, flounce

ole, olé *interj* bravo!

oleada *nf* (**a**) *(del mar)* wave (**b**) *(de protestas, atentados)* wave; **sentí una o. de indignación** I felt a surge of indignation

oleaginoso, -a *adj* oleaginous

oleaje *nm* swell, surge; **el fuerte o. impidió que saliéramos a la mar** the heavy swell prevented us from putting out to sea

oleandro *nm Bot* oleander

olefina *nf Quím* olefin

oleicultura *nf* olive oil production

óleo *nm* (**a**) *(material)* oil; **pintar al ó.** to paint in oils; **una pintura al ó.** an oil painting (**b**) *(cuadro)* oil painting (**c**) *Rel* **los santos óleos** the holy oils

oleoducto *nm* oil pipeline

oleómetro *nm* oil hydrometer, oleometer

oleosidad *nf* oiliness

oleoso, -a *adj* oily

oleosoluble *adj* oil-soluble

oler [45] **1** *vt* to smell; **desde aquí huelo el tabaco** I can smell the cigarette smoke from here

2 *vi* (**a**) *(despedir olor)* to smell (**a** of); **¡qué mal huele aquí!** it smells awful here!; **¡huele que apesta!** it stinks!; **te huele un poco el aliento** your breath smells a bit; **huele a quemado** it smells of burning; EXPR **o. que alimenta: este guisado huele que alimenta** this stew smells delicious; *Hum* **te huelen los pies que alimentan** your feet are humming; EXPR *Fam* **o. a cuerno quemado** to smell fishy; EXPR *Fam* **o. a rayos** to stink (to high heaven); EXPR *Fam* **o. a tigre** to stink; EXPR **o. a encerrado** to smell stuffy

(**b**) *(parecer)* **su cambio de actitud huele a soborno** his change of attitude smacks of bribery

3 olerse *vpr Fig* **olerse algo** to sense sth; **me huelo que está enfadado conmigo** I sense he's angry with me; **ya me olía yo algo así** I suspected as much; EXPR *Méx Fam* **olérselas** to have a suspicion; EXPR *Fam* **ya me olía la tostada** I could sense there was trouble coming; EXPR *Fam* **me huele a chamusquina** it smells a bit fishy to me, I don't like the look of this

oletear *vt Perú* to pry into

olfa *nmf Arg Fam Br* swot, *US* grind

olfatear *vt* (**a**) *(olisquear)* to sniff; *(rastro)* to scent (**b**) *Fig (barruntar)* to smell, to sense; **o. en** *(indagar)* to pry into

olfativo, -a *adj* olfactory

olfato *nm* (**a**) *(sentido)* (sense of) smell (**b**) *(sagacidad)* nose, instinct; **tener (buen) o. para algo** to be a good judge of sth

oliera *etc ver* **oler**

oligarca *nmf* oligarch

oligarquía *nf* oligarchy

oligárquico, -a *adj* oligarchic(al)

oligisto *nm Geol* oligist, crystallized haematite

oligoceno, -a *Geol* **1** *adj* Oligocene

2 *nm* **el o.** the Oligocene

oligoelemento *nm* trace element

oligofrenia *nf* severe mental handicap

oligofrénico, -a 1 *adj* severely mentally handicapped

2 *nm,f* severely mentally handicapped person

oligopolio *nm Econ* oligopoly

olimpiada, olimpíada *nf* (**a**) *(periodo de cuatro años)* Olympiad (**b**) *(juegos olímpicos)* **las olimpiadas** the Olympics, the Olympic Games

olímpicamente *adv Fam* **paso o. de ayudarlos** I'm damned if I'm going to help them; **pasa de sus padres o.** she totally ignores her parents; **despreció o. la oferta** he turned his nose up at the offer

olímpico, -a 1 *adj* (**a**) *Dep* Olympic (**b**) *(altanero)* Olympian, haughty; **me trataron con un desprecio o.** they looked down their noses at me

2 *nm Urug* = giant cheese and ham sandwich with salad, olives and egg

olimpismo *nm* Olympic movement

Olimpo *nm* **el O.** Mount Olympus

olisquear *vt* to sniff (at)

oliva *nf* olive ►► ***o. negra*** black olive; ***o. rellena*** stuffed olive; ***o. verde*** green olive

oliváceo, -a *adj* olive

olivar *nm* olive grove

olivarero, -a 1 *adj* olive; **el sector o.** the olive-growing industry

2 *nm,f* olive-grower

olivícola *adj* olive-growing

olivicultor, -ora *nm,f* olive-grower

olivicultura *nf* olive growing

olivo *nm* olive tree ►► ***o. silvestre*** wild olive tree

olla *nf* (**a**) *(cacerola)* pot ►► ***o. exprés*** pressure cooker; *Fig* ***una o. de grillos*** bedlam, a madhouse; **aquello era una o. de grillos** it was bedlam *o* a madhouse; ***o. a presión*** pressure cooker; *Fig* **el campo era una o. a presión** there was a pressure cooker atmosphere in the stadium

(**b**) *(cocido)* = meat and vegetable stew ►► *Culin* ***o. podrida*** = meat and vegetable stew containing also ham, poultry, sausages etc; *Urug* ***o. popular*** soup kitchen

(**c**) *Fam (cabeza)* head, nut; **tú estás mal de la o.** you're off your head; EXPR **se fue de la o., se le fue la o.** he lost it

(**d**) *Fam (en fútbol)* (penalty) area

(**e**) EXPR *Ven Fam* **montar la o.** to make the food; *Fam* **no tener con qué montar la o.** not to be able to make ends meet; EXPR *Andes, RP Fam* **parar la o.** to be the breadwinner

ollar *nm* nostril

olmeca *Hist* **1** *adj* Olmec

2 *nmf* Olmec

olmeda *nf,* **olmedo** *nm* elm grove

olmo *nm* elm (tree) ►► ***o. americano*** American elm tree

ológrafo, -a 1 *adj* holographical

2 *nm* holograph

olor *nm* smell (**a** of); **tener o. a** to smell of; **los niños acudieron al o. de la comida** the children were drawn to the smell of cooking; **miles de jóvenes aspirantes acuden a Hollywood al o. de la fama** thousands of young hopefuls come to Hollywood looking for fame; EXPR *Fam* **en o. de multitudes** enjoying popular acclaim; EXPR **vivir/morir en o. de santidad** to live/die like a saint ►► *RP Fam* ***o. a chivo*** BO; ***o. corporal*** body odour

oloroso, -a 1 *adj* fragrant

2 *nm* oloroso (sherry)

OLP *nf (abrev de* **Organización para la Liberación de Palestina**) PLO

olvidadizo, -a *adj* forgetful

olvidado, -a *adj* forgotten

olvidar 1 *vt* (**a**) *(en general)* to forget; **no consigo olvidarla** I can't forget her; **intenté o. aquellos años y rehacer mi vida** I tried to forget those years and rebuild my life (**b**) *(dejarse)* to leave; **olvidé las llaves en la oficina** I left my keys at the office; **Juan olvidó su bufanda al irse** Juan left his scarf behind when he left

2 olvidarse *vpr* (**a**) *(en general)* to forget; **olvidarse de algo/de hacer algo** to forget sth/to do sth; **me olvidé de su cumpleaños** I forgot her birthday; **olvídate de lo ocurrido** forget what happened; **se me olvidaba decirte que...** I almost forgot to tell you that...; **yo no me olvido de mis amigos** I don't forget my friends

(**b**) *(dejarse)* to leave; **me he olvidado el paraguas en el tren** I've left my umbrella on the train; **mira, se ha olvidado la cartera** look, he's forgotten his wallet

olvido *nm* (**a**) *(de un nombre, hecho)* **caer en el o.** to fall into oblivion; **enterrar en el o.** to cast into oblivion; **rescatar** *o* **sacar del o.** to rescue from oblivion (**b**) *(descuido)* oversight; **ha sido un o. imperdonable** it was an unforgivable oversight

Omán *n* Oman

omaní (*pl* **omaníes**) **1** *adj* Omani

2 *nmf* Omani

ombligo *nm* navel; **se te ve el o.** your belly button's showing; EXPR **mirarse el propio o.** to contemplate one's navel; **deja de mirarte el o.** stop navel-gazing, stop contemplating your navel EXPR **se cree el o. del mundo** he thinks the world revolves around him

ombliguero *nm* bellyband

ombú (*pl* **ombúes**) *nm* ombu

ombudsman *nm inv* ombudsman

OMC *nf (abrev de* **Organización Mundial del Comercio**) WTO

omega *nf* omega

omelet (*pl* **omelets**), **omelette** [ome'let] *nm Am* omelette

OMG *nm (abrev de* **Organismo Modificado Genéticamente**) GMO

ómicron *nf* omicron

ominoso, -a *adj* (**a**) *(abominable)* abominable (**b**) *(de mal agüero)* ominous

omisión *nf* omission

omiso, -a *adj* **hacer caso o. de algo** to ignore sth, to pay no attention to sth

omitir *vt* to omit

ómnibus (*pl* **ómnibus** *o* **omnibuses**) *nm* (**a**) *Esp (tren)* local train (**b**) *Cuba, Urug (urbano)* bus; *Andes, Cuba, Urug (interurbano, internacional) Br* coach, *US* bus ►► ***ó. de línea*** *Br* coach, *US* bus

omnímodo, -a *adj* all-embracing, absolute

omnipotencia *nf* omnipotence

omnipotente *adj* omnipotent

omnipresencia *nf* omnipresence

omnipresente *adj* omnipresent

omnisapiente *adj* omniscient
omnisciencia *nf* omniscience
omnisciente *adj* omniscient
omnívoro, -a 1 *adj* omnivorous
2 *nm,f* omnivore
omoplato, omóplato *nm* shoulder-blade, *Espec* scapula
OMS [oms] *nf* (*abrev de* **Organización Mundial de la Salud**) WHO
onagra *nf* evening primrose
onagro *nm (asno salvaje)* onager
onanismo *nm* onanism
ONCE ['onθe] *nf* (*abrev de* **Organización Nacional de Ciegos Españoles**) = Spanish association for the blind, famous for its national lottery
once 1 *núm* eleven; *ver también* **tres**
2 *nm* (**a**) *(equipo)* eleven; **los integrantes del o. colombiano** the Colombian eleven (**b**) *Andes* **onces** *(por la mañana)* mid-morning snack, *Br* elevenses; *(por la tarde)* mid-afternoon snack (**c**) *RP Fam* **en el o.** *(a pie)* on foot
onceavo, -a *núm (fracción)* eleventh; **la onceava parte** an eleventh
oncogén *nm* oncogene
oncogénico, -a *adj* oncogenic
oncología *nf* oncology
oncológico, -a *adj* oncological
oncólogo, -a *nm,f* oncologist
onda *nf* (**a**) *Fís, Rad* wave; **longitud de o.** wavelength ►► ***o. de choque*** shock wave, blast wave; ***o. corta*** short wave; ***o. electromagnética*** electromagnetic wave; ***o. expansiva*** shock wave; ***o. hertziana*** radio wave, Hertzian wave; ***o. larga*** long wave; ***o. luminosa*** *o* ***lumínica*** light wave; ***o. media*** medium wave; ***o. pura*** sine wave; ***o. sinusoidal*** sine wave; ***o. sísmica*** seismic wave; ***o. sonora*** sound wave
(**b**) *Fam* EXPR **estar en (la) o.** to be hip *o* with it; **este grupo está muy en (la) o.** this group is really hip; EXPR **me alegra saber que estamos en la misma o.** I'm glad to know we're on the same wavelength; EXPR **estar fuera de o.** to be behind the times; EXPR **¡qué buena o.!** that's cool!; EXPR **me da mala o.** I've got bad vibes about him/her/it; EXPR **tus primos tienen** *o RP* **son muy buena o.** your cousins are really cool; EXPR *RP* **de o.: esta es la playa de o.** this is the beach to be seen at; **siempre tiene el modelo de o.** she's always got the latest outfit; EXPR *RP* **hacer algo de o.** to do sth for the hell of it; EXPR *Méx, RP* **no me tires malas ondas** I don't want your bad vibes; EXPR *Méx, RP* **captar** *o* **agarrar la o.** *(entender)* to catch the drift; EXPR *Méx, RP* **¿qué o.?** how's it going?, how are things?; EXPR *Méx, RP* **sacar de o.** to take by surprise; *Méx, RP* **cuando me ves concentrada no me hables, que me sacás de o.** don't talk to me when you see me concentrating, you put me off
(**c**) *(en el agua)* wave
(**d**) *(del pelo)* wave
(**e**) *(en costura)* scallop; **bordado en o.** embroidered in scallops
ondeado, -a *adj* wavy
ondeante *adj* rippling
ondear 1 *vi (bandera)* to flutter, to fly; *(pelo)* to wave; **o. a media asta** to fly at half-mast
2 *vt (pañuelo, bandera)* to wave
ondero, -a *adj RP Fam Pey* trendy; **a Pedro hoy le gusta el tenis y mañana prefiere el golf, no le hagas caso, es muy o.** Pedro's into tennis one day and golf the next, he's very faddish
ondina *nf Mitol* undine, water nymph
ondulación *nf* (**a**) *(acción)* rippling (**b**) *(onda)* ripple; *(del pelo)* wave (**c**) *(movimiento)* undulation
ondulado, -a *adj (pelo)* wavy; *(agua)* rippling; *(campo, terreno)* rolling, undulating; *(patata frita)* crinkly, crinkle-cut
ondulante *adj* undulating
ondular 1 *vi (agua)* to ripple; *(terreno)* to undulate
2 *vt (pelo)* to wave
ondulatorio, -a *adj* wavelike, *Espec* undulatory
oneroso, -a *adj Formal* (**a**) *(pesado)* burdensome, onerous (**b**) *(caro)* costly, expensive
ONG *nf inv* (*abrev de* **Organización no Gubernamental**) NGO
ónice *nm o nf* onyx
onírico, -a *adj* dreamlike; **experiencia onírica** dreamlike experience
ónix *nm o nf* onyx
ONL *nf* (*abrev de* **Organización no Lucrativa**) *Br* non-profit(-making) *o US* not-for-profit organization
onomástica *nf Esp* name day
onomástico, -a 1 *adj* onomastic; **índice o.** name index
2 *nm Am* (**a**) *(cumpleaños)* birthday (**b**) *(santo)* name day
onomatopeya *nf* onomatopoeia
onomatopéyico, -a *adj* onomatopoeic
ontogénesis *nf inv,* **ontogenia** *nf Biol* ontogeny
ontogénico,-a *adj* ontogenic
ontología *nf* ontology
ontológico, -a *adj* ontological
ONU ['onu] *nf* (*abrev de* **Organización de las Naciones Unidas**) UN
onubense 1 *adj* of/from Huelva *(Spain)*
2 *nmf* person from Huelva *(Spain)*
onza[1] *nf* (**a**) *(unidad de peso)* ounce (**b**) *(de chocolate)* square
onza[2] *nf (guepardo)* cheetah
onzavo, -a *núm ver* **onceavo**
op. (*abrev de* **opus**) op
OPA ['opa] *nf* (*abrev de* **oferta pública de adquisición**) takeover bid; **lanzar una O. sobre** to launch a takeover bid for ►► ***O. hostil*** hostile takeover bid
opa[1] *Andes, RP Fam* 1 *adj* dumb, *Br* gormless
2 *nmf* dumb cluck, *Br* twit
opa[2] *interj RP Fam* (**a**) *(cuando se cae algo)* oops!, whoops!; *(expresando sorpresa)* hey!, hello! (**b**) *(hola)* hi!, *US* yo!
opacar *vt Am* (**a**) *(quitar brillo)* to mar; **su ausencia opacó las celebraciones** his absence cast a shadow over *o* marred the celebrations
(**b**) *(oscurecer)* to darken, to dull; **el polvo opacaba el brillo de la platería** the dust dulled the shine on the silverware
(**c**) *(eclipsar)* to overshadow, to outshine; **su belleza opacaba a todas las demás modelos** she outshone all the other models in her beauty, her beauty put all the other models in the shade
opacidad *nf también Fig* opacity
opaco, -a *adj* opaque
opalescencia *nf* opalescence
opalescente *adj* opalescent
opalina *nf* opaline
opalino, -a *adj* opaline
ópalo *nm* opal
opción *nf* (**a**) *(elección)* option; **no hay o.** there is no alternative; **no le quedó otra o. que dimitir** she had no option *o* choice but to resign
(**b**) *(derecho)* right; **dar o. a** to give the right to; **tener o. a** *(empleo, cargo)* to be eligible for; **ya no tienen o. al primer puesto** they've lost all chance of winning; **alquiler con o. a compra** rental with the option to buy ►► *Fin* ***opciones sobre acciones*** stock options; *Fin* ***o. de adquisición*** option to buy, purchase option; *Fin* ***o. de compra*** call option; *Fin* ***o. de compra de acciones*** stock option; *Fin* ***o. de futuro*** futures option; *Fin* ***o. de venta*** put option
opcional *adj* optional
opcionalmente *adv* optionally; **se puede visitar, o., el museo arqueológico** there is the option of a visit to the museum of archaeology; **el techo solar se ofrece o.** the sun roof is available as an optional extra
op. cit. (*abrev de* **opere citato**) op cit
open *nm Dep* Open (tournament); **O. de Australia/Francia/USA** *(en tenis)* Australian/French/US Open
OPEP [o'pep] *nf* (*abrev de* **Organización de Países Exportadores de Petróleo**) OPEC
ópera *nf* (**a**) *(composición)* opera; *(edificio)* opera house ►► ***ó. bufa*** comic opera, opera buffa; ***ó. rock*** rock opera (**b**) ***ó. prima*** *(novela, película)* first work
operable *adj* operable
operación *nf* (**a**) *(acción organizada)* operation ►► ***o. policial*** police operation; ***o. de rescate*** rescue operation; ***o. retorno*** = police operation to assist traffic at the end of popular holiday periods; ***o. salida*** = police operation to assist traffic at the beginning of popular holiday periods; ***o. de salvamento*** rescue operation
(**b**) *(quirúrgica)* operation; **o. (quirúrgica)** (surgical) operation; **una o. de corazón** a heart operation; **una o. a corazón abierto** open-heart surgery; **una o. a vida o muerte** a life-or-death operation; **el paciente debe someterse a una o.** the patient needs to have an operation; **le realizaron una o. de estómago** he had a stomach operation; **tuvo que ser sometida a una o. de urgencia** she had to undergo an emergency operation
(**c**) *(matemática)* operation

(d) *(militar)* operation; **operaciones conjuntas** joint operations ►► ***o. de limpia** o **de limpieza*** a mopping-up operation

(e) *Com, Fin* transaction; **una o. bursátil** a stock-market transaction; **una o. mercantil** *o* **comercial** a commercial transaction; **una o. de ingreso** a deposit; **una o. de reintegro** a withdrawal

operacional *adj* operational

operador, -ora 1 *nm,f* (a) *Informát* operator ►► ***o. del sistema*** SYSOP, systems operator (b) *Tel* operator (c) *Cine & TV (de la cámara)* cameraman, *f* camerawoman; *(del proyector)* projectionist; **un o. de sonido** a sound engineer (d) *(de una máquina)* operator

2 *nm* (a) *(empresa)* ***o. telefónico*** telephone operator *o* company; ***o. turístico*** tour operator (b) *Mat* operator ►► *Informát* ***o. lógico*** logical operator

operadora *nf Tel* telephone operator *o* company

operante *adj* operating, working

operar 1 *vt* (a) *(enfermo)* **o. a alguien (de algo)** to operate on sb (for sth); **ese es el médico que la operó** that's the surgeon who operated on her; **casi me tienen que o. de urgencia** I almost needed an emergency operation; **lo operaron del hígado** he had a liver operation; **la han operado de cáncer de pecho** she's had an operation for breast cancer; **de pequeño lo operaron de las amígdalas** he had his tonsils removed when he was a child

(b) *(cambio)* to bring about, to produce

(c) *Am (máquina)* to operate

2 *vi* (a) *(realizar una actividad)* to operate; **el ladrón operaba en esta zona** the thief operated in this area; **el técnico operó con gran precisión** the technician operated *o* worked with great precision (b) *Com & Fin* to deal (c) *Mat* to operate (d) *Mil* to operate

3 **operarse** *vpr* (a) *(enfermo)* to be operated on, to have an operation; **operarse de algo: se ha operado de un tumor** he's had an operation to remove a tumour; **me voy a o. del hígado** I'm going to have an operation on my liver; **se va a tener que o. del estómago** she's going to have to have a stomach operation; EXPR *Fam* **¡por mí como si se operan!** I couldn't care less what they do!

(b) *(cambio)* to occur, to come about

operario, -a *nm,f (trabajador)* worker; *(de máquina)* operator

operativa *nf* operations; **precisa agilidad en la o.** it requires operational agility

operatividad *nf (de ley, medida)* feasibility; *(de organización, dispositivo)* operational effectiveness; **los equipos de mejora y su o.** improvement teams and how they work

operativo, -a 1 *adj* (a) *(que funciona)* operative; **medidas operativas** operational measures; **el servicio será o. desde el viernes** the service will be operational from Friday; **una gran capacidad operativa** a large operating capacity (b) *Informát* operating; **el sistema o.** the operating system

2 *nm* operation; **un o. policial** a police operation

operatorio, -a *adj* operative

opérculo *nm* operculum

opereta *nf* operetta

operístico, -a *adj* operatic

opiáceo, -a 1 *adj* opiate

2 *nm* opiate

opinable *adj* debatable, arguable

opinar 1 *vt* to believe, to think; **o. de algo/alguien, o. sobre algo/alguien** to think about sth/sb; **¿qué opinas de la pena de muerte?** what are your views on *o* what do you think about the death penalty?; **ellos no lo veían necesario pero yo opinaba lo contrario** they didn't think it necessary but I held the opposite view; **ninguno de los consultados opina lo mismo** none of those consulted holds the same view; **el comité opinaba que era necesario invertir más** the committee was of the opinion *o* held the view that more investment was necessary; **o. bien de alguien** to think highly of sb; **opino de ella que es una excelente profesional** I think she's an excellent professional; **o. uno sobre algo** to give one's opinion about sth

2 *vi* to give one's opinion; **no te dejan o.** they don't allow you to express an opinion; **prefiero no o.** I would prefer not to comment; **sólo algunos se atrevieron a o. sobre este punto** only a few dared to express an opinion on this point

opinión *nf* opinion; **en mi o. no deberíamos ir** in my opinion, we shouldn't go; **es mi o. personal** that's my personal opinion; **¿cuál es tu o. al respecto?** what's your opinion *o* view on this matter?; **después de escuchar distintas opiniones sobre el tema...** after hearing different views on the matter...; **compartir una o.** to share a view *o* an opinion; **he cambiado de o.** I've changed my mind; **expresar** *o* **dar una o.** to give an opinion; **reservarse la o.** to reserve judgment; **ser de la o. de que** to be of the opinion that; **ser una cuestión de o.** to be a matter of opinion; **tener buena/mala o. de alguien** to have a high/low opinion of sb ►► ***la o. pública*** public opinion

opio *nm* opium; **el o. del pueblo** the opium of the people; EXPR *RP Fam* **ser un o.** to be a yawn

opíparamente *adv* sumptuously

opíparo, -a *adj* sumptuous

opondré *etc ver* **oponer**

oponente *nmf* opponent

oponer [50] 1 *vt* (a) *(resistencia)* to put up (b) *(argumento, razón)* to put forward, to give

2 **oponerse** *vpr (no estar de acuerdo)* to be opposed; **oponerse a algo** *(desaprobar, rechazar)* to be opposed to sth, to oppose sth; *(ser contrario a)* to be opposed to sth; **todos se opusieron al plan** everybody was opposed to the plan; **me opongo a creerlo** I refuse to believe it; **me opongo a que vengan ellos también** I'm opposed to having them come along too

Oporto *n* Oporto

oporto *nm* port (wine)

oportunamente *adv* opportunely, conveniently; **la decisión se dará a conocer o.** the decision will be announced in due course

oportunidad *nf* (a) *(momento adecuado)* opportunity; **aprovechar la o.** to seize the opportunity; **no pienso desaprovechar la o.** I don't intend to waste the opportunity; **ahora es la o. para planteárselo** now is the right moment to put it to her; **es una o. única** it's a unique opportunity

(b) *(posibilidad)* chance, opportunity; **me dio una segunda o.** he gave me a second chance; **a la primera o. que tenga se lo digo** I'll tell her just as soon as I get the chance *o* at the earliest opportunity; **me surgió esta o. y decidí aprovecharla** this opportunity arose and I decided to make the most of it

(c) *(ocasión, vez)* occasion, time; **en esa o. tuve que callarme, pero no lo haré más** on that occasion I had to keep quiet, but I won't in future; **como ya dijimos en otras oportunidades...** as we have already said on other occasions...

(d) *(conveniencia)* timeliness; **la o. de esta decisión se pudo comprobar unos meses después** the timeliness of this decision became apparent a few months later

(e) **oportunidades** *(en gran almacén)* bargains; **la sección de oportunidades** the bargains section

oportunismo *nm* opportunism

oportunista 1 *adj* opportunistic

2 *nmf* opportunist

oportuno, -a *adj* (a) *(pertinente)* appropriate; **me pareció o. callarme** I thought it best to say nothing

(b) *(propicio)* timely, opportune; **el momento o.** the right time; **en el momento menos o.** at the very worst time *o* moment; **su llegada fue muy oportuna** she arrived at an opportune moment; **se lo diré cuando sea o.** I'll tell him in due course *o* when the time is right; *Irónico* **¡ella siempre tan oportuna!** she really chooses her moments

(c) *(agudo)* sharp, acute; **has estado muy o. al contestarle así** it was very sharp of you to answer him like that

oposición *nf* (a) *(resistencia)* opposition (**a** to); **la o. de mis padres a que haga este viaje es total** my parents are totally opposed to me going on this trip

(b) *(política)* **la o.** the opposition; **los partidos de la o.** the opposition parties

(c) *(examen)* = competitive public examination for employment in the civil service, education, legal system etc; **o. a profesor** = public examination to obtain a state teaching post; **preparar oposiciones** to be studying for a public examination; **conseguir una plaza por o.** to obtain a post by sitting a public examination

opositar *vi* = to sit a public entrance examination; **o. a** *o* **para algo** to sit a public examination for sth

opositor, -ora *nm,f* (a) *(a un cargo)* = candidate in a public entrance examination (b) *(oponente)* opponent

oposum *nm* opossum

opresión *nf* (a) *(represión)* oppression (b) *(molestia, ahogo)* **sentía una o. en el pecho** he felt a tightness in his chest

opresivo, -a *adj* oppressive

opresor, -ora 1 *adj* oppressive

2 *nm,f* oppressor

oprimido, -a 1 *adj* oppressed

2 *nm,f* **los oprimidos** the oppressed

oprimir *vt* (**a**) *(apretar) (botón)* to press; *(garganta, brazo)* to squeeze (**b**) *(sujeto: zapatos, cinturón)* to pinch, to be too tight for; **la corbata le oprimía el cuello** his tie felt too tight (**c**) *(reprimir)* to oppress (**d**) *(angustiar)* to weigh down on, to burden; **me oprime la soledad** being on my own depresses me

oprobio *nm* shame, disgrace

optar *vi* (**a**) *(escoger)* **o. (por algo)** to choose (sth); **o. por hacer algo** to choose to do sth; **o. entre** to choose between (**b**) *(aspirar)* **o. a** to aim for, to go for; **optan al puesto siete candidatos** there are seven candidates for the job; **los que no son licenciados no pueden o. a este cargo** non-graduates may not apply for *o* are not eligible for this post

optativa *nf Educ* optional subject, *US* elective

optativamente *adv* optionally

optativo, -a *adj* optional, *US* elective

óptica *nf* (**a**) *(ciencia)* optics *(singular)* (**b**) *(tienda)* optician's (shop) (**c**) *(punto de vista)* point of view

óptico, -a 1 *adj* optic
2 *nm,f (persona)* optician

óptimamente *adv* ideally, in the best way

optimar *vt* to optimize

optimismo *nm* optimism

optimista 1 *adj* optimistic
2 *nmf* optimist

optimización *nf* optimization

optimizar *vt* to optimize

óptimo, -a *adj* optimum, optimal; **un alimento ó. para los niños** an ideal food for children

optómetra *nmf* optometrist, *Br* ophthalmic optician

optometría *nf* optometry

optometrista *nmf* optometrist, *Br* ophthalmic optician

opuesto, -a 1 *participio ver* **oponer**
2 *adj* (**a**) *(contrario)* opposed, contrary (**a** to); **los dos hermanos son opuestos en todo** the two brothers are completely different; **opiniones opuestas** contrary *o* opposing opinions; **ser o. a algo** to be opposed *o* contrary to sth
(**b**) *(del otro lado)* opposite; **el extremo o. a éste** the opposite end to this; **el coche venía en dirección opuesta** the car was coming the other way *o* in the opposite direction; EXPR **son dos polos opuestos** *(personas)* they are complete *o* polar opposites

opulencia *nf (riqueza)* opulence; *(abundancia)* abundance; **vivir en la o.** to live in luxury; **nadar en la o.** to be filthy rich

opulento, -a *adj (rico)* opulent; *(abundante)* abundant

opus *nm inv* (**a**) *Mús* opus (**b**) ***el O. Dei*** the Opus Dei, = traditionalist religious organization, whose members include many professional people and public figures

opúsculo *nm* short work

opusiera *etc ver* **oponer**

OPV *nf* (*abrev de* **Oferta Pública de Venta (de acciones)**) offer for sale, *US* public offering

oquedad *nf (cavidad)* hole; *(en pared)* recess

oquedal *nm* = forest of tall trees without undergrowth

oquis: de oquis *loc adv Méx Fam* (for) free

ORA *nf* (*abrev de* **Operación de Regulación del Aparcamiento**) = system of paid street parking in some parts of Spain

ora *conj Formal* **o.... o....** now... now...; **miraba, o. a un lado, o. al otro** she looked first one way, then the other

oración *nf* (**a**) *(rezo)* prayer; **esa habitación está reservada para la o.** that room is set aside for prayer; **rezar una o.** to say a prayer ►► ***o. fúnebre*** funeral oration (**b**) *Gram* sentence ►► ***o. compuesta*** compound *o* complex sentence; ***o. principal*** main clause; ***o. relativa*** relative clause; ***o. simple*** simple sentence; ***o. subordinada*** subordinate clause

oracional *adj Gram* clausal

oráculo *nm* (**a**) *(mensaje, divinidad)* oracle (**b**) *(persona)* fount of wisdom

orador, -ora *nm,f* speaker; **un gran o.** a great speaker *o* orator

oral 1 *adj (examen, tradición)* oral; **medicamento de administración o.** medicine to be taken orally
2 *nm (examen)* oral exam

órale *interj Méx Fam* (**a**) *(venga)* come on!; **ó., apúrate o llegaremos tarde** come on, hurry up or we'll be late (**b**) *(de acuerdo)* right!, OK!; **ó., te espero a las cinco** right, I'll expect you at five

oralidad *nf Ling* (**a**) *(en fonología)* orality (**b**) *(en adquisición del lenguaje)* orality, (spoken) language

oralmente *adv* orally; **este medicamento se administra o.** this medicine is taken orally

orangista 1 *adj* Orange
2 *nmf* Orangeman, *f* Orangewoman

orangután *nm* orang-outang

orar *vi* to pray; **o. por alguien** to pray for sb

orate *nmf* lunatic

oratoria *nf* oratory

oratorio, -a 1 *adj* oratorical
2 *nm* (**a**) *(capilla)* oratory (**b**) *Mús* oratorio

orbe *nm Literario* (**a**) *(mundo)* world, globe (**b**) *(esfera)* orb, sphere

orbicular *nm Anat* orbicularis muscle

órbita *nf* (**a**) *(de astro)* orbit; **ó. terrestre** Earth's orbit; **entrar/poner en ó.** to go/put into orbit; EXPR **le pegó tal bofetón que casi le pone en ó.** he gave him such a slap he nearly knocked him into the middle of next week
(**b**) *(de ojo)* **ó. (ocular)** eye socket, *Espec* orbit; **al verla casi se le salen los ojos de las órbitas** his eyes nearly popped out of his head when he saw her
(**c**) *(ámbito)* sphere, realm

orbital *nm Quím* orbital

orbitar *vi* to orbit

orca *nf* killer whale, orca

Órcadas *fpl* **las Ó.** the Orkney Islands, the Orkneys

órdago *nm* = all-or-nothing stake in the game of "mus"; *Fig* **una comida de ó.** a terrific *o* lovely meal; **lleva un enfado de ó.** he's absolutely raging

ORDEN[1] *nm* (**a**) *(secuencia, colocación correcta)* order; **un o. jerárquico** a hierarchy; **le gusta el o. y la limpieza** she likes order and cleanliness; *Mat* **el o. de los factores no altera el producto** the order of the factors does not affect the product; **en o.** *(bien colocado)* tidy, in its place; *(como debe ser)* in order; **poner en o. algo, poner o. en algo** *(cosas, habitación)* to tidy sth up; **tengo que poner mis ideas/mi vida en o.** I have to put my ideas/life in order, I have to sort out my ideas/life; **en** *o* **por o. alfabético/cronológico** in alphabetical/chronological order; **por o.** in order; **por o. de antigüedad/de tamaños** in order of seniority/size; *Cine & Teatro* **por o. de aparición** in order of appearance; EXPR **sin o. ni concierto** haphazardly ►► ***o. del día*** agenda
(**b**) *(normalidad, disciplina)* order; **acatar el o. establecido** to respect the established order; **llamar al o. a alguien** to call sb to order; **el o. natural de las cosas** the natural order of things; **mantener/restablecer el o.** to keep/restore order; **¡o. en la sala!** order!, order! ►► ***el o. público*** law and order
(**c**) *(tipo)* order, type; **dilemas de o. filosófico** philosophical dilemmas; **problemas de o. financiero** economic problems; **es una universidad de primer(ísimo) o.** it's a first-rate university; **del o. de** around, approximately, of *o* in the order of; **en otro o. de cosas** on the other hand ►► ***o. de magnitud*** order of magnitude
(**d**) *Biol* order
(**e**) *Arquit* order ►► ***o. corintio*** Corinthian order; ***o. dórico*** Doric order; ***o. jónico*** Ionic order
(**f**) *Rel* ***el o. sacerdotal*** *(sacramento)* holy orders

ORDEN[2] *nf* (**a**) *(mandato)* order; **¡es una o.!** that's an order!; *Mil* **¡a la o.!, ¡a sus órdenes!** (yes) sir!; *Am* **estoy a las/sus órdenes** I am at your service; *Am* **si no me queda bien, ¿la puedo cambiar? – cómo no, a sus** *o* **las órdenes** if it's not right, can I change it? – of course you can, we're at your disposal; *Am* **mi auto/casa está a la o.** my car/house is at your disposal; **cumplir órdenes** to obey orders; **dar órdenes (a alguien)** to give (sb) orders; **a mí nadie me da órdenes** I don't take orders from anyone; **hasta nueva o.** until further notice; **por o. de** by order of; **el local fue cerrado por o. del ayuntamiento** the premises were closed by order of *o* on the orders of the town council; **obedecer órdenes** to obey orders; **recibimos órdenes del jefe** we received orders from the boss; **sólo recibo órdenes de mis superiores** I only take orders from my superiors; **tener órdenes de hacer algo** to have orders to do sth ►► *Der* ***o. de arresto*** arrest warrant; *Der* ***o. de busca y captura*** warrant for search and arrest; *Der* ***o. de comparecencia*** summons; ***o. de desahucio*** eviction order; ***o. de desalojo*** eviction order; *Der* ***o. de detención*** arrest warrant; ***o. de detención europea*** European arrest warrant; *Mil* ***la o. del día*** *Mil* the order of the day; *Am (de reunión)* the agenda; EXPR **estar a la o. del día** *(muy habitual)* to be the order of the day; ***o. de embargo***

order for seizure; *Der* ***o. judicial*** court order; *CSur Der* ***o. de lanzamiento*** eviction order; *Bolsa* ***o. al mercado*** market order; *Der* ***o. de registro*** search warrant
(**b**) *Com* order ►► ***o. de compra*** purchase order; ***o. de pago*** payment order
(**c**) *(institución)* order ►► ***o. de caballería*** order of knighthood; ***o. mendicante*** mendicant order; ***o. militar*** military order; ***o. monástica*** monastic order
(**d**) *Rel* ***órdenes sagradas*** holy orders
(**e**) *Am (pedido)* order; **¿ya les tomaron la o.?** have you ordered yet?; **¿tiene la o. del médico?** have you got the form from your doctor?

---

ordenación *nf* (**a**) *(organización)* ordering, arranging; *(disposición)* order, arrangement; *(de recursos, edificios)* planning ►► ***o. del suelo*** town planning regulations, *US* zoning regulations; ***o. territorial*** *o* ***del territorio*** regional planning (**b**) *Rel* ordination

ordenada *nf Mat* ordinate

ordenadamente *adv (desfilar, salir)* in an orderly fashion *o* manner; *(colocar)* neatly

ordenado, -a *adj* (**a**) *(lugar, persona)* tidy; *(vida)* ordered (**b**) *(sacerdote)* ordained

ordenador *nm Esp* computer; **pasar algo a o.** to key sth up (on a computer) ►► ***o. analógico*** analogue computer; ***o. de a bordo*** onboard computer; ***o. central*** central computer; ***o. compatible*** compatible computer; ***o. digital*** digital computer; ***o. doméstico*** home computer; ***o. personal*** personal computer; ***o. portátil*** laptop computer; ***o. de sobremesa*** desktop computer

ordenamiento *nm* (**a**) *(código de leyes)* **el o. constitucional** the constitution; **el o. jurídico español** Spanish law (**b**) *Am (organización)* ordering, arranging; **el o. de sus pertenencias es responsabilidad de cada uno** each person is responsible for putting their own belongings in order

ordenanza 1 *nm* (**a**) *(de oficina)* office boy (**b**) *Mil* orderly
2 *nf* ordinance, law; **ordenanzas municipales** by-laws

ordenar 1 *vt* (**a**) *(poner en orden) (alfabéticamente, numéricamente)* to arrange, to put in order; *(habitación, papeles)* to tidy (up); **o. alfabéticamente** to put in alphabetical order; **o. en montones** to sort into piles; **o. por temas** to arrange by subject
(**b**) *Informát* to sort
(**c**) *(mandar)* to order; **te ordeno que te vayas** I order you to go; **me ordenó callarme** he ordered me to be quiet
(**d**) *Rel* to ordain
(**e**) *Am (pedir)* to order; **acabamos de o. el desayuno** we've just ordered breakfast
2 *vi* (**a**) *(mandar)* to give orders; EXPR **(yo) ordeno y mando: Ana es de las de (yo) ordeno y mando** Ana's the sort of person who likes telling everybody what to do (**b**) *Am (pedir)* to order; **¿ya eligieron?, ¿quieren o.?** are you ready to order?
3 ordenarse *vpr Rel* to be ordained

ordenata *nm Esp Fam* computer

ordeña *nf Am* milking

ordeñador, -ora *nm,f (persona)* milker

ordeñadora *nf (máquina)* milking machine

ordeñar *vt* to milk

ordeño *nm Esp* milking

ordinal 1 *adj* ordinal
2 *nm (número)* ordinal (number)

ordinariamente *adv* (**a**) *(normalmente)* ordinarily (**b**) *(groseramente)* coarsely, vulgarly

ordinariez *nf* vulgarity, coarseness; **decir/hacer una o.** to say/do something rude; **¡no digas ordinarieces!** don't be so coarse *o* vulgar!; **¡qué o.!** how vulgar!

ordinario, -a 1 *adj* (**a**) *(común)* ordinary, usual; **están más callados que de o.** they're quieter than usual; **de o. la veo todos los días** I usually *o* normally see her every day (**b**) *(vulgar)* coarse, vulgar (**c**) *(no selecto)* unexceptional; *(de poca calidad)* poor-quality, cheap (**d**) **correo o.** *Br* normal *o US* regular delivery; **tribunal o.** court of first instance
2 *nm,f* common *o* coarse person; **es un o.** he's terribly coarse *o* vulgar
3 *nm Rel* Ordinary

ordovícico, -a *Geol* **1** *adj* Ordovician
2 *nm* **el o.** the Ordovician

orear 1 *vt* to air
2 orearse *vpr (ventilarse)* to air

orégano *nm* oregano

oreja 1 *nf* (**a**) *(de persona, animal)* ear; **orejas de soplillo** sticky-out ears; **el perro puso las orejas tiesas** the dog pricked up his ears; **tirar a alguien de las orejas** to pull sb's ears *(traditionally done to a person celebrating their birthday)*; *Fig* to give sb a good telling-off; **tenía una sonrisa de o. a o.** he was grinning from ear to ear; EXPR *Fam* **agachar** *o* **bajar las orejas** *(en discusión)* to back down; EXPR *Am Fam* **le deben arder las orejas** his ears must be burning; EXPR *Fam* **calentarle a alguien las orejas** to box sb's ears; EXPR *Fam* **descubrir** *o* **enseñar la o.** to show one's true colours; EXPR *Fam* **con las orejas gachas** with one's tail between one's legs; EXPR *Am Fam* **parar la o.** to pay attention, to listen up; EXPR **ponerle las orejas coloradas a alguien** to tell sb off, to make sb feel uncomfortable; EXPR *Fam* **ver las orejas al lobo** to see what's coming
(**b**) *(de sillón)* wing
(**c**) *(de vasija)* handle
(**d**) ***o. de mar*** abalone
2 *nmf Méx Fam* informer, *Br* grass

orejera *nf (en gorra)* earflap; **orejeras** earmuffs

orejón, -ona 1 *adj* (**a**) *(orejudo)* big-eared, jug-eared (**b**) *Col (rudo)* coarse, uncouth
2 *nm (dulce)* dried apricot/peach; EXPR *RP Fam* **ser el último o. del tarro** to be the lowest of the low

orejudo, -a *adj* big-eared, jug-eared

orensano, -a 1 *adj* of/from Orense *(Spain)*
2 *nm,f* person from Orense *(Spain)*

orfanato, *Méx* **orfanatorio** *nm* orphanage

orfandad *nf* orphanhood

orfebre *nmf (de plata)* silversmith; *(de oro)* goldsmith

orfebrería *nf* (**a**) *(objetos) (de plata)* silver work; *(de oro)* gold work (**b**) *(oficio) (de plata)* silversmithing; *(de oro)* goldsmithing

orfelinato *nm* orphanage

Orfeo *n Mitol* Orpheus

orfeón *nm* choral group *o* society

organdí (*pl* **organdíes**) *nm* organdie

orgánico, -a *adj* (**a**) *(ser, química)* organic (**b**) *(estructura, crecimiento)* organic (**c**) **ley orgánica** constitutional law, organic law

organigrama *nm* (**a**) *(de organización, empresa)* organization chart (**b**) *Informát* flow chart *o* diagram

organillero, -a *nm,f* organ-grinder

organillo *nm* barrel organ

organismo *nm* (**a**) *Biol* organism ►► ***o. modificado genéticamente*** genetically modified organism (**b**) *Anat* organism (**c**) *(entidad)* organization, body

organista *nmf* organist

organización *nf* (**a**) *(orden)* organization
(**b**) *(organismo)* organization; **las organizaciones sindicales** the trade unions ►► ***o. de ayuda humanitaria*** humanitarian aid organization; ***o. benéfica*** charity, charitable organization; ***o. de consumidores*** consumer organization; ***O. para la Cooperación y el Desarrollo Económico*** Organization for Economic Cooperation and Development; ***O. de Estados Americanos*** Organization of American States; ***O. Internacional de Normalización*** International Standards Organization; ***O. Internacional del Trabajo*** International Labour Organization; ***O. para la Liberación de Palestina*** Palestine Liberation Organization; ***O. Mundial del Comercio*** World Trade Organization; ***O. Mundial de la Salud*** World Health Organization; ***O. de las Naciones Unidas*** United Nations Organization; ***o. no gubernamental*** non-governmental organization; ***O. de Países Exportadores de Petróleo*** Organization of Petroleum Exporting Countries; ***O. para la Seguridad y Cooperación en Europa*** Organization for Security and Cooperation in Europe; ***O. del Tratado del Atlántico Norte*** North Atlantic Treaty Organization

organizadamente *adv* in an organized way

organizado, -a *adj* organized

organizador, -ora 1 *adj* organizing
2 *nm,f* organizer

organizar [14] **1** *vt* (**a**) *(estructurar, ordenar)* to organize (**b**) *(fiesta, partido)* to organize (**c**) *Esp (pelea, lío)* to cause
2 organizarse *vpr* (**a**) *(persona)* to organize oneself (**b**) *Esp (pelea, lío)* to break out, to happen suddenly; **se organizó un verdadero follón a la salida** there was a real commotion as people left

organizativo, -a *adj* organizational

órgano *nm* (**a**) *(del cuerpo)* organ ►► ***ó. vital*** vital organ (**b**) *(instrumento musical)* organ ►► ***ó. electrónico*** electric organ (**c**) *(institución)* organ ►► ***ó. ejecutivo*** executive (**d**) *Fig (instrumento)* organ; **este periódico es el ó. del partido** this newspaper is the party organ (**e**) *Méx (planta)* organ pipe *(cactus)*

orgásmico, -a *adj* orgasmic

orgasmo *nm* orgasm

orgía *nf* orgy

orgiástico, -a *adj* orgiastic

orgullo *nm* (**a**) *(actitud)* pride; **no aguanto su o.** I can't bear his haughtiness *o* arrogance; EXPR **tragarse el o.** to swallow one's pride
(**b**) *(satisfacción)* pride; **es el o. de la familia** he's the pride of the family; **me llena de o. poder inaugurar este centro** it fills me with pride *o* I am very proud to be able to open this centre; **tuve el o. de conocerlo** I'm proud to say I knew him; EXPR **no caber en sí de o., reventar de o.** to be bursting with pride
(**c**) *(amor propio)* pride; **le picó el o. y aceptó el reto** it wounded his pride so he accepted the challenge

orgullosamente *adv* proudly

orgulloso, -a 1 *adj* proud; **estar o. de algo** to be proud of sth; **estoy muy o. de mi esfuerzo** I'm very proud of my effort; **estar o. de hacer algo** to be proud to do sth, to be proud of doing sth; **estaba o. de haberlo intentado** he was proud of having tried
2 *nm,f* proud person; **es un o.** he's very proud

orientación *nf* (**a**) *(dirección) (acción)* guiding; *(rumbo)* direction; **sentido de la o.** sense of direction
(**b**) *(posicionamiento) (acción)* positioning; *(lugar)* position; *(de edificio)* aspect; **una casa con o. al oeste** a house that faces west; **hay que ajustar la o. del sensor** the position *o* angle of the sensor needs adjusting; **¿cuál tiene que ser la o. de la antena?** which way should the aerial be pointing? ►► *Informát* ***o. horizontal*** horizontal *o* landscape orientation; *Informát* ***o. vertical*** vertical *o* portrait orientation
(**c**) *(enfoque)* orientation; **le dieron una o. práctica al curso** the course had a practical bias *o* slant
(**d**) *(información)* guidance, advice; **algunas orientaciones** some guidance ►► ***o. pedagógica*** = guidance on courses to be followed; ***o. profesional*** careers advice *o* guidance; *CSur* ***o. vocacional*** careers advice
(**e**) *(tendencia)* tendency, leaning; **un partido con una o. liberal** a party with liberal leanings *o* tendencies ►► ***o. sexual*** sexual orientation
(**f**) *(deporte de aventura)* orienteering

orientado, -a *adj Informát* **o. a objeto** object-oriented; **o. a usuario** user-oriented

orientador, -ora 1 *adj* guiding, directing
2 *nm,f* guide ►► ***o. psicológico*** (psychological) counsellor

oriental 1 *adj* (**a**) *(del este)* eastern; *(del Lejano Oriente)* oriental (**b**) *Am (uruguayo)* Uruguayan (**c**) *(de Oriente, Venezuela)* of/from Oriente
2 *nmf* (**a**) *(del Lejano Oriente)* oriental (**b**) *Am (uruguayo)* Uruguayan; *Hist* **los 33 orientales** = group of Uruguayans who played a key role in the wars of independence by regaining control, in April 1825, of the area that was then eastern Uruguay (**c**) *(persona de Oriente, Venezuela)* person from Oriente

orientalismo *nm* orientalism

orientalista *nmf* orientalist

orientar 1 *vt* (**a**) *(dar una posición)* to direct; **hay que o. el foco hacia abajo** the spotlight needs to be pointed downwards; **orientó la popa hacia el este** he pointed the stern eastwards; **mi ventana está orientada hacia el sur** my window faces south *o* is south-facing
(**b**) *(indicar una dirección)* to guide; **un lugareño les orientó** a local pointed them in the right direction
(**c**) *(aconsejar)* to give advice *o* guidance to; **necesito que me orienten sobre el mejor modelo** I need some advice about the best model
(**d**) *(enfocar)* **o. hacia** to direct towards *o* at; **orientaron las medidas a reducir la inflación** the measures were aimed at reducing inflation; **orientó sus investigaciones hacia la biogenética** he focused his research on biogenetics
2 orientarse *vpr* (**a**) *(dirigirse) (foco)* **orientarse a** to point towards *o* at
(**b**) *(encontrar el camino)* to find one's direction; **se orientó con las estrellas** he found his direction by the stars; **tardó un rato en orientarse** it took her a while to get her bearings; **yo me oriento muy bien** I find my way around pretty well
(**c**) *(encaminarse)* **orientarse hacia** to be aiming at; **las negociaciones se orientan a la liberación de los rehenes** the aim of the talks is to free the hostages

orientativo, -a *adj* illustrative, guiding

oriente *nm* (**a**) *(este)* east; **el O.** the East, the Orient; **Extremo o Lejano O.** Far East ►► ***O. Medio*** Middle East; ***O. Próximo*** Near East (**b**) *(de perla)* orient

orífice *nm* goldsmith

orificio *nm* hole, *Espec* orifice; *Tec* opening; **el cadaver tenía tres orificios de bala** there were three bullet holes in the body

oriflama *nf* oriflamme

origami *nm* origami

origen *nm* (**a**) *(principio)* origin; **en su o.** originally; **dar o. a** to give rise to; **sus palabras han dado o. a especulaciones** her statements have given rise to *o* caused speculation; **esta idea dio o. a la actual empresa** this idea was the origin of the company as it is today; **desde sus orígenes** from its origins; **tener su o. en** *(lugar)* to have one's origins in, to originate in; **esta leyenda tiene su o. en un hecho histórico** this legend has its origins in historical fact; **tiene su o. en el siglo XIX** it originated in the 19th century
(**b**) *(ascendencia)* origins, birth; **Alicia es colombiana de o.** Alicia is Colombian by birth; **de o. humilde** of humble origin
(**c**) *(causa)* cause; **el o. del problema** the cause *o* source of the problem
(**d**) *(de un producto)* origin; **los aceites de o. español** oils from Spain; **agua mineral envasada en o.** mineral water bottled at source
(**e**) *Mat* origin

original 1 *adj* (**a**) *(nuevo, primero)* original; **el texto o.** the original text; **en versión o.** in the original version
(**b**) *(no imitación)* original; **este es o. y esta la copia** this is original and this is the copy; **un Velázquez o.** an original Velázquez
(**c**) *(inusual)* original; **esa corbata es muy o.** that's a very original *o* unusual tie
(**d**) *(raro)* different, eccentric; **tú siempre tan o.** you always have to be different
(**e**) *(procedente)* **ser o. de** *(persona)* to be a native of; *(animal, planta)* to be native to
2 *nm* (**a**) *(primera versión)* original; **hay que entregar tres copias y el o.** you have to give them the original and three copies; **leer algo en el o.** to read sth in the original (**b**) *(manuscrito)* manuscript

originalidad *nf* (**a**) *(novedad)* originality (**b**) *(extravagancia)* eccentricity

originalmente *adv* originally

originar 1 *vt (conflicto, problema)* to give rise to, to cause; *(discusión, incendio, epidemia)* to start; *(crisis)* to spark (off), to precipitate
2 originarse *vpr (acontecimiento)* to (first) start; *(costumbre, leyenda)* to originate

originariamente *adv* originally

originario, -a *adj* (**a**) *(inicial, primitivo)* original (**b**) *(procedente)* **ser o. de** *(costumbre)* to have its origins in, to originate in; *(producto)* to originally come from; *(persona)* to be a native of; *(animal, planta)* to be native to

orilla *nf* (**a**) *(ribera) (de río)* bank; *(de mar, lago)* shore; **a orillas de** *(río)* on the banks of; **a orillas del mar** by the sea; *Fig* **fue aclamado en las dos orillas del Atlántico** he was acclaimed on both sides of the Atlantic (**b**) *(borde)* edge (**c**) *Méx, RP, Ven (de ciudad)* **orillas** outskirts

orillar 1 *vt* (**a**) *(dificultad, obstáculo)* to get around (**b**) *(tela)* to edge (**c**) *Méx (forzar)* to force; **la situación desesperante los orilló a poner en marcha el plan de emergencia** the desperate situation forced them to put the emergency plan into action
2 orillarse *vpr Esp, Méx (vehículo)* to pull over; *(persona)* to move to one side

orillero, -a *RP, Ven* **1** *adj* common, low-class
2 *nm,f* common *o* low-class person

orillo *nm Tex* selvage

orín *nm* (**a**) *(herrumbre)* rust (**b**) **orines** *(orina)* urine

orina *nf* urine

orinal *nm (de dormitorio)* chamberpot; *(para niños)* potty

orinar 1 *vi* to urinate
2 *vt* **el enfermo orinaba sangre** the patient was passing blood (in his urine)
3 orinarse *vpr* to wet oneself; **orinarse en la cama** to wet the bed

Orinoco *nm* **el O.** the Orinoco

orinoquense 1 *adj* of/from the River Orinoco area
2 *nmf* person from the River Orinoco area

orinoqueño, -a *adj, nm,f* = **orinoquense**

orita *adv Méx Fam* (right) now; **o. voy** I'm just coming

oriundo, -a 1 *adj* **ser o. de** *(persona)* to be a native of; *(planta)* to be native to; **utiliza plantas oriundas del Brasil** it uses plants native to Brazil; **aunque vive en Europa, el artista es o. de Chile** although he lives in Europe, the artist is a native of *o* is originally from Chile
2 *nm,f* (**a**) *(nativo)* native; **los oriundos del lugar** the locals, the local inhabitants (**b**) *Dep* = non-native soccer player whose mother or father is a native of the country he plays for

orla *nf* (**a**) *(adorno) (de tela, papel)* (decorative) border; *(de vestido)* trimming; *(de escudo)* border, *Espec* orle (**b**) *Esp (fotografía)* graduation photograph

orlar *vt (tela, papel)* to border; *(vestido)* to trim

orlón® *nm* Orlon®

ornamentación *nf* ornamentation

ornamental *adj (de adorno)* ornamental; *Fig (inútil)* merely decorative

ornamentar *vt* to decorate, to adorn

ornamento *nm* (**a**) *(objeto)* ornament (**b**) *Rel* **ornamentos** vestments

ornar *vt Formal* to decorate, to adorn

ornato *nm Formal* decoration

ornitología *nf* ornithology

ornitológico, -a *adj* ornithological

ornitólogo, -a *nm,f* ornithologist

ornitorrinco *nm* duck-billed platypus

oro *nm* 1 (**a**) *(metal)* gold; **un reloj de o.** a gold watch; **o. de 18 quilates** 18-carat gold; *Literario* **sus cabellos de o.** her golden hair; *Hum* **voy a guardar los oros** *(joyas de oro)* I'm going to put away my gold jewellery; **vestido de o. y negro** all dressed up, dressed up to the nines; EXPR **no lo haría ni por todo el o. del mundo** I wouldn't do it for all the tea in China; EXPR **guardar algo como o. en** *Esp* **paño** *o Am* **polvo** to treasure sth; EXPR **hacerse de o.** to make one's fortune; EXPR **no es o. todo lo que reluce** all that glitters is not gold; EXPR *Vulg* **o. del que cagó el moro** *(oro falso)* fool's gold; *(cosa de mala calidad)* trash; EXPR **pedir el o. y el moro** to ask for the moon; EXPR **prometer el o. y el moro** to promise the earth; EXPR *Am* **ser alguien o. en polvo** to be an absolute treasure ▸▸ ***o. amarillo*** yellow gold; ***o. en barras*** bullion; ***o. batido*** gold leaf; ***o. blanco*** white gold; ***o. laminado*** rolled gold; ***o. de ley*** standard gold, pure *o* real gold; ***o. molido*** powdered gold; ***o. negro*** oil, black gold; ***o. en polvo*** gold dust; ***o. rojo*** red gold; ***o. viejo*** old gold
(**b**) *Dep (medalla)* gold; **Kenia se llevó el o.** Kenya won (the) gold
(**c**) *(naipe)* any card of the "oros" suit
(**d**) **oros** *(palo)* = suit in Spanish deck of cards, with the symbol of a gold coin
(**e**) *(en escudo)* or
2 *adj inv* gold

orogénesis *nf inv* orogenesis

orogenia *nf* orogeny

orogénico, -a *adj* orogenic

orografía *nf* (**a**) *Geog* orography (**b**) *(relieve)* terrain

orográfico, -a *adj* orographic

orondo, -a *adj* (**a**) *(gordo)* rotund, plump (**b**) *(satisfecho)* pleased with oneself, smug

oronja *nf* Caesar's mushroom, Caesar's amanita ▸▸ ***o. verde*** death-cap

oropel *nm* (**a**) *(latón)* composition leaf, Dutch gold (**b**) *(decoración sin valor)* tinsel, flashy ornament (**c**) *(ostentación)* glitter, glitz; **un estilo de vida de mucho o.** a glitzy *o* flashy lifestyle; **se dejó deslumbrar por los oropeles de la fama** she let herself be dazzled by all the glamour and glitz of fame

oropéndola *nf* golden oriole

oroya *nf Am* = rope basket for crossing rivers

orozuz *nm* liquorice

orquesta *nf* (**a**) *(músicos)* orchestra ▸▸ ***o. de cámara*** chamber orchestra; ***o. sinfónica*** symphony orchestra (**b**) *(lugar)* orchestra pit

orquestación *nf* orchestration

orquestal *adj* orchestral

orquestar *vt* (**a**) *(música)* to orchestrate (**b**) *(campaña)* to orchestrate

orquestina *nf* dance band

orquídea *nf* orchid

orquitis *nf Med* orchitis

orsay ['orsai] *nm (en fútbol)* offside; **estar en o.** to be offside; EXPR **pillar a alguien en o.** to catch sb out

ortiga *nf* (stinging) nettle

ortigal *nf* bed of nettles

orto *nm* (**a**) *Astron* rising (**b**) *RP Vulg (ano) Br* arsehole, *US* asshole (**c**) *RP Vulg (suerte)* luck; **¡qué o. tiene!, se sacó la grande** the lucky bastard! he won the jackpot

ortocentro *nm Geom* orthocentre

ortodoncia *nf* orthodontics *(singular)*; **hacerse la o.** to have orthodontic work done

ortodóntico, -a *adj* orthodontic

ortodontista *nmf* orthodontist

ortodoxia *nf* orthodoxy

ortodoxo, -a 1 *adj* (**a**) *(aceptado, conforme)* orthodox (**b**) *Rel* Orthodox
2 *nm,f* (**a**) *(en partido político)* party-liner (**b**) *Rel* member of the Orthodox Church

ortoedro *nm Geom* rectangular prism

ortofonía *nf* speech therapy

ortofonista *nmf* speech therapist

ortogonal *adj* orthogonal

ortografía *nf* spelling, *Espec* orthography

ortográfico, -a *adj* spelling

ortopeda *nmf* orthopaedist

ortopedia *nf* orthopaedics *(singular)*

ortopédico, -a *adj* (**a**) *(zapato, corsé)* orthopaedic; **pierna ortopédica** artificial leg (**b**) *Fam Hum (deforme)* weird-looking, freaky; **llevaba un bolso muy o.** she was carrying a really weird-looking bag

ortopedista *nmf* orthopaedist

ortóptero, -a *Zool* 1 *adj* orthopteran
2 **ortópteros** *nmpl (orden)* orthoptera

ortosa *nf Geol* orthoclase

oruga *nf* (**a**) *(insecto)* caterpillar (**b**) *(vehículo)* caterpillar tractor

orujo *nm* = strong spirit made from grape pressings, similar to eau-de-vie

orureño, -a 1 *adj* of/from Oruro *(Bolivia)*
2 *nm,f* person from Oruro *(Bolivia)*

orvallo *nm Esp* drizzle

orza *nf* (**a**) *Náut* **o. (de la quilla)** centreboard (**b**) *(vasija)* pot *(of glazed earthenware, used especially for storing honey)*

orzar [10] *vt Náut* to luff

orzuelo *nm* stye

---

os *pron personal Esp* (**a**) *(complemento directo)* you; **me gustaría veros** I'd like to see you; **¿os atracaron en plena calle?** were you mugged in the middle of the street?; **al final os aprobarán a todos** you'll all pass *o* they'll pass all of you in the end
(**b**) *(complemento indirecto)* (to) you; **os lo dio** he gave it to you, he gave you it; **os tengo miedo** I'm afraid of you; **os lo ha comprado** *(vosotros se lo vendisteis)* she bought it from *o* off you; *(es para vosotros)* she bought it for you; **¿os han quitado el permiso?** have they taken your licence away from you?; **os estropearon el tocadiscos** they broke your record player; **os han pegado una paliza** they've thrashed you; **se os olvidará** you'll forget (about it); **os será de gran ayuda** it will be a great help to you
(**c**) *(reflexivo)* yourselves; **os vestís** you get dressed; **servíos una copa** pour yourselves a drink; **poneos los abrigos** put your coats on; **os podéis acostar en el sofá** you can lie down on the sofa
(**d**) *(recíproco)* each other; **os enamorasteis** you fell in love (with each other); **os estabais pegando** you were hitting each other
(**e**) *(con valor intensivo o expresivo)* **¿no os lo creéis?** don't you believe it?; **os lo comisteis todo** you ate the whole lot; **si se os echa a llorar no le hagáis caso** don't take any notice if he starts crying (on you)
(**f**) *(para formar verbos pronominales)* **¿os acordáis?** do you remember?; **poneos cómodos** make yourselves comfortable

---

osadía *nf* (**a**) *(valor)* boldness, daring (**b**) *(descaro)* audacity, temerity

osado, -a *adj* (**a**) *(valeroso)* daring, bold (**b**) *(descarado)* impudent, audacious

osamenta *nf* (**a**) *(esqueleto)* skeleton (**b**) *(conjunto de huesos)* bones

osar 1 *vi* to dare
2 *vt* to dare; **osó contestarme** he dared to answer me back

osario *nm* ossuary

Oscar *nm Cine* Oscar; **los Oscar(s)** *(la ceremonia)* the Oscars

oscarizado, -a *adj* Oscar-winning

OSCE *nf* (*abrev de* **Organización sobre** *o* **para la Seguridad y Cooperación en Europa**) OSCE

oscense 1 *adj* of/from Huesca *(Spain)*
2 *nmf* person from Huesca *(Spain)*

oscilación *nf* (**a**) *(de péndulo) (movimiento)* swinging; *(espacio recorrido)* swing (**b**) *(de llama)* flickering (**c**) *Fís* oscillation (**d**) *(variación)* fluctuation; **la o. de los precios** the fluctuation in prices

oscilador *nm* oscillator

oscilante *adj* oscillating

oscilar *vi* (**a**) *(moverse) (péndulo)* to swing; *(torre)* to sway; *(llama)* to flicker
(**b**) *Fís* to oscillate
(**c**) *(variar)* to vary, to fluctuate; **el precio oscila entre los mil y los dos mil pesos** the price ranges between one and two thousand pesos; **la temperatura osciló entre los 20 y los 30** the temperature fluctuated between 20° and 30°; **la longitud de estas serpientes oscila entre cinco y siete metros** these snakes vary *o* range in length between five and seven metres
(**d**) *(vacilar)* to vacillate, to waver; **oscila entre el pesimismo y la esperanza** she fluctuates between pessimism and hope

oscilatorio, -a *adj* swinging; *Fís* oscillating

oscilógrafo *nm* oscillograph

oscilograma *nm* oscillogram

osciloscopio *nm* oscilloscope

ósculo *nm Formal* kiss

oscuramente *adv* obscurely

oscurantismo, obscurantismo *nm* obscurantism

oscurantista, obscurantista 1 *adj* obscurantist
2 *nmf* obscurantist

oscurecer [46], **obscurecer** [46] **1** *vt* (**a**) *(habitación)* to darken; *(pantalla)* to make darker (**b**) *(mente)* to confuse, to cloud (**c**) *(deslucir)* to overshadow (**d**) *(mensaje, significado, sentido)* to obscure (**e**) *Arte & Fot* to darken, to make darker
2 *v impersonal (anochecer)* to get dark
3 oscurecerse *vpr* (**a**) *(cielo, habitación, imagen)* to darken, to grow dark (**b**) *(barniz, mezcla, madera)* to darken, to go *o* get darker; *(cabellos)* to go *o* get darker (**c**) *(futuro, perspectivas)* to look more gloomy (**d**) *Literario (rostro, mirada)* to darken

oscurecimiento *nm* darkening

oscuridad, obscuridad *nf* (**a**) *(falta de luz)* darkness; **me da miedo la o.** I'm afraid of the dark; **¿cómo puedes trabajar con esta o.?** how can you work in the dark like this?
(**b**) *(zona oscura)* **en la o.** in darkness, in the dark; **se perdieron en la o.** they got lost in the dark
(**c**) *(falta de claridad)* obscurity
(**d**) *(falta de fama)* obscurity; **con ese disco salieron de la o.** that record brought them out of obscurity

oscuro, -a *adj* (**a**) *(sin luz)* dark; **nos quedamos a oscuras** we were left in darkness *o* in the dark; *Fig* **en este tema estoy a oscuras** I'm ignorant about this subject; **¡qué oscura está esta habitación!** this room is very dark!; **una casa oscura y lúgubre** a dark and gloomy house
(**b**) *(nublado)* overcast; **se quedó una tarde oscura** the afternoon turned out overcast
(**c**) *(color, traje, piel, pelo)* dark
(**d**) *(poco claro)* obscure, unclear; **palabras de o. sentido** words whose meaning is unclear
(**e**) *(incierto)* uncertain, unclear; **tiene un origen o.** it's of uncertain origin
(**f**) *(intenciones, asunto)* shady
(**g**) *(porvenir, futuro)* gloomy
(**h**) *(de poca relevancia)* obscure, minor; **un o. funcionario** a minor official

óseo, -a *adj (estructura, fractura)* bone; *(consistencia)* bony; **esqueleto ó.** bony skeleton

osezno *nm* bear cub

osificación *nf* ossification

osificarse [60] *vpr* to ossify

Osiris *n Mitol* Osiris

osito *nm* ***o. de peluche*** teddy bear

Oslo *n* Oslo

osmio *nm Quím* osmium

osmosis, ósmosis *nf inv* (**a**) *Quím* osmosis (**b**) *(influencia)* osmosis

osmótico, -a *adj* osmotic

oso, -a *nm,f* bear, *f* she-bear; EXPR *Fam* **hacer el o.** to act the fool; EXPR *Esp* **¡anda la osa!** well I never!, upon my word!; EXPR *RP Fam* **hacerse el o.** to pretend one didn't hear/see etc; ►► ***o. blanco*** polar bear; ***o. de felpa*** teddy bear; ***o. hormiguero*** anteater; ***o. marino*** fur seal; ***la Osa Mayor*** the Great Bear; *Ven* ***o. melero*** anteater; ***la Osa Menor*** the Little Bear; ***o. negro*** black bear; *Ven* ***o. palmero*** giant anteater; ***o. panda*** panda; ***o. pardo*** brown bear; *(norteamericano)* grizzly bear; ***o. de peluche*** teddy bear; ***o. polar*** polar bear

osobuco *nm Culin* osso bucco

osornino, -a 1 *adj* of/from Osorno *(Chile)*
2 *nm,f* person from Osorno *(Chile)*

osteítis *nf inv Med* osteitis

ostensible *adj* obvious, evident; **con un gesto que hacía o. su impaciencia** with a gesture that made clear *o* betrayed her impatience

> **Falso amigo**: El adjetivo inglés **ostensible** no es la traducción del español **ostensible**. El término inglés **ostensible** significa "aparente".

ostensiblemente *adv* visibly, noticeably; **el consumo de tabaco se ha incrementado o.** there has been a noticeable *o* marked increase in tobacco consumption; **cojeaba o.** he had a pronounced limp

> **Falso amigo**: El adverbio inglés **ostensibly** no es la traducción del español **ostensiblemente**. En inglés **ostensibly** significa "aparentemente".

ostensivo, -a *adj* evident

ostentación *nf* ostentation, show; **hacer o. de algo** to show sth off, to parade sth

ostentar *vt* (**a**) *(poseer)* to hold, to have (**b**) *(exhibir)* to show off, to parade (**c**) *(cargo)* to hold, to occupy

ostentosamente *adv* ostentatiously

ostentoso, -a *adj* ostentatious

osteoartritis *nf inv Med* osteoarthritis

osteomielitis *nf Med* osteomyelitis

osteópata *nmf* osteopath

osteopatía *nf (terapia)* osteopathy

osteoplastia *nf* osteoplasty

osteoporosis *nf inv Med* osteoporosis

ostión *nm* (**a**) *Méx (ostra)* Portuguese oyster, Pacific oyster (**b**) *Chile (vieira)* scallop

ostionería *nf Méx* oyster bar, seafood restaurant

ostra 1 *nf* oyster; EXPR **aburrirse como una o.** to be bored stiff ►► ***o. perlífera*** pearl oyster
2 *interj Esp Fam* **¡ostras!** *(mostrando sorpresa)* good grief!, *Br* blimey!; *(mostrando disgusto o enfado)* dammit!

ostracismo *nm* ostracism; **un año en el o. político** a year in the political wilderness

ostrería *nf* oyster bar

ostrero *nm* (**a**) *(ostral)* oyster bed (**b**) *(ave)* oystercatcher

ostrogodo, -a 1 *adj* Ostrogothic
2 *nm,f* Ostrogoth

osuno, -a *adj* bear-like

OTAN ['otan] *nf* (*abrev de* **Organización del Tratado del Atlántico Norte**) NATO

otario, -a *RP Fam* **1** *adj* gullible, wet behind the ears
2 *nm,f* sucker

otear *vt (horizonte)* to survey, to scan; **oteó las casas del pueblo desde la torre** from the tower he surveyed *o* scanned the houses in the village

otero *nm* hillock

OTI ['oti] *nf* (*abrev de* **Organización de Televisiones Iberoamericanas**) = association of all Spanish-speaking television networks; **el festival de la O.** = televised song competition across the Spanish-speaking world

otitis *nf inv* inflammation of the ear, *Espec* otitis

otoción *nm* bat-eared fox

otomano, -a 1 *adj* Ottoman
2 *nm,f* Ottoman

otoñal *adj* autumn, autumnal, *US* fall; **viento o.** autumn wind

otoño *nm* autumn, *US* fall; **en o.** in (the) autumn, *US* in the fall; **cuando llegue el o.** when autumn *o US* the fall comes; **el último o.** last autumn, *US* last fall; **en el o. de la vida** in the autumn of one's life

otorgamiento *nm* (**a**) *(de favor, petición)* granting; *(de premio, beca)* awarding (**b**) *Der (de documento)* execution; *(documento)* legal document, instrument

otorgar [38] *vt* (**a**) *(favor, privilegio, préstamo)* to grant; *(honor, título)* to confer; *(premio, beca)* to award, to present (**b**) *Der* to sign, *Espec* to execute (**c**) *(ley)* to pass, *Espec* to promulgate

otorrino, -a *nm,f Fam* ENT specialist

otorrinolaringología *nf* otolaryngology, otorhinolaryngology

otorrinolaringólogo, -a *nm,f* ear, nose and throat specialist

otredad *nf Formal* otherness

OTRO, -A 1 *adj* (**a**) *(distinto)* another; **otros/otras** other; **o. chico** another boy; **el o. chico** the other boy; **(los) otros chicos** (the) other boys; **¿conoces o. sitio donde podamos ir?** do you know anywhere else we could go?; **no hay otra impresora como ésta** there's no other printer quite like this one; **dame otra cosa, no quiero zumo** could I have something else? I don't feel like juice; **no hace otra cosa que llorar** she does nothing but cry; **el o. día** *(pasado)* the other day; **al o. año volvimos a Acapulco** *(año siguiente)* we returned to Acapulco the following year; **otros pocos/muchos votaron a favor** a few/several of the others voted in favour

(**b**) *(nuevo)* another; **estamos ante o. Dalí** this is another Dali; **otros tres goles** another three goals; **vendrán otros dos amigos** another two friends will come; **yo hubiera hecho o. tanto** I would have done just the same; **otra vez** again

2 *pron* another (one); **el o.** the other one; **otros/otras** others; **los otros/las otras** the others; **¿nos tomamos otra?** shall we have another (one)?; **dame o.** give me another (one); **sé que sales con otra** I know you're seeing another woman *o* someone else; **¡pareces o.!** you look like a completely different person!; **mientras uno baila, el o. canta** while one of them dances, the other sings; **la semana que viene no, la otra** the week after next; **los perros se mordían el uno al o.** the dogs were biting each other; **nos ayudamos los unos a los otros** we all help each other *o* one another; **algún o. quedará** there's bound to be a couple left; **ningún o. corre tanto como él** no-one runs as fast as he does; **su calidad de impresión es mejor que ninguna otra** it prints better than anything else; **yo no lo hice, fue o.** it wasn't me, it was somebody else; **o. habría abandonado, pero no él** anyone else would have given up, but not him; **la razón no es otra que la falta de medios** the reason is quite simply a lack of resources; **póganos otra de lo mismo** (the) same again, please; **¡hasta otra!** I'll see you when I see you, see you again some time; **¡otra!** *(en conciertos)* encore!, more!; EXPR **o. que tal (baila): el padre era un mujeriego y el hijo es o. que tal (baila)** the father was a womanizer and his son's a chip off the old block; EXPR **¡o. que tal!, ¡es que no paran de preguntar!** there goes another one! they never stop asking questions!; EXPR *Am* **¡otra que!: ¡otra que 20 años, debe tener como 25!** what do you mean, 20? he must be about 25!; EXPR *Am* **no hay** *o* **me queda otra** I've got no choice *o* alternative

otrora *adv Formal* formerly

otrosí *adv Formal* besides, moreover

Ottawa [o'tawa] *n* Ottawa

OUA *nf Antes* (*abrev de* **Organización para la Unidad Africana**) OAU

ouija® ['wiχa] *nf (mesa)* ouija® board

out [aut] *adj* (**a**) *Dep (pelota)* out (**b**) *Fam (pasado de moda)* out, uncool; *(no al tanto de la moda)* behind the times

output ['autput] (*pl* **outputs**) *nm Informát* output

ova 1 *nf Bot* green algae
2 **ovas** *nfpl Zool* roe

ovación *nf* ovation; **ovaciones** cheering, applause

ovacionar *vt* to give an ovation to, to applaud

oval *adj* oval

ovalado, -a *adj* oval

óvalo *nm* oval

ovárico, -a *adj* ovarian

ovario *nm* ovary; EXPR *Esp muy Fam* **¡estoy hasta los ovarios!** I'm fed up to the back teeth!

oveja *nf* sheep, ewe; **contar ovejas** to count sheep; PROV **cada o. con su pareja** birds of a feather flock together ►► ***o. descarriada*** lost sheep; ***o. merina*** merino (sheep); *Fig* ***o. negra*** black sheep

ovejero, -a *nm,f* shepherd, *f* shepherdess

ovejuno, -a *adj* (**a**) *(leche, queso)* sheep's; **ganado o.** sheep (**b**) *(rasgos, comportamiento)* sheep-like, *Formal* ovine

overbooking [oβer'βukin] (*pl* **overbookings**) *nm* overbooking; *Fam* **yo no puedo llevarte porque tengo o. en el coche** I can't give you a *Br* lift *o US* ride, my car's already too full

overo *nm* = animal, especially a horse, with pale reddish fur

overol *nm Am (de peto) Br* dungarees, *US* overalls; *(completo)* overalls, *Br* boilersuit; *(para bebé)* rompers

ovetense 1 *adj* of/from Oviedo *(Spain)*
2 *nmf* person from Oviedo *(Spain)*

óvido, -a *Zool* 1 *adj* of the sheep family
2 *nm (animal)* animal of the sheep family
3 **óvidos** *nmpl (orden)* Ovidae

oviducto *nm Anat* oviduct

oviforme *adj* oviform, egg-shaped

ovillar 1 *vt* to roll *o* wind into a ball
2 **ovillarse** *vpr* to curl up into a ball

ovillo *nm* ball *(of wool etc)*; **hacerse un o.** to curl up into a ball

ovino, -a *adj* sheep, *Espec* ovine; **productos ovinos** sheep products; **enfermedades ovinas** sheep diseases, diseases of sheep

ovíparo, -a 1 *adj* oviparous
2 *nm,f* oviparous animal

ovni *nm* (*abrev de* **objeto volador no identificado**) UFO

ovogénesis *nf inv Biol* ovogenesis

ovoide *adj* ovoid

ovolactovegetariano, -a 1 *adj* lacto-vegetarian
2 *nm,f* lacto-vegetarian

ovulación *nf* ovulation

ovular 1 *adj* ovular
2 *vi* to ovulate

óvulo *nm* ovum

oxálico, -a *adj* oxalic

oxiacetilénico, -a *adj* oxyacetylene

oxiacetileno *nm* oxyacetylene

oxidable *adj* oxidizable

oxidación *nf* (**a**) *(de hierro)* rusting (**b**) *Quím* oxidation ►► ***o.-reducción*** oxidation-reduction

oxidado, -a *adj* (**a**) *(cubierto de herrumbre)* rusty (**b**) *Quím* oxidized

oxidante 1 *adj* oxidizing
2 *nm* oxidizing agent, oxidant

oxidar 1 *vt* (**a**) *(cubrir de herrumbre)* to rust (**b**) *Quím* to oxidize
2 **oxidarse** *vpr* (**a**) *(cubrirse de herrumbre)* to rust (**b**) *Quím* to oxidize (**c**) *(anquilosarse)* to get rusty

oxidasa *nf Bioquím* oxidase

óxido *nm* (**a**) *(herrumbre)* rust (**b**) *Quím* oxide ►► ***ó. de cinc*** zinc oxide; ***ó. férrico*** ferric oxide; ***ó. de hierro*** iron oxide; ***ó. nítrico*** nitric oxide; ***ó. nitroso*** nitrous oxide

oxigenación *nf Quím* oxygenation

oxigenado, -a *adj* (**a**) *Quím* oxygenated (**b**) *(cabello)* peroxide; **una rubia oxigenada** a peroxide blonde

oxigenar 1 *vt Quím* to oxygenate
2 **oxigenarse** *vpr* (**a**) *(airearse)* to get a breath of fresh air (**b**) *(cabello)* to bleach

oxígeno *nm* oxygen ►► ***o. líquido*** liquid oxygen

oxte *interj Esp* oh, for heaven's sake!; EXPR **sin decir ni o. ni moste** without (uttering) a word

oyamel *nm* oyamel fir

oye *ver* **oír**

oyente 1 *adj* **alumno o.** *Br* occasional student, *US* auditing student
2 *nmf* (**a**) *(de programa)* listener (**b**) *(alumno) Br* occasional student, *US* auditing student; **¿eres alumno oficial? – no, sólo voy de o.** are you an official student? – no, I'm just sitting in on classes

oyera *etc ver* **oír**

ozonizador *nm* ozone generator

ozono *nm* ozone; **la capa de o.** the ozone layer

ozonosfera *nf* ozonosphere

P, p

P, p [pe] *nf (letra)* P, p
P[1] *(abrev de* **peón***) (en notación de ajedrez)* P
P.[2] *(abrev de* **padre***)* Fr.
P/ *(abrev de* **Plaza***)* Sq.
p. *(abrev de* **página***)* p
P *(abrev de* **Paseo***)* = Av., Ave.
PA *nm (abrev de* **Partido Arnulfista***)* = Panamanian political party
pa *interj RP Fam* wow!, (good) heavens!; **¡pa!, mirá la hora que es** wow! *o* (good) heavens! look at the time!; **¿si me dolió? pa, ni te imaginás** did it hurt, you say? God, you've no idea
pa' *prep Fam* = colloquial form of "para"
p.a. **(a)** *(abrev de* **por ausencia***)* pp **(b)** *(abrev de* **por autorización***)* pp
pabellón *nm* **(a)** *(edificio)* pavilion; *(parte de un edificio)* block, section; **la feria está compuesta de varios pabellones** the fair consists of several exhibition halls *o* pavilions ▸▸ ***p. de aduanas*** customs house; ***p. de caza*** hunting lodge; ***p. de deportes*** sports hall; ***p. de maternidad*** maternity ward
(b) *(en parques, jardines)* summerhouse
(c) *(tienda de campaña)* bell tent
(d) *(dosel)* canopy
(e) *(bandera)* flag; **un barco de p. panameño** a ship sailing under the Panamanian flag, a ship registered in Panama; **navega bajo p. liberiano** it sails under the Liberian flag; *Fig* **ha defendido dos veces el p. de su país** she has represented her country twice; *Fig* **dejaron alto el p. de su país** they did their country proud ▸▸ ***p. de conveniencia*** flag of convenience
(f) *Mús* bell
(g) ***p. auditivo*** outer ear; ***p. de la oreja*** outer ear
(h) *Ven (platillo)* = dish consisting of portions of rice, fried or stewed meat and black beans ▸▸ ***p. con baranda*** = "pabellón" with slices of fried plantain
(i) *Ven (quirófano) Br* operating theatre, *US* operating room
pabilo, pábilo *nm* wick
Pablo *n pr* **San P.** St Paul
pábulo *nm* **dar p. a** to give rise to; **su conducta dio p. a toda clase de rumores** her behaviour gave rise to *o* encouraged all kinds of rumours; **él mismo dio p. a los rumores** he himself fed *o* fuelled the rumours; **la biblioteca fue p. de las llamas** the library was burned to the ground
PAC [pak] *nf UE (abrev de* **Política Agrícola Común***)* CAP
paca *nf* **(a)** *(paquete)* bale **(b)** *(roedor)* paca
pacana *nf* pecan
pacano *nm* **(a)** *(árbol)* pecan tree **(b)** *(fruto)* pecan (nut)
pácatelas *interj Méx Fam* **iba tan tranquila y ¡p.! el carro de atrás me pegó un llegue** I was driving along perfectly normally, when bang!, the car behind ran straight into me; **iba corriendo y ¡p.!, que se cae** he was running and fell smack on his face; **abrí el libro y ¡p.!, que se deshoja** I opened the book and, would you believe it!, the pages fell out
pacato, -a 1 *adj* **(a)** *(mojigato)* prudish **(b)** *(tímido)* shy
2 *nm,f (mojigato)* prude
pacay *(pl* **pacayes** *o* **pacaes***) nm Andes, Arg* **(a)** *(árbol)* pacay tree **(b)** *(fruto)* pacay fruit
pacense 1 *adj* of/from Badajoz *(Spain)*
2 *nmf* person from Badajoz *(Spain)*
paceño, -a 1 *adj* of/from La Paz
2 *nm,f* person from La Paz
pacer [42] *vi* to graze
pacha *nf Méx Fam* flask *o* bottle of booze
pachá *nm* pasha; EXPR *Fam* **vivir como un p.** to live like a lord
pachamanca *nf Perú* = meat cooked between hot stones or in a hole in the ground under hot stones
pachanga *nf Fam* **(a)** *(juerga)* rowdy celebration; **vamos a salir de p.** we're going out partying *o* on the town **(b)** *(fiesta)* rave-up **(c)** EXPR *RP* **María no estudia nada, está para la p.** María doesn't do any work, all she's interested in is having a good time
pachanguear *vi RP Fam* to go out partying, to go out on the town
pachanguero, -a *Fam* **1** *adj* **(a)** *Esp (música)* catchy; *(persona)* tacky **(b)** *Am (alegre)* lively, party-loving; **es muy p.** he loves going out partying
2 *nm,f Am* party animal, raver
pacharán *nm* = liqueur made from a mixture of anisette and aguardiente with sloes
pachas: a pachas *loc adv Esp Fam* **lo pagamos a p.** we went halves on it, we split the cost; **nos fumamos el cigarro a p.** we shared the cigarette
pacheco *nm Ven Fam* cold spell; **ya bajó p.** the cold weather's here; **¡hace un p.!** there's a real chill in the air!
pachichi *adj Méx Fam* gaga
pachón, -ona 1 *nm,f Fam* **es un p.** he's very laid back
2 *nm (perro)* = gun dog similar to Spanish pointer
pachorra *nf Fam* calmness; **hace todo con mucha p.** she does everything very calmly *o* slowly; **¡qué p. tiene el camarero!** the waiter's taking his time!
pachotada *nf Andes, Ven Fam* nasty remark, rude remark
pachucho, -a *adj Fam* **(a)** *(persona, animal)* under the weather, poorly **(b)** *(fruta)* overripe
pachuco, -a *Méx Fam Hist nm,f* **(a)** *(persona)* = young Mexican living in the southern USA in the 1950s **(b)** *(estilo)* = style of flashy dress fashionable in Mexico in the 1950s **(c)** *(proxeneta)* pimp, *f* madam
pachulí *(pl* **pachulíes***) nm* patchouli
pachuqueño, -a 1 *adj* of/from Pachuca *(Mexico)*
2 *nmf* person from Pachuca *(Mexico)*
paciencia *nf* patience; **¡p., que todo se arreglará!** be patient, it'll all get sorted out!; **¡qué p. hay que tener contigo!** you'd try the patience of a saint!; **se le acabó** *o* **se le agotó la p.** he lost his patience; **¡este niño va a acabar con mi p.!** I'm losing my patience with this child!; **armarse de p.** to summon up one's patience; **llevar algo con p.** to put up with sth, to be stoical about sth; **perder la p.** to lose one's patience; **tener p.** to be patient; EXPR **p. y barajar** hang on in there; EXPR **tener más p. que Job** *o* **que un santo** to have the patience of Job *o* a saint; PROV **con p. se gana el cielo** patience is a virtue
paciente 1 *adj* patient
2 *nmf* patient ▸▸ ***p. externo*** outpatient; ***p. interno*** in-patient
pacientemente *adv* patiently
pacienzudo, -a *adj Fam* patient
pacificación *nf* pacification
pacificador, -ora 1 *adj (actitud, tono)* placatory; *(esfuerzo, papel, proceso)* peacemaking; **medidas pacificadoras** measures to achieve peace; **las fuerzas pacificadoras de la ONU** the UN peacekeeping forces
2 *nm,f* pacifier, peacemaker
pacíficamente *adv* peacefully
pacificar [60] **1** *vt* **(a)** *(país)* to pacify **(b)** *(calmar)* to calm, to appease; **hicieron un esfuerzo por p. a los ánimos** they attempted to calm people down; **una serie de resoluciones encaminadas a p. a la oposición** a series of resolutions designed to appease the opposition
2 pacificarse *vpr (persona)* to calm down
Pacífico 1 *adj* **el océano P.** the Pacific Ocean
2 *nm* **el P.** the Pacific (Ocean)
pacífico, -a *adj (vida, relaciones, manifestación)* peaceful; *(persona)* peaceable

pacifismo *nm* pacifism

pacifista 1 *adj* pacifist
2 *nmf* pacifist

pack [pak] (*pl* **packs**) *nm* pack; **un p. de seis** a six-pack

paco, -a 1 *nm,f Andes, Pan Fam* cop
2 *nm* (**a**) *RP Fam (mentira)* fib, lie; **meter un p.** to tell a fib *o* lie (**b**) *Andes* = hybrid of alpaca and guanaco (**c**) *Ecuad Fam (metal)* = silver ore containing iron (**d**) *Ecuad Fam (de marihuana)* big stash

pacotilla 1 *nf Ven* junk, trash
2 **de pacotilla** *loc adj* trashy, third-rate

pacotillero, -a *nm,f Am Fam Br* pedlar, *US* peddler, hawker

pactar 1 *vt* to agree to; **p. un acuerdo** to reach an agreement; **los sindicatos han pactado no ir a la huelga** the unions have agreed not to go on strike
2 *vi* to strike a deal (**con** with)

pacto *nm* agreement, pact; **hacer/romper un p.** to make/break an agreement; **cumplir un p.** to fulfil an agreement; PROV **hacer un p. con el diablo** to make a pact with the devil ►► ***p. de no agresión*** non-aggression pact; ***P. Andino*** = agreement between Andean countries to promote economic development and cooperation; ***p. de*** *o* ***entre caballeros*** gentleman's agreement; ***p. electoral*** electoral pact; *Pol* ***p. a la griega*** = alliance of opposing forces in order to gain power; ***p. de recompra*** repurchase agreement; ***p. social*** social contract

padecer [46] 1 *vt* (**a**) *(sufrimiento)* to endure, to undergo; *(hambre, injusticia)* to suffer; *(enfermedad)* to suffer from; **p. inundaciones/un terremoto** to be hit by floods/an earthquake (**b**) *Formal (error, confusión)* **padece usted un error** you are mistaken, you are labouring under a misapprehension
2 *vi* to suffer; **p. del corazón/riñón** to suffer from *o* have a heart/kidney complaint; **padeció mucho por sus hijos** she suffered a lot for the sake of her children

padecimiento *nm* suffering

pádel *nm Dep* paddle tennis, = game similar to tennis, in which the ball may be bounced off walls at either end of the court

padezco *etc ver* **padecer**

padrastro *nm* (**a**) *(pariente)* stepfather (**b**) *(en el dedo)* hangnail

padrazo *nm Fam* doting *o* dedicated father

padre 1 *nm* (**a**) *(pariente)* father; **Cervantes es el p. de la novela moderna** Cervantes is the father of the modern novel; **Emilio p.** Emilio senior; EXPR *Fam* **cada uno es de su p. y de su madre** each one is different; EXPR *Fam* **de p. y muy señor mío** incredible, tremendous; EXPR *Esp Fam* **hacer p. a alguien** to make sb a happy man EXPR *Fam* **itu p.!** sod you!; EXPR *Fam Hum* **no tener p. ni madre ni perrito que le ladre** to be without *o* not to have a friend in the world ►► ***p. de familia*** head of the family; ***p. de la patria*** founding father; ***p. político*** father-in-law; ***p. soltero*** single parent
(**b**) *(sacerdote)* father ►► ***p. espiritual*** confessor; *Rel* ***Padres de la Iglesia*** Fathers of the Christian Church; *Rel* ***p. nuestro*** Lord's Prayer
(**c**) *Rel* **el P.** the Father
2 *adj inv Fam* (**a**) *Esp (tremendo)* incredible, tremendous; **se armó el lío p.** there was a terrible *o* huge fuss; **fue el cachondeo p.** it was a great laugh (**b**) *Méx (genial)* great, fantastic; **esa canción está muy p.** that song is really great *o* fantastic; **¡ay qué p.!** hey, that's great *o* fantastic!
3 **padres** *nmpl* (**a**) *(padre y madre)* parents (**b**) *(antepasados)* forefathers, ancestors; **las tradiciones de nuestros padres** the traditions of our forefathers *o* ancestors

padrenuestro *nm* Lord's Prayer; **decir un p.** to say an Our Father *o* the Lord's Prayer; EXPR **saberse algo como el p.** to know sth by heart, to have sth off pat; EXPR *Fam* **en un p.** in the twinkling of an eye

padrillo *nm RP* stallion

padrinazgo *nm* (**a**) *(cargo de padrino)* godfathership (**b**) *Fig (protección)* sponsorship, patronage

padrino *nm* (**a**) *(de bautismo)* godfather; **padrinos** *(padrino y madrina)* godparents (**b**) *(de boda)* = man, usually the bride's father, who gives away the bride at her wedding (**c**) *(en duelos, torneos)* second (**d**) *Fig (protector)* patron; **ése tiene un buen p. que pronto le colocará** he's got a good patron who'll soon find him a job

padrísimo, -a *adj Méx Fam* fantastic, great

padrón *nm* (**a**) *(censo)* census; *(para votar)* electoral roll *o* register (**b**) *CAm, Carib, Andes (caballo)* stallion (**c**) *Chile (de automóvil)* (vehicle) registration document (**d**) *Urug (de terreno)* (land) registration document

padrote *nm* (**a**) *Méx Fam (proxeneta)* pimp (**b**) *CAm, Ven (caballo)* stallion

padrotear *vt Fam* (**a**) *Méx (explotar)* to exploit (**b**) *Ven (mandonear)* to boss around

paella *nf* paella ►► ***p. marinera*** seafood paella; ***p. mixta*** mixed paella *(with meat or chicken and seafood)*; ***p. valenciana*** Valencia-style paella *(with chicken and seafood)*

paellera *nf* = large frying-pan for cooking paella

paf *interj* bang!, crash!

pág. (*abrev de* **página**) p

paga *nf (salario)* salary, wages; *(de niño)* pocket money; **día de p.** payday; **tenemos 14 pagas al año** we have 14 salary payments *o* wage packets a year; **hoy nos dan la p.** we get paid today ►► ***p. extra*** *o* ***extraordinaria*** = additional payment of a month's salary or wages in June and December; ***p. de Navidad*** = additional payment of a month's salary or wages at Christmas

pagable *adj* payable

pagadero, -a *adj* payable; **p. a 90 días/a la entrega** payable within 90 days/on delivery

pagado, -a *adj* paid; **p. de sí mismo** pleased with oneself, full of oneself

pagador, -ora 1 *adj* paying; **agente p.** payer
2 *nm,f* payer; *(de obreros)* paymaster; **ser buen/mal p.** to be a good/bad payer

pagaduría *nf* accounts office

págalo *nm* ***p. grande*** great skua; ***p. parásito*** arctic skua; ***p. pomarine*** pomarine skua; ***p. rabero*** long-tailed skua

paganini *nm Esp Fam* dummy *(who ends up paying)*

paganismo *nm* paganism

paganizar *vt* 1 to paganize
2 **paganizarse** *vpr* to be paganized

pagano, -a 1 *adj* pagan, heathen
2 *nm,f* (**a**) *Rel* pagan, heathen (**b**) *Esp Fam (que paga)* dummy *(who ends up paying)*

pagar [38] 1 *vt* (**a**) *(con dinero) (precio, alquiler, factura)* to pay; *(deuda, hipoteca)* to pay off; *(gastos, ronda)* to pay for; *(dividendo, indemnización)* to pay out; **pagó dos millones por la casa** she paid two million for the house; **su padre le paga los estudios** his father is supporting him through college/university; **yo pago la cena** I'll pay for dinner; **aún no hemos pagado el reportaje de la boda** we still haven't paid for the wedding photos; **los jubilados no pagan las medicinas** pensioners don't pay for prescriptions; **no iría aunque me lo pagaras** I wouldn't go (even) if you paid me; **¿cómo lo va a p.?** how would you like to pay?; EXPR *RP* **p. derecho de piso** to earn one's place in the job *o* office
(**b**) *(devolver) (ayuda, favor)* to repay; **¡que Dios se lo pague!** God bless you!
(**c**) *(expiar) (delito, consecuencias)* to pay for; **pagarás caro lo que me has hecho** I'll make you pay for what you did to me; *Fam* **me las pagarás (todas juntas)** you'll pay for this; EXPR **el que la hace la paga** he/she/*etc* will pay for it in the end; EXPR *Fam* **p. el pato/los platos rotos** to carry the can; EXPR *Fam* **pagarla con alguien** *(injustamente)* to take it out on sb
2 *vi* (**a**) *(con dinero)* to pay; **les pagaron puntualmente** they paid them promptly; **p. por adelantado** to pay in advance; **p. al contado** to pay (in) cash; **p. a plazos** to pay in instalments; **p. con tarjeta (de crédito)** to pay by credit card; **p. en especie** to pay in kind; **p. en pesos/libras** to pay in pesos/pounds; **p. en efectivo** *o* **en metálico** to pay (in) cash; **esta cantidad queda a p.** this amount is still outstanding *o* to be paid; EXPR **p. a alguien con la misma moneda** to give sb a taste of their own medicine
(**b**) *Am Fam (compensar)* to be worth it; **ese viaje tan largo no paga** such a long journey is not worth it; **no paga mandar el auto al taller otra vez** it's not worth (it) taking the car to the garage again; **no paga hacer trampa** it doesn't pay to cheat
3 **pagarse** *vpr* (**a**) *(costearse)* to pay for; **se paga los estudios** she's financing herself through college/university (**b**) **p. de algo** *(vanagloriarse)* to boast about sth

pagaré *nm Com* promissory note, IOU ►► ***p. del Tesoro*** Treasury note; ***p. a la vista*** demand note

pagel *nm (pez)* pandora

página *nf* (**a**) *(de libro, publicación)* page; **a toda p.** full-page ►► ***las páginas amarillas*** the Yellow Pages; ***p. central*** centrefold
(**b**) *(episodio)* chapter; **con su muerte se cierra una p. en la historia del teatro mexicano** his death closes a chapter in the history of Mexican theatre

(c) *Informát* page ▸▸ ***p. de búsqueda*** search engine; ***p. inicial*** *o* ***de inicio*** home page; ***p. personal*** personal home page; ***p. web*** web page

paginación *nf* pagination

paginar *vt* to paginate

pago, -a 1 *adj RP (trabajador)* paid

2 *nm* (a) *(de dinero)* payment; *Fig* reward, payment; **día de p.** payday; **en p. de** *o* **a** *(en recompensa por)* as a reward for; *(a cambio de)* in return for; **tener pagos atrasados** to be in arrears ▸▸ ***p. por adelantado*** advance payment; ***p. anticipado*** advance payment; ***p. al contado*** cash payment; ***p. a cuenta*** payment on account; ***p. domiciliado*** direct debit; ***p. en efectivo*** cash payment; ***p. a la entrega*** cash on delivery; ***p. escalonado*** progress payment; ***p. en especie*** payment in kind; ***p. fraccionado*** payment by instalments; ***p. inicial*** down payment; ***p. en metálico*** cash payment; ***p. a plazos*** payment by instalments; ***p. contra reembolso*** cash on delivery; ***p. por visión*** pay-per-view

(b) *(lugar)* **por estos pagos** around here; **¿qué hacías tú por aquellos pagos?** what were you doing around there *o* in those parts?

pagoda *nf* pagoda

págs. *(abrev de* **páginas***)* pp

pai *nm CAm, Méx* pie

paico *nm* wormseed

paila *nf* (a) *Andes, CAm, Carib (sartén)* frying pan (b) *Chile (huevos fritos)* fried eggs (c) *Chile Fam Hum (oreja)* lug

paíño *nm* ***p. europeo*** storm(y) petrel

paipái *(pl* **paipáis***)*, **paipay** *(pl* **paipays***) nm Esp* = rigid circular fan with handle

páirex *nm Perú* Pyrex®

pairo *nm* EXPR **estar al p.** to be marking time *o* sitting on the sidelines; EXPR **quedarse al p.** to be marking time *o* sitting on the sidelines; EXPR *Fam* **traer al p.: su opinión me trae al p.** I couldn't care less what she thinks

país *(pl* **países***) nm* (a) *(nación)* country; **el p. votó "no" en el referéndum** the country *o* nation voted "no" in the referendum; PROV **en el p. de los ciegos, el tuerto es rey** in the kingdom of the blind, the one-eyed man is king ▸▸ ***los países no alineados*** the non-aligned countries; ***los Países Bajos*** the Netherlands; ***los países bálticos*** the Baltic States; ***países desarrollados*** developed countries; ***P. de Gales*** Wales; ***p. natal*** native country, homeland; ***p. neutral*** neutral country; ***p. de origen*** country of origin; ***p. de reciente industrialización*** newly industrialized country; ***p. satélite*** satellite state; ***países subdesarrollados*** underdeveloped countries; ***el P. Valenciano*** the autonomous region of Valencia; ***el P. Vasco*** the Basque Country; ***países en vías de desarrollo*** developing countries

(b) *(tierra)* land; **en un p. muy lejano...** in a distant *o* far-off land...; **en el p. de las maravillas** in wonderland; **el p. de nunca-jamás** never-never land

paisa *Fam* 1 *adj Col* of/from Antioquia or its capital, Medellín

2 *nmf* (a) *Col (antioqueño)* person from Antioquia or its capital, Medellín (b) *Col, Méx, Ven (del mismo país)* compatriot, fellow countryman, *f* fellow countrywoman; *(de la misma región)* person from the same region; *(del mismo pueblo)* person from the same town (c) *Ven (como apelativo)* pal, *Br* mate, *US* buddy

paisaje *nm* (a) *(terreno)* landscape; *(vista panorámica)* scenery, view; **una de las características del p. de esta comarca** one of the features of the landscape of this area; **un p. montañoso/accidentado/costero** a mountainous/rugged/coastal landscape; **se pararon a contemplar el p.** they stopped to admire the view *o* scenery ▸▸ ***p. lunar*** moonscape, lunar landscape; ***p. natural*** unspoilt countryside

(b) *(pintura)* landscape

paisajismo *nm (en pintura)* landscape painting

paisajista 1 *adj* landscape; **pintor p.** landscape painter

2 *nmf* landscape painter

paisajístico, -a *adj* landscape; **belleza paisajística** natural beauty

paisanada *nf RP Fam* group of peasants

paisanaje *nm* (a) civilians (b) *RP Fam (paisanada)* group of peasants

paisano, -a 1 *adj (del mismo país)* from the same country; *(de la misma región)* from the same region; *(del mismo pueblo)* from the same town

2 *nm,f* (a) *(del mismo país)* compatriot, fellow countryman, *f* fellow countrywoman; *(de la misma región)* person from the same region; *(del mismo pueblo)* person from the same town (b) *(campesino)* country person, peasant

3 *nm (civil)* civilian; **ir** *o* **vestir de p.** *(militar)* to be in *o* wearing civilian clothes; *(policía)* to be in *o* wearing plain clothes; **traje de p.** *(de militar)* civilian cothes; *(de policía)* plain clothes; **un policía de p.** a plain-clothes policeman

paja[1] *nf* (a) *(hierba, caña)* straw; **casa con techo de p.** thatched house, house with a thatched roof; EXPR **por un quítame allá esas pajas** over nothing, over some silly little thing; EXPR **separar la p. del grano** to separate *o* sort out the wheat from the chaff; EXPR *RDom Fam* **no ser p. de coco** to be no easy task; PROV **ver la p. en el ojo ajeno y no la viga en el propio** to see the mote in one's neighbour's eye and not the beam in one's own ▸▸ *Andes, RP* ***p. brava*** = tall, thick grass that grows on the altiplano and the pampas

(b) *(para beber)* (drinking) straw

(c) *Fam (relleno)* waffle, padding; **has metido mucha p. en el trabajo** your essay's got too much waffle *o* padding in it

(d) *muy Fam (masturbación) Br* wank, *US* jerkoff; **hacerse una** *o Am* **la p.** to jerk off, *Br* to have a wank ▸▸ ***p. mental:* no son más que pajas mentales** it's just mental masturbation; **deja de hacerte pajas mentales y decídete** quit *o* stop jerking around and make your mind up

(e) *Col, Ven Fam (palabrería)* blather, waffle; **deja ya de hablar p.** stop blathering *o Br* wittering on

paja[2] *adj Perú Fam* wicked, brilliant

pajar *nm* hayloft

pájara *nf* (a) *Pey (mujer)* crafty *o* sly woman; **¡buena p. está esa hecha!** she's a crafty devil! (b) *(in cycling)* bonk

pajarear *vi* (a) *Andes, Méx (caballo)* to shy (b) *Chile (estar distraído)* to be absent-minded (c) *Méx (intentar enterarse)* to eavesdrop

pajarera *nf* aviary

pajarería *nf* pet shop

pajarero, -a 1 *adj Andes, Méx (caballo)* shy, skittish

2 *nm,f (vendedor)* bird dealer *o* seller

pajarita *nf* (a) *Esp (corbata)* bow tie ▸▸ ***p. de broche*** clip-on bow tie (b) *(de papel)* paper bird

pajarito *nm (pájaro pequeño)* small bird; **¡mira al p.!** *(al tomar una foto)* watch the birdie!; EXPR **comer como un p.** to eat like a bird, to eat practically nothing; EXPR **me lo ha contado** *o* **dicho un p.** a little bird told me; EXPR **morir** *o* **quedarse como un p.** to just fade away; EXPR **quedarse p.** to freeze to death, to be frozen stiff

pájaro *nm* (a) *(ave)* bird; **¡mira al p.!** *(al tomar una foto)* watch the birdie!; EXPR *RP Fam* **andar con** *o* **tener los pájaros volados** to be in a bad mood; EXPR **tener pájaros en la cabeza** to be scatterbrained *o* empty-headed; PROV **más vale p. en mano que ciento volando** a bird in the hand is worth two in the bush; PROV *RP* **p. que comió, voló** I've got to love you and leave you *(said when one has to leave immediately after eating)* ▸▸ ***p. bobo*** penguin; ***p. bobo real*** king penguin; ***p. carpintero*** woodpecker; ***p. del diablo*** European coot; ***p. de mal agüero*** bird of ill omen; ***p. mosca*** hummingbird; ***p. moscón*** penduline tit; ***p. moscón verde*** verdin

(b) *Fam (persona)* crafty devil, sly old fox; **¡menudo p. es ese!** he's a crafty devil!; EXPR **es un p. de cuenta** he's a nasty piece of work *o* a bad lot

pajarón, -ona *CSur Fam* 1 *adj* silly

2 *nm,f Br* twit, *US* goof

pajarraco *nm Pey* (a) *(pájaro)* big ugly bird (b) *(persona)* nasty piece of work

paje *nm* page

pajear *Andes, RP Vulg* 1 *vt Br* to wank off, *US* to jack off

2 **pajearse** *vpr Br* to wank, *US* to jack off

pajería *nf Andes, RP muy Fam* **es una p.** it's *Br* bloody *o US* goddamn stupid; **decir pajerías** to talk *Br* rubbish *o US* garbage

pajero, -a 1 *nm,f Vulg* (a) *(onanista) Br* wanker, *US* jerkoff (b) *(insulto) Br* wanker, *US* jerkoff

2 *nm Ven Fam (charla)* blather, waffle

pajillero, -a *nm,f Esp muy Fam* (a) *(onanista) Br* wanker, *US* jerk-off (b) *(prostituta)* = person who masturbates others for money

pajita, pajilla *nf* (drinking) straw

pajizo, -a *adj (color, pelo)* straw-coloured

pajolero, -a *adj Esp muy Fam* damn, blessed; EXPR **no tengo ni pajolera idea** I haven't the faintest *Br* bloody *o US* goddamn idea

pajón *nm Am (hierba)* scrub, coarse grass

pajonal *nm* (a) *Am (paja)* field of scrub (b) *Ven Fam (charla)* blather, waffle

pajuatada *nf Ven Fam* **es una p.** it's damn silly

pajuato, -a *Ven Fam* 1 *adj* (a) *(simple)* simple (b) *(mojigato)* prudish

2 *nm,f* (a) *(simple)* simpleton (b) *(mojigato)* prude

pajudo, -a *Ven muy Fam* **1** *adj* **ser p.** to be a bullshitter
2 *nm,f* bullshitter

pajuerano, -a *RP Fam Pey* **1** *adj* rustic, provincial
2 *nm,f* yokel

Pakistán, Paquistán *n* Pakistan

pakistaní = **paquistaní**

pala *nf* (**a**) *(herramienta)* spade; *(para recoger)* shovel ►► ***p. excavadora*** excavator, digger; ***p. mecánica*** power shovel; ***p. quitanieves*** *Br* snow plough, *US* snow plow (**b**) *(cubierto)* fish knife (**c**) *(de frontón)* racket; *(de ping-pong)* bat, *US* paddle; **jugar a las palas** *(en la playa)* to play beach tennis (**d**) *(de remo, hélice)* blade (**e**) *(diente)* (upper) front tooth

PALABRA *nf* (**a**) *(término, vocablo)* word; **con palabras no puedo expresar lo que sentía** words cannot express what I felt; **dilo con tus propias palabras** say it in your own words; **lo dijo, aunque no con esas palabras** she said it, though not in so many words; **no son más que palabras (vacías)** it's all talk; **buenas palabras** fine-sounding words; **no cruzaron p. en todo el camino** they didn't exchange a word throughout the journey; **dejar a alguien con la p. en la boca** to cut sb off in mid-sentence; **dirigir la p. a alguien** to speak to sb; **no le dirige la p. a su madre desde hace semanas** he hasn't spoken to his mother for weeks; **en cuatro** *o* **dos palabras** in a few words; **en otras palabras** in other words; **en una p.** in a word; **lo dijo todo a medias palabras** she only hinted at what she meant; **medir las palabras** to weigh one's words (carefully); **no habla ni (media) p. de español** she doesn't speak a word of Spanish; **yo de este tema no sé ni (media) p.** I don't know a thing about this subject; **no dijo p.** he didn't say a word; **p. por p.** word for word; **me has quitado la p. de la boca** you took the words right out of my mouth; **lo de comprar una casa son palabras mayores** buying a house is a very serious matter; **no hace falta llegar a palabras mayores** there is no need to get nasty about it; **le aguanto casi todo, pero eso ya son palabras mayores** I'll put up with almost anything from him, but that's going a bit (too) far; **sin mediar p.** without a single word; **tener la última p.** to have the last word; **tener unas palabras con alguien** to have words with sb; **tuvo que tragarse sus palabras** he had to eat his words; PROV **a palabras necias, oídos sordos** sticks and stones may break my bones (but words will never hurt me) ►► *Informát* ***p. clave*** keyword; ***p. compuesta*** compound word; *CSur* ***palabras cruzadas*** crossword; ***p. de Dios*** word of God
(**b**) *(juramento, promesa)* word; **es su p. contra la mía** it's her word against mine; **dar/empeñar la p.** to give/pledge one's word; **ella me dio su p.** she gave me her word; **dio (su) p. de que nada saldría mal** he gave his word that nothing would go wrong; **estar bajo p.** *(en juicio)* to be under oath; **faltó a su p.** he went back on his word, he broke *o* didn't keep his word; **mantuvo su p.** she kept her word; **no tiene p.** he's not a man of his word; **tienes mi p.** you have my word; **tomar la p. a alguien** to hold sb to their word ►► ***p. de honor*** word of honour; **¡p. (de honor)!** honestly!; **yo no sabía nada ¡p. (de honor)!** I didn't know anything, honestly! *o* I swear!
(**c**) *(habla)* speech; **con el susto perdió la p.** the shock left her speechless; **de p.** by word of mouth, verbally; **el trato se hizo de p.** it was a purely verbal agreement *o* a gentleman's agreement
(**d**) *(derecho de hablar)* **dar la p. a alguien** to give sb the floor; **pedir la p.** to ask for the floor; **¡pido la p.!** could I say something, please?; **tomar la p.** to take the floor
(**e**) **palabras** *(discurso)* words; **a continuación nuestro invitado nos dirigirá unas palabras** our guest will now say a few words

palabreado, -a *adj Am Fam* **Néstor ya está p. para ayudarme con la mudanza** Néstor has already agreed *o* promised to help me with the move

palabrear *vt Am Fam* to agree verbally to

palabreja *nf* strange word; **la flexibilización, ¡vaya p.!** flexibilization, what an ugly word!

palabrería *nf Fam* hot air, talk; **basta de palabrerías** that's enough talk

palabrero, -a **1** *adj* (**a**) *(muy hablador)* talkative (**b**) *(de poco fiar)* unreliable
2 *nm,f* (**a**) *(persona muy habladora)* chatterbox (**b**) *(persona de poco fiar)* unreliable person

palabro *nm* (**a**) *(palabra ofensiva)* offensive word (**b**) *(palabra rara)* strange word

palabrota *nf* swearword, rude word; **decir palabrotas** to swear

palabrotero, -a **1** *nm,f* **ser un p.** to swear a lot, to be foul-mouthed
2 *adj* **ser p.** to swear a lot, to be foul-mouthed

palacete *nm* mansion, small palace

palaciego, -a *adj (costumbres, rutina)* palace, court; **lujo p.** palatial luxury; **intrigas palaciegas** palace/court intrigues

palacio *nm* palace ►► ***el p. arzobispal*** the archbishop's palace; ***p. de congresos*** conference centre; ***p. de deportes*** sports hall; ***p. ducal*** duke's *o* ducal palace; ***p. de exposiciones*** exhibition centre; ***P. de Justicia*** Law Courts; ***p. real*** royal palace

palada *nf* (**a**) *(con pala)* spadeful, shovelful (**b**) *(con remo)* stroke

paladar **1** *nm* (**a**) *(en la boca)* palate (**b**) *(gusto)* palate, taste; **su arte no se ajusta al p. europeo** his art doesn't appeal to European taste
2 *nf o nm Cuba* = small restaurant in a private house

paladear *vt también Fig* to savour

paladeo *nm* savouring, relishing

paladín *nm* (**a**) *Hist* paladin, heroic knight (**b**) *Fig (adalid)* champion, defender

paladino, -a *adj (claro)* clear, obvious

paladio *nm Quím* palladium

palafito *nm* stilt house

palafrén *nm Hist* palfrey

palafrenero *nm Hist* groom

palanca *nf* (**a**) *(barra, mando)* lever; **tuvimos que hacer p. para levantar la piedra** we had to use a lever to lift the rock ►► ***p. de arranque*** kick-starter; ***p. de cambio*** *(de automóvil) Br* gear lever, gearstick, *US* gearshift, stick shift; ***p. de freno*** brake lever; ***p. de mando*** joystick
(**b**) *(trampolín)* diving board; *(en la parte más alta)* high board
(**c**) *Am Fam* **tener p.** *(enchufe)* to have friends in high places

palangana **1** *nf* (**a**) *(para fregar) Br* washing-up bowl, *US* dishpan; *(para lavarse) Br* washbasin, *US* washbowl (**b**) *Am (fuente, plato)* wooden platter
2 *nm Andes, CAm Fam (fanfarrón, descarado)* braggart, show-off

palanganear *vi Andes Fam* to brag, to boast

palanganero *nm* washstand

palangre *nm* (**a**) *(en pesca)* paternoster line (**b**) *Ven (en periodismo)* bribe *(paid to a newspaper or reporter to publish certain information)* (**c**) *Ven (negocio)* profitable sideline

palangrerismo, palangrismo *nm Ven* = practice of giving/accepting bribes in journalism

palangrero *nm (barco)* = fishing boat with a "palangre"

palangrista *nmf Ven* = journalist or newspaper accepting bribes for publishing information

palanqueado, -a *CSur, Ven Fam* **1** *adj* **siempre entra p.** all the jobs he gets are through pulling strings *o* through patronage
2 *nm,f* = person who gets a job through pulling strings; **llenaron todas las vacantes con palanqueados** all the vacancies were taken by people who had contacts

palanquear *vt CSur, Ven Fam* **está tratando de palanquearle un cargo a la hija** he's trying to use his influence to get his daughter a job

palanqueta *nf* jemmy, crowbar

palanquín *nm Náut* clew garnet

palapa *nf Méx* (**a**) *(palmera)* Cohune palm (**b**) *(quincho)* = open-air shelter with a palm roof

palatal *adj Ling* palatal

palatalización *nf Ling* palatalization

palatalizar [14] *vt Ling* to palatalize

palatinado *nm Hist* palatinate

palatino, -a *adj* (**a**) *(de paladar)* palatine (**b**) *(de palacio)* palace, court; **oficio p.** position at court

palazo *nm* **dar un p. a alguien** to hit sb with a shovel/spade

palco *nm* box *(at theatre)* ►► ***p. de autoridades*** VIP box; ***p. de honor*** VIP box; ***p. de platea*** ground-floor *o* parterre box; ***p. presidencial*** president's box *(in bullring)*; ***p. de proscenio*** stage box; ***p. real*** royal box

palé[1] *nm* pallet

palé®[2] *nm Esp* Monopoly

palear *vt Ven Fam* to swipe, *Br* to nick

palenque *nm* (**a**) *(estacada)* fence, palisade (**b**) *(recinto)* arena; **salir al p.** to enter the fray (**c**) *Méx (para peleas de gallos)* cockpit, cockfighting arena (**d**) *Andes, RP (para animales)* hitching post

palentino, -a **1** *adj* of/from Palencia *(Spain)*
2 *nm,f* person from Palencia *(Spain)*

paleobiología *nf* palaeobiology

paleoceno, -a *Geol* 1 *adj* Palaeocene
2 *nm* **el P.** the Palaeocene
paleocristiano, -a 1 *adj* early Christian
2 *nm (arte)* = early Christian art
paleógeno *nm* Palaeogene
paleografía *nf* palaeography
paleográfico, -a *adj* palaeographic
paleógrafo, -a *nm,f* palaeographer
paleolítico, -a 1 *adj* palaeolithic
2 *nm* **el P.** the Palaeolithic (period); **el P. inferior/superior** the Lower/Upper Palaeolithic
paleología *nf* = the study of ancient languages
paleontología *nf* palaeontology
paleontológico, -a *adj* palaeontological
paleontólogo, -a *nm,f* palaeontologist
paleozoico, -a 1 *adj* Palaeozoic
2 *nm* **el P.** the Palaeozoic
Palestina *n* Palestine
palestino, -a 1 *adj* Palestinian
2 *nm,f* Palestinian
palestra *nf Hist* arena; EXPR **salir** *o* **saltar a la p.** to enter the fray
palet (*pl* **palets**) *nm* pallet
paleta[1] *nf* (a) *(pala pequeña)* small shovel, small spade; *(de albañil)* trowel
(b) *(en máquina)* blade, vane
(c) *(de pintor)* palette; **la p. clara de los impresionistas** the light palette of the impressionists
(d) *(de frontón, ping-pong)* bat, *US* paddle; **jugar a las paletas** *(en la playa)* to play beach tennis
(e) *(para servir)* fish slice
(f) *(de remo, hélice)* blade
(g) *(diente)* (upper) front tooth
(h) *Informát* palette ►► ***p. flotante*** floating palette; ***p. de herramientas*** tool palette
(i) *Andes, CAm, Méx (pirulí)* lollipop; *Bol, Col, Perú (polo) Br* ice lolly, *US* Popsicle®
(j) *CSur (omóplato) (de persona)* shoulder blade; *CSur, Ven (de vaca)* shoulder
paleta[2] *Fam* 1 *adj Chile* helpful
2 *nmf* (a) *RP (carabina)* **es un p.** he's always tagging along where he's not wanted; **estar** *o* **ir de p.** to play chaperone *o Br* gooseberry (b) *Chile (persona servicial)* helpful person
paleta[3] *ver* **paleto**
paletada *nf* (a) *(con paleta)* shovelful, spadeful; *(de yeso)* trowelful (b) *Fam (acción o dicho de paleto)* **deja de decir paletadas** don't talk such ignorant nonsense; **la moda de esta temporada me parece una p.** I think this season's fashion is really tacky
paletilla *nf* (a) *(omóplato)* shoulder blade (b) *(carne)* shoulder
paletización *nf* palletization
paletizar *vt* to palletize
paleto, -a *Esp Pey* 1 *adj* coarse, uncouth
2 *nm,f* country bumpkin, yokel, *US* hick
paletó *nm Chile* long fitted jacket
paletón *nm* bit
paliacate *nm Méx* = large checked scarf worn on the head or around the neck
paliar *vt (atenuar) (dolor)* to ease, to relieve; *(cansancio)* to relieve
paliativo, -a 1 *adj* palliative
2 *nm Med* palliative
3 **sin paliativos** *loc adj* unmitigated; **una derrota sin paliativos** an unmitigated defeat
4 **sin paliativos** *loc adv* unreservedly; **condenó sin paliativos el asesinato** she condemned the murder unreservedly
palidecer [46] *vi* (a) *(ponerse pálido)* to go *o* turn pale (b) *(perder importancia)* to pale, to fade; **una obra que palidece ante la de su maestro** a work which pales beside that of his master
palidez *nf* paleness
pálido, -a *adj* (a) *(rostro, enfermo)* pale; **ponerse p.** to turn *o* go pale (b) *(color)* pale (c) *(insuficiente)* **ser un p. reflejo** *o* **una pálida imagen de** to be a pale reflection of; **el premio es un p. reconocimiento de su trabajo** the prize is meagre reward for her work
paliducho, -a *adj Fam (persona)* pale
palier[1] *nm Aut* bearing
palier[2] [pa'lje] (*pl* **paliers**) *nm RP (corredor)* landing

palillero, -a *nm* toothpick holder
palillo *nm* (a) *(mondadientes)* **p. (de dientes)** toothpick (b) *(baqueta)* drumstick (c) *(para comida china)* chopstick (d) *Fam (persona delgada)* matchstick; EXPR **está hecho un p.** he's as thin as a rake (e) **palillos** *(castañuelas)* castanets (f) *Chile (de tejer)* knitting needle (g) *Urug (pinza) Br* clothes peg, *US* clothes pin
palimpsesto *nm* palimpsest
palíndromo *nm* palindrome
palio *nm (dosel)* canopy; EXPR **recibir con** *o* **bajo p.** to receive with great pomp
palique *nm Esp Fam* chat, natter; **estar de p.** to be having a chat *o* natter; **se pasaron toda la mañana de p.** they spent the whole morning chatting *o* nattering
paliquear *vi Esp Fam* to chat, to natter
palisandro *nm* rosewood
palista *nmf Dep* (a) *(piragüista)* canoeist (b) *(pelotari)* pelota player
palito *nm* (a) **p. (de pescado)** *Br* fish finger, *US* fish stick ►► ***p. de cangrejo*** crab stick (b) *RP (helado) Br* ice lolly, *US* Popsicle®
palitroque *nm (palo)* small stick
paliza 1 *nf* (a) *(golpes)* beating; **le dieron una p.** they beat him up
(b) *(derrota)* thrashing; **¡menuda p. recibió el equipo!** the team got completely thrashed!
(c) *Fam (esfuerzo)* hard grind; **el viaje hasta la capital es una auténtica p.** the journey to the capital is a real killer; **nos dimos una p. tremenda para acabar a tiempo** we slogged our guts out to finish in time
(d) *Fam (rollo)* drag; EXPR **dar la p. (a alguien)** to go on (at sb); **lleva semanas dándome la p. con que tenemos que ir a esquiar** he's being going on at me *o* pestering me for weeks saying we've got to go skiing
2 *nmf inv Esp Fam* **ser un paliza(s)** to be a pain in the neck
palizada *nf* (a) *(valla)* fence (b) *(recinto cercado)* fenced enclosure
palla *nf Chile (canción)* = improvised song
pallar[1] *nm Andes* lima bean
pallar[2] *vi Chile (cantar)* = to sing improvised songs
palm *nm o nf* (*pl* **palm** *o* **palms**) palmtop
palma *nf* (a) *(de mano)* palm; EXPR **conocer algo como la p. de la mano** to know sth like the back of one's hand
(b) *(palmera)* palm (tree) ►► *Col* ***p. de cera*** wax palm; ***p. enana*** (European) fan palm, palmetto; ***p. real*** royal palm
(c) *(hoja de palmera)* palm leaf
(d) **palmas** *(aplausos)* clapping, applause; **batir** *o* **dar palmas** to clap (one's hands)
(e) EXPR **llevarse la p.** to be the best; *Irónico* **él es tonto, pero su hermano se lleva la p.** he's stupid but his brother takes the *Br* biscuit *o US* cake; **llevar** *o* **traer en palmas a alguien** to pamper sb
palmada *nf* (a) *(suave)* pat; *(más fuerte)* slap; **dar palmadas en la espalda a alguien** to pat/slap sb on the back (b) *(aplauso)* clap; **palmadas** clapping; **dar palmadas** to clap, to applaud (c) *Am (azote)* smack
palmadita *nf* pat; **dar palmaditas a alguien** to pat sb
palmar[1] 1 *adj* of the palm *(of the hand)*
2 *nm* palm grove
palmar[2] *Fam* 1 *vi* to kick the bucket, to croak
2 *vt* **palmarla** to kick the bucket, to croak
palmarés *nm inv* (a) *(historial)* record; **tiene un p. brillante como ajedrecista** he has a brilliant record as a chess player (b) *(lista)* list *o* roll of winners; **el golfista inscribió su nombre en el p. del torneo** the golfer added his name to the tournament's list of winners *o* roll of honour
palmario, -a *adj* obvious, clear
palmatoria *nf* candlestick
palmeado, -a *adj* (a) *(en forma de palma)* palm-shaped (b) *(hoja, raíz)* palmate (c) *(pata)* webbed
palmear 1 *vt* (a) *(aplaudir)* to applaud (b) *(espalda, hombro) (suavemente)* to pat; *(con más fuerza)* to slap (c) *(en baloncesto)* to tip in
2 *vi* (a) *(aplaudir)* to clap, to applaud (b) *(en baloncesto)* to tip in
palmeño, -a 1 *adj* of/from Las Palmas *(Spain)*
2 *nm,f* person from Las Palmas *(Spain)*
palmeo *nm (en baloncesto)* tip-in
palmera *nf* (a) *(árbol)* palm (tree); *(datilera)* date palm ►► ***p. de aceite*** oil palm; ***p. datilera*** date palm; ***p. real*** royal palm (b) *(pastel)* = flat, heart-shaped pastry
palmeral *nm* palm grove

palmesano, -a 1 *adj* of/from Palma (Majorca) *(Spain)*
2 *nm,f* person from Palma (Majorca) *(Spain)*

palmeta *nf (palo)* (schoolmaster's) cane

palmetazo *nm (con palmeta)* stroke

palmípedo, -a 1 *adj* web-footed
2 **palmípedas** *nfpl (grupo)* water fowl *(plural)*

palmita *nf* (**a**) *RP (pastel)* = flat, heart-shaped pastry (**b**) EXPR *Esp Fam* **llevar** *o* **traer a alguien en palmitas** to pamper sb

palmito *nm* (**a**) *(árbol)* palmetto, fan palm (**b**) *Culin* palm heart (**c**) *Esp Fam (buena planta)* good looks; EXPR **lucir el p.** to show off one's good looks

palmo *nm (distancia)* handspan; *también Fig* **p. a p.** bit by bit; EXPR **crecer a palmos** to shoot up; EXPR *Fam* **dejar a alguien con un p. de narices** to leave sb feeling disappointed *o* cheated

palmotear *vi* to clap

palmoteo *nm* clapping

palmtop *nm o nf* (*pl* **palmtops** *o* **palmtop**) palmtop

PALO *nm* (**a**) *(trozo de madera)* stick; **p. de escoba** broomhandle; **los palos de la tienda de campaña** the tent poles; EXPR *Fam* **como un p.** *(flaco)* as thin as a rake; PROV **de tal p., tal astilla** like father like son ►► *RP* ***p. de amasar*** rolling pin
(**b**) *(de golf)* club; *(de hockey)* stick
(**c**) *(de portería) (laterales)* post; *(larguero)* bar; **estrellaron tres disparos en los palos** they hit the woodwork three times
(**d**) *(mástil)* mast; EXPR *Fam* **a p. seco** *(sin nada más)* without anything else, on its own; *(bebida)* neat; EXPR **que cada p. aguante su vela** each of us is responsible for his/her own affairs ►► ***p. mayor*** mainmast; ***p. de mesana*** mizzenmast; ***p. de trinquete*** foremast
(**e**) *(golpe)* blow (with a stick); **dar de palos a alguien** to beat *o* hit sb (with a stick); **liarse a palos (con alguien)** to come to blows (with sb); **moler a alguien a palos** to thrash sb (with a stick); EXPR **dar palos de ciego** *(criticar)* to lash out (wildly); *(no saber qué hacer)* to grope around in the dark; EXPR *Andes, RP Fam* **ni a palos: eso no lo hago ni a palos** there's no way I'm going to do that; EXPR *Fam* **no dar** *o* **pegar un p. al agua** not to do a stroke of work
(**f**) *(mala crítica)* bad review; **se llevó muchos palos de la crítica** she was panned by the critics
(**g**) *Fam (desgracia, trauma)* blow; **¡qué p., me han suspendido!** what a drag, I've failed!; **se ha llevado muchos palos últimamente** he's had to put up with a lot recently
(**h**) *Fam (reparo)* **me da p. hacerlo/decirlo** I hate having to do/say it; **prefiero que se lo digas tú, a mí me da mucho p.** I'd rather you told him, I really don't want to
(**i**) *Fam (pesadez)* pain, drag; **da mucho p. ponerse a estudiar en verano** it's a pain *o* drag having to start studying during the summer
(**j**) *Fam (atraco, robo)* **darle un p. a alguien** *(por la calle)* to mug sb; **dar un p. en un banco** to stick up a bank
(**k**) *(de baraja)* suit
(**l**) *Imprenta (en letra)* stroke
(**m**) *(de cante flamenco)* = style of flamenco singing; EXPR *Fam* **tocar todos los palos** *(hacer de todo)* to do a bit of everything
(**n**) *(madera)* **de p.** wooden; **una cuchara de p.** a wooden spoon; *Am* **no ser de p.** not to be made of stone; *RP Fam* **los de afuera son de p.** outsiders have no say ►► ***p. de rosa*** rosewood
(**o**) *Am (árbol, arbusto)* tree ►► ***p. borracho*** silk floss tree; ***p. de Brasil*** brazil wood tree; ***p. dulce*** liquorice root; ***p. santo*** lignum vitae
(**p**) *Carib Fam (trago, copa)* drink
(**q**) *Am Fam (millón)* million; **esa casa vale dos palos y medio** this house is worth two and a half million ►► ***un p. verde*** a million bucks
(**r**) *Col, Méx, Pan, Ven Fam (como intensificador)* **p. de hombre** great man; **p. de mujer** real beauty; **p. de agua** *(aguacero)* downpour, deluge of rain
(**s**) EXPR *Cuba, Méx muy Fam* **echarse un p.** to have a screw, *Br* to have it off; *Ven Fam* **echar un p.** to have a drink; *Ven Fam* **ir** *o* **venir p. abajo** to go downhill, to go from bad to worse

paloduz *nm* liquorice

paloma *nf* (**a**) *(ave) (silvestre)* dove; *(urbana)* pigeon ►► ***p. bravía*** rock dove; ***p. mensajera*** carrier *o* homing pigeon; ***la p. de la paz*** the dove of peace; ***p. torcaz*** ringdove, woodpigeon; ***p. zurita*** stock dove (**b**) *Pol (persona)* dove (**c**) *Méx (marca)* tick (**d**) *Méx (cohete)* = triangular firework (**e**) *CAm, Méx, Ven Fam (vulva)* pussy (**f**) *Méx, Ven Fam (pene)* prick, cock

palomar *nm (pequeño)* dovecote; *(grande)* pigeon shed

palomazo *nm Méx Fam* unbilled appearance; **mi banda hizo un p. en el concierto de Santana** my band made an unbilled appearance at Santana's concert

palomear *vt Méx (marcar)* to tick, to mark with a tick

palomero *nm Fam (en fútbol)* goalhanger; *(en baloncesto)* cherry picker

palometa *nf* (**a**) *(pez)* pomfret (**b**) *(rosca)* butterfly nut, wing nut

palomilla 1 *adj Perú Fam* mischievous
2 *nf* (**a**) *(insecto)* grain moth (**b**) *(rosca)* butterfly nut, wing nut (**c**) *(soporte)* bracket (**d**) *CAm, Chile, Méx Fam (pandilla)* gang (**e**) *CAm, Chile, Méx Fam (chusma)* rabble, riff-raff (**f**) *Perú Fam (travieso)* little monkey

palomillada *nf Perú Fam* prank

palomillar *vi Perú Fam* to play pranks

palomino *nm* (**a**) *(ave)* young dove *o* pigeon (**b**) *Esp Fam (en calzoncillos)* skidmark

palomita *nf* (**a**) **palomitas (de maíz)** popcorn (**b**) *(en fútbol)* diving stop (**c**) *(bebida)* = drink made with anisette and water

palomo *nm* male dove *o* pigeon

palosanto *nm* lignum vitae

palote *nm* (**a**) *(trazo)* = practice stroke used by children learning to write (**b**) *RP (de amasar)* rolling pin

palpable *adj* (**a**) *(que se puede tocar)* touchable, palpable (**b**) *(evidente)* evident, clear; **el malestar en la empresa es p.** the unease within the company is evident; **había una tensión p. en la habitación** there was a noticeably strained atmosphere in the room

palpablemente *adv* clearly, palpably

palpación *nf* palpation

palpar 1 *vt* (**a**) *(tocar)* to feel, to touch; *(sujeto: doctor)* to palpate (**b**) *RP* **p. de armas a alguien** *(cachear)* to frisk sb, to search sb for weapons (**c**) *(percibir)* to feel; **se palpaba el descontento** the restlessness could be felt
2 *vi* to feel around

palpitación *nf* (**a**) *(de corazón)* beating; *(con fuerza)* throbbing; **una p.** *(de corazón)* a beat; *(con fuerza)* a throb (**b**) **palpitaciones** *(en párpados, dedo, etc.)* palpitations

palpitante *adj* (**a**) *(que palpita)* beating; *(con fuerza)* throbbing (**b**) *(interesante) (discusión, competición)* lively; *(interés, deseo, cuestión)* burning; **un asunto de p. actualidad** a highly topical issue

palpitar 1 *vi* (**a**) *(latir)* to beat; *(con fuerza)* to throb (**b**) *(sentimiento)* to be evident; **en su voz palpitaba el nerviosismo** her voice betrayed her nervousness
2 *v impersonal RP Fam (parecer)* **me palpita que no van a llegar a tiempo** I have a feeling they're not going to arrive on time; **ya me palpitaba yo que no iba a llamar** I had a feeling he wasn't going to call

pálpito *nm esp RP Fam* feeling, hunch; **tener un p.** to have a feeling

palta *nf Andes, RP (fruto)* avocado

paltero *nm RP* avocado tree

palto *nm Andes* avocado tree

paltó *nm Ven* (man's) jacket ►► ***p. levita*** frock coat

palúdico, -a *adj* malarial

paludismo *nm* malaria

palurdo, -a *Pey* 1 *adj* coarse, uncouth
2 *nm,f* country bumpkin, yokel, *US* hick

palustre 1 *adj* marsh; **terreno p.** marshy ground
2 *nm (paleta)* trowel

pamba, pambiza *nf Méx Fam* pummelling; **p. al que no sepa la respuesta** a cuffing for anyone who doesn't know the answer; **a Juan le dieron una p. por haber contado el secreto** Juan was clouted *o* clobbered for telling the secret

pamela *nf* sun hat

pamemas *nfpl Esp Fam* (**a**) *(tonterías)* nonsense (**b**) *(melindres)* fuss; **hacer p.** to make a great fuss

pamentero, -a *RP Fam* 1 *adj* exaggerated; **se puso muy p.** he got terribly worked up
2 *nm,f* **no seas pamentera** don't make such a fuss

pamento *nm RP Fam* fuss; **armar** *o* **hacer p.: es un cortecito de nada, no armes tanto p.** it's just a scratch, don't make such a fuss; **no me gusta Alicia, por cualquier cosita hace p.** I don't like Alicia, she makes a song and dance about the slightest thing

PAMI ['pami] *nm (abrev de* **Programa de Asistencia Médico Integral**) = Argentinian organization which provides for the welfare of pensioners and those who have retired

pampa[1] *nf* **la p.** the pampas ▸▸ ***p. húmeda*** humid pampas; ***p. seca*** dry pampas

pampa[2] **1** *adj* pampas Indian
2 *nmf* pampas Indian

pámpana *nf* vine leaf

pámpano *nm* (**a**) *(sarmiento, pimpollo)* vine tendril, vine shoot (**b**) *(hoja)* vine leaf

pampeano, -a **1** *adj* (**a**) *(de La Pampa)* of/from La Pampa *(Argentina)* (**b**) *(de las pampas)* of/from the pampas
2 *nm,f* (**a**) *(de La Pampa)* person from La Pampa *(Argentina)* (**b**) *(de las pampas)* inhabitant of the pampas

pampero, -a **1** *adj* of/from the pampas
2 *nm (viento)* = cold South wind from the pampas

pamplina *nf (planta)* chickweed

pamplinas *nfpl Fam (tontería)* trifle, unimportant thing; **¡no me vengas con p.!** don't try that nonsense with me!; **¡déjate de p. y cómete la sopa!** stop your nonsense and eat your soup!

pamplona *nf Urug* = grilled meat stuffed with olives and seasoning

pamplonés, -esa **1** *adj* of/from Pamplona *(Spain)*
2 *nm,f* person from Pamplona *(Spain)*

pamplonica **1** *adj* of/from Pamplona *(Spain)*
2 *nmf* person from Pamplona *(Spain)*

PAN [pan] *nm* (**a**) (*abrev de* **Partido de Acción Nacional**) = right-wing Mexican political party (**b**) (*abrev de* **Partido de Avanzada Nacional**) = centre-right Guatemalan political party

PAN *nm* (**a**) *(alimento)* bread; *(barra, hogaza)* loaf; **p. con mantequilla** bread and butter; **a p. y agua** on bread and water; EXPR **vivir a p. y agua** to be *o* live on the breadline; EXPR *Fam* **con su p. se lo coma** that's his/her problem; EXPR **contigo, p. y cebolla** you're all I need (in the world); EXPR **ganarse el p.** to earn a living; EXPR **llamar al p., p. y al vino, vino** to call a spade a spade; EXPR **no sólo de p. vive el hombre** man cannot live on bread alone; EXPR *Fam* **ser más bueno que el p., ser un p. bendito** to be kindness itself; EXPR *Fam* **estar más bueno que el p.** to be gorgeous; EXPR *Méx* **ser un p.**, *RP* **ser un p. de Dios** to be an absolute angel; EXPR *Fam* **ser p. comido** to be a piece of cake, to be as easy as pie; EXPR *Fam* **ser el p. nuestro de cada día** *(habitual)* to be commonplace, to be an everyday occurrence; EXPR **es p. para hoy y hambre para mañana** it's little more than a short-term solution; EXPR **venderse como p. caliente** to sell like hot cakes ▸▸ ***p. de ajo*** garlic bread; ***p. ázimo*** *o* ***ácimo*** unleavened bread; ***p. de azúcar*** sugar loaf; ***p. de barra*** French bread; *Rel* ***p. bendito*** communion bread; *Esp* ***p. Bimbo***® packaged sliced bread; ***p. de centeno*** rye bread; ***p. dulce*** *Méx (bollo)* bun; *RP (panetone)* panettone; ***p. francés*** French bread; *Chile* ***p. Frica*** hamburger bun; ***p. de hogaza*** large round loaf; ***p. integral*** *Br* wholemeal *o US* wholewheat bread; *Arg* ***p. lactal*** sliced bread; *Urug* ***p. de miga*** packaged sliced bread; ***p. de molde*** packaged sliced bread; ***p. moreno*** *(integral)* brown bread; *(con centeno)* black *o* rye bread; ***p. negro*** *(integral)* brown bread; *(con centeno)* black *o* rye bread; ***p. rallado*** breadcrumbs; *Col* ***p. tajado*** sliced bread; ***p. tostado*** *Esp (de paquete)* Melba toast; *Am (tostada)* toast; ***p. de Viena*** *RP* hot dog roll, finger roll; *Esp* = type of soft white bread made with the addition of milk
(**b**) ***p. de higo(s)*** = dessert consisting of dried figs squashed together with whole almonds to form a kind of round cake
(**c**) ***p. de oro*** gold leaf
(**d**) ***p. y quesillo*** *(planta)* shepherd's purse

pana[1] *nf* (**a**) *(tela)* corduroy; **pantalones/camisa de p.** corduroy trousers/shirt ▸▸ ***p. lisa*** velveteen
(**b**) *Chile (hígado)* liver
(**c**) *Chile Fam (avería)* breakdown; **quedar en p.** to have a breakdown; **no hay ropa limpia, la lavadora tiene una p.** there are no clean clothes, the washing-machine's out of order
(**d**) *Chile Fam (audacia)* guts; **le sobra p. para pelear** he's got the guts to fight; **achicar (a uno) la p.** to intimidate, to unnerve; **helársele** *o* **derretírsele a uno la p.** to lose one's nerve, *Br* to lose one's bottle

pana[2] *nmf Ecuad, Ven Fam* (**a**) *(amigo)* pal, *Br* mate, *US* buddy (**b**) *(como apelativo)* pal, *US* buddy; **¿qué hubo, p.?** how're you doing, pal?

panacea *nf* panacea

panaché *nm* **p. (de verduras)** mixed vegetables

panadería *nf* (**a**) *(tienda)* bakery, baker's; *(fábrica)* bakery (**b**) *(oficio)* bread-making

panadero, -a *nm,f* baker

panafricanismo *nm* Pan-Africanism

panafricano, -a *adj* Pan-African

panal *nm* honeycomb

Panamá *n* Panama

panamá *nm* panama (hat)

panameño, -a **1** *adj* Panamanian
2 *nm,f* Panamanian

Panamericana *nf* **la P.** the Pan-American Highway

panamericanismo *nm* Pan-Americanism

panamericano, -a *adj* Pan-American

panárabe *adj* Pan-Arab, Pan-Arabic

panarabismo *nm* Pan-Arabism

panavisión *nf* panavision

pancarta *nf* placard, banner; **p. de meta** finishing line *(with banner across)*

panceta *nf* bacon

panchitos *nmpl Esp Fam* salted peanuts

pancho, -a **1** *adj Fam* **se enteró del accidente y se quedó tan p.** he didn't bat an eyelid *o* turn a hair when he heard about the accident; **le dijeron que estaba despedido y se quedó tan p.** when they told him he was *Br* sacked *o US* fired he didn't seem the least bit concerned; **estaba tan p., sentado en el sofá** he was sitting on the couch without a care in the world; **no te quedes ahí tan p. y ayúdanos** don't just stand there, come and lend us a hand
2 *nm* (**a**) *RP (perrito caliente)* hot dog (**b**) *Méx Fam* **hacer Panchos** to make a fool of oneself

panchólares *nmpl Méx Fam* pesos

pancista *Fam* **1** *adj* opportunistic
2 *nmf* opportunist

pancita *nf Méx* tripe stew

pancito *nm Am* bread roll

páncreas *nm inv* pancreas

pancreático, -a *adj* pancreatic

pancreatitis *nf inv* pancreatitis

pancromático, -a *adj* panchromatic

panda **1** *adj* **oso p.** panda
2 *nm* panda ▸▸ ***p. gigante*** giant panda
3 *nf Esp Fam* (**a**) *(de amigos)* crowd, gang (**b**) *(de gamberros, delincuentes)* gang; **¡menuda p. de vagos están hechos!** what a bunch of layabouts they've become!

pandear **1** *vi* (**a**) *(madera)* to warp (**b**) *(pared)* to bulge, to sag
2 pandearse *vpr* (**a**) *(madera)* to warp (**b**) *(pared)* to bulge, to sag

pandemia *nf Med* pandemic

pandémico, -a *adj Med* pandemic

pandemónium *nm* pandemonium; **se armó un auténtico p.** there was absolute pandemonium, all hell broke loose

pandeo *nm* (**a**) *(de madera)* warping (**b**) *(de pared)* bulging, sagging

pandereta *nf* tambourine

pandero *nm* (**a**) *(instrumento)* tambourine (**b**) *Esp Fam (trasero) Br* bum, *US* butt (**c**) *Perú (compra cooperativa)* = communal savings scheme *(usually for buying cars)*

pandilla *nf* (**a**) *(de amigos)* crowd, gang (**b**) *(de gamberros, delincuentes)* gang; **¡vaya p. de holgazanes!** what a bunch of lazybones!

pandillero, -a *nm,f* member of a gang

pándit (*pl* **pándits**) *nm Rel* pundit

pando, -a *adj* (**a**) *(madera)* warped (**b**) *(pared)* bulging, sagging

pandorga *nf Par (cometa)* kite

panecillo *nm Esp* bread roll

panecito *nm Am* bread roll

panegírico, -a **1** *adj* panegyrical, eulogistic
2 *nm* panegyric, eulogy

panegirista *nmf* panegyrist

panel *nm* (**a**) *(pared, biombo)* screen (**b**) *(tablero)* board ▸▸ ***p. de control*** *(en máquina, computador)* control panel; ***p. de instrumentos*** *(en vehículo)* instrument panel; ***p. solar*** solar panel (**c**) *(de personas)* panel

panela *nf* (**a**) *CAm, Col, Méx, Ven (azúcar)* = brown-sugar loaf (**b**) *Méx (queso)* = type of fresh cheese (**c**) *Ven (pieza)* = rectangular bar or block

panera *nf* (**a**) *(para servir pan)* bread basket (**b**) *(para guardar pan) Br* bread bin, *US* bread box

panero, -a **1** *adj* **ser muy p.** to be very fond of bread
2 *nm Br* bread tray, *US* bread box

panetone *nm* panettone

paneuropeísmo *nm* Pan-Europeanism

paneuropeo, -a *adj* Pan-European

pánfilo, -a *Fam* **1** *adj* simple, foolish
2 *nm,f* fool, simpleton

panfletario, -a *adj* propagandist

panfletista *nmf* pamphleteer

panfleto *nm* (**a**) *(escrito)* polemical pamphlet (**b**) *(folleto)* (political) leaflet

panga *nf* (**a**) *Méx (barcaza)* ferry (**b**) *CAm, Méx (canoa)* small fishing boat

pangaré *adj CSur* pangare, mealy

pangermánico, -a *adj* Pan-German

pangermanismo *nm* Pan-Germanisn

pangolín *nm* pangolin, scaly anteater

paniaguado *nm Pey (enchufado)* protégé

pánico *nm* panic; **el p. se apoderó de la sala tras la explosión** panic gripped *o* seized the hall after the explosion; **¡que no cunda el p.!** don't panic!; **ser presa del p.** to be panic-stricken; **tener p. a** to be terrified of; **me dan p. los barcos** I'm terrified of sailing

panificación *nf* bread-making

panificadora *nf* (large) bakery

panislámico, -a *adj* Pan-Islamic

panislamismo *nm* Pan-Islamicism

panista *Méx* **1** *adj* relating to the PAN party
2 *nmf* PAN supporter

panizo *nm* millet

panocha *nf* (**a**) *(de maíz)* ear, cob (**b**) *Méx (de melaza)* brown sugar loaf (**c**) *Col, Méx Vulg (vulva)* cunt

panoja *nf* ear, cob

panoli *Fam* **1** *adj* foolish, silly
2 *nmf* fool, idiot

panoplia *nf* (**a**) *(tabla)* display panel (**b**) *(armas)* mounted display of weapons (**c**) *(conjunto, gama)* range, gamut; **se presentan a las elecciones una p. de partidos** a whole range of parties are running for election

panorama *nm* (**a**) *(vista)* panorama (**b**) *(visión general)* overview; **un p. de la música barroca** an overview of Baroque music (**c**) *(situación)* outlook; **el p. económico no es bueno** the economic outlook is not good

panorámica *nf* (**a**) *(vista)* panoramic view (**b**) *(en cine, televisión)* pan

panorámico, -a *adj* panoramic

panqué *nm* (**a**) *Cuba, Méx (crepe)* pancake (**b**) *Méx (pastel)* sponge cake

panqueca *nf Ven* pancake

panqueque *nm Am* pancake

pantagruélico, -a *adj* gargantuan, enormous

pantalán *nm Náut* wharf

pantaleta *nf*, **pantaletas** *nfpl CAm, Carib, Méx (bragas)* panties, *Br* knickers

pantalla *nf* (**a**) *(de cine, televisión, ordenador)* screen; **la p. grande** the big screen; **la pequeña p.** the small screen, television; **van a llevar a la p. la vida de Zapata** they're going to make a film about the life of Zapata; **mostrar en p.** to show on the screen; **una estrella de la p.** a TV/movie star ▸▸ ***p. acústica*** *(musical)* baffle; *(en carretera)* acoustic screen, = roadside screen to reduce traffic noise; *Informát* ***p. de ayuda*** help screen; *Am* ***p. chica*** small screen; ***p. de cristal líquido*** liquid crystal display; ***p. gigante*** big screen; *Informát* ***p. de matriz activa*** active matrix display; ***p. plana*** flat screen; ***p. de radar*** radar screen; *Informát* ***p. táctil*** touch screen
(**b**) *(de lámpara)* lampshade
(**c**) *(de chimenea)* fireguard
(**d**) *(encubridor)* front; **esta empresa les sirve de p. para sus actividades ilegales** this company serves as a front for their illegal activities
(**e**) *Andes, RP (abanico)* fan
(**f**) *Ven Fam (pose)* sham; **su casamiento es p.** his marriage is a sham

pantallar, pantallear *vi Ven Fam* to show off; **está siempre pantallando** she's always showing off

pantallazo *nm* (**a**) *Informát Fam* screen capture *o* dump (**b**) *RP Fam (sinopsis)* snapshot; **es un curso muy rápido, pero te da un p. del arte medieval** it's a very short course but it gives you a snapshot of mediaeval art

pantallero, -a *Ven Fam* **1** *adj* showy, flashy
2 *nm,f* show-off

pantalón *nm*, **pantalones** *nmpl* trousers, *US* pants; **se compró unos pantalones** he bought a pair of trousers *o US* pants; EXPR *Méx Fam* **amarrarse** *o* **fajarse** *o* **ponerse los pantalones** to take matters in hand; EXPR *Fam* **bajarse los pantalones** to climb down; EXPR *Fam* **llevar los pantalones** to wear the trousers *o US* pants ▸▸ *Am* ***p. acampanado*** bell-bottoms; *Col* ***p. de baño*** swimming trunks; ***pantalones bombachos*** baggy trousers; *(para golf)* plus fours; *RP* ***p. (de) bombilla*** drainpipe trousers *o US* pants; ***p. de campana*** bell-bottoms; *Esp* ***p. de chándal*** tracksuit *Br* bottoms *o US* pants; ***p. corto*** short trousers *o US* pants, shorts; ***p. de esquí*** ski pants; *Col, Cuba* ***pantalones interiores*** *(braga)* panties, *Br* knickers; ***p. largo*** (long) trousers *o US* (long) pants; *Méx* ***pantalones de mezclilla*** jeans; ***p. de montar*** jodhpurs; ***p. de pana*** cords; ***p. de peto*** *Br* dungarees, *US* overalls; ***p. de pinzas*** pleated trousers *o US* pants; ***p. (de) pitillo*** drainpipe trousers *o US* pants; ***p. tejano*** jeans; ***p. vaquero*** jeans

pantaloncillo *nm*, **pantaloncillos** *nmpl Col, Ven (calzoncillos) Br* underpants, *US* shorts

pantaloneta *nf CAm, Col* short trousers *o US* pants, shorts

pantanal *nm* marsh, bog

pantano *nm* (**a**) *(ciénaga)* marsh; *(laguna)* swamp (**b**) *(embalse)* reservoir

pantanoso, -a *adj* (**a**) *(cenagoso)* marshy, boggy (**b**) *(difícil)* tricky

panteísmo *nm* pantheism

panteísta **1** *adj* pantheistic
2 *nmf* pantheist

panteón *nm* (**a**) *(templo)* pantheon (**b**) *(mausoleo)* mausoleum, vault ▸▸ ***p. familiar*** family vault (**c**) *Andes, CAm, Carib, Méx (cementerio)* cemetery

panteonero *nm Andes, CAm, Carib, Méx* cemetery worker

pantera *nf* panther; EXPR *Méx* **ser una p.** to be fearless ▸▸ ***p. negra*** black panther

panti *nm Br* tights, *US* pantyhose

pantimedias *nfpl Méx Br* tights, *US* pantyhose

pantocrátor *nm Arte* Christ Pantocrator

pantógrafo *nm* pantograph

pantomima *nf* (**a**) *(mimo)* mime (**b**) *(farsa)* pantomime, acting

pantomimo *nm* mime artist

pantoque *nm Náut* bilge

pantorrilla *nf* calf

pantri, pantry *nm Ven* (**a**) *(comedor diario)* = family dining area off kitchen (**b**) *(comedor de formica)* = metal or plastic dining-table with chairs

pants *nmpl Méx* (**a**) *(pantalón)* tracksuit bottoms *o US* pants (**b**) *(traje)* track *o* jogging suit

pantufla *nf* slipper

panty (*pl* **pantis**) *nm Br* tights, *US* pantyhose

panza *nf* (**a**) *Fam (barriga)* belly (**b**) *(de rumiantes)* rumen (**c**) *(de avión, jarrón)* belly

panzada *nf Fam* (**a**) *(en el agua)* belly-flop; **darse una p.** to do a belly flop (**b**) *(hartazgo)* **se dieron una p. de marisco** they pigged out on shellfish; **nos dimos una p. de estudiar** we studied really hard

panzazo *nm Fam* belly-flop; **darse un p.** to do a belly flop

panzón, -ona *Fam* **1** *adj* (**a**) *Am (panzudo)* paunchy (**b**) *Méx (embarazada)* pregnant
2 *nm,f Am* paunch, potbelly

panzona *nf Méx Fam* pregnant woman

panzudo, -a *adj Fam* paunchy, potbellied

pañal *nm Br* nappy, *US* diaper; EXPR *Fam* **estar en pañales** *(en sus inicios)* to be in its infancy; *(sin conocimientos)* not to have a clue; EXPR *Fam* **dejar a alguien en pañales** to leave sb standing *o* behind

pañería *nf* (**a**) *(producto)* drapery (**b**) *(tienda) Br* draper's (shop), *US* dry goods store

paño *nm* (**a**) *(tela)* cloth, material
(**b**) *(trapo)* cloth; *(para polvo)* duster; *(de cocina)* tea towel; **pásale un p. al salón** dust the living room ▸▸ *Chile* ***p. de loza*** tea towel
(**c**) *(lienzo)* panel, length
(**d**) *(tapiz)* hanging, tapestry
(**e**) *Arquit (pared)* length (of wall)
(**f**) *(en la cara)* liver spot
(**g**) *Ven (toalla)* bath towel

(**h**) *Fam* EXPR **conocer el p.** to know the score; **ser el p. de lágrimas de alguien** to be a shoulder to cry on for sb; **en paños menores** in one's underthings; **paños calientes** half-measures

pañol *nm Náut* storeroom

pañolada *nf* = waving of handkerchiefs by crowd at bullfights and sporting events to signal approval or disapproval

pañolenci *nm RP* felt

pañoleta *nf* (**a**) *(de mujer)* shawl, wrap (**b**) *(de torero)* neckerchief

pañolón *nm* shawl

pañuelo *nm* (**a**) *(de nariz)* handkerchief ▸▸ ***p. de bolsillo*** pocket handkerchief; ***p. de mano*** pocket handkerchief; ***p. de papel*** paper handkerchief, tissue (**b**) *(para el cuello)* scarf, neckerchief; *(para la cabeza)* headscarf ▸▸ ***p. de cuello*** scarf, neckerchief

papa[1] *nm* pope; **el P. Juan Pablo II** Pope John Paul II ▸▸ ***el p. negro*** the black pope *(the head of the Jesuit order)*

papa[2] *nf* (**a**) *esp Am (tubérculo)* potato; EXPR *Fam* **ni p.: no saber ni p.** not to have a clue; *Fam* **no entendí ni p.** I didn't understand a word; EXPR *Ven Fam* **ponerse/estar las papas duras: se estan poniendo las papas duras** the going is getting tough; EXPR *Am Fam Hum* **quítate la p. de la boca** speak clearly; EXPR *RP Fam* **ser una p.** *(ser muy fácil)* to be a cinch, to be a pushover; EXPR *Ven Fam* **ser p. pelada** *(ser muy fácil)* to be a cinch *o* a pushover ▸▸ *Esp* ***papas bravas*** = sautéed potatoes served with spicy tomato sauce; *Urug* ***papas chip*** *Br* crisps, *US* (potato) chips; *Am* ***p. dulce*** sweet potato; *Am* ***papas fritas*** *(de sartén) Br* chips, *US* (French) fries; *(de bolsa) Br* crisps, *US* (potato) chips; EXPR *RP Fam* **ser un/una p. frita** to be a *Br* wally *o US* goofball; ***p. nueva*** new potato; ***p. temprana*** new potato

(**b**) *Am Fam (comida)* food; **cómete toda la p.** eat up all your food

(**c**) *CSur Fam (en la media)* hole

(**d**) *Méx Fam (mentira)* fib

papá *nm (utilizado por niño)* dad, daddy, *US* pop; *Am (utilizado por adulto)* dad; **invita también a tus papás** invite your *Br* mum *o US* mom and dad too ▸▸ ***P. Noel*** Father Christmas

papable *adj* **el p. cardenal Martini** Cardinal Martini, a candidate to be the next pope

papachado, -a *Méx* **1** *adj* pampered, spoilt
2 *nm,f* spoilt child

papachador, -ora *nm,f Méx* openly affectionate person

papachar *vt Méx* to cuddle, to pamper

papachento, -a *Méx* **1** *adj* **es muy p.** he loves being pampered, he loves being made a fuss of
2 *nm,f* **eres una papachenta** you love being pampered, you love being made a fuss of

papachero, -a *Méx* **1** *adj* demonstrative
2 *nm,f* openly affectionate person

papacho *nm Méx* hug, cuddle

papacito *nm CAm, Carib, Méx* daddy

papada *nf (de persona)* double chin; *(de animal)* dewlap

papado *nm* papacy

papagayo *nm* (**a**) *(animal)* parrot; EXPR **hablar como un p.** to be a chatterbox (**b**) *Carib, Méx (cometa)* kite (**c**) *Arg (orinal)* male urinal

papal *adj* papal

papalina *nf* (**a**) *(gorra)* = cap that covers the ears (**b**) *(cofia)* bonnet

papalote *nm CAm, Méx (cometa)* kite

papamoscas **1** *nm* flycatcher ▸▸ ***p. cerrojillo*** pied flycatcher; ***p. gris*** spotted flycatcher
2 *nmf inv RP Fam* sucker, simpleton

papamóvil *nm* popemobile

papanatas *nmf inv Fam* sucker, simpleton

Papanicolau *nm Am* smear test; **hacerse un P.** to have a smear test

papar *Fam* **1** *vt* (**a**) *RP (comer)* to eat (**b**) *Méx, RP* EXPR **p. moscas** *(estar despistado)* to daydream
2 *vi RP* to eat
3 paparse *vpr RP* to scoff

paparazzi [papa'ratsi] *nmf inv* paparazzi

paparruchas *nfpl Fam* nonsense; **¡p.!** *Br* codswallop!, *US* bunkum!

papaúpa *nmf Ven Fam* number one, kingpin

papaya *nf* (**a**) *(fruta)* papaya, pawpaw (**b**) *Ven Fam (cosa fácil)* cinch, piece of cake (**c**) *Cuba Vulg (vulva)* cunt

papayo *nm* papaya tree, pawpaw tree

papeado, -a *adj Ven Fam* sturdy, solid; **lo tiene al bebé bien p.** her baby's nice and chubby

papear *Esp, Ven Fam* **1** *vt* to eat, to scoff
2 *vi* to eat, *Br* to nosh

PAPEL *nm* (**a**) *(material)* paper; *(hoja)* sheet of paper; *(trozo)* piece of paper; **una bolsa de p.** a paper bag; **un p. en blanco** a blank sheet of paper; **espera un momento, que agarro lápiz y p.** wait a moment while I get a pencil and paper; **sobre el p.** *(teóricamente)* on paper; EXPR **perder los papeles** *(perder control)* to lose one's cool, to lose control; *RP, Ven Fam (estar desorientado)* to lose one's touch; EXPR **ser p. mojado** to be worthless ▸▸ *Esp* ***p. albal***® tin *o* aluminium foil; ***p. de aluminio*** tin *o* aluminium foil; *RP* ***p. de armar*** cigarette paper; ***p. de arroz*** rice paper; ***p. (de) barba*** untrimmed paper; ***p. biblia*** bible paper; ***p. de borrador*** scrap *o* waste paper; ***p. de calco*** *o* ***de calcar*** *(transparente)* tracing paper; *(entintado)* carbon paper; ***p. carbón*** *o RP* ***carbónico*** carbon paper; ***p. de carta*** notepaper; ***p. cebolla*** onionskin; ***p. celofán*** Cellophane®; ***p. de cera*** *(para envolver) Br* greaseproof paper, *US* wax paper; ***p. charol*** coloured tissue paper; *Chile* ***p. confort*** toilet paper; *Informát* ***p. continuo*** continuous paper; ***p. couché*** coated (magazine) paper; *Am* ***p. crepé*** crepe paper; *Col* ***p. crespón*** crepe paper; ***p. cuadriculado*** graph paper; ***p. cuché*** coated paper; ***p. ecológico*** acid-free paper; ***p. de embalar*** *o* ***de embalaje*** wrapping paper; ***p. de envolver*** wrapping paper; ***p. de estaño*** tin *o* aluminium foil; ***p. de estraza*** brown paper; ***p. de fumar*** cigarette paper; *RP* ***p. glasé*** coloured tissue paper; ***p. higiénico*** toilet paper; ***p. de lija*** sandpaper; ***p. maché*** papier-mâché; *CSur* ***p. madera*** brown paper; *RP* ***p. manteca*** *(para envolver) Br* greaseproof *o US* wax paper; ***p. milimetrado*** graph paper; *Chile* ***p. mural*** wallpaper; *Am* ***p. oficio*** foolscap; ***p. pautado*** *(para música)* (music) manuscript paper, staff paper; ***p. pentagramado*** *(para música)* (music) manuscript paper, staff paper; ***p. de periódico*** newspaper, newsprint; *RP* ***p. picado*** confetti; *Esp* ***p. pinocho*** crepe paper; ***p. pintado*** wallpaper; ***p. de plata*** tin *o* aluminium foil; ***p. reciclado*** recycled paper; ***p. de regalo*** wrapping paper; *Cuba* ***p. sanitario*** toilet paper; ***p. secante*** blotting paper; ***p. de seda*** tissue (paper); ***p. sellado*** stamped paper, = paper bearing an official stamp to show that the corresponding tax has been paid; *Informát* ***p. térmico*** thermal paper; ***p. timbrado*** stamped paper, = paper bearing an official stamp to show that the corresponding tax has been paid; *Guat, Ven* ***p. toilette*** *o* ***tualé*** toilet paper; *Quím* ***p. tornasol*** litmus paper; ***p. vegetal*** tracing paper

(**b**) *(en película, teatro)* role, part; **Bogart está insuperable en el p. de Rick** Bogart is superb as Rick; **hacer** *o* **representar el p. de** to play the role *o* part of ▸▸ ***p. principal*** main part; ***p. secundario*** minor part

(**c**) *(función)* role, part; **hace el p. de padre y de madre** he plays the role of both father and mother; **desempeña un p. crucial en la compañía** she plays a crucial role in the company; **¡vaya un p. que vamos a hacer con tantos lesionados!** we're going to make a poor showing with so many injuries!; **hacer (un) buen/mal p.** to make a good/poor showing

(**d**) *Fin (valores)* stocks and shares ▸▸ ***p. del Estado*** government bonds; ***p. moneda*** paper money, banknotes; ***p. de pagos (al Estado)*** = special stamps for making certain payments to the State

(**e**) *Esp Fam (1.000 pesetas)* = thousand pesetas

(**f**) **papeles** *(documentos, identificación)* papers; **los papeles del coche** the car's registration documents; **tener los papeles en regla** to have one's papers in order; **los sin papeles** undocumented immigrants

(**g**) *Fam* **los papeles** *(la prensa escrita)* the papers

---

papela *nf Esp Fam* (**a**) *(documentación)* ID (**b**) *(papelina)* wrap, = sachet of paper containing drugs

papeleo *nm* paperwork, red tape; **ya he acabado todo el p. del préstamo** I've done all the paperwork for the loan

papelera *nf* (**a**) *(cesto)* wastepaper basket, *Br* wastepaper bin; *(en la calle)* litter bin (**b**) *(fábrica)* paper mill (**c**) *Informát (en Windows)* recycle bin; *(en Macintosh) Br* wastebasket, *US* trash can

papelería *nf* stationer's (shop); **material** *o* **artículos de p.** stationery

papelero, -a **1** *adj* paper; **industria papelera** paper industry
2 *nm* (**a**) *CSur (papelera)* wastepaper basket, *Br* wastepaper bin (**b**) *Ven (desorden)* mess of papers

papeleta *nf* (**a**) *(boleto)* ticket, slip (of paper)

(**b**) *(de votación)* ballot paper ▸▸ ***p. en blanco*** blank ballot paper; ***p. nula*** void ballot paper

(**c**) *Educ* = slip of paper with university exam results

(**d**) *(problema)* **le tocó la p. de comunicarle que estaba despedido** she got lumbered with the job of telling him he was fired; **tiene una buena p. con la mujer en el hospital y el hijo en el paro** he has a lot on his plate with his wife in hospital and his son unemployed

papelillo *nm Ven* confetti

papelina *nf Fam* wrap, = sachet of paper containing drugs

papelitos *nmpl Urug* confetti

papelón *nm* (**a**) *Fam (mal papel)* spectacle; **hacer un p.** to make a fool of oneself, to be left looking ridiculous (**b**) *Andes, Ven (azúcar)* brown sugar loaf

papeo *nm Fam* grub

paperas *nfpl* mumps

papero, -a *adj Am* potato

papi *nm Fam* daddy, *US* pop

papiamento *nm* Papiamento *(a creole language spoken in the Dutch Antilles)*

papila *nf* papilla ▸▸ ***p. gustativa*** taste bud

papilar *adj* papillary

papilionáceo, -a *Bot* **1** *adj* papilonaceous
2 papilionáceas *nfpl (familia) Papilonaceae*

papilla *nf* (**a**) *(para niños)* baby food, *US* formula; EXPR *Fam* **echar** *o* **arrojar hasta la primera p.** to be as sick as a dog; EXPR *Fam* **hacer p. a alguien** to make mincemeat of sb; EXPR *Fam* **hecho(a) p.** *(cansado)* shattered, exhausted; *(roto)* smashed to bits, ruined (**b**) *Med* barium meal

papiloma *nm Med* papilloma

papión *nm* baboon

papiro *nm* (**a**) *(planta)* papyrus (**b**) *(escrito)* papyrus

papiroflexia *nf* origami

papirotazo *nm* flick *(of finger)*

papisa *nf* female pope ▸▸ ***la p. Juana*** Pope Joan

papismo *nm* papistry, popery

papista **1** *adj* papist; EXPR *Fam* **ser más p. que el Papa** to be more Catholic than the Pope
2 *nmf* papist

papo *nm Fam* (**a**) *(moflete)* jowls (**b**) *(de ave)* crop (**c**) *(descaro)* **tener mucho p.** to have a lot of cheek; **itiene un p. que se lo pisa!** he's got some cheek!

paporreta *nf Perú Fam* **de p.** *(de memoria)* parrot-fashion; **se sabía la lista de p.** she knew the list by heart

páprika, paprika *nf* paprika

papú (*pl* **papúes**) **1** *adj* Papuan
2 *nmf* Papuan

Papúa-Nueva Guinea *n* Papua New Guinea

paquebote *nm* packet boat

paquete[1], -a *adj RP Fam* smart, elegant; **es una mujer muy paqueta** she's a very smart dresser; **hoy estás muy p.** you're looking very elegant today; **tiene un apartamento muy p.** he's got a very chic apartment

paquete[2] *nm* (**a**) *(de libros, regalos)* parcel ▸▸ ***p. bomba*** parcel bomb; *Col, Ven Fam* ***p. chileno*** *(timo)* = deception involving the use of a fake wad of bank notes; *(estafa)* swindle; ***p. postal*** parcel
(**b**) *(de cigarrillos, folios)* pack, packet; *(de azúcar, arroz)* bag
(**c**) *(maleta, bulto)* bag
(**d**) *(en rugby)* pack
(**e**) *(en ciclismo)* pack
(**f**) *(en motocicleta)* passenger; **ir de p.** to ride pillion
(**g**) *(conjunto)* package ▸▸ *Bolsa* ***p. de acciones*** bundle *o* lot of shares; ***p. de medidas*** package of measures; ***p. turístico*** package tour
(**h**) *Informát* package ▸▸ ***p. integrado*** integrated package
(**i**) *Esp Fam (pañales) Br* nappies, *US* diapers
(**j**) *Fam (cosa fastidiosa)* **me ha tocado el p. de hacer...** I've been lumbered with doing...
(**k**) *Esp Fam (genitales masculinos)* packet, bulge; **marcar p.** to draw attention to one's packet *o* bulge
(**l**) *Fam (inútil)* **ser un p.** to be useless *o* hopeless
(**m**) *Méx Fam (problema)* major hurdle
(**n**) EXPR *Fam* **meter un p. a alguien** *(castigar)* to come down hard on sb; *Méx Fam* **darse p.** to put on airs

paquetear *vi RP Fam* to dress up smart; **anda siempre paqueteando** she's always very dressed up

paquetería *nf* (**a**) *(mercancía)* small goods; **empresa de p.** parcel delivery company (**b**) *(negocio)* small goods shop (**c**) *RP Fam (elegancia)* smartness, elegance

paqueterío *nm RP Fam* pile of parcels

paquidermo *nm* pachyderm

Paquistán = **Pakistán**

paquistaní (*pl* **paquistaníes**), **pakistaní** (*pl* **pakistaníes**) **1** *adj* Pakistani
2 *nmf* Pakistani

paquita *nf Chile Fam* female police officer

par **1** *adj* (**a**) *(número)* even; **echar algo a pares o nones** = to decide something between two people by a game in which each holds out a certain number of fingers behind their back, predicts whether the total will be odd or even, then reveals their hand to the other (**b**) *(igual)* equal
2 *nm* (**a**) *(de zapatos, pantalones)* pair; **a** *o* **en pares** in pairs, two by two
(**b**) *(de personas, cosas)* couple; EXPR *Fam Hum* **de tres pares de narices: está cayendo una tormenta de tres pares de narices** there's an almighty storm going on; **tengo un lumbago de tres pares de narices** I've got horrendous lumbago
(**c**) *(número indeterminado)* few, couple; **un p. de copas** a couple of *o* a few drinks; **un p. de veces** a couple of times, a few times; *Vulg* **es un tipo con un p. de cojones** *o* **huevos** he's got guts *o* balls
(**d**) *(número par)* even number
(**e**) *(en golf)* par; **dos bajo/sobre p.** two under/over par; **hacer p. en un hoyo** to par a hole
(**f**) *(noble)* peer
(**g**) *Fís* couple ▸▸ ***p. de fuerzas*** couple; ***p. de torsión*** torque
(**h**) **sin p.** *(sin comparación)* without equal, matchless; **de una belleza sin p.** incomparably beautiful
(**i**) **(abierto) de p. en p.** *(puerta, ventana, boca)* wide open
(**j**) *Tel* ***p. trenzado*** twisted pair
3 a la par *loc adv* (**a**) *(simultáneamente)* at the same time; **los dos llegaron a la p.** they both arrived at the same time (**b**) *(a igual nivel)* at the same level; **se han colocado a la p. de la competencia** they have put themselves on an equal footing with their competitors (**c**) *Fin* at par; **el dólar cotiza a la p. con el euro** the dollar is trading at par with the euro

PARA *prep* (**a**) *(indica destino, finalidad, motivación)* for; **es p. ti** it's for you; **significa mucho p. mí** it means a lot to me; **"¡qué suerte!", dije p. mí** "how lucky," I said to myself; **una mesa p. el salón** a table for the living room; **desayuno p. dos** breakfast for two; **crema p. zapatos** shoe polish; **pastillas p. dormir** sleeping pills; **están entrenados p. el combate** they have been trained for combat; **estudia p. dentista** she's studying to become a dentist; **esta agua no es buena p. beber** this water isn't fit for drinking *o* to drink; **p. conseguir sus propósitos** in order to achieve his aims; **lo he hecho p. agradarte** I did it to please you; **me voy p. no causar más molestias** I'll go so I don't cause you any more inconvenience; **te lo repetiré p. que te enteres** I'll repeat it so you understand; **resulta que se divorcian p. un mes más tarde volverse a casar** so they get divorced, only to remarry a month later; **p. con** towards; **es buena p. con los demás** she is kind towards other people; **¿p. qué?** what for?; **¿p. qué quieres un martillo?** what do you want a hammer for?, why do you want a hammer?; **¿p. qué has venido?** why are you here?; **¿p. quién trabajas?** who do you work for?
(**b**) *(indica dirección)* towards; **el próximo vuelo p. Caracas** the next flight to Caracas; **ir p. casa** to head (for) home; **salir p. el aeropuerto** to leave for the airport; **p. abajo** downwards; **p. arriba** upwards; **tira p. arriba** pull up *o* upwards; **p. atrás** backwards; **échate p. atrás** *(en asiento)* lean back; **p. delante** forwards; **ya vas p. viejo** you're getting old; **esta muchacha va p. pintora** this girl has all the makings of a painter
(**c**) *(indica tiempo)* for; **tiene que estar acabado p. mañana/p. antes de Navidad** it has to be finished by *o* for tomorrow/before Christmas; **faltan cinco minutos p. que salga el tren** the train leaves in five minutes; **tienen previsto casarse p. el 17 de agosto** they plan to get married on 17 August; **llevamos comida p. varios días** we have enough food for several days; *Andes, CAm, Carib, Méx* **diez p. las once** ten to eleven; *Andes, CAm, Carib, Méx* **un cuarto p. las once** (a) quarter to eleven; **va p. un año que no nos vemos** it's getting on for a year since we saw each other; **¿y p. cuándo un bebé?** and when are you going to start a family?; **p. entonces** by then
(**d**) *(indica comparación)* **tiene la estatura adecuada p. su edad** she is the normal height for her age; **está muy delgado p. lo que come** he's very thin considering how much he eats; **p. ser verano hace mucho frío** considering it's summer, it's very cold; **p. ser un principiante no lo hace mal** he's not bad for a beginner; **p. lo que me ha servido...** for all the use it's been to me...; **¡tanto esfuerzo p. nada!** all that effort for nothing!; **¿y tú quién eres p. tratarla así?** who do you think you are, treating her like that?; **yo no soy quien p. decir...** it's not for me to say...
(**e**) *(después de adjetivo y antes de infinitivo) (indica inminencia,*

propósito) to; **la comida está lista p. servir** the meal is ready to be served; **el atleta está preparado p. ganar** the athlete is ready to win
(**f**) *(indica opinión)* for; **p. Marx, la religión era el opio del pueblo** for Marx, religion was the opium of the people; **p. mí/ti/***etc.* as far as I'm/you're/*etc* concerned; **p. mí que no van a venir** it looks to me like they're not coming; **¿p. ti quién es más guapo?** who do you think is the most handsome?
(**g**) *(indica disposición, estado)* **no estoy p. fiestas** I'm not in the mood for parties; **el abuelo no está ya p. hacer viajes largos** grandfather's no longer up to going on long journeys; **¿hace día p. ir sin chaqueta?** is it warm enough to go out without a jacket on?
(**h**) *(indica consecuencia)* **p. su sorpresa, p. sorpresa suya** to her surprise; **p. alegría de todos** to everyone's delight; **p. nuestra desgracia** unfortunately for us
(**i**) EXPR **no es/fue/***etc.* **p. tanto** it's not/it wasn't/*etc* such a big deal; **no llores, que no es p. tanto** don't cry, it's not such a big deal, there's no need to cry about it; **dicen que les trataron mal, pero no fue p. tanto** they say they were ill-treated, but that's going a bit far; *Fam* **que p. qué: hace un calor que p. qué** it's absolutely boiling; **este plato pica que p. qué** this dish is really hot, *Br* this dish isn't half hot

> See the grammar box at **por** for discussion of the finer shades of meaning between **por** and **para**.

parabellum [para'βelum] *nf* **casquillos de nueve milímetros p.** 9 mm Parabellum cases

parabién (*pl* **parabienes**) *nm Formal* congratulations; **dar el p. a alguien** to congratulate sb; EXPR *RP* **estar de parabienes** to be in luck

parábola *nf* (**a**) *(alegoría)* parable (**b**) *Mat* parabola

parabólica *nf* satellite dish

parabólico, -a *adj* parabolic

parabrisas *nm inv Br* windscreen, *US* windshield

paraca *nmf Fam (paracaidista)* paratrooper, para; **los paracas** the Paras

paracaídas *nm inv* parachute; **saltar** *o* **tirarse en p.** to parachute; **un salto en p.** a parachute jump; **lanzar algo en p.** to parachute sth, to drop sth by parachute

paracaidismo *nm* (**a**) *(deporte)* parachuting, parachute jumping (**b**) *Méx (invasión)* parachute squatting

paracaidista 1 *adj* parachute; **brigada p.** paratroop brigade
2 *nmf* (**a**) *(deportivo)* parachutist (**b**) *(militar)* paratrooper (**c**) *Am Fam (persona no invitada)* **calcula más comida, que nunca falta algún paracaidista** make sure there's enough food for a few extra people as there are always one or two who drop in uninvited (**d**) *RP Fam Pey (advenedizo)* upstart (**e**) *Méx (invasor)* squatter

paracetamol *nm* paracetamol

parachispas *nm inv* (**a**) *(de chimenea)* fireguard (**b**) *(de contacto eléctrico)* spark arrester

parachoques *nm inv (de automóvil)* bumper, *US* fender; *(de tren)* buffer

parada *nf* (**a**) *(detención)* stop; **hicimos una p. para descansar** we stopped for a rest; **el tren hace p. en todas las estaciones** the train stops at every station; EXPR **hacer p. y fonda** *(para comer)* to stop for something to eat; *(para dormir)* to make an overnight stop ►► ***p. en boxes*** *(en automovilismo)* pit stop
(**b**) *(de autobús)* (bus) stop; *(de metro)* (subway) station; **la próxima p. es la mía** mine's the next stop, I get off at the next stop ►► ***p. discrecional*** request stop; ***p. de taxi*** taxi rank, taxi stand
(**c**) *Dep* save
(**d**) *(desfile)* parade
(**e**) ***p. nupcial*** courtship ritual
(**f**) *Arg, Ven* ***p. de manos*** handstand; **hacer un p. de manos** to do a handstand
(**g**) *Andes, RP Fam (engreimiento)* airs and graces; **son gente de mucha p.** they're very high and mighty *o* hoity-toity
(**h**) *Perú (mercado)* market stall
(**i**) EXPR *CSur Fam* **hacer p. de hacer algo** to move *o* make as if to do sth; **hizo p. de abrirme la puerta** he made as if to open the door for me
(**j**) *ver también* **parado**

paradero *nm* (**a**) *(de persona)* whereabouts; **están en p. desconocido** their present whereabouts are unknown; **averiguar el p. de** to ascertain the whereabouts of, to locate; **ignorar** *o* **no saber el p. de alguien** not to know where sb is (**b**) *Chile, Col, Méx, Perú (de autobús)* bus stop (**c**) *Méx (lugar)* area (**d**) *Ecuad (parador)* roadside inn

paradigma *nm* paradigm, example

paradigmático, -a *adj* paradigmatic

paradiña *nf* feint

paradisiaco, -a, paradisíaco, -a *adj* heavenly

parado, -a 1 *adj* (**a**) *(inmóvil) (vehículo)* stationary; *(persona)* still, motionless; *(fábrica, proyecto)* at a standstill *o* halt; **¡no te quedes ahí parado!** don't just stand there!
(**b**) *Esp (pasivo)* lacking in initiative; **tu hermano es muy p.** your brother lacks initiative
(**c**) *Esp (sin empleo)* unemployed, out of work; **estar p.** to be unemployed
(**d**) *Am (en pie)* standing; **estar p.** to be standing; **caer p.** to land on one's feet
(**e**) *Am (en posición vertical)* standing; **tenía los pelos parados** her hair was on end; *muy Fam* **tenerlo** *o* **tenerla parada** to have a stiffie; EXPR *Méx Fam* **estar p. de pestañas** to be in high dudgeon
(**f**) *Chile, PRico (orgulloso)* vain, conceited
(**g**) EXPR *Am* **está bien p. con el jefe** he's well in with the boss; **salir bien/mal p. de algo: el actual campeón salió muy bien p. en el sorteo** the current holder of the title had a lucky draw; **fue el que mejor p. salió del accidente** he was the one who came off best in the accident; **el conductor salió muy mal p.** the driver was badly hurt *o* injured; **la imagen de la empresa ha salido muy mal parada** the company's image has suffered a serious blow
2 *nm,f Esp (desempleado)* unemployed person; **los parados** the unemployed; **los parados de larga duración** the long-term unemployed

paradoja *nf* paradox

paradójicamente *adv* paradoxically

paradójico, -a *adj* paradoxical, ironical

paradón *nm Fam* great save

parador *nm* (**a**) *(mesón)* roadside inn (**b**) *Esp (hotel)* **p. (nacional)** = state-owned luxury hotel, usually a building of historic or artistic importance

paraestatal 1 *adj* semi-public
2 *nf Am* semi-public company

parafango *nm Ven* mudguard

parafernalia *nf* paraphernalia

parafina *nf* paraffin

parafinar *vt* to paraffin

parafrasear *vt* to paraphrase

paráfrasis *nf inv* paraphrase

paragolpes *nm inv RP* bumper, *US* fender

parágrafo *nm Am* paragraph

paraguas *nm inv* (**a**) *(para lluvia)* umbrella (**b**) *(escudo)* shield ►► ***p. nuclear*** nuclear umbrella; ***p. protector*** protective umbrella (**c**) *Fam (condón)* rubber

Paraguay *nm* **(el) P.** Paraguay

paraguaya *nf (fruta)* = fruit similar to peach

paraguayo, -a 1 *adj* Paraguayan
2 *nm,f* Paraguayan

paragüería *nf* umbrella shop

paragüero *nm* umbrella stand

paraíso *nm* (**a**) *Rel* Paradise ►► ***p. terrenal*** earthly Paradise (**b**) *(edén)* paradise; **en esta playa estoy en el p.** I'm in paradise on this beach; **estas montañas son el p. de los esquiadores** these mountains are a skier's paradise ►► ***p. fiscal*** tax haven (**c**) *Teatro* **asientos de p.** seats in the gods

paraje *nm* spot, place

paral *nm Ven* upright

paralaje *nm Astron* parallax

paralela *nf* (**a**) *(línea)* parallel (line) (**b**) *Dep* **paralelas** parallel bars ►► ***paralelas asimétricas*** asymmetric bars

paralelamente *adv* (**a**) *(en el espacio)* parallel; **la carretera discurre p. al río** the road runs parallel to the river (**b**) *(en el tiempo)* at the same time; **p., otro grupo se encarga de estudiar el presupuesto** at the same time, another group will study the budget

paralelepípedo *nm Geom* parallelepiped

paralelismo *nm* (**a**) *(semejanza)* similarity, parallels; **existe un cierto p. entre las dos propuestas** there is a certain similarity between the two proposals (**b**) *Mat* parallelism

paralelo, -a 1 *adj* (**a**) *(en el espacio)* parallel; **la cordillera corre paralela al mar** the mountain range runs parallel to the sea
(**b**) *(en el tiempo)* at the same time; **dos computadores funcionando en p.** two computers working in parallel
(**c**) *(semejante)* parallel, similar; **los dos políticos han seguido**

caminos paralelos the two politicians have followed similar paths
(**d**) *Elec* **estar en p.** to be in parallel
2 *nm* (**a**) *Geog* parallel (**b**) *(comparación)* comparison; **trazar un p. con** to draw a comparison *o* parallel with

paralelogramo *nm* parallelogram

paralenguaje *nm Ling* paralanguage

paralímpico, -a, paraolímpico, -a, parolímpico, -a *adj* Paralympic; **juegos paralímpicos** Paralympic games, Paralympics

paralingüístico, -a *adj Ling* paralinguistic

parálisis *nf inv* (**a**) *(enfermedad)* paralysis ►► ***p. agitada*** Parkinson's disease; ***p. cerebral*** cerebral palsy; ***p. facial*** facial paralysis; ***p. infantil*** polio; ***p. progresiva*** progressive *o* creeping paralysis (**b**) *(de país, economía)* paralysis

paralítico, -a **1** *adj* paralytic; **quedarse p.** to be paralysed
2 *nm,f* paralytic

paralización *nf* (**a**) *(parálisis)* paralysis (**b**) *(detención)* **los huelguistas persiguen la p. del transporte por carretera** the strikers are aiming to bring road transport to a halt; **la empresa ha anunciado la p. de la producción** the company has announced that production has been halted; **la amenaza de una p. de la economía** the threat of economic paralysis

paralizador, -ora, paralizante *adj* paralysing

paralizar [14] **1** *vt* (**a**) *(causar parálisis)* to paralyse; **un veneno que paraliza los músculos** a poison which paralyses the muscles; **el susto lo paralizó** he was paralysed with fear (**b**) *(detener)* to stop; **el transporte aéreo está paralizado** air traffic has come to a standstill
2 paralizarse *vpr* (**a**) *(pararse)* to become paralysed (**b**) *(producción, proyecto)* to come to a standstill; **la construcción del puente se ha paralizado indefinidamente** construction work on the bridge has been suspended indefinitely

paralogismo *nm* paralogism

paramagnético, -a *adj Fís* paramagnetic

paramagnetismo *nm Fís* paramagnetism

Paramaribo *n* Paramaribo

paramento *nm* (**a**) *(adorno)* adornment ►► ***paramentos sacerdotales*** ecclesiastic vestments *o* robes (**b**) *Constr* facing *(of a wall)*

parameño, -a, paramero, -a **1** *adj* upland
2 *nm,f* inhabitant of an upland area, uplander

paramera *nf* highland, upland area

paramero = **parameño**

parámetro *nm* (**a**) *(dato, valor)* parameter (**b**) *Mat* parameter

paramilitar **1** *adj* paramilitary
2 *nmf* paramilitary

páramo *nm* (**a**) *(terreno yermo)* highland, upland area; **los páramos** the highlands (**b**) *(lugar solitario)* wilderness (**c**) *Col, Ecuad, Ven Fam (llovizna)* drizzle (**d**) *Col, Ven (cordillera)* Andean highlands

Paraná *n* **el P.** the Parana

parangón *nm* paragon; **sin p.** unparalleled; **tener p. con** to be comparable with

parangonar *vt* (**a**) *(comparar)* to compare, to establish a parallel between; **no deseo p. su situación con la mía** I don't want to compare her situation with mine (**b**) *Imprenta* to justify

paraninfo *nm* assembly hall, auditorium

paranoia *nf* paranoia

paranoico, -a **1** *adj* paranoiac
2 *nm,f* paranoiac

paranormal *adj* paranormal

parante *nm RP* upright

paraolímpico, -a = **paralímpico**

parapente *nm* (**a**) *(actividad) (desde montaña)* paragliding, parapenting; *(a remolque de lancha motora)* parascending; **ir a hacer p.** to go parapenting (**b**) *(paracaídas)* parapente

parapentista *nmf* paraglider

parapetarse *vpr* (**a**) *(protegerse)* to take cover (**detrás** *o* **tras** behind) (**b**) *(escudarse)* **no te parapetes tras ninguna excusa** don't hide behind excuses

parapetear *Ven Fam* **1** *vt* (**a**) *(sujeto: médico)* **p. a alguien** to give sb a once-over (**b**) *(apuntalar)* to patch up
2 parapetearse *vpr* (**a**) *(reponerse)* to recover (**b**) *(arreglárselas)* to make do

parapeto *nm* (**a**) *(antepecho)* parapet (**b**) *(barandilla)* bannister (**c**) *(barricada)* barricade

paraplejia, paraplejía *nf Med* paraplegia

parapléjico, -a *Med* **1** *adj* paraplegic
2 *nm,f* paraplegic

parapolicial *adj* vigilante

parapsicología *nf* parapsychology

parapsicológico, -a *adj* parapsychological

parapsicólogo, -a *nm,f* parapsychologist

PARAR **1** *vi* (**a**) *(detenerse, interrumpirse)* to stop; **este tren para en todas las estaciones** this train stops at all stations; **¿paramos a** *o* **para comer algo?** shall we stop and *o* to have something to eat?; **párenos aquí** *(al taxista, conductor)* drop us off here; **no abra la lavadora hasta que (no) pare por completo** do not open the washing machine until it has come to a complete stop; **los obreros pararon diez minutos en señal de protesta** the workers stopped work for ten minutes as a protest; **¡no para callado/quieto un momento!** he won't be quiet/stay still for a single moment!; **p. de hacer algo** to stop doing sth; **no ha parado de llover desde que llegamos** it hasn't stopped raining since we arrived; **no para de molestarme** she keeps annoying me; **no para de llamarme por teléfono** he keeps ringing me up, he's always ringing me up; **no parará hasta conseguirlo** she won't stop until she gets it; *Fam* **no para** *(está siempre liado)* he's always on the go; *Fam* **hoy no he parado un momento** I've been on the go all day; *Fam* **ser un no p.** *(trabajo, vida)* to be hectic; **¡para ya!** stop it!; **¡para ya de hacer ruido!** stop that noise!; **un perro, dos gatos y para de contar** a dog, two cats and that's it; **p. en seco** to stop dead; **sin p.** non-stop
(**b**) *(alojarse)* to stay; **siempre paro en el mismo hotel** I always stay at the same hotel; *Fam* **solía p. en** *o* **por aquel bar** I used to hang out at that bar; **paro poco en** *o* **por casa** I'm not at home much
(**c**) *(acabar)* to end up; **¿en qué parará este lío?** where will it all end?; **ir a p. a** to end up in; **todos fuimos a p. al mismo lugar** we all ended up in the same place; **ese camino va a p. a la carretera** this path leads to the road; **¿dónde habrán ido a p. mis llaves?** where can my keys have got to?; EXPR **¡dónde iremos a p.!** *(¡es increíble!)* whatever next!; EXPR *Fam* **¡dónde va a p.!** *(¡no compares!)* there's no comparison!
(**d**) *(recaer)* **p. en manos de alguien** to come into sb's possession
(**e**) *Am (ir a la huelga)* to go on strike; **los médicos paran mañana** doctors are on strike tomorrow
2 *vt* (**a**) *(detener, interrumpir)* to stop; *(asalto)* to repel; *(golpe)* to parry; *(penalti, tiro)* to save; *(balón)* to stop; **para el motor** turn the engine off, stop the engine; **nos paró la policía** we were stopped by the police; **p. (a) un taxi** to hail *o* stop a taxi; **cuando le da por hablar no hay quien la pare** once she starts talking, there's no stopping her; EXPR *Perú, RP Fam* **pararle el carro a alguien** to put sb in his/her place; EXPR *Méx Fam* **pararle el gallo** *o* **macho a alguien** to put sb in his/her place
(**b**) *Am (poner de pie)* to stand; **pará a la nena, así la peino** stand her up so I can comb her hair
(**c**) *Am (levantar)* to raise; **paré el espejo para verme mejor** I lifted the mirror up so I could see myself better
3 pararse *vpr* (**a**) *(detenerse)* to stop; **se me ha parado el reloj** my watch has stopped; **pararse a hacer algo** to stop to do sth; **me paré a echar gasolina** I stopped to fill up with *Br* petrol *o US* gas; **no me paré a pensar si le gustaría o no** I didn't stop to think whether she'd like it or not
(**b**) *Am (ponerse de pie)* to stand up; **párense para cantar el himno** please stand to sing the hymn; *Méx* **pararse de puntas,** *CSur* **pararse en puntas de pie** to stand on tiptoe; *RP* **pararse de cabeza** to do a headstand; EXPR *RP Fam* **pararse para toda la vida** to be made for life
(**c**) *Am (levantarse)* to stand; **se le pararon los pelos** her hair stood on end; *muy Fam* **no se le para** *(el pene)* he can't get it up
(**d**) *Carib, Méx (salir de la cama)* to get up

---

pararrayos *nm inv (en un tejado)* lightning rod *o* conductor; **funciona como un p.** it acts as a lightning conductor

parasíntesis *nf inv Ling* parasynthesis

parasitario, -a *adj* parasitic

parasitismo *nm* parasitism

parásito, -a **1** *adj Biol* parasitic
2 *nm* (**a**) *Biol* parasite (**b**) *(persona)* parasite ►► ***p. social*** social parasite (**c**) *Tel* **parásitos** *(interferencias)* static

parasitología *nf* parasitology

parasitosis *nf inv* parasitosis

parasol *nm* (**a**) *(sombrilla)* parasol (**b**) *(en coche)* sunroof (**c**) *(en objetivo)* lens hood

paratifoidea *nf* paratyphoid

parcela *nf* (a) *(de tierra)* plot (of land) (b) *(de saber, poder)* area; **el ministro no quiere que nadie invada su p. de poder** the minister doesn't want anyone encroaching on his area of authority; **se agarra a su p. de poder** he's holding on to his power

parcelable *adj* divisible into plots

parcelación *nf* (a) *(de terreno)* parcelling out, division into plots (b) *(de saber, poder)* subdivision; **la creciente p. del poder en la región** the increasing subdivision of power in the region

parcelar *vt* to parcel out, to divide into plots

parcelario, -a *adj* of *o* relating to plots of land

parcero *nm Col Fam* pal, *US* buddy

parcha *nf Ven* passion fruit

parchado, -a *adj Am Fam* patched up; **no quiero éste todo p., me voy a comprar uno nuevo** I don't want this one all patched up, I'm going to buy myself a new one

parchar *vt Am Fam* to patch up; **no empecemos a p., es mejor comprar uno nuevo** let's not start trying to patch it up, it's better to buy a new one

parche *nm* (a) *(de tela, goma)* patch; **poner un p. a algo** to put a patch on sth; EXPR *Fam* **ioído** *o* **ojo al p.!** watch out ►► *Chile* ***p. curita*** *Br* sticking plaster, *US* band aid; ***p. de nicotina*** nicotine patch; ***p. poroso*** *Br* medicated plaster, *US* medicated band aid
(b) *(en el ojo)* eyepatch
(c) *(emplasto)* poultice
(d) *(solución transitoria)* makeshift solution; **la ley es sólo un p. al problema de la inmigración** this law merely provides a makeshift solution to the problem of immigration; **la empresa sobrevive poniendo parches a sus problemas** the company survives by papering over the cracks
(e) *Informát* patch
(f) *(piel de tambor)* drumhead
(g) *(tambor)* drum

parchear *vt* (a) *(neumático, pantalón)* to put a patch on, to patch (b) *(problema)* to patch up

parchís *nm inv Br* ludo, *US* Parcheesi®

parchita *nf Ven* passion fruit

parcial 1 *adj* (a) *(no total)* partial; **trabajar a tiempo p.** to work part-time (b) *(no ecuánime)* biased (c) *(examen)* end-of-term
2 *nm* (a) *(examen)* = end-of-term exam at university which counts towards the final qualification (b) *(en partido)* **el p. de la primera parte fue 43-50** the score at the end of the first half was 43-50; **tuvieron que remontar un p. de 3-0** they had to overcome a 3-0 deficit

parcialidad *nf* (a) *(tendenciosidad)* bias, partiality (b) *(bando)* faction

parcialmente *adv* (a) *(en parte)* partially, partly (b) *(de forma no ecuánime)* partially, in a biased way

parco, -a *adj (escaso)* meagre; *(cena)* frugal; *(explicación)* brief, concise; *(moderado)* sparing (**en** in); **es muy p. en palabras** he is a man of few words; **el director fue p. en detalles** the director gave few details

pardela *nf* shearwater ►► ***p. pichoneta*** Manx shearwater

pardiez *interj Anticuado o Hum* by Jove!

pardillo, -a 1 *adj Esp Fam* (a) *(ingenuo)* naive (b) *(palurdo)* **ser p.** to be a *Br* bumpkin *o US* hick
2 *nm,f Esp Fam* (a) *(ingenuo)* naive person (b) *(palurdo) Br* bumpkin, *US* hick
3 *nm (pájaro)* linnet ►► ***p. sizerín*** redpoll

pardo, -a 1 *adj* (a) *(color)* greyish-brown, dull brown (b) *Carib, RP Pey (mulato)* mulatto
2 *nm,f Carib, RP Pey (mulato)* mulatto
3 *nm* (a) *(color)* greyish-brown, dull brown (b) **el Pardo** *(palacio)* = royal palace in Madrid, formerly the official residence of General Franco

pardusco, -a, parduzco, -a *adj* brownish

pare *nm RP (señal)* stop sign

pareado 1 *adj* **chalet p.** semi-detached house
2 *nm* (a) *(verso)* couplet (b) *(vivienda)* semi-detached house

parear *vt* to pair

PARECER [46] 1 *nm* (a) *(opinión)* opinion; **somos de igual** *o* **del mismo p.** we are of the same opinion; **a mi/nuestro/***etc.* **p.** in my/our/*etc* opinion; **cambiar de p.** to change one's mind (b) *(apariencia)* **de buen p.** good-looking
2 *vi (semejar)* to look like; **parece un palacio** it looks like a palace; **parecía un sueño** it was like a dream
3 *v copulativo* to look, to seem; **pareces cansado** you look *o* seem tired; **en la tele parece más joven** she looks younger on the TV; **el casero parece buena persona** the landlord seems nice *o* seems like a nice person; **parece de metal** it looks like it's made of metal; **es alemán, pero no lo parece** he's German, but he doesn't look it; **¡pareces bobo!** are you stupid, or what?
4 *v impersonal* (a) *(indica opinión)* **me parece que...** I think that..., it seems to me that...; **me parece que viven juntos** I think *o* believe they live together; **me parece que no voy a aprobar** I don't think I'm going to pass; **me parece que sí/no** I think/don't think so; **el examen me pareció bastante complicado** I found the exam rather difficult, I thought the exam was rather difficult; **no me pareció interesante** I didn't find it interesting, I didn't think it was interesting; **¿qué te parece mi vestido?** what do you think of my dress?; **¿qué te parece si vamos a mi casa?** why don't we go to my place?, what do you say we go to my place?; **¿qué te parece la idea? – me parece bien/mal** what do you think of the idea? – it seems OK to me/I don't think much of it; **nada le parece bien** she's never happy with anything; **todo le parece bien** he always says yes to everything; **no me parece bien que llegues tan tarde** I'm not pleased about you arriving so late; **me parece mal que se experimente con animales** I don't agree with experiments on animals; **no me parece mal que venga** I don't see anything wrong with her coming; **haz lo que te parezca** *(lo que quieras)* do what you like; **haz lo que te parezca mejor** do as you see fit, do what you think best; **parece mentira que todavía no haya dimitido** it's incredible that he hasn't resigned yet; **es bastante caro, ¿no te parece?** it's rather expensive, don't you think?; **si te parece (bien) quedamos el lunes** we can meet on Monday, if that's all right by you; **podemos comer fuera, ¿te parece?** why don't we go out for a meal?, what do you say we go out for a meal?; **¿te parece bonito lo que has hecho?** are you pleased with yourself *o* satisfied now?
(b) *(tener aspecto de)* **parece que va a llover** it looks like (it's going to) rain; **parece que le gusta** it looks as if *o* it seems (that) she likes it; **no parece que le guste** he doesn't seem to like it, it seems (that) he doesn't like it; **parece (ser) que hay un pequeño malentendido** there seems to be a small misunderstanding, it seems (like) there's a small misunderstanding; **ahora parece (ser) que quieren echarse atrás** it now seems they want to pull out; **a lo que parece, al p.** apparently; **tienen mucho dinero, aunque no lo parezca** it may not seem like it, but they've got a lot of money; **eso parece** so it seems; **parece como si estuviéramos en invierno** it's as if it was still winter; **parece que fue ayer cuando nos conocimos** it seems like only yesterday that we met; **¿lo ha hecho? – parece que sí** has she done it? – it seems so *o* it seems she has; **¿te han invitado? – parece que no** have they invited you? – it seems not *o* it doesn't seem so; **parece que no, pero se tarda en llegar hasta aquí** you'd be surprised how long it takes you to get here; **según parece** apparently
5 **parecerse** *vpr* to be alike (**en** in); **se parecen mucho en sus gustos** they have very similar tastes; **no se parecen en nada** *(personas, cosas)* they are not at all alike; **parecerse a alguien** *(físicamente)* to look like sb; *(en carácter)* to be like sb; **nos parecemos bastante** *(físicamente)* we look quite similar; *(en carácter)* we're very similar; **no tenemos yate ni nada que se le parezca** we haven't got a yacht or anything (like that)

parecido, -a 1 *adj* similar; **p. a** similar to, like; **es p. a su padre** he resembles his father; **¡habráse visto cosa parecida!** have you ever heard *o* seen the like?; **bien p.** *(atractivo)* good-looking; **mal p.** *(feo)* ugly
2 *nm* resemblance (**con/entre** to/between); **el p. entre todos los hermanos es asombroso** there's a startling resemblance between all the brothers; **tiene un gran p. a John Wayne** he looks very like John Wayne; **cualquier p. es pura coincidencia** any similarity is purely coincidental

pared *nf* (a) *(de construcción)* wall; **entre cuatro paredes** cooped-up at home; **me pusieron contra la p.** they had me up against the wall; EXPR **las paredes oyen** walls have ears; EXPR **si las paredes hablasen...** if the walls could talk...; EXPR **subirse por las paredes** to hit the roof, to go up the wall; **está que se sube por las paredes** she's in an absolute rage, she's fit to be tied; EXPR *Fam* **como hablar a la p.** like talking to a brick wall ►► ***p. maestra*** main wall; ***p. mediana*** *o* ***medianera*** party wall
(b) *(de montaña)* face ►► ***p. artificial*** climbing wall
(c) *(de nariz, intestino)* wall; *(caja)* side ►► ***p. arterial*** arterial wall; ***p. celular*** cell wall
(d) *Dep* one-two; **hacer la p.** to play a one-two

paredón *nm* (a) *(muro)* (thick) wall (b) *(de fusilamiento)* (execution) wall; **llevar** *o* **mandar a alguien al p.** to order sb to be shot

pareja *nf* (**a**) *(par)* pair; **por parejas** in pairs; **formar parejas** to get into pairs
(**b**) *(de novios)* couple; **vivir en p.** to live together ▸▸ ***p. de hecho*** unmarried couple
(**c**) *(sentimental)* partner; *(en baile)* (dancing) partner; **no tiene p. estable** she doesn't have a steady partner
(**d**) *(de naipes)* pair
(**e**) *(guante, zapato)* other one; **la p. de este calcetín** the other sock of this pair
(**f**) *Esp* **una p.** *(de la Guardia Civil)* a pair of Civil Guards, a Civil Guard patrol

parejero, -a *Ven Fam* **1** *adj* (**a**) *(arribista)* pushy (**b**) *(presumido)* big-headed
2 *nm* (**a**) *(arribista)* (social) climber (**b**) *(presumido)* bighead

parejo, -a 1 *adj* (**a**) *(semejante)* similar (**a** to); **ir parejos** to be neck and neck (**b**) *esp Am (uniforme, liso)* even (**c**) *Méx (imparcial)* even-handed; **fue muy p. con todos sus hijos** he treated all his children equally
2 *adv Am* equally; **si nos esforzamos p. sacaremos la misma nota** if we both work as hard as each other we'll get the same *Br* marks *o US* grade; **las dos crecieron muy p.** they both grew at the same rate
3 al parejo *loc adv Méx* **corrían al p.** they were running neck and neck; **ha puesto a la música de su país al p. de los mejores ritmos caribeños** he has put his country's music on a par with the best of the Caribbean

paremia *nf Ling* proverb, saying

parénquima *nm Biol* (**a**) *(en vegetales)* parenchyma (**b**) *(en animales)* parenchyma

parentela *nf Fam* family, clan; **apareció con toda la p.** he turned up with the whole clan

parenteral *adj Med* **por vía p.** parenterally

parentesco *nm* (**a**) *(entre personas)* relationship; **les une una relación de p.** they are related to one another; **p. lejano/cercano** distant/close relationship ▸▸ ***p. político*** relationship by marriage (**b**) *(entre cosas)* tie, bond; **existe un claro p. entre ambas propuestas** the two proposals are clearly related

paréntesis *nm inv* (**a**) *(signo)* bracket; **abrir/cerrar el p.** to open/close brackets; **entre p.** *(texto)* in brackets, in parentheses; **y, entre p., tengo que decir que...** and, by the way, I must say that...; **poner algo entre p.** to put sth in brackets, to bracket sth ▸▸ ***p. angular*** angle bracket (**b**) *(intercalación)* digression (**c**) *(interrupción)* break; **hacer un p.** to have a break

pareo *nm (prenda)* wraparound skirt

parezco *etc ver* **parecer**

pargo *nm* (**a**) *(pez mediterráneo)* sea bream, porgy (**b**) *(pez caribeño)* snapper (**c**) *Ven Fam (homosexual)* queer

paria *nmf* pariah

parida *nf Esp Fam* **soltar paridas** to talk *Br* rubbish *o US* garbage; **eso que has dicho es una p.** you're talking *Br* rubbish *o US* garbage; **¡menuda p.!** what a lot of nonsense!

paridad *nf* (**a**) *(semejanza)* similarity (**b**) *(igualdad)* equality; **la p. entre hombres y mujeres** equality between men and women; **reclaman la p. de salarios** they are demanding equal pay (**c**) *Fin* parity; **la p. del dólar con el euro** the dollar euro exchange rate ▸▸ ***p. de cambio*** parity of exchange (**d**) *Informát* parity

parienta *nf Esp Fam* **la p.** *(cónyuge) Br* the missus *o* missis, *US* my old lady

pariente *nmf (familiar)* relation, relative; **p. cercano/lejano** close/distant relation *o* relative

> **Falso amigo**: El sustantivo inglés **parent** no es la traducción del español **pariente**. En inglés **parent** significa "padre" o "madre".

parietal *Anat* **1** *adj* parietal
2 *nm Anat* parietal

parihuela *nf* (**a**) *(camilla)* stretcher (**b**) *Méx, Perú* ***p. de mariscos*** seafood casserole

paripé *nm* EXPR *Esp Fam* **hacer el p.** to put on an act, to pretend

parir 1 *vi* (**a**) *(mujer)* to give birth, to have a baby; EXPR *Esp Fam* **poner algo/a alguien a p.** *Br* to slag sth/sb off, *US* to badmouth sth/sb; EXPR *Esp muy Fam* **¡la madre que lo parió!** son of a bitch!; EXPR *Esp muy Fam* **¡viva la madre que te parió!** *(en concierto, corrida de toros)* we love you! (**b**) *(yegua)* to foal; *(vaca)* to calve; *(oveja)* to lamb
2 *vt* (**a**) *(mujer)* to give birth to, to bear (**b**) *(animal)* to bear, to have

París *n* Paris

parisiense, parisién 1 *adj* Parisian
2 *nmf* Parisian

parisino, -a 1 *adj* Parisian
2 *nm,f* Parisian

parista *nmf Méx* striker

paritario, -a *adj* joint; **comisión paritaria** joint commission

paritorio *nm* delivery room

parka *nf* parka

parking ['parkin] (*pl* **parkings**) *nm Br* car park, *US* parking lot ▸▸ ***p. disuasorio*** park & ride

párkinson *nm Med* Parkinson's disease

parlamentar *vi* to negotiate

parlamentario, -a 1 *adj* parliamentary
2 *nm,f* member of parliament

parlamentarismo *nm* parliamentary system

parlamento *nm* (**a**) *(asamblea)* parliament ▸▸ ***el P. Europeo*** the European Parliament; ***el P. Latinoamericano*** the Latin American Parliament (**b**) *(negociación)* parley (**c**) *Teatro* speech

parlanchín, -ina *Fam* **1** *adj* chatty
2 *nm,f* chatterbox

parlante 1 *adj* talking
2 *nm Am* speaker

parlar *vi* (**a**) *Fam (persona)* to chatter (**b**) *(ave)* to talk

parlotear *vi Fam* to chatter

parloteo *nm Fam* chatter

PARM [parm] *nm* (*abrev de* **Partido Auténtico de la Revolución Mexicana**) PARM

parmesano, -a 1 *adj* **queso p.** Parmesan cheese
2 *nm (queso)* Parmesan

parnaso *nm Formal* parnassus

parné *nm Esp Fam* dough

paro[1] *nm* (**a**) *Esp (desempleo)* unemployment; **estar en (el) p.** to be unemployed; **lleva cinco meses en el p.** she's been unemployed for five months; **quedarse en p.** to be left unemployed ▸▸ ***p. cíclico*** cyclical unemployment; ***p. encubierto*** hidden unemployment; ***p. estructural*** structural unemployment; ***p. registrado*** registered unemployment, official unemployment
(**b**) *Esp (subsidio)* unemployment benefit, dole money; **apuntarse al p.** to sign on; **cobrar el p.** to claim *o* receive unemployment benefit
(**c**) *esp Am (huelga)* strike; *Am* **estar en** *o* **de p.** to be on strike; *Am* **hacer p.** to strike; **los trabajadores en p.** the strikers ▸▸ *Am* ***p. de brazos caídos*** sit-down (strike); *Am* ***p. cívico*** community protest; ***p. general*** general strike; *Am* ***p. indefinido*** indefinite strike; ***p. laboral*** industrial action
(**d**) *(cesación) (acción)* shutdown; *(estado)* stoppage; **los trabajadores realizaron un p. de diez minutos para condenar el último atentado** the workers staged a ten-minute stoppage in protest at the latest attack ▸▸ ***p. biológico*** = temporary halt to fishing at sea to preserve fish stocks; ***p. cardiaco*** cardiac arrest
(**e**) *Méx Fam (excusa)* excuse; **con el p. de que tiene mucho trabajo nunca sale** she never goes out, saying she's too busy
(**f**) *Méx Fam (favor)* favour; **hazme el p., dile que la llamaré luego** be a dear, tell her I'll call her later
(**g**) *RP* ***p. de manos*** handstand; **hacer un p. de manos** to do a handstand

paro[2] *nm (ave)* titmouse

parodia *nf (de texto, estilo)* parody; *(de película)* send-up, spoof; **hacer una p. de alguien** to do a send-up *o* take-off of sb

parodiar *vt (texto, estilo)* to parody; *(película)* to send up, to spoof; *(persona)* to send up, to take off

paródico, -a *adj* parodical

parodista *nmf* parodist

parolímpico, -a = **paralímpico**

parón *nm* sudden stoppage

parónimo *nm* paronym

paronomasia *nf* paronomasia, play on words

paroxismo *nm* paroxysm; **su furia llegó al p.** her rage reached a climax

paroxítono, -a *adj* paroxytone, = stressed on the penultimate syllable

parpadeante *adj (luz)* flickering

parpadear *vi* (**a**) *(pestañear)* to blink (**b**) *(luz)* to flicker; *(estrella)* to twinkle

parpadeo *nm* (**a**) *(pestañeo)* blinking (**b**) *(de luz)* flickering; *(de estrella)* twinkling

párpado *nm* eyelid

parque *nm* (**a**) *(terreno)* park ▸▸ ***p. acuático*** waterpark; ***p. de atracciones*** amusement park; *Esp* ***p. de bomberos*** fire station; *Col, RP* ***p. de diversiones*** amusement park; ***p. empresarial*** business park; *Chile* ***p. de entretenciones*** amusement park; ***p. eólico*** wind farm; ***p. infantil*** playground; ***p. nacional*** national park; ***p. natural*** nature reserve; ***p. tecnológico*** science park; ***p. temático*** theme park; ***p. zoológico*** zoo
(**b**) *(para bebés)* playpen
(**c**) *(vehículos)* fleet; **el p. automovilístico español ha crecido un 10 por ciento en el último año** the Spanish vehicle fleet has grown 10 percent over the last year ▸▸ *RP* ***p. automotor*** fleet; ***p. móvil*** fleet
(**d**) *Mil* **p. (de artillería)** (artillery) depot
(**e**) *CAm, Méx (municiones)* munitions

parqué *nm* (**a**) *(suelo)* parquet (floor) (**b**) *(en Bolsa)* floor

parqueadero *nm Col, Ecuad, Pan, Ven Br* car park, *US* parking lot

parquear *Bol, Carib, Col* **1** *vt* to park
2 parquearse *vpr* to park

parquedad *nf* (**a**) *(moderación)* moderation (**b**) *(prudencia)* frugality; **con p.** sparingly

parqueo *nm Bol, Col, Cuba* (**a**) *(acción)* parking (**b**) *(lugar) Br* car park, *US* parking lot (**c**) *(espacio)* parking space

parqués *nm Col Br* ludo®, *US* Parcheesi®

parquet [par'ke] (*pl* **parquets**) *nm* (**a**) *(suelo)* parquet (floor) (**b**) *(en Bolsa)* floor

parquímetro *nm* parking meter

parra *nf* grapevine; EXPR *Fam* **subirse a la p.** *(darse importancia)* to get above oneself; *(enfurecerse)* to hit the roof

parrafada *nf* (**a**) *(perorata)* lecture; **nos soltó una p. sobre los peligros de las drogas** he gave us a lecture on the dangers of drugs (**b**) *(charla)* chat; **quiero echar una p. con él para ver qué opina** I want to have a a chat with him to see what he thinks

párrafo *nm* paragraph

parral *nm* (**a**) *(emparrado)* vine arbour (**b**) *(terreno)* vineyard

parranda *nf Fam (juerga)* **irse** *o* **salir de p.** to go out on the town

parrandear *vi Fam* to go out on the town

parrandero, -a 1 *adj Fam* party-loving
2 *nm,f* party lover, party animal

parricida *nmf* parricide

parricidio *nm* parricide

parrilla *nf* (**a**) *(utensilio)* grill; **a la p.** grilled (**b**) *(restaurante)* grillroom, grill (**c**) *Dep* **p. (de salida)** (starting) grid (**d**) *TV* programme schedule (**e**) *(rejilla)* grate, grating (**f**) *Am (baca)* roof rack (**g**) *Am (portabultos)* pannier rack, carrier (**h**) *Urug (en cama)* base

parrillada *nf* (**a**) *(comida)* = dish of barbecued fish and seafood or mixed meats (**b**) *RP (restaurante)* steak restaurant, grillroom

parrillero, -a 1 *adj RP* grilling, barbecue; **queso p.** grilling cheese; **salchicha p.** grilling *o* barbecue sausage
2 *nm,f* (**a**) *(en parrillada)* cook, barbecue cook; **un aplauso para el p.** three cheers for the cook (**b**) *Ven (en moto)* passenger

párroco *nm* parish priest

parrón *nm Chile* vine arbour

parronal *nm Chile* vineyard

parroquia *nf* (**a**) *(iglesia)* parish church (**b**) *(jurisdicción)* parish (**c**) *(fieles)* parishioners, parish (**d**) *(clientela)* clientele

parroquial *adj* parish; **iglesia p.** parish church

parroquiano, -a *nm,f* (**a**) *(feligrés)* parishioner (**b**) *(cliente)* customer, regular

pársec *nm Astron* parsec

parsimonia *nf* deliberation, calmness; **con p.** unhurriedly

parsimonioso, -a *adj* unhurried, deliberate

> **Falso amigo**: El adjetivo inglés **parsimonious** no es la traducción del español **parsimonioso**. En inglés **parsimonious** significa "mezquino".

PARTE[1] *nm* (**a**) *(informe)* report; **dar p. (a alguien de algo)** to report (sth to sb); **dimos p. del incidente a la policía** we reported the incident to the police ▸▸ ***p. de accidente*** *(para aseguradora)* (accident) claim form; ***p. facultativo*** medical report; ***p. de guerra*** dispatch; ***p. médico*** medical report; ***p. meteorológico*** weather report
(**b**) *Anticuado (noticiario)* news bulletin
(**c**) *Andes (multa)* fine *(for a traffic offence)*

PARTE[2] *nf* (**a**) *(porción, elemento, división)* part; **hizo su p. del trabajo** he did his share of the work; **las partes del cuerpo** the parts of the body; **"El Padrino, Segunda p."** "The Godfather, Part Two"; **la mayor p. de la gente** most people; **la mayor p. de la población** most of the population; **la tercera p. de** a third of; **repartir algo a partes iguales** to share sth out equally; **fue peligroso y divertido a partes iguales** it was both dangerous and fun at the same time; **dimos la lavadora vieja como p. del pago** we traded in our old washing machine in part exchange; **en p.** to a certain extent, partly; **en gran p.** *(mayoritariamente)* for the most part; *(principalmente)* to a large extent; **en su mayor p. están a favor** they're mostly in favour, most of them are in favour; **esto forma p. del proyecto** this is part of the project; **forma p. del comité** she's a member of the committee; **cada uno puso de su p.** everyone did what they could; **por mi/tu/***etc.* **p.** for my/your/*etc* part; **por mi p. no hay ningún problema** it's fine as far as I'm concerned; **hubo protestas por p. de los trabajadores** the workers protested, there were protests from the workers; **lo hicimos por partes** we did it bit by bit; **¡vamos por partes!** *(al explicar, aclarar)* let's take one thing at a time!; *Am Fam Hum* **¡vamos por partes!, dijo Jack** one thing at a time, my friend!; **ser p. integrante de algo** to be *o* form an integral part of sth; **llevarse la mejor/peor p.** to come off best/worst; **tomar p. en algo** to take part in sth; EXPR **llevarse la p. del león** to get the lion's share; EXPR *CSur* **mandarse la p.** to put on airs; EXPR *Euf* **en salva sea la p.: le dio un puntapié en salva sea la p.** she gave him a kick up the rear; PROV **segundas partes nunca fueron buenas** things are never as good the second time round ▸▸ *Quim* ***p. por millón*** part per million; *Gram* ***p. de la oración*** part of speech
(**b**) *(lado, zona)* part; **la p. de abajo/de arriba, la p. inferior/superior** the bottom/top; **la p. trasera/delantera, la p. de atrás/de delante** the back/front; **el español que se habla en esta p. del mundo** the Spanish spoken in this part of the world; **viven en la p. alta de la ciudad** they live in the higher part of the city; **¿de qué p. de Argentina es?** what part of Argentina is he from?, whereabouts in Argentina is he from?; **la bala le atravesó el cerebro de p. a p.** the bullet went right through his brain; **por una p...., por otra...** on the one hand..., on the other (hand)...; **por otra p.** *(además)* what is more, besides ▸▸ *Méx* ***p. baja*** *(en béisbol)* end of the inning
(**c**) *(lugar, sitio)* part; **he estado en muchas partes** I've been lots of places; **¡tú no vas a ninguna p.!** you're not going anywhere!; **en alguna p.** somewhere; **en cualquier p.** anywhere; **en otra p.** elsewhere, somewhere else; **en** *o* **por todas partes** everywhere; **no lo veo por ninguna p.** I can't find it anywhere; **esto no nos lleva a ninguna p.** this isn't getting us anywhere; **2.000 pesos no van a ninguna p.** 2,000 pesos won't get you far; EXPR **en todas partes cuecen habas** it's the same wherever you go
(**d**) *(bando)* side; **las partes enfrentadas** *o* **en conflicto** the opposing parties *o* sides; **estar/ponerse de p. de alguien** to be on/to take sb's side; **¿tú de qué p. estás?** who's side are you on?; **es pariente mío por p. de padre** he's related to me on my father's side; **tener a alguien de p. de uno** to have sb on one's side
(**e**) *Der (en juicio, transacción)* party; **no hubo acuerdo entre las partes** the two sides were unable to reach an agreement; **las partes interesadas** the interested parties ▸▸ ***la p. acusadora*** the prosecution; ***p. compradora*** buyer; ***p. contratante*** party to the contract; ***p. vendedora*** seller
(**f**) *Euf (genitales)* **partes** privates; **partes pudendas** private parts; **recibió un balonazo en sus partes** a ball hit him in the privates
(**g**) *Méx (repuesto)* (spare) part, spare
(**h**) *(en frases)* **de p. de** on behalf of, for; **traigo un paquete de p. de Juan** I've got a parcel for you from Juan; **venimos de p. de la compañía de seguros** we're here on behalf of the insurance company, we're from the insurance company; **de p. de tu madre, que vayas a comprar leche** your mother says for you to go and buy some milk; **dale recuerdos de mi p.** give her my regards; **fue muy amable/generoso de tu p.** it was very kind/generous of you; **¿de p. de (quién)?** *(al teléfono)* who's calling, please?; **de un tiempo a esta p.** for some time now; **de un mes/unos años a esta p.** for the last month/last few years

parteluz *nm Arquit* mullion

partenaire [parte'ner] *nmf (pareja artística)* partner

partenariado *nm* partnership

partenogénesis *nf inv* parthenogenesis

Partenón *nm* **el P.** the Parthenon

partera *nf* midwife

partero *nm* male midwife

parterre *nm Esp* flowerbed

partición *nf* (**a**) *(reparto)* sharing out; *(de territorio)* partitioning (**b**) *(división)* divison (**c**) *Informát (de palabra)* hyphenation ▸▸ ***p. silábica*** syllabic division (**d**) *Informát (de disco duro)* partition

participación *nf* (**a**) *(colaboración, intervención)* participation; **hubo mucha p.** *(en actividad)* many people took part; *(en elecciones)* there was a high turnout; **anunció su p. en el torneo** he announced that he would be taking part *o* participating in the tournament; **han negado su p. en el atentado** they have denied taking part in the attack; **la p. cubana en los Juegos Olímpicos fue la mejor de las últimas décadas** Cuba's performance in the Olympic Games was the best in recent decades

(**b**) *(de lotería)* = ticket or receipt representing a share in a lottery number

(**c**) *(comunicación)* notice ▸▸ ***p. de boda*** wedding invitation

(**d**) *Econ (acción)* share, interest; *(inversión)* investment; **quieren una p. en los beneficios** they want a share in the profits ▸▸ ***p. mayoritaria*** majority interest; ***p. minoritaria*** minority interest

participante 1 *adj* participating; **los equipos participantes** the participating teams, the teams taking part

2 *nmf (que toma parte)* participant; *(en carrera)* entrant, competitor

participar 1 *vi* (**a**) *(colaborar, intervenir)* to take part, to participate (**en** in); **participaron diez corredores/equipos** ten runners/teams took part *o* participated; **todo el mundo participó con entusiasmo en la limpieza del río** everyone joined in enthusiastically in cleaning up the river

(**b**) *Econ* to have a share (**en** in); **varias personas participan en la empresa** several people have shares in the company

(**c**) *(recibir)* to receive a share (**de** of); **todos participan de los beneficios** everyone has a share in the profits

(**d**) *(compartir)* **p. de** to share; **no participo de tus ideas** I don't share your ideas

2 *vt* (**a**) *(comunicar)* **p. algo a alguien** to notify *o* inform sb of sth; **nos participaron la celebración de la boda** we received an announcement of the wedding (**b**) *Econ* **una empresa participada por varias sociedades** a company in which several firms hold equity interests

participativo, -a *adj* **es muy p. en clase** he participates a lot in class

partícipe 1 *adj* involved (**de** in); **hacer p. de algo a alguien** *(notificar)* to notify *o* inform sb of sth; *(compartir)* to share sth with sb; **somos partícipes de tu alegría** we share your happiness

2 *nmf* participant

participio *nm* participle ▸▸ ***p. pasado*** past participle; ***p. presente*** present participle

partícula *nf* (**a**) *(trozo pequeño)* particle, speck; **partículas de polvo** dust particles (**b**) *Fís* particle ▸▸ ***p. alfa*** alpha particle; ***p. beta*** beta particle; ***p. elemental*** elementary particle; ***p. subatómica*** subatomic particle (**c**) *Ling* particle

particular 1 *adj* (**a**) *(especial)* particular; **tiene su sabor p.** it has its own particular taste; **en casos particulares puede hacerse una excepción** we can make an exception in special cases; **es una persona muy p.** she's a very unusual person; **eso no tiene nada de p.** that's nothing special *o* unusual; **lo que tiene de p. es...** the unusual thing about it is...; **en p.** in particular

(**b**) *(privado)* private; **se vieron en su domicilio p.** they met at his private residence; **dar clases particulares** to teach privately; **domicilio p.** home address; **la casa tiene jardín p.** the house has its own *Br* garden *o US* yard

2 *nmf (persona)* member of the public; *Am* **de p.** *(de paisano) (policía)* in plain clothes; *(soldado)* in civilian clothes; **iba vestido de p.** *(policía)* he was in *o* wearing plain clothes; *(soldado)* he was in *o* wearing civilian clothes

3 *nm (asunto)* matter; **¿cuál es tu opinión sobre el p.?** what's your opinion on this (matter)?; **te llamaba sin otro p. que preguntarte por la operación de tu madre** I was just calling to ask about your mother's operation; **sin otro p., se despide atentamente** *(en carta) Br* yours faithfully, *US* sincerely yours

particularidad *nf* (**a**) *(rasgo)* particular feature, peculiarity; **tiene la p. de funcionar con energía solar** a particular feature of it is that it runs on solar energy (**b**) *(cualidad)* **la p. de su petición** the unusual nature of his request (**c**) **particularidades** *(pormenores)* details, finer points

particularismo *nm* **la lucha en torno a los particularismos étnicos y religiosos** the struggle over ethnic and religious differences *o* distinctions; **la tradición humanista que respeta los particularismos de cada grupo cultural** the humanistic tradition that respects the particularities *o* peculiarities of each cultural group

particularizar [14] 1 *vt* (**a**) *(caracterizar)* to characterize (**b**) *(concretar, precisar)* to specify

2 *vi* (**a**) *(detallar)* to go into details (**b**) *(personalizar)* **p. en alguien** to single sb out; **la responsabilidad es de todos, no particularices** everyone is responsible, don't single anybody out

3 **particularizarse** *vpr (caracterizarse)* **particularizarse por** to be characterized by

particularmente *adv* (**a**) *(especialmente)* particularly; **está p. molesto** he is particularly upset (**b**) *(en particular)* in particular; **me refiero p. a los productos orgánicos** I am referring in particular to organic products

partida *nf* (**a**) *(marcha)* departure

(**b**) *(en juego)* game; **una p. de ajedrez** a game of chess; **echar una p.** to have a game

(**c**) *(documento)* certificate ▸▸ ***p. de bautismo*** baptismal certificate; ***p. de defunción*** death certificate; ***p. de matrimonio*** marriage certificate; ***p. de nacimiento*** birth certificate

(**d**) *Com (mercancía)* consignment

(**e**) *Com (entrada)* item, entry

(**f**) *(expedición)* party; *(militar)* squad ▸▸ ***p. de caza*** hunting party; ***p. de reconocimiento*** reconnaissance party

(**g**) EXPR **por p. doble: hacer algo por p. doble** to do sth twice; **nos engañaron por p. doble** they fooled us twice over; **la familia real es hoy noticia por p. doble** the royal family is in the news today on two accounts; **un producto que es beneficioso para la salud por p. doble** a product which is doubly beneficial to health

partidario, -a 1 *adj* **ser p. de** to be in favour of; **es p. de medidas más radicales** he is in favour of *o* he supports more radical measures; **yo sería p. de invitarles a ellos también** I think we should invite them as well

2 *nm,f* supporter; **los partidarios de la paz** those in favour of peace

partidillo *nm* practice game *o Br* match

partidismo *nm* partisanship, bias

partidista *adj* partisan, biased

partido *nm* (**a**) *(político)* party; **p. político** political party; **un p. de izquierda(s)** a left-wing party; **el p. en el gobierno** the ruling party; **un p. de (la) oposición** an opposition party ▸▸ ***p. bisagra*** = minority party holding the balance of power

(**b**) *(deportivo)* game, *Br* match; **un p. de baloncesto/rugby** a game of basketball/rugby; **un p. de liga/copa** a league/cup game *o Br* match ▸▸ ***p. amistoso*** friendly; ***p. benéfico*** benefit game *o Br* match; ***p. de clasificación*** qualifying game *o Br* match, qualifier; ***p. de consolación*** consolation final; ***p. de desempate*** play-off; ***p. de dobles*** game of doubles, doubles game *o Br* match; ***p. de entrenamiento*** practice game *o Br* match; ***p. de las estrellas*** all-star game; ***p. de exhibición*** exhibition game *o Br* match; ***p. (de) homenaje*** testimonial (game); ***p. de ida*** *(en copa)* first leg; ***p. internacional*** international, *Br* international match; ***p. de vuelta*** *(en copa)* second leg

(**c**) *Am (partida)* game; **un p. de ajedrez** a game of chess

(**d**) *(futuro cónyuge)* **ser buen/mal p.** to be a good/bad match

(**e**) *Esp* ***p. judicial*** = area under the jurisdiction of a court of first instance

(**f**) EXPR **sacar p. de, sacarle p. a** to make the most of; **tomar p. por** *(ponerse de parte de)* to side with; *(decidir)* to decide on; **tomar p. por hacer algo** to decide to do sth

PARTIR 1 *vt* (**a**) *(dividir)* to divide, to split (**en** into); **parte el pastel en tres** cut the cake in three; **70 partido por 2 es igual a 35** 70 divided by two equals 35

(**b**) *(repartir)* to share out; **partió el dinero del premio con sus hermanos** he shared the prize money with his brothers; **partió el dinero del premio entre sus hermanos** he shared out the prize money between his brothers

(**c**) *(romper)* to break open; *(cascar)* to crack; *(cortar)* to cut; *(diente)* to chip; *(ceja, labio)* to split (open), to cut; **le partieron el brazo** they broke his arm; **le partieron la ceja/el labio** they split *o* cut her eyebrow/lip; **párteme un pedazo de pan** break me off a piece of bread; **párteme otra rodaja de melón** cut me another slice of melon; **p. una tarta por la mitad** *o* **en dos** to cut a cake in half; *Fam* **partirle la boca** *o* **la cara a alguien** to smash sb's face in

(**d**) *Fam (fastidiar)* **tener que salir de casa me parte por completo** it's a real pain having to go out; **aquel contratiempo nos partió la mañana** that setback ruined our morning for us

2 *vi* (**a**) *(marchar)* to leave, to set off (**de/para** from/for); **el buque partió de las costas británicas con rumbo a América** the ship set sail from Britain for America

(**b**) *(empezar)* **p. de** to start from; **p. de cero** to start from scratch; **la**

idea partió de un grupo de colegiales it was a group of schoolchildren that first had the idea; **partimos de la base de que todos saben leer** we are assuming that everyone can read; **partiendo de este hecho, Newton creó una nueva teoría** Newton built a new theory around this fact

(c) *(repartir)* to share out; PROV **el que parte y reparte se lleva la mejor parte** people always save the biggest part for themselves

3 **partirse** *vpr* (a) *(romperse)* to split; **se me ha partido una uña** one of my nails has split; **el vaso se partió al caer al suelo** the glass smashed when it hit the floor; **partirse en dos** to split *o* break in two

(b) *(rajarse)* to crack; **se partió la cabeza al caer de un andamio** he cracked his head when he fell from the scaffolding

(c) *Fam (desternillarse)* **partirse (de risa)** to crack up (with laughter); **¡yo me parto con sus hermanas/chistes!** his sisters/jokes really crack me up!; EXPR *muy Fam* **partirse el culo** to piss oneself (laughing)

4 **a partir de** *loc prep* starting from; **a p. de ahora** from now on; **a p. de aquí** from here on; **a p. de entonces** from then on, thereafter; **el autor creó el relato a p. de un hecho real** the author based the story on an actual event

---

partisano, -a 1 *adj* partisan
2 *nm,f* partisan

partitivo, -a 1 *adj* partitive
2 *nm* partitive

partitura *nf* score

parto *nm* (a) *(de bebé)* birth; **los días anteriores al p.** the days preceding the birth; **estar de p.** to be in labour; **asistir en un p.** to deliver a baby ►► ***p. sin dolor*** painless childbirth; ***p. inducido*** induced labour; ***p. múltiple*** multiple birth; ***p. de nalgas*** breech delivery *o* birth; ***p. natural*** natural childbirth; ***p. prematuro*** premature birth

(b) *(de proyecto)* **el acuerdo tuvo un p. muy largo** the agreement was a long time in the making; **este proyecto ha tenido un p. muy difícil** it was very difficult getting this project off the ground

parturienta *nf (de parto)* woman in labour; *(que ha parido)* woman who has just given birth

parva *nf Agr* unthreshed grain

parvada *nf* (a) *Agr* heap of unthreshed grain (b) *Andes, CAm, Méx (de pájaros)* flock (c) *Andes, CAm, Méx (de personas)* crowd

parvulario, -a 1 *nm* nursery school, kindergarten
2 *nm,f Chile Br* infant, *US* preschooler

parvulista *nmf* nursery (school) teacher

párvulo, -a *nm,f Br* infant, *US* preschooler

pasa *nf (fruta)* raisin; EXPR *Fam* **estar** *o* **quedarse hecho una p.** *(persona)* to become all shrivelled up ►► ***p. de Corinto*** currant; ***p. de Esmirna*** sultana; *RP* ***p. de uva*** raisin

pasable *adj* passable

pasaboca *nm Col* snack, appetiser

pasabordo *nm Col* boarding pass

pasacalle[1] *nm*, **pasacalles** *nm inv* street procession *(during town festival)*

pasacalle[2] *nm Col, Urug* banner *(hung across street)*

pasada *nf* (a) *(con trapo)* wipe; **dales una p. a los muebles con el trapo del polvo** give the furniture a wipe *o* run-over with the duster; **dale una p. con la plancha a los pantalones** just run the iron over the trousers, will you?; **dar una segunda p. a** *(con brocha)* to give a second coat to

(b) *(en costura)* stitch

(c) *(repaso)* read through; **dar una p. a un texto** to read a text through

(d) *(de vehículo)* **los alborotadores dieron varias pasadas en coche delante del cuartel** the troublemakers drove to and fro several times in front of the barracks; **el avión dio dos pasadas sobre el aeropuerto antes de aterrizar** the plane made two passes over the airport before landing

(e) **de p.** *(de paso)* on the way; *(sin detalles)* in passing; **vete a comprar el pan y de p. tráeme el periódico** go and buy the bread and get me the paper while you are at it; **decir algo de p.** to say sth in passing

(f) *Esp Fam (exageración)* **lo que le hiciste a Sara fue una p.** what you did to Sara was a bit much, you went too far doing that to Sara; **ese sitio es una p. de bonito** that's a really lovely spot; **me han regalado una p. de ordenador** I've been given this amazing computer; **le metieron diez puñaladas – ¡qué p.!** he was stabbed ten times – that's barbaric!

(g) **mala p.** dirty trick; **los frenos me jugaron una mala p.** the brakes let me down

pasadizo *nm* passage

pasado, -a 1 *adj* (a) *(terminado)* past; **p. un año** a year later; **son las nueve pasadas** it's gone nine (o'clock); **se pusieron en marcha pasada la medianoche** it was past *o* gone midnight when they set off; EXPR **lo p., p. está** let bygones be bygones; EXPR *Am* **lo p., pisado** let bygones be bygones

(b) *(último)* last; **el año/mes p.** last year/month; **ocurrió el p. martes** it happened last Tuesday

(c) *(podrido)* off, bad

(d) *(muy hecho) (pasta)* overcooked; *(filete, carne)* overdone

(e) *(anticuado)* old-fashioned, out-of-date

(f) *Fam* **estar p.** *(drogado)* to be stoned

(g) EXPR *Fam* **ese tío está p. de rosca** *o* **de revoluciones** he goes too far *o* over the top

2 *nm* (a) *(tiempo)* past; **tiene un p. muy sospechoso** he has a very suspect past (b) *Gram* past (tense); **en p.** in the past (tense)

pasador[1] *nm* (a) *(cerrojo)* bolt (b) *(para corbata)* tie pin *o* clip (c) *(para cinturón)* (belt) loop (d) *(colador)* colander, strainer (e) *(aguja para pelo)* slide (f) *Méx (horquilla)* hairpin, *Br* hairgrip, *US* bobby pin (g) *Perú (de zapato)* shoelace

pasador[2], **-ora** *nm,f Dep* passer

pasaje *nm* (a) *esp Am (billete)* ticket; **el p. cuesta 1.000 dólares** the ticket costs 1,000 dollars, the fare is 1,000 dollars ►► *Am* ***p. abierto*** open ticket; *Am* ***p. de ida*** *Br* single, *US* one-way ticket; *Am* ***p. de ida y vuelta*** *Br* return (ticket), *US* round-trip (ticket) (b) **el p.** *(pasajeros)* the passengers (c) *(calle)* passage; *(galería)* arcade (d) *(fragmento)* passage

pasajero, -a 1 *adj (amor)* short-lived, brief; *(moda)* passing; **una molestia pasajera** a passing discomfort; **es algo p.** it's (something) temporary, it'll pass
2 *nm,f* passenger; **"pasajeros al tren"** "all aboard"

pasamanería *nm (adornos)* decorative fringe

pasamanos *nm inv* (a) *(de escalera interior)* bannister; *(de escalera exterior)* handrail (b) *CSur (en transporte público)* handrail

pasamontañas *nm inv* balaclava (helmet)

pasante *nmf* (a) *(de abogado)* articled clerk (b) *Am (ayudante en prácticas)* assistant (c) *Méx (profesor)* probationary teacher

pasantía *nf* (a) *(función)* assistantship (b) *(tiempo)* probationary period, apprenticeship

pasapalo *nm Ven* snack, appetiser

pasaportar *vt Fam (matar)* to bump off

pasaporte *nm* passport; EXPR *Esp Fam* **dar (el) p. a alguien** *(echar)* to send sb packing; *(matar)* to bump sb off ►► ***p. diplomático*** diplomatic passport

pasapuré *nm*, **pasapurés** *nm inv* (a) *(chino)* conical sieve, chinois (b) *(con mango)* = hand-operated food mill, *Br* mouli-legumes

---

PASAR 1 *vt* (a) *(dar, transmitir)* to pass; *(noticia, aviso)* to pass on; **¿me pasas la sal?** would you pass me the salt?; **pásame toda la información que tengas** give me *o* let me have all the information you've got; **no se preocupe, yo le paso el recado** don't worry, I'll pass on the message to him; **páseme con el encargado** *(al teléfono)* could you put me through to *o* could I speak to the person in charge?; **le paso (con él)** *(al teléfono)* I'll put you through (to him); **Valdez pasó el balón al portero** Valdez passed the ball (back) to the keeper; **pasan sus conocimientos de generación en generación** they pass down their knowledge from one generation to the next; **el Estado le pasa una pensión** she gets a pension from the State; **p. harina por un cedazo** to sieve flour; **p. la leche por el colador** to strain the milk; **pasa la cuerda por ese agujero** pass the rope through this hole; **hay que p. las maletas por la máquina de rayos X** your luggage has to go through the X-ray machine; **pase las croquetas por huevo** coat the croquettes with egg; **p. el cepillo por el suelo** to scrub the floor; **pasa un paño por la mesa** give the table a wipe with a cloth; **unas vacaciones pasadas por agua** a *Br* holiday *o US* vacation when it rained the whole time; **se dedican a p. tabaco de contrabando/inmigrantes ilegales por la frontera** they smuggle tobacco/illegal immigrants across the border

(b) *(contagiar)* **p. algo a alguien** to give sb sth, to give sth to sb; **me has pasado el resfriado** you've given me your cold

(c) *(cruzar)* to cross; **p. la calle/la frontera** to cross the road/border; **pasé el río a nado** I swam across the river

(d) *(rebasar, sobrepasar)* to go through; **¿hemos pasado ya la frontera?** have we gone past *o* crossed the border yet?; **p. un semáforo en rojo** to go through a red light; **al p. el parque gire a su izquierda** once you're past the park, turn left, turn left after the park; **cuando el automóvil pase los primeros cinco años debe ir a revisión** the car should be serviced after five years; **ya ha pasado los veinticinco** he's over twenty-five now; **mi hijo me pasa ya dos centímetros** my son is already two centimetres taller than me

(**e**) *(adelantar) (corredores, vehículos)* to overtake; **pasa a esa furgoneta en cuanto puedas** overtake that van as soon as you can

(**f**) *(trasladar)* **p. algo a** to move sth to; **hay que p. todos estos libros al estudio** we have to take all these books through to the study, we have to move all these books to the study

(**g**) *(conducir adentro)* to show in; **el criado nos pasó al salón** the butler showed us into the living room

(**h**) *(hacer avanzar) (páginas de libro)* to turn; *(hojas sueltas)* to turn over; EXPR **p. página** to make a fresh start

(**i**) *(mostrar) (película, diapositivas, reportaje)* to show

(**j**) *(emplear) (tiempo)* to spend; **pasó dos años en Roma** he spent two years in Rome; **¿dónde vas a p. las vacaciones?** where are you going on holiday?, where are you going to spend your holidays?; **pasé la noche trabajando** I worked all night, I spent the whole night working; **he pasado muy buenos ratos con él** I've had some very good times with him

(**k**) *(experimentar)* to go through, to experience; **hemos pasado una racha muy mala** we've gone *o* been through a very bad patch; **p. frío/miedo** to be cold/scared; **¿has pasado la varicela?** have you had chickenpox?; **¿qué tal lo has pasado?** did you have a nice time?, did you enjoy yourself?; **pasarlo bien** to enjoy oneself, to have a good time; **¡que lo pases bien!** have a nice time!, enjoy yourself!; **lo hemos pasado muy mal últimamente** we've had a hard time of it recently; EXPR *Fam* **pasarlas canutas** to have a rough time

(**l**) *(superar)* to pass; **muy pocos pasaron el examen/la prueba** very few people passed the exam/test; **hay que p. un reconocimiento médico** you have to pass a medical; **no pasamos la eliminatoria** we didn't get through the tie

(**m**) *(consentir)* **p. algo a alguien** to let sb get away with sth; **que me engañes no te lo paso** I'm not going to let you get away with cheating me; **este profesor no te deja p. (ni) una** you can't get away with anything with this teacher; **p. algo por alto** *(adrede)* to pass over sth; *(sin querer)* to miss sth out

(**n**) *(transcribir)* **p. algo a limpio** to make a fair copy of sth, to write sth out neatly; **yo te lo paso a máquina** I'll type it up for you; **p. un documento** *Esp* **a ordenador** *o Am* **a la computadora** to type *o* key a document (up) on the computer

(**o**) *RP Fam (engañar)* to diddle; **están siempre tratando de pasarte con el vuelto** they always try to short-change you *o* diddle you over the change

2 *vi* (**a**) *(ir, moverse)* to pass, to go; **vimos p. a un hombre corriendo** we saw a man run past; **¿cuándo pasa el camión de la basura?** when do the *Br* dustmen *o US* garbage collectors come?; **deja p. a la ambulancia** let the ambulance past; **¿me deja p., por favor?** may I come past, please?; **pasó por mi lado** he passed by my side; **he pasado por tu calle** I went down your street; **el autobús pasa por mi casa** the bus passes in front of *o* goes past my house; **¿qué autobuses pasan por aquí?** which buses go past here?, which buses can you catch from here?; **el Támesis pasa por Londres** the Thames flows through London; **yo sólo pasaba por aquí** I was just passing by; **pasaba por allí y entré a saludar** I was in the area, so I stopped by to say hello; **p. de largo** to go straight by

(**b**) *(entrar)* to go/come in; **pasen por aquí, por favor** come this way, please; **lo siento, no se puede p.** sorry, you can't go in there/come in here; **pasamos a un salón muy grande** we entered a very large living room; **¿puedo p.?** may I come in?; **¿puedo p. al cuarto de baño?** can I use the bathroom?; **¡pase!**, *Méx* **¡pásale/pásele!** come in!; **hazlos p.** show them in; *RP* **p. al pizarrón** to go/come to the blackboard

(**c**) *(caber)* to go (**por** through); **por ahí no pasa este armario** this wardrobe won't go through there

(**d**) *(acercarse, ir un momento)* to pop in; **pasaré por mi oficina/por tu casa** I'll pop into my office/round to your place; **pasa por la farmacia y compra aspirinas** pop into the *Br* chemist's *o US* pharmacy and buy some aspirin; **pasé a verla al hospital** I dropped in at the hospital to see her; **pase a por el vestido** *o* **a recoger el vestido el lunes** you can come and pick the dress up on Monday

(**e**) *(suceder)* to happen; **¿qué pasa aquí?** what's going on here?; **¿qué pasa?** *(¿qué ocurre?)* what's the matter?; *Fam (al saludar a alguien)* how's it going?; *Méx Fam* **¿qué pasó?** *(¿qué tal?)* how's it going?; **¿qué pasa con esas cervezas?** where have those beers got to?, what's happened to those beers?; **no te preocupes, no pasa nada** don't worry, it's OK; **aquí nunca pasa nada** nothing ever happens here; **¿qué le pasa?** what's wrong with him?, what's the matter with him?; **¿le pasó algo al niño?** did something happen to the child?; **¿qué te pasa en la pierna?** what's wrong with your leg?; **eso te pasa por mentir** that's what you get for lying; **lo que pasa es que...** the thing is...; **pase lo que pase** whatever happens, come what may; **siempre pasa lo mismo, pasa lo de siempre** it's always the same; **dense la mano y aquí no ha pasado nada** shake hands and just forget the whole thing (as if it had never happened)

(**f**) *(terminar)* to be over; **pasó la Navidad** Christmas is over; **ya ha pasado lo peor** the worst is over now; **cuando pase el dolor** when the pain passes *o* stops; **la tormenta ya ha pasado** the storm is over now; **el efecto de estos fármacos pasa enseguida** these drugs wear off quickly

(**g**) *(transcurrir)* to go by; **pasaron tres meses** three months went by; **cuando pase un rato te tomas esta pastilla** take this tablet after a little while; **¡cómo pasa el tiempo!** time flies!

(**h**) *(cambiar)* **p. de... a...** *(de lugar, estado, propietario)* to go *o* pass from... to...; **pasamos del último puesto al décimo** we went (up) from last place to tenth; **pasa de la depresión a la euforia** she goes from depression to euphoria; **pasó a formar parte del nuevo equipo** he joined the new team; **p. a** *(nueva actividad, nuevo tema)* to move on to; **pasemos a otra cosa** let's move on to something else; **ahora pasaré a explicarles cómo funciona esta máquina** now I'm going to explain to you how this machine works; **Alicia pasa a (ser) jefa de personal** Alicia will become personnel manager; **p. de curso** *o* **al siguiente curso** = to pass one's end-of-year exams and move up a year

(**i**) *(ir más allá, sobrepasar)* **si pasas de 160, vibra el volante** if you go faster than 160, the steering wheel starts to vibrate; **yo creo que no pasa de los cuarenta años** I doubt she's older than forty; **no pasó de ser un aparatoso accidente sin consecuencias** the accident was spectacular but no-one was hurt

(**j**) *(conformarse, apañarse)* **p. (con/sin algo)** to make do (with/without sth); **tendrá que p. sin coche** she'll have to make do without a car; **¿cómo puedes p. toda la mañana sólo con un café?** how can you last all morning on just a cup of coffee?; **no sabe p. sin su familia** he can't cope without his family

(**k**) *(experimentar)* **hemos pasado por situaciones de alto riesgo** we have been in some highly dangerous situations

(**l**) *(tolerar)* **p. por algo** to put up with sth; **¡yo por ahí no paso!** I draw the line at that!

(**m**) *(ser considerado)* **pasa por ser uno de los mejores tenistas del momento** he is considered to be one of the best tennis players around at the moment; **hacerse p. por algo/alguien** to pretend to be sth/sb, to pass oneself off as sth/sb

(**n**) *Fam (prescindir)* **p. de algo/alguien** to want nothing to do with sth/sb; **paso de política** I'm not into politics; **¡ése pasa de todo!** he couldn't care less about anything!; **paso de ir al cine hoy** I don't fancy *o* can't be bothered going to the cinema today; **paso olímpicamente** *o* **ampliamente de hacerlo** I'm damned if I'm going to do it

(**o**) *(en naipes)* to pass

(**p**) *(servir, valer)* **puede p.** it'll do; **por esta vez pase, pero que no vuelva a ocurrir** I'll overlook it this time, but I don't want it to happen again

(**q**) *Méx Fam (gustar)* **me pasa ese cantante** I think that singer's great

3 pasarse *vpr* (**a**) *(acabarse, cesar)* **se me ha pasado el dolor** the pain has gone; **se le ha pasado la fiebre** his temperature has gone down *o* dropped; **se me ha pasado la gripe** I've got over my bout of flu; **se nos han pasado los efectos** the effects have worn off; **siéntate hasta que se te pase** sit down until you feel better; **si no se le pasa, habrá que ir al médico** if she doesn't get better, we'll have to go to the doctor; **se le ha pasado el enfado/sueño** he's no longer angry/sleepy; **ya se le ha pasado el berrinche** he's got over his tantrum; **se ha pasado la tormenta** the storm's over; **saldremos cuando se pase el calor** we'll go out when it's a bit cooler *o* not so hot; **¿ya se ha pasado la hora de clase?** is the class over already?; **los días se (me) pasan volando** the days seem to fly by

(**b**) *(emplear) (tiempo)* to spend; **se pasaron el día hablando** they spent all day talking; *Am* **se pasa molestando a los compañeros** he spends the whole time annoying his classmates; *Am* **se pasa al teléfono** she spends all her time on the phone

(**c**) *(cambiar)* **pasarse al enemigo/a la competencia** to go over to the enemy/competition; **me he pasado a la cerveza sin alcohol** I've gone over to drinking alcohol-free beer; **nos hemos pasado al edificio de al lado** we've moved into the building next door

(**d**) *(ir demasiado lejos)* **creo que nos hemos pasado** I think we've gone too far; **se han pasado ustedes, el museo queda al principio de la calle** you've come too far, the museum's at the beginning of the street; **nos hemos pasado de parada** we've missed our stop

(**e**) *(excederse, exagerar)* **te has pasado con el ajo** you've overdone the garlic, you've put too much garlic in; **no te pases con el ejercicio** don't overdo the exercise; **pasarse de generoso/bueno** to be far too generous/kind; **se pasa de listo** he's too clever by half, he's too clever for his own good; **habría un millón de personas – ¡no te pases!** there must have been a million people there – don't exaggerate!; **¡no te pases con la sal!** steady on with *o* go easy on the salt!

(**f**) *Fam (propasarse)* **pasarse (de la raya)** to go too far, *Br* to go OTT; **te has pasado diciéndole eso** what you said went too far *o* was just a bit much; **¡no te pases, que yo no te he insultado!** keep your hair on, I didn't insult you!; EXPR *Esp* **te has pasado varios** *o* **cinco pueblos** you've really gone and done it (this time)

(**g**) *(estropearse) (comida)* to go off; *(flores)* to fade

(**h**) *(cocerse en exceso) (arroz, pasta)* **procura que no se te pase la paella** try not to overcook the paella

(**i**) *(desaprovecharse)* **se me pasó la oportunidad** I missed my chance; **se le pasó el turno, señora** you've missed your turn, madam

(**j**) *(olvidarse)* **pasársele a alguien** to slip sb's mind; **¡que no se te pase!** make sure you don't forget!; **se me pasó decírtelo** I forgot to mention it to you

(**k**) *(no notarse)* **pasársele a alguien** to escape sb's attention; **no se le pasa nada** he never misses a thing; **se me pasó ese detalle** I didn't notice that detail, that detail escaped my attention

(**l**) *(omitir)* to miss out; **te has pasado una página** you've missed a page out

(**m**) *(divertirse)* **¿qué tal te lo estás pasando?** how are you enjoying yourself?, are you having a good time?; **pasárselo bien/mal** to have a good/bad time, to enjoy/not to enjoy oneself; **¡que te lo pases bien!** have a good time!, enjoy yourself!

(**n**) *(acercarse, ir un momento)* to pop in; **me pasaré por mi oficina/por tu casa** I'll pop into my office/round to your place; **pásate por la farmacia y compra aspirinas** pop into the *Br* chemist's *o US* pharmacy and buy some aspirin; **pásate por aquí cuando quieras** come round any time you like; **pásese a por el vestido** *o* **a recoger el vestido el lunes** you can come and pick the dress up on Monday

(**o**) *CSur Fam (lucirse)* **te pasaste con lo que le dijiste** what you said was brilliant; **la modista se pasó con el vestido de la novia** the dressmaker did a fantastic job with the bride's dress

---

pasarela *nf* (**a**) *(puente)* footbridge; *(para desembarcar)* gangway ▸▸ ***p. telescópica*** *(en aeropuerto)* jetty *(for boarding aircraft)* (**b**) *(en desfile de moda) Br* catwalk, *US* runway (**c**) *Informát* gateway ▸▸ ***p. de correo*** mail gateway

pasatiempo *nm* (**a**) *(hobby)* pastime, hobby (**b**) **pasatiempos** *(en periódico)* puzzles

PASCAL, Pascal *nm Informát* PASCAL, Pascal

pascana *nf Andes (mesón)* inn, tavern

pascua *nf* (**a**) *(de los cristianos)* Easter ▸▸ ***P. Florida*** Easter; ***P. de Resurrección*** Easter

(**b**) **Pascuas** *(Navidad)* Christmas *(singular)*; **¡felices Pascuas (y próspero año nuevo)!** Merry Christmas (and a Happy New Year)!

(**c**) *(de los judíos)* Passover

(**d**) EXPR *Fam* **estar como unas Pascuas** to be as pleased as Punch; **no va poder ayudarnos – ¡pues nos ha hecho la p.!** he's not going to be able to help us – well that's messed up our plans!; *Fam* **de Pascuas a Ramos** once in a blue moon; *Fam* **dile que no, ¡y santas Pascuas!** tell him no, and that's it *o* that's all there is to it

pascual *adj* Easter; **cordero p.** Paschal lamb

pascualina *nf RP, Ven* = tart with spinach and hard-boiled egg

pascuense 1 *adj* of/from Easter Island *(Chile)*

2 *nm,f* Easter Islander *(Chile)*

pase *nm* (**a**) *(permiso)* pass ▸▸ *Méx, Ven* ***p. de abordar*** boarding pass; *Mil* ***p. (de) pernocta*** overnight pass

(**b**) *(cambio de lugar)* **aprobaron su p. al departamento de contabilidad** they approved her transfer to the accounts department; **obtuvieron el p. a la final del campeonato** they qualified for the final of the championship; **no consiguió el p. a la fase de entrevistas** he didn't get through to the interview stage

(**c**) *Dep* pass ▸▸ ***p. adelantado*** *(en rugby)* forward pass; ***p. de la muerte*** *(en fútbol)* killer pass; ***p. de pecho*** chest-level pass; ***p. picado*** *o* ***de pique*** *(en baloncesto)* bounce pass

(**d**) *Taurom* pass

(**e**) *Esp (proyección)* showing, screening ▸▸ ***p. privado*** sneak preview

(**f**) *(desfile)* parade; **p. de modelos** fashion parade

(**g**) *(de mago)* sleight of hand; **dio** *o RP* **hizo un p. y apareció un conejo** he waved his magic wand and a rabbit appeared

(**h**) *Esp Fam* **eso tiene un p.** I/you/*etc* can live with that

(**i**) *Col (de conducción) Br* (driving) licence, *US* driver's license

(**j**) *Col, RP Fam (de cocaína)* line

paseandero, -a *nm,f Andes, RP Fam* **es muy paseandera** she's always out and about

paseante *nmf* person out for a stroll; **los paseantes que llenaban el parque** the crowds out for a stroll in the park

pasear 1 *vi (andando)* to go for a walk; *(a caballo)* to go for a ride; *(en coche)* to go for a ride *o* drive; **p. a caballo** to go horse riding

2 *vt* (**a**) *(sacar a paseo)* to take for a walk; *(perro)* to walk (**b**) *(hacer ostentación de)* to show off, to parade (**c**) *CAm (arruinar)* to spoil, to ruin

3 pasearse *vpr* (**a**) *(caminar)* to go for a walk (**b**) *Fam (ganar con facilidad)* **Colombia se paseó en la final** the final was a walkover for Colombia

paseíllo *nm Taurom* = parade of bullfighters when they come out into the ring before the bullfight starts

paseo *nm* (**a**) *(acción) (a pie)* walk; *(en coche)* drive, ride; *(a caballo)* ride; *(en barca)* row; **un p. en coche** a drive; **un p. a caballo** a (horse) ride; **dar un p.** *(a pie)* to go for a walk; *(a caballo)* to go for a ride; *(en coche)* to go for a drive *o* ride; **ir de p.** *(andar)* to walk ▸▸ ***p. espacial*** space walk

(**b**) *(distancia corta)* short walk; **sólo es un p. hasta el teatro** it's only a short walk to the theatre

(**c**) *(calle)* avenue ▸▸ ***p. marítimo*** promenade

(**d**) *Am (excursión)* trip, outing; **hacer un p.** to go on a trip *o* outing

(**e**) *RDom (arcén) Br* hard shoulder, *US* shoulder

(**f**) *Fam (cosa fácil)* walkover

(**g**) EXPR *Fam* **dar el p. a alguien** to bump sb off; *Fam* **mandar** *o* **enviar a alguien a p.** to send sb packing; *Fam* **¡vete a p.!** get lost!; *Fam* **mandó los estudios a p.** he said to hell with his studies

paseriforme *Zool* **1** *adj* passerine

2 *nm* passerine

3 paseriformes *nmpl (orden) Passeriformes*

pasero *nm Méx* = person who, for a fee, helps people cross the border into the USA illegally

pashmina *nf* pashmina

pasillo *nm* (**a**) *(en casa, edificio)* corridor; *(en avión)* aisle; **hacer (el) p.** to form a corridor *(for people to walk down)*; **abrirse p. entre la multitud** to make *o* force one's way through the crowd ▸▸ ***p. aéreo*** air corridor; ***p. deslizante*** travelator; ***p. de honor*** *(en fútbol)* guard of honour *(formed by the team about to play the champions to applaud them onto the pitch)*; ***p. móvil*** moving walkway; ***p. rodante*** moving walkway

(**b**) *Col, Ecuad, Pan (baile, música)* = folk song and dance

pasión *nf* (**a**) *(sentimiento)* passion; **la filatelia es la p. de su vida** stamp-collecting is his great passion; **una noche de p.** a night of passion; **hacer las cosas con p.** to do things passionately; **siente** *o* **tiene gran p. por los trenes** he really loves *o* adores trains; **siente** *o* **tiene gran p. por Isabel** he's passionately in love with Isabel; **tienes que dominar tus pasiones** you must master your passions

(**b**) *Rel* **la P.** the Passion

pasional *adj* passionate

pasionaria *nf* passion flower

pasito *adv Col* softly, quietly; **hablen más p.** could you talk more quietly?

pasiva *nf* (**a**) *Gram* passive (voice); **en p.** in the passive (voice) ▸▸ ***p. refleja*** reflexive passive (**b**) *ver también* **pasivo**

pasividad *nf* (**a**) *(falta de iniciativa)* passivity (**b**) *Urug Formal (pensión)* pension

pasivo, -a 1 *adj* (**a**) *(persona)* passive; **es muy p.** he's very passive (**b**) *Gram* passive; **la voz pasiva** the passive voice (**c**) *(población)* inactive; **las clases pasivas** = pensioners and people on benefit (**d**) *(haber)* (received) from a pension

2 *nm Com* liabilities, liabilities and equity ▸▸ ***p. corriente*** current liabilities; ***p. diferido*** deferred liabilities

3 *nm,f Urug (pensionista)* (old age) pensioner

pasma *Esp muy Fam* **1** *nf* **la p.** the cops, the pigs; **un coche de la p.** a cop car

2 *nmf* cop, pig

pasmado, -a 1 *adj* (**a**) *(asombrado)* astonished, astounded (**b**) *(atontado)* stunned (**c**) *(enfriado)* frozen stiff; **me quedé p. esperando el autobús** I nearly froze to death waiting for the bus

2 *nm,f* halfwit

pasmar 1 *vt* (**a**) *(asombrar)* to astound, to amaze (**b**) *(dejar atónito)* to stun (**c**) *(enfriar)* to freeze

2 pasmarse *vpr* (**a**) *(asombrarse)* to be astounded *o* amazed; **te vas a p. cuando te cuente lo que me ha pasado** you just won't believe it when I tell you what happened to me (**b**) *(atontarse)* to be stunned (**c**) *(enfriarse)* to freeze; **¡hace un frío que te pasmas!** it's freezing!

pasmarote *nmf Fam* halfwit, dumbo

pasmo *nm Fam* (a) *(asombro)* astonishment, amazement; **cuando se lo dije le dio un p.** she had a fit when I told her (b) *(de frío)* chill; **te va a dar un p.** you'll catch your death

pasmoso, -a *adj Fam* astounding, amazing; **tiene una habilidad pasmosa para cocinar** he's amazingly good at cooking

PASO 1 *nm* (a) *(con el pie)* step; *(huella)* footprint; **dar un p. adelante** *o* **al frente** to step forwards, to take a step forwards; **dar un p. atrás** *(al andar)* to step backwards, to take a step backwards; *(en proceso, negociaciones)* to take a backward step; **aprendí unos pasos de baile** I learnt a few dance steps; **oía pasos arriba** I could hear footsteps upstairs; **se veían sus pasos sobre la nieve** you could see its footprints in the snow; **a cada p.** *(cada dos por tres)* every other minute; **está a dos** *o* **cuatro pasos (de aquí)** it's just down the road (from here); **vivimos a un p. de la estación** we live just round the corner from *o* a stone's throw away from the station; **el ruso está a un p. de hacerse campeón** the Russian is on the verge of *o* just one small step away from becoming champion; **a pasos agigantados** at a terrific rate, at a rate of knots; **la economía crece a pasos agigantados** the economy is growing at a rate of knots; **el sida se propaga a pasos agigantados** AIDS is spreading like wildfire *o* at an alarming rate; **la ingeniería genética avanza a pasos agigantados** genetic engineering has made giant *o* enormous strides; **dar un p. en falso** *o* **un mal p.** *(tropezar)* to stumble; *(equivocarse)* to make a false move *o* a mistake; *Fig* **no dio ni un p. en falso** he didn't put a foot wrong; **seguir los pasos a alguien** *(perseguir, vigilar)* to tail sb; **seguir los pasos de alguien** *(imitar)* to follow in sb's footsteps; **volvimos sobre nuestros pasos** we retraced our steps

(b) *(acción)* passing; *(cruce)* crossing; *(camino de acceso)* way through, thoroughfare; **con el p. del tiempo** with the passage of time; **con el p. de los años** as the years go by; **el p. de la juventud a la madurez** the transition from youth to adulthood; **su p. fugaz por la universidad** his brief spell at the university; **el Ebro, a su p. por Zaragoza** the Ebro, as it flows through Zaragoza; **la tienda está en una zona de mucho p.** the shop is in a very busy area; *también Fig* **abrir p. a alguien** to make way for sb; **abrirse p.** *(entre la gente, la maleza)* to make one's way; **abrirse p. en la vida/en el mundo de la política** to get on *o* ahead in life/politics; **¡abran p.!** make way!; **ceder el p. (a alguien)** *(dejar pasar)* to let (sb) past; *(en automóvil)* to give way (to sb); **ceda el p.** *(en letrero) Br* give way, *US* yield; **cerrar** *o* **cortar el p. a alguien** to block sb's way; **de p.** *(de pasada)* in passing; *(aprovechando)* while I'm/you're/*etc* at it; **de p. que vienes, tráete las fotos de las vacaciones** you may as well bring the photos from your *Br* holiday *o US* vacation when you come; **la estación me pilla de p.** the station's on my way; **estar de p.** *(en un lugar)* to be passing through; **prohibido el p.** *(en letrero)* no entry; **salir al p. a alguien, salir al p. de alguien** *(acercarse)* to come up to sb; *(hacer detenerse)* to come and bar sb's way; **salir al p. de algo** *(rechazar)* to respond to sth ►► ***p. de cebra*** *Br* zebra crossing, = pedestrian crossing marked with black and white lines; *Méx* ***p. a desnivel*** *Br* flyover, *US* overpass; ***p. del Ecuador*** *(en barco)* crossing the line ceremony; *(en universidad)* = (celebration marking) halfway stage in a university course; ***p. elevado*** *Br* flyover, *US* overpass; ***p. fronterizo*** border crossing (point); ***p. a nivel*** *Br* level crossing, *US* grade crossing; ***p. a nivel con barrera*** *Br* gated level crossing, *US* protected grade crossing; ***p. a nivel sin barrera*** *Br* ungated level crossing, *US* unprotected grade crossing; *Chile* ***p. bajo nivel*** *Br* subway, *US* underpass; ***p. peatonal*** *o* ***de peatones*** pedestrian crossing; ***p. subterráneo*** *Br* subway, *US* underpass

(c) *(forma de andar)* walk; *(ritmo)* pace; **con p. cansino se dirigió a la puerta** he walked wearily towards the door; **a buen p.** at a good rate; **a este p.** *o* **al p. que vamos, no acabaremos nunca** at this rate *o* at the rate we're going, we'll never finish; **al p.** *(en equitación)* at a walk; **a p. lento** slowly; **a p. ligero** at a brisk pace; *Mil* at the double; **aflojar el p.** to slow down; **apretar el p.** to go faster, to speed up; **llevar el p.** to keep step; **marcar el p.** to keep time; EXPR **a p. de tortuga** at a snail's pace ►► *Mil* ***p. de la oca*** goose-step

(d) *Geog (en montaña)* pass; *(en el mar)* strait

(e) *(trámite, etapa, acontecimiento)* step; *(progreso)* step forward, advance; **antes de dar cualquier p. siempre me pregunta** she always asks me before doing anything; **dar los pasos necesarios** to take the necessary steps; **dar los primeros pasos hacia la paz** to take the first steps towards peace; **la aprobación de una constitución supondría un gran p. para la democracia** the passing of a constitution would be a big step forward for democracy; **explícamelo p. a** *o* **por p.** explain it to me step by step; **p. a** *o* **por p. se ganó la confianza de sus alumnos** she gradually won the confidence of her pupils; **salir del p.** to get out of trouble

(f) *(de llamadas telefónicas, consumo eléctrico)* unit

(g) *(en procesión)* float *(in Easter procession)*

(h) **pasos** *(en baloncesto)* travelling; **hacer pasos** to travel

2 *interj* make way!

pasodoble *nm* paso doble

pasota *Esp Fam* 1 *adj* **está muy p. últimamente** he's had a very couldn't-care-less attitude lately; **tiene un comportamiento muy p.** she behaves as if she couldn't care less

2 *nmf* **es un p.** he couldn't care less about anything

pasote *nm Esp Fam* **es un p. de película** that movie is just too much; **tu compañero de piso es un p. de divertido** your *Br* flatmate *o US* roommate is a scream

pasotismo *nm Esp Fam* couldn't-care-less attitude

paspadura *nf Andes, RP (en piel)* red/sore patch (on the skin)

pasparse *vpr* (a) *Andes, RP (piel)* to get chapped; **el bebé se paspó** the baby's got *Br* nappy *o US* diaper rash (b) *RP Fam (persona)* to get fed up; **vámonos de acá, me paspa esperar** let's go, I'm fed up of waiting; **se paspó y se fue** she got fed up and left

paspartú *nm* passe-partout

pasquín *nm* lampoon

pássim *adv* passim

passing-shot ['pasinʃot] (*pl* **passing-shots**) *nm (en tenis)* passing shot, pass

pasta *nf* (a) *(masa)* paste; *(de papel)* pulp ►► ***p. dentífrica*** *o* ***de dientes*** toothpaste

(b) *(espaguetis, macarrones)* pasta; **me encanta la p.** *o Am* **las pastas** I love pasta ►► ***pastas alimenticias*** pasta

(c) *(de pasteles)* pastry; *(de pan)* dough; **p. para croquetas** croquette mixture; ►► ***p. brisa*** choux pastry; ***p. de hojaldre*** puff pastry; ***p. quebrada*** shortcrust pastry

(d) *(pastelito)* shortcake *Br* biscuit *o US* cookie ►► *Esp* ***pastas de té*** = cookies served with tea *o* coffee

(e) *Esp Fam (dinero)* dough; EXPR **costar/ganar una p. gansa** to cost/earn a packet *o* fortune; EXPR **aflojar** *o* **soltar la p.** to cough up the money

(f) *(encuadernación)* **de p. dura/blanda** hardback/paperback

(g) *Chile (betún)* (shoe) polish

(h) *Fam* EXPR **ser de buena p.** to be good-natured; **tener p. de** to have the makings of

pastaflora *nf* fine puff pastry

pastafrola *nf RP* = pastry filled with quince jelly

pastaje *nm Col, Guat, RP* pasture

pastar *vi* to graze

pastear *vt RP* to spy on

pastel 1 *adj inv (color)* pastel; **colores p.** pastel colours

2 *nm* (a) *(dulce)* cake ►► ***p. de bodas*** wedding cake ***p. de cumpleaños*** birthday cake; ***p. de manzana*** apple pie

(b) *(salado)* pie; **un p. de carne** a meat pie ►► *Chile* ***p. de choclo*** = chicken stew with ground *Br* sweetcorn *o US* corn; *CSur* ***p. de papas*** ≃ shepherd's pie

(c) *Arte* pastel; **pintar al p.** to draw in pastels

(d) *Fam Euf (excremento)* **un p. de vaca** a cowpat

(e) *Fam (chapucería)* botch-up

(f) *PRico (plato, guiso)* = pork stew with manioc and bananas, typical at Christmas

(g) EXPR **descubrir el p.** *(enterarse)* to find out what's going on; *(destapar)* to reveal what's going on, to give the game away; **finalmente su mujer descubrió el p.** in the end his wife found out about his little game; **se descubrió el p.** the goings-on were discovered; **repartirse el p.** to share things out

pasteleo *nm Esp Fam* wheeling and dealing, jobbery

pastelería *nf* (a) *(establecimiento)* cake shop, patisserie (b) *(repostería)* pastries (c) *(oficio)* pastry-making

pastelero, -a 1 *adj* pastry; **crema pastelera** confectioner's custard; **la industria pastelera** the cake and biscuit manufacturing industry

2 *nm,f* (a) *(cocinero)* pastry cook (b) *(vendedor)* patisserie owner (c) *Fam (en deportes)* turncoat, = fan who is always changing his allegiance to the winning side (d) *Perú Fam (drogadicto)* junkie

pasteurización, pasterización *nf* pasteurization

pasteurizado, -a, pasterizado, -a *adj* pasteurized

pasteurizar [14], **pasterizar** [14] *vt* to pasteurize

pastiche *nm* pastiche

pastilla *nf* (a) *(medicina)* pill, tablet; **tome la p. dos veces al día** take the pills *o* tablets twice a day ►► ***p. para adelgazar*** slimming pill *o* tablet; ***p. para dormir*** sleeping pill *o* tablet

(**b**) *(píldora anticonceptiva)* pill; **estar tomando la p.** to be on the pill
(**c**) *(caramelo) Br* sweet, *US* candy ►► ***p. de menta*** mint, peppermint; ***p. para la tos*** cough drop
(**d**) *(de jabón)* bar
(**e**) *(de caldo)* cube
(**f**) *(de mantequilla)* pat
(**g**) *(de chocolate) (tableta)* bar; *(porción)* piece; *(de turrón)* bar
(**h**) *Aut* **p. (de freno)** (brake) shoe
(**i**) *Elec* microchip
(**j**) EXPR *Esp Fam* **ir a toda p.** *(vehículo)* to go at top speed, *Br* to go like the clappers; *(persona)* to go at the double; **tuve que ir a toda p. a la farmacia** I had to shoot *o* belt over to the chemist's; **pasó en su moto a toda p.** he zoomed *o* shot past on his motorbike; **tuvimos que acabar el trabajo a toda p.** we had to rush to get the job finished

pastillero, -a 1 *nm (caja)* pillbox
2 *nm,f Esp Fam (persona)* pill popper

pastinaca *nf* stingray

pastizal *nm* pasture

pasto *nm* (**a**) *(hierba)* fodder (**b**) *(sitio)* pasture; **una región de fértiles pastos** a region abounding in fertile pasture (**c**) *Am (césped)* lawn, grass; **cortar el p.** to mow the lawn, to cut the grass (**d**) EXPR **a todo p.** in abundance; **ser p. de las llamas** to go up in flames

pastón *nm Esp Fam* **vale un p.** it costs a fortune *o Br* a bomb; **nos costó un p.** it cost us a fortune *o Br* a bomb

pastor, -ora 1 *nm,f (de ganado)* shepherd, *f* shepherdess
2 *nm* (**a**) *(sacerdote)* minister; **p. protestante** Protestant minister (**b**) *(perro)* ***p. alemán*** Alsatian, German shepherd; ***p. belga*** Belgian sheepdog

pastoral 1 *adj* pastoral
2 *nf Rel (documento)* pastoral letter

pastorear 1 *vt* to put out to pasture
2 *vi* to pasture, to graze

pastoreo *nm* shepherding

pastoril *adj* pastoral, shepherd; **novela p.** pastoral novel

pastosidad *nf* (**a**) *(blandura)* pastiness (**b**) *(suavidad)* mellowness

pastoso, -a *adj* (**a**) *(blando)* pasty; *(arroz)* sticky (**b**) *(seco)* dry; **tener la boca pastosa** to have a furry tongue (**c**) *(voz)* mellow, rich

pastún 1 *adj* Pashtun
2 *nmf* Pashtun

pasudo, -a *Carib, Col, Méx* 1 *adj* fuzzy, frizzy
2 *nm,f* person with curly hair

pata 1 *nf* (**a**) *(pierna de animal)* leg; **las patas delanteras** the forelegs; **las patas traseras** the hindlegs; *Culin* **p. de pollo** chicken leg ►► *Esp Culin* ***p. negra*** = type of top-quality cured ham; EXPR *Esp* **ser (de) p. negra** *(excelente)* to be first-rate *o* top-class
(**b**) *(pie de animal)* foot; *(de perro, gato)* paw; *(de vaca, caballo)* hoof ►► ***p. de cabra*** crowbar, *Br* jemmy, *US* jimmy; ***pantalones de p. de elefante*** bell bottoms, flares; ***p. de gallo*** *(tejido)* hound's-tooth check (material); ***patas de gallo*** *(arrugas)* crow's feet; *RP* ***patas de rana*** *(para bucear)* flippers
(**c**) *Fam (de persona) (pierna)* leg; *Am (pie)* foot; *Am* **me torcí la p.** I twisted my ankle; *Am* **¡qué olor a p.!** what a stink of smelly feet in here!; **a cuatro patas** on all fours; **a p.** on foot; **ir a la p. coja** to hop; **salimos de allí por patas** we legged it out of there; *Esp Fam* **tener la p. chula** to have a gammy leg ►► ***p. de palo*** wooden leg
(**d**) *(de mueble, mesa)* leg; **una mesa de tres patas** a three-legged table
(**e**) *Chile Fam (etapa)* stage, leg
(**f**) EXPR *Esp Fam* **a la p. la llana** straightforwardly; **nos tratamos a la p. la llana** we were quite straight with each other; *RP Fam* **por abajo de la p.** at least; *Fam* **estirar la p.** to kick the bucket; *Esp Fam Hum* **estoy más liado que la p. de un romano** things are pretty hectic at the moment; *RP Fam* **hacer p. a alguien** to keep sb company; *Fam* **tener mala p.** to be unlucky; **¡qué mala p. tienes!** what rotten luck!; *Fam* **meter la p.** to put one's foot in it; *Fam* **poner algo patas arriba** *o Am* **para arriba** to turn sth upside down; *CSur Fam* **saltar en una p.** to jump for joy; *RP Fam* **ser p.** to be willing to go along; **si van al cine soy p.** if you're going to the cinema count me in; *Chile, Méx Fam* **ser p. de perro** to have itchy feet; *Am Fam* **tener patas** to have friends in high places
(**g**) *ver también* **pato**
2 *nm Perú Fam* (**a**) *(amigo)* pal, *Br* mate, *US* buddy (**b**) *(tipo)* guy, *Br* bloke
3 **patas** *nfpl Chile Fam (poca vergüenza)* cheek

pataca *nf* Jerusalem artichoke

patacón *nm* (**a**) *(moneda antigua)* old silver coin (**b**) *Chile (cardenal)* welt, bruise (**c**) *Chile (borrón)* blot (**d**) *Col, Ven (plátano)* = slice of fried plantain

patada *nf* (**a**) *(con el pie)* kick; *(en el suelo)* stamp; **dar una p. a algo/alguien** to kick sth/sb; **dar patadas** *(el feto)* to kick; **dar patadas en el suelo** to stamp one's feet; **echar a alguien a patadas de** to kick sb out of; *Am* **los agarraron a patadas** they gave them a kicking; **derribaron la puerta a patadas** they kicked the door down *o* in; *Fam* **había turistas a patadas** there were loads of tourists; EXPR *Am Fam* **a las patadas** really badly; **me trata a las patadas** he treats me really badly *o* like dirt; **se llevan a las patadas** they can't stand each other; EXPR *Fam* **me da cien patadas (que...)** it makes me mad (that...); EXPR **dar la p. a alguien** *(de un lugar, empleo)* to kick sb out, to give sb the boot; *Fam Hum* **le da patadas continuas al diccionario** he murders *o* butchers the (English/Spanish/*etc*) language; EXPR *Fam* **darse de patadas con algo** *(no armonizar)* to clash horribly with sth; EXPR *CSur Fam* **le dio una p. al hígado** it went straight to her liver; EXPR *Méx Fam* **de la p.: me cae de la p.** I can't stand her; **hace un frío de la p.** it's freezing; EXPR **en dos patadas** *(en seguida)* in two shakes; EXPR *RP Fam* **quedar como una p.** to look really bad; EXPR *Fam* **sentar como una p. (en el estómago)** to be like a kick in the teeth; EXPR *Fam* **me sentó como una p. en el culo** *Br* it really pissed me off, *US* I was really pissed about it; EXPR **tratar a alguien a patadas** to treat sb like dirt ►► *Méx* ***p. de ahogado*** desperate last effort; ***p. a seguir*** *(en rugby)* kick and chase
(**b**) *Am (descarga eléctrica)* (electric) shock; **el enchufe le dio una p.** he got a shock when he touched the plug
(**c**) *Am (retroceso)* kick

patagón, -ona 1 *adj* Patagonian (Indian)
2 *nm,f* Patagonian (Indian)

Patagonia *n* **la P.** Patagonia

patagónico, -a 1 *adj* Patagonian
2 *nm,f* Patagonian

patalear *vi* (**a**) *(en el aire)* to kick about; *(en el suelo)* to stamp one's feet; **el bebé lleva dos horas pataleando y llorando** the baby's been kicking and screaming for the last two hours (**b**) *(protestar)* to kick up a fuss, to scream and shout; **por mucho que pataleen no me van a convencer** no matter how much they scream and shout, they won't persuade me

pataleo *nm (en el aire)* kicking, thrashing about; *(en el suelo)* stamping; *Fam* **me queda el derecho al p.** all I can do now is complain

pataleta *nf Fam* tantrum; **le dio una p.** he threw a tantrum

patán 1 *adj* uncivilized, uncouth
2 *nm* (**a**) *(ignorante)* boor (**b**) *CSur (inútil)* good-for-nothing

Patas *nm Col, Méx Fam* **el P.** the devil

patasca *nf* (**a**) *Andes, Arg (guiso)* = pork and maize *o US* corn stew (**b**) *Pan, Perú (alboroto)* quarrel, row

patata *nf Esp* (**a**) *(tubérculo)* potato; EXPR *Fam* **ni p.: no entendí ni p.** I didn't understand a word of it; *Fam* **¡(di) p.!** *(en foto)* say cheese! ►► ***patatas bravas*** = sautéed potatoes served with spicy tomato sauce; *Fig* ***p. caliente*** hot potato; ***patatas fritas*** *(de sartén) Br* chips, *US* (French) fries; *(de bolsa) Br* crisps, *US* (potato) chips; ***p. nueva*** new potato; ***patatas paja*** potato straws; ***p. temprana*** early potato
(**b**) *Fam (cosa sin valor)* **ser una p.** to be useless; **esta impresora es una p.** this printer's a dud

patatal, patatar *nm* potato field

patatero, -a *Esp* 1 *adj* (**a**) *(de la patata)* potato; **una región patatera** a potato-growing area (**b**) *Fam* **la película fue un rollo p.** the movie was a real bore *o* drag
2 *nm,f* potato farmer

patatín: que si patatín, que si patatán *loc adv Fam* **estuvimos hablando que si p., que si patatán** we talked about this, that and the next thing; **no empieces que si p., que si patatán, hazlo** don't start making excuses, just do it!

patatús (*pl* **patatuses**) *nm Fam* fit; **cuando se entere le va a dar un p.** when he finds out he'll have a fit

paté *nm* pâté

pateador, -ora *nm,f* (**a**) *(en rugby)* kicker (**b**) *(en golf)* putter

pateadura *nf Andes, RP Fam* kicking; **le dieron una p. a la salida del estadio** he got his head kicked in when he came out of the stadium; **su comentario me cayó como una p.** her remark was like a kick in the teeth

patear 1 *vt* (**a**) *(dar un puntapié a)* to kick; **p. la pelota** to kick the ball
(**b**) *(en golf)* to putt
(**c**) *(pisotear)* to stamp on; EXPR *RP Fam* **patearle el chiquero a alguien** to spoil it *o* things for sb

(d) *Fam (andar por)* to traipse round; **he pateado varias tiendas buscando el libro** I traipsed round several shops looking for the book
(e) *CSur Fam (abandonar)* to dump, to ditch; **llevaban como cinco años juntos y él la pateó** after they'd been together for about five years, he dumped her
2 *vi* (a) *(patalear)* to stamp one's feet
(b) *Fam (andar)* to tramp
(c) *(en golf)* to putt
(d) *Am (cocear)* to kick
(e) *Am (arma)* to kick
(f) *Am (artefacto eléctrico)* **ojo con la lavadora, mirá que patea** careful with the washing machine, it can give you a shock
(g) EXPR *RP Fam* **p. para el otro lado** to swing the other way, to bat for the other side
3 **patearse** *vpr Fam (recorrer)* to tramp; **se pateó toda la ciudad buscando el disco** he tramped *o* traipsed all over town looking for the record

patena *nf* paten; EXPR *Esp* **limpio** *o* **blanco como una p.** as clean as a new pin

patentado, -a *adj* patent, patented

patentar *vt* (a) *(invento)* to patent (b) *CSur (vehículo)* to register

patente 1 *adj (descontento, indignación)* obvious, evident; *(demostración, prueba)* clear; **su dolor era p.** he was clearly in pain; **la declaración dejó p. el fracaso de la cumbre** it was obvious *o* clear from the statement that the summit had failed; **el nerviosismo se hizo p. en su actuación** her nervousness showed in her performance; **su enfado quedó p. con su respuesta** her reply made it clear she was angry
2 *nf* (a) *(de invento)* patent; **tiene la p. de este invento** he holds the patent on *o* for this invention; EXPR *RP Fam Hum* **sacar p. de algo: ese sacó p. de bobo** he's as stupid as they come ►► ***p. de invención*** patent
(b) *(autorización)* licence ►► *Hist* ***p. de corso*** letter(s) of marque; *Fig* **se cree que tiene p. de corso para hacer lo que quiera** she thinks she has carte blanche to do what she likes; ***p. de navegación*** certificate of registration
(c) *CSur (matrícula) Br* number plate, *US* license plate
(d) *CSur (impuesto) (de circulación)* road tax; *(de perro)* (dog) licence
(e) *Chile (cuota)* membership fee, *Br* subscription

patentizar *vt* to reveal

pateo *nm Fam* stamping; **el presidente fue recibido con un sonoro p.** the president was greeted with a loud stamping of feet

patera *nf* (a) *(barca)* small boat, dinghy *(as used by North African immigrants to cross the Strait of Gibraltar and enter Spain illegally)* (b) *ver también* **patero**

páter familias *nm Formal* paterfamilias

paternal *adj* fatherly, paternal

paternalismo *nm* paternalism

paternalista *adj* paternalistic

paternidad *nf* (a) *(calidad de padre)* fatherhood ►► ***p. responsable*** responsible parenthood (b) *Der* paternity; **prueba de p.** paternity test (c) *(creación)* authorship; **la p. del proyecto es suya** he devised the project

paterno, -a *adj* (a) *(del padre)* paternal (b) *(abuelo)* paternal, on one's father's side; **está emparentado con él por línea paterna** he's related to him on his father's side

patero, -a *nm,f Chile Fam (adulador)* bootlicker, toady

patético, -a *adj* (a) *(emocionante)* moving, pathetic (b) *(ridículo, grotesco)* pathetic; **su comportamiento fue p.** his behaviour was pathetic

patetismo *nm* pathos; **imágenes de gran p.** very moving pictures

patibulario, -a *adj (horroroso)* horrifying, harrowing

patíbulo *nm* scaffold, gallows; **lo condenaron al p.** he was sentenced to hang, he was sent to the gallows

paticojo, -a *Fam* 1 *adj* lame
2 *nm,f* lame person, cripple

patidifuso, -a *adj Fam* stunned, *Br* gobsmacked; **me quedé patidifusa** I was stunned *o Br* gobsmacked

patilla *nf* (a) *(de pelo)* sideboard, sideburn (b) *(de gafas)* arm (c) *(de hebilla)* prong (d) *Informát (de enchufe)* pin (e) *Col, Ven (sandía)* watermelon

patilludo, -a *adj* (a) *(con patillas)* **es p.** he has long thick sideburns (b) *RP Fam (harto)* fed up, sick; **me tenés p. con tus preguntas** I'm fed up *o* sick of your questions

patín *nm* (a) *(de hielo)* ice skate; *(de ruedas paralelas)* roller skate; *(en línea)* rollerblade; **me regalaron unos patines en línea** they gave me some rollerblades (b) *(patinete)* scooter ►► *Méx* ***p. del diablo*** scooter (c) *Esp (embarcación)* pedalo (d) *Méx Fam* **a p.** *(a pie)* on foot; **ir a p.** to hoof *o* leg it

pátina *nf* patina

patinada *nf Am (de coche)* skid; *(de persona)* slip; **el suelo estaba mojado y se dio una p.** the floor was wet and he slipped

patinador, -ora *nm,f* skater ►► ***p. artístico*** figure skater; ***p. sobre hielo*** ice skater; ***p. de velocidad*** speed skater

patinaje *nm* skating ►► ***p. artístico*** figure skating; ***p. sobre hielo*** ice skating; ***p. sobre ruedas*** roller skating; *(con patines en línea)* roller blading; ***p. de velocidad*** speed skating

patinar 1 *vi* (a) *(sobre hielo)* to skate, to ice-skate; *(sobre ruedas)* to roller-skate; *(con patines en línea)* to roller-blade; **¿quieres venir a p. sobre hielo?** do you want to come skating *o* ice-skating?
(b) *(resbalar) (coche)* to skid; *(persona)* to slip; **la bici patinó en una curva** the bike skidded on a bend; EXPR *Esp Fam* **le patinan las neuronas, le patina el embrague** he's going a bit funny in the head; EXPR *Esp Fam* **lo que diga me patina** I couldn't care less what he says, *Br* I don't give a monkey's what he says, *US* I don't give a rat's ass what he says
(c) *Esp Fam (equivocarse)* to make a mistake, to slip up; **patiné comprándome ese coche** buying that car was a really bad move
2 **patinarse** *vpr RP Fam (dinero)* to blow; **se patinó todo el sueldo en trajes** he blew all his salary on suits

patinazo *nm* (a) *(de coche)* skid; *(de persona)* slip; **el suelo estaba mojado y se dio un p.** the floor was wet and he slipped; **se dio un p. en una curva y se cayó de la moto** he skidded on a bend and fell off the motorbike (b) *Fam (equivocación)* blunder; **dar un p.** to bungle, to mess up

patinete *nm*, **patineta** *nf* (a) *(con manillar)* scooter (b) *Ven (sin manillar)* skateboard

patio *nm (de casa)* courtyard; *(de escuela)* playground; *(de cuartel)* parade ground; EXPR *Esp Fam* **¡cómo está el p.!** what a fine state of affairs!; **visto como está el patio...** considering the way things are... ►► ***p. de armas*** parade ground; *Esp* ***p. de butacas*** stalls; ***p. interior*** *(en edificio)* central courtyard; ***p. de luces*** central well, air shaft

patita *nf* EXPR *Fam* **poner a alguien de patitas en la calle** to kick sb out; EXPR *CSur Fam Hum* **patitas para qué te quiero: ahí viene la policía, ¡patitas para qué te quiero!** here come the police, time to leg it!

patitieso, -a *adj Fam* (a) *(de frío)* frozen stiff (b) *(de sorpresa)* stunned, *Br* gobsmacked; **dejar p.** to stun, to dumbfound; **me dejó p. con el anuncio** his announcement left me stunned; **quedarse p.** to be stunned *o Br* gobsmacked

patito *nm* **el p. feo** the ugly duckling; *Fam* **los dos patitos** *(el número 22)* all the twos, twenty-two

patituerto, -a *adj* bow-legged, bandy-legged

patizambo, -a *adj* knock-kneed

pato, -a 1 *nm,f (ave)* duck; EXPR *Fam* **¡al agua, patos!** *(en piscina)* in you jump!; EXPR *Méx Fam* **no te hagas p., págame lo que me debes** don't mess me around, just pay me what you owe me; EXPR *Fam* **pagar el p.** *Br* to carry the can, *US* to pick up the tab; EXPR *Arg, Chile, Méx Fam* **ser el p. de la boda** to be the one who pays the consequences, to be the one who foots the bill ►► ***p. almizlado*** muscovy duck; ***p. arlequín*** harlequin duck; ***p. colorado*** red-crested pochard; ***p. havelda*** long-tailed duck; ***p. mandarín*** mandarin duck; ***p. a la naranja*** duck à l'orange
2 *nm* (a) *Esp Fam (persona torpe)* clumsy oaf, clodhopper (b) *Chile (biberón)* (baby's) bottle (c) *Méx (orinal)* bed bottle

patochada *nf Fam* piece of nonsense, idiocy; **no dice más que patochadas** he just talks nonsense; **la última p. del Gobierno** the government's latest crazy plan

patógeno, -a 1 *adj* pathogenic; **agente p.** pathogen
2 *nm* pathogen

patojo, -a *nm,f Guat (niño)* kid, youngster

patología *nf* pathology

patológico, -a *adj* (a) *(de la patología)* pathological (b) *(enfermizo)* pathological; **tiene un miedo p. al dentista** she has a pathological fear of dentists

patólogo, -a *nm,f* pathologist

patón, -ona *adj Am Fam* **es muy p.** he's got enormous feet

patoso, -a *Esp Fam* 1 *adj* clumsy; **no sabe bailar, es muy p.** he can't dance, he's got two left feet; **hoy estoy muy p.** I'm being really clumsy today
2 *nm,f* clumsy idiot *o* oaf

patota *nf Fam* (**a**) *Perú, RP (de gamberros)* street gang (**b**) *Col (de amigos)* gang, crew

patotero, -a *Perú, RP Fam* 1 *adj* thuggish; **es muy p.** he's a real thug
2 *nm,f* young thug

patovica *nmf RP Fam* (**a**) *(guardaespaldas)* minder (**b**) *(en una discoteca)* bouncer

patraña *nf* yarn, cock-and-bull story

patria *nf* native country, fatherland; **la madre p.** the mother country, the motherland; **defender la p.** to defend one's country; **morir por la p.** to die for one's country; EXPR **hacer p.** to fly the flag ▸▸ ***p. chica*** home town; *Der* ***p. potestad*** parental authority

patriarca *nm* (**a**) *(en familia)* patriarch (**b**) *Rel* patriarch

patriarcado *nm* (**a**) *(organización social)* patriarchy (**b**) *Rel* patriarchate

patriarcal *adj* (**a**) *(de la familia)* patriarchal (**b**) *Rel* patriarchal

patriciado *nm* patriciate

Patricio *n pr* **San P.** St Patrick

patricio, -a 1 *adj* patrician
2 *nm,f* patrician

patrimonial *adj* hereditary

patrimonio *nm* (**a**) *(bienes) (heredados)* inheritance; *(propios)* wealth, assets; *(económico)* national wealth; **el p. natural de un país** a country's natural heritage; **el p. de la empresa asciende a mil millones de dólares** the company has net assets of one billion dollars; **los ríos son p. de todos** rivers are a heritage shared by all; **la paz no es p. exclusivo de los partidos políticos** peace is not the exclusive preserve of political parties; **p. personal** personal estate
(**b**) *(cultura)* heritage; **Granada es p. (mundial) de la humanidad** Granada is a world heritage site ▸▸ ***p. histórico-artístico*** artistic *o* cultural heritage; ***p. nacional*** national heritage

patrio, -a *adj* native; **el suelo p.** one's native soil; **el orgullo p.** national pride

patriota 1 *adj* patriotic
2 *nmf* patriot

patriotería *nf*, **patrioterismo** *nm Pey* jingoism, chauvinism

patriotero, -a *Pey* 1 *adj* jingoistic, chauvinistic
2 *nm,f* chauvinist

patriótico, -a *adj* patriotic

patriotismo *nm* patriotism

patrocinado, -a *adj* sponsored

patrocinador, -ora 1 *adj* sponsoring; **la empresa patrocinadora del encuentro** the company sponsoring the event
2 *nm,f (de proyecto, equipo, programa)* sponsor; *(de exposición, concierto)* sponsor, promoter

patrocinar *vt* (**a**) *(proyecto)* to sponsor, to finance; *(equipo, programa)* to sponsor; *(exposición, concierto)* to sponsor, to promote (**b**) *Méx Der (acusado)* to defend

patrocinio *nm* (**a**) *(de proyecto)* sponsorship, financing; *(de equipo, programa)* sponsorship; *(de exposición, concierto)* sponsorship, promotion; **una exposición con el p. del Ministerio de Cultura** an exhibition sponsored by the Ministry of Culture (**b**) *Méx Der (de acusado)* defence

patrón, -ona 1 *nm,f* (**a**) *(de obreros)* boss; *(de criados)* master, *f* mistress; *(empresario)* employer (**b**) *Esp (de pensión)* landlord, *f* landlady (**c**) *(santo)* patron saint
2 *nm* (**a**) *(de barco)* skipper (**b**) *(medida)* standard ▸▸ *Econ* ***p. internacional*** international standard; ***p. oro*** gold standard; ***p. de referencia*** reference gauge (**c**) *(en costura)* pattern

patrona *nf* (**a**) *CSur Fam* **la p.** *Br* the missus *o* missis, *US* my old lady (**b**) *ver también* **patrono**

patronal 1 *adj* (**a**) *(empresarial)* management; **organización p.** employers' organization (**b**) *(del santo patrón)* **fiestas patronales** = festival in honour of the local patron saint
2 *nf (organización)* employers' organization; **la p. del turismo** the tourist operators' association *o* organization; **negociaciones entre la p. y los sindicatos** negotiations between employers and the unions

patronato *nm (dirección)* board of trustees; *(con fines benéficos)* trust ▸▸ *Esp* ***p. de apuestas mutuas*** totalizator

patronazgo *nm* patronage

patronímico, -a 1 *adj* patronymic
2 *nm* patronymic

patronista *nmf* pattern cutter

patrono, -a *nm,f* (**a**) *(de obreros)* boss; *(de criados)* master, *f* mistress; *(empresario)* employer (**b**) *(santo)* patron saint

patrulla *nf* (**a**) *(de soldados, vigilantes)* patrol; **una p. de barcos** a sea patrol; **una p. de rescate** a rescue team ▸▸ ***p. urbana*** vigilante group (**b**) *(acción)* patrol; **hoy nos toca p. a nosotros** it's our turn (to be) on patrol today; **estar de p.** to be on patrol (**c**) *Méx (vehículo)* patrol car

patrullar 1 *vt* to patrol
2 *vi* to patrol; **p. por** to patrol

patrullera *nf* (**a**) *(barco)* patrol boat (**b**) *Chile (auto)* police (patrol) car, *US* cruiser

patrullero, -a 1 *adj* patrol; **barco p.** patrol boat
2 *nm* (**a**) *(barco)* patrol boat (**b**) *CSur (auto)* police (patrol) car, *US* cruiser

patuco *nm Esp* bootee

patudez *nf Chile Fam* cheek, *Br* brass neck

patudo, -a *adj* (**a**) *Am Fam (de pies grandes)* **es muy p.** he's got enormous feet (**b**) *Chile Fam (confianzudo)* cheeky, *US* fresh

patulea *nf Fam* (**a**) *(de niños)* rowdy mob (**b**) *(de criminales)* gang

paulatino, -a *adj* gradual

paulista 1 *adj* of/from São Paulo
2 *nmf* person from São Paulo

pauperismo *nm* pauperism

pauperización *nf* impoverishment

paupérrimo, -a *adj* very poor, impoverished

pausa *nf* (**a**) *(descanso)* pause, break; **con p.** unhurriedly; *Méx* **con toda p.** at a leisurely pace; **hacer una p.** *(al hablar)* to pause; *(en actividad)* to take a break ▸▸ ***p. publicitaria*** commercial break (**b**) *Ling* pause (**c**) *Mús* rest

pausadamente *adv* deliberately, slowly

pausado, -a *adj* deliberate, slow

pauta *nf* (**a**) *(modelo)* standard, model; **dar** *o* **marcar la p.** to set the standard; **seguir una p.** to follow an example (**b**) *(en un papel)* guideline

pautado, -a *adj (papel)* lined, ruled

pava *nf* (**a**) *Esp Fam (colilla)* dog end (**b**) *CAm (flequillo) Br* fringe, *US* bangs (**c**) *Chile, Perú (broma)* coarse *o* tasteless joke (**d**) *Arg (hervidor)* kettle (**e**) *Col, Ven Fam (mala suerte)* bad *o* tough luck; **tener p.** to be unlucky

pavada *RP Fam* 1 *nf* (**a**) *(estupidez)* **decir una p.** to say something stupid; **decir pavadas** to talk nonsense; **hacer una p.** to do something stupid; **hizo la p. de decírselo** she was stupid enough to tell him; **¡cuánta p. hay en el mundo!** people can be really stupid sometimes!
(**b**) *(cosa sin importancia)* silly little thing; **se pelearon por una p.** they had an argument over a silly little thing; **¡no es p.!** *(va en serio)* it's no joke!; **¿qué te ha pasado? – nada, una p.** what happened to you? – oh, it's nothing serious; **por hacer cuatro pavadas me cobró 500 pesos** he charged me 500 pesos for doing next to nothing
(**c**) *(cosa fácil)* **ser una p.** to be a piece of cake *o* a cinch
2 **pavada de** *loc adv* **p. de fiesta hicieron** they threw a terrific party; **p. de discusión hubo** there was one hell of an argument

pavear *vi Fam* (**a**) *Chile, Perú (burlarse)* to play a joke (**b**) *RP (hacer tonterías)* to fool around, to play the fool (**c**) *Ecuad, Pan (faltar a clase)* to play truant

pavés *nm* cobbles, cobblestones

pavesa *nf* ember

pavía *nf Esp* clingstone peach

pavimentación *nf (con asfalto)* surfacing; *(con losas)* paving; *(con baldosas)* tiling

pavimentado, -a *adj (con asfalto)* surfaced, asphalted; *(con losas)* paved; *(con baldosas)* tiled

pavimentar *vt (con asfalto)* to surface; *(con losas)* to pave; *(con baldosas)* to tile

pavimento *nm (de asfalto)* (road) surface; *(de losas)* paving; *(de baldosas)* tiling

pavisoso, -a *adj Fam* bland, wishy-washy

pavo, -a 1 *adj Fam Pey (persona)* wet, drippy
2 *nm,f* (**a**) *(ave)* turkey; EXPR *Esp Fam* **se le subió el p.** she went bright red ▸▸ ***p. real*** peacock, *f* peahen (**b**) *Fam Pey (persona sosa)* drip (**c**) *Esp Fam (hombre)* guy, *Br* bloke; *(mujer)* woman; *(mujer joven)* girl

3 *nm* (**a**) *Esp Fam (cinco pesetas)* five pesetas; **cinco/cien pavos** twenty five/five hundred pesetas (**b**) *Chile (cometa)* large kite (**c**) *Chile Fam (polizón)* stowaway; **viajó de p.** he stowed away

pavón *nm* (**a**) *(ave)* peacock (**b**) *(mariposa)* emperor moth (**c**) *(óxido)* bluing, bronzing

pavonado *nm* bluing

pavonar *vt* to blue

pavonearse *vpr* to boast, to brag (**de** about)

pavoneo *nm* showing off, boasting

pavor *nm* terror; **le tengo p. a los aviones** I'm terrified of flying

pavoroso, -a *adj* terrifying; **un incendio p.** a terrible fire

pavoso, -a *Ven Fam* 1 *adj* jinxed
2 *nm,f* jinx

pavote, -a *RP Fam* 1 *adj* dopey, goofy
2 *nm,f Br* wally, *US* dweeb

pay *nm Chile, Méx, Ven* pie ►► ***p. de limón*** lemon meringue pie; ***p. de manzana*** apple pie; ***p. de queso*** cheesecake

paya *nf* (**a**) *Chile* = improvised folk song (**b**) *ver también* **payo**

payada *nf CSur* (**a**) *(canto)* = improvised folk song (**b**) *Fam (invento)* waffle; **sus discursos son siempre la misma p.** her speeches are always the same old waffle; **si no saben, no escriban, pero no llenen la hoja con payadas** if you don't know what to write, don't write anything, don't try to fill up the page with waffle

payador, -ora *nm,f CSur* (**a**) *(cantor)* = singer of improvised songs (**b**) *Fam (improvisador)* fabulist; **no le prestes atención cuando habla de cine, es un p.** don't pay any attention to him when he starts talking about movies, he makes it all up

payanés, -esa 1 *adj* of/from Popayán *(Colombia)*
2 *nm,f* person from Popayán *(Colombia)*

payar *vi CSur* (**a**) *(cantar)* = to sing improvised songs (**b**) *Fam (inventar)* to waffle, to make things up; **como no había estudiado, payé bastante** I hadn't done any revision, so I just waffled *o* so I just made it up as I went along

payasada *nf* (**a**) *(graciosa)* piece of clowning; **hacer payasadas** to clown *o* fool around (**b**) *(grotesca)* **eso que has dicho/hecho es una p.** what you said/did is ludicrous

payasear *vi Am Fam* to clown *o* fool around

payaso, -a 1 *adj Fam Pey* **¡no seas p.!** stop clowning *o* fooling around!
2 *nm,f* (**a**) *(de circo)* clown (**b**) *Fam Pey (poco serio)* **¡mi profesor es un p.!** my teacher is a clown!, my teacher is always clowning around!

payés, -esa *nm,f* = peasant farmer from Catalonia or the Balearic Islands

payo, -a 1 *adj* (**a**) *Esp (no gitano)* = term used by gypsies to refer to non-gypsies (**b**) *Méx (campesino)* = typical of a peasant who has moved to the city
2 *nm,f* (**a**) *Esp (no gitano)* = term used by gypsies to refer to non-gypsies (**b**) *Méx (campesino)* = peasant who has moved to the city

paz *nf* (**a**) *(ausencia de guerra)* peace; **mantener la p.** to keep the peace; **poner p. entre** to reconcile, to make peace between; **y en p.** and that's that; **estar** *o* **quedar en p.** to be quits; EXPR **...y aquí p. y después gloria** ...and let that be an end to it
(**b**) *(tranquilidad)* peacefulness; **dejar a alguien en p.** to leave sb alone *o* in peace; **que en p. descanse, que descanse en p.** may he/she rest in peace
(**c**) *(acuerdo, convenio)* peace treaty; **la P. de Aquisgrán** the Treaty of Aix-la-Chapelle; **firmar la p.** to sign a peace treaty; **hacer las paces** to make (it) up
(**d**) *Rel* pax; **dar la p.** to make the sign of peace

pazguato, -a, *RP* **pazcuato, -a** *Fam* 1 *adj* (**a**) *(simple)* simple (**b**) *(mojigato)* prudish
2 *nm,f* (**a**) *(simple)* simpleton (**b**) *(mojigato)* prude

pazo *nm* = Galician mansion, belonging to noble family

PBI *nm Perú, RP* (*abrev de* **producto bruto interno**) GDP

PBN *nm Am* (*abrev de* **producto bruto nacional**) GNP

PC *nm* (**a**) (*abrev de* **personal computer**) PC (**b**) (*abrev de* **Partido Comunista**) CP

PCC *nm* (*abrev de* **Partido Comunista Cubano**) Cuban Communist Party

PCE *nm* (*abrev de* **Partido Comunista de España**) Spanish Communist Party

pche, pchs *interj* bah!

PCUS [pe'kus] *nm* (*abrev de* **Partido Comunista de la Unión Soviética**) Soviet Communist Party

PD (*abrev de* **posdata**) PS

PDC *nm* (*abrev de* **Partido Demócrata Cristiano**) Christian Democratic Party

PE *nm* (*abrev de* **Parlamento Europeo**) European Parliament

pe *nf* EXPR *Fam* **de pe a pa** from beginning to end

pea *nf Esp Fam (borrachera)* **agarrarse una p.** to get plastered *o Br* pissed

peaje *nm* (**a**) *(importe)* toll; **autopista de p.** *Br* toll motorway, *US* turnpike (**b**) *(lugar)* toll barrier

peal *nm Am (lazo)* lasso

pealar *vt Am* to lasso

peana *nf* (**a**) *(pedestal)* pedestal (**b**) *Esp Fam (pie)* big foot

peatón *nm* pedestrian

peatonal *adj* pedestrian; **calle p.** pedestrian street

peatonalización *nf* pedestrianization

peatonalizar *vt* to pedestrianize

pebete, -a *RP* 1 *nm,f* child
2 *nm (panecillo)* = small bun used for sandwiches

pebetero *nm* (**a**) *(para perfumes)* incense burner (**b**) *(para antorcha olímpica)* cauldron

pebre *nm o nf* (**a**) *(salsa)* = sauce made with green pepper and garlic (**b**) *(pimienta)* black pepper

peca *nf* freckle

pecado *nm* (**a**) *(en religión)* sin; **estar en p.** to be in sin; **morir en p.** to die unrepentant; **ser p.** to be a sin; EXPR **se dice el p. pero no el pecador** no names, no packdrill, I'm naming no names; EXPR *Fam* **de mis pecados: pero niña de mis pecados ¿cuántas veces tengo que decírtelo?** for goodness' sake, girl, how many times do I have to tell you? ►► ***pecados capitales*** deadly sins; ***p. mortal*** mortal sin; ***p. original*** original sin
(**b**) *(pena, lástima)* sin; **sería un p. no aprovechar este día de primavera** it would be a sin not to make the most of this spring day; **es un p. que no le guste la paella** it's such a pity she doesn't like paella

pecador, -ora 1 *adj* sinful
2 *nm,f* sinner

pecaminoso, -a *adj* sinful

pecán *nm (árbol)* pecan (tree)

pecar [60] *vi* (**a**) *(en religión)* to sin; **p. de obra/palabra/pensamiento** to sin in deed/word/thought (**b**) *(pasarse)* **p. de confiado/generoso** to be overconfident/too generous

pecarí (*pl* **pecaríes**), **pécari** *nm* peccary

pecblenda *nf* pitchblende

pecera *nf (rectangular)* fish tank; *(redonda)* fish bowl

pecero,-a *Fam* 1 *adj* PC
2 *nm,f* PC user

peceto *nm RP* eye round (of beef)

pechada *nf* (**a**) *Esp Fam (hartazgo)* **me di una p. de estudiar** I really studied hard; **se dio una p. de llorar** she cried her heart out (**b**) *CSur* **mandarse una p. con alguien** *(pedir)* to sponge *o* scrounge off sb

pechar 1 *vt* (**a**) *Andes, RP (empujar)* to push, to shove (**b**) *CSur Fam (pedir)* to scrounge, to bum; **se la pasa pechándole cigarrillos a todo el mundo** he's always bumming cigarettes off people
2 *vi* **p. con** to bear, to shoulder
3 **pecharse** *vpr RP* **pecharse a** *o* **con alguien** to bump into sb

pechazo *nm CSur Fam* (**a**) *(gorroneo)* **mandarse un p. con alguien** to sponge *o* scrounge off sb; **vive del p.** he's always sponging *o* on the scrounge (**b**) *(golpe) (entre dos personas)* bump; **nos dimos un p.** we bumped into one another; **me dí un p. contra la puerta** I walked straight into the door

pechblenda *nf* pitchblende

peche *adj Salv (flaco)* thin

pechera *nf* (**a**) *(de camisa)* shirt front; *(de blusa, vestido)* bust (**b**) *Fam (de mujer)* bosom

pechiazul *nm* bluethroat

pechina *nf Arquit* pendentive

pecho *nm* (**a**) *(tórax)* chest; **un dolor en el p.** a pain in the chest, a chest pain
(**b**) *(de mujer)* bosom; **tener poco p.** to have a small bust; **tener mucho p.** to have a big bust
(**c**) *(mama)* breast; **dar el p. a** to breast-feed
(**d**) *(interior)* heart; **guardaba mucha rabia en su p.** his heart was full of anger
(**e**) *Am (en natación)* breaststroke; **nadar p.** to do the breaststroke; **los 100 metros p.** the 100 metres breaststroke

(**f**) EXPR *Fam* **a lo hecho, p.: no me gusta, pero a lo hecho, p.** I don't like it but, what's done is done; *Fam* **tú lo hiciste, así que a lo hecho, p.** you did it, so you'll have to take the consequences; **a p. descubierto** *(sin defensas)* without protection *o* any form of defence; *(con sinceridad)* quite openly *o* candidly; *Fam* **echarse** *o* **meterse entre p. y espalda algo** *(comida)* to put *o* tuck sth away; *(bebida)* to knock sth back, to down sth; *Fam* **me partí el p. por ayudarle** I bent over backwards to help him; **sacar (el) p.** to thrust one's chest out; **tomarse algo a p.** *(ofenderse)* to take sth to heart; *(tomar con empeño)* to take sth seriously; **no te lo tomes tan a p.** you shouldn't take it so to heart; **se toma el trabajo muy a p.** she takes her work very seriously

pechuga *nf* (**a**) *(de ave)* breast *(meat)*; **p. de pollo** breast of chicken, chicken breast (**b**) *Fam (de mujer)* bosom, bust (**c**) *Andes, CAm, Ven Fam (descaro)* nerve, audacity

pechugón, -ona *Fam* **1** *adj* (**a**) *(con pechos grandes)* busty, buxom (**b**) *Andes, CAm, Ven (desvergonzado)* brazen, opportunistic
2 *nm,f Andes, CAm, Ven (desvergonzado)* shameless opportunist

pecíolo, peciolo *nm Bot* stalk

pécora *nf* (**a**) **ser una mala p.** to be a bitch *o* harpy (**b**) *Perú Fam (olor a pies)* stink of smelly feet

pecoso, -a *adj* freckly

pectina *nf* pectin

pectíneo *nm Anat* pectineus

pectoral 1 *adj* (**a**) *Anat* pectoral, chest; **músculos pectorales** pectorals (**b**) *Med* cough; **jarabe p.** cough syrup
2 *nm* (**a**) *Anat* pectoral (**b**) *Med* cough mixture *o* medicine (**c**) *Rel* pectoral cross

pecuario, -a *adj* livestock; **actividad pecuaria** livestock raising

peculado *nm esp Am* misappropriation of public funds

peculiar *adj* (**a**) *(característico)* typical, characteristic; **tiene el sabor p. de la cebolla** it has the characteristic *o* distinctive taste of onion; **trabajaba con su p. seriedad** he worked with characteristic seriousness (**b**) *(raro, curioso)* peculiar; **tiene una manera muy p. de hacer las cosas** she has a very peculiar *o* strange way of doing things

peculiaridad *nf* (**a**) *(cualidad)* uniqueness; **cada uno tiene sus peculiaridades** we all have our little ways *o* idiosyncracies (**b**) *(detalle)* particular feature *o* characteristic; **tiene la p. de que funciona con energía solar** a particular feature of it is that it runs on solar energy

peculio *nm* (**a**) *(dinero)* personal money (**b**) *Der* peculium

pecuniario, -a *adj* pecuniary

peda *nf Méx Fam* **anoche nos pusimos una buena p.** we got totally plastered *o Br* pissed last night

pedagogía *nf* teaching, pedagogy

pedagógico, -a *adj* teaching, pedagogical

pedagogo, -a *nm,f* (**a**) *(especialista)* educationalist (**b**) *(profesor)* teacher, educator

pedal *nm* (**a**) *(de coche, fuente)* pedal ►► ***p. acelerador*** accelerator; ***p. de(l) embrague*** clutch (pedal); ***p. de freno*** brake pedal (**b**) *(de piano, arpa)* pedal (**c**) *(de bicicleta)* pedal; **dar a los pedales** to pedal; **un as del p.** an ace cyclist (**d**) *Esp Fam (borrachera)* **agarrar un p.** to get plastered; **llevo un p. que no me aguanto** I'm completely plastered *o* out of my head

pedalada *nf* turn of the pedals; **con cada p. recorre cinco metros** with each turn of the pedals he travels five metres; **dar pedaladas** to pedal; **pedaladas rápidas/lentas** fast/slow pedalling

pedalear *vi* to pedal

pedaleo *nm* pedalling

pedanía *nf* district

pedante 1 *adj* pretentious
2 *nmf* pretentious person

pedantería *nf* (**a**) *(cualidad)* pretentiousness (**b**) *(dicho, hecho)* piece of pretentiousness

pedazo *nm* (**a**) *(trozo)* piece, bit; **un p. de pan** a piece of bread; **caerse a pedazos** *(deshacerse)* to fall to pieces; *(estar cansado)* to be dead tired, to be worn out; **hacer pedazos algo** to break sth to bits; *Fig* to destroy sth; **saltar en (mil) pedazos** to be smashed to pieces; EXPR **ser un p. de pan** to be an angel, to be a real sweetie
(**b**) *Fam (para enfatizar)* **¡p. de animal** *o* **de bruto!** stupid oaf *o* brute!; **¡p. de alcornoque!** you stupid idiot!; **¡qué p. de actor!** now there's an actor for you!

pederasta *nm* (**a**) *Der (contra menores)* paedophile (**b**) *(homosexual)* homosexual

pederastia *nf* (**a**) *Der (contra menores)* paedophilia (**b**) *(sodomía)* sodomy

pedernal *nm* flint; EXPR **duro como el** *o* **un p.** as hard as a rock

pederse *vpr Fam* to fart

pedestal *nm* pedestal, stand; EXPR **poner a alguien en un p.** to put sb on a pedestal; **la tiene en un p.** he's put her on a pedestal; EXPR **bajar del p.: desde que ganó el premio no hay quien lo baje del p.** since he won the prize, it's been impossible to get him down off his high horse

pedestre *adj* (**a**) *(a pie)* on foot; **una carrera p.** a foot race, a walking race (**b**) *(corriente)* pedestrian, prosaic

pediatra *nmf* paediatrician

pediatría *nf* paediatrics *(singular)*

pediátrico, -a *adj* pediatric

pedículo *nm* peduncle

pediculosis *nm inv Med* pediculosis

pedicura *nf* pedicure; **hacerle la p. a alguien** to give sb a pedicure; **hacerse la p.** to have a pedicure

pedicuro, -a *nm,f, Am* **pedicurista** *nmf* chiropodist, *US* podiatrist

pedida *nf Esp* = family ceremony in which the groom-to-be asks his future wife's parents for their daughter's hand in marriage, ≃ engagement party

pedido *nm* (**a**) *(de producto)* order; **hacer un p.** to place an order; **un p. en firme** a firm order; **sólo se fabrica sobre p.** they are manufactured exclusively to order ►► ***p. por correo*** mail order (**b**) *Am (petición)* request; **p. de arresto** arrest warrant; **a p. de** at the request of

pedigrí, pedigree [peði'ɣri] *nm* pedigree; **un perro con p.** a pedigree dog; *Fam* **un político/deportista con p.** a politician/sportsman with an impressive track record

pedigüeño, -a 1 *adj* **qué hermano más p. tengo** my brother's always asking for things
2 *nm,f (que pide)* **es un p.** he's always asking for things

pedinche *nmf Méx Fam* scrounger

PEDIR [47] **1** *vt* (**a**) *(solicitar)* to ask for; **p. algo a alguien** to ask sb for sth; **me pidió (mi) opinión** she asked me (for) my opinion; **p. un taxi (por teléfono)** to ring for a taxi; **p. a alguien que haga algo** to ask sb to do sth; **le pido que sea breve, por favor** I would ask you to be brief, please; **le pedí que saliera conmigo** I asked her out; **p. a alguien en matrimonio, p. la mano de alguien** to ask for sb's hand (in marriage); **p. prestado algo a alguien** to borrow sth from sb; **pide un millón por la moto** he's asking a million for the motorbike; **no tienes más que pedirlo** all you need to do is ask; **si no es mucho p.** if it's not too much to ask; EXPR *CAm, Méx* **p. raid** to hitch a ride *o Br* lift
(**b**) *(en bares, restaurantes)* to order; **¿qué has pedido de postre?** what have you ordered for dessert?
(**c**) *(mercancías)* to order; **p. algo a alguien** to order sth from sb
(**d**) *(exigir)* to demand; **¡pido que se me escuche!** I demand to be heard!; **le pedimos al gobierno una inmediata retirada de las tropas** we demand that the government withdraw its troops immediately; **la acusación pide veinte años de cárcel** the prosecution is asking for twenty years
(**e**) *(requerir)* to call for, to need; **los cactus piden poca agua** cacti don't need a lot of water; **esta cocina está pidiendo a gritos que la limpies** this kitchen is crying out for you to clean it
2 *vi* (**a**) *(mendigar)* to beg; **hay mucha gente pidiendo por la calle** there are a lot of beggars in the streets
(**b**) *(en bares, restaurantes)* to order; **¿han pedido ya?** have you ordered?
(**c**) *(rezar)* **p. por el alma de alguien** to pray for sb's soul
3 pedirse *vpr (escoger)* **¿qué pastel te pides tú?** which cake do you want?; **¡me pido primero para subir al columpio!** *(uso infantil) Br* bags I get first go on the swing!, *US* dibs on first go on the swing!

---

pedo 1 *adj inv Esp, Méx Fam* **estar p.** to be smashed *o Br* pissed
2 *nm* (**a**) *(ventosidad)* fart; **echarse** *o* **tirarse un p.** to fart
(**b**) *Fam (borrachera)* **agarrarse** *o Esp* **cogerse un p.** to get smashed *o Br* pissed; *RP* **estar en p.** to be smashed *o Br* pissed
(**c**) *Méx Fam (problema)* problem; **se armó un gran p.** there was a big free-for-all *o* bust-up
(**d**) EXPR *RP Fam* **al p.** *(inútilmente)* for nothing; *RP Fam* **a los pedos** *(rapidísimo)* in a flash, double quick; *RP Fam* **de p.** *(de casualidad)* by chance, *Br* by a fluke; *Méx muy Fam* **hacerla de p.** to be a pain; *RP Fam* **ni en p.** no way, never in a million years; *Méx muy Fam* **no hay p.** it's OK; *Méx muy Fam* **ponerse al p.** to square up *(for a fight)*
3 *nm,f Méx Fam* drunk

pedofilia *nf* paedophilia

pedófilo, -a *nm,f* paedophile

pedología *nf* pedology

pedorrear *vi Fam* to fart a lot

pedorrero, -a *Fam* **1** *adj* **es muy p.** he's always farting
2 *nm,f* **es un p.** he's always farting

pedorreta *nf Fam* raspberry *(sound)*

pedorro, -a *Fam* **1** *adj* **(a)** *(que se tira pedos)* **es muy p.** he's always farting **(b)** *(tonto, pesado)* **ser p.** to be a drag *o* pain
2 *nm,f* **(a)** *(que se tira pedos)* **es un p.** he's always farting **(b)** *(tonto, pesado)* drag, pain

pedrada *nf* **(a)** *(golpe)* **rompió la ventana de una p.** he smashed the window with a stone; **recibieron a la policía a pedradas** the police were met by a hail of stones; **el árbitro recibió una p. en la cabeza** the referee was hit on the head by a stone; **matar a pedradas a alguien** to stone sb to death; **pegar una p. a alguien** to hit sb with a stone; EXPR *Fam* **venir como p. en ojo de boticario** to be just what one needed
(b) *Méx Fam (indirecta)* snide remark; **tirar pedradas a alguien** to make snide remarks about sb

pedrea *nf* **(a)** *Esp (en lotería)* = group of smaller prizes in the Spanish national lottery **(b)** *(lucha)* stone fight

pedregal *nm* stony ground

pedregoso, -a *adj* stony

pedregullo *nm RP* gravel

pedrejón *nm* boulder, rock

pedrera *nf* stone quarry

pedrería *nf* precious stones

pedrero *nm (cantero)* stonecutter, quarryman

pedrisco *nm* hail

pedriza *nf (terreno)* rocky *o* stony ground

Pedro *n pr* **San P.** St Peter; *Fam Hum* **P. Botero** Old Nick

pedrusco *nm* **(a)** *(roca)* rough stone **(b)** *Esp Fam (piedra preciosa)* huge jewel

pedunculado, -a *adj Bot* pedunculate

pedúnculo *nm Bot* stalk, *Espec* peduncle

peeling ['pilin] *(pl* **peelings***)* *nm* face mask *o* pack

peerse *vpr* to fart

pega *nf* **(a)** *Esp (obstáculo)* difficulty, hitch; **la p. que tiene es que es muy caro** the only problem is it's very expensive; **le puso muchas pegas a nuestra propuesta** he kept raising objections to our proposal; **me pusieron muchas pegas para conseguir el visado** they made a lot of problems before they gave me a visa; **le veo muchas pegas al plan** I see a lot of problems with the plan
(b) de p. *(falso)* false, fake; **un Rolex de p.** a fake Rolex; **un electricista de p.** a bogus electrician
(c) *Andes, Cuba Fam (trabajo)* job; **está buscando p.** he's looking for work *o* a job

pegada *nf* **(a)** *(en boxeo)* punch; *(en fútbol)* kick; *(en tenis, golf)* shot; **un boxeador con una fuerte p.** a boxer with a powerful punch; **un delantero con buena p.** a forward with a good *o* powerful kick
(b) *(colocación)* **la campaña comenzó con la p. de carteles** the campaign started with posters being stuck *o* put up
(c) *RP Fam (acierto)* **¡qué p. fue comprar esa casa en aquel momento!** what a stroke of luck it was, buying that house when we did!; **fue una p. llamar antes de salir** it was lucky we phoned before we left

pegadizo, -a *adj* **(a)** *(música)* catchy **(b)** *(contagioso)* catching

pegado 1 *adj* **(a)** *(junto)* **nuestra oficina está pegada a la suya** our office is right next to theirs; **ha aparcado el coche demasiado p. al mío** he's parked his car too close to mine; **su novio estuvo p. a ella durante toda la fiesta** her boyfriend was glued to her side all through the party; **lleva cinco horas p. al televisor** he's been glued to the television for five hours
(b) *(con pegamento)* glued, stuck; **la suela está pegada al zapato** the sole is glued *o* stuck to the shoe
(c) *Esp Fam (asombrado)* amazed, flabbergasted; **me dejó p. con su respuesta** I was amazed *o* flabbergasted at his answer; **me quedé p. cuando me enteré** I was amazed *o* flabbergasted when I found out
(d) *Esp Fam* **estar p.** *(no saber)* not to have a clue; **en latín estoy p.** I'm hopeless at Latin
2 *nm (parche)* plaster

pegadura *nf Col, Ecuad (burla)* trick

pegajoso, -a *adj* **(a)** *(adhesivo)* sticky; **tengo las suelas pegajosas** the soles of my shoes are sticky **(b)** *(calor)* sticky; *(frío)* clammy **(c)** *Fam (persona)* clingy, clinging; **es muy p.** he's very clingy **(d)** *Méx (música)* catchy

pegamento *nm* glue

pegante *nm Col* glue

pegapega *nf Col, RP (de caza)* birdlime

PEGAR [38] *vt* **(a)** *(adherir)* to stick; *(con pegamento)* to glue; *(póster, cartel)* to fix, to put up; *(botón)* to sew on; **pegó la suela al zapato** he stuck the sole on the shoe
(b) *(arrimar)* **p. algo a** *o* **contra algo** to put *o* place sth against sth; **no pegues la silla tanto a la pared** don't put the chair so close up against the wall; **pega el coche un poco más a la acera** move the car in a bit closer to the *Br* pavement *o US* sidewalk
(c) *(golpear)* to hit; **el balón me pegó en la cara** the ball hit me in the face; **pega a su mujer/a sus hijos** he beats his wife/children
(d) *(dar) (bofetada, paliza, patada)* to give; **pegó un golpe sobre la mesa** he banged the table; **p. un golpe a alguien** to hit sb; **p. un susto a alguien** to give sb a fright; **p. un disgusto a alguien** to upset sb; **p. un tiro a alguien** to shoot sb
(e) *(realizar, producir)* **p. un bostezo** to yawn; **p. un grito** to cry out, to let out a cry; **no arreglas nada pegando gritos** it's no use shouting; **p. un respingo** to (give a) start; **pegaban saltos de alegría** they were jumping for joy; **p. un suspiro** to (give a) sigh; **p. fuego a algo** to set sth on fire, to set fire to sth
(f) *(contagiar)* **p. algo a alguien** to give sb sth, to pass sth on to sb; **le pegó el sarampión a su hermano** she gave her brother measles
(g) *(corresponder a, ir bien a)* to suit; **no le pega ese vestido** that dress doesn't suit her; **esta corbata pega con esa camisa** this tie goes with that shirt; **no le pega ese novio** that boyfriend isn't right for her
(h) *Informát* to paste
(i) *Fam (tener el hábito de)* **le pega mucho al vino** he likes his wine
(j) *RP Fam* **pegarla** *(acertar)* to be spot on; **la pegamos con esa idea** we were spot on with that idea
2 *vi* **(a)** *(adherir)* to stick
(b) *(golpear)* to hit; **la lluvia pegaba en la ventana** the rain was driving against the windowpane; **una bala pegó contra el techo** a bullet hit the ceiling; **la pelota pegó en el larguero** the ball hit the crossbar
(c) *(armonizar)* to go together, to match; **no pegan nada** they don't go together *o* match at all; **no pega mucho un bingo en este barrio** a bingo hall doesn't really fit *o* looks rather out of place in this part of town; **p. con** to go with; **un color que pegue (bien) con el rojo** a colour that goes (well) with red
(d) *Fam (ser fuerte) (sol)* to beat down; *(viento, aire)* to be strong; *(vino, licor, droga)* to be strong stuff, to pack a punch; **el aire pega de costado** there's a strong side wind; **¡cómo pega el sol!** it's absolutely scorching!
(e) *(estar al lado)* **p. a** *o* **con** to be right next to; **el restaurante pega con la estación** the restaurant's right next to the station
(f) *Fam (tener éxito, estar de moda)* to be in; **este grupo está pegando mucho últimamente** this group is massive at the moment; **una nueva generación de tenistas viene pegando fuerte** a new generation of tennis players is beginning to come through
3 pegarse *vpr* **(a)** *(adherirse)* to stick; *Fig* **se pega a la televisión y no hace otra cosa** he just sits in front of the television all day and never moves
(b) *(guiso, comida)* to stick; **se me ha pegado el arroz** the rice has stuck (to the pan)
(c) *(pelearse, agredirse)* to fight, to hit one another
(d) *(golpearse)* **pegarse (un golpe) con** *o* **contra algo** to bump into sth; **me he pegado con el pico de la mesa** I bumped into the corner of the table; **me pegué (un golpe) en la pierna/la cabeza** I hit *o* bumped my leg/head; *Esp Fam* **perdimos el control del coche y nos la pegamos contra un árbol** we lost control of the car and smashed into a tree
(e) *(contagiarse) (enfermedad)* to be passed on; *(canción)* to be catchy; **no te me acerques, que se te pegará el resfriado** don't come near me, you don't want to catch my cold off me; **se me pegó su acento** I picked up his accent; **se le ha pegado el sentido del humor británico** the British sense of humour has rubbed off on her
(f) *Fig (engancharse)* **pegarse a alguien** to stick to sb; **se nos pegó y no hubo forma de librarse de él** he attached himself to us and we couldn't get rid of him
(g) *(darse) (baño, desayuno)* to have; **no me importaría pegarme unas buenas vacaciones** I wouldn't mind (having) a good holiday; **nos pegamos un viaje de diez horas** we had a ten-hour journey; **me pegué un buen susto** I got a real fright; **¡vaya siesta te has pegado!** that was certainly a long siesta you had there!; **pegarse un tiro** to shoot oneself; *Fig* **como la elijan a ella, me pego un tiro** if they choose her, I'll kill myself; *Perú Fam* **pegarse una muñequeada** to get the fright of one's life
(h) *Esp Fam (pasarse)* to spend; **se pega todo el rato protestando**

she spends all her time complaining; **se pegó el fin de semana en la cama** he spent the weekend in bed
(**i**) *Esp Fam* **pegársela a alguien** *(engañar)* to have sb on; *(cónyuge)* to cheat on sb; *Esp Fam* **se la pega a su marido con el vecino** she's cheating on her husband with the man next door

---

pegatina *nf Esp* sticker

pego *nm* EXPR *Esp Fam* **dar el p.** to look like the real thing; **no es piel auténtica pero da el p.** it's not real fur but it looks just like it *o* just like the real thing

pegote *nm Fam* (**a**) *(masa pegajosa)* sticky mess; **este arroz está hecho un p.** this rice is a sticky mess; **tenía la moto llena de pegotes de barro** her motorbike was covered in mud splashes
(**b**) *(chapucería)* botch; **el final de la película es un p.** the ending just doesn't go with the rest of the movie
(**c**) *Esp (mentira)* **tirarse pegotes** to tell tall stories, to boast; **se tiró el p. diciendo que era jugador de baloncesto** he spun a yarn about being a basketball player
(**d**) *RP (persona)* **es un p. de la madre** he's tied to his mother's apron strings, he's a mummy's boy; **esos dos están siempre como un p.** those two are like Siamese twins, they're never apart

pegoteado, -a *adj CSur Fam* sticky

pegotear *CSur Fam* **1** *vt* to make sticky
2 pegotearse *vpr* to get oneself all sticky

pegual *nm CSur* cinch, girth

pegue *nm Méx Fam* charisma, sex appeal; **ese cantante tiene mucho p.** that singer's got a lot of charisma *o* sex appeal

pehuén *nm* monkey-puzzle tree

pehuenche 1 *adj* Pehuenche, = relating to an indigenous people who inhabited part of present-day Chile
2 *nmf* Pehuenche, = member of an indigenous people who inhabited part of present-day Chile

peinado, -a 1 *adj* **siempre va muy peinada** she always has her hair very nicely done; **va muy mal p.** his hair's a mess
2 *nm* (**a**) *(acción)* combing (**b**) *(estilo, tipo)* hairstyle; *(más elaborado)* hairdo (**c**) *(rastreo)* thorough search; **la policía hizo un p. de la zona** the police combed the area

peinador, -ora 1 *nm* (**a**) *(bata)* dressing gown, robe (**b**) *Bol, Chile, Cuba (tocador)* dressing table
2 *nm,f Am (peluquero)* hairdresser

peinadora *nf Ven (tocador)* dressing table

peinar 1 *vt* (**a**) *(cabello) (con peine)* to comb; *(con cepillo)* to brush; **¿quién te peina?** who does your hair? (**b**) *(caballo, gato)* to comb, to groom (**c**) *(rastrear)* to comb (**d**) *(en fútbol)* **p. la pelota** to flick the ball on with one's head
2 peinarse *vpr* (**a**) *(cabello) (con peine)* to comb one's hair; *(con cepillo)* to brush one's hair; **no salgas así, ipéinate!** don't go out like that, comb your hair!; **me peino en la peluquería del barrio** I get my hair done at the local hairdresser's
(**b**) *RP Fam (ilusionarse)* to get one's hopes up; *Fig* **no te peines, mirá que en esta foto no salís** don't get your hopes up, you're not going to be in on this one

peine *nm* comb; **pasarse el p.** to comb one's hair; EXPR *Esp Fam* **enterarse de** *o* **saber lo que vale un p.** to find out what's what *o* a thing or two

peineta *nf* (**a**) *(adorno)* = decorative comb worn in hair (**b**) *Chile (peine)* comb

peinilla *nf* (**a**) *Am (peine)* comb (**b**) *Col (machete)* machete

p. ej. (*abrev de* **por ejemplo**) e.g.

pejesapo *nm* monkfish, angler (fish), *US* goosefish

pejiguera *nf Esp Fam* drag, pain

Pekín *n* Peking, Beijing

pekinés, -esa = **pequinés**

pela *nf Esp Fam (peseta)* peseta; **está forrado de pelas** he's rolling in it; **no tengo pelas** I'm broke *o Br* skint; EXPR **la p. es la p.** money makes the world go round

pelacables *nm inv* wire stripper

pelada *nf* (**a**) *CSur Fam (calva)* blunder (**b**) *Andes, Cuba, RP Fam* **la P.** *(la muerte)* the Grim Reaper (**c**) *ver también* **pelado**

peladero *nm* (**a**) *Andes, Ven (terreno)* wasteland (**b**) *Chile (solar)* site, *US* lot

peladez *nf Méx (actitud)* rudeness; *(dicho grosero)* rude *o* coarse remark

peladilla *nf* sugared almond

pelado, -a 1 *adj* (**a**) *(cabeza)* shorn
(**b**) *(fruta)* peeled
(**c**) *(piel, cara)* **tengo la nariz pelada** my nose is peeling
(**d**) *(habitación, monte, árbol)* bare
(**e**) *(número)* exact, round; **el treinta p.** a round thirty
(**f**) *(mínimo)* **saqué un aprobado p.** I passed, but only just; **nos sirvieron un vino p., y ya está** they gave us a mingy glass of wine, and that was it
(**g**) *Fam (sin dinero)* broke, *Br* skint; **estar p.** to be broke *o Br* skint
(**h**) *CSur Fam (calvo)* bald
(**i**) *CAm, Méx Fam (grosero)* rude, foulmouthed
2 *nm Esp Fam (corte de pelo)* **iqué p. te han metido!** you've really been scalped!
3 *nm,f* (**a**) *Andes Fam (niño, adolescente)* kid (**b**) *Andes Fam (novio)* childhood sweetheart (**c**) *CAm, Méx Fam (persona humilde)* common person, *Br* pleb, *Br* oik; **la plaza estaba llena de pelados** the square was full of riffraff *o Br* plebs (**d**) *CSur Fam (calvo)* baldy

pelador, -ora *nm,f* peeler

peladura *nf* peeling; **p. de naranja** orange peel

pelagatos *nmf inv Fam Pey* nobody

pelágico, -a *adj* deep-sea, *Espec* pelagic

pelaje *nm* (**a**) *(de gato, oso, conejo)* fur; *(de perro, caballo)* coat (**b**) *Fam Pey (aspecto)* look; **no me gusta su p.** I don't like the look of him (**c**) *Fam Pey (calaña)* **gente de ese p.** people of that sort (**d**) *Fam (cantidad de pelo)* mop

pelambre *nm* (**a**) *(de pelo)* mane *o* mop of hair (**b**) *Chile Fam (chisme)* gossip; **un p.** a piece of gossip

pelambrera *nf Fam* long thick hair; **deberías cortarte esa p.** you should get that mop of hair cut

pelanas *nmf inv Fam* poor devil, wretch

pelandrún, -una *nm,f RP* rascal, rogue

pelandusca *nf Fam Pey* tart, slut

pelapapas *nm inv Am* potato peeler

pelapatatas *nm inv Esp* potato peeler

pelar 1 *vt* (**a**) *(fruta, patatas)* to peel; *(guisantes, marisco)* to shell
(**b**) *(cable)* to strip; *(caramelo)* to unwrap
(**c**) *(aves)* to pluck; *(conejos)* to skin; EXPR *Fam* **p. la pava** *(novios)* to flirt, to have a lovey-dovey conversation; EXPR **p. el diente** *CAm, Col (coquetear)* to flirt; *Carib (adular)* to flatter
(**d**) *Fam (persona)* to scalp; **me han pelado** I've been scalped; **lo pelaron al cero** he had his head shaved
(**e**) *Fam Fig (dejar sin dinero)* to clean out, to fleece
(**f**) *Méx Fam (hacer caso)* **no me pela** he doesn't pay any attention to me
2 *vi* EXPR *Fam* **hace un frío que pela** it's freezing cold; *RP Fam* **está que pela** *(caliente)* it's boiling (hot); *Ven Fam* **estar pelando** to be broke *o Br* skint
3 pelarse *vpr* (**a**) *(piel, espalda)* to peel; **te estás pelando** you're peeling; **se me está pelando la cara** my face is peeling
(**b**) *Fam (cortarse el pelo)* to have one's hair cut; **tengo que ir a que me pelen** I've got to go and get my hair cut
(**c**) *muy Fam* **pelársela** *(masturbarse) Br* to wank, *US* to jerk off
(**d**) *CSur Fam* **pelárselas** *(largarse)* to clear off, *Br* to scarper; **se las peló para Europa** he upped *Br* sticks *o US* stakes and went to Europe
(**e**) EXPR *Fam* **pelarse de frío** to be frozen stiff, to be freezing cold; *Fam* **corre que se las pela** she runs like the wind

pelas *nm inv Esp Fam (taxi)* cab

pelazón *nf Ven Fam* poverty; **aquí la p. es mucha** there's a lot of poverty here

peldaño *nm (escalón)* step; *(de escalera de mano)* rung

pelea *nf* (**a**) *(a golpes)* fight; **una p. cuerpo a cuerpo** a hand-to-hand fight (**b**) *(discusión)* row, quarrel (**c**) *(combate)* fight; **una p. de gallos** a cockfight

peleado, -a *adj* (**a**) *(disputado) (combate, campaña electoral)* fierce, hard-fought; *(partido, carrera)* close (**b**) *(enfadado)* **está p. con su novia** he's had a row with his girlfriend; **están peleados** they've fallen out, they're not on good terms

pelear 1 *vi* (**a**) *(a golpes)* to fight (**b**) *(a gritos)* to have a row *o* quarrel; **han peleado y ya no se quieren ver** they've had a row *o* quarrelled, and don't want to see each other any more (**c**) *(esforzarse)* to fight hard, to struggle; **ha peleado por sacar a su familia adelante** he's fought hard *o* struggled to keep his family; **ha peleado mucho por ese puesto** she has fought hard to get that job
2 pelearse *vpr* (**a**) *(a golpes)* to fight; **se pelearon a patadas** they fought and kicked each other
(**b**) *(a gritos)* to have a row *o* quarrel; **se pelearon por una estupidez** they had a row *o* they quarrelled over a stupid little thing

(c) *(enfadarse)* to fall out; **se ha peleado con su hermano** he's fallen out with his brother; **se ha peleado con su novia** he's had a row with his girlfriend

pelechar *vi* (a) *(echar plumas)* to grow feathers (b) *RP Fam (prosperar)* to make good

pelela *nf CSur* potty

pelele *nm* (a) *Fam Pey (persona)* puppet (b) *(muñeco)* guy, straw doll (c) *Esp (prenda de bebé)* romper suit, *Br* Babygro®

peleón, -ona *adj* (a) *(persona)* **es muy p.** he's always getting into fights (b) *Fam (vino)* rough

peletería *nf* (a) *(tienda)* fur shop, furrier's (b) *(oficio)* furriery (c) *(pieles)* furs; **artículos de p.** furs

peletero, -a 1 *adj* fur; **industria peletera** fur trade
2 *nm,f* furrier

peli *nf Esp Fam* movie, *Br* flick

peliagudo, -a *adj* tricky

pelicano, -a *adj* grey-haired

pelícano *nm* pelican

película 1 *nf* (a) *(de cine)* movie, *Br* film; **una p. de** *Esp* **vídeo** *o Am* **video** a video (movie); **una p. de Scorsese** a Scorsese movie *o Br* film; **echar** *o* **poner una p.** to show a movie *o Br* film ►► ***p. de acción*** action movie *o Br* film; ***p. de animación*** animated feature film; ***p. de ciencia ficción*** science fiction movie *o Br* film; ***p. de culto*** cult movie *o Br* film; ***p. de dibujos animados*** feature-length cartoon; ***p. de época*** period *o* costume drama; ***p. de gángsters*** gangster movie *o Br* film; ***p. de miedo*** horror movie *o Br* film; ***p. muda*** silent movie *o Br* film; ***p. del Oeste*** western; ***p. porno*** porn movie; *Esp* ***p. de suspense*** thriller; *Am* ***p. de suspenso*** thriller; ***p. de terror*** horror movie *o Br* film; ***p. X*** X-rated movie *o Br* film
(b) *(fotográfica)* film; **una p. en blanco y negro/color** a black-and-white/colour film ►► ***p. fotográfica*** photographic film; ***p. virgen*** unexposed film
(c) *(capa)* film
(d) *Fam (historia increíble)* (tall) story; **montarse una p.** to dream up an incredible story
2 **de película** *loc adj Fam* **tienen una casa de p.** they've got a dream house; **pasamos unas vacaciones de p.** we had the holiday of our dreams
3 **de película** *loc adv Fam* **canta/baila de p.** she's a fabulous singer/dancer

peliculero, -a *Fam* 1 *adj* (a) *(cinéfilo)* **es muy p.** *(que va al cine)* he's a keen moviegoer *o Br* filmgoer; *(entiende de cine)* he's a real movie *o Br* film buff (b) *(fantasioso)* **es muy p.** he's got a very vivid imagination
2 *nm,f* (a) *(cinéfilo) (que va al cine)* moviegoer, *Br* filmgoer; *(que entiende de cine)* movie *o Br* film buff (b) *(fantasioso)* **es un p.** he's got a very vivid imagination

peliculón *nm Fam* fantastic *o* great movie *o Br* film

peligrar *vi* to be in danger; **su vida no peligra** her life is not in danger; **el asesinato hace p. el alto el fuego** the murder is threatening the ceasefire

peligro *nm* (a) *(situación)* danger; **ya ha pasado el p.** the danger has passed; **correr p. (de)** to be in danger (of); **corremos el p. de que se enfade** there's a danger that he'll get angry; **estar/poner en p.** to be/put at risk; **una especie en p. de extinción** an endangered species; **un animal en p. de extinción** an animal threatened with extinction; **fuera de p.** out of danger; **¡p. de muerte!** *(en letrero)* danger!; **p. de incendio** *(en letrero)* fire hazard
(b) *(persona, objeto)* **ser un p.** to be dangerous; **ese cable eléctrico es un p.** that electric cable is dangerous; **un p. público** a public menace

peligrosamente *adv* dangerously

peligrosidad *nf* dangerousness

peligroso, -a *adj* dangerous

pelillo *nm* EXPR *Esp Fam* **¡(echemos) pelillos a la mar!** let's just forget about it!

pelín *nm Esp Fam* **un p.** a little bit; **es un p. caro** it's a bit on the expensive side; **estoy un p. cansado** I'm a little bit tired; **te has pasado un p.** you've gone a little bit too far

pelirrojo, -a 1 *adj* ginger, red-headed
2 *nm,f* redhead

pella *nf Esp Fam* **hacer pellas** *Br* to skive off (school), *US* to play hookey

pelleja *nf (piel)* hide, skin

pellejería *nf* (a) *(lugar)* tannery (b) *(pieles)* skins, hides (c) *Andes Fam* **pellejerías** *(dificultades)* difficulties

pellejo *nm* (a) *(piel)* skin; EXPR *Fam* **estar/ponerse en el p. de otro** to be/put oneself in someone else's shoes; **si yo estuviera en tu p....** if I were in your shoes... (b) *Fam (vida)* skin; **arriesgar** *o* **jugarse el p.** to risk one's neck; **salvar el p.** to save one's skin (c) *(padrastro)* hangnail (d) *(odre)* wineskin

pellica *nf (manta)* = coverlet made of fine skins

pelliza *nf* fur jacket

pellizcar [60] *vt* (a) *(persona)* to pinch (b) *(pan)* to pick at

pellizco *nm* (a) *(en piel)* pinch; **dar un p. a alguien** to give sb a pinch (b) *(pequeña cantidad)* little bit; *(de sal)* pinch; *Fam* **un buen p.** *(de dinero)* a tidy sum

pellón *nm Am (cojín)* saddle pad

pelma *Esp Fam* 1 *adj* annoying, tiresome
2 *nmf* bore, pain

pelmazo, -a *Fam* 1 *adj* annoying, tiresome
2 *nm,f* bore, pain

PELO *nm* (a) *(cabello)* hair; **hay un p. en la sopa** there's a hair in my soup; **la bañera estaba llena de pelos** the bathtub was full of hairs; **se me está cayendo el p.** I'm losing my hair; **tiene un p. rubio precioso** she has lovely fair hair; **llevar** *o* **tener el p. de punta** to have spiky hair; **cortarse el p.** *(uno mismo)* to cut one's (own) hair; *(en peluquería)* to have one's hair cut; **teñirse el p.** to dye one's hair; **llevar el p. recogido/suelto** to wear one's hair up/loose; EXPR **se le va a caer el p.** he'll be in big trouble; EXPR *Méx Fam* **de pelos** *(muy bien)* great; EXPR *Chile Fam* **echar el p.** to chill; EXPR *Fam* **estar hasta los pelos** to be fed up; EXPR **así te luce el p.: no estudias nada y así te luce el p. en los exámenes** you never study and it shows in your exam results; EXPR **de medio p.** second-rate; EXPR *Fam* **te voy a dar para el p.** I'm going to give you what for; EXPR **ser un hombre de p. en pecho** to be a real man; EXPR **por los pelos, por un p.** by the skin of one's teeth, only just; EXPR *CSur Fam* **andar** *o* **estar con los pelos de punta** to be strung-out; EXPR **poner a alguien los pelos de punta** to make sb's hair stand on end; **se me pusieron los pelos de punta** it made my hair stand on end; EXPR **con pelos y señales** with all the details; EXPR **no tiene pelos en la lengua** she doesn't mince her words; EXPR **no tiene un p. de tonto** he's nobody's fool; EXPR **soltarse el p.** to let one's hair down; EXPR **tirarse de los pelos** *(de desesperación)* to tear one's hair out; EXPR **tocar un p. (de la ropa) a alguien** *(hacerle daño)* to lay a finger on sb; **no le toqué un p.** I never touched her, I never laid a finger on her; EXPR **tomar el p. a alguien** to pull sb's leg; EXPR **traído por los pelos** *(argumento, hipótesis)* farfetched; EXPR **venir a p.** *(en la conversación, discusión)* to be relevant; **venir al p. a alguien** to be just right for sb; EXPR **no ver el p. a alguien** not to see hide nor hair of sb; EXPR *Fam* **¡y yo con estos pelos!: ¡mi novio ha llegado y yo con estos pelos!** my boyfriend's arrived and I am in such a state *o* look such a mess!
(b) *(pelaje) (de oso, conejo, gato)* fur; *(de perro, caballo)* coat; EXPR **a p.: montar (a caballo) a** *o RP* **en p.** to ride bareback; *Fam* **presentarse a un examen a p.** to go to an exam unprepared; *Esp muy Fam* **follar a p.** to ride bareback *(have unprotected sex)* ►► ***p. de camello*** *(tejido)* camel hair
(c) *(de melocotón)* down
(d) *(de una tela, tejido)* nap; *(de alfombra)* pile; **este jersey suelta mucho p.** *o* **muchos pelos** this jumper leaves a lot of hairs everywhere
(e) *Fam (pizca, poquito)* **échame un p. más de ginebra** could I have a smidgin *o* tad more gin?; **pasarse un p.** to go a bit too far; **no me gusta (ni) un p. ese tipo** I don't like that guy at all

---

pelón, -ona 1 *adj Fam* (a) *(sin pelo)* bald (b) *Méx (difícil)* tricky; **está p. pasar el examen si no estudiaste** you're going to have a job passing the exam if you haven't done any studying
2 *nm* (a) *RP (fruta)* nectarine (b) *Ven Fam (error)* blunder

pelona *nf CAm, Col, Méx Fam* **la P.** *(la muerte)* Death, the Grim Reaper

Peloponeso *n* **el P.** the Peloponnese

pelota[1] 1 *nf* (a) *(balón)* ball; **p. de golf/de tenis** golf/tennis ball; **jugar a la p.** to play ball; EXPR *Esp* **la p. está en el tejado** it's in the air; EXPR *Esp* **la p. está en su tejado** the ball is in their court; EXPR *CSur* **dar p. (a algo/alguien)** to pay attention (to sth/sb); **dame p. cuando te hablo** listen to me *o* pay attention when I'm talking to you; **la biodiversidad es una cuestión seria, hay que darle p.** biodiversity is a serious issue that deserves our attention; EXPR **devolver la p. a alguien** to put the ball back into sb's court; EXPR *Esp Fam* **hacer la p. (a alguien)** to suck up (to sb); EXPR **pasarse la p.** to pass the buck ►► ***p. base*** baseball; *Arg* ***p. al cesto*** = school sport similar to basketball played by teams of six players; ***p. de goma*** rubber bullet; ***p. mano*** = pelota played with the hand as opposed to a basket strapped to the hand; ***p. vasca*** pelota, jai alai (**b**) *muy Fam (testículo)* **pelotas** balls; EXPR **en pelotas,** *Esp* **en p. picada** *Br* starkers, *US* butt-naked; EXPR *RP* **¡las pelotas!** balls to that!; EXPR **no me sale de las pelotas** I can't be arsed; EXPR **estar hasta las pelotas: estoy hasta las pelotas de ellos** I've had it up to here with them; EXPR *RP* **tener las pelotas llenas (de algo/de alguien)** to be pissed off (about sth/with sb); EXPR *RP* **llenar las pelotas a alguien** to piss sb off; **claro que está de mal humor, le llenaron las pelotas todo el día** of course he's in a bad mood, *Br* they've been getting on his tits *o US* they've been on his ass all day; EXPR **rascarse** *o* **tocarse las pelotas: se pasa todo el día rascándose** *o* **tocándose las pelotas** he spends the whole day pissing about *o* around

(**c**) *Am (béisbol)* baseball

2 *nmf* EXPR *RP Fam* **ser un pelotas** to be a lazy so-and-so

pelota[2] *Esp Fam Pey* 1 *adj (adulador)* **es muy p.** he's always sucking up to people, he's a real creep

2 *nmf (persona)* creep, crawler

pelotari *nmf* pelota player

pelotazo *nm* (**a**) *(con pelota)* **rompió el espejo de un p.** she smashed the mirror with the ball; **me dieron un p. en la cabeza** they hit me on the head with the ball (**b**) *Esp Fam (copa)* drink; **un p. de ginebra** a gin (**c**) *Esp Fam (enriquecimiento)* **la cultura del p.** = ruthless obsession with money and power; **pegar un p.** to make a killing

pelotear *vi (en tenis)* to knock up; *(en fútbol)* to kick a ball about

peloteo *nm* (**a**) *(en tenis)* knock-up; *(en fútbol)* kickabout (**b**) *Esp Fam (adulación)* creeping; **se le da muy bien el p.** he's an expert at sucking up to people

pelotera *nf Fam* row; **cuando le negaron la solicitud montó una p.** she kicked up a row when her application was turned down

pelotero, -a 1 *adj Esp Fam Pey* **es muy p.** he's always sucking up to people

2 *nm,f* (**a**) *Esp Fam Pey (adulador)* creep, crawler (**b**) *Am (jugador de béisbol)* baseball player (**c**) *CSur (recogepelotas)* ball boy, *f* ball girl

pelotilla *nf Fam* (**a**) *Esp* **hacer la p. a alguien** *(adular)* to suck up to sb (**b**) *(bolita) (de moco)* bogey, *US* booger; *(de suciedad)* = ball of grime rubbed from skin

pelotillero, -a *Esp Fam Pey* 1 *adj* **es muy p.** he's always sucking up to people

2 *nm,f* creep, crawler

pelotón *nm* (**a**) *(de soldados)* squad ►► ***p. de ejecución*** firing squad; ***p. de fusilamiento*** firing squad

(**b**) *(de gente)* crowd; **la esperaba un p. de periodistas** there was a pack of journalists waiting for her ►► *Fam Hum* ***el p. de los torpes*** the incompetent brigade

(**c**) *(de ciclistas)* bunch, peloton; *Fig* **una empresa en el p. de cabeza de las ganancias** a company which is at the top end of the earnings league; *Fig* **un país que no consigue abandonar el p. de cola de los más pobres** a country that has consistently ranked among the world's poorest

pelotudear *vi RP Fam* to mess about *o* around

pelotudez *nf RP Fam* (**a**) *(acto)* damn stupid thing; *(dicho)* damn stupid remark; **hacer una p.** to do something damn stupid; **hacer pelotudeces** to behave like an idiot; **decir una p.** to say something damn stupid; **decir pelotudeces** to talk nonsense

(**b**) *(cosa insignificante)* stupid little thing; **se pelearon por una p.** they fell out over something really stupid; **le compré una p.** I bought her a silly little present

(**c**) *(pereza)* **ayer no hice nada, me dio un ataque de p.** I didn't do anything yesterday, I just couldn't be bothered *o Br* fagged

pelotudo, -a *adj RP Fam* (**a**) *(estúpido)* damn stupid (**b**) *(grande)* massive; **tengo que leer un libro p. para la próxima clase** I've got this really massive book to read for the next class; **se compraron una casa pelotuda** they bought a massive house

peltre *nm* pewter

peluca *nf* wig; **llevar p.** to wear a wig

peluche *nm* (**a**) *(material)* plush (**b**) *(muñeco)* cuddly toy; **osito de p.** teddy bear (**c**) EXPR *Méx Fam* **de peluches** *(muy bien)* great

peluco *nm Esp Fam (reloj)* watch

pelucón, -ona *adj Perú Fam* **es muy p.** he's got long hair

peluda *nf (pez)* scaldfish

peludo, -a 1 *adj (con pelo)* hairy (**b**) *Ven Fam (complicado)* tricky

2 *nm RP* (**a**) *(animal)* armadillo; EXPR *Fam* **caer como p. de regalo** to appear out of the blue (**b**) *Fam (borrachera)* **agarrar un p.** to get plastered

peluquearse *vpr Am Fam* to get *o* have one's hair done

peluquería *nf* (**a**) *(establecimiento)* hairdresser's (shop); **p. de caballeros** barber's, *Br* men's hairdresser's, *US* barbershop; **p. de señoras** ladies' hairdressers (**b**) *(oficio)* hairdressing

peluquero, -a *nm,f* hairdresser

peluquín *nm* toupee; EXPR *Esp Fam Hum* **ni hablar del p.** no way, José

pelusa[1] *nf* (**a**) *(de tela)* fluff (**b**) *(vello)* down (**c**) *(de polvo)* ball of fluff (**d**) *Esp Fam (celos)* **tener p. de** to be jealous of

pelusa[2] *nmf Chile Fam* urchin

pelviano, -a, pélvico, -a *adj* pelvic

pelvis *nf inv* pelvis

PEMEX ['pemeks] *nmpl* (*abrev de* **Petróleos Mexicanos**) = Mexican state oil company

---

PENA *nf* (**a**) *(lástima)* shame, pity; **es una p. (que no puedas venir)** it's a shame *o* pity (you can't come); **da p. no poder hacer nada** it's a shame *o* pity we can't do anything; **el pobre me da p.** I feel sorry for the poor guy; **me da p. ver lo pobres que son** it's awful to see how poor they are; **me da p. tener que irme ya** I hate to have to leave already; **¡qué p.!** what a shame *o* pity!; **¡qué p. de hijo tengo!** what a useless son I've got!

(**b**) *(tristeza)* sadness, sorrow; **sentía una gran p.** I felt terribly sad

(**c**) *(desgracia)* problem, trouble; **bebe para olvidar** *o* **ahogar las penas** he drinks to drown his sorrows; **me contó sus penas** she told me her troubles *o* about her problems

(**d**) *(dificultad)* struggle; **pasaron grandes penas durante la guerra** they suffered great hardship during the war; **subimos el piano a duras penas** we got the piano up the stairs with great difficulty; **con mi sueldo mantengo a duras penas a mi familia** my salary is barely enough for me to support my family; **consiguieron llegar a duras penas** they only just managed to get there

(**e**) *(castigo)* punishment; **le cayó** *o* **le impusieron una p. de treinta años** he was sentenced to *o* given thirty years; **cumplió p. en la prisión de Alcatraz** he served his sentence in Alcatraz; *Formal* **so** *o* **bajo p. de** *(bajo castigo de)* under penalty of; *(a menos que)* unless ►► ***p. capital*** death penalty; ***p. de cárcel*** prison sentence; ***p. máxima*** *(jurídica)* maximum sentence; *(en fútbol)* penalty; ***p. de muerte*** death penalty; ***p. de reclusión*** prison sentence

(**f**) *CAm, Carib, Col, Méx (vergüenza)* embarrassment; **me da p.** I'm embarrassed about it; **me da p. molestar** I'm terribly sorry to bother you; **tengo p. de hablar con ella** I'm too embarrassed to talk to her

(**g**) EXPR *Esp Fam* **de p.:** *(muy mal)* **lo pasamos de p.** we had an awful time; **dibuja/cocina de p.** he can't draw/cook to save his life, he's useless at drawing/cooking; **ese peinado le queda de p.** that haircut looks terrible on her; *Fam* **hecho una p.** in a real state; **(no) valer** *o* **merecer la p.** (not) to be worthwhile *o* worth it; **una película que merece la p.** a movie that's worth seeing; **vale la p. intentarlo** it's worth a try; **no merece la p. que te preocupes tanto** there's no point you getting so worried; **sin p. ni gloria** without distinction; **un jugador que pasó por el equipo sin p. ni gloria** a player who had an undistinguished career in the team; **el año acabó sin p. ni gloria** it was a wholly unremarkable year

---

penacho *nm* (**a**) *(de pájaro)* crest (**b**) *(adorno)* plume

penado, -a *nm,f* convict

penal 1 *adj* criminal; **derecho p.** criminal law

2 *nm* (**a**) *(prisión)* prison (**b**) *Am (penalti)* penalty

pénal *nm Andes* penalty

penalidad *nf* suffering, hardship; **sufrieron muchas penalidades** they suffered great hardship

penalista *nmf (abogado)* criminal lawyer

penalización *nf* (**a**) *(acción)* penalization (**b**) *(sanción)* penalty (**c**) *(en deporte)* penalty; **una p. de dos minutos** a two-minute penalty

penalizar [14] *vt* (**a**) *(sancionar)* to penalize (**b**) *(en deporte)* to penalize

penalti, penalty *nm* penalty; **cometer un p.** to give away a penalty; **ganar por penaltis** to win on penalties; **marcar de p.** to score a penalty; **parar un p.** to save a penalty; **señalar (un) p.** to award a penalty, to point to the spot; **transformar un p.** to score *o* convert a penalty; EXPR *Esp Fam* **casarse de p.** to have a shotgun wedding ►► ***p. córner*** *(en hockey)* penalty *o* short corner

penar 1 *vt (castigar)* to punish; **un delito penado con cárcel** an offence punishable by imprisonment

2 *vi (sufrir)* to suffer

penates *nmpl Mitol* household gods

penca[1] *nf* (**a**) *(de cactus)* fleshy leaf (**b**) *Méx (racimo)* bunch (**c**) *Urug (lotería)* sweepstake *(among friends or co-workers)* (**d**) *Chile Vulg (pene)* prick

penca[2] *adj Chile Fam* (**a**) *(hecho)* god-awful, really crap (**b**) *(objeto)* crap, crappy (**c**) *(persona)* crap (**d**) *(mujer)* **anda con una mina p.** he's going out with a real dog

pencar *vi Esp Fam* to work

pendanga *nf Ven* Surinam cherry

pendejada *nf Am muy Fam* (**a**) *(acto) Br* bloody *o US* goddamn stupid thing; *(dicho) Br* bloody *o US* goddamn stupid remark; **hacer una p.** to do something *Br* bloody *o US* goddamn stupid; **hacer pendejadas** to behave like a *Br* bloody *o US* goddamn idiot; **decir una p.** to say something *Br* bloody *o US* goddamn stupid; **decir pendejadas** to talk a load of *Br* bloody *o US* goddamn nonsense
(**b**) *(cosa insignificante) Br* bloody *o US* goddamn stupid little thing; **se pelearon por una p.** they fell out over something *Br* bloody *o US* goddamn stupid; **le compré una p.** I bought her some stupid piece of crap

pendejear *vi Méx Fam* to mess about *o* around

pendejo, -a 1 *nm muy Fam (pelo)* pube; EXPR *RP muy Fam Hum* **un p. tira más que una yunta de bueyes** sex appeal can move mountains
2 *nm,f* (**a**) *Méx Fam (cobarde)* coward (**b**) *Am muy Fam (tonto)* jerk, *Br* tosser; EXPR *Méx Fam* **hacerse p.** to act dumb (**c**) *RP muy Fam Pey (adolescente)* spotty teenager

pendencia *nf* (**a**) *(riña)* quarrel, fight (**b**) *Der* lis pendens, pending lawsuit

pendenciero, -a 1 *adj* **es muy p.** he's always getting into fights
2 *nm,f* **es un p.** he's always getting into fights

pendentif [penden'tif] *(pl* **pendentifs***) nm Andes* earring

pender *vi* (**a**) *(colgar)* to hang (**de** from); EXPR **p. de un hilo** to be hanging by a thread (**b**) *(amenaza, catástrofe)* **p. sobre** to hang over (**c**) *(sentencia)* to be pending; **el juicio pende ante el tribunal** the court is still considering the evidence

pendiente 1 *adj* (**a**) *(por resolver)* pending; *(deuda)* outstanding; **estar p. de** *(a la espera de)* to be waiting for; **tiene dos asignaturas pendientes** she has to retake two subjects; EXPR **estar p. de un hilo** to be hanging by a thread
(**b**) **estar p. de** *(atento a)* to keep an eye on; **estoy p. de conocer la respuesta** I'm anxious to know the reply; **vive p. del teléfono** she spends her life waiting for the phone to ring
(**c**) *(colgante)* hanging
2 *nm* (**a**) *Esp (adorno)* earring ▸▸ ***p. de clip*** clip-on earring (**b**) *Am (asunto)* unresolved matter; **la lista de pendientes es enorme** there is an enormous backlog of matters to be dealt with
3 *nf* (**a**) *(cuesta)* slope; **una calle con mucha p.** a very steep street; **el terreno está en p.** the ground slopes *o* is on a slope; **una p. del 20 por ciento** a 1:5 gradient (**b**) *(de tejado)* pitch

péndola *nf* (**a**) *(péndulo)* pendulum (**b**) *(reloj)* pendulum clock (**c**) *(de puente)* suspension cable

pendón[1] *nm (estandarte)* banner

pendón[2], **-ona** *nm,f Esp Fam* (**a**) *(golfa)* floozy (**b**) *(vago)* layabout, good-for-nothing

pendonear *vi Esp Fam* to hang out

pendoneo *nm Esp Fam* **les gusta ir de p. con sus amigos** they like hanging out with their friends; **en vez de trabajar se pasa todas las tardes de p.** instead of working he spends all his afternoons lazing around

pendular *adj (movimiento)* swinging, swaying

péndulo *nm* pendulum

pene *nm* penis

peneca *nmf Chile Fam* primary school pupil

penene *nmf Fam* = untenured teacher or lecturer

peneque *nm Méx* = fried, cheese-filled tortilla

penetrabilidad *nf* penetrability

penetración *nf* (**a**) *(introducción)* penetration; **no logró detener la p. del delantero por la banda** he couldn't stop the forward from advancing up the wing; **un país con escasa p. de Internet** a country with low Internet penetration ▸▸ *Econ* ***p. de mercado*** market penetration (**b**) *(sexual)* penetration (**c**) *(sagacidad)* astuteness, sharpness

penetrante *adj* (**a**) *(intenso) (dolor)* acute; *(olor)* sharp; *(frío)* biting; *(mirada)* penetrating; *(voz, sonido)* piercing (**b**) *(sagaz)* sharp, penetrating

penetrar 1 *vi* **el agua penetraba por la puerta** the water was seeping under the door; **la luz penetraba por entre las rendijas** the light came filtering through the cracks; **p. en** *o Am* **a** *(internarse en)* to enter; *(filtrarse por)* to get into, to penetrate; *(perforar)* to pierce; *(llegar a conocer)* to get to the bottom of; **cinco terroristas penetraron en el palacio** five terrorists got into the palace; **no consiguen p. en el mercado europeo** they have been unable to penetrate the European market
2 *vt* (**a**) *(introducirse en) (sujeto: arma, sonido)* to pierce, to penetrate; *(sujeto: humedad, líquido)* to permeate; *(sujeto: emoción, sentimiento)* to pierce; **la bala le penetró el corazón** the bullet pierced her heart; **el frío les penetraba hasta los huesos** they were chilled to the bone; **el grito le penetró los oídos** the scream pierced her eardrums; **han penetrado el mercado latinoamericano** they have made inroads into *o* penetrated the Latin American market
(**b**) *(secreto, misterio)* to get to the bottom of
(**c**) *(sexualmente)* to penetrate

peneuvista *Esp* 1 *adj* = of/relating to the Basque nationalist party PNV
2 *nmf* = member/supporter of the Basque nationalist party PNV

peni *nf Chile Fam Br* nick, *US* joint

penicilina *nf* penicillin

penillanura *nf Geog* erosion plain, peneplain

Peninos *n* **los montes P.** the Pennines

península *nf* peninsula ▸▸ ***la p. Arábiga*** the Arabian peninsula; ***la p. Ibérica*** the Iberian peninsula; ***la p. de Yucatán*** the Yucatan peninsula

peninsular 1 *adj* peninsular
2 *nmf* peninsular Spaniard

penique *nm* penny; **peniques** pence

penitencia *nf* (**a**) *(religiosa)* penance; **hacer p.** to do penance (**b**) *RP Fam (castigo)* punishment; **está en p.** he's in disgrace; **lo pusieron en p.** they punished him

penitenciaría *nf* prison, *US* penitentiary

penitenciario, -a *adj* prison; **régimen p.** prison regime

penitente *nmf* penitent

penol *nm Náut* yardarm

penoso, -a *adj* (**a**) *(trabajoso)* backbreaking; **llegaron a puerto tras una travesía penosa** they reached port after an arduous crossing (**b**) *(lamentable)* dreadful; **el arbitraje fue p.** the refereeing was dreadful; **tenía un aspecto p.** he was a sorry sight (**c**) *CAm, Carib, Col, Méx (embarazoso)* embarrassing (**d**) *CAm, Carib, Col, Méx (persona)* shy

penquista 1 *adj* of/from Concepción *(Chile)*
2 *nmf* person from Concepción *(Chile)*

pensado, -a *adj* **en el día/momento menos p.** when one least expects it; **no está p. para niños menores de cinco años** it's not designed *o* intended for children under five; **tener p.** to have in mind, to intend; **mal p.** twisted, evil-minded; **un mal p.** a twisted person; **bien p.** on reflection; **un sistema muy bien p.** a very well conceived *o* well thought-out system

pensador, -ora *nm,f* thinker

pensamiento *nm* (**a**) *(facultad)* thought; *(mente)* mind; **se debe potenciar la capacidad de p. en los alumnos** pupils should be encouraged to think; **sumido en sus pensamientos** deep in thought; **no me pasó por el p.** it never crossed my mind; **leer el p. a alguien** to read sb's mind *o* thoughts ▸▸ ***p. lateral*** lateral thinking
(**b**) *(idea)* idea, thought; **el p. socialdemócrata** social democratic thought *o* thinking ▸▸ *Pol* ***el p. único:*** **según el p. único...** according to the current free-market liberal-democratic consensus...
(**c**) *(sentencia)* maxim, saying
(**d**) *(flor)* pansy

pensante *adj* thinking

PENSAR [3] 1 *vi* to think; **p. en algo/alguien** to think about sth/sb; **p. en hacer algo** to think about doing sth; **¿en qué piensas** *o* **estás pensando?** what are you thinking (about)?; **hemos pensado en ti para este puesto** we thought of you for this position; **piensa en un número/buen regalo** think of a number/good present; **sólo piensas en comer/la comida** eating/food is all you think about; **sólo (de) p. en ello me pongo enfermo** it makes me sick just thinking *o* just to think about it; **p. para sí** to think to oneself; **p. sobre algo** to think about sth; **piensa sobre lo que te he dicho** think about what I've said to you; **sin p.** without thinking; **dar que p. a alguien** to give sb food for thought; **da que p. que nadie se haya quejado** it is somewhat surprising that nobody has complained; **p. en voz alta** to think aloud; **no pienses mal...** don't get the wrong idea...; **p. mal de alguien** to think badly *o* ill of sb; **pienso, luego existo** I think, therefore I am; PROV **piensa mal y acertarás: ¿quién habrá sido? – piensa mal y acertarás** who can it have been? – I think you know who it was; **¿le contará la verdad o no? – piensa mal y acertarás** will he tell her the truth or not? – it's not too hard to work that one out
2 *vt* (**a**) *(reflexionar sobre)* to think about *o* over; **piénsalo** think

about it, think it over; **después de pensarlo mucho** after much thought, after thinking it over carefully; **si lo piensas bien...** if you think about it...; **ahora que lo pienso...** come to think of it..., now that I think about it...; **cuando menos lo pienses, te llamarán** they'll call you when you least expect it; **¡ni pensarlo!** no way!; **pensándolo mejor, pensándolo bien** on second thoughts; **¡y p. que no es más que una niña!** and to think (that) she's just a girl!

(**b**) *(opinar, creer)* to think; **¿tú qué piensas?** what do you think?; **p. algo de algo/alguien** to think sth of *o* about sth/sb; **¿qué piensas de...?** what do you think of *o* about...?; **piensa de él que es un memo** she thinks he's an idiot; **pienso que sí/no** I think so/not; **pienso que no vendrá** I don't think she'll come; **pensaba que no la oíamos** she thought we couldn't hear her; **no vayas a p. que no me preocupa** don't think it doesn't bother me; **¡quién lo hubiera pensado!** who'd have thought it!

(**c**) *(idear)* to think up

(**d**) *(tener la intención de)* **p. hacer algo** to intend to do sth; **no pienso decírtelo** I have no intention of telling you; **¿qué piensas hacer?** what are you going to do?, what are you thinking of doing?; **¿estás pensando en mudarte de casa?** are you thinking of moving house?

(**e**) *(decidir)* to think; **¿has pensado ya el sitio donde vamos a cenar?** have you thought where we can go for dinner yet?

3 pensarse *vpr* **pensarse algo** to think about sth, to think sth over; **piénsatelo** think about it, think it over; **me lo pensaré** I'll think about it, I'll think it over; **mejor que te lo pienses dos veces** *o* **muy bien antes de hacerlo** I'd think twice *o* carefully before doing it if I were you; **me ofrecieron el trabajo y no me lo pensé (dos veces)** they offered me the job and I had no hesitation in accepting it; **claro que se lo dije, ¿qué te pensabas?** of course I told her, what did you think I was going to do?

---

pensativo, -a *adj* pensive, thoughtful

pensil, pénsil *nm* delightful garden

Pensilvania *n* Pennsylvania

pensión *nf* (**a**) *(dinero)* pension; **cobra la p. una vez al mes** he receives his pension once a month; **no ha empezado a cobrar la p. todavía** she isn't on a pension yet ►► ***p. alimentaria*** *o* ***alimenticia*** maintenance; ***p. asistencial*** = benefit paid to people with low incomes, *Br* ≃ income support; ***p. contributiva*** earnings-related pension; ***p. no contributiva*** non-contributory pension; ***p. de invalidez*** disability allowance; ***p. de jubilación*** retirement pension; ***p. retributiva*** earnings-related pension; ***p. vitalicia*** life pension; ***p. de viudedad*** widow's pension

(**b**) *(de huéspedes)* guest house; **media p.** *(en hotel)* half board; **estar a media p.** *(en colegio)* to have school dinners ►► ***p. completa*** full board

(**c**) *Chile (melancolía)* **estar con p.** to be feeling blue

pensionado *nm* (**a**) *Esp (internado)* boarding school (**b**) *CSur (residencia) Br* hall of residence, *US* dormitory

pensionarse *vpr Col* to qualify for a pension

pensionista *nmf* (**a**) *(jubilado)* pensioner (**b**) *(en pensión)* guest, lodger (**c**) *Esp (en internado)* boarder

pensum *nm inv Col* syllabus

pentaedro *nm* pentahedron

pentagonal *adj* pentagonal

pentágono *nm* (**a**) *(figura)* pentagon (**b**) **el P.** *(en Estados Unidos)* the Pentagon (**c**) *Méx (en béisbol)* home plate, home base

pentagrama *nm Mús* stave

pentámetro *nm (en poesía)* pentameter

Pentateuco *nm* **el P.** the Pentateuch

pentatlón, pentathlon *nm* pentathlon ►► ***p. moderno*** modern pentathlon

pentecostal *adj* Pentecostal

Pentecostés *nm* (**a**) *(cristiano)* Whitsun, Pentecost (**b**) *(judío)* Pentecost

penthouse [pent'χaus] *nm CSur, Ven* penthouse

pentotal *nm* Pentothal®

penúltimo, -a 1 *adj* penultimate, last but one
2 *nm,f* penultimate, last but one

penumbra *nf* (**a**) *(sombra, semioscuridad)* semi-darkness, half-light; **en p.** in semi-darkness (**b**) *Astron* penumbra

penuria *nf* (**a**) *(pobreza)* poverty; **vivieron muchos años en la p.** they lived in poverty for many years (**b**) *(escasez)* paucity, dearth; **pasar penurias** to suffer hardship

peña *nf* (**a**) *(roca)* crag, rock (**b**) *(monte)* cliff (**c**) *(club)* club; *(futbolística)* supporters' club; *(quinielística)* pool; **p. ciclista/taurina** club of cycling/bullfighting fans (**d**) *Esp Fam (grupo de amigos)* crowd; **fuimos toda la p. al cine** the whole crowd went to the cinema (**e**) *Esp Fam (gente)* people; **a pesar de la lluvia acudió mucha p.** loads of folk turned up despite the rain (**f**) *CSur (reunión)* fiesta

peñascal *nm* rocky *o* craggy place

peñasco *nm* large crag *o* rock

peñazo *nm Esp Fam* bore; **es un p. de libro** the book's deadly boring; **¡no seas p.!** don't be such a bore *o* so boring!

peñón *nm (monte)* rocky outcrop; **el P. (de Gibraltar)** the Rock (of Gibraltar)

peón *nm* (**a**) *(obrero)* unskilled labourer ►► *Taurom* ***p. de brega*** bullfighter's assistant; ***p. caminero*** roadworker, *Br* navvy (**b**) *(en granja)* farmhand, farm worker (**c**) *(en ajedrez)* pawn (**d**) *(peonza)* (spinning) top

peonada *nf* (**a**) *(día de trabajo)* day's work (**b**) *(sueldo)* day's wages (**c**) *(obreros)* gang of labourers (**d**) *(en granja)* group of farmhands

peonaje *nm* gang of labourers

peoneta = **pioneta**

peonía *nf* peony

peonza *nf* (spinning) top

PEOR 1 *adj* (**a**) *(comparativo)* worse (**que** than); **este disco es bastante p.** this record is quite a lot worse; **hace mucho p. tiempo en la montaña** the weather is much worse in the mountains; **he visto cosas peores** I've seen worse; **una televisión de p. calidad** a worse quality television; **es p. no decir nada** it's even worse not to say anything at all; **no hay nada p. que...** there's nothing worse than...; **podría haber sido p.** it could have been worse; **un cambio a p.** a change for the worse; **y lo que es p....** and what's worse...; EXPR **fue p. el remedio que la enfermedad** it only made things worse

(**b**) *(superlativo)* **el/la p....** the worst...; **el p. equipo de todos/del mundo** the worst team of all/in the world; **un producto de la p. calidad** an extremely poor quality product; **es lo p. que nos podía ocurrir** it's the worst thing that could happen to us; **es una persona despreciable, le deseo lo p.** he's a horrible person, I hate him; **lo p. fue que...** the worst thing was that...; **lo p. estaba aún por venir** the worst was still to come; **ponerse en lo p.** to expect the worst

2 *nmf* **el/la p.** the worst; **el p. de todos/del mundo** the worst of all/in the world; **el p. de los dos** the worse of the two; **en el p. de los casos** at worst, if the worst comes to the worst ►► *Am Fam Hum* ***p. es nada*** *(novio)* boyfriend; *(novia)* girlfriend; **vino con su p. es nada** he came with his other half

3 *adv* (**a**) *(comparativo)* worse (**que** than); **ahora veo p.** I can't see as well now; **el francés se me da p. que el inglés** I'm worse at French than I am at English; **las cosas me van p. que antes** things aren't going as well for me as before; **¿qué tal las vacaciones? – p. imposible** how were your holidays? – they couldn't have been worse; **está p. preparado que tú** he's not as well prepared as you; **lo hace cada vez p.** she's getting worse and worse at it; **está p.** *(el enfermo)* he has got worse; **estoy p.** *(de salud)* I feel worse; **p. para ti/él/***etc.* that's your/his/*etc* problem; **que se calle, y si no quiere, p. que p.** *o* **tanto p.** tell him to shut up, and if he doesn't want to, so much the worse for him; **y si además llueve, p. que p.** *o* **tanto p.** and if it rains too, that would be even worse

(**b**) *(superlativo)* worst; **el que lo hizo p.** the one who did it (the) worst; **esto es lo que se me da p.** this is what I'm worst at; **los exámenes p. presentados** the worst-presented exams

---

pepa[1] *nf* (**a**) *Andes, CAm, Carib, Méx (pepita)* pip; *(hueso)* stone

(**b**) *Méx, RP, Ven muy Fam (vulva)* pussy

(**c**) *Ven (en la piel)* blackhead

(**d**) *Ven (en telas)* spot; **a pepas** spotted

(**e**) EXPR *Fam* **¡viva la P.!: no tiene casi dinero, pero él, ¡viva la P.!, ¡a gastar!** he hardly has any money, but he just goes ahead and spends it anyway; *RP Fam* **fue un viva la P.** it was a free-for-all; **su casa siempre fue un viva la P.** their house was always a bit chaotic

pepa[2] = **pepón**

pepenador, -ora *CAm, Méx* **1** *adj* scavenging
2 *nm,f* scavenger *(on rubbish tip)*

pepenar *vt CAm, Méx Fam* (**a**) *(juntar)* to pick up (**b**) *(recolectar)* to collect

pepián, pipián *nm Andes, CAm, Méx* (**a**) *(salsa)* = sauce thickened with ground nuts or seeds (**b**) *(guiso)* = type of stew in which the sauce is thickened with ground nuts or seeds

pepinazo *nm Fam* **(a)** *(explosión)* explosion, blast **(b)** *Dep (disparo)* powerful shot, screamer; *(pase)* powerful pass

pepinillo *nm* gherkin

pepino *nm* cucumber; EXPR *Fam* **me importa un p.** I couldn't care less, I don't give a damn

pepita *nf* **(a)** *(de fruta)* pip **(b)** *(de oro)* nugget **(c)** *Méx (de calabaza)* pumpkin seed *(eaten as snack)*

pepito *nm Esp* **(a)** *(de carne)* grilled meat sandwich **(b)** *(dulce)* = long, cream-filled cake made of dough similar to doughnut

pepitoria *nf (guisado)* = fricassee made with egg yolk

pepón, -ona, pepa *adj Perú Fam* tasty, *Br* fit

pepona *nf* large cardboard doll

pepsina *nf* pepsin, pepsine

péptico, -a *adj* peptic

peque *nmf Fam (niño)* kid

pequeñez *nf* **(a)** *(cualidad)* smallness **(b)** *(cosa insignificante)* little thing; **se pelearon por una p.** they fell out over a tiny little thing

pequeñín, -ina 1 *adj* teeny, tiny
2 *nm,f* tot

pequeño, -a 1 *adj* **(a)** *(de tamaño)* small; **este traje me está** *o* **me queda p.** this dress is too small for me; **la casa se nos ha quedado pequeña** the house is too small for us now; **su jardín es un Versalles en p.** her garden is a miniature Versailles ►► ***pequeña burguesía*** petty bourgeoisie; ***pequeños comerciantes*** small businessmen; ***pequeña empresa*** small business; **la pequeña empresa** small businesses; ***p. empresario*** small businessman; ***pequeñas y medianas empresas*** small and medium-sized enterprises; ***la pequeña pantalla*** the small screen
(b) *(de estatura)* small; **la niña está muy pequeña para su edad** the girl is very small for her age
(c) *(en cantidad) (ingresos, cifras)* low
(d) *(en intensidad) (dolor)* slight; *(explosión)* small; *(problema)* small, slight; *(posibilidad)* slight; **de pequeña importancia** of little importance
(e) *(en duración) (discurso, texto)* short
(f) *(hermano)* little
2 *nm,f (niño)* little one; **de p.** as a child; **el p., la pequeña** *(benjamín)* the youngest, the baby

pequeñoburgués, -esa 1 *adj* petit bourgeois
2 *nm,f* petit bourgeois, *f* petite bourgeoise

pequeñuelo, -a 1 *adj* tiny, teeny
2 *nm,f* tot

pequinés, -esa, pekinés, -esa 1 *adj* Pekinese
2 *nm,f* Pekinese
3 *nm (perro)* Pekinese

PER [per] *nm (abrev de* **Plan de Empleo Rural***)* = Spanish government project to support rural employment

pera 1 *nf* **(a)** *(fruta)* pear ►► ***p. de agua*** dessert pear; ***p. limonera*** = type of pear which has a lemony taste
(b) *(de goma)* (rubber) bulb
(c) *(interruptor)* = light switch on cord
(d) *(en barba)* goatee
(e) *Esp Fam* **peras** *(tetas)* knockers
(f) *CSur Fam (mentón)* chin
(g) EXPR **partir peras** to fall out; **pedir peras al olmo** to ask (for) the impossible; *Fam* **ponerle a alguien las peras al cuarto** to put the squeeze on sb; *Esp Fam* **ser la p.** to be something else; *Fam* **ser una p. en dulce** to be a gem
2 *adj inv Esp Fam* posh; **niño p.** spoilt *o* posh brat

peral *nm* pear tree

peraleda *nf* pear orchard

peraltado, -a *adj (carretera)* banked

peralte *nm (de carretera)* banking

perborato *nm* perborate

perca *nf* perch ►► ***p. americana*** largemouth *o* black bass; ***p. sol*** pumpkinseed

percal *nm* percale; *Fam* **conocer el p.** to know the score *o* what's what

percalina *nf* percaline

percán *nm Chile* mould

percance *nm* mishap; **tuvo un p. con la moto** he had a minor motorcycle accident

per cápita *loc adj* per capita

percatarse *vpr* **p. (de algo)** to notice (sth); **no me percaté de que quería hablar conmigo** I didn't realize that she wanted to talk to me

percebe *nm* **(a)** *(marisco)* goose barnacle **(b)** *Fam (persona)* twit

percepción *nf* **(a)** *(por los sentidos)* perception ►► ***p. extrasensorial*** extrasensory perception **(b)** *(por la inteligencia)* view, perspective; **tenemos una p. de la realidad completamente diferente** we have a completely different view of *o* perspective on reality **(c)** *(cobro)* receipt; *(pago)* payment

perceptible *adj* **(a)** *(por los sentidos)* noticeable, perceptible **(b)** *(que se puede cobrar)* receivable, payable

perceptivo, -a *adj* sensory

perceptor, -ora 1 *adj* **(a)** *(que siente)* perceiving, sensing **(b)** *(que cobra)* collecting
2 *nm,f* **(a)** *(persona que siente)* perceiver **(b)** *(cobrador)* collector, receiver

percha *nf* **(a)** *(de armario)* (coat) hanger **(b)** *(de pared)* coat hook **(c)** *(de pie)* coat stand, hat stand **(d)** *(para pájaros)* perch **(e)** EXPR *Fam* **ser una buena p.** to have a good figure

perchero *nm* **(a)** *(de pared)* coat rack; *(de pie)* coat stand, hat stand **(b)** *Cuba (percha)* (coat) hanger

percherón, -ona *nm,f* shire horse

percibir *vt* **(a)** *(con los sentidos)* to perceive, to notice; *(por los oídos)* to hear **(b)** *(con la inteligencia)* to see, to grasp; **no percibió el tono amenazador de su carta** she failed to detect the menacing tone of his letter **(c)** *(cobrar)* to receive, to get

perclorato *nm* perchlorate

percudido, -a *adj Andes, RP* grimy, dirt-stained

percudirse *vpr Andes, RP* to get grimy, to become stained with dirt

percusión *nf* percussion

percusionista *nmf* percussionist

percusor = **percutor**

percutir *vt* **(a)** *(golpear)* to strike **(b)** *Med* to percuss

percutor, percusor *nm* hammer, firing pin

perdedor, -ora 1 *adj* losing; **el equipo p.** the losing team, the losers
2 *nm,f* loser; **es un mal p.** he's a bad loser

PERDER [66] 1 *vt* **(a)** *(extraviar)* to lose; **he perdido el paraguas** I've lost my umbrella
(b) *(dejar de tener) (dinero, amigo, empleo, interés)* to lose; **he perdido el contacto con ellos** I've lost touch with them; **la policía ha perdido la pista** *o* **el rastro de los secuestradores** the police have lost track of the kidnappers; **no sé nada de Ana, le he perdido la pista** *o* **el rastro** I don't know anything about Ana, I've lost touch with her; **el accidente le hizo p. la visión** he lost his sight in the accident; **ya hemos perdido toda esperanza de encontrarlo** we've now given up *o* lost all hope of finding him; **he perdido bastante práctica** I'm rather out of practice; **p. el equilibrio/la memoria** to lose one's balance/memory; **p. peso** to lose weight; **p. el miedo/el respeto a alguien** to lose one's fear of/respect for sb; **cientos de personas perdieron la vida** hundreds of people lost their lives; **no tienes/tiene/***etc.* **nada que p.** you have/he has/*etc* nothing to lose; EXPR *Esp* **más se perdió en Cuba** *o* **en la guerra** it's not as bad as all that, it's not the end of the world
(c) *(ser derrotado en) (batalla, partido, campeonato, elecciones)* to lose; **este error podría hacerle p. el partido** this mistake could lose her the game
(d) *(desperdiciar) (tiempo)* to waste; *(oportunidad, ocasión)* to miss; **no pierdas el tiempo con** *o* **en tonterías** don't waste your time on nonsense like that; **he perdido toda la mañana en llamadas de teléfono** I've wasted all morning making phone calls; **no pierda la ocasión de ver esta fantástica película** don't miss this wonderful movie; **no hay tiempo que p.** there's no time to lose
(e) *(no alcanzar) (tren, vuelo, autobús)* to miss
(f) *(tener un escape de) (agua)* to lose, to leak; **la bombona pierde aire** air is escaping from the cylinder; **ese camión va perdiendo aceite** this lorry is losing *o* leaking oil
(g) *(perjudicar)* to be the ruin of; **le pierde su pasión por el juego** his passion for gambling is ruining him
(h) *Urug (examen)* to fail
2 *vi* **(a)** *(salir derrotado)* to lose; **p. al póquer/billar** to lose at poker/billiards; **perdimos (por) dos a cero** we lost two-nil; **no te pelees con él, que llevas las de p.** don't get into a fight with him, you're bound to lose; **sabe/no sabe p.** he's a good/bad loser; **salir perdiendo** to lose out, to come off worse
(b) *(empeorar)* to go downhill; **este restaurante ha perdido mucho** this restaurant has really gone downhill; **estas alfombras pierden bastante al lavarlas** these carpets don't wash very well
(c) *(tener un escape) (de agua, aceite)* to have a leak; **esa bombona pierde** that gas cylinder is leaking; **una de las ruedas pierde por la válvula** the air's coming out of one of the tyres

(d) *(en frases)* **echar algo a p.** to spoil sth; **echarse a p.** *(alimento)* to go off, to spoil

3 perderse *vpr* **(a)** *(extraviarse)* to get lost; **me he perdido** I'm lost; **se han perdido las tijeras** the scissors have disappeared; **se me ha perdido el reloj** I've lost my watch; *Fig* **a mí no se me ha perdido nada por allí** I've no desire to go there

(b) *(desaparecer)* to disappear; **se perdió entre el gentío** she disappeared amongst the crowd; *Fam* **ipiérdete!** get lost!

(c) *(distraerse, no seguir el hilo)* **me he perdido, ¿podría repetir?** I'm lost, would you mind repeating what you just said?; **cuando empiezan a hablar de toros yo me pierdo** when they start talking about bullfighting, I get completely lost; **uno se pierde entre tantas siglas de partidos políticos** all these acronyms for the different political parties are so confusing; **explícamelo otra vez, que me he perdido** explain it to me again, you lost me

(d) *(desaprovechar)* **perderse algo** to miss out on sth; **ino te lo pierdas!** don't miss it!; **me he perdido el principio** I missed the beginning; **no te has perdido gran cosa** you didn't miss much

(e) *(desperdiciarse)* to be wasted

(f) *(por los vicios, las malas compañías)* to be beyond salvation

(g) *(anhelar)* **perderse por** to be mad about

---

perdición *nf* ruin, undoing; **esos amigos van a ser tu p.** those friends will be the ruin of you

pérdida *nf* **(a)** *(extravío)* loss; **en caso de p., entregar en ...** in the event of loss, deliver to...; *Esp* **no tiene p.** you can't miss it

(b) *(de vista, audición, peso)* loss ▸▸ ***p. del conocimiento*** loss of consciousness

(c) *(de tiempo, dinero)* waste

(d) *(escape)* leak

(e) *(muerte)* loss; **nunca se recuperó de la p. de su mujer** he never got over losing his wife ▸▸ ***pérdidas humanas*** loss of life

(f) *(en baloncesto)* turnover

(g) **pérdidas** *(financieras)* losses ▸▸ ***pérdidas y ganancias*** profit and loss

(h) **pérdidas (materiales)** *(daños)* damage; **las inundaciones han causado grandes pérdidas** the floods have caused extensive damage

(i) **pérdidas** *(de sangre)* hemorrhage

perdidamente *adv* hopelessly; **p. enamorado** hopelessly in love

perdido, -a 1 *adj* **(a)** *(extraviado)* lost; **lo podemos dar por p.** it is as good as lost; **estaba p. en sus pensamientos** he was lost in thought; EXPR *Esp Fam Hum* **estar más p. que un pulpo en un garaje** to be totally lost

(b) *(animal, bala)* stray

(c) *(tiempo)* wasted; *(ocasión)* missed

(d) *(remoto)* remote, isolated; **un pueblo p.** a remote *o* isolated village

(e) *(acabado)* done for; **iestamos perdidos!** we're done for!, we've had it!; EXPR **ide perdidos, al río!** in for a penny, in for a pound

(f) *Fam (de remate)* complete; **es idiota p.** he's a complete idiot; **es una esquizofrénica perdida** she's a complete schizophrenic

(g) *Esp Fam (sucio)* filthy; **se puso perdida de pintura** she got herself covered in paint; **lo dejaron todo p. de barro** they left it covered in mud

(h) *(enamorado)* **estar p. por** to be madly in love with

(i) *Méx Fam* **de perdida** *(al menos)* at least

2 *nm,f* reprobate

perdigón *nm* **(a)** *(bala)* pellet **(b)** *(ave)* partridge chick

perdigonada *nf* **(a)** *(tiro)* shot **(b)** *(herida)* gunshot wound

perdiguero *nm* gun dog ▸▸ ***p. de Burgos*** Spanish pointer

perdiz *nf* partridge; EXPR **y fueron felices y comieron perdices** and they all lived happily ever after; EXPR *RP Fam* **levantar la p.** to give the game away ▸▸ ***p. blanca*** ptarmigan; ***p. nival*** ptarmigan; ***p. pardilla*** grey partridge; ***p. roja*** red-legged partridge

perdón 1 *nm* **(a)** *(de ofensa, falta)* pardon, forgiveness; **el p. de los pecados** the forgiveness of sins; **pedir p.** to apologize; **ve a pedirle p. a tu abuela** go and apologize to your grandmother; **te pido mil perdones** I'm terribly sorry; **te pido p. por el daño que te he causado** I apologize *o* I'm sorry for the hurt I've caused you; **es un gilipollas, con p.** he's a jerk, if you'll forgive the expression; EXPR **no tener p. (de Dios)** to be unforgivable

(b) *(de delito)* pardon; **el gobierno estudia conceder el p. a los militares sublevados** the government is considering granting the officers involved in the uprising a pardon

(c) *(de deuda)* pardon; **el p. de la deuda externa** foreign debt pardon

2 *interj (lo siento)* sorry!; *(tras estornudar, eructar)* pardon (me)!; **p., ¿me deja pasar?** excuse me, can I get past?; **p., ¿podría repetir?** I'm sorry, could you say that again?; **se creó en 1873, p., fue en 1875** it was created in 1873, no, sorry, I mean 1875; **p. pero no me parece una buena idea** I'm sorry but I don't think it's a good idea

perdonable *adj* pardonable, forgivable

perdonar 1 *vt* **(a)** *(ofensa, falta)* to forgive; **perdonarle algo a alguien** to forgive sb for sth; **no le perdonó nunca que no la invitara a la boda** she never forgave him for not inviting her to the wedding; **su mujer no le perdona ni una** his wife keeps him on a short leash; **perdona que no te haya dirigido la palabra** I'm sorry I've been ignoring you; **p. los pecados** to forgive sins; **que Dios me perdone, pero su padre es un sinvergüenza** God forgive me for saying so, but his father is a good-for-nothing

(b) *(condena)* **p. algo a alguien** to let sb off sth; **perdonarle la vida a alguien** to spare sb their life; *Fam Pey* **va por ahí perdonándole la vida a todo el mundo** she goes around patronizing everybody

(c) *(deuda)* to pardon; **te perdono lo que me debes** I'll let you off what you owe me; **p. la deuda externa de un país** to pardon a country's foreign debt

(d) *(como fórmula de cortesía)* **perdone que le moleste** sorry to bother you; **perdona que no te haga caso, estoy muy cansada** I'm sorry I'm not paying much attention to what you're saying, I'm very tired; **perdona la pregunta, ¿estás casada?** forgive *o* pardon my asking, but are you married?; **perdona mi ignorancia, ¿qué es un atomizador?** sorry to be so ignorant, but what's an atomizer?

(e) *Fam (desperdiciar)* **no p. algo** not to miss sth; **no perdona su coñac y su puro después de la comida** he never misses his brandy and cigar after dinner

2 *vi* **los años no perdonan** the years take their toll; **un delantero que no perdona** a lethal forward; **perdona, no lo hice a idea** I'm sorry, I didn't do it on purpose; **perdone, ¿me deja pasar?** excuse me, can I get past?; **perdone, ¿le he hecho mucho daño?** I'm sorry, did I hurt you?; **ya perdonarás, pero yo estaba primero** I'm sorry *o* excuse me, but I was first; **perdona, pero creo que te equivocas** I'm sorry, but I think you're mistaken

perdonavidas *nmf inv Fam* bully

perdurabilidad *nf* **(a)** *(de lo duradero)* durability **(b)** *(de lo eterno)* eternal *o* everlasting nature

perdurable *adj* **(a)** *(que dura mucho)* long-lasting **(b)** *(que dura siempre)* eternal

perdurar *vi* **(a)** *(durar mucho)* to endure, to last; **todavía perdura el recuerdo de su última visita** her last visit still hasn't been forgotten **(b)** *(persistir)* to persist; **una costumbre que aún perdura** a custom that is still alive, a custom that survives to this day

perecedero, -a *adj* **(a)** *(productos)* perishable **(b)** *(naturaleza)* transitory

perecer [46] *vi* to perish, to die; **pereció en el rescate de las víctimas** he perished *o* died rescuing the victims; **todos los pasajeros perecieron en el accidente** all the passengers died in the accident

peregrina *nf (vieira)* scallop

peregrinación *nf*, **peregrinaje** *nm* **(a)** *(religiosa)* pilgrimage **(a** to); **una ruta de p.** a pilgrimage route **(b)** *(a un lugar)* trek; **este bar es el lugar de p. favorito de los estudiantes a la hora del almuerzo** students flock to this bar at lunchtime

peregrinar *vi* **(a)** *(a lugar sagrado)* to make a pilgrimage **(b)** *(por un lugar)* to trail, to trek; **estuvo peregrinando por varios hospitales buscando a su hijo** he trailed *o* trekked from hospital to hospital in search of his son

peregrino, -a 1 *adj* **(a)** *(ave)* migratory **(b)** *(idea, argumento)* strange, bizarre

2 *nm,f (persona)* pilgrim

perejil *nm* parsley

perengano, -a *nm,f (hombre)* so-and-so, what's-his-name; *(mujer)* so-and-so, what's-her-name; **siempre se queja, que si fulano no le habla, que si p. le molesta** she's always complaining: either somebody won't talk to her, or somebody won't leave her alone, there's always something

perenne *adj* **(a)** *(planta, hoja)* perennial; **un árbol de hoja p.** an evergreen tree **(b)** *(recuerdo)* enduring **(c)** *(continuo)* constant; **su p. mal humor** his permanently bad mood

perentoriamente *adv* peremptorily

perentorio, -a *adj* **(a)** *(urgente)* urgent, pressing **(b)** *(gesto, tono)* peremptory **(c)** *(improrrogable)* **plazo p.** fixed time limit

perestroika *nf* perestroika

pereza *nf* idleness; **me da p. ir a pie** I can't be bothered walking; **no lo hice por p.** I couldn't be bothered doing it; **sacudirse la p.** to wake oneself up; **sentir p.** to feel lazy

perezco *etc ver* **perecer**

perezosamente *adv* lazily

perezoso, -a 1 *adj* (**a**) *(vago)* lazy (**b**) *(lento)* slow, sluggish
2 *nm,f (vago)* lazy person, idler
3 *nm (animal)* sloth

perfección *nf* perfection; **es de una gran p.** it's exceptionally good; **a la p.** perfectly; **habla inglés a la p.** she speaks perfect English

perfeccionamiento *nm* (**a**) *(acabado)* perfecting (**b**) *(mejoramiento)* improvement; **un curso de p.** an advanced training course

perfeccionar *vt* (**a**) *(redondear)* to perfect (**b**) *(mejorar)* to improve

perfeccionismo *nm* perfectionism

perfeccionista 1 *adj* perfectionist
2 *nmf* perfectionist

perfectamente *adv* (**a**) *(sobradamente)* perfectly; **caben p. cinco personas** five people fit comfortably (**b**) *(muy bien)* fine; **¿cómo estás? – estoy p.** how are you? – I'm fine (**c**) *(de acuerdo)* **¡p.!** fine!, great!

perfectivo, -a *adj* perfective

perfecto, -a 1 *adj* (**a**) *(impecable, inmejorable)* perfect; **es el regalo p.** it's the perfect gift; **la sopa está perfecta** the soup is perfect *o* just right; **el televisor está en p. estado** the television is in perfect *o* immaculate condition (**b**) *(total)* absolute, complete; **es un p. idiota** he's an absolute *o* complete idiot; **es un p. desconocido** he's a complete unknown (**c**) *Gram* perfect
2 *adj Gram* perfect
3 *interj (de acuerdo)* fine!, great!

perfidia *nf* perfidy, treachery

pérfido, -a 1 *adj* perfidious, treacherous ►► *Hum* ***la pérfida Albión*** perfidious Albion
2 *nm,f* treacherous person

perfil *nm* (**a**) *(de cara, cuerpo)* profile; **una foto de p.** a photograph in profile; **en la foto salgo de p.** I appear in profile in the photo; **le vi de p.** I saw him in profile *o* from the side; **un p. griego** a Greek profile
(**b**) *(contorno)* outline, shape; **un p. aerodinámico** an aerodynamic shape
(**c**) *(característica)* characteristic; **el p. de un candidato** a candidate's profile; **un p. psicológico** a psychological profile; **buscan licenciados con un p. comercial** they are looking for graduates with a background in sales
(**d**) *Mat* cross section

perfilado, -a *adj* (**a**) *(rostro)* long and thin (**b**) *(nariz)* perfect, regular (**c**) *(de perfil)* in profile

perfilar *vt* 1 (**a**) *(trazar)* to outline (**b**) *(afinar)* to polish, to put the finishing touches to
2 **perfilarse** *vpr* (**a**) *(destacarse)* to be outlined; **se perfila como el ganador de las elecciones** he's beginning to look like he'll win the election (**b**) *(concretarse)* to shape up; **la ciudad se perfilaba en el horizonte** the city could be seen on the horizon

perforación *nf* (**a**) *(acción)* drilling, boring (**b**) *(de estómago, intestino)* perforation (**c**) *(taladro, hueco)* bore-hole (**d**) *(en sellos, papeles)* perforation (**e**) *(de oreja, ombligo)* piercing

perforador, -ora 1 *adj* drilling
2 *nm,f Andes Fam* = robber who breaks in by making a hole in the wall of the adjoining premises

perforadora *nf* (**a**) *(herramienta)* drill (**b**) *(para papel)* hole punch (**c**) *Informát* card punch

perforar 1 *vt* (**a**) *(agujerear)* to cut a hole/holes in; *(con taladro)* to drill a hole/holes in; **la bala le perforó el pulmón** the bullet pierced his lung; **están perforando un túnel** they are drilling a tunnel (**b**) *Informát* to punch
2 **perforarse** *vpr* (**a**) *(estómago, intestino)* to become perforated (**b**) *(para poner anillo)* **perforarse las orejas/la nariz** to have *o* get one's ears/nose pierced

performance *nf Am* performance

performativo, -a *adj Ling* performative

perfumador *nm* perfume atomizer

perfumar 1 *vt* to perfume
2 **perfumarse** *vpr* to put perfume on

perfume *nm* perfume

perfumería *nf* (**a**) *(tienda, arte)* perfumery (**b**) *(productos)* perfumes

perfumista *nmf* perfumer

perfusión *nf Med* perfusion

pergamino *nm* parchment

pergenio, -a *nm,f CSur Fam* rascal

pergeñar *vt (plan, idea)* to rough out; *(comida)* to whip up

pérgola *nf* pergola

periantio, perianto *nm Bot* perianth

perica *nf Fam (cocaína)* snow, coke

pericardio *nm Anat* pericardium

pericarpio *nm Bot* pericarp

pericia *nf* skill; **resolvió el caso con p.** he solved the case expertly *o* with expertise

pericial *adj* expert

Perico *n pr Fam* **P. (el) de los Palotes** anybody *o* whoever (you like)

perico *nm* (**a**) *(pájaro)* parakeet ►► ***p. monje*** monk parakeet (**b**) *Esp, RP, Ven Fam (cocaína)* snow, coke (**c**) *Col (café con leche)* white coffee (**d**) *Carib, Guat, Méx (charlatán)* big talker

pericón *nm* = dance and music typical of the River Plate region

pericote *nm Arg, Bol, Perú* large rat

peridoto *nm* peridot

periferia *nf (contorno)* periphery; *(alrededores)* outskirts

periférico, -a 1 *adj* peripheral; **barrio p.** outlying district
2 *nm* (**a**) *Informát* peripheral ►► ***p. de entrada*** input device; ***p. de salida*** output device; ***p. en serie*** serial device (**b**) *CAm, Méx (carretera) Br* ring road, *US* beltway

perifollo 1 *nm (planta)* chervil ►► ***p. oloroso*** sweet cicely
2 **perifollos** *nmpl Fam* frills (and fripperies)

perífrasis *nf inv* wordy explanation ►► *Gram* ***p. verbal*** compound verb

perifrástico, -a *adj* long-winded

perigeo *nm Astron* perigee

perihelio *nm Astron* perihelion

perilla *nf* (**a**) *(barba)* goatee; EXPR *Fam* **venir de p.** *o* **perillas** to be very handy *o* just the thing (**b**) *Am (de puerta)* doorknob; *(de aparato)* knob (**c**) *(interruptor)* = light switch on cord

perímetro *nm* perimeter

perimido, -a *adj RP* archaic

perinatal *adj* perinatal

periné, perineo *nm Anat* perineum

perinola *nf (juguete)* teetotum

periódicamente *adv* periodically

periodicidad *nf* periodicity; **se publica con una p. bianual** it is published twice yearly

periódico, -a 1 *adj* (**a**) *(regular)* regular, periodic (**b**) *Mat* recurrent
2 *nm* newspaper, paper ►► ***p. digital*** online newspaper, digital newspaper; ***p. del domingo*** Sunday paper; ***p. dominical*** Sunday paper; ***p. electrónico*** electronic newspaper; ***p. de la tarde*** evening paper; ***p. vespertino*** evening paper

> **Falso amigo**: El sustantivo inglés **periodical** no es la traducción del español **periódico**. En inglés **periodical** significa "publicación periódica, boletín".

periodicucho *nm Pey* rag, bad newspaper

periodiquero, -a *nm,f Méx* newspaper seller

periodismo *nm* journalism ►► ***p. amarillo*** gutter journalism; ***p. gráfico*** photojournalism; ***p. de investigación*** investigative journalism

periodista *nmf* journalist ►► ***p. gráfico*** press photographer

periodístico, -a *adj* journalistic

periodización *nf* periodization

periodo, período *nm* (**a**) *(espacio de tiempo)* period; **el primer p.** *(de partido)* the first half ►► ***p. contable*** accounting period; ***p. de gestación*** gestation period; *Com* ***p. de gracia*** days of grace; ***p. de incubación*** incubation period; ***p. de prácticas*** trial period; ***p. de prueba*** trial period; *Ind* ***p. de reflexión*** *(en disputa)* cooling-off period; ***p. refractario*** refractory period; ***p. de transición*** transition period
(**b**) *Mat* period
(**c**) *Fís* period
(**d**) *Geol* age ►► ***p. glacial*** ice age; ***p. interglacial*** interglacial period
(**e**) *(menstruación)* period; **estar con el p., tener el p.** to be having one's period
(**f**) *Ling* period

periostio *nm Anat* periosteum

peripatético, -a 1 *adj* (**a**) *Filosofía* Peripatetic (**b**) *Fam (ridículo)* ludicrous
2 *nm,f* Peripatetic

peripecia *nf* incident, adventure; **sus peripecias en la selva** his adventures in the jungle

periplo *nm* **(a)** *(viaje)* journey, voyage; **hicieron un p. por África** they journeyed around Africa **(b)** *(por mar)* voyage

peripuesto, -a *adj Fam* dolled-up, tarted-up

periquete *nm Fam* **en un p.** in a jiffy

periquito 1 *nm (ave)* parakeet; *(australiano)* budgerigar
2 *adj Esp Fam* = of/relating to Español Football Club

periscopio *nm* periscope

perista *nmf Esp Fam* fence, receiver of stolen goods

peristáltico, -a *adj Fisiol* peristaltic

peristilo *nm* peristyle

perita *nf* EXPR *Fam* **ser una p. en dulce** to be a gem

peritaje *nm*, **peritación** *nf* **(a)** *(trabajo)* expert work; **antes de comprar la casa encargaron un p.** before buying the house they got it surveyed **(b)** *(informe)* expert's report **(c)** *(estudios)* professional training

peritar *vt (casa)* to value; *(coche)* to assess the value of, to assess the damage to

perito 1 *adj* expert; **ser p. en algo** to be an expert in sth
2 *nm* **(a)** *(experto)* expert; **un p. en contabilidad** an accountancy expert ▸▸ ***p. agrícola*** agronomist; ***p. agrónomo*** agronomist; ***p. judicial*** legal expert; ***p. tasador de seguros*** loss adjuster **(b)** *(ingeniero técnico)* **p. (industrial)** = engineer who has done a three-year university course rather than a full five-year course

peritoneo *nm Anat* peritoneum

peritonitis *nf inv Med* peritonitis

perjudicado, -a 1 *adj* affected; **los agricultores fueron los más perjudicados** the farmers were the worst affected; **aquí soy yo el que sale p.** I'm the one who's losing out here; *Der* **la parte perjudicada** the injured party
2 *nm,f* **los perjudicados por la inundación** the people affected by the flood, the flood victims; *Der* **el p.** the injured party; **los perjudicados somos nosotros** we are the ones who are losing out

perjudicar [60] *vt* to damage, to harm; **el tabaco perjudica la salud** smoking damages your health; **esa decisión perjudica nuestros intereses** this decision damages our interests

perjudicial *adj* harmful (**para** to); **el exceso de colesterol es p. para la salud** too much cholesterol is damaging to your health; **la decisión es p. para nuestros planes** the decision upsets our plans

perjuicio *nm* harm, damage; **causar perjuicios (a)** to do harm *o* damage (to); **ir en p. de** to be detrimental to; **la reforma educativa favorece a algunas asignaturas en p. de otras** the education reform favours some subjects at the expense of others; **una indemnización por daños y perjuicios** compensation for damages; **sin p.: lo haré, sin p. de que proteste** I'll do it, but I retain the right to make a complaint about it; **urge la reforma de la ley, sin p. de la revisión de otras leyes** the law must be reformed as a matter of urgency, however this should not mean that the review of other laws is neglected

perjurar *vi* **(a)** *(jurar mucho)* **juró y perjuró que no había sido él** he swore blind that he hadn't done it **(b)** *(jurar en falso)* to commit perjury

perjurio *nm* perjury

perjuro, -a 1 *adj* perjured
2 *nm,f* perjurer

perla *nf* **(a)** *(joya)* pearl; EXPR **de perlas: su ayuda me viene de perlas** her help is just what I needed ▸▸ ***p. artificial*** artificial pearl; ***p. cultivada*** cultured pearl; ***p. de cultivo*** cultured pearl; ***p. natural*** natural pearl **(b)** *(maravilla)* gem, treasure; **la nueva señora de la limpieza es una p.** the new cleaning lady is a gem **(c)** *(frase desafortunada)* gem

perlado, -a *adj (de gotas)* beaded

perlocución *nf Ling* perlocution

permafrost *nm Geol* permafrost

permanecer [46] *vi* **(a)** *(en un lugar)* to stay; **los secuestradores todavía permanecen en la embajada** the hostage-takers are still *o* remain inside the embassy
(b) *(en un estado)* to remain, to stay; **permaneció enfermo dos semanas** he was ill for two weeks; **p. en silencio** to remain silent; **permanezcan en sus asientos hasta que el avión se haya parado por completo** please remain seated until the aircraft has come to a complete stop

permanencia *nf* **(a)** *(en un lugar)* staying, continued stay; **su larga p. en el poder ha sido muy negativa** their prolonged period in office has had very damaging consequences; **se está cuestionando su p. en el cargo de presidente** doubts are being raised as to whether he should continue as president; **su p. en primera división depende de una victoria en este partido** they need to win this game in order to stay in the first division
(b) *(en un estado)* continuation

permanente 1 *adj* permanent; **comisión p.** standing committee
2 *nf* perm; **hacerse la p.** to have a perm
3 *nm Méx* perm; **hacerse el p.** to have a perm

permanentemente *adv* permanently

permanezco *etc ver* **permanecer**

permanganato *nm Quím* permanganate

permeabilidad *nf* permeability

permeable *adj* permeable

pérmico,-a *Geol* **1** *adj* Permian
2 *nm* **el p.** the Permian

permisible *adj* permissible, acceptable

permisionario, -a *nm,f Méx* official agent

permisividad *nf* permissiveness

permisivo, -a *adj* permissive

permiso *nm* **(a)** *(autorización)* permission; **dar p. a alguien para hacer algo** to give sb permission to do sth; **pedir p. para hacer algo** to ask permission to do sth
(b) *(fórmula de cortesía)* **con p.** if I may, if you'll excuse me; **con p., ¿puedo pasar?** may I come in?
(c) *(documento)* licence, permit ▸▸ ***p. de armas*** gun licence; ***p. de circulación*** *Br* (vehicle) registration document, *US* vehicle license; ***p. de conducción*** *o* ***de conducir*** *Br* driving licence, *US* driver's license; ***p. de obras*** planning permission; ***p. de residencia*** residence permit; ***p. de trabajo*** work permit
(d) *(vacaciones)* leave; **estar de p.** to be on leave; **le concedieron un p. carcelario de tres días** he was allowed out of prison for three days ▸▸ ***p. por maternidad*** maternity leave; ***p. por paternidad*** paternity leave

permitido, -a *adj* permitted, allowed

permitir 1 *vt* **(a)** *(autorizar)* to allow, to permit; **p. a alguien hacer algo** to allow sb to do sth; **¿me permite?** may I?; **¿me permite su carnet de conducir, por favor?** may I see your *Br* driving licence *o US* driver's license, please?; **permítele venir** *o* **que venga con nosotros** let her come with us; **permíteme que te ayude** let me help you, allow me to help you; **si el tiempo lo permite** weather permitting; **no permitas que te tomen el pelo** don't let them mess you about; **¡no te permito que me hables así!** I won't have you talking to me like that!; **no se permite fumar** *(en letrero)* no smoking; **no se permite la entrada a menores de 18 años** *(en letrero)* no entry for under 18s; **sus padres no le permiten fumar en casa** his parents don't allow him to *o* won't let him smoke at home
(b) *(hacer posible)* to allow, to enable; **la nieve caída permitió abrir la estación de esquí** the fallen snow allowed *o* enabled the ski resort to be opened; **ese tractor permite roturar los campos más rápidamente** with this tractor the fields can be ploughed more quickly; **este modelo permite enviar y recibir faxes** this model allows you to send and receive faxes; **el cable permite enviar información a mayor velocidad** cable allows *o* enables information to be sent faster
2 permitirse *vpr* **no puedo permitírmelo** I can't afford it; **de vez en cuando se permite un cigarrillo** he allows himself a cigarette from time to time; **se permite demasiadas confianzas con las mujeres** he takes too many liberties with women; **me permito recordarle que...** let me remind you that...

permuta *nf (de bienes)* exchange; *(de trabajos)* job swap ▸▸ *Fin* ***p. de divisas*** currency swap

permutable *adj* exchangeable

permutación *nf* **(a)** *(permuta)* exchange **(b)** *Mat* permutation

permutar *vt* **(a)** *(intercambiar) (bienes, trabajos)* to exchange, to swap **(b)** *Mat* to permute

pernera *nf* trouser leg, *US* pant leg

pernicioso, -a *adj* damaging, harmful

pernil *nm* leg of ham

pernio *nm* hinge

perno *nm* bolt

pernoctar *vi* to stay overnight

PERO 1 *conj* **(a)** *(adversativo)* but; **el reloj es viejo, p. funciona bien** the watch is old but it keeps good time; **hablo portugués, p. muy poco** I speak some Portuguese, though not very much; **sí, p. no** yes and no (**b**) *(enfático) (en exclamaciones, interrogaciones)* **¿p. qué es todo este ruido?** what on earth is all this noise about?; **¡p. no se quede ahí; pase, por favor!** but please, don't stand out there, do come in!; **¡p. cómo vas a** *Esp* **conducir** *o Am* **manejar, si no puedes tenerte en pie!** how on earth are you going to drive if you can't even stand up properly!; **p., ¡tú por aquí!** well I never, fancy meeting you here!; **p. bueno ¿tú eres tonto?** are you stupid or something?; **ahora dice que no me va a pagar – ¡p. bueno!** now she says she's not going to pay me – no!; **¡p. si eso lo sabe todo el mundo!** come on, everyone knows that!; **¿salir ahora? ¡p. si ya es la medianoche!** go out now? but it's already midnight!; **¡p. si es un Picasso auténtico!** *(expresa sorpresa)* well I never, it's a genuine Picasso!

(**c**) *(antes de adverbios, adjetivos) (absolutamente)* **llevo años sin escribir nada, p. nada de nada** I haven't written anything at all for years, and when I say nothing I mean nothing; **estas peras están buenísimas, p. que buenísimas** these pears are completely and utterly delicious; **el clima allí es p. que muy frío** the climate there really is very cold indeed

2 *nm* snag, fault; **poner peros (a algo/alguien)** to raise questions (about sth/sb); **poner peros a todo** to find fault with everything; EXPR **no hay p. que valga** *o* **peros que valgan** there are no buts about it

---

perogrullada *nf* truism

perogrullesco, -a *adj* trite, hackneyed

Perogrullo *n* **una verdad de P.** a truism

perol *nm* (**a**) *(plato)* casserole (dish) (**b**) *Ven Fam (lata)* can (**c**) *Ven Fam (chatarra)* piece of junk (**d**) *Ven Fam (cachivache)* thing

perola *nf* saucepan

peroné *nm* fibula

peronismo *nm Pol* Peronism

peronista *Pol* 1 *adj* Peronist
2 *nmf* Peronist

perorar *vi Pey* to speechify

perorata *nf Pey* long-winded speech; **le soltó una p. sobre la inmoralidad** she gave him a long lecture on immorality

peróxido *nm* peroxide ►► ***p. de hidrógeno*** hydrogen peroxide

perpendicular 1 *adj* perpendicular; **ser p. a algo** to be perpendicular *o* at right angles to sth
2 *nf* perpendicular (line)

perpendicularmente *adv* perpendicularly

perpetración *nf* perpetration

perpetrar *vt* to perpetrate, to commit

perpetuación *nf* perpetuation

perpetuar [4] 1 *vt* to perpetuate
2 **perpetuarse** *vpr* to last, to endure

perpetuidad *nf* perpetuity; **a p.** in perpetuity; **presidente a p.** president for life; **condenado a p.** condemned to life imprisonment

perpetuo, -a *adj* (**a**) *(para siempre)* perpetual (**b**) *(vitalicio)* lifelong

Perpiñán *n* Perpignan

perplejidad *nf* perplexity, bewilderment; **me miró con p.** he looked at me in perplexity *o* bewilderment

perplejo, -a *adj* perplexed, bewildered; **la noticia me dejó p.** the news perplexed *o* bewildered me

perra *nf* (**a**) *(animal)* bitch; **dale de comer a la p.** feed the dog
(**b**) *Esp Fam (rabieta)* tantrum; **coger una p.** to throw a tantrum
(**c**) *Esp Fam (obsesión)* obsession; **ha cogido la p. de ir de crucero** she's become obsessed with the idea of going on a cruise
(**d**) *Esp Fam (dinero)* **tengo unas cuantas perras ahorradas** I've got a bit of money saved up; **me costó cuatro perras** it cost me next to nothing; **estoy sin una p.** I'm flat broke; EXPR **no tiene una p. gorda** *o* **chica** he hasn't got a bean; EXPR **no vale una p. gorda** *o* **chica** it isn't worth a bean; EXPR **¡para ti la p. gorda!** you win!
(**e**) *ver también* **perro**

perrada *nf Fam (acción mala)* dirty trick

perramus® *nm Arg* raincoat

perredista *Méx* 1 *adj* = of/relating to the PRD party
2 *nmf* = member or supporter of the PRD party

perrera *nf* (**a**) *(lugar)* kennels ►► ***p. municipal*** *Br* lost dogs' home, *US* dog pound, dog shelter (**b**) *(vehículo)* dogcatcher's van (**c**) *Méx (caseta)* kennel, *US* doghouse (**d**) *ver también* **perrero**

perrería *nf Fam* (**a**) *(acción)* **hacer perrerías a alguien** to do horrible things to sb; **estoy harto de aguantar las perrerías de mi jefe** I'm sick of putting up with the lousy treatment I get from my boss (**b**) *(insulto)* nasty remark; **le dijeron perrerías** they called him all sorts of names

perrero, -a *nm,f (persona)* dogcatcher

perrito *nm* (**a**) *(animal)* little dog (**b**) **p. (caliente)** hot dog (**c**) *Chile (pinza) Br* clothes peg, *US* clothes pin

---

PERRO, -A 1 *adj Fam* (**a**) *(asqueroso, desgraciado)* lousy; **¡qué vida más perra!** life's a bitch!; **llevan una vida muy perra** they have a lousy life; EXPR *RP Fam* **en la perra vida: en la perra vida le dije eso** I never said that to him (**b**) *(perezoso)* bone idle; **¡mira que eres p.!** you lazy so-and-so!

2 *nm* (**a**) *(animal)* dog; **comida para perros** dog food; **la caseta del p.** the dog kennel; **¡cuidado con el p.!** *(en letrero)* beware of the dog; **sacar a pasear al p.** to walk the dog, to take the dog for a walk; EXPR **allí no atan los perros con longaniza** the streets there aren't paved with gold; EXPR **andar** *o* **llevarse como el p. y el gato** to fight like cat and dog; EXPR *Fam* **de perros** *(tiempo, humor)* lousy; **hace un día de perros** the weather's foul today, it's lousy weather today; EXPR *RP Fam* **estar como p. en cancha de bochas** to be completely lost; EXPR *Fam* **echarle los perros a alguien** *(reprender)* to have a go at sb; EXPR **ser como el p. del hortelano (que ni come ni deja comer al amo)** to be a dog in the manger; EXPR *RP Fam* **está meado por los perros** he's jinxed; EXPR **el mismo p. con distinto collar: el nuevo régimen no es más que el mismo p. con distinto collar** the new regime may have a different name but nothing has really changed; EXPR *Fam* **¡a otro p. con ese hueso!** *Br* pull the other one!, *US* tell it to the marines!; EXPR **tratar a alguien como a un p.** to treat sb like a dog; EXPR **ser p. viejo** to be an old hand; PROV **muerto el p., se acabó la rabia** it's best to deal with problems at their source; PROV **a p. flaco todo son pulgas** the worse off you are, the more bad things seem to happen to you; PROV **p. ladrador, poco mordedor,** *RP* **p. que ladra no muerde** his/her bark is worse than his/her bite ►► ***p. callejero*** stray (dog); ***p. de caza*** hunting dog; ***p. cobrador*** retriever; ***p. de compañía*** pet dog; ***p. esquimal*** husky; ***p. faldero*** *(perrito)* lapdog; *Fig (persona)* lackey; ***p. guardián*** guard dog, watchdog; ***p. de lanas*** poodle; ***p. lazarillo*** *Br* guide dog, *US* seeing-eye dog; ***p. lobo*** Alsatian, German shepherd; *RP* ***p. ovejero*** sheepdog; ***p. pastor*** sheepdog; ***p. policía*** police dog; ***p. de las praderas*** *(roedor)* prairie dog; ***p. rastreador*** tracker dog; ***p. de raza*** pedigree dog; ***p. salchicha*** sausage dog; ***p. de Terranova*** Newfoundland; ***p. vagabundo*** stray dog
(**b**) *Fam (persona)* swine, dog
(**c**) *Chile (pinza) Br* clothes peg, *US* clothes pin

---

perruno, -a *adj* canine; **una vida perruna** a dog's life

persa 1 *adj* Persian
2 *nmf* Persian
3 *nm (idioma)* Persian, Farsi

per saecula saeculorum *loc adv Formal* for ever and ever

per se *loc adv Formal* per se

persecución *nf* (**a**) *(seguimiento)* pursuit (**b**) *(acoso)* persecution; **los primeros cristianos sufrieron p.** the first Christians were persecuted (**c**) *Dep* pursuit ►► ***p. por equipos*** team pursuit; ***p. individual*** individual pursuit

per sécula seculorum *adv Formal* for ever and ever

persecutorio, -a *adj* **complejo p.** persecution complex

perseguidor, -ora 1 *adj* (**a**) *(que sigue)* pursuing (**b**) *(que atormenta)* persecuting
2 *nm,f* (**a**) *(el que sigue)* pursuer (**b**) *(el que atormenta)* persecutor

perseguir [62] *vt* (**a**) *(seguir)* to pursue; *(a un corredor, ciclista)* to chase down
(**b**) *(tratar de obtener)* to pursue; **con esta medida, el gobierno persigue la contención de la inflación** the government's purpose in taking this measure is to curb inflation
(**c**) *(acosar)* to persecute; **lo persiguieron por sus ideas** he was persecuted for his beliefs; **lo persigue la mala suerte** she's dogged by bad luck; **los fantasmas de la niñez la persiguen** she is tormented by the ghosts of her childhood

perseverancia *nf* perseverance, persistence

perseverante *adj* persistent

perseverar *vi* to persevere (**en** with), to persist (**en** in)

Persia *n* Persia

persiana *nf (enrollable)* (roller) blind; *(con láminas)* (Venetian) blind; EXPR *Esp* **enrollarse como una p.** *o* **como las persianas: se enrolla como una p.** he could talk the hind legs off a donkey ►► ***p. enrollable*** roller blind; ***p. veneciana*** Venetian blind

pérsico, -a *adj* Persian

persignarse *vpr Rel* to cross oneself

persigo *etc ver* **perseguir**

persiguiera *etc ver* **perseguir**

persinado, -a *adj Méx Fam (mojigato)* prudish, strait-laced

persistencia *nf* persistence
persistente *adj* persistent
persistentemente *adv* persistently
persistir *vi* to persist (**en** in); **el riesgo de tormentas persistirá hasta la semana que viene** there will be a risk of storms until next week; **persiste en su idea de viajar al Nepal** she persists in her idea of going to Nepal
persona *nf* (**a**) *(individuo)* person; **vinieron varias personas** several people came; **cien personas** a hundred people; **la p. responsable** the person in charge; **las personas adultas** adults; **necesitan la mediación de una tercera p.** they need the mediation of a third party; **ser buena p.** to be nice; **ha venido el obispo en p.** the bishop came in person; **este niño es el demonio en p.** this child is the very devil; **de p. a p.** person to person, one to one; **por p.** per head ▸▸ ***p. mayor*** adult, grown-up; ***p. non grata*** persona non grata
(**b**) *Der* party ▸▸ ***p. física*** private individual; ***p. jurídica*** legal entity *o* person
(**c**) *Gram* person; **la segunda p. del singular** the second person singular
(**d**) *Rel* person
personación *nf Der* appearance
personaje *nm* (**a**) *(persona importante)* important person, celebrity; **acudieron personajes del mundo del cine** celebrities from the movie world came; **¡menudo p.!** *(persona despreciable)* what an unpleasant individual! (**b**) *(en novela, teatro)* character
personal 1 *adj (privado, íntimo)* personal; **una opinión/pregunta p.** a personal opinion/question; **mi teléfono p. es...** my home *o* private number is...; **para uso p.** for personal use; **p. e intransferible** non-transferable
2 *nm* (**a**) *(trabajadores)* staff, personnel ▸▸ ***p. administrativo*** administrative staff; ***p. de cabina*** cabin staff *o* crew; ***p. docente*** teaching staff; ***p. de planta*** staff; ***p. de tierra*** ground staff *o* crew; ***p. de ventas*** sales force *o* team (**b**) *Esp Fam (gente)* people; **el p. quería ir al cine** the gang wanted to go to the cinema
3 *nf (en baloncesto)* personal foul
personalidad *nf* (**a**) *(características)* personality; **tener p.** to have personality *o* character ▸▸ ***p. múltiple*** multiple personality (**b**) *(identidad)* identity (**c**) *(persona importante)* important person, celebrity (**d**) *Der* legal personality *o* status ▸▸ ***p. jurídica*** legal status
personalismo *nm* (**a**) *(parcialidad)* favouritism (**b**) *(egocentrismo)* self-centredness
personalizado, -a *adj* personalized; *(computador)* customized
personalizar [14] **1** *vi* (**a**) *(nombrar)* to name names; **no quiero p., pero...** I don't want to name names *o* mention any names, but... (**b**) *(aludir)* to get personal
2 *vt (adaptar)* to personalize, to customize; *(computador)* to customize
personalmente *adv* personally; **me encargaré yo p.** I'll deal with it myself *o* personally; **no la conozco p.** I don't know her personally; **les afecta p.** it affects them personally; **a mí, p., no me importa** it doesn't matter to me personally; **p., prefiero la segunda propuesta** personally I prefer the second proposal
personarse *vpr* (**a**) *(presentarse)* to turn up; **Señor López, persónese en caja central** would Mr López please go to the main sales desk (**b**) *Esp Der* to appear; **p. como parte en un juicio** = to take part in a trial in support of, but independent from, the state prosecution, to represent victims or special interests
personería *nf Arg* ***p. gremial*** trade union status; *Col, CSur* ***p. jurídica*** legal personality *o* status
personero, -a *nm,f Am* (**a**) *(representante)* representative (**b**) *(portavoz)* spokesperson
personificación *nf* (**a**) *(representación)* personification; **este niño es la p. del mal** this child is an absolute devil (**b**) *(prosopopeya)* personification
personificar *vt* (**a**) *(representar)* to personify; **este niño es la maldad personificada** this child is an absolute devil (**b**) *(atribuir rasgos humanos)* to personify
perspectiva *nf* (**a**) *(en dibujo)* perspective; **en p.** *(dibujo)* in perspective ▸▸ ***p. aérea*** aerial perspective; ***p. lineal*** linear perspective
(**b**) *(paisaje)* view
(**c**) *(punto de vista)* perspective; **según su p....** the way he sees it...
(**d**) *(futuro)* prospect; **en p.** in prospect; **tienen un viaje a África en p.** they have a trip to Africa in prospect
(**e**) *(posibilidad)* prospect; **la p. de tener que visitarla no me entusiasma** the prospect of having to visit her doesn't exactly thrill me

perspex®, pérspex® *nm inv* Perspex®, *US* Plexiglas®
perspicacia *nf* insight, perceptiveness; **actuó con p.** she acted shrewdly
perspicaz *adj* sharp, perceptive
persuadir 1 *vt* to persuade; **p. a alguien para que haga algo** to persuade sb to do sth
2 persuadirse *vpr* to persuade oneself; **persuadirse de algo** to become persuaded of sth
persuasión *nf* persuasion; **tiene mucha capacidad de p.** she's very persuasive
persuasiva *nf* persuasive power
persuasivo, -a *adj* persuasive
pertenecer [46] *vi* (**a**) **p. a** *(ser propiedad de)* to belong to; **este libro pertenece a la biblioteca de mi tío** this book is part of my uncle's library; **el león pertenece a la categoría de los felinos** the lion belongs to the cat family (**b**) *(corresponder a)* to be up to, to be a matter for; **es a él a quien pertenece presentar disculpas** it's up to him to apologize
perteneciente *adj* **p. a** belonging to
pertenencia 1 *nf* (**a**) *(propiedad)* ownership (**b**) *(afiliación)* membership; **su p. a la empresa lo invalida para participar en el concurso** he's not allowed to take part in the competition because he's a member of the company; **negó su p. a la banda armada** he denied belonging to the terrorist organization
2 pertenencias *nfpl (efectos personales)* belongings
pértiga *nf* (**a**) *(vara)* pole (**b**) *(disciplina)* **(salto con) p.** pole vault
pertiguista *nmf* pole vaulter
pertinacia *nf* (**a**) *(terquedad)* stubbornness (**b**) *(persistencia)* persistence
pertinaz *adj* (**a**) *(terco)* stubborn (**b**) *(persistente)* persistent
pertinencia *nf* (**a**) *(adecuación)* appropriateness (**b**) *(relevancia)* relevance
pertinente *adj* (**a**) *(adecuado)* appropriate; **se tomarán las medidas pertinentes** the appropriate measures will be taken; **si lo consideras p., llámale** telephone him if you think it's necessary (**b**) *(relativo)* relevant, pertinent; **ya he enviado todos los documentos pertinentes a la beca** I have already sent off all the forms relating to the grant
pertrechar 1 *vt* (**a**) *(ejército)* to supply with food and ammunition (**b**) *(equipar)* to equip
2 pertrecharse *vpr* **pertrecharse de** to equip oneself with
pertrechos *nmpl* (**a**) *(de ejército)* supplies and ammunition (**b**) *(utensilios)* gear
perturbación *nf* (**a**) *(desconcierto)* disquiet, unease (**b**) *(disturbio)* disturbance ▸▸ ***p. del orden público*** breach of the peace (**c**) *(mental)* mental imbalance (**d**) *Meteo* ***p. atmosférica*** atmospheric disturbance
perturbado, -a 1 *adj* (**a**) *(mental)* disturbed, mentally unbalanced (**b**) *(desconcertado)* perturbed
2 *nm,f* mentally unbalanced person
perturbador, -ora 1 *adj* unsettling
2 *nm,f* troublemaker
perturbar *vt* (**a**) *(trastornar)* to disrupt (**b**) *(alterar)* to disturb, to unsettle (**c**) *(enloquecer)* to perturb
Perú *nm* **(el) P.** Peru
peruanismo *nm* = word or expression peculiar to Peruvian Spanish
peruano, -a 1 *adj* Peruvian
2 *nm,f* Peruvian
perversidad *nf* wickedness
perversión *nf* perversion ▸▸ ***p. sexual*** sexual perversion
perverso, -a 1 *adj* evil, wicked
2 *nm,f* (**a**) *(depravado)* depraved person (**b**) *(persona mala)* evil person
pervertido, -a *nm,f* pervert
pervertidor, -ora 1 *adj* pernicious, corrupting
2 *nm,f* reprobate, corrupter ▸▸ ***p. de menores*** corrupter of minors
pervertir [63] **1** *vt* to corrupt
2 pervertirse *vpr* to become corrupt, to be corrupted
pervivencia *nf* survival
pervivir *vi* to survive
pesa *nf* (**a**) *(balanza, contrapeso)* weight (**b**) *(de reloj)* weight (**c**) *Dep* **pesas** weights; **levantamiento de pesas** weightlifting; **levantar pesas** to do weightlifting; *Fam* **hacer pesas** to lift weights, to do weight training

pesabebés *nm inv* baby scales

pesadamente *adv* **(a)** *(con gran peso)* heavily; **dejó caer el puño p. sobre la mesa** he brought his fist down heavily on the table **(b)** *(dificultosamente)* heavily; **respirar p.** to breathe heavily *o* with difficulty

pesadez *nf* **(a)** *(peso)* weight **(b)** *(sensación)* heaviness ►► ***p. de estómago*** full feeling in the stomach, bloated stomach **(c)** *(molestia, fastidio)* drag, pain **(d)** *(aburrimiento)* bore; **¡qué p. de película!** what a boring *o* tedious movie!

pesadilla *nf* **(a)** *(sueño)* nightmare **(b)** *(angustia)* nightmare

pesado, -a 1 *adj* **(a)** *(que pesa)* heavy
(b) *(industria, maquinaria)* heavy
(c) *(tiempo, día)* oppressive; **el día está p.** it's very close today
(d) *(comida)* heavy, stodgy
(e) *(ojos, cabeza)* heavy; **tengo el estómago p.** I feel bloated
(f) *(sueño)* deep
(g) *(lento)* slow-moving; **un hombre de andares pesados** a man with a ponderous gait
(h) *(tarea, trabajo)* difficult, tough
(i) *(aburrido)* boring
(j) *(molesto)* annoying, tiresome; **¡qué pesada eres!** you're so annoying!; **ponerse p.** to be a pain; EXPR *Fam* **¡eres más p. que una vaca en brazos!** you're such a pain in the neck!
2 *nm,f* bore, pain

pesadumbre *nf* grief, sorrow

pesaje *nm* **(a)** *(acción)* weighing **(b)** *(en deporte)* weigh-in

pésame *nm* sympathy, condolences; **dar el p.** to offer one's condolences; **mi más sentido p.** my deepest sympathies

PESAR[1] **1** *nm* **(a)** *(tristeza)* grief; **todos sentimos un hondo p. por su fallecimiento** we all felt a great sorrow at his death **(b)** *(arrepentimiento)* remorse; **no le daba ningún p.** she felt no remorse at all
2 a pesar de *loc prep* despite, in spite of; **a p. de las críticas** in spite of *o* despite all the criticism; **tuve que hacerlo a p. mío** I had to do it against my will; **muy a nuestro p., hubo que invitarles** we had to invite them, even though we really didn't want to; **muy a p. mío no puedo darte lo que me pides** I can't give you what you want, much as I'd like to; **a p. de que...** in spite of *o* despite the fact that...; **a p. de que me dolía, seguí jugando** I carried on playing in spite of *o* despite the pain; **a p. de todo** in spite of *o* despite everything; EXPR *Fam* **a p. de los pesares** in spite of *o* despite everything

PESAR[2] **1** *vt* **(a)** *(en balanza)* to weigh; **pésemelo, por favor** could you weigh it for me, please?
(b) *(examinar, calibrar)* to weigh up
2 *vi* **(a)** *(tener peso)* to weigh; **pesa cinco kilos** it weighs five kilos; **¿cuánto pesa?** how much *o* what does it weigh?; **esta maleta no pesa nada** this suitcase hardly weighs anything
(b) *(ser pesado)* to be heavy; **¡cómo** *o* **cuánto pesa!** it's really heavy!; **¡ya va pesando la edad!, ¡ya van pesando los años!** I'm getting old!
(c) *(recaer)* **pesa una orden de arresto sobre él** there is a warrant out for his arrest; **sobre ti pesa la decisión última** the final decision rests with you
(d) *(importar, influir)* to play an important part; **en su decisión pesaron muchas razones** a number of reasons influenced her decision
(e) *(doler, entristecer)* **me pesa tener que hacerlo** I regret having to do it; **me pesa tener que decirte esto** I'm sorry to have to tell you this; **no me pesa haber dejado ese trabajo** I have no regrets about leaving that job, I'm not at all sorry I left that job
(f) EXPR **mal que te pese** (whether you) like it or not
3 pesarse *vpr* to weigh oneself
4 pese a *loc prep* despite, in spite of; **pese a no conocerla...** although I didn't know her..., in spite of *o* despite the fact that I didn't know her...; **pese a que** in spite of *o* despite the fact that...; **el espectáculo, pese a que es caro, vale la pena** although the show's expensive, it's worth seeing, in spite of *o* despite the fact that the show's expensive, it's still worth seeing; **lo haré pese a quien pese** I'm going to do it, no matter who I upset

pesaroso, -a *adj* **(a)** *(arrepentido)* remorseful **(b)** *(afligido)* sad

PESC *nf UE (abrev de* **política exterior y de seguridad común***)* CSFP

pesca *nf* **(a)** *(acción)* fishing; **la p. de la ballena** whaling; **ir de p.** to go fishing ►► ***p. de altura*** deep-sea fishing; ***p. de arrastre*** trawling; ***p. de bajura*** coastal fishing; ***p. con caña*** angling; ***p. deportiva*** angling *(in competitions)*; ***p. submarina*** underwater fishing
(b) *(captura)* catch; EXPR *Fam* **toda la p.: tuvimos que preparar la tienda de campaña y toda la p.** we had to get the tent ready and all the rest of it; **vinieron Luis, su hermano y toda la p.** Luis, his brother and the rest of the crew all came

pescada *nf* hake

pescadería *nf* fishmonger's (shop)

pescadero, -a *nm,f* fishmonger

pescadilla *nf* whiting; EXPR *Esp Fam* **ser como la p. que se muerde la cola** to be a vicious circle

pescadito *nm* **p. (frito)** = dish consisting of small fried fish

pescado *nm* fish ►► ***p. azul*** oily fish; ***p. blanco*** white fish

pescador, -ora *nm,f (en barco)* fisherman, *f* fisherwoman; *(de caña)* angler ►► ***p. furtivo*** poacher

pescante *nm* **(a)** *(de carruaje)* driver's seat **(b)** *Náut* davit **(c)** *Teatro* hoist *(for lowering/lifting actors onto/from stage)*

pescar [60] **1** *vt* **(a)** *(peces)* to catch; **sólo consiguieron p. una bota** all they caught was an old boot
(b) *Fam (contraer)* to catch; **pescó una gripe** she caught the flu
(c) *Fam (pillar, atrapar)* to catch; **lo pescaron intentando entrar sin pagar** he got caught trying to get in without paying
(d) *Fam (conseguir)* to get, to land; **ha pescado un trabajo estupendo** she's landed a fantastic job; **pescó un buen marido** she landed herself a good husband
(e) *Fam (entender)* to pick up, to understand; **¿has pescado el chiste?** did you get the joke?; **cuando me hablan en francés no pesco ni una** I can't understand a word when they speak to me in French
2 *vi* to fish; **ir a p.** to go fishing

pescozada *nf*, **pescozón** *nm Fam* blow on the neck

pescuezo *nm* neck; EXPR *Fam* **retorcer el p. a alguien** to wring sb's neck

pese *ver* **pesar**

pesebre *nm* **(a)** *(para los animales)* manger **(b)** *(belén)* crib, Nativity scene

pesero *nm Méx* **(a)** *(vehículo)* collective taxi *(with a fixed rate and that travels a fixed route)* **(b)** *(persona)* collective taxi driver

peseta *nf Antes* peseta; *Esp* **no tengo ni una p., estoy sin una p.** I'm broke; EXPR *Esp Fam* **cambiar la p.** to puke; EXPR *Esp Fam* **mirar la p.** to watch one's money

pesetero, -a *Esp Fam Pey* **1** *adj* money-grubbing
2 *nm,f* moneygrubber

pésimamente *adv* terribly, awfully

pesimismo *nm* pessimism

pesimista 1 *adj* pessimistic
2 *nmf* pessimist

pésimo, -a 1 *superlativo ver* **malo**
2 *adj* terrible, awful

pesista *nmf Am* weightlifter

peso *nm* **(a)** *(en general)* weight; **tiene un kilo de p.** it weighs a kilo; **ganar/perder p.** to gain/lose weight; **vender algo al p.** to sell sth by weight; **de p.** *(razones)* weighty, sound; *(persona)* influential; EXPR **caer por su propio p.** to be self-evident; EXPR **pagar algo a p. de oro** to pay a fortune for sth; EXPR **valer su p. en oro** to be worth its/his/*etc* weight in gold ►► ***p. atómico*** atomic weight; ***p. bruto*** gross weight; *Fís* ***p. específico*** relative density, specific gravity; *Fig* **tiene mucho p. específico** he carries a lot of weight; *Quím* ***p. molar*** molar weight; ***p. molecular*** molecular weight; ***p. muerto*** dead weight; ***p. neto*** net weight
(b) *(sensación)* heavy feeling; **siento p. en las piernas** my legs feel heavy
(c) *(fuerza, influencia)* weight; **su palabra tiene mucho p.** his word carries a lot of weight; **el p. de sus argumentos está fuera de duda** there is no disputing the force of her arguments; **el vicepresidente ejerce mucho p. en la organización** the vice president carries a lot of weight in the organization
(d) *(carga, preocupación)* burden; **el p. de la culpabilidad** the burden of guilt; EXPR **quitarse un p. de encima** to take a weight off one's mind
(e) *(balanza)* scales
(f) *(moneda)* peso
(g) *Dep* shot; **lanzamiento de p.** shot put
(h) *(en boxeo)* weight ►► ***p. gallo*** bantamweight; ***p. ligero*** lightweight; ***p. medio*** middleweight; ***p. mosca*** flyweight; *también Fig* ***p. pesado*** heavyweight; ***p. pluma*** featherweight; ***p. semiligero*** light middleweight; ***p. semipesado*** light heavyweight; ***p. welter*** welterweight
(i) *Am Fam (dinero)* **en ese trabajo no gana un p.** she earns next to

nothing in that job; **no tengo un p.** I'm broke; **¿cuánto te costó? – no mucho, dos pesos** how much did it cost you? – not much *o* next to nothing

pespunte *nm* backstitch

pespuntear *vt* to backstitch

pesquería *nf* (**a**) *(sitio)* fishery, fishing ground (**b**) *(actividad)* fishing

pesquero, -a 1 *adj* fishing; **la flota pesquera** the fishing fleet
2 *nm* fishing boat

pesquis *nm inv Esp Fam* gumption, *Br* nous; **no tiene nada de p.** he has no gumption *o Br* nous whatsoever

pesquisa *nf* investigation, inquiry

pestaña *nf* (**a**) *(de párpado)* eyelash; EXPR *Fam* **quemarse las pestañas** to burn the midnight oil (**b**) *(de recortable)* flap (**c**) *Tec* flange

pestañear *vi* to blink; EXPR **sin p.** *(con serenidad)* without batting an eyelid; *(con atención)* without losing concentration once

pestañeo *nm* blinking

pestazo *nm Fam* stink, stench

peste *nf* (**a**) *(enfermedad epidémica)* plague; EXPR **huir de alguien como de la p.** to avoid sb like the plague ▸▸ ***p. aviar*** *o* ***aviaria*** fowl pest; ***p. bubónica*** bubonic plague; ***p. equina*** African horse sickness; ***la p. negra*** the Black Death; ***p. porcina*** *Br* swine fever, *US* hog cholera
(**b**) *Andes, RP Fam (resfriado)* cold; *(gripe)* flu; **se agarró una p. que anda rondando** she caught a flu bug that's going around
(**c**) *Fam (mal olor)* stink, stench
(**d**) *Fam (molestia)* pain (in the neck); **iqué p. de vecinos tenemos!** what a pain (in the neck) our neighbours are!
(**e**) EXPR *Fam* **decir** *o* **echar pestes de alguien** *Br* to slag sb off, *US* to badmouth sb; *Fam* **echar pestes** to curse, to swear

pesticida 1 *adj* pesticidal
2 *nm* pesticide

pestilencia *nf* stench

pestilente *adj* foul-smelling

pestillo *nm* (**a**) *(cerrojo)* bolt; **correr** *o* **echar el p. de la puerta** to bolt the door (**b**) *(pieza)* latch

pestiño *nm* (**a**) *(dulce)* honey-dipped fritter (**b**) *Esp Fam (aburrimiento)* bore; **imenudo p. de novela!** what a boring *o* dull novel!

pesto *nm (salsa)* pesto (sauce)

pestoso, -a *adj RP* foul-smelling

PET [pet] *nm Med* (*abrev de* **Positron Emission Tomography**) PET scan

petaca *nf* (**a**) *(para cigarrillos)* cigarette case; *(para tabaco)* tobacco pouch (**b**) *(para bebidas)* flask (**c**) *Méx (maleta)* suitcase (**d**) *Méx Fam* **petacas** *(nalgas)* buttocks (**e**) *Urug (polvera)* (powder) compact (**f**) *PRico (para lavar)* washing trough (**g**) EXPR *Fam* **hacer la p.** *(como broma)* to make an apple-pie bed

petaco *nm Esp Fam* pinball machine

pétalo *nm* petal

petanca *nf* petanque

petardo, -a 1 *nm,f Fam* (**a**) *(persona fea)* horror, ugly person (**b**) *(persona molesta)* pain (in the neck); **ino seas p.!** don't be a pain (in the neck)!
2 *nm* (**a**) *(cohete)* firecracker, *Br* banger (**b**) *Fam (aburrimiento)* bore; **iqué p. de película!** what a boring movie! (**c**) *Esp Fam (porro)* joint

petate 1 *nm* (**a**) *(bolsa)* kit bag; EXPR *Esp Fam* **liar el p.** *(marcharse)* to pack one's bags and go; EXPR *CAm, Méx Fam* **doblar** *o* **liar el p.** *(morir)* to kick the bucket (**b**) *Andes, CAm, Méx (estera)* palm leaf mat *(for sleeping on)*; EXPR *Méx Fam* **el p. del muerto: a mí no me espantan** *o* **asustan con el p. del muerto** you don't scare me, you're just bluffing
2 petates *nmpl RP Fam* gear, things; **vamos a poner orden aquí, juntá todos tus petates** let's tidy the place up, gather all your things together

petatearse *vpr CAm, Méx Fam* to kick the bucket

petenera *nf* = Andalusian popular song; EXPR *Esp Fam* **salir por peteneras** to go off at a tangent

petición *nf* (**a**) *(acción)* request; **el país formuló una p. de ayuda al exterior** the country made an appeal for foreign aid; **a p. de** at the request of; **a p. del público habrá dos representaciones más** by popular request there will be two further performances; **el presidente compareció ante la cámara a p. propia** the president appeared before the house at his own request; **certificado expedido a p. del interesado** certificate issued at the request of the person concerned ▸▸ ***p. de extradición*** extradition request; ***p. de indulto*** appeal for a reprieve; ***p. de mano*** = act of formally asking a woman's parents for her hand in marriage
(**b**) *Der (escrito)* petition

peticionante *Am* **1** *adj* petitioning
2 *nmf* petitioner

peticionar *vt Am* to petition

peticionario, -a 1 *adj* petitioning
2 *nm,f* petitioner

petimetre *nm* fop, dandy

petirrojo *nm* robin

petiso, -a, petizo, -a 1 *adj Andes, RP Fam* short
2 *nm* (**a**) *Andes, RP Fam (persona)* shorty (**b**) *RP (caballo)* small horse

petit: en petit comité *loc adv* **la decisión se tomó en p. comité** the decision was taken by a select few

petizo = **petiso**

peto *nm* (**a**) *(de prenda)* bib (**b**) *(de armadura)* breastplate (**c**) *(en béisbol)* chest protector (**d**) *Taurom* = protective padding for picador's horse

petrel *nm* petrel

pétreo, -a *adj* (**a**) *(de piedra)* stone; **un muro p.** a stone wall (**b**) *(como piedra)* stony

petrificación *nf* petrification

petrificado, -a *adj* (**a**) *(endurecido)* petrified (**b**) *(sorprendido)* petrified

petrificar [60] **1** *vt* (**a**) *(endurecer)* to petrify (**b**) *(sorprender)* to stun
2 petrificarse *vpr* (**a**) *(endurecerse)* to become petrified (**b**) *(sorprenderse)* to be stunned

petrodólar *nm* petrodollar

petroglifo *nm* petroglyph

petrografía *nf Geol* petrography

petróleo *nm* oil, petroleum ▸▸ ***p. crudo*** crude oil

> **Falso amigo**: El sustantivo inglés **petrol** no es la traducción del español **petróleo**. En inglés **petrol** significa "gasolina".

petrolera *nf* oil company

petrolero, -a 1 *adj* oil; **compañía petrolera** oil company
2 *nm* oil tanker

petrolífero, -a *adj* oil; **pozo p.** oil well

petrología *nf* petrology

petroprecio *nm Méx* price of oil

petroquímica *nf* petrochemistry

petroquímico, -a *adj* petrochemical

petulancia *nf* arrogance

petulante 1 *adj* opinionated, arrogant
2 *nmf* opinionated person; **es un p.** he's very opinionated

> **Falso amigo**: El adjetivo inglés **petulant** no es la traducción del español **petulante**. En inglés **petulant** significa "caprichoso".

petunia *nf* petunia

peúco *nm* bootee

peyorativo, -a *adj* pejorative

peyote *nm* peyote

pez¹ *nm (animal)* fish; EXPR **estar como p. en el agua** to be in one's element; EXPR *Esp Fam* **estar p. (en algo)** to have no idea (about sth); EXPR **el p. grande se come al chico** the big fish swallow up the little ones; PROV **por la boca muere el p.,** *RP* **el p. por la boca muere** silence is golden ▸▸ ***p. de agua dulce*** freshwater fish; ***p. de agua salada*** saltwater fish; ***p. de colores*** goldfish; EXPR *Fam* **me río yo de los peces de colores** I couldn't care less; ***p. erizo*** porcupine fish; ***p. espada*** swordfish; *Fam Fig* ***p. gordo*** big shot; ***p. luna*** sunfish; ***p. martillo*** hammerhead shark; ***p. piloto*** pilot fish; ***p. de río*** freshwater fish; ***p. sierra*** sawfish; ***p. volador*** flying fish

pez² *nf (sustancia)* pitch, tar

pezón *nm* (**a**) *(de pecho)* nipple (**b**) *(de planta)* stalk

pezonera *nf* nipple shield

pezuña *nf* (**a**) *(de animal)* hoof (**b**) *Fam (mano)* paw

PGB *nm Chile* (*abrev de* **producto geográfico bruto**) GDP

PGE *nmpl* (*abrev de* **Presupuestos Generales del Estado**) = Spanish National Budget, *Br* ≃ the Budget

pH *nm* pH

Phnom Penh [nom'pen] *n* Phnom Penh

pi *nm Mat* pi

piadosamente *adv* (**a**) *(con compasión)* kindheartedly (**b**) *(con devoción)* piously

piadoso, -a *adj* (**a**) *(compasivo)* kind-hearted (**b**) *(religioso)* pious

piafar *vi* to paw the ground

pial *nm Am* lasso

pialar *vt Andes, RP* to lasso

piamadre, piamáter *nf Anat* pia mater

Piamonte *nm* **(el) P.** Piedmont

pianissimo [pja'nisimo] *adv Mús* pianissimo

pianista *nmf* pianist

piano 1 *nm* piano; EXPR *Esp Fam* **como un p.: una mentira como un p.** a huge lie, an absolute whopper ►► ***p. bar*** piano bar; ***p. de cola*** grand piano; ***p. de media cola*** baby grand; ***p. vertical*** upright piano
2 *adv Mús* piano; EXPR *Méx, RP* **p., p.** take it easy

pianoforte *nm Mús* pianoforte

pianola *nf* Pianola®

piar [32] *vi* to cheep, to tweet

piara *nf* herd

piastra *nf* piastre, piaster

PIB *nm (abrev de* **producto** *Esp* **interior** *o Am* **interno bruto**) GDP

pibe, -a *nm,f Fam* (**a**) *Esp (hombre)* guy; *(mujer)* girl (**b**) *Arg (niño)* kid, boy; *(niña)* kid, girl

piberío *nm Arg* bunch of kids

pibil *nm* **al p.** = wrapped in banana skins, cooked in an underground oven, and served in an annatto seed and orange or lime juice sauce

pica *nf* (**a**) *(lanza)* pike; EXPR **poner una p. en Flandes** to do the impossible (**b**) *Taurom* goad, picador's spear (**c**) *(naipe)* spade (**d**) **picas** *(palo)* spades (**e**) *Imprenta (medida)* pica (**f**) *Fam (revisor)* ticket inspector (**g**) *RP Fam (tensión)* resentment; **hay p. entre los hinchas de estos dos cuadros** there's a lot of needle *o* ill-feeling between the fans of these two teams

picacera *nf Chile, Perú* pique, resentment

picacho *nm* summit, peak

picada *nf* (**a**) *RP (tapas)* appetizers, snacks (**b**) *RP Fam (carrera)* car race *(in street)* (**c**) *RP Br* mince, *US* ground beef (**d**) *Am (de avión)* nose dive; **hacer una p.** to dive; **caer en p.: el avión cayó en p.** the plane nose-dived; **la caída en p. del PIB** the sharp drop in GDP

picadero *nm* (**a**) *(de caballos)* riding school (**b**) *Fam (de soltero)* = apartment or house used for sexual encounters (**c**) *Fam (de drogadictos)* shooting gallery

picadillo *nm* (**a**) *(preparación)* **añada un p. de perejil y cebolla** add finely chopped parsley and onion; **hacer un p. de cebolla** to chop an onion finely; EXPR *Fam* **hacer p. a alguien** to beat sb to a pulp (**b**) *Chile (tapas)* appetizers, snacks

picado, -a 1 *adj* (**a**) *(marcado) (piel)* pockmarked; *(fruta)* bruised
(**b**) *(agujereado)* perforated; **p. de polilla** moth-eaten
(**c**) *(diente)* decayed; **tengo una muela picada** I've got a bad *o* rotten tooth
(**d**) *(triturado) (alimento)* chopped; *(tabaco)* cut; *Esp, RP* **carne picada** *Br* mince, *US* ground beef
(**e**) *(vino)* sour
(**f**) *(mar)* choppy
(**g**) *Fam (enfadado)* peeved, put out; **está p. porque no lo invitaron a la fiesta** he's peeved *o* put out because he wasn't invited to the party
(**h**) *Am (achispado)* tipsy
2 *nm* (**a**) *Esp (de avión)* nose dive; **hacer un p.** to dive; **caer en p.: el avión cayó en p.** the plane nose-dived; **la caída en p. del régimen** the collapse of the regime (**b**) *Col, RP Fam (de fútbol)* kickabout; **¿jugamos un p.?** shall we have a kickabout?

picador, -ora *nm,f* (**a**) *Taurom* picador (**b**) *(domador)* (horse) trainer (**c**) *(minero)* face worker

picadora *nf Esp, RP* mincer

picadura *nf* (**a**) *(de mosquito, serpiente)* bite; *(de avispa, escorpión)* sting (**b**) *(de viruela)* pockmark (**c**) *(de diente)* decay (**d**) *(tabaco)* (cut) tobacco

picaflor *nm Am* (**a**) *(colibrí)* hummingbird (**b**) *(galanteador)* flirt

picajoso, -a *adj Fam* touchy

picamaderos *nm inv* woodpecker

picana *nf Am* (**a**) *(para ganado)* goad (**b**) *(eléctrica)* electric cattle prod

picanear *vt Am* (**a**) *(ganado)* to goad (**b**) *(persona)* to torture with an electric cattle prod

picante 1 *adj* (**a**) *(comida)* spicy, hot (**b**) *(chiste, comedia)* saucy (**c**) *Chile Fam (ordinario)* common; **se fue a vivir a un barrio p.** she went to live in a downmarket area
2 *nm* (**a**) *(salsa)* hot sauce; **le puso demasiado p.** she made it too hot *o* spicy; **me gusta el p.** I like spicy food (**b**) *Andes (guiso)* spicy meat stew (**c**) *Chile Fam (ordinario)* pleb; **son unos picantes** they're plebs

picantería *nf Andes* (**a**) *(restaurante)* cheap restaurant (**b**) *(carrito)* = cart selling snacks

picapedrero *nm* stonecutter

picapica *nm* **(polvos de) p.** itching powder

picapleitos *nmf inv Fam Pey* shyster (lawyer)

picaporte *nm* (**a**) *(mecanismo)* latch (**b**) *(aldaba)* doorknocker

PICAR [60] **1** *vt* (**a**) *(sujeto: mosquito, serpiente)* to bite; *(sujeto: avispa, escorpión)* to sting; **me picó una avispa** I was stung by a wasp; **p. el cebo/anzuelo** *(pez)* to bite
(**b**) *(sujeto: ave) (comida)* to peck at; **la gaviota me picó (en) una mano** the seagull pecked my hand
(**c**) *(trocear) (verdura)* to chop; *(piedra, hielo)* to break up; *(pared)* to chip the plaster off; *Esp, RP (carne)* to mince
(**d**) *Méx (pinchar)* to prick
(**e**) *(dañar, estropear) (diente, caucho, cuero)* to rot; **esos caramelos terminarán picándote las muelas** *Br* those sweets *o US* that candy will rot your teeth
(**f**) *(aperitivo)* **p. unas aceitunas** to have a few olives as an aperitif; **vamos a p. algo antes de comer** let's have some nibbles before the meal; **está todo el día picando comida** she's always nibbling at something or other between meals
(**g**) *Esp Fam (enojar)* to annoy; **le encanta p. a su hermana** he loves needling his sister
(**h**) *(estimular) (persona, caballo)* to spur on; **aquello me picó la curiosidad** that aroused my curiosity
(**i**) *(perforar) (billete, ficha)* to punch
(**j**) *Fam (mecanografiar)* to type (up)
(**k**) *Taurom* to goad
(**l**) *Dep (con efecto) (balón, pelota)* to chip; *(bola de billar)* to screw
(**m**) *Am (botar) (balón, pelota)* to bounce
(**n**) *Mús (nota)* to play staccato
(**o**) *Méx Fam* **picarle** to get a move on; **pícale, que se nos hace tarde para el teatro** get a move on, we'll be late for the play; **ya píquenle con eso, o no acabarán nunca** you'd better get a move on with that or you'll never finish
(**p**) *Col (guiñar)* to wink; **picarle un ojo a alguien** to wink at sb
2 *vi* (**a**) *(escocer) (parte del cuerpo, herida, prenda)* to itch; **¿te pica?** does it itch?; **me pica mucho la cabeza** my head is really itchy; **me pican los ojos** my eyes are stinging
(**b**) *(estar picante) (alimento, plato)* to be spicy *o* hot; *(cebolla)* to be strong
(**c**) *(ave)* to peck
(**d**) *(pez)* to bite
(**e**) *(dejarse engañar)* to take the bait; **no creo que pique** I don't think he's going to fall for it *o* take the bait
(**f**) *(tomar un aperitivo)* to nibble; **cosas de** *o* **para p.** nibbles; **¿te pongo unas aceitunas para p.?** would you like some olives as an aperitif?
(**g**) *(sol)* to burn; **cuando más picaba el sol** when the sun was at its hottest
(**h**) *Fam (mecanografiar)* to type
(**i**) *Am (balón, pelota)* to bounce; **la pelota picó fuera** the ball went out
(**j**) *RP Fam (largarse)* to take off
(**k**) EXPR **p. (muy) alto** to have great ambitions
3 picarse *vpr* (**a**) *(echarse a perder) (vino)* to turn sour; *(fruta, muela, caucho, cuero)* to rot; **la manta se ha picado** the blanket is all moth-eaten
(**b**) *(oxidarse)* to go rusty
(**c**) *(embravecerse) (mar)* to get choppy
(**d**) *Fam (enfadarse)* to get in a huff; **se picó y ganó la carrera** he got nettled and went on to win the race; PROV **el que se pica, ajos come** if the cap fits, wear it
(**e**) *Fam (inyectarse droga)* to shoot up
(**f**) *RP Fam* **picárselas** *(largarse)* to take off; **si nos parece aburrido, nos las picamos** if we find it boring, we can always just take off

picardía 1 *nf* (**a**) *(astucia)* cunning, craftiness; **hace todo con mucha p.** she does everything with great cunning *o* very cunningly (**b**) *(travesura)* naughty trick, mischief (**c**) *(atrevimiento)* brazenness; **a ese chico le falta p. con las chicas** that boy isn't bold enough with the girls (**d**) *RP (lástima)* shame
2 picardías *nm inv (con falda)* baby-doll nightdress; *(con pantalón)* baby-doll pyjamas

picaresca *nf* (a) *Lit* **la p.** picaresque literature (b) *(modo de vida)* roguery (c) *(falta de honradez)* dishonesty

picaresco, -a *adj* (a) *Lit* picaresque (b) *(del pícaro)* mischievous, roguish

pícaro, -a 1 *adj* (a) *(astuto)* cunning, crafty; **¡qué p. es este gato!** this cat is very cunning *o* sly (b) *(travieso)* naughty, mischievous (c) *(atrevido) (persona)* bold, daring; *(comentario)* naughty, racy; *(sonrisa)* wicked, cheeky
2 *nm,f* (a) *Lit* rogue *(protagonist in picaresque novels)* (b) *(astuto)* sly person, rogue (c) *(travieso)* rascal (d) *(atrevido)* brazen person

picarón, -ona 1 *adj Fam* roguish, mischievous
2 *nm,f Fam* rogue, rascal
3 *nm Andes* doughnut

picassiano, -a *adj* Picassoesque

picatoste *nm* crouton

picazón *nf* (a) *(en el cuerpo)* itch (b) *(inquietud)* uneasiness

picha *nf* (a) *Esp Vulg* prick; EXPR **hacerse la p. un lío** to get in a total *Br* bloody *o US* goddamn muddle (b) *Col Fam* sleep *(in the eyes)*

pichana, pichanga *nf* (a) *Andes (escoba)* broom (b) *Chile (de fútbol)* kickabout

piche *adj Ven Fam* (a) *(podrido)* off, rotten (b) *(escaso)* measly

pichear 1 *vt (en béisbol)* to pitch
2 *vi (en béisbol)* to pitch

pícher, pitcher *nm (en béisbol)* pitcher

pichi[1] *nm Esp Br* pinafore (dress), *US* jumper

pichi[2] *RP Fam* 1 *adj* cheap and nasty
2 *nmf* poor wretch

pichí *nm CSur Fam* pee; **hacer p.** to have a pee

pichicata *nf Andes, RP Fam* (a) *(droga)* drugs; **mi vecina le da a la p.** my neighbour's a druggie (b) *(medicamento)* medicine *(that makes you drowsy)*; **lo peor de estar enfermo es tener que tomar tanta p.** the worst thing about being ill is having to take all those medicines that make you drowsy

pichicatear *Andes, RP Fam* 1 *vt* to drug
2 **pichicatearse** *vpr* to take drugs

pichicatero, -a *nm,f Andes, RP Fam* druggie

pichicato, -a *adj Méx Fam* stingy

pichichi *nm Esp Dep* top scorer

pichicho, -a *nm,f RP Fam* pooch

pichincha *nf RP Fam* snip, bargain

pichintún *nm Chile Fam* **un p. de** a smidgen of

pichirre *adj Ven Fam* skinflint

pichiruche, pichiruchi *nm Andes, RP Fam* nobody

picho, -a *adj Col* rotten

pichón *nm* (a) *(ave)* young pigeon; **tiro de p.** pigeon shooting (b) *Fam (apelativo cariñoso)* darling, sweetheart (c) *Méx Fam (ingenuo)* novice, *US* rookie

pichula *nf Chile, Perú Vulg* prick, cock

pichulear *vi RP Fam (regatear)* to haggle

pichuleo *nm RP Fam* haggling

pichuncho *nm Chile* = cocktail made with pisco and vermouth

Picio *n pr* EXPR *Fam* **ser más feo que P.** to be as ugly as sin

pickles ['pikles] *nmpl RP* pickles

pickup [pi'kap] *(pl* **pickups**) *nf Am* pick-up (truck)

picnic *(pl* **picnics**) *nm* picnic; **hacer un p.** to have a picnic

pico *nm* (a) *(de ave)* beak; EXPR *Méx Fam* **ser p. de gallo** to be a loudmouth
(b) *Fam (boca)* mouth, *esp Br* gob; **¡no se te ocurra abrir el p.!** keep your mouth shut!; **¡cierra el p.!** shut your trap!; EXPR **darle al p.** to talk a lot, to yak; EXPR *Fam* **irse del p.** to shoot one's mouth off; EXPR **ser** *o* **tener un p. de oro, tener mucho p.** to be a smooth talker, to have the gift of the gab
(c) *(punta, saliente)* corner
(d) *(de vasija)* lip, spout
(e) *(herramienta)* pick, pickaxe
(f) *(cumbre)* peak; *(montaña)* peak, mountain ►► ***los Picos de Europa*** = mountain range in the northern Spanish provinces of Asturias, León and Cantabria
(g) *(cantidad indeterminada)* **cincuenta y p.** fifty-odd, fifty-something; **llegó a las cinco y p.** he got there just after five; **pesa diez kilos y p.** it weighs just over ten kilos; EXPR **le costó** *o* **le salió por un p.** *(cantidad elevada)* it cost her a fortune
(h) *(ave)* ***p. menor*** lesser spotted woodpecker; ***p. picapinos*** great spotted woodpecker
(i) *Fam (de heroína)* fix; **meterse un p.** to give oneself a fix
(j) *Arg, Col Fam (beso)* kiss
(k) *Chile Vulg (pene)* cock, knob
(l) EXPR *Esp Fam* **andar/irse de picos pardos** to be/go out on the town; *Fam* **darse el p.** *(besarse) Br* to snog, *US* to suck face; *RP* **a p. seco** *(bebida)* neat

picogordo *nm* hawfinch

picoleto *nm Esp Fam Pey* = derogatory name for member of the Guardia Civil

picor *nm* itch; **tengo un p. en la espalda** my back itches, I've got an itchy back

picoso, -a *adj Méx* spicy, hot

picota *nf* (a) *(de ajusticiados)* pillory; EXPR **poner a alguien en la p.** to pillory sb (b) *(cereza)* = type of large cherry

picotazo *nm* peck; **la paloma le dio un p. en el dedo** the pigeon pecked him on the finger

picotear *vt* 1 (a) *(ave)* to peck (b) *Fam (comer)* to pick at
2 *vi Fam (comer)* to nibble, to pick

picoteo *nm* (a) *(de ave)* pecking (b) *Fam (de persona)* nibbling

pictografía *nf* pictography

pictograma *nm* pictogram

pictórico, -a *adj* pictorial

picudo, -a 1 *adj* (a) *(puntiagudo)* pointed (b) *Méx Fam (sagaz)* clever
2 *nm,f Méx Fam* **es un p., todo le sale bien** he's really clever, he's good at everything

pidén *nm* austral rail

pidgin ['piðjin] *(pl* **pidgins**) *nm* pidgin

pidiera *etc ver* **pedir**

pido *etc ver* **pedir**

pídola *nf Esp* leapfrog

PIE *nm* (a) *(de persona)* foot; **estos zapatos me hacen daño en los pies** these shoes hurt my feet; **a p.** on foot; **prefiero ir a p.** I'd rather walk *o* go on foot; **estar de** *o* **en p.** to be standing; **ponerse de** *o* **en p.** to stand up; **llevamos dos horas de p.** we've been on our feet for two hours; **llevo en p. desde las seis de la mañana** I've been up and about since six in the morning; **la oferta sigue en p.** the offer still stands; **echar p. a tierra** *(jinete)* to dismount; *(pasajero)* to alight; **se me fueron los pies** *(resbalé)* I slipped, I lost my footing; **se me iban los pies con la música** my feet were tapping along to the music; **perder/no hacer p.** *(en el agua)* to go/to be out of one's depth; *Formal* **a sus pies** at your service; **el ciudadano de a p.** the man in the street; **en p. de igualdad** on an equal footing; **en p. de guerra** on a war footing; EXPR **pies de barro: un héroe/líder con (los) pies de barro** a hero/leader with feet of clay; EXPR *Fam* **buscar (los) tres** *o* **cinco pies al gato** to overcomplicate matters; EXPR **de pies a cabeza** from head to toe; EXPR **con buen p.: empezar con buen p.** to get off to a good start; **terminar con buen p.** to end on a good note; EXPR **caer de p.** *(tener suerte)* to land on one's feet; EXPR **no dar p. con bola** to get everything wrong; EXPR **con el p. derecho: empezar con el p. derecho** to get off to a good start; EXPR **estar con un p. en el estribo** to be about to leave; EXPR **a pies juntillas** unquestioningly; EXPR **levantarse con el p. izquierdo** to get out of bed on the wrong side; EXPR **con mal p.: empezar con mal p.** to get off to a bad start; **terminar con mal p.** to end on a sour note; EXPR **nacer de p.** to be born lucky; EXPR **andar** *o* **ir con pies de plomo** to tread carefully; EXPR **pararle los pies a alguien** to put sb in their place; EXPR *Fam* **poner pies en polvorosa: al llegar la policía, puso pies en polvorosa** when the police arrived, you couldn't see him for dust *o* he legged it; EXPR **poner los pies en** *o* **sobre la tierra** to get a grip on reality; EXPR *Esp* **saber de qué p. cojea alguien** to know sb's weaknesses; EXPR *Fam* **salir con los pies por delante** to leave feet first *o* in a box; EXPR *Esp Fam* **salir por pies** to leg it; EXPR **no tener ni pies ni cabeza** to make no sense at all; EXPR **tener un p. en la tumba** to have one foot in the grave EXPR **no tenerse en p.: no me tengo de** *o* **en p.** I'm can't stand up a minute longer; **esa teoría no se tiene en p.** that theory doesn't stand up ►► ***p. de atleta*** athlete's foot; ***p. de cabra*** crowbar, *Br* jemmy, *US* jimmy; ***pies de cerdo*** (pig's) trotters; ***pies planos*** flat feet
(b) *(base) (de lámpara, micrófono)* stand; *(de copa)* stem; *(de montaña, árbol, escalera)* foot; **al p. de la página** at the foot *o* bottom of the page; **al p. de** *o* **a los pies de la cama/de la montaña** at the foot of the bed/mountain; **al p. de la letra** to the letter, word for word; **sigue las instrucciones al p. de la letra** follow the instructions to the letter; **copiar algo al p. de la letra** to copy sth word for word; **no hace falta que lo interpretes al p. de la letra** there's no need to interpret it literally; EXPR **al p. del cañón: ahí está, siempre al p. del cañón** there he is, always hard at work ►► ***p. de foto*** caption; ***p. de***

imprenta imprint; *Informát* ***p. de página*** footer
(**c**) *(medida)* foot; **mide tres pies de ancho** it's three foot *o* feet wide
(**d**) *Teatro* cue; *Fig* **dar p. a** *(críticas, comentarios)* to give rise to; *(sospechas)* to give cause for; *Fig* **dar p. a alguien para que haga algo** to give sb cause to do sth
(**e**) *Lit (de verso)* foot ►► ***p. quebrado*** = short line of four or five syllables alternating with longer lines
(**f**) ***p. de lobo*** *(planta)* clubmoss
(**g**) ***pies de gato*** *(botas)* rock boots
(**h**) *Chile (anticipo)* down payment

---

piedad *nf* (**a**) *(compasión)* pity; **tener p. de** to take pity on; **siento p. por los que sufren** I feel sorry for those who suffer; **ten p. de nosotros** have mercy on us (**b**) *(religiosidad)* piety (**c**) *Arte* Pietà

pied-de-poule [pjeð'pul] *nm CSur* hound's-tooth check

piedra *nf* (**a**) *(material, roca)* stone; **una casa/un muro de p.** a stone house/wall; **lavado a la p.** stonewashed; EXPR **¡uno no es/yo no soy de p.!** I'm only human!; EXPR **dejar a alguien de p.** to stun sb; EXPR **estar más duro que una p.** to be rock hard; EXPR *Fam* **menos da una p.** it's better than nothing; EXPR **no dejar p. por mover** *o* **sin remover** to leave no stone unturned; EXPR **no dejar p. sobre p.** to leave no stone standing; EXPR *Esp muy Fam* **pasarse por la p. a alguien** *(sexualmente)* to have it off with sb; EXPR **poner la primera p.** *(inaugurar)* to lay the foundation stone; *(sentar las bases)* to lay the foundations; EXPR **no quedar p. sobre p.: tras el terremoto no quedaba p. sobre p.** there wasn't a stone left standing after the earthquake; EXPR **quedarse de p.** to be stunned; EXPR **tirar la p. y esconder la mano** to play the innocent; EXPR **tirar la primera p.** to cast the first stone; EXPR **están tirando piedras contra su propio tejado** they're just harming themselves ►► ***p. de afilar*** whetstone, grindstone; *también Fig* ***p. angular*** cornerstone; ***p. arenisca*** sandstone; ***p. caliza*** limestone; ***p. filosofal*** philosopher's stone; ***p. fina*** precious stone; *RP* ***p. laja*** slate paving stone; ***p. de molino*** millstone; *Méx* ***p. poma*** pumice stone; ***p. pómez*** pumice stone; ***p. preciosa*** precious stone; ***p. semipreciosa*** semi-precious stone; ***p. de toque*** touchstone; *Fig* **fue la p. de toque del equipo** it was a chance to see how good the team was
(**b**) *(de mechero)* flint; **se le ha gastado** *o* **agotado la p.** the flint has worn down
(**c**) *(en vejiga, riñón, vesícula)* stone; **tiene una p. en el riñón/en la vesícula** she has a kidney stone/gallstone
(**d**) *(granizo)* hailstone; EXPR *RP Fam* **cayó p. sin llover** oh no, look who's here
(**e**) *(de molino)* millstone, grindstone
(**f**) *Fam* **p. (de hachís)** lump of hash
(**g**) *Col Fam* EXPR **tener una p. con alguien** to be hacked off with sb; **sacarle la p. a alguien** to hack sb off

piel *nf* (**a**) *(epidermis)* skin; **una persona de p. oscura** a dark-skinned person; EXPR **dejarse la p.** to sweat blood; EXPR **jugarse la p.** to risk one's neck; EXPR **salvar la p.** to save one's skin; EXPR *Fam* **ser de la p. del diablo,** *Am* **ser la p. de Judas** to be a little devil; EXPR **vender la p. del oso antes de cazarlo** to count one's chickens before they are hatched ►► ***p. de gallina*** gooseflesh, goose pimples, goose bumps; **se me pone la p. de gallina al ver esas imágenes** it sends a shiver down my spine when I see those pictures; ***p. roja*** redskin; **los pieles rojas** the redskins; *Fig* ***la p. de toro*** the Iberian Peninsula
(**b**) *Esp, Méx (cuero)* leather; **cazadora/guantes de p.** leather jacket/gloves ►► ***p. sintética*** imitation leather
(**c**) *(pelo)* fur; **abrigo de p.** fur coat
(**d**) *(cáscara) (de naranja, limón, manzana)* peel; *(de plátano)* skin **quítale la p. a la manzana** peel the apple

piélago *nm Literario (mar)* **el p.** the deep

pienso[1] *etc ver* **pensar**

pienso[2] *nm* feed ►► ***p. compuesto*** compound (feed)

piercing ['pirsin] (*pl* **piercings**) *nm* body piercing; **hacerse un p. en el ombligo** to have one's navel pierced

pierdo *etc ver* **perder**

pierna[1] *nf* (**a**) *(de persona, animal)* leg; **cruzar las piernas** to cross one's legs; **estirar las piernas** to stretch one's legs; EXPR *Fam* **dormir a p. suelta** to sleep like a log; EXPR *Fam* **salir por piernas** to leg it ►► ***p. ortopédica*** artificial leg (**b**) *(cocinada)* leg ►► ***p. de cordero*** *(plato)* gigot, leg of lamb

pierna[2] *adj RP Fam* **ser p.** to be game for anything

pieza *nf* (**a**) *(unidad)* piece; **una p. de ajedrez** a chesspiece; **una p. de fruta** a piece of fruit; **una p. dental** a tooth; **una vajilla de cien piezas** a hundred-piece dinner service; **una p. de coleccionista** a collector's item; **piezas de artillería** guns, artillery; **construyó el televisor p. a p.** he put the television together piece by piece; EXPR *Fam* **dejar/quedarse de una p.** to leave/be thunderstruck; EXPR *Am Fam* **es de una p.** she's a really decent person ►► ***p. arqueológica*** archaeological piece; *Fig* ***p. clave*** linchpin; ***p. de coleccionista*** collector's item; ***p. de museo*** museum piece, exhibit; *Fig* **esta máquina de escribir es una p. de museo** this typewriter's a museum piece
(**b**) *(de mecanismo)* part ►► ***p. de recambio*** spare part, *US* extra; ***p. de repuesto*** spare part, *US* extra
(**c**) *(de pesca)* catch; *(de caza)* kill
(**d**) *Irónico (persona)* **ser una (buena) p.** to be a fine one *o* a right one; **¡menuda p. está hecha Susana!** Susana's a fine one *o* right one!
(**e**) *(parche)* patch
(**f**) *(obra dramática)* play
(**g**) *(habitación)* room
(**h**) *Mús* piece
(**i**) *Der* ***p. de convicción*** piece of evidence *(used by the prosecution)*
(**j**) *(rollo de tela)* roll

piezoelectricidad *nf Elec* piezoelectricity

piezoeléctrico, -a *adj Elec* piezoelectric

pífano *nm* (**a**) *(instrumento)* fife (**b**) *(persona)* fife player

pifia *nf* (**a**) *Fam (error)* blunder; **hacer una p.** to make a blunder (**b**) *(en billar)* miscue (**c**) *Andes, Arg Fam (abucheo)* booing and hissing (**d**) *Andes, Arg Fam (burla)* joke

pifiada *nf RP Fam* blunder

pifiadera *nf Andes Fam* blunder

pifiar *vt* (**a**) *(fallar)* **el jugador pifió el remate** the player fluffed his shot; EXPR *Fam* **pifiarla** to mess up; **la pifié con el examen** I made a mess of the exam (**b**) *(en billar)* to miscue (**c**) *Andes, Arg Fam (abuchear)* to boo and hiss

pifión, -ona *Andes, Arg Fam* **1** *adj* mocking
2 *nm,f* scoffer

pigargo *nm* white-tailed eagle ►► ***p. cabeciblanco*** bald eagle

pigmentación *nf* pigmentation

pigmentar *vt* to pigment

pigmento *nm* pigment

pigmeo, -a *nm,f* pygmy

pignoración *nf Fin* hypothecation

pignorar *vt Fin* to hypothecate

pignoraticio, -a *adj Fin* **préstamo p.** collateral loan

pija *nf* (**a**) *esp RP Vulg (pene)* prick, cock (**b**) *ver también* **pijo**

pijada, pijería, pijotada *nf Esp Fam Pey* (**a**) *(dicho)* trivial remark; **¡no digas pijadas!** don't talk nonsense!
(**b**) *(objeto)* **le gustan mucho todas esas pijadas electrónicas** he really likes all those electronic gizmos
(**c**) *(cosa insignificante)* trifle; **le compramos una p. y ya está** we'll get him some stupid little knick-knack and that's it; **se pelearon por una p.** they fell out over some stupid little thing

pijama *nm* pyjamas; **un p.** a pair of pyjamas

pije *Chile Fam Pey* **1** *adj* posh
2 *nmf* rich kid

pijería = **pijada**

pijerío *nm Esp Fam Pey* **allí es donde va el p. de la ciudad** that's where all the town's rich kids go

pijije *nm* lesser yellowlegs

pijo, -a *Esp* **1** *adj Fam Pey* (**a**) *(esnob) (persona)* = who speaks and dresses in an affected way; **llevaba una chaqueta muy pija** he was wearing a typical rich kid jacket; **tenía un acento muy p.** he spoke with the affected accent of a trendy youth (**b**) *(refinado)* posh
2 *nm,f Fam Pey (persona)* = person who speaks and dresses in an affected way
3 *nm muy Fam (pene)* prick, cock

pijotada = **pijada**

pijotero, -a *adj Esp Fam* (**a**) *(molesto)* annoying, irritating (**b**) *(pijo) (persona)* = who speaks and dresses in an affected way; **llevaba una chaqueta muy pijotera** he was wearing a typical rich kid jacket

pijudo, -a *adj CAm Fam* wicked, awesome

pila 1 *nf* (**a**) *(generador)* battery; **funciona a** *o* **con pilas** it works *o* runs off batteries; EXPR *Fam* **cargar las pilas** to recharge one's batteries; EXPR *Fam* **ponerse las pilas** to get moving *o* cracking ►► ***p. alcalina*** alkaline battery; ***p. atómica*** atomic pile; ***p. botón*** watch battery; ***p. de larga duración*** long-life battery; ***p. recargable*** rechargeable battery; ***p. seca*** dry cell; ***p. solar*** solar cell
(**b**) *(montón)* pile; **una p. de libros** a pile of books
(**c**) *Fam (cantidad)* **una p. de** masses of; **tengo una p. de trabajo** I've got a mountain of *o* masses of work; **tiene una p. de deudas** he's up to his neck in debt

(**d**) *(recipiente) (para fregar)* sink; *(de agua bendita)* stoup, holy water font; *Andes (fuente)* fountain ►► ***p. bautismal*** (baptismal) font
(**e**) *Informát* stack
(**f**) *Arquit* pile
(**g**) *Cuba (grifo) Br* tap, *US* faucet
2 *adv RP Fam* masses; **la quiere p.** *o* **pilas** he loves her a hell of a lot; **tengo p.** *o* **pilas de ganas de verla** I'm really dying to see her; **hace p.** *o* **pilas que no voy al cine** I haven't been to the cinema for ages *o Br* yonks

pilar 1 *nm* (**a**) *(columna)* pillar; *(de puente)* pier (**b**) *(apoyo)* pillar; **uno de los pilares de la iglesia católica** one of the pillars of the Catholic Church (**c**) *(mojón)* milestone
2 *nmf (en rugby)* prop ►► ***p. derecho*** tight head prop; ***p. izquierdo*** loose head prop

pilastra *nf* pilaster

Pilatos *n pr* **(Poncio) P.** (Pontius) Pilate

pilchas *nfpl CSur Fam* gear

pilche *nm Andes* = cup or bowl made from a gourd

píldora *nf (pastilla)* pill; **la p. (anticonceptiva)** the (contraceptive) pill; **estar tomando la p.** to be on the pill ►► ***p. del día siguiente*** morning-after pill

pileta *nf RP* (**a**) *(piscina)* swimming pool (**b**) *(en baño)* washbasin; *(en cocina)* sink

piletón *nm RP* pool

pilila *nf Fam Br* willie, *US* peter

pilín *nm Col Fam* **un p.** a mite, a tiny bit

pillaje *nm* pillage

pillar 1 *vt* (**a**) *(tomar, atrapar)* to catch; **p. un taxi** to catch a taxi; **me pillas de casualidad** you were lucky to catch me; **¿a que no me pillas?** bet you can't catch me; **un árbol cayó y le pilló la pierna** a tree fell and trapped his leg
(**b**) *(sorprender)* to catch; **lo pillé leyendo mi diario** I caught him reading my diary; **el terremoto me pilló fuera del país** the earthquake struck while I was out of the country
(**c**) *(atropellar)* to knock down; **lo pilló un autobús** he got knocked down by a bus
(**d**) *Fam (pulmonía, resfriado)* to catch; **pillamos una borrachera tremenda** we got really drunk
(**e**) *Fam (chiste, explicación)* to get; **no lo pillo** I don't get it
(**f**) *Esp Fam (comprar)* to get
(**g**) *Esp Fam (droga)* to get (hold of)
2 *vi Esp (hallarse, coger)* **me pilla lejos** it's out of the way for me; **me pilla de camino** it's on my way
3 **pillarse** *vpr* (**a**) *(atraparse)* **pillarse los dedos** to catch one's fingers; *Fig* to get burned; **me pillé la camisa con la puerta** I caught my shirt on the door (**b**) *CSur Fam (orinarse)* to wet oneself

pillastre *nmf Fam* rogue, crafty person

pillería *nf Fam (acción)* prank, trick

pillín, -ina *nm,f Fam* little scamp, rascal

pillo, -a *Fam* 1 *adj* (**a**) *(travieso)* mischievous (**b**) *(astuto)* crafty
2 *nm,f* (**a**) *(pícaro)* rascal (**b**) *(astuto)* crafty person

pilluelo, -a *nm,f Fam* rascal, scamp

pilmama *nf Méx* nanny

pilón *nm* (**a**) *(pila) (para lavar)* basin; *(para animales)* trough
(**b**) *(torre eléctrica)* pylon
(**c**) *(pilar grande)* post
(**d**) *Méx Fam (azúcar)* sugarloaf
(**e**) *Méx (regalo)* **compra una docena y no olvides pedir el p.** buy a dozen and don't forget to ask for something extra thrown in for free; **si compra una docena lleva uno de p.** if you buy a dozen you get one thrown in for free
(**f**) *RP, Ven Fam (gran cantidad)* masses; **tiene un p.** *o* **pilones de libros** she's got stacks of books; **ganó un p.** *o* **pilones de plata** he earned a packet; **te quiero un p.** *o* **pilones** I love you a hell of a lot

piloncillo *nm Méx* brown sugar *(sold in cone-shaped blocks)*

pilongo, -a *adj* thin, lean

pilono *nm Arquit* pylon

píloro *nm Anat* pylorus

pilot [pi'lo] (*pl* **pilots**) *nm Urug* raincoat

pilotaje *nm* (**a**) *(de avión)* flying, piloting; **un aparato de fácil p.** a plane that is easy to fly (**b**) *(de automóvil, moto)* driving (**c**) *(de barco)* steering (**d**) *(pilotes)* pilings

pilotar, *Am* **pilotear** *vt* (**a**) *(avión)* to fly, to pilot (**b**) *(automóvil)* to drive; *(moto)* to ride (**c**) *(barco)* to steer

pilote *nm* pile

pilotear = **pilotar**

pilotín *nm RP (impermeable)* short raincoat

piloto 1 *nmf* (**a**) *(de avión)* pilot ►► ***p. comercial*** airline pilot; ***p. de pruebas*** test pilot (**b**) *(de automóvil, moto)* driver ►► ***p. de carreras*** racing driver; ***p. de pruebas*** test driver; ***p. de rallys*** rally driver (**c**) *(de barco)* pilot
2 *nm* (**a**) *(luz) (de coche)* tail light; *(de aparato)* pilot light; **se ha encendido el p. de la gasolina** the fuel warning light has come on (**b**) ***p. automático*** *(de avión, vehículo)* automatic pilot (**c**) *(llama)* pilot light (**d**) *Arg, Chile (impermeable)* raincoat
3 *adj inv* pilot; **casa p.** show house; **programa p.** pilot (programme); **proyecto p.** pilot project

pilsen® *nf Perú* lager

piltra *nf Esp Fam* pit, bed

piltrafa *nf* (**a**) *(de comida)* scrap (**b**) *Fam (persona débil)* wreck (**c**) *Fam (cosa inservible)* piece of junk; **estar hecho una p.** *(persona, coche)* to be a wreck; *(chaqueta, zapatos)* to be worn out

pilucho, -a *adj Chile Fam* naked, *Br* starkers

pimentero *nm* (**a**) *(planta)* pepper plant (**b**) *(vasija)* pepper shaker

pimentón *nm* (**a**) *(especia) (dulce)* paprika; *(picante)* cayenne pepper (**b**) *(pimiento)* pepper, capsicum

pimienta *nf* pepper ►► ***p. blanca*** white pepper; ***p. en grano*** peppercorns; ***p. molida*** ground pepper; ***p. negra*** black pepper

pimiento *nm (fruto)* pepper, capsicum; *(planta)* pimiento, pepper plant; EXPR *Fam* **ime importa un p.!** I couldn't care less!; EXPR *Fam* **iy un p.!: ¿me dejas tu coche? – iy un p.!** could you lend me your car? – get lost! *o* like hell I will! ►► ***p. morrón*** red pepper; ***p. de Padrón*** = small, green pepper; **p. rojo** red pepper; ***p. verde*** green pepper

pimpampum *nm Esp* shooting gallery

pimpante *adj Fam* (**a**) *(satisfecho)* well-pleased; **le informé del accidente y se quedó tan p.** when I told him about the accident he didn't turn a hair (**b**) *(garboso)* swish, smart

pimpinela *nf* pimpernel

pimplar *Esp Fam* 1 *vi* to booze
2 **pimplarse** *vpr* **se pimpló dos botellas él solo** he downed two bottles on his own

pimpollo *nm* (**a**) *(de rama, planta)* shoot; *(de flor)* bud (**b**) *Fam (persona atractiva) (hombre)* hunk; *(mujer)* babe (**c**) *Fam (niño hermoso)* angel, cherub

pimpón *nm* ping-pong, table-tennis

PIN *nm* (**a**) (*abrev de* **producto interior neto**) NDP (**b**) (*abrev de* **personal identification number**) PIN

pin (*pl* **pins**) *nm* (**a**) *Fam (insignia)* pin, lapel badge (**b**) *(de enchufe)* pin

pinacoteca *nf* art gallery

pináculo *nm* (**a**) *(de edificio)* pinnacle (**b**) *(cumbre, apogeo)* pinnacle, peak; **está en el p. de su carrera literaria** he's at the pinnacle *o* peak of his literary career (**c**) *(juego de naipes)* pinochle

pinar *nm* pine wood/grove

pinaza *nf* pine needles

pincel *nm* (**a**) *(para pintar)* paintbrush; *(para maquillar)* brush (**b**) *(estilo)* style

pincelada *nf* (**a**) *(con el pincel)* brushstroke; EXPR **a grandes pinceladas** in broad terms; EXPR **dar la última p. a algo** to put the finishing touches to sth (**b**) *(toque, detalle)* touch; **el autor describe con unas pocas pinceladas el ambiente de la época** the author conveys the atmosphere of the period in a few short sentences

pincha *nmf Esp Fam* DJ

pinchadiscos *nmf inv Esp Fam* DJ

pinchar 1 *vt* (**a**) *(punzar)* to prick; *(rueda)* to puncture; *(globo, balón)* to burst; **pincha la carne con el tenedor** prick the meat with the fork
(**b**) *(penetrar)* to pierce
(**c**) *(con chinchetas, alfileres)* **p. algo en la pared** to pin sth to the wall
(**d**) *(inyectar)* **p. a alguien** to give sb an injection *o* a jab
(**e**) *Fam (teléfono)* to tap
(**f**) *Fam (irritar)* to wind up; **deja de p. a tu hermana** stop winding your sister up
(**g**) *Fam (incitar)* **p. a alguien para que haga algo** to prod sb into doing sth
(**h**) *Esp Fam (discos)* to play; **pinchaba discos en un bar** he DJ'ed in a bar
2 *vi* (**a**) *(vehículo)* to get a puncture; **pinchó a cinco kilómetros de la meta** he got a puncture *o* flat tyre five kilometres from the finish
(**b**) *(barba)* to be prickly

(**c**) *Fam (fracasar)* to be a flop; **el director australiano pinchó con su última película** the Australian director's latest movie has been a flop; **la oposición pinchó en los barrios más acomodados** the opposition came to grief in the better-off areas
(**d**) *Informát* to click; **pinche aquí** click here
(**e**) *Esp Fam (disc jockey)* to DJ
(**f**) EXPR *Fam* **ni pincha ni corta** his opinion doesn't count for anything; **a mí no me preguntes, que en esto ni pincho ni corto** don't ask me, I don't have any say in the matter; *Fam* **p. en hueso** to go wide of the mark, to misfire
3 pincharse *vpr* (**a**) *(punzarse) (persona)* to prick oneself; **me pinché intentado coser el botón** I pricked myself trying to sew the button on
(**b**) *(rueda)* to get a puncture; *(globo, balón)* to burst; **se nos ha pinchado una rueda** we've got a puncture *o* flat tyre
(**c**) *Fam (irritarse)* to get annoyed
(**d**) **pincharse (algo)** *(medicamento)* to inject oneself (with sth); *Fam (droga)* to shoot (sth) up; **su hijo se pincha** her son's on drugs

> **Falso amigo**: El verbo inglés **to pinch** no es la traducción del español **pinchar**. En inglés **to pinch** significa "pellizcar", "apretar" o "afanar".

pinchazo *nm* (**a**) *(punzada)* prick; **se dio un p. con una aguja** he pricked himself with a needle
(**b**) *(inyección)* injection, *Br* jab, *US* shot
(**c**) *(marca)* needle mark
(**d**) *(de neumático)* puncture, flat; **sufrió un p. a los cinco kilómetros de carrera** he got a puncture *o* flat tyre five kilometers into the race
(**e**) *(dolor agudo)* stabbing pain, pang; **me ha dado un p. en la espalda** I felt a stabbing pain in my back
(**f**) *Fam (de teléfono)* tap
(**g**) *Fam (fracaso)* **el nuevo modelo ha sido un p.** the new model has been a flop; **la empresa no se ha recuperado de su p. en la Bolsa** the company hasn't recovered from the collapse of its share price

pinche[1] *nmf* (**a**) *(de cocina)* kitchen boy, *f* maid (**b**) *RP Fam (en oficina)* office junior; *Fig* **yo no sé nada, acá soy el p.** I don't know anything, I'm nobody round here (**c**) *Chile (horquilla)* hairgrip, hairpin

pinche[2] *adj Méx Fam* damn, *Br* bloody; **¡ese p. perro!** that damn *o Br* bloody dog!; **no es más que un p. campesino** he's just a lousy *o Br* bloody peasant

pinchito *nm (tapa)* bar snack, aperitif

pincho *nm* (**a**) *(punta)* (sharp) point (**b**) *(espina) (de planta)* prickle, thorn (**c**) *(varilla)* pointed stick (**d**) *Esp (tapa)* bar snack, aperitif ▸▸ ***p. moruno*** = marinated pork cooked on a skewer; ***p. de tortilla*** = small portion of Spanish omelette (**e**) *Fam (cuchillo)* knife

pinchurriento, -a *adj Méx Fam* measly, miserable

pindonguear *vi Esp Fam* to loaf about

pinga *nf Andes, Carib, Méx muy Fam* prick; EXPR *Ven muy Fam* **de p.** wicked, awesome

pingajo *nm Esp Fam* rag; EXPR **ir hecho un p.** to look a sight

pinganilla *nf Chile Fam* dandy

pingo *nm* (**a**) *Esp Fam (pingajo)* rag; EXPR **ir hecho un p.** to look a sight; EXPR **poner a alguien como un p.** to badmouth sb, *Br* to slag sb off (**b**) *Fam (persona despreciable)* rotter, dog (**c**) *RP (caballo vivo)* fast horse (**d**) *Chile, Perú (caballo malo)* nag (**e**) *Méx (diablo)* **el p.** the Devil (**f**) *Méx (niño)* little devil

pingonear *vi Fam* to loaf about

pingoneo *nm Fam* **estar de p.** to loaf about

ping-pong [pim'pon] *nm* ping-pong, table-tennis

pingüe *adj* plentiful; **pingües beneficios** a fat profit

pingüinera *nf Arg, Chile* penguin reserve

pingüino *nm* penguin ▸▸ ***p. emperador*** emperor penguin; ***p. enano*** little penguin; ***p. real*** king penguin

pinitos *nmpl Fam* (**a**) *(de bebé)* **Carlitos comienza a hacer p.** Carlitos is starting to walk (**b**) *(en actividad)* **ha comenzado a hacer sus p. en fotografía** he's started dabbling in photography; **desde sus primeros p. como cantante ha mejorado muchísimo** she's improved enormously since when she started out as a singer

pinnípedo, -a *Zool* **1** *adj* pinniped
2 *nm* pinniped
3 pinnípedos *nmpl (orden) Pinnipedia*

pino *nm* (**a**) *(árbol)* pine (tree); EXPR *Esp Fam* **en el quinto p.** in the back of beyond ▸▸ ***p. albar*** Scots pine, ***p. carrasco*** Aleppo pine; ***p. insigne*** Monterey pine; ***p. marítimo*** pinaster; ***p. piñonero*** stone pine; ***p. silvestre*** Scotch pine
(**b**) *Esp (ejercicio)* **hacer el p.** *(sin apoyar la cabeza en el suelo)* to do a handstand; *(apoyando la cabeza en el suelo)* to stand on one's head
(**c**) **Los Pinos** *(en México)* = official residence of the Mexican president

Pinocho *nm* Pinocchio

pinol, pinole, pinolillo *nm CAm, Méx (harina) Br* maize flour *US* corn flour

pinolate *nm CAm, Méx (bebida)* = flavoured non-alcoholic drink made from roasted *Br* maize flour *o US* corn flour

pinole, pinolillo = **pinol**

pinrel *nm Esp Fam* foot

pinsapo *nm* Spanish fir

pinta 1 *nf* (**a**) *(lunar)* spot
(**b**) *(aspecto)* **tiene p. de estar enfadado** he looks like he's annoyed; **tiene buena p.** it looks good; **ese cocido tiene muy buena p.** that stew looks delicious; **¡menuda p. tienes, todo lleno de barro!** you look a real sight, all covered in mud!; EXPR *Am* **echar** *o* **hacer** *o* **tirar p.** to show off; EXPR *RP* **ser alguien en p.** to be the spitting image of sb
(**c**) *(medida)* pint
(**d**) *Méx (pintada)* graffiti
(**e**) *Méx* **irse de p.** *(hacer novillos) Br* to play truant, *US* to play hooky
2 *nmf Urug Fam (hombre)* guy, *Br* bloke; *(mujer)* woman

pintada *nf* (**a**) *(en pared)* graffiti; **la fachada apareció llena de pintadas** the facade was covered in graffiti (**b**) *(ave)* guinea fowl ▸▸ ***p. vulturina*** vulturine guinea fowl

pintado, -a *adj* (**a**) *(coloreado)* coloured; **recién p.** *(en letrero)* wet paint
(**b**) *(maquillado)* made-up; **le gusta ir muy pintada** she likes to wear a lot of make-up
(**c**) *(moteado)* speckled
(**d**) *Am Fam (idéntico)* identical; **salió p. al padre** he's the spitting image of his father
(**e**) *RP Fam (perfecto)* **ese vestido te queda p.** you look great in that dress
(**f**) EXPR **el más p.: es capaz de timar al más p.** there's nobody he couldn't take in; **eso le puede pasar al más p.** it could happen to anyone *o* to the best of us; **venir que ni p.** to be just the thing; **el aumento de sueldo me viene que ni p.** this pay rise has come at just the right time; **el papel de malo le viene que ni p.** he could have been made for the role of the villain; *RP* **no puedo verle ni p.** I can't stand the sight of him

pintalabios *nm inv* lipstick

pintamonas *nmf inv Esp Fam* (**a**) *Pey (pintor)* dauber (**b**) *(persona poco importante)* **ser un p.** to be a nobody

pintar 1 *vt* (**a**) *(dibujo, pared)* to paint; **p. algo de verde/azul** to paint sth green/blue (**b**) *(dibujar)* to draw; **pintó una casa** she drew a house (**c**) *(describir)* to paint, to describe; **me pintó la escena con pelos y señales** he painted the scene in graphic detail
2 *vi* (**a**) *(con pintura)* to paint; **p. al óleo** to paint in oils
(**b**) *(escribir)* to write; **este bolígrafo no pinta** this pen isn't working
(**c**) *Fam (significar, importar)* **ella no pinta nada en esta empresa** she's nobody in this company; **aquí no pinto nada, me marcho mañana** there's no place for me here, I'm leaving tomorrow; **a mí no me preguntes, aquí no pinto nada** don't ask me, my opinion isn't worth anything round here; **¿qué pinto yo en este asunto?** what's any of this got to do with me?
(**d**) *(en juegos de cartas)* to be trumps; **pintan oros** "oros" are trumps; EXPR **pintan bastos** things are getting strained, the going's getting tough
(**e**) *Andes, RP Fam (situación)* **ese casamiento pinta muy bien** that marriage has every chance of succeeding; **las perspectivas pintan mal** things aren't looking good
(**f**) *RP Fam (aparecer)* **hace meses que no pinta nada** he hasn't been around for months; **pintá por casa esta noche** come round tonight
3 pintarse *vpr* (**a**) *(maquillarse)* to make oneself up; **pintarse las uñas** to paint one's nails; EXPR **se las pinta solo para engañar a los clientes** he's a past master at cheating his clients (**b**) *(manifestarse)* to show, to be evident

pintarrajear *Fam* **1** *vt* to daub
2 pintarrajearse *vpr* to plaster oneself in make-up

pintarroja *nf* dogfish

pintiparado, -a *adj* (**a**) *(igual)* identical (**a** to), exactly the same (**a** as) (**b**) *(muy a propósito)* just right, ideal; **me viene p. para decorar mi habitación** it's just perfect for my room; **es una ocasión pintiparada para darse a conocer** it's an ideal opportunity to become better known

Pinto *n* EXPR **estar entre P. y Valdemoro** to be unable to make up one's mind

pinto, -a *adj* speckled, spotted
pintón, -ona *adj RP (atractivo)* good-looking
pintor, -ora *nm,f* (**a**) *(artista)* painter (**b**) *(profesional)* painter ▸▸ ***p. de brocha gorda*** *(de oficio)* painter and decorator; *Pey (artista)* dauber
pintorcito *nm Arg (bata)* apron, pinafore
pintoresco, -a *adj* (**a**) *(bonito)* picturesque (**b**) *(extravagante)* colourful
pintura *nf* (**a**) *(técnica, cuadro)* painting; **la p. renacentista** Renaissance painting; EXPR **no poder ver algo/a alguien ni en p.** not to be able to stand the sight of sth/sb ▸▸ ***p. a la acuarela*** watercolour; ***p. al fresco*** fresco; ***p. mural*** mural painting; ***p. al óleo*** oil painting; ***p. rupestre*** cave painting
(**b**) *(materia)* paint ▸▸ ***p. acrílica*** acrylic paint; ***p. plástica*** emulsion (paint); ***p. al temple*** tempera
(**c**) *(descripción)* description, portrayal
(**d**) **pinturas** *(material para pintar)* crayons
pinturero, -a *Fam* **1** *adj* vain, conceited
2 *nm,f* show-off
PINU ['pinu] *nm (abrev de* **Partido Innovación y Unidad**) = Honduran political party
pinza *nf* (**a**) *(de tender ropa)* clothes peg, *US* clothes pin
(**b**) *(para el pelo) Br* hairgrip, *US* bobby pin
(**c**) *(para papeles)* paper clip
(**d**) **pinzas** *(instrumento)* tweezers; *(de cirujano)* forceps; *(para el hielo)* tongs; EXPR *Fam* **coger** *o Am* **agarrar algo con pinzas** to handle sth with great care; EXPR *RP* **tratar a alguien con pinzas** to treat sb with kid gloves
(**e**) *(de animal)* pincer, claw
(**f**) *(pliegue)* fold
(**g**) *(en costura)* dart; **un pantalón de pinzas** pleated trousers *o US* pants
pinzón *nm* chaffinch ▸▸ ***p. americano*** American tree sparrow; ***p. real*** brambling
piña[1] *nf* (**a**) *(del pino)* pine cone (**b**) *(fruta tropical)* pineapple ▸▸ ***p. colada*** piña colada (**c**) *(conjunto de gente)* close-knit group; **formar una p.** to rally round (**d**) *Fam (golpe)* knock, bash; **darse una p.** to have a crash (**e**) *RP, Ven Fam (puñetazo)* thump; **dar una p. a alguien** to thump sb (**f**) *Perú Fam (infortunio)* **¡qué p.!** how unlucky!
piña[2], **piñoso, -a** *adj Perú Fam* unlucky; **qué p. estoy hoy** I'm right out of luck today
piñal *nm Am* pineapple plantation
piñata *nf* = suspended pot full of sweets which blindfolded children try to break open with sticks at parties
piñazo *nm Fam* (**a**) *(golpe)* knock, bash; **darse un p.** to have a crash (**b**) *RP (puñetazo)* thump; **dar un p. a alguien** to thump sb
piño *nm Esp Fam (diente)* tooth
piñón *nm* (**a**) *(fruto)* pine nut *o* kernel; EXPR *Fam* **estar a partir un p. con alguien** to be hand in glove with sb (**b**) *(rueda dentada)* pinion; *(de bicicleta)* sprocket wheel ▸▸ ***p. fijo*** *(en bicicleta)* fixed wheel; EXPR **ser de p. fijo** to be fixed *o* rigid; EXPR **a p. fijo: solo él se mantuvo a p. fijo** he alone continued as he had begun
piñonero, -a *adj* **pino p.** stone pine
piñoso = **piña**[2]
Pío *n pr* **P. I/II** Pius I/II
pío[1] *interj* cheep; **¡p., p.!** cheep, cheep!; EXPR *Fam* **no decir ni p.: no ha dicho ni p. desde que llegó** we haven't heard a peep out of her since she arrived; **y al jefe, no le digas ni p. de lo que te he contado** and not a word of what I've told you to the boss
pío[2], **-a** *adj* pious
pío[3] *nm* **un p. p.** *(en lenguaje infantil)* a birdie
piocha *nf* (**a**) *Méx (barba)* goatee (beard); EXPR **por p.** per head (**b**) *Chile (distintivo)* badge
piojo[1] *nm* louse; **piojos** lice
piojo[2], **-a** **1** *adj Méx, RP Fam* (**a**) *(objeto, lugar)* lousy (**b**) *(persona)* stingy, tightfisted
2 *nm,f RP Fam Hum* ankle-biter, rug rat
piojoso, -a **1** *adj* (**a**) *(con piojos)* lousy, covered in lice (**b**) *Fam (sucio)* flea-bitten, filthy
2 *nm,f* (**a**) *(con piojos)* louse-ridden person (**b**) *Fam (sucio)* filthy person, *US* scuzzball
piola **1** *nf Am* cord; EXPR *RP Fam* **darle p. a alguien** to pay attention to sb
2 *adj RP Fam* (**a**) *(persona)* nice; **me gusta tu hermana, es muy p.** I like your sister, she's really nice (**b**) *(lugar)* cosy (**c**) EXPR **quedarse p.** to act the innocent
3 *nmf RP Fam* smart alec(k); **no te hagas el p.** stop being such a smart alec(k)
4 *adv RP Fam* very well; **ese vestido nuevo te queda muy p.** you look great in that new dress
piolet *(pl* **piolets**) *nm* ice axe
piolín *nm Andes, RP* cord
pión *nm Fís* pi-meson
pionero, -a **1** *adj* pioneer, pioneering
2 *nm,f* pioneer
pioneta, peoneta *nmf Chile* driver's mate
piorrea *nf* pyorrhoea
pipa **1** *nf* (**a**) *(para fumar)* pipe; **fumar en p.** to smoke a pipe; EXPR **fumar la p. de la paz** to smoke the pipe of peace
(**b**) *(pepita)* seed
(**c**) **pipas** *(de girasol)* sunflower seeds *(sold as a snack)*; EXPR **eso no te da ni para pipas** that's not even enough to buy a bag of peanuts!
(**d**) *(tonel)* barrel
(**e**) *(lengüeta)* reed
(**f**) *Fam (pistola)* piece
(**g**) *Méx (camión)* tanker; **una p. de agua** a water tanker
(**h**) *PRico Fam (barriga)* belly
2 *adv Fam* **pasarlo** *o* **pasárselo p.** to have a great time; *Fam* **en esta playa se está p.** it's great on this beach
pipermín *nm* peppermint liqueur
pipeta *nf* pipette
pipí *nm Fam (lenguaje infantil)* pee, *Br* wee-wee; **hacer p.** to have a pee *o Br* wee-wee; **el niño se ha hecho p.** the child's done a pee *o Br* wee-wee
pipián = **pepián**
pipiolo *nm Fam* (**a**) *(muchacho)* youngster (**b**) *(principiante)* novice, beginner
pipirigallo *nm (planta)* sainfoin
pipón, -ona *adj RP Fam (lleno)* stuffed; **estoy** *o* **he quedado p.** I'm stuffed
pique **1** *ver* **picar**
2 *nm* (**a**) *Fam (enfado)* grudge; **tener un p. con alguien** to have a grudge against sb; **su p. dura ya un año** it's already a year since they fell out
(**b**) *Fam (rivalidad)* **hay mucho p. entre ellas** there's a lot of rivalry *o* needle between them
(**c**) **irse a p.** *(barco)* to sink; *(negocio)* to go under; *(plan)* to fail
(**d**) *Am (rebote)* bounce; **después de dos piques, la pelota se salió de la cancha** the ball bounced twice before going out
(**e**) *RP Fam (aceleración)* acceleration; **este auto no tiene nada de p.** this car's got no acceleration
(**f**) *Chile Fam (visita)* **dar un p. por casa de alguien** to go round to sb's house
3 a los piques *loc adv RP Fam (muy rápido)* in a hurry
piqué *nm* piqué
piquera *nf Méx Fam* dive
piquero *nm Chile, Perú (ave)* booby
piqueta *nf* (**a**) *(herramienta)* pickaxe; *(de demolición)* mason's hammer *o* pick (**b**) *(en tienda de campaña)* metal tent-peg (**c**) *Arg, Chile (vino)* weak wine
piquete *nm* (**a**) *(herramienta)* peg, stake
(**b**) *(de huelguistas)* picket ▸▸ ***p. informativo*** = picket concerned with raising awareness and informing workers about the need for industrial action
(**c**) ***p. de ejecución*** firing squad
(**d**) *Col (picnic)* picnic
(**e**) *Col (comida)* = roast meat chopped into small pieces and accompanied by potatoes, banana and corn
(**f**) *Méx Fam (picadura, pinchazo) (de aguja)* prick; *(de insecto)* sting
(**g**) *Méx Fam (golpe)* prod; **dar un p. a alguien** to prod sb
(**h**) *Méx Fam (punzada)* stabbing pain
(**i**) *Méx Fam (de bebida)* shot
piqueteadero *nm Col Fam* = restaurant specialising in "piquetes"
piquituerto *nm* crossbill
pira *nf* pyre
pirado, -a *Fam* **1** *adj* crazy
2 *nm,f* loony, *Br* nutter
piragua *nf* canoe
piragüismo *nm* canoeing
piragüista *nmf* canoeist
piramidal *adj* pyramid-shaped, pyramidal

pirámide *nf* (**a**) *(monumento)* pyramid (**b**) *(figura)* pyramid ►► ***p. ecológica*** ecological pyramid; ***p. de población*** pyramid of population; ***p. trófica*** ecological pyramid

piraña[1] *nf (pez)* piranha

piraña[2], **pirañita** *nmf Perú Fam (niño)* street kid

pirar 1 *vi RP Fam* to go mad *o* crazy; **¿cómo que me dejás? ¿vos piraste?** what you mean you're leaving me? are you out of your mind?; **no intentes entender lo que quiere, piró** don't try to make sense of what he wants, he's off his head

2 pirarse *vpr Esp, RP Fam* to clear off; **nos piramos** we're off; **¿ya te piras?** are you off, then?; **me las piro, hasta mañana** I'll be off, see you tomorrow

pirata 1 *adj* (**a**) *(barco, ataque)* pirate (**b**) *(radio, edición, vídeo)* pirate; *(casete, grabación)* bootleg (**c**) *Am (profesional, servicio)* cowboy; **un electricista p.** a cowboy electrician

2 *nmf* (**a**) *(corsario)* pirate ►► ***p. aéreo*** hijacker; ***p. del aire*** hijacker; ***p. informático*** cracker, hacker (**b**) *Am (mal profesional)* cowboy

piratear 1 *vi* (**a**) *(asaltar barcos)* to be involved in piracy (**b**) *Informát* to crack

2 *vt* (**a**) *(propiedad intelectual)* to pirate (**b**) *Informát (programa) (desproteger)* to hack *o* crack into; *(hacer copia ilegal)* to pirate

pirateo *nm Fam (de programa informático, de vídeos)* piracy

piratería *nf* (**a**) *(de corsarios)* piracy ►► ***p. aérea*** hijacking (**b**) *(de programas, vídeos, ropa)* piracy ►► ***p. informática*** *(copias ilegales)* software piracy; *(acceso no autorizado)* hacking

pirca *nf Andes, Arg* dry-stone wall

pirenaico, -a *adj* Pyrenean

pírex® *nm* Pyrex®

pirincho *nm* guira cuckoo

pirindolo *nm Fam* decorative knob

Pirineo *nm* **el P., los Pirineos** the Pyrenees

pirinola *nf Méx* spinning top

piripi *adj Fam* tipsy

pirita *nf* pyrite

piro *nm Esp Fam* **darse el p.** *Br* to scarper, *US* to split

pirograbado *nm (técnica)* pokerwork

piromanía *nf* pyromania

pirómano, -a 1 *adj* pyromaniacal

2 *nm,f* pyromaniac

piropear *vt* **p. a alguien** to make flirtatious remarks to sb

piropo *nm* flirtatious remark; **decir** *o* **echar piropos a alguien** to make flirtatious remarks to sb

pirotecnia *nf* pyrotechnics *(singular)*

pirotécnico, -a 1 *adj* firework; **un montaje p.** a firework display

2 *nm,f* firework specialist

piroxeno *nm* pyroxene

pirrar *Fam* **1** *vt* **me pirran las albóndigas** I just adore *o* love meatballs

2 pirrarse *vpr* **p. por algo/alguien** to be dead keen on sth/sb

pírrico, -a *adj* Pyrrhic; **victoria pírrica** Pyrrhic victory

pirueta *nf* pirouette; EXPR **hacer piruetas** *(esfuerzo)* to perform miracles

piruja *nf Col, Méx muy Fam (prostituta)* whore, *US* hooker

pirujo *nm Méx muy Fam* womanizer

pirula *nf Esp Fam* (**a**) *(jugarreta)* dirty trick; **hacer una p. a alguien** to play a dirty trick on sb (**b**) *(escándalo)* **montar una p.** to make *o* cause a scene (**c**) *(maniobra ilegal)* **hacer una p.** to break the traffic regulations (**d**) *(pene) Br* willy, *US* johnson

piruleta *nf Esp* lollipop

pirulí *nm (golosina)* lollipop

pirulos *nmpl RP Fam (años)* **tiene como cincuenta p.** she's about fifty

pis *nm Fam* pee; **hacer p.** to have a pee; **hacerse p.** *(tener ganas)* to be dying *o* bursting for a pee; **el niño se ha hecho p.** the child's done a pee

pisacorbata *nm Col* tie-pin

pisada *nf* (**a**) *(acción)* footstep (**b**) *(huella)* footprint

pisadura *nf* footprint

pisapapeles *nm inv* paperweight

pisapuré *nm RP* hand-operated food mill

pisar 1 *vt* (**a**) *(con el pie)* to tread on; *(uvas)* to tread; **p. el freno** to put one's foot on the brake; **prohibido p. el césped** *(en cartel)* keep off the grass; EXPR *Andes, RP Fam* **p. el poncho: nadie me pisa el poncho bailando** nobody can beat me at dancing; EXPR *Andes, RP Fam* **dejarse p. el poncho** to be a doormat

(**b**) *(visitar)* to set foot in; **nunca he pisado su casa** I've never set foot in her house

(**c**) *(despreciar)* to trample on; **la conducta de este país pisa todas las leyes internacionales** this country's actions fly in the face of international law

(**d**) *(anticiparse a)* **p. un contrato a alguien** to beat sb to a contract; **p. una idea a alguien** to think of something before sb; **el periódico rival les pisó la noticia** the rival paper stole *o* pinched the story from them, the rival paper got in first with the news

(**e**) *Mús (puntear)* to pluck; *(tocar)* to strike

(**f**) *(hembra)* to cover

(**g**) *RP (aplastar)* to mash

(**h**) *RP Fam (atropellar)* to knock down, to run over

2 *vi* to tread, to step; **pisa con cuidado** tread carefully; EXPR **p. fuerte** to be firing on all cylinders; EXPR **venir pisando fuerte** to be on the road to success

3 pisarse *vpr* EXPR *RP Fam* **pisarse el palito** to give oneself away

pisaverde *nm Fam Anticuado* dandy

pisca *nf Méx (de maíz, café)* harvesting; *(de algodón)* picking

piscador, -ora *nm,f Méx (de maíz, café)* harvester; *(de algodón)* picker

piscar, pizcar *Méx* **1** *vt (maíz, café)* to harvest; *(algodón)* to pick

2 *vi* to harvest

pisciano, -a *Am* **1** *adj* Pisces; **ser p.** to be (a) Pisces

2 *nm,f* Pisces, Piscean; **los piscianos son...** Pisceans are...

piscícola *adj* piscicultural

piscicultor, -ora *nm,f* fish farmer

piscicultura *nf* fish farming

piscifactoría *nf* fish farm

pisciforme *adj* fish-shaped

piscina *nf* (**a**) *(para nadar)* swimming pool ►► ***p. al aire libre*** open-air swimming pool; ***p. climatizada*** heated swimming pool; ***p. cubierta*** covered *o* indoor swimming pool; ***p. infantil*** paddling pool; ***p. inflable*** paddling pool; ***p. olímpica*** Olympic-size swimming pool (**b**) *(para peces)* fishpond

Piscis 1 *adj inv (persona)* Pisces; *Esp* **ser P.** to be (a) Pisces

2 *nm (signo)* Pisces; *Am* **los de P. son...** Pisceans are...

3 *nmf inv (persona)* Pisces, Piscean; *Esp* **los P. son...** Pisceans are ...

pisco *nm* (**a**) *(bebida)* pisco, = Andean grape brandy ►► ***p. sour*** = cocktail of pisco, beaten egg and lemon juice (**b**) *Col (tipo)* guy

piscola *nm Chile* = pisco and cola

piscolabis *nm inv Esp Fam* snack

piso *nm* (**a**) *(planta) (de edificio)* floor; *(de autobús)* deck; *(de teatro)* circle; **primer p.** *Br* first floor, *US* second floor; **un autobús de dos pisos** a double-decker bus

(**b**) *(suelo) (de habitación)* floor; *(de carretera)* surface; EXPR *Am* **andar con el ánimo por el p.** to be very down *o* low

(**c**) *(capa)* layer; **un sandwich de dos pisos** a double-decker sandwich

(**d**) *(de zapato)* sole

(**e**) *Esp (apartamento)* apartment, *Br* flat ►► ***p. franco*** safe house; ***p. piloto*** show apartment *o Br* flat

(**f**) *Chile (taburete)* stool

pisotear *vt* (**a**) *(con el pie)* to trample on (**b**) *(humillar)* to scorn (**c**) *(oprimir)* to trample on

pisotón *nm Fam* stamp *(of the foot)*; **dar un p. a alguien** to stamp on sb's foot

pista *nf* (**a**) *(carretera)* unsurfaced road ►► ***p. forestal*** forest track; ***p. de tierra*** dirt road *o* track

(**b**) *(superficie, terreno)* ***p. de atletismo*** athletics track; ***p. de baile*** dance floor; *Esp* ***p. de cemento*** *(en tenis)* hard court; ***p. cubierta*** indoor track; **atletismo en p. cubierta** indoor athletics; ***p. de esquí*** piste, ski slope; ***p. de hielo*** ice rink; *Esp* ***p. de hierba*** *(en tenis)* grass court; ***p. de patinaje*** skating rink; *Esp* ***p. de tenis*** tennis court; *Esp* ***p. de tierra batida*** *(en tenis)* clay court

(**c**) *(para aviones)* ***p. de aterrizaje*** runway; **una p. de aterrizaje en mitad de la selva** a landing strip in the middle of the jungle

(**d**) *(de circo)* ring; ***p. de rodaje*** taxiway

(**e**) *Informát & Mús* track

(f) *(indicio)* clue; **te daré una p.** I'll give you a clue
(g) *(rastro)* trail, track; **estar sobre la p.** to be on the trail *o* track; **seguir la p. a alguien** to be on sb's trail

pistacho, *Méx* **pistache** *nm* **(a)** *(fruto)* pistachio **(b)** *(árbol)* pistachio tree

pistear *vt Méx Fam* **¿qué estás pisteando?** what are you having (to drink)?

pistilo *nm* pistil

pisto *nm* **(a)** *(guiso)* ratatouille **(b)** EXPR *Esp Fam* **darse p.** to show off **(c)** *CAm Fam (dinero)* dough **(d)** *Méx Fam (bebida alcohólica)* booze

pistola *nf* **(a)** *(arma) (con cilindro)* gun; *(sin cilindro)* pistol ►► ***p. de agua*** water pistol; ***p. de aire comprimido*** air pistol **(b)** *(pulverizador)* spray gun; **pintar a p.** to spray-paint **(c)** *(herramienta)* gun ►► ***p. de engrase*** grease gun **(d)** *(de pan)* French loaf

pistolera 1 *nf (funda)* holster
2 pistoleras *nfpl Fam (celulitis)* saddlebags

pistolerismo *nm* **el p. aún no ha desaparecido** people are still hiring gunmen

pistolero *nm* gunman ►► ***p. a sueldo*** hired gunman *o* killer

pistoletazo *nm* pistol shot ►► ***p. de salida*** *(en carrera)* shot from the starter's gun; *(de proyecto, campaña electoral)* starting signal

pistón *nm* **(a)** *Tec* piston **(b)** *Mús (corneta)* cornet; *(llave)* key **(c)** *(de arma)* percussion cap

pistonudo, -a *adj Esp Fam* wicked, awesome

pita *nf* **(a)** *(planta)* pita **(b)** *(hilo)* pita fibre

pitada *nf* **(a)** *(silbidos)* whistling; **despidieron al equipo con una sonora p.** the team were loudly whistled off the field **(b)** *(con bocina)* beep; **dar una p.** to beep one's horn **(c)** *Am Fam (calada)* drag, puff

Pitágoras *n pr* Pythagoras

pitagórico, -a 1 *adj* Pythagorean
2 *nm,f* Pythagorean

pitagorín, -ina *nm,f Fam* brain, *Br* swot

pitahaya, pitaya *nf CAm, Carib, Méx* **(a)** *(planta)* pitaya **(b)** *(fruta)* pitaya

pitanga *nf RP* Surinam cherry

pitanza *nf* **(a)** *Anticuado (ración de comida)* daily rations **(b)** *Fam (alimento)* grub **(c)** *Chile (broma)* joke

pitar 1 *vt* **(a)** *(arbitrar) (partido)* to referee **(b)** *(señalar) (falta)* to blow for; **el árbitro pitó penalti** the referee blew for a penalty **(c)** *(abuchear)* **p. a alguien** to whistle at sb in disapproval **(d)** *Am Fam (dar una calada a)* to puff (on)
2 *vi* **(a)** *(tocar el pito)* to blow a whistle; *(del coche)* to beep one's horn; **el coche pitaba para abrirse paso** the car beeped its horn to get through
(b) *(arbitrar)* to referee
(c) *Fam (funcionar) (cosa)* to work; *(persona)* to get on
(d) *Am Fam (dar caladas)* to smoke
(e) *Chile (burlarse de)* to make fun of
(f) *Esp Fam* EXPR **salir/irse pitando** to rush out/off like a shot, to dash out/off; **venir pitando** to come rushing

pitaya = **pitahaya**

pitazo *nm* **(a)** *Andes, RP, Ven (pitido)* whistle; **el árbitro dio un p.** the referee blew his whistle **(b)** *Ven Fam (chivatazo)* **dar el p. a alguien** to tip sb off

pitbull ['pitβul] *(pl* **pitbulls***) nm* pit bull (terrier)

pitcher = **pícher**

pitecántropo *nm* pithecanthropus

pitido *nm (con pito)* whistle; *(de aparato electrónico)* beep, bleep; **los pitidos de los coches** the honking of car horns; **tengo un p. en los oídos** I've got a whistling noise in my ears

pitillera *nf* cigarette case

pitillo *nm* **(a)** *(cigarrillo)* cigarette **(b)** *Col (paja)* drinking straw

pitiminí *(pl* **pitiminíes***)* **1** *nm (rosal)* fairy rose; **rosa de p.** fairy rose
2 de pitiminí *loc adj* **una boquita de p.** a dainty little mouth; **¡tú pide por esa boquita de p.!** here we go, I can see you're going to ask for the impossible!

pito *nm* **(a)** *(silbato)* whistle; **tener voz de p.** to have a very shrill voice; EXPR *RP Fam* **¿y vos qué p. tocás acá?** and what the hell are you doing here?; EXPR *RP* **hacerle p. catalán a alguien** to cock a snook at sb
(b) *(claxon)* horn; **tocar el p.** to sound one's horn
(c) ***p. real*** *(ave)* green woodpecker
(d) *Fam (cigarrillo)* smoke, *Br* fag
(e) *Fam (pene) Br* willie, *US* peter
(f) *esp Méx Vulg (pene)* cock
(g) EXPR *Fam* **entre pitos y flautas** what with one thing and another; *Fam* **por pitos o por flautas** for one reason or another; *Fam* **(no) me importa un p.** I couldn't give a damn; *Fam* **me toman por el p. del sereno** they don't pay me a blind bit of notice

pitoitoy *nm* red-breasted snipe

pitón¹ *nm* **(a)** *(cuerno)* horn **(b)** *(pitorro)* spout **(c)** *(en alpinismo)* piton **(d)** *muy Fam (pecho)* tit

pitón² *nm o nf (serpiente)* python

pitonazo *nm (herida)* gore

pitonisa *nf* fortune-teller

pitorrearse *vpr Esp Fam* **p. de alguien** to make fun of sb, *Br* to take the mickey out of sb

pitorreo *nm Esp Fam* **esta empresa es un p.** this company is a joke; **tomarse algo a p.** to treat sth as a joke; **¡ya basta de p.!** that's enough clowning around!

pitorro *nm* **(a)** *(de botijo)* spout **(b)** *Fam (pieza)* **¿para qué sirve este p.?** what's this button thing for?

pitote *nm Fam (jaleo)* row, fuss; **armar un p.** to kick up a row *o* fuss; **se armó un p. cuando se anunció el resultado** all hell broke loose when the result was announced

pitucada *nf CSur, Perú Fam* **la p.** the snobs

pituco, -a *CSur, Perú Fam* **1** *adj* **(a)** *(elegante)* posh **(b)** *(engreído)* snobby
2 *nm,f* snob

pitufo,-a *nm,f* **(a)** *Fam (persona pequeña)* shorty; *(niño)* ankle-biter, rug rat **(b) los pitufos**® the smurfs® **(c)** *Esp Fam (guardia)* = member of the local police force

pituitaria *nf* pituitary gland

pitusa *nm Cuba* jeans

pituso, -a *Fam* **1** *adj* sweet, cute
2 *nm,f* cute child

pituto *nm Chile Fam* pull, influence

piure *nm Chile* sea squirt

pívot *(pl* **pívots***) nmf (en baloncesto)* centre

pivotar *vi* **(a)** *(pieza)* to pivot **(b)** *(jugador)* to pivot

pivote *nmf* **(a)** *(eje)* pivot **(b)** *(en baloncesto)* centre

píxel *nm Informát* pixel

piyama *nm o nf Am (pijama)* pyjamas; **un p.** a pair of pyjamas

pizarra *nf* **(a)** *(roca, material)* slate **(b)** *(encerado) Br* blackboard, *US* chalkboard; **salir a la p.** to go up to the *Br* blackboard *o US* chalkboard

pizarral *nm* slate quarry

pizarrín *nm* slate pencil

pizarrón *nm Am Br* blackboard, *US* chalkboard

pizca *nf* **(a)** *(cantidad)* tiny bit; *(de sal)* pinch; **pásame una p. de pan** pass me a little bit of bread; **le falta una p. de velocidad para ser campeón** he's just slightly short of the pace you need to be a champion; EXPR *Fam* **ni p.** not one bit; **ahora no tengo ni p. de tiempo** I've got absolutely no time just now; **no me hace ni p. de gracia** I don't find it in the least bit funny
(b) *Méx (cosecha)* harvest, crop

pizcar = **piscar**

pizpireta *adj Fam (niña, mujer)* spirited, zippy

pizza ['pitsa] *nf* pizza

pizzería [pitse'ria] *nf* pizzeria, pizza parlour

pizzicato [pitsi'kato] *nm Mús* pizzicato

PJ *nm (abrev de* **Partido Justicialista***)* = Argentinian political party

PJF *nf (abrev de* **Policía Judicial Federal***)* = in Mexico, police force that acts under the orders of federal judges

PL *nm (abrev de* **Partido Liberal***)* = Columbian/Honduran political party

Pl. *(abrev de* **Plaza***)* square

placa *nf* **(a)** *(lámina)* plate; *(de madera)* sheet ►► ***p. de hielo*** patch of ice; **la moto patinó en una p. de hielo** the motorbike skidded on a patch of ice; ***p. solar*** solar panel
(b) *(inscripción)* plaque; **p. conmemorativa** commemorative plaque
(c) *(de policía)* badge
(d) *(de cocina)* ring ►► ***p. de vitrocerámica*** ceramic hob
(e) *Aut* **p. (de matrícula)** *Br* number plate, *US* license plate
(f) *Geol* plate ►► ***p. tectónica*** tectonic plate
(g) *Elec* board
(h) *Informát* board ►► ***p. base*** motherboard; ***p. lógica*** logic board; ***p. madre*** motherboard; ***p. de vídeo*** *o Am* ***video*** video board

(**i**) *Fot* plate
(**j**) *(en dientes)* **p. (bacteriana** *o* **dental)** plaque
(**k**) *(en garganta)* infected area, *Espec* plaque

placaje *nm Dep* tackle

placar[1] [60] *vt Dep* to tackle

placar[2], **placard** (*pl* **placares**) *nm RP (para ropa)* fitted wardrobe; *(de cocina)* fitted cupboard

placé *adj inv Andes, RP* **llegar p.** *(caballo)* to place

placebo *nm* placebo

pláceme *nm Formal* congratulations; **dar el p. a alguien** to congratulate sb

placenta *nf* placenta

placentero, -a *adj* pleasant

placer 1 *nm* pleasure; **los placeres de la carne** the pleasures of the flesh; **un viaje de p.** a pleasure trip; **ha sido un p. (conocerle)** it has been a pleasure (meeting you); **es un p. ayudarte** it's a pleasure to help you; **¿me concede este baile? – con p.** may I have this dance? – with pleasure; **es un p. anunciar que...** it is my pleasure to announce that...

2 a placer *loc adv* **comimos pasteles a p.** we ate as many cakes as we wanted; **marcar a p.** *(en fútbol, balonmano)* to score an easy goal

3 *vt* to please; **me place conversar** I take great pleasure in conversation; **nos place comunicarle que...** we are pleased to inform you that...; **si me place** if I want to, if I feel like it; **haz lo que te plazca** do as you please

plácet (*pl* **plácets**) *nm Formal (aprobación)* approval; **dar el p. a un embajador** to accept an ambassador's credentials

plácidamente *adv* placidly

placidez *nf (de persona)* placidness; *(de día, vida, conversación)* peacefulness

plácido, -a *adj (persona)* placid; *(día, vida, conversación)* peaceful

plafón *nm* (**a**) *(lámpara)* ceiling light *(that is flush with the ceiling)* (**b**) *(tablero)* soffit

plaga *nf* (**a**) *(de insectos)* plague ►► ***p. de langosta*** plague of locusts (**b**) *(desastre, calamidad)* plague; **el tabaco es una de las plagas modernas** smoking is one of the plagues of modern society; **la zona se vio afectada por una p. de robos** the area suffered a spate of robberies (**c**) *(de gente)* swarm; **una p. de turistas** a swarm of tourists

plagado, -a *adj (de insectos)* infested (**de** with); **p. de dificultades** beset *o* plagued with difficulties; **la ciudad está plagada de turistas** the city is overrun with tourists; **una declaración plagada de contradicciones** a statement riddled with contradictions

plagar [38] **1** *vt* **p. de** *(propaganda)* to swamp with; *(moscas)* to infest with

2 plagarse *vpr* **el centro se está plagando de bares** the town centre is becoming covered in bars

plagiar *vt* (**a**) *(copiar)* to plagiarize (**b**) *CAm, Col, Perú, Ven (secuestrar)* to kidnap

plagiario, -a *nm,f* (**a**) *(que copia)* plagiarist (**b**) *CAm, Col, Perú, Ven (secuestrador)* kidnapper

plagio *nm* (**a**) *(copia)* plagiarism (**b**) *CAm, Col, Perú, Ven (secuestro)* kidnapping

plaguicida 1 *adj* pesticidal

2 *nm* pesticide

plan *nm* (**a**) *(proyecto, programa)* plan; **hacer planes** to plan; **tenemos p. de visitarte la próxima semana** we're planning to call on you next week; **¿tienes algún p. para mañana por la tarde?** have you got any plans for tomorrow evening? ►► ***p. de acción*** action plan; ***p. de adelgazamiento*** diet; ***p. de ahorro*** savings plan; ***p. de amortización*** repayment plan; ***p. de choque*** emergency plan; ***p. de desarrollo*** development plan; ***p. de emergencia*** *(para el futuro)* contingency plan; *(como reacción)* emergency plan; ***p. de estudios*** syllabus; ***p. hidrológico*** water management plan; ***p. de jubilación*** pension scheme *o* plan; ***p. de pensiones*** pension scheme *o* plan; ***p. de pensiones contributivo*** contributory pension scheme *o* plan; *Hist* ***p. quinquenal*** five-year plan; ***p. de urbanismo*** urban development plan; ***p. de viabilidad*** feasibility plan; ***p. de vuelo*** flight plan

(**b**) *Fam (ligue)* date; **salieron a buscar un p.** they went out on the pull

(**c**) EXPR *Fam* **a todo p.** in the greatest luxury, with no expense spared; *Fam* **en p.**: **lo dijo en p. serio** he was serious about it; **si te pones en ese p....** if you're going to be like that about it...; **se puso en p. violento** he got *o* became violent; *Fam* **en p. de**: **lo dijo en p. de broma** he was only kidding, he meant it as a joke; **vamos a Perú en p. de turismo** we are going to Peru for a holiday; *Fam* **no es p.** it's just not on; **¡vaya p. de vida!** what a life!

plana *nf* (**a**) *(página)* page; **el anuncio saldrá a toda p.** it will be a full-page advert; **en primera p.** on the front page; EXPR **corregir** *o* **enmendar la p. a alguien** *(criticar)* to find fault with sb, to criticize sb; *(superar)* to go one better than sb (**b**) *(llanura)* plain (**c**) ***la p. mayor*** *(de ejército)* the general staff; *(de empresa, partido político)* the leading figures (**d**) *(ejercicio escolar)* writing exercise

plancha *nf* (**a**) *(para planchar)* iron; **pasar la p. a algo** to give sth a quick iron; **odio la p.** I hate ironing; **esas camisas necesitan una p.** those shirts need ironing ►► ***p. de vapor*** steam iron

(**b**) *(ropa planchada)* ironing
(**c**) *(para cocinar)* grill; **a la p.** grilled
(**d**) *(placa)* plate; *(de madera)* sheet
(**e**) *Fam (metedura de pata)* boob, blunder
(**f**) *(en fútbol)* dangerous tackle *(with studs showing)*; **entrar en p.** to go in studs first
(**g**) *Imprenta* plate
(**h**) *(al nadar)* **hacer la p.** to float on one's back
(**i**) *RP, Ven (lista)* slate, ticket
(**j**) *Méx Fam* EXPR **ser una p.** to be a pain in the neck; **darle p. a alguien** to stand sb up; **pegarse p.** to get a nasty shock

planchada *nf Am* ironing; **dale una p. a esa camisa** give that shirt an iron

planchado, -a 1 *adj Fam* (**a**) *RP (cansado)* (dead) beat, *Br* knackered (**b**) *Chile (sin plata)* broke, *Br* skint (**c**) *Urug (dormido)* dead to the world

2 *nm* ironing; **dale un p. a esa camisa** give that shirt an iron

planchadora *nf (máquina)* pressing machine

planchar 1 *vt* (**a**) *(ropa)* to iron; EXPR *Esp Fam Hum* **p. la oreja** *(dormir)* to get some shut-eye (**b**) *Fam (aplastar)* to flatten (**c**) *Fam (hundir psicológicamente)* to devastate; **se quedó planchado cuando escuchó la noticia** he was devastated when he heard the news

2 *vi* (**a**) *(con plancha)* to do the ironing (**b**) *RP Fam (caerse)* to crash to the floor (**c**) *CSur Fam (en baile)* **¿bailaste mucho anoche? – no, planché** did you dance a lot last night? – no, nobody asked me

planchazo *nm Fam* (**a**) *(sorpresa desagradable)* shock; **menudo p. se llevó cuando se enteró** she got a hell of a shock when she found out (**b**) *(en piscina)* belly-flop

plancton *nm* plankton

planeación *nf Col, Méx* planning

planeador *nm* glider

planeadora *nf (lancha)* speedboat

planeamiento *nm* (**a**) *(planificación)* planning (**b**) *(vuelo)* gliding

planear 1 *vt* to plan; **planean una fiesta para el viernes** they are planning a party for Friday; **planeo viajar a Asia en verano** I'm planning to travel to Asia this summer

2 *vi* (**a**) *(hacer planes)* to plan (**b**) *(planeador)* to glide (**c**) *(ave)* to glide, to soar

planeo *nm* (**a**) *(de planeador)* gliding (**b**) *(de ave)* gliding, soaring

planeta *nm* planet ►► ***p. exterior*** outer planet; ***p. interior*** inner planet; ***p. mayor*** major planet; ***el p. rojo*** *(Marte)* the Red Planet

planetario, -a 1 *adj* (**a**) *(de un planeta)* planetary (**b**) *(mundial)* world; **a nivel p.** on a global scale

2 *nm* planetarium

planetoide *nm Astron* planetoid

planicie *nf* plain

planificación *nf* planning ►► ***p. ambiental*** environmental planning; ***p. económica*** economic planning; ***p. familiar*** family planning; ***p. urbanística*** town planning

planificador, -ora 1 *adj* planning

2 *nm,f* planner

planificar [60] *vt* to plan

planilla *nf* (**a**) *Am (formulario)* form (**b**) *Am (nómina)* payroll; **estar en p.** to be on the payroll, to be a permanent member of staff (**c**) *Méx (lista)* slate, ticket

planimetría *nf* planimetry

planisferio *nm* planisphere

planning ['planin] (*pl* **plannings**) *nm* schedule, agenda

plano, -a 1 *adj* flat

2 *nm* (**a**) *(diseño, mapa)* plan; **el p. de una ciudad** the map of a city ►► ***p. acotado*** spot height map; ***p. de calles*** street map; ***p. de planta*** floor plan

(**b**) *(ámbito)* **en el p. político** politically; **una persona muy estable en el p. afectivo** a very emotionally stable person

(**c**) *Cine* shot; **primer p.** close-up; *también Fig* **en segundo p.** in the background ►► ***p. corto*** close-up; ***p. general*** pan shot; ***p. largo*** long shot

(d) *(en pintura)* **primer p.** foreground; **segundo p.** background
(e) *Mat* plane ►► *Geol* ***p. de falla*** fault plane; ***p. inclinado*** inclined plane
3 de plano *loc adv (golpear)* right, directly; *(negar)* flatly; *Fam* **cantar de p.** to make a full confession; **te equivocas de p.** you're completely wrong; **rechazó de p. la propuesta** she flatly rejected the proposal

planta *nf* **(a)** *(vegetal)* plant ►► ***p. acuática*** aquatic plant; ***p. anual*** annual; ***p. de interior*** house plant, indoor plant; ***p. medicinal*** medicinal plant; ***p. perenne*** perennial; ***p. transgénica*** transgenic plant; ***p. trepadora*** climbing plant
(b) *(fábrica)* plant ►► ***p. depuradora*** purification plant; ***p. desaladora de agua*** desalination plant; ***p. desalinizadora*** desalination plant; ***p. envasadora*** packaging plant; ***p. de envase*** packaging plant; *RP* ***p. faenadora de reses*** abattoir; ***p. de montaje*** assembly plant; ***p. de reciclaje*** recycling plant; ***p. de tratamiento de residuos*** waste treatment plant
(c) *(piso)* floor; **p. baja** *Br* ground floor, *US* first floor; **p. primera** *Br* first floor, *US* second floor
(d) *(plano)* plan; **un templo de p. rectangular** a temple built on a rectangular plan; **de nueva p.** brand new
(e) *(del pie)* sole
(f) EXPR *Fam* **tener buena p.** to be good-looking

plantación *nf* **(a)** *(terreno)* plantation **(b)** *(acción)* planting

plantado, -a *adj* **(a)** *(planta, árbol)* planted; **un terreno p. de trigo** a field planted with wheat; EXPR *Fam* **ser bien p.** to be good-looking **(b)** EXPR *Fam* **dejar p. a alguien** *(no acudir)* to stand sb up; **prometió prestarnos dinero pero luego nos dejó plantados** she promised to lend us some money but in the end she let us down

plantador, -ora 1 *nm,f (persona)* planter
2 *nm (herramienta)* dibble, dibber

plantadora *nf (máquina)* planter

plantar 1 *vt* **(a)** *(sembrar)* to plant (**de** with); *(semillas)* to sow; **plantaron la zona de eucaliptos** they planted the area with eucalyptus
(b) *(fijar) (tienda de campaña)* to pitch; *(poste)* to put in
(c) *Fam (dar)* **le plantó una bofetada/un beso** she gave him a slap in the face/a kiss
(d) *Fam (decir con brusquedad)* **le plantó cuatro frescas** she gave him a piece of her mind
(e) *Fam (dejar plantado)* **p. a alguien** *(no acudir)* to stand sb up; **plantó a su novio tras cinco meses de noviazgo** she ditched *o* dumped her boyfriend after they'd been going out together for five months
(f) *Fam (construcción, mueble, objeto)* to plonk; **plantó los pies en el sofá** she plonked her feet on the sofa
2 plantarse *vpr* **(a)** *(ponerse, colocarse)* to plant oneself; **el perro se plantó delante de la puerta** the dog planted itself in front of the door
(b) *Fam (presentarse)* to turn up; **se plantó en la fiesta con dos amigos** he turned up at the party with two friends
(c) *Fam (en un sitio con rapidez)* **plantarse en** to get to, to make it to; **nos podemos p. ahí en quince minutos** we'll be able to get there in fifteen minutes
(d) *(en una actitud)* **plantarse en algo** to stick to sth, to insist on sth; **se ha plantado y dice que no quiere venir** he's standing firm *o* digging his heels in and refusing to come
(e) *(en naipes)* to stick; **¡me planto!** stick!

plante *nm* **(a)** *(protesta)* **ayer hubo un p. en la fábrica** workers in the factory downed tools yesterday **(b)** *(plantón)* **dar** *o* **hacer un p. a alguien** to stand sb up

planteamiento *nm* **(a)** *(exposición)* **no entiendo el p. de esta pregunta** I don't understand the way this question is phrased; **hizo un p. realista de la situación** he gave a realistic assessment of the situation; **su p. del problema** the way she presented the problem
(b) *(enfoque)* approach; **no estoy de acuerdo con su p. radical** I don't agree with her radical approach; **tenemos planteamientos diferentes** we see things differently
(c) *Lit, Teatro* exposition; **p., nudo y desenlace** introduction, development and denouement

plantear 1 *vt* **(a)** *(formular) (problema matemático)* to set out
(b) *(exponer) (reivindicación)* to put forward; *(dificultad, duda, cuestión)* to raise; **me planteó sus preocupaciones** he put his concerns to me, he raised his concerns with me
(c) *(proponer) (solución, posibilidad)* to propose; **plantean una solución radical al cambio climático** they are proposing a radical solution to climate change; **nos plantearon la posibilidad de abandonar** they asked us to consider the possibility of withdrawing
(d) *(presentar) (problema)* to pose
2 plantearse *vpr* **plantearse algo** to consider sth, to think about sth; **se está planteando retirarse** she is considering retiring; **nunca me había planteado esa posibilidad** I had never considered that possibility; **se me planteó el dilema de elegir entre dos excelentes candidatos** I was confronted with the dilemma of choosing between two excellent candidates

plantel *nm* **(a)** *(criadero)* nursery bed **(b)** *(conjunto)* group; **lo respalda un p. de asesores** he is supported by a team of advisers **(c)** *Am (equipo)* team

planteo *nm Am (propuesta)* idea

plantificar [60] *vt Fam* **(a)** *(dar)* **le plantificó una bofetada/un beso** she gave him a slap in the face/a kiss **(b)** *(colocar)* to stick; **plantificaron a los niños en un internado** they stuck the children in a boarding school

plantígrado, -a *Zool* **1** *adj* plantigrade
2 *nm* plantigrade

plantilla *nf* **(a)** *(de empresa)* staff; **estar en p.** to be on the payroll, to be a permanent member of staff; **reducir la p.** to downsize **(b)** *(de equipo)* squad **(c)** *(para zapatos)* insole ►► ***p. ortopédica*** orthopaedic insole, *US* orthotic footbed **(d)** *(patrón)* pattern, template **(e)** *Informát* template **(f)** *CSur (soletilla)* = small, flat cake in the shape of a sole

plantillazo *nm Dep* dangerous tackle *(with studs showing)*

plantío *nm* bed *(for plants)*

plantón *nm* **(a)** *Fam (espera)* **perdona el p., no he podido llegar antes** I'm sorry for keeping you waiting, I couldn't get here any earlier; **dar un p. a alguien** to stand sb up; **estar de p.** to be kept waiting, to be cooling one's heels **(b)** *(estaca)* cutting **(c)** *Méx Fam (sentada)* sit-down protest

plántula *nf* plantlet

plañidera *nf* hired mourner

plañidero, -a *adj* plaintive, whining

plañido *nm* moan

plañir 1 *vt* to bewail
2 *vi* to moan, to wail

plaqueta *nf* **(a)** *(en la sangre)* platelet **(b)** *(de cerámica)* tile

plasma *nm* plasma ►► ***p. sanguíneo*** blood plasma

plasmación *nf* expression; **la ley es una p. de su preocupación por los inmigrantes** the law is an expression of their concern about immigrants; **la inauguración del museo supuso la p. de un sueño** the opening of the museum was the fulfilment of a dream

plasmar 1 *vt (reflejar) (sentimientos)* to give expression to; *(realidad)* to reflect; *(sueño)* to fulfil; **plasma su radicalismo en la novela** she expresses her radical views in the novel
2 plasmarse *vpr* to emerge, to take shape; **el acuerdo se plasmó en el último momento** the agreement took shape *o* gelled at the last moment; **su iniciativa se plasmó en un proyecto** his initiative turned into a project

plasta 1 *adj Fam* **(a)** *Esp (pesado)* **ser p.** to be a pain; **un tío p.** a real bore **(b)** *RP (perezoso)* **ser p.** to be a lazy slob
2 *nmf Fam* **(a)** *Esp (pesado)* pain, drag **(b)** *RP (perezoso)* lazy slob
3 *nf* **(a)** *(cosa blanda)* mess **(b)** *(cosa mal hecha)* botch-up

plástica *nf* **(a)** *Arte* plastic art **(b)** *(en escuela)* arts and crafts

plasticidad *nf* **(a)** *(moldeabilidad)* plasticity **(b)** *(expresividad)* expressiveness

plasticina® = **plastilina**

plástico, -a 1 *adj* **(a)** *(moldeable)* plastic **(b)** *(expresivo)* expressive
2 *nm* **(a)** *(material)* plastic **(b)** *(explosivo)* plastic explosive **(c)** *Fam (tarjeta de crédito)* plastic (money) **(d)** *Fam (disco)* disc

plastificación *nf (de carné, tarjeta)* lamination; *(de mesa, tela)* plastic-coating

plastificado, -a 1 *adj (carné, tarjeta)* laminated; *(mesa, tela)* plastic-coated
2 *nm (de carné, tarjeta)* lamination; *(de mesa, tela)* plastic-coating

plastificante *nm* plasticizer

plastificar [60] *vt (carné, tarjeta)* to laminate; *(mesa, tela)* to coat with plastic

plastilina®, *RP* **plasticina**® *nf* Plasticine®

plata *nf* **(a)** *(metal)* silver; EXPR *Fam* **hablar en p.** to speak bluntly ►► ***p. de ley*** sterling silver **(b)** *(objetos de plata)* silverware **(c)** *Dep (medalla)* silver; **Cuba se llevó la p.** Cuba took the silver **(d)** *Am Fam (dinero)* money; **¿tienes p.?** have you got any money?

plataforma *nf* **(a)** *(superficie elevada, estrado)* platform ▸▸ ***p. de lanzamiento*** launching *o* launch pad; ***p. petrolífera*** oil rig, oil platform
(b) ***p. espacial*** space station *o* platform
(c) *(vagón)* open *o* flatbed wagon
(d) *(punto de partida)* launching pad; **utilizó la sociedad como p. para defender sus intereses económicos** she used the company as a basis to further her financial interests
(e) *Geol* shelf ▸▸ ***p. continental*** continental shelf
(f) *Pol* platform, programme ▸▸ ***p. electoral*** electoral platform
(g) *(organización)* organization; **una p. estudiantil** a student organization
(h) *Informát* platform

platal *nm Am Fam* **un p.** a fortune, loads of money

platanal, platanar *nm* banana plantation

platanera *nf*, **platanero** *nm* banana tree

plátano *nm* **(a)** *(fruta)* banana **(b)** *(árbol de sombra)* plane tree

platea *nf* **(a)** *(en teatro) Br* stalls, *US* orchestra **(b)** *RP (butaca)* seat in the *Br* stalls *o US* orchestra

plateado, -a *adj* **(a)** *(con plata)* silver-plated **(b)** *(color)* silvery

platear *vt* to silver-plate

platelminto *nm* flatworm

platense 1 *adj* **(a)** *(de la ciudad)* of/from La Plata *(Argentina)* **(b)** *(de la región)* of/from the River Plate region
2 *nm,f* **(a)** *(de la ciudad)* person from La Plata *(Argentina)* **(b)** *(de la región)* person from the River Plate region

plateresco *nm* plateresque, = 16th century Spanish style of architecture and decoration

platería *nf* **(a)** *(arte, oficio)* silversmithing **(b)** *(tienda)* silversmith's (shop); *(taller)* silversmith's workshop **(c)** *(objetos)* silverware

platero, -a *nm,f* silversmith

plática *nf CAm, Méx* **(a)** *(charla)* talk, chat; **estar de p.** to chat **(b)** *(relato)* talk

platicador, -ora *adj CAm, Méx* conversational

platicar [60] *CAm, Méx* 1 *vi* to talk, to chat (**de** about)
2 *vt* to tell

platicón, -ona *CAm, Méx Fam* 1 *adj* talkative
2 *nm,f* chatterbox

platija *nf (pez)* plaice

platillo *nm* **(a)** *(plato pequeño)* small plate; *(de taza)* saucer **(b)** *(de una balanza)* pan **(c)** ***p. volador*** flying saucer; *Esp* ***p. volante*** flying saucer **(d)** *Mús* **platillos** cymbals **(e)** *Méx (comida)* meal, dish

platina *nf* **(a)** *(de tocadiscos)* turntable **(b)** *(de casete)* cassette deck **(c)** *(de microscopio)* stage **(d)** *Imprenta* platen, bedplate

platinado *nm* platinum plating

platinar *vt* to platinize

platino 1 *nm (metal)* platinum
2 **platinos** *nmpl Aut & Tec* contact points

plato *nm* **(a)** *(recipiente)* plate, dish; **lavar los platos** to wash the dishes, *Br* to do the washing-up; **estaba el mar como un p.** the sea was like a millpond; EXPR *Fam* **comer en el mismo p.** to be great friends; EXPR *Fam* **nada entre dos platos** nothing special; EXPR *Fam* **pagar los platos rotos** to carry the can; EXPR *Fam* **parece que no ha roto un p. en su vida** he looks as if butter wouldn't melt in his mouth ▸▸ ***p. hondo*** soup dish *o* plate; ***p. llano*** plate; *Méx*, RP ***p. playo*** plate; ***p. de postre*** dessert plate; ***p. sopero*** soup dish *o* plate
(b) *(parte de una comida)* course; **primer p.** first course, starter; **de primer p.** for starters; **segundo p.** second course, main course; EXPR *Fam* **ser p. de segunda mano** *o* **mesa** *(ser despreciado)* to be a second-class citizen; *(haber perdido la virginidad)* to be spoiled goods ▸▸ ***p. combinado*** = single-course meal which usually consists of meat or fish accompanied by French fries and sometimes vegetables; *Chile* ***p. de fondo*** main course; ***p. fuerte*** *(en una comida)* main course; *Fig* main part; **su actuación es el p. fuerte de la noche** her performance is the night's main event; ***p. principal*** main course
(c) *(comida)* dish; **mi p. favorito** my favourite meal ▸▸ ***p. del día*** dish of the day; ***p. precocinado*** pre-cooked meal; ***p. preparado*** ready-made meal; ***p. típico*** typical dish; ***p. único*** single-course meal
(d) *(de tocadiscos, microondas)* turntable
(e) *(de bicicleta)* chain wheel
(f) *(de balanza)* pan, scale
(g) *Dep* clay-pigeon
(h) EXPR *Am Fam* **ser un p.** to be a scream; **¡qué p.!** how hilarious!

plató *nm* set

Platón *n pr* Plato

platón *nm Méx* serving dish

platónico, -a *adj* platonic

platonismo *nm* Platonism

platudo, -a *adj Am Fam* loaded, rolling in it

plausibilidad *nf* **(a)** *(carácter admirable)* praiseworthiness **(b)** *(admisibilidad)* acceptability **(c)** *(posibilidad)* plausibility

plausible *adj* **(a)** *(admirable)* praiseworthy **(b)** *(admisible)* acceptable **(c)** *(posible)* plausible

playa *nf* **(a)** *(en el mar)* beach; **ir a la p. de vacaciones** to go on holiday to the seaside **(b)** *Am* ***p. de estacionamiento*** *(en ciudad) Br* car park, *US* parking lot

play-back ['pleiβak] *(pl* **play-backs***) nm* **cantar en** *o* **hacer p.** to mime (the lyrics)

playboy [plei'βoi] *(pl* **playboys***) nm* playboy

playera *nf* **(a)** *(zapato) (de deporte)* tennis shoe; *(de lona)* canvas shoe **(b)** *Méx (camiseta)* T-shirt

playero, -a 1 *adj* **(a)** *(de la playa)* beach; **toalla playera** beach towel **(b)** *(persona)* **es muy p.** he loves the beach
2 *nm RP Fam* = beach guard on assignment from the navy

playo, -a *adj Méx, RP (poco profundo)* shallow; **plato p.** plate

play-off ['plei'of] *(pl* **play-offs***) nm Dep* play-off

plaza *nf* **(a)** *(en una población)* square; **la p. del pueblo** the village *o* town square ▸▸ ***p. mayor*** main square; ***p. del mercado*** market square
(b) *(sitio)* place; **tenemos plazas limitadas** there are a limited number of places available ▸▸ ***p. de aparcamiento*** parking space; ***p. de garaje*** parking space *(in a private garage)*
(c) *(asiento)* seat; **un vehículo de dos/cinco plazas** a two-seater/five-seater vehicle
(d) *(puesto de trabajo)* position, job; **está buscando una p. de médico** he's looking for a position as a doctor; **han sido cubiertas todas las plazas** all the positions have been filled ▸▸ ***p. vacante*** vacancy
(e) *(mercado)* market, marketplace; **el producto que usted busca no está más en p.** the product you are looking for is no longer on the market
(f) *Taurom* **p. (de toros)** bullring
(g) *Com (zona)* area
(h) *(fortificación)* ***p. de armas*** parade ground; ***p. fuerte*** stronghold

plazca *etc ver* **placer**

plazo *nm* **(a)** *(de tiempo)* period (of time); **en el p. de un mes** within a month; **mañana termina el p. de inscripción** the deadline for registration is tomorrow; **tenemos de p. hasta el domingo** we have until Sunday; **hay un p. de dos semanas para inscribirse** there is a period of two weeks for registration; **a corto/medio** *o RP* **mediano/largo p.** in the short/medium/long term; **una solución a corto/largo p.** a short-/long-term solution; **en breve p.** within a short time; **invertir dinero a p. fijo** to invest money for a fixed term ▸▸ *Com* ***p. de entrega*** delivery time
(b) *(de dinero)* instalment; **comprar a plazos** to buy on *Br* hire purchase *o US* an installment plan; **pagar a plazos** to pay in instalments ▸▸ ***p. mensual*** monthly instalment

plazoleta, plazuela *nf* small square

PLD *nm (abrev de* **Partido de la Liberación Dominicana***)* = political party in the Dominican Republic

pleamar *nf* high tide

plebe 1 *nf* **(a)** **la p.** *(la masa)* the plebs **(b)** *Méx Fam* **la p.** *(los amigos)* the guys
2 *nmf Méx Fam* **los plebes** *(los niños)* the kids; **el p. no quiere dormir** the kid doesn't want to go to sleep

plebeyo, -a *adj* **(a)** *Hist* plebeian **(b)** *(vulgar)* common

plebiscitar *vt* to submit to a plebiscite

plebiscito *nm* plebiscite

plectro *nm* **(a)** *Mús* plectrum **(b)** *Literario (inspiración)* inspiration

plegable *adj (silla, mesa)* folding; *(cama)* foldaway

plegadera *nf* paperknife

plegamiento *nm Geol* fold

plegar [43] 1 *vt (papel)* to fold; *(mesita, hamaca)* to fold away
2 *vi Esp Fam (acabar)* to knock off
3 **plegarse** *vpr* **(a)** *(ceder)* **plegarse (a algo)** to give in *o* yield (to sth); **se pliega a todos sus caprichos** she gives in to all his whims **(b)** *Andes, CSur (unirse)* to join in; **muchos peatones se plegaron a la manifestación** many passers-by joined the demonstration

plegaria *nf* prayer

pleistoceno, -a *Geol* **1** *adj* Pleistocene
2 *nm* **el p.** the Pleistocene

pleitear *vi Der* to litigate, to conduct a lawsuit

pleitesía *nf* homage; **rendir p. a alguien** to pay homage to sb

pleito *nm* **(a)** *Der (litigio)* lawsuit; *(disputa)* dispute; **ganar/perder un p.** to win/lose a case *o* lawsuit; **poner un p. (a alguien)** to take legal action (against sb) **(b)** *Am (discusión)* argument **(c)** *Méx (de boxeo)* fight

plenamente *adv* completely, fully

plenario, -a 1 *adj* plenary
2 *nm* plenary (session)

plenilunio *nm* full moon

plenipotenciario, -a 1 *adj* plenipotentiary
2 *nm,f* plenipotentiary

plenitud *nf* **(a)** *(apogeo)* completeness, fullness; **en la p. de** at the height of; **el actor está en su p. artística** the actor is at the peak of his abilities, the actor is in his prime; **el corredor no se halla en p. de facultades** the runner is not at his best **(b)** *(abundancia)* abundance

pleno, -a 1 *adj* full, complete; **en p. día** in broad daylight; **en p. invierno** in the middle of winter; **en plena guerra** in the middle of the war; **la bomba cayó en p. centro de la ciudad** the bomb landed right in the city centre; **le dio en plena cara** she hit him right in the face; **en plena forma** on top form; **en plena naturaleza** in the middle of the country(side); **en p. uso de sus facultades** in full command of his faculties; **miembro de p. derecho** full member ►► ***p. empleo*** full employment; ***plenos poderes*** plenary powers
2 *nm* **(a)** *(reunión)* plenary meeting; **la reunión en p.** the meeting as a whole, everyone at the meeting **(b)** *Esp (en las quinielas)* = 14 correct forecasts on soccer pools ►► ***p. al quince*** = 15 correct forecasts on soccer pools entitling player to jackpot prize

pleonasmo *nm Ling* pleonasm

pleonástico, -a *adj Ling* pleonastic

pletina *nf* cassette deck

plétora *nf* plethora

pletórico, -a *adj* **p. de** full of; **está p. de salud** he's bursting with health; **está p. de felicidad** he's radiant with happiness

pleura *nf* pleural membrane

pleural *adj* pleural

pleuresía *nf Med* pleurisy

pleuritis *nf inv Med* pleurisy

plexiglás® *nm inv* Perspex®, *US* Plexiglas®

plexo *nm Anat* plexus ►► ***p. braquial*** brachial plexus; ***p. sacro*** sacral plexus; ***p. solar*** solar plexus

pléyade *nf (conjunto)* **una p. de historiadores** an illustrious company of historians

plica *nf (sobre sellado)* sealed envelope

pliego 1 *ver* **plegar**
2 *nm* **(a)** *(de papel, cartulina)* sheet **(b)** *(carta, documento)* sealed document *o* letter ►► ***p. de cargos*** list of charges *o* accusations; ***p. de condiciones*** specifications; ***p. de descargos*** list of rebuttals **(c)** *Imprenta* signature

pliegue 1 *ver* **plegar**
2 *nm* **(a)** *(en papel, piel)* fold **(b)** *(en un plisado)* pleat **(c)** *Geol* fold

plin *nm Esp Fam* **ia mí, p.!** I couldn't care less!

plinto *nm* **(a)** *Arquit* plinth **(b)** *(en gimnasia)* vaulting box

plioceno, -a *Geol* **1** *adj* Pliocene
2 *nm* **el p.** the Pliocene

plisado *nm* pleating

plisar *vt* to pleat

PLN *nm* (*abrev de* **Partido Liberación Nacional**) = Costa Rican political party

plomada *nf* **(a)** *Constr* plumb line **(b)** *Náut (de medición)* plumb line

plomazo *nm Fam* **(a)** *(persona, libro, película)* bore **(b)** *Méx (balazo)* bullet wound

plomería *nf Méx, RP, Ven* **(a)** *(negocio)* plumber's (workshop) **(b)** *(instalación)* plumbing

plomero *nm Méx, RP, Ven* plumber

plomizo, -a *adj (color, cielo)* leaden

plomo *nm* **(a)** *(metal)* lead; **sin p.** *(gasolina)* unleaded; *Fig* **caer a p.** to fall *o* drop like a stone **(b)** *(pieza de metal)* lead weight **(c)** *(fusible)* fuse; **se han fundido los plomos** the fuses have gone *o* blown **(d)** *Fam (pelmazo) (persona, libro, película)* bore; **ino seas p.!** don't be such a bore! **(e)** *(balas)* lead; **le llenaron el cuerpo de p.** they filled him full of lead; *Col* **dar p. a alguien** to shoot sb

plóter (*pl* **ploters**), **plotter** (*pl* **plotters**) *nm Informát* plotter

PLRA *nf* (*abrev de* **Partido Liberal Radical Auténtico**) = Paraguayan political party

plug-in [plu'ɣin] (*pl* **plug-ins**) *nm Informát* plug-in

pluma 1 *nf* **(a)** *(de ave)* feather; *(adorno)* plume, feather; **un sombrero con plumas** a feathered hat; **un edredón de plumas** a feather duvet; EXPR **ser ligero** *o Am* **liviano como una p.** to be as light as a feather
(b) *(de humo, vapor)* plume
(c) *(de grúa)* boom
(d) *(para escribir)* (fountain) pen; *(de ave)* quill (pen); *Carib, Méx (bolígrafo)* (ballpoint) pen; EXPR **dejar correr la p., escribir a vuela p.** to jot down; EXPR **vivir de la p.** to live by the pen ►► *Méx* ***p. atómica*** ballpoint (pen); ***p. estilográfica*** fountain pen; *Méx, Ven* ***p. fuente*** fountain pen
(e) *(estilo de escribir)* style
(f) *(escritor)* writer
(g) *Carib, Col, Méx (grifo) Br* tap, *US* faucet
(h) *Fam (amaneramiento)* **tener mucha p.** to be camp
2 *adj inv Dep* featherweight; **peso p.** featherweight

plumada *nf Am* = **plumazo**

plumaje *nm* **(a)** *(de ave)* plumage **(b)** *(adorno)* plume

plumazo *nm* stroke of the pen; **de un p.** *(al tachar)* with a stroke of one's pen; *Fig* at a stroke; **el nuevo presidente suprimió de un p. las barreras arancelarias** the new president abolished the tariff barriers with a stroke of his pen; **la empresa eliminó a sus rivales de un p.** the company got rid of its rivals at a stroke; **la decisión resuelve de un p. varios problemas** the decision solves several problems at a stroke *o* at once

plúmbeo, -a *adj* **(a)** *(de plomo)* lead **(b)** *(pesado)* tedious, heavy

plum-cake [plun'keik] (*pl* **plum-cakes**) *nm Esp* fruit cake

plumear *vt Arte* to hatch

plumero *nm* feather duster; EXPR *Fam* **se le ve el p.** you can see through him

plumier (*pl* **plumiers**) *nm* pencil box

plumífero *nm (anorak)* feather-lined anorak

plumilla *nf* **(a)** *(pluma)* nib **(b)** *Fam (periodista)* journo

plumín *nm* nib

plumón *nm* **(a)** *(de ave)* down **(b)** *Méx (rotulador)* felt-tip pen

plural 1 *adj* **(a)** *(múltiple)* pluralist **(b)** *Gram* plural
2 *nm Gram* plural; **primera persona del p.** first person plural ►► ***el p. mayestático*** the royal we; ***p. de modestia*** = use of the pronoun 'we' instead of 'I' as a gesture of modesty

pluralidad *nf* diversity

pluralismo *nm* pluralism

pluralista *adj* pluralist

pluralizar [14] **1** *vi (generalizar)* **no pluralices, yo no tuve nada que ver** don't say "we", I had nothing to do with it; **no pluralices, yo no he dicho que quiera ir** speak for yourself, I didn't say I wanted to go
2 *vt Ling* to pluralize

pluricelular *adj* multicellular

pluriempleado, -a 1 *adj* **estar p.** to have more than one job
2 *nm,f* = person with more than one job

pluriemplearse *vpr* to have more than one job

pluriempleo *nm* **el p. es común en la región** having more than one job is common in the region

plurilingüe *adj* multilingual

pluripartidismo *nm* multiparty system

pluripartidista *adj* multiparty; **un acuerdo p.** a multiparty agreement

plurivalente *adj* polyvalent

plus *nm* bonus ►► ***p. familiar*** family allowance; ***p. de peligrosidad*** danger money, *US* danger pay; ***p. de productividad*** productivity bonus

pluscuamperfecto, -a *Gram* **1** *adj* pluperfect
2 *nm* pluperfect

plusmarca *nf* record ►► ***p. mundial*** world record; ***p. personal*** personal best

plusmarquista *nmf* record-holder ►► ***p. mundial*** world record-holder

plusvalía *nf* **(a)** *Econ (aumento de valor)* appreciation; *(tras venta)* capital gain **(b)** *(concepto marxista)* surplus value

pluto, -a *adj Ecuad Fam (borracho)* plastered, *Br* pissed; **estar p.** to be plastered *o Br* pissed

plutocracia *nf* plutocracy

plutócrata *nmf* plutocrat

plutocrático, -a *adj* plutocratic

Plutón *n* Pluto

plutonio *nm Quím* plutonium

pluvial *adj* rain; **régimen p.** annual rainfall pattern

pluviometría *nf* measurement of rainfall, *Espec* pluviometry

pluviómetro *nm* rain gauge, *Espec* pluviometer

pluviosidad *nf* rainfall

pluvioso, -a *adj Formal* rainy

pluvisilva *nf* rainforest

PM *nf (abrev de* **policía militar**) MP

p.m. *(abrev de* **post meridiem**) p.m

PN *nm (abrev de* **Partido Nacional**) = Honduran political party

PNB *nm (abrev de* **producto nacional bruto**) GNP

PNN *nmf Esp (abrev de* **profesor no numerario**) = untenured teacher or lecturer

PNUD *nm (abrev de* **Programa de las Naciones Unidas para el Desarrollo**) UNDP

PNUMA *nm (abrev de* **Programa de las Naciones Unidas para el Medio Ambiente**) UNEP

PNV *nm (abrev de* **Partido Nacionalista Vasco**) = Basque nationalist party to the right of the political spectrum

P *(abrev de* **paseo**) ≃ Ave

p.o., p/o *(abrev de* **por orden**) pp

poblacho *nm Pey* godforsaken town

población *nf* **(a)** *(ciudad)* town, city; *(pueblo)* village **(b)** *(personas, animales)* population ►► ***p. activa*** working population; ***p. de derecho*** permanent population; ***p. flotante*** floating population; ***p. de riesgo*** group at risk **(c)** *(acción de poblar)* settlement **(d)** *Chile (barrio)* **p. (callampa)** shanty town

poblacional *adj* population; **aumento p.** population growth

poblada *nf Andes, Ven* **(a)** *(tumulto)* riot **(b)** *(gentío)* crowd **(c)** *(sedición)* rebellion, revolt

poblado, -a 1 *adj* **(a)** *(habitado)* inhabited; **una zona muy poblada** a densely populated area **(b)** *(lleno)* full; *(barba, cejas)* bushy

2 *nm (pueblo)* settlement ►► *Esp* ***p. de chabolas*** shanty town

poblador, -ora *nm,f* **(a)** *(habitante)* inhabitant **(b)** *(colono)* settler **(c)** *Chile (chabolista)* shanty town dweller

poblamiento *nm* settlement

poblano, -a 1 *adj* **(a)** *(de Puebla)* of/from Puebla *(Mexico)* **(b)** *Am (de un pueblo)* village; **médico p.** village doctor

2 *nm,f* **(a)** *(de Puebla)* person from Puebla *(Mexico)* **(b)** *Am (lugareño)* villager

poblar [64] 1 *vt* **(a)** *(establecerse en)* to settle, to colonize **(b)** *(habitar)* to inhabit; **pueblan esa laguna muchas especies** the lagoon is home to a great variety of species **(c)** *(llenar)* **p. (de)** *(plantas, árboles)* to plant (with); *(peces)* to stock (with)

2 **poblarse** *vpr* to fill up (**de** with); **las gradas se poblaron de banderas del equipo** banners supporting the team started to fill the stands; **la zona se pobló de aves tropicales** the area was colonized by tropical birds

pobre 1 *adj* **(a)** *(necesitado)* poor; **un país p.** a poor country; EXPR *Fam* **más p. que las ratas** as poor as a church mouse

(b) *(desdichado)* poor; **el p. bebé estaba llamando a su mamá** the poor little baby was calling for its mother; **¡p. hombre!** poor man!; **¡p. de mí!** poor me!; **p. de aquél que se atreva a comerse mi ración** woe betide anyone who dares to eat my portion; **p. de ti como te dejes engañar por sus encantos** God help you if you fall for her charms

(c) *(mediocre, defectuoso)* poor; **utilizó un razonamiento muy p.** the arguments she gave were very weak *o* poor

(d) *(escaso)* poor; **utiliza un léxico muy p.** she has a very poor vocabulary; **una dieta p. en proteínas** a diet lacking in protein; **esta región es p. en recursos naturales** this region lacks natural resources

(e) *(poco fértil)* poor

2 *nmf* **(a)** *(sin dinero)* poor person; **los pobres** the poor, poor people **(b)** *(infeliz)* **¡el p.!** poor thing!; **la p. está siempre luchando por dar de comer a sus hijos** the poor woman is forever struggling to keep her children fed; **el p. no consigue aprobar el examen** the poor thing just can't seem to pass the exam **(c)** *(mendigo)* beggar

pobrecía *nf Col* **(a)** *(clase baja)* **la p.** the poor **(b)** *(pobreza)* poverty

pobrerío *nm CSur Fam* **el p.** the poor

pobreza *nf* **(a)** *(de bienes)* poverty; **vivir en la p.** to live in poverty; **p. de espíritu** spiritual poverty **(b)** *(escasez)* poverty; **p. de ideas** poverty of ideas **(c)** *(de terreno)* barrenness

pocero *nm* well digger

pocha *nf (judía)* haricot bean

pochada *nf RP Fam* **decir una p.** to say something tacky; **hacer una p.** to do something tacky

pocho, -a 1 *adj* **(a)** *(persona)* off-colour **(b)** *(fruta)* over-ripe **(c)** *Méx Fam (americanizado)* Americanized **(d)** *RP Fam (ordinario)* tacky

2 *nm Méx Fam* = mixture of Spanish and English

pochoclo *nm Arg* popcorn

pochola *nf Col Fam* beer

pocholada *nf Esp Fam* **una p. de niño/vestido** a cute little child/dress

pocholo, -a *adj Esp Fam* cute

pocilga *nf* **(a)** *(porqueriza)* pigsty **(b)** *Fam (lugar sucio)* pigsty

pocillo *nm* **(a)** *RP (pequeño)* small cup **(b)** *Méx, Ven (grande)* enamel mug

pócima *nf* **(a)** *(poción)* potion **(b)** *Fam (bebida de mal sabor)* concoction

poción *nf* potion

POCO, -A 1 *adj (singular)* little, not much; *(plural)* few, not many; **de poca importancia** of little importance; **poca agua** not much water; **pocas personas lo saben** few *o* not many people know it; **hay pocos árboles** there aren't many trees; **tenemos p. tiempo** we don't have much time; **hace p. tiempo** not long ago; **dame unos pocos días** give me a few days; **esto ocurre pocas veces** this rarely happens, this doesn't happen often; **tengo pocas ganas de ir** I don't really *o* much feel like going; **me parece que le estás echando poca sal** I don't think you're putting enough salt in, I think you're putting too little salt in; **con lo p. que le gusta la ópera, y la han invitado a La Traviata** it's ironic, considering how she dislikes opera, that they should have invited her to see La Traviata

2 *pron* **(a)** *(escasa cantidad) (singular)* little, not much; *(plural)* few, not many; **hay p. que decir** there isn't much to say, there's very little to say; **queda p.** there's not much left; **tengo muy pocos** I don't have very many, I have very few; **pocos hay que sepan tanto** not many people know so much; **éramos pocos** there weren't very many of us, there were only a few of us; **lo p. que tengo se lo debo a él** I owe what little I have to him; **otro p.** a little (bit) more; **un p.** a bit; **¿me das un p.?** can I have a bit?; **lo hice un p. por ayudarles** in a way, I did it to help them; **me pasa un p. lo que a ti** it's a bit like that for me, too; **un p. de** a bit of; **un p. de sentido común** a bit of common sense; **compra un p. de pescado** buy some fish; **unos pocos** a few; **sólo unos pocos de ellos estaban de acuerdo** only a few of them agreed; **a p. que estudies, aprobarás** you'll only need to study a little bit in order to pass; **es una madre como hay pocas** there aren't many mothers like her around; **necesitamos, como p., veinte** we need at least twenty, we need twenty, minimum; **tener en p. a alguien** not to think much of sb

(b) *(breve tiempo)* **espera un p.** wait a minute; **me quedaré un p. más** I'll stay a bit longer; **a** *o* **al p. de...** shortly after...; **dentro de p.** soon, in a short time; **hace p.** a little while ago, not long ago; **tardaré muy p.** I won't be long; **queda p. para el verano** it's not long till summer now

3 *adv* **(a)** *(escasamente)* not much; **este niño come p.** this boy doesn't eat much; **es p. común** it's not very common; **es p. profesional** it's not very professional, it's unprofessional; **resulta p. práctico** it's not very practical, it's rather impractical; **es un p. triste** it's rather sad; **va un p. lento todavía** it's still going rather slowly; **p. antes/después** shortly before/after; **p. después oí un tiro** shortly *o* soon after, I heard a shot; **eran p. más de las dos** it was just gone two o'clock; EXPR *Fam* **¡no p.!: dice que no le gustan los caramelos – ¡no p.!** she says she doesn't like *Br* sweets *o US* candy – not much she doesn't!; **dice que no se lo habías contado – ¡no p.!** he says you never told him – the hell I didn't!

(b) *(infrecuentemente)* not often; **voy p. por allí** I don't go there very often; **voy muy p. por allí** I seldom go there

(c) *(en frases)* **p. a p.**, *RP* **de a p.** *(progresivamente)* little by little, bit by bit; **¡p. a p.!** *(despacio)* steady on!, slow down!; **p. más o menos** more or less; **es p. menos que imposible** it's next to *o* virtually impossible; **p. menos que me dijo que me largara** he only came and told me to get lost; *Méx* **¿a p. no?** *(¿no es verdad?)* isn't that right?; **es un robo la nueva alza a la gasolina, ¿a p. no?** putting the price of petrol up again like this is daylight robbery, don't you think?; **¿a p. no vas a venir?** *(expresa incredulidad)* don't tell me you're not coming!; **por p.** almost, nearly; **por p. no me caigo** I nearly fell

---

poda *nf* (**a**) *(acción)* pruning (**b**) *(tiempo)* pruning time

podadera, *Am* **podadora** *nf* garden shears

podar *vt* to prune

podenco *nm* hound

PODER[1] *nm* (**a**) *(mando, autoridad)* power; **la gente con más p. en la organización** the most powerful people in the organization; **estar en el p.** to be in power; **hacerse con** *o* **tomar el p.** to seize power; **perder el p.** to lose power; **el p. corrompe** power corrupts; **la separación de poderes** the separation of powers; EXPR **de p. a p.: un enfrentamiento de p. a p.** a heavyweight contest; **el partido se disputó de p. a p.** it was a close contest between two excellent sides ►► ***p. absoluto*** absolute power; ***el p. ejecutivo*** *(el gobierno)* the executive; ***los poderes fácticos*** the centres of power in society; ***el p. judicial*** *(los jueces)* the judiciary; ***el p. legislativo*** *(las cortes)* the legislature; ***poderes públicos*** (public) authorities

(**b**) *(posesión, control)* **estar en p. de alguien** to be in sb's hands; **obra en su p. un documento comprometedor** she has in her possession a compromising document; **tienen en su p. a varios rehenes** they have taken a number of hostages; **el pueblo cayó en p. del enemigo** the town fell to the enemy; **la casa pasó a p. del banco** ownership of the house was transferred to the bank

(**c**) *(capacidad)* power; **un producto con gran p. de limpieza** a very powerful cleaning product; **tener poderes (paranormales)** to be psychic, to have psychic powers ►► ***p. adquisitivo*** *(de salario)* purchasing power; *(de persona)* disposable income; ***p. calorífico*** calorific value; ***p. de convicción*** persuasive powers; ***p. de convocatoria:*** **tener p. de convocatoria** to be a crowd-puller; *Mil* ***p. de disuasión*** deterrent force; *Mil* ***p. disuasorio*** deterrent force

(**d**) *(autorización)* power, authorization; *(documento)* power of attorney; **dar poderes a alguien para que haga algo** to authorize sb to do sth; **tener plenos poderes para hacer algo** to be fully authorized to do sth; **por poderes** by proxy; **casarse por** *Esp* **poderes** *o Am* **p.** to marry by proxy ►► ***p. notarial*** power of attorney *(witnessed by a notary)*

PODER[2] [49] **1** *vi* (**a**) *(tener facultad, capacidad)* can, to be able to; **no puedo decírtelo** I can't tell you, I'm unable to tell you; **ahora mismo no podemos atenderle, llame más tarde** we can't *o* we are unable to take your call right now, please call later; **¿puedes correrte un poco, por favor?** could you move up a bit, please?; **al final pudo salir de allí** in the end she managed to get out of there; **¡así no se puede hacer nada!** we'll never get anywhere like this!; **de p. ir, sería a partir de las siete** if I manage to *o* can make it, it will be after seven; **en cuanto pueda** as soon as possible; **si puedo, te llamaré** I'll call you if I get the chance

(**b**) *(tener permiso)* can, may; **no puedo salir por la noche** I'm not allowed to *o* I can't go out at night; **¿podríamos ir con vosotros?** could we go with you?; **¿podría hablar un momento con usted?** could I have a word with you?; **¿se pueden hacer fotos?** can we *o* are we allowed to take photos?; **¿puedo fumar aquí?** may *o* can I smoke here?; **no se puede fumar** you're not allowed to smoke; **¿se puede?** may I come in?; **¿se puede saber dónde te habías metido?** might I know *o* would you mind telling me where you were?

(**c**) *(ser capaz moralmente)* can; **no podemos portarnos así con él** we can't treat him like that; **¿cómo puedes decir una cosa así?** how can you say such a thing?

(**d**) *(tener posibilidad, ser posible)* may, can; **puede volver de un momento a otro** she could come back any moment; **puedo haberlo perdido** I may have lost it; **podías haber cogido el tren** you could have caught the train; **puede estallar la guerra** war could *o* may break out; **¿dónde puede** *o* **podrá estar?** where can it have got to?; **¡habría podido invitarnos!, ¡podría habernos invitado!** *(expresa enfado)* she could *o* might have invited us!; **ya podemos despedirnos de un aumento de sueldo** we can forget our pay rise now

(**e**) *(tener fuerza)* **p. con** *(enfermedad, rival)* to be able to overcome; *(tarea, problema)* to be able to cope with; **¿puedes con todas las bolsas?** can you manage all those bags?; **no puedo con este baúl, ¿me ayudas a levantarlo?** I can't lift this trunk on my own, can you give me a hand?; **no p. con algo/alguien** *(no soportar)* not to be able to stand sth/sb; **no puedo con la hipocresía** I can't stand hypocrisy; **¡contigo no hay quien pueda!** you're impossible!; **no p. más** *(estar cansado)* to be too tired to carry on; *(estar harto de comer)* to be full (up); *(estar enfadado, harto)* to have had enough; EXPR **no puedo con mi alma** I'm ready to drop

(**f**) *Méx (doler)* to hurt

(**g**) *(en frases)* **a** *o* **hasta más no p.** as much as can be; **es avaro a más no p.** he's as miserly as can be; **llovía a más no p.** it was absolutely pouring down; **la pierna me dolía a más no p.** you can't imagine how much my leg was hurting; **no pude por menos que reírme** I had to laugh, I couldn't help but laugh; *Fam* **¡ya podrás, con una máquina como esa!** anyone could do it with a machine like that!

2 *v impersonal (ser posible)* may; **puede que llueva** it may *o* might rain; **puede que se haya equivocado** she may be wrong; **¿vendrás mañana? – puede** will you come tomorrow? – I may do; **puede que sí o puede que no** maybe, maybe not; **puede ser** perhaps, maybe; **si puede ser, a p. ser** if (at all) possible; **lo siento, pero no va a p. ser** I'm sorry, but it's not going to be possible; **puede ser que no lo sepa** she may not know; **¡no puede ser que sea ya tan tarde!** surely it can't be that late already!

3 *vt* (**a**) *(ser más fuerte que)* to be stronger than; **tú eres más alto, pero yo te puedo** you may be taller than me, but I could still beat you up; **mi coche le puede al tuyo** my car is faster than yours any day

(**b**) *Méx (doler)* **me puede mucho que me desprecies** it hurts me a lot that you look down on me; **le pudo su derrota, todavía no se repone** losing really got to her, she still hasn't got over it

poderhabiente *nmf* (**a**) *(representante)* agent (**b**) *Der* attorney, proxy

poderío *nm* (**a**) *(poder, fuerza)* power (**b**) *(riqueza)* riches

poderoso, -a 1 *adj* (**a**) *(con poder, riquezas)* powerful; EXPR **p. caballero es don dinero** money talks *o* makes the world go round (**b**) *(remedio, cura)* powerful (**c**) *(razón, motivo)* powerful, compelling

2 *nm,f* powerful person; **los poderosos** the powerful

podiatra *nmf Am* chiropodist, *US* podiatrist

podio, pódium *nm* (**a**) *(en deporte)* podium; *Fig* **subir al p.** to finish on the podium (**b**) *(en música)* podium (**c**) *Arquit* podium

podología *nf* chiropody, *US* podology

podólogo, -a *nm,f* chiropodist, *US* podiatrist

podómetro *nm* pedometer

podré *etc ver* **poder**

podredumbre *nf* (**a**) *(putrefacción)* putrefaction (**b**) *(inmoralidad)* corruption

podría *etc ver* **poder**

podrida *nf RP Fam* rumpus; **cuando se enteraron se armó una p.** when they found out, all hell broke loose; **supe que ayer hubo p. en tu casa** I heard there was a bit of a rumpus round at your place yesterday

podrido, -a 1 *participio ver* **pudrir**

2 *adj* (**a**) *(descompuesto)* rotten; EXPR *Fam* **estar p. de dinero** *o Am* **en plata** to be filthy rich

(**b**) *(corrupto)* rotten

(**c**) *RP Fam (harto)* fed up, sick; **estar p. de algo/alguien** to be fed up with sth/sb, to be sick of sth/sb; **me tienen p. con sus pedidos** I'm sick of their requests

(**d**) *RP Fam (aburrido)* fed up; **están podridos porque no tienen nada que hacer** they're fed up because they've got nothing to do

podrir = **pudrir**

poema *nm* poem; EXPR *Fam* **ser (todo) un p.: era todo un p. verlo llorar** it was heartbreaking to see him cry; **su cara era todo un p.** her face was a picture; *Am* **esa novela es un p.** that novel's a joke ►► *Mús* ***p. sinfónico*** symphonic *o* tone poem

poesía *nf* (**a**) *(género literario)* poetry (**b**) *(poema)* poem

poeta *nmf* poet

poética *nf* poetics *(singular)*

poético, -a *adj* poetic

poetisa *nf* (female) poet, poetess

poetizar [14] **1** *vt* to poeticize, to make poetic

2 *vi* to write poetry

pogromo, pogrom (*pl* **pogroms**) *nm* pogrom

póinter (*pl* **póinters**), **pointer** (*pl* **pointers**) *nm (perro)* pointer

póker = **póquer**

pola *nf Col Fam* beer

polaco, -a 1 *adj* (**a**) *(de Polonia)* Polish (**b**) *Esp Fam Pey (catalán)* = pejorative term for a Catalan

2 *nm,f* (**a**) *(de Polonia)* Polish (**b**) *Esp Fam Pey (catalán)* = pejorative term for a Catalan

3 *nm (lengua)* Polish

polaina *nf* (**a**) *(de cuero, sintética)* gaiter (**b**) *RP (de lana)* legwarmer

polar *adj* polar

polaridad *nf* polarity

polarización *nf* (**a**) *(de interés, atención)* concentration (**b**) *Fís & Fot* polarization

polarizador, -ora 1 *adj* polarizing; **filtro p.** polarizing filter
2 *nm Fís & Fot* polarizer
polarizar [14] 1 *vt* (**a**) *(miradas, interés, atención)* to concentrate (**b**) *Fís & Fot* to polarize
2 **polarizarse** *vpr (vida política, opinión pública)* to become polarized
polaroid® *nf inv* Polaroid®
polca *nf* polka
pólder *nm* polder
polea *nf* pulley
poleadas *nfpl* porridge
polémica *nf* controversy
polémico, -a *adj* controversial
polemista *nmf* polemicist
polemizar [14] *vi* to argue, to debate; **p. con alguien sobre algo** to debate sth with sb
polen *nm* pollen
polenta *nf* (**a**) *(comida)* polenta; EXPR *RP Fam* **¿comiste mucha p. cuando eras chico?** you're a strapping fellow, they must have fed you well when you were little (**b**) *RP Fam (energía)* drive, energy; **esa banda tiene mucha p.** they're an energetic band
polentear *vt RP Fam* to feed; **esos niños están muy bien polenteados** those kids are very well fed
polentón, -ona *adj RP Fam* **una película polentona** a meaty movie; **creo que lo va a lograr, es muy p.** I think he'll do it, he's a real go-getter
poleo *nm* (**a**) *(planta)* pennyroyal (**b**) *(infusión)* pennyroyal tea
pole-position ['polpo'siʃon] *(pl* **pole-positions***) nf Dep* pole position
polera *nf* (**a**) *Arg, Chile (polo)* polo shirt (**b**) *Urug (de cuello alto)* turtleneck *o Br* polo neck sweater
poli *Fam* 1 *nmf* cop ►► ***polis y cacos*** *(juego infantil)* cops and robbers
2 *nf* **la p.** the cops
poli- *pref* poly-
poliamida *nf* polyamide
poliandria *nf* polyandry
policarbonato *nm* polycarbonate
polichar *vt Col* to wax
polichinela *nm (títere)* puppet, marionette
policía 1 *nmf* police officer, policeman, *f* policewoman; **un p. de paisano** a plain-clothes policeman ►► *Ven Fam* ***p. acostado*** speed bump, *Br* sleeping policeman; ***p. municipal*** local policeman, *f* local policewoman; ***p. nacional*** = officer of the national police force; ***p. de tráfico*** traffic policeman, *f* traffic policewoman
2 *nf* **la p.** the police; **viene la p.** the police are coming ►► ***p. antidisturbios*** riot police; *Esp* ***p. autónoma*** = police force of one of Spain's autonomous regions; ***p. de barrio*** community police; *RP* ***p. caminera*** traffic police; ***p. judicial*** = division of police which carries out the orders of a court; *Méx* ***p. judicial federal*** = police force that acts under the orders of federal judges; ***p. militar*** military police; ***p. montada*** mounted police; ***p. municipal*** local police; ***p. nacional*** national police force; *Esp* ***p. de proximidad*** community police; ***p. secreta*** secret police; ***p. de tráfico*** traffic police; *Am* ***p. de tránsito*** traffic police; ***p. urbana*** local police; *Arg, Col, Méx* ***p. vial*** traffic police
policiaco, -a, policíaco, -a *adj* **película/novela policiaca** detective movie/story
policial *adj* police; **investigación p.** police investigation *o* enquiry; **la intervención p. puso fin al secuestro** the police intervened to bring the hostage situation to an end; **una novela p.** a detective story
policlínica *nf,* **policlínico** *nm* general hospital, polyclinic
policromado, -a *adj* polychrome
policromía *nf* polychromy
policromo, -a, polícromo, -a *adj* polychromatic
polideportivo, -a 1 *adj* multi-sport; *(gimnasio)* multi-use
2 *nm* sports centre
poliedro *nm* polyhedron
poliéster *nm inv* polyester
poliestireno *nm* polystyrene ►► ***p. expandido*** expanded polystyrene
polietileno *nm Br* polythene, *US* polyethylene
polifacético, -a *adj (persona)* multifaceted; *(actor)* versatile
polifásico, -a *adj Elec* polyphase, multiphase
poliflor® *nf Perú* floorwax
polifonía *nf* polyphony
polifónico, -a *adj* polyphonic
poligamia *nf* polygamy
polígamo, -a 1 *adj* polygamous
2 *nm,f* polygamist
poliglosia *nf Ling* polyglottism
políglota, -a, poligloto, -a 1 *adj* polyglot
2 *nm,f* polyglot
poligonal *adj* polygonal
polígono *nm* (**a**) *(figura)* polygon ►► ***p. regular*** regular polygon (**b**) *(terreno)* ***p. industrial*** *Br* industrial estate, *US* industrial area; ***p. residencial*** housing development, *Br* housing estate; ***p. de tiro*** firing range
poliinsaturado, -a *adj* polyunsaturated
polilla *nf* moth
polimerización *nf Quím* polymerization
polímero *nm Quím* polymer
polimorfismo *nm* polymorphism
polimorfo, -a *adj* polymorphous
Polinesia *n* Polynesia
polinesio, -a 1 *adj* Polynesian
2 *nm,f (persona)* Polynesian
3 *nm (lengua)* Polynesian
polinización *nf* pollination ►► ***p. cruzada*** cross-pollination
polinizar [14] *vt* to pollinate
polinomio *nm* polynomial
polio *nf inv* polio
poliomelítico, -a 1 *adj* with polio
2 *nm,f* polio victim
poliomielitis *nf inv* poliomyelitis
polípero, polipero *nm* polypary
polipiel *nf* artificial skin
pólipo *nm* (**a**) *(tumor)* polyp (**b**) *(animal)* polyp
polis *nf inv Hist* polis
polisacárido *nm Quím* polysaccharide
Polisario [poli'sarjo] *nm (abrev de* **Frente Popular para la Liberación de Sakiet el Hamra y Río de Oro***)* **el (Frente) P.** Polisario, = Western Sahara liberation front
polisemia *nf* polysemy
polisémico, -a *adj* polysemous, polysemic
polisílabo, -a 1 *adj* polysyllabic
2 *nm* polysyllable
polisíndenton *nm Ling* polysyndeton
polisón *nm* bustle
polista *nmf* polo player
polistel® *nm Perú* = brand of synthetic fabric
politécnico, -a *adj* polytechnic; **universidad politécnica** technical university
politeísmo *nm* polytheism
politeísta 1 *adj* polytheistic
2 *nmf* polytheist
política *nf* (**a**) *(arte de gobernar)* politics *(singular)*; **lleva treinta años dedicado a la p.** he has been in politics for the last thirty years; **hablar de p.** to discuss politics, to talk (about) politics
(**b**) *(modo de gobernar, táctica)* policy ►► *UE* ***P. Agrícola Común*** Common Agricultural Policy; ***la p. del avestruz*** burying one's head in the sand; **sigue con su p. del avestruz** he still prefers to bury his head in the sand; ***p. comercial*** trade policy; ***p. de empresa*** company policy; ***p. exterior*** foreign policy; ***p. fiscal*** fiscal policy; ***p. monetaria*** monetary policy; *UE* ***P. Pesquera Común*** Common Fisheries Policy; ***p. de tierra quemada*** scorched earth policy
políticamente *adv* politically; **p. correcto** politically correct
politicastro *nm Pey* bad politician
político, -a 1 *adj* (**a**) *(de gobierno)* political (**b**) *(prudente)* tactful (**c**) *(pariente)* **hermano p.** brother-in-law; **familia política** in-laws (**d**) *(geografía, mapa)* political
2 *nm,f* politician
politiquear *vi Pey* to politick
politiqueo *nm Pey* politicking
politiquero, -a *nm,f Pey* politicker
politización *nf* politicization

politizar [14] **1** *vt* to politicize
2 politizarse *vpr* to become politicized

politología *nf* political science

politólogo, -a *nm,f* political scientist

poliuretano *nm* polyurethane

polivalencia *nf (de vacuna, suero)* polyvalency; *(de sala, espacio, edificio)* versatility, adaptability; *(de sistema, jugador)* versatility

polivalente *adj (vacuna, suero)* polyvalent; *(sala, espacio, edificio)* multipurpose; *(sistema, jugador)* versatile

polivinilo *nm* polyvinyl resin

póliza *nf* **(a)** *(de seguro)* (insurance) policy; **p. de incendios/de vida** fire/life-insurance policy; **suscribir una p.** to take out a policy **(b)** *(sello)* = stamp on a document showing that a certain tax has been paid

polizón *nm* stowaway

polizonte *nm Fam* cop

polla *nf* **(a)** *Esp Vulg (pene)* cock, prick; **comer la p. a alguien** to suck sb's cock; EXPR **¡una p.!** *(no)* no fucking way!, *Br* not bloody likely!; EXPR **ni qué pollas: ¡qué sopa ni qué pollas!** to hell with soup!; EXPR **ser la p.** to be the absolute end; EXPR **porque me sale de la p.** because I *Br* bloody *o US* goddamn well want to; EXPR **¡me suda la p.!** I couldn't give a fuck *o Br* toss!; EXPR **pollas en vinagre: ¡ni excusas ni pollas en vinagre!** no excuses or that kind of shit!
(b) ***p. de agua*** *(ave)* moorhen
(c) *Arg (carrera)* horse race
(d) *Chile (lotería)* state lottery
(e) *ver también* **pollo**

pollada *nf* brood

pollera *nf* **(a)** *CSur (occidental)* skirt ►► ***p. acampanada*** full skirt; ***p. escocesa*** kilt; ***p. fruncida*** gathered skirt; ***p. pantalón*** culottes, divided skirt; ***p. plisada*** pleated skirt *(with accordion pleats)*; ***p. portafolio*** wrapover skirt; ***p. recta*** straight skirt; ***p. tableada*** pleated skirt *(with knife pleats)*; ***p. tubo*** pencil skirt; ***p. de volados*** ruffled skirt
(b) *Andes (indígena)* = long skirt worn in layers by Indian women
(c) *ver también* **pollero**

pollería *nf* poultry shop

pollero, -a *nm,f* **(a)** *(comerciante)* poulterer **(b)** *Méx Fam (en la frontera)* = person who smuggles illegal immigrants from Mexico to the US

pollerudo, -a *RP Fam* **1** *adj* wimpish
2 *nm,f* wimp

pollino, -a *nm,f* **(a)** *(asno)* donkey **(b)** *Fam (persona)* clod

pollito *nm* chick

pollo, -a 1 *nm,f* **(a)** *Anticuado o Hum (joven)* young shaver **(b)** *Méx Fam (inmigrante ilegal)* = illegal immigrant who is smuggled from Mexico into the US by a "pollero"
2 *nm* **(a)** *(animal)* chick ►► ***p. tomatero*** spring chicken **(b)** *(guiso)* chicken ►► ***p. al ajillo*** chicken fried with garlic; ***p. asado*** roast chicken; ***p. frito*** fried chicken; *Méx* ***p. rostizado*** roast chicken; *RP* ***p. al spiedo*** spit-roasted chicken **(c)** *Fam (escupitajo)* gob

polluela *nf* ***p. chica*** Baillon's crake

polluelo *nm* chick

polo *nm* **(a)** *(de la Tierra)* pole ►► ***p. celeste*** celestial pole; ***p. geográfico*** terrestrial pole; ***p. magnético*** magnetic pole; ***p. Norte*** North Pole; ***p. Sur*** South Pole; ***p. terrestre*** terrestrial pole
(b) *Elec* terminal; **p. negativo/positivo** negative/positive terminal; EXPR **ser polos opuestos** to be poles apart; EXPR **ser el p. opuesto de** to be the complete opposite of
(c) *(helado) Br* ice lolly, *US* Popsicle®
(d) *(camiseta)* polo shirt
(e) *(centro)* **p. de atracción** *o* **atención** centre of attraction
(f) *(deporte)* polo ►► *Am* ***p. acuático*** water polo

pololear *vi Chile Fam* to go out (together)

pololeo *nm Chile Fam* **(a)** *(trabajo)* small job **(b)** *(noviazgo)* **su p. con ella dura ya tres meses** he's been going out with her for three months

pololito *nm Chile Fam* small job

pololo, -a *nm,f Chile Fam* boyfriend, *f* girlfriend

polonesa *nf Mús* polonaise

Polonia *n* Poland

polonio *nm Quím* polonium

poltrón, -ona *adj Fam* lazy; **no seas p.** don't be such a lazy slob

poltrona *nf* **(a)** *(silla)* easy chair **(b)** **la p. (ministerial)** ministerial office; **su apego por la p.** his attachment to ministerial office

poltronear *vi Fam* to idle, to loaf around

polución *nf* **(a)** *(contaminación)* pollution ►► ***p. ambiental*** air pollution; ***p. atmosférica*** air pollution, atmospheric pollution **(b)** *(eyaculación)* ***p. nocturna*** wet dream

polucionar *vt* to pollute

polulo *nm Chile* popcorn

poluto, -a *adj* soiled, polluted

polvareda *nf* dust cloud; EXPR **levantar una gran p.** to cause a commotion

polvera *nf* powder compact

polvo *nm* **(a)** *(en el aire)* dust; **limpiar** *o* **quitar el p.** to do the dusting; **quitar el p. al televisor** to dust the TV ►► ***p. cósmico*** cosmic dust
(b) *(de un producto)* powder; **leche en p.** powdered milk; **canela en p.** ground cinnamon ►► *Fam* ***p. de ángel*** angel dust; *Am* ***p. de hornear*** baking powder; ***polvos (de) picapica*** itching powder; *RP* ***p. Royal®*** baking powder; ***polvos de talco*** talcum powder
(c) **polvos** *(maquillaje)* powder; **ponerse polvos** to powder one's face
(d) *muy Fam (coito)* screw, *Br* bonk; **echar un p.** to have a screw, *Br* to have it off; **¡qué p. tiene!** what a babe!
(e) EXPR *Fam* **estar hecho(a) p.** *(muy cansado)* to be dead beat *o Br* knackered; *(muy deprimido)* to be shattered *o Br* gutted; *Fam* **hacer p. algo** to smash sth; **estos zapatos me están haciendo p. los pies** these shoes are killing my feet; **el cambio de fecha me hace p.** the change of date is a bummer for me; *Fam* **quedarse hecho(a) p.** *(agotado)* to be dead beat *o Br* knackered; *(deprimido)* to be shattered *o Br* gutted; *Fam* **morder el p.** to be humiliated; *Fam* **hacer morder el p. a alguien** to make sb eat dirt

pólvora *nf* **(a)** *(sustancia explosiva)* gunpowder; EXPR **correr como la p.** to spread like wildfire; EXPR *Fam* **inventar la p.: me parece que has inventado la p.** that's not exactly news; **no ha inventado la p.** *(es tonto)* he's no genius **(b)** *(fuegos artificiales)* fireworks

polvoriento, -a *adj (superficie)* dusty; *(sustancia)* powdery

polvorilla *nmf Fam* **es un p.** *(inquieto)* he can't sit still for five minutes; *(de genio vivo)* he's a live wire

polvorín *nm* **(a)** *(almacén)* munitions dump **(b)** *Fam (lugar, situación)* powder keg

polvorita *adj RP Fam* **ser muy p.** to have a short fuse

polvorón *nm* = very crumbly shortbread biscuit

polvoroso, -a, *Am* **polvoso, -a** *adj* dusty

polyfom® *nm Urug* foam rubber

pomada *nf* ointment; EXPR *Méx, RP Fam* **hacer algo p.: si sigues toqueteando esa planta la vas a hacer p.** that plant's going to fall to bits if you keep touching it; **esos argumentos te los hacen p. en cinco minutos** they'll pull those arguments to pieces in next to no time; **hizo p. el auto** he wrote the car off; EXPR *Méx, RP Fam* **hacerse p.: se hizo p. con el accidente** he hurt himself really badly in the accident ►► *RP* ***p. para zapatos*** shoe polish

pomelo *nm* **(a)** *(fruto)* grapefruit **(b)** *(árbol)* grapefruit tree

pómez *adj* **piedra p.** pumice stone

pomo *nm* **(a)** *(de puerta, mueble)* handle, knob **(b)** *(de espada)* pommel **(c)** *Am (de pasta)* tube **(d)** *RP (de agua)* spray bottle **(e)** *Méx (pote)* jar **(f)** *Méx Fam (botella)* bottle **(g)** *RP Fam* EXPR **no veo un p.** I can't see a thing; **no sabe un p.** she hasn't got a clue

pompa 1 *nf* **(a)** *(suntuosidad)* pomp **(b)** *(ostentación)* show, ostentation **(c)** **p. (de jabón)** (soap) bubble
2 pompas *nfpl* **(a)** *Méx Fam* behind, bottom **(b)** ***pompas fúnebres*** *(servicio)* undertaker's; *(ceremonia)* funeral

pompeyano, -a 1 *adj* Pompeiian
2 *nm,f* Pompeiian

pompis *nm inv Fam* behind, bottom

pompón *nm* pompom

pomposamente *adv* **(a)** *(con suntuosidad)* splendidly, with great pomp **(b)** *(con ostentación)* showily **(c)** *(hablar)* pompously

pomposidad *nf* **(a)** *(suntuosidad)* splendour, pomp **(b)** *(ostentación)* showiness **(c)** *(en el lenguaje)* pomposity

pomposo, -a *adj* **(a)** *(suntuoso)* sumptuous, magnificent **(b)** *(ostentoso)* showy **(c)** *(lenguaje)* pompous

pómulo *nm* **(a)** *(hueso)* cheekbone **(b)** *(mejilla)* cheek

pon *ver* **poner**

ponchada *nf CSur* **una p. de** loads of; **esa casa le costó una p. (de plata)** that house cost her a packet

ponchadura *nf CAm, Carib, Méx* puncture, *US* blowout

ponchar **1** *vt* (**a**) *CAm, Carib, Méx (rueda)* to puncture (**b**) *Am (en béisbol)* to strike out
2 poncharse *vpr* (**a**) *CAm, Carib, Méx (rueda)* to blow; **se ponchó un neumático** a tyre blew (**b**) *Am (en béisbol)* to strike out

ponchazo *nm CSur Fam* EXPR **andar a los ponchazos: anda a los ponchazos con todo el mundo** he's at loggerheads with absolutely everyone; **anda a los ponchazos por la vida** life has been a constant battle for her

ponche *nm* (**a**) *(en fiesta)* punch (**b**) *(con leche y huevo)* eggnog (**c**) *Am (en béisbol)* strikeout

ponchera *nf* punch bowl

poncho *nm* poncho

ponderable *adj* (**a**) *(en peso)* weighable (**b**) *(en ponderación)* worthy of consideration

ponderación *nf* (**a**) *(alabanza)* praise (**b**) *(moderación)* deliberation; **una crítica hecha con p.** a carefully weighed *o* deliberated criticism (**c**) *(en estadística)* weighting

ponderado, -a *adj* (**a**) *(alabado)* praised; **el nunca bien p. director** the eternally underrated director (**b**) *(moderado)* considered (**c**) *(en estadística)* weighted

ponderar *vt* (**a**) *(alabar)* to praise (**b**) *(considerar)* to consider, to weigh up (**c**) *(en estadística)* to weight

ponderativo, -a *adj* (**a**) *(halagador)* praising (**b**) *(meditativo)* thoughtful, meditative

pondré *etc ver* **poner**

ponedero *nm* nesting box

ponedor, -ora **1** *adj* **gallina ponedora** layer, laying hen
2 *nm (ponedero)* nesting box

ponencia *nf* (**a**) *(conferencia)* lecture, paper; **una p. sobre ecología** a lecture *o* paper on ecology (**b**) *(informe)* report (**c**) *(comisión)* reporting committee

ponente *nmf* (**a**) *(en congreso)* speaker (**b**) *(relator)* reporter, rapporteur

PONER [50] **1** *vt* (**a**) *(situar, agregar, meter)* to put; **me pusieron en la última fila** I was put in the back row; **ponle un poco más de sal** put some more salt in it, add a bit of salt to it; **pon los juguetes en el armario** put the toys (away) in the cupboard; **¿dónde habré puesto la calculadora?** where can I have put *o* left the calculator?; **p. un anuncio en el periódico** to put an advert in the paper; **p. un póster en la pared** to put a poster up on the wall; **p. una inyección a alguien** to give sb an injection; **hubo que ponerle un bozal al perro** we had to put a muzzle on the dog, we had to muzzle the dog
(**b**) *(ropa, zapatos, maquillaje)* **p. algo a alguien** to put sth on sb; **ponle este pañal al bebé** put this *Br* nappy *o US* diaper on the baby
(**c**) *(servir)* **¿qué le pongo?** what can I get you?, what would you like?; **póngame una cerveza, por favor** I'd like *o* I'll have a beer, please; **¿cuánto le pongo?** how much would you like?; **póngame un kilo** give me a kilo
(**d**) *(contribuir, aportar)* to put in; **p. dinero en el negocio** to put money into the business; **p. algo de mi/tu/*etc.* parte** to do my/your/*etc* bit; **p. mucho empeño en (hacer) algo** to put a lot of effort into (doing) sth; **pon atención en lo que digo** pay attention to what I'm saying; **hay que p. más cuidado con** *o* **en la ortografía** you have to take more care over your spelling
(**e**) *(hacer estar de cierta manera)* **p. a alguien en un aprieto/de mal humor** to put sb in a difficult position/in a bad mood; **le has puesto colorado/nervioso** you've made him blush/feel nervous; **ponérselo fácil/difícil a alguien** to make things easy/difficult for sb; **lo puso todo perdido** she made a real mess; **el profesor nos puso a hacer cuentas** the teacher gave us some sums to do; **llegó y nos puso a todos a trabajar** she arrived and set us all to work; **pon la sopa a calentar** warm the soup up; **me pusieron de aprendiz de camarero** they had me work as a trainee waiter; **p. cara de tonto/inocente** to put on a stupid/an innocent face
(**f**) *(calificar)* **p. a alguien de algo** to call sb sth; **me pusieron de mentiroso** they called me a liar; **p. bien algo/a alguien** to praise sth/sb; **p. mal algo/a alguien** to criticize sth/sb
(**g**) *(oponer)* **p. obstáculos a algo** to hinder sth; **p. pegas a algo** to raise objections to sth
(**h**) *(asignar) (precio)* to fix, to settle on; *(multa)* to give; *(deberes, examen, tarea)* to give, to set; **le pusieron (de nombre) Mario** they called him Mario; **me han puesto (en el turno) de noche** I've been assigned to the night shift, they've put me on the night shift; **le pusieron un cinco en el examen** he got five out of ten in the exam
(**i**) *(comunicar) (telegrama, fax, giro postal)* to send; *(conferencia)* to make; *Esp* **¿me pones con él?** can you put me through to him?; *Esp* **no cuelgue, ahora le pongo** don't hang up, I'll put you through in a second
(**j**) *(conectar, hacer funcionar) (televisión, radio)* to switch *o* put on; *(despertador)* to set; *(instalación, gas)* to put in; *(música, cinta, disco)* to put on; **pon la lavadora** put the washing machine on; **pon el telediario** put the news on; **puse el despertador a las seis/el reloj en hora** I set my alarm clock for six o'clock/my watch to the right time; **¿te han puesto ya el teléfono?** are you on the phone yet?, have they connected your phone yet?; **ponlo más alto, que no se oye** turn it up, I can't hear it
(**k**) *(en el cine, el teatro, la televisión)* to show; **anoche pusieron un documental muy interesante** last night they showed a very interesting documentary; **¿qué ponen en la tele/en el Rialto?** what's on the TV/on at the Rialto?; **en el Rialto ponen una de Stallone** there's a Stallone movie on at the Rialto
(**l**) *(montar)* to set up; **p. la casa** to set up home; **p. un negocio** to start a business; **ha puesto una tienda** she has opened a shop; **han puesto una cocina nueva** they've had a new *Br* cooker *o US* stove put in; **hemos puesto moqueta en el salón** we've had a carpet fitted in the living room; **p. la mesa** to lay the table; **pusieron la tienda (de campaña) en un prado** they pitched their tent *o* put their tent up in a meadow
(**m**) *(decorar)* to do up; **han puesto su casa con mucho lujo** they've done up their house in real style
(**n**) *(suponer)* to suppose; **pongamos que sucedió así** (let's) suppose that's what happened; **pon que necesitemos cinco días** suppose we need five days; **poniendo que todo salga bien** assuming everything goes according to plan; **¿cuándo estará listo? – ponle que en dos días** when will it be ready? – reckon on it taking two days
(**o**) *Esp (decir)* to say; **¿qué pone ahí?** what does it say there?
(**p**) *(escribir)* to put; **¿qué pusiste en la segunda pregunta?** what did you put for the second question?
(**q**) *(huevo)* to lay
(**r**) *RP (demorar)* to take; **el tren pone media hora en llegar allá** the train takes half an hour to get there
2 *vi (gallina, aves)* to lay (eggs)
3 ponerse *vpr* (**a**) *(colocarse)* to put oneself; **ponerse de pie** to stand up; **ponerse de rodillas** to kneel (down); **ponerse de espaldas a la pared** to turn one's back to the wall; **ponerse de perfil** to turn sideways on; **¡no te pongas en medio!** you're in my way there!; **ponte en la ventana** stand by the window; **se pusieron un poco más juntos** they moved a bit closer together
(**b**) *(ropa, gafas, maquillaje)* to put on; **ponte la ropa** put your clothes on, get dressed; **¿qué te vas a p. para la fiesta?** what are you going to wear to the party?
(**c**) *(volverse de cierta manera)* to go, to become; **se puso de mal humor** she got into a bad mood; **se puso rojo de ira** he went red with anger; **se puso muy triste cuando se enteró de su muerte** he was very sad when he heard she had died; **las cosas se están poniendo muy difíciles** things are getting very difficult; **se ha puesto muy gordo** he's got very fat; **se puso colorado** he blushed; **te has puesto muy guapa** you look lovely; **ponerse malo** *o* **enfermo** to fall ill; **ponerse bien** *(de salud)* to get better; **¡cómo te pones por nada!** there's no need to react like that!; **¡no te pongas así!** *(no te enfades)* don't be like that!; *(no te pongas triste)* don't get upset!, don't be sad!
(**d**) *(iniciar)* **ponerse a hacer algo** to start doing sth; **se puso a nevar** it started snowing; **me he puesto a dieta** I've started a diet; **ponerse con algo** to start on sth; *Fam* **ya que te pones, haz café para todos** while you're at it, why don't you make enough coffee for everyone?
(**e**) *(llenarse)* **¡cómo te has puesto (de barro)!** look at you (you're covered in mud)!; **se puso de barro hasta las rodillas** he got covered in mud up to his knees; *Fam* **nos pusimos hasta arriba** *o* **hasta las orejas de pasteles** we stuffed our faces with cakes
(**f**) *(sol, luna)* to set; **el sol se pone por el oeste** the sun sets in the west; **al ponerse el sol** when the sun goes/went down
(**g**) *Esp (al teléfono)* **dile a tu marido que se ponga** tell your husband to come on; **ahora se pone** she's just coming, I'll put her on in a moment; **ponte, es de la oficina** here, it's somebody from the office for you
(**h**) *Esp (llegar)* **ponerse en** to get to; **nos pusimos en Santiago en dos horas** we made it to Santiago in two hours; **con esta moto te pones en los 150 sin enterarte** on this motorbike you're doing 150 before you even realize it
(**i**) *RP Fam (entregar dinero)* to chip in; **vamos, vamos, hay que ponerse para el regalo** come on, everybody's got to chip in for the present; **¿con cuánto te pusiste? – yo, con diez** how much did you put in? – ten

(j) *Andes, RP Fam (tener ocurrencias)* **¡se te pone cada cosa!** you get the strangest ideas!

(k) *Am Fam (parecer)* **se me pone que...** it seems to me that...

---

poney ['poni] *nm* pony

pongaje, pongueaje *nm Andes Hist* unpaid domestic service

pongo[1] *ver* **poner**

pongo[2], **-a** *nmf Andes* (a) *Hist* unpaid Indian domestic servant (b) *(sirviente)* domestic

poni *nm* pony

poniente *nm* (a) *(occidente)* West (b) *(viento)* west wind; **viento de p.** west wind

ponqué *nm Col, Ven* = fruit or custard-filled cake

pontevedrés, -esa 1 *adj* of/from Pontevedra *(Spain)*
2 *nm,f* person from Pontevedra *(Spain)*

pontificado *nm* papacy

pontifical *adj* papal

pontificar [60] *vi* to pontificate

pontífice *nm* (a) *(Papa)* Pope; **el Sumo P.** the Supreme Pontiff, the Pope (b) *(obispo)* bishop

pontificio, -a *adj (de los obispos)* episcopal; *(del Papa)* papal

pontón *nm* pontoon

pontonero *nm Mil* engineer *(specialist in bridge building)*

ponzoña *nf* (a) *(veneno)* venom, poison (b) *(cosa perjudicial)* venom

ponzoñoso, -a *adj* (a) *(venenoso)* venomous, poisonous (b) *(crítica, comentario)* venomous

pool *nm* (a) *Com* pool (b) *(billar)* pool

pop 1 *adj* pop
2 *nm* (a) *(música)* pop (b) *Urug (maíz)* popcorn ►► ***p. acaramelado*** toffee popcorn; ***p. salado*** salted popcorn

popa *nf* stern

pop-art *nm* pop art

pope *nm* (a) *Rel (ortodoxo)* pope (b) *Fam (persona influyente)* **un p. de la novela policiaca** a leading writer of detective stories; **uno de los popes de Internet** an Internet guru

popelín *nm*, **popelina** *nf* poplin

popis *Méx Fam* 1 *adj inv* posh
2 *nmf inv* posh person

popó *nm Méx* (a) *(lenguaje infantil) (excremento) Br* poo-poo, *US* poop (b) *(cosa sucia)* **no toques eso, es p.** don't touch that, it's dirty

popocho, -a *adj Col Fam* chubby

popoff *adj inv Méx Fam* ritzy, posh

poporopo *nm Guat* popcorn

popote *nm Méx* (drinking) straw

populachero, -a *adj Pey* (a) *(fiesta)* common, popular (b) *(discurso)* populist

populacho *nm Pey* **el p.** the mob, the masses

popular 1 *adj* (a) *(del pueblo) (creencia, movimiento, revuelta)* popular; **una insurrección/protesta p.** a popular uprising/protest; **la voluntad p.** the will of the people
(b) *(arte, música)* folk
(c) *(precios)* affordable
(d) *(lenguaje)* colloquial
(e) *(famoso)* popular; **hacerse p.** to catch on
(f) *(aceptado)* popular; **es muy p. en la oficina** she's very popular in the office
(g) *Esp Pol* = of/relating to the Partido Popular
2 *nmf Esp Pol* = member/supporter of the Partido Popular

popularidad *nf* popularity

popularización *nf* popularization

popularizar [14] 1 *vt* to popularize
2 **popularizarse** *vpr* to become popular

popularmente *adv* **p. conocido como...** more commonly known as...

populismo *nm* populism

populista 1 *adj* populist
2 *nmf* populist

populoso, -a *adj* populous, crowded

popurrí *nm* (a) *(de canciones)* medley (b) *(de cosas)* mishmash

popusa *nf Bol, Guat, Salv (tortilla)* = tortilla filled with cheese or meat

póquer, póker *nm* (a) *(juego)* poker (b) *(jugada)* four of a kind; **p. de ases** four aces ►► ***p. descubierto*** stud poker

poquito *nm* **un p.** a little bit

POR *prep* (a) *(indica causa)* because of; **llegó tarde p. el tráfico** she was late because of the traffic; **lo hizo p. amor** he did it out of *o* for love; **me disculpé p. llegar tarde** I apologized for arriving late; **miré dentro p. simple curiosidad** I looked inside out of pure curiosity; **accidentes p. conducción temeraria** accidents caused by reckless driving; **muertes p. enfermedades cardiovasculares** deaths from cardiovascular disease; **no quise llamar p. la hora (que era)** I didn't want to call because of the time; **cerrado p. vacaciones/reformas** *(en letrero)* closed for holidays/alterations; **p. mí no te preocupes** don't worry about me; *Esp* **fue p. eso p. lo que tuvimos tantos problemas,** *Am* **fue p. eso que tuvimos tantos problemas** that's why we had so many problems; **eso te pasa p. (ser tan) generoso** that's what you get for being so generous; **la razón p. (la) que dimite** the reason (why) she is resigning; **¿p. qué?** why?; **¿p. qué no vienes?** why don't you come?; **¿p. qué lo preguntas? – p. nada** why do you ask? – no reason; *Fam* **¿p.?** why?; **p. si** in case; **p. si se te olvida** in case you forget

(b) *(indica indicio)* **p. lo que me dices/lo que he oído no debe de ser tan difícil** from what you say/what I've heard, it can't be that difficult; **p. lo que tengo entendido, viven juntos** as I understand it, they live together, my understanding is that they live together; **p. lo visto, p. lo que se ve** apparently

(c) *(indica finalidad) (antes de infinitivo)* (in order) to; *(antes de sustantivo o pronombre)* for; **lo hizo p. complacerte** he did it to please you; **vine p. charlar un rato** I came to have a chat *o* for a chat; **escribo p. diversión** I write for fun; **lo hice p. ella** I did it for her; **vino un señor preguntando p. usted** a man was here asking for you; **corrí las mesas p. que tuvieran más espacio** I moved the tables along so they had more room

(d) *(indica inclinación, favor)* **sentía un gran amor/interés p. los animales** she had a great love of/interest in animals; **existía cierta fascinación p. lo oriental** there was a certain fascination with all things oriental; **tengo curiosidad p. saberlo** I'm curious to know; **votó p. los socialistas** he voted for the socialists; **la mayoría está p. la huelga** *o* **p. hacer huelga** the majority is in favour of a strike

(e) *(indica medio, modo)* by; **p. mensajero/fax/teléfono** by courier/fax/telephone; **estuvimos hablando p. teléfono** we were talking on the phone; **p. correo** by post, by mail; **se comunican p. Internet** they communicate via the Internet; **te mandé un mensaje p. correo electrónico** I sent you an e-mail; **te mandaré el archivo p. correo electrónico** I'll send you the file by e-mail, I'll e-mail the file to you; **p. escrito** in writing; **lo oí p. la radio** I heard it on the radio; **van a echar p. la tele un ciclo de Scorsese** they are going to have a season of Scorsese films on the TV; **conseguí las entradas/el empleo p. un amigo** I got the tickets/job through a friend; **funciona p. energía solar** it runs on *o* uses solar power; **nos comunicábamos p. señas** we communicated with each other by *o* using signs; **los discos están puestos p. orden alfabético** the records are arranged in alphabetical order; **p. la forma de llamar a la puerta supe que eras tú** I knew it was you from *o* by the way you knocked on the door; **lo agarraron p. el brazo** they seized him by the arm; **lo harás p. las buenas o p. las malas** you'll do it whether you like it or not

(f) *(indica agente)* by; **el récord fue batido p. el atleta cubano** the record was broken by the Cuban athlete

(g) *(indica tiempo aproximado)* **creo que la boda será p. abril** I think the wedding will be some time in April; **p. entonces** *o* **p. aquellas fechas yo estaba de viaje** I was away at the time

(h) *(indica tiempo concreto)* **p. la mañana/tarde** in the morning/afternoon; **p. la noche** at night; **ayer salimos p. la noche** we went out last night; **p. unos días** for a few days; **p. ahora** for the time being; **p. ahora no podemos hacer nada** for the time being, we can't do anything, there's nothing we can do for the moment

(i) *(antes de infinitivo) (indica tarea futura)* **los candidatos que quedan p. entrevistar** the candidates who have not yet been interviewed *o* who have still to be interviewed; **tengo todos estos papeles p. ordenar** I've got all these papers to sort out; **estuve p. ir, pero luego me dio pereza** I was about to go *o* on the verge of going, but then I decided I couldn't be bothered; **¡eso está p. ver!** that remains to be seen!; **está p. ver si eso es cierto** it remains to be seen whether that is the case

(j) *(indica lugar indeterminado)* **¿p. dónde vive?** whereabouts does he live?; **vive p. las afueras** he lives somewhere on the outskirts; **ese restaurante está p. el centro** that restaurant is in the town centre somewhere; **estará p. algún cajón/p. ahí** it'll be in a drawer somewhere/around somewhere (**k**) *(indica lugar o zona concretos)* **voy p. el principio/la mitad de la novela** I'm just starting/I'm halfway through the novel; **el agua nos llegaba p. las rodillas** the water came up to our knees; **había papeles p. el suelo** there were papers all over the floor; **estuvimos viajando p. Centroamérica** we were travelling around Central America; **p. todo el mundo** all over *o* throughout the world; **hay poca vegetación p. aquí/allí** there isn't much vegetation round here/there; **p. delante/detrás parece muy bonito** it looks very nice from the front/back; **sólo quedaba sitio p. delante/detrás** there was only room at the front/back; **los que van p. delante/detrás** the leaders/backmarkers; **está escrito p. detrás** there's writing on the back

(**l**) *(indica tránsito, trayectoria) (a través de)* through; **vamos p. aquí/allí** let's go this/that way; **¿p. dónde se entra/se sale?** where's the way in/out?; **iba paseando p. el bosque/la calle/el jardín** she was walking through the forest/along the street/in the garden; **pasar p. la aduana** to go through customs; **entraron p. la ventana** they got in through the window; **se cayó p. la ventana/la escalera** she fell out of the window/down the stairs

(**m**) *(indica movimiento) (en busca de)* for; *Esp* **a p.** for; **baja (a) p. tabaco** go down to the shops for some cigarettes, go down to get some cigarettes; **vino (a) p. las entradas** she came for the tickets; **fui (a) por ellos al aeropuerto** I went to pick them up at the airport

(**n**) *(indica cambio, sustitución, equivalencia)* for; **lo ha comprado p. poco dinero** she bought it for very little; **cambió el coche p. la moto** he exchanged his car for a motorbike; **un premio/cheque p. valor de 1.000 pesos** a prize of/cheque for 1,000 pesos; **él lo hará p. mí** he'll do it for me; **se hizo pasar p. policía** he pretended to be a policeman

(**o**) *(indica reparto, distribución)* per; **dos euros p. unidad** two euros each; **mil unidades p. semana** a thousand units a *o* per week; **20 kms p. hora** 20 km an *o* per hour; **hay un parado p. cada cinco trabajadores** there is one person unemployed for every five who have a job; **sólo vendemos las patatas p. sacos** we only sell potatoes by the sack; **uno p. uno** one by one

(**p**) *(indica multiplicación)* **dos p. dos igual a cuatro** two times two is four

(**q**) *(indica área geométrica)* by; **la habitación mide cinco p. tres metros** the room is five metres by three

(**r**) *(indica concesión)* **p. más *o* mucho que lo intentes no lo conseguirás** however hard you try *o* try as you might, you'll never manage it; **no me cae bien, p. (muy) simpático que te parezca** you may think he's nice, but I don't like him

(**s**) *(en cuanto a)* **p. mí/nosotros** as far as I'm/we're concerned; **p. nosotros no hay inconveniente** it's fine by us; **p. mí puedes hacer lo que quieras** as far as I'm concerned, you can do whatever you like

(**t**) *Am (durante)* for; **fue presidente p. treinta años** he was president for thirty years

---

porcelana *nf* (**a**) *(material)* porcelain, china (**b**) *(objeto)* piece of porcelain *o* china

porcentaje *nm* percentage; **nos dan un p. sobre las ventas** we get a percentage of the sales

porcentual *adj* percentage; **seis puntos porcentuales** six percentage points

porcentualmente *adv* in percentage terms

porche *nm (entrada)* porch; *(soportal)* arcade

porcino, -a *adj* pig; **excrementos porcinos** pig excrement; **el sector p.** the pig-farming industry; **ganado p.** pigs

porción *nf* (**a**) *(parte)* portion, piece (**b**) *(de comida)* portion, helping; **sirven porciones abundantes en este restaurante** they serve big portions in this restaurant

pordiosear *vi* to beg

pordiosero, -a 1 *adj* begging
2 *nm,f* beggar

porfa *adv Fam* please

porfía *nf* (**a**) *(disputa)* dispute (**b**) *(insistencia)* persistence; *(tozudez)* stubbornness; **a p.** determinedly

porfiado, -a *adj (insistente)* persistent; *(tozudo)* stubborn

porfiar [32] *vi* (**a**) *(disputar)* to argue obstinately (**b**) *(insistir)* **p. en algo** to insist on sth; **porfió en que lo había hecho él** he insisted that HE had done it (**c**) *(empeñarse)* **porfió en su postura inamovible** she remained stubbornly immovable in her opinion

pórfido *nm* porphyry

porfiria *nf Med* porphyria

porfiriano, -a *adj Méx* = relating to Porfirio Díaz, dictatorial ruler of Mexico 1877-1911

pormenor *nm* detail; **me explicó los pormenores del proyecto** she explained the details of the project to me

pormenorizadamente *adv* in detail

pormenorizado, -a *adj* detailed

pormenorizar [14] 1 *vt* to describe in detail
2 *vi* to go into detail

porno 1 *adj* porn, porno
2 *nm* porn ►► ***p. blando*** soft porn; ***p. duro*** hardcore porn

pornografía *nf* pornography

pornográfico, -a *adj* pornographic

pornógrafo, -a *nm,f* pornographer

poro *nm* (**a**) *(piel)* pore (**b**) *Chile, Méx (verdura)* leek

porongo *nm RP* gourd

pororó *nm RP* popcorn; EXPR *Fam* **hablar como un p.** to talk nineteen to the dozen; EXPR *Fam* **ser como un p.** to be a live wire

porosidad *nf* porousness, porosity

poroso, -a *adj* porous

poroto *nm* (**a**) *Andes, RP (judía)* kidney bean ►► ***p. blanco*** butter bean; ***p. de manteca*** butter bean; ***p. negro*** black bean; *Chile* ***p. verde*** green bean (**b**) EXPR *RP Fam* **anotarse un p.** to score a point; *RP Fam* **ser un p.** to be insignificant

porque *conj* (**a**) *(debido a que)* because; **¡p. sí/no!** just because!; **lo hice p. sí** I did it because I felt like it; **¡p. lo digas tú!** says who? **lo vas a hacer p. lo digo yo** you are going to do it because I say so; **p. haga mal tiempo no vamos a quedarnos en casa** we're not going to stay at home just because the weather's bad

(**b**) *(para que)* so that, in order that; **reza p. no nos descubran** pray that they don't find us out

porqué *nm* reason; **el p. de** the reason for

porquería 1 *nf* (**a**) *(suciedad)* filth; **la habitación está llena de p.** the room is absolutely filthy

(**b**) *Fam (cosa de mala calidad) Br* rubbish, *US* garbage; **es una p. de libro** the book is *Br* rubbish *o US* garbage; **una p. de moto** a useless bike; **¡qué p. de música escuchas!** that music you listen to is a load of *Br* rubbish *o US* garbage!

(**c**) **porquerías** *(comida) Br* rubbish, *US* garbage

(**d**) *(grosería)* vulgarity

POR/PARA

Apart from the respective uses of **por** and **para** which are given in the corresponding entries, there are certain contexts in which both prepositions can be used. In such cases, the use of **por** indicates the motivation behind the action (a paraphrase might be "motivado por del deseo de"), while **para** indicates the intended objective (a paraphrase might be "con la intención de"). As will be seen from the following pairs of examples, this is often simply a difference in emphasis which is not always easy to reproduce in English translation:

lo hizo por complacerte *he did it (because he wanted) to please you*
lo hizo para complacerte *he did it (in order) to please you*
me voy por no causar más molestias *I'm leaving because I don't want to cause more trouble*
me voy para no causar más molestias *I'm leaving so as not to cause more trouble*

In other cases the two options reflects a clearer difference in meaning:

tantos esfuerzos por nada *so much effort over nothing*
tantos esfuerzos para nada *so much effort (and all) for nothing*

2 **de porquería** *loc adj Andes, RP Fam* lousy, useless; **una moto de p.** a useless bike; **da unas clases de p.** his classes are lousy *o* useless; **son unos usureros de p.** they're a bunch of lousy loan sharks

porqueriza *nf* pigsty

porquero, -a *nm,f* swineherd

porra 1 *nf* (a) *(palo)* club; *(de policía) Br* truncheon, *US* nightstick
(b) *(masa frita)* = deep-fried pastry sticks
(c) *Esp Fam (apuesta)* sweepstake *(among friends or co-workers)*
(d) *Méx Dep (hinchada)* fans
(e) *Col, Méx (arenga)* chant; **echar porras a alguien** to cheer sb on; **las porras del Santa Fe se escuchan más fuerte** the Santa Fe supporters are starting to make themselves heard
(f) EXPR *Fam* **mandar a alguien a la p.** to tell sb to go to hell; **¡vete a la p.!** go to hell!, get lost!; *Fam* **¿por qué/dónde porras...?** why/where the hell...?; *Fam* **ni qué porras: ¡qué concierto ni qué porras, esta noche te quedas en casa!** I don't give a damn about the concert, you're staying in tonight!; *Fam* **¡y una p.!** no way!
2 *interj Fam* **¡porras!** hell!, damn it!

porrada, *RP* **porrotada** *nf Fam* **una p. (de)** loads (of); **tiene una p. de discos** she's got loads of records; **gana una p. de dinero** he earns loads of money, he earns a fortune

porrazo *nm* (a) *(golpe con la porra)* **un policía lo dejó inconsciente de un p. en la cabeza** a policeman knocked him unconscious with a blow from his *Br* truncheon *o US* nightstick; **la policía se abrió paso a porrazos** the policeman beat his way through the crowd with his *Br* truncheon *o US* nightstick
(b) *Fam (choque, caída)* bump; **me di un p. tremendo contra la puerta** I whacked myself on the door; **se dio un p. con la moto** he had a smash-up on his bike

porrero, -a *Fam* 1 *adj* **es muy p.** he's a real pothead *o* dopehead
2 *nm,f* pothead, dopehead

porreta *Fam* 1 *nmf* pothead, dopehead
2 **en porreta(s)** *loc adv (desnudo)* in the altogether, in one's birthday suit

porrillo: a porrillo *loc adv Fam* by the bucket; **tiene clientes a p.** she has tons *o* loads of customers; **gana dinero a p.** he earns loads of money, he earns a fortune

porrista 1 *nmf Méx (hincha)* fan, supporter
2 *nf Col, Méx (animadora)* cheerleader

porro *nm* (a) *Fam (de droga)* joint (b) *Am (puerro)* leek

porrón[1] *nm* (a) *(vasija)* = glass wine vessel used for drinking wine from its long spout (b) *Esp Fam* **un p. de** loads of; **tiene un p. de coches** she's got loads of cars; **murió hace un p. de años** she died donkey's years ago

porrón[2] *nm (ave)* pochard ►► ***p. coacoxtle*** canvasback; ***p. moñudo*** tufted duck; ***p. osculado*** goldeneye; ***p. pardo*** ferruginous duck

porrotada = **porrada**

porta *Anat* 1 *adj* **vena p.** portal vein
2 *nf* portal vein

portaaviones, portaviones *nm inv* aircraft carrier

portabebés *nm inv Br* carrycot, *US* portacrib®

portabicis *nm inv* bicycle rack *(on car)*

portabilidad *nf Informát* portability

portabultos *nm inv Méx* roof rack

portabustos *nm inv Méx* bra

portación *nf Arg, CAm, Cuba, Méx* **p. de armas** carrying of weapons *o* arms; **arrestado por p. ilegal de arma** arrested for carrying an illegal weapon

portada *nf* (a) *(de libro)* title page; *(de revista)* (front) cover; *(de periódico)* front page (b) *Informát (de página Web)* home page (c) *(de disco)* sleeve (d) *Arquit* façade, facade

portadocumentos *nm inv Andes, RP* document wallet

portador, -ora 1 *adj* carrying, bearing
2 *nm,f* (a) *(de noticia)* bearer; *(de virus)* carrier; **los portadores del virus del sida** carriers of the AIDS virus (b) *Com* bearer; **al p.** to the bearer

portadora *nf Tel* carrier

portaequipajes, portamaletas *nm inv* (a) *(en automóvil) (maletero) Br* boot, *US* trunk; *(baca)* roof *o* luggage rack (b) *(en autobús, tren)* luggage rack

portaesquís *nm inv* ski rack

portaestandarte *nm* standard-bearer

portafiltros *nm inv* filter holder

portafolio *nm*, **portafolios** *nm inv (carpeta)* file; *(maletín)* attaché case

portafusil *nm* rifle sling

portahelicópteros *nm inv* helicopter carrier

portal *nm* (a) *(entrada)* entrance hall; *(puerta)* main door; **viven en aquel p.** they live at that number (b) *(belén)* crib, Nativity scene; **el p. de Belén** the stable at Bethlehem (c) *Informát (página Web)* portal

portalada *nf* = large doors or gate giving access to interior courtyard from street

portalámparas *nm inv* socket

portalápiz *nm* pencil holder

portalibros *nm inv* = strap tied round books to carry them

portaligas *nm inv Am Br* suspender belt, *US* garter belt

portalón *nm* = large doors or gate giving access to interior courtyard from street

portamaletas = **portaequipajes**

portaminas *nm inv Br* propelling pencil, *US* mechanical pencil

portamisiles *adj inv* **buque p.** missile carrier

portamonedas *nm inv* purse

portante *nm (del caballo)* amble, ambling gait; EXPR *Fam* **agarrar** *o* **tomar** *o* **coger el p.: agarró el portante** she upped and went

portaobjeto *nm*, **portaobjetos** *nm inv (de microscopio)* slide

portapapeles *nm inv Informát* clipboard

portar 1 *vt* to carry; **no se permite p. armas** it is forbidden to carry weapons *o* arms
2 **portarse** *vpr* to behave; **portarse bien** to behave (well); **se ha portado bien conmigo** she has treated me well; **portarse mal** to misbehave, to behave badly; **pórtate bien** behave (yourself)!; **se portó muy mal con su hermano** he treated his brother very badly; *Fam* **anda, pórtate bien y tráeme un café** be a star and bring us a cup of coffee

portarretratos *nm inv* picture frame, photograph frame

portarrollos *nm inv (en baño)* toilet roll holder; *(en cocina)* kitchen towel holder

portátil 1 *adj* portable
2 *nm* laptop

portatrajes *nm inv* garment bag

portaviandas *nm inv* lunch box

portaviones = **portaaviones**

portavoz *nmf* (a) *(persona)* spokesperson, spokesman, *f* spokeswoman (b) *(medio de comunicación)* mouthpiece; **esa cadena de televisión es la p. del gobierno** that television channel is the voice *o* mouthpiece of the government

portazo *nm* (a) *(de puerta)* **oímos un p.** we heard a slam *o* bang; **dar un p.** to slam the door; **la puerta se cerró de un p.** the door slammed shut (b) *(negativa)* **dar un p. a algo** to flatly reject sth; **el general dio un p. al plan de paz** the general flatly rejected the peace plan

porte *nm* (a) *(gasto de transporte)* transport costs, carriage; **los portes corren a cargo del destinatario** transport *o* carriage is payable by the addressee ►► *Com* ***portes debidos*** *Br* carriage forward, *US* freight collect; **enviar algo a portes debidos** to send sth *Br* carriage forward *o US* freight collect; *Com* ***portes pagados*** *Br* carriage paid, *US* freight paid; **enviar algo a portes pagados** to send sth *Br* carriage paid *o US* freight paid
(b) *(transporte)* carriage, transport; **una empresa de portes y mudanzas** *Br* a removal firm, *US* a moving firm
(c) *(capacidad, tamaño)* size, capacity; *Am* **llegó una caja de este p.** *(muy grande)* a box arrived that was THIS big
(d) *(aspecto)* bearing, demeanour; **su padre tiene un p. distinguido** your father has a very distinguished air; **un edificio de p. majestuoso** a very grand-looking building
(e) *RP (permiso)* permit, licence; **¿usted tiene p. de armas?** do you have a gun licence?
(f) *RP (acción)* carrying; **se prohíbe el p. de armas** the carrying of weapons *o* arms is forbidden

porteador, -ora *nm,f* porter

portento *nm* (a) *(persona)* wonder, marvel; **es un p. tocando el piano** he's a wonderful piano player (b) *(hecho)* **es un p. que la casa siga en pie después del incendio** it's a wonder the house is still standing after the fire

portentoso, -a *adj* amazing, incredible; **tiene una inteligencia portentosa** she's amazingly *o* incredibly intelligent

porteño, -a 1 *adj* (**a**) *(de Buenos Aires)* of/from the city of Buenos Aires (**b**) *(de Valparaíso)* of/from Valparaiso *(Chile)* (**c**) *RP (del puerto)* port; **autoridad porteña** port authority
2 *nm,f* (**a**) *(de Buenos Aires)* person from the city of Buenos Aires (**b**) *(de Valparaíso)* person from Valparaiso *(Chile)*

portería *nf* (**a**) *(de casa, escuela) Br* caretaker's office *o* lodge, *US* super(intendent)'s office (**b**) *(de hotel, ministerio)* porter's office *o* lodge (**c**) *(deporte)* goal, goalmouth

portero, -a 1 *nm,f* (**a**) *(de casa) Br* caretaker, *US* super(intendent) (**b**) *(de hotel, ministerio) (en recepción)* porter; *(a la puerta)* doorman (**c**) *(de discoteca)* doorman (**d**) *(en fútbol, balonmano, hockey)* goalkeeper; *(en hockey)* goalminder
2 *nm* ***p. automático*** entryphone; ***p. eléctrico*** entryphone; ***p. electrónico*** entryphone

portezuela *nf (de coche)* door

porticado, -a *adj* **una plaza porticada** a square surrounded by an arcade

pórtico *nm* (**a**) *(fachada)* portico (**b**) *(arcada)* arcade

portilla *nf Náut* porthole

portillo *nm* (**a**) *(abertura)* opening, gap (**b**) *(puerta pequeña)* wicket gate

Port Moresby *n* Port Moresby

portón *nm* large door

portorriqueño, -a 1 *adj* Puerto Rican
2 *nm,f* Puerto Rican

portuario, -a *adj* (**a**) *(del puerto)* port; **ciudad portuaria** port (**b**) *(de los muelles)* dock; **trabajador p.** docker; **la zona portuaria** the docks (area)

Portugal *n* Portugal

portugués, -esa 1 *adj* Portuguese
2 *nm,f (persona)* Portuguese
3 *nm (lengua)* Portuguese

portuguesismo *nm* = Portuguese word or expression

porvenir *nm* future; **adivinar el p.** to foresee the future, to see into the future; **se está labrando su p.** she is carving out a future for herself

pos[1]**: en pos de** *loc prep* (**a**) *(detrás de)* behind; **corrió en p. de su amo** he ran after his master (**b**) *(en busca de)* after; **esfuerzos en p. de lograr la paz** efforts in pursuit of peace

pos-[2]**, post-** *pref* post-

posada *nf* (**a**) *(fonda)* inn, guesthouse (**b**) *CAm, Méx (fiesta)* Christmas party

posaderas *nfpl Fam* backside, bottom

posadero, -a *nm,f* innkeeper

posar 1 *vt* (**a**) *(objeto)* to put *o* lay down (**en** on); *(mano)* to rest (**en** *o* **sobre** on) (**b**) *(mirada)* to rest (**en** on)
2 *vi* to pose
3 **posarse** *vpr* (**a**) *(insecto, polvo)* to settle (**b**) *(pájaro)* to perch (**en** on); *(nave, helicóptero)* to land, to come down (**en** on)

posavasos *nm inv (de madera, plástico)* coaster; *(de cartón)* beer mat

posdata *nf* postscript

pose *nf* (**a**) *(para cuadro, retrato)* pose (**b**) *(actitud)* pose; **es solo una p.** it's just a pose; **adoptó una p. salomónica** he made out that he was very even-handed

poseedor, -ora 1 *adj (propietario)* owning, possessing; *(de cargo, acciones, récord)* holding
2 *nm,f (propietario)* owner; *(de cargo, acciones, récord)* holder; **es el p. del récord mundial** he is the world record-holder, he holds the world record

poseer [37] *vt* (**a**) *(ser dueño de)* to own; **posee una casa en las afueras** he has a house in the suburbs
(**b**) *(tener)* to have; **posee aire acondicionado** it has air conditioning, it is air-conditioned
(**c**) *(estar en poder de)* to have, to possess; *(puesto, marca)* to hold; **no poseo la llave del archivo** I don't have the key to the archive
(**d**) *(sexualmente)* to have; **la poseyó violentamente** he took her violently

poseído, -a 1 *adj* **p. por** possessed by
2 *nm,f* possessed person

Poseidón *n Mitol* Poseidon

posesión *nf* (**a**) *(acción, efecto)* possession; **la granja ha pasado a p. de sus antiguos dueños** ownership of the farm has passed back to its previous owners; **está en p. del récord del mundo** she holds the world record; **se cree en p. de la verdad** she believes herself to be in possession of the truth; **para solicitar el puesto es necesario estar en p. de un título universitario** in order to apply for the job you need to have a degree; **el acusado estaba en plena p. de sus facultades mentales** the accused was in full possession of his mental faculties; **tomar p. de un cargo** to take up a position *o* post
(**b**) *(cosa poseída)* possession; **tuvo que vender todas sus posesiones** she had to sell all her possessions; **las posesiones españolas en África** Spanish possessions in Africa

posesionar 1 *vt* to give possession of, to hand over
2 **posesionarse** *vpr* **posesionarse de** to take possession of, to take over

posesivo, -a 1 *adj* (**a**) *(persona)* possessive (**b**) *Gram* possessive
2 *nm Gram* possessive

poseso, -a 1 *adj* possessed
2 *nm,f* possessed person; **gritar como un p.** to scream like one possessed

poseyera *etc ver* **poseer**

posfranquismo *nm* = period after the death of Franco

posgrado, postgrado *nm* postgraduate course; **un p. en educación ambiental** a postgraduate course in environmental education; **estudios de p.** postgraduate studies

posgraduado, -a, postgraduado, -a 1 *adj* postgraduate
2 *nm,f* postgraduate

posguerra, postguerra *nf* post-war period

posibilidad *nf* (**a**) *(circunstancia)* possibility, chance; **no descartamos ninguna p.** we are not ruling anything out; **cabe la p. de que...** there is a chance *o* possibility that...; **tienes muchas posibilidades de que te admitan** you have a good chance of being accepted; **no hay ninguna p. de que aprueben la propuesta** there is no chance that they will approve the proposal
(**b**) *(opción)* possibility; **tienes tres posibilidades, ¿cuál eliges?** you've got three options, which will you choose?; **una p. sería que fuéramos en avión** one possibility would be for us to go by plane
(**c**) **posibilidades (económicas)** financial means *o* resources; **comprar una casa no entra dentro de nuestras posibilidades** we don't have the means *o* we can't afford to buy a house

posibilismo *nm* pragmatism

posibilitar *vt* to make possible; **las negociaciones posibilitaron el alto el fuego** the negotiations made a cease-fire possible

posible 1 *adj* possible; **es p. que llueva** it could rain; **es p. que sea así** that might be the case; **¿llegarás a tiempo? – es p.** will you arrive in time? – possibly *o* I may do; **ven lo antes p.** come as soon as possible; **dentro de lo p., en lo p.** as far as possible; **dentro de lo p. intenta no hacer ruido** as far as possible, try not to make any noise; **a** *o* **de ser p.** if possible; **hacer p. algo** to make sth possible; **su intervención hizo p. el acuerdo** his intervention made the agreement possible; **hacer (todo) lo p.** to do everything possible; **hicieron todo lo p. por salvar su vida** they did everything possible to save his life; **lo antes p.** as soon as possible; **¿cómo es p. que no me lo hayas dicho antes?** how could you possibly not have told me before?; **no creo que nos sea p. visitaros** I don't think we'll be able to visit you; **¡será p.!** I can't believe this!; **¿será p. que nadie le haya dicho nada?** can it be true that nobody told her anything about it?; **¡no es p.!** surely not!
2 **posibles** *nmpl* (financial) means

posiblemente *adv* possibly, perhaps; **p. no sepamos nada hasta mañana** we might not know anything until tomorrow; **¿se lo dirás? – p.** will you tell him? – possibly *o* perhaps

posición *nf* (**a**) *(postura física)* position ►► ***p. fetal*** foetal position; ***p. de loto*** lotus position
(**b**) *(puesto)* position; **quedó en (la) quinta p.** he was fifth; **el equipo ha recuperado posiciones con respecto al líder** the team has closed the gap on the leaders; **p. ventajosa** vantage point
(**c**) *(lugar)* position; **tomaron las posiciones enemigas** they took the enemy positions
(**d**) *(situación)* position; **no estoy en p. de opinar** I'm not in a position to comment; **estoy en una p. muy difícil** I'm in a very difficult position
(**e**) *(categoría) (social)* status; *(económica)* situation; **está en una p. económica difícil** he's in a difficult financial situation

posicionamiento *nm* position; **su p. con respecto a la crisis** his position on the crisis

posicionarse *vpr* to take a position *o* stance; **evitó p. en contra del candidato** he avoided declaring his opposition to the candidate

posidonia *nf* neptunegrass

positivado *nm Fot (de negativos)* printing

positivamente *adv* positively

positivar *vt Fot (negativos)* to print

positivismo *nm* **(a)** *(realismo)* pragmatism **(b)** *Filosofía* positivism

positivista *Filosofía* 1 *adj* positivist
2 *nmf* positivist

positivo, -a 1 *adj* **(a)** *(número respuesta, resultado)* positive; **el test dio p.** the test was positive; **saldo p.** credit balance **(b)** *(persona, actitud)* positive; **una experiencia muy positiva** a very positive experience **(c)** *Elec* positive
2 *nm Fot* print

positrón *nm Fís* positron

posmodernidad, postmodernidad *nf* post-modernity

posmodernismo, postmodernismo *nm* post-modernism

posmoderno, -a, postmoderno, -a 1 *adj* post-modernist
2 *nm,f* post-modernist

poso *nm* **(a)** *(sedimento)* sediment; *(de café)* grounds; **formar p.** to settle **(b)** *(resto, huella)* trace; **la discusión me dejó un p. amargo** the argument left a bitter taste in my mouth

posología *nf* dosage

posoperatorio, -a, postoperatorio, -a 1 *adj* post-operative
2 *nm (periodo)* post-operative period

pospalatal, postpalatal *adj Ling* postpalatal

posparto, postparto 1 *adj* postnatal
2 *nm* postnatal period

posponer [50] *vt* **(a)** *(relegar)* to put behind, to relegate **(b)** *(aplazar)* to postpone; **pospondremos la reunión para mañana** we will postpone the meeting until tomorrow

pospuesto, -a *participio ver* **posponer**

pospusiera *etc ver* **posponer**

post = **pos²**

posta 1 *adj RP Fam* cool
2 *nf* **(a)** *Am* **postas** *(carrera)* relay (race); EXPR *RP Fam* **pasarle la p. a alguien** to pass the baton to sb, to hand over to sb **(b)** *Chile, Perú (médica)* clinic **(c)** *RP Fam* **la p.** *(la verdad)* the truth
3 **a posta** *loc adv* on purpose

postal 1 *adj* postal
2 *nf* postcard

postdata *nf* postscript

poste *nm* **(a)** *(madero)* post, pole; EXPR *Fam* **no te quedes ahí como un p.** don't just stand there! ►► ***p. de alta tensión*** electricity pylon; ***p. kilométrico*** kilometre marker, ≃ milepost; *Am* ***p. restante*** *Br* poste restante, *US* general delivery; ***p. telegráfico*** telegraph pole **(b)** *(de portería)* post **(c)** *(en baloncesto)* centre

póster *(pl* **pósters)** *nm* poster

postergación *nf (aplazamiento)* postponement

postergar [38] *vt* **(a)** *(aplazar)* to postpone **(b)** *(relegar)* to put behind

posteridad *nf* posterity; **hagámonos una foto para la p.** let's take a photo for posterity; **pasar a la p.** to go down in history, to be remembered; **quedar para la p.** to be left to posterity

posterior *adj* **(a)** *(en el espacio)* rear, back; **p. a** behind; **la piscina está en la parte p. del hotel** the swimming pool is at the back *o* rear of the hotel **(b)** *(en el tiempo)* subsequent, later; **p. a** subsequent to, after; **fue un descubrimiento p. al de la penicilina** it was a discovery made after that of penicillin **(c)** *(vocal)* back

posteriori *ver* **a posteriori**

posterioridad *nf* **con p.** later, subsequently; **con p. a** later than, subsequent to

posteriormente *adv* subsequently, later (on); **p., se dieron la mano** later on they shook hands; **como se explicará p....** as will be explained further on *o* later...

postgrado = **posgrado**

postgraduado, -a = **posgraduado, -a**

postguerra = **posguerra**

postigo *nm* **(a)** *(contraventana)* shutter **(b)** *(puerta)* wicket gate

postilla *nf* scab

postillón *nm* postilion

postimpresionismo *nm* postimpressionism

postimpresionista 1 *adj* postimpressionist
2 *nmf* postimpressionist

postín *nm* **(a)** *(distinción)* cachet; **de p.** posh; **fue una boda de p.** it was a posh *o* fancy wedding **(b)** *(presunción)* showiness; **darse p.** to show off; **lleva una vida de p.** she lives flashily

postindustrial *adj* post-industrial

post-it® *nm inv* Post-it®

postizo, -a 1 *adj* **(a)** *(diente, pelo, bigote)* false; **dentadura postiza** false teeth, dentures **(b)** *(cuello, manga)* detachable **(c)** *(sonrisa)* false
2 *nm* hairpiece

postmodernidad = **posmodernidad**

postmodernismo = **posmodernismo**

postmoderno, -a = **posmoderno, -a**

post mórtem *adj* 1 postmortem
2 *nm* postmortem (examination)

postoperatorio, -a = **posoperatorio, -a**

postor, -ora *nm,f* bidder; **vender al mejor p.** to sell to the highest bidder

postpalatal = **pospalatal**

postparto = **posparto**

postproducción *nf Cine* post-production

postración *nf* prostration

postrado, -a *adj* prostrate

postrar 1 *vt* **la gripe lo postró en cama** he was laid up in bed with flu
2 **postrarse** *vpr* to prostrate oneself; **se postró ante el altar** he prostrated himself before the altar

postre 1 *nm (dulce, fruta)* dessert, *Br* pudding; **tomaré fruta de p.** I'll have fruit for dessert; **¿qué hay de p.?** what's for dessert?; EXPR **llegar a los postres** to come too late; EXPR **para p.** to cap it all
2 **a la postre** *loc adv* in the end; **votantes que, a la p., han hecho posible el triunfo electoral** voters who, at the end of the day, are to thank for them winning the election; **el que a la p. sería ganador pinchó en la primera vuelta** the eventual winner had a puncture on the first lap

postrero, -a *adj* last, final

> **Postrer** is used instead of **postrero** before singular masculine nouns (e.g. **el postrer día** the last day).

postrimerías *nfpl* final stages; **en las p. del siglo XIX** at the end *o* close of the 19th century; **marcaron el gol del empate en las p. del encuentro** they equalized in the dying moments of the game

PostScript® ['poskrip] *nm Informát* PostScript®

postulación *nf* **(a)** *(colecta)* collection **(b)** *(acción)* postulation **(c)** *Am Pol (candidatura)* nomination

postulado *nm* postulate

postulante, -a *nm,f* **(a)** *(en colecta)* collector **(b)** *Rel* postulant **(c)** *Am (candidato)* candidate **(d)** *CSur (concursante)* candidate, applicant

postular 1 *vt* **(a)** *(defender)* to call for **(b)** *Am (candidatar)* to nominate
2 *vi* **(a)** *(en colecta)* to collect; **p. para una causa** to collect for a cause **(b)** *CSur (para trabajo)* to apply
3 **postularse** *vpr CSur* **(a)** *(para cargo)* to stand, to run **(b)** *(para trabajo)* to apply (**para** *o Am* **a** for)

póstumamente *adv* posthumously

póstumo, -a *adj* posthumous; **un homenaje p.** a posthumous tribute; **recibió, a título p., la medalla al valor** he was posthumously awarded the medal for bravery

postura *nf* **(a)** *(posición)* position, posture; **ponte en una p. cómoda** get into a comfortable position, make yourself comfortable ►► ***p. del misionero*** missionary position
(b) *(actitud)* attitude, stance; **adoptar una p.** to adopt an attitude *o* a stance; **tienes que tomar p.** you have to take up a position; **defiende posturas muy radicales** he upholds very radical opinions *o* views
(c) *(en subasta)* bid
(d) *Am (uso)* **este vestido se me estropeó a la segunda p.** this dress fell to pieces the second time I wore it
(e) *Chile* ***p. de argollas*** *(celebración)* engagement party

posventa, postventa *adj inv Com* after-sales; **servicio p.** after-sales service

pota *nf Fam (vómito)* puke; **echar la p.** to puke (up)

potabilidad *nf* fitness for drinking

potabilización *nf* purification

potabilizador, -ora *adj* water-treatment; **planta potabilizadora** water-treatment plant, waterworks *(singular)*

potabilizadora *nf* water-treatment plant, waterworks *(singular)*

potabilizar *vt* to purify

potable *adj* **(a)** *(bebible)* drinkable; **agua p.** drinking water; **no p.** *(cartel)* not for drinking **(b)** *Fam (aceptable) (comida)* edible; *(novela)* readable; *(película)* watchable; *(chica)* passable

potaje *nm* **(a)** *(guiso)* vegetable stew **(b)** *Fam (brebaje)* potion, brew **(c)** *Fam (mezcla)* jumble, muddle

potar *vi Fam* to puke (up)
potasa *nf* potash
potásico, -a *adj* potassic; **cloruro/sulfato p.** potassium chloride/ sulphate
potasio *nm Quím* potassium
pote *nm* **(a)** *(cazuela)* pan **(b)** *(cocido)* stew **(c)** *RP (recipiente)* jar, pot
potencia *nf* **(a)** *(capacidad, fuerza)* power; **la p. de las aguas derribó el dique** the force of the water burst the dike; **este automóvil tiene mucha p.** this car is very powerful ▸▸ ***p. sexual*** sexual prowess
(b) *Fís* power ▸▸ ***p. acústica*** acoustic power; ***p. de un cohete*** rocket thrust; ***p. de una lente*** power of a lens
(c) *(país)* power; **las grandes potencias** the major (world) powers ▸▸ ***p. mundial*** world power; **es una p. mundial en la fabricación de automóviles** it's one of the major *o* main car manufacturers in the world; ***p. nuclear*** nuclear power
(d) *(posibilidad)* **en p.** potentially; **una campeona en p.** a potential champion
(e) *Mat* power; **elevar a la segunda p.** to raise to the second power, to square; **elevar a la tercera p.** to raise to the third power, to cube
potenciación *nf* promotion; **ayudar a la p. de algo** to promote sth, to encourage sth; **la p. del interés por la lectura** promoting interest in reading
potenciador *nm* enhancer
potencial 1 *adj* potential
2 *nm* **(a)** *(fuerza)* power **(b)** *(posibilidades)* potential **(c)** *Gram* conditional **(d)** *Elec* (electric) potential
potencialidad *nf* potentiality, potential
potencialmente *adv* potentially
potenciar *vt* to promote, to encourage; **medidas para p. el comercio justo** measures to promote fair trade; **el acuerdo potenciará los intercambios entre los países firmantes** the agreement will encourage *o* promote trade between the signatories; **una campaña para p. el acceso de la población a Internet** a campaign to promote public access to the Internet
potenciómetro *nm* potentiometer
potentado, -a *nm,f* tycoon, magnate; **un p. del sector bancario** a banking tycoon *o* magnate
potente *adj* **(a)** *(máquina, coche, nación)* powerful **(b)** *(grito)* powerful, loud; *(abrazo)* big **(c)** *Dep (disparo)* powerful; *(pase)* hard-hit **(d)** *(hombre)* virile
potestad *nf* authority, power; **tener p. sobre alguien** to have authority over sb; **tener p. para hacer algo** to have the authority *o* power to do sth
potestativo, -a *adj* optional
potiche *nm CSur* earthenware pot
potingue *nm Fam (cosmético)* potion
potito *nm* = jar of baby food
poto *nm* **(a)** *(árbol)* devil's ivy, hunter's robe **(b)** *Andes Fam (trasero)* bottom, backside **(c)** *Perú (vasija)* gourd, earthenware drinking vessel
potosí (*pl* **potosíes**) *nm Fam* **costar un p.** to cost a fortune; **valer un p.** to be worth one's weight in gold
potosino, -a 1 *adj* **(a)** *(boliviano)* of/from Potosí *(Bolivia)* **(b)** *(mexicano)* of/from San Luis Potosí *(Mexico)*
2 *nm,f* **(a)** *(boliviano)* person from Potosí *(Bolivia)* **(b)** *(mexicano)* person from San Luis Potosí *(Mexico)*
potra *nf* **(a)** *(yegua joven)* filly **(b)** *Fam (suerte)* luck; **¡qué p.!** how lucky can you get!; **tener p.** to be lucky *o Br* jammy
potrada *nf* = herd of young horses
potranco, -a *nm,f* = horse under three years of age
potrero *nm Am* field, pasture
potro *nm* **(a)** *(caballo joven)* colt **(b)** *(en gimnasia)* vaulting horse **(c)** *(aparato de tortura)* rack
poyo *nm (banco)* stone bench
poza *nf (de río)* pool, deep section of small river
pozal *nm* **(a)** *(brocal)* rim **(b)** *(cubo)* bucket
pozo *nm* **(a)** *(de agua)* well; EXPR **ser un p. de sabiduría** to be a fountain of knowledge *o* wisdom; EXPR *Fam* **ser un p. sin fondo** to be a bottomless pit ▸▸ ***p. artesiano*** artesian well; ***p. de extracción*** extraction shaft; ***p. negro*** cesspool; ***p. de petróleo*** oil well; ***p. petrolífero*** oil well; ***p. de ventilación*** ventilation shaft **(b)** *(de mina)* shaft **(c)** *RP (en vereda, carretera)* pothole
pozole *nm CAm, Carib, Méx (guiso)* = stew made with maize kernels, pork or chicken and vegetables

PP *nm (abrev de* **Partido Popular***)* = Spanish political party to the right of the political spectrum
pp. *(abrev de* **páginas***)* pp
p.p. **(a)** *(abrev de* **por poder***)* pp **(b)** *(abrev de* **porte pagado***)* c/p
PPA *nm (abrev de* **Partido Peronista Auténtico***)* = Argentinian political party which follows the ideology of Perón
PPC *nm (abrev de* **Partido Popular Cristiano***)* = Peruvian political party
ppp *Infomát (abrev de* **puntos por pulgada***)* dpi
PPS *nm (abrev de* **Partido Popular Socialista***)* = Marxist-Leninist political party in Mexico
práctica *nf* **(a)** *(experiencia)* practice; **te hace falta más p.** you need more practice; **con la p. adquirirás más soltura** you'll become more fluent with practice; **esto es algo que se aprende con la p.** it comes with practice
(b) *(ejercicio)* practice; *(de un deporte)* playing; **se dedica a la p. de la medicina** she practices medicine; **me han recomendado la p. de la natación** I've been advised to go swimming
(c) *(aplicación)* practice; **llevar algo a la p., poner algo en p.** to put sth into practice; **en la p.** in practice
(d) *(clase no teórica)* practical; **prácticas de laboratorio** lab sessions
(e) prácticas *(laborales)* training; **contrato en prácticas** work-experience contract
(f) *(costumbre)* practice; **ser p. establecida** to be standard practice
practicable *adj* **(a)** *(realizable)* practicable **(b)** *(transitable)* passable
prácticamente *adv (casi)* practically; **es p. imposible que lo consiga** there's practically *o* almost no chance of him doing it; **¿estás lista ya? – p.** are you ready yet? – almost *o* nearly
practicante 1 *adj* practising; **un católico no p.** a non-practising *o* lapsed Catholic
2 *nmf* **(a)** *(de deporte)* practitioner; *(de religión)* = practising member of a Church **(b)** *Med* = medical assistant who specializes in giving injections, checking blood etc **(c)** *RP (profesor)* student teacher
practicar [60] **1** *vt* **(a)** *(ejercitar)* to practise; *(deporte)* to play; **practica natación tres veces a la semana** she goes swimming three times a week; **es creyente pero no practica su religión** he's a believer, but he doesn't practise his religion; **estos viajes me vienen muy bien para p. el idioma** these trips are good for practising my language skills
(b) *(realizar)* to carry out, to perform; **le practicaron una operación de corazón** she had heart surgery; **le practicaron la autopsia** they carried out *o* performed an autopsy on him; **tuvieron que p. un hueco en la pared para poder salir** they had to make a hole in the wall to get out
(c) *(profesión)* to practise; **practica la abogacía desde hace diez años** she has been practising law for ten years
2 *vi* to practise; **es católico pero no practica** he's a Catholic, but not a practising one
practicidad *nf CSur* **me fascina la p. de esta herramienta** I'm fascinated by how useful *o* handy this tool is; **las deportistas adoptan este corte de pelo por su p.** sportswomen favour this hairstyle because it is very practical
práctico[1], -a *adj* **(a)** *(objeto, situación)* practical; *(útil)* handy, useful; **un regalo p.** a practical gift; **es muy p. vivir cerca del centro** it's very handy *o* convenient living near the centre
(b) *(curso, conocimientos)* practical; **un curso p. de fotografía** a practical photography course; **estudiaremos varios casos prácticos** we will study a number of practical examples
(c) *(persona) (pragmático)* practical; **es una persona muy práctica** she's a very practical *o* pragmatic person
(d) *RP (persona) (experimentado)* **estar p.** to be experienced, to have experience
práctico[2] *nm Náut* pilot
pradera *nf* area of grassland; *(en Norteamérica)* prairie ▸▸ *RP* ***p. artificial*** = area of grassland grown especially for grazing cattle; *RP* ***p. natural*** area of natural grassland
prado *nm* **(a)** *(para el ganado)* meadow **(b)** *Col (césped)* lawn, grass
Praga *n* Prague
pragmática *nf* **(a)** *Hist (edicto)* royal edict **(b)** *Ling* pragmatics *(singular)*
pragmático, -a 1 *adj* pragmatic
2 *nm,f* pragmatist
pragmatismo *nm* pragmatism
praguense 1 *adj* of/from Prague
2 *nmf* person from Prague
pral. *(abrev de* **principal***) Br* first floor, *US* second floor

praliné *nm* praline

prángana *Cuba, Méx Fam* **1** *adj* poor; **estoy bien p.** I'm completely broke
2 *nmf* miserable wretch; **ese novio tuyo es un p.** that boyfriend of yours is a dead loss
3 *nf* abject poverty; **viven en la p.** they live in abject poverty

praseodimio *nm Quím* praseodymium

praxis *nf inv* **(a)** *Formal (práctica)* praxis, practice **(b)** *(en teoría marxista)* praxis

PRD *nm* **(a)** *(abrev de* **Partido Revolucionario Democrático**) = Mexican political party **(b)** *(abrev de* **Partido Revolucionario Democrático**) = Panamanian political party **(c)** *(abrev de* **Partido Revolucionario Dominicano**) = political party in Dominican Republic

PRE *nm (abrev de* **Partido Rodolsista Ecuatoriano**) = Ecuadoran political party

pre- *pref* pre-

preacuerdo *nm* draft agreement; **llegar a un p.** to come to a preliminary agreement

prealerta *nf* = state of readiness in anticipation of natural disaster such as flooding, storms etc

preámbulo *nm* **(a)** *(introducción) (de libro)* foreword, preface; *(de congreso, conferencia)* introduction; **la recepción sirvió de lujoso p. a la cumbre** the reception provided a luxurious introduction to the summit **(b)** *(rodeo)* **sin más preámbulos...** without further ado...; **casi sin preámbulos me empezó a relatar su viaje** he more or less went straight into telling me about his trip

preaviso *nm* prior notice; **hay que dar un mes de p.** you have to give a month's notice

prebenda *nf* **(a)** *Rel* prebend **(b)** *(privilegio)* privilege; **denunciaron que los familiares del presidente disfrutan de prebendas** they condemned the fact that the president's relatives enjoy special privileges; **las prebendas de ser director** the perks of being a manager

preboste *nm* provost

precalentado, -a *adj* preheated

precalentamiento *nm Dep* warm-up

precalentar [3] *vt* **(a)** *(plato, horno)* to preheat **(b)** *Dep* to warm up

precámbrico, -a *Geol* **1** *adj* Precambrian
2 *nm* **el p.** the Precambrian

precampaña *nf Pol* run-up to the election campaign

precandidato, -a *nm,f Am* = person in the running to become a party's candidate for an election

precariedad *nf* precariousness; **viven en una situación de p. económica** they are living in a precarious financial situation; **la p. en el empleo** job insecurity

precario, -a *adj (salud, acuerdo)* precarious; **un empleo p.** a temporary job with poor pay and conditions; **la situación de su familia es muy precaria** her family's situation is very precarious; **inmigrantes que viven en condiciones precarias** immigrants living in poor conditions

precarización *nf* **la p. del empleo** the casualization of labour, the rise in temporary jobs with poor pay and conditions

precaución *nf* **(a)** *(prudencia)* caution, care; *Esp* **conduce** *o Am* **maneja con p.** drive carefully; **por p.** as a precaution; **tuvo la p. de desenchufar el aparato** he took the precaution of unplugging the appliance **(b)** *(medida)* precaution; **tomar precauciones** to take precautions

precautorio, -a *adj Méx* precautionary; **se decidió el desalojo p. de las comunidades vecinas** it was decided to evacuate the people who lived in the area as a precautionary measure

precaver 1 *vt* to guard against
2 precaverse *vpr* to take precautions; **precaverse de** *o* **contra** to guard (oneself) against

precavidamente *adv* cautiously

precavido, -a *adj* **(a)** *(prevenido)* prudent; **es muy p.** he always comes prepared **(b)** *(cauteloso)* wary

precedencia *nf (de tiempo, orden, lugar)* precedence, priority

precedente 1 *adj* previous, preceding; **en años precedentes** in previous years
2 *nm* precedent; **sentar (un) p.** to set a precedent; **que no sirva de p.** this is not to become a regular occurrence; **sin precedentes** unprecedented

preceder *vt* to go before, to precede

preceptista 1 *adj* preceptive
2 *nmf* follower of literary precepts

preceptiva *nf* rules

preceptivo, -a *adj* obligatory, compulsory

precepto *nm* precept

preceptor, -ora *nm,f* (private) tutor

preceptuar *vt Formal* to stipulate

preces *nfpl Formal* prayers

preciado, -a *adj* valuable, prized; **un metal muy p.** a highly-prized metal; **un bien muy p.** a highly-valued possession

preciarse *vpr* **cualquier aficionado que se precie sabe que...** any self-respecting fan knows that...; **cualquier película policiaca que se precie debe contener una persecución** any police movie worth its salt has a chase in it; **p. de** to pride oneself on; **se precia de haber descubierto al actor** he prides himself on having discovered the actor

precintado *nm* **(a)** *(de caja, paquete)* sealing **(b)** *(de bar, lugar)* sealing off

precintadora *nf* sealing machine

precintar *vt* **(a)** *(caja, paquete)* to seal **(b)** *(bar, lugar)* to seal off

precinto *nm* **(a)** *(en sello, envoltorio)* seal ►► ***p. de garantía*** protective seal **(b)** *(de caja, paquete)* sealing **(c)** *(de bar, lugar)* sealing off; **el juez ordenó el p. de la sala** the judge ordered the room to be sealed off

> **Falso amigo**: El sustantivo inglés **precinct** no es la traducción del español **precinto**. En inglés **precint** significa "zona comercial", "distrito" o "comisaría".

precio *nm* **(a)** *(en dinero)* price; **¿qué p. tiene esta corbata?** how much is this tie?; **subir los precios** to put prices up; **bajar los precios** to bring prices down; **ha subido el p. de la vivienda** house prices have gone up; **está muy bien de p.** it's very reasonably priced; **un p. prohibitivo** a prohibitively high price; EXPR *Andes Fam* **a p. de huevo** for next to nothing; EXPR **a p. de oro: la merluza está a p. de oro** hake has become ridiculously expensive; EXPR *RP* **hacer p. a alguien** to give sb a discount; **poner p. a** to put a price on; EXPR **poner p. a la cabeza de alguien** to put a price on sb's head; EXPR **no tener p.** to be priceless ►► *Bolsa* ***p. de apertura*** opening price; ***p. de catálogo*** list price; *Bolsa* ***p. de cierre*** closing price; ***p. de compra*** purchase price; *Bolsa* ***p. comprador*** bid price; ***p. al contado*** cash price; *Esp* ***p. de coste*** cost price; ***p. de costo*** cost price; **comprar algo a p. de costo** to buy sth at cost price; *Bolsa* ***p. de cotización*** quoted price; *Fin* ***el p. del dinero*** the cost of borrowing; *Bolsa* ***p. de ejercicio*** striking price; ***p. de fábrica*** factory price; ***p. indicativo*** guide price; ***p. de lanzamiento*** launch price; ***p. de lista*** list price; ***p. al por mayor*** trade price; ***p. de mercado*** market price; *Bolsa* ***p. nominal*** nominal price; *Bolsa* ***p. de oferta*** offer price; ***p. de saldo*** bargain price; ***p. de salida*** starting price; ***p. de salida a Bolsa*** issue price; ***p. simbólico*** nominal *o* token amount; ***p. tope*** top *o* ceiling price; ***p. por unidad*** unit price; ***p. unitario*** unit price; ***p. de venta (al público)*** retail price
(b) *(sacrificio)* price; **es el p. de la fama** it's the price of fame; **pagaron un p. muy alto por la victoria** they paid a very high price for victory, victory cost them dearly; **a cualquier p.** at any price; **al p. de** at the cost of

preciosidad *nf* **(a)** *(cosa, persona)* **ies una p.!** it's lovely *o* beautiful!; **su hija es una verdadera p.** their daughter is absolutely lovely *o* beautiful **(b)** *(como apelativo)* gorgeous

preciosismo *nm* preciousness

preciosista 1 *adj* affected
2 *nmf* affected writer

precioso, -a *adj* **(a)** *(bonito)* lovely, beautiful **(b)** *(valioso)* precious; **la salud es un bien p.** one's health is a precious thing

preciosura *nf Am* **(a)** *(cosa, persona)* **ies una p.!** it's lovely *o* beautiful!; **su hija es una verdadera p.** their daughter is absolutely lovely *o* beautiful **(b)** *(como apelativo)* gorgeous

precipicio *nm* **(a)** *(de montaña)* precipice **(b)** *(abismo)* **la compañía está al borde del p.** the company is on the verge of ruin *o* collapse

precipitación 1 *nf* **(a)** *(apresuramiento)* haste; **actuaron con p.** they acted hastily **(b)** *Quím* precipitation
2 precipitaciones *nfpl (lluvia)* rain, *Espec* precipitation; **precipitaciones en forma de nieve** snow; **intervalos nubosos con precipitaciones ocasionales** scattered cloud with occasional showers

precipitadamente *adv* hastily; **abandonó p. el lugar** he left hastily

precipitado, -a 1 *adj* hasty; **no seas p., reflexiona un poco** don't be too hasty, think it over a little
2 *nm Quím* precipitate

precipitar 1 *vt* (**a**) *(arrojar)* to throw *o* hurl down (**b**) *(acelerar)* to hasten, to speed up; **su dimisión precipitó las elecciones** his resignation hastened *o* precipitated the elections; **no precipitemos los acontecimientos** let's not rush things, let's not jump the gun; **la muerte de su mujer precipitó su vuelta** his wife's death caused him to return early (**c**) *Quím* to precipitate
2 *vi Quím* to precipitate
3 **precipitarse** *vpr* (**a**) *(caer)* to plunge (down); **se precipitó al vacío desde lo alto del edificio** he threw himself from the top of the building
(**b**) *(acelerarse)* **se precipitaron los acontecimientos** things happened very quickly
(**c**) *(apresurarse)* to rush (**hacia** towards); **el público se precipitó hacia las salidas de emergencia** the audience rushed towards the emergency exits
(**d**) *(obrar irreflexivamente)* to act rashly; **te precipitaste al anunciar los resultados antes de tiempo** you were rash to announce the results prematurely; **no nos precipitemos** let's not rush into anything, let's not be hasty

precisamente *adv* (**a**) *(con precisión)* precisely (**b**) *(justamente)* **¡p.!** exactly!, precisely!; **p. por eso** for that very reason; **p. tú lo sugeriste** in fact it was you who suggested it; **p. te andaba buscando** I was just looking for you; **p. esta mañana hemos discutido el asunto** just this morning we were talking about it; **no es que sea p. un genio** he's not exactly a genius

precisar 1 *vt* (**a**) *(determinar)* to fix, to set; *(aclarar)* to specify exactly; **el lugar está sin p.** the location has not yet been fixed *o* specified; **no puedo p. cuándo** I can't say exactly when (**b**) *(necesitar)* to need, to require; **se precisa una gran habilidad** much skill is needed *o* required; **empresa informática precisa ingeniero** *(en anuncio)* engineer required by computer firm
2 *vi* **p. de** to need; **el equipo precisa de su actuación** the team needs him to play

precisión *nf* accuracy, precision; **con p.** accurately, precisely; **instrumento de p.** precision instrument

preciso, -a *adj* (**a**) *(exacto)* precise; **nos dio instrucciones precisas** she gave us precise instructions; **llegaste en el momento p. en el que me marchaba** you arrived exactly as I was leaving; **en este p. instante no puedo atender la llamada** I can't take the call right now; **el accidente ocurrió en este p. lugar** the accident happened right here *o* on this very spot
(**b**) *(necesario)* **carecen de los medios precisos** they lack the necessary means; **ser p. (para algo/hacer algo)** to be necessary (for sth/to do sth); **fue p. llamar a los bomberos** the fire brigade had to be called; **es p. que vengas** you must come; **no es p. que madrugues** there's no need for you to get up early; **será p. que obtengan un permiso** it will be necessary for them to get a permit; **cuando sea p.** when necessary; **si es p., llámame** call me if necessary; **si es p., contrataremos a un consultor** if necessary, we will hire a consultant
(**c**) *(conciso)* exact, precise; **utiliza un lenguaje muy p.** he uses very precise language

preclaro, -a *adj Formal* illustrious, eminent

precocidad *nf* precociousness

precocinado, -a 1 *adj* pre-cooked
2 *nm* precooked dish

precolombino, -a *adj* pre-Columbian

preconcebido, -a *adj (idea)* preconceived; *(plan)* drawn up in advance

preconcebir [47] *vt* to draw up in advance

preconizar [14] *vt* to recommend, to advocate

precontrato *nm* pre-contract; **firmar un p.** to sign a pre-contract

precordillera *nf Andes* foothills of the Andes

precoz *adj* (**a**) *(persona)* precocious (**b**) *(lluvias, frutos)* early (**c**) *(diagnóstico)* early

precursor, -ora 1 *adj* precursory; **un movimiento p. del impresionismo** a movement which anticipated the Impressionists
2 *nm,f* precursor

predador, -ora 1 *adj* predatory
2 *nm* predator

predatorio, -a *adj (animal, instinto)* predatory

predecesor, -ora *nm,f* predecessor

predecibilidad *nf* predictability

predecible *adj* predictable

predecir [51] *vt* to predict

predestinación *nf* predestination

predestinado, -a *adj* predestined, destined (**a** to); **un artista p. a la fama** an artist predestined *o* destined to become famous

predestinar *vt* to predestine

predeterminación *nf* predetermination

predeterminado, -a *adj* predetermined

predeterminar *vt* to predetermine

predial *adj Am* property; **impuesto p.** property tax

prédica *nf* sermon; **su p. en defensa de los derechos del hombre** her harangue in defence of human rights

predicado *nm Gram* predicate

predicador, -ora *nm,f* preacher

predicamento *nm (estima)* esteem, regard; **un escritor que goza de mucho p. entre los jóvenes** a writer held in high regard *o* great esteem by young people, a writer regarded very highly by young people

> **Falso amigo**: El sustantivo inglés **predicament** no es la traducción del español **predicamento**. En inglés **predicament** significa "aprieto, apuro" o "dilema, conflicto".

predicar [60] 1 *vt* to preach
2 *vi* to preach; EXPR **p. con el ejemplo** to practice what one preaches, to set a good example; EXPR **es como p. en el desierto** it's like talking to a brick wall

predicativo, -a *Gram* 1 *adj* predicative
2 *nm* complement

predicción *nf* prediction, forecast ►► ***p. meteorológica*** weather forecast; ***p. del tiempo*** weather forecast

predice *ver* **predecir**

predicho, -a *participio ver* **predecir**

predigo *ver* **predecir**

predijera *etc ver* **predecir**

predilección *nf* particular preference (**por** for); **siento p. por la ópera** I'm particularly fond of opera; **es un poeta de mi p.** he's one of my favourite poets

predilecto, -a *adj* favourite

predio *nm* (**a**) *Der (terreno)* estate, property (**b**) *Am (edificio)* building

predisponer [50] *vt* (**a**) to predispose (**a** to); **p. a alguien en contra de/a favor de algo** to prejudice sb against/in favour of sth (**b**) *Med* to predispose

predisposición *nf* (**a**) *(aptitud)* **p. para** aptitude for; **no tiene p. para el tenis** he has no aptitude for tennis (**b**) *(tendencia)* **p. a** predisposition to; **tiene una gran p. a enfermar** he's very prone to getting sick, he's very susceptible to illness

predispuesto, -a 1 *participio ver* **predisponer**
2 *adj* predisposed (**a** to); **están predispuestos en contra mía** they're biased against me

predominancia *nf* predominance

predominante *adj (que prevalece) (color, emoción)* predominant; *(viento, actitudes)* prevailing

predominantemente *adv* predominantly

predominar *vi* to predominate, to prevail (**sobre** over); **una clase en la que predominan las mujeres** a class made up predominantly of women; **el pesimismo predomina entre los inversores** the mood among investors is predominantly one of pessimism; **en su cuadro predominan los elementos abstractos** his painting is dominated by abstract elements; **una reunión en la que predominó la unidad** a meeting at which unity prevailed; **una región en la que predomina el cereal** a region in which cereals are the main crop

predominio *nm* predominance; **p. de algo sobre algo** predominance of sth over sth; **había un p. de gente joven entre el público** the audience was made up predominantly of young people

preelectoral *adj* pre-election; **el periodo p.** the pre-election period, the run-up to the elections

preeminencia *nf* preeminence

preeminente *adj* preeminent

preescolar 1 *adj* preschool, nursery; **educación** *o* **enseñanza p.** nursery *o* preschool education
2 *nm* nursery school, kindergarten

preestablecido, -a *adj* pre-established

preestreno *nm* preview

preexistencia *nf* pre-existence

preexistente *adj* pre-existing

preexistir *vi* to pre-exist

prefabricado, -a *adj* prefabricated

prefabricar [60] *vt* to prefabricate

prefacio *nm* preface

prefecto *nm* (**a**) *Rel* prefect (**b**) *(en Perú)* civil governor (**c**) *(en Francia)* prefect

prefectura *nf* (**a**) *Rel* prefecture (**b**) *(en Perú)* civil governor's office (**c**) *RP (naval)* naval command (**d**) *(en Francia)* prefecture

preferencia *nf* (**a**) *(prioridad)* preference; **tener p.** *(vehículo)* to have right of way; **tienen p. los vehículos que vienen por la derecha** vehicles coming from the right have right of way *o* priority; **a la hora de pedir vacaciones tienen p. los más veteranos** when it comes to requesting holiday leave, the older members of staff have first choice; **dan p. a los jubilados** they give priority to the retired
(**b**) *(predilección)* preference; **es conocida su p. por la playa antes que la montaña** it is well known that he prefers the seaside to the mountains; **con** *o* **de p.** preferably; **tener p. por** to have a preference for
(**c**) *(en teatro, estadio)* **asientos de p.** = seats with the best view

preferencial *adj* preferential

preferente *adj* (**a**) *(prioritario)* preferential; **las personas mayores reciben un trato p.** older people receive preferential treatment (**b**) *(en transporte)* **clase p.** club class

preferentemente *adv* preferably

preferible *adj* preferable (**a** to); **es p. madrugar** it's better to get up early; **es p. que no vengas** it would be better if you didn't come; **un viaje en tren es p. a uno en autobús** travelling by train is preferable to travelling by bus; **lo p. sería que llamaras primero** it would be best if you could call first

preferiblemente *adv* ideally

preferido, -a 1 *adj* favourite
2 *nm,f* favourite; **es el p. de su madre** he's his mother's favourite

preferir [63] *vt* to prefer; **¿qué prefieres, vino o cerveza?** what would you prefer, wine or beer?; **lo prefiero con un poco de sal** I prefer it slightly salted; **prefiere no salir** she'd prefer not to go out, she'd rather not go out; **prefirió quedarse en casa** he preferred to stay at home; **p. algo a algo** to prefer sth to sth; **prefiero el pescado a la carne** I prefer fish to meat; **prefiero que me digan las cosas a la cara** I prefer people to say things to my face, I'd rather people said things to my face

prefigurar *vt* to prefigure

prefijar *vt* to fix in advance

prefijo *nm* (**a**) *Gram* prefix (**b**) *(telefónico) Br* dialling code, *US* area code

prefiriera *etc ver* **preferir**

preformateado, -a *adj Informát* pre-formatted

pregón *nm* (**a**) *(bando)* proclamation, announcement (**b**) *(en fiestas)* opening speech

pregonar *vt* (**a**) *(bando)* to proclaim, to announce (**b**) *(secreto)* to spread about; **no vayas por ahí pregonando la noticia** don't go spreading the news around (**c**) *(cualidades, virtudes)* to praise, to extol

pregonero, -a *nm,f* (**a**) *(de pueblo)* town crier (**b**) *(de fiestas)* = person who makes a "pregón" (**c**) *(bocazas)* blabbermouth

pregrabado, -a *adj* prerecorded

pregunta *nf* question; **hacer una p.** to ask a question; **¿te importa si te hago una p.?** do you mind if I ask you a question?; **¿te gustaría venir a la fiesta? – ¡qué p.!** would you like to come to the party? – what a question!; EXPR *Fam* **andar a la cuarta** *o* **última p.** to be broke; EXPR *Fam* **freír a preguntas a alguien** to bombard sb with questions ►► ***p. capciosa*** trick question; *Fam Hum* ***la p. del millón (de dólares)*** the sixty-four-thousand dollar question; ***p. retórica*** rhetorical question

preguntadera *nf Andes* barrage of questions

preguntar 1 *vt* to ask; **p. algo a alguien** to ask sb sth; **a mí no me lo preguntes** don't ask me; **si no es mucho p., ¿cuántos años tiene?** if you don't mind my asking, how old are you?; **esas cosas no se preguntan** you just don't ask questions like that
2 *vi* to ask; **a mí no me preguntes** don't ask me; **preguntan por ti** they're asking for you; **entre en la oficina y pregunte por Carolina** go into the office and ask for Carolina; **pregunté por sus padres** I asked after his parents; **eso es p. por p.** that's just asking for the sake of asking
3 **preguntarse** *vpr* to wonder; **me pregunto si habré hecho bien** I wonder if I've done the right thing

preguntón, -ona *Fam* 1 *adj* nosey
2 *nm,f* nosey person, *Br* nosey parker

prehistoria *nf* prehistory

prehistórico, -a *adj* (**a**) *(de la prehistoria)* prehistoric (**b**) *Fam (anticuado)* prehistoric

preimpresión *nf Imprenta* pre-press

preindustrial *adj* preindustrial

preinscripción *nf* pre-enrolment, pre-registration

prejubilación *nf* early retirement

prejuiciado, -a = **prejuicioso**

prejuicio *nm* prejudice; **están cargados de** *o* **tienen muchos prejuicios** they're very prejudiced; **tiene muchos prejuicios contra los inmigrantes** she has a lot of prejudices about immigrants ►► ***p. racial*** racial prejudice

prejuicioso, -a, prejuiciado, -a *Am* 1 *adj* prejudiced
2 *nm,f* **es un p.** he has a lot of prejudices

prejuzgar [38] 1 *vt* to prejudge
2 *vi* to prejudge

prelación *nf* priority, precedence; **tener p. sobre** to take precedence over, to have priority over

prelado *nm Rel* prelate

prelavado *nm* pre-wash

preliminar 1 *adj* preliminary; **quedó el primero en la ronda p.** he came first in the preliminary round
2 *nm* preliminary

preludiar *vt* **un fuerte viento preludiaba el invierno** a strong wind signalled the beginning *o* onset of winter, a strong wind heralded the coming of winter; **aquella discusión no preludiaba nada bueno** that argument did not bode well

preludio *nm* (**a**) *(anuncio)* prelude; **las lluvias eran el p. de la primavera** the rains signalled the beginning *o* onset of spring, the rains heralded the coming of spring (**b**) *Mús* prelude

premamá *adj inv (ropa)* maternity; **vestido p.** maternity dress

prematrimonial *adj* premarital; **relaciones prematrimoniales** premarital sex

prematuramente *adv* prematurely

prematuro, -a 1 *adj* (**a**) *(muerte, nacimiento)* premature (**b**) *(bebé)* premature (**c**) *(decisión)* premature; **todavía es p. realizar un anuncio oficial** it is still too early to make an official announcement
2 *nm,f* premature baby

premeditación *nf* premeditation; **actuó con p.** he acted with premeditation, it was a premeditated act; *Der* **con p. y alevosía** with malice aforethought; *Fam* **intentó hundir sus planes con p. y alevosía** he deliberately tried to ruin her plans

premeditadamente *adv* deliberately, with premeditation

premeditado, -a *adj* premeditated

premeditar *vt* to plan; **p. un crimen** to premeditate a crime

premenstrual *adj* premenstrual

premiación *nf Am (en escuela, club)* prizegiving; *(de cine, música)* awards ceremony

premiado, -a 1 *adj* (**a**) *(número)* winning (**b**) *(película, escritor)* prize-winning
2 *nm,f* winner, prizewinner

premiar *vt* (**a**) *(recompensar)* to reward; **premian la fidelidad con vales de descuento** they reward loyalty with discount vouchers; **la decisión premia la calidad sobre la originalidad** the decision places quality above originality
(**b**) *(dar un premio a)* to give a prize to; **fue premiado con un viaje al Caribe** he won a trip to the Caribbean; **fue premiado con el Óscar al mejor actor** he won *o* he was awarded the Oscar for best actor

premier *nmf* prime minister, premier

premio *nm* (**a**) *(en competición, sorteo)* prize; **dar** *o* **conceder un p.** to award a prize; **obtener** *o* **ganar un p.** to win a prize; **le tocó un p.** he won a prize; **el p. al mejor actor** the prize for best actor; **un p. consistente en una vuelta al mundo** a prize of a trip round the world ►► ***p. a la combatividad*** *(en ciclismo)* most aggressive rider classification; ***p. de consolación***, *RP* ***p. consuelo*** consolation prize; ***p. en efectivo*** cash prize; ***p. gordo*** first prize; ***p. en metálico*** cash prize, prize money; ***p. de la montaña*** *(en ciclismo) (competición)* king of the mountains competition; *(lugar)* = checkpoint at which cyclists can accrue points towards the king of the mountains competition; ***P. Nobel*** Nobel Prize; ***p. de la regularidad*** *(en ciclismo)* points competition
(**b**) *(recompensa)* reward; **recibió la medalla como p. a su valor** he received the medal as a reward for his bravery

(c) *(ganador)* prize-winner ▸▸ ***p. Nobel*** Nobel Prize winner; **este año tampoco ha sido el p. Nobel** he didn't win the Nobel Prize this year either

premioso, -a *adj* (a) *(apretado)* tight, constricting (b) *(lenguaje, estilo)* laboured

premisa *nf* premise; **partes de una p. falsa** you are starting from a false premise

premolar 1 *adj* premolar
2 *nm* premolar

premonición *nf* premonition; **tuve la p. de que íbamos a ganar** I had a premonition that we were going to win

premonitorio, -a *adj* portentous

premunido, -a *adj Andes* armed (**de** with); **llegó p. de su pasaporte** he arrived armed with his passport

premunirse *vpr Andes* **p. de** *(armas)* to arm oneself with; *(valor, paciencia)* to summon up

premura *nf* (a) *(urgencia)* urgency, haste; **con p.** urgently (b) *(escasez)* lack, shortage; **dada la p. de tiempo...** given the lack of time...

prenatal *adj* prenatal, antenatal

prenda *nf* (a) *(vestido)* garment, article of clothing; **prendas de abrigo/verano** warm/summer clothing ▸▸ ***p. interior*** undergarment; ***p. íntima*** undergarment, piece of underwear
(b) *(señal, garantía)* pledge; **dejar algo en p.** to leave sth as a pledge; **le dio el anillo en p. de su amor** he gave her the ring as a token *o* pledge of his love; **el regalo era una p. de su amistad** the gift was a token of his friendship
(c) *(en juego)* forfeit; **jugar a las prendas** to play forfeits
(d) *(virtud)* talent, gift
(e) *Fam (apelativo cariñoso)* darling, treasure
(f) EXPR **no doler prendas: no me duelen prendas reconocer que estaba equivocado** I don't mind admitting I was wrong; *Fam* **no soltar p.** not to say a word

prendar 1 *vt* to enchant
2 **prendarse** *vpr* **prendarse de alguien** to fall in love with sb; **me quedé prendado de aquel coche** I fell in love with that car

prendedor *nm* brooch

prender 1 *vt* (a) *(arrestar)* to arrest, to apprehend
(b) *(sujetar)* to fasten; **prendió el clavel en la solapa con un alfiler** she attached the carnation to her lapel with a pin
(c) *(fuego)* to light; **prendieron fuego a los matorrales** they set fire to the bushes, they set the bushes on fire
(d) *(agarrar)* to grip; **prendió con fuerza el brazo de su madre** he gripped his mother's arm tightly
(e) *esp Am (luz, interruptor)* to switch on; *(motor)* to start (up); **prende la luz, que no veo** turn *o* switch the light on, I can't see; **prendió un cigarrillo** she lit a cigarette
2 *vi* (a) *(arder)* to catch fire; **esta leña no prende** this wood won't catch fire (b) *(planta)* to take root (c) *(opinión)* to spread; **es una idea que ha prendido entre el público** it's an idea that has caught on among the public
3 **prenderse** *vpr* (a) *(arder)* to catch fire (b) *Am (luz, interruptor)* to switch itself on

prendido, -a *adj* (a) *(sujeto)* caught (b) *(encantado)* enchanted, captivated; **quedar p. de** to be captivated by

prenombrado, -a *adj Arg, Chile* aforementioned, aforesaid

prensa *nf* (a) *(periódicos, periodistas)* press; **compro la p. todos los días** I buy the newspapers every day; EXPR **tener buena/mala p.** to have a good/bad press ▸▸ ***la p. amarilla*** the gutter press, the tabloids; ***la p. del corazón*** gossip magazines; ***la p. deportiva*** the sports press; ***la p. diaria*** the daily press; ***la p. escrita*** the press; ***la p. especializada*** specialist publications; ***la p. rosa*** gossip magazines
(b) **la p.** *(los periodistas)* the press
(c) *(imprenta)* printing press; **entrar en p.** to go to press
(d) *(máquina)* press ▸▸ ***p. hidráulica*** hydraulic press

prensado *nm* pressing

prensar *vt* to press

prensil *adj* prehensile

prenupcial *adj* premarital

preñada *nf* pregnant woman

preñado, -a *adj* (a) *(hembra)* pregnant; **preñada de tres meses** three months pregnant; *Fam* **ha dejado preñadas a tres mujeres** he's got three women pregnant; *Fam* **se ha vuelto a quedar preñada** *(mujer)* she's expecting again; *Fam* **se quedó preñada de su novio** her boyfriend got her pregnant (b) *Literario (lleno)* **p. de** full of; **música preñada de pasión** music bursting with passion

preñar *vt* (a) *(hembra)* to make pregnant; *Fam* **ha preñado a tres mujeres** he's got three women pregnant (b) *Literario (llenar)* **p. de** to fill with

preñez *nf* pregnancy

preocupación *nf* concern, worry; **mi mayor p. es no perder el empleo** my main concern is not to lose my job; **su p. por el dinero ha llegado a alturas absurdas** his preoccupation with money has reached absurd heights; **para él no existen las preocupaciones** he doesn't have a care in the world

preocupado, -a *adj* worried, concerned (**por** about); **nuestro hijo nos tiene muy preocupados** we're very worried *o* concerned about our son

preocupante *adj* worrying; **lo p. es que no haya llamado todavía** the worrying thing is that she still hasn't phoned

preocupar 1 *vt* (a) *(inquietar)* to worry; **me preocupa no saber nada de él** I'm worried I haven't heard from him; **me preocupa que no haya llamado** I'm worried that she hasn't called; **no me preocupa que lo sepan otros** it doesn't worry me that other people know about it
(b) *(importar)* to bother; **sólo le preocupa su apariencia externa** he's only bothered about his appearance
2 **preocuparse** *vpr* (a) *(inquietarse)* to worry (**por** about); **no te preocupes** don't worry; **no te preocupes por ella** don't worry about her; **se preocupa por cualquier cosa** he worries *o* gets worried about the slightest thing
(b) *(encargarse)* **preocuparse de algo** to take care of sth; **preocuparse de hacer algo** to see to it that sth is done; **preocuparse de que...** to make sure that...; **me preocuparé de que nunca les falte nada** I will make sure that they never lack for anything

preolímpico, -a *Dep* 1 *adj* **torneo p.** Olympic qualifying competition
2 *nm* Olympic qualifying competition

prepa = **preparatoria**

prepalatal *adj Ling* prepalatal

preparación *nf* (a) *(disposición, elaboración)* preparation; **dedicó sus vacaciones a la p. de los exámenes** he spent his holidays preparing for the exams; **tiene un nuevo disco en p.** she's working on a new record
(b) *(de atleta)* training ▸▸ ***p. física*** *(entrenamiento)* physical training; *(estado)* physical condition
(c) *(formación) (práctica)* training; *(teórica)* education; **tiene una buena p. en idiomas** he has good language skills
(d) *(para microscopio)* specimen

preparado, -a 1 *adj* (a) *(dispuesto)* ready (**para** for); *(de antemano)* prepared (**para** for); **ya está todo p. para la inauguración** everything is now ready for the opening; **les sirvió un plato que ya tenía p.** he served them a dish which he had prepared earlier; **no estaba p. para la vida de soltero** he wasn't prepared for life as a single person; **preparados, listos, ¡ya!** ready, steady, go!, on your marks, get set, go!
(b) *(capacitado)* qualified; **no estoy p. para hacer este trabajo** I'm not qualified to do *o* for this job; **varios candidatos muy preparados** several well-qualified candidates
(c) *(plato)* ready-cooked
2 *nm (medicamento)* preparation

preparador, -ora *nm,f Dep (entrenador)* coach ▸▸ ***p. físico*** trainer

PREPARAR 1 *vt* (a) *(disponer, elaborar)* to prepare; *(trampa)* to set, to lay; *(maletas)* to pack; **estaban preparando un robo** they were planning a robbery; **voy a p. la cena/el arroz** I'm going to get dinner ready/cook the rice; **nos preparó una cena estupenda** she made *o* cooked a delicious evening meal for us; **¿quién prepara la comida en tu casa?** who does the cooking in your household?; **le hemos preparado una sorpresa** we've got a surprise for you
(b) *(examen, oposiciones, prueba)* to prepare for
(c) *(entrenar, adiestrar) (físicamente)* to train; *(tácticamente)* to coach; *(alumnos)* to coach; *(animales)* to train; **no nos habían preparado para solucionar este tipo de problemas** we hadn't been taught to solve this type of problem
2 **prepararse** *vpr* (a) *(disponerse)* to prepare oneself, to get ready (**para** for); **¡prepárate!** *(disponte)* get ready!; **como no esté terminado para mañana, prepárate** it had better be ready by tomorrow, or else...; **se prepara para el examen** she's preparing for the exam; **prepararse para hacer algo** to prepare *o* get ready to do sth; **prepárate para oír una buena/mala noticia** are you ready for some good/bad news?; **prepárate para aburrirte como una ostra** get ready *o* prepare yourself to be bored to death
(b) *(entrenarse) (equipo, deportista)* to train; **prepararse para algo/para hacer algo** to train for sth/to do sth; **se prepara para las olimpiadas** she's in training for the Olympics; **se preparó a fondo**

para el campeonato she prepared thoroughly for the championships (**c**) *(fraguarse) (tormenta, nevada)* to be on its way; **se estaba preparando una verdadera tormenta política** a major political storm was brewing *o* on its way

---

preparativo, -a 1 *adj* preparatory, preliminary
2 preparativos *nmpl* preparations; **están ultimando los preparativos para la cumbre** they are finalizing preparations for the summit

preparatoria, *Fam* **prepa** *nf Méx* = three-year course of studies for students aged 14-17, *Br* ≃ Sixth Form studies, *US* ≃ Senior High School studies

preparatorio, -a 1 *adj* preparatory
2 preparatorios *nmpl Urug* = last two years of secondary school, devoted to preparing for university, *Br* ≃ sixth form, *US* ≃ senior high school

prepizza *nf RP* pizza base

prepo *RP Fam* **1 a prepo** *loc adv* **terminó estudiando a p.** she ended up being forced to study against her will
2 de prepo *loc adv* **entraron de p.** they barged in without asking

preponderancia *nf* preponderance; **tener p. (sobre)** to predominate (over)

preponderante *adj (opinión, comportamiento)* prevailing; **desempeñó un papel p. en las negociaciones** he played a major role in the negotiations

preponderar *vi* to prevail; **preponderaba el optimismo** a mood of optimism prevailed

preposición *nf* preposition

preposicional *adj* prepositional

prepositivo, -a *adj Ling* prepositive

prepósito *nm Rel* ***p. general*** superior general

prepotencia *nf* (**a**) *(arrogancia)* arrogance; **nos hablaba con mucha p.** he spoke to us very arrogantly *o* overbearingly (**b**) *(poder)* dominance, power

prepotente *adj* (**a**) *(arrogante)* domineering, overbearing (**b**) *(poderoso)* very powerful

prepucio *nm* foreskin

prerrafaelista *nmf Arte* Pre-Raphaelite

prerrequisito *nm* prerequisite

prerrogativa *nf* prerogative

prerrománico *nm* early medieval architecture *(of 5th to 11th centuries)*

presa *nf* (**a**) *(captura) (de cazador)* catch; *(de animal)* prey; **hacer p. en alguien** to seize *o* grip sb; **ser p. de la emoción** to be overcome with excitement; **el público huyó p. del pánico** the audience fled in panic; **es p. fácil de los estafadores** she's easy prey for swindlers; **cayó p. de un espejismo** she was taken in by an illusion
(**b**) *(dique)* dam ►► ***la p. de Assuan*** *o* ***Asuán*** the Aswan Dam
(**c**) *(de carne)* piece
(**d**) *ver también* **preso**

presagiar *vt* **esas nubes presagian tormenta** there's going to be a storm, by the look of those clouds; **su silencio no presagia nada bueno** his silence gives little grounds for optimism

presagio *nm* (**a**) *(premonición)* premonition; **tengo el p. de que alguien va a morir** I have a premonition that somebody is going to die (**b**) *(señal)* omen; **un buen/mal p.** a good/bad omen

presbicia *nf Br* longsightedness, *US* farsightedness

presbiterianismo *nm* Presbyterianism

presbiteriano, -a 1 *adj* Presbyterian
2 *nm,f* Presbyterian

presbiterio *nm* presbytery

presbítero *nm Rel* priest

presciencia *nf* prescience, foreknowledge

prescindencia *nf Am* omission; **con p. de** without

prescindir *vi* (**a**) **p. de** *(renunciar a)* to do without; **no puedo p. de su ayuda** I can't do without her help; **prescindió del coche durante una semana** she did without the car for a week; **prescindieron del entrenador** they got rid of the coach; **decidieron p. de sus servicios** they decided to dispense with her services
(**b**) **p. de** *(omitir)* **prescinde de detalles, por favor** please leave out *o* skip the details; **prescindiendo de este capítulo, el resto está muy bien** apart from this chapter, the rest is very good; **prescindiendo de la normativa...** ignoring the regulations...

prescribir 1 *vt* (**a**) *(sujeto: médico)* to prescribe (**b**) *(ordenar)* to prescribe; **la ley prescribe pena de prisión para ese tipo de delitos** the law prescribes *o* stipulates a prison sentence for this type of crime, this type of crime carries a prison sentence according to the law
2 *vi Der (plazo, deuda)* to expire, to lapse; **estos delitos no prescriben** there is no statute of limitations on these crimes

prescripción *nf* (**a**) *(orden)* prescription; **por p. facultativa** on medical advice, on doctor's orders; **un fármaco de p. facultativa** a prescription-only drug (**b**) *Der (de plazo, deuda)* expiry, lapsing

prescrito, -a *participio ver* **prescribir**

presea *nf Méx* trophy

preselección *nf* **tuvimos que hacer una p.** we had to draw up a short list; **no pasó de la fase de p.** he didn't get beyond the initial selection stage

preseleccionar *vt (candidatos)* to shortlist; **preseleccionaron a 40 jugadores para formar una plantilla de 25** an initial pool of 40 players was selected, from which the 25 making up the final squad would be chosen

presencia *nf* (**a**) *(en lugar)* presence; **en p. de** in the presence of; **estamos en p. de un hecho histórico** we are witnessing an historic event; **no hables así en p. de tu abuela** don't speak like that in front of your grandmother; **hacer acto de p.** to attend; **se echó en falta su p.** her presence was missed; **critican la p. de las bases americanas** they are critical of the presence of American bases; **sospechan de la p. de un virus en la red** they suspect the presence of a virus in the network
(**b**) *(aspecto)* presence; **buena p.** smart appearance; **mucha/poca p.** great/little presence
(**c**) ***p. de ánimo*** presence of mind

presencial *adj* **testigo p.** eyewitness

presenciar *vt (asistir)* to be present at; *(ser testigo de)* to witness; **50.000 personas presenciaron la final en directo** 50,000 people were present at *o* attended the final

presentable *adj* presentable

presentación *nf* (**a**) *(aspecto exterior)* presentation; **una p. muy cuidada** *(de libro, plato)* a very meticulous *o* careful presentation; *(de persona)* an impeccable appearance ►► *Informát* ***p. preliminar*** preview
(**b**) *(entrega) (de dimisión)* tendering; *(de tesis, pruebas, propuesta)* submission; *(de moción)* proposal; **mañana concluye el plazo de p. de candidaturas** tomorrow is the last day for submitting applications
(**c**) *(entre personas)* introduction; **ya me encargo yo de hacer las presentaciones** I'll see to making the introductions
(**d**) *(de producto, persona)* presentation; **la p. de un libro/disco** the launch of a book/record; **la p. del nuevo jugador tuvo lugar ayer** the new player was introduced to the press for the first time yesterday ►► ***p. en sociedad*** coming out, debut
(**e**) *(de programa)* **la p. del telediario corre a cargo de María Gala** the news is presented *o* read by María Gala

presentador, -ora *nm,f* presenter

PRESENTAR 1 *vt* (**a**) *(mostrar, entregar)* to present; *(dimisión)* to tender, to hand in; *(tesis)* to submit, to hand in; *(pruebas, propuesta)* to submit; *(recurso, denuncia)* to lodge; *(solicitud)* to make; *(moción)* to propose; **presente su pasaporte en la ventanilla** show your passport at the window; **p. cargos/una demanda contra alguien** to bring charges/an action against sb; **¡presenten armas!** *(en ejército)* present arms!; **es un trabajo muy bien presentado** it is a very well presented piece of work
(**b**) *(dar a conocer)* to introduce; **me presentó a sus amigos** she introduced me to her friends; **Juan, te presento a Carmen** Juan, this is Carmen; **me parece que no nos han presentado** I don't think we've been introduced; **permítame que le presente a nuestra directora** allow me to introduce you to our manager, I'd like you to meet our manager; **no se conocían, pero yo los presenté** they didn't know each other, but I introduced them (to each other)
(**c**) *(anunciar) (programa de radio o televisión)* to present; *(espectáculo)* to compere; **la mujer que presenta el telediario** the woman who reads the news on TV
(**d**) *(proponer) (obra)* to enter; **p. una novela a un premio literario** to enter a novel for a literary prize; **p. una película a concurso** to enter a film at a film festival; **p. a alguien para algo** to propose sb for sth, to put sb forward for sth; **el partido presentará a la señora Cruz para la alcaldía** the party is putting Mrs Cruz forward for the office of mayor, Mrs Cruz will be the party's candidate for the office of mayor
(**e**) *(exhibir por primera vez) (planes, presupuestos)* to present; *(película)* to premiere; *(libro, disco)* to launch; **el club presentó a su último fichaje ante la prensa** the club introduced its new signing to the press

(f) *(ofrecer) (disculpas, excusas)* to make; *(respetos)* to pay; **nos presentó (sus) disculpas** he made his excuses to us

(g) *(tener) (aspecto, características, novedades)* to have; **este fondo de inversión presenta grandes ventajas** this investment fund offers *o* has big advantages; **la playa presenta un aspecto deplorable** the beach is in a terrible state; **presenta difícil solución** it's going to be difficult to solve; **el paciente presentaba síntomas de deshidratación** the patient presented symptoms of dehydration

2 **presentarse** *vpr* (a) *(personarse)* to turn up, to appear; **se presentó borracho a la boda** he turned up drunk at the wedding; **se presentó en la fiesta sin haber sido invitada** she turned up at the party without having been invited; **mañana preséntate en el departamento de contabilidad** go to the accounts department tomorrow; **presentarse ante el juez** to appear before the judge; **tiene que presentarse en la comisaría cada quince días** he has to report to the police station once a fortnight; **presentarse a un examen** to sit an exam

(b) *(darse a conocer)* to introduce oneself; **se presentó como un amigo de la familia** he introduced himself as a friend of the family; **permítame que me presente** allow me to introduce myself

(c) *(para un cargo)* to stand, to run (**a** for); **presentarse a un concurso** to go in for a competition; **se presenta a alcalde** he's running for mayor; **presentarse de candidato a las elecciones** to run in the elections

(d) *(ofrecerse voluntario)* to offer oneself *o* one's services; **muchos se presentaron (voluntarios) para colaborar** several people volunteered

(e) *(surgir) (problema, situación)* to arise, to come up; *(ocasión, oportunidad, posibilidad)* to arise; **si se te presenta algún problema, llámame** if you have any problems, call me; **en cuanto se me presente la ocasión, me voy al extranjero** I'm going to go abroad as soon as I get the chance

(f) *(tener cierto aspecto) (el futuro, la situación)* to look; **el porvenir se presenta oscuro** the future looks bleak; **la noche se presenta fresquita** it's looking rather cool this evening

---

presente 1 *adj* (a) *(asistente, que está delante)* present; **yo estuve p. el día que hicieron la reunión** I was present on the day of the meeting; **siempre está p. en mí su recuerdo** her memory is always present in my mind; **aquí p.** here present; **hacer p. algo a alguien** to notify sb of sth; **tener p.** *(recordar)* to remember; *(tener en cuenta)* to bear in mind; **lo tenemos p. en nuestros ruegos** we remember him in our prayers; **ten p. que acaba de salir del hospital** bear in mind that she has just left hospital; **Carlos Muñoz – ¡p.!** *(al pasar lista)* Carlos Muñoz – present!; EXPR **mejorando lo p.: es muy guapa, mejorando lo p.** she's very pretty, though not as pretty as you; **todos los hombres son idiotas, mejorando lo p.** I think all men are stupid, present company excepted

(b) *(en curso)* current; **del p. mes** of this month; **en las presentes circunstancias es mejor no decir nada** in the present circumstances it is best to say nothing

2 *nmf (en un lugar)* **los/las (aquí) presentes** everyone present; **invitó a los presentes a acudir a la próxima reunión** he invited everyone present to attend the next meeting

3 *nm* (a) *(tiempo actual)* present; **hasta el p.** up to now (b) *Gram* present ►► ***p. histórico*** historical present; ***p. de indicativo*** present indicative; ***p. de subjuntivo*** present subjunctive (c) *(regalo)* gift, present (d) *(corriente)* **el p.** *(mes)* the current month; *(año)* the current year

4 *nf (escrito)* **por la p. le informo...** I hereby inform you...; **por la p. se le comunica su nombramiento como tesorero** I am writing to inform you that you have been appointed treasurer

presentimiento *nm* presentiment, feeling; **tengo el p. de que...** I have the feeling that...

presentir [63] *vt* **p. que algo va a pasar** to have a feeling that something is going to happen; **p. lo peor** to fear the worst

preservación *nf* preservation; **la p. de especies en peligro de extinción** the protection of endangered species

preservante *nm Am* preservative

preservar 1 *vt* (a) *(proteger)* to protect (b) *Am (conservar)* to conserve, to maintain

2 **preservarse** *vpr* **preservarse de** to protect oneself *o* shelter from

preservativo, -a 1 *adj* protective

2 *nm* (a) *(condón)* condom ►► ***p. femenino*** female condom (b) *Am (conservante)* preservative

presidencia *nf* (a) *(de nación)* presidency; **el candidato a la p.** the presidential candidate; **la p. de la Unión Europea** the EU presidency; **durante la p. de Ford** during Ford's presidency, while Ford was president; **ocupar la p. del gobierno** to be the head of government

(b) *(de asamblea, empresa, reunión)* chairmanship; **ocupa la p. del banco** he is chairman of the bank; **la p. tiene la palabra** the chair has the floor ►► ***p. de honor*** honorary presidency

(c) *Méx* ***p. municipal*** *(corporación)* town council; *(edificio)* town hall

presidenciable *nmf esp Am* potential presidential candidate

presidencial *adj* presidential

presidencialismo *nm* presidential system

presidencialista 1 *adj* presidential

2 *nmf* supporter of the presidential system

presidente, -a *nm,f* (a) *(de nación)* president; **p. (del Gobierno)** prime minister

(b) *(de asamblea, jurado)* chairman, *f* chairwoman; *(de empresa)* chairman, *f* chairwoman, *US* president ►► ***p. de honor*** honorary president *o* chairman; ***p. de mesa*** *(en elecciones) Br* chief scrutineer, *US* chief canvasser; *RP (en exámenes)* chairman, *f* chairwoman *(of the panel)*

(c) *(del parlamento)* speaker

(d) *(de tribunal)* presiding judge ►► ***p. del tribunal supremo*** chief justice

(e) *Méx* ***p. municipal*** *(alcalde)* mayor

presidiario, -a *nm,f* convict

presidio *nm* (a) *(cárcel)* prison (b) *(pena)* prison sentence

presidir *vt* (a) *(ser presidente de) (nación)* to be president of; *(jurado, tribunal)* to preside over; *(asamblea, reunión)* to chair

(b) *(predominar sobre)* to dominate; **una gran chimenea preside el salón** a large fireplace dominates the living room; **la bondad preside todos sus actos** kindness prevails in everything she does; **la tristeza presidió el funeral** a feeling of sadness reigned over the funeral

presienta *etc ver* **presentir**

presilla *nf* (a) *(lazo)* loop (b) *(en costura)* buttonhole stitching (c) *(para cinturón)* loop (d) *Cuba (para el pelo)* hairpin

presintiera *etc ver* **presentir**

presintonía *nf (de radio)* pre-set station selector

presión *nf* (a) *(fuerza)* pressure; **una olla a p.** a pressure cooker; **tiene cierre a p.** you press it shut; **bajo p.** under pressure; **hacer p.** to press ►► ***p. arterial*** blood pressure; ***p. atmosférica*** atmospheric pressure; ***p. barométrica*** barometric pressure; ***p. de los neumáticos*** tyre pressure; *Econ* ***p. fiscal*** tax burden; ***p. sanguínea*** blood pressure

(b) *(coacción, influencia)* pressure; **la p. de la calle obligó a dimitir al presidente** pressure from the public forced the president to resign; **hacer** *o* **ejercer p. sobre** to pressurize; **meter p. a alguien** to put pressure on sb; **aceptó bajo p.** he accepted under pressure

(c) *(en baloncesto)* press; *(en fútbol, rugby)* pressure

presionar 1 *vt* (a) *(apretar)* to press; **presione la tecla de retorno** press *o* hit the return key (b) *(coaccionar)* to pressurize, to put pressure on; **lo presionaron para que aceptara** they put pressure on him to accept (c) *(en baloncesto)* to press; *(en fútbol, rugby)* to put pressure on

2 *vi (en baloncesto)* to press; *(en fútbol, rugby)* to put on the pressure

preso, -a 1 *adj* imprisoned; **estuvo p. durante tres años** he was imprisoned for three years

2 *nm,f* prisoner ►► ***p. común*** ordinary criminal; ***p. de conciencia*** prisoner of conscience; ***p. político*** political prisoner; ***p. preventivo*** remand prisoner

pressing ['presin] *nf* **hacer p.** *(en fútbol)* to put on the pressure

prestación *nf* (a) *(de servicio) (acción)* provision; *(resultado)* service ►► ***prestaciones por desempleo*** unemployment benefit; ***p. social*** social security benefit, *US* welfare; ***p. social sustitutoria*** = community service done as alternative to military service (b) **prestaciones** *(de vehículo)* performance features

prestado, -a 1 *adj* on loan; **dar algo p.** to lend sth; **pedir/tomar algo p.** to borrow sth

2 **de prestado** *loc adv* **desde que se quedó sin trabajo, vive de p.** she's been living off other people since she lost her job

prestamiento *nm Méx* loan

prestamista *nmf* moneylender

préstamo *nm* (a) *(acción) (de prestar)* lending; *(de pedir prestado)* borrowing; **ese libro está en p.** that book is out on loan; **una biblioteca sin permiso de p.** a non-lending library ►► *Fin* ***p. y arriendo*** lend-lease (b) *(cantidad)* loan; **pedir un p.** to ask for a loan ►► ***p. bancario*** bank loan; ***p. hipotecario*** mortgage; ***p. a plazo fijo*** fixed-term loan (c) *Ling* loanword

prestancia *nf* excellence, distinction

prestanombres *nm inv Méx Fam* front man

prestar 1 *vt* (a) *(dejar) (dinero, cosa)* to lend; **¿me prestas mil pesos?** could you lend me a thousand pesos?; **¿me prestas tu pluma?** can I borrow your pen?

(b) *(dar) (ayuda)* to give, to offer; *(servicio)* to offer, to provide; **prestaron ayuda a los accidentados** they offered assistance to the accident victims; **p. atención** to pay attention

(c) *(declaración, juramento)* to make; **prestó juramento ante el rey** she took an oath before the king

(d) *(transmitir encanto)* to lend; **la decoración presta un aire de fiesta** the decorations lend a festive tone

2 **prestarse** *vpr* (a) *(ser apto)* **prestarse (para)** to be suitable (for), to lend itself (to); **el lugar se presta para descansar** this is a good place to rest; **una casa que no se presta para hacer muchas reformas** a house which is not suitable for making many alterations to

(b) **prestarse a** *(ofrecerse a)* to offer to; **se prestó a ayudarme enseguida** she immediately offered to help me

(c) **prestarse a** *(acceder a)* to consent to; **no sé cómo se ha prestado a participar en esa película** I don't know how he consented to take part in that film

(d) **prestarse a** *(dar motivo a)* to be open to; **sus palabras se prestan a varias interpretaciones** her words are open to various interpretations

prestatario, -a *nm,f* borrower

presteza *nf* promptness, speed; **con p.** promptly, swiftly

prestidigitación *nf* conjuring

prestidigitador, -ora *nm,f* conjuror

prestigiado = **prestigioso**

prestigiar *vt* **su nombre prestigia la institución** his name lends prestige to the institution; **hace mucho tiempo que no nos prestigia con su presencia** he hasn't honoured us with his presence for a long time

prestigio *nm* prestige; **una tienda de p.** a prestigious store; **un cirujano de p. internacional** a surgeon of international renown; **una voz que goza de mucho p. entre los intelectuales** a figure who enjoys great prestige among intellectuals

prestigioso, -a, *Chile, Méx* **prestigiado, -a** *adj* prestigious

presto, -a *adj* 1 (a) *(dispuesto)* ready (**a** to); **estaban prestos a ayudar con lo que fuera** they were ready to help in whatever way they could (b) *(rápido)* prompt; **acudió p. a ver lo que pasaba** he came quickly to see what was happening (c) *Mús* presto

2 *nm Mús* presto

3 *adv Mús* presto

presumible *adj* probable, likely; **era p. que ocurriera así** it was always likely that it would turn out like that; **como era p., se llevó el primer premio** as (was to be) expected, he won first prize

presumiblemente *adv* presumably

presumido, -a 1 *adj* (a) *(jactancioso)* **ser p.** to be a show-off (b) *(vanidoso)* vain

2 *nm,f* (a) *(jactancioso)* show-off (b) *(vanidoso)* **ser un p.** to be vain

> **Falso amigo**: El adjetivo inglés **presumed** no es la traducción del español **presumido**. La oración inglesa "he is **presumed** dead" podría traducirse como "se le da por muerto".

presumir 1 *vt (suponer)* to presume, to assume; **presumo que no tardarán en llegar** I presume *o* suppose they'll be here soon; **es de p. que ya se hayan enterado de la noticia** presumably they've already heard the news; **ese escándalo era de p.** that scandal was only to be expected

2 *vi* (a) *(jactarse)* to show off; **presume de rico** he makes a show of being rich; **presume de artista** he likes to think he's an artist, he fancies himself as an artist; **presume de guapa** she thinks she's pretty; **pocos pueden p. de haber ganado tantos premios como ella** few can boast of having won as many prizes as she has (b) *(ser vanidoso)* to be vain

presunción *nf* (a) *(suposición)* presumption (b) *(jactancia)* boastfulness (c) *(vanidad)* vanity (d) *Der* presumption; **p. de inocencia** presumption of innocence

presuntamente *adv (supuestamente)* presumably, supposedly; *(en delito)* allegedly

presunto, -a *adj (supuesto)* presumed, supposed; *(criminal)* alleged, suspected; **el p. autor del asesinato** the suspected perpetrator of the murder, the person alleged to have committed the murder

presuntuosidad *nf (vanidad)* conceit; *(pretensión)* pretentiousness

> **Falso amigo**: El sustantivo inglés **presumptuousess** no es la traducción del español **presuntuosidad**. En inglés **presumptuousness** significa "impertinencia".

presuntuoso, -a 1 *adj (vanidoso)* conceited; *(pretencioso)* pretentious

2 *nm,f* conceited person

> **Falso amigo**: El adjetivo inglés **presumptuous** no es la traducción del español **presuntuoso**. En inglés **presumptuous** significa "impertinente".

presuponer [50] *vt* to presuppose

presuposición *nf* assumption

presupuestal = **presupuestario**

presupuestar *vt* **esta partida no estaba presupuestada** this item wasn't budgeted for; **me presupuestaron la reparación en 100 euros** they gave me an estimate of 100 euros for the repair; **han presupuestado la construcción del museo en cien millones de euros** they have calculated that the museum will cost a hundred million euros to build

presupuestario, -a, *Am* **presupuestal** *adj* budgetary; **déficit p.** budget deficit

presupuesto, -a 1 *participio ver* **presuponer**

2 *nm* (a) *(dinero disponible)* budget ►► ***presupuestos (generales) del Estado*** state budget, national budget (b) *(cálculo de costes)* estimate, quote; **pedir (un) p.** to ask for an estimate; **me han dado un p. de dos millones** they've given me an estimate of two million (c) *(suposición)* assumption

presurización *nf* pressurization

presurizado, -a *adj* pressurized

presurizar [14] *vt* to pressurize

presuroso, -a *adj* in a hurry; **acudió p. en nuestro auxilio** he hurried to our assistance; **realizó una visita presurosa a la ciudad** she paid a flying visit to the city

prêt-à-porter [pretapor'te] 1 *adj (ropa, moda)* ready-to-wear, *Br* off-the-peg

2 *nm* ready-to-wear *o Br* off-the-peg clothing

pretecnología *nf* craftwork, handicrafts

pretemporada *nf* pre-season

pretenciosidad *nf* pretentiousness

pretencioso, -a 1 *adj* pretentious

2 *nm,f* pretentious person

pretender *vt* (a) *(intentar, aspirar a)* **sólo pretendo ayudarte** I just want to help you; **pretendo comprarme una casa** I'm hoping to buy a house; **pretende llegar a presidente** he aims to become president; **no sé qué pretende con esa actitud** I don't know what he hopes to achieve with that attitude; **¿pretendes que te crea?** do you expect me to believe you?; **¿qué pretendes decir?** what do you mean?; **¿no pretenderás que te deje el dinero?** you don't really expect me to lend you the money, do you?

(b) *(simular)* to pretend; **pretende estar estudiando** he pretends he's studying

(c) *(afirmar)* to claim

(d) *(cortejar)* to court

pretendidamente *adv* supposedly

pretendido, -a *adj* supposed; **la pretendida bajada de precios no se ha producido todavía** the supposed fall in prices has yet to materialize; **la obra describe con p. realismo la guerra** the work provides a supposedly realistic portrayal of the war

pretendiente, -a 1 *nm,f* (a) *(aspirante)* candidate (**a** for) (b) *(a un trono)* pretender (**a** to)

2 *nm (a noviazgo, matrimonio)* suitor

pretensión *nf* (a) *(intención)* aim, intention; **tener la p. de** to intend to

(b) *(aspiración)* aspiration; **no tiene grandes pretensiones económicas** she doesn't have great financial aspirations *o* ambitions; **una película con pretensiones artísticas** a film with artistic pretensions; **sin pretensiones** unpretentious

(c) *(supuesto derecho)* claim (**a** *o* **sobre** to)

(d) **pretensiones** *(exigencias)* demands

pretensor *nm Aut* **cinturón de seguridad con p.** inertia-reel seatbelt

pretérito, -a 1 *adj Literario* past; **en tiempos pretéritos** in times past

2 *nm Gram* preterite, past ►► ***p. anterior*** past anterior; ***p. imperfecto*** imperfect; ***p. indefinido*** simple past; ***p. perfecto*** (present) perfect; ***p. perfecto simple*** (present) perfect simple; ***p. pluscuamperfecto*** pluperfect, past perfect

pretextar *vt* to claim; **pretextó un dolor de cabeza para no acudir** he claimed he had a headache in order to avoid having to go; **pretextó no saber nada del acuerdo** he claimed to know nothing about the agreement

pretexto *nm* pretext, excuse; **que nadie entre en este cuarto bajo ningún p.** under no circumstances is anyone to enter this room; **con el p. de que...** on the pretext that...; *Formal* **so p. de...** on the pretext of...

pretil *nm* parapet

pretina *nf* waistband

Pretoria *n* Pretoria

preuniversitario, -a *adj* preuniversity

prevalecer [46] *vi* to prevail (**sobre** over); **al final prevaleció la cordura** common sense prevailed in the end

prevaleciente *adj* prevailing, prevalent

prevaler [70] **1** *vi* to prevail (**sobre** over)

2 prevalerse *vpr* **prevalerse de** to take advantage of; **se prevalió de su ingenuidad** he took advantage of her naivety

prevaricación *nf Der* perversion of the course of justice

prevaricar [60] *vi Der* to pervert the course of justice

> **Falso amigo**: El verbo inglés **to prevaricate** no es la traducción del español **prevaricar**. En inglés **to prevaricate** significa "dar rodeos, andar con evasivas".

prevención *nf* (**a**) *(acción)* prevention; *(medida)* precaution; **una campaña de p. del sida** an AIDS prevention campaign; **en p. de** as a precaution against ►► ***p. laboral*** health and safety (**b**) *(prejuicio)* prejudice; **probó la sopa no sin cierta p.** she tried the soup, albeit rather reluctantly; **tener p. contra alguien** to be prejudiced against sb

prevengo *etc ver* **prevenir**

prevenido, -a *adj* (**a**) *(previsor)* **ser p.** to be well-prepared; **es muy p., tiene todos los teléfonos de emergencia a mano** he's very well-organized, he has all the emergency numbers to hand (**b**) *(avisado)* **estar p.** to be in the know; **ahora ya estás p., ten mucho cuidado con lo que vas diciendo por ahí** you've been warned, so be careful what you say

prevenir [71] **1** *vt* (**a**) *(evitar)* to prevent; **para p. la gripe** to prevent flu; **un medicamento que previene contra la malaria** a medicine that protects against malaria; PROV **más vale p. que curar** prevention is better than cure

(**b**) *(avisar)* to warn; **te prevengo de que la carretera es muy mala** be warned that the road is very bad

(**c**) *(prever)* to foresee, to anticipate

(**d**) *(predisponer)* **p. a alguien contra algo/alguien** to prejudice sb against sth/sb

2 prevenirse *vpr (tomar precauciones)* to take precautions; **prevenirse contra algo** to take precautions against sth

preventiva *nf Méx Br* amber *o US* yellow light

preventivo, -a 1 *adj (medicina, prisión)* preventive; *(medida)* precautionary; **tomaron medidas preventivas contra el contagio** they took precautionary measures to prevent infection

2 *nm,f Méx (policía)* policeman, *f* policewoman

prever [72] **1** *vt* (**a**) *(predecir)* to forecast, to predict; **él había previsto el terremoto** he had forecast *o* predicted the earthquake

(**b**) *(planear)* to plan; **prevén vender un millón de unidades del nuevo modelo** they plan to sell a million units of the new model; **tenía previsto ir al cine esta tarde** I was planning to go to the cinema this evening; **tenía previsto llamarte en cuanto supiera la noticia** I was intending to phone you as soon as I heard the news

(**c**) *(anticipar)* to foresee, to anticipate; **era una reacción que los médicos no habían previsto** it was a reaction the doctors hadn't foreseen; **se prevé una fuerte oposición popular a la ley** strong popular opposition to the law is anticipated *o* expected; **no se prevén grandes atascos en las carreteras** no major holdups on the roads are anticipated; **todo hace p. que nevará este fin de semana** all the signs are that it will snow this weekend

2 *vi* **como era de p.** as was to be expected

previa *nf RP Univ* = module that has to be passed in order to do a more advanced module

previamente *adv* previously

previene *etc ver* **prevenir**

previera *etc ver* **prever**

previniera *etc ver* **prevenir**

previó *etc ver* **prever**

previo, -a 1 *adj* (**a**) *(anterior)* prior; **se requiere la autorización previa de los padres** parents' prior consent is required; **sin p. aviso** without prior warning

(**b**) *(condicionado a)* subject to; **p. acuerdo de las partes interesadas** subject to the agreement of the interested parties; **p. pago de multa** on payment of a fine; **las maletas se podrán retirar previa entrega del resguardo** luggage will be returned on presentation of your receipt

2 *nm Cine* prescoring, playback

previsible *adj* foreseeable; **era p. que acabara cayéndose** it was only to be expected that she would end up falling

previsiblemente *adv* **llegarán p. antes del anochecer** they'll probably arrive before it gets dark; **p. durará dos semanas** it's likely to last two weeks

previsión *nf* (**a**) *(predicción)* forecast ►► ***p. meteorológica*** weather forecast; ***p. del tiempo*** weather forecast; ***p. de ventas*** sales forecast (**b**) *(visión de futuro)* foresight; **esto no entraba en mis previsiones** I hadn't foreseen *o* predicted this (**c**) *(precaución)* **en p. de** as a precaution against (**d**) *Andes, RP* ***p. social*** social security

previsional *adj Andes, RP* **gastos previsionales** social security spending

previsor, -ora, *Am* **previsivo, -a** *adj* prudent, farsighted

previsto, -a 1 *participio ver* **prever**

2 *adj (conjeturado)* predicted; *(planeado)* forecast, expected, planned; **salió tal y como estaba p.** it turned out just as planned

prez *nm o nf Literario* honour, glory

PRI [pri] *nm (abrev de* **Partido Revolucionario Institucional***)* = Mexican political party, the governing party from 1929 to 2000

prieto, -a *adj* (**a**) *(ceñido)* tight; **los zapatos me quedan muy prietos** my shoes are very tight; **íbamos muy prietos en el coche** it was a real squash in the car (**b**) *Cuba, Méx (moreno)* dark-skinned (**c**) *Méx (oscuro)* dark

priísta *Méx Pol* **1** *adj* relating to the "PRI"

2 *nmf* member/supporter of the "PRI"

prima *nf* (**a**) *(paga extra)* bonus ►► *Col* ***p. legal*** = additional payment of a month's salary or wages at Christmas; *Dep* ***primas a terceros*** = legal practice in soccer where one team gives another team financial inducement to beat a third team (**b**) *(de seguro)* premium ►► *Fin* ***p. de emisión*** issue premium; ***p. de riesgo*** risk premium (**c**) *(subvención)* subsidy (**d**) *ver también* **primo**

primacía *nf* (**a**) *(superioridad)* **la derrota puso fin a la p. del equipo en la liga** the defeat knocked the team off the top of the league; **defienden la p. de la estética sobre la técnica** they believe aesthetic qualities to be more important than technique (**b**) *(prioridad)* **esta tarea tiene p. sobre las demás** this task takes priority over the others

primado *nm Rel* primate

primadona *nf* prima donna

primar 1 *vi* to have priority (**sobre** over); **el interés colectivo prima sobre el personal** collective interests have priority over personal ones

2 *vt* (**a**) *(dar una prima a)* to give a bonus to; **la tienda prima la fidelidad de los clientes con vales de descuento** the store rewards customer loyalty with discount vouchers (**b**) *(dar prioridad a)* **el tribunal prima más el conocimiento del tema que la expresión oral** the examiners place greater importance on knowledge of the subject than oral expression

primaria 1 *nf (enseñanza)* primary education

2 primarias *nfpl (elecciones)* primaries

primario, -a *adj* (**a**) *(básico, elemental)* primary (**b**) *(primitivo)* primitive (**c**) *(era, enseñanza)* primary (**d**) *(elecciones)* primary

primate *nm* primate

primavera *nf* (**a**) *(estación)* spring; **en p.** in (the) spring; **cuando llegue la p.** when (the) spring comes; **la última p.** last spring; PROV **la p. la sangre altera** spring is in the air (**b**) *(juventud)* springtime (**c**) *(año)* **tiene diez primaveras** she is ten years old, she has seen ten summers (**d**) *(planta)* primrose

primaveral *adj* spring; **día p.** spring day

primer *ver* **primero**

primera 1 *nf* (**a**) *(marcha)* first (gear); **meter (la) p.** to go into first (gear) (**b**) *(en avión, tren)* first class; **viajar en p.** to travel first class (**c**) *Dep* first division; **subir a p.** to go up into the first division (**d**) **a la p.** at the first attempt; EXPR *Fam* **a las primeras de cambio** at the first opportunity (**e**) *ver también* **primero**

2 de primera *loc adj* first-class, excellent

primeramente *adv* first, in the first place

primeriza *nf (madre)* first-time mother

primerizo, -a 1 *adj* (**a**) *(principiante)* novice; **es p. en el vuelo en ala delta** he's a novice at hang-gliding (**b**) *(embarazada)* first-time
2 *nm,f (principiante)* beginner

PRIMERO, -A

Primer is used instead of **primero** before singular masculine nouns (e.g. **el primer hombre** the first man).

1 *núm adj* (**a**) *(en orden)* first; **el primer capítulo, el capítulo p.** chapter one; **los primeros diez párrafos, los diez párrafos primeros** the first ten paragraphs; **Carlos p.** *(escrito Carlos I)* Charles the First *(written Charles I)*; **el siglo p.** *(escrito el siglo I)* the first century *(written 1st century)*; **el primer piso** the *Br* first *o US* second floor; **a primera hora de la mañana** first thing in the morning; **en primera fila** in the front row; **en primer lugar, abre la caja** first (of all), open the box; **en primera página** on the front page ►► ***primeros auxilios*** first aid; **prestar primeros auxilios a alguien** to give sb first aid; ***primer bailarín*** leading dancer; ***primera bailarina*** prima ballerina; *Dep* ***primera base*** *(posición, jugador)* first base; ***primera comunión*** first communion; **hacer la primera comunión** to celebrate one's first communion; ***primera dama*** *Teatro* leading lady; *Pol (esposa)* first lady; ***primera división*** first division; *Dep* ***primer equipo*** first team; *Taurom* ***primer espada*** principal bullfighter; *Mil* ***primera línea*** front line; **estar en primera línea** *(de batalla)* to be on the front line; *(entre los mejores)* to be amongst the best; *RP* ***primera magistratura*** presidency; ***primer ministro*** prime minister; ***primer plano*** close-up; **en primer plano** in the foreground; ***primer plato*** first course, starter; ***primer violín*** first violin
(**b**) *(en importancia, calidad)* main; **la primera empresa del sector** the leading company in the sector; **el primer tenista del país** the country's top tennis player; **uno de los primeros objetivos del gobierno** one of the government's main aims; **el primer actor** the leading man; **la primera actriz** the leading lady; **productos de primera calidad** top-quality products; **deportistas de primera clase** *o* **categoría** *o* **fila** top-class sportsmen; **productos de primera necesidad** basic necessities; **lo p.** the most important *o* main thing; **lo p. es lo p.** first things first
2 *núm nm,f* (**a**) *(en orden)* **el p.** the first one; **el p. fue bueno** the first one was good; **llegó el p.** he came first; **el p. de la cola** the person at the front of the *Br* queue *o US* line; **¿quién es el p. de la cola?** who's first?; **es el p. de la clase** he's top of the class; **él fue el p. en venir** he was the first (person *o* one) to come; **no eres el p. que me pregunta eso** you're not the first person to ask me that
(**b**) *(mencionado antes)* **vinieron Pedro y Juan, el p. con...** Pedro and Juan arrived, the former with...
3 *adv* (**a**) *(en primer lugar)* first; **p. déjame que te explique una cosa** let me explain something to you first; **usted estaba p.** you were in front of me *o* first; **¿quién va** *o* **está p.?** who's first?; *Am* **p. que nada** first of all
(**b**) *(indica preferencia)* **p.... que...** rather... than...; **p. morir que traicionarle** I'd rather die than betray him
4 *nm* (**a**) *(en edificio) Br* first floor, *US* second floor
(**b**) *(curso universitario)* first year; **estudiantes de p.** first years; **estoy en p.** I'm a first year
(**c**) *(curso escolar)* = first year of primary school, *US* ≃ first grade
(**d**) *(día del mes)* **el p. de mayo** *(también escrito el 1 de mayo)* the first of May *(written 1 May)*
(**e**) *(en frases)* **a primeros de mes/año** at the beginning of the month/year; **a primeros de junio** at the beginning of June, in early June; **de p.** *(de primer plato)* for starters

primicia *nf* (**a**) *(fruto)* first fruit (**b**) *(noticia)* scoop, exclusive; **una gran p. informativa** a real scoop *o* exclusive

primigenio, -a *adj* original, primitive

primípara *Med* 1 *adj f* primiparous
2 *nf* primipara

primitiva *nf Esp (lotería)* = weekly state-run lottery, *Br* ≃ National Lottery

primitivismo *nm* (**a**) *(rudimentariedad)* primitiveness (**b**) *Arte* primitivism

primitivo, -a *adj* (**a**) *(arcaico, rudimentario)* primitive (**b**) *(original)* original (**c**) *Arte* primitivist

primo, -a 1 *adj* (**a**) *(número)* prime (**b**) *(materia)* raw
2 *nm,f* (**a**) *(pariente)* cousin ►► ***p. carnal*** first cousin; ***p. hermano*** first cousin; ***p. segundo*** second cousin (**b**) *Fam (tonto)* sucker; EXPR **hacer el p.** to be taken for a ride

primogénito, -a 1 *adj* first-born
2 *nm,f* first-born

primogenitura *nf* primogeniture

primor *nm* (**a**) *(persona)* treasure, marvel; *(cosa, trabajo)* fine thing; **hecho un p.** *(lugar)* spick and span; **su abuela cose que es un p.** his grandmother sews beautifully (**b**) *(esmero)* **con p.** with skill

primordial *adj* fundamental; **reducir el paro es un asunto p.** cutting unemployment is a top priority; **es p. que acabemos hoy** it's essential that we finish today

primorosamente *adv (con exquisitez)* finely, exquisitely

primoroso, -a *adj* (**a**) *(delicado)* exquisite, fine (**b**) *(hábil)* skilful

prímula *nf* primrose

primus® *nm inv Am* primus (stove)

princesa *nf* princess

principado *nm* principality ►► ***el P. de Asturias*** the Principality of Asturias; ***el P. de Mónaco*** the Principality of Monaco

principal 1 *adj* (**a**) *(más importante)* main, principal; **me han dado el papel p. de la obra de teatro** I've been given the leading *o* lead role in the play; **puerta p.** front door; **lo p.** the main thing (**b**) *Gram (oración)* main
2 *nm* (**a**) *(en edificio) Br* first floor, *US* second floor (**b**) *Fin* principal

principalmente *adv* principally, mainly

príncipe 1 *adj (edición)* first, original
2 *nm* prince ►► ***el P. de Asturias*** the Spanish crown prince; ***p. azul*** Prince Charming; ***p. consorte*** prince consort; ***p. heredero*** crown prince; ***p. regente*** prince regent; ***p. de las tinieblas*** Prince of Darkness

principesco, -a *adj* princely

principiante, -a 1 *adj* inexperienced; **se pone nervioso con los conductores principiantes** he gets nervous with inexperienced drivers; **para ser p., no lo hace mal** he's not bad for a beginner
2 *nm,f* beginner; **ha cometido un error de p.** he's made a really basic mistake

principiar *vt* to begin, to start

principio *nm* (**a**) *(comienzo)* beginning, start; **empieza por el p.** start at the beginning; **al p.** at first, in the beginning; **desde el p.** from the beginning; **se ha llegado a un p. de acuerdo** a preliminary agreement has been reached; **a principios de** at the beginning of; **en un p.** at first; **el p. del fin** the beginning of the end; **del p. al fin, desde el p. hasta el fin** from beginning to end, from start to finish
(**b**) *(fundamento, ley)* principle ►► ***p. de Arquímedes*** Archimedes' principle; *Filosofía* ***p. de causalidad*** causality principle; ***p. de incertidumbre*** uncertainty principle; ***p. de indeterminación*** uncertainty principle; ***p. del todo o nada*** all-or-nothing policy
(**c**) *(origen)* origin, source
(**d**) *(elemento)* element ►► ***p. activo*** active ingredient
(**e**) **principios** *(reglas de conducta)* principles; **un hombre de principios** a man of principles; **sin principios** unprincipled, unscrupulous; **por p.** on principle; **se negó a hacerlo por principios** she refused to do it on principle
(**f**) **principios** *(nociones)* rudiments, first principles; **tiene algunos principios de informática** she knows a bit about computing
(**g**) *(primera consideración)* **en p.: en p., me parece buena la idea** in principle, the idea seems good; **en p. quedamos en hacer una reunión el jueves** provisionally *o* unless you hear otherwise, we've arranged to meet on Thursday

principismo *nm Am* principlism

principista *Am* 1 *adj* principlist
2 *nmf* principlist

pringado, -a *nm,f Esp Fam* (**a**) *(desgraciado)* loser (**b**) *(iluso)* mug, sucker

pringar [38] 1 *vt* (**a**) *(ensuciar)* to make greasy (**b**) *(mojar)* to dip (**c**) *Fam (comprometer)* **p. a alguien en algo** to get sb mixed up in sth; **a mí no me pringues en tus asuntos** don't get me mixed up in your affairs (**d**) *Fam* **pringarla** *(fastidiar)* **¡ya la has pringado!** now you've done it! (**e**) *Fam* **pringarla** *(morir)* to peg out
2 *vi* (**a**) *Fam (pagar las culpas)* to carry the can; **al final he pringado yo por todos** I've ended up carrying the can for everyone (**b**) *Fam (trabajar)* to slog away, to graft; **nos tocó p. todo el fin de semana** we were landed with working all weekend
3 *v impersonal CAm, Méx, Ven* to drizzle
4 **pringarse** *vpr* (**a**) *(ensuciarse)* **pringarse de** *o* **con algo** to get covered in *o* with sth; **me he pringado las manos de tinta** I've got my hands covered in ink (**b**) *Fam (en asunto sucio)* to get one's hands dirty; **se ha pringado de lleno en el atraco** he's seriously mixed up in the robbery

pringoso, -a *adj (grasiento)* greasy; *(pegajoso)* sticky

pringue *nm (suciedad)* muck, dirt; *(grasa)* grease

prión *nm* prion

prior, -ora *nm,f Rel* prior, *f* prioress
priorato *nm Rel* priorate
priori *ver* **a priori**
prioridad *nf* (**a**) *(preferencia)* priority; **los jubilados tienen p.** pensioners have priority; **tienen como p. reducir el paro** their priority is to cut unemployment; **dan p. a las madres solteras** they give priority to single mothers (**b**) *Aut* right of way, priority; **tienen p. los vehículos que vienen por la derecha** vehicles coming from the right have right of way *o* priority
prioritario, -a *adj* priority; **ser p.** to be a priority; **objetivo p.** key objective *o* aim
priorizar *vt* to give priority to
prisa *nf (prontitud)* haste, hurry; *(rapidez)* speed; *(urgencia)* urgency; **¿por qué tantas prisas?** what's the hurry?; **con las prisas me olvidé de llamarte** in the rush I forgot to call you; **a toda p.** very quickly; **correr p.** to be urgent; **¿qué es lo que más p. corre?** which is most urgent?; **darse p.** to hurry (up); **de p.** quickly; **de p. y corriendo** in a slapdash way; **ir con p., llevar p.** to be in a hurry; **meter p. a alguien** to hurry *o* rush sb; **tener p.** to be in a hurry; EXPR **la p. es mala consejera** more haste, less speed; EXPR **sin p. pero sin pausa** slowly but steadily
prisión *nf* (**a**) *(cárcel)* prison ►► ***p. de máxima seguridad*** top-security prison; ***p. de régimen abierto*** open prison
(**b**) *(encarcelamiento)* imprisonment; **fue condenado a veinte años de p.** he was sentenced to twenty years imprisonment ►► ***p. incondicional*** remand without bail; ***p. mayor*** = prison sentence of between six years and twelve years; ***p. menor*** = prison sentence of between six months and six years; ***p. preventiva*** preventive custody
prisionero, -a *nm,f* prisoner; **caer p.** to be taken prisoner; **hacer p. a alguien** to take sb prisoner ►► ***p. de conciencia*** prisoner of conscience; ***p. de guerra*** prisoner of war; ***p. político*** political prisoner
prisma *nm* (**a**) *Geom* prism (**b**) *Fís* prism (**c**) *(perspectiva)* viewpoint, perspective
prismático, -a 1 *adj* prismatic
2 prismáticos *nmpl* binoculars
Pristina *n* Pristina
prístino, -a *adj Formal* pristine, original
priva *nf Esp Fam (bebida)* booze
privacía *nf Méx* privacy
privacidad *nf* privacy
privación *nf* (**a**) *(acción)* deprivation; **p. de libertad** loss of freedom (**b**) **privaciones** *(escasez)* hardship; **pasar** *o* **padecer privaciones** to suffer hardship
privada *nf Méx* private road
privadamente *adv* privately, in private
privado, -a 1 *adj* private; **en p.** in private
2 *nm Am (despacho)* private office
privar 1 *vt* (**a**) *(dejar sin)* **p. a algo/alguien de** to deprive sth/sb of; **un accidente la privó de la vista** she lost her sight in an accident; **una caída lo privó de conseguir el triunfo en la carrera** a fall robbed him of victory in the race
(**b**) *(prohibir)* **p. a alguien de hacer algo** to forbid sb to do sth; **le han privado de salir por las noches** he's forbidden to go out at night (**c**) *Méx (desmayar)* to knock unconscious
2 *vi Fam* (**a**) *(gustar)* **le privan los pasteles** he adores cakes (**b**) *(estar de moda)* to be in (fashion) (**c**) *Esp (beber)* to booze
3 privarse *vpr* (**a**) **privarse de** *(quedarse sin)* to go without; **me privo de comer dulces** I've stopped eating sweet things; **no me privo de nada** I don't deprive myself of anything (**b**) *Fam (desear)* **privarse por: se priva por salir de excursión** she's dying to go on a trip (**c**) *Méx (desmayarse)* to faint
privativo, -a *adj* (**a**) *(característico)* exclusive; **una facultad privativa del presidente** a power which belongs exclusively to the president (**b**) *(que priva)* **una pena privativa de libertad** a custodial sentence, a prison sentence
privatización *nf* privatization, sell-off
privatizador, -ora *adj* **política privatizadora** privatization policy; **un gobierno p.** a privatizing government
privatizar [14] *vt* to privatize, to sell off
privilegiado, -a 1 *adj* (**a**) *(favorecido)* privileged (**b**) *(excepcional)* exceptional
2 *nm,f* (**a**) *(afortunado)* privileged person (**b**) *(muy dotado)* very gifted person
privilegiar *vt* (**a**) *(persona)* to favour; **una reforma que privilegia al partido en el poder** a reform which favours the party in power (**b**) *(intereses)* to put first
privilegio *nm* privilege; **tengo el p. de presentar a...** I have the honour of introducing... ►► *Informát* ***privilegios de acceso*** access privileges
PRN *nm (abrev de* **Partido de la Renovación Nacional**) = Chilean political party
pro 1 *prep* **un grupo p. amnistía** a pro-amnesty group; **una asociación p. derechos humanos** a human rights organization
2 *nm* **los pros y los contras** the pros and cons; **hay que sopesar los pros y los contras** the pros and cons have to be weighed up
3 de pro *loc adj Formal* worthy; **un hombre de p.** a worthy man
4 en pro de *loc prep* for; **luchan en p. de los inmigrantes** they are fighting for *o* in support of the immigrants
proa *nf (de barco)* prow, bows; *(de avión)* nose; **poner p. a** to set sail for
probabilidad *nf* (**a**) *(posibilidad)* probability, likelihood; **existe la p. de que acabemos antes de tiempo** it's probable *o* likely that we'll finish early; **la p. de que sobreviva es muy escasa** there's little possibility *o* chance that he'll survive, it's highly unlikely that he'll survive; **con toda p. acabaremos mañana** in all probability *o* likelihood we'll finish tomorrow
(**b**) *Mat* probability
probable *adj* probable, likely; **es p. que llueva** it'll probably rain; **es p. que no diga nada** he probably won't say anything; **¿lo comprarás? – es p.** will you buy it? – probably; **es muy p. que no pueda acudir** it's very likely that I won't be able to attend; **lo más p. es que no pueda ir** she probably won't be able to go
probablemente *adv* probably; **¿vendrás a la fiesta? – p.** will you come to the party? – probably; **p. hayan ido al parque** they've probably gone to the park
probadamente *adv* **un tratamiento p. eficaz** a treatment proven to be effective
probado, -a *adj* (**a**) *(demostrado)* proven; **un vino de probada calidad** a wine of proven quality (**b**) *Der* proven
probador *nm* fitting room
probanza *nf Der* proof
probar [64] **1** *vt* (**a**) *(demostrar, indicar)* to prove; **eso prueba que tenía razón** that shows I was right
(**b**) *(comprobar)* to test, to check; **prueba tú mismo la potencia de mi coche** see for yourself how powerful my car is
(**c**) *(experimentar)* to try; **lo hemos probado todo** we've tried everything; **probaron a varios actores antes de encontrar el que buscaban** they tried *o* auditioned various actors before finding the one they were looking for
(**d**) *(ropa)* to try on; **p. una camisa** to try on a shirt
(**e**) *(degustar)* to taste, to try; **¿has probado alguna vez el caviar?** have you ever tasted *o* tried caviar?; **no prueba el vino desde hace meses** he hasn't touched wine for months; **no he probado bocado en todo el día** I haven't had a bite to eat all day
2 *vi* (**a**) *(tratar de)* **p. a hacer algo** to try to do sth; **prueba a nadar de espaldas** try swimming backstroke; **deja que pruebe yo** let me try; **por p. no se pierde nada** there's no harm in trying (**b**) *(degustar)* **p. de todo** to try a bit of everything
3 probarse *vpr (ropa)* to try on; **pruébate estos zapatos** try these shoes on; **¿me lo puedo probar?** can I try it on?
probeta 1 *adj inv* **bebé** *o* **niño p.** test-tube baby
2 *nf (para análisis, reacción)* test tube; *(para medir)* measuring cylinder
probidad *nf Formal* integrity
problema *nm* (**a**) *(dificultad)* problem; **el p. del terrorismo** the terrorist problem, the problem of terrorism; **los niños no causan más que problemas** children cause nothing but trouble *o* problems; **no quiero más problemas** I don't want any more trouble; **el p. es que no nos queda tiempo** the problem *o* thing is that we don't have any time left; *Am* **no te hagas p.** don't worry about it
(**b**) *(matemático)* problem; **resolver un p.** to solve a problem
problemática *nf* problems; **la p. del desempleo** the problems of unemployment
problemático, -a *adj* problematic; **es un niño muy p.** he's a very difficult child
probo, -a *adj Formal* upright, honest
probóscide *nf Zool* proboscis
procacidad *nf* (**a**) *(desvergüenza)* obscenity (**b**) *(acto)* indecent act
procaz *adj* indecent, obscene

procedencia *nf* (a) *(origen)* origin; **es de p. griega** it's of Greek origin (b) *(punto de partida)* point of departure; **con p. de** (arriving) from (c) *(pertinencia)* properness, appropriateness

procedente *adj* (a) *(originario)* **p. de** *(proveniente de)* originating in; *(avión, tren)* (arriving) from; **el vuelo p. de Lima** the flight (coming) from Lima (b) *(oportuno)* appropriate; *Der* fitting, right and proper

proceder[1] *vi* (a) *(originarse)* **p. de** to come from; **la sidra procede de la manzana** cider comes from apples; **esta costumbre procede del siglo XIX** this custom dates back to the 19th century

(b) *(actuar)* to act, to proceed (**con** with); **no procedió correctamente** he did not behave correctly; **hay que p. con cuidado en este asunto** we should proceed with care in this matter

(c) *(empezar)* to proceed (**a** with); **procedemos a leer el nombre de los ganadores** we will now read out the names of the winners; **vamos a p. a la votación** we will now proceed with the vote

(d) *(ser oportuno)* to be appropriate; **procede estudiar la propuesta con detenimiento** it would be wise to study the proposal carefully; **procede cambiar de táctica** it would be a good idea to change tactics

(e) *(legalmente)* **van a p. contra la empresa** they are going to start proceedings against the company

proceder[2] *nm* conduct, behaviour

procedimiento *nm* (a) *(método)* procedure, method (b) *Der* proceedings

proceloso, -a *adj Literario* stormy, tempestuous

prócer *nm Formal* great man

procesado, -a 1 *nm,f* accused, defendant

2 *nm* processing

procesador *nm Informát* processor ►► ***p. de coma flotante*** floating-point processor; ***p. RISC*** RISC processor; ***p. de textos*** word processor

procesal *adj (costas, alegaciones)* legal; *(derecho)* procedural

procesamiento *nm* (a) *Der* prosecution (b) *Informát* processing ►► ***p. de datos*** data processing; ***p. de textos*** word processing

procesar *vt* (a) *Der* to prosecute; **p. a alguien por algo** to prosecute sb for sth (b) *(productos, basuras)* to process (c) *Informát* to process

procesión *nf* procession; *Fam* **fuimos allí todos en p.** we all trooped over there; EXPR **la p. va por dentro** he/she is putting on a brave face

procesionaria *nf* processionary moth

proceso *nm* (a) *(fenómeno, operación)* process; **el p. de fabricación de la cerveza** the process of brewing beer; **el p. de paz** the peace process; **el paciente está en un p. de recuperación** the patient is in the process of recovering

(b) *(transcurso, intervalo)* course; **se esperan grandes cambios en el p. de un año** great changes are expected in the course of the year

(c) *Der (juicio)* trial; *(causa)* lawsuit; **abrir un p. contra alguien** to bring an action against sb

(d) *Med* **padece un p. gripal** he has the flu

(e) *Informát (de datos)* processing ►► ***p. por lotes*** batch processing; ***p. subordinado*** background process; ***p. de textos*** word processing

(f) *RP Pol* **el P.** *(dictadura)* = military dictatorship in Uruguay (1973-85) or Argentina (1976-1983)

proclama 1 *nf (política)* proclamation

2 **proclamas** *nfpl (amonestaciones)* banns

proclamación *nf* (a) *(anuncio)* notification (b) *(acto, ceremonia)* proclamation

proclamar 1 *vt* (a) *(nombrar)* to proclaim (b) *(anunciar)* to declare; **el presidente ha proclamado su inocencia en el escándalo** the president has declared his innocence in the scandal; **no es necesario proclamarlo a los cuatro vientos** you don't need to broadcast it

2 **proclamarse** *vpr* (a) *(nombrarse)* to proclaim oneself; **se proclamó defensor de los inmigrantes** he proclaimed himself champion of the immigrants (b) *(conseguir un título)* **proclamarse campeón** to become champion

proclítico, -a *adj Ling* proclitic

proclive *adj* **p. a** prone to; **es p. a los resfriados** she's prone to colds; **es p. a creerse todo lo que le cuentan** he tends to believe everything he's told; **un gobierno p. al gasto público** a government predisposed to public spending; **un escritor proclive a moralizar** a writer given to moralizing

proclividad *nf* proclivity; **la p. del peso a variar bruscamente** the tendency of the peso to fluctuate sharply

procónsul *nm* proconsul

proconsulado *nm (cargo)* proconsulate

procreación *nf* procreation

procrear 1 *vi* to procreate

2 *vt* to generate, to bear

procura *nf Am (busca)* search, hunt; **salieron en p. del asesino** the set off in search of the murderer

procuración *nf Der (poder)* power of attorney, proxy; **por p.** by proxy

procurador, -ora *nm,f* (a) *Der* attorney (b) *Esp Hist* ***p. en Cortes*** Member of Spanish Parliament *(in 19th century or under Franco)* (c) *Am* ***p. general del Estado*** *o* ***de la nación*** *o* ***de la república*** *Br* ≃ Director of Public Prosecutions, *US* ≃ Attorney General; *Méx* ***p. general de justicia*** Minister of Justice (d) *Méx (representante)* ***p. del consumidor*** ombudsman

procuraduría *nf* (a) *(oficio)* legal profession (b) *(oficina)* lawyer's practice (c) *Am* ***p. general del Estado*** *o* ***de la nación*** *o* ***de la república*** *Br* ≃ DPP's office, *US* ≃ Attorney General's office; *Méx* ***p. general de justicia*** Ministry of Justice

procurar 1 *vt* (a) *(intentar)* **p. hacer algo** to try to do sth; **procura llegar puntual** try to arrive on time; **p. que...** to make sure that...; **procuraré que no les falte nada** I'll try to make sure they have everything they need (b) *(proporcionar)* to get, to secure; **nos procurarán todos los medios necesarios** they will provide us with everything we need

2 **procurarse** *vpr* to get, to obtain; **se procuró un trabajo en el extranjero** she got herself a job abroad

Prode *nm Arg* = gambling game involving betting on the results of soccer matches, *Br* ≃ football pools

prodigalidad *nf* (a) *(derroche)* prodigality (b) *(abundancia)* profusion

prodigar [38] 1 *vt* **p. algo a alguien** to lavish sth on sb; **prodiga mucho cariño a sus nietos** she lavishes great affection on her grandchildren

2 **prodigarse** *vpr* (a) *(exhibirse)* to appear a lot in public; **se ha prodigado mucho últimamente** he's appeared a lot in public recently, he's been in the public eye a lot recently

(b) *(excederse)* **prodigarse en elogios** to be lavish with one's praise; **se prodigó en atenciones con sus invitados** she lavished attention on her guests; **se prodigó en insultos contra el presidente** he heaped abuse on the president

prodigio 1 *nm* (a) *(suceso)* miracle; **es un p. que haya sobrevivido** it's a miracle she survived (b) *(persona)* wonder, prodigy; **el bailarín es un p. de elasticidad** the dancer is unbelievably supple

2 *adj inv* **niño p.** child prodigy

prodigiosamente *adv* marvellously

prodigioso, -a *adj* (a) *(sobrenatural)* miraculous (b) *(extraordinario)* extraordinary; **es de una inteligencia prodigiosa** she is phenomenally intelligent

pródigo, -a 1 *adj* (a) *(derrochador)* extravagant; **el hijo p.** *(en la Biblia)* the prodigal son (b) *(generoso)* generous, lavish; **es muy p. con su familia** he's very generous to his family (c) *(abundante)* **una región pródiga en recursos naturales** a region rich in natural resources; **un país p. en abogados** a country with vast quantities of lawyers

2 *nm,f* spendthrift

producción *nf* (a) *(acción)* production; *(producto)* product; **se ha incrementado la p. de acero** steel production has increased; **un autor con una extensa p. poética** an author with an extensive poetic output ►► *Ind* ***p. en cadena*** mass production; *Ind* ***p. en serie*** mass production (b) *Cine & TV* production; **una p. de TVE** a TVE production

producir [18] 1 *vt* (a) *(productos agrícolas, recursos naturales)* to produce; **las abejas producen miel** bees produce honey

(b) *(manufacturar)* to produce

(c) *(generar) (calor, sonido)* to produce

(d) *(artista, campeón)* to produce; **un país que ha producido varios campeones mundiales** a country which has produced several world champions

(e) *(ocasionar)* to cause, to give rise to; **tu actuación me produce tristeza** your conduct makes me very sad; **un medicamento que produce náuseas** a medicine which causes nausea; **no me produjo muy buena impresión** it didn't make a very good impression on me

(f) *(interés)* to yield, to bear; **este negocio produce grandes pérdidas** this business is making huge losses; **la operación produjo muchas ganancias para el banco** the transaction yielded substantial profits for the bank

(g) *(en cine, televisión)* to produce

2 **producirse** *vpr* (a) *(ocurrir)* **el accidente se produjo a las nueve de la mañana** the accident occurred at nine o'clock in the morning; **se produjeron disturbios en varias ciudades** there were disturbances in

several cities; **el accidente se produjo por exceso de velocidad** the accident was caused by speeding; **se produjeron varios heridos** several people were injured; **tras su intervención se produjo un gran silencio** there was a long silence after her speech, a long silence followed her speech

(**b**) *Formal (comportarse)* to conduct oneself; **fue sancionado por producirse de manera violenta** he was banned for violent conduct

productividad *nf* productivity

productivo, -a *adj* (**a**) *(trabajador, método)* productive; *(encuentro)* productive, fruitful (**b**) *(inversión, negocio)* profitable

producto *nm* (**a**) *(bien, objeto)* product; **productos agrícolas** agricultural produce; **un p. derivado del petróleo** an oil derivative ▸▸ ***p. acabado*** finished product; ***p. alimenticio*** foodstuff; ***productos de belleza*** cosmetics; ***p. básico*** *(de primera necesidad)* staple; ***p. final*** end product; *Esp* ***p. interior bruto*** gross domestic product; *Am* ***p. interno bruto*** gross domestic product; ***p. líder*** product leader; ***p. manufacturado*** manufactured product; ***p. milagro*** miracle product; ***p. nacional bruto*** gross national product; ***p. de primera necesidad*** staple; ***p. químico*** chemical; ***productos de la tierra*** agricultural *o* farm produce

(**b**) *(ganancia)* profit

(**c**) *(resultado)* result, product; **el accidente fue p. de un despiste del conductor** the accident was caused by a lapse of attention on the part of the driver; **la obra es el p. de un gran esfuerzo colectivo** the work is the product of a great collective effort

(**d**) *Mat* product

productor, -ora 1 *adj* producing; **país p. de petróleo** oil-producing country; **células productoras de dopamina** dopamine-producing cells

2 *nm,f* (**a**) *(fabricante)* producer; **productores de papel** paper manufacturers (**b**) *(de productos agrícolas)* farmer; **productores de plátanos** banana growers; **productores agrícolas** farmers (**c**) *(en cine, televisión)* producer

productora *nf (de cine, televisión)* production company

produjera *etc ver* **producir**

produzco *ver* **producir**

proemio *nm (de libro)* preface, prologue

proeza *nf* exploit, deed; **realizó la p. de cruzar el Atlántico en solitario** she accomplished the feat of a solo crossing of the Atlantic

prof. (*abrev de* **profesor**) *(en colegio, academia)* teacher; *(en universidad) Br* lecturer, *US* professor

profanación *nf* desecration

profanar *vt* to desecrate

profano, -a 1 *adj* (**a**) *(no sagrado)* profane, secular; **literatura/música profana** secular literature/music (**b**) *(ignorante)* ignorant, uninitiated; **soy p. en la materia** I'm a layman when it comes to that subject, I know nothing about the subject

2 *nm,f* layman, *f* laywoman; **soy un p. en cuestiones de economía** I'm a layman when it comes to economics, I know nothing about economics

profe *nmf Fam (de colegio)* teacher; *(de universidad)* lecturer

profecía *nf* prophecy

proferir [5] *vt (palabras, sonidos)* to utter; *(insultos)* to hurl; **los manifestantes profirieron gritos en contra del gobierno** the demonstrators shouted abuse against the government

profesar 1 *vt* (**a**) *(religión)* to follow (**b**) *(arte, oficio)* to practise (**c**) *(admiración, amistad)* to feel; **profesa un gran amor hacia** *o* **por los animales** she has a great love of animals

2 *vi Rel* to take one's vows

profesión *nf* (**a**) *(empleo, ocupación)* profession; *(en formularios)* occupation; **de p.** by profession; **ser de la p.** to be in the same profession ▸▸ ***p. liberal*** liberal profession (**b**) *(declaración)* declaration, avowal ▸▸ *Rel* ***p. de fe*** profession *o* declaration of faith

profesional 1 *adj* (**a**) *(de la profesión)* professional (**b**) *(eficaz)* professional; **es un albañil muy p.** he's a very professional bricklayer (**c**) *(deportista)* professional

2 *nmf* (**a**) *(trabajador liberal)* professional (**b**) *(deportista)* professional (**c**) *(practicante de actividad)* professional; **un p. del crimen** a professional criminal; *Hum* **un p. del pesimismo** a professional pessimist

profesionalidad *nf* professionalism

profesionalismo *nm* professionalism

profesionalización *nf* professionalization

profesionalizar [14] 1 *vt* to professionalize

2 **profesionalizarse** *vpr* to turn professional

profesionalmente *adv* professionally

profesionista *nmf Méx* professional

profeso, -a 1 *adj* professed

2 *nm,f* professed monk, *f* professed nun

profesor, -ora *nm,f* (**a**) *(de colegio, academia)* teacher; *(de autoescuela, esquí)* instructor; **p. de historia/música** history/music teacher ▸▸ ***p. agregado*** *(de secundaria)* teacher *(with permanent post)*; ***p. particular*** (private) tutor; ***p. suplente*** *Br* supply teacher, *US* substitute teacher

(**b**) *(de universidad) Br* lecturer, *US* professor ▸▸ ***p. asociado*** = university lecturer with part-time contract; ***p. ayudante*** = university lecturer who is also studying for their PhD; ***p. emérito*** professor emeritus, emeritus professor; ***p. invitado*** visiting lecturer; ***p. titular*** *Br* lecturer, *US* professor *(with tenure)*

profesorado *nm* (**a**) *(plantilla)* teaching staff, *US* faculty; **hay mucho malestar entre el p.** there is a lot of discontent among the teaching staff (**b**) *(profesión)* teaching profession; **ejerce el p. desde hace diez años** he has been a teacher for ten years

profeta *nm* prophet; EXPR **nadie es p. en su tierra** no man is prophet in his own land

profético, -a *adj* prophetic

profetisa *nf* prophetess

profetizar [14] *vt* to prophesy

profiero *etc ver* **proferir**

profiláctico, -a 1 *adj* prophylactic

2 *nm* prophylactic, condom

profilaxis *nf inv* prophylaxis

proforma, pro forma *adj* pro forma

prófugo, -a 1 *adj* fugitive

2 *nm,f* fugitive; **un p. de la justicia** a fugitive from justice

3 *nm Mil* = person evading military service

profundamente *adv* deeply; **lamento p. lo que ha pasado** I deeply regret what has happened; **dormía p.** she was fast asleep; **una tradición p. arraigada** a deep-rooted tradition

profundidad *nf* (**a**) *(de mar, lago, río)* depth; *(de hoyo, raíces, herida)* depth; **¿cuál es la p. de esta piscina?** how deep is this swimming pool?; **tiene dos metros de p.** it's two metres deep; **de poca p.** shallow; **se encontraba a poca p. cuando ocurrió el accidente** it was near the surface when the accident occurred; **hallaron los restos del barco en las profundidades del océano** they found the remains of the ship in the depths of the ocean

(**b**) *(de habitación, sala)* depth; **la cocina tiene una p. de cuatro metros** the kitchen is four metres deep ▸▸ *Fot* ***p. de campo*** depth of field

(**c**) *(de libro, idea, pensamiento)* depth; **conocer un tema en p.** to know a subject in depth; **discutieron el problema en p.** they discussed the problem in depth

profundización *nf* (**a**) *(de estudio, conocimientos)* **un curso con un alto nivel de p. en el tema** a course that goes into the subject in depth (**b**) *(de actividad, relaciones)* strengthening; **trabajar por la p. de la democracia en la región** to work to strengthen democracy in the region

profundizar [14] 1 *vt (hoyo, conocimientos)* to deepen

2 *vi* (**a**) *(en excavación)* to dig deeper

(**b**) *(en estudio, conocimientos)* to go into depth; **p. en un tema** *(estudiar)* to study a topic in depth; *(debatir)* to discuss a topic in depth; **no profundizó demasiado en los personajes secundarios** he didn't really develop the secondary characters

(**c**) *(en actividad)* **piden seguir profundizando en la unidad monetaria** they are calling for monetary union to continue to be strengthened

profundo, -a *adj* (**a**) *(mar, lago, río)* deep; *(hoyo, raíces, herida)* deep; **navegaban por aguas profundas** they were sailing in deep waters; **es un lago muy poco p.** it's a very shallow lake; **la España profunda** = backward, traditional Spain

(**b**) *(habitación, sala)* deep

(**c**) *(respeto, admiración, tristeza)* profound, deep; *(alegría, dolor)* intense; *(sueño)* deep

(**d**) *(voz)* deep

(**e**) *(mirada)* deep and meaningful

(**f**) *(libro, idea, pensamiento)* profound

(**g**) *Gram (estructura)* deep

profusamente *adv* profusely; **una técnica p. empleada en la medicina moderna** a widely-used technique in modern medicine; **un libro p. ilustrado** a lavishly illustrated book

profusión *nf* profusion

profuso, -a *adj* profuse

progenie *nf Formal* (**a**) *(familia)* lineage (**b**) *(descendencia)* offspring

progenitor, -ora *nm,f* father, *f* mother; **progenitores** parents

progesterona *nf* progesterone

prognato, -a *adj Espec* prognathous; **los Austrias más prognatos** the Hapsburgs with the most prominent lower jaws

programa *nm* (**a**) *(de radio, televisión)* programme ►► ***p. concurso*** game show; ***p. de entrevistas*** talk show
(**b**) *(de lavadora, lavavajillas)* cycle ►► ***p. de lavado*** wash cycle
(**c**) *(proyecto)* programme ►► ***p. electoral*** platform; ***p. espacial*** space programme; ***p. de intercambio*** exchange (programme)
(**d**) *(folleto)* programme ►► ***p. de mano*** programme
(**e**) *(de actividades)* schedule, programme; **¿cuál es el p. para esta tarde?** what's the plan for this afternoon?; *Hum* **la tormenta no estaba en el p.** the storm wasn't part of the programme, the storm wasn't supposed to happen ►► ***p. de fiestas*** programme of events *(during annual town festival)*
(**f**) *(de curso, asignatura)* syllabus
(**g**) *Informát* program ►► *Informát* ***p. de dibujo*** paint program; ***p. de maquetación*** page layout program
(**h**) *(en patinaje artístico)* ***p. libre*** free skating
(**i**) *RP Fam (ligue)* pick-up; **empezaron a llegar, cada uno con su p.** they began to arrive, each with his or her pick-up

programable *adj* programmable

programación *nf* (**a**) *(de fiestas) (acción)* programming, scheduling; *(programa)* programme (**b**) *(de vídeo)* programming (**c**) *(televisiva)* scheduling; **la p. del lunes** Monday's programmes (**d**) *Informát* programming ►► ***p. lineal*** linear programming

programador, -ora 1 *nm,f Informát (persona)* programmer
2 *nm (aparato)* programmer; **el p. de la calefacción/del vídeo** the heating/video programmer

programar 1 *vt* (**a**) *(actividades, proyecto)* to plan; **han programado una reunión para el lunes** they have scheduled a meeting for Monday (**b**) *(en televisión)* to schedule; *(en cine)* to put on; **suelen p. documentales por las tardes** they usually put on *o* show documentaries in the afternoons (**c**) *(máquina, vídeo)* to programme (**d**) *Informát* to program
2 *vi Informát* to program

programático, -a *adj (de programa electoral)* **una propuesta programática** a manifesto proposal; **los partidos llegaron a un acuerdo p.** the parties reached an agreement on policy

progre *Fam* **1** *adj (liberal)* liberal; *(moderno)* trendy, hip; **los miembros más progres del partido** the more liberal members of the party; **tengo unos padres muy progres** I have really trendy parents
2 *nmf* progressive

progresar *vi* to progress, to make progress; **p. en** to make progress in

progresía *nf Fam (liberales)* liberals; *(modernos)* trendies

progresión *nf* progression, advance ►► ***p. aritmética*** arithmetic progression; ***p. geométrica*** geometric progression; *Fig* **crecer en p. geométrica** to increase exponentially

progresismo *nm* progressivism

progresista 1 *adj* progressive
2 *nmf* progressive

progresivo, -a *adj* (**a**) *(que progresa)* progressive (**b**) *(gradual)* gradual; **se espera un aumento p. de las temperaturas** a gradual rise in temperatures is expected (**c**) *(impuesto)* progressive (**d**) *Gram* progressive, continuous

progreso *nm* (**a**) *(adelanto, avance)* progress; **los progresos de la ciencia** scientific progress *o* advances; **hacer progresos** to make progress (**b**) *(en política)* progress; **se ha erigido en defensor del p.** he has appointed himself a champion of progress

progubernamental *adj* pro-government

prohibición *nf (efecto)* ban; *(acción)* banning; **han levantado la p. de pescar en el mar del Norte** they have lifted the ban on fishing in the North Sea; **un tratado de p. de pruebas nucleares** a nuclear test ban treaty; **está a favor de la p. de la caza del zorro** she's in favour of banning fox-hunting; **lo hizo a pesar de la p. expresa de sus jefes** he did it in spite of the fact that his bosses had expressly forbidden him to

prohibicionista *nmf* prohibitionist

prohibido, -a *adj* **un libro p.** a banned book; **la fruta prohibida** the forbidden fruit; **está p. fumar aquí** this is a no-smoking area, smoking is prohibited here; **está prohibida la venta de alcohol a menores** *(en letrero)* it is illegal to sell alcoholic drinks to anyone under the age of 18; **p. aparcar/fumar** *(en letrero)* no parking/smoking, parking/smoking prohibited; **p. fijar carteles** *(en letrero)* stick no bills; **prohibida la entrada** *(en letrero)* no entry

prohibir *vt* (**a**) *(impedir, proscribir)* to forbid; **p. a alguien hacer algo** to forbid sb to do sth; **te prohíbo que vayas a la fiesta** I forbid you to go to the party; **el médico me ha prohibido fumar** the doctor has told me to stop smoking; **tengo prohibido el alcohol** I've been told I mustn't touch alcohol; **se prohíbe el paso** *(en letrero)* no entry
(**b**) *(por ley) (de antemano)* to prohibit; *(a posteriori)* to ban; **a partir de ahora se prohíbe fumar en los lugares públicos** smoking in public places has now been banned; **se prohíbe la entrada a menores de 18 años** *(en letrero)* over 18s only

prohibitivo, -a *adj* (**a**) *(norma, ley)* prohibitive (**b**) *(precio)* prohibitive

prohijar *vt* (**a**) *(niño)* to adopt (**b**) *(ideas, doctrinas)* to adopt

prohombre *nm Formal* great man

prójima *nf Fam* tart, slut

prójimo *nm* fellow human being, neighbour; **intenta ayudar al p. siempre que puede** try to help your neighbour whenever you can; **ama a tu p. como a ti mismo** *(cita bíblica)* love your neighbour as yourself

prolapso *nm Med* prolapse

prole *nf* offspring; **llegaron nuestros amigos con toda su p.** our friends arrived with all their offspring in tow

> **Falso amigo**: El verbo inglés **to quit** no es la traducción del español **quitar**. En inglés **to quit** significa "abandonar", "dejar", "irse" o "dimitir".

prolegómenos *nmpl (de una obra)* preface; **se produjo una pelea en los p. del partido** a fight broke out just before the kick-off

proletariado *nm* proletariat

proletario, -a 1 *adj* proletarian
2 *nm,f* proletarian

proliferación *nf* proliferation; **p. nuclear** nuclear proliferation

proliferar *vi* to proliferate

prolífico, -a *adj* (**a**) *(animal)* prolific (**b**) *(artista)* prolific

prolijamente *adv* (**a**) *(a fondo)* exhaustively (**b**) *RP (con pulcritud)* tidily, neatly

prolijidad *nf* (**a**) *(extensión)* long-windedness; **un relato de gran p.** a very long-winded account (**b**) *RP (pulcritud)* tidiness, neatness

prolijo, -a *adj* (**a**) *(extenso)* long-winded (**b**) *(esmerado)* meticulous (**c**) *(detallado)* exhaustive; **una explicación prolija en detalles** an exhaustively detailed explanation (**d**) *RP (pulcro)* tidy, neat

PROLOG, Prolog *nm Informát* PROLOG, Prolog

prologar *vt* **prologó el libro un famoso escritor** the preface to the book was written by a famous author

prólogo *nm* (**a**) *(de libro)* preface, foreword (**b**) *(de obra de teatro)* prologue (**c**) *(de acto)* prelude; **se celebró una cena como p. al congreso** a dinner was held as a prelude to the conference (**d**) *(en ciclismo)* prologue

prologuista *nmf* author of prefaces; **el p. del libro** the person who wrote the preface to the book

prolongación *nf*, **prolongamiento** *nm* (**a**) *(de espera, visita, conversación)* prolongation; *(de contrato)* extension (**b**) *(de cuerda, tubo)* lengthening; *(de carretera)* extension

prolongado, -a *adj* (**a**) *(alargado)* long (**b**) *(en el tiempo)* lengthy

prolongamiento = **prolongación**

prolongar [38] **1** *vt* (**a**) *(en el tiempo) (espera, visita, conversación)* to prolong; *(contrato)* to extend; **los médicos no quieren p. su sufrimiento** the doctors do not wish to prolong her suffering (**b**) *(en el espacio) (cuerda, tubo)* to lengthen; *(carretera)* to extend
2 prolongarse *vpr* (**a**) *(en el tiempo)* to go on, to continue; **la reunión se prolongó más de lo previsto** the meeting went on for longer than expected; **la familia no quiere que se prolongue su agonía** the family do not wish his suffering to be prolonged
(**b**) *(en el espacio)* to extend; **la nueva línea se prolonga hasta el aeropuerto** the new route extends to the airport, the new route now goes as far as the airport

promediar 1 *vt* (**a**) *(calcular promedio de)* to average out (**b**) *(dividir en dos partes)* to divide in two; **procura p. la carne para dos días** try to divide the meat up so it lasts for two days
2 *vi* **cuando promediaba el verano** halfway *o* midway through the summer

promedio *nm* **(a)** *(media)* average; **escribe un p. de cinco libros al año** on average, he writes five books a year; **hacer** *o* **sacar el p. de algo** to find the average of sth ►► ***p. de goles*** goal average **(b)** *(punto medio)* midpoint

promesa *nf* **(a)** *(compromiso)* promise; **me hizo la p. de que no se lo diría a nadie** he promised me not to tell anyone; **cumplir (con) una p.** to keep a promise; **faltar a una p.** to break a promise **(b)** *(persona)* promising talent; **una joven p. del tenis chileno** a promising young talent of Chilean tennis

promesero, -a *nm,f Andes, RP* pilgrim

prometedor, -ora *adj* promising

prometer 1 *vt* **(a)** *(dar palabra)* to promise; **(te) lo prometo** I promise; **prometo hablar con ella** I promise to talk to her; **te prometo que no miento** I promise you I'm not lying; *Fam* **no aguanto más, te lo prometo** I'm telling you, I can't take any more

(b) *(cargo)* **el presidente prometió su cargo ante el rey** the president was sworn in before the king

(c) *(augurar)* to promise; **este libro promete ser entretenido** this book promises to be entertaining

2 *vi (tener futuro)* **el programa de fiestas promete** the programme for the celebrations looks promising; **esto promete** this is promising

3 prometerse *vpr* **(a)** *(novios)* to get engaged **(b)** *Fam* **prometérselas: se las promete muy felices** he thinks he's got it made; **se las prometían muy felices pero se llevaron un chasco** they had high hopes but they were in for a disappointment

prometido, -a 1 *adj* **(a)** *(para casarse)* engaged **(b)** *(asegurado)* **lo p.** what has been promised, promise; **cumplir lo p.** to keep one's promise; EXPR **lo p. es deuda** a promise is a promise

2 *nm,f* fiancé, *f* fiancée

prometio *nm Quím* promethium

prominencia *nf* **(a)** *(abultamiento)* protuberance **(b)** *(elevación)* rise **(c)** *(importancia)* prominence

prominente *adj* **(a)** *(abultado)* protruding **(b)** *(elevado)* prominent **(c)** *(importante)* prominent

promiscuidad *nf* promiscuity

promiscuo, -a *adj* **(a)** *(persona)* promiscuous **(b)** *(confuso) (colectivo)* motley

promisorio, -a *adj* promissory

promoción *nf* **(a)** *(de producto, candidato)* promotion ►► ***p. de ventas*** sales promotion **(b)** *(ascenso)* promotion **(c)** *(en deportes)* promotion; **van a jugar la p.** they will play off to decide who is promoted **(d)** *(curso)* class, year; **compañeros de p.** classmates; **la p. del 91** the class of 91

promocional *adj* promotional

promocionar 1 *vt* **(a)** *(producto, candidato)* to promote **(b)** *(empleado)* to promote

2 *vi Dep* to play off

3 promocionarse *vpr* to put oneself forward, to promote oneself

promontorio *nm* promontory

promotor, -ora 1 *adj* promoting

2 *nm,f* **(a)** *(constructor)* developer ►► ***p. inmobiliario*** *Br* property *o US* real estate developer **(b)** *(de boxeador, cantante)* promoter **(c)** *(organizador)* organizer; *(de una rebelión)* instigator; **¿quién fue el p. de la idea?** who initiated the idea? ►► ***p. de conciertos*** concert promoter

promover [41] *vt* **(a)** *(iniciar)* to initiate, to bring about; *(impulsar)* to promote; **una campaña para p. la lectura** a campaign designed to promote reading **(b)** *(ocasionar)* to cause; **sus declaraciones promovieron gran indignación** his statements caused *o* provoked considerable indignation **(c)** *(ascender)* **p. a alguien a** to promote sb to

promulgación *nf (de ley, decreto)* passing, enactment

promulgar [38] *vt (ley, decreto)* to pass, to enact

pronación *nf Anat* pronation

pronador, -ora *adj Anat* pronator

pronombre *nm Gram* pronoun ►► ***p. demostrativo*** demonstrative pronoun; ***p. indefinido*** indefinite pronoun; ***p. interrogativo*** interrogative pronoun; ***p. personal*** personal pronoun; ***p. posesivo*** possessive pronoun; ***p. relativo*** relative pronoun

pronominal *Gram* **1** *adj* pronominal

2 *nm* pronominal verb

pronosticar [60] *vt* to predict, to forecast; **han pronosticado sol para el fin de semana** sunshine is forecast for the weekend; **los sindicatos pronostican un año conflictivo** the unions are predicting trouble in the year ahead

pronóstico *nm* **(a)** *(predicción)* forecast ►► ***p. del tiempo*** weather forecast **(b)** *Med* prognosis; **de p. leve** suffering from a mild condition; **de p. grave** in a serious condition; **de p. reservado** under observation

prontitud *nf* promptness; **respondió con p.** she answered promptly

pronto, -a 1 *adj* **(a)** *(rápido)* quick, fast; *(respuesta)* prompt, early; *(curación, tramitación)* speedy; **p. pago** prompt payment **(b)** *RP (preparado)* ready; **¿demorás mucho? – no, ya estoy p.** are you going to be long? – no, I'm ready; **prontos, listos, ¡ya!** ready, steady, go!, on your marks, get set, go!

2 *adv* **(a)** *(rápidamente)* quickly; **tan p. como** as soon as; **lo más p. posible** as soon as possible **(b)** *Esp (temprano)* early; **salimos p.** we left early; **llegó muy p. a la cita** she arrived very early for the appointment **(c)** *(dentro de poco)* soon; **¡hasta p.!** see you soon!; **ya verás cómo encontrarás casa p.** you'll soon find a house, don't worry; **p. se acabará el año** the year will soon be over

3 *nm Fam* **tiene unos prontos de rabia inaguantables** he gets these sudden fits of rage which are really unbearable; **le dio un p. y se fue** something got into him and he left

4 al pronto *loc adv* at first

5 de pronto *loc adv* **(a)** *(imprevistamente)* suddenly; **el ladrón apareció de p. en la salida** the robber suddenly appeared in the exit **(b)** *Andes, RP (tal vez)* perhaps, maybe; **de p. se perdieron** perhaps *o* maybe they got lost

6 por de pronto, por lo pronto *loc adv (de momento)* for the time being; *(para empezar)* to start with; **por de** *o* **lo p. pon los niños a dormir, luego hablaremos** for the moment just put the children to bed, we'll talk later

prontuariar *vt Andes, RP Der* to open a file on

prontuario *nm* **(a)** *(resumen)* summary **(b)** *Andes, RP Der* police record

pronunciación *nf* pronunciation

pronunciado, -a *adj* **(a)** *(facciones)* pronounced **(b)** *(curva)* sharp; *(pendiente, cuesta)* steep **(c)** *(tendencia)* marked

pronunciamiento *nm* **(a)** *(golpe)* (military) coup **(b)** *Der* pronouncement **(c)** *RP (anuncio, declaración)* statement

pronunciar 1 *vt* **(a)** *(palabra, sílaba)* to pronounce; **no sabe p. la erre** he can't pronounce the 'rr' sound; **no pronunció palabra en toda la reunión** she didn't utter a word during the whole meeting **(b)** *(discurso)* to deliver, to make **(c)** *(acentuar, realzar)* to accentuate **(d)** *Der* to pronounce, to pass

2 pronunciarse *vpr* **(a)** *(definirse)* to state an opinion (**sobre** on); **el rey todavía no se ha pronunciado sobre el tema** the king has not yet made any pronouncement on the subject; **el presidente se pronunció a favor del proyecto** the president declared that he was in favour of the project **(b)** *(sublevarse)* to stage a coup

propagación *nf* **(a)** *(extensión, divulgación)* spreading; **cortaron varios árboles para evitar la p. del fuego** they cut down several trees to stop the fire from spreading **(b)** *(de especies, ondas)* propagation

propagador, -ora 1 *adj* **(a)** *(difusor)* spreading **(b)** *(de razas, especies)* propagating

2 *nm,f* **(a)** *(difusor)* spreader **(b)** *(de razas, especies)* propagator

propaganda *nf* **(a)** *(publicidad)* advertising; **hacer p. de algo** to advertise sth; **un folleto de p.** an advertising leaflet **(b)** *(prospectos)* publicity leaflets; *(por correo)* junk mail; **repartir p.** to distribute advertising leaflets; *(en la calle)* to hand out advertising leaflets ►► ***p. electoral*** *(folletos)* election literature; *(anuncios, emisiones)* election campaign advertising **(c)** *(política, religiosa)* propaganda

propagandista *nmf* propagandist

propagandístico, -a *adj* **(a)** *(de producto)* advertising; **campaña propagandística** advertising campaign **(b)** *(de ideas políticas o religiosas)* propaganda; **actividad propagandística** propaganda activity

propagar [38] **1** *vt* **(a)** *(extender, divulgar)* to spread **(b)** *(especies, ondas)* to propagate; **los fuertes vientos propagaron el fuego** the strong winds caused the fire to spread

2 propagarse *vpr* **(a)** *(extenderse, divulgarse)* to spread; **la noticia se propagó rápidamente** the news spread quickly; **el incendio se propagó de forma incontrolada** the fire spread uncontrollably **(b)** *(especies, ondas)* to propagate

propalar *vt* to divulge

propano *nm* propane

proparoxítono, -a *adj Ling* proparoxytone, = stressed on the third-last syllable

propasarse *vpr* **(a)** *(excederse)* to go too far (**con** with); **creo que te propasas con el tabaco** I think you overdo it with the smoking **(b)** *(sexualmente)* **p. con alguien** to make indecent advances to sb

propelente *nm* propellant

propender *vi* to tend, to be inclined

propensión *nf* tendency, propensity; **un niño con p. a encerrarse en sí mismo** a boy with a tendency to retreat into himself; **los fumadores tienen mayor p. a desarrollar determinadas enfermedades** smokers show a greater tendency to develop certain diseases; **tiene p. a resfriarse** she's prone to catching colds; **tiene cierta p. a creer en milagros** he's inclined to believe in miracles

propenso, -a *adj* **p. a algo/a hacer algo** prone to sth/to doing sth

propergol *nm* propellant

propiamente *adv (adecuadamente)* properly; *(verdaderamente)* really, strictly; **p. dicho** strictly speaking

propiciar *vt (favorecer)* to be conducive to; *(causar)* to bring about, to cause; **su actitud desafiante ha propiciado el enfrentamiento** her defiant attitude has helped bring about the confrontation; **la rotura de cristales propició la intervención de la policía** the smashing of windows caused the police to intervene

propiciatorio, -a *adj* propitiatory

propicio, -a *adj (favorable)* propitious, favourable; *(adecuado)* suitable, appropriate; **un bar no es un entorno p. para el estudio** a bar is not a suitable place for studying in

propiedad *nf* **(a)** *(derecho)* ownership; *(bienes)* property; **la casa es p. de sus padres** the house belongs to *o* is owned by her parents; **pertenecer en p. a alguien** to rightfully belong to sb; **tener algo en p.** to own sth ►► ***p. horizontal*** condominium, horizontal property; ***p. industrial*** patent rights; ***p. inmobiliaria*** real estate; ***p. intelectual*** copyright; ***p. privada*** private property; ***p. pública*** public ownership

(b) *(facultad)* property; **las propiedades de una sustancia** the properties of a substance; **con propiedades medicinales** with medicinal properties

(c) *(exactitud)* accuracy; **expresarse** *o* **hablar con p.** to use words properly; **empleaste esa expresión con mucha p.** you used exactly the right expression there

propietario, -a 1 *adj* proprietary

2 *nm,f* **(a)** *(de bienes)* owner **(b)** *(de cargo)* holder

propileno *nm Quím* propylene

propina *nf* **(a)** *(de empleado)* tip; **dar p. (a alguien)** to tip (sb); **dejó 50 céntimos de p.** he left a tip of 50 cents; EXPR **de p.** *(por añadidura)* on top of that **(b)** *(de niño)* pocket money

propinar *vt (paliza)* to give; **le propinó una patada en la pierna** he kicked him in the leg; **me propinó un susto increíble** she gave me a terrible shock

propincuidad *nf Formal* propinquity, proximity

propio, -a 1 *adj* **(a)** *(en propiedad)* own; **tiene coche p.** she has a car of her own, she has her own car; **se requiere vehículo p.** *(en anuncio laboral)* own car required

(b) *(de la misma persona)* **lo vi con mis propios ojos** I saw it with my own eyes; **me lo dijo en mi propia cara** he said it to my face; **actuó en defensa propia** she acted in self-defence; **por tu p. bien** for your own good

(c) *(peculiar)* **p. de** typical *o* characteristic of; **el monzón es p. de esta época** the monsoon is characteristic of this season; **es muy p. de él llegar tarde** it's absolutely typical of him to arrive late; **no es p. de él** it's not like him

(d) *(adecuado)* suitable, right (**para** for); **recitó un poema p. para la ocasión** she recited a suitable poem for the occasion

(e) *(correcto)* proper, true

(f) *(en persona)* himself, *f* herself; **el p. compositor** the composer himself

(g) *(semejante)* true to life; **en ese retrato quedaste muy p.** that portrait is a very good likeness of you

(h) *Gram* proper

(i) lo p. *(lo mismo)* the same; **Elena se retiró a descansar y su compañero hizo lo p.** Elena went to have a rest and her companion did the same

2 *nmpl* **a propios y extraños** all and sundry; **con su victoria sorprendió a propios y extraños** his victory surprised everyone

3 **de propio** *loc adv (expresamente)* **fui de p. a la ciudad para verla** I went to the city just to see her

própolis, propóleo *nm* propolis

proponer [50] 1 *vt* **(a)** *(sugerir)* to propose, to suggest; **han propuesto varias ideas** they have put forward a number of ideas; **propongo ir al cine** I suggest going to the cinema; **me propuso un trato** he proposed a deal; **me propuso que fuéramos al teatro** she suggested going to the theatre

(b) *(candidato)* to put forward; **lo han propuesto para secretario general del partido** he has been put forward as a candidate for party chairman

2 **proponerse** *vpr* **proponerse hacer algo** to plan *o* intend to do sth; **se ha propuesto perder diez kilos** she has decided to lose ten kilos; **el nuevo juez se ha propuesto acabar con la delincuencia** the new judge has set himself the task of putting an end to crime; **consigue todo lo que se propone** she achieves everything she sets out to; **no me proponía ofender a nadie** it wasn't my intention to offend anyone

proporción *nf* **(a)** *(relación)* proportion; **en p. a** in proportion to; **guardar p. (con)** to be in proportion (to); **los dos edificios no guardan p. entre sí** the two buildings are out of proportion

(b) *Mat* proportion ►► ***p. aritmética*** arithmetic proportion; ***p. geométrica*** geometric proportion

(c) proporciones *(tamaño)* size; *(importancia)* extent, scale; **un incendio de grandes proporciones** a major fire; **el escándalo alcanzó proporciones mayúsculas** the scandal reached huge proportions; **un desastre de proporciones gigantescas** a massive disaster

proporcionado, -a *adj (tamaño, sueldo)* commensurate (**a** with); *(medidas)* proportionate (**a** to); **un sueldo p. al trabajo realizado** a salary commensurate with the work performed; **un castigo p. a la falta** a punishment that fits the crime; **bien p.** well-proportioned

proporcional *adj* proportional (**a** to); **dos valores inversamente proporcionales** two inversely proportional values

proporcionalidad *nf* proportionality; **no hay p. entre lo que pide y lo que ofrece** what he's asking for is out of proportion to what he's offering

proporcionalmente *adv* proportionally (**a** to); **el presupuesto se reparte p. a la población de cada región** the budget is divided in proportion to the population of each region

proporcionar *vt* **(a)** *(facilitar)* **p. algo a alguien** to provide sb with sth; **las autoridades proporcionaron alojamiento a todos los refugiados** the authorities provided all the refugees with accommodation; **proporcionamos el material necesario a los alumnos** we provide *o* supply students with the necessary materials

(b) *(ajustar)* **p. algo a algo** to adapt sth to sth; **deben p. los gastos a los ingresos** they ought to adjust their spending to their income

(c) *(producir)* **este niño sólo proporciona disgustos** that child causes nothing but trouble; **esta música proporciona paz y tranquilidad** this music produces a sensation of peace and tranquility

proposición *nf* **(a)** *(propuesta)* proposal; **una p. de matrimonio** a proposal of marriage; **hacer proposiciones a alguien** to proposition sb ►► ***proposiciones deshonestas*** improper advances **(b)** *Gram* clause **(c)** *(en lógica)* proposition

propósito 1 *nm* **(a)** *(intención)* intention; **mi p. era llamarte cuando llegara** I had intended to phone you when I arrived; **tengo el p. de dejar el alcohol** I intend to give up alcohol; **hizo el p. de no volver a fumar** she made a resolution *o* resolved not to smoke again; **con el p. de** in order to; **con este p.** to this end

(b) *(objetivo)* purpose; **el p. de las medidas es contener la inflación** the purpose *o* aim of the measures is to control inflation; **una ley con el único p. de ayudar a los más débiles** a law the sole purpose of which is to help the weakest

2 **a propósito** *loc adv* **(a)** *(adecuado)* suitable; **tu ayuda nos viene muy a p.** your help is coming just at the right time

(b) *(adrede)* on purpose; **hacer algo a p.** to do sth on purpose *o* deliberately; **no lo hice a p.** I didn't do it on purpose; **lo dijo a p. para que nos enfadáramos** he said it deliberately to annoy us

(c) *(por cierto)* by the way; **a p. de viajes, ¿has estado en Japón?** speaking of travelling, have you been to Japan?

3 **a propósito de** *loc prep* with regard to, concerning; **ha habido un gran debate público a p. de la ley** there has been considerable public debate concerning the law

propuesta *nf (proposición)* proposal; *(de empleo)* offer; **me hicieron una p. de trabajo** they made me a job offer; **la p. de Juan como tesorero fue aprobada por unanimidad** Juan's nomination as treasurer was approved unanimously; **se guardó un minuto de silencio, a p. del presidente** there was a minute's silence at the suggestion of the president ►► ***p. de ley*** bill; ***p. no de ley*** = motion for debate presented to parliament by someone other than the government

propuesto, -a *participio ver* **proponer**

propugnar *vt* to advocate, to support

propulsante *nm* propellant

propulsar *vt* **(a)** *(vehículo)* to propel **(b)** *(plan, actividad)* to promote

propulsión *nf* propulsion ►► ***p. a chorro*** jet propulsion; ***p. a reacción*** jet propulsion

propulsor, -ora 1 *adj* propulsive

2 *nm,f (persona)* promoter

3 *nm* **(a)** *(dispositivo)* engine **(b)** *(combustible)* propellant

propusiera *etc ver* **proponer**

prorrata *nf* quota, share; **a p.** pro rata

prorratear *vt* to divide proportionally

prorrateo *nm* sharing out (proportionally)

prórroga *nf* (**a**) *(de plazo, tiempo)* extension; **les concedieron dos semanas de p. para la entrega del proyecto** they were given a two-week extension for handing in the project (**b**) *(en deporte) Br* extra time, *US* overtime (**c**) *(de estudios, servicio militar)* deferment; **le concedieron una p. por estudios** *(del servicio militar)* he was granted a deferment for his studies

prorrogable *adj* **un permiso de trabajo p. por dos años** a work permit which can be extended by two years; **un plazo no p.** a deadline which cannot be extended

prorrogar [38] *vt* (**a**) *(alargar)* to extend; **han prorrogado el plazo dos semanas más** the deadline has been extended by a further two weeks (**b**) *(aplazar)* to defer, to postpone

prorrumpir *vi* **p. en** to burst into; **el público prorrumpió en aplausos** the public broke into applause

prosa *nf* (**a**) *(en literatura)* prose; **en p.** in prose (**b**) *Andes Fam (petulancia)* pomposity; **echar** *o* **tirar p.** to give oneself airs

prosaico, -a *adj (trivial)* mundane, prosaic; *(materialista)* materialistic

prosapia *nf* lineage, ancestry

proscenio *nm Teatro* proscenium

proscribir *vt* (**a**) *(prohibir)* to ban (**b**) *(desterrar)* to banish

proscripción *nf* (**a**) *(prohibición)* banning (**b**) *(destierro)* banishment, exile

proscrito, -a, *RP* **proscripto, -a** **1** *participio ver* **proscribir**
 2 *adj* (**a**) *(prohibido)* banned (**b**) *(desterrado)* banished
 3 *nm,f* (**a**) *(fuera de la ley)* outlaw (**b**) *(desterrado)* exile

prosecución *nf Formal* continuation; **aprobaron la p. de la huelga** they voted to continue the strike

proseguir [62] **1** *vt* to continue; **prosiguió sus estudios en el extranjero** she continued her studies aboad
 2 *vi* to go on, to continue (**con** with); **prosiguen los ataques a colonos** the attacks on settlers are continuing; **la tormenta impidió p. con el concierto** the storm prevented the concert from continuing; **prosigue con tu relato, por favor** please go on *o* continue with your account

proselitismo *nm* proselytism; **hacer p.** to proselytize

proselitista **1** *adj* proselytizing
 2 *nmf* proselytizer

prosélito, -a *nm,f* proselyte

prosificar *vt* to turn into prose

prosigo *etc ver* **proseguir**

prosiguiera *etc ver* **proseguir**

prosista *nmf* (**a**) *(escritor)* prose writer (**b**) *Andes Fam (petulante)* pompous ass

prosodia *nf* (**a**) *Gram* prosody (**b**) *Lit* prosody

prosódico, -a *adj* (**a**) *Gram* orthoepic (**b**) *Lit* prosodic

prosopopeya *nf* (**a**) *Lit* prosopopeia, personification (**b**) *(solemnidad)* ceremoniousness, pomposity

prospección *nf* (**a**) *(de terreno)* prospecting; **están realizando prospecciones en busca de petróleo** they are prospecting for oil ►► ***p. geológica*** geological prospecting; ***p. petrolífera*** oil prospecting (**b**) *(estudio)* research ►► ***p. de mercados*** market research

prospectar *vt* to prospect

prospectivo, -a *adj* exploratory

prospecto *nm* (**a**) *(folleto)* leaflet ►► *Fin* ***p. de emisión*** *(de acciones)* prospectus (**b**) *(de medicamento)* = leaflet giving directions for use

prosperar *vi* (**a**) *(mejorar)* to prosper, to thrive (**b**) *(triunfar)* to be successful; **la idea no prosperó** the idea was unsuccessful

prosperidad *nf* (**a**) *(mejora)* prosperity (**b**) *(éxito)* success

próspero, -a *adj* prosperous, flourishing; **¡p. Año Nuevo!** Happy New Year!

prostaglandina *nf Fisiol* prostaglandin

próstata *nf* prostate

prosternarse *vpr Formal* to prostrate oneself

prostíbulo *nm* brothel

próstilo *Arquit* **1** *adj* prostyle
 2 *nm* prostyle

prostitución *nf* (**a**) *(actividad)* prostitution (**b**) *(de ideales, valores)* betrayal

prostituir [34] **1** *vt* (**a**) *(sexualmente)* to prostitute (**b**) *(ideales, valores)* to betray
 2 prostituirse *vpr* (**a**) *(sexualmente)* to prostitute oneself (**b**) *(envilecerse)* to prostitute oneself

prostituta *nf* prostitute

prostituto *nm* male prostitute

protactinio *nm Quím* protactinium

protagonismo *nm* (**a**) *(importancia)* significance, importance; **buscan un mayor p. de las mujeres en la política** their aim is for women to play a more prominent role in politics; **han criticado su afán de p.** his desire to be the centre of attention *o* in the limelight has been criticized; **el atentado restó p. a la cumbre de presidentes** the attack diverted attention from the presidential summit
 (**b**) *(en suceso)* key role; **los militares tuvieron un p. destacado en la caída del régimen** the military played a key role in the downfall of the regime

protagonista *nmf* (**a**) *(de libro, película)* main *o* central character; *(de obra de teatro)* lead, leading role; **un actor que sólo acepta papeles de p.** an actor who only accepts leading roles
 (**b**) *(de suceso)* **los protagonistas de la revolución** the chief actors in the revolution; **ser p. de** *(acontecimiento histórico)* to play a leading part in; *(accidente)* to be one of the main people involved in; *(entrevista, estudio)* to be the subject of

protagonizar [14] *vt* (**a**) *(película, obra)* to play the lead in, to star in; *(libro)* to be the main character in (**b**) *(acontecimiento histórico)* to play a leading part in; *(accidente)* to be one of the main people involved in; *(entrevista, estudio)* to be the subject of

protección *nf* protection; **diez guardaespaldas se encargan de la p. del juez** ten bodyguards are responsible for protecting the judge; **sexo sin p.** unprotected sex ►► ***p. civil*** civil defence; *Informát* ***p. contra copia*** copy protection; ***p. de datos*** data protection; *Informát* ***p. de hardware*** dongle

proteccionismo *nm Econ* protectionism

proteccionista *Econ* **1** *adj* protectionist
 2 *nmf* protectionist

protector, -ora **1** *adj* protective; **pintura protectora** weatherproof paint; **casco p.** crash helmet
 2 *nm,f (persona)* protector
 3 *nm (objeto) (en boxeo)* gumshield ►► ***p. labial*** lip salve; *Informát* ***p. de pantalla*** *(salvapantallas)* screensaver

protectorado *nm* protectorate

proteger [52] **1** *vt* (**a**) *(persona, animal, objeto)* to protect (**de** *o* **contra** from *o* against); **el sombrero me protege del sol** the hat protects me from the sun, the hat keeps the sun off me; **la roca nos protegía del viento** the rock protected us against the wind; **los guardaespaldas la protegieron de los fans** the bodyguards shielded her from the fans; **un organismo para p. la fauna** an organization set up to protect wildlife, a wildlife organization
 (**b**) *Econ (productos)* to protect
 (**c**) *Informát* to protect
 2 protegerse *vpr* to take cover *o* refuge (**de** *o* **contra** from); **se protegió del fuerte sol con un sombrero** she wore a hat to protect herself from the strong sun; **se protegieron del bombardeo en un refugio** they took refuge from the bombing in a shelter; **se protegió la cara con las manos** he shielded *o* protected his face with his hands

protege-slips *nm inv* panty liner

protegido, -a **1** *adj* (**a**) *(especie)* protected (**b**) *Informát* protected; **p. contra copia** copy-protected; **p. contra escritura** write-protected
 2 *nm,f* protégé, *f* protégée

proteico, -a *adj* (**a**) *Literario (cambiante)* protean (**b**) *(de la proteína)* protein; **necesidades proteicas** protein requirements

proteína *nf* protein

proteínico, -a *adj* protein; **deficiencia proteínica** protein deficiency

protésico, -a **1** *adj* prosthetic
 2 *nm,f* prosthetist ►► ***p. dental*** dental technician

prótesis *nf inv* (**a**) *Med* prosthesis; *(miembro)* artificial limb; **p. auditiva** hearing aid; **p. dental** dentures (**b**) *Gram* prothesis

protesta *nf* (**a**) *(queja)* protest; **se manifestaron en p. por la realización de pruebas nucleares** they demonstrated in protest at the nuclear tests; **bajo p.** under protest; **en señal de p.** in protest (**b**) *(manifestación)* protest (**c**) *Der* objection; **se admite la p.** objection sustained; **p. denegada** objection overruled (**d**) *Méx (promesa)* oath

protestante **1** *adj* Protestant
 2 *nmf* Protestant

protestantismo *nm* Protestantism

protestar 1 *vi* (**a**) *(quejarse)* to protest (**por/contra** about/against); **los manifestantes protestaban contra la detención del líder sindical** the demonstrators were protesting against the arrest of the union leader; **protestaron por el mal servicio** they complained about the poor service; **haz lo que te digo sin p.** do what I tell you without complaining; **deja ya de p.** stop complaining
(**b**) *Der* **¡protesto!** *(en juicio)* objection!
2 *vt* (**a**) *Com* to protest (**b**) *Méx (prometer)* **el presidente protestó su cargo ante el congreso** the president was sworn in before parliament

protesto *nm Com* protest ▸▸ ***p. de letra*** noting bill of exchange

protestón, -ona *Fam* 1 *adj* **es muy p.** *(que se queja)* he's always complaining; *(que refunfuña)* he's always moaning
2 *nm,f (que se queja)* complainer, awkward customer; *(que refunfuña)* grumbler, moaner

prótido *nm* protide

protocolario, -a *adj* ceremonial; **fue una visita protocolaria** it was a ceremonial visit

protocolo *nm* (**a**) *(ceremonial)* protocol; **como exige el p.** as required by protocol; **seguir el p.** to follow protocol (**b**) *Der* = documents handled by a solicitor (**c**) *Informát* protocol ▸▸ ***p. de comunicación*** communications protocol; ***p. de Internet*** Internet protocol (**d**) *(acta)* protocol ▸▸ ***el P. de Kioto*** the Kyoto agreement (**e**) *Méx (de experimento)* protocol

protohistoria *nf* protohistory

protomártir *nm* protomartyr

protón *nm* proton

protoplasma *nm* protoplasm

protoplasmático, -a, protoplásmico, -a *adj* protoplasmic

prototípico, -a *adj* prototypical

prototipo *nm* (**a**) *(modelo)* archetype; **el p. de ejecutivo agresivo** the archetypal aggressive executive; **es el p. del egoísmo** he's selfishness personified (**b**) *(primer ejemplar)* prototype

protozoo *nm* protozoan, protozoon

protráctil *adj* protractile

protuberancia *nf* protuberance, bulge ▸▸ ***p. solar*** solar prominence

protuberante *adj* protuberant; **nariz p.** big nose

provecho *nm* (**a**) *(beneficio)* benefit; **sólo busca el p. personal** all he is interested in is personal gain; **sus explicaciones nos fueron de gran p.** we found her explanations very helpful; **en p. propio** in one's own interest, for one's own benefit; **hacer p. a alguien** to do sb good; **sacar p. de** *(aprovecharse de)* to make the most of, to take advantage of; *(beneficiarse de)* to benefit from, to profit from; **no saqué nada de p. de su conferencia** I didn't learn *o* gain anything useful from her lecture; **¡buen p.!** enjoy your meal!; **un hombre de p.** a useful member of society
(**b**) *RP (eructo)* burp; **ya hizo p.** she has already burped

provechosamente *adv* (**a**) *(ventajosamente)* advantageously (**b**) *(lucrativamente)* profitably

provechoso, -a *adj* (**a**) *(ventajoso)* beneficial, advantageous; **sus consejos nos fueron muy provechosos** we found his advice very helpful (**b**) *(lucrativo)* profitable

provecto, -a *adj Formal (persona)* elderly; **la edad provecta** old age; **un hombre de edad provecta** a man advanced in years

proveedor, -ora 1 *nm,f* supplier
2 *nm Informát* ***p. de acceso (a Internet)*** Internet access provider; ***p. de servicios Internet*** Internet service provider

proveer [37] 1 *vt* (**a**) *(abastecer)* to supply, to provide; **p. a alguien de algo** to provide *o* supply sb with sth; **la empresa provee de acceso a Internet al ministerio** the company acts as Internet service provider for the Ministry (**b**) *(puesto, cargo)* to fill
2 *vi* **¡Dios proveerá!** God will provide!
3 **proveerse** *vpr* **proveerse de** *(ropa, víveres)* to stock up on; *(medios, recursos)* to arm oneself with

proveniente *adj* **p. de** (coming) from

provenir [71] *vi* **p. de** to come from; **sus problemas económicos provienen de su afición al juego** his financial problems all have their roots in his fondness for gambling

provenzal 1 *adj* Provençal
2 *nmf (persona)* Provençal
3 *nm (lengua)* Provençal

proverbial *adj* proverbial

proverbio *nm* proverb; *Rel* **Proverbios** Proverbs

providencia *nf* (**a**) *Rel* **la (Divina) P.** (Divine) Providence (**b**) *(medida)* measure, step; **tomaron providencias para evitar un atentado** measures were taken to prevent an attack (**c**) *Der* ruling; **el juez dictó varias providencias** the judge issued several orders

providencial *adj* (**a**) *(de la Providencia)* providential (**b**) *(oportuno)* fortunate; **fue p. que pasara por ahí una ambulancia** it was most fortunate that an ambulance should happen to be passing by; **una p. tormenta ayudó a contener el incendio** a timely storm helped to stop the fire from spreading

provídente *adj* provident

próvido, -a *adj Literario* munificent; **la mano próvida del Señor** the Lord's providing hand

proviene *etc ver* **provenir**

provincia 1 *nf* (**a**) *(división administrativa)* province (**b**) *Rel* province
2 **provincias** *nfpl (no la capital)* the provinces; **la gente de provincias** people who live in the provinces; **hacer una gira por provincias** to go on a tour of the provinces

provincial 1 *adj* provincial
2 *nmf Rel* provincial

provincianismo *nm* provincialism

provinciano, -a 1 *adj* (**a**) *(de la provincia)* provincial (**b**) *Pey (de mentalidad cerrada)* provincial, parochial (**c**) *Pey (rústico)* provincial, old-fashioned
2 *nm,f* (**a**) *Pey (de mentalidad cerrada)* **ser un p.** to be very parochial (**b**) *Pey (rústico) Br* country bumpkin, *US* hick

proviniera *etc ver* **provenir**

provisión *nf* (**a**) *(suministro)* supply, provision ▸▸ ***p. de fondos*** advance (**b**) **provisiones** *(alimentos)* provisions (**c**) *(disposición)* measure (**d**) *(de una plaza)* filling (**e**) *Urug (almacén) Br* grocer's shop, *US* grocery store

provisional, *Am* **provisorio, -a** *adj* provisional

provisionalidad *nf* provisional nature

provisionalmente *adv* provisionally

provisorio = **provisional**

provisto, -a *participio ver* **proveer**

provitamina *nf* provitamin

provocación *nf* (**a**) *(desplante)* provocation; **recibieron instrucciones de evitar las provocaciones** they were instructed to avoid provocation; **el delantero respondió con una patada a las provocaciones del defensa** the forward reacted to the defender's provocation by kicking him
(**b**) *(de incendio)* starting; *(de revuelta)* instigation; **le achacaron la p. del incidente** he was accused of causing the incident

provocador, -ora 1 *adj* (**a**) *(ofensivo)* provocative (**b**) *(vestido)* provocative
2 *nm,f* agitator

provocadoramente *adv* provocatively

provocar [60] 1 *vt* (**a**) *(incitar)* to provoke; **¡no me provoques!** don't provoke me!
(**b**) *(causar) (accidente, muerte)* to cause; *(incendio, rebelión)* to start; *(sonrisa, burla)* to elicit; **una placa de hielo provocó el accidente** the accident was caused by a sheet of black ice; **p. las iras de alguien** to anger sb; **provocó las risas de todos** he made everyone laugh; **el polvo me provoca estornudos** dust makes me sneeze; **su actitud me provoca más lástima que otra cosa** her attitude makes me pity her more than anything else
(**c**) *(excitar sexualmente)* to lead on; **le gusta p. a los chicos con su ropa** she likes to tease the boys with her clothes
2 *vi Carib, Col, Méx Fam (apetecer)* **¿te provoca ir al cine?** would you like to go to the movies?, *Br* do you fancy going to the cinema?; **¿te provoca un vaso de vino?** would you like a glass of wine?, *Br* do you fancy a glass of wine?; **¿qué te provoca?** what would you like to do?, *Br* what do you fancy doing?

provocativo, -a *adj* (**a**) *(ofensivo)* provocative (**b**) *(insinuante)* provocative

proxeneta *nmf* pimp, *f* procuress

proxenetismo *nm* pimping, procuring

próximamente *adv* (**a**) *(pronto)* soon, shortly (**b**) *(en cartelera)* coming soon

proximidad 1 *nf* (**a**) *(en el tiempo)* closeness, proximity; **dada la p. de las elecciones** as the elections are imminent
(**b**) *(en el espacio)* closeness, proximity; **lo que más me gusta de esta casa es su p. al centro** what I like best about this house is that it's so close to the centre

2 proximidades *nfpl (de ciudad)* surrounding area; *(de lugar)* vicinity; **el avión cayó al mar en las proximidades de las Bahamas** the plane crashed into the sea in the vicinity of the Bahamas

próximo, -a *adj* (**a**) *(en el tiempo)* near, close; **en fecha próxima** shortly; **las vacaciones están próximas** the holidays are nearly here
(**b**) *(en el espacio)* near, close; **una casa próxima al río** a house near the river; **el colegio está muy p. al centro** the school is very near to the centre
(**c**) *(en número)* close; **un número de muertos p. al centenar** a death toll approaching one hundred
(**d**) *(siguiente)* next; **el p. año** next year; **el p. domingo** next Sunday; **la próxima vez** next time; **me bajo en la próxima** I'm getting off at the next stop; **gira en la próxima a la derecha** take the next right

proxy ['proksi] *nm Informát* proxy

proyección *nf* (**a**) *(de película)* screening, showing; **una p. de diapositivas** a slide show
(**b**) *(de mapa)* projection ▸▸ ***p. cartográfica*** map projection; ***p. cilíndrica*** cylindrical projection; ***p. cónica*** conical projection; ***p. ortogonal*** orthogonal projection
(**c**) *Mat* projection
(**d**) *(lanzamiento)* throwing forwards
(**e**) *(trascendencia)* importance; **con p. de futuro** with a promising future; **la p. internacional de una empresa** the international presence *o* profile of a company

proyeccionista *nmf Cine* projectionist

proyectar 1 *vt* (**a**) *(luz)* to shine, to direct; *(sombra)* to cast
(**b**) *(mostrar) (película)* to project, to screen; *(diapositivas)* to show
(**c**) *(viaje, operación)* to plan; **proyectan ir de vacaciones a la playa** they are planning to go on holiday to the seaside
(**d**) *(edificio)* to plan; *(puente, obra)* to design
(**e**) *(arrojar)* to throw forwards; **la fuente proyectaba un chorro de agua** a jet of water was spurting out of the fountain
(**f**) *Mat* to project
(**g**) *Psi* to project
2 proyectarse *vpr (sombra, silueta)* to be cast

proyectil *nm* projectile, missile ▸▸ ***p. dirigido*** guided missile; ***p. teledirigido*** guided missile

proyectista *nmf* designer

proyecto *nm* (**a**) *(plan)* plan; **tener en p. hacer algo** to be planning to do sth; **tengo el p. de viajar cuando me jubile** I'm planning to travel when I retire
(**b**) *(programa)* project; **un p. de investigación** a research project
(**c**) *(diseño) (de edificio)* design; *(de pieza, maquinaria)* plan
(**d**) *(borrador)* draft ▸▸ ***p. de ley*** bill
(**e**) *Educ* ***p. de fin de carrera*** final project *(completed after the end of architecture or engineering degree)*; ***p. de investigación*** *(de un grupo)* research project; *(de una persona)* dissertation

proyector, -ora 1 *adj* projecting
2 *nm* (**a**) *(de cine, diapositivas)* projector ▸▸ ***p. cinematográfico*** film projector; ***p. de diapositivas*** slide projector (**b**) *(foco)* searchlight; *(en el teatro)* spotlight

prozac® *nm* Prozac®

PRSC *nm (abrev de* **Partido Reformista Social Cristiano**) = political party in the Dominican Republic

prudencia *nf* (**a**) *(cuidado, cautela)* care; *(previsión, sensatez)* good sense, prudence; **habló con mucha p.** she chose her words very carefully; **conduce con p.** she's a careful driver (**b**) *(moderación)* moderation; **con p.** in moderation

prudencial *adj* (**a**) *(sensato)* sensible; **dejé pasar un tiempo p. antes de irme** I waited a prudent amount of time before leaving (**b**) *(moderado)* moderate; **una cantidad p. de vino** a moderate amount of wine

prudenciarse *vpr CAm, Col, Méx* to be cautious

prudente *adj* (**a**) *(cuidadoso)* careful; *(previsor, sensato)* sensible, prudent; **lo más p. sería esperar** the most sensible thing would be to wait; **se mostró muy p. en sus declaraciones** she was very careful about what she said; **es muy p. conduciendo** he's a very careful driver
(**b**) *(razonable)* reasonable; **a una hora p.** at a reasonable time; **a una distancia p.** at a safe distance

prudentemente *adv* (**a**) *(cuidadosamente)* carefully, cautiously (**b**) *(juiciosamente)* prudently

PRUEBA 1 *ver* **probar**
2 *nf* (**a**) *(demostración)* proof; **no existe ninguna p. de que haya copiado en el examen** there is no proof that he copied during the exam; **dio pruebas irrefutables de que era inocente** she gave irrefutable proof of her innocence, she proved beyond doubt that she was innocent; **no tengo pruebas** I have no proof; **¡ahí tienes la p.!** that proves it!
(**b**) *Der* piece of evidence; **pruebas** evidence, proof; **fue absuelto por falta de pruebas** he was acquitted owing to a lack of evidence; **presentar pruebas** to submit evidence; **a las pruebas me remito** the evidence will bear me out ▸▸ ***pruebas indiciarias*** circumstantial evidence; ***pruebas de indicios*** circumstantial evidence; ***pruebas instrumentales*** documentary evidence
(**c**) *(manifestación, señal)* sign; **eso es p. de que les importa** this proves they care, this is a sign that they care; **a mitad de carrera empezó a dar pruebas de cansancio** halfway through the race she started to show signs of tiring; **en** *o* **como p. de mi amistad** in *o* as proof of friendship; **le hice el regalo como p. de agradecimiento/mi amor** I gave her the present as a token of my gratitude/love
(**d**) *(examen académico)* test; **el examen consta de una p. escrita y otra oral** the exam has an oral part and a written part ▸▸ ***p. de acceso*** entrance examination; ***p. de aptitud*** aptitude test
(**e**) *(comprobación, ensayo, experimento)* test; **hicimos la p. de cambiar las pilas** we tried changing the batteries; **¡haga usted la p.!** try it and see!; **hacerle a alguien una p.** to test sb, to give sb a test; EXPR *RP Fam* **hacer la p.: te voy a abandonar para siempre – hacé la p.** I'm going to walk out and leave you for good – go on, then! ▸▸ ***p. del ADN*** DNA test; ***p. del alcohol*** Breathalyser® test; **hacer la p. del alcohol a alguien** to breathalyse sb; ***p. de (la) alcoholemia*** Breathalyser® test; ***p. antidopaje*** drugs test; ***p. antidoping*** drugs test; **hacer la p. antidoping a alguien** to test sb for drugs; ***p. del embarazo*** pregnancy test; **hacerse la p. del embarazo** to take a pregnancy test; *Fig* ***la p. de fuego*** the acid test; ***p. nuclear*** nuclear test; ***pruebas nucleares*** nuclear testing; ***p. de (la) paternidad*** paternity test; ***p. de resistencia*** endurance test; ***la p. del sida*** AIDS test; **hacerle a alguien la p. del sida** to test sb for AIDS; **hacerse la p. del sida** to have an AIDS test; ***p. de sonido*** sound check
(**f**) *(trance)* ordeal, trial; **la distancia fue una dura p. para su relación** being separated really put their relationship to the test
(**g**) *Dep* event; **la p. de los 110 metros vallas** the 110 metres hurdles; **la p. de lanzamiento de jabalina** the javelin; **una p. ciclista** a cycling race ▸▸ ***p. clásica*** classic; ***p. clasificatoria*** heat; ***p. eliminatoria*** heat; ***p. de saltos*** *(de equitación)* show jumping (competition)
(**h**) *Imprenta* proof; **corregir pruebas, hacer corrección de pruebas** to proofread
(**i**) *Fot* ***p. negativa*** negative; ***p. positiva*** print
(**j**) *Am (ejercicio)* acrobatic feat
3 a prueba *loc adj (trabajador)* on trial; *(producto comprado)* on approval; **a p. de agua** waterproof; **a p. de balas** bulletproof; **a p. de bombas** bombproof; *Hum* **tiene un estómago a p. de bombas** she has an iron stomach; **fe a toda p.** *o* **a p. de bombas** unshakeable faith; **paciencia a toda p.** *o* **a p. de bombas** unwavering patience; **poner algo/a alguien a p.** to put sth/sb to the test; **poner a p. la paciencia de alguien** to try sb's patience

prurigo *nm Med* prurigo

prurito *nm* (**a**) *Med* itch, itching (**b**) *(afán, deseo)* urge; **su p. de modernidad es inaguantable** he is obsessively driven to be modern

Prusia *n Hist* Prussia

prusiano, -a *Hist* **1** *adj* Prussian
2 *nm,f* Prussian

PS (**a**) *(abrev de* **post scríptum**) PS (**b**) *(abrev de* **Partido Socialista**) = Socialist Party

PSC *nm (abrev de* **Partido Social Cristiano**) = Ecuadoran political party

pseudo- *pref* pseudo-

pseudociencia *nf* pseudoscience

pseudofármaco *nm* = product claiming medical benefits, but not subject to legal tests of effectiveness

pseudónimo *nm* pseudonym

PSI *nm Informát (abrev de* **Proveedor de Servicios Internet**) ISP

psi *nf* psi

psico- *pref* psycho-

psicoanálisis *nm inv* psychoanalysis

psicoanalista *nmf* psychoanalyst

psicoanalítico, -a *adj* psychoanalytic(al)

psicoanalizar [14] **1** *vt* to psychoanalyze
2 psicoanalizarse *vpr* to be psychoanalyzed

psicodélico, -a *adj* psychedelic

psicodrama *nm* psychodrama

psicofármaco *nm* psychotropic *o* psychoactive drug

psicofonía *nf* seance
psicolingüística *nf* psycholinguistics *(singular)*
psicología *nf* (**a**) *(ciencia)* psychology ►► ***p. clínica*** clinical psychology; ***p. cognitiva*** cognitive psychology; ***p. infantil*** child psychology; ***p. del trabajo*** occupational psychology
(**b**) *(forma de pensar)* psychology; **la p. de los niños** the psychology of children, the way children think
(**c**) *(comprensión)* **tiene mucha p. para las negociaciones** he understands the psychology of negotiating; **hay que tener mucha p. para tratar con niños** to deal with children you need to understand how their minds work
psicológicamente *adv* psychologically
psicológico, -a *adj* psychological
psicólogo, -a *nm,f* (**a**) *(profesional)* psychologist ►► ***p. clínico*** clinical psychology; ***p. cognitivo*** cognitive psychologist; ***p. infantil*** child psychologist; ***p. del trabajo*** occupational psychologist
(**b**) *(persona perceptiva)* **el entrenador es un p. excepcional** the coach has an exceptional understanding of how players' minds work
psicometría *nf* psychometrics *(singular)*
psicomotor, -triz, psicomotor, -ora *adj* psychomotor
psicomotricidad *nf* psychomotricity
psicópata *nmf* psychopath
psicopatía *nf* psychopathy, psychopathic personality
psicopático, -a *adj* psychopathic
psicopatología *nf* psychopathology
psicopedagogo, -a *nm,f* educational psychologist
psicosis *nf inv* (**a**) *(enfermedad)* psychosis ►► ***p. maníaco-depresiva*** manic-depressive psychosis (**b**) *(miedo)* psychosis; **la expansión de la enfermedad ha provocado una p. colectiva** the spread of the disease has sparked collective psychosis
psicosomático, -a *adj* psychosomatic
psicotécnico, -a 1 *adj* psychotechnical
2 *nm,f* psychotechnician
3 *nm (prueba)* psychotechnical test
psicoterapeuta *nmf* psychotherapist
psicoterapéutico, -a *adj* psychotherapeutic
psicoterapia *nf* psychotherapy
psicótico, -a 1 *adj* psychotic
2 *nm,f* psychotic
psicotrópico, -a *adj* psychotropic, psychoactive
psique *nf* psyche
psiquiatra *nmf* psychiatrist
psiquiatría *nf* psychiatry
psiquiátrico, -a 1 *adj* psychiatric
2 *nm* psychiatric *o* mental hospital
psíquico, -a *adj* psychic
psiquis *nf inv* psyche
psitacosis *nf inv Med* psittacosis
psoas *nm inv Anat* psoas
PSOE [pe'soe, 'soe] *nm (abrev de* **Partido Socialista Obrero Español**) = Spanish political party to the centre-left of the political spectrum
psoriasis *nf inv* psoriasis
pta. (*pl* **ptas.**) (*abrev de* **peseta**) pta
PTB *nm Perú (abrev de* **producto territorial bruto**) GDP
pte. (*abrev de* **presidente**) Pres
pterodáctilo [tero'ðaktilo] *nm* pterodactyl
ptomaína [toma'ina] *nf Biol* ptomaine
púa *nf* (**a**) *(de planta)* thorn; *(de erizo)* barb, quill (**b**) *(de peine)* spine, tooth; *(de tenedor)* prong (**c**) *Mús* plectrum (**d**) *(de tocadiscos)* needle (**e**) *Esp Antes Fam (peseta)* peseta
pub [paβ, paf] (*pl* **pubs**) *nm (bar)* bar *(open late, usually with music)*; *(de estilo irlandés)* pub
púber *Formal* 1 *adj* adolescent
2 *nmf* adolescent
pubertad *nf* puberty
púbico, -a, pubiano, -a *adj* pubic
pubis *nm inv* (**a**) *(área)* pubes (**b**) *(hueso)* pubic bone
publicación *nf* (**a**) *(acción)* publication; **una revista de p. semanal** a weekly magazine (**b**) *(escrito, revista)* publication
públicamente *adv* publicly
publicano *nm Hist* publican
publicar [60] *vt* (**a**) *(libro, revista)* to publish; **el escritor está a punto de p. una nueva novela** the writer is about to have a new novel published (**b**) *(difundir)* to publicize; *(noticia)* to make known, to make public; *(aviso)* to issue; *(ley)* = to bring a law into effect by publishing it in the official government gazette
publicidad *nf* (**a**) *(difusión)* publicity; **dar p. a algo** to publicize sth; **han preferido no dar p. al nombramiento** they have chosen not to make the appointment public
(**b**) *Com (promoción)* advertising; *(en televisión)* adverts, commercials; **una campaña de p.** an advertising campaign ►► ***p. directa*** direct mailing; ***p. estática*** billboards; ***p. subliminal*** subliminal advertising
(**c**) *(folletos)* advertising material; **no me gusta recibir p. por correo** I don't like being sent junk mail
publicista *nmf* advertising agent
publicitario, -a 1 *adj* advertising; **pausa publicitaria** commercial break
2 *nm,f* advertising agent
público, -a 1 *adj* (**a**) *(colegio, transporte, teléfono, servicio)* public; **personaje p.** public figure; **un acto p. en honor al escritor fallecido** a public ceremony in honour of the late writer; **ese andamio es un peligro p.** that scaffolding is a danger to the public; **eso es de dominio p.** that's public knowledge; **en p.** in public; **no le gusta hablar en p.** she doesn't like speaking in public; **hacer algo p.** to make sth public
(**b**) *(del Estado)* public; **el sector p.** the public sector; **un funcionario p.** a public sector worker
(**c**) *(conocido)* public; **ser p.** to be common knowledge
2 *nm* (**a**) *(en espectáculo)* audience; *(en encuentro deportivo)* crowd; **una película dirigida al p. infantil** a movie aimed at young audiences; **para todos los públicos** *o CSur* **para todo p.** (suitable) for all ages; *(película) Br* ≃ U, *US* ≃ G; **muy poco p. asistió al encuentro** very few people attended the game; **tiene un p. fiel** she has a loyal following
(**b**) *(comunidad)* public; **el gran p.** the (general) public; **abierto al p.** open to the public
publirreportaje *nm (en televisión)* promotional film; *(en revista)* advertising spread
pucará *nf Andes, Arg Hist* Indian hill fortress
pucha *interj Andes, RP Fam Euf* (**a**) *(lamento) Br* sugar!, *US* shoot!; **¡p.!, ¡cómo pasa el tiempo!** jeez, it's getting late!; **¡p. digo, ya son las 12!** *Br* sugar *o US* shoot! it's 12 o'clock already! (**b**) *(sorpresa)* wow; **¡p. que llegaste rápido!** wow, you got here fast!; **¿50 años? ¡la p.!** 50 years old? get away! *o* never! (**c**) *(enojo) Br* sugar!, *US* shoot!; **¡la p.!, perdí las llaves** *Br* sugar *o US* shoot! I've lost my keys!
pucherazo *nm Fam* electoral fraud
puchero *nm* (**a**) *(recipiente)* cooking pot (**b**) *(comida)* stew (**c**) *(gesto)* pout; **hacer pucheros** to pout
puchito: de a puchitos *loc adv Andes, RP Fam* bit by bit
pucho *Fam* 1 *nm* (**a**) *Andes, RP (cigarrillo)* cigarette, *Br* fag (**b**) *Andes, RP (colilla)* cigarette butt (**c**) *Chile, Ecuad (hijo menor)* youngest child (**d**) EXPR *RP* **sobre el p.** in the nick of time
2 **de a puchos** *loc adv Andes, RP* bit by bit; **fue comiendo de a puchos hasta terminar el plato** she went on taking tiny mouthfuls until the plate was empty; **está pagando la deuda, pero de a puchos** she is paying off the debt, but only bit by bit *o* in dribs and drabs
puck ['puk] (*pl* **pucks**) *nm (en hockey)* puck
pudding ['puðin] (*pl* **puddings**) *nm* (plum) pudding
pudendo, -a *adj* **partes pudendas** private parts
pudibundez *nf* prudishness
pudibundo, -a *adj* prudish
púdico, -a *adj* modest, demure
pudiente 1 *adj* wealthy, well-off
2 *nmf* wealthy person
pudiera *etc ver* **poder**
pudin (*pl* **púdines**), **pudín** (*pl* **pudines**) *nm* (**a**) *(dulce)* pudding (**b**) *(salado)* terrine ►► ***p. de carne*** meat loaf; ***p. de salmón*** salmon terrine
pudor *nm* (**a**) *(recato)* shyness; *(vergüenza)* (sense of) shame; **no se ducha en público por p.** he's too embarrassed *o* shy to have a shower in front of other people (**b**) *(modestia)* modesty
pudoroso, -a *adj* (**a**) *(recatado)* modest, demure (**b**) *(modesto)* modest, shy
pudrición *nf* (**a**) *(putrefacción)* rotting (**b**) *RP Fam (aburrimiento)* deadly bore; **esa película es una p.** that movie is deadly boring
pudridero *nm Br* rubbish dump, *US* garbage dump

pudrir 1 *vt* (a) *(descomponer)* to rot; **el calor pudre los alimentos** hot weather makes food go off (b) *RP Fam (cansar)* **la pudrieron tanto con sus quejas, que al final se mandó mudar** she got so fed up with their complaints that in the end she left

2 **pudrirse** *vpr* (a) *(descomponerse)* to rot; *Fam* **pudrirse en la cárcel** *(preso)* to rot in jail (b) *RP Fam (aburrirse)* to be bored stiff; **no es una película para niños, se van a p.** it's not a movie for children, they'll be bored stiff (c) EXPR *Fam* **¡ahí te pudras!** to hell with you!

pueblada *nf Andes, RP* rebellion, uprising

pueblerino, -a 1 *adj Pey* rustic, provincial; **tiene unos modales muy pueblerinos** he behaves like a real yokel *o US* hick

2 *nm,f* (a) *(habitante)* villager (b) *Pey (paleto)* yokel

pueblo 1 *ver* **poblar**

2 *nm* (a) *(población) (pequeña)* village; *(grande)* town; *Pey* **ser de p.** to be a *Br* country bumpkin *o US* hick; PROV *Am* **p. chico, infierno grande** village life can be very claustrophobic ►► ***p. abandonado*** ghost town; ***p. fantasma*** ghost town; *Perú* ***p. joven*** shanty town; ***p. de mala muerte*** one-horse town; *Am* ***p. nuevo*** shanty town

(b) *(nación, ciudadanos)* people; **la voluntad del p.** the will of the people; **el p. español** the Spanish people ►► ***el p. elegido*** the chosen people

(c) *(proletariado)* **el p.** the (common) people; **el p. llano** the common people, ordinary people

puedo *etc ver* **poder**

puente *nm* (a) *(construcción)* bridge; EXPR **tender un p.** to offer a compromise ►► ***p. de barcas*** pontoon (bridge); ***p. basculante*** balance *o* bascule bridge; ***p. colgante*** suspension bridge; ***p. ferroviario*** rail bridge; ***p. giratorio*** swing bridge; ***p. levadizo*** drawbridge; ***p. de peaje*** toll bridge; ***p. peatonal*** footbridge; ***p. de pontones*** pontoon (bridge)

(b) *(días festivos)* ≃ long weekend *(consisting of a public holiday, the weekend and the day in between)*; **hacer p.** = to take an extra day off to join a public holiday with the weekend

(c) *(en barco)* bridge ►► ***p. de mando*** bridge

(d) ***p. aéreo*** *(civil)* air shuttle; *(militar)* airlift

(e) *(en dientes)* bridge

(f) *(de gafas)* bridge

(g) *(en instrumento de cuerda)* bridge

(h) *(del pie)* arch

(i) *(en gimnasia)* arch, back bridge

(j) *(Informát)* bridge

(k) *(para arrancar un coche)* **hacer un p.** to hot-wire a car

puentear *vt Elec (circuito)* to bridge; *(para arrancar un coche)* to hot-wire

puenting *nm* bungee-jumping; **hacer p.** to go bungee-jumping

puercada *nf CAm, Méx, RDom* disgusting thing

puerco, -a 1 *adj Fam* (a) *(sucio)* filthy (b) *(malintencionado)* nasty, mean

2 *nm,f* (a) *(animal)* pig, *f* sow ►► ***p. espín*** porcupine (b) *Fam (persona malintencionada)* swine (c) *Fam (persona sucia)* pig

3 *nm Méx (carne)* pork

puercoespín *nm* porcupine

puericultor, -ora *nm,f* nursery nurse

puericultura *nf* childcare

pueril *adj* childish

puerilidad *nf* childishness

puérpera *nf Med* woman who has just given birth

puerperal *adj Med* puerperal

puerperio *nm Med* puerperium

puerro *nm* leek

PUERTA 1 *nf* (a) *(de casa, habitación, vehículo, armario)* door; *(de jardín, ciudad, aeropuerto)* gate; **te acompaño hasta la p.** I'll see you out; **cerrar la p. a alguien** to close the door on sb; **echar la p. abajo** to knock the door down; **te espero en la** *o* **a la p. del cine** I'll wait for you outside the entrance to the cinema; **llaman a la p.** there's somebody at the door; **viven en la p. de al lado** they live next door; **no obstruyan las puertas** *(en letrero)* keep the doors clear; **un turismo de cuatro puertas** a four-door saloon; **servicio (de) p. a p.** door-to-door service; **de p. en p.** from door to door; **se gana la vida vendiendo de p. en p.** he's a door-to-door salesman; **su despacho y el mío están p. con p.** his office is right next to mine; **a p. cerrada** *(reunión)* behind closed doors; *(juicio)* in camera; *(partido)* behind closed gates, in an empty stadium; EXPR **a las puertas de** *(muy cerca de)* on the verge of; **se quedó a las puertas de batir el récord** she came within an inch of beating the record; **a las puertas de la muerte** at death's door; EXPR **de puertas adentro: no me importa lo que hagas de puertas adentro** I don't care what you do in the privacy of your own home; EXPR **de puertas afuera: de puertas afuera parecía una persona muy amable** he seemed like a nice person to the outside world; EXPR *Esp* **coger la p. y marcharse** to up and go; EXPR *Fam* **dar p. a alguien** to give sb the boot, to send sb packing; EXPR **dar a alguien con la p. en las narices** to slam the door in sb's face; EXPR *RP Fam* **en p.: parece que hay casorio en p.** I think I can hear wedding bells (ringing); EXPR **estar en puertas** *(acercarse)* to be knocking on the door, to be imminent; EXPR **estar en puertas de hacer algo** to be about to do sth, to be on the verge of doing sth; EXPR *Méx Fam* **no hallar la p.: ya no hallo la p.** *(no aguanto más)* I can't take any more; **Alma no halla la p. con las exigencias de su jefa** *(no tiene tregua)* Alma doesn't get a moment's peace with her boss's constant demands; EXPR **salir por la p. grande** to make a triumphant exit ►► ***p. blindada*** reinforced door; ***p. corredera*** sliding door; ***p. corrediza*** sliding door; ***p. de embarque*** *(en aeropuerto)* departure gate; ***p. falsa*** secret door; ***p. giratoria*** revolving door; ***p. contra incendios*** fire door; ***p. principal*** *(en casa)* front door; *(en hotel, museo, hospital)* main door *o* entrance; ***p. de servicio*** service entrance; ***p. trasera*** *(en casa)* back door; *(en hotel, museo, hospital)* rear entrance; ***p. vidriera*** glass door

(b) *(posibilidad)* gateway, opening; **dejó una p. abierta a otras sugerencias** she left the door open to other suggestions; **cerró la p. a cualquier negociación** he closed the door on *o* put an end to any prospect of negotiation; **se le cerraban todas las puertas** he found all avenues blocked

(c) *Dep (portería)* goal, goalmouth; **hubo varios tiros** *o* **remates a p.** there were several shots on goal; **marcar a p. vacía** to put the ball into an empty net; **fallar un gol a p. vacía** to miss an open goal; **va a sacar de p. el guardameta** the goalkeeper is going to take the goal kick

(d) *Dep (en esquí, piragüismo)* gate

(e) *Informát* gate

2 *interj Esp Fam (¡largo!)* the door's over there!, get out!

---

puerto *nm* (a) *(de mar)* port; **llegar a p.** to come into port; EXPR **llegar a buen p.** to come through safely ►► ***p. deportivo*** marina; ***P. España*** Port of Spain; ***p. fluvial*** river port; ***p. franco*** free port; ***p. libre*** free port; ***p. natural*** natural harbour; ***p. pesquero*** fishing port; ***P. Príncipe*** Port-au-Prince; ***P. Rico*** Puerto Rico

(b) *(de montaña)* pass; **subir/bajar un p.** to go up/down a mountain pass ►► ***p. de primera categoría*** *(en ciclismo)* first category climb; ***p. puntuable*** *(en ciclismo)* category climb

(c) *Informát* port ►► ***p. de la impresora*** printer port; ***p. del módem*** modem port; ***p. paralelo*** parallel port; ***p. del ratón*** mouse port; ***p. serie*** serial port

(d) *(refugio)* haven

puertorriqueño, -a 1 *adj* Puerto Rican

2 *nm,f* Puerto Rican

pues 1 *conj* (a) *(entonces, en ese caso)* then; **¿no quieres ir? p. te quedas en casa** you don't want to go? well, stay at home then; **¿no querías trabajo? p. ya lo tienes** you said you wanted some work, didn't you? well, now you've got it; **¿no quieres escucharme? ¡p. te arrepentirás!** you won't listen to me, eh? well, you'll regret it!; **¿qué quieres hacer, p.?** what do you want to do, then?

(b) *(enfático)* **¡p. ya está!** well, that's it!; **¡p. claro!** but of course!; **p. no** certainly not; **¡p. vaya amigo que tienes!** some friend he is!; **¡p. haberlo dicho antes!** well, you could have said so earlier!; **¿no te gustan? ¡p. a mí me encantan!** you don't like them? I LOVE them!

(c) *(como comodín)* **p., como iba diciendo** anyway, as I was saying; **p. nada, cuando tengas noticias de ellos me avisas** right, well let me know when you hear from them; **¿p. qué te pasa? – p. nada** so what's the matter then? – nothing; **p. ¿qué quieres que te diga?, a mí no me gustó** what do you want me to say? I didn't like it

(d) *(dado que)* since, as; **no pude verlo, p. olvidé las gafas** I couldn't really see it, because I'd forgotten my glasses

2 *adv (por lo tanto)* therefore, so; **creo, p., que...** so, I think that...; **repito, p., que hace bien** anyway, as I said before, I think he's doing the right thing

puesta *nf* (a) *(acción) (de un motor)* tuning ►► ***p. al día*** updating; ***p. en circulación*** *(de moneda)* introduction; ***p. en común*** pooling; **hacer una p. en común de algo** to pool sth; ***p. en escena*** staging, production; **una p. en escena muy tradicional** a very traditional production; ***p. en funcionamiento*** *(de máquina)* start-up; ***p. de largo*** debut (in society); ***p. en marcha*** *(de máquina)* starting, start-up; *(de acuerdo, proyecto)* implementation; **la p. en marcha del euro** the introduction of the euro; ***p. en órbita*** putting into orbit; ***p. a punto*** *(de una técnica)* perfecting; *(de un motor)* tuning; **este coche necesita una p. a punto** this car needs tuning; ***p. en servicio*** *(de máquina, tren)* introduction; **con la p. en servicio de trenes más rápidos la duración del viaje se reducirá** the journey time will be cut when the

new trains come into service *o* when the new trains are introduced
(**b**) *(de ave)* laying
(**c**) *(de un astro)* setting ▸▸ ***p. de sol*** sunset

puestero, -a *nm,f Am* stallholder

puesto, -a 1 *participio ver* **poner**
2 *adj* (**a**) *(objeto)* **llevaba p. el sombrero** he was wearing his hat; **iba sólo con lo p.** all she had with her were the clothes on her back; **dejaron la mesa puesta** they didn't clear the table; EXPR *muy Fam* **los tiene bien puestos** he's got guts *o* balls
(**b**) *(persona)* **ir muy p.** *(arreglado)* to be all dressed up; *Fam* **estar muy p. en algo** to be well up on sth
(**c**) *Fam (drogado)* high, stoned; *(borracho)* drunk, smashed
3 *nm* (**a**) *(empleo)* post, position; **escalar puestos** to work one's way up ▸▸ ***p. de trabajo*** job; ***p. vacante*** opening, vacancy
(**b**) *(en fila, clasificación)* place
(**c**) *(lugar)* place; **¡cada uno a sus puestos!** to your places, everyone!; **¿quieres que te cambie el p.?** do you want me to swap places *o* seats with you?
(**d**) *(tenderete)* stall, stand ▸▸ **p. de escucha** *(en tienda)* listening post
(**e**) *(de control)* post ▸▸ ***p. de la Cruz Roja*** Red Cross post; ***p. de mando*** command post; ***p. de observación*** observation post; ***p. de policía*** police station; ***p. de socorro*** first-aid post; ***p. de vigilancia*** sentry post
(**f**) *RP (de ganado)* cattle station
(**g**) *Col, Méx (estanco)* tobacconist's
4 **puesto que** *loc conj* since, as; **preferimos este modelo, p. que además de ser eficaz es barato** we chose this model, since it is not only efficient but also cheap

pueyo *nm* hummock

puf[1] (*pl* **pufs**) *nm* pouf, pouffe

puf[2] *interj (expresando molestia)* humph; *(expresando repugnancia)* ugh; *(expresando cansancio)* phew

pufo *nm Fam* swindle, swizz

púgil *nm* (**a**) *(boxeador)* boxer (**b**) *Hist* bare-fist boxer *(in ancient Rome)*

pugilato *nm* (**a**) *(pelea)* fist fight (**b**) *(disputa)* battle

pugilismo *nm* boxing

pugilista *nm* boxer

pugilístico, -a *adj* boxing; **combate p.** boxing match

pugna *nf* (**a**) *(batalla, pelea)* fight, battle
(**b**) *(desacuerdo, disputa)* confrontation, clash; **una p. entre partidarios y detractores de la ley** a clash between supporters and opponents of the law; **mantener una p. con alguien por algo** to vie *o* compete with sb for sth; **estar en p. con alguien** to clash with sb; **dos empresas en p. por conseguir un contrato** two companies fighting to win a contract

pugnacidad *nf Literario* pugnacity

pugnar *vi* (**a**) *(luchar)* to fight; **pugnaban por ser los primeros en llegar al polo Norte** they were battling to be the first people to reach the North Pole (**b**) *(esforzarse)* to struggle, to fight (**por** for); **pugnan por conseguir la mayor cantidad de votos** they are fighting to win the most votes

pugnaz *adj Literario* pugnacious, aggressive

puja *nf* (**a**) *(en subasta) (acción)* bidding; *(cantidad)* bid (**b**) *(lucha)* struggle

pujante *adj* thriving, flourishing

pujanza *nf* vigour, strength

pujar 1 *vi* (**a**) *(en subasta)* to bid higher (**por** for) (**b**) *(luchar)* to struggle (**por** to) (**c**) *Am (en parto)* to push
2 *vt* to bid

pujo *nm Med* tenesmus

pulcritud *nf* (**a**) *(limpieza)* neatness, tidiness (**b**) *(esmero)* great care, meticulousness; **hacer algo con p.** to do sth meticulously *o* with great care

pulcro, -a *adj* (**a**) *(aseado)* neat, tidy (**b**) *(esmerado)* very careful, meticulous

pulga *nf (insecto)* flea; EXPR *Fam* **tener malas pulgas** to be bad-tempered, *Br* to be stroppy; EXPR *Am Fam* **estar con** *o* **tener la p. detrás de la oreja** to be suspicious *o* distrustful; EXPR *RP Fam* **andar con** *o* **tener pocas pulgas** to be in a bad mood, *Br* to be in a strop

pulgada *nf* inch

pulgar 1 *adj* **dedo p.** *(de mano)* thumb; *(de pie)* big toe
2 *nm (dedo) (de mano)* thumb; *(de pie)* big toe

Pulgarcito *n pr* Tom Thumb

pulgón *nm* greenfly, aphid

pulgoso, -a *adj* flea-ridden

pulido, -a 1 *adj* (**a**) *(piedra, madera, cristal)* polished (**b**) *(trabajo, estilo, texto)* polished
2 *nm (de piedra, madera, cristal)* polishing; **durante el p. del suelo** while polishing the floor; **procedieron al p. de la superficie** they proceeded to polish the surface

pulidor, -ora 1 *adj* polishing
2 *nm Urug* scouring powder

pulidora *nf* polisher

pulimentar *vt (piedra, madera, cristal)* to polish

pulimento *nm* (**a**) *(acción)* polishing (**b**) *(sustancia)* polish

pulir 1 *vt* (**a**) *(lustrar) (piedra, madera, cristal)* to polish (**b**) *(perfeccionar) (trabajo, estilo, texto)* to polish
2 **pulirse** *vpr Fam (dinero)* to blow, to throw away; **se pulió el sueldo en una semana** he blew his wages in a week; **nos pulimos una botella de whisky** we polished off *o* put away a bottle of whisky

pulla *nf* gibe, dig

pullman ['pulman] (*pl* **pullmans**) *nm* luxury coach

pullover [pu'loβer] (*pl* **pullovers**) *nm* pullover

pulmón *nm* lung; **a pleno p.** *(gritar)* at the top of one's voice; *(respirar)* deeply; EXPR **tener buenos pulmones** *(vozarrón)* to have a powerful voice; EXPR **ser el p. de algo: ese parque es el p. de la ciudad** that park is the lungs of the city; **Silva es el p. del equipo** Silva covers more ground than anyone else in the team ▸▸ ***p. de acero*** iron lung; ***p. artificial*** iron lung

pulmonado *nm Zool* pulmonate

pulmonar *adj* pulmonary, lung; **enfermedad p.** lung disease, pulmonary disease

pulmonía *nf* pneumonia

pulóver *nm* pullover

pulpa *nf* (**a**) *(de fruta)* flesh, pulp (**b**) *(de papel)* pulp (**c**) *Urug (corte de carne)* fillet

pulpejo *nm* (**a**) *(del cuerpo)* fleshy part (**b**) *(del caballo)* bulb

pulpería *nf Am Hist* general store

pulpero, -a *nm,f Am Hist* general store owner

púlpito *nm* pulpit

pulpo *nm* (**a**) *(animal)* octopus (**b**) *Esp Fam Pey (hombre)* **es un p.** he can't keep his hands off women (**c**) *(correa elástica)* spider strap

pulque *nm CAm, Méx* pulque, = fermented agave cactus juice

pulquería *nf CAm, Méx* "pulque" bar

pulquero, -a *nm,f CAm, Méx* owner of a "pulque" bar

pulsación *nf* (**a**) *(del corazón)* beat; **100 pulsaciones por minuto** 100 beats per minute, 100 bpm; **le aumentaron las pulsaciones** her heart rate went up (**b**) *(en máquina de escribir)* keystroke, tap; *(en piano)* touch; **pulsaciones por minuto** keystrokes per minute

pulsador *nm* button, push button

pulsar *vt* (**a**) *(botón, timbre, teclas de ordenador)* to press; *(teclas de piano)* to play; *(cuerdas de guitarra)* to pluck (**b**) *(opinión pública)* to sound out

púlsar *nm Astron* pulsar

pulseada *nf RP* **echar una p. (con alguien)** to arm-wrestle (with sb); *Fig* **la patronal ganó la p.** the employers won the battle of wills

pulsear *vi RP* (**a**) *(echar pulseada)* to arm-wrestle (**con** with) (**b**) *(pelear)* **p. con alguien** to pit one's strength against sb

pulsera *nf* bracelet

pulsión *nf* drive

pulso *nm* (**a**) *(latido)* pulse; **tomar el p. a alguien** to take sb's pulse; *Fig* **tomar el p. a algo/alguien** to sound sth/sb out
(**b**) *(firmeza)* **tener buen p.** to have a steady hand; **levantaron el piano a p.** they lifted up the piano with their bare hands; **dibujar a p.** to draw freehand; EXPR **se lo ha ganado a p.** *(algo bueno)* he's earned it; *(algo malo)* he deserves it
(**c**) *(lucha)* **echar un p. (con alguien)** to arm-wrestle (with sb); *Fig* **mantener un p. con alguien** to be locked in struggle with sb; *Fig* **las negociaciones se han convertido en un p. entre patronal y sindicatos** the negotiations have turned into a battle of wills between management and the unions
(**d**) *(cuidado)* tact
(**e**) *Tel* pulse
(**f**) *Col, Cuba, Méx (pulsera)* bracelet

pulsómetro *nm* pulsometer

pulular *vi* (**a**) *(insectos)* to swarm (**b**) *(personas)* to mill around; **miles de turistas pululaban por el centro de la ciudad** the city centre was swarming with thousands of tourists

pulverización *nf* (**a**) *(de sólido)* pulverization (**b**) *(de líquido)* spraying (**c**) *(aniquilación)* crushing (**d**) *(de récord)* breaking, smashing

pulverizador *nm (para perfume, insecticida, limpiacristales)* spray; *(para pintura)* spray gun; **un envase con p.** a spray bottle

pulverizar [14] *vt* (**a**) *(sólido)* to pulverize (**b**) *(líquido)* to spray (**c**) *(aniquilar)* to crush, to pulverize (**d**) *(récord)* to break, to smash

pum *interj* bang!

puma *nm* (**a**) *(animal)* puma (**b**) **los Pumas** *(en rugby)* the Pumas *(Argentinian rugby union team)*

pumba *interj* wham!, bang!

pumita *nf Geol* pumice

PUN [pun] *nm* (*abrev de* **Partido Unión Nacional**) = Costa Rican political party

puna *nf Andes* (**a**) *(llanura)* Andean plateau (**b**) *(mal de altura)* altitude sickness

punción *nf* puncture ►► ***p. lumbar*** spinal tap

pundonor *nm* pride

puneño, -a 1 *adj* of/from the Puna region *(Andes)*
2 *nm,f* person from the Puna region *(Andes)*

punga *RP Fam* 1 *nmf (persona)* pickpocket
2 *nf (acción)* pickpocketing

punguear *vi RP Fam* to pick pockets

punguista *nmf RP Fam* dip, pickpocket

punible *adj* punishable

punición *nf Formal* punishment

púnico, -a *adj* Punic

punitivo, -a *adj* punitive

punk [pank] (*pl* **punks**) 1 *adj* punk
2 *nmf (persona)* punk
3 *nm (estilo musical)* punk

punki 1 *adj* punk
2 *nmf* punk

PUNTA 1 *adj inv* **hora p.** rush hour; **velocidad p.** top speed
2 *nf* (**a**) *(extremo) (de cuchillo, lápiz, aguja)* point; *(de pan, pelo, nariz)* end; *(de dedo, cuerno, flecha, pincel)* tip; *(de zapato)* toe; *(de pistola)* muzzle; *(de sábana, pañuelo)* corner; **este zapato me aprieta en la p.** this shoe's squashing the ends of my toes; **p. fina/gruesa** *(de bolígrafo)* fine/thick point; **lo sujetó con la p. de los dedos** she held it with the tips of her fingers; **tengo las puntas (del pelo) abiertas** *o RP* **florecidas** I've got split ends; **en la otra p. de la ciudad** on the other side of town; **en la otra p. de la mesa** at the other end of the table; **se dio en la rodilla con la p. de la mesa** she banged her knee on the corner of the table; **lleva el pelo de p.** he has spiky hair; **recorrimos Chile de p. a p.** we travelled from one end of Chile to the other; **acabado en p.** *(objeto, instrumento)* pointed; **a p. de pistola** at gunpoint; **sacar p. a un lápiz** to sharpen a pencil; EXPR *Fam* **a p. (de) pala: tiene libros a p. (de) pala** he has loads of books; **vinieron turistas a p. (de) pala** loads of tourists came, tourists came by the busload; EXPR **estar de p. con alguien** to be on edge with sb; EXPR **ir de p. en blanco** to be dressed up to the nines; EXPR *Fam* **sacarle p. a algo** to read too much into sth; EXPR **tener algo en la p. de la lengua** to have sth on the tip of one's tongue ►► ***p. de flecha*** arrowhead; *Fig* ***la p. del iceberg*** the tip of the iceberg; *Fig* ***p. de lanza*** spearhead; **los obreros de la capital fueron la p. de lanza de la revolución** the industrial workers of the capital spearheaded the revolution; *Perú, Ven* ***p. trasera*** rump tail; ***p. de velocidad:*** **tiene una gran p. de velocidad** he's very pacey, *Br* he has a good turn of pace
(**b**) *(pizca)* touch, bit; *(de sal)* pinch
(**c**) *(clavo)* small nail
(**d**) *Dep (zona de ataque)* attack; *(jugador de ataque)* forward; **jugar en p.** to play in attack, to be a forward; **jugar como media p.** to play just in behind the strikers
(**e**) *Geog* point, headland
(**f**) *CSur* **en puntas de pie** on tiptoe; **andar en puntas de pie** to (walk on) tiptoe
(**g**) *RP Fam* **una p.** *(mucho)* loads; **se casó hace una p. de años** he got married donkey's years ago; **tiene una p. de primos** she's got loads of cousins
(**h**) EXPR *Am* **a p. de** *(a fuerza de)* by dint of; **lo convencí a p. de amenazas** I threatened him into doing it

puntada *nf* (**a**) *(pespunte)* stitch; EXPR *RP Fam* **no dan p. sin hilo** they never do anything without a reason (**b**) *RP (dolor)* stabbing pain; **me dio una p. en el corazón** I felt a stabbing pain in my heart (**c**) *Méx (broma)* witticism

puntaje *nf Am (calificación)* mark, *US* grade; *(en concursos, competiciones)* score

puntal *nm* (**a**) *(madero)* prop (**b**) *(en mina)* shore, leg (**c**) *(apoyo)* mainstay; **el sector agrario es uno de los puntales de la región** farming is one of the mainstays of the regional economy (**d**) *Andes, CAm, Méx (aperitivo)* snack

puntapié *nm* kick; **darle** *o* **pegarle un p. a alguien** to kick sb; **echar a alguien a puntapiés** to kick sb out; EXPR **tratar a alguien a puntapiés** to be nasty to sb ►► ***p. a botepronto*** *(en rugby)* drop kick; ***p. colocado*** *(en rugby)* place kick; ***p. a lateral*** *(en rugby)* touch kick

puntarenense 1 *adj* of/from Punta Arenas *(Chile)*
2 *nmf* person from Punta Arenas *(Chile)*

puntazo *nm Fam* **iqué p. de fiesta!** what a great party!

punteado, -a 1 *adj (línea)* dotted
2 *nm Mús* plucking

puntear *vt* (**a**) *Mús* to pluck (**b**) *(trazar puntos en)* to dot (**c**) *(cuenta)* to check entry by entry (**d**) *Col, Perú, RP (encabezar)* to lead, to march at the front of

punteo *nm* (**a**) *Mús* plucking (**b**) *(de cuenta)* checking

puntera *nf* (**a**) *(de zapato)* toecap; *(de calcetín)* toe (**b**) *ver también* **puntero**

puntería *nf* (**a**) *(destreza)* marksmanship; **afinar la p.** to aim carefully; **tener buena p.** to be a good shot; **tener mala p.** to be a bad shot (**b**) *(orientación para apuntar)* aim

puntero, -a 1 *adj* leading; **una de las empresas punteras en el sector** one of the leading companies in the industry; **un país p. en agricultura biológica** a world leader in organic farming
2 *nm* (**a**) *(para señalar)* pointer (**b**) *Informát* pointer (**c**) *Andes, RP, Méx (persona)* leader; *(animal)* leading animal (**d**) *Andes (de reloj)* hand
3 *nm,f CSur Dep* winger; **p. izquierdo/derecho** left/right winger

puntestero, -a 1 *adj* of/from Punta del Este *(Uruguay)*
2 *nm,f* person from Punta del Este *(Uruguay)*

puntiagudo, -a *adj* pointed

puntilla 1 *nf* (**a**) *(encaje)* point lace (**b**) *Taurom* = short-bladed dagger used to administer the coup de grâce to the bull; **dar la p.** to finish off the bull; *Fig* to give the coup de grâce; **aquello fue la p.** that was what did it
2 **de puntillas,** *Am* **en puntillas** *loc adv* on tiptoe; **andar de** *o Am* **en puntillas** to (walk on) tiptoe; **ir de** *o Am* **en puntillas** to tiptoe

puntillazo *nm Taurom* coup de grâce *(given to the bull using the "puntilla")*

puntillero *nm Taurom* = bullfighter who administers the coup de grâce

puntillismo *nm Arte* pointillism

puntillista *Arte* 1 *adj* pointillist
2 *nmf* pointillist

puntillo *nm* pride

puntilloso, -a *adj* (**a**) *(susceptible)* touchy (**b**) *(meticuloso)* punctilious

PUNTO 1 *nm* (**a**) *(marca)* dot, spot; *(en geometría)* point; **recorte por la línea de puntos** cut along the dotted line ►► ***p. de fuga*** vanishing point
(**b**) *(signo ortográfico) (al final de frase) Br* full stop, *US* period; *(sobre i, j, en dirección de correo electrónico)* dot; **dos puntos** colon; *Fam* **no vas a ir, y p.** you're not going, and that's that; EXPR **poner los puntos sobre las íes** to dot the i's and cross the t's ►► *Bol, Perú* ***p. acápite*** semicolon; ***p. y aparte*** *Br* full stop *o US* period, new paragraph; ***p. y coma*** semicolon; ***p. final*** *Br* full stop, *US* period; EXPR **poner p. final a algo** to bring sth to an end; ***p. y seguido*** *Br* full stop, *US* period *(no new paragraph)*; ***puntos suspensivos*** suspension points
(**c**) *(unidad) (en juegos, competiciones, exámenes, bolsa)* point; **ganar/perder por seis puntos** to win/lose by six points; **ganar por puntos** *(en boxeo)* to win on points; **el índice Dow Jones ha subido seis puntos** the Dow Jones index is up six points; **los tipos de interés bajarán un p.** interest rates will go down by one (percentage) point ►► ***p. de break*** break point; ***p. de juego*** game point; ***p. de partido*** match point; ***p. porcentual*** percentage point; ***p. de set*** set point
(**d**) *(asunto, parte)* point; **pasemos al siguiente p.** let's move on to the next point; **te lo explicaré p. por p.** I'll explain it to you point

by point; **tenemos los siguientes puntos a tratar** we have the following items on the agenda ►► ***p. débil*** weak point; ***p. fuerte*** strong point

(e) *(lugar)* spot, place; **éste es el p. exacto donde ocurrió todo** this is the exact spot where it all happened; **hay retenciones en varios puntos de la provincia** there are delays at several different points across the province ►► ***p. de apoyo*** *(en palanca)* fulcrum; *Ling* ***p. de articulación*** point of articulation; ***los puntos cardinales*** the points of the compass, *Espec* the cardinal points; ***p. ciego*** *(en el ojo)* blind spot; ***p. de encuentro*** meeting point; *Dep* ***p. fatídico*** penalty spot; ***p. G*** g-spot; ***p. de mira*** *(en armas)* sight; EXPR **está en mi p. de mira** *(es mi objetivo)* I have it in my sights; ***p. negro*** *(en la piel)* blackhead; *(en carretera)* accident blackspot; ***p. neurálgico*** *(de ser vivo, organismo)* nerve centre; **la plaza mayor es el p. neurálgico de la ciudad** the main square is the town's busiest crossroads; **éste es el p. neurálgico de la negociación** this is the central issue at stake in the negotiations; ***p. de partida*** starting point; ***p. de penalti*** *o* ***penalty*** penalty spot; ***p. de referencia*** point of reference; ***p. de reunión*** meeting point; *Com* ***p. de venta:*** **en el p. de venta** at the point of sale; **tenemos puntos de venta en todo el país** we have (sales) outlets across the country; ***p. de venta autorizado*** authorized dealer; ***p. de venta electrónico*** electronic point of sale; ***p. de vista*** point of view, viewpoint; **bajo mi p. de vista...** in my view...; **desde el p. de vista del dinero...** in terms of money...

(f) *(momento)* point, moment; **lo dejamos en este p. del debate y seguimos tras la publicidad** we'll have to leave the discussion here for the moment, we'll be back after the break; **al p.** at once, there and then; **en p.** exactly, on the dot; **a las seis en p.** at six o'clock on the dot, at six o'clock sharp; **son las seis en p.** it's (exactly) six o'clock; **estar a p.** to be ready; **estuve a p. de cancelar el viaje** I was on the point of cancelling the trip; **estamos a p. de firmar un importante contrato** we are on the verge *o* point of signing an important contract; **estaba a p. de salir cuando...** I was about to leave when...; **estuvo a p. de morir ahogada** she almost drowned; **llegar a p. (para hacer algo)** to arrive just in time (to do sth) ►► ***p. crítico*** critical moment *o* point; *(de reactor)* critical point; **alcanzar el p. crítico** *(reactor)* to go critical

(g) *(estado, fase)* state, condition; **estando las cosas en este p.** things being as they are; **llegar a un p. en que...** to reach the stage where...; **estar en su p.** to be just right; **¿cómo quiere el filete? – a p.** *o* **al p.** how would you like your steak? – medium, please; **poner a p.** *(motor)* to tune; *(sistema, método)* to fine-tune ►► ***p. de congelación*** freezing point; ***p. culminante*** high point; ***p. de ebullición*** boiling point; *Fin* ***p. de equilibrio*** break-even point; ***p. de fusión*** melting point; ***p. muerto*** *(en automóviles)* neutral; *(en negociaciones)* deadlock; **ir en p. muerto** *(automóvil)* to freewheel; **estar en un p. muerto** *(negociaciones)* to be deadlocked; ***p. de nieve:*** **batir a p. de nieve** to beat until stiff

(h) *(grado)* degree; **de todo p.** *(completamente)* absolutely; **hasta cierto p.** to some extent, up to a point; **el ruido era infernal, hasta el p. de no oír nada** *o* **de que no se oía nada** the noise was so bad that you couldn't hear a thing; **hasta tal p. que** to such an extent that

(i) *(cláusula)* clause

(j) *(puntada) (en costura, en cirugía)* stitch; *(en unas medias)* hole; **tienes** *o* **se te ha escapado un p. en el jersey** you've pulled a stitch out of your jumper, you've got a loose stitch on your jumper; **le dieron diez puntos en la frente** he had to have ten stitches to his forehead; **coger puntos** to pick up stitches ►► ***p. atrás*** backstitch; ***p. de cadeneta*** chain stitch; ***p. de cruz*** cross-stitch; ***p. del revés*** purl; *Med* ***p. de sutura*** suture

(k) *(estilo de tejer)* knitting; **un jersey de p.** a knitted sweater; **prendas de p.** knitwear; **hacer p.** to knit ►► ***p. de ganchillo*** crochet

(l) *(pizca, toque)* touch; **son comentarios un p. racistas** they are somewhat racist remarks

(m) *Arquit* **de medio p.** *(arco, bóveda)* semicircular

(n) *Esp Fam (borrachera ligera)* **cogerse/tener un p.** to get/be merry

(o) *Esp Fam (reacción, estado de ánimo)* **le dan unos puntos muy raros** he can be really weird sometimes; **le dio el p. generoso** he had a fit of generosity

(p) *Esp Fam (cosa estupenda)* **¡qué p.!** that's great *o* fantastic!

(q) EXPR *RP Fam* **agarrar a alguien de p.** to tease sb, *Br* to take the mickey out of sb

2 **punto com** *nf (empresa)* dotcom

puntuable *adj* **un esprint p. para la clasificación final** a sprint that counts towards the final classification

puntuación *nf* (a) *(calificación)* mark; *(en concursos, competiciones)* score (b) *(ortográfica)* punctuation

puntual 1 *adj* (a) *(en el tiempo)* punctual; **es muy p.** she's very punctual (b) *(exacto, detallado)* detailed (c) *(aislado)* isolated, one-off

2 *adv* punctually, on time; **llegó p.** he arrived punctually *o* on time

puntualidad *nf* (a) *(en el tiempo)* punctuality; **la p. suiza** strict punctuality (b) *(exactitud)* exactness

puntualización *nf* clarification; **me gustaría hacer unas puntualizaciones** I'd like to make a few points

puntualizar [14] *vt (aclarar)* to specify, to clarify; **hay que p. que no estaba solo** it should be made clear *o* pointed out that he wasn't alone; **quisiera p. que éste es un caso aislado** I would like to make it clear *o* stress that this is an isolated case

puntualmente *adv (en el momento justo)* punctually, promptly

puntuar [4] 1 *vt* (a) *(calificar)* to mark, *US* to grade (b) *(escrito)* to punctuate

2 *vi* (a) *(calificar)* to mark, *US* to grade; **puntúa muy bajo** he gives very low marks *o US* grades, he marks very low (b) *(entrar en el cómputo)* to count (**para** towards) (c) *(obtener puntos)* to score, to score points; **el Atlético lleva tres partidos sin p.** Atlético has lost the last three games

puntudo, -a *adj Chile* (a) *(puntiagudo) (nariz, pico)* pointed; *(cuchillo, artefacto)* sharp (b) *(delicado) (tema)* thorny; *(persona)* prickly

punzada *nf* (a) *(pinchazo)* prick (b) *(dolor intenso)* stabbing pain; **sentí una p. en el pecho** I felt a stabbing pain in my chest; **me da punzadas la espalda** I get this stabbing pain in my back (c) *(de remordimiento)* pang, twinge; **sentí una p. de remordimiento** I felt a pang of remorse

punzante *adj* (a) *(que pincha)* sharp (b) *(intenso)* sharp, stabbing (c) *(mordaz)* caustic

punzar [14] *vt* (a) *(pinchar)* to prick (b) *(sujeto: dolor)* to stab (c) *(sujeto: actitud)* to wound

punzó *adj inv Andes, RP* red

punzón *nm* (a) *(para telas, cuero)* punch (b) *(para monedas, medallas)* die

puñado *nm* handful; **a puñados** by the handful; **había policías/ratas a puñados** the place was swarming with police/rats

puñal *nm* dagger; EXPR **poner a alguien el p. en el pecho** to hold a gun to sb's head

puñalada *nf (acción)* stab; *(herida)* stab wound; **lo mataron a puñaladas** they stabbed him to death; EXPR **coser a puñaladas** to stab repeatedly; *Fam Fig* **una p. trapera** *o* **por la espalda** a stab in the back

puñeta 1 *nf* (a) *Fam (fastidio, lata)* drag, pain; **¡qué p. tener que trabajar el domingo!** what a drag *o* pain having to work on a Sunday!

(b) *(bocamanga)* border

(c) EXPR *Fam* **hacer la p.** to be a pain; *Fam* **irse a hacer puñetas** *(planes)* to go up in smoke; **¡vete a hacer puñetas!** get lost!; *Fam* **mandar a alguien a hacer puñetas** to tell sb to get lost; *Fam* **¡no me vengas ahora con puñetas!** don't give me that nonsense!

2 *interj Fam* **¡p.!, ¡puñetas!** damn it!; **¡cállate, p.!** shut up, damn it!

puñetazo *nm* punch; **acabaron a puñetazos** they ended up brawling; **darle un p. a alguien** to punch sb; **dio un p. en la mesa** he thumped his fist on the table; **rompió la puerta de un p.** he smashed a hole in the door with his fist

puñete *nm Chile Fam* thump

puñetería *nf Fam* (a) *(molestia)* pain (b) *(menudencia)* trifle, unimportant thing

puñetero, -a *Esp Fam* 1 *adj* (a) *(molesto)* **no seas p.** don't be rotten *o* a swine

(b) *(difícil)* tricky, awkward; **nos puso un examen muy p.** he set us a very tricky exam

(c) *(enfático)* **la puñetera lavadora no quiere funcionar** the damn washing machine won't work; **tiene la puñetera manía de poner la música a todo volumen** he has the *Br* bloody *o US* goddamn annoying habit of playing music at full volume; **no me hacen ni p. caso** they don't take a blind bit of notice of me; **¡cállate de una puñetera vez!** shut up, for Christ's sake!

2 *nm,f* pain; **la puñetera de su hermana** his *Br* bloody *o US* goddamn sister

puño *nm* (a) *(mano cerrada)* fist; **apretar los puños** to clench one's fists; **saludar con el p. cerrado** *o* **alzado** *o* **en alto** to give a clenched fist salute; EXPR *Fam* **como un p.: una verdad como un p.** an undeniable fact; EXPR **de su p. y letra** in his/her own handwriting; EXPR **meter** *o* **tener a alguien en un p.** to have sb under one's thumb; EXPR **estoy con el corazón en un p.** my heart's in my mouth

(b) *(de manga)* cuff

(c) *(empuñadura) (de espada)* hilt; *(de paraguas)* handle

(d) *Náut* ***p. de la escota*** clew

pupa 1 *nf* (**a**) *Fam (erupción)* blister (**b**) *Fam (daño)* **me he hecho p. en el dedo** I've hurt my finger; **tengo p. en la rodilla** my knee's sore (**c**) *Zool (crisálida)* pupa
2 **pupas** *nm inv* **ser un pupas** to be accident-prone

pupila *nf* (**a**) *(de ojo)* pupil (**b**) *ver también* **pupilo**

pupilente *nm o nf Méx* contact lens

pupilo, -a 1 *adj RP* **está p.** he's a boarder
2 *nm,f* (**a**) *(discípulo)* pupil (**b**) *(huérfano)* ward (**c**) *RP (interno)* boarder

pupitre *nm* desk

pupusa *nf CAm* maize dumpling

pura *Fam* 1 *nf CSur* **la p.** *(la verdad)* the honest truth
2 **por las puras** *loc adv Andes* just for the sake of it, for no reason

puramente *adv* (**a**) *(únicamente)* purely, simply; **este jarrón es p. decorativo** this vase is purely for decoration (**b**) *(con pureza)* purely, chastely

purasangre 1 *adj* thoroughbred
2 *nm inv* thoroughbred

puré *nm* thick soup; EXPR *Fam* **estar hecho p.** to be beat *o Br* knackered ►► ***p. de patatas*** mashed potatoes; ***p. de tomate*** tomato purée

pureta *Fam* 1 *adj* fogeyish
2 *nmf* old fogey

puretera *nf*, **puretero** *nm RP* (potato) masher

pureza *nf* (**a**) *(de atmósfera, aire)* purity; **la p. de las líneas del edificio** the building's clean lines (**b**) *(de conducta, persona)* purity; **nadie dudaba de la p. de su amor por ella** nobody doubted the purity of his love for her

purga *nf* (**a**) *Med* purgative (**b**) *(depuración)* purge

purgaciones *nfpl Med* gonorrhoea

purgante 1 *adj* purgative
2 *nm* purgative

purgar [38] 1 *vt* (**a**) *Med* to purge (**b**) *(radiador, tubería)* to drain (**c**) *(condena)* to serve (**d**) *(depurar)* to purge
2 **purgarse** *vpr* to take a purge

purgatorio *nm* purgatory

puridad: en puridad *loc adv* strictly speaking; **un problema que, en p., no es responsabilidad suya** a problem that, strictly speaking, is not his responsibility

purificación *nf* purification; **p. del agua** water treatment

purificador, -ora 1 *adj* purifying; **el fuego p.** the purifying fire
2 *nm* (**a**) *Rel* purificator (**b**) *Am (de agua)* purifier

purificar [60] *vt* (**a**) *(agua, sangre, aire)* to purify; *(mineral, metal)* to refine (**b**) *Rel (persona)* to purify; *(pecados)* to wash away

purina *nf Quím* purine

purismo *nm* purism

purista 1 *adj* purist; **una corriente p.** a purist tendency
2 *nmf* purist

puritanismo *nm* puritanism

puritano, -a 1 *adj* (**a**) *Rel* puritan (**b**) *(mojigato)* puritanical
2 *nm,f* (**a**) *Rel* puritan (**b**) *(mojigato)* puritan

puro, -a 1 *adj* (**a**) *(limpio, sin mezcla)* pure; *(oro)* solid; **este jersey es de pura lana** this sweater is 100 percent wool
(**b**) *(atmósfera, aire)* clear
(**c**) *(conducta, persona)* decent, honourable; **un alma pura** a pure soul; **la mirada pura de un niño** the clear *o* pure gaze of a child
(**d**) *(mero)* sheer; *(verdad)* plain; **por pura casualidad** by pure chance; **me quedé dormido de p. cansancio** I fell asleep from sheer exhaustion; **fue una pura coincidencia** it was pure coincidence; **p. y duro: y ésta es la realidad pura y dura** and that is the harsh reality of the matter; **este trabajo es una esclavitud pura y dura** this job is nothing more (nor less) than slavery
2 *nm* (**a**) *(cigarro)* cigar ►► ***p. habano*** Havana (cigar) (**b**) EXPR *Esp Fam* **meterle un p. a alguien** *(regañina)* to give sb a row *o* rocket; *(castigo)* to throw the book at sb; **si te descubren te caerá un buen p.** if you're found out, you'll be in for it

púrpura 1 *adj inv* purple
2 *nm (color)* purple
3 *nf (molusco)* = type of Mediterranean mollusc

purpurado *nm Rel* cardinal

purpúreo, -a *adj* purple

purpurina *nf* (**a**) *(polvos)* glitter *(in metallic paint)* (**b**) *(pintura)* metallic paint

purulencia *nf* purulence

purulento, -a *adj* purulent

pus *nm* pus

PUSC [pusk] *nm (abrev de* **Partido Unidad Social Cristiana**) = Costa Rican political party

puse *etc ver* **poner**

pusiera *etc ver* **poner**

pusilánime 1 *adj* faint-hearted; **tiene un carácter p.** he's a weak character
2 *nmf* faint-hearted person; **la carrera no fue para los pusilánimes** the race was not for the faint-hearted

pústula *nf* pustule

puta *nf* (**a**) *muy Fam* whore; **ir** *o* **irse de putas** to go whoring; EXPR **¡me cago en la p.!** *(indica enfado, contrariedad)* fucking hell!, fuck it!; EXPR **pasarlas putas** to have a really shit time; EXPR **ser más p. que las gallinas** to be a real old tart *o Br* slag *o Br* slapper; EXPR *RP* **de la gran p.: hace un frío de la gran p.** it's *Br* bloody *o US* goddamn freezing; **se armó un lío de la gran p.** it was *Br* bloody *o US* goddamn chaos
(**b**) *ver también* **puto**

putada *nf muy Fam* **es una p. tener que madrugar todos los días** it's a pain in the *Br* arse *o US* ass having to get up so early every day; **hacerle una p. a alguien** to be a mean bastard to sb; **¡qué p.!** what a bummer!

putaparió *nm RP Fam* = hot red chilli pepper

putativo, -a *adj* putative

putazo *nm Méx muy Fam* **se agarraron a putazos** they beat the shit out of each other

puteada *nf RP muy Fam (insulto)* swear word

puteado, -a *adj muy Fam* **tengo la espalda puteada** my back is fucked; **está p. en el trabajo** they're fucking him around at work; **está p. porque no tiene dinero** he can't do a fucking thing because he's got no money

putear *muy Fam* 1 *vt* (**a**) *(fastidiar)* **p. a alguien** to screw *o Br* bugger sb around; **me está puteando el dolor de espalda** my back is *Br* bloody *o US* goddamn killing me; **lo putean mucho en el trabajo** he gets screwed *o Br* buggered around a lot at work (**b**) *Am (insultar)* **p. a alguien** to call sb for everything, to call sb every name under the sun
2 *vi* (**a**) *(salir con prostitutas)* to go whoring (**b**) *Am (decir malas palabras)* to eff and blind; **es muy desagradable, se pasa puteando** he's very unpleasant, he never stops effing and blinding

puteo *nm muy Fam* (**a**) *(fastidio)* **es un p.** it's a pain in the *Br* arse *o US* ass (**b**) *(con prostitutas)* **ir de p.** to go whoring

puterío *nm muy Fam* (**a**) *(prostitución)* whoring (**b**) *RP (discusión, problema)* **no quiero volver a trabajar con ella, es mucho p.** I don't want to work with her again, it's too much of a pain in the *Br* arse *o US* ass; **basta de puteríos, tratemos de disfrutar las vacaciones** that's enough *Br* bloody *o US* goddamn rows, let's try to enjoy our holiday

putero *nm muy Fam* (**a**) *(persona)* **es un p.** he goes whoring a lot (**b**) *Méx, RP (prostíbulo)* whorehouse (**c**) *RP (relajo) Br* bloody *o US* goddamn chaos; **cuando llegué, aquello era un p.** when I arrived, the place was total *Br* bloody *o US* goddamn chaos

puticlub *nm Fam* pick-up joint

putiza *nf Méx Vulg* (**a**) *(paliza)* **le pusieron una buena p.** they kicked the shit out of him (**b**) **en p.** *(a toda velocidad)* at breakneck speed; **los de las motos pasaron en p.** the motorcyclists came tearing past like *Br* bloody *o US* goddamn maniacs

puto, -a 1 *adj* (**a**) *Vulg (maldito)* fucking; **vámonos de una puta vez** let's just fucking well leave; **¡cállate de una puta vez!** shut the fuck up!; **tiene la puta manía de poner la música a todo volumen** she's got the fucking annoying habit of turning the music up full blast; **¡todos a la puta calle!** get the fuck out of here all of you!; *Esp muy Fam* **no tengo ni puta idea** I haven't got a *Br* bloody *o US* goddamn clue
(**b**) *muy Fam (difícil) Br* bloody *o US* goddamn difficult
(**c**) *Chile muy Fam (promiscuo)* **es muy p.** he really screws around
(**d**) EXPR *muy Fam* **de puta madre** *(estupendo) Br* bloody *o US* goddamn brilliant; **me parece de puta madre** that's *Br* bloody *o US* goddamn marvellous; **nos lo pasamos de puta madre** we had a *Br* bloody *o US* goddamn marvellous time; *Vulg* **¡me cago en su puta madre!** *(insultando a alguien)* fucking bastard/bitch!; *(indicando enfado, contrariedad)* fucking hell!, fuck it!; *Vulg* **¡la puta madre que te parió!** you fucking bastard/bitch!; *Vulg* **de puta pena** *(muy mal)* fucking terrible *o* awful; **esa tía me cae de puta pena** I fucking hate that girl; *Vulg* **en la puta vida: en la puta vida hice eso** I never did that in my fucking life
2 *nm muy Fam* (**a**) *(prostituto)* rent boy (**b**) *RP (homosexual) Br* poof, *US* faggot (**c**) *Chile muy Fam (hombre promiscuo)* **es un puta** he really screws around

putón *nm muy Fam* **un p. (verbenero)** a cheap slut

putrefacción *nf* rotting, putrefaction

putrefacto, -a *adj* rotting

pútrido, -a *adj* putrid

putt [pat] (*pl* **putts**) *nm* (**a**) *(golpe)* putt (**b**) *(palo)* putter

putter ['pater] (*pl* **putters**) *nm (palo)* putter

puya *nf* (**a**) *(punta de vara)* goad (**b**) *(palabras)* gibe, dig; **lanzar una p.** to make a gibe, to have a dig

puyar *vi Chile, Col, Pan (bregar)* to work hard

puyazo *nm* (**a**) *(golpe)* jab *(with goad)* (**b**) *Fam (palabras)* gibe, dig

puzzle ['puθle], **puzle** *nm* jigsaw puzzle

PVC *nm* (*abrev de* **cloruro de polivinilo**) PVC

PVP *nm* (*abrev de* **precio de venta al público**) retail price ►► ***P. recomendado*** RRP

PYME ['pime] *nf* (*abrev de* **Pequeña y Mediana Empresa**) SME

Pyongyang *n* Pyongyang

pyrex® *nm* Pyrex®

Pza., pza. (*abrev de* **plaza**) Sq

Q, q

Q, q [ku] *nf (letra)* Q, q

Qatar *n* Qatar

qatarí (*pl* **qataríes**) **1** *adj* Qatari
2 *nmf* Qatari

q.e.p.d. (*abrev de* **que en paz descanse**) RIP

Qosqo *n Perú* Cuzco

Quáker® *nm Am* porridge

quántum (*pl* **quanta**) *nm Fís* quantum

quark (*pl* **quarks**) *nm Fís* quark

quásar *nm Astron* quasar

QUE 1 *pron relativo* **(a)** *(sujeto) (persona)* who, that; *(cosa)* that, which; **la mujer q. me saluda** the woman (who *o* that is) waving to me; **el q. me lo compró** the one *o* person who bought it from me; **el hombre, q. decía llamarse Simón, era bastante sospechoso** the man, who said he was called Simón, seemed rather suspicious; **¿hay alguien q. tenga un encendedor?** does anyone have a lighter?; **la moto q. me gusta** the motorbike (that) I like; **hace natación, q. es muy sano** she swims, which is very good for your health; **la salsa fue lo q. más me gustó** the sauce was the bit I liked best; **el q. más y el q. menos** every last one of us/them, all of us/them without exception

(b) *(complemento directo) (se puede omitir en inglés) (persona)* who, whom; *(cosa)* that, which; **el hombre q. conociste ayer** the man (who *o* whom) you met yesterday; **la persona/el lugar q. estás buscando** the person/the place you're looking for; **eres de los pocos a los q. invitaron** you're one of the few people (who) they invited; **esa casa es la q.** *o* **esa es la casa q. me quiero comprar** that house is the one (that) I want to buy, that's the house (that) I want to buy; **eso es todo lo q. sé** that's all *o* everything I know

(c) *(complemento indirecto) (se puede omitir en inglés)* **al q., a la q., a los/las q.** (to) who, (to) whom; **ese es el chico al q. presté dinero** that's the boy (who) I lent some money to, that's the boy (to) whom I lent some money

(d) *(complemento circunstancial)* **la playa a la q. fui** the beach where I went, the beach I went to; **la mujer con/de la q. hablas** the woman (who) you are talking to/about; **la mesa en la q. escribes** the table on which you are writing, the table you are writing on; **la manera** *o* **forma en q. lo dijo** the way (in which) she said it; **(en) q.** *(indicando tiempo)* when; **el día (en) q. me fui** the day (when) I left; **el año (en) q. nos conocimos** the year (when) we first met

(e) *(en frases)* **en lo q. tú te arreglas, yo recojo la cocina** I'll tidy the kitchen up while you're getting ready

2 *conj* **(a)** *(con oraciones de sujeto)* that; **es importante q. me escuches** it's important that you listen to me, it's important for you to listen to me; **q. haya pérdidas no significa que vaya a haber despidos** the fact that we've suffered losses doesn't mean anyone is going to lose their job; **sería mejor q. no se lo dijeras** it would be better if you didn't tell her; **se suponía q. era un secreto** it was supposed to be a secret

(b) *(con oraciones de complemento directo)* that; **me ha confesado q. me quiere** he has told me that he loves me; **creo q. no iré** I don't think (that) I'll go; **procura q. no se te escape el perro** try and make sure (that) the dog doesn't get away from you; **intentamos q. todos estén contentos** we try to keep everybody happy; **me dijeron q. me quedara en casa** they told me to stay at home; **me dijeron q. dónde iba** they asked me where I was going

(c) *(después de preposición)* **estoy convencido de q. es cierto** I'm convinced (that) it's true; **con q. esté listo el jueves es suficiente** as long as it's ready by Thursday, that'll be fine; **estoy en contra de q. siga en el cargo** I'm opposed to him continuing in his job; **sin q. nadie se entere** without anyone realizing; **el hecho de q....** the fact that...

(d) *(comparativo)* than; **es más rápido q. tú** he's quicker than you; **alcanza la misma velocidad q. un tren convencional** it can go as fast as a conventional train; **trabaja el doble de horas q. yo** she works twice as many hours as me; **antes morir q. vivir la guerra otra vez** I'd rather die than live through the war again

(e) *(indica causa, motivo)* **hemos de esperar, q. todavía no es la hora** we'll have to wait, (as) it isn't time yet; **no quiero café, q. luego no duermo** I won't have any coffee, it stops me from sleeping; **baja la voz, q. nos van a oír** lower your voice or they'll hear us; **el dólar ha subido, q. lo oí en la radio** the dollar has gone up, I heard it on the radio

(f) *(indica consecuencia)* that; **tanto me lo pidió q. se lo di** he asked me for it so insistently that I gave it to him; **¡esta habitación huele q. apesta!** this room stinks!; **mira si es grande q. no cabe por la puerta** it's so big it won't go through the door

(g) *(indica finalidad)* so (that); **ven aquí q. te vea** come over here so (that) I can see you

(h) *(indica deseo, mandato)* that; **espero q. te diviertas** I hope (that) you have fun; **¡q. te diviertas!** have fun!; **quiero q. lo hagas** I want you to do it; *Fam* **¡q. se vaya a la porra!** she can go to hell!; **por favor, q. nadie se mueva de aquí** please don't anybody go away from here; **¡q. llamen a un médico!** get them to call a doctor!

(i) *(para reiterar, hacer hincapié)* **¡q. te doy un bofetón!** do that again and I'll slap you!; **¿no vas a venir? – ¡q. sí!** aren't you coming? – of course I am!; **¿pero de verdad no quieres venir? – ¡q. no!** but do you really not want to come? – definitely not!; **¡q. me dejes!** just leave me alone!; **¡q. pases te digo!** but do come in, please!

(j) *(para expresar contrariedad, enfado)* **¡q. tenga una que hacer estas cosas a sus años!** that she should have to do such things at her age!

(k) *(en oraciones interrogativas) (para expresar reacción a lo dicho)* **¿q. quiere venir? pues que venga** so she wants to come? then let her; **¿q. te han despedido?** *(con tono de incredulidad)* you're telling me they've sacked you?; **¿cómo q. dónde está? ¡donde siempre!** what do you mean where is it? it's where it always is!

(l) *(para explicar)* **es q....** the thing is (that)..., it's just (that)...; **es q. yo ya tengo perro** the thing is (that) *o* it's just (that) I already have a dog; **¿es q. te da vergüenza?** are you embarrassed (or what)?, is it that you're embarrassed?

(m) *(indica hipótesis)* if; **q. no quieres hacerlo, pues no pasa nada** it doesn't matter if you don't want to do it; **¿q. llueve? nos quedamos en casa** if it rains, we'll just stay at home; **¿tú q. él qué harías?** what would you do if you were him *o* (if you were) in his shoes?

(n) *(indica disyunción)* or; **quieras q. no, harás lo que yo mando** you'll do what I tell you, whether you like it or not; **han tenido algún problema q. otro** they've had the odd problem

(o) *(indica reiteración)* **estuvieron charla q. te charla toda la mañana** they were nattering away all morning; **se pasó el día llora q. te llora** she cried and cried all day, she didn't stop crying all day

> The relative pronouns "that", "who", "which" and "whom" can be left out of English sentences when they refer to the object of the relative clause. However, in Spanish, the equivalent pronouns **que** or **quien** can never be omitted:
> **el hombre que vi**
> *the man (that/whom/who) I saw*
> **la casa que compraron**
> *the house (that/which) they bought*
> **tiene unos vecinos a los que no aguanta**
> *he's got some neighbours (who/whom/that) he can't stand*

QUÉ 1 *adj* **(a)** *(interrogativo) (en general)* what; *(al elegir, al concretar)* which; **¿q. hora es?** what's the time?; **disculpa, no sabía q. hora era** sorry, I didn't realize the time; **¿q. chaqueta prefieres?** which jacket do you prefer?; **¿para q. empresa trabaja?** which company do you work for?; **¿a q. distancia?** how far away?

(b) *(exclamativo)* **¡q. fallo!** what a mistake!; **¡q. día llevo!** what a day I'm having!; **¡q. casa más bonita!** what a lovely house!; **¡q. horror!** how awful!; **¡q. suerte!** that's lucky!, how fortunate!

2 *pron* (a) *(interrogativo)* what; **¿q. te dijo?** what did he tell you?; **¿q. hay en la caja?** what's in the box?; **no sé q. hacer** I don't know what to do; **¿para q. has venido?** why have you come?, what have you come for?; **¿con q. limpias los espejos?** what do you use to clean the mirrors?, what do you clean the mirrors with?; *Fam* **¿q. te costó?** *(¿cuánto?)* what did it cost you?; **¿q.?** *(¿cómo dices?)* sorry?, pardon?; **¡Carlos! – ¿q.?** *(contestando a una llamada)* Carlos! – what?; **quiero el divorcio – ¿q.?** *(expresando incredulidad)* I want a divorce – (you want) what?; **¿que le diga q.?** you want me to say WHAT to her?; *Esp* **¿bueno q.?, ¿nos vamos?** right, shall we go, then?; **¿y q.?** so what?

(b) *(exclamativo)* **¡q. sé yo!** how should I know!; **me ofrecieron casa, trabajo y q. sé yo cuántas cosas más** they offered me a house, a job and heaven knows what else; *Fam* **¡q. va!** *(en absoluto)* not in the least, not at all; *Fam* **¿cansado? – ¡q. va!** are you tired? – not at all!

3 *adv* (a) *(exclamativo)* how; **¡q. horrible/divertido!** how horrible/funny!; **¡q. tonto eres!,** *Fam* **¡q. tonto que eres!** how stupid you are!, you're so stupid!; **¡q. casa más bonita!** what a lovely house!; **¡q. bien te sale la pasta!,** *Fam* **¡q. bien que te sale la pasta!** you're so good at cooking pasta!; **¡q. tarde es ya!** *Fam* **¡q. tarde que es ya!** is it really that late?; **¿ya estás aquí?, ¡q. rápido has vuelto!** *o Fam* **¡q. rápido que has vuelto!** are you back already? that was quick!

(b) *(interrogativo)* **¿q. tal?** how are things?, how are you doing?; *Fam* **¿q. hay?,** *CAm, Col, Méx, Ven* **¿q. hubo?,** *Ven* **¿q. más?,** *Ven* **¿q. pasó?** how are you doing?; **¿q. tal la fiesta/película?** how was the party/movie?; **¿por q.?** why?

(c) *(expresa gran cantidad)* **¡q. de...!** what a lot of...!; **¡q. de gente hay aquí!** what a lot of people there are here!, there are so many people here!

(d) *Am* **¿q. tan/tanto?** *(¿cuánto?)* how much?; **¿q. tanto gastaste?** how much did you spend?

Quebec *nm* **(el) Q.** Quebec

quebequés, -esa 1 *adj* Quebecois

2 *nm,f* Quebecois, Quebecker

quebracho *nm* quebracho

quebrada *nf* (a) *(desfiladero)* gorge (b) *Am (arroyo)* stream (c) *Méx Fam (oportunidad)* **Edgar quiere que le pases q. y le presentes a tu amiga** Edgar's hoping you'll do him a favour and introduce him to your friend; **el profe nos dio q. para entregar el trabajo hasta la semana próxima** the teacher gave us an extension till next week on handing in the work

quebradero *nm* **q. de cabeza** headache, problem; **la preparación del viaje les ha dado muchos quebraderos de cabeza** the preparations for the trip have given them a lot of headaches

quebradizo, -a *adj* (a) *(frágil)* fragile, brittle (b) *(débil)* frail (c) *(voz)* wavering, faltering

quebrado, -a 1 *adj* (a) *(terreno)* rough, rugged; *(línea)* crooked (b) *(fraccionario)* **número q.** fraction (c) *Lit* broken (d) *Méx (pelo)* curly (e) *Cuba (hoja de tabaco)* full of holes

2 *nm (fracción)* fraction

quebrantado, -a *adj* frail

quebrantahuesos *nm inv* bearded vulture, lammergeyer

quebrantamiento *nm* (a) *(incumplimiento)* breaking (b) *(de moral, resistencia)* breaking; **produjo el q. de su salud** it caused her health to fail

quebrantar 1 *vt* (a) *(promesa, ley)* to break; *(obligación)* to fail in (b) *(rocas)* to crack (c) *(moral, resistencia) (romper)* to break; *(debilitar)* to weaken

2 **quebrantarse** *vpr* (a) *(rocas)* to crack (b) *(moral, resistencia) (romperse)* to break; *(debilitarse)* to weaken

quebranto *nm* (a) *(pérdida)* loss; **la devaluación supuso un q. importante para la empresa** the devaluation caused the company significant losses (b) *(debilitamiento)* weakening, debilitation (c) *(pena)* grief

quebrar [3] 1 *vt* (a) *(objeto)* to break; **tanto peso puede q. la plancha de vidrio** all that weight may cause the sheet of glass to break

(b) *(situación, proceso)* to break; **el terrorismo pretende q. la estabilidad constitucional** the terrorists are trying to destroy the constitutional order

(c) *(debilitar) (voz, salud)* to weaken

(d) *(cintura)* to bend; **al hacer este ejercicio, no se debe q. la cintura** when doing this exercise you should avoid bending at the waist; **a fuerza de q. la cintura, atrae todas las miradas** the way she swings her hips attracts a lot of attention

(e) *Col, Méx Fam (matar)* to do in

2 *vi* (a) *(empresa)* to go bankrupt (b) *Méx (torcer)* to turn; **en la esquina, quebré a la izquierda** I turned left at the corner

3 **quebrarse** *vpr* (a) *(romperse)* to break; **se quebró una pierna** she broke a leg; *Méx Fig* **quebrarse la cabeza** to rack *o US* cudgel one's brains

(b) *(voz)* to break, to falter; **se le quebró la voz** her voice faltered

(c) *Am (darse por vencido)* to give in, to throw in the towel; **se quiebra ante cualquier dificultad** she gives in at the slightest sign of difficulty

(d) *Méx Fam (morirse) Br* to snuff it, *US* to check out

quebrazón *nf CAm, Chile, Méx* (a) *(rotura) (de objeto, mercancía)* breakage; **se notaba la q. de su voz** you could hear her voice faltering (b) *(quiebra)* bankruptcy

queche *nm* ketch

quechua, quichua 1 *adj* Quechuan

2 *nmf (persona)* Quechua

3 *nm (idioma)* Quechua

quechuismo *nm* = word or phrase of Quechuan origin

queda *nf* **toque de q.** curfew

quedada *nf Fam* (a) *(tomadura de pelo)* wind-up; **estoy harto de tus quedadas** I'm fed up of you always winding me up (b) *(encuentro)* meetup

quedado, -a *adj CSur, Ven Fam* lackadaisical; **es muy q., por eso nunca consiguió un buen empleo** he's got no initiative, that's why he's never found a decent job

quedamente *adv Literario* quietly, softly

QUEDAR 1 *vi* (a) *(permanecer)* to remain, to stay; **nuestros problemas quedaron sin resolver** our problems remained unsolved; **los tipos de interés han quedado al mismo nivel** interest rates have stayed *o* remained at the same level; **no le quedaron secuelas del accidente** he suffered no after-effects from the accident; *Andes, RP* **en el apuro, quedaron los abrigos** the coats got left behind *o* forgotten in the rush; **quedo a su entera disposición para cualquier consulta** *(en cartas)* I am available to answer any enquiries you may have; **todo quedó en un buen susto** she suffered nothing worse than a shock; **el viaje quedó en proyecto** the trip never got beyond the planning stage; **¡esto no puede** *o* **no va a q. así!** I'm not going to let it rest at this!; **todos nuestros problemas han quedado atrás** all our problems are behind us now

(b) *(haber aún)* to be left, to remain; **¿queda azúcar?** is there any sugar left?; **no queda azúcar** there isn't any sugar left; **no nos queda leche** we're out of milk; **queda gente dentro haciendo el examen** there are still some people left inside doing the exam; **queda poco del casco antiguo de la ciudad** little remains of the old part of the city; **nos quedan 50 pesos** we have 50 pesos left; **lo que quede dáselo al perro** give whatever's left over to the dog; **no me quedan ganas de seguir hablando** I don't feel like talking any more; **me queda la esperanza de volver algún día** I can only hope that one day I will return; EXPR *Am* **no queda otra** there's nothing else for it; **voy a tener que vender el auto para pagar las cuentas, no queda otra** I'm going to have to sell the car to pay the bills, there's nothing else for it

(c) *(faltar)* **¿cuánto queda para Buenos Aires?** how much further is it to Buenos Aires?; **quedan dos vueltas para que termine la carrera** there are two laps to go until the end of the race; **queda poco/un mes para las vacaciones** there's not long to go/there's a month to go until the holidays, it's not long/it's a month until the holidays; **queda mucho para mi cumpleaños** my birthday's a long way off; **me quedan dos días para terminar el trabajo** I have two days (left) to finish the work; **sólo me queda despedirme hasta la próxima semana** all that remains is for me to say goodbye until next week; **q. por hacer** to remain to be done; **queda por fregar el suelo** the floor has still to be cleaned; **nos quedan bastantes sitios por visitar** we still have quite a lot of places to visit

(d) *(mostrarse, dar cierta imagen)* **q. bien/mal (con alguien)** to make a good/bad impression (on sb); **le gusta q. bien con todo el mundo** he likes to keep everyone happy; **quedaste estupendamente trayendo flores** you made a very good impression by bringing flowers; **voy a q. fatal si no voy** it'll look really bad if I don't go; **no me hagas q. mal** don't show me up; **quedaste como un mentiroso** you ended up looking like *o* you came across like a liar; **quedó como un idiota** he ended up *o* he was left looking stupid

(e) *(resultar)* **el trabajo ha quedado perfecto** the job turned out perfectly; **el cuadro queda muy bien ahí** the picture looks great there; **el salón te ha quedado muy bonito** the living-room has turned out lovely, you've made a great job of the living-room; **q. claro** to be clear; **no quiero que llegues después de las once, ¿queda claro?** I don't want you back later than eleven, is that clear?; **q. en** *(llegar, acabar)* to end in; **q. en quinto lugar, q. el quinto** to come fifth; **q. en nada** to come to nothing; *RP Fam* **quedamos en veremos** we left it open

(f) *(sentar)* **te queda un poco corto el traje** your suit is a bit too short; **esta falda me queda un poco justa** this skirt is a bit tight; **¡qué bien te queda ese traje!** that dress really suits you!, you look great in that dress!; **esa camisa te queda mal** that shirt doesn't suit you; **¿te quedan bien los zapatos?** do the shoes fit you?; **q. bien/mal con algo** to go well/badly with sth; *Méx* **este pantalón no me queda** these *Br* trousers *o US* pants don't suit me; *Méx* **esas cortinas le quedan mal al salón** those curtains don't go well in the living-room

(g) *(citarse)* **q. (con alguien)** to arrange to meet (sb); **¿cuándo/dónde quedamos?** when/where shall we meet?; **hemos quedado el lunes** we've arranged to meet on Monday; **he quedado con Juan para jugar al tenis** I've arranged to play tennis with Juan

(h) *(acordar)* **q. en algo** to agree on sth; **q. en** *o Am* **de hacer algo** to agree to do sth; **¿en qué has quedado?** what have you decided to do?; **q. en que...** to agree that...; **quedé con ellos en que iría** I told them I'd go; **¿en qué quedamos?** what's it to be, then?

(i) *(estar situado)* to be; **queda por las afueras** it's somewhere on the outskirts; **¿por dónde queda?** whereabouts is it?

(j) *(asignatura)* **me queda el inglés de primero** I still haven't passed first-year English; **¿cuántas te han quedado?** how many subjects from last year do you have to resit this year?

2 *vt RP Fam* **quedarla: no apuestes todo a una sola posibilidad porque si no sale, la quedás** don't put all your eggs in one basket because if it doesn't work out, you've had it; **¿quién la queda?** *(en juego)* who's counting?

3 *v impersonal* **por mí que no quede** don't let me be the one to stop you; **que no quede por falta de dinero** we don't want it to fall through for lack of money; **por probar que no quede** we should at least try it

4 **quedarse** *vpr* (a) *(permanecer)* to stay, to remain; **todos le pidieron que se quedara** everyone asked her to stay; **va a tener que quedarse en el hospital** he is going to have to stay *o* remain in hospital; **¿por qué no te quedas un rato más?** why don't you stay on a bit longer?; **hoy me quedaré en casa** I'm going to stay at home *o* stay in today; **me quedé estudiando hasta tarde** I stayed up late studying; **me quedé en la cama hasta tarde** I slept in; **se quedó de pie mirándome** she stood there watching me

(b) *(terminar en un estado)* **quedarse ciego/sordo** to go blind/deaf; **quedarse viudo** to be widowed; **quedarse soltero** to remain single *o* a bachelor; **quedarse sin dinero** to be left penniless; **me quedé dormido** I fell asleep; **se quedó un poco triste** she was *o* felt rather sad; *Esp* **se ha quedado/se está quedando muy delgada** she's become/she's getting very thin; **al verla se quedó pálido** he turned pale when he saw her; *Esp* **la pared se ha quedado limpia** the wall is clean now; **quedarse atrás** to fall behind

(c) *(comprar, elegir)* to take; **me quedo éste** I'll take this one

(d) **quedarse con** *(retener, guardarse)* to keep; **quédese con la vuelta** *o* **el cambio** keep the change; **alguien se ha quedado con mi paraguas** someone has taken my umbrella; **no me quedé con su nombre** I can't seem to remember his name

(e) **quedarse con** *(preferir)* to go for, to prefer; **de todos los pescados me quedo con el salmón** I prefer salmon to any other sort of fish, when it comes to fish, I'd go for salmon every time

(f) *Fam (persona)* to kick the bucket; *Am (máquina)* to pack up; **anduvo bien los primeros kilómetros y de pronto se quedó** it was fine for the first few miles, then all of a sudden it packed up

(g) *Esp Fam* **quedarse con alguien** *(burlarse de)* to wind sb up; **te estás quedando conmigo** you're having me on!

---

quedo, -a 1 *adj* quiet, soft

2 *adv* quietly, softly

quehacer *nm* task; **quieren acercar al gran público al q. científico** they want to bring the work of scientists to a wider public; **quehaceres domésticos** *o* **de la casa** housework

queimada *nf* = punch typical of Galicia, made from spirits and sugar, which is set alight to burn off some of the alcohol before being drunk

queja *nf* (a) *(lamento)* moan, groan (b) *(protesta)* complaint; **presentar una q.** *(formalmente)* to make *o* lodge a complaint; **tener q. de algo/alguien** to have a complaint about sth/sb; **no tienes ningún motivo de q.** you've got nothing to complain about, you've no cause for complaint; **no me ha dado ningún motivo de q.** I've got no complaints about him

quejarse *vpr* (a) *(lamentarse)* to groan, to moan; **últimamente se queja mucho de la espalda** recently she's been complaining a lot that her back hurts

(b) *(protestar)* to complain; *(refunfuñar)* to moan; **siempre está quejándose del frío que hace en este país** he's always complaining about how cold it is in this country; **se quejó por la lentitud de la conexión** he complained about how slow the connection was; **no sé de qué te quejas** I don't know what you're complaining about; EXPR *Fam* **q. de vicio** to complain about nothing

quejica *Fam Pey* 1 *adj* whining, whingeing; **es muy q.** he's always whining *o* whingeing; **no seas q. y ponte a trabajar** stop whining *o* whingeing and get some work done

2 *nmf* whinger

quejicoso, -a *adj & nm,f* = **quejica**

quejido *nm* cry, moan; **dar quejidos** to moan

quejigo *nm* gall oak

quejoso, -a 1 *adj* **estar q. de** *o* **por** to be unhappy *o* dissatisfied with

2 *nm,f* (a) *Méx, RP Fam Pey (quejumbroso)* whinger (b) *Méx (demandante)* plaintiff

quejumbroso, -a *adj* (a) *(lastimero)* pitiful (b) *(quejica)* whining, whingeing

queli *nf Esp Fam* pad

quelite *nm Méx* fat hen, pigweed

quelonio *Zool* 1 *nm* chelonian

2 **quelonios** *nmpl (orden) Chelonia*

quema *nf* burning; **los soldados procedieron a la q. del pueblo** the soldiers set fire to the village; **prohibida la q. de rastrojos** stubble burning prohibited; EXPR **huir de la q.** to get out before it is too late; EXPR **salvarse de la q.** to escape the carnage *o* rout

quemada = **quemadura**

quemadero *nm* **q. (de basuras)** waste incineration site

quemado, -a 1 *adj* (a) *(por fuego)* burnt; *(por agua hirviendo)* scalded; **huele a q.** it smells of burning; **unidad de quemados** *(en hospital)* burns unit

(b) *Am (bronceado)* tanned; **estaba preciosa, bien quemada y con un vestido blanco** she looked fabulous with her lovely tan and in her white dress

(c) *Fam* **estar q.** *(agotado)* to be burnt-out; *(harto)* to be fed up; **está muy q. con sus compañeros de trabajo** he's completely fed up with his colleagues at work

2 *nm* tan; **estaba preciosa, con un vestido blanco que le realzaba el q.** she looked fabulous in a white dress that brought out her tan

quemador *nm Br* gas ring, *US* burner

quemadura, *Méx* **quemada** *nf* (a) *(lesión) (por fuego)* burn; *(por agua hirviendo)* scald; *Andes, RP (por sol)* sunburn; **hacerse una q.** to burn/scald oneself; **q. de segundo grado/de primer grado** second-degree/first-degree burn; **cúbrete el rostro, que las quemaduras en la nariz son muy frecuentes** cover your face or your nose is likely to get sunburnt

(b) *(señal)* burn mark; **me hizo una q. en la camisa** it left a burn mark on my shirt

quemar 1 *vt* (a) *(sol, con fuego, calor)* to burn; *(con líquido hirviendo)* to scald; **quemaron una bandera americana** they set fire to an American flag; **has quemado los macarrones** you've burnt the macaroni; **quemaban a los herejes en la hoguera** heretics were burnt at the stake; EXPR **q. etapas** *(ir rápido)* to come on in leaps and bounds, to progress rapidly; *(ir demasiado rápido)* to cut corners; EXPR **q. el último cartucho** to play one's last card

(b) *(calorías)* to burn up; *(grasa)* to burn off

(c) *(plantas)* **la helada quemó las plantas** the frost killed the plants; **el sol quemó las plantas** the plants withered in the sun

(d) *(malgastar)* to run through, to fritter away; **quemó sus ahorros en pocos meses** she ran through her savings in just a few months

(e) *Fam (desgastar)* to burn out

(f) *CAm, Méx (delatar)* to denounce, to inform on

(g) *Carib, Méx (estafar)* to swindle

(h) *RP Fam (balear)* to shoot

(i) *RP Fam (dejar mal a)* **q. a alguien** to make sb look bad; **me quemaron con la publicación de esa noticia** they really landed me in it by publishing that story

2 *vi* (a) *(estar caliente)* to be (scalding) hot; **ten cuidado que la sopa quema** be careful, the soup's (scalding) hot (b) *Fam (desgastar)* **la política quema** politics burns you out

3 **quemarse** *vpr* (a) *(por fuego)* to burn down; *(por calor)* to burn; *(por agua hirviendo)* to get scalded; **se quemó con una sartén** he burnt himself on a frying pan; **se ha quemado la lasaña** the lasagne's burnt; **¡te quemas!** *(al buscar algo)* you're burning!

(b) *(por el sol) (abrasarse)* to get (sun)burnt; *Am (broncearse)* to get a tan; **en un mes de playa se quemó divinamente** after a month at the seaside he had a wonderful tan

(c) *Fam (desgastarse)* to burn out; **se quemó tras quince años en las canchas de tenis** after fifteen years as a tennis player he was burnt out

(d) *Esp Fam (hartarse)* to get fed up; **acabó quemándose por culpa**

de las críticas de su jefe she ended up getting fed up with her boss's criticisms

(**e**) *RP Fam (quedar mal)* to make oneself look bad; **si largás en la mitad del proyecto te quemás para siempre** if you leave halfway through the project you'll be blowing your chances with them for good

quemarropa: a quemarropa *loc adv* (**a**) *(desde cerca)* **le dispararon a q.** he was shot at point-blank range (**b**) *(por sorpresa)* point-blank; **le hicieron la pregunta a q.** they asked him point-blank

quemazón *nf* (**a**) *(ardor)* burning (sensation); *(picor)* itch (**b**) *RP (quemo)* embarrassment

quemo *nm RP Fam* **ser un q.** *(situación)* to be dead embarrassing; **dejé de salir con Pedro porque es un q.** I stopped going out with Pedro because he's just so embarrassing *o* he makes me cringe; **ir a ese club es un q.** I wouldn't be seen dead at that club

quena *nf* = type of Andean flute

quepa *etc ver* **caber**

quepis *nm inv* kepi

quepo *ver* **caber**

queque *nm Andes, CAm, Méx* sponge (cake)

queratina *nf* keratin

queratotomía, queratomía *nf* keratotomy

querella *nf* (**a**) *Der (acusación)* charge; **presentar** *o* **poner una q. contra alguien/por algo** to bring an action against sb/for sth (**b**) *(conflicto)* dispute

querellante *nmf Der* plaintiff

querellarse *vpr Der* to bring an action (**contra** against)

querencia *nf* (**a**) *(tendencia)* homing instinct (**b**) *Taurom* = preference of the bull for a particular part of the bullring

querendón, -ona *adj Am Fam* loving, affectionate

QUERER [53] **1** *vt* (**a**) *(amar)* to love; **te quiero** I love you; **lo quiero como a un hermano** I love him like a brother; **es muy querida por todo el mundo** she is much loved by everyone; **me quiere, no me quiere** *(deshojando margarita)* she loves me, she loves me not; **¡por lo que más quieras, cállate!** for heaven's sake shut up!; **q. bien a alguien** to care a lot about sb; **q. mal a alguien** to wish sb ill; PROV **quien bien te quiere te hará llorar** you have to be cruel to be kind

(**b**) *(desear)* to want; **quiero una bicicleta** I want a bicycle; **dime lo que quieres** tell me what you want; **lo único que quiero** *o* **todo lo que quiero es un poco de comprensión** all I want *o* all I ask for is a little understanding; **¿qué es lo que quieres ahora?** *(con tono de enojo)* what do you want now?, what is it now?; **haz lo que quieras** do what you want *o* like, do as you please *o* like; **q. hacer algo** to want to do sth; **quiere explicártelo, te lo quiere explicar** she wants to explain it to you; **no quiso ayudarnos** she didn't want to help us; **era muy tarde pero tú querías quedarte** it was very late, but you insisted on staying *o* would stay *o* wanted to stay; **quisiera informarme** *o* **que me informaran sobre vuelos a Nueva York** I'd like some information about flights to New York; **quisiera hacerlo, pero...** I'd like to do it, but...; **¡eso quisiera yo saber!** that's what I want to know!; **¡ya quisieran muchos tener tu suerte!** a lot of people would be very grateful to be as lucky as you!; **el maldito clavo no quiere salir** the damn nail won't *o* refuses to come out; **q. que alguien haga algo** to want sb to do sth; **quiero que lo hagas tú** I want you to do it; **q. que pase algo** to want sth to happen; **queremos que las cosas te vayan bien** we want things to go well for you; **el azar quiso que nos volviéramos a ver** fate decreed that we should see each other again; **como quien no quiere la cosa** as if it were nothing; **¿qué quieres que te diga?, a mí me parece caro** to be honest, it seems expensive to me, what can I say? it seems expensive to me; **¡qué quieres que haga!** what am I supposed to do?; **alto, guapo y todo lo que tú quieras, pero no me gusta** sure, he's tall, handsome and all that, but I don't find him attractive; PROV **el que algo quiere, algo le cuesta** no pain, no gain

(**c**) *(en preguntas, ofrecimientos, ruegos) (con amabilidad)* **¿quieren ustedes algo más/algo de postre?** would you like anything else/anything for dessert?; **¿quieres un pitillo?** do you want a cigarette?; **¿quiere decirle a su amigo que pase?** could you tell your friend to come in, please?; **¿querrías explicarme qué ha pasado aquí?** would you mind explaining what happened here?; **¿quieres por esposo a Francisco?** do you take Francisco to be your lawfully wedded husband?

(**d**) *(pedir)* **q. algo (por)** to want sth (for); **¿cuánto quieres por la casa?** how much do you want for the house?

(**e**) *Irónico (dar motivos para)* **tú lo que quieres es que te pegue** you're asking for a smack; **¿quieres que te atropelle el tren o qué?** do you want to get run over by a train or something?

(**f**) *(en naipes) (aceptar apuesta)* **quiero tus cinco mil** I'll see your five thousand

2 *vi* to want; **ven cuando quieras** come whenever you like *o* want; **cuando quieras** *(estoy listo)* ready when you are; **no me voy porque no quiero** I'm not going because I don't want to; **si quieres, lo dejamos** we can forget about it if you like; **quieras o no, quieras que no** (whether you) like it or not; **pásame el martillo, ¿quieres?** pass me the hammer, would you?; **déjame en paz, ¿quieres?** leave me alone, will you?; *Fam* **le pedí que lo dejara, pero que si quieres** I asked him to stop, but would he?; **queriendo** on purpose; **ha sido queriendo** he did it on purpose; **hacer algo sin q.** to do sth accidentally; **lo siento, ha sido sin q.** sorry, it was an accident; **q. decir** to mean; **¿qué quieres decir con eso?** what do you mean by that?; **¿sabes lo que quiere decir "procrastination"?** do you know what "procrastination" means?; **"NB" quiere decir "nota bene"** "NB" stands for "nota bene"; EXPR *Fam* **está como quiere** *(en una situación ideal)* he's got it made; *(es guapísimo)* he's gorgeous; PROV **q. es poder** where there's a will there's a way

3 *v impersonal (haber atisbos de)* **parece que quiere llover** it looks like rain

4 *nm (amor)* love; **las cosas del q.** matters of the heart

5 quererse *vpr* to love each other; **se quieren con locura** they are madly in love

---

queretano, -a 1 *adj* of/from Querétaro *(Mexico)*

2 *nm,f* person from Querétaro *(Mexico)*

querido, -a 1 *adj* (**a**) *(en cartas)* dear; **Querido Juan** Dear Juan; **Queridos padres** Dear Mum and Dad; **Mi q. amigo** Dear friend (**b**) *(amado)* **la pena que causa la muerte de alguien q.** the pain of losing a loved one *o* someone dear to you; **el alcalde era q. por todos** the mayor was loved by everyone; **una ciudad especialmente querida para el cantante** a city that is particularly close to the singer's heart

2 *nm,f* (**a**) *(amante)* lover (**b**) *(apelativo afectuoso)* darling

quermes *nm inv* kermes

quermés *nf inv*, **quermese** *nf* (*pl* **quermeses**) kermis

queroseno, *Am* **querosén,** *Am* **querosene** *nm* kerosene

querré *etc ver* **querer**

querubín *nm* cherub

quesadilla *nf* (**a**) *CAm, Méx (salada)* quesadilla, = filled fried tortilla (**b**) *Ecuad (dulce)* = sweet, cheese-filled pasty

quesera *nf* (**a**) *(recipiente)* cheese dish (**b**) *ver también* **quesero**

quesería *nf* cheese shop

quesero, -a 1 *adj* (**a**) *(del queso)* cheese; **la industria quesera** the cheese-making industry (**b**) *(aficionado)* **es muy q.** he loves cheese

2 *nm,f* (**a**) *(fabricante)* cheese maker (**b**) *(vendedor)* cheese seller

quesillo *nm Ven* = dessert made with egg yolk and syrup, similar to crème caramel

quesito *nm* cheese portion *o* triangle

queso *nm* (**a**) *(producto lácteo)* cheese; EXPR *Fam* **a mí no me las das con q.** don't you try and fool me ►► ***q. azul*** blue cheese; ***q. de bola*** Dutch cheese; ***q. brie*** Brie; ***q. de cabrales*** = Asturian cheese similar to Roquefort; ***q. camembert*** Camembert; *Andes, RP* ***q. de cerdo*** head cheese, *Br* brawn; ***q. crema*** cream cheese; ***q. emmental*** Emmental; ***q. fresco*** cottage cheese; ***q. gorgonzola*** Gorgonzola; ***q. gouda*** Gouda; ***q. gruyère*** Gruyère; ***q. manchego*** = hard yellow cheese made in La Mancha; ***q. mozzarella*** mozzarella (cheese); ***q. parmesano*** Parmesan (cheese); ***q. en porciones*** cheese triangles; *CAm, Méx* ***q. de puerco*** head cheese, *Br* brawn; ***q. rallado*** grated cheese; ***q. roquefort*** Roquefort; ***q. de tetilla*** = soft mound-shaped Galician cheese; ***q. de untar*** cheese spread

(**b**) *Fam (pie)* foot; **te huelen los quesos** you've got cheesy feet

(**c**) *Ven Fam (estafa)* fiddle

(**d**) *RP Fam (bobo)* thickhead, dummy

quetzal *nm* (**a**) *(ave)* quetzal (**b**) *(moneda)* quetzal

quevedos *nmpl Anticuado* pince-nez

quia *interj Fam* bah!; **¿vendrás? – ¡q., estoy muy ocupado!** will you come? – bah! I'm too busy!

quiche [kiʃ] *nf* quiche

quiché 1 *adj* Quiché

2 *nm* Quiché

quichua = **quechua**

quicio *nm* (**a**) *(de puerta, ventana)* jamb *(on hinge side)* (**b**) EXPR **sacar de q. a alguien** to drive sb mad; **me saca de q. que utilice tantas palabrotas** I really hate it when she uses so much bad language; **sacar las cosas de q.** to blow things (up) out of all proportion

quico *nm (maíz tostado)* = toasted, salted maize kernel; EXPR *Fam* **ponerse como el q.** to stuff one's face

quid (*pl* **quids**) *nm* crux; **el q. de la cuestión** the crux of the matter

quiebra *nf* (**a**) *(ruina)* bankruptcy; *(en Bolsa)* crash; **ir a la q.** to go bankrupt; **declararse en q.** to go into liquidation ►► *Der* ***q. fraudulenta*** fraudulent bankruptcy (**b**) *(pérdida)* collapse; **q. moral** moral bankruptcy (**c**) *(grieta)* fissure, crack

quiebre *nm Andes, RP* breakdown

quiebro 1 *ver* **quebrar**
2 *nm* (**a**) *(ademán)* swerve; **hizo un q. con la cintura y sorteó al defensa** he beat the defender with a swerve to one side (**b**) *Mús* trill

QUIEN *pron* (**a**) *(relativo) (sujeto)* who; *(complemento)* who, *Formal* whom; **fue mi hermano q. me lo explicó** it was my brother who explained it to me; **él fue q. me robó** he's the one who robbed me; **era Rosario a q. vi/de q. no me fiaba** it was Rosario (who) I saw/didn't trust; **buscaba a alguien con q. hablar** I was looking for someone to talk to; **el atracador, a q. nadie reconoció, logró escapar** the mugger, who nobody recognized, was able to escape; **gane q. gane, el partido está siendo memorable** whoever wins, it has been an unforgettable game
(**b**) *(indefinido)* **q. lo encuentre que se lo quede** whoever finds it can keep it; **quienes quieran verlo que se acerquen** whoever wants to see it will have to come closer; **q. no sabe nada de esto es tu madre** one person who knows nothing about it is your mother; **hay q. lo niega** there are those who deny it; **al billar no hay q. le gane** he's unbeatable at billiards; **q. más q. menos** everyone; **q. más q. menos, todo el mundo se lo esperaba** that's what everyone expected, to some extent or other; EXPR *CAm, Méx, Ven Fam* **q. quita y...** *(tal vez)* maybe...; *(ojalá)* let's hope...; **visita nuestra página, q. quita y te gusta** visit our website, you may like it *o* maybe you'll like it; **¿mañana sales de viaje? q. quita y te vaya bien** so you're off on a trip tomorrow? I hope it all goes well

QUIÉN *pron* (**a**) *(interrogativo) (sujeto)* who; *(complemento)* who, *Formal* whom; **¿q. es ese hombre?** who's that man?; **¿quiénes son ustedes/ellos?** who are you/they?; **no sé q. viene** I don't know who's coming; **no sé a q. creer** I don't know who to believe; **¿q. puede ser** *o* **q. será a estas horas?** who *o* whoever can it be at this hour?; **¿a quiénes has invitado?** who *o Formal* whom have you invited?; **¿con q. estás saliendo?** who are you going out with?; **¿de q. es esto?** whose is this?; **hay una carta para ti – ¿de q.?** there's a letter for you – who from?; **¿q. es?** *(en la puerta)* who is it?; *(al teléfono)* who's calling?; **¡tú no eres q. para darme órdenes!** who are you to give me orders?, who do you think you are giving me orders?; **yo no soy q. para decir si es mi mejor novela** it's not for me to say whether it's my best novel
(**b**) *(exclamativo)* **¡q. pudiera verlo!** if only I could see it!; **¡q. sabe!** who knows?

> In conversational English a preposition is frequently placed at the end of a sentence beginning with an interrogative pronoun. In Spanish the preposition must always come at the beginning of the sentence before the interrogative pronoun:
> **¿con quién quiere hablar?**
> *who does he want to speak to?*
> **¿de quién conseguiste esto?**
> *who/whom did you get this from?*
> The same contrast is found in the use of relative pronouns in the two languages:
> **el hombre con quien hablaba**
> *the man (that/who) I was talking to*

quienquiera (*pl* **quienesquiera**) *pron* whoever; **q. que venga** whoever comes

quiero *etc ver* **querer**

quieto, -a *adj* (**a**) *(parado)* still; **¡estate q.!** keep still!; **¡q. ahí!** don't move!; **¡las manos quietas!** keep your hands to yourself! (**b**) *(tranquilo)* quiet; **desde que se fue el director el trabajo está q.** things have been a lot quieter at work since the boss left

quietud *nf* (**a**) *(inmovilidad)* stillness (**b**) *(tranquilidad)* quietness (**c**) *RP (reposo)* rest

quif *nm* kif

quihubo *interj CAm, Col, Méx, Ven Fam* how are you doing?

quijada *nf* jaw

quijotada *nf* quixotic deed

quijote *nm (soñador)* do-gooder; **don Q.** Don Quixote

quijotería *nf* quixotism

quijotesco, -a *adj* quixotic

quijotismo *nm* quixotism

quilate *nm* (**a**) *(de piedras preciosas, perlas)* carat (**b**) *(de oro)* carat; **oro de 24 quilates** 24-carat gold

quilla *nf (de barco)* keel

quillango *nm Arg, Chile* fur blanket

quillay *nm Arg, Chile* soapbark tree

quilo = **kilo**

quilombo *nm RP muy Fam* (**a**) *(burdel)* whorehouse (**b**) *(lío, desorden)* **¡tu mesa es un q.!** your desk's a *Br* bloody *o US* goddamn mess!; **se armó un gran q.** all hell broke loose

quiltro, -a *nm,f Chile Fam* mongrel

quimba *nf* (**a**) *Andes (contoneo)* swaying (**b**) *Col, Ecuad, Ven (calzado)* peasant shoe

quimbambas *nfpl* EXPR *Fam* **en las q.** in the back of beyond

quimbar *vi Andes (contonearse)* to sway

quimbombó *nm Cuba* okra, gumbo

quimera *nf* (**a**) *(ilusión)* chimera; **la q. de una Europa unida** the chimera of a united Europe; **tus ideas no son más que una q.** your ideas are pie in the sky (**b**) *Mitol* Chimera

quimérico, -a *adj* fanciful, unrealistic; **hizo unos cálculos quiméricos** she made some fanciful *o* far-fetched calculations

química *nf* (**a**) *(ciencia)* chemistry; **un licenciado en química(s)** a chemistry graduate ►► ***q. agrícola*** agrochemistry; ***q. física*** physical chemistry; ***q. industrial*** industrial chemistry; ***q. inorgánica*** inorganic chemistry; ***q. orgánica*** organic chemistry
(**b**) *(sustancias artificiales)* chemicals; **es pura q.** it's full of chemicals
(**c**) *Fam (atracción, entendimiento)* chemistry; **no hay q. entre los dos políticos** there's no chemistry between the two politicians
(**d**) *ver también* **químico**

químicamente *adv* chemically

químico, -a 1 *adj* chemical
2 *nm,f (científico)* chemist

quimioterapia *nf* chemotherapy

quimono *nm* kimono

quina *nf (extracto)* quinine; EXPR *Fam* **ser más malo que la q.** to be truly horrible; EXPR *Fam* **tragar q.** to grin and bear it

quincajú *nm* kinkajou, honey bear

quincalla *nf* trinket

quincallería *nf (chatarra)* trinkets

quincallero, -a *nm,f Br* ironmonger, *US* hardware dealer

quince *núm* fifteen; **q. días** a fortnight; *UE* **los Q.** the Fifteen; EXPR **dar q. y raya a alguien** to get the better of sb; *Fam* EXPR **del q.: un constipado del q.** a stinking cold; *ver también* **tres**

quinceañero, -a 1 *adj* teenage
2 *nm,f* teenager

quinceavo, -a *núm (fracción)* fifteenth; *ver también* **octavo**

quincena *nf* fortnight; **la segunda q. de agosto** the second fortnight *o* half of August

quincenal *adj* fortnightly

quincenalmente *adv* fortnightly, every two weeks

quincha *nf*, **quinchado** *nm Andes, RP* (**a**) *(entramado)* wickerwork (**b**) *(pared)* = wall made of reeds and adobe

quinchar *vt Andes, RP* to thatch

quincho *nm* (**a**) *Andes, RP (techo)* thatched roof (**b**) *Andes, RP (refugio)* thatched shelter (**c**) *RP Fam Euf (lío)* **se armó un q. de novela** there was a terrific hullabaloo; **la fiesta fue un q.** the party was utter chaos

quincuagenario, -a 1 *adj* **un político q.** a politician in his fifties
2 *nm,f* **Emilio es q.** Emilio is in his fifties

quincuagésimo, -a *núm* fiftieth; *ver también* **octavo**

quinesioterapeuta, quinesiterapeuta *nmf* kinesitherapist

quinesioterapia, quinesiterapia *nf* kinesitherapy

quingombó *nm Cuba* okra, gumbo

quingos *nmpl Col, Perú* zigzag

quiniela *nf* (**a**) *Esp (boleto)* pools coupon; **quiniela(s)** *(apuestas) Br* (football) pools, *US* sports lottery; **jugar a las quinielas** *Br* to do the pools, *US* to play the sports lottery; **echar una q.** to hand in one's *Br* pools coupon *o US* sports lottery ticket; **hacer una q.** *Br* to do the

pools, *US* to play the sports lottery; **le tocó la q.** she won the *Br* pools *o US* sports lottery; *Fig* **ser una q.** to be a lottery ►► ***q. hípica*** = gambling pool based on the results of horse races
(**b**) *Méx, RP (juego de azar)* lottery

quinielista *nmf Esp* = person who does the football pools

quinielístico, -a *adj Esp Br* (football) pools, *US* sports lottery; **peña quinielística** (football) pools syndicate

quinielón *nm Esp* = 15 correct forecasts on football pools entitling player to jackpot prize

quinientos, -as *núm* five hundred; *ver también* **treinta**

quinina *nf* quinine

quino *nm (árbol)* cinchona (tree)

quinoa, quínoa *nf Andes, Arg* quinoa

quinoto *nm* kumquat; EXPR *RP muy Fam* **romper los quinotos** to be a pain in the *Br* arse *o US* butt

quinqué *nm* oil lamp

quinquenal *adj* five-year; **plan q.** five-year plan

quinquenio *nm* (**a**) *(periodo)* five years; **el q. 2000-2004** the five-year period 2000-2004 (**b**) *(paga)* = five-yearly salary increase

quinqui *nmf Esp Fam (macarra)* lout, *Br* yob

quinta *nf* (**a**) *(finca)* country house (**b**) *Mil* call-up year; **entrar en quintas** to be called up; **Juan es de mi q.** *(tiene mi edad)* Juan is my age (**c**) *Mús* fifth (**d**) *(marcha)* fifth (gear); **meter (la) q.** to go into fifth (gear) (**e**) *ver también* **quinto**

quintacolumnista *nmf* fifth columnist

quintaesencia *nf* quintessence; **es la q. del pop británico** it's quintessential British pop; **es la q. de la sencillez** it's simplicity itself

quintal *nm* quintal, = weight measure equivalent to 46 kilos; EXPR **pesar un q.** to weigh a ton ►► ***q. métrico*** quintal, = weight measure equivalent to 100 kilos

quintanense 1 *adj* of/from Quintana Roo *(Mexico)*
2 *nmf* person from Quintana Roo *(Mexico)*

quintar *vt Mil* to draft, to call up

quinteto *nm* quintet

quintillizo, -a 1 *adj* quintuplet
2 *nm,f* quintuplet

quinto, -a 1 *núm* fifth; EXPR *Fam* **en el q. infierno** *o Esp* **pino: vive en el q. infierno** *o Esp* **pino** she lives in the back of beyond *o* in the middle of nowhere; EXPR *Esp Vulg* **en el q. coño: vive en el q. coño** she lives *Br* bloody *o US* goddamn miles from anywhere ►► *también Fig* ***quinta columna*** fifth column; ***quinta esencia*** quintessence; *ver también* **octavo**
2 *nm* (**a**) *(parte)* fifth (**b**) *(piso) Br* fifth floor, *US* sixth floor (**c**) *Mil* = person who has been chosen (by lots) to do military service (**d**) *(curso universitario)* fifth year (**e**) *(curso escolar)* = fifth year of primary school, *US* ≃ fifth grade (**f**) *Esp (de cerveza)* = small bottle of beer containing 0.2 litres

quintral *nm Arg, Chile* mistletoe

quintuplicar [60] **1** *vt* to increase fivefold
2 quintuplicarse *vpr* to increase fivefold

quíntuplo, -a, quíntuple 1 *adj* quintuple
2 *nm* quintuple

quinua, quínua *nf Andes, Arg* quinoa

quiosco *nm* (**a**) *(de periódico, revistas)* newspaper stand *o* kiosk; *(de refrescos)* kiosk; *(de helados)* ice cream stand; *(de lotería)* = kiosk where lottery tickets are sold ►► ***q. de música*** bandstand (**b**) *RP (estanco)* tobacconist's

quiosquero, -a *nm,f* = person selling newspapers, drinks etc from a kiosk

quipe *nm Andes* knapsack

quipos, quipus *nmpl Andes* quipus, = knotted cords used for record keeping by the Incas

quique *nm Chile* grison

quiqui, kiki *nm Esp muy Fam* **echar un q.** to do it, to get it on

quiquiriquí (*pl* **quiquiriquíes** *o* **quiquiriquís**) **1** *nm* (**a**) *(canto)* crowing (**b**) *(mechón)* **llevas un q.** your hair's sticking up at the front
2 *interj* cock-a-doodle-do!

quirófano *nm* operating *Br* theatre *o US* room

quiromancia *nf* palmistry, chiromancy

quiromántico, -a 1 *adj* chiromantic
2 *nm,f* palm reader, palmist

quiromasaje *nm* massage

quiromasajista *nmf* masseur, *f* masseuse

quiropráctica *nf* chiropractic

quiropráctico, -a 1 *adj* chiropractic
2 *nm,f* chiropractor

quiropraxia *nf* chiropractic

quiróptero *Zool* **1** *nm* chiropteran
2 quirópteros *nmpl (orden) Chiroptera*

quirquincho *nm Andes, Arg* armadillo

quirúrgico, -a *adj* surgical

quise *etc ver* **querer**

quisiera *etc ver* **querer**

quisque, quisqui *nm* **cada q.** everyone; **que cada q. se ocupe de sus asuntos** everyone should mind their own business; **todo q.** everyone; **aquí todo q. hace lo que le da la gana** everyone just does whatever they like round here; **por mí, como si se entera todo q.** personally, I don't care if the whole world knows it

quisquilla 1 *nf (camarón) Br* shrimp, *US* prawn
2 *nmf Fam (susceptible)* touchy person; **ser un q.** to be touchy

quisquilloso, -a 1 *adj* (**a**) *(detallista)* pernickety (**b**) *(susceptible)* touchy, oversensitive
2 *nm,f* (**a**) *(detallista)* nit-picker (**b**) *(susceptible)* touchy person; **ser un q.** to be touchy

quiste *nm* cyst ►► ***q. hidatídico*** hydatid (cyst); ***q. ovárico*** ovarian cyst; ***q. sebáceo*** sebaceous cyst

quístico, -a *adj* cystic

quita *nf Der* acquittance, release

quitaesmalte *nm* nail-polish remover

quitaipón: de quitaipón *loc adj Fam* removable

quitamanchas *nm inv* stain remover

quitameriendas *nm inv* meadow saffron

quitamiedos *nm inv* (**a**) *(en carretera)* crash barrier (**b**) *(para evitar caída)* railing

quitamultas *nm inv Fam* = very lightweight crash helmet worn by motorcyclists not wishing to wear a proper helmet but wanting to avoid being fined

quitanieves 1 *adj* **máquina q.** *(con pala)* snowplough; *(por succión)* snowblower
2 *nm inv (con pala)* snowplough; *(por succión)* snowblower

quitapenas *nm inv Fam (licor)* pick-me-up

QUITAR 1 *vt* (**a**) *(retirar, extraer, apartar)* to remove; *(ropa, zapatos)* to take off; *Esp* **q. la mesa** *(despejar)* to clear the table; **al q. la tapa de la olla salió un delicioso olor** when she took the lid off the pot, a delicious smell came out; **le han quitado un tumor del pecho** they've removed a tumour from her breast; **quita tus cosas de la cama** take your things off the bed; **quita tus cosas de en medio** clear your things up (out of the way); **voy a q. el polvo de los muebles** I'm going to dust the furniture; **quitarle algo a alguien** *(arrebatar, privar de)* to take sth away from sb; **me quitó la carta de las manos** she took the letter from my hands; **durante la guerra le quitaron la casa** they took her house away from her during the war; **le han quitado la custodia de los niños** they've taken away custody of the children from her; **eso fue lo que dijo, sin q. ni poner nada** that's what he said, word for word; EXPR **por un quítame allá esas pajas** for no reason, over nothing; EXPR *Méx* **no q. el dedo del renglón** to keep coming back to the same point
(**b**) *(eliminar, suprimir)* to remove; **quité la mancha con jabón** I removed the stain *o* got the stain out with soap; **han quitado mi programa favorito de la tele** they've taken my favourite programme off the TV; **ese ministerio lo han quitado** they've done away with *o* got rid of that ministry; **el médico me ha quitado el tabaco** *(prohibido)* the doctor has told me to stop smoking
(**c**) *(robar)* to take, to steal; **me han quitado la cartera** someone has taken *o* stolen my wallet; **le quitaron el puesto** they've taken his job away from him
(**d**) *(mitigar del todo) (dolor, ansiedad)* to take away, to relieve; *(sed)* to quench; **el aperitivo me ha quitado el hambre** the snack has taken away my appetite
(**e**) *(ocupar) (tiempo, espacio)* to take up; **me quitan mucho tiempo los niños** the children take up a lot of my time; **el trabajo me quita tiempo para el deporte** my job doesn't leave me much time for sport; **el armario va a q. mucho sitio ahí** the wardrobe's going to take up a lot of space there
(**f**) *(restar)* to take away; **a esa cifra quítale el 20 por ciento** take away 20 percent from that figure; **no quiero q. mérito** *o* **valor a lo que ha hecho** I don't want to take away from *o* detract from what she

has done; **le quitó importancia al hecho** he played it down

(**g**) *(impedir)* **esto no quita que sea un vago** that doesn't change the fact that he's a layabout; **que me mude de ciudad no quita que nos sigamos viendo** just because I'm moving to another city doesn't mean we won't still be able to see each other

(**h**) *(exceptuar)* **quitando el queso, me gusta todo** apart from cheese, I like everything

(**i**) *(desconectar) (aparato)* to switch off; **quita el gas antes de salir** turn the gas off before leaving

2 *vi* (**a**) *(apartarse)* to get out of the way; **iquita (de ahí), que no veo!** get out of the way, I can't see!

(**b**) **de quita y pon** *(asa, tapa, capucha)* removable

(**c**) *Fam (expresando incredulidad)* **iquita!, iquite!** don't talk rubbish!; **¿casarme yo? iquita, quita, estoy muy bien como estoy!** me, get married? you must be joking, I'm quite happy as I am!; **iquita, yo no me lo creo!** pull the other one *o* come off it, you don't expect me to believe that, do you?

3 quitarse *vpr* (**a**) *(apartarse)* to get out of the way; **iquítate de en medio!** get out of the way!

(**b**) *(ropa, gafas, pendientes)* to take off; **quítese el abrigo** take your coat off

(**c**) *(librarse de) (fiebre, dolor, temores)* to get rid of; **no puedo quitármelo de la cabeza** I can't get it out of my head; **quitarse a alguien de encima** *o* **de en medio** to get rid of sb

(**d**) *(desaparecer) (sujeto: mancha)* to come out; *(sujeto: dolor, granos, sarpullido)* to go away; **no se le quita la fiebre** her temperature won't go down; **se me ha quitado el hambre** I'm not hungry any more

(**e**) *(dejar, abandonar)* **quitarse de algo** *(el tabaco, la bebida)* to give sth up; **me quité de fumar** I gave up *o* stopped smoking

(**f**) *Fam* **quitarse de en medio** *(suicidarse)* to kill oneself, *Br* to top oneself; **quitarse la vida** to take one's own life

---

quitasol *nm* parasol, sunshade

quitasueño *nm Fam* headache, worry

quite *nm* (**a**) *Dep* parry (**b**) *Taurom* = attempt to distract the bull from attacking one of the other bullfighters (**c**) EXPR **estar al q.** *(alerta)* to keep one's ears/eyes open; **estaré al q. por si necesitas mi ayuda** I'll be on hand in case you need my help; EXPR **salir al q.: salió al q. para defender a su hermano** he sprang to his brother's defence

quiteño, -a 1 *adj* of/from Quito *(Ecuador)*

2 *nm,f* person from Quito *(Ecuador)*

quitina *nf Biol* chitin

Quito *n* Quito

quitrín *nm Am* = two-wheeled open carriage

quiubo, quiúbole *interj CAm, Col, Méx, Ven Fam* how are you doing?

quivi *nm* kiwi

quizá, quizás *adv* perhaps, maybe; **¿vienes? – q.** are you coming? – perhaps *o* maybe *o* I may do; **q. llueva mañana** it may rain tomorrow; **q. no lo creas** you may not believe it; **q. sí** maybe, perhaps; **q. no** maybe not, perhaps not

quórum *nm* quorum; **hay q.** we have a quorum, we are quorate; **no hay q.** we are inquorate; **la votación se suspendió por falta de q.** the vote was postponed because there wasn't a quorum

R, r

R, r [*Esp* 'erre, *Am* 'ere] *nf (letra)* R, r

R (**a**) (*abrev de* **rey**) *(en notación de ajedrez)* K (**b**) (*abrev de* **Residencia**) boarding house

rabadilla *nf* (**a**) *(de persona)* tailbone (**b**) *(de ave)* parson's nose

rabanero, -a *Fam* **1** *adj (vulgar)* coarse, vulgar
2 *nm,f (vulgar)* coarse *o* vulgar person

rabanillo *nm* wild radish

rábano *nm* radish; EXPR *Fam* **me importa un r.** I couldn't care less, I don't give a damn; EXPR **¡y un r.!** no way!; EXPR **tomar** *o Esp* **coger el r. por las hojas** to get the wrong end of the stick

Rabat *n* Rabat

rabear *vi* to wag its tail

rabel *nm* rebec

rabí (*pl* **rabís** *o* **rabíes**) *nm* rabbi

rabia *nf* (**a**) *(enfermedad)* rabies *(singular)*
(**b**) *(enfado)* rage; **me da r.** it makes me mad; **me da r. no haber podido ayudarles** it's so annoying *o* frustrating not having been able to help them; **¡qué r.!** how annoying!; **¡qué r. que no haya podido despedirme de ella!** I'm so annoyed I wasn't able to say goodbye to her!; **"¡déjame!", dijo con r.** "leave me alone," she said angrily; **¿dónde dejo esto? – donde más r. te dé** where shall I put this? – wherever you like; **compra el que más r. te dé** buy whichever one you like *o* fancy
(**c**) *(antipatía)* **me tienen r.** they've got something against me
(**d**) *(furia)* fury; **el equipo empezó a atacar con r.** the team started attacking furiously

rabiar *vi* (**a**) *(sufrir)* **r. de dolor** to writhe in pain
(**b**) *(enfadarse)* to be furious; **estar a r. (con alguien)** to be furious (with sb); **hacer r. a alguien** *(enfadar)* to make sb furious; **sólo lo dije para hacerte r.** I only said it to annoy you
(**c**) *(desear)* **r. por algo/hacer algo** to be dying for sth/to do sth
(**d**) EXPR *Fam* **a r.: llovía a r.** it was pouring down; **me gusta a r.** I'm wild *o* crazy about it; **el público aplaudió a r.** the audience went wild; **pica que rabia** *(comida)* it's incredibly hot

rabicorto, -a *adj* short-tailed

rábida *nf* = Muslim frontier fort

rabieta *nf Fam* tantrum; **le dio una r.** she threw a tantrum

rabihorcado *nm* frigate bird

rabijunco *nm* yellow-billed tropicbird

rabilargo, -a **1** *adj* long-tailed
2 *nm (ave)* azure-winged magpie

rabillo *nm* (**a**) *(de hoja, fruto)* stalk (**b**) *(del ojo)* corner; **mirar algo con** *o* **por el r. del ojo** to look at sth out of the corner of one's eye

rabinato *nm* rabbinate

rabínico, -a *adj* rabbinical, rabbinic

rabino *nm* rabbi

rabión *nm* rapid

rabiosamente *adv* (**a**) *(mucho)* terribly; **era r. atractiva** she was drop-dead gorgeous (**b**) *(con enfado)* furiously; **lo miró r.** he looked at her furiously, he gave her a furious look

rabioso, -a *adj* (**a**) *(enfermo de rabia)* rabid (**b**) *(furioso)* furious (**c**) *(muy intenso)* terrible; **tenía un dolor r.** I was in excruciating pain; **tengo unas ganas rabiosas de que vuelva** I'm absolutely dying for her to get back; **de rabiosa actualidad** *(libro, emisión)* extremely topical (**d**) *(chillón)* loud, gaudy

rabo *nm* (**a**) *(de animal)* tail; EXPR **irse** *o* **salir con el r. entre las piernas** to go off with one's tail between one's legs ▸▸ *Culin* ***r. de buey*** oxtail; *Culin* ***r. de toro*** = dish of stewed bull's tail (**b**) *(de hoja, fruto)* stalk (**c**) *muy Fam (pene)* prick, cock

rabón, -ona *adj* (**a**) *(con rabo corto)* short-tailed (**b**) *(sin rabo)* tailless

rabona *nf RP Fam* **hacerse la r.** *Br* to bunk off, *US* to play hooky

rabonearse *vpr RP Fam Br* to bunk off, *US* to play hooky

rabudo, -a *adj* long-tailed

rábula *nm Pey* shyster *(lawyer)*

racanear *Fam* **1** *vt* to be stingy with
2 *vi* (**a**) *(ser tacaño)* to be stingy (**b**) *(holgazanear)* to loaf about

racaneo *nm*, **racanería** *nf Fam* stinginess

rácano, -a *Fam Pey* **1** *adj* (**a**) *(tacaño)* mean, stingy (**b**) *(holgazán)* idle, lazy
2 *nm,f* (**a**) *(tacaño)* mean *o* stingy devil (**b**) *(holgazán)* lazybones

RACE ['rraθe] *nm* (*abrev de* **Real Automóvil Club de España**) = Spanish automobile association, *Br* ≃ AA, RAC, *US* ≃ AAA

racha *nf* (**a**) *(época)* **buena/mala r.** good/bad patch; **estamos pasando una buena r.** *(en deportes, juegos de azar)* we're on a winning streak, we're on a roll; *(en empresa)* things are going well for us at the moment; **una r. de buena suerte** a run of good luck, a lucky streak; **una mala r. de resultados económicos** a string of poor financial results; **rompieron una r. de seis derrotas consecutivas** they ended a run of six consecutive defeats; **a rachas** in fits and starts
(**b**) *(ráfaga)* gust (of wind)

racheado, -a *adj* gusty, squally

rachear *vi* to gust

racial *adj* racial

racimo *nm (de uvas, plátanos, flores)* bunch

raciocinio *nm* (**a**) *(razón)* (power of) reason (**b**) *(razonamiento)* reasoning

ración *nf* (**a**) *(porción)* portion; *(en bar, restaurante)* = portion of a dish served as a substantial snack; **contiene dos raciones** *(en envase de alimento)* serves two (**b**) *(cantidad correspondiente)* share; **terminó su r. de trabajo** she finished her share of the work (**c**) *(cantidad de alimentos)* **poner a alguien a media r.** to put sb on short rations

racionado, -a *adj* rationed

racional *adj* (**a**) *(dotado de razón)* rational (**b**) *(lógico)* rational (**c**) *Mat* rational

racionalidad *nf* rationality

racionalismo *nm Filosofía* rationalism

racionalista *Filosofía* **1** *adj* rationalistic
2 *nmf* rationalist

racionalización *nf* rationalization

racionalizar [14] *vt* (**a**) *(expresar racionalmente)* to rationalize (**b**) *(gastos)* to rationalize (**c**) *Mat* to rationalize

racionalmente *adv* rationally

racionamiento *nm* rationing

racionar *vt* to ration

racismo *nm* racism

racista **1** *adj* racist
2 *nmf* racist

raconto *nm RP Fam* account

rácor *nm Cine* **no hay r., hay una falta de r.** there's a lack of continuity

rada *nf* roadstead, inlet

radar, rádar (*pl* **radares**) *nm* radar ▸▸ ***r. de seguimiento*** tracking radar

radiación *nf* radiation ▸▸ ***r. alfa*** alpha radiation; ***r. beta*** beta radiation; *Astron* ***r. cósmica*** cosmic radiation; *Astron* ***r. de fondo*** background radiation; ***r. gamma*** gamma radiation; ***r. nuclear*** nuclear radiation; ***r. solar*** solar radiation; ***r. ultravioleta*** ultraviolet radiation

radiactividad *nf* radioactivity

radiactivo, -a *adj* radioactive

radiado, -a *adj* (**a**) *(mensaje)* radioed; **programa r.** radio programme (**b**) *(radial)* radiate

radiador *nm* (**a**) *(para calefacción)* radiator ▸▸ ***r. eléctrico*** electric radiator (**b**) *(en vehículo)* radiator

radial *adj* (**a**) *(del radio)* radial (**b**) *(en forma de estrella)* radial (**c**) *Am (de la radio)* radio

radián *nm* radian

radiante *adj* (**a**) *(brillante)* brilliant; **lucía un sol r.** the sun was shining brightly (**b**) *(alegre)* radiant; **la novia estaba r.** the bride was radiant; **estar r. de felicidad** to be beaming with joy

radiar *vt* (**a**) *(irradiar)* to radiate (**b**) *Fís* to irradiate (**c**) *Med* to give X-ray treatment to (**d**) *(emitir por radio)* to broadcast (**e**) *Am (hacer el vacío a)* to cold-shoulder; **traté de integrarme, pero desde el principio me radiaron** I tried to join in, but they made me feel unwelcome right from the start

radicación *nf* (**a**) *(situación)* location; **pese a su r. gallega, la asociación está abierta a gentes de toda España** despite being based in Galicia, membership of the association is open to people from all over Spain (**b**) *Mat* evolution

radical 1 *adj* (**a**) *(drástico)* radical (**b**) *(no moderado)* radical (**c**) *Arg Pol* = relating to the Unión Cívica Radical (**d**) *Gram* root (**e**) *Bot* root
2 *nmf* (**a**) *(que no es moderado)* radical (**b**) *Arg Pol* = member or supporter of the Unión Cívica Radical
3 *nm* (**a**) *Gram* root (**b**) *Mat* square root sign (**c**) *Quím* radical ▸▸ ***r. libre*** free radical

radicalismo *nm* (**a**) *(intransigencia)* inflexibility, unwillingness to compromise (**b**) *(de ideas políticas)* radicalism (**c**) *Arg Pol* = political ideology or movement of the Unión Cívica Radical

radicalización *nf (de postura)* hardening, radicalization; *(de huelga, conflicto)* intensification

radicalizar [14] 1 *vt (postura)* to harden, to make more radical; *(huelga, conflicto)* to intensify
2 **radicalizarse** *vpr (persona, postura)* to become more radical; *(huelga, conflicto)* to intensify

radicalmente *adv* radically

radicando *nm Mat* radicand

radicar [60] 1 *vi* (**a**) *(consistir)* **r. en** to lie in; **el éxito de su proyecto radica en su sencillez** the success of her project lies in its simplicity (**b**) *(estar situado)* to be (located) (**en** in)
2 **radicarse** *vpr (establecerse)* to settle (**en** in)

radícula *nf Bot* radicle

radiestesia *nf* radiesthesia

radiestesista *nmf* radiesthesist

radio[1] *nm* (**a**) *(de circunferencia)* radius; **en un r. de** within a radius of ▸▸ ***r. de acción*** range; **el bombardero tiene un r. de acción de 2.000 kilómetros** the bomber has a range of 2,000 kilometres; **el general queda fuera del r. de acción del juez** the general is beyond the judge's jurisdiction; **la empresa quiere ampliar su r. de acción** the company wants to expand the area in which it trades
(**b**) *(de rueda)* spoke
(**c**) *Quím* radium
(**d**) *Anat* radius
(**e**) *Andes, CAm, Carib, Méx (transistor)* radio ▸▸ ***r. despertador*** clock radio

radio[2] *nf* (**a**) *(medio)* radio; **oír algo por la r.** to hear sth on the radio ▸▸ *CRica, Cuba, Pan Fam* ***r. bemba:*** **enterarse de algo por r. bemba** to hear sth on the grapevine *o* on the bush telegraph; *Esp Fam* ***r. macuto:*** **enterarse de algo por r. macuto** to hear sth on the grapevine *o* on the bush telegraph; ***r. pirata*** pirate radio (**b**) *Esp, CSur (transistor)* radio ▸▸ ***r. despertador*** clock radio

radioactividad *nf* radioactivity

radioactivo, -a *adj* radioactive

radioaficionado, -a *nm,f* radio ham

radioastronomía *nf* radio astronomy

radiobaliza *nf* radio beacon

radiobiología *nf* radiobiology

radiocarbono *nm* radiocarbon

radiocasete *nm* radio cassette (player)

radiocompás (*pl* **radiocompases**) *nm* radio compass

radiocomunicación *nf* radio communication

radiocontrol *nm* remote control

radiodespertador *nm* clock radio

radiodiagnóstico *nm* radiological diagnosis

radiodifusión *nf* broadcasting

radioemisora, *Am* **radiodifusora** *nf* radio station, radio transmitter

radioenlace *nm* radio link

radioescucha *nmf* listener

radiofaro *nm* radio beacon

radiofonía *nf* radio *(technology)*

radiofónico, -a *adj* radio; **programa r.** radio programme

radiofórmula *nf Esp* = radio which only plays hits and formulaic pop music

radiofrecuencia *nf* radio frequency

radiogoniometría *nf* radiogoniometry

radiogoniómetro *nm* direction finder

radiograbador *nm,* **radiograbadora** *nf CSur* radio cassette

radiografía *nf* (**a**) *(técnica)* radiography (**b**) *(fotografía)* X-ray; **le hicieron una r. del tobillo** they X-rayed her ankle

radiografiar [32] *vt* to X-ray

radiográfico, -a *adj* X-ray; **un análisis r.** an X-ray analysis

radiógrafo, -a *nm,f* radiographer

radiograma *nm* radiogram

radioisótopo *nm* radioisotope

radiola *nf Andes* radiogram

radiología *nf* radiology

radiológico, -a *adj* X-ray, radiological; **examen r.** X-ray examination

radiólogo, -a *nm,f* radiologist

radiomensaje *nm RP (buscapersonas)* pager

radiomensajería *nf* radio messages

radiometría *nf* radiometry

radiómetro *nm* radiometer

radionavegación *nf* radio navigation

radionovela *nf* radio serial

radiooperador, -ora *nm,f* radio operator

radiopatrulla *nm* (radio) patrol car

radiorreceptor *nm* radio (receiver)

radiorreloj *nm* clock radio

radioscopia *nf* radioscopy

radioscópico, -a *adj* radioscopic

radioso, -a *adj Am* radiant

radiosonda *nf* radiosonde

radiotaxi *nm* (**a**) *(taxi)* taxi *(fitted with two-way radio)* (**b**) *(aparato de radio)* = taxi-driver's two-way radio

radiotelecomunicación *nf* radio communication

radiotelefonía *nf* radiotelephony

radioteléfono *nm* radiotelephone

radiotelegrafía *nf* radiotelegraphy

radiotelegrafista *nmf* wireless operator

radiotelégrafo *nm* radiotelegraph

radiotelescopio *nm* radio telescope

radiotelevisión *nf* **empresa de r.** broadcasting company

radioterapeuta *nmf* radiotherapist

radioterapia *nf* radiotherapy

radiotransmisión *nf* broadcasting

radiotransmisor *nm* radio transmitter

radioyente *nmf* listener

radique *etc ver* **radicar**

radón *nm Quím* radon

RAE ['rrae] *nf* (*abrev de* **Real Academia Española**) Spanish Royal Academy

raer [54] *vt* (**a**) *(raspar)* to scrape (off) (**b**) *(desgastar)* to wear out; *(por los bordes)* to fray

ráfaga *nf* (**a**) *(de aire, viento)* gust (**b**) *(de disparos)* burst (**c**) *(de luces)* flash

rafia *nf* raffia

rafting ['rraftin] *nm Dep* rafting; **hacer r.** to go rafting

raglán = **ranglan**

ragout [rra'ɣu] (*pl* **ragouts**) *nm* ragout

ragtime [rraɣ'taim] *nm* ragtime

ragú *nm* ragout

raid (*pl* **raids**) *nm* (**a**) *Mil* raid (**b**) *CAm, Méx (autoestop)* **pedir r.** to hitch a *Br* lift *o US* ride

raído, -a *adj (desgastado)* threadbare; *(por los bordes)* frayed

raigambre *nf* (**a**) *(tradición)* tradition; **de r.** traditional; **una costumbre que tiene mucha r. en el país** a custom that is deeply rooted in the country's tradition (**b**) *(origen)* roots; **una familia de r. aristocrática** a family with aristocratic roots

raigo *etc ver* **raer**

raigón *nm* (**a**) *Bot* thick root (**b**) *(de diente)* root

raíl, rail *nm* rail

raite *nm Méx Fam* (**a**) *(paseo)* ride; **me voy a dar un r. con la moto** I'm going for a ride on the motorbike (**b**) *(aventón) Br* lift, *US* ride; **¿me das un r. a la estación?** could you give me a *Br* lift *o US* ride to the station?

raíz 1 *nf* (**a**) *(de planta)* root; **la solución tiene que ser de r.** the solution has to attack the heart of the problem; **arrancar algo de r.** *(planta)* to root sth out completely; **el gobierno cortó de r. el levantamiento** the government nipped the uprising in the bud; **eliminaron de r. el problema del terrorismo** the problem of terrorism was stamped out; **echar raíces** *(árbol, planta)* to take root; *(persona)* to put down roots ►► ***r. tuberosa*** tuberous root
(**b**) *(de pelo, muela)* root
(**c**) *(origen)* origin; **de raíces humildes** of humble origins; **la costumbre tiene su r. en la España del siglo XV** the custom has its roots *o* origin in 15th century Spain
(**d**) *(causa)* root; **el dinero es la r. de todos sus males** money is at the root of all her problems
(**e**) *Ling* root
(**f**) *Informát* root
(**g**) *Mat* root ►► ***r. cuadrada*** square root; ***r. cúbica*** cube root
2 **a raíz de** *loc prep* as a result of, following; **se produjo un gran escándalo a r. de sus declaraciones** his statements caused outrage

raja *nf* (**a**) *(hendidura) (en cerámica, puerta)* crack; *(en tela)* tear, rip; *(en piel)* gash; **le ha salido una r. al plato** the plate has cracked; **me he hecho una r. en la camisa** I've torn *o* ripped my shirt; **me hice una r. en la mano con un cuchillo** I cut *o* gashed my hand with a knife (**b**) *(rodaja)* slice; **una r. de queso/melón** a slice of cheese/melon (**c**) *Vulg (vagina)* crack (**d**) *muy Fam* **r. del culo** (bum) crack

rajá (*pl* **rajás** *o* **rajaes**) *nm* raja; EXPR *Fam* **vivir como un r.** to live like a lord *o* king

rajadera *nf Perú Fam* backbiting

rajado, -a *nm,f Fam (cobarde)* chicken; **¡eres un r.!** *(siempre te echas atrás)* you're always backing *o* pulling out at the last minute!; *(nunca participas)* you never join in anything!

rajadura *nf* crack

rajar 1 *vt* (**a**) *(cerámica, puerta)* to crack; *(tela)* to tear, to rip; *(piel)* to gash; **le rajaron un neumático** he had one of his tyres slashed
(**b**) *Esp (melón, sandía)* to slice
(**c**) *Fam (herir con navaja)* to slash, to cut (up); **dame el dinero o te rajo** hand over the money or I'll cut you up
(**d**) *Col, PRico (aplastar, apabullar)* to crush, to defeat
(**e**) *Andes, RP Fam (echar)* to chuck out
(**f**) *Andes, RP Fam (criticar)* to knock, to pull to pieces
(**g**) *Andes Fam (reprobar)* to fail
(**h**) *Ven Fam (beber)* to knock back
2 *vi Fam* (**a**) *Esp (hablar)* to natter, to witter on; **estuvo toda la tarde rajando por teléfono** he spent the whole afternoon nattering on the phone (**b**) *Andes, Carib, RP Fam (huir) Br* to scarper, *US* to hightail it (**c**) *Andes, Carib, RP Fam* **rajando** *(a toda velocidad)* at top speed; **se comió la sopa rajando** she guzzled the soup down as fast as she could
3 **rajarse** *vpr* (**a**) *(partirse) (cerámica, puerta)* to crack; *(tela)* to tear, to rip; **se me rajó la camisa** my shirt ripped
(**b**) *Esp Fam (echarse atrás)* to back *o* pull out; **ahora ya es muy tarde para que te rajes** it's too late for you to back out now
(**c**) *Andes, CAm, RP Fam (gastar)* to blow; **se rajó todo el sueldo en una semana** she blew all her wages in one week
(**d**) *Andes, Carib, RP Fam (escaparse)* to rush *o* run off
(**e**) *Bol, CAm, Chile, Perú Fam (obsequiar)* **se rajó con un anillo de brillantes** he splashed out on a diamond ring
(**f**) *Andes Fam (esforzarse)* to slog one's guts out; **se rajó para que él pudiese terminar los estudios** she slogged her guts out so that he could finish his studies
(**g**) *Chile, Col Fam (suspender)* to fail, *US* to flunk; **si no estudia para el examen, va a rajarse** if she doesn't revise, she'll come a cropper in the exam

rajatabla: a rajatabla *loc adv* to the letter, strictly; **cumplió sus órdenes a r.** he followed his orders to the letter

raje *nm Fam* (**a**) *RP (huída)* **pegar(se) el r.** *Br* to scarper, *US* to hightail it; **ya es tarde, ¿nos pegamos el r.?** it's getting late, shall we split?; EXPR **dar el r. a alguien** to give sb the boot (**b**) *Perú (crítica)* backbiting

rajón, -ona 1 *nm,f Fam* (**a**) *Perú (criticón)* gossip (**b**) *CAm, Chile, Perú (dadivoso)* generous giver
2 *nm* (**a**) *(rasguño)* rip, tear (**b**) *CAm, Méx (fanfarrón)* braggart

ralea *nf Pey* (**a**) *(clase)* breed, ilk; **de baja r.** *(persona)* ill-bred (**b**) *(calidad)* **es un mueble de mala r.** it's a poor-quality piece of furniture

ralear *vi (tela)* to wear thin; *(pelo)* to thin

ralentí *nm* (**a**) *Aut* **al r.** ticking over (**b**) *Cine* **al r.** in slow motion

ralentización *nf* slowing down

ralentizar 1 *vt* to slow down
2 **ralentizarse** *vpr* to slow down

rallado, -a 1 *adj* grated; **pan r.** breadcrumbs
2 *nm* grating

rallador *nm* grater ►► ***r. de queso*** cheese grater

ralladura *nf* grating ►► ***r. de limón*** grated lemon rind

rallar *vt* to grate

rally ['rrali] (*pl* **rallys**) *nm* rally

ralo, -a *adj (pelo, barba)* sparse, thin; *(bosque)* sparse; **tener los dientes ralos** to have several teeth missing

RAM [rram] *nf Informát (abrev de* **random access memory**) RAM ►► ***R. caché*** cache RAM; ***R. dinámica*** dynamic RAM

rama *nf* (**a**) *(de planta)* branch; **la r. materna de mi familia** my mother's side of the family; **algodón en r.** raw cotton; **canela en r.** cinnamon sticks; EXPR *Fam* **andarse** *o* **irse por las ramas** to wander off the point, to go off at a tangent; EXPR **ir de r. en r.** *(sin rumbo fijo)* to jump from one thing to another (**b**) *(de ciencia)* branch (**c**) *(de colectivo)* wing; **la r. más radical del partido** the radical wing of the party

ramadán *nm* Ramadan

ramaje *nm* branches

ramal *nm (de carretera, ferrocarril)* branch; *(de cordillera)* branch

ramalazo *nm Fam* (**a**) *(ataque)* fit; **cuando le da el r. puede decir cualquier barbaridad** he's capable of talking absolute nonsense when the mood takes him; **le dio el r. religioso** she suddenly went all religious (**b**) *(amaneramiento)* **tener r.** to be limp-wristed

rambla *nf* (**a**) *(río)* watercourse (**b**) *(avenida)* avenue, boulevard (**c**) *Urug (paseo marítimo)* promenade

ramera *nf* whore, *US* hooker

ramificación *nf* (**a**) *(de árbol)* ramification (**b**) *(de arterias, nervios)* branch (**c**) *(de cordillera)* embranchment, branch; *(de ferrocarril, carretera)* branch (**d**) *(consecuencia)* ramification

ramificarse [60] *vpr* (**a**) *(árbol)* to branch out (**b**) *(arterias, nervios)* to branch (**c**) *(cordillera)* to branch; *(ferrocarril, carretera)* to branch (**d**) *(empresa)* **el grupo se ramifica en cinco áreas de negocio** the group is made up of five divisions

ramillete *nm* (**a**) *(de flores)* bunch (**b**) *(conjunto)* handful; **acudió rodeado de un r. de bellezas** he arrived surrounded by a bevy of beauties

ramio *nm* ramie

ramo *nm* (**a**) *(de flores)* bunch; **recibió el premio y un r. de rosas** she received the award and a bouquet of roses (**b**) *(rama)* branch; **un r. de olivo** an olive branch (**c**) *(sector)* industry; **el r. de la construcción** the building industry (**d**) *CSur* **comercio de ramos generales** general store

ramonear 1 *vt (podar)* to prune
2 *vi (animales)* = to graze on the leaves of trees or bushes

ramoso, -a *adj* **un árbol r.** a densely branched tree

rampa *nf* (**a**) *(para subir y bajar)* ramp ►► ***r. de lanzamiento*** launch(ing) pad (**b**) *(cuesta)* steep incline

rampante *adj Arquit* rampant

rampla *nf Chile* (**a**) *(rampa)* ramp (**b**) *(carretilla)* wheelbarrow

ramplón, -ona *adj* vulgar, coarse

ramplonería *nf (cualidad)* vulgarity, coarseness

ramplús (*pl* **rampluses**) *nm Ven* block of wood

rana *nf* (**a**) *(animal)* frog; EXPR *Fam* **cuando las ranas críen pelo: te devolverá el libro cuando las ranas críen pelo** you'll be waiting till the cows come home for him to give you that book back; EXPR *Fam* salir r. to be a major disappointment ►► *r. de San Antonio* European tree frog (b) *(juego)* = game in which the players throw coins or counters into the mouth of a metal frog

rancagüino, -a 1 *adj* of/from Rancagua *(Chile)*
2 *nm,f* person from Rancagua *(Chile)*

ranchera *nf* (a) *(canción)* = popular Mexican song (b) *(automóvil) Br* estate (car), *US* station wagon

ranchería *nf*, **rancherío** *nm Col, Méx, RP, Ven* (a) *(en el campo)* = group of labourers' dwellings (b) *(en la ciudad)* shanty town

ranchero, -a 1 *adj* (a) *(del rancho)* ranch; **la vida ranchera** life on a ranch (b) *Méx Fam (tímido)* shy
2 *nm,f* (a) *(propietario)* rancher (b) *(trabajador)* ranch hand

rancho *nm* (a) *(comida)* mess; EXPR *Fam* **hacer** *o* **formar r. aparte: ésos siempre hacen** *o* **forman r. aparte** they always form their own little clique (b) *(granja del Oeste)* ranch (c) *CSur, Ven (en la ciudad)* shack, shanty (d) *Méx (pequeña finca)* = small farmhouse and outbuildings (e) *RP (en el campo)* farm labourer's cottage (f) *RP (en la playa)* = thatched beachside building

ranciedad *nf (mal estado) (de mantequilla, aceite)* rancidness; *(de pan)* staleness

rancio, -a *adj* (a) *(en mal estado) (mantequilla, aceite)* rancid; *(pan)* stale (b) *(antiguo)* ancient; **de r. abolengo** of noble lineage (c) *(añejo)* **vino r.** mellow wine (d) *(antipático)* sour, unpleasant

rand *nm* rand

randa *nf (encaje)* lace trimming

ranglan, raglán *adj* **manga r.** raglan sleeve

rango *nm* (a) *(social)* standing (b) *(jerárquico)* rank; **de alto r.** high-ranking (c) *Ling* rank (d) *Andes, CAm, PRico (esplendor)* pomp, splendour (e) *RP (juego)* leapfrog

Rangún *n* Rangoon

ranita *nf* ***r. de San Antonio*** tree frog

ranking ['rrankin] (*pl* **rankings**) *nm* **el r. de las 30 empresas con más facturación** the list of the 30 companies with the highest turnover; **el r. del ATP** the ATP rankings; **el r. de accidentes laborales** the industrial accidents league table; **ocupa el sexto puesto en el r. mundial** it is ranked sixth in the world

ranúnculo *nm* buttercup

ranura *nf* (a) *(abertura) (para monedas)* slot; *(debajo de la puerta, ventana)* gap (b) *(surco)* groove (c) *Informát* slot ►► ***r. de expansión*** expansion slot

rap *nm* rap; **música r.** rap music

rapacidad *nf* rapacity, greed

rapado, -a 1 *adj (pelado)* shaven
2 *nm,f* skinhead
3 *nm* crew cut

rapapolvo *nm Esp Fam* **dar** *o* **echar un r. a alguien** to tear a strip off sb

rapar 1 *vt* (a) *Fam (cabeza)* to shave; **lo raparon** they gave him a crew cut; **lo raparon al cero** they gave him a skinhead (b) *(barba, bigote)* to shave off (c) *Col Fam (arrebatar)* to snatch
2 **raparse** *vpr Fam* **se rapó la cabeza al cero** he shaved all his hair off

rapaz[1] 1 *adj* (a) *(que roba)* rapacious, greedy (b) **ave r.** bird of prey, raptor
2 *nf* bird of prey, raptor

rapaz[2], **-aza** *nm,f Fam (muchacho)* lad, *f* lass

rape[1] *nm (pez)* monkfish

rape[2]**: al rape** *loc adv* **cortar el pelo al r. a alguien** to give sb a crew cut

rapé *nm* snuff

rapear *vi* to rap

rápel (*pl* **rapels**), **rappel** (*pl* **rappels**) *nm Dep* abseiling, rappelling; **hacer r.** to abseil, to rappel

rapero, -a *nm,f* rapper

rápidamente *adv* quickly

rapidez *nf* speed; **con r.** quickly; **ya está listo – ¡qué r.!** it's ready – that was quick!

rápido, -a 1 *adj (veloz)* quick, fast; *(vehículo, comida)* fast; *(beneficio, decisión, vistazo)* quick; **ser r. de reflejos** to have quick reflexes
2 *adv* quickly, fast; **no conduzcas tan r.** don't drive so fast; **no hables tan r., no te entiendo** don't talk so fast, I can't understand you; **más r.** quicker; **¡ven, r.!** come, quick!; **¡hazlo/termina r.!** hurry up!; **si vamos r. puede que lleguemos a tiempo** if we're quick *o* if we hurry we may get there on time
3 *nm* (a) *(tren)* express train (b) **rápidos** *(de río)* rapids

rapidógrafo *nm Col* Rotring® (pen)

rapiña *nf* (a) *(robo)* pillaging (b) **ave de r.** bird of prey

rapiñar *vt* to steal

raponazo *nm Col Fam (de bolsos)* bag-snatching; **me robaron el pasaporte de un r.** I had my passport snatched

raponear *vi Col Fam* to snatch bags

raponero, -a *nm,f Col Fam (de bolsos)* bag-snatcher

raposo, -a *nm,f* fox, *f* vixen

rappel = **rápel**

rapsoda *nm Hist* rhapsode, rhapsodist

rapsodia *nf* rhapsody

raptar *vt* to abduct, to kidnap

rapto *nm* (a) *(secuestro)* abduction, kidnapping (b) *(ataque)* fit; **en un r. de entusiasmo se abrazó a su jefe** in a fit of enthusiasm he hugged his boss

raptor, -ora *nm,f* abductor, kidnapper

raque *nm* beachcombing

raqueta *nf* (a) *(de tenis, squash, badminton)* racket; *(de ping pong)* bat, *US* paddle (b) *(para la nieve)* snowshoe (c) *(en casino)* rake (d) *(tenista)* tennis player (e) *(en carretera)* = slip road to allow cars to cross oncoming traffic or do a U-turn

raquianestesia *nf Med* epidural (anaesthetic)

raquídeo, -a *adj Anat* **bulbo r.** medulla oblongata

raquis *nm inv Anat* vertebral column

raquítico, -a 1 *adj* (a) *(canijo)* scrawny (b) *(escaso)* miserable (c) *Med* rachitic
2 *nm,f Med* rickets sufferer

raquitismo *nm Med* rickets

rara avis *nf* **ser una r.** to be rather unusual

raramente *adv* (a) *(rara vez)* rarely, seldom; **r. la verás sonreír** you rarely *o* seldom see her smile (b) *(con rareza)* strangely, oddly

rareza *nf* (a) *(cualidad de raro)* rareness, rarity (b) *(objeto raro)* rarity (c) *(infrecuencia)* infrequency (d) *(extravagancia)* idiosyncrasy, eccentricity

rarificar *Fís* 1 *vt* to rarefy
2 **rarificarse** *vpr* to become rarefied

raro, -a *adj* (a) *(extraño)* strange, odd; **¡qué r.!** how strange *o* odd!; **¡qué r. que no haya llamado!** it's very strange *o* odd that she hasn't called; **es r. que no nos lo haya dicho** it's odd *o* funny that she didn't tell us; **ya me parecía r. que no hubiera dicho nada** I thought it was strange *o* odd that he hadn't said anything; **no sé qué le pasa últimamente, está** *o* **la noto muy rara** I don't know what's up with her lately, she's been acting very strangely
(b) *(excepcional)* unusual, rare; *(visita)* infrequent; **rara vez** rarely; **es r. el día que viene a comer** she very rarely comes round for lunch; **r. es el que no fuma** very few of them don't smoke
(c) *(extravagante)* odd, eccentric
(d) *(escaso)* rare
(e) *Quím* rare

ras 1 **a(l) ras** *loc adv* to the brim; **lleno a** *o* **al r.** *(recipiente)* full to the brim; **una cucharada llena a** *o* **al r.** *(cucharada)* a level tablespoon; **la bala le pasó al r.** *(muy cerca)* the bullet missed him by a hair's breadth
2 **a(l) ras de** *loc prep* level with; **a r. de tierra** *o* **del suelo** at ground level; **volar a r. de tierra** to fly low

rasante 1 *adj* (a) *(vuelo)* low-level (b) *(tiro)* low
2 *nf (inclinación)* gradient; **cambio de r.** *(formando una elevación)* rise in the road; *(formando una depresión)* dip in the road; *(en letrero)* blind summit

rasar *vt* to skim, to graze

rasca 1 *adj RP Fam* (a) *(ordinario)* tacky (b) *(de mala calidad)* shoddy
2 *nf* (a) *Esp Fam (frío)* **hace mucha r.** it's absolutely freezing (b) *Andes, Ven Fam (borrachera)* **tener/pegarse una r.** to be/get plastered *o* smashed

rascacielos *nm inv* skyscraper

rascado, -a *adj Andes, Ven Fam* plastered, smashed

rascador *nm* (a) *(herramienta)* scraper (b) *(para las cerillas)* striking surface

rascar [60] 1 *vt* (a) *(con uñas, clavo)* to scratch (b) *(con espátula)* to scrape (off); *(con cepillo)* to scrub (c) *(instrumento)* to scrape away at (d) *Fam (obtener) (dinero)* to scrape together
2 *vi* to be rough, to scratch

3 rascarse *vpr* **(a)** *(con uñas)* to scratch oneself; EXPR *Fam* **rascarse el bolsillo** to fork out; EXPR *Fam* **rascarse la barriga** to twiddle one's thumbs, to laze around; EXPR *RP muy Fam* **se pasa todo el día rascándose las bolas** *Br* he does bugger all all day, *US* he doesn't do shit all day **(b)** *RP Fam (perder el tiempo)* to lounge around

rascón *nm* water rail

rascuache *adj Méx Fam* crummy

RASD [rrasð] *nf (abrev de* **República Árabe Saharaui Democrática***)* Democratic Arab Republic of the Western Sahara

rasear *vt Dep* **r. la pelota** to pass the ball along the ground

rasera *nf* fish slice

rasero *nm* strickle; EXPR **medir por el mismo r.** to treat alike

rasgado, -a *adj (boca)* wide; **ojos rasgados** almond(-shaped) eyes

rasgadura *nf* **(a)** *(en tela)* rip, tear **(b)** *(acción)* ripping, tearing

rasgar [38] **1** *vt* to tear; **r. un sobre** to tear open an envelope
2 rasgarse *vpr* to tear; EXPR **rasgarse las vestiduras** to kick up a fuss

rasgo *nm* **(a)** *(característica)* trait, characteristic **(b)** *(del rostro)* feature; **tiene un rostro de rasgos asiáticos** he has Asian features **(c)** *(acto elogiable)* act **(d)** *(trazo)* flourish, stroke **(e) a grandes rasgos** *(en términos generales)* in general *o* broad terms; **explicar algo a grandes rasgos** to outline sth

rasgón *nm* tear

rasgue *etc ver* **rasgar**

rasguear *vt (guitarra)* to strum

rasgueo *nm* strumming

rasguñar 1 *vt* to scratch
2 rasguñarse *vpr* to scratch oneself; **se rasguñó la rodilla** she scraped *o* grazed her knee

rasguño, *Am* **rasguñón** *nm* scratch; **sin un r.** without a scratch

rasilla *nf (ladrillo)* = type of thin, hollow brick

raso, -a 1 *adj* **(a)** *(terreno)* flat **(b)** *(cucharada)* level **(c)** *(cielo)* clear **(d)** *(a poca altura)* low **(e)** *Mil* **soldado r.** private
2 *nm (tela)* satin
3 al raso *loc adv* in the open air; **pasar la noche al r.** to sleep rough

raspa 1 *nf (espina)* bone; *(espina dorsal)* backbone; EXPR *Esp Fam* **no dejó ni la r.** he cleaned his plate
2 *nmf Méx Fam (grosero)* lout, *Br* yob; **no te juntes con ésos, son pura r.** don't hang out with that lot, they're a bunch of louts *o Br* yobs

raspado *nm* **(a)** *Med* scrape **(b)** *(de pieles)* scraping **(c)** *Méx (refresco)* = drink of flavoured crushed ice

raspador *nm* scraper

raspadura *nf* **(a)** *(señal)* scratch **(b)** *(partícula) (de yeso, pintura)* flake; **raspaduras de limón** grated lemon peel *o* zest

raspaje *nm RP Med* scrape

raspar 1 *vt* **(a)** *(rascar) (pintura)* to scrape off; *(pared)* to scrape **(b)** *(rasguñar)* to graze, to scrape **(c)** *(causar picor)* to burn; **este aguardiente raspa la garganta** this liquor burns your throat **(d)** *Ven Fam (en un examen)* to fail, *US* to flunk
2 *vi* to be rough, to scratch; **esta lana raspa** this wool scratches
3 rasparse *vpr* to graze, to scrape; **se raspó el codo** she grazed *o* scraped her elbow

raspón *nm* **(a)** *(herida)* graze, scrape; **se hizo un r. en la rodilla** she grazed *o* scraped her knee **(b)** *Am (en vehículo)* scratch

rasponazo *nm (señal, herida)* graze, scrape; **se hizo un r. en la rodilla** she grazed *o* scraped her knee

rasposo, -a *adj* **(a)** *(áspero)* rough **(b)** *RP Fam (gastado)* tatty, threadbare

rasque *etc ver* **rascar**

rasqueta *nf* **(a)** *(herramienta)* scraper **(b)** *Am (para caballo)* currycomb

rasquetear *vt* **(a)** *Am (caballo)* to brush down, to curry **(b)** *Andes, RP (rascar)* to scrape

rasta *adj Fam (rastafari)* Rasta; **pelo** *o* **peinado r.** dreadlocks

rastacuero, -a *nm,f Am Fam* nouveau riche

rastafari 1 *adj* Rastafarian
2 *nmf* Rastafarian

rasterizado *nm Informát* rasterizing

rasterizar *vt Informát* to rasterize

rastra *nf* **(a)** *Agr (rastrillo)* rake; *(azada)* hoe; *(grada)* harrow **(b)** *(ristra)* = string of dried fruit **(c)** *RP (de cinturón)* = decorative buckle of a gaucho's belt

rastras: a rastras *loc adv también Fig* **llevar algo/a alguien a r.** to drag sth/sb along; **se llevaron a los manifestantes a r.** they dragged the demonstrators away; **trajeron el piano a r.** they dragged the piano in; **tuvo que llevarlo a r. al colegio** she had to drag him kicking and screaming to school; **llegaron casi a r.** *(agotados)* they were on their last legs when they arrived

rastreador, -ora 1 *adj* tracker; **perro r.** tracker dog
2 *nm,f* **(a)** *(que rastrea)* tracker **(b)** *Informát* crawler
3 *nm* ***r. de minas*** minesweeper

rastrear *vt* **(a)** *(bosque, zona)* to search, to comb; **los submarinistas rastrearon el canal en busca del cuerpo** divers dredged the canal in search of the body **(b)** *(persona, información)* to track

rastreo *nm* **(a)** *(de bosque, zona)* search; *(de río)* dredging **(b)** *(de información)* trawling through

rastrero, -a *adj* **(a)** *(despreciable)* despicable **(b)** *(planta)* creeping, trailing

rastrillada *nf Bol, RP (huella)* track, trail

rastrilladora *nf* mechanical rake

rastrillaje *nm RP* thorough *o* systematic search

rastrillar *vt* **(a)** *(allanar)* to rake (over) **(b)** *(recoger)* to rake up **(c)** *Méx (disparar)* to fire **(d)** *RP (peinar)* to comb, to scour

rastrillo *nm* **(a)** *(instrumento)* rake **(b)** *(mercado)* flea market; *(benéfico) Br* jumble *o US* rummage sale **(c)** *(puerta, reja)* portcullis **(d)** *Méx (cuchilla de afeitar)* razor

rastro *nm* **(a)** *(pista)* trail; **seguir el r. de alguien** to trail sb; **perder el r. de alguien** to lose track of sb **(b)** *(vestigio)* trace; **desapareció sin dejar r.** he vanished without trace; **no hay** *o* **queda ni r. de él** there's no sign of him; **cuando llegamos no había ni r. de cerveza** when we got there there wasn't a drop of beer left **(c)** *(mercado)* flea market **(d)** *Méx (matadero)* abattoir, slaughterhouse

rastrojero *nm Arg* pick-up (truck)

rastrojo *nm* stubble

rasurador *nm,* **rasuradora** *nf Méx* shaver, electric razor

rasurar 1 *vt* to shave
2 rasurarse *vpr* to shave

rata[1] *nf* rat; EXPR *RP Fam* **hacerse la r.** *Br* to bunk off, *US* to play hooky ►► ***r. de agua*** water vole *o* rat; ***r. de alcantarilla*** *(animal)* brown rat; *Fam (persona despreciable)* swine; ***r. campestre*** black rat; ***r. canguro*** kangaroo rat; *Fam* ***r. de sacristía*** *(persona)* fanatical churchgoer

rata[2] *Fam* **1** *adj* stingy, mean
2 *nmf* stingy *o* mean person; **ser un r.** to be stingy *o* mean

ratafía *nf* ratafia

rataplán *nm* rat-a-tat-tat

ratear *vt* **(a)** *Fam (robar)* to swipe, *Br* to nick **(b)** *Econ (prorratear)* to divide proportionally

ratel *nm* ratel, honey badger

ratería *nf Fam* **(a)** *(robo)* pilfering, stealing; **hacer raterías** to swipe *o Br* nick stuff **(b)** *(tacañería)* stinginess, meanness; **el regalo que me han hecho es una r.** the present they gave me is really cheap and nasty

ratero, -a *nm,f* petty thief

raticida *nm* rat poison

ratificación *nf* ratification

ratificar [60] **1** *vt (anuncio, declaraciones)* to confirm; *(convenio)* to ratify
2 ratificarse *vpr* **ratificarse en** to stand by, to stick to

ratificatorio, -a *adj* ratifying

rating ['rreitin] *(pl* **ratings***) nm* **(a)** *Fin* credit rating **(b)** *Am (de audiencia)* ratings

ratio *nf* ratio

rato *nm* while; **estuvimos hablando mucho r.** we were talking for quite a while; **te llamaré en que tenga un r. (libre)** I'll call you as soon as I've got a free moment; **hace un r. estaba en la oficina** she was in the office just a short while ago; **a cada r. viene a hacerme preguntas** he keeps coming and asking me questions (all the time); **al poco r. (de)** shortly after; **al r. me di cuenta de que no le había dado mi teléfono** a bit later I realized I hadn't given her my phone number; *Méx* **¿vamos a comer algo? – al r.** shall we go and have something to eat? – in a while; **a ratos** at times; **a ratos perdidos** at odd moments; **un buen r.** *(momento agradable)* a good time; *(mucho tiempo)* a good while, quite some time; **pasamos un buen r. con ellos** we had a good time with them; **¡hasta otro r.!,** *Méx* **¡nos vemos al r.!** see you soon!; **con esto hay para r.** this should keep us going for a while; **va para r.**

it will take some (considerable) time; **tenemos lluvia para r.** the rain will be with us for some time; **pasar el r.** to kill time, to pass the time; **pasar un mal r.** to suffer; **me hizo pasar un mal r.** he made me suffer; **ratos libres** spare time; *Esp Fam* **un r. (largo): se enfadó un r. largo** she was dead annoyed; *Esp Fam* **hay que saber un r. (largo) de economía para ocupar ese puesto** you have to know loads about economics in that job

ratón *nm* (a) *(animal)* mouse; EXPR *Urug Fam* **estar lleno de** *o* **tener muchos ratones** to fancy oneself ►► ***r. de biblioteca*** *(persona)* bookworm; ***r. de campo*** fieldmouse; ***r. de las mieses*** harvest mouse (b) *Esp Informát* mouse ►► ***r. óptico*** optical mouse (c) *Ven Fam (resaca)* hangover

ratona *nf (ave)* house wren

ratoncito *nm* ***el r. Pérez*** ≃ the tooth fairy

ratonear *Fam* **1** *vt Arg* to turn on
2 *vi Chile* to slave away
3 ratonearse *vpr Arg* to get turned on

ratonera *nf* (a) *(madriguera)* mousehole (b) *(para cazar)* mousetrap (c) *Fam (trampa)* trap (d) *Andes, RP (casucha)* hovel

ratonero *nm (ave)* buzzard

raudal *nm* (a) *(de agua)* torrent (b) *(gran cantidad)* abundance; *(de lágrimas)* flood; *(de desgracias)* string; EXPR **a raudales** in abundance, by the bucket; **salía gente a raudales** people were pouring *o* streaming out; **tiene dinero a raudales** he's got pots of money; **hubo emoción a raudales en la prórroga** it was a thrill a minute during *Br* extra time *o US* overtime

raudo, -a *adj* fleet, swift; **acudió r. a abrir la puerta** he rushed to open the door

raulí *nm* southern beech

ravioli *nm* (piece of) ravioli; **raviolis** ravioli

raya 1 *ver* **raer**
2 *nf* (a) *(línea)* line; *(en tejido)* stripe; **a rayas** striped; **una camisa a** *o* **de rayas** a striped shirt
(b) *Esp, Andes, RP (del pelo) Br* parting, *US* part; **hacerse la r.** to part one's hair; **se peina con la r.** *Esp* **en el** *o Andes, RP* **al medio** she has a *Br* centre parting *o US* center part; **lleva la r. al** *Esp* **lado** *o Andes, RP* **costado** he has a *Br* side parting *o US* side part
(c) *(de pantalón)* crease
(d) *(límite)* limit; EXPR *Fam* **pasarse de la r.** to go too far; **te has pasado de la r., ¿por qué le pegaste?** you went too far, why did you hit him?; EXPR **mantener** *o* **tener a r. a alguien** to keep sb in line; EXPR **poner a r.** to check, to hold back
(e) *(señal) (en disco, superficie)* scratch
(f) *(pez)* ray, skate
(g) *(guión)* dash
(h) *Fam (de cocaína)* line
(i) *Am Fam (del trasero)* crease; **estuve tantas horas sentada que se me borró la r.** I was sitting down for so long I couldn't feel my backside *o Br* bum any more
(j) *Méx (sueldo)* pay, wages
(k) *CAm, Carib, Perú (juego)* hopscotch

rayado, -a 1 *adj* (a) *(a rayas) (tela)* striped; *(papel)* ruled (b) *(disco, superficie)* scratched (c) *CSur Fam (loco)* **estar r.** to be a headcase *o Br* nutter
2 *nm (rayas)* stripes

rayador *nm (ave)* black skimmer

rayano, -a *adj* **r. en** verging *o* bordering on; **un optimismo r. en la irresponsabilidad** optimism verging on the irresponsible

rayar 1 *vt* (a) *(con marcas) (disco, superficie)* to scratch; **le rayaron el coche con una llave** they scratched his car with a key
(b) *(escribiendo)* to scribble on; **el bebé rayó la pared con un rotulador** the baby scribbled on the wall with a felt-tip pen
(c) *(trazar líneas en)* to rule lines on
(d) *Méx, RP (detener)* to stop suddenly
(e) *Esp Fam (molestar)* to rub up the wrong way
2 *vi* (a) *(aproximarse)* **r. en algo** to border *o* verge on sth; **su cortesía raya en el servilismo** his politeness borders on servility; **raya en los cuarenta** he's pushing forty
(b) *(lindar)* **r. con** to border on, to be next to
(c) *(alba)* to break; **al r. el alba** at the break of day
(d) *Am (espolear a caballo)* to spur on one's horse
(e) *Méx (pagar)* to pay; *(cobrar)* to get paid
3 rayarse *vpr* (a) *(disco, superficie)* to get scratched; **se me han rayado dos discos** two of my records have got scratched; *Fam* **parece que te has rayado** you're like a broken record (b) *CSur muy Fam (volverse loco)* to go crazy *o Br* off one's head

raye *nm RP Fam* **tener un r.** to be crazy *o Br* a nutter; **no te preocupes por lo que dice, ¡tiene un r.!** don't take any notice of what he says, he's crazy *o Br* a nutter!

rayo 1 *ver* **raer**
2 *nm* (a) *(de luz)* ray; **un r. de sol** a ray of sunlight; **los rayos solares calientan la Tierra** the sun's rays heat the Earth
(b) *Fís* beam, ray ►► ***rayos alfa*** alpha rays; ***rayos beta*** beta rays; ***rayos catódicos*** cathode rays; ***rayos cósmicos*** cosmic rays; ***rayos gamma*** gamma rays; ***rayos infrarrojos*** infrared rays; ***r. láser*** laser beam; ***rayos ultravioleta*** ultraviolet rays; ***rayos uva*** UVA rays; ***rayos X*** X-rays
(c) *Meteo* bolt of lightning; **le dan miedo los rayos** she's scared of lightning; **un r. cayó en el edificio** the building was struck by lightning; EXPR **caer como un r.** to be a bombshell; EXPR *Fam* **¡que lo parta un r.!** he can go to hell!, to hell with him!; **siempre lo mismo, ellos a lo suyo, y al abuelo, que lo parta un r.** it's always the same, they do their own thing and grandpa can go hang for all they care; EXPR *Esp Fam* **huele a rayos** it stinks to high heaven; EXPR *Esp Fam* **sabe a rayos** *(comida)* it tastes foul; **le supo a rayos que no la invitaras** she was none too impressed about you not inviting her
(d) *(persona)* **ser un r.** to be like greased lightning; **pasar como un r.** to flash by
(e) *CSur (de rueda)* spoke
3 *interj Fam* **¡rayos (y centellas)!** heavens above!

rayón *nm (fibra)* rayon

rayuela *nf (juego)* hopscotch

raza *nf* (a) *(humana)* race; **la r. humana** the human race; **la r. blanca** whites, white people (b) *(animal)* breed; **de (pura) r.** *(caballo)* thoroughbred; *(perro)* pedigree (c) *Méx Pey (populacho)* **la r.** the masses (d) *Méx Fam (grupo)* gang, guys; **cuando llegué, la r. ya estaba instalada** the guys were already there when I arrived (e) *Perú (descaro)* cheek, nerve

razia, razzia *nf* raid

RAZÓN *nf* (a) *(causa, motivo, argumento)* reason; **la r. de la huelga/de que estén en huelga** the reason for the strike/why they are on strike; **no entiendo la r. de su marcha** I don't understand why she's leaving; **no hay r. para enfadarse** there's no reason to get angry; **la r. por la que voy** the reason (why) I'm going; **atender a razones** to listen to reason; **con mayor r. si...** all the more so if...; **¡con r. no quería venir!** no wonder he didn't want to come!; **y con r.** and quite rightly so; **en** *o* **por r. de** *(en vista de)* in view of; *(a causa de)* because of; **por razones de salud/seguridad** for health/safety reasons; **r. de más para quedarse/protestar** all the more reason to stay/protest; **tiene razones para estar enojado** he has good cause *o* good reason to be angry; **tenemos razones para creer que...** we have reason *o* cause to believe that...; **sus razones tendrá para hacer eso** she must have her reasons for doing something like that ►► *Pol* ***razones de Estado*** reasons of state; ***r. de ser*** raison d'être; **su actitud no tiene r. de ser** her attitude is completely unjustified
(b) *(verdad)* **la r. estaba de su parte,** *Formal* **le asistía la r.** he was in the right, he had right on his side; **r. no le falta** he's quite right; **con r. o sin ella** rightly or wrongly; **dar la r. a alguien** to admit that sb is right; **llevar** *o* **tener r.** to be right; **llevas** *o* **tienes toda la r.** you're quite right; **tener r. en** *o* **al hacer algo** to be right to do sth; **no tener r.** to be wrong; **quitar la r. a alguien** *(demostrar su equivocación)* to prove sb wrong
(c) *(juicio, inteligencia)* reason; **entrar en r.** to see reason; **no hay quien le haga entrar en r.** no one can make him see reason; **perder la r.** to lose one's reason *o* mind
(d) *(información)* **se vende casa: r. aquí** *(en letrero)* house for sale: enquire within; **dar r. de** to give an account of; **se recompensará a quien dé r. de su paradero** there is a reward for anyone giving information regarding his whereabouts ►► *Com* ***r. social*** trade name *(of company)*
(e) *Mat* ratio; **a r. de** at a rate of; **salimos** *o* **tocamos a r. de 300 pesos por persona** it worked out at 300 pesos per person
(f) *Col, Méx, Ven (recado)* message; **Diego no está, ¿quiere dejarle r.?** Diego's not in, do you want to leave a message?; **viajo mañana, ¿tiene r. para su madre?** I'm leaving tomorrow, do you have any messages for your mother?; **pídale a su padre que mande r.** ask her father to send us his news

---

razonable *adj* reasonable

razonablemente *adv* reasonably

razonadamente *adv* rationally

razonado, -a *adj* reasoned

razonamiento *nm* reasoning

razonar 1 *vt (argumentar)* to reason out
2 *vi (pensar)* to reason; **el anciano ya no razona** the old man has lost his reason; **es imposible r. con él** there's no reasoning with him
razzia = **razia**
RDA *nf Antes* (*abrev de* **República Democrática Alemana** *o* **de Alemania**) GDR
RDSI *nf Tel* (*abrev de* **Red Digital de Servicios Integrados**) ISDN
re *nm (nota musical)* D; *(en solfeo)* re; *ver también* **do**
re- *pref* (**a**) *(indica repetición)* re-; **reexplicar** to re-explain, to explain again (**b**) *Fam (uso enfático)* **rebién** wonderfully *o* marvellously well; **iba muy repeinada** she had an incredibly smart hairdo
reabastecer *vt (avión)* to refuel; *(tropas)* to reprovision, to resupply
reabierto, -a *participio ver* **reabrir**
reabrir 1 *vt* to reopen; **el juez reabrió el caso** the judge reopened the case
2 **reabrirse** *vpr* to reopen
reabsorber 1 *vt* to reabsorb
2 **reabsorberse** *vpr* to be reabsorbed
reabsorción *nf* reabsorption
reacción *nf* (**a**) *(respuesta)* reaction; **tuvo una r. rara/buena** she reacted strangely/well (**b**) *Fís & Quím* reaction ►► *también Fig* ***r. en cadena*** chain reaction; ***r. nuclear*** nuclear reaction; ***r. química*** chemical reaction; ***r. redox*** redox reaction; ***r. termonuclear*** thermonuclear reaction (**c**) *(a vacuna, alérgica)* reaction (**d**) *Av* **avión/motor a r.** jet plane/engine
reaccionar *vi* (**a**) *(responder)* to react; **no supo cómo r.** she didn't know how to react; **la economía reaccionó con las medidas del gobierno** the economy responded to the government's measures; **reaccionó con violencia ante las amenazas** he reacted violently to the threats (**b**) *Fís & Quím* to react; **r. con algo** to react with sth (**c**) *(paciente)* to respond; **no reaccionó al tratamiento** she didn't respond to treatment
reaccionario, -a 1 *adj* reactionary
2 *nm,f* reactionary
reacio, -a *adj* reluctant; **ser r. a hacer algo** to be reluctant to do sth; **es muy r. a hacer reclamaciones** he's very reluctant to complain; **se mostró r. a firmar el acuerdo** he was reluctant to sign the agreement; **ser r. a los cambios** to be resistant to change
reaclimatación *nf* reacclimatization
reactancia *nf Elec* reactance
reactivación *nf (de economía)* recovery
reactivar 1 *vt* to revive; **r. la economía** to kick-start the economy
2 **reactivarse** *vpr* to recover
reactivo, -a 1 *adj* reactive
2 *nm Quím* reagent
reactor *nm* (**a**) *(avión)* jet (plane *o* aircraft) ►► ***r. de despegue vertical*** jump jet (**b**) *(propulsor)* jet engine (**c**) *(nuclear)* reactor ►► ***r. de agua presurizada*** pressurized water reactor; ***r. nuclear*** nuclear reactor; ***r. nuclear refrigerado por gas*** gas-cooled reactor; ***r. nuclear reproductor*** breeder reactor
readaptación *nf* readjustment
readaptar 1 *vt* to adapt
2 **readaptarse** *vpr* to readjust
readmisión *nf* readmission
readmitir *vt* to accept *o* take back
reafirmar 1 *vt* to confirm; **r. a alguien en algo** to confirm sb in sth
2 **reafirmarse** *vpr* to assert oneself; **reafirmarse en algo** to become confirmed in sth
reagrupación *nf* (**a**) *(reunión)* regrouping (**b**) *(reorganización)* reorganization
reagrupamiento *nm* (**a**) *(reunión)* regrouping; **el r. familiar de los refugiados** the reuniting of refugee families ►► ***r. espontáneo*** *(en rugby)* maul (**b**) *(reorganización)* reorganization
reagrupar *vt* (**a**) *(reunir)* to regroup (**b**) *(reorganizar)* to reorganize
reajustar *vt* (**a**) *(ajustar de nuevo)* to readjust (**b**) *(corregir) (precios, impuestos, salarios)* to make changes to, to adjust; *(sector)* to streamline
reajuste *nm* (**a**) *(cambio)* readjustment; **r. ministerial** cabinet reshuffle (**b**) *Econ (de precios, impuestos, salarios)* change, adjustment; *(de sector)* streamlining ►► ***r. de plantilla*** downsizing
real 1 *adj* (**a**) *(verdadero)* real; **existe un peligro r. de que explote** there is a real danger that it may explode; **una historia r.** a true story (**b**) *(de la realeza)* royal ►► ***R. Academia Española (de la Lengua)*** = institution that sets lexical and syntactical standards for Spanish; ***r. decreto*** = name given to acts passed by the Spanish parliament when appearing in the official gazette; *Hist* royal decree; EXPR *Fam* **por r. decreto: tenemos que volver a casa a las diez por r. decreto** it has been decreed that we should be back home by ten o'clock
2 *nm* (**a**) *(moneda) (de Brasil)* real; *Hist (de España)* = old Spanish coin worth one quarter of a peseta; EXPR **cuatro reales: lo compró por cuatro reales** she bought it for next to nothing; EXPR **no tener un r.** not to have a penny to one's name; EXPR **no valer un r.** to be worthless (**b**) EXPR **sentar el r., sentar los reales** *(ejército)* to set up camp; *(persona)* to settle down
realce 1 *ver* **realzar**
2 *nm* (**a**) *(esplendor)* glamour; **el maquillaje pone de r. su belleza** make-up enhances *o* highlights her beauty; **la presencia del rey dio r. al acto** the king's presence lent the occasion an air of particular importance ►► *Informát* ***r. de imagen*** image enhancement (**b**) *(en arquitectura, escultura)* relief (**c**) *(bordado)* detail (in relief)
realengo, -a *adj* (**a**) *Hist (de la Corona)* belonging to the Crown (**b**) *CAm, Carib, Méx (sin dueño)* ownerless (**c**) *Ven (de la calle)* street; **niños realengos** street children (**d**) *Ven (vago)* idle (**e**) *Col, Ven (sin cargas)* unencumbered
realero *nm Ven Fam* fortune
realeza *nf* (**a**) *(monarcas)* royalty (**b**) *(grandeza)* magnificence
realidad *nf* (**a**) *(mundo real)* reality ►► *Informát* ***r. virtual*** virtual reality (**b**) *(situación)* reality; **la r. social de hoy en día** today's social reality (**c**) *(verdad)* truth; **la r. es que me odia** the fact is, she hates me; **en r.** actually, in fact; **parece tímido, cuando en r. no lo es** he seems shy, but actually he isn't; **hacerse r.** to come true; **aspira a convertir en r. sus sueños** she is hoping to make her dreams come true
realimentación *nf* feedback
realismo *nm* (**a**) *(pragmatismo)* realism; **analizó con r. la situación** he made a realistic analysis of the situation (**b**) *(en arte, literatura)* realism; **con mucho r.** very realistically ►► *Lit* ***r. mágico*** magic(al) realism (**c**) *Hist (monarquismo)* royalism (**d**) *Filosofía* realism
realista 1 *adj* (**a**) *(pragmático)* realistic (**b**) *(en arte, literatura)* realist (**c**) *Hist (monárquico)* royalist (**d**) *Filosofía* realist
2 *nmf* (**a**) *(pragmático)* realist (**b**) *(en arte, literatura)* realist (**c**) *Hist (monárquico)* royalist (**d**) *Filosofía* realist
reality show [rre'aliti'ʃou] (*pl* **reality shows**) *nm* **los reality shows** reality TV
realizable *adj* (**a**) *(factible)* feasible (**b**) *Fin* realizable
realización *nf* (**a**) *(ejecución) (de esfuerzo, viaje, inversión)* making; *(de operación, experimento, trabajo)* performing; *(de encargo)* carrying out; *(de plan, reformas)* implementation; *(de desfile)* organization
(**b**) *(cumplimiento) (de sueños, deseos)* fulfilment, realization
(**c**) *Fin* **r. de beneficios** profit-taking
(**d**) *(satisfacción personal)* self-fulfilment
(**e**) *(película, programa)* production
(**f**) *(actividad) (en cine)* direction; *(en televisión)* editing
(**g**) *Ling* realization
realizado, -a *adj (satisfecho)* fulfilled; **sentirse r.** to feel fulfilled
realizador, -ora *nm,f* (**a**) *(de cine)* director (**b**) *(de televisión)* editor
realizar [14] 1 *vt* (**a**) *(ejecutar) (esfuerzo, viaje, inversión)* to make; *(operación, experimento, trabajo)* to perform; *(encargo)* to carry out; *(plan, reformas)* to implement; *(desfile)* to organize (**b**) *(hacer real)* to fulfil, to realize; **realizó su sueño** he fulfilled his dream (**c**) *Fin (bienes)* to sell off, *Espec* to realize; **r. beneficios** to realize one's profits (**d**) *(película)* to direct; *(programa)* to edit
2 **realizarse** *vpr* (**a**) *(hacerse real) (sueño, predicción, deseo)* to come true; *(esperanza, ambición)* to be fulfilled (**b**) *(en un trabajo, actividad)* to find fulfilment; **quiere buscar trabajo fuera de casa para realizarse** she wants to look for a job outside the home so she can feel more fulfilled
realmente *adv* (**a**) *(en realidad, verdad)* really; **si r. lo hizo él, habría que darle un premio** if he really did it himself, he deserves a prize
(**b**) *(muy)* really; **estaba r. enfadado** he was really angry; **es un paisaje r. precioso** the scenery is really beautiful
(**c**) *(sinceramente)* really, honestly; **r., no sé qué pensar** I really *o* honestly don't know what to think; **r., creo que te pasaste** I really *o* honestly think you went too far; **r., como no te pongas a estudiar no sé cómo vas a aprobar** if you don't start doing some work, I honestly *o* really don't know how you're going to pass
realojamiento, realojo *nm* rehousing
realojar *vt* to rehouse
realojo = **realojamiento**
realquilado, -a 1 *adj* sublet
2 *nm,f* subtenant
realquilar *vt* to sublet

realzar [14] *vt (destacar)* to enhance; **el fondo neutro realza el retrato** the neutral background brings out the portrait *o* makes the portrait stand out better

reanimación *nf* (**a**) *(física, moral)* recovery (**b**) *Med* resuscitation

reanimar 1 *vt* (**a**) *(físicamente)* to revive (**b**) *(moralmente)* to cheer up; **r. la situación económica** to improve the economy (**c**) *Med* to resuscitate

2 **reanimarse** *vpr* (**a**) *(físicamente)* to revive (**b**) *(moralmente)* to cheer up

reanudación *nf (de conversación, actividad)* resumption; *(de amistad)* renewal

reanudar 1 *vt (conversación, actividad)* to resume; *(amistad)* to renew

2 **reanudarse** *vpr (conversación, actividad)* to resume; *(amistad)* to be renewed; **los vuelos a la región se reanudarán la próxima semana** flights to the area will be resumed next week

reaparecer [46] *vi (enfermedad, persona)* to reappear; *(artista, deportista)* to make a comeback

reaparición *nf (de enfermedad, persona)* reappearance; *(de artista, deportista)* comeback

reapertura *nf* reopening

rearmar *vt* to rearm

rearme *nm* rearmament; **el r. moral de la sociedad** the moral regeneration of society

reasegurar *vt* to reinsure

reaseguro *nm* reinsurance

reasentamiento *nm* resettlement

reasentarse *vpr* to resettle

reasumir *vt* to resume, to take up again

reata *nf* (**a**) *(de caballos, mulas)* single file; **de r.** (in) single file (**b**) *Méx (para ganado)* lasso; *Fam* **es bien r. para bailar** she's a really good dancer

reavivar 1 *vt* (**a**) *(fuego)* to rekindle (**b**) *(odio, polémica, interés)* to revive; **r. los enfrentamientos** to cause renewed clashes

2 **reavivarse** *vpr* (**a**) *(fuego)* to be rekindled (**b**) *(odio, polémica, interés)* to be revived

rebaba *nf* jagged edge

rebaja *nf* (**a**) *(acción)* reduction (**b**) *(descuento)* discount; **hacer una r. a alguien** to give sb a discount; **me hicieron una r. del 5 por ciento** they gave me a 5 percent discount, they gave me 5 percent off (**c**) *(en tienda)* sale; **las rebajas** the sales; **las rebajas de enero** the January sales; **estar de rebajas** to have a sale on; **grandes rebajas** *(en letrero)* massive reductions

rebajado, -a *adj* (**a**) *(precio)* reduced (**b**) *(humillado)* humiliated (**c**) *(acera, bordillo)* lowered (**d**) *(diluido)* diluted (**con** with) (**e**) *RP (pelo)* layered

rebajamiento *nm* reduction

rebajar 1 *vt* (**a**) *(precio)* to reduce; **han rebajado los precios a la mitad** prices have been reduced *o* cut by half; **te rebajo 10 euros** I'll knock 10 euros off for you; **me rebajaron el 10 por ciento** they gave me 10 percent off

(**b**) *(humillar)* to humiliate, to put down; **se siente inferior, toda la vida lo rebajaron** he feels inferior, people have always put him down throughout his life

(**c**) *(intensidad)* to tone down

(**d**) *(altura)* to lower; *(acera, bordillo)* to lower

(**e**) *(diluir)* to dilute

(**f**) *Mil* to exempt

(**g**) *RP (adelgazar)* to lose; **rebajé 3 kilos en un mes** I lost 3 kilos in a month

(**h**) *RP (pelo)* to layer

2 *vi RP (adelgazar)* to lose weight

3 **rebajarse** *vpr (persona)* to humble oneself; **rebajarse ante alguien** to grovel to sb; **rebajarse a hacer algo** to lower oneself *o* stoop to do sth; **no tiene intención de rebajarse a pedirle disculpas** he has no intention of stooping so low as to apologize to her

rebalsar *RP* 1 *vt* **el agua rebalsará la tina** the bathtub will overflow; EXPR **ser la gota que rebalsa el vaso** to be the last straw, to be the straw that broke the camel's back

2 *vi* to overflow; **dos por tres el río rebalsa** the river is always bursting its banks

3 **rebalsarse** *vpr* to overflow; **dos por tres el río se rebalsa** the river is always bursting its banks

rebanada *nf* slice

rebanar 1 *vt* (**a**) *(pan)* to slice (**b**) *(dedo)* to cut *o* slice off; *(cabeza)* to cut off

2 **rebanarse** *vpr* to cut *o* slice off; **se rebanó un dedo con un cuchillo** he sliced a finger off with a knife

rebañaduras *nfpl (sobras)* scrapings

rebañar *vt (plato)* to clean; *(con pan)* to mop up

rebaño *nm* (**a**) *(de ovejas)* flock; *(de vacas, cabras)* herd (**b**) *(de fieles)* flock

rebasar 1 *vt* (**a**) *(sobrepasar)* to exceed, to surpass; **el agua rebasó el borde de la bañera** the bath overflowed; **la inflación rebasó la barrera del 5 por ciento** inflation passed the 5 percent mark; **el caza rebasó la barrera del sonido** the fighter plane broke the sound barrier; **la pelota rebasó la línea de gol** the ball went over *o* crossed the goal line; **nunca rebasa el límite de velocidad** she never speeds, she never drives over the speed limit; **las ventas rebasaron las predicciones** sales were higher than predicted; **un debate que rebasa el ámbito de lo político** a debate that goes beyond politics

(**b**) *CAm, Méx (corredor, vehículo)* to pass, to overtake

2 *vi CAm, Méx (adelantar)* to overtake

rebatible *adj* (**a**) *(argumento)* refutable (**b**) *RP (abatible) (silla, mesa)* folding; *(cama)* foldaway

rebatiña *nf* scramble, fight

rebatir *vt* to refute

rebato *nm* alarm; **tocar a r.** to sound the alarm

rebeca *nf* cardigan

rebeco *nm* chamois

rebelarse *vpr* to rebel (**contra** against); **se rebelaron contra las órdenes de sus superiores** they refused to obey the orders of their superior officers; **un grupo de jóvenes que se rebela contra el racismo** a group of young people who reject racism

rebelde 1 *adj* (**a**) *(sublevado)* rebel; **ejército r.** rebel army (**b**) *(desobediente)* rebellious (**c**) *(difícil de dominar) (pelo)* unmanageable; *(tos)* persistent; *(mancha)* stubborn; *(pasiones)* unruly (**d**) *Der* defaulting

2 *nmf* (**a**) *(sublevado, desobediente)* rebel (**b**) *Der* defaulter

rebeldía *nf* (**a**) *(cualidad)* rebelliousness (**b**) *(acción)* act of rebellion; **sus compañeros los animaron a la r.** their colleagues encouraged them to rebel (**c**) *Der* default; **declarar a alguien en r.** to declare sb in default; **lo juzgaron en r.** he was tried in his absence

rebelión *nf* rebellion; **una r. militar** a military rebellion *o* uprising

rebenque *nm RP (fusta)* (riding) crop, whip

reblandecer [46] 1 *vt* to soften

2 **reblandecerse** *vpr* to get soft

reblandecimiento *nm* softening

rebobinado *nm* rewinding

rebobinar *vt* to rewind

reboce *etc ver* **rebozar**

rebollo *nm* Pyrenean oak

reborde *nm (de piscina)* edge; *(de bandeja)* rim

rebosadero *nm* (**a**) *(desagüe)* overflow (**b**) *Chile, Hond Min* large mineral deposit

rebosante *adj (lleno)* brimming, overflowing (**de** with); **r. de alegría** brimming with joy; **estaba r. de felicidad** she was glowing *o* radiant with happiness; **r. de salud** glowing with health; **un vaso r. de vino** a glass full to the brim with wine; **volvió al país r. de nuevas ideas** she returned to the country brimming with new ideas

rebosar 1 *vt (estar lleno de)* to be overflowing with; **rebosaba alegría** she was brimming with joy; **rebosaba salud** he was glowing with health

2 *vi* to overflow; **r. de** *(estar lleno de)* to be overflowing with; **rebosaba de alegría** she was brimming with joy; **rebosaba de salud** he was glowing with health; **estar (lleno) a r.** to be full to overflowing; **el castillo rebosaba de turistas** the castle was overflowing with tourists; **rebosaba de satisfacción** she was glowing with satisfaction

rebotado, -a *adj Fam* (**a**) *(cura)* = who has given up the cloth *o* left the priesthood (**b**) *(enfadado) Br* cheesed off, *US* pissed

rebotar 1 *vi* (**a**) *(botar)* to bounce, to rebound (**en** off) (**b**) *Informát* to bounce

2 **rebotarse** *vpr Esp Fam (irritarse)* to get *Br* cheesed off *o US* pissed; **se rebotó porque no la invitaste** she was none too impressed about you not inviting her

rebote *nm* (**a**) *(bote)* bounce; EXPR **de r.** *(indirectamente)* by chance, indirectly; **este es un problema que me ha llegado a mí de r.** this is a problem that's been passed on to me by someone else; **la huelga**

provocó problemas, de r., en otros sectores the strike had a knock-on effect on other industries
(**b**) *Dep* rebound; **de r.** on the rebound ►► ***r. defensivo*** *(en baloncesto)* defensive rebound; ***r. ofensivo*** *(en baloncesto)* offensive rebound
(**c**) *Informát* bounce
(**d**) EXPR *Esp Fam (enfado)* **coger** *o* **pillarse un r.** to get *Br* cheesed off *o US* pissed

reboteador, -ora *nm,f Dep (en baloncesto)* rebounder

rebotear *vi Dep* to rebound

rebotica *nf Anticuado (en farmacia)* back room

rebozado, -a *adj* breaded, = coated in flour, egg and breadcrumbs; **llegué a casa r. de** *o* **en barro** I got home covered in mud

rebozar [14] *vt* to coat in flour, egg and breadcrumbs

rebozo *nm Am* wrap, shawl; **sin r.** *(con franqueza)* frankly

rebozuelo *nm* chanterelle

rebrotar *vi* (**a**) *Bot* to sprout (**b**) *(fenómeno)* to reappear; **la violencia ha rebrotado en la región** there has been a new outbreak of violence in the region

rebrote *nm* (**a**) *Bot* sprout, shoot (**b**) *(de fenómeno)* reappearance; **intentan contener el r. de la violencia** they are attempting to contain the renewed outbreaks of violence

rebufo *nm (de vehículo)* slipstream; **ir al r. de algo/alguien** to travel along in sth's/sb's wake; **el piloto español se puso al r. del líder de la carrera** the Spanish driver slipstreamed the race leader

rebujar *Fam* **1** *vt* (**a**) *(amontonar)* to bundle (up) (**b**) *(arropar)* to wrap up (warmly)
2 rebujarse *vpr (arroparse)* to wrap oneself up; *(encogerse)* to huddle up; **se rebujó entre las mantas** he snuggled up under the blankets

rebujo *nm (montón) (de hilos, pelos)* tangled mass; *(de papeles)* ball

rebullir 1 *vi* to stir, to begin to move
2 rebullirse *vpr* to stir, to begin to move

rebusca *nf* (**a**) *(desechos)* useless part (**b**) *(fruto)* gleanings

rebuscado, -a *adj (lenguaje)* obscure, recherché; **una explicación rebuscada** a roundabout explanation; **el final de la película es muy r.** the ending of the movie is very contrived

rebuscamiento *nm (de lenguaje)* obscurity; *(de explicación)* roundabout nature

rebuscar [60] **1** *vi* to search (around); **no me gusta que rebusques en mis cajones** I don't like you poking around in *o* going through my drawers; **rebusqué por todas partes pero no lo encontré** I searched everywhere but I couldn't find it
2 rebuscarse *vpr Andes, RP Fam* to get by; **no consigo trabajo pero me rebusco** I can't find a job but I get by; **rebuscárselas** to get by; **gana muy poco pero se las rebusca** she earns very little but she gets by

rebusque *nm Andes, RP Fam* job on the side; **además del empleo, siempre tiene algún r.** as well as his main job, he's always got some job on the side

rebuznar *vi* to bray

rebuzno *nm* bray; **soltar un r.** to bray; **se escuchaba el r. de un burro** you could hear a donkey braying *o* the braying of a donkey

recabar *vt* (**a**) *(pedir, reclamar)* to ask for; **todos los ciudadanos tienen derecho a r. justicia ante los tribunales** every citizen has the right to expect justice from the courts
(**b**) *(conseguir)* **no han conseguido r. ayuda para su proyecto** they haven't managed to get any assistance for their project; **recaban apoyos para su propuesta** they are seeking support for their proposal; **recaban información para un estudio de mercado** they are gathering information for market research

recadero, -a *nm,f (de mensajes)* messenger; *(de encargos)* errand boy, *f* errand girl

recado *nm* (**a**) *(mensaje)* message; **le dejé un r. en el contestador** I left a message (for her) on her answering machine; **si no estoy, deja r.** if I'm not in, leave a message; **dele el r. de que no voy a poder acudir a la reunión** let her know I won't be able to come to the meeting
(**b**) *(encargo, tarea)* errand; **hacer recados** to run errands; **tengo que hacer un r. en el centro** I have to go into town for something
(**c**) *(material)* ***r. de escribir*** writing materials *o* things; ***r. de fumar*** smokers' requisites
(**d**) *CSur (para el caballo)* saddle and trappings
(**e**) *Nic, RDom Culin* mincemeat filling

recaer [13] *vi* (**a**) *(enfermo)* to (have a) relapse
(**b**) *(reincidir)* **r. en** to relapse into; **ha vuelto a r. en la bebida** he's started drinking again
(**c**) *(ir a parar) (sospechas)* to fall (**en** *o* **sobre** on); **la responsabilidad recayó en su hermano mayor** the responsibility fell to his older brother; **el premio recayó en un escritor uruguayo** the prize went to a Uruguayan writer
(**d**) *(tratar)* **r. sobre algo** to be about sth, to deal with sth
(**e**) *(acento)* to fall; **el acento recae en la última sílaba** the accent falls *o* is on the last syllable

recaída *nf* relapse; **tener una r.** to have a relapse

recaigo *etc ver* **recaer**

recalar 1 *vt (mojar)* to soak
2 *vi* (**a**) *Náut* to put in (**en** at) (**b**) *Fam (aparecer, pasar)* to drop *o* look in (**en** *o* **por** at); **en vacaciones siempre recaló por mi pueblo** when he was on *Br* holiday *o US* vacation he always stopped off at my home town
3 recalarse *vpr (mojarse)* to get soaked

recalcar [60] *vt* to stress, to emphasize; **recalcó la importancia del acuerdo** he stressed *o* emphasized the importance of the agreement; **recalcó que era simplemente una propuesta** she stressed *o* emphasized that it was merely a suggestion

recalcitrante *adj* (**a**) *(obstinado) (persona, mancha, actitud)* stubborn (**b**) *(incorregible)* recalcitrant

recalentado, -a *adj* warmed up, reheated

recalentamiento *nm* overheating; **el r. del planeta** global warming; **el r. de la economía** the overheating of the economy

recalentar [3] **1** *vt* (**a**) *(volver a calentar)* to warm up, to reheat (**b**) *(calentar demasiado)* to overheat
2 recalentarse *vpr* to overheat; **se ha recalentado el motor** the engine has overheated

recalificación *nf* reclassification *(of land for planning or development purposes)*

recalificar *vt* to reclassify *(land for planning or development purposes)*; **recalificaron una zona verde como urbanizable** they reclassified *o US* rezoned a park as land that could be developed

recalzar *vt* (**a**) *Agr* to earth up (**b**) *Arquit* to reinforce

recamado *nm* overlay

recamar *vt* to overlay

recámara *nf* (**a**) *(de arma de fuego)* chamber; EXPR **guardar** *o* **tener algo en la r.** to have sth in reserve *o* up one's sleeve (**b**) *(habitación)* dressing room (**c**) *CAm, Col, Méx (dormitorio)* bedroom

recamarera *nf CAm, Col, Méx* chambermaid

recambiar *vt* to replace

recambio *nm* (**a**) *(acción)* replacement (**b**) *(repuesto)* spare; *(para pluma, cuaderno)* refill; **rueda de r.** spare wheel

recapacitar *vi* to reflect, to think; **recapacitó sobre su decisión** he thought his decision over

recapado *nm Arg* remoulding, retreading

recapar *vt Arg* to remould, to retread

recapitalización *nf* recapitalization

recapitulación *nf* recap, summary

recapitular *vt* to recapitulate, to summarize

recargable *adj (batería, pila)* rechargeable; *(encendedor)* refillable

recargado, -a *adj (estilo)* overelaborate; **un vestido r. de lazos** a dress bedecked with too many ribbons

recargar [38] **1** *vt* (**a**) *(volver a cargar) (encendedor, recipiente, pluma)* to refill; *(batería, pila)* to recharge; *(fusil, camión)* to reload; EXPR *Fam* **r. las pilas** *o* **baterías** *(recobrar fuerzas)* to recharge one's batteries
(**b**) *(cargar demasiado)* to overload; **recargó el baúl de libros** she put too many books in the trunk; **nos han recargado de trabajo** we've been overloaded with work
(**c**) *(adornar en exceso)* to overdecorate; **recargó el vestido con demasiados lazos** she overdid the ribbons on the dress
(**d**) *(cantidad)* **r. 1.000 pesos a alguien** to charge sb 1,000 pesos extra
(**e**) *(aire, ambiente)* to make stuffy
2 recargarse *vpr* (**a**) *(batería, pila)* to recharge (**b**) *(aire, ambiente)* to get stuffy (**c**) *Méx (apoyarse)* to lean; **no te recargues en** *o* **sobre** *o* **contra la puerta** don't lean on *o* against the door

recargo *nm* extra charge, surcharge; **pagaron un r. del 15 por ciento** they paid a 15 percent surcharge; **nos añadieron un r. por pagar fuera de plazo** they charged us extra for paying after the due date

recatadamente *adv* modestly, demurely

recatado, -a *adj (pudoroso)* modest, demure

recatarse *vpr* **r. (de hacer algo)** to hold back (from doing sth); **sin r.** openly, without reserve

recato *nm* **(a)** *(pudor)* modesty, demureness **(b)** *(reserva)* **no tuvo ningún r. en admitir su culpa** he openly admitted his guilt; **sin r.** openly, without reserve **(c)** *(cautela)* prudence, caution

recauchado = **reencauchado**

recauchadora = **reencauchadora**

recauchar = **reencauchar**

recauchutado, -a 1 *adj* **(a)** *(neumático)* remoulded, retreaded; **un neumático r.** a remould, a retread **(b)** *RP (objeto)* patched up **(c)** *RP Fam (persona)* **está muy recauchutada** she's had more than a few nips and tucks

2 *nm* remould, retread

recauchutaje *nm* **(a)** *Am (lugar)* tyre centre **(b)** *Am (acción)* remoulding, retreading **(c)** *RP (reparación)* patching up **(d)** *RP Fam (cirugía plástica)* **pasó por un buen r.** she had a few nips and tucks

recauchutar *vt* **(a)** *(neumático)* to remould, to retread **(b)** *RP (objeto)* to patch up **(c)** *RP Fam (persona)* to give a few nips and tucks

recaudación *nf* **(a)** *(acción)* collection, collecting; **r. de impuestos** tax collection **(b)** *(cantidad)* takings; *(en teatro)* box office takings; *(en estadio)* gate

recaudador, -ora *nm,f* **r. (de impuestos)** tax collector

recaudar *vt* to collect

recaudería *nf Méx* greengrocer's

recaudo *nm* **(a)** *Chile, Guat, Méx (condimentos)* spices and condiments **(b)** EXPR **a buen r.: los asesinos están a buen r.** the killers are in safe hiding; **poner algo a buen r.** to put sth in a safe place

recayera *etc ver* **recaer**

rece *etc ver* **rezar**

recelar 1 *vt* **(a)** *(sospechar)* to suspect; **recelo que no dice la verdad** I suspect that he's not telling the truth **(b)** *(temer)* to fear

2 *vi* to be mistrustful, to be suspicious; **recelo de él/de sus intenciones** I'm suspicious of him/of his intentions

recelo *nm* suspicion; **el policía nos miró con r.** the policeman looked at us suspiciously; **la decisión creó r. entre los inversores** the decision made investors wary; **sentir r.** to be suspicious

receloso, -a *adj* mistrustful, suspicious; **los empresarios están recelosos de la apertura a otros mercados** businessmen are wary of opening up to other markets

recensión *nf* review, write-up

recepción *nf* **(a)** *(de carta, paquete)* receipt; *Com* **pagar a la r.** to pay on delivery; *Com* **el pago se efectuará a la r. del envío** payment will be made on receipt of the goods **(b)** *(de hotel)* reception; **te veré en r.** I'll see you in reception **(c)** *(fiesta)* reception; **ofrecer una r. a alguien** to lay on a reception for sb **(d)** *(de sonido, imagen)* reception **(e)** *(en béisbol)* catch; *(en fútbol americano)* reception

recepcionar *vt Am* to receive

recepcionista *nmf* receptionist

receptáculo *nm* receptacle

receptividad *nf* receptiveness **(a** to); **mostró una gran r. a nuestras propuestas** she was very receptive to our proposals

receptivo, -a *adj* receptive

receptor, -ora 1 *adj* receiving; **un país r. de inmigrantes** a country that welcomes immigrants

2 *nm,f* **(a)** *(paciente)* recipient ►► ***r. de órgano*** *(en transplante)* organ recipient; ***r. universal*** universal recipient **(b)** *Ling* recipient **(c)** *(en béisbol)* catcher; *(en fútbol americano)* receiver

3 *nm* **(a)** *(aparato)* receiver **(b)** *Biol* receptor

recesión *nf* **(a)** *(económica)* recession **(b)** *(suspensión)* recess

recesivo, -a *adj* **(a)** *Econ* recessionary **(b)** *Biol* recessive

receso *nm* **(a)** *(separación)* withdrawal **(b)** *(descanso) (en juicio)* adjournment; *(parlamentario)* recess; *(en teatro)* interval; *(en reunión)* break

receta *nf* **(a)** *(de cocina)* recipe; **la r. del éxito** the recipe for success **(b)** *(médica)* prescription; **sin r. médica** over the counter

recetar *vt* to prescribe

recetario *nm* **(a)** *(de cocina)* recipe book **(b)** *(de médico)* prescription pad

rechace *nm Dep* clearance

rechazar [14] *vt* **(a)** *(no aceptar)* to reject; *(oferta, invitación)* to turn down, to reject

(b) *(negar)* to deny; **el gobierno rechazó las acusaciones de corrupción** the government rejected *o* denied the accusations of corruption; **rechazó que vaya a presentarse a la presidencia** he denied that he was going to run for the presidency

(c) *(órgano)* to reject; **el paciente rechazó el órgano** the patient rejected the organ

(d) *(repeler) (a una persona)* to push away; *(a atacantes)* to drive back, to repel; **rechazaron el ataque de los enemigos** they repelled the enemy attack

(e) *Dep* to clear; **el portero rechazó la pelota y la mandó fuera** the goalkeeper tipped the ball out of play

rechazo *nm* **(a)** *(no aceptación)* rejection; *(hacia ley, político)* disapproval; **mostró su r.** he made his disapproval clear; **los ciudadanos mostraron su r. al racismo** the people made plain their rejection of racism; **r. a hacer algo** refusal to do sth; **provocar el r. de alguien** to meet with sb's disapproval **(b)** *(negación)* denial **(c)** *Dep* clearance

rechifla *nf* **(a)** *(abucheo)* hissing, booing; **el público le dedicó una sonora r.** he was roundly booed by the audience **(b)** *(burla)* derision, mockery

rechiflar 1 *vt* to hiss at, to boo

2 rechiflarse *vpr* to mock; **rechiflarse de alguien** to mock sb

rechinar 1 *vt* **rechinó los dientes** he gnashed *o* ground his teeth

2 *vi* **(a)** *(puerta)* to creak; *(dientes)* to grind; *(frenos, ruedas)* to screech; *(metal)* to clank **(b)** *(dando dentera)* to grate

3 rechinarse *vpr CAm, Méx (comida)* to burn

rechistar *vi* to answer back; **lo vas a hacer sin r.** you'll do it, and I don't want to hear any arguments

rechoncho, -a *adj Fam* tubby, chubby

rechulo, -a *adj Méx Fam* absolutely lovely

rechupete: de rechupete *Fam* **1** *loc adj* **este asado está de r.** this roast is yummy

2 *loc adv* **nos lo pasamos de r.** we had a brilliant *o* great time

recibí *nm* **(a)** *(documento)* receipt, confirmation of receipt **(b)** *(sello)* "received" stamp

recibidor *nm* entrance hall

recibimiento *nm* reception, welcome; **tuvieron un caluroso r.** they were given a warm welcome *o* reception; **el equipo tuvo un r. multitudinario** crowds of people turned out to welcome the team

---

RECIBIR 1 *vt* **(a)** *(tomar, aceptar, admitir)* to receive; *(carta, regalo, premio, llamada, respuesta)* to receive, to get; *(propuesta, sugerencia)* to receive; *(castigo)* to be given; *(susto)* to get; *(clase, instrucción)* to have; **r. una paliza** to get beaten up; **recibió un golpe en la cabeza** he was hit on the head, he took a blow to the head; **un sector que recibe muchas ayudas del gobierno** an industry which receives substantial government aid; **recibió el Premio Nobel de Literatura** he won *o* was awarded the Nobel Prize for Literature; **el anuncio fue muy bien recibido** the announcement was welcomed; **recibieron la orden de detener al general** they received *o* were given the order to arrest the general; **he recibido una carta suya** *o* **de ella** I've received *o* had a letter from her; **recibió la noticia con alegría** he was very happy about the news; **r. consejos de alguien** to receive advice from sb, to be given advice by sb; **recibí orden de que no la molestaran** I received orders that she was not to be disturbed; **estoy recibiendo clases de piano** I'm having *o* taking piano classes; **estos pilares reciben todo el peso del techo** these pillars take the weight of the whole roof; *Formal* **reciba mi más cordial** *o* **sincera felicitación** please accept my sincere congratulations

(b) *(persona, visita)* to receive; **lo recibieron con un cálido aplauso** he was received with a warm round of applause; **¿cuándo cree que podrá recibirnos?** when do you think she'll be able to see us?

(c) *(ir a buscar)* to meet; **fuimos a recibirla al aeropuerto** we went to meet her at the airport

(d) *(captar) (ondas de radio, televisión)* to get; **aquí no recibimos la CNN** we don't get CNN here; **torre de control a V-5, ¿me recibe?** ground control to V-5, do you read me?

2 *vi (atender visitas) (médico, dentista)* to hold surgery; *(rey, papa, ministro)* to receive visitors; **el médico no recibe hoy** the doctor isn't seeing any patients today

3 recibirse *vpr Am (graduarse)* to graduate, to qualify **(de** as); **se recibió de lingüista hace poco tiempo** she recently graduated in linguistics

---

recibo *nm* **(a)** *(recepción)* receipt; **al r. de tu carta...** on receipt of your letter...; **acusar r. de** to acknowledge receipt of

(b) *(documento) (de compra)* receipt

(c) *(del gas, de la luz)* bill

(d) EXPR **ser de r.: su actuación no fue de r.** their performance wasn't up to scratch; **no sería de r. ocultarle la situación** it wouldn't be right not to tell her the situation; **no es de r. que ahora nos traten así** it's not on for them to treat us like that

reciclable *adj* recyclable

reciclado, -a 1 *adj* recycled
2 *nm* recycling

reciclador, -ora *nm,f Col* = person who collects and sorts *Br* rubbish *o US* garbage

reciclaje *nm* (**a**) *(de residuos)* recycling (**b**) *(de personas)* retraining

reciclar *vt* (**a**) *(residuos)* to recycle (**b**) *(personas)* to retrain

recidiva *nf Med* reappearance *(of illness)*

recidivar *vi Med* to reappear *(of illness)*

recién *adv* (**a**) *(con participio) (hace poco)* recently, newly; **el pan está r. hecho** the bread is freshly baked; **r. pintado** *(en letrero)* wet paint ▸▸ ***los r. casados*** the newly-weds; ***los r. llegados*** *(los nuevos)* the newcomers; *(los que acaban de llegar)* those who have/had just arrived; ***el r. nacido*** the newborn baby
(**b**) *Am (apenas)* just now, recently; **regresó r. ayer** she only *o* just got back yesterday
(**c**) *Am (ahora mismo)* (only) just; **r. me entero** I've (only) just heard; **r. me llamaron para avisarme** they (only) just called to let me know
(**d**) *Am (sólo)* only; **r. el martes sabremos el resultado** we'll only know the result on Tuesday, we won't know the result until Tuesday; **r. me pasaron a buscar a las nueve** they only came to collect me at nine, they didn't come and collect me until nine

reciente *adj* (**a**) *(acontecimiento)* recent; **todavía tiene muy r. su divorcio** she still hasn't got over her divorce; **su muerte está demasiado r. para hablar de su sucesor** it's too soon after his death to talk about his successor (**b**) *(pintura, pan)* fresh

recientemente *adv* (**a**) *(hace poco)* recently (**b**) *(en los últimos tiempos)* recently, of late

recinto *nm* (**a**) *(zona cercada)* enclosure; **el r. amurallado de la ciudad** the walled part of the city (**b**) *(área)* place, area; *(alrededor de edificios)* grounds; **me dan miedo los recintos cerrados** I'm frightened of enclosed spaces; **le prohibieron el acceso a recintos deportivos** he was banned from sports grounds; **el r. diplomático** the embassy grounds ▸▸ ***r. ferial*** fairground *(of trade fair)*

recio, -a 1 *adj* (**a**) *(persona)* robust (**b**) *(voz)* gravelly (**c**) *(objeto)* sturdy (**d**) *(material, tela)* tough, strong (**e**) *(lluvia, viento)* harsh
2 *adv (trabajar, soplar, llover)* hard; *Méx* **hablar r.** to talk in a loud voice

recipiendario, -a *nm,f Formal* newly elected member

recipiente *nm* container; **necesito un r. para poner la fruta** I need something to put the fruit in

> **Falso amigo**: El sustantivo inglés **recipient** no es la traducción del español **recipiente**. En inglés **recipient** significa "destinatario" o "receptor".

reciprocidad *nf* reciprocity; **en r. a** in return for

recíproco, -a *adj* (**a**) *(sentimiento)* mutual; *(acción)* reciprocal; **la admiración entre ellos es recíproca** they have a mutual admiration for each other (**b**) *Ling* reciprocal

recitación *nf* recitation, recital

recitador, -ora 1 *adj* reciting
2 *nm,f* reciter

recital *nm* (**a**) *(de música clásica)* recital; *(de pop, rock)* concert (**b**) *(de lectura)* reading

recitar *vt* to recite

recitativo, -a *adj* recitative

reclamación *nf* (**a**) *(petición)* claim, demand (**b**) *(queja)* complaint; **hacer una r.** to make a complaint (**c**) *(a un seguro)* claim

reclamante 1 *adj* claiming
2 *nmf* claimant

reclamar 1 *vt* (**a**) *(pedir, exigir)* to demand, to ask for; **le he reclamado todo el dinero que me debe** I've demanded that he return to me all the money he owes me; **reclamó ante un tribunal una indemnización** she went to court to claim compensation; **la multitud reclamaba que cantara otra canción** the crowd clamoured for her to sing another song
(**b**) *(necesitar)* to demand, to require; **el negocio reclama toda mi atención** the business requires *o* demands all my attention; **este conflicto reclama una solución inmediata** this conflict calls for an immediate solution
(**c**) *(llamar)* to ask for; **te reclaman en la oficina** they're asking for you at the office
(**d**) *Der* **r. a alguien** to summon sb to appear before the court
2 *vi (protestar)* to protest; *(quejarse)* to complain; **reclamó contra la sanción** he protested against the suspension; **reclamaron por los malos tratos recibidos** they complained about the ill-treatment they had received

reclame *nm Am* advertisement

reclamo *nm* (**a**) *(para atraer)* inducement ▸▸ ***r. publicitario*** advertising gimmick (**b**) *(para cazar)* decoy, lure (**c**) *(de ave)* call (**d**) *(en texto)* note, reference mark (**e**) *Am (queja)* complaint; **cuente el vuelto antes de retirarse de la ventanilla, después no aceptamos reclamos** check your change before leaving, mistakes cannot be rectified later (**f**) *Am (reivindicación)* claim; **los reclamos de los trabajadores** the workers' demands

reclinable *adj* reclining

reclinar 1 *vt* to lean; **reclinó la tabla contra la pared** she leant the board against the wall; **reclinó la cabeza en** *o* **sobre su hombro** he leant his head against *o* on her shoulder
2 **reclinarse** *vpr* to lean back (**contra** against)

reclinatorio *nm* prie-dieu, prayer stool

recluir [34] 1 *vt* to shut *o* lock away, to imprison; **recluyeron a los prisioneros en una cárcel de máxima seguridad** they put the prisoners in a maximum security prison
2 **recluirse** *vpr* to shut oneself away; **se recluyó en un pueblo remoto** she hid herself away in a remote village

reclusión *nf* (**a**) *(encarcelamiento)* imprisonment (**b**) *(encierro)* seclusion

recluso, -a *nm,f (preso)* prisoner

> **Falso amigo**: El sustantivo inglés **recluse** no es la traducción del español **recluso**. En inglés **recluse** significa "solitario".

reclusorio *nm Méx* prison

recluta *nmf (soldado) (obligatorio)* conscript; *(voluntario)* recruit

reclutamiento *nm* (**a**) *(de soldados) (obligatorio)* conscription; *(voluntario)* recruitment (**b**) *(de trabajadores)* recruitment

reclutar *vt* (**a**) *(soldados) (obligatoriamente)* to conscript; *(voluntariamente)* to recruit (**b**) *(trabajadores)* to recruit (**c**) *RP (ganado)* to round up

recluyo *etc ver* **recluir**

recobrar 1 *vt (recuperar)* to recover; **r. el tiempo perdido** to make up for lost time; **r. el conocimiento** *o* **el sentido** to regain consciousness, to come round; **r. el juicio** to regain one's sanity; **la región ha recobrado la calma tras los disturbios** peace has returned to the area after the disturbances
2 **recobrarse** *vpr (de enfermedad)* to recover (**de** from); **tardé un rato en recobrarme del susto** it was a while before I got over the shock *o* recovered from the shock; **la empresa aún no se ha recobrado de la crisis** the company still hasn't recovered from the crisis

recocer [15] 1 *vt* (**a**) *(volver a cocer)* to recook (**b**) *(cocer demasiado)* to overcook (**c**) *(metal)* to anneal
2 **recocerse** *vpr Fam (persona)* to get all steamed up

recocha *nf Col Fam* **hacer r.** to party

recochinearse *vpr Fam* **r. de alguien** to laugh at sb, *Br* to take the mickey out of sb; **no te recochinees de él, sólo lleva un mes en el trabajo** don't laugh at him *o Br* take the mickey out of him, he's only been in the job a month

recochineo *nm Fam* **decir algo con r.** to say sth to really rub it in

recodo *nm* bend

recogedor *nm* dustpan

recogelatas *nmf inv Ven Fam* tramp, *US* bum

recogemigas *nm inv* crumb scoop

recogepelotas *nmf inv* ball boy, *f* ball girl

RECOGER [52] 1 *vt* (**a**) *(coger, levantar)* to pick up; **recogí los papeles del suelo** I picked the papers up off the ground; **recogieron el agua con una fregona** they mopped up the water
(**b**) *(reunir, retener)* to collect, to gather; **están recogiendo firmas/dinero para...** they are collecting signatures/money for...; **este trasto no hace más que r. polvo** this piece of junk is just gathering dust
(**c**) *(ordenar, limpiar) (mesa)* to clear; *(casa, habitación, cosas)* to tidy *o* clear up
(**d**) *(ir a buscar)* to pick up, to fetch; **iré a r. a los niños a la escuela** I'll pick the children up from school; **¿a qué hora paso a recogerte?** what time shall I pick you up?; **¿a qué hora recogen la basura?** what time do they collect the rubbish?
(**e**) *(recolectar) (mies, cosecha)* to harvest; *(fruta, aceitunas)* to pick; *(setas, flores)* to pick, to gather; *(beneficios)* to reap; **ahora empieza a**

r. los frutos de su trabajo now she's starting to reap the rewards of her work

(**f**) *(mostrar) (sujeto: foto, película)* to show; *(sujeto: novela)* to depict; **su ensayo recoge una idea ya esbozada por Spinoza** her essay contains an idea already hinted at by Spinoza; **una comedia que recoge el ambiente de los ochenta** a comedy which captures the atmosphere of the eighties; **la exposición recoge su obra más reciente** the exhibition brings together his latest works

(**g**) *(acoger) (mendigo, huérfano, animal)* to take in; **en el albergue recogen a los sin techo** the hostel takes in homeless people

(**h**) *(plegar) (velas, sombrillas)* to take down; *(cortinas)* to tie back

(**i**) *(prenda) (acortar)* to take up, to shorten; *(estrechar)* to take in

2 *vi (ordenar, limpiar)* to tidy *o* clear up; **cuando acabes de r....** when you've finished tidying *o* clearing up...

3 recogerse *vpr* (**a**) *(a dormir, meditar)* to retire; **aquí la gente se recoge pronto** people go to bed early here (**b**) **recogerse el pelo** *(en moño)* to put one's hair up; *(en trenza)* to tie one's hair back

---

recogida *nf* (**a**) *(acción)* collection; **hacer una r. de firmas** to collect signatures ►► ***r. de basuras*** refuse collection; ***r. de datos*** data capture; ***r. de equipajes*** baggage reclaim; ***r. selectiva en origen*** *(de basura)* waste segregation (**b**) *(cosecha)* harvest, gathering (**c**) *(de fruta)* picking; **la r. de la uva** the grape harvest

recogido, -a *adj* (**a**) *(vida)* quiet, withdrawn; *(lugar)* secluded; **lleva una vida recogida** he leads a quiet life (**b**) *(cabello)* tied back

recogimiento *nm* (**a**) *(concentración)* concentration, absorption (**b**) *(retiro)* withdrawal, seclusion

recoja *etc ver* **recoger**

recolección *nf* (**a**) *(cosecha)* harvest, gathering (**b**) *(recogida)* collection; *(de fruta)* picking ►► *RP* ***r. de residuos*** refuse *o US* garbage collection

> **Falso amigo**: El sustantivo inglés **recollection** no es la traducción del español **recolección**. En inglés **recollection** significa "recuerdo".

recolectar *vt* (**a**) *(cosechar)* to harvest, to gather; *(fruta)* to pick (**b**) *(reunir)* to collect

recolector, -ora 1 *adj* (**a**) *(maquinaria, época)* harvesting (**b**) *(que vive de la recolección)* **sociedad recolectora** foraging society; **hombre r.** forager

2 *nm,f (de cosecha)* harvester; *(de fruta)* picker; *Am (de basura) Br* dustcart, rubbish truck, *US* garbage truck

recoleto, -a *adj* quiet, secluded

recolocación *nf* **la difícil r. de...** the difficulty in finding new jobs for...

recolocar *vt* to find a new job for

recombinación *nf Biol* recombination

recomendable *adj* **es un hotel muy r.** this hotel can be highly recommended; **es r. pedir cita previa** it is advisable to make an appointment; **no es r.** it's not a good idea; **esa zona no es r.** it's not a very nice area; **va con gente poco r.** he keeps bad company

recomendación *nf* (**a**) *(consejo)* recommendation; **siguió sus recomendaciones al pie de la letra** he followed her advice to the letter; **por r. de alguien** on sb's advice *o* recommendation (**b**) *(referencia)* (**carta de**) **r.** letter of recommendation (**c**) *(enchufe)* recommendation; **le dieron el trabajo porque tenía r. del jefe** the boss got him the job

recomendado¹, -a *nm,f Pey* = person who gets a job, passes an exam etc through influence or connections; **es un r. del jefe** he's got the boss looking out for him

recomendado², -a *adj Am (carta, paquete)* registered; **enviar un paquete r.** to send a parcel by registered *Br* post *o US* mail

recomendar [3] *vt* (**a**) *(aconsejar)* to recommend; **el médico me ha recomendado reposo** the doctor has recommended that I rest, the doctor has advised me to rest; **me han recomendado este restaurante** this restaurant has been recommended to me; **r. a alguien que haga algo** to recommend that sb do sth, to advise sb to do sth; **te lo recomiendo** I recommend it to you; **se recomienda precaución** caution is advised; **no recomendada para menores de 18** *(película)* not suitable for persons under 18

(**b**) *(a trabajador)* to recommend; **lo recomendaron para el puesto** he was recommended for the job

recomenzar [17] **1** *vt* to begin *o* start again, to recommence

2 *vi* to begin *o* start again, to recommence

recompensa *nf* reward; **en** *o* **como r. por** as a reward for; **se ofrece r.** *(en letrero)* reward; **no recibió ninguna r. por su trabajo** she got nothing in return for her work

recompensar *vt* to reward; **se recompensará** *(en letrero)* reward

recomponer [50] *vt* to repair, to mend

recompra *nf (de acciones)* buy-back, repurchase; *(de productos)* buying back; **una campaña de r. de ordenadores viejos** a trade-in scheme for old computers

recompuesto, -a *participio ver* **recomponer**

reconcentrar 1 *vt* (**a**) *(reunir)* to bring together (**b**) *(concentrar)* **r. algo en** to centre *o* concentrate sth on; **reconcentró su atención en la tesis** she focused her attention on her thesis (**c**) *(solución)* to concentrate, to make more concentrated

2 reconcentrarse *vpr* to concentrate (**en** on); **se reconcentró en el estudio** he concentrated on his studies

reconciliable *adj* reconcilable

reconciliación *nf* reconciliation

reconciliador, -ora 1 *adj* reconciliatory

2 *nm,f* reconciler

reconciliar 1 *vt* to reconcile

2 reconciliarse *vpr* **se reconciliaron rápidamente después de la discusión** they soon made (it) up after their argument; **se ha reconciliado con su padre** he is reconciled with his father; **tardaron años en reconciliarse** it was years before they were reconciled

reconcomer 1 *vt* **los celos lo reconcomen** he's consumed with jealousy; **me reconcomen los nervios** I'm a bundle of nerves

2 reconcomerse *vpr* to get worked up; **reconcomerse de celos** to be consumed with jealousy; **se reconcomía de envidia** she was consumed with envy

recóndito, -a *adj* hidden, secret; **viajó hasta el pueblo más r. del país** she travelled to the remotest village in the country; **en lo más r. de mi corazón** in the depths of my heart

reconducción *nf* (**a**) *(desviación)* redirection (**b**) *(devolución)* return

reconducir [18] *vt* (**a**) *(desviar)* to redirect (**b**) *(devolver)* to return

reconfortante *adj* (**a**) *(anímicamente)* comforting; **es r. saber que no les pasó nada** it's good *o* a relief to know that they're all right (**b**) *(físicamente)* revitalizing

reconfortar *vt* (**a**) *(anímicamente)* to comfort (**b**) *(físicamente)* to revitalize

reconocer [19] **1** *vt* (**a**) *(identificar)* to recognize; **con esa barba no te reconocía** I didn't recognize you with that beard; **reconocí su voz** I recognized her voice; **el buen vino se reconoce por el color** you can tell a good wine by its colour

(**b**) *(admitir)* to admit; **reconozco que estaba equivocada** I accept *o* admit that I was mistaken; **hay que r. que lo hace muy bien** you have to admit that she's very good at it; **por fin le reconocieron sus méritos** they finally recognized her worth; **lo reconocieron como el mejor atleta del siglo** he was acknowledged as the greatest athlete of the century

(**c**) *(examinar)* to examine; **el doctor la reconocerá enseguida** the doctor will see you in a moment

(**d**) *(inspeccionar)* to survey; *Mil* to reconnoitre

(**e**) *(agradecer)* to acknowledge; **reconocieron su trabajo con un ascenso** they acknowledged his work *o* showed their appreciation of his work by promoting him; **reconoció su esfuerzo con un regalo** he gave her a present in recognition of all her hard work

(**f**) *Der (hijo)* to recognize; *(firma)* to authenticate; *(sindicato, partido, derecho)* to recognize; **no reconoce la autoridad del rey** he doesn't recognize *o* acknowledge the king's authority

2 reconocerse *vpr* (**a**) *(identificarse) (mutuamente)* to recognize each other; **reconocerse en alguien** to see oneself in sb (**b**) *(confesarse)* **reconocerse culpable** to admit one's guilt

reconocible *adj* recognizable; **es una seta fácilmente r. por su color** this mushroom is easily recognizable *o* recognized by its colour

reconocido, -a *adj* (**a**) *(admitido)* recognized, acknowledged; **un empresario de reconocida trayectoria** a businessman with a proven track record (**b**) *(agradecido)* grateful; **le estamos muy reconocidos por su ayuda** we're very grateful to him for his help

reconocimiento *nm* (**a**) *(identificación)* recognition ►► *Informát & Ling* ***r. del habla*** speech recognition; *Informát* ***r. óptico de caracteres*** optical character recognition; *Informát* ***r. de voz*** voice recognition

(**b**) *(admisión) (de error, culpa)* admission; *(de méritos, autoridad)* recognition

(**c**) *(examen, inspección)* examination ►► ***r. médico*** medical examination *o* checkup

(**d**) *(inspección)* surveying; *Mil* reconnaissance; **hacer un r.** to reconnoitre; **hizo un viaje de r. antes de irse a vivir a Perú** he went on a reconnaissance trip before moving to Peru; **un vuelo/avión de r.** a reconnaissance flight/plane
(**e**) *(agradecimiento)* gratitude; **en r. por** in recognition of
(**f**) *(respeto)* recognition
(**g**) *Der (de hijo)* recognition; *(de firma)* authentication; *(de sindicato, partido, derecho)* recognition

reconozco *etc ver* **reconocer**

reconquista *nf* (**a**) *(de territorio, ciudad)* reconquest, recapture (**b**) *Hist* **la R.** = the Reconquest of Spain, when the Christian Kings retook the country from the Muslims

reconquistar *vt* (**a**) *(territorio, ciudad)* to recapture, to reconquer (**b**) *(título, amor)* to regain, to win back

reconsiderar *vt* to reconsider

reconstitución *nf* reconstitution

reconstituir [34] 1 *vt* (**a**) *(rehacer)* to reconstitute (**b**) *(reproducir)* to reconstruct
2 **reconstituirse** *vpr (país, organización)* to rebuild itself

reconstituyente 1 *adj* tonic
2 *nm* tonic

reconstrucción *nf* (**a**) *(de edificios, país)* rebuilding (**b**) *(de sucesos)* reconstruction

reconstruir [34] *vt* (**a**) *(edificio, país)* to rebuild (**b**) *(suceso)* to reconstruct

reconvención *nf* reprimand, reproach

reconvenir [71] *vt* to reprimand, to reproach

reconversión *nf* restructuring ▸▸ ***r. industrial*** rationalization of industry, industrial conversion

reconvertir [63] *vt (reestructurar)* to restructure; *(industria)* to rationalize

Recopa *nf* Cup-Winners' Cup

recopilación *nf* (**a**) *(acción)* collection, gathering (**b**) *(libro)* collection, anthology; *(disco)* compilation; *(de leyes)* code

recopilador, -ora *nm,f (de escritos, leyes)* compiler

recopilar *vt* (**a**) *(recoger)* to collect, to gather (**b**) *(escritos, leyes)* to compile

recopilatorio, -a 1 *adj* **un disco r.** a compilation (record)
2 *nm* compilation

recórcholis *interj Fam (expresa sorpresa)* good heavens!; *(expresa admiración)* gosh!; *(expresa enfado)* for heaven's sake!

récord (*pl* **récords**) 1 *adj* record; **en un tiempo r.** in record time
2 *nm* record; **batir un r.** to break a record; **establecer un r.** to set a (new) record; **tener el r.** to hold the record

recordación *nf (acción)* remembering

recordar [64] 1 *vt* (**a**) *(acordarse de)* to remember; **no recuerdo dónde he dejado las llaves** I can't remember where I left the keys; **recuerdo que me lo dijo** I remember him telling me; **no recordaba yo un invierno tan frío** I don't remember a winter as cold as this
(**b**) *(traer a la memoria)* to remind; **recuérdame que cierre el gas** remind me to turn the gas off; **te recuerdo que el plazo termina mañana** don't forget that the deadline is tomorrow; **tienes que ir al dentista esta tarde – ¡no me lo recuerdes!** you have to go to the dentist this afternoon – don't remind me!
(**c**) *(por asociación)* to remind; **me recuerda a un amigo mío** he reminds me of a friend of mine; **me recuerda aquella vez que nos quedamos sin luz** it reminds me of that time when the electricity got cut off
2 *vi* (**a**) *(acordarse)* to remember; **si mal no recuerdo** as far as I can remember (**b**) *(traer a la memoria)* **ese pintor recuerda a Picasso** that painter is reminiscent of Picasso (**c**) *Méx (despertar)* to wake up
3 **recordarse** *vpr Méx (despertarse)* to wake up

recordatorio *nm* (**a**) *(aviso)* reminder (**b**) *(estampa)* = card given to commemorate sb's first communion, a death etc

recordista *nmf Am* record holder

recordman *nm Dep* record holder

recorrer 1 *vt* (**a**) *(atravesar) (lugar, país)* to travel through *o* across, to cross; *(ciudad)* to go round; **recorrieron la sabana en un camión** they drove round the savannah in a truck; **recorrió la región a pie** he walked round the region; **recorrieron el perímetro de la isla** they went round the island
(**b**) *(distancia)* to cover; **recorrió los 42 km en tres horas** he covered *o* did the 42 km in three hours
(**c**) *(con la mirada)* to look over; **lo recorrió de arriba a abajo con la mirada** she looked him up and down
2 **recorrerse** *vpr* (**a**) *(atravesar) (lugar, país)* to travel through *o* across, to cross; *(ciudad)* to go round; **se recorrió el desierto en solitario** he crossed the desert on his own (**b**) *(distancia)* to cover

recorrida *nf Am* (**a**) *(ruta, itinerario)* route; **hacer una r. turística** to go sightseeing (**b**) *(viaje)* journey; **una r. a pie por la ciudad** a walk round the city; **una breve r. por la prehistoria** a brief overview of prehistory; **hacer una r. (mental) por algo** to run over sth (in one's head)

recorrido *nm* (**a**) *(ruta, itinerario)* route; **hacer un r. turístico** to go sightseeing (**b**) *(viaje)* journey; **un r. a pie por la ciudad** a walk round the city; **un breve r. por la prehistoria** a brief overview of prehistory; **hacer un r. (mental) por algo** to run over sth (in one's head) (**c**) *(en golf)* round (**d**) *(en esquí)* run (**e**) *(en estadística)* range

recortable 1 *adj* cutout; **un animal r.** a cutout figure of an animal
2 *nm* cutout (figure)

recortada *nf (escopeta)* sawn-off shotgun

recortado, -a *adj* (**a**) *(cortado)* cut (**b**) *(borde)* jagged

recortar 1 *vt* (**a**) *(cortar) (lo que sobra)* to cut off *o* away; *(figuras)* to cut out (**b**) *(pelo, flequillo)* to trim (**c**) *(reducir)* to cut; **hay que r. gastos** we'll have to cut (down) our expenditure (**d**) *Dep* to sidestep; **recortó a un defensa** he sidestepped a defender
2 **recortarse** *vpr (perfil)* to stand out, to be silhouetted (**en** against); **el perfil del castillo se recortaba en el horizonte** the castle was silhouetted against the horizon

recorte *nm* (**a**) *(pieza cortada)* trimming; *(de periódico, revista)* cutting, clipping (**b**) *(reducción)* cut, cutback ▸▸ ***recortes de personal*** job cuts; ***r. presupuestario*** budget cut; ***r. salarial*** wage *o* pay cut (**c**) *(cartulina)* cutout (**d**) *Dep* sidestep (**e**) *Méx Fam (crítica)* nasty *o* snide remark; **no me gustan tus amigos, están siempre en el r.** I don't like your friends, they're always being nasty about *o Br* slagging off other people

recoser *vt* (**a**) *(volver a coser)* to sew (up) again (**b**) *(zurcir)* to mend, to darn

recostar [64] 1 *vt* to lean (back); **recostó la cabeza en el cojín** she leaned her head back against *o* on the cushion; **recostó la escalera en la pared** he leaned the ladder against the wall
2 **recostarse** *vpr (tumbarse)* to lie down; **se recostó sobre mi hombro** he leaned on *o* against my shoulder

recoveco *nm* (**a**) *(rincón)* nook, hidden corner; **se conoce todos los recovecos de la carretera** he knows all the road's twists and turns (**b**) *(complicación)* **recovecos** ins and outs; **sin recovecos** uncomplicated (**c**) *(lo más oculto)* **los recovecos del alma** the innermost recesses of the soul

recreación *nf* recreation

recrear 1 *vt* (**a**) *(volver a crear, reproducir)* to recreate; **la novela recrea fielmente el ambiente de la época** the novel faithfully recreates the atmosphere of the time (**b**) *(entretener)* to amuse, to entertain; **r. la vista** to be a joy to behold
2 **recrearse** *vpr* (**a**) *(entretenerse)* to amuse oneself, to entertain oneself (**en** with); **recrearse haciendo algo** to amuse *o* entertain oneself by doing sth (**b**) *(regodearse)* to take delight *o* pleasure (**en** in) (**c**) *(reinventarse)* to re-create oneself

recreativo, -a *adj* recreational; **máquina recreativa** arcade machine; **salón r.** amusement arcade

recreo *nm* (**a**) *(entretenimiento)* recreation, amusement; **embarcación de r.** pleasure boat (**b**) *Educ (en primaria)* playtime; *(en secundaria)* break (**c**) *Educ (patio)* playground

recriar [32] *vt (animales)* to breed, to raise

recriminación *nf* reproach, recrimination

recriminar 1 *vt* to reproach; **le recriminó que no hubiera ayudado** he reproached her for not helping
2 **recriminarse** *vpr (mutuamente)* to reproach each other

recriminatorio, -a *adj* reproachful, recriminatory

recrudecer [46] 1 *vt (conflicto, crisis económica)* to intensify; *(tormenta, incendio)* to make worse
2 **recrudecerse** *vpr (conflicto, crisis económica)* to worsen; *(tormenta, incendio)* to grow worse

recrudecimiento *nm (de crisis)* worsening; *(de criminalidad)* upsurge; **el r. de la huelga ha obligado a intervenir al gobierno** the escalation of the strike has forced the government to intervene

recta *nf* (**a**) *(línea)* straight line (**b**) *(en carretera)* straight stretch of road; *(en pista de carreras)* straight ▸▸ ***la r. final*** *(en pista de carreras)* the home straight; *(de competición, campaña electoral)* the closing *o* final stages; **entrar en la r. final** *(corredor)* to enter the home straight; *(competición, campaña electoral)* to enter its closing *o* final stages (**c**) *ver también* **recto**

rectal *adj* rectal

rectamente *adv (con rectitud)* rightly, justly

rectangular *adj* (**a**) *(de forma)* rectangular (**b**) *(de ángulos rectos)* right-angled

rectángulo *nm* rectangle

rectificable *adj* rectifiable

rectificación *nf* (**a**) *(de error)* rectification; *(en periódico)* correction (**b**) *Elec* rectification (**c**) *(en baloncesto)* double pump

rectificador *nm Elec* rectifier

rectificar [60] *vt* (**a**) *(error)* to rectify, to correct (**b**) *(conducta, actitud)* to improve (**c**) *(ajustar)* to put right (**d**) *Elec* to rectify

rectilíneo, -a *adj* (**a**) *(en línea recta)* straight; **una carretera rectilínea** a straight road (**b**) *(carácter, actitud)* rigid

rectitud *nf* (**a**) *(de línea)* straightness (**b**) *(de conducta)* rectitude, uprightness

recto, -a 1 *adj* (**a**) *(sin curvas)* straight (**b**) *(vertical)* straight; **ese cuadro no está r.** that picture isn't straight (**c**) *(íntegro)* upright, honourable (**d**) *(justo, verdadero)* true, correct (**e**) *(literal)* literal, true (**f**) *Mat* **un ángulo r.** a right angle

2 *nm* (**a**) *Anat* rectum ►► ***r. abdominal*** abdominal rectus; ***r. anterior*** anterior rectus (**b**) *Imprenta (de página)* recto

3 *adv* straight on *o* ahead; **todo r.** straight on *o* ahead

rector, -ora 1 *adj* governing, guiding; **el principio r. de una política** the guiding principle of a policy

2 *nm,f* (**a**) *(de universidad) Br* vice-chancellor, *US* president (**b**) *(dirigente)* leader, head

3 *nm Rel* rector

rectorado *nm* (**a**) *(cargo) Br* vice-chancellorship, *US* presidency (**b**) *(lugar) Br* vice-chancellor's office, *US* president's office

rectoría *nf* (**a**) *(cargo)* rectorate, rectorship (**b**) *(casa)* rectory

rectoscopia *nf* rectal examination

recua *nf* (**a**) *(de animales)* pack, drove (**b**) *Fam (de personas)* crowd

recuadrar *vt* to (put in a) box

recuadro *nm* box

recubierto, -a *participio ver* **recubrir**

recubrimiento *nm (cubrimiento)* covering; *(con pintura, barniz)* coating

recubrir *vt (cubrir)* to cover; *(con pintura, barniz)* to coat; **recubrió la tarta de chocolate** he iced the cake with chocolate; **recubrió el agujero con escayola** she covered up the hole with plaster, she plastered over the hole

recuece *etc ver* **recocer**

recuento *nm (por primera vez)* count; *(otra vez)* recount; **hubo que proceder al r. de los votos** the votes had to be recounted, a recount was needed ►► ***r. espermático*** *o* ***de espermatozoides*** sperm count

recuerdo 1 *ver* **recordar**

2 *nm* (**a**) *(rememoración)* memory; **quedar en el r. (de)** to be remembered (by); **traer recuerdos a alguien de algo** to bring back memories of sth to sb; **tengo muy buen/mal r. de ese viaje** I have very fond/bad memories of that trip

(**b**) *(objeto) (de viaje)* souvenir; *(de persona)* keepsake; **me quedé su agenda como r.** I kept her diary as a keepsake

(**c**) **recuerdos** *(saludos)* regards; **dale recuerdos a tu hermana (de mi parte)** give my regards to your sister, give your sister my regards; **Javier te manda recuerdos** Javier sends his regards; **recuerdos de Isabel** Isabel says hello

recuesto *etc ver* **recostar**

recuezo *etc ver* **recocer**

recular *vi* (**a**) *(retroceder)* to move back; **el camión reculó para dejar pasar al autobús** the truck moved back *o* reversed to let the bus through (**b**) *Fam (ceder)* to back down

recuperable *adj (información, objeto)* recoverable, retrievable; **esta clase es r.** you can catch *o* make this class up later

recuperación *nf* (**a**) *(de lo perdido, la salud, la economía)* recovery; *(de información)* retrieval; *(de espacios naturales)* reclamation

(**b**) *(rehabilitación) (de local, edificio)* refurbishment ►► ***r. paisajística*** improving the visual environment

(**c**) *Informát (de información dañada)* recovery ►► ***r. de datos*** data recovery

(**d**) *(reciclaje)* recovery

(**e**) *(examen)* resit; **(clase de) r.** = extra class for pupils or students who have to resit their exams

(**f**) *(fisioterapia)* physiotherapy

(**g**) *(en baloncesto)* steal

recuperar 1 *vt* (**a**) *(recobrar) (lo perdido)* to recover; *(espacios naturales)* to reclaim; *(horas de trabajo)* to make up; *(conocimiento)* to regain; **r. el tiempo perdido** to make up for lost time; **recuperó la salud** she got better, she recovered; **recuperó la vista** she regained her sight, she got her sight back; **no recuperaron el dinero invertido** they didn't get back *o* recoup the money they invested; **recuperó la libertad tras diez años en la cárcel** he regained his freedom after ten years in prison; **haremos un descanso para r. fuerzas** we'll have a break to get our strength back

(**b**) *(rehabilitar) (local, edificio)* to refurbish

(**c**) *Informát (información dañada)* to recover

(**d**) *(reciclar)* to recover

(**e**) *(examen)* to resit; **tengo que r. la física en septiembre** I have to resit physics in September

(**f**) *(en baloncesto)* to steal

2 **recuperarse** *vpr* (**a**) *(enfermo)* to recover, to recuperate (**b**) *(de una crisis)* to recover; *(negocio)* to pick up; **recuperarse de algo** *(divorcio, trauma)* to get over sth; **tardé en recuperarme del susto** it took me a while to recover from *o* get over the shock

recurrencia *nf* recurrence

recurrente 1 *adj* (**a**) *Der* appellant (**b**) *(repetido)* recurrent

2 *nmf Der* appellant

recurrir 1 *vt Der* to appeal against

2 *vi* (**a**) *(utilizar)* **r. a alguien** to turn *o* go to sb; **r. a algo** *(violencia, medidas)* to resort to sth; **r. a un diccionario** to consult a dictionary (**b**) *Der* to appeal; **recurrirá contra la sentencia** she will appeal against the judgement

> **Falso amigo**: El verbo inglés **to recur** no es la traducción del español **recurrir**. En inglés **to recur** significa "repetirse" o "reaparecer".

recursivo, -a *adj Ling* recursive

recurso *nm* (**a**) *(medio)* resort; **como último r.** as a last resort; **es un hombre de recursos** he's very resourceful; **el único r. que le queda es llamar a su hermano** his only remaining alternative *o* option is to call his brother

(**b**) *Der* appeal; **presentar r. (ante)** to appeal (against) ►► ***r. de alzada*** appeal (against an official decision); ***r. de amparo*** appeal for protection; ***r. de apelación*** appeal; ***r. de casación*** High Court appeal; ***r. contencioso administrativo*** = court case brought against the State; ***r. de súplica*** = appeal to a higher court for reversal of a decision

(**c**) *(bien, riqueza)* resource; **no tiene recursos, así que su familia le da dinero** he doesn't have his own means, so he gets money from his family ►► ***r. energético*** energy resource; ***recursos financieros*** financial resources; ***recursos hídricos*** water resources; ***recursos humanos*** human resources; ***recursos minerales*** mineral resources; ***recursos naturales*** natural resources; *Econ* ***recursos propios*** equity; ***recursos renovables*** renewable resources; ***recursos no renovables*** non-renewable resources

(**d**) *Informát* resource

recusable *adj* rejectable, refusable

recusación *nf* (**a**) *Der (de juez, testigo)* challenge (**b**) *Dep (de árbitro)* rejection (**c**) *(rechazo)* rejection

recusar *vt* (**a**) *Der (juez, testigo)* to challenge (**b**) *Dep (árbitro)* to reject (**c**) *(rechazar)* to reject, to refuse

red *nf* (**a**) *(de pesca, caza)* net; *también Fig* **echar** *o* **tender las redes** to cast one's net; EXPR **caer en las redes de alguien** to fall into sb's trap ►► ***r. de arrastre*** dragnet; ***r. de deriva*** drift net

(**b**) *(en tenis, voleibol, fútbol)* net; **subir a la r.** *(en tenis)* to go into the net

(**c**) *(para cabello)* hairnet

(**d**) *(sistema)* network, system; *(de electricidad, agua)* mains *(singular)*; **una r. de traficantes** a network *o* ring of traffickers; **conectar algo a la r.** to connect sth to the mains ►► ***r. de distribución*** distribution network; ***r. eléctrica*** mains *(singular)*; ***r. ferroviaria*** rail network; ***r. hidrográfica*** river system *o* network; *Biol* ***r. trófica*** food chain; ***r. viaria*** road network *o* system

(**e**) *(organización) (de espionaje)* ring; *(de narcotraficantes)* network; *(de tiendas, hoteles)* chain

(**f**) *Informát* network; **la R.** *(Internet)* the Net; **lo encontré en la R.** I found it on the Net; **la R. de redes** *(Internet)* the Internet ►► ***r. en anillo*** ring network; ***r. de área extensa*** wide area network; ***r. de área local*** local area network; ***r. ciudadana*** freenet; ***r. de datos*** (data) network; ***r. local*** local (area) network; ***r. neuronal*** neural network; ***r. troncal*** backbone

redacción *nf* (a) *(acción)* writing; *(de periódico)* editing; **la r. de la enciclopedia llevó diez años** it took ten years to write *o* produce the encyclopedia (b) *(estilo)* wording (c) *(equipo de redactores)* editorial team *o* staff (d) *(oficina)* editorial office (e) *(escrito escolar)* essay

redactar 1 *vt* to write; **r. un contrato/un tratado** to draw up a contract/a treaty; **tenemos que redactarlo de forma más clara** we have to word it more clearly
2 *vi* to write

redactor, -ora *nm,f Prensa (escritor)* writer; *(editor)* editor ►► ***r. jefe*** editor-in-chief

redada *nf (de policía) (en un solo lugar)* raid; *(en varios lugares)* round-up; **hicieron una r. en el barrio** they carried out a raid in *o* raided the neighbourhood

redaños *nmpl (valor)* spirit; **no tener r. para hacer algo** not to have the courage to do sth

redecilla *nf* (a) *(de pelo)* hairnet (b) *Zool* reticulum

rededor: en rededor *loc adv Literario* around

redefinir *vt* to redefine

redención *nf* (a) *(salvación)* redemption (b) *(de esclavo)* redemption (c) *(de penas)* reduction (d) *Fin (de hipoteca)* repayment, redemption

redentor, -ora *nm,f* (a) *(persona)* redeemer (b) *Rel* **el Redentor** the Redeemer

redescubrir *vt* to rediscover

redibujar *vt Informát* to redraw

redicho, -a *adj Fam* affected, pretentious

rediez *interj Fam (expresa sorpresa, admiración)* my goodness!; *(expresa enfado)* for heaven's sake!

redil *nm* fold, pen; EXPR **volver al r.** to return to the fold

redimible *adj* redeemable

redimir 1 *vt* (a) *(librar, liberar)* to free, to deliver; *(esclavo)* to redeem; **r. a alguien de la pobreza** to free *o* deliver sb from poverty (b) *Rel* to redeem (**de** from) (c) *Fin (hipoteca)* to repay, to redeem (d) *Com (recomprar)* to redeem
2 **redimirse** *vpr* (a) *(librarse)* to free *o* release oneself (b) *Rel* to redeem oneself

rediós *interj Fam (expresa sorpresa, admiración)* my goodness!; *(expresa enfado)* for heaven's sake!

redireccionar *vt Informát* to readdress

redistribución *nf* redistribution

redistribuir [34] *vt* to redistribute

rédito *nm* interest, yield

redituable *adj* interest-yielding

redituar [4] *vt* to yield

redivivo, -a *adj Rel* risen (from the dead); **este chico es su tío redivivo** this boy is the spitting image of his uncle

redoblado, -a *adj (esfuerzo)* renewed, redoubled

redoblamiento *nm (de esfuerzos)* redoubling

redoblar 1 *vt (aumentar)* to redouble; **redoblaron las medidas de seguridad** security measures were stepped up *o* tightened
2 *vi (tambor)* to roll

redoble *nm (de tambor)* roll, drum roll

redoblona *nf Méx, RP Br* accumulator, *US* parlay

redoma *nf* (a) *(frasco)* flask (b) *Ven (rotonda) Br* roundabout, *US* traffic circle

redomado, -a *adj (mentiroso, jugador)* inveterate; **es un vago r.** he's bone idle

redonda 1 *nf* (a) *Mús Br* semibreve, *US* whole note (b) *Imprenta* roman character; **en r.** in roman (type) (c) *ver también* **redondo**
2 **a la redonda** *loc adv* **en 15 kilómetros a la r.** within a 15 kilometre radius; **la explosión se oyó en muchos kilómetros a la r.** the explosion was heard for miles around

redondeado, -a *adj* rounded

redondear *vt* (a) *(hacer redondo)* to round, to make round (b) *(negocio, acuerdo)* to round off (c) *(cifra, precio) (al alza)* to round up; *(a la baja)* to round down

redondel *nm* (a) *(círculo)* circle, ring (b) *Taurom* bullring

redondeo *nm (de cifra, precio) (al alza)* rounding up; *(a la baja)* rounding down

redondez *nf* (a) *(cualidad)* roundness (b) **redondeces** *(curvas de mujer)* curves

redondilla 1 *adj* roman
2 *nf* octosyllabic quatrain

redondo, -a 1 *adj* (a) *(circular, esférico)* round; **girar en r.** to turn round; EXPR **caerse r.** to collapse in a heap; **me caí r. en la cama** I collapsed into bed
(b) *(perfecto)* excellent; **fue una compra redonda** it was an excellent buy; **salir r.** *(examen, entrevista)* to go like a dream; *(pastel)* to turn out perfectly
(c) *(rotundo)* categorical; **se negó en r. a escucharnos** she refused point-blank to listen to us
(d) *(cantidad)* round; **mil pesos redondos** a round thousand pesos
2 *nm (de carne)* topside

redor: en redor *loc adv Literario* around

reducción *nf* (a) *(disminución)* reduction; **piden la r. de la jornada laboral** they are asking for working hours to be shortened; **se ha producido una r. de los precios de 5 puntos porcentuales** prices have gone down *o* fallen by 5 percent ►► ***r. al absurdo*** reductio ad absurdum; ***r. de condena*** remission; ***r. fiscal*** tax cut; ***r. de gastos*** cost cutting; **han anunciado una r. de gastos** they have announced that they are going to cut costs; ***r. de precios*** *(acción)* price-cutting; *(resultado)* price cut; ***r. tributaria*** tax cut
(b) *(sometimiento) (de rebelión)* suppression; *(de ejército)* defeat
(c) *Med (de fractura)* reduction
(d) *Quím* reduction
(e) *Hist* = settlement of Indians converted to Christianity
(f) *RP (de cadáver)* exhumation *(for reburial of bones in smaller container)*

reduccionismo *nm* reductionism

reduccionista *adj* reductionist

reducible *adj* reducible

reducido, -a *adj* (a) *(pequeño)* small; **un espacio muy r.** a very limited space; **lo compré a un precio r.** I bought it at a reduced price (b) *(limitado)* limited; **hay un número r. de plazas** there is a limited number of places

reducidor, -ora *nm,f* (a) *Am (de cabezas)* headshrinker (b) *Andes, RP (de objetos robados)* receiver of stolen goods, fence

---

REDUCIR [18] 1 *vt* (a) *(disminuir)* to reduce; *(gastos, costes, impuestos, plantilla)* to cut; *(producción)* to cut (back on); **nos han reducido el sueldo** our salary has been cut; **reduzca la velocidad** *(en letrero)* reduce speed now; **r. algo a algo** to reduce sth to sth; **el edificio quedó reducido a escombros** the building was reduced to a pile of rubble; **r. algo al mínimo** to reduce sth to a minimum; **r. algo a** *o* **en la mitad** to reduce sth by half; **tú todo lo reduces a tener dinero** the only thing you care about is money; **r. a la mínima expresión** to cut down to the bare minimum
(b) *(fotocopia)* to reduce
(c) *(someter) (país, ciudad)* to suppress, to subdue; *(atracador, ladrón, sublevados)* to overpower
(d) *Mat (unidades de medida)* to convert (**a** to); *(fracciones, ecuaciones)* to cancel out
(e) *Med (hueso)* to set
(f) *Quím* to reduce
(g) *Culin (guiso, salsa)* to reduce
(h) *Andes, RP (objetos robados)* to receive, to fence
(i) *RP (cadáver)* to exhume *(for reburial in smaller container)*
2 *vi* (a) *(en el automóvil)* **r. (de marcha** *o* **velocidad)** to change down; **reduce a tercera** change down into third (gear) (b) *Culin (guiso, salsa)* to reduce
3 **reducirse** *vpr* (a) *(disminuir)* to go down, to fall, to decrease; **se ha reducido la diferencia** the gap has closed; **los salarios se han reducido un 2 por ciento** salaries have gone down *o* fallen *o* decreased by 2 percent
(b) **reducirse a** *(limitarse a)* **toda su ayuda se redujo a unas palabras de ánimo** her help amounted to nothing more than a few words of encouragement; **me he reducido a lo esencial** I've concentrated on the bare essentials
(c) **reducirse a** *(equivaler a)* to boil *o* come down to; **todo se reduce a una cuestión de dinero** it all boils *o* comes down to money

---

reductasa *nf Bioquím* reductase

reductible *adj* reducible

reducto *nm* (a) *(fortificación)* redoubt (b) *(refugio)* stronghold, bastion

reductor, -ora *Quím* 1 *adj* reducing
2 *nm* reducer

redujera *etc ver* **reducir**

redundancia *nf* **eso es una r.** that's redundant *o* superfluous; **valga la r.** if you'll forgive me for using two words that sound so similar in the same sentence

redundante *adj* redundant, superfluous

redundar *vi* **redunda en beneficio nuestro** it is to our advantage; **la reforma redunda en perjuicio de los más débiles** the reform is to the detriment of the weakest

reduplicación *nf* **(a)** *(intensificación)* redoubling **(b)** *(repetición)* reduplication **(c)** *Ling* reduplication

reduplicar [60] *vt* **(a)** *(intensificar)* to redouble **(b)** *(duplicar)* to reduplicate **(c)** *Ling* to reduplicate

reduzco *etc ver* **reducir**

reedición *nf* **(a)** *(nueva edición)* new edition **(b)** *(reimpresión)* reprint

reedificación *nf* rebuilding

reedificar *vt* to rebuild

reeditar *vt* **(a)** *(publicar nueva edición de)* to bring out a new edition of **(b)** *(reimprimir)* to reprint

reeducar [60] *vt* to re-educate

reelaborar *vt (trabajo)* to redo

reelección *nf* re-election

reelecto, -a *adj* re-elected

reelegir [55] *vt* to re-elect

reembolsable, rembolsable *adj (gastos)* reimbursable; *(fianza)* refundable; *(deuda)* repayable

reembolsar, rembolsar *vt (gastos)* to reimburse; *(fianza)* to refund; *(deuda)* to repay

reembolso, rembolso *nm (de gastos)* reimbursement; *(de fianza, dinero)* refund; *(de deuda)* repayment; **contra r.** cash on delivery

reemplazante, remplazante *nmf* replacement

reemplazar, remplazar [14] *vt* **(a)** *(persona)* to replace; **Pérez reemplaza a Ramírez al frente del Ministerio de Defensa** Pérez is replacing Ramírez as Minister of Defence; **será difícil de r.** she will be difficult to replace

(b) *(pieza)* to replace; **reemplazaron el motor con** *o* **por uno nuevo** they replaced the engine (with a new one); **el correo electrónico ha reemplazado al tradicional** e-mail has replaced *o* superseded conventional mail

reemplazo, remplazo *nm* **(a)** *(sustitución)* replacement **(con** *o* **por** with); **buscan un r. para el presidente** they are looking for a replacement for the president, they are looking for someone to replace the president **(b)** *Mil* call-up, draft; **el r. de 1998** the 1998 draft; **soldado de r.** = person doing military service

reemprender *vt* to start again; **reemprendieron la marcha tras un breve descanso** they started walking again after a short rest

reencarnación *nf* reincarnation

reencarnar **1** *vt* to reincarnate

2 reencarnarse *vpr* to be reincarnated; **reencarnarse en algo/alguien** to be reincarnated as sth/sb

reencauchado, -a, recauchado, -a *adj Andes, Ven* remoulded, retreaded; **un neumático r.** a remould, a retread

reencauchadora, recauchadora *nf Andes, Ven* tyre centre

reencauchar, recauchar *vt Andes, Ven* to remould, to retread

reencontrar [64], **rencontrar** [64] **1** *vt* to find again

2 reencontrarse *vpr (varias personas)* to meet again

reencuentro, rencuentro *nm* reunion

reengancharse *vpr Mil* to re-enlist

reenganche *nm Mil (acción)* re-enlistment

reenviar [32] *vt* **(a)** *(devolver)* to return, to send back **(b)** *(reexpedir)* to forward, to send on

reenvío *nm* **(a)** *(devolución)* return, sending back **(b)** *(reexpedición)* forwarding

reescribir *vt* to rewrite

reestrenar *vt* **(a)** *(película)* to rerun, to rerelease **(b)** *(obra)* to revive

reestreno *nm* **(a)** *(película)* rerun, rerelease; **cine de r.** second-run cinema; **reestrenos, películas de r.** *(en cartelera)* rereleases **(b)** *(obra)* revival

reestructuración *nf* restructuring

reestructurar *vt* to restructure

reexpedición *nf (de cartas)* forwarding

reexpedir [47] *vt* to forward, to send on

reexportación *nf* re-exportation

reexportar *vt* to re-export

refacción *nf* **(a)** *Andes, CAm, RP, Ven (reforma)* refurbishment; **la r. de la casa llevó dos meses** the refurbishment of the house took two months; **cerrado para refacciones** *(en letrero)* closed for refurbishment **(b)** *Andes, CAm, RP, Ven (reparación)* restoration **(c)** *Méx (recambio)* spare part

refaccionar *vt Andes, CAm, Ven* **(a)** *(reformar)* to refurbish **(b)** *(reparar)* to restore

refaccionaria *nf Méx (tienda)* car spare parts shop; *(taller)* garage

refajo *nm* underskirt, slip

refanfinflar *vt Esp Fam Hum* **me la refanfinfla** I don't care two hoots

refectorio *nm* refectory

referencia *nf* **(a)** *(mención)* reference; **hacer r. a** to make reference to, to refer to **(b)** *(remisión)* reference ►► *Informát* ***r. circular*** circular reference **(c)** *(base de comparación)* reference; **con r. a** with reference to; **tomar algo como r.** to use sth as a point of reference **(d) referencias** *(información)* information; *(para puesto de trabajo)* references

referéndum *(pl* **referendums** *o* **referendos)** *nm* referendum; **someter algo a r.** to hold a referendum on sth; **fue aprobado en r.** it was approved in a *o* by referendum

referente **1** *adj* **r. a** concerning, relating to; **en lo r. a tu pregunta...** as regards your question...

2 *nm Ling* referent

referí *nmf Am* referee

referir [63] **1** *vt* **(a)** *(narrar)* to tell, to recount **(b)** *(remitir)* **r. a alguien a** to refer sb to **(c)** *(relacionar)* **r. algo a** to relate sth to **(d)** *Com (convertir)* **r. algo a** to convert sth into

2 referirse *vpr* **(a) referirse a** *(estar relacionado con)* to refer to; **por** *o* **en lo que se refiere a...** as far as... is concerned **(b) referirse a** *(aludir, mencionar)* **¿a qué te refieres?** what do you mean?; **¿te referías a ella?** were you referring to her?, did you mean her?; **no me refiero a ti, sino a ella** I don't mean you, I mean her; **se refirió brevemente al problema de la vivienda** he briefly mentioned the housing problem

refilón: de refilón *loc adv* **(a)** *(de pasada)* briefly; **mencionar algo de r.** to mention sth in passing; **leer una revista de r.** to flick through a magazine **(b)** *(de lado)* sideways; **mirar/ver algo de r.** to look at/see sth out of the corner of one's eye

refinado, -a **1** *adj* **(a)** *(de buen gusto)* refined **(b)** *(inteligencia, crueldad)* supreme

2 *nm* refining

refinamiento *nm* **(a)** *(de petróleo, aceite, azúcar)* refining **(b)** *(de objeto, sistema)* refinement **(c)** *(de modales)* refinement

refinanciación *nf* refinancing

refinanciar *vt* to refinance

refinar *vt* **(a)** *(petróleo, aceite, azúcar)* to refine **(b)** *(objeto, sistema)* to refine **(c)** *(modales)* to refine

refinería *nf* refinery

refiriera *etc ver* **referir**

refitolero, -a *Carib Fam* **1** *adj (zalamero)* fawning

2 *nm,f (zalamero)* flatterer

reflación *nf Econ* reflation

reflacionar *vt Econ* to reflate

reflacionario, -a *adj Econ* reflationary

reflectante **1** *adj* reflective

2 *nm* reflector

reflectar *vt* to reflect

reflector, -ora **1** *adj* reflective

2 *nm* **(a)** *(foco)* spotlight; *Mil* searchlight **(b)** *(telescopio)* reflector **(c)** *(aparato que refleja)* reflector

reflejar **1** *vt* **(a)** *(onda, rayo)* to reflect; *Fig* **no me veo reflejado en esa descripción** I don't see myself in that description **(b)** *(sentimiento, duda)* to show; **su rostro reflejaba el cansancio** his face looked tired; **esa pregunta refleja su ignorancia** that question shows *o* demonstrates his ignorance; **su voz reflejaba su nerviosismo** his nervousness showed in his voice

2 reflejarse *vpr* **(a)** *(onda, rayo)* to be reflected **(en** in) **(b)** *(sentimiento, duda)* to be reflected **(en** in); **la felicidad se refleja en su mirada** her gaze radiates happiness; **su inexperiencia se refleja en su trabajo** her inexperience shows up in her work

reflejo, -a **1** *adj (movimiento, dolor)* reflex; **acto r.** reflex action

2 *nm* **(a)** *(luz)* reflection; **me cegó el r. del sol** I was blinded by the sun's reflection

(b) *(imagen, manifestación)* reflection; **la novela es un fiel r. de la realidad** the novel is a faithful reflection of reality

(c) *Anat* reflex; *también Fig* **tener buenos reflejos** to have good *o* quick reflexes ▸▸ ***r. condicional*** *o* ***condicionado*** conditioned reflex *o* response

(**d**) **reflejos** *(de peluquería)* highlights; **hacerse** *o* **darse reflejos** to have highlights put in (one's hair)

réflex *Fot* 1 *adj inv* reflex, SLR

2 *nf inv (cámara)* reflex *o* SLR camera

reflexión *nf* (**a**) *(meditación)* reflection; **sin previa r.** without thinking (**b**) *(razonamiento)* thought; **me hizo unas reflexiones sobre el asunto** he made a few remarks on the matter to me, he shared some of his thoughts on the matter with me (**c**) *(de onda, rayo)* reflection

reflexionar 1 *vi* to think (**sobre** about), to reflect (**sobre** on); **reflexiona bien antes de tomar una decisión** think carefully before taking a decision; **actuó sin r.** she acted without thinking

2 *vt* to think about, to consider

reflexivo, -a *adj* (**a**) *(que piensa)* reflective, thoughtful (**b**) *Gram* reflexive

reflexología *nf* reflexology

reflexoterapia *nf* reflexology

reflorecimiento *nm* resurgence, rebirth

reflotamiento *nm*, **reflotación** *nf Econ (de empresa, banco)* saving; **un acuerdo para el r. del sector** an agreement aimed at saving the industry

reflotar *vt* (**a**) *(barco)* to refloat (**b**) *Econ (empresa, banco)* to save, to bail out

refluir [34] *vi* to flow back *o* out

reflujo *nm* ebb (tide)

refocilarse *vpr* **r. haciendo algo** to take delight in doing sth; **r. en la desgracia ajena** to gloat over others' misfortune

reforestación *nf* reforestation, *Br* reafforestation

reforestar *vt* to reforest, *Br* to reafforest

reforma *nf* (**a**) *(modificación)* reform ▸▸ ***r. agraria*** land reform, agrarian reform; ***r. electoral*** electoral reform; ***reformas estructurales*** structural reforms; ***r. fiscal*** tax reform

(**b**) *(en local, casa)* alterations; **hacer reformas en** to do up; **he gastado los ahorros en hacer reformas en mi casa** I've spent all my savings on doing up the house; **cerrado por reformas** *(en letrero)* closed for alterations

(**c**) *Hist* **la R.** the Reformation

reformado, -a 1 *adj* (**a**) *(modificado)* altered (**b**) *(mejorado)* improved (**c**) *(rehecho)* reformed

2 *nm,f* Protestant

reformador, -ora 1 *adj* reforming

2 *nm,f* reformer

reformar 1 *vt* (**a**) *(cambiar)* to reform (**b**) *(local, casa)* to do up (**c**) *(criminal)* to reform

2 **reformarse** *vpr* to mend one's ways

reformatorio *nm Br* youth custody centre, *US* reformatory

reformismo *nm* reformism

reformista 1 *adj* reformist

2 *nmf* reformist

reformular *vt* to reformulate, to put another way

reforzado, -a *adj* reinforced

reforzar [31] *vt* (**a**) *(hacer resistente)* to reinforce; **reforzaron los pilares del puente** they reinforced the piers of the bridge (**b**) *(intensificar)* to strengthen; **han reforzado las medidas de seguridad en torno al palacio** they have tightened security around the palace (**c**) *Fot* to intensify

refracción *nf* refraction

refractar *vt* to refract

refractario, -a *adj* (**a**) *(material)* heat-resistant, refractory; *(plato, fuente)* ovenproof (**b**) *(opuesto)* **r. a** averse to; **es r. a los cambios** he's opposed to change (**c**) *(inmune)* **r. a** immune to

refrán *nm* proverb, saying; **como dice el r.,...** as the saying goes,..., as they say,...

> **Falso amigo**: El sustantivo inglés **refrain** no es la traducción del español **refrán**. En inglés **refrain** significa "estribillo" o "cantinela".

refranero *nm* = collection of proverbs or sayings

refregar [43] *vt* (**a**) *(frotar)* to scrub (**b**) *(restregar)* **se lo estuvo refregando toda la noche** he was rubbing it in all evening; **les refregó la derrota en sus narices** he really rubbed it in about the defeat

refregón *nm Fam (refregamiento)* scrubbing

refreír [56] *vt* (**a**) *(volver a freír)* to re-fry (**b**) *(freír en exceso)* to over-fry

refrenar 1 *vt* to curb, to restrain

2 **refrenarse** *vpr* to hold back, to restrain oneself

refrendar *vt* (**a**) *(aprobar)* to endorse, to approve (**b**) *(legalizar)* to endorse, to countersign

refrendo *nm* (**a**) *(aprobación)* endorsement, approval (**b**) *(firma)* countersignature

refrescante *adj* refreshing; **una bebida r.** a refreshing drink

refrescar [60] 1 *vt* (**a**) *(enfriar)* to refresh; *(bebidas)* to chill (**b**) *(conocimientos)* to brush up; **r. la memoria a alguien** to refresh sb's memory (**c**) *Informát* to refresh

2 *vi (bebida)* to be refreshing

3 *v impersonal* **esta noche refrescará** it will get cooler tonight

4 **refrescarse** *vpr* (**a**) *(enfriarse)* to cool down; **voy a darme una ducha para refrescarme** I'm going to have a shower to cool off (**b**) *(tomar aire fresco)* to get a breath of fresh air (**c**) *(mojarse con agua fría)* to splash oneself down (**d**) *Informát* to refresh

refresco *nm* (**a**) *(bebida)* soft drink; **un r. de naranja** an orangeade (**b**) *Mil* **de r.** new, fresh (**c**) *Informát* refresh ▸▸ ***r. de pantalla*** (screen) refresh

refresquería *nf CAm, Carib, Méx* = shop which sells soft drinks

refría *etc ver* **refreír**

refriega 1 *ver* **refregar**

2 *nf (lucha)* scuffle; *Mil* skirmish

refriegue *etc ver* **refregar**

refriera *etc ver* **refreír**

refrigeración *nf* (**a**) *(aire acondicionado)* air-conditioning (**b**) *(de alimentos)* refrigeration (**c**) *(de máquinas, motores)* cooling; **(sistema de) r.** cooling system ▸▸ ***r. por agua*** water-cooling; ***r. por aire*** air-cooling

refrigerado, -a *adj* (**a**) *(local)* air-conditioned (**b**) *(alimentos)* refrigerated (**c**) *(líquido, gas)* cooled

refrigerador, -ora 1 *adj (líquido, sistema)* cooling

2 *nm* (**a**) *(frigorífico)* refrigerator, fridge, *US* icebox (**b**) *(de máquinas, motores)* cooling system

3 *nf CAm, Perú* refrigerator, fridge, *US* icebox

refrigerante 1 *adj* (**a**) *(para alimentos)* refrigerating (**b**) *(para motores)* cooling

2 *nm (para motor)* coolant

refrigerar *vt* (**a**) *(local)* to air-condition (**b**) *(alimentos)* to refrigerate (**c**) *(máquina, motor)* to cool

refrigerio *nm* refreshments; **se servirá un r.** refreshments will be served

refrito, -a 1 *participio ver* **refreír**

2 *adj (frito de nuevo)* re-fried; *(demasiado frito)* over-fried

3 *nm* (**a**) *(sofrito)* = lightly fried onions, garlic and usually also tomato, used as a basis for sauces, stews etc (**b**) *Fam (cosa rehecha)* rehash; **es un r. de varias novelas** it's a rehash of various other novels

refucilo *nm RP* flash of lightning

refuerce *etc ver* **reforzar**

refuerzo 1 *ver* **reforzar**

2 *nm* (**a**) *(acción)* reinforcement (**b**) *(de tela, cuero)* backing (**c**) *Mil* **refuerzos** reinforcements; **soldados de r.** reinforcements (**d**) *RP (bocadillo)* filled roll

refugiado, -a 1 *adj* refugee

2 *nm,f* refugee ▸▸ ***r. político*** political refugee

refugiar 1 *vt* to give refuge to

2 **refugiarse** *vpr* to take refuge; **refugiarse de algo** to shelter from sth; **se refugió en la bebida** he took *o* sought refuge in drink

refugio *nm* (**a**) *(lugar)* shelter, refuge ▸▸ ***r. antiaéreo*** air-raid shelter; ***r. antinuclear*** nuclear bunker; ***r. atómico*** nuclear bunker; ***r. de montaña*** *(muy básico)* mountain shelter; *(albergue)* mountain refuge; ***r. subterráneo*** bunker, underground shelter (**b**) *(amparo, consuelo)* refuge, comfort; **la gente busca r. en la religión** people seek refuge in religion (**c**) *Aut* traffic island (**d**) ***r. fiscal*** tax shelter; ***r. tributario*** tax shelter

refulgencia *nf Literario* brilliance

refulgente *adj Literario* brilliant, refulgent

refulgir [24] *vi Literario* to shine brightly

refundición *nf* (**a**) *(de metales)* re-casting (**b**) *(unión)* merging, bringing together (**c**) *Lit* adaptation

refundir *vt* (**a**) *(fundir de nuevo)* to re-cast (**b**) *(unir)* to bring together (**c**) *Lit* to adapt (**d**) *CAm, Col, Méx, Perú Fam (extraviar)* to lose, to mislay

refunfuñar *vi* to grumble

refunfuñón, -ona 1 *adj* grumpy
2 *nm,f* grumbler
refusilo *nm RP* flash of lightning
refutable *adj* refutable
refutación *nf* refutation
refutar *vt* to refute
regadera *nf* (a) *(para regar)* watering can; EXPR *Esp Fam* **estar como una r.** to be as mad as a hatter (b) *Col, Méx, Ven (ducha)* shower
regadío *nm (sistema)* irrigation; **cultivos de r.** irrigated *o* irrigation crops; **tierras de r.** irrigated land
regaladamente *adv* **vivían r.** they had a comfortable *o* an easy life
regalado, -a *adj* (a) *(muy barato)* dirt-cheap; **precios regalados** giveaway prices
(b) *(como regalo)* **todos estos libros son regalados** all these books are presents *o* were given to me; **te lo doy r.** I'm giving it away to you; **no lo quiero ni r.** I wouldn't want it even if you were giving it away
(c) *(agradable)* comfortable, easy; **llevaba una existencia regalada** he led a very comfortable *o* easy life
(d) *Am Fam (muy fácil)* dead easy; **las pruebas que pone siempre son regaladas** the tests she sets are always dead easy
(e) *RP Fam (desprotegido)* **no aceptes trabajar sin contrato, porque quedás r.** don't agree to work without a contract, because that leaves you without a leg to stand on; **no tenían seguro, estaban muy regalados** they weren't insured, so they were very vulnerable; **no te metas por callejones oscuros, no andes regalada** don't put yourself at risk by going down dark alleyways
regalar 1 *vt* (a) *(dar) (de regalo)* to give *(as a present)*; *(gratis)* to give away; **¿qué le regalarás para Navidad?** what are you going to give *o* get her for Christmas?; **me regalaron un reloj para mi cumpleaños** I got a watch for my birthday; **si lo quieres, te lo regalo** if you'd like it, you can have it for free *o* I'll give it to you; **si compras dos, te regalan una** if you buy two, you get one free
(b) *(agasajar)* **r. a alguien con algo** to shower sb with sth; **les regalaron con muchas atenciones** they showered them with attentions; **esta música regala los oídos** this music is a joy to listen to
(c) *Andes, CAm, Carib, Méx (prestar)* to lend
(d) *Méx, RP (facilitar)* **el referí les regaló el triunfo** the referee handed them the victory on a plate; **ese profesor regala los exámenes** the exams that teacher sets are dead easy
2 **regalarse** *vpr* **me he regalado un viaje a París** I've treated myself to a trip to Paris
regalía *nf* (a) *(privilegio real)* royal prerogative (b) *CAm, Carib (regalo)* present

> **Falso amigo**: El sustantivo inglés **regalia** no es la traducción del español **regalía**. En inglés **regalia** significa "galas".

regaliz *nm* liquorice; **pastillas de r.** liquorice pastilles ►► ***r. de palo*** liquorice sticks
regalo *nm* (a) *(obsequio)* present, gift; *(en rifa)* prize; **r. de Navidad/de cumpleaños** Christmas/birthday present; **me hicieron muchos regalos para mi cumpleaños** I got lots of presents for my birthday; **por ese precio, es un auténtico r.** at that price, it's a real giveaway; **de r.** *(gratuito)* free; **compras tres y te dan uno de r.** if you buy three, you get one free
(b) *(placer)* joy, delight; **esa voz es un r. para los oídos** that voice is a delight to listen to
regalón, -ona *adj* (a) *CSur Fam (niño)* **el niño r. de su madre** the apple of his mother's eye (b) *RP (animal)* devoted
regalonear *vt CSur Fam* to pamper, to make a fuss of
regañadientes: a regañadientes *loc adv Fam* unwillingly, reluctantly
regañar 1 *vt (reprender)* to tell off; **me regañaron por acabarme toda la cerveza** I got a row for finishing all the beer
2 *vi Esp (pelearse)* to fall out; **ha regañado con su hermana** he's fallen out with his sister; **están regañados** they've fallen out
regañina *nf (reprimenda)* telling-off; **me echaron una r. por volver a casa tarde** I got told off for coming home late
regaño *nm* telling-off
regañón, -ona 1 *adj* **es muy r.** he's always telling people off for nothing
2 *nm,f* **es un r.** he's always telling people off for nothing
regar [43] *vt* (a) *(con agua) (planta, campo)* to water; *(calle)* to hose down; **regaron la comida con un buen vino tinto** they washed down the meal with a good red wine
(b) *(sujeto: río)* to flow through; **el río que riega la región** the river which flows through the region
(c) *(sujeto: vasos sanguíneos)* to supply with blood; **esta arteria riega de sangre los pulmones** this artery supplies blood to the lungs
(d) *(desparramar)* to sprinkle, to scatter; **regaron el suelo de papeles** they scattered papers all over the floor
(e) *Méx Fam* **regarla** *(meter la pata)* to put one's foot in it
regata *nf* (a) *Náut* regatta, yacht race (b) *(reguera)* irrigation channel
regate *nm Dep* sidestep; **hizo un r. al defensa** he sidestepped the defender
regateador, -ora *nm,f (con precios)* haggler
regatear 1 *vt* (a) *(escatimar)* to be sparing with; **no ha regateado esfuerzos** he has spared no effort (b) *Dep* to beat, to sidestep; **regateó al portero y marcó** he rounded the keeper and scored (c) *(precio)* to haggle over
2 *vi* (a) *(negociar el precio)* to barter, to haggle (b) *Náut* to race
regateo *nm* bartering, haggling
regatista *nmf Dep* participant *(in a regatta or yacht race)*
regato *nm* brook, rivulet
regatón *nm* tip, ferrule
regazo *nm* lap
regencia *nf* (a) *(reinado)* regency (b) *(administración)* running, management
regeneración *nf* (a) *(recuperación, restablecimiento)* regeneration (b) *(reciclado)* recycling (c) *(de delincuente, degenerado)* reform
regeneracionismo *nm Hist* regenerationism, = Spanish 19th century political reform movement
regenerar 1 *vt* (a) *(recuperar, restablecer)* to regenerate (b) *(reciclar)* to recycle (c) *(delincuente, degenerado)* to reform
2 **regenerarse** *vpr* (a) *(recuperarse, restablecerse)* to regenerate (b) *(delincuente, degenerado)* to reform
regenerativo, -a *adj* regenerative
regenta *nf* wife of the regent
regentar *vt* (a) *(país)* to run, to govern (b) *(negocio)* to run, to manage (c) *(puesto)* to hold *(temporarily)*
regente 1 *adj* regent
2 *nmf* (a) *(de un país)* regent (b) *(administrador) (de tienda)* manager; *(de colegio)* governor (c) *Méx (alcalde)* mayor, *f* mayoress
reggae ['rriɣi, 'rreɣi] *nm* reggae
regicida *nmf* regicide *(person)*
regicidio *nm* regicide *(crime)*
regidor, -ora *nm,f* (a) *Teatro* stage manager; *Cine & TV* assistant director (b) *(concejal)* councillor
régimen *(pl* **regímenes**) *nm* (a) *(sistema político)* regime; **r. parlamentario** parliamentary system
(b) *(normas)* rules; **alojarse en un hotel en r. de media pensión** to stay at a hotel (on) half-board; **una cárcel en r. abierto** an open prison; **estar en r. abierto** *(preso)* to be allowed to leave the prison during the day
(c) *(dieta)* diet; **estar a r.** to be on a diet; **ponerse a r.** to go on a diet; **seguir un r.** to follow a diet ►► ***r. de adelgazamiento*** slimming diet; ***r. alimenticio*** diet
(d) *(rutina)* pattern ►► ***r. climático*** climate; ***r. hidrológico*** rainfall pattern; ***r. de lluvias*** rainfall pattern; ***r. de marea*** tide range; ***r. de vida*** lifestyle
(e) *Ling* government
(f) *Tec (de motor)* speed
regimiento *nm* (a) *Mil* regiment (b) *(multitud)* army; **en su casa cabe un r.** you could fit an army in her house
regio, -a *adj* (a) *(real)* royal (b) *Andes, RP (genial)* great, fabulous
regiomontano, -a 1 *adj* of/from Monterrey *(Mexico)*
2 *nm,f* person from Monterrey *(Mexico)*
región *nf* (a) *(área)* region (b) *(administrativa)* region (c) *Mil* district ►► ***r. aérea*** aerial zone; ***r. militar*** military zone; ***r. naval*** naval zone (d) *Anat* region, area
regional *adj* regional
regionalismo *nm* (a) *(ideología)* regionalism (b) *Ling* regionalism
regionalista 1 *adj* regionalist
2 *nmf* regionalist
regionalización *nf* regionalization
regionalizar [14] *vt* to regionalize
regir [55] 1 *vt* (a) *(gobernar)* to rule, to govern (b) *(administrar)* to run, to manage (c) *Ling* to take; **este verbo rige la preposición "de"** this verb takes the preposition "de" (d) *(determinar)* to govern; **las leyes que rigen los intercambios comerciales** the laws governing trade; **las normas básicas que rigen la convivencia en una sociedad**

the basic rules governing how people live together in a society

2 *vi* (**a**) *(ley)* to be in force; **rige una moratoria sobre la caza de ballenas** a moratorium on whaling is in force; **rige el toque de queda en la zona** a curfew is in force in the area; **la ley regirá con efecto retroactivo** the law will apply retrospectively (**b**) *(funcionar)* to work; **este reloj no rige** this watch doesn't work (**c**) *Fam (persona)* **la abuela ya no rige** grandma has gone a bit gaga

3 **regirse** *vpr* **regirse por** to be guided by; **su gestión se rige por criterios de eficacia** his approach to management is guided by *o* based on the principle of efficiency; **los valores por los cuales se rige la magistratura** the values which guide judges; **las votaciones se rigen por el criterio de la unanimidad** voting is governed by *o* based on the principle of unanimity

registrado, -a *adj* (**a**) *(grabado, anotado)* recorded (**b**) *(patentado, inscrito)* registered (**c**) *Am (certificado)* registered

registrador, -ora 1 *adj* registering; **un barómetro r.** a recording barometer; **una caja registradora** a cash register

2 *nm,f* registrar ▸▸ ***r. de la propiedad*** land registrar, recorder of deeds

registradora *nf Am* cash register

registrar 1 *vt* (**a**) *(zona, casa, persona)* to search; **registraban a todos los que entraban al estadio** everybody entering the stadium was searched; EXPR *Fam* **a mí, que me registren** don't look at me!

(**b**) *(datos, hechos)* to register, to record; **la empresa ha registrado un aumento de las ventas** the company has recorded an increase in sales, the company's sales have gone up; **esta enciclopedia registra muchos términos técnicos** this encyclopedia contains a lot of technical terms

(**c**) *(grabar)* to record

(**d**) *Am (certificar)* to register

2 **registrarse** *vpr* (**a**) *(producirse)* **se ha registrado un aumento de los accidentes laborales** there has been an increase in accidents at work; **no se registraron víctimas mortales** there were no fatalities; **se registró una inflación superior a la prevista** the inflation figures were higher than predicted; **se registró un temblor de 7 grados en la escala de Richter** an earth tremor measuring 7 on the Richter Scale was recorded

(**b**) *(en censo)* to register; *(en hotel)* to check in

registro *nm* (**a**) *(oficina)* registry (office) ▸▸ ***r. catastral*** land register; ***r. civil*** registry (office); ***r. de comercio*** trade register office; ***r. mercantil*** trade register office; ***r. parroquial*** parish register; ***r. de la propiedad*** land registry office; ***r. de la propiedad industrial*** trademark registry office; ***r. de la propiedad intelectual*** copyright registry office

(**b**) *(libro)* register; **inscribir a alguien en el r. civil** to register sb in the register of births, marriages and deaths ▸▸ *Com* ***r. de caja*** cash book

(**c**) *(inscripción)* registration; **llevar el r. de algo** to keep a record of sth

(**d**) *(inspección)* search; **una orden de r.** a search warrant; **procedieron al r. de la fábrica** they carried out a search of the factory; **efectuaron un r. domiciliario** they searched his/her/*etc* home

(**e**) *(de libro)* bookmark

(**f**) *Informát (en base de datos)* record

(**g**) *Ling* register

(**h**) *Mús (notas)* register

(**i**) *Mús (en órgano)* stop, register; *Fig* **tocar todos los registros** to pull out all the stops

(**j**) *Tec (abertura)* inspection hatch

(**k**) *Tec (llave)* stopcock

regla *nf* (**a**) *(para medir)* ruler, rule ▸▸ ***r. de cálculo*** slide rule

(**b**) *(norma)* rule; **las reglas del juego** the rules of the game; **en r.** in order; **ir en contra de las reglas** to be against the rules; **poner algo en r.** to put sth in order; **por r. general** as a rule, generally; **salirse de la r.** to overstep the mark *o* line ▸▸ ***r. de oro*** golden rule; ***reglas ortográficas*** spelling rules

(**c**) *Mat* **las cuatro reglas** addition, subtraction, multiplication and division ▸▸ ***r. de tres*** rule of three; EXPR *Fam* **por la misma r. de tres...** by the same token...

(**d**) *Fam (menstruación)* period; **tener la r.** to have one's period; **le ha venido la r. hoy** her period started today

(**e**) *Rel* rule

reglaje *nm (de motor)* tuning; *(de suspensión)* adjustment; **los faros necesitan un r.** the headlights need adjusting

reglamentación *nf* (**a**) *(acción)* regulation (**b**) *(reglas)* rules, regulations

reglamentar *vt* to regulate

reglamentario, -a *adj* (**a**) *(arma, uniforme)* regulation; **el tiempo r.** normal time (**b**) *Der* statutory

reglamento *nm (normas)* regulations, rules; **balón de r.** *(en fútbol)* regulation football

reglar *vt* to regulate

regleta *nf (para enchufes)* multiple socket adaptor

regocijar 1 *vt* to delight

2 **regocijarse** *vpr* to rejoice (**de** *o* **con** in)

regocijo *nm* joy, delight; **recibieron la noticia con r.** they received the news with delight

regodearse *vpr* to take delight (**en** *o* **con** in); **se regodea en** *o* **con las desgracias ajenas** he takes delight in other people's misfortunes

regodeo *nm* delight; **se equivocó de nombres, para r. de todos** he mixed up the names, much to everyone's delight

regoldar [6] *vi* to belch

regordete *adj* chubby, tubby

regrabable *adj Informát* rewritable

regresar 1 *vi (yendo)* to go back, to return; *(viniendo)* to come back, to return; **¿cuándo regresará?** when will she be back?; **regresó a su casa después de dos meses en el extranjero** she returned home after two months abroad

2 *vt Andes, CAm, Carib, Méx* (**a**) *(objeto) (devolver)* to give back (**b**) *(persona) (mandar de vuelta)* to send back

3 **regresarse** *vpr Andes, CAm, Carib, Méx (yendo)* to go back, to return; *(viniendo)* to come back, to return

> **Falso amigo**: El verbo inglés **to regress** no es la traducción del español **regresar**. En inglés **to regress** significa "involucionar, sufrir una regresión".

regresión *nf* (**a**) *(de economía, exportaciones)* downturn (**b**) *(de epidemia)* regression (**c**) *Psi (en el tiempo)* regression

regresivo, -a *adj* regressive

regreso *nm* (**a**) *(a un lugar)* return; **estar de r.** to be back; **¿conoces el camino de r.?** do you know the way back?; **durante el r.** on the way back; **os llamaré al r. de mis vacaciones** I'll ring you when I'm back from my *Br* holiday *o US* vacation; **el r. de un país a la democracia** a country's return to democracy (**b**) *Andes, CAm, Carib, Méx (de dinero, producto)* return

regué *etc ver* **regar**

regüelda *etc ver* **regoldar**

regüeldo *nm* belch

reguera *nf* irrigation ditch

reguero *nm* (**a**) *(rastro) (de sangre, agua)* trickle; *(de harina, arena)* trail; **el huracán dejó tras de sí un r. de muertes** the hurricane left a trail of fatalities in its wake; EXPR **correr como un r. de pólvora** to spread like wildfire (**b**) *(canal)* irrigation ditch

regulable *adj* adjustable

regulación *nf* (**a**) *(de actividad, economía)* regulation ▸▸ ***r. de empleo*** workforce reduction (**b**) *(de nacimientos, tráfico)* control (**c**) *(de mecanismo)* adjustment

regulado, -a *adj (controlado)* regulated, controlled

regulador, -ora 1 *adj* regulatory; **un organismo r. de la competencia** a body that regulates competition; **un acuerdo r. del comercio mundial** an agreement regulating world trade

2 *nm* regulator, controller ▸▸ ***r. de flujo*** flow regulator agent; ***r. de intensidad*** *(de la luz)* dimmer; *Aut* ***r. de velocidad*** cruise control

regular[1] 1 *adj* (**a**) *(uniforme)* regular; **de un modo r.** regularly; **hay un servicio de autobús r. a la capital** there is a regular bus service to the capital (**b**) *(mediocre)* average; **una actuación r.** an undistinguished *o* a rather average performance (**c**) *(normal)* normal, usual; *(de tamaño)* medium; **por lo r.** as a rule, generally (**d**) *Gram* regular (**e**) *Geom* regular (**f**) *Rel* regular

2 *nm Mil* regular

3 *adv (no muy bien)* so-so; **lleva unos días r., tiene un poco de fiebre** she's been so-so the last few days, she's got a bit of a temperature; **me encuentro r.** I feel a bit under the weather; **¿qué tal el concierto? – r.** how was the concert? – so-so *o* nothing special

regular[2] *vt* (**a**) *(actividad, economía)* to regulate; **la normativa regula estos casos** the regulations govern these cases (**b**) *(mecanismo)* to adjust; *(temperatura)* to regulate, to control; *(tráfico)* to control; **las presas regulan el cauce del río** the dams regulate the flow of the river

regularidad *nf* regularity; **con r.** regularly

regularización *nf* (**a**) *(normalización)* return to normal (**b**) *(legalización)* regularization

regularizar [14] 1 *vt* (**a**) *(devolver a la normalidad)* to get back to normal (**b**) *(legalizar)* to regularize
2 **regularizarse** *vpr (volver a la normalidad)* to return to normal
regularmente *adv* (**a**) *(frecuentemente)* regularly (**b**) *(normalmente)* normally, usually
regulativo, -a *adj* regulative
regurgitación *nf* regurgitation
regurgitar 1 *vt* to regurgitate
2 *vi* to regurgitate
regusto *nm* (**a**) *(sabor)* aftertaste; **esa salsa deja un r. ácido** that sauce has an acidic aftertaste (**b**) *(sensación)* aftertaste; **sus palabras me dejaron un r. amargo** her words left a bitter taste in my mouth (**c**) *(semejanza, aire)* flavour; **la decoración tiene un claro r. barroco** there's an obvious baroque flavour to the décor
rehabilitación *nf* (**a**) *(de toxicómano, delincuente)* rehabilitation (**b**) *(de órgano lesionado)* rehabilitation (**c**) *(en un puesto)* reinstatement (**d**) *(de local, edificio)* refurbishment (**e**) *(de reputación)* restoration
rehabilitador, -ora 1 *adj* **médico r.** rehabilitation doctor
2 *nm,f* rehabilitation doctor
rehabilitar *vt* (**a**) *(toxicómano, delincuente)* to rehabilitate (**b**) *(órgano lesionado)* to rehabilitate (**c**) *(en un puesto)* to reinstate (**d**) *(local, edificio)* to refurbish (**e**) *(reputación)* to restore
rehacer [33] 1 *vt* (**a**) *(volver a hacer)* to redo, to do again (**b**) *(reconstruir)* to rebuild; **tuvo que r. su vida** he had to rebuild his life
2 **rehacerse** *vpr* (**a**) *(recuperarse)* to recuperate, to recover; **tardó en rehacerse de la pérdida de su mujer** he took a long time to recover from the loss of his wife (**b**) *(recuperar la compostura)* to recover; **le costó rehacerse del susto** it took him a long time to get over the shock
rehecho, -a *participio ver* **rehacer**
rehén (*pl* **rehenes**) *nm* hostage
rehíce *etc ver* **rehacer**
rehiciera *etc ver* **rehacer**
rehilamiento *nm Ling* = pronunciation in Argentina and Uruguay of Spanish "ll" and "y" as [ʒ], the voiced fricative of "pleasure"
rehilar *vt Ling* = in Argentina and Uruguay, to pronounce Spanish "ll" and "y" as [ʒ]
rehilete *nm* (**a**) *(flechilla)* dart (**b**) *Taurom* banderilla (**c**) *(dicho malicioso)* dig, gibe (**d**) *Méx (juguete)* (toy) windmill
rehiletero *nm Taurom* banderillero, = bullfighter's assistant who sticks "banderillas" into the bull
rehogar [38] *vt* = to fry over a low heat
rehuir [34] *vt* to avoid
rehumedecer [46] *vt* to soak
rehusar 1 *vt* to refuse; **rehusó la invitación** he turned down the invitation; **rehusó colaborar con nosotros** she refused to work with us
2 *vi* to refuse
rehuya *etc ver* **rehuir**
rehuyera *etc ver* **rehuir**
reidor, -ora *adj* **es una chica reidora** she's always laughing, she laughs a lot
Reikiavik *n* Reykjavik
reimplantar *vt* (**a**) *(reintroducir)* to reintroduce (**b**) *Med* to implant again
reimportación *nf* reimporting
reimportar *vt* to reimport
reimpresión *nf* (**a**) *(tirada)* reprint (**b**) *(acción)* reprinting
reimpreso, -a *adj* reprinted
reimprimir *vt* to reprint
reina 1 *adj (prueba, etapa)* blue-ribbon
2 *nf* (**a**) *(monarca)* queen ►► ***la r. de las fiestas*** = young woman chosen each year to preside at the various local celebrations, ≃ carnival queen; ***la r. madre*** the Queen Mother (**b**) *(en ajedrez)* queen (**c**) *(en naipes)* queen (**d**) *(abeja)* queen (**e**) *(apelativo)* love, darling; **ven aquí, mi r.** come here, princess
reinado *nm* reign
reinante *adj* (**a**) *(monarquía, persona)* reigning, ruling (**b**) *(viento, ambiente, silencio)* prevailing
reinar *vi* (**a**) *(gobernar)* to reign (**b**) *(caos, confusión, pánico)* to reign; **el silencio reinó en la sala durante varios minutos** the hall fell completely silent for several minutes; **en esta casa reina la alegría** everyone is always happy in this house (**c**) *(triunfar)* **el bien reinó sobre el mal** good triumphed over evil
reincidencia *nf (en un vicio)* relapse; *(en un delito)* reoffending, recidivism
reincidente 1 *adj* **un joven r.** a young reoffender; **un comportamiento r.** recidivist behaviour
2 *nmf* reoffender, recidivist
reincidir *vi (en falta, error)* to relapse (**en** into); *(en delito)* to reoffend; **r. en un delito** to reoffend, to commit the same crime again
reincorporación *nf* return (**a** to)
reincorporar 1 *vt (a puesto)* to reinstate (**a** in)
2 **reincorporarse** *vpr* **¿cuándo te reincorporas?** *(al trabajo)* when will you be coming back *o* returning to work?; *(al ejército)* when will you be returning from leave?; **se reincorporó al equipo tras una larga lesión** he returned to the team after a long lay-off through injury
reineta *nf* = type of apple with tart flavour, used for cooking and eating
reingresar *vi* to return (**en** to); **reingresó en el servicio tras unas largas vacaciones** he returned to work after a long *Br* holiday *o US* vacation; **el paciente volvió a r. tras un fallo cardiaco** the patient was readmitted to hospital after suffering heart failure
reinicializar [14], **reiniciar** *vt Informát (ordenador)* to reboot, to restart; *(impresora)* to reset
reino *nm* (**a**) *(territorio, estado)* kingdom; **el r. de los cielos** the kingdom of Heaven ►► *Hist* ***r. de taifa*** = independent Muslim kingdom in Iberian peninsula; ***el R. Unido (de Gran Bretaña e Irlanda del Norte)*** the United Kingdom (of Great Britain and Northern Ireland) (**b**) *Biol* kingdom ►► ***r. animal*** animal kingdom; ***r. mineral*** mineral kingdom; ***r. vegetal*** vegetable kingdom (**c**) *(ámbito, dominio)* realm
reinona *nf Fam* queen
reinserción *nf* **la r. (laboral) de los desempleados de larga duración** getting the long-term unemployed back to work; **r. (social)** social rehabilitation, reintegration into society
reinsertado, -a *nm,f* former criminal
reinsertar *vt* (**a**) *(en sociedad)* to reintegrate, to rehabilitate; **el objetivo del plan es r. a los terroristas en la sociedad** the aim of the plan is to reintegrate terrorists into society; **tenemos que r. a los parados de larga duración** we have to get the long-term unemployed back to work (**b**) *(en ranura)* to reinsert
reinstalación *nf* (**a**) *(en lugar)* reinstallation (**b**) *(en puesto)* reinstatement
reinstalar *vt* (**a**) *(en lugar)* to reinstall (**b**) *(en puesto)* to reinstate
reinstaurar *vt* to re-establish
reintegración *nf* (**a**) *(a puesto)* reinstatement (**a** in) (**b**) *(de gastos)* reimbursement, refund; *(de préstamo)* repayment
reintegrar 1 *vt* (**a**) *(a un puesto)* to reinstate (**a** in) (**b**) *(gastos)* to reimburse, to refund; *(préstamo)* to repay (**c**) *(documento)* to put a fiscal stamp on
2 **reintegrarse** *vpr* to return (**a** to); **se reintegró a la vida laboral** she returned to work, she found a new job
reintegro *nm* (**a**) *(a un puesto)* reinstatement (**b**) *(de gastos)* reimbursement, refund; *(de préstamo)* repayment; *(en banco)* withdrawal (**c**) *(en lotería)* **le tocó el r.** he won back the price of his ticket
reinversión *nf* reinvestment
reinvertir [63] *vt* to reinvest
reír [56] 1 *vi* to laugh; EXPR **r. a mandíbula batiente** to laugh one's head off; EXPR *Irónico* **no me hagas r.: ¿se ha puesto a dieta? – ¡no me hagas r.!** has she gone on a diet? – don't make me laugh!; PROV **quien ríe el último ríe mejor** he who laughs last laughs longest
2 *vt* to laugh at; **¡no le rías las gracias!** don't laugh at his antics!
3 **reírse** *vpr* to laugh (**de** at); **se ríe por cualquier cosa** he'll laugh at anything; **se ríe de sus propios chistes** she laughs at her own jokes; **no te rías, es un asunto muy serio** don't laugh, it's a very serious matter; **se rió en mi propia cara** she laughed in my face; **reírse por lo bajo** to snicker, to snigger; **¡me río yo de los sistemas de seguridad!** I laugh at security systems!, security systems are no obstacle to me!; **sí, tú ríete de lo feo que es, pero es millonario** you can laugh as much as you like at how ugly he is, but the fact is he's a millionaire
reiteración *nf* reiteration, repetition
reiteradamente *adv* repeatedly
reiterado, -a *adj* repeated; **te lo he dicho reiteradas veces** I've told you repeatedly
reiterar 1 *vt* to reiterate, to repeat
2 **reiterarse** *vpr* **reiterarse en** to reaffirm; **me reitero en lo dicho** I stand by what I have said
reiterativo, -a *adj* repetitive

reivindicación *nf* (a) *(acción)* **estamos a la espera de la r. del atentado** no one has yet claimed responsibility for the attack (b) *(resultado)* claim, demand; **el salario mínimo es una r. histórica de los sindicatos** a minimum wage is one of the trade unions' traditional demands; **el país ha abandonado sus reivindicaciones territoriales** the country has renounced its territorial claims ►► ***r. salarial*** pay claim

reivindicar [60] 1 *vt* (a) *(derechos, salario)* to claim, to demand; **reivindican el derecho a sindicarse** they are demanding the right to join a union (b) *(atentado, secuestro)* to claim responsibility for; **la banda reivindicó el atentado** the group claimed responsibility for the attack (c) *(herencia, territorio)* to lay claim to (d) *(reputación, memoria)* to defend

2 **reivindicarse** *vprAm* (a) *(recuperarse)* to vindicate oneself; **en el próximo partido, el equipo buscará reivindicarse** in the next game, the team will be looking to restore its reputation; **reivindicarse con alguien** to restore one's reputation with sb (b) *(responsabilizarse de)* to claim responsibility for; **la banda se reivindicó el atentado** the group claimed responsibility for the attack

reivindicativo, -a *adj* **dio un discurso r.** he gave a speech in which he made a series of demands; **jornada reivindicativa** day of protest; **plataforma reivindicativa** pressure group

reja *nf* (a) *(barrotes)* bars; *(en el suelo)* grating; *(rejilla en ventana)* grille; EXPR **estar entre rejas** to be behind bars (b) *(del arado)* ploughshare

rejego, -a *adj Méx Fam (terco)* pigheaded

rejilla *nf* (a) *(enrejado)* grid, grating; *(de ventana)* grille; *(de ventilación)* grating; *(de cocina)* grill *(on stove)*; *(de horno)* gridiron; *(de confesionario)* screen ►► *Aut* ***r. del radiador*** radiator grille

(b) *(celosía)* lattice window/screen

(c) *(en sillas, muebles)* **una silla de r.** a chair with a wickerwork lattice seat

(d) *(para equipaje)* luggage rack

(e) *TV* **r. (de programación)** programme schedule

rejo *nm* (a) *Zool* sting (b) *Bot* radicle (c) *Cuba, Ven (cuero)* = strip of raw leather

rejón *nm Taurom* = pike used by mounted bullfighter

rejoneador, -ora *nm,f Taurom* = bullfighter on horseback who uses the "rejón"

rejonear *Taurom* 1 *vt* = to wound with a "rejón"

2 *vi* = to fight the bulls on horseback using a "rejón"

rejoneo *nm Taurom* = use of the "rejón"

rejuntarse *vpr Fam (pareja)* to shack up together; **r. con alguien** to shack up with sb

rejuvenecedor, -ora *adj (efecto)* rejuvenating

rejuvenecer [46] 1 *vt* to rejuvenate; **esa ropa te rejuvenece mucho** those clothes make you look a lot younger

2 *vi* **las vacaciones rejuvenecen** holidays rejuvenate you; **la cirugía estética rejuvenece** plastic surgery makes you look younger

3 **rejuvenecerse** *vpr* to be rejuvenated; **desde que se afeitó se ha rejuvenecido diez años** shaving his beard off has made him look ten years younger

rejuvenecimiento *nm* rejuvenation; **el r. de la población** the drop in the average age of the population

relación 1 *nf* (a) *(nexo)* relation, connection; **con r. a, en r. con** in relation to, with regard to; **no hay ninguna r. entre los dos secuestros** the two kidnappings are unrelated *o* unconnected; **guardar r. con algo** to be related to sth; **no guardar r. con algo** to bear no relation to sth; **r. calidad-precio** value for money

(b) *(comunicación, trato)* relations, relationship; **mantener relaciones con alguien** to keep in touch with sb; **tener** *o* **mantener buenas relaciones con alguien** to be on good terms with sb ►► ***relaciones comerciales*** *(vínculos)* business links; *(comercio)* trade; ***relaciones diplomáticas*** diplomatic relations; **han roto las relaciones diplomáticas** they have broken off diplomatic relations; ***relaciones internacionales*** international relations; ***relaciones laborales*** industrial relations; ***r. de pareja:*** **los problemas de las relaciones de pareja** relationship problems; **dice que no necesita de la r. de pareja** she says she doesn't need to be in a relationship with anybody; ***relaciones de parentesco*** kinship; ***relaciones personales*** personal relationships; ***relaciones públicas*** *(actividad)* public relations, PR

(c) *(lista)* list

(d) *(descripción)* account

(e) *(informe)* report

(f) **relaciones** *(noviazgo)* relationship; **llevan cinco años de relaciones** they've been going out together for five years; **un cursillo sobre las relaciones de pareja** a course on being in a relationship; **relaciones prematrimoniales** premarital sex; **mantener relaciones prematrimoniales** to have premarital sex; **relaciones sexuales** sexual relations

(g) **relaciones** *(contactos)* contacts, connections; **tener buenas relaciones** to be well connected

(h) *Mat* ratio

2 *nmf inv* ***relaciones públicas*** *(persona)* public relations officer, PR officer

relacionado, -a *adj* (a) *(emparentado)* related; **r. con** related to, connected with (b) *(concerniente)* concerning, regarding; **le interesa todo lo r. con el calentamiento global** he's interested in anything to do with global warming

relacional *adj* relational

relacionar 1 *vt* (a) *(vincular)* to relate (**con** to), to connect (**con** with); **estar bien relacionado** to be well connected; **la policía relacionó la explosión con las protestas contra los experimentos con animales** the police linked the explosion to the protests against animal experiments (b) *(enumerar)* to list, to enumerate

2 **relacionarse** *vpr (alternar)* to mix (**con** with); **no se relacionaba con los lugareños** he didn't have anything to do with the locals

relacionista *nmf Andes, RP* public relations officer

relajación *nf*, **relajamiento** *nm* (a) *(de tensión)* relaxation; **la r. de un músculo** the relaxation of a muscle (b) *(de severidad)* relaxation; **la r. de la moral** the decline in moral standards

relajadamente *adv* relaxedly

relajado, -a 1 *adj* (a) *(tranquilo)* relaxed (b) *RP Fam (picante)* dirty, crude; *(grosero)* crude; **me hace ponerme roja, es muy r.** he makes me blush, he's so crude (c) *RP Fam (indisciplinado)* lax; **mi casa está hecha un desastre, ando muy relajada** my house is a complete mess, I've let things slip

2 *nm,f RP Fam* **es un r., le dice cosas a todas las mujeres que pasan** he's really crude, he makes lewd remarks to any woman that goes by

relajamiento = **relajación**

relajante 1 *adj* relaxing

2 *nm* relaxant

relajar 1 *vt* (a) *(distender)* to relax; **una ducha te relajará** a shower will relax you *o* help you relax (b) *(hacer menos estricto)* to relax (c) *PRico (burlarse de)* to make fun of, to mock (d) *RP (rezongar)* to scold, to tell off; **me fui porque se pasaba relajándome** I left him because he was always pulling me to pieces; **su madre descubrió el secreto y la relajó toda** her mother discovered the secret and gave her an almighty row

2 **relajarse** *vpr* (a) *(distenderse)* to relax; **siéntate y relájate** sit down and relax (b) *(hacerse menos estricto)* **se han relajado las restricciones a la inmigración** immigration restrictions have been relaxed (c) *RP (desordenarse)* to get out of hand; **en cuanto la maestra sale del salón, se relajan** as soon as the teacher leaves the room, they go wild

relajo *nm* (a) *Esp (descanso)* rest; **pasamos unos días de r. en la playa** we had a restful few days at the seaside

(b) *Am Fam (alboroto)* **se armó un r.** there was an almighty row; **esta mesa es un r.** this table is a complete mess; **tiene un r. en la cabeza** he doesn't know whether he's coming or going; EXPR **r. pero con orden** it's OK to be relaxed about things, but only up to a point

(c) *Méx, RP (complicación)* nuisance, hassle; **aquí hacer cualquier trámite es un r.** going through any official procedure here is a hassle

(d) *CAm, Carib, Méx (broma)* joke; **de** *o* **por r.** as a joke; *Méx* **echar r.** to fool around

relamer 1 *vt* to lick repeatedly

2 **relamerse** *vpr* (a) *(persona)* to lick one's lips; **relamerse de gusto** to smack one's lips; **se relamía de gusto al pensar en...** he savoured the thought of... (b) *(animal)* to lick its chops

relamido, -a *adj* prim and proper

relámpago *nm (descarga)* flash of lightning; *(destello)* flash; **hubo muchos relámpagos** there was a lot of lightning; **un viaje r.** a quick trip; **una visita r.** a flying visit; EXPR **pasar como un r.: el coche pasó como un r.** the car flashed *o* zoomed past; **el Papa pasó por la ciudad como un r.** the Pope zoomed through the city

relampagueante *adj* flashing

relampaguear 1 *v impersonal* **relampagueó** lightning flashed

2 *vi* to flash

relampagueo *nm* (a) *Meteo* lightning (b) *(destello)* flashing

relanzamiento *nm* relaunch

relanzar [14] *vt* to relaunch

relatar *vt (suceso)* to relate, to recount; *(historia)* to tell

relatista *nmf Ecuad* short story writer

relativamente *adv* relatively

relatividad *nf* relativity

relativismo *nm* relativism

relativista 1 *adj* relativistic
2 *nmf* relativist

relativizar [14] *vt* to play down

relativo, -a 1 *adj* (a) *(no absoluto)* relative; **mayoría relativa** relative majority; **todo es r.** it's all relative; **su estudio tiene un r. valor científico** her study's scientific value is relative
(b) *(relacionado, tocante)* **r. a** relating to; **un debate r. al problema del desempleo** a debate on the problem of unemployment; **el precio debería ser r. a la calidad** the price should be in proportion to the quality; **en lo r. a...** regarding..., in relation to...
(c) *Gram (pronombre, adjetivo, adverbio)* relative
(d) *Gram (oración)* relative
2 *nm Gram* relative

relato *nm (exposición)* account, report; *(cuento)* tale, story; **hizo un r. de su viaje** she gave an account of her trip

relator *nm* (a) *Pol* rapporteur (b) *RP (comentarista)* commentator

relave *nm Chile* tailings

relax *nm inv* (a) *(relajación)* relaxation (b) *(sección de periódico)* personal services section

relé *nm Elec* relay ►► ***r. fotoeléctrico*** photoelectric relay

releer [37] *vt* to re-read

relegación *nf* relegation

relegar [38] *vt* to relegate (**a** to); **r. algo al olvido** to banish sth from one's mind; **fue relegado al olvido** it was consigned to oblivion; **r. algo a segundo plano** to push sth into the background

relente *nm* (night) dew

relevamiento *nm RP (de datos, información)* collection

relevancia *nf* importance

> **Falso amigo**: El sustantivo inglés **relevance** no es la traducción del español **relevancia**. En inglés **relevance** significa "pertinencia".

relevante *adj* outstanding, important

> **Falso amigo**: El adjetivo inglés **relevant** no es la traducción del español **relevante**. En inglés **relevant** significa "pertinente" o "correspondiente".

relevar 1 *vt* (a) *(sustituir)* to relieve, to take over from; *(en deporte)* to substitute; **el presidente lo relevó por una mujer** the president replaced him with a woman; **los bomberos recién llegados relevaron a sus agotados compañeros** the firemen who had just arrived relieved *o* took over from their exhausted colleagues; **¿quién lo va a r. cuando se jubile?** who's going to take over from him when he retires?
(b) *(destituir)* to dismiss (**de** from), to relieve (**de** of); **lo relevaron de la presidencia del partido** they dismissed him as leader of the party
(c) *(eximir)* to free (**de** from)
(d) *(en relevos)* to take over from
2 **relevarse** *vpr (turnarse)* to take turns; **se relevan en el cuidado de los niños** they take turns looking after the children

relevista *nmf Dep* relay runner

relevo *nm* (a) *(sustitución, cambio)* change; **tomar el r.** to take over; **el r. de la guardia** the changing of the guard
(b) *(sustituto, grupo)* relief; **el r. del presidente estuvo presente en la reunión** the person who was taking over from the president was present at the meeting
(c) **relevos** *(carrera)* relay (race); **el r. jamaicano** the Jamaican relay team; **tomar el r.** *(de atleta)* to take the baton; **España tomó el r. de Francia como principal destino turístico** Spain took over from *o* replaced France as the most popular tourist destination

releyera *etc ver* **releer**

relicario *nm* (a) *Rel* reliquary (b) *(estuche)* locket

relieve *nm* (a) *Geog* terrain; **una región con un r. muy accidentado** a region with very rugged terrain (b) *Arte* **alto r.** high relief; **bajo r.** bas-relief; **en r.** in relief (c) *(elevación)* **la pieza tiene un centímetro de r.** the part protrudes by a centimetre (d) *(importancia)* importance; **de r.** important; **para dar r. al acontecimiento...** to lend importance to the event...; **poner de r.** to underline, to highlight

religión *nf* religion; **la r. judía/musulmana** the Jewish/Muslim religion

religiosamente *adv* religiously; **paga r. sus facturas** he pays his bills religiously

religiosidad *nf* religiousness; **con r.** religiously; **cumple con r. su horario** she sticks religiously to her working hours

religioso, -a 1 *adj* religious
2 *nm,f (monje)* monk; *(monja)* nun

relinchar *vi* to neigh, to whinny

relincho *nm* neigh

reliquia *nf (restos)* relic; *(familiar)* heirloom; **esta costumbre es una r. de la Edad Media** this custom is a relic from the Middle Ages; *Fam Hum* **esta computadora es una r.** this computer is a museum piece

rellano *nm* (a) *(de escalera)* landing (b) *(de terreno)* shelf

rellenar *vt* (a) *(volver a llenar)* to refill; **rellenaron el agujero con cemento** they filled the hole back up with cement (b) *(documento, formulario)* to fill in *o* out (c) *(pollo)* to stuff; *(tarta, pastel)* to fill; **rellenó los canelones de** *o* **con atún** she filled the cannelloni with tuna (d) *(cojín, almohadón)* to stuff

relleno, -a 1 *adj* (a) *(lleno)* stuffed (**de** with); *(tarta, pastel)* filled (**de** with); **aceitunas rellenas** stuffed olives (b) *(gordo)* plump; **un señor bastante r.** a rather portly gentleman
2 *nm* (a) *(de pollo)* stuffing; *(de pastel)* filling (b) *(de cojín, almohadón)* stuffing
3 **de relleno** *loc adj* **páginas de r.** padding; **necesitamos poner algo de r.** we need to pad it out a bit; **esta actuación es de r.** this act is just a filler

reloj *nm (de pared, en torre)* clock; *(de pulsera)* watch; *Ind (para fichar)* time clock; **hacer algo contra r.** to do sth against the clock; EXPR **funcionar como un r.** to go like clockwork; EXPR *Fam* **es un r.** *(es puntual)* you can set your watch by him ►► ***r. de agua*** water clock; ***r. analógico*** analogue watch; ***r. de arena*** hourglass; ***r. atómico*** atomic clock; ***r. biológico*** body clock, biological clock; ***r. de bolsillo*** pocket watch; ***r. checador*** time clock; ***r. de cuarzo*** quartz clock; ***r. de cuco*** *o Am* ***cucú*** cuckoo clock; ***r. de cuerda*** wind-up watch; ***r. despertador*** alarm clock; ***r. digital*** digital watch; *Informát* ***r. interno*** internal clock; ***r. de pared*** grandfather clock; ***r. de péndulo*** pendulum clock; ***r. de pulsera,*** *RP* ***r. pulsera,*** *Col, Méx* ***r. de pulso*** watch, wristwatch; ***r. de sol*** sundial

relojear *vt RP Fam* to eye up

relojería *nf* (a) *(tienda)* watchmaker's (shop) (b) *(arte)* watchmaking; **de r.** *(mecanismo)* clockwork; *también Fig* **bomba de r.** time bomb

relojero, -a *nm,f (de relojes de pulsera)* watchmaker; *(de relojes de pared)* clockmaker

reluciente *adj* shining, gleaming; **dejó el jarrón r.** she polished the vase until it was gleaming; **tiene la cocina r.** her kitchen is spotless

relucir [39] *vi* (a) *(resplandecer)* to shine; **sacar algo a r.** to bring sth up, to mention sth; EXPR **sacar a r. los trapos sucios** to wash one's dirty linen in public; **el año pasado salió a r. que tenía una amante** it came to light last year that he had a mistress; **el problema de la inflación salió a r. en el debate** the problem of inflation came up in the course of the debate
(b) *(destacar)* to stand out; **no reluce precisamente por su simpatía** he isn't exactly famous for his friendly personality

reluctancia *nf Fís* reluctance

relumbrante *adj* dazzling, resplendent

relumbrar *vi* to shine brightly

relumbrón *nm* (a) *(golpe de luz)* flash; **el r. del sol le cegó** he was blinded by the glare of the sun (b) *(oropel)* tinsel; **de r.: un trabajo de r.** a job that's not as important as it sounds; **ha ganado varios premios de r.** he's won several prizes, none of which really mean anything

reluzca *etc ver* **relucir**

rem *nm Fís* rem

rema *nf Ling* rheme

remachado *nm (del clavo)* clinching

remachar *vt* (a) *(clavo)* to clinch (b) *(poner remaches a)* to rivet (c) *(recalcar)* to stress; **remachó que era un acuerdo provisional** he stressed that it was a provisional agreement

remache *nm* (a) *(acción)* clinching (b) *(clavo)* rivet

remador, -ora *nm,f* rower

remake [rri'meik] (*pl* **remakes**) *nm* remake

remallar *vt* to mend *(fishing net)*

remanente *nm* (a) *(de géneros)* surplus stock; *(de productos agrícolas)* surplus (b) *(en cuenta bancaria)* balance (c) *(de beneficios)* net profit

remangado, -a, arremangado, -a *adj* (a) *(mangas)* rolled-up (b) *(persona)* **estaba r.** he had his sleeves rolled up

remangar [38], **arremangar** [38] **1** *vt (pantalones)* to roll up; *(falda)* to hitch up; **remanga la camisa** roll up your (shirt) sleeves

2 remangarse *vpr (falda)* to hitch up; **remangarse (los pantalones)** to roll up one's trouser legs; **remangarse (la camisa)** to roll up one's (shirt) sleeves

remanguillé: a la remanguillé *loc adj Fam* **la casa estaba a la r.** the house was in an awful mess

remansarse *vpr* to (form a) pool

remanso *nm* still pool; **un r. de paz** an oasis of peace

remar *vi* to row

remarcar [60] **1** *vt (recalcar)* to underline, to stress

2 *vi Col, CRica, CSur (aumentar los precios)* to put up prices

> **Falso amigo**: El verbo inglés **to remark** no es la traducción del español **remarcar**. En inglés **to remark** significa "comentar, observar".

rematadamente *adv* absolutely, utterly; **lo hizo r. mal** he did it absolutely terribly; **está r. loco** he's stark raving mad

rematado, -a *adj* utter, complete; **es tonto r.** he's a complete idiot

rematador, -ora *nm,f* **(a)** *(futbolista)* finisher **(b)** *Andes, RP (en subasta)* auctioneer

rematar 1 *vt* **(a)** *(acabar)* to finish; **remató su actuación cantando su éxito más famoso** she rounded off the performance by singing her best-known hit; EXPR **para r.** to cap *o* crown it all

(b) *(matar)* to finish off; **tuvieron que r. al caballo de un tiro** they had to shoot the horse to put it out of its misery

(c) *Dep* **r. un córner** *(con el pie)* to shoot from a corner; *(con la cabeza)* to head a corner; **remató a gol un centro de su compañero** he turned in a cross from his team-mate

(d) *(liquidar, vender)* to sell off cheaply

(e) *(costura, adorno)* to finish off; **remató la tarta con trocitos de fruta** he decorated the cake with some pieces of fruit

(f) *(adjudicar en subasta)* to knock down

(g) *Andes, RP (subastar)* to auction

2 *vi* **(a)** *(acabar)* **la casa remata con una veleta** the house is topped by a weather vane **(b)** *Dep (con el pie)* to shoot; **r. a puerta** *(con el pie)* to shoot at goal; **r. de cabeza** to head at goal

remate *nm* **(a)** *(fin, colofón)* end; **el premio es el r. de un año excelente para el director** the prize rounds off *o* crowns an excellent year for the director; EXPR **de r.: es una tonta de r.** she's a complete *o* utter idiot; EXPR **para r.** to cap *o* crown it all **(b)** *(costura)* overstitch **(c)** *Arquit* top **(d)** *Dep (con el pie)* shot; **r. a puerta** *(con el pie)* shot at goal; **r. de cabeza** header (at goal) **(e)** *(liquidación)* sale **(f)** *Andes, RP (subasta)* auction

rematista *nmf Perú, PRico* auctioneer

rembolsable *ver* **reembolsable**

rembolsar *ver* **reembolsar**

rembolso *ver* **reembolso**

remecer [40] *vt Chile, Méx* to shake

remedar *vt (imitar)* to imitate; *(por burla)* to ape, to mimic

remediable *adj* remediable; **fácilmente r.** easily remedied

remediar *vt* **(a)** *(daño)* to remedy, to put right; *(problema)* to solve; **al fin se remedió su situación** her situation was finally resolved; **un mejunje que se solía beber para r. la impotencia** a concoction that people used to drink as a cure for impotence; **ya no se puede r.** there's nothing to be done about it, it can't be helped; **no sé qué remedias con insultarla** I don't know what good you hope to do by insulting her

(b) *(peligro)* to avoid, to prevent; **si puedes remediarlo, no vayas ese día** don't go on that day if you can help it; **no lo puedo r.** I can't help it; **no pudo r. que muchos militantes abandonaran el partido** he couldn't prevent many of the rank and file from leaving the party; **si alguien no lo remedia, vamos a perder el tren** if somebody doesn't do something, we're going to miss the train

remedio *nm* **(a)** *(solución)* solution, remedy; **este error ya no tiene r.** there's no longer anything that can be done about this mistake; **poner r. a algo** to do something about sth; **no tiene r.** *(persona)* he's a hopeless case; *(problema)* nothing can be done about it; **sin r.** *(sin cura, solución)* hopeless; EXPR **es peor el r. que la enfermedad** the solution is worse than the problem

(b) *(alternativa)* alternative; **no hay** *o* **queda más r. que...** there's nothing for it but...; **no le quedó otro r. que pedir perdón** she had no choice but to apologize; **no tener más r. (que hacer algo)** to have no alternative *o* choice (but to do sth); **¿vas a invitarla? – ¡qué r.!** are you going to invite her? – what else can I do?; **como último r.** as a last resort

(c) *(medicamento)* remedy, cure; **un r. contra el sida** a cure for AIDS ▸▸ ***r. casero*** home remedy; **conozco un r. casero para quitar las manchas de vino** I know a home remedy for getting rid of wine stains

(d) *(consuelo)* comfort, consolation; **el mejor r. contra la depresión es el trabajo** the best cure for depression is work

(e) *RP (fármaco)* medicine

remedo *nm (imitación)* imitation; *(por burla)* parody

remembranza *nf* memory, remembrance

rememoración *nf* recollection

rememorar *vt* to remember, to recall

remendado, -a *adj (con parches)* patched; *(zurcido)* darned, mended

remendar [3] *vt (con parches)* to patch, to mend; *(zurcir)* to darn, to mend

remendón, -ona *adj* **zapatero r.** cobbler

remera *nf RP (prenda)* T-shirt

remero, -a *nm,f (persona)* rower

remesa *nf (de productos)* shipment, consignment; *(de dinero)* remittance

remeter *vt* to tuck in

remezón *nm* **(a)** *Andes, RP (de barco)* rocking **(b)** *Andes (temblor)* earth tremor **(c)** *Chile Fam (reprimenda)* telling-off

remiendo 1 *ver* **remendar**

2 *nm* **(a)** *(parche)* patch; *(zurcido)* darn **(b)** *Fam (apaño)* **este cuarto de baño va a necesitar algún r.** this bathroom is going to need a bit of work on it; **hizo un r. para que la moto siguiera funcionando** he patched up the motorbike to keep it on the road

remilgado, -a, *Méx* **remilgoso, -a** *adj* **(a)** *(afectado)* affected **(b)** *(escrupuloso)* squeamish; *(con comida)* fussy, finicky

remilgo *nm* **(a)** *(afectación)* affectation **(b)** *(escrúpulos)* squeamishness; *(con comida)* fussiness; **hacer remilgos a algo** to turn one's nose up at sth

remilgoso = **remilgado**

reminiscencia *nf* **(a)** *(recuerdo)* reminiscence; **tener reminiscencias de** to be reminiscent of **(b)** *(influencia)* influence; **una iglesia con reminiscencias barrocas** a church with baroque influences, a church reminiscent of the baroque style

remirado, -a *adj* **(a)** *(meticuloso)* meticulous **(b)** *(melindroso)* fussy, finicky

remirar *vt* **(a)** *(volver a mirar)* to look at again **(b)** *(examinar)* to look closely at, to examine

remise *nm RP* taxi *(in private car without meter)*

remisero, -a *nm,f RP* taxi driver *(of private car without meter)*

remisible *adj* remissible

remisión *nf* **(a)** *(envío)* **ordenó la r. del proyecto al Senado** he ordered that the bill should be brought before the Senate **(b)** *(en texto)* cross-reference, reference; **una r. a otra palabra** a cross-reference to another word **(c)** *(perdón)* remission, forgiveness; *Der* **la r. de una pena** the reduction of a sentence; **sin r.** without hope of a reprieve **(d)** *(de enfermedad)* remission; *(de dolor)* easing off

remiso, -a *adj (reacio)* reluctant; **se mostró r. a los cambios** he was resistant to the changes; **es r. a intervenir** he is reluctant to intervene

remite *nm* = sender's name and address

remitente *nmf* sender

remitido *nm* announcement, notice *(paid for, in the press)*

remitir 1 *vt* **(a)** *(enviar)* to send; **adjunto le remito mi currículum vítae** I enclose my CV; **remití el paquete por correo** I sent the parcel by mail **(b)** *(trasladar)* to refer; **remitiré tu solicitud al jefe** I'll refer your application to the boss **(c)** *(perdonar)* to forgive, to remit

2 *vi* **(a)** *(en texto)* to refer **(a** to) **(b)** *(tormenta, viento)* to subside; *(lluvia, calor)* to ease off; *(temperatura)* to go down **(c)** *(fiebre)* to go down; *(dolor)* to go away; *(enfermedad)* to go into remission

3 remitirse *vpr* **(a) remitirse a** *(atenerse a)* to abide by; **me remito a la decisión del presidente** I will abide by the president's decision **(b) remitirse a** *(referirse a)* to refer to; **me remito a los hechos** the facts speak for themselves

remo *nm* **(a)** *(pala) (de barco de remos)* oar; *(de canoa, kayak)* paddle; **llegaron a la orilla a r.** they rowed to the shore **(b)** *(deporte)* rowing

remoción *nf* **(a)** *(de personal)* dismissal, sacking **(b)** *Andes, RP (de heridos)* transport **(c)** *Andes, RP (de escombros)* removal

remodelación *nf* **(a)** *(de edificio, plaza)* renovation **(b)** *(de gobierno, organización)* reshuffle; **r. ministerial** cabinet reshuffle

remodelar *vt* **(a)** *(edificio, plaza)* to renovate; **r. algo para convertirlo en** to convert sth into **(b)** *(gobierno, organización)* to reshuffle

remojar *vt* (a) *(mojar)* to soak (b) *Fam (celebrar bebiendo)* to celebrate with a drink; **esta noticia hay que remojarla** this news calls for a drink

remojo *nm (agua)* **poner algo en** *o* **a r.** to leave sth to soak; **estar en r.** to be soaking

remojón *nm (en la piscina, el mar)* dip; *(bajo la lluvia)* soaking, drenching; **me di un r. rápido en la piscina** I went for a quick dip in the pool

remolacha *nf Br* beetroot, *US* beet ►► ***r. azucarera*** (sugar) beet

remolachero, -a 1 *adj Br* beetroot, *US* beet; **el sector r.** the *Br* beetroot *o US* beet sector
2 *nm,f Br* beetroot grower, *US* beet grower

remolcador, -ora 1 *adj (vehículo)* **lancha remolcadora** tug, tugboat; **camión r.** *Br* breakdown van *o* truck, *US* tow truck
2 *nm* (a) *(barco)* tug, tugboat (b) *(camión) Br* breakdown van *o* truck, *US* tow truck

remolcar [60] *vt* (a) *(barco)* to tug (b) *(coche)* to tow

remoler [41] *vi Chile, Perú Fam* to live it up, to have a ball

remolienda *nf Chile, Perú Fam* binge, spree

remolino *nm* (a) *(de agua)* eddy, whirlpool; *(de viento)* whirlwind; *(de humo)* swirl (b) *(de gente)* throng, mass (c) *(de ideas)* confusion (d) *(de pelo)* cowlick (e) *RP (juguete)* (toy) windmill

remolón, -ona *Fam* 1 *adj* lazy
2 *nm,f* **hacerse el r.** to shirk, to be lazy

remolonear *vi Fam (perder el tiempo)* to shirk, to be lazy; *(en la cama)* to laze about in bed

remolque *nm* (a) *(acción)* towing; **nos llevaron a r. hasta el garaje** they towed us to the garage; EXPR **a r. de: la política exterior del país va a r. de la estadounidense** the country's foreign policy is led by that of the United States; **va a r. de lo que dice su hermano** he goes along with whatever his brother says (b) *(vehículo)* trailer

remonta *nf Mil* (a) *(conjunto de caballos)* supply of remounts (b) *(establecimiento)* remount establishment

remontada *nf Fam Dep* comeback; **la r. del equipo en la liga** the team's rapid climb back up the league table

remontar 1 *vt* (a) *(pendiente, río)* to go up; *(obstáculo)* to get over, to overcome; *(puestos)* to go up, to climb up; **remontaron un parcial de 3-0** they overcame a 3-0 deficit; **r. (el) vuelo** *(avión, ave)* to soar; **la empresa no consigue r.** the company hasn't been able to pull itself out of the crisis (b) *RP (cometa)* to fly
2 **remontarse** *vpr* (a) *(ave, avión)* to soar, to climb high (b) *(gastos)* **remontarse a** to amount *o* come to (c) **remontarse a** *(datar de)* to go *o* date back to; **la disputa se remonta al siglo XIX** the dispute dates back to the 19th century (d) *(retroceder en el tiempo)* **si nos remontamos 300 años...** if we go back 300 years... (e) *RP Fam (entusiasmarse)* to get carried away

remonte *nm* ski lift

remoquete *nm Fam (apodo)* nickname

rémora *nf* (a) *(pez)* remora (b) *(impedimento)* hindrance; **la falta de inversiones constituye una r. para el desarrollo del país** the lack of investment is hindering the country's development

remorder [41] *vt* **me remuerde (la conciencia) haberle mentido** I feel guilty *o* bad about lying to him; **le remuerde (la conciencia) no haberles ayudado** she feels guilty *o* bad about not helping them

remordimiento *nm* remorse; **tener remordimientos (de conciencia) por algo** to feel remorse about sth; **le mentí y luego sentí remordimientos** I lied to her and felt bad about it later

remotamente *adv* remotely; **no se parecen ni r.** they don't look even remotely like each other; **me recuerda r. a mi país** it vaguely reminds me of my own country

remoto, -a *adj* (a) *(en el espacio)* remote; **visitantes de tierras remotas** visitors from far-off lands (b) *(en el tiempo)* distant, remote (c) *(posibilidad, parecido)* remote; **no tengo ni la más remota idea** I haven't got the faintest idea (d) *Informát* remote

remover [41] 1 *vt* (a) *(agitar) (sopa, café)* to stir; *(ensalada)* to toss (b) *(tierra)* to turn over, to dig up; EXPR **r. Roma con Santiago** to leave no stone unturned (c) *(obstáculo)* to remove (d) *(recuerdos, pasado)* to stir up, to rake up; **prefieren no r. el asunto** they would rather not rake up the matter (e) *esp Am (despedir)* to dismiss, to sack
2 **removerse** *vpr (moverse)* to fidget; **se removía inquieto en la cama** he was tossing and turning in his bed

remozar *vt (edificio, fachada)* to renovate; *(equipo)* to give a new look to

remplazante = **reemplazante**

remplazar = **reemplazar**

remplazo = **reemplazo**

remuelco *etc ver* **remolcar**

remuelo *etc ver* **remoler**

remuerda *etc ver* **remorder**

remuevo *etc ver* **remover**

remunerable *adj* remunerable

remuneración *nf* (a) *(acción)* remuneration (b) *(cantidad)* remuneration; **cobra una alta r. por sus servicios** she charges a high fee for her services; **r.: a convenir** *o* **negociar** *(en anuncio)* salary *o* remuneration to be agreed, salary negotiable

remunerado, -a *adj* paid; **bien r.** well paid; **mal r.** badly paid; **no r.** unpaid

remunerar *vt* (a) *(pagar)* to remunerate (b) *(recompensar)* to reward; **se remunerará** *(en cartel)* reward

remunerativo, -a *adj* remunerative

renacentista 1 *adj* Renaissance; **pintor r.** Renaissance painter
2 *nmf (artista)* Renaissance artist

renacer [42] *vi* (a) *(flores, hojas)* to grow again (b) *(sentimiento, interés)* to return, to revive; **renació la esperanza de llegar a un acuerdo** hopes of reaching an agreement were revived *o* rekindled; **me siento r.** I feel reborn, I feel like I have a new lease of life; **renació de sus cenizas** it rose from its ashes

Renacimiento *nm* **el R.** the Renaissance

renacimiento *nm* (a) *(de flores, hojas)* budding (b) *(de sentimiento, interés)* revival, return; **r. espiritual** spiritual rebirth

renacuajo 1 *nm (animal)* tadpole
2 *nmf Fam (niño)* tiddler

renal *adj* renal, kidney; **infección r.** kidney infection

renazco *etc ver* **renacer**

rencilla *nf* (long-standing) quarrel, feud

renco, -a 1 *adj* lame
2 *nm,f* lame person

rencontrar *ver* **reencontrar**

rencor *nm* resentment, bitterness; **espero que no me guardes r.** I hope you don't feel bitter towards me; **le guardo mucho rencor** I feel a lot of resentment towards him; **me guarda r. por lo que le hice** he bears me a grudge because of what I did to him

rencoroso, -a 1 *adj* resentful; **es muy r.** he's very resentful
2 *nm,f* resentful person; **ser un r.** to be resentful

rencuentro *ver* **reencuentro**

rendición *nf* surrender ►► ***r. incondicional*** unconditional surrender

> **Falso amigo**: El sustantivo inglés **rendition** no es la traducción del español **rendición**. En inglés **rendition** significa "interpretación".

rendido, -a *adj* (a) *(agotado)* exhausted, worn out; **estoy r. de tanto caminar** I'm exhausted *o* worn out from all that walking (b) *(sumiso)* submissive; *(admirador)* servile, devoted

rendidor, -ora *adj RP (inversión, acciones)* profitable; *(producto)* long-lasting; *(estudiante)* hard-working; **un champú muy r.** a shampoo that goes a long way; **comprar en grandes cantidades es más r.** buying in bulk is cheaper

rendija *nf* crack, gap

rendimiento *nm* (a) *(de inversión, negocio)* yield, return; *(de tierra, cosecha)* yield ►► ***r. bruto*** gross yield; ***r. del capital*** capital yield
(b) *(de motor, máquina)* performance; *(de trabajador, fábrica)* productivity; **trabajar a pleno r.** to work flat out (c) *(de estudiante, deportista)* performance

rendir [47] 1 *vt* (a) *(cansar)* to wear out, to tire out; **este trabajo rinde a cualquiera** this work is enough to wear anyone out
(b) *(rentar)* to yield
(c) *(vencer)* to defeat, to subdue
(d) *(entregar, dar) (arma, alma)* to surrender; **rindió su alma a Dios** she surrendered her soul to God; **r. cuentas a alguien de algo** to give an account of sth to sb; **no tiene que r. cuentas a nadie** he doesn't have to answer to anybody for his actions, he isn't accountable to anybody for his actions
(e) *(ofrecer)* to give, to present; *(pleitesía)* to pay; **r. culto a** to worship; **r. homenaje** *o* **tributo a alguien** to pay tribute to sb; **le rindieron honores de Jefe de Estado** he was accorded the same treatment as a Head of State
(f) *Méx* **r. protesta** to be sworn in
(g) *RP (examen)* to take, *Br* to sit
2 *vi* (a) *(inversión, negocio)* to be profitable

(**b**) *(motor, máquina)* to perform well; *(trabajador, fábrica)* to be productive

(**c**) *(deportista, estudiante)* **este atleta ya no rinde como antes** this athlete isn't as good as he used to be; **el niño no está rindiendo en los estudios** the boy isn't doing well at school

(**d**) *(dar de sí)* **esta pintura rinde mucho** a little of this paint goes a long way; **me rinde mucho el tiempo** I get a lot done (in the time)

(**e**) *RP (hacer examen)* to take *o Br* sit an exam

3 rendirse *vpr* (**a**) *(entregarse)* to give oneself up, to surrender; **los atracadores se rindieron a la policía** the bank robbers gave themselves up to the police; **¡ríndete!** give yourself up! (**b**) *(ceder, abandonar)* to give in, to give up; **no te rindas ahora, que ya casi has acabado** don't give in *o* up now, you've almost finished; **rendirse a la evidencia** to bow to the evidence; **¡me rindo!** *(en adivinanza)* I give in *o* up!

renegado, -a 1 *adj* renegade

2 *nm,f* renegade

renegar [43] 1 *vt (negar)* to deny categorically; **negó y renegó que hubiera estado allí** he repeatedly and categorically denied that he had been there

2 *vi* (**a**) **r. de** *(fe)* to renounce (**b**) **r. de** *(familia)* to disown; *(principios)* to abandon, to renounce (**c**) *Fam (gruñir)* to grumble

renegociación *nf* renegotiation

renegociar *vt* to renegotiate

renegrido, -a 1 *adj* grimy, blackened

2 *nm* shiny cowbird

renegué *ver* **renegar**

Renfe ['rrenfe] *nf* (*abrev de* **Red Nacional de los Ferrocarriles Españoles**) = Spanish state railway company

renglón *nm* (**a**) *(línea)* line; **escribir a alguien unos renglones** to drop sb a line; EXPR **a r. seguido** straight after; **la insultó y a r. seguido le pidió disculpas** he insulted her and then said sorry in the same breath (**b**) *Méx (colección)* line

rengo, -a *Andes, RP* 1 *adj* lame

2 *nm,f* lame person

renguear *vi Andes, RP* to limp, to hobble

renguera *nf Andes, RP* limp

reniego *etc ver* **renegar**

renio *nm Quím* rhenium

reno *nm* reindeer

renombrado, -a *adj* renowned, famous

renombrar *vt Informát* to rename

renombre *nm* renown, fame; **una marca de r.** a well-known make; **un empresario de r. internacional** an internationally famous businessman

renovabilidad *nf (de recurso natural)* renewability

renovable *adj* renewable

renovación *nf* (**a**) *(de mobiliario, local)* renewal; **se ha producido una r. del personal** changes have been made to the staff (**b**) *(de carné, contrato, suscripción)* renewal (**c**) *(de ataques, esfuerzos)* renewal (**d**) *(restauración)* restoration (**e**) *(revitalización)* revitalization (**f**) *Pol (reforma)* reform

renovado, -a *adj* (**a**) *(carné, contrato)* renewed (**b**) *(ataques, esfuerzos)* renewed; **con renovados bríos** with renewed energy

renovador, -ora 1 *adj* (**a**) *(que renueva)* innovative (**b**) *Pol (que reforma)* reformist

2 *nm,f* (**a**) *(persona que renueva)* innovator (**b**) *Pol (persona que reforma)* reformer

renovar [41] 1 *vt* (**a**) *(cambiar) (mobiliario, local)* to renovate; *(personal, plantilla)* to make changes to, to shake out; **r. el vestuario** to buy new clothes, to update one's wardrobe; **la empresa ha renovado su imagen** the company has brought its image up to date (**b**) *(carné, contrato)* to renew (**c**) *(ataques, esfuerzos)* to renew (**d**) *(restaurar)* to restore (**e**) *(revitalizar)* to revitalize (**f**) *Pol (reformar)* to reform

2 renovarse *vpr* **¡renovarse o morir!**, *Am* **¡renovarse es vivir!** adapt or die!

renqueante *adj* (**a**) *(cojo)* limping, hobbling (**b**) *(con dificultades)* struggling; **la r. economía del país** the country's struggling economy

renquear *vi* (**a**) *(cojear)* to limp, to hobble (**b**) *(tener dificultades)* to struggle along

renqueo *nm, Am* **renquera** *nf* limp

renta *nf* (**a**) *(ingresos)* income; **vivir de las rentas** to live off one's (private) income; *Fam* **sacan un disco de éxito y luego, a vivir de las rentas** they bring out one hit record and then sit back and live off the profits ►► ***r. per cápita*** per capita income; ***r. gravable*** taxable income; ***r. por habitante*** per capita income; ***r. imponible*** taxable income; ***r. nacional*** national income; ***r. del trabajo*** earned income; ***r. vitalicia*** life annuity

(**b**) *(alquiler)* rent

(**c**) *(beneficios)* return ►► ***r. del capital*** capital yield

(**d**) *(intereses)* interest ►► ***r. fija*** fixed (interest) rate; **acciones de r. fija** fixed-interest shares; ***r. variable*** variable (interest) rate; **acciones de r. variable** variable-interest shares; **los mercados de r. variable** the equity markets

(**e**) *(deuda pública)* national *o* public debt

rentabilidad *nf* profitability; **el negocio tiene muy poca r.** the business is not very profitable; **un bono de alta r.** a bond offering a high yield *o* return

rentabilizar [14] *vt* to make profitable; **rentabilizaron la inversión inicial en dos años** it took them two years to make a profit on their initial investment; **al gobierno le costó r. sus éxitos en las urnas** the government struggled to turn its achievements into votes *o* into success at the polls

rentable *adj* profitable; **la manera más r. de hacerlo es...** the most cost-efficient way of doing it is...; **sólo es** *o* **sale r. si viajas más de tres veces diarias** it's only worth it if you make more than three journeys a day

rentado, -a *adj* (**a**) *Méx (alquilado) (apartamento)* rented; **un carro r.** a hire car (**b**) *RP (remunerado)* paid

rentar 1 *vt* (**a**) *(rendir)* to produce, to yield; **esa inversión no me renta mucho** my earnings on that investment aren't very high (**b**) *Méx (alquilar)* to rent; *(vehículo)* to hire; **se renta** *(en letrero)* to let

2 *vi* to be profitable

rentista *nmf* person of independent means

renuencia *nf* reluctance, unwillingness

renuente *adj* reluctant, unwilling (**a** to); **se mostró r. a la negociación** she was reluctant *o* unwilling to enter into negotiations

renuevo 1 *etc ver* **renovar**

2 *nm Bot* shoot

renuncia *nf* (**a**) *(abandono)* giving up; **demandan que el grupo anuncie su r. a la violencia** they are demanding that the group renounce the use of violence (**b**) *(dimisión)* resignation; **presentó su r.** he handed in his (letter of) resignation

renunciar *vi* (**a**) **r. a algo** *(abandonar, prescindir de)* to give sth up; **r. a un proyecto** to abandon a project; **r. al tabaco** to give up *o* stop smoking; **r. a la violencia** to renounce the use of violence

(**b**) *(dimitir)* to resign; **renunció a su cargo de secretario** he resigned his position as secretary

(**c**) *(rechazar)* **r. a hacer algo** to refuse to do sth; **r. a algo** *(premio, oferta)* to turn sth down; **renunció a recibir ayuda del extranjero** he refused to accept help from abroad

(**d**) *(en naipes)* to revoke

renuncio *nm* (**a**) *(en naipes)* revoke (**b**) EXPR **pillar a alguien en (un) r.** to catch sb out

reñidero *nm* pit ►► ***r. de gallos*** cockpit

reñido, -a *adj* (**a**) *(enfadado)* **está r. con su madre** he's fallen out with his mother; **están reñidos** they've fallen out

(**b**) *(disputado) (combate, campaña electoral)* fierce, hard-fought; *(partido, carrera)* close

(**c**) *(incompatible)* **estar r. con** to be at odds with, to be incompatible with; **la técnica no está reñida con la creatividad** good technique is not incompatible with creativity, it is possible to have good technique and be creative at the same time

reñir [47] 1 *vt (regañar)* to tell off; **les riñeron por hablar en clase** they were told off for talking in class

2 *vi* (**a**) *(discutir)* to argue; **¡niños, dejad de r.!** stop arguing, children! (**b**) *(enemistarse)* to fall out (**con** with); **riñeron por una tontería** they fell out over something really silly

reo[1] *nmf* (**a**) *(culpado)* offender, culprit (**b**) *(acusado)* accused, defendant

reo[2], **-a** *RP Fam* 1 *adj (en aspecto)* scruffy; *(en modales)* loutish, *Br* yobbish

2 *nm,f (en aspecto) Br* scruff, *US* bum; *(en modales)* lout, *Br* yob

reoca *nf* EXPR *Fam* **ser la r.** *(gracioso)* to be a scream; *(genial)* to be really cool; *(el colmo)* to be the absolute limit

reojo: de reojo *loc adv* **mirar algo/a alguien de r.** to look at sth/sb out of the corner of one's eye

reología *nf* rheology

reordenación *nf* restructuring

reordenar *vt* to restructure

reorganización *nf (reestructuración)* reorganization; *(del gobierno)* reshuffle

reorganizar [14] *vt (reestructurar)* to reorganize; *(gobierno)* to reshuffle

reorientar 1 *vt (carrera, vida)* to give a new direction to; *(empresa, energías, interés)* to re-focus (**hacia** on), to redirect (**hacia** towards)
2 **reorientarse** *(carrera, vida)* to take a new direction; *(empresa, energías, interés)* to refocus (**hacia** on)

reóstato, reostato *nm* rheostat

Rep. *(abrev de* **República***)* Rep

repajolero, -a *adj Fam* **no tengo ni repajolera idea** I haven't the foggiest; **no le hizo ni repajolera gracia** she didn't find it the slightest bit funny

repámpanos *interj Fam (expresa sorpresa)* good heavens!; *(expresa enfado)* for heaven's sake!

repampimflar *vt Fam* **me la repampimfla** I don't give a damn

repanchigarse [38], **repanchingarse** [38] *vpr Fam* to sprawl out

repanocha *nf* EXPR *Fam* **ser la r.** *(gracioso)* to be a scream; *(genial)* to be really cool; *(el colmo)* to be the absolute limit

repantigarse [38], **repantingarse** [38] *vpr Fam* to sprawl out

reparable *adj (remediable)* repairable

reparación *nf* (**a**) *(arreglo)* repair; **necesita varias reparaciones** it needs several things repairing; **en r.** under repair; **reparaciones** *(taller)* repair shop (**b**) *(compensación)* redress; **reclamó una r. por la ofensa de que fue objeto** he sought redress for the wrong done to him

reparador, -ora *adj (descanso, sueño)* refreshing

reparar 1 *vt* (**a**) *(vehículo, aparato)* to repair, to fix; **llevar algo a r.** to take sth to be repaired *o* fixed (**b**) *(error, daño)* to make amends for, to make up for (**c**) *(fuerzas)* to restore
2 *vi (percatarse)* **r. en (la cuenta de) algo** to notice sth; **no reparó en que una de las ruedas estaba pinchada** he didn't notice that one of the tyres had a puncture; **¿reparaste en la cara que pusieron?** did you see their expression?; **no repara en los posibles obstáculos** she doesn't realize the possible pitfalls; **no r. en gastos** to spare no expense

reparo *nm* (**a**) *(objeción)* objection; **no tengo ningún r. en negociar con ellos** I have no objection to doing business with them; **poner reparos a algo** to raise objections to sth (**b**) *(apuro)* **con reparos** with hesitation *o* reservations; **me da r.** I feel awkward about it; **no tener reparos en hacer algo** to have no qualms *o* scruples about doing sth; **sin reparos** without reservation, with no holds barred

reparón, -ona *adj Fam* fault-finding, carping

repartición *nf* (**a**) *(reparto)* sharing out (**b**) *Andes, RP (departamento)* department

repartidor, -ora 1 *adj* delivery; **camión r.** delivery lorry
2 *nm,f (de butano, carbón)* delivery man, *f* delivery woman; *(de leche)* milkman, *f* milklady; *(de periódicos)* paperboy, *f* papergirl; **es r. de publicidad** *(en la calle)* he hands out advertising leaflets; *(en buzones)* he distributes advertising leaflets

repartija *nf CSur Fam* share-out; **antes que se muriera ya había empezado la r.** they had already started carving up his estate before he died

repartimiento *nm (de tierras, recursos)* distribution

repartir 1 *vt* (**a**) *(dividir)* to share out, to divide; **repartió los terrenos entre sus hijos** she divided the land amongst her children; **la riqueza está mal repartida** there is an uneven distribution of wealth
(**b**) *(distribuir) (leche, periódicos, correo)* to deliver; *(naipes)* to deal (out); **repartimos a domicilio** we do home deliveries; *Fam* **repartió puñetazos a diestro y siniestro** he lashed out with his fists in every direction
(**c**) *(esparcir) (pintura, mantequilla)* to spread; **reparte bien la salsa** pour the sauce evenly; **repartieron la carga por todo el camión** they spread the load over the whole of the truck *o Br* lorry
(**d**) *(asignar) (trabajo, órdenes)* to give out, to allocate; *(papeles)* to assign; **nos vamos a r. las tareas** we're going to share the jobs out between us
2 *vi (en juego de naipes)* to deal; **ahora reparto yo** it's my turn to deal
3 **repartirse** *vpr* (**a**) *(dividirse)* to divide up, to share out; **se repartieron el botín** they divided up *o* shared out the loot (**b**) *(distribuirse)* to spread out; **las tropas se repartieron por el bosque** the troops spread out across the wood

reparto *nm* (**a**) *(división)* division; **hacer el r. de algo** to divide sth up, to share sth out; **el r. de la riqueza** the distribution of wealth ►► *Esp Econ* ***r. de beneficios*** profit sharing; *Econ* ***r. de dividendos*** dividend payout; ***r. del trabajo*** division of labour; *Am Econ* ***r. de utilidades*** profit sharing
(**b**) *(distribución) (de leche, periódicos, correo)* delivery; *(de naipes)* dealing; **el camión del r.** the delivery van; **se dedica al r. de publicidad** he distributes advertising leaflets ►► ***r. a domicilio*** home delivery
(**c**) *(asignación)* giving out, allocation ►► ***r. de premios*** prize-giving
(**d**) *Cine & Teatro* cast; **actor de r.** supporting actor
(**e**) *Cuba (barrio)* neighbourhood, area

repasador *nm RP (trapo)* tea towel

repasar *vt* (**a**) *(revisar)* to go over, to check; **hay que r. las cuentas para detectar el error** we'll have to go through all the accounts to find the mistake; **hoy repasaremos la segunda lección** we'll go over lesson two again today (**b**) *(estudiar)* to revise (**c**) *(zurcir)* to darn, to mend

repaso *nm* (**a**) *(revisión)* check; **hacer un r. de algo** to check sth over (**b**) *(estudio)* revision; **dar un r. a algo** to revise sth (**c**) *(de ropa)* **dar un r. a algo** *(remendar)* to darn *o* mend sth; *(planchar)* to give sth a quick iron; **necesita un r.** *(remiendo)* it needs darning *o* mending; *(planchado)* it needs a quick iron (**d**) *Fam* **dar un r. a alguien** *(regañar)* to give sb a stern telling-off; *(apabullar)* to thrash sb

repatear *vt Fam* **me repatea que...** it really annoys me that...; **ese tipo me repatea** I can't stand that guy

repatriación *nf* (**a**) *(de persona)* repatriation (**b**) *(de capitales)* repatriation

repatriado, -a 1 *adj* (**a**) *(persona)* repatriated (**b**) *(capitales)* repatriated
2 *nm,f* repatriate

repatriar [32] 1 *vt* (**a**) *(persona)* to repatriate (**b**) *(capitales)* to repatriate
2 **repatriarse** *vpr* (**a**) *(persona)* to be repatriated (**b**) *(capitales)* to be repatriated

repe *adj Esp Fam* **este cromo lo tengo r.** I've got a swap for this picture card, I've two copies of this picture card

repecho *nm* short steep slope

repeinado, -a *adj* **iba repeinada** she had had her hair all done up

repelar *Méx* 1 *vt (exasperar)* to exasperate, to irritate
2 *vi (rezongar, refunfuñar)* to grumble

repelencia *nf* repulsion

repelente 1 *adj* (**a**) *Fam (niño)* **es un niño r.** he's a disgusting little goody-goody (**b**) *(odioso)* disgusting (**c**) *(de insectos)* repellent
2 *nm* **r. (contra insectos)** insect repellent

repeler 1 *vt* (**a**) *(ataque)* to repel (**b**) *(sustancia)* **una tela que repele las manchas** a stain-resistant fabric; **el poste repelió el balón** the ball was kept out by the post (**c**) *(repugnar)* to repulse, to disgust; **ese olor me repele** I find that smell disgusting *o* repulsive
2 **repelerse** *vpr (mutuamente)* to repel

repelús, repeluzno *nm Fam* (**a**) *(escalofrío)* shiver; **me dio un r.** it sent a shiver down my spine (**b**) **me da r.** *(miedo)* it gives me the shivers; *(repugnancia)* I find it revolting *o* disgusting

repensar *vt* to think over

repente 1 *nm (arrebato)* fit; **le dio un r.** she had a fit
2 **de repente** *loc adv* (**a**) *(súbitamente)* suddenly; **se puso a llover de r.** it suddenly started raining; **todo sucedió de r.** it all happened very suddenly (**b**) *RP, Ven (tal vez)* maybe, perhaps; **de r. cambió de idea** maybe *o* perhaps he changed his mind, he might have changed his mind

repentinamente *adv* suddenly

repentino, -a *adj* sudden; **su muerte repentina sorprendió a todos** her sudden death surprised everybody

repera *nf* EXPR *Fam* **ser la r.** *(gracioso)* to be a scream; *(genial)* to be really cool; *(el colmo)* to be the limit

repercusión *nf* (**a**) *(de sonido)* reverberation (**b**) *(eco)* impact; **el tratado tuvo r. en todo el mundo occidental** the treaty had an impact throughout the Western world (**c**) *(consecuencia)* repercussion; **el atentado tendrá graves repercusiones en el proceso de paz** the attack will have serious repercussions on the peace process

repercutir 1 *vi* (**a**) *(resonar)* to resound, to reverberate (**b**) **r. en algo** *(afectar)* to affect sth; **sus problemas repercuten en su rendimiento** his problems are affecting his performance
2 *vt (gastos)* **r. algo en alguien** to pass sth on to sb

repertorio *nm* (**a**) *(obras)* repertoire (**b**) *(serie)* selection (**c**) *Informát* **r. de instrucciones** instruction set

repesca *nf* (**a**) *Educ* resit (**b**) *Dep* repechage

repescar [60] *vt* (**a**) *Educ* **r. a alguien** to allow sb a resit (**b**) *Dep* **r. a alguien** to allow sb into the repechage

repetición *nf (de acción, dicho)* repetition; *(de programa)* repeat; **una r. de los resultados de 2002** a repeat of the 2002 results; **la r. (de la jugada)** the (action) replay; **la r. de las jugadas más interesantes** the highlights; **fusil de r.** repeater, repeating firearm

repetidamente *adv* repeatedly

repetido, -a *adj* (**a**) *(reiterado)* repeated; **se lo he dicho repetidas veces** I've told him time and again, I've told him repeatedly (**b**) *(duplicado)* **tengo este libro r.** I've got two copies of this book

repetidor, -ora 1 *adj Educ* **alumno r.** = pupil repeating a year
2 *nm,f Educ* = pupil repeating a year
3 *nm (de radio, televisión)* repeater

repetir [47] 1 *vt* (**a**) *(hacer, decir de nuevo)* to repeat; *(ataque)* to renew; **vas a tener que r. la redacción** you're going to have to rewrite it; **repíteme tu apellido** could you repeat your surname?, could you tell me your surname again?; **el bebé repite todo lo que dicen sus padres** the baby repeats everything his parents say; **te lo he repetido mil veces** I've told you a thousand times; **te lo voy a r.: no quiero ir** I'm going to tell you one more time: I don't want to go; **no me gustaría r. una experiencia así** I wouldn't like to repeat an experience like that
(**b**) *Educ* **repitió tercero** he repeated his third year
(**c**) *(en comida)* to have seconds of; **voy a r. postre** *(en un restaurante)* I'm going to have another dessert; *(en casa)* I'm going to have some more dessert *o* another helping of dessert
2 *vi* (**a**) *Educ* to repeat a year (**b**) *(sabor, alimento)* **r. a alguien** to repeat on sb; **el ajo repite mucho** garlic really repeats on you; **me está repitiendo la cebolla** the onion is repeating on me (**c**) *(de comida)* to have seconds; **esta ensalada me encanta, voy a r.** I love this salad, I'm going to have some more of it
3 **repetirse** *vpr* (**a**) *(acontecimiento)* to recur; **este fenómeno se repite cada verano** this phenomenon recurs *o* is repeated every summer; **una oportunidad así no se repetirá** you/we/*etc* won't get another opportunity like this; **¡y que no se vuelva a r.!** and don't let it happen again! (**b**) *(persona)* to repeat oneself

repetitivo, -a *adj* repetitive

repicar [60] 1 *vt (campanas)* to ring; *(tambor)* to beat
2 *vi (campanas)* to ring; *(tambor)* to sound

repintar 1 *vt* to repaint
2 **repintarse** *vpr (maquillarse)* to put on heavy make-up

repipi *Fam Pey* 1 *adj* **un niño r.** a precocious brat
2 *nmf* precocious brat

repique 1 *ver* **repicar**
2 *nm* peals, ringing; **el r. de las campanas se oía en todo el pueblo** the ringing of the bells could be heard throughout the village

repiquetear 1 *vt (campanas)* to ring loudly
2 *vi (campanas)* to peal (out); *(tambor)* to beat; *(timbre)* to ring; *(lluvia, dedos)* to drum

repiqueteo *nm (de campanas)* pealing; *(de tambor)* beating; *(de timbre)* ringing; *(de lluvia, dedos)* drumming

repisa *nf* (**a**) *(estante)* shelf; *(sobre chimenea)* mantelpiece (**b**) *Arquit* bracket

repitiera *etc ver* **repetir**

repito *etc ver* **repetir**

replana *nf Perú* slang *(especially that used by criminals)*

replantar *vt* (**a**) *(parque)* to replant (**b**) *(planta) (en jardín, huerto)* to transplant; *(en maceta)* to repot

replanteamiento *nm* (**a**) *(de situación, problema)* restatement (**b**) *(de cuestión) (parafraseo)* rephrasing; **el r. de una cuestión** raising an issue again

replantear 1 *vt* (**a**) *(situación, problema)* to restate (**b**) *(cuestión) (de nuevo)* to raise again; *(parafrasear)* to rephrase
2 **replantearse** *vpr (situación, problema, cuestión)* to reconsider; **se replanteó su participación en el acto** he reconsidered taking part in the event

replay [rriplei] (*pl* **replays**) *nm* replay

replegar [43] 1 *vt* (**a**) *(tropas)* to withdraw; **el entrenador replegó a sus jugadores tras el gol** the coach got his team to play deeper after the goal (**b**) *(alas)* to fold
2 **replegarse** *vpr* (**a**) *(tropas)* to withdraw; *(jugadores)* to play deeper (**b**) **replegarse (en sí mismo)** *(persona)* to withdraw into oneself

repleto, -a *adj (habitación, autobús)* packed; **estoy r.** *(de comida)* I'm full (up); **el centro estaba r. de turistas** the town centre was packed with tourists

réplica *nf* (**a**) *(respuesta)* reply (**b**) *(copia)* replica (**c**) *(de terremoto)* aftershock

replicación *nf Biol* replication

replicar [60] 1 *vt* (**a**) *(responder)* to answer (**b**) *(objetar)* to answer back, to retort
2 *vi (objetar)* to answer back; **hazlo ya, y sin r.** do it now, and no arguments!

> **Falso amigo**: El verbo inglés **to replicate** no es la traducción del español **replicar**. En inglés **to replicate** significa "reproducir" o "reproducirse".

replicón, -ona *Fam* 1 *adj* argumentative
2 *nm,f* argumentative person; **es un r.** he's always answering back

repliego *etc ver* **replegar**

repliegue *nm* (**a**) *(retirada)* withdrawal (**b**) *(pliegue)* fold

repoblación *nf* (**a**) *(con gente)* resettlement (**b**) *(con animales)* repopulation; *(con peces)* restocking; *(con árboles)* replanting ►► ***r. forestal*** reafforestation

repoblador, -ora *nm,f* resettler

repoblar [64] *vt* (**a**) *(con gente)* to resettle (**b**) *(con animales)* to repopulate; *(con peces)* to restock; *(con árboles)* to replant, to reforest

repollito *nm Andes, RP* **r. de Bruselas** Brussels sprout

repollo *nm* cabbage ►► *RP* ***r. colorado*** red cabbage

repolludo, -a *adj Fam (rechoncho)* chubby

reponer [50] 1 *vt* (**a**) *(sustituir) (existencias, trabajador)* to replace; **repuso el dinero en la caja** he put the money back in the till, he returned the money to the till
(**b**) *(restituir) (en un cargo)* to reinstate; **repusieron al secretario en su cargo** the secretary was reinstated in his post
(**c**) *(película)* to re-run; *(obra)* to revive; *(serie)* to repeat
(**d**) *(replicar)* to reply; **repuso que le parecía muy bien** he replied that he thought it was a very good idea
(**e**) *(recuperar)* **haremos una parada para r. fuerzas** we'll make a stop to get our strength back
2 **reponerse** *vpr* to recover (**de** from); **el atleta se está reponiendo rápidamente de su lesión** the athlete is making a quick recovery from his injury; **tardé mucho en reponerme del susto** it took me a long time to recover from *o* to get over the shock

repóquer *nm* **un r. de ases** five aces *(when playing with two decks)*

reportaje *nm* (**a**) *(en radio, televisión) (programa)* report; *Am (entrevista)* interview (**b**) *(en periódico) (artículo)* feature; *Am (entrevista)* interview ►► ***r. de boda*** wedding photos; ***r. fotográfico*** illustrated feature; ***r. gráfico*** illustrated feature

reportar 1 *vt* (**a**) *(traer)* to bring; **no le ha reportado más que problemas** it has caused him nothing but problems; **el negocio reporta muchos beneficios** the business generates a lot of profit, the business is very profitable (**b**) *Andes, CAm, Méx, Ven (informar)* to report (**c**) *CAm, Méx (denunciar)* to report (to the police); **reportó el ataque en la delegación** she reported the attack to the police
2 **reportarse** *vpr* (**a**) *(reprimirse)* to control oneself (**b**) *CAm, Méx, Ven (presentarse)* to report (**a** to)

reporte *nm Andes, CAm, Méx, Ven (informe)* report; *(noticia)* news item *o* report; **recibí reportes de mi hermano** I had some news from my brother; **el r. del tiempo** the weather report *o* forecast

reportear *Chile, Méx* 1 *vt* to report on, to cover; **reporteó la entrega del premio** he reported on *o* covered the prizegiving ceremony
2 *vi* **fue a r. al Medio Oriente** he went to work as a reporter in the Middle East

reportero, -a *nm,f* reporter ►► ***r. gráfico*** press photographer

reposabrazos *nm inv* armrest

reposacabezas *nm inv* headrest

reposadamente *adv* **conversamos/caminamos r.** we had a leisurely conversation/walk

reposado, -a *adj (persona)* calm; *(actividad, trabajo)* leisurely

reposapiés *nm inv* footrest

reposar 1 *vi* (**a**) *(descansar)* to (have a) rest; **le gusta r. después de comer** she likes to have a rest after lunch (**b**) *(sedimentarse)* to stand; **deja que repose el agua** allow the water to settle; **la masa tiene que r. durante media hora** the dough needs to stand for half an hour (**c**) *(yacer)* to lie; **su cuerpo reposa en el cementerio de la ciudad** her body lies in the town cemetery
2 *vt* (**a**) *(apoyar)* to lean; **reposó la cabeza en su hombro** he leaned his head on her shoulder (**b**) *(digerir)* **todavía no he reposado la comida** I still haven't digested my meal

reposera *nf RP Br* sun-lounger, *US* beach recliner

reposición *nf* (**a**) *(de película)* rerun; *(de obra)* revival; *(de serie)* repeat (**b**) *(de existencias, pieza)* replacement

repositorio *nm* repository

reposo *nm* (**a**) *(descanso)* rest; **en r.** *(cuerpo, persona)* at rest; *(máquina)* not in use; *Culin* **dejar algo en r.** to leave sth to stand; **guardar** *o* **hacer r.** to rest; **recomendó r. absoluto** she recommended a complete rest (**b**) *Fís* rest; **electrones en r.** electrons at rest

repostaje *nm* refuelling

repostar 1 *vi (avión)* to refuel; *(coche)* to fill up
2 *vt* (**a**) *(gasolina)* to fill up with; **repostamos combustible** we refuelled (**b**) *(provisiones)* to stock up on

repostería *nf* (**a**) *(establecimiento)* confectioner's (shop) (**b**) *(oficio)* confectionery (**c**) *(productos)* confectionery, cakes and pastries

repostero, -a 1 *nm,f (persona)* confectioner
2 *nm Andes (armario)* larder, pantry

reprender *vt (a niños)* to tell off; *(a empleados)* to reprimand

reprensible *adj* reprehensible

reprensión *nf (a niños)* telling-off; *(a empleados)* reprimand

represa *nf* (**a**) *(dique)* dam (**b**) *Am (de presa)* reservoir

represalia *nf* reprisal; **tomar represalias** to retaliate, to take reprisals; **un ataque en** *o* **como r. por el asesinato de su líder** an attack made in retaliation *o* in reprisal for the assassination of their leader

represaliar *vt* **r. a alguien (por algo)** to take reprisals against sb (for sth)

represar *vt (agua)* to dam

representable *adj (obra de teatro)* performable

representación *nf* (**a**) *(símbolo, imagen, ejemplo)* representation; **no me hago una r. clara de lo que ocurrió** I haven't got a clear picture of what happened; **la paloma es una r. de la paz** the dove is a symbol of peace
(**b**) *(delegación)* representation; **en r. de** on behalf of; **acudió a la reunión en r. de sus compañeros** he attended the meeting on behalf of his colleagues, he represented his colleagues at the meeting
(**c**) *Pol* ***r. mayoritaria*** majority rule; ***r. proporcional*** proportional representation
(**d**) *Teatro* performance; **una obra de difícil r.** a difficult play to perform; **r. única** one-night stand
(**e**) *Com* representation; **tener la r. de** to act as a representative for

representante 1 *adj* representative
2 *nmf (delegado)* representative; **ganó el festival el r. irlandés** the contestant representing Ireland won the contest; **r. (artístico)** agent; **r. (comercial)** (sales) rep ►► ***r. sindical*** union rep *o* representative

representar *vt* (**a**) *(simbolizar, ejemplificar)* to represent; **este cuadro representa la Última Cena** this painting depicts the Last Supper; **la coma representa los decimales** the comma indicates decimal places; **Dalí representa perfectamente el surrealismo** Dali is the ultimate surrealist painter
(**b**) *(actuar en nombre de)* to represent; **el delegado sindical representaba a sus compañeros** the shop steward represented his fellow workers; **ha participado en dos festivales representando a su país** she has represented her country at two festivals; **representa a varios artistas** she acts as an agent for several artists
(**c**) *(aparentar)* to look; **representa unos cuarenta años** she looks about forty; **representa muchos menos años de los que tiene** she looks a lot younger than she is
(**d**) *(significar)* to mean; **representa el 50 por ciento del consumo interno** it accounts for 50 percent of domestic consumption; **diez millones no representan nada para él** ten million is nothing to him; **representa mucho para él** it means a lot to him
(**e**) *Teatro (función)* to perform; *(papel)* to play
(**f**) *Com* to represent

representatividad *nf* **este sindicato no tiene r. entre los trabajadores del sector** this union is not representative of the workers in the industry

representativo, -a *adj* (**a**) *(simbolizador)* **ser r. de algo** to represent sth; **un grupo r. de la población general** a group that represents the population as a whole; **un escándalo r. del clima de corrupción en el que vive el país** a scandal which reflects *o* is representative of the climate of corruption in the country
(**b**) *(característico, relevante)* **r. (de)** representative (of); **este cuadro es poco r. de su estilo** this painting is not very representative of his style

represión *nf* (**a**) *(política)* repression (**b**) *Psi* repression

represivo, -a *adj* repressive

represor, -ora 1 *adj* repressive
2 *nm,f* oppressor

reprimenda *nf* reprimand; **recibieron una r. por su comportamiento** they were reprimanded for their behaviour

reprimido, -a 1 *adj* repressed
2 *nm,f* repressed person; **ser un r.** to be repressed

reprimir 1 *vt* (**a**) *(llanto, risa)* to suppress (**b**) *(minorías, disidentes)* to repress
2 **reprimirse** *vpr* **reprimirse (de hacer algo)** to restrain oneself (from doing sth)

reprise (*pl* **reprises**), **reprís** *nm* acceleration

reprivatización *nf* privatization *(of an industry that had previously been nationalized)*

reprivatizar *vt* to privatize *(an industry that had previously been nationalized)*

reprobable *adj* reprehensible

reprobación *nf* reproof, censure

reprobar [64] *vt* (**a**) *(desaprobar)* to censure, to condemn (**b**) *Am (estudiante, examen)* to fail

reprobatorio, -a *adj* reproving

réprobo, -a 1 *adj* damned
2 *nm,f* lost soul

reprochable *adj* reproachable

reprochar 1 *vt* **r. algo a alguien** to reproach sb for sth; **le reprocharon que no hubiera ayudado** they reproached him for not helping
2 **reprocharse** *vpr* **reprocharse algo** *(uno mismo)* to reproach oneself for sth

reproche *nm* reproach; **hacer un r. a alguien** to reproach sb; **el único r. que se le puede hacer es que es un proyecto demasiado ambicioso** the only reproach that can be made of it is that it is too ambitious a project; **sus declaraciones le valieron muchos reproches** her statements earned her a great deal of criticism

reproducción *nf* (**a**) *(procreación)* reproduction; **tratamiento de r. asistida** fertility treatment ►► ***r. asexual*** asexual reproduction; ***r. sexual*** sexual reproduction (**b**) *(copia)* reproduction; **es una r. exacta del original** it is an exact replica of the original (**c**) *(repetición)* recurrence; **preocupa la r. de la enfermedad** there is concern about the possibility of the disease recurring (**d**) *(de sonido)* playback

reproducible *adj* reproducible

reproducir [18] 1 *vt* (**a**) *(repetir)* to reproduce; *(gestos)* to copy, to imitate (**b**) *(copiar)* to reproduce; **reprodujo su declaración por escrito** he put his statement into writing (**c**) *(representar)* to depict; **la novela reproduce fielmente la atmósfera del periodo** the novel faithfully recreates the atmosphere of the period (**d**) *(sonido)* to play back
2 **reproducirse** *vpr* (**a**) *(volver a suceder)* to recur; **anoche se reprodujeron los choques armados en la frontera** last night there were renewed armed clashes on the border (**b**) *(procrear)* to reproduce

reproductor, -ora 1 *adj* reproductive; *Anat* **el aparato r.** the reproductive system; **un aparato r. de DVD** a DVD player
2 *nm,f (animal)* breeding animal
3 *nm* ***r. de discos compactos*** compact disc player, CD player; ***r. de DVD*** DVD player; ***r. de vídeo*** video player

reprografía *nf* reprographics *(singular)*; **(servicio de) r.** copying service

reprogramación *nf Econ* ***r. de la deuda*** *(aplazamiento)* debt rescheduling; *(reorganización)* debt restructuring

reprogramar *vt Econ (deuda) (aplazar)* to reschedule; *(reorganizar)* to restructure

repruebo *etc ver* **reprobar**

reptar *vi (soldado, cocodrilo)* to crawl; *(serpiente)* to slither

reptil *nm* reptile

república *nf* republic ►► ***r. bananera*** banana republic; ***la R. Centroafricana*** the Central African Republic; ***la R. Checa*** the Czech Republic; ***la R. del Congo*** the Republic of the Congo; *Antes* ***la R. Democrática Alemana*** *o* ***de Alemania*** the German Democratic Republic; ***la R. Democrática del Congo*** the Democratic Republic of Congo; ***la R. Dominicana*** the Dominican Republic; ***la R. Eslovaca*** the Slovak Republic; ***r. federal*** federal republic; *Antes* ***la R. Federal Alemana*** *o* ***de Alemania*** the Federal Republic of Germany; *Antes* ***la R. Federal de Yugoslavia*** the Yugoslav Federal Republic; ***la R. de Irlanda*** the Republic of Ireland; ***la R. Irlandesa*** the Irish Republic; ***la R. Oriental del Uruguay*** = the official name of Uruguay; ***la R. Popular China*** the People's Republic of China; ***la R. Popular de Corea*** the Democratic People's Republic of Korea; ***la R. de Sudáfrica*** the Republic of South Africa

republicanismo *nm* republicanism

republicano, -a 1 *adj* republican
2 *nm,f* republican
3 *nm (ave)* sociable weaver

repudiación *nf* repudiation

repudiar *vt* (a) *(condenar)* to condemn (b) *(esposa)* to repudiate, to disown (c) *(herencia)* to renounce

repudio *nm* (a) *(condena)* condemnation (b) *(de esposa)* repudiation, disowning (c) *(de herencia)* renouncement

repudrir 1 *vt* to (cause to) rot away
2 **repudrirse** *vpr* (a) *(pudrirse)* to rot away (b) *Fam (consumirse)* to pine away; **se repudría de tristeza** she was consumed with sadness

repueblo *etc ver* **repoblar**

repuesto, -a 1 *participio ver* **reponer**
2 *adj* recovered (**de** from)
3 *nm* (a) *(recambio)* spare part; **de r.** spare, in reserve; **la rueda de r.** the spare wheel (b) *(provisión extra)* reserve

repugnancia *nf (asco)* disgust; **me da** *o* **produce r.** I find it disgusting; **sentir r. hacia algo** to find sth disgusting

repugnante *adj* (a) *(sabor, olor)* disgusting, revolting (b) *(acción, comportamiento)* disgusting

repugnar *vi* **me repugna ese olor/su actitud** I find that smell/her attitude disgusting; **me repugna hacerlo** I'm loath to do it; **unas fotografías que repugnan** disgusting photographs

repujado, -a 1 *adj* embossed
2 *nm* embossed work

repujar *vt* to emboss

repulir 1 *vt* (a) *(pulir)* to polish (b) *(acicalar)* to smarten up
2 **repulirse** *vpr* to smarten up

repulsa *nf (censura)* condemnation; **se produjo una manifestación de r. por el atentado** there was a demonstration in condemnation of the attack

repulsión *nf* (a) *(repugnancia)* repulsion; **me produce r.** it makes me sick (b) *Fís* repulsion

repulsivo, -a *adj* (a) *(asqueroso)* repulsive (b) *Fís* repulsive

repuntar 1 *vt Chile (animales)* to round up
2 *vi* (a) *Fin (valor)* to rally, to recover (b) *(marea)* to turn (c) *Am (mejorar)* to improve

repunte *nm* (a) *Fin (de valores, precios)* rally, recovery; **un r. de la inflación** a slight rise in inflation; **la economía ha tenido un r. al alza** the economy has rallied; **se ha producido un r. de los precios** there has been a slight price rise *o* a rise in prices; **un r. navideño de las ventas** a slight upturn in sales over the Christmas period (b) *(de marea)* turning

repusiera *etc ver* **reponer**

reputación *nf* reputation; **un cirujano de muy buena r.** a surgeon with a very good reputation; **tiene muy mala r.** he has a very bad reputation; **tiene r. de ser un hábil negociador** he has a reputation for being a skilful negotiator

reputado, -a *adj* highly reputed; **uno de los economistas más reputados del país** one of the most highly reputed economists in the country

reputar *vt* to consider

requebrar [3] *vt (piropear)* to make flirtatious remarks to

requemado, -a *adj* burnt

requemar 1 *vt* (a) *(comida)* to burn (b) *(planta, tierra)* to scorch (c) *(reconcomer)* **los celos lo requeman** he's consumed with jealousy
2 **requemarse** *vpr (quemarse)* to get burnt, to burn

requerimiento *nm* (a) *(demanda)* request; **no liberaron al niño a pesar de los requerimientos de su padre** they refused to free the child in spite of his father's pleas; **el informe fue elaborado a r. de la comisión** the report was written at the request of the committee (b) *Der (intimación)* writ, injunction; *(aviso)* summons *(singular)*; **acudió a r. del juez** she appeared after being summonsed by the judge

> **Falso amigo**: El sustantivo inglés **requirement** no es la traducción del español **requerimiento**. En inglés **requirement** significa "requisito".

requerir [63] *vt* (a) *(necesitar)* to require; **es un asunto que requiere mucha diplomacia** it is a matter which requires a great deal of tact; **se requieren conocimientos de francés** a knowledge of French is essential (b) *(ordenar)* **r. a alguien (para) que haga algo** to demand that sb do sth (c) *Der* to order; **el juez requirió la extradición del terrorista** the judge ordered the extradition of the terrorist

requesón *nm* = ricotta-type cheese

requete- *pref Fam* **requetebién** wonderfully *o* marvellously well; **requetegrande** absolutely enormous, *Br* ginormous; **todo está muy requetepensado** it's all been incredibly carefully thought out

requeté *nm Hist* (a) *(organización)* **el R.** the Carlist militia (b) *(persona)* Carlist militiaman

requiebro 1 *ver* **requebrar**
2 *nm* flirtatious remark

réquiem (*pl* **requiems**) *nm* (a) *Rel* requiem (b) *Mús* requiem

requiero *etc ver* **requerir**

requilorio *nm Fam* **déjate de tantos requilorios** stop being so excessively formal

requintar *vt CAm, Col, Méx (apretar)* to tighten, to squeeze

requinto *nm (guitarra)* = small four-stringed guitar

requiriente *nmf* plaintiff

requiriera *etc ver* **requerir**

requisa *nf* (a) *(expropiación)* requisition; *(en aduana)* seizure (b) *(inspección)* inspection (c) *Am (registro)* search

requisar *vt (expropiar)* to requisition; *(en aduana)* to seize

requisición *nf (expropiación)* requisition

requisito *nm* requirement; **cumplir los requisitos** to fulfil the requirements; **reúne todos los requisitos** it meets *o* satisfies all the requirements; **un r. previo** prerequisite; **el dominio del alemán es r. indispensable** a knowledge of German is essential

res (*pl* **reses**) *nf* (a) *(animal)* beast, animal ►► ***r. vacuna*** head of cattle (b) *Am* **reses** *(ganado vacuno)* cattle

resabiado, -a *adj* (a) *(experimentado)* **estar r.** to be hardened (b) *(mal acostumbrado)* **un caballo r.** a vicious horse

resabiar 1 *vt* to teach bad habits
2 **resabiarse** *vpr* (a) *(adquirir vicios)* to acquire bad habits (b) *(enfadarse)* to get annoyed

resabido, -a *adj Fam Pey (sabelotodo)* **es un r.** he's such a *Br* know-all *o US* know-it-all

resabio *nm* (a) *(sabor)* nasty aftertaste; **la bebida me dejó un r. en la boca** the drink left a nasty aftertaste in my mouth; **el asunto me dejó un r. en la boca** the affair left a bad taste in my mouth (b) *(vicio)* bad habit *(left over from an earlier time)*; **aún le quedan resabios machistas** he can still be a bit of a male chauvinist sometimes

resaca *nf* (a) *(de las olas)* undertow; **hay mucha r.** the undertow is very strong (b) *Fam (de borrachera)* hangover; **estar con r.** to have a hangover; **todavía dura la r. de la victoria** they're still suffering from the hangover of their victory

resacoso, -a *adj Fam* **estar r.** to have a hangover

resalado, -a *adj Fam* charming

resaltador *nm Col, RP (rotulador fluorescente)* highlighter

resaltar 1 *vi* (a) *(destacar)* to stand out; **resalta en el equipo por su velocidad** he stands out as one of the fastest players in the team (b) *(en edificios) (cornisa, ventana)* to stick out
2 *vt (destacar)* to highlight; **hacer r. algo** to emphasize sth, to stress sth; **el orador resaltó la contribución del difunto a la ciencia** the speaker highlighted the contribution to science made by the deceased

resalte, resalto *nm* (a) *(saliente)* projection (b) *Esp (en la carretera)* speed bump, *Br* sleeping policeman

resarcimiento *nm* compensation

resarcir [74] 1 *vt* **r. a alguien (de)** to compensate sb (for); **la aseguradora lo resarció por los daños sufridos** the insurance company paid him compensation *o* compensated him for the damage caused
2 **resarcirse** *vpr (daño, pérdida)* to be compensated (**de** for); **se resarció de la derrota del mes pasado** he gained revenge for his defeat the previous month

resbalada *nf Am Fam* slip; **dar** *o* **pegar una r.** to slip

resbaladizo, -a *adj* (a) *(suelo, terreno)* slippery (b) *(asunto)* tricky

resbalar 1 *vi* (a) *(caer)* to slip (**con** *o* **en** on) (b) *(deslizarse)* to slide (**por** along); **le resbalaban las lágrimas por el rostro** tears ran *o* trickled down her cheeks; **los coches resbalaban sobre el hielo** the cars were sliding on the ice (c) *(estar resbaladizo)* to be slippery; **este suelo resbala** this floor is slippery (d) *Fam (equivocarse)* to slip up
2 *vt Fam* **sus problemas me resbalan** his problems leave me cold; **le resbala todo lo que le digo** everything I say to him goes in one ear and out the other; **¡me resbala lo que diga de mí!** I couldn't care less what she says about me!
3 **resbalarse** *vpr* to slip (over); **me resbalé y me caí** I slipped and fell; **se resbaló con una piel de plátano** he slipped on a banana skin

resbalín *nm Chile Fam* slide

resbalón *nm* (a) *(caída)* slip; **dar** *o* **pegar un r.** to slip (b) *(indiscreción)* slip

resbalosa *nf* = heel-tapping dance typical of Argentina and Peru

resbaloso, -a *adj* (a) *(resbaladizo)* slippery (b) *Méx Fam (insinuante)* flirty

rescatador, -ora *nm,f* rescuer

rescatar *vt* (a) *(liberar, salvar)* to rescue (b) *(pagando rescate)* to ransom (c) *(recuperar) (herencia)* to recover

rescate *nm* (a) *(liberación, salvación)* rescue (b) *(dinero)* ransom; **pagaron un millón de dólares de r.** they paid a ransom of a million dollars (c) *(recuperación)* recovery

rescatista *nmf Méx* rescuer

rescindible *adj* rescindable

rescindir *vt* to rescind, to cancel

rescisión *nf* cancellation

rescoldo *nm* (a) *(brasa)* ember (b) *(resto)* lingering feeling, flicker; **todavía quedaban en él rescoldos de pasión** feelings of passion still lingered within him

resecamiento *nm* **evita el r. de la piel** it prevents your skin from drying out

resecar [60] 1 *vt* (a) *(piel)* to dry out (b) *(tierra)* to parch
2 **resecarse** *vpr* (a) *(piel)* to dry out (b) *(tierra)* to become parched

resección *nf Med* resection

reseco, -a *adj* (a) *(piel, garganta, pan)* very dry (b) *(tierra)* parched (c) *(flaco)* emaciated

resembrar [3] *vt* to resow

resentido, -a 1 *adj* bitter, resentful; **estar r. con alguien** to be really upset with sb
2 *nm,f* bitter *o* resentful person; **ser un r.** to be bitter *o* resentful

resentimiento *nm* resentment, bitterness

resentirse [63] *vpr* (a) *(debilitarse)* to be weakened; *(salud)* to deteriorate; **la calidad de su trabajo se resintió por la falta de motivación** her work deteriorated through lack of motivation (b) *(sentir)* **r. de** to be suffering from; **aún se resiente de aquel golpe** she's still suffering from the effects of that blow; **se resiente de la rodilla** he's got a bad knee, his knee is giving him trouble (c) *(ofenderse)* to be offended

reseña *nf* (a) *(crítica) (de libro, concierto, película)* review; *(de partido, conferencia)* report; **hizo** *o* **escribió una r. de la película** she reviewed the movie, she wrote a review of the movie (b) *(descripción)* description; **hizo una r. de su atacante** she gave a description of her attacker

reseñar *vt* (a) *(criticar) (libro, concierto, película)* to review; *(partido, conferencia)* to report on (b) *(describir)* to describe

reseque *etc ver* **resecar**

resero *nm RP (pastor)* herdsman

reserva 1 *nf* (a) *(de hotel, avión)* reservation; **no tenemos r.** we don't have a reservation; **he hecho la r. de las entradas** I've booked the tickets; **tengo una r. en el restaurante** I've reserved *o* booked a table at the restaurant ►► ***r. anticipada*** advance booking
(b) *(provisión)* reserves; **tenemos una r. de carbón para el invierno** we're stocked up with coal for the winter; **tener algo de r.** to keep sth in reserve; **agotó sus reservas de agua** he used up his water supply *o* his reserves of water ►► ***reservas energéticas*** energy reserves; ***reservas hídricas*** water reserves; ***reservas minerales*** mineral reserves
(c) *Econ* reserve ►► ***reservas de divisas*** foreign currency reserves; ***la R. Federal*** *(en Estados Unidos)* the Federal Reserve; ***reservas monetarias*** monetary reserves; ***reservas de oro*** gold reserves
(d) *(objeción, cautela)* reservation; **aceptaron el acuerdo, pero con reservas** they accepted the agreement, with some reservations; **sin reservas** without reservation; **tener reservas** to have reservations
(e) *(discreción)* discretion; **puedes hablar sin reservas** you can speak openly; **con la mayor r.** in the strictest confidence
(f) *(de indígenas)* reservation
(g) *(de animales, plantas)* reserve ►► ***r. de caza*** game preserve; ***r. forestal*** forest park; ***r. natural*** nature reserve
(h) *Mil* reserve; **pasar a la r.** to become a reservist
(i) *Biol (de grasa, energía)* reserves
2 *nmf Dep* reserve, substitute
3 *nm (vino)* vintage (wine) *(at least three years old)*
4 **a reserva de** *loc prep* pending; **a r. de un estudio más detallado...** pending a more detailed analysis...

reservación *nf Méx* reservation

reservado, -a 1 *adj* (a) *(mesa, plaza)* reserved (b) *(tema, asunto)* confidential (c) *(persona)* reserved
2 *nm (en restaurante)* private room; *(en tren)* reserved compartment

reservar 1 *vt* (a) *(billete, habitación)* to book, to reserve; **r. por adelantado** to book in advance; **reservado** *(en cartel)* reserved (b) *(guardar, apartar)* to set aside; **reservan la primera fila para los críticos** the front row is reserved for the critics; **¿me puedes r. un sitio a tu lado?** could you save a seat for me next to you?; **reservó la buena noticia para el final** she saved the good news till last (c) *(callar) (opinión, comentarios)* to reserve
2 **reservarse** *vpr* (a) *(esperar)* **reservarse para** to save oneself for; **me estoy reservando para el postre** I'm saving myself for the dessert (b) *(guardar para sí) (secreto)* to keep to oneself; *(dinero, derecho)* to retain (for oneself); **me reservo mi opinión sobre este asunto** I'm reserving judgement on this matter

reservista *Mil* 1 *adj* reserve; **militar r.** officer in the reserve
2 *nmf* reservist

resfriado, -a 1 *adj* **estar r.** to have a cold
2 *nm* cold; **coger un r.** to catch a cold

resfriarse [32] *vpr (constiparse)* to catch a cold

resfrío *nm Andes, RP* cold; **agarrarse un r.** to catch a cold

resguardar 1 *vt* to protect; **la sombrilla nos resguarda del sol** the parasol shades us from the sun
2 *vi* to protect (**de** against)
3 **resguardarse** *vpr (en un portal)* to shelter (**de** from); *(con abrigo, paraguas)* to protect oneself (**de** against); **se resguardaron de la lluvia debajo de un árbol** they sheltered from the rain under a tree

resguardo *nm* (a) *(documento) (de compra, carné)* receipt; *(de ingreso en un banco)* counterfoil; **conserve el r. de compra** please keep your receipt (b) *(protección)* protection; **al r. de** safe from; **estaban en un portal, al r. de la lluvia** they were sheltering from the rain in a doorway (c) *Méx, RP (control)* control

residencia *nf* (a) *(establecimiento) (de oficiales)* residence; **r. (de ancianos)** old people's home; **r. (de estudiantes)** *Br* hall of residence, *US* dormitory ►► ***r. de animales*** kennels; ***r. universitaria*** *Br* hall of residence, *US* dormitory
(b) *(vivienda)* residence; **su r. de verano** their summer residence
(c) *(localidad, domicilio)* residence; **fijaron su r. en la costa** they took up residence on the coast; **certificado de r.** = official document confirming one's residence in a country, city etc; **permiso de r.** residence permit
(d) *(permiso para extranjeros)* residence permit
(e) *(hotel)* boarding house
(f) *(hospital)* hospital
(g) *(estancia)* stay; **durante su r. en Alemania conoció a mucha gente** she met a lot of people while she was in Germany

residencial 1 *adj* residential; **barrio r.** *(lujoso)* residential area
2 *nm* (a) *CSur (pensión)* boarding house (b) *(edificio, urbanización)* = name given to up-market apartments or estates; **R. Louvre** ≃ Louvre Court

residente 1 *adj* (a) *(ciudadano)* resident (b) *(médico)* **médico r.** *Br* house officer, *US* intern (c) *Informát* resident
2 *nmf* (a) *(habitante)* resident (b) *(médico, veterinario) Br* house officer, *US* intern

residir *vi* (a) *(vivir)* to reside (b) *(radicar)* to lie, to reside (**en** in); **el atractivo del proyecto reside en su bajo costo** the attractive thing about the project is its low cost; **el poder legislativo reside en el Congreso** legislative power lies with *o* rests with Congress

residual *adj* residual; **aguas residuales** sewage

residuo *nm* (a) **residuos** *(material inservible)* waste ►► ***residuos industriales*** industrial waste; ***residuos nucleares*** nuclear waste; ***residuos radiactivos*** radioactive waste; ***residuos sólidos*** solid waste; ***residuos tóxicos*** toxic waste (b) *Quím* residue (c) *Mat* remainder

resiembro *etc ver* **resembrar**

resiento *etc ver* **resentirse**

resignación *nf* resignation; **se tomaron la derrota con r.** they accepted the defeat with resignation

resignadamente *adv* with resignation

resignarse *vpr* **r. (a hacer algo)** to resign oneself (to doing sth); **no se resignaba a seguir viviendo en la miseria** she refused to resign herself to carrying on living in poverty

resina *nf* resin

resinoso, -a *adj* resinous

resintiera *etc ver* **resentirse**

resistencia *nf* **(a)** *(fuerza)* strength **(b)** *(aguante, oposición)* resistance; *(para correr, hacer deporte)* stamina; **ofrecer** *o* **oponer r.** to put up resistance ▸▸ ***r. activa*** active resistance; ***r. pasiva*** passive resistance **(c)** *Elec* resistance **(d)** *Fís* resistance **(e)** *Hist* **la R.** the Resistance

resistente *adj (fuerte) (material)* strong, tough; *(tela)* tough, hard-wearing; *(estructura)* strong; *(persona, animal)* tough; *(planta)* tough, hardy; *(bacteria)* resistant; **r. al calor** heat-resistant; **r. al frío** resistant to the cold; **r. a los antibióticos** resistant to antibiotics; **hacerse r. (a)** to build up a resistance (to)

resistir 1 *vt* **(a)** *(peso, dolor, críticas)* to withstand, to take; *(ataque)* to withstand; **la presa no resistió la fuerza de las aguas** the dam could not withstand the force of the water; **resiste muy mal el calor** he can't take the heat **(b)** *(tentación, impulso, deseo)* to resist **(c)** *(tolerar)* to tolerate, to stand; **no lo resisto más** I can't stand it any longer

2 *vi* **(a)** *(ejército, ciudad)* **r. (a algo/a alguien)** to resist (sth/sb)

(b) *(persona, aparato)* to keep going; **ese corredor resiste mucho** that runner has a lot of stamina; **el tocadiscos aún resiste** the record player's still going strong; **r. a algo** to stand up to sth, to withstand sth

(c) *(mesa, dique)* to take the strain; **este puente ya no resiste en pie** this bridge is on its last legs; **r. a algo** to withstand sth

(d) *(mostrarse firme) (ante tentaciones)* to resist (it); **¡ya no resisto más!** I can't stand it any longer!; **r. a algo** to resist sth

3 resistirse *vpr* **resistirse (a algo)** to resist (sth); **por más que empujo esta puerta se resiste** however hard I push, this door refuses to give way; **resistirse a hacer algo** to refuse to do sth; **me resisto a creerlo** I refuse to believe it; **se resiste a marcharse de la ciudad** she refuses to leave the town; **el presidente se está resistiendo a abandonar el cargo** the president is unwilling to give up his post; **no hay hombre que se le resista** no man can resist her; **a este escritor no hay género que se le resista** there is no literary genre to which this writer cannot turn his hand; **se le resisten los idiomas** she just can't get the hang of languages

resma *nf Imprenta* ream

resol *nm* (sun's) glare; **hace r.** it's cloudy but very bright

resoli, resolí *nm* = liqueur typical of Cuenca, containing aniseed and cinnamon

resollar [64] *vi (jadear)* to pant; *(respirar)* to breathe

resolución *nf* **(a)** *(solución) (de una crisis)* resolution; *(de un crimen)* solution ▸▸ *Informát* ***r. de problemas*** troubleshooting **(b)** *(firmeza)* determination, resolve **(c)** *(decisión)* decision; *(de tribunal)* ruling; *(de Naciones Unidas)* resolution; **tomar una r.** to take a decision **(d)** *Informát (de imagen)* resolution

resoluto, -a *adj* resolute

resolutorio, -a *adj* resolute

resolver [41] **1** *vt* **(a)** *(solucionar) (duda, crisis)* to resolve; *(problema, caso, crucigrama, acertijo)* to solve **(b)** *(partido, disputa, conflicto)* to settle; **una canasta en el último segundo resolvió el partido a favor del equipo visitante** a basket in the last second of the game secured victory for the visitors **(c)** *(decidir)* **r. hacer algo** to decide to do sth; **resolvió llamar a la policía** she decided to call the police

2 resolverse *vpr* **(a)** *(solucionarse) (duda, crisis)* to be resolved; *(problema, caso)* to be solved; **el secuestro se resolvió con la liberación de los rehenes** the hijacking was resolved *o* brought to an end with the release of the hostages **(b)** *(decidirse)* **resolverse a hacer algo** to decide to do sth **(c)** *(terminar)* **el huracán se resolvió en una tormenta tropical** the hurricane ended up as a tropical storm

resonancia *nf* **(a)** *(sonido)* resonance **(b)** *Mús* resonance **(c)** *Fís* resonance ▸▸ ***r. magnética*** magnetic resonance imaging; **le hicieron una r. magnética** they gave him an MRI scan **(d)** *(importancia)* repercussions; **tener r.** to cause a stir; **el escándalo tuvo mucha r. en la prensa** the scandal caused quite a stir in the press

resonante *adj* **(a)** *(que suena, retumba)* resounding **(b)** *(importante)* important

resonar [64] *vi* to resound, to echo; **aún resuenan en mi mente sus gritos de dolor** her cries of pain are still ringing in my head

resoplar *vi (de cansancio)* to pant; *(de enfado)* to snort

resoplido *nm (por cansancio)* pant; *(por enfado)* snort

resorción *nf Med* resorption

resorte *nm* **(a)** *(muelle)* spring **(b)** *(medio)* means; **tocar todos los resortes** to pull out all the stops **(c)** *Méx (elástico)* elastic **(d)** *Méx (órbita)* responsibility; **ese delito es del r. de la justicia penal** that crime falls under the jurisdiction of criminal law

> **Falso amigo**: El sustantivo inglés **resort** no es la traducción del español **resorte**. En inglés **resort** significa "recurso", "centro turístico" o "refugio".

resortera *nf Méx* catapult, *US* slingshot

respaldar 1 *vt* **(a)** *(proyecto, empresa)* to back, to support; **varios intelectuales respaldan la candidatura del escritor** several intellectuals are backing *o* supporting the writer as a candidate **(b)** *(tesis)* to back up, to support; **el descubrimiento respalda su teoría** the discovery backs up *o* supports his theory

2 respaldarse *vpr* **(a) respaldarse en** *(la espalda)* to fall back on; **se respaldó en el sillón** she sat back in her armchair **(b)** *(apoyarse)* **se respalda siempre en sus padres** he's always leaning on his parents (for support)

respaldo *nm* **(a)** *(de asiento)* back; **asiento r. abatible** reclining seat **(b)** *(apoyo)* backing, support; **cuenta con el r. de todo el partido** he has the backing *o* support of the entire party

respectar *v impersonal* **por** *o* **en lo que a mí respecta, la fiesta puede celebrarse** as far as I'm concerned, the party can go ahead; **expuso sus reservas por** *o* **en lo que respecta a la unión monetaria** he expressed his reservations concerning Monetary Union

respectivamente *adv* respectively

respectivo, -a *adj* respective; **en lo r. a** with regard to

respecto 1 al respecto, a este respecto *loc adv* in this respect; **no sé nada al r.** I don't know anything about it; **no tengo nada que añadir al r.** I have nothing to add on the matter; **a este r. dijo que ya se había aprobado un paquete de ayudas a la región** with regard to this subject, he said that an aid package for the area had already been approved

2 (con) respecto a, respecto de *loc prep* regarding

respetabilidad *nf* respectability

respetable 1 *adj* **(a)** *(venerable)* respectable **(b)** *(considerable)* considerable; **le tocó una r. cantidad de dinero** he won a considerable sum of money

2 *nm Fam* **el r.** *(en concierto)* the audience; *(en encuentro deportivo, toros)* the crowd

respetar *vt* **(a)** *(persona, costumbre, deseos)* to respect; *(norma)* to observe; *(la palabra)* to honour; **hay que r. a los ancianos** you should show respect for the elderly; **no respeta las señales de tráfico** he takes no notice of traffic signs; **el accidente se produjo porque no respetó un ceda el paso** the accident happened because he ignored a *Br* give way *o US* yield sign; **hacerse r.** to earn (people's) respect

(b) *(no destruir)* to spare; **respeten las plantas** *(en letrero)* keep off the flowerbeds

respeto *nm* **(a)** *(consideración)* respect **(a** *o* **por** for); **el r. a los derechos humanos** respect for human rights; **trata a sus profesores con mucho r.** he shows a great deal of respect towards his teachers, he is very respectful towards his teachers; **es una falta de r.** it shows a lack of respect; **me parece una falta de r. hacia sus compañeros** I think it shows a lack of consideration towards his colleagues; **faltar al r. a alguien** to be disrespectful to sb; **con su acción se ganó el r. de todos** what he did earned him everybody's respect; **dentro de la iglesia hay que guardar r.** you must be respectful inside the temple; **sus opiniones no me merecen demasiado r.** I have very little respect for her opinions; **siento mucho r. por él** I respect him greatly; **por r. a** out of consideration for

(b) *(miedo)* **tener r. a las alturas** to be afraid of heights

(c) respetos *(saludos)* respects; **le presentaron sus respetos** they paid him their respects

respetuosamente *adv* respectfully

respetuoso, -a *adj* respectful **(con** of)

respingado, -a *adj Am* turned up

respingar [38] *vi (protestar)* to make a fuss, to complain

respingo *nm* **(a)** *(movimiento)* start, jump; **dar un r.** to start **(b)** *(contestación)* shrug *(of annoyance or disdain)*; **dio un r. al escuchar mi propuesta** he reacted to my proposal with a disdainful/angry shrug

respingón, -ona *adj (nariz)* turned up, retroussé; *(trasero, pecho)* pert

respiración *nf* **(a)** *(humana, animal)* breathing, *Espec* respiration; **contener la r.** to hold one's breath; **quedarse sin r.** *(agotado)* to be out of breath; *(asombrado)* to be stunned ▸▸ ***r. artificial*** artificial respiration; ***r. asistida*** artificial respiration; ***r. boca a boca*** mouth-to-mouth resuscitation, the kiss of life; **hacer la r. boca a boca a alguien** to give sb mouth-to-mouth resuscitation *o* the kiss of life **(b)** *(ventilación)* ventilation

respiradero *nm* **(a)** *(hueco)* vent **(b)** *(conducto)* ventilation shaft

respirador *nm* **r. (artificial)** *(máquina)* respirator, ventilator

respirar 1 *vt* (a) *(aire)* to breathe; **respirábamos el aire puro de la montaña** we breathed in the pure mountain air; **en esa casa se respira el amor por la música** a love of music pervades that house; **en la ciudad se respira el ambiente carnavalesco** the carnival atmosphere pervades the city (b) *(mostrar)* to exude; **el equipo respiraba optimismo** the team was radiating *o* exuding optimism

2 *vi* (a) *(aire)* to breathe; **respira hondo** breathe deeply, take a deep breath; **aún respira** she's still breathing; EXPR **no dejar r. a alguien** not to allow sb a moment's peace

(b) *(ventilarse) (vino)* to breathe; **levanta el capó para que respire el motor** lift the *Br* bonnet *o US* hood so that the engine can cool down

(c) *(sentir alivio)* to breathe again; **ahora que han aparecido los niños ya podemos r.** now that the children have turned up we can breathe again

(d) *(relajarse)* to have a breather; **sin r.** *(sin descanso)* without a break; *(atentamente)* with great attention; **después de tanto trabajo necesito r.** I need a breather after all that work; **con tanto trabajo no puedo ni r.** I'm absolutely overwhelmed with work at the moment

respiratorio, -a *adj* respiratory

respiro *nm* (a) *(descanso)* rest; **no he tenido ni un momento de r. en toda la mañana** I haven't had a moment's rest all morning; **no me da ni un r.** he never gives me a moment's rest; **dame un r., ¿no ves que estoy ocupado?** give me a break, can't you see I'm busy?

(b) *(alivio)* relief, respite; **las ayudas públicas han dado un r. a la crisis de la empresa** the government aid has provided temporary relief to the struggling company; **les dieron un r. para la devolución de la deuda** they gave them a bit longer to pay off the debt

resplandecer [46] *vi* (a) *(brillar)* to shine (b) *(destacar)* **resplandecía por su belleza** she was dazzlingly beautiful (c) *(brillar)* **su rostro resplandecía de alegría** her face shone *o* glowed with happiness

resplandeciente *adj* (a) *(brillante) (sol, luna, estrellas)* sparkling; *(plata)* shiny, gleaming; *(vestimenta, color)* resplendent; **el salón quedó r.** the living-room was sparkling clean (b) *(sonrisa)* beaming; **su cara estaba r. de orgullo** she glowed with pride

resplandor *nm* (a) *(luz)* brightness; *(de fuego)* glow (b) *(brillo)* gleam

---

RESPONDER 1 *vt (contestar)* to answer; *(con insolencia)* to answer back; **respondió que sí/que no** she said yes/no; **respondió que lo pensaría** she said that she'd think about it

2 *vi* (a) *(contestar)* **r. (a algo)** *(pregunta, llamada, carta, saludo)* to answer (sth); **no responde nadie** *(al llamar)* there's no answer; **responde al nombre de Toby** he answers to the name of Toby

(b) *(replicar)* to answer back; **¡no respondas a tu madre!** don't answer your mother back!

(c) *(reaccionar)* to respond (**a** to); **el paciente no responde al tratamiento** the patient isn't responding to the treatment; **la nueva máquina responde bien** the new machine is performing well; **los mandos no (me) responden** the controls aren't responding; **el delantero no respondió a las provocaciones de su marcador** the forward didn't react to his marker's attempts to provoke him

(d) *(responsabilizarse)* **si te pasa algo yo no respondo** I can't be held responsible if anything happens to you; **r. de algo/por alguien** to answer for sth/for sb; **yo respondo de su inocencia/por él** I can vouch for his innocence/for him; **responderá de sus actos ante el parlamento** she will answer for her actions before Parliament; **¡no respondo de mis actos!** I can't be responsible for what I might do!; **yo no respondo de lo que pueda pasar si se autoriza la manifestación** I won't be held responsible for what might happen if the demonstration is authorized

(e) *(corresponder)* **las medidas responden a la crisis** the measures are in keeping with the nature of the crisis; **un producto que responde a las necesidades del consumidor medio** a product which meets the needs of the average consumer; **no ha respondido a nuestras expectativas** it hasn't lived up to our expectations

(f) *(ser consecuencia de)* **r. a algo** to reflect sth; **las largas listas de espera responden a la falta de medios** the long waiting lists reflect the lack of resources

---

respondón, -ona 1 *adj* **es muy r.** he answers back too much

2 *nm,f* **es un r.** he answers back too much

responsabilidad *nf* (a) *(obligación)* responsibility; *Der* liability; **es r. suya atender el teléfono** it's her job to answer the phone; **exigir r. a alguien por algo** to call sb to account for sth; **no quiero que recaiga sobre mí esa r.** I don't want that responsibility to fall on my shoulders; **tener la r. de algo** to be responsible for sth; **los padres tienen la r. de alimentar a los hijos** fathers are responsible for feeding their children; **no tuve ninguna r. en el accidente** I was not in the least to blame for the accident ▸▸ *Der* ***r. atenuada*** diminished responsibility; *Der* ***r. civil*** civil liability; ***r. limitada*** limited liability; *Der* ***r. penal*** criminal liability; ***responsabilidades del puesto*** *(en un empleo)* job description

(b) *(cualidad)* responsibility; **tiene un gran sentido de la r.** she has a strong sense of responsibility

(c) *(importancia)* responsibility; **puesto de r.** senior position; **no quiero tareas de tanta r.** I don't want to do tasks which involve so much responsibility

responsabilizar [14] 1 *vt* **r. a alguien (de algo)** to hold sb responsible (for sth)

2 **responsabilizarse** *vpr* to accept responsibility (**de** for); **la empresa se responsabilizó del accidente** the company accepted responsibility for the accident; **no nos responsabilizamos de ningún daño por uso indebido del producto** we do not accept liability for any harm caused by incorrect use of the product

responsable 1 *adj* (a) *(de algo)* responsible (**de** for); *Der* liable; **soy r. de mis actos** I'm responsible for my actions; **fue r. del accidente** he was responsible for the accident; **hacerse r. de** *(responsabilizarse de)* to take responsibility for; *(atentado, secuestro)* to claim responsibility for (b) *(sensato)* responsible; **es muy r.** she's very responsible

2 *nmf* (a) *(culpable, autor)* person responsible; *Der* liable person; **los responsables** those responsible/liable; **tú eres el r. de...** you're responsible/liable for... (b) *(encargado)* person in charge; **soy el r. de la sección de ventas** I'm in charge of the sales department

responso *nm* prayer for the dead

respuesta *nf* (a) *(contestación)* answer, reply; *(en exámenes)* answer; **en r. a** in reply to; **r. afirmativa** affirmative reply (b) *(reacción)* response ▸▸ *Biol* ***r. inmunitaria*** immune response

resquebrajadizo, -a *adj* **es muy r.** *(loza)* it cracks very easily; *(madera)* it splits very easily

resquebrajadura *nf (en piedra, loza, plástico)* crack; *(en madera)* split

resquebrajamiento *nm* (a) *(grieta) (en piedra, loza, plástico)* crack; *(en madera)* split (b) *(cuarteamiento)* cracking; *(desmoronamiento)* crumbling

resquebrajar 1 *vt (piedra, loza, plástico)* to crack; *(madera)* to split

2 **resquebrajarse** *vpr (piedra, loza, plástico)* to crack; *(madera)* to split; **se está resquebrajando la sociedad** society is beginning to fall apart *o* crumble

resquemor *nm* resentment, bitterness

resquicio *nm* (a) *(abertura)* chink; *(grieta)* crack; **un r. legal** a loophole in the law

(b) *(pizca)* glimmer; **el mal tiempo no deja r. alguno a la esperanza de encontrar supervivientes** the bad weather does not permit even a glimmer of hope of finding survivors; **el comunicado de la organización revelaba sin r. de duda su actitud beligerante** the communiqué made by the organization left not the slightest trace of doubt as to its belligerent attitude

resta *nf* subtraction; **las restas se me dan muy mal** I'm no good at subtraction

restablecer [46] 1 *vt (paz, orden, confianza)* to restore; *(relaciones diplomáticas)* to re-establish

2 **restablecerse** *vpr* (a) *(curarse)* to recover (**de** from) (b) *(reinstaurarse)* to be re-established

restablecimiento *nm* (a) *(reinstauración) (de paz, orden, confianza)* restoration; *(de relaciones diplomáticas)* re-establishment (b) *(cura)* recovery

restallar 1 *vt* (a) *(látigo)* to crack (b) *(lengua)* to click

2 *vi* (a) *(látigo)* to crack (b) *(lengua)* to click

restallido *nm (de látigo)* crack

restante *adj* remaining; **lo r.** the rest

restañar *vt (herida)* to staunch

restar 1 *vt* (a) *Mat* to subtract; **r. una cantidad de otra** to subtract one figure from another; **a esa cantidad réstale los gastos de envío** subtract *o* deduct the postage and packing from that figure

(b) *(quitar, disminuir)* **r. importancia a algo** to play down the importance of sth; **r. méritos a algo/a alguien** to detract from sth/sb; **su participación en el escándalo le resta legitimidad** her involvement in the scandal detracts from her legitimacy

2 *vi* (a) *(faltar)* to be left; **me resta envolver los regalos** I still have to wrap up the presents; **sólo restan tres días** only three days are left; **sólo me resta agradecerles su ayuda** all that remains is for me to thank you for your help (b) *(en tenis)* to return

restauración *nf* (**a**) *(de muebles, arte, edificio)* restoration (**b**) *(de monarquía, democracia)* restoration (**c**) *(rama de hostelería)* **el sector de la r.** the restaurant sector

restaurador, -ora *nm,f* (**a**) *(de muebles, arte)* restorer (**b**) *(hostelero)* restaurateur

restaurante, *Am* **restaurant,** *Am* **restaurán** *nm* restaurant ▸▸ ***r. de carretera*** *Br* transport café, *US* truck stop

restaurar *vt* (**a**) *(muebles, arte, edificio)* to restore (**b**) *(monarquía, democracia)* to restore (**c**) *(recuperar)* to restore; **r. fuerzas** to get one's strength back

restinga *nf* sandbar

restitución *nf* return

restituir [34] **1** *vt* (**a**) *(devolver) (objeto)* to return; *(derechos)* to restore (**b**) *(en cargo)* to reinstate; **r. a alguien en un puesto** to reinstate sb in a post (**c**) *(salud)* to restore

2 restituirse *vpr* **restituirse a** *(regresar)* to return to

resto *nm* (**a**) **el r.** *(lo que queda)* the rest; **el r. se fue a bailar** the rest (of them) went dancing; **me da igual lo que opine el r.** I don't care what the rest of them think *o* what the others think; **... y el r. de la historia ya la sabes** ... and you already know the rest of the story; EXPR *Fam* **echar el r.: tenemos que echar el r.** we have to give it our all

(**b**) *Mat* **el r.** the remainder

(**c**) **restos** *(sobras)* leftovers; *(cadáver)* remains; *(ruinas)* ruins; **encontraron los cuerpos entre los restos del naufragio** the bodies were found amidst the wreckage of the ship ▸▸ ***restos mortales*** (mortal) remains

(**d**) *(en tenis)* return (of serve); **al r., Jiménez** Jiménez to receive

restorán *nm RP* restaurant

restregar [43] **1** *vt* (**a**) *(frotar)* to rub hard; *(para limpiar)* to scrub (**b**) *(refregar)* **se lo estuvo restregando toda la noche** he was rubbing it in all evening; **les restregó la derrota en sus narices** he really rubbed it in about the defeat

2 restregarse *vpr (frotarse)* to rub; **al gato le gusta restregarse contra las piernas de su amo** the cat likes to rub against its owner's legs

restregón *nm (frotamiento)* hard rub; *(para limpiar)* scrub

restricción *nf* restriction; **no hay restricciones de edad** there's no age limit; **restricciones de agua** water rationing, water restrictions; **restricciones eléctricas** power cuts; **han impuesto restricciones a la importación de vehículos extranjeros** restrictions have been placed on the importing of foreign vehicles; **esta opción permite navegar por Internet sin restricciones horarias** this option allows you unmetered access to the Net twenty-four hours a day

restrictivo, -a *adj* restrictive

restriego *etc ver* **restregar**

restringido, -a *adj* limited, restricted

restringir [24] *vt* to limit, to restrict

resucitación *nf* resuscitation

resucitar 1 *vt* (**a**) *(persona)* to bring back to life; **Jesús resucitó a varios muertos** Jesus raised several people from the dead; EXPR *Fam* **r. a un muerto: tómate un trago de este licor, resucita a un muerto** have some of this to drink, it's potent stuff; **¡este olor resucita a un muerto!** it smells wonderful in here! (**b**) *(costumbre)* to resurrect, to revive

2 *vi (persona)* to rise from the dead

resuello 1 *ver* **resollar**

2 *nm (jadeo)* pant, panting; **quedarse sin r.** to be out of breath

resueltamente *adv* resolutely, determinedly

resuelto, -a 1 *participio ver* **resolver**

2 *adj* (**a**) *(solucionado)* solved (**b**) *(decidido)* determined; **estar r. a hacer algo** to be determined to do sth

resuelve *nmf Ven Fam Hum* casual lover

resuelvo *etc ver* **resolver**

resueno *etc ver* **resonar**

resultado *nm* (**a**) *(efecto)* result; **el r. de sus gestiones fue un acuerdo de paz** their efforts resulted in a peace agreement; **los resultados económicos han sido muy positivos** the economic results have been very positive; **como r.** as a result; **dar r.** to work (out), to have the desired effect; **estos zapatos me han dado un r. buenísimo** these shoes have turned out to be really good; **dar buen r.** to work well; **el edificio es r. de muchos años de trabajo** the building is the result *o* fruit of many years' work; **el cambio tuvo por r. una mejora en el juego** the substitution led to an improvement in their game; **el experimento no ha tenido el r. esperado** the experiment has not had the expected result; **r. final** end result

(**b**) *(de análisis, competición)* result

(**c**) *(marcador)* score; **¿cuál es el r.?** what's the score?

resultando *nm Der* conclusion

resultante 1 *adj* resultant

2 *nf* resultant

resultar 1 *vi* (**a**) *(salir)* to (turn out to) be; **¿cómo resultó?** how did it turn out?; **resultó un éxito** it was a success; **el viaje resultó ser una maravilla** the journey was wonderful; **toda la confusión resultó ser un malentendido** all the confusion turned out to be because of a misunderstanding; **r. en** *(dar como resultado)* to result in; **r. herido/muerto** to be injured/killed; **resultó ileso** he was uninjured; **nuestro equipo resultó vencedor** our team came out on top; **su idea no resultó** his idea didn't work; **intentaré convencerle, pero no creo que resulte** I'll try to talk him round, but I don't think it will work

(**b**) *(originarse)* **r. de** to come of, to result from; **de aquella reunión no resultó nada** nothing came of that meeting

(**c**) *(ser)* to be; **esta oficina resulta demasiado pequeña para tanta gente** this office is too small for so many people; **resulta sorprendente** it's surprising; **me resultó imposible terminar antes** I was unable to finish earlier; **me resulta muy simpática** I find her very nice; **este tema me está resultando ya aburrido** this topic is beginning to bore me; **resulta mejor comprar a granel** it's better to buy in bulk; **r. útil** to be useful; **resultó ser mentira** it turned out to be a lie

2 *v impersonal (suceder)* **resultó que era un impostor** he turned out to be an impostor; **ahora resulta que no quiere alquilarlo** now it seems that she doesn't want to rent it; **al final resultó que tenía razón** in the end it turned out that she was right; **ahora va a r. que la culpa es mía** so now it's suddenly all going to be my fault; **resulta que su marido ha tenido un accidente** it seems her husband has had an accident

resultas: a resultas de, de resultas de *loc prep* as a result of; **murió a** *o* **de r. de las heridas recibidas** he died as a result of his injuries

resultón, -ona *adj Fam (person)* sexy, desirable; **el coche es muy r.** the car looks great

resumen *nm* summary; **hazme un r. de lo que pasó** give me a summary of what happened; **van a emitir el r. de la ceremonia inaugural** the highlights of the opening ceremony are going to be broadcast; **en r.** in short

resumidero *nm Am* drain, sewer

resumido, -a *adj* brief; **en resumidas cuentas** in short

resumir 1 *vt (abreviar)* to summarize; *(discurso)* to sum up

2 *vi* to sum up; **resume, no queda mucho tiempo** just give us a summary, there's not much time left; **resumiendo, que estamos muy contentos con los resultados** to sum up *o* in short, we are very happy with the results

3 resumirse *vpr* (**a**) *(abreviarse)* **se resume en pocas palabras** it can be summed up in a few words (**b**) **resumirse en** *(saldarse con)* to result in

> **Falso amigo**: El verbo inglés **to resume** no es la traducción del español **resumir**. En inglés **to resume** significa "reanudar" o "continuar".

resurgimiento *nm* resurgence

resurgir [24] *vi* **el equipo ha resurgido tras una mala racha** the team has bounced back *o* returned to form after a bad patch; **el movimiento pacifista resurgió con fuerza en aquella década** the pacifist movement experienced a major resurgence during that decade; **la empresa ha resurgido de sus cenizas** the company has risen from the ashes; **han resurgido los combates en la frontera** there have been renewed outbreaks of fighting along the border

resurrección *nf* resurrection

retablo *nm* (**a**) *(en iglesia)* altarpiece (**b**) *Teatro* tableau

retacado, -a *adj Méx Fam* packed, crammed

retacar *Méx Fam* **1** *vt* to cram; **no se puede r. las calles con puestos de comida rápida** you can't just cram the streets with fast-food stands; **la basura suele r. las coladeras** the drains tend to get blocked up with *Br* rubbish *o US* garbage

2 retacarse *vpr* to stuff oneself

retacear *vt RP* (**a**) *(recortar) (presupuesto)* to cut; *(recursos)* to cut back on (**b**) *(escatimar)* to skimp on

retaceo *nm RP* cut, cutback; EXPR **sin retaceos** openly

retachar *Méx Fam* **1** *vt* to return; **préstame tu lápiz, ahorita te lo retacho** lend me your pencil, I'll give it back to you in a moment; **lo retacharon al hospital porque le dio otro ataque** they took him back to hospital because he had another attack; **me dio un golpe, pero se**

lo retaché he hit me, but I hit him back

2 **retacharse** *vpr* (a) *(retornar)* to go/come back, to return; **tuve que retacharme a la casa porque me había olvidado la cartera** I had to go back to the house because I'd left my wallet behind (b) *(volverse contra)* **quería perjudicarme, pero se le retachó** he wanted to harm me, but it backfired on him; **no eches maldiciones, se te van a r.** don't curse anybody, the curses will return to haunt you

retache *nm Méx Fam* **de r.** back; **manda de r. a ese niño a su casa, tiene fiebre** send this child back home, he's got a temperature; **lleva este queso de r. a la tienda, está averiado** take this cheese back to the shop, it's off

retaco *nm Fam* **es un r.** he's short and fat

retacón, -ona *RP Fam* 1 *adj* short and fat
2 *nm,f* **es un r.** he's short and fat

retador, -ora *nm,f Am* challenger

retaguardia *nf* (a) *Mil (tropa)* rearguard (b) *Mil (territorio)* rear; **tienen dos acorazados en r.** they have two battleships at their rear (c) *Fam (parte trasera)* rear, back

retahíla *nf* string, series *(singular)*; **tenían que memorizar una r. de nombres de reyes** they had to memorize a long list of kings' names; **una r. de insultos** a stream of insults

retal *nm* remnant

retama *nf* broom ►► ***r. de olor*** Spanish broom; ***r. de los tintoreros*** dyer's-greenweed

retar *vt* (a) *(desafiar)* to challenge (**a** to); **me retó a una carrera** she challenged me to a race (b) *RP (reñir)* to tell off (c) *Chile (insultar)* to insult, to abuse

retardado, -a 1 *adj* (a) *(atrasado)* delayed (b) *RP Pey (persona)* (mentally) retarded
2 *nm,f RP Pey (persona)* moron, cretin, *US* retard

retardador, -ora 1 *adj* retardant
2 *nm* retardant

retardar 1 *vt* (a) *(retrasar)* to delay (b) *(frenar)* to hold up, to slow down
2 **retardarse** *vpr (retrasarse)* to be delayed

retardo *nm* (a) *(atraso)* delay (b) *RP Pey (mental)* **tener un r.** to be (mentally) retarded

retazo *nm* (a) *(resto)* remnant (b) *(pedazo)* fragment; **una conferencia hecha de retazos** a speech patched together from bits and pieces of other speeches

retel *nm* = special fishing net used for catching crayfish

retén *nm* (a) *(de soldados)* reserve; **un r. de bomberos** a squad of firefighters (b) *(de cosas)* stock (c) *Am (de menores)* reformatory, reform school

retención *nf* (a) *(en comisaría)* detention (b) *(en el sueldo)* deduction; **las retenciones fiscales han disminuido** the amount of tax deducted from wages at source has gone down (c) *(de tráfico)* hold-up, delay (d) *Med* retention

retener [67] *vt* (a) *(detener)* to hold back; *(en comisaría)* to detain; **no me retuvo mucho tiempo** he didn't keep me long; **r. el tráfico** to hold up the traffic
(b) *(contener) (impulso, ira)* to hold back, to restrain; *(aliento)* to hold
(c) *(conservar)* to retain; **las hojas retienen la humedad** leaves retain moisture
(d) *(quedarse con)* to hold on to, to keep
(e) *(memorizar)* to remember
(f) *(deducir del sueldo)* to deduct; **el fisco me retiene el 20 por ciento del sueldo** 20 percent of my salary goes in tax
(g) *(apoderarse de) (sueldo)* to withhold

retengo *etc ver* **retener**

retentiva *nf* memory

retentivo, -a *adj* retentive

Retevisión [reteβi'sjon] *nf* (*abrev de* **Red Técnica Española de Televisión**) = Spanish national broadcasting network

reticencia *nf* (a) *(resistencia)* reluctance; **con reticencias** reluctantly; **aceptó el puesto, pero con muchas reticencias** he accepted the post, albeit with a great deal of reluctance *o* very reluctantly; **tengo algunas reticencias** I have some reservations (b) *(insinuación)* insinuation

reticente *adj* (a) *(reacio)* reluctant; **el gobierno es r. a las privatizaciones** the government is reluctant to privatize; **se mostró r. a dar su opinión** he was reluctant to give his opinion (b) *(con insinuaciones)* full of insinuation

> **Falso amigo**: El adjetivo inglés **reticent** no es la traducción de **reticente**. En inglés **reticent** significa "reservado".

rético, -a 1 *adj* Rhaetian, Rhaeto-Romanic
2 *nm* Rhaetian, Rhaeto-Romanic

retícula *nf* reticle

reticular *adj* reticulate

retículo *nm* (a) *(tejido)* reticulum (b) *Zool* reticulum (c) *(en óptica)* reticle, reticule

retiene *ver* **retener**

retina *nf* retina; **desprendimiento de r.** detached retina, retinal detachment

retinitis *nf inv Med* retinitis

retintín *nm* (a) *(ironía)* sarcastic tone; **con r.** sarcastically (b) *(tintineo)* ringing; **aún tengo el r. de las campanas en el oído** I can still hear the bells ringing in my ears

retinto, -a *adj* dark brown

retirada *nf* (a) *Mil (retroceso)* retreat; **batirse en r.** to beat a retreat; **cubrir la r.** to cover the retreat; **tocar la r.** to sound the retreat
(b) *(de carné, pasaporte)* withdrawal
(c) *(de fondos)* withdrawal
(d) *(de acusación)* withdrawal
(e) *(de moneda, producto)* withdrawal; **el ayuntamiento es responsable de la r. de las basuras** the town council is responsible for refuse collection; **han ordenado la r. del mercado del producto** they have ordered the product to be withdrawn from *o* taken off the market
(f) *(de competición, actividad)* withdrawal; **el presidente ordenó la r. del embajador** the president ordered the ambassador to be recalled; **piden la r. de las tropas de la región** they are asking for the troops to be withdrawn from the region; **su r. de la política sorprendió a todos** her retirement from politics surprised everybody; **el deportista ha anunciado su r. de los terrenos de juego** the sportsman has announced his retirement from the game

retirado, -a 1 *adj* (a) *(jubilado)* retired (b) *(solitario)* isolated, secluded; **un pueblecito r. de la civilización** a little village miles away from anywhere
2 *nm,f (jubilado)* retired person, *US* retiree

RETIRAR 1 *vt* (a) *(quitar, sacar)* to remove (**a** from); *(moneda, producto)* to withdraw (**de** from); *(carné, pasaporte)* to take away (**a** from); *(ayuda, subvención, apoyo)* to withdraw (**a** from); *(ejército, tropas)* to withdraw (**de** from); *(embajador)* to withdraw, to recall (**de** from); **r. dinero del banco/de la cuenta** to withdraw money from the bank/one's account; **el entrenador retiró a Claudio del terreno de juego/del equipo** the manager took Claudio off/left Claudio out of the team; **me ha retirado el saludo** she's not speaking to me
(b) *(apartar, quitar de en medio) (objeto)* to move away; *(nieve)* to clear; *(mano)* to withdraw; **habrá que r. ese armario de ahí** we'll have to move that wardrobe (away) from there; **retira el dedo o te cortarás** move your finger back or you'll cut yourself
(c) *(recoger, llevarse)* to pick up, to collect; **puede pasar a r. sus fotos el jueves** you can pick your photos up *o* collect your photos on Thursday
(d) *(retractarse de) (insultos, acusaciones, afirmaciones)* to take back; *(denuncia)* to drop; **iretira eso que** *o* **lo que dijiste!** take that back!, take back what you said!
(e) *(jubilar) (a empleado)* to retire; **una lesión lo retiró de la alta competición** an injury forced him to retire from top-flight competition
2 **retirarse** *vpr* (a) *(jubilarse)* to retire
(b) *(abandonar, irse) (de elecciones, negociaciones)* to withdraw (**de** from); *(de competición)* to pull out (**de** of); *(atleta, caballo)* to drop out (**de** of); *(en ciclismo, automovilismo)* to retire (**de** from); **se retiró de la reunión** she left the meeting; **se retira (del terreno de juego) López** López is coming off
(c) *(ejército, tropas) (de campo de batalla)* to retreat (**de** from); *(de país, zona ocupada)* to withdraw (**de** from), to pull out (**de** of)
(d) *(irse a dormir)* to go to bed; *(irse a casa)* to go home
(e) *(apartarse)* to move away (**de** from); **retírate, que no dejas pasar** move out of the way, people can't get past; **se retiró el pelo de la cara** she brushed the hair out of her eyes

---

retiro *nm* (a) *(jubilación)* retirement (b) *(pensión)* pension (c) *(refugio)* retreat (d) *(religioso)* retreat

reto *nm* (a) *(desafío)* challenge (b) *RP (regaño)* telling-off, talking-to

retobado, -a *adj* (a) *Méx (obstinado)* stubborn, obstinate (b) *Méx, RP (indómito)* wild, unruly

retobarse *vpr RP* to get angry *o* irritated; **se retobó la yegua** the horse reared up; **lo regañé y se me retobó** I told him off and he snapped back at me

retobo *nm* (**a**) *Col, Hond (desecho)* refuse (**b**) *Chile, Perú (arpillera)* sackcloth

retocado *nm* **r. *fotográfico*** photo retouching; *Informát* **r. *de imagen*** image retouching

retocar [60] **1** *vt (prenda de vestir)* to alter; *(proyecto, escrito)* to make a few final adjustments to; *(fotografía, imagen)* to retouch; **r. la pintura** to touch up the paintwork

2 retocarse *vpr* **se retocó un poco antes de salir** she touched up her make-up before going out

retoce *etc ver* **retozar**

retomar *vt* to take up again; **r. la conversación** to pick up the conversation

retoñar *vi* (**a**) *(planta)* to sprout, to shoot (**b**) *(situación, problema)* to reappear

retoño *nm* (**a**) *(planta)* sprout, shoot (**b**) *Fam (hijo)* **vino con sus dos retoños** he came with his two little ones; **mis retoños** my offspring

retoque 1 *ver* **retocar**

2 *nm (toque)* touching-up; *(de prenda de vestir)* alteration; **hacer un r. a algo** *(foto, con pintura)* to touch sth up; *(prenda de vestir)* to alter sth; **dar los últimos retoques a algo** to put the finishing touches to sth ►► ***r. fotográfico*** photo retouching

retorcer [15] **1** *vt* (**a**) *(torcer) (brazo, alambre)* to twist; *(ropa, cuello)* to wring; **¡le voy a r. el pescuezo como lo vea!** I'll wring his neck if I get my hands on him! (**b**) *(tergiversar)* to twist

2 retorcerse *vpr (persona)* **se retorcía de risa** she was doubled up with laughter, she was in stitches; **se retorcía de dolor** he was writhing (about) in agony

retorcido, -a *adj* (**a**) *(torcido) (brazo, alambre)* twisted; *(ropa)* wrung out (**b**) *(estilo, lenguaje)* involved, convoluted (**c**) *(enrevesado)* devious; **¿por qué eres siempre tan r.?** why do you always have to be so devious? (**d**) *(malintencionado)* twisted, warped

retorcijón = **retortijón**

retorcimiento *nm* (**a**) *(de brazo, alambre) (de ropa)* wringing out (**b**) *(de estilo, lenguaje)* convolutedness (**c**) *(carácter enrevesado)* deviousness (**d**) *(mala intención)* twisted nature, warped nature

retórica *nf* (**a**) *(arte)* rhetoric (**b**) *(habla rebuscada)* rhetoric, bombast

retórico, -a 1 *adj* (**a**) *(figura, lenguaje, estilo)* rhetorical (**b**) *(rebuscado)* bombastic

2 *nm,f (persona)* rhetorician

retornable *adj* returnable; **no r.** non-returnable

retornar 1 *vt* to return

2 *vi* to return

retorno *nm* (**a**) *(regreso)* return; **a su r.** on her return, when she got back (**b**) *(devolución)* return (**c**) *Informát* return ►► ***r. de carro*** carriage return; ***r. manual*** hard return

retorromano, -a 1 *adj* Rhaeto-Romanic

2 *nm* Rhaeto-Romanic

retorta *nf* retort

retortero *nm Fam* EXPR **andar al r.** to be extremely busy; EXPR **tener al r.: tiene todo el cuarto al r.** his room is utter chaos; EXPR **traer a alguien al r.** to keep sb on the go

retortijón, retorcijón *nm* stomach cramp; **me dio un r.** I got a stomach cramp

retostado, -a *adj* dark brown

retostar [64] *vt* to toast brown

retozar [14] *vi* (**a**) *(niños, cachorros)* to gambol, to frolic (**b**) *(amantes)* to romp about

retozo *nm* (**a**) *(de niños, cachorros)* gambolling, frolicking (**b**) *(de amantes)* romp

retozón, -ona *adj (niño, cachorro)* playful

retracción *nf* (**a**) *Econ (del mercado)* shrinking; *(de la demanda)* reduction, fall; **se ha producido una r. de las inversiones** there has been a drop in investments (**b**) *Med* retraction

retractable *adj* retractable

retractación *nf* retraction

retractarse *vpr (de una promesa)* to go back on one's word; *(de una opinión)* to take back what one has said; **me retracto de lo dicho** I take back what I said; **se retractó de su declaración** she took back what she had said; **se retractó públicamente de sus acusaciones** he publicly withdrew his accusations

retráctil *adj (antena, brazo mecánico)* retractable; *(uña)* retractile

retraer [68] **1** *vt* (**a**) *(uñas, cuernos)* to retract, to draw in (**b**) *(disuadir)* **r. a alguien de hacer algo** to persuade sb not to do sth

2 retraerse *vpr* (**a**) *(encogerse)* to retract (**b**) *(aislarse, retroceder)* to withdraw, to retreat; **se retrae cuando hay extraños** he becomes very withdrawn *o* he goes into his shell in the company of strangers (**c**) *Econ (demanda, inversiones)* to fall

retraído, -a *adj* withdrawn, retiring

retraigo *etc ver* **retraer**

retraimiento *nm* (**a**) *(acción)* withdrawal (**b**) *(carácter)* shyness, reserve

retranca *nf* (**a**) *Fam (intención disimulada)* **le hizo una pregunta con r.** his question had an ulterior motive (**b**) *Col, Cuba (de carruaje)* brake

retransmisión *nf* (**a**) *(de mensaje, señal)* transmission (**b**) *(emisión)* broadcast; **r. en directo/en diferido** live/recorded broadcast; **una r. deportiva** a sports programme *o* broadcast; **a continuación, r. deportiva** coming up, sport

retransmisor *nm* transmitter

retransmitir *vt* (**a**) *(mensaje, señal)* to transmit (**b**) *(emitir)* to broadcast; **r. algo en directo** to broadcast sth live; **r. algo en diferido** to broadcast a recording of sth

retrasado, -a 1 *adj* (**a**) *(país, industria)* backward (**b**) *(reloj)* slow; **llevo el reloj r.** my watch is slow; **ese reloj va r.** that clock is slow (**c**) *(tren)* late, delayed; **vamos muy retrasados en el proyecto** we're very behind (schedule) with the project (**d**) *(persona)* retarded, backward; **un paciente r. (mental)** a mentally retarded patient

2 *nm,f* (**a**) *(discapacitado)* **r. (mental)** mentally retarded person (**b**) *Fam (como insulto)* moron, cretin, *US* retard

retrasar 1 *vt* (**a**) *(aplazar)* to postpone; **retrasaron la fecha de la reunión** the meeting was postponed, they put back the date of the meeting

(**b**) *(demorar)* to delay, to hold up

(**c**) *(hacer más lento)* to slow down, to hold up; *(pago, trabajo)* to set back

(**d**) *(reloj)* to put back; **habrá que r. los relojes una hora** the clocks will have to be put back an hour

(**e**) *Dep (balón)* to pass back

2 *vi (reloj)* to be slow

3 retrasarse *vpr* (**a**) *(llegar tarde)* to be late; **el vuelo se ha retrasado una hora** the flight is an hour late

(**b**) *(quedarse atrás)* to fall behind; **se retrasaron un mes en la entrega** they were a month late with the delivery

(**c**) *(aplazarse)* to be postponed; **la reunión se ha retrasado una hora** the meeting has been put back an hour

(**d**) *(demorarse)* to be delayed; **me he retrasado por el tráfico** I've been held up in the traffic

(**e**) *(reloj)* to lose time; **mi reloj se retrasa cinco minutos al día** my watch loses five minutes a day

retraso *nm* (**a**) *(demora)* delay; **el vuelo ha sufrido un pequeño r.** the flight has been slightly delayed; **perdón por el r.** I'm sorry about the delay; **llegar con (quince minutos de) r.** to be (fifteen minutes) late; **los trenes circulan hoy con (una hora de) r.** trains are running (an hour) late today; **el gobierno anunció el r. de las elecciones** the government announced that the elections were to be put back *o* postponed

(**b**) *(por sobrepasar un límite)* **el proyecto lleva dos semanas de r.** the project is two weeks behind schedule; **llevo en mi trabajo un r. de veinte páginas** I'm twenty pages behind with my work

(**c**) *(subdesarrollo)* backwardness; **llevar (siglos de) r.** to be (centuries) behind

(**d**) ***r. mental*** mental deficiency; **tener un r. mental** to be mentally retarded

retratar 1 *vt* (**a**) *(fotografiar)* to photograph (**b**) *(dibujar)* to do a portrait of (**c**) *(describir)* to portray; **la película retrata fielmente la época** the movie paints an accurate picture of the era

2 retratarse *vpr* (**a**) *(fotografiarse)* to have one's photograph taken (**b**) *(ser dibujado)* to have one's portrait painted (**c**) *Fam (pagar)* to cough up

retratista *nmf* (**a**) *(pintor)* portrait artist *o* painter (**b**) *(fotógrafo)* (portrait) photographer

retrato *nm* (**a**) *(dibujo, pintura)* portrait; **r. de medio cuerpo** head-and-shoulders portrait; **r. de cuerpo entero** full-length portrait; **ser el vivo r. de alguien** to be the spitting image of sb ►► *Andes, RP* ***r. hablado*** Identikit® picture, *Br* Photofit® picture; ***r. robot*** Identikit® picture, *Br* Photofit® picture

(b) *(fotografía)* portrait (photograph)
(c) *(descripción)* portrayal; **hace un r. muy fiel de las costumbres de entonces** she paints a very accurate picture of the customs of the time

retrechero, -a *adj* **(a)** *Fam (astuto)* cunning, crafty **(b)** *(atractivo)* attractive, charming

retreparse *vpr* to lean back

retreta *nf Mil* retreat; **tocaron r.** they sounded the retreat

retrete *nm* **(a)** *(taza)* toilet **(b)** *(habitación)* toilet, *US* bathroom

retribución *nf* **(a)** *(pago)* payment; **retribuciones salariales** salaries **(b)** *(recompensa)* reward **(c)** *Am (de favor)* **en r. del favor que me hizo, le mandé un ramo de flores** I sent her a bunch of flowers to thank her for *o* in return for the favour she did me

> **Falso amigo**: El sustantivo inglés **retribution** no es la traducción del español **retribución**. En inglés **retribution** significa "represalias".

retribuido, -a *adj (trabajo)* paid; **no r.** unpaid

retribuir [34] *vt* **(a)** *(pagar)* to pay **(b)** *(recompensar)* to reward **(c)** *Am (favor, obsequio)* to return, to repay

retributivo, -a *adj* **la política retributiva** pay policy; **un premio r.** a cash prize

retro *adj Fam* **(a)** *(estilo, moda)* retro **(b)** *Pol* reactionary

retroacción *nf Elec* feedback

retroactivamente *adv* retroactively

retroactividad *nf (de ley)* retroactivity; *(del pago)* backdating

retroactivo, -a *adj (ley)* retrospective, retroactive; *(pago)* backdated; **con efecto** *o* **con carácter r.** retroactively

retroalimentación *nf* feedback ►► *Elec* ***r. negativa*** negative feedback; *Elec* ***r. positiva*** positive feedback

retroceder *vi* **(a)** *(moverse hacia atrás)* to go back; **tuvo que r. para salir del garaje** he had to back out of the garage; **la lluvia de piedras obligó a r. a la policía** the shower of stones forced the police to move back; **retrocedió dos puestos en la clasificación** he dropped *o* fell two places in the table **(b)** *(ante obstáculo)* to back down; **no retrocederé ante nada** there's no stopping me now

retroceso *nm* **(a)** *(movimiento hacia atrás)* backward movement; **supuso un r. en las negociaciones** it caused a setback in the negotiations **(b)** *(de fusil, cañón)* recoil **(c)** *(de tropas)* retreat **(d)** *(en la economía)* recession **(e)** *(en enfermedad)* deterioration; **el paciente ha experimentado un r.** the patient's condition has deteriorated

retrocohete *nm* retro-rocket

retroflexo, -a *adj Ling* retroflex

retrógrado, -a 1 *adj* **(a)** *Pey (anticuado)* backward-looking, hidebound; *(en política)* reactionary **(b)** *(movimiento)* retrograde
2 *nm,f (anticuado)* backward-looking *o* hidebound person; *(en política)* reactionary

retropropulsión *nf* jet propulsion

retroproyector *nm* overhead projector

retrospección *nf* retrospection

retrospectiva *nf* retrospective; **en r.** in retrospect

retrospectivamente *adv* in retrospect

retrospectivo, -a *adj* retrospective; **echar una mirada retrospectiva a** to look back over

retrotraer [68] **1** *vt (relato)* to set in the past; **una historia que nos retrotrae a la Rusia zarista** a story which takes us back to tsarist Russia
2 retrotraerse *vpr (al pasado)* to cast one's mind back, to go back; **mi memoria ahora se retrotrae constantemente a 1968** my mind keeps going back to 1968

retroventa *nf Der* resale

retrovirus *nm inv Med* retrovirus

retrovisor *nm* rear-view mirror; **r. interior** rear-view mirror; **r. lateral** wing mirror

retrucar [29] **1** *vi* **(a)** *(en billar)* **la bola retrucó** he got a double-kiss **(b)** *Perú, RP, Ven Fam (responder)* to answer back
2 *vt Perú, RP, Ven Fam (replicar)* to retort

retruécano *nm* pun, play on words

retuerzo *ver* **retorcer**

retuesto *etc ver* **retostar**

retumbante *adj* resounding

retumbar *vi* **(a)** *(resonar)* to resound; **sus gritos retumbaban en la cueva** his shouts echoed *o* resounded around the cave; **las paredes retumbaban con cada explosión** the walls shook with each explosion; *Fam* **me retumban los oídos** my ears are ringing **(b)** *(hacer ruido)* to thunder, to boom; **el trueno retumbó en la sala** the thunder rumbled through the hall

retuviera *etc ver* **retener**

reubicación *nf Am* relocation

reubicar *vt Am* to relocate

reuma, reúma *nm o nf* rheumatism

reumático, -a 1 *adj* rheumatic
2 *nm,f* rheumatic

reumatismo *nm* rheumatism

reumatología *nf* rheumatology

reumatólogo, -a *nm,f* rheumatologist

reunido, -a *adj (en reunión)* **ahora no puede ponerse, está r.** he can't come on the phone at the moment, he's in a meeting; **estuvieron reunidos toda la mañana** they were in a meeting all morning

reunificación *nf* reunification

reunificar [60] **1** *vt* to reunify
2 reunificarse *vpr* to reunify

reunión *nf* **(a)** *(encuentro) (profesional)* meeting; *(de amigos, familiares)* get-together, gathering; **hacer** *o* **celebrar una r.** to have *o* hold a meeting ►► ***r. atlética*** athletics meeting, *US* track and field meet **(b)** *(tras largo tiempo)* reunion; **una r. familiar/de veteranos** a family/veterans' reunion **(c)** *(asistentes)* meeting **(d)** *(recogida)* gathering, collection

reunir [57] **1** *vt* **(a)** *(juntar) (personas)* to bring together; **la fiesta de homenaje reunió a todos los amigos del artista** the party in his honour brought all the artist's friends together
(b) *(objetos, información)* to collect, to bring together; *(fondos)* to raise; **reunió una gran fortuna** he amassed a large fortune
(c) *(tener) (requisitos, condiciones)* to meet, to fulfil; *(cualidades)* to possess, to combine; **el plan reúne todas las condiciones para ser aceptado** the plan meets *o* fulfils all the criteria for acceptance; **no reúne los requisitos necesarios para el puesto** she doesn't meet the requirements for the post
(d) *(volver a unir)* to put back together
2 reunirse *vpr (congregarse, juntarse)* to meet; **reunirse con alguien** to meet (up with) sb; **el presidente se reunirá con los sindicatos** the president will meet (with) the unions; **se reunió con su familia tras cinco años de separación** he was reunited with his family after being apart from them for five years

reutilizable *adj* reusable

reutilización *nf* reuse

reutilizar [14] *vt* to reuse

reválida *nf* **(a)** *Antes (examen)* = qualifying exam for higher stages of secondary education, taken at 14 and 16 **(b)** *(confirmación)* **pasó la r. del título** he successfully defended the title **(c)** *Am (de estudios, título)* recognition

revalidar *vt* **(a)** *Esp (en deportes)* to successfully defend; **el ciclista revalidó su título mundial** the cyclist successfully defended his world title **(b)** *Am (estudios, diploma)* to validate; **para poder trabajar en otro país tiene que r. el título** in order to work in another country she has to have her degree validated *o* recognized

revalorización *nf* **(a)** *(aumento del valor)* appreciation **(b)** *(de moneda)* revaluation **(c)** *(restitución del valor)* favourable reassessment

revalorizar [14] **1** *vt* **(a)** *(aumentar el valor de)* to increase the value of **(b)** *(moneda)* to revalue **(c)** *(restituir el valor de)* to reassess in a favourable light
2 revalorizarse *vpr* **(a)** *(aumentar de valor)* to appreciate **(b)** *(moneda)* to be revalued; **la libra se revalorizó frente al dólar** the pound rose against the dollar **(c)** *(recuperar valor)* to be reassessed favourably; **un artista que se ha revalorizado en los últimos años** an artist who has undergone a favourable reappraisal in recent years

revaluación *nf* **(a)** *(evaluación)* reappraisal, reassessment **(b)** *(de moneda)* revaluation

revaluar 1 *vt* **(a)** *(evaluar)* to reappraise, to reassess **(b)** *(moneda)* to revalue
2 revaluarse *vpr (moneda)* to be revalued; **la libra se revaluó frente al dólar** the pound rose against the dollar

revancha *nf* **(a)** *(venganza)* revenge; **tienen muchas ganas de r.** they are hungry for revenge; **tomarse la r.** to take revenge **(b)** *(partido, partida)* rematch; **el equipo derrotado pidió la r.** the losers asked for a rematch

revanchismo *nm* vengefulness

revanchista *adj (actitud, espíritu)* vengeful

revelación *nf* (**a**) *(de documento, secreto)* revelation (**b**) *(sorpresa)* revelation; **el cineasta tailandés fue la r. del festival** the Thai director was the revelation *o* discovery of the festival; **el equipo r. de la temporada** the team that has been the revelation of the season (**c**) *Rel* revelation

revelado *nm Fot* developing

revelador, -ora 1 *adj (aclarador)* revealing, revelatory
2 *nm Fot* developer

revelar 1 *vt* (**a**) *(descubrir)* to reveal; **se negó a r. la localización de la bomba** he refused to reveal *o* disclose the whereabouts of the bomb (**b**) *(manifestar)* to show; **sus acciones revelan una gran generosidad** his actions show great generosity (**c**) *Fot* to develop
2 revelarse *vpr* (**a**) *(descubrirse)* **revelarse como** to show oneself to be; **se reveló como un poeta excepcional** he showed himself to be an exceptional poet (**b**) *(resultar)* **sus esfuerzos se han revelado inútiles** their efforts proved useless

revendedor, -ora *nm,f* ticket tout

revender *vt* (**a**) *(productos, bienes)* to resell (**b**) *(entradas)* to tout

revenirse [71] *vpr* (**a**) *(ponerse correoso)* to go soggy (**b**) *(avinagrarse)* to turn sour

reventa *nf* (**a**) *(de productos, bienes)* resale (**b**) *(de entradas)* touting; **las autoridades han prohibido la r. de entradas** the authorities have banned ticket touting; **compré las entradas en la r.** I bought the tickets from a tout

reventadero *nm Chile* = place where the waves break

reventado, -a *adj Fam (cansado)* shattered, whacked

reventador *nm (boicoteador)* troublemaker

reventar [3] **1** *vt* (**a**) *(hacer estallar)* to burst; **el hielo reventó las tuberías** the ice burst the pipes
(**b**) *(romper)* to break; *(echar abajo)* to break down; *(con explosivos)* to blow up
(**c**) *Andes, RP Fam (golpear)* **si no me devolvés eso te reviento** if you don't give that back to me I'm going to thump you one
(**d**) *(hacer fracasar)* to ruin, to spoil; *Com* **r. los precios** to make massive price cuts
(**e**) *(boicotear)* to disrupt
(**f**) *Fam (cansar mucho)* to shatter; **el jinete reventó al caballo** the jockey rode the horse into the ground
(**g**) *Fam (fastidiar)* to get; **me revienta que...** it really gets me that...; **me revienta que nunca cuenten conmigo** it bugs the hell out of me that they never include me
2 *vi* (**a**) *(estallar) (globo, neumático)* to burst; **el jarrón reventó al estrellarse contra el suelo** the vase shattered when it hit the ground; *Fig* **si no se lo digo, reviento** I'd have exploded if I hadn't said anything to him; *Fam* **por mí, como si revienta** he can drop dead as far as I'm concerned
(**b**) *(estar lleno)* **r. de** to be bursting with; *Fam* **estoy que reviento** *(estoy lleno)* I'm stuffed; **el estadio reventaba de espectadores** the stadium was packed to the rafters; **la sala estaba (llena) a r.** the room was bursting at the seams
(**c**) *(desear mucho)* **r. por hacer algo** to be bursting to do sth; **reventaba por contarnos el último cotilleo** she was dying *o* bursting to tell us the latest gossip
(**d**) *Fam (cansarse mucho)* **trabajaron hasta r.** they worked their socks off
(**e**) *Fam (perder los nervios)* to explode (**de** with); **al final reventó de impaciencia** her impatience finally got the better of her
3 reventarse *vpr* (**a**) *(explotar)* to explode; *(rueda, tuberías)* to burst; **no te revientes los granos** don't squeeze your spots; *Andes, RP* **venía mirando para otro lado y me reventé contra la puerta** I was looking the other way and banged into the door (**b**) *Fam (cansarse)* to get whacked, to tire oneself to death; **se reventó a limpiar** she tired herself to death *o Br* slogged her guts out doing the cleaning

reventón *nm* (**a**) *(pinchazo)* blow-out, *Br* puncture, *US* flat; **sufrimos un r.** we had a *Br* puncture *o US* flat (**b**) *(estallido)* burst; **dar un r.** to burst (**c**) *Arg, Chile Min* outcrop (**d**) *Méx Fam (fiesta)* wild party

reverberación *nf* (**a**) *(de sonido)* reverberation (**b**) *(de luz, calor)* reflection

reverberante *adj* (**a**) *(sonido)* reverberating (**b**) *(luz)* reflecting

reverberar *vi* (**a**) *(sonido)* to reverberate (**b**) *(luz, calor)* to reflect; **el sol reverberaba sobre las aguas** the sunlight glinted on the water

reverbero *nm CAm, Cuba, Ecuad (cocinilla)* cooking stove

reverdecer [46] **1** *vt* (**a**) *(campos)* to turn green again (**b**) *(interés, sentimientos)* to revive
2 *vi* (**a**) *(campos)* to turn green again (**b**) *(interés, sentimientos)* to revive

reverencia *nf* (**a**) *(respeto)* reverence (**b**) *(saludo) (inclinación)* bow; *(flexión de piernas)* curtsy; **hacer una r.** *(con la cabeza)* to bow; *(inclinarse)* to curtsy (**c**) *(tratamiento)* **su R.** Your/His Reverence

reverencial *adj* reverential

reverenciar *vt* to revere

reverendísimo, -a *adj* Right Reverend

reverendo, -a 1 *adj* (**a**) *(forma de tratamiento)* reverend; **el r. padre** the reverend father; **la reverenda madre** the reverend mother (**b**) *Am (enorme)* **eso es un r. disparate** that's absolute nonsense
2 *nm* reverend

reverente *adj* reverent

reversa *nf Méx* reverse

reversibilidad *nf* reversibility

reversible *adj* reversible

reverso *nm (parte de atrás)* back; *(de moneda, medalla)* reverse; **ver al r.** see back, see other side; EXPR **ser el r. de la medalla** to be the other side of the coin

reverter [66] *vi* to overflow

revertir [63] **1** *vt Am (invertir)* **r. la situación** to reverse the situation
2 *vi* (**a**) *(resultar)* **r. en** to result in; **r. en beneficio/perjuicio de** to be to the advantage/detriment of (**b**) *(volver)* **r. a** to revert to (**c**) *Der (propiedad)* to revert; **la obra revertirá al Estado después de cincuenta años** the work will revert to the State after fifty years

revés (*pl* **reveses**) *nm* (**a**) *(parte opuesta) (de papel, mano)* back; *(de tela)* other side, wrong side; **al r.** *(en dirección o sentido equivocado)* the wrong way round; *(en forma opuesta, invertido)* the other way round; **escribe las eses al r.** she writes the letter "s" backwards *o* back to front; **te has puesto los guantes al r.** you've put your gloves on inside out; **todo lo entiende al r.** she's always getting the wrong end of the stick; **no estoy triste, al r. estoy contentísima** I'm not sad, on the contrary, I'm very happy; **lo hizo al r. de como le dije** she did the opposite of what I told her to; **del r.** *(lo de detrás, delante)* the wrong way round, back to front; *(lo de dentro, fuera)* inside out; *(lo de arriba, abajo)* upside down; **volver algo del r.** to turn sth around; **me puso el estómago del r.** it turned my stomach
(**b**) *(contratiempo)* setback, blow; **sufrir un r.** to suffer a setback
(**c**) *(bofetada)* slap
(**d**) *Dep (en tenis)* backhand; **un golpe de r.** a backhand; **tiene un buen r.** she has a good backhand
(**e**) *Cuba (gusano)* tobacco weevil

revestimiento *nm (por fuera)* covering; *(por dentro)* lining; *(con pintura)* coating ►► ***r. de fachadas*** facing

revestir [47] **1** *vt* (**a**) *(recubrir)* to cover; *(con pintura)* to coat; *(con forro)* to line; **revistieron las paredes de corcho** they put cork panels on the walls; **revistieron el patio de cemento** the courtyard was cemented over
(**b**) *(poseer)* **el incidente no revistió importancia** the incident was not important; **la herida no reviste importancia** the wound isn't serious; **el acto revistió gran solemnidad** it was a very solemn occasion
(**c**) *(adornar)* to dress up (**de** in), to adorn (**de** with)
(**d**) *(disfrazar)* to disguise, to cover up
2 revestirse *vpr* (**a**) *(dotarse)* **revestirse de paciencia** to summon up one's patience; **se revistió de la seriedad que requería la situación** she showed the seriousness required by the situation; **el acto se revistió de gran solemnidad** the event was marked by great solemnity (**b**) *(sacerdote)* to put on one's vestments

reviene *etc ver* **revenirse**

reviento *etc ver* **reventar**

revierta *etc ver* **revertir**

reviniera *etc ver* **revenirse**

revirado, -a *adj RP* bad-tempered; **no le hagas caso, que hoy anda medio r.** don't pay any attention to him, he's in a bad mood today

revirarse *vpr RP Fam* to fly into a rage

revire *nm RP Fam* rage, bad mood

revirtiera *etc ver* **revertir**

revisación *nf RP* (**a**) *(médica, odontológica)* examination (**b**) *(registro)* search

revisar *vt* (**a**) *(repasar)* to go over again; **revisé el examen antes de entregarlo** I went over the exam again before handing it in
(**b**) *(examinar)* to check; *Am (pruebas, galeradas)* to correct; *Am (paciente)* to examine; **déjame que revise la cuenta del supermercado** let me check the supermarket receipt; **un auditor vino a r. las cuentas de la empresa** an auditor came to audit the company's accounts; **me tengo que r. la vista** I have to get my eyes tested; **le revisaron el**

equipaje they searched her luggage; **tengo que llevar el coche a que lo revisen** I have to take the car in to have it serviced; **revíseme los frenos** could you check my brakes?

(c) *(modificar)* to revise; **han revisado sus previsiones de crecimiento** they've revised their growth forecasts

(d) *Am (registrar)* to search; **revisaban a todos antes de subir al avión** they searched everyone before they boarded the plane; EXPR *Fam* **a mí, que me revisen** don't look at me!

revisión *nf* (a) *(repaso)* revision; **pidió la r. del examen** he asked for the exam to be remarked

(b) *(examen)* check; *(de vehículo)* service; **llevar el coche a una r.** to have one's car serviced ►► ***r. de cuentas*** audit; ***r. médica*** check-up; **me tengo que hacer una r. médica** I have to have a check-up; ***r. de la vista*** eye test

(c) *(modificación)* review; **han hecho una r. de las cifras de crecimiento** the growth figures have been revised; **el gobierno anunció una r. de su política de empleo** the government announced a review of its employment policy; **r. de los precios** price review *o* change

(d) *CAm, Méx (registro)* search

revisionismo *nm* revisionism

revisionista 1 *adj* revisionist

2 *nmf* revisionist

revisor, -ora *nm,f (en tren, autobús)* ticket inspector ►► ***r. de cuentas*** auditor

revista 1 *ver* **revestir**

2 *nf* (a) *(publicación)* magazine; *(académica)* journal ►► *CSur* ***r. de chistes*** (children's) comic; ***r. del corazón*** gossip magazine *(with details of celebrities' lives)*; *Am* ***r. de historietas*** (children's) comic; ***r. pornográfica*** pornographic magazine

(b) *(espectáculo teatral)* revue ►► ***r. musical*** musical revue

(c) *(inspección)* **pasar r. a** *(tropas)* to inspect, to review; **el informe pasa r. a la situación del sector agrícola** the report reviews the situation of the farming sector; **un estudio que pasa r. a las transformaciones de final de siglo** a study which reviews *o* looks at the transformations undergone at the turn of the century

revistar *vt (tropas)* to review, to inspect

revistero *nm (mueble)* magazine rack

revistiera *etc ver* **revestir**

revitalización *nf* revitalization

revitalizar [14] *vt* to revitalize

revival [rri'βaiβal] *nm* revival

revivificar [60] *vt* to revive

revivir 1 *vi* (a) *(muerto)* to revive, to come back to life (b) *(sentimientos)* to revive, to be rekindled; **su pasión por el deporte revivió al cabo de muchos años** his passion for sport revived after several years

2 *vt* (a) *(recordar) (sujeto: acontecimiento)* to revive memories of; **revivieron su época de estudiantes** they recalled their time as students (b) *(muerto)* to revive, to bring back to life (c) *(sentimientos)* to revive, to rekindle

revocable *adj* revocable

revocación *nf (de sentencia, testamento)* revocation

revocar [60] *vt* (a) *(sentencia, testamento)* to revoke (b) *(pared) (interior)* to plaster; *(exterior)* to render

revocatoria *nf Am* revocation

revolcar [69] 1 *vt* to throw to the ground, to upend; **el caballo revolcó a la amazona** the horse threw its ride

2 **revolcarse** *vpr* (a) *(por el suelo)* to roll around; **el perro se revolcaba en la arena** the dog rolled around in the sand; **nos revolcamos por los suelos de risa** we rolled around (on the ground) with laughter; **se revolcaba de dolor** she was writhing in pain (b) *Fam (amantes)* to roll around *(kissing and canoodling)*

revolcón *nm* (a) *(caída)* tumble, fall; EXPR **darle un r. a alguien** *(vencerle)* to thrash *o* hammer sb (b) *Fam (juegos amorosos)* **darse un r.** to roll around *(kissing and canoodling)*

revolear *vt Méx, RP* to whirl around; EXPR **r. la cartera** to walk the streets, to work as a prostitute; EXPR **r. la pata** to be full of life *o* verve

revolotear *vi* (a) *(pájaro, mariposa)* to flutter (about) (b) *(persona)* to flit about

revoloteo *nm* (a) *(de pájaro, mariposa)* fluttering (about) (b) *(de persona)* flitting about; **me está poniendo nervioso su r. cerca de mi mesa** she's getting on my nerves flitting around my desk like that

revoltijo, revoltillo *nm* jumble

revoltoso, -a 1 *adj* (a) *(soldado, estudiante)* rebellious (b) *(niño)* naughty

2 *nm,f* (a) *(soldado, estudiante)* troublemaker (b) *(niño)* rascal

revolución *nf* (a) *(cambio profundo)* revolution ►► *Hist* ***la R. Francesa*** the French Revolution; *Hist* ***la R. Industrial*** the Industrial Revolution; ***r. de palacio*** palace revolution (b) *(giro, vuelta)* revolution, rev; **33 revoluciones por minuto** 33 revolutions per minute

revolucionar *vt* (a) *(agitar) (crear conflicto en)* to cause uproar in; *(crear excitación en)* to cause a stir in; **¡no revoluciones a los niños!** don't get the children all excited! (b) *(transformar)* to revolutionize (c) *Tec (motor)* to rev (up)

revolucionario, -a 1 *adj* (a) *(de la revolución)* revolutionary (b) *(innovador)* revolutionary

2 *nm,f* revolutionary

revolvedor *nm Cuba* vat, cauldron

revolver [41] 1 *vt* (a) *(mezclar) (líquido)* to stir; *(ensalada)* to toss; *(objetos)* to mix; *Am (dados)* to shake; *CSur (baraja)* to shuffle; **la travesía me ha revuelto el estómago** the crossing has made me sick in my stomach; PROV **r. Roma con Santiago** to leave no stone unturned

(b) *(desorganizar)* to turn upside down, to mess up; *(cajones)* to turn out; **los niños revolvieron la casa** the children left the house in a complete mess; **lo dejaron todo revuelto** they turned the place upside down

(c) *(irritar)* to upset; **me revuelve el estómago** *o* **las tripas** it makes my stomach turn

(d) *(alterar)* **r. los ánimos** to cause feelings to run high

2 *vi* **r. en** *(armario, pasado)* to rummage around in; **¿quién ha estado revolviendo en mis cajones?** who's been rummaging around in my drawers?

3 **revolverse** *vpr* (a) *(moverse) (en un sillón)* to shift about; *(en la cama)* to toss and turn (b) *(volverse)* to turn around; **revolverse contra alguien** to turn on sb (c) *(mar, río)* to become rough; *(tiempo)* to turn; **se ha revuelto el día** the weather has turned

> **Falso amigo**: El verbo inglés **to revolve** no es la traducción del español **revolver**. En inglés **to revolve** significa "girar" o "considerar".

revólver *(pl* **revólveres***) nm* revolver; EXPR *RP* **hacer algo con un r. en el pecho** to do sth with a gun held to one's head; EXPR *RP* **poner un r. en el pecho a alguien** to hold a gun to sb's head

revoque 1 *ver* **revocar**

2 *nm* (a) *(de pared) (interior)* plastering; *(exterior)* rendering (b) *(material) (interior)* plaster; *(exterior)* render

revuelco *etc ver* **revolcar**

revuelo *nm* (a) *(agitación)* commotion; **armar** *o* **causar un gran r.** to cause a stir (b) *(revoloteo)* fluttering (c) *Am (de gallo)* thrust with the spur

revuelque *etc ver* **revolcar**

revuelta *nf* (a) *(disturbio)* riot (b) *(curva)* bend, turn

revuelto, -a 1 *participio ver* **revolver**

2 *adj* (a) *(desordenado) (habitación)* upside down, in a mess; *(pelo)* dishevelled; **tengo el estómago r.** I feel sick in my stomach

(b) *(trastornado)* restless; *(época)* troubled, turbulent; **los estudiantes andan un poco revueltos** the students are rather restless; **los ánimos están muy revueltos** people are really on edge

(c) *(mezclado)* mixed up; **viven revueltos las gallinas y las personas** chickens and people all live under the same roof; **viven todos revueltos** they live on top of one another

(d) *(clima)* unsettled; *(aguas)* choppy, rough; **el río baja muy r.** the river is very turbulent

3 *nm (plato)* scrambled eggs; **r. de espárragos** = scrambled eggs with asparagus

revuelvo *etc ver* **revolver**

revulsión *nf* revulsion

revulsivo, -a 1 *adj (fármaco)* **un fármaco r.** a counter-irritant, *Espec* a revulsive

2 *nm* (a) *(fármaco)* counter-irritant, *Espec* revulsive (b) *(estímulo)* kick-start, stimulus; **el gol fue el r. que necesitaba el equipo** the goal kick-started the team; **la nueva empresa fue un r. para la competencia** the new company spurred the competition into action

rey *nm* (a) *(monarca)* king; **los Reyes** the King and Queen; **el r. de la selva** the king of the jungle; EXPR **hablando del r. de Roma** talk *o* speak of the devil ►► ***los Reyes Católicos*** = the Spanish Catholic monarchs Ferdinand V and Isabella; ***los Reyes Magos*** the Three

Kings, the Three Wise Men; **¿qué les vas a pedir a los Reyes (Magos)?** ≃ what are you going to ask Father Christmas for?; ***r. de la montaña*** *(en ciclismo)* king of the mountains; *CAm, Méx* ***r. de los zopilotes*** *(ave)* king vulture
(**b**) **(Día de) Reyes** Epiphany *(6 January, day on which children receive presents)*
(**c**) *(en ajedrez)* king
(**d**) *(en naipes)* king
(**e**) *(apelativo)* love, darling

reyerta *nf* fight, brawl

reyezuelo *nm (ave)* **r. (sencillo)** goldcrest

rezagado, -a 1 *adj* **la atleta se quedó rezagada** the athlete fell behind; **las empresas del país se están quedando rezagadas** the country's businesses are beginning to lag behind; **venían rezagados 3 kilómetros más atrás** they were lagging 3 kilometres behind
2 *nm,f* straggler; **ya espero yo a los rezagados** I'll wait for the stragglers

rezagarse [38] *vpr* to fall behind

rezago *nm Am* **los rezagos sociales del país** the country's social backwardness

rezar [14] 1 *vt* (**a**) *(oración)* to say; **r. un Padrenuestro/un Avemaría** to say an Our Father/a Hail Mary; **r. el rosario** to say *o* to recite the rosary (**b**) *(decir)* to read, to say; **el cartel reza: "prohibido el paso"** the sign says "no entry"; **como reza el artículo segundo de la ley** as stated in article two of the law
2 *vi* (**a**) *(orar)* to pray (**a** to); **r. por algo/alguien** to pray for sth/sb; **le reza a la Virgen** she prays to the Virgin (**b**) *(decir)* to read, to say (**c**) *Fam (tener que ver)* **esto no reza conmigo** that has nothing to do with me

rezo *nm* (**a**) *(acción)* praying; **el r. del rosario** the saying *o* recitation of the rosary (**b**) *(oración)* prayer

rezongar [38] 1 *vi (refunfuñar)* to grumble, to moan
2 *vt Urug (regañar)* to scold, to tell off

rezongo *nm Urug* telling-off

rezongón, -ona 1 *adj* **es muy r.** he's always grumbling *o* moaning
2 *nm,f* grumbler, moaner

rezumar 1 *vt* (**a**) *(transpirar)* to ooze; **las paredes rezumaban agua** the walls were running with damp (**b**) *(manifestar)* **rezumaba entusiasmo** he was bubbling with enthusiasm
2 *vi* to ooze *o* seep out

RF *nf* (*abrev de* **radiofrecuencia**) rf

RFA *nf Antes* (*abrev de* **República Federal Alemana** *o* **de Alemania**) FRG

RGB *Informát* (*abrev de* **red, green and blue**) RGB

Rh *nm* (*abrev de* **Rhesus**) Rh; **Rh. positivo/negativo** Rh positive/negative

rhesus *nm* rhesus monkey

Rhin = **Rin**

ría 1 *ver* **reír**
2 *nf* (**a**) *(accidente geográfico)* ria, = long narrow sea inlet (**b**) *(en pista de atletismo)* water jump

riachuelo *nm* brook, stream

Riad, Riyad *n* Riyadh

riada *nf* (**a**) *(de agua)* flood (**b**) *(de solicitudes)* flood; *(de preguntas)* barrage; *(de personas)* crowd

rial *nm* rial

ribazo *nm (terreno inclinado)* slope; *(del río)* sloping bank

ribeiro *nm* = wine from the province of Orense, Spain

ribera *nf* (**a**) *(orilla) (de río)* bank; *(de lago, mar)* shore (**b**) *(vega)* fertile plain; **la r. del Ebro** the banks of the Ebro

ribereño, -a 1 *adj (de río)* riverside; *(de lago)* lakeside; *(de mar)* coastal; **una aldea ribereña** a village on the banks of a river/on the shore of a lake; **los países ribereños del Mediterráneo** the Mediterranean countries
2 *nm,f* = person who lives by a river or a lake or the sea

ribete *nm* (**a**) *(cinta)* edging, trimming (**b**) **ribetes** *(rasgos)* touches, nuances; **una política de izquierdas con ribetes revolucionarios** a leftist policy with revolutionary elements; **tener ribetes de poeta** to be something of a poet

ribeteado, -a *adj* edged, trimmed

ribetear *vt* to edge, to trim

riboflavina *nf Biol* riboflavin

ribonucleico, -a *adj Biol* **ácido r.** ribonucleic acid

ribosoma *nm Biol* ribosome

ricachón, -ona *nm,f Pey* filthy *o* stinking rich person

ricamente *adv* (**a**) *(con riqueza)* richly; **viven r.** they live in luxury; **un palacio r. decorado** a richly decorated palace (**b**) *Fam (a gusto)* **estar tan r.** to be quite happy; **me lo dijo así, tan r.** she told me just like that; **dormí muy r.** I slept like a baby

rice *etc ver* **rizar**

ricino *nm (planta)* castor oil plant

ricitos *nmf inv Fam (como apelativo)* curly locks

rico, -a 1 *adj* (**a**) *(adinerado)* rich; **un país r.** a rich country
(**b**) *(abundante)* rich (**en** in); **una dieta rica en proteínas** a protein-rich diet, a diet rich in proteins; **esta región es rica en recursos naturales** this region is rich in natural resources
(**c**) *(fértil)* fertile, rich
(**d**) *(sabroso)* delicious; **la sopa está muy rica** the soup is really delicious; **¡qué r.!** this is delicious!
(**e**) *(simpático)* cute; **¡qué perrito tan r.!** what a cute little dog!
(**f**) *(bello, de calidad) (telas, tapices, vocabulario)* rich
(**g**) *Andes, CAm, Carib, Méx (agradable)* lovely; **¡qué clima más r. hace aquí!** the climate here is lovely!
2 *nm,f* (**a**) *(adinerado)* rich person; **los ricos** the rich; **los nuevos ricos** the nouveaux riches (**b**) *Fam (apelativo)* **¡oye, r.!** hey, sunshine!; **¿por qué no te callas, r.?** shut up, you!
3 *adv Andes, CAm, Carib, Méx (bien)* well; **qué r. toca el piano** she plays the piano so well; **qué r. se está aquí en la playa** it's lovely here on the beach

rictus *nm inv* **un r. de dolor** a wince *o* grimace of pain; **un r. de ironía** an ironic smirk; **un r. de desprecio** a disdainful sneer; **un r. de amargura** a bitter expression

ricura *nf Fam* (**a**) *(persona)* delight, lovely person; **¡qué r. de niño!** what a lovely *o* delightful child! (**b**) *(apelativo)* **¡oye, r.!** hey, sunshine!; **¿por qué no te callas, r.?** shut up, you! (**c**) *(guiso)* **¡qué r. de sopa!** what delicious soup!

ridiculez *nf* (**a**) *(payasada)* silly thing; **esa corbata es una r.** that tie is ridiculous; **¡no digas ridiculeces!** don't talk nonsense! (**b**) *(nimiedad)* **cuesta una r.** it costs next to nothing; **se pelearon por una r.** they fell out over nothing; **me pagan una r.** I'm paid a pittance (**c**) *(cualidad)* ridiculousness

ridiculizar [14] *vt* to ridicule

ridículo, -a 1 *adj* (**a**) *(sombrero, traje)* ridiculous; **quedas r. con esos pantalones** you look ridiculous in those *Br* trousers *o US* pants (**b**) *(afirmación, situación)* ridiculous; **eso que ha dicho es r.** what she said was ridiculous; **acéptalo, ¡no seas r.!** take it, don't be ridiculous *o* silly! (**c**) *(precio, suma, sueldo)* laughable, ridiculously low
2 *nm* ridicule; **hacer el r.** to make a fool of oneself; **hizo el r. más espantoso** he made an utter fool of himself; **poner** *o* **dejar en r. a alguien** to make sb look stupid; **quedar en r. (delante de alguien)** to end up looking like a fool (in front of sb); **no tiene sentido del r.** he doesn't get embarrassed easily

ríe *ver* **reír**

riego 1 *ver* **regar**
2 *nm (de campo)* irrigation; *(de jardín)* watering; **ella se encarga del r. del jardín** she's in charge of watering the garden ►► ***r. por aspersión*** sprinkling; ***r. sanguíneo*** (blood) circulation

riegue *etc ver* **regar**

riel *nm* (**a**) *(de vía)* rail (**b**) *(de cortina)* (curtain) rail

rielar *vi* to shimmer

rienda *nf* (**a**) *(de caballería)* rein; EXPR **aflojar las riendas** to slacken the reins; EXPR **a r. suelta: comer a r. suelta** to eat one's fill; **hablar a r. suelta** to talk nineteen to the dozen; **se reía a r. suelta** she was laughing uncontrollably; EXPR **dar r. suelta a** to give free rein to; **dio r. suelta a su imaginación** she gave free rein to her imagination; **dio r. suelta a su ira** he made no attempt to control his anger
(**b**) *(dirección)* **llevar** *o* **tener las riendas** to hold the reins, to be in control; **a la muerte de su padre, tomó las riendas del negocio** she took over the business when her father died; **él lleva las riendas de la casa** he's the boss in the household

riera *etc ver* **reír**

riesgo *nm* risk; **hay r. de inundaciones** there's a danger of flooding; **a r. de** at the risk of; **saltó por el barranco (aun) a r. de matarse** he jumped across the ravine even though he was risking his life; **se lo contó, a r. de que se enfadara** she told him, despite the risk of him getting annoyed; **a todo r.** *(seguro, póliza)* comprehensive; **aseguró la casa a todo r.** she took out comprehensive home insurance; **correr (el) r. de** to run the risk of; **corremos el r. de no llegar a tiempo** we are in danger of not arriving in time; **¿para qué correr riesgos**

innecesarios? why should we take unnecessary risks?; **existe el r. de que no queden localidades** there's a risk *o* danger that there won't be any tickets left

riesgoso, -a *adj Am* risky

rifa *nf* raffle ►► ***r. benéfica*** charity raffle

rifar 1 *vt* to raffle; **rifan un todoterreno** they're giving away a four-wheel drive in a prize draw
2 rifarse *vpr* **(a)** *(sortear)* **nos rifamos la botella de vodka** we drew lots to see who got the bottle of vodka
(b) *(disputarse)* to fight over, to contest; **a mi prima se la rifan los chicos** the boys are always running after *o* fighting over my cousin
(c) *RP Fam (malgastar)* to blow; *(desperdiciar)* to waste; **se rifó el sueldo en una semana** he blew his wages in a week; **te estás rifando los mejores años de tu vida** you're throwing away the best years of your life
(d) *Urug Fam (tema, capítulo)* **rifarse algo** not to study sth, to give sth a miss

rifirrafe *nm Fam* tiff; **tuvieron un pequeño r.** they had a tiff

rifle *nm* rifle

rift *nm Geol* rift valley

Riga *n* Riga

rige *ver* **regir**

rigidez *nf* **(a)** *(de objeto, material)* rigidity; *(de tela)* stiffness **(b)** *(de pierna, brazo)* stiffness **(c)** *(del rostro)* stoniness **(d)** *(severidad)* strictness, harshness; **la r. de la disciplina militar** the harshness *o* severity of military discipline; **aplican las normas con r.** they apply the rules strictly

rígido, -a *adj* **(a)** *(objeto, material)* rigid; *(tela)* stiff **(b)** *(pierna, brazo)* stiff; **pon el brazo r.** tense your arm, hold your arm stiff **(c)** *(rostro)* stony **(d)** *(severo, inflexible) (normas)* strict, harsh; *(carácter)* inflexible; *(horario)* strict

rigiera *etc ver* **regir**

rigodón *nm* rigadoon

rigor *nm* **(a)** *(severidad)* strictness; **criticaron el r. de la pena** they criticized the severity *o* harshness of the sentence; **con r.** strictly
(b) *(exactitud)* accuracy, rigour; **a este análisis le falta r.** this analysis isn't rigorous enough; **esta teoría no tiene ningún r. científico** this theory is totally lacking in scientific rigour; **me dieron las instrucciones de r.** they gave me the usual instructions; **nos cayó la bronca de r.** we got the inevitable telling-off; **es de r. en esas ocasiones** it's de rigueur on such occasions; **en r.** strictly (speaking)
(c) *(inclemencia)* harshness; **los rigores del invierno** the rigours of winter; **los rigores del verano** the harshness of the summer climate
(d) *(rigidez)* ***r. mortis*** rigor mortis
(e) EXPR *Fam* **es el r. de las desdichas** she was born unlucky

rigurosamente *adv* **(a)** *(severamente)* strictly; **aplicó la ley r.** she applied the law strictly **(b)** *(exactamente)* rigorously; **es r. cierto** it's the exact truth

rigurosidad *nf* **(a)** *(severidad)* strictness; **aplicó la ley con r.** she applied the law strictly **(b)** *(exactitud)* accuracy, rigour; **a este análisis le falta r.** this analysis isn't rigorous enough **(c)** *(inclemencia)* harshness; **la r. del clima** the harshness of the climate

riguroso, -a *adj* **(a)** *(severo)* strict; **el árbitro estuvo muy r.** the referee was very strict; **vestía de luto r.** she was in strict mourning; **sigue una dieta rigurosa** he's on a strict diet; **someten el proceso de fabricación a un r. control** the manufacturing process is strictly *o* tightly controlled; **las entradas se darán en r. orden de llegada** the tickets will be issued strictly on a first come first served basis
(b) *(exacto)* rigorous; **un análisis r.** a rigorous analysis
(c) *(inclemente)* harsh; **ha sido un invierno r.** it has been a harsh winter

rijo *etc ver* **regir**

rijoso, -a *adj* **(a)** *(pendenciero)* **es un tipo r.** he's always getting into fights **(b)** *(lujurioso)* lustful

rilarse *vpr Fam* to back *o* pull out

rima *nf* **(a)** *(concordancia)* rhyme ►► ***r. asonante*** assonant rhyme; ***r. consonante*** consonant rhyme **(b)** *(composición)* poem; **rimas** verse

rimar 1 *vt* to rhyme
2 *vi* to rhyme (**con** with)

rimbombancia *nf* **(a)** *(de estilo, frases)* pomposity **(b)** *(de desfile, fiesta)* razzmatazz

rimbombante *adj* **(a)** *(estilo, frases)* pompous **(b)** *(desfile, fiesta)* spectacular

rímel *nm* mascara

rimero *nm* heap, pile

rimmel® ['rrimel] *nm* mascara

Rin, Rhin *nm* **el R.** the Rhine

rin *nm* **(a)** *Carib, Col, Méx (llanta)* rim **(b)** *Perú (cabina telefónica)* phone box, *US* phone booth

rincón *nm* **(a)** *(esquina)* corner *(inside)* **(b)** *(lugar apartado)* corner; **vive en un r. apartado del mundo** she lives in a remote spot; **lo guardo en algún r. de mi memoria** I keep it tucked away in a corner of my memory; **recorrimos todos los rincones de la ciudad** we explored every nook and cranny of the city **(c)** *(lugar pequeño)* corner; **te he dejado un r. para que guardes tus cosas** I've given you a corner to keep your things in

rinconada *nf* corner

rinconera *nf* corner piece

rindiera *etc ver* **rendir**

rindo *etc ver* **rendir**

ring [rrin] (*pl* **rings**) *nm* (boxing) ring

ringla *nf,* **ringlera** *nf* line, row

ringorrango *nm Fam* **(a)** *(de estilo)* flourish **(b)** *(adorno)* frill, frippery

rinitis *nf inv Med* rhinitis ►► ***r. alérgica*** allergic rhinitis

rinoceronte *nm* rhinoceros, rhino

rinofaringe *nf Anat* nasopharynx

rinoplastia *nf Med* rhinoplasty; **le hicieron una r.** they operated on his nose

riña *nf* **(a)** *(discusión)* quarrel **(b)** *(pelea)* fight ►► *RP* ***r. de gallos*** cockfight

riñera *etc ver* **reñir**

riño *etc ver* **reñir**

riñón *nm* **(a)** *(órgano)* kidney; EXPR *Fam* **costar un r.** to cost a fortune; EXPR *Fam* **tener el r. bien cubierto** to be well-heeled; EXPR *Fam* **valer un r.** to be worth a fortune ►► ***r. artificial*** kidney machine **(b)** **riñones** *(región lumbar)* lower back; **dolor de riñones** lower back pain

riñonada *nf* **(a)** *(región lumbar)* lower back **(b)** *(guisado)* kidney stew

riñonera *nf* **(a)** *(pequeño bolso) Br* bum bag, *US* fanny pack **(b)** *(faja)* back support

río¹ *etc ver* **reír**

río² *nm* **(a)** *(corriente de agua, de lava)* river; **ir r. arriba/abajo** to go upstream/downstream; **se han escrito ríos de tinta sobre el tema** people have written reams on the subject; PROV **a r. revuelto, ganancia de pescadores** it's an ill wind that blows nobody any good; PROV **cuando el r. suena, agua lleva** there's no smoke without fire ►► ***el R. Bravo*** the Rio Grande; ***el R. Grande*** the Rio Grande; ***R. de Janeiro*** Rio de Janeiro; ***R. de la Plata*** River Plate
(b) *(gran cantidad) (de cartas)* flood; *(de insultos)* stream; **un r. de gente** a mass of people

rioja *nm* rioja (wine)

riojano, -a 1 *adj* **(a)** *(de Argentina)* = of/from the Argentinian city or province of La Rioja **(b)** *(de España)* = of/from the Spanish region of La Rioja
2 *nm,f* **(a)** *(de Argentina)* = person from the Argentinian city or province of La Rioja **(b)** *(de España)* = person from the Spanish region of La Rioja

rioplatense 1 *adj* of/from the River Plate region
2 *nmf* person from the River Plate region

R.I.P. [rrip] (*abrev de* **requiescat in pace**) RIP

ripiado, -a *adj Andes, RP* gravel-covered

ripiar *vt* **(a)** *Carib, Col (destrozar)* to tear to pieces **(b)** *Andes, RP (pavimentar)* to cover with gravel

ripio *nm* **(a)** *Lit (en verso)* = word or phrase included to complete a rhyme; *(en escrito)* padding; EXPR **no perder r.** to be all ears **(b)** *(cascote)* rubble **(c)** *Andes, RP* gravel

riqueza *nf* **(a)** *(fortuna)* wealth; **la redistribución de la r.** the redistribution of wealth
(b) *(cosas de valor)* **el cofre estaba lleno de oro y riquezas** the chest was full of gold and riches
(c) *(abundancia)* richness; **una región de gran r. minera** a region rich in mineral resources; **tiene gran r. de vocabulario** she has a very rich vocabulary; **un alimento con gran r. vitamínica** a food rich in vitamins; **la r. de la decoración llamaba la atención** the lavish décor was striking

risa *nf* laughter; **se oía una r. en el piso de arriba** somebody could be heard laughing in the flat above; **r. floja** *o* **tonta** giggle; **una película de r.** a comedy; **unos precios de r.** laughably low prices; **tiene una r. muy contagiosa** she has a very infectious laugh; **se oían risas** laughter could be heard; **¡qué r.!** how funny!; **me da r.** I find it funny; **se me**

escapó la r. I burst out laughing; **me entró la r.** I got the giggles; **estaba muerta de risa** she was in stitches; **tiene el ordenador muerto de r.** his computer's gathering dust; **contener la r.** to keep a straight face; **fue una r. verle imitar a los profesores** it was hilarious *o* a scream watching him take off the teachers; **no es cosa de r.** it's no laughing matter; **provocó las risas del público** it made the audience laugh; **tomar algo a r.** to take sth as a joke; EXPR *Fam* **caerse** *o* **morirse** *o* **partirse** *o RP* **matarse de r.** to die laughing, to split one's sides (laughing); EXPR *Fam* **mearse de r.** to piss oneself laughing ▸▸ ***r. enlatada*** canned laughter; ***risas grabadas*** canned laughter

RISC [rrisk] *Informát* (*abrev de* **reduced instruction set computer**) RISC

riscal *nm* craggy place

risco *nm* crag

risible *adj* laughable

risita *nf* giggle

risotada *nf* guffaw; **soltar una r.** to guffaw

risotto [rri'soto], **risoto** *nm* risotto

ristra *nf* string; **soltó una r. de insultos** he let out a stream of insults ▸▸ ***r. de ajos*** string of garlic

ristre: en ristre *loc adj* at the ready; **cabalgaba, lanza en r.** he rode along, lance at the ready; **salió al escenario, guitarra en r.** he came out onto the stage, guitar at the ready

risueño, -a *adj* (**a**) *(alegre)* smiling (**b**) *(próspero)* bright, promising; **la agricultura ecológica tiene un r. porvenir** organic farming has a bright *o* rosy future

Rita *n* EXPR *Fam Hum* **santa R., R., lo que se da no se quita** a present's a present; EXPR *Hum Fam* **¡que lo haga R. (la cantaora)!** no way am I doing that!

rítmico, -a *adj* rhythmic

ritmo *nm* (**a**) *(compás, repetición)* rhythm, beat; **esa canción tiene mucho r.** that song's got a very strong beat *o* rhythm; **llevaba el r. con los pies** she was tapping the rhythm *o* keeping time with her feet ▸▸ ***r. cardíaco*** heartbeat

(**b**) *(velocidad)* pace; **la economía está creciendo a un buen r.** the economy is growing at a healthy pace *o* rate; **llevan un r. de trabajo agotador** they have a punishing work rate; **este r. de vida me supera** this hectic lifestyle's too much for me; **a este r. no vamos a acabar nunca** at this rate we're never going to finish; **acelerar el r.** to speed up; **el ciclista francés impuso su r.** the French cyclist dictated the pace

rito *nm* (**a**) *Rel* rite ▸▸ ***r. iniciático*** initiation rite (**b**) *(costumbre)* ritual (**c**) *Chile (manta)* heavy poncho

ritual 1 *adj* ritual

2 *nm* ritual

ritualismo *nm* ritualism

rival 1 *adj* rival

2 *nmf* rival

rivalidad *nf* rivalry

rivalizar [14] *vi* to compete; **r. con alguien por algo** to compete with sb for sth; **rivalizan en belleza** they rival each other in beauty

rivera *nf* brook, stream

riverense 1 *adj* of/from Rivera *(Uruguay)*

2 *nmf* person from Rivera *(Uruguay)*

Riyad = **Riad**

riyal *nm* riyal

rizado, -a 1 *adj* (**a**) *(pelo)* curly (**b**) *(mar)* choppy

2 *nm (en peluquería)* **hacerse un r.** to have one's hair curled

rizador *nm* curling tongs

rizar [14] **1** *vt* (**a**) *(pelo)* to curl (**b**) *(mar)* to make choppy (**c**) **r. el rizo** *(avión)* to loop the loop; *(complicar)* to overcomplicate (things); **para r. el rizo hizo un doble salto mortal** as if all that wasn't impressive enough, he performed a double somersault

2 rizarse *vpr* (**a**) *(pelo)* to curl (**b**) *(mar)* to get choppy

rizo *nm* (**a**) *(de pelo)* curl (**b**) *(de avión)* loop (**c**) *(tela)* towelling, terry (**d**) *Náut* reef

rizoma *nm Bot* rhizome

rizoso, -a *adj (pelo)* (naturally) curly

RM *nf* (*abrev de* **Resonancia Magnética**) MRI

RN *nm* (*abrev de* **Renovación Nacional**) = Chilean political party

RNE *nf* (*abrev de* **Radio Nacional de España**) = Spanish state radio station

roano, -a *adj (caballo)* roan

roast-beef [rros'βif] (*pl* **roast-beefs**) *nm* roast beef

robacarros, robacoches *nmf inv CAm, Méx* car thief

róbalo, robalo *nm* sea bass

robar 1 *vt* (**a**) *(objeto)* to steal; *(casa)* to burgle; *(banco)* to rob; **r. a alguien** to rob sb; **me han robado la moto** my motorbike's been stolen; **nos robaron el partido** we were robbed; **le robó el corazón** she stole his heart; PROV *Fam* **el que roba a un ladrón, tiene cien años de perdón** it's no crime to steal from a thief

(**b**) *(niño, mujer)* to abduct, to kidnap

(**c**) *(tiempo)* to take up; **te robaré sólo un minuto** I'll only take up a minute of your time; **la contabilidad me roba mucho tiempo** doing the accounts takes up a lot of my time

(**d**) *(espacio)* to take away; **con esta reforma le robamos unos metros al garaje** this alteration will take a few square metres away from the garage

(**e**) *(naipe)* to draw

(**f**) *(cobrar caro)* to rob; **en esa tienda te roban** the prices in that shop are daylight robbery

2 *vi* (**a**) *(sustraer)* to steal; **han robado en una tienda del centro** there's been a robbery in a shop in the town centre (**b**) *(tomar un naipe)* to draw

robellón *nm (seta)* saffron milk cap

roble *nm* (**a**) *(árbol, madera)* oak; **un armario de r.** an oak wardrobe; EXPR **ser** *o* **estar fuerte como un r.** to be as strong as an ox (**b**) *(persona)* strong person

robledal *nm* oak wood

robledo *nm* oak grove

roblón *nm* (**a**) *(clavo)* rivet (**b**) *(en tejado)* ridge

robo *nm* (**a**) *(atraco)* robbery; *(hurto)* theft; *(en casa)* burglary ▸▸ ***r. a mano armada*** armed robbery (**b**) *(cosa robada)* stolen goods (**c**) *Fam* **ser un r.** *(precios)* to be daylight robbery; **¡qué r.!** what a rip-off!

robot (*pl* **robots**) *nm* robot; EXPR **actuar como un r.** to behave like a machine *o* robot ▸▸ ***r. articulado*** articulated robot; ***r. de cocina*** food processor; ***r. industrial*** industrial robot

robótica *nf* robotics *(singular)*

robotización *nf* automation

robotizar [14] *vt* to automate

robustecer [46] **1** *vt* to strengthen

2 robustecerse *vpr* to get stronger

robustecimiento *nm* strengthening

robustez *nf* robustness

robusto, -a *adj* robust

roca *nf* rock; EXPR **ser (como) una r.** to be as hard as nails ▸▸ ***r. metamórfica*** metamorphic rock; ***r. sedimentaria*** sedimentary rock; ***r. volcánica*** volcanic rock

rocalla *nf* rubble

Rocallosas *nfpl Am* **las R.** the Rockies

rocalloso, -a *adj Am* **las montañas Rocallosas** the Rocky Mountains

rocambolesco, -a *adj* fantastic, incredible; **nos sucedió una aventura rocambolesca** the most incredible series of things happened to us; **protagonizó una huída rocambolesca de la prisión** his escape from the prison involved a string of bizarre events

rocanrolero, -a *adj (ritmo, música)* rock and roll

roce 1 *ver* **rozar**

2 *nm* (**a**) *(contacto)* rubbing; **el r. de la seda contra su piel** the brushing of the silk against her skin; **el r. de su mano en la mejilla** the touch of his hand on her cheek; **el r. de la silla con la pared ha desgastado la pintura** the back of the chair has worn away some of the paint on the wall; **me ha salido una ampolla del r. del zapato** I've got a blister from my shoe rubbing against my foot; **el r. del viento en la piedra** the weathering effect of the wind on the stone

(**b**) *(rozadura)* **el pantalón tiene roces en las rodillas** the *Br* trousers *o US* pants are worn at the knees; **la pared está llena de roces** the wall has had the paint scraped off it in several places

(**c**) *(rasguño) (en piel)* graze; *(en madera, zapato)* scuffmark; *(en metal)* scratch

(**d**) *(trato)* close contact; **con el r. se han ido tomando cariño** being in close contact has made them grow fond of each other

(**e**) *(desavenencia)* brush, quarrel; **tener un r. con alguien** to have a brush with sb

(**f**) *RP (modales)* **tener r.** to have good social skills

rochabús *nm Perú Fam* water cannon truck

rochar *vt Chile Fam* to catch; **te roché que querías irte sin despedirte de mí** I caught you trying to leave without saying goodbye to me

rochela *nf Col, Ven Fam (bullicio)* racket

rociada *nf* **(a)** *(rocío)* dew **(b)** *(aspersión)* sprinkling **(c)** *(de insultos, perdigones)* shower

rociador *nm* ***r. contra incendios*** sprinkler

rociar [32] **1** *vt* **(a)** *(arrojar gotas a)* to sprinkle; *(con espray)* to spray; **le roció la cabeza con colonia** she sprayed cologne on his head **(b)** *(arrojar cosas a)* **r. algo/alguien (con)** to shower sth/sb (with); **rociaron a los novios con arroz** they showered the newly-weds with rice **(c)** *(con vino)* **rociaron la cena con un tinto** they washed the meal down with a red wine
2 *v impersonal (caer rocío)* **roció anoche** a dew fell last night

rociero, -a *nm,f* = participant in the "Rocío" pilgrimage to Almonte, Huelva

rocín *nm* **(a)** *(caballo)* nag **(b)** *Bol (buey)* ox

rocinante *nm* nag

rocío *nm* **(a)** *(agua)* dew **(b)** **el R.** *(romería)* = annual pilgrimage to Almonte, Huelva

rock **1** *adj inv* rock
2 *nm* rock ►► ***r. and roll*** rock and roll; ***r. duro*** hard rock; ***r. psicodélico*** psychedelic rock

rocker *nm Fam* rocker

rockero, -a, roquero, -a **1** *adj* rock; **grupo r.** rock group
2 *nm,f* **(a)** *(músico)* rock musician **(b)** *(fan)* rock fan

rococó **1** *adj inv* rococo
2 *nm* rococo

rocódromo *nm* indoor climbing centre

rocola *nf Andes, CAm, Méx, Ven* jukebox

Rocosas *nfpl* **las R.** the Rockies

rocoso, -a *adj* rocky; **las montañas Rocosas** the Rocky Mountains

rocote, rocoto *nm Andes* = large green chilli pepper

roda *nf Náut* stem

rodaballo *nm* turbot

rodada *nf* tyre track

rodado, -a **1** *adj* **(a)** *(por carretera)* road; **tráfico r.** road traffic **(b)** *(piedra)* rounded **(c)** EXPR **estar muy r.** *(persona)* to be very experienced; **venir r. para** to be the perfect opportunity to
2 *nm* **(a)** *RP (vehículo)* vehicle **(b)** *Chile (de tierra)* landslide; *(de nieve)* avalanche

rodador *nm* **(a)** *(ciclista)* = cyclist who is particularly good on flat stretches of road **(b)** *Am (insecto)* gnat

rodaja *nf* slice; **cebolla en rodajas** sliced onion; **cortar algo en rodajas** to cut sth in slices, to slice sth

rodaje *nm* **(a)** *(filmación)* shooting **(b)** *(de motor)* running-in; **el coche está en r.** we're running the car in **(c)** *(experiencia)* experience **(d)** *(de avión)* taxiing

rodamiento *nm* bearing ►► ***r. de bolas*** ball-bearing

Ródano *nm* **el R.** the Rhône

rodante *adj* rolling

rodapié *nm Br* skirting board, *US* baseboard

rodar [64] **1** *vi* **(a)** *(deslizarse)* to roll; **la moneda rodó y se metió debajo de la cama** the coin rolled under the bed
(b) *(circular)* to travel, to go; **rodaban a más de 180 km/h** they were doing more than 180 km/h
(c) *(girar)* to turn
(d) *(caer)* to tumble (**por** down); **rodó escaleras abajo** she tumbled down the stairs; *Fam* **echar algo a r.** *(malograr)* to ruin sth
(e) *(ir de un lado a otro)* to go around; **ha rodado por todo el mundo** he's been all over the world
(f) *Cine* to shoot; **¡silencio, se rueda!** we're rolling!
2 *vt* **(a)** *(hacer girar)* to roll **(b)** *Cine* to shoot; **rodó varias comedias** he filmed several comedies **(c)** *(automóvil)* to run in **(d)** *(avión)* to taxi

Rodas *n* Rhodes

rodear **1** *vt* **(a)** *(poner o ponerse alrededor de)* to surround (**de** with); **le rodeó el cuello con los brazos** she put her arms around his neck; **¡ríndete, estás rodeado!** surrender, we have you *o* you're surrounded!; **vive rodeado de libros** he's always surrounded by books
(b) *(estar alrededor de)* to surround; **el misterio que rodea la investigación** the mystery surrounding the investigation; **todos los que la rodean hablan muy bien de ella** everyone around her speaks very highly of her
(c) *(dar la vuelta a)* to go around
(d) *(eludir) (tema)* to skirt around
(e) *Am (ganado)* to round up
2 rodearse *vpr* **rodearse de** to surround oneself with; **se rodeó de amigos** he surrounded himself with friends

rodela *nf* buckler, round shield

rodeo *nm* **(a)** *(camino largo)* detour; **dar un r.** to make a detour **(b)** *(evasiva)* **rodeos** evasiveness; **andar** *o* **ir con rodeos** to beat about the bush; **habló sin rodeos** he didn't beat about the bush **(c)** *(espectáculo)* rodeo **(d)** *(reunión de ganado)* rounding up

rodera *nf* tyre mark

rodete *nm* **(a)** *(de tela)* round pad **(b)** *(moño)* bun

rodilla *nf* knee; **estaba de rodillas** he was on his knees; *Fig* **te lo pido de rodillas** I'm begging you; **doblar** *o* **hincar la r.** *(arrodillarse)* to go down on one knee; *Fig* to bow (down), to humble oneself; **ponerse de rodillas** to kneel (down)

rodillazo *nm* **me dio un r. en el estómago** he kneed me in the stomach

rodillera *nf* **(a)** *(protección)* kneepad **(b)** *(remiendo)* knee patch **(c)** *(abultamiento)* **tienes rodilleras en el pantalón** your *Br* trousers *o US* pants have gone baggy at the knees

rodillo *nm* **(a)** *(para amasar)* rolling pin **(b)** *(para pintar)* (paint) roller **(c)** *(para asfaltar)* road roller; *Fam* **el gobierno utilizó el r. parlamentario para aprobar la ley** the government steamrollered the bill through parliament **(d)** *(pieza cilíndrica) (en máquina de escribir, imprenta)* roller

rodio *nm Quím* rhodium

rododendro *nm* rhododendron

rodoviario *nm Chile* coach terminal

rodrigón *nm* supporting cane *(for plant)*

rodríguez *nm inv Fam* = man who stays at home working while his family goes away on holiday; **estar** *o* **quedarse de r.** to be left at home while one's family is away on *Br* holiday *o US* vacation

roedor, -ora **1** *adj* rodent; **animal r.** rodent
2 *nm* rodent
3 roedores *nmpl (orden)* rodents

roedura *nf* **(a)** *(acción)* gnawing **(b)** *(señal)* gnaw mark

roentgen ['rrengen] (*pl* **roentgens**) *nm Fís* roentgen

roer [58] *vt* **(a)** *(con dientes)* to gnaw (at); EXPR **ser duro de r.** to be a tough nut to crack **(b)** *(gastar)* to eat away (at) **(c)** *(atormentar)* to nag *o* gnaw (at); **le roe la conciencia por lo mal que se ha portado** her appalling behaviour is gnawing (at) her conscience

rogar [16] **1** *vt (implorar)* to beg; *(pedir)* to ask; **r. a alguien que haga algo** to beg/ask sb to do sth; **te lo ruego, no se lo cuentes a ella** don't tell her, I beg you; **le ruego (que) me perdone** I beg your forgiveness; **ruego a Dios que...** I pray to God that...; **se ruega silencio** *(en letrero)* silence, please
2 *vi* to pray; **ruega a la Virgen por nosotros** pray to the Virgin for us; EXPR **hacerse (de) r.** to play hard to get

rogativa *nf* rogation

rogatoria *nf Der* = request made by a court of one country to that of another country

rogué *etc ver* **rogar**

roigo *etc ver* **roer**

rojear *vi* to turn red

rojez *nf* **(a)** *(cualidad)* redness **(b)** *(en la piel)* (red) blotch

rojillo, -a *Fam* **1** *adj* **es muy r.** he's a real lefty
2 *nm,f* lefty

rojizo, -a *adj* reddish

rojo, -a **1** *adj* **(a)** *(de color)* red; **ponerse r.** *(ruborizarse)* to blush; *(semáforo)* to turn red **(b)** *(izquierdista)* red; **tiene ideas bastante rojas** she has rather left-wing ideas **(c)** *Hist (en Guerra Civil española)* Republican **(d)** *Andes (vino)* red
2 *nm,f* **(a)** *(izquierdista)* red **(b)** *Hist (en Guerra Civil española)* Republican
3 *nm* **(a)** *(color)* red; **el r. es mi color favorito** red is my favourite colour; *Méx Fam* **¡(di) r.!** *(en foto)* say cheese! ►► ***r. blanco*** white heat
4 al rojo *loc adj (metal)* red-hot; **al r. blanco** white-hot; **la situación está al r. vivo** the situation is at boiling point

rol (*pl* **roles**) *nm* **(a)** *(papel)* role; **desempeña un r. muy importante en su familia** he plays a very important role in his family **(b)** *Náut* muster

rola *nf* **(a)** *Méx Fam* number, song **(b)** *ver también* **rolo**

rolar *vi* **(a)** *(embarcación)* to roll **(b)** *(viento) (en sentido de las agujas de reloj)* to veer; *(en sentido contrario a las agujas del reloj)* to back **(c)** *Chile, Perú (relacionarse)* to mix, to socialize

roldana, *Méx* **rondana** *nf* pulley wheel

rolete: a rolete *loc adv RP Fam* **gana plata a r.** she earns a packet; **tienen libros a r.** they've got loads *o* stacks of books

rollito *nm Culin* ***r. (de) primavera*** spring roll

rollizo, -a *adj* chubby, plump

ROLLO 1 *nm* **(a)** *(cilindro)* roll; *(cuerda, cable)* coil ►► ***r. de papel higiénico*** toilet roll; ***r. de pergamino*** scroll; *Culin* ***r. de primavera*** spring roll

(b) *(carrete fotográfico)* roll of film; *(de película de cine)* reel

(c) *Fam (pesadez, aburrimiento)* drag, bore; *(molestia, latazo)* pain; **¡qué r.!** *(aburrimiento)* what a drag *o* bore!; *(molestia)* what a pain!; **un r. de discurso/tío** an incredibly boring speech/guy; **el r. de costumbre** the same old story; **¡corta el r. ya!** shut up, you're boring me to death!; **soltar el r.** to go on and on; **tener mucho r.** to witter on; **es un r. macabeo** *o* **patatero** *(muy aburrido)* it's a real bore *o* drag

(d) *Fam (embuste)* tall story; **nos metió un r. diciéndonos que...** he gave us some story *o* spiel about... ►► ***r. macabeo*** *(mentira)* ridiculous spiel; ***r. patatero*** *(mentira)* ridiculous spiel

(e) *Fam (tema, historia)* stuff; **el r. ese de la clonación** all that stuff about cloning, all that cloning business; **¿de qué va el r.?** what's it all about?; **¡vamos, suelta el r.!** come on, out with it!

(f) *Esp Fam (ambiente, tipo de vida)* scene; **el r. de la droga/de las discotecas** the drug/nightclub scene; **no me va ese r.** it's not my scene, I'm not into all that

(g) *Esp Fam (relación)* **tener un r. (con alguien)** to have a fling (with sb); **tengo buen r. con él** we're good *Br* mates *o US* buddies; **tengo mal r. con él** we're not the best of *Br* mates *o US* buddies; **venga, colega, tírate el r. y déjanos pasar** go on, be a pal and let us in

(h) *Esp Fam (sensación)* **esta música me da muy buen r.** this music really does something for me; **le daba mal r. quedarse sola** she was really uncomfortable about being left on her own

(i) *Ven (rulo)* roller, curler

(j) *RP Fam (pliegue de grasa)* spare tyre

(k) EXPR *RP Fam* **largar el r.** *(vomitar)* to throw up

2 *adj inv Esp Fam (aburrido)* boring; **yo lo encuentro un poco r.** I think he's a bit of a bore

rolo, -a 1 *adj Col Fam* from Bogota

2 *nm* **(a)** *Ven (porra) Br* truncheon, *US* nightstick **(b)** *Ven (rodillo)* ink roller **(c)** *Ven Fam (aprovechador)* smart guy **(d)** *Col Fam (bogotano)* person from Bogota

ROM [rrom] *nf Informát* (*abrev de* **read only memory**) ROM

Roma *n* Rome; PROV **R. no se construyó en una hora** Rome wasn't built in a day

romana *nf* **(a)** *(para pesar)* steelyard **(b)** *ver también* **romano**

romance 1 *adj* Romance

2 *nm* **(a)** *(idilio)* romance **(b)** *Ling* Romance language **(c)** *Lit* romance

romancear *vt Chile* to court, to woo

romancero *nm Lit* collection of romances

romanche *nm* Romans(c)h

romaní 1 *adj* Romany

2 *nmf (persona)* Romany

3 *nm (lengua)* Romany

románico, -a 1 *adj* **(a)** *(arte)* Romanesque **(b)** *(lengua)* Romance

2 *nm (arte)* **el Románico** the Romanesque style

romanista *nmf* **(a)** *Der* Romanist **(b)** *(lingüista)* Romance scholar

romanización *nf* Romanization

romanizar [14] *vt* to Romanize

romano, -a 1 *adj* Roman

2 *nm,f* Roman

romanticismo *nm* **(a)** *Arte, Hist & Lit* Romanticism **(b)** *(sentimentalismo)* romanticism

romántico, -a 1 *adj* **(a)** *Arte & Lit* Romantic **(b)** *(sentimental)* romantic

2 *nm,f* **(a)** *Arte & Lit* Romantic **(b)** *(sentimental)* romantic

romanza *nf Mús* ballad

rómbico, -a *adj Geom* rhombic

rombo *nm* **(a)** *(figura)* rhombus; *Imprenta* lozenge **(b)** *(naipe)* diamond **(c)** **rombos** *(palo)* diamonds

romboedro *nm Geom* rhombohedron

romboidal *adj Geom* rhomboid, rhomboidal

romboide *nm Geom* rhomboid

romboideo, -a *adj Geom* rhomboid, rhomboidal

romeo *nm* sweetheart

romeral *nm* rosemary patch

romería *nf* **(a)** *(peregrinación)* pilgrimage **(b)** *(fiesta)* = open-air festivities to celebrate a religious event **(c)** *(mucha gente)* **los fines de semana el centro es una r.** the centre is packed at weekends; **la entrada del hospital era una r. de gente** there were crowds of people outside the hospital entrance

romero, -a 1 *nm,f (peregrino)* pilgrim

2 *nm (arbusto, condimento)* rosemary

romo, -a *adj* **(a)** *(sin filo)* blunt **(b)** *(de nariz)* snub-nosed

rompebolas, rompehuevos, rompepelotas *RP muy Fam* 1 *adj inv Br* bloody *o US* goddamn annoying

2 *nmf inv* pain in the *Br* arse *o US* butt

rompecabezas *nm inv* **(a)** *(juego)* jigsaw **(b)** *Fam (problema)* puzzle

rompecocos *CSur muy Fam* 1 *adj inv Br* bloody *o US* goddamn annoying

2 *nmf inv* pain in the *Br* arse *o US* butt

rompecorazones *nmf inv Fam* heartbreaker

rompedero *nm Arg Fam* ***r. de cabeza*** puzzle

rompehielos *nm inv* icebreaker

rompehuevos = **rompebolas**

rompenueces *nm inv* nutcracker

rompeolas *nm inv* breakwater

rompepelotas = **rompebolas**

romper 1 *vt* **(a)** *(partir, fragmentar)* to break; *(hacer añicos)* to smash; *(rasgar)* to tear; **r. algo en pedazos** to break/smash/tear sth to pieces; *Mil* **¡rompan filas!** fall out!; EXPR *Fam* **r. la baraja** to get annoyed; EXPR *Fam* **o jugamos todos, o se rompe la baraja** either we all play, or nobody does

(b) *(estropear)* to break

(c) *(desgastar)* to wear out

(d) *(interrumpir) (monotonía, silencio, hábito)* to break; *(hilo del discurso)* to break off; *(tradición)* to put an end to, to stop

(e) *(terminar)* to break off

(f) *(incumplir)* to break; **rompió su promesa de ayudarnos** she broke her promise to help us

(g) **r. el par** *(en golf)* to break par

(h) **r. el servicio de alguien** *(en tenis)* to break sb's serve

(i) *RP Fam (fastidiar)* **no me rompas** give me a break; **no (me) rompas la paciencia** you're trying my patience; *muy Fam* **r. las pelotas** *o* **las bolas** *o* **los huevos a alguien** to get on sb's tits; *muy Fam* **dejá de r. las pelotas** *o* **las bolas** *o* **los huevos** stop being such a pain in the *Br* arse *o US* ass

2 *vi* **(a)** *(terminar una relación)* **r. (con alguien)** to break up *o* split up (with sb); **rompió con su novia** he broke up *o* split up with his girlfriend; **ha roto con su familia** she has broken off contact with her family; **r. con la tradición** to break with tradition; **rompió con el partido** she broke with the party

(b) *(empezar) (día)* to break; *(hostilidades)* to break out; **al r. el alba** *o* **día** at daybreak; **r. a hacer algo** to suddenly start doing sth; **r. a llorar** to burst into tears; **r. a reír** to burst out laughing

(c) *(olas)* to break

(d) *Fam (tener éxito)* to be a hit; **un cantante que rompe** a singer who's all the rage; EXPR **de rompe y rasga: es una mujer de rompe y rasga** she's a woman who knows what she wants *o* knows her own mind

(e) *RP Fam (molestar)* to be a pain; **¡no rompas!** give me a break!

3 **romperse** *vpr* **(a)** *(partirse)* to break; *(rasgarse)* to tear; **se rompió en mil pedazos** it smashed to pieces; **se ha roto una pierna** he has broken a leg

(b) *(estropearse)* to break; **se ha roto la tele** the TV is broken

(c) *(desgastarse)* to wear out; **se me están rompiendo las mangas** my sleeves are getting worn

(d) *(quebrantarse)* to break down; **se ha roto el consenso entre los partidos** the consensus between the parties has broken down

(e) *RP Fam (esforzarse)* to put oneself out; **no te rompiste demasiado para ese examen, ¿cómo sacaste tan buena nota?** you hardly killed yourself studying for the exam, so how did you get such good marks?

rompevientos *nm RP* **(a)** *(jersey) Br* polo neck, *US* turtleneck **(b)** *(anorak)* windcheater

rompible *adj* breakable

rompiente *nm* = place where the waves break

rompimiento *nm Am* break

rompope, rompopo *nm Méx* = type of eggnog with cinnamon or vanilla

ron *nm* rum

roncador *nm* bastard grunt, roncador grunt

roncar [60] *vi* to snore; EXPR *Am Fam* **r. los motores: a mi auto ahora le roncan los motores** my car's running beautifully now

roncha *nf* lump *(on skin)*; **me han salido unas ronchas en la espalda** my back has come out in a rash; **le salió una r. por la picadura del tábano** he got a bump on his skin from the horsefly bite; EXPR *Fam* **levantar ronchas** to create bad feeling

ronco, -a *adj* (a) *(persona)* hoarse; **me he quedado r.** I've gone hoarse (b) *(voz)* hoarse; *(sonido)* harsh

ronda *nf* (a) *(de vigilancia)* patrol; **los agentes hacían la r.** the police officers were patrolling *o Br* on the beat; **salir de r.** to go out on patrol
(b) *(de visitas)* **hacer la r.** to do one's rounds; **salir de r.** *(músico)* to go (out) serenading
(c) *(de conversaciones, en el juego)* round
(d) *Fam (de bebidas)* round; **pagar una r.** to buy a round
(e) *(avenida)* avenue ►► ***r. de circunvalación*** *Br* ring road, *US* beltway
(f) *Dep (carrera ciclista)* tour ►► ***la r. francesa*** the Tour de France
(g) *CSur (corro)* circle, ring

rondador *nm Andes (instrumento)* = type of panpipes

rondalla *nf* group of minstrels

rondana = **roldana**

rondar 1 *vt* (a) *(vigilar)* to patrol; **rondaban las calles en parejas** they patrolled the streets in pairs (b) *(parecer próximo)* **me está rondando un resfriado** I've got a cold coming on; **le ronda el sueño** he's about to drop off; **me ronda una idea por** *o* **en la cabeza** I've been turning over an idea in my head
2 *vi* (a) *(vigilar)* to patrol; **rondaban en parejas** they patrolled in pairs (b) *(merodear)* to wander (**por** around) (c) *(edad, cifra)* to be around; **ronda los cuarenta años** he's about forty; **las pérdidas rondan los tres millones** the losses are in the region of three million (d) *(cortejar)* to serenade

rondero, -a *nm,f Perú* voluntary watchman, *f* voluntary watchwoman

rondín *nm Andes* (a) *(vigilante)* watchman, guard (b) *(armónica)* mouth organ

rondó *nm Mús* rondo

rondón *nm Fam* **entrar de r.** to barge in

ronero, -a *adj Cuba* rum; **la producción ronera** rum production

ronque *etc ver* **roncar**

ronquear *vi* to be hoarse

ronquera *nf* hoarseness

ronquido *nm* snore; **me despertaron sus ronquidos** I was woken by his snoring

ronroneante *adj* purring

ronronear *vi (gato, motor)* to purr

ronroneo *nm* purr; **el r. del motor era un sonido agradable** the purring of the engine was pleasant to listen to

ronzal *nm* halter

ronzar [14] *vt* to munch

roña 1 *adj Fam (tacaño)* stingy, tight
2 *nmf Fam (tacaño)* skinflint
3 *nf* (a) *(suciedad)* filth, dirt (b) *Fam (tacañería)* stinginess, tightness (c) *(enfermedad de animal)* mange (d) *(herrumbre)* rust (e) *Méx (juego)* catch

roñería, roñosería *nf Fam* stinginess, tightness

roñica *Fam* 1 *adj* stingy, tight
2 *nmf* skinflint

roñosería = **roñería**

roñoso, -a 1 *adj* (a) *(sucio)* dirty; **la habitación estaba roñosa** the room was filthy (b) *Fam (tacaño)* tight, stingy (c) *Carib, Méx (ofendido)* resentful
2 *nm,f Fam* skinflint, tightwad

ropa *nf* (a) *(de vestir)* clothes; **me gusta la r. que lleva** I like the clothes she wears; **el cubo de la r. sucia** the dirty laundry *o* clothes basket; **ligero de r.** scantily clad; EXPR **lavar la r. sucia en público** to wash one's dirty linen in public ►► ***r. de abrigo*** warm clothes; ***r. blanca*** *(sábanas, toallas y manteles)* linen; *(para lavadora)* whites; ***r. de cama*** bed linen; ***r. de color*** coloureds; ***r. deportiva*** sportswear; ***r. de diseño*** designer clothes; *RP* ***r. de fajina*** work clothes; ***r. hecha*** ready-to-wear clothes; ***r. para el hogar*** linen and curtains; ***r. interior*** underwear; ***r. interior femenina*** lingerie; ***r. íntima*** underwear; ***r. de invierno*** winter clothing; ***r. de sport*** casual clothes; ***r. sucia*** *(para lavar)* laundry, washing; ***r. de trabajo*** work clothes; ***r. usada*** second-hand *o* old clothes
(b) ***r. vieja*** *(plato)* = stew made from leftovers

> **Falso amigo**: El sustantivo inglés **rope** no es la traducción del español **ropa**. En inglés **rope** significa "cuerda, soga".

ropaje *nm* robes

ropavejero, -a *nm,f* secondhand clothes dealer

ropavieja *nf (plato)* = stew made from leftovers

ropero *nm* (a) *(armario)* wardrobe; *(habitación)* walk-in wardrobe; **tiene un r. muy anticuado** *(ropas)* she wears very old-fashioned clothes; EXPR *RP Fam* **ser un r.** to be built like a tank (b) *(guardaropa)* cloakroom (c) *(de caridad)* = charitable organization that distributes old clothes to the poor

ropón *nm* (a) *(ropa)* robe, gown (b) *Chile, Col (de amazona)* riding skirt

roque 1 *adj Fam* **estar r.** to be out for the count; **quedarse r.** to drop *o* nod off
2 *nm (en ajedrez)* castle

roquedal *nm* rocky place

roquefort [roke'for] *nm* Roquefort

roquero, -a = **rockero**

rorcual *nm (cetáceo)* rorqual, finback ►► ***r. jiboso*** humpback whale

rorro *nm Fam* baby

rosa 1 *adj* (a) *(de color)* pink; EXPR **verlo todo de color (de) r.** to see everything through rose-tinted spectacles (b) *(del corazón)* **la prensa r.** gossip magazines; **una novela r.** a romance, a romantic novel
2 *nm (color)* pink; **el r. es mi color favorito** pink is my favourite colour
3 *nf* rose; EXPR **estar (fresco) como una r.** to be as fresh as a daisy ►► ***r. del desierto*** desert rose; ***r. de Jericó*** damask rose; ***r. silvestre*** wild rose; ***r. de los vientos*** compass rose

rosáceo, -a *adj* pinkish

rosado, -a 1 *adj* (a) *(de color rosa)* pink (b) *(vino)* rosé
2 *nm (vino)* rosé

rosal *nm (arbusto)* rose bush

rosaleda *nf* rose garden

rosarino, -a 1 *adj* of/from Rosario *(Argentina)*
2 *nm,f* person from Rosario *(Argentina)*

rosario *nm* (a) *(rezo)* rosary; **rezar el r.** to say one's rosary; EXPR *Fam* **acabar como el r. de la aurora** to degenerate into chaos (b) *(cuentas)* rosary (beads) (c) *(serie)* string; **un r. de desgracias** a string of disasters; **lanzó un r. de acusaciones contra el gobierno** he made a litany of accusations against the government

rosbif (*pl* **rosbifs**) *nm* roast beef

rosca *nf* (a) *(de tornillo)* thread; **un tapón de r.** a screw top; **un tornillo de r.** a screw; EXPR *Fam* **pasarse de r.** *(persona)* to go over the top
(b) *(forma) (de anillo)* ring; *(espiral)* coil
(c) *(de pan)* = ring-shaped bread roll; *Méx (bizcocho)* sponge cake; EXPR *Esp Fam* **hacerle la r. a alguien** to suck up to sb; EXPR *Fam* **nunca se come una r.** he never gets off with anyone ►► *Am* ***r. de Reyes*** = ring-shaped pastry eaten on 6 January
(d) *(en fútbol)* curl, bend; **pase/remate de r.** curling pass/shot
(e) *Andes, RP Fam (círculo de personas)* clique
(f) *Chile (almohadilla)* pad
(g) *CSur Fam (discusión, pelea)* fight

roscar [60] *vt* to thread

rosco *nm* (a) *(de pan)* = ring-shaped bread roll; EXPR *Esp Fam* **nunca se come un r.** he never gets off with anyone ►► ***r. de vino*** = ring-shaped Christmas sweet (b) *Fam (cero)* zilch; **sacó un r. en el examen** he got a big O in the exam

roscón *nm* = ring-shaped bread roll ►► ***r. de Reyes*** = ring-shaped pastry eaten on 6 January

rosedal *nm Am* rose garden

roseta *nf* (a) *(rubor)* flush (b) **rosetas** *(palomitas)* popcorn (c) *(de regadera)* rose, sprinkler; *(de ducha)* shower head (d) *Arg (pan)* round bread loaf

rosetón *nm* (a) *Arquit (ventana)* rose window (b) *(adorno)* ceiling rose

rosque *etc ver* **roscar**

rosquete 1 *adj Perú Fam Pey* queer
2 *nm Am* large doughnut

rosquilla *nf* ring doughnut; EXPR *Fam* **venderse como rosquillas** to sell like hot cakes

rosticería *nf Chile, Méx* = shop selling roast chicken

rostizar *vt Méx* to spit-roast

rostro *nm* (**a**) *(cara)* face; **tenía un r. triste** he had a sad face ▸▸ ***r. pálido*** paleface (**b**) *Fam (caradura)* **tener (mucho) r.** to have a (lot of) nerve; *Hum* **tiene un r. que se lo pisa** she's got a hell of a nerve; **iqué r. tiene!, no nos quiere ayudar a limpiar** what a nerve, she refuses to help us with the cleaning; **échale r., ya verás cómo lo consigues** just give it a go and you'll do it, I'm sure

> **Falso amigo**: El sustantivo inglés **rostrum** no es la traducción del español **rostro**. En inglés **rostrum** significa "estrado".

rotación *nf* (**a**) *(giro)* rotation (**b**) *(alternancia)* rota; **por r.** in turn ▸▸ ***r. de cultivos*** crop rotation; ***r. de personal*** staff turnover (**c**) *(en voleibol)* rotation

rotacismo *nm Ling* rhotacism

rotafolios *nm inv* flip chart

rotar 1 *vt* (**a**) *(hacer girar)* to rotate (**b**) *(cultivos)* to rotate
2 *vi* (**a**) *(girar)* to rotate, to turn (**b**) *(alternar, turnarse)* to rotate (**c**) *(cultivos)* to rotate
3 **rotarse** *vpr (turnarse)* to take turns; **los tres grupos se van rotando** the three groups take turns; **nos rotamos en el cuidado de los niños** we take turns looking after the children

rotario, -a 1 *adj* Rotary
2 *nm,f* Rotarian

rotativa *nf* rotary press

rotativo, -a 1 *adj* (**a**) *(movimiento)* rotary (**b**) *(turno)* **trabajan en turnos rotativos** they work a rotating shift pattern (**c**) *(cultivo)* **el cultivo r.** crop rotation
2 *nm* newspaper

rotatorio, -a *adj* (**a**) *(movimiento)* rotary (**b**) *(turno)* **trabajan en turnos rotatorios** they work a rotating shift pattern (**c**) *(cultivo)* **el cultivo r.** crop rotation

rotería *nf Chile Fam Pey* (**a**) *(chusma)* rabble, plebs (**b**) *(horterada)* **eso es una r.** that's really common

rotisería *nf CSur* delicatessen

roto, -a 1 *participio ver* **romper**
2 *adj* (**a**) *(partido, rasgado)* broken; *(tela, papel)* torn; *(zapato)* worn out (**b**) *(estropeado)* broken (**c**) *(deshecho) (vida)* destroyed; *(corazón)* broken (**d**) *Fam (exhausto)* shattered; **la carrera me dejó r.** I was shattered after the race (**e**) *Chile Fam Pey (ordinario)* common (**f**) *Chile Fam Pey (pobre)* penniless
3 *nm,f Chile Fam* (**a**) *(tipo)* guy; *(mujer)* woman (**b**) *Pey (trabajador)* worker (**c**) *Pey (persona ordinaria)* pleb, *Br* oik
4 *nm Esp (en tela)* tear, rip; **tengo un r. en el calcetín** there's a hole in my sock; EXPR *Fam* **vale** *o* **sirve lo mismo para un r. que para un descosido** *(persona)* he can turn his hand to all sorts of different things

rotograbado *nm Imprenta* rotogravure

rotonda *nf* (**a**) *(en calle, carretera)* roundabout (**b**) *(plaza)* circus (**c**) *(edificio)* rotunda

rotor *nm* rotor

rotoso, -a *Andes, RP* 1 *adj* ragged, in tatters
2 *nm,f* scarecrow

rotring® ['rrotrin] (*pl* **rotrings**) *nm* Rotring® pen

rottweiler [rrot'bailer] (*pl* **rottweilers**) *nm* Rottweiler

rótula *nf* (**a**) *Anat* kneecap (**b**) *Tec* ball-and-socket joint

rotulación *nf* (**a**) *(de mapa, gráfico)* labelling (**b**) *(de calle, carretera)* signposting

rotulador *nm* felt-tip pen ▸▸ ***r. fluorescente*** highlighter (pen)

rotular *vt* (**a**) *(con rotulador)* to highlight (**b**) *(carta, artículo)* to head with fancy lettering (**c**) *(mapa, gráfico)* to label (**d**) *(calle, carretera)* to signpost

rotulista *nmf* sign-painter

rótulo *nm* (**a**) *(letrero)* sign ▸▸ ***r. luminoso*** *(de neón)* neon sign (**b**) *(encabezamiento)* headline, title

rotundamente *adv* (**a**) *(categóricamente)* categorically; **rechazó r. que tuviera nada que ver con el escándalo** he categorically denied having anything to do with the scandal (**b**) *(completamente)* completely; **la nueva empresa fracasó r.** the new company was a total *o* complete failure

rotundidad *nf* firmness, categorical nature; **con r.** categorically

rotundo, -a *adj* (**a**) *(negativa, persona)* categorical (**b**) *(lenguaje, estilo)* emphatic, forceful (**c**) *(completo)* total; **un r. fracaso** a total *o* complete failure; **tuvo un r. éxito** it enjoyed a resounding success, it was hugely successful (**d**) *(cuerpo)* rotund; **una mujer de formas rotundas** a curvaceous woman

rotura *nf (de hueso)* fracture; *(en tela)* rip, hole; **sufre una r. de ligamentos** he has torn ligaments; **la r. de la correa del ventilador obligó a interrumpir el viaje** the fan belt snapped *o* went, making it necessary to interrupt the journey ▸▸ ***r. del servicio*** *(en tenis)* service break

roturación *nf* ploughing

roturadora *nf* Rotavator®

roturar *vt* to plough

rough [rraf] *nm (en golf)* rough

roulotte [rru'lot] *nf Br* caravan, *US* trailer

round [rraun(d)] (*pl* **rounds**) *nm Dep* round

router ['rruter] (*pl* **routers**) *nm Informát* router

roya *nf (hongo)* rust

royal® *nm Andes, RP* baking powder

royalty [rro'jalti] (*pl* **royalties**) *nm* royalty

royera *etc ver* **roer**

roza *nf* groove

rozadura *nf* (**a**) *(señal)* scratch, scrape (**b**) *(herida)* graze; **estos zapatos me hacen rozaduras en los tobillos** these shoes are rubbing my ankles

rozagante *adj Esp* **estar r.** *(satisfecho)* to be extremely pleased; *(con buen aspecto)* to look lovely

rozamiento *nm* (**a**) *(fricción)* rubbing (**b**) *Fís* friction; **el r. del aire** air resistance

rozar [14] 1 *vt* (**a**) *(frotar)* to rub; *(suavemente)* to brush; **la rueda está rozando con la horquilla** the wheel is rubbing against the fork of the bicycle; **separa la silla para que no roce la pared** move the chair away from the wall a bit so that it doesn't rub against it; **me roza el zapato en la parte de atrás** my shoe is rubbing my heel; **la rozó con el brazo ligeramente** his arm brushed against her
(**b**) *(pasar cerca de)* to skim, to shave; **la bala lo pasó rozando** the bullet missed him by a hair's breadth; **la pelota rozó el poste** the ball shaved the post
(**c**) *(estar cerca de)* to border on; **roza los cuarenta** he's almost forty; **su talento roza lo divino** he is touched by genius; **tu plan roza la locura** your plan is verging *o* bordering on madness
(**d**) *(desgastar)* to wear out
(**e**) *Agr* to clear
(**f**) *Méx (irritar)* to irritate; **no puedo usar tejidos sintéticos porque me rozan** I can't wear synthetics, they irritate my skin
2 *vi* **r. con** *(tocar)* to brush against; *(relacionarse con)* to touch on; **no dejes que el sofá roce con la pared** don't let the sofa rub against the wall
3 **rozarse** *vpr* (**a**) *(tocarse)* to touch (**b**) *(pasar cerca)* to brush past each other (**c**) *(rasguñarse)* to graze oneself (**con** on); **me rozé la mano con la pared** I grazed my hand on the wall (**d**) *(tener trato)* **rozarse con** to rub shoulders with

rpm (*abrev de* **revoluciones por minuto**) rpm

RR.HH. (*abrev de* **recursos humanos**) HR

Rte. (*abrev de* **remitente**) sender

RTF *Informát* (*abrev de* **rich text format**) RTF

RTVE *nf* (*abrev de* **Radiotelevisión Española**) = Spanish state broadcasting company

rúa *nf* street

ruana *nf* (**a**) *Andes (cerrado)* poncho (**b**) *RP (abierto)* wrap-around poncho

Ruanda *n* Rwanda

ruandés, -esa 1 *adj* Rwandan
2 *nm,f (persona)* Rwandan
3 *nm (lengua)* Rwanda

ruano, -a *adj* roan

rubeola, rubéola *nf* German measles, *Espec* rubella

rubí (*pl* **rubíes** *o* **rubís**) *nm* ruby

rubia *nf* (**a**) *Fam Anticuado (moneda)* peseta (**b**) *ver también* **rubio**

rubiácea *Bot* 1 *nf* rubiaceous plant
2 **rubiáceas** *nfpl (familia) Rubiaceae*; **de la familia de las rubiáceas** of the family *Rubiaceae*

rubiales *Esp Fam* 1 *adj inv* blond(e), fair-haired
2 *nmf inv* blond *o* fair-haired guy, *f* blonde

Rubicón *nm* EXPR **pasar el R.** to cross the Rubicon

rubicundo, -a *adj* ruddy

rubidio *nm Quím* rubidium

rubio, -a 1 *adj* (**a**) *(pelo, persona)* blond, *f* blonde, fair; **r. platino** platinum blonde (**b**) *(tabaco)* **tabaco r.** Virginia tobacco *(as opposed to black tobacco)* (**c**) *(cerveza)* **cerveza rubia** lager
2 *nm,f* (**a**) *(persona rubia)* blond, *f* blonde, fair-haired person; **rubia** *Esp* **platino** *o Am* **platinada** platinum blonde (**b**) *Am Fam (como apelativo)* blondie; **¿cuándo se va la rubia?** when's the blonde woman leaving?
3 *nm (tabaco)* Virginia tobacco *(as opposed to black tobacco)*; *(cigarrillo)* = cigarette containing Virginia tobacco

rublo *nm* rouble

rubor *nm* (**a**) *(vergüenza)* embarrassment; **causar r. a alguien** to embarrass sb (**b**) *(sonrojo)* blush (**c**) *Am (colorete)* blusher

ruborizado, -a *adj* flushed

ruborizar [14] 1 *vt* (**a**) *(hacer enrojecer)* to make blush (**b**) *(avergonzar)* to embarrass
2 **ruborizarse** *vpr* to blush

ruboroso, -a *adj* (**a**) *(cara)* blushing, red (**b**) *(persona)* **es muy r.** he blushes very easily

rúbrica *nf* (**a**) *(de firma)* flourish (**b**) *(título)* title (**c**) *(conclusión)* close, conclusion; **poner r. a algo** to conclude sth, to bring sth to a close *o* conclusion

rubricar [60] *vt* (**a**) *(firmar)* to sign (**b**) *(confirmar)* to confirm (**c**) *(concluir)* to complete

rubro *nm Am* (**a**) *(rótulo)* heading; **buscar por rubros: hoteles, posadas, restaurantes** search by category: hotels, boarding houses, restaurants
(**b**) *(campo)* area, field; **las acciones implementadas en el r. "desarrollo social" fueron exitosas** the measures carried out in the area of *o* under the category of "social development" were successful; **preparamos empresas líderes en su r.** we provide training for companies which are leaders in their field
(**c**) *Cont* item; **r. presupuestal 2003: educación, salud, seguridad pública** 2003 budget headings: education, health, law and order

ruca *nf Chile* (**a**) *(indígena)* = Mapuche hut (**b**) *(moderna)* shack (**c**) *ver también* **ruco**

rucio, -a 1 *adj* (**a**) *(gris)* grey (**b**) *Chile (rubio)* blond, *f* blonde, fair
2 *nm,f Chile (rubio)* blond, *f* blonde, fair-haired person
3 *nm (animal)* ass, donkey

ruco, -a *adj* (**a**) *CAm (gastado)* worn out (**b**) *Méx Fam (viejo)* old

ruda *nf* (**a**) *(planta)* rue (**b**) *ver también* **rudo**

rudeza *nf* (**a**) *(tosquedad)* roughness (**b**) *(brusquedad)* sharpness, brusqueness; *(grosería)* rudeness, coarseness; **trata a sus padres con mucha r.** she treats her parents very brusquely (**c**) *(rigurosidad, dureza)* harshness

rudimentario, -a *adj* rudimentary

rudimento 1 *nm Biol* rudiment
2 **rudimentos** *nmpl* rudiments; **aprendió los rudimentos del inglés en la escuela** he learned the rudiments of English at school

rudo, -a *adj* (**a**) *(tosco, basto)* rough (**b**) *(brusco)* sharp, brusque; *(grosero)* rude, coarse; **es muy r. en el trato** he's very brusque with people (**c**) *(riguroso, duro)* harsh; **un trabajo r.** a hard *o* tough job

rueca *nf* distaff

rueda *nf* (**a**) *(pieza)* wheel; EXPR **chupar r.** *(en motociclismo)* to slipstream; *(en ciclismo)* to tag on behind another cyclist, to slipstream; EXPR **ir a la r. de alguien** *(en ciclismo)* to be on sb's wheel; EXPR **ir sobre ruedas** to go smoothly ►► *Arg* ***r. de auxilio*** spare wheel; *RP* ***r. de carro*** cartwheel; *Andes* ***r. de Chicago*** *Br* big wheel, *US* Ferris wheel; ***r. delantera*** front wheel; ***r. dentada*** cogwheel; ***la r. de la fortuna*** *(de hechos)* the wheel of fortune; *Méx (noria) Br* big wheel, *US* Ferris wheel; *Chile, Urug* ***r. gigante*** *Br* big wheel, *US* Ferris wheel; ***r. hidráulica*** waterwheel; *Dep* ***r. lenticular*** disc wheel; ***r. de molino*** millstone; ***r. de recambio*** spare wheel; ***r. de repuesto*** spare wheel; ***r. trasera*** rear wheel
(**b**) *(corro)* circle ►► ***r. de prensa*** press conference; ***r. de presos*** identification parade; ***r. de reconocimiento*** identification parade
(**c**) *(rodaja)* slice; **una r. de merluza** a hake steak
(**d**) *(en baloncesto)* = basketball drill in which each player in turn takes a shot at the basket

ruedo 1 *ver* **rodar**
2 *nm* (**a**) *Taurom* bullring; **dar la vuelta al r.** to do a lap of honour round the bullring; EXPR **echarse al r.** to enter the fray (**b**) *Am (dobladillo)* hem

ruego 1 *ver* **rogar**
2 *nm* request; **sus ruegos no ablandaron a su captor** her pleas failed to soften her captor; **accedieron a mis ruegos** they acceded to my requests; **fui a verla a r. suyo** I went to see her at her request; **ruegos y preguntas** any other business

rufián *nm* villain

rufianesca *nf* **la r.** the underworld

rufianesco, -a *adj* villainous

rufo, -a *adj Literario* **ir** *o* **estar r.** to be as pleased as punch

rugby ['rruγbi, *CSur* 'rraγbi] *nm* rugby ►► ***r. a siete*** sevens; ***r. a trece*** rugby league

rugido *nm* (**a**) *(de animal)* roar; **oímos el r. de un león** we heard a lion roar (**b**) *Literario (de mar, viento)* roar, roaring; **el r. del viento era ensordecedor** the roaring of the wind was deafening (**c**) *(de persona)* bellow; **dar un r.** to bellow (**d**) *(de tripas)* rumble

rugir [24] *vi* (**a**) *(animal)* to roar (**b**) *Literario (mar, viento)* to roar (**c**) *(persona)* to bellow (**d**) *(tripas)* to rumble; **me rugen las tripas** my tummy's rumbling

rugosidad *nf* (**a**) *(cualidad)* roughness (**b**) *(arruga) (de piel)* wrinkle; *(de tejido)* crinkle

rugoso, -a *adj* (**a**) *(áspero)* rough (**b**) *(con arrugas) (piel)* wrinkled; *(tejido)* crinkled

ruibarbo *nm* rhubarb

ruido *nm* (**a**) *(sonido)* noise; **escuchamos un r.** we heard a noise; **desde aquí se escuchan los ruidos de la fiesta** you can hear the noise of the party from here; **esta lavadora hace mucho r.** this washing machine is very noisy; **esta impresora hace un r. muy raro** this printer is making a very strange noise; **¡no hagas r.!** be quiet!; EXPR **mucho r. y pocas nueces** much ado about nothing ►► ***r. de fondo*** background noise; *Pol* ***r. de sables:*** **se oye r. de sables** there has been some sabre-rattling
(**b**) *(alboroto)* row; **hacer** *o* **meter r.** to cause a stir
(**c**) *Tel* noise ►► ***r. blanco*** white noise; ***r. en la línea*** line noise

ruidosamente *adv* noisily

ruidoso, -a *adj* (**a**) *(que hace ruido)* noisy (**b**) *(escandaloso)* sensational; **llevaba una corbata ruidosa** he was wearing a very loud tie

ruin *adj* (**a**) *(vil)* contemptible (**b**) *(avaro)* mean (**c**) *Cuba (en celo) Br* on heat, *US* in heat

ruina *nf* (**a**) *(quiebra)* ruin; **su negocio es una r.** his business is swallowing up his money; **la caída de la Bolsa causó su r.** the collapse of the Stock Exchange ruined him; **dejar en** *o* **llevar a la r. a alguien** to ruin sb; **estar en la r.** to be ruined; **la epidemia ha supuesto la r. de muchos ganaderos** the epidemic has ruined many cattle farmers; **vamos a la r.** we are going to wrack and ruin
(**b**) *(destrucción)* destruction; **el alcohol será su r.** drink will be the ruin *o* ruination of him
(**c**) **ruinas** *(de una construcción)* ruins; **un puente en ruinas** a bridge in ruins; **amenazar r.** *(edificio)* to be about to collapse
(**d**) *(persona)* wreck; **estar hecho una r.** to be a wreck

ruindad *nf* (**a**) *(cualidad)* meanness, baseness (**b**) *(acto)* vile deed

ruinoso, -a *adj* (**a**) *(poco rentable)* ruinous; **la situación del sector textil es ruinosa** the textile industry is in a disastrous *o* ruinous state (**b**) *(edificio)* ramshackle, dilapidated

ruiseñor *nm* nightingale

rujo *etc ver* **rugir**

rular *vi Fam* (**a**) *(funcionar)* to go, to work; **esta tele no rula** this telly is bust (**b**) *(deslizarse)* to roll

rulemán *nm RP* roller-bearing

rulero *nm RP (para el pelo)* roller, curler

ruleta *nf* roulette ►► ***r. rusa*** Russian roulette

ruletear *vi CAm, Méx Fam (en taxi)* to drive a taxi

ruletero *nm CAm, Méx Fam (de taxi)* taxi driver

rulo *nm* (**a**) *(para el pelo)* roller, curler (**b**) *(rizo)* curl (**c**) *Chile (secano)* unirrigated land (**d**) EXPR *RP* **hacerse rulos** *(ilusión)* to get excited; *(aprontarse)* to start preparing oneself

rulot *(pl* **rulots** *o* **rulotes**) *nf Br* caravan, *US* trailer

ruma *nf Andes, Ven* heap, pile

Rumanía, Rumania *n* Romania

rumano, -a 1 *adj* Romanian
2 *nm,f (persona)* Romanian
3 *nm (lengua)* Romanian

rumba *nf* (**a**) *(baile)* rumba (**b**) *Carib, Perú (juerga)* party

rumbear *vi* (**a**) *(bailar)* to dance the rumba (**b**) *Am (orientarse)* to get one's bearings (**c**) *Andes, RP* **r. para** to be heading for (**d**) *Carib, Perú Fam (andar de juerga)* to party

rumbero, -a 1 *adj* (**a**) *(de la rumba)* rumba; **ritmo r.** rumba beat (**b**) *Col, Perú Fam (cumbiambero)* party-loving
2 *nm,f Col, Perú Fam (cumbiambero)* party animal

rumbo *nm* (**a**) *(dirección) (al navegar)* course; **ir con r. a** to be heading for; **zarparon con r. a lo desconocido** they set out into the unknown; **cambió el r. de su vida** it changed the course of her life; **corregir el r.** to correct one's course; **habrá que corregir el r. de la empresa** we will have to change the company's direction; **mantener el r.** to maintain one's course; **perder el r.** *(barco)* to go off course; *Fig (persona)* to lose one's way; **puso r. al sur/a Terranova** he set a course for the south/for Newfoundland; **el r. de los acontecimientos** the course of events; **caminar sin r. (fijo)** to wander aimlessly; *Fig* **tomar otro r.** to take a different tack; **no me gusta el r. que están tomando las negociaciones** I don't like the direction *o* turn the negotiations have taken
(**b**) *(ostentación)* lavishness
(**c**) *CAm (juerga)* binge

rumboso, -a *adj Fam (generoso, suntuoso)* lavish

rumiante 1 *adj* ruminant
2 *nm* ruminant

rumiar 1 *vt* (**a**) *(masticar)* to chew (**b**) *(pensar)* to ruminate on, to chew over; **rumió la propuesta durante varios días** he chewed over the proposal for several days (**c**) *(mascullar)* to mutter
2 *vi (masticar)* to ruminate, to chew the cud

rumor *nm* (**a**) *(ruido sordo)* murmur; **el r. de las olas** the murmur of the waves; **un r. de voces** the sound of voices (**b**) *(chisme)* rumour; **corre un r.** there's a rumour going round; **corre el r. de que va a dimitir** it is rumoured that he's going to resign

rumorearse *v impersonal* **se rumorea que...** it is rumoured that...

runa 1 *nf* rune
2 *nmf Andes Pey (indígena)* = Indian man or woman

runfla *nf Méx Fam* gang

rúnico, -a *adj* runic

runrún *nm* (**a**) *(ruido)* hum; **se escuchaba un r. de voces** a hum of voices could be heard (**b**) *(chisme)* rumour

runrunear *vi* to hum

runruneo *nm (ruido)* hum; **el r. del motor era imperceptible** the hum of the engine was barely audible

rupestre *adj* (**a**) *(de las rocas)* rock (**b**) *(pinturas)* cave; **arte r.** cave paintings

rupia *nf* rupee

ruptor *nm Elec* contact breaker

ruptura *nf (de relaciones, conversaciones)* breaking-off; *(de pareja)* break-up; *(de contrato)* breach; **se han lamentado de la r. del consenso entre los partidos políticos** they have lamented the breakdown of the consensus among the political parties; **acusan al ejército de la r. de la tregua** they are accusing the army of breaking the truce; **su separación fue una r. amistosa** they remained friends after breaking up; **su última novela marca una r. con su estilo anterior** his latest novel marks a break with his previous style

rural 1 *adj* rural
2 *nf RP* van

ruralismo *nm (vocablo)* = word used by country people

Rusia *n* Russia

ruso, -a 1 *adj* Russian
2 *nm,f (persona)* Russian
3 *nm (lengua)* Russian

rústica *nf* **en r.** *(encuadernación)* paperback

rusticidad *nf* roughness, coarseness

rústico, -a *adj* (**a**) *(del campo)* country; **casa rústica** country cottage (**b**) *(tosco)* rough, coarse

ruta *nf* (**a**) *(itinerario)* route; **en r. (hacia)** en route (to); **en r.** *(en carretera)* on the road; **la seguridad en r.** road safety ►► ***r. aérea*** air route, airway; ***r. comercial*** trade route; ***r. marítima*** sea *o* shipping lane; ***r. turística*** scenic route; ***r. de vuelo*** flight path
(**b**) *(trayectoria)* way, course; **ha escogido una r. muy arriesgada para conseguir sus objetivos** he has chosen a very risky way of achieving his goals
(**c**) *RP (carretera)* road

rutenio *nm Quím* ruthenium

rutero, -a *adj (en carretera)* on-the-road

rutherfordio [rruter'fordjo] *nm Quím* rutherfordium

rutilante *adj* (**a**) *(brillante) (luna)* bright; *(estrellas)* bright, sparkling; *(belleza)* dazzling (**b**) *(destacado)* outstanding, brilliant

rutilar *vi* to shine brightly

rutilo *nm Geol* rutile

rutina *nf* (**a**) *(costumbre)* routine; **de r.** routine; **por r.** out of habit; **intenta romper con la r. diaria** she's trying to break away from her daily routine (**b**) *Informát* routine (**c**) *(serie de ejercicios)* routine

rutinariamente *adv* routinely

rutinario, -a *adj* (**a**) *(actividad, vida)* routine (**b**) *(persona)* **es muy r.** he likes to stick to his routine

Rvda. (*abrev de* **Reverenda**) Rev *(Mother etc)*

Rvdo. (*abrev de* **Reverendo**) Rev *(Father etc)*

S, s

S, s ['ese] *nf (letra)* S, s
S (*abrev de* **sábado**) S, Sat
S. (**a**) (*abrev de* **San**) St (**b**) (*abrev de* **Sur**) S
s (*abrev de* **segundo**) s
s. (**a**) (*abrev de* **san**) St (**b**) (*abrev de* **siglo**) C; **el s. XIX** the 19th century, the C19 (**c**) (*abrev de* **siguiente**) following
S.A. *nf* (*abrev de* **sociedad anónima**) *Br* ≃ PLC, *US* ≃ Inc
sáb. (*abrev de* **sábado**) Sat
sábado *nm* Saturday; **¿qué día es hoy? – (es) s.** what day is it (today)? – (it's) Saturday; **cada s., todos los sábados** every Saturday; **cada dos sábados, un s. sí y otro no** every other Saturday; **caer en s.** to be on a Saturday; **te llamo el s.** I'll call you on Saturday; **¡hasta el s.!** see you on Saturday!; **el próximo s., el s. que viene** next Saturday; **el s. pasado** last Saturday; **el s. por la mañana/tarde/noche** Saturday morning/afternoon/night; **el s. 5 de enero** Saturday the 5 January; **en s.** on Saturdays; **nací en s.** I was born on a Saturday; **este s.** *(pasado)* last Saturday; *(próximo)* this (coming) Saturday; **¿trabajas los sábados?** do you work (on) Saturdays?; **trabajar un s.** to work on a Saturday; **un s. cualquiera** on any Saturday ►► ***s. inglés*** = half day's work on Saturday *(as part of a five and a half day working week)*; ***S. Santo*** Easter Saturday
sábalo *nm (pez)* shad
sabana *nf* savannah; EXPR *Ven Fam* **estar en la s.** to be in clover; EXPR *Ven Fam* **ponerse en la s.** to get rich overnight
sábana *nf* sheet; EXPR *Fam* **se le pegan las sábanas** she's not good at getting up; **se me han pegado las sábanas** I overslept ►► ***s. de abajo*** bottom sheet; ***s. de arriba*** top sheet; ***s. bajera*** bottom sheet; *Esp* ***s. de cuatro picos*** fitted sheet; ***s. encimera*** top sheet; ***la S. Santa (de Turín)*** the Turin Shroud
sabandija 1 *nf* (**a**) *(animal)* creepy-crawly, bug (**b**) *Pey Fam (persona)* worm
2 *nmf RP Fam (niño)* little monkey, little tyke
sabanear *vi Carib, Col, Ven* to herd cattle on the savannah
sabanera *nf CAm, Col, Ven (serpiente)* savannah snake
sabanero *nm Carib, Col, Ven (ganadero)* cowboy, cattle drover
sabañón *nm* chilblain
sabático, -a *adj (de descanso)* sabbatical; **año s.** sabbatical (year)
sabatino, -a *adj (del sábado)* Saturday; **dimos el paseo s.** we went on our Saturday walk
sabedor, -ora *adj* **s. de que nunca sería elegido, se presentó a la elección** knowing that he would never be elected, he presented himself as a candidate; **sabedores de su gusto por la cocina, le regalaron un recetario** knowing he loved cooking, they gave him a recipe book
sabelotodo *Fam* **1** *adj inv* **niños s.** little *Br* know-alls *o US* know-it-alls; **tus amigos s.** your *Br* know-all *o US* know-it-all friends
2 *nmf Br* know-all, *US* know-it-all

SABER [59] **1** *nm* knowledge; *Formal* **según mi/nuestro/***etc.* **leal s. y entender** to the best of my/our/*etc* knowledge; PROV **el s. no ocupa lugar** you can never know too much
2 *vt* (**a**) *(conocer)* to know; **ya lo sé** I know; **no lo sé** I don't know; **yo no sabía nada de eso** I didn't know anything about that; **no sabía que eras médico** I didn't know you were a doctor; **ya sé lo que vas a decir** I know what you're going to say; **de haberlo sabido (antes)** *o* **si lo llego a s., me quedo en casa** if I'd known, I'd have stayed at home; **es de** *o* **por todos sabido que...** it's common knowledge that..., everyone knows that...; **hacer s. algo a alguien** to inform sb of sth, to tell sb sth; **para que lo sepas, somos amigos** we're friends, for your information; **¿sabes qué (te digo)?, que no me arrepiento** you know what, I don't regret it; **si lo sabré yo, que tengo cuatro hijos** you're telling me! I've got four children!; **sin yo saberlo, sin saberlo yo** without my knowledge; *Fig* **no sabía dónde meterme** I didn't know where to put myself; **no sabe lo que (se) hace** she doesn't know what she's doing; **no sabe lo que tiene** he doesn't realize just how lucky he is; *Fam* **te ha llamado un tal Antonio no sé cuántos** there was a call for you from Antonio something or other; **no sé qué decir** I don't know what to say; **¡qué sé yo!, ¡y yo qué sé!** how should I know!; **¡qué sé yo la de veces que me caí de la bici!** heaven knows how many times I fell off my bike!; *Irónico* **como te pille vas a s. lo que es bueno** just wait till I get my hands on you!; *Irónico* **cuando hagas la mili sabrás lo que es bueno** you'll be in for a nasty surprise when you do your military service; **tener un no sé qué** to have a certain something; *Fam* **y no sé qué y no sé cuántos** and so on and so forth
(**b**) *(ser capaz de)* **s. hacer algo** to be able to do sth, to know how to do sth; **¿sabes cocinar?** can you cook?; **no sé nadar** I can't swim, I don't know how to swim; **sabe hablar inglés/montar en bici** she can speak English/ride a bike; **sabe perder** he's a good loser; **su problema es que no saben beber** *(beben demasiado)* their problem is they don't know when to stop drinking
(**c**) *(enterarse de)* to learn, to find out; **lo supe ayer/por los periódicos** I found (it) out yesterday/in the papers; **supe la noticia demasiado tarde** I only heard the news when it was too late; **¿sabes algo de Juan?, ¿qué sabes de Juan?** have you had any news from *o* heard from Juan?; **¿sabes algo de cuándo será el examen?** have you heard anything about when the exam's going to be?
(**d**) *(entender de)* to know about; **sabe mucha física** he knows a lot about physics
3 *vi* (**a**) *(tener sabor)* to taste (**a** of); **a mí me sabe a fresa** it tastes of strawberries to me; **sabe mucho a cebolla** it has a very strong taste of onions, it tastes very strongly of onions; **esto no sabe a nada** this has no taste to it, this doesn't taste of anything; **s. bien/mal** to taste good/bad; **¡qué bien sabe este pan!** this bread's really tasty!, this bread tastes really good!; **esta agua sabe** this water has a funny taste; EXPR *Fam* **s. a cuerno quemado** *o* **a rayos** to taste disgusting *o* revolting
(**b**) *(sentar)* **le supo mal** *(le enfadó)* it upset *o* annoyed him; **me sabe mal mentirle** I feel bad about lying to him; EXPR *Fam* **s. a cuerno quemado** *o* **a rayos: sus comentarios me supieron a cuerno quemado** *o* **a rayos** I thought his comments were really off
(**c**) *(tener conocimiento)* to know; **no sé de qué me hablas** I don't know what you're talking about; **sé de una tienda que vende discos de vinilo** I know of a shop that sells vinyl records; **que yo sepa** as far as I know; **¡quién sabe!, ¡vete (tú) a s.!, ¡vaya usted a s.!** who knows!; **pues, sabes, a mí no me importaría** I wouldn't mind, you know; **es vecino mío, ¿sabes?** he's my neighbour, you know; EXPR *Méx Fam* **¡sepa Pancha!, ¡sepa la bola!** who knows?
(**d**) *(entender)* **s. de algo** to know about sth; **¿tú sabes de mecánica?** do you know (anything) about mechanics?; **ése sí que sabe** he's a canny one
(**e**) *(tener noticia)* **s. de alguien** to hear from sb; **no sé de él desde hace meses** I haven't heard (anything) from him for months; **s. de algo** to learn of sth; **supe de su muerte por los periódicos** I learnt of her death in the papers; **no quiero s. (nada) de ti** I don't want to have anything to do with you
(**f**) *(parecer)* **eso me sabe a disculpa** that sounds like an excuse to me; **este postre me ha sabido a poco** I could have done with the dessert being a bit bigger; **las vacaciones me han sabido a muy poco** my holidays weren't nearly long enough, I could have done with my holidays being a lot longer
(**g**) *Am (soler)* **s. hacer algo** to be in the habit of doing sth
4 saberse *vpr* (**a**) *(uso transitivo enfático) (conocer)* **saberse algo** to know sth; **se sabe todas las capitales de Latinoamérica** she knows (the names of) all the capitals in Latin America; EXPR **sabérselas todas** to know all the tricks; **se cree que se las sabe todas** he thinks he knows it all *o* has all the answers
(**b**) *(uso impersonal) (conocerse)* **¿se sabe si ha habido víctimas mortales?** is it known whether anyone was killed?; **aún no se sabe qué pasó** it is still not known what happened; **llegar a saberse** to come to light; **nunca se sabe** you never know; **¿se puede s. porque**

no me avisasteis? would you mind explaining why you didn't tell me?
(**c**) *(uso copulativo) (tener certeza de ser)* **él ya se sabía ganador del torneo** he already knew that he had won the tournament
5 a saber *loc conj (es decir)* namely

sabiamente *adv* wisely

sabido, -a *adj* **como es (bien) s.** as everyone knows; **es s. que este sistema operativo falla mucho** this operating system is known to be crash-prone

sabiduría *nf* (**a**) *(conocimientos)* knowledge, learning; **la s. popular** folklore, popular wisdom (**b**) *(prudencia)* wisdom; **actuó con mucha s.** she acted very wisely

sabiendas: a sabiendas *loc adv* knowingly; **utilizaron una sustancia tóxica a s.** they knowingly used a toxic substance; **aprobaron el proyecto a s. de su alto costo** they approved the project knowing that the cost would be high; **presentó la propuesta a s. de que sería derrotada** she presented the bill knowing full well that it would be defeated

sabihondez = **sabiondez**

sabihondo, -a = **sabiondo**

sabina *nf (arbusto)* juniper

sabio, -a 1 *adj* (**a**) *(sensato, inteligente)* wise (**b**) *(docto)* learned (**c**) *(amaestrado)* trained
2 *nm,f* (**a**) *(sensato, inteligente)* wise person; EXPR **de sabios es rectificar** a wise man acknowledges his mistakes (**b**) *(docto)* learned person

sabiondez, sabihondez *nf Br* know-all *o US* know-it-all attitude

sabiondo, -a, sabihondo, -a *Fam* **1** *adj Br* know-all, *US* know-it-all
2 *nm,f Br* know-all, *US* know-it-all

sablazo *nm* (**a**) *Fam (de dinero)* **sablazos** scrounging; EXPR **dar** *o* **pegar un s. a alguien** to scrounge money off sb (**b**) *(golpe)* blow with a sabre (**c**) *(herida)* sabre wound

sable *nm* (**a**) *(arma)* sabre (**b**) *Náut* batten (**c**) *(en heráldica)* sable (**d**) *Cuba (pez)* cutlass fish

sableador, -ora *nm,f Fam* scrounger

sablear *vi Fam* to scrounge money

sablista *nmf Fam* scrounger

saboneta *nf* pocket watch

sabor *nm* (**a**) *(gusto)* taste, flavour; **tener s. a algo** to taste of sth; **tiene un s. dulce/picante** it tastes sweet/spicy; **no conviene mezclar sabores** it's not a good idea to mix flavours; **con s. a limón** lemon-flavoured
(**b**) *(impresión)* **dejó mal s. (de boca)** it left a nasty taste in my mouth; **dejó buen s. (de boca)** it left me with a warm feeling inside; **aquella conversación me dejó un s. amargo** that conversation left me with a bitter taste in my mouth
(**c**) *(estilo)* flavour; **una obra de s. clásico** a play with a classical flavour

saborear *vt* (**a**) *(comida)* to savour (**b**) *(victoria, momento)* to savour

saboreo *nm* savouring

saborizante *nm* flavouring

sabotaje *nm* sabotage; **el accidente fue debido a un s.** the accident was caused by sabotage

saboteador, -ora *nm,f* saboteur

sabotear *vt* to sabotage

sabré *etc ver* **saber**

sabroso, -a 1 *adj* (**a**) *(gustoso)* tasty
(**b**) *(sustancioso)* tidy, considerable
(**c**) *(comentario) (gracioso)* juicy, tasty
(**d**) *(malicioso)* mischievous
(**e**) *Carib, Col, Méx (grato)* pleasant, nice; **tu compañía es muy sabrosa** you're very good company
(**f**) *Carib, Col, Méx (entretenido)* entertaining; **su último libro es s.** his latest book is entertaining *o* is a good read; **nadar es muy s.** swimming is good fun
(**g**) *Carib, Col, Méx (contagioso)* contagious; **tiene una risa sabrosa** she has a contagious laugh; **ese ritmo es muy s.** that beat is very catchy
(**h**) *Carib, Col, Méx Fam (hermoso)* lovely, gorgeous
2 *adv Carib, Col, Méx* (**a**) *(en forma, bien)* on form; **hoy me siento s.** I'm feeling good *o* on form today (**b**) *(con habilidad)* well; **juega muy s.** she plays very well; **baila s.** he's a good dancer

sabrosón, -ona *adj Carib, Col, Méx Fam* (**a**) *(gustoso)* tasty (**b**) *(grato)* pleasant, nice (**c**) *(entretenido)* entertaining (**d**) *(contagioso)* contagious (**e**) *(hermoso)* lovely, gorgeous

sabrosura *Carib, Col, Méx Fam* **1** *nf* (**a**) *(gusto)* tastiness (**b**) *(desenfado)* nerve, *Br* cheek
2 *interj* gorgeous!

sabueso *nm* (**a**) *(perro)* bloodhound (**b**) *Fam (detective)* sleuth

saca *nf* (**a**) *(bolsa, saco)* sack ►► ***s. de correo*** *Br* postbag, *US* mailbag (**b**) *Carib, Col (de ganado)* herd

sacabocados *nm inv* punch

sacabotas *nm inv* boot-jack

sacacorazones *nm inv (de manzana)* (apple) corer

sacacorchos *nm inv* corkscrew

sacacuartos, sacadineros, sacaperras 1 *nm inv Fam (oferta, libro)* rip-off; **este coche es un s.** this car is a drain on our finances
2 *nmf inv (persona)* scrounger

sacada *nf Andes, RP Fam* **la s. de plata de una cuenta es hoy más fácil gracias a los cajeros automáticos** getting money out of the bank is easier today, thanks to ATMs; **la s. de la mesa siempre genera discusiones entre ellos** clearing the table always leads to arguments between them

sacadineros = **sacacuartos**

sacadura *nf Chile (acción de sacar)* removal

sacalagua *nmf Am* light-skinned mestizo

sacaleches *nm inv* breast pump

sacamuelas *nm inv Fam Pey* dentist

sacaperras = **sacacuartos**

sacapuntas *nm inv* pencil sharpener

SACAR [60] **1** *vt* (**a**) *(poner fuera, hacer salir, extraer)* to take out; *(pistola, navaja, espada)* to draw; *(naipe, ficha)* to play; *(carbón, oro, petróleo)* to extract; **s. agua de un pozo** to draw water from a well; **sacó la lengua** she stuck her tongue out; **¡saca las manos de los bolsillos!** take your hands out of your pockets!; **sacó la mano/la cabeza por la ventanilla** he stuck his hand/head out of the window; **habrá que s. los zapatos a la terraza** we'll have to put our shoes out on the balcony; **¿de qué carpeta has sacado estos papeles?** which folder did you take these papers out of?; **¿cómo lo vamos a s. de ahí?** how are we going to get him out of there?; **me sacaron de allí/a la calle por la fuerza** they threw me out of there/into the street by force; **s. a alguien a bailar** to ask sb to dance; **s. a pasear al perro** to walk the dog, to take the dog for a walk; **nos sacaron algo de comer** they gave us something to eat; EXPR *Ven Fam* **s. la piedra a alguien** to make sb mad
(**b**) *(quitar)* to remove (**de** from); *(manchas)* to get out, to remove (**de** from); *(espinas)* to get *o* pull out (**de** from); **el dentista me sacó una muela** I had a tooth out at the dentist's; **sacarle sangre a alguien** to draw blood from sb; *RP* **¿quién me sacó el diccionario?** who's taken my dictionary?
(**c**) *(obtener) (carné, certificado, buenas notas)* to get; *(entradas, billetes, pasajes)* to get, to buy; *(datos, información)* to get, to obtain; *(premio)* to win; **¿qué sacaste en el examen de inglés?** what did you get for *o* in your English exam?; **saqué un ocho** I got eight out of ten; **s. beneficios (a** *o* **de un negocio)** to make a profit (from a business); **s. dinero del banco** to get *o* take some money out of the bank; **¿de dónde has sacado esa idea?** where did you get that idea (from)?; **lo que sigue está sacado de la Constitución** the following is an extract from the Constitution; **la sidra se saca de las manzanas** cider is made from apples; **de esta pizza no sacas más de seis raciones** you won't get more than six portions from this pizza; **¿y qué sacamos con reñirle?** what do we gain by telling him off?, what's the point in telling him off?; **¿y yo qué saco?** what's in it for me?
(**d**) *(librar, salvar)* **s. a alguien de algo** to get sb out of sth; **gracias por sacarme del apuro** thanks for getting me out of trouble; **5.000 pesos no nos van a s. de pobres** 5.000 pesos isn't exactly enough for us never to have to work again
(**e**) *(realizar) (foto)* to take; *(fotocopia)* to make; *RP (apuntes, notas)* to take; **siempre me sacan fatal en las fotos** I always look terrible in photos; **juntaos, que no os saco a todos** move closer together, I can't fit you all in the photo like that
(**f**) *(sonsacar)* **s. algo a alguien** to get sth out of sb; **no me sacarán nada** they won't get anything out of me
(**g**) *(nuevo producto, modelo, libro)* to bring out; *(disco)* to release; **ha sacado un nuevo disco/una nueva novela** he has a new record/novel out
(**h**) *(manifestar)* **s. (a relucir) algo** to bring sth up; **yo no fui el que sacó el tema** it wasn't me who brought the matter up in the first

place; **sacó su mal humor a relucir** he let his bad temper show
(**i**) *(resolver, encontrar)* to do, to work out; *(crucigrama)* to do, to solve; **s. la cuenta/la solución** to work out the total/the answer; **s. la respuesta correcta** to get the right answer; **siempre está sacando defectos a la gente** she's always finding fault with people
(**j**) *(deducir)* to gather, to understand; **s. una conclusión** to come to a conclusion; **s. algo en consecuencia de algo** to conclude *o* deduce sth from sth; **lo leí tres veces, pero no saqué nada en claro** *o* **limpio** I read it three times, but I couldn't make much sense of it
(**k**) *(aventajar en)* **sacó tres minutos a su rival** he was three minutes ahead of his rival; **mi hijo ya me saca la cabeza** my son's already a head taller than me
(**l**) *(en medios de comunicación)* to show; **sacaron imágenes en el telediario** they showed pictures on the news; **sacaron imágenes en el periódico** they printed pictures in the newspaper; **la sacaron en** *o* **por televisión** she was on television
(**m**) *Esp (prenda) (de ancho)* to let out; *(de largo)* to let down
(**n**) *Am (camisa, zapatos)* to take off; **sácale la ropa al niño** get the child undressed
(**o**) *(en deportes) (en tenis, voleibol)* to serve; **s. un córner/una falta** to take a corner/free kick
(**p**) **s. adelante** *(hijos)* to provide for; *(negocio, proyecto)* to make a go of; **sacó sus estudios adelante** she successfully completed her studies; **no sé cómo vamos a s. adelante la empresa** I don't know how we're going to keep the company going; **saca adelante a su familia con un mísero salario** he supports his family on a miserable salary
2 *vi (en fútbol, baloncesto, hockey)* to put the ball into play; *(en tenis, voleibol)* to serve; **s. de banda/de esquina/de puerta** to take a throw-in/corner/goal kick
3 **sacarse** *vpr* (**a**) *(poner fuera)* **se sacó la cartera del bolsillo** he took his wallet out of his pocket; EXPR *Fam* **sacarse algo de la manga** to make sth up (on the spur of the moment)
(**b**) *(carné, título, certificado)* to get; **se sacó el pasaporte la semana pasada** she got her passport last week
(**c**) *Am (ropa, lentes, aros)* to take off; **sáquese la camisa** take your shirt off
(**d**) *Am (ganar)* **se sacó la lotería** he won the lottery

sacárido *nm Quím* saccharide

sacarina *nf* saccharine

sacarosa *nf* sucrose

sacerdocio *nm* (**a**) *Rel* priesthood (**b**) *(dedicación)* vocation

sacerdotal *adj* priestly

sacerdote, -isa 1 *nm,f (pagano)* priest, *f* priestess
2 *nm (cristiano)* priest; **mujer s.** woman priest

sachar *vt* to weed

saciar 1 *vt (satisfacer) (sed)* to quench; *(hambre, curiosidad)* to satisfy; *(ambición)* to fulfil; **acudieron al festival para s. su sed de música** they went to the festival to quench their thirst for music
2 **saciarse** *vpr (de comida, bebida)* to have had one's fill; *(de conocimientos, poder)* to be satisfied; **nunca se sacia de ver la televisión** she never tires of watching television; **su ambición no se sacia con nada** his ambition knows no bounds

saciedad *nf (sensación)* **comió hasta la s.** she ate until she couldn't eat any more; **repetir algo hasta la s.** to repeat sth over and over

saco 1 *nm* (**a**) *(bolsa)* sack; **un s. de carbón/patatas** a sack of coal/potatoes; EXPR **caer en s. roto** to fall on deaf ears; EXPR **echar en s. roto: espero que no eches en s. roto mis consejos** I hope you take good note of my advice; EXPR **ser (como) un s. sin fondo** to be (like) a bottomless pit ►► ***s. de arena*** sandbag; ***s. de dormir*** sleeping bag; ***s. de dormir (tipo) momia*** mummy sleeping bag; ***s. terrero*** sandbag
(**b**) *Fam (persona)* EXPR **ser un s. de huesos** to be all skin and bones; EXPR **ser un s. de mentiras** to be full of lies
(**c**) *Biol* sac, bag ►► ***s. lacrimal*** lacrimal sac; ***s. vitelino*** yolk sac
(**d**) *Am (abrigo)* coat
(**e**) *Am (de tela)* jacket; *(de punto)* cardigan; *RP* **s. largo** overcoat, three-quarter-length coat ►► *Am* ***s. sport*** sports jacket
(**f**) EXPR *Esp muy Fam* **mandar a alguien a tomar por s.** to tell sb to get screwed *o Br* stuffed; *Esp muy Fam* **¡que le den por s.!** screw him!, *Br* he can get stuffed!
2 **a saco** *loc adv* **entraron a s. en el pueblo** they sacked *o* pillaged the village; **los asaltantes entraron a s. en el palacio presidencial** the attackers stormed the presidential palace; **el periodista entró a s. con las preguntas** the journalist didn't beat about the bush with his questions

sacón *nm RP* overcoat, three-quarter-length coat

sacralizar [14] *vt* to consecrate, to make sacred

sacramentado, -a *adj* **estar s.** to have received the last rites

sacramental *adj* (**a**) *Rel* sacramental (**b**) *(palabras, fórmula)* ceremonial

sacramentar *vt* to administer the last rites to

sacramento *nm* sacrament; **administrar un s.** to administer a sacrament; **recibir un s.** to receive a sacrament; **los últimos sacramentos** the last rites

sacrificar [60] 1 *vt* (**a**) *(animal) (para consumo)* to slaughter; *(por enfermedad)* to slaughter, to destroy (**b**) *(a los dioses)* to sacrifice (**a** to) (**c**) *(renunciar a)* to sacrifice, to give up; **sacrificó la carrera por su familia** she gave up her career for her family
2 **sacrificarse** *vpr* **sacrificarse (para hacer algo)** to make sacrifices (in order to do sth); **sacrificarse por alguien** to make sacrifices for sb

sacrificio *nm* (**a**) *(de animal) (para consumo)* slaughter; *(por enfermedad)* slaughter, destruction (**b**) *(a los dioses)* sacrifice ►► ***el s. del altar*** the sacrifice of the altar (**c**) *(renuncia)* sacrifice; **me costó muchos sacrificios** I had to make a lot of sacrifices

sacrilegio *nm* (**a**) *(religioso)* sacrilege (**b**) *(blasfemia)* sacrilege

sacrílego, -a 1 *adj* sacrilegious
2 *nm,f* sacrilegious person

sacristán, -ana *nm,f* (**a**) *(ayudante de sacerdote)* sacristan, sexton (**b**) *Am Fam (entrometido)* busybody

sacristía *nf* sacristy

sacro, -a 1 *adj* (**a**) *(sagrado)* holy, sacred ►► *Hist* ***el Sacro Imperio Romano (Germánico)*** the Holy Roman Empire (**b**) *Anat* sacral; **el hueso s.** the sacrum
2 *nm Anat* sacrum

sacrosanto, -a *adj* sacrosanct

sacuanjoche *nm CAm* frangipani

sacudida *nf* (**a**) *(movimiento)* shake; *(de la cabeza)* toss; *(de tren, coche)* jolt; **el avión dio una fuerte s.** the plane shuddered *o* lurched (**b**) *(terremoto)* tremor (**c**) *(conmoción)* shock; **la noticia le produjo una fuerte s.** the news gave her a deep shock (**d**) *(calambre)* **s. (eléctrica)** electric shock; **le dio una s. al tocar el enchufe** she got a shock when she touched the socket

sacudidor *nm* carpet beater

sacudir 1 *vt* (**a**) *(agitar)* to shake; **el terremoto sacudió la ciudad** the earthquake shook the city
(**b**) *(quitar) (agitando)* to shake off; *(frotando)* to brush off; **s. el polvo a una mesa** to dust a table
(**c**) *(golpear) (alfombra)* to beat; *(mantel, chaqueta)* to shake out; *Fam (persona)* to whack; **sacude bien las migas del mantel** shake all the crumbs off the tablecloth; **le sacudió una bofetada** she slapped him
(**d**) *(conmover)* to shake, to shock; **su asesinato sacudió a la población** people were shaken by his assassination
2 *vi RP* to shake oneself, to give oneself a shake; **hay que s. bien, si no queda todo el polvo** you have to give yourself a good shake, or you stay covered in dust
3 **sacudirse** *vpr* (**a**) *(librarse) (de responsabilidad, tarea)* to get out of; **se sacudió a sus perseguidores (de encima)** she shook off her pursuers; **no consigo sacudírmelo (de encima)** I can't seem to get rid of him (**b**) *(apartar)* **la vaca se sacudía las moscas con el rabo** the cow was swishing the flies away with its tail; **sacúdete las migas de la falda** shake the crumbs off your skirt

sacudón *nm Am* (**a**) *(sacudida)* shake; **no sintieron el s. que advertía de un movimiento sísmico de intensidad** they did not notice the tremor that heralded a major earthquake (**b**) *(golpe)* blow; **el banco había sufrido su primer gran s.** the bank had suffered its first major blow (**c**) *(revuelo)* upheaval, turmoil; **hubo un s. en los mercados bursátiles** there was upheaval on the Stock Market

SAD *nf Esp Dep* (*abrev de* **Sociedad Anónima Deportiva**) = abbreviation indicating that a sports club is a public limited company

S.A. de C.V. *nf Méx* (*abrev de* **sociedad anónima de capital variable**) variable capital corporation

sádico, -a 1 *adj* sadistic
2 *nm,f* sadist

sadismo *nm* sadism

sadomasoquismo *nm* sadomasochism

sadomasoquista 1 *adj* sadomasochistic
2 *nmf* sadomasochist

saduceo, -a *Hist* 1 *adj* Sadducean
2 *nm,f* Sadducee

saeta *nf* (**a**) *(flecha)* arrow (**b**) *(de reloj)* hand; *(de brújula)* needle (**c**) *(copla)* = flamenco-style song sung on religious occasions

safacón *nm RDom (papelera)* wastepaper basket *o* bin

safari *nm* (**a**) *(expedición)* safari; **ir de s., hacer un s.** to go on a safari ▸▸ ***s. fotográfico*** photo safari (**b**) *(zoológico)* safari park

saga *nf* (**a**) *Lit* saga (**b**) *(familia)* dynasty

sagacidad *nf* astuteness, shrewdness

sagaz *adj* astute, shrewd

sagitariano, -a *Am* **1** *adj* Sagittarian; **ser s.** to be (a) Sagittarian *o* Sagittarius
2 *nm,f* Sagittarian, Sagittarius; **los sagitarianos son...** Sagittarians are...

Sagitario **1** *adj inv* Sagittarian; *Esp* **ser S.** to be (a) Sagittarian *o* Sagittarius
2 *nm (signo)* Sagittarius; **los de S. son...** Sagittarians are...
3 *nmf (persona)* Sagittarian, Sagittarius; *Esp* **los S. son...** Sagittarians are...

sagrado, -a *adj* (**a**) *Rel* holy, sacred ▸▸ ***el Sagrado Corazón*** the Sacred Heart; ***las Sagradas Escrituras*** Holy Scripture, the Holy Scriptures; ***la Sagrada Familia*** the Holy Family (**b**) *(merecedor de respeto)* sacred; **para mí, la familia es sagrada** my family is sacred to me

sagrario *nm (tabernáculo)* tabernacle

Sáhara ['saχara], **Sahara** [sa'ara] *nm* **el (desierto del) S.** the Sahara (Desert) ▸▸ ***el S. Occidental*** Western Sahara

saharaui [saχa'rawi] **1** *adj* Saharawi; **el pueblo s.** the Saharawi people
2 *nmf* Saharawi

sahariana *nf* [saa'rjana] *(prenda)* safari jacket

sahariano, -a [saχa'rjano, -a, saa'rjano, -a] **1** *adj* Saharan
2 *nm,f* Saharan

sahino = **saíno**

sahumado, -a *adj Am Fam (achispado)* tight, tipsy

sahumador *nm (para perfumes)* incense burner

sahumar **1** *vt* = to perfume or purify with aromatic smoke
2 sahumarse *vpr* = to be perfumed or purified with aromatic smoke

sahumerio *nm* (**a**) *(acción)* = perfuming or purifying with aromatic smoke (**b**) *(humo)* aromatic smoke (**c**) *(sustancia)* incense

SAI ['sai] *nm Informát* (*abrev de* **sistema de alimentación ininterrumpida**) UPS

saín *nm (de animal)* animal fat

sainete *nm (teatro)* = short, popular comic play

saíno, sahino *nm Am* peccary

sajar *vt (grano)* to lance; *(quiste)* to cut open

sajón, -ona **1** *adj* Saxon
2 *nm,f* Saxon

sake, saki *nm* sake

sal **1** *nf* (**a**) *(condimento)* salt; **echar s. a** *(guiso)* to add salt to; **sin s.** *(mantequilla)* unsalted ▸▸ ***s. de cocina*** cooking salt; ***s. común*** cooking salt; ***s. fina*** table salt; ***s. de fruta*** fruit salts; ***s. gema*** rock salt; *Esp* ***s. gorda*** *(condimento)* cooking salt; *(humor soez)* coarse humour; ***s. gruesa*** *(en la cocina)* cooking salt; *(como descripción)* coarse salt; ***s. marina*** sea salt; ***s. de mesa*** table salt
(**b**) *Quím* salt ▸▸ ***s. amónica*** sal ammoniac
(**c**) *(gracia)* wit; *(garbo)* verve; **tiene mucha s. bailando** she dances with great verve; EXPR **es la s. de la vida** it's one of the things that make life worth living
(**d**) *CAm, Carib, Méx (desgracia)* misfortune, bad luck; EXPR **echar la s. a alguien** to put a jinx on sb
2 sales *nfpl* (**a**) *(para reanimar)* smelling salts (**b**) *(para baño)* **sales (de baño)** bath salts

sala *nf* (**a**) *(habitación)* room; *(de una casa)* lounge, living-room; *(de hospital)* ward ▸▸ ***s. capitular*** chapter house; ***s. de embarque*** *(en aeropuerto)* departure lounge; ***s. de espera*** waiting room; ***s. de estar*** lounge, living-room; ***s. de juntas*** boardroom; ***s. de lectura*** reading room; ***s. de máquinas*** engine room; *Cine* ***s. de montaje*** cutting room; ***s. de operaciones*** *Br* operating theatre, *US* operating room; ***s. de partos*** delivery room; ***s. de profesores*** staff (common) room; ***s. de proyección*** projection room; ***s. de tránsito*** *(en aeropuerto)* transfer lounge; ***s. de urgencias*** *Br* casualty ward, *US* emergency room; ***s. VIP*** VIP lounge
(**b**) *(local) (de conferencias, conciertos)* hall; *(de cine)* screen; *(de teatro)* auditorium; **un cine de ocho salas** an eight-screen cinema *o* multiplex ▸▸ ***s. de bingo*** bingo hall; ***s. de conciertos*** *(de música moderna)* concert venue; *(de música clásica)* concert hall; ***s. de exposiciones*** art gallery; ***s. de fiestas*** discotheque; ***s. X*** = porn cinema, *US* X-rated movie house
(**c**) *Der (lugar)* court(room); *(magistrados)* bench ▸▸ ***s. de lo civil*** civil court; ***s. de lo penal*** criminal court

salacidad *nf Formal* salaciousness

salacot (*pl* **salacots** *o* **salacotes**) *nm* pith helmet

saladillo, -a *adj* salted

saladito *nm RP* savoury snack *o* appetizer

salado, -a *adj* (**a**) *(con sal)* salted; *(con demasiada sal)* salty; **estar s.** to be salty; **agua salada** salt water; **bacalao s.** salt(ed) cod
(**b**) *(opuesto a lo dulce)* savoury; **me gusta más lo s.** I prefer savoury food
(**c**) *Esp (gracioso, simpático)* amusing; *(encantador)* charming; **tu amigo es muy s.** your friend is very amusing; **¡qué bebé más s.!** what a charming baby!
(**d**) *CAm, Carib, Méx (desgraciado)* unlucky; EXPR **estar s.** to have lousy luck
(**e**) *CSur Fam (caro)* pricey

salamanca *nf RP (animal)* = type of salamander considered by some cultures to be an evil spirit

salamandra *nf* (**a**) *(animal)* salamander (**b**) *(estufa)* = salamander stove

salamanquesa, *Andes* **salamanqueja** *nf* Moorish gecko

salame **1** *nm CSur (salami)* salami
2 *nmf RP Fam (tonto)* idiot

salami *nm* salami

salamín *nm RP (salami)* = type of thin salami

salar[1] *vt* (**a**) *(para conservar)* to salt (**b**) *(para cocinar)* to add salt to (**c**) *CAm, Carib, Méx (echar a perder)* to spoil, to ruin; *(causar mala suerte)* to bring bad luck to

salar[2] *nm* salt flat

salarial *adj* **congelación s.** pay freeze; **incremento s.** pay rise; **política s.** wage(s) policy

salario *nm* salary, wages ▸▸ ***s. base*** *o* ***básico*** basic wage; ***s. bruto*** gross wage; ***s. mínimo (interprofesional)*** minimum wage; ***s. neto*** net wage; *Esp* ***s. social*** = benefit paid by local authorities to low-income families

salaz *adj Formal* salacious

salazón **1** *nf* (**a**) *(de alimentos)* salting (**b**) *CAm, Cuba, Méx Fam (mala suerte)* bad luck
2 salazones *nfpl (carne)* salted meat; *(pescado)* salted fish

salcedo *nm* willow grove

salchicha *nf* sausage ▸▸ ***s. de Fráncfort*** frankfurter, *US* wiener

salchichería *nf* sausage shop

salchichero, -a *nm,f* (**a**) *(fabricante)* sausage maker (**b**) *(vendedor)* sausage seller

salchichón *nm* = cured pork sausage similar to salami

salchichonería *nf Méx* delicatessen

salchipapa *nf Perú* = dish of sliced frankfurter with French fries

saldar **1** *vt* (**a**) *(pagar) (cuenta)* to close; *(deuda)* to settle (**b**) *(arreglar, finalizar)* to settle (**c**) *Com (vender)* to sell off
2 saldarse *vpr (acabar)* **la pelea se saldó con once heridos** eleven people were injured in the brawl; **el partido se saldó con una victoria local** the game resulted in a home win

saldo *nm* (**a**) *(de cuenta)* balance; **s. a favor/en contra** credit/debit balance; **la balanza comercial entre los dos países arroja un s. favorable a Japón** the trade balance between the two countries is tipped in Japan's favour ▸▸ ***s. acreedor*** credit balance; ***s. anterior*** balance brought forward; ***s. de caja*** cash balance; ***s. deudor*** debit balance; ***s. disponible*** balance available; ***s. medio*** average (bank) balance; ***s. negativo*** debit balance
(**b**) *(de deudas)* settlement
(**c**) *(de partido, enfrentamiento)* result, outcome; **la iniciativa tuvo un s. positivo** on balance, the outcome of the initiative was positive; **el accidente tuvo un s. de cinco muertos** the accident left five people dead; **los incidentes arrojaron un s. de cincuenta detenidos** the incidents ended with fifty arrests
(**d**) **saldos** *(restos de mercancías)* remnants
(**e**) **saldos** *(rebajas)* sale; **de s.** bargain

saldré *etc ver* **salir**

saledizo *Arquit* **1** *adj* projecting, overhanging
2 *nm* overhang

salegar *nm* salt lick

salero *nm* **(a)** *(recipiente)* saltcellar, *US* salt shaker **(b)** *Fam (gracia)* wit; *(garbo)* verve; **con Juan nos reímos siempre, tiene mucho s.** Juan always makes us laugh, he's very witty; **baila con mucho s.** she dances with great verve; **cuenta chistes con s.** she's really good at telling jokes

saleroso, -a *adj Fam (gracioso)* witty; *(garboso)* vivacious

salesiano, -a 1 *adj* Salesian
2 *nm,f* Salesian

salgo *etc ver* **salir**

salicilato *nm Quím* salicylate

salicílico, -a *adj Quím* **ácido s.** salicylic acid

sálico, -a *adj Hist* **ley sálica** Salic law

SALIDA *nf* **(a)** *(partida, marcha)* departure; **tenían prevista la s. al amanecer** they intended to leave at dawn; **el tren con destino a Santiago va a efectuar su s. por la vía 4** the Santiago train is about to depart from platform 4; **salidas nacionales/internacionales** *(en aeropuerto)* national/international departures
(b) *(lugar para salir) (de edificio, recinto)* exit, way out; *(de red de cables, cañerías)* outlet; **gira en la próxima s.** turn off at the next exit; **la región no tiene s. al mar** the region has no outlet to the sea; **s. 20** *(en autopista)* junction 20; **¿dónde está la s.?** where's the way out?; **s.** *(en letrero)* exit, way out; **esta calle no tiene s.** this road's a dead end; **todas las salidas de Caracas estaban colapsadas** traffic was at a standstill on all the roads leading out of Caracas; **dar s. a** *(sentimientos)* to vent, to let out; *(ideas)* to find an outlet for ►► ***s. de emergencia*** emergency exit; ***s. de humos*** air vent; ***s. de incendios*** fire exit
(c) *(en deportes, carreras)* start; **dar la s. a una carrera** to start a race ►► ***s. nula*** false start
(d) *(viaje)* trip; **una s. al extranjero** a trip abroad; **hicimos una s. al campo de un día** we went out for the day to the country, we went on an outing to the country for a day
(e) *(aparición) (de revista, nuevo modelo, producto)* appearance; **a la s. del sol** at sunrise; **su s. a escena fue recibida con aplausos** her entry on stage was greeted with applause, she was applauded as she came on stage; **esta llave regula la s. del agua** this *Br* tap *o US* faucet controls the flow of water ►► *Com* ***s. a bolsa*** *(de empresa)* flotation
(f) *(momento)* **quedamos a la s. del trabajo** we agreed to meet after work; **te espero a la s. del cine** I'll meet you after the movie
(g) *(solución)* way out; **es preciso encontrar una s. al problema/a esta situación** we need to find a way round the problem/a way out of this situation; **si no hay otra s.** if there's no alternative
(h) *(ocurrencia)* witty remark; *(pretexto)* excuse; **tener salidas** to be witty; **desde luego tiene cada s....** she certainly comes out with some witty remarks ►► ***s. de tono*** out-of-place remark
(i) *Com (producción)* output; *(posibilidades)* market; **dar s. a** *(producto)* to find an outlet for; **este producto tiene mucha s.** *(posibilidades de venta)* there's a big market for this product; *(se vende)* this product sells well; **este producto no tiene s.** *(posibilidades de venta)* there's no market for this product; *(no se vende)* this product doesn't sell
(j) salidas *(en contabilidad)* outgoings
(k) *Informát* output
(l) *Dep (partido fuera de casa)* away game
(m) salidas *(posibilidades laborales)* openings, opportunities; **carreras con salidas** university courses with good job prospects
(n) *Am* ***s. de baño*** bathrobe; *Am* ***s. de playa*** beach robe

salido, -a 1 *adj* **(a)** *(saliente)* projecting, sticking out; *(ojos)* bulging; **dientes salidos** buckteeth **(b)** *(animal)* on heat **(c)** *muy Fam (excitado)* horny; **estar s.** to be horny **(d)** *Ven Fam (atrevido)* pushy, interfering
2 *nm,f* **(a)** *muy Fam (excitado)* horny bugger **(b)** *Ven Fam (atrevido)* busybody

salidor, -ora *adj Andes, RP* **es muy s.** he loves going out

saliente 1 *adj* **(a)** *(destacable)* salient **(b)** *(presidente, ministro)* outgoing
2 *nm* projection

salina *nf* **(a)** *Min* salt mine **(b) salinas** *(en el mar)* saltworks *(singular)* **(c)** *ver también* **salino**

salinera *nf Min* salt mine

salinidad *nf* salinity

salinizar *vt* to salinize

salino, -a *adj* saline

SALIR [61] **1** *vi* **(a)** *(ir fuera)* to go out; *(venir fuera)* to come out; **¡sal aquí fuera!** come out here!; **no pueden s., están atrapados** they can't get out, they're trapped; **¿salimos al jardín?** shall we go out into the garden?; **salieron al balcón** they went out onto the balcony; **salió a la puerta** she came/went to the door; **s. a escena** *(actor)* to come/go on stage; **s. a pasear/tomar el aire** to go out for a walk/for a breath of fresh air; **s. a hacer la compra/de compras** to go shopping; **s. de** to go/come out of; **me lo encontré al s. del cine** I met him as I was coming out of the cinema; **¡sal de aquí!** get out of here!; **¡sal de ahí!** come out of there!; **salimos por la escalera de incendios/la puerta trasera** we left via the fire escape/through the back door; EXPR *Fam* **porque me sale/no me sale de las narices** because I damn well feel like it/damn well can't be bothered; EXPR *muy Fam* **porque me sale/no me sale de los huevos** because I bloody well feel like it/because I can't be arsed
(b) *(marcharse)* to leave (**para** for); **cuando salimos de Quito/del país** when we left Quito/the country; **salí de casa/del trabajo a las siete** I left home/work at seven; **¿a qué hora** *o* **cuándo sale vuestro vuelo?** when does your flight leave?; **¿a qué hora** *o* **cuándo sales de trabajar?** what time do you leave *o* finish work?; **s. corriendo** to run off; *Fam* **s. pitando** to leg it; **s. de vacaciones** to go (away) on *Br* holiday *o US* vacation; **s. de viaje** to go away (on a trip)
(c) *(ser novios)* to go out (**con** with); **están saliendo** they are going out (together); **¿desde cuándo llevan saliendo?** how long have they been going out (together)?
(d) *(ir a divertirse)* to go out; **suelo s. el fin de semana** I usually go out at the weekend; **salen mucho a cenar** they eat out a lot
(e) *(librarse)* **s. de la droga** to get off drugs; **Marisa ha salido de la depresión** Marisa has got over *o* come through her depression; **s. de la miseria** to escape from poverty; **s. de un apuro** to get out of a tight spot; **le he ayudado a s. de muchos líos** I've helped him out of a lot of tricky situations; **no sé si podremos s. de ésta** I don't know how we're going to get out of this one; **con este dinero no vamos a s. de pobres** this money isn't exactly enough for us never to have to work again
(f) *(desembocar) (calle, sendero, carretera)* **¿a dónde sale esta calle?** where does this street come out?
(g) *(separarse)* **este anillo sale fácilmente** this ring comes off easily; **este corcho no sale** this cork won't come out
(h) *(resultar)* to turn out; **ha salido muy estudioso** he's turned out to be very studious; **¿cómo salió la fiesta?** how did the party go?; **¿qué salió en la votación?** what was the result of the vote?; **a mí me sale un total de 35.000 pesos** I've got a total of 35,000 pesos, I make it 35,000 pesos in total; **salió (como) senador por California** he was elected (as) senator for California; **salió elegida actriz del año** she was voted actress of the year; **salió herido/ileso del accidente** he was/wasn't injured in the accident; **s. premiado** to be awarded a prize; **s. bien/mal** *(examen, entrevista)* to go well/badly; *(plato, dibujo)* to turn out well/badly; **¿qué tal te ha salido?** how did it go?; **me ha salido bien/mal** *(examen, entrevista)* it went well/badly; *(plato, dibujo)* it turned out well/badly; *(cuenta)* I got it right/wrong; **normalmente me sale a la primera** I normally get it right first time; **a mí la paella no me sale tan bien como a ti** my paella never turns out as well as yours does; **¿te salen las cuentas?** do all the figures tally?; **s. ganando/perdiendo** to come off well/badly
(i) *(en sorteo, juego) (número, nombre)* to come up; **no me ha salido un as en toda la partida** I haven't got *o* had a single ace in the whole game
(j) *(proceder)* **s. de** to come from; **el vino sale de la uva** wine comes from grapes; **salió de él (lo de) regalarte unas flores** it was his idea to get you the flowers
(k) *(surgir, brotar) (luna, estrellas)* to come out; *(sol)* to rise; *(flores, hojas)* to come out; *(dientes)* to come through; **le han salido varias flores al rosal** the rose bush has got several flowers now; **le están saliendo canas** he's getting grey hairs, he's going grey; **le están saliendo los dientes** her teeth are starting to come through, she's teething; **me salen los colores con tanto cumplido** all these compliments are making me blush; **le ha salido un sarpullido en la espalda** her back has come out in a rash; **te está saliendo sangre** you're bleeding; **me ha salido un grano en la nariz** I've got a spot on my nose
(l) *(aparecer) (publicación, producto, modelo)* to come out; *(disco)* to come out, to be released; *(moda, ley)* to come in; *(trauma, prejuicios)* to come out; *(tema, asunto)* to come up; **una revista que sale los jueves** a magazine that comes out on Thursdays; **su nuevo disco saldrá al mercado en otoño** her new record comes out *o* will be released in the autumn; **salieron (a relucir) todos sus miedos** all his fears came out; **¡qué bien sales en esta foto!** you look great in this photo!; **ha salido en los periódicos/en la tele** it's been in the papers/on TV; **s. de/en** *(en película, serie, obra de teatro)* to appear as/in;

salía de extra en "Ben-Hur" he appeared as *o* was an extra in "Ben-Hur"; **s. en defensa de alguien** to come to sb's defence
(**m**) *(presentarse, ofrecerse) (ocasión, oportunidad)* to turn up, to come along; *(puesto, empleo)* to come up; *(problema)* to arise; *(contratiempo)* to occur; **le ha salido una plaza de profesor en Tegucigalpa** a job has come up for him as a teacher in Tegucigalpa; EXPR **a lo que salga, salga lo que salga** whatever happens
(**n**) *(costar)* **salimos a 20 dólares por cabeza** it came to *o* worked out at $20 each; **¿por cuánto me saldría una moto de segunda mano?** how much would a second-hand motorbike cost me *o* come to?; **en botella te saldrá más barata la cerveza** the beer works out cheaper if you buy it bottled; **s. caro** *(económicamente)* to be expensive; *(por las consecuencias)* to be costly
(**o**) *(decir u obrar inesperadamente)* **nunca se sabe por dónde va a s.** you never know what she's going to come out with/do next; **el jefe sale con cada tontería...** the boss comes out with some really stupid remarks; **salió con que era un incomprendido y nadie le hacía caso** he claimed he was misunderstood and that no one ever took any notice of him; **¿y ahora nos sales con ésas?** now you tell us!
(**p**) *(parecerse)* **s. a alguien** to take after sb; **eres un vago, en eso has salido a tu padre** you're a layabout, just like your father
(**q**) *(en juegos)* to lead; **te toca s. a ti** it's your lead; **salió con un as** she led with an ace; **salen blancas** *(en damas, ajedrez)* white goes first
(**r**) *(desaparecer)* to come out; **la mancha de vino no sale** the wine stain won't come out
(**s**) *Informát (instrucción)* to quit, to exit; **s. de un programa** to quit *o* exit a program
(**t**) **s. adelante** *(persona, empresa)* to get by; *(proyecto, propuesta, ley)* to be successful; **la familia lo está pasando muy mal para s. adelante** the family is struggling to get by *o* to make ends meet
2 **salirse** *vpr* (**a**) *(marcharse)* **salirse (de)** to leave; **muchos se salieron del partido** many people left the party; **la obra era tan mala que nos salimos (del teatro) a la mitad** the play was so bad that we left (the theatre) halfway through; **me salí del agua porque tenía frío** I came out of the water because I was cold
(**b**) *(irse fuera, traspasar)* **salirse de** *(límites)* to go beyond; **no te salgas del margen al escribir** stay inside the margin when you're writing; **el balón se salió del terreno de juego** the ball went out of play; **salirse del presupuesto** to overrun the budget; **eso se sale de mis competencias** that's outside my authority; **tiene una inteligencia que se sale de lo normal** she is exceptionally intelligent; **salirse del tema** to digress
(**c**) *(filtrarse) (líquido, gas)* to leak, to escape (**por** through); *(humo, aroma)* to come out (**por** through); **este grifo se sale** this *Br* tap *o US* faucet is leaking; **a esta rueda se le sale el aire** the air's getting out of *o* escaping from this tyre
(**d**) *(rebosar)* to overflow; *(leche)* to boil over; **el río se salió del cauce** the river broke its banks
(**e**) *(desviarse)* **salirse (de algo)** to come off (sth); **el autobús se salió de la carretera** the bus came off *o* left the road
(**f**) *(desprenderse, soltarse) (tornillo, tapón, anillo)* **salirse (de algo)** to come off (sth); **este anillo se me sale** this ring's too big for me; **se te sale la camiseta por detrás** your shirt's not tucked in properly at the back
(**g**) **salirse con la suya** to get one's (own) way

---

salitre *nm* (**a**) *Quím* saltpetre (**b**) *(sustancia salina)* salt residue
salitrera *nf* saltpetre bed *o* deposit
salitrero, -a *nm,f* saltpetre miner
saliva *nf* saliva; EXPR *Fam* **gastar s. (en balde)** to waste one's breath; EXPR **tragar s.** to bite one's tongue
salivación *nf* salivation
salivadera *nf Andes, RP* spittoon
salivajo = **salivazo**
salival *adj* salivary
salivar 1 *adj* salivary
2 *vi* (**a**) *(segregar saliva)* to salivate (**b**) *Am (escupir)* to spit
salivazo, salivajo *nm* blob of spit; **echar un s.** to spit
salmantino, -a 1 *adj* of/from Salamanca *(Spain)*
2 *nm,f* person from Salamanca *(Spain)*
salmer *nm Arquit* voussoir
salmista *nmf* psalmist
salmo *nm* psalm; *Rel* **Salmos** Psalms
salmodia *nf* (**a**) *Rel* singing of psalms (**b**) *(letanía)* drone
salmodiar *vt* to sing in a monotone
salmón 1 *adj (color)* salmon (pink)
2 *nm* (**a**) *(color)* salmon (pink) (**b**) *(pez)* salmon ►► ***s. ahumado*** smoked salmon
salmonela, salmonella [salmo'nela] *nf* salmonella *(bacterium)*
salmonelosis, salmonellosis [salmone'losis] *nf inv* salmonella *(illness)*
salmonera *nf* salmon ladder
salmonero, -a *adj* salmon; **río s.** salmon river
salmonete *nm* red mullet
salmuera *nf* brine
salobre *adj* salty
salobreño, -a *adj* saline
salobridad *nf* saltiness
Salomón *n* **las islas S.** the Solomon Islands
salomónico, -a *adj* (**a**) *(decisión, solución)* balanced, equitable (**b**) *(columna)* spiral
salón *nm* (**a**) *(en vivienda)* lounge, sitting room; **revolucionario de s.** armchair revolutionary; **intelectual de s.** armchair intellectual
(**b**) *(para reuniones, ceremonias)* hall ►► ***s. de actos*** assembly hall, assembly room; ***s. de baile*** ballroom; *RP* ***s. de fiestas*** function room; ***s. de sesiones*** committee room
(**c**) *(mobiliario)* lounge suite
(**d**) *(feria)* show, exhibition ►► ***s. del automóvil*** motor show; ***s. de la informática*** computer fair
(**e**) *(establecimiento)* shop ►► ***s. de belleza*** beauty parlour, beauty salon; ***s. de masaje*** massage parlour; ***s. recreativo*** amusement arcade; ***s. de té*** tearoom
salpicadera *nf Méx Br* mudguard, *US* fender
salpicadero *nm Esp* dashboard
salpicado, -a *adj* **una tela salpicada de flores** a fabric dotted with flowers; **un discurso s. de anécdotas** a speech peppered with anecdotes; **el viaje estuvo s. de dificultades** the journey was punctuated by difficulties
salpicadura *nf* (**a**) *(acción)* splashing, spattering (**b**) *(mancha)* spot, spatter; **tengo las botas llenas de salpicaduras de barro** my boots are spattered all over with mud
salpicar [60] 1 *vt* (**a**) *(con líquido)* to splash, to spatter; **me salpicó de agua/barro** he splashed water/mud over me; **te has salpicado la chaqueta** you've spattered your jacket
(**b**) *(espolvorear)* to sprinkle (**de** with); **salpicó el cocido de perejil** he sprinkled parsley on the stew; **salpicó de referencias literarias su discurso** he peppered his speech with literary allusions
(**c**) *(reputación)* **el escándalo salpicó al presidente** the scandal cast a cloud over *o* tainted the presidency
2 *vi* to spit; **el aceite caliente salpica** hot oil tends to spit
salpicón *nm* (**a**) *(plato)* = cold dish of chopped fish or meat, seasoned with pepper, salt, vinegar and onion (**b**) *Col, Ecuad (refresco)* fruit juice
salpimentar [3] *vt* to season (with salt and pepper)
salsa *nf* (**a**) *(condimento)* sauce; *(de carne)* gravy; *Fig* **en su (propia) s.** in one's element ►► ***s. agridulce*** sweet-and-sour sauce; ***s. bearnesa*** Béarnaise sauce; ***s. bechamel*** *o* ***besamel*** béchamel sauce; *Col, CSur* ***s. blanca*** white sauce; *RP* ***s. golf*** cocktail sauce; ***s. mahonesa*** *o* ***mayonesa*** mayonnaise; ***s. Perrins®*** Worcester sauce; ***s. picante*** hot sauce; *Méx* ***s. ranchera*** = chilli sauce made with green chilli peppers, tomatoes, onions and coriander; ***s. rosa*** ≃ Thousand Island dressing, *US* ≃ French dressing; ***s. de soja*** soy sauce; ***s. tártara*** tartar sauce; ***s. de tomate*** tomato sauce; ***s. verde*** *(salsa de perejil)* parsley sauce; *Méx (ají)* chilli sauce made with tomatillos
(**b**) *(interés)* spice; **ser la s. de la vida** to make life worth living
(**c**) *(música, baile)* salsa
salsamentaría *nf Col (tienda)* = shop selling cold meats, sausages etc
salsera *nf* gravy boat
salsero, -a *Am* 1 *adj* salsa
2 *nm,f* salsa fan
salsifí (*pl* **salsifíes**) *nm* salsify ►► ***s. de España*** black salsify; ***s. negro*** black salsify
saltador, -ora 1 *adj* jumping; **un animal s.** a jumping animal
2 *nm,f Dep* jumper ►► ***s. de altura*** high jumper; ***s. de esquí*** ski jumper; ***s. de longitud*** long jumper; ***s. de pértiga*** pole vaulter; ***s. de triple salto*** triple jumper
saltamontes *nm inv* grasshopper
saltante *adj Chile* outstanding, noteworthy

SALTAR 1 *vt* (a) *(obstáculo, valla, verja)* to jump (over); **si salta los 2,35 ganará la prueba** if he jumps *o* clears 2.35 metres, he'll win the competition
(b) *(omitir)* to skip, to miss out; **me saltaron al nombrar los candidatos** they missed me out of the list of candidates
(c) *(romper violentamente)* **s. una cerradura** to force a lock; **s. un ojo a alguien** to poke sb's eye out; *Informát* **s. la protección de un programa** to break a program's protection, to crack a program
(d) *CSur (sofreír)* to sauté, to fry lightly
2 *vi* (a) *(brincar, lanzarse)* to jump; **los chicos saltaron al otro lado de la tapia** the children jumped over the wall; **saltó de** *o* **desde una ventana** she jumped out of *o* from a window; **Bubka fue el primero en s. por encima de los 6 metros** Bubka was the first person to clear 6 metres; **s. de alegría** to jump for joy; **s. a la cuerda** *o Esp* **comba** to skip; **s. en paracaídas** to parachute; **s. al río** to jump into the river; **s. a tierra** to jump to the ground; **s. del** *o* **desde el trampolín** to dive off the springboard; **s. al vacío** to leap into space; **los jugadores saltan al campo** the players are coming out onto the field; **s. de un tema a otro** to jump (around) from one subject to another; **saltábamos de la euforia al desánimo** our mood was swinging backwards and forwards between euphoria and dejection; **s. sobre algo/alguien** *(abalanzarse)* to jump on sth/sb; EXPR *Fam RP* **s. en una pata** to be over the moon
(b) *(levantarse de repente)* to jump up; **s. de la silla/cama** to jump out of one's seat/out of bed
(c) *(salir disparado) (objeto)* to jump, to shoot; *(corcho, válvula)* to pop out; *(botón)* to pop off; *(aceite)* to spurt; *(esquirlas, astillas, chispas)* to fly
(d) *(explotar)* to explode, to blow up; **el automóvil saltó por los aires** the car was blown into the air; **han saltado los plomos** *o CSur* **tapones** the fuses have blown
(e) *(romperse)* to crack; **fregando los platos me saltó un vaso** I broke one of the glasses when I was doing the washing-up
(f) *(decir inesperadamente)* **"de eso nada", saltó ella** "no way," she blurted out; **s. con** to suddenly come out with; **saltó con una impertinencia** he suddenly came out with an impertinent remark; **cuando le pasaron la factura saltó con que no tenía dinero** when they gave her the bill, she suddenly said she didn't have any money
(g) *(reaccionar bruscamente)* to explode; **s. a la mínima** to be quick to lose one's temper
(h) *(alarma)* to go off; *(botón)* to jump out; *(mecanismo, termostato, interruptor)* to activate; **hacer s. la alarma** to set off the alarm
(i) *(agua, cascada)* **s. por** to gush down, to pour down
(j) *(venir)* **me salta a la memoria aquel momento inolvidable cuando...** that unforgettable moment springs to mind, when...
(k) EXPR **está a la que salta** *(para aprovechar ocasión)* she's always on the lookout; *(para señalar error ajeno)* she never misses a chance to criticize
3 **saltarse** *vpr* (a) *(omitir) (intencionadamente)* to skip, to miss out; *(accidentalmente)* to miss out; **ese trozo sáltatelo, que es muy aburrido** miss that bit out *o* skip that bit, it's very boring; **nos saltamos el desayuno** we skipped breakfast, we didn't have any breakfast
(b) *(salir despedido)* to pop off; **se me ha saltado un botón** one of my buttons has popped off; **se le saltaban las lágrimas** tears were welling up in her eyes
(c) *(no respetar) (cola, semáforo)* to jump; *(señal de stop)* to drive straight past; *(ley, normas)* to break
(d) *Fam Informát* **saltarse la protección de un programa** to break a program's protection, to crack a program

---

saltarín, -ina 1 *adj* fidgety
2 *nm,f* fidget

salteado, -a *adj* (a) *(sofrito)* sautéed (b) *(espaciado)* **en días salteados** every other day; **se sentaron en pupitres salteados** they sat at alternate desks

salteador, -ora *nm,f* **s. (de caminos)** highwayman, highway robber

saltear 1 *vt* (a) *(asaltar)* to rob (b) *(sofreír)* to sauté
2 **saltearse** *vpr RP (intencionadamente)* to skip, to miss out; *(accidentalmente)* to miss out; **están peleados, ¿no viste que al saludar se lo salteó?** they've fallen out, didn't you see how she missed him out when she was saying hello to everybody?; **siempre se saltea alguna línea, por eso las cuentas le dan mal** he always misses out a line or two, that's why he's no good at keeping accounts

salteño, -a 1 *adj* (a) *(en Argentina)* of/from Salta *(Argentina)* (b) *(en Uruguay)* of/from Salto *(Uruguay)*
2 *nm,f* (a) *(en Argentina)* person from Salta *(Argentina)* (b) *(en Uruguay)* person from Salto *(Uruguay)*

salterio *nm* (a) *Rel (de salmos)* psalter (b) *Mús* psaltery

saltillense 1 *adj* of/from Saltillo *(Mexico)*
2 *nmf* person from Saltillo *(Mexico)*

saltimbanqui *nmf* (a) *(artista)* acrobat (b) *Fam (persona inquieta)* **este niño es un s.** the boy has got ants in his pants, the boy can't keep still for a moment

salto *nm* (a) *(brinco)* jump; *(grande)* leap; *(al agua)* dive; **cruzó la grieta de un s.** he jumped across the crevice; **dar** *o* **pegar un s.** to jump; *(grande)* to leap; **dar saltos de alegría** *o* **contento** to jump for joy; **cuando se enteró de la noticia pegó un s. de alegría** when she heard the news she was absolutely thrilled; **el corazón le dio un s. cuando escuchó el disparo** her heart skipped a beat when she heard the shot; **la empresa ha decidido dar el s. a Internet** the company has decided to go on line; EXPR **vivir a s. de mata** to live from one day to the next ►► *Am* ***s. alto*** high jump; ***s. de altura*** high jump; ***s. del ángel*** swallow dive; ***s. entre dos*** *(en baloncesto)* jump ball; ***saltos de esquí*** ski jumping; *Am* ***s. con garrocha*** pole vault; ***s. inicial*** *(en baloncesto)* tip-off; *Am* ***s. largo*** long jump; ***s. de longitud*** long jump; ***s. mortal*** somersault; ***s. en paracaídas*** parachute jump; ***s. con pértiga*** pole vault
(b) *(omisión)* gap; **en este texto hay un s. de varios párrafos** there are several paragraphs missing from this text
(c) *(progreso)* leap forward; **el nuevo modelo supone un significativo s. cualitativo** this model represents a significant qualitative leap forward; **con esta victoria el equipo da un s. importantísimo** this victory is a big leap forward for the team; **un s. hacia atrás** a major step backwards; **finalmente dio el s. a la fama** he finally made his big breakthrough
(d) *(despeñadero)* precipice ►► ***s. de agua*** waterfall; *Geol* ***s. de falla*** fault plane
(e) *(prenda)* ***s. de cama*** *(liviano)* négligée
(f) *Informát* ***s. hipertextual*** hypertext link; ***s. de línea automático*** wordwrap; ***s. de página*** page break

saltón, -ona *adj* (a) *(ojos)* bulging; **dientes saltones** buckteeth (b) *Chile, Col (medio crudo)* half-cooked

salubre *adj* healthy

salubridad *nf* healthiness

salud 1 *nf* (a) *(de ser vivo)* health; **su estado de s. no le permite viajar** his state of health does not allow him to travel; **el sistema de s. de un país** a country's health system; **estar bien/mal de s.** to be well/unwell; **beber** *o* **brindar a la s. de alguien** to drink to sb's health; **tiene una s. de hierro** she has an iron constitution ►► ***s. mental*** mental health; ***s. pública*** public health
(b) *(de nación, democracia)* health; **el sistema goza de un buen estado de s.** the system is in excellent health
2 *interj (para brindar)* cheers!; *Am (después de estornudar)* bless you!; **is., camaradas!** greetings, comrades!

saluda *nm* = type of unsigned note written on a standard form for communicating with officials

saludable *adj* (a) *(sano)* healthy (b) *(beneficioso)* beneficial

saludar 1 *vt* (a) *(por cortesía)* to greet; **ni siquiera nos saludó** she didn't even say hello (to us); **me saludó con la mano** he waved to me (in greeting); **saluda a Ana de mi parte** give my regards to Ana; **le saluda atentamente** *(en carta)* yours faithfully; **siempre que vamos a Lima pasamos a saludarlos** whenever we go to Lima we drop in to say hello; **tuvo que salir a s. al público varias veces** he had to come back on stage to take a bow several times
(b) *(soldado, policía)* to salute
(c) *(acoger favorablemente)* to welcome; **los sindicatos saludaron el acuerdo como una victoria de los trabajadores** the unions hailed the agreement as a victory for the workers
2 *vi* to say hello; **salió a s. varias veces** she came on stage to take a bow several times
3 **saludarse** *vpr* to greet one another; **ni siquiera se saludan** they don't even acknowledge each other

saludes *nfpl Andes, CAm, Méx (saludos)* greetings

saludo *nm* (a) *(por cortesía)* greeting; **Ana te manda saludos** *(en carta)* Ana sends you her regards; *(al teléfono)* Ana says hello; **dale saludos de mi parte** give her my regards; **saludos a Aitana** say hello to Aitana for me; **un s. afectuoso** *(en cartas)* yours sincerely; **saludos (cordiales)** *(en cartas)* best wishes *o* regards; **me ha retirado el s.** she's not speaking to me
(b) *(de soldado, policía)* salute

salutación *nf* greeting

salva *nf (de cañonazos)* salvo; **fue recibido con la tradicional s. de 21 cañonazos** he was received with the traditional 21-gun salute; **una s. de aplausos** a round of applause

salvación *nf* (**a**) *(remedio, solución)* **no tener s.** to be beyond hope; **las lluvias fueron la s. de los agricultores** the rains were the farmers' salvation (**b**) *Rel* salvation

salvada *nf PRico Fam* good fortune *o* luck

salvado *nm* bran

Salvador *nm* (**a**) *Rel* **el S.** the Saviour (**b**) *(país)* **El S.** El Salvador

salvador, -ora 1 *adj* saving; **una medida salvadora** a saving measure
2 *nm,f (persona)* saviour; **fue el s. de la empresa** he was the white knight who saved the company

salvadoreño, -a 1 *adj* Salvadoran
2 *nm,f* Salvadoran

salvaguarda = **salvaguardia**

salvaguardar *vt* to safeguard

salvaguardia, salvaguarda *nf* (**a**) *(defensa)* protection (**b**) *(salvoconducto)* safe-conduct, pass

salvajada *nf* (**a**) *(acción) (en guerra)* atrocity; **las salvajadas cometidas por las tropas** the atrocities committed by the troops; **el despido de tantos trabajadores ha sido una s.** it was outrageous to sack all those workers (**b**) *(dicho)* **¡menuda s.!** what a terrible thing to say!; **su discurso estaba lleno de salvajadas racistas** his speech was full of racist abuse

salvaje 1 *adj* (**a**) *(animal)* wild (**b**) *(planta, terreno)* wild (**c**) *(pueblo, tribu)* savage (**d**) *(cruel, brutal)* brutal, savage; **se escuchó una explosión s.** there was a massive explosion; **el capitalismo s.** ruthless capitalism (**e**) *(incontrolado)* **acampada s.** unauthorized camping; **una huelga s.** an unofficial strike, a wildcat strike; **vertidos salvajes** illegal dumping
2 *nmf* (**a**) *(primitivo)* savage
(**b**) *(bruto)* brute; **unos salvajes prendieron fuego a un inmigrante** some inhuman brutes set fire to an immigrant; **la s. de tu hermana ha suspendido todas las asignaturas** your thick sister has failed every subject; **es un s., se comió un pollo él sólo** he's an animal, he ate a whole chicken by himself; **eres un s., ¿cómo tratas así a tu madre?** you're a monster, how can you treat your mother like that?

salvajismo *nm* (**a**) *(de pueblo, tribu)* savagery (**b**) *(brutalidad)* brutality; **el s. de los hinchas futbolísticos** the barbaric behaviour of the football fans

salvamanteles *nm inv (plano)* table mat; *(con pies)* trivet

salvamento *nm* rescue; **equipo de s.** rescue team ►► ***s. marítimo*** sea rescue

salvapantallas *nm inv Informát* screensaver

salvar 1 *vt* (**a**) *(librar de peligro)* to save; **nos salvó del peligro** he saved us from danger; **la subvención los salvó de la ruina** the subsidy saved them from ruin; **el portero salvó el gol en el último instante** the goalkeeper saved the goal at the last moment; **me has salvado de tener que ir a visitarla** you've saved me from having to go and visit her
(**b**) *(rescatar)* to rescue; **salvaron todo lo que pudieron del edificio en llamas** they rescued all they could from the blazing building
(**c**) *(superar) (dificultad)* to overcome; *(obstáculo)* to go over *o* around; **el caballo salvó el foso de un salto** the horse jumped (across) the ditch; **un puente salva la distancia entre las dos orillas** a bridge spans the river; **la atleta salvó los 2 metros** the athlete cleared 2 metres
(**d**) *(recorrer)* to cover; **salvaron la distancia entre las dos ciudades en tres días** they covered the distance between the two cities in three days
(**e**) *(exceptuar)* **salvando algunos detalles** except for a few details; **salvando las distancias** allowing for the obvious differences
(**f**) *Rel* to save
(**g**) *Urug (aprobar)* to pass
2 salvarse *vpr* (**a**) *(librarse)* to escape; **la biblioteca se salvó del incendio** the library escaped being destroyed by the fire; **se salvó de morir ahogado** he escaped drowning; **se salvó gracias a que llevaba paracaídas** he survived because he was wearing a parachute; **no te vas a s. de tener que limpiar** you won't get out of having to clean up; EXPR **sálvese quien pueda** every man for himself
(**b**) *(exceptuarse)* **sus amigos son inaguantables, ella es la única que se salva** her friends are unbearable, she's the only one who's OK
(**c**) *Rel* to be saved

salvataje *nm Andes, RP* rescue

salvavidas 1 *adj inv* **bote s.** lifeboat; **chaleco s.** life jacket
2 *nm inv* (**a**) *(chaleco)* life jacket (**b**) *(flotador)* life belt
3 *nmf inv RP* lifeguard

salve[1] *interj* hail!

salve[2] *nf* = prayer or hymn to the Virgin Mary

salvedad *nf* exception; **hacer una s.** to make an exception; **vinó toda la familia, con la s. de la abuela** the whole family came, with the exception of the grandmother; **es el mismo modelo, con la s. de que ahora funciona con diesel** it's the same model, except that this one runs on diesel

salvelino *nm (pez)* char

salvia *nf* sage

salvo[1] *prep* except; **todos, s. los enfermos** everyone except (for) the sick; **s. ella, nadie más conocía el camino** apart from her, nobody else knew the way, nobody knew the way except for her; **s. que llueva** unless it rains; **s. que estés ocupado, ¿por qué no vienes a visitarnos?** if you're not busy, why don't you come and visit us?; **s. error u omisión** errors and omissions excepted

salvo[2]**, -a 1** *adj* **sano y s.** safe and sound
2 *nm* **estar a s.** to be safe; **los marineros se encuentran ya a s. en tierra firme** the sailors are now safely back on land; **poner algo a s.** to put sth in a safe place; **poner a alguien a s.** to lead sb to safety; **ponerse a s.** to reach safety

salvoconducto *nm* safe-conduct, pass

samán *nm Col, Ven* rain-tree

samario *nm Quím* samarium

samaritano, -a 1 *adj* Samaritan
2 *nm,f* Samaritan; **el buen s.** the Good Samaritan

samba *nf* samba

sambayón *nm RP* zabaglione

sambenito *nm Fam* **poner** *o* **colgar a alguien el s. de borracho/tacaño** to brand sb a drunk/a miser; **intenta quitarse el s. de corrupto** he is trying to shake off his reputation as a crook; **desde hace tiempo arrastra el s. de vago** for a long time he has had the reputation of being a layabout

sambumbia *nf Méx (de piña)* = cordial made from pineapple and sugar

samoano, -a 1 *adj* Samoan
2 *nm,f (persona)* Samoan
3 *nm (lengua)* Samoan

Samoa Occidental *n* Western Samoa

samovar *nm* samovar

samoyedo, -a 1 *adj* (**a**) *(pueblo)* Samoyedic (**b**) **perro s.** Samoyed
2 *nm,f* Samoyed

sampablera *nf Ven Fam* uproar

sampán *nm* sampan

sampleado *nm Mús* sampling

samplear *vt Mús* to sample

sámpler *nm Mús* sampler

samurái (*pl* **samuráis**) *nm* samurai

san[1] *adj*

> **santo** is shortened to **san** when it comes before a man's name, except before the names Domingo, Tomás, Tomé and Toribio.

Saint ►► *Urug* ***S. Antonio*** *(mariquita) Br* ladybird, *US* ladybug; ***S. Bernardo*** *(perro)* Saint Bernard; ***S. Cristóbal y Nieves*** *(federación)* Saint Kitts and Nevis; ***S. José*** *(santo)* Saint Joseph; *(de Costa Rica)* San José; *Andes, Méx* ***S. Lunes*** = imaginary saint's day cited as an excuse for not going to work on Monday; **estaba festejando el San Lunes** he had a bad attack of lazyitis and didn't go to work on Monday; ***S. Marino*** San Marino; *RP* ***S. Pablo*** *(ciudad)* São Paulo; ***S. Petersburgo*** Saint Petersburg; ***S. Salvador*** San Salvador

san[2] *nm Ven* = popular savings scheme

Sana, Sanaa *n* Sanaa

sanable *adj* curable

sanador, -ora *nm,f* healer

sanamente *adv (con sinceridad)* sincerely, earnestly

sanar 1 *vt (persona)* to cure; *(herida)* to heal
2 *vi (persona)* to get better; *(herida)* to heal

sanata *nf Arg Fam* (**a**) *(cantinela)* yarn (**b**) *(mentira)* lie

sanatorio *nm* (**a**) *(para tratamientos largos)* sanatorium ►► ***s. psiquiátrico*** psychiatric hospital (**b**) *RP (hospital)* private clinic, private hospital

sanción *nf* (**a**) *(multa)* fine; **la s. por desobedecer el reglamento** the penalty for breaking the rules; **imponer sanciones (económicas) a** *(a un país)* to impose (economic) sanctions on; *Dep* **le han impuesto una**

s. de un partido he has been suspended *o* banned for one game (**b**) *(aprobación)* approval; **el parlamento dio su s. al proyecto** parliament approved the plan

sancionable *adj* punishable; **una falta s. con penalti** a penalty offence; **un delito s. con la pena de...** an offence punishable by...

sancionar *vt* (**a**) *(multar)* to fine; *(a un país)* to impose sanctions on; **lo sancionaron con una multa** they fined him; **lo sancionaron por desobedecer el reglamento** he was punished for breaking the rules; *Dep* **le han sancionado con tres partidos de suspensión** he has been suspended *o* banned for three games (**b**) *(aprobar)* to approve, to sanction

sancochar *vt (cocer)* to parboil

sancocho *nm* (**a**) *Andes (comida)* = stew of beef, chicken or fish, vegetables and green bananas (**b**) *RP Fam (chapucería)* hash, mess

sanctasanctórum *nm* (**a**) *(lugar)* sanctum (**b**) *(en Biblia)* holy of holies

sanctus ['santus] *nm inv Rel* Sanctus

sandalia *nf* sandal

sándalo *nm* sandalwood

sandez *nf* silly thing; **decir sandeces** to talk nonsense

sandía *nf* watermelon

sandial, sandiar *nm* watermelon field/patch

sandinismo *nm* Sandinista movement

sandinista 1 *adj* Sandinista
2 *nmf* Sandinista

sánduche, sánguche *nm* (**a**) *(con pan de molde) (sin tostar)* sandwich; *(tostado)* toasted sandwich ►► ***s. mixto*** cheese and ham sandwich; *Urug* ***s. olímpico*** = giant cheese and ham sandwich with salad, olives and egg (**b**) *Am (con pan de barra)* sandwich *(made with French bread)*

sandunga *nf* (**a**) *Fam (gracia)* wit; *(garbo)* verve; **le echa mucha s. al baile** she dances with great verve (**b**) *Méx (baile)* = type of Mexican dance

sandunguero, -a *adj Fam (gracioso)* witty; *(garboso)* vivacious

sándwich ['sanwitʃ, 'sanwis] (*pl* **sándwiches**) *nm* (**a**) *(con pan de molde) (sin tostar)* sandwich; *(tostado)* toasted sandwich ►► ***s. mixto*** cheese and ham sandwich (**b**) *Am (con pan de barra)* sandwich *(made with French bread)* (**c**) *Urug (feriado)* = long weekend created when a holiday falls on a Tuesday or Thursday, and the working day in between is made a holiday too

sandwichera [sanwi'tʃera] *nf* toasted sandwich maker

sandwichería *nf* sandwich bar

saneado, -a *adj* (**a**) *(amortizado) (totalmente)* written off; *(parcialmente)* written down (**b**) *(economía)* sound, healthy; *(cuenta)* regularized

saneamiento *nm* (**a**) *(limpieza) (de tierras)* drainage; *(de edificio)* disinfection (**b**) *(fontanería)* plumbing; **artículos de s.** bathroom furniture (**c**) *(de río)* clean-up (**d**) *(de activos) (amortización total)* write-off; *(reconocimiento de minusvalías)* write-down (**e**) *(de moneda)* stabilization; *(de economía)* refloating; *(de empresa)* turnaround; *(de cuenta)* regularization; **el s. de las cuentas públicas** the reform *o* restructuring of public finances

sanear *vt* (**a**) *(higienizar) (tierras)* to drain; *(edificio)* to disinfect (**b**) *(río)* to clean up (**c**) *(amortizar totalmente)* to write off; *(reconocer minusvalías)* to write down (**d**) *(moneda)* to stabilize; *(economía)* to refloat; *(empresa)* to turn around; *(cuenta)* to regularize; **s. las cuentas públicas** to reform *o* restructure public finances

sanedrín *nm Hist* Sanhedrin

sanfermines *nmpl* = festival held in Pamplona in July during which bulls are run through the streets of the town

sanforizado, -a *Am* **1** *adj* Sanforized®
2 *nm* = Sanforizing® process

sangrado *nm Imprenta* indentation

sangrante *adj* (**a**) *(herida)* bleeding (**b**) *(situación, injusticia)* shameful, outrageous

sangrar 1 *vi* to bleed; **me sangra la nariz** my nose is bleeding
2 *vt* (**a**) *(sacar sangre a)* to bleed (**b**) *(árbol)* to tap (**c**) *Fam (robar)* to bleed dry (**d**) *Imprenta* to indent

SANGRE *nf* (**a**) *(fluido)* blood; **una camisa manchada de s.** a bloodstained shirt; **te está saliendo s.** you're bleeding; **la s. de Cristo** *(en Misa)* the blood of Christ; **animales de s. caliente/fría** warm-blooded/cold-blooded animals; **ha corrido mucha s. en este conflicto** there has been a lot of bloodshed in this conflict; **dar** *o* **donar s.** to give blood; **echar s.** *(sangrar)* to bleed; **echaba s.** *o* **le salía s. por la boca/la nariz** her mouth/nose was bleeding; **hacer s. (a alguien)** to draw (sb's) blood; **me he hecho s. en el dedo** I've cut my finger; EXPR **a s. y fuego: arrasaron el pueblo a s. y fuego** they brutally razed the village to the ground; EXPR *Fam* **chupar la s. a alguien** to bleed sb dry; EXPR **s., sudor y lágrimas: me costó s., sudor y lágrimas terminarlo** I sweated blood to get it finished; EXPR **dar la s. por algo/alguien** *(morir)* to give one's life for sth/sb; EXPR **encender la s. a alguien** to make sb's blood boil; EXPR **hacerse mala s. (por algo)** to get worked up (about sth); EXPR **se me/le/***etc.* **heló la s. en las venas** my/his/her/*etc* blood ran cold; EXPR **hervir la s.: me hierve la s. cuando veo estas cosas** it makes my blood boil when I see things like that; EXPR **no llegó la s. al río** it didn't get too nasty; EXPR **llevar** *o Am* **tener** *o Am* **traer algo en la s.** to have sth in one's blood; EXPR *RP* **con la s. en el ojo** full of rancour; EXPR *Fam* **quemar la s. a alguien** to make sb's blood boil; EXPR *Fam* **se le subió la s. a la cabeza** he saw red; EXPR **sudar s.** to sweat blood; EXPR **tener la s. caliente** to be hot-blooded; EXPR **tener s. de horchata** *(ser tranquilo)* to be as cool as a cucumber; *(ser demasiado frío)* to have a heart of stone; EXPR *Fam* **tener mala s.** to be malicious; EXPR **no tiene s. en las venas** he's got no life in him; EXPR **la s. tira (mucho)** blood is thicker than water ►► ***s. azul*** blue blood; ***s. fría*** sangfroid; **a s. fría** in cold blood
(**b**) *(linaje)* blood; **gentes de s. noble/real** people with noble/royal blood; **ser de la misma s.** *(familiares)* to be from the same family

sangría *nf* (**a**) *(bebida)* sangria (**b**) *(matanza)* bloodbath (**c**) *(ruina)* drain; **los continuos accidentes laborales son una s. para la empresa** the constant accidents among its employees are a drain on the company's resources (**d**) *Med* bloodletting (**e**) *Imprenta* indentation

sangriento, -a *adj* (**a**) *(ensangrentado, cruento)* bloody (**b**) *(despiadado, hiriente)* cruel

sangriligero, -a *adj CAm, Col, Méx Fam (persona)* nice

sangripesado, -a, sangrón, -ona *adj CAm, Col, Méx Fam (persona)* nasty

sanguaraña *nf* (**a**) *(baile)* = Peruvian folk dance (**b**) *Ecuad, Perú (rodeo)* **sanguarañas** evasiveness; **hablar sin sanguarañas** to come straight to the point

sánguche = **sánduche**

sanguijuela *nf* (**a**) *(gusano)* leech (**b**) *Fam (persona)* leech

sanguina *nf* (**a**) *(para dibujar)* red chalk (**b**) *(naranja)* blood orange

sanguinario, -a *adj* bloodthirsty

sanguíneo, -a *adj* blood; **presión sanguínea** blood pressure

sanguinero *nm* buckthorn

sanguinolento, -a *adj* (**a**) *(que echa sangre)* bleeding (**b**) *(bañado en sangre)* bloody; *(manchado de sangre)* bloodstained (**c**) *(ojos)* bloodshot

sanidad *nf* (**a**) *(salubridad)* health, healthiness (**b**) **s. (pública)** *(sistema)* public health service; **los gastos en s.** public health spending ►► ***s. privada*** private health care (**c**) *(ministerio)* **S.** Department of Health

> **Falso amigo**: El sustantivo inglés **sanity** no es la traducción del español **sanidad**. En inglés **sanity** significa "cordura" o "sensatez".

sanitario, -a 1 *adj* health; **política sanitaria** health policy; **personal s.** health workers; **reforma sanitaria** reform of the health care system
2 *nm,f* (**a**) *(auxiliar)* health (care) worker; **un s. de la Cruz Roja** a Red Cross worker (**b**) *RP (plomero)* plumber
3 *nm* (**a**) *(retrete)* toilet, *US* bathroom (**b**) **sanitarios** *(bañera, lavabo, retrete)* bathroom furniture

sanjacobo *nm* = two slices of steak or ham with a slice of cheese in between, fried in breadcrumbs

sanjuanino, -a 1 *adj* of/from San Juan *(Argentina)*
2 *nm,f* person from San Juan *(Argentina)*

sano, -a *adj* (**a**) *(no enfermo)* healthy; **tiene una corazón muy s.** he has a very healthy heart
(**b**) *(saludable)* healthy; **un ejercicio/clima muy s.** a very healthy exercise/climate; **hacer vida sana** to have a healthy lifestyle
(**c**) *(positivo) (principios, persona)* sound; *(ambiente, educación)* healthy, wholesome; **una diversión sana** a healthy pastime; **un ambiente familiar muy s.** a very healthy home environment
(**d**) *(entero)* intact, undamaged; **no quedó ni un vaso s.** not a glass was left unbroken *o* undamaged; **s. y salvo** safe and sound

> **Falso amigo**: El adjetivo inglés **sane** no es la traducción del español **sano**. En inglés **sane** significa "cuerdo" o "juicioso".

sansalvadoreño, -a 1 *adj* of/from San Salvador
2 *nm,f* person from San Salvador

sánscrito, -a 1 *adj* Sanskrit
2 *nm* Sanskrit

sanseacabó *interj Fam* that's an end to it!; **he dicho que no y s.** I said no, and that's final *o* that's that

sansón *nm* **es un s.** he's as strong as an ox

santabárbara *nf* magazine *(on ship)*

santafecino, -a, santafesino, -a 1 *adj* of/from Santa Fe *(Argentina)*
2 *nm,f* person from Santa Fe *(Argentina)*

santanderino, -a 1 *adj* of/from Santander *(Spain)*
2 *nm,f* person from Santander *(Spain)*

santería *nf* (**a**) *(beatería)* sanctimoniousness (**b**) *(religión)* santeria, = Afro-Cuban religion (**c**) *Am (tienda)* = shop selling religious mementos such as statues of saints

santero, -a *nm,f* (**a**) *(en ermita, santuario)* = caretaker of a hermitage/shrine (**b**) *(curandero)* = faith healer who calls on the saints to assist with the healing process

Santiago[1] *n pr* St James

Santiago[2] *n* ***S. de Chile*** Santiago; ***S. de Compostela*** Santiago de Compostela

santiaguense *adj, nmf* = **santiaguero**

santiaguero, -a 1 *adj* of/from Santiago de Cuba
2 *nm,f* person from Santiago de Cuba

santiagueño, -a 1 *adj* of/from Santiago del Estero *(Argentina)*
2 *nm,f* person from Santiago del Estero *(Argentina)*

santiagués, -esa 1 *adj* of/from Santiago de Compostela *(Spain)*
2 *nm,f* person from Santiago de Compostela *(Spain)*

santiaguino, -a 1 *adj* of/from Santiago (de Chile)
2 *nm,f* person from Santiago (de Chile)

santiamén *nm Fam* **en un s.** in a flash

santidad *nf* (**a**) *(cualidad)* saintliness, holiness (**b**) **Su S.** *(el Papa)* His Holiness

santificación *nf* sanctification

santificar [60] *vt* (**a**) *(consagrar)* to sanctify; **santificado sea tu nombre** *(en Padrenuestro)* hallowed be thy name (**b**) *(respetar)* **s. las fiestas** to observe feast days

santiguarse [11] *vpr* to cross oneself

SANTO, -A 1 *adj* (**a**) *(sagrado)* holy ►► *Hist* ***la Santa Alianza*** the Holy Alliance; ***la santa cena*** the Last Supper; ***el S. Grial*** the Holy Grail; ***los Santos Inocentes*** the Holy Innocents; ***los santos lugares*** the holy places; ***la Santa Madre Iglesia*** the Holy Mother Church; ***el S. Oficio*** the Holy Office; ***el S. Padre*** the Holy Father; *Am* ***s. patrono*** patron saint; ***los santos sacramentos*** the Sacraments; ***la Santa Sede*** the Holy See
(**b**) *(virtuoso)* saintly; **su padre era un s. varón** her father was a saintly man
(**c**) *(antes de nombre propio)* ***Santa Claus*** Santa Claus; *Méx, Ven* ***Santa Clos*** Santa Claus; ***Santa María*** Saint Mary; ***S. Tomás*** Saint Thomas
(**d**) *(en nombres geográficos)* ***S. Domingo*** Santo Domingo; ***Santa Elena*** Saint Helena; ***S. Tomé*** São Tomé; ***S. Tomé y Príncipe*** São Tomé and Príncipe
(**e**) ***santa Rita*** *(planta)* bougainvillea
(**f**) *Fam (dichoso, maldito)* damn; **todo el s. día** all day long; **no paró de nevar en todo el s. día** it went on snowing all day long; **el teléfono lleva sonando toda la santa mañana** the damn phone hasn't stopped ringing all morning; **él siempre hace su santa voluntad** he always does whatever he damn well likes
(**g**) *Fam (beneficioso)* miraculous; **esta infusión es cosa santa** this herbal tea works wonders
2 *nm,f* saint; **su madre era una santa** her mother was a saint ►► ***s. patrón*** patron saint; ***santa patrona*** patron saint
3 *nm* (**a**) *(onomástica)* saint's day; **hoy es su s.** it's his saint's day today
(**b**) *Fam (ilustración)* illustration
(**c**) *(contraseña)* **s. y seña** password
(**d**) *Chile (parche)* patch
(**e**) EXPR **¿a s. de qué?** why on earth?, for what earthly reason?; **¿a s. de qué me llamas a casa?** why on earth are you calling me at home?; **desnudar a un s. para vestir a otro** to rob Peter to pay Paul; **se le fue el s. al cielo** he completely forgot; **llegar y besar el s.: fue llegar y besar el s., nos dieron el permiso a los dos días** it couldn't have been easier, we got the licence within two days; **fue llegar y besar el s., marcó a los dos minutos de su debut** he was an instant success, he scored within two minutes of his debut; **no es s. de mi devoción** he's not my cup of tea; **¡por todos los santos!** for heaven's sake!; **quedarse para vestir santos** to be left on the shelf; **tener el s. de cara** to have luck on one's side

santón *nm* (**a**) *Rel* holy man (**b**) *(persona influyente)* guru

santoral *nm* (**a**) *(libro)* = book containing lives of saints (**b**) *(onomásticas)* = list of saints' days

santuario *nm* (**a**) *(templo)* shrine (**b**) *(lugar venerable)* holy place (**c**) *(de animales)* sanctuary (**d**) *(de exiliados, terroristas)* refuge (**e**) *Col (tesoro)* buried treasure

santurrón, -ona *Pey* 1 *adj* sanctimonious
2 *nm,f* sanctimonious person; **ser un s.** to be sanctimonious

santurronería *nf Pey* sanctimoniousness

saña *nf* viciousness, malice; **con s.** viciously, maliciously

sañudo, -a *adj* vicious, malicious

sao *nm Cuba (sabana)* = small savannah with clusters of trees or bushes

São Paulo *n* São Paulo

sapan *nm* sappanwood

sapear *vt Ven Fam* to snitch *o* rat on

sapelli *nm* sapele

sapiencia *nf Formal* knowledge

sapito *nm Urug* **hacer sapitos** *(juego)* to play ducks and drakes

sapo *nm* (**a**) *(anfibio)* toad; EXPR **echar sapos y culebras** to rant and rave; EXPR *RP* **estar** *o* **sentirse como** *o* **ser s. de otro pozo** to be *o* feel like a fish out of water ►► ***s. partero*** midwife toad (**b**) *Chile (suerte)* fluke, stroke of luck (**c**) *Pan Fam (canalla)* scoundrel, rascal (**d**) *Ven Fam (delator)* snitch, rat

sapolio *nm Perú* scouring powder

saque 1 *ver* **sacar**
2 *nm* (**a**) *(en fútbol)* ***s. de banda*** throw-in; ***s. de centro*** kick-off; *Andes, RP* ***s. de costado*** throw-in; ***s. de esquina*** corner (kick); ***s. de fondo*** goal kick; ***s. de honor*** = ceremonial kick-off by celebrity; ***s. inicial*** kick-off; *CSur* ***s. lateral*** throw-in; ***s. de meta*** goal kick; ***s. neutral*** drop ball; ***s. de puerta*** goal kick; *CSur* ***s. de valla*** goal kick
(**b**) *(en rugby)* **s. de banda** line-out
(**c**) *(en tenis, voleibol)* serve; **tener buen s.** to have a good serve
(**d**) *Fam (apetito)* **tener buen s.** to have a hearty appetite

saqueador, -ora *nm,f* looter

saquear *vt* (**a**) *(ciudad, población)* to sack (**b**) *(tienda)* to loot; *Fam (nevera, armario)* to raid

saqueo *nm* (**a**) *(de ciudad)* sacking (**b**) *(de tienda)* looting; *Fam (de nevera, armario)* raiding

SAR [sar] *nm (abrev de* **Servicio Aéreo de Rescate**) = Spanish air rescue service

S.A.R. *(abrev de* **Su Alteza Real**) HRH

Sarajevo *n* Sarajevo

sarampión *nm* measles

sarao *nm* (**a**) *(fiesta)* party (**b**) *Fam (jaleo)* row, rumpus; **se armó un s. enorme cuando llegó la policía** there was a huge ruckus when the police arrived

sarape, zarape *nm Guat, Méx* serape

sarasa *nm Fam Pey* queer, *US* fag

sarcasmo *nm* sarcasm

sarcásticamente *adv* sarcastically

sarcástico, -a 1 *adj* sarcastic
2 *nm,f* sarcastic person; **ser un s.** to be sarcastic

sarcófago *nm* sarcophagus

sarcoma *nm Med* sarcoma

sardana *nf* = traditional Catalan dance and music

sardina *nf* (**a**) *(pez)* sardine; EXPR **como sardinas en lata** packed like sardines (**b**) *ver también* **sardino**

sardinada *nf* barbecue of grilled sardines

sardinel *nm Col, Perú (bordillo) Br* kerb, *US* curb

sardinero, -a *adj* sardine; **barco s.** sardine fishing boat

sardino, -a *Col Fam* 1 *adj* (**a**) *(joven)* wet behind the ears (**b**) *(novato)* green
2 *nm,f* kid

sardo, -a 1 *adj* Sardinian
2 *nm,f (persona)* Sardinian
3 *nm (lengua)* Sardinian

sardónico, -a *adj* sardonic

sarga *nf* (**a**) *(tela)* serge; *(para decorar)* wall hanging (**b**) *(arbusto)* willow

sargazo *nm* sargasso, gulfweed

Sargazos *nmpl* **el mar de los S.** the Sargasso Sea

sargenta = **sargentona**

sargentear *vi Fam* to boss people around; **él es muy simpático, pero ella no me cae nada bien, siempre está sargenteando** he's very nice but I don't like her, she's always bossing people around

sargento 1 *nmf* (**a**) *Mil* sergeant ▸▸ ***s. primero*** *Br* staff sergeant, *US* sergeant-major (**b**) *Fam Pey (mandón)* dictator, little Hitler
2 *nm (herramienta)* small clamp

sargentona, *Am* **sargenta** *nf Fam Pey* battle-axe, dragon

sari *nm* sari

sarmentoso, -a *adj* **tiene las manos sarmentosas** she has long and bony fingers

sarmiento *nm* vine shoot

sarna *nf* (**a**) *(en personas)* scabies; PROV **s. con gusto no pica** I'm/he's/*etc* more than happy to put up with it (**b**) *(en animales)* mange

sarnoso, -a 1 *adj* (**a**) *(persona)* scabby (**b**) *(perro)* mangy
2 *nm,f (persona)* scabies sufferer

sarpullido *nm* rash; **le ha salido un s. en la espalda** her back has come out in a rash

sarraceno, -a *Hist* 1 *adj* Saracen
2 *nm,f* Saracen

Sarre *n* (**a**) **el S.** *(río)* the Saar (**b**) **el S.** *(región)* the Saarland

sarrio *nm* chamois

sarro *nm* (**a**) *(en dientes)* tartar (**b**) *(en tuberías)* scale, fur

sarta *nf (de objetos)* string; **una s. de insultos/mentiras** a string of insults/lies

sartal *nm Andes* string

sartén *nf, Am nm o nf* frying pan, *US* fry-pan; EXPR *Fam* **tener la s. por el mango** to call the shots

sartorio *nm Anat* sartorius

sastre, -a *nm,f* tailor

sastrería *nf* (**a**) *(oficio)* tailoring (**b**) *(taller)* tailor's (shop); *(en cine, teatro)* wardrobe (department)

Satanás, Satán *n* Satan

satanelo *nm* northern quoll

satánico, -a *adj* (**a**) *(de Satanás)* satanic (**b**) *(diabólico)* demonic

satanismo *nm* Satanism

satélite 1 *adj inv* satellite; **las ciudades s. de Barcelona** the towns around Barcelona; **estado s.** satellite (state)
2 *nm* satellite ▸▸ ***s. artificial*** (artificial) satellite; ***s. espía*** spy satellite; ***s. geoestacionario*** geostationary satellite; ***s. meteorológico*** weather satellite; ***s. de telecomunicaciones*** telecommunications satellite

satén, *CAm, Méx* **satín** *nm* (**a**) *(tela) (de seda)* satin; *(de algodón)* sateen (**b**) *(árbol)* satinwood

satinado, -a 1 *adj (papel)* glossy; *(tela)* satiny; *(pintura)* satin
2 *nm (de papel)* glossy finish; *(de tela, pintura)* satin finish

satinar *vt (papel)* to give a glossy finish to; *(tela, pintura)* to give a satin finish to

sátira *nf* satire

satírico, -a 1 *adj* satirical
2 *nm,f* satirist

satirizar [14] *vt* to satirize

sátiro *nm* (**a**) *Mitol* satyr (**b**) *(lujurioso)* lecher (**c**) *RP (violador)* monster

satisfacción *nf* (**a**) *(agrado, gusto)* satisfaction; **espero que todo sea de su s.** *o* **esté a su s.** I hope everything is to your satisfaction; **ha sido una s. poder ayudaros** I'm glad I've been able to help you; **me dio mucha s.** I found it very satisfying; **darle a alguien la s. de hacer algo** to give sb the satisfaction of doing sth; **darse la s. de hacer algo** to allow oneself the pleasure of doing sth; **nos mostró sus trofeos con s.** he took great pleasure in showing us his trophies; **sentir una gran s. personal** to feel a sense of fulfilment *o* satisfaction ▸▸ ***s. laboral*** job satisfaction
(**b**) *(de deseo)* fulfilment; **el viaje era la s. de sus sueños** the trip was the fulfilment of her dreams
(**c**) *(de ofensa, daño)* satisfaction
(**d**) *(de deuda)* payment, settlement

satisfacer [33] 1 *vt* (**a**) *(saciar)* to satisfy; **s. el hambre/la curiosidad** to satisfy one's hunger/curiosity; **s. la sed** to quench one's thirst; **satisfizo su sueño de viajar a Australia** he fulfilled his dream of travelling to Australia; **su explicación no nos satisfizo** we weren't satisfied with his explanation
(**b**) *(gustar, agradar)* to please; **me satisface anunciar...** I am pleased to announce...
(**c**) *(deuda)* to pay, to settle; *(pago)* to make
(**d**) *(ofensa, daño)* to redress
(**e**) *(duda, pregunta)* to answer
(**f**) *(cumplir) (requisitos, exigencias)* to meet; **un producto que satisface nuestras necesidades** a product which meets *o* satisfies our needs
2 **satisfacerse** *vpr* (**a**) *(conformarse)* to be satisfied; **no se satisfacen con nada** nothing seems to satisfy them (**b**) *(de agravio)* to obtain satisfaction

satisfactoriamente *adv* satisfactorily

satisfactorio, -a *adj* (**a**) *(suficientemente bueno)* satisfactory (**b**) *(gratificante)* rewarding, satisfying

satisfago *etc ver* **satisfacer**

satisfecho, -a 1 *participio ver* **satisfacer**
2 *adj* (**a**) *(complacido, contento)* satisfied; **darse por s.** to be satisfied; **su explicación no me dejó s.** his explanation didn't satisfy me (**b**) *(saciado)* full; **estar** *o* **quedarse s.** *(de comida)* to be full; **dejar s. a alguien** to satisfy sb; **tiene satisfechas todas sus necesidades** all his needs *o* requirements have been met *o* satisfied (**c**) *(orgulloso)* smug; **s. de sí mismo** self-satisfied

sátrapa *nm* (**a**) *(rico)* **vivir como un s.** to live like a lord (**b**) *(dictador)* dictator, little Hitler (**c**) *Hist* satrap

satsuma *nf* satsuma

saturación *nf* (**a**) *Quím* saturation; *Fig* **hasta la s.** ad nauseam (**b**) *(de mercado, espacio aéreo)* saturation

saturado, -a *adj* (**a**) *(persona)* **estar s. de trabajo** to be up to one's neck in work; **estoy s. de comida** I've had as much as I can to eat; **estoy s. de deporte en televisión** I've had my fill of TV sport (**b**) *(mercado, espacio aéreo)* saturated; **las líneas telefónicas están saturadas** the telephone lines are saturated; **el mercado está saturado de imitaciones** the market is saturated with imitations (**c**) *Quím* saturated (**de** with)

saturar 1 *vt* (**a**) *(persona)* **ya me he saturado de cultura** I've had my fill of culture, I've had a bellyful of culture; **la cena me ha saturado** the dinner has left me full up (**b**) *(mercado)* to saturate, to glut; *(espacio aéreo)* to saturate (**c**) *Quím* to saturate
2 **saturarse** *vpr* to become saturated (**de** with); **me he saturado de pasteles** I've stuffed myself with cakes; **el mercado se ha saturado de imitaciones** the market has been saturated *o* flooded with imitations

saturnal *adj* Saturnian

saturnino, -a *adj Med* lead

saturnismo *nm Med* lead poisoning

Saturno *n* Saturn

sauce *nm* willow ▸▸ ***s. llorón*** weeping willow

sauceda *nf,* **saucedal** *nm* willow grove

saúco *nm* elder(berry)

saudade *nf Literario* nostalgia

saudí (*pl* **saudíes**), **saudita** 1 *adj* Saudi
2 *nmf* Saudi

sauna *nf, Am nm o nf* sauna; *Fam* **esto es una s.** it's like a sauna in here

saurio *nm* lizard

savia *nf* (**a**) *(de planta)* sap (**b**) *(vitalidad)* vitality; **s. nueva** new blood

sávila *nf Méx* aloe vera

savoir faire [saβuar'fer] *nm* savoir-faire

savora® *nf RP* Savora® mustard

saxífraga *nf Bot* saxifrage

saxo 1 *nm (instrumento)* sax ▸▸ ***s. alto*** alto sax; ***s. tenor*** tenor sax
2 *nmf (persona)* sax player ▸▸ ***s. alto*** alto sax player; ***s. tenor*** tenor sax player

saxofón, saxófono 1 *nm (instrumento)* saxophone
2 *nmf (persona)* saxophonist

saxofonista *nmf* saxophonist

saxófono = **saxofón**

saya *nf Anticuado* petticoat

sayal *nm Anticuado* sackcloth

sayo *nm Anticuado* smock

sazón 1 *nf* (**a**) *(madurez)* ripeness; **en s.** ripe (**b**) *(sabor)* seasoning, flavouring
2 *nm Am* flair for cooking; **tener buen s.** to be a great cook
3 **a la sazón** *loc adv* then, at that time; **Blánquez, que a la s. era presidente de la entidad,...** Blánquez, who was president of the organization at that time,...

sazonado, -a *adj* seasoned; **un plato s. de especias** a dish seasoned with spices

sazonar *vt* to season; **sazonó su discurso de anécdotas** he peppered his speech with anecdotes

scalextric® [eska'lekstrik] *nm* (**a**) *(cruce vial) Br* spaghetti junction, = traffic interchange with several overpasses and underpasses (**b**) *(juguete)* Scalextric® set

schop [ʃop] (*pl* **schops**) *nm CSur* (**a**) *(jarra)* beer mug (**b**) *(cerveza)* (mug of) beer

schopería [ʃope'ria] *nf CSur* beer hall

scon, scone [es'kon] *nm CSur* scone

scooter [es'kuter] (*pl* **scooters**) *nm* (motor) scooter

Scotch® [es'kotʃ], **escoch** *nm Andes, RP Br* Sellotape®, *US* Scotch tape®

scout [es'kaut] (*pl* **scouts**) 1 *adj* **un grupo s.** a scout troop
2 *nmf* (boy) scout, *f* girl guide

script [es'kript] (*pl* **scripts**) 1 *nm también Informát* script
2 *nf* script girl

scruchante [eskru'tʃante] *nmf RP* housebreaker

SCSI [es'kasi] *Informát* (*abrev de* **small computer system interface**) SCSI

SDRAM *nf Informát* (*abrev de* **synchronous dynamic random access memory**) SDRAM

SE (*abrev de* **Sudeste**) SE

S.E. (*abrev de* **Su Excelencia**) HE

SE *pron personal* (**a**) *(reflexivo) (de personas) (singular)* himself, *f* herself; *(plural)* themselves; *(usted mismo/misma)* yourself; *(ustedes mismos/mismas)* yourselves; **se está lavando, está lavándose** he/she is washing (himself/herself); **se lavó los dientes** he/she cleaned his/her teeth; **se hizo una casa en la montaña** *(él mismo)* he built (himself) a house in the mountains; *(mandó hacerla)* he had a house built in the mountains
(**b**) *(de cosas, animales) (singular)* itself; *(plural)* themselves; **el perro se lame** the dog is licking itself; **se lame la herida** it's licking its wound
(**c**) *(reflexivo impersonal)* oneself, yourself; **uno se mira en el espejo y piensa...** one looks at oneself in the mirror and thinks..., you look at yourself in the mirror and think...; **hay que afeitarse todos los días** one has to shave every day, you have to shave every day
(**d**) *(recíproco)* each other, one another; **se aman** they love each other *o* one another; **se escriben cartas** they write to each other *o* one another; **se han enamorado** they have fallen in love (with each other *o* one another)
(**e**) *(impersonal, con valor pasivo)* **a esta oficina se viene a trabajar** you come to this office to work; **lo que se siente al perder un amigo** what you feel when you lose a friend; **se pasa muy bien en la universidad** university's great, it's great at university; **se empeñan en subir los impuestos** they insist on putting taxes up; **se espera mucho de él** a lot is expected of him; **¿cómo se dice "juez" en inglés?** how do you say "juez" in English?, what's the English for "juez"?; **en esta sociedad ya no se respeta a los ancianos** in our society old people are no longer respected; **se ha suspendido la reunión** the meeting has been cancelled; **se dice que...** it is said that..., people say that...; **se prohíbe fumar** *(en letrero)* no smoking; **se habla español** *(en letrero)* Spanish spoken; **se busca cocinero** *(en letrero)* cook wanted; **se vende casa** *(en letrero)* house for sale; **rómpase en caso de incendio** *(en letrero)* break glass in the event of a fire
(**f**) *(con verbos pronominales, con valor enfático)* **¿a qué se refiere?** what is he referring to?; **se levantaron y se fueron** they got up and left; **se averió la máquina** the machine broke down; **todos se rieron** everyone laughed; **se lo bebió de un trago** she drank it down in one gulp; **espero que se diviertan** I hope they enjoy themselves
(**g**) *(como complemento indirecto) (de personas) (singular)* (to) him, *f* (to) her; *(plural)* (to) them; *(a usted, ustedes)* (to) you; **se lo dio** he gave it to him/her/*etc*; **se lo dije, pero no me hizo caso** I told him/her/*etc* but he/she/*etc* didn't listen; **si usted quiere, yo se lo arreglo en un minuto** if you like, I'll sort it out for you in a minute
(**h**) *(como complemento indirecto) (de cosas, animales) (singular)* (to) it; *(plural)* (to) them; **el gato tenía una herida en la pata, pero se la curamos** the cat had hurt its paw, but we cleaned the wound for it

---

sé (**a**) *ver* **saber** (**b**) *ver* **ser**

sebáceo, -a *adj* sebaceous

sebo *nm* (**a**) *(grasa untuosa)* grease (**b**) *(para jabón, velas)* tallow; EXPR *RP Fam* **hacer s.** to laze around (**c**) *(suciedad)* grease (**d**) *Chile (regalo)* = christening present from godparents

seborrea *nf* seborrhoea; **un champú contra la s.** a shampoo for greasy hair

seboso, -a *adj* (**a**) *(grasiento)* greasy, oily (**b**) *(mugriento)* greasy (**c**) *Fam (gordo)* tubby, podgy

secadero *nm* drying room

secado *nm* drying

secador *nm* (**a**) *(aparato)* dryer, drier; **s. (de pelo)** hairdryer (**b**) *CAm (trapo)* tea towel

secadora *nf* (**a**) *(de ropa)* clothes dryer, tumble-drier (**b**) *Méx (de pelo)* hairdryer

secamanos *nm inv (aparato)* hand-drier

secamente *adv (contestar)* brusquely

secano *nm (sistema)* unirrigated *o* dry land; **cultivos de s.** = crops suitable for unirrigated land

secante 1 *adj* (**a**) *(que seca)* drying; **papel s.** blotting paper (**b**) *Geom* secant; **línea s.** secant
2 *nf Geom* secant
3 *nmf Dep* man marker

secar [60] 1 *vt* (**a**) *(platos, manos, niño)* to dry (**b**) *(planta, tierra)* to dry up; **el sol secó los campos** the sun parched the fields (**c**) *(enjugar)* to wipe away; *(con fregona)* to mop up (**d**) *Dep (jugador)* to mark (**e**) *RP Fam (fastidiar)* to get on sb's nerves; **por favor, no me dejes sola con ella porque me seca** please don't leave me alone with her, she drives me up the wall
2 *vi* to dry; **déjalo ahí a s.** leave it there to dry
3 **secarse** *vpr* (**a**) *(planta, pozo)* to dry up; **se ha secado el rotulador** the felt-tip pen has dried up; **se me ha secado la piel** my skin has got very dry (**b**) *(vajilla, suelo, ropa)* to dry; **nos secamos al sol** we dried off in the sunshine; **me sequé las manos en la toalla** I dried my hands with the towel

secarropas *nf RP* tumble-drier

sección *nf* (**a**) *(parte)* section; *(departamento)* department; **la s. de discos** the record department ►► ***s. de cuerda(s)*** string section; ***s. de necrológicas*** *(en periódico)* obituary section; ***s. rítmica*** rhythm section; ***s. de viento(s)*** wind section (**b**) *(corte)* section ►► ***s. longitudinal*** longitudinal section; ***s. transversal*** cross-section (**c**) *Geom* section (**d**) *Mil* section

seccional *nf RP* (**a**) *(policial)* police district, *US* police precinct (**b**) *(gremial)* section

seccionar *vt* (**a**) *(cortar)* to cut off; **la máquina le seccionó un dedo** the machine cut off one of his fingers (**b**) *(dividir)* to section

secesión *nf* secession

secesionismo *nm* secessionism

secesionista 1 *adj* secessionist
2 *nmf* secessionist

seco, -a 1 *adj* (**a**) *(ropa, lugar)* dry; **el pantalón todavía no está s.** the *Br* trousers *o US* pants aren't yet dry; **tiene la piel seca/el cabello s.** she has dry skin/hair; **consérvese en un lugar s.** *(en etiqueta)* keep in a dry place
(**b**) *(higos)* dried; **flores secas** dried flowers
(**c**) *(clima, país)* dry
(**d**) *(marchito)* withered
(**e**) *(pozo, fuente)* dry, dried up
(**f**) *(persona, actitud)* brusque (**con** to); **estuvo muy s. con su madre** he was very short with his mother; **me contestó con un no s.** she answered me with a curt "no"
(**g**) *(flaco)* thin, lean; **se está quedando s.** he's getting skinny
(**h**) *(vino, licor)* dry
(**i**) *(ruido)* dull; *(tos)* dry; *(voz)* sharp; **un golpe s.** a thud
(**j**) *Fam (sediento)* thirsty; **estar s.** to be thirsty
(**k**) *Fam (muerto)* stone-dead; *(pasmado)* stunned; **dejar a alguien s.** *(matar)* to kill sb stone-dead; *(pasmar)* to stun sb; *RP Fam (agotar)* to leave sb drained
(**l**) **parar en s.** *(bruscamente)* to stop dead
2 *nm* (**a**) *Perú (guiso)* = meat stew served with rice and a garlic,

lemon and coriander sauce (**b**) *Col (plato principal)* main dish
3 **a secas** *loc adv* simply, just; **llámame Juan a secas** just call me Juan; **no comas pan a secas** don't eat just bread

secoya = **secuoya**

secreción *nf* secretion

secreta *nf* (**a**) *Rel* secret (**b**) *Fam* **la s.** *(policía)* the secret police

secretamente *adv* secretly

secretar *vt* to secrete

secretaría *nf* (**a**) *(oficina administrativa)* secretary's office
(**b**) *(organismo político)* secretariat ▸▸ ***S. de Estado*** *(en España)* = government department under the control of a *Br* junior minister *o US* under-secretary; *(en Latinoamérica)* ministry; *(en Estados Unidos)* State Department
(**c**) *(cargo administrativo)* post of secretary
(**d**) *(cargo político) (en España)* post of *Br* junior minister *o US* under-secretary; *(en Latinoamérica)* office of *Br* minister *o US* secretary; *(en Estados Unidos)* office of Secretary of State

secretariado *nm* (**a**) *(estudios)* secretarial skills; **estudia s.** she's doing a secretarial course (**b**) *(cargo)* post of secretary (**c**) *(organismo)* secretariat

secretario, -a 1 *nm,f* (**a**) *(administrativo)* secretary ▸▸ ***s. de dirección*** secretary to the director; ***s. particular*** private secretary; ***s. personal*** personal assistant; ***s. de prensa*** press secretary
(**b**) *(político) (en Latinoamérica) Br* minister, *US* secretary ▸▸ ***s. de embajada*** embassy secretary; ***s. de Estado*** *(en España) Br* junior minister, *US* under-secretary; *(en Latinoamérica) Br* minister, *US* secretary; *(en Estados Unidos)* Secretary of State; ***s. general*** General Secretary
2 *nm* secretary bird

secretear *Fam* 1 *vi* to whisper, to talk secretively
2 **secretearse** *vpr* to whisper, to talk secretively

secreteo *nm Fam* whispering

secreter *nm* bureau, writing desk

secretismo *nm* (excessive) secrecy

secreto, -a 1 *adj* secret
2 *nm* (**a**) *(noticia, información)* secret; **guardar un s.** to keep a secret; **mantener algo en s.** to keep sth secret; **ser un s. a voces** to be an open secret; **no es ningún s. que el país atraviesa una crisis** it's no secret that the country is going through a crisis; **la mecánica no tiene ningún s. para él** mechanics holds no secrets for him ▸▸ ***s. bancario*** banking confidentiality; ***s. de confesión*** secrecy of the confessional; ***s. de Estado*** State secret; ***s. profesional*** professional secret; ***s. sumarial*** *o* ***del sumario:*** **decretar el s. sumarial** *o* **del sumario** = to deny access to information relating to a judicial inquiry
(**b**) *(sigilo)* secrecy; **en s.** in secret; **me dijo en s. que iba a divorciarse** she told me in secret that she was going to get divorced; **llevaban con mucho s. los preparativos de la fiesta** they kept the preparations for the party very secret

secretor, -ora *adj* secretory

secta *nf* sect

sectario, -a 1 *adj* sectarian
2 *nm,f* (**a**) *(miembro de secta)* sect member (**b**) *(fanático)* fanatic

sectarismo *nm* sectarianism

sector *nm* (**a**) *(división)* section; **todos los sectores de la sociedad** the whole of society
(**b**) *Econ* sector, industry; **el líder del s.** the industry leader ▸▸ ***s. cuaternario*** leisure industries *o* sector; ***s. exterior*** foreign sector; ***s. primario*** primary sector; ***s. privado*** private sector; ***s. público*** public sector; ***s. secundario*** secondary sector; ***s. servicios*** service industries *o* sector; ***s. terciario*** service industries *o* sector
(**c**) *(zona)* sector, area; **en el s. norte de la ciudad** in the northern area *o* part of the city
(**d**) *Geom* sector

sectorial *adj* sectoral

secuaz *nmf Pey* minion

secuela *nf* consequence; **las secuelas del terremoto** the aftermath of the earthquake; **el accidente no le dejó secuelas** the accident didn't do him any permanent damage

secuencia *nf* (**a**) *(serie)* sequence (**b**) *Cine* sequence (**c**) *Mús* sequence (**d**) *Informát* sequence

secuenciador *nm* (**a**) *Mús* sequencer (**b**) *Informát* sequencer

secuencial *adj* sequential

secuenciar *vt* to arrange in sequence

secuestrado, -a 1 *adj (raptado)* kidnapped; *(avión, barco, pasajero)* hijacked
2 *nm,f* hostage

secuestrador, -ora *nm,f (de persona)* kidnapper; *(de avión, barco)* hijacker

secuestrar *vt* (**a**) *(raptar)* to kidnap; *(avión, barco)* to hijack (**b**) *(bienes, publicación)* to seize

secuestro *nm* (**a**) *(rapto)* kidnapping (**b**) *(de avión, barco)* hijack (**c**) *(de bienes, publicación)* seizure

secular *adj* (**a**) *(seglar)* secular, lay; **clero s.** secular clergy (**b**) *(centenario)* centuries-old, age-old

secularización *nf* secularization

secularizar [14] *vt* to secularize

sécula seculórum *loc adv* **(per) s.** for ever (and ever)

secundar *vt* to support, to back (up); **s. una propuesta** to second a proposal

secundaria *nf (educación)* secondary

secundario, -a 1 *adj* (**a**) *(en orden)* secondary (**b**) *(de menor importancia)* minor; **actor s.** supporting actor (**c**) *Geol* secondary
2 *nm Geol* **el Secundario** the Secondary (era)

secuoya, secoya *nf* sequoia, redwood ▸▸ ***s. gigante*** giant sequoia *o* redwood

sed 1 *ver* **ser**
2 *nf* thirst; **las palomitas dan s.** popcorn makes you thirsty; **tener s.** to be thirsty; **saciar la s.** to quench one's thirst; **los familiares de la víctima tienen s. de venganza** the victim's family is thirsty for revenge

seda *nf* silk; EXPR **ir como una** *o* **la s.** to go smoothly ▸▸ ***s. artificial*** rayon, artificial silk; ***s. cruda*** raw silk; ***s. dental*** dental floss; ***s. natural*** pure silk

sedación *nf Med* sedation; *(con música)* soothing, calming

sedal *nm* fishing line

sedán *nm Br* saloon, *US* sedan

sedante, sedativo, -a 1 *adj Med* sedative; *(música)* soothing
2 *nm* sedative

sedar *vt (con medicamentos)* to sedate; *(sujeto: música)* to soothe, to calm

sedativo, -a = **sedante**

sede *nf* (**a**) *(de organización, empresa)* headquarters; *(de Gobierno)* seat; *(de congreso, Juegos Olímpicos)* venue (**de** for); **el país s. del próximo mundial de fútbol** the country hosting the next World Cup ▸▸ ***s. social*** *(oficina principal)* headquarters, head office; *(de club)* headquarters (**b**) *Rel* see

sedentario, -a *adj* sedentary

sedentarismo *nm* sedentary lifestyle; **el s. avanza** people are adopting an increasingly sedentary lifestyle

sedente *adj Arte* seated

sedería *nf* (**a**) *(negocio)* silk trade (**b**) *(tejidos)* silks, silk goods (**c**) *(tienda)* silk shop

sedero, -a 1 *adj* silk; **la industria sedera** the silk industry
2 *nm,f* (**a**) *(tejedor)* silk weaver (**b**) *(comerciante)* silk trader

sedicente *adj* self-styled; **un s. historiador** a self-styled historian

sedición *nf* sedition

sedicioso, -a 1 *adj* seditious
2 *nm,f* rebel

sediento, -a *adj (de agua)* thirsty; **s. de justicia/venganza** thirsty for justice/revenge

sedimentación *nf* settling, *Espec* sedimentation

sedimentar 1 *vt* to deposit
2 **sedimentarse** *vpr* to settle

sedimentario, -a *adj* sedimentary

sedimento *nm* (**a**) *(poso)* sediment (**b**) *Literario (huella)* residue

sedoso, -a *adj* silky

seducción *nf* (**a**) *(cualidad)* seductiveness (**b**) *(atracción)* attraction, charm; *(sexual)* seduction

seducir [18] *vt* (**a**) *(atraer)* to attract, to charm; **sedujo a sus compañeros con su simpatía** he won over his colleagues with his personal charm; **¿te seduce la idea de ir a la playa?** how do you like the idea of going to the beach?; **la idea no me seduce demasiado** I'm not too keen on the idea (**b**) *(sexualmente)* to seduce (**c**) *(persuadir)* **s. a alguien para que haga algo** to charm sb into doing sth

seductor, -ora 1 *adj* (a) *(atractivo)* attractive, charming; *(idea)* seductive (b) *(sexualmente)* seductive (c) *(persuasivo)* persuasive, charming

2 *nm,f* seducer

sedujera *etc ver* **seducir**

seduzco *etc ver* **seducir**

sefardí (*pl* **sefardíes**), **sefardita** 1 *adj* Sephardic

2 *nmf (persona)* Sephardi

3 *nm (lengua)* Sephardi

segada *nf (en fútbol)* scything tackle

segador, -ora *nm,f (agricultor)* reaper

segadora *nf (máquina)* reaping machine

segar [43] *vt* (a) *Agr* to reap (b) *(cortar)* to cut off; **la sierra le segó la mano** the saw cut off his hand (c) *(esperanzas)* to dash; **la epidemia segó la vida de cientos de personas** the epidemic claimed the lives of hundreds of people

seglar 1 *adj* secular, lay

2 *nm* lay person

segmentación *nf* (a) *(de óvulo)* division (b) *(de mercados)* segmentation

segmentar *vt (recta)* to cut *o* divide into segments

segmento *nm* (a) *Geom* segment (b) *Zool* segment (c) *(trozo)* piece (d) *(de mercado)* segment

segoviano, -a 1 *adj* of/from Segovia *(Spain)*

2 *nm,f* person from Segovia *(Spain)*

segregación *nf* (a) *(separación, discriminación)* segregation ▸▸ ***s. racial*** racial segregation (b) *(secreción)* secretion

segregacionismo *nm* policy of racial segregation

segregacionista 1 *adj* segregationist; **política s.** policy of racial segregation

2 *nmf* segregationist

segregar [38] 1 *vt* (a) *(separar, discriminar)* to segregate (b) *(secretar)* to secrete

2 **segregarse** *vpr (separarse)* to cut oneself off

segué *etc ver* **segar**

segueta *nf* fretsaw

seguida: en seguida *loc adv (inmediatamente)* immediately, at once; *(pronto)* very soon; **lo haré en s., antes de que se me olvide** I'll do it straight away before I forget; **llegará en s.** he'll be here any minute now; **vino a las seis, pero se fue en s.** he came at six, but he left soon after; **en s. lo atiendo** I'll be with you in a minute *o* directly; **en s. vuelvo** I'll be right back; **cruza el puente y en s. verás la casa a la derecha** cross the bridge and you'll see the house on your right; *Am* **en s. de comer no se debe hacer ejercicio** you should not exercise immediately after a meal

seguidamente *adv* then, next; **s. procederemos a anunciar los resultados** we shall now proceed to announce the results; **saludó a su familia y, s., a sus compañeros** he first greeted his family and then his colleagues; **fue arrestado en Francia y s. deportado a España** she was arrested in France and immediately deported to Spain

seguidilla *nf* (a) *Lit* = poem containing four or seven verses used in popular songs (b) *(cante flamenco)* = mournful flamenco song

seguido, -a 1 *adj* (a) *(consecutivo)* consecutive; **diez años seguidos** ten years in a row; **llamó a la puerta cinco veces seguidas** she knocked at the door five times; **llegaron los tres seguidos** the three of them arrived one after the other

(b) *(sin interrupción)* continuous; **llevan reunidos cuatro horas seguidas** they've been in the meeting for four hours without a break *o* for four solid hours; **ha nevado durante dos semanas seguidas** it's been snowing for two weeks solid; **viajaron durante todo el día s.** they travelled the whole day without a break

(c) *(inmediatamente después)* **s. de** followed by; **sopa, seguida de carne** soup, followed by meat

2 *adv* (a) *(sin interrupción)* continuously (b) *(en línea recta)* straight on; **todo s.** straight on *o* ahead; **por ahí s. llegarás a la autopista** go straight on *o* ahead and you'll get to the *Br* motorway *o US* highway (c) *Am (a menudo)* often

seguidor, -ora *nm,f* follower; **tiene muchos seguidores** he has a considerable following; **los seguidores del equipo inglés protagonizaron muchas peleas** the England fans were involved in a number of fights

seguimiento *nm* (a) *(de persona)* following; *(de clientes)* follow-up (b) *(por radio, radar)* tracking (c) *(de noticia)* following (d) *(de elecciones, enfermedad)* monitoring; **efectuar el s. de una epidemia** to monitor the course of an epidemic

SEGUIR [62] 1 *vt* (a) *(ir detrás de, tomar la ruta de)* to follow; **tú ve delante, que yo te sigo** you go ahead, I'll follow *o* I'll go behind; **síganme, por favor** follow me, please; **la generación que nos sigue** *o* **que sigue a la nuestra** the next generation, the generation after us; **sigue este sendero hasta llegar a un bosque** follow this path until you come to a forest; **s. el rastro de alguien/algo** to follow sb's/sth's tracks; **siga la flecha** *(en letrero)* follow the arrow

(b) *(perseguir)* to follow; **me parece que nos siguen** I think we're being followed; **s. a alguien de cerca** to tail sb; **parece que le siguen los problemas** trouble seems to follow him around wherever he goes; PROV **el que la sigue la consigue** where there's a will there's a way

(c) *(estar atento a, imitar, obedecer)* to follow; **seguían con la vista la trayectoria de la bola** they followed the ball with their eyes; **no seguimos ese programa** we don't follow that programme; **s. algo de cerca** *(su desarrollo, sus resultados)* to follow *o* monitor sth closely; **siempre sigue los dictámenes de la moda** she always follows the latest fashion; **los que siguen a Keynes** followers of Keynes; **el cuadro sigue una línea clásica** the painting is classical in style; **s. las órdenes/instrucciones de alguien** to follow sb's orders/instructions; **sigue mi consejo y habla con ella** take my advice and talk to her; **siguiendo sus indicaciones, hemos cancelado el pedido** we have cancelled the order as instructed

(d) *(reanudar, continuar)* to continue, to resume; **yo seguí mi trabajo/camino** I continued with my work/on my way; **él siguió su discurso** he continued *o* resumed his speech

(e) *(comprender) (explicación, profesor, conferenciante)* to follow; **me costaba seguirle** I found her hard to follow; **¿me sigues?** do you follow?, are you with me?

(f) *(mantener, someterse a)* to follow; **hay que s. un cierto orden** you have to follow *o* do things in a certain order; **seguiremos el procedimiento habitual** we will follow the usual procedure; **es difícil seguirle (el ritmo), va muy deprisa** it's hard to keep up with him, he goes very quickly; **los aspirantes elegidos seguirán un proceso de formación** the chosen candidates will receive *o* undergo training

(g) *(cursar)* **sigue un curso de italiano** he's doing an Italian course; **sigue la carrera de medicina** she's studying medicine

2 *vi* (a) *(proseguir, no detenerse)* to continue, to go on; **¡sigue, no te pares!** go *o* carry on, don't stop!; **aquí se baja él, yo sigo** *(al taxista)* he's getting out here, I'm going on; **siga con su trabajo** carry on with your work; **el sendero sigue hasta la cima** the path continues *o* carries on to the top; **"sigue la crisis en la bolsa de Tokio"** "Tokyo stock market crisis continues"; **debes s. haciéndolo** you should keep on *o* carry on doing it; **¿vas a s. intentándolo?** are you going to keep trying?; **se seguían viendo de vez en cuando** they still saw each other from time to time, they continued to see each other from time to time; **s. adelante (con algo)** *(con planes, proyectos)* to go ahead (with sth)

(b) *(mantenerse, permanecer)* **sigue enferma/en el hospital** she's still ill/in hospital; **¿qué tal sigue la familia?** how's the family getting on *o* keeping?; **todo sigue igual** everything's still the same, nothing has changed; **sigue el buen tiempo en el sur del país** the good weather in the south of the country is continuing; **sigo trabajando en la fábrica** I'm still working at the factory; **¿la sigues queriendo?** do you still love her?; **sigo pensando que está mal** I still think it's wrong; **sigue habiendo dudas sobre...** doubts remain about...; **¡buen trabajo, sigue así!** good work, keep it up!; **si seguimos jugando así, ganaremos la liga** if we carry on *o* keep playing like that, we'll win the league; *Fam* **a s. bien** *(como despedida)* take care, look after yourself; **de s. así las cosas, si las cosas siguen así** if things go on like this, the way things are going

(c) *(tomar un camino)* **el resto siguió por otro camino** the rest went another way; **seguiremos hacia el este** we'll go east then; **siga todo recto** go straight on; **siga hasta el siguiente semáforo** carry on till you get to the next set of traffic lights

(d) *(sucederse, ir después)* to follow; **lo que sigue es una cita del Corán** the following is a quotation from the Koran; **s. a algo** to follow sth; **la lluvia siguió a los truenos** the thunder was followed by rain; **¿cómo sigue el chiste?** how does the joke go on *o* continue?; **el proceso de selección se realizará como sigue:...** the selection process will be carried out as follows:...; **sigue en la página 20** *(en periódico, libro)* continued on page 20

(e) *Col (para dar permiso)* please do; **con permiso, ¿puedo entrar? – siga** excuse me, can I come in? – please do

3 **seguirse** *v impersonal (deducirse)* to follow; **seguirse de algo** to follow *o* be deduced from sth; **de esto se sigue que estás equivocado** it therefore follows that you are wrong

seguiriya *nf* = mournful flamenco song

según 1 *prep* (a) *(de acuerdo con)* according to; **s. el ministro, fue un accidente** according to the minister, it was an accident; **s. su opinión, ha sido un éxito** in her opinion *o* according to her, it was a success; **s. pone aquí, ahora hay que apretar la tecla de retorno** according to what it says here, now you have to press the return key; **s. Nietzsche,...** according to Nietzsche,...; **el Evangelio s. San Juan** the Gospel according to St John

(b) *(dependiendo de)* depending on; **s. la hora que sea** depending on the time; **s. el tiempo que haga iremos a la montaña** depending on what the weather's like, we may go to the mountains; **s. como te vaya en el examen, podemos ir a celebrarlo** depending on how you do in the exam, we could go out for a celebration

2 *adv* (a) *(como)* (just) as; **todo permanecía s. lo recordaba** everything was just as she remembered it; **actuó s. se le recomendó** he did as he had been advised; **hazlo s. creas** do as you see fit; **lo hice s. y como** *o* **s. y conforme me dijiste** I did it exactly *o* just like you told me; **s. parece, no van a poder venir** apparently, they're not going to be able to come

(b) *(a medida que)* as; **entrarás en forma s. vayas entrenando** you'll get fit as you train

(c) *(dependiendo)* **s. se mire** depending on how you look at it; **¿te gusta la pasta? – s.** do you like pasta? – it depends; **lo intentaré s. esté de tiempo** I'll try to do it, depending on how much time I have; **s. qué días la clase es muy aburrida** some days the class is really boring

segunda *nf* (a) *(marcha)* second (gear); **meter (la) s.** to go into second (gear)

(b) *(en avión, tren)* second class; **viajar en s.** to travel second class

(c) *(mala categoría)* **de s.** second-rate

(d) *Dep* second division; **bajar a s.** to be relegated to the second division

(e) **segundas** *(intenciones)* **con segundas (intenciones)** with an ulterior motive; **¿me lo dices con segundas?** are you telling me this for any particular reason?

(f) EXPR *Ven Fam* **hacerle la s. a alguien** to stand in for sb

(g) *ver también* **segundo**

segundero *nm* second hand

segundo, -a 1 *núm* second; **de segunda mano** second-hand; **contraer segundas nupcias** to remarry; **casarse de segundas** to remarry ►► *Dep* ***la segunda base*** *(posición)* second base; *Dep* ***el/la segunda base*** *(jugador)* second base; ***s. equipo*** *(en deporte)* second team; ***la Segunda Guerra Mundial*** the Second World War, World War Two; ***segunda lengua*** second language; ***segunda línea*** *(en rugby)* lock (forward), second row (forward); ***segunda oportunidad*** second chance; ***segunda parte*** second half; ***s. violín*** second violin; ***segunda vivienda*** second home

2 *nm,f* (a) *(mencionado antes)* **vinieron Pedro y Juan, el s. con...** Pedro and Juan arrived, the latter with...

(b) *(ayudante)* number two ►► ***s. de a bordo*** *Náut* first mate; *Fig* second-in-command; *ver también* **octavo**

3 *nm* (a) *(piso) Br* second floor, *US* third floor (b) *(cantidad de tiempo)* second; **tres segundos** *(en baloncesto)* three-seconds violation (c) *(curso universitario)* second year (d) *(curso escolar)* = second year of primary school, *US* ≃ second grade

segundón, -ona 1 *nm,f* **ser el eterno s.** to be one of life's eternal bridesmaids

2 *nm (hijo)* second son

segur *nf (hacha)* axe

seguramente *adv* probably; **s. iré, pero aún no lo sé** the chances are I'll go, but I'm not sure yet; **s. te veré en la fiesta** I expect I'll see you at the party; **¿crees que dirán que sí? – s.** do you think they'll agree? – I should think so

> **Falso amigo**: El adverbio inglés **securely** no es la traducción del español **seguramente**. En inglés **securely** significa "a buen recaudo" o "firmemente".

seguridad *nf* (a) *(ausencia de peligro)* safety; **la s. de los pasajeros es nuestra prioridad** passenger safety is our priority; **de s.** *(cinturón, cierre)* safety ►► ***s. vial*** road safety

(b) *(protección)* security; **s. en el trabajo** safety at work *o* in the workplace ►► ***s. ciudadana*** public safety; ***s. privada*** security firms; ***S. Social*** Social Security

(c) *(estabilidad, firmeza)* security; **una inversión que ofrece s.** a safe *o* secure investment

(d) *(certidumbre)* certainty; **con s.** for sure, definitely; **no lo sé con s.** I don't know for sure *o* for certain; **con toda s.** with absolute certainty; **tener la s. de que** to be certain that

(e) *(confianza)* confidence; **habla con mucha s.** she speaks very confidently; **s. en sí mismo** self-confidence; **mostrar una falsa s.** to put on a show of confidence

SEGURO, -A 1 *adj* (a) *(sin peligro)* safe; **el medio de transporte más s.** the safest means of transport; **¿es éste un lugar s.?** is it safe here?; **aquí estaremos seguros** we'll be safe here; **es una inversión segura** it's a safe investment; **prefiero ir sobre s.** I'd rather play (it) safe; **más vale ir sobre s. y llamar antes** we'd better ring first, to be safe

(b) *(protegido, estable)* secure; **un trabajo s.** a secure job; **esta mesa no está segura** this table isn't very steady; **¿irán las botellas seguras ahí atrás?** are the bottles safe in the back there?

(c) *(fiable, infalible)* reliable; **un método s. para combatir** *o* **contra los catarros** a sure-fire cure for colds

(d) *(indudable, cierto)* definite, certain; **creo que sí, pero no es s.** I think so, but I'm not certain *o* but it's not definite; **su nombramiento es s.** he's certain to be given the post; **ya sabemos la fecha segura de su llegada** we've now got a definite date for his arrival; **no es s. que vengan** they're not definitely coming, they're not certain to come; **lo puedes dar por s.** you can be sure of it; **ya daban la victoria por segura** they were sure that they had won; **tener por s. que...** to be sure (that)...; **ten por s. que vendrá** you can be sure (that) she'll come; **¿crees que nos ayudará? – a buen s., de s.** do you think she'll help us? – I'm sure she will; **a buen s. que pone alguna pega** he's certain to find something wrong with it

(e) *(convencido)* sure; **¿estás s.?** are you sure?; **no estoy muy s.** I'm not too sure; **estar s. de algo** to be sure about *o* of sth; **estoy s. de ello** I'm sure of it; **estamos seguros de que te gustará** we're sure you'll like it; **no estoy s. de habérselo dicho** I'm not sure I told him; **estaba segura de vencer** she was confident of winning

(f) *(con confianza en uno mismo)* self-assured, self-confident; **se le ve un tipo muy s.** he's very self-assured *o* self-confident; **ser s. de sí mismo, ser una persona segura de sí misma** to be self-assured *o* self-confident

2 *nm* (a) *(contrato)* insurance; **contratar** *o* **hacerse un s.** to take out insurance ►► ***s. de accidentes*** accident insurance; ***s. de asistencia en viaje*** travel insurance; ***s. del automóvil*** car insurance; ***s. de cambio*** exchange rate hedge; ***s. de la casa*** buildings insurance; ***s. de enfermedad*** private health insurance; ***s. de hogar*** buildings insurance; ***s. de*** *o* ***contra incendios*** fire insurance; ***s. médico*** private health insurance; ***s. multirriesgo*** comprehensive insurance; ***s. mutuo*** joint insurance; ***s. de responsabilidad civil*** liability insurance; ***s. a todo riesgo*** comprehensive insurance; ***s. a terceros*** liability insurance; ***s. de viaje*** travel insurance; ***s. de vida*** life insurance *o* assurance

(b) *Fam* **el s.** *(la seguridad social) Br* ≃ the National Health, *US* ≃ Medicaid; **ir al s.** to go to the hospital; **ese tratamiento no lo cubre el s.** ≃ you can't get that treatment on *Br* the National Health *o US* Medicaid ►► ***s. de desempleo*** unemployment benefit; ***s. de incapacidad*** disability benefit; ***s. de invalidez*** disability benefit; ***s. de paro*** unemployment benefit

(c) *(dispositivo)* safety device; *(de armas)* safety catch; *(en automóvil)* door lock catch; **echa** *o* **pon el s.** lock the car door

(d) *CAm, Méx (imperdible)* safety pin

3 *adv* for sure, definitely; **¿vienes s.?** are you definitely coming?; **no lo sé s.** I don't know for sure; **s. que vendrá** she's bound *o* certain *o* sure to come; **s. que suspendo** I'm bound *o* certain *o* sure to fail; **s. que ahora va y se lo cuenta todo a ella** I bet she's going to go and tell her everything; **¿s. que no necesitas nada? – sí, sí, s.** are you sure you don't need anything? – yes, I'm sure

seibó *nm Col, Ven* sideboard

seis *núm* six; **el (Torneo de las) S. Naciones** *(en rugby)* the Six Nations (Championship); *ver también* **tres**

seiscientos, -as 1 *núm* six hundred; *ver también* **treinta**

2 *nm inv (automóvil)* Seat® 600 (car)

seísmo *nm* earthquake

SELA ['sela] *nm (abrev de* **Sistema Económico Latinoamericano***)* SELA

selaginela *nf* clubmoss, selaginella

selección *nf* (a) *(acción)* selection; **hizo una s. de los cuadros más interesantes** he made a selection of the most interesting paintings; **una prueba de s. de candidatos** a candidate selection test; **test de s. múltiple** multiple-choice test ►► ***s. natural*** natural selection; ***s. de personal*** recruitment (b) *(equipo)* team; **s. (nacional)** national team

seleccionable *adj* eligible for selection (for a team)

seleccionado *nm Dep* **el s. cubano** the Cuban (national) team

seleccionador, -ora 1 *adj (de personal)* recruiting
2 *nm,f* (**a**) *(de personal)* recruiter (**b**) *Dep* **s. (nacional)** national coach *o* manager

seleccionar *vt* to pick, to select

selectividad *nf* (**a**) *(selección)* selectivity (**b**) *Esp (examen)* = former university entrance examination

selectivo, -a *adj* selective

selecto, -a *adj* select

selector, -ora 1 *adj* selecting
2 *nm* (**a**) *(mando)* dial, knob (**b**) *Informát* chooser

selenio *nm Quím* selenium

selenita 1 *nf* selenite
2 *nmf (habitante)* moon dweller

self-service [self'serβis] *nm* self-service restaurant

sellado, -a 1 *adj* (**a**) *(cerrado herméticamente)* sealed (**b**) *(documento)* sealed; *(pasaporte, carta)* stamped
2 *nm* (**a**) *(proceso de cerrar herméticamente)* sealing (**b**) *(de documento)* sealing; *(de pasaporte, carta)* stamping

sellador, -ora *nm,f* (**a**) *(persona)* stamper (**b**) *(instrumento)* seal

sellar *vt* (**a**) *(timbrar)* to stamp (**b**) *(cerrar)* to seal (**c**) *(pacto, labios)* to seal; **sellaron el pacto con un abrazo** they sealed the pact with an embrace

sello *nm* (**a**) *(timbre)* stamp ►► ***s. de correos*** postage stamp; ***s. postal*** postage stamp (**b**) *(tampón)* rubber stamp; *(marca)* stamp ►► ***s. de caucho*** rubber stamp (**c**) *(lacre)* seal (**d**) *(sortija)* signet ring (**e**) *(carácter)* hallmark; **ese libro lleva el s. de su autor** this book is unmistakably the work of its author (**f**) *(compañía)* ***s. discográfico*** record label; ***s. editorial*** imprint; ***s. independiente*** independent record label (**g**) *Andes, Ven (de una moneda)* reverse

Seltz, seltz *nm* **(agua de) S.** Seltzer (water)

selva *nf (jungla)* jungle; *(bosque)* forest; **una s. de libros** mountains of books ►► ***la S. Lacandona*** the Lacandon Rainforest; ***la S. Negra*** the Black Forest; ***s. tropical*** tropical rainforest; ***s. virgen*** virgin forest

selvático, -a *adj* woodland; **zona selvática** woodland area

sema *nm Ling* seme

semáforo *nm* (**a**) *(en calle)* traffic lights; **el s. está (en) rojo** the lights are red; **saltarse un s.** to jump the lights; **gira a la derecha en el próximo s.** turn right at the next traffic lights ►► ***s. sonoro*** pelican crossing *(with audible signal)* (**b**) *Ferroc* railway signal

semana *nf* week; **entre s.** during the week; **fin de s.** weekend; **la s. próxima** *o* **que viene** next week; **dos veces por s.** twice a week, twice weekly; **me deben tres semanas de alquiler** they owe me three weeks' rent ►► ***s. laboral*** *Br* working week, *US* workweek; ***S. Santa*** Easter; *Rel* Holy Week

semanada *nf Am* (weekly) pocket money

semanal *adj* weekly

semanalmente *adv* every week, once a week; **se publica s.** it's published weekly

semanario *nm (publicación semanal)* weekly

semántica *nf* semantics *(singular)*

semánticamente *adv* semantically

semántico, -a *adj* semantic

semantista *nmf* semanticist

semblante *nm* countenance, face

semblantear *vt* (**a**) *Arg (calibrar)* to assess (**b**) *Méx Fam (encarar)* to look straight in the eye

semblanza *nf* portrait, profile; **el orador nos hizo una breve s. del homenajeado** the speaker gave us a brief portrait of the guest of honour

sembradero *nm Col* sown field

sembradío *nm* arable land

sembrado, -a 1 *adj* (**a**) *(plantado)* sown (**b**) *(lleno)* **s. de errores** plagued with mistakes; **s. de minas** mined
2 *nm* sown field

sembrador, -ora 1 *adj* sowing
2 *nm,f (persona)* sower

sembradora *nf (máquina)* seed drill

sembrar [3] *vt* (**a**) *(plantar)* to sow (**con** *o* **de** with); PROV **quien siembra vientos recoge tempestades** as you sow, so shall you reap
(**b**) *(llenar)* to scatter, to strew; **sembró la habitación de confeti** she showered the room with confetti
(**c**) *(confusión, pánico)* to sow; **el anuncio del gobierno sembró el pánico** the government's announcement sowed panic; **los resultados financieros han sembrado la inquietud entre los inversores** the financial results have spread unease among investors

sembrío *nm Andes* sown field

semejante 1 *adj* (**a**) *(parecido)* similar (**a** to); **son de una edad s.** they are (of) a similar age; **su plan es s. al nuestro** her plan is similar to ours
(**b**) *(tal)* such; **jamás aceptaría s. invitación** I would never accept such an invitation; **una propuesta de s. talante** a proposal of this nature, such a proposal; **no sé cómo pudo mover s. piedra** I don't know how he managed to shift such a heavy rock; **¡cómo pudo decir s. tontería!** how could he say something so stupid!; **¡s. mentiroso! ¡cómo puede decir eso!** what a liar! how can he say that!
2 *nm* fellow (human) being

semejanza *nf* similarity; **a s. de sus padres, prefiere el campo a la ciudad** he prefers the countryside to the city, just like his parents; **a s. de lo que ocurrió en el partido de ida, el encuentro fue violento** like the first leg, the return game, too, was marred by violence

semejar 1 *vt* to resemble
2 semejarse *vpr* to be alike, to resemble each other; **semejarse a algo/alguien** to resemble sth/sb

semen *nm* semen

semental 1 *adj* stud; **toro s.** stud bull
2 *nm* (**a**) *(animal)* stud; *(caballo)* stallion (**b**) *Fam (persona)* stud

sementera *nf* (**a**) *(tierra)* sown land (**b**) *(siembra)* sowing

semestral *adj* (**a**) *(en frecuencia)* six-monthly, semiannual (**b**) *(en duración)* six-month; *Educ* **asignatura s.** one-semester course

semestralmente *adv* every six months, semiannually

semestre *nm* (**a**) *(periodo)* period of six months; **cada s.** every six months; **el primer s. del año** the first half of the year (**b**) *Univ* semester

semi- *pref* semi-

semiabierto, -a *adj* half-open

semiacabado, -a *adj* half-finished, semi-finished

semiárido, -a *adj* semi-arid

semiautomático, -a *adj* semiautomatic

semibreve *nf Mús Br* semibreve, *US* whole note

semicerrado, -a *adj* half-closed

semicircular *adj* semicircular

semicírculo *nm* semicircle

semicircunferencia *nf* semicircumference

semiconductor *nm* semiconductor

semiconsciencia *nf* semiconsciousness

semiconsciente *adj* semiconscious

semiconserva *nf* semipreserve

semiconsonante *nf* semiconsonant

semicorchea *nf Mús Br* semiquaver, *US* sixteenth note

semiderruido, -a *adj* crumbling

semidesconocido, -a 1 *adj* almost unknown
2 *nm,f* **es un s.** he is almost unknown

semidesértico, -a *adj* semidesert; **un clima s.** a semidesert climate

semidesierto, -a 1 *adj (calle, playa)* almost deserted; *(sala, oficina)* almost empty
2 *nm* semidesert

semidesnatado, -a *adj* semi-skimmed

semidesnudo, -a *adj* half-naked

semidiós, -osa *nm,f* demigod, *f* demigoddess

semidirecto, -a 1 *adj* **tren s.** = through train, a section of which becomes a stopping train
2 *nm (tren)* = through train, a section of which becomes a stopping train

semidormido, -a *adj* half-asleep

semienterrado, -a *adj* half-buried

semiesfera *nf* hemisphere

semiesférico, -a *adj* semispherical

semifinal *nf* semifinal

semifinalista 1 *adj* semifinalist; **equipo s.** semifinalist
2 *nmf* semifinalist

semifusa *nf Mús Br* hemidemisemiquaver, *US* sixty-fourth note

semiinconsciente *adj* semiconscious, half-unconscious

semilíquido, -a *adj* semiliquid

semilla *nf* (**a**) *(de planta)* seed; EXPR **sembrar la s. de la discordia** to sow the seeds of discord (**b**) *(origen)* seed; **el control de la tierra es la s. del conflicto en la región** control of land is at the root of the conflict in the region

semillero *nm* (**a**) *(para plantar)* seedbed (**b**) *(para guardar)* seed box (**c**) *(fuente, criadero)* seedbed, breeding ground; **esa universidad es un s. de economistas** that university is a seedbed of economists; **la herencia familiar es un s. de discordias** the family inheritance is a bone of contention

semimembranoso *nm Anat* semimembranosus

seminal *adj* seminal

seminario *nm* (**a**) *(escuela para sacerdotes)* seminary (**b**) *(curso, conferencia)* seminar (**c**) *(departamento)* department, school

seminarista *nm* seminarist

seminola 1 *adj* Seminole
2 *nmf* Seminole

seminuevo, -a *adj* almost new

semioctava *nf Mús* half octave, semioctave

semioculto, -a *adj* partially hidden

semiología *nf* (**a**) *Ling* semiology (**b**) *Med* semiology

semiólogo, -a *nm,f* (**a**) *Ling* semiologist (**b**) *Med* semiologist

semiótica *nf* (**a**) *Ling* semiotics *(singular)* (**b**) *Med* semiotics *(singular)*

semipermeable *adj* semi-permeable

semipesado, -a *Dep* 1 *adj* light heavyweight; **peso s.** light heavyweight
2 *nm* light heavyweight

semipiso *nm RP* = *Br* flat *o US* apartment occupying half of one floor

semiprecioso, -a *adj* semi-precious

semirrecta *nf Geom* half-line

semirremolque *nm* semitrailer

semiseco, -a *adj* medium dry

semisótano *nm* = level of building partially below ground level

semita 1 *adj* Semitic
2 *nmf* Semite

semitendinoso *nm Anat* semitendinosus

semítico, -a *adj* Semitic

semitismo *nm* Semitism

semitono *nm Mús* semitone

semitransparente *adj* translucent

semivocal *nf Ling* semivowel

sémola *nf* semolina

sempiterno, -a *adj Formal* eternal

Sena *nm* **el S.** the Seine

senado *nm* (**a**) *(asamblea)* senate (**b**) *(edificio)* senate, *US* senate house

senador, -ora *nm,f* senator

senatorial *adj* (**a**) *(del senado)* senate; **comité s.** senate committee (**b**) *(de senador)* senatorial

sencillamente *adv* (**a**) *(fácilmente)* simply, easily; **esto se soluciona muy s.** there's a very simple solution to this (**b**) *(vestir)* simply (**c**) *(hablar, comportarse)* unaffectedly, naturally (**d**) *(francamente)* **s., porque no quiero** quite simply, because I don't want to; **su actuación fue s. excepcional** her performance was simply outstanding

sencillez *nf* (**a**) *(facilidad)* simplicity (**b**) *(de decoración, vestido)* simplicity; **vestir con s.** to dress simply (**c**) *(de lenguaje, estilo)* simplicity (**d**) *(campechanía)* unaffectedness, naturalness

sencillo, -a 1 *adj* (**a**) *(fácil)* simple; **no fue s. convencerla** it was not easy to convince her (**b**) *(sin lujo) (decoración, vestido)* simple (**c**) *(claro, natural) (lenguaje, estilo)* simple (**d**) *(campechano)* natural, unaffected; **es muy s. en el trato** he's very natural *o* unaffected (**e**) *(billete) Br* single, *US* one-way (**f**) *(no múltiple)* single; **habitación sencilla** single room
2 *nm* (**a**) *(disco)* single (**b**) *Andes, CAm, Méx Fam (cambio)* loose change

senda *nf* (**a**) *(camino)* path; **siguió la s. del mal** he went astray, he chose the path of evil (**b**) *Urug (carril)* lane

senderismo *nm* hiking, trekking, *Br* hillwalking

senderista *nmf* (**a**) *(caminante)* hiker, *Br* hillwalker (**b**) *(miembro de Sendero Luminoso)* = follower of the Peruvian guerrilla movement, the Shining Path

sendero *nm* path ►► ***S. Luminoso*** Shining Path

sendos, -as *adj pl* **llegaron con s. paquetes** they each arrived with a parcel; **los conferenciantes leyeron sendas ponencias** the speakers each read a paper

senectud *nf Formal* old age

Senegal *nm* **(el) S.** Senegal

senegalés, -esa 1 *adj* Senegalese
2 *nm,f* Senegalese

senescencia *nf Formal* senescence

senil *adj* senile

senilidad *nf* senility

sénior (*pl* **séniors**) 1 *adj* (**a**) *Dep* senior (**b**) *(padre)* senior; **Joaquín Sánchez s.** Joaquín Sánchez Senior
2 *nm Dep* senior

seno *nm* (**a**) *(pecho)* breast; **senos** breasts, bosom
(**b**) *(amparo, cobijo)* refuge, shelter; **acogieron en su s. a los refugiados** they gave shelter to *o* took in the refugees; **nació en el s. de una familia acaudalada** she was born into a wealthy family; **que Dios lo acoja en su s.** may the Lord take them unto Himself
(**c**) *(útero)* **s. (materno)** womb
(**d**) *(de una organización)* heart; **en el s. de** within; **hay tensiones en el s. del partido** the party is riven by internal dissension
(**e**) *(concavidad)* hollow
(**f**) *Mat* sine
(**g**) *(de la nariz)* sinus

sensación *nf* (**a**) *(percepción)* feeling, sensation; **una s. de dolor** a painful sensation; **nos embargó una s. de tristeza** we were overcome by a feeling of sadness; **tengo** *o* **me da la s. de que estoy perdiendo el tiempo** I get the feeling *o* have a feeling I'm wasting my time
(**b**) *(efecto)* sensation; **causar s.** to cause a sensation; **causar una gran s. a alguien** to make a great impression on sb
(**c**) *(premonición)* feeling; **tengo la s. de que...** I have a feeling that...

sensacional *adj* sensational

sensacionalismo *nm* sensationalism

sensacionalista *adj* sensationalist

sensatez *nf* (common) sense; **pongo en duda la s. de esta propuesta** I would have to question the wisdom of this proposal; **con s.** sensibly

sensato, -a *adj* sensible

sensibilidad *nf* (**a**) *(percepción)* feeling; **no tiene s. en los brazos** she has no feeling in her arms
(**b**) *(emotividad)* sensitivity; **tener la s. a flor de piel** to be easily hurt, to be very sensitive; **estas imágenes pueden herir la s. del espectador** some viewers may find these images disturbing
(**c**) *(inclinación)* feeling; **s. artística/musical** feeling for art/music; **tiene una s. especial para la poesía** she has a special feeling for poetry
(**d**) *(de instrumento, película)* sensitivity; **un termómetro de gran s.** a very sensitive thermometer

sensibilización *nf* (**a**) *(concienciación) (acción)* awareness-raising; *(resultado)* increased awareness; **una campaña de s. sobre los peligros del tabaco** a campaign to raise awareness about the dangers of tobacco (**b**) *(a un estímulo)* sensitization

sensibilizar [14] *vt* (**a**) *(concienciar)* to raise the awareness of; **una campaña para s. a la población sobre el problema de la violencia doméstica** a campaign to raise public awareness of the problem of domestic violence; **estamos muy sensibilizados ante el problema** we are very aware of the problem (**b**) *(a un estímulo)* to sensitize

sensible *adj* (**a**) *(susceptible)* sensitive; **yo soy más s. al frío que mi hermano** I feel the cold more than my brother; **una planta muy s. a los cambios de temperatura** a plant which is very sensitive to changes in temperature; **mis ojos son muy sensibles a la luz** my eyes are very sensitive to the light
(**b**) *(emocionalmente)* sensitive; **no se lo digas directamente, es muy s.** don't just tell her straight out, she's very sensitive
(**c**) *(evidente)* perceptible; *(importante)* significant; **pérdidas sensibles** significant losses; **muestra una s. mejoría** he has shown a notable improvement; **se espera una subida s. de las temperaturas** a significant rise in temperatures is expected; **hay una s. diferencia entre las dos culturas** the two cultures are perceptibly different
(**d**) *(instrumento, película)* sensitive

> **Falso amigo**: El adjetivo inglés **sensible** no es la traducción del español **sensible**. En inglés **sensible** significa "sensato", "práctico" o "considerable".

sensiblemente *adv* noticeably; **esta película es s. mejor que su anterior** this movie is considerably better than her last one; **has adelgazado s.** you've noticeably lost weight; **las temperaturas han subido s.** temperatures have risen quite noticeably

sensiblería *nf Pey* mushiness, sloppiness

sensiblero, -a *adj Pey* mushy, sloppy

sensitiva *nf* sensitive plant

sensitivo, -a *adj* (a) *(de los sentidos)* sensory (b) *(receptible)* sensitive

sensor *nm* sensor

sensorial *adj* sensory

sensual *adj* sensual

sensualidad *nf* sensuality; **la s. de una mirada/un baile** the sensuality of a look/a dance

sentada *nf* (a) *(protesta)* sit-in; **hacer una s.** to stage a sit-in (b) *Fam* **hacer algo de una s.** to do sth at one sitting *o* in one go

sentaderas *nfpl Méx Fam* behind, rump

sentado, -a *adj* (a) *(juicioso)* sensible, steady

(b) *(en asiento)* seated; **estar s.** to be sitting down; **espérame s. en recepción** sit and wait for me in reception; *Fam* **si crees que te voy a dejar dinero, puedes esperar s.** if you think I'm going to lend you some money, you've got another think coming

(c) *Bot* stemless

(d) *(establecido)* **dar algo por s.** to take sth for granted, to assume sth; **di por s. que ibas a venir** I took it for granted that you would be coming; **las autoridades dan por s. que es el líder de la banda** the authorities are assuming that he is the leader of the gang; **doy por s. que estás de acuerdo con mi idea** I'm assuming you agree with my idea; **dejar s. que...** to make it clear that...; **dejó s. que no estaba satisfecho con la solución** he made it clear that he was not satisfied with the solution

sentador, -ora *adj RP* becoming; **esa falda es muy s.** that dress is very becoming; **las vacaciones al aire libre suelen ser sentadoras** outdoor holidays always tend to do you a power of good

sentar [3] **1** *vt* (a) *(en asiento)* to sit; **te sentaremos al lado de mi madre** we'll sit you next to my mother (b) *(establecer)* to establish; **s. las bases para** to lay the foundations of; **sus estudios sentaron las bases de la física moderna** his research laid the foundations of modern physics; **s. precedente** to set a precedent

2 *vi* (a) *(ropa, color)* to suit; **no le sienta bien** it doesn't suit her; **ese peinado te sienta genial** that hairstyle suits you wonderfully

(b) *(comida)* **s. bien/mal a alguien** to agree/disagree with sb; **algunos consideran que una copita de vino sienta bien** some people think a glass of wine is good for you; **el café no me sienta bien** coffee disagrees with me

(c) *(vacaciones, medicamento)* **s. bien a alguien** to do sb good; **te sentaría bien tomar el aire** it would do you good to get a breath of fresh air

(d) *(comentario, consejo)* **le sentó bien** she appreciated it; **le sentó mal** it upset her; **le sentó mal que no la consultáramos** she was upset that we hadn't consulted her

3 sentarse *vpr* to sit down; **sentarse a la mesa** to sit at the table; **sentarse a hacer algo** to sit down and do sth; **siéntate** take a seat; **siéntate donde quieras** sit wherever you like

sentencia *nf* (a) *(judicial)* sentence; **dictar** *o* **pronunciar s.** to pass *o* pronounce sentence; **visto para s.** ready for judgement ►► ***s. absolutoria*** acquittal; ***s. condenatoria*** guilty verdict (b) *(proverbio, máxima)* maxim

sentenciado, -a *nm,f* **un s. a muerte/a cadena perpetua** a person who has been sentenced to death/to life

sentenciar *vt* (a) *(judicialmente)* to sentence; **s. a alguien a algo** to sentence sb to sth; **lo sentenciaron a tres años/cadena perpetua** he was sentenced to three years/life, he was given a three-year/life sentence; **lo sentenciaron a muerte** he was sentenced to death

(b) *(condenar, juzgar)* to condemn; **está sentenciado** it's doomed

(c) *(competición, partido)* to decide, to settle; **el gol que sentenció el encuentro** the goal which decided the game

sentencioso, -a *adj* sententious

sentido, -a 1 *adj* (a) *(profundo)* heartfelt; **mi más s. pésame** with deepest sympathy (b) *(sensible)* **ser muy s.** to be very sensitive (c) *(ofendido)* hurt, offended; **quedó muy s. por tu respuesta** he was very hurt by your reply (d) *RP (lesionado)* hurt; **el talonador no puede seguir jugando, está s.** the hooker is unable to carry on playing, he's hurt

2 *nm* (a) *(capacidad para percibir)* sense; **s. del tacto** sense of touch; **con los cinco sentidos** *(completamente)* heart and soul; **no tengo ningún s. del ritmo** I have no sense of rhythm; **tiene un s. muy particular de la sinceridad** he has a very peculiar notion of sincerity; EXPR **poner los cinco sentidos en algo** to give one's all to sth ►► ***s. común*** common sense; **tener s. común** to have common sense; ***s. del deber*** sense of duty; ***s. del humor*** sense of humour; ***s. de la orientación*** sense of direction; ***s. del ridículo*** sense of the ridiculous

(b) *(consciencia)* consciousness; **perder/recobrar el s.** to lose/regain consciousness; **sin s.** unconscious

(c) *(significado)* meaning, sense; **esta frase tiene varios sentidos** this sentence has several possible interpretations; **esta expresión tiene un s. peyorativo** this expression has a pejorative sense; **una frase de doble s.** a phrase with a double meaning; **en s. figurado** in the figurative sense; **en ese s.** *(respecto a eso)* as far as that's concerned; **en ese s., tienes razón** in that sense, you're right; **tener s.** to make sense; **no tiene s. escribirle si no sabe leer** there's no point writing to him if he can't read; **no tiene s. que salgamos si llueve** there's no sense in going out if it's raining; **dijo que para ella la vida ya no tenía s.** she said that life no longer had any meaning for her; **sin s.** *(ilógico)* meaningless; *(inútil, irrelevante)* pointless; **doble s.** double meaning; **un sin s.** nonsense

(d) *(dirección)* direction; **los trenes circulaban en s. opuesto** the trains were travelling in opposite directions; **de s. único** one-way; **de doble s.** two-way; **en el s. de las agujas del reloj** clockwise; **en el s. contrario al de las agujas del reloj** *Br* anticlockwise, *US* counterclockwise

sentimental 1 *adj* (a) *(persona)* sentimental; **se puso s.** he got sentimental (b) *(que expresa ternura)* sentimental; **esa medalla tiene mucho valor s.** that medal has great sentimental value (c) *(amoroso)* **aventura s.** love affair; **compañero s.** partner; **problemas sentimentales** relationship problems; **relación s.** relationship; **ruptura s.** break-up

2 *nmf* **es un s.** he's very sentimental

sentimentalismo *nm* sentimentality

sentimentalmente *adv* **está s. unido a una famosa actriz** he's romantically involved with a famous actress

sentimentaloide *adj Pey* mushy, sloppy

sentimiento *nm* (a) *(estado afectivo)* feeling; **s. de culpabilidad/soledad** feeling of guilt/loneliness; **me inspira un s. de rabia** it makes me furious; **le acompaño en el s.** my condolences; **dile que la acompaño en el s.** please give her my condolences

(b) **sentimientos** *(parte afectiva de persona)* feelings; **¡no tienes sentimientos!** you have no feelings!; **dejarse llevar por los sentimientos** to get carried away; **es una persona de buenos sentimientos** he's a kind-hearted person; **no juegues con los sentimientos de otros** don't play with other people's emotions *o* feelings

(c) *(sentido)* sense; **lo hizo por un s. del deber** she did it out of a sense of duty

(d) *(amor)* **nunca le contó sus sentimientos** he never declared his feelings to her

sentina *nf* (a) *(cloaca)* sewer (b) *(antro)* den of iniquity (c) *Náut* bilge

SENTIR [63] **1** *nm* (a) *(sentimientos)* feelings (b) *Formal (opinión)* **me gustaría conocer su s. sobre este tema** I'd like to know your feelings *o* what you feel about this matter; **el s. popular** public opinion

2 *vt* (a) *(percibir, experimentar, notar)* to feel; **¿no sientes calor con tanta ropa?** aren't you hot with all those clothes on?; **no siento los pies del frío que hace** it's so cold I can't feel my feet; **sentía cierta tensión en el ambiente** I could sense *o* feel a degree of tension in the atmosphere; **sentimos mucha alegría/pena al enterarnos** we were very happy/sad when we found out; **siempre dice lo que siente** he always says what he thinks; **los trabajadores hicieron s. su disconformidad** the workers made plain their disagreement; *Méx* **s. bonito/feo** to feel well/unwell

(b) *(lamentar)* to regret, to be sorry about; **sentimos mucho la muerte de su amigo** we deeply regret the death of your friend; **lo siento (mucho)** I'm (really) sorry; **no sabes cuánto lo siento** I can't tell you how sorry I am; **por él es por quien más lo siento** it's him I'm really sorry for; **siento que no puedas venir** I'm sorry you can't come; **siento no poder ayudarte** I'm sorry I can't help you; **siento haberle hecho esperar** sorry to keep you waiting; **sentimos mucho (tener que) comunicarle que...** *(en cartas)* we regret to inform you that...

(c) *(presentir)* to sense; **siento que hay algo que no va bien** I have a feeling *o* I sense that something's not quite right

(d) *(oír)* to hear; **sentí pasos** I heard footsteps; **no te sentí entrar** I didn't hear you come in

(e) *Am (olor, gusto)* **siento mal olor** there's a bad smell; **por el resfrío, no le siente gusto a la comida** she can't taste the food because of her cold

3 *vi* to feel; **el frío ya se deja s.** you can really feel the cold now; **la antipatía entre ellos aún se deja s.** the dislike between them is still noticeable; **sin s.** without noticing

4 sentirse *vpr* **(a)** *(encontrarse, considerarse)* to feel; **¿te sientes mal/bien?** are you feeling ill/all right?; **ya me siento mejor** I feel better now; **me siento feliz/mareada** I feel happy/sick; **después de la ducha me siento otro/otra** I feel like a new man/woman after my shower; **se siente superior** she feels superior; **me sentía obligado a ayudarle** I felt obliged to help him; **no me siento con ganas de hacer nada** I don't feel like doing anything; **me sentía morir** I felt like I was dying
(b) *Am (ofenderse)* to take offence; **se sintió mucho por lo que dijiste** he took great offence at what you said

---

seña 1 *nf* **(a)** *(gesto, indicio, contraseña)* sign, signal **(b)** *RP (señal)* deposit; **dejé una s. para que me guardaran la blusa hasta mañana** I left a deposit so they would keep the blouse for me until tomorrow; **para los arreglos de más de veinte libras, pedimos una s. del cincuenta por ciento** for repairs in excess of twenty pounds, we ask for a 50 percent deposit
2 señas *nfpl* **(a)** *(dirección)* address; **señas personales** (personal) description
(b) *(gesto)* signs; **hablar por señas** to talk in sign language; **hacer señas (a alguien)** to signal (to sb); **me hizo señas para que me sentara** he signalled to me to sit down
(c) *(indicio)* signs; **dar señas de algo** to show signs of sth; **todavía no ha dado señas de cansancio** he still hasn't shown any signs of getting tired
(d) *(detalle)* details; **para** *o* **por más señas** to be precise

---

SEÑAL *nf* **(a)** *(gesto, sonido, acción)* signal; **la s. convenida eran tres golpes en la puerta** the signal they agreed on was three knocks on the door; **cuando dé la s. empujamos todos a la vez** when I give the signal, everyone push together; **hacerle una s. a alguien para que haga algo** to signal to sb to do sth; **el guardia nos hizo una s. de** *o* **para que pasáramos** the guard signalled to us to go through ►► ***s. de alarma*** alarm signal; ***las señales horarias*** *(en la radio)* the time signal, *Br* the pips; ***señales de humo*** smoke signals; ***s. de peligro*** danger sign; ***s. de salida*** starting signal; ***s. de socorro*** distress signal
(b) *Ferroc* signal
(c) *(tono telefónico)* tone ►► ***s. de comunicando*** *Br* engaged tone, *US* busy signal; *Méx* ***s. de libre*** *Br* dialling *o US* dial tone; ***s. de llamada*** ringing tone; ***s. de*** *o* ***para marcar*** *Br* dialling *o US* dial tone; ***s. de ocupado*** *Br* engaged tone, *US* busy signal; ***s. de portadora*** carrier signal
(d) *(símbolo)* sign; **una s. de prohibido adelantar** a no overtaking sign; **en s. de** as a mark *o* sign of; **en s. de duelo/buena voluntad** as a sign of mourning/goodwill ►► ***s. de circulación*** road sign; ***s. de la cruz*** sign of the Cross; ***s. indicadora (de dirección)*** *(en carretera)* signpost; ***s. de tráfico*** road sign
(e) *(indicio)* sign; **esto es s. de que están interesados** this is a sign that *o* this shows they're interested; **dar señales de vida** to show signs of life; **el temporal no daba señales de remitir** the storm showed no sign of abating; **ser buena/mala s.** to be a good/bad sign
(f) *(marca, huella)* mark; **hice** *o* **puse una s. en las cajas con ropa** I marked *o* put a mark on the boxes with clothes inside; **el cuerpo presentaba señales de descomposición** the body showed signs of decomposition; **no quedó ni s. de él** there was no sign of him left; **no dejó ni s.** she didn't leave a trace
(g) *(cicatriz)* scar, mark; **te va a quedar s.** you'll have a scar
(h) *(fianza)* deposit; **dar** *o* **dejar una s.** to leave a deposit

---

señaladamente *adv* **(a)** *(especialmente)* especially **(b)** *(claramente)* clearly, distinctly; **su reacción fue s. hostil** her reaction was distinctly hostile

señalado, -a *adj* **(a)** *(importante) (fecha)* special; *(personaje)* distinguished **(b)** *(con cicatrices)* scarred, marked **(c)** *(lugar, hora)* agreed, arranged

señalar 1 *vt* **(a)** *(marcar)* to mark; *(hora, temperatura)* to indicate, to show; **el termómetro señalaba 10 grados** the thermometer showed 10 degrees; **la brújula debe s. el norte** the compass should indicate north; **cuando el reloj señale las doce** when the clock says twelve; **las elecciones de aquel año señalaron el comienzo de la transición** that year's elections marked the beginning of the transition
(b) *(apuntar)* to point out; **nos señaló con el dedo** he pointed at us; **no quiero s. a nadie, pero...** I don't want to point the finger at anyone, but...; **la flecha señala el camino** the arrow indicates the path; **me señaló los errores que había cometido** he showed me *o* pointed out to me the mistakes I had made
(c) *(ser el inicio de)* to mark, to signal; **las lluvias señalan la llegada del monzón** the rains signal *o* announce the arrival of the monsoon
(d) *(recalcar)* to point out; **me gustaría s. que...** I'd like to point out that...
(e) *(fijar)* to set, to fix; **aún no han señalado el día de la boda** they haven't yet fixed the date of the wedding; **señaló su valor en 1.000 dólares** he set *o* fixed its value at 1,000 dollars
(f) *(ganado)* to brand
2 señalarse *vpr (destacar)* to distinguish oneself (**por** for); **el montañero se señaló por su valor en el rescate** the mountaineer distinguished himself for his bravery in the rescue

señalero *nm Urug* indicator, *US* turn signal

señalización *nf* **(a)** *(conjunto de señales)* signs ►► ***s. vial*** *o* ***viaria*** road signs **(b)** *Ferroc* signals **(c)** *(colocación de señales)* signposting

señalizador *nm Chile* indicator, *US* turn signal

señalizar [14] *vt* **(a)** *(carretera, ciudad)* to signpost **(b)** *Ferroc* to signal

señar *vt RP* to put a deposit on; **¿puedo s. esta blusa y la vengo a buscar mañana?** may I leave a deposit on this blouse and come back for it tomorrow?

señera *nf* Catalan national flag

señero, -a *adj Formal* **(a)** *(solitario)* solitary **(b)** *(único)* unique, extraordinary; **una figura s. de la literatura hispanoamericana** an outstanding figure in Spanish American literature

seño *nf Fam* **la s.** *(maestra)* miss, the teacher; **la s. nos manda muchos deberes** the teacher gives us a lot of homework; **¡s.!** miss!

SEÑOR, -ORA 1 *adj* **(a)** *(refinado)* noble, refined
(b) *Fam (antes de sustantivo) (gran)* real; *(excelente)* wonderful, splendid; **tienen una señora casa/un s. problema** that's some house/problem they've got
2 *nm* **(a)** *(tratamiento) (antes de apellido, nombre, cargo)* Mr; **el s. López** Mr López; **los señores Ruiz** Mr and Mrs Ruiz; **¿están los señores (Ruiz) en casa?** are Mr and Mrs Ruiz in?; **dile al s. Miguel que gracias** say thanks to Miguel from me; **¡s. presidente!** Mr President!; **el s. director les atenderá enseguida** the manager will see you shortly
(b) *(tratamiento) (al dirigir la palabra)* Sir; **pase usted, s.** do come in, do come in, Sir; **¡oiga s., se le ha caído esto!** excuse me! you dropped this; **señores, debo comunicarles algo** gentlemen, there's something I have to tell you; **¿qué desea el s.?** what would you like, Sir?; **sí, s.** yes, Sir; **Muy s. mío, Estimado s.** *(en cartas)* Dear Sir; **Muy señores míos** *(en cartas)* Dear Sirs
(c) *(hombre)* man; **llamó un s. preguntando por ti** there was a call for you from a man; **el s. de la carnicería** the man from the butcher's; **en el club sólo dejaban entrar a (los) señores** they only let men into the club; **un s. mayor** an elderly gentleman; **señores** *(en letrero)* men, gents
(d) *(caballero)* gentleman; **es todo un s.** he's a real gentleman; **vas hecho un s. con ese traje** you look like a real gentleman in that suit
(e) *(dueño)* owner; *Formal* **¿es usted el s. de la casa?** are you the head of the household?
(f) *Formal (de criado, esclavo)* master
(g) *(noble, aristócrata)* lord ►► *Hist* ***s. feudal*** feudal lord; ***s. de la guerra*** warlord
(h) *(en religión)* **el S.** the Lord; **Nuestro S.** Our Lord; **¡S., ten piedad!** Lord, have mercy upon us!
(i) *(indica énfasis)* **sí s., eso fue lo que ocurrió** yes indeed, that's exactly what happened; **¡sí s., así se habla!** excellent, that's what I like to hear!; **no s., estás muy equivocado** oh no, you're completely wrong; **a mí no me engañas, no s.** you can't fool ME
3 *interj* Good Lord!; **¡S., qué manera de llover!** Good Lord, look how it's raining!

SEÑORA *nf* **(a)** *(tratamiento) (antes de apellido, nombre, cargo)* Mrs; *(al dirigir la palabra)* Madam; **la s. López** Mrs López; **¡s. presidenta!** Madam President!; **¿qué desea la s.?** what would you like, Madam?; **la s. presidenta les atenderá enseguida** the president will see you shortly; **¡señoras y señores!** Ladies and Gentlemen!; **Estimada s.** *(en cartas)* Dear Madam; **¿es usted s. o señorita?** are you a Mrs or a Miss?
(b) *(mujer)* lady; **llamó una s. preguntando por ti** there was a call for you from a lady; **la s. de la tienda** the woman from the shop; **una s. mayor** an elderly lady; **s. de compañía** female companion; **señoras** *(en letrero)* women, ladies
(c) *(dama)* lady; **es toda una s.** she's a real lady
(d) *(dueña)* owner; **la s. de la casa** the lady of the house
(e) *(ama)* mistress
(f) *(esposa)* wife; **el señor Ruiz y s.** Mr and Mrs Ruiz; **la s. de Peralta** Mrs Peralta; **mi s. esposa** my (good) wife
(g) *Rel* **Nuestra S.** Our Lady

(**h**) *(indica énfasis)* **sí s., eso fue lo que ocurrió** yes indeed, that's exactly what happened; **¡sí s., así se habla!** excellent, that's what I like to hear!; **no s., estás muy equivocada** oh no, you're completely wrong; **a mí no me engañas, no s.** you can't fool ME

---

señorear *vt (dominar)* to control, to rule

señoría *nf* lordship, *f* ladyship; **su s.** *(a un noble)* Your Lordship, *f* Your Ladyship; *(a un parlamentario)* the Honourable gentleman, *f* the Honourable lady; *(a un ministro)* the Right Honourable gentleman, *f* the Right Honourable lady; *(a un juez)* your Honour

señorial *adj* (**a**) *(majestuoso)* stately (**b**) *(del señorío)* lordly

señorío *nm* (**a**) *(dominio)* dominion, rule (**b**) *(distinción)* nobility (**c**) *Fam (personas distinguidas) Br* nobs

señorita *nf* (**a**) *(soltera, tratamiento)* Miss; **la s. Ana Martel** Miss Ana Martel; **s. Ana, no me pase ninguna llamada** Miss Martel, please don't put any further calls through; **¿es usted señora o s.?** are you a Mrs or a Miss?; **Estimada s.** *(en cartas)* Dear Madam

(**b**) *(joven)* young lady; **tu hija está hecha toda una s.** your daughter's turned into quite a young lady; **busco a la s. que me atendió ayer** I'm looking for the young lady who served me yesterday

(**c**) *(maestra)* **la s.** miss, the teacher; **la s. nos manda muchos deberes** the teacher gives us a lot of homework; **¡s.!** miss!

(**d**) *ver también* **señorito**

señoritingo, -a *nm,f Pey* spoilt brat

señorito, -a 1 *adj Fam Pey (refinado)* snooty, stuck-up

2 *nm,f* (**a**) *Anticuado (hijo del amo)* master, *f* mistress; **s. Gabriel, ¿le preparo el caballo?** master Gabriel, shall I get your horse ready?; **la señorita Paloma dijo que volvería a las ocho** mistress Paloma said she would return at eight (**b**) *Fam Pey (niñato)* rich kid

señorón, -ona *Pey* 1 *adj* high and mighty, *US* high-hat

2 *nm,f* personage, *Br* nob

señuelo *nm* (**a**) *(reclamo)* decoy (**b**) *(cebo, trampa)* bait, lure (**c**) *Arg, Bol (novillos)* = group of young lead bulls

seo *nf (catedral)* cathedral

sep. (*abrev de* **septiembre**) Sep, Sept

sepa *etc ver* **saber**

sépalo *nm Bot* sepal

separable *adj* separable, detachable

separación *nf* (**a**) *(de elementos)* separation; **es conveniente la s. entre el poder judicial y el ejecutivo** it's best for the judiciary to be independent from the government ►► *Imprenta* ***s. de colores*** colour separation; ***s. de poderes*** separation *o* division of powers

(**b**) *(en el tiempo)* separation; **se reunieron tras una s. de tres meses** they were reunited after a three month separation; **se le hizo muy difícil la s. de su compañera durante tanto tiempo** he found it very hard being apart from his partner for so long

(**c**) *(matrimonial)* separation ►► *Der* ***s. de bienes*** separate estates *(in matrimony)*; ***s. matrimonial*** separation

(**d**) *(distancia)* space, distance; **deja más s. entre los coches** leave more space between the cars; **hay demasiada s. entre las plantas** the plants are too far apart

(**e**) *(de cargo)* dismissal; **fue anunciada su s. del cargo de presidente** his removal from presidential office was announced

separadamente *adv* separately

separado, -a 1 *adj* (**a**) *(apartado)* separate; **está muy s. de la pared** it's too far away from the wall; **por s.** separately (**b**) *(del cónyuge)* separated

2 *nm,f* separated person

separador, -ora 1 *adj* separating

2 *nm,f* separator

3 *nm* (**a**) *Tec* separator (**b**) *Med* retractor (**c**) *(en carpeta)* divider

---

SEPARAR 1 *vt* (**a**) *(alejar, dividir, aislar)* to separate (**de** from); **lo han separado de sus hijos** they've taken his children away from him; **tuvo que venir la policía para separarlos** the police had to be called to break them up *o* separate them; **el muro que separa los dos campos** the wall separating *o* that separates the two fields; **s. algo en grupos/partes iguales** to divide sth into groups/equal parts; **son muchas las cosas que nos separan** there are many differences between us; **quiere s. su vida privada de su vida pública** she wants to keep her private life separate from her public life

(**b**) *(apartar, dejar espacio entre)* to move away (**de** from); **separe el cuerpo del volante** keep your body away from the steering wheel; **separa un poco las sillas** move the chairs apart a bit; **separa bien las piernas** open your legs wide

(**c**) *(desunir, quitar)* **las hojas se han pegado y no las puedo s.** the pages have stuck together and I can't separate them *o* get them apart; **separe la carne del caldo** remove the meat from the stock; **no separaba los ojos del reloj** she never took her eyes off the clock

(**d**) *(reservar)* to put aside

(**e**) *(destituir)* **s. de** to remove *o* dismiss from; **fue separado del cargo** he was removed (from his post), he was dismissed (from his job); **separaron al coronel del servicio** the colonel was removed from active service

2 **separarse** *vpr* (**a**) *(apartarse)* to move apart; **separaos un poco** move apart a bit; **separarse de** to move away from; **sepárese un poco del micrófono** don't speak too close to the microphone; **no se separen del grupo** don't leave the group, stay together with the group; **no se separaba de mí** he didn't leave my side; **jamás se separa de su osito de peluche** she never goes anywhere without her teddy bear; **es la primera vez que se separa de sus padres** it's the first time he's been away from his parents

(**b**) *(ir por distinto lugar) (personas)* to separate, to part company; *(caminos, vías, carreteras)* to diverge; **aquí se separan nuestros caminos** this is where we each go our separate way, this is where we part company

(**c**) *(matrimonio)* to separate (**de** from); *(novios, grupo musical, entidades)* to split up (**de** with); **se ha separado de su marido** she has separated from her husband

(**d**) *(independizarse) (territorio, comunidad)* to break away (**de** from)

(**e**) *(desprenderse)* to come away *o* off

---

separata *nf* pull-out supplement

separatismo *nm* separatism

separatista 1 *adj* separatist

2 *nmf* separatist

separo *nm Méx* cell

sepelio *nm* burial

SEPI ['sepi] *nf* (*abrev de* **Sociedad Estatal de Participaciones Industriales**) = Spanish governmental organization that promotes industry

sepia 1 *adj (color)* sepia

2 *nm (color)* sepia

3 *nf (molusco)* cuttlefish

sepiolita *nf Geol* sepiolite

sepsis *nf inv Med* sepsis

septentrión *nm Literario* north

septentrional 1 *adj* northern

2 *nmf* northerner

septeto *nm* septet

septicemia *nf Med* septicaemia

séptico, -a *adj* septic

septiembre, setiembre *nm* September; **el 1 de s.** 1 September; **uno de los septiembres más lluviosos de la última década** one of the rainiest Septembers in the last decade; **a principios/mediados/finales de s.** at the beginning/in the middle/at the end of September; **el pasado/próximo (mes de) s.** last/next September; **en s.** in September; **en pleno s.** in mid-September; **este (mes de) s.** *(pasado)* (this) last September; *(próximo)* next September, this coming September

septillizo, -a *nm,f* septuplet

séptimo, -a, sétimo, -a *núm* seventh ►► ***el s. arte*** the seventh art, the movies, the cinema; *ver también* **octavo**

septuagenario, -a 1 *adj* septuagenarian

2 *nm,f* septuagenarian

septuagésimo, -a *núm* seventieth; *ver también* **octavo**

septuplicar [60] 1 *vt* to multiply by seven

2 **septuplicarse** *vpr* to increase sevenfold

séptuplo *nm* septuple

sepulcral *adj* (**a**) *(del sepulcro)* **arte s.** funerary art; **una escultura s.** a funerary sculpture (**b**) *(profundo) (voz)* lugubrious; *(frío)* deathly; **reinaba un silencio s.** it was as silent as the grave

sepulcro *nm* tomb

sepultar *vt* (**a**) *(enterrar)* to bury (**b**) *(cubrir)* to bury; **el corrimiento de tierras sepultó a diez personas** the landslide buried ten people; **la avalancha sepultó el pueblo** the avalanche buried the village

sepultura *nf* (**a**) *(enterramiento)* burial; **dar s. a** to bury; **recibir s.** to be buried; **recibió cristiana s.** he received a Christian burial (**b**) *(fosa)* grave

sepulturero, -a *nm,f* gravedigger

seque *etc ver* **secar**

sequedad *nf* (**a**) *(falta de humedad)* dryness (**b**) *(antipatía)* brusqueness; **me recibió con s.** he gave me a brusque welcome

sequía *nf* **(a)** *(falta de agua)* drought **(b)** *Col (sed)* thirst

séquito *nm* **(a)** *(comitiva)* retinue, entourage; **el cantante llegó con un s. de cincuenta personas** the singer arrived with a fifty-strong entourage **(b)** *(sucesión)* **trajo consigo un s. de consecuencias** it had a whole range of consequences

SER [2]

The auxiliary verb **ser** is used with the past participle of a verb to form the passive (e.g. **la película fue criticada** the movie was criticized).

1 *v aux (para formar la voz pasiva)* to be; **fue visto por un testigo** he was seen by a witness; **la propuesta es debatida** *o* **está siendo debatida en el parlamento** the proposal is being debated in parliament

2 *v copulativo* **(a)** *(con adjetivos, sustantivos, pronombres) (indica cualidad, identidad, condición)* to be; **es alto/gracioso** he's tall/funny; **soy chileno/chiapaneco** I'm Chilean/from Chiapas; **es azul/difícil** it's blue/difficult; **sé discreta/paciente** be discreet/patient; **es un amigo/el dueño** he's a friend/the owner; **son unos amigos míos** they're friends of mine; **es el cartero/tu madre** it's the postman *o US* mailman/your mother; **soy yo, ábreme** open up, it's me; **soy Víctor** *(al teléfono)* it's Víctor; **la casa es aquella de ahí** the house is that one over there; **es un tipo muy simpático** he's a very nice guy; **¿es eso verdad?** is that true?; **eso no es cierto** that isn't true; **es obvio que le gustas** it's obvious that he likes you; **no es necesario ir** it isn't necessary to go; **es posible que llueva** it may rain; **no está mal para s. de segunda mano** it's not bad considering it's second-hand; **no pierde sus derechos por s. inmigrante** just because he's an immigrant doesn't mean he doesn't have any rights; **te lo dejo en la mitad por s. tú** seeing as *o* because it's you, I'll let you have it half-price; **por s. usted, señora, 15 euros** to you, madam, 15 euros; **que seas muy feliz** I wish you every happiness, I hope you'll be very happy; **¡será imbécil el tipo!** the guy must be stupid!; **este restaurante ya no es lo que era** this restaurant isn't as good as it used to be *o* isn't what it used to be; *RP Fam* **s. loco por algo** to be wild about sth

(b) *(con sustantivos, adjetivos) (indica empleo, dedicación, estado civil, religión)* to be; **soy abogado/actriz** I'm a lawyer/an actress; **son estudiantes** they're students; **para s. juez hay que trabajar mucho** you have to work very hard to be *o* become a judge; **es padre de tres hijos** he's a father of three; **es soltero/casado/divorciado** he's single/married/divorced; **era viuda** she was a widow; **son budistas/protestantes** they are Buddhists/Protestants; **el que fuera gobernador del estado** the former governor of the state; EXPR *Am Fam* **¿tú eres o te haces?** are you stupid or what?; EXPR *RP Fam* **¿vos sos o te hacés?** are you stupid or what?

(c) *(con de) (indica material, origen, propiedad)* **s. de** *(estar hecho de)* to be made of; *(provenir de)* to be from; *(pertenecer a)* to belong to; **un juguete que es todo de madera** a completely wooden toy, a toy made completely of wood; **¿de dónde eres?** where are you from?; **estas pilas son de una linterna** these batteries are from a torch; **¿es de usted este abrigo?** is this coat yours?, does this coat belong to you?; **los juguetes son de mi hijo** the toys are my son's; **portarse así es de cobardes** only cowards behave like that, it's cowardly to behave like that

(d) *(con de) (indica pertenencia a grupo)* **s. de** *(club, asociación, partido)* to be a member of; **¿de qué equipo eres?** *(aficionado)* which team *o* who do you support?; **soy del Barcelona** I support Barcelona; **s. de los que...** to be one of those people who...; **ése es de los que están en huelga** he is one of those on strike; **no es de las que se asustan por cualquier cosa** she's not one to get scared easily

3 *vi* **(a)** *(ocurrir, tener lugar)* to be; **fue aquí** it was here; **¿cuándo es la boda?** when's the wedding?; **la final era ayer** the final was yesterday; **¿cómo fue lo de tu accidente?** how did your accident happen?; **¿qué fue de aquel amigo tuyo?** what happened to that friend of yours?; **¿qué es de Pablo?** how's Pablo (getting on)?

(b) *(constituir, consistir en)* to be; **fue un acierto que nos quedáramos en casa** we were right to stay at home; **lo importante es decidirse** the important thing is to reach a decision; **su ambición era dar la vuelta al mundo** her ambition was to travel round the world; **tratar así de mal a la gente es buscarse problemas** treating people so badly is asking for trouble

(c) *(con fechas, horas)* to be; **¿qué (día) es hoy?** what day is it today?, what's today?; **hoy es jueves** today's Thursday, it's Thursday today; **¿qué (fecha) es hoy?** what's the date today?, what date is it today?; **mañana será 15 de julio** tomorrow (it) will be 15 July; **¿qué hora es?** what time is it?, what's the time?; **son las tres (de la tarde)** it's three o'clock (in the afternoon), it's three (pm); **serán** *o* **deben de s. las tres** it must be three (o'clock)

(d) *(con precios)* to be; **¿cuánto es?** how much is it?; **son 300 pesos** that'll be 300 pesos; **¿a cómo son esos tomates?** how much are those tomatoes?

(e) *(con cifras, en operaciones)* to be; **ellos eran unos 500** there were about 500 of them; **11 por 100 son 1.100** 11 times 100 is 1,100

(f) *(servir, ser adecuado)* **s. para** to be for; **este trapo es para (limpiar) las ventanas** this cloth is for (cleaning) the windows; **este libro es para niños** this book is for children; **la ciudad no es para mí** the city isn't for me

(g) *(con de más infinitivo) (indica necesidad, posibilidad)* **es de desear que...** it is to be hoped that...; **era de esperar que pasara algo así** it was to be expected that something like that would happen; **es de suponer que aparecerá** presumably, he'll turn up; **es de temer cuando se enoja** she's really scary when she gets angry

(h) *(para recalcar, poner énfasis)* **ése es el que me lo contó** he's the one who told me; **lo que es a mí, no me llamaron** they certainly didn't call me, they didn't call me, anyway; **¿es que ya no te acuerdas?** don't you remember any more, then?, you mean you don't remember any more?

(i) *(indica excusa, motivo)* **es que no me hacen caso** but *o* the thing is they don't listen to me; **es que no vine porque estaba enfermo** the reason I didn't come is that I was ill, I didn't come because I was ill, you see; **¿cómo es que no te han avisado?** how come they didn't tell you?

(j) *Literario (existir)* **Platón, uno de los grandes sabios que en el mundo han sido** Plato, one of the wisest men ever to walk this earth

(k) *(en frases)* **a no s. que venga** unless she comes; **tengo que conseguirlo (sea) como sea** I have to get it one way or another; **hay que evitar (sea) como sea que se entere** we have to prevent her from finding out at all costs *o* no matter what; **hazlo cuando sea** do it whenever; **de no s./haber sido por...** if it weren't/hadn't been for...; **de no s. por él no estaríamos vivos** if it weren't for him, we wouldn't be alive; **de no s. así** otherwise; **de s. así** if that should happen; **déjalo donde sea** leave it anywhere *o* wherever; **érase una vez, érase que se era** once upon a time; **dile lo que sea, da igual** tell her anything *o* whatever, it doesn't make any difference; **haré lo que sea para recuperar mi dinero** I will do whatever it takes *o* anything to get my money back; **se enfadó, y no era para menos** she got angry, and not without reason; **no sea que..., no vaya a s. que...** in case...; **la llamaré ahora no sea que luego me olvide** I'll call her now in case I forget later; **Estados Unidos y Japón, o sea, las dos economías mundiales más importantes** the United States and Japan, that is to say *o* in other words, the two most important economies in the world; **50 euros, o sea unas 8.300 pesetas** 50 euros, that's about 8,300 pesetas; **o sea que no quieres venir** so you don't want to come then?; **por si fuera poco** as if that wasn't enough; **habla con quien sea** talk to anyone; **sea quien sea no abras la puerta** don't open the door, whoever it is; **si no fuera/hubiera sido por...** if it weren't/hadn't been for...; *Am* **siendo que...** seeing that *o* as..., given that...; *Am* **siendo que tienes la plata, cómprate el vestido más caro** seeing as *o* since you've got the money, buy yourself the more expensive dress

4 *v impersonal (indica tiempo)* to be; **es muy tarde** it's rather late; **era de noche/de día** it was night/day

5 *nm* **(a)** *(ente)* being; **seres de otro planeta** beings from another planet ►► ***s. humano*** human being; ***S. Supremo*** Supreme Being; ***los seres vivos*** living things

(b) *(persona)* person; **sus seres queridos** his loved ones

(c) *(existencia)* **mis padres me dieron el s.** my parents gave me my life

(d) *(esencia, naturaleza)* being; **la quiero con todo mi s.** I love her with all my being *o*

---

seráfico, -a *adj Literario (angélical)* seraphic

serafín *nm* **(a)** *Rel* seraph **(b)** *(animal)* ***s. de platanar*** silky anteater

serbal *nm* sorb, service tree

Serbia *n* Serbia

serbio, -a 1 *adj* Serbian
2 *nm,f* Serbian
3 *nm (lengua)* Serbian

serbobosnio, -a 1 *adj* Bosnian Serb
2 *nm,f* Bosnian Serb

serbocroata 1 *adj* Serbo-Croat
2 *nmf (persona)* Serbo-Croat
3 *nm (lengua)* Serbo-Croat

serenamente *adv (tranquilamente)* calmly, serenely

serenar 1 *vt (calmar)* to calm
2 serenarse *vpr (calmarse)* to calm down; *(tiempo)* to clear up; *(viento)* to die down; *(aguas)* to grow calm

serenata *nf* (a) *Mús* serenade (b) *Fam (ruido)* **con toda esta s. de ambulancias es imposible concentrarse** with all this wailing of ambulances, it's impossible to concentrate; EXPR **dar la s.** to pester

serendipidad *nf* serendipity

serenense 1 *adj* of/from La Serena *(Chile)*
2 *nmf* person from La Serena *(Chile)*

serenidad *nf* (a) *(tranquilidad)* calm; **no perdió nunca la s.** he never lost his calm (b) *(quietud)* tranquillity, serenity

serenísimo, -a *adj* **su Alteza Serenísima** His Serene Highness, *f* Her Serene Highness

sereno, -a 1 *adj* (a) *(sobrio)* sober (b) *(tranquilo)* calm, serene (c) *(cielo)* clear; *(tiempo)* fine
2 *nm* (a) *Anticuado (vigilante)* nightwatchman (b) *(humedad)* night dew

serial *nm, CSur nf* serial ▸▸ ***s. radiofónico*** *o CSur* ***radiofónica*** radio serial

serialización *nf* serialization

serializar *vt* to serialize

seriamente *adv* seriously; **tuve que hablar muy s. con ella** I had to have a very serious talk with her

seriar *vt* to put in order

sericultor, -ora *nm,f* sericulturist

sericultura *nf* sericulture

serie *nf* (a) *(sucesión, conjunto)* series *(singular)*; *(de mentiras)* string; **ha escrito una s. de artículos sobre el tema** he has written a series of articles on the topic; **me dijo una s. de cosas** he told me a number of things
(b) *(de televisión)* series *(singular)*; **película de s. B** B-movie
(c) *(de sellos, monedas)* set; *(de grabados)* series
(d) *(producción)* run, batch; **este coche es de la primera s. que se fabricó** this car is from the first batch that was produced; **fabricación en s.** mass production; **con ABS de s.** with ABS as standard
(e) *Elec* **en s.** in series

seriedad *nf* (a) *(gravedad, importancia)* seriousness; **viste con demasiada s.** he dresses too formally (b) *(responsabilidad)* sense of responsibility; *(formalidad)* reliability; **¡qué falta de s.!** it's disgraceful!

serif, sérif *nm Imprenta* serif; **sans s.** sans serif

serigrafía *nf* (silk) screen printing

serigrafiado, -a *adj* (silk) screen printed

serio, -a 1 *adj* (a) *(grave)* serious; **es una persona muy seria** he's a very serious person; **estar s.** to look serious; **me lanzó una mirada seria** she gave me a serious look; **me tuve que poner muy seria con mis alumnos** I had to get very serious with my pupils
(b) *(importante)* serious; **es una enfermedad muy seria** it's a very serious illness; **me dio un susto muy s.** I got a very nasty shock; **una seria amenaza para la paz mundial** a serious threat to world peace
(c) *(responsable)* responsible; *(cumplidor, formal)* reliable; **son muy serios, cumplirán los plazos** they're very reliable, they'll meet the deadlines; **no son gente seria** they're very unreliable; **¡esto no es s.!** this is ridiculous!; **lo que no es s. es que ahora digan que necesitan dos meses más** what's really unacceptable is that now they're saying they need another two months
(d) *(sobrio)* sober; **un traje s.** a formal suit; **sólo ve programas serios** she only watches serious programmes
2 en serio *loc adv* seriously; **lo digo en s.** I'm serious; **en s., me ha tocado la lotería** seriously, I've won the lottery; **¿vas en s.?** are you (being) serious?; **tomarse algo/a alguien en s.** to take sth/sb seriously; **ponte a estudiar en s.** get down to some serious study

sermón *nm* (a) *(discurso)* sermon (b) *(bronca, perorata)* lecture; **echarle un s. a alguien** to lecture sb, to give sb a lecture

sermonear *vt* to give a lecture *o* ticking-off to; **me sermoneó por estar fumando** he gave me a ticking-off for smoking

serodiagnóstico *nm Med* serodiagnosis

serología *nf* serology

seropositivo, -a 1 *adj* HIV-positive
2 *nm,f* HIV-positive person; **ser un s.** to be HIV-positive

seroso, -a *adj* serous

serotonina *nf Bioquím* serotonin

sérox = **xérox**

serpentear *vi* (a) *(río, camino)* to wind, to snake (b) *(culebra)* to wriggle

serpenteo *nm* (a) *(de río, camino)* winding, meandering (b) *(de culebra)* wriggling

serpentín *nm* ***s. calentador*** heating coil; ***s. refrigerante*** cooling coil

serpentina *nf* streamer

serpiente *nf (culebra)* snake ▸▸ ***s. de agua*** water snake; ***s. de cascabel*** rattlesnake; *Fin* ***s. monetaria*** monetary snake; ***s. pitón*** python; *Prensa* ***s. de verano*** = story of questionable importance that attracts comment in newspapers during the summer months when more important news is scarce

serrado, -a *adj* (a) *(cortado)* sawn (b) *(con dientes)* serrated

serraduras *nfpl* sawdust

serrallo *nm* seraglio

serranía *nf* mountainous region

serranilla *nf Lit* = poem describing an encounter between a knight and a country girl

serrano, -a 1 *adj* (a) *(de la sierra)* mountain, highland; **aire/pueblo s.** mountain air/village (b) *Fam (hermoso)* **¡vaya cuerpo s.!** what a great bod!; *Irónico* **¡vaya cuerpo s. tengo!** I feel like death warmed up!
2 *nm,f Am* person from the mountains

serrar [3] *vt* to saw (up)

serrato *nm Anat* serratus

serrería *nf* sawmill

serreta *nf* ***s. chica*** smew; ***s. grande*** goosander; ***s. mediana*** red-breasted merganser

serrín *nm* sawdust

serrote *nm Méx* hand saw

serruchar *vt Am* to saw with a hand saw; EXPR *RP Fam* **serrucharle el piso a alguien** = to criticize another person's work in the hope of getting their job

serrucho 1 *nm* (a) *(herramienta)* hand saw (b) *Cuba (pez)* sawfish (c) *Col* **hacer s.** to be on the fiddle
2 al serrucho *loc adv Cuba Fam* **ir al s.** to go halves

serval *nm* serval

service *nm RP* customer service

servicentro *nm CAm, CSur* service station

servicial *adj* attentive, helpful

SERVICIO *nm* (a) *(prestación, asistencia, sistema)* service; **se ha suspendido el s. en la línea 1 de autobús** the number 1 bus isn't running today; **hubo que recurrir a los servicios de una agencia inmobiliaria** we had to use the services of *Br* an estate agent *o US* a real estate office; **el s. postal/hospitalario** the postal/hospital service; **lleva muchos años al s. de la empresa** she has worked for the company for several years; **estamos a su s. para lo que necesite** we are at your service if you need anything; **hacer** *o* **prestar un buen s. a alguien** *(prenda, utensilio, aparato)* to serve sb well; **nos ha ofrecido sus servicios** he has offered us his services; **por los servicios prestados** for services rendered; **prestar s. como** *o* **de** to serve as ▸▸ ***s. de asistencia técnica*** technical support; ***s. de atención al cliente*** customer service department; ***s. discrecional*** private service; ***s. a domicilio*** home delivery service; *Informát* ***s. de filmación*** service bureau; ***s. de habitaciones*** room service; ***servicios informativos*** *(de cadena de radio, televisión)* news service; ***s. de inteligencia*** intelligence service; ***s. en línea*** on-line service; ***s. de mensajería*** courier service; ***s. militar*** military service; **hacer el s. militar** to do one's military service; ***servicios mínimos*** *(en huelga)* skeleton service; ***s. de paquetería*** parcel service; ***s. posventa*** after-sales service; ***s. de prensa*** press department; ***s. público*** public service; ***s. religioso*** religious service; ***s. secreto*** secret service; ***servicios sociales*** social services; ***s. técnico*** technical assistance; ***s. de urgencias*** *Br* casualty department, *US* emergency room; ***s. de veinticuatro horas*** round-the-clock service
(b) *(funcionamiento)* service; **entrar en s.** to come into service; **estar fuera de s.** *(máquina)* to be out of order
(c) *(servidumbre)* servants; **el s. está fatal hoy en día** you just can't find the staff these days ▸▸ ***s. doméstico*** domestic help
(d) *(turno)* duty; **estar de s.** to be on duty ▸▸ ***s. activo*** *(en el ejército)* active service *o* duty
(e) *(en tenis, squash)* serve, service; **primer/segundo s.** first/second serve *o* service; **al s., Ríos** Ríos to serve; **mantener el s.** to hold one's serve
(f) *(cubierto)* place setting
(g) *(juego de tazas, platos)* **s. de café/té** coffee/tea set; **s. de mesa** dinner service
(h) *(en restaurante) (atención al cliente)* service; *(recargo)* service charge; **dan un s. pésimo** the service is awful; **el s. está incluido** service is included; **s. no incluido** service is not included

(i) **servicios** *(sector terciario)* services; **una empresa de servicios** a services company; **el sector servicios** the services sector
(j) *Esp (WC)* toilet, *US* bathroom; **¿dónde están los servicios?** where are the toilets?, *US* where's the bathroom?; **el s. de señoras/caballeros** the ladies/gents

servidor, -ora 1 *nm,f* (a) *(criado)* servant (b) *(en cartas)* **su seguro s.** yours faithfully (c) *(yo)* yours truly, me; **¿quién es el último? – s.** who's last? – I am; **Lola López – servidora** *(al pasar lista)* Lola López – here!; **s. de usted** at your service
2 *nm Informát* server ▸▸ ***s. de archivos*** file server; ***s. espejo*** mirror site; ***s. de impresora*** printer server; ***s. de listas*** list server; ***s. proxy*** proxy server; ***s. de terminales*** terminal server; ***s. Web*** Web server

servidumbre *nf* (a) *(criados)* servants (b) *(dependencia, esclavitud)* servitude

servil *adj* (a) *(obsequioso)* servile (b) *(humilde)* menial

servilismo *nm (comportamiento)* servile attitude

servilleta *nf* (a) *(de tela, papel)* napkin, *Br* serviette; **una s. de papel** a paper napkin *o Br* serviette (b) *Méx Fam (servidor)* servant; **aquí tienes a tu s. para lo que se te ofrezca** your wish is my command

servilletero *nm* napkin *o Br* serviette ring

servilmente *adv* servilely

serviola *nf (pez)* amberjack

SERVIR [47] 1 *vt* (a) *(comida, bebida)* to serve; **todavía no nos han servido** we haven't been served yet; **la cena se servirá** *o* **será servida a las ocho** dinner will be served at eight; **sírvanos dos cervezas** two beers, please; **¿te sirvo más patatas?** would you like some more potatoes?; **¿me sirve un poco más, por favor?** could I have a bit more, please?; **s. mesas** *Br* to wait at table, *US* to wait tables; **la polémica está servida** the gloves are off
(b) *(prestar servicio a)* to serve; **¿en qué puedo servirle?** *(en tienda, mostrador)* what can I do for you?; **s. a la patria/a Dios** to serve one's country/God; *Formal* **para servirle, para s. a usted** *(como respuesta)* at your service
(c) *(suministrar) (mercancías)* to supply; **le serviremos el pedido en el acto** we'll bring you your order immediately; **nuestra empresa sirve a toda la zona** our company serves *o* supplies the whole area
(d) **voy servido** *(en naipes)* stick, I'm sticking; *Fig (tengo de sobra)* I've got plenty
2 *vi* (a) *(prestar servicio)* to serve; **sirvió de ministro en el gobierno socialista** he served as *o* was a minister in the socialist government; **s. en el ejército** to serve in the Army
(b) *(valer, ser útil)* **esta batidora ya no sirve/aún sirve** this mixer is no good any more/can still be used; **esta mesa no me sirve, necesito una mayor** this table's no good *o* use to me, I need a bigger one; **s. de algo** *(cumplir la función de)* to serve as sth; **el desván le sirve de oficina** he uses the attic as an office, the attic serves as his office; **la radio me servía de distracción** the radio kept me entertained *o* served to entertain me; **s. de guía** to act as a guide; **s. para** *(utensilio, máquina, objeto)* to be for; **¿para qué sirve esto?** what's this for?; **este líquido sirve para limpiar la plata** this liquid is for cleaning silver; **¿te sirven estos papeles para algo?** are these papers any use to you?; **este pegamento no sirve para la madera** this glue is no good for wood; **yo no serviría para sacerdote** I wouldn't be any good as a priest; **no sirve para estudiar** he's no good at studying; **no s. de** *o* **para nada** to be useless; **nuestro esfuerzo no sirvió de** *o* **para nada** our effort was in vain; **de nada sirve que se lo digas** it's no use telling him; **¿de qué sirve quejarse si no nos hacen caso?** what's the point in *o* what's the good of complaining if they never take any notice of us?
(c) *(como criado)* to be in service; **tuvo que ponerse a s.** she had to go into service; **s. en palacio/en una casa** to be a servant at a palace/in a household
(d) *(en tenis, squash)* to serve
3 **servirse** *vpr* (a) *(aprovecharse, utilizar)* **servirse de algo** to make use of sth; **servirse de alguien** to use sb
(b) *(comida, bebida)* to help oneself; **¿no te sirves más?** is that all you're having?; **sírvase usted mismo** *(en letrero)* self-service; **me serví un coñac** I poured myself a brandy, I helped myself to a glass of brandy; **que cada uno se sirva lo que prefiera** help yourselves to whatever you like; **sírvase (bien) frío** *(en etiqueta)* serve chilled
(c) *Formal (tener a bien)* **se ha servido ayudarnos** she has been good enough to help us; **sírvase llamar cuando quiera** please call whenever you wish; **sírvanse cerrar la puerta** *(en letrero)* please close the door

servo *nm Tec* servo

servoasistido, -a *adj Aut* servo; **dirección servoasistida** power steering

servodirección *nf* power steering

servofreno *nm* servo brake

servomecanismo *nm* servomechanism

servomotor *nm* servomotor

sesada *nf* (a) *(de animal)* brains (b) *(para comer)* fried brains

sésamo *nm* (a) *(planta)* sesame (b) EXPR **iábrete, Sésamo!** open, Sesame!

sesear *vi* = to pronounce "c" and "z" as "s", as in Andalusia and Latin America

sesenta *núm* sixty; *ver también* **treinta**

sesentavo, -a *núm* sixtieth; *ver también* **octavo**

sesentón, -ona *Fam* 1 *adj* **un señor s.** a man in his sixties
2 *nm,f* man in his sixties, *f* woman in her sixties; **es un s.** he's in his sixties

seseo *nm* = pronunciation of "c" and "z" as an "s", as in Andalusian and Latin American dialects

sesera *nf Fam* (a) *(cabeza)* nut, *Br* bonce (b) *(inteligencia)* brains; **iqué poca s. tienes!** where's your common sense!

sesgado, -a *adj* (a) *(en diagonal)* slanted; **un corte s.** a diagonal cut, a crosswise cut (b) *(subjetivo)* biased

sesgar [38] *vt (tela)* to cut on the bias; **la senda discurría sesgando los cultivos de la ladera** the path wandered up the hillside, cutting across the fields

sesgo *nm* (a) *(oblicuidad)* slant; **al s.** *(en diagonal)* on a slant; *(costura)* on the bias (b) *(rumbo)* course, path; **preocupa el s. que está tomando el conflicto** the conflict has taken a worrying turn

sesgue *etc ver* **sesgar**

sesión *nf* (a) *(reunión)* meeting, session; *(de juicio)* sitting, session; **abrir/levantar la s.** to open/adjourn the meeting ▸▸ ***s. informativa*** *(para presentar algo)* briefing; *(después de una misión)* debriefing; ***s. plenaria*** *(de congreso)* plenary (session); *(de organización)* plenary (assembly)
(b) *(proyección, representación)* show, performance ▸▸ ***s. continua*** continuous performance; ***s. doble*** double bill, double feature; ***s. golfa*** late-night showing; ***s. de madrugada*** late-night showing; ***s. matinal*** matinée; ***s. de noche*** evening showing; ***s. de tarde*** afternoon matinée
(c) *(de actividad)* session; **s. de espiritismo** séance; **s. fotográfica** photo session

sesionar *vi* to be in session

seso *nm* (a) *(cerebro)* brain; **le volaron de un tiro la tapa de los sesos** with one shot they blew his brains out (b) *(sensatez)* brains, sense (c) **sesos** *(para comer)* brains (d) EXPR *Fam* **calentarse** *o* **devanarse los sesos** to rack one's brains; *Fam* **perder el s.: ha perdido el s. por ella** he's madly in love with her; *Fam* **sorber el s.** *o* **los sesos a alguien** to brainwash sb; *Fam* **tiene poco s.** he's not very bright

sesquicentenario *nm Formal* 150th anniversary

sestear *vi (dormir una siesta)* to have a nap

sesteo *nm (de persona)* nap

sestercio *nm Hist* sesterce

sesudo, -a *adj Fam* (a) *(sensato)* wise, sensible (b) *(inteligente)* brainy

set *(pl* **sets***)* *nm* (a) *(conjunto)* set (b) *Dep* set

seta *nf Esp* mushroom; EXPR **como setas: los teléfonos móviles proliferan como setas** mobile phones are everywhere nowadays ▸▸ ***s. de cardo*** oyster mushroom; ***s. comestible*** edible mushroom; ***s. venenosa*** poisonous mushroom, toadstool

setecientos, -as *núm* seven hundred; *ver también* **treinta**

setenta *núm* seventy; *ver también* **treinta**

setentavo, -a *núm* seventieth; *ver también* **octavo**

setentón, -ona *Fam* 1 *adj* **un señor s.** a man in his seventies
2 *nm,f* man in his seventies, *f* woman in her seventies; **es un s.** he's in his seventies

setiembre = **septiembre**

sétimo, -a = **séptimo**

seto *nm (valla)* fence; **s. (vivo)** hedge

setter ['seter] *(pl* **setters***)* *nm* setter ▸▸ ***s. inglés*** English setter; ***s. irlandés*** Irish setter

seudo- *pref* pseudo-

seudónimo *nm* pseudonym

Seúl *n* Seoul

s.e.u.o. *(abrev de* **salvo error u omisión***)* E & OE

severamente *adv* severely; **lo castigaron s.** he was severely punished; **fue criticado s.** it was harshly *o* severely criticized; **la sequía afectó s. al norte del país** the drought severely affected the north of the country

severidad *nf* (**a**) *(de persona)* strictness; *(de castigo)* severity, harshness (**b**) *(de clima)* harshness, severity; *(de enfermedad)* seriousness (**c**) *(de gesto, aspecto)* sternness

severo, -a *adj* (**a**) *(persona)* strict; *(castigo)* severe, harsh (**b**) *(clima)* harsh, severe; *(enfermedad)* serious (**c**) *(gesto, aspecto)* stern

seviche *nm* = raw fish marinated in lemon and garlic

sevichada *nf* = get-together where the main or only course is "seviche"

sevicia *nf Formal* excessive *o* undue cruelty

Sevilla *n* Seville; PROV **quien** *o* **el que se fue a S., perdió su silla** you shouldn't have gone away if you wanted to keep your place/seat

sevillana *nf* = Andalusian dance and song

sevillano, -a 1 *adj* Sevillian
2 *nm,f* Sevillian

sexagenario, -a 1 *adj* sexagenarian
2 *nm,f* sexagenarian

sexagesimal *adj* sexagesimal

sexagésimo, -a *núm* sixtieth; *ver también* **octavo**

sex-appeal [seksa'pil] *nm* sex appeal

sexar *vt* to sex

sexenal *adj* **plan s.** six-year plan

sexenio *nm* six-year period

sexi = **sexy**

sexismo *nm* sexism

sexista 1 *adj* sexist
2 *nmf* sexist

sexo *nm* (**a**) *(género)* sex; **el s. masculino/femenino** the male/female sex; **el bello s., el s. débil** the fair sex; **el s. fuerte** the stronger sex; **un organismo de s. masculino** a male organism; EXPR **esto es como hablar del s. de los ángeles** there's no point in having this discussion (**b**) *(genitales)* genitals (**c**) *(sexualidad)* sex ►► ***s. oral*** oral sex; ***s. sin protección*** unprotected sex; ***s. sin riesgo*** safe sex; ***s. seguro*** safe sex

sexología *nf* sexology

sexólogo, -a *nm,f* sexologist

sex-shop [sek'ʃop] (*pl* **sex-shops**) *nm* sex shop

sex-symbol (*pl* **sex-symbols**) *nmf* sex symbol

sextante *nm* sextant

sexteto *nm* (**a**) *Mús* sextet (**b**) *Lit* sestina

sextillizo, -a 1 *adj* sextuplet
2 *nm,f* sextuplet

sexto, -a 1 *núm* sixth ►► ***s. sentido*** sixth sense; *ver también* **octavo**
2 *nm* (**a**) *(piso) Br* sixth floor, *US* seventh floor (**b**) *(curso universitario)* sixth year; **estudiantes de s.** sixth-year students; **estoy en s.** I'm in my sixth year (**c**) *(curso escolar)* = last year of primary school, *US* ≃ sixth grade

sextuplicar [60] **1** *vt* to multiply by six
2 sextuplicarse *vpr* to increase sixfold

séxtuplo, -a 1 *adj* sixfold
2 *nm* sextuple

sexuado, -a *adj* sexed

sexual *adj* sexual; **educación/vida s.** sex education/life

sexualidad *nf* sexuality

sexualmente *adv* sexually

sexy, sexi *adj Fam* sexy

Seychelles [sei'ʃels] *nfpl* **las (islas) S.** the Seychelles

SGAE *nf* (*abrev de* **Sociedad General de Autores de España**) = society that safeguards the interests of Spanish authors, musicians etc

SGBD *nm Informát* (*abrev de* **Sistema de Gestión de Bases de Datos**) DBMS

sgto. *nm* (*abrev de* **sargento**) Sgt

sha [sa, ʃa] *nm* shah

shakesperiano, -a [ʃespi'rjano, -a] *adj* Shakespearian

shareware ['ʃerwer] *nm Informát* shareware

sheriff ['ʃerif, 'tʃerif] (*pl* **sheriffs**) *nm* sheriff

sherpa ['serpa, 'ʃerpa] *nm* Sherpa

shiatsu ['ʃiatsu] *nm* shiatsu

shií [ʃi'i] (*pl* **shiíes**) **1** *adj* Shiite
2 *nmf* Shiite

shock [ʃok] (*pl* **shocks**) *nm* (**a**) *Med* shock (**b**) *(emocional)* shock; **me llevé un s. cuando me enteré** I had a shock when I found out

shopping ['ʃopin] (*pl* **shoppings**) *nm RP* shopping centre, *US* shopping mall

short [ʃor, ʃort] (*pl* **shores**) *nm Am* shorts ►► ***s. de baño*** swimming trunks

shorts [ʃorts] *nmpl* shorts

show [ʃou, tʃou] (*pl* **shows**) *nm* show; EXPR *Fam* **montar un s.** to cause a scene

showman ['ʃouman] (*pl* **showmans** *o* **showmen**) *nm* showman

SI *nm* (*abrev de* **Sistema Internacional**) SI

si[1] (*pl* **sis**) *nm* *(nota musical)* B; *(en solfeo)* ti; *ver también* **do**

SI[2] **1** *conj* (**a**) *(condicional)* if; **si no te das prisa perderás el tren** if you don't hurry up you'll miss the train; **si viene él yo me voy** if he comes, then I'm going; **si tuviera dinero me compraría una casa** if I had a lot of money, I'd buy a house; **si hubieses venido te habrías divertido** if you had come, you would have enjoyed yourself; **si lo llego a saber** *o* **si lo sé me quedo en casa** if I had known, I would have stayed at home; **¡si me lo llegas a decir antes...!** if only you'd told me earlier...!; **quisiera que nos viéramos hoy si es posible** I'd like us to meet today, if possible; **si es tan amable de esperar un momento** if you'd be so kind as to wait a moment; **¿y si no nos dejan entrar?** what if they don't let us in?; **¿y si lo dejamos por hoy?** why don't we call it a day?
(**b**) *(en oraciones interrogativas indirectas)* if, whether; **ignoro si lo sabe** I don't know if *o* whether she knows; **pregúntale si van a venir a arreglar la fotocopiadora** ask her if *o* whether they're going to come and fix the photocopier; **no sabía si llorar o reír** I didn't know whether to laugh or to cry; **¿que si me gusta el caviar? ¡pues claro!** do I like caviar? you bet!
(**c**) *(indica protesta o énfasis)* but; **¡si te dije que no lo hicieras!** but I told you not to do it!; **¡si apenas le conoces!** but you hardly know him!; **¡si será imbécil el tipo!** the guy must be stupid!; **no, si no me importa que hablen de mí, pero...** no, it's not that I mind them talking about me, but...
2 si bien *loc conj* although, even though; **si bien la música es buena, el guión es flojo** although the music is good, the script is weak; **aceptó la oferta, si bien con poco entusiasmo** she accepted the offer, if rather unenthusiastically
3 si no *loc conj* if not, otherwise; **corre, que si no, llegamos tarde** run, or we'll be late

SÍ (*pl* **síes**) **1** *adv* (**a**) *(en respuestas)* yes; **¿vendrás? – sí** will you come? – yes, I will; **¿aún te duele? – sí** does it still hurt? – yes, it does; **claro que sí** of course; **yo digo que sí, que se lo digamos** I say we tell her; **dijo que sí con la cabeza** she nodded; **sí, quiero** *(en una boda)* I do; **¡sí, mi sargento/capitán/teniente!** yes, Sergeant/Captain/Lieutenant!
(**b**) *(para sustituir a frases afirmativas)* **creo que sí** I think so; **¿vendrá a verte? – me gustaría que sí** will she come to see you? – I'd like her to *o* I'd like it if she did; **¿están de acuerdo? – algunos sí** do they agree? – some do; **a mí no me harán caso, pero a ti sí** they won't take any notice of me, but they will of you; **¿de verdad que me sienta bien? – ¡que sí, mujer!** does it really suit me? – yes, I've told you it does!; **¿lo conseguirá? – tal vez sí, tal vez no** will he get it? – maybe he will, maybe he won't; **un día sí y otro no** every other day; **no creo que puedas hacerlo – ¡a que sí!** I don't think you can do it – I bet I can!; **pero no me negarás que la obra es divertida – eso sí** but you can't deny that the play's entertaining – that's true
(**c**) *(enfático)* **sí debo decirte que la operación es de alto riesgo** what I must tell you is that the operation is extremely risky; **tú no estás embarazada – ¡te digo que sí lo estoy!** you're not pregnant – oh yes I am!; **sí que** really, certainly; **¡esto sí que es vida!** this is the life!; **sí que me gusta** I (certainly) do like it; **éste sí que me gusta** this one I DO like; **¿usted vio lo que pasó? – sí señor, sí que lo vi** did you see what happened? – yes indeed, I certainly did; *Irónico* **¡sí, sí!** *(no me lo creo)* oh sure!; **es champán francés– ¡sí, sí, francés! aquí dice hecho en Italia** it's French champagne – sure it is, it says here it was made in Italy!
(**d**) *(en frases)* **me quedo con ello, eso sí, con una condición...** I'll buy it, but on one condition...; **eso sí que no** certainly not, no way; **van a subir la gasolina – ¡pues sí que...!** petrol prices are going up – what a pain!; *Irónico* **¿un caniche? ¡pues sí que entiendes tú mucho de perros!** a poodle? as if you knew anything about dogs!; **¿sí?** *(al contestar el teléfono)* hello?; *(¿en serio?)* really?; *(¿de acuerdo?)* all right?; **la han despedido – ¿ah sí?** she's been sacked – really?
2 *pron personal* (**a**) *(reflexivo) (de personas) (singular)* himself, *f*

herself; *(plural)* themselves; *(usted)* yourself, *pl* yourselves; **lo quiere todo para sí (misma)** she wants everything for herself; **acercó la silla hacia sí** he drew the chair nearer (himself); **lo solucionará por sí sola** *o* **por sí misma** she'll solve it by herself *o* on her own; **"menudo lío", dijo para sí** "what a mess," he said to himself; **tenían ante sí un inmenso reto** they were faced with a huge challenge
(**b**) *(reflexivo) (de cosas, animales)* itself, *pl* themselves; **la Tierra gira sobre sí misma** the Earth revolves on its own axis
(**c**) *(reflexivo impersonal)* oneself; **cuando uno piensa en sí mismo** when one thinks about oneself, when you think about yourself
3 *nm* (**a**) *(voto afirmativo)* aye; **gana el sí** the ayes have it (**b**) *(consentimiento)* consent; **dar el sí** to give one's consent; **esperaba un sí por respuesta** I had expected the answer to be yes
4 de por sí *loc adv (cosa)* in itself; **el tema es de por sí complejo** the subject is already complex in itself; **ella ya es de por sí bastante charlatana** she's already talkative enough as it is
5 en sí *loc adv* **me interesa el concepto en sí** I'm interested in the concept in itself; **la ciudad en sí carece de interés** the city itself is of no interest

---

siamés, -esa 1 *adj* Siamese; **hermanos siameses** Siamese twins
2 *nm,f* (**a**) *(de Siam)* Siamese person (**b**) *(gemelo)* Siamese twin
3 *nm (gato)* Siamese

sibarita 1 *adj* luxury-loving, *Literario* sybaritic; **tiene un estómago muy s.** he's a real gourmet
2 *nmf* bon vivant, *Literario* sybarite

sibarítico, -a *adj* luxury-loving, *Literario* sybaritic

sibaritismo *nm* love of luxury, *Literario* sybaritism

Siberia *n* Siberia

siberiano, -a 1 *adj* Siberian
2 *nm,f* Siberian

sibila *nf Mitol* Sibyl

sibilante *adj* sibilant

sibilino, -a *adj* (**a**) *(profético)* sibylline (**b**) *(incomprensible)* mysterious, cryptic

sic *adv* sic

sicalíptico, -a *adj* saucy

sicario *nm* hired assassin

SICAV [si'kaβ] *nf Fin* (*abrev de* **sociedad de inversión de capital variable**) ICVC, investment company with variable capital

Sicilia *n* Sicily

siciliano, -a 1 *adj* Sicilian
2 *nm,f* Sicilian

siclo *nm Hist (moneda)* shekel

sicoanálisis, sicoanalista *etc* = **psicoanálisis, psicoanalista** *etc*

sicodélico, -a = **psicodélico**

sicodrama = **psicodrama**

sicofanta *nf*, **sicofante** *nm* slanderer

sicofármaco = **psicofármaco**

sicofonía = **psicofonía**

sicología, sicológico, -a *etc* = **psicología, psicológico** *etc*

sicometría = **psicometría**

sicomoro, sicómoro *nm (planta)* sycamore

sicomotor = **psicomotor**

sicomotricidad = **psicomotricidad**

sicópata = **psicópata**

sicopatía = **psicopatía**

sicosis = **psicosis**

sicosomático, -a = **psicosomático**

sicotécnico, -a = **psicotécnico**

sicoterapia = **psicoterapia**

sicótico, -a = **psicótico**

sicotrópico, -a = **psicotrópico**

sicu, siku *nm Andes, Arg* panpipes

SID *nf* (*abrev de* **Servicio de Información de Defensa**) = Uruguayan defence intelligence department

sida, SIDA *nm* (*abrev de* **síndrome de inmunodeficiencia adquirida**) AIDS; **tener (el) s.** to have AIDS

SIDE *nf* (**a**) (*abrev de* **Secretaría de Inteligencia del Estado**) = Argentinian national intelligence department (**b**) (*abrev de* **Servicio de Investigación de Delitos Económicos**) = Chilean economic crime investigation department

sidecar [siðe'kar] (*pl* **sidecares**) *nm* sidecar

sideral *adj* (**a**) *(espacio, tiempo)* sidereal (**b**) *RP Fam (precio)* astronomical

siderometalúrgico, -a *adj* iron and steel manufacturing; **industria siderometalúrgica** iron and steel manufacturing industry

siderurgia *nf* iron and steel industry

siderúrgico, -a *adj* iron and steel; **el sector s.** the iron and steel industry

sidoso, -a 1 *adj* suffering from AIDS
2 *nm,f* AIDS sufferer

sidra *nf Br* cider, *US* hard cider

sidrería *nf Br* cider *o US* hard cider bar

siega *nf* (**a**) *(acción)* reaping, harvesting (**b**) *(época)* harvest (time)

siego *etc ver* **segar**

siembra *nf* (**a**) *(acción)* sowing (**b**) *(época)* sowing time

siembro *etc ver* **sembrar**

SIEMPRE *adv* (**a**) *(en todo momento, todo el tiempo)* always; **s. cenamos a las diez** we always have supper at ten; **tú s. quejándote** you're always complaining; **anda s. cambiando de opinión** she's forever *o* always changing her mind; **como s.** as usual; **hemos quedado en el bar de s.** we've arranged to meet at the usual bar; **la misma historia de s.** the same old story; **lo de s.** the usual; **somos amigos de s.** we've always been friends; **de s. se ha hecho así** it's always been done that way; **es así desde s.** it has always been that way; **hasta s.** *(hasta dentro de mucho)* farewell; *(hasta dentro de poco)* see you again soon; **te odiaré para s.** I'll hate you forever; **nos quedamos a vivir allí para s.** we settled down there for good; **por s. jamás** for ever and ever; **s. que** *(cada vez que)* whenever; *(a condición de que)* provided that, as long as; **ven a verme s. que necesites ayuda** come and see me if you ever need any help; **llámame, s. que no sea muy tarde** call me, as long as it's not too late; **prefiero ir contigo, s. que no te moleste** I'd rather go with you, if that's all right (by you) *o* if you don't mind; **s. y cuando** provided that, as long as
(**b**) *(en cualquier caso, en último extremo)* always; **s. es mejor estar preparado** it's always better to be prepared; **si no hay autobuses s. podemos ir a pie** if there aren't any buses, we can always walk
(**c**) *Am (todavía)* still; **s. viven allí** they still live there, they're still living there
(**d**) *Méx Fam (enfático)* **s. sí quiero ir** I do still want to go; **s. no me marcho** I'm still not leaving; **¿s. aceptaste la oferta?** did you accept the offer in the end *o* after all?; **s. sí que era un tumor** it did actually turn out to be a tumour

---

siempreviva *nf* everlasting flower, immortelle

sien *nf* temple

siena 1 *adj* sienna
2 *nm* sienna

siento *etc* (**a**) *ver* **sentar** (**b**) *ver* **sentir**

sierpe *nf Anticuado* serpent

sierra *nf* (**a**) *(herramienta)* saw ►► ***s. de calar*** jigsaw; ***s. circular*** circular saw; ***s. eléctrica*** power saw; ***s. de mano*** hand saw (**b**) *(cordillera)* mountain range; **la s. de Guadarrama** the Guadarrama mountains (**c**) *(región montañosa)* mountains; **se van a la s. los fines de semana** they go to the mountains at the weekend (**d**) ***S. Leona*** Sierra Leone

sierraleonés, -esa 1 *adj* Sierra Leonean
2 *nm,f* Sierra Leonean

sierro *etc ver* **serrar**

siervo, -a *nm,f* (**a**) *(esclavo)* serf ►► ***s. de la gleba*** serf (**b**) *Rel* servant

sieso *nm Esp muy Fam (ano) Br* arsehole, *US* asshole

siesta *nf* siesta, nap; **dormir** *o* **echarse la s.** to have an afternoon nap; **no me llames a la hora de la s.** don't call me at siesta time

siete 1 *núm* seven; EXPR **guardar algo bajo s. llaves** to keep sth under lock and key; EXPR **tener s. vidas (como los gatos)** to have nine lives ►► ***los s. grandes*** the G7 countries; ***las s. maravillas del mundo*** the Seven Wonders of the World; ***las s. y media, el s. y medio*** = card game, related to blackjack and pontoon, in which players aim to get seven and a half points; ***los s. pecados capitales*** the seven deadly sins; *ver también* **tres**
2 *nm (roto)* tear *(right-angled in shape)*
3 *nf* EXPR *RP Fam* **de la gran s.** amazing, incredible; *Euf* **la gran s.!** *Br* sugar!, *US* shoot!

sietemesino, -a 1 *adj* premature *(by two months)*
2 *nm,f* premature baby *(by two months)*

sífilis *nf inv* syphilis

sifilítico, -a 1 *adj* syphilitic
2 *nm,f* syphilis sufferer

sifón *nm* (a) *(agua carbónica)* soda (water) (b) *(botella)* siphon (bottle) (c) *(de WC)* trap, U-bend (d) *(tubo)* siphon

sifosis *nf inv Med* kyphosis

sifrino, -a *Ven Fam Pey* 1 *adj* posh
2 *nm,f* rich kid

SIG [siχ] *nm Informát (abrev de* **sistema de información geográfica**) GIS

sig. *(abrev de* **siguiente**) following

siga *etc ver* **seguir**

sigilo *nm* (a) *(secreto)* secrecy; **actuar con s.** to be secretive (b) *(al robar, escapar)* stealth; **con s.** stealthily; **se me acercó con mucho s.** he crept up to me

sigilosamente *adv* (a) *(secretamente)* secretly (b) *(robar, escapar)* stealthily

sigiloso, -a *adj* (a) *(discreto)* secretive (b) *(al robar, escapar)* stealthy

sigla *nf (leída deletreando)* abbreviation; *(leída silábeando)* acronym; **¿qué significan las siglas CIA?** what do the letters CIA stand for?; **VHF es la s.** *o* **son las siglas de "very high frequency"** VHF is the abbreviation for *o* stands for "very high frequency"

siglo *nm* (a) *(cien años)* century; **el s. XX** the 20th century ►► ***el s. de las Luces*** the Age of Enlightenment; ***el S. de Oro*** the Golden Age *(of Spanish literature)* (b) *Fam (mucho tiempo)* **hace siglos que no la veo** I haven't seen her for ages; EXPR **por los siglos de los siglos** for ever and ever

signar 1 *vt (firmar)* to sign
2 **signarse** *vpr* to cross oneself

signatario, -a 1 *adj* signatory
2 *nm,f* signatory

signatura *nf* (a) *(en biblioteca)* catalogue number (b) *(firma)* signature (c) *Imprenta* signature

significación *nf* (a) *(importancia)* significance (b) *(significado)* meaning

significado, -a 1 *adj* important; **un s. defensor de los derechos humanos** a noted *o* renowned champion of human rights
2 *nm* (a) *(sentido)* meaning (b) *Ling* signifier

significante *nm Ling* signifiant

significar [60] 1 *vt* (a) *(querer decir)* to mean; **la luz roja significa que está en funcionamiento** the red light means (that) it's in operation; **¿qué significa "shrapnel"?** what does "shrapnel" mean? (b) *(suponer, causar)* to mean; **eso significaría una subida de los precios** that would mean a price rise; **hacer eso significaría nuestra ruina** if we did that it would be our ruin (c) *(expresar)* to express
2 *vi (tener importancia)* **no significa nada para mí** it means nothing to me
3 **significarse** *vpr (hacerse notar)* **significarse por algo** to be known for sth; **se significó como pacifista** he showed himself to be a pacifist

significativamente *adv* significantly

significativo, -a *adj* significant; **fue muy s. que no pidiera disculpas** it was very significant that she did not apologize; **expresó su enfado con un s. gesto** he showed his anger in a meaningful gesture; **no se han producido cambios significativos en el estado del paciente** there have been no significant changes in the patient's condition

signo *nm* (a) *(señal)* sign; **el acuerdo nace bajo el s. del fracaso** the agreement is doomed to failure ►► *Ling* ***s. lingüístico*** linguistic sign
(b) *(del zodiaco)* (star) sign; **¿de qué s. eres?** what (star) sign are you? ►► ***s. del zodiaco*** sign of the zodiac
(c) *(en la escritura)* mark ►► ***s. de admiración*** exclamation mark; ***s. de dividir*** *o* ***de división*** division sign; ***s. de exclamación*** exclamation mark; ***s. igual*** *Br* equals sign, *US* equal sign; ***s. de interrogación*** question mark; ***s. más*** plus sign; ***s. menos*** minus sign; ***s. de multiplicar*** *o* ***de multiplicación*** multiplication sign; ***s. negativo*** negative sign; ***s. ortográfico*** *(acento, diéresis)* diacritic; *(punto, coma)* punctuation mark; ***s. porcentual*** percentage sign; ***s. de puntuación*** punctuation mark
(d) *(símbolo)* symbol; **un yate es s. de riqueza** a yacht is a symbol of wealth

sigo *etc ver* **seguir**

siguiente 1 *adj* (a) *(posterior)* next; **me llamó al día s.** she called me the next *o* following day; **el día s. a la catástrofe** the day after the disaster; **eso está explicado en el capítulo s.** that is explained in the next chapter (b) *(a continuación)* following; **Juan me contó la s. historia** Juan told me the following story; **lo s.** the following
2 *nmf* **el s.** the next one; **¡(el) s.!** next, please!

siguiera *etc ver* **seguir**

sij *(pl* **sijs**) 1 *adj* Sikh
2 *nmf* Sikh

siku = **sicu**

sílaba *nf* syllable ►► ***s. átona*** atonic *o* unstressed syllable; ***s. tónica*** tonic *o* stressed syllable

silabario *nm* = reader in which words are divided into syllables

silabear 1 *vt* to spell out syllable by syllable
2 *vi* to read syllable by syllable

silabeo *nm* syllabication, syllabification

silábico, -a *adj* syllabic

silba *nf* hissing

silbante *adj (respiración)* whistling

silbar 1 *vt* (a) *(melodía)* to whistle; *(como piropo)* to wolf-whistle at; **silbó una melodía** he whistled a tune (b) *(abuchear)* to whistle at; **los espectadores silbaron al árbitro** the crowd whistled at the referee; **el público silbó y abucheó al cantante** the audience hissed and booed at the singer
2 *vi* (a) *(melodía)* to whistle; **el dardo le pasó silbando** the dart whistled past him (b) *(abuchear)* to whistle, to catcall (c) *(oídos)* to ring; **me silban los oídos** my ears are ringing

silbatina *nf Andes, RP* hissing

silbato *nm* whistle; **tocar el s.** to blow the whistle

silbido *nm* (a) *(sonido)* whistle; **llamó al perro con un s.** she called the dog with a whistle; **el s. del viento** the whistling of the wind; **se oía el s. del ventilador** you could hear the whirring of the fan
(b) *(para abuchear)* whistle, catcall; **los silbidos del público eran ensordecedores** the whistling of the crowd was deafening; **su actuación fue recibida con silbidos y abucheos** her performance was greeted with hissing and booing
(c) *(de serpiente)* hiss; **la cobra emite un s. agudo antes de atacar** the cobra emits a sharp hissing sound *o* hiss before attacking

silbo *nm* (a) *(silbido)* whistle (b) *(para abuchear)* whistle (c) *(de serpiente)* hiss

silenciador *nm* (a) *(de arma)* silencer (b) *(de coche, moto) Br* silencer, *US* muffler

silenciar *vt* (a) *(acallar) (persona, protestas)* to silence; **silenciaron a los testigos ofreciéndoles dinero** they silenced the witnesses with bribes, they bought the witnesses off; **los bombarderos silenciaron las baterías enemigas** the bombers silenced the enemy batteries (b) *(ocultar, omitir) (hecho, escándalo)* to hush up; **la prensa silenció el atentado** the press hushed up the attack

silencio *nm* (a) *(ausencia de sonido)* silence; **el s. reinaba en la habitación** there was complete *o* absolute silence in the room; **¡s.!** silence!, quiet!; **¡s. en la sala!** silence in court!; **en s.** in silence; **estar en s.** to be silent; **tienes que guardar s. en clase** you have to keep quiet in class; **guardó s. sobre el escándalo** he kept silent about the scandal; **guardaron un minuto de s.** they held a minute's silence; **imponer s. a alguien** to make sb be silent; **romper el s.** to break the silence ►► ***s. administrativo*** = lack of official response to a request, claim etc within a given period, signifying refusal or tacit assent, depending on circumstances
(b) *Mús* rest

silenciosamente *adv* silently, quietly

silencioso, -a *adj* (a) *(persona)* silent, quiet (b) *(motor, coche)* quiet

silente *adj Formal* silent, quiet

sílex *nm inv* flint

sílfide *nf* sylph; EXPR **está hecha una s.** she's really slim

silfo *nm* sylph

silicato *nm* silicate

sílice *nf* silica

silícico, -a *adj* silicic

silicio *nm* silicon

silicona *nf* silicone

silicosis *nf inv* silicosis

silla *nf* (a) *(asiento)* chair ►► ***s. eléctrica*** electric chair; ***s. giratoria*** swivel chair; ***s. de manos*** sedan chair; *Esp* ***s. de niño*** pushchair; ***s. de pista*** courtside seat; ***s. plegable*** folding chair; ***s. de la reina*** = seat made by two people joining hands; ***s. de ruedas*** wheelchair; ***s. de tijera*** folding chair (b) *(para caballo)* **s. (de montar)** saddle

sillar *nm* (a) *Arquit* ashlar (b) *(lomo)* horse's back, saddle

sillería *nf* (**a**) *(sillas)* set of chairs (**b**) **la s. del coro** the choir stalls (**c**) *Arquit* masonry

silleta *nf Andes, Ven (silla)* chair, seat

sillín *nm* saddle, seat

sillita *nf (cochecito)* pushchair

sillón *nm* armchair ►► ***s. de orejas*** wing chair

silo *nm* (**a**) *(para trigo)* silo (**b**) *(para misiles)* silo

silogismo *nm* syllogism

silogístico, -a *adj* syllogistic

silueta *nf* (**a**) *(cuerpo)* figure; **esta falda realza la s.** this skirt shows off your figure (**b**) *(contorno)* outline; **se veía la s. del castillo** you could see the outline *o* silhouette of the castle (**c**) *(dibujo)* silhouette

silúrico, -a *Geol* **1** *adj* Silurian
2 *nm* **el s.** the Silurian (period)

siluro *nm* wels, *Br* wels catfish

silvestre *adj* wild

silvia *nf* wood anemone

silvicultor, -ora *nm,f* forestry worker

silvicultura *nf* forestry

silvina *nf* silvite

sima *nf* (**a**) *(cavidad)* chasm (**b**) *Geol (capa)* sima

simbiosis *nf inv* (**a**) *Biol* symbiosis (**b**) *(de personas, organismos)* symbiosis

simbiótico, -a *adj* symbiotic

simbólicamente *adv* symbolically

simbólico, -a *adj* symbolic

simbolismo *nm* (**a**) *(significado)* symbolism (**b**) *(movimiento)* Symbolism

simbolista 1 *adj* symbolist
2 *nmf* symbolist

simbolizar [14] *vt* to symbolize

símbolo *nm* symbol

simbología *nf* system of symbols

simetría *nf* symmetry

simétrico, -a *adj* symmetrical

simiente *nf* seed

simiesco, -a *adj* simian, apelike

símil *nm* (**a**) *(paralelismo)* similarity, resemblance; **establecer un s.** to draw a comparison (**b**) *Lit* simile (**c**) *(material)* ***s. piel*** artificial leather

similar *adj* similar (**a** to)

similor *nm* ormolu

similitud *nf* similarity

simio, -a *nm,f* simian, ape

SIMM [sim] *nm Informát* (*abrev de* **single in-line memory module**) SIMM

simón *nm* (**a**) *(coche de caballos)* = horse-drawn carriage for hire (**b**) *Ven Fam (moneda)* one bolivar

simonía *nf* simony

simoniz® *nf Perú* car wax

simonizar *vt Perú Fam* to wax, *US* to simonize

simpatía *nf* (**a**) *(cordialidad)* friendliness
(**b**) *(cariño)* affection; **un actor que despierta muchas simpatías** a well-liked actor; **tomar** *o Esp* **coger s. a alguien** to take a liking to sb; **ganarse** *o* **granjearse la s. de** to win the affection of; **inspirar s.** to inspire affection; **tener s. a, sentir s. por** to like
(**c**) **simpatías** *(apoyo)* sympathy; **de todos son conocidas sus simpatías por el régimen** her sympathies for the regime are well known
(**d**) *Anat* sympathy

> **Falso amigo**: La acepción más frecuente del sustantivo español **simpatía** ("cordialidad") no se traduce al inglés como **sympathy**. Los sentidos más habituales de **sympathy** son "compasión" o "comprensión".

simpático, -a *adj* (**a**) *(persona) (agradable)* nice, likeable; *(abierto, cordial)* friendly; **me cae muy s.** I think he's very nice, I find him very likeable; **estuvo muy s. conmigo** he was very friendly to me; **hacerse el s.** to come over all friendly (**b**) *(ocasión)* agreeable, pleasant (**c**) *(anécdota, comedia)* amusing, entertaining (**d**) *Anat* sympathetic

> **Falso amigo**: Salvo en la acepción de anatomía, el adjetivo inglés **sympathetic** no es la traducción del español **simpático**. En inglés **sympathetic** significa "comprensivo", "compasivo".

simpatizante 1 *adj* sympathizing
2 *nmf* sympathizer

simpatizar [14] *vi (persona)* to hit it off, to get on (**con** with); *(cosa)* to sympathize (**con** with); **no tardaron mucho en s.** they hit it off *o* took to each other straight away; **simpatiza con la ideología comunista** she has communist sympathies; *CSur Fam* **los nuevos vecinos no me simpatizan** I don't like the new neighbours much

simple 1 *adj* (**a**) *(sencillo, tonto)* simple
(**b**) *(fácil)* easy, simple; **es muy s., metes la moneda y ya está** it's quite simple, all you have to do is insert the coin
(**c**) *(sin complicación)* simple; **una decoración s.** a simple decoration
(**d**) *(único, sin componentes)* single; **dame una s. razón** give me one single reason
(**e**) *(mero)* **es un s. trabajador** he's a simple *o* an ordinary worker; **no le pedí más que un s. favor** I merely asked her a favour; **nos basta con su s. palabra** his word is enough for us by itself; **por s. estupidez** through sheer stupidity
(**f**) *Mat* prime
(**g**) *Quím* simple
(**h**) *Ling (verbo)* simple
2 *nmf (persona)* simpleton

simplemente *adv* simply; **tiene s. un resfriado** she's just got a cold; **s. por eso ya se merecería un ascenso** for that alone he would deserve promotion; **su actuación fue, s., vergonzosa** his behaviour was, quite simply, disgraceful; **es s. genial** it's simply *o* just brilliant; **s. quería que supieras que lo siento** I just wanted you to know that I'm sorry

simpleza *nf* (**a**) *(de persona)* simple-mindedness (**b**) *(dicho)* **decir simplezas** to talk foolish nonsense (**c**) *(hecho)* **confiar en ellos fue una s.** it was a foolish mistake to trust them (**d**) *(insignificancia)* trifle

simplicidad *nf* simplicity; **un aparato de una s. increíble** an incredibly simple device

simplificación *nf* simplification

simplificar [60] **1** *vt* (**a**) *(procedimiento, trámite)* to simplify (**b**) *Mat* to simplify
2 simplificarse *vpr* to be simplified

simplismo *nm* oversimplification

simplista 1 *adj* simplistic
2 *nmf* simplistic person; **ser un s.** to be simplistic

simplón, -ona *Fam* **1** *adj* naive
2 *nm,f* naive person; **ser un s.** to be naive

simposio, simposium *nm* symposium (**sobre** on)

simulación *nf* (**a**) *(fingimiento)* pretence, simulation (**b**) *Informát* simulation ►► *Am* ***s. por computadora*** computer simulation; *Esp* ***s. por ordenador*** computer simulation

simulacro *nm* simulation ►► ***s. de combate*** mock battle; ***s. de incendio*** fire drill

simulado, -a *adj* (**a**) *(fingido)* feigned; **su tristeza era simulada** he was only pretending to be sad (**b**) *(de prueba)* simulated

simulador *nm* simulator ►► ***s. de vuelo*** flight simulator

simular *vt* (**a**) *(aparentar)* to feign; **s. una enfermedad** to pretend to have an illness; **simuló que no me había visto** he pretended not to have seen me (**b**) *(copiar, emular)* to simulate

simultáneamente *adv* simultaneously

simultanear *vt* to do at the same time; **simultanea el trabajo con los estudios** she combines her work with her studies

simultaneidad *nf* simultaneousness

simultáneo, -a *adj* simultaneous

simún *nm* simoom

SIN *nf* (**a**) (*abrev de* **Servicio de Inteligencia Nacional del Perú**) = Peruvian national intelligence department (**b**) (*abrev de* **Servicio de Inmigración y Naturalización**) INS *(US Immigration and Naturalization Service)*

SIN **1** *prep* (**a**) *(con sustantivos)* without; **la gente s. empleo** the jobless, people without a job; **buscan gente s. experiencia previa** they are looking for people with no *o* without previous experience; **organizaciones s. ánimo de lucro** non-profit-making organizations; **s. alcohol** alcohol-free; **s. conservantes ni aditivos** *(en etiqueta)* free from preservatives and additives, no preservatives or additives; **estoy s. una peseta** I'm completely out of money; **estamos s. vino** we're out of wine; **muchos se quedaron s. casa** a lot of people were left homeless, a lot of people lost their homes; **cantar/tocar s. acompañamiento** to sing/play unaccompanied; **aceptó la oferta, no s. ciertas reticencias** she accepted the offer, albeit with some reservations *o* though not without some reservations; **s. más (ni más)** just like that
(**b**) *(con infinitivos, subordinadas)* without; **se marcharon s.**

despedirse they left without saying goodbye; **lleva tres noches s. dormir** she hasn't slept for three nights; **sigo s. entenderlo** I still don't understand; **s. (contar) las novelas ha escrito cinco libros** he has written five books, not counting his novels; **está s. hacer** it hasn't been done yet; **dejó una ópera s. terminar** he left one opera unfinished; **llovió todo el día s. parar** it rained non-stop all day; **los mercenarios se retiraron, no s. antes saquear varias aldeas** the mercenaries withdrew, but not before they had looted several villages; **s. que** without; **s. que nadie se enterara** without anyone noticing; **no me voy de aquí s. que me lo expliquen** I'm not leaving without an explanation, I'm not leaving until I get an explanation

2 **sin embargo** *loc conj* (**a**) *(no obstante)* however, nevertheless; **es, sin s., uno de los mejores jugadores del equipo** he is, however *o* nevertheless, one of the best players in the team; **te engaña y, sin s., te quiere** he cheats on you, and yet he loves you; **sin s., es un buen chico** he's a good lad though

(**b**) *(por el contrario)* on the other hand; **los ingresos han aumentado y, sin s., los gastos se han mantenido al mismo nivel** income has increased, while on the other hand expenses have remained largely the same

---

sinagoga *nf* synagogue

Sinaí *nm* **el S., la península del S.** the Sinai Peninsula; **el monte S.** Mount Sinai

sinalefa *nf Lit* elision

sinaloense 1 *adj* of/from Sinaloa *(Mexico)*
2 *nmf* person from Sinaloa *(Mexico)*

sinapismo *nm (emplasto)* mustard plaster, *Espec* sinapism

sinapsis *nf inv Fisiol* synapse

sinartrosis *nf inv Anat* synarthrosis

sinceramente *adv* sincerely; **te felicitó s.** (I offer you) my most sincere congratulations; **s., preferiría no ir** to be honest, I'd rather not go

sincerarse *vpr (hablar abiertamente)* to talk openly (**con** to); *(revelar sentimientos)* to open one's heart (**con** to); **se sinceró con la prensa** he talked openly to the press

sinceridad *nf* sincerity; **con toda s.** in all honesty *o* sincerity

sincero, -a *adj* sincere; **para serte s.,...** to be honest *o* frank,...

sinclinal *Geol* 1 *adj* synclinal
2 *nm* syncline

síncopa *nf* (**a**) *(en palabra)* syncope (**b**) *Mús* syncopation

sincopado, -a *adj* syncopated

sincopar *vt* to syncopate

síncope *nm* (**a**) *Med* blackout; **le dio un s.** he blacked out (**b**) *Lit* syncope

sincrético, -a *adj* syncretic

sincretismo *nm* syncretism

sincronía *nf* (**a**) *(simultaneidad)* simultaneity (**b**) *Ling* synchrony

sincrónico, -a *adj* (**a**) *(simultáneo)* simultaneous; *(coordinado)* synchronous (**b**) *Ling* synchronic

sincronismo *nm (simultaneidad)* simultaneity

sincronización *nf* synchronization

sincronizar [14] *vt (coordinar)* to synchronize; **sincronizaron los relojes** they synchronized their watches

síncrono, -a *adj Informát* synchronous

sindicación *nf* (**a**) *(afiliación)* union affiliation (**b**) *Andes, RP, Ven (inculpación)* accusation, charge

sindicado, -a *adj* (**a**) *(trabajador)* **estar/no estar s.** to belong/not to belong to a (*Br* trade *o US* labor) union, to be/not to be unionized (**b**) *Fin (préstamo, crédito)* syndicated (**c**) *Andes, RP, Ven (inculpado)* accused, charged

sindical *adj* (*Br* trade *o US* labor) union; **dirigente s.** union leader; **organización s.** *Br* trade-union *o US* labor-union organization

sindicalismo *nm* unionism, *Br* trade unionism

sindicalista 1 *adj* union
2 *nmf* union member, *Br* trade unionist

sindicalización *nf* unionization

sindicar[1] [60], **sindicalizar** [14] 1 *vt* to unionize
2 **sindicarse** *vpr* to join a union

sindicar[2] *vt Andes, RP, Ven* to accuse; **s. a alguien de algo** to accuse sb of sth

sindicato *nm* (**a**) *(de trabajadores)* union, *Br* trade union, *US* labor union ►► ***s. amarillo*** yellow union, = conservative trade union that leans towards the employers' interests; *Méx* ***s. blanco*** = union which serves the interests of the employers rather than of the workers; *Méx* ***s. charro*** = union which serves the interests of the employers rather than of the workers; ***s. de estudiantes*** students' union; ***s. obrero*** blue-collar union; *Esp* ***s. vertical*** = workers' and employers' union during the Franco period
(**b**) *Fin* ***s. de bancos*** banking syndicate

sindicatura *nf (de una quiebra)* receivership

síndico *nm* (**a**) *(representante)* community representative (**b**) *(administrador)* (official) receiver (**c**) *Econ* trustee ►► ***s. de la Bolsa*** Chairman of the Stock Exchange

síndrome *nm* syndrome ►► ***s. de abstinencia*** withdrawal symptoms; ***s. de Down*** Down's syndrome; ***s. del edificio enfermo*** sick building syndrome; ***s. de Estocolmo*** Stockholm syndrome; ***s. de estrés postraumático*** post-traumatic stress disorder; ***s. de fatiga crónica*** ME, myalgic encephalomyelitis; ***s. de inmunodeficiencia adquirida*** acquired immune deficiency syndrome; ***s. de la muerte súbita infantil*** sudden infant death syndrome, cot death; ***s. premenstrual*** premenstrual syndrome, premenstrual tension; ***s. del túnel carpiano*** carpal tunnel syndrome; ***s. tóxico*** = toxic syndrome caused by ingestion of adulterated rapeseed oil in Spain in the 1980s

sinécdoque *nf* synecdoche

sinecura *nf* sinecure

sine die 1 *adj* **un aplazamiento s.** an indefinite postponement
2 *adv* indefinitely

sine qua non *loc adj* **es condición s. para poder participar** it is a sine qua non for participation

sinéresis *nf inv* syneresis

sinergia *nf* synergy

sinergismo *nm* synergism

sinestesia *nf* synaesthesia

sinfín *nm* **un s. de problemas** no end of problems; **recibió un s. de regalos** she got hundreds of presents

sínfisis *nf Anat* **s. púbica** pubic symphysis

sinfonía *nf* symphony; **una s. de luz y color** a symphony of light and colour

sinfónica *nf* symphony orchestra

sinfónico, -a *adj* symphonic

sinfonola *nf Méx* jukebox

singani *nm Bol* grape brandy

Singapur *n* Singapore

singapurense 1 *adj* Singaporean
2 *nmf* Singaporean

singar *vi Ven muy Fam* to screw

singladura *nf* (**a**) *Náut (distancia)* day's run (**b**) *Náut (día)* nautical day (**c**) *(dirección)* course; **se inicia una nueva s. en la compañía** the company is entering a new era

single ['singel] *nm* (**a**) *(disco)* single (**b**) *CSur (habitación)* single room

singular 1 *adj* (**a**) *(raro)* peculiar, odd; **un hombre s.** a peculiar man (**b**) *(único)* unique; **tiene dotes singulares de cantante** she has unique talent as a singer (**c**) **s. batalla** single combat (**d**) *Gram* singular
2 *nm Gram* singular; **en s.** in the singular

singularidad *nf* (**a**) *(rareza, peculiaridad)* peculiarity, oddness; **una de las singularidades de esta especie** one of the special characteristics of this species (**b**) *(exclusividad)* uniqueness

singularizar [14] 1 *vt (distinguir)* to distinguish, to single out
2 *vi (particularizar)* **¡no singularices!** it's not just me/you/*etc*, you know!
3 **singularizarse** *vpr* to stand out, to be conspicuous (**por** because of); **la iglesia se s. por su planta circular** the church stands out for its circular floor plan

singularmente *adv* (**a**) *(raramente)* oddly (**b**) *(únicamente)* uniquely

sinhueso *nf Fam* **la s.** the tongue; EXPR **darle a la s.** to rabbit on

siniestra *nf Anticuado* left hand

siniestrabilidad *nf* accident rate

siniestrado, -a 1 *adj (edificio)* ruined, destroyed; **el coche s. viajaba en dirección contraria** the car that caused the accident was driving on the wrong side of the road; **los pilotos consiguieron salir del avión s.** the pilots managed to escape from the wreckage of the plane
2 *nm,f* (accident) victim

siniestralidad *nf* accident rate

siniestro, -a 1 *adj* (**a**) *(malo)* sinister (**b**) *(desgraciado)* disastrous (**c**) *(izquierdo)* left
2 *nm* (**a**) *(daño, catástrofe)* disaster; *(accidente de coche)* accident;

(incendio) fire; *(atentado)* terrorist attack (**b**) *(en seguros)* loss ►► ***s. total*** total loss; **mi taxi fue declarado s. total** my cab was declared a write-off

sinnúmero *nm* **un s. de problemas** no end of problems; **recibieron un s. de quejas** they received countless *o* innumerable complaints

sino[1] *nm* fate, destiny; **ése parece ser mi s.** that seems to be my fate *o* destiny

sino[2] *conj* (**a**) *(para contraponer)* **no lo hizo él, s. ella** he didn't do it, she did; **no sólo es listo, s. también trabajador** he's not only clever but also hardworking; **no vino, s. que dejó un recado** he didn't come, he left a message; **no sólo uno, s. tres** not one, but three
(**b**) *(para exceptuar)* **¿quién s. tú lo haría?** who else but you would do it?; **no quiero s. que se haga justicia** I only want justice to be done; **esto no hace s. confirmar nuestras sospechas** this only serves to confirm our suspicions

sínodo *nm* synod

sinología *nf* Sinology

sinólogo, -a *nm,f* Sinologist

sinonimia *nf* synonymy

sinónimo, -a 1 *adj* synonymous; **ser s. de algo** to be synonymous with sth
2 *nm* synonym

sinopsis *nf inv* (**a**) *(resumen)* synopsis (**b**) *Urug (corto)* trailer

sinóptico, -a *adj* synoptic; **cuadro s.** tree diagram

sinovial *adj Anat* synovial

sinovitis *nf inv Med* synovitis

sinpa *nm Fam* **hacer un s.** to leg it without paying, *Br* to do a runner

sinrazón *nf (falta de sentido)* senselessness; **es una s. que lo hagas tú solo** it's ridiculous that you should do it on your own

sinsabores *nmpl* trouble, upsetting experiences; **ese trabajo me causó muchos s.** the job gave me a lot of headaches; **no tardó en descubrir los s. de la vida adulta** she soon discovered the disappointments of adult life

sinsentido *nm* **eso es un s.** that doesn't make sense; **decir un s.** to say something that doesn't make sense

sinsonte *nm* mockingbird

sintáctico, -a *adj* syntactic

sintagma *nm* syntagma, syntagm ►► ***s. nominal*** noun phrase; ***s. verbal*** verb phrase

sintagmático, -a *adj* syntagmatic

sintasol® *nm* linoleum, lino

sintaxis *nf inv* syntax

síntesis *nf inv* (**a**) *(resumen)* synthesis; **en s.** in short; **esta obra hace una s. de sus ideas sobre el tema** this work draws together his ideas on the subject ►► *Ling* ***s. del habla*** speech synthesis (**b**) *Filosofía* synthesis (**c**) *Quím* synthesis (**d**) *Med* synthesis

sintéticamente *adv* synthetically

sintético, -a *adj* (**a**) *(artificial)* synthetic (**b**) *(conciso)* concise

sintetizador, -ora 1 *adj* synthesizing
2 *nm* synthesizer

sintetizar [14] *vt* (**a**) *(resumir)* to summarize; *(reunir)* to draw together (**b**) *(fabricar artificialmente)* to synthesize (**c**) *Filosofía* to synthesize (**d**) *Quím* to synthesize

sintiera *etc ver* **sentir**

sintoísmo *nm* Shintoism

sintoísta 1 *adj* Shintoist
2 *nmf* Shintoist

síntoma *nm* (**a**) *(de enfermedad)* symptom; **presenta síntomas de congelación en el pie** his foot shows signs of frostbite (**b**) *(señal, signo)* sign; **hay síntomas de mejoría en la economía** there are signs of improvement in the economy

sintomático, -a *adj* symptomatic

sintomatología *nf* symptoms

sintonía *nf* (**a**) *(música)* theme tune, *Br* signature tune; **la s. del telediario** the TV news theme (tune) (**b**) *(conexión)* tuning; **están ustedes en la s. de Radio 4** this is Radio 4 (**c**) *(compenetración)* harmony; **sus ideas están en s. con las mías** her ideas are in line with mine; **sus ideas están en sintonía con la voluntad de la mayoría** her ideas are in tune with the wishes of the majority

sintonización *nf* (**a**) *(conexión)* tuning (**b**) *(compenetración)* **la s. entre los dos es perfecta** the two of them are really on the same wavelength

sintonizador *nm* tuner, tuning dial

sintonizar [14] 1 *vt (conectar)* to tune in to; **sintonizan ustedes Radio 4** this is Radio 4
2 *vi* (**a**) *(conectar)* to tune in (**con** to) (**b**) *(compenetrarse)* **sintonizaron muy bien** they clicked straight away; **s. en algo (con alguien)** to be on the same wavelength (as sb) about sth

sinuosidad *nf* bend, wind

sinuoso, -a *adj* (**a**) *(camino)* winding (**b**) *(movimiento)* sinuous (**c**) *(disimulado)* devious

sinusitis *nf inv* sinusitis

sinusoide *nf* sinusoid

sinvergüenza 1 *adj* (**a**) *(canalla)* shameless (**b**) *(fresco, descarado)* cheeky
2 *nmf* (**a**) *(canalla)* scoundrel; **ser un s.** to be shameless (**b**) *(fresco, descarado)* cheeky person; **ser un s.** to be a cheeky rascal *o* so-and-so; **ese s. me ha quitado el bocadillo** that cheeky rascal *o* so-and-so stole my sandwich

sinvergüenzada *nf Am Fam* dirty trick

Sión *n* Zion

sionismo *nm* Zionism

sionista 1 *adj* Zionist
2 *nmf* Zionist

sioux ['siu(k)s] 1 *adj inv* Sioux
2 *nmf inv* Sioux

siquiatra, siquiatría *etc* = **psiquiatra, psiquiatría** *etc*

síquico, -a = **psíquico**

siquiera 1 *conj (aunque)* even if; **ven s. por pocos días** do come, even if it's only for a few days
2 *adv (por lo menos)* at least; **dime s. tu nombre** (you could) at least tell me your name; **no tiene s. dónde dormir** he doesn't even have a place to sleep; **ni (tan) s.** not even; **no me permiten ni (tan) s. fumar** they don't even let me smoke; **ni (tan) s. me hablaron** they didn't even speak to me; **¿te saludó? – ni (tan) s. eso** did she say hello to you? – no, not even that; **no quiso ni (tan) s. saludarlo** she would not so much as say hello to him

siquis = **psiquis**

sirena *nf* (**a**) *Mitol* mermaid, siren (**b**) *(señal)* siren

sirga *nf* towrope

Siria *n* Syria

siriar *vt Perú Fam* to chat up

sirimiri *nm* drizzle

siringa *nf Andes Bot* rubber tree

sirio, -a 1 *adj* Syrian
2 *nm,f* Syrian

sirlero, -a *nm,f Fam* = thug who carries a knife

siroco *nm (viento)* sirocco; EXPR *Fam* **dar el s.: le ha dado el s.** she's had a brainstorm

sirope *nm* golden syrup ►► ***s. de chocolate*** *(para helado)* chocolate sauce; ***s. de fresa*** *(para helado)* strawberry sauce

sirviente, -a *nm,f* servant

sirviera *etc ver* **servir**

sirvo *etc ver* **servir**

sisa *nf* (**a**) *(de manga)* armhole (**b**) *(de dinero)* pilfering

sisal *nm* sisal

sisar *Esp* 1 *vt* to pilfer
2 *vi* to pilfer

sisear 1 *vt* to hiss
2 *vi* to hiss

siseo *nm (de serpiente, cinta magnética, aire)* hiss; *(de tela, brisa)* rustle; **el s. del público le puso muy nervioso** the hissing from the audience really flustered him

sísmico, -a *adj* seismic; **zona sísmica** earthquake zone

sismo *nm* earthquake

sismográfico, -a *adj* seismographic

sismógrafo *nm* seismograph

sismología *nf* seismology

sisón, -ona 1 *adj* pilfering
2 *nm,f (ladrón)* pilferer, petty thief
3 *nm (ave)* little bustard

sistema 1 *nm* (**a**) *(conjunto ordenado)* system ►► ***s. de apertura retardada*** time lock; ***s. de apoyo*** support system; ***el s. bancario*** the banking system; *Astron* ***s. binario*** *(de estrellas)* binary system; ***s. cegesimal*** *(de unidades)* CGS system; ***s. de coordenadas*** coordinate system; ***s. decimal*** decimal system; *TV* ***s. dual*** bilingual broadcasting;

s. fiscal tax system; ***el S. Ibérico*** the Iberian chain; ***s. impositivo*** tax system; ***s. internacional de unidades*** SI system; ***s. métrico (decimal)*** metric (decimal) system; ***S. Monetario Europeo*** European Monetary System; ***s. montañoso*** mountain chain *o* range; ***s. periódico (de los elementos)*** periodic table (of elements); ***s. planetario*** planetary system; ***s. político*** political system; ***s. de referencia*** frame of reference; ***s. de seguridad*** security system; ***s. solar*** solar system; ***s. de transportes*** transport system; ***s. tributario*** tax system

(**b**) *Anat* system ►► ***s. cardiovascular*** cardiovascular system; ***s. circulatorio*** circulatory system; ***s. endocrino*** endocrine system; ***s. inmunológico*** immune system; ***s. linfático*** lymphatic system; ***s. nervioso*** nervous system; ***s. nervioso central*** central nervous system

(**c**) *(método, orden)* method; **trabajar con s.** to work methodically

(**d**) *Informát* system ►► ***s. de alimentación ininterrumpida*** uninterruptible power supply; ***s. de almacenamiento*** storage system; ***s. de archivos jerárquicos*** hierarchical file system; ***s. de autor*** authoring system; ***s. binario*** binary system; ***s. experto*** expert system; ***s. de gestión de bases de datos*** database management system; ***s. hexadecimal*** hexadecimal system, base 16; ***s. multiprocesador*** multiprocessor system; ***s. multiusuario*** multi-user system; ***s. de nombres de dominio*** domain name system; ***s. operativo*** operating system

(**e**) *Ling* system

2 por sistema *loc adv* systematically; **me lleva la contraria por s.** he always argues with everything I say

sistemáticamente *adv* (**a**) *(de manera sistemática)* systematically (**b**) *(invariablemente)* invariably; **me despierto s. a las ocho** I invariably wake up at eight o'clock

sistemático, -a *adj* (**a**) *(que sigue sistema)* systematic (**b**) *(persona)* systematic

sistematización *nf* systematization

sistematizar [14] *vt* to systematize

sistémico, -a *adj* systemic

sístole *nf Fisiol* systole

sitar *nm* sitar

sitiado, -a *adj* besieged

sitiador, -ora 1 *adj* besieging

2 *nm,f* besieger

sitial *nm Formal* seat of honour

sitiar *vt* (**a**) *(cercar)* to besiege; **sitiaron el castillo** they laid siege to *o* besieged the castle (**b**) *(acorralar)* to surround

sitio *nm* (**a**) *(lugar)* place; **lo tengo que haber dejado en algún s.** I must have left it somewhere; **estuve una hora buscando un s. para aparcar** it took me an hour to find somewhere to park; **cambiar de s. (con alguien)** to change places (with sb); **cambié los muebles de s.** I changed the furniture round; **en cualquier s.** anywhere; **en ningún s.** nowhere; **en otro s.** elsewhere; **en todos los sitios** everywhere; EXPR *Fam* **en el s.: un camión lo atropelló y lo dejó en el s.** he was hit by a truck and died on the spot; **le dio un ataque al corazón y se quedó en el s.** she had a heart attack and dropped dead on the spot; EXPR *Fam* **poner a alguien en su s.** to put sb in their place

(**b**) *(asiento)* place, seat; **está sentado en mi s.** you're sitting in my place *o* seat; **no queda ni un s. (libre)** there isn't a single free seat; **¿me guardas un s.?** will you save me a place *o* seat?

(**c**) *(espacio)* room, space; **aquí hay s. para tres personas** there's room *o* space for three people here; **no va a haber s. para todos** there isn't going to be enough room *o* space for everybody; **hacer s. a alguien** to make room for sb; **ocupa mucho s.** it takes up a lot of room *o* space; **no queda más s.** there's no more room; **no tengo s. para tantos libros** I don't have enough room *o* space for all those books

(**d**) *(cerco)* siege

(**e**) *Informát* site ►► ***s. web*** website

(**f**) *Méx (granja)* small farm

(**g**) *Méx (parada de taxis)* taxi *Br* rank *o US* stand

(**h**) *Chile (terreno) Br* plot of land, *US* lot

sito, -a *adj* located

situación *nf* (**a**) *(circunstancias)* situation; *(legal, social)* status; **estar en s. de hacer algo** *(en general)* to be in a position to do sth; *(enfermo, borracho)* to be in a fit state to do sth; **estar en una s. privilegiada** to be in a privileged position ►► ***s. económica*** economic situation; ***s. límite*** extreme *o* critical situation

(**b**) *(ubicación)* location; **la tienda está en una s. muy céntrica** the shop is in a very central location

situado, -a *adj* (**a**) *(ubicado)* located; **estar bien s.** *(casa)* to be conveniently located (**b**) *(acomodado)* comfortably off; **estar bien s.** to be well-placed

situar [4] **1** *vt* (**a**) *(colocar)* to place, to put; *(edificio, ciudad)* to site, to locate; **los arqueólogos sitúan el antiguo teatro en el centro de la ciudad** archaeologists place the ancient theatre in the centre of the town; **situó la acción de la novela en la Edad Media** he set the novel in the Middle Ages; **me suena pero no lo sitúo** he sounds familiar, but I can't place him

(**b**) *(en clasificación)* **su victoria les sitúa en el primer puesto** their win moves them up to first place; **la nueva obra lo sitúa entre los artistas más importantes de su generación** his latest work places him among the most important artists of his generation

2 situarse *vpr* (**a**) *(colocarse)* to take up position; **los agentes se situaron en las cercanías del banco** the police officers took up position in the vicinity of the bank

(**b**) *(ubicarse)* to be located; **está cerca de la plaza, ¿te sitúas?** it's near the square, do you know where I mean?

(**c**) *(desarrollarse) (acción)* to be set; **la acción se sitúa en la Segunda Guerra Mundial** the action is set during the Second World War

(**d**) *(acomodarse, establecerse)* to get oneself established

(**e**) *(en clasificación)* to be placed; **se situó en el tercer puesto** he was placed third

siútico, -a *adj Chile Fam* stuck-up

S.J. *(abrev de* **Societatis Jesu**) SJ

skateboard [es'keitβor] (*pl* **skateboards**), *RP* **skate** [es'keit] *nm* (**a**) *(tabla)* skateboard (**b**) *(deporte)* skateboarding

skay [es'kai] *nm* Leatherette®

sketch [es'ketʃ] (*pl* **sketches**) *nm (escena)* sketch

skin head [es'kinχeð] (*pl* **skin heads**) *nmf* skinhead

S.L. *nf (abrev de* **sociedad limitada**) *Br* ≃ Ltd, *US* ≃ Inc

slack [es'lak] (*pl* **slacks**) *nm Col* slacks; **llevaba un s. blanco** he was wearing white slacks

slalom [es'lalom] (*pl* **slaloms**) *nm Dep* slalom ►► ***s. especial*** special slalom; ***s. gigante*** giant slalom

Slam [es'lam] *nm Dep* **el Gran S.** the Grand Slam

sleeping [es'lipin] (*pl* **sleepings**) *nm Andes, Méx* sleeping bag

slip [es'lip] (*pl* **slips**) *nm* (**a**) *(calzoncillo)* briefs *(men's)*; **compré un s.** I bought some briefs, I bought a pair of briefs (**b**) *(bañador)* swimming trunks; **trae un s.** bring some swimming trunks, bring a pair of swimming trunks

S.M. *(abrev de* **Su Majestad**) HM

smash [es'maʃ] (*pl* **smashes**) *nm Dep* smash

SME *nm (abrev de* **Sistema Monetario Europeo**) EMS

SMI *nm (abrev de* **Sistema Monetario Internacional**) IMS

smog [es'moɣ] (*pl* **smogs**) *nm* smog

s/n *(abrev de* **sin número**) = abbreviation used in addresses after the street name, where the building has no number

snob [es'noβ] **1** *adj* **es muy s.** he's always trying to look trendy and sophisticated

2 *nmf* = person who wants to appear trendy and sophisticated

snobismo [esno'βismo] *nm* **sólo lo hace por s.** he's just doing that because he thinks it's trendy and sophisticated

snorkel [es'norkel] (*pl* **snorkels**) *nm* (**a**) *(actividad)* snorkelling; **hacer s.** to go snorkelling (**b**) *(tubo)* snorkel

snowboard [es'nouβor] (*pl* **snowboards**) *nm* (**a**) *(tabla)* snowboard (**b**) *(deporte)* snowboarding

SO *(abrev de* **Sudoeste**) SW

so 1 *prep* under; **so pena de muerte/excomunión** on pain of death/excommunication; **so pretexto de** under the pretext of

2 *adv* **¡so tonto!** you idiot!

3 *interj* **¡so, caballo!** whoa!

soasar *vt* to roast lightly

soba *nf Fam (paliza, derrota)* hiding; **dar una s. a alguien** to give sb a good hiding

sobaco *nm* armpit

sobado, -a *adj* (**a**) *(cuello, puños)* worn, shabby; *(libro)* dog-eared (**b**) *(argumento, tema)* well-worn, hackneyed (**c**) *Esp Fam (dormido)* asleep; **me quedé s. viendo la televisión** I crashed out in front of the TV

sobadora *nf RP* bread kneading machine

sobajar, sobajear *vt Andes, CAm, Méx, Ven* (**a**) *(humillar)* to humiliate (**b**) *(sobar)* to paw

sobao *nm (dulce)* = small, flat, square sponge cake

sobaquera *nf* (**a**) *(refuerzo)* = reinforcement added to the underarm of a garment (**b**) *(apertura)* armhole (**c**) *(para pistola)* shoulder holster

sobaquina *nf Fam* body odour, BO

sobar **1** *vt* (**a**) *(toquetear)* to finger, to paw (**b**) *Fam (persona)* to paw, to touch up (**c**) *(ablandar)* to soften (**d**) *Fam (pegar, derrotar)* to give a hiding (**e**) *Méx, RP (frotar)* to scrub (**f**) *RP (amasar)* to knead
2 *vi Esp Fam Br* to kip, *US* to catch some zees

sobe, sobeo *nm* (**a**) *Fam (toqueteo)* pawing, touching up (**b**) *(correa)* strap

soberanamente *adv* (**a**) *(independientemente)* independently, free from outside interference (**b**) *(enormemente)* **aburrirse s.** to be bored stiff

soberanía *nf* sovereignty; **la s. popular** the sovereignty of the people

soberano, -a **1** *adj* (**a**) *(independiente)* sovereign (**b**) *(belleza, calidad)* supreme, unrivalled (**c**) *Fam (grande)* massive; **una soberana paliza** an almighty thrashing; **decir/hacer una soberana tontería** to say/do something unbelievably stupid; **fue un s. aburrimiento** it was mindnumbingly boring
2 *nm,f* sovereign

soberbia *nf* (**a**) *(arrogancia)* pride, arrogance (**b**) *(magnificencia)* grandeur, splendour

soberbio, -a **1** *adj* (**a**) *(arrogante)* proud, arrogant (**b**) *(magnífico)* superb, magnificent
2 *nm,f (persona)* proud *o* arrogant person; **es un s.** he's proud *o* arrogant

sobetear *vt Fam* **no sobetees esa manzana** stop playing with that apple

sobeteo *nm Fam* **de tanto s. has dejado el vaso sucísimo** you've messed around with that glass so much you've made it filthy

sobón, -ona *Fam* **1** *adj* touchy-feely; **es muy s.** he's a great one for hugging and kissing
2 *nm,f* groper

sobornable *adj* bribable

sobornar *vt* to bribe

soborno **1** *nm* (**a**) *(acción)* bribery (**b**) *(dinero, regalo)* bribe; **aceptar un s.** to accept a bribe
2 de soborno *loc adj Bol, Chile* additional

sobra *nf* (**a**) **de s.** *(en exceso)* more than enough; *(de más)* superfluous; **tenemos dinero de s.** we have more than enough money; **tengo una raqueta de s.** I've got a spare racket; **me voy, aquí estoy de s.** I'm off, it's obvious I'm not wanted here; **lo sabemos de s.** we know it only too well; **sabes de s. que no miento** you know perfectly well *o* full well that I'm not lying; **tengo motivos de s. para no hablarle** I've got plenty of reasons for not talking to her
(**b**) **sobras** *(de comida)* leftovers; *(de tela)* remnants

sobradamente *adv* **un pintor s. conocido** a very well-known artist; **como es s. conocido...** as I/we/*etc* know all too well...; **te conoce s.** she knows you inside out

sobrado, -a **1** *adj* (**a**) *(de sobra)* **con sobrada experiencia** with ample experience; **tengo sobradas sospechas para desconfiar de él** I've more than enough reasons to suspect him (**b**) *(con suficiente)* **estar s. de dinero/tiempo** to have more than enough money/time (**c**) *Chile (enorme)* enormous, huge
2 sobrados *nmpl Andes* leftovers

sobrador, -ora *adj Andes, RP Fam* snotty, stuck-up

sobrante **1** *adj* remaining; **con el dinero s. se irán de vacaciones** with the money that's left over they plan to go on *Br* holiday *o US* vacation; **los huesos sobrantes se pueden utilizar para una sopa** the leftover bones can be used for stock
2 *nm* surplus

sobrar **1** *vi* (**a**) *(quedar, restar)* to be left over, to be spare; **nos sobró comida** we had some food left over; **no me sobró ni un centavo** I didn't have a penny left; **nos van a s. un par de días** we'll have a couple of days left
(**b**) *(haber de más)* **parece que van a s. bocadillos** it looks like there are going to be too many *o* more than enough sandwiches; **sobra una silla** there's one chair too many
(**c**) *(estar de más)* to be superfluous; **lo que dices sobra** that goes without saying; **aquí sobra alguien** someone here is not welcome
2 *vt Andes, RP Fam* **s. a alguien** to look down on sb, to patronize sb

sobrasada *nf* = Mallorcan spicy pork sausage that can be spread

sobre[1] *nm* (**a**) *(para cartas)* envelope (**b**) *(para alimentos, medicamentos)* sachet, packet (**c**) *Fam (cama)* **irse al s.** to hit the sack (**d**) *Am (bolsa)* clutch bag (**e**) *Urug* **s. de dormir** sleeping bag

SOBRE[2] **1** *prep* (**a**) *(encima de)* on (top of); **el libro está s. la mesa** the book is on (top of) the table; **aún hay nieve s. las montañas** there's still snow on the mountains; **fui apilando las tejas una s. otra** I piled the tiles up one on top of the other; **una cruz roja s. fondo blanco** a red cross on *o* against a white background; **varios policías saltaron s. él** several policemen fell upon him; **seguimos s. su pista** we're still on her trail; EXPR *Andes, RP* **s. la hora: ¿tomamos algo antes de que subas al tren? – imposible, ya estoy s. la hora** shall we have a bite to eat before you catch the train? – I can't, I'm already tight for time; **llegamos muy s. la hora** we arrived with very little time to spare
(**b**) *(por encima de)* over, above; **el puente s. la bahía** the bridge across *o* over the bay; **en estos momentos volamos s. la isla de Pascua** we are currently flying over Easter Island; **la catedral destaca s. los demás edificios** the cathedral stands out over *o* above the other buildings; **a 3.000 metros s. el nivel del mar** 3,000 metres above sea level
(**c**) *(en torno a)* on; **la Tierra gira s. sí misma** the Earth revolves on its own axis
(**d**) *(indica superioridad)* **su opinión está s. las de los demás** his opinion is more important than that of the others; **una victoria s. alguien** a win over sb
(**e**) *(indica relación, contraste, efecto)* **el impuesto s. la renta** income tax; **tiene muchas ventajas s. el antiguo modelo** it has a lot of advantages over the old model; **su efecto s. la quemadura es inmediato** its effect on the burn is immediate; **no tienen influencia s. ellos** they have no influence over them
(**f**) *(acerca de)* about, on; **discuten s. política** they are arguing about politics; **un libro s. el amor** a book about *o* on love; **una conferencia s. el desarme** a conference on disarmament
(**g**) *(aproximadamente)* about; **llegarán s. las diez/s. el jueves** they'll arrive at about ten o'clock/around Thursday; **tiene s. los veinte años** she's about twenty; **los solicitantes deben de ser s. dos mil** there must be about two thousand applicants
(**h**) *(indica acumulación)* upon; **nos contó mentira s. mentira** he told us lie upon lie *o* one lie after another
(**i**) *(indica inminencia)* upon; **la desgracia estaba ya s. nosotros** the disaster was already upon us
2 sobre todo *loc adv* above all; **afectó s. todo a la industria turística** it particularly affected the tourist industry; **y, s. todo, no le digas nada a ella** and, above all, don't say anything to her

sobreabundancia *nf* surplus

sobreabundante *adj* excessive

sobreabundar *vi* to abound

sobreactuar *vi* to overact

sobrealimentación *nf* (**a**) *(de persona)* overeating (**b**) *(de motor)* supercharching, turbocharging

sobrealimentar **1** *vt* (**a**) *(alimentar en exceso)* to overfeed (**b**) *(motor)* to supercharge, to turbocharge
2 sobrealimentarse *vpr* to overeat

sobreañadido *nm* unnecessary addition

sobreañadir *vt* **s. algo a algo** to add sth on top of sth

sobrecalentamiento *nm* overheating

sobrecalentar [3] *vt* to overheat

sobrecama *nf* bedspread

sobrecarga *nf* (**a**) *(exceso de carga)* excess load (**b**) *(saturación)* overload; **s. de trabajo** excessive workload; **s. muscular** muscle strain; **por s. en las líneas le rogamos marque dentro de unos minutos** all our lines are busy at the moment, please try again later (**c**) *(eléctrica)* surge

sobrecargado, -a *adj* (**a**) *(con peso)* overloaded; **estar s. de trabajo** to be overburdened with work, to have an excessive workload (**b**) *(con decoración)* overdone

sobrecargar [38] *vt* (**a**) *(con peso)* to overload (**de** with); *(con trabajo)* to overburden (**de** with) (**b**) *(decoración)* to overdo

sobrecargo *nm* (**a**) *Náut* supercargo (**b**) *Av* flight attendant (**c**) *Com* surcharge

sobrecogedor, -ora *adj* (**a**) *(terrorífico)* frightening, startling (**b**) *(impresionante)* shocking, harrowing

sobrecoger [52] **1** *vt* (**a**) *(asustar)* to frighten, to startle (**b**) *(impresionar)* to shock
2 sobrecogerse *vpr* (**a**) *(asustarse)* to be frightened, to be startled; **se sobrecogió al oír el trueno** she was startled when she heard the thunder (**b**) *(impresionarse)* to be shocked

sobrecogimiento *nm* (**a**) *(susto)* fright (**b**) *(impresión)* shock

sobrecoste, sobrecosto *nm* extra cost

sobrecubierta *nf* (**a**) *(de libro)* (dust) jacket (**b**) *(de barco)* upper deck
sobrecuello *nm (de sacerdote)* dog collar
sobredicho, -a *adj Formal* aforementioned, above-mentioned
sobredimensionar *vt* to blow up out of all proportion
sobredorar *vt (dorar)* to gild
sobredosis *nf inv* overdose
sobreentender = **sobrentender**
sobreentendido, -a = **sobrentendido**
sobreesdrújula = **sobresdrújula**
sobreesdrújulo, -a = **sobresdrújulo**
sobreestimar = **sobrestimar**
sobreexcitación = **sobrexcitación**
sobreexcitado, -a = **sobrexcitado**
sobreexcitar = **sobrexcitar**
sobreexplotación *nf (de campos, cultivos)* overfarming; *(minera)* overmining; **s. de los recursos marítimos** overfishing; **s. de los recursos naturales** overexploitation of natural resources
sobreexplotar *vt (campos, cultivos)* to overfarm; *(recursos mineros)* to overmine; **s. los recursos marítimos** to overfish; **s. los recursos naturales** to overexploit *o* drain natural resources
sobreexponer = **sobrexponer**
sobreexposición = **sobrexposición**
sobrefalda *nf* overskirt
sobrefusión *nf* supercooling
sobregiro *nm Com* overdraft
sobrehilado *nm (en costura)* overcast stitching, whipstitching
sobrehilar *vt* to whipstitch
sobrehumano, -a *adj* superhuman
sobreimpresión *nf* superimposing
sobreimprimir *vt* to superimpose
sobrellevar *vt* to bear, to endure; **sobrelleva la desgracia con mucha resignación** he is bearing his misfortune with great resignation
sobremanera *adv Formal* exceedingly; **me place s. que recurran a nuestros servicios** I'm exceedingly pleased that you should have decided to use our services
sobremesa *nf* = time after midday meal, usually between three and five o'clock in the afternoon, when people stay at the table talking, playing cards etc; **quedarse de s.** to stay at the table *(talking, playing cards etc)*; **la programación de s.** afternoon TV (programmes)
sobrenadar *vi* to float
sobrenatural *adj* supernatural; **poderes sobrenaturales** supernatural powers
sobrenombre *nm* nickname
sobrentender [66], **sobreentender** [66] **1** *vt* to understand, to deduce
2 sobrentenderse *vpr* **se sobrentiende que vendrán** it is understood that they'll come; **se sobrentiende que ellos correrán con los gastos** it goes without saying that they will pay the expenses
sobrentendido, -a, sobreentendido, -a *adj* implied, implicit; **eso está s.** that goes without saying
sobrepaga *nf* bonus
sobreparto *nm* confinement *(after childbirth)*
sobrepasar **1** *vt* (**a**) *(exceder)* to exceed; **su sueldo no sobrepasa el de sus compañeros** his pay is no higher than that of his colleagues; **sobrepasó la barrera del sonido** it broke the sound barrier; **en este caso, la realidad sobrepasa a la ficción** in this instance, reality is stranger than fiction
(**b**) *(aventajar)* **me sobrepasa en altura** he's taller than me; **lo sobrepasa en inteligencia** she's more intelligent than he is
2 sobrepasarse *vpr* (**a**) *(excederse)* to go over the top; **se sobrepasaron en el dinero gastado** they went over the top in the amount they spent (**b**) *(propasarse)* to go too far (**con** with); **sobrepasarse con alguien** *(sexualmente)* to take liberties with sb
sobrepelliz *nf* surplice
sobrepesca *nf* overfishing
sobrepeso *nm* excess weight; **tuve que pagar por s. de equipaje** I had to pay for excess baggage; *Am* **no pudo competir porque está con s.** he couldn't compete because he's overweight
sobreponer [50] **1** *vt* (**a**) *(poner encima)* to put on top (**b**) *(anteponer)* **s. algo a algo** to put sth before sth
2 sobreponerse *vpr* **sobreponerse a algo** to overcome sth; **todavía no se ha sobrepuesto a la pérdida de su amada** he still hasn't recovered from losing the woman he loved

sobreposición *nf* superimposing
sobreprecio *nm* extra charge, surcharge
sobreprima *nf* additional premium
sobreproducción *nf Econ* overproduction
sobreproteger [52] *vt* to overprotect
sobrepuesto, -a **1** *participio ver* **sobreponer**
2 *adj* superimposed
3 *nm Am (panal)* = honeycomb formed after the hive is full
sobrepujar *vt* to outdo, to surpass
sobrero *nm Taurom* = bull kept in reserve in case it is needed in a bullfight
sobresábana *nf Col* top sheet
sobresaliente **1** *adj (destacado)* outstanding
2 *nm (nota)* = mark of between 9 and 10 out of 10, ≃ excellent, ≃ A
3 *nmf* (**a**) *Taurom* reserve bullfighter (**b**) *Teatro* understudy
sobresalir [61] *vi* (**a**) *(en tamaño)* to jut out, to stick out; **arreglaron la baldosa que sobresalía del pavimento** they have fixed the slab which was sticking out from the *Br* pavement *o US* sidewalk; **el tejado sobresale varios metros** the roof juts out several metres; **la enagua le sobresale por debajo de la falda** her petticoat is showing beneath her skirt; **su cabeza sobresalía entre la masa** his head stuck out above the rest of the crowd
(**b**) *(descollar)* to stand out; **sobresale por su inteligencia** he is outstandingly intelligent
sobresaltar **1** *vt* to startle
2 sobresaltarse *vpr* to be startled; **se sobresaltó al oír el portazo** she was startled when she heard the door slam
sobresalto *nm* start, fright; **dar un s. a alguien** to startle sb, to give sb a fright; **vive en un continuo s. por la frágil salud de sus padres** because of his parents' delicate health he lives in a constant state of alert
sobresaturar *vt* to supersaturate
sobrescribir *vt* to overwrite
sobrescrito, -a *participio ver* **sobrescribir**
sobresdrújula, sobreesdrújula *nf* = word stressed on the fourth-last syllable
sobresdrújulo, -a, sobreesdrújulo, -a *adj* = stressed on the fourth-last syllable
sobreseer [37] *vt Der* to discontinue, to dismiss
sobreseimiento *nm Der* discontinuation, dismissal
sobrestante *nm* foreman
sobrestimar, sobreestimar **1** *vt* to overestimate
2 sobrestimarse *vpr* to overestimate one's own abilities
sobresueldo *nm* bonus; **cobrar un s.** to earn some extra income
sobretasa *nf* surcharge
sobretiempo *nm Andes* (**a**) *(en trabajo)* overtime (**b**) *(en deporte) Br* extra time, *US* overtime
sobretodo *nm* overcoat
sobrevalorado, -a *adj* (**a**) *(artista, obra)* overrated (**b**) *(casa, acciones, moneda)* overvalued
sobrevalorar **1** *vt* (**a**) *(artista, obra)* to overrate (**b**) *(casa, acciones, moneda)* to overvalue
2 sobrevalorarse *vpr* to have too high an opinion of oneself
sobrevenir [71] *vi* to occur; **sobrevino la guerra** the war intervened; **estaban en el extranjero cuando sobrevino la epidemia** they were abroad when the epidemic broke out *o* occurred; **no supieron reaccionar cuando sobrevino el desastre** they failed to react when the disaster struck *o* occurred; **la enfermedad le sobrevino durante las vacaciones** he was struck down by the illness during the holidays
sobreventa *nf* overbooking ▸▸ ***s. de billetes*** overbooking
sobrevida *nf Am* survival
sobreviviente **1** *adj* surviving
2 *nmf* survivor
sobrevivir *vi* to survive; **s. a un accidente** to survive an accident; **sobrevivió a sus hijos** she outlived her children
sobrevolar [64] *vt* to fly over
sobrexcitación, sobreexcitación *nf* overexcitement
sobrexcitado, -a, sobreexcitado, -a *adj* overexcited
sobrexcitar, sobreexcitar **1** *vt* to overexcite
2 sobrexcitarse *vpr* to get overexcited
sobrexponer [50], **sobreexponer** [50] *vt* to overexpose
sobrexposición, sobreexposición *nf* overexposure

sobriedad *nf* (a) *(moderación)* restraint, moderation; *(sencillez)* simplicity, sobriety (b) *(no embriaguez)* soberness

sobrino, -a *nm,f* nephew, *f* niece; **mis sobrinos** my nieces and nephews ►► ***sobrina nieta*** grandniece, great niece; ***s. nieto*** grandnephew, great nephew; ***sobrina segunda*** second cousin; ***s. segundo*** second cousin

sobrio, -a *adj* (a) *(moderado)* restrained; *(no excesivo)* simple; **es s. en el vestir** he dresses simply (b) *(austero) (decoración, estilo)* sober (c) *(no borracho)* sober

sobros *nmpl CAm, Méx* leftovers

socaire 1 *nm Náut* lee
2 **al socaire de** *loc adv* under the protection of

socarrado, -a *adj* burnt, scorched

socarrar 1 *vt (quemar)* to burn, to scorch
2 **socarrarse** *vpr* to burn, to get scorched

socarrón, -ona *adj* ironic

socarronería *nf* irony, ironic humour

sócate *nm Ven* socket

socavar *vt* (a) *(debilitar)* to undermine (b) *(excavar por debajo)* to dig under

socavón *nm* (a) *(hoyo)* hollow; *(en la carretera)* pothole (b) *Min* gallery

sochantre *nm* precentor

sociabilidad *nf* (a) *(simpatía)* sociability (b) *Urug (vida social)* socializing; **hacer s.** *(charlar)* to chat; *(alternar)* to socialize

sociable *adj* sociable

social *adj* (a) *(clase, organización, lucha)* social (b) *(vida, actividad)* social (c) *Econ* **capital s.** share capital; **sede s.** headquarters, head office

socialdemocracia *nf* social democracy

socialdemócrata 1 *adj* social democratic
2 *nmf* social democrat

sociales *nfpl* (a) *Educ Fam* social sciences (b) *Arg (vida social)* socializing; **hacer s.** *(charlar)* to chat; *(alternar)* to socialize (c) *RP (columna social)* society column

socialismo *nm* socialism

socialista 1 *adj* socialist
2 *nmf* socialist

socialización *nf Econ* nationalization

socializar [14] *vt Econ* to nationalize

socialmente *adv* socially

sociata *nmf Esp Fam Pey* = supporter of the PSOE (Spanish Socialist Party)

sociedad *nf* (a) *(de seres vivos)* society; **las hormigas viven en s.** ants are social creatures ►► ***la s. civil*** civil society; ***s. de consumo*** consumer society; ***s. de la información*** information society; ***la s. del ocio*** the leisure society; ***s. plural*** plural society; ***s. postindustrial*** post-industrial society
(b) *(mundo elegante)* society; **entrar** *o* **presentarse en s.** to come out, to make one's debut; **alta s.** high society; **notas de s.** society column
(c) *(asociación)* society ►► ***s. deportiva*** sports club; ***s. gastronómica*** dining club, gourmet club; ***la S. de Jesús*** the Society of Jesus; ***s. literaria*** literary society; ***s. médica*** private health care company; *Hist* ***la S. de Naciones*** the League of Nations; ***la S. Protectora de Animales*** *Br* ≃ the RSPCA, *US* ≃ the SPCA
(d) *Com & Fin (empresa)* company ►► ***s. anónima*** *Br* public (limited) company, *US* incorporated company; ***s. de cartera*** holding (company); ***s. colectiva*** general partnership; ***s. comanditaria*** *o* ***en comandita*** general and limited partnership; ***s. cooperativa*** co-operative; ***s. industrial*** industrial society; ***s. de inversión*** investment company; ***s. de inversión de capital variable*** investment company with variable capital, SICAV; ***s. de inversión mobiliaria*** investment trust; ***s. limitada*** private limited company; ***s. mercantil*** trading corporation; ***s. mixta*** joint venture; ***s. de responsabilidad limitada*** private limited company

socio, -a *nm,f* (a) *Com* partner; **hacerse s. de una empresa** to become a partner in a company ►► ***s. capitalista*** *Br* sleeping partner, *US* silent partner; ***s. comanditario*** *Br* sleeping partner, *US* silent partner; ***s. comercial*** trading partner; ***s. fundador*** founding partner; ***s. mayoritario*** majority shareholder
(b) *(miembro)* member; **hacerse s. de un club** to join a club ►► ***s. honorario*** *o* ***de honor*** honorary member; ***s. de número*** full member; ***s. vitalicio*** life member
(c) *Fam (amigo)* mate

socio- *pref* socio-

sociobiología *nf* sociobiology

sociocultural *adj* sociocultural

socioeconomía *nf* socioeconomics *(singular)*

socioeconómico, -a *adj* socioeconomic

sociolecto *nm Ling* sociolect, social dialect

sociolingüística *nf* sociolinguistics *(singular)*

sociolingüístico, -a *adj* sociolinguistic

sociología *nf* sociology

sociológico, -a *adj* sociological

sociólogo, -a *nm,f* sociologist

sociopolítico, -a *adj* sociopolitical

soco, -a *adj Chile, PRico (manco)* **es s.** he only has one arm

socorrer *vt* to help

socorrido, -a *adj (útil)* useful, handy; **los huevos fritos son un plato muy s.** fried eggs is a very handy dish

socorrismo *nm (primeros auxilios)* first aid; *(en la playa)* lifesaving; *(en la montaña)* mountain rescue

socorrista *nmf (en ambulancia)* first-aider; *(en la playa)* lifeguard; *(en montaña)* mountain rescue worker

socorro 1 *nm* help, assistance; **una llamada de s.** a call for help, an SOS; *Av & Náut* a distress call; **acudieron en s. del barco** they came to the ship's aid *o* assistance; **prestar s. a alguien** to offer sb help *o* assistance
2 *interj* help!

socotroco, zocotroco *nm RP Fam* (a) *(golpe)* belt, wallop (b) *(bulto)* hunk, lump; **le pedí un pedazo de pan y me dio un tremendo s.** I asked him for a piece of bread and he gave me a huge great hunk

Sócrates *n pr* Socrates

socrático, -a *adj* Socratic

soda *nf (bebida)* soda water

sodero *nm RP* = man who delivers soda water to people's homes

sódico, -a *adj* sodium; **cloruro s.** sodium chloride

sodio *nm* sodium

sodomía *nf* sodomy

sodomita *nmf* sodomite

sodomizar [14] *vt* to sodomize

soez *adj* vulgar

sofá *nm* sofa, couch ►► ***s.-cama*** sofa bed

sófero, -a *adj Perú Fam* massive, *US* humongous

Sofía *n* Sofia

sofisma *nm* sophism

sofista 1 *adj* sophistic
2 *nmf* sophist

sofisticación *nf* (a) *(refinamiento)* sophistication (b) *(complejidad)* sophistication

sofisticado, -a *adj* (a) *(refinado)* sophisticated (b) *(complejo)* sophisticated

sofisticar [60] **1** *vt* (a) *(quitar naturalidad a)* to make too sophisticated (b) *(falsificar)* to adulterate, to doctor
2 **sofisticarse** *vpr* to get sophisticated

sofístico, -a *adj* specious, fallacious

soflama *nf Pey (discurso)* harangue

sofocación *nf (asfixia)* suffocation

sofocado, -a *adj* (a) *(por cansancio)* out of breath; *(por calor)* suffocating (b) *(por vergüenza)* embarrassed (c) *(por disgusto)* upset

sofocante *adj (calor)* suffocating, stifling

sofocar [60] **1** *vt* (a) *(ahogar, abrasar)* to suffocate, to stifle (b) *(incendio)* to put out, to smother (c) *(rebelión)* to suppress, to quell (d) *(agobiar) (con trabajo)* to overburden (e) *(avergonzar)* to embarrass
2 **sofocarse** *vpr* (a) *(ahogarse, abrasarse)* to suffocate (b) *(agobiarse) (con trabajo)* to overburden (c) *(avergonzarse)* to get embarrassed (d) *(disgustarse)* **¡no te sofoques!** there's no need to get upset about it!

sofoco *nm* (a) *(ahogo)* breathlessness; **le dio un s.** he got out of breath (b) *(bochorno)* hot flush (c) *(vergüenza)* embarrassment; **pasar un s.** to be embarrassed (d) *(disgusto)* **llevarse un s.** to get upset

sofocón *nm Fam* **llevarse un s.** *(un disgusto)* to get really upset

sofoque *etc ver* **sofocar**

sófora *nf* pagoda tree

sofreír [56] *vt* to fry lightly over a low heat

sofrenar *vt* (**a**) *(retener)* to rein in suddenly, to check (**b**) *(refrenar)* to restrain, to control

sofrío, sofriera *etc ver* **sofreír**

sofrito, -a 1 *participio ver* **sofreír**
2 *nm* = lightly fried onions, garlic, and usually also tomato, used as a base for sauces, stews etc

sofrología *nf* relaxation therapy

soft ['soft] *nm Informát Fam* software

software ['sofwer] *nm Informát* software; **paquete de s.** software package ►► ***s. de comunicaciones*** communications software; ***s. de dominio público*** public domain software; ***s. integrado*** integrated software; ***s. de sistema*** system software

soga *nf (cuerda)* rope; *(para ahorcar)* noose; EXPR **estar con la s. al cuello** to be in dire straits; EXPR **mentar la s. en casa del ahorcado** to really put one's foot in it *(by mentioning a sensitive subject)*

soguear *vt* (**a**) *Ecuad (atar)* to tie with a long rope (**b**) *Col (burlarse de)* to make fun of

sois *ver* **ser**

soja, soya *nf* (**a**) *(planta, fruto)* soya bean, *US* soy bean (**b**) *(proteína)* soya

sojuzgar [38] *vt* to subjugate

sol *nm* (**a**) *(astro)* sun; **al salir/ponerse el s.** at sunrise/sunset; **de s. a s.** from dawn to dusk ►► ***s. de medianoche*** midnight sun; ***s. naciente*** rising sun; ***s. poniente*** setting sun
(**b**) *(rayos, luz)* sunshine, sun; **estar/ponerse al s.** to be in/move into the sun; **entraba el s. por la ventana** sunlight was coming in through the window; **¡cómo pega** *o* **pica el s.!** the sun's really hot!; **estaba leyendo a pleno s.** he was reading in the sun; **hace s.** it's sunny; **quemado por el s.** sunburnt; EXPR **hace un s. de justicia** it's blazing hot; **tomar el s.** to sunbathe; EXPR *Fam* **siempre se arrima al s. que más calienta** he is loyal to whoever offers him the best deal; EXPR **no dejar a alguien ni a s. ni a sombra** to follow sb around wherever they go
(**c**) *Fam (ángel, ricura)* darling, angel; **tu hermana es un s.** your sister's an angel
(**d**) *(nota musical)* G; *(en solfeo)* soh; *ver también* **do**
(**e**) *(moneda)* sol
(**f**) *Taurom* = seats in the sun, the cheapest in the bullring
(**g**) ***s. y sombra*** *(bebida)* = mixture of brandy and anisette

solado *nm*, **soladura** *nf* flooring

solador *nm* floorer

soladura = **solado**

solamente *adv* only, just; **s. he venido a despedirme** I've only *o* just come to say goodbye; **come s. fruta y verdura** she only *o* just eats fruit and vegetables; **es s. un bebé** he's only *o* just a baby; **s. le importa el dinero** she's only interested in money, all she cares about is money; **trabajo veinte horas a la semana – ¿s.?** I work twenty hours a week – is that all?; **no s.... sino (también)...** not only... but (also)...; **no s. me insultaron sino que además me golpearon** they didn't only insult me, they beat me too, not only did they insult me, they beat me too; **con s.** *o* **s. con una llamada basta para obtener el crédito** all you need to do to get the loan is to make one phone call; **con s.** *o* **s. con accionar la palanca...** by simply operating the lever...; **s. con que te disculpes me conformo** all you need to do is apologize and I'll be happy, all I ask is that you apologize; **s. de pensarlo me pongo enfermo** just thinking about it makes me ill; **s. que...** only...; **lo compraría, s. que no tengo dinero** I would buy it, only I haven't got any money

solana *nf* (**a**) *(lugar)* sunny spot (**b**) *(galería)* sun lounge

solanácea 1 *nf* solanaceous plant
2 **solanáceas** *nfpl (familia) Solanaceae*; **de la familia de las solanáceas** of the family *Solanaceae*

solano *nm* east wind

solapa *nf* (**a**) *(de prenda)* lapel (**b**) *(de libro, sobre)* flap

solapadamente *adv* underhandedly, deviously

solapado, -a *adj* underhand, devious

solapamiento *nm* overlapping

solapar *vt* to cover up

solar[1] *adj* solar; **energía s.** solar energy, solar power; **los rayos solares** the sun's rays

solar[2] *nm* (**a**) *(terreno)* vacant lot, undeveloped plot (of land) (**b**) *Cuba (casa de vecindad)* tenement

solariego, -a *adj* ancestral

solario, solárium (*pl* **solariums**) *nm* solarium

solaz *nm Formal* (**a**) *(entretenimiento)* amusement, entertainment (**b**) *(descanso)* rest

solazar [14] *Formal* 1 *vt (entretener)* to amuse, to entertain
2 **solazarse** *vpr* to amuse *o* entertain oneself

solazo *nm Fam* scorching *o* blazing sunshine

soldada *nf* pay

soldadera *nf Méx Hist* = woman who accompanied the soldiers during the Mexican Revolution

soldadesca *nf* rowdy *o* unruly gang of soldiers

soldadito *nm* ***s. de plomo*** tin soldier

soldado *nm* soldier ►► ***s. de caballería*** cavalryman; ***s. de infantería*** infantryman; ***s. de marina*** marine; ***s. de plomo*** tin soldier; ***s. de primera*** *Br* lance corporal, *US* private first class; ***s. raso*** private

soldador, -ora 1 *nm,f (persona)* welder
2 *nm (aparato) (con material adicional)* soldering iron; *(sin material adicional)* welder, welding equipment

soldadura *nf* (**a**) *(acción) (con estaño)* soldering; *(por arco, oxiacetilénica)* welding ►► ***s. autógena*** autogenous welding (**b**) *(juntura) (con estaño)* soldered joint; *(por arco, oxiacetilénica)* weld (**c**) *(de fractura)* knitting (together)

soldar [64] 1 *vt (metal) (con estaño)* to solder; *(por arco, con oxiacetileno)* to weld
2 *vi (huesos)* to knit
3 **soldarse** *vpr (huesos)* to knit (together)

soleá (*pl* **soleares**) *nf* = type of flamenco song and dance

soleado, -a *adj* sunny

solear *vt* to put in the sun

solecismo *nm* solecism

soledad *nf* (**a**) *(falta de compañía)* solitude; **vive en completa s.** he lives in complete solitude; **necesito un poco de s.** I need to be alone for a while; **se dedicó a escribir en la s. del exilio** he started writing in the solitude of exile (**b**) *(melancolía)* loneliness; **enfermó de s.** she grew sick with loneliness

solemne *adj* (**a**) *(con pompa, importante)* formal, solemn (**b**) *(serio)* solemn; **una promesa s.** a solemn promise (**c**) *(enorme)* utter, complete; **hacer/decir una s. tontería** to do/say something incredibly stupid

solemnemente *adv* solemnly

solemnidad 1 *nf* (**a**) *(suntuosidad)* pomp, solemnity; **la inauguración se celebró con gran s.** the inauguration took place with great solemnity (**b**) *(acto)* ceremony; **s. de María** Solemnity of Mary
2 **de solemnidad** *loc adv* **malo de s.** really bad; **son pobres de s.** they're really poor; **fue aburrido de s.** it was deadly boring

solemnizar [14] *vt* (**a**) *(celebrar)* to celebrate, to commemorate (**b**) *(dar solemnidad a)* to lend an air of solemnity to

solenodonte *nm* Cuban solenodon

solenoide *nm Elec* solenoid

sóleo *nm Anat* soleus

soler [41] *vi* **s. hacer algo** to do sth usually; **solemos comer fuera los viernes** we usually eat out on Fridays; **aquí suele llover mucho** it usually rains a lot here; **solía ir a la playa cada día** I used to go to the beach every day; **solíamos vernos más** we used to see more of each other; **como se suele hacer en estos casos** as is customary in such cases; **como se suele decir en estos casos, que les vaya muy bien** as people usually say at times like these, I hope it goes very well for you; **este restaurante suele ser bueno** this restaurant is usually good

solera *nf* (**a**) *(tradición)* tradition; **una familia/marca de s.** a long-established family/brand; **un barrio con mucha s.** a neighbourhood with a lot of local character (**b**) **vino de s.** *(añejo)* vintage wine (**c**) *RP (vestido)* sun dress (**d**) *Chile (de acera) Br* kerb, *US* curb

solero *nm RP (vestido)* sun dress

soletilla *nf* sponge finger

solfa *nf Fam (paliza)* thrashing; EXPR **poner algo en s.** to make fun of sth, *Br* to take the mickey out of sth; EXPR *RP* **tomarse algo en s.** not to take sth too seriously

solfatara *nf Geol* solfatara

solfear *vt Mús* to sol-fa

solfeo *nm Mús* music reading; **estudiar s.** to learn to read music; **estudia primero/segundo/tercero de s.** he's in his first/second/third year of music theory; **saber s.** to be able to read music

solicitada *nf Arg* = article inserted in a newspaper and paid for by the writer

solicitante *nmf* applicant ►► ***s. de asilo*** asylum seeker

solicitar *vt* (**a**) *(pedir) (información, permiso)* to request, to ask for; *(puesto, préstamo, beca)* to apply for; **s. algo a alguien** *(pedir) (información, permiso)* to request sth from sb, to ask sb for sth; *(puesto, préstamo, beca)* to apply to sb for sth; **me han solicitado que lo haga** they've requested that I do it
(**b**) *(persona)* to ask for; **le solicita el director de ventas** the sales manager wants to see you; **estar muy solicitado** to be very popular, to be very sought after
(**c**) *Anticuado (cortejar)* to woo

solícito, -a *adj* solicitous, obliging; **siempre fue muy solícita conmigo** she was always very kind and helpful towards me; **acudió s. a atender a los heridos** anxious to help, he came forward to take care of the injured

solicitud *nf* (**a**) *(petición) (de información, permiso)* request; *(de puesto, préstamo, beca)* application; **a s. de** at the request of; **en estos momentos no podemos atender su s.** we are unable to respond to your request at this time (**b**) *(documento)* application form (**c**) *(atención)* attentiveness; **con s.** attentively

sólidamente *adv* solidly

solidariamente *adv* (**a**) *(con solidaridad)* **actuaron s.** they showed great solidarity (**b**) *Der* severally

solidaridad *nf* solidarity; **lo hago por s. con los despedidos** I am doing it out of solidarity with the people who have been sacked; **mostrar s. con alguien** to show solidarity with sb; **fueron a la huelga en s. con otros compañeros del sector** they came out on strike in sympathy with other workers in the industry

solidario, -a *adj* (**a**) *(adherido) (actitud)* supportive (**con** of); **un gesto s.** a gesture of solidarity; **contamos con el apoyo s. de nuestros compañeros en otras fábricas** we have the support of our fellow workers in other factories; **ser s. con alguien** to show solidarity with sb; **nos hacemos solidarios de su causa** we join with you in their cause
(**b**) *Der (obligación, compromiso)* mutually binding
(**c**) *Tec (pieza)* integral

solidarizar [14] **1** *vt* to make jointly responsible *o* liable
2 solidarizarse *vpr (unirse)* to express *o* show one's solidarity (**con** with); **se solidarizaron con sus compañeros en huelga** they expressed their solidarity with their striking fellow workers; **nos solidarizamos con los manifestantes** we support the demonstrators

solideo *nm Rel* skullcap

solidez *nf* (**a**) *(de terreno, construcción)* solidity (**b**) *(de relación)* strength (**c**) *(de argumento, conocimiento, idea)* soundness

solidificación *nf* solidification

solidificar [60] **1** *vt* to solidify
2 solidificarse *vpr* to solidify

sólido, -a 1 *adj* (**a**) *(cuerpo)* solid; **un cuerpo s.** a solid (**b**) *(relación)* strong (**c**) *(fundamento)* firm; *(argumento, conocimiento, idea)* sound, solid (**d**) *(color)* fast
2 *nm* solid

soliloquio *nm* soliloquy

solio *nm* canopied throne

solipsismo *nm Filosofía* solipsism

solista 1 *adj* solo
2 *nmf* soloist

solitaria *nf (tenia)* tapeworm

solitario, -a 1 *adj* (**a**) *(persona, vida)* solitary; **una vida triste y solitaria** a sad and lonely life; **navegar en s.** to sail solo (**b**) *(lugar)* lonely, deserted; **es una calle muy solitaria** it's a very solitary street; **esto está muy s.** this place is deserted
2 *nm,f (persona)* loner
3 *nm* (**a**) *(diamante)* solitaire (**b**) *(juego) Br* patience, *US* solitaire; **hacer un s.** to play a game of *Br* patience *o US* solitaire

soliviantar 1 *vt* (**a**) *(excitar, incitar)* to stir up; **s. a alguien contra algo** to stir sb up against sth (**b**) *(indignar)* to exasperate
2 soliviantarse *vpr* (**a**) *(rebelarse)* to rise up, to rebel; **soliviantarse contra algo** to rise up against sth, to rebel against sth (**b**) *(indignarse)* to get annoyed

solla *nf* plaice

sollozar [14] *vi* to sob

sollozo *nm* sob

SOLO[1], -A **1** *adj* (**a**) *(sin nadie, sin compañía)* alone; **me gusta estar s.** I like being alone *o* on my own *o* by myself; **¿vives sola?** do you live alone *o* on your own *o* by yourself?; **lo hice yo s.** I did it on my own *o* by myself; **me quedé s.** *(todos se fueron)* I was left on my own; *(nadie me apoyó)* I was left isolated; **se quedó s. a temprana edad** he was on his own from an early age; **quería estar a solas** she wanted to be alone *o* by herself; **ya hablaremos tú y yo a solas** we'll have a talk with just the two of us, we'll have a talk alone; *Fam* **es gracioso/simpático como él s.** he's really funny/nice; EXPR **estar/quedarse más s. que la una** to be/be left all on one's own; PROV **más vale estar s. que mal acompañado** better to be alone than to be with the wrong people
(**b**) *(solitario)* lonely; **me sentía s.** I felt lonely
(**c**) *(sin nada)* on its own; *(café)* black; *(whisky)* neat; **¿quieres el café s. o con leche?** would you like your coffee black or with milk?; **le gusta comer el arroz s.** he likes to eat rice on its own
(**d**) *(único)* single; **no me han comprado ni un s. regalo** they didn't buy me a single present; **ni una sola gota** not a (single) drop; **dame una sola razón** give me one reason; **queda una sola esperanza** only one hope remains
(**e**) *(mero, simple)* very, mere; **la sola idea de suspender me deprime** the very *o* mere idea of failing depresses me; **el s. hecho de que se disculpe ya le honra** the very fact that he is apologizing is to his credit
2 *nm* (**a**) *Mús* solo; **un s. de guitarra** a guitar solo (**b**) *Fam (café)* black coffee

---

SÓLO, SOLO[2] *adv*

Note that the accented form should be used whenever there is a risk of confusion with the adjective.

only, just; **s. he venido a despedirme** I've only *o* just come to say goodbye; **come s. fruta y verdura** she only *o* just eats fruit and vegetables; **es s. un bebé** he's only *o* just a baby; **s. le importa el dinero** she's only interested in money, all she cares about is money; **trabajo veinte horas a la semana – ¿s.?** I work twenty hours a week – is that all?; **no s.... sino (también)...** not only... but (also)...; **no s. me insultaron sino que además me golpearon** they didn't only insult me, they beat me too, not only did they insult me, they beat me too; **con s.** *o* **s. con una llamada basta para obtener el crédito** all you need to do to get the loan is to make one phone call; **con s.** *o* **s. con accionar la palanca...** by simply operating the lever...; **s. con que te disculpes me conformo** all you need to do is apologize and I'll be happy, all I ask is that you apologize; **s. de pensarlo me pongo enfermo** just thinking about it makes me ill; **s. que...** only...; **lo compraría, s. que no tengo dinero** I would buy it, only I haven't got any money; **s. se vive una vez** you only live once

---

solomillo *nm* (**a**) *(carne)* sirloin (**b**) *(filete)* sirloin steak

solsticio *nm* solstice ►► ***s. de invierno*** winter solstice; ***s. de verano*** summer solstice

---

SOLTAR [64] **1** *vt* (**a**) *(desasir)* to let go of; **soltó la maleta sobre la cama** she dropped the suitcase onto the bed; **¡suéltame!** let me go!, let go of me!
(**b**) *(dejar ir, liberar) (preso, animales)* to release; *(freno)* to release; *(acelerador)* to take one's foot off; **han soltado a los presos** the prisoners have been released; **no sueltes al perro** don't let the dog off the leash; **ve soltando el embrague poco a poco** let the clutch out gradually; *Fam* **no suelta (ni) un** *Esp* **duro** *o Am* **centavo** you can't get a penny out of her; *Fam* **si yo pillo un trabajo así, no lo suelto** if I got a job like that I wouldn't let go of it *o* I'd make sure I hung on to it
(**c**) *(desatar) (cierre)* to unfasten; *(enganche)* to unhook; *(nudo, cuerda)* to untie; *(hebilla, cordones)* to undo; *(tornillo, tuerca)* to unscrew
(**d**) *(aflojar) (nudo, cordones, tornillo)* to loosen
(**e**) *(desenrollar) (cable, cuerda)* to let *o* pay out; **ve soltando cuerda hasta que yo te diga** keep letting out *o* paying out more rope until I tell you to stop
(**f**) *(desprender) (calor, olor, gas)* to give off; **este tubo de escape suelta demasiado humo** this exhaust pipe is letting out a lot of smoke; **estas hamburguesas sueltan mucha grasa** a lot of fat comes out of these burgers when you fry them; **este gato suelta mucho pelo** this cat loses a lot of hair
(**g**) *(dar) (golpe)* to give; *(risotada, grito, suspiro)* to give, to let out; **s. una patada a alguien** to give sb a kick, to kick sb; **s. un puñetazo a alguien** to punch sb; **¡a que te suelto un bofetón!** watch it or I'll smack you in the face!
(**h**) *(decir bruscamente)* to come out with; **me soltó que me fuera al infierno** he turned round and told me to go to hell; *Fam* **¡venga, suelta lo que sepas!** come on out with it!; *Fam* **nos soltó un sermón sobre la paternidad responsable** she gave us *o* came out with this lecture about responsible parenting
(**i**) *(laxar)* **esto te ayudará a s. el vientre** this will help to loosen your bowels

2 soltarse *vpr* (a) *(desasirse)* to let go; *(escaparse, zafarse)* to break free; **agárrate a mí y no te sueltes** hold on to me and don't let go; **se soltó de sus ataduras** he broke free from his bonds; **se ha soltado el perro** the dog has slipped its leash; **logró soltarse de las esposas** he managed to get out of his handcuffs

(b) *(desatarse) (nudo, cuerda, cordones)* to come undone; **se soltó el moño** she let her bun down; **se soltó el nudo de la corbata** he loosened his tie; EXPR *Fam* **soltarse el pelo** *o Ven* **el moño** to let one's hair down

(c) *(desprenderse)* to come off; **se ha soltado el pomo de la puerta** *(está totalmente desprendido)* the doorknob has come off; *(se ha aflojado)* the doorknob has come loose; **se me soltó la horquilla** my hairgrip came out

(d) *(ganar desenvoltura)* to get the hang of it, to get confident; **soltarse a** *Esp* **conducir** *o Am* **manejar** to get the hang of driving, to get confident about one's driving; **soltarse con** *o* **en algo** to get the hang of sth; **no termino de soltarme con el francés** I just can't seem to get the hang of French

(e) *Fam (perder timidez)* to let go; **una vez que se soltó a hablar ya no paró** once she started talking she didn't stop

---

soltería *nf (de hombre)* bachelorhood; *(de mujer)* spinsterhood; **lleva muy mal la s.** he really doesn't enjoy being a bachelor; **está felicísima con su s.** she's very happy to be single

soltero, -a 1 *adj* single, unmarried; **estar s.** to be single; **soltera y sin compromiso** single and unattached

2 *nm,f* bachelor, *f* single woman; **apellido de soltera** maiden name

solterón, -ona 1 *adj* unmarried

2 *nm,f* old bachelor, *f* spinster, *f* old maid; **es un s. empedernido** he's a confirmed bachelor

soltura *nf* (a) *(fluidez)* fluency; **habla inglés con s.** she speaks fluent English; **monta a caballo con mucha s.** he's a confident horse rider; **ha adquirido mucha s. al escribir a máquina** he has become a very fluent typist (b) *(facilidad, desenvoltura)* assurance; **tiene mucha s. para el trato con la gente** she's very good with people

solubilidad *nf* solubility

soluble *adj* (a) *(que se disuelve)* soluble; **s. en agua** water-soluble (b) *(que se soluciona)* solvable

solución *nf* (a) *(remedio)* solution; **pegarle una bofetada no es s.** slapping her is not the solution *o* answer; **no veo s. para este lío** I can't see any way out of this mess; **este problema no tiene s.** there's no solution to this problem; *Fam* **este niño no tiene s.** this child is impossible

(b) *(de problema matemático)* solution

(c) *(disolución)* solution ▸▸ ***s. acuosa*** aqueous solution; ***s. limpiadora*** *(para lentillas)* cleansing solution; ***s. salina*** saline solution

(d) *(interrupción)* **sin s. de continuidad** without interruption; **pasaron del invierno al verano sin s. de continuidad** they went straight from winter to summer; **la corrupción pasó sin s. de continuidad de la dictadura a la democracia** the corruption continued uninterrupted *o* seamlessly from dictatorship to democracy

solucionar 1 *vt* (a) *(dificultad)* to solve; *(disputa)* to resolve (b) *(problema matemático)* to solve

2 **solucionarse** *vpr* to be solved; **con la violencia no se soluciona nada** violence does not solve anything

solvencia *nf* (a) *(económica)* solvency (b) *(fiabilidad)* reliability

solventar *vt* (a) *(pagar)* to settle (b) *(resolver)* to resolve

solvente 1 *adj* (a) *(económicamente)* solvent (b) *(fiable)* reliable

2 *nm* solvent

soma *nm Biol* soma

somalí *(pl* **somalíes***)* 1 *adj* Somali

2 *nmf (persona)* Somali

3 *nm (lengua)* Somali

Somalia *n* Somalia

somanta *nf Fam* beating; **le dieron una s. de palos** they gave him a beating; **como no te estés quieto te vas a llevar una s. de palos** if you don't keep quiet you're going to get a good hiding

somatén *nm Hist* = armed vigilante group called out in emergencies

somático, -a *adj* somatic

somatización *nf Med* somatization

somatizar [14] *vt Med* to somatize

sombra *nf* (a) *(proyección) (fenómeno, silueta)* shadow; *(zona)* shade; **a la s.** in the shade; **a la s. de un árbol** in the shade of a tree; **a la s. de su padre** *(bajo su protección)* under the protection of his father; **su s. se reflejaba en la pared** his shadow fell on the wall; **las higueras dan muy buena s.** fig trees give a lot of shade; **dar s. a** to cast a shadow over; *Fam* **pasó un año a la s.** *(en la cárcel)* he spent a year in the slammer; **el asesino desapareció en las sombras de la noche** the murderer disappeared into the shadows of the night; EXPR *Vulg* **me cago en tu s.** screw you!; EXPR *Fam* **no se fía ni de su propia s.** he wouldn't trust his own mother; EXPR **hacer s. a alguien** to overshadow sb; EXPR **se ríe de su propia s.** she makes a joke of everything; EXPR **ser la s. de alguien** to be like sb's shadow; EXPR *Fam* **tener mala s.** to be mean *o* nasty; **iqué mala s.! ¿por qué no le has dicho la verdad?** that was mean of you! why didn't you tell her the truth? ▸▸ ***sombras chinescas*** *(marionetas)* shadow puppets; **hacer sombras chinescas** *(con las manos)* to make shadow pictures

(b) *(en pintura)* shade

(c) ***s. de ojos*** eye shadow

(d) *(anonimato)* background; **permanecer en la s.** to stay in the background

(e) *(imperfección)* stain, blemish; **tiene un currículum sin sombras** she has an unblemished record

(f) *(atisbo, apariencia)* trace, touch; **una s. de felicidad se asomó en su rostro** the flicker of a happy smile appeared on his face; **sin s. de duda** without a shadow of a doubt; **no es ni s. de lo que era** he's a shadow of his former self

(g) *(suerte)* **buena/mala s.** good/bad luck

(h) *Taurom* = most expensive seats in bullring, located in the shade

(i) *(oscuridad, inquietud)* darkness; **su muerte sumió al país en la s.** his death plunged the country into darkness

(j) *(misterio)* mystery; **las sombras que rodean al secuestro del embajador** the mystery surrounding the ambassador's kidnapping

(k) *Chile (sombrilla)* parasol

sombrajo *nm* sunshade

sombreado, -a 1 *adj* shady

2 *nm* shading

sombrear *vt* (a) *(dibujo)* to shade (b) *(dar sombra)* to shade

sombrerera *nf (caja)* hatbox

sombrerería *nf* (a) *(fábrica)* hat factory (b) *(tienda)* hat shop; *(para señoras)* milliner's

sombrerero, -a *nm,f* (a) *(fabricante)* hat maker, hatter; *(para señoras)* milliner (b) *(vendedor)* hatter; *(para señoras)* milliner

sombrerete *nm (de chimenea)* cowl, bonnet

sombrerillo *nm (de seta)* cap

sombrero *nm* (a) *(prenda)* hat; **llevar** *o* **usar s.** to wear a hat; EXPR **pasar el s.** to pass round the hat; EXPR **quitarse el s. (ante alguien)** to take one's hat off (to sb) ▸▸ ***s. de ala ancha*** wide-brimmed hat, broad-brimmed hat; *Am* ***s. alón*** wide-brimmed hat, broad-brimmed hat; ***s. canotier*** straw hat, boater; ***s. de copa*** top hat; ***s. cordobés*** Spanish hat; ***s. de fieltro*** felt hat; ***s. hongo*** *Br* bowler hat, *US* derby; ***s. jarano*** sombrero; ***s. de paja*** straw hat; ***s. de palma*** palm leaf hat; ***s. de teja*** shovel hat; ***s. de tres picos*** three-cornered hat

(b) *(de seta)* cap

sombrilla *nf* (a) *(quitasol)* sunshade, parasol (b) *Col (paraguas)* umbrella (c) *Méx Fam* **me vale s.** I couldn't care less

sombrío, -a *adj* (a) *(oscuro)* gloomy, dark (b) *(triste, lúgubre)* sombre, gloomy; **el futuro de la fábrica es s.** the future of the factory is grim *o* bleak

someramente *adv* (a) *(superficialmente)* superficially (b) *(brevemente)* briefly

somero, -a *adj* (a) *(superficial)* superficial (b) *(breve)* brief (c) *(aguas)* shallow

someter 1 *vt* (a) *(dominar, subyugar)* to subdue; **los sometieron a su autoridad** they forced them to accept their authority; **no consiguieron s. a la guerilla** they were unable to subdue *o* put down the guerrillas

(b) *(presentar)* **s. algo a la aprobación de alguien** to submit sth for sb's approval; **s. algo a votación** to put sth to the vote; **sometieron sus conclusiones a la comisión** they submitted *o* presented their conclusions to the committee

(c) *(subordinar)* **someto mi decisión a los resultados de la encuesta** my decision will depend on the results of the poll; **sometió su opinión a la de la mayoría** she went along with the opinion of the majority

(d) *(a interrogatorio, presiones)* **s. a alguien a algo** to subject sb to sth; **s. a alguien a una operación** to operate on sb; **sometieron la estructura a duras pruebas de resistencia** the structure was subjected to stringent strength tests; **sometieron la ciudad a un fuerte bombardeo** the city was subjected to heavy bombing

2 **someterse** *vpr* (a) *(rendirse)* to surrender

(b) *(conformarse)* **someterse a algo** *(autoridad, voluntad)* to submit to sth; **me someteré a la opinión de la mayoría** I will submit to *o* accept the opinion of the majority; **se somete a los caprichos de su**

marido she gives in to her husband's whims
(**c**) *(exponerse)* **someterse a algo** *(interrogatorio, pruebas)* to undergo sth; **someterse a un chequeo médico/una operación** to undergo *o* have a check-up/an operation; **se sometió voluntariamente al experimento** he underwent the experiment voluntarily; **se sometió a radiaciones peligrosas** she subjected *o* exposed herself to dangerous radiation

sometimiento *nm* (**a**) *(dominio)* subjugation (**b**) *(a autoridad, ley)* submission (**c**) *(a interrogatorio, pruebas)* subjection

somier (*pl* **somieres**) *nm (de muelles)* bedsprings; *(de tablas)* slats *(of bed)*

somnífero, -a 1 *adj* somniferous
2 *nm* sleeping pill

somnolencia, soñolencia *nf* sleepiness, drowsiness; **me produce s.** it makes me sleepy *o* drowsy

somnoliento, -a, soñoliento, -a *adj* sleepy, drowsy

somocismo *nm Pol* = regime of former Nicaraguan dictator Somoza

somocista *Pol* **1** *adj* = relating to the regime of former Nicaraguan dictator Somoza
2 *nmf* = supporter of former Nicaraguan dictator Somoza

somontano, -a *adj* mountainside

somormujo *nm* grebe ►► ***s. lavanco*** great crested grebe

somos *ver* **ser**

son 1 *ver* **ser**
2 *nm* (**a**) *(sonido)* sound; **se escuchaba el s. de una gaita** the sound of bagpipes could be heard; EXPR **bailar al s. que tocan: ese baila al s. que le tocan los de arriba** he does whatever his bosses tell him to do (**b**) *(canción y baile)* = Cuban song and dance of African origin
3 en son de *loc prep* **lo dijo en s. de burla/disculpa** she said it as a taunt/by way of an apology; **venir en s. de paz** to come in peace; **venir en s. de guerra** to come with warlike intentions

sonado, -a *adj* (**a**) *(renombrado)* famous; **va a ser un fracaso s.** it's going to be a spectacular *o* resounding failure; **fue una fiesta sonada** the party caused quite a stir (**b**) *Fam (loco)* crazy (**c**) *(boxeador)* punch drunk (**d**) *RP Fam (fastidiado)* **estar s.** to be done for, to have had it; **si no cobramos mañana estoy sonada** if we don't get paid tomorrow I'm done for *o* I've had it

sonaja 1 *nf* (**a**) *(chapa)* metal disc (**b**) *(sonajero)* rattle
2 sonajas *nfpl* tambourine

sonajero *nm* rattle

sonambulismo *nm* sleepwalking

sonámbulo, -a 1 *adj* sleepwalking; **es s.** he walks in his sleep; **iba como s.** it was as if he was in a trance; *Fam* **hoy estoy s.** I'm totally out of it today
2 *nm,f* sleepwalker

sonante *adj* **dinero contante y s.** hard cash

SONAR[1] [64] **1** *vi* (**a**) *(producir sonido) (timbre, teléfono, campana, despertador, alarma)* to ring; **sonó una explosión** there was an explosion; **sonó un disparo** a shot rang out; **sonaba a lo lejos una sirena** you could hear (the sound of) a siren in the distance; **hicieron s. la alarma** they set off the alarm; **sonaron las diez (en el reloj)** the clock struck ten; **suena (a) hueco** it sounds hollow; **suena a los Beatles** it sounds like the Beatles; **suena falso/a chiste** it sounds false/like a joke; *Fig* **no me gusta nada como suena esto** I don't like the sound of this at all; **(así** *o* **tal) como suena** *(literalmente)* literally, in so many words; **me llamó mentirosa, así como suena** she literally called me a liar; **su nombre se escribe como suena** you spell her name like it sounds; EXPR *Fam* **s. la flauta: sonó la flauta y aprobé el examen** it was a fluke that I passed the exam; **si suena la flauta...** with a bit of luck...
(**b**) *(ser conocido, familiar)* **me suena** it rings a bell; **esa cara me suena** I know that face, I've seen that face somewhere before; **¿te suena de algo este número de teléfono?** does this telephone number mean anything to you *o* ring a bell?; **no me suena su nombre** I don't remember hearing her name before; **un nombre que suena mucho en círculos políticos** a name that is often mentioned in political circles
(**c**) *(pronunciarse)* to be pronounced; **la letra "h" no suena** the "h" is silent
(**d**) *(mencionarse, citarse)* to be mentioned; **su nombre suena como futuro ministro** his name is being mentioned as a future minister
(**e**) *(rumorearse)* to be rumoured; **suena por ahí que lo van a echar** it is rumoured that he is going to be sacked
(**f**) *CSur Fam (fracasar)* to come a cropper, *US* to mess up; **si no te preparás para ese examen vas a s.** if you don't revise for the exam you're going to come a cropper; **no supieron llevar la empresa correctamente y sonaron** they mismanaged the company and came to grief
(**g**) *RP Fam (morir)* to kick the bucket
2 *vt* **s. la nariz a alguien** to wipe sb's nose
3 sonarse *vpr* **sonarse (la nariz)** to blow one's nose

---

sonar[2], sónar *nm Náut* sonar

sonata *nf* sonata

sonatina *nf* sonatina

sonda *nf* (**a**) *Med* catheter (**b**) *Tec* probe ►► ***s. espacial*** space probe (**c**) *(para medir profundidad)* sounding line ►► ***s. acústica*** echo sounder (**d**) *Min* drill, bore

sondar *vt* (**a**) *Med* to put a catheter in (**b**) *(medir profundidad)* to sound (**c**) *Min (terreno)* to test, to bore; *(roca)* to drill

sondear *vt* (**a**) *(sonsacar)* to sound out; **sondéalo, a ver si te cuenta qué planean** sound him out, maybe he'll tell you what they're planning; **sondeó el parecer de todos los miembros del comité** he sounded out the opinions of all the committee members (**b**) *(medir profundidad)* to sound (**c**) *Min (terreno)* to test, to bore; *(roca)* to drill

sondeo *nm* (**a**) *(encuesta)* (opinion) poll, survey; **voy a hacer un s. para ver a quién le interesa la propuesta** I'm going to ask around to find out who thinks it's a good idea ►► ***s. de opinión*** opinion poll (**b**) *(excavación)* drilling, boring (**c**) *(del espacio)* exploration

sonero, -a *nm,f* = musician who performs "son" music

soneto *nm* sonnet

sónico, -a *adj* sonic

sonidista *nmf Am* sound engineer, sound technician

sonido *nm* sound

soniquete *nm (sonido)* monotonous noise

sonora *nf Gram* voiced consonant

sonorense 1 *adj* of/from Sonora *(Mexico)*
2 *nmf* person from Sonora *(Mexico)*

sonoridad *nf* (**a**) *(armonía, sonido)* sonority (**b**) *(acústica)* acoustics (**c**) *(resonancia)* resonance

sonorización *nf* soundtrack recording

sonorizar [14] *vt* (**a**) *(con amplificadores)* to provide a sound system for (**b**) *Cine (poner sonido a)* to add the soundtrack to (**c**) *Gram* to voice

sonoro, -a 1 *adj* (**a**) *(del sonido)* sound; *(película)* talking; **ondas sonoras** sound waves; **banda sonora** sound track (**b**) *(ruidoso, resonante, vibrante)* resonant (**c**) *Gram* voiced
2 *nm (cine)* talking pictures, talkies

sonotone® *nm* hearing aid

sonreír [56] **1** *vi* (**a**) *(reír levemente)* to smile; **me sonrió** she smiled at me (**b**) *(ser favorable)* **s. a alguien** to smile on sb; **le sonrió la fortuna** fortune smiled on him
2 sonreírse *vpr* to smile

sonriente *adj* smiling; **estás muy s. hoy** you're looking very cheerful today

sonriera *etc ver* **sonreír**

sonrisa *nf* smile; **una s. de felicidad/triste** a happy/sad smile ►► *Arte* ***la s. etrusca*** Mona Lisa smile

sonrojar 1 *vt* to cause to blush
2 sonrojarse *vpr* to blush

sonrojo *nm* blush, blushing

sonrosado, -a *adj* rosy

sonrosar *vt* **el aire fresco le ha sonrosado las mejillas** the fresh air has brought some colour to his cheeks

sonsacar [60] *vt* **s. algo a alguien** to extract sth from sb; **s. a alguien** to pump sb for information

sonsear *vi Am* to fool around, to act foolishly

sonsera *nf Am (tontería)* nonsense, silliness; **decir/hacer una s.** to say/do something silly

sonso, -a *Am* **1** *adj* foolish, silly
2 *nm,f* fool, idiot

sonsonete *nm* (**a**) *(ruido)* tapping (**b**) *(entonación)* monotonous intonation; **leía el poema con s.** he read the poem in a monotone *o* drone (**c**) *(cantinela)* old tune

soñado, -a *adj* (**a**) *(de ensueño)* dream; **mi casa soñada** my dream house (**b**) *RP Fam (hermoso)* lovely, gorgeous

soñador, -ora 1 *adj* dreamy
2 *nm,f* dreamer

soñar [64] **1** *vt* (**a**) *(en sueños)* to dream; **eso lo has debido s.** you must have dreamed it; **soñé que podía volar** I dreamed (that) I could fly; EXPR **¡ni soñarlo!, ¡ni lo sueñes!** not on your life!; **¿me dejas dar una vuelta en tu coche? – ¡ni soñarlo** *o* **ni lo sueñes!** can I go for a drive in your car? - not on your life!; **¿invitarla a ella a la fiesta? ¡ni soñarlo** *o* **ni lo sueñes!** invite HER to the party? no way! *o* no chance!
(**b**) *(desear)* to dream; **nunca soñé que me pudiera pasar a mí** I never dreamed it could happen to me
2 *vi* (**a**) *(en sueños)* to dream; **anoche soñé con ella** I dreamed about her last night; **soñé con que estaba en una isla desierta** I dreamed (that) I was on a desert island; **estás soñando despierto** you're daydreaming; EXPR **que sueñes con los angelitos** sweet dreams!
(**b**) *(desear)* to dream; **sueña con una moto** he dreams of having a motorbike; **sueña con que le ofrezcan el puesto** she dreams of being offered the job

soñarrera *nf Fam* **tener una s.** to feel drowsy

soñolencia = **somnolencia**

soñoliento, -a = **somnoliento**

sopa *nf* (**a**) *(guiso)* soup; EXPR *Esp Fam* **andar a la s. boba** to scrounge; EXPR *Esp Fam* **dar sopas con hondas a alguien** to knock the spots off sb; EXPR *Méx Fam* **dar a alguien una s. de su propio chocolate** to give sb a taste of his/her own medicine; EXPR *Fam* **estar hasta en la s.: últimamente ese cantante está hasta en la s.** that singer has been everywhere you look, recently; EXPR *Fam* **me lo encuentro hasta en la s.** I bump into him wherever I go; EXPR *Fam* **estar como una s.** to be sopping wet; EXPR *Méx Fam* **no haber más que una s.** to be Hobson's choice ►► ***s. de ajo*** garlic soup; ***s. de cebolla*** onion soup; ***s. de fideos*** noodle soup; *Am* ***s. inglesa*** trifle; ***s. instantánea*** instant soup; ***s. juliana*** vegetable soup; ***s. de letras*** *(alimento)* alphabet soup; *(pasatiempo)* wordsearch; ***s. de pollo*** chicken soup; ***s. de sobre*** packet soup; ***s. de verduras*** vegetable soup
(**b**) *(de pan)* sop, piece of soaked bread; **no hagas sopas en la salsa** don't dip your bread into the sauce

sopaipilla *nf Chile* = pumpkin fritter in syrup

sopapa *nf RP* plunger

sopapina *nf Fam* slapping

sopapo *nm Fam* slap; **dar un s. a alguien** to slap sb

sopar, sopear *vt (pan)* to dip, to dunk

sopas *interj Méx Fam* crash!, wallop!

sope *nm Méx* = fried corn tortilla, with beans and cheese or other toppings

sopear = **sopar**

sopera *nf (recipiente)* soup tureen

sopero, -a *adj* soup; **plato s.** soup plate

sopesar *vt* (**a**) *(calcular el peso de)* to try the weight of (**b**) *(los pros y los contras de)* to weigh up

sopetón: de sopetón *loc adv* suddenly, abruptly; **"¿te gustaría venir?", me preguntó de s.** "would you like to come along?" he suddenly asked me

sopicaldo *nm* thin soup

sopla *interj Fam Br* crikey!, *US* jeez!

soplado, -a **1** *adj Fam (borracho)* pickled
2 *nm (del vidrio)* glassblowing

soplador, -ora *nm* (**a**) **s. (de vidrio)** glass-blower (**b**) *Ecuad Teatro* prompter

soplagaitas *nmf inv Fam (estúpido, pesado) Br* prat, *US* jerk

soplamocos *nm inv Fam* slap round the face

soplar **1** *vt* (**a**) *(vela, fuego)* to blow out
(**b**) *(para enfriar)* to blow on
(**c**) *(ceniza, polvo)* to blow off
(**d**) *(globo)* to blow up
(**e**) *(vidrio)* to blow
(**f**) *(ficha)* to take
(**g**) *Fam (en examen)* to prompt; **me sopló las respuestas** he whispered the answers to me
(**h**) *Fam (denunciar)* **le sopló a la policía la hora del atraco** he informed the police of the time of the robbery
(**i**) *Esp Fam (hurtar)* to pinch, *Br* to nick; **s. algo a alguien** to pinch *o Br* nick sth off sb
2 *vi* (**a**) *(echar aire)* to blow; **sopla más fuerte** blow harder; **el viento soplaba con fuerza** the wind was blowing hard; EXPR **ver de qué lado sopla el viento** to see which way the wind blows (**b**) *Esp Fam (beber)* to booze (**c**) *Fam (en examen)* **lo expulsaron por s.** he was thrown out for whispering the answers (**d**) EXPR *RP Fam* **no ser s. y hacer botellas** to be no easy thing
3 soplarse *vpr* (**a**) *Esp Fam (comer)* to gobble up; *(beber)* to knock back; **se sopló tres botellas de vino** she polished off three bottles of wine (**b**) *Méx Fam (aguantar)* to put up with; **tuve que soplarme un sermón larguísimo** I had to sit through a really long sermon

soplete *nm* (**a**) *(para soldar)* blowlamp, blowtorch (**b**) *CSur (para pintar)* spray gun

soplido *nm* blow, puff; **apagó la vela de un s.** she blew the candle out

soplillo *nm* (**a**) *(para fuego)* fan, blower (**b**) *Fam* **orejas de s.** sticky-out ears

soplo *nm* (**a**) *(soplido)* blow, puff; **apagó la vela de un s.** she blew the candle out; **un s. de viento se le llevó el globo** a gust of wind snatched the balloon away from him
(**b**) *(instante)* breath, moment; **se me ha pasado la tarde en un s.** the afternoon seems to have flown by; **las vacaciones pasaron como un s.** the holidays flew by, the holidays were over in no time at all
(**c**) *Fam (chivatazo)* tip-off; **dar el s.** to squeal, *Br* to grass
(**d**) *Med* murmur ►► ***s. cardíaco*** heart murmur

soplón, -ona *nm,f Fam (criminal) Br* grass, *US* rat; *(escolar) Br* telltale, *US* tattletale

soponcio *nm Fam* (**a**) *(desmayo)* fainting fit; **le dio un s.** she passed out (**b**) *(enfado)* fit; **le va a dar un s. cuando vea mis notas** she's going to have a fit when she sees my marks; **como se entere, me da un s.** I'll go nuts if he finds out

sopor *nm* drowsiness

soporífero, -a *adj* (**a**) *(somnífero)* soporific (**b**) *(aburrido)* soporific

soportable *adj* bearable, endurable

soportal *nm (pórtico)* porch; **soportales** arcade

soportar **1** *vt* (**a**) *(sostener)* to support
(**b**) *(resistir, tolerar)* to stand; **¡no lo soporto!** I can't stand him/it!; **no sé cómo soportas que te hablen así** I don't know how you put up with them talking to you like that; **no soporta que le griten** he can't bear being shouted at
(**c**) *(sobrellevar)* to endure, to bear; **el niño soportó el castigo sin inmutarse** the child took his punishment without turning a hair
(**d**) *Informát* to support
2 soportarse *vpr (mutuamente)* to stand one another

soporte *nm* (**a**) *(apoyo)* support; **es el s. de su familia** he's the mainstay of the family ►► ***s. técnico*** technical support
(**b**) *Informát* medium; **el documento se facilita en s. informático** the document is available in electronic form; **una edición en s. electrónico** an electronic edition ►► ***s. físico*** hardware; ***s. lógico*** software; ***el s. magnético*** magnetic (storage) media
(**c**) *Mktg* **s. (publicitario)** (media) vehicle

sopotocientos, -as *adj Ven Fam* hundreds of; **¡ya te dije eso sopotocientas veces!** I've told you hundreds of times!

soprano *nmf* soprano ►► ***s. coloratura*** coloratura soprano

sor *nf Rel* sister; **s. Virginia** Sister Virginia

sorber **1** *vt* (**a**) *(beber)* to sip; *(haciendo ruido)* to slurp (**b**) *(absorber)* to soak up, to absorb; **sorbía las palabras del conferenciante** *(escuchaba atentamente)* she drank in the speaker's words (**c**) *(atraer)* to draw *o* suck in
2 sorberse *vpr* **no te sorbas los mocos** don't sniff

sorbete *nm* (**a**) *(postre)* sorbet (**b**) *CAm (helado)* ice cream

sorbetería *nf CAm* ice cream parlour

sorbo *nm* (**a**) *(acción)* gulp, swallow; *(pequeño)* sip; **beber a sorbos** to sip (**b**) *(trago)* mouthful; *(pequeño)* sip; **¿quieres un s.?** would you like a drop *o* sip? (**c**) *(cantidad pequeña)* drop

sorda *nf* (**a**) *Gram* voiceless consonant (**b**) *ver también* **sordo**

sordera *nf* deafness

sordidez *nf* (**a**) *(miseria)* squalor (**b**) *(obscenidad, perversión)* sordidness

sórdido, -a *adj* (**a**) *(miserable)* squalid (**b**) *(obsceno, perverso)* sordid

sordina *nf (en instrumentos de viento, cuerda)* mute; *(en pianos)* damper; **con s.** *(hablar)* under one's breath; *(en secreto)* on the quiet

sordo, -a **1** *adj* (**a**) *(que no oye)* deaf; **quedarse s.** to go deaf; **¡no chilles, que no estoy s.!** there's no need to shout, I'm not deaf!; EXPR **estar s. como una tapia, estar más s. que una tapia** to be (as) deaf as a post; EXPR **permanecer s. a** *o* **ante algo** to be deaf to sth (**b**) *(pasos)* quiet, muffled (**c**) *(ruido, dolor)* dull (**d**) *Gram* voiceless, unvoiced
2 *nm,f (persona)* deaf person; **los sordos** the deaf; EXPR **hacerse el s.** to turn a deaf ear; **el jefe se hacía el s. cuando oía hablar de aumentos de sueldo** the boss pretended not to hear when people mentioned pay rises

sordomudez *nf* deaf-mutism

sordomudo, -a 1 *adj* deaf and dumb
2 *nm,f* deaf-mute

sorete *nm RP Vulg* turd; EXPR **caer soretes de punta** to tip down

sorgo *nm* sorghum

soriano, -a 1 *adj* of/from Soria *(Spain)*
2 *nm,f* person from Soria *(Spain)*

soriasis *nf inv* psoriasis

sorna *nf* **con s.** ironically, mockingly

sorocharse *vpr* **(a)** *Andes, Arg (enfermar)* to get altitude sickness **(b)** *Chile (ruborizarse)* to blush, to flush

soroche *nm* **(a)** *Andes, Arg (mal de altura)* altitude sickness **(b)** *Chile (rubor)* blush, flush

sorete *nm RP muy Fam* turd

sorprendente *adj* surprising

sorprendentemente *adv* surprisingly

sorprender 1 *vt* **(a)** *(asombrar, extrañar)* to surprise; **me sorprende verte por aquí** I'm surprised to see you here; **no me sorprende que se haya marchado** I'm not surprised she's left; **me sorprendió con su pregunta** I was surprised by her question
(b) *(atrapar, pillar)* **s. a alguien (haciendo algo)** to catch sb (doing sth)
(c) *(coger desprevenido)* to catch; **nos sorprendió la tormenta** we got caught in the storm; **el temporal nos sorprendió en mar abierto** the storm caught us out at sea
(d) *(descubrir)* to discover
2 **sorprenderse** *vpr* to be surprised; **no sé de qué te sorprendes** I don't know what you're surprised about; **se sorprendió mucho de verme ahí** he was very surprised to see me there

sorprendido, -a *adj* surprised; **se quedó muy s. cuando se lo conté** he was very surprised when I told him; **el primer s. fui yo** nobody was more surprised than me

sorpresa *nf* **(a)** *(impresión)* surprise; **¡qué s.!** what a surprise!; **¡qué s. verte por aquí!** what a surprise, seeing you here!; **dar una s. a alguien** to surprise sb; **llevarse una s.** to get a surprise; **por s.** unexpectedly; **el enemigo atacó la fortaleza por s.** the enemy made a surprise attack on the fort; **pillar a alguien por s.** to catch sb by surprise
(b) *(regalo)* surprise
(c) *(en función de adjetivo)* **ataque s.** surprise attack; **examen s.** surprise exam

sorpresivamente *adv* unexpectedly

sorpresivo, -a *adj* unexpected

sortear 1 *vt* **(a)** *(rifar)* to raffle; *(echar a suertes)* to draw lots for; **van a s. un viaje** there will be a prize draw to win a *Br* holiday *o US* vacation
(b) *(esquivar)* to dodge; **logró s. todos los obstáculos** he managed to negotiate all the obstacles; **sortearon todas las dificultades que encontraron** they got *o* worked around all the difficulties they came up against; **sorteó hábilmente sus preguntas** he skilfully avoided *o* sidestepped her questions
(c) *Mil* **s. a alguien** = to decide by lots where someone will be posted for their military service
2 **sortearse** *vpr* **se sortearon quién iría primero** they drew lots to decide who would go first; **se sorteará un viaje al Caribe** there will be a draw for a *Br* holiday *o US* vacation in the Caribbean

sorteo *nm* **(a)** *(lotería)* draw; *(rifa)* raffle; **haremos un s. con los premios** we'll raffle the prizes; **por s.** by drawing lots **(b)** *Mil* = draft lottery for compulsory military service

sortija *nf* **(a)** *(anillo)* ring **(b)** *(rizo)* hair ringlet

sortilegio *nm* **(a)** *(hechizo)* spell; **echar un s. a** to cast a spell on **(b)** *(atractivo)* charm, magic

SOS *nm* SOS; **lanzar un S.** to send an SOS

sos *CAm, RP* = **eres**; *ver* **ser**

sosa *nf* **(a)** *Quím* soda ►► ***s. cáustica*** caustic soda **(b)** *ver también* **soso**

sosaina *Fam* 1 *adj (sin gracia)* dull
2 *nmf* dull person, bore

sosegado, -a *adj* **(a)** *(persona)* calm, placid; **lleva una vida sosegada** he leads a quiet life **(b)** *(aguas)* placid, calm

sosegar [43] 1 *vt* to calm
2 **sosegarse** *vpr* **(a)** *(persona)* to calm down **(b)** *(aguas)* to grow calm

soseras *nmf inv Fam* dull person, bore

sosería *nf* **(a)** *(cualidad)* lack of sparkle **(b)** *(dicho, acción)* **es una s.** it's really dull *o* boring

sosia *nmf*, **sosias** *nmf inv* double, lookalike

sosiego 1 *ver* **sosegar**
2 *nm* calm; **todavía no he tenido un minuto de s.** I haven't had a moment's peace yet

soslayar *vt (dificultad)* to avoid, to get around; *(pregunta)* to avoid, to sidestep

soslayo: de soslayo *loc adv* **la miró de s.** he looked at her out of the corner of his eye; **la foto está colgada de s.** the photo is hanging crooked; **abordó la polémica de s.** she referred obliquely to *o* made a glancing reference to the controversy

soso, -a 1 *adj* **(a)** *(insípido)* bland, tasteless; **esta sopa está sosa** this soup needs more salt; **el guiso ha quedado muy s.** the stew hasn't got much flavour **(b)** *(sin gracia)* dull, insipid
2 *nm,f* dull person, bore

sospecha *nf* suspicion; **despertar** *o* **levantar sospechas** to arouse suspicion; **tengo la s. de que...** I have a suspicion that..., I suspect that...; **tengo fundadas sospechas de que miente** I have reason to suspect that he's lying

sospechar 1 *vt (creer, suponer)* to suspect; **sospecho que no lo terminará** I doubt whether she'll finish it
2 *vi* **s. de** to suspect

sospechosamente *adv* suspiciously

sospechoso, -a 1 *adj* suspicious; **me parece s. que no haya venido** it strikes me as suspicious that he hasn't come
2 *nm,f* suspect

sostén *nm* **(a)** *(apoyo)* support **(b)** *(sustento)* main support; *(alimento)* sustenance **(c)** *(prenda de vestir)* bra, brassiere

---

SOSTENER [67] 1 *vt* **(a)** *(sujetar) (edificio, estructura, lo que se tambalea)* to support, to hold up; *(objeto, puerta, bebé)* to hold; **cuatro columnas sostienen todo el peso de la cúpula** four columns take *o* support the entire weight of the dome; **sosténgame esto, por favor** hold this for me, please; **si no nos llegan a s. nos hubiéramos peleado** if they hadn't held us back, we'd have started fighting; **sólo les sostiene su inquebrantable optimismo** the only thing that keeps them going is their unshakeable optimism
(b) *(dar manutención a, sustentar)* to support
(c) *(mantener) (idea, opinión, tesis)* to defend; *(promesa, palabra)* to keep; **sostienen su oferta/invitación** their offer/invitation still stands; **s. que...** to maintain that...
(d) *(tener) (conversación)* to have; *(reunión, negociaciones)* to hold, to have; **s. correspondencia con alguien** to correspond with sb; **durante semanas sostuvo una agria polémica** he was involved in a bitter dispute which lasted several weeks
(e) *Fig (aguantar)* **el corredor no podía s. aquel ritmo de carrera** the athlete couldn't keep up with the pace of the race; **era una situación imposible de s.** the situation was untenable; **le sostuve la mirada** I held her gaze
(f) *Mús* **s. una nota** to hold a note
2 **sostenerse** *vpr* **(a)** *(tenerse en pie) (persona)* to stay on one's feet; *(edificio, estructura)* to stay up; *(en el aire)* to hang; **con ese clavito no se va a s.** it'll never stay up on that little nail; **es muy pequeño y aún le cuesta sostenerse de pie/sentado** he's only little and he still has difficulty standing up/sitting up; **esa teoría/ese argumento no se sostiene** that theory/argument doesn't hold water
(b) *(sustentarse)* to survive; **no puede sostenerse con tan poco dinero/alimento** she can't survive on so little money/food; **la organización se sostiene a base de donaciones** the organization depends on donations for its survival
(c) *(permanecer)* to continue, to remain; **sostenerse en el poder** to remain in power; **se sostienen los intentos por llegar a un acuerdo de paz** the attempts to reach a peace agreement are continuing
(d) *(mantenerse)* **me sostengo en lo que he dicho** I stand by what I said

---

sostenibilidad *nf (de desarrollo)* sustainability

sostenible *adj (objeto, desarrollo)* sustainable; *(idea, argumento)* tenable

sostenido, -a 1 *adj* **(a)** *(persistente)* sustained **(b)** *Mús* sharp; **do s.** C sharp
2 *nm Mús* sharp

sostenimiento *nm* **(a)** *(apoyo)* support **(b)** *(sustento)* sustenance

sostiene, sostuviera *etc ver* **sostener**

sota 1 *nf (carta)* jack *(in Spanish deck of cards)*
2 *nm Chile (capataz)* foreman, overseer

sotabanco *nm (ático)* attic

sotabarba *nf* double chin

sotana *nf* cassock

sótano *nm* basement, cellar; **planta s.** basement
sotavento *nm* leeward; **a s.** to leeward
soterrado, -a *adj* (**a**) *(enterrado)* buried (**b**) *(oculto)* hidden
soterrar [3] *vt* (**a**) *(enterrar)* to bury (**b**) *(ocultar)* to hide
soto *nm* (**a**) *(con matorrales)* thicket (**b**) *(con árboles)* grove
sotobosque *nm* undergrowth
sotto voce [soto'βotʃe] *adv* sotto voce
soufflé [su'fle] *(pl* **soufflés***)* *nm* soufflé
soul 1 *adj* soul
2 *nm* soul (music)
soutien [su'tjen], **sutién** *(pl* **sutienes***)* *nm Urug* bra
souvenir [suβe'nir] *(pl* **souvenirs***)* *nm* souvenir
soviet *(pl* **soviets***)* *nm* soviet ►► *Antes* ***el S. Supremo*** the Supreme Soviet
soviético, -a 1 *adj (de la URSS)* Soviet
2 *nm,f* Soviet
soy *ver* **ser**
soya = **soja**
SP (*abrev de* **servicio público**) = sign indicating public transport vehicle
spaghetti [espa'ɣeti] = **espagueti**
spanglish [es'panglis] *nm* Spanglish
spaniel [es'paniel] *(pl* **spaniels***)* *nm* spaniel
sparring [es'parrin] *(pl* **sparrings***)* *nm Dep* sparring partner
speed [es'pið] *nm (droga)* speed
spiedo [es'pieðo] *nm RP* spit; **pollo al s.** spit-roast chicken
spinnaker [espi'naker] *(pl* **spinnakers***)* *nm Náut* spinnaker
SPM *nm Med* (*abrev de* **síndrome premenstrual**) PMT
sport [es'por]**: de sport** *loc adj* **chaqueta de s.** sports jacket; **ropa de s.** casual clothes
spot [es'pot] *(pl* **spots***)* *nm* (**a**) *(anuncio)* (TV) advert; **un s. publicitario** a (television) commercial (**b**) *CSur (foco)* spotlight
spray [es'prai] *(pl* **sprays***)* *nm* (**a**) *(líquido)* spray; **desodorante/pintura en s.** spray deodorant/paint; **pintadas hechas con s.** spray-painted grafitti (**b**) *(envase)* spray, spray can
sprint [es'prin] *(pl* **sprints***)* *nm* sprint; **la carrera se decidió al s.** the race was decided in the final sprint ►► *Dep* ***s. especial*** *(en ciclismo)* hot spot sprint
sprintar [esprin'tar] *vi* to sprint
sprinter [es'printer] *(pl* **sprinters***)* *nmf* sprinter
squash [es'kwas] *nm Dep* squash
Sr. (*abrev de* **señor**) Mr
Sra. (*abrev de* **señora**) Mrs
Sres. (*abrev de* **señores**) Messrs
Sri Lanka *n* Sri Lanka
S.R.L. (*abrev de* **Sociedad de Responsabilidad Limitada**) Ltd
Srta. (*abrev de* **señorita**) Miss
S.S.[1] (**a**) (*abrev de* **Su Santidad**) HH (**b**) (*abrev de* **Seguridad Social**) = Social Security
S.S.[2] *nfpl Hist* **las S.** the SS
SS. MM. *nmpl* (*abrev de* **Sus Majestades**) their Royal Highnesses
Sta. (*abrev de* **santa**) St
staccato [esta'kato] *nm Mús* staccato
stage [es'taʃ] *nm* (**a**) *(cursillo)* work placement (**b**) *Dep* pre-season training camp
stand [es'tan] *(pl* **stands***)* *nm* stand
standing [es'tandin] *(pl* **standings***)* *nm* standing, social status; **un apartamento de alto s.** a luxury flat; **una compañía de alto s.** a top company
starter [es'tarter] *(pl* **starters***)* *nm* choke; **abrir el s.** to pull out *o* open the choke; **cerrar el s.** to push in *o* close the choke
statu quo [es'tatu'kwo] *nm* status quo
status [es'tatus] *nm inv* status
step [es'tep] *(pl* **steps***)* *nm* step (aerobics)
stick [es'tik] *(pl* **sticks***)* *nm (de hockey)* hockey stick
Sto. (*abrev de* **santo**) St
stock [es'tok] *(pl* **stocks***)* *nm Com* stock
stop [es'top] *(pl* **stops***)* *nm* (**a**) *(señal)* stop sign; **saltarse un s.** to drive straight past a stop sign (**b**) *(en telegrama)* stop
strapless [es'traples] *adj inv Am* strapless
strass [es'tras] *nm inv* paste, strass
stress [es'tres] *nm inv* stress
strike [es'traik] *nm (en béisbol)* strike
strip-tease [es'triptis, estrip'tis] *nm* striptease; **hacer un s.** to strip
stronismo [estro'nismo] *nm* = regime and ideology of Paraguayan dictator General Stroessner (1954-89); **durante el s.** under Stroessner, when Stroessner was in power
stronista [estro'nista] **1** *adj* relating to the Stroessner regime
2 *nmf* supporter of the Stroessner regime
su *(pl* **sus***)* *adj posesivo (de él)* his; *(de ella)* her; *(de cosa, animal)* its; *(de uno)* one's; *(de ellos, ellas)* their; *(de usted, ustedes)* your; **su libro** his/her/your/their book; **sus libros** his/her/your/their books; **su hocico** its snout; *Fam* **debe de tener sus buenos millones en el banco** she must have a good few million in the bank
suahili [swa'χili], **suajili** *nm (lengua)* Swahili
suave 1 *adj* (**a**) *(al tacto) (piel, toalla)* soft; *(jabón)* mild
(**b**) *(no brusco) (movimiento)* smooth; *(curva, cuesta)* gentle; **tiene la dirección muy s.** it has very smooth steering
(**c**) *(sabor)* mild; *(olor)* mild, slight; *(color)* soft; **este curry está bastante s.** this curry is quite mild
(**d**) *(apacible) (clima)* mild; *(brisa)* gentle; *(persona, carácter)* gentle
(**e**) *(fácil, lento) (tarea, ritmo)* gentle
(**f**) *(dócil)* meek; **está s. como un cordero** she's as meek as a lamb
(**g**) *Méx Fam (agradable)* pleasant; **dimos un paseo bien s.** we had a very pleasant stroll
(**h**) EXPR *Méx Fam* **estar s.** to be enough; **ya está s. de tanto barullo** that's enough of that racket; *Méx Fam* **dar la s. a alguien** to suck up to sb
2 *adv Méx Fam (de acuerdo)* all right, fine; **¿salimos a pasear? – s.** shall we go out for a walk? – fine

> **Falso amigo**: El adjetivo inglés **suave** no es la traducción del español **suave**. El inglés **suave** significa "fino", "zalamero" o "elegante".

suavemente *adv (acariciar)* gently; *(hablar)* softly
suavidad *nf* (**a**) *(al tacto) (de piel, toalla)* softness; *(de jabón)* mildness; **la acarició con s.** he caressed her gently (**b**) *(falta de brusquedad) (de movimiento)* smoothness; *(de curva, cuesta)* gentleness (**c**) *(de sabor, olor)* mildness; *(de color)* softness (**d**) *(de clima)* mildness; *(de brisa)* gentleness; *(de carácter)* gentleness (**e**) *(de tarea, ritmo)* gentleness (**f**) *(docilidad)* meekness
suavizante, *CAm* **suavizador, -ora 1** *adj (para ropa, cabello)* conditioning
2 *nm* conditioner ►► ***s. para la ropa*** fabric conditioner *o* softener
suavizar [14] **1** *vt* (**a**) *(poner blando)* to soften; *(ropa, cabello)* to condition; **suaviza el cutis** it leaves your skin soft (**b**) *(sabor, color)* to tone down (**c**) *(dificultad, tarea)* to ease; *(conducción)* to make smoother; *(clima)* to make milder; *(condena)* to reduce the length of (**d**) *(moderar)* **tienes que s. el discurso para no ofender a nadie** you should tone down the speech so you don't offend anyone
2 suavizarse *vpr* (**a**) *(ponerse blando)* to soften (**b**) *(dificultad, tarea)* to become easier; *(clima)* to become milder; **sus relaciones se han suavizado** their relations have improved (**c**) *(hacerse dócil)* to mellow
Suazilandia *n* Swaziland
sub- *pref* sub-
sub-21 *adj Dep* under-21
suba *nf CSur* price rise
subacuático, -a *adj (planta)* subaquatic; *(medicina, mundo)* underwater, subaquatic; *(deporte, fotografía)* underwater
subafluente *nm* minor tributary
subalimentación *nf* undernourishment
subalimentado, -a *adj* undernourished
subalimentar *vt* to undernourish
subalpino, -a *adj* subalpine
subalquilar *vt* to sublet, to sublease
subalterno, -a 1 *adj* (**a**) *(empleado)* auxiliary (**b**) *(secundario)* secondary
2 *nm,f (empleado)* subordinate
3 *nm Taurom* bullfighter's assistant
subarrendador, -ora *nm,f* subletter
subarrendar [3] *vt* to sublet, to sublease
subarrendatario, -a *nm,f* subtenant
subarriendo *nm* (**a**) *(acción)* subletting (**b**) *(contrato)* sublease (agreement)
subártico, -a *adj* subarctic

subasta *nf* (a) *(venta pública)* auction; **sacar algo a s.** to put sth up for auction; **vender en s.** to auction off, to sell at auction (b) *(contrata pública)* tender; **sacar algo a s.** to put sth out to tender

subastador, -ora *nm,f* auctioneer

subastar *vt (cuadro, jarrón)* to auction; *(contrato, obras)* to put out to tender

subatómico, -a *adj* subatomic

subcampeón, -ona *nm,f* runner-up

subcampeonato *nm* second place, runner-up's position

subclase *nf* subclass

subcomandante *nmf* = military rank below that of commander

subcomisario, -a *nm,f* deputy superintendent

subcomisión *nf* subcommittee

subcomité *nm* subcommittee

subconjunto *nm Mat* subset

subconsciencia *nf* subconscious

subconsciente 1 *adj* subconscious
2 *nm* subconscious ►► ***s. colectivo*** collective unconscious

subconsumo *nm Econ* underconsumption

subcontinente *nm* subcontinent

subcontratación *nf* subcontracting

subcontratar *vt* to subcontract

subcontratista *nmf* subcontractor

subcontrato *nm* subcontract

subcultura *nf* subculture

subcutáneo, -a *adj* subcutaneous

subdelegación *nf* subdelegation

subdelegado, -a *nm,f* subdelegate

subdesarrollado, -a *adj* underdeveloped

subdesarrollo *nm* underdevelopment

subdirección *nf (de empresa)* post of deputy director; *(de comercio)* post of assistant manager

subdirector, -ora *nm,f (de empresa)* deputy director; *(de comercio)* assistant manager

subdirectorio *nm Informát* subdirectory

súbdito, -a *nm,f* (a) *(de monarca)* subject (b) *(ciudadano)* citizen, national

subdividir 1 *vt* to subdivide
2 **subdividirse** *vpr* (a) *(ley, documento)* to be subdivided (**en** into) (b) *(células)* to subdivide (**en** into)

subdivisión *nf* subdivision

subdominante *adj Mús* subdominant

subempleado, -a *adj* (a) *(trabajador)* underemployed (b) *(recursos)* underutilized, underemployed

subemplear *vt* (a) *(trabajador)* to underemploy (b) *(recursos)* to underutilize, to underemploy

subempleo *nm* (a) *(de trabajador)* underemployment (b) *(de recursos)* underutilization, underemployment

subespecie *nf* subspecies

subestación *nf Elec* substation

subestimar 1 *vt* to underestimate
2 **subestimarse** *vpr* to underestimate oneself

subfamilia *nf Biol* subfamily

subfusil *nm* automatic rifle

subgénero *nm* subgenus

subgrupo *nm* subgroup

subibaja *nm* seesaw

subida *nf* (a) *(cuesta)* hill (b) *(ascensión)* ascent, climb; **el tenista australiano se impuso en sus subidas a la red** the Australian player showed his superiority when he came to the net (c) *(aumento)* increase, rise; **se espera una s. de las temperaturas** temperatures are expected to rise ►► ***s. de sueldo*** pay rise, *US* raise (d) EXPR *RP Fam* **una s. al carro** an attempt to jump on the bandwagon

subido, -a 1 *adj* (a) *(intenso)* strong, intense; **s. de tono** *(atrevido)* risqué; *(impertinente)* impertinent (b) *Fam (en cantidad)* **tiene el guapo s.** he really fancies himself; **está de un imbécil s.** he has been acting like an idiot recently
2 *nm,f* EXPR *RP Fam* **ser un s. al carro** to have climbed on the bandwagon, to be an opportunist

subidón *nm Fam (de drogas)* high

subíndice *nm* subscript

subinspector, -ora *nm,f* deputy inspector

subintendente *nmf* assistant superintendent

SUBIR 1 *vt* (a) *(poner arriba) (libro, cuadro)* to put up; *(telón)* to raise; *(persiana)* to roll up; *(ventanilla)* to wind up, to close; **he subido la enciclopedia de la primera a la última estantería** I've moved the encyclopedia up from the bottom shelf to the top one; **sube el cuadro un poco** move the picture up a bit *o* a bit higher; **¿me ayudas a s. las bolsas?** could you help me take the bags up?; **ayúdame a s. la caja** *(a lo alto)* help me get the box up; *(al piso de arriba)* help me carry the box upstairs
(b) *(montar)* **s. algo/a alguien a** to lift sth/sb onto
(c) *(alzar) (bandera)* to raise; **s. la mano** to put one's hand up, to raise one's hand
(d) *(ascender) (calle, escaleras)* to go/come up; *(escalera de mano)* to climb; *(pendiente, montaña)* to go up; **subió las escaleras a toda velocidad** she ran up *o* climbed the stairs as fast as she could; **subió la calle a todo correr** he ran up the street as fast as he could
(e) *(aumentar) (precio, impuestos)* to put up, to increase; *(música, volumen, radio)* to turn up; **subió la voz** *o* **el tono para que se le oyera** she raised her voice so she could be heard; **sube la voz** *o* **el tono, no te oigo** speak up, I can't hear you; **s. el fuego de la cocina** to turn up the heat; **s. la moral a alguien** to lift sb's spirits, to cheer sb up
(f) *(hacer ascender de categoría)* to promote
(g) *Mús* to raise the pitch of
(h) *Fam Informát* to upload
2 *vi* (a) *(a piso, azotea)* to go/come up; **¿podrías s. aquí un momento?** could you come up here a minute?; **subo enseguida** I'll be up in a minute; **s. corriendo** to run up; **s. en ascensor** to go/come up in the *Br* lift *o US* elevator; **s. por la escalera** to go/come up the stairs; **s. (a) por algo** to go up and get sth; **s. a la red** *(en tenis)* to come (in) to the net
(b) *(montar) (en avión, barco)* to get on; *(en coche)* to get in; *(en moto, bicicleta, tren)* to get on; *(en caballo)* to get on, to mount; *(en árbol, escalera de mano, silla)* to climb up; **s. a** *(coche)* to get in(to); *(moto, bicicleta, tren, avión)* to get on; *(caballo)* to get on, to mount; *(árbol, escalera de mano)* to climb up; *(silla, mesa)* to get *o* climb onto; *(piso)* to go/come up to; **s. a bordo** to go on board; **es peligroso s. al tren en marcha** it is dangerous to board the train while it is moving
(c) *(aumentar)* to rise, to go up; *(hinchazón, cauce)* to rise; *(fiebre)* to raise, to go up; **los precios subieron** prices went up *o* rose; **subió la gasolina** the price of petrol went up *o* rose; **el euro subió frente a la libra** the euro went up *o* rose against the pound; **las acciones de C & C han subido** C & C share prices have gone up *o* risen; **han subido las ventas** sales are up; **este modelo ha subido de precio** this model has gone up in price, the price of this model has gone up; **el coste total no subirá del millón** the total cost will not be more than *o* over a million; **no subirá de tres horas** it will take three hours at most, it won't take more than three hours; **está subiendo la marea** the tide is coming in; **el jefe ha subido mucho en mi estima** the boss has gone up a lot in my estimation
(d) *(cuenta, importe)* **s. a** to come *o* amount to
(e) *Culin (crecer)* to rise
(f) *Fam (ir, venir)* to come/go up; **subiré a la capital la próxima semana** I'll be going up to the capital next week; **sube a vernos este fin de semana** come up to see us this weekend
(g) *(ascender de categoría)* to be promoted (**a** to); *Dep* to be promoted, to go up (**a** to); **el Atlético subió de categoría** Atlético went up
3 **subirse** *vpr* (a) *(ascender) (en avión, barco)* to get on; *(en coche)* to get in; *(en moto, bicicleta, tren)* to get on; *(en caballo)* to get on, to mount; *(en árbol, escalera de mano, silla)* to climb up; **subirse a** *(coche) (moto, bicicleta, tren, avión)* to get on; *(caballo)* to get on, to mount; *(árbol, escalera de mano)* to climb up; *(silla, mesa)* to get *o* climb onto; *(piso)* to go/come up to; EXPR **subirse por las paredes** to go up the wall, to hit the roof; EXPR **subírsele a la cabeza a alguien: el éxito/alcohol se le subió a la cabeza** the success/alcohol went to her head; EXPR *RP Fam* **subirse al carro** to jump on the bandwagon
(b) *(alzarse)* **subirse las mangas** to roll one's sleeves up; **subirse los calcetines** to pull one's socks up; **subirse los pantalones** to pull one's *Br* trousers *o US* pants up; **subirse la cremallera** to do one's *Br* zip *o US* zipper up
(c) *Fam (ir, venir)* to go/come up; **súbete a esquiar con nosotros** come up and do some skiing with us

---

súbitamente *adv* suddenly, all of a sudden

súbito, -a *adj* sudden; **de s.** suddenly, all of a sudden

subjefe, -a *nm,f (de comercio)* assistant manager

subjetividad *nf* subjectivity

subjetivismo *nm* subjectivism

subjetivo, -a *adj* subjective
sub júdice [suβ'juðiθe] *adj Der* sub judice
subjuntivo, -a 1 *adj* subjunctive
2 *nm* subjunctive
sublema *nm Urug Antes (de partido político)* fraction
sublevación *nf*, **sublevamiento** *nm* uprising
sublevar 1 *vt* (**a**) *(amotinar)* to stir up (**b**) *(indignar)* to infuriate
2 **sublevarse** *vpr* (**a**) *(amotinarse)* to rise up, to rebel (**b**) *(indignarse)* to get infuriated
sublimación *nf* (**a**) *(exaltación)* exaltation (**b**) *Psi* sublimation (**c**) *Quím* sublimation
sublimado *nm Quím* sublimate ►► ***s. corrosivo*** corrosive sublimate
sublimar *vt* (**a**) *(exaltar)* to exalt (**b**) *Psi* to sublimate (**c**) *Quím* to sublimate
sublime *adj* sublime
sublimidad *nf* sublimity
subliminal *adj* subliminal
sublingual *adj* sublingual
submarinismo *nm* scuba diving
submarinista *nmf* (**a**) *(buceador)* scuba diver (**b**) *(tripulante)* submariner
submarino, -a 1 *adj* undersea, submarine; **fotografía submarina** underwater photography
2 *nm* (**a**) *(nave)* submarine ►► ***s. atómico*** atomic submarine; ***s. nuclear*** nuclear submarine (**b**) *Fam (infiltrado)* mole (**c**) *RP (merienda)* = drink of hot milk with a lump of melted chocolate (**d**) *RP (tortura)* = method of torture in which the victim's head is held underwater
submúltiplo, -a 1 *adj* submultiple
2 *nm* submultiple
submundo *nm* world, scene; **el s. de las drogas** the drugs world *o* scene
subnormal 1 *adj* (**a**) *(retrasado)* mentally retarded (**b**) *Fam Pey (imbécil)* moronic
2 *nmf* (**a**) *(retrasado)* mentally retarded person (**b**) *Fam Pey (imbécil)* moron, cretin
subnormalidad *nf* **una campaña de prevención de la s.** a campaign aimed at preventing children from being born with a mental handicap; **la actitud de la sociedad ante la s.** society's attitude to the mentally retarded
suboficial *nmf Mil* non-commissioned officer ►► ***s. de marina*** petty officer
suborden *nm Biol* suborder
subordinación *nf* (**a**) *(sometimiento)* subordination (**b**) *Gram* subordination
subordinado, -a 1 *adj* (**a**) *(sometido)* subordinate (**a** to) (**b**) *Gram* subordinate
2 *nm,f* subordinate
subordinante *Gram* 1 *adj* subordinating
2 *nf* main
subordinar 1 *vt* (**a**) *(someter)* to subordinate (**b**) *Gram* to subordinate
2 **subordinarse** *vpr* to be subordinate (**a** to)
subproducto *nm* by-product
subprograma *nm Informát* subprogram
subrayado, -a 1 *adj* (**a**) *(con línea)* underlined (**b**) *(en cursiva)* italicized, in italics
2 *nm* underlining
subrayar *vt* (**a**) *(palabra, texto)* to underline (**b**) *(destacar)* to underline
subreino *nm Biol* subkingdom
subrepticiamente *adv* surreptitiously
subrepticio, -a *adj* surreptitious
subrogación, *Chile* **subrogancia** *nf Der* subrogation
subrogar [38] *vt Der* to subrogate
subrutina *nf Informát* subroutine
subsahariano, -a 1 *adj* sub-Saharan
2 *nm,f* sub-Saharan African
subsanable *adj* (**a**) *(solucionable)* solvable (**b**) *(corregible)* rectifiable
subsanación *nf (de errores)* correction
subsanar *vt* (**a**) *(problema)* to resolve; *(error)* to correct; **le mandó un ramo de flores para s. su falta de cortesía** he sent her a bouquet of flowers to make amends for his discourtesy (**b**) *(disculpar)* to excuse
subscribir = **suscribir**
subscripción = **suscripción**
subscriptor, -ora = **suscriptor**
subscrito, -a = **suscrito**
subsecretaría *nf* (**a**) *(en España)* under-secretaryship (**b**) *(en Latinoamérica)* deputy ministership
subsecretario, -a *nm,f* (**a**) *(administrativo)* assistant secretary (**b**) *(de ministro) (en España)* under-secretary (**c**) *(de ministro) (en Latinoamérica)* deputy minister
subsector *nm* subsector
subsecuentemente *adv* subsequently
subsidiar *vt* to subsidize
subsidiariedad *nf* subsidiarity
subsidiario, -a *adj* (**a**) *(empresa)* subsidiary (**b**) *Der* ancillary
subsidio *nm* benefit, allowance ►► ***s. de desempleo*** unemployment benefit; ***s. de enfermedad*** sick pay; ***s. de invalidez*** disability allowance
subsiguiente *adj* subsequent
subsiguientemente *adv* immediately afterwards
subsistema *nm* subsystem
subsistencia *nf* (**a**) *(vida)* subsistence (**b**) *(conservación)* continued existence (**c**) **subsistencias** *(provisiones)* provisions
subsistente *adj* surviving
subsistir *vi* (**a**) *(vivir)* to live, to exist (**b**) *(sobrevivir)* to survive
subsónico, -a *adj* subsonic
substancia, substancial *etc* = **sustancia, sustancial** *etc*
substantivar, substantivo, -a *etc* = **sustantivar, sustantivo** *etc*
substitución, substituir *etc* = **sustitución, sustituir** *etc*
substracción, substraer *etc* = **sustracción, sustraer** *etc*
substrato = **sustrato**
subsuelo *nm* (**a**) *(terreno)* subsoil (**b**) *Andes, RP (sótano)* basement
subte *nm RP Br* underground, *US* subway; **en s.** by *Br* underground *o* *US* subway
subteniente *nmf* sub-lieutenant
subterfugio *nm* subterfuge; **sin subterfugios** without subterfuge
subterráneo, -a 1 *adj* subterranean, underground
2 *nm* (**a**) *(túnel)* underground tunnel (**b**) *RP (metro) Br* underground, *US* subway
subtipo *nm Biol* subtype
subtitular *vt* (**a**) *(película)* to subtitle; **una película subtitulada** a subtitled movie *o Br* film (**b**) *(libro, capítulo)* to subtitle
subtítulo *nm* (**a**) *(de película)* subtitle (**b**) *(de libro, capítulo)* subtitle
subtotal *nm* subtotal
subtropical *adj* subtropical
suburbano, -a 1 *adj* suburban
2 *nm (tren)* suburban train
suburbial *adj* **barrio s.** poor suburb
suburbio *nm* (**a**) *(barrio pobre)* poor suburb (**b**) *Ecuad (barrio de chabolas)* shanty-town

> **Falso amigo**: Aunque tanto **suburb** como **suburbio** se refieren a un barrio situado a las afueras de una población, sus connotaciones son diametralmente opuestas, ya que con el sustantivo **suburb** se hace referencia a la zona en la que habitan las clases acomodadas, y no las familias más modestas, quienes viven en un **suburbio**.

subvalorar *vt* to undervalue, to underrate
subvención *nf* (**a**) *(para proteger precios, una industria)* subsidy (**b**) *(para un proyecto)* grant; **la orquesta recibe una s. del ayuntamiento** the orchestra receives financial support *o* a grant from the town council
subvencionar *vt* (**a**) *(precios, industria)* to subsidize (**b**) *(proyecto, actividad cultural, estudios)* to provide financial support for; **el proyecto está subvencionado por el gobierno** the project is financed by a government grant
subversión *nf* subversion
subversivo, -a *adj* subversive
subvertir [63] *vt* to subvert
subyacente *adj* underlying

SUBJUNTIVO

This is a basic, though not exhaustive, list of the uses of the subjunctive in Spanish:

A) In subordinate clauses starting with **que**:

1.- Where the verb in the main clause implies an intention to influence the conduct of another person, whether directly (**conseguir, intentar, necesitar**) or through a command (**insistir, mandar, ordenar**), prohibition (**prohibir**), or wish (**desear, pedir**), or by giving advice (**aconsejar**), permission (**permitir, invitar**) and so on :

te ordeno que vengas aquí *I order you to come here*

2.- When the verb in the main clause conveys a feeling: **aburrir, apenar, disgustar, divertir, encantar, gustar, molestar, perdonar, sentir, temer**:

me alegro que estés bien *I'm glad you're well*
¿te importa que fume? *do you mind if I smoke?*
a todos nos sorprendió que decidiera marcharse *we were all surprised that he decided to leave*

3.- When the verb in the main clause expresses an evaluation or value judgement, normally of the form: **ser/estar/parecer** + ADJECTIVE/NOUN/ADVERB + **que**:

es extraño que tarde tanto *it's odd he should be so late*

When the verb in the main clause expresses certainty or a truth, on the other hand, the verb in the subordinate clause is in the indicative:

es cierto que la luna es redonda *it's true that the moon is round*

4.-When the verb in the main clause suggests doubt about the possibility or likelihood of what is contained in the subordinate clause: **dudar que, es improbable que, no pensar, no creer, no suponer, no imaginar**:

no creo que Mario esté aquí *I don't think Mario is here* but: **creo que Mario está aquí** *I think Mario is here*

B) After conjunctions

1.- With **donde** or **como** if they do not refer to a concrete place or manner:

hazlo como quieras *do it the way you want* but: **hazlo como te digo** *do it the way I tell you*

déjalo donde puedas *leave it wherever you can* but: **no estaba donde lo puse ayer** *it wasn't where I put it yesterday*

2.- With conjunctions referring to a hypothetical or future time: **cuando, mientras que, hasta que, después que, cada vez que, antes de que** (this last conjunction is always followed by the subjunctive):

cuando vengas, te lo diré *I'll tell you when you come* but: **cuando vas a su casa nunca le encuentras allí** *when you go to his house you never find him at home*

no te irás hasta que no me digas la verdad *you're not leaving until you tell me the truth*

3.- With conjunctions which indicate conditions, such as **a no ser que, con tal de que, a condición de que, en caso de que**:

no pensaba ir, a no ser que necesiten mi ayuda *I wasn't thinking of going, unless they need my help*
¡cómpraselo! ¡con tal de que deje de llorar! *buy it for him! anything to stop him crying!*

Where **si** refers to an unlikely or impossible condition, the subjunctive is also required:

si fuera sueca muy probablemente tendría el pelo rubio *if she was/were Swedish she would most likely have blonde hair*

4.- Conjunctions which express the purpose of an action (eg **para que, a fin de que, con el objeto de que**) are always followed by the subjunctive:

los padres trabajan mucho para que los hijos puedan estudiar *the parents work hard so that their children can study*

5.- With conjunctions indicating contrast, such as **aunque** or **a pesar de que**, the subjunctive is used when referring to the future. In the present both options may be possible, though reference to a "hypothetical present" requires the subjunctive:

aunque me lo pida de rodillas, no voy a ir *even if he asks me on his knees, I'm not going to go*

Where the sentence refers to present matters of fact, the choice between subjunctive and indicative is mainly a matter of emphasis. The indicative is appropriate where a simple statement of contrast is desired:

aunque las ballenas son mamíferos, parecen peces *although whales are mammals they look like fish*

Where the subjunctive is used, the effect is to emphasize the contrast, which usually requires the translation "even though":

sí, pero aunque sea español, vive en Francia *yes, but even though he's Spanish he lives in France*

subyacer *vi (estar oculto)* **en su obra subyace la amargura** there's an underlying bitterness in his work; **bajo su apariencia tímida subyace una gran inteligencia** beneath his timid exterior lies a very sharp mind; **s. bajo algo** to underlie sth

subyugación *nf* subjugation

subyugado, -a *adj* (**a**) *(sometido)* subjugated (**b**) *(cautivado)* **s. por** captivated by, enthralled by

subyugar [38] *vt* (**a**) *(someter)* to subjugate (**b**) *(cautivar)* to captivate

succión *nf* suction

succionar *vt (sujeto: raíces)* to suck up; *(sujeto: bebé)* to suck

sucedáneo, -a 1 *adj* ersatz, substitute
2 *nm* (**a**) *(sustituto)* substitute; **un s. del café** a coffee substitute ▸▸ ***s. de chocolate*** ersatz chocolate (**b**) *(mala copia)* **ser un s. de** to be an apology for

suceder 1 *v impersonal (ocurrir)* to happen; **sucedió el año pasado** it happened last year; **nunca nos había sucedido nada igual** we'd never had anything like it happen to us before; **suceda lo que suceda** whatever happens; **sucedió que me olvidé de poner el despertador** what happened was that I forgot to set the alarm clock; **lo peor que nos podía s. es que...** the worst that could happen to us is that...; **sucedió que estábamos un día en el campo cuando...** it so happens that we were in the country one day when...; **llevaré provisiones para varios días por lo que pueda s.** I'll take enough provisions for a few days just in case anything happens; **¿qué te sucede?** what's the matter (with you)?
2 *vt (sustituir)* to succeed (**en** in); **al presidente socialista le sucedió un conservador** the socialist president was succeeded by a conservative; **sucedió a su padre en el trono** he succeeded his father to the throne
3 *vi (venir después)* **s. a** to come after, to follow; **la primavera sucede al invierno** spring follows winter; **a la guerra sucedieron años muy tristes** the war was followed by years of misery

sucedido *nm* event

sucesión *nf* (**a**) *(serie)* succession; **sufrieron una s. de desgracias** they had a series of mishaps
(**b**) *(cambio) (de monarca)* succession; *(de cargo importante)* succession, changeover; **la s. al trono** the succession to the throne
(**c**) *(descendencia)* **morir sin s.** to die without issue; **no tuvo s.** he had no heirs ▸▸ ***s. intestada*** intestate succession; ***s. testada*** testate succession; ***s. universal*** universal succession
(**d**) *Der (legado)* estate, inheritance; **impuesto de s.** *o* **sobre sucesiones** inheritance tax
(**e**) *Mat* sequence

sucesivamente *adv* successively; **y así s.** and so on

sucesivo, -a *adj* (**a**) *(consecutivo)* successive, consecutive; **viajó hasta allí en cinco días sucesivos** he travelled there on five successive days *o* on five days in succession (**b**) *(siguiente)* **en días sucesivos les informaremos** we shall inform you over the next few days; **en lo s.** in future

suceso *nm* (**a**) *(acontecimiento)* event (**b**) *(hecho delictivo)* crime; *(incidente)* incident; **(sección de) sucesos** *(en prensa)* = section of newspaper dealing with accidents, crimes, disasters etc

> **Falso amigo**: El sustantivo inglés **success** no es la traducción del español **suceso**. En inglés **success** significa "éxito".

sucesor, -ora 1 *adj* succeeding
2 *nm,f* successor

sucesorio, -a *adj* succession; **impuesto s.** inheritance tax

suche 1 *adj Méx, Ven* unripe
2 *nm* (**a**) *Chile, Nic Fam Pey* menial (**b**) *Ecuad, Perú (árbol)* white frangipani

suciedad *nf* (**a**) *(falta de limpieza)* dirtiness; *(al comer, trabajar)* messiness (**b**) *(porquería)* dirt, filth; **esta cocina está llena de s.** this kitchen is filthy

sucintamente *adv* succinctly

sucinto, -a *adj* (**a**) *(conciso)* succinct (**b**) *(pequeño, corto)* skimpy; **una falda sucinta** a skimpy skirt

sucio, -a 1 *adj* (**a**) *(sin limpieza)* dirty; **estar s.** to be dirty; **tiene muy sucia la cocina** his kitchen is very dirty; **la ropa sucia** the dirty clothes
(**b**) *(al comer, trabajar)* messy; **ser s.** to be messy
(**c**) *(que se ensucia)* **el blanco es un color muy s.** white is a colour that really shows the dirt
(**d**) *(color)* dirty; **un pantalón de un color blanco s.** off-white *Br* trousers *o US* pants
(**e**) *(lenguaje)* dirty, filthy
(**f**) *(conciencia)* bad, guilty
(**g**) **en s.** *(escribir)* in rough
2 *adv* **jugar s.** to play dirty
3 *nm Ven Fam* stain, dirty mark

suco *nm Andes, Ven (terreno)* muddy ground

Sucre *n* Sucre

sucre *nm (moneda)* sucre

sucrense 1 *adj* of/from Sucre *(Bolivia or Venezuela)*
2 *nmf* person from Sucre *(Bolivia or Venezuela)*

sucucho *nm RP Fam* hovel

suculento, -a *adj* (**a**) *(delicioso)* tasty; *(jugoso)* succulent (**b**) *Bot* succulent

sucumbir *vi* (**a**) *(rendirse, ceder)* to succumb; **la ciudad sucumbió a los ataques enemigos** the city succumbed to the enemy attacks; **sucumbí a la tentación** I succumbed *o* gave in to temptation (**b**) *(fallecer)* to die; *(desaparecer)* to disappear

sucursal *nf (de banco)* branch; *(de empresa)* office

sudaca *Esp Fam* 1 *adj* = pejorative term used to refer to people from Latin America
2 *nmf* = pejorative term for a person from Latin America

sudadera *nf* (**a**) *(prenda)* sweatshirt (**b**) *Fam (sudor)* **no se abrigó después de una s. y se enfrió** she didn't wrap up after having worked up a sweat and caught a cold; **nos pegamos una s. para subir el piano** we sweated buckets getting the piano upstairs (**c**) *Col (chándal)* tracksuit

sudado *nm Andes* = dish of steamed fish and vegetables

Sudáfrica *n* South Africa

sudafricano, -a 1 *adj* South African
2 *nm,f* South African

Sudamérica *n* South America

sudamericano, -a 1 *adj* South American
2 *nm,f* South American

Sudán *n* Sudan

sudanés, -esa 1 *adj* Sudanese
2 *nm,f* Sudanese

sudar 1 *vi* (**a**) *(transpirar)* to sweat; *Fam* **sudaban a chorros** they were dripping sweat (**b**) *(pared)* to run with condensation (**c**) *(trabajar duro)* **sudaron mucho por (conseguir) ese trofeo** they had to sweat blood to win this trophy (**d**) EXPR *Esp muy Fam* **me la suda** *Br* I don't give a monkey's, *US* I don't give a rat's ass
2 *vt* (**a**) *(empapar)* to soak in sweat; **sudó las sábanas** he soaked the sheets in sweat (**b**) *Fam (trabajar duro por)* to sweat blood for (**c**) EXPR **s. la gota gorda** *(transpirar mucho)* to sweat buckets; *(esforzarse)* to sweat blood; **s. tinta** to sweat blood

sudario *nm* shroud

sudcaliforniano, -a 1 *adj* of/from Baja California Sur *(Mexico)*
2 *nm,f* person from Baja California Sur *(Mexico)*

sudestada *nf CSur* = rainy, southeasterly wind in Argentina

sudeste, sureste 1 *adj (posición, parte)* southeast, southeastern; *(dirección, viento)* southeasterly
2 *nm* southeast ▸▸ ***el Sudeste*** *o* ***Sureste asiático*** Southeast Asia

sudista *Hist* 1 *adj* Southern *(in US Civil War)*
2 *nmf* Southerner *(in US Civil War)*

sudoeste, suroeste 1 *adj (posición, parte)* southwest, southwestern; *(dirección, viento)* southwesterly
2 *nm* southwest

sudor *nm* (**a**) *(transpiración)* sweat; **con el s. de mi frente** by the sweat of my brow ▸▸ ***s. frío*** cold sweat; **me entran sudores fríos de pensarlo** *(me entra miedo)* it makes me break out in a cold sweat *o* it sends a shiver down my spine just to think of it
(**b**) *(de pared)* condensation
(**c**) **sudores** *(esfuerzos)* toil, labour; **me costó muchos sudores conseguirlo** it cost me a lot of trouble to get hold of it

sudoración *nf* sweating, perspiration

sudoriento, -a *adj* sweaty

sudorífero, -a 1 *adj* sudoriferous, sudorific
2 *nm* sudorific

sudoríparo, -a *adj* sweat; **glándula sudorípara** sweat gland

sudoroso, -a *adj* sweaty

sudsudeste, sudsureste *nm* south-southeast

sudsudoeste, sudsuroeste *nm* south-southwest

sudsureste = **sudsudeste**

sudsuroeste = **sudsudoeste**

Suecia *n* Sweden

sueco, -a 1 *adj* Swedish
2 *nm,f (persona)* Swede; EXPR *Fam* **hacerse el s.** *(fingir no entender)* to pretend not to understand, to play dumb; *(fingir no ver)* to pretend not to see
3 *nm (lengua)* Swedish

suegro, -a *nm,f* father-in-law, *f* mother-in-law; **suegros** parents-in-law, in-laws

suela *nf* (**a**) *(de zapato)* sole; **media s.** half-sole; EXPR *Fam* **estar como una s.: este filete está como una s.** this steak's as tough as old boots; EXPR *Fam* **no le llega a la s. del zapato** he can't hold a candle to her (**b**) *(cuero)* coarse leather (**c**) *(de taco de billar)* cue tip (**d**) *(de grifo)* washer

sueldo[1] *ver* **soldar**

sueldo[2] *nm (salario)* pay, wages; *(de profesional, oficinista)* salary; **a s.** *(asesino)* hired; *(empleado)* salaried; **me han subido el s.** they've given me a pay rise *o US* raise; **pidió una semana sin s.** he asked for a week's unpaid leave ►► ***s. base*** basic pay, basic wage; *(de profesional, oficinista)* basic salary; ***s. mínimo*** minimum wage; ***s. neto*** take-home *o* net pay

suelo[1] *etc ver* **soler**

suelo[2] *nm* (**a**) *(pavimento) (en interiores)* floor; *(en el exterior)* ground; EXPR *Fam* **arrastrarse por el s.** to grovel, to humble oneself; EXPR *Fam* **besar el s.** to fall flat on one's face; EXPR **echar algo por el s.** to ruin sth; EXPR *Fam* **estar por los suelos** *(persona, precio)* to be at rock bottom; *(productos)* to be dirt cheap; **tienen la moral por los suelos** their morale has hit rock bottom; EXPR **poner** *o* **tirar por los suelos** to run down, to criticize; **venir** *o* **venirse al s.** *(caer)* to fall down, to collapse; *(fracasar)* to fail
(**b**) *(terreno, territorio)* soil; *(para edificar)* land; **en s. colombiano** on Colombian soil; **el precio del s. urbano** land prices in urban areas ►► ***s. no urbanizable*** land which is unsuitable for development; ***s. urbanizable*** land suitable for development

suelta *nf (liberación)* release; **concluyeron la protesta con una s. de palomas** they brought the protest to a close with a release of white doves

suelto, -a 1 *ver* **soltar**
2 *adj* (**a**) *(animal, criminal)* loose; **las vacas pastaban sueltas por el prado** the cows grazed freely in the meadow; **andar s.** *(animal)* to be on the loose; *(criminal)* to be at large
(**b**) *(tornillo, cuerda)* loose; *(cordones)* undone; **deja el cinturón un poco más s.** loosen your belt a little
(**c**) *(vestido)* loose, loose-fitting; **la falda me queda muy suelta** the skirt is very loose on me
(**d**) *(separado)* separate; *(desparejado)* odd; **no los vendemos sueltos** we don't sell them separately; **guardo algunos números sueltos de esa revista** I've kept a few odd numbers of that magazine
(**e**) *(no envasado)* loose; **venden los tornillos sueltos** they sell the screws loose *o* singly
(**f**) *(dinero)* **¿tienes 25 céntimos sueltos?** have you got 25 cents in loose change?
(**g**) *(arroz)* fluffy
(**h**) *(lenguaje, estilo)* fluent, fluid
(**i**) *(desenvuelto)* comfortable, at ease
(**j**) *(con diarrea)* **estar s.** to have loose bowels
3 *nm* (**a**) *(calderilla)* loose change; **¿llevas s.?** do you have any change? (**b**) *(en periódico)* short item

sueno *etc ver* **sonar**

sueñecito *nm* snooze; **echarse un s.** to have a snooze

SUEÑO 1 *ver* **soñar**
2 *nm* (**a**) *(ganas de dormir)* sleepiness; *(por medicamento, alcohol)* drowsiness; **tener s.** to be sleepy; **(estoy que) me caigo** *o* **me muero de s.** I'm falling asleep on my feet; **tienes cara de s.** you look sleepy; **algunos medicamentos me dan s.** certain medicines make me drowsy; **con la tele** *o* **viendo la tele me entra s.** watching TV makes me sleepy; **¡qué s.!** I'm really tired *o* sleepy!; **el café le quita el s.** coffee wakes her up
(**b**) *(estado de dormir)* sleep; **s. ligero/pesado** light/heavy sleep; **tener el s. ligero/pesado** to be a light/heavy sleeper; *Esp* **coger el s.** to get to sleep; **conciliar el s.** to get to sleep; **descabezar** *o* **echar un s.** to have a nap; **no pierdas el s. por él/ello** don't lose any sleep over him/it; **no me quita el s.** I'm not losing any sleep over it; **tengo s. atrasado** I've got a lot of sleep to catch up on ►► ***s. eterno*** eternal rest; ***s. REM*** REM sleep
(**c**) *(imagen mental)* dream; **un mal s.** a bad dream; **tener un s.** to have a dream; **tuve un s. contigo** I had a dream about you; **en sueños** in a dream; **entre sueños oí que te ibas** I was half-asleep when I heard you go; **ni en sueños** no way, under no circumstances; **ni en sueños haría yo eso** no way *o* under no circumstances would I ever do a thing like that, I wouldn't dream of doing a thing like that
(**d**) *(objetivo, maravilla, quimera)* dream; **hacer eso es el s. de toda una vida** doing this is my dream come true; **el s. de su vida era dar la vuelta al mundo** her dream was to travel round the world; **esta casa es un s.** this house is a dream; **el hombre/la casa de sus sueños** the man/house of her dreams, her dream man/house; **una medalla olímpica, el s. dorado de cualquier deportista** an Olympic medal, every sportsman's dream *o* what every sportsman dreams about; **un s. hecho realidad** a dream come true; **un s. imposible** a pipe dream

suero *nm* (**a**) *(solución salina)* saline solution ►► ***s. artificial*** saline solution; ***s. fisiológico*** saline solution; ***s. de la verdad*** truth drug (**b**) *(de la sangre)* serum ►► ***s. linfático*** lymphatic fluid (**c**) *(de la leche)* whey

sueroterapia *nf* serotherapy

suerte *nf* (**a**) *(azar)* chance; **echar** *o* **tirar algo a** *Esp* **suertes** *o Am* **a la s.** to draw lots for sth; EXPR **la s. está echada** the die is cast
(**b**) *(fortuna)* luck; **te deseo buena s.** I wish you good luck; **es una s. que estés aquí** it's lucky you're here; **estar de s.** to be in luck; **¡qué s.!** that was lucky!; **¡qué s. tuviste!** you were so lucky!; **¡qué s. que traje el paraguas!** how lucky that I brought my umbrella!; **por s.** luckily; **probar s.** to try one's luck; **tener (buena) s.** to be lucky; **tiene la s. de vivir cerca de la playa** he's lucky enough to live near the beach; **tener mala s.** to be unlucky; **tuve muy mala s. con las preguntas que me tocaron** I was very unlucky with the questions that came up; EXPR **tener la s. de espaldas** to be having a run of bad luck; EXPR **tentar a la s.** to tempt fate; EXPR **tocar** *o* **caer en s. a alguien** to fall to sb's lot; **me ha tocado** *o* **caído en s. ser el primero** fate decreed that I should be the first one ►► ***la s. del principiante*** beginner's luck
(**c**) *(destino)* fate; **abandonaron el barco a su s.** they abandoned the boat to its fate
(**d**) *(clase)* **toda s. de** all manner of; **conocí a toda s. de personas** I met all sorts of people; **ser una s. de...** to be a kind *o* sort of...
(**e**) *(manera)* manner, fashion; **de s. que** in such a way that
(**f**) *Taurom* = any of the three stages ("tercios") of a bullfight
(**g**) *Perú (billete de lotería)* lottery ticket

suertero, -a 1 *adj CSur Fam* lucky, *Br* jammy
2 *nm,f Perú* lottery ticket seller

suertudo, -a *Fam* 1 *adj* lucky, *Br* jammy
2 *nm,f* lucky *o Br* jammy devil

sueste *nm* sou'wester

suéter (*pl* **suéteres**) *nm* sweater

suevo, -a *Hist* 1 *adj* Suevic
2 *nm,f (pueblo)* **los suevos** the Suevi, = Germanic tribe which invaded Spain in the 5th century AD

sufí (*pl* **sufíes**) 1 *adj* sufic
2 *nmf* sufi

suficiencia *nf* (**a**) *(capacidad)* proficiency (**b**) *(idoneidad)* suitability; *(de medidas, esfuerzos)* adequacy (**c**) *(presunción)* smugness, self-importance; **me miró con un aire de s.** he looked at me smugly

suficiente 1 *adj* (**a**) *(bastante)* enough; *(medidas, esfuerzos)* adequate; **no llevo (dinero) s.** I don't have enough (money) on me; **no tienes la estatura s.** you're not tall enough; **con 20 litros habrá más que s.** 20 litres will be more than enough; **¡ya es s.!, ¡silencio!** that's enough! silence! (**b**) *(presuntuoso)* smug, full of oneself
2 *nm (nota)* pass *(between 5 and 5.9 out of 10)*

suficientemente *adv* enough, sufficiently; **esta cocina no está s. limpia** this kitchen is not clean enough; **es lo s. inteligente como para no arriesgarse** she's intelligent enough not to take the risk; **no me quedó s. claro lo que quería decir** it wasn't clear enough to me what he meant

sufijo *nm* suffix

sufismo *nm* Sufism

suflé *nm* soufflé

sufragar [38] 1 *vt (costes)* to defray; *(estudios)* to meet the cost of
2 *vi Am (votar)* to vote

sufragio *nm* (**a**) *(sistema)* suffrage ►► ***s. directo*** direct suffrage; ***s. indirecto*** indirect suffrage; ***s. restringido*** restricted suffrage; ***s. universal*** universal suffrage (**b**) *(voto)* vote (**c**) *(oración)* suffrage

sufragismo *nm Hist* suffragette movement

sufragista *Hist* 1 *adj* suffragette; **movimiento s.** suffragette movement
2 *nmf* suffragette

sufrible *adj* bearable, endurable

sufrido, -a *adj* (**a**) *(resignado)* patient, uncomplaining; *(durante mucho tiempo)* long-suffering (**b**) *(resistente) (tela)* hardwearing; **un color muy s.** a colour that doesn't show the dirt

sufridor, -ora *adj* easily worried

sufrimiento *nm* suffering; **una droga para aliviar el s. de los enfermos terminales** a drug to alleviate the suffering of the terminally ill; **el hijo les está costando muchos sufrimientos** their son is causing them a lot of heartache

sufrir 1 *vt* (**a**) *(padecer)* to suffer; *(accidente)* to have; **sufre frecuentes ataques epilépticos** she often has epileptic fits; **sufrió persecución por sus ideas** she suffered persecution for her ideas; **no sufrió daños** it wasn't damaged; **sufrió una agresión/un atentado** he was attacked/an attempt was made on his life; **sufrí una vergüenza increíble** I felt incredibly embarrassed; **la empresa ha sufrido pérdidas** the company has reported *o* made losses; **el ejército invasor sufrió numerosas bajas** the invading army suffered numerous casualties

(**b**) *(soportar)* to put up with, to bear; **tengo que s. sus manías** I have to put up with his idiosyncrasies; **a tu jefe no hay quien lo sufra** your boss is impossible to put up with

(**c**) *(experimentar)* to undergo, to experience; **la Bolsa sufrió una caída** the stock market fell; **las temperaturas sufrirán un descenso** temperatures will fall

2 *vi (padecer)* to suffer; **sufrió mucho antes de morir** she suffered a lot before she died; **sufre mucho si su hijo no lo llama** he gets very anxious if his son doesn't call him; **s. de** *(enfermedad)* to suffer from; **s. del estómago/riñón** to have stomach/kidney trouble *o* a stomach/kidney complaint

sugerencia *nf* suggestion; **me gustaría hacer una s.** I'd like to make a suggestion; **a s. de alguien** at sb's suggestion

sugerente *adj* (**a**) *(evocador)* evocative (**b**) *(atractivo)* attractive

sugerir [63] *vt* (**a**) *(proponer)* to suggest; **me sugirió visitar el país en verano** he suggested I should visit the country in summer; **¿qué sugieres que hagamos?** what do you suggest we do?; **sugirió que diéramos la vuelta** he suggested we (should) turn back

(**b**) *(evocar)* to evoke; **¿qué te sugiere este poema?** what does this poem remind you of?; **aquella batalla le sugirió el tema de su próximo libro** that battle gave him the idea for his next book

sugestión *nf* (**a**) *(acción)* suggestion; **tiene mucho poder de s.** she has great powers of suggestion (**b**) *(sugerencia)* suggestion

sugestionable *adj* impressionable

sugestionar 1 *vt* to influence

2 **sugestionarse** *vpr* (**a**) *(obsesionarse)* to get ideas into one's head (**b**) *Psi* to use autosuggestion

sugestivo, -a *adj* attractive

> **Falso amigo**: El adjetivo inglés **suggestive** no es la traducción del español **sugestivo**. En inglés **suggestive** significa "sugerente" o "insinuante".

sugiero *etc ver* **sugerir**

sugiriera *etc ver* **sugerir**

suiche *nm Col, Ven* switch

suicida 1 *adj* suicidal

2 *nmf (por naturaleza)* suicidal person; *(persona que se ha suicidado)* person who has committed suicide; *(persona que ha intentado suicidarse)* person who attempted to commit suicide

suicidarse *vpr* to commit suicide

suicidio *nm* (**a**) *(de persona)* suicide ►► ***s. asistido*** assisted suicide (**b**) *(locura)* suicide; **invertir en esa empresa sería un s.** it would be suicide to invest in that company

sui géneris *adj inv* peculiar, unusual; **tiene un concepto muy s. de la amistad** she has her own peculiar notion of friendship; **es un artista muy s.** he's a very idiosyncratic artist; **un sistema democrático s.** a system of democracy unlike any other

suite [suit] *nf* (**a**) *(habitación)* suite ►► ***s. nupcial*** bridal suite (**b**) *Mús* suite (**c**) *Informát* suite

Suiza *n* Switzerland

suizo, -a 1 *adj* Swiss

2 *nm,f* Swiss

3 *nm Esp (dulce)* = type of sugared bun

sujeción *nf* (**a**) *(acción)* **un neumático con una excelente s. al firme** a tyre with excellent road-holding properties; **los pilares de s. del puente se hundieron** the supporting pillars of the bridge collapsed (**b**) *(sometimiento)* subjection

sujetacorbata *nm Am* tie clip

sujetador *nm Esp (sostén)* bra, brassiere; *(de bikini)* (bikini) top ►► ***s. de aros*** underwired bra; ***s. deportivo*** sports bra

sujetalibros *nm inv* book end

sujetapapeles *nm inv* paper clip

sujetar 1 *vt* (**a**) *(agarrar) (para mantener en su sitio)* to hold in place; *(sobre una superficie, con un peso)* to hold down; *(para que no se caiga)* to hold up; **sujeta la cuerda al poste** tie the rope to the post; **s. con clavos/cola** to fasten with nails/glue; **sujeta los papeles con un clip** fasten the papers together with a paper clip; **le sujetó el pelo con una goma** she tied his hair back with an elastic band; **intentó escapar, pero la sujetaron firmemente** she tried to escape, but they kept a firm grip on her; **si no lo llegan a s., la mata** if they hadn't held him back, he would have killed her

(**b**) *(sostener)* to hold; **sujétame esta bolsa un momento** hold this bag for a moment, will you?

(**c**) *(someter)* to control

2 **sujetarse** *vpr* (**a**) *(agarrarse)* **se sujeta el pelo con una horquilla** she keeps her hair in place with a hairclip; **sujétate bien o te caerás** hold on tight or you'll fall; **sujetarse a** to hold on to; **sujétate al pasamanos** hold on to the handrail

(**b**) *(aguantarse)* to stay in place; **esta pegatina no se sujeta** this sticker won't stick properly

(**c**) *(someterse)* **sujetarse a** *(normas)* to comply with, to abide by; *(autoridad)* to submit to

sujeto, -a 1 *adj* (**a**) *(agarrado)* fastened; **las cuerdas están bien sujetas** the ropes are secure *o* are firmly fastened (**b**) *(sometido)* subject (**a** to); **este proyecto está s. a modificaciones** this plan is subject to modifications

2 *nm* (**a**) *(de frase)* subject ►► ***s. agente*** actor (**b**) *(individuo)* individual; **un s. sospechoso** a suspicious individual ►► *Econ* ***s. pasivo*** taxpayer (**c**) *Filosofía* subject

sulfamida *nf Farm* sulphonamide

sulfatar 1 *vt* to sulpherize

2 **sulfatarse** *vpr (pilas)* to leak

sulfato *nm* sulphate ►► ***s. de cobre*** copper sulphate

sulfhídrico, -a *adj Quím* **ácido s.** hydrogen sulphide

sulfito *nm* sulphite

sulfurar 1 *vt* (**a**) *Fam (encolerizar)* to infuriate (**b**) *Quím* to sulphurate

2 **sulfurarse** *vpr Fam (encolerizarse)* to get mad; **¡no te sulfures!** don't get mad!

sulfúrico, -a *adj* sulphuric

sulfuro *nm* sulphide

sulfuroso, -a *adj Quím* sulphurous

sulky *nm RP* = a light two-wheeled horse-drawn vehicle

sultán *nm* sultan

sultana *nf* sultana

sultanato, sultanado *nm* sultanate

suma 1 *nf* (**a**) *(operación matemática)* addition; **hacer una s.** to do an addition

(**b**) *(conjunto) (de conocimientos, datos)* total, sum; *(de dinero)* sum; **es la s. del trabajo de varios investigadores** it is the product of the work of several researchers; **la s. de los gastos asciende a 4.000 pesos** total expenditure was 4,000 pesos ►► *Informát* ***s. de comprobación*** checksum; *Informát* ***s. de control*** checksum

2 **en suma** *loc adv (en resumen)* in short

sumamente *adv* extremely; **es s. agradable** he's extremely pleasant

sumando *nm Mat* addend

sumar 1 *vt* (**a**) *(varias cantidades)* to add together; **súmale diez** add ten (**b**) *(dar como resultado)* to add up to, to make; **tres y cinco suman ocho** three and five make *o* are eight (**c**) *(añadir)* to add; **súmale a eso todas las mentiras que nos ha dicho** to that we also have to add all the lies he's told us; **s. y sigue** *(en contabilidad)* carried forward; *Fam* here we go again! (**d**) *(costar)* to come to

2 **sumarse** *vpr* (**a**) *(agregarse)* **la epidemia se suma ahora a la larga sequía** the epidemic comes on top of the long drought; **y a eso se suman las pocas ganas que tengo de trabajar** and on top of that I don't feel at all like working

(**b**) *(adherirse)* to join (**a** in); **sumarse a la opinión de alguien** to adhere to sb's opinion; **los mineros se sumaron a la manifestación** the miners joined (in) the demonstration

sumarial *adj* pertaining to an indictment; **decretar el secreto s.** = to deny access to information relating to a judicial inquiry

sumariamente *adv* summarily, without delay

sumario, -a 1 *adj* (**a**) *(conciso)* brief (**b**) *Der* summary
2 *nm* (**a**) *(resumen)* summary (**b**) *Der* examining magistrate's report; **el juez que instruye el s.** the examining magistrate
sumarísimo, -a *adj Der* swift, expeditious
Sumatra *n* Sumatra
sumergible 1 *adj* (**a**) *(reloj, cámara)* waterproof (**b**) *(barco)* submersible
2 *nm* submersible
sumergido, -a *adj* (**a**) *(bajo el agua)* submerged; **el país está sumergido en el caos** the country is enveloped in chaos (**b**) *(ilegal)* black; **la economía sumergida** the black economy *o* market
sumergir [24] 1 *vt* (**a**) *(hundir)* to submerge; *(con fuerza)* to plunge; *(bañar)* to dip; **s. en el caos** to plunge into chaos (**b**) *(abstraer)* to immerse; **el libro sumerge al lector en otra época** the book immerses the reader in another age
2 **sumergirse** *vpr* (**a**) *(hundirse)* to submerge; *(con fuerza)* to plunge; **el coche se sumergió en el río** the car sank to the bottom of the river (**b**) *(abstraerse)* to immerse oneself (**en** in); **se sumergió en sus pensamientos** he immersed himself in his thoughts
sumerio, -a 1 *adj* Sumerian
2 *nm,f* Sumerian
sumersión *nf* submergence, immersion
sumidero *nm* drain ►► *Informát* ***s. térmico*** heat sink
sumiller (*pl* **sumillers**) *nm* sommelier, wine waiter
suministrador, -ora *nm,f* supplier
suministrar *vt* (**a**) *(productos, electricidad, armas)* to supply; **s. algo a alguien** to supply sb with sth, to supply sth to sb (**b**) *(información)* to supply; **s. algo a alguien** to supply sb with sth, to supply sth to sb
suministro *nm* (**a**) *(productos)* supply (**b**) *(acción)* supplying ►► ***s. de agua*** water supply; ***s. eléctrico*** electricity supply, power supply; ***s. de gas*** gas supply
sumir 1 *vt* (**a**) *(abismar)* **s. a alguien en** to plunge sb into; **la noticia nos sumió en la desolación** we were plunged into despair by the news; **el vino lo sumió en un estado de somnolencia** the wine left him feeling drowsy; **sus declaraciones nos sumieron en la confusión** his statement threw us into confusion
(**b**) *(sumergir)* to submerge
(**c**) *(enterrar)* to bury
(**d**) *Méx Fam (hundir)* to make a dent in; **¡sume la panza!** tuck that belly in!
2 **sumirse** *vpr* (**a**) **sumirse en** *(depresión, desesperación, sueño)* to sink into (**b**) **sumirse en** *(estudio, tema)* to immerse oneself in (**c**) **sumirse en** *(sumergirse en)* to be submerged in
sumisamente *adv* submissively
sumisión *nf* (**a**) *(obediencia) (acción)* submission; *(cualidad)* submissiveness; **con s.** submissively (**b**) *(rendición)* surrender
sumiso, -a *adj* submissive
súmmum *nm* **el s. de** the height of; **esto es el s.** this is wonderful *o* magnificent; **este hotel es el s. de la elegancia** this hotel is the height of elegance; **su hermana es el s. de la imbecilidad** her sister's a complete and utter moron
sumo[1]**, -a** *adj* (**a**) *(supremo)* highest, supreme ►► ***s. pontífice*** supreme pontiff; ***s. sacerdote*** high priest (**b**) *(gran)* extreme, great; **lo aprecio en grado s.** I think extremely highly of him; **con s. cuidado** with extreme *o* great care; **a lo s.** at most; **tendrá a lo s. veinte años** she can't be more than twenty
sumo[2] *nm (deporte)* sumo (wrestling)
suní (*pl* **suníes**), **sunní** (*pl* **sunníes**) 1 *adj* Sunni
2 *nmf* Sunnite, Sunni Muslim
sunita, sunnita 1 *adj* Sunni
2 *nmf* Sunnite, Sunni Muslim
suntuario, -a *adj* luxury; **unas vacaciones suntuarias** a luxury *Br* holiday *o US* vacation
suntuosamente *adv* sumptuously, magnificently; **una habitación s. decorada** a sumptuously decorated room
suntuosidad *nf* sumptuousness, magnificence
suntuoso, -a *adj* sumptuous, magnificent
supe *ver* **saber**
supeditación *nf* subordination
supeditar 1 *vt* (**a**) *(subordinar)* to subordinate (**a** to); **supedita sus intereses a los del partido** he subordinates his personal interests to those of the party (**b**) *(someter)* **estar supeditado a** to be dependent on; **el proyecto está supeditado al presupuesto disponible** the project depends on the available budget
2 **supeditarse** *vpr* (**a**) *(subordinarse)* to subordinate (**a** to); **cualquier otra consideración debe supeditarse a este objetivo** any other consideration must be made subordinate to that goal (**b**) *(someterse)* **supeditarse a** to submit to; **supeditarse a las órdenes de alguien** to submit to sb's orders; **supeditarse a unas normas** to abide by the rules
super- *pref* (**a**) *(por encima de)* super- (**b**) *Fam (muy)* **es supermajo** he's really nice; **superfácil** really *o* dead easy; **esta sopa está superbuena** this soup is lovely!
súper[1] 1 *adj (gasolina) Br* four-star, *US* regular
2 *nf Br* four-star (petrol), *US* regular
súper[2] 1 *adj Fam (genial)* great, super; **se ha comprado una moto s.** he's bought himself a super motorbike
2 *adv Fam* **pasarlo s.** to have a great time
súper[3] *nm Fam (supermercado)* supermarket
superable *adj (problema)* surmountable
superabundancia *nf* excess
superabundante *adj* excessive
superabundar *vi* to abound
superación *nf* (**a**) *(de problema)* overcoming; **afán de s.** desire to excel (**b**) *(de límite)* exceeding; *(récord)* breaking
superar 1 *vt* (**a**) *(aventajar)* to beat; **s. algo/a alguien en algo** to beat sth/sb for sth; **nos superan en número** they outnumber us; **me supera en altura/inteligencia** he's taller/cleverer than me
(**b**) *(sobrepasar) (récord)* to break; **queremos s. los resultados del año pasado** we want to improve on *o* beat last year's results; **me superó por dos décimas de segundo** she beat me by two tenths of a second
(**c**) *(adelantar)* to overtake, to pass; **superó a su rival en la recta final** she overtook her rival on the home straight
(**d**) *(época, técnica)* **estar superado** to have been superseded
(**e**) *(complejo, crisis, enfermedad)* to overcome, to get over; **no ha superado la pérdida de su mujer** he has not overcome the loss of his wife; **tener algo superado** to have got over sth
(**f**) *(examen, prueba)* to pass
2 **superarse** *vpr* (**a**) *(mejorar)* to better oneself; **se supera día a día** he goes from strength to strength (**b**) *(lucirse)* to excel oneself; *Irónico* **esta vez te has superado** you've excelled yourself this time
superávit (*pl* **superávit, superávits**) *nm* surplus
supercarburante *nm* high-grade fuel
superchería *nf* (**a**) *(engaño)* fraud, hoax (**b**) *(superstición)* superstition
superclase *nf Biol* superclass
superconductividad *nf Fís* superconductivity
superconductor *nm Fís* superconductor
supercopa *nf (en Europa)* European Supercup; *(en España)* = cup contested by the league champions and the winner of the cup at the end of the season, *Br* ≃ Charity Shield
supercuenta *nf Fin* high-interest account
superdirecta *nf Aut* overdrive
superdotado, -a 1 *adj* extremely gifted
2 *nm,f* extremely gifted person; **es un s.** he's extremely gifted
superego *nm Psi* superego
superestrato *nm Ling* superstratum, superstrate
superestrella *nf* superstar
superestructura *nf* superstructure
superficial *adj* (**a**) *(poco profundo) (capa, herida)* superficial (**b**) *(frívolo) (persona, conversación)* superficial
superficialidad *nf* (**a**) *(de herida)* superficiality (**b**) *(frivolidad)* superficiality
superficialmente *adv* superficially; **lo conozco sólo s.** I know him only superficially
superficie *nf* (**a**) *(parte exterior)* surface; **la s. de la Tierra** the Earth's surface; **transporte de s.** surface transport; **salir a la s.** to come to the surface, to surface (**b**) *(extensión)* area; **tiene una s. de 2.500 metros cuadrados** it covers 2,500 square metres ►► ***s. comercial*** floor space; ***s. de trabajo*** work surface; ***s. de venta*** floor space
superfino, -a *adj* superfine
superfluo, -a *adj (innecesario)* superfluous; *(gasto)* unnecessary
supergigante *nm Dep* super giant slalom, Super G
superhéroe *nm* superhero
superhombre *nm* superman
superíndice *nm* superscript
superintendencia *nf* (**a**) *(cargo)* superintendence (**b**) *(oficina)* superintendent's office

superintendente *nmf* superintendent

superior, -ora 1 *adj* (a) *(de arriba)* top; **los pisos superiores tienen mejores vistas** the upper floors have better views; **la parte s. (de algo)** the top (of sth); **la mitad s.** the top *o* upper half
(b) *(mayor)* higher (**a** than); **ser s. en número, ser numéricamente s.** to have a numerical advantage; **temperaturas superiores a los 12 grados** temperatures above 12 degrees; **una cifra s. a 100** a figure greater than 100; **lo venden a un precio un 30 por ciento s. al del mercado** they are selling it at 30 percent above the market price; **por un periodo no s. a tres años** for a period not exceeding three years
(c) *(mejor)* superior (**a** to); **es s. a la media** it's above average; **una mujer de inteligencia s. a la media** a woman of above-average intelligence; **no me creo s. a nadie** I don't consider myself superior to anyone
(d) *(excelente)* excellent; **productos de calidad s.** superior-quality products
(e) *Fam* **es s. a mí** *o* **a mis fuerzas** *(no lo puedo soportar)* it's too much for me
(f) *Biol* **los mamíferos superiores** the higher mammals
(g) *Anat* upper; **el labio/la mandíbula s.** the upper lip/jaw
(h) *Geog* upper
(i) *Educ* higher
(j) *Rel* superior
(k) *Geol* upper; **el Paleolítico s.** the Upper Palaeolithic
2 *nm,f Rel* superior, *f* mother superior
3 *nm (jefe)* superior

superioridad *nf* (a) *(preeminencia, ventaja)* superiority; *Dep* **estar en s. numérica** to have a numerical advantage (b) *(suficiencia)* superiority; **con un tono de s.** in a superior tone

superlativo, -a 1 *adj* (a) *(belleza, inteligencia)* exceptional (b) *Gram* superlative
2 *nm Gram* superlative

superligero, -a 1 *adj (en boxeo)* **peso s.** super lightweight
2 *nm,f (en boxeo)* super lightweight

supermán *nm* superman

supermercado *nm* supermarket

superministro, -a *nm,f* = powerful government minister in charge of more than one department

supernova *nf* supernova

supernumerario, -a 1 *adj* (a) *(que está de más)* supernumerary, extra (b) *(funcionario)* on temporary leave
2 *nm,f* (a) *(trabajador)* supernumerary (b) *(del Opus)* lay member

superordenador *nm Esp Informát* supercomputer

superpesado, -a 1 *adj* (a) *(en boxeo)* **peso s.** superheavyweight (b) *Fam (que pesa mucho)* **es s.** it weighs a ton (c) *Fam (muy aburrido)* dead boring
2 *nm,f (en boxeo)* superheavyweight

superpetrolero *nm* supertanker

superpluma 1 *adj (en boxeo)* **peso s.** super-featherweight
2 *nmf (en boxeo)* super-featherweight

superpoblación *nf* overpopulation

superpoblado, -a *adj* overpopulated

superponer [50] *vt (poner encima)* to put on top (**a** of)

superposición *nf* superimposition

superpotencia *nf* superpower

superproducción *nf* (a) *Econ* overproduction (b) *(película)* big-budget movie

superpuesto, -a 1 *participio ver* **superponer**
2 *adj* superimposed

supersónico, -a *adj* supersonic

superstición *nf* superstition

supersticioso, -a *adj* superstitious

supérstite *adj Der* surviving

supervalorar *vt (artista, obra)* to overrate; *(casa, acciones)* to overvalue

superventas *nm inv* best-seller

supervigilancia *nf Andes, CAm, Carib* supervision, oversight

supervigilar *vt Andes, CAm, Carib* to supervise, to oversee

supervisar *vt* to supervise

supervisión *nf* supervision

supervisor, -ora 1 *adj* supervisory
2 *nm,f* supervisor

supervivencia *nf* survival

superviviente 1 *adj* surviving
2 *nmf* survivor

superwelter 1 *adj (en boxeo)* **peso s.** light-middleweight
2 *nmf (en boxeo)* light-middleweight

superyó *nm Psi* superego

supiera *etc ver* **saber**

supinador *nm Anat* supinator

supino, -a 1 *adj* (a) *(tendido)* supine (b) *(excesivo)* utter
2 *nm Gram* supine

suplantación *nf* **s. (de personalidad)** impersonation

suplantador, -ora *nm,f* impostor

suplantar *vt* (a) *(ilegítimamente)* to impersonate, to pass oneself off as (b) *CSur (legítimamente)* to replace

suplementario, -a *adj* (a) *(esfuerzo)* extra; *(ingresos)* supplementary, extra (b) *(ángulo)* supplementary

suplementero, -a *nm,f Chile* newspaper vendor

suplemento *nm* (a) *(añadido)* supplement ▸▸ ***s. de sueldo*** bonus; ***s. vitamínico*** vitamin supplement (b) *(complemento)* attachment (c) *(recargo)* supplement (d) *(publicación)* supplement ▸▸ ***s. dominical*** Sunday supplement

suplencia *nf* **hacer una s.** *(profesor)* to do *Br* supply teaching *o US* substitute teaching; *(médico)* to do a locum

suplente 1 *adj* substitute, stand-in; **profesor s.** substitute teacher, *Br* supply teacher; **equipo s.** reserve team
2 *nmf* (a) *(sustituto)* substitute, stand-in; *(de médico) Br* locum, *US* covering doctor; *(de juez, presidente)* deputy (b) *Teatro* understudy (c) *Dep* substitute

supletorio, -a 1 *adj* additional, extra
2 *nm Tel* extension

súplica *nf* (a) *(ruego)* plea, entreaty (b) *Der* petition

suplicante 1 *adj (que ruega)* entreating, pleading; **me pidió en un tono s. que la perdonara** she asked me in pleading tones to forgive her
2 *nmf* petitioner

suplicar [60] *vt* (a) *(rogar)* **s. algo (a alguien)** to plead for sth (with sb); **s. a alguien que haga algo** to beg sb to do sth; **déjame verla, te lo suplico** let me see her, I beg of you (b) *Der* to appeal to

suplicatorio *nm Der* (a) *(a tribunal superior)* = request by lower court for assistance from a higher court (b) *(a órgano legislativo)* = request by court for the parliamentary immunity of the accused to be waived

suplicio *nm* (a) *(tortura)* torture (b) *Fam (molestia)* torture; **es un s.** it's torture; **¡qué s.!** what a nightmare *o* pain!; **estos niños son un auténtico s.** these children are a real pain in the neck

suplique *etc ver* **suplicar**

suplir *vt* (a) *(sustituir)* to stand in for, to substitute for; **suple en la tienda a su hermano** he's standing in for his brother in the shop
(b) *(compensar)* **s. algo (con)** to make up *o* compensate for sth (with); **suple su timidez con una gran tenacidad** he makes up for his shyness with great tenacity; **el festival intentará s. con buen cine la falta de estrellas americanas** the festival will try to make up for the lack of American stars with good cinema
(c) *(añadir)* to supply
(d) *Andes, RP (proporcionar)* to provide, to supply; **siempre nos suplieron de todo lo necesario** they always provided us with everything we needed; **allí suplen agua potable** they supply drinking water there

supo *ver* **saber**

SUPONER [50] 1 *nm* **imagino que nos invitarán – eso es un s.** I imagine they'll invite us – that's pure conjecture *o* you can't say for sure; **imagina, y es un s., que te quedas sin dinero** imagine, for the sake of argument, that you didn't have any money
2 *vt* (a) *(creer, presuponer)* to suppose; **supongo que ya habrán llegado** I suppose *o* expect (that) they'll have arrived by now; **supongo que tienes razón** I suppose *o* guess you're right; **supongo que sí/no** I suppose *o* expect so/not; **supongamos que me niego** supposing I refuse; **es de s. que se disculparán** I would expect them to apologize; **es de s. una nueva bajada de los tipos de interés** a further drop in interest rates seems likely, we can expect a further drop in interest rates; **al final lo perdí todo – era de s.** in the end I lost everything – it was only to be expected *o* that's hardly surprising; **nada hacía s. que...** there was nothing to suggest that...; **todo hacía s. que se llegaría a un acuerdo** everything pointed to an agreement; **suponiendo que...** supposing *o* assuming that...; **suponiendo que no te moleste** as long as *o* assuming it doesn't bother you

(b) *(implicar)* to involve, to entail; **una dieta así supone mucho sacrificio** a diet like that involves a lot of sacrifices; **esto nos supone un cambio de planes** this involves *o* entails *o* means a change of plan for us; **no me supuso ningún esfuerzo** it was no trouble (for me)

(c) *(significar)* to mean; **supone mucho para mí** it means a lot to me; **este descubrimiento supone un importante avance para la ciencia** this discovery constitutes a major advance for science

(d) *(conjeturar)* to imagine; **lo suponía** I guessed as much; **te suponía mayor** I thought you were older

3 suponerse *vpr (uso pasivo, impersonal)* **se supone que habíamos quedado a las ocho** we were supposed *o* meant to meet at eight; **se supone que es la mejor película del año** it's supposed *o* meant to be the movie of the year; **se supone que todos tenemos los mismos derechos** we're all supposed to have the same rights; **a un soldado el valor se le supone** you expect soldiers to be brave, bravery is something that goes with being a soldier

---

suposición *nf* assumption

supositorio *nm* suppository

supra- *pref* supra-

supranacional *adj* supranational

suprarrenal *adj* suprarenal

supremacía *nf* **(a)** *(superioridad)* supremacy **(b)** *(preferencia)* precedence; **tener s. sobre algo** to take precedence over sth

supremo, -a 1 *adj* **(a)** *(jefe, autoridad)* supreme **(b)** *(calidad)* supreme; **una mujer de suprema belleza** a woman of supreme *o* outstanding beauty **(c)** *(momento, instante)* supreme

2 *nm Der* **el Supremo** *Br* ≃ the High Court, *US* ≃ the Supreme Court

supresión *nf* **(a)** *(de ley, impuesto, derecho)* abolition; *(de sanciones, restricciones)* lifting **(b)** *(de palabras, texto)* deletion **(c)** *(de puestos de trabajo, proyectos)* axing

supresor, -ora *nm,f* supressor

suprimir *vt* **(a)** *(eliminar)* to get rid of; *(ley, impuesto, derecho)* to abolish; *(sanciones, restricciones)* to lift; *(gastos)* to cut out; **hay que s. todo lo superfluo** we have to get rid of everything that's superfluous; **han suprimido las retransmisiones deportivas** they have cancelled the sports broadcasts

(b) *(palabras, texto)* to delete; **suprime los detalles y ve al grano** forget the details and get to the point

(c) *(puestos de trabajo, proyectos)* to axe

supuestamente *adv* supposedly

supuesto, -a 1 *participio ver* **suponer**

2 *adj* **(a)** *(hipotético)* supposed; *(culpable, asesino)* alleged; **no se ha confirmado el s. ataque al corazón del presidente** there has been no confirmation of the president's supposed *o* alleged heart attack **(b)** *(falso)* false; **actuó bajo un nombre s.** he acted under a false *o* assumed name

3 *nm* supposition, assumption; **en el s. de que venga** assuming (that) he comes; **esto no es más que un s.** this is no more than a supposition; **en estos supuestos no es válido el principio general** in these cases the general rule does not apply; **partimos del s. de que todo va a salir bien** we're working on the assumption that everything will turn out right; **supuestos de cancelación** grounds for cancellation

4 por supuesto *loc adv* of course; **¿te gusta? – por s.** do you like it? – of course; **¿la invitarás? – por s. que sí/no** are you going to invite her? – of course I am/of course not; **por s. que puedes venir** of course you can come; **por s. que si te deja de interesar, te puedes retirar** of course if you lose interest, you can always back out; **dar algo por s.** to take sth for granted; **doy por s. que te interesa** I take it for granted that you're interested

supuración *nf* suppuration

supurar *vi* to suppurate, to fester

supusiera *etc ver* **suponer**

sur 1 *adj inv (posición, parte)* south, southern; *(dirección)* southerly; *(viento)* south, southerly; **la cara s. de la montaña** the mountain's south face; **la costa s.** the south coast; **tiempo soleado en la mitad s. del país** it will be sunny in the southern half of the country; **partieron con rumbo s.** they headed south; **un frente frío que se desplaza en dirección s.** a cold front which is moving south *o* southwards

2 *nm* **(a)** *(zona)* south; **está al s. de Buenos Aires** it's (to the) south of Buenos Aires; **la fachada da al s.** the building faces south *o* is south-facing; **viento del s.** south *o* southerly wind; **habrá lluvias en el s. (del país)** there will be rain in the south (of the country); **ir hacia el s.** to go south *o* southwards **(b)** *(punto cardinal)* South **(c)** *(viento)* south wind, southerly

sura *nf* sura

Suráfrica *n* South Africa

surafricano, -a 1 *adj* South African

2 *nm,f* South African

Suramérica *n* South America

suramericano, -a 1 *adj* South American

2 *nm,f* South American

surazo *nm CSur* strong southerly wind

surcar [60] *vt* **(a)** *(tierra)* to plough **(b)** *(aire, agua)* to cut *o* slice through; **el velero surcaba las olas** the sailing boat cut through *o* ploughed the waves; **una bandada de ocas surcaba los cielos** a flock of geese flew across the sky **(c)** *(cara, rostro)* to line; **profundas arrugas surcaban su cara** her face was deeply lined *o* wrinkled

surco *nm* **(a)** *(de arado)* furrow **(b)** *(de rueda)* rut **(c)** *(en disco)* groove **(d)** *(arruga)* line, wrinkle

surcoreano, -a 1 *adj* South Korean

2 *nm,f* South Korean

sureño, -a 1 *adj* southern; *(viento)* southerly

2 *nm,f* southerner

sureste = **sudeste**

surf, surfing *nm* surfing; **hacer s.** to surf

surfear *Fam Informát* **1** *vt* to surf

2 *vi* to surf

surfing = **surf**

surfista *nmf* surfer

surgimiento *nm (aparición)* emergence

surgir [24] *vi* **(a)** *(brotar)* to emerge, to spring; **un manantial surgía entre las rocas** a spring emerged among the rocks, water sprang from among the rocks

(b) *(aparecer)* to appear; **surgió de detrás de las cortinas** he emerged from behind the curtains; **el rascacielos surgía entre los edificios del centro** the skyscraper rose *o* towered above the buildings in the city centre

(c) *(producirse)* to arise; **se lo preguntaré si surge la ocasión** I'll ask her if the opportunity arises; **la idea surgió cuando...** the idea occurred to him/her/*etc* when...; **nos surgieron varios problemas** we ran into a number of problems; **me han surgido varias dudas** I have a number of queries; **nos ha surgido una dificultad de última hora** a last-minute difficulty has arisen *o* come up; **están surgiendo nuevos destinos turísticos** new tourist destinations are emerging *o* appearing; **un banco surgido como resultado de la fusión de otros dos** a bank that came into being *o* emerged as a result of the merger of two other banks; **un movimiento surgido tras la guerra fría** a movement which emerged after the cold war

> **Falso amigo**: El verbo inglés **to surge** no es la traducción del español **surgir**. En inglés **to surge** significa "incrementarse repentinamente" o "abalanzarse".

suricato *nm* slender-tailed meerkat

Surinam *n* Surinam

surinamés, -esa 1 *adj* Surinamese

2 *nm,f* Surinamese

surmenaje *nm* exhaustion, fatigue

suroeste = **sudoeste**

surque *etc ver* **surcar**

surrealismo *nm* surrealism

surrealista 1 *adj* **(a)** *(en arte, literatura, cine)* surrealist **(b)** *(absurdo)* surreal

2 *nmf* surrealist

sursureste *nm* south-southeast

sursuroeste *nm* south-southwest

surtido, -a 1 *adj* **(a)** *(bien aprovisionado)* well-stocked; **una tienda bien surtida de telas** a shop with a wide selection of cloth **(b)** *(variado)* assorted

2 *nm* **(a)** *(gama)* range **(b)** *(de galletas, bombones)* assortment

surtidor *nm* **(a)** *(de gasolina)* pump **(b)** *(de un chorro)* spout; *(de ballena)* blowhole

surtir 1 *vt* **(a)** *(proveer)* to supply (**de** with) **(b)** *(producir)* **s. efecto** to have *o* produce an effect; **sus amenazas surtieron el efecto deseado** her warnings had the desired effect; **las medidas surtieron efecto** the measures proved effective; **este medicamento surte efecto a la media**

hora de tomarlo this medicine takes effect half an hour after being taken
2 *vi (brotar)* to spout, to spurt (**de** from)
3 **surtirse** *vpr (proveerse)* **surtirse de** to stock up on

surumpe *nm Bol, Perú* snow blindness

suruví, surubí *nm (moteado)* spotted sorubim; *(atigrado)* barred sorubim, tiger shovelnose catfish

survietnamita 1 *adj* South Vietnamese
2 *nmf* South Vietnamese

susceptibilidad *nf (sensibilidad)* oversensitivity; **eres de una s. exagerada** you're much too thin-skinned

susceptible *adj* (**a**) *(sensible)* oversensitive (**b**) *(modificable)* **el proyecto es s. de cambios** changes may be made to the project; **un plan s. de mejora** a plan that can be improved on

suscitar *vt (discusión)* to give rise to; *(dificultades)* to cause, to create; *(interés, simpatía, sospechas)* to arouse; *(dudas)* to raise

suscribir, subscribir 1 *vt* (**a**) *(firmar)* to sign; *Formal* **el que suscribe** the undersigned
(**b**) *(ratificar, apoyar)* to endorse; **suscribo sus opiniones** I subscribe to her opinion; **suscribo lo dicho por el presidente** I endorse *o* second the president's remarks
(**c**) *Fin (acciones)* to subscribe for; *(póliza)* to take out
(**d**) *(a publicación)* **s. a alguien a una revista** to get *o* buy sb a subscription to a magazine
2 **suscribirse** *vpr* (**a**) *(a publicación)* to subscribe (**a** to) (**b**) *Com* **suscribirse a** to take out an option on

suscripción, subscripción *nf* (**a**) *(a publicación)* subscription (**b**) *Fin (de acciones)* subscription; **oferta pública de s. de acciones** public offering of shares; **debe acreditar la s. de una póliza de seguros** you must provide proof of insurance; **es obligatoria la s. de un seguro** it is obligatory to take out insurance

suscriptor, -ora, subscriptor, -ora *nm,f* subscriber

suscrito, -a, subscrito, -a 1 *participio ver* **suscribir**
2 *adj* **estar s. a** to subscribe to

susodicho, -a *adj* above-mentioned

suspender 1 *vt* (**a**) *(colgar)* to hang (up); **lo suspendieron de una cuerda/de un clavo** they hung it from a rope/nail
(**b**) *Esp (examen, asignatura)* to fail; **me suspendieron la Historia** I failed History
(**c**) *(interrumpir)* to suspend; *(reunión, sesión)* to adjourn; **suspendieron las obras de la central nuclear** construction work on the nuclear power plant was suspended; **se suspendió el partido a causa de la lluvia** the game was called off *o* postponed because of the rain; **se han suspendido los vuelos hasta nueva orden** flights have been cancelled until further notice
(**d**) *(sancionar) (trabajador)* to suspend; *Am (alumno)* to suspend; **s. a alguien de empleo y sueldo** to suspend sb without pay
2 *vi Esp (alumno)* to fail

suspense *nm Esp* suspense

suspensión *nf* (**a**) *(interrupción)* postponement; *(de servicio)* suspension; *(de reunión, sesión)* adjournment; **las fortísimas lluvias llevaron a la s. del servicio de correos** the heavy rains led to the postal service being suspended ►► ***s. de pagos*** temporary receivership, *Br* ≃ administration order, *US* ≃ Chapter 11; **declarar la s. de pagos** *Br* ≃ to petition for an administration order, *US* ≃ to file for Chapter 11
(**b**) *(sanción) (de trabajador)* suspension; *Am (de alumno)* suspension ►► ***s. de empleo y sueldo*** suspension without pay
(**c**) *Aut* suspension ►► ***s. hidráulica*** hydraulic suspension
(**d**) *(mezcla)* suspension; **en s.** in suspension
(**e**) *(en baloncesto, balonmano)* **pase/tiro en s.** jump pass/shot

suspensivo, -a *adj* **puntos suspensivos** suspension points

suspenso, -a *adj* 1 (**a**) *(colgado)* **s. de** hanging from (**b**) *Esp (no aprobado)* **estar s.** to have failed (**c**) *(embelesado)* mesmerized
2 *nm* (**a**) *Esp (nota)* fail; **sacar un s.** to fail (**b**) *Am (suspense)* suspense (**c**) **en s.** *(interrumpido)* pending; **la aprobación de la ley ha quedado en s.** the bill is pending; **el tribunal ha dejado en s. la ejecución de la condena** the court suspended the sentence

suspensores *nmpl* (**a**) *Andes (tirantes) Br* braces, *US* suspenders (**b**) *Andes, RP (suspensorio)* jockstrap

suspensorio *nm* jockstrap

suspicacia *nf* suspicion

suspicaz *adj* suspicious

suspirado, -a *adj* longed-for, yearned-for

suspirar *vi* (**a**) *(dar suspiros)* to sigh; **s. de** to sigh with (**b**) *(desear)* **s. por algo/por hacer algo** to long for sth/to do sth; **s. por alguien** to have a crush on sb

suspiro *nm* (**a**) *(aspiración)* sigh; **dar un s.** to heave a sigh; EXPR **dio** *o* **exhaló el último s.** he breathed his last (**b**) *(instante)* **en un s.** in no time at all; EXPR **durar lo que un s.** to be short-lived (**c**) *Andes, Ven (merengue)* = type of round meringue (**d**) *Am (flor)* morning glory

sustancia *nf* (**a**) *(materia)* substance ►► *Anat* ***s. blanca*** white matter; *Anat* ***s. gris*** grey matter; ***s. química*** chemical (**b**) *(esencia)* essence; **sin s.** lacking in substance; **este artículo no tiene mucha s.** this article lacks substance (**c**) *(de alimento)* nutritional value (**d**) *Filosofía* substance

sustancial *adj* (**a**) *(de la sustancia)* substantial, significant (**b**) *(importante)* substantial

sustancialmente *adv* substantially, significantly

sustanciar *vt* (**a**) *(resumir)* to summarize (**b**) *Der* to substantiate

sustancioso, -a *adj* (**a**) *(importante)* substantial (**b**) *(nutritivo)* substantial

sustantivación *nf Gram* nominalization, use as a noun

sustantivar *vt Gram* to nominalize, to use as a noun

sustantivo, -a 1 *adj (importante)* substantial, significant
2 *nm Gram* noun

sustentamiento *nm*, **sustentación** *nf* (**a**) *(soporte, base)* support (**b**) *(alimento)* sustenance, nourishment (**c**) *(afirmación)* defence (**d**) *Av* lift

sustentar 1 *vt* (**a**) *(sostener, mantener)* to support; **sustenta a toda la familia con su salario** he supports his entire family on his salary (**b**) *(defender) (argumento, teoría)* to defend; *(opinión)* to hold, to subscribe to (**c**) *(apoyar)* to base; **sustenta sus teorías en una premisa errónea** his theories are founded on a false premise
2 **sustentarse** *vpr* (**a**) *(sostenerse, mantenerse)* to support oneself; **no se sustenta solo** he can't support himself (**b**) *(apoyarse)* **su ilusión se sustenta en vanas promesas** her hopes are based *o* founded on empty promises

sustento *nm* (**a**) *(alimento)* sustenance; *(mantenimiento)* livelihood; **ganarse el s.** to earn one's living (**b**) *(apoyo)* support; **su teoría carece de s.** her theory has no foundation

sustitución *nf* (**a**) *(cambio)* replacement; *(de jugador)* substitution; **trabajar haciendo sustituciones** to work as a stand-in; **aprobaron la s. del sistema informático por uno más moderno** they approved the replacement of the computer system by a more up-to-date one; **la s. del presidente por alguien sin experiencia fue un error** replacing the president with a person who had no experience was a mistake; **entró al terreno de juego en s. del defensa francés** he went onto the field as a replacement for the French defender
(**b**) *Der* subrogation

sustituible *adj* replaceable

sustituir [34] *vt* to replace; **sustituyó a su secretaria** he replaced his secretary, he got a new secretary; **la sustituyó como presidenta de la empresa** he took her place as president of the company; **lo sustituyeron por uno mejor** they replaced it with a better one; **sustituyó al portero titular por uno más joven** he replaced the first-team goalkeeper with a younger player; **han sustituido la moneda nacional por el dólar** the national currency has been replaced by the dollar; **tuve que sustituirle durante su enfermedad** I had to stand in *o* substitute for her while she was ill

sustitutivo, -a, sustitutorio, -a 1 *adj* substitute
2 *nm* substitute

sustituto, -a *nm,f (persona)* substitute, replacement (**de** for); *(profesor)* stand-in; *(médico) Br* locum, *US* covering doctor; **ha sido designado s. de Pérez en la presidencia** he has been appointed to stand in *o* substitute for Pérez as president

susto *nm* fright; **tenía cara de s.** he looked frightened; **dar** *o* **pegar un s. a alguien** to give sb a fright; **darse** *o* **pegarse un s.** to get a fright; **iqué s. (me di)!** I got the fright of my life!; **iqué s. me has dado!** you gave me a real fright!; **reponerse del s.** to get over the shock; **después del s. del accidente...** after the shock of the accident...; **ime has dado un s. mortal** *o* **de muerte!** you nearly scared me to death!; **nos dimos un s. mortal** *o* **de muerte cuando nos enteramos de que...** we got the shock of our lives when we found out that...; EXPR *Fam* **no ganar para sustos** to have no end of troubles

sustracción *nf* (**a**) *(robo)* theft (**b**) *Mat* subtraction

sustraendo *nm Mat* subtrahend

sustraer [68] 1 *vt* (**a**) *(robar)* to steal (**b**) *Mat* to subtract
2 **sustraerse** *vpr* **sustraerse a** *o* **de** *(obligación, problema)* to avoid; **le resultó muy difícil sustraerse a las presiones políticas** he found it very difficult to escape from *o* avoid the political pressures

sustrato *nm* (**a**) *(terreno)* substratum (**b**) *Ling* substratum, substrate

susurrador, -ora, susurrante *adj* (**a**) *(voz)* whispering (**b**) *(viento, agua)* murmuring

susurrar 1 *vt* to whisper; **me susurró la respuesta al oído** she whispered the answer in my ear

2 *vi* (**a**) *(persona)* to whisper (**b**) *(viento, agua)* to murmur

susurro *nm* (**a**) *(palabras)* whisper; **"¡ahora!", dijo en un s.** "now!," she whispered (**b**) *(de agua, viento)* murmur

sutién = **soutien**

sutil *adj* (**a**) *(crítica, inteligencia)* subtle (**b**) *(delicado) (velo, tejido)* delicate, thin; *(brisa)* gentle; *(hilo, línea)* fine

sutileza *nf* (**a**) *(de crítica, inteligencia)* subtlety (**b**) *(delicadeza) (de velo, tejido)* delicacy, thinness; *(de brisa)* gentleness; *(de hilo, línea)* fineness

sutilmente *adv* (**a**) *(con sutileza)* subtly (**b**) *(delicadamente)* delicately

sutura *nf* (**a**) *Med* suture; **le dieron cinco puntos de s.** he had five stitches (**b**) *Anat* suture (**c**) *Bot* suture

suturar *vt* to stitch

suyo[1], -a 1 *adj posesivo (de él)* his; *(de ella)* hers; *(de uno)* one's (own); *(de ellos, ellas)* theirs; *(de usted, ustedes)* yours; **este libro es s.** this book is his/hers/*etc*; **un amigo s.** a friend of his/hers/*etc*; **no es asunto s.** it's none of his/her/*etc* business; *RP* **¡permiso! – (es) s.** may I? – go ahead; EXPR *Fam* **es muy s.** he's a law unto himself

2 *pron posesivo* **el s.** *(de él)* his; *(de ella)* hers; *(de cosa, animal)* its (own); *(de uno)* one's own; *(de ellos, ellas)* his/her/*etc* lot *o* side; *(de usted, ustedes)* yours; **de s.** in itself; **hacer s.** to make one's own; *Fam* **los suyos** *(su familia)* his/her/*etc* folks; *(su bando)* his/her/*etc* lot *o* side; EXPR **lo s.: lo s. es el teatro** he/she/*etc* should be on the stage; *Fam* **lo s. sería volver** the proper thing to do would be to go back; *Fam* **les costó lo s.** it wasn't easy for him/her/them; EXPR **hacer de las suyas** to be up to his/her/*etc* usual tricks; EXPR **una de las suyas** one of his/her/*etc* tricks; EXPR *Fam* **ésta es la suya** this is the chance he's been waiting for *o* his big chance

suyu, suyo[2] *nm Hist* = administrative district in the Inca Empire

svástica [es'βastika] *nf* swastika

SWAPO ['swapo] *nm* (*abrev de* **South West African People's Organization**) SWAPO

Swazilandia [swaθi'landia] *n* Swaziland

swing [swin] (*pl* **swings**) *nm* (**a**) *Mús* swing (**b**) *Dep* swing

switch [switʃ] (*pl* **switches**) *nm Am* switch

T, t

T, t [te] *nf (letra)* T, t

T (**a**) (*abrev de* **torre**) (*en notación de ajedrez*) R (**b**) (*abrev de* **tara**) t

t (**a**) (*abrev de* **tonelada**) t (**b**) (*abrev de* **tomo**) vol

taba *nf* (**a**) *(juego)* jacks; **jugar a la t.** *o* **a las tabas** to play jacks (**b**) *(hueso)* ankle bone

tabacal *nm* tobacco plantation

tabacalero, -a 1 *adj* tobacco; **la industria tabacalera** the tobacco industry
 2 *nm,f* tobacco grower *o* farmer

tabaco 1 *nm* (**a**) *(planta)* tobacco plant; **una plantación de t.** a tobacco plantation
 (**b**) *(picadura)* tobacco ►► ***t. de liar*** rolling tobacco; ***t. de mascar*** chewing tobacco; ***t. negro*** black *o* dark tobacco; ***t. de pipa*** pipe tobacco; ***t. en*** *o* ***de polvo*** snuff; ***t. rubio*** Virginia tobacco
 (**c**) *(cigarrillos)* cigarettes; **una cajetilla de t.** a pack *o Br* packet of cigarettes; **el t. perjudica seriamente la salud** smoking can seriously damage your health
 2 *adj inv (color)* light brown

tabalear *vi (con los dedos)* to drum

tabanco *nm* (**a**) *(puesto)* mobile food stall (**b**) *CAm (desván)* attic

tábano *nm* (**a**) *(insecto)* horsefly (**b**) *Fam (persona pesada)* pain (in the neck)

tabaquera *nf* (**a**) *(para tabaco)* tobacco tin; *(para cigarrillos)* cigarette case (**b**) *ver también* **tabaquero**

tabaquería *nf Am Br* tobacconist's (shop), *US* cigar store

tabaquero, -a 1 *adj* tobacco; **la industria tabaquera** the tobacco industry
 2 *nm,f* tobacco grower *o* farmer

tabáquico, -a *adj (hábito)* smoking

tabaquismo *nm* smoking, smoking habit; **el aumento del t. entre los jóvenes** the increase in smoking among young people; **factores de riesgo como el t. y el alcohol** risk factors such as smoking and alcohol abuse ►► ***t. pasivo*** passive smoking

tabardillo *nm Esp Fam* (**a**) *(insolación)* sun-stroke; **le dio** *o* **cogió un t.** he got sunstroke (**b**) *(persona alocada)* tearaway

tabardo *nm* (coarse) cloak

tabarra *nf Fam (molestia)* pain; EXPR **dar la t.** to be a pest *o* a pain, to play up; **¡deja ya de darme la t.!** stop being a pest *o* a pain!; EXPR **dar la t. con algo** to go on and on about sth

tabasco® *nm* Tabasco® *(sauce)*

tabasqueño, -a 1 *adj* of/from Tabasco *(Mexico)*
 2 *nm,f* person from Tabasco *(Mexico)*

taberna *nf (tasca)* bar *(old-fashioned in style)*; *(antigua, tradicional)* tavern, inn

tabernáculo *nm* tabernacle

tabernario, -a *adj (lenguaje)* coarse

tabernero, -a *nm,f* (**a**) *(propietario)* landlord, *f* landlady (**b**) *(encargado)* bartender, barman, *f* barmaid

tabica *nf (de escalón)* riser

tabicar [60] *vt* to wall up

tabique *nm* (**a**) *(pared)* partition (wall) (**b**) *Anat* septum ►► ***t. nasal*** nasal septum (**c**) *Méx (ladrillo)* brick

tabla 1 *nf* (**a**) *(de madera)* plank, board; *(de mármol, piedra)* slab; **un puente de tablas** a plank bridge; **la ventana estaba tapada con tablas** the window was boarded up; **lo escondió bajo una t. del suelo** he hid it under a floorboard; EXPR **t. de salvación** salvation; **tú fuiste mi t. de salvación** you were my salvation; **nuestro partido no será la t. de salvación del gobierno** our party will not bale the government out; EXPR **hacer t. rasa** to wipe the slate clean; EXPR **hacer t. rasa de algo: intentó hacer t. rasa de su pasado** she tried to wipe out *o* obliterate her past; **el presidente hizo t. rasa de las instituciones democráticas** the president did away with *o* swept away the institutions of democracy ►► ***t. de cocina*** chopping board; ***t. de lavar*** washboard; *Rel* ***las tablas de la ley*** the tablets of the law; ***t. de patés*** selection of pâtés; ***t. de planchar*** ironing board; ***t. de quesos*** cheeseboard; *Dep* ***t. de saltos*** *(trampolín)* diving board
 (**b**) *(en deportes)* board ►► ***t. de snowboard*** snowboard; ***t. de surf*** surfboard; ***t. de windsurf*** windsurfing board, sailboard
 (**c**) *(del inodoro)* seat
 (**d**) *Arte* panel
 (**e**) *(lista, gráfico)* table; *Informát* table; **Manchester sigue primero en la t. de clasificación** Manchester is still at the top of the league table ►► ***t. de conversión*** conversion table; ***t. de materias*** table of contents; ***t. periódica (de los elementos)*** periodic table (of the elements)
 (**f**) *Mat* table; **la t. del 3** the 3 times table ►► ***t. de multiplicar*** multiplication table
 (**g**) *(de gimnasia)* exercise routine
 (**h**) *(pliegue)* pleat; **una falda de tablas** a pleated skirt
 (**i**) *Ven Fam (billete)* = 100 bolivar note
 2 tablas *nfpl* (**a**) *(en ajedrez)* **hizo tablas con el campeón del mundo** he drew with the world champion; **quedamos en tablas** *(en ajedrez, juego)* the game ended in stalemate; *(en enfrentamiento)* we reached a stalemate
 (**b**) *(escenario, teatro)* **las tablas** the stage; **su regreso a las tablas** his return to the stage; **pisar las tablas** to tread the boards; **salir** *o* **subir a las tablas** to go on stage; **tener (muchas) tablas** to be an experienced actor; *Fig* to be an old hand
 (**c**) *Taurom* = fence surrounding a bullring

tablada *nf RP* stockyard, cattle yard

tablado *nm (de teatro)* stage; *(de baile)* dance floor; *(para hablar, presidir un acto)* platform

tablao *nm* **t. (flamenco)** *(local)* = club where flamenco dancing and singing are performed

tablazón *nf (tablas)* boards, planking; *(de embarcación)* timbers

tableado, -a 1 *adj (falda)* pleated
 2 *nm (de falda)* pleats, pleating

tablear *vt* (**a**) *(madero)* to divide into planks (**b**) *(tela)* to pleat

tablero *nm* (**a**) *(tabla)* board; *(de mesa)* top; *(de juego)* board ►► ***t. de ajedrez*** chessboard; ***t. de anuncios*** *Br* notice board, *US* bulletin board; ***t. de damas*** *Br* draughtboard, *US* checkerboard; ***t. de dibujo*** drawing board
 (**b**) *(marcador)* scoreboard
 (**c**) *(en baloncesto)* backboard; **tirar al t.** to do *o* shoot a lay-up
 (**d**) **t. (de mandos)** *(de avión)* instrument panel; *(de coche)* dashboard
 (**e**) *Col (pizarra) Br* blackboard, *US* chalkboard

tableta *nf* (**a**) *(de chocolate, turrón)* bar (**b**) *(pastilla)* tablet (**c**) *Informát* tablet ►► ***t. gráfica*** graphics tablet

tabletear *vi* to rattle

tableteo *nm* rattling

tablilla *nf* (**a**) *(para entablillar)* splint (**b**) *Méx (de chocolate)* bar

tabloide *nm* tabloid

tablón *nm* (**a**) *(tabla)* plank ►► ***t. de anuncios*** *Br* notice board, *US* bulletin board; *Informát* ***t. de anuncios electrónico*** bulletin board system (**b**) *(viga)* beam (**c**) *Fam (borrachera)* **agarrar un t.** to get smashed *o* blind drunk (**d**) *Andes, Méx, Ven (parcela)* plot (of land) (**e**) *RP (pliegue)* large pleat

tabú (*pl* **tabúes** *o* **tabús**) **1** *adj* taboo; **es un tema t.** that subject is taboo
 2 *nm* taboo

tabuco *nm (casa)* hovel; *(habitación)* poky little room

tabulación *nf* (**a**) *(de texto)* tab-settings (**b**) *(de datos, cifras)* tabulation

tabulador *nm* (**a**) *(tecla)* tabulator, tab (key) (**b**) *(carácter)* tab character

tabular[1] *adj* tabular

tabular[2] **1** *vt* (**a**) *(texto)* to set the tabs for (**b**) *(datos, cifras)* to tabulate
 2 *vi (en un texto)* to set the tabs

taburete *nm* stool

TAC [tak] *nm Med* (*abrev de* **tomografía axial computerizada**) *(sistema)* CAT; *(escáner)* CAT scan.

taca 1 *nf (marisco)* = type of edible shellfish, found in Chile
 2 *nm Urug Fam* ***t. t.*** cash on the nail

tacada *nf (en billar) (golpe)* stroke; *(carambolas)* break; EXPR **hacer algo de una t.** *(de un tirón)* to do sth in one go

tacañear *vi* to be mean *o* miserly

tacañería *nf* meanness, miserliness

tacaño, -a 1 *adj* mean, miserly
 2 *nm,f* mean *o* miserly person; **ser un t.** to be mean *o* miserly

tacataca, tacatá *nm* baby-walker

taca-taca *nm Chile Br* table football, *US* foosball

tacha *nf* (**a**) *(mancilla)* blemish; **sin t.** *(reputación)* unblemished, untarnished; *(comportamiento)* beyond reproach; **es un hombre sin t.** he has an unblemished record (**b**) *(defecto, tara)* flaw, fault; **sin t.** flawless, faultless

tachadura *nf* crossing out; **una página llena de tachaduras** a page full of crossings out *o* of things crossed out

tachán *interj* hey presto!

tachar *vt* (**a**) *(borrar)* to cross out, to scratch (out); **su nombre había sido tachado de la lista** her name had been crossed off the list
 (**b**) *(acusar)* **t. a alguien de algo: lo tacharon de mentiroso/cobarde** he was branded a liar/coward; **la tacharon de elitista** she was accused of being elitist; **t. algo de algo: el libro fue tachado de pornográfico** the book was labelled as pornographic
 (**c**) *Der (testigo)* to challenge

tachero *nm RP Fam (taxista)* taxi driver

tachines *nmpl Esp Fam Hum (pies)* feet

tacho *nm* (**a**) *Andes, RP (metálico, de hojalata)* tin; *(de plástico)* container; *(papelera) Br* waste-paper bin *o* basket, *US* waste basket; EXPR *Fam* **irse al t.** to go down the drain, to go to pot ►► ***t. de la basura*** *(en cocina) Br* waste *o* rubbish bin, *US* garbage *o* trash can; *(en la calle) Br* rubbish bin, *US* garbage *o* trash can (**b**) *RP Fam (sartén, olla)* pan (**c**) *RP Fam (taxi)* taxi (**d**) *Am (para dulce)* sugar evaporator

tachón *nm* (**a**) *(tachadura)* crossing out; **una página llena de tachones** a page full of crossings out *o* of things crossed out (**b**) *(clavo)* stud

tachonado, -a *adj (salpicado)* studded (**de** with); **un cielo t. de estrellas** a sky filled *o* studded with stars

tachonar *vt* (**a**) *(poner clavos)* to decorate with studs (**b**) *(salpicar)* to stud (**de** with)

tachuela *nf* (**a**) *(clavo)* tack; *(en chaqueta, baúl)* stud (**b**) *Dep (elevación)* small climb

tacita *nf (de té, café)* cup; EXPR *Fam* **tener algo como una t. de plata** to keep sth spotless *o* as clean as a new pin ►► ***la T. de Plata*** = Cádiz

tácitamente *adv* tacitly

tácito, -a *adj (acuerdo)* tacit; *(norma, regla)* unwritten

taciturno, -a *adj (persona)* silent, taciturn; *(carácter, actitud)* gloomy

tackle *nm Am (en rugby)* tackle

tackleador, -ora *nm,f Am (en rugby)* tackler

tacklear *vt Am (en rugby)* to tackle

taclear *vt Méx* to tackle

taco *nm* (**a**) *(tarugo)* plug; *(para tornillo)* Rawlplug®; *(en calzado deportivo)* stud
 (**b**) *(cuña)* wedge ►► ***tacos de salida*** *(en atletismo)* starting block
 (**c**) *(montón) (de billetes de banco)* wad; *(de billetes de autobús, metro)* book; *(de hojas)* pile, stack
 (**d**) *(de billar)* cue
 (**e**) *Esp (de jamón, queso)* cube; **jamón/queso (cortado) en tacos** diced ham/cheese
 (**f**) *Esp Fam (palabrota)* swearword; **decir tacos** to swear
 (**g**) *Esp Fam (confusión)* mess, muddle; **armarse un t. (con algo)** to get into a muddle (over sth); EXPR **armar el t.** *(triunfar)* to bring the house down
 (**h**) *Esp Fam* **tiene veinte tacos** he's twenty
 (**i**) *Esp Fam* **un t. de** *(mucho)* loads of; **tiene un t. de dinero** she's got loads of money, she's loaded
 (**j**) *(tortilla de maíz)* taco; EXPR *Méx Fam* **a mí, mis tacos** I mind my own business; EXPR *Méx Fam* **darse t.** to show off; EXPR *Méx Fam* **echarse un t. de ojo** to get an eyeful; EXPR *Méx Fam* **hacerse t.** to wrap up (warm); EXPR *Méx Fam* **hacer t. a alguien** to wrap sb up; EXPR *Méx Fam* **ponerle mucha crema a los tacos** to exaggerate
 (**k**) *Méx (bocado)* snack
 (**l**) *Andes, RP (tacón)* heel; **zapatos de t. alto** high heels, high-heeled shoes; **zapatos de t. bajo** low-heeled shoes ►► ***t. aguja*** stiletto heel; ***t. chino*** wedge heel; ***t. corrido*** wedge heel; ***t. tanque*** wedge heel
 (**m**) *Chile (obstrucción)* obstruction, blockage
 (**n**) *Chile (embotellamiento)* traffic jam

tacógrafo *nm* tachograph

tacómetro *nm* tachometer, rev counter

tacón *nm* (**a**) *(pieza)* heel; **zapatos de t. alto** high heels, high-heeled shoes; **zapatos de t. bajo** low-heeled shoes ►► ***t. de aguja*** stiletto heel (**b**) **tacones** *(zapatos)* (high) heels; **no me gusta llevar tacones** I don't like wearing high heels

taconazo *nm* (**a**) *(golpe)* stamp (of the heel); **dar un t.** *(en el suelo)* to stamp one's foot; *(haciendo chocar los tacones)* to click one's heels (**b**) *Dep* back heel; **dar un t. al balón** to back-heel the ball

taconear *vi* (**a**) *(bailarín)* to stamp one's feet (**b**) *Mil* to click one's heels

taconeo *nm (de bailarín)* foot-stamping

táctica *nf* (**a**) *(plan)* tactics; **decidí cambiar de t.** I decided to change (my) tactics; **t. defensiva** defensive tactics *o* strategy (**b**) *Mil* tactics

táctico, -a 1 *adj* tactical
 2 *nm,f Mil* tactician

táctil *adj* tactile; **pantalla t.** touch screen

tacto *nm* (**a**) *(sentido)* (sense of) touch (**b**) *(textura)* feel; **áspero/suave al t.** rough/soft to the touch; **adivinó lo que era por el t.** he guessed what it was by the feel of it (**c**) *(delicadeza)* tact; **con t.** tactfully; **hay que tratarla con mucho t.** she needs to be handled very carefully; **tener t.** to be tactful; **no tiene ningún t.** she's completely tactless (**d**) *Med* manual examination

tacuache *nm Cuba* lie

tacuara *nf CSur* = kind of strong bamboo

TAE ['tae] *nm o nf Fin* (*abrev de* **tasa anual equivalente**) APR

taekwondista [taekwon'dista] *nmf* taekwondo practitioner

taekwondo [tae'kwondo] *nm* taekwondo

tafetán, *Méx, RP* **tafeta** *nm* taffeta

tafilete *nm* morocco leather

tagalo, -a 1 *adj* Tagalog
 2 *nm,f (persona)* Tagalog
 3 *nm (lengua)* Tagalog

tagarnina *nf* golden thistle

tagarote *nm* barbary falcon

tagua *nf* (**a**) *Andes (planta)* ivory nut palm (**b**) *Andes (ave)* coot (**c**) *Am* **hacer taguas** to dive

taguara *nf Ven Fam* bar

tahalí (*pl* **tahalíes** *o* **tahalís**) *nm* baldric

Tahití *n* Tahiti

tahitiano, -a 1 *adj* Tahitian
 2 *nm,f* Tahitian

tahona *nf* (**a**) *(panadería)* bakery (**b**) *(molino)* flour mill

tahúr, -ura *nm,f* cardsharp

tai-chi *nm* tai chi

taifa *nf Hist* = independent Muslim kingdom in Iberian peninsula

taiga *nf* taiga

tailandés, -esa 1 *adj* Thai
 2 *nm,f (persona)* Thai
 3 *nm (lengua)* Thai

Tailandia *n* Thailand

taima *nf* (**a**) *(astucia)* cunning, craftiness (**b**) *Chile (obstinación)* stubbornness, obstinacy

taimado, -a 1 *adj* (**a**) *(astuto)* cunning, crafty (**b**) *Chile (obstinado)* stubborn, obstinate
 2 *nm,f* (**a**) *(astuto)* cunning *o* crafty person (**b**) *Chile (obstinado)* stubborn *o* obstinate person

taíno, -a 1 *adj* Taino
 2 *nm,f (persona)* Taino
 3 *nm (idioma)* Taino

Taipei *n* Taipei

taita *nm Andes, Arg, Ven Fam* = term of respect for an older male member of the community

Taiwán [tai'wan] *n* Taiwan

taiwanés, -esa [taiwa'nes, -esa] **1** *adj* Taiwanese
2 *nm,f* Taiwanese

tajada *nf* **(a)** *(de comida) (trozo)* piece; *(rodaja)* slice; **una t. de pollo** a piece *o* slice of chicken; **partió el melón en tajadas** he cut the melon into slices **(b)** *Fam (parte)* share, cut; **todo el mundo quiere sacar t.** everyone wants to get in on the act; **sacar t. de algo** to get something out of sth **(c)** *Esp Fam (borrachera)* **agarrarse** *o* **cogerse una t.** to get plastered

tajadera *nf* **(a)** *(tabla)* chopping board **(b)** *(cuchillo)* chopping knife

tajado, -a *adj* **(a)** *(escarpado)* steep, sheer **(b)** *Esp Fam (borracho)* plastered, smashed

tajador *nm* **(a)** *(para cortar carne)* chopping board **(b)** *Perú (sacapunta)* pencil sharpener

tajalápiz *nm Col* pencil sharpener

tajamar *nm* **(a)** *(de embarcación)* cutwater **(b)** *(de puente)* cutwater **(c)** *CAm, Andes (dique)* dike, seawall **(d)** *Arg (embalse)* reservoir

tajante *adj (respuesta)* categorical; *(rechazo, negativa)* categorical, outright; *(tono)* emphatic; **fue t. al negar las acusaciones** she categorically *o* flatly denied the accusations; **contestó de modo t.** she was categorical in her reply

tajantemente *adv (responder)* categorically; *(rechazar, negar)* categorically, flatly; **se negaba t. a colaborar** she flatly refused to collaborate

tajar **1** *vt* **(a)** *(cortar)* to cut *o* slice up; *(en dos)* to slice in two **(b)** *Col, Perú (sacar punta)* to sharpen
2 tajarse *vpr Fam* to get plastered *o* smashed

tajear *vt CSur* to slash

tajín *nm Culin* tagine

Tajo *nm* **el (río) T.** the (River) Tagus

tajo *nm* **(a)** *(corte)* deep cut; **hizo un t. en el asado** she made a cut in the meat; **se hizo un t. en la mano** he cut his hand; **le hizo un t. con la navaja** he slashed her with the knife **(b)** *Esp Fam (trabajo)* work; **volver al t.** to go back to work **(c)** *(de carnicero)* butcher's block, chopping block **(d)** *(asiento)* stool **(e)** *(acantilado)* precipice **(f)** *(en mina)* face **(g)** *RP (en falda, abrigo)* slit

---

TAL **1** *adj* **(a)** *(semejante)* such; **¡jamás se vio cosa t.!** you've never seen anything like it!; **en t. caso** in that case, if that were the case; **dijo cosas tales como...** he said things like...

(b) *(tan grande)* such; **lo dijo con t. seguridad que...** he said it with such conviction that...; **me enojé de t. modo que...** I got so angry that...; **su miedo era t. que..., t. era su miedo que...** so great *o* such was her fear that..., she was so afraid that...

(c) *(mencionado)* **yo no he dicho t. cosa** I never said any such thing, I never said anything of the sort; **tales noticias resultaron falsas** the news turned out to be untrue; **ese t. Félix es un antipático** that Félix is really unpleasant

(d) *(sin especificar)* such and such; **a t. hora** at such and such a time; **quedamos t. día en t. sitio** we agreed to meet on a certain day in a certain place

(e) *(desconocido)* **te ha llamado un t. Pérez** a Mr Pérez called for you; **hay un t. Jiménez que te puede ayudar** there's someone called Mr Jiménez who can help you

2 *pron* **(a)** *(semejante cosa)* such a thing; **yo no dije t.** I never said any such thing, I never said anything of the sort; **como t.** *(en sí)* as such; **t. y cual, t. y t.** this and that; **y t.** *(etcétera)* and so on; **trajeron vino, cerveza y t.** they brought wine and beer and so on *o* and stuff

(b) *(semejante persona)* **si eres un profesional, actúa como t.** if you're a professional, then act like one

(c) EXPR **que si t., que si cual** this, that and the other; **ser t. para cual** to be two of a kind

3 *adv* **¿qué t....?** how...?; **¿qué t. (estás)?** how are you (doing)?, how's it going?; **¿qué t. el viaje?** how was the journey?; **¿qué t. es ese hotel?** what's that hotel like?; **¿qué t. si nos tomamos algo?** why don't we have something to drink?; **¿qué t. un descanso?** what about a break?; **t. (y) como** just as *o* like; **todo está t. y como lo dejamos** everything is just as we left it; **t. y como están las cosas...** as things stand..., the way things are...; **t. y como suele ocurrir...** as is usual...; **déjalo t. cual** leave it (just) as it is; *Fam* **una bebida, t. que una cerveza** a drink, like a beer

4 con tal de *loc conj* as long as, provided; **con t. de volver pronto...** as long as *o* provided we're back early...; **haría lo que fuera con t. de entrar en el equipo** I'd do anything to get into the team, I'd do anything as long as *o* provided I got into the team; **lo haré con t. (de) que me des tiempo** I'll do it as long as *o* provided you give me time

5 tal vez *loc adv* perhaps, maybe; **¿vienes? – t. vez** are you coming? – perhaps *o* maybe *o* I may do; **t. vez vaya** I may go; **t. vez llueva mañana** it may rain tomorrow; **t. vez no lo creas** you may not believe it; **pensé que t. vez mereciera la pena intentarlo** I thought it might be worth trying; **t. vez sí** maybe, perhaps; **t. vez no** maybe not, perhaps not

---

tala **1** *nf (de árbol)* felling; *(de bosque)* clearing
2 *nm Bol, RP (árbol)* hackberry tree

talabarte *nm* baldric

talabartería *nf* saddlery

talabartero, -a *nm,f* saddler

talacha, talache *nf Méx* **(a)** *(herramienta)* mattock **(b)** *Fam (trabajo)* work **(c)** *Fam (ocupación)* dirty work

talachero, -a *nm,f Méx Fam* handyman, *f* handywoman

taladradora *nf* **(a)** *(para pared, madera)* drill; **t. eléctrica** electric drill **(b)** *(para papel)* paper punch

taladrar *vt (madera, metal, suelo)* to drill; **taladra la pared aquí para poner el tornillo** drill a hole in the wall here for the screw; **este ruido te taladra los tímpanos** this noise goes right through you

taladro *nm* **(a)** *(taladradora)* drill ►► ***t. de aire comprimido*** pneumatic drill; ***t. manual*** hand drill; ***t. mecánico*** power drill; ***t. neumático*** pneumatic drill; ***t. de percusión*** hammer drill **(b)** *(agujero)* drill hole; **hacer un t. en la pared** to drill a hole in the wall

talaje *nm Chile* pasture

tálamo *nm* **(a)** *Formal (cama)* **t. nupcial** marriage bed **(b)** *Anat* thalamus **(c)** *Bot* thalamus

talán *nm* ding-dong

talante *nm* **(a)** *(humor)* mood; **estar de buen/mal t.** to be in a good/bad mood **(b)** *(carácter)* character, disposition; **tiene buen/mal t.** he's good-natured/he's an unpleasant type; **manifestó un t. conciliador ante sus rivales** he showed a conciliatory disposition towards his rivals **(c)** *(disposición)* **hacer algo de buen/mal t.** to do sth willingly/reluctantly *o* unwillingly

talar[1] *adj (vestidura)* ankle-length, long

talar[2] *vt (árbol)* to fell; *(bosque)* to clear

talasemia *nf Med* thalassemia

talasoterapia *nf* thalassotherapy

talayot, talayote *nm (monumento megalítico)* talayot

talco *nm* **(a)** *(mineral)* talc **(b)** *(cosmético)* **(polvos de) t.** talcum powder, talc

talega *nf* **(a)** *(saco)* sack; *(cantidad)* sack, sackful; **la t. del pan** the bread bag, = cloth bag for carrying and storing bread **(b)** *Chile (bolsa)* (plastic) bag

talegazo *nm Fam (golpe)* nasty fall; **darse un t.** to have a nasty fall

talego *nm* **(a)** *(saco)* sack; *(cantidad)* sack, sackful **(b)** *Esp Fam (1.000 pesetas)* = 1,000 pesetas; **cuesta 5 talegos** it costs 5,000 pesetas **(c)** *Esp Fam (cárcel)* slammer, *Br* nick, *US* pen; **ir al t.** to go to jail, *Br* to get sent down **(d)** *Col (bolsa)* (plastic) bag ►► ***t. de dormir*** sleeping bag

taleguilla *nf* = trousers worn by bullfighter

talento *nm* **(a)** *(don natural)* talent; **tiene mucho t.** she's very talented; **un músico/pintor de gran t.** a highly talented *o* gifted musician/painter; **tiene t. para la pintura** she has a talent for painting **(b)** *(inteligencia)* intelligence; **un alumno con** *o* **de t.** a bright pupil **(c)** *(persona con don natural)* talent; **un t. del golf** a golfing wizard *o* ace **(d)** *Hist (moneda)* talent

talentoso, -a, talentudo, -a *adj* talented

talero *nm CSur (fusta)* riding crop

Talgo ['talgo] *nm (abrev de* **tren articulado ligero Goicoechea Oriol***)* = Spanish intercity high-speed train

talibán **1** *adj* Taliban
2 *nmf* Taliban

talidomida *nf Farm* thalidomide

talio *nm Quím* thallium

talión *nm* **la ley del t.** the rule of an eye for an eye (and a tooth for a tooth); **no cree en la ley del t.** she doesn't believe in an eye for an eye (and a tooth for a tooth)

talismán *nm* talisman

talla *nf* **(a)** *(medida)* size; **¿qué t. usas?** what size are you?; **¿qué t. de camisa usas?** what size shirt are you?, what size shirt do you take?; **yo uso la t. XL** I take size XL; **unos pantalones de la t. 44** a pair of

size 44 trousers; **gorros de t. única** one-size caps; **no es de mi t.** it's not my size
(**b**) *(estatura)* height; **¿qué t. tiene el bebé?** what does the baby measure?; **es de mi t.** she's my height
(**c**) *(valor, capacidad)* stature; **hay pocos atletas de la t. del cubano** there are few athletes to match the Cuban; **políticos de gran t. moral** politicians of considerable moral stature; EXPR **dar la t.** to be up to it; **no dio la t. como representante del colegio** he wasn't up to the task of representing his school
(**d**) *(figura tallada) (en madera)* carving; *(en piedra)* sculpture, carving; *(en metal)* sculpture
(**e**) *(tallado) (de madera)* carving; *(piedra)* sculpting, carving; *(de metal)* sculpting; *(de piedras preciosas)* cutting

tallado, -a 1 *adj (madera)* carved; *(piedra)* sculpted, carved; *(metal)* sculpted; *(piedras preciosas)* cut; **una virgen tallada en mármol/bronce** a virgin sculpted in marble/bronze
2 *nm (de madera)* carving; *(piedra)* sculpting, carving; *(de metal)* sculpting; *(de piedras preciosas)* cutting

tallador *nm* (**a**) *(de piedra)* (stone) carver; *(de metal)* engraver (**b**) *Am (en juego de naipes)* banker

talladura *nf (en madera)* carving; *(en metal)* engraving

tallar 1 *vt* (**a**) *(esculpir) (madera)* to carve; *(piedra)* to sculpt, to carve; *(metal)* to sculpt; *(piedra preciosa)* to cut; **talló un corazón en el árbol** he carved a heart in the tree trunk (**b**) *(medir)* to measure (the height of) (**c**) *Méx (limpiar)* to scrub (**d**) *Méx (masajear)* to rub
2 **tallarse** *vpr Méx Fam* to slave (away)

tallarines *nmpl* (**a**) *(en cocina china)* noodles (**b**) *(en cocina italiana)* tagliatelle

talle *nm* (**a**) *(cintura)* waist; **de t. estrecho** narrow-waisted; **t. de avispa** wasp waist (**b**) *(figura, cuerpo)* figure (**c**) *(en sastrería)* neck to waist measurement; **se llevan las chaquetas de t. largo** long-waisted jackets are the fashion (**d**) *Chile, Guat, Méx (corsé)* corset (**e**) *RP (talla)* size

taller *nm* (**a**) *(lugar de trabajo) (de ebanista, artesano)* workshop, studio; *(de artista)* studio ►► ***t. de artesanía*** craft studio; ***t. de confección*** dressmaker's workshop; ***t. de costura*** dressmaker's workshop; ***t. de encuadernación*** bindery; ***talleres gráficos*** print shop, printing works
(**b**) *(de reparación de vehículos)* garage, repair shop ►► ***t. de bicicletas*** bicycle (repair) shop; ***t. de chapa y pintura*** body shop; ***t. mecánico*** garage, repair shop; ***t. de reparaciones*** garage, repair shop
(**c**) *(sección de fábrica)* shop ►► ***t. de montaje*** assembly shop
(**d**) *(cursillo, seminario)* workshop; **t. de teatro/títeres** theatre/puppet workshop

Tallin *n* Tallin

tallista *nmf (de madera)* wood carver; *(de piedras preciosas)* cutter

tallo *nm* (**a**) *(de planta, flor)* stem, stalk ►► ***t. herbáceo*** herbaceous stalk; ***t. leñoso*** woody stalk; ***t. rastrero*** creeping stalk, trailing stalk; ***t. trepador*** climbing stalk (**b**) *(brote)* sprout, shoot; **echar tallos** to put out shoots (**c**) *Col (col)* cabbage

talludito, -a *adj Fam* **se casó con un tipo ya t.** the guy she married was no spring chicken; **estar** *o* **ser t.** to be getting on (a bit)

talludo, -a *adj* (**a**) *(planta)* thick-stemmed (**b**) *(alto)* tall (**c**) *Fam (mayor)* **estar** *o* **ser t.** to be getting on (a bit)

talmente *adv* **es t. como su hermano** he's just *o* exactly like his brother; **parecía t. que le iba a pegar un tortazo** it looked for all the world as if he was going to slap her

Talmud *nm* **el T.** the Talmud

talmúdico, -a *adj* Talmudic

talo *nm Bot* thallus

talofita *Bot* 1 *adj* thallophytic
2 *nf (planta)* thallophyte
3 **talofitas** *nfpl (grupo)* thallophytes

talón *nm* (**a**) *(de pie)* heel; EXPR **pisarle los talones a alguien** to be hot on sb's heels ►► ***t. de Aquiles*** Achilles' heel
(**b**) *(de zapato)* heel; **unos zapatos con el t. abierto** a pair of shoes with open heels
(**c**) *(cheque)* cheque; *(matriz)* stub; **extender un t. (a alguien)** to write (sb) a cheque, to make out a cheque (to sb) ►► ***t. bancario*** banker's cheque; ***t. en blanco*** blank cheque; ***t. cruzado*** crossed cheque; ***t. devuelto*** bounced cheque; ***t. sin fondos*** bad cheque; ***t. nominativo*** = cheque made out to a specific person; **envíe un t. nominativo a favor de...** send a cheque payable to..., send a cheque made out to the order of...; ***t. al portador*** bearer cheque
(**d**) *(de neumático)* rim

> **Falso amigo**: El sustantivo inglés **talon** no es la traducción del español **talón**. En inglés **talon** significa "garra" o "uña extremadamente larga".

talonador, -ora *nm,f (en rugby)* hooker

talonario *nm (de cheques)* chequebook; *(de recibos)* receipt book; **un t. de vales** a book of vouchers

talonazo *nm* **le dio un t. en la espinilla** she kicked him in the shin with her heel

taloneador, -ora *nm,f (en rugby)* hooker

talonear 1 *vi* (**a**) *Am (espolear)* to spur on one's horse (**b**) *Méx Fam (prostituirse)* to work the streets
2 *vt* (**a**) *Am (espolear)* to spur on, to dig one's spurs into (**b**) *Méx Fam (apresurar)* to pressure, to hassle; **tuve que acelerar porque el del carro de atrás me andaba taloneando** I had to accelerate because the car behind was right on top of me *o esp US* was tailgating me

talonera *nf* heelpiece

talquino, -a 1 *adj* of/from Talca *(Chile)*
2 *nm,f* person from Talca *(Chile)*

taltuza *nf* gopher

talud *nm* (**a**) *(inclinación)* bank, slope, *Espec* talus ►► *Geog* ***t. continental*** continental slope (**b**) *RP (en cancha de fútbol)* stands behind the goal

talvez *adv Am* perhaps, maybe; **¿vienes? – t.** are you coming? – perhaps *o* maybe *o* I may do; **t. vaya** I may go; **t. llueva mañana** it may rain tomorrow; **t. no lo creas** you may not believe it; **t. sí** maybe, perhaps; **t. no** maybe not, perhaps not

tamal *nm* (**a**) *(comida)* tamale ►► ***t. de cazuela*** = meat stew in thick tomato sauce (**b**) *Méx (intriga, embrollo)* intrigue (**c**) *Méx (bulto)* package, bundle; EXPR *Fam* **estar hecho un t.** to be all wrapped *o* bundled up; **traía al niño hecho un t.** she was carrying the baby with her, all wrapped *o* bundled up

tamalada *nf* = gathering where different types of tamale are served

tamalero, -a *nm,f* tamale seller

tamango *nm CSur* = type of rudimentary, home-made leather boot

tamañito, -a *adj Cuba, Méx* **dejar a alguien t.** to cut sb down to size

tamaño, -a 1 *adj* such; **¡cómo pudo decir tamaña estupidez!** how could he say such a stupid thing!; **jamás vi tamaña osadía** I've never seen such audacity
2 *nm* size; **lo tenemos en varios tamaños** we have it in various sizes; **¿de qué t. lo quiere?** what size would you like?; **son del mismo t.** they're the same size; **de gran t.** large; **de pequeño t.** small, small-sized; **de t. mediano** medium, medium-sized; **países de mayor/menor t. que el nuestro** countries larger/smaller than ours; **del t. de** the size of; **hay teléfonos del t. de un paquete de tabaco** there are telephones the size of *o* as small as a packet of cigarettes; **del mismo t. que** the same size as; **¿por qué no te metes con alguien de tu mismo t.?** why don't you pick on someone your own size? ►► *Informát* ***t. de archivo*** file size; ***t. carné*** *o* ***carnet*** passport-size; **una fotografía (de) t. carné** a passport-size photograph; ***t. familiar*** family-size; **un paquete (de) t. familiar** a family-size pack; ***t. gigante*** giant-size; **tarrinas de helado (de) t. gigante** giant-size tubs of ice cream; *Imprenta* ***t. de letra*** point size, size of typeface; ***t. de muestra*** sample size; ***t. natural*** life size; **esculturas de t. natural** life-size sculptures

támara *nf* date palm

tamarindo *nm* (**a**) *(fruta)* tamarind ►► *Ven* ***t. chino*** star fruit, carambola (**b**) *Méx Fam (policía de tránsito)* traffic cop

tamarisco *nm* tamarisk

tamarugal *nm Arg, Chile* carob grove

tamarugo *nm Arg, Chile* carob tree

tamaulipeco, -a 1 *adj* of/from Tamaulipas *(Mexico)*
2 *nm,f* person from Tamaulipas *(Mexico)*

tambache *nm Méx Fam* (**a**) *(bulto)* bundle (**b**) *(chanchullo)* dirty trick

tambaleante *adj* (**a**) *(persona)* staggering; *(mueble, estante)* wobbly, unsteady; **salió con paso t.** he staggered *o* tottered out (**b**) *(gobierno, economía)* shaky, tottering

tambalearse *vpr* (**a**) *(persona)* to stagger, to sway; *(mueble, estante)* to wobble, to be unsteady; **el borracho caminaba tambaleándose** the drunk was staggering *o* lurching along; **el golpe hizo que se tambaleara** he staggered under the blow (**b**) *(gobierno, economía)* to totter; **las bases de la democracia se tambalean** the foundations of democracy are crumbling

tambaleo *nm (de persona)* staggering, swaying; *(de mueble, estante)* wobble

tambero, -a *nm,f* (a) *RP (granjero)* dairy farmer (b) *Andes (dueño) (de una tienda)* storekeeper; *(de un tenderete)* stall holder

también *adv* (a) *(igualmente)* too, also; **yo t. vivo en Chile, yo vivo en Chile t.** I live in Chile too *o* as well; **yo t.** me too; **dormí muy bien – yo t.** I slept very well – me too *o* so did I; **t. a mí me gusta** I like it too; **¿tú t. quieres helado?** do you want some ice cream as well *o* too?; **yo soy minero y mi padre t.** I'm a miner and so is my father
(b) *(además)* also, too; **trabaja t. de taxista** he also works as a taxi driver; **sabes cantar y bailar, pero no tocar el piano – sí, t.** you can sing and you can dance, but you can't play the piano – yes, I can do that too; **cose, cocina y t. plancha** he sews, cooks and irons too *o* as well
(c) *(en usos enfáticos)* **nadie nos dio ayuda, t. es verdad que no la pedimos** no one helped us, but then again, we didn't ask for help; *Fam* **le eché un broncazo increíble – ¡tú t.!** I gave him a real telling off – was that really necessary?; *RP* **perdieron el examen – y t., si fueron sin estudiar** they failed the exam – no wonder *o* that's hardly surprising, if they didn't do any revision

tambo *nm* (a) *Andes Hist* = Incan wayside lodging and storage place (b) *Andes (posada)* wayside inn (c) *Andes (tienda)* shop; *(tenderete)* stall (d) *RP (granja)* dairy farm (e) *Méx (recipiente)* drum (f) *Méx Fam (cárcel)* slammer, *Br* nick, *US* pen (g) EXPR *Andes, Ven* **andar del timbo al t.** to chase around all over the place

tambor 1 *nm* (a) *(instrumento de percusión)* drum; **tocar el t.** to play the drum; EXPR **a t. batiente** triumphantly (b) *(recipiente)* drum; **un t. de detergente** a drum of washing powder (c) *(de revólver)* cylinder (d) *(de lavadora)* drum (e) *(de frenos)* drum (f) *(para bordar)* tambour (g) *(para enrollar cable)* drum (h) *Arquit (de cúpula)* tambour, drum
2 *nmf (tamborilero)* drummer ▸▸ ***t. mayor*** drum major

tambora *nf Cuba Fam* (a) *(mentira)* fib (b) *(tapacubos)* hub cap

tamborear *vi* to drum one's fingers

tamboril *nm* small drum

tamborilear *vi* (a) *(con los dedos)* to drum one's fingers (b) *Mús* to drum

tamborileo *nm* drumming

tamborilero, -a *nm,f* drummer

tamborrada *nf Esp* = procession accompanied by drummers

Támesis *nm* **el (río) T.** the (River) Thames

tamil 1 *adj* Tamil
2 *nmf (persona)* Tamil
3 *nm (lengua)* Tamil

tamiz *nm* (a) *(cedazo)* sieve; **pasar algo por un t.** to sieve sth (b) *(selección)* **la prueba es un t. para eliminar a los peores** the test is designed to weed out the weaker candidates

tamizar [14] *vt* (a) *(cribar)* to sieve (b) *(seleccionar)* to screen (c) *(luz)* to filter; **la luz entraba tamizada por los visillos** the light filtered through the net curtains

tamo *nm* (a) *(de lino)* lint (b) *(de semilla)* grain dust (c) *(de polvo)* fluff *(that accumulates under bed, sofa)*

támpax® *nm inv* Tampax®

tampoco *adv* (a) *(igualmente no, además no)* neither, not... either; **ella no va y tú t.** she's not going and neither are you *o* and you aren't either; **yo no voy – yo t.** I'm not going – neither am I *o* me neither; **yo t. lo veo** I can't see it either; **no me gusta éste ni ése t.** I don't like this one or this one either; **t. dice nada en las instrucciones** it doesn't say anything in the instructions either
(b) *(en usos enfáticos)* **¡t. nos íbamos a presentar sin un regalo!** we were hardly going to turn up without a present!; **t. es que me importe mucho** it's not as if it matters much to me; **t. vendría mal descansar un poco** it wouldn't be a bad idea to have a little rest, a little rest wouldn't come amiss

tampón *nm* (a) *(de tinta) (sello)* stamp; *(almohadilla)* ink pad (b) *(para menstruación)* tampon

tam-tam *nm* (a) *(tambor)* tom-tom (b) *(sonido)* drumming

tamujo *nm* = type of spurge

tan 1 *adv* (a) *(mucho)* so; **t. grande/deprisa (que...)** so big/quickly (that...); **¡es un viaje t. largo!** it's such a long journey!; **¡qué película t. larga!** what a long film!; **¿t. aburrido te parece?** do you really find it that boring?; **t. es así que...** so much so that...; **de t. amable que es, se hace inaguantable** she's so kind it can get unbearable
(b) *(en comparaciones)* **t.... como...** as... as...; **no es t. tonto como parece** he's not as stupid as he seems
(c) *Am* **qué t.** *(cuán)* how; **¿qué t. confiables son estos datos?** how reliable are these figures?
2 tan sólo *loc adv* only; **t. sólo pido hablar con él** all I ask is to speak to him

tana *nf* (a) *(animal)* terrestrial *o* large tree shrew (b) *ver también* **tano**

tanaceto *nm* tansy

tanagra *nf* (a) *(ave)* tanager (b) *(escultura)* Tanagra figurine

tanate *nm* (a) *CAm, Méx (bolso)* leather bag (b) *CAm (trasto)* bundle; **cargar con los tanates** to pack one's bags

tanatorio *nm* = building where relatives and friends of a dead person can stand vigil over the deceased in a private room on the night before the burial

tanda *nf* (a) *(grupo)* **como éramos demasiados, entramos en dos tandas** there were too many of us, so we went in in two groups *o* parties; **hoy entrevistamos a una nueva t. de candidatos** today we interviewed another batch *o* group of candidates; **hizo tres tandas de galletas** he made three batches of biscuits; **tengo varias tandas de ropa para lavar** I've got several loads of washing to do; **una t. de inyecciones** a course of injections; **recibió una t. de latigazos** he got a series of lashes with the whip; **tengo una buena t. de ejercicios que hacer** I've got a pile of exercises to do ▸▸ *Dep* ***t. de penalties*** penalty shoot-out
(b) *RP (corte publicitario)* commercial break
(c) *Méx (compra cooperativa)* = communal savings scheme
(d) *Méx (turno)* shift

tándem *(pl* **tándemes)** *nm* (a) *(bicicleta)* tandem (b) *(pareja)* duo, pair; **forman un t. difícil de vencer** together *o* as a team they are hard to beat; **el t. Costa-Ríos se impuso en la final** the doubles tandem of Costa and Ríos won in the final

tandeo *nm Méx* selective water restrictions, water rationing

tanga *nm* tanga

tangana *nf Fam* punch-up, free-for-all

tángana *nf Ven Fam* punch-up, free-for-all

tanganazo *nm Col, Ven Fam* whack, wallop

Tanganica *nm* **el lago T.** Lake Tanganyika

tangar [38] *vt Fam* to rip off

tangará *nm* ***t. escarlata*** scarlet tanager; ***t. overo*** magpie tanager

tangencial *adj* (a) *Geom* tangential (b) *(marginal)* incidental, tangential (a to); **esta cuestión es meramente t. al tema que nos ocupa** this issue is purely incidental to the subject we're discussing

tangente 1 *adj* tangential
2 *nf* tangent; EXPR **irse** *o* **salirse por la t.** to change the subject

Tánger *n* Tangiers

tangible *adj* (a) *(material)* tangible (b) *(evidente)* tangible; **el jefe quiere resultados tangibles** the boss wants tangible *o* concrete results

tango *nm* (a) *(argentino)* tango; **bailar t.** to (dance the) tango (b) *(flamenco)* tango flamenco

tanguear *vi (bailar)* to (dance the) tango; *(cantar)* to sing tango(s)

tanguería *nf* tango club

tanguero, -a 1 *adj* **es muy t.** he loves the tango
2 *nm,f (aficionado)* tango enthusiast

tanguista *nmf (cantante)* tango singer

tánico, -a *adj Quím* tannic

tanino *nm Quím* tannin

tano, -a *RP Fam Pey* **1** *adj* wop
2 *nm,f* wop

tanque *nm* (a) *(carro de combate)* tank (b) *(vehículo cisterna)* tanker (c) *(en vehículo)* tank (d) *(de gas, oxígeno)* tank; *Ecuad (bombona)* cylinder (e) *RP (en edificio)* tank, cistern; *(para riego)* tank, reservoir (f) *Esp Fam (de cerveza)* mug, jug

tanquear *vi Col* to fill up (with *Br* petrol *o US* gas), *Br* to tank up

tanqueta *nf* armoured car

tanta *nm* fork-marked mouse lemur

tantalio *nm Quím* tantalum

tántalo *nm* (a) *Zool* ***t. americano*** wood stork (b) *Quím* tantalum

tantarantán *nm* (a) *(de tambor)* rat-a-tat-tat, drumming sound (b) *Fam (golpe)* resounding blow

tantas *nfpl Fam* **eran las t.** it was very late

tanteador *nm (marcador)* scoreboard

tantear 1 *vt* (a) *(probar, sondear)* to test (out); *(contrincante, fuerzas)* to size up; **tantéalo, a ver cómo anda de humor** sound him out to see what sort of mood he's in first; EXPR **t. el terreno** to see how the land lies, to test the waters (b) *(calcular) (peso, precio, cantidad)* to make a rough calculation of, to guess; *(posibilidades)* to weigh up (c) *(palpar)* to feel (d) *Taurom* to test

2 *vi* **(a)** *(andar a tientas)* to feel one's way **(b)** *Der* to exercise the right of first refusal *o* the right of pre-emption **(c)** *(anotar los tantos)* to score, to keep the score

tanteo *nm* **(a)** *(prueba, sondeo)* testing out; *(de contrincante, fuerzas)* sizing up **(b)** *(cálculo aproximado)* rough calculation, estimate; *(de posibilidades)* weighing up; **a t.** roughly **(c)** *(puntuación)* score **(d)** *Der* ***(derecho de) t.*** (right of) first refusal, (right of) pre-emption **(e)** *Taurom* testing

tantito, -a *Méx* **1** *adj (poquito)* very little; **tenemos tantita agua** we have very little water, we don't have much water

2 *adv (poquito)* a little bit; **ha llovido t.** it has rained a little bit

TANTO,-A **1** *adj* **(a)** *(gran cantidad) (singular)* so much; *(plural)* so many; **t. dinero** so much money, such a lot of money; **tanta gente** so many people; **tiene t. entusiasmo/tantos amigos que...** she's so enthusiastic/has so many friends that...; *Fam* **nunca había visto t. niño junto en mi vida** I'd never seen so many children in one place; **de t. gritar se quedó afónico** he lost his voice from all that shouting, he shouted so much that he lost his voice; **¡t. quejarse del tiempo y luego se mudan a Alaska!** they never stop complaining about the weather and then they move to Alaska!

(b) *(cantidad indeterminada) (singular)* so much; *(plural)* so many; **nos daban tantas pesos al día** they used to give us so many pesos per day; **hay cuarenta y tantos candidatos** there are forty-odd *o* forty or so candidates; **tiene treinta y tantos años** she's thirty-something *o* thirty-odd; **nos conocimos en el año sesenta y tantos** we met in nineteen sixty-something

(c) *(en comparaciones)* **t.... como** as much... as; **tantos... como** as many... as; **hoy no hay tanta gente como ayer** there aren't as many people today as yesterday

2 *pron* **(a)** *(tan gran cantidad) (singular)* so much; *(plural)* so many; **tenemos t. de qué hablar** we have so much *o* such a lot to talk about; **¿cómo puedes tener tantos?** how can you have so many?; **éramos tantos que faltó comida** there were so many of us we ran out of food; EXPR **ser uno de tantos** to be nothing special

(b) *(cantidad indeterminada) (singular)* so much; *(plural)* so many; **si el petróleo está a t. el barril...** if oil costs so much a barrel...; **a tantos de agosto** on such and such a date in August; **debe de andar por los cuarenta y tantos** he must be forty-odd; **ocurrió en el sesenta y tantos** it happened in nineteen sixty something

(c) *(igual cantidad) (singular)* as much; *(plural)* as many; **tantos** as many; **tantos como desees** as many as you like; **había mucha gente aquí, pero allí no había tanta** there were a lot of people here, but there weren't as many there; **otro t.** as much again, the same again; **otro t. le ocurrió a los demás** the same thing happened to the rest of them; **ponme otro t.** same again, please; EXPR *Fam* **ni t. ni tan calvo** there's no need to go to extremes; EXPR *Esp* **t. monta, monta t.** it makes no difference, it's all the same to me/him/*etc*

3 *adv* **(a)** *(mucho)* **t. (que...)** *(cantidad)* so much (that...); *(tiempo)* so long (that...); **no bebas t.** don't drink so much; **de eso hace t. que ya no me acordaba** it's been so long since that happened that I don't even remember; **la aprecia t. que...** he's so fond of her that...; **ya no llueve t.** it's not raining as much *o* so hard now; **ya no vienen t. por aquí** they don't come here so often *o* as much any more; **la quiero, pero no t.** I like her, but not that much; **quizás tardemos una hora en llegar – ¡no t.!** it may take us an hour to get there – it won't take that long!; **¿nos denunciarán? – no creo que la cosa llegue a t.** will they report us? – I don't think it will come to that; **no es para t.** *(no es tan grave, malo)* it's not too serious; *(no te enfades)* there's no need to get so upset about it, it's not such a big deal; **¿el mejor escritor de la historia? yo creo que no es para t.** the best writer ever? I don't see what all the fuss is about myself; **faltan unos cien kilómetros todavía – ¿t.?** there are still a hundred kilometres to go – as much as that?; **t. (es así) que...** so much so that...; **odia las fiestas, t. es así que no celebra ni su cumpleaños** he hates parties, so much so that he doesn't even celebrate his own birthday; **t. más cuanto que...** all the more so because...; **t. mejor/peor** so much the better/worse; **si no nos quieren invitar, t. peor para ellos** if they don't want to invite us, that's their loss; **¡y t.!** absolutely!, you bet!; **hay cosas más importantes en la vida – y t.!** there are more important things in life – there certainly are! *o* that's too true!

(b) *(en comparaciones)* **t. como** as much as; **me gusta t. como a ti** I like it (just) as much as you do; **la casa está deteriorada, pero no t. como para demolerla** the house is in a poor state of repair, but not so as you'd want to demolish it; **t. hombres como mujeres** both men and women; **t. si estoy en casa como si no** whether I'm at home or not

(c) *Am* **qué t.** *(cuánto)*: **¿qué t. lo conoces?** how well do you know him?; **no importa qué t. sepan de tecnología** it doesn't matter how much they know about technology

4 *nm* **(a)** *(punto)* point; *(gol)* goal; **marcar un t.** to score ►► ***t. directo de saque*** *(en tenis)* ace; ***t. de saque*** *(en tenis)* service point

(b) *(ventaja)* point; **apuntarse un t. (a favor)** to earn a point in one's favour

(c) *(poco)* **un t.** a bit, rather; **es un t. pesada** she's a bit of a bore *o* rather boring; **se le ve un t. triste** he seems rather sad

(d) *(cantidad indeterminada)* **un t.** so much, a certain amount; **te cobran un t. por la reparación y otro por el desplazamiento** they charge you so much *o* a certain amount for the repair work and on top of that a call-out charge; **un t. así** *(acompañado de un gesto)* this much ►► ***t. por ciento*** percentage; **¿qué t. por ciento de IVA llevan los libros?** what percentage *Br* VAT *o US* sales tax do you pay on books?

5 al tanto *loc adv* **siempre está al t. de todo** she always knows everything that's going on; **no estoy al t. de lo que ha pasado** I'm not up to date with what happened; **mantener a alguien al t. de algo** *(informado)* to keep sb up to date on *o* informed about sth; **te mantendremos al t.** we'll keep you informed; **mantenerse al t. (de algo)** to keep up to date (on sth), to keep oneself informed (about sth); **poner a alguien al t. (de algo)** to inform sb (about sth)

6 en tanto que *loc conj* **(a)** *(mientras, hasta que)* while; **espera en t. que acabamos** wait while we finish

(b) *(mientras, pero)* while, whereas; **él dimitió en t. que los demás siguieron en el cargo** he resigned while *o* whereas the others remained in their posts

7 en tanto que *loc prep (como)* as; **en t. que director, me corresponde la decisión** as manager, it's for me to decide

8 entre tanto *loc adv (mientras)* meanwhile; **haz las camas y entre t., yo lavo los platos** you make the beds and, meanwhile, I'll do the dishes

9 hasta tanto *loc conj (hasta que)* until; **hasta t. no se reúnan** until they meet

10 por (lo) tanto *loc conj* therefore, so

tantra *nm* tantra

tantrismo *nm* tantrism

tanza *nf RP* (fishing) line

Tanzania *n* Tanzania

tanzano, -a **1** *adj* Tanzanian

2 *nm,f* Tanzanian

tañer [65] *vt* **(a)** *(instrumento de cuerda)* to strum **(b)** *(campana)* to ring

tañido *nm* **(a)** *(de guitarra, arpa)* strumming **(b)** *(de campana)* ringing; **se oye el t. de las campanas** you can hear the bells ringing

taoísmo *nm* Taoism

taoísta **1** *adj* Taoist

2 *nmf* Taoist

tapa *nf* **(a)** *(para cerrar) (de caja, estuche, olla, ataúd, cofre, baúl, piano, pupitre, maletero)* lid; *(de frasco)* top; *Andes, RP (de botella, bolígrafo)* top; *Fam* **levantarle** *o* **volarle a alguien la t. de los sesos** to blow sb's brains out; EXPR *RP Fam* **poner la t. a alguien** to leave sb speechless ►► ***t. del depósito*** *Br* filler cap, *Br* petrol *o US* gas (tank) cap; ***t. del distribuidor*** distributor cap; ***t. del objetivo*** lens cap

(b) *(portada) (de libro, CD)* cover; *(de disco)* sleeve; **un libro de tapas de piel** a leather-bound book; **un libro de t. dura** a hardback; **tapas de plástico** PVC cover

(c) *Esp (de comida)* snack, tapa; **una t. de queso** a couple of slices of cheese; **un bar de tapas** a tapas bar; **comer de tapas** to have a meal consisting of tapas; **ir(se) de tapas** to go out for some tapas

(d) *(de zapato)* heel plate

(e) *(trozo de carne)* topside

tapabarros *nm Andes* mudguard

tapacubos *nm inv* hubcap

tapadera *nf* **(a)** *(tapa)* lid **(b)** *(para encubrir)* front; **utilizan la tienda como t. para sus negocios sucios** they use the shop as a front for their illegal activities

tapadillo: de tapadillo *loc adv Fam* on the sly

tapado, -a **1** *adj Andes, Méx, Ven (persona)* stupid, dull

2 *nm* **(a)** *CSur (abrigo)* overcoat **(b)** *Méx Fam (candidato)* = electoral candidate for a party before his or her identity has been revealed **(c)** *Bol (tesoro) (escondido)* hidden treasure; *(enterrado)* buried treasure **(d)** *Andes, Méx, Ven (persona)* **ser un t.** to be a bit dim *o* thick

tapadura *nf Chile (empaste)* filling

tapajuntas *nm inv* fillet *(on door or window)*

tápalo *nm Méx* shawl

tapaojos *nm inv Andes, Méx, Ven (anteojeras) Br* blinkers, *US* blinders

tapaporos *nm inv* primer, sealant

tapar 1 *vt* (a) *(cerrar) (olla)* to put the lid on, to cover; *(caja)* to put the lid on, to close; *(ataúd, cofre, baúl)* to close (the lid of); *(frasco, botella)* to put the top on
(b) *(ocultar, cubrir)* to cover; *(no dejar ver)* to block (out); *(rellenar)* to fill; **tapó el monitor con una funda** she put a cover on *o* over the monitor; **colgaba cuadros para t. las grietas** he hung pictures to hide *o* cover the cracks; **un velo le tapaba el rostro** a veil covered *o* hid her face; **la fábrica nos tapa la vista** the factory blocks our view; **apártate, que me tapas la tele** move over, you're blocking the TV; **tapó el agujero con yeso** she filled the hole with plaster; **un montón de cajas tapa la salida de emergencia** a pile of boxes is blocking the emergency exit; **me tapó los ojos** *(con las manos)* he put his hands over my eyes; *(con venda)* he blindfolded me; EXPR **t. la boca a alguien** to silence sb, to shut sb up; **le han tapado la boca con amenazas** they've silenced him with threats; **con su brillante actuación tapó la boca a sus detractores** with her brilliant performance she silenced her critics
(c) *(abrigar)* to cover up; *(en la cama)* to tuck in; **lo tapó con una manta** she covered him with a blanket, she put a blanket over him
(d) *(encubrir)* to cover up; **trató de t. sus errores** he tried to cover up his mistakes
(e) *Am (taponar)* to block; **no tires basura al wáter, que tapa los caños** don't throw rubbish down the toilet, it blocks the pipes
(f) *Chile (empastar)* to fill
2 **taparse** *vpr* (a) *(cubrirse)* to cover (up); **se tapó la boca con la mano** she put her hand over her mouth; **se tapó la nariz y saltó a la piscina** he held his nose and jumped into the swimming pool; **me tapo los oídos con algodones** I plug my ears with cotton wool
(b) *(abrigarse) (con ropa)* to wrap up; *(en la cama)* to tuck oneself in; **me tapé con una manta** I pulled a blanket over me; **tápate bien el cuello, no vayas a resfriarte** put something round your neck or you'll catch cold
(c) *Am (taponarse)* to get blocked (up); **en estas casas tan viejas, los caños se tapan con mucha facilidad** in old houses like these, the pipes get blocked (up) very easily

tapara *nf Col, Ven* = vessel made from a gourd; EXPR *Fam* **vaciarse como una t.** to pour one's heart out

taparo *nm Col, Ven, Méx* gourd tree

taparrabo *nm*, **taparrabos** *nm inv* (a) *(de hombre primitivo)* loincloth (b) *(tanga)* tanga

tapatío, -a 1 *adj* of/from Guadalajara *(Mexico)*
2 *nm,f* person from Guadalajara *(Mexico)*

tape[1] ['teip] *nm Cuba (cinta adhesiva)* sticky tape, adhesive tape

tape[2] *nmf RP (indio)* = pejorative term for an Indian

tapear *vi Esp Fam* to have some tapas

tapeo *nm Esp Fam* **ir de t.** to go out for some tapas; **bar de t.** tapas bar

táper *(pl* **tápers***) nm esp Am* Tupperware® *(container)*

tapera *nf RP* hut, shack

tapete *nm* (a) *(paño) (sobre mesa, mueble)* runner; *(sobre sofá)* antimacassar; *(en mesa de billar, para cartas)* baize; EXPR **sobre el t.: estar sobre el t.** to be up for discussion; **poner algo sobre el t.** to put sth up for discussion ►► ***t. verde*** *(mesa de juego)* card table (b) *Am (alfombra)* carpet ►► ***t. de entrada*** doormat

tapia *nf* (stone) wall; EXPR **estar (sordo) como una t.** to be as deaf as a post

tapial *nm (tapia)* mud wall

tapiar *vt* (a) *(puerta, pared, hueco)* to wall up, to brick up (b) *(terreno, finca, solar)* to put a wall round, to wall in

tapice *etc ver* **tapizar**

tapicería *nf* (a) *(de muebles, automóvil)* upholstery; **tela de t.** upholstery fabric (b) *(tienda)* upholsterer's (c) *(tapices)* tapestries (d) *(oficio)* upholstery; *(arte)* tapestry making

tapicero, -a *nm,f* (a) *(de muebles)* upholsterer (b) *(de tapices)* tapestry maker

tapilla *nf Chile (de taco)* heel

tapioca *nf* tapioca

tapir *nm* tapir

tapisca *nf CAm, Méx Br* maize harvest, *US* corn harvest

tapiscar [60] *vt CAm, Méx* to harvest

tapiz *nm* (a) *(para la pared)* tapestry ►► *Chile, Méx* ***t. de empapelar*** wallpaper (b) *(sobre suelo, césped, senda)* carpet; **el jardín es un t. de flores** the garden is carpeted with flowers ►► ***t. rodante*** *(aparato)* treadmill

tapizado, -a 1 *adj* (a) *(mueble, automóvil)* upholstered (**en** *o* **con** with) (b) *(pared)* covered (**en** *o* **con** with)
2 *nm* (a) *(de mueble, automóvil)* upholstery (b) *(tapices)* tapestries

tapizar [14] *vt* (a) *(mueble, automóvil)* to upholster; *(pared)* to hang with tapestries (b) *(suelo, césped, senda)* to carpet; **el jardín estaba tapizado de hojas** the garden was carpeted with leaves

tapoatafa *nm* brush-tailed phascogale

tapón *nm* (a) *(para tapar) (botellas, frascos)* stopper; *(bañera, lavabo)* plug; *(de corcho)* cork; *(de metal, plástico)* cap, top; *(para el oído)* earplug; **quitarle el t. al lavabo** to pull the plug out of the sink ►► ***t. de rosca*** screw top
(b) *(obstáculo)* **hay un t. de suciedad en el tubo** the pipe is blocked with dirt; **tengo un t. de cera** my ear is blocked (up) with wax; **le pusieron unos tapones de algodón en la nariz** they plugged his nostrils with cotton wool; **se formó un t. de gente a la entrada** a knot of people blocked the entrance
(c) *(atasco)* traffic jam
(d) *Fam (persona baja)* shorty
(e) *(en baloncesto)* block; **poner un t.** to block a shot
(f) *Am (plomo)* fuse

taponado, -a *adj (nariz, oídos, conducto)* blocked

taponamiento *nm* (a) *(de tubo)* blockage; **este t. de oídos me da dolor de cabeza** my ears are blocked and it's giving me a headache (b) *(de herida)* staunching

taponar 1 *vt* (a) *(cerrar) (botella)* to put the top on; *(lavadero)* to put the plug in; *(agujero)* to stop up, to plug; *(nariz, oídos, salida, tubería)* to block (b) *(herida)* to staunch
2 **taponarse** *vpr (nariz, oídos, conducto)* to get blocked, to block up; **se le taponaron los oídos** her ears blocked up

taponazo *nm (al descorchar)* pop

taponero, -a 1 *adj* cork; **la industria taponera** the cork industry
2 *nm,f* cork maker

tapsia *nf* turpeth root

tapujo *nm* subterfuge; **hacer algo con/sin tapujos** to do sth deceitfully/openly; **no se anda con tapujos al decir lo que piensa** she makes no bones about saying what she thinks

taqueado, -a *adj Col, Ven Fam* stuffed *o* crammed (full)

taquear 1 *vt Col, Ven Fam (atiborrar)* **no taquees ese armario** don't stuff too many things into that cupboard
2 *vi* (a) *Am Fam (jugar billar)* to play billiards, to play *o US* shoot pool (b) *Méx (comer)* to eat tacos
3 **taquearse** *vpr Col, Ven Fam (de comida)* to stuff oneself

taquera *nf (en billar)* cue stand

taquería *nf Méx (quiosco)* taco stall; *(restaurante)* taco restaurant

taquete *nm Méx (tarugo)* plug; *(para tornillo)* Rawlplug®

taquicardia *nf* tachycardia

taquigrafía *nf* shorthand, stenography

taquigrafiar [32] *vt* to write (down) in shorthand

taquigráfico, -a *adj* shorthand, stenographic

taquígrafo, -a *nm,f* shorthand writer, stenographer

taquilla *nf* (a) *(ventanilla) (de estación, estadio, museo)* ticket office; *(de cine, teatro, circo)* box office; **las entradas cuestan doce euros, once en t.** tickets cost twelve euros, eleven on the door
(b) *(recaudación)* takings; **la obra hizo** *o* **tuvo buena t.** the play did well at the box office; **la película fue un éxito de t.** the movie was a box-office hit
(c) *(armario)* locker
(d) *(casillero)* set of pigeonholes
(e) *CAm (bar)* bar, tavern
(f) *Chile (clavo)* small nail, tack

taquillero, -a 1 *adj* **es un espectáculo t.** the show is a box-office hit; **es un actor/cantante muy t.** he's a big box-office attraction *o* draw
2 *nm,f* ticket clerk

taquillón *nm* = type of small sideboard usually found in hallway

taquimeca *nf Fam* shorthand typist

taquimecanografía *nf* shorthand and typing

taquimecanógrafo, -a *nm,f* shorthand typist

taquímetro *nm (en topografía)* tacheometer

tara[1] *nf* (**a**) *(defecto)* defect; **artículos con t.** seconds; **el niño nació con una t. física/mental** the child was born with a physical/mental handicap (**b**) *(peso)* tare

tara[2] *nf* (**a**) *Col (serpiente)* poisonous snake (**b**) *Ven (langosta)* green grasshopper

tarabilla 1 *nf (ave)* stonechat ▸▸ ***t. norteña*** whinchat
2 *nmf Fam (persona)* chatterbox

taracea *nf* (**a**) *(técnica)* marquetry, inlay; **muebles de t.** inlaid furniture (**b**) *(incrustación)* inlay

taraceado *nm (incrustación)* inlay

taracear *vt* to inlay

tarado, -a 1 *adj* (**a**) *(defectuoso)* defective (**b**) *Pey (tonto)* stupid (**c**) *Andes, RP (nervioso)* flustered; *(distraído)* muddled; **manejá vos por favor, hoy estoy t., dormí muy mal** you drive, I'm not with it today, I slept really badly
2 *nm,f Pey* idiot

tarambana *Fam* **1** *adj* good-for-nothing
2 *nmf* waster, good-for-nothing

taranta *nf (de flamenco)* = flamenco folk song from Andalusia and Murcia

tarantela *nf* tarantella

tarantín *nm CAm, Cuba* thingummy, thingumajig

tarántula *nf* tarantula

tarar 1 *vt* (**a**) *(mercancía, vehículo)* to tare (**b**) *Andes, RP Fam (persona)* to turn into an idiot; **no le hables al niño como si fuera un bebé, que lo vas a t.** don't talk to the boy as if he were a baby, you'll turn him into an idiot
2 tararse *vpr (por nerviosismo)* to get flustered; *(por distracción)* to get muddled; **siempre que le preguntan sobre eso se tara, no sabe qué contestar** whenever anyone asks her about it she gets flustered and doesn't know what to say; **yo con el miedo me taro, quedo sin reacción** when I'm scared I just seize up, I can't react

tararear *vt* to hum; **¿me la puedes t.?** can you hum it to me?

tarareo *nm* humming, singing

tararí 1 *nm (sonido de trompeta)* blare
2 *interj Fam* **it. (que te vi)!** *(de eso nada)* no way, José!

tararira *nf (pez)* = type of freshwater fish

tarasca *nf* (**a**) *(figura)* = dragon figure in Corpus Christi processions (**b**) *Fam (mujer)* hag (**c**) *Chile, CRica Fam (boca)* big mouth *o esp Br* gob

tarascada *nf* (**a**) *(mordedura)* bite (**b**) *Fam (respuesta)* rude reply

tarascar [60] *vt* to bite

tarascón *nm RP* bite

tardanza *nf* lateness; **disculpen mi t.** I'm sorry I'm late; **me extraña su t.** I'm surprised she's late

tardar 1 *vi* (**a**) *(con complemento de tiempo)* to take; **tardó un año en hacerlo** she took a year to do it; **de Bilbao a Santander tardamos dos horas** it took us two hours to get from Bilbao to Santander; **el motor tarda mucho en enfriarse** the engine takes a long time to cool down; **aguarda aquí, no tardo un minuto** wait here, I won't be a minute; **¿por qué tardará tanto?** what can be taking him so long?; **¿cuánto tardarás (en hacerlo)?** how long will it take you (to do it)?; **¿cuánto se tarda en conseguir un pasaporte?** how long does it take to get a passport?
(**b**) *(sin complemento de tiempo) (retrasarse)* to be late; *(ser lento)* to be slow; **nos vemos a las siete, ¡y no tardes!** I'll see you at seven, don't be late!; **ahora vuelvo, no tardo** I'll be back in a minute, I won't be long; **t. en hacer algo** to take a long time to do sth; **tardó en darse cuenta** it took him a while *o* he took a while to realize; **no tardaron en hacerlo** they were quick to do it; **no tardará en llegar** he won't be long (in coming); **la reserva natural tardará en recuperarse del desastre** it will be some time before the nature reserve recovers from the disaster
2 tardarse *vpr Méx* **espera, no me tardaré** wait, I won't be long
3 a más tardar *loc adv* at the latest; **lo necesito para el jueves a más t.** I need it by Thursday at the latest
4 sin tardar *loc adv* promptly

tarde 1 *nf (hasta las cinco)* afternoon; *(después de las cinco)* evening; **a las tres de la t.** at three in the afternoon; **a las siete de la t.** at seven in the evening; **a primera/última hora de la t.** early/late in the afternoon; **los periódicos de la t.** the evening papers; **buenas tardes** *(hasta las cinco)* good afternoon; *(después de las cinco)* good evening; *Esp* **por la t.**, *Am* **en la t.**, *Arg* **a la t.**, *Urug* **de t.** *(hasta las cinco)* in the afternoon; *(después de las cinco)* in the evening; **llegamos a Chicago mañana** *Esp* **por la** *o Am* **en la** *o Arg* **a la** *o Urug* **de t.** we arrive in Chicago tomorrow afternoon; EXPR **de t. en t.** from time to time; **sólo de t. en t. aparecen futbolistas como éste** footballers like this don't come along every day; EXPR **muy de t. en t.** very occasionally; **salimos a cenar muy de t. en t.** we eat out only very occasionally
2 *adv* (**a**) *(a hora avanzada)* late; **nos quedamos charlando hasta t.** we stayed up late talking; **no te levantes tan t.** don't get up so late
(**b**) *(con retraso, a destiempo)* late; **el tren salió más t. de lo habitual** the train left later than usual; **nos casamos muy t.** we got married quite late (in life); **(demasiado) t.** too late; **ya es (demasiado) t. para eso** it's too late for that now; **llegar t.** to be late; **llegamos diez minutos t.** we arrived ten minutes late; **llegué t. a la reunión** I was late getting to the meeting; **como muy t. el miércoles** by Wednesday at the latest; **se está haciendo t.** it's getting late; **corre, no se te vaya a hacer t.** hurry or you'll be late; **se me hizo un poco t. y perdí el avión** I was a bit late and I missed the plane; **t. o temprano** sooner or later; EXPR **t., mal y nunca: la ayuda humanitaria llegaba t., mal y nunca** the humanitarian aid was too little, too late; PROV **más vale t. que nunca** better late than never; PROV **nunca es t. si la dicha es buena** better late than never

tardecita *nf CSur* dusk; **saldremos de t.** we'll leave at dusk

tardíamente *adv* belatedly

tardío, -a *adj* (**a**) *(que ocurre demasiado o muy tarde) (decisión, medidas, respuesta)* belated; *(fruto)* late, late-ripening; **el nuestro fue un amor t.** ours was a late-blossoming romance; **tendremos un otoño t.** *Br* autumn *o US* fall will be late this year (**b**) *(de la última época)* late; **sus novelas tardías son las mejores** her late novels are the best ones; **latín t.** Late Latin

tardo, -a *adj* (**a**) *(lento)* slow (**b**) *(torpe)* dull; **t. de oído** hard of hearing

tardón, -ona *Fam* **1** *adj* (**a**) *(impuntual)* **¡mira que eres t.!** you're always late! (**b**) *(lento)* slow
2 *nm,f Fam* (**a**) *(impuntual)* = person who is always late; **es un t.** he's always late (**b**) *(lento)* slowcoach

tarea *nf* (**a**) *(trabajo)* task; **fue una ardua t.** it was a hard task; **mantener limpia la ciudad es t. de todos** keeping the city clean is everyone's responsibility; **las tareas del campo** agricultural *o* farm work ▸▸ ***tareas domésticas*** household chores, housework (**b**) *(escolar)* homework; **hace la t.** she's doing her homework (**c**) *Informát* task

tarifa *nf* (**a**) *(precio)* charge; *(en transportes)* fare; *(de médico, abogado)* fee; *(de servicio telefónico, postal)* rate ▸▸ ***t. del agua*** water charges; ***t. de alta*** joining fee; ***t. apex*** Apex fare; ***t. de cancelación de reserva*** cancellation fee; ***t. eléctrica*** electricity charges; ***t. de la electricidad*** electricity charges; ***t. máxima*** peak rate; ***t. nocturna*** *(eléctrica)* off-peak (electricity) rate; *(en taxis)* night rate; *Informát* ***t. plana*** flat rate; ***t. reducida*** *(eléctrica)* cheap rate; *(de transporte)* reduced fare; ***t. única*** flat rate
(**b**) *Com (arancel)* tariff ▸▸ *UE* ***t. exterior común*** common external tariff
(**c**) *(lista)* price list

tarifar 1 *vt (poner precio)* to price
2 *vi Fam (pelear)* to have a row; **salió tarifando con su hermano** she ended up having a row with her brother

tarificación *nf* pricing

tarima *nf* (**a**) *(plataforma)* platform (**b**) *(suelo de madera)* wooden floorboards ▸▸ ***t. flotante*** raised wooden floor

tarja *nf CAm, Méx (tarjeta)* visiting card, *US* calling card

tarjar *vt Chile (tachar)* to cross out

tarjeta *nf* (**a**) *(para presentación, pagos, transporte)* card ▸▸ ***t. bancaria*** bank card; ***t. de cliente*** customer card; ***t. de compra*** store card, charge card; ***t. de crédito*** credit card; ***t. de débito*** debit card; ***t. de embarque*** boarding pass; ***t. de felicitación*** greetings card; *Com* ***t. de fidelización*** loyalty card; ***t. identificativa*** identity badge; ***t. de inmigración*** landing card; ***t. inteligente*** smart card; ***t. magnética*** card with a magnetic strip; ***t. monedero*** electronic wallet; ***t. multiviaje*** travel pass; ***t. de Navidad*** Christmas card; ***t. postal*** postcard; *Tel* ***t. (de) prepago*** pre-paid card; ***t. sanitaria*** = card bearing national insurance number and doctor's address; ***t. teléfonica*** phonecard; ***t. de teléfono*** phonecard; ***t. de visita*** visiting card, *US* calling card
(**b**) *(en deportes)* card ▸▸ ***t. amarilla*** yellow card; ***t. roja*** red card
(**c**) *Informát* card ▸▸ ***t. aceleradora*** acceleration card; ***t. de ampliación*** expansion card; ***t. caché*** cache card; ***t. de expansión*** expansion card; ***t. lógica*** logic card; ***t. perforada*** punched card; ***t. de registro*** registration card; ***t. de sonido*** sound card; ***t. de vídeo*** video card

tarjetahabiente *nmf Am* card holder

tarjetazo *nm Perú Fam* = use of a personal recommendation to obtain a favour

tarjetero, -a 1 *adj Fam* **el árbitro tiene fama de t.** the referee has a reputation for booking players
2 *nm (cartera)* credit-card wallet; *(caja)* card holder *(for business cards)*

tarjetón *nm Col (para votar)* ballot paper

tarlatana *nf Tex* tarlatan

tarot *nm* tarot; **las cartas del t.** the tarot cards; **echar el t. a alguien** to read sb's tarot cards

tarquín *nm* mud, slime

tarra *nm Esp Fam* old codger

tarraconense 1 *adj* of/from Tarragona *(Spain)*
2 *nmf* person from Tarragona *(Spain)*

tarrina *nf (envase)* tub

tarro *nm* (**a**) *(recipiente) (de cristal)* jar; *(de barro)* jar, pot ►► *RP* ***t. de la basura*** *Br* rubbish bin, *US* garbage *o* trash can (**b**) *Esp Fam (cabeza)* nut, *Br* bonce; **me duele el t.** I've got a headache; **ése está mal del t.** that guy's nuts (**c**) *Zool* ***t. blanco*** *(ave)* shelduck (**d**) *Chile Fam (sombrero)* top hat (**e**) *Cuba, Méx (cuerno)* horn (**f**) EXPR *RP Fam* **tener t.** to be lucky

tarsana *nf CRica, Ecuad, Perú (corteza)* soapbark, quillai bark

tarsero *nm Zool* tarsier

tarso *nm* tarsus

tarta *nf* (**a**) *(de bizcocho)* cake ►► ***t. de cumpleaños*** birthday cake; ***t. helada*** ice cream gâteau; ***t. nupcial*** wedding cake; ***t. de queso*** cheesecake; ***t. al whisky*** = ice cream gâteau with whisky (**b**) *(con base de pasta dura)* tart ►► ***t. de manzana*** apple tart; ***t. de puerros*** leek tart; ***t. de queso*** *(salada)* quiche

tártago *nm Bot* spurge

tartaja *Fam* 1 *adj* **ser t.** to have a stammer *o* stutter
2 *nmf* stammerer, stutterer; **ser un t.** to have a stammer *o* stutter

tartajear *vi Fam* to stammer, to stutter

tartajeo *nm Fam* stammer, stutter

tartaleta, *RP* **tarteleta** *nf* tartlet; **t. de frutas** fruit tartlet

tartamudear *vi* to stammer, to stutter

tartamudeo *nm,* **tartamudez** *nf* stammer, stutter

tartamudo, -a 1 *adj* stammering, stuttering; **ser t.** to have a stammer *o* stutter
2 *nm,f* stammerer, stutterer

tartán[1] *nm (tela escocesa)* tartan

tartán[2] *nm Dep* tartan

tartana *nf* (**a**) *Fam (coche viejo)* banger (**b**) *(carruaje)* trap

tartárico, -a *adj Quím* tartaric

tártaro, -a 1 *adj* (**a**) *(pueblo)* Tartar (**b**) *Culin (bistec, salsa, estilo)* tartar(e); **filete a la tártara** steak tartar(e)
2 *nm,f (persona)* Tartar

tarteleta = **tartaleta**

tartera *nf (fiambrera)* lunch box

tartesio, -a *Hist* 1 *adj* Tartessian
2 *nm,f* Tartessian, = member of a pre-Roman people who lived in the South of Spain

tartufo *nm Formal Pey* hypocrite, Tartuffe

tarugo *nm* (**a**) *(de madera)* block of wood (**b**) *(de pan)* hunk *(of stale bread)* (**c**) *Fam (necio)* blockhead (**d**) *Fam (persona chaparra)* **es un t.** he's short and squat, he's a fireplug of a man

tarumba *adj Fam* crazy; **volver t. a alguien** to drive sb crazy; **volverse t.** to go crazy

tasa *nf* (**a**) *(índice)* rate ►► *Fin* ***t. anual equivalente*** annual percentage rate; *Fin* ***t. básica*** basic rate; ***t. de cambio*** exchange rate; ***t. de crecimiento*** growth rate; *Fin* ***t. de descuento*** discount rate; ***t. de desempleo*** unemployment rate; **una t. de desempleo del 10 por ciento** 10 percent unemployment; ***t. de fecundidad*** fertility rate; ***t. de inflación*** rate of inflation, inflation rate; ***t. de interés*** interest rate; ***t. de interés bancario*** bank rate; ***t. de interés fijo*** fixed interest rate; ***t. de interés hipotecario*** mortgage rate; ***t. de interés variable*** variable interest rate; ***t. mínima*** basic rate; ***t. de mortalidad*** death *o* mortality rate; ***t. de natalidad*** birth rate; ***t. de paro*** unemployment rate; *Fin* ***t. preferencial*** prime (lending) rate; *Fin* ***t. de rentabilidad*** rate of return
(**b**) *(impuesto)* tax ►► ***tasas de aeropuerto*** airport tax; ***t. municipal*** ≃ *Br* council tax, ≃ *US* municipal tax
(**c**) *Educ* **tasas** tuition fees
(**d**) *(tasación)* valuation
(**e**) *(medida)* **gastar (dinero) sin t.** to spend (money) freely; **beber sin t.** to drink heavily

tasación *nf* valuation; **hacer la t. de un inmueble** to value a property

tasador, -ora 1 *adj* evaluating
2 *nm,f* valuer ►► ***t. de la propiedad*** surveyor; ***t. de seguros*** insurance adjuster

tasajear *vt Andes, Carib, Méx* (**a**) *(trozar)* to cut up (**b**) *(herir)* to slash

tasajo *nm (carne seca)* jerked beef

tasar *vt* (**a**) *(valorar) (obra de arte, objeto de valor, inmueble)* to value; *(daños, avería)* to calculate; **tasaron la casa en diez millones** they valued the house at ten million (**b**) *(fijar precio)* to fix a price for (**c**) *(restringir)* to restrict, to ration; **habrá que tasarle el alcohol** we'll have to restrict *o* ration the amount he drinks

tasca *nf* (**a**) *(bar)* cheap bar; **ir de tascas** to go round a few bars, *Br* to go on a pub crawl (**b**) *Perú (oleaje)* turbulent coastal waters

tascar [59] *vt (sujeto: vaca, caballo, oveja)* to chomp, to munch; **t. el freno** to champ at the bit

Tasmania *n* Tasmania

tasquear *vi* to go round a few bars, *Br* to go on a pub crawl

tasqueo *nm* **ir de t.** to go round a few bars, *Br* to go on a pub crawl

tata 1 *nf* (**a**) *Esp (niñera)* nanny (**b**) *ver también* **tato**
2 *nm Am Fam (papá)* dad, *US* pop

tatami *nm Dep* tatami, judo/karate mat

tatarabuelo, -a *nm,f* great-great-grandfather, *f* great-great-grandmother; **tatarabuelos** great-great-grandparents

tataranieto, -a *nm,f* great-great-grandson, *f* great-great-granddaughter; **tataranietos** great-great-grandchildren

tate *interj Fam* (**a**) *(¡ya comprendo!)* now I get it! (**b**) *(¡cuidado!)* watch out!

tatemar *vt Méx* to roast lightly

ta-te-ti *nm RP Br* noughts and crosses, *US* tic-tac-toe

tato, -a *nm,f Fam (hermano)* big brother, *f* big sister

tatú (*pl* **tatúes** *o* **tatús**) *nm Bol, RP (armadillo)* armadillo

tatuador, -ora *nm,f* tattooist

tatuaje *nm* (**a**) *(dibujo)* tattoo (**b**) *(acción)* tattooing

tatuar [4] 1 *vt* to tattoo
2 *vi* to do tattoos
3 **tatuarse** *vpr* to have a tattoo done; **se tatuó un corazón en el brazo** he had a heart tattooed on his arm

taula *nf (monumento megalítico)* = megalithic standing stones in the shape of a T, found on the Balearic Islands

taumaturgia *nf* miracle-working

taumaturgo, -a *nm,f* miracle-worker

taurina *nf Quím* taurine

taurino, -a 1 *adj* (**a**) *(de los toros)* bullfighting; **temporada taurina** bullfighting season (**b**) *Am (de Tauro)* Taurus; **ser t.** to be (a) Taurus
2 *nm,f Am* Taurus, Taurean; **los taurinos son...** Taureans are...

tauro 1 *adj inv* Taurus; *Esp* **ser t.** to be (a) Taurus, to be a Taurean
2 *nm (signo)* Taurus; **los de T. son...** Taureans are...
3 *nmf inv (persona)* Taurus, Taurean; *Esp* **los t. son...** Taureans are...

taurómaco, -a *nm,f* expert on bullfighting

tauromaquia *nf* bullfighting

tautología *nf* tautology

tautológico, -a *adj* tautological

taxativo, -a *adj* strict

taxi *nm* taxi, cab; **fui en t.** I took a taxi *o* cab; **tomar** *o Esp* **coger un t.** to take a taxi *o* cab ►► ***t. aéreo*** = helicopter or small plane hired for short journeys; *Andes* ***t. colectivo*** = taxi for up to five passengers, with a fixed route

taxidermia *nf* taxidermy

taxidermista *nmf* taxidermist

taxiflet (*pl* **taxiflets** *o* **taxifletes**) *nm RP Br* (removal) van, *US* moving truck

taximetrero, -a, *nm,f,* **taximetrista** *nmf RP* taxi driver

taxímetro *nm* taximeter

taxista *nmf* taxi driver

taxón *nm* taxon

taxonomía *nf* taxonomy

taxonómico, -a *adj* taxonomic

taxonomista *nmf* taxonomist

Tayikistán *n* Tadzhikistan

tayiko, -a 1 *adj* Tadzhiki
2 *nm,f* Tadzhik

taza *nf* (**a**) *(para beber) (recipiente)* cup; *(contenido)* cup, cupful; **una t. de agua y tres de arroz** one cup of water and three of rice ►► ***t. de café*** *(recipiente)* coffee cup; *(contenido)* cup of coffee; **¿te apetece una t. de café?** would you like *o Br* do you fancy a cup of coffee?; ***t. de té*** *(recipiente)* teacup; *(contenido)* cup of tea
(**b**) *(de retrete)* bowl
(**c**) *(de fuente)* basin, bowl
(**d**) *Chile, Perú (palangana)* washbasin
(**e**) *RP (tapacubos)* hubcap
(**f**) *RP (de sostén)* cup

tazón *nm* bowl

TC *nm* (*abrev de* **Tribunal Constitucional**) constitutional court

TCP/IP *nm Informát* (*abrev de* **transmission control protocol/Internet protocol**) TCP/IP

TE *pron personal* (**a**) *(complemento directo)* you; **le gustaría verte** she'd like to see you; **¿te atracaron en plena calle?** were you mugged in the middle of the street?; **te han aprobado** you've passed
(**b**) *(complemento indirecto)* (to) you; **te lo dio** he gave it to you, he gave you it; **te tiene miedo** he's afraid of you; **te lo ha comprado** *(tú se lo has vendido)* she bought it from *o* off you; *(es para ti)* she bought it for you; **te extrajeron sangre** they took some of your blood; **¿te quitaron una maleta?** did they steal one of your suitcases?; **te rompieron el brazo** they broke your arm; **te pegaron una paliza** they beat you up; **se te olvidará** you'll forget (about it); **te será de gran ayuda** it will be a great help to you
(**c**) *(reflexivo)* yourself; **sírvete un whisky** pour yourself a whisky; **ívístete!** get dressed!; **sírvete más arroz** take some more rice; **ponte el abrigo, que nos vamos** put your coat on, we're going; **puedes acostarte en el sofá** you can lie down on the sofa
(**d**) *(con valor impersonal)* **si te dejas pisar, estás perdido** if you let people walk all over you, you've had it
(**e**) *(con valor intensivo o expresivo)* **¿no te lo crees?** don't you believe it?; **cómetelo todo** eat it all up; **si se te echa a llorar, no le hagas caso** don't take any notice if he starts crying (on you)
(**f**) *(para formar verbos pronominales)* **¿te acuerdas?** do you remember?; **ponte cómodo** make yourself comfortable

---

té *nm* (**a**) *(planta)* tea
(**b**) *(infusión)* tea; **¿quieres un té?** would you like a cup of tea?; **me invitaron a tomar el té** they invited me over for tea; EXPR *Fam* **darle el té a alguien** to pester sb ►► ***té en bolsitas*** teabags; ***té con limón*** lemon tea; *RP* ***té de manzanilla*** camomile tea; ***té de México*** saltwort; ***té en saquitos*** teabags; ***té de tilo*** lime blossom tea; *RP* ***té de yuyos*** = type of herbal tea
(**c**) *esp Am (reunión)* tea party

tea *nf (antorcha)* torch

teatral *adj* (**a**) *(de teatro)* theatre; **actor t.** stage actor; **autor t.** playwright; **grupo t.** theatre *o* drama group; **obra t.** play; **temporada t.** theatre season (**b**) *(exagerado)* theatrical

teatralidad *nf* (**a**) *(carácter teatral)* theatricality (**b**) *(exageración)* exaggeration, over-dramatization

teatralización *nf (adaptación)* dramatization

teatralizar [14] *vt* (**a**) *(adaptar para el teatro)* to dramatize (**b**) *(exagerar)* to exaggerate

teatrero, -a *adj* (**a**) *(aficionado al teatro)* keen on (the) theatre (**b**) *Fam (exagerado)* **ino seas tan t.!** don't be such a drama queen!

teatro *nm* (**a**) *(espectáculo, género)* theatre; **el t. de Brecht** Brecht's plays *o* theatre; **el t. de vanguardia** avant-garde theatre; **una obra de t. clásico** a classical play; **un autor de t.** a playwright; **un grupo de t.** a theatre *o* drama group; **ir al t.** to go to the theatre; **dedicó toda su vida al t.** she devoted her whole life to the stage; **la vuelta al t. de Olivier** Olivier's return to the stage ►► *Lit* ***t. del absurdo*** theatre of the absurd; ***t. aficionado*** amateur dramatics; ***t. callejero*** street theatre; ***t. de guiñol*** puppet theatre; ***t. lírico*** opera and light opera; ***t. de marionetas*** puppet theatre; ***t. de repertorio*** repertory theatre; *RP* ***t. de revista*** *Br* music hall, *US* variety, vaudeville; ***t. de títeres*** puppet theatre; ***t. de variedades*** *Br* music hall, *US* variety, vaudeville
(**b**) *(edificio)* theatre; **lograron llenar el t.** they managed to fill the theatre; *Fig* **cuando la diva salió a saludar, el t. se vino abajo** when the diva came out to take a bow she brought the house down ►► ***t. al aire libre*** open-air theatre; ***t. de la ópera*** opera house; ***t. romano*** amphitheatre
(**c**) *Fam (fingimiento, exageración)* play-acting; **no le pasaba nada, era todo puro t.** there was nothing the matter with him, it was just play-acting; **hacer t.** to play-act; **echarle mucho t., tener mucho t.** to be a drama queen
(**d**) *Fig (escenario)* scene; **el Marne fue el t. de la batalla** the Marne was the scene of the battle ►► ***t. de operaciones*** theatre of operations

tebano, -a *Hist* **1** *adj* Theban
2 *nm,f* Theban

tebeo *nm Esp* (children's) comic; **personajes de t.** cartoon characters; EXPR *Fam* **estar más visto que el t.** to be old hat

teca *nf (árbol)* teak

tecali *nm Méx (mineral)* Mexican alabaster

techado *nm* roof; **un t. de paja** a thatched roof

techador, -ora *nm,f* roofer

techar *vt* to roof; **t. una casa con paja** to thatch (the roof of) a house

techo 1 *nm* (**a**) *(tejado) (fuera del edificio)* roof; *(dentro del edificio)* ceiling; **un t. de paja** a thatched roof; **hay que pintar el t. de la cocina** the kitchen ceiling needs painting; **el t. de la tienda de campaña está flojo** the roof of the tent is sagging ►► ***t. descapotable*** *(en coche)* convertible roof; *Av & Meteo* ***t. de nubes*** cloud ceiling; ***t. solar*** *(en coche)* sunroof
(**b**) *(casa, hogar)* house; **al menos tenemos t. y comida** at least we have food and a roof over our heads; **compartía t. con unos alemanes** he shared a house *o* a place with some Germans; **bajo t.** under cover; **dormir bajo t.** to sleep with a roof over one's head, to sleep indoors; **quedarse sin t.** to become homeless
(**c**) *(límite)* ceiling; **superó el t. de los 8,90 en salto de longitud** he broke through the 8.9 metre barrier in the long jump; **Escocia aspira a elevar su t. competencial** Scotland is aiming to acquire a greater level of devolved power; **tocar t.** *(inflación, precios)* to level off and start to drop; **la crisis ha tocado t.** the worst of the recession is behind us
(**d**) *Av (altura máxima)* ceiling
(**e**) *(jugador más alto)* tallest player
2 sin techo *nmf* homeless; **los sin t.** the homeless

techumbre *nf* roof; **una t. de paja** a thatched roof

teckel ['tekel] *nm (perro)* dachshund

tecla *nf* (**a**) *(de computadora, máquina de escribir, calculadora)* key; **pulsar** *o* **tocar una t.** to press *o* strike a key; EXPR **tocar muchas teclas** *(contactar)* to pull lots of strings; *(abarcar mucho)* to have too many things on the go at once ►► ***t. alt*** alt key; ***t. de bloqueo de mayúsculas*** shift lock key, caps lock key; ***t. de borrado*** delete key; ***t. de comando*** command key; ***t. de control*** control key; ***teclas de cursor*** cursor keys; ***t. (de) enter*** enter key; ***t. de escape*** escape key; ***t. fin*** end key; ***t. de función*** function key; ***t. de mayúsculas*** shift key; ***t. de mayúsculas fijas*** caps lock key; ***t. de opción*** option key; ***t. de retorno*** return key
(**b**) *(de instrumento musical)* key; **pulsar** *o* **tocar una t.** to press *o* strike a key
(**c**) *(botón)* button; **aprieta esta t. para rebobinar la cinta** press this button to rewind the tape

tecladista *nmf Am* keyboard player

teclado *nm* (**a**) *(de computadora)* keyboard; *(de máquina de escribir)* keys; *(de calculadora)* keypad ►► ***t. ergonómico*** ergonomic keyboard; ***t. expandido*** *o* ***extendido*** expanded *o* enhanced keyboard; ***t. numérico*** (numeric) keypad (**b**) *(de instrumento musical)* keyboard

tecleado *nm (en computadora)* keying; *(en máquina de escribir)* typing; *(en un instrumento musical)* playing, fingerwork

teclear 1 *vi* (**a**) *(en computadora, máquina de escribir)* to type
(**b**) *(en instrumento musical)* to play
(**c**) EXPR *RP Fam* **quedar tecleando: desde que perdió el trabajo, toda la familia quedó tecleando** since he lost his job, the whole family has been in the doldrums; **después de la crítica feroz que hizo la dirección, el proyecto quedó tecleando** after the fierce criticism it received from management, the project was put on hold; *RP Fam* **dejar a alguien tecleando: la noticia de su muerte me dejó tecleando** the news of her death left me dazed; **la reducción de gastos en la empresa dejó varios proyectos tecleando** the firm's cost-cutting exercise left several projects hanging in the air
2 *vt (en computadora)* to key (in), to type (in); *(en máquina de escribir)* to type; *(en calculadora)* to key (in); **teclee su número secreto** key in *o* enter your PIN number

tecleo *nm* (**a**) *(acción) (en computadora)* typing, keying; *(en máquina de escribir)* typing; *(ruido)* clacking, clatter (**b**) *(en instrumento musical)* playing

teclista *nmf* (**a**) *(músico)* keyboard player (**b**) *Imprenta* keyboarder

tecnecio *nm Quím* technetium

técnica *nf* (**a**) *(procedimiento)* technique; **en Florencia aprendió la t. pictórica del fresco** in Florence he learned the fresco technique; **tiene mucha t.** she has very good technique, she's very skilful ►► ***técnicas de reproducción asistida*** assisted reproduction techniques; ***técnicas de venta*** sales techniques
(**b**) *(tecnología)* technology; **los grandes avances de la t.** great advances in technology
(**c**) *(en baloncesto)* technical foul; **el árbitro le pitó una t. al entrenador** the referee blew the whistle for a technical foul by the trainer
(**d**) *ver también* **técnico**

técnicamente *adv* technically; **t., el ganador es el candidato demócrata** technically, the democratic candidate is the winner

tecnicismo *nm* (**a**) *(cualidad)* technical nature (**b**) *(término)* technical term

técnico, -a 1 *adj* (**a**) *(estudio, palabra, diccionario)* technical; **hubo un problema t.** there was a technical hitch *o* problem (**b**) *(persona)* technically proficient, with a good technique; **es un futbolista muy t.** he's a very technical player
2 *nm,f* (**a**) *(mecánico)* technician; **un t. en iluminación** a lighting technician; **vino el t. a arreglar la lavadora** the repairman came to fix the washing machine ►► ***t. agrícola*** agronomist; ***t. electricista*** electrical engineer; ***t. de laboratorio*** laboratory *o* lab technician; ***t. de sonido*** sound technician (**b**) *(entrenador)* coach, *Br* manager (**c**) *(experto)* expert

tecnicolor® *nm* Technicolor®

tecnificación *nf (en deporte)* competitive training; *(en agricultura)* modernization

tecnificar [60] *vt (persona)* to give technical training to; *(actividad)* to modernize

tecno 1 *adj inv* techno; **música t.** techno (music)
2 *nm inv* techno (music)

tecnocracia *nf* technocracy

tecnócrata 1 *adj* technocratic
2 *nmf* technocrat

tecnología *nf* technology; **de alta t.** high-tech; **las nuevas tecnologías** new technologies ►► ***t. espacial*** space technology; ***tecnologías de la información*** information technology; ***t. punta*** state-of-the-art technology; ***t. de las telecomunicaciones*** telecommunications technology

tecnológico, -a *adj* technological

tecnólogo, -a *nm,f* technologist

tecolote *nm CAm, Méx* (**a**) *(búho)* owl (**b**) *Fam (policía)* cop *(on night patrol)*

tecomate *nm CAm, Méx* = vessel made from a gourd

tecorral *nm CAm, Méx* stone wall

tectónica *nf* tectonics *(singular)* ►► *Geol* ***t. de placas*** plate tectonics

tectónico, -a *adj* tectonic

tedéum *nm inv* Te Deum

tedio *nm* (**a**) *(aburrimiento)* boredom, tedium (**b**) *(apatía)* apathy

tedioso, -a *adj* tedious

tee [ti] *nm* (**a**) *(lugar)* tee (**b**) *(taco)* tee (peg)

teflón® *nm* Teflon®

Tegucigalpa *n* Tegucigalpa

tegucigalpense 1 *adj* of/from Tegucigalpa *(Honduras)*
2 *nmf* person from Tegucigalpa *(Honduras)*

tegumento *nm Anat* integument

Teherán *n* Teheran

tehuacanazo *nm Méx Fam* = method of torture in which a bottle of mineral water is shaken vigorously, then opened and applied to one of the victim's nostrils

tehuelche *nmf* native of Patagonia

Teide *nm* **el T.** (Mount) Teide

teína *nf* caffeine *(contained in tea)*

teip, teipe *nm Carib* Sellotape®

teísmo *nm* theism

teísta 1 *adj* theist
2 *nmf* theist

teja *nf* (**a**) *(de tejado)* tile; **un techo de tejas** a tiled roof; **color t.** brick red ►► ***t. árabe*** Spanish tile, *US* tapered Mission tile (**b**) *(dulce)* = type of biscuit which is curved in shape (**c**) *(sombrero)* shovel hat

tejadillo *nm* = small roof over doorway, window etc

tejado *nm* roof

tejamanil *nm Carib, Col, Méx* shingle

tejano, -a 1 *adj* (**a**) *(de Texas)* Texan (**b**) *(tela, falda, chaqueta)* denim
2 *nm,f (persona)* Texan

tejanos *nmpl (pantalones)* jeans

tejar[1] **1** *vt* to tile
2 *vi* to tile

tejar[2] *nm* tile factory

Tejas *n* Texas

tejedor, -ora 1 *adj* (**a**) *(que teje)* weaving (**b**) *Chile, Perú Fam (intrigante)* scheming, conniving
2 *nm,f* (**a**) *(persona que teje)* weaver (**b**) *Chile, Perú Fam (persona intrigante)* schemer, conniver
3 *nm Zool* (**a**) *(insecto acuático)* pondskater (**b**) *(ave)* ***t. familiar*** village weaver

tejedora *nf (máquina)* knitting machine

tejeduría *nf* (**a**) *(técnica)* weaving (**b**) *(taller)* weaving mill

tejemaneje *nm Fam* (**a**) *(maquinación)* intrigue; **lo logró a base de tejemanejes** he achieved it by scheming; **es un t. para poder ascender** it's a ruse *o* scheme to get promoted (**b**) *(ajetreo)* to-do, fuss

tejer 1 *vt* (**a**) *(hilos, mimbre)* to weave; **tejió una cesta de mimbre** she made a wicker basket; **artículos tejidos a mano** hand-woven goods (**b**) *(labor de punto)* to knit; **t. algo a ganchillo** to crochet sth (**c**) *(telaraña, capullo)* to spin (**d**) *(labrar) (porvenir)* to carve out; *(ruina)* to bring about (**e**) *(tramar)* **t. un plan** to forge a plot
2 *vi* (**a**) *(hacer punto)* to knit; **t. a ganchillo** to crochet; EXPR **t. y destejer** to chop and change (**b**) *(araña, gusano)* to spin (**c**) *CSur, Perú Fam (conspirar)* to scheme, to plot

tejido *nm* (**a**) *(tela)* fabric, material; *Ind* textile ►► ***t. de punto*** knitted fabric; ***t. sintético*** synthetic fabric
(**b**) *(en seres vivos)* tissue ►► ***t. adiposo*** fatty tissue, *Espec* adipose tissue; ***t. blando*** soft tissue; ***t. cartilaginoso*** cartilaginous tissue; ***t. conjuntivo*** connective tissue; ***t. epitelial*** epithelial tissue; ***t. muscular*** muscular tissue; ***t. nervioso*** nerve tissue; ***t. óseo*** bone tissue, *Espec* osseous tissue
(**c**) *(estructura, sistema)* fabric; **el t. social/industrial del país** the social/industrial fabric of the country; **el t. asociativo de la sociedad** the network of associations in society
(**d**) *Am (de lana)* knitting; **¿dónde habré dejado mi t.?** where can I have left my knitting? ►► ***t. de alambre*** chicken wire
(**e**) *Am (labor)* knitting; **prefiero el t. a la costura** I prefer knitting to sewing

tejo[1] *nm (árbol)* yew

tejo[2] *nm* (**a**) *(juego)* hopscotch (**b**) *(pieza para juegos)* = disc of clay, metal or stone used in certain throwing games; EXPR *Esp Fam* **tirar los tejos a alguien** to make a pass at sb; **se pasó toda la fiesta tirándole los tejos a Silvia** he spent the whole party making passes at Silvia; **creo que te está tirando los tejos** I think he's coming on to you

tejocote *nm Méx* Mexican hawthorn tree

tejolote *nm Méx* stone pestle

tejón *nm* badger

tejonera *nf* badger's set

tejuelo *nm (en libro)* = label on spine of library books with abbreviated information about subject matter and author

tel. *(abrev de* **teléfono***)* tel.

tela 1 *nf* (**a**) *(tejido)* fabric, material; *(retal)* piece of material; **t. de algodón** cotton; **t. estampada/lisa** printed/plain material *o* fabric; **está hecho de una t. ligera** it's made out of a light fabric; **le pusieron una t. encima** they covered it with some cloth; **una funda de t.** a fabric cover; **un libro encuadernado en t.** a clothbound book; EXPR **haber mucha t. que cortar: hay mucha t. que cortar en relación con esto** there's plenty that could be said about this; EXPR **poner algo en t. de juicio** to call sth into question ►► *Am* ***t. adhesiva*** (sticking) plaster; ***t. de araña*** spider's web, cobweb; ***t. asfáltica*** asphalt roofing/flooring; *Méx* ***t. de costal*** sackcloth; *RP* ***t. esponja*** towelling; ***t. metálica*** wire netting; ***t. de saco*** sackcloth; ***t. tejana*** denim; ***t. vaquera*** denim
(**b**) *(lienzo, pintura)* canvas
(**c**) *Fam (dinero)* dough; **costó mucha t.** it cost a bundle *o Br* a packet
(**d**) *Fam (cosa complicada)* **el examen era t.** the exam was really tricky; **tener (mucha) t.** *(ser difícil)* to be (very) tricky; **hay t. (para rato)** *(trabajo)* there's no shortage of things to do; EXPR **¡fue t. marinera!** it was a nightmare!

(**e**) *Fam (para enfatizar)* **ser t. de fácil** to be a piece of cake, *Br* to be dead easy; **es t. de guapa** she's really gorgeous
2 *adv Esp Fam (muchísimo)* **me gusta t.** I really love it

telar *nm* (**a**) *(máquina)* loom (**b**) *Teatro* gridiron (**c**) **telares** *(fábrica)* textile mill

telaraña *nf* spider's web, cobweb; **un mosquito cayó en la t.** a fly got caught in the spider's web; **había telarañas en el techo** there were cobwebs on the ceiling; EXPR **tener telarañas en los ojos** to be blind ►► *Informát* ***la t. mundial*** the world wide web

Tel Aviv *n* Tel Aviv

tele *nf Fam (aparato, sistema)* TV, *Br* telly; **¿qué ponen** *o* **echan** *o* **dan en la t.?** what's on TV?

teleadicto, -a *nm,f* TV addict

teleapuntador *nm Br* Autocue®, *US* Teleprompter®

telearrastre *nm* button lift, ski-tow

teleaudiencia *nf Am* TV audience, viewers

telebanca *nf* telephone banking, home banking

telebanco *nm* telephone bank, home bank

telebasura *nf Fam* junk TV

telecabina *nf* cable car

telecentro *nm* telecentre

teleco *Fam* **1** *nmf (estudiante)* telecommunications student
2 *nf* (**a**) *(empresa)* telco (**b**) *(estudios)* telecommunications

telecomedia *nf* sitcom

telecompra *nf* teleshopping, home shopping

telecomunicación *nf* (**a**) *(comunicación)* telecommunication (**b**) *(sistema)* **telecomunicaciones** telecommunications

telecontrol *nm* remote control

teledetección *nf* remote sensing

telediario *nm Esp* television news; **el t. de la tarde/de las nueve** the afternoon/nine o'clock television news

teledifusión *nf* broadcasting

teledirigido, -a *adj (avión, coche)* remote-controlled; *(misil)* guided

teledirigir [24] *vt* to operate by remote control

teleeducación *nf* telelearning

teléf. *(abrev de* **teléfono**) tel.

telefax *nm inv* (**a**) *(aparato)* fax (**b**) *(mensaje)* fax

teleférico *nm* cable car

telefilme (*pl* **telefims**), **telefilm** (*pl* **telefilms**) *nm* TV movie *o Br* film

telefonazo *nm Fam (llamada)* buzz, *Br* ring; **dar** *o* **pegar un t. a alguien** to give sb a buzz *o Br* ring

telefonear **1** *vt* to phone, *Br* to ring; **me telefoneó para contármelo** she phoned me to tell me
2 *vi* to phone; **no nos dejan t. al extranjero** we're not allowed to phone abroad

telefonema *nm Am* telephone call

telefonía *nf* telephony ►► ***t. básica*** basic telephony; ***t. celular*** cellphones; **el mercado de la t. celular** the cellphone market; ***t. fija*** fixed telephony; ***t. móvil*** mobile telephony; **el mercado de la t. móvil** the mobile phone market

telefónica *nf (empresa)* telecommunications company

telefónicamente *adv* by phone

telefónico, -a *adj* telephone; **llamada telefónica** telephone call

telefonillo *nm (portero automático)* entryphone

telefonista *nmf* telephonist, (telephone) operator

teléfono *nm* (**a**) *(aparato, sistema)* telephone, phone; **la recepcionista atiende también el t.** the receptionist also answers the telephone; **coger el t.** to answer *o* pick up the phone; **descolgar el t.** to answer the phone; **estar al t.** to be on the phone; **hablaré con ella por t.** I'll speak to her on the phone; **está hablando por t.** she's on the phone; **llamar por t. a alguien** to phone sb; **te llaman por t.** there's someone on the phone for you; **tengo que llamar por t.** I've got to make a phone call; **ponerse al t.** to come to the phone; **ponte al t., es para ti** come to the phone, it's for you; **tener t.** to be on the phone, to have a phone; **¿tienes t.?** are you on the phone? ►► ***t. celular*** cellular phone, cellphone; *RP* ***t. descompuesto*** *(juego)* Chinese whispers; ***t. erótico*** telephone sex line; ***t. inalámbrico*** cordless phone; ***t. inteligente*** cellphone; *Informát* ***t. por Internet*** Internet phone; ***t. sin manos*** phone with hands-free facility; ***t. de manos libres*** phone with hands-free facility; ***t. modular*** cellphone; *Am* ***t. monedero*** payphone; ***t. móvil*** mobile phone; ***t. público*** public phone; ***t. rojo*** hot line
(**b**) *(número)* telephone number; **no tengo tu t.** I haven't got your number; **dar el t. a alguien** to give one's telephone number to sb ►► *Esp* ***t. 900*** ≃ freephone number

telefotografía *nf* telephotography

telegénico, -a *adj* telegenic

telegrafía *nf* telegraphy

telegrafiar [32] **1** *vt* to telegraph
2 *vi* to telegraph

telegráficamente *adv* (**a**) *(por telégrafo)* by telegraph (**b**) *(escuetamente)* telegraphically

telegráfico, -a *adj* (**a**) *(de telegrafía)* telegraphic (**b**) *(escueto)* telegraphic

telegrafista *nmf* telegraphist

telégrafo *nm* (**a**) *(medio, aparato)* telegraph (**b**) **telégrafos** *(oficina)* telegraph office

telegrama *nm* telegram

teleimpresor *nm* teleprinter

telejuego *nm* television game show

telekinesia *nf,* **telekinesis** *nf inv* telekinesis

telele *nm Fam* **le dio un t.** *(desmayo)* he passed out, he fainted; *(enfado, ataque de nervios)* he had a fit

telemando *nm* remote control

telemarketing *nm* telemarketing

telemática *nf* telematics *(singular)*

telemático, -a *adj* telematic

telematizar [14] *vt* to introduce telematics into

telemetría *nf* telemetry

telémetro *nm (en topografía, construcción)* telemeter; *(en armamento, fotografía)* rangefinder

telenovela *nf* TV soap opera

teleobjetivo *nm* telephoto lens

teleología *nf* teleology

teleósteo, -a *Zool* **1** *adj* teleost
2 *nm (pez)* teleost
3 **teleósteos** *nmpl (grupo)* Teleostei

telepatía *nf* telepathy; **dice que se comunican por t.** *o* **que tienen t.** she says they communicate telepathically

telepático, -a *adj* telepathic

telepedido *nm* teleorder

teleplatea *nf CSur* television audience, viewers

teleprocesar *vt Informát* to teleprocess

teleproceso *nm Informát* teleprocessing

telequinesia *nf,* **telequinesis** *nf inv* telekinesis

telera *nf (pan)* = large oval brown loaf

telerruta *nf* = telephone service giving traffic information

telescópico, -a *adj* (**a**) *(lente, mira, planeta)* telescopic (**b**) *(antena, paraguas, trípode)* telescopic

telescopio *nm* telescope ►► ***t. reflector*** reflecting telescope; ***t. de refracción*** refracting telescope

teleserie *nf* TV series

telesilla *nm* chairlift

telespectador, -ora *nm,f* viewer

telesquí (*pl* **telesquís** *o* **telesquíes**) *nm* button lift, ski-tow

teletexto *nm* Teletext®

teletienda *nf* television home shopping programme; **comprar algo en** *o* **por t.** to buy sth from a home shopping programme

teletipo *nm* (**a**) *(aparato)* teleprinter (**b**) *(texto)* Teletype®

teletonta *nf Fam* box, *US* idiot box

teletrabajador, -ora *nm,f* teleworker

teletrabajo *nm* teleworking

teletransportar *vt* to teleport

televendedor, -ora *nm,f* telesales assistant

televenta *nf* (**a**) *(por teléfono)* telesales (**b**) *(por televisión)* teleshopping, home shopping

televidente *nmf* viewer

televigilancia *nf* video surveillance

televisado, -a *adj* televised

televisar *vt* to televise

televisión *nf* (**a**) *(medio, sistema)* television; **¿qué ponen hoy en** *o* **por la t.?** what's on television *o* TV today?; **millones de personas lo vieron por t.** millions of people watched it on television; **ve demasiada t.** she watches too much television ▸▸ ***t. para abonados*** subscription television; ***t. de alta definición*** high-definition television; *Esp* ***t. autonómica*** regional television; ***t. en blanco y negro*** black-and-white television; ***t. por cable*** cable television; ***t. a la carta*** TV on demand; ***t. en color*** colour television; ***t. digital*** digital television; ***t. interactiva*** interactive television; ***t. de pago*** pay TV; ***t. panorámica*** widescreen TV; ***t. privada*** privately owned television; ***t. pública*** public television; ***t. por*** *o* ***vía satélite*** satellite television
(**b**) *(aparato)* television; **encender** *o* **poner la t.** to switch on the television
(**c**) *(empresa)* television company; **las televisiones privadas** private television companies

televisivo, -a *adj* television; **concurso t.** television game show

televisor *nm* television (set) ▸▸ ***t. en blanco y negro*** black-and-white television; ***t. en color*** colour television

televisora *nf Am* television company

télex *nm inv* telex; **enviar** *o* **mandar algo por t.** to telex sth

telgopor *nm Arg* (expanded) polystyrene

telilla *nf* (**a**) *(tela fina)* fine cloth (**b**) *(en superficie de líquido)* skin

telnet (*pl* **telnets**) *nm Informát* telnet

telo *nm RP Fam* = hotel where rooms are let by the hour

telón *nm (de escenario) (delante)* curtain; *(detrás)* backcloth; **subir/bajar el t.** to raise/to lower the curtain ▸▸ *Hist* ***el t. de acero*** the Iron Curtain; *Teatro* ***t. de boca*** front *o* house curtain; ***t. de fondo*** backdrop; **hubo elecciones con la corrupción política como t. de fondo** the elections took place against the backdrop of political corruption

telonero, -a 1 *adj* supporting; **grupo t.** support (band)
2 *nm,f (cantante, artista)* supporting artist; *(grupo, banda)* support (band)

telson *nm Zool* telson

telúrico, -a *adj* telluric

telurio, teluro *nm Quím* tellurium

tema *nm* (**a**) *(asunto)* subject; **será mejor no sacar/tocar ese t.** it would be best not to bring up that subject; **¿de qué t. quieres que hablemos?** what do you want to talk about?; **el t. de la película son las drogas** the film deals with drugs; **alejarse** *o* **salirse del t.** to wander off the subject; **cambiar de t.** to change the subject; *Fam* **el t. es que necesita ayuda** the fact of the matter is she needs help ▸▸ ***temas de actualidad*** current affairs; ***t. de conversación*** talking point, topic of conversation; ***t. espinoso*** thorny issue
(**b**) *(lección, unidad)* topic; **en el examen entran cinco temas** the exam covers five topics
(**c**) *(canción)* track, song; **una versión de un viejo t.** a cover of an old song
(**d**) *Mús (melodía básica)* theme; **el t. principal de la suite** the main theme of the suite
(**e**) *Ling* theme

temario *nm* (**a**) *(de asignatura)* syllabus; *(de oposiciones)* = list of topics for public examination (**b**) *(de reunión, congreso)* agenda

temascal, temazcal *nm Méx* steam bath

temática *nf* subject matter; **poesía de t. social** poetry dealing with social issues

temático, -a *adj* (**a**) *(del tema, asunto)* thematic; **parque t.** theme park (**b**) *Ling (vocal)* thematic

temazcal = **temascal**

tembladera *nf* (**a**) *(temblor)* trembling fit; **le dio** *o* **entró una t.** she started trembling, she got the shakes (**b**) *(pez)* electric ray (**c**) *(enfermedad)* scrapie

tembladeral *nm CSur* quaking bog

temblar [3] *vi* (**a**) *(persona) (de miedo, por nervios)* to tremble, to shake (**de** with); *(de frío)* to shiver (**de** with); **la fiebre le hacía t.** the fever made her shiver; **me tiemblan las piernas** my legs are shaking; **le temblaba la voz de la emoción** her voice was trembling with emotion; *Fig* **tiemblo por lo que pueda pasarle** I shudder to think what could happen to him; *Fig* **tiemblo sólo de pensarlo** I shudder just thinking about it; EXPR *Fam* **dejar algo temblando** *(la despensa, la nevera, una botella)* to leave sth almost empty; EXPR **dejar a alguien temblando** *(asustar, preocupar)* to leave sb quaking in their boots, to give sb a fright; EXPR **t. como un flan** to shake like a jelly
(**b**) *(suelo, edificio, máquina)* to shudder, to shake; **tembló la tierra** the ground shook; **tiembla la imagen del televisor** the television picture is shaky

tembleque *nm* trembling fit; **le dio** *o* **entró un t.** he started trembling, he got the shakes; **me dio** *o* **entró un t. en las piernas** my legs started shaking; **tiene t. en las manos** he has a tremor in his hands

temblequear *vi* (**a**) *(persona) (de miedo, por nervios)* to tremble; *(de frío)* to shiver (**b**) *(suelo, edificio, máquina)* to shudder, to shake

temblón, -ona *adj* shaky, trembling

temblor *nm* (**a**) *(del cuerpo) (por miedo, nervios)* shaking, trembling; *(por frío, fiebre)* shivering; **le dio** *o* **entró t. de piernas** his legs started shaking; **la fiebre le produjo temblores** the fever made him start shaking *o* shivering; *Fig* **me dan temblores sólo de pensarlo** it makes me shudder just to think about it (**b**) *(terremoto)* **t. (de tierra)** earth tremor (**c**) *(de máquina, motor)* shudder

tembloroso, -a *adj* (**a**) *(persona, manos, piernas)* trembling, shaky; *(voz)* trembling, quavering; *(labios)* quivering (**b**) *(luz, llama)* flickering, quivering

temer 1 *vt* (**a**) *(tener miedo de) (persona)* to fear, to be afraid of; *(represalias, consecuencias, reacción)* to fear, to be afraid of; **yo no te temo** I'm not afraid of you; **temo herir sus sentimientos** I'm afraid of hurting her feelings; **temen que los despidan** they are afraid of losing their jobs; *Fam* **cuando se pone a hablar le temo** my heart sinks whenever he opens his mouth
(**b**) *(sospechar)* to fear; **temo que vamos a tener que trabajar mucho** I fear we're going to have to work hard; **tememos lo peor** we fear the worst
2 *vi* to be afraid (**a** of); **le teme mucho al fuego** she's very afraid of fire; **no temas** don't worry; **t. por** to fear for; **los médicos temen por su vida** the doctors fear for her life; **ser de t.** *(ser temible)* to be formidable *o* fearsome; **el equipo polaco es de t.** the Polish team are formidable opponents; **estos críos son de t.** these kids are a menace; **es de t. que...** it is to be feared that...; **son de t. nuevos atentados** further attacks are to be feared
3 **temerse** *vpr* **temerse que** to be afraid (that), to fear (that); **me temo que no vendrá** I'm afraid (that) she won't come; **mucho me temo que fue todo un malentendido** I'm afraid it was all a misunderstanding; **¿queda leche? – me temo que no** is there any milk left? – I'm afraid not; **temerse lo peor** to fear the worst

temerariamente *adv (obrar, comportarse)* rashly, recklessly; *(juzgar, opinar)* rashly; *(conducir)* recklessly, carelessly

temerario, -a *adj (persona, conducta)* rash, reckless; *(juicio, opinión)* rash; **conducción temeraria** careless *o* reckless driving

temeridad *nf* (**a**) *(cualidad)* recklessness; **con t.** recklessly (**b**) *(acción)* **fue una t. hacer eso** it was reckless of you/him/*etc* to do that

temerosamente *adv (con temor)* fearfully

temeroso, -a *adj (con temor)* fearful; **se escondían temerosos** they hid in fear; **estar t. de algo/alguien** to fear sth/sb; **t. de Dios** God-fearing

temible *adj* fearsome

temor *nm* fear (**a** *o* **de** of); **el t. a las represalias** the fear of reprisals; **le tiene t. a la oscuridad** she's scared of the dark; **tengo el t. de que no sepan volver** I'm afraid they won't know how to get back; **por t. a** *o* **de** for fear of; **por t. a cometer un error** for fear of making a mistake ▸▸ *Rel* ***t. de Dios*** fear of God

témpano *nm* **t. (de hielo)** ice floe; EXPR **como un t.** chilled to the bone; **tenía las orejas como témpanos** my ears were frozen stiff

témpera *nf Arte* tempera

temperado, -a *adj* temperate

temperamental *adj* (**a**) *(vehemente, enérgico)* spirited; *(impulsivo)* impulsive (**b**) *(cambiante)* temperamental

temperamento *nm* (**a**) *(modo de ser)* temperament; **es una persona de t. impulsivo/dócil** he has a very impulsive/docile temperament; **tiene t. de ganador** he has a winner's temperament; **tiene un t. muy fuerte** *(mal genio)* she has a quick temper
(**b**) *(vehemencia, energía)* spirit; **los argentinos son jugadores con t.** the Argentinians are spirited players; **tiene mucho t.** she has a lot of spirit

temperancia *nf Formal* temperance

temperar 1 *vt (moderar)* to temper
2 *vi Col, Ven (cambiar de aires)* to have a change of air

temperatura *nf (atmosférica, corporal)* temperature; **se espera un aumento/descenso de las temperaturas** temperatures are expected to rise/fall; **tomar la t. a alguien** to take sb's temperature ▸▸ ***t. ambiental*** *o* ***ambiente*** room temperature; **sírvase a t. ambiente** serve at room temperature; *Cine & Fot* ***t. de(l) color*** colour temperature; *Fís* ***t. crítica*** critical temperature; ***t. máxima*** highest temperature; ***t. mínima*** lowest temperature

temperie *nf* weather (conditions)

tempero *nm Agr* = readiness of the soil for sowing

tempestad *nf* storm; **se levantó una fuerte t.** a fierce storm blew up; **levantar una t. de protestas** to raise a storm of protest; EXPR **una t. en un vaso de agua** *Br* a storm in a tea cup, *US* a tempest in a teapot ►► ***t. de arena*** sandstorm; ***t. de nieve*** snowstorm

tempestuoso, -a *adj* (a) *(día, viento, mar)* stormy (b) *(relaciones, asamblea, vida)* stormy, tempestuous

templa *nf Arte* distemper

templadamente *adv (con calma)* calmly

templado, -a 1 *adj* (a) *(agua, leche, comida) (tirando a frío)* lukewarm; *(tirando a caliente)* warm (b) *(clima, zona)* temperate; *(temperaturas)* mild; **tenemos una mañana templada en Cartagena** it's a mild morning here in Cartagena (c) *(sereno) (persona, carácter, ánimos)* calm, composed; *(nervios)* steady (d) *(moderado)* moderate
2 *nm Tec (del acero)* tempering

templanza *nf* (a) *(serenidad)* composure (b) *(moderación)* moderation (c) *(benignidad) (del clima)* mildness

templar 1 *vt* (a) *(entibiar) (lo frío)* to warm (up); *(lo caliente)* to cool down; **templaban las manos al calor de la hoguera** they warmed their hands at the bonfire
(b) *(calmar) (nervios, ánimos)* to calm; *(ira, pasiones)* to restrain; *(voz)* to soften; **t. la pelota** *o* **el balón** *(en fútbol)* to slow the game down
(c) *Tec (metal, cristal, vidrio)* to temper
(d) *(instrumento musical)* to tune; EXPR **t.gaitas** to calm things down
(e) *(tensar)* to tighten (up)
(f) *Andes (matar)* to kill
2 *vi* (a) *(tiempo, día)* to get milder; *(viento)* to lighten, to moderate (b) *Taurom* = to control the movement of the cape to accompany the bull's charge (c) *Cuba Fam (copular)* to screw
3 **templarse** *vpr* (a) *(entibiarse) (lo frío)* to warm up; *(lo caliente)* to cool down; **deja que se temple el café un poco** wait until the coffee cools down a little (b) *(calmarse) (nervios, ánimos)* to calm down; *(voz)* to soften; *(persona)* to control oneself (c) *Chile (enamorarse)* to fall in love (d) *Ecuad, Guat, Hond (morir)* to die

templario *nm* Templar

Temple *nm Hist* **el T.** (the Order of) the Templars

temple *nm* (a) *(entereza)* composure; **actuó con mucho t., tuvo mucho t.** she acted with great restraint
(b) *(estado de ánimo)* mood; **estar de buen/mal t.** to be in a good/bad mood
(c) *Tec (de metal, vidrio, cristal)* tempering; *(enfriamiento)* quenching, quench hardening
(d) *(pintura)* **(pintura al) t.** *(témpera)* tempera; *(para paredes)* distemper; **pintar al t.** *(con témpera)* to paint in tempera; *(en paredes)* to distemper
(e) *Taurom* = in bullfighting, skilful use of the cape to control the bull's movements

templete *nm (en parque, jardín)* pavilion; *(para banda de música)* bandstand; *(para sepulcro, mausoleo)* mausoleum; *(para figura, escultura, imagen)* niche

templo *nm* (a) *(edificio) (no cristiano)* temple; *(católico, protestante)* church; EXPR *Fam* **como un t.** huge; **eso es una verdad como un t.** that's an undeniable fact (b) *(lugar mitificado)* temple; **un t. de la música rock** a temple of rock

tempo *nm* (a) *Mús* tempo (b) *(de película, novela)* pace, tempo

temporada *nf* (a) *(periodo concreto)* season; **la t. de lluvias** the rainy season; **en la t. de primavera-verano se llevará el amarillo** yellow will be the colour to wear in the spring-summer season; **la t. de exámenes** exams *o* exam time; **de t.** *(fruta, trabajo, ropa)* seasonal; **estamos en t. de sandías, es t. de sandías** this is the watermelon season, watermelons are in season; **los kiwis están fuera de t.** kiwis are out of season; **de fuera de t.** off-season ►► ***t. alta*** high season; ***t. baja*** low season; ***la t. blanca*** the snow season; ***t. de caza*** hunting season; ***t. media*** mid-season; ***t. turística*** tourist *o* holiday season
(b) *(periodo indefinido)* time; **pasé una t. en el extranjero** I spent some time abroad; **tras una t. como profesor, se puso a traducir** after a stint *o* spell of teaching, he went into translating; **por temporadas** off and on

temporal[1] 1 *adj* (a) *(no permanente) (situación, actividad, ubicación)* temporary; *(bienes, vida)* worldly; **un contrato t. (de trabajo)** a temporary *o* fixed-term contract; **este trabajo es solamente t.** this job is only temporary (b) *(del tiempo)* time; **el factor t.** the time factor (c) *Rel (poder)* temporal
2 *nm (tormenta)* storm; *(racha prolongada de lluvias)* rainy spell; **t. de lluvia** rainstorm; **t. de nieve** snowstorm

temporal[2] *Anat* 1 *adj* temporal
2 *nm (hueso)* temporal

temporalero = **temporero**

temporalidad *nf (transitoriedad)* temporary nature; **hay que reducir la t. en el empleo** we need to reduce the number of temporary contracts

temporalmente, *Am* **temporariamente** *adv (por algún tiempo)* temporarily; **viven aquí t.** they are living here temporarily; **estaba contratado t.** he was hired on a temporary basis

temporario, -a *adj Am* temporary

temporero, -a, *Méx* **temporalero, -a** 1 *adj* seasonal
2 *nm,f* seasonal worker

temporizador *nm* timer

tempranamente *adv* early

tempranero, -a *adj* (a) *(persona)* early-rising; **ser t.** to be an early riser (b) *(acontecimiento, fruto)* early; **el verano ha sido t.** summer has come early

tempranito *adv Fam (muy temprano)* early; **esta noche, me iré t. a la cama** I'm going to have an early night tonight

temprano, -a 1 *adj* early; **a una edad temprana, a temprana edad** at an early age; **fruta temprana** early fruit
2 *adv* (a) *(por la mañana, por la noche)* early; **me levanto por la mañana t.** I get up early in the morning; **esta noche t. llegaremos a Caracas** we arrive in Caracas early tonight
(b) *(muy pronto, antes de tiempo)* early; **llegué t. a trabajar** I was early for work; **iremos t. para evitar colas** we'll go early to avoid the queues; **almorzaremos t.** we will have an early lunch; **es t. para saberlo** it's too soon to say

temucano, -a 1 *adj* of/from Temuco *(Chile)*
2 *nm,f* person from Temuco *(Chile)*

ten[1] *ver* **tener**

ten[2] *nm* EXPR **t. con t.: tener t. con t.** *(tacto)* to be tactful

tenacidad *nf* (a) *(perseverancia)* tenacity (b) *(persistencia)* persistence (c) *(resistencia)* toughness

tenacillas *nfpl (para rizar el pelo)* curling tongs; *(para depilar)* tweezers; *(para agarrar terrones de azúcar, dulces)* tongs

tenaz *adj* (a) *(perseverante) (persona, empeño, actitud)* tenacious (b) *(persistente) (mancha, grasa)* stubborn; *(dolor, dolencia)* chronic (c) *(resistente)* tough (d) *Col Fam (terrible)* terrible, awful; **iuy, t.!** *(¡no me digas!)* you don't say!

tenaza *nf,* **tenazas** *nfpl* (a) *(de carpintería, bricolaje)* pincers; *(para cocina, chimenea)* tongs; **agarró el filete con unas tenazas** he took hold of the steak with a pair of tongs; EXPR **ni con tenazas: no le pudimos sacar la información ni con tenazas** try as we might, we couldn't squeeze the information out of him; **no se puede agarrar ni con tenazas** it's absolutely filthy (b) *(de cangrejo, langosta)* pincer

tenazmente *adv* (a) *(con perseverancia)* tenaciously (b) *(con persistencia)* stubbornly

tenca *nf (pez)* tench

tendajón *nm Méx* small store

tendal *nm* (a) *(armazón)* (clothes) airer; *(cuerda)* clothes line (b) *Cuba, Ecuad (para café)* drying floor (c) *Am Fam (desorden, caos)* **estuvieron los niños y como siempre, dejaron un t.** the children were here and, as usual, they left the place a mess; **es muy bonita, siempre que pasa queda el t.** she's a stunner, wherever she goes she causes a commotion

tendalada *nf Chile Fam* devastation; **después del tornado, quedó la t.** the tornado left a trail of destruction

tendedero, tendedor *nm* (a) *(armazón fijo)* (clothes) airer; *(armazón plegable)* clothes horse; *(cuerda)* clothes line (b) *(lugar)* drying place

tendencia *nf* (a) *(inclinación)* tendency; **un diario de marcada t. conservadora** a very conservative newspaper; **tener t. a hacer algo** to tend *o* have a tendency to do sth; **tiene t. a meterse en líos** she tends to get herself into trouble; **tiene t. a la depresión** he has a tendency to depression
(b) *(corriente)* trend; **las últimas tendencias de la moda** the latest fashion trends; **hay tendencias reformistas dentro del partido** there are reformist tendencies within the party ►► *Econ* ***tendencias del mercado*** market trends

tendenciosidad *nf* tendentiousness

tendencioso, -a *adj* tendentious

tendente, tendiente *adj* **t. a** *(inclinado a)* prone to; *(encaminado a)* intended *o* designed to; **era una persona t. a las depresiones** he was prone to depression; **medidas tendentes a mejorar la economía** measures intended *o* designed to improve the economy

tender [66] **1** *vt* **(a)** *(tumbar)* to lay (out); **lo tendieron en una camilla** they laid him out on a stretcher
(b) *(colgar) (ropa)* to hang out; **voy a t. las sábanas** I'm going to hang out the sheets; **tendió la ropa en una silla frente a la chimenea** she spread the clothes on a chair in front of the fireplace
(c) *(extender, colocar) (manta)* to stretch (out); *(mantel)* to spread; *Am (cama)* to make; *Am (mesa)* to set, to lay
(d) *(entre dos puntos) (cable, tuberías, vía)* to lay; *(puente)* to build; *(cuerda)* to stretch
(e) *(dar) (cosa)* to hand; **le tendió una cuerda para que subiera por ella** he threw her a rope so she could climb up; **t. la mano a alguien** *(extender la mano)* to hold out one's hand to sb, to offer sb one's hand; **ella fue la única que me tendió una** *o* **la mano** *(me ayudó)* she was the only person to lend *o* give me a hand
(f) *(trampa, emboscada)* to lay; **la policía tendió una trampa al sospechoso** the police laid a trap for the suspect
2 *vi* **(a)** *(tener inclinación)* **t. a hacer algo** to tend to do sth; **tiende a enojarse con facilidad** he tends to get annoyed easily; **t. a la depresión** to be prone to depression; **un azul que tiende a violeta** a blue which is almost violet; **la inflación tiende a la baja** inflation is trending down **(b)** *Mat* **cuando x tiende a 1** as x tends to 1
3 tenderse *vpr (tumbarse)* to stretch out, to lie down (**en** on); **nos tendimos al sol** we stretched out in the sun

ténder *nm Ferroc* tender

tenderete *nm (puesto)* stall

tendero, -a *nm,f* storekeeper, shopkeeper

tendido, -a 1 *adj* **(a)** *(extendido, tumbado)* stretched out **(b)** *(colgado) (ropa)* on the line; **recoger la ropa tendida** to take the washing in (off the line)
2 *nm* **(a)** *(instalación) (de cable, vía, tuberías)* laying; *(de puente)* construction ►► ***t. eléctrico*** *(cables)* power lines **(b)** *Taurom* front rows; *Fig* **saludar al t.** *(monarca, personaje público)* to wave to the crowd ►► ***t. de sol*** = area of stands in bullring which is in the sun; ***t. de sombra*** = area of stands in bullring which is in the shade

tendiente = **tendente**

tendiera *etc ver* **tender**

tendinitis *nf inv* tendinitis

tendón *nm* tendon ►► ***t. de Aquiles*** Achilles' tendon

tendré *etc ver* **tener**

tenebrismo *nm* tenebrism

tenebrista 1 *adj* tenebrist
2 *nmf* tenebrist

tenebrosidad *nf* **(a)** *(oscuridad)* darkness, gloom **(b)** *(carácter siniestro)* sinisterness

tenebroso, -a *adj* **(a)** *(oscuro)* dark, gloomy **(b)** *(siniestro) (asunto, lugar, personaje)* shady, sinister; *(porvenir, perspectiva, situación)* grim, dismal; **su t. rostro** his gloomy face

tenedor[1] *nm (utensilio)* fork; **un restaurante de un t./de cinco tenedores** = restaurant with lowest/highest rating according to Spanish restaurant classification system

tenedor[2]**, -ora** *nm,f (poseedor)* holder ►► ***t. de acciones*** shareholder; *Com* ***t. de libros*** bookkeeper; ***t. de póliza*** policy-holder

teneduría *nf Com* **t. (de libros)** bookkeeping

tenencia *nf* **(a)** *(posesión)* possession ►► ***t. de drogas*** possession of drugs; ***t. ilícita de armas*** illegal possession of arms **(b)** *(de puesto)* ***t. de alcaldía*** deputy mayor's office **(c)** *Méx (impuesto)* road tax

TENER [67] **1** *vt* **(a)** *(poseer, disfrutar de) (objeto, cualidad, elemento, parentesco)* to have; **no tengo televisor/amigos** I haven't got *o* I don't have a television/any friends; **¿tienes un bolígrafo?** have you got *o* do you have a pen?; **¿tiene usted hora?** have you got the time?; **tenemos un mes para terminarlo** we've got a month in which to finish it; **tiene el pelo corto, ojos azules y gafas** she has (got) short hair, blue eyes and she wears glasses; **muchos no tienen trabajo** *o* **empleo** a lot of people are out of work; **el documental no tiene mucho interés** the documentary is not very interesting; **¿cuántas habitaciones tiene?** how many rooms has it got *o* does it have?; **¿tienes hermanos?** have you got *o* do you have any brothers or sisters?; **tengo un hermano** I've got *o* I have a brother; **t. un niño** to have a baby; **no tienen hijos** they haven't got *o* don't have any children; *RP Fam* **t. algo a bocha** *(en gran cantidad)* to have tons *o* loads of sth; EXPR **¿conque ésas tenemos?, ¿ahora no quieres ayudar?** so that's the deal, is it? you don't want to help now, then; EXPR **no las tiene todas consigo** he is not too sure about it; EXPR *muy Fam* **tenerlos bien puestos** to have guts; PROV **tanto tienes, tanto vales** you are what you own
(b) *(padecer, realizar, experimentar)* to have; **t. fiebre** to have a temperature; **tiene cáncer/el sida** she has (got) cancer/AIDS; **doctor, ¿qué tengo?** what's wrong with me, doctor?; **no tienes nada (grave)** it's nothing (serious), there's nothing (seriously) wrong with you; **tuvieron una pelea/reunión** they had a fight/meeting; **tengo las vacaciones en agosto** my holidays are in August; **mañana no tenemos clase** we don't have to go to school tomorrow, there's no school tomorrow; **¡que tengan buen viaje!** have a good journey!; **no he tenido un buen día** I haven't had a good day; **tiene lo que se merece** she's got what she deserves
(c) *(medida, años, sensación, sentimiento)* to be; **tiene 3 metros de ancho** it's 3 metres wide; **¿cuántos años tienes?** how old are you?; **tiene diez años** she's ten (years old); *Am* **tengo tres años aquí** I've been here for three years; **t. hambre/miedo** to be hungry/afraid; **t. suerte/mal humor** to be lucky/bad-tempered; **tengo un dolor de espalda terrible** I have a terrible backache; **tengo alergia al polvo** I'm allergic to dust; **me tienen cariño/envidia** they're fond/jealous of me; **le tiene lástima** he feels sorry for her; **tengo ganas de llorar** I feel like crying
(d) *(hallarse o hacer estar en cierto estado)* **tenía la cara pálida** her face was pale; **tienes una rueda pinchada** you've got a *Br* puncture *o US* flat; **tienes la corbata torcida** your tie isn't straight; **me tuvo despierto** it kept me awake; **eso la tiene despistada/preocupada** that has her confused/worried; **esto la tendrá ocupada un rato** this will keep her busy for a while; **un psicópata tiene atemorizada a la población** a psychopath is terrorizing the population; **nos tuvieron una hora en comisaría** they kept us at the police station for an hour; **me tuvo esperando una hora** she kept me waiting an hour; **nos tuvieron toda la noche viendo vídeos** they made us watch videos all night; **la tienen como** *o* **de encargada en un restaurante** she's employed as a manageress in a restaurant
(e) *(sujetar)* to hold; **tenlo por el asa** hold it by the handle; **¿puedes tenerme esto un momento?** could you hold this for me a minute?; **ten los brazos en alto** hold your arms up high
(f) *(tomar)* **ten el libro que me pediste** here's the book you asked me for; **¡aquí tienes!, ¡ten!** here you are!; **ahí tienes la respuesta** there's your answer
(g) *(recibir) (mensaje, regalo, visita, sensación)* to get; **tuve una carta suya** I got *o* had a letter from her; **el que llegue primero tendrá un premio** whoever arrives first will get a prize; **tendrás noticias mías** you'll hear from me; **tenemos invitados/a la familia a cenar** we've got guests/the family over for dinner; **tendrá una sorpresa** he'll get a surprise; **tenía/tuve la impresión de que...** I had/got the impression that...; **tuve una verdadera desilusión** I was really disappointed
(h) *(valorar, estimar)* **t. en mucho/poco a alguien** to think a lot/not to think very much of sb; **me tienen por tonto** they think I'm stupid; *Formal* **t. a bien hacer algo** to be kind enough to do sth; **les ruego tengan a bien considerar mi candidatura para el puesto de...** I would be grateful if you would consider my application for the post of...
(i) *(guardar, contener)* to keep; **¿dónde tienes las joyas/el dinero?** where do you keep the jewels/money?; **¿dónde tendré las gafas?** where can my glasses be?; **la botella tenía un mensaje** the bottle had a message inside; **esta cuenta no tiene fondos** there are no funds in this account
(j) *RP Fam* **tenerla con algo/alguien** to go on about sth/sb; **icómo la tenés con tu vecino!** you're always going on about your neighbour!; **icómo la tiene con el auto que se va a comprar!** he's always going on about the car he's going to buy!; **icómo la tiene el jefe contigo!** the boss really has it in for you!
2 *v aux* **(a)** *(antes de participio) (haber)* **teníamos pensado ir al teatro** we had thought of going to the theatre, we had intended to go to the theatre; **¿cuánto tienes hecho de la tesis?** how much of your thesis have you (got) done?; **te tengo dicho que no pises los charcos** I've told you before not to step in puddles; **tengo entendido que se van a casar** I understand (that) they are going to get married
(b) t. que: *(indica obligación)* **t. que hacer algo** to have to do sth; **tenía/tuve que hacerlo** I had to do it; **¿tienes que irte?** do you have to go?, have you got to go?; **tienes que esforzarte más** you must try harder; **tiene que ser así** it has to be this way; **tenemos que salir de aquí** we have (got) to *o* need to get out of here, we must get out of here; **teníamos que haber hecho esto antes** we should have *o* ought to have done this before; **no tienes que disculparte** you needn't apologize, you don't need to apologize; **si quieres algo, no tienes más que pedirlo** if you want something, all you have to do is ask; **no tienes por qué venir, si no quieres** you don't have to come if you don't want to
(c) t. que: *(indica propósito, consejo)* **tenemos que ir a cenar un día** we ought to *o* should go for dinner some time; **tienes que ir a ver esa película** you must see that movie; **tenías que haber visto cómo corría**

you should have seen him run; **tendrías que dejar de fumar** you ought to give up smoking

(**d**) **t. que:** *(indica probabilidad)* **ya tienen que haber llegado** they must have *o* should have arrived by now; **las llaves tienen que andar por aquí** the keys must be round here somewhere; **tendría que haber terminado hace rato** she should have *o* ought to have finished some time ago; **tenía que ser él, no podía ser otro** it had to be him, it couldn't have been anyone else

(**e**) **t. que ver: t. que ver con algo/alguien** to have to do with sth/sb; **actitudes que tienen que ver con la falta de educación** attitudes which are related to a lack of education; **se apellida Siqueiros, pero no tiene que ver con el pintor** his surname is Siqueiros, but he's got nothing to do with the painter; **¿qué tiene eso que ver conmigo?** what has that got to do with me?; **no t. nada que ver con algo/alguien** to have nothing to do with sth/sb; **lo que digo no tiene nada que ver con eso** what I'm saying has nothing to do with that; **aunque los dos vinos sean Rioja, no tienen nada que ver** even if both wines are Riojas, there's no comparison between them; **¿qué tiene que ver que sea mujer para que haga bien su trabajo?** what's her being a woman got to do with whether or not she does a good job?; **es un poco tarde, ¿no? – ¿y qué tiene que ver?** it's a bit late, isn't it? – so what?; **t. que ver en algo** to be involved in sth; **dicen que la CIA tuvo que ver en ello** rumour has it the CIA were involved; **¿has tenido tú algo que ver en esto?** have you had something to do with this?

3 tenerse *vpr* (**a**) *(sostenerse)* **tenerse de pie** *o* **en pie** *(persona, objeto)* to stand upright; **tenerse sentado** to sit up; **no se tiene de la borrachera (que lleva)** he's so drunk he can't stand up (straight); *Fam* **tengo un hambre que no me tengo** I'm so hungry I feel faint

(**b**) *(considerarse)* **se tiene por listo** he thinks he's clever; **me tengo por una persona honrada** I see myself as *o* consider myself an honest person

(**c**) *(reprimirse, contenerse)* **tente, no vayas a hacer una tontería** control yourself, don't do anything silly

---

tenería *nf* tannery

tengo *ver* **tener**

tenia *nf* tapeworm

tenida *nf* (**a**) *(reunión)* = meeting of a Masonic lodge (**b**) *Chile (traje)* outfit

teniente[1] *nmf* (**a**) *Mil* lieutenant ►► ***t. coronel*** lieutenant colonel; ***t. general*** lieutenant general; ***t. de navío*** lieutenant (**b**) *(sustituto)* deputy ►► ***t. (de) alcalde*** deputy mayor

teniente[2] *adj Fam (sordo)* **estar t.** to be a bit deaf

tenis 1 *nm inv (deporte)* tennis; **un partido de t.** a game of tennis; **jugar al t.** to play tennis ►► ***t. sobre hierba*** grass-court tennis; ***t. de mesa*** table tennis

2 *nmpl (calzado)* tennis shoes

tenista *nmf* tennis player

tenístico, -a *adj* tennis; **campeonato t.** tennis championship

tenor[1] *Mús* **1** *adj* tenor; **saxo t.** tenor sax

2 *nm* tenor

tenor[2] *Formal* **1** *nm (estilo)* tone; **el t. de su discurso fue relajado** his speech was relaxed in tone; **profirió insultos como éste y otros de parecido t.** he uttered insults like this and others in a similar vein; **a este t.** *(de la misma manera)* in the same vein

2 a tenor de *loc prep (a juzgar por)* judging by; *Der (de acuerdo con)* in accordance with; **a t. de lo visto en el campo, el resultado es justo** judging by what we've just seen on the field *o Br* pitch, it's a fair result; **a t. de sus declaraciones** judging by his statements; **a t. de lo dispuesto en el artículo III** in accordance with the provisions of Article 3

tenora *nf Mús* shawm

tenorio *nm* ladies' man, Casanova

tensado *nm* tautening

tensar 1 *vt* (**a**) *(cable, cuerda)* to tauten; *(arco)* to draw; *(músculo, cuerpo)* to tense (**b**) *(situación, relación, ambiente)* to make tense, to strain; *(persona)* to make tense

2 tensarse *vpr* (**a**) *(cable, cuerda)* to tauten (**b**) *(situación, relación, ambiente)* to become tense *o* strained; *(persona)* to become tense

tensímetro, tensiómetro *nm* blood pressure gauge, *Espec* sphygmomanometer

tensioactivo, -a *adj* **agente t.** surfactant

tensión *nf* (**a**) *(estado emocional)* tension; **estar en t.** to be tense; **los jugadores soportan una gran t.** the players are under a lot of pressure ►► ***t. nerviosa*** nervous tension; *Med* ***t. premenstrual*** premenstrual tension, PMT

(**b**) *(enfrentamiento)* tension; **hubo muchas tensiones entre ellos** there was a lot of tension between them

(**c**) *(de cuerda, cable)* tension; **en t.** tensed; **puso sus músculos en t.** he tensed his muscles ►► ***t. superficial*** surface tension

(**d**) *Elec* voltage; **alta t.** high voltage

(**e**) *Med* **t. (arterial)** blood pressure; **tener la t. (arterial) alta/baja** to have high/low blood pressure; **tener una subida/bajada de t.** to suffer a rise/drop in blood pressure; **tomar la t. a alguien** to take sb's blood pressure

tenso, -a *adj* (**a**) *(cuerda, cable)* taut; *(arco)* drawn; *(músculo, cuerpo)* tense (**b**) *(situación, relación, ambiente)* tense, strained; *(persona)* tense; **estar t. con alguien** to be tense with sb; **ponerse t.** to become tense

tensó, tensón *nf Lit* tenson

tensor, -ora 1 *adj* tightening

2 *nm* (**a**) *(dispositivo)* turnbuckle (**b**) *(músculo)* tensor (**c**) *Mat* tensor

tentación *nf* (**a**) *(impulso)* temptation; **caer en la t.** to give in to temptation; **no caí en la t. de probar otro bombón** I resisted the temptation to try another chocolate; *Rel* **no nos dejes caer en la t.** lead us not into temptation; **tener la t. de hacer algo** to be tempted to do sth; **tuve la t.** *o* **me daban tentaciones de abrir los regalos** I was tempted to open the presents

(**b**) *(persona, cosa)* temptation; **las tartas del escaparate eran una t.** the cakes in the window were a temptation

(**c**) *RP (de risa)* the giggles; **su forma de hablar me da mucha t.** the way he speaks gives me the giggles

tentaculado, -a *adj* tentacled

tentacular *adj* tentacular

tentáculo *nm* (**a**) *(de animal)* tentacle (**b**) *(de organización, grupo)* tentacle; **los tentáculos del poder** the tentacles of power

tentadero *nm Taurom* bull ring

tentado, -a *adj* (**a**) *(de tentación)* tempted; **estar t. de hacer algo** to be tempted to do sth; **estuve t. de darle un puñetazo** I was tempted to punch him (**b**) *RP (de risa)* **no pudo contestar porque estaba tentada** she was trying so hard to stop herself laughing that she couldn't reply

tentador, -ora *adj* tempting; **la idea es muy tentadora** it's a very tempting idea

tentar [3] **1** *vt* (**a**) *(incitar)* to tempt; **no me tientes, que no tengo dinero para irme de viaje** don't tempt me, I don't have enough money to go travelling; **lo tentó el diablo** he was tempted by the devil; **t. a alguien con algo** to tempt sb with sth; **t. a alguien a hacer algo** to tempt sb to do sth; EXPR **t. al diablo** *o* **a la suerte** to tempt fate

(**b**) *(atraer)* to tempt; **es gente a la que no le tienta el lujo** he's the sort of person who isn't tempted by luxury; **me tienta mucho la idea** I find the idea very tempting

(**c**) *(palpar)* to feel; **se tentó los bolsillos en busca del encendedor** he felt his pockets for the lighter

(**d**) *Taurom* = to goad (a young bull) with a spear to test its mettle

2 tentarse *vpr RP* to want to laugh; **si nos mirábamos, nos íbamos a tentar** if we looked at each other, we'd want to laugh

tentativa *nf* attempt; **superó el listón en** *o* **a la segunda t.** he got over the bar at the second attempt ►► ***t. de asesinato*** attempted murder; ***t. de delito*** attempted crime; ***t. de suicidio*** suicide attempt

tentativo, -a *adj* tentative

tentempié *nm* (**a**) *(aperitivo)* snack (**b**) *(tentetieso)* tumbler doll, wobble doll

tentetieso *nm* tumbler doll, wobble doll

tenue *adj* (**a**) *(fino) (tela, velo)* fine (**b**) *(débil) (luz, voz, sonrisa)* faint; *(niebla, lluvia)* fine; **hizo un gesto t. de asentimiento** he gave a faint nod of assent (**c**) *(poco sólido) (relación, argumentación)* tenuous

teñido, -a 1 *adj (tela, pelo)* dyed

2 *nm* dyeing

teñir [47] **1** *vt* (**a**) *(tintar) (tela, pelo)* to dye; **t. algo de rojo/verde** to dye sth red/green

(**b**) *(manchar)* to stain; **la sangre teñía sus manos** her hands were stained with blood; **el trabajo en la mina les tiñe el rostro de negro** the work in the mine blackens their faces

(**c**) *(matizar)* to tinge sth (**de** with); **tiñe su prosa de melancolía** her prose is tinged with melancholy; **el ambiente festivo tiñe las calles por estas fechas** at this time of year the streets are filled with a festive atmosphere

2 teñirse *vpr* **teñirse (el pelo)** to dye one's hair; **se tiñe de rubio** he dyes his hair blond

teocali, teocalli *nm Hist* teocalli
teocracia *nf* theocracy
teocrático, -a *adj* theocratic
teodicea *nf Filosofía* theodicy
teodolito *nm* theodolite
teogonía *nf* theogony
teologal *adj* theological; **las virtudes teologales** the theological virtues
teología *nf* theology ►► ***t. de la liberación*** liberation theology
teológico, -a *adj* theological
teologizar [14] *vi* to theologize
teólogo, -a *nm,f* theologian
teorema *nm* theorem ►► ***el t. de Pitágoras*** Pythagoras' theorem
teorético, -a *adj Formal* theoretical
teoría *nf* (a) *(especulación)* theory; **la teoría se le da bien, pero la práctica...** he's good at the theory but in practice...; **en t.** in theory; **en t. han venido a ayudar** in theory they have come to help
(b) *(hipótesis)* theory; **mi t. es que...** my theory is that...; **hay quien tiene** *o* **sostiene la t. de que...** there are people who maintain that... ►► ***la t. del big bang*** the big bang theory; *Mat* ***la t. del caos*** chaos theory; *Biol* ***t. celular*** cell theory; ***t. de la comunicación*** communication theory; *Mat* ***t. de conjuntos*** set theory; ***t. del conocimiento*** epistemology; ***t. cuántica*** quantum theory; ***la t. de la evolución*** the theory of evolution; *Mat* ***t. de grupos*** group theory; ***t. de la información*** information theory; ***t. monetaria*** monetary theory; *Mat* ***t. de números*** number theory; ***la t. de la relatividad*** the theory of relativity
teóricamente *adv* (a) *(en teoría)* theoretically; **ellos son t. superiores** in theory they are better (b) *(desde la teoría, de modo teórico)* theoretically
teórico, -a 1 *adj (caso, conocimientos, examen)* theoretical; **clases teóricas** theory classes
2 *nm,f (persona)* theorist
3 *nm (examen de conducir)* written exam
teorizador, -ora *adj* theorizing
teorizar [14] *vi* to theorize (**sobre** about)
teosofía *nf* theosophy
teósofo, -a *nm,f* theosophist
TEP [tep] *nm Med (abrev de* **tomografía por emisión de positrones***)* *(técnica)* PET; *(escáner)* PET scan
tepache *nm* = non-alcoholic drink made from fermented pineapple peelings and unrefined sugar, typical of Mexico
tepachería *nf* establishment which serves tepache
tepalcate *nm Méx Hist* shard
tépalo *nm Bot* tepal
tepe *nm* sod, piece of turf
tepetate *nm Méx* (a) *(roca)* limestone (b) *(arcilla)* caliche
tepiqueño, -a 1 *adj* of/from Tepic *(Mexico)*
2 *nm,f* person from Tepic *(Mexico)*
tepuy *nm Ven* table mountain
tequeño *nm Ven* cheese fritter
tequesquite *nm Méx* natural salt
tequi *nm Esp Fam (taxi)* cab, taxi
tequila *nm o nf* tequila
tequio *nm Méx Hist* = forced labour imposed on the Indians by the Spanish as tribute
terapeuta *nmf* (a) *(médico)* doctor (b) *(fisioterapeuta)* physiotherapist
terapéutica *nf* (a) *(ciencia)* therapeutics *(singular)* (b) *(tratamiento)* therapy
terapéutico, -a *adj* therapeutic
terapia *nf* therapy; **está en t. con un psicólogo** he's in therapy with a psychologist ►► ***t. combinada*** combination therapy; ***t. de electrochoque*** electroshock therapy *o* treatment; ***t. genética*** *o* ***génica*** gene therapy; ***t. de grupo*** group therapy; *Méx, RP* ***t. intensiva*** intensive care; ***t. ocupacional*** occupational therapy; ***t. de rehidratación oral*** oral rehydration therapy; ***t. de relajación*** relaxation therapy
terapista *nmf Andes, Méx* therapist
teratogénico, -a, teratógeno, -a *adj Biol* teratogenic
teratología *nf Biol* teratology
terbio *nm Quím* terbium
tercena *nf Ecuad (carnicería)* butcher's (shop)
tercer *ver* **tercero**
tercera *nf* (a) *(marcha)* third (gear); **meter (la) t.** to go into third (gear) (b) *Mús* third (c) *ver también* **tercero**
tercería *nf (mediación)* mediation
tercerización *nf Am Com* outsourcing
tercerizar [14] *vt Am Com* to outsource
tercermundismo *nm* (a) *(del Tercer Mundo)* underdevelopment (b) *(de servicios, sistema, funcionamiento)* backwardness
tercermundista *adj* (a) *(del Tercer Mundo)* third-world; **un país t.** a third-world country (b) *(servicios, sistema, funcionamiento)* appalling; **¡este servicio es t.!** this service is appalling *o* a disgrace!
tercero, -a

Tercer is used instead of **tercero** before masculine singular nouns (e.g. **el tercer piso** the third floor).

1 *núm* third; EXPR *Esp* **a la tercera va la vencida,** *Am* **la tercera es la vencida** third time lucky ►► *Dep* ***la tercera base*** *(posición)* third base; *Dep* ***el/la tercera base*** *(jugador)* third base; ***la tercera edad*** senior citizens; **durante la tercera edad** in old age; **pensionistas de la tercera edad** *Br* old age pensioners, *US* retirees; *Hist* ***el tercer estado*** the third estate; ***el Tercer Mundo*** the Third World; *Pol* ***la tercera vía*** the third way; *ver también* **octavo**
2 *nm* (a) *(piso)* third floor; **el t. izquierda** the third floor *Br* flat *o US* apartment on the left
(b) *(curso universitario)* third year
(c) *(curso escolar)* = third year of primary school, *US* ≃ third grade
(d) *(mediador, parte interesada)* third party; **seguro a terceros** third-party insurance, liability insurance; **me enteré por un t.** I found out from a third party *o* from another person ►► ***el t. en discordia*** the third party
terceto *nm* (a) *(estrofa)* tercet (b) *Mús* trio
tercia *nf* (a) *Rel* tierce (b) *ver también* **tercio**
terciado, -a *adj (mediano)* medium-sized
terciador, -ora 1 *adj* mediating, arbitrating
2 *nm,f* mediator, arbitrator
terciana *nf,* **tercianas** *nfpl* tertian fever, tertian
terciar 1 *vt* (a) *(poner en diagonal) (objeto, mueble)* to place diagonally; *(sombrero)* to tilt; **el sofá estaba terciado en medio del salón** the sofa was placed diagonally across the middle of the sitting room (b) *(dividir)* to divide into three (c) *(decir)* to interject; **"a mí no me metas en esto", terció ella** "don't mix me up in this," she interjected (d) *Col, Méx (una carga)* to carry on one's back; **terció el bulto** he carried the pack on his back (e) *Andes, Cuba, Méx (aguar)* to water down
2 *vi* (a) *(mediar)* to mediate (**en** in); **Estados Unidos terció en el conflicto** the United States mediated in the conflict (b) *(participar)* to intervene, to take part; **t. en la conversación** to join in the conversation
3 terciarse *vpr* to arise, to come up; **si se tercia** if the opportunity arises
terciario, -a 1 *adj* (a) *(asunto, prioridad)* tertiary; **el sector t.** the tertiary sector (b) *Geol* Tertiary
2 *nm Geol* **el Terciario** the Tertiary (era)
terciarización *nf Am Com* outsourcing
terciarizar [14] *vt Am Com* to outsource
tercio, -a 1 *nm* (a) *(tercera parte)* third; **hay un t. de entrada en el estadio** the stadium is one-third full; **dos tercios de la población** two-thirds of the population; EXPR *Méx* **hacer mal t.** *Br* to play gooseberry, *US* to be a fifth wheel
(b) *Mil* regiment; *Hist* tercio; **t. de la guardia civil** Civil Guard division
(c) *Taurom* = any of the three stages of a bullfight; EXPR **cambiar de t.** *(de tema)* to change the subject; *(de método)* to change tack; EXPR **cambio de t.** *(de tema)* change of subject; *(de método)* change of tack
(d) *(de cerveza)* bottle of beer *(0.33 litre)*; *ver también* **octavo**
2 *nm,f Ven Fam (individuo)* guy, *Br* bloke
terciopelo *nm* velvet; **un vestido de t.** a velvet dress
terciopersonal *adj Gram* **un verbo t.** = verb only used in the third person
terco, -a 1 *adj* (a) *(testarudo)* stubborn; EXPR **t. como una mula** as stubborn as a mule (b) *Ecuad (indiferente)* cold, aloof
2 *nm,f* stubborn person; **ser un t.** to be stubborn
tereré *nm Arg, Par (mate)* cold maté
Teresa *n pr* **Santa T.** St Theresa (of Avila); **la madre T. (de Calcuta)** Mother Teresa (of Calcutta)
teresiana *nf (monja)* Theresian; **las teresianas** *(colegio)* the Theresians

tergal® *nm* = type of synthetic fibre containing polyester
tergiversación *nf* distortion
tergiversador, -ora 1 *adj* distorting
2 *nm,f* **es un t.** he always distorts *o* twists the facts
tergiversar *vt* to distort, to twist
terma *nm Perú* water-heater
termal *adj* thermal; **fuente de aguas termales** hot spring
termas *nfpl* **(a)** *(baños)* hot baths, spa **(b)** *Hist* **termas (romanas)** (Roman) baths
termes = **termita**
térmico, -a *adj* **(a)** *(de la temperatura)* temperature; **descenso t.** drop in temperature **(b)** *(energía)* thermal **(c)** *(aislante, material)* thermal
terminación *nf* **(a)** *(finalización)* completion; **la fecha de t. del edificio** the date of completion of the building; **los meses que quedan para la t. del curso académico** the months remaining before the end of the academic year **(b)** *(parte final)* end, termination ►► ***t. nerviosa*** nerve ending **(c)** *Gram* ending
terminado, -a *adj (trabajo)* finished, done
terminador *nm Informát* terminator
terminal 1 *adj* **(a)** *(enfermedad)* terminal; **es un enfermo (en fase) t.** he's terminally ill **(b)** *Bot* terminal
2 *nm* **(a)** *Informát* terminal ►► *Am* ***t. de computadora*** computer terminal; *Esp* ***t. de ordenador*** computer terminal; ***t. de videotexto*** videotext terminal **(b)** *Elec* terminal; **t. negativo/positivo** negative/ positive terminal
3 *nf (de aeropuerto)* terminal; *(de autobuses)* terminus; **en la t. nacional/internacional** in the national/international terminal ►► ***t. aérea*** air terminal; ***t. de carga*** freight terminal; ***t. de contenedores*** container terminal; ***t. de pasajeros*** passenger terminal; *Am* ***t. pesquera*** fish warehouse; ***t. de vuelo*** air terminal
4 *nm Am* ***t. pesquero*** fish warehouse
terminante *adj (prohibición, negativa)* categorical; *(prueba)* conclusive; **contestó con un "no" t.** he replied with a categorical "no"
terminantemente *adv (prohibir, negarse)* categorically; **está t. prohibido** it is strictly forbidden

TERMINAR 1 *vt (acabar)* to finish; **termina la cerveza, que nos vamos** finish your beer, we're going; **terminamos el viaje en San Francisco** we ended our journey in San Francisco; **dar por terminado algo** *(discurso, reunión, discusión, visita)* to bring sth to an end *o* a close; **está sin t.** it isn't finished; EXPR *RP Fam* **¡terminala!** that's enough!
2 *vi* **(a)** *(acabar)* to end, to finish; *(tren, autobús, línea de metro)* to stop, to terminate; **¿cómo termina la historia?** how does the story end *o* finish?; **todo ha terminado** it's all over; **deja que termine, déjame t.** *(al hablar)* let me finish; **t. con la pobreza/la corrupción** to put an end to poverty/corruption; **¿has terminado con las tijeras?** have *o* are you finished with the scissors?; **han terminado con toda la leche que quedaba** they've finished off *o* used up all the milk that was left; **t. con algo/alguien** *(arruinar, destruir)* to destroy sth/sb; *(matar)* to kill sth/sb; **t. de hacer algo** to finish doing sth; **terminamos de desayunar a las nueve** we finished having breakfast at nine; **t. en** *(objeto)* to end in; **termina en punta** it ends in a point; **las sílabas que terminan en vocal** syllables that end in a vowel; **para t., debo agradecer...** *(en discurso)* finally, I would like to thank...
(b) *(reñir)* to finish, to split up (**con** with); **¡hemos terminado!** it's over!
(c) *(en cierto estado o situación)* to end up; **terminamos de mal humor/un poco deprimidos** we ended up in a bad mood/(feeling) rather depressed; **terminó loco** he ended up going mad; **vas a t. odiando la física** you'll end up hating physics; **este chico terminará mal** this boy will come to a bad end; **este asunto terminará mal** no good will come of this matter; **terminó de camarero/en la cárcel** he ended up as a waiter/in jail; **la discusión terminó en pelea** the argument ended in a fight; **t. por hacer algo** to end up doing sth
(d) *(llegar a)* **no termino de entender lo que quieres decir** I still can't quite understand what you mean; **no terminábamos de ponernos de acuerdo** we couldn't quite seem to come to an agreement; **no termina de gustarme** I just *o* simply don't like it
3 terminarse *vpr* **(a)** *(finalizar)* to finish; **¿cuándo se termina el curso?** when does the course finish?
(b) *(agotarse) (repuestos, víveres)* to run out; **se han terminado las cerillas** the matches have run out; **se nos ha terminado el azúcar** we've run out of sugar, the sugar has run out
(c) *(acabar) (comida, revista)* to finish off; **¿te has terminado el desayuno?** have you finished your breakfast?; **me terminé la novela en una noche** I finished off the novel in one night

TÉRMINO *nm* **(a)** *(fin)* end; **al t. de la reunión se ofrecerá una rueda de prensa** there will be a press conference at the conclusion of the meeting; **dar t. a algo** *(discurso, reunión, discusión)* to bring sth to a close; *(visita, vacaciones)* to end; **llegó a su t.** it came to an end; **llevar algo a buen t.** to bring sth to a successful conclusion; **poner t. a algo** *(relación, amenazas)* to put an end to sth; *(discusión, debate)* to bring sth to a close
(b) *(plano, posición)* **en primer t.** *(en cuadros, fotografías)* in the foreground; **quedar** *o* **permanecer en un segundo t.** *(pasar inadvertido)* to remain in the background; **su carrera como modelo ha quedado en un segundo t. y ahora se dedica al cine** her modelling career now takes second place to her acting; **en último t.** *(en cuadros, fotografías)* in the background; *(si es necesario)* as a last resort; *(en resumidas cuentas)* in the final analysis
(c) *(punto, situación)* point; **llegados a este t. hay que tomar una decisión** we have reached the point where we have to take a decision ►► ***t. medio*** *(media)* average; *(arreglo)* compromise, happy medium; **por t. medio** on average
(d) *(palabra)* term; **lo dijo, aunque no con** *o* **en esos términos** that's what he said, although he didn't put it quite the same way; **en términos generales** generally speaking; **en términos de Freud** in Freud's words; **los términos del acuerdo/contrato** the terms of the agreement/contract
(e) *Mat (de fracción, silogismo, ecuación)* term
(f) *(relaciones)* **estar en buenos/malos términos (con)** to be on good/bad terms (with)
(g) *(territorio)* **t. (municipal)** = area under the jurisdiction of a town council
(h) *(plazo)* period; **en el t. de un mes** within (the space of) a month
(i) *(de línea férrea, de autobús)* terminus
(j) *(linde, límite)* boundary

terminología *nf* terminology
terminológico, -a *adj* terminological
termita *nf*, **termes** *nm inv* termite
termitero *nm* termite mound *o* nest
termo *nm* **(a)** *(para bebida, comida)* Thermos® *(flask)* **(b)** *(calentador de agua)* water heater
termoadhesivo, -a *adj* thermoadhesive
termoaislante *adj* heat insulating
termobárico, -a *adj Fís* thermobaric
termodinámica *nf* thermodynamics *(singular)*
termodinámico, -a *adj* thermodynamic
termoelectricidad *nf* thermoelectricity
termoeléctrico, -a *adj* thermoelectric
termoestable *adj* thermostable
termofón *nm Urug* water heater
termografía *nf* thermography
termógrafo *nm* thermograph
termometría *nf* thermometry
termométrico, -a *adj* thermometric
termómetro *nm* thermometer; **poner el t. a alguien** to take sb's temperature ►► ***t. centígrado*** centigrade *o* Celsius thermometer; ***t. clínico*** clinical thermometer; ***t. de mercurio*** mercury thermometer
termonuclear *adj* thermonuclear
termopar *nm Elec* thermocouple
termopila *nf Elec* thermopile
termoplástico, -a *adj* thermoplastic
termoquímica *nf* thermochemistry
termorregulación *nf* **(a)** *(con termostato)* thermostatic control **(b)** *Biol* body temperature regulation, *Espec* thermoregulation
termorregulador 1 *adj* **(a)** *Tec* thermostatic **(b)** *Biol* **organismos termorreguladores** organisms that regulate body temperature
2 *nm (termostato)* thermostat
termosfera *nf* thermosphere
termosifón *nm* water heater
termostato *nm* thermostat
termotanque *nm RP* water heater
termoterapia *nf* heat treatment, *Espec* thermotherapy
terna *nf* **(a)** *(trío)* trio; **la t. de expertos seleccionados** the chosen trio of experts **(b)** *(de candidatos)* = shortlist of three candidates **(c)** *Taurom* = trio of bullfighters heading the bill in a bullfighting session
ternario, -a *adj* ternary

ternasco *nm* suckling lamb

ternera *nf (carne) (blanca)* veal; *(de más de 4 meses)* beef

ternero, -a *nm,f (animal)* calf

terneza *nf* (a) *(cualidad)* tenderness (b) *(expresión de afecto)* sweet nothing

ternilla *nf* (a) *(en bistec)* gristle (b) *Anat* cartilage

terno *nm* (a) *(trío)* trio (b) *(traje)* three-piece suit

ternura *nf* tenderness; **con t.** tenderly; **sentir t. por algo/alguien** to feel tenderness towards sth/sb

tero *nm* (a) *(ave)* pied lapwing (b) **los teros** *(en rugby)* the Teros *(nickname of Uruguayan rugby team)*

terquedad *nf* (a) *(testarudez)* stubbornness; **con t.** stubbornly (b) *Ecuad (indiferencia)* coldness, aloofness

terracota *nf* terracotta

terrado *nm* (a) *(en edificio)* terrace roof (b) *Fam (cabeza)* nut; **estar mal del t.** to have a screw loose

terraja[1] *nf (herramienta)* diestock

terraja[2] *RP Fam* 1 *adj* (a) *(decoración, ropa, canción)* tacky, *Br* naff (b) *(persona)* flashy, tacky
2 *nmf (persona)* **es un t.** he's tacky

terrajada *nmf RP Fam* **esos zapatos son una t.** those shoes are tacky

terraje *nm* = rent on arable land

terral *nm* (a) *(viento)* wind from inland (b) *Am (polvareda)* dust cloud

terramicina *nf Farm* Terramycin®

Terranova *n* Newfoundland

terranova *nmf (perro)* Newfoundland

terraplén *nm* embankment

terráqueo, -a *adj* **globo t.** globe

terrario, terrarium *nm* terrarium

terrateniente *nmf* landowner

terraza *nf* (a) *(balcón)* balcony ►► ***t. cerrada*** glazed balcony (b) *(de café)* terrace; **la gente sentada en las terrazas de verano** the people sitting out in the pavement cafés (c) *(bancal)* terrace; **cultivo en terrazas** terrace farming (d) *(azotea)* terrace roof (e) *Fam (cabeza)* nut

terrazgo *nm* (a) *(tierra)* plot of land (b) *(renta)* land rent

terrazguero *nm* tenant farmer

terrazo *nm* terrazzo

terregoso, -a *adj* covered in clods

terremoteado, -a *adj Chile* affected by an earthquake

terremoto *nm* earthquake; *Fam* **este niño es un t.** this boy is a menace

terrenal *adj (vida)* earthly; *(bienes, preocupaciones)* worldly

TERRENO, -A 1 *adj Formal (vida)* earthly; *(bienes, preocupaciones)* worldly
2 *nm* (a) *(suelo)* land; *(por su relieve)* terrain; *(por su composición, utilidad agrícola)* soil; **grandes extensiones de t.** large tracts of land; **t. montañoso/abrupto** mountainous/rugged terrain; **t. arenoso/volcánico** sandy/volcanic soil; **el t. era irregular** the ground was uneven; EXPR **ser t. abonado (para algo)** to be fertile ground (for sth) ►► ***t. agrícola*** farmland; ***t. cultivable*** arable land; ***t. edificable*** land suitable for development; ***t. rústico*** land unsuitable for development; ***t. urbanizable*** land suitable for development; ***t. no urbanizable*** land unsuitable for development
(b) *(parcela, solar)* plot (of land); **tenemos unos terrenos en el pueblo** we have some land in the village
(c) *(en deportes)* **t. (de juego)** field, *Br* pitch; **los jugadores saltaron al t. de juego** the players came out onto the field *o Br* pitch
(d) *(ámbito)* field; **en el t. de la música/medicina** in the field of music/medicine; **tiene muchos problemas en el t. personal** she has a lot of problems in her private life; **ha habido muchos avances en este t.** there have been considerable advances in this field
(e) *(territorio)* ground; **estar** *o* **encontrarse en su propio t.** to be on home ground; **estar en** *o* **pisar t. conocido/desconocido/firme** to be on familiar/unfamiliar/solid ground; **llevar algo/a alguien a su t.: sabe llevar las conversaciones a su t.** he knows how to steer conversations round to what interests him; **la campeona supo llevar a su t. a la tenista holandesa** the champion was able to impose her own terms on the Dutch player; **sabe llevar cualquier canción a su t.** he is capable of making any song his own; EXPR **ceder t.** to give ground; EXPR **ganar t.** to gain ground; **le está ganando t. a su rival** he's gaining ground on his rival; EXPR **perder t. (ante alguien)** to lose ground (to sb); EXPR **preparar el t. (para algo/a alguien)** to pave the way (for sth/sb); EXPR **reconocer** *o* **tantear el t.** to see how the land lies; EXPR **sabe el t. que pisa** she knows what she is about; EXPR **sobre el t.: estudiar algo sobre el t.** to study something in the field; **resolveremos los problemas sobre el t.** we'll solve the problems as we go along

térreo, -a *adj* earthy

terrera *nf* greater short-toed lark ►► ***t. marismeña*** lesser short-toed lark

terrero, -a *adj (de tierra)* **saco t.** sandbag

terrestre *adj* (a) *(del planeta)* terrestrial; **la corteza t.** the Earth's crust; **globo t.** globe; **superficie t.** Earth's surface (b) *(de la tierra)* land; **animales terrestres** land animals; **televisión t.** terrestrial television; **transporte t.** land transport; **transporte de viajeros por vía t. o aérea** overland and air transportation of passengers

terrible *adj* (a) *(malo)* terrible; **la guerra es siempre t.** war is always a terrible thing; **un año t. para la economía del país** a terrible year for the country's economy; **este niño es t.** this boy is a terror; **es t. no poder hacer nada por ellos** it's terrible not to able to do anything for them (b) *(mucho)* terrible; **tengo un hambre/frío t.** I'm terribly hungry/cold

terriblemente *adv* terribly; **los delitos han aumentado t.** crime has risen terribly; **me duele t. el estómago** I've got terrible stomach ache

terrícola 1 *adj* **las naves terrícolas** spaceships from Earth
2 *nmf* earthling

terrier *nmf* terrier ►► ***t. escocés*** Scottish terrier

terrina *nf* terrine

territorial *adj (soberanía, unidad, ordenamiento)* territorial; **está en peligro la integridad t. del país** the territorial integrity of the country is in jeopardy

territorialidad *nf* (a) *(de animal)* territorial behaviour (b) *Der* territoriality

territorio *nm* territory; **fuera del t. brasileño** outside of Brazilian territory; **por todo el t. nacional** across the country, nationwide; **los territorios ocupados** *(de Palestina)* the Occupied Territories

terrón *nm* (a) *(de tierra)* clod of earth (b) **t. (de azúcar)** sugar lump

terror *nm* (a) *(miedo)* terror; **de t.** *(cine, película)* horror; **dar t. a alguien: le da t.** it terrifies her; **me da t. pensar en las vacaciones con los niños** I shudder to think what the holidays with the children will be like; **tener t. a algo/alguien** to be terrified of sth/sb; **sembrar el t.** to spread terror
(b) *(persona)* terror; **esa banda de delincuentes es el t. del pueblo** this gang of criminals is terrorizing the village
(c) **el T.** *Hist (en la revolución francesa)* the Terror

terrorífico, -a *adj* terrifying

terrorismo *nm* terrorism ►► ***t. de Estado*** state terrorism

terrorista 1 *adj* terrorist
2 *nmf* terrorist

terroso, -a *adj* (a) *(color, textura)* earthy (b) *(con tierra)* muddy

terruño *nm* (a) *(terreno)* plot of land (b) *Fam (patria)* homeland

tersar *vt* to make smooth

terso, -a *adj* (a) *(piel, superficie) (liso)* smooth; *(brillante)* glossy (b) *(estilo, lenguaje)* polished

tersura *nf* (a) *(de piel, superficie) (suavidad)* smoothness; *(brillo)* polish (b) *(de estilo, lenguaje)* polish

tertulia *nf* (a) *(reunión)* = regular informal social gathering where issues of common interest are discussed; *(en radio, TV)* talk show; **estar de t.** to sit chatting ►► ***t. literaria*** literary circle; ***t. radiofónica*** radio talk show; ***t. televisiva*** TV talk show (b) *RP (en teatro)* dress circle

tertuliano, -a *nm,f (en reunión)* = participant in a "tertulia"; *(en la radio, TV)* participant *(in a talk show)*

tertuliar *vi Am* to hold discussions, to debate

tesauro *nm* thesaurus

tesela *nf* tessera

teselado *nm* mosaic

tesina *nf* (undergraduate) dissertation

tesis *nf inv* (a) *(teoría, idea)* view, thesis; **defiende la t. de que...** he holds the view that...; **es una t. muy interesante** that's a very interesting theory; **novela de t.** novel with a message, didactic novel
(b) *Filosofía* thesis; **t., antítesis y síntesis** thesis, antithesis and synthesis
(c) *Educ* thesis; **leer la t.** ≃ to have one's viva (voce), *US* to defend one's dissertation ►► ***t. doctoral*** doctoral *o* PhD thesis

tesitura *nf* (**a**) *(situación)* circumstances, situation; **ante esta t. hemos decidido marcharnos** in view of the circumstances we have decided to leave (**b**) *Mús* tessitura, pitch

tesla *nf Fís* tesla

teso *nm (de cerro)* hilltop

tesobono *nm Méx* = Mexican government bond denominated in US dollars

tesón *nm* tenacity, perseverance; **trabajar con t.** to work steadily

tesonero, -a *adj* tenacious, persistent

tesorería *nf* (**a**) *(cargo)* treasurership (**b**) *(oficina)* treasurer's office (**c**) *Com* liquid capital

tesorero, -a *nm,f* treasurer

tesoro *nm* (**a**) *(botín)* treasure; **el cofre del t.** the treasure chest (**b**) *(hacienda pública)* treasury, exchequer; **el T.** the Treasury ►► ***t. público*** the Treasury (**c**) *(persona valiosa)* gem, treasure; **este niño es un t.** this boy is a real gem (**d**) *(apelativo)* darling, **ven t.** come here, darling (**e**) *(diccionario)* thesaurus

test [tes(t)] (*pl* **tests**) *nm* (**a**) *(psicológico)* test; **hacer un t.** to do *o* take a test ►► ***t. de inteligencia*** intelligence *o* IQ test; ***t. de personalidad*** *(en revista)* personality questionnaire *o* quiz; ***t. psicológico*** psychological test
(**b**) *(médico)* test; **voy al médico a hacerme unos tests** I'm going to have some tests done at the doctor's ►► ***t. del embarazo*** pregnancy test
(**c**) *(prueba)* test; **vamos a hacer un t. de sonido** we're going to do a sound check; **hacer un t. a alguien** to give sb a test ►► ***t. de alcoholemia*** breathalyser test
(**d**) *(examen)* test; **tipo t.** *(examen, pregunta)* multiple-choice

testa *nf* head ►► ***t. coronada*** *(monarca)* crowned head, monarch

testado, -a *adj (persona)* testate; *(herencia)* testamentary

testador, -ora *nm,f* testator, *f* testatrix

testaferro *nm* front man

testamentaría *nf* (**a**) *(documentos)* documentation *(of a will)* (**b**) *(bienes)* estate, inheritance

testamentario, -a 1 *adj* testamentary; **las disposiciones testamentarias** the terms of the will
2 *nm,f* executor

testamento *nm* (**a**) *(documento)* will; **hacer t.** to make a will ►► ***t. cerrado*** sealed will; ***t. hológrafo*** *o* ***ológrafo*** holograph will (**b**) *Rel* **Antiguo/Nuevo T.** Old/New Testament (**c**) *Fam (texto largo)* screed; **¿tengo que leerme este t.?** do I have to read this screed?

testar 1 *vi* to make a will; **testó en favor de sus nietos** she left everything to her grandchildren
2 *vt (probar)* to test

testarazo *nm Fam* (**a**) *Dep* header (**b**) *(golpe) (dado)* head butt; *(recibido)* bump *o* bash on the head; **darse un t.** to bang *o* bash one's head

testarudez *nf* stubbornness; **con t.** stubbornly

testarudo, -a 1 *adj* stubborn
2 *nm,f* stubborn person; **ser un t.** to be stubborn

testear *vt CSur* to test

testera *nf* (**a**) *(frente, fachada)* front (**b**) *(de animal)* forehead (**c**) *(adorno para caballos)* crownpiece

testicular *adj* testicular

testículo *nm* testicle

testificación *nf* testimony; **es la t. de su talento** it bears witness to her talent

testificar [60] **1** *vt* (**a**) *(dar testimonio de)* **t. que...** to testify that... (**b**) *(probar, indicar)* to testify to, to bear witness to; **sus acciones testifican su ignorancia** her actions testify to *o* bear witness to her ignorance
2 *vi* to testify, to give evidence; **t. a favor/en contra de alguien** to testify in favour of/against sb

testigo 1 *nmf* (**a**) *(en juicio, de acción)* witness; **ser t. de algo** to witness sth; **fue t. del accidente** he witnessed the accident; **tú eres t. de que estuve allí** you are my witness that I was there; **un castillo que ha sido t. de innumerables batallas** a castle that has witnessed countless battles; **pongo a Dios** *o* **al cielo por t.** as God *o* Heaven is my witness; *RP* **salir de t. a alguien** *(en juicio)* to be a witness for sb; *(en casamiento)* to be a witness for *o* at sb's wedding ►► ***t. de cargo*** witness for the prosecution; ***t. de descargo*** witness for the defence; ***t. de Jehová*** Jehovah's Witness; ***t. ocular*** eyewitness; ***t. presencial*** eyewitness
(**b**) *(en boda)* witness
2 *nm Dep* baton

testimonial *adj* (**a**) *(documento, prueba)* testimonial (**b**) *(presencia, retribución)* token, symbolic

testimoniar *vt* (**a**) *(ser testigo de)* to testify to, to bear witness to; **como lo testimonia el resultado de las elecciones** as the election result demonstrates (**b**) *(agradecimiento)* to demonstrate

testimonio *nm* (**a**) *(en juicio)* testimony; **prestar t.** to give evidence (**b**) *(prueba)* proof; **como t. de** as proof of; **como t. de nuestro agradecimiento** as a token of our gratitude; **dar t. de algo** to bear witness to sth; **los cuadros dan t. de su calidad artística** the paintings testify to his quality as an artist

testosterona *nf* testosterone

testuz *nm o nf* (**a**) *(frente)* brow (**b**) *(nuca)* nape

teta 1 *nf* (**a**) *Fam (de mujer)* tit; **dar la t.** to breast-feed; EXPR **dos tetas tiran más que cien carretas** sex appeal can move mountains (**b**) *(de animal)* teat
2 *adj inv Fam* ace, wicked; **la tarta estaba t.** the cake was wicked
3 *adv Fam* **lo pasamos t.** we had an ace *o* a wicked time

tetamen *nm muy Fam* tits

tétanos *nm inv,* **tétano** *nm* tetanus

tetera *nf* (**a**) *(para servir)* teapot (**b**) *(hervidor)* kettle

tetería *nf* tea-room

tetero *nm Col, Ven (biberón)* baby's bottle

tetilla *nf* (**a**) *(de hombre, animal)* nipple (**b**) *(de biberón)* teat

tetina *nf* teat

tetón *nm* stub, stump

tetona *adj f Fam* busty, top-heavy; **es muy t.** she's got big jugs

tetrabrik® (*pl* **tetrabriks**) *nm* tetrabrik®; **un t. de leche** a carton of milk

tetracampeón, -ona 1 *adj* **el equipo t.** the four-times winners *o* champions
2 *nm,f* four-times winner *o* champion

tetraciclina *nf Farm* tetracycline

tetraédrico, -a *adj* tetrahedral

tetraedro *nm* tetrahedron

tetrágono *nm* tetragon

tetralogía *nf Lit* tetralogy

tetramorfo *nm* Tetramorph

tetraplejía, tetraplejia *nf* quadriplegia, tetraplegia

tetrapléjico, -a 1 *adj* quadriplegic, tetraplegic
2 *nm,f* quadriplegic, tetraplegic

tétrico, -a *adj* gloomy

tetudo, -a *adj Fam* busty, top-heavy; **es muy tetuda** she has big boobs

teutón, -ona *Hist* **1** *adj* Teutonic
2 *nm,f* Teuton

teutónico, -a *adj Hist* Teutonic

Texas ['teχas] *n* Texas

textil 1 *adj* textile
2 *nm* textile
3 *nf RP* textile mill

texto *nm* (**a**) *(palabras)* text ►► ***t. cifrado*** cipher text; *Informát* ***t. oculto*** hidden text; *Informát* ***t. simulado*** Greek text (**b**) *(pasaje)* passage (**c**) *(libro)* text; **los textos sagrados** the sacred texts *o* writings

textual *adj* (**a**) *(coherencia, análisis)* textual; **una cita t.** a direct quotation (**b**) *(exacto)* exact; **dijo, palabras textuales, que era horroroso** her exact words were "it was terrible"

textualmente *adv* literally, word for word; **dijo t. que le parecía fabuloso** his exact words were "I think it's fabulous"

textura *nf* (**a**) *(de superficie, tela, material)* texture (**b**) *(de texto, discurso)* texture

texturación *nf* texturing

tez *nf* complexion; **una mujer de t. morena** a woman with a dark complexion

tezontle *nm Méx* = dark red volcanic rock used for building

tfno. (*abrev de* **teléfono**) tel.

thatcherismo [θatʃe'rismo] *nm Pol* Thatcherism

thinner, tíner ['tiner] *nm Am* paint thinner

thriller ['θriler] (*pl* **thrillers**) *nm* thriller

TI *nf(pl) Informát* (*abrev de* **Tecnología(s) de la Información**) IT

ti *pron personal (después de prep)* (**a**) *(en general)* you; **siempre pienso en ti** I'm always thinking about you; **me acordaré de ti** I'll remember you
(**b**) *(reflexivo)* yourself; **sólo piensas en ti (mismo)** you only think about yourself
(**c**) *(en frases)* **¡a ti qué!** so what?, why should you care?; **para ti** *(tú crees)* as far as you're concerned, in your opinion; **por ti** as far as you're concerned; **si por ti no hay inconveniente, lo hacemos mañana** if it's fine by you we can do it tomorrow

tiamina *nf* thiamin(e)

tianguis *nm inv CAm, Méx* open-air market

tianguista *nmf CAm, Méx* stallholder *(in an open-air market)*

TIAR [tjar] *nm (abrev de* **Tratado Interamericano de Asistencia Recíproca**) Inter-American Treaty of Reciprocal Assistance

tiara *nf* tiara

tiarrón, -ona *nm,f Fam* hulk

Tíber *nm* **el T.** the Tiber

tiberio *nm Fam* hullabaloo, uproar

Tíbet, Tibet *nm* **el T.** Tibet

tibetano, -a 1 *adj* Tibetan
2 *nm,f (persona)* Tibetan
3 *nm (lengua)* Tibetan

tibia *nf* shinbone, *Espec* tibia; **me dio una patada en la t.** she kicked me in the shin

tibiarse *vpr CAm, Ven* to get annoyed *o* irritated

tibieza *nf* (**a**) *(de líquido)* tepidness, lukewarmness (**b**) *(de reacción, posición)* lukewarmness, half-heartednesss; **"de acuerdo", dijo con t.** "all right," she said half-heartedly *o* without enthusiasm

tibio, -a *adj* (**a**) *(líquido)* tepid, lukewarm (**b**) *(reacción, posición)* lukewarm, half-hearted; **el libro tuvo una tibia acogida en la prensa** the book received *o* had a lukewarm reception from the press (**c**) *Col, Perú, Ven (enojado)* annoyed, irritated (**d**) *Fam* EXPR **poner t. a alguien** to speak ill of sb; **ponerse t. de algo** *(comer)* to stuff one's face with sth; *(beber)* to down bucketfuls of sth

tiburón *nm* (**a**) *(pez)* shark ►► ***t. ballena*** whale shark; ***t. peregrino*** basking shark (**b**) *Fin Fam* raider

tic *nm* (**a**) *(involuntario)* tic ►► ***t. nervioso*** nervous tic (**b**) *(manía)* mannerism

ticket ['tiket, 'tike] *(pl* **tickets**) *nm* (**a**) *(billete)* ticket (**b**) *(recibo)* **t. (de compra)** receipt

tico, -a *Am Fam* **1** *adj* Costa Rican
2 *nm,f* Costa Rican

tictac, tic-tac *nm* tick-tock

tie-break ['taiβrek] *(pl* **tie-breaks**) *nm Dep* tie-break

tiemblo *etc ver* **temblar**

TIEMPO *nm* (**a**) *(transcurso, rato, momento)* time; **en poco** *o* **dentro de poco t. lo sabremos** we will soon know; **tardé** *o* **me llevó bastante t.** it took me quite a while *o* quite a long time; **es una tarea que lleva mucho t.** it's a very time-consuming task; **¡cómo pasa el t.!** time flies!; **todo el t.** all the time; **estuvo todo el t. de pie** he was standing up the whole time; **al mismo t.** at the same time; **al poco t., poco t. después** soon after(wards); **podríamos discutirlo al t. que comemos** we could discuss it while we eat; **antes de t.** *(nacer)* prematurely; *(florecer, celebrar)* early; **muchos llegaron antes de t.** a lot of people arrived early; **a t. completo** full-time; **a t. parcial** part-time; **a su (debido) t.** in due course; **cada cosa a su t.** everything in due course *o* in good time; **a un t.** at the same time; **empujaron todos a un t.** they all pushed together *o* at the same time; **cada cierto t.** every so often; **¿cada cuánto t. tiene que tomarlo?** how often *o* frequently does he have to take it?; **con el t.** in time; **de t. en t.** from time to time, now and then; **de un t. a esta parte** recently, for a while now; **dar t. al t.** to give things time; **el t. lo dirá** time will tell; **ganar t.** to save time; **hacer t.** to pass the time; *RP* **hacerse t.** to make time, to find time; **matar el t.** to kill time; **perder el t.** to waste time; **no hay t. que perder** there's no time to lose; EXPR **el t. es oro** time is money; EXPR **el t. todo lo cura** time is a great healer ►► *Informát* ***t. de acceso*** access time; *Informát* ***t. de búsqueda*** search time; ***t. de cocción*** cooking time; *Fot* ***t. de exposición*** exposure time; ***t. libre:*** **no me queda mucho t. libre** I don't have much free *or* spare time any more; **te dan t. libre para asuntos personales** they give you time off for personal matters; ***t. de ocio*** leisure time; *Informát* ***t. real*** real time; *Informát* ***t. de respuesta*** response time; ***t. universal coordinado*** Coordinated Universal Time
(**b**) *(periodo disponible, suficiente)* time; **¡se acabó el t.! pueden ir entregando los exámenes** time's up, start handing in your papers!; **a t. (para algo/de hacer algo)** in time (for sth/to do sth); **no llegamos a t. de ver el principio** we didn't arrive in time to see *o* for the beginning; **estar a t. de hacer algo** to be in time to do sth; **si quieres apuntarte, aún estás a t.** if you want to join in, you still have time *o* it's not too late; **con t. (de sobra)** with plenty of time to spare, in good time; **¿nos dará t.?** will we have (enough) time?; **no me dio t. a** *o* **no tuve t. de decírselo** I didn't have (enough) time to tell her; **dame t. y yo mismo lo haré** give me (a bit of) time and I'll do it myself; **me faltó t. para terminarlo** I didn't have (enough) time to finish it; *Fam Irónico* **le faltó t. para ir y contárselo a todo el mundo** she wasted no time in telling everyone about it; **sacar t. para hacer algo** to find (the) time to do sth; **¿tienes t. para tomar algo?** do you have time for a drink?; **tenemos todo el t. del mundo** we have all the time in the world
(**c**) *(periodo largo)* long time; **¿cuánto t. hace (de eso)?** how long ago (was that)?; **¿cuánto t. hace que no vas al teatro?** how long is it since you went to the theatre?; **¡cuánto t. sin verte!** it's been ages since I saw you!, I haven't seen you for ages!; **hace t. que** it is a long time since; **hace t. que no vive aquí** he hasn't lived here for some time; **hace mucho t. que no lo veo** I haven't seen him for ages; **t. atrás** some time ago; *Méx* **tener t. de algo: tiene t. de estudiar lingüística** she's been studying linguistics for a long time; **tómate tu t. (para hacerlo)** take your time (over it *o* to do it)
(**d**) *(época)* time; **aquél fue un t. de paz y felicidad** those were peaceful and happy times, it was a time of peace and happiness; **corren** *o* **son malos tiempos para el estudio del latín** it isn't a good time to be studying Latin; **en estos tiempos que corren** these days; **del t.** *(fruta)* of the season; **las ideas de nuestro t.** the ideas of our time *o* day; **el hombre de nuestro t.** modern man; **el mejor boxeador de todos los tiempos** the greatest ever boxer, the greatest boxer of all time; **mi álbum favorito de todos los tiempos** my all-time favourite album, my favourite ever album; **en aquellos tiempos, por aquel t.** in those days, back then, at that time; **en los buenos tiempos** in the good old days; **en mis tiempos** in my day *o* time; **Johnson, en otro t. plusmarquista mundial,...** Johnson, once the world record-holder *o* the former world record-holder,...; **en tiempo(s) de Napoleón** in Napoleon's times *o* day; **eran otros tiempos (entonces)** things were different (back) then; **¡qué tiempos aquellos!** those were the days!; **en tiempos** *(antiguamente)* in former times; EXPR **en tiempos de Maricastaña** donkey's years ago; EXPR **ser del t. del** *Perú, RP* **ñaupa** *o Chile* **ñauca** to be ancient, to be as old as the hills
(**e**) *(edad)* age; **¿qué t. tiene?** how old is he?
(**f**) *(clima)* weather; **¿qué tal está el t.?, ¿qué tal t. hace?** what's the weather like?; **buen/mal t.** good/bad weather; **hizo buen/mal t.** the weather was good/bad; **nos hizo un t. horrible** we had terrible weather; **del t.,** *Méx* **al t.** *(bebida)* at room temperature; **estas cervezas están del t.** these beers aren't cold *o* haven't been chilled; **si el t. lo permite** *o* **no lo impide** weather permitting; EXPR **hace un t. de perros** it's a foul day; EXPR **poner al mal t. buena cara** to put a brave face on things
(**g**) *Dep (mitad)* half; *(cuarto)* quarter; **primer/segundo t.** first/second half ►► ***t. añadido*** injury *o* stoppage time; ***t. de descuento*** injury *o* stoppage time; ***t. muerto*** time-out; ***t. reglamentario*** normal time
(**h**) *(marca) (en carreras)* time; **consiguió un t. excelente** his time was excellent; **lograron clasificarse por tiempos** they qualified as fastest losers ►► ***t. intermedio*** split time *(at halfway point)*; ***t. parcial*** split time; ***t. récord*** record time; **en un t. récord** in record time
(**i**) *(movimiento)* movement; **levantó las pesas en dos tiempos** he lifted the weights in two movements; **motor de cuatro tiempos** four-stroke engine
(**j**) *Gram* tense ►► ***t. compuesto*** compound tense; ***t. simple*** simple tense
(**k**) *Mús (ritmo)* tempo; *(movimiento)* movement; *(compás)* time

tienda *nf* (**a**) *(establecimiento)* shop, store; **ir de tiendas** to go shopping ►► *Andes, CAm, Méx* ***t. de abarrotes*** *Br* grocer's shop, *US* grocery store; ***t. de alimentación*** *Br* grocer's shop, *US* grocery store; ***t. de antigüedades*** antique shop; ***t. de artículos de regalo*** gift shop; *Méx* ***t. de departamentos*** department store; ***t. de deportes*** sports shop; ***t. libre de impuestos*** duty-free shop; ***t. de modas*** clothes shop *o* store; ***t. de muebles*** furniture shop *o* store; ***t. de ropa*** clothes shop *o* store; ***t. de ultramarinos*** *Br* grocer's shop, *US* grocery store
(**b**) *(de plástico, lona)* **t. (de campaña)** tent; **montar/desmontar la t.** to pitch/take down one's tent ►► ***t. (de campaña) canadiense*** ridge tent; *Med* ***t. de oxígeno*** oxygen tent

tiendo *etc ver* **tender**

tiene *etc ver* **tener**

tienta 1 *nf Taurom* trial *(of the bulls)*
2 **a tientas** *loc adv* blindly; **andar a tientas** to grope along; **buscar algo a tientas** to grope about *o* around for sth

tiento 1 *ver* **tentar**
2 *nm* (a) *(cuidado)* care; *(en el trato con la gente)* tact; **puedes decírselo, pero hay que ir con t.** you can tell him, but watch *o* be careful how you do it
(b) *(prueba)* **dar un t. a algo** to try sth; **dio un t. a la botella** he took a swig from the bottle
(c) *(de ciego)* white stick
(d) *(de equilibrista)* balancing pole
(e) *CSur (correa)* leather strip
(f) *(en flamenco)* = variety of flamenco music and dance

tiernamente *adv* tenderly

tierno, -a 1 *adj* (a) *(carne)* tender (b) *(pan)* fresh (c) *(afectuoso)* tender, affectionate; **estar t. con alguien** to be tender *o* affectionate with *o* towards sb (d) *(emotivo)* **una escena tierna** a moving scene (e) *(joven) (brote, criatura)* tender (young); **desde su más tierna edad** from a tender age (f) *Chile, Ecuad (fruto, hortaliza)* unripe
2 *nm Am* baby

TIERRA *nf* (a) *(planeta)* **la T.** (the) Earth
(b) *(superficie)* land; **viajar por t.** to travel by land; **t. adentro** inland; EXPR **poner t. (de) por medio** to make oneself scarce ►► *Am* ***t. caliente*** = in Latin America, climate zone up to an altitude of approximately 1,000 metres; ***t. firme*** *(por oposición al mar)* land, dry land; *(terreno sólido)* hard ground; *Am* ***t. fría*** = in Latin America, climate zone above the altitude of approximately 2,000 metres; ***T. del Fuego*** Tierra del Fuego; ***t. de nadie*** no-man's-land; ***t. prometida*** Promised Land; ***T. de Promisión*** Promised Land; ***T. Santa*** the Holy Land; ***la t. del Sol Naciente*** the land of the Rising Sun; *Am* ***t. templada*** = in Latin America, climate zone between the altitudes of approximately 1,000 and 2,000 metres; ***t. virgen*** virgin land
(c) *(suelo)* ground; **trabajan bajo t.** they work underground; **caer a t.** to fall to the ground; **dar en t. con algo** *(tirar)* to knock sth down *o* to the ground; **quedarse en t.** *(viajero)* to miss the boat/train/plane/ *etc*; **muchos aviones se han quedado en t. por la niebla** many planes have been grounded because of the fog; **tocar t.** *(avión)* to touch down; **tomar t.: tomó t. en un campo** he landed in a field; **tomaremos t. en el aeropuerto de Barajas en diez minutos** we will be landing at Barajas airport in ten minutes; EXPR **besar la t.** to fall flat on one's face; EXPR **echar** *o* **tirar algo por t.** *(esperanzas, planes, carrera)* to ruin sth; *(argumentos, teoría)* to demolish sth; EXPR *Fam* **it., trágame!, itrágame t.!** I wish the earth would swallow me up!; EXPR **era como si se lo hubiera tragado la t.** he had vanished without a trace; EXPR **venir** *o* **venirse a t.** to come to nothing
(d) *(materia)* earth; *(para nutrir plantas)* soil; **se me ha metido t. en los zapatos** I've got some earth in my shoes; **esta t. no es buena para cultivar** this soil isn't good for growing things; **un camino de t.** a dirt track; **política de t. quemada** scorched earth policy; *Formal* **dar t. a alguien** to bury sb; EXPR **echar t. a** *o* **sobre un asunto** to hush up an affair ►► ***t. batida*** *(en tenis)* clay; ***t. vegetal*** topsoil, loam
(e) *(en agricultura)* land; **cultivar la t.** to farm the land ►► ***t. cultivable*** arable land; ***t. de cultivo*** arable land; ***t. de labor*** arable land; ***t. de labranza*** arable land
(f) *(lugar de origen) (país)* homeland, native land; *(región)* home *o* native region; **este chico es de mi t.** this lad is from where I come from; **vino/queso de la t.** local wine/cheese ►► ***t. natal*** homeland, native land
(g) *(terrenos, países)* **es el dueño de estas tierras** he's the owner of this land; **en tierras del rey** on the King's land; **en tierras mexicanas** on Mexican soil; **por estas tierras** round these parts, down this way; **ver otras tierras** to travel, to see the world
(h) *Elec* **(toma de) t.** *Br* earth, *US* ground; **estar conectado a t., tener toma de t.** to be *Br* earthed *o US* grounded
(i) *Quím* ***t. rara*** rare earth
(j) *Am (polvo)* dust

tierral, tierrero *nm Am (polvareda)* dust cloud

tieso, -a *adj* (a) *(rígido)* stiff; **quedarse t.** *(de frío)* to be frozen stiff; **me quedé t. del susto** I was scared stiff; **tiene las orejas tiesas** his ears are pricked; *muy Fam* **se le puso tiesa** he got a hard-on
(b) *(erguido)* erect
(c) *Fam (engreído)* haughty; **iba muy tiesa con su vestido nuevo** she was parading around in her new dress
(d) *Fam (distante)* distant
(e) *Fam (sin dinero)* broke
(f) *Fam (muerto)* stone dead; **dejar t. a alguien** to bump sb off; **quedarse t.** to croak

tiestazo *nm Col Fam* bang, wallop

tiesto *nm* (a) *(maceta)* flowerpot; **¿me riegas los tiestos?** will you water my plants for me? (b) *Chile (vasija)* pot

tiesura *nf (rigidez)* rigidity, stiffness

TIFF [tif] *nm Informát (abrev de* **Tagged Image File Format**) TIFF

tifo = **tifus**

tifoideo, -a *adj* typhoid; **fiebres tifoideas** typhoid fever

tifón *nm* typhoon

tifosi *nmpl Dep* tifosi *(Italian soccer fans)*

tifus *nm inv* typhus ►► ***t. exantemático*** epidemic typhus

tigre *nm* (a) *(animal)* tiger; **los tigres económicos del sudeste asiático** the tiger economies of South-East Asia ►► ***t. de Bengala*** Bengal tiger; *Pol* ***t. de papel*** paper tiger (b) *Esp Fam (WC) Br* bog, *US* john; EXPR *Fam* **huele a t.** it stinks (c) *Am (jaguar)* jaguar

tigresa *nf* (a) *(animal)* tigress (b) *Fam (mujer)* vamp

tigrillo *nm Andes, CAm, Méx, Ven (Felis pardalis)* ocelot; *(Felis wiedi)* margay; *(Felis tigrina)* oncilla, tiger cat

TIJ [tiχ] *nm (abrev de* **Tribunal Internacional de Justicia**) ICJ, International Court of Justice

tijera *nf* (a) *(para cortar)* scissors; *(de jardinero, esquilador)* shears; **unas tijeras** (a pair of) scissors/shears; **de t.** *(escalera, silla)* folding; EXPR **meter la t. a** *(censurar)* to cut, to take the scissors to ►► ***tijeras de podar*** secateurs (b) *Dep* **de t.: meter un gol de t.** to score with a bicycle *or* scissors kick

tijereta *nf* (a) *(insecto)* earwig (b) *(en fútbol)* (overhead) bicycle *or* scissors kick (c) *Andes, RP (ave)* scissortail

tijeretazo *nm* (a) *(con la tijera)* snip (b) *(en fútbol)* bicycle *or* scissors kick

tijeretear *vt* to cut up

tijuanense 1 *adj* of/from Tijuana *(Mexico)*
2 *nmf* person from Tijuana *(Mexico)*

tila *nf* (a) *(flor)* lime blossom, linden flower (b) *(infusión)* lime blossom tea, linden flower tea

tílburi *nm* chaise, tilbury

tildar *vt* **t. a alguien de algo** to brand *o* call sb sth; **le tildaron de colaboracionista** she was branded a collaborator

tilde *nf* (a) *(acento gráfico)* accent (b) *(de la ñ)* tilde

tiliche *nm CAm, Méx* trinket, knick-knack

tilico, -a *adj Méx Fam* skinny

tilín *nm* tinkle, tinkling; EXPR *Fam* **hacer t.: me hace t.** I like the look of him/her/it; **no me hizo mucho t.** he/she/it didn't do much for me

tilingada, tilinguería *nf RP Fam* empty-headedness, imbecility

tilingo, -a *RP Fam* 1 *adj* empty-headed, halfwitted
2 *nm,f* halfwit, airhead

tilinguería = **tilingada**

tilinguerío *nm RP Fam* **estaba todo el t. del barrio** all the local airheads *o* halfwits were there

tilma *nf Méx* woollen blanket

tilo *nm* (a) *(árbol)* lime *o* linden tree (b) *(madera)* lime (c) *CSur (infusión)* lime blossom tea, linden flower tea

tilonorrinco *nm* bowerbird

timador, -ora *nm,f* confidence trickster, swindler

timar *vt* (a) *(estafar)* **t. a alguien** to swindle sb; **t. algo a alguien** to swindle sb out of sth (b) *(engañar)* to cheat, to con; **¿cinco mil por eso? ¡te han timado!** five thousand for that? you've been done *o* had!

timba *nf* (a) *(partida)* card game *(in gambling den)* (b) *(lugar)* gambling den (c) *CAm, Méx Fam (barriga)* belly

timbal *nm* (a) *(de orquesta)* kettledrum (b) *(tamboril)* small drum (c) *Culin* timbale

timbalero, -a *nm,f* timpanist

timbear *vi RP Fam* to gamble

timbero, -a *RP Fam* 1 *adj* **es muy t.** he loves gambling
2 *nm,f* gambler

timbó *nm* timbo, = tropical tree with light wood, used for making canoes

timbrado, -a *adj* (a) *(sellado)* stamped (b) *(sonido)* clear

timbrar 1 *vt* (a) *(documento)* to stamp (b) *(voz)* **t. la voz** to adjust the tone of one's voice
2 *vi Andes, CAm, Méx* to ring

timbrazo *nm* loud ring; **dale un t.** give it a good ring

timbre *nm* (**a**) *(aparato)* bell; **tocar el t.** to ring the bell ►► ***t. de alarma*** alarm (bell) (**b**) *(de instrumento)* timbre; **el t. de su voz** the sound of her voice; **un t. metálico** a metallic ring (**c**) *(sello) (de documentos)* (official) stamp; *(de impuestos)* seal; *CAm, Méx (de correos)* stamp (**d**) *(en escudo de armas)* crest

tímidamente *adv* (**a**) *(con vergüenza)* shyly (**b**) *(con vacilación)* timidly

timidez *nf* (**a**) *(vergüenza)* shyness; **hablaba con t.** he spoke shyly (**b**) *(vacilación)* timidity; **se acercó con t.** she approached timidly

tímido, -a 1 *adj* (**a**) *(vergonzoso)* shy (**b**) *(vacilante)* timid
2 *nm,f* shy person; **ser un t.** to be shy

timo *nm* (**a**) *(estafa)* swindle; **¡qué t.!** what a rip-off! ►► ***el t. de la estampita*** = confidence trick in which the victim buys a pile of pieces of paper thinking them to be bank notes; *Fam* **¡eso es el t. de la estampita!** it's a complete rip-off! (**b**) *Anat* thymus

timolina *nf Perú* disinfectant

timón *nm* (**a**) *(de barco) (palanca)* tiller, helm; *(rueda)* wheel, helm; *(pieza articulada)* rudder; **estar al t.** to be at the helm (**b**) *(gobierno)* helm; **ella lleva el t. de la empresa** she's at the helm of the company (**c**) *Andes, Cuba (volante)* steering wheel

timonear *vi* to steer

timonel *nm Náut* helmsman; *(en barca de remo)* cox

Timor *n* Timor ►► ***T. Oriental*** East Timor

timorato, -a *adj* (**a**) *(mojigato)* prudish (**b**) *(tímido)* fearful

timorés, -esa 1 *adj* Timorese
2 *nm,f* Timorese

timpánico, -a *adj* tympanic

tímpano *nm* (**a**) *Anat* eardrum, *Espec* tympanum (**b**) *Mús (tamboril)* small drum; *(de cuerda)* hammer dulcimer (**c**) *Arquit* tympanum

tina *nf* (**a**) *(tinaja)* pitcher (**b**) *(gran cuba)* vat (**c**) *CAm, Col, Méx (bañera)* bathtub

tinaco *nm* (**a**) *Méx (tinaja)* (large) pitcher (**b**) *CAm, Méx (depósito de agua)* water tank

tinaja *nf* (large) pitcher

tinamú (**tinamúes** *o* **tinamús**) *nm (ave)* tinamou

tinca *nf Chile, Perú Fam* (**a**) *(corazonada)* feeling, hunch (**b**) *(empeño)* **ponerle t. a algo** to put one's heart into sth

tincada *nf Chile, Perú Fam* feeling, hunch

tincar [60] *vi Chile, Perú Fam* **me tinca que va a llegar tarde** I have the feeling *o* something tells me he's going to be late; **me tinca buena película** I get the feeling *o* something tells me it's probably a good movie

tinción *nf* dyeing

tíner = **thinner**

tinerfeño, -a 1 *adj* of/from Tenerife *(Spain)*
2 *nm,f* person from Tenerife *(Spain)*

tingladillo *nm Náut* **de t.** clinker-built

tinglado *nm* (**a**) *(armazón)* platform; EXPR *Fam* **todo el t.** the whole caboodle
(**b**) *Fam (desorden)* chaos; **¡qué t. de papeles tengo en la mesa!** I've got such a clutter *o* jumble of papers on my desk!; **armaron un t. terrible para cambiar la instalación eléctrica** they made a real meal out of rewiring the house
(**c**) *Fam (asunto)* business; **tienen montado un t. extraño esos dos** those two are up to some sort of funny business; EXPR **dirigir** *o* **manejar el t.** to rule the roost
(**d**) *(cobertizo)* shed

tinieblas *nfpl* (**a**) *(oscuridad)* darkness, murk; **estábamos en t.** we were in darkness (**b**) *(confusión)* confusion, uncertainty; **estar en t. sobre algo** to be in the dark about sth

tino *nm* (**a**) *(puntería)* good aim; **tener mucho t.** to be a good shot
(**b**) *(habilidad)* skill; **tú que tienes más t., ¿me ayudas a abrirlo?** you're better at this kind of thing, can you help me open it?
(**c**) *(juicio)* sense, good judgement; *(prudencia)* moderation; **¡qué poco t. tienes!** you've got no sense!; **hacer algo con buen t.** to show good judgement in doing sth; **gastar sin t.** to spend money recklessly

tinque *etc ver* **tincar**

tinta *nf* (**a**) *(para escribir)* ink; EXPR **medias tintas: andarse con medias tintas** to be wishy-washy; **no me gustan las medias tintas** I don't like half-measures *o* doing things by halves; EXPR **cargar** *o* **recargar las tintas** to exaggerate; EXPR **saberlo de buena t.** to have it on good authority ►► ***t. china*** Indian ink; ***t. indeleble*** indelible ink; ***t. invisible*** invisible ink; ***t. simpática*** invisible ink
(**b**) *(de calamar)* ink
(**c**) *RP (para pelo)* dye; **hacerse la t.** to dye one's hair

tintar *vt* to dye

tinte *nm* (**a**) *(sustancia)* dye; **t. de pelo** hair dye (**b**) *(operación)* dyeing (**c**) *(tintorería)* dry cleaner's; **llevar algo al t.** to take sth to the dry cleaner's, to get sth dry-cleaned (**d**) *(rasgo)* overtone, suggestion; **declaraciones de claro t. antisemita** remarks with clearly anti-semitic overtones; **una novela de tintes autobiográficos** a novel with autobiographical overtones *o* elements

tinterillo, -a *nm,f Perú Fam Pey* shyster (lawyer)

tintero *nm (frasco)* ink pot; *(fijo en la mesa)* inkwell; EXPR **dejarse algo en el t.** to leave sth unsaid

tintín *nm* (**a**) *(de vasos)* clink, clinking (**b**) *(de campanilla)* tinkle, tinkling

tintinear *vi* to jingle, to tinkle

tintineo *nm* tinkle, tinkling

tinto, -a 1 *adj* (**a**) *(vino)* red (**b**) *Literario (teñido)* dyed (**c**) *(manchado)* stained; **una espada tinta en sangre** a blood-stained sword
2 *nm* (**a**) *(vino)* red wine ►► *Esp* ***t. de verano*** red wine spritzer (**b**) *Col, Ven (café)* black coffee

tintorera *nf* (**a**) *(tiburón)* blue shark (**b**) *ver también* **tintorero**

tintorería *nf* dry cleaner's

tintorero, -a *nm,f* dry cleaner

tintorro *nm Fam* cheap red wine, *Br* red plonk

tintura *nf* (**a**) *Quím* tincture ►► ***t. de yodo*** (tincture of) iodine (**b**) *(tinte)* dye; *(proceso)* dyeing

tiña *nf* (**a**) *Med* ringworm, *Espec* tinea (**b**) *Fam (suciedad)* filth

tiñera *etc ver* **teñir**

tiño *etc ver* **teñir**

tiñoso, -a *adj* (**a**) *Med* suffering from ringworm (**b**) *Fam (tacaño)* stingy

tío, -a *nm,f* (**a**) *(familiar)* uncle, *f* aunt; **mis tíos** my aunt and uncle; **la tía Sara** Aunt Sara; EXPR *Fam* **¡cuéntaselo a tu tía!** pull the other one!; EXPR *Fam* **no hay tu tía: no hay tu tía, no puedo abrir el cajón** this drawer just refuses to open; **por más que se lo pido, no hay tu tía** I've asked him and asked him, but he's not having any of it ►► ***tía abuela*** great-aunt; ***t. abuelo*** great-uncle; ***tía carnal*** aunt *(blood relative)*; ***t. carnal*** uncle *(blood relative)*; ***el t. Sam*** Uncle Sam; ***t. segundo*** first cousin once removed
(**b**) *Esp Fam (hombre)* guy, *Br* bloke; *(mujer)* woman; *(mujer joven)* girl; **¡cómo sois los tíos!** you men are all the same!; **t. bueno** hunk; **tía buena** gorgeous woman *o Br* bird; **¡tía buena!** *(piropo)* hello gorgeous!
(**c**) *Esp Fam (apelativo) (hombre)* pal, *Br* mate; **¡tía, déjame en paz!** leave me alone, will you?; **¡tía, qué guapa estás!** wow, you look fantastic!

tiovivo *nm* merry-go-round, *US* carousel; **subir al t., montar en t.** to have a go on the merry-go-round

tipa *nf* (**a**) *(árbol)* tipu tree, pride of Bolivia (**b**) *ver también* **tipo**

tiparraco, -a = **tipejo**

tipazo *nm Fam (de mujer)* fantastic figure; *(de hombre)* good build; **con este t. toda la ropa le queda bien** with a figure like that everything looks good on her

tipear *Am* 1 *vt* to type
2 *vi* to type

tipejo, -a, tiparraco, -a *nm,f Fam Pey* individual, character

tipeo *nm Am* typing

típicamente *adv* typically

típico, -a *adj* (**a**) *(característico)* typical (**de** of); **es un plato t. de Francia** this is a typical French dish; **es un rasgo t. de los orientales** it is a characteristic of orientals; **es t. de** *o* **en él llegar tarde** it's typical of him to arrive late; **es la típica frase de saludo** it's the traditional *o* customary greeting; **¿y qué hiciste – pues lo t.** so what did you do? – all the usual *o* typical things
(**b**) *(traje, restaurante)* traditional

tipificación *nf* (**a**) *(de producto, delito)* classification (**b**) *(normalización)* standardization (**c**) *(paradigma, representación)* epitome

tipificar [60] *vt* (**a**) *(clasificar)* to classify; **está tipificado como delito** it is a statutory offence (**b**) *(normalizar)* to standardize; **productos tipificados** standardized products (**c**) *(representar)* to epitomize, to typify

tipismo *nm* local colour

tiple 1 *nmf (cantante)* soprano
2 *nm* (**a**) *(voz)* soprano (**b**) *(guitarra)* treble guitar

tipo, -a 1 *nm,f Fam (hombre)* guy, *Br* bloke; *(mujer)* woman; *(mujer joven)* girl
2 *nm* (**a**) *(clase)* type, sort; **no es mi t.** he's not my type; **todo t. de** all sorts of; **vinieron personas de todo t.** all sorts of people came; **no me gustan las películas de ese t.** I don't like movies like that *o* those sorts of movies
(**b**) *(cuerpo) (de mujer)* figure; *(de hombre)* build; **tiene muy buen t.** she has a very good body; EXPR *Fam* **jugarse el t.** to risk one's neck; EXPR *Fam* **aguantar** *o* **mantener el t.** to keep one's cool, not to lose one's head; EXPR **dar el t.** to be up to standard *o* scratch
(**c**) *Econ* rate ▸▸ ***t. básico*** *(de interés)* base rate; *(de impuestos)* basic rate; ***t. de cambio*** exchange rate, rate of exchange; ***t. de descuento*** discount rate; ***t. impositivo*** tax rate; ***t. de interés*** interest rate; ***t. de interés bancario*** bank rate; ***t. de interés fijo*** fixed interest rate; ***t. de interés hipotecario*** mortgage rate; ***t. de interés variable*** variable *o* floating interest rate; ***t. marginal*** marginal rate; ***t. mínimo*** minimum rate; ***t. preferencial*** prime (lending) rate
(**d**) *Imprenta* type
(**e**) *Biol* type
3 *adj inv* (**a**) *(estándar)* **el boliviano/la dieta t.** the average Bolivian/ diet (**b**) **un pantalón t. pitillo** a pair of drainpipe trousers; **una película t. Rambo** a Rambo-style movie
4 *adv RP Fam (aproximadamente)* like; **llegaron t. nueve** they arrived at, like, nine o'clock; **se casó hace t. cinco años** she got married something like five years ago

tipografía *nf* (**a**) *(procedimiento)* typography, printing (**b**) *(taller)* printing works *(singular)* (**c**) *Informát* typography

tipográfico, -a *adj* typographical, printing; **industria tipográfica** printing industry

tipógrafo, -a *nm,f* printer, typographer

tipología *nf* typology

Tipp-Ex® ['tipeks] *nm inv* Tipp-Ex®

típula *nf* daddy-longlegs

tíquet (*pl* **tíquets**), **tique** *nm* (**a**) *(billete)* ticket (**b**) *(recibo)* **t. (de compra)** receipt

tiquismiquis *Fam* 1 *adj inv (maniático)* pernickety
2 *nmf inv (maniático)* fusspot
3 *nmpl* (**a**) *(reparos)* **andar con t.** to fuss over little things (**b**) *(bagatelas)* trifles

tira 1 *nf* (**a**) *(banda cortada)* strip; **cortar algo en tiras** to cut sth into strips; **hacer algo tiras** *(trapo, papel)* to tear sth to pieces
(**b**) *(tirante)* strap
(**c**) *(de viñetas)* **t. (cómica)** comic *o* cartoon strip
(**d**) EXPR *Fam* **la t.: me gustó la t.** I really loved it; **¿tienes juguetes? – ¡la t.!** have you got any toys? – loads (of them)!; **la t. de** loads of; **hace la t. que no viene por aquí** it's ages since she's been here
(**e**) *Méx Fam* **la t.** *(la policía)* the law, *US* the heat
(**f**) *RP (de asado)* short ribs
2 *nm* **t. y afloja: firmaron el acuerdo tras meses de t. y afloja** they signed the agreement after months of hard bargaining; **el t. y afloja que mantienen británicos y españoles en el tema de Gibraltar** the wrangling between Britain and Spain over Gibraltar
3 *nmf* (**a**) *Méx (policía)* cop (**b**) *RP Fam (detective)* plain-clothes cop

tirabeque *nm* mangetout, *US* snow pea

tirabuzón *nm* (**a**) *(rizo)* curl (**b**) *(sacacorchos)* corkscrew

tirachinas *nm inv Br* catapult, *US* slingshot

tirada *nf* (**a**) *(lanzamiento)* throw; **estuvo dos tiradas sin jugar** she missed two goes; EXPR **de** *o* **en una t.** in one go (**b**) *Imprenta (número de ejemplares)* print run; **este diario tiene una t. de 100.000 ejemplares** this paper has a circulation of 100,000 (**c**) *Imprenta (reimpresión)* reprint (**d**) *Fam (distancia)* **hay una buena t. hasta allí** it's a fair way away (**e**) *Méx Fam (objetivo)* target, goal (**f**) *ver también* **tirado**

tiradero *nf* (**a**) *Méx (vertedero) Br* rubbish tip *o* dump, *US* garbage dump; *Fig* **su mesa es un t. de papeles** you can't see her desk for the heaps of paper on it (**b**) *Ven Fam (casa de citas)* brothel

tirado, -a *Fam* 1 *adj* (**a**) *(barato)* dirt cheap
(**b**) *(fácil)* simple, dead easy; **un crucigrama t.** a dead easy crossword; **estar t.** to be a cinch
(**c**) *(débil, cansado)* worn-out
(**d**) *(miserable)* seedy
(**e**) *(abandonado, plantado)* **dejar t. a alguien** to leave sb in the lurch; **el taxista les dejó tirados en medio del campo** the taxi driver left them stranded in the middle of the countryside; EXPR *Méx Fam* **estar t. a la calle** to be in bad shape
2 *nm,f (persona)* slacker

tirador, -ora 1 *nm,f* (**a**) *(persona)* marksman, *f* markswoman; **ser un buen t.** to be a good marksman (**b**) *(en esgrima)* fencer
2 *nm* (**a**) *(mango)* handle (**b**) *(de campanilla)* bell rope (**c**) *(tirachinas) Br* catapult, *US* slingshot (**d**) *Bol, RP* **tiradores** *(tirantes) Br* braces, *US* suspenders

tirafondo *nm* screw

tiragomas *nm inv* catapult

tiraje *nm Am* (**a**) *(de publicación)* print run; **este diario tiene un t. de 100.000 ejemplares** this paper has a circulation of 100,000 (**b**) *(de chimenea)* draft; **tener buen t.** to draw well

tiralevitas *nmf Pey* creep, crawler

tiralíneas *nm inv* ruling pen, = pen used with bottled ink for drawing geometrical figures, plans etc

tiramisú *nm* tiramisu

Tirana *n* Tirana

tiranía *nf* (**a**) *(de gobierno, dictador)* tyranny (**b**) *(del reloj, de la moda)* tyranny

tiranicida *Formal* 1 *adj* tyrannicidal
2 *nmf* tyrannicide

tiranicidio *nm Formal* tyrannicide

tiránico, -a *adj* tyrannical

tiranizar [14] *vt* to tyrannize

tirano, -a 1 *adj* (**a**) *(gobierno)* tyrannical (**b**) *(padre, amor)* tyrannical
2 *nm,f* (**a**) *(gobernante)* tyrant (**b**) *(persona dominante)* **eres un t.** you're a tyrant
3 *nm* kingbird ▸▸ ***t. real*** eastern kingbird

tiranosaurio *nm* tyrannosaurus

tirantas *nfpl Col* (**a**) *(para pantalones) Br* braces, *US* suspenders (**b**) *(de blusa, vestido)* straps

tirante 1 *adj* (**a**) *(estirado) (cuerda, goma)* taut; **me noto la piel t.** my skin feels taut *o* tight; **la coleta está demasiado t.** this pigtail is too tight (**b**) *(violento, tenso) (situación, relaciones)* tense; **estar t. con alguien** to be tense with sb
2 *nm* (**a**) *(de tela)* strap; **camiseta de tirantes** *Br* vest, *US* undershirt; **un sostén sin tirantes** a strapless bra (**b**) **tirantes** *(para pantalones) Br* braces, *US* suspenders (**c**) *Arquit* brace

tirantez *nf* (**a**) *(de cuerda, goma)* tension (**b**) *(de situación, relaciones)* tension, tenseness; **existe cierta t. entre ellos** there is a certain tension between them

TIRAR 1 *vt* (**a**) *(lanzar)* to throw; **tiraron las gorras al aire** they threw their caps (up) in the air; **t. algo a alguien** *(para que lo agarre)* to throw sth to sb; *(para hacer daño)* to throw sth at sb; **tírame una manzana** throw me an apple; **le tiró un beso** she blew him a kiss; **le tiraban piedras a la policía** they were throwing stones at the police
(**b**) *(dejar caer) (objeto)* to drop; *(líquido) (derramar)* to spill; **no tiren los papeles al suelo** don't throw *o* drop the wrappers on the ground; **tiró las maletas y se tumbó en la cama** she dropped her suitcases and lay down on the bed; **me has tirado salsa en el traje** you've spilt some sauce on my suit
(**c**) *(derribar) (botella, lámpara)* to knock over; *(muro, tabique, edificio)* to knock down; **tiró la lámpara con un codo al pasar** she knocked over the lamp with her elbow as she went by; **la violencia del choque la tiró al suelo** the force of the collision knocked *o* hurled her to the floor; **esta pared habrá que tirarla** we're going to have to knock this wall down
(**d**) *(desechar)* to throw away *o* out; **t. algo a la basura** to throw sth out; **tíralo a la papelera** throw it in the wastepaper basket; **esto está para tirarlo** you/we/*etc* should throw this away *o* out; **eso es t. el dinero** that's a complete waste of money
(**e**) *(arrastrar)* **un carro tirado por dos bueyes** an ox-drawn cart
(**f**) *(disparar) (balas, misiles, disparos)* to fire; *(bomba)* to drop; *(petardo, cohete)* to let off; *(dardos, flechas)* to shoot; *Fam* **t. una foto** to take a picture
(**g**) *(jugar) (carta)* to play; *(dado)* to throw
(**h**) *(en deportes) (falta, penalti)* to take; *(balón)* to pass
(**i**) *(imprimir)* to print
(**j**) *(trazar) (línea)* to draw
(**k**) *Fam (suspender)* to fail, *US* to flunk; **me han tirado en geografía** I've failed *o US* flunked geography
2 *vi* (**a**) *(disparar)* to shoot; **t. al aire** to fire shots into the air; **t. a dar** to shoot to wound, not to kill; **t. a matar** *(con arma)* to shoot to kill; *(con comentario)* to go for the jugular
(**b**) *(estirar, arrastrar)* **t. (de algo)** to pull (sth); **el ciclista colombiano tiraba del pelotón** the Colombian cyclist was pulling the bunch along; **me tiró del pelo** she pulled my hair; **t.** *(en letrero)* pull; **me**

tiró del brazo/de la manga she tugged at my arm/sleeve; EXPR *RP* **t. parejo: esto no es justo, o tiramos parejo o yo me retiro** this is not fair, either we all pull together or I'm dropping out

(**c**) *(estar tirante)* to be tight; **la chaqueta me tira de atrás** the jacket's a bit tight at the back

(**d**) *(en deportes) (con el pie)* to kick; *(con la mano)* to throw; *(a meta, canasta)* to shoot; **t. a gol** *o Am* **al arco** *o Esp* **a puerta** to shoot, to have a shot at goal

(**e**) *(dirigirse)* to go (**hacia** *o* **para** towards), to head (**hacia** *o* **para** for *o* towards); *Fam* **¡tira!** *(para empezar a moverse)* get moving!; *Fam* **¡tira que llegamos tarde!** let's get a move on or we'll be late!; **tiramos hacia la izquierda** we turned left; *Fam* **tira para arriba, que ahora subo yo** you go on up, I'll come up in a minute; **tira por esa calle** go up *o* take that street

(**f**) *(jugar)* to go, to have one's go; **te toca t. a ti** *(en naipes, dados, billar)* it's your go

(**g**) *(cigarrillo, chimenea)* to draw; **este tabaco no tira** these cigarettes aren't drawing properly

(**h**) *Fam (funcionar)* to go, to work; **el motor no tira** the engine isn't working properly; **el coche tira bien** the car runs well

(**i**) *(durar)* to last; **estos zapatos tirarán otro año** these shoes will last another year

(**j**) *Fam (atraer)* **la familia tira mucho** blood is thicker than water; **la tierra siempre tira de uno** your homeland never loses its pull on you; **tirarle a alguien: me tira la vida del campo** country life appeals to me; **no le tira la profesión de su padre** his father's profession doesn't appeal to him; **no le tira viajar** she doesn't feel the urge to travel; **t. de alguien** to exert a pull on sb

(**k**) *Fam (apañárselas)* **aún puedo t. con este abrigo un par de inviernos** this coat should do me for another couple of winters yet; **ir tirando** to get by; **voy tirando** I'm OK, I've been worse

(**l**) *(tener aspecto de o tendencia a)* **t. a: tira a gris** it's greyish; **tira a su abuela** she takes after her grandmother; **este programa tira a (ser) hortera** this programme is a bit on the tacky side; **el tiempo tira a mejorar** the weather looks as if it's getting better; **es un reformista tirando a radical** he's somewhere between a reformist and a radical; **es verde tirando a azul** it's a bluey green; **es tirando a delgado** if anything, he's rather thin; **tira para deportista** he has the makings of a sportsman

(**m**) *Fam (hacer uso)* **t. de algo** to use sth; **cuando no hay dinero hay que t. del ingenio** when you don't have any money, you have to rely on your wits; **hubo que t. de los ahorros** we had to draw on our savings

(**n**) *Ven Vulg (copular)* to fuck

3 tirarse *vpr* (**a**) *(lanzarse) (al aire)* to jump (**a** into); *(al agua)* to dive (**a** into); **se tiró de** *o* **desde lo alto del muro** she jumped down from the wall; **tirarse del trampolín** to dive off the springboard; **se tiró de un sexto piso** he threw himself from the sixth floor; **se tiró por la ventana** she jumped out of the window; **tirarse en paracaídas** to parachute; **tirarse sobre alguien** to jump on top of sb; EXPR *RP, Ven* **tirarse al agua (de traje)** to take the plunge

(**b**) *(tumbarse)* to stretch out; **tirarse en el suelo/en la cama** to stretch out on the ground/bed

(**c**) *Fam (en fútbol)* to dive; EXPR **tirarse a la piscina** to make a theatrical dive

(**d**) *Fam (pasar tiempo)* to spend; **se tiraba todo el día viendo la tele** she'd be in front of the telly all day long, she'd spend the whole day in front of the telly; **se tiró siete años para hacer la carrera** he took seven years to get his degree

(**e**) *Fam (expulsar)* **tirarse un pedo** to fart; **tirarse un eructo** to burp; **tirarse un farol** to bluff

(**f**) *muy Fam (sexualmente)* **tirarse a alguien** to lay sb, *Br* to have it off with sb

(**g**) *RP Fam* **tirárselas de: se las tira de intelectual/elegante** he fancies himself as an intellectual/a dandy

tirilla 1 *nf* (**a**) *(de camisa)* neckband (**b**) *Chile (vestido)* ragged *o* tattered clothing

2 tirillas *nmpl* **ser un tirillas** to be a weakling *o* weed

tirio, -a *Hist* **1** *adj* Tyrian

2 *nm,f* Tyrian; EXPR **tirios y troyanos** all sides; **en su discurso atacó a tirios y troyanos** he attacked all and sundry in his speech

tirita *nf Br* (sticking-)plaster, *US* Bandaid®; **ponerse una t.** to put a *Br* plaster *o US* Bandaid® on

tiritar *vi* to shiver (**de** with); EXPR *Fam* **dejar algo tiritando: has dejado la botella tiritando** you haven't left much of that bottle

tiritona, tiritera *nf* **le dio una t.** he had a fit of shivering

TIRO *nm* (**a**) *(disparo) (con arma)* shot; **le dieron un t. en el brazo** he was shot in the arm; **se oyó un t.** a shot rang out, there was a shot; **lo mataron de un t.** he was shot dead; **pegar un t. a alguien** to shoot sb; **pegarse un t.** to shoot oneself; **se liaron a tiros** they started shooting at each other; EXPR *RP* **como (un) t.** *(partir, salir)* like a shot; **ir como (un) t.** to tear along, *US* to barrel along; EXPR *Fam* **ni a tiros: este cajón no se abre ni a tiros** this drawer just refuses to open; **esta cuenta no me sale ni a tiros** however hard I try I don't seem to be able to get this sum right; EXPR *Fam* **a t. hecho: fui a esa tienda a t. hecho** I went to that shop on purpose; EXPR **no van por ahí los tiros** you're a bit wide of the mark there; EXPR **saber por dónde van los tiros** to know what's really going on; EXPR **me salió el t. por la culata** it backfired on me; EXPR *Fam* **sentar como un t. a alguien** *(comentario)* to go down badly with sb; *(comida)* to disagree with sb; *(ropa, indumentaria)* to look awful on sb; **su reacción me sentó como un t.** her reaction really upset me ►► ***t. de gracia*** coup de grâce

(**b**) *(disparo) (con balón)* shot; **hubo varios tiros a gol** there were several shots at goal; *Fam* **echar unos tiros** *(en baloncesto)* to play hoops ►► *Am* ***t. al arco*** *(en fútbol)* shot at goal; ***t. de dos (puntos)*** *(en baloncesto)* two-point basket; ***t. de campo*** *(en baloncesto)* field goal; *Am* ***t. de esquina*** corner; ***t. libre*** *(en fútbol)* free kick; *(en baloncesto)* free throw; ***t. libre directo*** *(en fútbol)* direct free kick; ***t. libre indirecto*** *(en fútbol)* indirect free kick; ***t. a la media vuelta*** *(en baloncesto)* turn-around jump shot; ***t. en suspensión*** *(en baloncesto)* jump shot; ***t. de tres (puntos)*** *(en baloncesto)* three-pointer

(**c**) *(actividad)* shooting; **hacer prácticas de t.** to practise one's shooting ►► ***t. con arco*** archery; ***t. al blanco*** *(deporte)* target shooting; *(lugar)* shooting range; ***t. al plato*** clay pigeon shooting

(**d**) *(huella, marca)* bullet mark; *(herida)* gunshot wound; **tiene un t. en la pierna** he has a gunshot wound in his leg

(**e**) *(alcance)* range; **a t. de** within range of; **a t. de piedra (de)** a stone's throw away (from); **ponerse/estar a t.** *(de arma)* to come/be within range; *(de persona)* to come/be within one's reach; **si se me pone a t. no dejaré escapar la ocasión** if the chance comes up, I won't miss it

(**f**) *(de chimenea, horno) (conducto)* flue; *(corriente)* draft; **tener buen t.** to draw well

(**g**) *(de pantalón)* = distance between crotch and waist; **este pantalón me queda corto/largo de t.** these *Br* trousers *o US* pants are a bit tight/baggy at the crotch; EXPR **de tiros largos: vestirse** *o* **ponerse de tiros largos** to dress up to the nines

(**h**) *(de caballos)* team

(**i**) *Fam (raya de cocaína)* line

(**j**) *Chile Fam* **al t.** in a flash, at once; **me respondió al t.** she answered me in a flash

tiroideo, -a *adj* thyroid; **glándula tiroidea** thyroid (gland)

tiroides *nm inv* thyroid (gland)

Tirol *nm* **(el) T.** the Tyrol

tirolés, -esa 1 *adj* Tyrolean; **sombrero t.** Tyrolean hat

2 *nm,f* Tyrolean

tirón *nm* (**a**) *(estirón)* pull; **le dio un t. de orejas** she tweaked his ears; **dar tirones (de algo)** to tug *o* pull (at sth); EXPR *Fam* **de un t.** in one go; **dormir diez horas de un t.** to sleep ten hours straight through

(**b**) *(muscular)* pull; **me ha dado un t.** I've pulled a muscle; **sufrir un t.** to pull a muscle

(**c**) *(robo)* **el t.** bag-snatching; **le dieron un t.** she had her bag snatched

(**d**) *Fam (atractivo)* **tiene mucho t. entre los jóvenes** she's a big hit with young people

(**e**) *(aceleración)* **les salvó el t. de las fiestas navideñas** they were saved by the Christmas spending spree; **la economía ha crecido debido al t. del euro** the economy has grown due to the impetus given by the euro

(**f**) *Fam (distancia)* **hay un buen t. hasta allá** it's quite a trek (to get there)

tironear 1 *vt* to tug *o* pull (at)

2 *vi* to tug, to pull; **no tironees que se rompe** don't pull at it or it'll tear; *RP* **cuando querés algo, pedilo, no tironees** if you want something, ask for it, don't grab

tirotear 1 *vt* to fire at

2 *vi* to shoot

3 tirotearse *vpr* to fire at each other

tiroteo *nm (tiros)* shooting; *(intercambio de disparos)* shootout; **en el t. murieron dos personas** two people were killed in the shooting

Tirreno *nm* **el (mar) T.** the Tyrrhenian Sea

tirria *nf Fam* **le tengo t.** I can't stand him

tisana *nf* herbal tea

tísico, -a *Med* **1** *adj* consumptive, tubercular; **estar t.** to have consumption *o* tuberculosis
2 *nm,f* consumptive

tisis *nf inv Med* consumption, tuberculosis

tisú *nm (tela)* lamé

titán *nm* **(a)** *Mitol* Titan **(b)** *(gigante)* giant; *(persona excepcional)* giant, titan; **un duelo de titanes** a battle of titans

titánico, -a *adj* titanic

titanio *nm Quím* titanium

títere *nm* **(a)** *(muñeco)* puppet; **títeres** *(guiñol)* puppet show; EXPR **no dejar t. con cabeza** *(destrozar)* to destroy everything in sight; *(criticar)* to spare nobody; **no quedó t. con cabeza** no one was spared **(b)** *Pey (persona)* puppet

titi *nf muy Fam (chica) Br* bird, *US* broad

tití *(pl* **titís** *o* **tities)** *nm (mono)* marmoset

titiaro *nm Ven* lady finger banana, fig banana

Titicaca *nm* **el lago T.** Lake Titicaca

titilación *nf Literario* **(a)** *(de estrella, luz)* flickering **(b)** *(temblor)* trembling

titilar *vi Literario* **(a)** *(estrella, luz)* to flicker **(b)** *(temblar)* to tremble

titileo *nm Literario* **(a)** *(de estrella, luz)* flickering **(b)** *(temblor)* trembling

titipuchal *nm Méx Fam* **un t. de** heaps of, *US* a whole mess of

titiritar *vi* to shiver **(de** with)

titiritero, -a *nm,f* **(a)** *(de títeres)* puppeteer **(b)** *(acróbata)* acrobat

tito *nm (de aceituna, cereza) Br* stone, *US* pit

titubeante *adj (actitud)* hesitant; *(voz)* faltering, hesitant

titubear *vi (dudar)* to hesitate; *(al hablar)* to falter, to hesitate

titubeo *nm (duda, al hablar)* hesitation, hesitancy; **tras muchos titubeos** after much hesitation

titulación *nf (académica)* qualifications

titulado, -a 1 *adj (diplomado)* qualified; *(licenciado)* with a degree; **t. en enfermería/ciencias económicas** with a degree in nursing/economics; **abogado t.** law graduate
2 *nm,f (diplomado)* holder of a qualification; *(licenciado)* graduate; **para recién titulados** *(diplomados)* for those newly qualified; *(licenciados)* for recent graduates ►► ***t. superior*** (university) graduate

titular 1 *adj (profesor)* tenured; **miembro t.** full member; **el equipo t.** the first team; **el juez t.** = the judge assigned to a particular court
2 *nmf* **(a)** *(poseedor)* holder; **t. de una tarjeta de crédito/cuenta corriente** credit card/current account holder **(b)** *(profesor)* tenured lecturer; **el t. de la cátedra** the holder of the chair **(c)** *(jugador)* first-team player
3 *nm Prensa* headline; **con grandes titulares** splashed across the front page
4 *vt (libro, cuadro)* to call, to title
5 titularse *vpr* **(a)** *(llamarse)* to be titled *o* called; **¿cómo se titula la película?** what's the title of the movie? **(b)** *(licenciarse)* to graduate **(en** in); *(diplomarse)* to obtain a qualification **(en** in); **se tituló por la universidad de Cuernavaca** she graduated from *o* did her degree at Cuernavaca university

titularidad *nf* **(a)** *(de bienes)* ownership; *(de derechos)* possession; **una empresa de t. estatal** a state-owned company **(b)** *(de puesto)* **asumió la t. del cargo** she assumed *o* took up the post; **perder la t.** *(deportista)* to lose one's first-team place

titulitis *nf inv Fam* = over-reliance on academic qualifications

titulización *nf Bolsa* securitization

título 1 *nm* **(a)** *(de obra, película)* title ►► *Cine* ***títulos de crédito*** credits; ***t. de página*** running head, page title
(b) *(licenciatura)* degree; *(diploma)* diploma; **tiene muchos títulos** she has a lot of qualifications ►► ***t. académico*** academic degree; ***t. universitario*** university degree
(c) *(de concurso, competición)* title; **el t. de la liga/de campeón** the league/championship title
(d) *(de derecho, obligación) (documento)* deed; ***t. de propiedad*** title deed
(e) *Fin* security ►► ***t. de acción*** *Br* share *o US* stock certificate; ***títulos no cotizados*** unlisted securities; ***t. de deuda pública*** government bond
(f) t. (nobiliario *o* **de nobleza)** title
(g) *(derecho)* title, right
2 a título (de) *loc prep* **a t. de amigo** as a friend; **a t. de ejemplo podemos destacar...** by way of example we can point to...; **participar a t. individual** to take part on an individual basis; **lo digo a t. individual** I'm speaking purely for myself; **a t. orientativo** by way of guidance, for your guidance

tiza *nf (material)* chalk; **una t.** a piece of chalk

Tiziano *n pr* Titian

tiznado, -a *adj* blackened

tiznadura *nf* **(a)** *(acción)* blackening, dirtying **(b)** *(mancha)* black mark

tiznajo *nm Fam* smudge, stain

tiznar 1 *vt* to blacken
2 tiznarse *vpr* **(a)** *(ponerse negro)* to get blackened; **tiznarse la cara** *(a propósito)* to blacken one's face; *(por accidente)* to get one's face blackened; **se tiznó el vestido** her dress got all black **(b)** *Arg (emborracharse)* to get drunk

tizne *nm o nf* soot

tiznón *nm* black stain

tizón *nm (al rojo)* ember; *(frío)* half-burnt stick

tizona *nf Literario* sword

tlacote *nm Méx* spot, pimple

tlapalería *nf Méx* ironmonger's (shop)

tlaxcalteca 1 *adj* of/from Tlaxcala *(Mexico)*
2 *nmf* person from Tlaxcala *(Mexico)*

TLC *nm (abrev de* **Tratado de Libre Comercio)** NAFTA

TNLC *nm (abrev de* **Tratado Norteamericano de Libre Comercio)** NAFTA

TNT *nm (abrev de* **trinitrotolueno)** TNT

toalla *nf* **(a)** *(para secarse)* towel; EXPR **arrojar** *o* **tirar la t.** to throw in the towel ►► ***t. de baño*** bath towel; ***t. de ducha*** bath towel; *Am* ***t. femenina*** sanitary *Br* towel *o US* napkin; *Am* ***t. higiénica*** sanitary *Br* towel *o US* napkin; *CAm* ***t. húmeda*** wet wipe, moist towelette; ***t. de manos*** hand towel; *Am* ***t. sanitaria*** sanitary *Br* towel *o US* napkin **(b)** *(tejido)* towelling; **tela de t.** towelling

toallero *nm (barra)* towel *Br* rail *o US* bar; *(anilla)* towel ring

toallita *nf* **(a)** *(para la cara)* face cloth **(b)** *(refrescante)* towelette **(c)** *(para bebés)* baby *o* wet wipe

toallón *nm RP (de baño)* bath towel; *(de playa)* beach towel

toba *nf* **(a)** *Fam (golpe)* flick **(b)** *Fam (colilla)* cigarette butt *o* stub, *Br* dog end **(c)** *(caliza)* tufa

tobera *nf (de horno)* air inlet; *(de propulsor)* nozzle

tobillera *nf* ankle support

tobillero, -a *adj* ankle-length; **falda tobillera** ankle-length skirt; **pantalones tobilleros** ankle-length *Br* trousers *o US* pants

tobillo *nm* ankle

tobo *nm Ven* bucket, pail

tobogán *nm* **(a)** *(rampa)* slide; *(en parque de atracciones)* helter-skelter; *(en piscina)* chute, flume **(b)** *(trineo)* toboggan; *(pista)* toboggan run

toca *nf* **(a)** *(de monja)* wimple **(b)** *(de dama antigua)* headdress

tocadiscos *nm inv* record player

tocado, -a 1 *adj* **(a)** *Fam (loco)* **t. (del ala)** soft in the head **(b)** *Fam (afectado negativamente)* affected **(c)** *(con sombrero)* wearing a hat; **iba tocada con una pamela** she was wearing a sun hat **(d)** *(fruta)* bad, rotten **(e)** *(jugador)* injured
2 *nm* **(a)** *(prenda)* headgear **(b)** *(peinado)* hairdo **(c)** *(en esgrima)* hit

tocador *nm* **(a)** *(mueble)* dressing table **(b)** *(habitación) (en lugar público)* powder room; *(en casa)* boudoir ►► ***t. de señoras*** *(aseo)* powder room

tocamientos *nmpl* **(a)** *Der* sexual assault **(b)** *Euf (masturbación)* touching oneself

tocante *adj* **(en lo) t. a** regarding; **y en lo t. al ascenso salarial...** and regarding the pay rise...

tocapelotas *nmf inv muy Fam* jerk, *Br* piss-artist

TOCAR [60] **1** *vt* **(a)** *(entrar en contacto con, alterar)* to touch; *(palpar)* to feel; **por favor, no toquen las esculturas** please do not touch the sculptures; **el médico le tocó el estómago** the doctor felt her stomach; **yo no lo tocaría, así está muy bien** I wouldn't touch a thing, it's fine as it is; **tócalo, verás qué suave es** touch it and see how soft it is; **¡no se te ocurra t. al niño!** don't you dare lay a finger on the child!; **el corredor cayó al t. la valla con un pie** the athlete fell when his foot struck *o* clipped the hurdle; **el balón tocó el poste** the ball touched *o* clipped the post; **no ha tocado la comida** he hasn't touched his food; **¡esos libros, ni tocarlos!** don't you go near those

books!; EXPR **t. madera** to touch wood
(**b**) *(hacer sonar) (instrumento, canción)* to play; *(bombo)* to bang; *(sirena, alarma)* to sound; *(campana, timbre)* to ring; *(bocina, claxon)* to hoot, to toot; *(silbato)* to blow; **el reloj tocó las doce** the clock struck twelve
(**c**) *(abordar) (asunto, tema)* to touch on; **lo tocó por encima** he touched on it briefly; **no toques ese tema** don't mention that subject
(**d**) *(concernir)* **por lo que a mí me toca** as far as I'm concerned; **en** *o* **por lo que toca al asunto de los ascensos** as far as the matter of promotions is concerned; **t. a alguien de cerca** to concern sb closely
(**e**) *(conmover)* to touch; **la historia la tocó hondo** the story touched her deeply
2 *vi* (**a**) *(entrar en contacto)* to touch; **no t.** *(en letrero)* don't touch; **no t., alto voltaje** *(en letrero)* high voltage: do not touch
(**b**) *(estar próximo)* **t. con algo** *(pared, mueble)* to be touching sth; *(país, jardín)* to border (on) sth; **la mesa toca con la pared** the table is touching the wall; **nuestra casa toca con la suya** our house is right next to theirs
(**c**) *(llamar)* **t. a la puerta/ventana** to knock on *o* at the door/window
(**d**) *(campanas, timbre)* to ring
(**e**) *(en un reparto)* **t. a alguien: le tocó la mitad** he got half of it; **a ti te toca la casa** you get the house; **a mí me toca fregar la cocina** I've got to mop the kitchen; **tocamos a dos trozos cada uno** there's enough for two slices each; **tocamos a mil cada uno** *(nos deben)* we're due a thousand each; *(debemos)* it's a thousand each; **te toca a ti hacerlo** *(turno)* it's your turn to do it; *(responsabilidad)* it's up to you to do it; **te toca tirar a ti** *(en juegos)* it's your go; **¿a quién le toca?** whose turn is it?
(**f**) *(caer en suerte)* **me ha tocado la lotería/el gordo** I've won the lottery/the jackpot; **me tocaron seis millones a** *o* **en la lotería** I won six million in the lottery; **le ha tocado sufrir mucho** he has had to suffer a lot
(**g**) *(llegar el momento)* **hoy toca limpiar** it's cleaning day today; **ahora toca divertirse** now it's time to have some fun; **le toca dar a luz la semana que viene** she's due to have the baby next week; **ya me toca ir al dentista** it's time for me to go to the dentist; **¿cuándo te toca renovar el permiso?** when do you have to renew your licence?; *Fam Hum* **si te dicen que salgas, a salir tocan** if they tell you to go out, then you'd better go out
(**h**) *(rayar)* **t. en algo** to verge *o* border on sth; **eso ya toca en lo imaginario** that's verging on the imaginary
3 tocarse *vpr* (**a**) *(palpar)* to touch; **no te toques la cicatriz** don't touch the scar
(**b**) *(estar en contacto)* to touch; **las dos mesas se tocan** the two tables are touching
(**c**) *(cubrirse la cabeza)* to cover one's head; **se tocó con un sombrero de fieltro** he donned a felt hat

---

tocata 1 *nm Fam (tocadiscos)* record player
2 *nf Mús* toccata

tocateja: a tocateja *loc adv* **pagar a t.** to pay up front in cash

tocayo, -a *nm,f* namesake; **es mi t.** he has the same name as me, he's my namesake; **somos tocayos** we have the same (first) name

tochimbo *nm Andes* smelting furnace

tocho 1 *adj inv Fam (grande)* huge
2 *nm* (**a**) *Fam (cosa grande)* massive *o* huge great thing; *(libro)* massive tome; **tengo que estudiar este t. de apuntes** I've got to study this wad *o Br* wodge of notes (**b**) *(hierro)* iron ingot

tocinera *nf Esp muy Fam* police van, *US* paddy wagon

tocineta *nf Col, Ven* smoked bacon

tocino *nm* (**a**) *(para cocinar)* pork *o* bacon fat *(in a piece)* ▸▸ ***t. entreverado*** = pork fat containing streaks of meat (**b**) *Méx (beicon)* bacon (**c**) *(dulce)* ***t. de cielo*** = rich custard dessert

toco *nm RP Fam* **un t. de** tons *o* loads of; **tiene un t. de libros** she's got tons *o* zillions of books; **tienen un t. de guita** they've got tons *o* heaps of dough; **te extraño tocos** I miss you heaps *o* big time

tocología, tocoginecología *nf* obstetrics *(singular)*

tocólogo, -a, tocoginecólogo, -a *nm,f* obstetrician

tocomocho *nm* = confidence trick involving the sale of a lottery ticket, claimed to be a certain winner, for a large amount of money

tocón, -ona *Fam* **1** *adj* **no seas t.** keep your hands to yourself
2 *nm,f* **es un t.** he can't keep his hands to himself
3 *nm* stump

tocororo *nm* Cuban trogon *(national bird of Cuba)*

tocuyo *nm Andes, Arg* coarse cotton cloth

todavía *adv* (**a**) *(con afirmación)* still; *(con negación)* yet, still; **están t. aquí** they are still here; **¿pero vive t.?** but is she still alive?; **t. no** not yet; **t. no lo he recibido** I still haven't got it, I haven't got it yet; **¿t. no ha llegado?** hasn't she arrived yet?, has she still not arrived?
(**b**) *(con más énfasis)* still; **he hecho todo lo que me ha pedido y t. no está contento** I've done everything he asked and he still isn't happy
(**c**) *(incluso)* even; **t. más** even more; **¡t. querrá más!** I hope he's not going to ask for more!

todito, -a *Fam* **1** *adj* **se comió todita la comida** she ate every last bit of food
2 *pron* every last bit of it, the whole lot

TODO, -A **1** *adj* (**a**) *(el conjunto o total de)* all; **t. el día** all day; **t. el libro** the whole book, all (of) the book; **t. el vino** all (of) the wine; **todas las manzanas** all the apples; **todos los americanos** all Americans; **toda esta planta está dedicada al impresionismo** all (of) *o* the whole of this floor is devoted to impressionism; **t. un día está dedicado a visitar la ciudad** a whole day is devoted to visiting the city; **todos ellos se marcharon** they all left; **toda su ilusión es conocer Europa** her greatest wish is to visit Europe; **por todas partes** everywhere; **t. el mundo,** *Méx* **t. mundo** everybody; **en t. momento** at all times; **ilustraciones a t. color** full-colour illustrations; **un seguro a t. riesgo** a comprehensive insurance policy; **subimos la calle a toda velocidad** we went up the street as fast as we could *o* at top speed; **t. Buenos Aires habla de ello** the whole of *o* all of Buenos Aires is talking about it
(**b**) *(cada, cualquier)* every; **todos los días/lunes** every day/Monday; **como t. mexicano sabe...** as every Mexican knows..., as all Mexicans know...; **t. edificio de más de veinte años pasará una revisión** all buildings that are more than twenty years old will be inspected; **t. aquel que** *o* **t. el que viole las normas** anybody *o* anyone who breaks the rules; **todos aquellos que** *o* **todos los que están en huelga** all those (who are) on strike
(**c**) *(para enfatizar)* **es t. un hombre** he's every inch a man; **ya es toda una mujer** she's a grown woman now; **fue t. un éxito** it was a great success; **se produjo t. un cúmulo de casualidades** there was a whole series of coincidences
(**d**) *(del todo)* **el jardín estaba t. descuidado** the garden was completely *o* all neglected; **se puso toda enojada** she got all annoyed
2 *pron* (**a**) *(singular)* everything; **lo vendió t.** he sold everything, he sold it all; **t. está listo** everything is ready, it's all ready; **t. es poco tratándose de sus hijos** nothing is too much when it comes to her children; **se enoja por t.** he gets angry at the slightest thing; **eso es t.** that's all ▸▸ *Esp* ***t. a cien*** *(tienda) Br* ≃ pound shop, *US* ≃ nickel-and-dime store
(**b**) **todos** *(todas las personas)* everybody, everyone; *(todas las cosas)* all of them; **todos vinieron** everybody *o* everyone came, they all came; **quiero agradecer a todos su cooperación** I would like to thank you all *o* everybody *o* everyone for your cooperation; **¿estamos todos?** are we all here?, is everybody *o* everyone here?; **todos están rotos** they're all broken, all of them are broken; **me los ha dado todos** she's given me all of them, she's given me them all
(**c**) *(otras frases)* **ante t.** *(sobre todo)* above all; *(en primer lugar)* first of all; **con t. (y con eso)** all the same; **de t.** everything (you can think of); **tenemos de t.** we have everything; **puede pasar de t.** anything could happen; **después de t.** after all; **del t.** completely; **no estoy del t. contento** I'm not entirely happy; **no lo hace mal del t.** she doesn't do it at all badly; **en t. y por t.** entirely; **está en t.** he thinks of everything; **pese a t., a pesar de t.** in spite of *o* despite everything; **t. lo más** at (the) most; **y t.: me invitó a cenar y t.** she even asked me to dinner; **se presentó en la fiesta con muletas y t.** he turned up at the party, crutches and all; EXPR **de todas todas** without a shadow of a doubt; EXPR **fue t. uno: subirse al barco y marearse fue t. uno** no sooner had he got on the boat than he felt sick
3 *nm* whole; **jugarse el t. por el t.** to stake everything
4 *adv (totalmente)* **el camarero era t. amabilidad** the waiter was all friendliness, the waiter was extremely friendly; **esa chica es t. huesos** that girl is all skin and bones; EXPR **soy t. oídos** I'm all ears
5 a todo esto *loc adv (mientras tanto)* meanwhile; *(a propósito)* by the way

---

todopoderoso, -a 1 *adj* almighty
2 *nm* **el Todopoderoso** the Almighty

todoterreno 1 *adj inv (vehículo)* all-terrain
2 *nm* (**a**) *(vehículo)* four-wheel drive (vehicle), all-terrain vehicle (**b**) *Fam (persona)* all-rounder

tofe, toffee ['tofe] *nm* coffee-flavoured toffee

tofo *nm Chile (arcilla)* fireclay

tofu *nm* tofu

toga *nf* (**a**) *(romana)* toga (**b**) *(de académico)* gown; *(de magistrado)* robes (**c**) *(en el pelo)* **hacerse la t.** = to wrap one's wet hair round one's head and cover it with a towel to dry, in order to straighten out curls

togado, -a *adj* robed

Togo *n* Togo

toilette [twa'let] **1** *nm CSur* toilet, lavatory
2 *nf Anticuado* **hacer la t.** to perform one's toilet(te)

toisón *nm* ***t. de oro*** *(insignia)* golden fleece *(emblem of Order of the Golden Fleece)*

tojo *nm* gorse; **cayó entre unos tojos** he fell into some gorse

tojosa *nf Cuba* = grey dove found in Central America

Tokio *n* Tokyo

toldillo *nm Col (mosquitero)* mosquito net

toldo *nm* (**a**) *(de tienda, balcón)* awning (**b**) *(de playa)* sunshade (**c**) *(de camión)* tarpaulin

toledano, -a **1** *adj* of/from Toledo *(Spain)*
2 *nm,f* person from Toledo *(Spain)*

tolerable *adj* (**a**) *(aguantable)* tolerable; **el dolor es t.** the pain is bearable (**b**) *(perdonable)* acceptable

tolerado, -a *adj (película)* suitable for all ages, *Br* ≃ U, *US* ≃ G

tolerancia *nf* (**a**) *(respeto)* tolerance (**b**) *(a medicamentos, dolor)* tolerance (**a** of) (**c**) *Tec (en material, producto)* tolerance; **margen de t.** (margin of) tolerance

tolerante **1** *adj* tolerant
2 *nmf* tolerant person

tolerar *vt* (**a**) *(consentir, aceptar)* to tolerate; **t. que alguien haga algo** to tolerate sb doing sth; **no tolero esa actitud** I won't tolerate that sort of attitude; **no tolero a los que mienten así** I can't stand *o* abide people who lie like that; **¡cómo toleras que te hable así!** how can you let him talk to you like that!
(**b**) *(aguantar) (altas temperaturas)* to stand, to tolerate; *(medicinas)* to tolerate; **esta planta tolera muy bien la sequedad** this plant survives very well in dry conditions

toletazo *nm Am* (**a**) *(físico)* blow with a club; **le dieron un t.** they hit him with a club, they clubbed him (**b**) *(moral)* blow, shock

tolete *nm* (**a**) *(escálamo)* thole, tholepin (**b**) *CAm, Carib, Col, Méx (porra)* cudgel, club

toletole *nm Fam* hubbub, uproar

tollina *nf Fam* beating, hiding

tolteca **1** *adj* Toltec, Toltecan
2 *nmf* Toltec

tolueno *nm Quím* toluene

toluqueño, -a **1** *adj* of/from Toluca *(Mexico)*
2 *nm,f* person from Toluca *(Mexico)*

tolva *nf* hopper

tolvanera *nf* dust storm

toma **1** *nf* (**a**) *(acción de tomar)* ►► ***t. de conciencia*** realization; **la t. de conciencia tardó mucho tiempo** it took some time for people to become aware of the true situation; ***t. de decisiones*** decision-making; ***t. de posesión*** *(de gobierno, presidente)* investiture; **la t. de posesión será el día 25** *(de cargo)* he will take up his post on the 25th; ***t. de posición*** *o* ***posiciones*** position taking; **alabaron la t. de posición del presidente en este tema** they praised the position taken by the president on this matter
(**b**) *(de biberón, papilla)* feed
(**c**) *(de medicamento)* dose
(**d**) *(de ciudad)* capture; **la t. del castillo** the storming of the castle
(**e**) *(de agua, aire)* inlet ►► *Am Elec* ***t. de contacto*** power point, socket; *Elec* ***t. de corriente*** power point, socket; *Elec* ***t. de tierra*** *Br* earth, *US* ground
(**f**) *Cine & TV (plano)* take ►► ***t. falsa*** outtake
(**g**) *Col (cauce)* irrigation ditch
(**h**) *Chile (presa)* dam
2 *nm Fam* **t. y daca** give and take

tomacorriente *nm Am* power point, socket

tomado, -a *adj* (**a**) *(voz)* hoarse (**b**) *Am Fam (persona)* tight, tanked up

tomador, -ora **1** *adj Andes, PRico, RP (que bebe)* drinking
2 *nm,f* (**a**) *Com* drawee (**b**) *Andes, PRico, RP (bebedor)* (heavy) drinker, drunkard

tomadura *nf* ***t. de pelo*** *(broma)* hoax; **¡esto es una t. de pelo!** *(es indignante)* this is a joke!

tomahawk [toma'χauk] (*pl* **tomahawks**) *nm* tomahawk

TOMAR **1** *vt* (**a**) *(agarrar)* to take; **me tomó de un brazo** he took me by the arm; **tomó el dinero y se fue** she took the money and left; **tómalo, ya no me hace falta** take *o* have it, I no longer need it; **toma el libro que me pediste** here's the book you asked me for; *Fam* **¡toma ésa!** *(expresa venganza)* that'll teach you!, chew on that!
(**b**) *(sacar, obtener)* to take; **este ejemplo lo tomé del libro** I took this example from the book; **fue al sastre para que le tomara las medidas** he went to the tailor's to have his measurements taken; **toma unos planos de la casa** *(con cámara)* take a few shots of the house; **t. fotos (a** *o* **de)** to take photos (of); **t. declaración a alguien** to take a statement from sb; **tomarle la lección a alguien** to test sb on what they've learned at school; **t. unas muestras de orina/sangre (a alguien)** to take some urine/blood samples (from sb); **t. la tensión/temperatura a alguien** to take sb's blood pressure/temperature
(**c**) *(ingerir) (alimento, medicina, droga)* to take; **¿qué quieres t.?** *(beber)* what would you like (to drink)?; *Esp (comer)* what would you like (to eat)?; **¿quieres t. algo (de beber)?** would you like something to drink?; *Esp* **¿quieres t. algo (de comer)?** would you like something to eat?; **tomé sopa** I had soup; **no tomo alcohol** I don't drink (alcohol)
(**d**) *(exponerse a)* **t. el sol,** *Am* **t. sol** to sunbathe; **salir a t. el aire,** *Am* **salir a t. aire** to go out for a breath of fresh air; **salir a t. el fresco** to go out for a breath of fresh air; *RP* **t. frío** to catch a chill; **tomó frío, por eso se engripó** she caught a chill, that's why she came down with flu
(**e**) *(desplazarse mediante) (autobús, tren)* to catch; *(taxi, ascensor, telesilla)* to take; **tomaré el último vuelo** I'll be on the last flight; **podríamos t. el tren** we could go by train; **tomaron un atajo** they took a short-cut
(**f**) *(recibir)* to take; **toma lecciones de piano** she is taking *o* having piano lessons; **he tomado un curso de jardinería** I've taken *o* done a course on gardening; **toma mi consejo y...** take my advice and...; **¿tomas a María por esposa?** do you take María to be your lawfully wedded wife?
(**g**) *(apuntar) (datos, información)* to take down; **t. apuntes** *o* **notas** to take notes; **t. algo por escrito** to take *o* write sth down; **el secretario iba tomando nota de todo** the secretary noted everything down
(**h**) *(baño, ducha)* to take, to have
(**i**) *(adoptar) (medidas, precauciones, decisión)* to take; *(actitud, costumbre, modales)* to adopt; **t. la determinación de hacer algo** to determine *o* decide to do sth; **el Presidente debe t. una postura sobre este asunto** the President should state his opinion on this matter
(**j**) *(adquirir, cobrar) (velocidad)* to gain, to gather; **las cosas están tomando mejor aspecto con este gobierno** things are looking up under this government; **el avión fue tomando altura** the plane climbed; **t. confianza** to grow in confidence, to become more assured; **la obra ya está tomando forma** the play is beginning to take shape; **t. fuerzas** to gather one's strength; **voy tomándole el gusto a esto del esquí acuático** water-skiing is starting to grow on me; **t. interés por algo** to get *o* grow interested in sth; **tomarle manía/cariño a** to take a dislike/a liking to; **las negociaciones tomaron un rumbo favorable** the negotiations started to go better
(**k**) *(asumir, encargarse de)* **t. el control** to take control; **el copiloto tomó el mando** the copilot took over; **él tomó sobre sí** *o* **sobre sus espaldas toda la responsabilidad** he assumed full responsibility
(**l**) *(reaccionar a)* to take; **¿qué tal tomó la noticia?** how did she take the news?; **las cosas hay que tomarlas como vienen** you have to take things as they come; **tómalo con calma** take it easy
(**m**) *(llevar) (tiempo)* to take; **me tomó mucho tiempo limpiarlo todo** it took me a long time to clean it all
(**n**) *(contratar)* to take on
(**o**) *(invadir)* to take; **las tropas tomaron la ciudad** the troops took *o* seized the city; **los estudiantes tomaron la universidad** the students occupied the university
(**p**) *Fam* **tomarla con alguien** to have it in for sb
(**q**) *(confundir)* **t. a alguien por algo/alguien** to take sb for sth/sb; **¿por quién me tomas** *o* **has tomado?** what do you take me for?; **lo tomé por el jefe** I took *o* mistook him for the boss; **¿tú me tomas por tonto o qué?** do you think I'm stupid or something?
2 *vi* (**a**) *(encaminarse)* to go; **toma a la derecha/izquierda** turn *o* go right/left; **tomamos hacia el sur** we headed south; **toma por ahí/por ese camino** go that way/down that road
(**b**) *(en imperativo) (al dar algo)* **¡toma!** here you are!; **toma, dale esto a tu madre** here, give this to your mother
(**c**) *Fam (como interjección)* **¡toma!** *(expresa sorpresa)* good grief!, *Br* blimey!; **necesito unas vacaciones – ¡t.! ¡y yo!** I need a *Br* holiday *o US* vacation – what, and I don't?; **¡t. ya!, ¡qué golazo!** how's that for a goal?
(**d**) *Am (beber alcohol)* to drink

3 tomarse *vpr* (a) *(medicina, drogas)* to take; **cuando te lo hayas tomado todo podrás ir a jugar** you can go and play once you've eaten it all up; **se tomó dos cervezas** he had two beers; *Esp* **se tomó dos bocadillos** he had two sandwiches

(b) *(tiempo, vacaciones, día libre)* to take; **puedes tomarte todo el tiempo que necesites** take as long as you need; **se ha tomado la tarde libre** she's taken the afternoon off

(c) *(reaccionar a, interpretar)* to take; **tómatelo con calma** take it easy; **tomarse algo bien/(a) mal** to take sth well/badly; **era una broma, no te lo tomes a mal** it was a joke, don't take it the wrong way; **tomarse algo en serio/a broma** to take sth seriously/as a joke

(d) *(emplear)* **tomarse la libertad de hacer algo** to take the liberty of doing sth; **tomarse la molestia de hacer algo** to go to *o* take the trouble of doing sth; **no hace falta que te tomes tantas molestias** there's no need for you to go to so much trouble

(e) *RP Fam* **tomárselas, tomarse los vientos** to clear off; **¡nos las tomamos!** we're off!; **¿ya se las toman?** are you off, then?

Tomás *n pr* **Santo T. de Aquino** St Thomas Aquinas

tomatal *nm* tomato field

tomate *nm* (a) *(fruto)* tomato; EXPR **ponerse como un t.** to go as red as a *Br* beetroot *or US* beet ►► ***t. cereza*** cherry tomato; ***t. frito*** = unconcentrated puree made by frying peeled tomatoes; ***t. de pera*** plum tomato; *RP, Ven* ***t. (de) perita*** plum tomato (b) *Méx (tomatillo)* tomatillo, husk tomato (c) *Fam (en calcetín)* hole (d) *Fam (jaleo)* uproar, commotion

tomatera *nf* tomato plant

tomatero, -a 1 *adj (pollo)* young and tender

2 *nm,f* tomato seller

tomatillo *nm* tomatillo, husk tomato

tomavistas *nm inv* cine camera

tómbola *nf* tombola

tómbolo *nm Geol* tombolo, = sand bar linking small island to mainland or another island

tomillo *nm* thyme

tomismo *nm* Thomism

tomista *nmf* Thomist

tomo *nm* (a) *(volumen)* volume (b) *(libro)* tome (c) EXPR *Fam* **de t. y lomo: es un mentiroso/un canalla de t. y lomo** he's a real liar/swine; **un resfriado de t. y lomo** a heavy cold

tomografía *nf* tomography ►► *Med* ***t. axial computarizada*** computerized axial tomography; *Med* ***t. por emisión de positrones*** positron emission tomography

ton: sin ton ni son *loc adv Fam* for no apparent reason

tonada *nf* (a) *(melodía)* tune (b) *Am (acento)* (regional) accent

tonadilla *nf* = song in popular Spanish style

tonadillero, -a *nm,f* = singer/writer of "tonadillas"

tonal *adj* tonal

tonalidad *nf* (a) *Mús* key (b) *(de color)* tone

tonel *nm (recipiente)* barrel; EXPR **estar/ponerse como un t.** to be/become (like) an elephant *o* a whale

tonelada *nf* tonne; **pesar una t.** to weigh a ton ►► ***t. métrica*** metric ton, tonne

tonelaje *nm* tonnage

tonelería *nf* (a) *(fabricación)* barrelmaking, cooperage (b) *(taller)* barrel shop, cooperage

tonelero, -a *nm,f* cooper

tóner *nm* toner

Tonga *n* Tonga

tongo *nm* (a) *Fam (engaño)* **en la pelea hubo t.** the fight was fixed (b) *Andes Fam (sombrero hongo) Br* bowler hat, *US* derby

tongonear *Col, Ven Fam* **1** *vt* to swing

2 tongonearse *vpr* to swing one's hips

tonguear *vt RP Fam* to con

tónica *nf* (a) *(tendencia)* trend; **la falta de confianza inversora ha sido la t. general hoy en la bolsa** lack of investor confidence set the tone on the stock exchange today (b) *(bebida)* tonic water (c) *Mús* tonic

tónico, -a 1 *adj* (a) *(reconstituyente)* revitalizing (b) *Gram* tonic; **sílaba tónica** stressed syllable (c) *Mús* tonic

2 *nm* (a) *(reconstituyente)* tonic (b) *(cosmético)* skin toner

tonificación *nf* invigoration

tonificante, tonificador, -ora *adj* invigorating

tonificar [60] *vt* to invigorate

tonillo *nm Pey (retintín)* sarcastic tone of voice

tonina *nf* (a) *(atún)* tuna (b) *(delfín)* dolphin

tono *nm* (a) *(de sonido)* tone; **bajar el t.** to lower one's voice; **dar el t.** to set the tone ►► ***t. continuo*** *(de teléfono) Br* dialling *o US* dial tone; *Andes, RP* ***t. de discado*** *o* ***de discar*** *(de teléfono) Br* dialling *o US* dial tone; ***t. de llamada*** *(de teléfono) Br* dialling *o US* dial tone; ***t. de marcado*** *o* ***de marcar*** *(de teléfono) Br* dialling *o US* dial tone; ***t. de ocupado*** *Br* engaged tone, *US* busy signal

(b) *(de palabras, escrito, discurso)* tone; **el t. con el que lo dijo** the tone she said it in, the tone in which she said it; **¡no me hables en ese t.!** don't speak to me in that tone (of voice)!; **habló con t. serio** he spoke in a serious tone of voice; **lo dijo en t. de broma** she said it jokingly; **la novela es de t. humorístico** the novel is humorous in tone; **bajar de t.** to quieten down; **cambiar de t.: la reunión fue cambiando de t.** the tone *o* atmosphere of the meeting gradually changed; **aquí el texto cambia de t.** at this point in the text the tone changes; **subir el t., subir de t.** *(volumen, ruido)* to get *o* grow louder; *(situación)* to get angrier; **el murmullo/la protesta subió de t.** the murmuring/the protests grew louder; **la conversación subió de t.** the conversation got more heated; **subido de t.** *(atrevido, picante)* risqué; *(impertinente)* impertinent

(c) *(de color)* shade, tone; **en tonos ocres/pastel** in ochre/pastel shades *o* tones; **t. de piel** complexion

(d) *(de músculo)* tone ►► ***t. muscular*** muscle tone

(e) *Mús (tonalidad)* key; *(altura)* pitch; *(intervalo)* tone, *US* step ►► ***t. agudo*** high pitch; ***t. grave*** low pitch; ***t. mayor*** major key; ***t. menor*** minor key; ***t. puro*** simple tone

(f) *Informát* ***t. continuo*** continuous tone

(g) *(en frases)* **a t.: cortinas y cojines a t.** matching curtains and cushions; **estar a t. con** to suit; **un traje/discurso a t. con las circunstancias** a dress/speech appropriate to *o* in keeping with the circumstances; EXPR *Fam* **ponerse a t.** *(emborracharse)* to get in the mood; EXPR **de buen t.** elegant, tasteful; EXPR **ser de buen t.** to be the done thing; **no es de buen t. mencionar la guerra** it is not done to mention the war; EXPR **de mal t.** crass, vulgar; EXPR *Fam* **darse t.** to give oneself airs; EXPR **fuera de t.** out of place

tonsura *nf* (a) *(ceremonia)* tonsure; **hacerse la t.** to have one's hair tonsured (b) *(coronilla)* tonsure

tonsurado *nm (sacerdote)* priest

tonsurar *vt* (a) *(clérigo)* to tonsure (b) *(pelo)* to cut (c) *(lana)* to shear

tontada *nf* **hacer tontadas** to act the fool; **decir tontadas** to talk nonsense; **¡vaya t.!** *(idea)* what an idiotic idea!

tontaina *Fam* **1** *adj* daft

2 *nmf* daft idiot

tontamente *adv* foolishly, stupidly; **se reía t.** she laughed foolishly

tontear *vi* (a) *(hacer el tonto)* to fool about (b) *(coquetear)* **t. (con alguien)** to flirt (with sb)

tontería, *Am* **tontera** *nf* (a) *(estupidez)* stupid thing; **ha sido una t. no presentarse al examen** it was stupid not to take the exam; **decir una t.** to say something stupid; **eso son tonterías** that's nonsense; **decir tonterías** to talk nonsense; **hacer una t.** to do something stupid; **hizo la t. de decírselo** she was stupid enough to tell him; **¡cuánta t. hay en el mundo!** people can be really stupid sometimes!

(b) *(cosa sin importancia o valor)* trifle; **no es ninguna t.** *(va en serio)* it's serious; *(no está mal)* it's not bad at all; **¿qué te ha pasado? – nada, una t.** what happened to you? – oh, it's nothing serious; **por hacer cuatro tonterías me ha cobrado 1.000 pesos** he charged me 1,000 pesos for doing next to nothing

tonto, -a 1 *adj* (a) *(persona) (estúpido)* stupid; *(menos fuerte)* silly; **pero ¿seré t.? otra vez me he vuelto a confundir** I must be stupid or something, I've gone and got it wrong again; **nos toman por tontos** they think we're idiots; **¿estás t.? para qué me pegas?** don't be stupid! what are you hitting me for?; **no seas t., no hay por qué preocuparse** don't be silly, there's no need to worry; EXPR **ser t. de capirote** *o* **remate** to be daft as a brush; EXPR **ser más t. que Abundio** to be as thick as two short planks

(b) *(retrasado mental)* dim, backward

(c) **ponerse t.** *(pesado, insistente)* to be difficult; *(arrogante)* to get awkward, *Br* to get stroppy

(d) *(sin sentido) (risa)* mindless; *(esfuerzo)* pointless; **fue una caída tonta** it was so silly, falling over like that; EXPR **a lo t.: lo perdí a lo t.** I stupidly lost it; **me tropecé a lo t.** I tripped over like an idiot; **me he ido haciendo con una extensa colección de sellos a lo t.** I've built up a sizeable stamp collection without hardly realising it

2 *nm,f* idiot; **los listos y los tontos de la clase** the bright ones and the dim ones in the class; **el t. del pueblo** the village idiot; EXPR **hacer el t.** *(juguetear)* to mess around; *(no actuar con inteligencia)* to be stupid *o* foolish; **estoy haciendo el t. intentando convencerle** I'm wasting my time trying to convince him; EXPR **hacerse el t.** to act innocent; EXPR **a tontas y a locas** without thinking ▸▸ ***t. útil*** useful idiot

tontolaba *Esp Fam* 1 *adj* dopey, *Br* gormless
2 *nmf Br* twerp, *US* dumb cluck

tontorrón, -ona 1 *adj* daft
2 *nm,f* daft idiot

tontuna *nf Fam (atontamiento)* **iqué t. tengo hoy!** I feel so dopey today!

toña *nf Fam* **(a)** *(borrachera)* **agarrar una t.** to get smashed *o Br* pissed **(b)** *(golpe)* thump, wallop; **iqué t. se ha dado!** what a thump he gave himself!

top (*pl* **tops**) *nm (prenda)* cropped top

topacio *nm* topaz

topada *nf* headbutt

topadora *nf RP* bulldozer

topar 1 *vi* **(a)** *(chocar)* **t. con** *o* **contra** to knock *o* bump into **(b)** *(encontrarse)* **t. con alguien** to bump into sb; **t. con algo** to come across sth **(c)** *Andes, Méx (en juego)* to wager, to bet
2 **toparse** *vpr* **toparse con** *(persona)* to bump into; *(cosa)* to come across; **se toparon con el enemigo** they came up against the enemy

tope 1 *nm* **(a)** *(límite máximo)* limit; *(de plazo)* deadline; **pusieron como t. diez por persona** each person was allowed no more than ten; **un t. máximo de 20 millones** a maximum of 20 million; EXPR *Fam* **a t.** *(de velocidad, intensidad)* flat out; *(lleno)* packed; **abrir el grifo a t.** to turn the tap on full; **la calefacción estaba a t.** the heating was on full blast; **estoy a t. de trabajo** I'm up to my neck in work; **disfrutar a t.** to have a whale of a time; EXPR **estar hasta los topes** to be bursting at the seams
(b) *Ferroc* buffer
(c) *(freno)* **poner t. a** to rein in, to curtail
(d) *(pieza)* block; *(para puerta)* doorstop
(e) *Méx (para velocidad)* speed bump, *Br* sleeping policeman
2 *adj inv* **(a)** *(máximo) (sueldo, velocidad)* top, maximum; *(edad)* maximum; **fecha t.** deadline **(b)** *Esp Fam (genial)* fab, *Br* brill
3 *adv Esp Fam (muy)* mega, really; **un bar t. enrollado** a megacool bar

topera *nf* molehill

topetazo *nm*, **topetada** *nf*, **topetón** *nm* bump; **darse un t. en la cabeza** to bump one's head

topetear *vi* to butt

topetón = **topetazo**

tópico, -a 1 *adj* **(a)** *Med* topical **(b)** *(manido)* clichéd
2 *nm* cliché

> **Falso amigo**: El sustantivo inglés **topic** no es la traducción del español **tópico**. En inglés **topic** significa "tema, asunto".

topillo *nm* pine vole

topless ['toples] *nm inv* **(a)** *(práctica)* topless sunbathing; **en t.** topless; **hacer t., ponerse en t.** to go topless **(b)** *(bar)* topless bar

topo *nm* **(a)** *(animal)* mole **(b)** *(infiltrado)* mole **(c)** *Esp (lunar en tela)* polka dot; **una falda de topos** a polka-dot skirt **(d)** *Fam (ciego)* **es un t.** he's as blind as a bat **(e)** *Imprenta* bullet **(f)** *Andes (alfiler)* large pin **(g)** *Col (pendiente)* ear stud

topocho, -a *adj Ven* chubby, plump

topografía *nf* topography ▸▸ ***t. aérea*** aerial surveying

topográfico, -a *adj* topographical

topógrafo, -a *nm,f* topographer

topolino *nm Anticuado* platform shoe

topología *nf* topology

toponimia *nf* **(a)** *(nombres)* place names **(b)** *(ciencia)* toponymy

toponímico, -a 1 *adj* toponymic; **estudio t.** place-name study, *Espec* toponymic study
2 *nm (topónimo)* place name, *Espec* toponym

topónimo *nm* place name

toque 1 *ver* **tocar**
2 *nm* **(a)** *(golpe)* knock; **dio unos toques en la puerta** she knocked on the door; **jugar al primer t.** *(en fútbol)* to play one-touch soccer
(b) *(detalle, retoque)* touch; **el t. femenino** the feminine touch; **dar los últimos toques a algo** to put the finishing touches to sth
(c) *Fam (aviso)* **dar un t. a alguien** *(llamar)* to give sb a shout; *(llamar la atención)* to talk to sb, to have a few words with sb; **si te enteras de algo, dame un t.** if you hear anything, give me a shout ▸▸ ***t. de atención*** warning; **le dio un t. de atención por llegar tarde** she had a word with him about coming in late
(d) *(sonido) (de campana)* chime; *(de tambor)* beat; *(de sirena)* blast ▸▸ ***t. de diana*** reveille; ***t. de difuntos*** *(con campanas)* death knell; ***t. de queda*** curfew; ***t. de retreta*** last post

toquetear *Fam* 1 *vt (manosear) (cosa)* to fiddle with; *(persona)* to fondle
2 *vi (sobar)* to fiddle about

toqueteo *nm (a cosa)* fiddling; *(a persona)* fondling

toquilla *nf* shawl

tora *nf (libro)* Torah

torácico, -a *adj* thoracic

torada *nf* herd of bulls

toral 1 *adj* **(a)** *(arco)* main **(b)** *Méx (tema, avance)* major, significant
2 *nm (arco)* main arch

tórax *nm inv* thorax; **una radiografía de t.** a chest X-ray

torbellino *nm* **(a)** *(remolino) (de aire)* whirlwind; *(de agua)* whirlpool; *(de polvo)* dustcloud **(b)** *(mezcla confusa) (de actividad, emociones)* whirlwind; **su vida es un t.** her life is a whirlwind of activity **(c)** *(persona inquieta)* whirlwind; **es un t. de energías** she is a bundle of energy

torcaz *adj* **paloma t.** ringdove, wood pigeon

torcedura *nf* **(a)** *(torsión)* twist **(b)** *(esguince)* sprain

torcer [15] 1 *vt* **(a)** *(retorcer) (cuerpo, cuerda)* to twist; **ime vas a t. el brazo!** you're twisting my arm!; EXPR **t. el gesto** to pull a face
(b) *(doblar) (aguja, alambre)* to bend
(c) *(girar)* to turn; **torció la cabeza** she turned her head
(d) *(desviar)* **t. la vista** to look away; **t. el curso de los acontecimientos** to divert *o* change the course of events
(e) *(persona)* to corrupt
2 *vi (girar)* to turn; **el camino tuerce a la izquierda** the road turns to the left; **al llegar al cruce tuerce a la derecha** when you get to the crossroads, turn right
3 **torcerse** *vpr* **(a)** *(retorcerse) (cuerpo, cuerda)* to twist; **torcerse el tobillo** to twist one's ankle
(b) *(doblarse) (aguja, alambre)* to bend
(c) *(no quedar derecho)* **me tuerzo al andar/escribir** I can't walk/write in a straight line; **se ha torcido el cuadro** the painting's not straight
(d) *(ir mal) (esperanzas, negocios, día)* to go wrong; *(persona)* to go astray; **por si se tuercen las cosas** in case things go wrong

torcida *nf Dep* = Brazilian soccer fans

torcido, -a *adj* **(a)** *(no derecho) (cuello, cable)* twisted; *(nariz)* bent; **llevas la corbata torcida** your tie's not straight; **ese cuadro está t.** that picture's not straight; **la rueda de la bicicleta está torcida** the bicycle wheel is bent; **te ha salido un nueve t.** that nine has come out a bit crooked; **me miró con el gesto t.** she frowned at me
(b) *(doblado) (clavo, alambre)* bent
(c) *(retorcido) (intención)* twisted; *(interpretación)* mistaken
(d) *Guat (desafortunado)* unfortunate

torcijón *nm* stomach cramp

tordillo, -a 1 *adj* dappled, dapple-grey
2 *nm,f* dapple-grey

tordo, -a 1 *adj* dappled
2 *nm,f (caballo)* dapple
3 *nm* **(a)** *(pájaro)* thrush **(b)** *Arg, CAm, Chile (estornino)* starling

toreador, -ora *nm,f* bullfighter

torear 1 *vt* **(a)** *(toro)* to fight **(b)** *Fam (eludir)* to dodge; **siempre está toreando el tráfico** he's always dodging in and out of the traffic; **lleva meses toreando a Hacienda** he's been dodging the tax inspector for months **(c)** *Fam (provocar)* **t. a alguien** to mess sb about; **iése a mí no me torea!** I'm not going to let him mess me about *o* around!
2 *vi (torero)* to fight bulls; **toreó con arte** he gave a very skilful display of bullfighting

toreo *nm* bullfighting

torera *nf* **(a)** *(prenda)* bolero (jacket); EXPR **saltarse algo a la t.** to flout sth **(b)** *ver también* **torero**

torería *nf* **(a)** *(toreros)* bullfighters **(b)** *(orgullo)* pride

torero, -a 1 *adj (gesto, actitud)* haughty
2 *nm,f* bullfighter

toril *nm* bullpen *(in bullring)*

torillo *nm* little button quail

torio *nm Quím* thorium

torito *nm* (a) *RP (insecto)* rhinoceros beetle (b) *Ecuad (flor)* = variety of orchid (c) *Chile (sombrajo)* awning (d) *Cuba (pez)* horned boxfish *o* trunkfish

tormenta *nf* (a) *(en la atmósfera)* storm; *Fig* **esperar a que pase la t.** to wait until things have calmed down; EXPR **fue una t. en un vaso de agua** it was *Br* a storm in a teacup *o US* a tempest in a teapot ►► ***t. de arena*** sandstorm; ***t. eléctrica*** electrical storm; ***t. de ideas*** brainstorming session; ***t. magnética*** magnetic storm; ***t. de nieve*** snowstorm; ***t. de polvo*** dust storm; ***t. de verano*** summer storm

(b) *(avalancha) (de cambios, críticas)* storm; **aquella decisión desató una t. de protestas** that decision unleashed a storm of protest; **recibió una t. de felicitaciones** she was deluged *o* showered with congratulations

(c) *(crisis)* storm; **la t. desatada por su dimisión** the storm unleashed by her resignation; **la situación ha desatado una pequeña t. diplomática** the situation has sparked a minor diplomatic storm *o* row ►► *Fin* ***t. monetaria*** monetary crisis

tormento *nm* (a) *(dolor físico)* torment, agony

(b) *(angustia)* torment, anguish; **el t. de un amor no correspondido** the torment *o* anguish of unrequited love; **después de varios días de t., conseguí quitarme de encima de mi tío** after several agonising days, I managed to get rid *o Br* shot of my uncle; **ser un t.** *(persona)* to be a torment; *(cosa)* to be torture

(c) *(torture)* torture; **fue sometido a t.** he was subjected to torture

tormentoso, -a *adj* (a) *(cielo, día)* stormy (b) *(relación)* stormy; *(época)* troubled, turbulent

torna *nf (vuelta)* return; EXPR **volver las tornas** to turn the tables; EXPR **se han vuelto las tornas** the boot is on the other foot

tornadizo, -a *adj* fickle

tornado *nm* tornado

tornamesa *nm o nf Chile, Méx* record deck, turntable

tornar *Literario* **1** *vt* (a) *(convertir)* to make; **los celos lo tornaron insoportable** jealousy made him unbearable; **t. algo en algo** to turn sth into sth; **los estudiantes tornaron el encuentro en un grito de protesta** the students turned the meeting into a noisy protest (b) *(devolver)* to return

2 *vi* (a) *(regresar)* to return (b) *(volver a hacer)* **t. a hacer algo** to do sth again

3 tornarse *vpr* (a) *(volverse)* to turn; **el cielo se tornó gris** the sky turned grey; **su expresión se tornó grave** her expression *o* face became serious (b) *(convertirse)* **tornarse en** to turn into; **su alegría se tornó en estupor** his delight turned to astonishment

tornasol *nm* (a) *(girasol)* sunflower (b) *(reflejo)* sheen; **los tornasoles de la tela** the sheen of the fabric (c) *Quím* litmus; **papel de t.** litmus paper

tornasolado, -a *adj (color, reflejo)* iridescent; *(seda)* shot

torneado, -a 1 *adj* (a) *(madera)* turned (b) *(brazos, piernas)* shapely

2 *nm (de madera)* turning

tornear *vt* to turn

torneo *nm* (a) *(en deportes, naipes)* tournament, *US* tourney ►► *Antes* ***el T. de las Cinco Naciones*** *(en rugby)* the Five Nations (Championship); ***el T. de las Seis Naciones*** *(en rugby)* the Six Nations (Championship) (b) *(medieval)* tournament

tornero, -a *nm,f (con madera)* lathe operator

tornillería *nf* (a) *(tornillos)* screws (b) *(técnica)* screw manufacturing

tornillo *nm* (a) *(con punta)* screw; *(con tuerca)* bolt; EXPR **apretar los tornillos a alguien** to put the screws on sb; EXPR *Fam* **le falta un t.** he has a screw loose ►► ***t. de banco*** vice (b) *Fam (beso)* French kiss

torniquete *nm* (a) *Med* tourniquet (b) *(en entrada)* turnstile

torniscón *nm Fam* (a) *(pellizco)* pinch (b) *(bofetada)* slap in the face

torno 1 *nm* (a) *(de dentista)* drill (b) *(de alfarero)* (potter's) wheel (c) *(de carpintero)* lathe ►► ***t. de banco*** vice (d) *(para pesos)* winch

2 en torno a *loc prep* (a) *(alrededor de)* around, round; **el cordón policial en t. al edificio** the police cordon around *o* round the building; **la familia se reunía en t. al televisor** the family gathered round *o* around the television

(b) *(acerca de)* **la polémica en t. a esta decisión** the controversy surrounding this decision; **el misterio que gira en t. a su muerte** the mystery surrounding her death; **el debate giró en t. al tema del euro** the debate revolved around the subject of the euro

(c) *(aproximadamente)* around, about; **la tasa de desempleo se sitúa en t. al 10 por ciento** unemployment stands at around 10 percent; **ocurrió en t. a finales de siglo** it happened somewhere around the turn of the century

toro *nm* (a) *(animal)* bull; EXPR **agarrar** *o Esp* **coger el t. por los cuernos** to take the bull by the horns; EXPR **estar hecho un t., ser como un t.** to be built like a house *o* tank; EXPR **ver los toros desde la barrera** to watch from the wings; EXPR **nos va a pillar el t.** we're going to be late; EXPR **a t. pasado** with hindsight ►► ***t. bravo*** fighting bull; ***t. de lidia*** fighting bull; ***t. mecánico*** bucking bronco; ***T. Sentado*** *(jefe indio)* Sitting Bull

(b) *(lidia)* **los toros** bullfighting; **ir a los toros** to go to a bullfight

(c) *Geom* torus

(d) *(carretilla elevadora)* forklift truck

(e) *Cuba (pez)* horned boxfish *o* trunkfish

toronja *nf* grapefruit

toronjil *nm* lemon balm

toronjo *nm (árbol)* grapefruit (tree)

Toronto *n* Toronto

torpe *adj* (a) *(sin destreza) (persona)* clumsy; *(dedos, andares)* clumsy, awkward; **sus movimientos son torpes** her movements are clumsy; **escrito en torpes trazos infantiles** written with clumsy childish handwriting; **t. con las manos** *(que rompe las cosas) esp Br* ham-fisted, *US* ham-handed; *(que deja caer las cosas)* butter-fingered; **con los años estoy t. ya** I'm getting clumsy as I get older; **es muy t. en dibujo** he's not very good at drawing; **es muy t.** *Esp* **conduciendo** *o Am* **manejando** he's a terrible driver

(b) *(sin tacto) (gestos, palabras, comportamiento)* clumsy

(c) *(sin inteligencia)* slow, dim-witted

torpedear *vt* (a) *(embarcación)* to torpedo (b) *(iniciativa, proyecto)* to torpedo

torpedero, -a 1 *adj* **lancha torpedera** torpedo boat

2 *nm* torpedo boat

torpedo *nm* (a) *(proyectil)* torpedo (b) *(pez)* electric ray

torpemente *adv* (a) *(moverse, escribir)* clumsily, awkwardly (b) *(actuar, hablar)* clumsily

torpeza *nf* (a) *(falta de destreza)* clumsiness (b) *(falta de tacto)* clumsiness; **tuvimos problemas por su t. al llevar el tema** we had problems because of her clumsy handling of the issue (c) *(acción inconveniente)* **fue una t. hacerlo/decirlo** it was a clumsy thing to do/say; **cometer una t.** to make a blunder (d) *(falta de inteligencia)* slowness

torpor *nm* torpor, sluggishness

torrado *nm* toasted chickpea

torrar 1 *vt* to roast

2 torrarse *vpr Fam* to be roasting

torre *nf* (a) *(en fortaleza, castillo, iglesia)* tower; *(que sobresale de una muralla)* turret; *(en punta afilada)* spire ►► ***t. albarrana*** bastion, flanking tower; ***la T. de Babel*** the Tower of Babel; ***t. del homenaje*** keep; ***t. de marfil*** ivory tower; ***t. del vigía*** *(de observación)* observation tower

(b) *(estructura) (de alta tensión)* pylon; *(transmisora, de teléfono móvil)* mast ►► ***t. de control*** control tower; ***t. de perforación*** drilling rig, oil derrick; ***t. de refrigeración*** cooling tower; ***t. del reloj*** clock tower

(c) *(en ajedrez)* rook, castle

(d) *Informát* tower (computer)

(e) *(vivienda)* **t. (de apartamentos)** high-rise (apartment) block, *Br* tower block; **una t. de 15 pisos** a 15-storey block

(f) *Esp (casa)* detached house *(with garden)*

torrefacción *nf* roasting

torrefacto, -a *adj* dark-roast, high-roast; **café t.** dark-roast *o* high-roast coffee

torreja *nf* (a) *Am (dulce)* French toast *(sweetened)* (b) *Perú (buñuelo)* fritter (c) *Chile (rodaja)* slice

torrencial *adj* torrential

torrencialmente *adv* **llueve t.** there is torrential rain

torrente *nm* (a) *(de agua)* torrent ►► ***t. sanguíneo*** bloodstream (b) *(de gente, palabras)* stream, flood; *(de dinero, energía)* masses; **las nuevas normas han dado lugar a un t. de críticas** the new rules have provoked a flood of criticism; **es un t. de vitalidad** he is bursting with vitality

torrentera *nf* (a) *(cauce)* watercourse, gully (b) *(torrente)* torrent

torrentoso, -a *adj* (a) *(torrencial)* torrential (b) *Am (impetuoso)* fast-flowing

torreón *nm* large fortified tower

torrero, -a *nm,f (de faro)* lighthouse keeper

torreta *nf* (a) *(para armas)* turret (b) *(eléctrica)* pylon

torrezno *nm* = chunk of fried bacon

tórrido, -a *adj* (**a**) *(clima, zona)* torrid (**b**) *(verano, tarde)* sweltering, torrid

torrija *nf* French toast *(sweetened)*

torsión *nf* (**a**) *(del cuerpo, brazo)* twist, twisting (**b**) *Tec* torsion

torso *nm* torso

torta *nf* (**a**) *Esp (de harina)* = flat, round plain cake; EXPR *Fam* **ni t.** *(nada)* not a thing; **no veo ni t.** I can't see a thing; EXPR *Fam* **nos costó la t. un pan** it cost us an arm and a leg
(**b**) *CSur, Ven (dulce)* cake; EXPR *RP Fam* **le salió una t. de plata** it cost him an arm and a leg ►► ***t. de cumpleaños*** birthday cake; ***t. helada*** ice cream gâteau
(**c**) *Andes, CAm, Carib, RP (salada)* pie ►► ***t. pascualina*** spinach and egg pie
(**d**) *Méx (sandwich)* filled roll
(**e**) *Méx (tortilla)* flat omelette, frittata; ***t. de huevos*** plain omelette
(**f**) *RP* ***t. frita*** doughnut-shaped fritter
(**g**) *Fam (bofetada)* slap (in the face); **dar** *o* **pegar una t. a alguien** to slap sb (in the face)
(**h**) *Fam (golpe, accidente)* thump; **darse** *o* **pegarse una t.** *(al caer)* to bang oneself; *(con el coche)* to have a smash; *Fig* **había tortas para entrar** people were fighting to get in

tortada *nf (pastel)* = type of meat and egg pie

tortazo *nm Fam* (**a**) *(bofetón)* slap (in the face); **dar** *o* **pegar un t. a alguien** to slap sb (in the face); **liarse a tortazos** to come to blows (**b**) *(accidental) (golpe)* thump, wallop; *(en vehículo)* smash-up; **darse** *o* **pegarse un t.** to give oneself a thump; *(en vehículo)* to have a smash; **se dieron un t. en la carretera de Guadalajara** they had a smash-up on the road to Guadalajara

tortear *vt Méx muy Fam (manosear)* to feel up

tortellini [torte'lini] *nm* tortellini

tortería *nf Méx* sandwich shop, *US* luncheonette

torticeramente *adv* dishonestly

torticero, -a *adj* underhand; **métodos torticeros** underhand methods

tortícolis *nf inv* **tener t.** to have a stiff neck, to have a crick in one's neck

tortilla *nf* (**a**) *(de huevo)* omelette; **una t. de espárragos** an asparagus omelette; EXPR **hacer algo t.** to smash sth up; EXPR **hacerse t.** to get smashed up; EXPR **dar la vuelta a la t.** to turn everything upside down; **la crisis financiera dio la vuelta a la t.** the financial crisis turned everything upside down; EXPR **se ha dado la vuelta la t., se ha vuelto la t.** the boot is on the other foot ►► ***t. (a la) española*** Spanish *o* potato omelette; *Esp* ***t. (a la) francesa*** French *o* plain omelette; *Esp* ***t. paisana*** = omelette made with potatoes, vegetables and chorizo; *Am* ***t. de papas*** Spanish *o* potato omelette; ***t. de patatas*** Spanish *o* potato omelette
(**b**) *(de maíz)* tortilla, = thin maize pancake

tortillera *nf* (**a**) *muy Fam* dyke, lezzy (**b**) *ver también* **tortillero**

tortillería *nf* = shop selling (corn) tortillas

tortillero, -a *nm,f* (**a**) *(vendedor)* tortilla seller (**b**) *(fabricante)* tortilla maker

tortita *nf* (**a**) *(alimento)* small pancake (**b**) *(juego)* **hacer tortitas** ≃ to play pat-a-cake

tórtola *nf* (**a**) *(ave)* turtledove ►► ***t. turca*** collared dove (**b**) *ver también* **tórtolo**

tortolito, -a *nm,f* (**a**) *Fam (enamorado)* lovebird; **están como dos tortolitos** they're like two lovebirds (**b**) *(inexperto)* novice

tórtolo, -a *nm,f Fam (enamorado)* lovebird

tortuga *nf* (**a**) *(animal) (terrestre)* tortoise, *US* turtle; *(marina)* turtle; *(fluvial)* terrapin; EXPR **ser una t.** *(ser lento)* to be a snail; EXPR **ir a paso de t.** to go at a snail's pace (**b**) *Urug (pan)* bun

tortuguismo *nm CAm, Méx* (**a**) *(actitud)* slowness, inertia (**b**) *(medida de presión) Br* go-slow, *US* slowdown

tortuosamente *adv* deviously

tortuosidad *nf* (**a**) *(de camino)* tortuousness, windiness (**b**) *(de método, mente)* deviousness; *(de relaciones)* tortuousness; **la t. de las relaciones entre ambos países** the tortuousness of relations between the two countries

tortuoso, -a *adj* (**a**) *(camino)* tortuous, winding (**b**) *(método, mente)* devious; *(relaciones)* tortuous

tortura *nf* (**a**) *(física)* torture; **métodos de t.** torture methods, methods of torture (**b**) *(angustia)* torture; **la espera fue una t.** the wait was torture; **¡este tráfico es una t.!** this traffic is a nightmare!

torturado, -a *nm,f* torture victim

torturador, -ora 1 *adj* torturing
2 *nm,f* torturer

torturar 1 *vt* (**a**) *(físicamente)* to torture (**b**) *(angustiar)* to torture, to torment; **no me tortures más y dímelo** stop torturing me, just tell me; **la torturaba pensar en dónde estaría su hijo** she was tortured *o* tormented by the thought of where her son might be
2 torturarse *vpr* to torture oneself

torunda *nf (de algodón)* swab

torvamente *adv* fiercely

torvisco *nm* spurge flax

torvo, -a *adj* fierce

torzamos *etc ver* **torcer**

tos *nf* cough; **el niño tiene t.** the child has a cough; **me dio la t.** I started coughing; EXPR *Méx Fam* **hacerla de t.** to be difficult *o* awkward ►► ***t. ferina*** whooping cough; ***t. perruna*** hacking cough; ***t. seca*** dry cough

toscamente *adv* (**a**) *(hacer, confeccionar)* crudely (**b**) *(comportarse)* roughly, coarsely

toscano, -a 1 *adj* Tuscan
2 *nm,f* Tuscan
3 *nm RP* cigar

tosco, -a *adj* (**a**) *(acabado, herramienta)* crude (**b**) *(persona, modales)* rough, coarse

toser *vi* to cough; EXPR **no hay quien le tosa** *(no acepta críticas)* he won't listen to a word of criticism; *(no tiene rival)* he has no rivals, he is unbeatable

tosferina *nf* whooping cough

tósigo *nm* poison

tosquedad *nf* (**a**) *(de objeto)* crudeness (**b**) *(de persona, modales)* roughness

tostada *nf* (**a**) *(de pan)* **una t.** a piece of toast; **¿quieres tostadas?** would you like some toast?; **tostadas con mantequilla** buttered toast (**b**) *Méx (de tortilla)* tostada, = flat fried tortilla; EXPR *Méx Fam* **¡me lleva la t.!** it gets my goat!

tostadero *nm* (**a**) *(de café)* roaster (**b**) *(lugar caluroso)* oven; **mi pueblo en verano es un t.** it's like an oven in my village in summer

tostado, -a 1 *adj* (**a**) *(pan)* toasted; *(almendras, café)* roasted (**b**) *(color)* brownish (**c**) *(piel)* tanned (**d**) *Ven Fam (persona)* crazy, nuts
2 *nm* (**a**) *(de café)* roasting (**b**) *Arg (sándwich)* toasted sandwich

tostador *nm*, **tostadora** *nf* toaster

tostar [64] **1** *vt* (**a**) *(dorar, calentar) (pan)* to toast; *(café, almendras)* to roast; *(carne)* to brown (**b**) *(broncear)* to tan
2 tostarse *vpr* (**a**) *(broncearse)* to get brown; **tostarse al sol** to sunbathe (**b**) *Fam (de calor)* to be boiling (hot)

tostón *nm* (**a**) *Fam (rollo, aburrimiento)* bore, drag; **este libro es un t.** this book is a drag *o* bore; **dar el t. a alguien** to pester sb, to go on and on at sb (**b**) *Fam (persona molesta)* pain; **¡qué t. de niño!** that child's a real pain! (**c**) *(de pan)* crouton (**d**) *(cochinillo)* roast sucking pig (**e**) *Carib (de plátano)* fried plantain chip

total 1 *adj* (**a**) *(cifra, coste, gasto)* total; **el importe t. de las inversiones** the total amount of the investments (**b**) *(confianza, rechazo, ruptura)* total, complete; **actúa con t. libertad** she acts completely freely, she has complete freedom of action; **su influencia en ellos es t.** he has overwhelming influence over them (**c**) *Fam (fantástico)* fab, *Br* brill
2 *nm* (**a**) *(suma)* total; **el t. de visitantes del museo alcanzó los tres millones** the total number of visitors to the museum reached three million; **me da un t. de 580** I make it 580 ►► *Cont* ***t. actualizado*** running total (**b**) *(totalidad, conjunto)* whole; **el t. del grupo** the whole group; **en t.** in total, in all; **nos costó 200 dólares en t.** it cost us 200 dollars in total *o* all; **en t. fuimos más de treinta personas** in total there were more than thirty of us
3 *adv* (**a**) *(en resumen)* basically, in a word; **t., que me marché** so anyway, I left; **t., que te has quedado sin trabajo, ¿no?** basically, you're out of a job, then? (**b**) *(en realidad)* anyway; **t., ¿qué más da?** what difference does it make anyway?; **llévatelo, t. ¿para qué lo quiero yo?** take it, what good is it to me, after all?

totalidad *nf* **la t. de: la t. del presupuesto** the entire budget; **tendrán acceso a la t. del sistema** they will have access to the entire *o* whole system; **la práctica t. de la cámara votó a favor** virtually the whole house voted in favour; **la t. de los profesores** all (of) the teachers; **en su t.** in its entirety; **desconocemos el asunto en su t.** we know absolutely nothing about the matter; **los accionistas son italianos en su t.** all the shareholders are Italian

totalitario, -a, totalitarista *adj* totalitarian

totalitarismo *nm* totalitarianism

totalizador, -ora *adj* all-encompassing, totalizing

totalizar [14] *vt (puntos)* to obtain, to score; **el equipo totalizó 70 goles en la temporada** the team notched up 70 goals during the season

totalmente *adv* totally, completely; **el país ha cambiado t. en los últimos años** the country has changed completely in the last few years; **una publicación t. gratuita** a completely free publication; **es t. imposible** it's totally impossible; **¿crees que ganaremos? – t.** do you think we'll win? – definitely *o* absolutely

tótem (*pl* **tótems** *o* **tótemes**) *nm* totem

totémico, -a *adj* totemic

totemismo *nm* totemism

totogol *nm Col, CRica* = gambling game involving betting on the results of soccer matches, *Br* ≃ football pools

totopo, totoposte *nm CAm, Méx* tortilla chip

totora *nf Andes, RP* totora reed

totoral *nm Andes, RP* totora reed marsh

totovía *nf* woodlark

totuma, tutuma *nf Am* calabash, gourd

totumo *nm Am* calabash tree

Tour [tur] *nm (carrera ciclista)* **el T. (de Francia)** the Tour (de France)

tour [tur] (*pl* **tours**) *nm* (**a**) *(gira, viaje)* tour; **hacer un t.** to go on *o* do a tour ►► ***t. operador*** tour operator (**b**) ***t. de force*** tour de force

tournedós [turne'ðo] *nm inv* tournedos

tournée [tur'ne] *nf* tour; **estar de t.** to be on tour

toxemia *nf Med* toxaemia

toxicidad *nf* toxicity

tóxico, -a 1 *adj* toxic, poisonous
2 *nm* poison

toxicodependiente 1 *adj* drug-dependent
2 *nmf* drug dependent (person)

toxicología *nf* toxicology

toxicológico, -a *adj* toxicological

toxicólogo, -a *nm,f* toxicologist

toxicomanía *nf* drug addiction

toxicómano, -a 1 *adj* addicted to drugs; **su hijo t.** their drug addict son
2 *nm,f* drug addict

toxina *nf* toxin ►► ***t. botulínica*** botulin

toxoplasmosis *nm Med* toxoplasmosis

tozudez *nf* stubbornness

tozudo, -a 1 *adj* stubborn
2 *nm,f* stubborn person; **ser un t.** to be stubborn

traba *nf* (**a**) *(obstáculo)* obstacle; **poner trabas a alguien** to put obstacles in sb's way; **necesito trabajar sin trabas de ningún tipo** I need to be able to work without any kind of constraints (**b**) *(para coche)* chock (**c**) *(de mesa)* crosspiece (**d**) *RP (seguro)* bolt (**e**) *RP* ***t. de corbata*** tie-pin

trabado, -a *adj* (**a**) *(unido) (salsa)* smooth; *(discurso)* coherent (**b**) *(atascado)* jammed (**c**) *RP (asegurado)* locked (**d**) *RP Fam (por drogas, alcohol)* **estar t.** to be wrecked *o Br* off one's face (**e**) *Gram (sílaba)* ending in a consonant

trabajado, -a *adj* (**a**) *(obra)* well-crafted; *(plan, proyecto)* carefully thought out; **la novela tiene un estilo muy t.** the novel has a highly wrought *o* polished style (**b**) *(músculo)* developed

trabajador, -ora 1 *adj* hard-working; **es muy t.** he's a hard worker, he works hard
2 *nm,f* worker ►► ***t. autónomo*** self-employed person; ***t. cualificado*** skilled worker; ***t. por cuenta ajena*** employee; ***t. por cuenta propia*** self-employed person; ***t. manual*** manual worker; ***t. social*** social worker; ***t. a tiempo parcial*** part-timer, part-time worker
3 *nm Chile (ave)* heron

TRABAJAR 1 *vi* (**a**) *(tener un empleo)* to work; **no trabajes tanto** you shouldn't work so hard; **t. a tiempo parcial/completo** to work part time/full time; **¿de qué trabaja?** what does she do (for a living)?; **trabaja de** *o* **como taxista** he's a taxi driver, he works as a taxi driver; **t. de autónomo** to be self-employed; **t. de voluntario** to do voluntary work; **t. en una empresa** to work for a firm; **trabaja en personal** she works in personnel; **trabaja para una multinacional** she works for a multinational; **t. por horas** to work by the hour; **t. por cuenta propia/ajena** to be self-employed/an employee; *Am* **t. afuera** to work outside the home; *Am* **t. en casa** to work at *o* from home
(**b**) *(realizar una tarea)* to work; **tiene que t. más si quiere aprobar** she has to work harder if she wants to pass; **ponerse a t.** to get to work; **está trabajando en un nuevo guión** he's working on a new script; **trabajamos mucho con empresas japonesas** we do a lot of business with Japanese companies
(**c**) *(actor, actriz)* to act; **trabajaba en "Vértigo"** she was in "Vertigo"; **¡qué bien trabajan todos!** the acting is really good!
(**d**) *(funcionar)* to work; **la central nuclear trabaja ya a pleno rendimiento** the nuclear power station is now operating at maximum capacity; **los pulmones son los que trabajan** it demands a lot of your lungs; **hacer t. una máquina** to load a machine; **hacer t. un músculo** to exercise a muscle
2 *vt* (**a**) *(hierro, barro, madera, cuero)* to work; *(la tierra, el campo)* to work; *(masa)* to knead
(**b**) *(vender) (producto, género, marca)* to sell, to stock; **sólo trabajamos esta marca** we only sell *o* stock this brand
(**c**) *(mejorar)* to work on *o* at; **debes t. la pronunciación** you need to work on *o* at your pronunciation; **t. los músculos** to build up one's muscles
(**d**) *Fam (convencer)* **t. a alguien (para que haga algo)** to work on sb (to get them to do sth)
3 **trabajarse** *vpr Fam* (**a**) *(intentar lograr)* to work for; **el puesto que ocupa se lo ha trabajado** she has worked hard for her current job
(**b**) *(convencer)* **trabajarse a alguien (para que haga algo)** to work on sb (to get them to do sth); **si te lo trabajas un poco te dejará el dinero** if you work on him a bit he'll lend you the money

---

TRABAJO *nm* (**a**) *(tarea, actividad, práctica)* work; **tengo mucho t. que hacer** I've got a lot of work to do; **una casa tan grande da mucho t.** a big house like that is a lot of work; **uno de los últimos trabajos de Diego Rivera** one of Diego Rivera's last works; **recibió un Óscar por su t. en "Cabaret"** she received an Oscar for (her performance in) "Cabaret"; **¡buen t.!** good work!; **hacer un buen t.** to do a good job; EXPR **ser un t. de chinos** *(minucioso)* to be a fiddly *o* finicky job; *(pesado)* to be hard work ►► ***t. de campo*** fieldwork; ***t. de* o *en equipo*** teamwork; ***t. físico*** physical work, manual labour; ***trabajos forzados* o *forzosos*** hard labour; ***t. intelectual*** intellectual work; ***t. manual*** manual labour; ***trabajos manuales*** *(en el colegio)* arts and crafts; ***t. remunerado*** paid work; ***t. social*** social work; ***t. sucio*** dirty work; ***t. temporal*** temporary work; ***t. por turnos*** shiftwork; ***t. voluntario*** voluntary work
(**b**) *(empleo)* job; **buscar/encontrar t.** to look for/find work *o* a job; **no tener t., estar sin t.** to be out of work; **me he quedado sin t.** I've been left without a job, I'm out of work; **tener un t. fijo** to have a permanent job
(**c**) *(lugar)* work; **en el t.** at work; **ir al t.** to go to work; **¿quieres que pase a recogerte al t.?** do you want me to pick you up from work?
(**d**) *(escrito) (por estudiante)* essay, paper; **hacer un t. sobre algo/alguien** to write an essay on sth/sb
(**e**) *(esfuerzo)* effort; **lograron sacar el armario con mucho t.** they managed to remove the wardrobe, but not without a lot of effort *o* but it was no easy task; **costar mucho t. (a alguien)** to take (sb) a lot of effort; **me cuesta mucho t. levantarme por las mañanas** I find it a real struggle getting up in the morning; **cuesta t. admitir que uno se ha equivocado** it's not easy to admit that you're wrong; **tomarse el t. de hacer algo** to go to *o* take the trouble of doing sth
(**f**) *Econ & Pol* labour
(**g**) *Fís* work
(**h**) *Literario* **trabajos** *(apuros)* hardships; **pasar trabajos** to suffer hardships

---

trabajoadicto, -a *nm,f* workaholic

trabajosamente *adv* laboriously; **el anciano se metió t. en el coche** the old man laboriously manoeuvred himself into the car; **lucharon t. por liberar a los detenidos** they fought tirelessly for the prisoners' release

trabajoso, -a *adj* (**a**) *(difícil)* laborious, difficult; **un proceso más t.** a more laborious process (**b**) *Col (exigente)* demanding

trabalenguas *nm inv* tongue twister

trabar 1 *vt* (**a**) *(unir) (palabras, ideas)* to join; **t. varios argumentos** to tie several arguments together; **un discurso bien trabado** a well-constructed speech
(**b**) *(iniciar) (conversación, amistad)* to strike up; **trabaron amistad en 1987** they became friends in 1987; **el acuerdo trabado entre ambos países** the agreement established between the two countries
(**c**) *(salsa)* to thicken
(**d**) *(sujetar) (en general)* to immobilize; *(puerta, ventana) (abierta)* to wedge open; *(cerrada)* to wedge shut; *(preso)* to shackle; **troncos**

de madera trabados entre sí tree trunks lashed together
(**e**) *RP (con cerrojo)* to bolt; *(con llave)* to lock; *(con tranca)* to bar
(**f**) *(obstaculizar)* to obstruct, to hinder; **las negociaciones quedaron trabadas** the negotiations became deadlocked
2 trabarse *vpr* (**a**) *(enredarse)* to get tangled; **la cuerda se trabó en unas ramas** the rope got tangled in some branches (**b**) *(atascarse) (puerta, cerrojo)* to jam, to get jammed (**c**) *(espesarse) (salsa)* to thicken (**d**) *(al hablar)* to stutter; **se le trabó la lengua** he tripped over his tongue (**e**) *RP Fam (por drogas, alcohol)* to get fuddled

trabazón *nf* (**a**) *(unión)* assembly (**b**) *(de salsa)* thickening (**c**) *(conexión)* link, connection; **le falta t. al argumento de la obra** the plot is disjointed *o* doesn't hang together

trabe *nf* beam, joist

trabilla *nf (de pantalón)* belt loop

trabucar 1 *vt* to mix up
2 trabucarse *vpr* (**a**) *(persona) (liarse)* to get things mixed up; *(al hablar)* to stutter; **se le trabucó la lengua** he tripped over his tongue (**b**) *(cosas, fechas)* to get mixed up

trabuco *nm (arma de fuego)* blunderbuss

traca *nf* string of firecrackers; EXPR *Fam* **de t.: una caída de t.** a spectacular fall

trácala *nf Méx, Ven Fam* trick

tracalada *nf Col, Méx* crowd

tracalear *vi Méx, Ven Fam* to trick, to diddle

tracalero, -a *Méx, Ven Fam* **1** *adj* cheating
2 *nm,f* cheat

tracción *nf* (**a**) *(de vehículo)* **vehículo de t. animal** vehicle drawn by an animal ►► ***t. a las cuatro ruedas*** four-wheel drive; ***t. delantera*** front-wheel drive; ***t. trasera*** rear-wheel drive (**b**) *Tec (fuerza)* traction

trace *etc ver* **trazar**

tracería *nf Arquit* tracery

tracio, -a *Hist* **1** *adj* Thracian
2 *nm,f* Thracian

tracoma *nm* trachoma

tracto *nm* tract ►► ***t. digestivo*** digestive tract; ***t. intestinal*** intestinal tract; ***t. urinario*** urinary tract

tractocamión *nm Méx Br* articulated lorry, *US* semitrailer

tractor *nm* tractor ►► ***t. oruga*** caterpillar tractor

tractorada *nf* tractor protest

tractorista *nmf* tractor driver

tradescantia *nf* wandering Jew, spiderwort

tradición *nf* tradition; **es t. vestirse de negro para ir a un entierro** it is the tradition *o* it is traditional to wear black for a funeral; **se hace por t.** it's done *o* people do it out of tradition ►► ***t. escrita*** written tradition; ***t. oral*** oral tradition

tradicional *adj* traditional; **como es ya t. en cada partido de fútbol** as has become traditional at every soccer game

tradicionalismo *nm* traditionalism

tradicionalista 1 *adj* traditionalist
2 *nmf* traditionalist

tradicionalmente *adv* traditionally

trading ['treiðin] *nm Bolsa* trading

traducción *nf* translation ►► ***t. automática*** machine translation; ***t. directa*** translation into one's own language; ***t. inversa*** translation out of one's own language; ***t. simultánea*** simultaneous translation

traducible *adj* translatable

traducir [18] **1** *vt* (**a**) *(a otro idioma)* to translate; **t. algo del alemán al castellano** to translate sth from German into Spanish (**b**) *(expresar)* to express, to convey; **una actitud corporal que traduce aplomo y seguridad** a posture that conveys composure and self-confidence
2 *vi* to translate (**de/a** from/into)
3 traducirse *vpr* (**a**) *(a otro idioma)* to be translated (**por** by *o* as) (**b**) **traducirse en** *(ocasionar)* to translate into; **la subida de la inflación se traduce en una pérdida de poder adquisitivo** the rise in inflation translates into a loss of purchasing power

traductor, -ora 1 *adj* translating
2 *nm,f* translator ►► ***t. jurado*** *o* *RP* ***público*** = translator qualified to work in court and translate legal documents

traductorado *nm RP* degree in translation

TRAER [68] **1** *vt* (**a**) *(llevar de un lugar a otro)* to bring; **no traigan diccionario al examen** don't bring a dictionary into the exam; **trae a tus amigos** bring your friends (along); **voy a t. los libros a casa** I'm going to take the books home; **me trajo un recuerdo de París** she brought me a souvenir (back) from Paris; **tráiganos otra botella de vino, por favor** could we have *o* could you bring us another bottle of wine, please?; **nos trajeron del aeropuerto al hotel en coche** they took us from the airport to the hotel by car, they drove us from the airport to the hotel; **el buen tiempo trajo muchos turistas este año** the good weather brought a lot of tourists (with it) this year; **¿qué te trae por aquí/por Bogotá?** what brings you here/to Bogotá?
(**b**) *(llevar encima, consigo)* to carry; **traía una pistola** he was carrying a gun, he had a gun on him; **¿qué traes ahí?** what have you got there?; **traigo un cansancio enorme** I'm extremely tired
(**c**) *(llevar puesto)* to wear; **traía un traje nuevo** he was wearing a new suit
(**d**) *(contener)* to have; **trae un artículo interesante** it has an interesting article in it; **¿qué trae ese sobre?** what's in that envelope?
(**e**) *(provocar) (ruina, pobreza, enfermedades)* to bring; *(consecuencias)* to carry, to have; *(cambios)* to bring about; **esto trajo muchos problemas** this caused a lot of problems; **me trajo suerte** it brought me luck; **aquella decisión trajo como consecuencia la caída de la monarquía** that decision led to the fall of the monarchy; **traerá consigo una bajada de precios** it will lead to *o* mean a drop in prices
(**f**) *Fam Informát* to download
(**g**) *Fam (en un estado determinado)* **este tipo me trae frito/loco** that guy is being such a pain/is driving me up the wall
2 *vi* **¡trae!** bring *o* give it here!; **¡trae!, yo te lo arreglo** bring it here! I'll fix it for you
3 traerse *vpr* (**a**) *(llevar con uno)* to bring (along); **se trajo un cuaderno/a unos amigos** she brought (along) a notebook/some friends; EXPR *muy Fam* **me la trae floja** I couldn't give a shit *o Br* toss
(**b**) *Fam (tramar)* **me pregunto qué se traerán (entre manos) esos dos** I wonder what those two are up to
(**c**) EXPR *Fam* **traérselas** *(trabajo, asunto, persona)* to be a real handful; **este niño se las trae** that kid is a real handful; **tiene un carácter que se las trae** she has a right old temperament
(**d**) *Fam Informát* to download

traficante *nmf (de drogas, armas)* trafficker, dealer ►► ***t. de armas*** arms dealer *o* trafficker; ***t. de drogas*** drugs dealer *o* trafficker; ***t. de esclavos*** slave trader

traficar [60] *vi (comerciar)* to traffic, to deal (**en/con** in); **jóvenes que trafican con drogas** young people who deal in drugs; **mafias que trafican con seres humanos** criminal gangs who traffic *o* trade in human beings

tráfico *nm* (**a**) *(de vehículos)* traffic; **una carretera cortada al t.** a road closed to traffic; **infracción de t.** driving offence ►► ***t. aéreo*** air traffic; ***t. marítimo*** maritime traffic; ***t. rodado*** road traffic
(**b**) *(comercio)* traffic; **luchar contra el t. ilegal de inmigrantes** to fight the illegal trade in immigrants ►► ***t. de armas*** arms dealing *o* trafficking; ***t. de drogas*** drug dealing *o* trafficking; ***el t. de esclavos*** the slave trade; ***t. de estupefacientes*** drug trafficking *o* dealing; ***t. de influencias*** influence peddling, *US* graft; ***t. sexual*** sex trafficking

traga *RP Fam* **1** *adj* **ser t.** to be *Br* swotty *o US* a grind
2 *nmf Br* swot, *US* grind

tragaderas *nfpl* EXPR *Fam* **tener (buenas) t.** *(comer mucho)* to eat like a horse; *(ser crédulo)* to swallow anything; *(ser tolerante)* to be able to put up with a lot

tragadero *nm Fam* (**a**) *(sumidero)* plughole (**b**) *(garganta)* throat, gullet

tragafuegos *nm inv* fire-eater

trágala *nm* (**a**) *Hist (canción)* = early 19th century satirical anti-government song (**b**) *(imposición)* imposition; **tuvimos que aceptar el t. de la dirección** we had to accept the solution imposed by management

tragaldabas *nmf inv Fam* greedy guts, human dustbin

tragaluz *nm* skylight

tragamonedas, traganíqueles *nf inv Am Fam* slot machine, one-armed bandit

tragaperras *nf inv Fam* slot machine, one armed-bandit

tragar [38] **1** *vt* (**a**) *(ingerir)* to swallow; **tragó la pastilla con dificultad** she swallowed the pill with difficulty; **t. agua** *(en mar, piscina)* to swallow water; **t. saliva** to swallow, to gulp
(**b**) *Fam (creer)* to swallow; **creo que no ha tragado la historia** I don't think she swallowed the story; **le hicieron t. el cuento** they managed to make him believe the story
(**c**) *(absorber)* to swallow up; **ese desagüe traga el agua sucia** the dirty water goes down that drain
(**d**) *Fam (soportar)* to put up with; **¡lo que hay que t. por los hijos!** the things you have to put up with for the sake of the children!; **yo**

creo que Ana no me traga I don't think Ana likes me; **no la puedo t., no la trago** I can't stand her

(e) *Fam (consumir mucho)* to devour, to guzzle; **¡cómo traga gasolina este coche!** *Br* this car really guzzles petrol!, *US* this car is a real gas-guzzler!

(f) *RP Fam (estudiar)* to bone up on, *Br* to swot up (on)

2 *vi* (a) *(ingerir)* to swallow; **me cuesta t.** I can't swallow properly, I have trouble swallowing

(b) *Fam (comer)* **¡cómo traga tu primo!** your cousin can certainly put it away!

(c) *Fam (creerse)* **¿crees que tragará?** do you think he'll swallow it?

(d) *Fam (acceder)* to give in; **ahora no lo acepta pero acabará tragando** she refuses to accept it right now, but she'll give in in the end

(e) *(absorber)* **esa alcantarilla no traga** that drain's blocked

(f) *RP Fam (estudiar) Br* to swot, *US* to grind

3 **tragarse** *vpr* (a) *(ingerir)* to swallow; **me he tragado una espina** I've swallowed a bone; **el mar se tragó la lancha** the sea swallowed up *o* engulfed the boat

(b) *Fam (comer)* to guzzle; **se tragó tres huevos fritos** he guzzled three fried eggs; **se tragó a Caperucita entera** he swallowed Little Red Riding Hood whole

(c) *(contener) (lágrimas)* to choke back; **se tragó su orgullo y pidió perdón** he swallowed his pride and apologized; **se tuvo que t. sus propias palabras** he had to eat his words

(d) *(consumir)* to swallow up, to devour; **el proyecto se tragó casi todo el presupuesto** the project swallowed up *o* devoured almost the entire budget

(e) *Fam (creerse)* to swallow; **¿crees que se lo tragará?** do you think she'll swallow it?; EXPR **se tragó el cuento** he swallowed the story; EXPR *Ven* **t. un paquete** to fall for it, to be taken in

(f) *Fam (sufrir) (discurso, espectáculo)* to sit through; **me tragué un programa horrible** I sat through an awful programme; **se traga lo que le echen en la tele** he'll watch whatever's on the TV

(g) *Fam (soportarse)* **no se tragan** they can't stand each other

tragasables *nmf inv* sword-swallower

tragedia *nf* (a) *(obra)* tragedy (b) *(género)* tragedy; **la t. griega** Greek tragedy (c) *(hecho desgraciado)* tragedy; **el viaje acabó en t.** the trip ended in tragedy; **la t. personal que se esconde tras su aparente felicidad** the personal tragedy that lies concealed beneath his happy exterior

trágicamente *adv* tragically

trágico, -a 1 *adj* (a) *(obra, género)* tragic (b) *(suceso, final, consecuencias)* tragic; *Fam* **ponerse t.** to be melodramatic

2 *nm,f* tragedian

tragicomedia *nf* tragicomedy

tragicómico, -a *adj* tragicomic

trago *nm* (a) *(de líquido)* drink; **¿me das un trago de cerveza?** could I have a drink *o* sip of your beer?; **beber algo a grandes tragos** to gulp sth down; **sólo un traguito** just a sip; **de un t.** in one gulp

(b) *Fam (copa)* drink; **echar** *o* **tomar un t.** to have a quick drink

(c) *Am Fam* **el t.** *(la bebida)* the booze; **le gusta demasiado el t.** he's too fond of the booze

(d) *(situación difícil) Fam* **ser un t. para alguien** to be tough on sb; *Fam* **pasar un mal t.** to have a tough time of it; **pasó muy mal t. con el accidente de su hijo** she went through a very tough time over her son's accident; **le tocó el t. amargo de anunciar los despidos** he had the unpleasant task of announcing the redundancies; **su ausencia resultaría un t. amargo para todos** his absence would be a bitter blow for all of them

tragón, -ona *Fam* 1 *adj* greedy

2 *nm,f* **¡tu primo es un t.!** your cousin can certainly put it away!

trague *etc ver* **tragar**

traición *nf* (a) *(infidelidad)* betrayal; **claudicar sería una t. a nuestros camaradas** if we gave in, we would be betraying our comrades; **le mataron a t.** he was treacherously murdered; **temía un disparo a t.** he was afraid of being shot by someone on his own side (b) *(contra el Estado)* treason; **alta t.** high treason

traicionar *vt* (a) *(amigo, ideal, país)* to betray; **tuvo que t. a sus aliados para salvarse** she had to betray her allies to save her own life; **no quiero t. la confianza que puso en mí** I do not want to betray the trust he placed in me; **se siente traicionado por los políticos** he feels betrayed by politicians

(b) *(provocar fracaso)* **a veces le traiciona su timidez** his shyness sometimes gets the better of him

(c) *(descubrir)* to give away; **su acento/aquel gesto lo traicionó** his accent/that gesture gave him away; **lo traicionó el subconsciente** his subconscious gave him away

traicionero, -a 1 *adj* (a) *(aliado, amigo)* treacherous; **eso fue un golpe t.** that was a bit below the belt (b) *(tiempo, corriente)* treacherous, dangerous; **las montañas pueden ser muy traicioneras** mountains can be very treacherous (c) *(gesto, lágrimas)* revealing, telltale

2 *nm,f* traitor

traída *nf* bringing, carrying ►► ***t. de agua*** water supply

traído, -a *adj* worn-out; EXPR **t. y llevado** much discussed, well-worn; **el tan t. y llevado acuerdo entre socialistas y liberales** the much discussed agreement between the socialists and the liberals

traidor, -ora 1 *adj* (a) *(persona) (contra amigos, camaradas)* treacherous; *(contra el Estado)* treasonous (b) *(tiempo, corriente)* treacherous, dangerous (c) *(gesto, lágrimas)* revealing, telltale

2 *nm,f* traitor; **es un t. a la patria** he's a traitor to his country

traigo *etc ver* **traer**

trail *nm Dep* trails riding

tráiler *(pl* **tráilers***) nm* (a) *Cine* trailer (b) *(remolque)* trailer; *(camión) Br* articulated lorry, *US* semitrailer (c) *Méx (casa rodante) Br* caravan, *US* trailer ►► ***t. park*** *Br* caravan site, *US* trailer park

trailero, -a *nm,f CAm, Méx Br* lorry driver, *US* truck driver

traílla *nf (correa)* leash

traína *nf* purse seine (net)

trainera *nf* = small boat, for fishing or rowing in races

traje 1 *ver* **traer**

2 *nm* (a) *(con chaqueta)* suit; *(de una pieza)* dress ►► ***t. de astronauta*** space suit; ***t. de baño*** *(para hombre o mujer)* swimming costume, bathing suit *o Br* costume; *(para hombre)* swimming trunks; *(para mujer)* swimsuit; ***t. de bucear*** *o* ***buceo*** wet suit; ***t. de chaqueta*** woman's two-piece suit; ***t. espacial*** space suit; ***t. de etiqueta*** evening dress; ***t. de faralaes*** = typical Andalusian frilly dress; ***un t. de gala*** a dress suit; **llevar t. de gala** to wear formal dress; ***t. de hombre rana*** diving suit; ***t. de luces*** matador's outfit; ***t. de noche*** evening dress; ***t. de novia*** wedding dress; ***t. pantalón*** trouser suit; ***t. sastre*** woman's two-piece suit; ***t. de submarinismo*** wet suit

(b) *(regional, disfraz)* costume ►► ***t. de época*** period dress; ***t. típico*** *(de un país)* national dress

(c) *(ropa)* clothes ►► ***t. de calle*** business suit, *Br* lounge suit; ***t. de diario*** everyday clothes; ***t. de paisano*** *(de militar)* civilian clothes; *(de policía)* plain clothes

trajeado, -a *adj* (a) *(con traje)* **ir t.** to wear a suit; **bien t.** well-dressed (b) *Fam (arreglado)* spruced up

trajear 1 *vt* to dress in a suit

2 **trajearse** *vpr* to wear a suit

trajera *etc ver* **traer**

trajín *nm (ajetreo)* bustle; **esta mañana hay mucho t. en la oficina** it's a bit hectic in the office this morning; **el t. de los días de mercado** the hustle and bustle of market days; **con tanto t., se me olvidó** it was all so hectic that I forgot

trajinar 1 *vi Fam Fig* to bustle about; **me paso todo el día trajinando** I spend all day rushing around

2 **trajinarse** *vpr muy Fam* **trajinarse a alguien** *(sexualmente) Br* to roger sb, *US* to bone sb

tralla *nf* (a) *(látigo)* whip (b) *Fam (presión)* **dar** *o* **meter t. a alguien** *(presionar)* to pester sb; *(criticar)* to slate sb

trallazo *nm* (a) *(chasquido)* lash, crack (b) *Fam (reprensión)* tongue-lashing (c) *Fam Dep (disparo)* screamer, powerful shot

trama *nf* (a) *(de historia)* plot ►► ***t. argumental*** plot, storyline (b) *(confabulación)* plot, intrigue; **una oscura t. financiera** a shadowy web of financial intrigue (c) *(de hilos)* weft (d) *Imprenta* screen (e) *(de pantalla)* raster (f) *(papel adhesivo)* screen tone

tramado *nm Imprenta* halftone grid

tramar *vt* (a) *(planear)* to plot; *(complot)* to hatch; **un plan tramado por sus enemigos** a plot hatched by her enemies; **estar tramando algo** to be up to something (b) *(hilo)* to weave

tramitación *nf* processing; **se ha aplazado la t. de la extradición** the extradition process has been delayed; **está en t.** it is being processed

tramitar *vt* (a) *(sujeto: autoridades) (pasaporte, solicitud)* to process; **tardaron tres días en t. el crédito** it took them three days to do all the paperwork for the loan; **me están tramitando la renovación de la licencia** my application for a new licence is being processed

(b) *(sujeto: solicitante)* to be in the process of applying for; **estamos tramitando el divorcio** we are in the process of getting a divorce

trámite *nm* (a) *(gestión)* formal step; **sólo quedan un par de trámites más** there are only a few formalities left; **los trámites burocráticos** the bureaucratic procedures; **los trámites burocráticos para crear**

una empresa the paperwork involved in setting up a company; **agilizar/iniciar los trámites** to speed up/to start the bureaucratic process; **estaban en trámites de separación** they were in the process of getting separated; **de t.** *(acto, asunto)* routine; **es sólo cuestión de t.** it's purely routine, it's just a formality

(**b**) *(tramitación)* processing; **admitir una denuncia a t.** to agree to consider a complaint; **el permiso de obras está pendiente de t.** a decision on the planning permission is pending; **por t. de urgencia** urgently

tramo *nm* (**a**) *(de carretera, ruta)* section, stretch; **el t. final de la carrera** the final stretch of the race

(**b**) *(de escalera)* flight (of stairs)

(**c**) *(de tarifa)* band; *(de edad)* bracket, band; **el t. de edad entre los 35 y 40 años** the 35-40 age bracket; **el t. superior del impuesto sobre la renta** the higher rate income tax band ►► *Bolsa* ***t. minorista*** retail tranche

tramontana *nf* tramontane, = cold, dry north wind in Catalonia and Majorca

tramoya *nf* (**a**) *Teatro* stage machinery (**b**) *(enredo)* intrigue

tramoyista *nmf* (**a**) *Teatro* stagehand (**b**) *(tramposo)* schemer

trampa *nf* (**a**) *(para cazar)* trap; **la t. del fuera de juego** *(en fútbol)* offside trap

(**b**) *(trampilla)* trapdoor

(**c**) *(engaño)* trick; **caer en la t.** to fall into the trap; **tender una t. (a alguien)** to set *o* lay a trap (for sb); EXPR **sin t. ni cartón: ha ganado el premio sin t. ni cartón** he won the prize fair and square; **en este espectáculo no hay t. ni cartón** everything you see in this show is for real

(**d**) *(en juegos)* **eso es t.** that's cheating; **hacer trampas** to cheat

(**e**) *(deuda)* debt

(**f**) *(en golf)* hazard

> **Falso amigo**: El sustantivo inglés **tramp** no es la traducción del español **trampa**. En inglés **tramp** significa "vagabundo", "fulana" o "carguero".

trampantojo *nm Arte* trompe-l'oeil

trampear *vi Fam* (**a**) *(estafar)* to scrounge money (**b**) *(ir tirando)* to struggle along

trampero, -a *nm,f* trapper

trampilla *nf (puerta)* trapdoor

trampolín *nm* (**a**) *(de piscina)* diving board; *(flexible)* springboard (**b**) *(en esquí)* ski jump (**c**) *(en gimnasia)* springboard (**d**) *(medio)* springboard; **le sirvió como t. para iniciar su carrera política** she used it as a springboard to launch her political career; **esa actuación fue su t. a la fama** that performance catapulted her to fame

> **Falso amigo**: El sustantivo inglés **trampoline** no es la traducción del español **trampolín**. En inglés **trampoline** significa "cama elástica".

trampolinista *nmf* diver

tramposo, -a **1** *adj* cheating; **no seas tan t.** don't be such a cheat

2 *nm,f* cheat

tranca *nf* (**a**) *(de puerta)* bar; **poner una t. en la puerta** to bar the door; EXPR *Fam* **a trancas y barrancas** with great difficulty; **terminó la carrera a trancas y barrancas** he finished his degree, but it was a struggle

(**b**) *(arma)* cudgel, stick

(**c**) *Fam (borrachera)* **agarrar una t.** to get plastered

(**d**) *Esp muy Fam (pene)* dong

(**e**) *Méx (en verja)* gate

(**f**) *Ven Fam (embotellamiento)* (traffic) jam

(**g**) *Ven Fam (discusión)* fuss, ruckus

trancar [60] **1** *vt* (**a**) *(puerta) (con barra)* to bar; *Am (con cerrojo)* to bolt

(**b**) *Am (frenar) (tránsito)* to block, to hold up; **los agricultores en manifestación trancaron la circulación hacia el este** the protesting farmers held up east-bound traffic; **si no tienes credencial, te trancan en la puerta** if you don't have a pass, you get stopped at the door; **si no pagas por fuera, te trancan el trámite** if you don't slip them a bribe, your application stays at the bottom of the pile

(**c**) *Am (atascar)* to jam; **hay un papel arrugado trancando la impresora** there's a crumpled piece of paper jamming the printer

2 trancarse *vpr Am* (**a**) *(atascarse) (máquina)* to jam, to get jammed; **la llave se trancó en la cerradura** the key stuck in the lock (**b**) *(detenerse) (proceso, actividad burocrática)* to be held up

trancazo *nm* (**a**) *(golpe)* blow (with a cudgel *o* stick) (**b**) *Fam (gripe)* bout of (the) flu

trance *nm* (**a**) *(situación crítica)* difficult situation; **ya había pasado por trances parecidos** she had already been through similar difficulties; **pasar por un mal t.** to go through a bad patch; **ahora se encuentra en el t. de tener que ayudar a un rival** now he finds himself in the position of having to help out a rival; EXPR **a todo t.** at all costs

(**b**) *(estado hipnótico)* trance; **entrar en t.** to go into a trance

(**c**) *(música)* trance

(**d**) *(proceso)* **en t. de: una cultura/lengua en t. de desaparición** a culture/language that is in the process of dying out; **en t. de muerte** on the point of death *o* dying

tranco *nm* stride; **llegó en dos trancos** he got there in a couple of strides

trancón *nm Col* traffic jam

tranque *nm CSur* reservoir

tranquera *nf* (**a**) *(estacada)* stockade, palisade (**b**) *Am (en alambrado)* gate

tranqui *interj Fam* don't worry!, cool it!

tranquilamente *adv* (**a**) *(con calma)* calmly; **piénsalo t.** take your time to think it over (**b**) *(con frescura)* coolly; **me lo dijo tan t.** he told me without batting an eyelid (**c**) *(sin dificultad)* easily; **me puedo comer tres hamburguesas t.** I can easily eat three hamburgers; **cuesta t. dos millones** it costs at least two million, it easily costs two million

tranquilidad *nf* (**a**) *(sosiego) (de lugar, calle, tarde, vida)* calm, peacefulness; *(de ambiente, tono de voz)* quietness, calmness; *(de mar)* calmness; *(de movimientos, paso)* unhurriedness, calmness; **¡qué t. se respira aquí!** it's so peaceful here!; **el presidente pidió t. a los ciudadanos** the President called on citizens to remain calm; **piénsalo con t.** take your time to think it over; **se tomó la noticia con mucha t.** she took the news very calmly

(**b**) *(falta de preocupaciones)* peace of mind; **para mayor t.** to be on the safe side; **para tu t.** to put your mind at rest

(**c**) *(de carácter)* calmness, calm

(**d**) *(despreocupación)* calm; **me extrañó la aparente t. con la que siguió su camino** I was surprised by how calmly she seemed to just carry on; **puedes llamar por teléfono con toda t.** please feel free to use the phone; **¿puedo servirme más? – ¡con toda t.!** can I have some more? – feel free!

(**e**) *(de conciencia)* clearness; **la t. que te da saber que has hecho lo que debías** the peace of mind you get from knowing you've done what you had to do

tranquilizador, -ora *adj (música, color)* soothing; *(influencia)* calming

tranquilizante **1** *adj* (**a**) *(música, color)* soothing; **no deja de ser t. que siga sin haber cambios en el estado del enfermo** it is reassuring, however, that the patient's condition has not changed (**b**) *(medicamento)* tranquilizing

2 *nm* tranquilizer

tranquilizar [14] **1** *vt* (**a**) *(calmar)* to calm (down); **una enfermera la tranquilizó** a nurse calmed her down; **me tranquiliza saber que está a salvo** it's a relief to know she's safe, I feel much better now I know she's safe (**b**) *(dar confianza a)* to reassure; **su presencia la tranquiliza** his presence reassures her *o* is reassuring to her

2 tranquilizarse *vpr* (**a**) *(calmarse)* to calm down; **¡tranquilízate!** calm down! (**b**) *(ganar confianza)* to feel reassured; **se tranquilizó al oírla llegar** he was relieved when he heard her arrive

tranquillo *nm Esp Fam* **coger el t. a algo** to get the knack of sth

tranquilo, -a *adj* (**a**) *(sosegado) (lugar, calle, tarde, vida)* quiet, peaceful; *(ambiente, tono de voz)* quiet, calm; *(mar)* calm; *(paso, movimientos)* unhurried; **pasé un día muy t. en casa** I had a very quiet *o* peaceful day at home; **es un barrio muy t.** it's a very quiet *o* peaceful neighbourhood; **en el pueblo duermo muy t.** I always sleep very peacefully in the village

(**b**) *(sin preocupaciones) (persona)* relaxed, calm; **iba t. a la entrevista** I went to the interview feeling calm; **prefiero vivir t.** I prefer the quiet life; **¡(tú) t.!** don't you worry!; **no estoy t. hasta que no llega a casa** I can't relax until she gets home; **por fin puedo respirar t.** at last I can breathe easily; EXPR **dejar a alguien t.** to leave sb alone

(**c**) *(por carácter)* calm; **es muy t.** he's very calm

(**d**) *(despreocupado)* **¿pero cómo es que estás tan t., sabiendo lo que está pasando?** how can you be so calm, knowing what's happening?; **lo escuchó y se quedó tan t.** he listened to it without batting an eyelid

(**e**) *(sin culpabilidad) (mente)* untroubled; *(conciencia)* clear; **tengo la conciencia tranquila** my conscience is clear

tranquis *adj inv Esp Fam* **it.! que no pasa nada** don't worry! there's no problem; **estamos aquí de t.** *o* **en plan t.** we're just taking it easy here

transa *nf Méx, RP Fam* deal

transacción *nf* **(a)** *Com* transaction ▸▸ ***t. bancaria*** bank transaction; ***t. comercial*** commercial transaction; ***t. electrónica*** electronic transaction **(b)** *Der* settlement (of action)

transalpino, -a, trasalpino, -a *adj* transalpine

transaminasa *nf Bioquím* transaminase

transandino, -a, trasandino, -a *adj* trans-Andean

transar *Fam* **1** *vi* **(a)** *Am (transigir)* to compromise, to give in; **a veces hay que t. en ciertos aspectos** sometimes you have to give way on certain issues **(b)** *Am (negociar)* to come to an arrangement, to reach a compromise **(c)** *RP (droga)* to deal

2 *vt (acciones)* to deal in, to trade

transatlántico, -a, trasatlántico, -a 1 *adj* transatlantic

2 *nm Náut* (ocean) liner

transbordador, trasbordador *nm* **(a)** *Náut* ferry **(b)** *Av* **t. (espacial)** space shuttle

transbordar, trasbordar *vi* to change (trains)

transbordo, trasbordo *nm* change; **hacer t.** to change (trains)

transcendencia, transcendental = **trascendencia, trascendental**

transceptor *nm* transceiver

transcontinental *adj* transcontinental

transcribir, trascribir *vt* **(a)** *(texto, conversación)* to transcribe **(b)** *Mús* to transcribe

transcripción, trascripción *nf* **(a)** *(de texto, conversación)* transcription ▸▸ ***t. de cintas*** transcription of cassette tapes; ***t. fonética*** phonetic transcription **(b)** *Mús* transcription

transcriptor, -ora, trascriptor, -ora 1 *nm,f (persona)* transcriber

2 *nm (aparato)* transcriber

transcrito, -a, *RP* **transcripto, -a, trascrito, -a** *adj* transcribed

transcurrido, -a, trascurrido, -a *adj (tiempo)* intervening; **durante los diez años transcurridos desde entonces** during the intervening ten years, during the ten years since (then); **transcurridos tres días...** three days later..., after three days...

transcurrir, trascurrir *vi* **(a)** *(tiempo)* to pass, to go by; **transcurrieron quince años hasta que volvieron a encontrarse** fifteen years went by *o* passed before they met again, they did not meet again until fifteen years later; **según transcurría el tiempo se iban calentando los ánimos** as time went by tempers started to fray

(b) *(ocurrir)* to take place, to happen; **la acción transcurre durante la guerra** the action takes place during the war; **la manifestación transcurrió sin incidentes** the demonstration went off *o* passed off without incident

transcurso, trascurso *nm* **(a)** *(paso de tiempo)* passing; **será necesario esperar al t. de tres años hasta tener resultados** it will be necessary to wait for three years before obtaining results; **con el t. del tiempo,...** with the passing of time,..., as time passes,...

(b) *(periodo de tiempo)* **en el t. de** in the course of; **todo sucedió en el t. de una tarde** it all happened in the course of a single afternoon; **durante el t. de la representación** during the course of the performance

transductor *nm Fís* transducer

transepto *nm Arquit* transept

transeúnte 1 *adj* passing

2 *nmf* **(a)** *(paseante)* passer-by **(b)** *(residente temporal)* temporary resident

transexual 1 *adj* transsexual

2 *nmf* transsexual

transexualidad *nf*, **transexualismo** *nm* transsexuality, transsexualism

transferencia, trasferencia *nf* **(a)** *(de datos, recursos, poderes)* transfer ▸▸ *Informát* ***t. de ficheros*** file transfer **(b)** *(de dinero)* transfer; **quiero hacer una t. de 1.000 euros a esta cuenta** I'd like to transfer 1,000 euros to this account ▸▸ ***t. bancaria*** credit transfer, (bank) draft; ***t. electrónica de fondos*** electronic funds transfer **(c)** *Psi* transference

transferible, trasferible *adj* **(a)** *(datos, derechos, recursos)* transferable **(b)** *(deportista)* transfer-listed; **ser t.** to be on the transfer list

transferir [63], **trasferir** [63] *vt* **(a)** *(datos, recursos, poderes)* to transfer **(b)** *Informát* to download

transfiguración, trasfiguración *nf* transfiguration

transfigurar, trasfigurar 1 *vt* to transfigure

2 transfigurarse *vpr* to become transfigured

transformacional *adj Ling* transformational

transformación, trasformación *nf* **(a)** *(en general)* transformation; **nuestra sociedad ha experimentado una profunda t.** our society has undergone a profound transformation; **la t. del deporte en un mercado del ocio** the transformation of sport into a leisure industry; **las industrias de t.** processing industries **(b)** *(en rugby)* conversion

transformador, -ora, trasformador, -ora 1 *adj* transforming

2 *nm Elec* transformer

transformar, trasformar 1 *vt* **(a)** *(convertir)* **t. algo (en)** to convert *o* turn sth (into); **un convento transformado en hotel** a convent converted into a hotel; **t. la ansiedad en energía positiva** to transform one's anxiety into constructive energy; **las penas lo han transformado en un alcohólico** his troubles have turned him into an alcoholic

(b) *(cambiar radicalmente)* to transform; **el turismo ha transformado a nuestro país** tourism has transformed our country

(c) *(en rugby)* to convert

(d) *(en fútbol)* **t. un penalty** to convert a penalty

2 transformarse *vpr* **(a)** *(convertirse)* **transformarse en algo** to turn into sth, to become sth; **el pañuelo se transformó en una paloma** the handkerchief turned into a dove; **el local se ha transformado en toda una institución** the place has become quite an institution; **la zona se ha transformado en un campo de batalla** the area has become a battleground

(b) *(cambiar radicalmente)* to be transformed; **con la oscuridad todo parece transformarse** when darkness falls everything seems changed *o* transformed; **en un año la jovencita se había transformado** in just one year the young girl had undergone a transformation

transformismo, trasformismo *nm* **(a)** *(teoría)* evolutionism **(b)** *(artístico)* **espectáculo de t.** quick-change act; *(de hombre en mujer)* drag act

transformista, trasformista 1 *nmf* quick-change artist

2 *nm* drag artist

transfronterizo, -a *adj* cross-border

tránsfuga, trásfuga *nmf* **(a)** *Pol* defector **(b)** *Am Fam Hum (sinvergüenza)* rascal

transfuguismo, trasfuguismo *nm Pol* defection *(to another party)*

transfundir, trasfundir 1 *vt* **(a)** *(líquido)* to transfuse; **le transfundieron un litro de sangre** they gave him a transfusion of a litre of blood **(b)** *Formal (noticia)* to spread

2 transfundirse *vpr Formal (noticia)* to spread

transfusión, trasfusión *nf* transfusion; **le hicieron una t. de sangre** *o* **sanguínea** they gave him a blood transfusion

transfusor, trasfusor *nm (aparato)* transfuser

transgénico, -a 1 *adj* transgenic; **alimentos transgénicos** genetically modified foods, GM foods

2 transgénicos *nmpl* GM foods

transgredir, trasgredir *vt* to transgress

transgresión, trasgresión *nf* transgression

transgresor, -ora, trasgresor, -ora *nm,f* transgressor

transiberiano *nm* trans-Siberian railway

transición *nf* transition; **un país en t.** a country in transition; **simplificar la t. a un nuevo sistema** to simplify the transition to a new system; **periodo de t.** transition *o* transitional period ▸▸ ***t. democrática*** transition to democracy

transido, -a *adj* stricken **(de** with); **t. de dolor** racked with pain; **t. de pena** grief-stricken

transigencia *nf* **(a)** *(espíritu negociador)* willingness to compromise **(b)** *(tolerancia)* tolerance

transigente *adj* **(a)** *(que cede)* willing to compromise **(b)** *(tolerante)* tolerant

transigir [24] *vi* **(a)** *(ceder)* to compromise **(en** on); **estoy dispuesto a t. en ese punto** I am willing to compromise on that point; **no pienso t.** I have no intention of giving in **(b)** *(ser tolerante)* to be tolerant **(con** with); **con tal de evitar discusiones transige con lo que sea** he'll put up with anything to avoid an argument

transistor *nm* **(a)** *Elec* transistor **(b)** *(radio)* transistor

transitable *adj (camino, sendero)* passable; *(carretera)* open to traffic; **la zona afectada por el corte de luz no está t.** the area affected by the power cut is closed to traffic

transitar *vi* to go (along); **los peatones/los vehículos transitan libremente por el centro** pedestrians/vehicles can move around the city centre quite freely

transitario, -a *nm,f Com* forwarding agent

transitividad *nf* transitivity

transitivo, -a *adj* transitive

tránsito *nm* (**a**) *(de vehículos)* traffic; **está cerrado el t. de vehículos** it is closed to traffic ►► ***t. rodado*** road traffic
(**b**) *(paso)* **el t. entre la Edad Media y el Renacimiento** the transition from the Middle Ages to the Renaissance; **es sólo un área de t.** it is just a transit area; **los extranjeros que están de t. en el país** foreigners who are in the country for a short time; **aviones en t. entre América y Europa** planes en route between America and Europe; **pasajeros en t. hacia Roma** *(en aeropuerto)* passengers with connecting flights to Rome
(**c**) *(movimiento)* movement; **facilita el t. intestinal** it facilitates bowel movement; **una calle de mucho t.** a busy street
(**d**) *Formal (muerte)* passing on; **pocos llorarán su t.** few will mourn her passing on

transitoriedad *nf* (**a**) *(de régimen, medida)* temporary nature (**b**) *(de la vida)* transience

transitorio, -a *adj* (**a**) *(régimen, medida)* transitional, interim; *(periodo)* transitional; *(residencia)* temporary; **una solución de carácter t.** a temporary solution; **el euro estuvo unos años en fase transitoria** the euro went through a transitional phase that lasted several years (**b**) *(pasajero)* transitory; **en esta vida transitoria** in this transitory *o* transient life

translación = **traslación**

translaticio = **traslaticio**

transliteración *nf* transliteration

transliterar *vt* to transliterate

translúcido, -a = **traslúcido**

translucir = **traslucir**

transmediterráneo, -a, trasmediterráneo, -a *adj* transmediterranean

transmigración *nf* transmigration

transmigrar *vi* to transmigrate

transmisible, trasmisible *adj* (**a**) *(enfermedad)* transmittable (**b**) *(título, posesiones)* transferrable

transmisión, trasmisión *nf* (**a**) *(de sonido, onda, movimiento)* transmission
(**b**) *(de señal, datos)* transmission; **una red de t. de datos** a data transmission network
(**c**) *(de noticias, mensaje)* passing on, conveying; **las dificultades de t. verbal de los sentimientos** the difficulties of conveying feelings in words
(**d**) *(de enfermedad, bacteria, virus)* transmission; **enfermedades de t. sexual** sexually transmitted diseases ►► ***t. del pensamiento*** telepathy
(**e**) *(programa)* broadcast; *(servicio)* broadcasting; **durante la t. del partido** while the game was being broadcast
(**f**) *(de derechos, poderes)* transfer ►► *Am* ***t. de mando*** transfer of power
(**g**) *Aut* transmission

transmisor, -ora, trasmisor, -ora 1 *adj* transmitting
2 *nm* transmitter

transmisor-receptor *nm* transceiver, walkie-talkie

transmitir, trasmitir 1 *vt* (**a**) *(sonido, onda, movimiento)* to transmit; **neuronas que transmiten mensajes sensoriales** neurons that transmit sensory data
(**b**) *(por radio, ordenador) (señal, datos)* to transmit, to send
(**c**) *(programa)* to broadcast; **t. un programa en directo** to broadcast a programme live
(**d**) *(mensaje, noticias, saludos)* to pass on, to convey; **ésas fueron las palabras que le transmitió su hermano** those were the words her brother conveyed to her
(**e**) *(enfermedad, bacteria, virus)* to transmit; *(optimismo, pesimismo, energía)* to convey, to communicate
(**f**) *(derechos, poderes)* to transfer
2 **transmitirse** *vpr (enfermedad)* to be transmitted

transmutable, trasmutable *adj* transmutable

transmutación, trasmutación *nf* transmutation

transmutar, trasmutar *vt* to transmute

transnacional, trasnacional 1 *adj* transnational
2 *nf* transnational (company)

transoceánico, -a *adj* transoceanic

transparencia, trasparencia *nf* (**a**) *(de líquido, material)* transparency
(**b**) *(de intenciones)* obviousness; *(de argumento)* clarity
(**c**) *(de elecciones, proceso)* openness, transparency; **es esencial mantener una absoluta t. en la gestión** it is essential that management be seen to be completely above-board; **garantizar la t. de los comicios** to guarantee fair elections; **falta de transparencia** lack of openness
(**d**) *(para retroproyector)* transparency
(**e**) *Cine* **transparencias** back projection
(**f**) *(tejido)* see-through fabric

transparentar, trasparentar 1 *vt (dejar ver)* to show
2 **transparentarse** *vpr* (**a**) *(ser transparente) (tela)* to be see-through; *(cristal, líquido)* to be transparent (**b**) *(verse)* to show through; **se transparentan sus intenciones/sentimientos** her intentions/feelings are obvious

transparente, trasparente 1 *adj* (**a**) *(líquido, material)* transparent; *(tela)* see-through; **una superficie t. a los rayos ultravioleta** a surface that is transparent to ultra-violet rays (**b**) *(intención, gesto)* clear (**c**) *(elecciones, proceso)* open, visibly fair; **negocios poco transparentes** murky business dealings
2 *nm* blind

transpirable, traspirable *adj* breathable

transpiración, traspiración *nf* (**a**) *(sudoración)* perspiration (**b**) *Bot* transpiration

transpirar, traspirar 1 *vi* (**a**) *(persona)* to perspire; *(material)* to breathe (**b**) *Bot* to transpire
2 *vt (exudar, exhalar)* to exude

transpirenaico, -a, traspirenaico, -a *adj* trans-Pyrenean

transplantar = **trasplantar**

transplante = **trasplante**

transponer = **trasponer**

transportable *adj* portable

transportación *nf Méx* transport, *US* transportation

transportador *nm* (**a**) *(para transportar)* ***t. aéreo*** cableway; ***t. de cinta*** conveyor belt (**b**) *(para medir ángulos)* protractor

transportar 1 *vt* (**a**) *(trasladar) (mercancías, pasajeros)* to transport; **transportaba una maleta en cada mano** he was carrying a suitcase in each hand; **esta música me transporta a la infancia** this music takes me back to my childhood (**b**) *(embelesar)* to captivate
2 **transportarse** *vpr (embelesarse)* to go into raptures

transporte *nm* transport, *US* transportation; **para el tratamiento y t. de residuos urbanos** for treating and transporting urban waste; **la empresa me paga los gastos de t.** the company pays my travel expenses; **mi medio de t. habitual** my usual means of transport; **empresas de t. por carretera** road transport companies, *Br* hauliers, *US* haulers; **carros de t. de tropas** troop carriers, armoured personnel carriers; **aviones de t. militar** military transport planes; **servicios de t. de viajeros** passenger transport services ►► ***t. aéreo*** air transport; ***t. blindado*** transport in armoured vehicles; ***t. por carretera*** road transport; ***t. colectivo*** public transport, *US* mass transit; ***t. marítimo*** maritime transport; ***t. de mercancías*** freight transport; ***t. público*** public transport, *US* mass transit; ***t. terrestre*** land transport; ***t. urgente*** courier service

transportista *nmf Com* carrier, shipper

transposición = **trasposición**

transpuesto, -a = **traspuesto**

transubstanciación, transustanciación *nf Rel* transubstantiation

transversal, trasversal 1 *adj* (**a**) *(línea)* transverse; **un corte t.** a cross section; **la calle t. a la Avenida de la Paz** the street that crosses the Avenida de la Paz (**b**) *Educ* **asignatura** *o* **materia t.** = underlying, value-based educational objective specified in the Spanish school curriculum
2 *nf* (**a**) *(calle)* **en la t. a la Avenida de la Paz** on the street that crosses the Avenida de la Paz (**b**) *Mat* transversal

transversalmente, trasversalmente *adv* crosswise

transverso, -a, trasverso, -a *adj* transverse

tranvía *nm Br* tram, *US* streetcar

Trapa *nf* **un monje de la T.** a Trappist monk

trapacear *vi* to be dishonest

trapacería *nf* **hacer trapacerías** to be dishonest

trapacero, -a *adj* dishonest, deceitful

trapajoso, -a *adj* (**a**) *(lengua)* clumsy, stumbling; *(pronunciación)* stumbling, halting (**b**) *(aspecto)* ragged

trápala 1 *nmf* (**a**) *(hablador)* chatterbox (**b**) *(embustero)* liar, cheat
2 *nf* (**a**) *(de gente)* racket, din (**b**) *Fam (embuste)* fib

trapalear *vi* (**a**) *Fam (mentir)* to fib (**b**) *(hablar mucho)* to chatter, to jabber

trapatiesta *nf Fam* racket, din

trape *nm Chile (cuerda)* woven cord

trapeador, -ora *nm,f Andes, CAm, Méx* mop

trapear *vt Andes, CAm, Méx (suelo)* to mop

trapecio 1 *adj Anat* **músculo t.** trapezius (muscle)
2 *nm* (**a**) *Geom Br* trapezium, *US* trapezoid (**b**) *(de gimnasia, circo)* trapeze (**c**) *Anat* trapezius

trapecista *nmf* trapeze artist

trapense 1 *adj* Trappist
2 *nmf* Trappist

trapería *nf (tienda)* old-clothes shop

trapero, -a 1 *adj CSur Fam (aficionado a la ropa)* clothes-mad, obsessed with clothes
2 *nm,f* (**a**) *(ropavejero) Br* rag-and-bone man, *US* junkman (**b**) *CSur Fam (aficionado a la ropa)* clothes horse, fashion nut

trapezoidal *adj* trapezoidal

trapezoide *nm Geom Br* trapezoid, *US* trapezium

trapiche *nm* (**a**) *(de aceituna)* olive press (**b**) *(de azúcar)* sugar mill

trapichear *vi Fam* to be on the fiddle; **t. con** to deal in, to peddle

trapicheo *nm Fam* (**a**) *(negocio sucio)* shady activity; **trapicheos** shady business; **se dedica al t. de droga** he deals drugs (**b**) *(tejemaneje)* scheme; **estoy harto de sus trapicheos** I'm sick of his scheming

trapichero, -a *nm,f Fam* peddler, dealer

trapillo: de trapillo *loc adv Fam* **vestir de t.** to wear any old thing

trapío *nm* (**a**) *(garbo)* grace, style; **una mujer de t.** a woman with style (**b**) *Taurom* good bearing

trapisonda *nf* (**a**) *(riña)* row, commotion (**b**) *(enredo)* scheme

trapisondear *vi* (**a**) *(reñir)* to kick up a row (**b**) *(liar, enredar)* to scheme

trapo 1 *nm* (**a**) *(trozo de tela)* rag; **una pelota de t.** a ball of cloth
(**b**) *(gamuza, bayeta)* cloth; **¿tienes un t. limpio?** have you got a clean cloth?; **con que pases un t. es suficiente** just give it a wipe, that'll be enough; EXPR *Fam* **estar hecho un t.** *(cansado)* to be shattered; EXPR *Fam* **como un t.: poner a alguien como un t.** to tear sb to pieces; **tratar a alguien como un t.** to treat sb like dirt; EXPR **entrar al t.** to go on the attack; **prefirió ir a la defensiva y no entrar al t.** he preferred to stay on the defensive rather than going on the attack; EXPR *Fam* **los trapos sucios: no empecemos a sacar los trapos sucios** let's not start washing our dirty linen in public; **no quiero que se saquen los trapos sucios (a relucir) en mi boda** I don't want people digging up old family quarrels at my wedding; **los trapos sucios se lavan en casa** you shouldn't wash your dirty linen in public; EXPR *Fam* **a todo t.** *(velocidad)* at full pelt; *(potencia)* (at) full blast ►► ***t. de cocina*** *Br* tea towel, *US* dish towel; *RP* ***t. de piso*** floor cloth; ***t. del polvo*** dust cloth, *Br* duster; ***t. de secar (los platos)*** *Br* tea towel, *US* dish towel
(**c**) *Taurom* cape
2 trapos *nmpl Fam (ropa)* clothes; **todo el día pensando en trapos** all day thinking about clothes

trapón *nm Méx (trapo)* dishcloth

tráquea *nf* windpipe, *Espec* trachea

traqueotomía *nf Med* tracheotomy

traquetear 1 *vi* (**a**) *(tren, carro)* to rattle (**b**) *(persona)* to bustle (around)
2 *vt* to shake

traqueteo *nm (de tren, carro)* rattling

tras *prep* (**a**) *(detrás de)* behind; **escondido t. unos matorrales** hidden behind some bushes
(**b**) *(después de)* after; **uno t. otro** one after the other; **día t. día** day after day; **t. unos momentos de silencio habló el juez** after a few moments' silence, the judge spoke; **t. decir esto, se marchó** after saying that, she left
(**c**) *(en pos de)* **andar t. algo** to be after sth; **se fue t. la gloria** he went in search of fame; **fue t. ella** he went after her
(**d**) *Fam (encima de)* **t. quedarse con todo, se enfada** she keeps the whole lot for herself and she still gets angry

trasalpino, -a = **transalpino**

trasandino, -a = **transandino**

trasatlántico, -a = **transatlántico**

trasbordador = **transbordador**

trasbordar = **transbordar**

trasbordo = **transbordo**

trascendencia, transcendencia *nf* importance, significance; **esta decisión tendrá una gran t.** this decision will be of major significance; **un tema de tanta t.** such an important issue

trascendental, transcendental *adj* (**a**) *(importante) (cambio, paso, hecho)* momentous; **un tema de t. importancia** a tremendously important issue; **estos hallazgos pueden ser trascendentales en el futuro** these discoveries may turn out to be exceptionally important in the future
(**b**) *(filosófico, elevado)* transcendental; *Fam* **ponerse t.** to wax philosophical
(**c**) *Filosofía* transcendental

trascendentalismo *nm* transcendentalism

trascendente, transcendente *adj* (**a**) *(importante)* momentous (**b**) *Filosofía* transcendent

trascender [66], **transcender** [66] **1** *vi* (**a**) *(noticia) (difundirse)* to become known; **la noticia trascendió a la prensa** the news leaked out to the press; **el enfermo, según trascendió ayer, se halla grave** the patient's condition, it emerged yesterday, is serious; **sólo ha trascendido que se prepara un desembarco** all we have heard so far is that a landing is being prepared; **que no trascienda** don't let on about it, don't let it get about
(**b**) *(efectos, consecuencias)* to spread (**a** to); **el cambio ha trascendido a amplias capas de la población** the change has spread to a large part of the population
(**c**) *(sobrepasar)* **t. de** to transcend, to go beyond; **un tema que trasciende del ámbito familiar** a subject that extends beyond the family circle
2 *vt (ir más allá de)* to go beyond, to transcend; **una costumbre que trasciende las fronteras** a custom that goes beyond national borders; **un problema que trascendió el ámbito nacional** a problem that went beyond the national level

trascendido *nm RP* leak

trascribir = **transcribir**

trascripción = **transcripción**

trascriptor, -ora = **transcriptor**

trascrito, -a = **transcrito**

trascurrido = **transcurrido**

trascurrir = **transcurrir**

trascurso = **transcurso**

trasegar [43] **1** *vt* (**a**) *(objetos, papeles)* to rummage about *o* amongst (**b**) *(bebida, líquido)* to decant (**c**) *Fam (beber)* to knock back
2 *vi Fam (beber)* to knock it back

trasera 1 *nf* rear
2 traseras *nfpl (de una casa)* back; **en las traseras de** at the back of, *US* in back of

trasero, -a 1 *adj (asiento)* back, rear; *(puerta) (de casa)* back, rear; *(de coche)* rear; *(patas)* hind, back
2 *nm* backside

trasferencia = **transferencia**

trasferible = **transferible**

trasferir = **transferir**

trasfiguración = **transfiguración**

trasfigurar = **transfigurar**

trasfondo *nm* (**a**) *(contexto)* background; **el t. histórico de la novela** the historical background of the novel (**b**) *(de palabras, intenciones)* undertone

trasformación = **transformación**

trasformador, -ora = **transformador**

trasformar = **transformar**

trasformismo = **transformismo**

trasformista = **transformista**

trásfuga = **tránsfuga**

trasfuguismo = **transfuguismo**

trasfundir = **transfundir**

trasfusión = **transfusión**

trasfusor = **transfusor**

trasgo *nm* goblin, imp

trasgredir = **transgredir**

trasgresión = **transgresión**

trasgresor, -ora = **transgresor**

trashumancia *nf* seasonal migration *(of livestock)*

trashumante *adj* seasonally migratory

trashumar *vi* to migrate seasonally

trasiego 1 *ver* **trasegar**
2 *nm* (**a**) *(de personas)* comings and goings; **hay un constante t. de enfermeros, médicos y visitas** there's a continual coming and going of nurses, doctors and visitors (**b**) *(de bebida, líquido)* decanting

trasiegue *etc ver* **trasegar**

traslación, translación *nf Astron* passage

trasladar 1 *vt* (**a**) *(desplazar) (objeto)* to move; *(herido)* to take, to move; *(detenido, sede)* to transfer, to move; **trasladamos los muebles a otra habitación** we moved the furniture to another room; **trasladaron su cuartel general a Túnez** they transferred *o* moved their headquarters to Tunis; **fue trasladada al hospital en una ambulancia** she was taken to hospital in an ambulance; **sus restos mortales fueron trasladados a su ciudad natal** his remains were transferred to his home town
(**b**) *(empleado, funcionario)* to transfer
(**c**) *(reunión, fecha)* to postpone, to move back
(**d**) *(petición, información)* to refer, to pass on
(**e**) *(reproducir)* **t. algo al papel** to transfer sth onto paper; **la novela que han trasladado ahora al cine** the novel which has now been transferred to the big screen
(**f**) *(traducir)* to translate
2 trasladarse *vpr* (**a**) *(mudarse)* to move; **me traslado de casa** I'm moving house (**b**) *(desplazarse)* to move, to shift; **las batallas comerciales se han trasladado a Internet** the battle for sales has moved over *o* shifted to the Internet

traslado *nm* (**a**) *(de objeto)* move; *(de sede)* move, transfer; **unas cajas se perdieron durante el t.** some boxes got lost during the move *o Br* removal; **una empresa de traslados** *Br* a removal company, *US* a moving firm; **se encargarán del t. de los muebles** they'll take charge of moving the furniture; **tras el t. de la capital de Bonn a Berlín** after the capital was moved *o* relocated from Bonn to Berlin
(**b**) *(de detenido)* transfer; **el t. de los heridos fue problemático** there were problems moving the wounded
(**c**) *(de empleado, funcionario)* transfer
(**d**) *(de petición, información)* **dar t. a una solicitud** to pass on *o* refer a petition
(**e**) *Der (copia) (de alegatos)* notice; *(de escrito)* copy

traslapar *vt* to overlap

traslúcido, -a, translúcido, -a *adj* translucent

traslucir [39], **translucir** [39] **1** *vt* to show, to reveal; **el entusiamo que traslucen sus declaraciones** the enthusiasm revealed by *o* that shines through her statements
2 *vi* **dejar t.: su expresión/comentario dejaba t. su pesimismo** her expression/remark revealed *o* betrayed her pessimism
3 traslucirse *vpr* (**a**) *(sentimiento, actitud)* to be revealed; **una visión crítica que no se trasluce en el texto** a critical vision that does not come out clearly in the text; **tras su sonrisa se trasluce una gran tristeza** a great sadness can be seen *o* detected behind his smile (**b**) *(ropa, tela)* to show through

trasluz *nm* **al t.** against the light; **lo miró al t.** she held it up *o* looked at it against the light

trasmallo *nm* trammel

trasmano: a trasmano *loc adv* out of the way; **la tienda me pilla muy a t.** the shop is completely out of my way

trasmediterráneo, -a = **transmediterráneo**

trasmisible = **transmisible**

trasmisión = **transmisión**

trasmisor, -ora = **transmisor**

trasmitir = **transmitir**

trasmutación = **transmutación**

trasmutar = **transmutar**

trasnacional = **transnacional**

trasnochada *nf* late night; **estoy cansadísima, llevo tres trasnochadas seguidas** I'm dead tired, I've had three late nights in a row

trasnochado, -a *adj* (**a**) *(teoría, ideas, costumbre)* outdated (**b**) *Andes (somnoliento)* sleepy

trasnochador, -ora 1 *adj* **ser muy t.** to be a night owl
2 *nm,f* night owl

trasnochar 1 *vi* to stay up late, to go to bed late
2 trasnocharse *vpr Andes* to stay up late; **me trasnoché leyendo ese libro** I stayed up late reading that book

trasnoche *nm CSur* (**a**) *(en cine)* late night movie (**b**) *(trasnochada)* late night

traspapelar 1 *vt (papeles, documentos)* to mislay, to misplace
2 traspapelarse *vpr* to get mislaid *o* misplaced

trasparencia = **transparencia**

trasparentar = **transparentar**

trasparente = **transparente**

traspasar *vt* (**a**) *(atravesar) (sujeto: puñal, bala)* to go through, to pierce; *(sujeto: líquido)* to soak through; **la bala le traspasó el muslo** the bullet went through his thigh; **la tinta traspasó el papel** the ink soaked through the paper; **el sudor le traspasaba la ropa** the sweat was soaking through his clothes
(**b**) *(pasar al otro lado de)* **t. la puerta** to go through the doorway; **t. una valla saltando** to jump over a fence; **no consiguió t. el muro de silencio que le rodeaba** she was unable to break through the wall of silence that surrounded her; **t. el umbral de los ochenta años** to enter one's ninth decade, to reach one's eighties
(**c**) *(exceder) (fronteras, límites)* to go beyond; **llegó a t. la barrera del millón de votos** she broke through the one-million-vote barrier
(**d**) *(transferir) (jugador, objeto)* to transfer; *(negocio)* to sell *(as a going concern)*; *(competencias)* to devolve; **se traspasa (negocio)** *(en cartel)* (business) for sale
(**e**) *(cambiar de sitio)* to move
(**f**) *(afectar mucho)* to devastate

> **Falso amigo**: El verbo inglés **to trespass** no es la traducción del español **traspasar**. En inglés **to trespass** significa "entrar sin autorización".

traspaso *nm* (**a**) *(transferencia) (de jugador)* transfer; *(de negocio)* sale (as a going concern) ▸▸ ***t. de competencias*** devolution (**b**) *(precio) (de jugador)* transfer fee; *(de negocio)* takeover fee

traspatio *nm Am (patio de atrás)* backyard

traspié *nm* (**a**) *(resbalón, tropiezo)* trip, stumble; **dar un t.** to trip (up), to stumble (**b**) *(error)* blunder, slip; **dar** *o* **tener un t.** to slip up, to make a mistake

traspiración = **transpiración**

traspirar = **transpirar**

traspirenaico, -a = **transpirenaico**

trasplantar, transplantar *vt* (**a**) *(órgano)* to transplant; **le han trasplantado el hígado** he's had a liver transplant (**b**) *(planta)* to transplant (**c**) *(sistema, ideas)* to transplant

trasplante, transplante *nm* (**a**) *(de órgano)* transplant ▸▸ ***t. de corazón*** heart transplant; ***t. de órganos*** organ transplant (**b**) *(de planta)* transplant

trasponer [50], **transponer** [50] **1** *vt* (**a**) *(cambiar el orden de) (letras, palabras)* to transpose (**b**) *(norma, directiva)* to transpose; **t. una directiva europea a la legislación española** to transpose a European directive into Spanish law (**c**) *(puerta, umbral)* to cross (**d**) *(sujeto: sol)* to disappear behind
2 trasponerse *vpr* (**a**) *(adormecerse)* to doze off (**b**) *(ocultarse)* to disappear

trasportín *nm* (**a**) *(de bicicleta) (rejilla)* (rear) rack; *(caja)* = box mounted on rear rack (**b**) *(asiento)* fold-down seat

trasposición, transposición *nf* transposition

traspuesto, -a, transpuesto, -a *adj (dormido)* **estar t.** to be dozing; **quedarse t.** to doze off

traspunte *nm Teatro* callboy

trasquilado, -a *adj* EXPR **salir t.** to come off badly

trasquiladura *nf* shearing

trasquilar *vt* (**a**) *(ovejas)* to shear (**b**) *(persona) Fam* **me trasquilaron (el pelo)** they gave me a terrible haircut

trasquilón *nm Fam* **hacerle un t. a alguien** to give sb a terrible haircut; **tener el pelo cortado a trasquilones** to have one's hair cut unevenly

trastabillar, trastabillear *vi* (**a**) *(al andar)* to stagger (**b**) *(al hablar)* to stumble over one's words

trastabillón *nm Am* slip, stumble

trastada *nf Fam* (**a**) *(travesura)* prank; **hacer trastadas** to play pranks (**b**) *(jugarreta)* dirty trick; **hacer una t. a alguien** to play a dirty trick on sb

trastazo *nm* bump, bang; **darse** *o* **pegarse un t.** to bang *o* bump oneself

traste *nm* (a) *Mús* fret (b) *Andes, CAm, Carib, Méx (utensilio de cocina)* cooking utensil; **fregar los trastes** to wash the dishes (c) *CSur Fam (trasero)* bottom, *US* tush (d) EXPR **dar al t. con algo** to ruin sth; **irse al t.** to fall through

trasteado *nm Mús* frets

trastear 1 *vi* (a) *(revolver)* to move things around; **¿quién ha estado trasteando en mi armario?** who's been rummaging around in my wardrobe? (b) *(hacer travesuras)* to play pranks
2 *vt* (a) *Taurom* to tease with the red cape (b) *Mús* to fret (c) *Fam (persona)* to manage, to manipulate

trastero, -a 1 *adj* **cuarto t.** junk *o* lumber room
2 *nm* (a) *(depósito)* junk *o* lumber room (b) *Méx (aparador)* sideboard

trastienda *nf* (a) *(de tienda)* backroom (b) *(de persona)* **tiene mucha t.** he's a wily one, you have to watch yourself with him

trasto *nm* (a) *(utensilio inútil)* piece of junk; **trastos** junk; **la habitación está llena de trastos** the room is full of junk; EXPR **tirarse los trastos a la cabeza** to have a flaming row
(b) *Fam (persona traviesa)* menace, nuisance; **pero ¡qué t. estás hecho!** you're a right little menace, aren't you!
(c) *Fam (persona inútil)* **ser un t. (viejo)** to be no use to anyone
(d) *Fam* **trastos** *(pertenencias, equipo)* things, stuff; **llévate tus trastos** take your stuff with you

trastocar [69] 1 *vt* (a) *(planes, expectativas, costumbres)* to disrupt, to upset; **este retraso me trastoca todos los planes** this delay has disrupted *o* upset all my plans (b) *(enloquecer)* **t. a alguien** to drive sb mad, to unbalance sb's mind
2 **trastocarse** *vpr (enloquecer)* to go mad

trastornado, -a *adj (loco, desequilibrado)* disturbed, unbalanced; **esa mujer lo tiene t.** he's crazy *o* nuts about that woman

trastornar 1 *vt* (a) *(volver loco)* to drive mad (b) *(inquietar)* to worry, to trouble (c) *(alterar) (planes, orden)* to disrupt; *(vida)* to turn upside down; **el cambio de trabajo lo trastornó mucho** the change of job caused him a lot of disruption (d) *(estómago)* to upset
2 **trastornarse** *vpr (volverse loco)* to go mad

trastorno *nm* (a) *(mental, físico)* disorder; *(digestivo)* upset ▸▸ ***t. alimentario*** *o* ***alimenticio*** eating disorder; ***t. depresivo*** depressive disorder; ***t. obsesivo-compulsivo*** obsessive-compulsive disorder
(b) *(alteración)* **causar trastornos** *o* **un t.** *(huelga, nevada)* to cause trouble *o* disruption; *(guerra)* to cause upheaval; **ven cuando quieras, no me causa ningún t.** come whenever you like, you won't be putting me out

trastrocamiento *nm (de plan, sistema, orden)* disruption; *(de valores, sentido, lenguaje)* distortion; **el t. de las alianzas entre los países de la región** the reconfiguration of the alliances between the different countries

trastrocar [69] 1 *vt (plan, sistema, orden)* to disrupt; *(valores, sentido, lenguaje)* to distort; **t. la mentira en verdad** to turn lies into truth
2 **trastrocarse** *vpr* to turn

trasuntar *vt Formal* to reflect; **los cambios en la ganadería trasuntan el desarrollo tecnológico general** the changes in livestock farming are a reflection of *o* reflect more general technological development

trasunto *nm Formal* reflection; **es fiel t. de la realidad** it is a true reflection of reality

trasvasar *vt* (a) *(agua de río)* to transfer (b) *(líquido)* to decant (c) *(fondos, información, personal)* to transfer

trasvase *nm* (a) *(entre ríos)* transfer (b) *(de líquido)* decanting (c) *(de fondos, información, personal)* transfer

trasversal = **transversal**

trasversalmente = **transversalmente**

trasverso = **transverso**

trata *nf (de esclavos)* slave trade ▸▸ ***t. de blancas*** white slave trade

tratable *adj* (a) *(persona)* easy-going, friendly (b) *(enfermedad)* treatable

tratadista *nmf* treatise writer, essayist

tratado *nm* (a) *(convenio)* treaty ▸▸ ***T. de Libre Comercio*** NAFTA Treaty; ***el T. de Maastricht*** the Maastricht Treaty; ***t. de paz*** peace treaty; ***t. de no proliferación*** non-proliferation treaty; ***el T. de Roma*** the Treaty of Rome (b) *(escrito)* treatise

tratamiento *nm* (a) *(de paciente, enfermedad)* treatment; **estoy en t.** I'm receiving treatment ▸▸ ***t. capilar*** hair restoration treatment; ***t. de choque:*** **le administraron un t. de choque a base de vitaminas y hierro** he was given massive doses of vitamins and iron; ***t. combinado*** combined treatment; ***t. del dolor*** pain relief; ***t. de fertilidad*** fertility treatment
(b) *(hacia persona)* treatment; **el humillante t. dado a la institución por parte de las autoridades** the humiliating treatment the institution received at the hands of the authorities
(c) *(título)* form of address; EXPR **apear el t. a alguien** to address sb more informally
(d) *(de tema)* treatment; **la película tiene un t. más lírico del problema que la novela** the problem is given a more lyrical treatment in the movie than in the novel
(e) *(de material, producto)* treatment ▸▸ ***t. de residuos*** waste treatment *o* processing
(f) *Informát* processing ▸▸ ***t. de datos*** data processing; ***t. de imagen*** image processing; ***t. por lotes*** batch processing; ***t. de textos*** word processing

tratante *nmf* dealer ▸▸ ***t. de blancas*** white slave trader; ***t. de vinos*** wine merchant

TRATAR 1 *vt* (a) *(portarse con, manejar)* to treat; **¿qué tal te trataron?** how were you treated?; **no la trates tan mal** don't be so nasty to her; **la vida no la ha tratado bien** life has not been kind to her; **te dejo los discos, pero trátamelos bien** I'll let you borrow the records, but look after them *o* be careful with them for me
(b) *(paciente, enfermedad, herida)* to treat; **la están tratando de cáncer, le están tratando un cáncer** she's being treated for cancer; **el médico que la trata** the doctor who is treating her
(c) *(tener relación con)* to have dealings *o* contact with; **era compañera de clase pero la traté muy poco** she was in my class, but I didn't have much to do with her
(d) *(llamar, dirigirse a)* **t. a alguien de usted/tú** = to address sb using the "usted" form/the "tú" form; **no hace falta que me trates de señor** there's no need to call me "sir"; **t. a alguien de tonto** to call sb an idiot
(e) *(tema, asunto)* to treat; **el tema que trata la obra** the subject of the book; **hay que t. este asunto con cuidado** this matter needs to be dealt with carefully; **eso lo tienes que t. con el jefe** that's something you'll have to discuss with the boss
(f) *(agua, sustancia, tejido, alimento)* to treat
(g) *Informát (datos, información)* to process
(h) *Bol (insultar)* to insult, to swear at
2 *vi* (a) *(intentar)* **t. de hacer algo** to try to do sth; **trata de comprenderlo, por favor** please try to understand; **trataré de no equivocarme** I'll try not to get it wrong; **sólo trataba de que estuvieras más cómodo** I was only trying to make you more comfortable
(b) *(versar)* **t. de** *o* **sobre** to be about; **¿de qué trata el documental?** what's the documentary about *o* on?; **la ponencia trata sobre contaminación acústica** the paper is about *o* on noise pollution
(c) *(tener relación)* **t. con alguien** to have dealings with sb; **en mi trabajo tengo que t. con todo tipo de gente** I have to deal with all sorts of people in my job; **trata con gente muy rara** she mixes with some very strange people; EXPR *RP* **t. a alguien con pinzas** to handle sb with kid gloves
(d) *(comerciar)* to deal (**en** in)
3 **tratarse** *vpr* (a) *(relacionarse)* **tratarse con** to deal with; **en mi trabajo me trato con todo tipo de gente** I deal with all sorts of people in my job; **se trata con gente muy rara** she mixes with some very strange people; **no se trata con su padre** he has no contact with his father
(b) *(considerado incorrecto) (versar)* **tratarse de** to be about; **¿de qué se trata?** *(libro, película)* what's it about?
(c) *(ser cuestión de, ser el caso de)* **tratarse de** to be a question *o* matter of; **se trata de encontrar una solución** it's a question of finding a solution, what we have to do is find a solution; **necesito hablar contigo – ¿de qué se trata?** I need to talk to you – what about?; **¿problemas con la familia? – no, no se trata de eso** are you having problems with your family? – no, that's not it; **tratándose de él, haremos una excepción** we'll make an exception in his case *o* seeing as it's him; **se trata de un hombre moreno de mediana estatura** he's a dark man of average height
(d) *(mutuamente)* **se tratan fatal (el uno al otro)** they're horrible to each other; **tratarse de usted/tú** = to address each other using the "usted" form/the "tú" form
(e) *(sujeto: enfermo, paciente)* to be treated (**de** for)

tratativas *nfpl CSur* negotiation

trato *nm* (a) *(acuerdo)* deal; **cerrar** *o* **hacer un t.** to do *o* make a deal; **¡t. hecho!** it's a deal!
(b) *(relación)* **con el t. continuo se conoce más a una persona** you get to know a person better when you deal with them on a day-to-day basis; **no busco el t. con él** I don't seek out his company; **no tengo mucho t. con ellos** I don't have much to do with them; **no querer**

tratos con alguien to want (to have) nothing to do with sb ►► ***t. carnal*** sexual relations

(**c**) *(negociación)* **estar en tratos con alguien** to be in talks *o* negotiation with sb

(**d**) *(manera de tratar)* treatment; **dar un t. preferente a alguien** to give sb preferential treatment; **le dan muy buen t.** they treat him very well; **malos tratos** battering, physical abuse

(**e**) *(comportamiento)* **una persona de t. agradable/fácil** a pleasant/ easygoing person

(**f**) *(título)* title, form of address

trauma *nm* trauma; **superar los traumas infantiles** to overcome childhood traumas

traumático, -a *adj* traumatic

traumatismo *nm Med* trauma ►► ***t. craneal*** cranial trauma

traumatizante *adj* traumatic

traumatizar [14] **1** *vt* to traumatize

2 traumatizarse *vpr* to be devastated; **el pobre está traumatizado con lo ocurrido** the poor guy is devastated by what happened

traumatología *nf Med* (**a**) *(disciplina)* traumatology (**b**) *(departamento)* trauma department

traumatólogo, -a *nm,f Med* trauma specialist, traumatologist

travellers ['traβelers] *nmpl* travellers' cheques

travelling ['traβelin] *(pl* **travellings**) *nm Cine* travelling shot

través 1 a través de *loc prep* (**a**) *(medio)* through; **lo supe a t. de Marta** I learnt of it through *o* from Marta; **se dirigen a sus clientes a t. de Internet** they communicate with their customers via the Internet; **la difusión de la cultura a t. de los libros** the spreading *o* diffusion of culture through books

(**b**) *(lugar)* through; **a t. del cristal** through the glass; **la luz pasa a t. de las rendijas** the light passes *o* travels through the slits; **a t. de una línea telefónica** over *o* through a telephone line

(**c**) *(tiempo)* over; **los cambios sufridos a t. de los años** the changes there have been over the years; **costumbres transmitidas a t. de generaciones** customs passed on *o* handed down over generations

2 al través *loc adv* crossways

3 de través *loc adv* (**a**) *(transversalmente)* crossways; **una viga puesta de t.** a beam set crossways (**b**) *(de lado)* crosswise, sideways; **mirar de t.** to give a sidelong glance

travesaño *nm* (**a**) *Arquit* crosspiece (**b**) *(peldaño)* rung (**c**) *Dep* crossbar

travesear *vi (andar inquieto)* to lark about

travesero, -a *adj* **flauta travesera** flute

travesía *nf* (**a**) *(viaje) (por mar)* voyage, crossing; *(por aire)* flight; *(por tierra)* journey; **durante los cinco días de t. en barco** during the five-day sea crossing (**b**) *(calle) (entre otras dos)* cross-street, connecting street; *(en pueblo)* = main road through a town

travestí *(pl* **travestís** *o* **travesties**), **travesti** *nmf* (**a**) *(que se viste de mujer)* transvestite (**b**) *(artista)* drag artist

> **Falso amigo**: El sustantivo inglés **travesty** no es la traducción del español **travestí**. En inglés **travesty** significa "farsa, parodia burda".

travestido, -a *nm,f* (**a**) *(que se viste de mujer)* transvestite, cross-dresser (**b**) *(artista)* drag artist

travestirse [47] *vpr* to cross-dress

travestismo *nm* transvestism

travesura *nf* prank; **hacer travesuras** to play pranks, to get up to mischief

traviata *nf RP* = sandwich made with crackers instead of bread

traviesa *nf Ferroc Br* sleeper, *US* tie *(on track)*

travieso, -a 1 *adj* mischievous

2 *nm,f* mischievous person; **este niño es un t.** that boy is a real mischief

trayecto *nm* (**a**) *(distancia)* distance; *(ruta)* route; **un t. muy corto** a short distance; **todas las estaciones del t.** all the stations along the way; **el avión que cubría el t. París-Bonn** the plane that used to fly the Paris-Bonn route; **final de t.** end of the line (**b**) *(viaje)* journey, trip; **se puede realizar el t. en una hora** the journey *o* trip can be done in an hour

trayectoria *nf* (**a**) *(recorrido)* trajectory, path; **describe una t. elíptica** it follows an elliptical path ►► ***t. de vuelo*** flight path (**b**) *(evolución)* **t. (profesional)** (professional) career; **su larga t. como actor/político** his long acting/political career; **la accidentada t. de la empresa** the company's chequered history

traza *nf* (**a**) *(aspecto)* appearance; **un hombre con mala t.** *o* **malas trazas** an unpleasant-looking man; **tener** *o* **llevar trazas de hacer algo** to show signs of doing sth; **no lleva trazas de dejar de llover** it doesn't look as if it's going to stop raining; **por las trazas yo diría que no es de aquí** by the look of her, I'd say she wasn't from around here

(**b**) *(boceto, plano)* plan, design

(**c**) *(habilidad)* **tener buena/mala t. (para algo)** to be good/no good (at sth)

(**d**) *RP (señal)* trace

(**e**) *Ven (polilla)* carpet moth

trazado, -a 1 *adj* designed, laid out

2 *nm* (**a**) *(trazo)* outline, sketching (**b**) *(diseño) (de carretera)* route; *(de ciudad, edificio)* plan, design (**c**) *(recorrido)* route; **una variante de t. de la línea actual** an alternative route for the existing line

trazador *nm* (**a**) *Informát* ***t. de gráficos*** plotter (**b**) *(sustancia marcadora)* tracer ►► ***t. radiactivo*** tracer

trazar [14] *vt* (**a**) *(línea)* to draw, to trace; *(plano, mapa)* to draw; *(ruta)* to plot (**b**) *(plan, estrategia)* to draw up; *(objetivo)* to set (**c**) *(describir)* **t. las líneas generales del proyecto** to give an outline of the project; **trazó un dramático panorama de la situación** she drew an alarming picture of the situation; **t. un paralelismo entre dos cosas** to draw a parallel between two things

trazo *nm* (**a**) *(al escribir, dibujar)* line; **hizo un dibujo con cuatro trazos** she drew a simple outline; **estaba escrito con trazos gruesos** it was written in a crude hand (**b**) *(de dibujo, rostro)* line; **a grandes trazos** in broad outline; **éste es, a grandes trazos, el argumento de la obra** that is the broad outline of the plot (**c**) *(de letra)* stroke

TRC *nm (abrev de* **tubo de rayos catódicos**) CRT

trébol *nm* (**a**) *(planta)* clover ►► ***t. de cuatro hojas*** four-leaf clover (**b**) *(naipe)* club (**c**) **tréboles** *(palo)* clubs (**d**) *(en una carretera)* cloverleaf junction

trece *núm* thirteen; EXPR **se mantuvo** *o* **siguió en sus t.** she stuck to her guns; *ver también* **tres**

treceavo, -a *núm (fracción)* thirteenth; *ver también* **octavo**

trecho *nm* (**a**) *(espacio)* distance; *(tiempo)* time, while; **aún queda un buen t. para llegar** there's still quite a way to go until we get there (**b**) *(tramo)* stretch; EXPR **de t. en t.** every so often

tregua *nf* (**a**) *(en guerra)* truce, ceasefire (**b**) *(descanso, respiro)* respite; **no dar t.** to give no respite; **no daban t. a la presa** they gave their prey no respite; **sin t.** relentlessly; **trabajar sin t.** to work tirelessly *o* non-stop

treinta 1 *adj inv* (**a**) *(para contar)* thirty; **tiene t. años** she's thirty (years old) (**b**) *(para ordenar)* (number) thirty; **la página t.** page thirty

2 *pron* (**a**) *(en fechas)* thirtieth; **el t. de agosto** the thirtieth of August; **hoy estamos a t.** today's the thirtieth; **acabaremos el día t.** we'll finish on the thirtieth; **los años t.** the thirties

(**b**) *(en direcciones)* **calle Mayor (número) t.** (number) thirty, calle Mayor

(**c**) *(referido a grupos)* **invité a muchos y vinieron t.** I invited a lot of people and thirty came; **somos t.** there are thirty of us; **participaron los t.** all thirty of them took part

(**d**) *(en temperaturas)* **estamos a t. grados** the temperature is thirty degrees

3 *nm (número)* thirty; **el t.** (number) thirty; **doscientos t.** two hundred and thirty; **t. y tres** thirty-three

treintañero, -a *Fam* **1** *adj* thirtysomething

2 *nm,f* thirtysomething

treintavo, -a *núm (fracción)* thirtieth; **la treintava parte** a thirtieth

treintena *nf* thirty; **andará por la t.** he must be about thirty; **una t. de personas/coches** *(unos treinta)* about thirty people/cars; *(treinta)* thirty people/cars

trekking ['trekin] *nm* hiking; **hacer t.** to go hiking

tremebundo, -a *adj* terrifying

tremedal *nm* quagmire

tremenda *nf* **tomar(se) algo a la t.** to overreact to sth; **no hay que tomárselo tan a la t.** there's no sense in overreacting, there's no need to take it so much to heart

tremendamente *adv* tremendously; **me preocupa/gusta t.** it worries me/I like it tremendously; **es t. importante** it's tremendously important

tremendismo *nm* (**a**) *(exageración)* alarmism (**b**) *Lit* = graphic Spanish post-war realism

tremendista 1 *adj (exagerado)* alarmist

2 *nmf (exagerado)* alarmist

tremendo, -a *adj* **(a)** *(enorme)* tremendous, enormous; **una caída/un éxito t.** a tremendous *o* huge fall/success; **se llevó un disgusto t.** he was terribly upset
(b) *(horrible)* terrible; **un espectáculo t.** a terrible *o* horrific sight; **tengo un dolor de cabeza t.** I've got a terrible headache
(c) *(enfadado)* **ponerse t.** to get very angry
(d) *(increíble)* **¡ese niño es t.!** that boy is a handful!; **cuando se enfada es t.** he's really scary when he gets angry

trementina *nf* turpentine

tremolina *nf* commotion, ruckus; **se armó una t.** there was a commotion

trémolo *nm Mús* tremolo

trémulo, -a *adj (voz)* trembling; *(luz)* flickering

tren *nm* **(a)** *(vehículo)* train; **el t. en Suiza funciona muy bien** the railways in Switzerland are very efficient; **ir en t.** to go by rail *o* train; EXPR **ir a buen t.** to be going well; EXPR **perder el t. de algo: hemos perdido el t. de las nuevas tecnologías** we have missed the boat *o* bus as far as the new technologies are concerned; **no podemos permitirnos perder el t. de Europa** we can't afford to get left behind by the rest of Europe; EXPR **subirse al t. de algo: la empresa debe subirse al t. del progreso** the company must keep pace with progress; **era un oportunista que se subió al t. del posmodernismo** he was an opportunist who jumped on the postmodernist bandwagon; EXPR *Fam* **como para parar un t.: estar como (para parar) un t.** to be stunning, to be a smasher; **nos dieron comida como para parar un t.** they gave us enough food to feed an army; EXPR *RP Fam* **seguirle el t. a alguien** to keep up with sb ►► ***t. de alta velocidad*** high-speed train; ***t. de carga*** freight *o* goods train; ***t. de cercanías*** local train, suburban train; ***t. correo*** mail train; ***t. de cremallera*** rack *o* cog railway train; ***t. directo*** through train; ***t. expreso*** express train; ***t. fantasma*** ghost train; ***t. de largo recorrido*** long-distance train; ***t. de mercancías*** freight *o* goods train; ***t. mixto*** passenger and goods train; ***t. nocturno*** overnight train, night train; ***t. ómnibus*** local train; ***t. rápido*** fast train; ***t. semidirecto*** = train that stops only at certain stations, *US* limited train
(b) *Tec* line ►► ***t. de aterrizaje*** undercarriage, landing gear; ***t. desbastador*** roughing mill; ***t. de lavado*** car wash
(c) *(estilo)* EXPR **a todo t.: un banquete a todo t.** a banquet with all the trimmings, a lavish banquet; **vivir a todo t.** to live in style; EXPR *RP Fam* **en t. de: ya que estamos en t. de diversión, podríamos ir a bailar** seeing as we're out for a good time, we could go dancing; **parecían en t. de aventura** they seemed to be up for a bit of adventure ►► ***t. de vida*** lifestyle

trena *nf Fam* slammer, *Br* nick, *US* pen

trenca *nf* duffle coat

trence *etc ver* **trenzar**

trencilla *nm Dep Fam* ref, referee

trencito *nm Urug Fam (chuleta)* crib

trenza *nf* **(a)** *(de pelo)* plait, *esp US* braid; *(de fibras)* braid **(b)** *(dulce)* = sweet bun made of plaited dough **(c)** *RP (pelea)* quarrel, fight

trenzado, -a 1 *adj* plaited
2 *nm* **(a)** *(peinado)* plait, *esp US* braid **(b)** *(de fibras)* plaiting, braiding **(c)** *(en danza)* entrechat

trenzar [14] **1** *vt* **(a)** *(pelo)* to plait, *esp US* to braid **(b)** *(fibras)* to plait, to braid
2 trenzarse *vpr* **(a)** *(el pelo)* to plait, *esp US* to braid **(b)** *RP Fam (enredarse, enzarzarse)* to get caught up in, to get entangled in; **trenzarse en una pelea** to get into a fight

trepa *nmf Esp Fam Pey* social climber

trepado *nm (en papel)* perforations

trepador, -ora 1 *adj* **planta trepadora** climbing plant
2 *nm,f Fam* social climber
3 *nm* **(a)** *(ave)* **t. (azul)** nuthatch **(b)** *(garfio)* climbing iron

trepanación *nf* trepanation, trephination

trepanar *vt* to trepan, to trephine

trépano *nm* **(a)** *Med* trepan, trephine **(b)** *(perforadora)* drill

trepar 1 *vt* to climb
2 *vi* **(a)** *(animal, persona)* to climb; **t. a un árbol** to climb a tree **(b)** *Fam (socialmente)* to be a social climber; **trepó en la empresa descaradamente** she quite unashamedly climbed the company ladder **(c)** *(planta)* to climb

treparriscos *nm inv* wallcreeper

trepidación *nf* shaking, vibration

trepidante *adj* **(a)** *(ritmo, actividad)* frenetic, frantic; **fue un partido t.** it was a thrilling game **(b)** *(vehículo)* shaking, vibrating; *(manos)* shaking, trembling

trepidar *vi* **(a)** *(vehículo)* to shake, to vibrate; *(manos)* to shake, to tremble **(b)** *Chile (vacilar)* to hesitate, to waver

tres 1 *adj inv* **(a)** *(para contar)* three; **tiene t. años** she's three (years old) ►► ***t. puertas*** *(vehículo)* three door (model); **(b)** *(para ordenar)* (number) three; **la página t.** page three
2 *pron* **(a)** *(en fechas)* third; **el t. de agosto** the third of August; **hoy estamos a t.** today's the third; **acabaremos el día t.** we'll finish on the third; **el siglo III** *(pronunciado tres)* the 3rd century
(b) *(en direcciones)* **calle Mayor (número) t.** (number) three, calle Mayor
(c) *(en horas)* **las t.** three o'clock; **son las t. (de la mañana/de la tarde)** it's three o'clock (in the morning/in the afternoon); **el tren sale a y t.** the train departs at three minutes past
(d) *(referido a grupos)* **invité a diez y sólo vinieron t.** I invited ten and only three came; **somos t.** there are three of us; **de t. en t.** in threes; **estaban aquí los t.** the three of them were here
(e) *(en temperaturas)* **estamos a t. bajo cero** the temperature is three below zero
(f) *(en puntuaciones)* **empatar a t.** to draw three all; **t. a cero** three-nothing, *Br* three-nil, *US* three-zero
(g) *(en naipes)* three; **el t. de diamantes** the three of diamonds; **echar** *o* **tirar un t.** to play a three
(h) EXPR **a la de t.** on the count of three; *Fam* **de t. al cuarto** cheap, third-rate; **t. cuartos de lo mismo** the same thing; *Fam* **no ver t. en un burro** to be as blind as a bat; *Fam* **no le convencimos ni a la de t.** there was no way we could convince him; **como que t. y dos son cinco** as sure as eggs is eggs
3 *nm* **(a)** *(número)* three; **el t.** (number) three; **doscientos t.** two hundred and three; **treinta y t.** thirty-three **(b)** ***t. cuartos*** *(abrigo)* three-quarter-length coat; *Col* ***t. en línea*** *Br* noughts and crosses, *US* tic-tac-toe; ***t. en raya*** *Br* noughts and crosses, *US* tic-tac-toe

trescientos, -as *núm* three hundred; *ver también* **treinta**

tresillo *nm* **(a)** *(sofá)* three-piece suite **(b)** *(juego de naipes)* ombre **(c)** *Mús* triplet **(d)** *(sortija)* ring (with three stones)

treta *nf* ruse, trick

trezavo, -a *núm* thirteenth; *ver también* **octavo**

tri- *pref* tri-

tríada *nf* triad

trial *nm Dep* trials riding ►► ***t. indoor*** indoor trials riding

triangulación *nf* triangulation

triangular 1 *adj* triangular
2 *nm Dep (torneo)* three-way tournament
3 *vi Dep (hacer pases)* = to pass the ball among three or more players

triángulo *nm* **(a)** *(figura)* triangle; **el t. de las Bermudas** the Bermuda Triangle ►► ***t. equilátero*** equilateral triangle; ***t. escaleno*** scalene triangle; ***t. isósceles*** isosceles triangle; ***t. de peligro*** *(en vehículo)* warning triangle; ***t. rectángulo*** right-angled triangle **(b)** *(en relaciones)* **t. (amoroso)** love triangle **(c)** *(en música)* triangle

triásico, -a *Geol* **1** *adj* Triassic
2 *nm* **el t.** the Triassic (period)

triate *nmf Méx* triplet

triatleta *nmf* triathlete

triatlón *nm* triathlon

tribal *adj* tribal

tribalismo *nm* tribalism

tribu *nf* **(a)** *(étnica)* tribe ►► ***t. urbana*** = identifiable social group, such as punks or yuppies, made up of young people living in urban areas **(b)** *Fam (familia)* tribe; **se fue con toda la t. al campo** she went out into the country with the whole tribe

tribulación *nf* tribulation

tribuna *nf* **(a)** *(para orador)* rostrum, platform ►► *Prensa* ***t. libre*** open forum **(b)** *(para desfile, procesión)* platform; *(del jurado)* jury box **(c)** *Dep (localidad)* stand; *(graderío)* grandstand ►► ***t. de prensa*** press box **(d)** *(en iglesia)* gallery

tribunal *nm* **(a)** *(de justicia)* court; **llevar a alguien/acudir a los tribunales** to take sb/to go to court ►► ***T. de Apelación*** Court of Appeal; ***T. Constitucional*** Constitutional Court; ***T. de Cuentas*** *(español)* ≃ National Audit Office; *(europeo)* Court of Audit; ***T. Europeo de Derechos Humanos*** European Court of Human Rights; ***T. Internacional de Justicia*** International Court of Justice; *UE* ***T. de Justicia Europeo*** European Court of Justice; ***T. de la Rota***

Sacra Romana Rota; ***el T. Supremo*** *Br* ≃ the High Court, *US* ≃ the Supreme Court; ***T. Tutelar de Menores*** Juvenile Court
(**b**) *(de examen)* board of examiners; *(de concurso)* panel

tribuno *nm* (**a**) *Hist* tribune ►► ***t. de la plebe*** tribune (**b**) *(orador)* orator

tributable *adj* taxable

tributación *nf* (**a**) *(impuestos)* tax (**b**) *(sistema)* taxation ►► ***t. conjunta*** joint taxation

tributar 1 *vt (homenaje)* to pay; **t. respeto/admiración a** to have respect/admiration for
2 *vi (pagar impuestos)* to pay taxes

tributario, -a 1 *adj* tax; **sistema t.** tax system; **derecho t.** tax law
2 *nm,f* taxpayer
3 *nm (río)* tributary

tributo *nm* (**a**) *(impuesto)* tax (**b**) *(precio, sacrificio)* price; **ése es el t. que hay que pagar** that's the price you have to pay (**c**) *(homenaje)* tribute; **rendir t. a alguien** to pay tribute to sb (**d**) *Hist (del vasallo)* tribute

tricampeón, -ona *nm,f* three-times champion

tricéfalo, -a *adj* three-headed

tricentenario *nm* tricentenary

tríceps *nm inv* triceps

triciclo *nm* tricycle

tricolor 1 *adj* tricolour, three-coloured
2 *nf* tricolour

tricomona *nf (parásito)* trichomonad; **tricomonas** *(enfermedad)* trichomoniasis, trich

tricornio *nm* three-cornered hat *(associated in Spain with the Civil Guard, who wear these hats)*

tricot (*pl* **tricots**) *nm* (**a**) *(actividad)* knitting (**b**) *(tejido)* knitted fabric (**c**) *(prenda)* knitted garment; **tricots Marín** Marín Knitwear

tricota *nf RP (cerrado)* sweater; *(abierto)* knitted jacket, cardigan

tricotar 1 *vt* to knit
2 *vi* to knit

tricotosa *nf* knitting machine

tricromía *nf Imprenta* trichromatism

tridente *nm* trident

tridimensional *adj* three-dimensional, 3-D

triedro, -a 1 *adj* trihedral
2 *nm* trihedron

trienal *adj* triennial, three-yearly

trienio *nm* (**a**) *(tres años)* three-year period; **el t. 1997-1999** the three years from 1997 to 1999 (**b**) *(paga)* = three-yearly salary increase

trifásico, -a *adj Elec* three-phase

triforio *nm Arquit* triforium

trifulca *nf Fam* row, squabble

trifurcación *nf* trifurcation

trifurcarse [60] *vpr* to branch into three

trigal *nm* wheat field

trigémino, -a *Anat* 1 *adj* trigeminal
2 *nm* trigeminal nerve

trigésimo, -a *núm* thirtieth; *ver también* **octavo**

triglicérido *nm* triglyceride

triglifo *nm* triglyph

trigo *nm* wheat; EXPR **no ser t. limpio: la niña no era t. limpio** the girl was a bad lot; **la invitación no era t. limpio** there was something fishy about the invitation ►► ***t. candeal*** bread wheat, white wheat; ***t. duro*** durum wheat, hard wheat; ***t. sarraceno*** buckwheat

trigonometría *nf* trigonometry

trigonométrico, -a *adj* trigonometric(al)

trigueño, -a *adj* (**a**) *(pelo)* light brown, corn-coloured; *(piel)* golden-brown (**b**) *Am (persona)* light brown-skinned

triguero, -a 1 *adj* (**a**) *(producción)* wheat (**b**) *(terreno)* wheat-producing
2 *nm (ave)* corn bunting

trilateral *adj* trilateral

trile *nm* = card game run by a "trilero" person who runs a game such as find-the-lady, the shell game etc, in which people bet on guessing the correct card, shell etc, out of three

trilingüe *adj* trilingual

trilita *nf* trinitrotoluene, TNT

trilla *nf* (**a**) *Agr (acción)* threshing (**b**) *Agr (tiempo)* threshing time *o* season (**c**) *Andes, PRico Fam (paliza)* thrashing, beating

trillado, -a *adj (tema)* well-worn, hackneyed; *(eslogan)* trite, hackneyed; *(camino)* well-trodden; **fuera de los caminos trillados** off the beaten track

trillador, -ora 1 *adj* threshing
2 *nm,f (persona)* thresher

trilladora *nf* threshing machine

trillar *vt* (**a**) *(mies)* to thresh (**b**) *(idea)* to overuse

trillizo, -a *nm,f* triplet

trillo *nm* (**a**) *(instrumento)* thresher (**b**) *CAm, Carib (vereda)* path

trillón *nm Br* trillion, *US* quintillion

trillonésimo, -a *núm Br* trillionth, *US* quintillionth; **la trillonésima parte** one *Br* trillionth *o US* quintillionth

trilobite *nm* trilobite

trilogía *nf* trilogy

trimarán *nm* trimaran

trimestral *adj (pago, revista)* quarterly; **exámenes/notas trimestrales** end-of-term exams/marks

trimestralmente *adv* quarterly, every three months

trimestre *nm* (**a**) *(tres meses)* quarter, three months (**b**) *Educ* term; **primer/segundo/tercer t.** autumn/winter/spring term

trimotor 1 *adj* three-engined
2 *nm* three-engined aeroplane

trinar *vi* to chirp, to warble; EXPR *Fam* **está que trina** he's fuming

trinca *nf* (**a**) *(trío)* trio (**b**) *Chile (juego)* pitching pennies

trincar [60] 1 *vt Fam* (**a**) *(agarrar)* to grab; **han trincado al ladrón** they've caught *o* nabbed the thief (**b**) *(descubrir)* to catch, to nab (**c**) *(beber)* to guzzle, to knock back
2 **trincarse** *vpr (bebida)* to guzzle, to knock back

trincha *nf* strap

trinchador *nm Méx* sideboard

trinchante *nm RP* sideboard

trinchar *vt* to carve

trinche *nm Andes, Méx (tenedor)* fork

trinchera *nf* (**a**) *(en la guerra)* trench (**b**) *(abrigo)* trench coat

trinchero, -a 1 *adj* carving; **plato t.** carving dish
2 *nm* carving board

trineo *nm (pequeño)* sledge; *(grande)* sleigh

Trinidad *nf* (**a**) **la (Santísima) T.** the (Holy) Trinity (**b**) ***T. y Tobago*** Trinidad and Tobago

trinidad *nf* threesome

trinitaria *nf* wild pansy, heartsease

trinitario, -a 1 *adj* Trinitarian
2 *nm,f* Trinitarian

trinitrotolueno *nm* trinitrotoluene

trino *nm* (**a**) *(de pájaros)* chirp, warble; **se oía el t. de los pájaros** you could hear the birds chirping *o* warbling (**b**) *(de notas musicales)* trill

trinomio *nm Mat* trinomial

trinque[1] *etc ver* **trincar**

trinque[2] *nm Fam* liquor

trinquete *nm* (**a**) *Náut* foremast (**b**) *Tec (lengüeta)* pawl (**c**) *Méx Fam (fraude)* rip-off; **hacer t.** to cheat, to rip off

trinquis *nm inv Fam* swig

trío *nm* (**a**) *(de personas)* trio, threesome; *(de naipes)* three of a kind (**b**) *Mús (composición)* trio

tripa *nf* (**a**) *Esp Fam (barriga)* gut, belly; **está echando t.** he's getting a potbelly *o* a bit of a gut; **tiene mucha t.** he's got a huge gut *o* belly on him
(**b**) *(de embarazada)* bump, bulge
(**c**) *(vientre)* stomach; **me duele la t.** I've got a stomachache; **dolor de t.** stomachache
(**d**) **tripas** *(intestino)* gut, intestine; **primero se le quitan las tripas al pescado** first, gut the fish; **te suenan las tripas** your stomach's rumbling; EXPR *Fam* **echar las tripas** to throw up, to puke; EXPR *Fam* **revolverle las tripas a alguien** to turn sb's stomach; EXPR *Fam* **hacer de tripas corazón** to pluck up one's courage; EXPR *Fam* **¿qué t. se te ha roto?** what's up with you, then?, what's bugging you?
(**e**) *Fam* **tripas** *(interior)* insides; **quiero ver las tripas de la máquina** I want to see the workings of the machine

tripanosoma *nm Med* trypanosome

tripanosomiasis *nf inv Med* trypanosomiasis

tripartito, -a *adj* tripartite

tripazo *nm Fam* belly flop; **darse un t.** to do a belly flop

tripear *vi Méx Fam* to freak out

tripero, -a *nm,f* (a) *(vendedor)* tripe seller (b) *Fam (glotón)* pig, greedy guts

tripi *nm Fam (de LSD)* tab

triple 1 *adj* triple ►► ***la t. corona*** *(en rugby)* the Triple Crown; ***t. salto*** triple jump
2 *nm* (a) *(tres veces)* **el t.** three times as much; **el t. de gente/libros** three times as many people/books; **el t. de grande/bueno** three times as big/good; **tardé el t. en terminarlo** it took me three times as long to finish it (b) *Elec* three-way adapter (c) *(en baloncesto)* three-pointer (d) *(en béisbol)* triple

triplicación *nf* tripling, trebling

triplicado *nm* **por t.** in triplicate; **las solicitudes deberán presentarse por t.** applications must be submitted in triplicate

triplicar [60] 1 *vt* to triple, to treble; **las exportaciones de frutas triplican las de carne** exports of fruit are three times *o* treble those of meat
2 **triplicarse** *vpr* to triple, to treble

triplo *nm Mat* **12 es el t. de 4** 12 is 4 multiplied by 3

trípode *nm* tripod

Trípoli *n* Tripoli

tripón, -ona *Fam* 1 *adj* potbellied
2 *nm,f* (a) *Esp (panzón)* potbellied person; **ser un t.** to have a potbelly (b) *Ven (niño)* kid

tríptico *nm* (a) *Arte* triptych (b) *(folleto)* leaflet *(folded twice to form three parts)*

triptongo *nm Gram* triphthong

tripudo, -a *Fam* 1 *adj* potbellied
2 *nm,f Esp (panzón)* potbellied person; **ser un t.** to have a potbelly

tripulación *nf* crew ►► ***t. de tierra*** ground crew; ***t. de vuelo*** flight crew

tripulado, -a *adj* manned; **no t.** unmanned

tripulante *nmf* crew member; **el capitán avisó a los tripulantes** the captain informed the crew ►► ***t. de cabina de pasajeros*** cabin crew member

tripular *vt* (a) *(conducir) (avión)* to fly; *(barco)* to steer (b) *Chile (mezclar)* to mix

trique 1 *nm Col, Cuba (juego) Br* noughts and crosses, *US* tic-tac-toe
2 **triques** *nmpl Méx Fam* stuff

triquina *nf Med* trichina

triquinosis *nf inv Med* trichinosis

triquiñuela *nf Fam* trick, ruse; **mediante triquiñuelas legales** by means of legal tricks *o* dodges

triquitraque *nm* (a) *(apagado)* creaking; *(fuerte)* rattling (b) *(cohete)* firecracker, jumping jack

tris *nm Fam* (a) *Col (poquito)* tiny bit (b) EXPR **estar en** *o Andes, RP* **a un t. de hacer algo: estuve en un t. de pegarle un tortazo** I very nearly slapped him; **estuvo en un t. de irse a pique** it came within inches of sinking; **por un t.: no me fui/no solté un par de voces por un t.** I very nearly walked out/shouted

triscar *vi (retozar)* to gambol, to frisk about

trisílabo, -a *Gram* 1 *adj* trisyllabic
2 *nm* three-syllable word

trisomía *nf Biol* trisomy

trisque *etc ver* **triscar**

triste *adj* (a) *(entristecido) (persona)* sad; **¿por qué estás t.?** why are you looking so sad?; **esa canción me pone t.** that song makes me feel sad; **no te pongas t.** don't be sad; **era un hombre t. y amargado** he was a sad and embittered man
(b) *(que entristece) (noticia, suceso)* sad; *(día, tiempo, paisaje)* gloomy, dreary; *(color, vestido, luz)* dull, dreary; **tiene los ojos tristes** she has sad eyes
(c) *(deplorable)* sad; **es t. que una empresa como ésa tenga que cerrar** it's sad *o* a shame that a firm like that should have to close down
(d) *(doloroso)* sorry; **los jueces ofrecen un t. espectáculo** the judges present a sorry spectacle; **el equipo hizo un t. papel** the team gave a poor showing
(e) *(humilde)* poor; **un t. viejo** a poor old man; **no es más que un t. empleado** he's nothing but a humble worker
(f) *(insignificante)* **un t. sueldo** a miserable salary; **nos dio dos tristes aceitunas** he gave us two measly olives; **es un t. consuelo** it's small consolation, it's cold comfort; **ni un t....** not a single...; **ni una t. excusa** not one single excuse; **no tengo ni una t. radio** I haven't even got a lousy radio

tristemente *adv* sadly; **el t. famoso penal** the notorious jail

tristeza *nf* (a) *(de persona)* sadness; **me miró con t.** he looked at me sadly (b) *(de día, tiempo, paisaje)* gloominess, dreariness; *(de color, vestido, luz)* dullness (c) **tristezas** *(sucesos)* **no me cuentes tus tristezas** I don't want to hear all your woes

tristón, -ona *adj* rather sad *o* miserable

tritio *nm Fís* tritium

tritón *nm* (a) *(animal)* newt (b) *Mitol* Triton

trituración *nf* grinding, crushing

triturador, -ora 1 *adj* grinding, crushing
2 *nm (de basura)* waste disposal unit; *(de papeles)* shredder; *(de ajos)* garlic press ►► ***t. de papel*** (document *o* paper) shredder

trituradora *nf* crushing machine, grinder ►► ***t. de basura*** waste-disposal unit; ***t. de papel*** (document *o* paper) shredder

triturar *vt* (a) *(moler, desmenuzar)* to crush, to grind; *(papel)* to shred (b) *(mascar)* to chew (c) *(destrozar)* to crush; **¡como lo pille, lo trituro!** if I get my hands on him, I'll make mincemeat of him!

triunfador, -ora 1 *adj (equipo)* winning; *(ejército)* victorious; **resultar t.** to win
2 *nm,f* winner

triunfal *adj* (a) *(arco, desfile, marcha)* triumphal (b) *(gesto)* triumphant, of triumph; *(sonrisa)* triumphant; *(noche, concierto, temporada)* hugely successful; **el ejército hizo su entrada t.** the army made its triumphant entry; **su regreso t. al escenario** his triumphant return to the stage

triunfalismo *nm* triumphalism

triunfalista *adj* triumphalist

triunfalmente *adv* triumphantly

triunfante *adj* victorious; **salir t.** to win, to emerge triumphant *o* victorious

triunfar *vi* (a) *(ejército, equipo, campeón, partido)* to win, to triumph; **nuestro partido triunfó en las elecciones** our party won the elections
(b) *(artista, músico)* to succeed, to be successful; **lo que quiere es t. en televisión** her ambition is to make it *o* succeed in television
(c) *(creencia)* to prevail; *(propuesta)* to win through; **al final triunfó la sensatez** in the end common sense won the day *o* prevailed

triunfo *nm* (a) *(de ejército)* triumph, victory; *(en encuentro, elecciones)* victory, win; **desde el t. de la revolución** since the triumph of the revolution; **un asombroso t. diplomático** an astonishing triumph *o* feat of diplomacy
(b) *(de artista, músico)* triumph
(c) *(en juegos de naipes)* trump; **sin t.** no trump; EXPR **tener todos los/varios triunfos en la mano** to hold all the/several trump cards
(d) *Fam (gran esfuerzo)* **le costó un t. convencerlo** she had the devil of a job persuading him
(e) *Arg, Perú (danza)* = lively folk dance

triunvirato *nm* triumvirate

triunviro *nm* triumvir

trivalente *adj* trivalent

trivial *adj* trivial

trivialidad *nf* (a) *(hecho)* trivial detail; **no hay que preocuparse por trivialidades como ésa** you shouldn't worry about trivial *o* little things like that (b) *(dicho)* trivial remark; **escribe trivialidades** he writes trivial stuff (c) *(cualidad)* triviality

trivialización *nf* trivialization

trivializar [14] *vt* to trivialize

trizar [14] 1 *vt CSur (vaso, espejo)* to shatter; *(tela, papel)* to tear to shreds; *(acuerdo, ilusiones, relaciones)* to wreck, to shatter
2 **trizarse** *vpr (vaso, espejo)* to shatter; *(tela, papel)* to be torn to shreds; *(acuerdo, ilusiones, relaciones)* to be wrecked, to be shattered

trizas *nfpl* **hacer t. algo** *(juguete, caja)* to smash sth to pieces; *(vaso, espejo)* to shatter sth; *(tela, papel)* to tear sth to shreds; *(obra, película)* to tear *o* pull sth to pieces; **hacer t. a alguien** *(abatir)* to shatter *o* devastate sb; *(cansar)* to shatter sb; *(vencer)* to demolish sb; *(criticar)* to tear *o* pull sb to pieces; **estar hecho t.** *(abatido)* to be shattered *o* devastated; *(cansado)* to be shattered

trobalco = **tobralco**

trocaico *nm Lit* trochaic

trocánter *nm Anat* trochanter

trocar [69] 1 *vt* (a) *(transformar)* **t. algo en algo** to convert *o* transform sth into sth; **consiguieron t. las sospechas iniciales de la gente en apoyo incondicional** they managed to convert people's initial suspicion into unconditional support (b) *(intercambiar)* to swap, to exchange; **t. las armas por buenas palabras** to lay down one's arms and talk (c) *(malinterpretar)* to mix up
2 **trocarse** *vpr* (a) *(transformarse)* **trocarse en algo** to change *o* turn into sth (b) *(intercambiarse)* to get swapped over; **los papeles se habían trocado** the papers had got swapped over

trocear *vt* to cut up (into pieces)

trocha *nf* (a) *(camino)* path (b) *Am Ferroc* gauge

troche: a troche y moche *loc adv* **repartía puñetazos/invitaciones a t. y moche** he was dishing out punches *Br* left right and centre *o US* left and right/he was handing out invitations to all and sundry

trócola *nf* pulley

trofeo *nm* trophy ►► ***t. de caza*** trophy

trófico, -a *adj Biol* **la cadena trófica** the food chain

troglodita 1 *adj* (a) *(cavernícola)* cave-dwelling (b) *Fam (bárbaro, tosco)* rough, brutish
2 *nmf* (a) *(cavernícola)* cave dweller (b) *Fam (bárbaro, tosco)* brute

troika *nf* troika

troj, troje *nf* granary

troja *nf RP Fam* **acá hay una t. de lugares para ver** there are loads of places to see here; **te quiero trojas** I love you to bits

troje = **troj**

trola *nf Fam (mentira)* fib

trole *nm* (a) *(barra)* trolley (b) *(trolebús)* trolleybus

trolebús *nm* trolleybus

trolero, -a *Fam* 1 *adj* **ser t.** to be a fibber
2 *nm,f* fibber

trolley ['trolei] *nm Am* trolleybus

trolo *nm RP muy Fam* queer, *US* fag

tromba *nf (en el mar)* waterspout; EXPR **en t.: entrar en t.** to burst in; **salir en t.** to surge *o* charge out; **los grupos políticos salieron en t. a pedir explicaciones al gobierno** political groups responded en masse, demanding explanations from the government; **se lanzaron en t. contra él** they hurled themselves upon him en masse ►► ***t. de agua*** *(lluvia)* downpour, deluge; *(riada)* torrent, deluge

trombo *nm Med* clot, *Espec* thrombus

trombón 1 *nm (instrumento)* trombone ►► ***t. de varas*** slide trombone
2 *nmf (músico)* trombonist

trombosis *nf inv Med* thrombosis ►► ***t. coronaria*** coronary thrombosis

trompa 1 *nf* (a) *(de elefante)* trunk; *(de oso hormiguero)* snout; *(de insecto)* proboscis
(b) *Anat* tube ►► ***t. de Eustaquio*** Eustachian tube; ***t. de Falopio*** Fallopian tube
(c) *(instrumento)* horn
(d) *Fam (nariz) Br* hooter, *US* schnozzle
(e) *Fam (borrachera)* **coger** *o* **pillar una t.** to get plastered
(f) *Andes, RP Fam (boca)* mouth
(g) *Andes, RP Fam (gesto)* grumpy look; **¿se puede saber por qué estás con esa t.?** what are you looking so grumpy for?
2 *nmf (músico)* horn player
3 *adj Fam (borracho)* plastered

trompada *nf Fam (puñetazo)* thump, punch

trompazo *nm* (a) *(golpe)* bang; **darse** *o* **pegarse un t. con algo** to bang into sth (b) *Am (puñetazo)* punch

trompear *Am Fam* 1 *vt* to thump, to punch
2 **trompearse** *vpr* to have a scrap *o* fight

trompe-l'oeil [trompe'loi] *nm* trompe-l'oeil

trompeta 1 *nf* (a) *(instrumento)* trumpet (b) *(planta)* trumpet vine
2 *nmf* trumpeter

trompetazo *nm (de trompeta)* trumpet blast; *(de corneta)* bugle blast

trompetería *nf* (a) *(trompetas)* trumpet section (b) *(de órgano)* trumpets

trompetero, -a 1 *adj (mosquito)* whining
2 *nm (pez)* boarfish

trompetilla *nf* (a) *(del oído)* ear trumpet (b) *Méx, Ven Fam* **tirar t.** to blow a raspberry

trompetista *nmf* trumpeter

trompicar *vi* to stumble

trompicón *nm* stumble; **iba dando trompicones** he was stumbling *o* lurching along; **a trompicones** in fits and starts

trompo *nm* (a) *(juguete)* spinning top (b) *(de coche)* spin (c) *Esp Antes Fam (billete)* 1,000 peseta note

trompudo, -a *adj Am* (a) *(de labios gruesos)* thick-lipped (b) *(malhumorado)* bad-tempered

trona *nf* high chair

tronada *nf* thunderstorm

tronado, -a *adj Fam (loco)* crazy

tronador, -ora *adj* thundering

tronar [64] 1 *v impersonal* to thunder; **está tronando** it's thundering
2 *vt* (a) *Chile Fam (volar)* to blow up
(b) *Méx (hacer estallar)* to let off; **a fin de año la gente truena cohetes** people let off fireworks at New Year
(c) *Méx Fam (destruir, acabar con)* to get rid of, to do away with; **el gobierno quiere t. a la institución** the government wants to do away with the institution; **este remedio es para t. anginas** this medicine is to get rid of sore throats
(d) *Méx Fam (suspender)* to fail
3 *vi Méx* (a) *(estallar)* **a punto de t.** about to explode (b) *(despotricar)* to rant on; **siempre está tronando por algo** he's always ranting on about something (c) *Fam (cortar)* **t. con alguien** to split up with sb, to break up with sb (d) *(estropearse)* **esta planta estaba a punto de t.** this plant had almost had it

troncal *adj* **asignatura t.** compulsory *o* core subject; **carretera t.** trunk road

troncha *nf Am* (a) *(tajada)* chunk, piece (b) *Fam (suerte)* good luck

tronchante *adj Fam* hilarious

tronchar 1 *vt (partir)* to snap
2 **troncharse** *vpr* (a) *(rama, tallo)* to snap (b) *Fam* **troncharse (de risa)** to split one's sides laughing

troncho *nm (de lechuga, coliflor)* stalk

tronco[1] *nm* (a) *(de árbol)* trunk; *(talado y sin ramas)* log; EXPR *Fam* **como un t.: dormir como un t.** to sleep like a log; **estar como un t.** to be dead to the world
(b) *(dulce)* **t. (de Navidad)** yule log
(c) *(de persona)* trunk
(d) *(origen común) (en una familia)* stock; *Ling* branch ►► ***Univ t. común*** compulsory subjects
(e) *Geom (sección)* frustum ►► ***t. de cono*** truncated cone
(f) *Anat* ***t. arterial*** arterial trunk; ***t. braquiocefálico*** brachiocephalic trunk; ***t. celíaco*** *Br* coeliac *o US* celiac trunk

tronco[2]**, -a** 1 *nm,f Fam* (a) *Esp (hombre)* pal, *Br* mate (b) *Esp (mujer)* **mira, tronca, yo sólo te digo que no te aguanto** look, darling, what I'm telling you is that I can't stand you; **¿qué tal, tronca?** how's it going? (c) *Am (persona estúpida)* thicko; *(persona torpe)* bungler, *US* klutz
2 *adj Am (estúpido)* thick; *(torpe)* clumsy, *US* klutzy

tronera *nf* (a) *(en castillo)* embrasure; *(en barco)* (gun) port, porthole (b) *(ventana)* small window (c) *(en billar)* pocket

tronío *nm Fam* (a) *(clase)* style; **tener mucho t.** to have style; **una fiesta de t.** a chic *o* smart party (b) *(despilfarro)* **comportarse/vivir con mucho t.** to throw one's money around

trono *nm* (a) *(asiento)* throne (b) *(dignidad)* throne; **heredero del t.** heir to the throne; **subir al t.** to ascend the throne; **una situación apoyada desde el t.** a situation supported by the crown (c) *Fam (en baño)* throne

tropa *nf* (a) *Mil (no oficiales)* rank and file; **las dependencias de t.** the soldiers' quarters
(b) *(ejército)* troops; **la retirada de la t. enemiga** the withdrawal of enemy troops; **las tropas británicas/de tierra** British/ground troops; **las tropas de la OTAN** NATO forces *o* troops ►► ***tropas de asalto*** assault troops, storm troops; ***tropas mecanizadas*** mechanized troops; ***t. profesional*** professional soldiers
(c) *Fam (multitud)* troop; **una t. de madridistas** a horde of Real Madrid supporters; **se presentó con toda la t.** he turned up with the whole tribe
(d) *RP (ganado)* herd, drove

tropear *vi RP* to herd

tropecientos, -as *adj Fam* hundreds (and hundreds) of, umpteen

tropel *nm* (a) *(de personas)* horde, crowd; **un t. de fans enardecidos** a horde of excited fans; **en t.** in a mad rush, en masse; **salieron de clase en t.** they poured out of the classroom (b) *(de cosas)* mass, heap (c) *RP (de ganado)* herd, drove

tropelía *nf (acción violenta)* atrocity; *(abuso)* outrage

tropero *nm RP* cattle drover

tropezar [17] **1** *vi* (**a**) *(con los pies)* to trip *o* stumble (**con** on, over); **tropecé con el bordillo y me caí** I tripped on the *Br* kerb *o US* curb and fell over; EXPR **t. dos veces con la misma piedra** to make the same mistake twice; **el hombre es el único animal que tropieza dos veces con la misma piedra** man is the only animal that doesn't learn from its mistakes
(**b**) *(por casualidad)* **t. con alguien** to bump *o* run into sb
(**c**) *(enfrentarse)* **t. con** *(obstáculo, problema)* to come up against; **tropezaron con la negativa de la dirección a colaborar** they came up against management's refusal to collaborate
(**d**) *(chocar)* **t. con** to bump into; **tropezó con una farola** she bumped into a lamppost
(**e**) *(equivocarse)* to slip up, to make a mistake
2 tropezarse *vpr Fam (dos personas)* to bump into each other; **tropezarse con alguien** to bump into sb

tropezón *nm* (**a**) *(con los pies)* trip, stumble; **dar un t.** to trip up, to stumble; **a tropezones** *(hablar)* haltingly; *(moverse)* in fits and starts (**b**) *(desacierto)* slip-up, mistake (**c**) *Culin* **tropezones** = finely chopped ham, boiled egg etc added as a garnish to soups or other dishes

tropical *adj* tropical

trópico *nm* tropic ►► ***t. de Cáncer*** Tropic of Cancer; ***t. de Capricornio*** Tropic of Capricorn

tropiece *etc ver* **tropezar**

tropiezo **1** *ver* **tropezar**
2 *nm* (**a**) *(con los pies)* trip, stumble; **dar un t.** to trip up, to stumble (**b**) *(contratiempo)* setback; **tener un t.** to suffer a setback; **realizamos la gira sin ningún t.** we finished the tour without a hitch
(**c**) *(discusión)* run-in; **tener un t. con alguien** to have a run-in with sb
(**d**) *(equivocación)* slip-up, mistake; **los tropiezos de la vida que me han ayudado a crecer** the mistakes in life that have helped me to grow as a person

tropilla *nf RP* troop

tropismo *nm Biol* tropism

tropo *nm* figure of speech, trope

troposfera *nf* troposphere

troqué *etc ver* **trocar**

troquel *nm* (**a**) *(para monedas, medallas)* die (**b**) *(para cartón, papel)* die cutter

troquelado *nm* (**a**) *(de moneda)* minting, striking; *(de medallas)* striking, die-casting (**b**) *Imprenta* die-cutting

troquelar *vt* (**a**) *(monedas)* to mint, to strike; *(medallas)* to strike, to die-cast (**b**) *(cartón, papel)* to die-cut

trotacalles *nmf inv Fam* lazy bum

trotaconventos *nmf inv* procuress

trotador, -ora *adj* trotting

trotamundos *nmf inv* globe-trotter

trotar *vi* (**a**) *(caballo, persona)* to trot (**b**) *Fam (andar mucho)* to dash *o* run around; **llevo toda la mañana trotando de aquí para allá** I've been dashing around all morning, I've been toing and froing all morning (**c**) *RP, Ven (ejercitarse)* to jog

trote *nm* (**a**) *(de caballo)* trot; **al t.** *(trotando)* at a trot; *(muy deprisa)* in a rush; **el pony se alejó al t.** the pony went off at a trot, the pony trotted off; **debían de llevar prisa porque iban al t.** they must have been in a hurry because they were rushing along
(**b**) *Fam (ajetreo)* **esa caminata fue mucho t. para mí** that walk was really hard going for me; EXPR **no estar para (estos) trotes** not to be up to it *o* to that kind of thing
(**c**) *Fam (uso)* **le he dado un buen t. a esta chaqueta** I've got good wear out of this jacket; **una tela de mucho t.** a hard-wearing material; **estos pantalones son para todo t.** these trousers are for everyday use

trotón, -ona *adj* trotter

trotskismo [tros'kismo] *nm* Trotskyism

trotskista [tros'kista] **1** *adj* Trotskyite, Trotskyist
2 *nmf* Trotskyite, Trotskyist

trotsko [tros'ko] *Fam* **1** *adj* Trot, Trotskyist
2 *nmf* Trot

troupe [trup] *nf* troupe

trova *nf Lit* ballad

trovador *nm* troubadour

trovadoresco, -a *adj* troubadour; **la poesía trovadoresca** troubadour lyrics

Troya *n* Troy; **el caballo de T.** the Trojan horse; EXPR **allí fue T.** there was a great to-do; EXPR **arda T.** to blazes with it!

troyano, -a **1** *adj* Trojan
2 *nm,f* Trojan

trozar *vt Am (carne)* to cut up; *(res, tronco)* to butcher, to cut up

trozo *nm* (**a**) *(de pan, tela, metal)* piece; **cortar algo en trozos** to cut sth into pieces (**b**) *(de camino)* stretch; **hacer algo a trozos** to do sth bit by bit (**c**) *(de obra)* extract; *(de película)* snippet

trucado, -a *adj* **una baraja/fotografía trucada** a trick deck/photograph; **dados trucados** *(cargados)* loaded dice

trucaje *nm* (**a**) *(visual)* trick effect; *Cine* trick photography; **t. (fotográfico)** trick photography (**b**) *(de motor)* souping up

trucar [60] *vt (contador)* to tamper with; *(motor)* to soup up

trucha *nf* (**a**) *(pez)* trout ►► ***t. arco iris*** rainbow trout; ***t. de arroyo*** brook trout; ***t. asalmonada*** salmon trout; ***t. de mar*** sea trout; *Culin* ***t. a la navarra*** = fried trout stuffed with ham
(**b**) *CAm (tenderete)* stand, kiosk
(**c**) *RP Fam (cara)* face; **por las truchas me dio la impresión de que venían a robar** from the look of them I got the impression they were planning to rob the place; **¿por qué estás con esa t.?** why the long face?, why so glum?

truchero, -a *adj* **río t.** trout river

trucho, -a *adj RP Fam* (**a**) *(falso)* bogus (**b**) *(de mala calidad)* dodgy, rubbishy

truco *nm* (**a**) *(trampa, engaño)* trick; **un t. de magia** a magic trick; **el viejo t. de hacerse pasar por extranjero** the old trick of pretending to be foreign; **la baraja no tiene t.** it's a perfectly normal pack of cards
(**b**) *(técnica hábil)* knack; **el t. está en saber no dejarlo demasiado tiempo en el horno** the secret is not to leave it in the oven for too long; **tiene t.** there's a knack to it; **no tiene t.** there's no secret *o* trick to it; EXPR *Hum* **este es el t. del almendruco** that's the trick; EXPR **pillarle el t. (a algo)** to get the knack *o* hang (of sth) ►► ***t. publicitario*** advertising gimmick
(**c**) *RP (juego de naipes)* = type of card game
(**d**) *Chile (golpe)* punch, thump

truculencia *nf* horror, terror

truculento, -a *adj* gruesome

> **Falso amigo**: El adjetivo inglés **truculent** no es la traducción del español **truculento**. En inglés **truculent** significa "agresivo".

trueco *etc ver* **trocar**

trueno **1** *ver* **tronar**
2 *nm* (**a**) *(por descarga eléctrica)* clap of thunder; **truenos** thunder; EXPR **abrir la caja de los truenos** to cause a storm (**b**) *(ruido)* thunder; **se oía el t. de las voces/del torrente** you could hear the boom of voices/the thunder of the torrent; **truenos** thunder, thundering

trueque **1** *ver* **trocar**
2 *nm* (**a**) *(de productos, bienes)* barter (**b**) *(intercambio)* exchange, swap

trufa *nf* (**a**) *(hongo)* truffle (**b**) *(bombón)* truffle; **helado de t.** = dark chocolate ice cream

trufar *vt* (**a**) *(alimento)* to stuff with truffles; **pavo trufado** turkey with truffle stuffing (**b**) *(escrito, discurso)* to fill; **un libro trufado de anécdotas** a book full of anecdotes

truhán, -ana **1** *adj* crooked
2 *nm,f* rogue, crook

truismo *nm* truism

trujamán *nm* counsellor, adviser

trullo *nm Fam* slammer, *Br* nick, *US* pen

truncado, -a *adj (cono, columna)* truncated

truncamiento *nm* (**a**) *Geom* truncation (**b**) *(de vida, carrera)* cutting short (**c**) *(de texto, frase)* truncation

truncar [60] **1** *vt* (**a**) *Geom* to truncate (**b**) *(frustrar) (vida, carrera)* to cut short; *(planes)* to spoil, to ruin; *(ilusiones)* to dash (**c**) *(cortar) (rama)* to cut off; *(texto, frase)* to truncate
2 truncarse *vpr (vida, carrera)* to be cut short; *(planes)* to be spoiled *o* ruined; *(ilusiones)* to be dashed

trunco, -a *adj Am* incomplete

truque *etc ver* **trucar**

trusa *nf* (**a**) *Carib (traje de baño)* swimsuit (**b**) *Perú (short)* briefs (**c**) *RP (faja)* girdle

trust [trus(t)] (*pl* **trusts**) *nm* trust, cartel

TS *nm* (*abrev de* **Tribunal Supremo**) = Spanish Supreme Court

tsé-tsé *adj inv* **mosca t.** tsetse fly

tsunami *nm* tsunami

Tte. (*abrev de* **teniente**) Lt, Lieut

tu *adj posesivo* your; **tu casa** your house; **tus libros** your books

TÚ 1 *pron personal* (**a**) *(sujeto)* you; **tú eres el más alto** you're the tallest; **¿quién dijo eso? – ¡tú!** who said that? – you did!; **nosotros estamos invitados, tú no** we're invited, but you're not *o* but not you; **tendrás que hacerlo tú mismo** you'll have to do it (all by) yourself; **he aprobado y tú también** I've passed and so have you; **tú te llamas Juan** you're called Juan, your name is Juan

(**b**) *(predicado)* you; **¿eres tú?** *(cuando llaman)* is it you?; **el invitado eres tú** you're the guest

(**c**) *(complemento con preposición o conjunción)* you; **es más alta que tú** she's taller than you; **trabaja tanto como tú** she works as hard as you (do); **entre tú y yo** between you and me, just between the two of us; **excepto/según tú** apart from/according to you; **hablar** *o* **tratar de tú a alguien** = to address sb as "tú", i.e. not using the formal "usted" form; EXPR **de tú a tú: hablar con/tratar a alguien de tú a tú** to talk to/treat sb as an equal

(**d**) *(vocativo)* **¡eh, tú!** hey, you!; **¡tú, apártate!** you, get out of the way, get out of the way, you

(**e**) *(impersonal)* you; **tú cuando votas piensas que va a servir de algo** when you vote you think it's going to make a difference

2 *nm* ***tú y yo*** = set of table linen for two people

> Because Spanish verbs are inflected, subject pronouns such as **tú** are largely redundant. In fact, they are normally omitted, with no loss in clarity about who is being referred to:
> **¿qué vas a hacer ahora?**
> *what are you going to do now?*
> The personal subject pronouns are used in cases where an explicit contrast is needed:
> **tú tendrás que hacer la prueba, pero nosotros no**
> *you'll have to do the test, but we won't*

tualé *nm* (**a**) *CSur (baño)* toilet, lavatory (**b**) *RP Anticuado (mueble)* dressing table

tuareg 1 *adj inv* Tuareg

2 *nmf inv* Tuareg

tuba *nf* tuba

tubazo *nm RP, Ven Fam* buzz, *Br* bell *(telephone call)*

tubectomía *nf Med* tubectomy

tuberculina *nf* tuberculin

tubérculo *nm* (**a**) *(planta)* tuber, root vegetable (**b**) *(tumor)* tubercle

tuberculosis *nf inv* tuberculosis

tuberculoso, -a 1 *adj* (**a**) *(bacilo, infección)* tuberculous, tubercular (**b**) *(persona)* **está t.** he has tuberculosis; **murió t.** he died of tuberculosis

2 *nm,f* tuberculosis sufferer, person with tuberculosis

tubería *nf* (**a**) *(tubo)* pipe; **t. de agua** water pipe; **t. principal** main (**b**) *(conjunto de tubos)* pipes

tuberosa *nf* tuberose

tuberoso, -a *adj* tuberous

tubillón *nm* dowel

tubino® *nm Perú* bobbin *(of sewing thread)*

tubo 1 *nm* (**a**) *(cilindro hueco)* tube; **un t. de cartón** a cardboard tube ►► ***t. fluorescente*** fluorescent light strip; ***t. de rayos catódicos*** cathode ray tube; *Elec* ***t. de vacío*** vacuum tube

(**b**) *(tubería)* pipe ►► ***t. del desagüe*** drainpipe; ***t. de escape*** exhaust (pipe)

(**c**) *(recipiente)* tube ►► ***t. de ensayo*** test tube

(**d**) *Anat* tract ►► ***t. digestivo*** digestive tract, alimentary canal

(**e**) *Esp Fam (de cerveza)* = tall glass of beer

(**f**) *Chile (rulo)* curl

(**g**) *RP, Ven (de teléfono)* receiver

(**h**) EXPR *Esp Fam* **por un t.: tiene dinero por un t.** he's got loads of money; **comimos por un t.** we ate a hell of a lot; *RP Fam* **como por un t.** *(fácilmente)* easily; **siempre le sale todo como por un t.** he never has any trouble with anything

2 *adj inv* **falda t.** tube skirt; **pantalón t.** *Br* drainpipe trousers, *US* drainpipe pants

tubolux, tuboluz *nm RP* fluorescent tube

tubular 1 *adj* tubular

2 *nm* bicycle tyre; **ganó por un t.** *(en esprint)* he won by the width of a tyre

túbulo *nm* tubule

tucán *nm* toucan

tucano, -a 1 *adj* Tucano

2 *nm,f (persona)* Tucano

3 *nm (lengua)* Tucano

tuco, -a 1 *adj* (**a**) *CAm, Ecuad, PRico (sin brazo)* one-armed (**b**) *Ven Fam (sin brazo)* one-armed; *(sin pierna)* one-legged

2 *nm,f* (**a**) *CAm (tocayo)* namesake (**b**) *Ven Fam (sin brazo)* one-armed person; *(sin pierna)* one-legged person

3 *nm* (**a**) *CAm, Ecuad, PRico, Ven (fragmento)* piece, fragment (**b**) *Perú (ave)* owl (**c**) *RP (salsa)* = pasta sauce similar to bolognese

tuco-tuco *nm* tucotuco, tucutucu

tudesco, -a 1 *adj* German

2 *nm,f* German

tuerca 1 *nf* nut; EXPR **apretar las tuercas a alguien** to tighten the screws on sb; EXPR **otra** *o* **una nueva vuelta de t.: la subida de los carburantes ha supuesto otra vuelta de t. para los ya sufridos agricultores** the rise in the price of fuel puts further pressure on the already suffering farmers; **la respuesta del gobierno es una nueva vuelta de t. en el contencioso pesquero** the government's response has raised the stakes in the fishing dispute ►► ***t. mariposa*** wing nut, butterfly nut

2 *adj RP Fam* car-mad

tuerce[1] *etc ver* **torcer**

tuerce[2] *nm Guat (mala suerte)* bad luck, misfortune

tuero *nm Guat (juego)* hide-and-seek

tuerto, -a 1 *adj (sin un ojo)* one-eyed; *(ciego de un ojo)* blind in one eye

2 *nm,f* **ser t.** *(sin un ojo)* to have only one eye; *(ciego de un ojo)* to be blind in one eye

tuerzo *etc ver* **torcer**

tueste *nm* (**a**) *(de café) (acción)* roasting; *(resultado)* roast ►► ***t. natural*** medium roast; ***t. torrefacto*** dark roast (**b**) *(de pan)* toasting (**c**) *(de carne)* browning

tuesto *etc ver* **tostar**

tuétano *nm* (**a**) *(del hueso)* (bone) marrow (**b**) *(meollo)* crux, heart; EXPR **hasta el t.** *o* **los tuétanos** to the core; **es catalán hasta el t.** he's Catalan through and through, he's Catalan to the core; **se comprometió con el proyecto hasta los tuétanos** he put his heart and soul into the project; **mojado hasta los tuétanos** soaked through *o* to the skin

tufarada *nf* waft

tufillas *nmf inv Fam* grouch

tufillo *nm Fam* (**a**) *(mal olor)* whiff (**b**) *(aire sospechoso)* **el t. xenófobo que se desprende de sus textos** the undercurrent of xenophobia in her writings; **el t. sensacionalista de su reportaje** the sensationalist tone *o* flavour of his report

tufo *nm* (**a**) *Fam (mal olor)* stink, stench; **hay un t. a sudor horrible** there's a foul smell of sweat (**b**) *(emanación)* fumes (**c**) *Fam (aire sospechoso)* **desconfiaba del t. clerical de sus palabras** I distrusted the clerical undertones of his remarks; **una decisión con un cierto t. electoralista** a decision that smacks of electioneering

tugurio *nm (casa)* hovel; *(bar)* dive

tul *nm* tulle

tula *nf (juego infantil)* tag

tulio *nm Quím* thulium

tulipa *nf* (**a**) *(de lámpara)* glass (lamp)shade (**b**) *(tulipán)* tulip

tulipán *nm* tulip

tulipero *nm* tulip tree

tullido, -a 1 *adj* paralysed, crippled

2 *nm,f* cripple

tullir *vt* to paralyse, to cripple

tumba *nf* (**a**) *(sepultura)* grave, tomb; EXPR **a t. abierta** *(a toda velocidad)* (at) full tilt, flat out; *(sin cautela)* all out; **se lanzó a t. abierta a defender los derechos de los sospechosos** he went all out to defend the suspects' rights; **en la entrevista hace una confesión a t. abierta** she confesses everything openly in the interview; EXPR **ser una t.: soy una t.** I won't say a word

(**b**) *Col, Cuba (tala)* felling

tumbaburros *nm inv Méx* (**a**) *Fam Hum (diccionario)* dictionary (**b**) *(de vehículo)* bull bars

tumbadero *nm* (**a**) *Cuba, Méx, PRico (terreno)* clearing (**b**) *Ven (corral)* branding yard

tumbado *nm Ecuad* ceiling

tumbar 1 *vt* (**a**) *(derribar)* to knock over *o* down; *Fam* **tiene un olor que tumba** the smell of it really knocks you out *o* over (**b**) *(reclinar)* **t. al paciente** lie the patient down (**c**) *Fam (en examen)* to fail (**d**) *Fam (derrotar)* to thrash; **el Real tumbó al Deportivo** Real thrashed Deportivo
2 **tumbarse** *vpr* to lie down; **leía tumbada en el sofá** she was stretched out on the sofa, reading

tumbo *nm* jolt, jerk; **dar tumbos** *o* **un t.** *(vehículo)* to jolt, to jerk; **ir dando tumbos** *(al caminar)* to lurch along; **el autobús va dando tumbos** the bus lurches from side to side; **un pobre hombre que va dando tumbos por la vida** a poor man who stumbles from one problem to another in life; **la economía europea va dando tumbos** the European economy is lurching from crisis to crisis

tumbona *nf Br* sun-lounger, *US* (beach) recliner

tumefacción *nf* swelling, *Espec* tumefaction

tumefacto, -a *adj* swollen, *Espec* tumid

tumescencia *nf* swelling, *Espec* tumescence

tumor *nm* tumour ▸▸ ***t. benigno*** benign tumor; ***t. cerebral*** brain tumour; ***t. maligno*** malignant tumor

tumoración *nf* (**a**) *(tumor)* tumour (**b**) *(hinchazón)* lump, swelling

tumoral *adj Med (proceso, célula, tejido)* tumorous, tumoral

túmulo *nm* (**a**) *(montículo)* burial mound, barrow, tumulus (**b**) *(catafalco)* catafalque

tumulto *nm* (**a**) *(alboroto)* commotion, tumult; **la presencia del cantante causó un t.** the presence of the singer caused a commotion (**b**) *(disturbio)* riot, disturbance (**c**) *(multitud)* crowd, throng; **intentó abrirse paso entre el t. de periodistas** she tried to make her way through the throng of reporters; **se formó un t. frente a la casa** a crowd formed in front of the house

tumultuoso, -a *adj* (**a**) *(calle)* crowded, teeming; *(espectáculo, reunión)* rowdy, tumultuous (**b**) *(mar, aguas)* rough, stormy

tuna *nf* (**a**) *(agrupación musical)* = group of student minstrels (**b**) *Am (higo chumbo)* prickly pear (**c**) *ver también* **tuno**

> **Falso amigo**: El sustantivo inglés **tuna** no es la traducción del español **tuna**. En inglés **tuna** significa "atún".

tunante, -a 1 *adj* **¡el muy t.!** the rascal!
2 *nm,f* rascal, rogue

tunco, -a 1 *adj Méx (sin una mano)* one-handed; *(sin un brazo)* one-armed
2 *nm CAm, Méx (puerco)* pig

tunda *nf Fam* (**a**) *(paliza)* beating, thrashing; **dar una t. a alguien** to beat *o* thrash sb (**b**) *(esfuerzo)* drag; **nos hemos dado** *o* **pegado una buena t.** it was a hell of a job *o* a real drag

tundra *nf* tundra

tunecino, -a 1 *adj* Tunisian
2 *nm,f* Tunisian

túnel *nm* tunnel; *Dep* **hacerle un t. a alguien** *Br* to nutmeg sb; EXPR **salir del t.: a ver cómo conseguimos salir del t.** we'll have to see how we can get out of this fix; **estamos empezando a salir del t.** we are beginning to see the light at the end of the tunnel ▸▸ ***t. aerodinámico*** wind tunnel; ***T. del Canal de la Mancha*** Channel Tunnel; *Aut* ***t. de lavado*** car wash; ***t. del tiempo*** time tunnel; ***t. de vestuarios*** *(en estadio)* tunnel; ***t. de viento*** wind tunnel

Túnez *n* (**a**) *(capital)* Tunis (**b**) *(país)* Tunisia

tungsteno *nm Quím* tungsten

túnica *nf* tunic

Tunicia *n Antes* Tunisia

tuno, -a 1 *adj* **es muy t.** he's a proper rascal
2 *nm,f* (**a**) *(tunante)* rascal, rogue (**b**) *(músico)* student minstrel

tuntún *nm* **al (buen) t.** without thinking; **no contestes al t.** don't just answer off the top of your head; **siempre echa la sal al t.** she never measures the amount of salt she puts in

tupa *nmf Pol Fam* = member of a Uruguayan Marxist urban guerrilla group of the 1960s and 70s, Tupamaro

tupamaro, -a 1 *adj* Tupamaro
2 *nm,f* = member of a Uruguayan urban guerrilla group of the 1960s and 70s, Tupamaro

tupé *nm* (**a**) *(mechón)* quiff (**b**) *(postizo)* toupee (**c**) *Fam (atrevimiento)* cheek, nerve

tupelo *nm* tupelo

tupí 1 *adj* Tupi
2 *nmf (persona)* Tupi
3 *nm (lengua)* Tupi

tupido, -a 1 *adj* (**a**) *(vegetación, bosque)* thick, dense; *(cejas)* bushy; *(velo)* thick; **en lo más t. del bosque** in the heart of the forest; **una tupida red de intereses** a dense network of interests; EXPR **corramos un t. velo** let's draw a veil over that (**b**) *RP Fam (de comida)* stuffed; **comí demasiado, estoy tupida** I've eaten too much, I'm stuffed
2 *adv RP Fam* **trabajamos t., toda la semana** we worked solid all week; **fue difícil, me preguntaron t.** it was difficult, they gave me a real grilling

tupí-guaraní (*pl* **tupí-guaraní** *o* **tupí-guaraníes**) 1 *adj* Tupi-Guaranian
2 *nm,f (persona)* Tupi-Guarani
3 *nm (lengua)* Tupi-Guarani

tupinambo *nm* Jerusalem artichoke

tupir *vt* to pack tightly

tupperware® [taper'wer] *nm* Tupperware®

turba *nf* (**a**) *(combustible)* peat (**b**) *(muchedumbre)* mob

turbación *nf* (**a**) *(desconcierto)* agitation, distress (**b**) *(vergüenza)* confusion, embarrassment

turbador, -ora *adj (belleza, presencia)* disturbing, unsettling; *(sonrisa)* disconcerting

turbamulta *nf* crowd, mob

turbante *nm* turban

turbar 1 *vt* (**a**) *(calma, silencio)* to disturb (**b**) *(emocionar)* to upset; *(avergonzar)* to fluster, to embarrass; **la noticia lo turbó visiblemente** he was visibly upset by the news; **bajó los ojos, turbada por la insistencia de aquel hombre** she lowered her eyes, flustered *o* embarrassed by the man's insistence
2 **turbarse** *vpr (emocionarse)* to get upset; *(avergonzarse)* to get embarrassed; **al oír las palabras del ángel la Virgen se turbó** Mary was deeply troubled at the angel's words

turbera *nf* peat bog

turbidez *nf* (**a**) *(de líquido) (un poco)* cloudiness; *(mucho)* murkiness; *(con barro)* muddiness (**b**) *(de negocio, vida)* shadiness

turbina *nf* turbine ▸▸ ***t. eólica*** wind turbine; ***t. hidráulica*** water turbine

turbio, -a 1 *adj* (**a**) *(líquido) (un poco)* cloudy; *(mucho)* murky; *(con barro)* muddy (**b**) *(vista)* blurred (**c**) *(negocio, vida)* shady (**d**) *(época, periodo)* turbulent, troubled
2 *adv* **ver t.** to have blurred vision

turbión *nm* downpour

turbo 1 *nm* (**a**) *(sistema)* turbocharger; EXPR *Fam* **poner el t.** to put one's foot down (on the accelerator) (**b**) *(vehículo)* turbo
2 *adj inv* turbo

turbocompresor *nm* turbocharger

turbodiesel *adj* **motor t.** turbodiesel engine

turboeje *nm* axial-flow turbine

turboeléctrico, -a *adj* turboelectric

turbogenerador *nm* turbogenerator

turbohélice *nf* turboprop

turbopropulsión *nf* turbopropulsion

turbopropulsor *nm* turboprop

turborreactor *nm* turbojet (engine)

turbosina *nf Méx* aviation fuel, jet fuel

turbulencia *nf* (**a**) *(de fluido)* turbulence (**b**) **t. (atmosférica)** turbulence; **una zona de turbulencias** an area of turbulence (**c**) *(de época, situación)* turbulence; *(de sentimientos)* turmoil (**d**) *(alboroto)* uproar, clamour

turbulento, -a *adj* (**a**) *(aguas)* turbulent (**b**) *(época, situación)* turbulent, troubled; *(sentimientos)* troubled (**c**) *(persona)* unruly, rebellious

turco, -a 1 *adj* (**a**) *(de Turquía)* Turkish (**b**) *Andes, CSur, Ven Fam (del Medio Oriente)* Arab, = term used to refer, sometimes pejoratively, to all immigrants of Middle Eastern origin (**c**) *Ven Fam (tacaño)* stingy
2 *nm,f* (**a**) *(de Turquía)* Turk (**b**) *Andes, CSur, Ven Fam (del Medio Oriente)* Arab, = term used to refer, sometimes pejoratively, to any immigrant of Middle Eastern origin
3 *nm* (**a**) *(lengua)* Turkish (**b**) *Arcaico* **el Gran T.** the Turks

turcochipriota 1 *adj* Turkish-Cypriot
2 *nmf* Turkish-Cypriot

turcomano, -a 1 *adj* Turkmen
2 *nm,f (persona)* Turkmen
3 *nm (lengua)* Turkmen

turf *nm* **el t.** *(pista) Br* the racecourse, *US* the racetrack; *(hipódromo) Br* the racecourse, *US* the racetrack; *(deporte)* the turf, horseracing

turfístico, -a *adj RP* (horse)racing

turgencia *nf* (a) *(de formas, muslos)* roundedness; *(de pecho)* fullness, plumpness (b) **turgencias** bulges

turgente *adj (formas, muslos)* well-rounded; *(pecho)* full

túrgido, -a *adj* turgid

turismo *nm* (a) *(actividad)* tourism; **hacer t. (por)** to go touring (round); **nos dedicaremos a hacer t. por la ciudad** we'll go sightseeing around the city ►► ***t. de aventura*** adventure tourism; ***t. de calidad*** quality *Br* holidays *o US* vacations; ***t. ecológico*** ecotourism; ***t. ecuestre*** riding holidays; ***t. rural*** rural tourism, country holidays; **casas** *o* **viviendas de t. rural** rural holiday properties; ***t. sexual*** sex tourism; ***t. verde*** green tourism
(b) *Aut* private car ►► ***t. de competición*** touring car

turista 1 *nmf* tourist; **estoy aquí de t.** I'm here on *Br* holiday *o US* vacation
2 *adj inv* **clase t.** tourist *o* economy class

turistear *vi Am Fam* to do some sightseeing

turístico, -a *adj* tourist; **atracción turística** tourist attraction

Turkmenistán *n* Turkmenistan

turmalina *nf* tourmaline

túrmix® *nf inv* blender, liquidizer

turnar 1 *vt Méx (enviar)* to dispatch
2 **turnarse** *vpr* to take turns, to take it in turns (**con** with); **se turna con él para vigilar la calle** they take (it in) turns to watch the street; **normalmente nos turnamos** we usually take (it in) turns

turnedó *nm* tournedos

turno *nm* (a) *(de trabajo)* shift; **trabajar por turnos** to work shifts; **t. de día/noche** day/night shift; **tiene el t. de noche** he's on the night shift, he's on nights; **t. partido** split shift; **de t.** on duty; **el médico de t.** the doctor on duty, the duty doctor; **el gracioso de t.** the inevitable smart alec ►► ***t. de oficio*** = order in which lawyers are assigned legal-aid cases
(b) *(vez)* turn, go; **cuando le llegue el t. hará como todos** when it's his turn he'll do the same as everyone else; **hacer algo por turnos** to take (it in) turns to do sth ►► ***t. de preguntas*** question time
(c) *(orden)* **hay un t. establecido para las vacaciones** there's a rota for *Br* holidays *o US* vacations

turolense 1 *adj* of/from Teruel *(Spain)*
2 *nmf* person from Teruel *(Spain)*

turón *nm* polecat

turpial *nm* troupial ►► ***t. norteño*** northern oriole

turquesa 1 *adj inv (color)* turquoise
2 *nm (color)* turquoise
3 *nf (mineral)* turquoise

Turquestán *n* Turkestan, Turkistan

Turquía *n* Turkey

turro, -a *RP Fam* 1 *adj* dim-witted, slow
2 *nm,f* dimwit

turrón *nm* = Christmas sweet similar to nougat, made with almonds and honey ►► ***t. de Alicante*** = hard "turron", containing whole almonds; ***t. blando*** = soft "turron", made with ground almonds; ***t. duro*** = hard "turron", containing whole almonds; ***t. de Jijona*** = soft "turron", made with ground almonds

turronero, -a 1 *adj* **empresa turronera** "turrón" manufacturer; **maestro t.** master "turrón" maker
2 *nm,f* "turrón" maker

turulato, -a *adj Fam* (a) *(pasmado)* flabbergasted, dumbfounded; **la noticia lo dejó t.** he was flabbergasted *o* dumbfounded by the news (b) *(atontado)* in a world of one's own, on another planet

tururú *interj Fam* get away!, you must be joking!

tusa *nf* (a) *CAm, Carib, Col (mazorca)* maize husk, *US* cornhusk (b) *Andes, Cuba (cigarro)* cigar rolled in a maize husk *o US* cornhusk (c) *Chile (crines)* mane (d) *Col (de viruela)* pockmark (e) *CAm (prostituta)* prostitute

tusar *vt Col, RP, Ven* (a) *(caballo)* to clip; *(oveja)* to shear (b) *Fam (persona)* **me tusaron (el pelo)** they gave me a terrible haircut

tusilago *nm* skin, *Espec* pellicle

tuso, -a 1 *adj* (a) *Col (de viruela)* pockmarked (b) *PRico (de rabo corto)* short-tailed (c) *PRico (sin rabo)* tailless
2 *interj Am Fam (para llamar al perro)* here, boy!

tute *nm* (a) *(juego)* = card game similar to whist (b) *Fam (trabajo intenso)* hard slog; EXPR **darse** *o* **pegarse un (buen) t.** *(trabajar)* to slog one's guts out; EXPR **darle** *o* **pegarle un (buen) t. a algo** to get full use out of sth

tutear 1 *vt* = to address as "tú", i.e. not using the formal "usted" form
2 **tutearse** *vpr* = to address each other as "tú", i.e. not using the formal "usted" form

tutela *nf* (a) *(de tutor) (de los padres)* custody; *(de otras personas)* guardianship; **perdió la t. de sus hijos** she lost custody of her children; **el niño quedó bajo la t. de su tío** the child remained in the care of *o* under the guardianship of his uncle; **se educó bajo la t. de su abuelo** he was brought up in the care of his grandfather; **estar bajo t. judicial** to be a ward of court
(b) *(supervisión)* supervision; *(protección)* protection; **la t. de los derechos de las mujeres** the protection of women's rights
(c) *Pol* tutelage

tutelaje *nm* (a) *Der* guardianship (b) *(supervisión)* supervision; *(protección)* protection

tutelar 1 *adj* (a) *Der* tutelary (b) *(protector)* tutelary; **los dioses tutelares del hogar** the gods of the hearth
2 *vt* (a) *(supervisar)* to supervise, to oversee; **un proceso tutelado por la Administración** a process supervised by the Administration; **hacer prácticas tuteladas en una empresa** to do supervised work experience in a firm; **casa tutelada** *(para mujeres maltratadas)* refuge; *(para ancianos)* sheltered housing (b) *(derechos)* to protect (c) *Pol* to protect

tuteo *nm* = use of "tú" form of address, as opposed to formal "usted" form

> The informal second person singular pronoun **tú** is used much more freely in Spanish than the equivalents in French and German, and this tendency has been increasingly marked in recent years.
> In Spain **tú** can in fact be regarded as the normal form of address. **Usted** and its corresponding verb forms are reserved for addressing older people who are not close family members, customers and one's superiors at work (if the relationship is on a formal footing). There is, however, some variation in usage – for example, advertisements may use **usted** as well as **tú** (unless they are aimed at young people). Again, in a telephone conversation two people previously unknown to each other might begin using **usted** and later switch to using **tú** without any explicit agreement to do so.
> In Latin America, on the other hand, the use of **usted** is much commoner than in Spain. The plural form **vosotros** is basically restricted to Spain, but may be found in especially formal contexts in Latin American, such as in religious liturgy.

tuti fruti, tutifruti *nm* tutti-frutti

tutiplén: a tutiplén *loc adv Fam* galore, a gogo; **tenía abrigos y zapatos a t.** she had coats and shoes galore; **repartió mamporros a t.** he clouted people left, right and centre *o US* left and right

tutor, -ora *nm,f* (a) *Der* guardian (b) *(profesor) (privado)* tutor; *(en colegio, instituto) Br* form *o US* class teacher; *(en universidad)* tutor

tutoría *nf* (a) *Der* guardianship, tutorship (b) *Educ (sesión con tutor)* tutorial session, tutorial; *(cargo de tutor)* tutorship

tutorial *nm Informát* tutorial

tutsi 1 *adj* Tutsi
2 *nmf* Tutsi

tutú *nm* (a) *(vestido)* tutu (b) *RP (coche)* brrm-brrm

tutuma = **totuma**

tuturuto, -a *Col, Ecuad, Ven Fam* 1 *adj* stunned, dumbfounded
2 *nm,f* stunned *o* dumbfounded person

tuviera *etc ver* **tener**

tuxtleco, -a 1 *adj* of/from Tuxtla Gutiérrez *(Mexico)*
2 *nm,f* person from Tuxtla Gutiérrez *(Mexico)*

tuya *nf* northern white cedar

tuyo, -a 1 *adj posesivo* yours; **este libro es t.** this book is yours; **un amigo t.** a friend of yours; **no es asunto t.** it's none of your business
2 *pron posesivo* **el t.** yours; **el t. es rojo** yours is red; **los tuyos están**

en la mesa yours are on the table; *Fam* **los tuyos** *(tu familia)* your folks; *(tu bando)* your lot, your side; EXPR **lo t.: lo t. es el teatro** *(lo que haces bien)* you should be on the stage; *Fam* **te costó lo t.** it wasn't easy for you; EXPR *Fam* **ésta es la tuya** this is the chance you've been waiting for *o* your big chance

TV *nf* (*abrev de* **televisión**) TV

TVE *nf* (*abrev de* **Televisión Española**) = Spanish state television network

tweed [twið] *nm* tweed

twist [twist] *nm inv* twist *(dance)*

txistu *nm* = Basque flute

txistulari *nmf* = Basque flute player

U, u

U, u [u] *nf (letra)* U, u
u *conj* or; *ver también* **o**
UA *nf* (*abrev de* **Union Africana**) AU
Uagadugú *n* Ouagadougou
ubérrimo, -a *adj Formal (tierra)* extremely fertile; *(vegetación)* luxuriant, abundant
ubicación *nf* location; **la u. de la nueva empresa está aún por decidir** the location of the new firm has yet to be decided
ubicado, -a *adj* (**a**) *(edificio)* located, situated (**b**) *Am (persona) (en sala)* **estoy mal ubicada acá, la columna me tapa parte de la pantalla** this isn't a good place to sit, the column is blocking out part of the screen (**c**) *RP (persona) (en cargo)* **está muy bien u. en esa empresa** he's very well placed *o* he's got a very good job in that firm
ubicar [60] **1** *vt* (**a**) *(situar) (edificio, fábrica)* to locate; **un lugar donde u. su empresa** a location for your firm
(**b**) *Am (colocar) (mueble)* to put, to place; *(persona)* to put; **a mi tía la ubicaremos al lado de tu madre** we'll put *o* sit my aunt next to your mother
(**c**) *Am (encontrar)* to find, to locate; **no veo su ficha por acá, pero en cuanto la ubique le aviso** I can't see your card here, but as soon as I find it I'll let you know; **hay que u. a la familia del accidentado** we have to locate the victim's family; **¿cómo te ubico?** where can I get hold of *o* contact you?
(**d**) *Am (identificar)* **¿González?, no lo ubico** González? I can't quite place him; **¿cuál es tu calle? ¿cómo la ubico?** what street are you in? how can I find it?
(**e**) *Chile (candidato)* to nominate
2 ubicarse *vpr* (**a**) *(edificio)* to be situated, to be located
(**b**) *Am (persona)* to get one's bearings; **¿ya te ubicás en la ciudad?** are you finding your way around the city all right?; **me voy a mudar, en este barrio no termino de ubicarme** I'm going to move, I just don't feel at home in this part of town
(**c**) *RP (encontrar empleo)* to find *o* get a job; **al poco tiempo se ubicó** she soon found a job
ubicuidad *nf* ubiquity; EXPR **el don de la u.: tiene el don de la u.** he seems to be everywhere at once
ubicuo, -a *adj* ubiquitous
ubique *etc ver* **ubicar**
ubre *nf* udder
ucase *nm* ukase
UCD *nf* (*abrev de* **Unión de Centro Democrático**) = former Spanish political party at the centre of the political spectrum
UCI ['uθi] *nf* (*abrev de* **unidad de cuidados intensivos**) ICU
UCN *nf* (*abrev de* **Unión del Centro Nacional**) = Guatemalan political party
UCP *nf Informát* (*abrev de* **unidad central de proceso**) CPU
UCR *nf* (*abrev de* **Unión Cívica Radical**) = Argentinian political party
Ucrania *n* the Ukraine
ucraniano, -a **1** *adj* Ukrainian
2 *nm,f* Ukrainian
UCS *nf* (*abrev de* **Unión Cívica y Solidaridad**) = Bolivian political party
Ud. *abrev de* **usted**
UDC *nf* (*abrev de* **universal decimal classification**) UDC
UDI[1] *nf* (*abrev de* **Unión Demócrata Independiente**) = Chilean political party
UDI[2] *nf* (*abrev de* **Unidad de Inversión**) = Mexican indexed unit of account
Uds. *abrev de* **ustedes**
UE *nf* (*abrev de* **Unión Europea**) EU
UEFA ['wefa] *nf* (*abrev de* **Union of European Football Associations**) UEFA
UEM [wem] *nf UE* (*abrev de* **unión económica y monetaria**) EMU
UEO *nf* (*abrev de* **Unión Europea Occidental**) WEU
UF *nf* (*abrev de* **Unidad de Fomento**) = Chilean indexed unit of account
uf *interj (expresa cansancio, calor)* phew!; *(expresa fastidio)* tut!; *(expresa repugnancia)* ugh!
ufa *interj* huh!
ufanarse *vpr* **u. de algo** to boast about sth
ufano, -a *adj* (**a**) *(satisfecho)* proud, pleased with oneself; **iba muy u. con su traje nuevo** he looked very proud in his new suit (**b**) *(engreído)* boastful, conceited (**c**) *(lozano)* luxuriant, lush
ufología *nf* ufology
ufólogo, -a *nm,f* ufologist
Uganda *n* Uganda
ugandés, -esa **1** *adj* Ugandan
2 *nm,f* Ugandan
ugetista **1** *adj* = of or belonging to the UGT
2 *nmf* = member of the UGT
ugrofinés, -esa *adj Ling* Finno-Ugric
UGT *nf* (*abrev de* **Unión General de los Trabajadores**) = major socialist trade union in Spain
uh *interj Am* (**a**) *(duración)* **¿y esperaste mucho? – iuh, años!** have you been waiting long? – oh! ages!
(**b**) *(cantidad)* **¿y tenía mucha fiebre? – iuh, volaba!** did she have a very high temperature? – huh! sky-high!
(**c**) *(duda)* **¿cuál prefieres? ¿éste o aquél? – uh, no sé, déjame ver** which do you prefer? this one or that one? – mmm, I don't know, let me see
(**d**) *(decepción)* **¿cómo te fue? – uh, más o menos** how did it go? – huh!, all right
UHF *nf* (*abrev de* **ultra-high frequency**) UHF
UHT *adj* (*abrev de* **ultra-heat-treated**) UHT
ujier *nm* usher
újule *interj Méx Fam* well well!
ukelele *nm* ukelele
Ulan-Bator *n* Ulan-Bator
úlcera *nf Med* ulcer ▸▸ ***ú. de decúbito*** pressure sore; ***ú. de estómago*** stomach ulcer; ***ú. gástrica*** stomach ulcer; ***ú. gastroduodenal*** stomach ulcer; ***ú. péptica*** peptic ulcer; ***ú. perforada*** perforated ulcer
ulceración *nf* ulceration
ulcerar **1** *vt* to ulcerate
2 ulcerarse *vpr* to ulcerate
ulceroso, -a *adj* ulcerous
ulema *nm* ulema
Ulises *n Mitol* Ulysses
Ulster *nm* **(el) U.** Ulster
ulterior *adj* (**a**) *(en el tiempo)* subsequent (**b**) *(en el espacio)* further
ulteriormente *adv* subsequently
ultimación *nf* conclusion, completion
últimamente *adv* recently, of late
ultimar *vt* (**a**) *(terminar)* to conclude, to complete (**b**) *Am (asesinar)* to kill
ultimátum (*pl* **ultimátums** *o* **ultimatos**) *nm* ultimatum

ÚLTIMO, -A **1** *adj* (**a**) *(en una serie, en el tiempo)* last; **mi última esperanza/oportunidad** my last hope/chance; **hizo un ú. intento** he made one last *o* final attempt; **ú. aviso para los pasajeros...** *(por megafonía)* (this is the) last *o* final call for passengers...; **decisiones de última hora** last-minute decisions; **a última hora, en el ú. momento** at the last moment; **como ú. recurso** as a last resort; **a lo ú.**

in the end; **lo ú. antes de acostarme** last thing before I go to bed; **en una situación así es lo ú. que haría** it's the last thing I'd do in a situation like that; **por ú.** lastly, finally; **ser lo ú.** *(lo final)* to come last; *(el último recurso)* to be a last resort; *(el colmo)* to be the last straw ►► ***la Última Cena*** the Last Supper; ***los últimos sacramentos*** the last sacraments; ***última voluntad*** last wish(es)

(**b**) *(más reciente)* latest, most recent; **una exposición de sus últimos trabajos** an exhibition of her most recent work; **las últimas noticias son inquietantes** the latest news is very worrying; **en los últimos días/meses** in recent days/months; **la última vez que lo vi** the last time I saw him, when I last saw him; *Fam* **es lo ú. en electrodomésticos** it's the latest thing in electrical appliances ►► ***última hora*** *(como título)* latest, stop press; **noticias de última hora** last-minute news

(**c**) *(más bajo)* bottom; *(más alto)* top; *(de más atrás)* back; **la última línea de la página** the bottom *o* last line of the page; **el ú. piso** the top floor; **la última fila** the back row

(**d**) *(más remoto)* furthest, most remote; **el ú. rincón del país** the remotest parts of the country

(**e**) *(definitivo)* **es mi última oferta** it's my last *o* final offer; **tener la última palabra en algo** to have the last word on sth

(**f**) *(primordial)* ultimate; **medidas cuyo fin ú. es...** measures that have the ultimate goal of...

(**g**) *RP (uso adverbial)* last; **empezaron últimos, por eso todavía no terminaron** they started last, that's why they haven't finished yet; **salí última porque me quedé conversando** I was the last to leave because I stayed behind talking

2 *nm,f* (**a**) *(en fila, carrera)* **el ú.** the last (one); **el ú. de la fila** the last person in the *Br* queue *o US* line; **el ú. de la clase** the bottom of the class; **es el ú. al que pediría ayuda** he's the last person I'd ask for help; **llegar/terminar el ú.** to come/finish last; **ser el ú. en hacer algo** to be the last to do sth; **a últimos de mes** at the end of the month; **¿nos tomamos la última?** shall we have one for the road?; EXPR **estar en las últimas** *(muriéndose)* to be on one's deathbed; *(sin dinero)* to be down to one's last penny; *(sin provisiones)* to be down to one's last provisions; *(botella, producto)* to have almost run out; EXPR *Fam* **ir a la última** to wear the latest fashion

(**b**) *(en comparaciones, enumeraciones)* **este ú....** the latter...

---

ultra *Pol* **1** *adj* extremist
2 *nmf* extremist

ultracentrifugación *nf* ultracentrifugation

ultracongelación *nf* deep-freezing

ultracongelado, -a 1 *adj* deep-frozen
2 ultracongelados *nmpl* deep-frozen food

ultraconservador, -ora 1 *adj* ultraconservative
2 ultraconservative *nm,f*

ultracorrección *nf* hypercorrection

ultraderecha *nf* far right

ultraderechista 1 *adj* far right
2 *nmf* extreme right-winger

ultrafino, -a *adj* ultra-thin

ultraísmo *nm Lit* Ultraism, = "pure poetry" movement of the 1920s in Spain and Latin America

ultraizquierda *nf* far left

ultraizquierdista 1 *adj* far left
2 *nmf* extreme left-winger

ultrajante *adj* insulting, offensive

ultrajar *vt* to insult, to offend

ultraje *nm* insult

ultraligero *nm* microlight

ultramar *nm* overseas; **productos de u.** overseas goods; **territorios de u.** overseas territories

ultramarino, -a 1 *adj* overseas; **territorios ultramarinos** overseas territories
2 ultramarinos *nmpl* (**a**) *(comestibles)* groceries; **tienda de u.** grocer's (shop) (**b**) *(tienda)* grocer's (shop)

ultramicroscopio *nm* ultramicroscope

ultramoderno, -a *adj* ultramodern

ultramontano, -a 1 *adj* (**a**) *(reaccionario)* reactionary (**b**) *Rel* ultramontane
2 *nm,f* (**a**) *(reaccionario)* reactionary (**b**) *Rel* ultramontane

ultranza: a ultranza 1 *loc adj* die-hard, hardline; **el liberalismo a u.** die-hard liberalism
2 *loc adv* to the last; **defender sus valores a u.** to defend one's values to the last *o* at any price

ultrarrojo, -a *adj* infrared

ultrasecreto, -a *adj* top-secret

ultrasónico, -a *adj* ultrasonic

ultrasonido *nm* ultrasound

ultrasur *Dep* **1** *adj inv* **peña u.** = group of soccer hooligans who support Real Madrid
2 *nmf inv* = member of group of soccer hooligans who support Real Madrid

ultratumba *nf* **de u.** from beyond the grave

ultravioleta (*pl* **ultravioleta** *o* **ultravioletas**) *adj* ultraviolet

ulular *vi (viento, lobo)* to howl; *(búho)* to hoot

ululato *nm Literario* (**a**) *(del viento)* howl (**b**) *(del búho)* hoot

umbilical *adj* **cordón u.** umbilical cord

umbra *nf Astron* umbra

umbral *nm* (**a**) *(de puerta)* threshold; **pisar el u.** to cross the threshold
(**b**) *(principio)* threshold; **en el u.** *o* **los umbrales del siglo XXI** on the threshold of the 21st century; **estamos en los umbrales de una nueva era** we are on the threshold of a new era
(**c**) *(nivel básico)* threshold; **llegar al u. del pleno empleo** to reach the threshold of full employment ►► ***u. de audición*** hearing threshold; ***u. del dolor*** pain barrier; ***u. de la pobreza*** poverty line; *Fin* ***u. de rentabilidad*** break-even point; ***u. de sensibilidad*** sensitivity threshold

umbría *nf* northward slope *(usually in the shade)*

umbrío, -a, umbroso, -a *adj* shady

UN, UNA[1] (*mpl* **unos**, *fpl* **unas**) *art indeterminado*

> **Un** is used instead of **una** before feminine nouns which begin with a stressed "a" or "ha" (e.g. **un águila** an eagle; **un hacha** an axe).

(**a**) *(singular)* a; *(ante sonido vocálico)* an; **un hombre/tren** a man/train; **una mujer/mesa** a woman/table; **una hora** an hour; **tengo un hambre enorme** I'm extremely hungry; **un Picasso auténtico** a genuine Picasso; **un niño necesita cariño** children need *o* a child needs affection

(**b**) *(plural)* some; **tengo unos regalos para tí** I have some presents for you; **llegaremos en unos minutos** we will arrive in a few minutes; **había unos coches mal estacionados** there were some badly parked cars; **son unas personas muy amables** they are very kind people; **tiene unas ganas enormes de viajar** he is extremely keen to travel; **unas tijeras/gafas** a pair of scissors/glasses; **llevaba unas gafas de sol** she was wearing sunglasses

(**c**) *(ante números) (indica aproximación)* **había unos doce muchachos** there were about *o* some twelve boys there

(**d**) *(con valor enfático)* **¡me dio una pena!** I felt so sorry for her!; **se te ocurren unas ideas...** you have some really odd ideas...

> The indefinite article is omitted in Spanish when unmodified nouns are used generically, as in the following cases:
> Referring to professions:
> **es ingeniero** *he's an engineer*
> but
> **es un ingeniero muy conocido** *he's a well-known engineer*
> After the verb **ser** in certain expressions: (eg **es parte de, es cuestión de, es víctima de, no es problema**)
> After the verbs **buscar** and **tener**:
> **busco trabajo/esposa** *I'm looking for a flat/a wife*
> **¿tienes gato?** *have you got a cat?*

---

una[2] 1 *nf* (**a**) **la una** *(hora)* one o'clock; *ver también* **tres** (**b**) **a una** *(a la vez, juntos)* together; **todos a una** *(a la vez)* everyone at once
2 *pron Fam (con valor enfático)* **lleva paraguas, que está cayendo una...** take your umbrella, *Br* it's tipping (it) down *o US* it's pouring rain; **dijo una de tonterías** she talked such a load of rubbish; **te va a caer una buena como no apruebes** you'll really be in for it if you fail; *ver también* **uno**

UNAM [u'nam] *nf (abrev de* **Universidad Nacional Autónoma de México**) National Autonomous University of Mexico

unánime *adj* unanimous

unánimemente *adv* unanimously

unanimidad *nf* unanimity; **por u.** unanimously

unción *nf* unction

uncir [74] *vt* to yoke

UNCTAD [un'taδ] *nf (abrev de* **United Nations Conference on Trade and Development**) UNCTAD

undécimo, -a *núm* eleventh; *ver también* **octavo**

underground ['anderɣraun] *adj inv* underground

UNED [u'neð] *nf (abrev de* **Universidad Nacional de Educación a Distancia**) = Spanish open university

Unesco [u'nesko] *nf (abrev de* **United Nations Educational, Scientific and Cultural Organization**) UNESCO

ungir [24] *vt* (**a**) *(con ungüento)* to put ointment on (**b**) *Rel (enfermo)* to anoint

ungüento *nm* ointment

ungulado, -a 1 *adj* hoofed, *Espec* ungulate
2 *nm* hoofed animal, *Espec* ungulate animal

únicamente *adv* only, solely

unicameral *adj* single-chamber

unicameralismo *nm* unicameralism

unicato *nm Am* monopoly

Unicef [uni'θef] *nm o f (abrev de* **United Nations Children's Fund**) UNICEF

unicelular *adj* single-cell, unicellular

unicidad *nf* uniqueness

único, -a 1 *adj* (**a**) *(solo)* only; *(precio, función, moneda)* single; **es la única forma que conozco de hacerlo** it's the only way I know of doing it; **la única alternativa posible** the only possible alternative; **hijo ú.** only child, only son; **hija única** only child, only daughter; **su caso no es ú.** his is not the only case; **es lo ú. que quiero** it's all I want; **lo ú. es que...** the only thing is (that)..., it's just that...; **única y exclusivamente** only, exclusively
(**b**) *(excepcional)* unique; **una oportunidad única para conocer otros países** a unique opportunity to get to know other countries; **eres ú.** you're one of a kind
2 *pron* **el ú./la única** the only one

unicornio *nm* unicorn ▸▸ ***u. marino*** narwhal

unidad *nf* (**a**) *(cohesión, acuerdo)* unity; **la fundación fracasó por falta de u.** the foundation failed for lack of unity; **necesitamos u. de acción** we need unity of action, we need to act as one; **no había u. de criterio sobre el tema** there was no consensus of opinion on the topic
(**b**) *(elemento)* unit; **25 pesos la u.** 25 pesos each; **quiero comprar seis unidades** I'd like to buy six ▸▸ ***la u. familiar*** the family unit
(**c**) *(sección)* unit; **el jefe de la u. de cirugía** the head of the surgery unit ▸▸ *Informát* ***u. aritmético-lógica*** arithmetic logic unit; *Informát* ***u. de CD-ROM*** CD-ROM drive; *Informát* ***u. central de proceso*** central processing unit; *Informát* ***u. de coma flotante*** floating point unit; *Informát* ***u. de control*** control unit; ***u. de cuidados intensivos*** intensive care unit; ***u. didáctica*** teaching unit; *Informát* ***u. de disco*** disk drive; *Informát* ***u. de entrada-salida*** input/output device; ***u. móvil*** mobile unit; *CSur* ***u. de tratamiento intensivo*** intensive care unit; ***u. de vigilancia intensiva*** intensive care unit
(**d**) *(medida)* unit ▸▸ *Antes UE* ***u. de cuenta europea*** European Currency Unit; ***u. de longitud*** unit of length; ***u. de medida*** measurement unit, unit of measure; ***u. monetaria*** monetary unit; ***u. de tiempo*** unit of time
(**e**) *(el uno)* **la u.** (the number) one
(**f**) *Mil* unit ▸▸ ***u. de combate*** combat unit
(**g**) *Am (vehículo)* vehicle; **cinco unidades resultaron dañadas durante los disturbios** five vehicles were damaged during the disturbances

unidimensional *adj* one-dimensional

unidireccional *adj* (**a**) *(calle)* one-way (**b**) *(antena, micrófono)* unidirectional

unido, -a *adj (junto, reunido)* united; *(familia, amigos)* close; **todos los miembros de la familia están muy unidos** all the members of the family are very close

unifamiliar *adj* **vivienda u.** house *(detached, semi-detached or terraced)*

unificación *nf* (**a**) *(unión)* unification; **la u. de Alemania** the unification of Germany (**b**) *(uniformización)* standardization

unificador, -ora *adj* (**a**) *(que une)* unifying; **el papel del cristianismo como elemento u. de Occidente** the role of Christianity in unifying the West (**b**) *(que uniformiza)* standardizing

unificar [60] **1** *vt* (**a**) *(unir)* to unite, to join; *(países)* to unify; **el nuevo mando militar unificado** the new unified military command; **la Alemania unificada** united Germany (**b**) *(uniformar) (tarifas, precios)* to standardize; **los intentos de u. la legislación internacional sobre el tema** attempts to unify *o* harmonize international legislation on the issue
2 unificarse *vpr* (**a**) *(unirse)* to unite, to join together; *(países)* to unify (**b**) *(uniformar)* to become standardized

uniformado, -a *adj (policía, soldado)* uniformed; **ir u.** to wear uniform

uniformar 1 *vt* (**a**) *(normas, productos)* to standardize (**b**) *(empleado, alumno)* to put into uniform
2 uniformarse *vpr* (**a**) *(normas, productos)* to become standardized (**b**) *(empleado, alumno)* to wear a uniform

uniforme 1 *adj (movimiento, temperatura, criterios)* uniform; *(superficie)* even; **el litoral tiene un clima bastante u.** the coast has a fairly uniform climate
2 *nm* uniform; **ir de u.** to be in uniform; **un policía de u.** a uniformed policeman, *f* policewoman ▸▸ ***u. escolar*** school uniform; *RP* ***u. de fajina*** fatigues; ***u. de gala*** dress uniform

uniformemente *adv* uniformly

uniformidad *nf (de movimiento, criterios, temperatura)* uniformity; *(de superficie)* evenness; **la tendencia a la u. que amenaza a nuestra sociedad** the trend towards uniformity that is threatening our society

uniformización *nf* standardization

uniformizar [14] **1** *vt* to standardize, to make uniform
2 uniformizarse *vpr* to be standardized, to be made uniform

unigénito, -a 1 *adj Formal (hijo)* only
2 *nm Rel* **el U.** the Son of God

unilateral *adj* unilateral

unilateralmente *adv* unilaterally

unión *nf* (**a**) *(asociación)* union; **en u. con** *o* **de** together with; **acudió a la ceremonia en u. de su familia** she attended the ceremony together with her family ▸▸ ***u. aduanera*** customs union; ***U. Africana*** African Union; *Méx* ***la U. Americana*** the United States; ***la U. Europea*** the European Union; ***U. Monetaria*** Monetary Union; *Antes* ***U. Soviética*** Soviet Union
(**b**) *(acción)* joining, union; **un compuesto es el resultado de la u. de dos palabras** a compound is the result of the joining of two words; **la u. de las dos empresas** the union *o* merger of the two companies
(**c**) *(juntura, adherimiento)* join, joint
(**d**) *(cohesión)* unity; **hay que potenciar la u. entre los ciudadanos** we must foster a sense of unity among citizens; EXPR **la u. hace la fuerza** unity is strength
(**e**) *(matrimonio)* marriage, union ▸▸ ***u. de hecho*** unmarried couple

unionismo *nm Pol* unionism

unionista *Pol* **1** *adj* unionist
2 *nmf* unionist

unipersonal *adj (régimen, gobierno)* one-man; *(hogar)* single-person; *(espectáculo)* one-man, *f* one-woman; **sociedad u.** sole proprietorship; **verbo u.** impersonal verb

---

UNIR 1 *vt* (**a**) *(juntar) (pedazos, piezas, habitaciones)* to join; *(empresas, estados, facciones)* to unite; *Informát (archivos)* to merge; **unió los dos palos con una cuerda** he joined *o* tied the two sticks with a piece of string; **debemos u. fuerzas** we must combine forces
(**b**) *(relacionar) (personas)* **aquella experiencia les unió mucho** that experience made them very close; **les une una fuerte amistad** they are very close friends, they share a very close friendship; **les une su pasión por la música** they share a passion for music; **los lazos que nos unen** the ties that bind us; *Formal* **u. a dos personas en (santo) matrimonio** to join two people in (holy) matrimony
(**c**) *(comunicar) (ciudades, terminales, aparatos)* to connect, to link; **la línea férrea que une la capital a** *o* **con la costa** the railway between *o* which links the capital and the coast
(**d**) *(combinar)* to combine; **en su obra une belleza y técnica** her work combines beauty with technique; **u. algo a algo** *(añadir)* to add sth to sth; **a la desinformación hay que u. también el desinterés de la gente** in addition to the lack of information, we have to take into account people's lack of interest
(**e**) *(mezclar)* to mix *o* blend in; **una la mantequilla con el azúcar** cream together the butter and the sugar
2 unirse *vpr* (**a**) *(juntarse) (personas, empresas, grupos)* to join together; *(factores, circunstancias)* to come together; **se unieron para derrocar al gobierno** they joined together *o* joined forces to bring down the government; **en él se unen rapidez y habilidad** he combines speed with skill; **a la falta de interés se unió el mal tiempo** the lack of interest was compounded by the bad weather; **unirse a algo/alguien** to join sth/sb; **también ellos se han unido a la huelga** they too have joined the strike; **¡únete a la fiesta!** join in the party!; **unirse en matrimonio** *(casarse)* to be joined in wedlock *o* matrimony
(**b**) *(encontrarse) (líneas, caminos)* to meet

---

unisex *adj inv* unisex

unisexual *adj* unisexual

unísono *nm* **al u.** in unison

UNITA [u'nita] *nf (abrev de* **Unión Nacional para la Independencia Total de Angola**) UNITA

unitario, -a 1 *adj* (**a**) *(criterio, estado, proyecto)* single (**b**) *(por unidad)* unit; **precio u.** unit price (**c**) *Rel* Unitarian
2 *nm,f Rel* Unitarian

unitarismo *nm Rel* Unitarianism

univalente *adj Quím* univalent

universal 1 *adj* (**a**) *(total) (acceso, idioma, sufragio)* universal; **un principio de validez u.** a universally valid principle (**b**) *(mundial)* world; **historia u.** world history; **literatura u.** world literature; **un artista de fama u.** a world-famous artist
2 universales *nmpl Filosofía* universals

universalidad *nf* universality

universalismo *nm* universalism

universalizar [14] **1** *vt* to make widespread
2 universalizarse *vpr* to become widespread

universalmente *adv* universally; **un principio reconocido u.** a universally acknowledged principle

universiada *nf Dep* **la U.** the World Student Games

universidad *nf* (**a**) *(centro educativo)* university ►► ***u. a distancia*** = distance learning university, *Br* ≃ Open University; ***u. de verano*** university summer school (**b**) *(enseñanza superior)* university; **la reforma de la u.** university reform

universitario, -a 1 *adj* university; **estudiante u.** university student
2 *nm,f* (**a**) *(estudiante)* university student (**b**) *(profesor)* university lecturer (**c**) *(licenciado)* university graduate

universo *nm* (**a**) *(cosmos)* universe ►► ***u. abierto*** open universe; ***u. cerrado*** closed universe; ***u. estacionario*** stationary universe; ***u. en expansión*** expanding universe (**b**) *(mundo)* world; **el u. literario de Proust** Proust's literary universe

univitelino, -a *adj Fisiol* monozygotic

unívoco, -a *adj* (**a**) *(correspondencia)* one-to-one (**b**) *(término, expresión)* univocal

UNIX ['unıks] *nm Informát (abrev de* **Uniplexed Information and Computing System**) UNIX

unjo *etc ver* **ungir**

UNO, -A

Un is used instead of **uno** before singular masculine nouns (e.g. **un perro** a dog; **un coche** a car).

1 *adj* (**a**) *(indefinido)* one; **un día volveré** one *o* some day I'll return; **unos cuantos** a few
(**b**) *(numeral)* one; **un hombre, un voto** one man, one vote; **una hora y media** an hour and a half, one and a half hours; **treinta y un días** thirty-one days; **cincuenta y una páginas** fifty-one pages
(**c**) *(después de sustantivo) (con valor ordinal)* one; **la fila/página u.** row/page one; *ver también* **tres**
2 *pron* (**a**) *(indefinido, numeral)* one; **toma u.** take one; **u. de ellos** one of them; **de u. en u., u. a u., u. por u.** one by one; **u. contra u.** *(en baloncesto)* one on one; **u. más u.** *(en baloncesto)* one and one; **juntar varias cosas en una** to combine several things into one; **más de u. piensa que es una mala decisión** more than a few people *o* no small number of people think it's a bad decision; **u. de tantos** one of many; **unos estaban a favor, otros en contra** some were in favour, others (were) against; **u. a otro, el u. al otro** each other, one another; **se miraron el u. al otro** they looked at each other *o* one another; **(los) unos a (los) otros** each other, one another; **se odian los unos a los otros** they hate each other *o* one another; **u. y otro** *(ambos)* both (of them); **unos y otros** *(todos)* all of them; **¡a la una, a las dos y a las tres!** *(en carrera)* ready, steady, go!; *(al saltar, lanzarse)* one, two, three!; EXPR **lo u. por lo otro** it all evens out in the end; EXPR **una de dos** it's either one thing or the other; EXPR **una y no más** once was enough, once bitten, twice shy
(**b**) *Fam (cierta persona)* someone, somebody; **hablé con u. que te conoce** I spoke to someone *o* somebody who knows you; **conocí a una de Tijuana** I met a woman from Tijuana; **me lo han contado unos** certain people told me so
(**c**) *(yo)* one; **u. ya no está para estos trotes** one isn't really up to this sort of thing any more
(**d**) *(con valor impersonal)* you; **se trabaja mucho, pero u. se termina acostumbrando** it's hard work but you get used to it eventually; **hay que tener confianza en u. mismo** you have to believe in yourself
3 *nm* (number) one; **el u.** number one; **el número termina en u.** the number ends in a one; *ver también* **tres**

UNRG *nf (abrev de* **Unidad Nacional Revolucionaria de Guatemala**) = former guerrilla coalition, now a political party

untadura *nf* (**a**) *(con ungüento)* anointing (**b**) *(con grasa)* greasing, oiling

untar 1 *vt* (**a**) *(mantequilla, crema)* to spread; **una margarina más fácil de u.** a margarine that's easier to spread; **u. el pan con paté** to spread pâté on the bread; **u. el molde con mantequilla** butter the baking tin (**b**) *(piel, cara)* to smear (**con** *o* **de** with) (**c**) *Fam (sobornar)* to grease the palm of, to bribe; **untarle la mano a alguien** to grease sb's palm
2 untarse *vpr* (**a**) *(embadurnarse)* **untarse la piel/cara (con** *o* **de)** to smear one's skin/face (with) (**b**) *Fam (enriquecerse)* to line one's pockets

unto *nm* (**a**) *(grasa)* grease (**b**) *Chile (betún)* shoe polish

untuosidad *nf* greasiness, oiliness

untuoso, -a *adj* greasy, oily

untura *nf* (**a**) *(ungüento)* ointment (**b**) *(grasa)* grease

unzo *etc ver* **uncir**

uña *nf* (**a**) *(de mano)* fingernail, nail; **hacerse las uñas** to do one's nails; **comerse** *o* **morderse las uñas** to bite one's nails; EXPR **dejarse las uñas en algo** to put a lot of hard work into sth; **con uñas y dientes** *(agarrarse)* doggedly; *(defender)* fiercely; EXPR *Fam* **estar de uñas** to be in a foul mood; EXPR **estar de uñas con alguien** to be at daggers drawn with sb; EXPR **enseñar** *o* **sacar las uñas** to bare one's teeth; EXPR **ser u. y carne** to be as thick as thieves ►► ***u. encarnada*** ingrown *o* ingrowing (finger)nail; ***uñas postizas*** false fingernails
(**b**) *(de pie)* toenail; **cortarse las uñas de los pies** to cut one's toenails ►► ***u. encarnada*** ingrown *o* ingrowing toenail
(**c**) *(garra)* claw; **el gato enseñó** *o* **sacó las uñas** the cat got its claws out ►► ***u. de gato*** *(planta)* cat-claw vine
(**d**) *(pezuña)* hoof; EXPR **a u. de caballo** at top speed
(**e**) *Méx (para instrumento musical)* plectrum

uñalarga *nmf Perú Fam* pickpocket

uñero *nm* (**a**) *(inflamación)* whitlow (**b**) *(uña encarnada)* ingrowing nail (**c**) *(en libro)* thumb index

uñeta *nf Chile* plectrum

UP[1] *nf (abrev de* **Unión Patriótica**) = Colombian political party

UP[2] *nf Hist (abrev de* **Unidad Popular**) = coalition of left wing Chilean political parties

upa *interj Fam* upsy-daisy!

upar *vt Fam* to lift up

uperisación = **uperización**

uperisado, -a = **uperizado**

uperisar = **uperizar**

uperización, uperisación *nf* U.H.T. treatment

uperizado, -a, uperisado, -a *adj (leche)* U.H.T.

uperizar [14], **uperisar** *vt* to give U.H.T. treatment to

UPN *nf (abrev de* **Unión del Pueblo Navarro**) = Navarrese nationalist party

UR *nf (abrev de* **Unidad Reajustable**) = indexed monetary unit in Uruguay

Ural *nm* **el U.** the River Ural

Urales *nmpl* **los U.** the Urals

uralita® *nf Constr* = material made of asbestos and cement, usually corrugated and used mainly for roofing

uranio *nm Quím* uranium ►► ***u. empobrecido*** depleted uranium; ***u. enriquecido*** enriched uranium

Urano *nm* Uranus

urbanícola *nmf* city-dweller

urbanidad *nf* politeness, courtesy; **las normas de u.** the rules of politeness

urbanismo *nm* town planning, city planning

urbanista *nmf* town planner, city planner

urbanístico, -a *adj* **boom u.** development boom; **desarrollo u.** urban development; **plan u.** urban development plan; **planeamiento u.** town planning, city planning

urbanita *nmf Hum* urbanite, townie

urbanizable *adj* **suelo u.** land available for development

urbanización *nf* (**a**) *(zona residencial)* (private) housing development (**b**) *(acción)* development, urbanization; **la u. de la zona** the development of the area

urbanizado, -a *adj (zona)* built-up; *(suelo)* developed

urbanizador, -ora 1 *adj* developing
2 *nm,f* developer

urbanizar [14] *vt* (**a**) *(construir)* to develop (**b**) *(dotar de servicios a)* to service; **suelo urbanizado** serviced land

urbano, -a *adj* urban, city; **autobús u.** city bus; **guardia u.** (local) policeman, *f* (local) policewoman

urbe *nf* large city

urca *nf (embarcación)* hooker

urdidera *nf* warping frame

urdidor, -ora 1 *adj* warping
2 *nm,f* warper
3 *nm* warping frame

urdimbre *nf* (**a**) *(de hilos)* warp (**b**) *(plan)* plot

urdir *vt* (**a**) *(plan)* to plot, to forge (**b**) *(hilos)* to warp

urdu, urdú *nm (lengua)* Urdu

urea *nf* urea

uremia *nf* uraemia

uréter *nm* ureter

uretra *nf* urethra

uretritis *nf inv* urethritis

urgencia *nf* (**a**) *(cualidad)* urgency; **debido a la u. de la situación** owing to the urgency of the situation; **con u.** urgently; **necesitan con u. alimentos y medicinas** they urgently need food and medicine; **en caso de u.** in case of emergency; **asuntos de u.** urgent matters
(**b**) *(necesidad)* urgent need; **tener una u.** to have an emergency
(**c**) *(en hospital) (caso)* emergency (case); **urgencias (médicas)** *(departamento) Br* casualty (department), accident and emergency (department), *US* emergency room

urgente *adj* (**a**) *(asunto, caso)* urgent (**b**) *(correo)* express

urgentemente *adv* urgently

urgir [24] 1 *v impersonal* to be urgently needed; **urge ayuda médica para los víctimas** medical help for the victims is urgently needed; **urge recoger medicinas para los damnificados** there is an urgent need to collect medicines for the victims; **me urge verla** I urgently need to see her
2 *vt (instar)* to urge; **la urgió a que le escuchara** he urged her to listen to him; **urgida por la desesperación** driven by desperation

úrico, -a *adj* uric

urinario, -a 1 *adj* urinary
2 *nm* urinal, *US* comfort station ▸▸ ***urinarios públicos*** (men's) public toilets, *US* (men's) public restrooms

urjo *etc ver* **urgir**

URL *nm Informát* (*abrev de* **uniform resource locator**) URL

urna *nf* (**a**) *(caja de cristal)* glass display case; **vivir en una u. de cristal** to live in splendid isolation (**b**) *(para votar)* ballot box; **acudir a las urnas** to go to the polls; **lo decidido ayer en las urnas** the result of yesterday's ballot (**c**) *(vasija)* urn ▸▸ ***u. cineraria*** urn *(for somebody's ashes)* (**d**) *Ven (ataúd)* coffin

URNG *nf* (*abrev de* **Unidad Revolucionaria Nacional Guatemalteca**) = former guerrilla coalition, now a political party

uro *nm* aurochs, urus

uroción *nm* grey fox

urogallo *nm* capercaillie

urogenital *adj* urogenital

urología *nf* urology

urólogo, -a *nm,f* urologist

urraca *nf* (**a**) *(ave)* magpie (**b**) *(persona)* magpie

urso, -a *nm,f RP Fam* (**a**) *(referido a físico)* bear of a man/woman (**b**) *(referido a actitud)* bear

URSS [urs] *nf Antes* (*abrev de* **Unión de Repúblicas Socialistas Soviéticas**) USSR

ursulina *nf* (**a**) *(monja)* Ursuline (nun) (**b**) *(mujer recatada)* prudish woman

urticaria *nf* nettle rash, *Espec* urticaria

urubú (*pl* **urubúes**) *nm* black vulture

Uruguay *nm* (**a**) *(país)* **(el) U.** Uruguay (**b**) *(río)* **el U.** the river Uruguay

uruguayo, -a 1 *adj* Uruguayan
2 *nm,f* Uruguayan

urutaú (*pl* **urutaúes**) *nm* great potoo

USA ['usa] *nmpl* (*abrev de* **United States of America**) USA; **los U.** the USA, the US

usado, -a *adj* (**a**) *(de segunda mano)* used (**b**) *(gastado)* worn; **una cartera ya muy usada** a very worn briefcase

usanza *nf* **una mujer vestida a la u. del XVI** a woman dressed in the style of the 16th century; **a la vieja** *o* **antigua u.** in the old style; **es un caballero a la antigua u.** he's a gentleman in the old style

usar 1 *vt* (**a**) *(aparato, herramienta, término)* to use; **¿sabes u. esta máquina?** do you know how to use this machine?; **una cafetera sin u.** an unused coffee pot; **es un método muy usado en literatura** it's a widely-used method in literature; **u. algo como** *o* **de: un cobertizo pequeño que se usa como** *o* **de almacén** a small shed which is used as a store; **de u. y tirar** *(producto)* disposable
(**b**) *(ropa, lentes)* to wear; **no uso maquillaje** I don't wear make-up; **estos guantes están sin u.** these gloves haven't been worn; **siempre uso la talla 40** I always wear size 40
(**c**) *Am (persona)* to use; **cuídate de ella, suele u. a la gente que se deja** watch out with her, she tends to use people if they let her
2 *vi* **u. de** to use, to make use of; **quien siempre usa de la verdad** whoever abides by the truth
3 **usarse** *vpr* (**a**) *(aparato, herramienta, término)* to be used; **ya casi no se usan las máquinas de escribir** people hardly use typewriters any more (**b**) *(ropa, lentes)* to be worn; **ya no se usan esos zapatos** those shoes are no longer worn *o* in fashion

usía *nmf Anticuado* Your Lordship, *f* Your Ladyship

usina *nf Andes, RP* plant ▸▸ ***u. eléctrica*** power station, power plant; ***u. nuclear*** nuclear power station, nuclear power plant

USO ['uso] *nf* (*abrev de* **Unión Sindical Obrera**) = centre-right Spanish union

---

USO *nm* (**a**) *(utilización)* use; **mascarillas para u. de los pasajeros** masks for the use of passengers; **está prohibido el u. de cámaras en el interior del museo** cameras may not be used inside the museum; **u. y abuso de los medicamentos** use and abuse of medicines; **un fármaco de u. común** a commonly used drug; **objetos de u. cotidiano** objects of daily use; **productos de u. exclusivo en hospitales** products used exclusively in hospitals; **de u. externo** *o* **tópico** *(medicamento)* for external use only; **de u. personal** for personal use; **en u.** in use; **una expresión aún en u.** an expression still in use; **estar en buen u.** to be in good condition; **fuera de u.** out of use, obsolete; **hacer u. de** *(tecnología, método, lengua)* to make use of, to use; *(prerrogativa, derecho)* to exercise; **hacer u. de la fuerza** to use force; **hacer buen u. de algo** to make good use of sth, to put sth to good use; **hacer mal u.** *o* **u. indebido de algo** to misuse sth; **tener el u. de la palabra** to have the floor ▸▸ ***u. de razón*** power of reason; **llevo haciéndolo desde que tenía u. de razón** I've been doing it for as long as I can remember
(**b**) *(aplicación, función)* use; **el nailon tiene muchos usos** nylon has several uses
(**c**) *(costumbre)* custom; **al u.: los políticos/textos al u. en nuestros días** the kind of politicians/texts that are in favour nowadays; **en aquella época los trajes al u....** the dresses that were fashionable in those days...; **al u. andaluz** in the Andalusian style; **al u. de** in the style of
(**d**) *Ling* usage; **es un u. exclusivamente argentino** it is an exclusively Argentinian usage
(**e**) *(desgaste)* wear and tear; **con el u.** *o* **del u. la moqueta va perdiendo lustre** the carpet is becoming shabby through use; **ha tenido mucho u. esa chaqueta** I've/he's/*etc* had a lot of use out of that jacket

---

USTED *pron personal*

While the singular suggests formality in most countries, **ustedes** is the standard form of the second person plural in Latin America

(**a**) *(sujeto)* you; **ustedes** you *(plural)*; **contesten ustedes a las preguntas** please answer the questions; **tendrá que hacerlo u. mismo** you'll have to do it (all by) yourself; **he aprobado y u. también** I passed and so did you; **como ustedes quieran** as you wish; **¿cómo se llama u.?** what's your name?
(**b**) *(predicado)* you; **ustedes** you *(plural)*; **¿quién es u.?** who are you?; **los invitados son ustedes** you're the guests
(**c**) *(con preposición o conjunción)* you; **ustedes** you *(plural)*; **esto es para u.** this is for you; **me gustaría hablar con u.** I'd like to talk to you; **trabaja tanto como u.** she works as hard as you (do); **de u./ustedes** *(posesivo)* yours; **¿es de u. este paraguas?** is this umbrella yours?; **hablar** *o* **tratar de u. a alguien** = to address sb using the formal "usted" form; **muchas gracias – (gracias) a u.** thank you very much – (no,) thank YOU
(**d**) *(vocativo)* **¡oiga, u., se le ha caído esto!** excuse me, you dropped this

Because Spanish verbs are inflected, subject pronouns such as **usted** are largely redundant. In fact, they are normally omitted, with no loss in clarity about who is being referred to:
¿qué va a hacer ahora? *what are you going to do now?*
The personal subject pronouns are used in cases where an explicit contrast is needed:
usted tendrá que hacer la prueba, pero nosotros, no
you'll have to do the test, but we won't

usual *adj* usual; **lo u. es hacerlo así** people usually do it this way; **no es u. verlo por aquí** it's unusual to see him here

usualmente *adv* usually

usuario, -a *nm,f* user ►► *Informát* ***u. final*** end user; ***u. registrado*** registered user

usufructo *nm Der* usufruct, use

usufructuar [4] *vt Der* to have the usufruct *o* use of

usufructuario, -a *Der* 1 *adj* usufructuary
2 *nm,f* usufructuary

usura *nf* usury

usurario, -a *adj* usurious

usurero, -a *nm,f* (**a**) *(prestamista)* usurer (**b**) *Pey (aprovechado)* **es un u.** he rips you off

usurpación *nf* usurpation; **lo acusaron de u. de personalidad** he was accused of impersonation

usurpador, -ora 1 *adj* usurping
2 *nm,f* usurper

usurpar *vt* to usurp

uta[1] *nf* = skin disease of the face suffered by Peruvian rubber plantation workers

uta[2] *interj Méx Fam Br* blast!, *US* shucks!

utensilio *nm (instrumento)* tool, implement; *(de cocina)* utensil; **utensilios de limpieza** cleaning equipment; **utensilios de pesca** fishing tackle

uterino, -a *adj* uterine

útero *nm* womb, uterus

UTI ['uti] *nf CSur* (*abrev de* **Unidad de Tratamiento Intensivo**) ICU

útil 1 *adj* useful; **hacer algo ú. para la sociedad** to do sth useful for society; **guardo todo lo que me es ú. para mis investigaciones** I keep everything that is useful for my investigations; **este hallazgo podría ser muy ú. en el tratamiento del cáncer** this discovery may be useful in the treatment of cancer; **es ú. para cargar maletas** it comes in handy for carrying suitcases; **50.000 metros cuadrados de superficie ú.** a usable area of 50,000 square metres; **todavía está ú.** it's still usable *o* serviceable
2 *nm (herramienta)* tool; *(de labranza)* implement; **útiles de cocina** kitchen utensils; *Am* **útiles escolares** school writing materials; **útiles de pesca** fishing tackle

utilería *nf* (**a**) *(útiles)* equipment (**b**) *Cine & Teatro* props (**c**) *RP Fam* **de u.** *(lugar, objeto)* fake, phoney

utilero, -a *nm,f Cine & Teatro* property *o* prop man, *f* property *o* prop mistress

utilidad 1 *nf* (**a**) *(cualidad)* usefulness; **dudo de su u.** I doubt it will be much use; **el libro me fue de gran u.** the book was very useful (**b**) *(beneficio)* profit (**c**) *Informát* utility (program)
2 **utilidades** *nfpl Am Econ* profits

utilitario, -a 1 *adj* (**a**) *(persona)* utilitarian (**b**) *(vehículo)* run-around, utility
2 *nm* run-around (car), utility (car)

utilitarismo *nm* utilitarianism

utilitarista 1 *adj* utilitarian
2 *nmf* utilitarian

utilización *nf* use; **está prohibida la u. de antibióticos para la cría de vacuno** the use of antibiotics in cattle breeding is prohibited; **el tratamiento de las aguas residuales para su posterior u.** the treatment of waste water for subsequent use; **de fácil u.** easy to use; **una interfaz de fácil u.** a user-friendly interface

utilizar [14] *vt* (**a**) *(expresión, método, producto)* to use (**b**) *(compañero, amigo)* to use; **te está utilizando** he's using you

utillaje *nm* tools

utillero *nm Dep* boot boy

útilmente *adv* usefully

utopía *nf* utopia

utópico, -a *adj* utopian

UV ['uβe] (*abrev de* **ultravioleta**) UV

uva *nf* grape; EXPR **de uvas a peras** once in a blue moon; EXPR *Fam* **estar de mala u.** to be in a foul mood; EXPR **tener mala u.** to be a bad sort, to be a nasty piece of work; EXPR **nos van a dar las uvas** we're going to be here for ever!, this is taking for ever! ►► ***u. blanca*** white grape; ***u. de gato*** white stonecrop ***u. pasa*** raisin; ***uvas de la suerte*** = grapes eaten for good luck as midnight chimes on New Year's Eve

UVI ['uβi] *nf* (*abrev de* **unidad de vigilancia intensiva**) ICU

úvula *nf* uvula

uvular *adj* uvular

uxoricida *Formal* 1 *adj* uxoricidal, wife-murdering
2 *nm* uxoricide

uxoricidio *nm Formal* uxoricide

Uzbekistán *n* Uzbekistan

uzbeko, -a 1 *adj* Uzbek
2 *nm,f* Uzbek

V, v

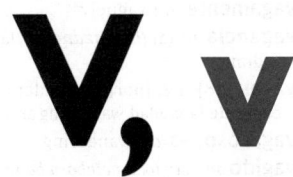

V, v [*Esp* 'uβe, *Am* be'korta] *nf (letra)* V, v; **v doble** W

V (*abrev de* **viernes**) F

v. (*abrev de* **véase**) v., vide

va *etc ver* **ir**

vaca *nf* **(a)** *(animal)* cow; *Fam* **la enfermedad** *o* **el mal de las vacas locas** mad cow disease; EXPR *Fam* **estar como una v.** to be huge ▸▸ *Fam* ***las vacas flacas*** lean years; *Fam* ***las vacas gordas*** years of plenty; *RP* ***vacas de invernada*** beef cattle; ***v. lechera*** dairy cow; ***v. marina*** manatee; ***v. sagrada*** sacred cow
(b) *(carne)* beef
(c) *Carib, Perú, RP Fam (fondo común)* kitty; **hacer una v. para comprar vino** to make a kitty to buy wine

vacacional *adj Br* holiday, *US* vacation; **periodo v.** holiday period

vacacionar *vi Am Br* to holiday, *US* to vacation; **vacacionan en la costa** they spend their *Br* holidays *o US* vacations on the coast

vacaciones *nfpl* holiday, *Br* holidays, *US* vacation; **tomar** *o Esp* **coger (las) v.** to take one's holidays; **me voy a tomar unas v. en primavera** I'm going to take a *Br* holiday *o US* vacation in the spring; **estar/irse de v.** to be/go on *Br* holiday *o US* vacation; **diez días de v.** ten days' *Br* holiday *o US* vacation ▸▸ ***v. fiscales*** tax holiday; ***v. de verano*** summer *Br* holiday *o US* vacation

vacacionista *nmf Am Br* holidaymaker, *US* vacationer

vacada *nf* herd of cows

vacante **1** *adj (puesto, plaza)* vacant; **el puesto que dejó v. en el equipo** the vacancy he left in the team; **queda v. el cargo de secretario general** the post of secretary general has fallen vacant
2 *nf* vacancy; **cubrir** *u* **ocupar una v.** to fill a vacancy

vacar [60] *vi* to become vacant

vacas *nfpl Fam Br* hols, *US* vacation

vaciado[1] *nm* **(a)** *(de recipiente)* emptying **(b)** *(de escultura)* casting, moulding

vaciado[2]**, -a** *Méx Fam* **1** *adj (gracioso)* funny
2 *adv (gracioso)* funny

vaciamiento *nm* **(a)** *(de bienes)* asset-stripping, plundering **(b)** *Med* emptying

vaciar [32] **1** *vt* **(a)** *(botella, bolsillo, cajón)* to empty (**de** of); *(líquido)* to pour; **vacía las bolsas de la compra** take the shopping out of the bags; **v. el agua de la botella** to pour the water out of the bottle **(b)** *(dejar hueco)* to hollow (out) **(c)** *(escultura)* to cast, to mould **(d)** *(empresa)* to asset-strip, to plunder
2 vaciarse *vpr* to empty; **en verano se vacía la ciudad** the city empties out in summer

vaciedad *nf* **(a)** *(tontería)* vapid remark; **decir vaciedades** to blather **(b)** *(de palabras, vida)* emptiness

vacilación *nf* **(a)** *(duda)* hesitation; *(al elegir)* indecision; **entró en el edificio sin v.** she entered the building without hesitation **(b)** *(oscilación)* wobbling; *(de la luz)* flickering

vacilada *nf Fam* joke, *Br* wind-up

vacilante *adj* **(a)** *(dudoso, indeciso)* hesitant; *(al elegir)* indecisive; **habló con tono v.** she spoke hesitantly **(b)** *(luz)* flickering; *(pulso)* irregular; *(paso)* swaying, unsteady

vacilar **1** *vi* **(a)** *(dudar)* to hesitate; **contestó sin v.** she replied without hesitation; **vacilaba entre ambas opciones** he hesitated *o* wavered between the two options; **no vaciles más y subscríbete** why wait? get your subscription today
(b) *(voz, principios, régimen)* to falter
(c) *(fluctuar) (luz)* to flicker; *(pulso)* to be irregular
(d) *(oscilar) (mueble, persona)* to wobble
(e) *Fam (causar sensación)* to be really cool; **una moto de esas vacila mucho** a bike like that is really cool
(f) *Esp, Carib, Méx Fam (bromear)* **está vacilando** he's pulling your leg *o* kidding, *Br* he's taking the mickey
(g) *CAm, Carib, Méx Fam (parrandear)* to party
2 *vt Fam* **(a)** *Esp, Carib, Méx* **v. a alguien** *(tomar el pelo)* to pull sb's leg, *Br* to take the mickey out of sb; **me estás vacilando** you're pulling my leg **(b)** *Carib (mirar con atención)* to get a load of, to check out; **vacílate ese carro** get a load of that car, check out that car

vacile *nm Fam* **(a)** *Esp, Carib, Méx (tomadura de pelo)* joke, *Br* wind-up; **estar de v.** *(de broma)* to be kidding *o* joking, *Br* to be taking the mickey **(b)** *Esp (cosa buena)* **¡una Harley Davidson!, ¡qué v.!** a Harley Davidson! cool! *o* awesome!

vacilón, -ona *Fam* **1** *adj* **(a)** *(fanfarrón)* swanky **(b)** *Esp, Carib, Méx (bromista)* jokey, teasing; **eres tan v.** you're such a tease **(c)** *CAm, Carib, Méx (juerguista)* fond of partying; **ser muy v.** to be a party-lover **(d)** *(bueno)* cool, awesome; **una moto muy vacilona** a really cool bike
2 *nm,f* **(a)** *(fanfarrón)* show-off, poser **(b)** *Esp, Carib, Méx (bromista)* joker, tease
3 *nm CAm, Carib, Méx* **(a)** *(fiesta)* party; **estar en el v.** to be in clover **(b)** *(tomadura de pelo)* leg-pull

vacío, -a **1** *adj* **(a)** *(recipiente, vivienda, espacio)* empty; **una sala casi vacía** an almost empty hall; **la ciudad estaba vacía** the city was empty *o* deserted **(b)** *(palabras, gesto, promesa)* empty; **v. de** *(contenido)* devoid of **(c)** *(vida, existencia)* empty
2 *nm* **(a)** *(espacio libre)* **se lanzó al v.** she threw herself into the void; **caer en el v.** *(palabras)* to fall on deaf ears; EXPR **hacer el v. a alguien** to cold-shoulder sb
(b) *Fís* vacuum; **envasar al v.** to vacuum-pack
(c) *(abismo, carencia)* void; **su muerte ha dejado un gran v.** his death has left a big gap *o* void ▸▸ ***v. existencial*** existential void; ***v. legal*** legal vacuum; *Pol* ***v. de poder*** power vacuum
(d) *(hueco)* space, gap; **tener un v. en el estómago** to feel hungry
(e) *RP (carne)* flank steak
3 de vacío *loc adv* **irse/volver de v.** *(persona)* to go/come back empty-handed; *(vehículo)* to go/come back empty

vacuidad *nf* vacuity, vacuousness

vacuna *nf* vaccine; **ponerse** *o RP* **darse una v.** to have a vaccination ▸▸ ***v. polivalente*** polyvalent vaccine; ***v. triple*** triple vaccine; ***v. viva*** live vaccine

vacunación *nf* vaccination; **campaña de v.** vaccination campaign

vacunar **1** *vt* to vaccinate
2 vacunarse *vpr* to get vaccinated (**contra** against); **¿te has vacunado contra la hepatitis?** have you been vaccinated against hepatitis?; **ya estoy vacunado contra ese tipo de críticas** now I'm immune to that sort of criticism

vacuno, -a **1** *adj* bovine; **ganado v.** cattle
2 *nm* cattle; **carne de v.** beef

vacuo, -a *adj* vacuous

vacuola *nf* vacuole

vade *nm* **(a)** *(carpeta)* folder **(b)** *(mueble)* desk

vadear *vt* **(a)** *(río)* to ford **(b)** *(dificultad)* to overcome

vademécum (*pl* **vademécums**) *nm* vade mecum, handbook

vade retro *interj Hum (márchate)* stay away from me!; EXPR **¡v., Satanás!** get thee behind me, Satan!

vado *nm* **(a)** *(en acera)* lowered kerb ▸▸ ***v. permanente*** *(en letrero)* keep clear at all times **(b)** *(de río)* ford

Vaduz *n* Vaduz

vagabundear *vi* **(a)** *(ser un vagabundo)* to lead a vagrant's life **(b)** *(vagar)* **v. (por)** to wander (around), to roam

vagabundeo *nm* **(a)** *(de vagabundo)* vagrancy **(b)** *(sin rumbo)* wandering

vagabundería *nf Ven* dirty dealings

vagabundo, -a 1 *adj (persona)* vagrant; *(perro)* stray
2 *nm,f* **(a)** *(sin domicilio)* tramp, vagrant, *US* bum **(b)** *Ven (sinvergüenza)* crook
vagamente *adv* vaguely
vagancia *nf* **(a)** *(holgazanería)* laziness, idleness **(b)** *(vagabundeo)* vagrancy
vagar [38] *vi* **v. (por)** to wander (around), to roam; **vagando por las calles de la ciudad** wandering around *o* roaming the streets of the city
vagaroso, -a *adj* wandering
vagido *nm* cry *(of a newborn baby)*
vagina *nf* vagina
vaginal *adj* vaginal
vaginitis *nf inv* vaginitis
vago, -a 1 *adj* **(a)** *(persona)* lazy, idle; EXPR *Fam Hum* **ser más v. que la chaqueta de un guardia** to be bone-idle **(b)** *(imagen, recuerdo)* vague **(c)** *Med* **nervio v.** vagus nerve
2 *nm,f* lazy person, idler; **ser un v.** to be lazy *o* idle
3 *nm* **hacer el v.** to laze around
vagón *nm (de pasajeros)* carriage, coach; *(de mercancías)* wagon ►► ***v. cisterna*** tanker, tank wagon; ***v. de mercancías*** goods wagon *o* van; ***v. de pasajeros*** passenger car; ***v. de primera*** first-class carriage; ***v. restaurante*** dining car, restaurant car; ***v. de segunda*** second-class carriage
vagoneta 1 *nf* wagon
2 *adj RP Fam* lazy
vaguada *nf* valley floor
vague *etc ver* **vagar**
vaguear *vi Fam* to laze around
vaguedad *nf* **(a)** *(cualidad)* vagueness **(b)** *(dicho)* vague remark; **decir vaguedades** to talk in vague terms
vaguería *nf Fam* laziness, idleness; **no lo ha hecho simplemente por v.** he hasn't done it out of pure laziness
vaguitis *nf inv Fam* **tener v.** to be feeling lazy
vaharada *nf* whiff
vahído *nm* blackout, fainting fit; **me dio un v.** I blacked out *o* fainted
vaho 1 *nm* **(a)** *(vapor)* steam; **los cristales están cubiertos de v.** the windows are steamed up **(b)** *(aliento)* breath
2 **vahos** *nmpl Med* **hacer vahos** to inhale *(medicinal vapours)*
vaina *nf* **(a)** *(en planta)* pod
(b) *(de espada)* scabbard
(c) *Col, Perú, Ven muy Fam (problema)* pain; **iqué v.!** what a pisser!
(d) *Col, Perú, Ven muy Fam (cosa)* **cualquier v.** anything
(e) *Col, Perú, Ven muy Fam (tontería)* **idéjate de vainas!** stop pissing around!
(f) *Col, Perú, Ven muy Fam (persona o cosa molesta)* pain; **ése es un v.** he's a pain; **ser una v. seria** to be a real pain
(g) EXPR *Col, Perú, Ven muy Fam* **de v.** by fluke; **ni de v.** no way
vainica *nf* hemstitch
vainilla *nf* **(a)** *(esencia)* vanilla; **yogur de v.** vanilla yogurt **(b)** *Am (vainica)* drawnwork
vainillina *nf* vanillin
vainita *nf Carib* green bean
vaivén *nm* **(a)** *(balanceo) (de barco)* swaying, rocking; *(de péndulo, columpio)* swinging **(b)** *(fluctuación)* **vaivenes** ups and downs; **los vaivenes de la economía** the ups and downs of the economy
vajilla *nf* crockery; **lavar la v.** to wash the dishes; **una v.** a dinner service ►► ***v. de plata*** silverware; ***v. de porcelana*** china
valdepeñas *nm inv* Valdepeñas, = Spanish wine from the La Mancha region, usually red
valdiviano, -a 1 *adj* of/from Valdivia *(Chile)*
2 *nm,f* person from Valdivia *(Chile)*
valdré *etc ver* **valer**
vale[1] 1 *nm* **(a)** *(bono, cupón)* coupon, voucher ►► ***v. de compra*** *(por devolución)* credit note; *(como premio)* (gift) voucher; ***v. de descuento*** discount coupon *o* voucher; ***v. de regalo*** gift token **(b)** *(comprobante)* receipt **(c)** *(pagaré)* IOU **(d)** *(entrada gratuita)* free ticket
2 *interj Esp* **(a)** *(de acuerdo)* O.K.!, all right!; **¿quieres un helado? – iv.!** do you want an ice cream? – O.K. *o* all right!; **por mí, v.** it's fine *o* O.K. by me; **¿v.?** O.K.?, all right?; **tú te quedas aquí, ¿v.?** you stay here, right? **(b)** *(basta)* **iv. (ya)!** that's enough!; **¿v. así** *o* **v. con eso o quieres un poco más?** is that enough or do you want a bit more?
vale[2] *nm Méx, Ven Fam (amigo)* pal, *Br* mate, *US* buddy
valedero, -a *adj* valid
valedor, -ora *nm,f* **(a)** *(protector, defensor)* protector **(b)** *Méx Fam (amigo)* pal, *Br* mate, *US* buddy
valemadres, valemadrista *Méx muy Fam* 1 *adj* cynical
2 *nm* total cynic
valemadrismo *nm Méx muy Fam* cynicism
valemadrista = **valemadres**
valencia *nf Quím* valency ►► ***v. química*** chemical valency
valenciana *nf Méx Br* cuff, *US* turn-up
valenciano, -a 1 *adj* Valencian
2 *nm,f* Valencian
3 *nm (idioma)* Valencian
valentía *nf* **(a)** *(valor)* bravery **(b)** *(hazaña)* act of bravery
Valentín *n pr* **San V.** St Valentine
valentón, -ona *nm,f* **hacerse el v.** to boast of one's bravery
valentonada *nf* boast, brag

VALER [70] 1 *vt* **(a)** *(costar) (precio)* to cost; *(tener un valor de)* to be worth; **¿cuánto vale?** how much does it cost?, how much is it?; **¿cuántos pesos vale un dólar?, ¿cuánto vale un dólar en pesos?** how many pesos are there to the dollar?; **este cuadro vale mucho dinero** this painting is worth a lot of money; EXPR **v. su peso en oro** to be worth its/his/*etc* weight in gold
(b) *(suponer)* to earn; **su generosidad le valió el afecto de todos** her generosity earned her everyone's affection; **esta victoria puede valerles el campeonato** this win may be enough for them to take the championship; **aquello nos valió muchos disgustos** that cost us a lot of trouble
(c) *(merecer)* to deserve; **esta noticia bien vale una celebración** this news deserves a celebration
(d) *(en exclamaciones)* EXPR **iválgame Dios!** good God *o* heavens!
2 *vi* **(a)** *(tener valor, merecer aprecio) (persona, película, obra)* to be good; **él era el que más valía en el equipo** he was the most valuable member of the team; **ha demostrado que vale** he's shown his worth; **el muchacho vale mucho** the lad's very good; **su mujer vale más que él** his wife's worth more than him; **la obra vale poco/no vale nada** the play isn't up to much/is no good at all; **hacer v. algo** *(derechos, autoridad, poder)* to assert sth; **el equipo local hizo v. su superioridad** the home team made its superiority count; **hacerse v.** to show one's worth
(b) *(servir)* **eso aún vale** you can still use that; **tíralo, ya no vale** throw it away, it's no use any more; **¿te vale este martillo/este sobre?** is this hammer/this envelope any use to you?; **v. de algo: sus consejos me valieron de mucho** her advice proved of great value *o* use to me; **de nada le valdrán** *o* **no le valdrán de nada sus artimañas** all his tricks will be no good *o* of no use to him; **de nada vale insistir** *o* **que insistamos** there's no point (in) insisting, it's no use insisting; **¿de qué vale contratar un seguro si no cubre estos casos?** what's the use of *o* the point in taking out an insurance policy if it doesn't cover cases like these?; **v. para algo** *(objeto, instrumento, aparato)* to be for sth; *(persona, trabajador)* to be good at sth; **¿para qué vale?** *(cosa)* what's it for?; **no vale para nada** he's/she's/it's useless; **yo no valgo para mentir** I'm useless *o* no good at telling lies
(c) *(ser válido) (documento, carnet, argumentos, norma)* to be valid; *(respuesta)* to be correct; **eso no vale** *(en juegos)* that's not allowed; **no me valen esas razones** I don't consider those reasons to be acceptable *o* valid; **esta moneda ya no vale** this coin is no longer legal tender; **vale el gol** the goal stands; **vale la canasta** the basket still counts; **no vale el gol/la canasta** the goal/basket has been disallowed; **esta carrera vale para el campeonato del mundo** this race counts towards the world championship; **valga la expresión** if you'll pardon the expression; **valga la redundancia** if you'll forgive me for using two words that sound so similar in the same sentence; EXPR **no hay ... que valga: no hay disculpa que valga** there are no excuses
(d) *(equivaler)* **vale por 1.000 pesos** it's worth 1,000 pesos; **vale por una camiseta de regalo** it can be exchanged for a free T-shirt
(e) *Esp (ser la talla)* to be the right size, to fit; **ya no me vale la falda** the skirt doesn't fit me any more
(f) *Méx Fam (no importar)* to be irrelevant; **lo que él piense me vale** I couldn't care less what he thinks
(g) más vale: más vale que te calles/vayas it would be better if you shut up/left; **más vale que no trate de engañarnos** he'd better not try to cheat us; **la llamaré – imás te vale!** I'll call her – you'd better!; EXPR **más vale tarde que nunca** better late than never
3 *nm Formal* worth, value
4 **valerse** *vpr* **(a)** *(servirse)* **valerse de algo/alguien** to use sth/sb; **se valió de su apellido/sus amistades para triunfar** she used her name/

connections to achieve success (**b**) *(desenvolverse)* **valerse (solo** *o* **por sí mismo)** to manage on one's own (**c**) *Méx (estar permitido)* to be allowed; **no se vale mentir** lying's not allowed

valeriana *nf* valerian, allheal ►► ***v. griega*** Jacob's ladder

valerosidad *nf* bravery, courage

valeroso, -a *adj* brave, courageous

Valeta *nf* **La V.** Valletta, Valeta

valetudinario, -a *Formal* **1** *adj* valetudinary
2 *nm,f* valetudinarian

valgo *etc ver* **valer**

Valhalla = **Walhalla**

valía *nf (de persona)* worth; *(de objeto)* value, worth; **ha demostrado su v.** she has proved her worth; **un científico de reconocida v.** a scientist of recognised worth

validación *nf (de documento, pasaporte)* validation; **un paso más en la v. de la teoría de la relatividad** another step towards the validation of the theory of relativity

validar *vt* (**a**) *(documento, tarjeta de crédito, hipótesis, resultado)* to validate; **varios ensayos clínicos validan la eficacia de este medicamento** various clinical trials have validated *o* confirmed the effectiveness of this medicine (**b**) *Am (gol)* to give, to allow

validez *nf* (**a**) *(de documento, pasaporte)* validity; **periodo de v.** period of validity; **dar v. a** to validate; **tener v.** to be valid; **ambos diplomas tienen la misma v. oficial** both diplomas have the same official validity (**b**) *(de argumento, teoría)* validity; **este proyecto confirma la v. científica de su enfoque** this project confirms the scientific validity of his approach; **tener v.** to be valid

valido, -a *nm,f Hist* royal adviser

válido, -a *adj* (**a**) *(documento, pasaporte)* valid (**b**) *(argumento, teoría)* valid

valiente 1 *adj* (**a**) *(valeroso)* brave, courageous (**b**) *Irónico (menudo)* **¡en v. lío te has metido!** you've got yourself into a fine mess!; **¡v. amigo estás hecho!** some friend you are!
2 *nmf* brave person

valientemente *adv* bravely, courageously

valiera *etc ver* **valer**

valija *nf* (**a**) *(maleta)* case, suitcase ►► ***v. diplomática*** diplomatic bag (**b**) *(de correos)* mailbag (**c**) *Urug (maletero) Br* boot, *US* trunk

valijero, -a *nm,f* (**a**) *(de diplomacia)* courier (**b**) *RP (en placard)* top cupboard (**c**) *Urug (maletero) Br* boot, *US* trunk

valimiento *nm (protección)* protection

valioso, -a *adj* (**a**) *(joya, documento)* valuable (**b**) *(consejo, tiempo)* valuable (**c**) *(intento, esfuerzo)* worthy

valium® *nm* Valium®

valla *nf* (**a**) *(cerca)* fence; **poner una v. alrededor de un terreno** to fence off a piece of land ►► ***v. electrificada*** electric fence; ***v. publicitaria*** billboard, *Br* hoarding (**b**) *Dep* hurdle; **los 110 metros vallas** the 110 metres hurdles (**c**) *Col, PRico (gallinero)* cockpit

valladar *nm* (**a**) *(cercado)* fence (**b**) *Dep* **es un v. para su equipo** he's a pillar of his team's defence

vallado *nm* fence

vallar *vt* to fence, to put a fence round; **un solar vallado** a fenced plot; **han vallado el terreno** the land has been fenced in

valle *nm* (**a**) *(entre montañas)* valley ►► ***v. de lágrimas*** vale of tears (**b**) *(de curva, línea)* trough

vallenato *nm* = a style of popular music from Colombia

vallisoletano, -a 1 *adj* of/from Valladolid *(Spain)*
2 *nm,f* person from Valladolid *(Spain)*

valón, -ona 1 *adj* Walloon
2 *nm,f (persona)* Walloon
3 *nm (lengua)* Walloon

valona *nf (crines)* mane

valonar *vt Andes (crines)* to crop

VALOR *nm* (**a**) *(precio, utilidad, mérito)* value; **ha subido el v. del peso frente al dólar** the peso has risen against the dollar; **tiene v. sentimental** it is of sentimental value; **tiene más v. arqueológico que artístico** it is of more archaeological than artistic value; **de (mucho) v.** (very) valuable; **no había nada de v. en la casa** there was nothing of value in the house; **joyas por v. de...** jewels worth...; **sin v.** worthless; **tener v.** *(ser valioso)* to be valuable; *(ser válido)* to be valid; **sin el sello oficial carece de** *o* **no tiene v.** it is not valid without the official seal; **tener mucho/poco v.** to be very/not very valuable ►► *Econ* ***v. activo neto*** net asset value; *Fin* ***v. actual neto*** net present value; ***v. adquisitivo*** purchasing power; *Am Econ* ***v. agregado*** added value; ***v. alimenticio*** food value; *Econ* ***v. añadido*** added value; *Fin* ***v. asegurado*** insured value; ***v. biológico*** biological value; ***v. calórico*** *(de comida)* calorific value; ***v. catastral*** = value of a property recorded in the land register, *Br* ≃ rateable value, *US* ≃ assessed value; ***v. comercial*** commercial value; *Fin* ***v. contable*** book price *o* value; ***v. de mercado*** market value; ***v. nominal*** face *o* nominal value; ***v. nutritivo*** nutritional value; *Fin* ~ ***realizable neto*** net realizable value; *Fin* ***v. de reposición*** replacement value; *Fin* ***v. de rescate*** surrender value
(**b**) *Mat* value
(**c**) *Mús* value
(**d**) *(importancia)* importance; **su opinión es de enorme v. para nosotros** her opinion is of great value *o* importance to us; **dar v. a** to give *o* attach importance to; **quitar v. a algo** to take away from sth, to diminish sth
(**e**) *(valentía)* bravery; **se necesita v. para hacer una cosa así** you need to be brave *o* it takes courage to do a thing like that; **armarse de v.** to pluck up one's courage; **le eché v., y le confesé la verdad** I plucked up my courage and told her the truth; EXPR **¡v. y al toro!** go for it!
(**f**) *(desvergüenza)* cheek, nerve; **¡hace falta v. para decir eso!** what a cheek *o* nerve saying a thing like that!; **tener el v. de hacer algo** to have the cheek *o* nerve to do sth
(**g**) *(personaje)* **un joven v. del atletismo/teatro** an up-and-coming young athlete/actor
(**h**) **valores** *(principios)* values
(**i**) *Fin* **valores** *(de inversión)* securities ►► ***valores en cartera*** investment portfolio; ***valores de crecimiento*** growth stock; ***valores inmuebles*** real estate; ***valores negociables*** negotiable securities; ***valores de renta fija*** fixed-interest *o* fixed-income securities; ***valores de renta variable*** variable-interest *o* variable-income securities, equities

valoración *nf* (**a**) *(tasación) (de obra de arte)* valuation; *(de pérdidas, daños)* assessment, estimation; **hicieron una v. de los daños** they assessed the damage
(**b**) *(evaluación) (de mérito, cualidad, ventajas)* evaluation, assessment; **¿cuál es su v. sobre el nuevo defensa del equipo?** what is your assessment of the team's new defender? **el ministro hizo ayer una v. positiva de los datos del paro** the minister yesterday described the job figures as encouraging

valorar *vt* (**a**) *(tasar) (obra de arte)* to value; *(daños)* to assess, to estimate; **la casa está valorada en 25 millones** the house is valued at 25 million
(**b**) *(evaluar)* to evaluate, to assess; **su actuación ha sido valorada muy positivamente** her performance has been judged very favourably; **el peor valorado entre todos los candidatos** the least favoured among the candidates
(**c**) *(apreciar)* to value; **no saben v. el trabajo de los enseñantes** they do not value the work that teachers do; **valoran mucho los conocimientos de inglés** they value a knowledge of English very highly

valorización *nf* increase in value

valorizar [14] **1** *vt* to increase the value of
2 valorizarse *vpr* to increase in value

valquiria *nf* Valkyrie

vals *nm* waltz

valsar *vi* to waltz

valuar [4] *vt* to value

valva *nf Zool* valve

válvula *nf* (**a**) *(para regular el paso)* valve ►► *Anat* ***v. aórtica*** aortic valve; ***v. de escape*** means of letting off steam; **el futbol les sirve de v. de escape** soccer is a way for them to let off steam; *Anat* ***v. mitral*** mitral valve; *Anat* ***v. pulmonar*** pulmonary valve; ***v. de seguridad*** safety valve; *Anat* ***v. tricúspide*** tricuspid valve (**b**) **v. (de vacío)** *(de radio)* valve, *US* vacuum tube

vamos 1 *ver* **ir**
2 *adv (introduce inciso, matiz o conclusión)* **tendrás que hacer la compra tú, v., si no es mucha molestia** you'll have to do the shopping yourself, if it's not too much trouble, of course; **se trata de un amigo, v., de un conocido** he's a friend, well, more of an acquaintance, really; **v., que al final la fiesta fue un desastre** anyway, in the end the party was a disaster

vampiresa *nf Fam* vamp, femme fatale

vampirismo *nm* vampirism

vampiro *nm* (**a**) *(personaje)* vampire (**b**) *(murciélago)* vampire bat (**c**) *Pey (aprovechado)* bloodsucker, leech

vanadio *nm Quím* vanadium

vanagloria *nf* boastfulness

vanagloriarse *vpr* to boast (**de** about); **v. de hacer algo** to boast of doing sth

vanamente *adv* (**a**) *(inútilmente)* in vain (**b**) *(con vanidad)* vainly

Vancouver *n* Vancouver

vandálico, -a *adj* vandalistic; **un acto v.** an act of vandalism

vandalismo *nm* vandalism

vándalo, -a 1 *adj Hist* Vandal
2 *nm,f Hist* Vandal
3 *nm (salvaje)* vandal; **son unos vándalos** they're vandals

vanesa *nf* vanessa

vanguardia *nf* (**a**) *Mil* vanguard (**b**) *(cultural)* avant-garde, vanguard; **la literatura/música de v.** avant-garde literature/music; **las vanguardias del siglo XX** the avant-gardes of the 20th century; **estar** *o* **ir a la v. de** to be at the forefront of; **van a la v. de los avances tecnológicos** they are at the forefront of *o* at the cutting edge of technological progress

vanguardismo *nm* (**a**) *(movimiento)* avant-garde; **los vanguardismos del siglo pasado** the avant-gardes of the last century (**b**) *(cualidad)* avant-gardism

vanguardista 1 *adj* avant-garde
2 *nmf* member of the avant-garde

vanidad *nf* (**a**) *(orgullo)* vanity; **se niega a admitir sus pequeños defectos por v.** he refuses out of vanity to admit his little defects (**b**) *(inutilidad)* futility (**c**) *(del mundo)* vanity; **v. de vanidades** vanity of vanities

vanidoso, -a 1 *adj* vain, conceited
2 *nm,f* vain *o* conceited person; **es un v.** he's vain *o* conceited

vano, -a 1 *adj* (**a**) *(inútil) (intento, ilusiones)* vain; **hubiera sido una pretensión vana por mi parte** it would have been a vain hope on my part; **vanas esperanzas** empty hopes; **todos nuestros esfuerzos fueron vanos** all our efforts were in vain (**b**) *(vacío) (palabras, promesas)* empty (**c**) *(persona)* vain, conceited
2 *nm (de puerta)* doorway
3 en vano *loc adv* in vain; **intenté consolarle, pero fue en v.** I tried to console him but it was in vain; **no en v.: han de pasar por unas pruebas durísimas, no en v. son un cuerpo de élite** they have to pass some very tough exams, they're not an elite corps for nothing

Vanuatú *n* Vanuatu

vapor *nm* (**a**) *(de agua)* steam; **al v.** steamed; **verduras (cocidas) al v.** steamed vegetables; **barco de v.** steamer, steamship; **máquina de v.** steam engine ►► ***v. de agua*** water vapour (**b**) *(emanación)* vapour; **los vapores de gases nocivos/de productos volátiles** the vapours of noxious gases/volatile products (**c**) *(barco)* steamer, steamship

vaporeta® *nf* vaporetto®, = cleaning appliance that uses high-pressure steam

vaporizador *nm* (**a**) *(pulverizador)* spray (**b**) *(para evaporar)* vaporizer

vaporizar [14] **1** *vt* (**a**) *Fís* to vaporize (**b**) *(pulverizar)* to spray
2 vaporizarse *vpr Fís* to vaporize

vaporosidad *nf* diaphanous quality

vaporoso, -a *adj* (**a**) *(tela, vestido)* diaphanous, sheer (**b**) *(ducha, baño)* steamy

vapulear *vt* (**a**) *(golpear)* to beat, to thrash; *(zarandear)* to shake about; **v. los derechos de alguien** to trample on sb's rights (**b**) *(criticar)* to slate; **la crítica vapuleó la obra** the critics slated the work (**c**) *Fam (vencer)* to thrash, to give a hiding to

vapuleo *nm* (**a**) *(golpes)* beating, thrashing; *(zarandeo)* shaking about; *(falta de respeto)* abuse (**b**) *(crítica)* slating (**c**) *Fam* **dar un v. a alguien** *(vencerlo)* to thrash sb, to give sb a hiding

vaque *etc ver* **vacar**

vaquería *nf* (**a**) *(de leche)* dairy (**b**) *Arg Fam (tienda de vaqueros)* jeans shop

vaqueriza *nf* cowshed

vaquerizo, -a *nm,f* cowboy, *f* cowgirl

vaquero, -a 1 *adj (tela)* denim; **cazadora vaquera** denim jacket; **tela vaquera** denim; **pantalón v.** jeans
2 *nm,f (persona)* cowboy, *f* cowgirl; **una película de vaqueros** a western, a cowboy movie
3 *nm (pantalón)* jeans; **unos vaqueros** (a pair of) jeans

vaqueta *nf RP* leather, calfskin

vaquilla *nf* (**a**) *(vaca)* heifer; *(toro)* young bull (**b**) ***v. de S. Antón*** *Br* ladybird, *US* ladybug

vaquillona *nf CSur* heifer

vaquita *nf RP* ***v. de San Antón*** *o* ***Antonio*** *Br* ladybird, *US* ladybug

vara *nf* (**a**) *(rama, palo)* stick
(**b**) *(tallo)* stem, stalk
(**c**) *(pértiga)* pole
(**d**) *(bastón de mando)* rod, staff
(**e**) *(de trombón)* slide
(**f**) *Taurom* = pike used by picador; EXPR *Fam* **dar la v.** to be a pain (in the neck); *Fam* **dar la v. a alguien para que haga algo** to go on at sb to do sth
(**g**) *(medida)* yard ►► ***v. de medir*** yardstick; **no se utiliza la misma v. de medir para todos** not everyone is measured by the same yardstick

varada *nf (de barco)* beaching

varadero *nm* dry dock

varado, -a *adj* (**a**) *(barco) (encallado)* aground, stranded; *(en el dique seco)* in dry dock; **hay una ballena varada en el puerto** there's a beached whale in the harbour
(**b**) *CSur Fam (persona)* **estar** *o* **quedar v.** to be left stranded; **se rompió el auto y quedamos varados en mitad de la carretera** the car broke down and we were left stranded in the middle of the road; **estamos varados en el pasado** we are trapped in the past

varadura *nf (de barco)* running aground

varamiento *nm Am (de ballena)* beaching

varano *nm* monitor lizard

varapalo *nm* (**a**) *(paliza)* hiding (**b**) *(crítica)* slating; **dar un v. a algo/alguien** to slate sth/sb

varar 1 *vt* to beach
2 *vi* to run aground
3 vararse *vpr* (**a**) *(barco, ballena)* to be beached (**b**) *Am (averiarse)* to break down

varazón *nf Am* beaching; **todos los años hay alguna v. de ballenas/peces** whales get beached/fish get washed up every year

varear *vt* (**a**) *(árbol, fruto)* **v. las aceitunas** = to beat the branches of olive trees with a wooden pole to bring down the ripe olives (**b**) *(lana)* to beat

varejón *nm Am (palo delgado)* thin pole

vareo *nm* (**a**) *(de árbol, fruto)* = technique for harvesting olives by beating the branches of the tree with a wooden pole to shake the fruit loose (**b**) *(de lana)* beating

variabilidad *nf* changeability, variability

variable 1 *adj* changeable, variable
2 *nf Mat* variable ►► ***v. aleatoria*** random variable

variación *nf* (**a**) *(cambio)* variation; *(del tiempo)* change (**de** in); **en cuanto a la Bolsa, apenas ha habido v. esta semana** there has been hardly any change in the stock market this week; **¡v. izquierda!** left turn! ►► ***v. magnética*** magnetic variation *o* deviation (**b**) *Mús* variation; **variaciones sobre el mismo tema** variations on a theme

variado, -a *adj* (**a**) *(diverso)* varied; **fue un día muy v.** it was a very varied day (**b**) *(galletas, bombones)* assorted

variante 1 *adj* variant
2 *nf* (**a**) *(variación)* variation; *(versión)* version; **una v. virulenta de salmonella** a virulent variant of salmonella (**b**) *(de palabra, pronunciación)* variant ►► ***v. ortográfica*** variant spelling (**c**) *(de carretera)* by-pass; *(de vía de tren)* bypass line (**d**) *(en quiniela)* draw or away win
3 variantes *nfpl* mixed pickles

varianza *nf (en estadística)* variance

variar [32] **1** *vt* (**a**) *(modificar)* to alter, to change; **fue necesario v. el rumbo** it was necessary to change course (**b**) *(dar variedad a)* to vary; **me gusta v. el camino al trabajo** I like to vary my route to work
2 *vi* (**a**) *(cambiar)* to change; **las circunstancias varían a lo largo del año** the circumstances change over the year; **ha variado de color** it has changed colour; **para v.** for a change; **está lloviendo, para v.** it's raining for a change (**b**) *(ser diferente)* to vary, to differ (**de** from); **las causas varían de un país a otro** the causes vary from one country to another

várice *nf Am* varicose vein

varicela *nf* chickenpox

varicosidad *nf* varicosity

varicoso, -a *adj* varicose

variedad 1 *nf* (**a**) *(diversidad)* variety; **hay gran v. de modelos** there is a wide variety of models (**b**) *(de planta)* variety; *(de animal)* breed

2 variedades *nfpl Teatro* variety, music hall; **artista de variedades** *Br* variety *o US* vaudeville artist

varilla[1] *nf (barra delgada)* rod; *(de abanico, paraguas)* spoke, rib; *(de gafas)* arm

varilla[2] *nf Ven Fam* (**a**) *(contrariedad)* pain; **es una v. tener que esperar** it's a pain having to wait

(**b**) *(cosa)* **cualquier v.** anything

(**c**) *(situación)* situation; **no aguanto más esta v., voy a buscar otro empleo** I can't stand this situation any more, I'm going to look for another job

(**d**) *(tontería)* **¡deja ya de varillas!** stop fooling around!

(**e**) *(persona o cosa molesta)* pain; **Juan es una v., siempre quiere algo** Juan's a pain, he's always after something

(**f**) *(insulto)* gibe, dig; **es insoportable, siempre sale con alguna v.** she's unbearable, she always has to have a gibe at somebody

varillaje *nm (de abanico, paraguas)* spokes, ribbing

variopinto, -a *adj* diverse

varios, -as 1 *adj (diversos)* several; **pantalones de v. colores** trousers in several *o* different colours; **hay varias maneras de hacerlo** there are several *o* various ways of doing it; **los motivos son v.** there are various reasons; **apareció en artículos v. del periódico** it appeared in various articles in the paper

2 *pron pl* several; **delante de v. de sus compañeros** in front of several colleagues; **el accidente lo vimos v.** quite a few of us saw the accident

varita *nf* (**a**) *(palo)* wand ►► ***v. mágica*** magic wand (**b**) *RP Fam (policía de tránsito)* traffic policeman

variz (*pl* **varices** *o* **várices**) *nf* varicose vein

varón 1 *adj* **dos hijos varones** two sons

2 *nm (hombre)* male, man; *(chico)* boy; **sexo: v.** sex: male; **tuvo dos varones y una hembra** she had two boys and a girl; **un santo v.** a saint

varonil *adj* (**a**) *(del varón)* masculine, male (**b**) *(viril)* manly, virile; **un hombre muy v.** a very manly man; **una mujer un tanto v.** a rather mannish woman

Varsovia *n* Warsaw

varsoviano, -a 1 *adj* of/from Warsaw *(Poland)*

2 *nm,f* person from Warsaw *(Poland)*

vasallaje *nm* (**a**) *(servidumbre)* servitude (**b**) *(impuesto)* liege money

vasallo, -a *nm,f* (**a**) *(siervo)* vassal (**b**) *(súbdito)* subject

vasar *nm* kitchen shelf

vasco, -a 1 *adj* Basque

2 *nm,f (persona)* Basque

3 *nm (lengua)* Basque

vascofrancés, -esa 1 *adj* of/from the French Basque provinces

2 *nm* French Basque

Vascongadas *nfpl* **las V.** the (Spanish) Basque Country

vascongado, -a 1 *adj* Basque

2 *nm,f* Basque

vascuence *nm (lengua)* Basque

vascular *adj* vascular

vasculitis *nf inv* vasculitis

vasectomía *nf* vasectomy

vasectomizar [14] *vt* to give a vasectomy to

vaselina *nf* (**a**) *(producto)* Vaseline® (**b**) *(en fútbol)* lob

vasija *nf* (**a**) *(de barro)* earthenware vessel (**b**) *(de reactor nuclear)* containment vessel

vaso *nm* (**a**) *(recipiente)* glass; **un v. de plástico** a plastic cup ►► ***vasos comunicantes*** communicating vessels; **un sistema de vasos comunicantes entre todos los ámbitos de la sociedad** a network of interconnections between all sectors of society; ***v. de papel*** paper cup; ***v. de precipitados*** beaker

(**b**) *(contenido)* glass; **se bebió un v. entero** he drank a whole glass; **un v. de vino** a glass of wine

(**c**) *(conducto)* vessel ►► ***vasos capilares*** capillaries; ***v. linfático*** lymphatic vessel; ***vasos sanguíneos*** blood vessels

(**d**) *(jarrón)* vase

(**e**) *Bot* vein

vasoconstricción *nf* vasoconstriction

vasoconstrictor, -ora 1 *adj* vasoconstrictor

2 *nm* vasoconstrictor

vasodilatación *nf* vasodilation

vasodilatador, -ora 1 *adj* vasodilator

2 *nm* vasodilator

vástago *nm* (**a**) *(descendiente)* descendant; **sus vástagos** her offspring (**b**) *(brote)* shoot; *Col, CRica, Ven (de banana)* banana stalk (**c**) *(varilla)* rod

vastedad *nf* (**a**) *(de extensión, territorio)* vastness (**b**) *(de conocimientos, cultura)* vastness

vasto, -a *adj* (**a**) *(extensión, territorio)* vast (**b**) *(conocimientos, cultura)* vast

vate *nm Formal* bard

váter *nm* toilet

Vaticano *n* **el V.** the Vatican

vaticano, -a *adj* Vatican

vaticinador, - ora 1 *adj* prophetic

2 *nm,f* prophet

vaticinar *vt* (**a**) *(predecir)* to predict, to forecast; **los expertos vaticinan una subida del dólar** the experts are predicting *o* forecasting a rise in the dollar (**b**) *(adivino)* to prophesy

vaticinio *nm* (**a**) *(predicción)* prediction, forecast; **acertaron los vaticinios más pesimistas** the most pessimistic predictions *o* forecasts turned out to be right (**b**) *(adivinación)* prophecy

vatímetro *nm* wattmeter

vatio *nm* watt

vaya 1 *ver* **ir**

2 *interj* (**a**) *(expresa sorpresa)* well!; **¡v.! ¡tú por aquí!** fancy seeing you here!; **¡v., v.! no me esperaba eso de ti** well, I certainly didn't expect that from you!

(**b**) *(expresa admiración)* **¡v. moto!** what a motorbike!; **¡v. si me gusta!** you bet I like it!; *Irónico* **¡v. (un) amigo!** some friend he is!; **¡v. con la dichosa cuestecita!** so much for this being a little hill!, some little hill this is!

(**c**) *(expresa contrariedad, disgusto)* oh no!; **¡v., me equivoqué otra vez!** oh, no, I've got it wrong again!; **¡v.! ¡ya te has manchado las manos otra vez!** honestly, you've gone and got your hands dirty again!; **¡v. por Dios!** *o Esp* **¡v., hombre! para una vez que compro gambas, me las dan pasadas** can you believe it *o* honestly, the one time I buy some prawns, they're off!

3 *adv* (**a**) *(introduce matiz o conclusión)* **tenían sus diferencias, v., que no se aguantaban** they had their differences, in fact, to be honest they couldn't stand each other (**b**) *(bueno, bien)* not bad, O.K.

V. B. (*abrev de* **visto bueno**) *(en documento)* approved

Vd. (*abrev de* **usted**) you

Vda. (*abrev de* **viuda**) widow

Vds. (*abrev de* **ustedes**) you

ve[1] *ver* **ir**

ve[2] *nf (letra)* v; *Am* **ve corta** v *(to distinguish from b)*

véase *ver* **ver**

vecinal *adj* (**a**) *(relaciones, trato)* neighbourly (**b**) *(asociación)* neighbourhood; *(camino, impuestos)* local

vecindad *nf* (**a**) *(barrio)* neighbourhood (**b**) *(cualidad)* neighbourliness; **un gesto de buena v.** a neighbourly gesture (**c**) *(alrededores)* vicinity (**d**) *Méx (vivienda)* = communal dwelling where poor families each live in a single room and share bathroom and kitchen with others

vecindario *nm* (**a**) *(barrio)* neighbourhood (**b**) *(vecinos)* neighbourhood, residents; **lo sabe todo el v.** the whole neighbourhood knows

vecino, -a 1 *adj* (**a**) *(cercano)* neighbouring; **lo trajeron de un pueblo v.** they brought it from a neighbouring village

(**b**) *(contiguo)* neighbouring; **el país v.** the neighbouring country; **v. a** next to; **una tienda vecina al restaurante** a shop next (door) to *o* adjacent to the restaurant

(**c**) *(parecido)* similar

2 *nm,f* (**a**) *(de la misma casa, calle)* neighbour; **es mi v.** he's a neighbour of mine; *Méx Fam* **el v. del norte** our northern neighbour *(the United States)*

(**b**) *(habitante) (de un barrio)* resident; *(de una localidad)* inhabitant; **las asociaciones de vecinos** the residents' associations; **una localidad de 500 vecinos** a village of 500 inhabitants; **Juan García, v. de Guadalajara** Juan García of Guadalajara

vector, -ora 1 *adj Med* vector

2 *nm* (**a**) *Fís & Tec* vector (**b**) *Med* vector

vectorial *adj* vectorial

veda *nf* (**a**) *(prohibición)* ban *(on hunting and fishing)*; **levantar la v.** to open the season (**b**) *(periodo)* close season

vedado, -a 1 *adj* prohibited
2 *nm* reserve ►► **v. de caza** game reserve

vedar *vt* (**a**) *(prohibir)* to prohibit, to ban; **tiene vedada la entrada al club** he has been banned from the club; **la política es un tema vedado en tales reuniones** politics is a taboo subject in such meetings (**b**) *(impedir)* to prevent; **la valla veda el paso a la propiedad** the fence bars the way into the estate (**c**) *(caza, pesca)* to prohibit, to ban

vedette [be'ðet] *nf* (**a**) *(en cabaret)* cabaret star (**b**) *(persona destacada)* star; **una v. del fútbol argentino** one of the stars of Argentinian soccer

védico, -a *adj* Vedic

vedija *nf (de lana, pelo)* tuft

vedismo *nm* Vedism

vega *nf* (**a**) *(terreno fértil)* fertile plain (**b**) *Cuba (tabacal)* tobacco plantation

vegetación 1 *nf* vegetation
2 **vegetaciones** *nfpl Med* adenoids

vegetal 1 *adj* (**a**) *(vida, célula)* plant; **el mundo v.** the plant kingdom (**b**) *(aceite, extracto)* vegetable; **sándwich v.** salad sandwich
2 *nm* vegetable; *Fam* **se convirtió en un v.** he became a vegetable

vegetalianismo *nm* veganism

vegetaliano, -a 1 *adj* vegan
2 *nm,f* vegan

vegetar *vi* (**a**) *(planta)* to grow (**b**) *Fam (persona)* to vegetate

vegetarianismo *nm* vegetarianism

vegetariano, -a 1 *adj* vegetarian
2 *nm,f* vegetarian ►► **v. estricto** vegan

vegetativo, -a *adj* vegetative

veguero, -a 1 *nm,f (labrador)* farmworker
2 *nm (cigarro)* = cigar made from a single tobacco leaf

vehemencia *nf* (**a**) *(pasión, entusiasmo)* vehemence (**b**) *(irreflexión)* impulsiveness, impetuosity

vehemente *adj* (**a**) *(apasionado, entusiasta)* vehement (**b**) *(irreflexivo)* impulsive, impetuous

vehicular *Formal* 1 *adj* **lengua v.** teaching language; **el tráfico v.** vehicular traffic
2 *vt* to serve as a vehicle for

vehículo *nm* (**a**) *(medio de transporte)* vehicle ►► **v. espacial** spacecraft; **vehículos industriales** industrial vehicles; **v. lanzador** launching vehicle; **v. pesado** heavy goods vehicle (**b**) *(medio de propagación) (de enfermedad)* carrier; *(de ideas)* vehicle

veinte *núm* twenty; **los (años) v.** the twenties; EXPR *Méx Fam* **caerle el v. a alguien: al final le cayó el v.** he finally got the point, the penny finally dropped; *ver también* **treinta**

veinteañero, -a 1 *adj* = in one's twenties
2 *nm,f* = person in his/her twenties; **para veinteañeros** for people in their twenties, for twenty-somethings

veinteavo, -a *núm (fracción)* twentieth; **la veinteava parte** a twentieth

veintena *nf* **una v. de...** *(unos veinte)* about twenty...; *(veinte)* twenty...; **andará por la v.** he must be about twenty

veinticinco *núm* twenty-five; *ver también* **treinta**

veinticuatro *núm* twenty-four; *ver también* **treinta**

veintidós *núm* twenty-two; *ver también* **treinta**

veintinueve *núm* twenty-nine; *ver también* **treinta**

veintiocho *núm* twenty-eight; *ver también* **treinta**

veintiséis *núm* twenty-six; *ver también* **treinta**

veintisiete *núm* twenty-seven; *ver también* **treinta**

veintitantos, -as *núm Fam* twenty-odd; **el v. de julio** the twenty-somethingth of July

veintitrés *núm* twenty-three; *ver también* **treinta**

veintiuna *nf (juego) Br* pontoon, *US* blackjack, *US* twenty-one

veintiuno, -a *núm*

> **Veintiún** is used instead of **veintiuno** before masculine nouns (e.g. **veintiún hombres** twenty-one men).

twenty-one; *ver también* **treinta**

vejación *nf,* **vejamen** *nm* humiliation; **las vejaciones que sufrió como inmigrante** the humiliations he suffered as an immigrant

> **Falso amigo**: El sustantivo inglés **vexation** no es la traducción del español **vejación**. En inglés **vexation** significa "disgusto" o "enfado".

vejar *vt* to humiliate

vejatorio, -a *adj* humiliating

vejestorio *nm Fam Pey* (**a**) *(persona)* old codger *o Br* crock (**b**) *Am (cosa)* old thing *o* relic

vejete *nm Fam* old guy *o Br* bloke

vejez *nf* old age; **pasó su v. en París** she spent her later years *o* old age in Paris; EXPR *Fam* **¡a la v., viruelas!** fancy that, at his/her age!

vejiga *nf* (**a**) *(órgano)* bladder ►► **v. de la bilis** gall bladder; *Zool* **v. natatoria** swim *o* air bladder; **v. de la orina** (urinary) bladder (**b**) *(ampolla)* blister (**c**) *RP, Ven Fam (idiota)* idiot, *Br* twit

vejuco, -a, vejucón, -ona *Ven Fam Pey* 1 *adj* old
2 *nm,f* old man, *f* old woman

vela 1 *nf* (**a**) *(para dar luz)* candle; **ponerle una v. a un santo** to light a candle for a saint; EXPR **estar a dos velas** not to have two halfpennies to rub together; EXPR **poner una v. a Dios y otra al diablo** to hedge one's bets; EXPR *Fam* **quedarse a dos velas** to be left none the wiser; EXPR *Fam* **¿quién te ha dado v. en este entierro?** *Br* who asked you to stick your oar in?, *US* who asked you to butt in? ►► **v. perfumada** scented candle
(**b**) *(de barco)* sail; **a toda v.** under full sail ►► **v. cangreja** gaff sail; **v. cuadra** square sail; **v. latina** lateen sail; **v. mayor** mainsail
(**c**) *(deporte)* sailing; **hacer v.** to go sailing ►► **v. deportiva** sailing
(**d**) *(vigilia)* vigil; **pasar la noche en v.** *(adrede)* to stay awake all night; *(desvelado)* to have a sleepless night
(**e**) *Taurom (cuerno)* horn
2 **velas** *nfpl Fam (mocos)* **ir con las velas colgando** to have snot hanging out of one's nose

velada *nf* evening; **una v. musical** a musical soirée, an evening of music

veladamente *adv* **le amenazaron v. con el despido** they made veiled threats to sack him; **le acusó v. de ser el culpable** she insinuated he was the guilty one

velado, -a *adj* (**a**) *(amenaza, crítica)* veiled (**b**) *(carrete)* damaged by exposure to sunlight

velador, -ora 1 *nm* (**a**) *(mesa)* pedestal table (**b**) *Andes, Méx (mesilla de noche)* bedside table (**c**) *Méx, RP (lámpara)* bedside lamp
2 *nm,f Méx (sereno)* night watchman

veladora *nf* (**a**) *Méx (vela)* candle (**b**) *Méx, RP (lámpara)* bedside lamp

velamen *nm* sails

velar[1] *adj Anat & Ling* velar

velar[2] 1 *vi* (**a**) *(cuidar)* **velan por la salud de los ciudadanos** they keep a watch on *o* look after the health of the nation's citizens; **velan por la seguridad del Estado** they are responsible for national security; **veló por que se cumpliera el acuerdo** he saw to it *o* ensured that the agreement was kept (**b**) *(no dormir)* to stay awake
2 *vt* (**a**) *(de noche) (muerto)* to keep a vigil over; *(enfermo)* to sit up with; **pasó la noche velando a su hijo enfermo** she sat up all night watching over her sick child; **v. las armas** to carry out the vigil of arms (**b**) *(ocultar)* to mask, to veil (**c**) *(carrete)* to damage by exposure to light, to fog
3 **velarse** *vpr (carrete)* to be damaged by exposure to light

velatorio *nm* (**a**) *(acto)* wake, vigil (**b**) *(lugar)* chapel of rest; *Fam* **esto parece un v.** it's like a wake here

velcro® *nm* Velcro®

veleidad *nf* (**a**) *(inconstancia)* fickleness (**b**) *(antojo, capricho)* whim

veleidoso, -a *adj* (**a**) *(inconstante)* fickle (**b**) *(caprichoso)* capricious

velero *nm (pequeño)* sailing boat; *(grande)* sailing ship

veleta 1 *nf* weather vane
2 *nmf Fam (persona)* **es un v.** he's very fickle

velís *nm Méx* suitcase

velista *nmf* yachtsman, *f* yachtswoman

veliz *nf Méx* suitcase

vello *nm (pelo)* hair; *(pelusilla)* down ►► **v. púbico** *o* **pubiano** pubic hair

vellocino *nm* fleece ►► **el v. de oro** the Golden Fleece

vellón *nm* (**a**) *(lana)* fleece (**b**) *(aleación)* = alloy of silver and copper; **monedas de v.** = coins made of a silver and copper alloy

vellosidad *nf (de pelo)* hairiness; *(de pelusilla)* downiness

velloso, -a, velludo, -a *adj (con pelo)* hairy; *(con pelusilla)* downy

velo *nm* (**a**) *(tela)* veil (**b**) *(prenda)* veil; **v. de monja** wimple; EXPR *Fam* **correr** *o* **echar un (tupido) v. sobre algo** to draw a veil over sth; EXPR **tomar el v.** to take the veil (**c**) *(cosa ligera)* veil; **un v. de humo** a veil of smoke; **un v. de envidia** a trace of envy (**d**) **v. del paladar** soft palate

velocidad *nf* (**a**) *(rapidez)* speed, *Espec* velocity; **íbamos a gran v.** we were going very fast; **¿a qué v. van?** what speed are they going at?, how fast are they going?; **a toda v.** *(en vehículo)* at full speed; **lo tuvimos que hacer a toda v.** we had to do it as fast as we could; **de alta v.** high-speed; **a la v. del rayo** as quick as lightning; **reducir la v.** to slow down ►► ***v. de crucero*** cruising speed; *Fís* ***v. límite*** terminal velocity; ***la v. de la luz*** the speed of light; ***v. máxima*** top speed; *Informát* ***v. de proceso*** processing speed; ***v. punta*** top speed; *Informát* ***v. de refresco*** refresh rate; *Informát* ***v. de reloj*** clock speed; ***la v. del sonido*** the speed of sound; ***v. supersónica*** supersonic speed; *Fís* ***v. terminal*** terminal velocity; *Informát* ***v. de transferencia*** transfer rate; *Informát* ***v. de transmisión*** *(en módem)* baud rate; ***v. de vuelo*** airspeed
(**b**) *Aut (marcha)* gear; **cambiar de v.** to change gear

velocímetro *nm* speedometer

velocípedo *nm* velocipede

velocista *nmf* sprinter

velódromo *nm* cycle track, velodrome

velomotor *nm* moped

velón *nm* (**a**) *(lámpara)* oil lamp (**b**) *Andes, RP (vela)* thick candle

velorio *nm* wake, vigil

veloz *adj* fast, quick

velozmente *adv* quickly, rapidly

ven *ver* **venir**

vena *nf* (**a**) *(vaso sanguíneo)* vein; **en v.: inyectarse en v.** *(substancia)* to be injected into a vein; *Fam* EXPR **llevar algo en las venas** to have sth in one's blood ►► ***v. cava*** vena cava; ***v. hepática*** hepatic vein; ***v. porta*** portal vein; ***v. pulmonar*** pulmonary vein; ***v. safena*** saphenous vein; ***v. subclavia*** subclavian vein; ***v. yugular*** jugular (vein)
(**b**) *(veta)* vein
(**c**) *Fam (ánimo)* mood; EXPR **darle la v.: si le da la v.** if the mood takes him; **cuando le da la v. se pone a cantar** when the mood takes her she'll start singing; EXPR *Fam* **estar en v.** *(inspirado)* to be feeling inspired; *(dispuesto)* to be in the right mood; *(en forma)* to be on form; **cuando está en v., escribe con mucho romanticismo** when he feels inspired, he writes very romantically; **no estaba en v. de conversación** she wasn't in the mood for conversation; **el equipo está en v. de aciertos** the team are on a winning streak ►► ***v. poética*** poetic vein
(**d**) *(don)* vein, streak; **tener v. de pintor** to have a gift for painting

venablo *nm* javelin

venado *nm (animal)* deer; *(carne)* venison

venalidad *nf* venality

vencedero, -a *adj Fin* payable

vencedor, -ora 1 *adj (equipo)* winning; *(ejército)* victorious
2 *nm,f (en competición)* winner; *(en batalla)* victor; **en una guerra civil no hay vencedores ni vencidos** in a civil war there are neither victors nor vanquished

vencejo *nm* swift ►► ***v. moro*** little swift; ***v. pálido*** pallid swift; ***v. real*** alpine swift

vencer [40] **1** *vt* (**a**) *(derrotar) (rival)* to beat; *(enemigo)* to defeat; **consiguió v. al cáncer** he won his battle against cancer
(**b**) *(superar) (miedo, obstáculos)* to overcome; *(tentación)* to resist; **venció al cansancio/sueño** she overcame her exhaustion/sleepiness; **lo venció el cansancio** he was overcome by tiredness
(**c**) *(aventajar)* **v. a alguien a** *o* **en algo** to outdo *o* beat sb at sth; **nadie lo vence a contar anécdotas** no one can beat him when it comes to telling stories
(**d**) *(hacer ceder)* to break, to snap; **el peso de los libros venció la estantería** the weight of the books caused the bookshelf to collapse
2 *vi* (**a**) *(equipo, partido)* to win; *(ejército)* to be victorious; **dejarse v. por el desánimo/la apatía** to let oneself be discouraged/to give in *o* succumb to apathy
(**b**) *(imponerse, prevalecer)* to prevail; **al final venció el sentido común** common sense prevailed in the end
(**c**) *(caducar) (garantía, contrato)* to expire; *(deuda, pago)* to fall due, to mature; *(bono)* to mature; *Am (medicamento)* to reach *o* pass its expiry date; **el plazo para entregar las solicitudes vence el 15 de mayo** the closing date *o* the deadline for sending in applications is 15th May
3 vencerse *vpr* (**a**) *(estante, cama)* to give way, to collapse (**b**) *Am (medicamento)* to pass its expiry date

vencido, -a 1 *adj* (**a**) *(derrotado)* defeated; **darse por v.** to give up (**b**) *(caducado) (garantía, contrato)* expired; *(deuda, pago)* due, mature; *(bono)* mature; *Am (medicamento)* past its expiry date
2 *nm,f (en deporte)* loser; **siempre hay un vencedor y un v.** there's always a winner and a loser; **los vencidos** *(en deporte)* the losers; *(en guerra)* the defeated, the vanquished; **el bando de los vencidos** the losing side

vencimiento *nm* (**a**) *(término) (de garantía, contrato, plazo)* expiry; *(de deuda, pago)* falling due, maturity; *(de bono)* maturity; **al v. del préstamo** when the loan falls due *o* matures; **deuda con v. a un año** debt with a maturity of one year; **opciones que pueden ejercitarse en cualquier momento hasta la fecha de v.** options that can be exercised at any time up to maturity
(**b**) *(de estante, suelo)* collapse

venda *nf* bandage, dressing; **una v. de gasa** a gauze bandage; EXPR **caérsele la v. de los ojos: cuando se le caiga la v. de los ojos** when the scales fall from his eyes; EXPR **tener una v. en** *o* **delante de los ojos** to be blind

vendaje *nm* (**a**) *(vendas)* bandaging, dressing (**b**) *Andes, Carib (dinero extra)* bonus

vendar *vt* to bandage, to dress; **v. los ojos a alguien** to blindfold sb; **tenía los ojos vendados** he was blindfolded

vendaval *nm* gale

vendedor, -ora 1 *adj* selling
2 *nm,f (en general)* seller; *(de coches, seguros)* salesman, *f* saleswoman; *(en tienda)* shop *o* sales assistant; *(en terminología legal)* vendor; **el mayor v. de juguetes del país** the biggest seller of toys in the country ►► ***v. ambulante*** street vendor; ***v. a domicilio*** door-to-door salesman; ***v. de periódicos*** newspaper seller

vender 1 *vt* (**a**) *(productos)* to sell; **v. algo a** *o* **por** to sell sth for; **venden naranjas a 20 pesos el kilo** they're selling oranges for 20 pesos a kilo; **se vende** *(en letrero)* for sale; **este modelo se vende mucho** this model is selling very well; **es capaz de v. a su madre** he'd sell his own mother; EXPR **v. su alma al diablo: es capaz de v. su alma al diablo por triunfar** he'd sell his soul to the Devil if that's what it took to be successful; EXPR **v. caro algo** not to give sth up without a fight; **el equipo vendió caro su título** the team did not give up its title without a fight; **la oposición venderá caro su apoyo** the opposition will demand a high price for its support; EXPR **no v. ni una escoba** to get absolutely nowhere; EXPR *Fam* **v. la moto a alguien: les vendió la moto de que iban a ser estrellas** he fooled them into believing they were going to be stars; **nos quieren v. la moto de que no van a subir los impuestos** they want us to swallow the story that they're not going to increase taxes; EXPR *RP* **v. salud** to be bursting with health
(**b**) *(idea, proyecto)* to sell
(**c**) *(amigo, familia)* to betray
2 *vi (producto, autor)* to sell; **eso no vende hoy día** that doesn't sell these days
3 venderse *vpr* (**a**) *(dejarse sobornar)* to sell out; **se ha vendido a las multinacionales** he has sold out to the multinationals; EXPR **venderse caro: te vendes muy caro** you're a hard man to find (**b**) *(descubrirse)* to give oneself away

vendetta *nf* vendetta

vendido, -a 1 *adj* sold; EXPR **estar** *o* **ir v.** not to stand a chance
2 *nm,f* **ser un v.** to have sold out

vendimia *nf* grape harvest

vendimiador, -ora *nm,f* grape picker

vendimiar 1 *vt* to harvest
2 *vi* to pick grapes

vendré *etc ver* **venir**

venduta *nf Cuba, RDom (tienda)* = small fruit and vegetable shop

Venecia *n* Venice

veneciano, -a 1 *adj* Venetian
2 *nm,f* Venetian

veneno *nm* (**a**) *(sustancia tóxica)* poison; *(de serpiente, insecto)* venom; **ese whisky es un v.** that whisky's lethal (**b**) *(mala intención)* venom; **el v. de sus palabras** the venom in his words

venenosidad *nf* poisonousness

venenoso, -a *adj* (**a**) *(sustancia, gas, planta)* poisonous; *(serpiente)* poisonous, venomous; **el monóxido de carbono es v.** carbon monoxide is poisonous (**b**) *(comentario, palabras)* venomous, malicious

venera *nf* (**a**) *(concha)* scallop shell (**b**) *(insignia)* scallop

venerable *adj* venerable

veneración *nf* (**a**) *(de familiar, famoso)* worship; **siente verdadera v. por su madre** he positively worships his mother (**b**) *(de dios, santo)* veneration, worship

venerador, -ora 1 *adj* venerational
2 *nm,f* venerator

venerar *vt* (**a**) *(familiar, famoso)* to worship (**b**) *(dios, santo)* to venerate, to worship

venéreo, -a *adj* venereal; **enfermedad venérea** venereal disease, VD

venereología *nf* venereology

venero *nm* (**a**) *(manantial)* spring, fountain (**b**) *Formal (origen)* fount; **un v. de datos** a fount *o* mine of information (**c**) *(de mineral)* seam, vein

venezolano, -a 1 *adj* Venezuelan
2 *nm,f* Venezuelan

Venezuela *n* Venezuela

venga *interj Esp Fam* (**a**) *(para animar)* come on!; **iv., vámonos!** come on, let's go!; **iv., pruébalo, que te va a gustar!** go on, try it, you'll like it! (**b**) *(para rechazar)* **iv. ya!, iv., hombre!** come off it! (**c**) *(expresando insistencia)* **v. a: yo con dolor de cabeza y él, v. a hablar** I had this headache but of course he just went on and on talking

vengador, -ora 1 *adj* avenging
2 *nm,f* avenger

venganza *nf* revenge, vengeance; **lo hicieron en v. por la muerte de su compatriota** they did it in revenge for the death of their countryman ▸▸ *Hum* ***la v. de Moctezuma*** Montezuma's revenge

vengar [38] **1** *vt* to avenge
2 vengarse *vpr* to take revenge (**de** on); **me vengaré de él algún día** I'll take my revenge *o* I'll get my own back on him some day; **se vengó en sus hijos** she took her revenge on his children

vengativo, -a *adj* vengeful, vindictive

vengo *etc ver* **venir**

vengue *etc ver* **vengar**

venia *nf* (**a**) *(permiso)* permission; **con la v.** *(al tomar la palabra)* by your leave (**b**) *(perdón)* pardon (**c**) *RP, Ven (saludo militar)* salute

venial *adj* venial

venialidad *nf* veniality

venida *nf* (**a**) *(llegada)* arrival (**b**) *(regreso)* return

venidero, -a *adj (generación)* future; **en años venideros** in years to come

VENIR [71] **1** *vi* (**a**) *(desplazarse, aproximarse)* to come; **ayer vino a casa** she came to visit us yesterday; **¿de dónde vienes?** where have you been?; **vengo del mercado** I've come from *o* been to the market; **v. a/de hacer algo** to come to do sth/from doing sth; **¿a qué has venido?** why have you come?, what have you come for?; **ven a ayudarme** come and help me; **voy y vengo** I'll be right back; **he venido (a) por Marta** I've come for Marta; **vinieron (a) por mí al aeropuerto** they picked me up at the airport; **todos veníamos muy cansados** we were all very tired; **vino hablando todo el camino** she spent the whole journey talking; **el año/mes que viene** next year/month; *RP* **v. al teléfono** to come to the phone

(**b**) *(llegar)* to arrive; *(regresar)* to get back; **aún no ha venido** *(llegado)* she hasn't arrived yet; *(regresado)* she's not back yet; **vendré tarde** I'll be late (back); **¿han venido los del gas?** has the gas man come yet?; **cuando venga el verano** when summer arrives

(**c**) *(pasar, ocurrir)* **en aquel año vino una recesión** there was a recession that year; **¿qué viene ahora?** what comes next?; **después de este programa viene una película** after this programme there's a movie

(**d**) *(proceder, derivarse)* **v. de algo** to come from sth; **viene de familia rica** she's from *o* she comes from a rich family; **el talento para la música le viene de familia** the gift for music runs in the family; **¿de qué árbol viene el caucho?** from what tree do we get rubber?; **de ahí viene que te duela la espalda** that's why your back is hurting; **viniendo de ella no me sorprende** it doesn't surprise me, coming from her

(**e**) *Fam (decir, soltar)* **v. a alguien con algo** to come to sb with sth; **no me vengas con exigencias** don't come to me making demands; **ino me vengas con ésas!** don't give me that!; **vino con que le hacía falta el dinero** he said he needed the money

(**f**) *(hallarse)* to be; **su foto viene en primera página** his photo is *o* appears on the front page; **¿dónde viene la sección de deportes?** where's the sports section?; **el texto viene en inglés** the text is in English; **vienen en todos los tamaños** they come in every size; **las anchoas vienen en lata** anchovies come in tins

(**g**) *(acometer, sobrevenir)* **me viene sueño** I'm getting sleepy; **me venían ganas de vomitar** I kept wanting to be sick; **le vinieron ganas de reír** he was seized by a desire to laugh; **me ha venido el periodo** my period has started; **le vino una tremenda desgracia** he suffered a great misfortune

(**h**) *(ropa, calzado)* **¿qué tal te viene?** does it fit all right?; **el abrigo le viene pequeño** the coat is too small for her; **este trabajo le viene un poco ancho** *o* **grande** he's not really up to this job

(**i**) *(convenir)* **v. bien/mal a alguien** to suit/not to suit sb; **el diccionario me vendrá muy bien** the dictionary will come in very useful; **¿qué tal te viene el lunes?** how's Monday for you?, how does Monday suit you?; **mañana no me viene bien** tomorrow isn't a good day for me, I can't make it tomorrow; **no te vendrían mal unas vacaciones** you could use a *Br* holiday *o US* vacation

(**j**) *(indica aproximación o resultado)* **viene a costar un millón** it costs almost a million; **esto viene a significar...** this effectively means...; **¿cómo has venido a parar aquí?** how did you end up here?; **v. a ser** to amount to; **viene a ser lo mismo** it doesn't make much difference; **v. a menos** *(negocio)* to go downhill; *(persona)* to go down in the world; **son una familia venida a menos** they're a family which has gone down in the world

(**k**) *Fam (orgasmo)* **me viene** I'm coming

(**l**) **¿a qué viene...?:¿a qué viene esto?** what do you mean by that?, what's that in aid of?; **¿a qué viene tanta amabilidad?** why all this kindness?, what's all this kindness in aid of?

2 *v aux* (**a**) *(antes de gerundio) (haber estado)* **v. haciendo algo** to have been doing sth; **vengo diciéndolo desde hace tiempo** I've been saying so for some time now; **las peleas vienen sucediéndose desde hace tiempo** fighting has been going on for some time; **el desempleo viene siendo el mayor problema** unemployment has been the major problem

(**b**) *(antes de participio) (haber sido)* **los cambios vienen motivados por la presión de la oposición** the changes have resulted from pressure on the part of the opposition; **un espectáculo que viene precedido de gran polémica** a show which has been surrounded by controversy

3 venirse *vpr* (**a**) *(venir)* to come; **¿te vienes?** are you coming?; **vente a casa si quieres** come over to my place if you like; **venirse abajo** *(techo, estante, edificio)* to collapse; *(ilusiones, planes)* to be dashed; *(persona)* to go to pieces; **ila que se nos viene encima!** we're really in for it!

(**b**) *(volver)* to come back (**de** from); **se vino de Argentina para montar un negocio** he came back from Argentina to start a business

(**c**) *Cuba, Méx muy Fam (tener un orgasmo)* to come

---

venopunción *nf* venipuncture; **sala** *o* **unidad de v.** injecting room

venosidad *nf* **tiene venosidades en la nariz** he's got a lot of blood vessels showing through on his nose

venoso, -a *adj* venous

venpermutar *vt Col* to offer for sale or exchange; **excelente lote se venpermuta por inmueble** prime plot of land for sale, or will exchange for a building

venta *nf* (**a**) *(acción)* sale; **de v. en tiendas especializadas** on sale in specialist shops *o* at specialist retailers; **estar en v.** to be for sale; **poner a la v.** *(casa)* to put up for sale; *(producto)* to put on sale; **salir a la v.** *(producto)* to go on sale; **el equipo de ventas** the sales team ▸▸ ***v. ambulante*** street vending; ***v. automatizada*** vending-machine sale; ***v. por catálogo*** mail-order selling; ***v. al contado*** cash sale; ***v. por correo*** mail order selling; ***v. por correspondencia*** mail order selling; ***v. a crédito*** credit sale; ***v. directa*** direct selling; ***v. a domicilio*** door-to-door selling; ***v. al por mayor*** wholesale; ***v. al por menor*** retail; ***v. piramidal*** pyramid selling; ***v. sobre plano*** sale of customized goods; ***v. a plazos*** sale by instalments, *Br* hire purchase; ***v. pública*** public auction; ***v. telefónica*** telephone sales

(**b**) *(cantidad)* sales; **la v. de hoy ha sido importante** sales have been strong today; **han aumentado/caído las ventas** sales have risen/fallen; **una novela que arrasa en ventas** a novel with phenomenal sales

(**c**) *(posada)* country inn

(**d**) **La V.** *(centro arqueológico)* = ancient Olmec city near the town of Villahermosa, Mexico

(**e**) *Chile (puesto en fiestas)* refreshment stand

ventaja *nf* (**a**) *(hecho favorable)* advantage; **tiene la v. de que es más manejable** it has the advantage of being easier to handle; **tenemos que sacarle las ventajas a la situación** we might as well look on the bright side ▸▸ *Com* ***v. competitiva*** competitive advantage; ***ventajas fiscales*** tax breaks; **invertir en cultura ofrece ventajas fiscales** there are tax advantages to investing in culture

(**b**) *(en competición)* lead; **dar v. a alguien** to give sb a start; **le dieron dos metros de v.** they gave him a two-metre start; **llevar v. a alguien** to have a lead over sb; **saca tres minutos de v. al pelotón** he has a three-minute lead over the pack, he's three minutes ahead of *o* clear of the pack

(**c**) *(en tenis)* advantage; **v. Hingis** advantage Hingis

ventajero, -a *RP* **1** *adj* opportunist
2 *nm,f* opportunist

ventajista 1 *adj* opportunist
2 *nmf* opportunist

ventajosamente *adv* favourably, to good effect; **permitirá a la empresa posicionarse v. en el mercado europeo** it will allow the company to position itself favourably in the European market; **puede ser empleado v. en el tratamiento de...** it can be used to good effect *o* with good results in the treatment of...

ventajoso, -a 1 *adj* (a) *(acuerdo, condiciones)* advantageous, favourable; **estar en una situación ventajosa** to be in a favourable position (b) *Col (ventajista)* opportunist
2 *nm,f Col* opportunist

ventana *nf* (a) *(en casa)* window; EXPR **echar** *o* **tirar algo por la v.** to let sth go to waste, to throw sth away; **estás tirando por la v. muchos años de investigación** you're throwing away many years of research ▸▸ ***v. de guillotina*** sash window; ***v. de socorro*** emergency exit (window)
(b) *Informát* window ▸▸ ***v. activa*** active window; ***v. de diálogo*** dialog *o Br* dialogue box
(c) *(de nariz)* ***v. de la nariz*** nostril

ventanaje *nm* windows

ventanal *nm* large window

ventanazo *nm (golpe)* **se oyó un v.** a window banged (shut)

ventanilla *nf* (a) *(de vehículo, sobre)* window
(b) *(taquilla, mostrador)* counter; **puede recoger las entradas en v.** tickets can be picked up at the box office; **estuve toda la mañana de v. en v.** I spent the whole morning going from one office to another ▸▸ ***v. única*** one-stop service, = Spanish system, designed to simplify citizens' dealings with the administration, whereby official documents can be obtained from a single office
(c) *(en sobre)* window

ventanillo *nm* (a) *(ventana pequeña)* small window (b) *(mirilla)* peephole (c) *(de barco)* porthole

ventarrón *nm Fam* strong *o* blustery wind

ventear 1 *v impersonal* to be very windy; **está venteando** it's very windy
2 *vt (aire)* to sniff
3 *vi (animal)* to sniff

ventero, -a *nm,f* innkeeper

ventilación *nf* ventilation; **la mala v. de los edificios modernos** the bad ventilation of modern buildings; **un local sin apenas v.** premises with practically no ventilation; **sistemas de v. para cocinas** ventilation systems for kitchens ▸▸ ***v. artificial*** artificial respiration; ***v. asistida*** artificial respiration; ***v. mecánica*** artificial respiration

ventilador *nm* (a) *(aparato)* fan ▸▸ ***v. de aspas*** ceiling fan; ***v. eléctrico*** electric fan (b) *(abertura)* air vent, ventilator (c) *(en coche)* fan

ventilar 1 *vt* (a) *(airear) (habitación)* to air, to ventilate; *(ropa, colchón)* to air
(b) *Fam (resolver)* to clear up, to sort out; **en cuanto ventile este asunto me voy** I'm going as soon as I clear up *o* sort out this matter
(c) *Fam (discutir)* to air; **le encanta v. sus problemas en público** she likes to air her problems in public
(d) *(difundir)* to make public; **va ventilando por ahí todos los secretos de los demás** she goes round telling *o* blabbing everyone else's secrets
2 **ventilarse** *vpr* (a) *(airearse)* to air; **voy a salir a ventilarme un poco** I'm going to pop out for a breath of fresh air (b) *Fam (terminarse) (botella)* to knock back, to polish off; *(comida, libro)* to polish off; **se ventiló el pastel en un periquete** he wolfed down the cake in next to no time (c) *Fam (resolver)* to clear up, to sort out; *(asesinar)* to rub out

ventisca *nf* blizzard, snowstorm

ventiscar [60], **ventisquear** *v impersonal* **está ventiscando** there's a blizzard *o* snowstorm

ventisquero *nm* (a) *(lugar)* = depression where the snow accumulates (b) *(nieve)* snowdrift

ventolera *nf* (a) *(viento)* gust of wind (b) *Fam (idea extravagante)* wild idea; **le ha dado la v. de hacerlo** she has taken it into her head to do it; **como le dé la v. se irá** when the mood takes him he'll up and go

ventolina *nf* breeze

ventorrillo *nm* small inn

ventosa *nf* (a) *(de animal)* sucker (b) *(de vidrio)* cupping glass (c) *(de goma)* suction pad

ventosear *vi* to break wind

ventosidad *nf* wind, flatulence; **expulsar una v.** to break wind; **los garbanzos producen ventosidades** chickpeas cause flatulence

ventoso, -a *adj* windy

ventral *adj* ventral

ventresca *nf* belly *(of fish)*

ventricular *adj* ventricular

ventrículo *nm* ventricle

ventrílocuo, -a *nm,f* ventriloquist

ventriloquía *nf* ventriloquism

ventrudo, -a *adj Fam* paunchy

ventura *nf Literario* (a) *(felicidad)* happiness; **le desearon toda suerte de venturas** they wished her every happiness
(b) *(suerte)* fortune; **por v.** fortunately; **por v. no sufrieron ningún contratiempo** fortunately, there were no mishaps
(c) *(azar)* **a la (buena) v.** without planning *o* a fixed plan; **emprendieron el camino a la v.** they set off without any fixed plan; *Anticuado* **¿piensa, por v., que le engaño?** perchance you think I am deceiving you?

venturoso, -a *adj* happy, fortunate

vénula *nf Anat* venule

Venus 1 *nm (planeta)* Venus
2 *n Mitol* Venus

venus *nf* (a) *(mujer)* beauty (b) *(estatua)* statue of Venus

venusiano, -a *adj* Venusian

venza *etc ver* **vencer**

veo-veo *nm* I-spy

VER [72] 1 *nm* (a) *(aspecto)* **estar de buen v.** to be good-looking (b) *(opinión)* **a mi v.** the way I see it
2 *vt* (a) *(percibir con los ojos)* to see; *(mirar)* to look at; *(televisión, programa, espectáculo deportivo)* to watch; *(película, obra, concierto)* to see; **¿ves algo?** can you see anything?; **yo no veo nada** I can't see a thing; **he estado viendo tu trabajo** I've been looking at your work; **¿vemos la tele un rato?** shall we watch some TV?; **esta serie nunca la veo** I never watch this series; **¿has visto el museo?** have you been to the museum?; **yo te veo más delgada** you look thinner to me; *Méx Fam* **¿qué me ves?** what are you looking at?; **este edificio ha visto muchos sucesos históricos** this building has seen a lot of historic events; **los jubilados han visto aumentadas sus pensiones** pensioners have had their pensions increased; **v. a alguien hacer algo** to see sb doing sth; **los vi actuar en el festival** I saw them acting at the festival; **te vi bajar del autobús** I saw you getting off the bus; **los vieron discutir** *o* **discutiendo** they were seen arguing; **¡nunca** *o* **jamás he visto cosa igual!** I've never seen the like of it!; **¡si vieras qué bien lo pasamos!** if only you knew what a good time we had!; **¡si vieras qué cara se le puso!** you can't imagine her face!; EXPR **v. venir algo/a alguien: este problema ya lo veía venir** I could see this problem coming; **lo veo venir** I can see what he's up to; EXPR **verlas venir: él prefiere quedarse a verlas venir** he prefers to wait and see; EXPR **¡quién lo ha visto y quién lo ve!** it's amazing how much he's changed!; EXPR **si no lo veo, no lo creo** I'd never have believed it if I hadn't seen it with my own eyes; EXPR **si te he visto no me acuerdo: pero ahora, si te he visto, no me acuerdo** but now he/she/*etc* doesn't want to know
(b) *(entender, apreciar, considerar)* to see; **ya veo que estás de mal humor** I can see you're in a bad mood; **¿no ves que trata de disculparse?** can't you see *o* tell she's trying to apologize?; **¿ves lo que quiero decir?** do you see what I mean?; **ahora lo veo todo claro** now I understand everything; **a todo le ve pegas** he sees problems in everything; **yo no le veo solución a este problema** I can't see a solution to this problem; **¿tú cómo lo ves?** how do you see it?; **yo lo veo así** I see it this way *o* like this; **es una manera de v. las cosas** that's one way of looking at it; **yo no lo veo tan mal** I don't think it's that bad; **ahí donde la ves, era muy guapa de joven** she was very pretty when she was young, you know; **dejarse v. (por un sitio)** to show one's face (somewhere); **¿te gusta? – ¡a v.!** do you like it? – of course I do!; EXPR **¡habráse visto!: ¡habráse visto qué cara dura/mal genio tiene!** you'd never believe what a cheek/temper he has!; EXPR **¡hay que v.!** *(indica sorpresa)* would you believe it!; *(indica indignación)* it makes me mad!; **¡hay que v. qué lista es!** you wouldn't believe how clever she is!; **¡hay que v. cuánto se gasta estando de vacaciones!** it's amazing how much you spend when you're on *Br* holiday *o US* vacation!; EXPR **para que veas: no le tengo ningún rencor, ¡para que veas!** I don't bear him any hard feelings, in case you were wondering; EXPR *Fam* **no poder v. a alguien (ni en pintura): no lo puedo ver** I can't stand (the sight of) him
(c) *(imaginar)* to see; **ya veo tu foto en los periódicos** I can (just) see

your photo in the newspapers; **francamente, yo no la veo casada** to be honest, I can't see her getting married

(**d**) *(comprobar)* to see; **ir a v. lo que pasa** to go and see what's going on; **ve a v. si quedan cervezas** go and see if *o* have a look if there are any beers left; **veré qué puedo hacer** I'll see what I can do; **queda por v. si ésta es la mejor solución** it remains to be seen whether this is the best solution; **eso está por v., eso habrá que verlo** that remains to be seen; **veamos** let's see

(**e**) *(tratar, estudiar) (tema, problema)* to look at; **el lunes veremos la lección 6** we'll do lesson 6 on Monday; **como ya hemos visto en anteriores capítulos...** as we have seen in previous chapters...

(**f**) *(reconocer) (sujeto: médico, especialista)* to have *o* take a look at; **necesitas que te vea un médico,** *Andes, RP* **hazte v. por un médico** you ought to see a doctor; *Andes, RP* **el televisor no funciona, tengo que hacerlo v.** the television's not working, I must get it seen to *o* get someone to have a look at it

(**g**) *(visitar, citarse con)* to see; **tienes que ir a v. al médico** you ought to see the doctor; **ven a vernos cuando quieras** come and see us any time you like; **mañana vamos a v. a mis padres** we're seeing my parents tomorrow; **hace siglos que no la veo** I haven't seen her for ages; **últimamente no los veo mucho** I haven't seen much of them recently

(**h**) *Der (juzgar)* **v. un caso** to hear a case

(**i**) *(en juegos de naipes)* to see; **las veo** I'll see you

3 *vi* (**a**) *(percibir con los ojos)* to see; **v. bien/mal** to have good/poor eyesight; **no veo bien de cerca/de lejos** I'm long-sighted/short-sighted; **¿ves bien ahí?** can you see all right from there?; EXPR *Fam* **que no veo: tengo un hambre/sueño que no veo** I'm incredibly hungry/tired; EXPR *Fam* **que no veas: hace un frío/calor que no veas** it's incredibly cold/hot; **los vecinos arman un ruido que no veas** the neighbours are unbelievably noisy; EXPR **hasta más v.** *(adiós)* see you soon

(**b**) *(hacer la comprobación)* to see; **la casa está en muy buenas condiciones – ya veo** the house is in very good condition – so I see; **es muy sencillo, ya verás** it's quite simple, you'll see; **creo que me queda uno en el almacén, iré a v.** I think I have one left in the storeroom, I'll just go and see *o* look; **vendrá en el periódico – voy a v.** it'll be in the newspaper – I'll go and see *o* look; **tú sigue sin estudiar y verás** you'll soon see what happens if you carry on not studying; **¿ves?, te lo dije** (you) see? I told you so; EXPR **v. para creer** seeing is believing

(**c**) *(decidir)* **¿lo harás? – ya veré** will you do it? – I'll see; **ya veremos** we'll see

(**d**) *(en juegos de naipes)* **¡veo!** I'll see you!

(**e**) *(como muletilla)* **verás, tengo algo muy importante que decirte** listen *o* look, I've got something very important to say to you; **¿qué ha pasado? – pues, verás, yo estaba...** what happened? – well, you see, I was...

(**f**) **a v.: a v. cuánto aguantas en esa postura** let's see how long you can hold that position; **a v. cuándo vienes a vernos** you must come and see us some time; **no subas al tejado, a v. si te vas a caer** don't go up on the roof, you might fall; **¡a v. si tienes más cuidado con lo que dices!** you should be a bit more careful what you say!; **¿a v.?** *(mirando con interés)* let me see, let's have a look; *Col* **¡a v.!** *(al teléfono)* hello?; **a v., ¿qué te pasa?** let's see, what's wrong?; **a v., antes de empezar...** let's see, right, before starting...; **vamos a v.** let's see

4 verse *vpr* (**a**) *(como reflexivo) (mirarse, imaginarse)* to see oneself; **verse en el espejo** to see oneself in the mirror; **yo me veo más gordo** I think I've put on weight; **ya me veo cargando el camión yo solo** I can see myself having to load the *Br* lorry *o US* truck on my own

(**b**) *(como impersonal, pasivo) (percibirse)* **desde aquí se ve el mar** you can see the sea from here; **somos muy felices – eso ya se ve** we're very happy – you can see that *o* you can tell; **se te ve más joven/contenta** you look younger/happier; **¿se me ve algo?** *(se transparenta?)* is my underwear showing through?; **¡se ve cada cosa en esta oficina!** it all happens in this office!; **por lo que se ve** apparently; **véase** *(en textos)* see

(**c**) *(como recíproco) (citarse, encontrarse)* to meet, to see each other; **nos vimos en Navidad** we met *o* saw each other at Christmas; **nos vemos muy a menudo** we see a lot of each other; **¿a qué hora nos vemos?** when shall we meet?; **hace mucho que no nos vemos** we haven't seen each other for a long time; **¡nos vemos!** see you!

(**d**) *(como auxiliar) (ser)* **los impuestos se verán incrementados en un 2 por ciento** taxes will be increased by 2 percent

(**e**) *(hallarse)* to find oneself; **si te ves en un apuro, llámame** if you find yourself in trouble, call me; **se vio forzado a dimitir** he was forced to resign

(**f**) *(enfrentarse)* **vérselas con algo/alguien: Argentina se las verá con México en la semifinal** Argentina will clash with *o* meet Mexico in the semifinals; **hubo de vérselas con todo tipo de adversidades** she came up against *o* met (with) all kinds of adversity; **si busca bronca tendrá que vérselas conmigo** if he's looking for trouble, he'll have to reckon with me; EXPR **vérselas y deseárselas para hacer algo** to have a real struggle doing sth

5 *interj RP* **¿viste?, ¿vio?** you see?, know what I mean?; **prefiero el vino, ¿vio?** I prefer wine, actually; **cambié de idea, ¿viste?** I changed my mind, you see

---

vera *nf* (**a**) *(orilla) (de río)* bank; *(de camino)* edge, side (**b**) *(lado)* side; **se sentó a la v. de su padre** she sat at her father's side; **ven aquí, a mi v.** come here, beside me; **a la v. del camino** at the side of the road (**c**) *(árbol)* verawood, Maracaibo lignum-vitae

veracidad *nf* truthfulness; **no dudo de la v. de esa anécdota** I don't doubt the truth of the story

veracruzano, -a 1 *adj* of/from Veracruz *(Mexico)*
2 *nm,f* person from Veracruz *(Mexico)*

veranda *nf* verandah

veraneante *nmf Br* holidaymaker, *US* (summer) vacationer

veranear *vi* **v. en** to spend one's summer *Br* holidays *o US* vacation in; **hace años que no veraneo** I haven't had a summer *Br* holiday *o US* vacation for years

veraneo *nm* summer *Br* holidays *o US* vacation; **su lugar de v. habitual es La Plata** she usually spends the summer in La Plata; **irse de v.** *Br* to go on (one's summer) holiday, *US* to vacation

veranero, -a *adj CRica* summer

veraniego, -a *adj (actividades, temperatura)* summer; **ropa veraniega** summer clothes; **vas muy v.** you look very summery

veranillo *nm* Indian summer ►► ***el v. de San Juan*** *(en el hemisferio sur)* = warm spell around 24th June; ***el v. de San Martín*** *(en el hemisferio norte)* = warm spell around 11th November

verano *nm* (**a**) *(estación)* summer; **en v.** in summer; **cuando llegue el v.** when summer comes; **el último v.** last summer (**b**) *(estación seca)* dry season

veras 1 *nfpl* truth; **lo dijo entre bromas y v.** she was only half-joking
2 de veras *loc adv (verdaderamente)* really; *(en serio)* seriously; **de v., yo no quería hacerte daño** I really didn't want to hurt you; **esta vez va de v.** this time it's serious *o* for real

veraz *adj* truthful

verazmente *adv* truthfully

verba *nf* loquaciousness, talkativeness

verbal *adj* verbal

verbalizar [14] *vt* to verbalize

verbalmente *adv* verbally

verbena *nf* (**a**) *(fiesta)* street party; **la v. de S. Juan** = street party on the night of 24th June, St John's day (**b**) *(planta)* verbena

verbenero, -a *adj* **ambiente v.** festive atmosphere

verbigracia *adv Formal* for example, for instance

Verbo *nm* **el V.** *(Rel)* the Word

verbo *nm* (**a**) *Gram* verb ►► ***v. atributivo*** copula, copulative verb; ***v. auxiliar*** auxiliary verb; ***v. copulativo*** copula, copulative verb; ***v. impersonal*** impersonal verb; ***v. intransitivo*** intransitive verb; ***v. modal*** modal verb; ***v. pronominal*** pronominal verb; ***v. reflexivo*** reflexive verb; ***v. transitivo*** transitive verb
(**b**) *(lenguaje)* language; **posee un v. elocuente** he is exceedingly eloquent, he makes eloquent use of language

verborrea *nf* verbal diarrhoea, verbosity

verbosidad *nf* verbosity

verboso, -a *adj* verbose

VERDAD 1 *nf* (**a**) *(realidad, afirmación real)* truth; **decir la v.** to tell the truth; **di la v., ¿a ti qué te parece?** tell the truth *o* be honest, what do you think?; **a decir v.** to tell the truth; **estás faltando a la v.** you're not telling the truth; **¿es v.?** is that true *o* right?; **eso no es v.** that isn't true *o* so; **¿no es v.?** isn't that so?; **bien es v. que..., v. es que...** it's certainly true that...; **si bien es v. que...** while it is true that...; **en v.** truly, honestly; **cree que está en posesión de la v.** she thinks she's always right about everything; **ser la pura v.** to be the absolute truth; EXPR **cantarle** *o* **decirle a alguien cuatro verdades** to tell sb a few home truths; EXPR **ir con la v. por delante** to be honest and up-front; EXPR **las verdades del barquero** home truths; EXPR *Fam* **es una v. como un puño** *o* **templo** it's an undeniable fact; **todo lo que dice son verdades como puños** she always speaks the truth, however unpalatable ►► ***v. a medias*** half-truth; ***v. de Perogrullo*** truism, platitude

(**b**) *(con valor enfático)* **la v., no me importa** to tell the truth *o* to be honest, I don't care; **la v. es que no lo sé** to be honest, I don't know, I don't really know; **la v. es que nunca me ha gustado** the truth is I've never liked her; **la v. es que la sopa está buenísima** the soup's actually really good

(**c**) *(buscando confirmación)* **no te gusta, ¿v.?** you don't like it, do you?; **está bueno, ¿v.?** it's good, isn't it?; **¿v. que me quieres?** you do love me, don't you?

(**d**) *(principio aceptado)* fact; **su libro no es fiel a la v. histórica** his book doesn't accurately reflect historical fact

2 **de verdad** *loc adv (en serio)* seriously; *(realmente)* really; **me gusta – ¿de v.?** I like it – (do you) really? *o* seriously?; **de v. que no sé qué decir** I honestly *o* really don't know what to say

3 **de verdad** *loc adj (auténtico)* real; **un héroe de v.** a real hero

verdaderamente *adv* (**a**) *(de verdad)* really; **v., no sé cómo lo soportas** I really *o* honestly don't know how you put up with him; **iqué tonto es! – v.** he's so stupid! – you can say that again! (**b**) *(muy)* truly, really; **una historia v. increíble** a truly amazing story

verdadero, -a *adj* (**a**) *(cierto, real) (historia)* true; *(nombre)* real; *(intenciones)* real, true; **la verdadera razón de su comportamiento fue otra** the real reason for his behaviour was different; **el v. protagonista de la tragedia** the person who was really the key figure in the tragedy; **distinguir entre lo v. y lo falso** to distinguish between what is true and what is false

(**b**) *(enfático)* real; **fue un v. lío** it was a real mess

verde 1 *adj* (**a**) *(de color)* green; EXPR *Fam* **poner v. a alguien** *(por la espalda)* to run sb down, *Br* to slag sb off, *US* to dump on sb; *(delante)* to tear into sb, to tear sb to pieces; EXPR *RP Fam* **estar v. de envidia** to be green with envy

(**b**) *(poco maduro) (fruta)* unripe, green; *Fam (persona)* green, wet behind the ears; **el proyecto está aún v.** the project is still very much in its early stages

(**c**) *(ecologista)* Green, green

(**d**) *(obsceno)* blue, dirty

(**e**) *Esp Antes Fam* **billete v.** = 1,000 peseta note

2 *nm (color)* green; **el v. es mi color favorito** green is my favourite colour; **cruzar con el semáforo en v.** to cross when the lights are green ►► ***v. agua*** pale blue-green; ***v. botella*** bottle green; *RP* ***v. cotorra*** bright green; ***v. esmeralda*** emerald green; ***v. lima*** lime green; ***v. manzana*** apple green; ***v. mar*** sea green; ***v. musgo*** moss green; ***v. oliva*** olive (green)

3 *nmpl* **los Verdes** *(partido)* the Greens

verdear *vi* (**a**) *(parecer verde)* to look green (**b**) *(plantas)* to turn *o* go green

verdecer [46] *vi* to turn *o* go green

verdecillo *nm* (**a**) *(planta)* golden tree-trumpet (**b**) *(ave)* serin

verdemar 1 *adj* sea-green

2 *nm* sea green

verderón *nm* greenfinch ►► ***v. pintado*** painted bunting; ***v. serrano*** citril finch

verdín *nm* (**a**) *(de plantas, algas)* slime (**b**) *(moho)* mould, mildew (**c**) *(musgo)* moss (**d**) *(cardenillo)* verdigris

verdinegro, -a *adj* very dark green

verdolaga *nf* purslane

verdor *nm* (**a**) *(color)* greenness (**b**) *(exuberancia)* lushness

verdoso, -a *adj* greenish

verdugo *nm* (**a**) *(de preso)* executioner; *(que ahorca)* hangman (**b**) *(tirano)* tyrant (**c**) *(gorro)* balaclava (**d**) *(de planta)* shoot

verdulera *nf* (**a**) *Fam (mujer vulgar)* fishwife (**b**) *ver también* **verdulero**

verdulería *nf* greengrocer's (shop)

verdulero, -a *nm,f (tendero)* greengrocer

verdura *nf* (**a**) *(comestible)* vegetables, greens; **es importante comer verdura(s)** it's important to eat vegetables *o* greens; **carne con verduras** meat and vegetables (**b**) *(color verde)* greenness

verdusco, -a *adj* dirty green

verecundia *nf Formal* shame

vereda *nf* (**a**) *(senda)* path; EXPR **entrar en v.** to toe the line; EXPR *Fam* **hacer entrar** *o* **meter a alguien en v.** to bring sb into line (**b**) *CSur, Perú (acera) Br* pavement, *US* sidewalk (**c**) *Col (distrito)* area, district

veredicto *nm* verdict

verga *nf* (**a**) *Zool* penis (**b**) *esp Am muy Fam (de hombre)* cock (**c**) *Náut* yard

vergatal *nm Méx Fam* **v. de** *(muchos)* tons of, loads of; **había un v. de gente en la discoteca** there were tons of people at the club

vergazo *nm CAm (golpe)* thump

vergel *nm* lush, fertile place

vergonzante *adj* shameful, disgraceful

vergonzosamente *adv* (**a**) *(sin honra)* shamefully, disgracefully (**b**) *(con timidez)* bashfully

vergonzoso, -a 1 *adj* (**a**) *(deshonroso)* shameful, disgraceful (**b**) *(tímido)* bashful

2 *nm,f* bashful person; **ser un v.** to be bashful

vergüenza 1 *nf* (**a**) *(deshonra)* shame; **sentir v.** to feel ashamed; **me da v. confesar que...** I'm ashamed to admit that...; **tener poca v., no tener v.** to be shameless; **¡eres la v. de la familia!** you're a disgrace to your family!

(**b**) *(bochorno)* embarrassment; **dar v. a alguien** to embarrass sb; **me da v. decírtelo** I'm embarrassed to tell you; **¡qué v.!** how embarrassing!; **sentir** *o* **pasar v.** to feel embarrassed; **ser de v.** to be disgraceful *o* a disgrace; **el trato que reciben es de v.** the way they're treated is disgraceful *o* a disgrace; **ese programa da v. ajena** that programme is cringe-making *o* embarrassingly bad; EXPR **el de la v.: ¿quién quiere el de la v.?** who wants the last one?

(**c**) *(timidez)* bashfulness; **perder la v.** to lose one's inhibitions

(**d**) *(deshonra, escándalo)* disgrace; **¡es una v.!** it's disgraceful!; **¡qué v.!** what a disgrace!

2 **vergüenzas** *nfpl Fam Euf (genitales)* private parts, privates

vericueto 1 *nm (camino abrupto)* rough track

2 **vericuetos** *nmpl (recovecos)* ins and outs; **se perdió por los vericuetos del barrio** he got lost in all the little backstreets of the area; **conoce todos los vericuetos burocráticos** he knows all the ins and outs *o* the inner workings of the bureaucracy

verídico, -a *adj (información)* true; *(hecho, suceso)* real; **la historia se basa en hechos verídicos** the story is based on real *o* true events; **detalles verídicos** true-life details; **la escuela que aparece en la película es verídica** the school that appears in the movie actually exists

verificable *adj* verifiable

verificación *nf* (**a**) *(de verdad, autenticidad, hipotesis)* verification; *(de acuerdo de paz)* monitoring; **software de v. de voz** voice recognition software (**b**) *(de funcionamiento)* checking, testing; *(de buen estado)* checking

verificador, -ora 1 *nm,f (de acuerdo de paz)* monitor, observer; *(de funcionamiento, buen estado)* checker

2 *nm Informát* ***v. ortográfico*** spell-checker

verificar [60] 1 *vt* (**a**) *(verdad, autenticidad)* to verify, to check; **el encargado de v. el alto el fuego** the person whose job it is to monitor *o* verify the observance of the ceasefire; **tengo que v. unos datos** I have to check a few facts (**b**) *(funcionamiento)* to check, to test; *(buen estado)* to check (**c**) *(llevar a cabo)* to carry out

2 **verificarse** *vpr* (**a**) *(tener lugar)* to take place; **cuando se verifica la venta** when the sale takes place *o* is completed (**b**) *(resultar cierto) (predicción)* to come true; *(temores)* to prove well-founded

verificativo *nm Méx* **tener v.** to take place

verija *nf Chile (ijada)* flank, side

verismo *nm* (**a**) *(realismo)* realism (**b**) *(en ópera)* verismo

verja *nf* (**a**) *(puerta)* iron gate (**b**) *(valla)* railings (**c**) *(en ventana)* grille

verme *nm* (intestinal) worm

vermicida, vermífugo 1 *adj* vermifugal

2 *nm* vermifuge

vermis *nm inv* vermis

vermouth [ber'mu] (*pl* **vermouths**) *nm* vermouth

vermú, vermut (*pl* **vermuts**) *nm* (**a**) *(bebida)* vermouth (**b**) *(aperitivo)* aperitif (**c**) *esp Andes, RP (en cine)* early-evening showing; *(en teatro)* early-evening performance

vernáculo, -a *adj* vernacular

vernal *adj* vernal, spring

verónica *nf* (**a**) *Taurom* veronica, = pass in which bullfighter holds the cape with both hands (**b**) *(planta)* veronica, speedwell

verosímil *adj* (**a**) *(creíble)* believable, credible; **la trama de la historia tiene que ser v.** the plot of the story has to be believable (**b**) *(probable)* likely, probable; **la hipótesis más v.** the most likely hypothesis

verosimilitud *nf* (**a**) *(credibilidad)* credibility; **para dar mayor v. a la situación** to make the situation more believable (**b**) *(probabilidad)* likeliness, probability; **una opción que cobra cada vez más v.** an option which is becoming more and more likely

verraco *nm* boar

verraquear *vi Fam* (**a**) *(animal)* to grunt (**b**) *(niño)* to shriek, to howl

verraquera *nf Fam* crying fit, tantrum

verruga *nf* (**a**) *(en pies, manos)* verruca, wart; *(en cara)* wart (**b**) *(en planta)* wart

verrugosidad *nf* wart-like growth

verrugoso, -a *adj* warty; **un sapo de piel v.** a toad with warty skin

versado, -a *adj* versed (**en** in); **muy v. en temas esotéricos** well-versed in esoteric subjects

versal *Imprenta* **1** *adj* capital
2 *nf* capital (letter)

versalita *Imprenta* **1** *adj* **letra v.** small capitals
2 *nf* small capital

versallesco, -a *adj* **(a)** *(jardín, palacio)* in the style of Versailles; **jardines de estilo v.** gardens in the style of Versailles **(b)** *(gesto, saludo)* affectedly polite

versallismo *nm* ostentatious luxury

versar *vi* **(a)** *(tratar)* **v. sobre** to be about, to deal with **(b)** *PRico (versificar)* to versify

versátil *adj* **(a)** *(voluble)* changeable, fickle **(b)** *(polifacético)* versatile

versatilidad *nf* **(a)** *(volubilidad)* changeability, fickleness **(b)** *(adaptabilidad)* versatility

versero, -a *RP Fam* **1** *adj* smooth-tongued, fast-talking
2 *nm,f Br* patter merchant, *US* schmoozer

versículo *nm* verse *(in the Bible)*

versificación *nf* versification

versificador, -ora *nm,f* versifier

versificar [60] **1** *vi* to write (in) verse
2 *vt* to put into verse

versión *nf* **(a)** *(de hecho, obra)* version; *(en música pop)* cover (version); **¿cuál es su v. de lo ocurrido?** what is his version of what happened? ▸▸ *Informát* ***v. alfa*** alpha version; *Informát* ***v. beta*** beta version; *Informát* ***v. impresa*** hard copy
(b) *(traducción)* translation, version ▸▸ *Cine* ***v. original*** original language version; *Cine* ***v. original subtitulada*** original language version with subtitles; **en ese cine ponen películas en v. original subtituladas** at that cinema they show movies (in their original language) with subtitles

versionar, versionear *vt Fam (en música pop)* to cover

verso *nm* **(a)** *(género)* verse; **en v.** in verse ▸▸ ***v. blanco*** blank verse; ***v. libre*** free verse **(b)** *(unidad rítmica)* line *(of poetry)* **(c)** *Imprenta (de página)* verso **(d)** *RP Fam (mentira)* fib, lie; **no le creas, todo lo que te dijo es v.** don't you believe him, everything he told you is lies; **hacerle** *o* **meterle el v. a alguien** to spin sb a yarn *o* line

versus *prep Formal* versus

vértebra *nf* vertebra ▸▸ *Anat* ***v. cervical*** cervical vertebra; ***v. dorsal*** thoracic *o* dorsal vertebra; ***v. lumbar*** lumbar vertebra

vertebración *nf* structural cohesion; **el principal factor de v. de una sociedad avanzada** the principal element in the structural cohesion of an advanced society; **los sistemas internos que hacen posible la v. de la empresa** the internal systems which make it possible for the company to function as a whole

vertebrado, -a 1 *adj* **(a)** *(animal)* vertebrate **(b)** *(coherente)* coherent
2 *nm (animal)* vertebrate

vertebrador, -ora *adj* structuring; **el argumento v. de la novela** the central plotline of the novel; **el concepto v. de nuestro movimiento político** the central ideological principle of our political movement

vertebral *adj* vertebral

vertebrar 1 *vt* to form the backbone of, to structure; **lo que vertebra la narración** what forms the backbone of *o* structures the narrative
2 vertebrarse *vpr* **nuestra reclamación se vertebra en dos aspectos** our complaint falls under two headings; **la región se vertebra en tres niveles administrativos** the region has a three-tier administrative structure

vertedero *nm* **(a)** *(de basuras) Br* rubbish tip *o* dump, *US* garbage dump **(b)** *(de pantano)* drain, spillway

vertedor *nm (desagüe, conducto)* drain

verter [66] **1** *vt* **(a)** *(derramar) (sal)* to spill; *(lágrimas)* to shed; **mucha sangre se ha vertido ya** much blood has already been shed *o* spilt
(b) *(echar) (líquido)* to pour (out); *(basura, residuos)* to dump; **vertió la harina en el saco** she poured the flour into the sack; **los ríos vierten sus aguas en el mar** rivers flow into the sea
(c) *(vaciar)(recipiente)* to empty
(d) *(traducir)* to translate (**a** into)
(e) *(expresar) (opinión)* to express; **las acusaciones/críticas vertidas por el periódico** the accusations/criticisms made by the newspaper
2 *vi* **v. a** *o* **en** to flow into
3 verterse *vpr (derramarse)* to spill

vertical 1 *adj* **(a)** *Geom* vertical **(b)** *(derecho) (línea, despegue)* vertical; **el respaldo estaba casi v.** the back was almost vertical; **poner en posición v.** to place in an upright position; **en v.: se hace una incisión en v.** a vertical incision is made **(c)** *(en crucigrama)* down; **3 v.** 3 down **(d)** *(formato, orientación)* portrait **(e)** *(estructura)* hierarchical
2 *nm Astron* vertical circle
3 *nf Geom* vertical (line); **forma un ángulo recto con la v.** it forms a right angle to the vertical

verticalazo *nm Andes, RP Fam* dictat, order from on high

verticalidad *nf* verticality, vertical position

verticalista *adj Andes, RP Pol* authoritarian; **su forma de hacer las cosas es demasiado v.** their way of doing things is too authoritarian

verticalmente *adv* vertically

vértice *nm* **(a)** *Geom (de ángulo, plano)* vertex; *(de cono, pirámide)* apex; **los vértices de un triángulo** the points *o Espec* vertices of a triangle ▸▸ ***v. geodésico*** triangulation pillar **(b)** *(de curva)* vertex

vertido 1 *nm (deliberado)* dumping; *(accidental)* spillage, spilling ▸▸ ***v. de residuos*** waste dumping
2 vertidos *nmpl (residuos)* waste ▸▸ ***vertidos radiactivos*** radioactive waste

vertiente *nf* **(a)** *(pendiente)* slope
(b) *(zona geográfica)* drainage basin *o* area; **la v. del pacífico** the Pacific drainage basin *o* area
(c) *(aspecto)* side, aspect; **la crisis presentaba diversas vertientes** there were several aspects to the crisis; **el desarrollo del romanticismo en su doble v. artística e ideológica** the development of romanticism in its twin aspects, artistic and ideological
(d) *CSur (manantial)* spring

vertiginosamente *adv* at a dizzying speed, vertiginously; **la población ha aumentado v.** the population has increased dramatically

vertiginoso, -a *adj (aumento, desarrollo)* dramatic, spectacular; *(velocidad)* dizzying; **la historia se desarrolla a un ritmo v.** the story develops at a frenetic pace; **la caída del líder fue v.** the leader's fall from power was spectacularly abrupt

vértigo *nm* **(a)** *(enfermedad)* vertigo; *(mareo)* dizziness; **trepar me da v.** climbing makes me dizzy; **sólo de pensarlo me da v.** just thinking about it makes me feel dizzy; **sentir** *o* **tener v.** to feel dizzy; **prefiero no subir, tengo v.** I'd rather not go up, I'm afraid of heights; EXPR **de v.** *(velocidad, altura)* dizzy, giddy; *(cifras)* mind-boggling
(b) *(apresuramiento)* mad rush, hectic pace; **el v. de la ciudad** the hectic pace of city life

vesícula *nf* **(a)** *Anat (de la bilis)* gall bladder ▸▸ ***v. biliar*** gall bladder **(b)** *(bolsa)* vesicle ▸▸ ***v. seminal*** seminal vesicle **(c)** *(de suero)* blister **(d)** *(en planta)* vesicle

vesicular *adj* vesicular

vespa® *nf* Vespa®, motor scooter

véspero *nm Literario* Vesper, evening star

vespertino, -a 1 *adj* evening; **diario v.** evening (news)paper
2 *nm (periódico)* evening (news)paper

vespino® *nm* moped

vesre *nm RP Fam* reverse slang; **hablar al v.** to talk back to front

vestal *nf* vestal (virgin)

vestíbulo *nm* **(a)** *(de casa)* (entrance) hall; *(de hotel, oficina)* lobby, foyer **(b)** *Anat (cavidad, del oído)* vestibule

vestido, -a 1 *adj* dressed; **una mujer muy bien vestida** a very well-dressed woman; **iba v. con ropa de trabajo** he was dressed in *o* wearing his work clothes; **ir v. de** *(blanco, negro)* to be dressed in; *(marinero, príncipe)* to be dressed as; **iba vestida de monja** she was dressed as a nun, she was in nun's clothing
2 *nm* **(a)** *(indumentaria)* clothes, clothing; **el v. a través de los siglos** clothing *o* costume through the ages
(b) *(prenda femenina)* dress ▸▸ *RP* ***v. maternal*** maternity dress; ***v. de novia*** wedding dress; ***v. premamá*** maternity dress
(c) *Col (traje de hombre)* suit ▸▸ *Col* ***v. de baño*** swimsuit; *Col* ***v. de baño enterizo*** one-piece swimsuit; *Col* ***v. de baño de dos piezas*** two-piece swimsuit, bikini; *Col* ***v. deportivo*** tracksuit

vestidor *nm* **(a)** *(en casa)* dressing room **(b)** *CAm, Méx (en club) Br* changing *o US* locker room

vestiduras *nfpl* **(a)** *(ropa)* clothes; EXPR **rasgarse las v.** to kick up a fuss **(b)** *(sacerdotales)* vestments

vestier *nm* **(a)** *Col (en club) Br* changing *o US* locker room **(b)** *Ven (en casa)* dressing room

vestigio *nm (de otras épocas, civilizaciones)* trace, vestige; **se destruyó todo v. de vida** every trace of life was destroyed; **los últimos vestigios del colonialismo** the last vestiges of colonialism

vestimenta *nf* clothes, clothing; **sofocadas de calor bajo sus vestimentas negras** suffocating with heat in their black clothes; **su extravagante v.** his outlandish garb

VESTIR [47] **1** *vt* (a) *(poner ropa a)* to dress; **viste al niño y vámonos** dress the child *o* get the child dressed and let's go; PROV **vísteme despacio que tengo prisa** more haste, less speed

(b) *(disfrazar)* **v. a alguien de algo** to dress sb up as sth

(c) *(llevar puesto)* to wear; **el sospechoso viste unos tejanos negros** the suspect is wearing black jeans

(d) *(diseñar ropa para)* to dress, to make clothes for; **el modisto que viste a la familia real** the fashion designer who dresses *o* makes the clothes for the royal family

(e) *(proporcionar ropa a)* to clothe; **v. a los pobres** to clothe the poor

(f) *(cubrir) (casa, paredes, salón)* to decorate

(g) *Literario (encubrir)* **v. algo de** to disguise sth with

2 *vi* (a) *(llevar ropa)* to dress; **aún estoy sin v.** I'm not dressed yet; **siempre viste muy bien** she always dresses very well; **tiene gusto para v.** she has good dress sense; **v. de algo** to wear sth; EXPR **el mismo que viste y calza** the very same!

(b) *(ser elegante)* to be smart; **este abrigo/color viste mucho** this coat/colour looks very smart; **de v.** *(ropa, calzado)* smart

(c) *Fam (estar bien visto)* **ya no viste tanto vivir en el campo** it's no longer considered so desirable to live in the country

3 vestirse *vpr* (a) *(ponerse ropa)* to get dressed, to dress; **vístete y vete** get dressed and go; **vestirse a la moda** to dress fashionably; **se vistió de luto/de blanco** she dressed in *o* wore mourning/white; **vestirse de largo** *(para fiesta)* to wear evening dress; **el Teatro Real se vistió ayer de largo para atender el estreno** the Theatre Royal was all decked out yesterday for the premiere

(b) *(disfrazarse)* **vestirse de algo** to dress up as sth; **se vistió de payaso** he dressed (up) as a clown

(c) *(comprar la ropa)* **vestirse en** to buy one's clothes at

(d) *Literario (cubrirse)* **vestirse de** to be covered in; **el cielo se vistió de nubes** the sky clouded over

vestón *nm Chile* jacket

vestuario *nm* (a) *(ropa)* clothes, wardrobe (b) *(de actores)* costumes; **premio al mejor v.** award for the best costumes (c) *(para cambiarse) (en deportes) Br* changing room, *US* locker room; *(en teatro)* dressing room

Vesubio *nm* **el V.** (Mount) Vesuvius

veta *nf* (a) *(de mineral)* seam (b) *(en madera)* grain; *(en mármol)* vein (c) *(en jamón, tocino)* streak

vetar *vt* to veto; **le han vetado la entrada en ese casino** he has been banned from that casino

veteado, -a 1 *adj (madera)* grained; *(mármol)* veined; **flores de color lila veteadas de blanco** lilac flowers with little streaks of white

2 *nm (de madera)* grain; *(de mármol)* veins, veining

vetear *vt* (a) *(hacer vetas en)* to grain (b) *Ecuad (azotar)* to whip

veteranía *nf (experiencia)* long experience; *(antigüedad)* seniority

veterano, -a 1 *adj* (a) *(militar)* veteran (b) *(en otra actividad)* experienced; **es más v. que yo** he's more experienced than me; **una de las directoras de cine más veteranas** a movie director with one of the longest track records in the business (c) *CSur Fam (maduro)* **estamos veteranos, nos cansamos pronto** we're getting on a bit now, we get tired easily

2 *nm,f* (a) *(militar)* veteran (b) *(en otra actividad)* veteran; **es ya un v. en estas lides** he's an old hand at these things (c) *CSur Fam (maduro)* older person; **es una veterana muy simpática** she's a very sweet old thing

veterinaria *nf (ciencia)* veterinary science

veterinario, -a 1 *adj* veterinary

2 *nm,f (persona)* vet, *Br* veterinary surgeon, *US* veterinarian

veto *nm* veto; **poner v. a algo** to veto sth

vetustez *nf Formal* antiquity, great age

vetusto, -a *adj Formal* ancient, very old

VEZ *nf* (a) *(ocasión)* time; **¿te acuerdas de una v. (en) que fuimos a pescar?** do you remember that time we went fishing?; **¿has estado allí alguna v.?** have you ever been there?; **hay veces (en) que es mejor callarse** there are times when *o* sometimes it's better to keep quiet; **a mi/tu/su v.: él a su v. se lo dijo a su mujer** he, in turn, told his wife; **yo a mi v. haré lo que pueda** I, for my part, will do whatever I can; **a la v.** at the same time; **a la v. podríamos hacer la compra** we could do the shopping at the same time; **así a la v. que leo, estudio** this way, while I'm reading, I'm also studying; **de una (sola) v.** in one go; **de una v. (para siempre** *o* **por todas)** once and for all; **icállate de una v.!** why don't you just shut up!; **vete de una v.** just go, for heaven's sake; **érase una v.** once upon a time; **ha llamado otra v.** she called again; **déjalo para otra v.** leave it for another time; **otra v. será** maybe next time; **por enésima v.** for the umpteenth time; **por esta v. pase** I'll let you off this time *o* just this once; **por primera v., por v. primera** for the first time; **por última v.** for the last time; *Formal* **toda v. que** since; **una v. más** once again; **una v. que hayas terminado** once you've finished; **una v. dorada la carne..., una v. que la carne está dorada...** once the meat is golden brown

(b) *(para expresar frecuencia)* **una v.** once; **una v. al día/mes** once a day/month; **dos veces** twice; **tres veces** three times; **te lo he dicho muchas/mil veces** I've told you many/a thousand times; **alguna que otra v.** occasionally; **a veces, algunas veces** sometimes, at times; **cada v.** every time; **cada v. que lo veo** every time (that) I see him; **cada v. más** more and more; **cada v. menos** less and less; **cada v. la veo más/menos feliz** she seems happier and happier/less and less happy; **resulta cada v. más difícil** it's getting harder and harder; **de v. en cuando** from time to time, now and again; **muy de v. en cuando** very occasionally; **muchas veces** *(con frecuencia)* often; **pocas veces** rarely, seldom; **rara v.** rarely, seldom; **repetidas veces** repeatedly, time and again; **una y otra v.** time and again

(c) *(substitución)* **en v. de** instead of; **en v. de trabajar tanto deberías salir un poco más** you should go out more instead of working so hard; **hacer las veces de** *(persona)* to act as; *(objeto, aparato, mueble)* to serve as

(d) *(en multiplicaciones, divisiones)* time; **es tres veces mayor** it's three times as big; **estas pilas producen diez veces más energía que las normales** these batteries produce ten times as much energy as ordinary ones

(e) *(turno)* turn; **¿quién da** *o* **lleva la v.?** who's the last in the *Br* queue *o US* line?; **voy a pedir la v.** I'm going to ask who's last

v.g., v.gr. *(abrev de* **verbigracia***)* e.g.

VGA *Informát (abrev de* **video graphics array***)* VGA

v.gr. = **v.g.**

VHF *nf (abrev de* **very high frequency***)* VHF

VHS *nm (abrev de* **video home system***)* VHS

vi *ver* **ver**

VÍA 1 *nf* (a) *(ruta)* route; **por v. aérea** *(en general)* by air; *(correo)* (by) airmail; **por v. marítima** by sea; **por v. terrestre** overland, by land; *Fam* **solucionar/conseguir algo por la v. rápida** to solve/get sth as quickly as possible; EXPR **dar** *o* **dejar v. libre a algo/alguien** *(dejar paso)* to give way to sth/sb; *(dar permiso)* to give sth/sb the go-ahead; **dar** *o* **dejar v. libre a alguien** *(dar libertad de acción)* to give sb carte blanche; EXPR **tener v. libre** *(proyecto)* to have received the go-ahead; **tener v. libre para hacer algo** to have carte blanche to do sth ►► ***v. de comunicación*** communication route; ***v. férrea*** *(ruta)* railway line; ***v. fluvial*** waterway; ***la V. Láctea*** the Milky Way

(b) *(calzada, calle)* road; **en mitad** *o* **en medio de la v.** in the middle of the road; **las vías de acceso a la ciudad** the roads leading into the city; *Andes* **calle de doble/una v.** two-way/one-way street ►► ***v. pública*** public thoroughfare; ***v. de servicio*** service *o US* frontage road

(c) *(de ferrocarril) (raíl)* rails, track; *(andén)* platform; **salirse de la v.** to be derailed; **un tramo de v. única/de doble v.** a single-track/double-track stretch of line; **este tren efectuará su salida por la v. 6** this train will depart from platform 6 ►► ***v. ancha*** broad gauge; ***v. estrecha*** narrow gauge; ***v. muerta*** siding; **haber entrado** *o* **estar en v. muerta** *(proyecto, negociaciones)* to have come to a standstill

(d) *Anat, Med* tract; **por v. intravenosa** intravenously; **por v. oral** orally; **por v. parenteral** parenterally; **esta enfermedad se transmite por v. sexual** this disease is sexually transmitted ►► ***las vías respiratorias*** the respiratory tract; ***las vías urinarias*** the urinary tract

(e) *(proceso)* **estar en vías de hacer algo** to be in the process of doing sth; **el conflicto parece estar en vías de solucionarse** it seems like the conflict is on the way to being solved *o* is nearing a solution; **el proyecto se halla en vías de negociación** the project is currently under discussion; **un paciente en vías de recuperación** a patient who is on the road *o* on his way to recovery; **un país en vías de desarrollo** a developing country; **una especie en vías de extinción** an endangered species

(f) *(opción, medio)* channel, path; **primero es necesario agotar la v. diplomática** we have to exhaust all the diplomatic options first; **por la v. del diálogo** by means of (a) dialogue, by talking (to each other); **por**

la v. de la violencia by using violence; **por la v. de la meditación** through meditation; **por v. oficial/judicial** through official channels/the courts
(g) *(en barco)* ***v. de agua*** leakage, hole *(below the water line)*
(h) *Der* procedure ►► ***v. de apremio*** notification of distraint; ***v. ejecutiva*** enforcement procedure; ***v. sumaria*** summary procedure
2 *nm inv* ***v. crucis*** *Rel* Stations of the Cross, Way of the Cross; *(sufrimiento)* ordeal
3 *prep* via; **volaremos a Sydney v. Bangkok** we are flying to Sydney via Bangkok; **una conexión v. satélite** a satellite link

viabilidad *nf* viability, feasibility
viabilizar [14] *vt* to make viable
viable *adj* viable, feasible
viaducto *nm* viaduct
viajado, -a *adj* well-travelled; **el más v. de todos nosotros** the one who's travelled most of all of us
viajante *nmf* travelling salesperson ►► ***v. de comercio*** commercial traveller
viajar *vi* (a) *(trasladarse, irse)* to travel (**en** by) (b) *(circular)* to run; **el tren viajaba a toda velocidad** the train was going at full speed
viaje *nm* (a) *(en general)* journey, trip; *(en barco)* voyage; **¡buen v.!** have a good journey *o* trip!; **fue un v. agotador** it was an exhausting journey; **hay once días de v.** it's an eleven-day journey; **en sus viajes al extranjero** on his journeys *o* travels abroad; **los viajes de Colón** the voyages of Columbus; **estar/ir de v.** to be away/go away (on a trip) ►► ***v. astral*** astral projection; ***v. de aventura*** adventure holiday; ***viajes espaciales*** space travel; ***v. de Estado*** state visit; ***v. de estudios*** *(en colegio, universidad)* class trip; ***v. de ida*** outward journey; ***v. de ida y vuelta*** *esp Br* return journey *o* trip, *US* round trip; ***v. marítimo*** sea voyage; ***v. de negocios*** business trip; ***v. de novios*** honeymoon; ***v. oficial*** official visit; ***v. organizado*** organized trip; ***v. de placer*** pleasure trip; *Méx* ***v. redondo*** *esp Br* return journey *o* trip, *US* round trip; ***v. relámpago*** lightning trip *o* visit; ***v. de vuelta*** return journey
(b) *(recorrido)* trip; **di** *o* **hice varios viajes para trasladar los muebles** it took me several trips to move all the furniture; EXPR *RP* **de un v.** *(de una vez)* in one go
(c) *Fam (alucinación)* trip
(d) *Fam (golpe)* bang, bump
viajero, -a 1 *adj (persona)* travelling; *(ave)* migratory; **soy muy v.** I love travelling
2 *nm,f (en general)* traveller; *(en transporte público)* passenger
vial 1 *adj* road; **seguridad v.** road safety
2 *nm (frasco)* phial
vialidad *nf* **el pésimo estado de la v.** the appalling state of the roads *o* highways; **departamento de v.** highway(s) department
vianda *nf* (a) *(comida)* food (b) *Méx, RP (tentempié)* packed lunch (c) *Méx, RP (fiambrera)* lunchbox
viandante *nmf* (a) *(peatón)* pedestrian (b) *(transeúnte)* passer-by
viaraza *nf* (a) *Am (acción repentina, ganas)* **le dio la v. de hacerlo** she took it into her head to do it (b) *RP (ataque de cólera)* fit of rage; **le vino la v.** he saw red
viario, -a *adj* road; **red viaria** road network
viático *nm* (a) *Rel* last rites, viaticum (b) *(dieta)* expenses allowance
víbora *nf* (a) *(serpiente)* adder, viper (b) *(persona mala)* viper; **es una v.** she has a vicious tongue
viborear *vi Méx Fam* to bitch, to backbite
viborera *nf* viper grass
vibra *nf Am Fam* vibes
vibración *nf* (a) *(oscilación)* vibration (b) *Fam* **vibraciones** *(sensación)* vibes; **María me da buenas/malas vibraciones** I get good/bad vibes off Maria
vibrador *nm* vibrator
vibráfono *nm* vibraphone
vibrante *adj* (a) *(aparato)* vibrating (b) *(música, espectáculo)* vibrant (c) *Ling* rolled, trilled
vibrar *vi* (a) *(onda, aparato)* to vibrate; *(edificio)* to shake (b) *(voz, rodillas)* to shake (c) *(persona)* to be thrilled; **el concierto hizo v. al público** the concert had an electrifying effect on the audience; **el teatro entero vibraba con la música** the whole theatre was thrilled by the music
vibrátil *adj* vibratile
vibratorio, -a *adj* vibratory
vicaría *nf* (a) *(cargo)* vicarship, vicariate (b) *(residencia)* vicarage; EXPR *Fam* **pasar por la v.** to tie the knot

vicario *nm* vicar ►► ***v. apostólico*** vicar apostolic; ***el v. de Cristo*** the Vicar of Christ
vicealmirantazgo *nm* vice-admiralty
vicealmirante *nm* vice-admiral
vicecanciller *nmf* (a) *(de gobierno)* vice-chancellor (b) *Am (de asuntos exteriores)* deputy foreign minister
vicecónsul *nm* vice-consul
viceconsulado *nm* (a) *(cargo)* vice-consulship (b) *(oficina)* vice-consulate
vicegobernador, -ora *nm,f* vice-governor
Vicente *n pr* EXPR *Fam* **¿dónde va V.? donde va la gente** he/she always follows the crowd
vicepresidencia *nf (de país, asociación)* vice-presidency; *(de comité, empresa)* vice-chairmanship
vicepresidente, -a *nm,f (de país, asociación)* vice-president; *(de comité, empresa)* vice-chairman, *US* vice-president
vicerrector, -ora *nm,f* deputy vice-chancellor *(of a university)*
vicerrectorado *nm* (a) *(cargo)* = post of deputy vice-chancellor of a university (b) *(lugar)* deputy vice-chancellor's office
vicesecretario, -a *nm,f* assistant secretary
vicetiple *nf* chorus girl
viceversa *adv* vice versa
vichada, bichada *nf RP Fam* **echar una v. a algo** to have a quick look at sth, *Br* to have a shufty at sth
vichar, bichar *RP Fam* **1** *vt* to peek at, to sneak a look at
2 *vi* to peek, to sneak a look
vichyssoise [bitʃi'swas] *nf* vichyssoise
viciado, -a *adj* (a) *(aire) (enrarecido)* stuffy; *(contaminado)* polluted (b) *(proceso, situación)* spoiled, blighted
viciar 1 *vt* (a) *(persona) (enviciar)* to get into a bad habit; *(pervertir)* to corrupt
(b) *(aire) (de habitación)* to make stuffy; *(contaminar)* to pollute
(c) *(deformar) (tuerca)* to ruin, to twist *o* bend out of shape; *(zapato)* to ruin, to spoil (the shape of); *(proceso, sistema)* to blight, to spoil
(d) *(falsear)* to distort, to twist; **los enfrentamientos personales viciaron el debate** personal animosities distorted the debate
(e) *Der (invalidar)* to invalidate
2 **viciarse** *vpr* (a) *(persona) (enviciarse)* to get into a bad habit; *(pervertirse)* to become *o* get corrupted; **es muy fácil viciarse con estos bombones** it's very easy to get addicted to these chocolates (b) *(aire) (de habitación)* to get stuffy; *(contaminarse)* to get polluted (c) *(deformarse) (tuerca)* to be bent *o* twisted out of shape; *(zapato)* to lose its shape, to be ruined
vicio *nm* (a) *(libertinaje)* vice; **el v. y la virtud** virtue and vice
(b) *(actividad inmoral)* vice; **gasta todo lo que gana en vicios** he spends everything he earns on his vices
(c) *(afición excesiva)* **fuma mucho, pero quiere dejar el v.** she smokes a lot, but she wants to give up (the habit); *Fam* **para mí, viajar es un v.** I'm addicted to travelling; EXPR *Fam* **de v.** *(fenomenal)* brilliant; **esta tarta está de v.** this cake is yummy *o* scrumptious; **nos lo pasamos de v.** we had a great *o* fantastic time; EXPR **quejarse** *o* **llorar de v.** to complain for no (good) reason
(d) *(mala costumbre)* bad habit, vice; **vicios posturales** bad postural habits
(e) *(defecto, error)* defect; **tiene un v. al andar** he walks in a strange way ►► ***v. de dicción*** incorrect use of language; *Der* ***v. de forma*** minor procedural irregularity
vicioso, -a 1 *adj* (a) *(depravado)* depraved (b) *(enviciado)* **es un jugador muy v.** he's heavily addicted to gambling
2 *nm,f* (a) *(depravado)* depraved person; **ser un v.** to be depraved (b) *(enviciado)* addict; *Fam* **es un v. de las novelas policíacas** he's addicted to detective novels

> **Falso amigo**: El adjetivo inglés **vicious** no es la traducción del español **vicioso**. En inglés **vicious** significa "brutal", "despiadado" o "cruel".

vicisitudes *nfpl* (a) *(sucesos)* setbacks, mishaps; **tras muchas v. alcanzamos la costa** after many setbacks we reached the coast (b) *(altibajos)* ups and downs, *Literario* vicissitudes; **el relato de las v. de una familia de emigrantes** the story of the ups and downs *o* *Literario* vicissitudes in the life of a family of emigrants
víctima *nf* (a) *(por mala suerte o negligencia)* victim; *(en accidente, guerra)* casualty; **ser v. de la represión/la injusticia** to be the victim of repression/injustice; **fue v. de su propia ambición** she was the

victim of her own ambition; **resultó v. de su propio engaño** he was hoist with his own petard, his scheme backfired on him; **falleció v. de un infarto** he died of a heart attack ▸▸ ***v. mortal*** fatality; **hubo tres víctimas mortales** three people were killed

(**b**) *(en sacrificio)* victim; EXPR **hacerse la v.** to play the martyr ▸▸ ***v. propiciatoria*** scapegoat

victimado, -a *nm,f Am* (murder) victim

victimar *vt Am* to kill, to murder

victimario, -a *nm,f* (**a**) *Formal (que hace víctimas)* victimizer (**b**) *Am* killer, murderer

victimismo *nm* **dejémonos de victimismos** let's stop trying to play the victim

victorense 1 *adj* of/from Ciudad Victoria *(Mexico)*

2 *nmf* person from Ciudad Victoria *(Mexico)*

victoria *nf* victory; **se adjudicó la v. en los 100 metros** she won the 100 metres; EXPR **cantar v.** to claim victory ▸▸ *Dep* ***v. local*** home win; ***v. moral*** moral victory; ***v. pírrica*** Pyrrhic victory; *Dep* ***v. visitante*** away win

victoriano, -a *adj* Victorian

victoriosamente *adv* victoriously

victorioso, -a *adj* victorious

victrola, vitrola *nf Am* gramophone, *US* phonograph

vicuña *nf* vicuña

vid *nf* vine

vid. (*abrev de* **véase**) v., vide

VIDA *nf* (**a**) *(estado fisiológico, hecho de existir)* life; **¿hay v. en otros planetas?** is there life on other planets?; **el cuerpo sin v. de un soldado** the lifeless body of a soldier; **el conflicto se cobró muchas vidas** many lives were lost in the conflict; **aquello le costó la v.** that cost him his life; **dar la v. por** to give one's life for; **estar con v.** to be alive; **va a ser una operación a v. o muerte** the operation may save his life but it may also kill him; **estar entre la v. y la muerte** to be at death's door; **perder la v.** to lose one's life; **quitar la v. a alguien** to kill sb; **quitarse la v.** to take one's (own) life; **salir con v.** to come out alive; **como si la v. le fuera en ello** as if his/her life depended on it; **ser una cuestión** *o* **un asunto de v. o muerte** to be a matter of life and death; EXPR **enterrarse en v.** to forsake the world; EXPR **pasar a mejor v.** *Euf (persona)* to pass away; *(prenda, aparato, utensilio)* to have had it; EXPR **la otra v.** the next life; EXPR **tenía la v. pendiente de un hilo** her life was hanging by a thread; EXPR **tener siete vidas (como los gatos)** to have nine lives; PROV **mientras hay v. hay esperanza** hope springs eternal ▸▸ ***v. artificial*** artificial life; ***la v. eterna*** eternal life; ***v. extraterrestre*** extraterrestrial life; ***v. intrauterina*** intrauterine life

(**b**) *(periodo de existencia)* life; **trabajó toda su v.** he worked all his life; **una v. plagada de éxitos** a lifetime of success; **de mi/tu/***etc.* **v.** of my/your/*etc* life; **el amor/la oportunidad de su v.** the love/chance of his life; **un amigo de toda la v.** a lifelong friend; **le conozco de toda la v.** I've known him all my life; **de toda la v. las novias van de blanco** brides have worn white since time immemorial, brides have always worn white; **de por v.** for life; **en v. de** during the life *o* lifetime of; **eso no lo hubieras dicho en v. de tu padre** you would never have said that while your father was alive; **así no vas a aprobar en la** *o* **tu v.** you'll never pass like that; **¡en mi** *o* **la v. vi cosa igual!** I'd never seen such a thing in all my life!; **pasarse la v. haciendo algo** to spend one's life doing sth; **se pasa la v. quejándose** he does nothing but complain all the time; EXPR **hacer la v. imposible a alguien** to make sb's life impossible; EXPR *Am* **toda la v.:** *(sin duda)* **¿prefieres África a Europa? – ¡toda la v.!** do you prefer Africa to Europe? – every time! *o* you bet!; EXPR **la v. da muchas vueltas** you never know what life has got in store for you; EXPR **la v. y milagros de alguien** sb's life story

(**c**) *Com (de maquinaria, aparato, automóvil)* life; **tiene una v. útil de veinte años** it has a useful life of twenty years, it's designed to last for twenty years ▸▸ ***v. en estantería*** shelf life; ***v. media*** average life, mean lifetime

(**d**) *(forma de vivir, faceta cotidiana)* life; **su v. es el teatro** the theatre is her life; **¿cómo es tu v. diaria?** what would be a typical day in your life?; **la v. política del país** the country's political life; **¿no te gustaría cambiar de v.?** wouldn't you like to change your life *o* the way you live?; **yo hago** *o* **vivo mi v. como todo el mundo** I just get on with my life like everyone else; **lleva una v. muy tranquila** she leads *o* lives a very peaceful life; **¡así es la v.!** that's life!, such is life!; **¡esto (sí que) es v.!** this is the life!; **una mujer de v. alegre** a loose woman; **¿qué es de tu v.?** how's life?; **¡qué v. ésta!** what a life!; **la buena v.** the good life; EXPR **darse** *o* **pegarse la gran v., darse** *o* **pegarse la v. padre** to live the life of Riley; EXPR **llevar una v. de perros** to lead a dog's life ▸▸ ***v. amorosa*** love life; ***v. de familia*** family life; ***v. privada*** private life; ***v. pública*** public life; ***v. sentimental*** love life; ***v. sexual*** sex life; ***v. social*** social life; **hacer v. social (con)** to socialize (with)

(**e**) *(animación)* life; **este pueblo tiene mucha v.** this town is very lively; **estar lleno de v.** to be full of life; **Brando da v. al personaje del padre** Brando plays the father ▸▸ ***v. nocturna*** nightlife

(**f**) *(necesidades materiales)* **la v. está muy cara en Japón** the cost of living is very high in Japan; *Fam* **está la v. muy achuchada** money's very tight; **ganarse la v.** to earn a living; **con este trabajo me gano bien la v.** I make a good living from this job

(**g**) *(apelativo cariñoso)* darling; **¡mi v.!, ¡v. mía!** my darling!

---

vidalita *nf* = plaintive folk song from Argentina or Uruguay

vidente 1 *adj* sighted; **no v.** blind, sightless

2 *nmf* (**a**) *(adivino)* clairvoyant (**b**) *(no ciego)* sighted person; **no v.** blind *o* sightless person; **los no videntes** the blind

vídeo, *Am* **video** *nm (aparato)* video, VCR; *(sistema)* video; *(cinta)* video(tape); *(videoclip)* (pop) video; **en v.** on video; **grabar en v.** to videotape, to record on video ▸▸ ***v. casero*** home video; ***v. comunitario*** = system enabling one video to be shown simultaneously on different television sets in the same block of flats; ***v. digital*** digital video; ***v. doméstico*** home video; ***v. interactivo*** interactive video; *Informát* ***v. inverso*** reverse video

videoaficionado, -a *nm,f* = person who makes amateur videos

videocámara *nf (grande)* video camera; *(pequeña)* camcorder

videocasete *nm* video, videocassette

videocinta *nf* video, videotape

videoclip *nm* (pop) video

videoclub *nm* video (rental) shop *o US* store

videoconferencia *nf* videoconference; **videoconferencias** videoconferencing

videoconsola *nf* game(s) console

videodisco *nm* videodisk

videoedición *nf* video editing

videografía *nf* (**a**) *(técnica)* video recording (**b**) *(vídeos)* videos

videográfico, -a *adj* video; **material v.** video material

videoinstalación *nf* videoinstallation

videojuego *nm* video game

videolibro *nm* video book

videomarcador *nm* electronic scoreboard

videopelícula *nf* video movie *o Br* film

videoportero *nm* video entryphone system

videoteca *nf* video library

videoteléfono *nm* videophone

videoterminal *nm* video terminal

videotexto *nm,* **videotex** *nm inv (por señal de televisión)* teletext; *(por línea telefónica)* videotext, viewdata

vidorra *nf Fam* **pegarse una gran v.** to live the life of Riley

vidorria *nf Fam* (**a**) *Méx, Ven (mala vida)* dog's life (**b**) *Ven (buena vida)* easy life

vidriado, -a 1 *adj* glazed

2 *nm* (**a**) *(técnica)* glazing (**b**) *(material)* glaze

vidriar *vt* to glaze

vidriera *nf* (**a**) *(puerta)* glass door; *(ventana)* glass window (**b**) *(en catedrales)* stained-glass window (**c**) *Am (escaparate)* shop window (**d**) *ver también* **vidriero**

vidriería *nf* glassworks *(singular)*

vidrierista *nmf Am* window dresser

vidriero, -a *nm,f* (**a**) *(que fabrica cristales)* glass manufacturer (**b**) *(que coloca cristales)* glazier

vidrio *nm* (**a**) *(material)* glass ▸▸ ***v. ahumado*** smoked *o* dark glass; ***v. blindado*** armoured glass; ***v. esmerilado*** frosted *o* ground glass; ***v. pyrex***® Pyrex® glass; ***v. de seguridad*** security glass

(**b**) *(objeto)* glass; **un v.** a piece of glass; **cuidado con los vidrios desparramados por el piso** careful of the bits of glass scattered on the floor; **está el suelo lleno de vidrios rotos** the floor is covered in broken glass; EXPR **pagar los vidrios rotos** to carry the can

(**c**) *(de ventana)* window (pane); *Am (de anteojos)* lens; *Am (de coche)* window; **bajar el v.** *(ventanilla)* to roll down the window; EXPR *Am* **todo depende del v. a través del que se mira** it all depends how you look at it ▸▸ *Am* ***v. eléctrico*** electric window

vidrioso, -a *adj* (a) *(material)* brittle (b) *(tema, asunto)* thorny, delicate (c) *(ojos)* glazed

vidurria *nf RP Fam* easy life

vieira *nf* scallop

vieja *nf* (a) *(pescado) (de las Canarias)* parrotfish; *(con tentáculos)* blenny (b) *Col, Méx, Ven Fam (mujer, chica)* woman, *Br* bird (c) *ver también* **viejo**

viejerío *nm Fam* (a) *Col, Méx, Ven* crowd *o* bunch of women *o Br* birds (b) *RP Pey* bunch of oldies *o Br* wrinklies *o US* oldsters

viejero *nm Col, Méx, Ven Fam* womanizer

viejo, -a 1 *adj* (a) *(en edad)* old; **está muy v. para su edad** he looks very old for his age; **ya soy** *o* **estoy v. para estas cosas** I'm a bit old for that sort of thing; **esa ropa te hace más v.** those clothes make you look older; **hacerse v.** to get *o* grow old; **de v. fue cuando empezó a viajar** it was only as an old man that he started to travel; **morirse de v.** to die from old age; EXPR *RP Fam* **ser más v. que andar a pie** to be as old as the hills, to have come out of the ark

(b) *(usado) (ropa, aparato)* old; **estas botas están ya viejas** these boots are worn out *o* past it now; **una radio vieja** an old radio; **una librería de v.** a second-hand bookshop

(c) *(antiguo)* old; **viejas canciones** old songs; **un v. conocido** an old acquaintance; **es un chiste muy v.** it's a really old joke

(d) *RP (de toda la vida)* **baila muy bien, es tanguero v.** he dances very well, he's always loved tango; **a ese no le creas, que es mentiroso v.** don't you believe him, he's a born liar

2 *nm,f* (a) *(anciano)* old man, *f* old lady; **los viejos** the elderly; **los viejos del pueblo** the old people in the village; **llegar a v.** to live to be an old man ►► *RP Fam* ***el v. de la bolsa*** the bogeyman; *Chile* ***el V. de Pascua*** Father Christmas; *Chile* ***el V. Pascuero*** Father Christmas; ***v. verde*** dirty old man

(b) *Fam (padre)* old man; *(madre)* old girl; **mis viejos** my folks

(c) *Am Fam (apelativo) (amigo)* pal, *Br* mate, *US* buddy; *(amiga)* girl, *US* girlfriend; **¿qué hay de nuevo, v.?** what's new, *Br* mate *o US* buddy?

(d) *Méx, RP Fam (apelativo) (esposo, esposa) Br* love, *US* honey

(e) *RP Fam (apelativo) (cariñoso o paternalista) Br* love, *US* honey; **¿querés un caramelo, mi v.?** *Br* do you want a sweet, love?, *US* do you want a piece of candy, honey?

Viena *n* Vienna

viene *etc ver* **venir**

vienés, -esa 1 *adj* Viennese

2 *nm,f* Viennese

viento *nm* (a) *(aire)* wind; **v. del norte** north *o* northerly wind; **navegábamos a favor del v.** we were sailing with the wind behind us; **navegar contra el v.** to sail into the wind; **hace v.** it's windy; **mis esperanzas se las llevó el v.** my hopes flew out of the window; EXPR **proclamar algo a los cuatro vientos** to shout sth from the rooftops; EXPR **contra v. y marea** through hell or high water, no matter the difficulties; **defender algo/a alguien contra v. y marea** to defend sth/sb in spite of everything; EXPR **despedir** *o* **echar a alguien con v. fresco** to send sb packing; EXPR *Fam* **tomar vientos: ¡vete a tomar vientos!** get lost!, lose yourself!; **lo mandó a tomar vientos** she told him to get lost; EXPR **v. en popa** splendidly, very nicely; **todo marcha v. en popa** everything's going swimmingly *o* very nicely ►► ***vientos alisios*** trade winds; ***v. de cara*** headwind; ***v. contrario*** headwind; ***v. de costado*** crosswind; ***v. dominante*** prevailing wind; ***v. flojo*** gentle breeze; ***v. fuerte*** high winds; ***v. de lado*** crosswind; ***v. solar*** solar wind

(b) *(cuerda)* guy (rope)

(c) *Mús* wind; **la sección de v.** the wind section

(d) *Náut (rumbo)* course, bearing

vientre *nm* (a) *(de persona) (cavidad con órganos)* abdomen; *(región)* stomach, belly; **hacer de v.** to have a bowel movement; **bajo v.** lower abdomen (b) *(de embarazada)* womb; *Rel* **el fruto de tu v.** the fruit of thy womb (c) *(de vasija)* belly, rounded part

vier. *(abrev de* **viernes***)* Fri

viera *etc ver* **ver**

viernes *nm inv* Friday ►► ***V. Santo*** Good Friday; *ver también* **sábado**

vierto *etc ver* **verter**

viese *etc ver* **ver**

Vietnam *n* Vietnam

vietnamita 1 *adj* Vietnamese

2 *nmf (persona)* Vietnamese

3 *nm (lengua)* Vietnamese

viga *nf (de madera)* beam, rafter; *(de metal)* girder ►► ***v. maestra*** main beam

vigencia *nf (de ley, contrato)* validity; **durante el primer año de v. de esta normativa** during the first year these regulations were in force; **el periodo de v. de una patente/de un contrato** the duration of a patent/contract; **no estoy seguro de la v. de la tarifa** I'm not sure if the rate is still applicable; **entrar en v.** *(ley)* to come into force; *(contrato, tarifa)* to come into effect, to take effect; **estar en v.** *(ley)* to be in force; *(contato, tarifa)* to apply, to be effective; **esa costumbre ha perdido v./todavía tiene v.** that custom has fallen out of use/is still observed

vigente *adj (ley)* in force; *(contrato, tarifa)* current; *(campeón)* reigning; *(costumbre)* in use; **según la normativa v....** according to the current regulations *o* the regulations currently in force...; **el contrato estará v. durante tres años** the contract will run *o* be valid for three years; **la tregua sigue v.** the ceasefire is still in force

vigésimo, -a *núm* twentieth; *ver también* **octavo**

vigía 1 *nmf* lookout

2 *nf (atalaya)* watchtower

vigilancia *nf* (a) *(cuidado)* vigilance ►► ***v. intensiva*** intensive care (b) *(control)* surveillance; **equipo de v.** *(aparatos)* surveillance equipment; **están al cargo de la v. en todo el edificio** they are in charge of security for the whole building; **tras la fuga aumentaron la v.** after the escape security was increased (c) *(vigilantes)* guards, security

vigilante 1 *adj* vigilant; **conviene mantenerse vigilantes** it's best to stay on your guard *o* remain alert

2 *nmf* guard ►► ***v. jurado*** security guard; ***v. nocturno*** nighwatchman

vigilar 1 *vt* (a) *(presos, banco)* to guard; **el guarda que vigila la salida** the guard on the exit (b) *(observar, cuidar) (enfermo)* to watch over; *(niños, bolso)* to keep an eye on; *(proceso)* to oversee; **vigila que nadie toque esto** make sure no one touches this (c) *(espiar)* to watch; **me vigilan desde hace días** they've been watching me for days

2 *vi* to keep watch; **él vigilaba mientras los demás dormían** he kept watch while the others slept; **v. por algo** to (keep a) watch over sth; **el estado vigila por la salud/seguridad de los ciudadanos** the State looks after *o* watches over people's health/security

vigilia *nf* (a) *(vela)* wakefulness; *(periodo)* period of wakefulness; **pasó varias noches de v.** she had several sleepless nights; **la mente se recupera durante el sueño del esfuerzo hecho durante la v.** the mind uses sleep to recharge its batteries after the efforts of the day

(b) *(insomnio)* sleeplessness

(c) *(víspera)* eve; **la v. de la Inmaculada** the eve of the feast of the Immaculate Conception

(d) *Rel (abstinencia)* abstinence

vigor *nm* (a) *(fuerza)* vigour

(b) *(vigencia)* **en v.** *(ley, reglamento)* in force; *(contrato, tarifa)* current; **el acuerdo en v.** the agreement in force, the current agreement; **el contrato/la tarifa ya no está en vigor** the contract is no longer valid/the rate is no longer valid *o* applicable; **entrar en v.** to come into force, to take effect; **con la entrada en v. de la nueva normativa, la situación va a cambiar** when the new regulations come into force *o* take effect, the situation will change

vigorizador, -ora, vigorizante *adj (medicamento)* fortifying; *(actividad)* invigorating

vigorizar [14] *vt (medicamento)* to fortify; *(actividad)* to invigorate

vigorosamente *adv* vigorously

vigoroso, -a *adj* (a) *(robusto)* vigorous (b) *(lenguage, estilo)* vigorous, forceful; *(actuación)* spirited, powerful

viguería *nf* girders, beams

vigués, -esa 1 *adj* of/from Vigo *(Spain)*

2 *nm,f* person from Vigo *(Spain)*

vigueta *nf* joist

VIH *nm (abrev de* **virus de la inmunodeficiencia humana***)* HIV

vihuela *nf* vihuela, = guitar-like musical instrument

vikingo, -a 1 *adj* Viking

2 *nm,f* Viking

vil *adj* vile, despicable; *Hum* **el v. metal** filthy lucre

vilano *nm* seedhead

vileza *nf* (a) *(acción)* vile *o* despicable act (b) *(cualidad)* vileness

vilipendiar *vt* (a) *(ofender)* to vilify, to revile (b) *(humillar)* to humiliate

vilipendio *nm* (a) *(ofensa)* vilification (b) *(humillación)* humiliation

vilipendioso, -a *adj* (a) *(ofensivo)* vilifying (b) *(humillante)* humiliating

villa *nf* (**a**) *(población)* small town; EXPR *Méx* **el que se fue a la v. perdió su silla** you shouldn't have gone away if you wanted to keep your place/seat ▸▸ *Arg, Bol* ***v. miseria*** shanty town; ***v. olímpica*** Olympic village (**b**) *(casa)* villa, country house ▸▸ ***v. romana*** Roman villa

Villadiego *n Fam* EXPR **tomar** *o RP* **tomarse** *o Esp* **coger las de V.** to take to one's heels

villahermosino, -a 1 *adj* of/from Villahermosa *(Mexico)*
2 *nm,f* person from Villahermosa *(Mexico)*

villanaje *nm (gente)* peasants, peasantry

villancico *nm* Christmas carol

villanía *nf* (**a**) *(acto)* vile *o* despicable act (**b**) *(cualidad)* vileness

villano, -a 1 *adj* villainous
2 *nm,f* (**a**) *(malvado)* villain (**b**) *(plebeyo)* peasant

villero, -a *Arg* 1 *adj* shanty town
2 *nm,f* shanty dweller

villorrio *nm Pey* one-horse town, backwater

vilmente *adv* vilely, despicably

Vilna *n* Vilnius

vilo: en vilo *loc adv* (**a**) *(suspendido)* in the air, suspended; **sostener algo en v.** to hold sth up (**b**) *(inquieto)* **con el corazón en v.** on tenterhooks; **tener el alma en v.** to be on tenterhooks; **la población sigue los sucesos con el alma en v.** the population is anxiously following events; **mantener** *o* **tener a alguien en v.** to keep sb in suspense

vinagre *nm* vinegar; **en v.** pickled ▸▸ ***v. de jerez*** sherry vinegar; ***v. de malta*** malt vinegar; ***v. de manzana*** apple *o* cider vinegar

vinagrera *nf* (**a**) *(vasija)* vinegar bottle (**b**) **vinagreras** *(para aceite y vinagre)* cruet set (**c**) *Andes (ardor de estómago)* heartburn

vinagreta *nf* vinaigrette, French dressing

vinajera *nf* cruet, = vessel holding wine or water in Catholic mass

vinatería *nf* (**a**) *(tienda)* wine shop (**b**) *(negocio)* wine trade

vinatero, -a 1 *adj* wine
2 *nm,f (vendedor)* wine merchant, vintner; *(fabricante)* wine maker

vinaza *nf (residuo)* stillage, vinasse

vinazo *nm* strong, heavy wine

vinca *nf* periwinkle

vincha *nf Andes, RP* hairband

vinchuca *nf* kissing bug, cone-nose bug

vinculación *nf* link, connection; **fue detenido por su presunta v. con el tráfico de drogas** he was arrested because of suspected links with drug-trafficking

vinculante *adj* binding

vincular 1 *vt* (**a**) *(enlazar)* to link; **estar vinculado a** *(tener vínculos con)* to be linked to, to have links with; *(depender de)* to be linked to (**b**) *(obligar)* **este tratado vincula a los países firmantes** this treaty is binding for the countries that have signed it (**c**) *Informát* to attach
2 **vincularse** *vpr (enlazarse)* **vincularse con** *o* **a** to form links with

vínculo *nm* (**a**) *(lazo) (entre hechos, países)* link; *(personal, familiar)* tie, bond; **mantenían vínculos comerciales con Oriente Medio** they maintained commercial *o* trading links with the Middle East; **los unía un v. muy profundo** they shared a very deep bond ▸▸ ***vínculos de parentesco*** family ties (**b**) *Informát* link (**c**) *Der* entail

vindicación *nf* (**a**) *(venganza)* vengeance, revenge (**b**) *(defensa, rehabilitación)* vindication

vindicar [60] *vt* (**a**) *(vengar)* to avenge, to revenge (**b**) *(defender, rehabilitar)* to vindicate (**c**) *(reivindicar)* to claim, to demand

vindicatorio, -a, vindicativo, -a *adj* (**a**) *(vengativo)* vindictive (**b**) *(rehabilitador)* vindicatory (**c**) *(reivindicativo)* **dio un discurso v.** he gave a speech in which he made a series of demands

vindicta *nf* revenge, vengeance ▸▸ ***v. pública*** exemplary punishment

vinería *nf Am* wine shop

vinero, -a *Am* 1 *adj* wine; **la producción vinera** wine production
2 *nm,f (vendedor)* wine merchant, vintner; *(fabricante)* wine maker

vinícola *adj (país, región)* wine-producing; **industria v.** wine industry

vinicultor, -ora *nm,f* wine producer

vinicultura *nf* wine production, wine-growing

viniera *etc ver* **venir**

vinificación *nf* fermentation, *Espec* vinification

vinilo *nm* vinyl

vino 1 *ver* **venir**
2 *nm* (**a**) *(bebida)* wine; **se tomaron un v.** they had a glass of wine; **ir de vinos** to go out for a few glasses of wine; EXPR **tiene mal v.** he turns nasty when he's had one too many ▸▸ ***v. añejo*** mature wine; ***v. blanco*** white wine; ***v. de la casa*** house wine; ***v. clarete*** light red wine; ***v. dulce*** sweet wine; ***v. espumoso*** sparkling wine; ***v. generoso*** full-bodied wine; ***v. de Jerez*** sherry; ***v. de mesa*** table wine; ***v. de Oporto*** port; ***v. peleón*** cheap wine, *Br* plonk; *Andes* ***v. rojo*** red wine; ***v. rosado*** rosé; ***v. seco*** dry wine; ***v. tinto*** red wine
(**b**) *(recepción)* **un v. español** a cheese and wine reception
3 *adj inv* **color v.** wine-coloured; **unos zapatos color v.** wine-coloured shoes

viña *nf* vineyard; *Rel* **la v. del Señor** the faithful; EXPR **de todo hay en la v. del Señor** it takes all sorts (to make a world)

viñador, -ora *nm,f (dueño)* vineyard owner; *(como productor de vino)* wine grower; *(trabajador)* vineyard worker

viñamarino, -a 1 *adj* of/from Viña del Mar *(Chile)*
2 *nm,f* person from Viña del Mar *(Chile)*

viñatero, -a *CSur* 1 *adj* wine-producing
2 *nm,f (dueño)* wine grower; *(trabajador)* vineyard worker

viñátigo *nm* Madeira bay persea

viñedo *nm* (large) vineyard

viñeta *nf* (**a**) *(de tebeo)* cartoon frame; **el texto va acompañado de unas viñetas** the text is accompanied by a cartoon (**b**) *(de libro)* vignette

vio *ver* **ver**

viola 1 *nf* viola
2 *nmf* viola player

violáceo, -a 1 *adj* violet
2 *nm* violet

violación *nf* (**a**) *(de persona)* rape (**b**) *(de ley, derechos)* violation, infringement; **v. del espacio aéreo panameño** violation of Panama's airspace ▸▸ *Der* ***v. de domicilio*** unlawful entry (**c**) *(en baloncesto)* violation

violado, -a 1 *adj* violet
2 *nm* violet

violador, -ora *nm,f* (**a**) *(de persona)* rapist (**b**) *(de ley, derechos)* violator

violar *vt* (**a**) *(persona)* to rape (**b**) *(ley, derechos)* to violate, to infringe; *(domicilio)* to break into

violencia *nf* (**a**) *(agresividad)* violence; **reaccionó con v.** she reacted violently; **emplear la v. contra la población desarmada** to use violence against an unarmed population ▸▸ ***v. callejera*** street violence; ***v. doméstica*** domestic violence; ***v. física*** physical violence (**b**) *(de viento, pasiones)* force (**c**) *(incomodidad)* awkwardness

violentamente *adv* violently

violentar 1 *vt* (**a**) *(incomodar)* **v. a alguien** to make sb feel awkward (**b**) *(forzar) (cerradura)* to force; *(domicilio)* to break into
2 **violentarse** *vpr* to feel awkward

violentismo *nm Andes* violent agitation, (political) violence

violentista *Andes* 1 *adj* violent; **una escalada v.** a spiral of violence
2 *nmf* violent social agitator

violento, -a 1 *adj* (**a**) *(persona, deporte, acción)* violent; **muerte violenta** violent death; **se hicieron con el parlamento por medios violentos** they took control of the parliament by violent means
(**b**) *(intenso) (pasión, tempestad)* intense, violent; *(viento)* fierce; **los despertó una violenta sacudida del wagón** they were awoken when the carriage gave a violent jolt
(**c**) *(incómodo)* awkward; **aquello lo puso en una situación muy violenta** that put him in a very awkward situation; **me resulta v. hablar con ella** I feel awkward talking to her
2 *nmpl* **los violentos** the men of violence

violeta 1 *nf (flor)* violet
2 *adj inv* violet
3 *nm (color)* violet

violetera *nf* violet seller

violín 1 *nm* violin; EXPR *RP Fam* **meter v. en bolsa** to hold one's tongue, to shut up; EXPR *Méx Fam* **pintar a alguien un v.** *Br* to stick two fingers up at sb, *US* to flip sb the bird
2 *nmf* violinist

violinista *nmf* violinist

violón 1 *nm* double bass
2 *nmf* double bass player

violonchelista, violoncelista *nmf* cellist

violonchelo, violoncelo 1 *nm* cello
2 *nmf* cellist

VIP [bip] *nmf* (*abrev de* **very important person**) VIP

viperino, -a *adj (lengua)* venomous

viracocha *nm Hist* = name given to the Spanish Conquistadores among the ancient Incas

virada *nf* (**a**) *(vuelta)* turn (**b**) *Náut* tack

virador *nm* toner

viraje *nm* (**a**) *(en coche)* swerve; **hacer un v.** to swerve (**b**) *(en barco)* tack; **hacer un v.** to change tack (**c**) *Fot* toning (**d**) *(cambio)* change of direction

viral *adj* viral

virar 1 *vt* (**a**) *(girar)* to turn (round) (**b**) *Fot* to tone
2 *vi* (**a**) *(girar)* to turn (round); *Náut* to tack; **v. en redondo** to turn round (**b**) *(cambiar) (persona)* to do a volte-face *o* U-turn; *(ideas, política)* to change radically

virgen 1 *adj (persona, selva, tierra)* virgin; *(cinta)* blank; *(película)* unused
2 *nmf (persona)* virgin
3 *nf* (**a**) *(imagen)* Madonna (**b**) *Rel* **la V.** the Virgin (Mary); *Fam* **¡V. Santa!** good heavens!; *Fam* **¡la V.!** *Br* blimey!, *US* jeez!

virginal *adj* virginal

virginiano, -a *Am* **1** *adj* Virgo; **ser v.** to be (a) Virgo
2 *nm,f* Virgo; **los virginianos son...** Virgos are...

virginidad *nf* virginity

virgo 1 *adj inv* **V.** Virgo; *Esp* **ser V.** to be (a) Virgo
2 *nm* (**a**) *(virginidad)* virginity; *(himen)* hymen (**b**) *(signo del zodiaco)* **V.** Virgo; *Am* **los de V. son...** Virgos are ...
3 *nmf inv (persona)* **V.** Virgo; *Esp* **los V. son...** Virgos are ...

virguería *nf Fam* **es una v.** *(diseño, objeto)* it's a work of art; **hacer virguerías** to do *o* work wonders; **hace virguerías con la guitarra** he's a wizard with the guitar; **hace virguerías con el balón** he works *o* performs miracles with the ball

virguero, -a *adj Fam (diseño, objeto)* fantastic, superb; *(persona)* **es un tío v. con el ordenador** the guy's a genius on the computer

vírgula, virgulilla *nf Imprenta (guión ondulado)* swung dash; *(sobre la ñ)* tilde

vírico, -a *adj* viral

viril *adj* virile, manly

virilidad *nf* virility

virilmente *adj* in a manly way, virilely

virola *nf* (**a**) *(de bastón, paraguas)* ferrule (**b**) *(árbol)* virole (**c**) *RP (en arreo de caballo)* silver disc

virolento, -a *adj* pockmarked

virolo, -a *adj Méx, Ven Fam Hum* cross-eyed

virología *nf* virology

virológico, -a *adj* virological

virólogo, -a *nm,f* virologist

virreina *nf* vicereine

virreinal *adj* viceregal

virreinato, virreino *nm* viceroyalty

virrey *nm* viceroy

virtiera *etc ver* **verter**

virtual *adj* (**a**) *(posible)* possible, potential; **le preocupaba el v. fracaso del proyecto** he was worried by the possible failure of the project (**b**) *(casi real)* **se le considera el v. ganador de las elecciones** he's considered to have virtually *o* practically won the elections already (**c**) *Informát* virtual

virtualidad *nf* potential

virtualmente *adv* virtually

virtud 1 *nf* (**a**) *(moral)* virtue; **la v. se opone al vicio** virtue is opposed to vice ▸▸ ***v. cardinal*** cardinal virtue; ***v. teologal*** theological virtue
(**b**) *(cualidad)* virtue; **la principal v. de este método es que...** the principal virtue of this method is that...
(**c**) *(poder, facultad)* power; **una planta con virtudes curativas** a plant with medicinal properties; **tener la v. de** to have the power *o* ability to; **dicho acuerdo tiene al menos la v. de interesar a la gente en el tema** this agreement at least has the virtue of getting people interested in the topic
2 **en virtud de** *loc prep* by virtue of; **es una de las principales potencias económicas en v. de su población** it's one of the major economic powers by virtue of its population; **en v. del tratado de París, cedieron varios territorios** under the Paris treaty they ceded several territories

virtuosamente *adv* virtuously

virtuosismo *nm* virtuosity

virtuosista *adj* virtuoso

virtuoso, -a 1 *adj (persona, comportamiento)* virtuous
2 *nm,f (genio)* virtuoso

viruela *nf* (**a**) *(enfermedad)* smallpox (**b**) *(pústula)* pockmark; **picado de viruelas** pockmarked

virulé: a la virulé *Fam* **1** *loc adj* **un ojo a la v.** a black eye; **iba con el sombrero a la v.** her hat was on crooked
2 *loc adv Br* skew-whiff, *US* skew-gee

virulencia *nf* (**a**) *(de epidemia, crítica, conflicto)* virulence, ferocity (**b**) *(de virus, microorganismo)* virulence

virulento, -a *adj* (**a**) *(epidemia, crítica, conflicto)* virulent, fierce (**b**) *(virus, microorganismo)* virulent

virus *nm inv* (**a**) *(microorganismo)* virus ▸▸ ***v. de Ébola*** Ebola virus; ***v. de la inmunodeficiencia humana*** human immunodeficiency virus; ***v. del sida*** AIDS virus (**b**) *Informát* virus ▸▸ ***v. informático*** computer virus

viruta *nf* (**a**) *(de madera)* shaving; EXPR *Fam* **echando virutas: se fue echando virutas** he rushed off (**b**) *Fam (dinero)* dough

vis *nf* **tener v. cómica** to be able to make people laugh

visado *nm Am* **visa** *nf* visa ▸▸ ***v. de entrada*** entry visa; ***v. de salida*** exit visa

visaje *nm* face, grimace; **hacer visajes** to make faces

visar *vt (pasaporte)* to put a visa in

vis a vis 1 *nm* face-to-face meeting; *(con el cónjuge)* conjugal visit
2 *loc adv* face to face

víscera *nf* internal organ; **vísceras** *(órganos internos)* entrails; *(como comida)* offal

visceral *adj* (**a**) *(odio, miedo)* visceral; **un sentimiento/una reacción v.** a gut feeling/reaction; **es muy v.** he always goes with his gut reactions (**b**) *Med* visceral

visceralmente *adv* viscerally

visco *nm* birdlime

viscosa *nf* viscose

viscosidad *nf* (**a**) *(cualidad) (de denso)* viscosity; *(de baboso)* sliminess (**b**) *Fís* viscosity

viscosilla *nf (con algodón)* viscose-cotton; *(con lana)* viscose-wool

viscoso, -a *adj* (**a**) *(denso)* viscous; *(baboso)* slimy (**b**) *Fís* viscous

visera *nf* (**a**) *(de gorra)* peak (**b**) *(de casco, suelta)* visor; **se puso la mano a modo de v.** she shaded her eyes with her hand (**c**) *(de automóvil)* sun visor (**d**) *Cuba (anteojeras) Br* blinkers, *US* blinders

visibilidad *nf* visibility; **no hay mucha v.** visibility is poor

visible *adj* (**a**) *(objeto, defecto)* visible; **es v. a varios metros** it is visible at several metres (**b**) *(evidente) (temblor, sentimiento)* visible; **se fue con v. satisfacción** she left visibly pleased (**c**) *(presentable)* **estar v.** to be decent *o* presentable

visiblemente *adv* visibly

visigodo, -a 1 *adj* Visigothic
2 *nm,f* Visigoth

visigótico, -a *adj* Visigothic

visillo *nm* net curtain, lace curtain

visión *nf* (**a**) *(capacidad)* vision, sight; **presenta una evidente pérdida de v.** there has been a noticeable loss of vision ▸▸ ***v. artificial*** artificial sight; ***v. binocular*** binocular vision
(**b**) *(acción)* seeing, witnessing; **tan sólo la v. de tal espectáculo ya le daba deseos de huir** just witnessing such a spectacle was enough to make him want to flee
(**c**) *(alucinación)* vision; **ver visiones** to be seeing things
(**d**) *(interpretación)* view; **una v. clara de la situación** a clear view *o* appreciation of the situation ▸▸ ***v. de conjunto*** overall view *o* appreciation; ***v. de futuro*** vision

visionado *nm Cine (acción)* viewing; *(sesión)* screening

visionar *vt Cine* to view *(during production or before release)*

visionario, -a 1 *adj* visionary
2 *nm,f* visionary

visir *nm* vizier

visirato *nm* vizierate

visita *nf* (**a**) *(a casa, hospital) (en general)* visit; *(breve)* call; **estar de v.** to be visiting *o* on a visit; **hacer una v. a alguien** to visit sb, to pay sb a visit; **horas de v.** visiting hours; **ir de v.** to go visiting ▸▸ ***v. de cortesía*** courtesy visit *o* call; ***v. de cumplido*** courtesy visit *o* call; ***v. relámpago*** flying visit
(**b**) *(de turismo)* visit; **hacer una v. a un museo** to visit *o* go to a museum ▸▸ ***v. guiada*** guided tour; ***v. turística:* hacer una v. turística de la ciudad** to do some sightseeing in the city

(**c**) *(de médico)* **pasar v.** to see one's patients ►► ***visitas médicas*** doctor's rounds
(**d**) *(visitante)* visitor; **tener v.** *o* **visitas** to have visitors
(**e**) *Informát (a página Web)* hit

Visitación *nf Rel* **la V.** the Visitation

visitador, -ora 1 *adj* fond of visiting; **es muy v.** he's a great one for visiting
2 *nm,f* (**a**) *(de laboratorio)* medical sales representative ►► ***v. médico*** medical representative (**b**) *(visitante)* visitor ►► *Am* ***v. social*** social worker

visitante 1 *adj Dep* visiting, away; **el equipo v.** the away team, the visitors
2 *nmf* visitor

visitar 1 *vt* (**a**) *(amigo, enfermo)* to visit (**b**) *(ciudad, museo)* to visit (**c**) *(sujeto: médico)* to visit, to call on; **el médico visitó al paciente** the doctor called on *o* visited the patient
2 visitarse *vpr* to visit each other

visiteo *nm* frequent visiting

vislumbrar 1 *vt* (**a**) *(entrever)* to make out, to discern (**b**) *(adivinar)* to discern, to have an inkling of
2 vislumbrarse *vpr* (**a**) *(entreverse)* to be barely visible (**b**) *(adivinarse)* to become a little clearer; **ya se vislumbra una posible solución** we are nearing a possible solution

vislumbre *nf* (**a**) *(de lugar, objeto)* glimpse; *(de luz)* glimmer (**b**) *(indicio)* glimpse

viso *nm* (**a**) *(reflejo) (de tejido)* sheen; *(de metal)* glint; **hacer visos** to have a sheen, to shimmer; *Chile* **hacerse visos** *(en el pelo)* to have highlights put in (one's hair)
(**b**) *(apariencia)* **esta ocupación carece de todo v. de legalidad** this activity lacks the slightest semblance of legality; **tener visos de: tiene visos de verdad** it seems pretty true; **tiene visos de hacerse realidad** it looks like it could become a reality
(**c**) *(enagua)* petticoat, underskirt
(**d**) *(de prenda)* lining

visón *nm* (**a**) *(animal)* mink (**b**) *(piel)* mink (**c**) *(abrigo)* mink (coat)

visor *nm* (**a**) *(en cámara)* viewfinder ►► ***v. de diapositivas*** slide viewer (**b**) *(de arma)* sight (**c**) *(en fichero)* file tab

> **Falso amigo**: El sustantivo inglés **visor** no es la traducción del español **visor**. El inglés **visor** significa "visera".

víspera *nf* (**a**) *(día antes)* day before, eve; **la v. de la Asunción** the eve of (the feast of) the Assumption; **en vísperas de** on the eve of (**b**) *Rel* **vísperas** evensong, vespers

VISTA 1 *adj ver* **visto**
2 *nf* (**a**) *(sentido)* (sense of) sight; *(visión)* eyesight; *(ojos)* eyes; **tiene buena/mala v., está bien/mal de la v.** she has good/poor eyesight; **la luz me hace daño a la v.** the light hurts my eyes; **se me nubló la v.** my eyes clouded over; **perder la v.** to lose one's sight, to go blind; **de v.: conocer a alguien de v.** to know sb by sight; **¡hasta la v.!** see you!; **a v. de pájaro: Cartagena a v. de pájaro** a bird's-eye view of Cartagena; EXPR **hacer la v. gorda** to turn a blind eye; EXPR **no perder de v. algo/a alguien** *(vigilar)* not to let sth/sb out of one's sight; *(tener en cuenta)* not to lose sight of sth/sb, not to forget about sth/sb; EXPR **perder de v. algo/a alguien** *(dejar de ver)* to lose sight of sth/sb; **perder de v. a alguien** *(perder contacto)* to lose touch with sb; EXPR **perderse de v.** *(en la distancia)* to disappear (from sight); EXPR **salta a la v.** *(es evidente)* it's blindingly *o* patently obvious; **salta a la v. que es novato** he is very obviously a beginner; **salta a la v. su juventud** *(sorprende)* one thing that strikes you is how young she is; EXPR **tener una v. de águila** *o* **de lince** to have an eagle eye ►► ***v. cansada*** *(por la edad)* long-sightedness; *(por el esfuerzo)* eyestrain
(**b**) *(mirada)* gaze; **dirigió la v. hacia la pantalla** she turned her eyes *o* gaze to the screen; **alzar/apartar/bajar la v.** to look up/away/down; **fijar la v. en** to fix one's eyes on, to stare at; **a primera** *o* **simple v.** *(aparentemente)* at first sight, on the face of it; **volver la v. atrás** to look back
(**c**) *(observación)* watching
(**d**) *(panorama)* view; **una habitación con vistas** a room with a view; **con vistas al mar** with a sea view ►► ***v. aérea*** aerial view; ***v. panorámica*** panoramic view
(**e**) *(perspicacia, discreción)* **tiene v. para las antigüedades** she has a good eye for antiques; **hay que tener más v. al decir las cosas** you have to me more careful what you say
(**f**) *Der* hearing ►► ***v. oral*** oral proceedings
(**g**) *Com & Fin* **a la v.** at sight; **a pagar a 30 días v.** payable within 30 days
(**h**) *(plazo)* **a dos meses v. de las elecciones** *(antes)* two months before the elections; *(después)* two months after the elections
3 *nm (empleado de aduanas)* customs officer *(responsible for checking baggage)*
4 a la vista *loc adj* (**a**) *(visible)* visible; **está a la v.** *(muy cerca)* it's staring you in the face; **¡barco/tierra a la v.!** ship/land ahoy!; **no dejen objetos de valor a la v. dentro del autocar** do not leave valuables lying around where they can be seen inside the coach
(**b**) *(en perspectiva)* **no tengo planes a la v.** I have no immediate plans; **tenemos varios proyectos a la v.** there are a number of possible projects on the horizon
5 a la vista de *loc prep* (**a**) *(delante de)* in full view of; **ocurrió a la v. de todos** it happened in full view of everybody; **está a la v. de todos** it's there for everybody to see
(**b**) *(en vista de)* in view of; **a la v. de los resultados financieros...** in view of the financial results...
6 con vistas a *loc prep (con la intención de)* with a view to; **se reunirán con vistas a negociar un nuevo convenio con la patronal** they will meet with a view to negotiating a new agreeement with the employers; **el ahorro con vistas al futuro** saving for the future
7 en vista de *loc prep* in view of, considering; **en v. de lo ocurrido...** considering what has happened...; **en v. de que** since, seeing as

vistazo *nm* glance, quick look; **echar** *o* **dar un v. a algo** to have a quick look at sth

viste *etc* **1** *ver* **ver**
2 *ver* **vestir**

vistiera *etc ver* **vestir**

visto, -a 1 *participio ver* **ver**
2 *ver* **vestir**
3 *adj* **estar bien v.** *(costumbre, acción)* to be considered good manners; *(persona)* to be well regarded; **estar mal v.** *(costumbre, acción)* to be frowned upon; *(persona)* to be looked down on; **estar muy v.** to be old hat; **ese modelo está muy v.** that model's really old *o* ancient; **ese bar ya lo tengo muy v.** I've already been to that bar loads of times; **está v. que: está v. que hoy no tendremos tranquilidad** it's quite clear that *o* obviously we're not going to get any peace today; EXPR **es lo nunca v.** you've never seen anything like it; EXPR **ni v. ni oído** in the twinkling of an eye; EXPR **fue v. y no v.** it happened just like that, it was over in a flash
4 *nm* ***v. bueno*** *(en documento)* approved; ***el v. bueno*** *(aprobación)* the go-ahead; **dar el v. bueno (a algo)** to give (sth) the go-ahead
5 por lo visto *loc adv* apparently; **por lo v. no han aceptado la idea** apparently they haven't accepted the idea, they don't seem *o* appear to have accepted the idea
6 visto que *loc conj* seeing as, given that; **v. que tienen poco interés en ayudarnos...** given that they have scant interest in helping us...

vistosamente *adv* brightly, colourfully; **información presentada v.** information attractively presented

vistosidad *nf* brightness, colourfulness

vistoso, -a *adj* eye-catching

visual 1 *adj* visual
2 *nf* line of sight

visualización *nf* (**a**) *(gráfica)* visualization (**b**) *(mental)* visualization (**c**) *Informát* display

visualizador *nm Informát* viewer

visualizar [14] **1** *vt* (**a**) *(ver)* **este aparato permite v. la estructura interna del órgano** this device allows us to see the internal structure of the organ; **el asesinato no está visualizado en la pantalla** the actual killing is not shown on screen (**b**) *(mentalmente)* to visualize (**c**) *Informát* to view
2 visualizarse *vpr Informát (datos)* to be displayed

visualmente *adv* visually

vital *adj* (**a**) *(órgano, función)* vital; **energía v.** vital *o* life energy; **un instinto v.** a vital instinct (**b**) *(esencial)* vital; **su testimonio es v. en este juicio** her testimony is vital to this trial; **es de v. importancia que vengas** it is vitally important for you to come (**c**) *(lleno de vitalidad)* full of life, vivacious

vitalicio, -a 1 *adj (miembro, pensión, senador)* life, for life; **cargo v.** position held for life; **renta vitalicia** life annuity; **ha sido nombrado director con carácter v.** he has been made a director for life
2 *nm* (**a**) *(pensión)* life annuity (**b**) *(seguro)* life insurance policy

vitalidad *nf* vitality

vitalismo *nm* (**a**) *(optimismo)* vitality (**b**) *Filosofía* vitalism

vitalista *adj* (**a**) *(entusiasta)* dynamic (**b**) *Filosofía* vitalist

vitalizar [14] *vt* to vitalize

vitamina *nf* vitamin

vitaminado, -a *adj* with added vitamins, vitamin-enriched
vitamínico, -a *adj* vitamin; **complejo v.** vitamin complex
vitaminosis *nf inv* vitamin deficiency
vitela *nf* vellum
vitelina *nf (proteína)* vitellin
vitelino, -a *adj* vitelline
vitelo *nm* yolk, *Espec* vitellus
vitícola *adj (región, industria)* grape-producing
viticultor, -ora *nm,f* grape grower, viticulturist
viticultura *nf* grape growing, viticulture
vitivinícola *adj* wine-producing; **región v.** wine-producing region; **producción v.** wine production
vitivinicultura *nf* grape growing, viticulture
vito *nm* = lively, fast-moving Andalusian music and dance
vitola *nf* **(a)** *(de puro)* cigar band **(b)** *(aspecto)* appearance
vítor *nm* cheer; **los vítores de la multitud** the cheers *o* cheering of the crowd
vitorear *vt* to cheer
vitoriano, -a **1** *adj* of/from Vitoria *(Spain)*
2 *nm,f* person from Vitoria *(Spain)*
vitral *nm* stained-glass window
vitraux [bi'tro] *nm inv CSur* stained-glass window
vítreo, -a *adj* vitreous
vitrificación *nf* **(a)** *(de cerámica)* vitrification **(b)** *(de madera)* sealing
vitrificar [60] *vt* **(a)** *(cerámica)* to vitrify **(b)** *(madera)* to seal
vitrina *nf* **(a)** *(en casa)* display cabinet **(b)** *(en tienda)* showcase, glass case **(c)** *Am (escaparate)* shop window
vitrinear *vi Chile Fam* to window-shop
vitrinista *nmf Chile, Ven* window dresser
vitriólico,-a *adj* vitriolic
vitriolo *nm* vitriol
vitro *ver* **in vitro**
vitrocerámica *nf* **(cocina** *o* **placa de) v.** ceramic hob
vitrola = **victrola**
vituallas *nfpl* provisions
vituperable *adj* reprehensible
vituperación *nf* condemnation
vituperar *vt* to criticize harshly, to condemn
vituperio *nm* harsh criticism, condemnation
viuda *nf* **(a)** *(planta)* mourning bride **(b)** *Imprenta* widow **(c)** ***v. negra*** *(araña)* black widow **(d)** *ver también* **viudo**
viudedad *nf* **(a)** *(viudez) (de mujer)* widowhood; *(de hombre)* widowerhood; **pensión de v.** widow's/widower's pension **(b)** *(pensión)* widow's/widower's pension
viudez *nf (de mujer)* widowhood; *(de hombre)* widowerhood
viudo, -a **1** *adj* **(a)** *(persona)* widowed; **estar v.** to be a widower; **estar viuda** to be a widow; **quedar v.** to be widowed **(b)** *(legumbres)* plain; **teníamos patatas viudas para cenar** we had potatoes on their own for dinner
2 *nm,f* widower, *f* widow
viva **1** *nm* cheer; **dar vivas a alguien** to cheer sb
2 *interj* hurrah!; **¡v. el rey!** long live the King!
vivac *nm* bivouac; **hacer v.** to bivouac
vivacidad *nf* vivaciousness
vivalavirgen *Fam* **1** *adj* **ser muy v.** to be totally irresponsible
2 *nmf inv* **es un v.** he just doesn't give a damn about anything
vivales *nmf inv* crafty person; **ser un v.** to be crafty
vivamente *adv* **(a)** *(relatar, describir)* vividly **(b)** *(afectar, emocionar)* deeply
vivaque *nm* bivouac
vivaquear *vi* to bivouac
vivar[1] *nm (de conejos)* warren
vivar[2] *vt Andes, RP, Ven* to cheer
vivaracho, -a *adj* lively, vivacious
viva voce *loc adv* aloud, out loud
vivaz *adj* **(a)** *(despierto)* alert, lively **(b)** *Bot (planta)* = with perennial underground organs
vivencia *nf* **(a)** *(experiencia)* experience; **un libro lleno de vivencias personales** a book full of personal experiences **(b)** *(acción)* experience; **la v. de lo místico** experience of the mystical
vivencial *adj* **un hecho v.** a life experience; **recuerdos vivenciales de la niñez** memories of childhood experiences
víveres *nmpl* provisions, food (supplies); EXPR *RP Fam* **cortarle los v. a alguien: como no estudiaba, su padre le cortó los v.** as he wasn't studying, his father left him to fend for himself financially; **me cansó su arrogancia, así que le corté los v.** I've had enough of his arrogance, so I'm through with him as a friend
vivero *nm* **(a)** *(de plantas)* nursery **(b)** *(de peces)* fish farm; *(de moluscos)* bed **(c)** **v. (de empresas)** business incubator
viveza *nf* **(a)** *(de colorido, descripción)* vividness **(b)** *(de deseo)* intensity; *(de color, tono)* brightness **(c)** *(de persona, discusión, ojos)* liveliness; **discutían con v.** they were having a lively discussion **(d)** *(de ingenio, inteligencia)* sharpness ►► *Ecuad, Perú, RP* ***v. criolla*** native cunning *o* wit
vivián *Ven Fam Hum* **1** *adj* freeloading, scrounging
2 *nmf* freeloader, scrounger
vívidamente *adv* vividly
vívido, -a *adj* vivid
vividor, -ora *nm,f* **(a)** *(que disfruta)* **es un v.** he likes the high life **(b)** *(aprovechado)* parasite, scrounger
vivienda *nf* **(a)** *(casa)* home; **tuvieron que abandonar sus viviendas debido a las inundaciones** they had to abandon their homes because of the floods; **primera/segunda v.** first/second home; **la carestía de las viviendas en la capital** the high cost of housing in the capital ►► ***v. habitual*** normal place of residence; *Col, CRica, Méx, Perú* ***v. de interés social*** = low-cost home subsidized by the government, *Br* ≃ council house/flat; ***v. de protección oficial*** = low-cost home subsidized by the government, *Br* ≃ council house/flat; ***v. pública de alquiler*** = low-cost home subsidized by the government, *Br* ≃ council house/flat; ***v. de renta limitada*** = government-subsidized home with fixed maximum rent; ***v. secundaria*** second home; ***viviendas sociales*** = low-cost housing subsidized by the government, *Br* ≃ council housing/flats; ***v. unifamiliar*** house *(detached, semi-detached or terraced)*
(b) *(alojamiento)* housing; **plan de v.** housing plan
viviente *adj* living
vivificante *adj (que da vida)* life-giving; *(que reanima)* revitalizing
vivificar [60] *vt (dar vida)* to give life to; *(reanimar)* to revitalize
vivíparo, -a *adj* viviparous

VIVIR **1** *vi* **(a)** *(tener vida, existir)* to live; **vivió noventa años** she lived for ninety years; **v. para algo/alguien** to live for sth/sb; **sólo vive para trabajar/para su hija** she only lives for her work/her daughter; **¡esto no es v.!** this is no way to live!, this is no sort of a life!; **no dejar v. a alguien** not to give sb any peace; **su recuerdo vivirá eternamente** his memory will live forever; **v. bien** *(en armonía)* to be happy; **¿quién vive?** who goes there?; EXPR **v. para ver** who'd have thought it?
(b) *(estar vivo)* to be alive; **todavía vive** she's still alive *or* living; **su padre ya no vive** her father is no longer alive
(c) *(residir)* to live; **¿dónde vives?** where do you live?; **vivo con mis padres** I live with my parents; **vivo en un apartamento con más gente** I share an apartment *or Br* a flat; **en el tercero no vive nadie** the third floor is unoccupied; **v. solo** to live alone *o* on one's own; **viven en pareja** they live together
(d) *(subsistir)* **cada día es** *o* **está más difícil v.** it's harder and harder to get by these days; **v. bien** *(económicamente)* to live well; **alcanzar** *o* **dar para v.** *(sueldo, pensión)* to be enough to live on; **con lo que saco de las clases no me alcanza para v.** what I earn from teaching isn't enough for me to live on *o* isn't enough to make ends meet; **¿da para v. esto de la pintura?** can you make a living from painting?; **v. de** to live on; **viven de un solo sueldo/de lo que les da el estado** they live off a single income/off the State; **viven de la agricultura** they make their living from farming
2 *vt* **(a)** *(experimentar)* to experience, to live through; **vivió la guerra** he lived through the war; **he vivido momentos difíciles** I've gone through *o* had some difficult times; **se vivieron momentos de tensión en las gradas** there were some moments of tension on the terraces
(b) *(sentir)* to live; **cuando se pone a bailar se nota que lo vive** you can tell she really lives it when she's dancing
3 *nm* **es un amante del buen v.** he enjoys the good life

---

vivisección *nf* vivisection
viviseccionar *vt* **(a)** *(animal)* to practice vivisection on **(b)** *(institución, teoría, prejuicio)* to dissect, to examine minutely
vivisector, -ora *nm,f* vivisector
vivito, -a *adj Fam* EXPR **v. y coleando** alive and kicking

vivo, -a 1 *adj* (a) *(ser, lengua)* living
(b) *(tras verbo)* alive; **estar v.** *(persona, costumbre, recuerdo)* to be alive; **su recuerdo sigue v. entre los suyos** his memory lives on among his family; **quemar v. alguien** to burn sb alive
(c) *(intenso) (dolor, deseo, olor)* intense; *(luz, color, tono)* bright; *(genio)* quick, hot; *(paso, ritmo)* lively; **un v. interés por algo** a lively interest in sth
(d) *(con vitalidad) (gestos, ojos)* lively; *(descripción, recuerdo)* vivid; **es el v. retrato de su padre** he's the spitting image of his father
(e) *(despierto)* quick, sharp; *(astuto)* shrewd, sly
2 *nm,f* **los vivos** the living
3 *nm* **en v.** *(en directo)* live; *(sin anestesia)* without anaesthetic; **haremos el programa en v.** we will do the programme live

Viyella®, *Am* **viyela** *nf* Viyella®

vizcacha *nf* viscacha

vizcaíno, -a 1 *adj* Biscayan, of/from Vizcaya *(Spain)*
2 *nm,f* Biscayan, person from Vizcaya *(Spain)*

vizcondado *nm* viscountcy

vizconde, -esa *nm,f* viscount, *f* viscountess

V.O. (*abrev de* **versión original**) original language version; **V.O. subtitulada** subtitled version

vocablo *nm* word, term

vocabulario *nm* vocabulary

vocación *nf* (a) *(religiosa)* vocation; **me falta v.** I lack vocation (b) *(inclinación) (médica, educativa)* vocation; **tener v. artística** to be a born artist; **un partido con v. de gobierno** a party with its sights on government

vocacional 1 *adj* vocational
2 *nf Méx Fam* technical college

vocal 1 *adj* vocal
2 *nmf (de consejo, tribunal)* member
3 *nf* vowel ▸▸ ***v. abierta*** open vowel; ***v. cerrada*** closed vowel; ***v. débil*** weak vowel; ***v. fuerte*** strong vowel

vocalía *nf* (a) *(cargo)* post of commitee member (b) *(comité)* committee

vocálico, -a *adj* vowel; **sonido v.** vowel sound

vocalista *nmf* vocalist

vocalización *nf* (a) *(pronunciación)* diction (b) *(de consonante)* vocalization (c) *Mús* vocalization

vocalizar [14] 1 *vi* (a) *(con claridad)* to enunciate clearly (b) *(en fonética)* to vocalize (c) *Mús* to vocalize
2 **vocalizarse** *vpr* to vocalize, to be vocalized

vocativo *nm Ling* vocative

voceador, -ora 1 *adj* loud, vociferous
2 *nm,f* (a) *(que grita)* loud *o* vociferous person (b) *Col, Ecuad, Méx (diariero)* newspaper seller

vocear 1 *vt* (a) *(gritar)* to shout out, to call out (b) *(llamar)* to shout *o* call to; **me voceó** she called out to me (c) *(vitorear)* to cheer (d) *(pregonar) (mercancía)* to hawk; *(secreto)* to publicize
2 *vi (gritar)* to shout

voceras *nm Fam* loudmouth

vocerío *nm* shouting

vocero, -a *nm,f esp Am* spokesperson, spokesman, *f* spokeswoman

vocho *nm Méx Fam (vehículo)* beetle

vociferador, -ora, vociferante *adj* vociferous, clamorous

vociferar *vi* to shout

vocinglero, -a *adj* vociferous, loud-mouthed

vodevil *nm* variety (show), *Br* music hall, *US* vaudeville

vodevilesco, -a *adj* farcical, vaudevillesque

vodka ['boðka] *nm o nf* vodka

voile *nm RP* voile, net

vol. (*abrev de* **volumen**) *(en bebida alcohólica)* vol

volada *nf* (a) *(de ave)* short flight (b) *RP (ocasión favorable)* event; **aprovechar la v.** to take advantage of the occasion; **¿por qué no aprovechan la v. y van hasta los Alpes?** why don't you make the most of the opportunity and go to the Alps as well? (c) EXPR *Méx Fam* **de v.: el tiempo se va de v.** time flies past; *RP Fam* **a las voladas** *(rápidamente)* in a flash

voladito, -a *adj Imprenta* superscript; **en letras voladitas** in superscript

voladizo, -a 1 *adj* projecting
2 *nm* ledge

volado, -a 1 *adj* (a) *(que sobresale)* projecting (b) *Imprenta* superscript (c) *Fam (ido)* **estar v.** to be away with the fairies (d) *Esp Fam (con prisa)* **estoy v.** I'm in a hurry (e) *RP Fam (enojado)* **andar v.** to be annoyed; EXPR **andar con los pájaros volados** to be near the end of one's tether
2 *nm* (a) *RP, Ven (de vestido)* ruffle, flounce (b) EXPR *Méx* **echar volados** to toss a coin
3 *adv Col, Méx Fam* **subió v.** *(con prisa)* he flew *o* rushed upstairs

volador, -ora 1 *adj* flying
2 *nm* (a) *(pez)* flying fish (b) *(calamar)* short-finned squid (c) *(cohete)* rocket (d) *Bol (cometa)* kite

voladura *nf (en guerras, atentados)* blowing up; *(de edificio en ruinas)* demolition *(with explosives)*; *Min* blasting

volandas 1 **en volandas** *loc adv* **levantar a alguien en v.** to lift sb off the ground; **la multitud lo llevó en v.** the crowd carried him through the air
2 **a las volandas** *loc adv Col, Méx, Perú* very quickly; **hace todo a las v.** he does everything in a rush

volandera *nf* (a) *(arandela)* washer (b) *(de molino)* grindstone, millstone

volandero, -a *adj* (a) *(que pende)* hanging (b) *(pájaro)* fledged, ready to fly (c) *(lectura, repaso)* cursory; *(imagen)* fleeting

volantazo *nm* **dar un v.** to swerve

volante 1 *adj* (a) *(que vuela)* flying (b) *(no fijo)* **el congreso tiene una sede v.** each year the conference takes place in a different place; **meta v.** *(en ciclismo)* hot spot sprint
2 *nm* (a) *(para conducir)* (steering) wheel; **estar** *o* **ir al v.** to be at the wheel; **es un as del v.** he's an ace driver (b) *(automovilismo)* motor racing (c) *(de tela)* frill, flounce; **una falda de volantes** a frilly skirt (d) *Esp (del médico)* (referral) note (e) *(en bádminton)* shuttlecock (f) *Am (de propaganda)* leaflet (g) *CSur (en fútbol)* winger

volantín *nm Carib, Chile* kite

volapié *nm Taurom* = method of killing the bull in which the matador runs at the bull and thrusts a sword into its neck while it is standing still

---

VOLAR [64] 1 *vi* (a) *(pájaro, insecto, avión, pasajero)* to fly; **v. a** *(una altura)* to fly at; *(un lugar)* to fly to; **volamos a 5.000 pies de altura** we're flying at 5,000 feet; **v. en avión/helicóptero** to fly in a plane/helicopter; **echar(se) a v.** to fly away *o* off; **hacer v. una cometa** to fly a kite; **salir volando** to fly off; EXPR **v. alto** to go far
(b) *(papeles, sombrero, ceniza)* to blow away; **hubo una pelea y empezaron a v. sillas y botellas** there was a fight and the chairs and bottles started to fly; **salir volando** to blow away; **v. por los aires** *(estallar)* to be blown into the air
(c) *(correr)* to fly, to rush (off); **v. a hacer algo** to rush off to do sth; **hacer algo volando** to do sth at top speed; **me visto volando y nos vamos** I'll get dressed quickly and we can go; **itráeme volando algo para tapar la herida!** bring me something to bandage the wound with immediately *o* now!; **me voy volando** I must fly *o* dash
(d) *(pasar deprisa) (días, años)* to fly by; *(rumores)* to spread quickly; **el tiempo pasa volando** time flies; **aquí las noticias vuelan** news travels fast around here
(e) *Fam (desaparecer)* to disappear, to vanish; **los aperitivos volaron en un santiamén** the snacks disappeared *o* vanished in an instant
(f) *Arquit* to project, to jut out
(g) *RP Fam* **está que vuela** *(de fiebre)* he has a raging temperature; *(de enojo)* he's fuming with rage
2 *vt* (a) *(hacer estallar) (en guerras, atentados)* to blow up; *(caja fuerte, puerta)* to blow open; *(edificio en ruinas)* to demolish *(with explosives)*; *(en minería)* to blast
(b) *(hacer volar) (cometa)* to fly
(c) *(la caza)* to rouse
(d) *Imprenta (letra)* to raise
(e) *Am Fam* **v. algo a alguien** *(robar)* to swipe *o Br* nick sth from sb; **ten cuidado porque a mí allí me volaron la cartera** be careful because I had my wallet swiped *o Br* nicked there
3 **volarse** *vpr (papeles, sombrero, globo)* to blow away; **se me voló la gorra** my cap blew away

---

volatería *nf* birds, fowl

volátil *adj* (a) *Quím* volatile (b) *(carácter, situación, precio)* volatile; **el ambiente es muy v.** the atmosphere is very *o* highly volatile

volatilidad *nf* (a) *Quím* volatility (b) *(de carácter, situación, precio)* volatility

volatilizar [14] 1 *vt* to volatilize
2 **volatilizarse** *vpr* (a) *Quím* to volatilize, to evaporate (b) *Fam (desaparecer)* to vanish into thin air

volatín *nm* acrobatic jump; **hacer volatines** to do acrobatics
volatinero, -a *nm,f* acrobat
vol-au-vent [bolo'βan] (*pl* **vol-au-vents**) *nm Am Culin* vol-au-vent
volcado, -a 1 *adj (dedicado)* **estar v. en algo** to be dedicated *o* deeply committed to sth; **están volcados en ayudar a la gente** they are devoted to helping people
2 *nm Informát* ***v. de pantalla*** screen dump; ***v. de pantalla en impresora*** hard copy
volcán *nm Geol* volcano; **su corazón era un v. de pasión** his heart was bursting with passion; EXPR **estar sobre un v.** to be sitting on a time bomb
volcánico, -a *adj* volcanic
volcanología *nf* vulcanology
volcar [69] 1 *vt* (**a**) *(tirar) (botella, jarrón)* to knock over; *(carretilla)* to tip (up); *(leche, vino)* to spill (**b**) *(vaciar) (bolso, recipiente)* to empty (out); *(contenido)* to empty out
2 *vi (coche, camión)* to overturn; *(barco)* to capsize
3 **volcarse** *vpr* (**a**) *(botella, jarrón) (caerse)* to fall over; *(ser tirado)* to be knocked over
(**b**) *(coche, camión)* to overturn; *(barco)* to capsize
(**c**) *(en amabilidad)* to bend over backwards (**con** for); **mientras estuvimos en su casa se volcó con nosotros** while we were in her house she bent over backwards *o* did everything she could to make us feel welcome
(**d**) *(dedicarse)* **se vuelca en sus hijos** she's completely devoted to her children; **se vuelca en su trabajo** she throws herself into her work
volea *nf* volley; **golpear de v.** to volley
volear 1 *vt* (**a**) *Dep* to volley (**b**) *Agr* to scatter
2 *vi Dep* to volley
voleibol, *Am* **vóleibol** *nm* volleyball
voleo *nm* **a** *o* **al v.** randomly; **escogió uno a v.** he chose one at random; **sembrar a v.** to sow seed by hand, to scatter the seed
voley *nm* ***v. playa*** beach volleyball
volframio *nm Quím* wolfram
volibol *nm Méx* volleyball
volición *nf* volition
volitivo, -a *adj* voluntary
volleyball ['boleiβol] *nm Am* volleyball
volován *nm* vol-au-vent
volqué *etc ver* **volcar**
volqueta *nf Urug* container, bin
volquete *nm* (**a**) *(camión)* dumper truck, *US* dump truck (**b**) *Arg (contenedor)* container, bin
voltaico, -a *adj* voltaic
voltaje *nm* voltage; **alto v.** high voltage
voltamperio *nm* volt-ampere
volteado *nm Col, Méx Fam* queer, *Br* poof, *US* fag
volteador, -ora *nm,f* acrobat
voltear 1 *vt* (**a**) *(dar la vuelta a) (heno, crepe)* to toss; *(tortilla)* to turn over; *(campana)* to ring; **el toro volteó al torero** the bull tossed the bullfighter
(**b**) *Am (derribar) (objeto)* to knock over; *(gobierno)* to overthrow, to bring down; **gesticulaba tanto que terminó volteando el florero** she was waving her hands about so much she ended up knocking over the vase
(**c**) *Andes, CAm, Carib, Méx (poner del revés) (boca abajo)* to turn upside down; *(lo de dentro fuera)* to turn inside out; *(lo de detrás delante)* to turn back to front; **después que esponje, se voltea la masa** once the dough has risen, turn it over; **voltea la página** turn the page
(**d**) *Andes, CAm, Carib, Méx (cabeza, espalda)* to turn; **voltéate hacia la profesora y espera las instrucciones** (turn to) face the teacher and wait for the instructions
2 *vi* (**a**) *Méx (doblar la esquina)* to turn; **al llegar a Insurgentes, volteas a la izquierda** when you get to Insurgentes, turn left
(**b**) *Méx (volcar)* to overturn; **un auto verde volteó ayer por la noche en esta esquina** a green car overturned on this corner last night
(**c**) *Andes (girar)* to turn (round); **las personas volteaban para ver de dónde venían los gritos** people turned round to see where the shouting was coming from
3 **voltearse** *vpr* (**a**) *Andes, CAm, Carib, Méx (volverse)* to turn around; **te volteas tanto que deshaces la cama** you turn over so much that you mess up the bed
(**b**) *Andes, CAm, Carib, Méx (cambiar de idea) (políticamente)* to change sides; **se volteó contra su familia** she turned against her family
(**c**) *Méx (vehículo)* to overturn
(**d**) *RP Vulg* **voltearse a alguien** to screw sb, *US* to bone sb
voltereta *nf (en el suelo)* handspring; *(en el aire)* somersault; **dar una v.** to do a somersault ►► ***v. lateral*** cartwheel
voltímetro *nm* voltmeter
voltio *nm* (**a**) *(electricidad)* volt (**b**) *Fam (paseo)* walk, stroll; **dar un v.** to go for a walk *o* stroll
volubilidad *nf* changeability, fickleness
voluble *adj (persona)* changeable, fickle

> **Falso amigo**: El adjetivo inglés **voluble** no es la traducción del español **voluble**. En inglés **voluble** significa "locuaz".

volumen *nm* (**a**) *(nivel, cantidad)* volume ►► *Econ* ***v. de contratación*** trading volume; ***v. de negocio*** turnover; ***v. de ventas*** turnover
(**b**) *(de sonido)* volume; **subir/bajar el v.** to turn up/down the volume; **sube el v. que no te oímos** speak up, please, we can't hear you; **a todo v.** at full volume
(**c**) *(espacio ocupado)* size, bulk; **ocupa poco v.** it doesn't take up a lot of space; **el sofá tiene un v. excesivo para la habitación** the sofa is too big for the room
(**d**) *(tomo)* volume
volumétrico, -a *adj* volumetric
voluminoso, -a *adj (tomo, objeto)* bulky; *(bibliografía, colección)* voluminous, extensive; **es demasiado v. para ese cuarto** it's too big for this room
voluntad *nf* (**a**) *(determinación)* will, willpower; **tiene mucha/poca (fuerza de) v.** she has a very strong/weak will; **no lo conseguirá por falta de v.** she'll never manage it because she hasn't got the willpower; **pone mucha v. en su trabajo** she's a very willing worker ►► ***v. férrea*** iron will; ***v. de hierro*** iron will
(**b**) *(deseo)* will, wishes; **no existe la v. política de resolver el problema** there isn't the political will to solve the problem; **expresaron su v. de entregar las armas** they said they were willing to hand over their weapons; **no era esa mi v.** that wasn't my intention, that's not what I wanted; **contra la v. de alguien** against sb's will; **no podemos ir contra la v. popular** we cannot go against the popular will; **hágase tu v.** Thy will be done; **al final impuso su v.** she got her way in the end; **por causas ajenas a mi v.** for reasons beyond my control; **por v. de alguien: fue arquitecto por v. de su padre** he was an architect because that's what his father wanted; **dimitió por v. propia** she resigned of her own free will *o* of her own volition; **última v.** last will and testament; EXPR *Fam* **hizo su santa v.** he did just as he pleased
(**c**) *(intención)* intention; **buena v.** goodwill; **gentes de buena v.** people of goodwill; **mala v.** ill will
(**d**) *(albedrío)* free will; **puedes usarlo a v.** you can use it as much as you like; **lo dejo a tu v.** I'll leave it up to you; **¿qué le debo? – la v.** what do I owe you? – whatever you think fit
voluntariado *nm* (**a**) *(actividad)* voluntary work; *Esp* **la ley del v.** = law governing voluntary work (**b**) *(voluntarios)* volunteers
voluntariamente *adv* voluntarily
voluntariedad *nf* voluntary nature; **demostrar la v. de una acción** to demonstrate that an action is voluntary
voluntario, -a 1 *adj (acto, contribución)* voluntary; **la asistencia a la conferencia es voluntaria** attendance at the lecture is voluntary; **ofrecerse v.** to volunteer; **presentarse v.** to volunteer
2 *nm,f* volunteer
voluntarioso, -a *adj* willing
voluntarismo *nm* (**a**) *(voluntad)* willingness; **había más v. que conocimientos** they were more willing (to help/participate/*etc*) than knowledgeable (**b**) *Psi* voluntarism
voluptuosamente *adv* voluptuously
voluptuosidad *nf* voluptuousness
voluptuoso, -a *adj* voluptuous
voluta *nf* (**a**) *(en columna)* volute (**b**) *(de humo)* spiral

VOLVER [41] 1 *vt* (**a**) *(dar la vuelta a)* to turn round; *(lo de arriba abajo)* to turn over; *(lo de dentro fuera)* to turn inside out; **vuelve la tele hacia aquí, que la veamos** turn the TV round this way so we can see it; **ayúdame a v. el colchón** help me turn the mattress over; **v. la hoja** *o* **página** to turn the page; **al v. la esquina** when we turned the corner
(**b**) *(cabeza, ojos, mirada)* to turn; **vuelve la espalda** turn your back to me
(**c**) *(convertir en)* **eso lo volvió un delincuente** that made him a

criminal, that turned him into a criminal; **la lejía volvió blanca la camisa** the bleach turned the shirt white

(**d**) *Méx* **v. el estómago** to throw up

2 *vi* (**a**) *(persona) (ir de vuelta)* to go back, to return; *(venir de vuelta)* to come back, to return; **yo allí/aquí no vuelvo** I'm not going back there/coming back here; **vuelve, no te vayas** come back, don't go; **¿cuándo has vuelto?** when did you get back?; **al v. pasé por el supermercado** I stopped off at the supermarket on the *o* my way back; **no vuelvas tarde** don't be late (back); **ya he vuelto a casa** I'm back home; **v. atrás** to go back; **cuando vuelva del trabajo** when I get back from work; **aún no ha vuelto del trabajo** she isn't back *o* hasn't got back from work yet; **ha vuelto muy morena de la playa** she's come back from the seaside with a nice tan

(**b**) *(mal tiempo, alegría, tranquilidad)* to return; **cuando vuelva el verano** when it's summer again; **todo volvió a la normalidad** everything went back *o* returned to normal; **vuelve la minifalda** miniskirts are back

(**c**) *(reanudar)* **v. a la tarea** to return to one's work; **v. al trabajo/al colegio** to go back to work/school; **volviendo al tema que nos ocupa...** to go back to the matter we are discussing...; **vuelve a leerlo** read it again; **tras el verano volvió a dar clases en la universidad** once the summer was over she started teaching at the university again; **vuelve a ponerlo en su sitio** put it back; **vuelve a dormirte** go back to sleep; **v. con alguien** *(reanudar relación)* to go back to sb; EXPR **v. a nacer** to be reborn

(**d**) **v. en sí** to come to, to regain consciousness

3 volverse *vpr* (**a**) *(darse la vuelta, girar la cabeza)* to turn round; **se volvió hacia mí** she turned towards me; **se volvió de espaldas a mí** he turned away from me, he turned his back on me; **vuélvete boca abajo/arriba** turn over so you're lying face down/up; **volverse atrás** *(de una afirmación, promesa)* to go back on one's word; *(de una decisión)* to change one's mind, to back out

(**b**) *(ir de vuelta)* to go back, to return; *(venir de vuelta)* to come back, to return; **nos volvimos a mitad de camino** we turned back halfway there; **vuélvete a casa** go home

(**c**) *(convertirse en)* to become; **volverse anarquista** to become an anarchist; **todo se volvió muy complicado** it all got very complicated; **volverse loco/pálido** to go mad/pale; **volverse contra** *o* **en contra de alguien** to turn against sb; EXPR *Fam* **todo se le volvía decir que...** all he could say was...

---

vómer *nm Anat* vomer

vomitar 1 *vt* to vomit, to bring up; **v. sangre** to cough up *o* vomit blood

2 *vi* to vomit, to be sick; **tengo ganas de v.** (I think) I'm going to be sick; **cuando me dan** *o* **entran ganas de v.** when I feel like I'm going to vomit *o* be sick; **cuando oigo cosas así me dan** *o* **entran ganas de v.** when I hear things like that I want to throw up

vomitera *nf Fam* **me dio una v.** I threw up

vomitivo, -a 1 *adj* (**a**) *Med* emetic (**b**) *Fam (asqueroso)* sick-making

2 *nm* emetic

vómito *nm* (**a**) *(acción)* **esta sustancia provoca el v.** this substance causes you to vomit; **he tenido vómitos** I've been vomiting; **provocarse el v.** to make oneself sick (**b**) *(sustancia)* vomit ►► *Andes* ***v. negro*** yellow fever

vomitona *nf Fam* (**a**) *(acción)* **me dio una v.** I threw up (**b**) *(sustancia)* vomit

vomitorio, -a 1 *adj Med* emetic

2 *nm* (**a**) *Med* emetic (**b**) *(en estadio)* vomitory (**c**) *Hist (en circos, plazas)* vomitory

voracidad *nf* voraciousness, voracity

vorágine *nf* (**a**) *(confusión)* confusion, whirl; **atrapado en la v. de la gran ciudad** trapped in the hectic whirl of life in the big city (**b**) *(remolino)* whirlpool

voraz *adj* (**a**) *(persona, apetito)* voracious (**b**) *(fuego, enfermedad)* raging

vorazmente *adv* voraciously

vormela *nf* marbled polecat

vórtice *nm* (**a**) *(de agua)* whirlpool, vortex (**b**) *(de aire)* whirlwind (**c**) *(de huracán)* vortex, eye

vos *pron personal Am* (**a**) *(sujeto)* you; **¿quién dijo eso? – ¡v.!** who said that? – you did!; **vas a tener que hacerlo v. mismo** you'll have to do it (all by) yourself

(**b**) *(objeto, atributo)* you; **¿sos v.?** *(cuando llaman)* is it you?

(**c**) *(complemento con preposición o conjunción)* you; **entre v. y yo** between you and me, just between the two of us; **excepto/según v.** apart from/according to you; **hablar** *o* **tratar de v. a alguien** = to address sb as "vos", i.e. not using the formal "usted" form

(**d**) *(vocativo)* **iche, v.!** hey, you!; **¡v., correte!** you, get out of the way!, get out of the way, you!

(**e**) *(impersonal)* you; **v. cuando votás pensás que va a servir de algo** when you vote you think it's going to make a difference

V.O.S.E. (*abrev de* **versión original subtitulada en español**) = original language version with Spanish subtitles

vosear *vt* to address as "vos"

voseo *nm* = practice of using the "vos" pronoun instead of "tú"

VOSOTROS, -AS *Esp pron personal* (**a**) *(sujeto)* you *(plural)*; **v. bailáis muy bien** you dance very well; **¿quién va primero? – v.** who's first? – you are; **v. los americanos** you Americans; **nosotros estamos invitados, v. no** we're invited, but you're not *o* but not you; **algunos de v./todos v. deberíais ir** some of you/all of you ought to go; **tendréis que hacerlo v. mismos** you'll have to do it yourselves; **hemos aprobado y v. también** we passed and so did you

(**b**) *(predicado)* you *(plural)*; **¿sois v.?** is it you?; **los invitados sois v.** you're the guests

(**c**) *(complemento con preposición o conjunción)* you *(plural)*; **os lo ha dicho a v.** she said it to you; **de v.** *(vuestro)* yours; **todo esto es de v.** all this is yours; **yo iré con v.** I'll go with you; **son más fuertes que v.** they're stronger than you (are); **arregladlo entre v.** sort it out amongst yourselves; **por v. me imagino que no habrá ningún problema** I imagine there's no problem as far as you're concerned; **excepto/incluso v.** except/including you

(**d**) *(vocativo)* you *(plural)*; **¡eh, v., apartaos de ahí!** hey, you (lot), get away from there!

> Because Spanish verbs are inflected, subject pronouns such as **vosotros** are largely redundant. In fact, they are normally omitted, with no loss in clarity about who is being referred to:
>
> **¿dónde vais?** *where are you going?*
>
> The personal subject pronouns are used in cases where an explicit contrast is needed:
>
> **vosotros tendreís que hacer la prueba, pero nosotros no** *you'll have to do the test, but we won't*

---

votación *nf* vote; **lo aprobaron por v.** it was passed *o* approved by vote; **decidir algo por v., someter algo a v.** to put sth to the vote; **fue elegido por v. popular/secreta** he was elected by popular/secret ballot; **un nuevo sistema de v.** a new voting system ►► ***v. a mano alzada*** show of hands

VOSEO

Voseo means the use of the **vos** form instead of **tú** in the second person singular. This is the norm in the River Plate region, but it is also found in other areas of Latin America. In Chile and areas of Bolivia, Peru and Venezuela, **tú** is also used, indicating slightly less informality. The forms **vos** and **tú** are both found in Central America, ranging from mostly **vos** in Costa Rica to mostly **tú** in Panama.

Vos is typically used with a special form in the present tense of verbs ending in **-ar** and **-er**. This is like the Peninsular Spanish **vosotros** form without the **i** (**sabés** instead of **sabéis, hablás** instead of **habláis**). Verbs ending in **-ir** use the **vosotros** form itself (**decís, repetís** etc). Although this is the norm in the River Plate region, other forms may be found, such as the informal Chilean forms **sabís** and **hablís**.

In the imperative form, the final **-d** is dropped: **escuchá** instead of **escuchad**, **tené** instead of **tened**, **decí** instead of **decid**. Note that if a pronoun is added at the end of this imperative, the stress then falls on the second last syllable and the written accent is omitted: **lavate, levantate, bebelo**. There is no possessive adjective or subject or object personal pronoun form of **vos** – the **tu** forms are used instead: **tu/tus** (adj) and **tu** (subject pronoun) and **te** (object pronoun). The only difference is in the personal pronoun used after a preposition – **vos** is used instead of **tí** (eg **es para vos, voy con vos**).

votante *nmf* voter

votar 1 *vt* (a) *(candidato)* to vote for; *(ley)* to vote on; **v. a un partido** to vote for a party; **¿qué has votado, sí o no?** how did you vote, yes or no? (b) *(aprobar)* to pass, to approve *(by vote)*

2 *vi* to vote; **v. a favor de/en contra de alguien** to vote for/against sb; **v. en blanco** to return an unmarked ballot paper; **v. por** *(emitir un voto por)* to vote for; *(estar a favor de)* to be in favour of; **yo voto por ir a la playa** I'm for going to the beach; **v. por que...** to vote (that)...

voto *nm* (a) *(en elección)* vote; **tres votos a favor/en contra** three votes in favour/against; **personas con derecho a v.** those with the right to vote; **tiene más del 20 por ciento de la intención de v.** he has the support of more than 20 percent of people intending to vote; **pide el v. para el partido conservador** she's asking people to vote for the conservative party ►► ***v. afirmativo*** vote in favour; ***v. en blanco*** unmarked ballot; ***v. de calidad*** casting vote; ***v. de castigo*** vote against one's own party; ***v. cautivo*** captive vote; ***v. de censura*** vote of no confidence; ***v. de confianza*** vote of confidence; ***v. por correo*** postal vote; ***v. por correspondencia*** postal vote; ***v. nulo*** spoilt ballot; ***v. secreto*** secret ballot; ***v. útil*** tactical voting

(b) *(derecho a votar)* **el v.** the vote; **obtuvieron el v. tras la guerra** they got the vote after the war; **tener v.** to have a vote

(c) *Rel* vow; **hacer v. de** to vow to ►► ***v. de castidad*** vow of chastity; ***v. de pobreza*** vow of poverty; ***v. de silencio*** vow of silence

(d) *(ruego)* prayer, plea; **hacer votos por** to pray for; **hago votos por su pronta recuperación** I wish him a speedy recovery; **votos de felicidad** best wishes

(e) *Chile, Cuba, Méx, RP (papeleta electoral)* ballot paper

voucher ['bautʃer] *nm Am* voucher

vox populi *nf* **ser v. que...** to be common knowledge that...

voy *ver* **ir**

voyeur [bwa'jer] (*pl* **voyeurs**) *nmf* voyeur

voyeurismo [bwaje'rismo] *nm* voyeurism

voyeurista [bwaje'rista], **voyeurístico, -a** [bwaje'ristiko, -a] *adj* voyeuristic

VOZ *nf* (a) *(sonido, habla)* voice; **tiene la v. aguda** she has a shrill voice; **tiene muy buena v.** she has a fine *o* very good voice; **la v. de la conciencia** the voice of conscience; **canta bien pero le falta v.** she's a good singer, but her voice lacks power; **mudó la v.** his voice broke; **me quedé sin v.** I lost my voice; **tener la v. tomada** to be hoarse; **le temblaba la v.** her voice was trembling; **aclarar** *o* **aclararse la v.** to clear one's throat ►► ***v. en off*** *Cine* voice-over; *Teatro* voice offstage

(b) *(tono)* **en v. alta** aloud; **en v. baja** softly, in a low voice; **hablaban en v. baja** they spoke in a low voice; **muchos comentan, en v. baja, que ha sido un fracaso** many people are saying under their breath that it's been a failure; **a v. en cuello** *o* **grito** at the top of one's voice; **alzar la v. (a alguien)** to raise one's voice (to sb); **bajar la v.** to lower one's voice; **levantar la v. a alguien** to raise one's voice to sb; **¡levanta la v.!** speak up!; **a media v.** in a low voice, under one's breath; **de viva v.: informó de viva v. a los periodistas** he told the journalists personally; **quiero agradecérselo de viva v.** I want to thank her in person ►► ***v. de mando*** order, command

(c) *(grito)* shout; **dar una v. a alguien** to give sb a shout; **¡qué voces! ¿por qué hablan tan alto?** what a racket! why do they have to speak so loud?; **dar voces** to shout; **decir algo a voces** to shout sth; **llamar a alguien a voces** to shout to sb; **dar la v. de alarma** *o* **alerta** to raise the alarm; EXPR **estar pidiendo algo a voces** to be crying out for sth

(d) *(opinión)* voice; *(derecho a opinar)* say; **cada vez se oyen más voces discrepantes** more and more voices are being raised in disagreement; **la v. de la experiencia/del pueblo** the voice of experience/of the people; **tener v. y voto** to have a say; EXPR **no tener ni v. ni voto** to have no say in the matter; EXPR *Fam* **la v. de su amo: han acusado a la televisión pública de no ser más que la v. de su amo** public television has been accused of being little more than a mouthpiece for the government

(e) *(cantante)* voice; **una de las mejores voces del país** one of the best voices in the country; **una pieza para dos voces** a piece for two voices; EXPR **llevar la v. cantante** to call the tune

(f) *(rumor)* rumour; **corre la v. de que va a dimitir** people are saying that she's going to resign; **¡corre la v.!** pass it on!

(g) *(vocablo)* word

(h) *Gram* voice ►► ***v. activa*** active voice; ***v. pasiva*** passive voice

vozarrón *nm* loud voice

VPO *nf* (*abrev de* **vivienda de protección oficial**) = low-cost housing subsidized by the government, *Br* ≃ council house

VRAM [uβe'rram] *nf Informát* (*abrev de* **video random access memory**) VRAM

VTR *nf* (*abrev de* **videotape recording**) VTR

VTV *nf RP* (*abrev de* **Verificación Técnica Vehicular**) = annual technical inspection for motor vehicles of five years or more; *Br* ≃ MOT

vudú (*pl* **vudús** *o* **vudúes**) *nm* voodoo

vuduista 1 *adj* voodoo

2 *nmf* voodooist, voodoo practitioner

vuecencia *pron personal Arcaico* your Excellency

vuelapluma: a vuelapluma *loc adv* **escribir algo a v.** to dash sth off

vuelco 1 *ver* **volcar**

2 *nm* (a) *(vuelta)* **dar un v.** *(coche)* to overturn; EXPR **me dio un v. el corazón** my heart missed *o* skipped a beat

(b) *(cambio)* twist; **ese v. político resultaría peligroso** this political turnabout *o* upset would be dangerous; **dar un v.** *(relaciones, vida)* to change completely; *(empresa)* to go to ruin; **esto demuestra el v. que ha dado nuestra sociedad** this shows how much our society has changed

vuelo 1 *ver* **volar**

2 *nm* (a) *(de pájaro, insecto)* flight; **alzar** *o* **emprender** *o* **levantar el v.** *(ave)* to take to the air; *(irse de casa)* to fly the nest; **coger** *o* **cazar algo al v.** *(en el aire)* to catch sth in flight; *(rápido)* to catch on to sth very quickly; EXPR **en un v.** in next to no time; EXPR **de altos vuelos** *(boda, ceremonia)* grand; *(conferencia)* prestigious; *(proyecto, programa)* ambitious; EXPR **cortar los vuelos a alguien** to clip sb's wings; EXPR **no se oía el v. de una mosca** you could have heard a pin drop; EXPR *Am* **a v. de pájaro** in overview, in broad outline

(b) *(de avión)* flight ►► *RP* ***v. de cabotaje*** internal flight; ***v. chárter*** charter flight; ***v. sin escalas*** direct flight; ***v. espacial*** space flight; ***v. libre*** hang-gliding; ***v. sin motor*** gliding; ***vuelos nacionales*** domestic flights; ***v. nocturno*** overnight flight; ***v. rasante*** low-level flight; ***v. de reconocimiento*** reconnaissance flight; ***v. regular*** scheduled flight; ***v. supersónico*** supersonic flight

(c) *(de vestido)* fullness; **una falda de v.** a full skirt

(d) *Arquit* projection

vuelque *etc ver* **volcar**

VUELTA *nf* (a) *(giro) (hecho)* turn; *(acción)* turning; **dar una v.** to turn round; **dar vueltas: la Tierra da vueltas sobre su eje** the Earth spins on its axis; **la Luna da vueltas alrededor de la Tierra** the Moon goes round the Earth; **dar vueltas en la cama** to toss and turn in bed; **este autobús da mucha(s) vuelta(s)** this bus goes all over the place; **la cabeza me da vueltas** my head's spinning; **dar una v. a algo, dar vueltas a algo** *(girándolo)* to turn sth round; *(recorriéndolo)* to go round sth; **le dio dos vueltas a la llave** she turned the key twice; **dio una v. a la manzana/al mundo** he went round the block/world; **dar la v.** to turn back; **darse la v.,** *CSur* **darse v.** *(de pie)* to turn round; *(tumbado)* to turn over; **media v.** *Mil* about-turn; *(en automóvil)* U-turn; **dar media v.** *Mil* to do an about-turn; *(en automóvil)* to do a U-turn; EXPR **andar a vueltas con algo** *(gestionándolo)* to be working on sth; *(insistiendo en ello)* to go on about sth; EXPR **buscarle las vueltas a alguien** to look for a chance to catch sb out; EXPR *Fam* **dar la v. a la tortilla** to turn the tables; EXPR *Fam* **darle cien** *o* **mil vueltas a alguien** to knock spots off sb; **esta bici le da cien vueltas a la tuya** this bike is miles better than yours; EXPR **darle vueltas a algo** *(pensarlo mucho)* to turn sth over in one's mind; **no le des más vueltas** stop worrying about it, just forget about it; **no paro de darle vueltas** I can't stop thinking about it; EXPR *Fam* **poner a alguien de v. y media** *(criticar)* to call sb all the names under the sun; *(regañar)* to give sb a good telling-off ►► ***v. de campana:*** **dar una v./dos vueltas de campana** *(vehículo)* to turn over once/twice; *RP* ***v. carnero*** somersault; *Arg* ***v. al mundo*** *(noria) Br* big wheel, *US* Ferris wheel

(b) *(parte opuesta)* back, other side; **a la v.** on the back, on the other side; **a la v. de la esquina** round the corner; **a la v. de la página** over the page; **el filete lo quiero v. y v.** I'd like my steak very rare; **dar la v. a,** *CSur* **dar v.** *(colchón, tortilla, disco, naipe)* to turn over; **dar (la) v. (a) la página** to turn the page (over); **dar (la) v. (a) un jersey/calcetín** *(ponerlo del derecho)* to turn a sweater/sock the right way out; *(ponerlo del revés)* to turn a sweater/sock inside out; **dar (la) v. (a) un vaso** *(ponerlo boca arriba)* to turn a glass the right way up; *(ponerlo boca abajo)* to turn a glass upside down; EXPR **no tiene v. de hoja** there are no two ways about it; EXPR *CSur* **esto no tiene v.** there's no getting away from it

(c) *(regreso)* return; **la v. al trabajo/colegio siempre es dura** it's never easy going back to work/school; **v. al colegio** *(como título, en letrero)* back to school; **el vuelo de v.** the return flight; **en el camino de v.** on the way back; **de v. en el hotel, tomé un baño** once I was back at the hotel, I had a bath; **estar de v. (de)** to be back (from); **a la v.: pasaré a visitarte a la v.** I'll visit you on the *o* my way back; **te veré a la v.** I'll see you when I get back; **¡hasta la v.!** see you when you get back!; EXPR **estar de v. de algo** to be blasé about sth; **estar de v. de todo** to have seen it all before

(**d**) *(viaje de regreso)* return journey; **¿para qué fecha tienes la v.?** when are you coming back?; **no he cerrado la v. todavía** I haven't booked the return journey yet *(with open return ticket)*; **un billete de ida y v.** *Br* a return (ticket), *US* a round-trip (ticket)

(**e**) *(fin)* **a la v. de** *(tras)* at the end of, after; **a la v. de unos años** at the end of *o* after a few years; **a la v. de publicidad...** *(en televisión)* after the break...

(**f**) *(devolución)* return; **te lo presto, pero lo quiero de v. mañana** I'll lend it to you, but I want it back tomorrow; *RP Fam* **¿me prestás tu lapicera? – sí, pero tiene una v.** can you lend me your pencil? – yes, but I'll be wanting it back; **a v. de correo** by return of post

(**g**) *(paseo)* **dar una v.** *(a pie)* to go for a walk; *(en bicicleta, motocicleta)* to go for a ride; *(en automóvil)* to go for a drive *o* spin; **dar vueltas** *(en automóvil)* to drive round and round; **date una v. por aquí cuando quieras** come round whenever you like; **el vigilante se dio una v. por la oficina** the guard had a look round the office

(**h**) *(a circuito, estadio)* lap; **deberán dar veinte vueltas al circuito** they will have to run twenty laps ►► ***v. de calentamiento*** *(en automovilismo)* warm-up lap; ***v. de honor*** lap of honour; *Taurom* ***v. al ruedo*** bullfighter's lap of honour

(**i**) *(carrera ciclista)* ***v. ciclista*** tour; **la V. (Ciclista) a España** the Tour of Spain

(**j**) *(curva)* bend; **la carretera da muchas vueltas** the road twists and turns a great deal

(**k**) *(dinero sobrante)* change; **quédese con la v.** keep the change

(**l**) *(ronda)* *(de elecciones, competición deportiva)* round; **la primera/segunda v.** the first/second round

(**m**) *(cambio, avatar)* change; **dar la** *o* **una v.** to turn around completely; **las vueltas que da la vida** how things change!

(**n**) *(de pantalón)* *Br* turn-up, *US* cuff; *(de manga)* cuff

(**o**) *(en labor de punto)* row

(**p**) *RP* **de v.** *(otra vez)* again; **me lo preguntó de v.** he asked me again

---

vueltero, -a *adj RP Fam* (**a**) *(indeciso)* dithering (**b**) *(difícil)* difficult, tricky

vuelto, -a 1 *participio ver* **volver**

2 *adj* turned

3 *nm Am* change; **me dieron mal el v.** I was given the wrong change

vuelvepiedras *nm inv* turnstone

vuelvo *etc ver* **volver**

vuestro, -a *Esp* 1 *adj posesivo* your; **v. libro/amigo** your book/friend; **este libro es v.** this book is yours; **un amigo v.** a friend of yours; **no es asunto v.** it's none of your business

2 *pron posesivo* **el v.** yours; **los vuestros están en la mesa** yours are on the table; *Fam* **los vuestros** *(vuestra familia)* your folks; *(vuestro bando)* your lot, your side; EXPR **lo v. es el teatro** *(lo que hacéis bien)* you should be on the stage; *Fam* **os costó lo v.** *(mucho)* it wasn't easy for you; EXPR *Fam* **ésta es la vuestra** this is the chance you've been waiting for *o* your big chance

vulcanismo *nm* vulcanism

vulcanización *nf* vulcanization

vulcanizadora *nf Méx, Perú* tyre shop

vulcanizar [14] *vt* to vulcanize

Vulcano *n Mitol* Vulcan

vulcanología *nf* vulcanology

vulcanológico, -a *adj* vulcanological

vulcanólogo, -a *nm,f* vulcanologist

vulgar *adj* (**a**) *(no refinado)* vulgar, common (**b**) *(corriente, común)* ordinary, common; EXPR **v. y corriente** common or garden (**c**) *(lenguaje)* vernacular, vulgar; **el latín v.** vulgar Latin (**d**) *(no técnico)* non-technical, lay; **sólo conozco el nombre v. de estas plantas** I only know the common name of these plants

vulgaridad *nf* (**a**) *(cualidad)* vulgarity (**b**) *(objeto, hecho vulgar)* **hacer/decir una v.** to do/say something vulgar; **llevar tantas joyas me parece una v.** I think it's terribly vulgar to wear so much jewellery

vulgarismo *nm* vulgarism

vulgarización *nf* popularization

vulgarizar [14] 1 *vt* to popularize

2 **vulgarizarse** *vpr* to become popular *o* common

vulgarmente *adv* (**a**) *(groseramente)* vulgarly; **como v. se dice...** as they say... (**b**) *(comúnmente)* commonly, popularly; **v. conocido como...** commonly *o* popularly known as...

vulgata *nf Rel* Vulgate

vulgo 1 *nm* **el v.** *(plebe)* the masses, the common people; *(no expertos)* the lay public

2 *adv Formal* commonly known as; *Viola tricolor*, **v. pensamiento** *Viola tricolor*, commonly known as the pansy

vulnerabilidad *nf* vulnerability

vulnerable *adj* vulnerable

vulneración *nf* (**a**) *(de prestigio, reputación)* harming, damaging; *(de intimidad)* invasion (**b**) *(de ley, pacto)* violation, infringement

vulnerar *vt* (**a**) *(prestigio, reputación)* to harm, to damage; *(intimidad)* to invade (**b**) *(ley, pacto)* to violate, to break

vulpeja *nf* vixen

vulva *nf* vulva

vulvitis *nf inv Med* vulvitis

W, w

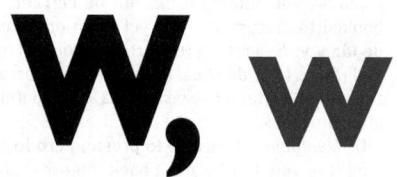

W, w *nf (letra)* W, w
wafle, waffle ['bafle] *nm Am* waffle
waflera [ba'flera] *nf Am* waffle iron *o* maker
Walhalla, Valhalla [bal'χala] *n Mitol* Valhalla
walkie-talkie [*Esp* 'walki'talki, *Am* 'woki'toki] *nm* walkie-talkie
walkiria [bal'kiria] *nf* Valkyrie
walkman® ['walman] (*pl* **walkmans**) *nm* Walkman®, personal stereo
WAN [wan] *nf Informát* (*abrev de* **wide area network**) WAN
WAP [wap] *nm Informát* (*abrev de* **Wireless Application Protocol**) WAP
warrant ['warrant] (*pl* **warrants**) *nm Com & Fin (de acciones)* warrant
Washington ['wasinton] *n* Washington
washingtoniano, -a [wasinto'njano, -a] *adj* Washington, Washingtonian
wáter [*Esp* 'bater, *Am* 'water] *nm* toilet
waterpolista [waterpo'lista] *nmf* water polo player
waterpolo [water'polo] *nm* water polo
watio ['batio] *nm* watt
WC [*Esp* uβe'θe, *Am* doβleβe'se, *Méx* doβleu'se] *nm* (*abrev de* **water closet**) WC
Web, web [weβ] *Informát* **1** *nf (World Wide Web)* **la W.** the Web **2** *nm o nf (página web)* website
weber ['beβer] (*pl* **webers**) *nm Fís* weber
Wellington ['welinton] *n* Wellington
welter ['welter, 'belter] **1** *adj* **peso w.** welterweight **2** *nmf* welterweight
western ['wester] (*pl* **westerns**) *nm Cine* western
whiskería [wiske'ria] *nf* = bar where hostesses chat with clients
whisky ['wiski] *nm* whisky; *RP Fam* **¡(decí) w.!** *(en foto)* (say) cheese! ►► ***w. escocés*** Scotch whisky; ***w. de malta*** malt whisky
winchester® ['wintʃester] (*pl* **winchesters**) *nm* Winchester®
windsurf ['winsurf], **windsurfing** ['winsurfin] *nm* windsurfing; **hacer w.** to go windsurfing
windsurfista [winsur'fista] *nmf* windsurfer
wing [win] *nm CSur Dep* wing
wok [wok] *nm* wok
wolframio [bol'framjo], **wolfram** [bol'fram] (*pl* **wolframs**) *nm* wolfram
WWW (*abrev de* **World Wide Web**) WWW

X, x

X *(abrev de* **miércoles)** W, Wed

X, x ['ekis] **1** *nf* **(a)** *(letra)* X, x **(b)** *Cine* **película X** X-rated movie; **sala X** = cinema that shows porn movies
 2 *nmf* **la señora X** Mrs X

xenofilia *nf* xenophilia

xenófilo, -a 1 *adj* xenophilic
 2 *nm,f* xenophile

xenofobia *nf* xenophobia

xenófobo, -a 1 *adj* xenophobic
 2 *nm,f* xenophobe

xenón *nm Quím* xenon

xenotrasplante *nm Med* xenotransplantation

xerocopia *nf* photocopy

xerocopiar *vt* to photocopy

xerófilo, -a *adj Bot* xerophilous

xerófito, -a *adj Bot* xerophytic

xeroftalmia *nf Med* xerophthalmia

xerografía *nf* xerography, photocopying

xerografiar *vt* to photocopy

xérox, sérox *nf Perú* **(a)** *(fotocopia)* Xerox® **(b)** *(fotocopiadora)* Xerox® machine

xifoides *nm Anat* xiphoid process *o* cartilage

xileno *nm* xylene

xilófago, -a *adj Zool* xylophagous

xilofón, xilófono *nm* xylophone

xilofonista *nmf* xylophone player

xilófono = **xilofón**

xilografía *nf* **(a)** *(técnica) (en el sentido de la fibra)* woodcut (printing); *(a contrafibra)* wood engraving **(b)** *(impresión) (en el sentido de la fibra)* woodcut; *(a contrafibra)* wood engraving

xilol *nm* xylene

Xunta ['ʃunta] *nf* = autonomous government of the region of Galicia

Y, y

Y, y [i'ɣrjeɣa] *nf (letra)* Y, y

Y *conj* **(a)** *(indica enlace)* and; **una computadora y una impresora** a computer and a printer; **un chico alto y guapo** a tall, handsome boy; **mi padre y mi hermano** my father and brother

(b) *(indica acumulación, intensidad)* and; **horas y horas de espera** hours and hours of waiting; **yo miraba y miraba, pero no te veía** I looked and looked, but couldn't see you; **¡y pensar que sólo era un niño!** and just to think he was only a boy!

(c) *(pero)* and yet; **sabía que era imposible y seguía intentándolo** she knew it was impossible and yet she kept on trying; **ella venga a hablar y yo sin decir nada** she talked and talked while I never said a word

(d) *(más)* and; **tres y dos son cinco** three and two are five

(e) *(en preguntas)* what about; **¿y tu mujer?** what about your wife?; **yo no tengo dinero, ¿y tú?** I haven't got any money, have you?, I haven't got any money, what about you?; **yo me llamo Pedro, ¿y tú?** I'm called Pedro, what about you?, my name's Pedro, what's yours?; **¿y yo qué?** what about me?; **me acompañó a casa... – ¿y? ¿qué pasó después?** he walked me home... – yes, and...? what happened next?; **¿y si nos quedamos?** *(como sugerencia)* why don't we stay?

(f) *Fam (indica desinterés)* **no me queda dinero – ¿y (qué)?** I haven't got any money left – so (what)?; **¿y a mí qué?** what do I care?, what's it to me?

(g) *(en números)* **tres y medio** three and a half; **treinta y tres** thirty-three; **trescientos treinta y dos** three hundred and thirty-two

(h) *RP Fam (en diálogo)* **¿llegaron a tiempo? – y sí, corrimos como locos y llegamos justito** did you arrive on time? – well, we ran like crazy and got there just in time; **¿pero él te pidió consejo? – y no, si se cree que lo sabe todo** but did he ask your advice? – well no, he thinks he knows it all already; **¿vos sabías lo que estaba pasando? – y claro, si vivimos en la misma casa** did you know what was going on? – of course, we live in the same house

---

YA **1** *adv* **(a)** *(en el pasado)* already; **ya me lo habías contado** you had already told me; **¿llamaron** *o* **han llamado ya?** have they called yet?; **¿habrán llegado ya?** will they have arrived yet *o* by now?; **ya dejó de llover** it has stopped raining; **ya en 1926** as long ago as 1926

(b) *(expresando sorpresa)* already; **¿ya has vuelto?** are you back already?; **son las siete – ¿ya?** it's seven o'clock – already?

(c) *(en presente)* now; **bueno, yo ya me voy** right, I'm off now; **ya es hora de cenar** it's time for dinner; **ya eres mayor para esas cosas** you're too old for that sort of thing; **¡ya voy!** I'm coming!

(d) *(inmediatamente)* at once; **hay que hacer algo ya** something has to be done now *o* at once; *Fam* **desde ya** right now; **hay que empezar desde ya** we have to start right now *o* away; **desde ya considérate invitado** consider yourself invited as of now; **ya mismo** right away

(e) *(en frases negativas)* **yo ya no estaba segura de nada** I was no longer sure of anything; **ya no es así** it's not like that any more, it's no longer like that; **ya no me duele** it doesn't hurt any more, it no longer hurts; **para entonces ya no quedarán entradas** there won't be any tickets left by then

(f) *(en el futuro)* **ya te llamaré** I'll give you a ring some time; **ya hablaremos** we'll talk later; **ya nos habremos ido** we'll already have gone; **ya me dirás si te gustó** you can tell me later if you liked it; **ya verás** you'll (soon) see; **ya verás cuando se enteren** just wait till they find out; **¡ya te agarraré yo a ti!** I'll get you sooner or later!

(g) *(con valor enfático o intensivo)* **ya entiendo/lo sé** I understand/know; **sin el uniforme ya parece otro** he looks completely different without his uniform on; **¡ya está! ¿ves qué fácil?** that's it *o* there you are, see how easy it is?; **¡ya no aguanto más!** I can't take any more!, I've had enough!; **¿es éste tu coche? – ¡ya me gustaría a mí!** *o* **¡ya quisiera yo!** is this your car? – I wish *o* if only!; **ya podías haberlo dicho antes** you could have said so before; **ya puedes hacer las maletas y largarte** I suggest you pack your bags and leave; **¿qué haces despierto? – ya ves, que no puedo dormir** what are you doing awake? – well, I can't get to sleep, you see; **te matas a trabajar y, ya ves, luego se olvidan de ti** you work yourself to death and then what happens...? they forget about you

2 *conj* **(a)** *(distributiva)* **ya sea por unas cosas ya sea por otras, siguen pasando hambre** for one reason or another, they are still going hungry; **manden sus datos ya sea por carta o por correo electrónico** send in your details (either) by post or by e-mail

(b) *(adversativa)* **ya no... sino..., no ya... sino...** not only... but...; **confían no ya en clasificarse sino en llegar a la final** they are not only confident of qualifying but also of reaching the final

3 *interj (indica asentimiento)* right!; *(indica comprensión)* yes!; **¡ya! no me eches más leche** that's enough milk, thanks!; **preparados, listos, ¡ya!** ready, steady, go!, on your marks, get set, go!; *Irónico* **¡ya, ya!** sure!, yes, of course!

4 ya que *loc conj* since; **ya que has venido, ayúdame con esto** since you're here, give me a hand with this; **ya que te pones, podías hacer también la cena** you could get dinner ready while you're at it; **ya que eres tan listo, dime...** if you're so clever *o* since you're so smart, tell me...

---

yabirú *nm* jabiru stork

yac *nm* yak

yacaré *nm* cayman

yacente, yaciente *adj (tumbado)* lying; *(estatua)* reclining, recumbent

yacer [73] *vi* **(a)** *(estar tumbado)* to lie; **varios heridos yacían en el suelo** several of the injured were lying on the ground **(b)** *(estar enterrado)* to lie; **aquí yace...** here lies... **(c)** *Anticuado (tener relaciones sexuales)* to lie together; **y. con** to lie with

yaciente = **yacente**

yacija *nf* **(a)** *(lecho)* bed **(b)** *(tumba)* grave **(c)** EXPR **ser de mala y.** *(dormir mal)* to be a restless sleeper; *(ser mala persona)* to be a ne'er-do-well

yacimiento *nm* **(a)** *(minero)* deposit ►► ***y. mineral*** mineral deposit; ***y. de petróleo*** oilfield; ***y. petrolífero*** oilfield **(b)** *(arqueológico)* site

yago *etc ver* **yacer**

yagua *nf Andes, Carib, Méx* **(a)** *(planta)* royal palm **(b)** *(tejido)* = fibrous tissue of the royal palm tree

yagual *nm CAm, Méx* = padded ring for carrying things on the head

yaguar = **jaguar**

yaguarondi *nm* jaguarundi

yaguasa *nf* jabiru (stork), black-necked stork,

yaguré *nm Am* skunk

yak *nm* yak

Yakarta *n* Jakarta

yámbico, -a *adj Lit* iambic

yambo *nm* **(a)** *Lit* iamb **(b)** *(árbol)* rose apple

Yankilandia, Yanquilandia *n Am Fam Hum* Gringoland, the States

yanomami **1** *adj (indio)* Yanomami

2 *nmf (indio)* Yanomami

yanqui **1** *adj* **(a)** *Hist* Yankee **(b)** *Fam (estadounidense)* American; **un político y.** an American politician

2 *nmf* **(a)** *Hist* Yankee **(b)** *Fam (estadounidense)* Yank

Yanquilandia = **Yankilandia**

yanquismo *nm Am* pro-Americanism

yantar *Anticuado* **1** *nm* fare, food

2 *vt* to eat

Yaoundé = **Yaundé**

yapa *nf Andes, RP Fam* **dar algo de y.** to throw sth in as an extra

yarará *nf* fer-de-lance

yaraví *(pl* **yaravíes** *o* **yaravís***) nm Am* = type of melancholy Indian song
yarda *nf* yard
yatay *nm* yatay palm
yate *nm* yacht
yatismo *nm RP* yachting
Yaundé, Yaoundé [jaun'de] *n* Yaoundé
yaya *nf* **(a)** *Perú (insecto)* mite **(b)** *(árbol) Cuba, PRico* lancewood
yayo, -a *nm,f Fam* grandad, *f* grandma; **los yayos** grandma and grandad
yazco *etc ver* **yacer**
yazgo *etc ver* **yacer**
yedra *nf* ivy
yegua 1 *nf* **(a)** *(animal)* mare **(b)** *CAm (colilla)* cigarette butt **(c)** *CSur muy Fam (mujer)* cow, bitch
2 *adj CSur Fam* **la muy y.** the old cow
yeguada *nf* **(a)** *(de animales)* herd of horses; **tiene una gran y.** he's got a lot of horses **(b)** *CAm, PRico (disparate)* stupid thing
yeguarizo, -a *RP* **1** *adj* **ganado y.** horses
2 *nm* horse
yeísmo *nm* = pronunciation of Spanish "ll" as "y", widespread in practice
yeísta *nmf* = person who pronounces Spanish "ll" as "y"
yelmo *nm* helmet
yema *nf* **(a)** *(de huevo)* yolk **(b)** *(de planta)* bud, shoot **(c)** *(de dedo)* fingertip **(d)** *(dulce)* = sweet made from sugar and egg yolk
Yemen *nm* **(el) Y.** Yemen
yemení *(pl* **yemeníes***)*, **yemenita 1** *adj* Yemeni
2 *nmf* Yemeni
yen *nm* yen
yerba[1] = **hierba**
yerba[2] *nf* **(a)** *Méx, Ven Fam (marihuana)* grass, weed **(b)** *RP (mate)* maté; **y. mate** (yerba) maté leaves
yerbal, yerbatal *nm RP (campo)* field of maté
yerbatero, -a 1 *adj RP (producción)* maté; *(terreno)* maté-producing
2 *nm,f Andes, Carib* **(a)** *(curandero)* healer **(b)** *(vendedor de hierbas)* herbalist
yerbera *nf RP* = jar for storing maté leaves
yerbero, -a *nm,f Méx* **(a)** *(curandero)* healer **(b)** *(vendedor)* herbalist
Yereván *n* Yerevan
yergo *etc ver* **erguir**
yermo, -a 1 *adj* **(a)** *(estéril)* barren **(b)** *(despoblado)* uninhabited
2 *nm* wasteland
yerno *nm* son-in-law
yerra *nf RP* cattle branding
yerro 1 *ver* **errar**
2 *nm Literario* mistake, error
yerto, -a *adj* rigid, stiff; **y. de frío** frozen stiff
yesca *nf* tinder
yesería *nf (fábrica)* gypsum kiln
yesero, -a 1 *adj* plaster; **producción yesera** plaster production
2 *nm,f* **(a)** *(fabricante)* plaster manufacturer **(b)** *(obrero)* plasterer
yeso *nm* **(a)** *Geol (mineral)* gypsum **(b)** *(para paredes)* plaster **(c)** *esp Am (vendaje)* plaster **(d)** *Arte (escultura)* plaster cast
yesquero *nm RP* cigarette lighter
yeta *RP Fam* **1** *adj* jinxed; **ser y.** to be jinxed
2 *nmf* jinxed person; **es un y.** he's jinxed, he's got a jinx on him
3 *nf* **tener y.** to be jinxed
yetatore *nmf RP Fam* **(a)** *(de mala suerte)* unlucky person **(b)** *(que trae mala suerte)* jinx, jonah
yeti *nm* yeti
yeyé *adj inv Fam* groovy *(used of sixties-style music, clothes, people etc)*
yeyo *nm Ven Fam* funny turn; **casi me da un y.** I nearly passed out *o* keeled over
yeyuno *nm Anat* jejunum
Yibuti *n* Djibouti
yiddish, yidish *nm* Yiddish
yihad [ji'χað] *nf* jihad
yira *nf RP Fam Pey* whore
yirar *vi RP Fam* to work the streets, *Br* to be on the game
yiro *nm RP Fam* **estar en el y.** to work the streets, *Br* to be on the game
yiu-yitsu *nm* ju-jitsu

YO 1 *pron personal* **(a)** *(sujeto)* I; **yo me llamo Luis** I'm called Luis, my name is Luis; **¿quién dijo eso? – yo** who said that? – I did *o* me; **¡eh, usted! – ¿quién? ¿yo?** hey, you! – who, me?; **algunos hacen deporte, yo no** some of them do sports, but I don't *o* but not me; **yo mismo lo preparé todo** I got it ready (all by) myself; **he aprobado – yo también** I passed – me too *o* so did I
(b) *(predicado)* **soy yo** it's me; **el invitado soy yo** I'm the guest
(c) *(complemento con preposición o conjunción)* me; **es más alta que yo** she's taller than me *o* than I am; **se fueron antes/después que yo** they left before/after me, they left before/after I did; **excepto/incluso yo** except/including me
(d) **yo que tú/él/***etc.* if I were you/him/*etc*
2 *nm Psi* **el yo** the ego

> Because Spanish verbs are inflected, subject pronouns such as **yo** are largely redundant. In fact, they are normally omitted, with no loss in clarity about who is being referred to:
> **no voy a ir a la fiesta** *I'm not going to go to the party*
> The personal subject pronouns are used in cases where an explicit contrast is needed:
> **yo tendré que hacer la prueba, pero tú no** *I'll have to do the test, but you won't*

yodado, -a *adj* iodized
yodar *vt* to iodize
yodo *nm Quím* iodine
yodoformo *nm* iodoform
yoduro *nm* iodide ►► ***y. de plata*** silver iodide
yoga *nm* yoga
yoghourt [jo'ɣur] *(pl* **yoghourts***)*, **yoghurt** [jo'ɣur] *(pl* **yoghurts***) nm* yoghurt; **un y. de fresa** a strawberry yoghurt
yogui *nmf* yogi
yóguico, -a *adj* yogic; **posturas yóguicas** yoga positions
yogur, yogurt *(pl* **yogurts***) nm* yoghurt
yogurtera *nf* yoghurt maker
yola *nf* yawl
yonque *nm Méx Fam* scrapyard, *US* wrecker's yard
yonqui *nmf Fam* junkie
yóquey *nm* jockey
york *nm* (boiled) ham
yorkshire ['jorksair] *nm (perro)* Yorkshire terrier
yoruba 1 *adj* Yoruba
2 *nmf (persona)* Yoruba
3 *nm (lengua)* Yoruba
yoyó *nm* **(a)** *(juguete)* yoyo **(b)** *Urug (bizcocho)* = caramel-filled, chocolate-covered sponge biscuit
yuan *nm* yuan
yubarta *nf* humpback whale
yuca *nf* **(a)** *(planta)* yucca **(b)** *(alimento)* cassava, manioc
yucal *nm* yucca field
Yucatán *n* **(el) Y.** (the) Yucatan
yucateco, -a 1 *adj* Yucatecan
2 *nm,f* Yucatecan
yudo *nm* judo
yudoka *nmf* judo player, judoka
yugo *nm* **(a)** *(para animales)* yoke **(b)** *(atadura)* yoke; **sacudir el y.** to throw off the yoke; **el y. del matrimonio** the ties of marriage
Yugoslavia *n* Yugoslavia
yugoslavo, -a 1 *adj* Yugoslavian
2 *nm,f* Yugoslav
yugular[1] **1** *adj* jugular
2 *nf* jugular
yugular[2] *vt* **(a)** *(persona)* to cut *o* slit the throat of **(b)** *(enfermedad)* to retard the progress of; *(síntoma)* to suppress **(c)** *(desarrollo)* to stifle; *(levantamiento)* to stifle, to suppress
yuju *interj Fam* yoo-hoo!, yippee!
Yungas *nmpl Andes* = warm, humid valleys
yunque *nm* **(a)** *(de hierro)* anvil **(b)** *(hueso)* anvil

yunta *nf* (**a**) *(de bueyes, vacas)* yoke, team (**b**) *Ven* **yuntas** *(gemelos)* cufflinks (**c**) EXPR *CSur Fam* **ser (buena) y.** to make a good pair; *RP Fam* **hacer (buena) y.** to be on the best of terms, to get along well

yunyún *nm RDom* = iced fruit drink

yupi *interj Fam* yippee!

yuppie ['jupi], **yupi** *nmf* yuppie

Yurex® *nm Méx Br* Sellotape®, *US* Scotch® tape

yute *nm* jute

yuxtaponer [50] **1** *vt* to juxtapose
2 yuxtaponerse *vpr* to be juxtaposed (**a** with)

yuxtaposición *nf* juxtaposition

yuxtapuesto, -a *participio ver* **yuxtaponer**

yuyal *nm CSur* patch of weeds

yuyería *nf RP* herbalist's

yuyero, -a *nm,f RP* herbalist

yuyo *nm* (**a**) *CSur (mala hierba)* weed; *(hierba medicinal)* medicinal herb (**b**) *Andes (hierba silvestre)* wild herb

Z, z

Z, z ['θeta, *Am* 'seta] *nf (letra)* Z, z

zacatal *nm CAm, Méx* pasture

zacate *nm CAm, Méx* fodder

zácate *interj RP Fam* all of a sudden, suddenly; **íbamos caminando y, ¡z.!, una explosión** we were walking along when, all of a sudden, there was an explosion

zacatecano, -a 1 *adj* of/from Zacatecas *(Mexico)*
2 *nm,f* person from Zacatecas *(Mexico)*

zafacón *nm RDom Br* rubbish bin, *US* trash can

zafado, -a *Fam* **1** *adj* **(a)** *Am (loco)* nuts, crazy **(b)** *Andes, RP (atrevido)* barefaced, cheeky, *Br* brass-necked
2 *nm,f* **(a)** *Am (loco)* nutcase **(b)** *Andes, RP (atrevido)* cheeky devil

zafar 1 *vi RP Fam (salir bien parado)* to come out on top; **zafamos de milagro** we got away by the skin of our teeth
2 zafarse *vpr* **(a)** *(librarse) (de tarea, obligación)* to get out of it; *(soltarse)* to escape; **zafarse de** *(persona)* to get rid of; *(obligación)* to get out of **(b)** *Méx (articulación)* to become dislocated

zafarrancho *nm* **(a)** *Náut* clearing of the decks ►► *Mil **z. de combate*** call to action stations **(b)** *(destrozo)* mess **(c)** *(riña)* row, fracas **(d)** *Fam (limpieza general)* spring cleaning

zafiedad *nf* roughness, uncouthness

zafio, -a *adj* rough, uncouth

zafiro *nm* sapphire

zafra *nf* **(a)** *(cosecha)* sugar cane harvest **(b)** *(fabricación)* sugarmaking **(c)** *Am (temporada)* harvest season **(d)** *Min* slag

zaga *nf* **(a) a la z.** *(detrás)* behind, at the back; **ir a la z. de alguien** *(en carrera, competición)* to trail (behind) sb; *(en desarrollo, proceso)* to lag behind sb; **no irle a la z. a alguien** to be every bit as good as sb, to be just as good as sb; **son buenos, pero nuestro equipo no les va a la z.** they're good, but our team are every bit as good as them; **quedar a la z.** to get left behind; **todos alabaron su comportamiento, y su profesor no se quedó a la z.** everybody praised her behaviour and her teacher was no exception
(b) *Dep* defence

zagal, -ala *nm,f* **(a)** *(muchacho)* lad, *f* lass **(b)** *(pastor)* shepherd, *f* shepherdess

zagaletón, -ona *nm,f Ven Fam* **(a)** *(adolescente)* lad, *f* lass **(b)** *(vago)* layabout, good-for-nothing

zaguán *nm* (entrance) hall

zaguero, -a *nm,f Dep* defender; *(en rugby)* fullback

zaherir *vt* **(a)** *(herir)* to hurt **(b)** *(burlarse de)* to mock

zahiriente *adj* wounding, hurtful

zahones *nmpl* chaps

zahorí *(pl* **zahoríes***)* *nmf* **(a)** *(de agua)* water diviner **(b)** *(clarividente)* mind reader

zahúrda *nf (pocilga)* pigsty

zaino, -a, zaíno, -a *adj* **(a)** *(caballo)* chestnut **(b)** *(res)* black

Zaire *n Antes* Zaire

zaireño, -a 1 *adj* Zairean
2 *nm,f* Zairean

zalagarda *nf (pelea)* skirmish

zalamería *nf* flattery, fawning

zalamero, -a 1 *adj* flattering, fawning
2 *nm,f* flatterer

zalema 1 *nf (reverencia)* salaam
2 zalemas *nfpl (lisonjas)* flattery

zamacuco, -a *nm,f* **(a)** *(tonto)* fool, idiot **(b)** *(persona solapada)* sly *o* crafty person; **ser un z.** to be sly *o* crafty

zamacueca *nf* = folk-dance typical of Chile and Argentina

zamaquear *vt Perú Fam* to shake

zamarra *nf (de piel de oveja)* sheepskin jacket; *(de piel)* leather jacket

zamarrear *vt* to shake

zamarro 1 *nm* **(a)** *Ecuad (pantalón)* jeans **(b)** *(chaqueta) (de piel de oveja)* sheepskin jacket; *(de piel)* leather jacket
2 zamarros *nmpl Andes* chaps

zamba *nf* **(a)** *(baile)* = popular South American dance **(b)** *ver también* **zambo**

zambardo *nm Chile* awkward *o* clumsy person

Zambeze *nm* **el Z.** the Zambezi (River)

Zambia *n* Zambia

zambo, -a 1 *adj (piernas, persona)* knock-kneed
2 *nm,f* **(a)** *(persona)* knock-kneed person **(b)** *Am (hijo de una persona negra y otra india)* = person who has one Black and one Indian parent

zambomba 1 *nf (instrumento)* = type of rustic percussion instrument
2 *interj Fam* wow!

zambombazo *nm Fam* **(a)** *(ruido)* bang **(b)** *Dep (disparo)* screamer, powerful shot

zambra *nf* **(a)** *(fiesta morisca)* Moorish festival **(b)** *(baile gitano)* = Andalusian gypsy dance

zambucar *vt Fam* to hide, to conceal

zambullida *nf (salto)* dive; **darse una z.** *(baño)* to go for a dip; **darle a alguien una z.** to duck sb

zambullir 1 *vt* to dip, to submerge
2 zambullirse *vpr (en agua)* to dive **(en** into); *(en actividad)* to immerse oneself **(en** in)

zambullón *nm Andes, RP (salto)* dive; **darse un z.** *(baño)* to go for a dip

zamburiña *nf (marisco)* = type of scallop

Zamora *n* EXPR **Z. no se ganó en una hora** Rome wasn't built in a day

zamorano, -a 1 *adj* of/from Zamora *(Spain)*
2 *nm,f* person from Zamora *(Spain)*

zampabollos *nmf inv Fam* human dustbin

zampar *Fam* **1** *vt Am* **(a)** *(meter)* to shove, to stick; **zampó la mano arriba de la torta** she slapped *o* smacked her hand down on top of the cake; **le zampé un piñazo en el estómago** I belted him one in the stomach **(b)** *(decir)* to say (right out); **le zampé todo lo que venía guardándome hace tiempo** I let rip at him with everything I'd been keeping to myself for so long
2 *vi* **¡cómo zampa!** look at him stuffing his face!
3 zamparse *vpr* to wolf down, *Br* to scoff; **se lo ha zampado todo** she's eaten the lot!

zampatortas *nmf inv Fam* **(a)** *(glotón)* human dustbin **(b)** *(torpe)* numbskull, blockhead

zampoña *nf* panpipes

zampullín *nm* grebe ►► ***z. chico*** little grebe; ***z. cuellinegro*** eared *o* black-necked grebe; ***z. cuellirojo*** horned *o* Slavonian grebe

zampuzar [10] *vt* to hide quickly

zanahoria 1 *nf (verdura)* carrot
2 *nmf Andes, RP, Ven Fam (ingenuo)* sucker; *(aburrido, sin vicios)* nerd

zanahorio, -a *adj Col Fam* square, nerdy

zanate *nm* grackle, crow blackbird

zanca *nf* **(a)** *(de ave)* leg, shank **(b)** *Hum (de persona)* shank

zancada *nf* stride; **caminaba dando grandes zancadas** he walked with huge strides; EXPR **en dos zancadas: te lo traigo en dos zancadas** I'll fetch it for you in two shakes (of a lamb's tail)

zancadilla *nf* trip; **poner una** *o* **la z. a alguien** *(con los pies)* to trip sb (up); *(estratagema)* to put a spoke in sb's wheel

zancadillear *vt* **z. a alguien** *(con los pies)* to trip sb (up); *(con estratagemas)* to put a spoke in sb's wheel

zancajo *nm* heel bone

zanco *nm* stilt

zancón, -ona *adj Col, Méx, Ven (traje)* too short

zancuda *nf* wader

zancudo, -a 1 *adj* (a) *(ave)* wading (b) *Fam (persona)* long-legged
2 *nm Am* mosquito

zanfoña *nf* hurdy-gurdy

zanganear *vi Fam* to laze *o* loaf about

zanganeo *nm Fam* lazing *o* loafing about

zanganería *nf Fam* laziness, idleness

zángano, -a 1 *nm,f Fam (persona)* lazy oaf, idler
2 *nm (abeja)* drone

zangolotear *Fam* 1 *vt* to shake
2 *vi* to wander around doing nothing

zangolotino, -a *adj Fam* babyish, childish

zanguango, -a 1 *adj* lazy, idle
2 *nm,f* idler

zanja *nf* ditch

zanjar *vt (poner fin a)* to put an end to, to settle; **zanjó el asunto diciendo que...** she put an end to the matter by saying that...; **la discusión se zanjó con una solución de compromiso** they put an end to the argument by reaching a compromise solution

zanjón *nm Andes, RP, Ven* gully, ravine

Zanzíbar *n* Zanzibar

zapa *nf (pala)* spade; EXPR **labor de z.: les acusó de hacer labor de z.** she accused them of undermining her

zapador, -ora *nm,f* sapper

zapallito *nm CSur Br* courgette, *US* zucchini

zapallo *nm* (a) *Andes, RP* **z. (italiano)** *Br* courgette, *US* zucchini (b) *Andes, RP (calabaza)* pumpkin (c) *RP Fam (bobo)* mug, *Br* wally

zapán *nm* Manila cherry

zapapico *nm* pickaxe

zapar *vi* to dig tunnels

zaparrastroso = **zarrapastroso**

zapata *nf* (a) *(cuña)* wedge (b) *(de freno)* brake shoe (c) *(de grifo)* rubber washer

zapatazo *nm* (a) *(golpe)* stamp (of the foot); **dar zapatazos** to stamp one's feet; EXPR **tratar a alguien a zapatazos** to kick sb around (b) *(en fútbol)* kick, boot

zapateado *nm* = type of flamenco dance where the dancers stamp their feet rhythmically

zapatear *vi* to stamp one's feet

zapateo *nm* rhythmic stamping ►► *RP* ***z. americano*** tap-dancing

zapatería *nf* (a) *(tienda)* shoe shop (b) *(taller)* shoemaker's ►► ***z. de viejo*** cobbler's, shoe repair shop (c) *(oficio)* shoemaking

zapatero, -a 1 *adj* (a) *(del zapato)* **industria zapatera** shoe-making industry (b) *(legumbres)* hard, tough
2 *nm,f* (a) *(fabricante)* shoemaker (b) *(reparador)* cobbler; **tengo que llevar estas botas al z.** I've got to take these boots to the cobbler's; EXPR **¡z. a tus zapatos!** mind your own business! ►► ***z. remendón*** cobbler; ***z. de viejo*** cobbler (c) *(vendedor)* shoe seller
3 *nm (insecto)* pondskater

zapateta *nf* = shoe-slap accompanied by a jump in certain dances

zapatilla *nf* (a) *(de baile)* shoe, pump; *(de estar en casa)* slipper; *(de deporte)* sports shoe, trainer, *US* sneaker; *(de torero)* bullfighter's shoe ►► ***zapatillas de lona*** canvas shoes; ***zapatillas de tenis*** tennis shoes (b) *(de grifo)* washer (c) *Méx (de tacón)* high-heeled shoe

zapatillazo *nm* whack *(with a slipper)*

zapatismo *nm* (a) *Pol* Zapatism (b) *Hist* = movement led by the Mexican revolutionary Emiliano Zapata

zapatista 1 *adj* (a) *Pol* Zapatista (b) *Hist* Zapatista, = relating to the Mexican revolutionary Emiliano Zapata (1879-1919)
2 *nmf* (a) *Pol* Zapatista, = member of the Zapatista Front, a mainly indigenous rebel group in the Southern Mexican state of Chiapas (b) *Hist* = follower or supporter of the Mexican revolutionary Emiliano Zapata (1879-1919)

zapato *nm* (a) *(prenda)* shoe; **ponerse los zapatos** to put one's shoes on; EXPR **saber dónde le aprieta el z. a alguien** to know how to deal with sb; EXPR *Fam Hum* **sácate el z. de la boca** *(por articular mal)* stop mumbling and speak clearly; *(por tener la boca llena)* don't talk with your mouth full ►► ***z. bajo*** low-heeled shoe; *RP* ***z. chato*** low-heeled shoe; ***z. de cordones*** lace-up (shoe); *RP* ***z. de fútbol*** soccer *o Br* football boot; *Ven* ***z. de goma*** trainer, *US* sneaker; ***z. plano*** flat(-heeled) shoe; ***z. de plataforma*** platform shoe; ***z. de salón*** *Br* court shoe, *US* pump; *CSur* ***z. de taco alto*** high-heeled shoe; ***z. de tacón*** high-heeled shoe
(b) *Urug (cuna) Br* carrycot, *US* portacrib

zape *interj Fam (sorpresa)* wow!

zapear *vi Fam* to channel-hop

zapeo *nm Fam (sin finalidad concreta) Br* channel-hopping, *US* channel surfing; *(para evitar anuncios)* zapping

zaperoco *nm Ven Fam* uproar, pandemonium

zapote *nm (árbol)* sapodilla (tree); *(fruto)* sapodilla (plum)

zapoteca 1 *adj* Zapotec, Zapotecan
2 *nmf* Zapotec, Zapotecan

zapping ['θapin] *nm inv Fam (sin finalidad concreta)* channel *Br* hopping *o US* surfing; *(para evitar anuncios)* zapping; **hacer z.** *(sin finalidad concreta) Br* to channel-hop, *US* to channel-surf; *(para evitar anuncios)* to zap

zar *nm* tsar, czar

zarabanda *nf* (a) *(danza)* saraband (b) *Fam (jaleo)* commotion, uproar

zaragata *nf Fam (jaleo)* row, *US* ruckus

zaragatero, -a *Fam* 1 *adj* argumentative, quarrelsome
2 *nm,f* troublemaker

Zaragoza *n* Saragossa, Zaragoza

zaragozano, -a 1 *adj* of/from Saragossa *(Spain)*
2 *nm,f* person from Saragossa *(Spain)*

zarajo *nm* = lamb intestines, rolled round two crossed sticks and fried

zaranda *nf* sieve, strainer

zarandajas *nfpl Fam* nonsense, trifles; **¡déjate de z.!** stop talking nonsense!; **siempre me está hablando de psicología, psicoterapia y otras z.** she's always talking to me about psychology, psychotherapy or some such nonsense

zarandeado, -a *adj* eventful, turbulent

zarandear 1 *vt* to shake
2 **zarandearse** *vpr* (a) *(bambolearse, agitarse)* to shake; **el vagón se zarandeaba mucho** the carriage was bumping up and down a lot (b) *Am (contonearse)* to swing one's hips

zarandeo *nm* (a) *(sacudida)* shaking; **le dio un buen z.** she shook him hard; **se mareó el niño con tanto z.** being shaken around so much made the boy feel ill (b) *Am (contoneo)* swinging of the hips

zarape = **sarape**

zarapito *nm* ***z. esquimal*** Eskimo whimbrel; ***z. real*** curlew; ***z. trinador*** whimbrel

zaraza *nf* chintz

zarcero *nm* melodious warbler ►► ***z. escita*** booted warbler; ***z. pálido*** olivaceous warbler

zarcillo *nm* (a) *(pendiente)* earring (b) *(en planta)* tendril

zarco, -a *adj* light blue

zarigüeya *nf* opossum

zarina *nf* tsarina, czarina

zarismo *nm* tsarism, czarism; **el fin del z.** the end of the Tsars *o* Czars

zarista 1 *adj* Tsarist, Czarist
2 *nmf* Tsarist, Czarist

zarpa *nf* (a) *(de animal) (uña)* claw; *(mano)* paw (b) *Fam (de persona)* paw, hand; **echar la z. a algo** to get one's paws *o* mitts on sth

zarpar *vi* to weigh anchor, to set sail

zarpazo *nm* swipe *(with a paw)*; **el león le dio un z.** the lion swiped at him with its paw; **de un solo z.** with a single swipe *o* blow of its paw

zarpear *vt CAm, Méx* to splash *o* splatter with mud

zarrapastroso, -a, *CSur* **zaparrastroso, -a** *Fam* 1 *adj* scruffy, shabby
2 *nm,f* scruff

zarza *nf* bramble, blackberry bush

zarzamora *nf* blackberry

zarzaparrilla *nf* sarsaparilla

Zarzuela *nf* **la Z.** = palace which is the official residence of the Spanish royal family in Madrid

zarzuela *nf* (a) *Mús* zarzuela, = Spanish light opera (b) *(plato)* = fish and/or seafood stew

zarzuelista *nmf* composer of "zarzuelas"

zarzuelístico, -a *adj* = of/relating to "zarzuelas"

zas *interj* (**a**) *(onomatopeya)* wham!, bang! (**b**) *(indica sorpresa)* **en cuanto se de la vuelta, ¡z.!, salimos corriendo** as soon as she turns round we run for it, right?

zascandil *nm Fam (adulto)* good-for-nothing; *(niño)* little rascal

zascandilear *vi Fam* to mess around *o* about, to slack (around)

zascandileo *nm Fam* messing about *o* around, slacking (around)

zedilla *nf* cedilla

zéjel *nm Lit* = verse form of Arabic origin consisting of an initial refrain and a variable number of four-line stanzas

zelote, zelota *nmf* Zealot

zen 1 *adj inv* Zen
2 *nm* Zen

zenit *nm* (**a**) *Astron* zenith (**b**) *(punto culminante)* peak, zenith; **ha llegado al z. de su carrera** she is at the peak *o* pinnacle of her career

zepelín (*pl* **zepelines**), **zeppelín** (*pl* **zeppelines**) *nm* zeppelin

zeta *Esp Fam* 1 *adj inv* **coche z.** *(de policía)* police patrol car
2 *nm (de policía)* police patrol car

zeugma *nf Ling* zeugma

Zeus *n Mitol* Zeus

zigoto *nm* zygote

zigurat (*pl* **zigurats**) *nm* ziggurat

zigzag (*pl* **zigzags** *o* **zigzagues**) *nm* zigzag

zigzagueante *adj (carretera)* winding; **una línea z.** a zigzag

zigzaguear *vi* to zigzag

zigzagueo *nm (de carretera, sendero)* twisting and turning

Zimbabue *n* Zimbabwe

zimbabuense 1 *adj* Zimbabwean
2 *nmf* Zimbabwean

zinc *nm* zinc

zíngaro, -a 1 *adj* gypsy
2 *nm,f* gypsy

zíper *nm CAm, Méx Br* zip, *US* zipper

zipizape *nm Fam* squabble, set-to; **se armó un z.** a squabble broke out, there was a set-to

zis, zas *interj* bang! bang!

zloty [es'loti] *nm (moneda)* zloty

zócalo *nm* (**a**) *(de pared)* skirting board (**b**) *(de edificio)* plinth (**c**) *(pedestal)* pedestal (**d**) *Geol* basement, pedestal (**e**) *Informát* socket (**f**) *Méx (plaza)* main square

zocato, -a *adj* (**a**) *(fruto)* overripe (**b**) *Fam (zurdo)* left-handed (**c**) *Am (pan)* stale

zoco *nm* souk, Arabian market

zocotroco = **socotroco**

zodiac® *nf* = rubber dinghy with outboard motor

zodiacal *adj* zodiacal

zodiaco, zodíaco *nm* zodiac; **los signos del z.** the signs of the zodiac, the star signs

zombi, zombie 1 *adj Fam (atontado)* zonked
2 *nmf (en vudú)* zombie; *Fam* **iba como un z. por la calle** she was walking along the street like a zombie

zompopo *nm CAm (hormiga)* = type of large-headed leafcutter ant

zona *nf* (**a**) *(espacio, área)* zone, area; **una z. montañosa/turística** a mountainous/tourist area; **la z. norte/sur de la isla** the northern/southern part of the island; **en las zonas más aisladas/pobres** in the most remote/poorest areas; **¿vives por la z.?** *(por aquí)* do you live around here?; **ésta la z. de copas de la ciudad** this is the centre of the city's nightlife ▸▸ ***z. azul*** *(de estacionamiento)* restricted parking zone; ***z. de carga y descarga*** loading bay; ***z. catastrófica*** disaster area; ***z. centro*** city centre, *US* downtown; ***z. cero*** *(en Nueva York)* ground zero; ***z. climática*** climatic zone; ***z. comercial*** shopping area; ***z. conflictiva*** trouble spot; ***z. de conflicto*** *(en guerra)* war zone, battle zone; ***z. edificada*** built-up area; ***z. erógena*** erogenous zone; ***z. euro*** euro zone; ***z. de exclusión*** exclusion zone; *Com* ***z. franca*** free-trade zone; ***z. de no fumadores*** no-smoking area; ***z. glacial*** glacial region; ***z. de guerra*** war zone; ***z. húmeda*** wetland area; ***z. intermareal*** intertidal zone; *Meteo* ***z. de inversión*** thermal *o* temperature inversion zone; ***z. de libre comercio*** free-trade zone; ***z. de marca*** *(en rugby)* in-goal area; ***z. militar*** military area *o* zone; *Esp* ***z. nacional*** *(en la guerra)* = the area controlled by Nationalist forces during the Spanish Civil War; ***z. peatonal*** pedestrian area; ***z. protegida*** *(natural)* conservation area; ***z. residencial*** residential area; ***z. roja*** *Esp (en la guerra)* = term used by Nationalists to refer to Republican-controlled areas during the Spanish Civil War; *Am (de prostitución)* red-light district; ***Z. Rosa*** *(en México DF)* = elegant tourist and shopping area in Mexico City; ***z. de seguridad*** *(entre países)* buffer zone; ***z. templada*** temperate zone; *Am Anticuado* ***z. de tolerancia*** red-light district; ***z. tórrida*** tropics, *Espec* torrid zone; ***z. de urgente reindustrialización*** = region given priority status for industrial investment, *Br* ≃ enterprise zone; ***z. verde*** *(grande)* park, green area; *(pequeña)* lawn
(**b**) *(en baloncesto) (área)* key
(**c**) *(en baloncesto) (violación)* three-seconds violation

zonal *adj (desarrollo, planificación)* area; **hospital z.** area hospital; *Dep* **defensa z.** zone *o* zonal defence; **plano z.** map of the area

zoncear *vi Am* to fool *o* mess around

zoncería, zoncera *nf Am* (**a**) *(cualidad)* silliness, stupidity (**b**) *(hecho, dicho)* **decir/hacer una z.** to say/do something silly *o* stupid; **eso son zoncerías** that's nonsense

zonificación *nf* zoning

zonificar *vt* to zone

zonzo, -a 1 *adj Am* (**a**) *(tonto)* foolish, silly (**b**) *(atontado)* dopey
2 *nm,f Am* fool, idiot
3 *nm Bol* = dish made with yucca and cheese

zoo *nm* zoo

zoofilia *nf* bestiality

zoófito *nm* zoophyte

zoogeografía *nf* zoogeography

zoolatría *nf* animal worship, *Espec* zoolatry

zoología *nf* zoology

zoológico, -a 1 *adj* zoological
2 *nm* zoo

zoólogo, -a *nm,f* zoologist

zoom [θum] (*pl* **zooms**) *nm Fot* zoom lens

zoomórfico, -a *adj* zoomorphic

zoonosis *nf inv* zoonosis

zooplancton *nm* zooplankton

zootecnia *nf* animal husbandry, *Espec* zootechnics

zopenco, -a *Fam* 1 *adj* idiotic, daft
2 *nm,f* idiot, nitwit

zopilote *nm CAm, Méx* black vulture

zoquete 1 *adj Fam* thick, dense
2 *nm CSur (calcetín)* ankle sock
3 *nmf Fam (tonto)* blockhead, idiot

zorcico *nm* = Basque folk dance

zorimbo, -a *Méx Fam* 1 *adj* silly, *Br* daft
2 *nm,f* crackpot, nitwit

zoroastrismo *nm* Zoroastrianism

zorongo *nm* = type of flamenco music, song and dance

zorra *nf* (**a**) *Esp Fam Pey (ramera)* whore, tart, *US* hooker (**b**) *RP (remolque)* trailer (**c**) *ver también* **zorro**

zorrear *vi Méx Fam* to spy, to keep watch

zorrera *nf* (**a**) *(madriguera)* foxhole (**b**) *(habitación)* smoke-filled room (**c**) *ver también* **zorrero**

zorrería *nf Fam* craftiness, cunning

zorrero, -a *nm,f* fox hunter

zorrillo *nm CAm, Méx* skunk

zorrino *nm Andes, RP* skunk

zorro, -a 1 *adj* (**a**) *(astuto)* foxy, crafty (**b**) *Esp muy Fam (para enfatizar)* **no tengo ni zorra (idea)** I haven't got a *Br* bloody *o US* goddamn clue
2 *nm,f* fox, *f* vixen; EXPR **por querer saber la zorra perdió la cola** curiosity killed the cat ▸▸ ***z. ártico*** arctic fox; ***z. azul*** blue fox; ***z. plateado*** silver fox
3 *nm* (**a**) *(persona astuta)* fox (**b**) *(piel)* fox (fur) (**c**) ***z. marino*** thresher shark
4 **zorros** *nmpl (utensilio)* feather duster; EXPR *Fam* **hecho unos zorros** *(cansado, maltrecho)* whacked, done in; *(objeto, ropa, habitación)* in a mess

zorruno, -a *adj* foxlike; *Fam* **oler a z.** to smell sweaty

zorzal *nm* (**a**) *(ave)* song thrush ▸▸ ***z. alirrojo*** redwing; ***z. charlo*** mistle thrush; ***z. real*** fieldfare (**b**) *(hombre astuto)* sly *o* cunning person (**c**) *Chile (tonto)* simpleton

zotaco, -a *Méx Fam* 1 *adj* short
2 *nm,f* shorty

zotal® *nm* = very powerful disinfectant
zote *Fam* **1** *adj* dopey
2 *nmf* dope, clod
zozobra *nf* **(a)** *(inquietud)* anxiety, worry; **sufrieron momentos de z.** they had an anxious time **(b)** *(naufragio) (de barco)* sinking, foundering; *(de empresa, planes)* ruin, end
zozobrante *adj* **(a)** *(barco)* foundering, sinking **(b)** *(economía, situación)* foundering **(c)** *(persona)* anxious, worried
zozobrar *vi* **(a)** *(barco)* to founder, to sink **(b)** *(proyecto, empresa)* to founder
zuavo *nm* Zouave
zueco *nm* clog
zulo *nm (para secuestrado)* = concealed room in which a hostage is imprisoned; *(para armas)* cache
zulú (*pl* **zulúes**) **1** *adj* Zulu
2 *nmf (persona)* Zulu
3 *nm (lengua)* Zulu
zumaque *nm* **(a)** *(planta)* sumach ►► ***z. venenoso*** poison sumach, poison ivy **(b)** *Fam (vino)* wine
zumba *nf* **(a)** *(cencerro)* = bell worn by lead animal **(b)** *(juguete)* bull-roarer **(c)** *(broma)* teasing, joking **(d)** *Andes, Méx, PRico (zurra)* beating, thrashing
zumbado, -a *Fam* **1** *adj* screwy, *Br* bonkers
2 *nm,f* nut, crackpot
zumbador *nm* buzzer
zumbar 1 *vi* **(a)** *(producir ruido) (insecto)* to buzz; *(máquinas)* to whirr, to hum; **me zumban los oídos** my ears are buzzing; **le estarán zumbando los oídos de tanto hablar de él** his ears must be burning with people talking about him so much **(b) zumbando: pasar zumbando** to shoot past; **salir zumbando** to dash off; **venir zumbando** to come running
2 *vt Fam (golpear)* to beat, to thump
zumbido *nm (de insecto)* buzz, buzzing; *(de máquinas)* whirr, whirring; **tengo un z. en los oídos** my ears are buzzing
zumbo *nm CAm, Col* = vessel made from a gourd
zumbón, -ona *Fam* **1** *adj* **un tipo z.** a joker, a tease
2 *nm,f* joker, tease
zumo *nm Esp* juice; **z. de naranja** orange juice
zunchar *vt* to fasten with a metal band *o* hoop
zuncho *nm (cinta)* metal band *o* hoop; *(refuerzo)* reinforcing ring ►► *Andes* ***z. plástico*** strapping tape
zunzún *nm* emerald hummingbird
zunzunito *nm* bee hummingbird
zurcido *nm*, **zurcidura** *nf* **(a)** *(acción)* darning **(b)** *(remiendo)* darn
zurcidor, -ora *nm,f* darner, mender
zurcir [74] *vt* to darn, to mend; EXPR *Fam* **¡anda y que te zurzan!** on your bike!, get lost!; **¡que le zurzan!** he can get lost!, *Br* he can take a running jump!
zurda *nf* **(a)** *(mano)* left hand **(b)** *(pierna)* left foot **(c)** *ver también* **zurdo**
zurdazo *nm Dep (con la mano)* left; *(con el pie)* powerful left-foot shot
zurdo, -a 1 *adj (mano, pierna)* left; *(persona)* left-handed; *(boxeador)* southpaw
2 *nm,f (persona)* left-handed person; *(boxeador)* southpaw
zurear *vi* to coo
zureo *nm* cooing
Zurich, Zúrich ['θurik] *n* Zurich
zurito *nm Esp* = small glass of wine
zurra *nf Fam* beating, hiding; **¡te voy a dar una z.!** I'm going to tan your hide!; EXPR **darse una z.** *(a trabajar, estudiar)* to slog one's guts out
zurracapote *nm* = a type of wine punch, drunk hot or cold
zurrapa *nf* **(a)** *(poso)* dregs, sediment **(b)** *Fam (de excremento)* skid mark
zurrar *vt Fam* **(a)** *(persona)* to beat, to thrash **(b)** *(piel)* to tan; EXPR *Esp Fam* **z. la badana a alguien** to tan sb's hide
zurraspa *nf Fam (de excremento)* skid mark
zurriagazo *nm* whipping
zurriago *nm* whip
zurrón *nm* shoulder bag
zurullo *nm* **(a)** *(cosa blanda)* round, soft lump **(b)** *muy Fam (excremento)* turd
zurzo *etc ver* **zurcir**
zutano, -a *nm,f (hombre)* so-and-so, what's-his-name; *(mujer)* so-and-so, what's-her-name
zuzo *interj* shoo!

SUPPLEMENT
SUPLEMENTO

SPANISH COMMUNICATION GUIDE

Letters

When sending a letter or other written communication, particular attention should be paid to the grammar and spelling as these are sensitive topics. Spelling mistakes and grammatical errors in a letter are considered very bad form, even in private correspondence.

The style should be simple and clear. Use paragraphs to make your ideas easier to follow.

Layout

Sender's name and address, normally in the top left corner. On company headed paper, the name of the company and its address are centred at the top of the letter. The sender's name and address are usually only included at the top of the letter in administrative and business letters.

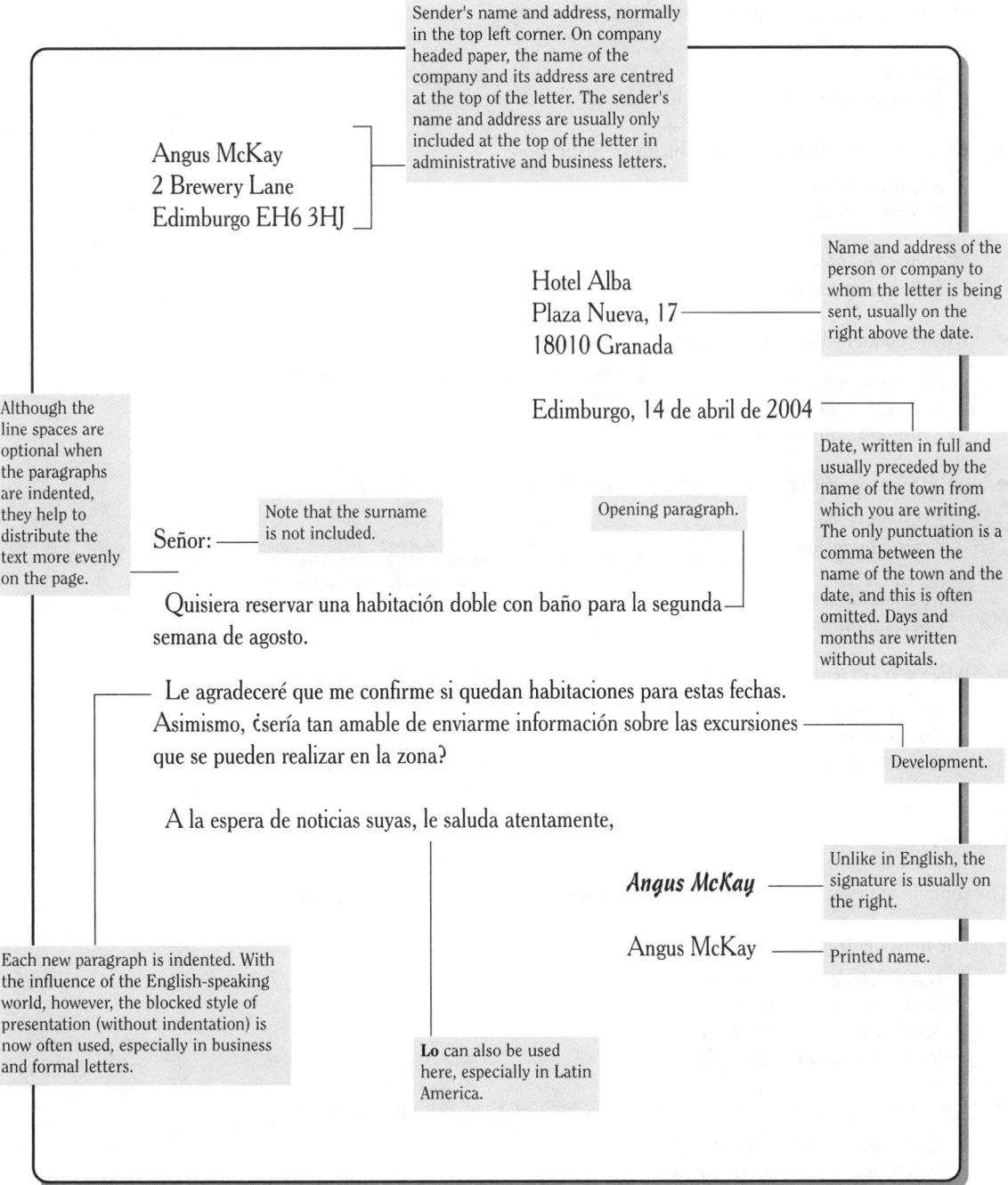

Angus McKay
2 Brewery Lane
Edimburgo EH6 3HJ

Name and address of the person or company to whom the letter is being sent, usually on the right above the date.

Hotel Alba
Plaza Nueva, 17
18010 Granada

Edimburgo, 14 de abril de 2004

Date, written in full and usually preceded by the name of the town from which you are writing. The only punctuation is a comma between the name of the town and the date, and this is often omitted. Days and months are written without capitals.

Although the line spaces are optional when the paragraphs are indented, they help to distribute the text more evenly on the page.

Señor:

Note that the surname is not included.

Opening paragraph.

Quisiera reservar una habitación doble con baño para la segunda semana de agosto.

Le agradeceré que me confirme si quedan habitaciones para estas fechas. Asimismo, ¿sería tan amable de enviarme información sobre las excursiones que se pueden realizar en la zona?

Development.

A la espera de noticias suyas, le saluda atentamente,

Angus McKay

Unlike in English, the signature is usually on the right.

Angus McKay

Printed name.

Each new paragraph is indented. With the influence of the English-speaking world, however, the blocked style of presentation (without indentation) is now often used, especially in business and formal letters.

Lo can also be used here, especially in Latin America.

Beginnings

The opening greetings and endings used in letters written in Spanish follow certain well-established rules:

- If you do not know the person you are writing to, whether you know their name or not, or if you know them only slightly:

  Estimado señor
  Estimada señora

  When preceded by another word (**Estimado**, **Muy**, **Distinguido**), *señor* and *señora* are written in lower case.

  Señor, Señora
  Señorita

  Señorita is used for an unmarried young woman, but it is somewhat old-fashioned nowadays. If in doubt, use **Señora**.

  Muy señor mío
  Distinguido señor

  More formal.

- When you are unsure whether the recipient of the letter is male or female and when the letter is addressed to a company rather than to an individual:

  Estimados señores
  Señores
  Muy señores míos

- When writing to the head of a company or institution:

  Señor Director
  Señora Directora

  Señor Presidente
  Señora Presidenta

- When you know the person you are writing to and want to sound less formal:

  Estimado señor (López)
  Estimada señora (Martín)
  Estimada señorita (Alsina)

  The abbreviations **Sr.**, **Sra.**, **Srta.** can be used before the surname

- When you are writing to a colleague you do not know or know only slightly:

  Estimado colega
  Estimada colega

  Querido amigo
  Querida amiga

  The titles **Querido amigo** and **Querida amiga** are still slightly formal and are not used between friends but between colleagues or acquaintances.

- When you are writing to a relative, to a friend or to a colleague with whom you are on first name terms:

  Querido Federico
  Querida Rosa
  Queridos tíos

Endings

The complimentary close should correspond in form and tone to the opening greeting.

- The most neutral endings are:

  Le/Lo saluda atentamente
  Se despide atentamente
  Reciba un cordial saludo de
  Reciba un atento saludo de

- If you want to end on a more respectful note, such as when writing to a superior:

  Quedo a su entera disposición.
  Reciba un respetuoso saludo de
  Respetuosamente le/lo saluda

- If you want to show your gratitude:

  Agradeciendo de antemano su atención
  Le hago partícipe de mi más sincero agradecimiento. (formal)

- Simplified and more informal endings are becoming more common. The following endings can be found more and more in everyday business letters, e-mails and faxes:

  Atentamente
  Cordialmente (more friendly)
  Un afectuoso saludo (even more friendly)

- The following endings are used when writing to friends or relatives:

  Polite:

  Un saludo
  Saludos
  Afectuosamente

  Friendly:

  Un (fuerte) abrazo
  Abrazos
  Con (mucho) cariño
  Hasta pronto
  Saludos a Pedro
  Besos a todos
  Muchos besos
  Un beso

  Informal:

  Un abrazote
  Un besazo —— Used particularly in Spain.

Addresses

- In Spanish addresses you will often find no word for "street", only the actual name of the street, unless it is called, for example, "Avenida" or "Paseo". You can also see the abbreviation C/ for "Calle". The house number comes after the street name, and the postcode precedes the name of the town or city.

  Gran Vía, 13
  28005 Madrid

- Some countries use different names to refer to "street". In Perú "Jirón" is often used, and in Colombia a street can be referred to as "Carrera", followed by a number, which is the street number.

  Carrera 3, 17

- You will often see a number followed by superscript ª or º, given after the house number. This indicates which floor of a building the apartment is situated on. For example, the third floor in the following example:

  Gran Vía, 13 3ª

  If a third number is given, this refers to the door number:

  Gran Vía, 13, 3º 1ª

- In Latin America this information is often given in full:

  Insurgentes 28, 3er. piso, despacho 305

  or sometimes the floor number is omitted:

  Insurgentes 28, despacho 305 or
  Insurgentes 28-305

The websites of the various postal services in Spanish-speaking countries are a useful source of information regarding addresses and post codes/zip codes in particular. Here are some useful addresses:

Spain: www.correos.es
Mexico: http://rtn.net.mx/sepomex
Argentina: www.correoargentino.com.ar

Envelopes

Don and **Doña** (and their abbreviated forms **D.** and **Dña.**) are used only when also giving the first name (**Don Ricardo Ugarte**) and where the letter is rather formal. This usage is regarded as somewhat old-fashioned in Latin America. Even in Spain, it is often sufficient to write the name and address of the recipient.

The recipient's name and address are written towards the right hand side of the lower half of the envelope.

Note that **calle** can be omitted from the street name (but not **avenida**, **plaza**, etc.).

It is standard practice to write a return address on the back of the envelope at the top, in case the letter gets lost.

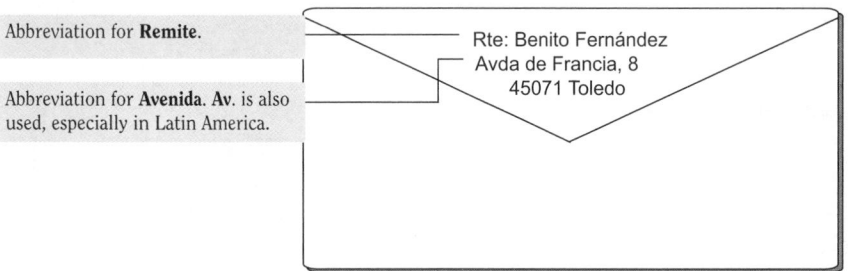

Abbreviation for **Remite**.

Abbreviation for **Avenida**. **Av.** is also used, especially in Latin America.

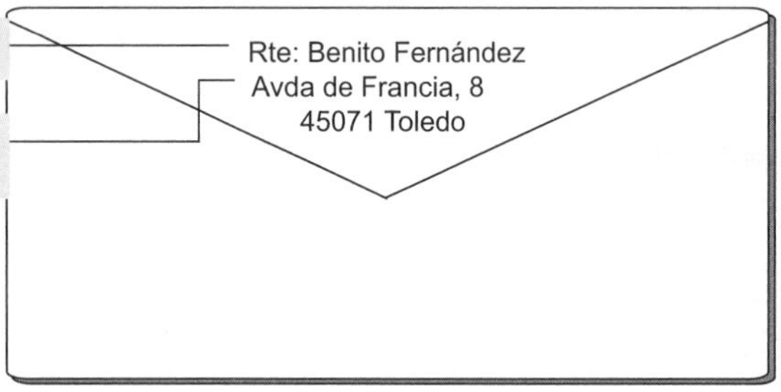

Model letters and cards

Chatty letter to a friend/relative

When writing to friends and relatives, as in English, you are free to write in pretty much any way you like.

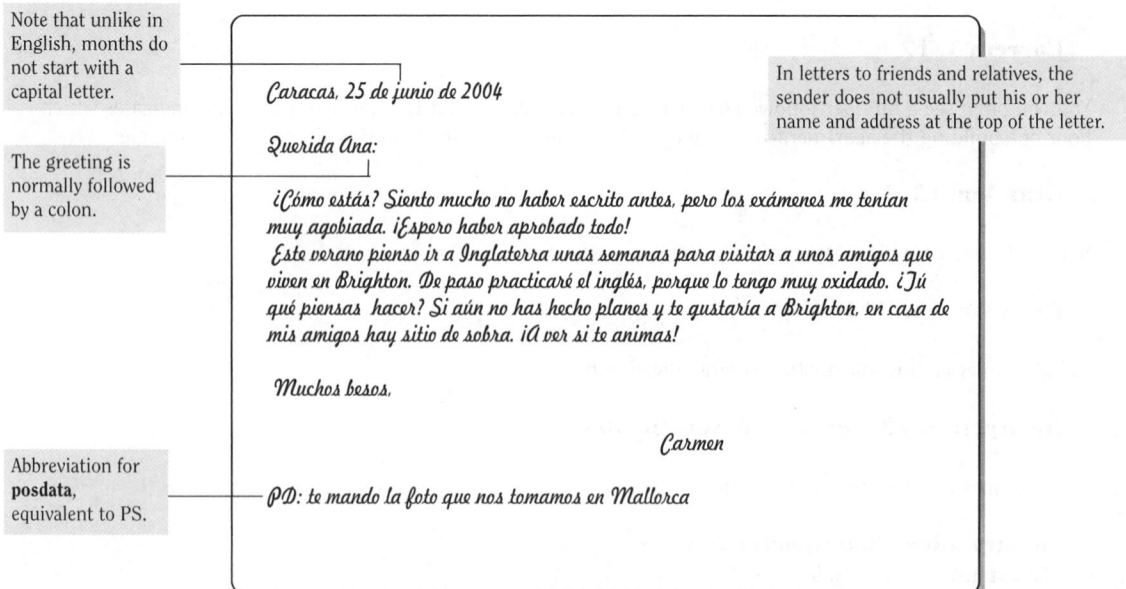

Note that unlike in English, months do not start with a capital letter.

The greeting is normally followed by a colon.

Abbreviation for **posdata**, equivalent to PS.

In letters to friends and relatives, the sender does not usually put his or her name and address at the top of the letter.

Caracas, 25 de junio de 2004

Querida Ana:

¿Cómo estás? Siento mucho no haber escrito antes, pero los exámenes me tenían muy agobiada. ¡Espero haber aprobado todo!
Este verano pienso ir a Inglaterra unas semanas para visitar a unos amigos que viven en Brighton. De paso practicaré el inglés, porque lo tengo muy oxidado. ¿Tú qué piensas hacer? Si aún no has hecho planes y te gustaría a Brighton, en casa de mis amigos hay sitio de sobra. ¡A ver si te animas!

Muchos besos,

Carmen

PD: te mando la foto que nos tomamos en Mallorca

Postcards

It is not unusual in the Spanish-speaking world for people to send a postcard in an envelope. Apart from the additional writing space this provides, it is a way of guaranteeing extra privacy.

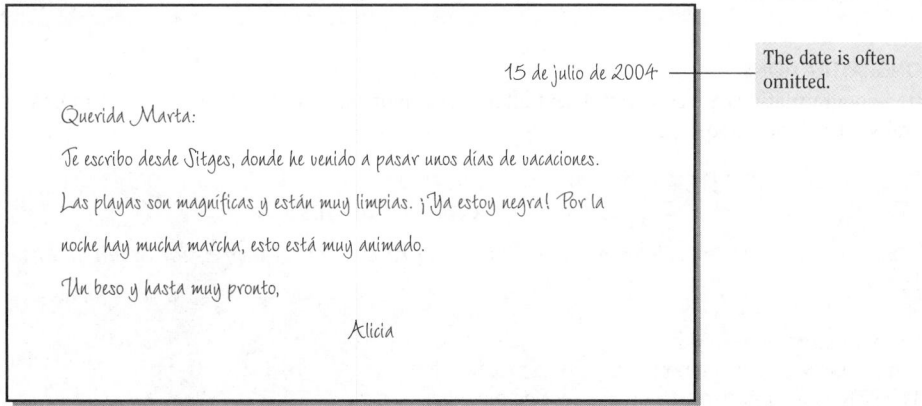

> 15 de julio de 2004
>
> Querida Marta:
>
> Te escribo desde Sitges, donde he venido a pasar unos días de vacaciones. Las playas son magníficas y están muy limpias. ¡Ya estoy negra! Por la noche hay mucha marcha, esto está muy animado.
>
> Un beso y hasta muy pronto,
>
> Alicia

The date is often omitted.

Greeting cards

▪ SEASON'S GREETINGS

The use of greeting cards is not so widespread in Spanish-speaking countries as in Britain and the United States. Greeting cards are usually sent for Christmas. They are mostly sent to friends and relatives who live far away, and business acquaintances. They are always posted and are never handed to the recipient.

Useful phrases:

(When two pronoun or verb forms are given in a phrase, the first form is for Spain and the second for Latin America)

Feliz Navidad y próspero 2005
Felices Fiestas
Felices Pascuas
¡Feliz Año Nuevo!

Te deseo lo mejor en el año que empieza.
Les deseo una feliz Navidad en compañía de los suyos.
Espero que el nuevo año os/les traiga a todos salud y felicidad.

▪ BIRTHDAYS AND SAINT'S DAYS

Birthday cards are not as popular in Spain and Latin America as in English-speaking countries. As with other types of greeting cards, they are mostly sent to friends and relatives who live far away rather than to people who you see regularly. Birthday cards are not usually handed directly to the recipient and presents are not systematically accompanied by a card.

It is traditional for people to celebrate their saint's day as well as their birthday. A person's saint's day is the day in the church calendar commemorating the saint after whom the person is named.

> *Querido Pedro:*
>
> *¡Feliz cumpleaños!*
> *Siento mucho no poder ir a tu fiesta, pero quiero que sepas que brindaré a tu salud ese día. Felicidades también de parte de Pilar.*
>
> *Un fuerte abrazo,*
>
> *Manolo*

Useful phrases:

¡Feliz cumpleaños!	¡Felicidades!
Felicidades, y que cumplas muchos más.	María y yo te deseamos un cumpleaños muy feliz.
¡Feliz santo!	Muchas felicidades en el día de tu santo.

▪ CONGRATULATIONS

Written congratulations are sometimes sent after the announcement of a birth, engagement or wedding, or on other, generally formal, occasions.

Useful phrases:

(When two pronoun or verb forms are given in a phrase, the first form is for Spain and the second for Latin America)

For an engagement or a wedding:
Mi más sincera felicitación por vuestro/su próximo enlace.
Recibid/Reciban nuestros mejores deseos de felicidad.
Os/Les deseamos que seáis/sean muy felices. *(less formal)*
Julián y yo queremos felicitaros/felicitarles y desearos/desearles lo mejor. *(less formal)*

For a birth:
Nuestra más sincera enhorabuena por el nacimiento de vuestro/su hijo.
Felicidades a los dos por la llegada al mundo de vuestra/su hija.

For a success/promotion:
Te felicito por el premio y espero sinceramente que continúen tus éxitos.
Me alegro mucho de que hayas aprobado los exámenes.
Reciba mi más sincera felicitación por tan merecido ascenso. *(formal)*

Letter of complaint

If you want your letter of complaint to be effective, in Spanish as in English, it is essential to remain polite and not simply to use the letter to give full vent to your anger.

For serious complaints, or if a first letter has been ignored, it is standard practice to send this type of letter by recorded delivery ("correo certificado con acuse de recibo").

Blanca Mendieta
Reina Leonor 28, 1º 4ª
09001 Burgos

Mudanzas Ramos
Plaza Cádiz, 6
09007 Burgos

Burgos, 4 de abril de 2004

Señores:

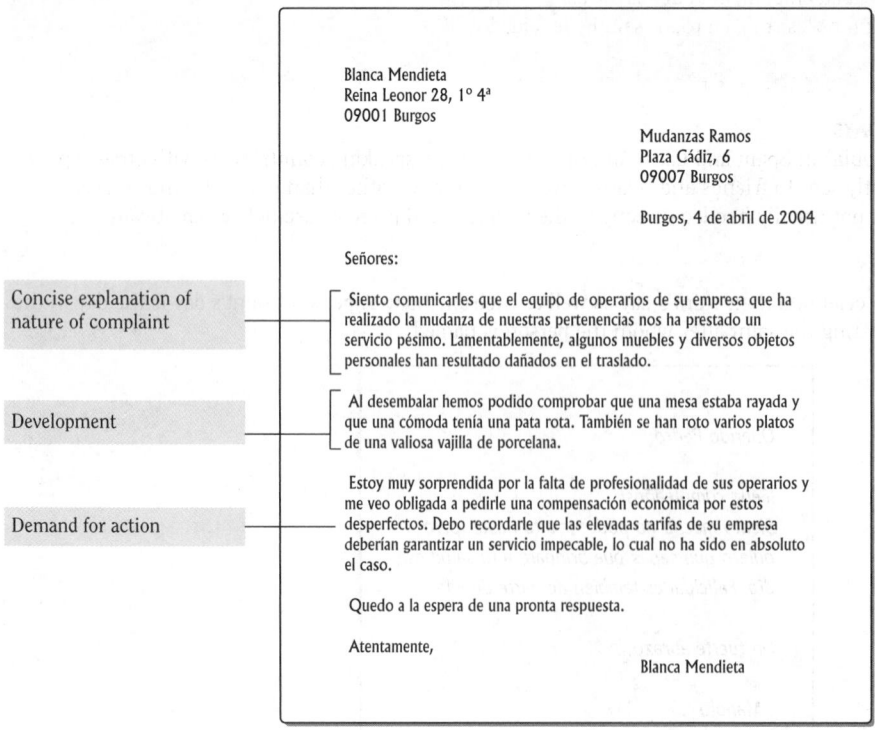

[Concise explanation of nature of complaint]
Siento comunicarles que el equipo de operarios de su empresa que ha realizado la mudanza de nuestras pertenencias nos ha prestado un servicio pésimo. Lamentablemente, algunos muebles y diversos objetos personales han resultado dañados en el traslado.

[Development]
Al desembalar hemos podido comprobar que una mesa estaba rayada y que una cómoda tenía una pata rota. También se han roto varios platos de una valiosa vajilla de porcelana.

[Demand for action]
Estoy muy sorprendida por la falta de profesionalidad de sus operarios y me veo obligada a pedirle una compensación económica por estos desperfectos. Debo recordarle que las elevadas tarifas de su empresa deberían garantizar un servicio impecable, lo cual no ha sido en absoluto el caso.

Quedo a la espera de una pronta respuesta.

Atentamente,

Blanca Mendieta

Useful phrases:

Me dirijo a ustedes para protestar por ...
Deseo expresarle mi más enérgica queja por ...
Le escribo para expresar mi protesta por el mal funcionamiento de ...
Rogamos se subsane de inmediato esta situación.
Siento comunicarles que he recibido un pésimo servicio por parte de su empresa.
Les ruego (que) anulen mi pedido y me reembolsen la cantidad de ...
Estamos francamente sorprendidos por su falta de profesionalidad.

Apologizing

Even if you have already apologized by telephone, in some situations (for example, if you have missed a formal appointment) you may feel that a letter of apology is in order.

Elvira Pozas
Minerva, 8 1°
41710 Utrera

ALTER S.L.
A/A de la Sra. Ana Ruiz
Teide, 14
41002 Sevilla

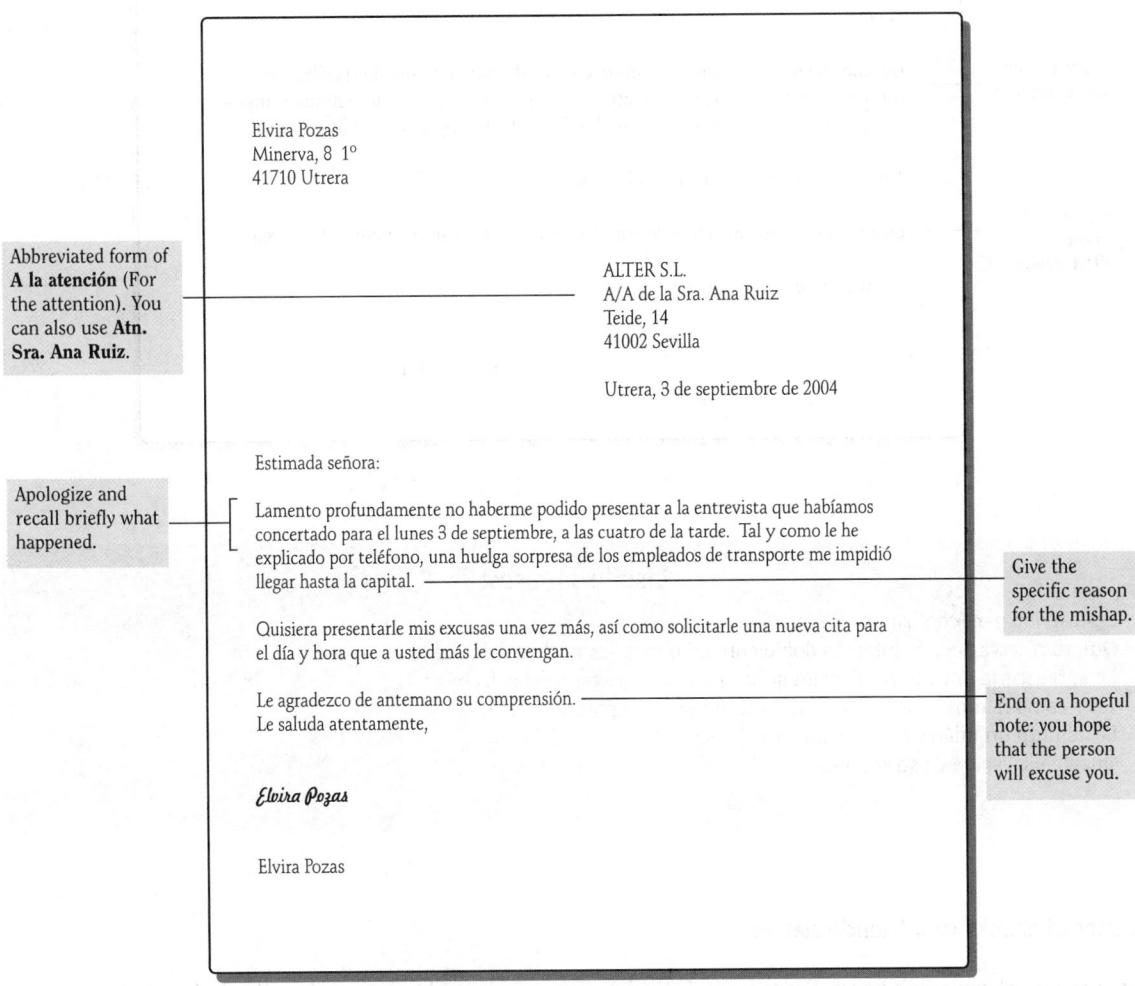

Abbreviated form of **A la atención** (For the attention). You can also use **Atn. Sra. Ana Ruiz.**

Utrera, 3 de septiembre de 2004

Estimada señora:

Lamento profundamente no haberme podido presentar a la entrevista que habíamos concertado para el lunes 3 de septiembre, a las cuatro de la tarde. Tal y como le he explicado por teléfono, una huelga sorpresa de los empleados de transporte me impidió llegar hasta la capital.

Apologize and recall briefly what happened.

Give the specific reason for the mishap.

Quisiera presentarle mis excusas una vez más, así como solicitarle una nueva cita para el día y hora que a usted más le convengan.

Le agradezco de antemano su comprensión.
Le saluda atentamente,

End on a hopeful note: you hope that the person will excuse you.

Elvira Pozas

Elvira Pozas

Useful phrases:

No sabe cuánto lamento este malentendido.
Siento mucho lo ocurrido.
Le pido disculpas una vez más.
Le ruego tenga a bien aceptar mis excusas. *(formal)*

Making a reservation

The standard procedure is to make the reservation by telephone and then to confirm the booking in writing.

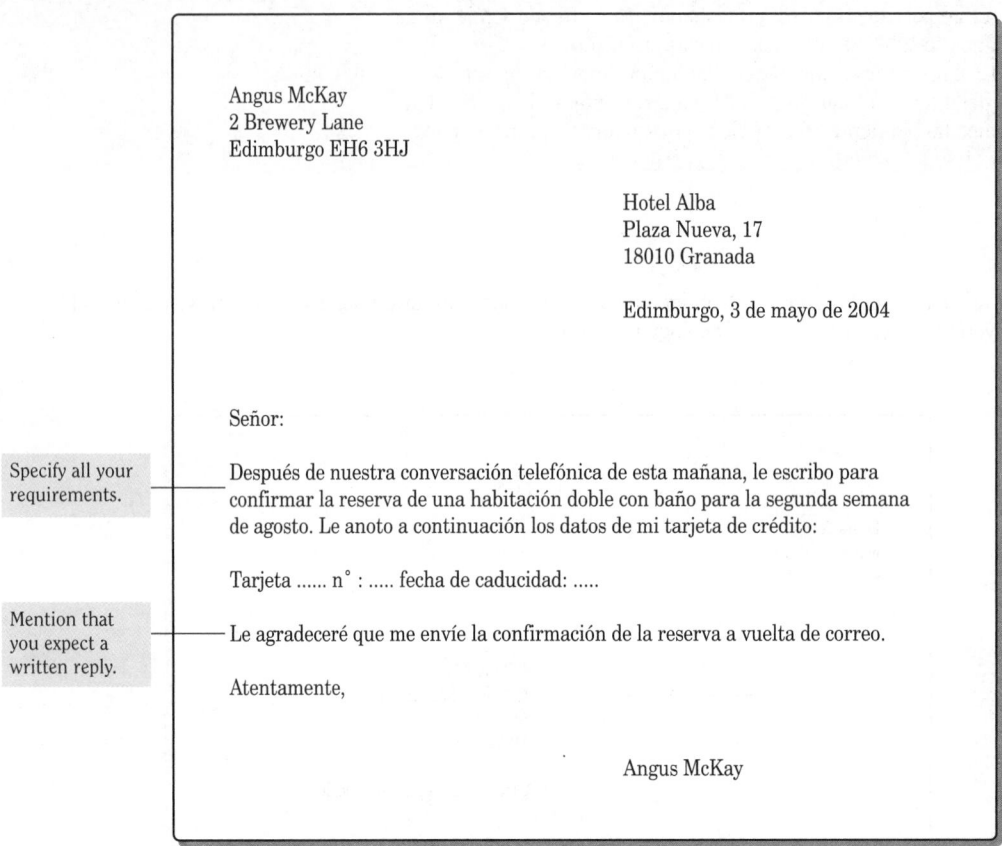

Angus McKay
2 Brewery Lane
Edimburgo EH6 3HJ

Hotel Alba
Plaza Nueva, 17
18010 Granada

Edimburgo, 3 de mayo de 2004

Señor:

Specify all your requirements.

Después de nuestra conversación telefónica de esta mañana, le escribo para confirmar la reserva de una habitación doble con baño para la segunda semana de agosto. Le anoto a continuación los datos de mi tarjeta de crédito:

Tarjeta ...... n° : ..... fecha de caducidad: .....

Mention that you expect a written reply.

Le agradeceré que me envíe la confirmación de la reserva a vuelta de correo.

Atentamente,

Angus McKay

Useful phrases:

Les escribo para confirmar mi reserva.
Quiero reservar una habitación doble con baño para las noches del ... al ... inclusive.
Le agradecería que me confirmara si hay habitaciones para estas fechas.
Tal y como hemos convenido, le adjunto un talón al portador de ...
Le adjunto un talón de ... en concepto de depósito.
Quedo a la espera de su respuesta.

Letter of thanks to a friend/relative

After staying at someone's house, Spanish and Latin American people tend to convey their thanks by telephone rather than sending a thank-you letter. In certain circumstances, however, you may feel that a letter will be appreciated.

A written thank-you letter is still considered obligatory for wedding or christening presents or for more formal situations.

This type of letter should be sent as soon after the event as possible.

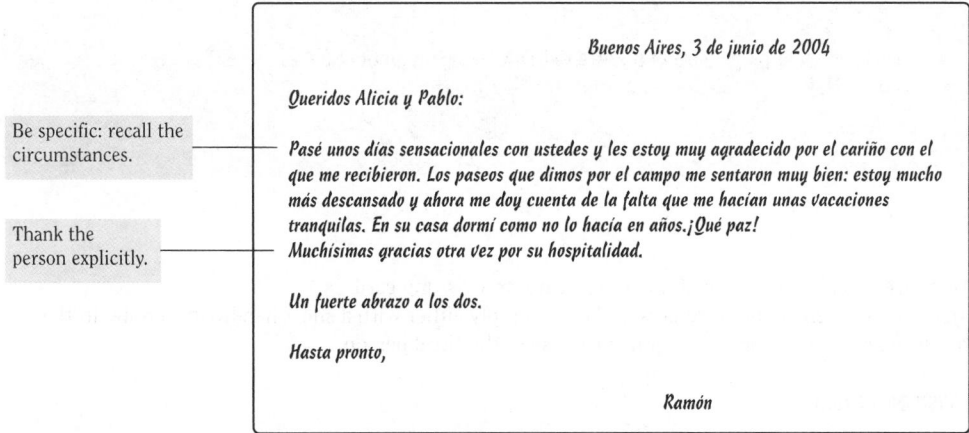

Be specific: recall the circumstances.

Thank the person explicitly.

Buenos Aires, 3 de junio de 2004

Queridos Alicia y Pablo:

Pasé unos días sensacionales con ustedes y les estoy muy agradecido por el cariño con el que me recibieron. Los paseos que dimos por el campo me sentaron muy bien: estoy mucho más descansado y ahora me doy cuenta de la falta que me hacían unas vacaciones tranquilas. En su casa dormí como no lo hacía en años.¡Qué paz!
Muchísimas gracias otra vez por su hospitalidad.

Un fuerte abrazo a los dos.

Hasta pronto,

Ramón

Useful phrases:

(When two pronoun or verb forms are given in a phrase, the first form is for Spain and the second for Latin America)

Muchísimas gracias por su obsequio.
Muchas gracias por la magnífica cubertería que nos habéis regalado/nos regalaron.
María y yo queremos darte las gracias por la preciosa medalla que has regalado/que regalaste a Lucía con motivo de su bautizo.
Te agradezco tu ayuda de todo corazón.
Os/Les agradecemos la atención que habéis tenido/que tuvieron al recibir a nuestro hijo en vuestra/su casa.
Queremos hacerles partícipes de nuestro más profundo agradecimiento. *(formal)*

Invitations and replies

▪ Letter

Informal invitations, for dinner parties with friends or family gatherings, are made by the telephone. If you are organizing a party or want to invite friends or relatives to visit for a few days, you can send a letter of invitation.

Montevideo, 25 de mayo de 2004

Querido Bernardo:

¿Te gustaría venir a pasar unos cuantos días en el campo con nosotros? Vamos a alquilar una casa en Villa Serrana con unos amigos entre el 7 y el 15 de agosto. Juan prometió que también viene y nos gustaría mucho que te unieras al grupo.
Te adjunto un mapa de la zona.
¡Contéstame rápido!
Abrazos,

Flora

Useful phrases:

Vamos a organizar una escapada a la playa para el puente del Día de la Independencia.
El 25 de enero hacemos una fiesta para celebrar el cumpleaños de José.
Te esperamos.

▪ Cards

More formal invitations are usually made with an invitation card or a visiting card.
These invitations are always written in the third person. You can reply either with a short handwritten note, in the first person, or on a visiting card, which always requires the use of the third person.

Invitation on a visiting card

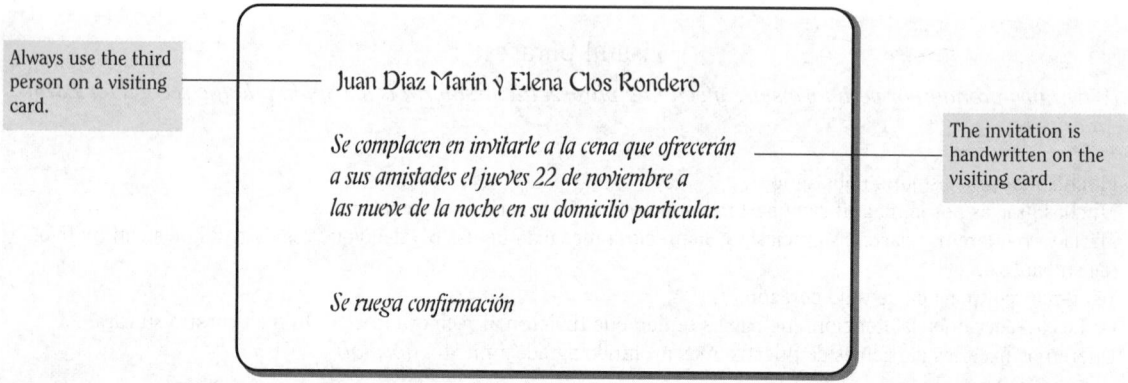

Always use the third person on a visiting card.

Juan Díaz Marín y Elena Clos Rondero

Se complacen en invitarle a la cena que ofrecerán a sus amistades el jueves 22 de noviembre a las nueve de la noche en su domicilio particular.

Se ruega confirmación

The invitation is handwritten on the visiting card.

Useful phrases:

Pedro Alvar Lope y señora tienen el honor de invitarle...
José Lacalle Millán y Adela Sanz Orozco agradecerán su asistencia a la cena que ofrecerán a sus amistades el próximo ...

Invitation card

These are usually made by a printer, who can suggest standard formulas.

Pedro Martín Codina y Marta Gómez Varela

Se complacen en invitarles a la ceremonia de bautizo de su hija

Ana

que tendrá lugar en la iglesia de la Concepción el próximo 14 de abril a las cinco de la tarde. Posteriormente se servirá una merienda en el restaurante Samoa.

Lima, marzo de 2004

Se ruega confirmación

Useful phrases:

Damos una fiesta el día 7 de mayo a partir de las nueve de la noche. ¡Contamos contigo!
La señorita Marisa Leal recibirá a sus amistades en la residencia particular de sus padres el 15 del presente mes, a partir de las diez de la noche. *(formal)*
Voy a ofrecer una cena con ocasión del aniversario de boda de mis padres y espero poder contar con su grata presencia. *(formal)*
Se ruega confirmar la asistencia. (R.S.V.P. *is also used in Latin America*)

▪ Wedding invitation

Álvaro Alonso Serra
Josefa Sala Guerra Tessier

Eduardo Gálvez Bas
Rosa Conesa Alpuente

For traditional weddings, the invitation is made by the parents of the couple.

tienen el gusto de comunicarles
el enlace matrimonial de sus hijos

Javier y Teresa

y se complacen en invitarles a la ceremonia religiosa que se celebrará el sábado 16 de junio a las siete de la tarde en la capilla de la Barrosa (Chiclana), así como a la cena que se servirá a continuación en el Hotel Fuentemar.

S.R.C.

Abbreviation for **Se ruega contestación.** (**R.S.V.P.** *is also used in Latin America)*

Francisco Liñán 16
Chiclana de la Frontera
Cádiz

Francesc Macià 8
Sabadell
Barcelona

The addresses of the couple's parents are given.

Useful phrases:

Las familias González-Martos y Badía-Sau tienen el placer de invitarles al enlace matrimonial de sus hijos Antonio y Celia el ... en la iglesia ...
Luis Nahum y Carla Onetti se complacen en invitarlos a su casamiento, que se celebrará el ... a las ... en la Oficina del Registro Civil de Punta Arenas. A continuación se servirá un aperitivo en ...

Declining an invitation

Replies to invitations need to be handwritten and sent as quickly as possible. If you are unable to accept the invitation, you need to give the reason.

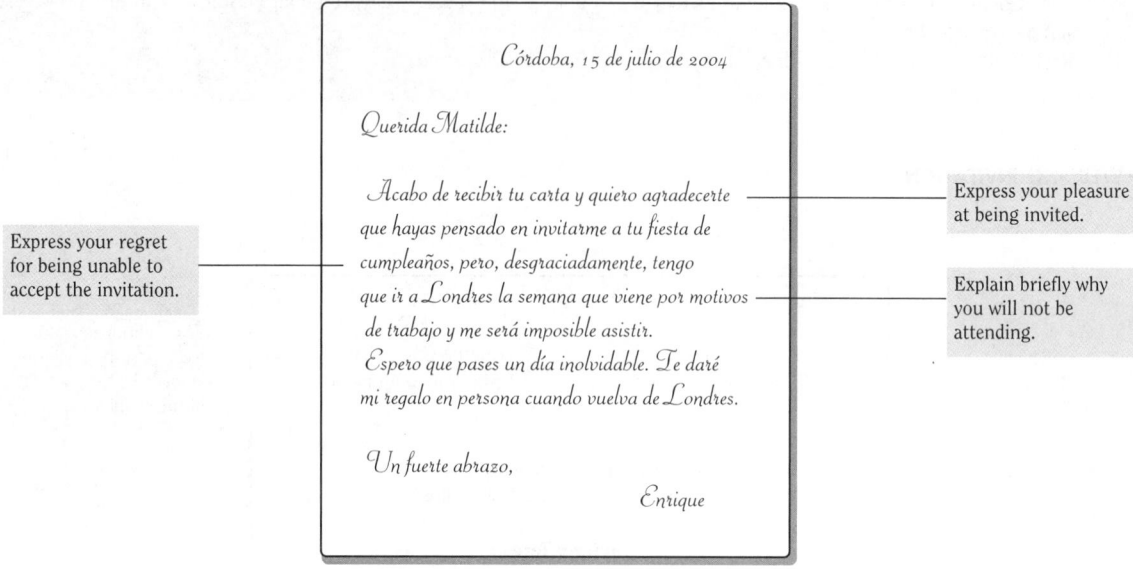

> Córdoba, 15 de julio de 2004
>
> Querida Matilde:
>
> Acabo de recibir tu carta y quiero agradecerte que hayas pensado en invitarme a tu fiesta de cumpleaños, pero, desgraciadamente, tengo que ir a Londres la semana que viene por motivos de trabajo y me será imposible asistir.
> Espero que pases un día inolvidable. Te daré mi regalo en persona cuando vuelva de Londres.
>
> Un fuerte abrazo,
>
> Enrique

Express your regret for being unable to accept the invitation.

Express your pleasure at being invited.

Explain briefly why you will not be attending.

Useful phrases:

(When two pronoun or verb forms are given in a phrase, the first form is for Spain and the second for Latin America)

Siento mucho no poder ir a tu fiesta, pero en esa misma fecha debo estar sin falta en Bogotá por asuntos de trabajo.
Me habría encantado ir a tu cena de despedida, pero desgraciadamente ya he aceptado/acepté una invitación anterior.
Sentimos no poder ir a vuestra/su fiesta y esperamos poder reunirnos con vosotros/ustedes en otra ocasión.
Lamento tener que declinar su amable invitación por tener de antemano un compromiso ineludible. *(formal)*

Accepting an invitation

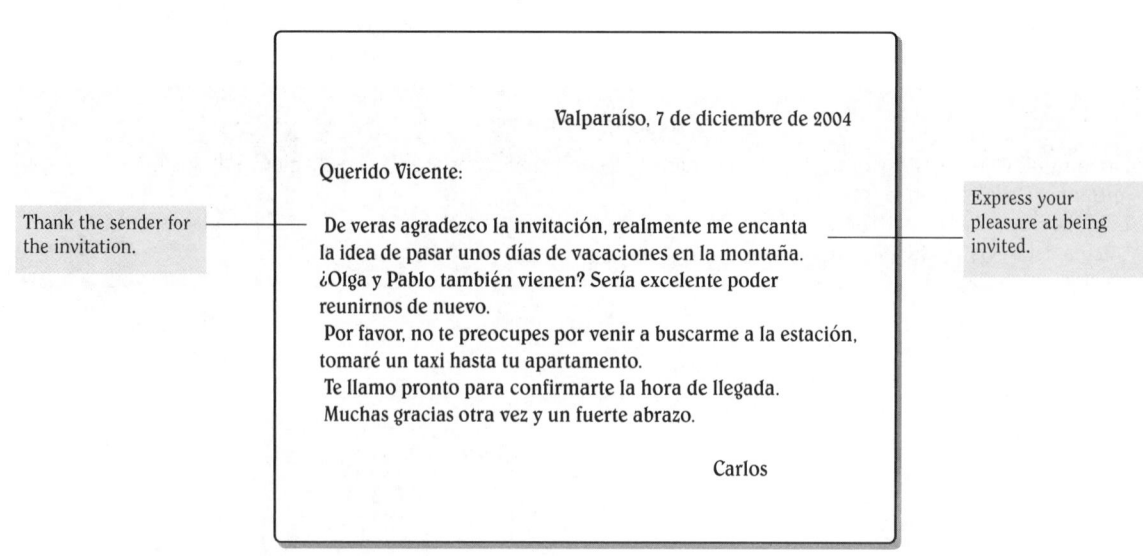

> Valparaíso, 7 de diciembre de 2004
>
> Querido Vicente:
>
> De veras agradezco la invitación, realmente me encanta la idea de pasar unos días de vacaciones en la montaña. ¿Olga y Pablo también vienen? Sería excelente poder reunirnos de nuevo.
> Por favor, no te preocupes por venir a buscarme a la estación, tomaré un taxi hasta tu apartamento.
> Te llamo pronto para confirmarte la hora de llegada.
> Muchas gracias otra vez y un fuerte abrazo.
>
> Carlos

Thank the sender for the invitation.

Express your pleasure at being invited.

Useful phrases:

(When two pronoun or verb forms are given in a phrase, the first form is for Spain and the second for Latin America)

Os/Les agradezco muchísimo que me hayáis/hayan invitado a vuestra/su casa de campo.
Aceptamos encantados vuestra/su invitación.
Tengo muchas ganas de volver a verte.
Agradecemos la invitación a la boda de Juan, a la que estaremos encantados de asistir.

Announcements

▪ Wedding announcement

In Spain and Latin America it is customary, when two people are about to be married, to send wedding announcements ("participaciones de boda") to relatives, friends and acquaintances, whereas only family and close friends receive an invitation. The invitation is usually enclosed with the announcement.

There is no need to include the date or place of the ceremony, as they are given in the invitation.

Wedding announcement sent by the couple themselves

Tenemos el gusto de participarles nuestro próximo enlace matrimonial, que se celebrará durante la primera quincena de junio en la iglesia parroquial de Villanueva.

Javier y Teresa

Wedding announcement sent by the parents of the couple

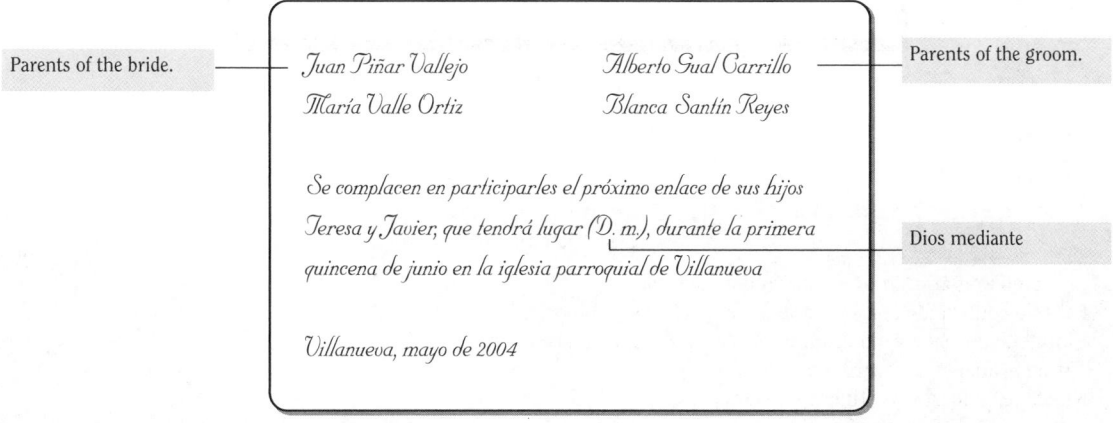

Parents of the bride. — *Juan Piñar Vallejo*
María Valle Ortiz

Alberto Gual Carrillo — Parents of the groom.
Blanca Santín Reyes

Se complacen en participarles el próximo enlace de sus hijos Teresa y Javier, que tendrá lugar (D. m.), durante la primera quincena de junio en la iglesia parroquial de Villanueva

(D. m.) — Dios mediante

Villanueva, mayo de 2004

Announcement of a birth

Dolores Vallejo Sahuquillo y Jeremías Reina Albesa

Se complacen en comunicarles el nacimiento de su hijo Gonzalo, que tuvo lugar el pasado 12 de abril.
Maracaibo, abril de 2004

Announcement of a death

An announcement of a death is usually written by a relative or colleague of the deceased.

Alfredo Cortezo Armengol
Ha fallecido cristianamente en Murcia el día 6 de agosto de 2004, a la edad de 87 años. Su esposa, sobrinos y familia comunican que el sepelio se celebrará hoy, día 8 de agosto, a las 10 horas, en la iglesia de San Francisco.

Emilia Muñoz Rivas
Falleció en Paysandú el 4 de marzo de 2004. Su esposo, hijos y familia invitan al entierro que tendrá lugar hoy, 6 de marzo, a las 9 horas en Cementerio Central.

Useful phrases:

Sus familiares ruegan una oración por su alma.
Falleció confortado con los Santos Sacramentos y la bendición apostólica.
El funeral por su eterno descanso se celebrará el ..., a las ..., en la iglesia ...
Tus compañeros te recordarán siempre.
Nunca te olvidaremos. Tu esposa y amigos.

Change of address

When people move to a new address, it is customary to send a visiting card to friends and acquaintances to inform them of the new address.

Esteban Rubio Pérez
Susana Fuentes García

Os ofrecemos nuestro nuevo domicilio
Paseo de la Ribera 34, 4º 1ª
Tel. (957) 41 96 18 *14004 Córdoba*

Handwritten on the visiting card.

Letter of condolence

There is no standard model for the expression of condolences, especially where friends and relatives are concerned. What matters most is to be sincere and to express your sympathy.

Monterrey, 3 de marzo del 2004

Querido Fernando:

Queremos expresarte nuestra tristeza por la muerte de tu padre. Sabemos que estaban muy unidos y podemos imaginar los difíciles momentos por los que estarás pasando. Todo el mundo apreciaba a Juan por su honestidad y su altruismo. Vamos a sentir enormemente su ausencia.
Si nos necesitas no dudes en decírnoslo, estamos a tu disposición.

Recibe un fuerte abrazo y todo nuestro cariño.

Antonio y Sofía

Express your support.

Name the person who died and, if you knew them, recall their qualities.

You can offer your help.

Useful phrases:

Te acompaño en el sentimiento.
Siento muchísimo la muerte de tu esposa.
Reciba mi más sentido pésame. *(formal)*
Deseo transmitirle mi sentimiento de profundo pesar. *(formal)*
Quiero expresarle mi más profundo dolor por tan sensible pérdida. *(formal)*
Le expreso mis más sinceras condolencias en estos difíciles momentos. *(formal)*

Asking for a brochure/information

When asking for information, specify all your requirements in order to receive the relevant documentation.

William Browston
29 Bletchley Road
Worthing
West Sussex
BN14 7QY

Oficina de Turismo
Plaza Porticada, 4
39001 Santander

Worthing, 4 de abril de 2004

Estimados señores:

Voy a pasar mis vacaciones (del 1 al 15 de julio) en Cantabria y quisiera pedirles que me envíen una lista de hoteles y pensiones de Santander o de cualquier localidad cercana.

Asimismo, les agredecería que me enviaran información sobre actividades culturales que puedan realizarse en la zona durante estas fechas.

Les doy las gracias de antemano por su atención.

En espera de su respuesta, les saluda atentamente,

William Browston

Useful phrases:

Le agredecería que me informara sobre ...
¿Podrían indicarme qué edificios de Gaudí están abiertos al público?
¿Serían tan amables de enviarme la lista de cámpings de esta región?
Muchas gracias por su amabilidad.

Business correspondence

Business to business (general)

Business correspondence in Spanish has become somewhat less formal in style under the influence of the English language.

ADEC CONSULTORES
Riera, 43
08301 Mataró
Barcelona

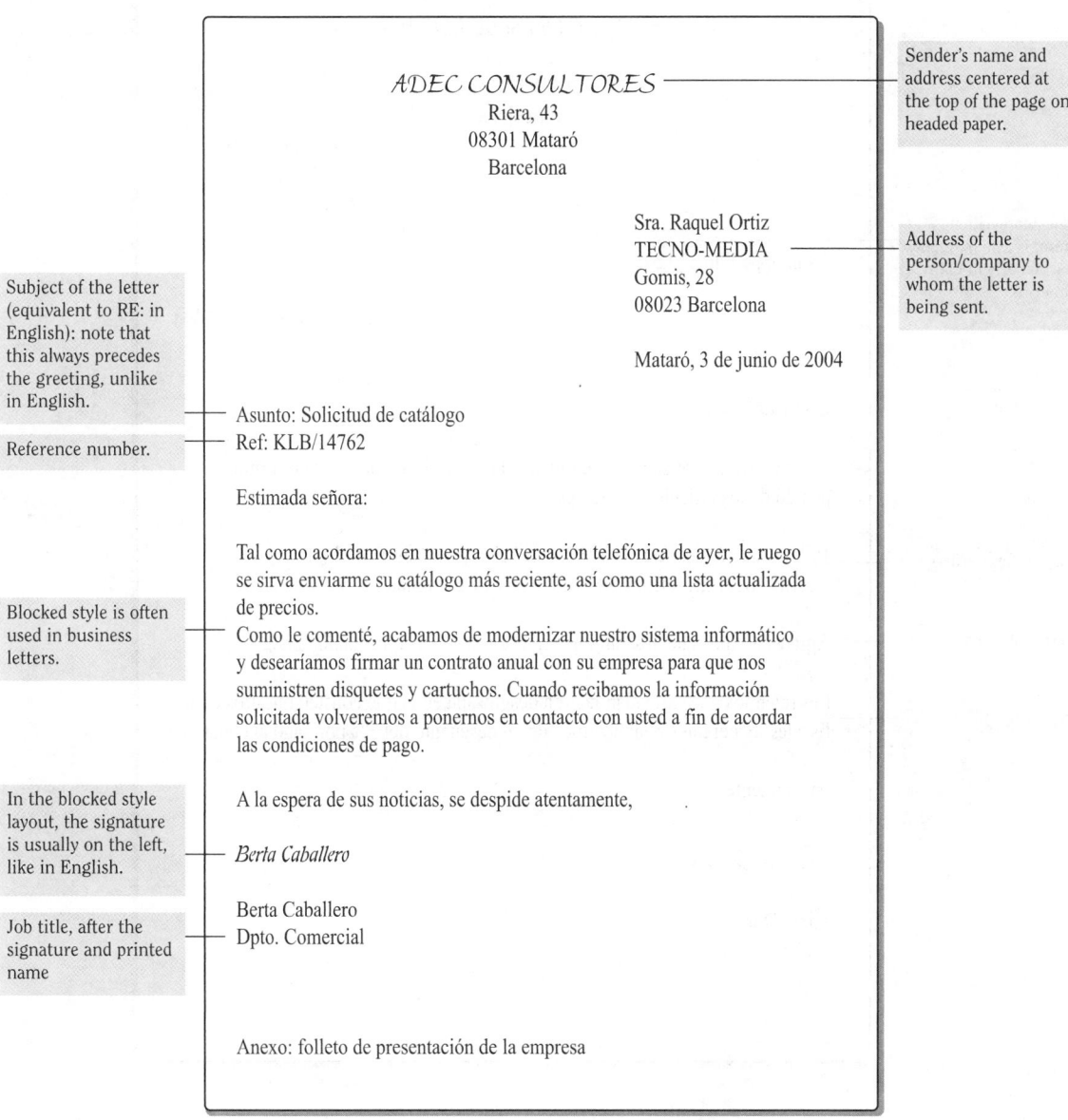

Sender's name and address centered at the top of the page on headed paper.

Sra. Raquel Ortiz
TECNO-MEDIA
Gomis, 28
08023 Barcelona

Address of the person/company to whom the letter is being sent.

Mataró, 3 de junio de 2004

Subject of the letter (equivalent to RE: in English): note that this always precedes the greeting, unlike in English.

Asunto: Solicitud de catálogo
Ref: KLB/14762

Reference number.

Estimada señora:

Blocked style is often used in business letters.

Tal como acordamos en nuestra conversación telefónica de ayer, le ruego se sirva enviarme su catálogo más reciente, así como una lista actualizada de precios.
Como le comenté, acabamos de modernizar nuestro sistema informático y desearíamos firmar un contrato anual con su empresa para que nos suministren disquetes y cartuchos. Cuando recibamos la información solicitada volveremos a ponernos en contacto con usted a fin de acordar las condiciones de pago.

A la espera de sus noticias, se despide atentamente,

In the blocked style layout, the signature is usually on the left, like in English.

Berta Caballero

Berta Caballero
Dpto. Comercial

Job title, after the signature and printed name

Anexo: folleto de presentación de la empresa

Useful phrases:

En respuesta a su carta del ...
Acusamos recibo de su carta del ...
Le agradecemos su interés y quedamos a su entera disposición.

Placing an order

The letter placing an order needs to specify the items required, as well as the conditions of delivery and payment.

ADEC CONSULTORES
Riera, 43
08301 Mataró
Barcelona

Sra. Dña. Raquel Ortiz
TECNO-MEDIA
Gomis, 28
08023 Barcelona

Asunto: pedido n° 12035

> The abbreviation **núm.** is also frequent, particularly in Latin America.

Mataró, 19 de junio de 2004

Estimada señora:

Tras nuestra conversación telefónica del pasado 17 de junio, le confirmo el pedido de los artículos siguientes:

> List of items ordered.

10 lotes de 20 disquetes DD/HD, ref. 12345, 18 € sin IVA el lote
2 cartuchos IBM, ref. 12698, 33,35 € sin IVA la unidad

> Terms of delivery.

Agradeceremos que nos suministren estos artículos quincenalmente.

> Payment terms.

Les rogamos que extiendan factura desglosada en la que consten nuestros datos fiscales. Esperamos beneficiarnos de un descuento del 5% por pago al contado.

Atentamente,

Jaime Durán

Jaime Durán
Jefe de Compras

Useful phrases:

Rogamos (que) nos envíen los artículos siguientes ...
Les remitimos el pedido n°...
Agradeceremos que se sirvan anotar el siguiente pedido ...

Informing a customer

TECNO-MEDIA
Gomis, 28
08023 Barcelona
http:\\www.tecnomedia.com

Barcelona, 10 de junio de 2004

Señor:

Tenemos el placer de informarle que a partir de este mes puede consultar nuestro catálogo y realizar su pedido directamente desde nuestro sitio Web.

La seguridad de nuestro sitio web está garantizada. Si desea beneficiarse de nuestros servicios en línea, bastará con que se registre en la siguiente dirección:

http:\\www.tecnomedia.com

Esperamos que este nuevo servicio sea de su entera satisfacción.

Le saluda atentamente,

Alicia Cabezas

Alicia Cabezas
Responsable del sitio web

Useful phrases:

Le informamos de que ...
Queremos anunciarle que ...
Quedamos a su entera disposición para cualquier consulta que desee hacernos.
Le rogamos (que) tome nota de nuestra nueva dirección.
La tienda abrirá sus puertas el ... en nuestra nueva dirección.

Dealing with a customer complaint

When replying to a customer complaint, it is necessary to give an explanation of what happened. If the complaint is justified, the company must apologize and offer a solution.

EXPORT S.A.
Av. de Mayo 500, piso 6
C1042AAB Buenos Aires

Buenos Aires, 7 de noviembre de 2004

Señor:

Reference to letter of complaint.

Acusamos recibo de su atenta carta del pasado 29 de octubre, en la que nos reclama que el pedido núm. 2983 no le ha llegado completo. Tras realizar las averiguaciones oportunas, podemos confirmar que se embarcó toda la mercancía tal como certifica nuestro agente en Corrientes, quien supervisó personalmente el embarque.

Explanation of cause of problem.

En consecuencia, lamentamos comunicarle que no podemos hacernos responsables de la pérdida. Probablemente se deba a un robo efectuado durante el almacenaje tras el desembarque, por lo que le aconsejamos que se ponga en contacto con su asegurador.

Sin otro particular, se despide atentamente,

Cristina Duarte

Cristina Duarte
Directora de Ventas

Useful phrases:

Lamentamos sinceramente este error.
Le rogamos disculpe las molestias que le hayamos podido ocasionar.
Le reiteramos nuestra más sincera disculpa y quedamos a su entera disposición.
Hemos tomado medidas para que no vuelva a producirse tan lamentable situación.
Esperamos solucionar cuanto antes este contratiempo.

Invoice

A company is free to choose the layout of its invoices, provided all the essential information is included.

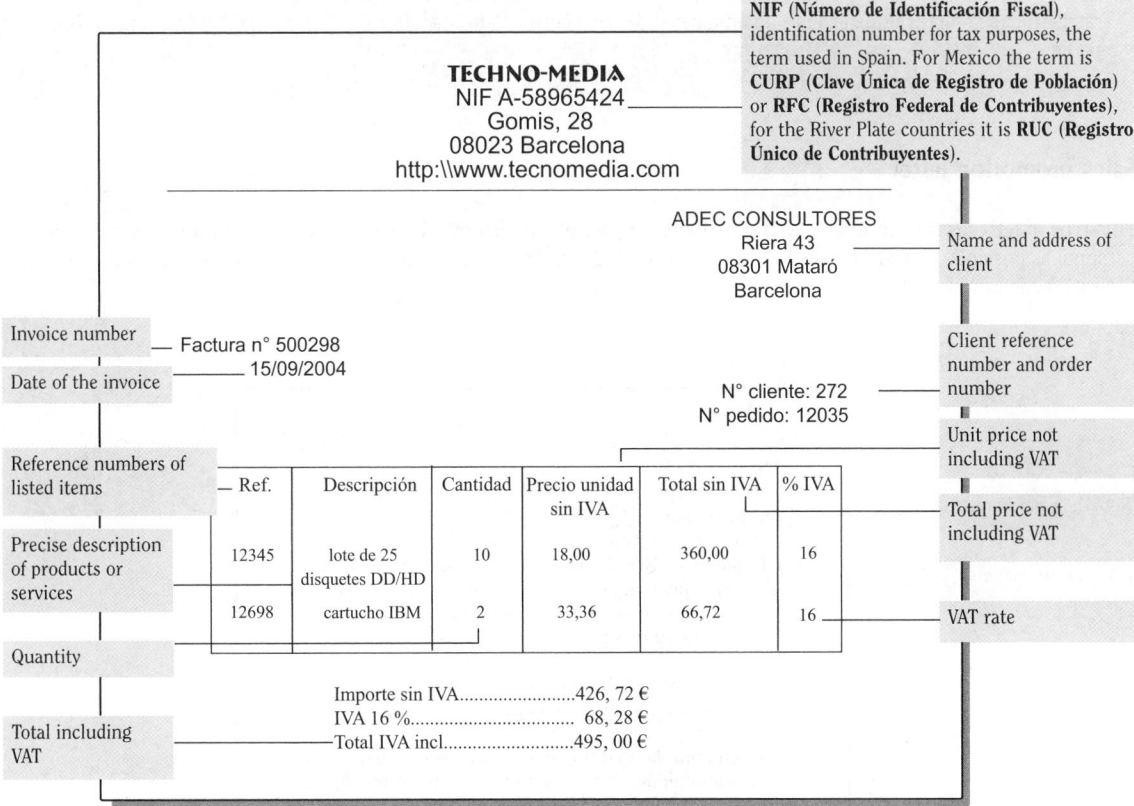

TECHNO-MEDIA
NIF A-58965424
Gomis, 28
08023 Barcelona
http:\\www.tecnomedia.com

NIF (Número de Identificación Fiscal), identification number for tax purposes, the term used in Spain. For Mexico the term is **CURP (Clave Única de Registro de Población)** or **RFC (Registro Federal de Contribuyentes)**, for the River Plate countries it is **RUC (Registro Único de Contribuyentes)**.

ADEC CONSULTORES
Riera 43
08301 Mataró
Barcelona

Name and address of client

Invoice number — Factura n° 500298

Date of the invoice — 15/09/2004

N° cliente: 272
N° pedido: 12035

Client reference number and order number

Ref.	Descripción	Cantidad	Precio unidad sin IVA	Total sin IVA	% IVA
12345	lote de 25 disquetes DD/HD	10	18,00	360,00	16
12698	cartucho IBM	2	33,36	66,72	16

Reference numbers of listed items — Ref.

Precise description of products or services — Descripción

Quantity — Cantidad

Unit price not including VAT — Precio unidad sin IVA

Total price not including VAT — Total sin IVA

VAT rate — % IVA

Importe sin IVA........................426, 72 €
IVA 16 %................................. 68, 28 €
Total IVA incl...........................495, 00 €

Total including VAT — Total IVA incl.

Reply to invoice

You only need to reply to an invoice if you are contesting it.

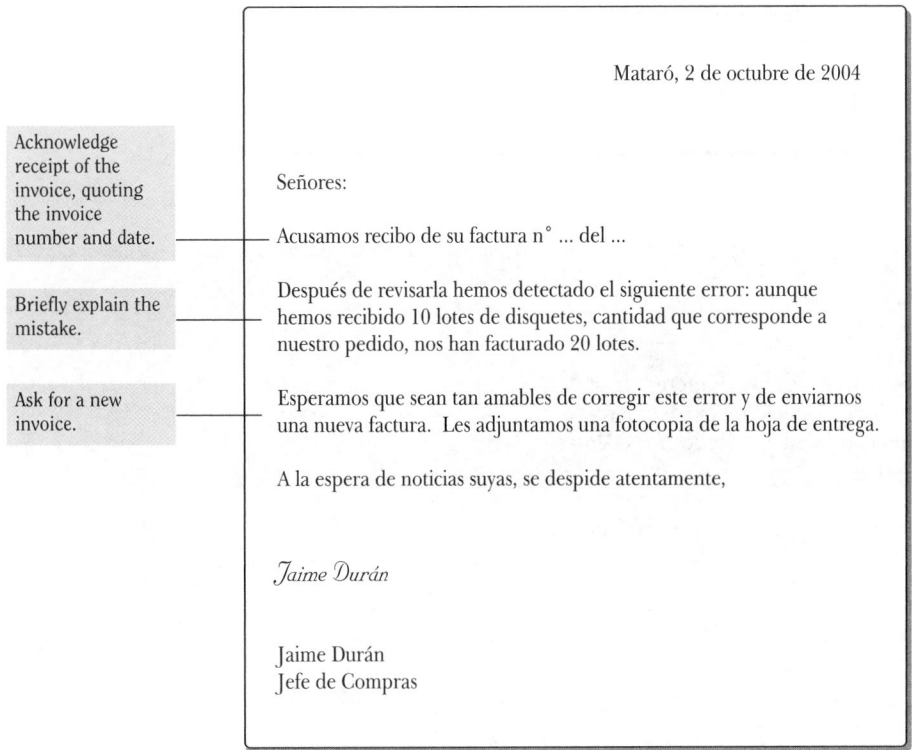

Mataró, 2 de octubre de 2004

Señores:

Acusamos recibo de su factura n° ... del ...

Después de revisarla hemos detectado el siguiente error: aunque hemos recibido 10 lotes de disquetes, cantidad que corresponde a nuestro pedido, nos han facturado 20 lotes.

Esperamos que sean tan amables de corregir este error y de enviarnos una nueva factura. Les adjuntamos una fotocopia de la hoja de entrega.

A la espera de noticias suyas, se despide atentamente,

Jaime Durán

Jaime Durán
Jefe de Compras

Acknowledge receipt of the invoice, quoting the invoice number and date. — Acusamos recibo de su factura n° ... del ...

Briefly explain the mistake. — Después de revisarla hemos detectado el siguiente error...

Ask for a new invoice. — Esperamos que sean tan amables de corregir este error y de enviarnos una nueva factura...

Useful phrases:

Acusamos recibo de su factura n° ...
Revisada la mercancía, hemos descubierto que cinco piezas presentaban desperfectos.
Tras verificar la factura que acaban de enviarnos, hemos constatado que su importe no corresponde a nuestro pedido.

Sales promotion letter

This type of letter is sent to many potential clients as part of a mailshot. The style is very direct and tries to sound as personal as possible. In addition to the standard greetings, various other greetings might be used: Apreciado cliente, Estimado consumidor, etc.

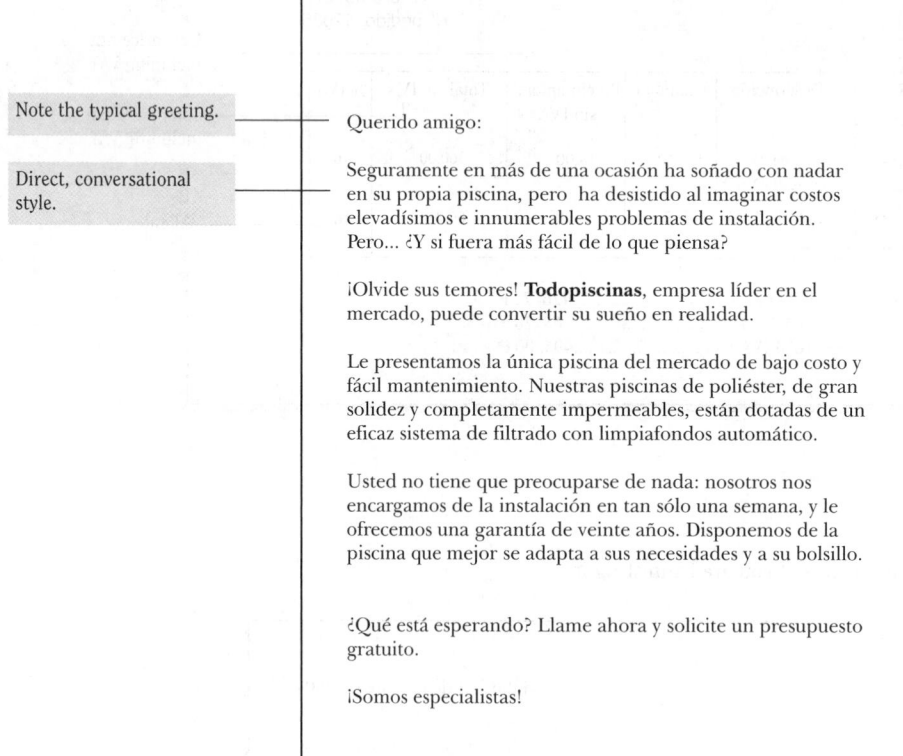

Note the typical greeting.

Direct, conversational style.

Querido amigo:

Seguramente en más de una ocasión ha soñado con nadar en su propia piscina, pero ha desistido al imaginar costos elevadísimos e innumerables problemas de instalación. Pero... ¿Y si fuera más fácil de lo que piensa?

¡Olvide sus temores! **Todopiscinas**, empresa líder en el mercado, puede convertir su sueño en realidad.

Le presentamos la única piscina del mercado de bajo costo y fácil mantenimiento. Nuestras piscinas de poliéster, de gran solidez y completamente impermeables, están dotadas de un eficaz sistema de filtrado con limpiafondos automático.

Usted no tiene que preocuparse de nada: nosotros nos encargamos de la instalación en tan sólo una semana, y le ofrecemos una garantía de veinte años. Disponemos de la piscina que mejor se adapta a sus necesidades y a su bolsillo.

¿Qué está esperando? Llame ahora y solicite un presupuesto gratuito.

¡Somos especialistas!

Useful phrases:

Estamos seguros de que ...
Nos complace anunciarles que ...
Esperamos que esta información sea de su interés.
Le ofrecemos la mejor relación calidad-precio del mercado.
Esperamos contar pronto con usted entre nuestros clientes.

Employment

Cover letter

A cover letter ("carta de presentación") is quite formal in its presentation. It should be printed or typed unless the employer specifically asks that it be handwritten. (Some Spanish companies use the services of a graphologist to analyse applicants' handwriting.) The letter should be concise, properly structured in paragraphs and have the standard opening and closing formulas. You should cover the following points:

- Point out what you consider important in your CV
- Add information about your goals and aspirations
- Explain why you are interested in the company
- Convince the reader that you are the right person for the job

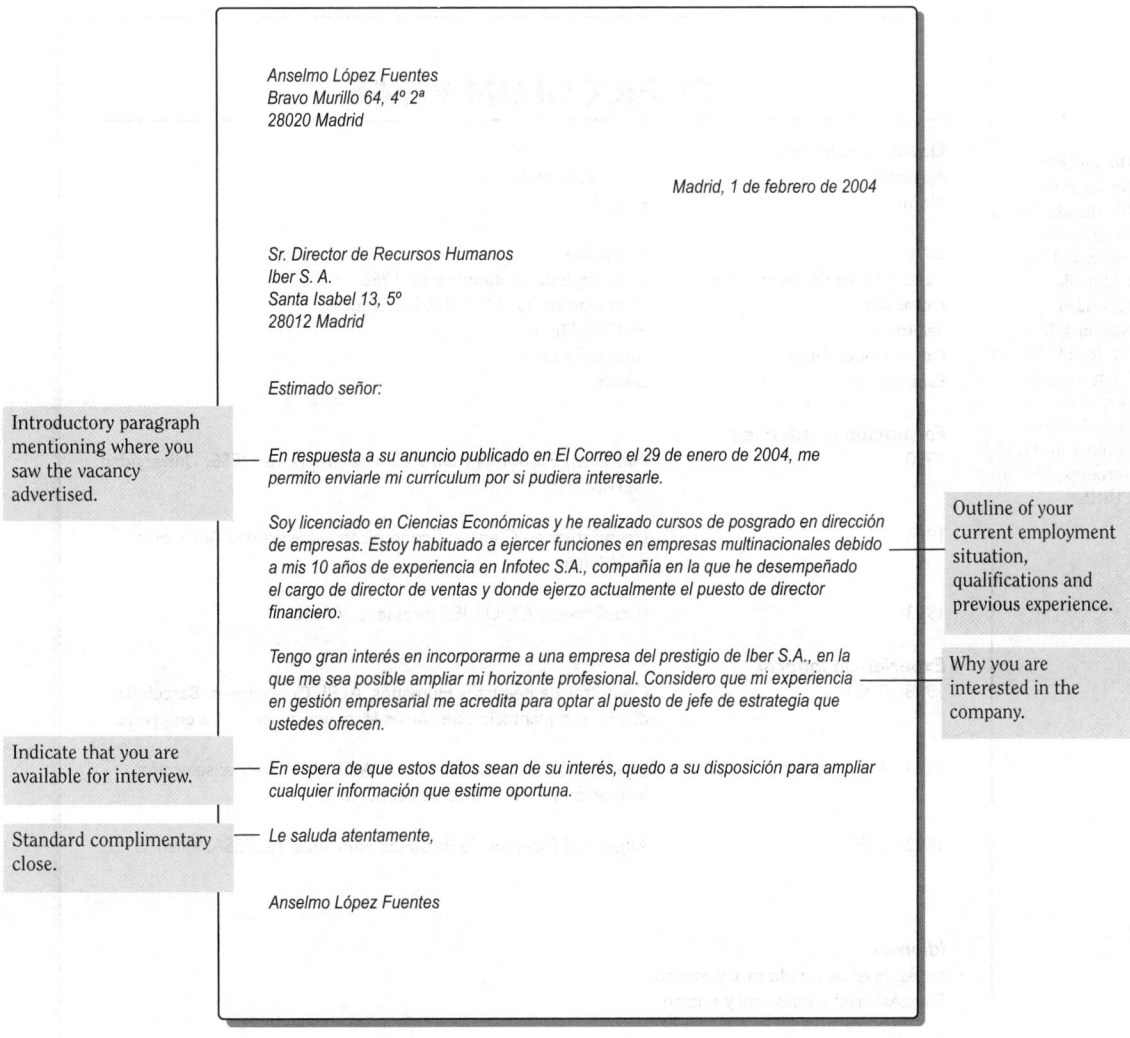

Anselmo López Fuentes
Bravo Murillo 64, 4º 2ª
28020 Madrid

Madrid, 1 de febrero de 2004

Sr. Director de Recursos Humanos
Iber S. A.
Santa Isabel 13, 5º
28012 Madrid

Estimado señor:

Introductory paragraph mentioning where you saw the vacancy advertised.

En respuesta a su anuncio publicado en El Correo el 29 de enero de 2004, me permito enviarle mi currículum por si pudiera interesarle.

Outline of your current employment situation, qualifications and previous experience.

Soy licenciado en Ciencias Económicas y he realizado cursos de posgrado en dirección de empresas. Estoy habituado a ejercer funciones en empresas multinacionales debido a mis 10 años de experiencia en Infotec S.A., compañía en la que he desempeñado el cargo de director de ventas y donde ejerzo actualmente el puesto de director financiero.

Why you are interested in the company.

Tengo gran interés en incorporarme a una empresa del prestigio de Iber S.A., en la que me sea posible ampliar mi horizonte profesional. Considero que mi experiencia en gestión empresarial me acredita para optar al puesto de jefe de estrategia que ustedes ofrecen.

Indicate that you are available for interview.

En espera de que estos datos sean de su interés, quedo a su disposición para ampliar cualquier información que estime oportuna.

Standard complimentary close.

Le saluda atentamente,

Anselmo López Fuentes

Useful phrases:

Me dirijo a ustedes para solicitar el puesto de secretaria anunciado en *El Correo de Quito* el ...
Cuento con varios años de experiencia en una empresa con sucursales en todo el territorio nacional.
A lo largo de mis cinco años de experiencia en la empresa X, he adquirido sólidos conocimientos de ...
A la espera de que mi candidatura sea de su interés, reciba un cordial saludo de ...
Quedo a la espera de su atenta respuesta a fin de concertar una entrevista personal.

Curriculum vitae

The presentation of a CV in Spanish is in many ways similar to a British CV or American résumé. The following differences should be respected:

- Only mention hobbies if they add something personal to your profile or if they are particularly relevant to the job. It is assumed that everybody likes reading, going to the cinema, listening to music and travelling.
- Do not include referees on your CV: references are not commonly used in Spain and Latin America except for certain occupations where personal recommendation would be expected, such as catering, cleaning, child care, construction, etc.

▪ **EXPERIENCED (SPANISH)**

CURRÍCULUM VITAE

Datos personales

Apellidos	Marín Rebolledo
Nombre	Rodolfo
DNI	46481603
Lugar y fecha de nacimiento	Valencia, 5 de septiembre de 1966
Domicilio	Campoamor 25, 4° 1ª, 46022 Valencia
Teléfono	963 572736
Correo electrónico	rmarin@ya.com
Estado civil	casado

Documento Nacional de Identidad. In Latin America the equivalent is **Cédula de Identidad Nacional**. In Mexican CVs you'll often see the personal identification number for tax purposes, **RFC** or **CURP**.

Formación académica

1990	Máster en Economía y Dirección de Empresas - IESE, Universidad de Navarra
1988	Licenciatura en Ciencias Económicas - Universidad Autónoma de Valencia
1983	Bachillerato y COU - IES Picassent, Valencia.

Experiencia laboral

1998 - 2003	Consultor de Recursos Humanos, ALPE Consultores, Barcelona: diseño e implantación de planes formativos, asesoría a empresas
1994 - 1997	Director de Recursos Humanos, ACTESA, Valencia: selección, formación y administración del personal
1992 - 1993	Adjunto al Director de Recursos Humanos, ACTESA, Valencia

Idiomas

Inglés: nivel avanzado oral y escrito
Francés: nivel medio oral y escrito

Otros datos de interés

Conocimientos a nivel de usuario de Microsoft Office
Disponibilidad para viajar

CURRÍCULUM VITAE

DATOS PERSONALES

Nombre y apellidos	Jill Farmer
Lugar y fecha de nacimiento	Boston, 17 de junio de 1962
Nacionalidad	estadounidense
Estado civil	soltera
Domicilio	Bolívar 134, Caracas
Teléfono	(02) 551.63.60
Correo electrónico	jfarmer@inicia.ve

If you are not Spanish, specify your nationality.

FORMACIÓN ACADÉMICA

1988	MBA, Harvard Business School
1984	MS (equivalente a maestría) en Economía y Gestión, Universidad de Boston
1980	High school diploma (equivalente a bachillerato superior)

EXPERIENCIA LABORAL

Desde 1996 — **ACT Venezolana S.A., Caracas**
Dirección Corporativa Adjunta al Consejero Delegado
· Diseño de estrategias comerciales
· Diversificación y desarrollo de los mercados existentes
· Apertura de 3 nuevos mercados (Francia, Italia, Grecia)
· Mejora de objetivos entre 80 y 120%

1988-1996 — **ICN Europa, Amsterdam**
Directora Comercial
· Responsable de la política comercial
· Selección y dirección de un equipo de 25 personas
· Definición de objetivos comerciales
· Captación de inversiones

1983-1987 — **ENSA Tecnología Química, Madrid**
Responsable de ventas
· Seguimiento y apoyo de tareas comerciales
· Apertura de nuevas cuentas
· Coordinación de un equipo de 6 personas

IDIOMAS

Inglés: lengua materna
Español: bilingüe
Francés: nociones

▪ EXPERIENCED (BRITISH)

Mary Grant

198 Francis Avenue
Leicester LE4 9PQ
Gran Bretaña
Tel : 00 44 1493 767 33 36
e-mail: mgrant@USA.net

32 años, soltera
Nacionalidad británica

ESTUDIOS REALIZADOS

1989 - 1993	MA (equivalente a licenciatura) en Gestión, Universidad de Edimburgo.
1989	A Levels (equivalente a bachillerato superior): economía, matemáticas, historia y francés (Instituto Harfield Comprehensive, Leicester).

EXPERIENCIA LABORAL

Desde septiembre de 1997	Directora de exportaciones, Gannett UK Ltd, Leicester (fabricación y distribución de productos cosméticos) * seguimiento y control de 40 representantes y 10 agentes * negociación con los puntos de venta * estudios de mercado
1994 - 1997	Responsable de exportaciones en Europa, Simon & Co plc, Leicester (confección de prendas deportivas) * captación de clientes * control de ventas * apertura de dos nuevos mercados (Francia e Italia)

OTRAS ACTIVIDADES

1993 - 1994	Profesora de inglés (academia Brighton, León)

IDIOMAS

Inglés: lengua materna
Castellano: bilingüe (madre española)
Francés: nivel medio

INFORMÁTICA

Conocimientos a nivel de usuario, entorno Windows, Word, Excel y Access

IGNACIO MENÉNDEZ BRAVO

DATOS PERSONALES
Nacido el 7/1/80
Lugar: Puebla
Estado civil: soltero
Nacionalidad: mexicana

DIRECCIÓN ACTUAL
Paseo del Río 14
C.P. 71010 Puebla
Tel.: 01 (2) 434 55 21
imenendez@uni3.com

Formación

2002 – 2003	Maestría en Mercadotecnia Internacional (Programa All-America impartido por la CONCAMIN, Confederación de Cámaras Industriales de México)
1998 – 2002	Diplomado en Estudios Empresariales, Universidad Autónoma de Guadalajara
1994 – 1998	Bachillerato Instituto Ignacio Zaragoza

Experiencia profesional

enero – agosto 2004	CIES S.L., Puebla Coordinador comercial: preparación de ofertas y promociones, seguimiento de pedidos
octubre – diciembre 2003	Arco S.A., Polígono Industrial Malpica, Puebla Prácticas en el departamento de mercadotecnia: seguimiento de clientes y proveedores
julio – septiembre 2003	Vendedor en Electrodomésticos Torres, Puebla

Idiomas
Inglés: hablado y escrito
Francés: nivel medio

Formación complementaria

septiembre 2002	Curso de Gestión Económica Financiera (Cepyme)
julio – agosto 2000	Diploma de instructor de tiempo libre, EPAJ (Escuela Poblana de Actividades pata Jóvenes), Tehuacán
agosto 93 – junio 94	Curso académico en Inglaterra

▪ RECENT GRADUATE (AMERICAN)

Martha Jacobs
493 Huntington Avenue
Boston
MA 02575
Estados Unidos
Tel: (617) 267-1680
E-mail: mjacobs@totem.com

25 años, soltera
Nacionalidad estadounidense

Equivalent to **Summa Cum Laude**. For Spain, use **matrícula de honor**.

ESTUDIOS

2000–2002	Diploma de traductora técnica Universidad McGill, Montreal
1996–2000	BA (equivalente a licenciatura) en inglés y español, mención honorífica Universidad de Boston
1995	High school diploma (equivalente a bachillerato superior)

EXPERIENCIA PROFESIONAL

2001–2002	*Editorial Kendall,* Montreal Trabajos de traducción por cuenta propia
junio–septiembre 2000	*Sociedad AX Networks*, Boston Prácticas en el departamento de traducción: adaptación de programas de software para el mercado europeo
1995–1996	*Colegio A. Bello*, Lima Asistente de inglés

IDIOMAS

Inglés: lengua materna
Español: bilingüe (2 años en Lima)
Francés: nivel medio

CONOCIMIENTOS INFORMÁTICOS

Word, Excel, Powerpoint y Access

INTERESES

Alpinismo, violín

▪ Recent graduate (British)

Stephen Forbes
81 Lincoln Walk
Stevenage
Herts, SE19 2DN
Tel: 0044 1283 456789
e-mail: sforbes@teaser.org.uk

23 años, soltero
Nacionalidad británica

Formación

2000–2004	BSc (equivalente a licenciatura) en Biología, Universidad de Swansea, Gran Bretaña.
2000	A Levels (equivalente a bachillerato superior): Matemáticas, Química, Biología y Español, Instituto Whitton Comprehensive, Bristol, Gran Bretaña.

Experiencia profesional

julio–septiembre 2004	Prácticas laborales en el servicio de hematología del hospital Frenchay de Bristol: realización de hemogramas.
octubre 2004–noviembre 2005	Profesor de inglés, Academia de idiomas Babel, Osaka, Japón.

Idiomas

Inglés: lengua materna
Castellano: fluido
Portugués: nociones

Conocimientos complementarios

Dominio de Word, Excel y AS-400
Carné de conducir

The name of this document varies from country to country. **Licencia de manejo** is used in Mexico, for example, while **permiso de conductor** is used in the River Plate area.

Faxes

Faxes, which are by definition a form of rapid communication, can generally be drafted in a more casual and concise way than letters.

The endings of faxes are usually short and simplified.

Business

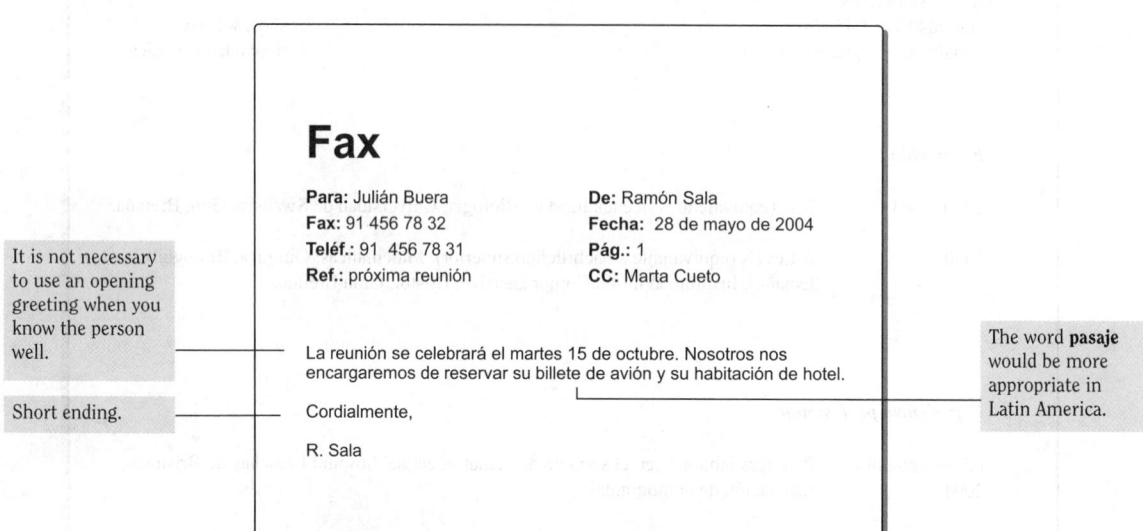

It is not necessary to use an opening greeting when you know the person well.

Short ending.

The word **pasaje** would be more appropriate in Latin America.

Fax

Para: Julián Buera
Fax: 91 456 78 32
Teléf.: 91 456 78 31
Ref.: próxima reunión

De: Ramón Sala
Fecha: 28 de mayo de 2004
Pág.: 1
CC: Marta Cueto

La reunión se celebrará el martes 15 de octubre. Nosotros nos encargaremos de reservar su billete de avión y su habitación de hotel.

Cordialmente,

R. Sala

Booking a hotel room

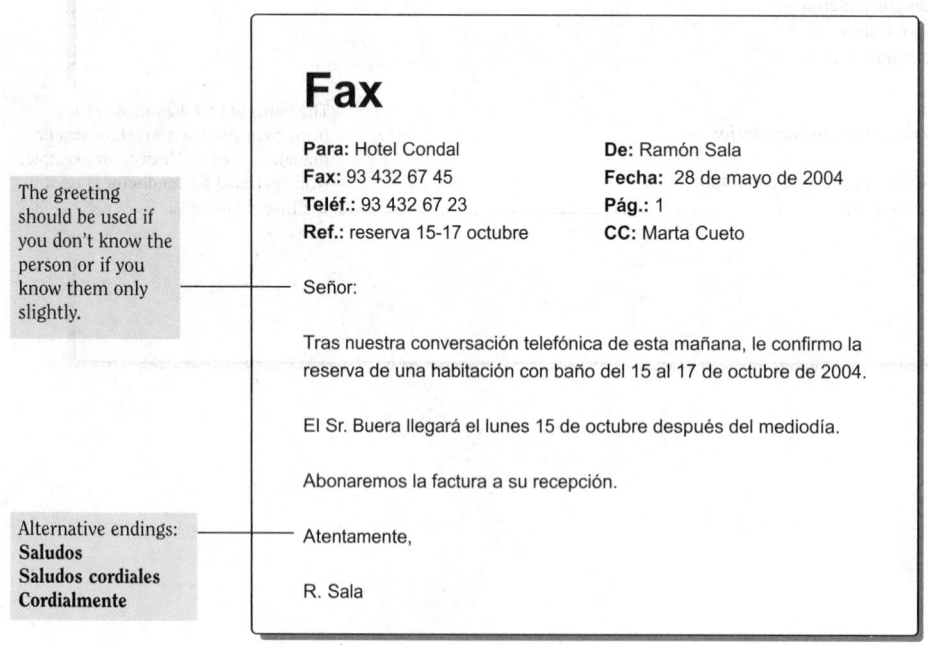

The greeting should be used if you don't know the person or if you know them only slightly.

Alternative endings:
Saludos
Saludos cordiales
Cordialmente

Fax

Para: Hotel Condal
Fax: 93 432 67 45
Teléf.: 93 432 67 23
Ref.: reserva 15-17 octubre

De: Ramón Sala
Fecha: 28 de mayo de 2004
Pág.: 1
CC: Marta Cueto

Señor:

Tras nuestra conversación telefónica de esta mañana, le confirmo la reserva de una habitación con baño del 15 al 17 de octubre de 2004.

El Sr. Buera llegará el lunes 15 de octubre después del mediodía.

Abonaremos la factura a su recepción.

Atentamente,

R. Sala

E-mail

- E-mail addresses are made up of two parts, the first being the user's name and the second being the domain name. The two parts are separated by the symbol @ (pronounced "arroba" in Spanish).
- E-mail is becoming more and more widely used in the working environment of the Spanish-speaking world, although it is probably not yet as well established a method of business correspondence as it is in the English-speaking world.
- E-mails in Spanish are often written in slightly less telegraphic style than tends to be the case in English, this being mainly due to the fact that Spanish contains fewer of the abbreviated forms that characterize so much of this type of communication in English. Endings are usually rather informal.
- The same rules of "netiquette" apply as in English, so avoid typing entire words in capital letters as this is equivalent to shouting.

To a friend

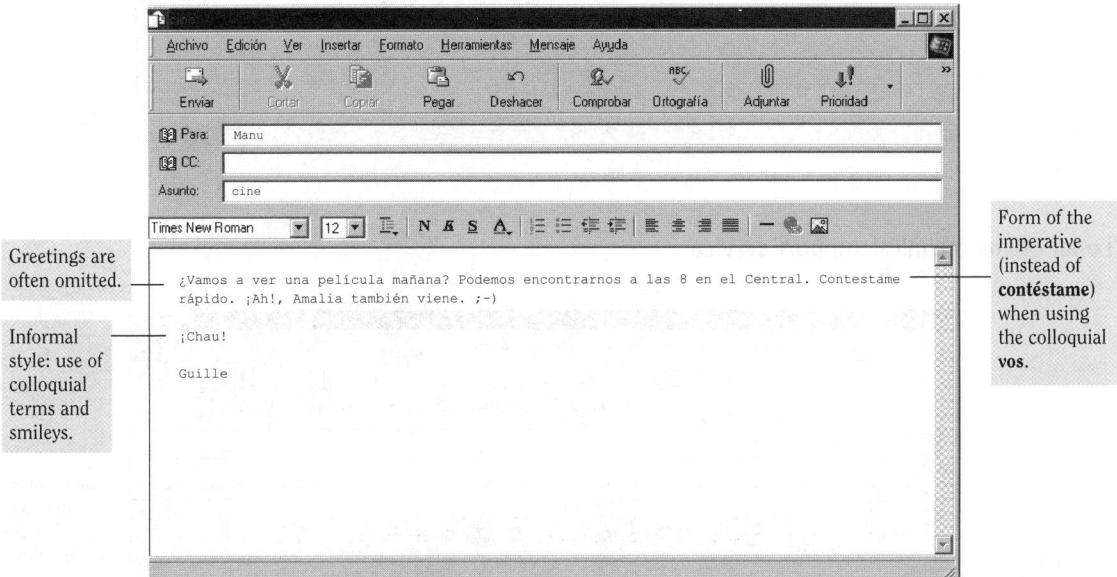

Greetings are often omitted.

Informal style: use of colloquial terms and smileys.

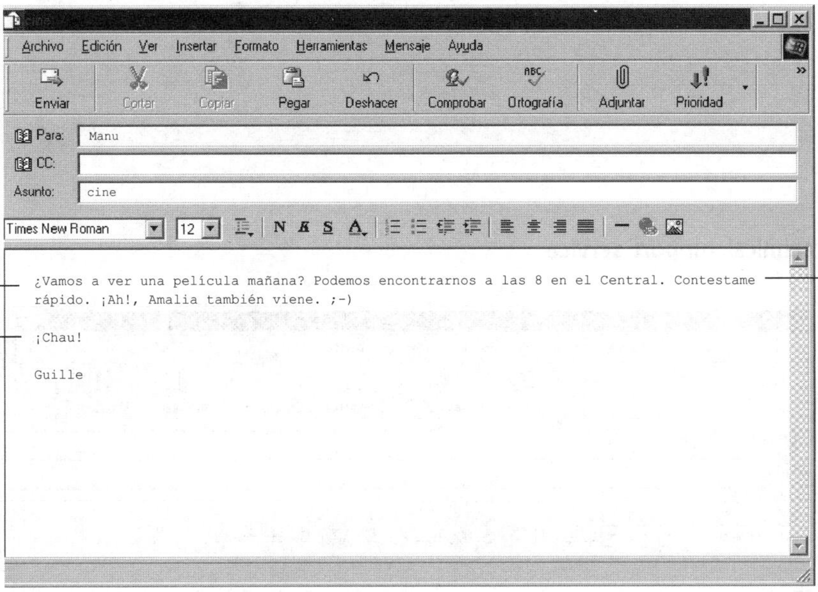

Form of the imperative (instead of **contéstame**) when using the colloquial **vos**.

To a business colleague

Informal greeting. It can also be omitted.

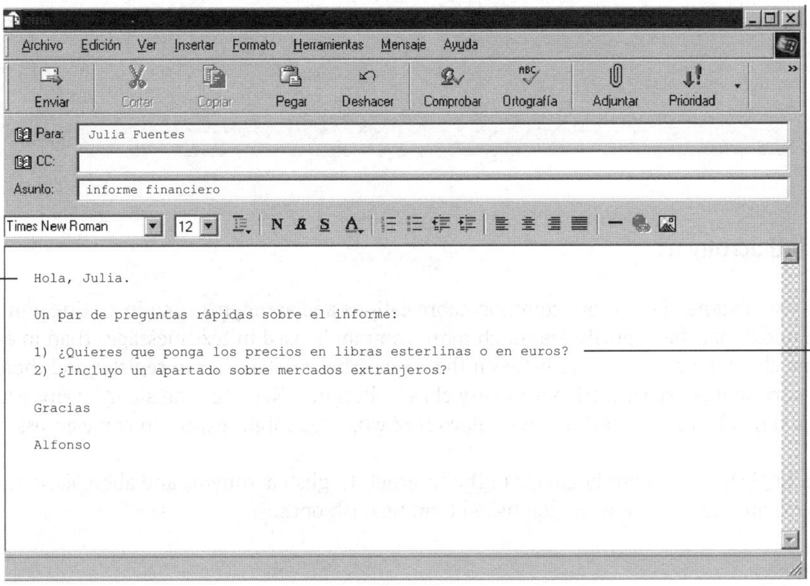

The message is brief and to the point.

Business to business

The style is almost as formal as in a letter.

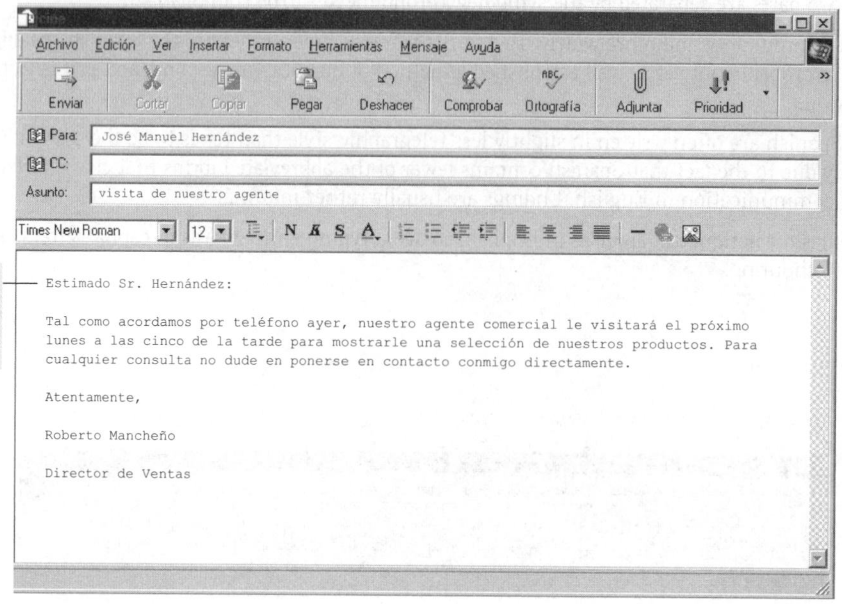

To an online technical support service

The problem is summarized clearly in the subject line.

Informal opening is preferred.

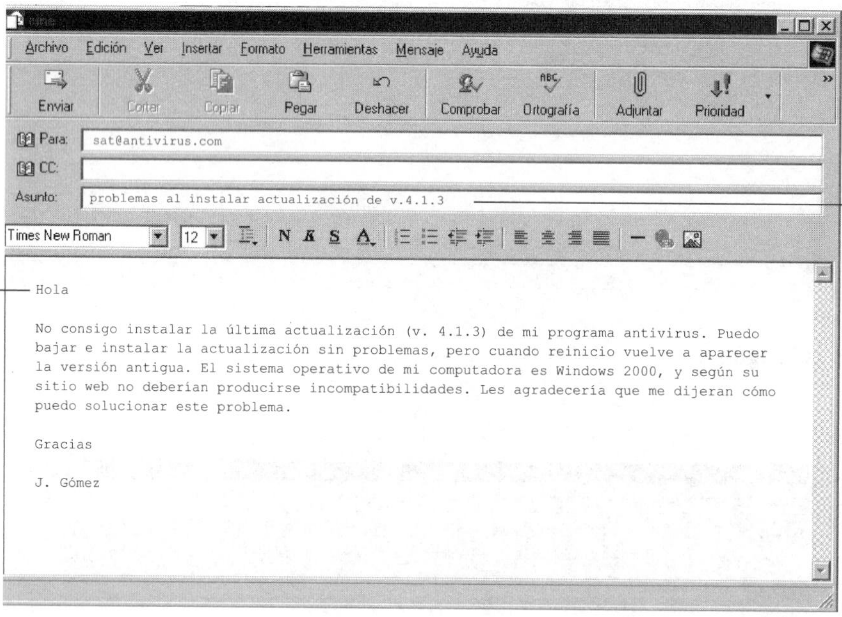

Abbreviations and acronyms

The following is a list of some of the more common abbreviations and acronyms used in texting, e-mails and online chat. It should be noted that the majority are much more commonly used in text messages than in e-mails, with their frequency in online chat falling somewhere between these two. They are familiar in register and therefore should only be used in casual correspondence with friends or very close colleagues. New "texting slang" terms are being invented all the time, so the terms listed only seek to give a flavour of what you might expect to come across.

Note that because English is the main language of the Internet, English acronyms and abbreviations (see section in English supplement) are much more well established than Spanish ones.

When writing text messages in Spanish, you should bear in mind the following basic rules:

- Accents are not used.
- Vowels are omitted from the most common words (e.g. "donde" becomes "dnd").
- The letter "h", which is not pronounced in Spanish, is always omitted (e.g. "hola" becomes "ola").
- The letter "ll" is replaced by "y" and "ch" is replaced by "x". Thus, for example, "botella" becomes "boteya" and "chica" becomes "xica".
- Question marks and exclamation marks are used in the same way as in English, i.e. they are only written at the end of a sentence, and not also at the beginning as in conventional written Spanish.

A2	adiós
bboo	besos
cnd	cuando, cuándo
dnd	donde, dónde
find	fin de semana
kdms	quedamos, quedemos
ke	que, qué
ktl?	¿qué tal?
LAP	lo antes posible
M1Ml	mándame un mensaje luego
mjr	mejor
mñn	mañana
muxo	mucho
q	que, qué
salu2	saludos
tb	también
tq	te quiero
x	por
xa	para
xdon	perdón
xq	porque, por qué

Smileys

Smileys, or emoticons, are a regular feature of casual e-mail correspondence. As with abbreviations, they are probably used more in English than in Spanish, but it is worth illustrating some of the most common ones here. It must be remembered of course that these symbols should only ever appear in the context of casual correspondence.

:-)	Happy; I'm making a joke
:-))	Very happy
:-D	Laughing out loud
:-(	Unhappy
:-((	Very unhappy
:'-(	Crying
:-((	Angry
:-C	Extremely unhappy
:-O	Very surprised; shocked
;-)	Winking
:-|	Frowning
|-)	Sleeping
:-¡	Smoking
:-	Sceptical
(-O	Yawning
:-*	Kiss

Advertisements

Many small ads are not abbreviated in Spanish-speaking countries, but those which are can seem rather cryptic if you are not familiar with the abbreviations and style used. Here are some examples that you could find in Spain and River Plate.

Accommodation to rent

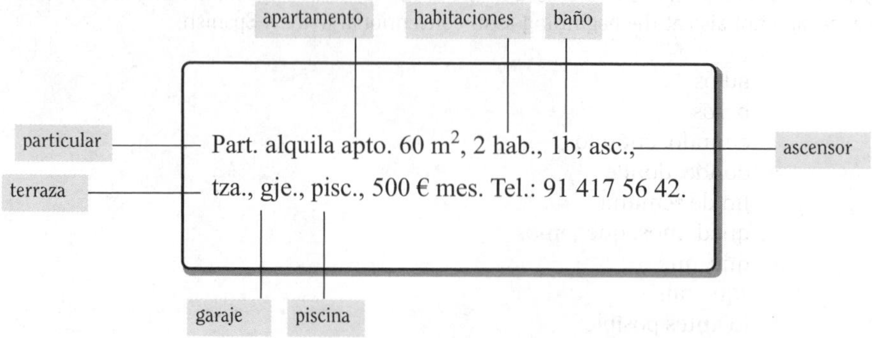

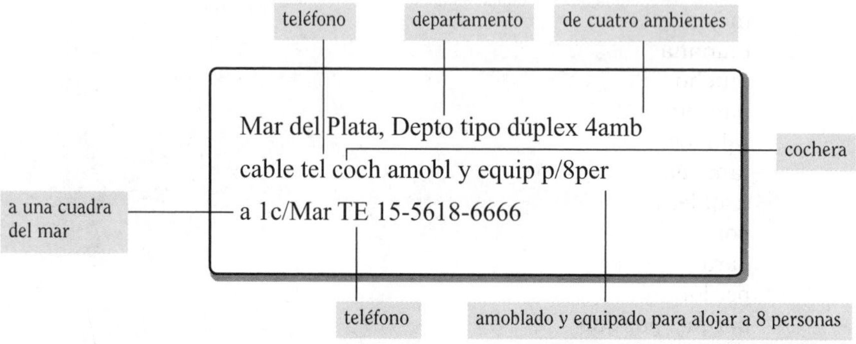

Offering goods for sale

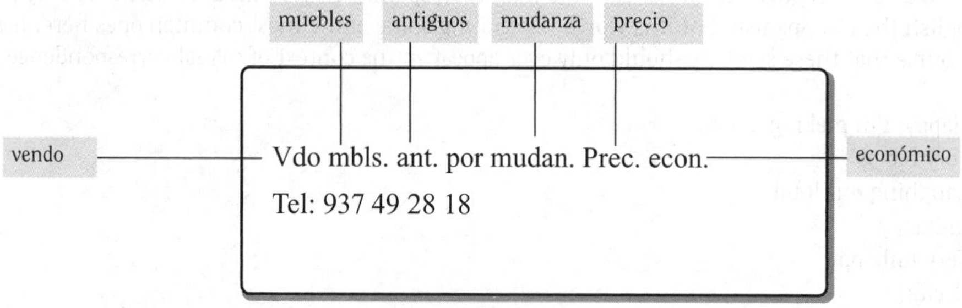

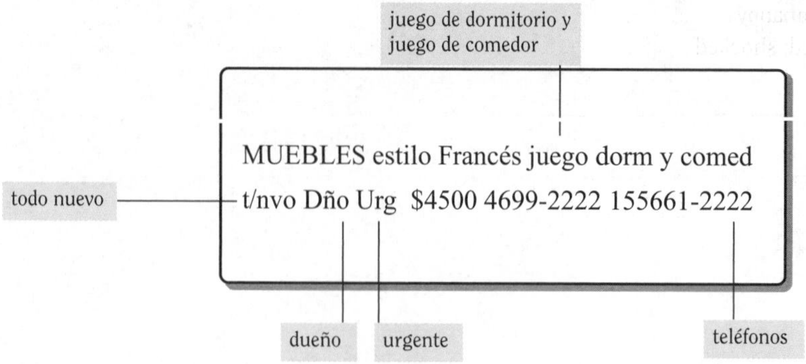

Personal advertisement

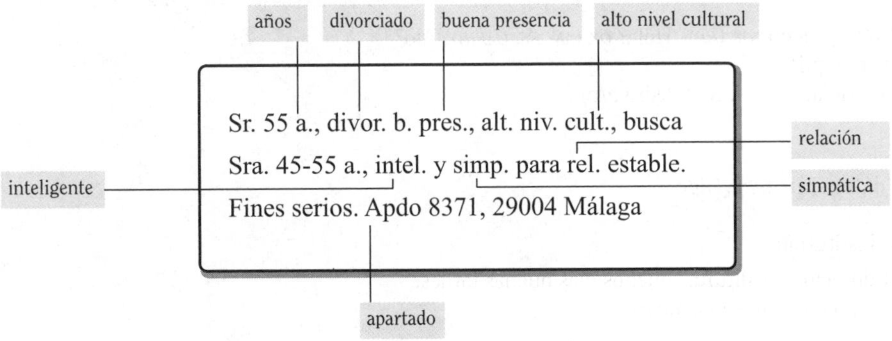

Job advertisement

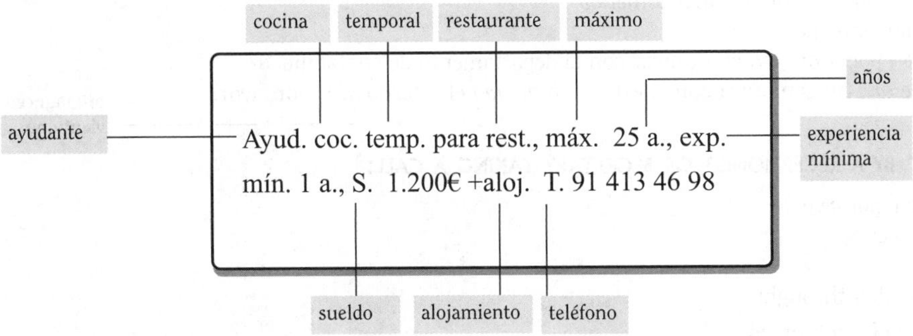

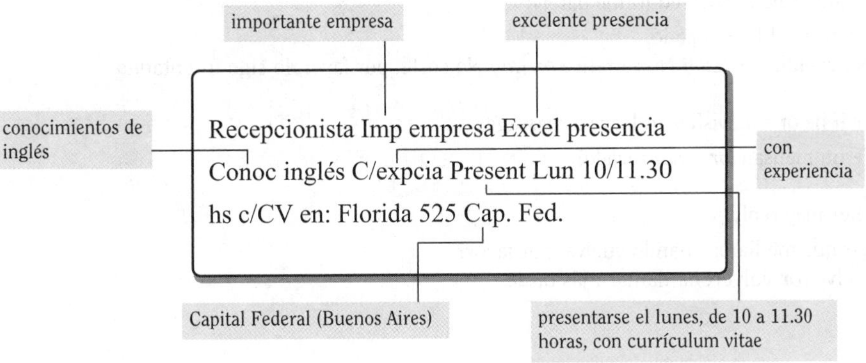

Telephone calls

Pronunciation of telephone numbers

When giving their telephone numbers, Spanish people either say the numbers one by one or, preferably, in pairs: 91 417 43 22: "noventa y uno, cuatro uno siete, cuatro tres, dos dos" or "noventa y uno cuatro diecisiete cuarenta y tres veintidós". This can be a little confusing and you may have to ask them to repeat, one number at a time.

Typical Phrases

▪ **Asking for information from the operator or switchboard:**

– ¿Me podría dar el número de los bomberos, por favor?
– ¿Me puede dar el número de Pablo Castillo Díaz, de Linares? No sé la calle.
– ¿Cuál es el prefijo *or* (*MÉX*) la clave de Italia, por favor?
– ¿Qué prefijo *or* (*MÉX*) clave tengo que marcar para llamar al extranjero *or* (*AM*) exterior?

▪ Answering the telephone:

Informally:
– (*ESP*) ¿Sí? *or* (*MÉX*) ¿Bueno? *or* (*RP*) ¿Hola? *or* (*ANDES, CARIB*) ¿Alo?
(To which the caller replies:
– ¿Está Miguel? *or* Hola, Miguel. Soy Pedro *etc*)

More formally:
– ¿Diga? *or* ¿Sí, dígame? *or* (*RP*) ¿Oigo?

In a company or institution:
– Ministerio de Educación y Cultura, ¿buenos días/buenas tardes?
– MC Traducciones, ¿en qué puedo ayudarle?

▪ Asking to speak to someone:

– Quisiera hablar con la señora Carmen Jiménez.
– ¿El señor Bustamante, por favor?
– ¿Me puede (*ESP*) poner *or* (*AM*) comunicar con el departamento de contabilidad?
– ¿Me (*ESP*) pone *or* (*AM*) comunica con la extensión *or* (*RP*) el interno 321, por favor?

pronounced **trescientos vientiuno**

▪ Phrases used by a receptionist or secretary taking a call:

– ¿Quién le llama, por favor?
– ¿De parte de quién?

When putting a caller through:
– Le paso *or* (*MÉX*) Lo comunico.
– No cuelgue *or* (*ESP*) No se retire *or* (*RP*) No corte.

When the caller cannot be connected immediately:
– *(ESP)* Comunica *or (AM)* Da ocupado.
– No contesta. No cuelgue *or (ESP)* No se retire *or (RP)* No corte, por favor, lo sigo intentando.

Asking the caller if he or she wishes to leave a message:
– ¿Quiere dejarle un mensaje *or (ESP)* recado?

To which the caller may reply:
– ¿Le podría decir que me llame cuando vuelva, por favor?
– No, gracias. Vuelvo *(or* volveré*)* a llamar más tarde.

▪ Recorded messages:

If you have to deal with the answering machine, the usual recorded message while waiting to get through is:

– Todas nuestras líneas están ocupadas en estos momentos. Por favor, espere *(or* siga a la espera*)* y en breve atenderemos su llamada.

If you have to leave a message, you will hear the following standard set of sentences:

– Ha llamado al número ... En estos momentos no podemos atender su llamada. Deje su nombre y su número de teléfono después de la señal y nos pondremos en contacto con usted lo antes posible. Gracias
– Este es el contestador de ... *or* (*MÉX*) Esta es la contestadora de... En estos momentos no estoy en casa. Por favor, deja *or* (*RP*) dejá tu mensaje después de la señal.
– Sergio Ruiz y María Aguirre. Deja *or* (*RP*) Dejá tu mensaje.

GUÍA DE COMUNICACIÓN EN INGLÉS

La correspondencia

La presentación de una carta ha de ser siempre esmerada, se trate de una carta comercial o personal. Cada país tiene sus propias pautas y códigos. Esta guía tiene la finalidad de facilitarle la redacción de una carta en inglés. En ella podrá encontrar consejos útiles sobre la disposición de cada parte, las fórmulas de introducción y de cortesía o el formato de la dirección, al igual que muchos modelos de cartas y sugerencias de expresiones que se pueden emplear en la correspondencia personal o comercial, el correo electrónico y los documentos enviados por fax.

Presentación de la carta

Hay dos tipos de presentación: la presentación tradicional, que está reservada a las cartas personales manuscritas y según la cual cada párrafo empieza con una sangría, y otra presentación más corriente, que se utiliza para todas las cartas mecanografiadas y según la cual los párrafos van alineados a la izquierda y separados entre sí por una línea en blanco (véanse los modelos y las notas siguientes).

▪ESTILO

La correspondencia administrativa o comercial, influida por el fax y el correo electrónico, obliga a utilizar un estilo directo y conciso. Se empleará preferiblemente un tono cordial y respetuoso, y se evitarán las abreviaturas o las contracciones como **don't**, **I've** o **she'd** en lugar de **do not**, **I have** o **she had/would**, que habrán de utilizarse únicamente en la correspondencia personal o la comunicación oral. La correspondencia personal, al igual que el correo electrónico y el fax, se caracteriza por un estilo más espontáneo y un registro de lengua menos formal.

▪ORGANIZACIÓN

Cada párrafo estará formado por tres o cuatro frases como máximo y tratará un solo tema. Hay que evitar mezclar el pasado y el presente dentro de una misma oración y respetar las reglas de concordancia entre los tiempos verbales.

Al contestar una carta, puede ser útil identificar en el original los puntos principales tratados por el remitente y las fórmulas que se pueden volver a utilizar.

Fórmulas de saludo y despedida

La fórmula de despedida varía en función de la fórmula de saludo utilizada. Consulte el cuadro que figura en el reverso.

▪Fórmula de saludo

▪Fórmula de despedida

Cuando no conocemos el nombre de la persona a la que nos dirigimos:

Dear Sir
Dear Madam

Cuando no sabemos si se trata de un hombre o de una mujer:
Dear Sir or Madam
o
Dear Sir/Madam

Cuando nos dirigimos a una empresa o a una entidad sin indicar el nombre del destinatario:
Dear Sirs *(Br)*
Gentlemen *(US)*

Yours faithfully *(Br)*

En inglés norteamericano, la fórmula de cortesía es siempre en sentido contrario:
Faithfully yours *(US)*

Cuando conocemos el nombre de la persona a la que nos dirigimos:

Dear Mr Jameson
Dear Mrs Lucas
Dear Miss Crookshaw
Dear Ms Greening

(La abreviatura Ms se utiliza cada vez más cuando nos dirigimos a una mujer porque así se evita indicar si se trata de una mujer casada (Mrs) o no (Miss).)

Dear Dr Illingworth

En los Estados Unidos, la abreviatura termina generalmente con un punto: Mr., Mrs., Ms., Dr.

Cuando nos dirigimos al director de un periódico:
Sir

a un concejal británico:
Dear Councillor Henderson
Dear Councillor Mr/Mrs/Ms Adams

a un diputado británico:
Dear Mr/Mrs Brown

a un gobernador:
Dear Governor Almanza

a un miembro del Congreso estadounidense:
Sir/Madam
Dear Congressman/Congresswoman Fox
Dear Senator Mitcham

al Primer Ministro:
Dear Sir/Madam
Dear Prime Minister

al Presidente de Estados Unidos:
Sir/Madam
Dear Mr/Madam President

Yours sincerely *(Br)*
Sincerely yours *(US)*
Sincerely *(US)*

Tono más amistoso:
Yours very sincerely *(Br)*

Estilo menos formal:
With best wishes
With kind regards
Kindest regards

Menos frecuente:
Yours respectfully *(Br)*
Respectfully yours *(US)*
Respectfully *(US)*

Cuando nos dirigimos a un pariente o a un amigo:

Dear Bill
Dear Marjorie
Dear Graham and Barbara
Dear all
Dear Mum and Dad
Dear Uncle Ralph/Auntie Ann
My dear Hector
Dearest/My dearest Jill

Muy familiar:
Hi John!
Hello there

With love
Love
Love from
Love and best wishes

Más afectuoso:
With all my/our love
Much love

Más familiar:
Lots of love

Más formal:
Yours
All the best *(Br)*
Best wishes
Regards

Familiar:
See you soon
Cheers *(Br)*
Bye for now

▪ PRESENTACIÓN DE UNA CARTA MECANOGRAFIADA

Los párrafos van alineados a la izquierda, sin sangría y separados por una línea en blanco.

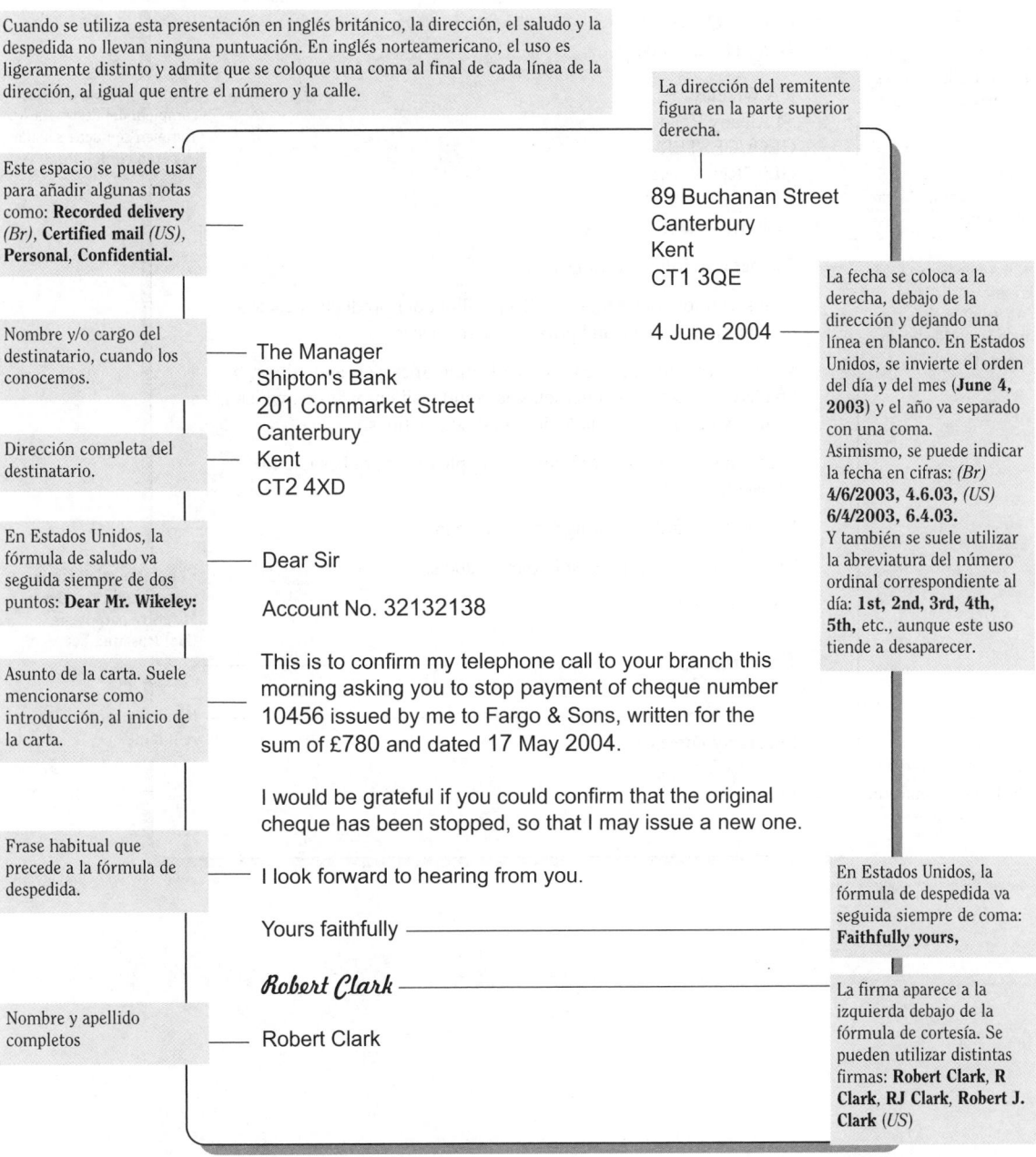

Cuando se utiliza esta presentación en inglés británico, la dirección, el saludo y la despedida no llevan ninguna puntuación. En inglés norteamericano, el uso es ligeramente distinto y admite que se coloque una coma al final de cada línea de la dirección, al igual que entre el número y la calle.

La dirección del remitente figura en la parte superior derecha.

Este espacio se puede usar para añadir algunas notas como: **Recorded delivery** *(Br)*, **Certified mail** *(US)*, **Personal**, **Confidential.**

89 Buchanan Street
Canterbury
Kent
CT1 3QE

4 June 2004

La fecha se coloca a la derecha, debajo de la dirección y dejando una línea en blanco. En Estados Unidos, se invierte el orden del día y del mes (**June 4, 2003**) y el año va separado con una coma. Asimismo, se puede indicar la fecha en cifras: *(Br)* **4/6/2003, 4.6.03,** *(US)* **6/4/2003, 6.4.03.** Y también se suele utilizar la abreviatura del número ordinal correspondiente al día: **1st, 2nd, 3rd, 4th, 5th,** etc., aunque este uso tiende a desaparecer.

Nombre y/o cargo del destinatario, cuando los conocemos.

The Manager
Shipton's Bank
201 Cornmarket Street
Canterbury
Kent
CT2 4XD

Dirección completa del destinatario.

En Estados Unidos, la fórmula de saludo va seguida siempre de dos puntos: **Dear Mr. Wikeley:**

Dear Sir

Account No. 32132138

Asunto de la carta. Suele mencionarse como introducción, al inicio de la carta.

This is to confirm my telephone call to your branch this morning asking you to stop payment of cheque number 10456 issued by me to Fargo & Sons, written for the sum of £780 and dated 17 May 2004.

I would be grateful if you could confirm that the original cheque has been stopped, so that I may issue a new one.

Frase habitual que precede a la fórmula de despedida.

I look forward to hearing from you.

Yours faithfully

En Estados Unidos, la fórmula de despedida va seguida siempre de coma: **Faithfully yours,**

Robert Clark

La firma aparece a la izquierda debajo de la fórmula de cortesía. Se pueden utilizar distintas firmas: **Robert Clark**, **R Clark**, **RJ Clark**, **Robert J. Clark** *(US)*

Nombre y apellido completos

Robert Clark

▪PRESENTACIÓN DE UNA CARTA EN PAPEL CON MEMBRETE

The Carpet Bazaar

El membrete de la empresa va en el centro o a la derecha.

5-7 Murray Road
NORWICH NO2 2RN
Tel: 01793 58607 Fax: 01793 44607
E-mail: carpetbazaar@flying.com
Website: www.carpetbazaar.com

Referencias

Our ref: CAR/402

En este tipo de carta la fecha va alineada a la izquierda.

Date: 11 July 2004

F A Wikeley
54 Albany Road
GLOUCESTER
GL9 7RN

Nombre y dirección completa del destinatario. También se puede señalar su cargo completo.

En inglés norteamericano: **Dear Mr. Wikeley:**

Dear Mr Wikeley

Asunto de la carta. El asunto puede ir precedido de la indicación **Re:** aunque no es aconsejable.

Carpet and kilim catalogue

Thank you for your enquiry of 2 July about our products. I enclose our current catalogue and price list as requested.

We are constantly adding to our collection of carpets and kilims. If you have access to the internet, you could visit our website, which is regularly updated to include our latest acquisitions.

If you require any further information, please do not hesitate to contact us.

We look forward to hearing from you soon.

Thank you for your interest in our products.

Yours sincerely

Rosanna Lee

El nombre puede ir precedido de **Mr, Mrs** o **Ms** entre paréntesis: **(Ms) Rosanna Lee**

Rosanna Lee
Managing Director

Nombre y cargo del remitente.

O bien: **Enclosure** (documentos adjuntos o anexos)

Encs

▪Presentación de una carta manuscrita a un amigo

Cada párrafo lleva sangría.

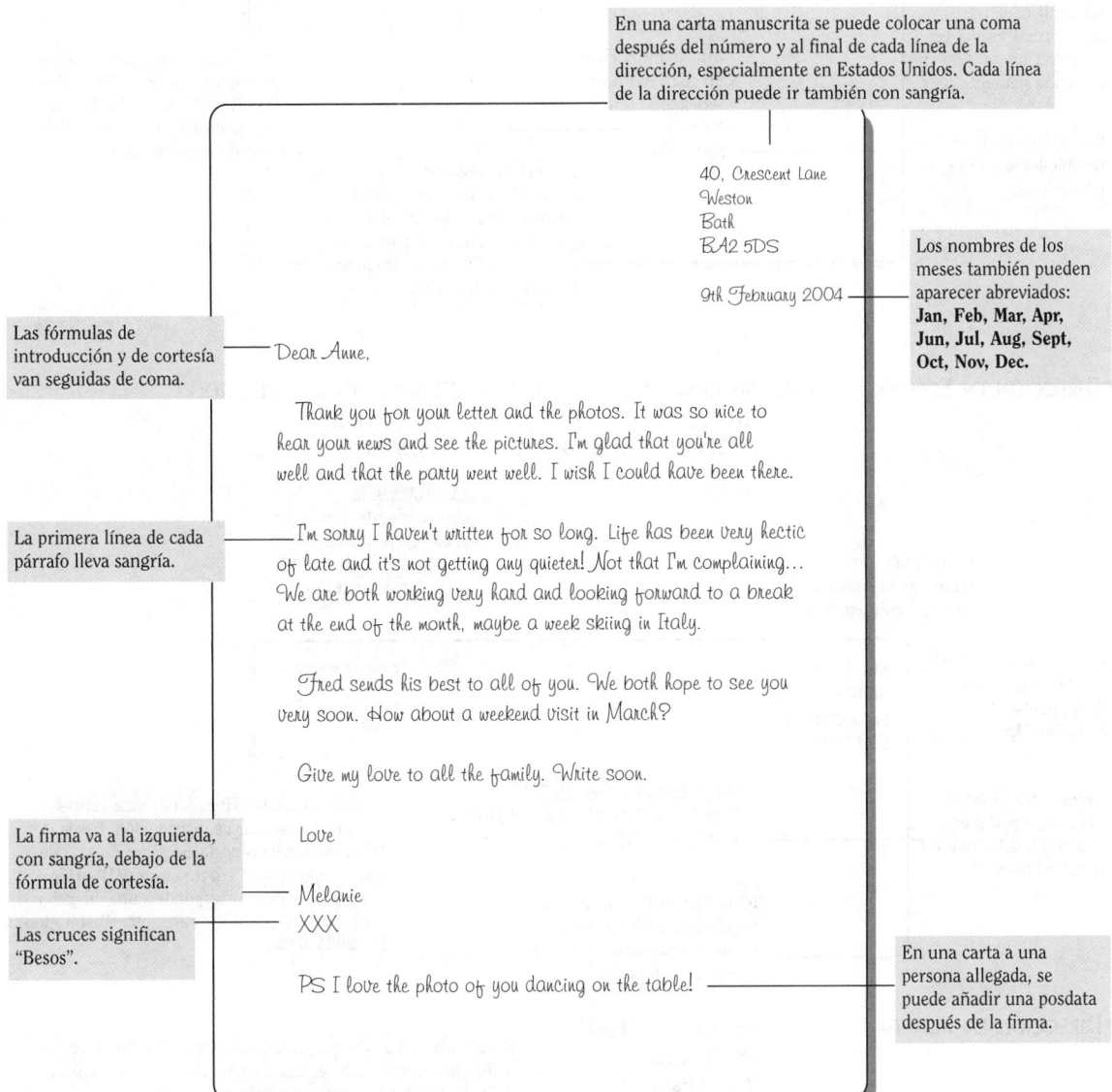

En una carta manuscrita se puede colocar una coma después del número y al final de cada línea de la dirección, especialmente en Estados Unidos. Cada línea de la dirección puede ir también con sangría.

40, Crescent Lane
Weston
Bath
BA2 5DS

9th February 2004

Los nombres de los meses también pueden aparecer abreviados: **Jan, Feb, Mar, Apr, Jun, Jul, Aug, Sept, Oct, Nov, Dec.**

Las fórmulas de introducción y de cortesía van seguidas de coma.

Dear Anne,

Thank you for your letter and the photos. It was so nice to hear your news and see the pictures. I'm glad that you're all well and that the party went well. I wish I could have been there.

La primera línea de cada párrafo lleva sangría.

I'm sorry I haven't written for so long. Life has been very hectic of late and it's not getting any quieter! Not that I'm complaining... We are both working very hard and looking forward to a break at the end of the month, maybe a week skiing in Italy.

Fred sends his best to all of you. We both hope to see you very soon. How about a weekend visit in March?

Give my love to all the family. Write soon.

Love

La firma va a la izquierda, con sangría, debajo de la fórmula de cortesía.

Melanie
XXX

Las cruces significan "Besos".

PS I love the photo of you dancing on the table!

En una carta a una persona allegada, se puede añadir una posdata después de la firma.

Sobres y direcciones

La dirección tiene que ser lo más precisa posible. Los sitios web de los servicios postales de cada país pueden ser útiles para encontrar la dirección completa de algún particular, de un organismo o empresa, incluso el código postal exacto.

Reino Unido: www.royalmail.com
Canadá: www.canadapost.ca
Irlanda: www.anpost.ie
Estados Unidos: www.usps.gov
Australia: www.auspost.com.au
Nueva Zelanda: www.nzpost.co.nz

Es aconsejable no incluir ningún signo de puntuación y escribir la dirección con mayúsculas especialmente si se trata de Estados Unidos o de Canadá (véanse los modelos siguientes).

▪Dirección en el Reino Unido:

Mr (Mrs, Ms, Dr, etc.), nombre (o inicial), apellido
(Nombre del lugar y/o) número, calle
Población
CONDADO o CIUDAD PRINCIPAL
CÓDIGO POSTAL

Hay que escribir la dirección en el centro del sobre, ligeramente hacia la izquierda.

En la parte de atrás del sobre se puede indicar la dirección del remitente, aunque esto no es muy frecuente.

También se puede utilizar la abreviatura **Rd.** La lista de las abreviaturas usadas en las direcciones figura en la página siguiente.

Mr Richard Hunt
26 Ashley Road
Worksop
NOTTS
S81 7JD

El código postal (**postcode**) se escribe en mayúsculas.

Si se trata de una de las ciudades principales, como LONDRES o LIVERPOOL, basta con indicar el código postal y el nombre de la ciudad en mayúsculas.

El condado se escribe preferiblemente en mayúsculas y puede ir abreviado. La relación de las abreviaturas usadas para los condados del Reino Unido figura en la página siguiente.

▪Dirección en Estados Unidos:

Mr. (Mrs., Ms., Dr., etc.), NOMBRE (y/o INICIAL), APELLIDO
(NOMBRE DEL LUGAR y/o) NÚMERO, CALLE
POBLACIÓN, ESTADO y CÓDIGO POSTAL

La localidad, la abreviatura del estado y el código postal (**ZIP code**) van uno detrás del otro en la misma línea.

La dirección del remitente se coloca en la parte superior izquierda.

Las abreviaturas y las iniciales van seguidas de un punto: **Mr., Mrs., Ms., Dr.**

Ms. S. Gulliver
3448 Kabel Dr
New Orleans
LA70131

La localidad, el estado y el código postal van uno detrás del otro en la misma línea.

Ms. WENDY ROBINSON
11867 CRESTA VERDE DRIVE
ST LOUIS, MO 63145

El código postal (**ZIP code**) de cinco cifras identifica un sector de distribución. Desde 1983, los servicios postales colocan detrás de este código otro de cuatro cifras (**ZIP+4**) que es optativo y que corresponde a una dirección o a un apartado postal, por ejemplo: **Washington DC 2026-0123**.

MO = **Missouri**. La lista de las abreviaturas usadas para los estados norteamericanos figura en la página siguiente.

▪Dirección en Irlanda:

Mrs Kathleen Ryan
48 The Glen
Roden Park
Rathfarnham
Dublin 14
(Ireland)

O bien: **Republic of Ireland**.

En Irlanda no hay código postal, excepto en Dublín, donde se utiliza una cifra de 1 a 18 para designar los distintos sectores de la ciudad. En las direcciones rurales, se emplea la abreviatura **Co.** para indicar el condado en el que está domiciliado el destinatario; por ejemplo, **Co. Clare** significa condado de Clare.

▪Dirección en Canadá:

Mr & Mrs Fitzgerald
28 Alpine Boulevard
St Albert AB T8N 2M7
(Canada)

AB = **Alberta**. La lista de las abreviaturas usadas para las provincias y los territorios de Canadá figura en las páginas siguientes.

Las dos primeras letras del código postal canadiense representan la provincia o el territorio.

▪Dirección en Australia:

Gareth Connolly
55 Elizabeth Street
Potts Point
NSW 2020
(Australia)

Abreviatura del estado o del territorio (consultar la lista en las páginas siguientes).

▪Dirección en Nueva Zelanda:

Mr J Hall
3 Bridge Avenue
Te Atatu
Auckland 8
(New Zealand)

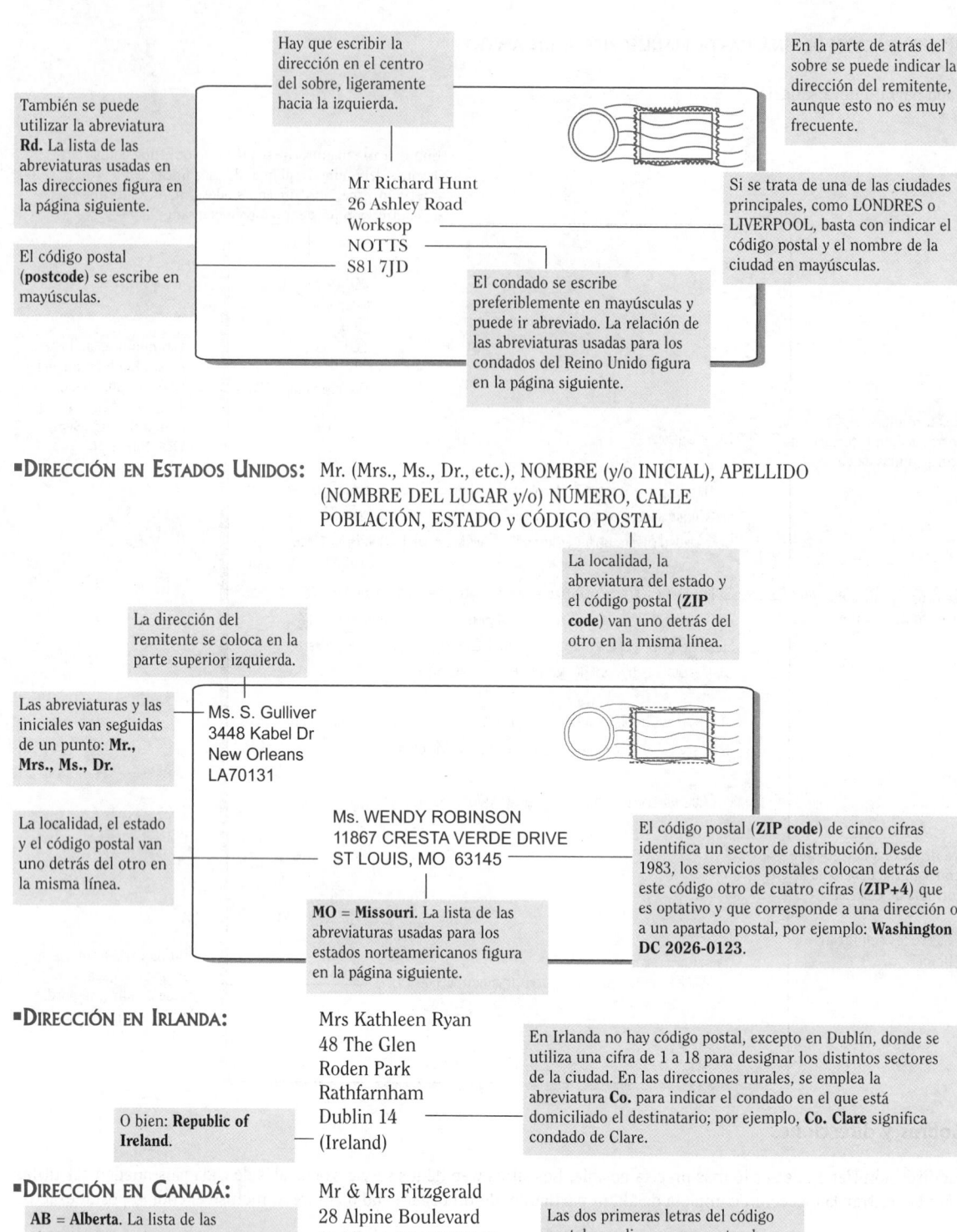

▪Abreviaturas usadas en las direcciones

Las abreviaturas siguientes se emplean habitualmente en las direcciones. Pueden figurar tanto en el encabezamiento de la carta como en el sobre.

Apt	Apartment	**Mtn**	Mountain
Av o **Ave**	Avenue	**Pde**	Parade
Blvd	Boulevard	**Pk**	Park
Cl	Close	**Pl**	Place
Cres	Crescent	**Plz**	Plaza
Ct	Court	**Rdg**	Ridge
Dr	Drive	**Rd**	Road
Est	Estate	**Rm**	Room
Gdns	Gardens	**Sq**	Square
Gr	Grove	**St**	Street
Hts	Heights	**Ter**	Terrace
La	Lane		

Las abreviaturas **N** (North), **S** (South), **W** (West), **E** (East), **NE** (Northeast), **NW** (Northwest), **SE** (Southeast) y **SW** (Southwest) también son muy usuales, especialmente en las direcciones de Estados Unidos y Canadá.

Por ejemplo, en Nueva York:

351 W 32ND ST
NEW YORK, NY 10001

Esta dirección se lee: **three hundred and fifty-one West Thirty-second Street**

en Montreal:

123 MAIN ST NW
MONTREAL QC H3Z 2Y7

Esta dirección se lee: **one hundred and twenty-three Main Street Northwest**

▪Abreviaturas de los condados del Reino Unido

Generalmente en los nombres de los condados que terminan en –shire se mantiene la primera sílaba a la que se le agrega una "**s**": **Beds = Bedfordshire, Berks = Berkshire, Bucks = Buckinghamshire, Cambs = Cambridgeshire, Gloucs = Gloucester, Herts = Hertfordshire, Lancs = Lancashire, Lincs = Lincolnshire, Notts = Nottinghamshire, Staffs = Staffordshire, Wilts = Wiltshire.**

Excepciones:
Northants = Northamptonshire, Oxon = Oxfordshire

Los condados siguientes no se abrevian: **Avon, Cleveland, Greater Manchester, Humberside, Kent, Merseyside, Tyne and Wear.**

▪Abreviaturas de los estados norteamericanos

AK	Alaska	**MT**	Montana
AL	Alabama	**NC**	North Carolina
AR	Arkansas	**ND**	North Dakota
AZ	Arizona	**NE**	Nebraska
CA	California	**NH**	New Hampshire
CO	Colorado	**NJ**	New Jersey
CT	Connecticut	**NM**	New Mexico
DC	District of Columbia	**NV**	Nevada
DE	Delaware	**NY**	New York
FL	Florida	**OH**	Ohio
GA	Georgia	**OK**	Oklahoma
HI	Hawaii	**OR**	Oregon
IA	Iowa	**PA**	Pennsylvania
ID	Idaho	**RI**	Rhode Island
IL	Illinois	**SC**	South Carolina
IN	Indiana	**SD**	South Dakota
KS	Kansas	**TN**	Tennessee
KY	Kentucky	**TX**	Texas
LA	Louisiana	**UT**	Utah
MA	Massachusetts	**VA**	Virginia
MD	Maryland	**VT**	Vermont
ME	Maine	**WA**	Washington
MI	Michigan	**WI**	Wisconsin
MN	Minnesota	**WV**	West Virginia
MO	Missouri	**WY**	Wyoming
MS	Mississippi		

▪ABREVIATURAS DE LAS PROVINCIAS Y LOS TERRITORIOS CANADIENSES

AB	Alberta
BC	British Columbia
MB	Manitoba
NB	New Brunswick
NF	Newfoundland
NS	Nova Scotia
NT	Northwest Territories
NU	Nunavut
ON	Ontario
PE	Prince Edward Island
QC	Quebec
SK	Saskatchewan
YT	Yukon

▪ABREVIATURAS DE LOS ESTADOS Y TERRITORIOS AUSTRALIANOS

ACT	Australian Capital Territory
NSW	New South Wales
NT	Northern Territory
QLD	Queensland
SA	South Australia
TAS	Tasmania
VIC	Victoria
WA	Western Australia

Modelos de cartas

Carta a un amigo

23, Juniper Close,
Lower Benefield,
Wykeham,
WE8 5AF

7th April 2004

> The y of nunca se escriben en las fechas aunque haya que pronunciarlos; **16th May** se lee: **the sixteenth of May**.

Dear Andres,

How are things with you? I hope you're well and not too unhappy that your holidays are now over! I guess it's time to go back to work and start saving for the next trip.

> O bien:
> **How are you?** Otras expresiones corrientes: **Thank you for your letter.**
> Y/o: **It was lovely/great/nice to hear from you.**
> **I'm sorry/Sorry I haven't written for so long.**

> Se suelen usar las contracciones: **you're, don't, I've, etc.**

It was great to see you in Bilbao, even if it was for such a short time. Let's hope that we can spend more time together next time. I'm planning a trip to Spain next month and will be spending a few days in both Bilbao and Madrid. Any chance of staying with you for a couple of nights? I haven't finalized dates yet, but will let you know as soon as I have. Probably around 16th May.

> Estilo telegráfico: **Any chance of ...** en lugar de **Is there any chance of ...**

The weather here is absolutely beautiful! Yes, it can be good in England! I'm making the most of it and walking every day, getting in training for the trek to Nepal in August.

Cheryl and Pedro send their love. They are both well and are sorry to have missed you.

> O bien:
> **X and Y send you (their) best wishes.**
> **X asks me to give you his/her love/best wishes.**
> **X sends his/her love/regards.**

> Estilo telegráfico: se omite el pronombre personal.

Anyway, that's about all for now. Will no doubt be in touch again very soon. Say hello to your parents from me. Take care of yourself and don't work too hard!

> O bien:
> **I look forward to seeing/hearing from you soon.**
> **Do write.**
> **Write soon.**
> **Do keep in touch.**
> **Hope to hear from you soon.**
> **Let me/us have your news.**

> O bien:
> **Please remember me to ...**
> **Give my love/my regards/my best wishes to ...**

With love,
Joanna
XXX

Postales

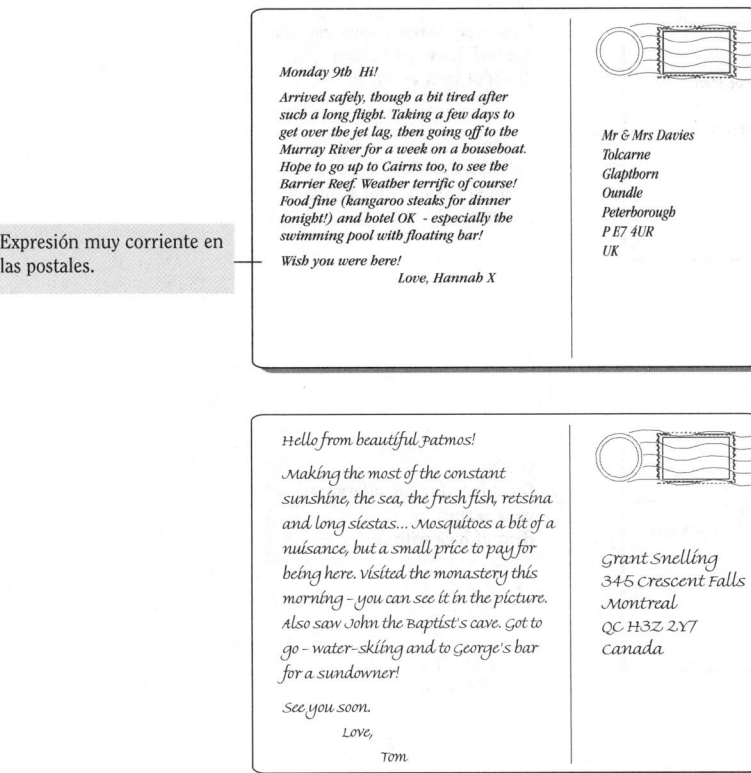

Monday 9th Hi!
Arrived safely, though a bit tired after such a long flight. Taking a few days to get over the jet lag, then going off to the Murray River for a week on a houseboat. Hope to go up to Cairns too, to see the Barrier Reef. Weather terrific of course! Food fine (kangaroo steaks for dinner tonight!) and hotel OK - especially the swimming pool with floating bar!
Wish you were here!
Love, Hannah X

Mr & Mrs Davies
Tolcarne
Glapthorn
Oundle
Peterborough
P E7 4UR
UK

Expresión muy corriente en las postales.

Hello from beautiful Patmos!
Making the most of the constant sunshine, the sea, the fresh fish, retsina and long siestas... Mosquitoes a bit of a nuisance, but a small price to pay for being here. Visited the monastery this morning - you can see it in the picture. Also saw John the Baptist's cave. Got to go - water-skiing and to George's bar for a sundowner!
See you soon.
Love,
Tom

Grant Snelling
345 Crescent Falls
Montreal
QC H3Z 2Y7
Canada

Tarjetas

▪Tarjetas de fin de año

En los países anglosajones las tarjetas de fin de año se mandan siempre antes de Navidad y no sólo en el ámbito de las relaciones profesionales, de compromiso o cuando la familia o los amigos están lejos, sino de forma mucho más general.

Haydn and Ann,

Merry Christmas and a Happy New Year!

Best wishes,

Harry and Dinah

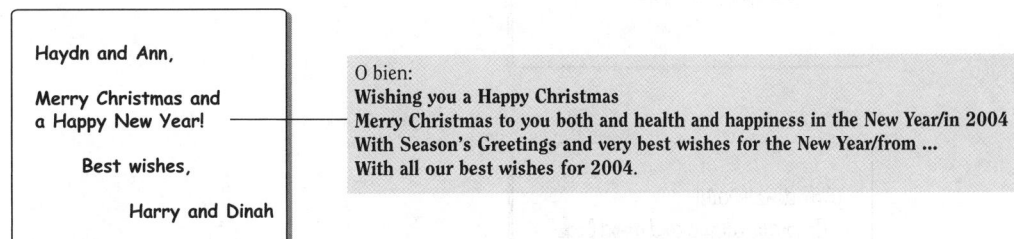

O bien:
Wishing you a Happy Christmas
Merry Christmas to you both and health and happiness in the New Year/in 2004
With Season's Greetings and very best wishes for the New Year/from ...
With all our best wishes for 2004.

▪Para felicitar el cumpleaños

En los países anglosajones se acostumbra mandar muchas más tarjetas de cumpleaños que en España o Hispanoamérica (y no sólo cuando el homenajeado vive lejos y no se lo va a ver personalmente). También se puede entregar la tarjeta personalmente con o sin regalo.

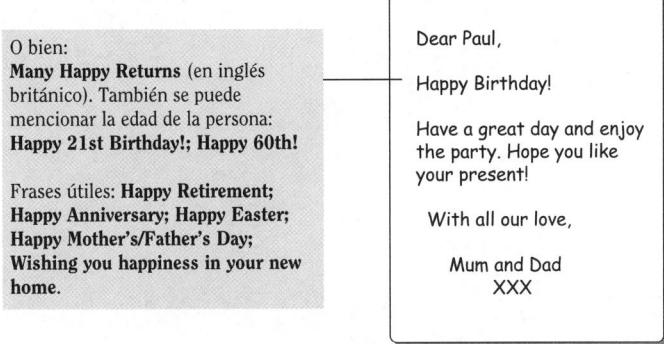

O bien:
Many Happy Returns (en inglés británico). También se puede mencionar la edad de la persona: **Happy 21st Birthday!; Happy 60th!**

Frases útiles: **Happy Retirement; Happy Anniversary; Happy Easter; Happy Mother's/Father's Day; Wishing you happiness in your new home.**

Dear Paul,

Happy Birthday!

Have a great day and enjoy the party. Hope you like your present!

With all our love,

Mum and Dad
XXX

▪Para desearle a alguien que se mejore pronto

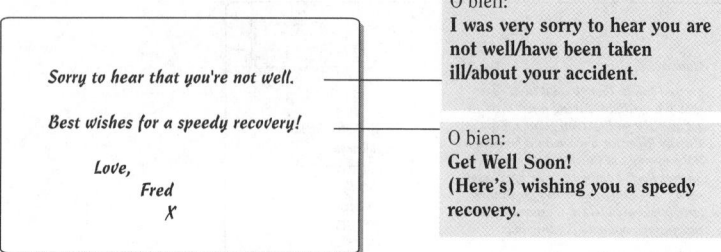

Sorry to hear that you're not well.

Best wishes for a speedy recovery!

Love,
Fred
X

O bien:
I was very sorry to hear you are not well/have been taken ill/about your accident.

O bien:
Get Well Soon!
(Here's) wishing you a speedy recovery.

▪Para desear buena suerte

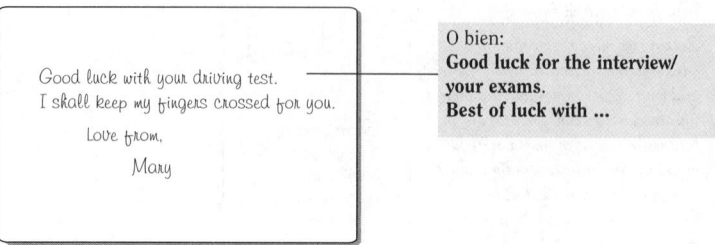

Good luck with your driving test.
I shall keep my fingers crossed for you.
Love from,
Mary

O bien:
Good luck for the interview/ your exams.
Best of luck with ...

▪Para felicitar a alguien

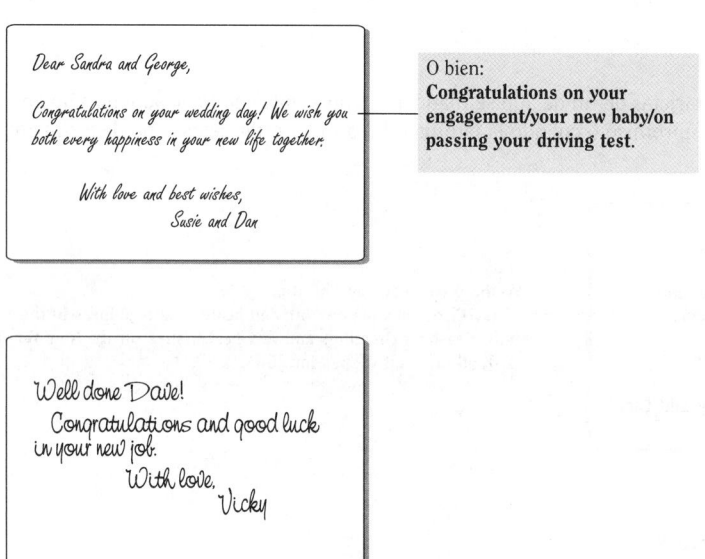

Dear Sandra and George,

Congratulations on your wedding day! We wish you both every happiness in your new life together.

With love and best wishes,
Susie and Dan

O bien:
Congratulations on your engagement/your new baby/on passing your driving test.

Well done Dave!
Congratulations and good luck in your new job.
With love,
Vicky

Invitaciones y respuestas

▪INVITACIÓN A UNA BODA

La invitación a un acontecimiento importante puede imprimirse en una tarjeta o bien escribirse en una hoja.

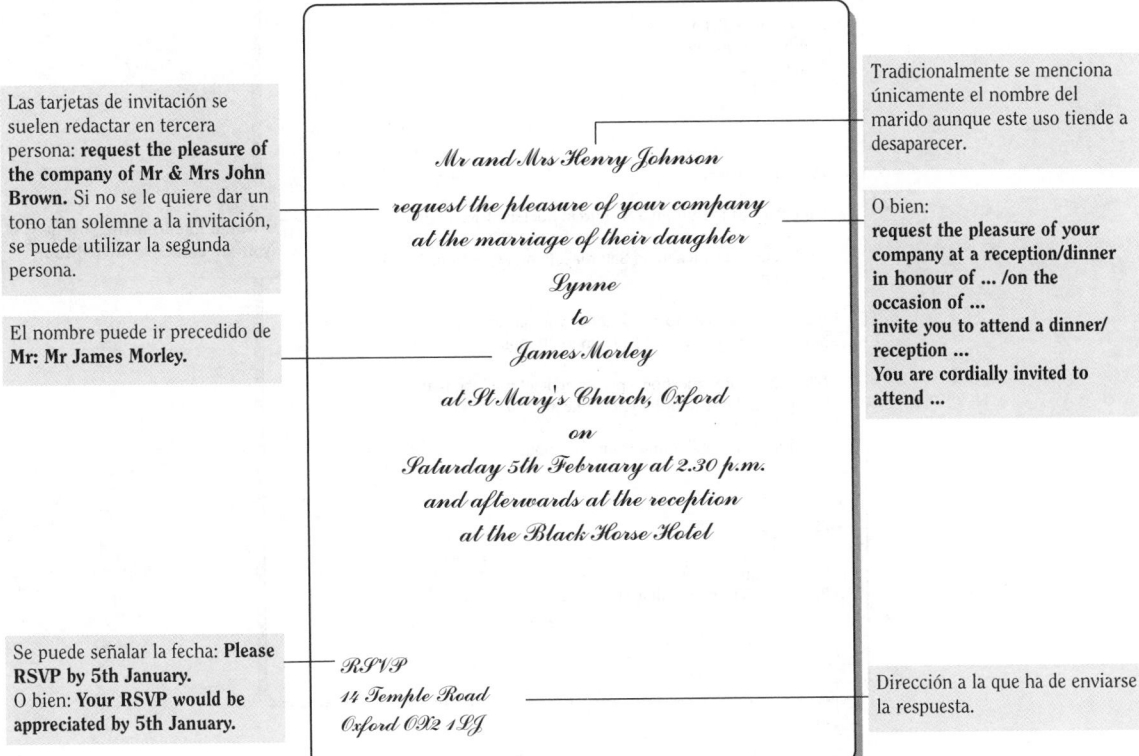

Las tarjetas de invitación se suelen redactar en tercera persona: **request the pleasure of the company of Mr & Mrs John Brown.** Si no se le quiere dar un tono tan solemne a la invitación, se puede utilizar la segunda persona.

El nombre puede ir precedido de **Mr: Mr James Morley.**

Mr and Mrs Henry Johnson
request the pleasure of your company
at the marriage of their daughter
Lynne
to
James Morley
at St Mary's Church, Oxford
on
Saturday 5th February at 2.30 p.m.
and afterwards at the reception
at the Black Horse Hotel

RSVP
14 Temple Road
Oxford OX2 1LJ

Tradicionalmente se menciona únicamente el nombre del marido aunque este uso tiende a desaparecer.

O bien:
request the pleasure of your company at a reception/dinner in honour of ... /on the occasion of ...
invite you to attend a dinner/ reception ...
You are cordially invited to attend ...

Se puede señalar la fecha: **Please RSVP by 5th January.**
O bien: **Your RSVP would be appreciated by 5th January.**

Dirección a la que ha de enviarse la respuesta.

▪PARA ACEPTAR UNA INVITACIÓN FORMAL

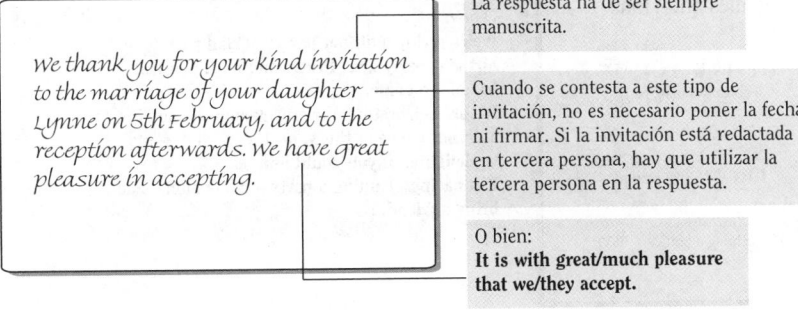

We thank you for your kind invitation to the marriage of your daughter Lynne on 5th February, and to the reception afterwards. We have great pleasure in accepting.

La respuesta ha de ser siempre manuscrita.

Cuando se contesta a este tipo de invitación, no es necesario poner la fecha ni firmar. Si la invitación está redactada en tercera persona, hay que utilizar la tercera persona en la respuesta.

O bien:
It is with great/much pleasure that we/they accept.

▪PARA RECHAZAR UNA INVITACIÓN FORMAL

We thank you for your kind invitation to your daughter's wedding, and to the reception afterwards, but regret that we are unable to attend.

O, en tercera persona:
Mr and Mrs Hall thank Mr and Mrs Johnson for their kind invitation to their daughter's wedding, and to the reception afterwards, but regret that they will be unable to attend.

▪Carta de invitación a un congreso

November 11, 2004

Mr. Faraday Peters
114 Roanoke Drive
Blacksburg,
VA 23501

Dear Mr. Peters,

On behalf of the Virginia Arthurian Society, I would like to extend to you an invitation to speak at our seminar during the VAS annual conference in Chicago on Saturday, February 8 from 10:00am to 12:00pm.

We would like you to speak about your latest research and your recent publications. You would have up to 20 minutes to speak.

If you have any questions, please contact me by email at vas@excalibur.edu or by telephone at (540) 567-1123.

I look forward to hearing from you soon.

Sincerely,

Henry Hunt

Henry Hunt
President, Virginia Arthurian Society

O bien:
I would like to invite you to ...
You are cordially invited to ...

▪Tarjeta de invitación a una fiesta entre amigos

James and Fiona

INVITE YOU TO
a house-warming party

ON: Friday 13th September
AT: 45 Rowan Crescent
FROM: 8pm onwards

Please bring a bottle RSVP

O bien:
We're giving a dinner party/cocktail party/ birthday party next Friday and hope you will be able to come.
We are celebrating our engagement by holding a dinner dance at the ... on the ..., and would be delighted if you could join us.
I'm having/planning a party – come along, and bring a friend.

▪Respuesta a una invitación a una fiesta entre amigos

46 Hatton Street
Bath
BA5 2GA

23 August 2004

Dear James and Fiona,

Thank you so much for the invitation to your house-warming party. I'd love to come. It will be great to see you and, of course, your new home.

If you need any help with food, I'd be only too glad to bring something along, as well as a bottle, of course!

Thanks once again for the kind invitation. I look forward to seeing you.

Love,

Emily

O bien:
I'd love to come to your party. It was good of you to invite me.
Thank you for your invitation to dinner/for the weekend – I look forward to it very much.
Thank you so much for your invitation, but I'm afraid I/we won't be able to come.
I was/We were delighted to get your invitation but unfortunately I/we can't come.

Agradecimientos

▪Tras haber pasado unos días en casa de unos amigos

40 The Crescent
5152 Crafers
SA Australia

2 September 2004

Dear Mrs Hepplewhite

I am writing to thank you for extending such a warm welcome to myself and my wife during our recent stay with you in Edinburgh. We greatly appreciated your help and advice, not to mention your hospitality and your cooking!

We were both very taken with the city and enjoyed the festival immensely. Thank you so much for guiding us through both the streets and the festival programme. We are already planning to return next year.

I hope you and your family are all well. Remember you are always more than welcome to come and stay with us in Australia. We would love the opportunity to return your hospitality and of course we have the Adelaide Festival to tempt you with.

We look forward to hearing from you and thank you once again for everything.

With best wishes

Tony and Diana Sedgwick

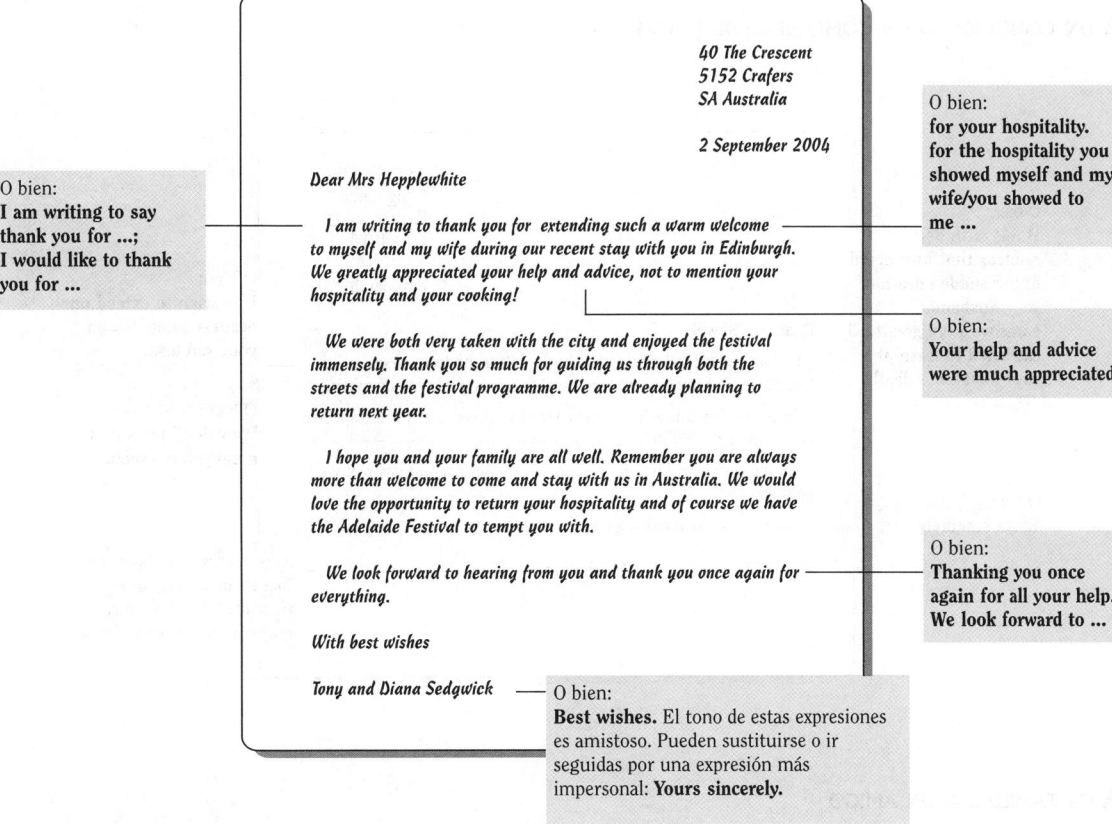

O bien:
I am writing to say thank you for ...; I would like to thank you for ...

O bien:
for your hospitality. for the hospitality you showed myself and my wife/you showed to me ...

O bien:
Your help and advice were much appreciated.

O bien:
Thanking you once again for all your help. We look forward to ...

O bien:
Best wishes. El tono de estas expresiones es amistoso. Pueden sustituirse o ir seguidas por una expresión más impersonal: **Yours sincerely.**

▪Por un regalo

167 Ecclesall Road
SouthSheffield
S11 9PN

31st May 2004

Dear Gay and Ralph

Thank you so much for the beautiful crystal decanter and wine glasses you sent us as a wedding present. They will look wonderful on our dinner table and I intend to make good use of them.

I was so glad that you could come to the wedding. I hope you enjoyed it as much as we did. It was quite a hectic day really, but of course a wonderful one! Give my thanks to Tracey for the catering, everyone said how delicious the food was.

We had a lovely honeymoon and are now busy settling in to our new home. You must come very soon for a meal to try out the glasses.

Many thanks once again!

With much love,

Katie

XXX

O bien:
I can't thank you enough for ... Thank you very much for ...

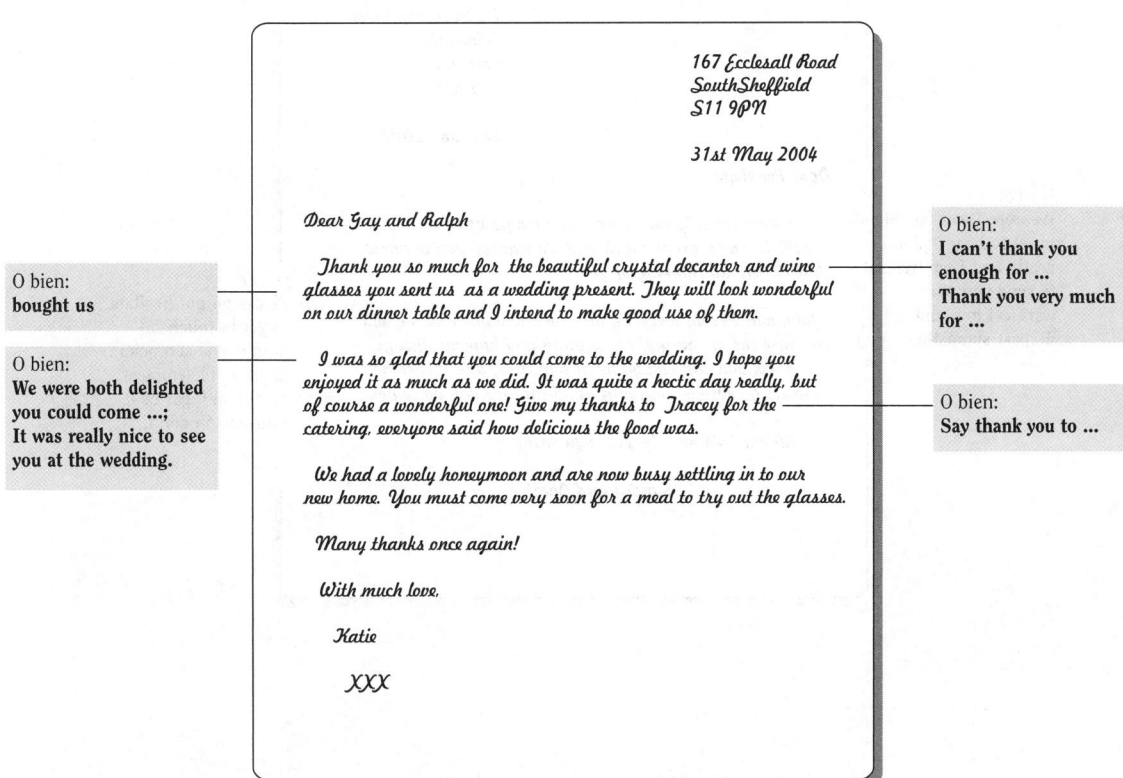

O bien:
bought us

O bien:
We were both delighted you could come ...; It was really nice to see you at the wedding.

O bien:
Say thank you to ...

Pésame

Para dar el pésame es preferible mandar una carta breve escrita a mano. También se puede mandar una tarjeta impresa, añadiéndole unas palabras manuscritas.

▪A UN CONOCIDO O UN COMPAÑERO DE TRABAJO

35 Daisy Hill
Long Eaton
Kent
CT3 4LT8

8th March 2004

Dear Mrs Sitwell,

I was very sad to hear of your husband's death last Tuesday, and I write to offer my sincere condolences to you and your daughter.

I am sure you know how much Mr Sitwell was liked and respected in the village. He will be greatly missed.

All the staff here join me in sending you our deepest sympathy on your sad loss.

Kindest regards,

Roger White

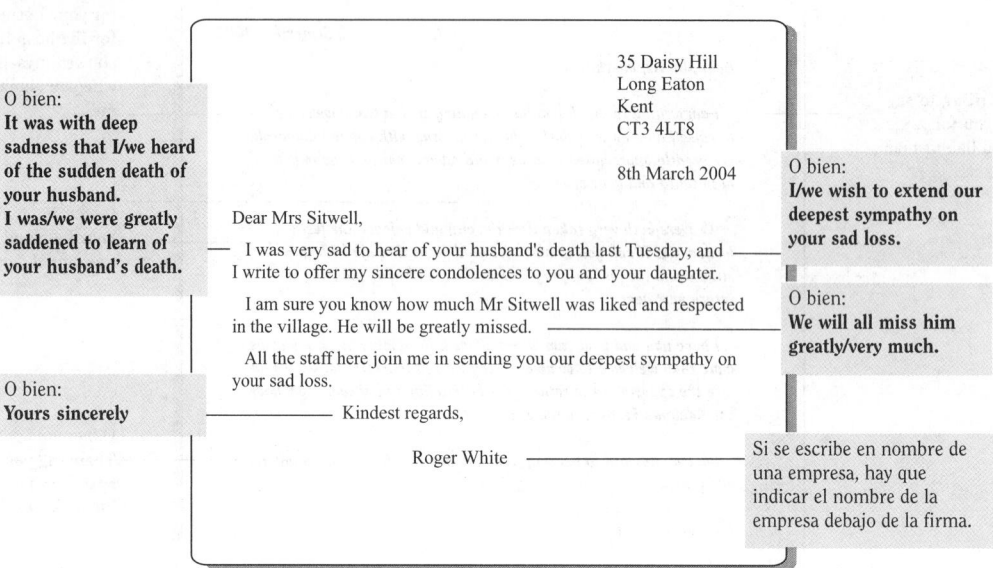

O bien:
It was with deep sadness that I/we heard of the sudden death of your husband.
I was/we were greatly saddened to learn of your husband's death.

O bien:
I/we wish to extend our deepest sympathy on your sad loss.

O bien:
We will all miss him greatly/very much.

O bien:
Yours sincerely

Si se escribe en nombre de una empresa, hay que indicar el nombre de la empresa debajo de la firma.

▪A UN FAMILIAR O UN AMIGO

14 Trevelyan Close
Falmouth
Cornwall
FA5 8LC

7th June 2004

Dear Penelope,

We were terribly sad to hear the tragic news of John's death. It was a great shock and we wanted you to know that we are all thinking of you.

John was dearly loved by all who knew him and we will treasure the memory of his warmth and humour always. You know you can call on us at any time, and please don't hesitate if there is anything at all that we can do to help.

All our love and deepest sympathy

Sandra and Derek

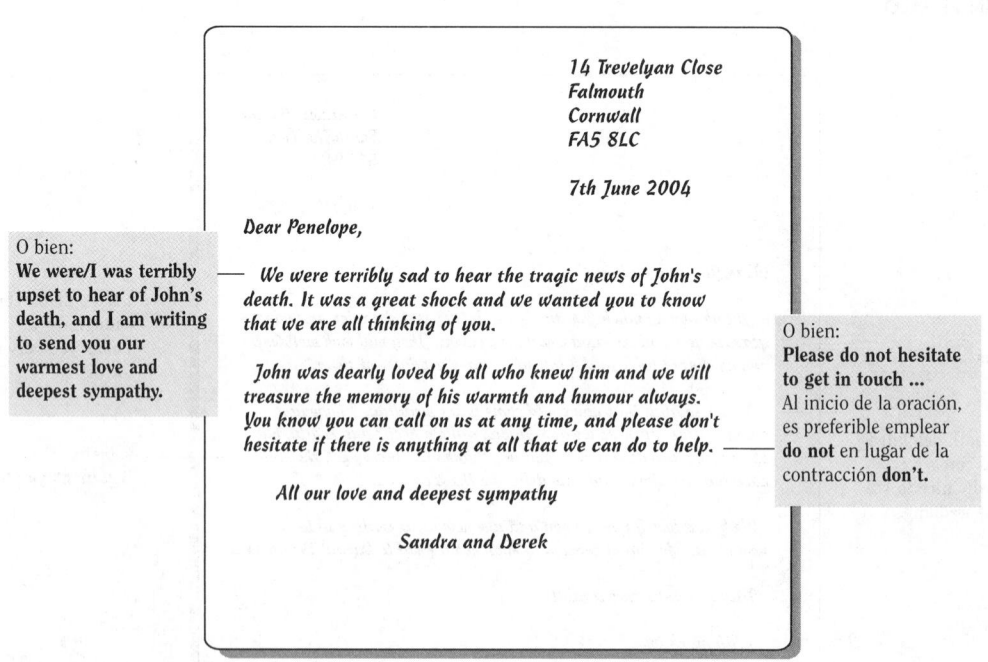

O bien:
We were/I was terribly upset to hear of John's death, and I am writing to send you our warmest love and deepest sympathy.

O bien:
Please do not hesitate to get in touch ...
Al inicio de la oración, es preferible emplear **do not** en lugar de la contracción **don't.**

Reservas

Las reservas de entradas o de habitaciones en los hoteles se hacen cada vez más por Internet y correo electrónico. Si se hace una reserva por teléfono, es aconsejable confirmarla por escrito. Bien sea una carta o un mensaje electrónico, el cuerpo del texto es el mismo. Es importante señalar por escrito todas las condiciones: fecha, número de noches, tipo y número de habitaciones o de entradas, etc.

▪Carta para hacer una reserva

Paseo de la Ribera 34, 4º
14004 Córdoba
Spain

17 November 2004

The Rocky Lodge
Calgary
Alberta
A5G 4MX

Dear Sir or Madam

I am writing to enquire about the possibility of reserving a double room with bath for three nights from December 19 to 21 inclusive.

I would be grateful if you could let me know by return of post if you have any vacancies for those dates. Could you please send me details of your prices and, if at all possible, some information on local events and sites in your area.

Thanking you in advance.

Yours faithfully

James Gulliver

O bien:
I would like to book ***(Br)*** **...**

O bien:
booking ***(Br)***

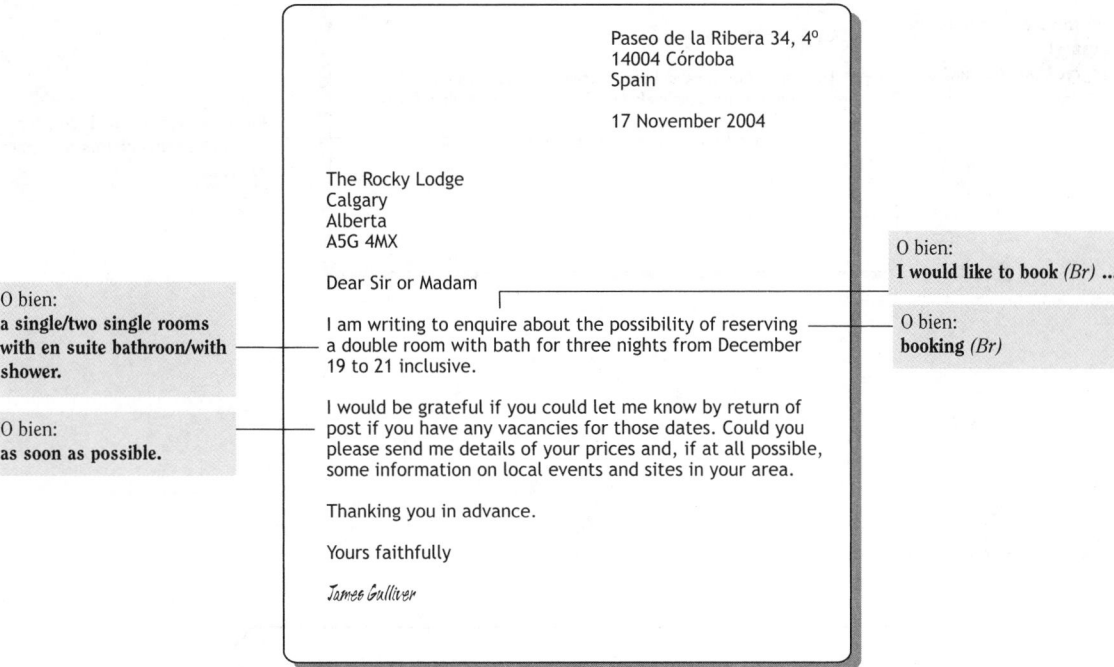

O bien:
a single/two single rooms with en suite bathroon/with shower.

O bien:
as soon as possible.

▪Carta para confirmar una reserva

54, Kabel Dr
New Orleans
LA 70131
USA

Tel: 504-152 52-0042

November 17, 2004

The Manager
The Rocky Lodge
Calgary
Alberta
A5G 4MX

Dear Sir:

Following our telephone conversation this morning, I am writing to confirm the reservation of your restaurant and bar facilities for the afternoon and evening of December 24.

There will be 200 guests in total, for a four-course meal with wine. I look forward to receiving the menus you are sending and will get back to you with our choices as soon as possible. I would appreciate written confirmation of the price agreed.

Do not hesitate to contact me at the above telephone number, if you need to discuss any further details.

Thanking you in advance.

Sincerely yours,

Harry Benson

O bien:
17 November 2004 ***(Br)***

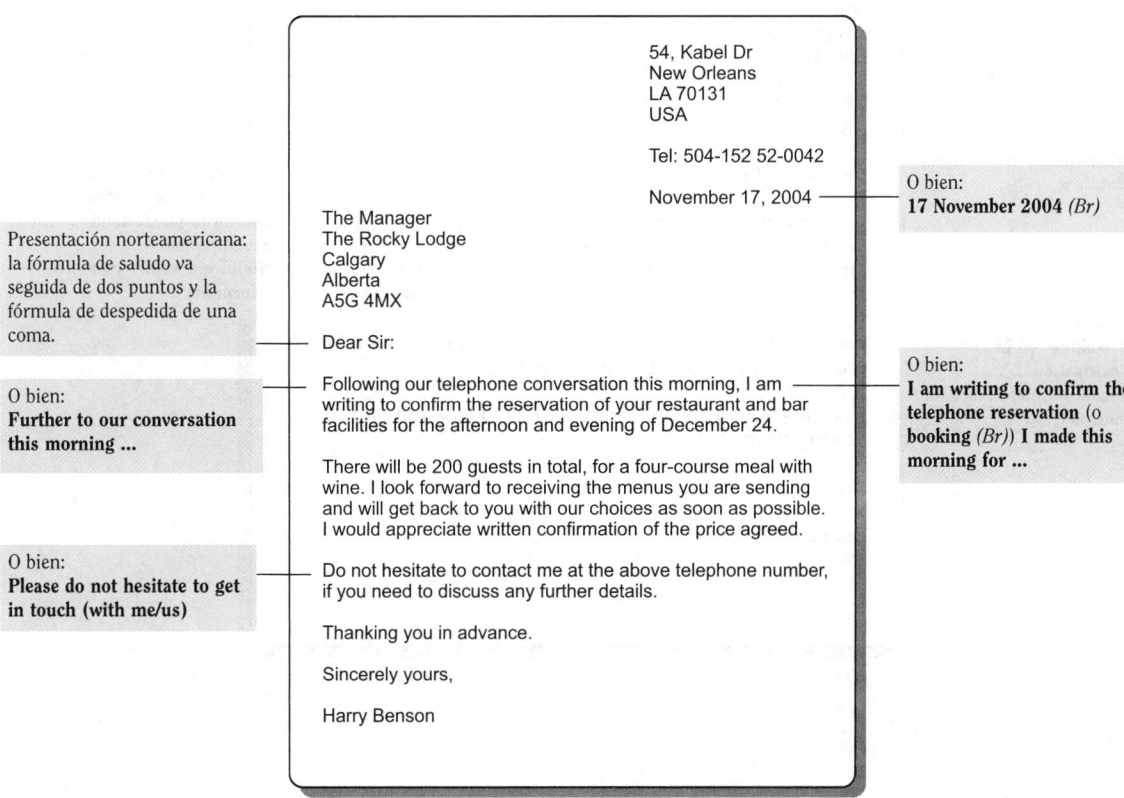

Presentación norteamericana: la fórmula de saludo va seguida de dos puntos y la fórmula de despedida de una coma.

O bien:
Further to our conversation this morning ...

O bien:
I am writing to confirm the telephone reservation (o **booking** ***(Br)***) **I made this morning for ...**

O bien:
Please do not hesitate to get in touch (with me/us)

▪CARTA PARA ANULAR UNA RESERVA

19 Clumber Park Road
Pitlochry
Tayside
PH16 5JS

17th November 2004

The Rocky Lodge
Calgary
Alberta
A5G 4MX

Dear Sir or Madam

I am afraid I must cancel the reservation I made with you for a twin room for three nights from 19th to 21st December 2004.

I apologize for any inconvenience caused.

Yours faithfully

James Gulliver

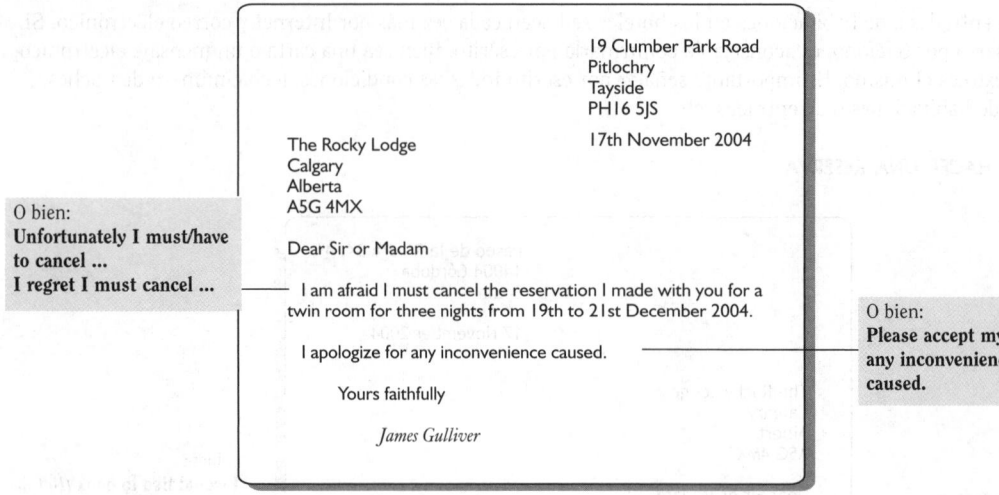

O bien:
Unfortunately I must/have to cancel ...
I regret I must cancel ...

O bien:
Please accept my apologies for any inconvenience this may have caused.

Solicitud de información

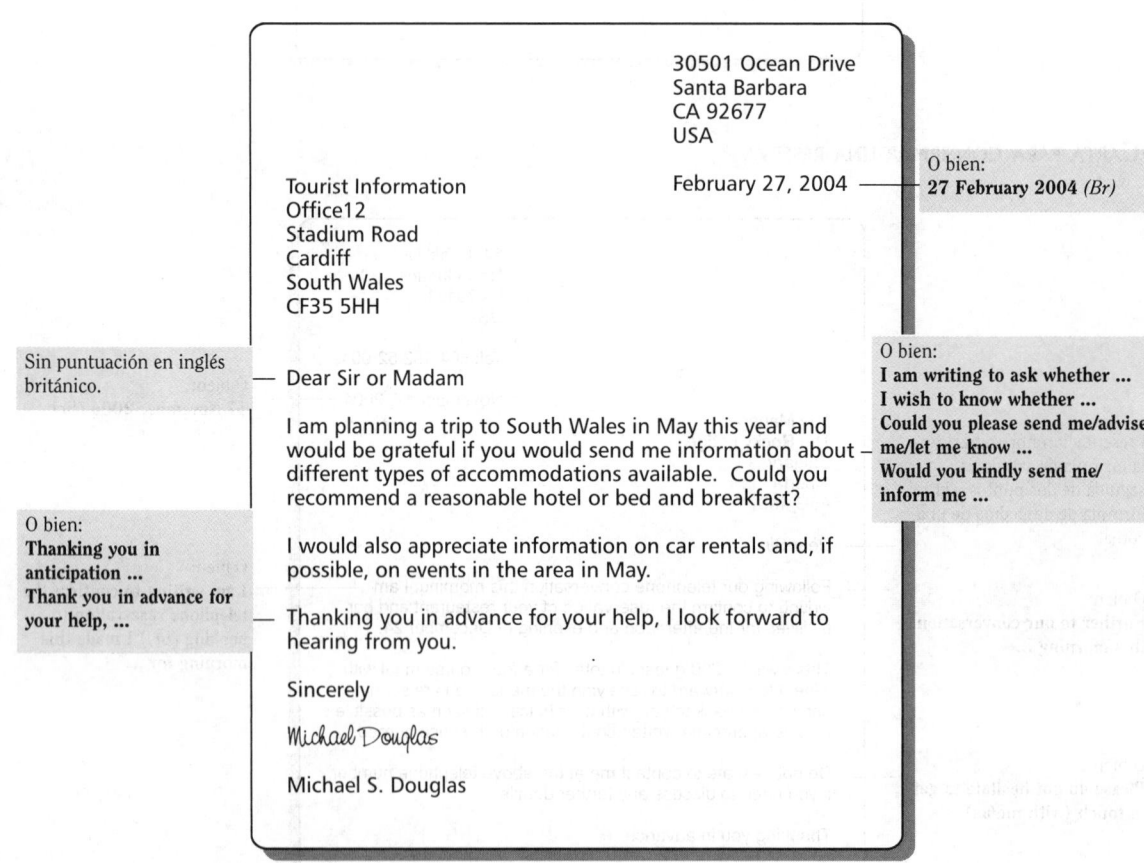

30501 Ocean Drive
Santa Barbara
CA 92677
USA

February 27, 2004

Tourist Information
Office12
Stadium Road
Cardiff
South Wales
CF35 5HH

Dear Sir or Madam

I am planning a trip to South Wales in May this year and would be grateful if you would send me information about different types of accommodations available. Could you recommend a reasonable hotel or bed and breakfast?

I would also appreciate information on car rentals and, if possible, on events in the area in May.

Thanking you in advance for your help, I look forward to hearing from you.

Sincerely

Michael Douglas

Michael S. Douglas

O bien:
27 February 2004 *(Br)*

Sin puntuación en inglés británico.

O bien:
I am writing to ask whether ...
I wish to know whether ...
Could you please send me/advise me/let me know ...
Would you kindly send me/ inform me ...

O bien:
Thanking you in anticipation ...
Thank you in advance for your help, ...

Solicitud de catálogo

Biggin House
22 Clifton Drive
Woodstock
OX23 1RH

1 November 2004

Trekkers &Co.
38 Walsingham Street
London
W1C 4ME

Dear Sir or Madam

Could you please send me a copy of your latest catalogue of walking gear and a current price list to the above address.

I would also appreciate it if you could send me a list of retailers and distributors of your products in the Oxford area.

Thanking you in advance.

Yours faithfully

Dominique Fox

(Mrs) Dominique Fox

Solicitud de presupuesto

24 Oldhay Close
Fulflood
Winchester
SO23 5BY

14th January 2004

Mr J. Fargo
Fargo & Sons
93 Hickory Street
Truro
CO1 3GH

Dear Mr Fargo

I have recently purchased a property in your area and am looking for a reliable builder to undertake extensive renovations. You have come highly recommended and I hope you will be available to work for me during the coming months.

I attach a detailed list of the work I have envisaged. Could you please send me an estimate for the renovations listed? I would also like to know how long the work might take.

O bien:
I would be grateful if you could send ...

I look forward to hearing from you.

O bien:
I look forward to doing business with you.

Yours sincerely

Kenneth McLough

Kenneth McLough

Reclamaciones

Si no conocemos el nombre del destinatario, hay que dirigir la carta al **Customer Services Manager.** Si se trata de una empresa pequeña o familiar, se puede dirigir la carta al director: **The Manager.**

12, Biggles Close
Woodbridge
Suffolk
CB12 3DF

The Customer Services Manager
East Coast Trains
King's Cross Station
London
NO1 4YY

4th August 2004

Dear Sir or Madam

I am writing to complain about the inconvenience caused to me last week by your company's inadequate performance.

O bien:
I wish to complain about ...
I wish to complain most strongly about ...

I was travelling on the 9.30 train from London to York on 1st August. The train was due to arrive in York at midday. It did not arrive until 5 o'clock in the afternoon, making me miss an important meeting. Added to this inconvenience, there were too few announcements informing passengers of what was happening.

I am more than disappointed with the service I received and feel I am entitled to compensation that reflects adequately the inconvenience suffered.

O bien:
The service I received was extremely unsatisfactory ...
I am extremely unhappy with the service I received ...

O bien:
I trust/hope that you will see your way to offering adequate compensation for the inconvenience suffered/ caused.

O bien:
I look forward to receiving a reasonable offer of compensation.

I look forward to receiving your response within the next 14 days.

Es aconsejable señalar el plazo dentro del cual se desea recibir una repuesta.

Yours faithfully

G. Roberts

Mr G. Roberts

---

3 Pennybrook Lane
Dollis Hill
London
NW2 6HG

The Customer Services Manager
Blotto & Co.
34 Vine Street
Ashford
Kent
KE8 5HB

1st September 2004

Dear Sir or Madam

Order 324B

Motivo de la queja: indicar el número de pedido, el código del modelo o la información necesaria para identificar la mercancía.

I received the above order from you on 30 August 2004. I regret to inform you that there were several items missing from the shipment and other items do not correspond to the original order.

O bien:
The goods I received were badly damaged.
The goods you sent me were damaged in transit/were damaged on receipt.
The goods you sent me had the following defects: ...

I enclose a list of the wines I have received, as well as a photocopy of the original order form and invoice. I trust you will remedy the situation as quickly as possible.

I look forward to hearing from you within the next 7 days.

Yours faithfully

Jackson Brattel

Mr Jackson Brattel

La correspondencia comercial

En la correspondencia comercial hay que usar un estilo directo, conciso y cortés. La ortografía y la gramática tienen que ser irreprochables.

En los países anglosajones la carta de negocios va siempre mecanografiada. Los párrafos van alineados a la izquierda, sin sangría y separados por una línea en blanco. En inglés británico, la fecha, las direcciones y las fórmulas de saludo y de despedida no llevan ningún signo de puntuación. En inglés norteamericano, se coloca una coma antes del año en la fecha, un punto después de las abreviaturas Mr., Ms., etc., dos puntos después de la fórmula de saludo y una coma después de la fórmula de despedida.

Para concertar una entrevista

LOOK NOW
Sant Josep, 25
08302 Mataró, Barcelona, Spain
E-mail: looknow@moda.es
Tel: (00 34) 93 744 5600
Fax: (00 34) 93 753 2126

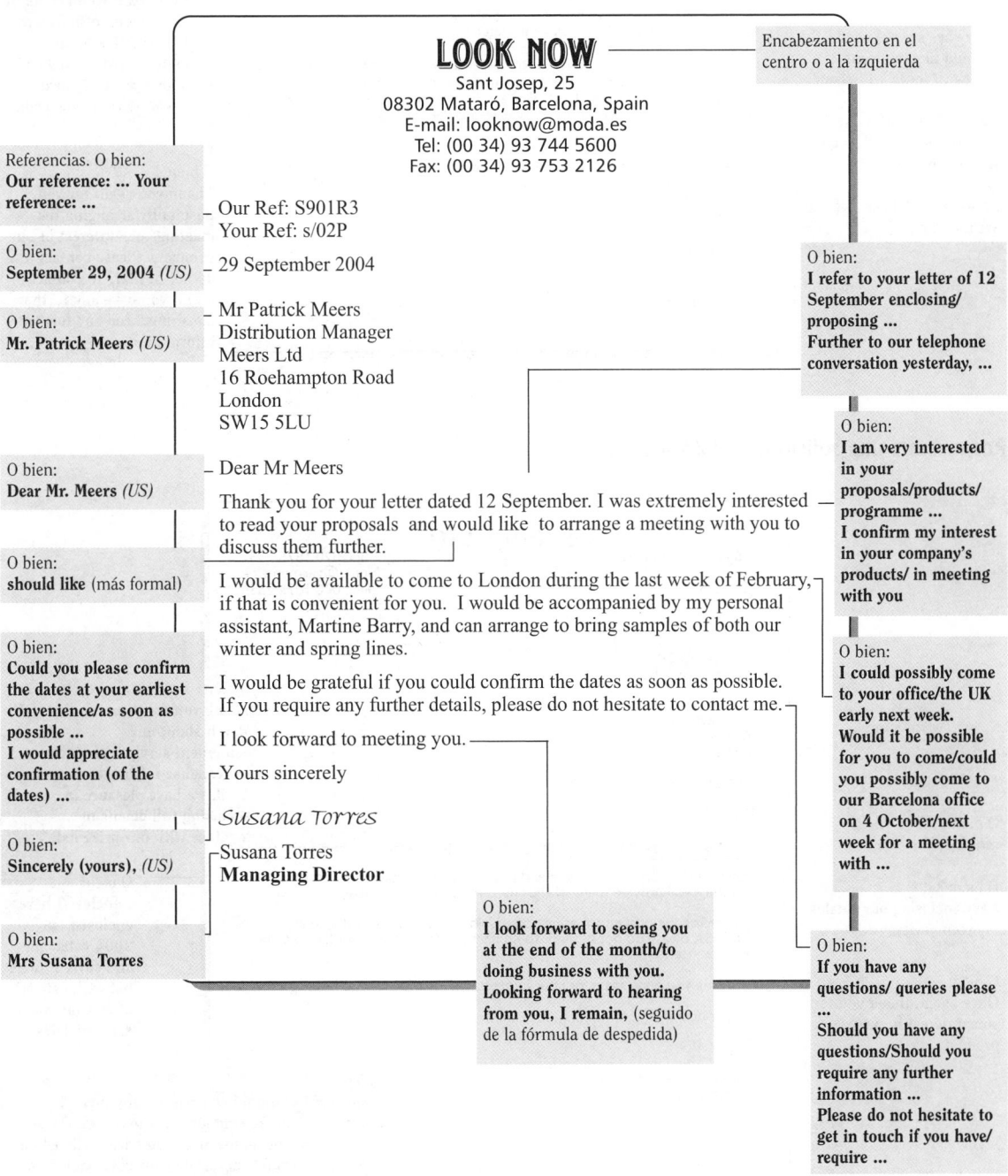

Encabezamiento en el centro o a la izquierda

Referencias. O bien:
Our reference: ... Your reference: ...

Our Ref: S901R3
Your Ref: s/02P

O bien:
September 29, 2004 *(US)*

29 September 2004

O bien:
Mr. Patrick Meers *(US)*

Mr Patrick Meers
Distribution Manager
Meers Ltd
16 Roehampton Road
London
SW15 5LU

O bien:
Dear Mr. Meers *(US)*

Dear Mr Meers

O bien:
I refer to your letter of 12 September enclosing/ proposing ...
Further to our telephone conversation yesterday, ...

Thank you for your letter dated 12 September. I was extremely interested to read your proposals and would like to arrange a meeting with you to discuss them further.

O bien:
I am very interested in your proposals/products/ programme ...
I confirm my interest in your company's products/ in meeting with you

O bien:
should like (más formal)

I would be available to come to London during the last week of February, if that is convenient for you. I would be accompanied by my personal assistant, Martine Barry, and can arrange to bring samples of both our winter and spring lines.

O bien:
I could possibly come to your office/the UK early next week. Would it be possible for you to come/could you possibly come to our Barcelona office on 4 October/next week for a meeting with ...

O bien:
Could you please confirm the dates at your earliest convenience/as soon as possible ...
I would appreciate confirmation (of the dates) ...

I would be grateful if you could confirm the dates as soon as possible. If you require any further details, please do not hesitate to contact me.

O bien:
If you have any questions/ queries please ...
Should you have any questions/Should you require any further information ...
Please do not hesitate to get in touch if you have/ require ...

I look forward to meeting you.

O bien:
I look forward to seeing you at the end of the month/to doing business with you.
Looking forward to hearing from you, I remain, (seguido de la fórmula de despedida)

Yours sincerely

O bien:
Sincerely (yours), *(US)*

Susana Torres

Susana Torres
Managing Director

O bien:
Mrs Susana Torres

Después de una entrevista

Meers Ltd

16 Roehampton Road
London
SW15 5LU

Tel: 020 1876 2332
E-mail: Meers@garments.uk
Fax: 020 1876 2334

Our Ref: s/02P
Your Ref: S901R3

Ms Susana Torres
Managing Director
Look Now
Sant Josep, 25
08302 Mataró, Barcelona
Spain

2 March 2004

Dear Ms Torres

Following our meeting of 28 February, I would like to thank you for your hospitality and confirm that we will send you a completed contract at the beginning of next week.

I am also pleased to confirm that the bulk discounts we discussed will be applicable for an order of 50 or more items. Once you have completed the order forms we left with you, please send them to our head office and the consignment will be dispatched within 14 days. The invoice will be delivered with your order. We would appreciate payment within 28 working days.

Thank you once again for your hospitality and continued interest in our products. We look forward to receiving your order and to doing business with you in the future.

Yours sincerely

Patrick Meers

Patrick Meers
Distribution Manager

En los países anglosajones, después de un primer contacto, se suele preferir llamar a las personas por su nombre. En tal caso, habría que empezar la carta diciendo **Dear Susana.**

O bien:
I would like to thank you for affording me the opportunity to meet with you and your staff.

O bien:
I would like to arrange another meeting with you to discuss matters/the proposal/ details further, and suggest next Friday/you could come to our London office on ...
I should like to discuss matters further and will phone you early next week/ write to you again.

O bien:
There are several points that I would like to discuss further. Firstly, ... Secondly, ...
I agree fully with your proposal to ..., and would like to confirm ...
O:
As we agreed/discussed on Wednesday ...

O bien:
Thank you again for your hospitality/arranging the meeting/your interest in our company. Please contact me/ do not hesitate to contact me, if you have any further questions/need any further information.

Respuesta a una solicitud de información

Meers Ltd

16 Roehampton Road
London
SW15 5LU

Tel: 020 1876 2332
E-mail: Meers@garments.uk
Fax: 020 1876 2334

Our Ref: s/02P
Your Ref: S901R3

Mr Richard Delacroix
8 Fallowfield Road
Walsall
WS5 3DL

17 March 2004

Dear Mr Ramos

Thank you for your recent enquiry about our products.

I enclose our current catalogue and price list and am confident that this literature will provide many of the answers you have requested.

If there is additional information you would like to have regarding our products, please do not hesitate to contact us. We will be most happy to be of assistance.

Thanking you once again for your interest, we look forward to hearing from you.

Yours sincerely

Margaret Meers

Margaret Meers
Assistant Manager

O bien:
Thank you for your enquiry of 13 March about our equipment/services/products ...
In response to your enquiry of 7 April, we have pleasure in enclosing full details of ..., together with our price list.

O bien:
inquiry *(US)*

O bien:
I enclose/I have enclosed our 2004 catalogue and current price list with details of discounts and delivery dates.

O bien:
I am enclosing our catalogue for your review.

O bien:
Once again, thank you for your interest in our products.

O bien:
If you require/Should you require any further information, please contact me. I look forward to hearing from you soon. After you have reviewed our material, we would appreciate your comments, and we will look forward to answering any questions you have about our products.

Respuesta a una reclamación

La carta de disculpa sigue la misma estructura que la carta de reclamación.

WOODS OF COVENTRY

21 Regina Drive
Coventry
CV9 2EQ
Tel: 02476 621699
E-mail: woods@mymail.uk

Mr Jackson Bratte
13 Pennybrook Lane
Dollis Hill
London
NW2 6HG

7 September 2004

Dear Mr Bratte

Order 324B

Thank you for your letter of 3 September, bringing to our attention the delay in the delivery of your computers for the above order.

Acuse de recibo de la carta de reclamación del cliente.

O bien:
I refer to your letter dated 3 September 2004 which arrived this morning with the consignment of damaged boxes you advised you would be returning to us.

I should like to apologize for the delay and the inconvenience this has caused you.

O bien:
I apologise most sincerely for the inconvenience this has caused you/your company and have dispatched this morning a replacement consignment of ... which will reach you by ...

We have experienced supply problems from our factory which have now been remedied. The computers are expected to arrive at our depot later this week and I shall contact you on their arrival to arrange a speedy delivery.

Explicación breve y detalle de las medidas tomadas para resolver el problema. O bien:
To compensate for the inconvenience cause to you/your company, we would like ...

Thank you for your patience and I look forward to advising you later this week.

O bien:
Once more please accept my sincerest apologies.
Please accept my/our sincere apologies once again.

Yours sincerely

Herbert Winner

Herbert Winner
Customer Services Manager

Mailing

BRACON SA
Paseo de la Havana, 10
28070 Madrid, Spain
Tel: (00 34) 91 280 3344 E-mail: bracon@tele.es
Nico Software Inc

Presentación de la empresa y asunto de la carta. Otras frases útiles:
Our firm recently received an extremely favourable review from/in ... which we hope may be of some interest to you.
It is our great pleasure to inform you that our new product line is ready for your inspection.

98 Howard Street
Manchester
M28 2SG

13 December 2004

Dear Sir or Madam

O bien:
To whom it may concern: *(Br)*
Gentlemen: *(US)*

Publishing Opportunities in Europe

We are an established publisher of European trade and business journals with high visibility throughout Europe. We are currently offering special advertising rates and benefits to new customers.

This is an excellent opportunity for your company to increase its share of the IT market in the dynamic European marketplace.

Introducción de los argumentos destinados a despertar el interés del lector. Otras frases útiles:
Since our service lends itself so well you your type of business, we would appreciate having an opportunity to speak with you or one of your representatives about ...

Please find enclosed two copies of our journals, with our compliments. If you wish to pursue our offer or require any further information, please contact our enquiry line on Freefone 900 30 33 41. I look forward to hearing from you and to our possible future partnership.

O bien: **We will look forward to seeing you soon.**

Invitación para que el lector contacte con la empresa. Otras frases útiles:
Please contact me at [nº de teléfono]**, so that we can arrange a convenient time to meet. I will be looking forward to your call.**
Please feel free to either drop in or make an appointment with one of our staff at any time.
Thank you for being a customer of our firm.
We invite you to call for an appointment to visit our display room/factory/shop.

Yours faithfully

Enrique Salas

Enrique Salas
Sales Director

Pedido

O bien:
Gentlemen: *(US)*
To whom it may concern:
Esta última expresión se utiliza en inglés británico en la correspondencia administrativa cuando no se conoce el nombre del destinatario.

O bien:
The enclosed order is based on your current price list, assuming our usual discount of ... on bulk orders.

Campoamor, 25
46022 Valencia, Spain
Tel: 00 34 963 572736

23 June 2004

Brooke's Books
188 Belvidere Road
Glasgow
G64 2JP

Dear Sir or Madam

Please send me the following items from your summer catalogue:

10 copies of "Learn English the Easy Way", Intermediate, Scot Press. Ref: 4356K
10 copies of "Improve your Ps and Qs", Scot Press. Ref 5367Q

I enclose a cheque made payable to you for £267.50, which includes the cost of postage and packaging.

I look forward to receiving confirmation of my order, and would be obliged if you would advise me in advance of the planned delivery date.

Yours faithfully

Rodolfo Marín

Rodolfo Marin

O bien:
We would like to place an order for the following items, in the sizes and quantities specified below.
I refer to your letter of 5 June enclosing your catalogue for 2004. I would like to place an order for/to order ...
Please find enclosed our order no. 471 for ...
I wish to order ... as advertised in the July issue of ...

O bien:
I enclose a cheque to the amount of £ ... *(Br)*
I am enclosing a check in the amount of $ ... *(US)*

▪Respuestas

- Thank you for your order no ... It is receiving our immediate attention and will be dispatched to you by ... Please allow 28 days for delivery.
- This is to acknowledge receipt of your order no. ... dated ..., and to advise you that the goods will be dispatched within 7 working days.
- We acknowledge receipt of your order of 12 July, which will be dispatched within 14 days.
- We cannot accept responsibility for goods damaged in transit.
- I hope we may continue to receive your valued custom.

O bien:
- We regret that we will be unable to fulfil your order for ...
- We regret that the goods you ordered are temporarily out of stock/we no longer stock the goods you ordered.

Factura

BROOKE'S BOOKS
188 Belvidere Road
Glasgow G64 2JP
Tel: 0141 762 0854

INVOICE

Invoice No: I459
Date: 9 July 2004
Order No: 321SB

To: Ana Martin
Avenida Turina 39,
Valencia 46013
SPAIN

10 copies of "Learn English the Easy Way", Intermediate, Scot Press. Ref: 4356K @ £12.25 each	£122.50
10 copies of "Improve your Ps and Qs", Scot Press. Ref 5367Q @ £13.50 each	£135.00
Postage and packaging	£ 10.00
Total due:	**£267.50** (incl. VAT)

Payment would be appreciated within 14 days of receipt.

Thanking you in advance.

O bien:
Payment is to be made 14 days after receipt of the invoice.

■Carta de reclamación por falta de pago

Our records indicate that payment on your account is overdue to the amount of £ ... If the amount has already been paid, please disregard this notice. If you have not yet posted your payment, please use the enclosed envelope to send payment in full.

Thank you in advance for your anticipated co-operation in this matter.

O bien:
in the amount of ... *(US)*

O bien:
mailed *(US)*

■Segunda reclamación

On 12 July 2004 we notified you of your overdue account for order no. ...

To date we still have not received payment for the above order.

Please give this matter your most urgent attention. Payment must be made within the next ten days.

Envío del pago

Watts On-Line

44 Ballyree Drive
Bangor
County Down
BT19 7RQ
Tel: 028 9145 0859

D George
Weldom Ltd
44-48 Eastham Street
Edinburgh
EH14 2AG

14 October 2004

Dear Mr George

Thank you for the prompt delivery of our order no. C0078.

Please find enclosed a cheque for £567.50 in payment of your invoice no. B556 of 10 October 2004.

We look forward to doing further business with you in the near future.

Yours sincerely

Brendan McMullan

Brendan McMullan
Buying assistant

O bien:
We apologise most sincerely for the non-payment/delayed payment of invoice no. ... We enclose a cheque for ... in full payment of ...

O bien:
in full/final payment of ...

O bien:
to the amount of ... *(Br)*
in the amount of ... *(US)*

O bien:
We enclose a cheque for ... in settlement of your invoice no. ... Enclosed is our payment to the amount of ... which should clear up any balance in our account with you.

Búsqueda de empleo

Carta de presentación

En los países anglosajones la carta de presentación se manda siempre mecanografiada, salvo si el anuncio especifica que la carta sea manuscrita. El papel de la carta tiene que ser el mismo que el del currículum.

Como en cualquier carta de negocios, el estilo ha de ser claro, conciso y cortés. Hay que dirigir la carta a la persona responsable, indicando su nombre y cargo si se conocen. No hay que dejar de mencionar las referencias del anuncio y el cargo en el que se está interesado. Si no se adjunta el currículum con la carta, esta deberá contener toda la información útil sobre el candidato: historial académico, experiencia profesional, aptitudes y títulos. Si la carta va acompañada de un currículum, no merece la pena repetir la información que figura en él; en este caso habrá que atraer la atención del lector, poniendo énfasis en la capacitación profesional y demostrando que uno tiene las cualidades requeridas. Se pueden volver a usar algunas palabras clave del anuncio para captar su atención.

La experiencia y los títulos que se mencionan deberán corresponder al cargo ofrecido.

El candidato tendrá que mostrar en la carta que conoce la empresa y que esta le interesa. Además, es preciso explicar por qué su experiencia y sus aptitudes se ajustan al perfil buscado. Es importante señalar que está disponible para una entrevista.

Solicitud por correo electrónico

El currículum y la carta de solicitud pueden enviarse por correo electrónico. Es preferible mandar asimismo una copia impresa por correo normal.

▪Solicitud de prácticas

Avenida de Palencia 13
47010 Valladolid
Spain

Tel: 00 34 983 4532 20
E-mail: crodriguez@wahadoo.es

Datos del remitente a la derecha.

Ms Sarah Hamilton
Personnel Manager
Hill's Press
18 Douglas Avenue
Worsley
MANCHESTER
M28 2SG

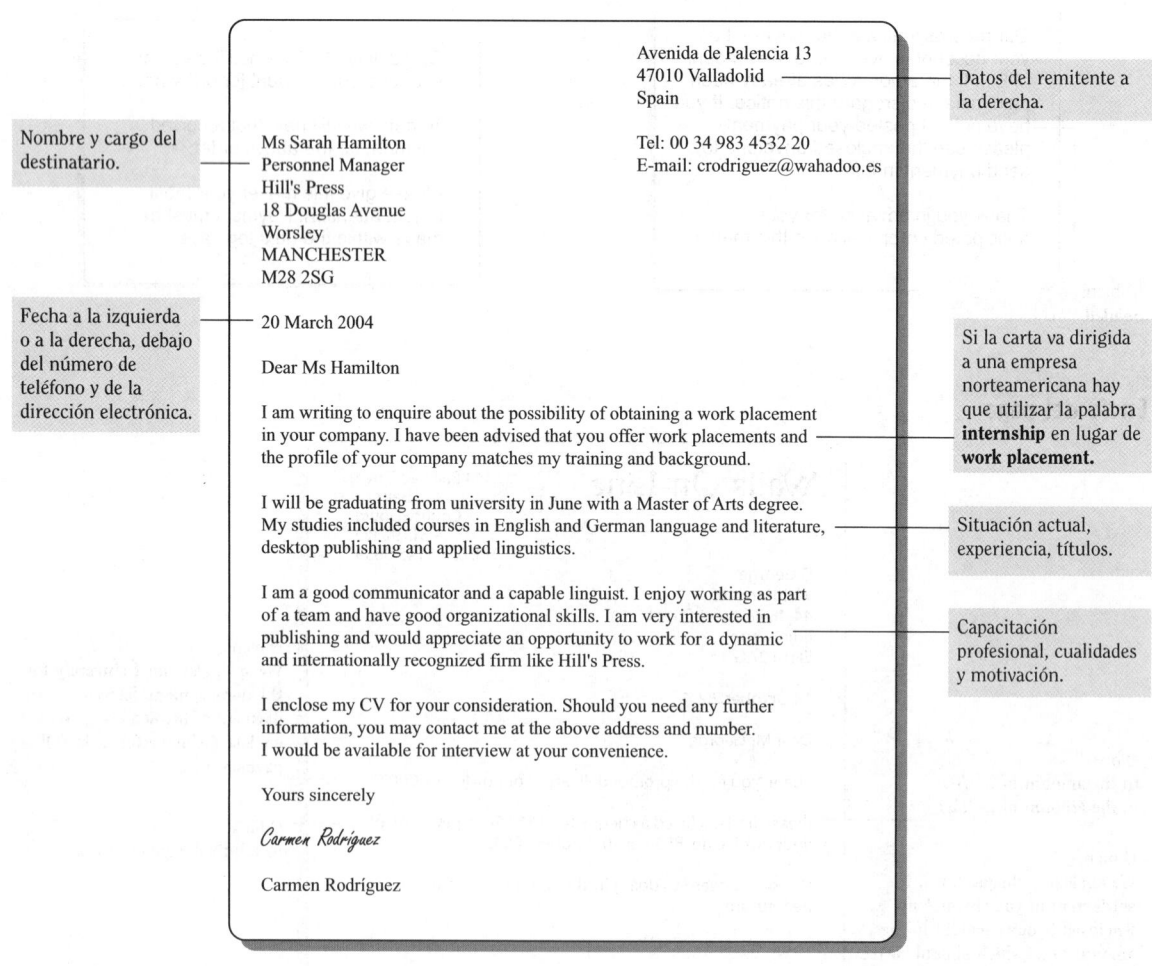

Nombre y cargo del destinatario.

20 March 2004

Fecha a la izquierda o a la derecha, debajo del número de teléfono y de la dirección electrónica.

Dear Ms Hamilton

I am writing to enquire about the possibility of obtaining a work placement in your company. I have been advised that you offer work placements and the profile of your company matches my training and background.

*Si la carta va dirigida a una empresa norteamericana hay que utilizar la palabra **internship** en lugar de **work placement.***

I will be graduating from university in June with a Master of Arts degree. My studies included courses in English and German language and literature, desktop publishing and applied linguistics.

Situación actual, experiencia, títulos.

I am a good communicator and a capable linguist. I enjoy working as part of a team and have good organizational skills. I am very interested in publishing and would appreciate an opportunity to work for a dynamic and internationally recognized firm like Hill's Press.

Capacitación profesional, cualidades y motivación.

I enclose my CV for your consideration. Should you need any further information, you may contact me at the above address and number.
I would be available for interview at your convenience.

Yours sincerely

Carmen Rodríguez

Carmen Rodríguez

▪Candidatura espontánea

29 Bletchley Road
Worthing
West Sussex
BN14 7QY

Tel: 01903 990092

Alexander Maxwell
Personnel Manager
Kingsway Ltd
24-28 Finchley Rd
London
N2 0TT

13 December 2004

Dear Mr Maxwell

I wish to enquire about any vacancy you may have in your Sales Department. Your customer services manager, Don Griffiths, suggested I wrote to you.

As you can see from the enclosed CV, I have a good educational background and twelve years' experience in sales, both as sales representative and sales executive.

I am currently working for a software company in Kent, where I have acquired essential IT skills. I believe this combined experience in sales and computing would be ideal for the job profile.

Should you consider my application favourably, I should be pleased to attend an interview at any time.

Yours sincerely

William Brownston

Enclosure

O bien:
I would like to/I wish to inquire about the possibility of becoming a ... at your factory/ facility/in your company.

Es conveniente mencionar, si se conoce, a alguien que trabaja en la empresa.

O bien:
I have been/I was given your address by a colleague of mine/ of yours, [nombre de la persona] **who has reason to believe you may be recruiting staff (for your sales team). I am seeking a position in sales/publishing at a (high technology) company such as yours.**

O bien:
As you will note from the enclosed CV *(Br)*/resumé *(US)*, I have specialized in/majored in *(US)* physics and have participated in significant research.

O bien:
at your convenience. I would like to learn more about ..., and I will contact your office early next week to arrange an appointment at your convenience.

Respuesta a un anuncio

Ave. Toluca 740
Col. Olivares
CP 01780 Mexico D.F.
México

Mr D Smithwick
Chief Analyst
Dunworkin Investments
Threadneedle Street
London
E3 6PG
UK

19 May 2004

Dear Mr Smithwick

Financial Analyst

I would like to apply for the above post as advertised in "The Guardian" of 14 May, and I enclose my CV for your attention.

I am an experienced financial analyst and consultant, having worked extensively in this sector in Mexico and Monterrey, and as a lecturer at Mexico university. I am currently looking for a position that will allow me to develop my skills and experience in a small, dynamic commercial team such as Dunworkin Investments.

I believe that my financial and academic background would be of benefit to your company. Should you consider me suitable for the post, I can provide the names of three referees.

I thank you for your consideration and remain at your disposal for any further information. I look forward to meeting you in the near future.

Your sincerely

H. de la Fuente

Héctor de la Fuente
Financial Investment Analyst

Enc.

O bien:
**I should like to apply for the above post as recently advertised in the July issue of .../which was advertised in today's Daily Post.
I am writing to apply for the above post/for the post of ... as advertised in ...
I am writing in response to your advertisement in ... for ...
I would like to be considered for the above post which your company advertised in ...**

Asunto de la carta: función o cargo.

O bien:
and (I) enclose my (current) CV *(Br)*/resumé *(US)* for your consideration.

O bien:
The position seems to fit very well with my education, experience, and career interests. According to the advertisement, your position requires excellent communication skills and an MA degree in ...

O bien:
I am confident that I can perform the job effectively and am excited about the idea of working for a dynamic firm. I know your firm seeks only the brightest staff for its team. I also know that I have the training and ability it takes to ... My degree in ... and my internship experiences have taught me how to ...

O bien:
Thank you for considering my application/for your consideration. If you would like to schedule an interview, please call me at ... I will be available at your convenience. I would appreciate the chance to meet with you. You may reach me at the above telephone number or e-mail address.

O bien:
I look forward to talking with you/to discussing matters with you (at a future interview).

Expresiones útiles

I know how to/I can operate a cash register/a computer/power equipment
I am computer literate/a good communicator/a good organizer
I am a capable linguist/can speak fluent English and German
I have good computer/IT/language/editing/communication/organizational skills
I can learn new tasks and enjoy/can accept a challenge
I enjoy working/can work with a variety of people
I work well in a team, and can also work under pressure
I perform well under stress/am good with difficult customers
I can handle multiple tasks simultaneously

Curriculum vitae

Hoy en día un buen currículum destaca si es conciso (dos páginas como máximo). Es aconsejable mencionar la experiencia profesional y los títulos según el cargo y la empresa de que se trate.

El currículum puede seguir un orden cronológico directo o inverso. En este caso, se empieza por el empleo más reciente y se termina por el más antiguo. Esta presentación es la más corriente. Cuando se aspira a un cargo o un sector profesional preciso, también se puede redactar un currículum adaptado al mismo, en el que se insiste más sobre los conocimientos, la capacitación y los resultados alcanzados que sobre la trayectoria profesional.

Se suelen omitir los artículos (**a**, **an** y **the**) y, por otra parte, se pueden usar verbos para describir experiencias, por ejemplo, **managed**, **organized**, **supervised**, **designed**, **co-ordinated**, **developed**, etc. Si se envía el currículum por correo electrónico o si es probable que la empresa lo vaya a digitalizar, es conveniente utilizar sustantivos o palabras clave que el software pueda reconocer, por ejemplo, **management**, **organization**, **supervision**, **design**, **co-ordination**, **development of**, etc.

Es preferible no indicar las referencias en el currículum. Si la empresa las pide, es mejor imprimirlas en una hoja aparte.

Si se manda el currículum por correo electrónico, es preferible escoger un tipo de caracteres sencillo y un cuerpo intermedio, entre 10 y 14 puntos. No hay que incluir tablas o gráficos, ni utilizar caracteres en cursiva o subrayados.

▪ TITULADO BRITÁNICO CON POCA EXPERIENCIA

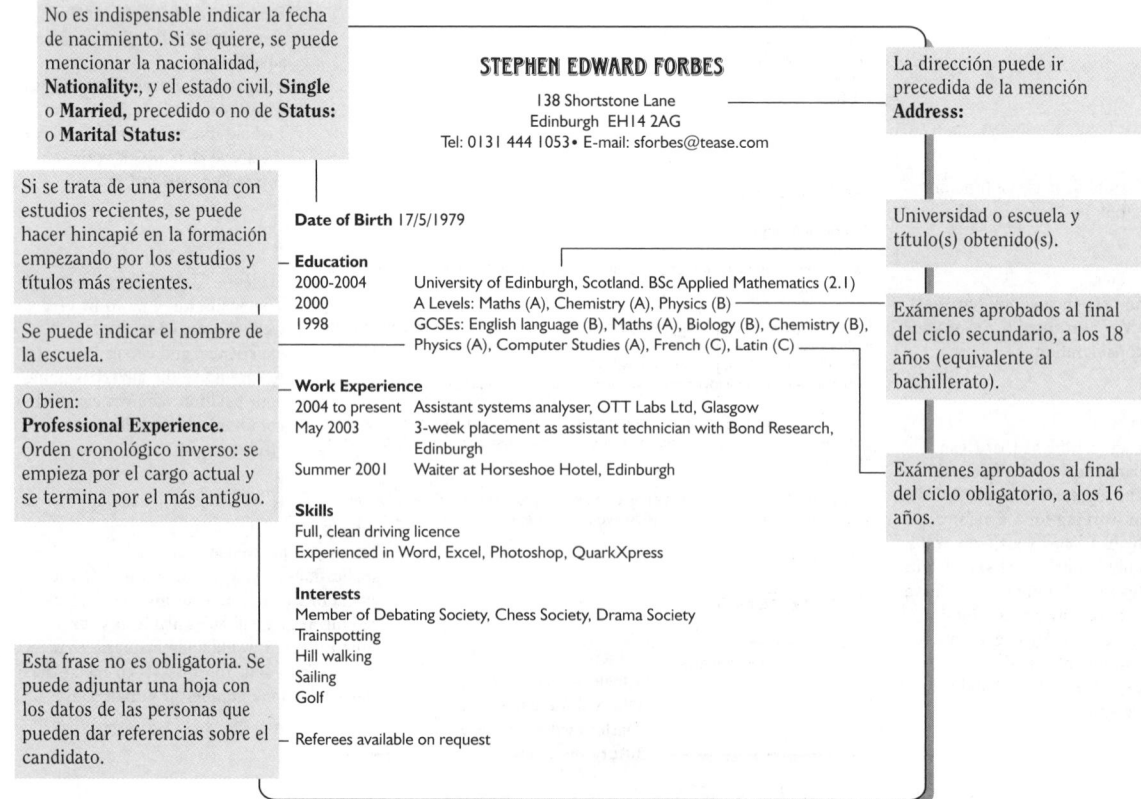

No es indispensable indicar la fecha de nacimiento. Si se quiere, se puede mencionar la nacionalidad, **Nationality:**, y el estado civil, **Single** o **Married,** precedido o no de **Status:** o **Marital Status:**

La dirección puede ir precedida de la mención **Address:**

STEPHEN EDWARD FORBES
138 Shortstone Lane
Edinburgh EH14 2AG
Tel: 0131 444 1053• E-mail: sforbes@tease.com

Date of Birth 17/5/1979

Si se trata de una persona con estudios recientes, se puede hacer hincapié en la formación empezando por los estudios y títulos más recientes.

Universidad o escuela y título(s) obtenido(s).

Education

2000-2004	University of Edinburgh, Scotland. BSc Applied Mathematics (2.1)
2000	A Levels: Maths (A), Chemistry (A), Physics (B)
1998	GCSEs: English language (B), Maths (A), Biology (B), Chemistry (B), Physics (A), Computer Studies (A), French (C), Latin (C)

Se puede indicar el nombre de la escuela.

Exámenes aprobados al final del ciclo secundario, a los 18 años (equivalente al bachillerato).

Exámenes aprobados al final del ciclo obligatorio, a los 16 años.

O bien: **Professional Experience.** Orden cronológico inverso: se empieza por el cargo actual y se termina por el más antiguo.

Work Experience

2004 to present	Assistant systems analyser, OTT Labs Ltd, Glasgow
May 2003	3-week placement as assistant technician with Bond Research, Edinburgh
Summer 2001	Waiter at Horseshoe Hotel, Edinburgh

Skills
Full, clean driving licence
Experienced in Word, Excel, Photoshop, QuarkXpress

Interests
Member of Debating Society, Chess Society, Drama Society
Trainspotting
Hill walking
Sailing
Golf

Referees available on request

Esta frase no es obligatoria. Se puede adjuntar una hoja con los datos de las personas que pueden dar referencias sobre el candidato.

▪ Británico con experiencia en un cargo intermedio

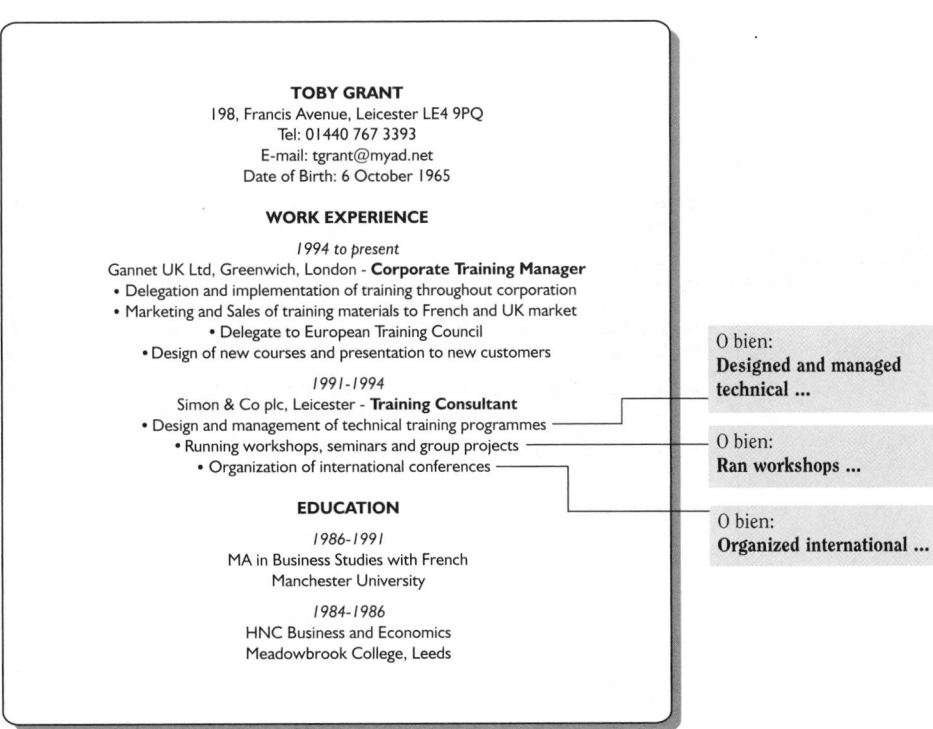

TOBY GRANT
198, Francis Avenue, Leicester LE4 9PQ
Tel: 01440 767 3393
E-mail: tgrant@myad.net
Date of Birth: 6 October 1965

WORK EXPERIENCE

1994 to present
Gannet UK Ltd, Greenwich, London - **Corporate Training Manager**
• Delegation and implementation of training throughout corporation
• Marketing and Sales of training materials to French and UK market
• Delegate to European Training Council
• Design of new courses and presentation to new customers

1991-1994
Simon & Co plc, Leicester - **Training Consultant**
• Design and management of technical training programmes
• Running workshops, seminars and group projects
• Organization of international conferences

EDUCATION

1986-1991
MA in Business Studies with French
Manchester University

1984-1986
HNC Business and Economics
Meadowbrook College, Leeds

O bien:
Designed and managed technical ...

O bien:
Ran workshops ...

O bien:
Organized international ...

▪ Titulado estadounidense con poca experiencia

Henry J. Scutter
1379 Pilgrim Street
Annapolis, MD 20000
(301) 444-5555
hjs@bingo.edu

●

OBJECTIVE
Position utilizing writing and computer skills; special interest in training

EDUCATION
B.S., Spanish with French Minor, 2003
University of Colorado, Boulder, CO
Overall GPA: 2.8/4.0
Study Abroad, Spring semester 2001
Center for European Studies Madrid, Spain
Full course load including Spanish, European History and Art History

COMPUTER SKILLS
Languages: JAVA, HTML
Software: Microsoft Word, Excel, PowerPoint

LANGUAGE SKILLS
Fluent in Spanish, conversational French

TECHNICAL EXPERIENCE
Student Computer Assistant, University of Colorado, Boulder, CO
September 2000-present (10 hours/week)
▫ Assist students with computer problems
▫ Minor installation and repair

WRITING EXPERIENCE
Writer / Editor, Colorado Student Newspaper, 1999-2003
▫ Editor of Events Page
▫ Wrote articles on campus topics weekly
▫ Wrote book reviews

ACTIVITIES & AWARDS
Boulder Chess Club, 2000-present
Dean's List: Fall 2000-Spring 2001

O bien:
TARGET

GPA = Grade Point Average o calificación media. Esta mención no es obligatoria.

▪ESTADOUNIDENSE CON EXPERIENCIA EN UN CARGO INTERMEDIO

JESSICA O'GARA
725 Boulder Henry Dr.,
Blacksburg, VA 24060
(540) 961-6666
jogara@vt.edu

OBJECTIVE
Product Designer/Manager

EXPERIENCE
Computer Consultant and Systems Designer, Systems Go Inc, Blacksburg, VA, 1997-present
Troubleshoot hardware and software problems
Design and test new operating systems
Head up large team of consultants

Assistant Systems Consultant, Benson Inc, Redmond, WA, 1993-1997
Created Web pages and customized computer systems for clients in the Redmond area

Intern, JCN Corp., Redmond, WA, June-August 1993
Worked as software design engineer intern.

EDUCATION
Bachelor of Science Degree in Computer Science, May 1993
Virginia Polytechnic Institute & State University (Virginia Tech), Blacksburg, VA

COMPUTER SKILLS
Languagues and Software : B, CC, Java, HTML, Excel, Word
Operating Systems : Unix, Windows, Mac OS

ACTIVITIES
Society of Manufacturing Engineers
Aircraft Owners and Pilots Association

O bien:
WORK EXPERIENCE
EMPLOYMENT HISTORY

No es necesario incluir esta sección cuando se quiere poner énfasis en la experiencia profesional.

▪TITULADO MEXICANO SIN EXPERIENCIA

Claudia Quiroga Ramos
RESUMÉ

PERSONAL DETAILS

CURRENT ADDRESS:	10 Poniente No. 1909 Colonia Santiago Puebla Puebla C.p. 72130 Mexico
TELEPHONE:	01 (2) 234 55 21
E-MAIL:	qr@yahoo.com
DATE OF BIRTH:	3rd May 1980
PLACE OF BIRTH:	Puebla
NATIONALITY:	Mexican
MARITAL STATUS:	Single

ACADEMIC RECORD

1998 - 2003	Universidad de las Américas, Puebla, Mexico Degree in International Relations
1995 - 1998	High School leaving certificate, Instituto Salvador Allende, Puebla
1992 - 1995	Secondary, Instituto Salvador Allende, Puebla
1986 - 1992	Primary, Escuela Primaria Oficial "2 de Abril", Puebla

EXTRACURRICULAR ACTIVITIES

1999	Participant in the 4th International Congress of the Americas Universidad de las Américas, Puebla
LANGUAGES	Spanish English
INTERESTS	Swimming Reading Listening to music

No es obligatorio mencionar la nacionalidad ni la edad. Estos datos, al igual que el estado civil, se suelen obviar.

CURRICULUM VITAE

Personal details

Surnames	Marín Rebolledo
First name	Rodolfo
Date and place of birth	Valencia, 5 September, 1966
Home address	Campoamor 25, 4º 1ª, 46022 Valencia
Telephone	963 572736
E-mail address	rmarin@ya.com
Marital status	married

Education and Qualifications

1990	Master's degree in economics and business management - IESE, University of Navarra
1988	Degree in economics - Universidad Autónoma de Valencia
1983	Secondary and High School education - IES Picassent, Valencia.

Employment History

1998 - 2004	Human Resources Consultant, ALPE Consultores, Barcelona: design and implementation of training schemes, business consultancy
1994 - 1997	Human Resources Manager, ACTESA, Valencia: recruitment, training and management of staff
1991 - 1993	Assistant to the Human Resources Manager, ACTESA, Valencia

Languages

English: advanced oral and written skills
French: intermediate-level oral and written skills

Other relevant details

Competent user of Microsoft Office
Free to travel

Abreviaturas y acrónimos usuales en la correspondencia

a/c	account (cuenta)
ack.	acknowledge (acuse de recibo)
add.	addendum (adición o apéndice)
AGM	annual general meeting (junta general anual)
am, a.m.	ante meridiem, morning (antes del mediodía, de la mañana)
AOB	any other business (ruegos y preguntas)
approx.	approximately (aproximadamente)
APR	annual percentage rate (TAE o tipo anual efectivo)
asap, a.s.a.p.	as soon as possible (lo antes posible)
av.	average (media)
bal.	balance (saldo)
b/d	bankers draft (cheque de banco)
bc., bcc.	blind (carbon) copy (CCC o copia invisible (o ciega) de cortesía)
b/e	bill of exchange (letra de cambio)
bk	bank; book (banco; libro)
bkcy, bkpt	bankruptcy, bankrupt (quiebra; en quiebra)
B/L, bl	bill of lading (conocimiento de embarque)
b/s	bill of sale (escritura de compraventa)
BST	British Summer Time (hora oficial de verano en el Reino Unido)
c.	circa (alrededor de)
CB	cash book (libro de caja)
cc	carbon copy (copia a)
CEO	chief executive officer (director gerente, consejero delegado)
CET	Central European Time (hora de Europa Central)
CFO	chief financial officer (director financiero)
chq	cheque
c.i.f., CIF	cost, insurance, freight (coste, seguro y flete)
C/O	care of; carried over; cash order (en el domicilio de; sigue; orden de caja)
Co	company; county (empresa; condado)
COD	cash on delivery (entrega contra reembolso)
Conf	confirm; conference (confirmar; conferencia)
Contd, cont'd	continued (continuación)
CV	curriculum vitae
DD	direct debit (domiciliación bancaria, *(AM)* débito bancario)
del.	delivery; delivered (entrega; entregado)
Dir	director
Dr	Doctor
E&OE	errors and omissions accepted (salvo error u omisión)
eg	for example (por ejemplo)
EGM	extraordinary general meeting (junta general extraordinaria)
enc(s)	enclosure(s) (documentos adjuntos o anexos)
ETA	estimated time of arrival (hora de llegada estimada)
FAO	for the attention of (a la atención de)
ff	following (a continuación de)
HM	His/Her Majesty (Su Majestad)
ie, i.e.	in other words (es decir)
Inc., Incorp.	incorporated (S.A.)
incl.	included, including (adjunto(a)(s) o incluido(a)(s))
infm., info	information (información)
inst	of this month (del corriente, del mes corriente)
L/C	letter of credit (carta de crédito)
Ltd	limited company (sociedad limitada)
MD	managing director (director gerente)
mgr.	manager (jefe o responsable)
mtg.	meeting (reunión o junta)
NB	nota bene (nota)
OD	overdraft (saldo negativo o deudor)
OHP	overhead projector (retroproyector)
ono	or nearest offer (negociable)
p.a.	per annum (al año o anual)
p&p	postage and packing (gastos de envío)
PAYE	pay as you earn (retención en nómina del impuesto sobre la renta)
P/L	profit and loss (pérdidas y ganancias)
PLC	public limited company (S.A.)
pm, p.m.	post meridiem (después del mediodía, de la tarde o de la noche)
p.o.	postal order (giro postal)
pp	post procurationem, on behalf of (en nombre de)
pps	additonal postscript (postdata adicional)
Pres.	president (presidente)
Prof.	professor (catedrático o profesor)
ps	postcript (postdata)
PTO	please turn over (sigue)
rc'd	received (recibido)
re	with reference to (asunto o referido a)
Ref	reference (referencia)
req, reqd	required (requerido)
retd	retired (jubilado)
sae	stamped addressed envelope (sobre franqueado)
sase	self-addressed stamped envelope (sobre franqueado con la dirección del remitente
SO	standing order (domiciliación bancaria, *(AM)* débito bancario)
tbc	to be confirmed (por confirmar)
ult.	ultimo, last (último(a))
viz	namely (o sea, es decir)
VP	vice-president (vicepresidente)
yf	Yours faithfully (atentamente)
ys	Yours sincerely (atentamente)

El fax

Estos son algunos consejos para redactar documentos que se envían por fax:

• deben mencionarse únicamente las informaciones esenciales,

• se puede adoptar un estilo telegráfico y emplear abreviaturas y acrónimos en lugar de ciertas palabras o incluso expresiones enteras, aunque es preciso utilizar las abreviaturas reconocidas como tales (véase p. 72),

• hay que cuidar el tono general del mensaje ya que los mensajes breves y fácticos pueden resultar fríos. Es aconsejable terminar con una fórmula de cortesía amistosa como, por ejemplo, "**Best Wishes**".

En una empresa

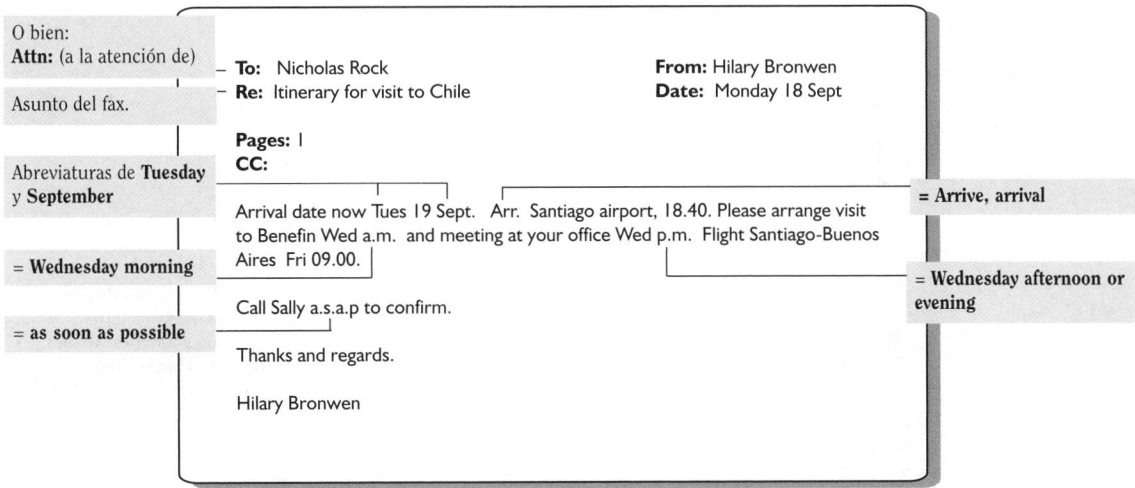

O bien:
Attn: (a la atención de)

Asunto del fax.

Abreviaturas de **Tuesday** y **September**

= **Wednesday morning**

= **as soon as possible**

To: Nicholas Rock
Re: Itinerary for visit to Chile

From: Hilary Bronwen
Date: Monday 18 Sept

Pages: 1
CC:

Arrival date now Tues 19 Sept. Arr. Santiago airport, 18.40. Please arrange visit to Benefin Wed a.m. and meeting at your office Wed p.m. Flight Santiago-Buenos Aires Fri 09.00.

Call Sally a.s.a.p to confirm.

Thanks and regards.

Hilary Bronwen

= **Arrive, arrival**

= **Wednesday afternoon or evening**

Para confirmar una reserva

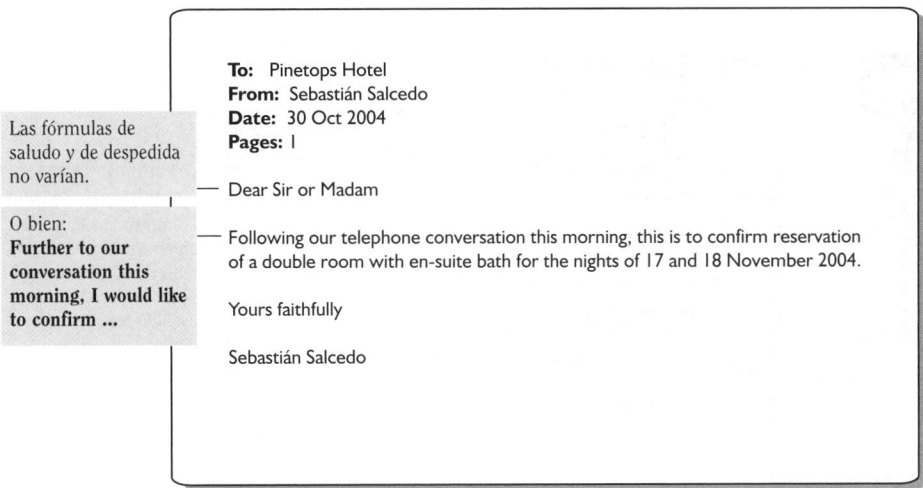

Las fórmulas de saludo y de despedida no varían.

O bien:
Further to our conversation this morning, I would like to confirm ...

To: Pinetops Hotel
From: Sebastián Salcedo
Date: 30 Oct 2004
Pages: 1

Dear Sir or Madam

Following our telephone conversation this morning, this is to confirm reservation of a double room with en-suite bath for the nights of 17 and 18 November 2004.

Yours faithfully

Sebastián Salcedo

El correo electrónico

El correo electrónico es un medio de comunicación rápido, por lo que el estilo de los mensajes suele ser familiar y telegráfico, y el uso de abreviaturas y acrónimos muy frecuente. Según la netiqueta, es decir, el código de conducta de la red, no es aconsejable escribir un mensaje todo en mayúsculas porque eso podría interpretarse como un signo de mal humor.

Se suelen omitir las fórmulas de introducción clásicas (**Dear ...**). Si uno conoce bien a su interlocutor, puede empezar con una expresión familiar como **Hello** o **Hi**, seguida del nombre de la persona.

Mensaje interno

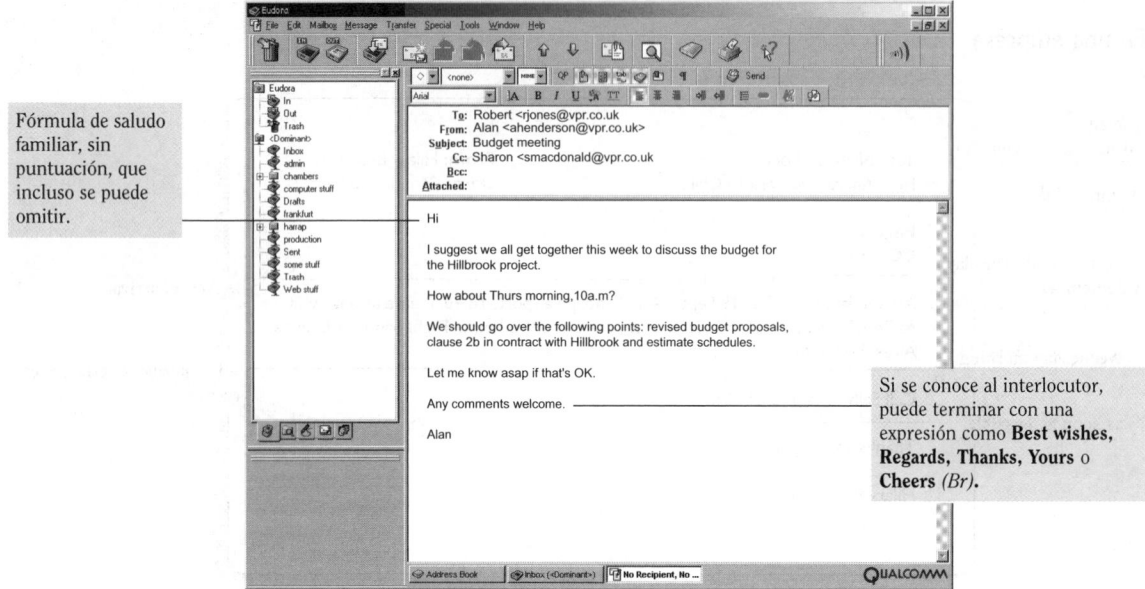

Fórmula de saludo familiar, sin puntuación, que incluso se puede omitir.

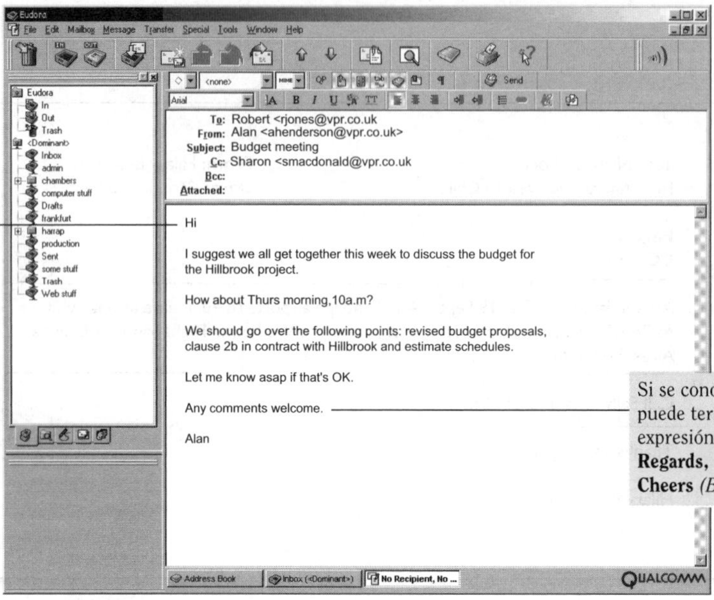

Si se conoce al interlocutor, puede terminar con una expresión como **Best wishes, Regards, Thanks, Yours** o **Cheers** *(Br)*.

Mensaje de una empresa a otra

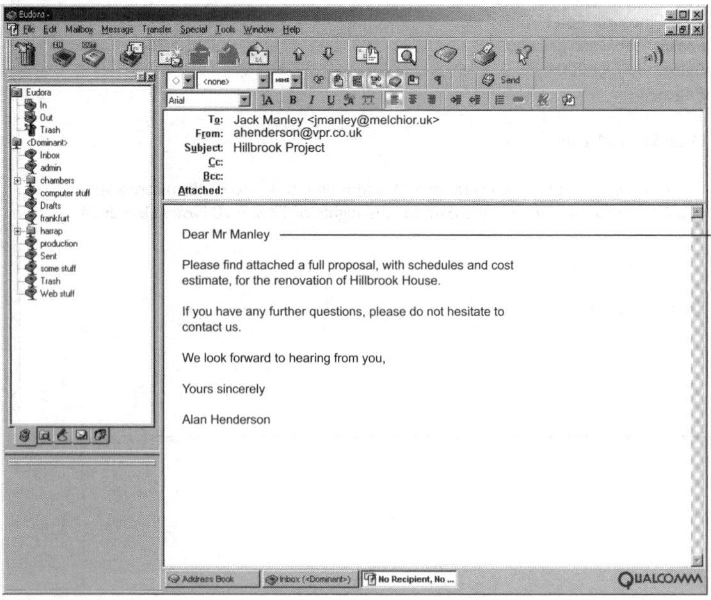

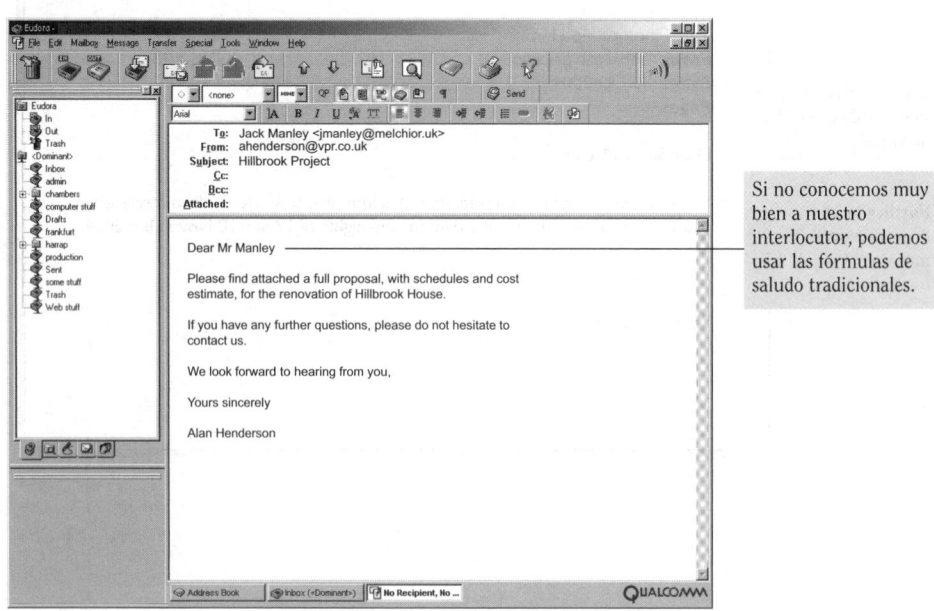

Si no conocemos muy bien a nuestro interlocutor, podemos usar las fórmulas de saludo tradicionales.

Reserva

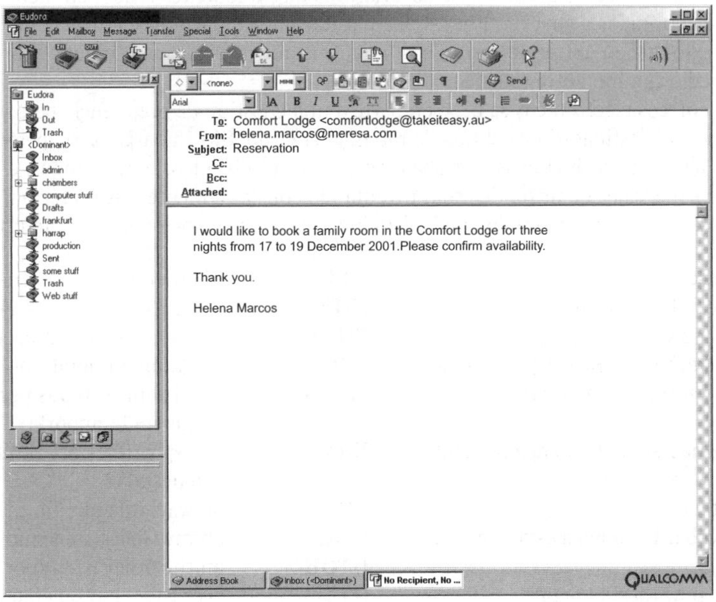

Mensaje al proveedor de acceso

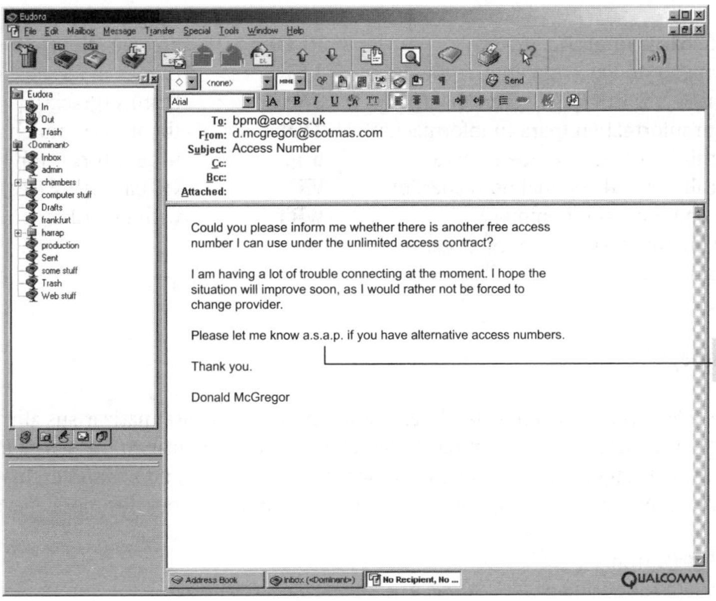

= as soon as possible

Abreviaturas y acrónimos

Incluimos a continuación una lista con algunas de las abreviaturas más frecuentes usadas en mensajes de texto (mensajes SMS), correos electrónicos y chats en línea. Cabe resaltar que la mayoría se emplean de forma mucho más habitual en mensajes de texto que en correos electrónicos, mientras que la frecuencia con que aparecen en los chats en línea se encuentra a medio camino entre estos dos.
El uso de abreviaturas en correos electrónicos se debe en parte a una cuestión de preferencia personal, y también depende mucho de quién sea el destinatario y del tipo de mensaje enviado. Sin embargo, sería perfectamente posible emplear cualquiera de las abreviaturas incluidas más abajo en correos electrónicos entre amigos, especialmente si ambos son aficionados a los mensajes de texto. Se están inventando constantemente nuevos términos pertenecientes a la jerga propia de los mensajes de texto, de modo que la lista incluída a continuación es tan sólo una muestra.

Adv	advice (consejo)
AFAICT	as far as I can tell (por lo que yo sé)
AFAIK	as far as I know (que yo sepa)
AFK	away from keyboard (*indica que alguien abandona momentáneamente el ordenador*)
AIUI	as far as I understand (si lo he entendido bien)
B4	before (antes)
BAK	back at keyboard (vuelvo a estar frente al teclado)
BBFN	bye bye for now (hasta luego)
BBL	be back later (luego vuelvo)
BTW	by the way (por cierto)
cld	could
Doc	document (documento)
EOF	end of file (fin del archivo)
F2F	face to face (cara a cara)
FAQ	frequently asked questions (preguntas más frecuentes)
FOC	free of charge (gratuito, gratis)
Foll	following, to follow (siguiente, sigue)
FWIW	for what it's worth (por si sirve de algo)
FYI	for your information (para tu información)
HTH	hope this helps (espero que te sirva)
IIRC	if I recall correctly (si mal no recuerdo)
IMO	in my opinion (en mi opinión)
IMHO	in my humble opinion (en mi modesta opinión)
IOW	in other words (en otras palabras)
ISTM	it seems to me (me parece)
ITRO	in the region of (alrededor de)
LOL	laughing out loud (me desternillo)
MYOB	mind your own business (no te metas en lo que no te importa)
NRN	no reply necessary (no hace falta respuesta)
NW!	no way! (¡de ningún modo!)
OMG	oh my God! (¡Dios mío!)
OTOH	on the other hand (por otra parte)
OTT	over the top (exagerado)
PD	public domain (dominio público)
PLS	please (por favor)
POV	point of view (punto de vista)
prhps	perhaps (tal vez)
ROTFL	rolling on the floor laughing (me parto de risa)
RTFM	read the fucking manual (léete el puto manual)
RUOK	are you OK? (¿estás bien?)
TIA	thanks in advance (gracias por adelantado)
TNX	thanks (gracias)
TVM	thanks very much (muchas gracias)
urgt	urgent (urgente)
VR	virtual reality (realidad virtual)
WRT	with regard to (en lo que se refiere a)

Emoticones o "smileys"

Los iniciados en el uso de la red recurren generalmente a los emoticones para matizar sus afirmaciones. Estos símbolos diminutos, que se logran con determinados caracteres el teclado, forman una carita que se aprecia inclinando la cabeza hacia la izquierda. Al igual que las abreviaturas, estos símbolos son exclusivos de la correspondencia entre amigos. Estos son algunos de los ejemplos más comunes de emoticones:

:-)	alegría; ironía
:-))	mucha alegría
:-D	carcajadas
:-(	tristeza; desacuerdo
:-((	mucha tristeza
:'-(	llanto
:-||	ira
:-C	mucha ira
:-O	sorpresa; conmoción
;-)	guiño
:-|	cejas fruncidas
|-)	sueño
:-¡	fumador
:-	duda
|-O	bostezos
:-*	un beso

Los anuncios clasificados

Leer un anuncio en un idioma extranjero puede resultar difícil al no conocer las abreviaturas utilizadas. Los ejemplos y listas siguientes dan las formas abreviadas que aparecen con más frecuencia en los anuncios clasificados.

Ofertas de empleo

Colombian student seeks au pair work, NE London, Aug-Dec 01. References. Contact Maria Montes, tel. 0207 405 405, a.m. only.

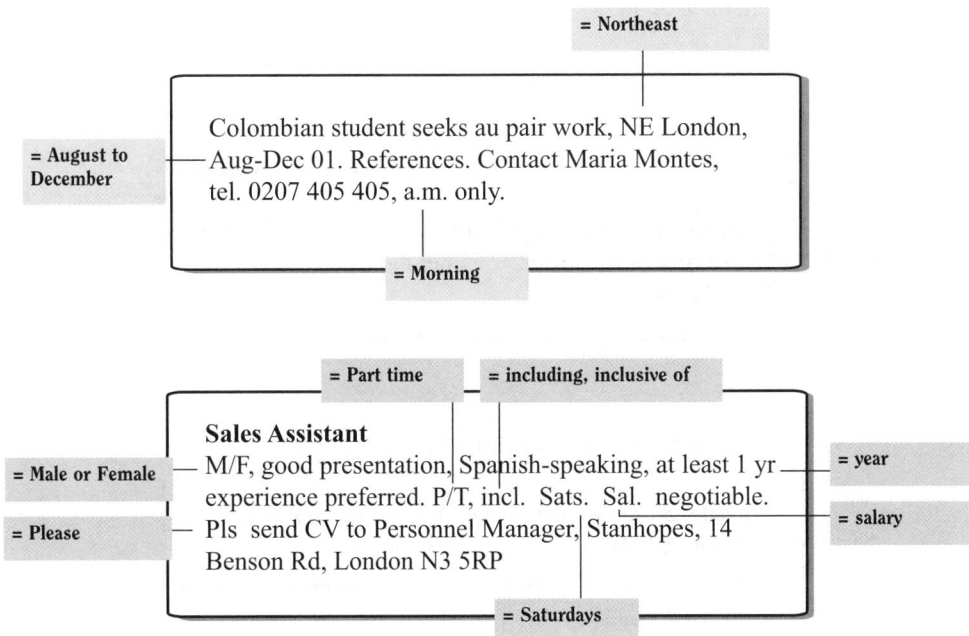

- NE = Northeast
- Aug-Dec = August to December
- a.m. = Morning

Sales Assistant
M/F, good presentation, Spanish-speaking, at least 1 yr experience preferred. P/T, incl. Sats. Sal. negotiable. Pls send CV to Personnel Manager, Stanhopes, 14 Benson Rd, London N3 5RP

- P/T = Part time
- incl. = including, inclusive of
- M/F = Male or Female
- yr = year
- Sal. = salary
- Pls = Please
- Sats. = Saturdays

Venta

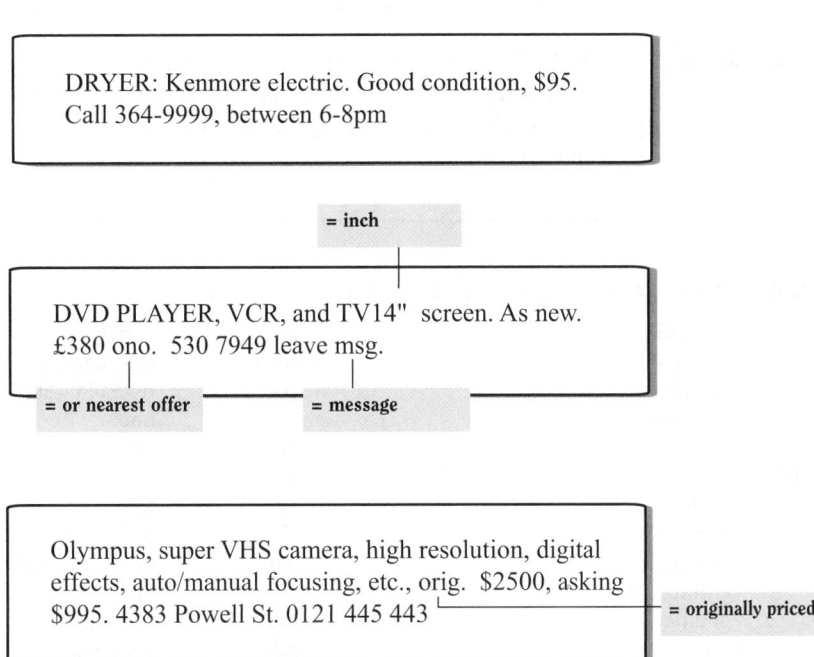

DRYER: Kenmore electric. Good condition, $95.
Call 364-9999, between 6-8pm

DVD PLAYER, VCR, and TV14" screen. As new. £380 ono. 530 7949 leave msg.

- " = inch
- ono = or nearest offer
- msg. = message

Olympus, super VHS camera, high resolution, digital effects, auto/manual focusing, etc., orig. $2500, asking $995. 4383 Powell St. 0121 445 443

- orig. = originally priced

Inmobiliaria

Lg. rm. to rent in shared house, SE London, £100 per wk., plus bills. Deposit reqd. Suit NS student.
Tel: 0206 555655

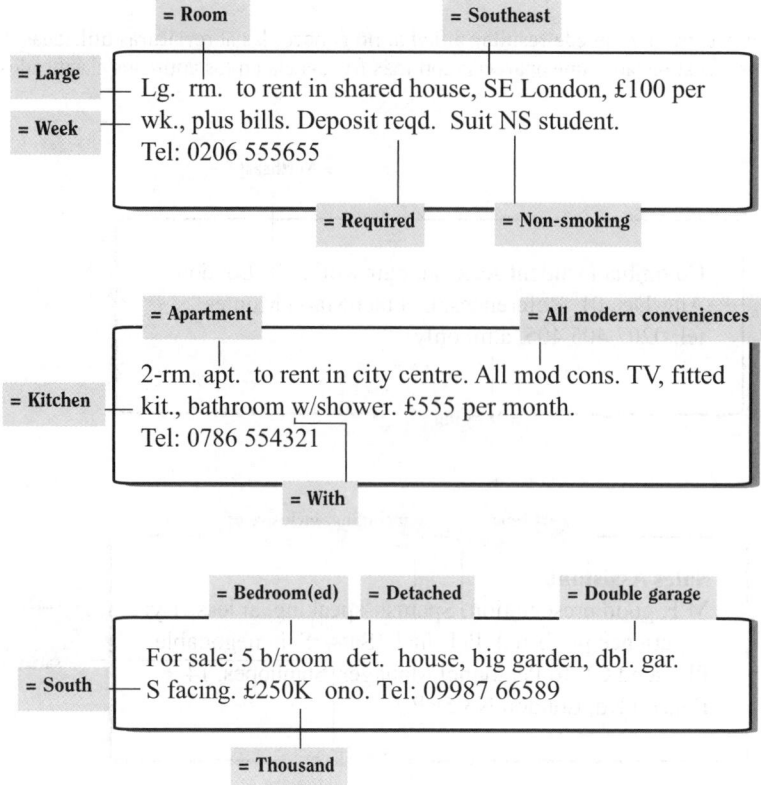

- = Large
- = Room
- = Southeast
- = Week
- = Required
- = Non-smoking

2-rm. apt. to rent in city centre. All mod cons. TV, fitted kit., bathroom w/shower. £555 per month.
Tel: 0786 554321

- = Apartment
- = All modern conveniences
- = Kitchen
- = With

For sale: 5 b/room det. house, big garden, dbl. gar.
S facing. £250K ono. Tel: 09987 66589

- = Bedroom(ed)
- = Detached
- = Double garage
- = South
- = Thousand

Encuentros/Amistades

SWM, 37YO, Aquarius. Caring, strong, romantic.
I like art, design, travel, photography & Autumn. WLTM a lady 30ish-50ish, for outings, possibly more.
London area.

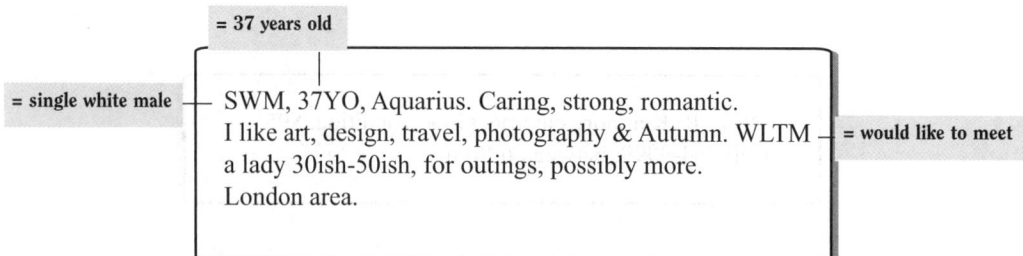

- = single white male
- = 37 years old
- = would like to meet

Abreviaturas usadas en los anuncios clasificados

AC	air conditioning	**gar.**	garage
adj.	adjoining	**GCH**	gas central heating
appt.	appointment	**H/CW**	hot/cold water
apt.	apartment	**hr.**	hour
avail.	available	**kit.**	kitchen
bedrm., BR	bedroom	**m.**	month
bldg.	building	**nr.**	near
bsmt.	basement	**obo**	or best offer
bus.	business	**ono**	or nearest offer
c/h	central heating	**opt.**	optional
cond.	condition	**pkg.**	parking
dbl.	double	**ref.**	reference
del.	deliver; delivery	**rm.**	room
det.	detached	**sal.**	salary
din.	dining	**sgl.**	single
dr.	door	**terr.**	terrace
ea.	each	**unfurn.**	unfurnished
elec.	electric	**vac.**	vacancy
exch.	exchange	**wk.**	week
fl.	floor	**wpm**	words per minute
ft.	foot, feet	**yr**	year
furn.	furniture, furnished		

▪Abreviaturas usadas en los anuncios de encuentros

A	Asian
B	Black
Bi	Bisexual
C	Christian
D	Divorced
F	Female
G	Gay
GSHO	Good Sense of Humour
H	Hispanic
ISO	In Search Of
LTR	Long Term Relationship
M	Male
NA	Native American
NBM	Never Been Married
ND	Non Drinker
NS	Non Smoker
P	Professional
S	Single
SD	Social Drinker
SI	Similar Interests
SOH	Sense of Humour
W	White
W/	With
Wi	Widowed
WLTM	Would Like To Meet
YO	Years Old

El teléfono

Pronunciación de los números de teléfono

20995 Two oh double nine five *(Br)*
Two zero double nine five *(US)*

Para pedir información

- Can I have directory enquiries *(Br) or* directory assistance *(US)* please?
- I'm trying to get through to a London number
- What is the (country) code for Canada?
- How do I get an outside line?

Para pedir hablar con alguien

Hello,

- could I speak to ...?
- can I speak to ...?
- I'd like to speak to ...
- (could I have) extension 593 please?

Para contestar a una llamada

- Robert McQueen speaking, can I help you?
- Hello, this is ...
- Yes, speaking (*para confirmar que se es la persona solicitada*)
- Hold on/hold please, I'll (just) get him/her.
- I'm sorry, he's/she's not here. Can I take a message?
- I'm afraid he's away on business/out of the office/off sick/on holiday/on vacation *(US)*

Para dejar un mensaje

En un contestador:

- I'm returning your call.
- I'll be in London next week, perhaps we can ...
- I'd like to talk to you about ...
- Could you call me back, so we can discuss ...?

A otra persona:

- Could you ask him/her to call me on ...?
- Could you tell him/her I won't be able to ...?
- I'll call back later.
- I need to speak to him/her urgently.
- Please ask him/her to confirm. Thank you.

Para pedir confirmación

- Could you spell that please?
- Could you speak a bit more slowly please?
- I'm sorry I didn't catch that. Could you repeat that please?
- Let me check, 11 a.m. Wednesday 10th. Yes, that's fine.

Para terminar una llamada

- Thank you, I look forward to seeing you on Wednesday. Goodbye.
- Thank you for your help.

Mensaje de un contestador automático

- We are unable to take your call at the moment. Please leave a message after the tone.
- I am not here at the moment. Please leave a message after the tone.

SPANISH FALSE FRIENDS

Below is a list of the Spanish false friends on the English-Spanish side in this dictionary.

actual

The most common senses of the English adjective actual are not translated by the Spanish word actual. In Spanish actual means "present", "modern" or "topical".

actually

The most common senses of the English adverb actually are not translated by the Spanish word actualmente. In Spanish actualmente means "these days" or "at the moment".

adept

The Spanish word adepto is not a translation for the English word adept. In Spanish adepto means "follower" (noun) or supporting (adjective).

affluent

The Spanish adjective afluente is not a translation for the English word afluent. In Spanish afluente means "fluent".

alcove

The Spanish noun alcoba is not a translation for the English word alcove. In Spanish alcoba means "bedroom".

amenity

The Spanish noun amenidad is not a translation for the English word amenity. In Spanish amenidad means "entertaining qualities" or "pleasantness".

bland

The Spanish adjective blando is not a translation for the English word bland. In Spanish blando means "soft", "tender", "weak" or "lenient".

candid

The Spanish adjective cándido is not a translation for the English word candid. In Spanish cándido means "ingenuous, naive".

candour

The Spanish noun candor is not a translation for the English word candour. In Spanish candor means "innocence, naivety".

carpet

The Spanish noun carpeta is not a translation for the English word carpet. In Spanish carpeta means "file, folder".

casket

The Spanish noun casquete is not a translation for the English word casket. In Spanish casquete means "skullcap".

casualty

The Spanish noun casualidad is not a translation for the English word casualty. In Spanish casualidad means "coincidence".

china

The Spanish noun china is not a translation for the English word china. In Spanish china means "Chinese woman" or "small stone, pebble", and in Latin America it can also mean an "Indian woman" or "servant".

commodious

The Spanish adjective cómodo is not a translation for the English word commodious. In Spanish cómodo means "comfortable", "convenient", "easy" or "lazy".

coloured

The Spanish word colorado is not a translation for the English word coloured. In Spanish colorado means "red".

commodity

The Spanish noun comodidad is not a translation for the English word commodity. In Spanish comodidad means "comfort" or "convenience".

complacency

The Spanish noun complacencia is not a translation for the English word complacency. In Spanish complacencia means "pleasure, satisfaction" or "indulgence".

complexion

The Spanish noun complexión is not a translation for the English word complexion. In Spanish complexión means "build".

compositor

The Spanish noun compositor is not a translation for the English word compositor. In Spanish compositor means "composer".

comprehensive

The Spanish adjective comprensivo is not a translation for the English word comprehensive. In Spanish comprensivo means "understanding".

compromise

The Spanish noun compromiso is not a translation for the English word compromise. In Spanish compromiso means "commitment", "agreement" or "engagement".

concourse

The Spanish noun concurso is not a translation for the English word concourse. In Spanish concurso means "competition".

confection

The Spanish noun confección is not a translation for the English word confection. In Spanish confección means "tailoring, dressmaking" or "preparation, making".

consistent

The Spanish adjective consistente is not a translation for the English word consistent. In Spanish consistente means "solid" or "sound, convincing".

constipated

The Spanish word constipado is not a translation for the English word constipated. In Spanish constipado means "suffering from a cold".

construe

The Spanish verb construir is not a translation for the

English word construe. In Spanish construir means "to build","to manufacture" or "to construct".

couplet

The Spanish noun cuplé is not a translation for the English word couplet. In Spanish cuplé means "saucy popular song".

deception

The Spanish noun decepción is not a translation for the English word deception. In Spanish decepción means "disappointment".

dejection

The Spanish noun deyección is not a translation for the English word dejection. In Spanish deyección means "debris" or "excretion".

depart

The Spanish verb departir is not a translation for the English word depart. In Spanish departir means "to talk, to converse".

derogatory

The Spanish adjective derogatorio is not a translation for the English word derogatory. In Spanish derogatorio means "repealing" or "rescinding".

desperado

The Spanish word desesperado is not a translation for the English word desperado. In Spanish desesperado means "desperate".

destitution

The Spanish noun destitución is not a translation for the English word destitution. In Spanish destitución means "dismissal".

devolve

The Spanish verb devolver is not a translation for the English word devolve. In Spanish the main meaning of devolver is "to give back, to return" or "to throw up".

disgust

The Spanish words disgusto and disgustar are not translations for the English word disgust. In Spanish disgusto means "annoyance" or "disappointment" and disgustar means "to upset".

duress

The Spanish noun dureza is not a translation for the English word duress. In Spanish dureza means "hardness", "harshness" or "strength".

egregious

The Spanish adjective egregio is not a translation for the English word egregious. In Spanish egregio means "illustrious".

embarkation

The Spanish noun embarcación is not a translation for the English word embarkation. In Spanish embarcación means "boat".

embarrassed

The Spanish adjective embarazado is not a translation for the English word embarrassed. In Spanish embarazado means "pregnant".

enrol

The Spanish verb enrollar is not a translation for the English word enrol. In Spanish enrollar means "to roll up" or "to bamboozle".

equivocation

The Spanish noun equivocación is not a translation for the English word equivocation. In Spanish equivocación means "mistake".

escalator

The Spanish noun escalador is not a translation for the English word escalator. In Spanish escalador means "climber".

escapade

The Spanish noun escapada is not a translation for the English word escapade. In Spanish escapada means "escape" or "quick trip".

eventual

The Spanish adjective eventual is not a translation for the English word eventual. In Spanish eventual means "temporary" or "possible".

eventually

The Spanish adverb eventualmente is not a translation for the English word eventually. In Spanish eventualmente means "by chance" or "possibly".

exit

The Spanish noun éxito is not a translation for the English word exit. In Spanish éxito means "success".

expedite

The Spanish verb expedir is not a translation for the English word expedite. In Spanish expedir means "to send" or "to issue".

extemporaneous

The Spanish adjective extemporáneo is not a translation for the English word extemporaneous. In Spanish extemporáneo means "unseasonable" or "inopportune".

fabric

The Spanish noun fábrica is not a translation for the English word fabric. In Spanish fábrica means "factory".

fastidious

The Spanish adjective fastidioso is not a translation for the English word fastidious. In Spanish fastidioso means "annoying" or "boring".

fatality

The most common sense of the English noun fatality is not translated by the Spanish word fatalidad. In Spanish fatalidad means "fate" or "misfortune".

figurine

The Spanish noun figurín is not a translation for the English word figurine. In Spanish figurín means "fashion sketch".

finality

The Spanish noun finalidad is not a translation for the English word finality. In Spanish finalidad means "aim, purpose".

flan

The Spanish noun flan is not a translation for the English word flan. In Spanish flan means "crème caramel".

fracas

The Spanish noun fracaso is not a translation for the English word fracas. In Spanish fracaso means "failure".

fume

The Spanish verb fumar is not a translation for the English word fume. In Spanish fumar means "to smoke".

fund

The Spanish verb fundar is not a translation for the English word fund. In Spanish fundar means "to found".

gaffe
The Spanish noun gafe is not a translation for the English word gaffe. In Spanish gafe means "jinxed person".

genial
The Spanish adjective genial is not a translation for the English word genial. In Spanish genial means "great" or "of genius".

geniality
The Spanish noun genialidad is not a translation for the English word geniality. In Spanish genialidad means "genius" or "stroke of genius".

genially
The Spanish adverb genialmente is not a translation for the English word genially. In Spanish genialmente means "brilliantly".

genteel
The Spanish adjective gentil is not a translation for the English word genteel. In Spanish gentil means "kind, nice".

gratification
The Spanish noun gratificación is not a translation for the English word gratification. In Spanish gratificación means "reward" or "bonus".

hermit
The Spanish noun ermita is not a translation for the English word hermit. In Spanish ermita means "country chapel" or "hermitage".

impudent
The Spanish adjective impúdico is not a translation for the English word impudent. In Spanish impúdico means "immodest, indecent".

inhabitable
The Spanish adjective inhabitable is not a translation for the English word inhabitable. In Spanish inhabitable means "uninhabitable".

inhabited
The Spanish adjective inhabitado is not a translation for the English word inhabited. In Spanish inhabitado means "uninhabited".

invidious
The Spanish adjective envidioso is not a translation for the English word invidious. In Spanish envidioso means "envious".

journal
The Spanish noun jornal is not a translation for the English word journal. In Spanish jornal means "day's wage".

lance
The Spanish noun lance is not a translation for the English word lance. In Spanish lance means "event", "dispute" or "predicament".

large
The Spanish adjective largo is not a translation for the English word large. In Spanish the main meaning of largo is "long".

largely
The Spanish adverb largamente is not a translation for the English word largely. In Spanish largamente means "for a long time", "easily" or "generously".

librarian
The Spanish noun librero is not a translation for the English word librarian. In Spanish librero means "bookseller" or (in parts of Latin America) "bookcase".

library
The Spanish noun librería is not a translation for the English word library, except in the computing sense. In Spanish librería means "bookshop" or (in Spain) "bookcase".

literate
The Spanish word literato is not a translation for the English word literate. In Spanish literato means "writer, author".

luxury
The Spanish noun lujuria is not a translation for the English word luxury. In Spanish lujuria means "lust".

mantle
The Spanish noun mantel is not a translation for the English word mantle. In Spanish mantel means "tablecloth".

measure
The Spanish noun mesura is not a translation for the English word measure. In Spanish mesura means "moderation", "courtesy" or "dignity".

mime
The Spanish verb mimar is not a translation for the English word mime. In Spanish mimar means "to spoil, to pamper".

misery
The Spanish noun miseria is not a translation for the English word misery. In Spanish miseria means "poverty", "meanness" or "hardship".

morose
The Spanish word moroso is not a translation for the English word morose. In Spanish moroso means "defaulter, bad debtor".

mundane
The Spanish word mundano is not a translation for the English word mundane. In Spanish mundano means "worldly" or "high society".

notice
The Spanish noun noticia is not a translation for the English word notice. In Spanish noticia means "(piece of) news".

notorious
The Spanish adjective notorio is not a translation for the English word notorious. In Spanish notorio means "widely-known" or "obvious".

obsequies
The Spanish noun obsequio is not a translation for the English word obsequies. In Spanish obsequio means "gift, present".

occurrence
The Spanish noun ocurrencia is not a translation for the English word occurrence. In Spanish the main meanings of ocurrencia are "bright idea" and "witty remark".

officious
The Spanish adjective oficioso is not a translation for the English word officious. In Spanish oficioso means "unofficial".

ostensible
The Spanish adjective ostensible is not a translation for the English word ostensible. In Spanish ostensible means "obvious, evident".

ostensibly
The Spanish adverb ostensiblemente is not a translation for the English word ostensibly. In Spanish ostensiblemente means "visibly, noticeably".

parent
The Spanish noun pariente is not a translation for the English word parent. In Spanish pariente means "relation, relative".

parsimonious
The Spanish adjective parsimonioso is not a translation for the English word parsimonious. In Spanish parsimonioso means "unhurried, deliberate".

periodical
The Spanish noun periódico is not a translation for the English noun periodical. In Spanish periódico means "newspaper".

petrol
The Spanish noun petróleo is not a translation for the English word petrol. In Spanish petróleo means "oil, petroleum".

petulant
The Spanish adjective petulante is not a translation for the English word petulant. In Spanish petulante means "opinionated, arrogant".

pinch
The Spanish verb pinchar is not a translation for the English word pinch. In Spanish the main meanings of pinchar are "to prick" and "to pierce".

precinct
The Spanish noun precinto is not a translation for the English word precinct. In Spanish precinto means "seal" or "sealing (off)".

predicament
The Spanish noun predicamento is not a translation for the English word predicament. In Spanish predicamento means "esteem, regard".

presumed
The Spanish adjective presumido is not a translation for the English word presumed. In Spanish presumido means "show-offish" or "vain".

presumptuous
The Spanish adjective presuntuoso is not a translation for the English word presumptuous. In Spanish presuntuoso means "conceited" or "pretentious".

presumptuousness
The Spanish noun presuntuosidad is not a translation for the English word presumptuousness. In Spanish presuntuosidad means "conceit".

prevaricate
The Spanish verb prevaricar is not a translation for the English word prevaricate. In Spanish prevaricar means "to pervert the course of justice".

prole
The Spanish noun prole is not a translation for the English word prole. In Spanish prole means "offspring".

quit
The Spanish verb quitar is not a translation for the English word quit. In Spanish the main meanings of quitar are "to remove", "to take off" or "to take away".

recipient
The Spanish noun recipiente is not a translation for the English word recipient. In Spanish recipiente means "container".

recluse
The Spanish noun recluso is not a translation for the English word recluse. In Spanish recluso means "prisoner".

recollection
The Spanish noun recolección is not a translation for the English word recollection. In Spanish recolección means "harvest" or "collection".

recur
The Spanish verb recurrir is not a translation for the English word recur. In Spanish recurrir means "to appeal (against)", "to turn (to)" or "resort (to)".

refrain
The most common sense of the English noun refrain is not translated by the Spanish word refrán. In Spanish refrán means "proverb, saying".

regalia
The Spanish noun regalía is not a translation for the English word regalia. In Spanish regalía means "royal prerogative".

regress
The most common sense of the English verb to regress is not translated by the Spanish word regresar. In Spanish regresar means "to go back, to return".

relevant
The Spanish adjective relevante is not a translation for the English word relevant. In Spanish relevante means "outstanding, important".

remark
The Spanish verb remarcar is not a translation for the English word remark. In Spanish remarcar means "to underline, to stress".

rendition
The Spanish noun rendición is not a translation for the English word rendition. In Spanish rendición means "surrender".

replicate
The Spanish verb replicar is not a translation for the English word replicate. In Spanish replicar means "to answer, to retort".

requirement
The Spanish noun requerimiento is not a translation for the English word requirement. In Spanish requerimiento means "request".

resort
The Spanish noun resorte is not a translation for the English word resort. In Spanish resorte means "spring" or "means".

resume
The most common senses of the English verb resume are not translated by the Spanish word resumir. In Spanish resumir means "to summarize" or "to sum up".

reticent
The Spanish adjective reticente is not a translation for the English word reticent. In Spanish reticente means "reluctant" or "full of insinuation".

retribution
The Spanish noun retribución is not a translation for the English word retribution. In Spanish retribución means "payment" or "reward".

revolve
The Spanish verb revolver is not a translation for the English

word revolve. In Spanish revolver means "to stir", "to mix", "to turn upside down" or "to upset".

rope
The Spanish noun ropa is not a translation for the English word rope. In Spanish ropa means "clothes".

rostrum
The Spanish noun rostro is not a translation for the English word rostrum. In Spanish rostro means "face".

sane
The Spanish adjective sano is not a translation for the English word sane. In Spanish sano means "healthy", "sound" or "intact".

sanity
The Spanish noun sanidad is not a translation for the English word sanity. In Spanish sanidad means "health" or "health service".

scenario
In the contexts of films and the theatre, the Spanish word escenario is not a translation for the English word scenario. In Spanish escenario means "stage", "setting" or "scene".

scenery
The Spanish word escenario is not a translation for the English word scenery. In Spanish escenario means "stage", "setting" or "scene".

securely
The Spanish adverb seguramente is not a translation for the English word securely. In Spanish seguramente means "probably".

sensible
The Spanish adjective sensible is not a translation for the English word sensible. In Spanish sensible means "sensitive" or "significant".

spade
The Spanish noun espada is not a translation for the English word spade. In Spanish the main meaning of espada is "sword".

stamp
The Spanish noun estampa is not a translation for the English word stamp. In Spanish estampa means "illustration", "appearance" or "image".

stretch
The Spanish verb estrechar is not a translation for the English word stretch. In Spanish estrechar means "to narrow", "to make closer" or "to squeeze".

suave
The Spanish word suave is not a translation for the English word suave. In Spanish suave means "soft", "mild", "smooth" or "gentle".

suburb
Although suburbio and suburb both refer to a residential district outside the centre of a city, they suggest quite different ideas. A suburbio would be where poorer people live, rather than the middle-classes of the suburb.

success
The Spanish noun suceso is not a translation for the English word success. In Spanish suceso means "event", "crime" or "incident".

suggestive
The Spanish word sugestivo is not a translation for the English word suggestive. In Spanish sugestivo means "attractive".

surge
The Spanish verb surgir is not a translation for the English word surge. In Spanish surgir means "to emerge", "to appear" or "to arise".

sympathetic
The most common senses of the English adjective sympathetic are not translated by the Spanish word simpático. In Spanish simpático means "likeable", "agreeable" or "amusing".

sympathy
The most common sense of the English noun sympathy (i.e. "compassion, understanding") is not translated by the Spanish word simpatía. The most common sense of simpatía is "friendliness".

talon
The Spanish noun talón is not a translation for the English word talon. In Spanish talón means "heel" or "cheque".

topic
The Spanish noun tópico is not a translation for the English word topic. In Spanish tópico means "cliché".

tramp
The Spanish noun trampa is not a translation for the English word tramp. In Spanish the main meanings of trampa are "trap" or "trick".

trampoline
The Spanish noun trampolín is not a translation for the English word trampoline. In Spanish trampolín means "diving board", "springboard" or "ski jump".

travesty
The Spanish noun travesti is not a translation for the English word travesty. In Spanish travesti means "transvestite" or "drag artist".

trespass
The Spanish verb traspasar is not a translation for the English word trespass. In Spanish traspasar means "to go through", "to go through" or "to transfer".

truculent
The Spanish adjective truculento is not a translation for the English word truculent. In Spanish truculento means "gruesome".

tuna
The Spanish noun tuna is not a translation for the English word tuna. In Spanish tuna means "group of student minstrels" or (in Latin America) "prickly pear".

vexation
The Spanish noun vejación is not a translation for the English word vexation. In Spanish vejación means "humiliation".

vicious
The most common senses of the English adjective vicious are not translated by the Spanish word vicioso. In Spanish vicioso means "depraved" or "addicted".

visor
The Spanish noun visor is not a translation for the English word visor. In Spanish visor means "viewfinder", "sight" or "file tab".

voluble
The Spanish adjective voluble is not a translation for the English word voluble. In Spanish voluble means "changeable, fickle".

which [illegible] "to recommend, to request".

rope
The Spanish noun ropa is not a translation for the English word rope. In Spanish ropa means "clothes".

[illegible]
The Spanish noun [illegible] is not a translation for the English word [illegible]. In Spanish [illegible].

sane
The Spanish adjective sano is not a translation for the English word sane. In Spanish sano means "healthy" [illegible] "fine".

sanity
The Spanish noun sanidad is not a translation for the English word sanity. In Spanish sanidad means "health" or "health services".

scenario
In the [illegible] [illegible] escenario [illegible] In Spanish escenario means "stage", "setting" or "scene".

scholar
The Spanish noun escolar is not a translation for the English word scholar. In Spanish escolar means [illegible] "pupil" or "school".

sensibly
The Spanish adverb sensiblemente is not a translation for the English word sensibly. In Spanish sensiblemente means "noticeably".

sensible
The Spanish adjective sensible is not a translation for the English word sensible. In Spanish sensible means "sensitive" or "noticeable".

[illegible]
The Spanish noun [illegible] is not a translation for the English word [illegible]. In Spanish [illegible].

[illegible]
The Spanish [illegible] is not a translation for the English word [illegible]. In Spanish [illegible].

sort
The Spanish verb sortear is not a translation for the English word sort. In Spanish sortear means "to draw lots", [illegible] or "to overcome".

suave
The Spanish word suave is not a translation for the English word suave. In Spanish suave means "soft", "smooth" or "gentle".

[illegible]
[illegible]

success
The Spanish noun suceso is not a translation for the English word success. In Spanish suceso means "event", "crime" or "incident".

suggestive
The Spanish adjective sugestivo is not a translation for the English word suggestive. In Spanish sugestivo means "attractive".

surge
The Spanish verb surgir is not a translation for the English word surge. In Spanish surgir means "to emerge", "to appear" or "to arise".

sympathetic
The most common senses of the English adjective sympathetic are not expressed by the Spanish word simpático. In Spanish simpático means "likeable", "agreeable" or "pleasant".

sympathy
The most common sense of the English noun sympathy ("compassion and understanding") is not translated by the Spanish word simpatía. The most common sense of simpatía is "friendliness".

[illegible]
The Spanish noun [illegible] is not a translation for the English word [illegible]. In Spanish [illegible].

topic
The Spanish noun tópico is not a translation for the English word topic. In Spanish tópico means "cliché".

tramp
The Spanish noun trampa is not a translation for the English word tramp. In Spanish the main meanings of trampa are "trap" or "trick".

trampoline
The Spanish noun trampolín is not a translation for the English word trampoline. In Spanish trampolín means "diving board", "springboard" or "ski jump".

travesty
The Spanish noun [illegible] is not a translation for the English word travesty. In Spanish [illegible].

trespass
The Spanish verb traspasar is not a translation for the English word trespass. In Spanish traspasar means "to go through" or "to transfer".

truculent
The Spanish adjective truculento is not a translation for the English word truculent. In Spanish truculento means [illegible].

tuna
The Spanish noun tuna is not a translation for the English word tuna. In Spanish tuna means [illegible] (in Latin America) [illegible].

versatile
The Spanish adjective versátil is not a translation for the English word versatile. In Spanish versátil means [illegible].

vicious
The most common senses of the English adjective vicious are not translated by the Spanish word vicioso. In Spanish vicioso means [illegible].

vase
The Spanish noun vaso is not a translation for the English word vase. In Spanish vaso means "glass", [illegible].

volatile
The Spanish adjective volátil is not a translation for the English word volatile. In Spanish volátil means "changeable, fickle".

FALSOS AMIGOS INGLESES

A continuación se incluye la lista de los falsos amigos que aparecen en la parte de español-inglés de este diccionario.

actual
El adjetivo inglés actual no es la traducción del español actual en sus acepciones más frecuentes. En inglés actual significa "verdadero, real".

actualmente
El adverbio inglés actually no es la traducción del español actualmente. En inglés actually significa "en realidad" o "de hecho".

adepto
La palabra inglesa adept no es la traducción del español adepto. En inglés adept significa "experto".

afluente
El adjetivo inglés affluent no es la traducción del español afluente. En inglés afluent significa "opulento, acomodado".

alcoba
El sustantivo inglés alcove no es la traducción del español alcoba. En inglés alcove significa "hueco".

amenidad
El sustantivo inglés amenity no es la traducción del español amenidad. En inglés amenity significa "servicio".

blando
El adjetivo inglés bland no es la traducción del español blando. En inglés blando significa "soso" o "insulso".

cándido
El adjetivo inglés candid no es la traducción del español cándido. En inglés candid significa "sincero, franco".

candor
El sustantivo inglés candour no es la traducción del español candor. En inglés candour significa "sinceridad, franqueza".

carpeta
El sustantivo inglés carpet no es la traducción del español carpeta. En inglés carpet significa "alfombra".

casquete
El sustantivo inglés casket no es la traducción del español casquete. En inglés, casket significa "cofre" o "ataúd".

casualidad
El sustantivo inglés casualty no es la traducción del español casualidad. En inglés, casualty significa "víctima".

china
El sustantivo inglés china no es la traducción del español china. En inglés, china significa "loza" o "porcelana".

colorado
El adjetivo coloured no es la traducción del español colorado. En inglés, coloured significa "coloreado" o "de color".

comodidad
El sustantivo inglés commodity no es la traducción del español comodidad. En inglés, commodity significa "bien de consumo" o "materia prima".

cómodo
El adjetivo inglés commodious no es la traducción del español cómodo. En inglés, commodious significa "amplio, espacioso".

complacencia
El sustantivo inglés complacency no es la traducción del español complacencia. En inglés, complacency significa "autocomplacencia".

complexión
El sustantivo inglés complexion no es la traducción del español complexión. En inglés complexion significa "tez" o "cariz".

compositor
El sustantivo inglés compositor no es la traducción del español compositor. En inglés, compositor significa "cajista".

comprensivo
El adjetivo inglés comprehensive no es la traducción del español comprensivo. En inglés comprehensive significa "detallado, completo" o " rotundo".

compromiso
El sustantivo inglés compromise no es la traducción del español compromiso. En inglés, compromise significa "solución negociada" o "solución intermedia".

concurso
El sustantivo inglés concourse no es la traducción del español concurso. En inglés, concourse significa "vestíbulo" o "concurrencia".

confección
El sustantivo inglés confection no es la traducción del español confección. En inglés, confection significa "dulce" o "creación".

consistente
El adjetivo inglés consistent no es la traducción del español consistente. En inglés, consistent significa "coherente" o "invariable, constante".

constipado
El adjetivo inglés constipated no es la traducción del español constipado. En inglés constipated significa "estreñido".

construir
El verbo inglés to construe no es la traducción del español construir. En inglés to construe significa "interpretar".

cuplé
El sustantivo inglés couplet no es la traducción del español cuplé. En inglés, couplet significa "pareado".

decepción
El sustantivo inglés deception no es la traducción del español decepción. En inglés deception significa "engaño".

departir
El verbo inglés to depart no es la traducción del español departir. En inglés to depart significa "salir" o "desviarse".

derogatorio
El adjetivo inglés derogatory no es la traducción del español derogatorio. En inglés, derogatory significa "despectivo".

desesperado
El término inglés desperado no es la traducción del español desesperado. En inglés, desperado significa "forajido".

destitución
El sustantivo inglés destitution no es la traducción del español destitución . En inglés, destitution significa "indigencia".

devolver
El verbo inglés to devolve no es la traducción del español devolver. En inglés to devolve significa "transferir, traspasar" o "recaer".

deyección
El sustantivo inglés dejection no es la traducción del español deyección. En inglés dejection significa "abatimiento".

disgustar
El verbo inglés to disgust no es la traducción del español disgustar. En inglés to disgust significa "repugnar".

disgusto
El sustantivo inglés disgust no es la traducción del español disgusto. En inglés disgust significa "asco, repugnancia".

dureza
El sustantivo inglés duress no es la traducción del español dureza. En inglés, duress significa "coacción".

egregio
El adjetivo inglés egregious no es la traducción del español egregio. En inglés egregious significa "atroz".

embarazada
El adjetivo inglés embarrassed no es la traducción del español embarazada. En inglés embarrassed significa "avergonzado" o "azorado, violento".

embarcación
El sustantivo inglés embarkation no es la traducción del español embarcación. En inglés embarkation significa "embarque".

enrollar
El verbo inglés to enrol no es la traducción del español enrollar. En inglés, to enrol significa "inscribir".

envidioso
El adjetivo inglés invidious no es la traducción del español envidioso. En inglés, invidious significa "odioso" o "ingrato".

equivocación
El sustantivo inglés equivocation no es la traducción del español equivocación. En inglés, equivocation significa "evasivas, ambigüedades".

ermita
El sustantivo inglés hermit no es la traducción del español ermita. En inglés hermit significa "ermitaño".

escalador
El sustantivo inglés escalator no es la traducción del español escalador. En inglés, escalator significa "escalera mecánica".

escapada
El sustantivo inglés escapade no es la traducción del español escapada. En inglés escapade significa "aventura, correría".

escenario
El sustantivo inglés scenery no es la traducción de la palabra española escenario. En inglés scenery significa "decorado" o "paisaje". Por otra parte, en el contexto de cine o teatro el sustantivo inglés scenario significa "argumento".

espada
El sustantivo inglés spade no es la traducción del español espada. En inglés spade significa "pala" o "pica".

estampa
El sustantivo inglés stamp no es la traducción del español estampa. En inglés el sentido básico de stamp es "sello".

estrechar
El verbo inglés to stretch no es la traducción del español estrechar. En inglés el sentido básico de to stretch es "estirar" o "extender".

eventual
El adjetivo inglés eventual no es la traducción del español eventual. En inglés eventual significa "final".

eventualmente
El adverbio inglés eventually no es la traducción del español eventualmente. En inglés eventually significa "finamente, al final".

éxito
El sustantivo inglés exit no es la traducción del español éxito. En inglés, exit significa "salida".

expedir
El verbo inglés to expedite no es la traducción del español expedir. En inglés, to expedite significa "acelerar, apresurar".

extemporáneo
El adjetivo inglés extemporaneous no es la traducción del español extemporáneo. En inglés, extemporaneous significa "improvisado".

fábrica
El sustantivo inglés fabric no es la traducción de la palabra española fábrica. En inglés fabric significa "tejido" o "estructura".

fastidioso
El adjetivo inglés fastidious no es la traducción del español fastidioso. En inglés, fastidious significa "meticuloso, puntilloso" o "quisquilloso".

fatalidad
Salvo en la acepción de "cualidad de fatal", el sustantivo fatality no es la traducción del español fatalidad. El sentido más frecuente del inglés fatality es "víctima mortal".

figurín
El sustantivo inglés figurine no es la traducción del español figurín. En inglés, figurine significa "figurilla, estatuilla".

finalidad
El sustantivo inglés finality no es la traducción del español finalidad. En inglés, finality significa "rotundidad, irrevocabilidad".

flan
El sustantivo inglés flan no es la traducción del español flan. En inglés flan significa "tarta".

fracaso
El sustantivo inglés fracas no es la traducción del español fracaso. En inglés, fracas significa "gresca, refriega".

fumar
El verbo inglés to fume no es la traducción del español fumar. En inglés to fume significa "despedir gases" o "echar humo".

fundar
El verbo inglés to fund no es la traducción del español fundar. En inglés to fund significa "financiar".

gafe
El sustantivo inglés gaffe no es la traducción del español gafe. En inglés gaffe significa "desliz, metedura de pata".

genial
El adjetivo inglés genial no es la traducción del español genial. En inglés genial significa "cordial, amable".

genialidad
El sustantivo inglés geniality no es la traducción del español genialidad. En inglés geniality significa "cordialidad, amabilidad".

genialmente
El adverbio inglés genially no es la traducción del español genialmente. En inglés genially significa "cordialmente, amablemente".

gentil
El adjetivo inglés genteel no es la traducción del español gentil. En inglés genteel significa "fino, afectado" o "respetable".

gratificación
El sustantivo inglés gratification no es la traducción del español gratificación. En inglés, gratification significa "satisfacción".

impúdico
El adjetivo inglés impudent no es la traducción del español impúdico. En inglés, impudent significa "desvergonzado, insolente".

inhabitable
El adjetivo inglés inhabitable no es la traducción del español inhabitable. En inglés inhabitable significa "habitable".

inhabitado
El adjetivo inglés inhabited no es la traducción del español inhabitado. En inglés inhabited significa "habitado".

intoxicar
El verbo inglés to intoxicate no es la traducción del español intoxicar. En inglés to intoxicate significa "embriagar" o "emborrachar".

jornal
El sustantivo inglés journal no es la traducción del español jornal. En inglés, journal significa "revista, boletín" o "diario".

lance
El sustantivo inglés lance no es la traducción del español lance. En inglés lance significa "lanza".

largamente
El adverbio inglés largely no es la traducción del español largamente. En inglés largely significa "en gran medida" o "principalmente".

largo
El adjetivo inglés large no es la traducción del español largo. En inglés large significa "grande".

librería
Excepto en la acepción de informática, el sustantivo inglés library no es la traducción del español librería. En inglés library significa "biblioteca".

librero
El sustantivo inglés librarian no es la traducción del español librero. En inglés librarian significa "bibliotecario".

literato
El adjetivo inglés literate no es la traducción del español literato. En inglés literate significa "que sabe leer y escribir" o "culto, instruido".

lujuria
El sustantivo inglés luxury no es la traducción del español lujuria. En inglés luxury significa "lujo".

mantel
El sustantivo inglés mantle no es la traducción del español mantel. En inglés mantle significa "manto", "manguito incandescente" o "capa".

mesura
El sustantivo inglés measure no es la traducción del español mesura. En inglés measure significa "medida" o "indicador".

mimar
El verbo inglés to mime no es la traducción del español mimar. En inglés to mime significa "hacer mímica" o "representar con gestos".

miseria
El sustantivo inglés misery no es la traducción del español miseria. En inglés misery significa "tristeza, infelicidad".

moroso
El término inglés morose no es la traducción del español moroso. En inglés morose significa "hosco, huraño".

mundano
El adjetivo inglés mundane no es la traducción del español mundano. En inglés mundane significa "prosaico" o "banal".

noticia
El sustantivo inglés notice no es la traducción del español noticia. En inglés notice significa "aviso", "cartel" o "atención".

notorio
El adjetivo español notorio se traduce al inglés como notorious únicamente si las connotaciones de aquél son negativas, ya que en inglés notorious significa "famoso por algo negativo, infame".

obsequio
El sustantivo inglés obsequies no es la traducción del español obsequio. En inglés obsequies significa "exequias".

ocurrencia
El sustantivo inglés occurrence no es la traducción del español ocurrencia. En inglés ocurrence significa "suceso" o "incidencia".

oficioso
El adjetivo inglés officious no es la traducción del español oficioso. En inglés officious significa "excesivamente celoso" o "entrometido".

ostensible
El adjetivo inglés ostensible no es la traducción del español ostensible. El término inglés ostensible significa "aparente".

ostensiblemente
El adverbio inglés ostensibly no es la traducción del español

ostensiblemente. En inglés ostensibly significa "aparentemente".

pariente

El sustantivo inglés parent no es la traducción del español pariente. En inglés parent significa "padre" o "madre".

parsimonioso

El adjetivo inglés parsimonious no es la traducción del español parsimonioso. En inglés parsimonious significa "mezquino".

periódico

El sustantivo inglés periodical no es la traducción del español periódico. En inglés periodical significa "publicación periódica, boletín".

petróleo

El sustantivo inglés petrol no es la traducción del español petróleo. En inglés petrol significa "gasolina".

petulante

El adjetivo inglés petulant no es la traducción del español petulante. En inglés petulant significa "caprichoso".

pinchar

El verbo inglés to pinch no es la traducción del español pinchar. En inglés to pinch significa "pellizcar", "apretar" o "afanar".

precinto

El sustantivo inglés precinct no es la traducción del español precinto. En inglés precint significa "zona comercial", "distrito" o "comisaría".

predicamento

El sustantivo inglés predicament no es la traducción del español predicamento. En inglés predicament significa "aprieto, apuro" o "dilema, conflicto".

presumido

El adjetivo inglés presumed no es la traducción del español presumido. La oración inglesa "he is presumed dead" podría traducirse como "se le da por muerto".

presuntuosidad

El sustantivo inglés presumptuousess no es la traducción del español presuntuosidad. En inglés presumptuousness significa "impertinencia".

presuntuoso

El adjetivo inglés presumptuous no es la traducción del español presuntuoso. En inglés presumptuous significa "impertinente".

prevaricar

El verbo inglés to prevaricate no es la traducción del español prevaricar. En inglés to prevaricate significa "dar rodeos, andar con evasivas".

prole

El sustantivo inglés prole no es la traducción del español prole. En inglés prole significa "proletariado".

quitar

El verbo inglés to quit no es la traducción del español quitar. En inglés to quit significa "abandonar", "dejar", "irse" o "dimitir".

recipiente

El sustantivo inglés recipient no es la traducción del español recipiente. En inglés recipient significa "destinatario" o "receptor".

recluso

El sustantivo inglés recluse no es la traducción del español recluso. En inglés recluse significa "solitario".

recolección

El sustantivo inglés recollection no es la traducción del español recolección. En inglés recollection significa "recuerdo".

recurrir

El verbo inglés to recur no es la traducción del español recurrir. En inglés to recur significa "repetirse" o "reaparecer".

refrán

El sustantivo inglés refrain no es la traducción del español refrán. En inglés refrain significa "estribillo" o "cantinela".

regalía

El sustantivo inglés regalia no es la traducción del español regalía. En inglés regalia significa "galas".

regresar

El verbo inglés to regress no es la traducción del español regresar. En inglés to regress significa "involucionar, sufrir una regresión".

relevancia

El sustantivo inglés relevance no es la traducción del español relevancia. En inglés relevance significa "pertinencia".

relevante

El adjetivo inglés relevant no es la traducción del español relevante. En inglés relevant significa "pertinente" o "correspondiente".

remarcar

El verbo inglés to remark no es la traducción del español remarcar. En inglés to remark significa "comentar, observar".

rendición

El sustantivo inglés rendition no es la traducción del español rendición. En inglés rendition significa "interpretación".

replicar

El verbo inglés to replicate no es la traducción del español replicar. En inglés to replicate significa "reproducir" o "reproducirse".

requerimiento

El sustantivo inglés requirement no es la traducción del español requerimiento. En inglés requirement significa "requisito".

resorte

El sustantivo inglés resort no es la traducción del español resorte. En inglés resort significa "recurso", "centro turístico" o "refugio".

resumir

El verbo inglés to resume no es la traducción del español resumir. En inglés to resume significa "reanudar" o "continuar".

reticente

El adjetivo inglés reticent no es la traducción de reticente. En inglés reticent significa "reservado".

retribución

El sustantivo inglés retribution no es la traducción del español retribución. En inglés retribution significa "represalias".

revolver

El verbo inglés to revolve no es la traducción del español revolver. En inglés to revolve significa "girar" o "considerar".

ropa
El sustantivo inglés rope no es la traducción del español ropa. En inglés rope significa "cuerda, soga".

rostro
El sustantivo inglés rostrum no es la traducción del español rostro. En inglés rostrum significa "estrado".

sanidad
El sustantivo inglés sanity no es la traducción del español sanidad. En inglés sanity significa "cordura" o "sensatez".

sano
El adjetivo inglés sane no es la traducción del español sano. En inglés sane significa "cuerdo" o "juicioso".

seguramente
El adverbio inglés securely no es la traducción del español seguramente. En inglés securely significa "a buen recaudo" o "firmemente".

sensible
El adjetivo inglés sensible no es la traducción del español sensible. En inglés sensible significa "sensato", "práctico" o "considerable".

simpatía
La acepción más frecuente del sustantivo español simpatía ("cordialidad") no se traduce al inglés como sympathy. Los sentidos más habituales de sympathy son "compasión" o "comprensión".

simpático
Salvo en la acepción de anatomía, el adjetivo inglés sympathetic no es la traducción del español simpático. En inglés sympathetic significa "comprensivo", "compasivo".

suave
El adjetivo inglés suave no es la traducción del español suave. El inglés suave significa "fino", "zalamero" o "elegante".

suburbio
Aunque tanto suburb como suburbio se refieren a un barrio situado a las afueras de una población, sus connotaciones son diametralmente opuestas, ya que con el sustantivo suburb se hace referencia a la zona en la que habitan las clases acomodadas, y no las familias más modestas, quienes viven en un suburbio.

suceso
El sustantivo inglés success no es la traducción del español suceso. En inglés success significa "éxito".

sugestivo
El adjetivo inglés suggestive no es la traducción del español sugestivo. En inglés suggestive significa "sugerente" o "insinuante".

surgir
El verbo inglés to surge no es la traducción del español surgir. En inglés to surge significa "incrementarse repentinamente" o "abalanzarse".

talón
El sustantivo inglés talon no es la traducción del español talón. En inglés talon significa "garra" o "uña extremadamente larga".

tópico
El sustantivo inglés topic no es la traducción del español tópico. En inglés topic significa "tema, asunto".

trampa
El sustantivo inglés tramp no es la traducción del español trampa. En inglés tramp significa "vagabundo", "fulana" o "carguero".

trampolín
El sustantivo inglés trampoline no es la traducción del español trampolín. En inglés trampoline significa "cama elástica".

traspasar
El verbo inglés to trespass no es la traducción del español traspasar. En inglés to trespass significa "entrar sin autorización".

travestí
El sustantivo inglés travesty no es la traducción del español travestí. En inglés travesty significa "farsa, parodia burda".

truculento
El adjetivo inglés truculent no es la traducción del español truculento. En inglés truculent significa "agresivo".

tuna
El sustantivo inglés tuna no es la traducción del español tuna. En inglés tuna significa "atún".

vejación
El sustantivo inglés vexation no es la traducción del español vejación. En inglés vexation significa "disgusto" o "enfado".

vicioso
El adjetivo inglés vicious no es la traducción del español vicioso. En inglés vicious significa "brutal", "despiadado" o "cruel".

visor
El sustantivo inglés visor no es la traducción del español visor. El inglés visor significa "visera".

voluble
El adjetivo inglés voluble no es la traducción del español voluble. En inglés voluble significa "locuaz".

DICTIONARY
DICCIONARIO

English-Spanish
Inglés-Español

A, a

A, a [eɪ] *n* (a) *(letter)* A, a *f* (b) IDIOMS **to get from A to B** ir de un lugar a otro; **from A to Z** de principio a fin ►► ***A to Z*** *(street guide) Esp* callejero *m*, *Am* guía *f* de la ciudad; **an A to Z of gardening** una guía completa de jardinería

A [eɪ] *n* (a) *(first, most important) Br* ***A road*** ≃ carretera *f* nacional *or* general; ***A-side*** *(of record)* cara *f* A, primera cara *f*
(b) *Sch (grade)* sobresaliente *m*; **to get an A** *(in exam, essay)* sacar un sobresaliente
(c) *Br* ***A level*** = examen final o diploma en una asignatura de los estudios preuniversitarios
(d) ***A bomb*** bomba *f* atómica
(e) *Mus* la *m*
(f) **A4** *(paper format)* A4, Din-A4
(g) (*abbr* **ampere**) A

A [ə, *stressed* eɪ] *indefinite art*

Antes de vocal o "h" muda **an** [ən, *stressed* æn].

(a) *(in general)* un, una; **a man** un hombre; **a woman** una mujer; **an hour** una hora; **I haven't got a television** no tengo televisión; **do they all have a knife and fork?** ¿tienen todos cuchillo y tenedor?; **can I have a quick wash?** ¿me puedo lavar en un momento?; **he is an Englishman/a father/a lawyer** es inglés/padre/abogado; **he's a nice person** es (una) buena persona; **she's a friend (of mine)** es amiga mía; **she didn't give me a penny** no me dio ni un centavo; **he was hailed as a new Pele** fue aclamado como el nuevo Pelé; **a dog has four legs** los perros tienen cuatro patas; **I've spent many a happy hour with them** he pasado muchas horas felices con ellos
(b) *(referring to personal attribute)* **he has a red nose** tiene la nariz roja; **I have a sore throat** me duele la garganta, tengo dolor de garganta; **she has a sharp tongue** tiene la lengua afilada
(c) *(expressing prices, rates)* **30 pence a kilo** 30 peniques el kilo; **three times a week/a year** tres veces a la semana/al año; **50 kilometres an hour** 50 kilómetros por hora
(d) *(replacing number one)* **a hundred** cien; **a thousand** mil; **a quarter** un cuarto; **two and a half** dos y medio; **a third of the participants** un tercio de los participantes; **two girls and a boy** dos chicas y un chico
(e) *(expressing time)* **the exam is on a Monday** el examen cae en lunes; **a week on Thursday** el jueves de la semana que viene; **a quarter of an hour** un cuarto de hora; **half an hour** media hora
(f) *(a certain)* **a Mr Watkins phoned** llamó un tal Sr. Watkins; **there was a bitterness in her words** había una cierta amargura en sus palabras
(g) *(referring to people collectively)* **a good cook never uses too much salt** un buen cocinero no usa demasiada sal; **a policeman should never drink on duty** los policías no deben beber cuando están de servicio
(h) *(referring to work of art)* **it's a Renoir** es un Renoir; **a well-known Goya** un Goya muy conocido
(i) *(referring to family)* **you can tell he's a Kennedy** se nota que es un Kennedy
(j) *(in exclamations)* **what an idiot!** ¡qué idiota!

A-1 [eɪ'wʌn] *adj* (a) *(first-class, perfect)* **everything's A.** está todo perfecto (b) *(in health)* **to be A.** tener una salud de hierro (c) *Naut* en excelente estado

AA [eɪ'eɪ] **1** *n* (a) (*abbr* **Alcoholics Anonymous**) AA, Alcohólicos *mpl* Anónimos (b) *Br* (*abbr* **Automobile Association**) = asociación automovilística británica, *Esp* ≃ RACE *m*, *Arg* ≃ ACA *m* (c) *US* (*abbr* **Associate in Arts**) ≃ diplomado(a) *m,f* en Filosofía y Letras
2 *adj* (*abbr* **anti-aircraft**) antiaéreo(a)

AAA [eɪeɪ'eɪ] *n US* (*abbr* **American Automobile Association**) = asociación automovilística estadounidense

Aachen ['ɑːkən] *n* Aquisgrán

AAC&U ['eɪeɪsiːən'djuː] *n* (*abbr* **Association of American Colleges and Universities**) = asociación estadounidense de escuelas superiores y universidades

aardvark ['ɑːdvɑːk] *n* cerdo *m* hormiguero

AB [eɪ'biː] *n* (a) *US Univ* (*abbr* **artium baccalaureus**) *(qualification)* licenciatura *f* en Filosofía y Letras; *(person)* licenciado(a) *m,f* en Filosofía y Letras (b) *Naut* (*abbr* **able-bodied seaman**) marinero *m* de primera

ABA [eɪbiː'eɪ] *n* (*abbr* **American Bar Association**) = asociación estadounidense de juristas

abaci *pl of* **abacus**

aback [ə'bæk] *adv* **to be taken a. (by)** quedarse desconcertado(a) (por)

abacus ['æbəkəs] (*pl* **abacuses** ['æbəkəsɪz] *or* **abaci** ['æbəsaɪ]) *n* ábaco *m*

abaft [ə'bɑːft] *adv Naut* a popa

abalone [æbə'ləʊnɪ] *n* oreja *f* de mar

abandon [ə'bændən] **1** *vt* (a) *(leave) (person, object, place)* abandonar; **to a. ship** abandonar el barco; **to a. sb to their fate** abandonar a alguien a su suerte
(b) *(give up) (search, studies, idea, attempt)* abandonar; *(match)* suspender; *Comptr (file, routine)* cancelar; **to a. all hope (of doing sth)** abandonar toda esperanza (de hacer algo)
(c) **to a. oneself to despair** abandonarse a la desesperación
2 *n* **with gay** *or* **reckless a.** como loco(a)

abandoned [ə'bændənd] *adj* (a) *(house, car)* abandonado(a); **to feel a.** sentirse abandonado(a) (b) *Old-fashioned (dissolute)* disoluto(a), licencioso(a)

abase [ə'beɪs] *vt* **to a. oneself** humillarse, degradarse

abashed [ə'bæʃt] *adj* **to be a.** estar avergonzado(a) *or* abochornado(a) *or Andes, CAm, Carib, Méx* apenado(a); **she seemed not (in) the least a.** no parecía estar avergonzada *or Andes, CAm, Carib, Méx* apenada en lo más mínimo

abate [ə'beɪt] *vi (storm, wind, flood)* amainar; *(pain)* remitir, calmarse; *(noise, anger, enthusiasm)* disminuir, atenuarse

abatement [ə'beɪtmənt] *n Formal (of storm)* amaine *m*; *(of pain)* remisión *f*; *(of noise, anger, enthusiasm)* disminución *f*, atenuación *f*

abattoir ['æbətwɑː(r)] *n* matadero *m*

abbess ['æbes] *n* abadesa *f*

abbey ['æbɪ] *n* abadía *f*

abbot ['æbət] *n* abad *m*

abbreviate [ə'briːvɪeɪt] *vt* (a) *(word, title)* abreviar (b) *(speech, remarks)* abreviar; **the chairman asked him to a. his remarks as time was short** el presidente le pidió que abreviara porque quedaba poco tiempo

abbreviation [əbriːvɪ'eɪʃən] *n (shortening of word, title)* abreviación *f*; *(short form)* abreviatura *f*

ABC [eɪbiː'siː] *n* (a) *(alphabet)* abecedario *m*; **an A. of gardening** una guía básica de jardinería (b) (*abbr* **American Broadcasting Corporation**) cadena *f* ABC *(de radio y televisión estadounidense)* (c) (*abbr* **Australian Broadcasting Corporation**) = radiotelevisión pública australiana

ABD [eɪbiː'diː] *n US Univ* (*abbr* **all but dissertation**) = estudiante de doctorado al que sólo le falta la tesis para obtener el título de doctor

abdicate ['æbdɪkeɪt] **1** *vt* (a) *(throne)* abdicar (b) *(responsibility)* desatender, abandonar; *(right)* renunciar a
2 *vi (monarch)* abdicar

abdication [æbdɪ'keɪʃən] *n* (a) *(of throne)* abdicación *f* (b) *(of responsibility)* descuido *m*, abandono *m*; *(of right)* renuncia *f*

abdomen ['æbdəmən] *n Anat & Zool* abdomen *m*

abdominal [əb'dɒmɪnəl] *adj Anat* abdominal

abduct [əb'dʌkt] *vt* raptar, secuestrar

abduction [əb'dʌkʃən] *n* rapto *m*, secuestro *m*

abductor [əb'dʌktə(r)] *n* **(a)** *(of person)* secuestrador(ora) *m,f*, raptor(ora) *m,f* **(b)** *Anat* abductor *m*

abeam [ə'bi:m] *adv* **(a)** *Av* en ángulo recto con el fuselaje **(b)** *Naut* en ángulo recto con la quilla

Abel ['eɪbəl] *pr n* Abel

Aberdonian [æbə'dəʊnɪən] **1** *n* persona de Aberdeen *(Escocia)*
2 *adj* de Aberdeen *(Escocia)*

aberrant [ə'berənt] *adj Formal (behaviour)* aberrante

aberration [æbə'reɪʃən] *n* **(a)** *(action, idea)* anomalía *f*, aberración *f*; **mental a.** desvarío, despiste; **in a moment of a.** en un momento de ofuscación **(b)** *Astron* aberración *f*

abet [ə'bet] *(pt & pp* **abetted***) vt Law* **to aid and a. sb** ser cómplice de alguien; **to be accused of aiding and abetting sb** ser acusado(a) de complicidad con alguien

abeyance [ə'beɪəns] *n* **to be in a.** *(of law, custom)* estar en desuso; **to fall into a.** *(of law, custom)* caer en desuso

abhor [əb'hɔ:(r)] *(pt & pp* **abhorred***) vt* aborrecer

abhorrence [əb'hɒrəns] *n Formal* aversión *f*, aborrecimiento *m* (**of** hacia *or* por); **to have an a. of sth/sb, to hold sth/sb in a.** aborrecer algo/a alguien

abhorrent [əb'hɒrənt] *adj Formal* aborrecible, repugnante; **it is a. to me** me resulta repugnante

abide [ə'baɪd] **1** *vt (tolerate)* soportar; **I can't a. him** no lo soporto
2 *vi Literary (live, stay)* habitar en, morar en; *Rel* **a. with me** quédate *or* permanece junto a mí

▸ **abide by** *vt insep (promise)* cumplir; *(rule, decision)* acatar, atenerse a

abiding [ə'baɪdɪŋ] *adj (interest, impression)* duradero(a); **my a. memory of Spain is...** mi recuerdo más destacado de España es...

ability [ə'bɪlɪtɪ] *n* **(a)** *(talent, skill)* aptitud *f*, habilidad *f*; **a person of real a.** una persona de gran valía; **he lacks a.** le falta maña; **he did it to the best of his a.** lo hizo lo mejor que supo; **children of all abilities** niños de todos los niveles de aptitud; **someone of her a. should have no problems** una persona con su capacidad no debería tener problema
(b) *(capability)* capacidad *f*; **we now have the a. to record all calls** ahora podemos grabar todas las llamadas; **he has no a. to concentrate** no tiene capacidad de concentración

abject ['æbdʒekt] *adj* **(a)** *(very bad)* deplorable; **a. poverty** pobreza extrema **(b)** *(lacking self-respect)* **to look a.** tener un aspecto lamentable; **an a. apology** una humilde disculpa; **a. cowardice** cobardía ruin

abjectly ['æbdʒektlɪ] *adv* **(a)** *(very badly)* **they failed a.** fracasaron por completo **(b)** *(without self-respect)* con mezquindad, miserablemente

abjure [əb'dʒʊə(r)] *vt Formal (religion, belief)* abjurar (de), renegar de; *(claim)* renunciar a

ablative ['æblətɪv] *Gram* **1** *n* ablativo *m* ▸▸ ***a. absolute*** ablativo *m* absoluto
2 *adj* ablativo(a)

ablaze [ə'bleɪz] *adj* **(a)** *(on fire)* **to be a.** estar ardiendo *or* en llamas; **to set sth a.** prender fuego a algo **(b)** *(bright, shining)* **her eyes were a. with passion** sus ojos ardían de pasión; **the garden was a. with colour** el jardín resplandecía de colorido

ABLE ['eɪbəl] *adj* **(a)** **to be a. to do sth** *(have the capability)* ser capaz de hacer algo, poder hacer algo; *(manage)* conseguir *or* poder hacer algo; **are you a. to use this program/speak Spanish?** ¿sabes usar este programa/hablar español?; **I was a. to speak to him myself** conseguí *or* pude hablar con él; **she was a. to see exactly what was happening** pudo ver exactamente lo que estaba sucediendo; **I won't be a. to pay until next week** no voy a poder pagar hasta la semana que viene; **the computer is a. to do several million calculations per second** *Esp* el ordenador *or Am* la computadora es capaz de realizar varios millones de cálculos por segundo; **please donate whatever you are a.** por favor, contribuya con lo que pueda; **do you feel a. to do it?** ¿te sientes capaz de hacerlo?; **I haven't been a. to do it yet** todavía no he podido hacerlo; **I'm delighted to be a. to tell you that...** me complace poder comunicarle que...; **she's better a. to do it than I am** ella está más capacitada para hacerlo que yo
(b) *(competent) (person)* capaz; *(piece of work, performance)* logrado(a), conseguido(a); **thanks to your a. assistance...** gracias a tu ayuda...

able-bodied ['eɪbəl'bɒdɪd] *adj* **every a. person helped in the search** todos los que estaban en condiciones de ayudar participaron en la búsqueda ▸▸ *Naut* ***a. seaman*** marinero *m* de primera

ablutions [əb'lu:ʃənz] *npl Formal or Hum* abluciones *fpl*

ably ['eɪblɪ] *adv* hábilmente; **a. assisted by** hábilmente ayudado por

ABM [eɪbi:'em] *n Mil (abbr* **antiballistic missile***)* misil *m* antibalístico

abnegation [æbnə'geɪʃən] *n Formal* **(a)** *(self-denial)* abnegación *f* **(b)** *(of responsibility)* abandono *m*

abnormal [æb'nɔ:məl] *adj (growth, behaviour, interest)* anormal, anómalo(a); **there's nothing a. about that** eso no tiene nada de anormal

abnormality [æbnɔ:'mælɪtɪ] *n* anormalidad *f*, anomalía *f*

abnormally [æb'nɔ:məlɪ] *adv* anormalmente; **a. large/quiet/helpful** excepcionalmente grande/tranquilo/útil

aboard [ə'bɔ:d] **1** *adv* a bordo; **to go a.** subir a bordo; **all a.!** *(boat)* ¡todo el mundo a bordo!; *(train)* ¡pasajeros, al tren!; **welcome a.!** *(onto ship, aircraft)* ¡bienvenidos(as) a bordo!; *(onto team)* ¡bienvenido(a)!
2 *prep (ship, aircraft)* a bordo de; *(bus, train)* en; **a. ship** a bordo (del barco)

abode [ə'bəʊd] *n* **(a)** *Literary* morada *f*; *Hum* **welcome to my humble a.** bienvenido a mi humilde morada **(b)** *Law* **of no fixed a.** sin domicilio fijo; **right of a.** derecho de residencia

abolish [ə'bɒlɪʃ] *vt (law, custom, distinction)* abolir, suprimir; *(slavery, death penalty)* abolir

abolition [æbə'lɪʃən] *n (of law, custom, distinction)* abolición *f*, supresión *f*; *(of slavery, death penalty)* abolición *f*

abolitionist [æbə'lɪʃənɪst] *Hist* **1** *n* abolicionista *mf*
2 *adj* abolicionista

abominable [ə'bɒmɪnəbəl] *adj* deplorable, abominable; **her handwriting is a.** tiene una letra malísima *or* lamentable; **the coffee was a.** el café estaba deplorable ▸▸ ***the a. snowman*** el abominable hombre de las nieves

abominably [ə'bɒmɪnəblɪ] *adv* **(a)** *(to behave, spell)* deplorablemente, abominablemente; **to treat sb a.** tratar a alguien de manera deplorable **(b)** *(as intensifier)* tremendamente; **it was a. difficult** fue tremendamente difícil

abominate [ə'bɒmɪneɪt] *vt Formal* abominar (de)

abomination [əbɒmɪ'neɪʃən] *n* **(a)** *(thing, action)* abominación *f*, horror *m* **(b)** *(disgust)* repugnancia *f*, aversión *f*; **to hold sth in a.** aborrecer *or* abominar algo

aboriginal [æbə'rɪdʒənəl] **1** *adj* **(a)** *(inhabitant)* aborigen, indígena **(b)** *(in Australia)* aborigen
2 *n* = **Aborigine**

Aborigine [æbə'rɪdʒɪnɪ] *n* aborigen *mf (de Australia)*

abort [ə'bɔ:t] **1** *n Comptr (program)* cancelación *f*
2 *vt* **(a)** *Med* **the foetus was aborted in the 14th week of pregnancy** se provocó un aborto en la 14a semana de embarazo **(b)** *(project, mission, flight)* interrumpir, suspender **(c)** *Comptr* cancelar
3 *vi* **(a)** *Med (woman)* abortar **(b)** *(abandon project, mission, flight)* abortar

abortifacient [əbɔ:tɪ'feɪʃənt] *Med* **1** *n* abortivo *m*
2 *adj* abortivo(a)

abortion [ə'bɔ:ʃən] *n* **(a)** *(termination of pregnancy)* aborto *m (provocado)*; **to have an a.** abortar, tener un aborto; **a. on demand** aborto libre; **a. clinic/law** clínica/ley abortista **(b)** *Med (miscarriage)* aborto *m* (espontáneo) **(c)** *very Fam (person)* feto *m*, cardo *m*; *(animal)* engendro *m*

abortionist [ə'bɔ:ʃənɪst] *n (practitioner)* abortista *mf*

abortive [ə'bɔ:tɪv] *adj (attempt, plan)* fallido(a), malogrado(a)

abound [ə'baʊnd] *vi* abundar (**in** *or* **with** en)

ABOUT [ə'baʊt] **1** *prep* **(a)** *(regarding)* sobre, acerca de; **a book a. France** un libro sobre Francia; **what's this book a.?** ¿de qué trata *or Am* se trata este libro?; **what's all the fuss a.?** ¿a qué viene tanto alboroto?; **what's so clever a. that?** ¿qué tiene eso de ingenioso?; **he wants to see you a. the missing money** quiere verte para hablar del dinero desaparecido; **to talk/argue a. sth** hablar/discutir de *or* sobre algo; **what are you talking a.?** *(that's ridiculous)* ¿qué dices?; **to complain/laugh a. sth** quejarse/reírse de algo; **to be angry a. sth** estar *esp Esp* enfadado *or esp Am* enojado por algo; **I'm sorry a. yesterday** siento lo de ayer; **he said something a. buying a new TV** dijo algo de comprar un televisor nuevo; **he's being very awkward a. it** está poniéndose muy difícil con respecto a este asunto; *Fam* **get me a beer and be quick a. it** ponme una cerveza y rapidito; **we must do something a. this problem** tenemos que hacer algo con este problema *or* para solucionar este problema; **there's nothing we can do a. it** no podemos hacer nada (al respecto); **he's always complaining, but he never does anything a. it** siempre se está quejando, pero nunca hace nada; **there's something a. her I don't like** tiene algo que no me gusta; **tell me all a. it** cuéntame, cuéntamelo todo; **the good/bad thing a....** lo bueno/malo de...; **what is it you don't like a. her?** ¿qué es lo que no te gusta de ella?; **how** *or* **what a. a cup of tea?** ¿te *Esp* apetece *or Carib, Col, Méx* provoca un té?, ¿quieres *or CSur* querés un té?; **I fancy a beer, how** *or* **what a. you?** me *Esp* apetece *or Carib, Col, Méx* provoca una cerveza, ¿y a ti?, *CSur* yo me tomaría una cerveza, ¿y vos?; **well how a. that!** ¡vaya!; **and what a. me?** ¿y yo qué?; **it's a good plan, but what a. the funding?** es un buen plan, pero ¿y la financiación?; *Br Fam* **could you get me one too, while you're a. it?** ¿me podrías traer otro para mí, ya que estás?

(**b**) *(introducing topic)* **a. the rent... we can't pay it this month** en cuanto al alquiler *or Méx* la renta,... es que no podemos pagar este mes; **it's a. the accident...** *(on phone)* llamaba por lo del accidente...; *(in person)* venía por lo del accidente...

(**c**) *(in various parts of)* por; **to walk a. the town** caminar por la ciudad; **papers were scattered a. the room** había papeles diseminados por toda la habitación; **you can't go a. the place spreading rumours** no puedes ir por ahí difundiendo rumores; *Br Formal* **do you have a piece of paper a. you?** ¿tiene un papel encima?

(**d**) *Literary (encircling)* **she put her arms a. his neck** le rodeó el cuello con los brazos; **he wore a sash a. his waist** una faja le ceñía la cintura

2 *adv* (**a**) *(in different directions, places)* **to run a.** correr de aquí para allá; **to walk a.** caminar *or* pasear por ahí; **they heard someone moving a. in the attic** oyeron a alguien moverse por el ático; **to follow sb a.** perseguir a alguien; **they sat a. (doing nothing) all afternoon** se pasaron la tarde sentados (sin hacer nada); **there were books scattered all a.** había libros esparcidos por todas partes

(**b**) *(in opposite direction)* **to turn/whirl a.** dar la vuelta, volver, *Andes, CAm, Carib, Méx* devolverse

(**c**) *(in the general area)* **is Jack a.?** ¿está Jack por ahí?; **he/it must be a. somewhere** debe de estar *or* andar por ahí; **there was nobody a.** no había nadie (por allí); **there's a nasty bug a.** hay una epidemia por ahí; **have you got the flu too? there's a lot of it a.** ¿tú también tienes la gripe? todo el mundo la tiene; **it's good to see you up and a. again** *(recovered)* ¡qué alegría verte otra vez en pie!

(**d**) *(approximately)* más o menos; **a. thirty** unos treinta; **she's a. thirty** anda por los treinta, tiene unos trienta años; **at a. one o'clock** alrededor de la una, a eso de la una; **a. a week** una semana más o menos; **she's a. as tall as you** es más o menos como tú de alta; **this is a. as good as it gets** pues esto es de lo mejor; **I've just a. finished** estoy a punto de acabar *or* terminar; **that's a. it for the moment** *(we've almost finished)* prácticamente hemos terminado; **that's a. enough** con eso basta; **I've had just a. enough of your cheek!** ¡ya me estoy hartando de tu descaro!; **a. time!** ¡ya era hora!

(**e**) *(on the point of)* **to be a. to do sth** estar a punto de hacer algo; **I'm not a. to...** *(have no intention of)* no tengo la más mínima intención de...

---

about-face [ə'baʊt'feɪs], *Br* **about-turn** [ə'baʊt'tɜːn] **1** *n* (**a**) *Mil* media vuelta *f*; **a.!** ¡media vuelta! (**b**) *(radical change)* giro *m* radical *or* de 180 grados; **to do an a.** dar un giro radical *or* de 180 grados

2 *vi* (**a**) *Mil* dar media vuelta (**b**) *(change opinion)* dar un giro radical *or* de 180 grados

---

ABOVE [ə'bʌv] **1** *n* **the a.** *(information)* lo anterior

2 *npl* **the a.** *(people)* los arriba mencionados; **all of the a. are covered by this policy** la presente póliza cubre a todos los arriba mencionados

3 *adj* de arriba; **the a. diagram** el diagrama de arriba; **for the a. reasons** por las razones arriba mencionadas

4 *prep* (**a**) *(physically)* por encima de; **the sky a. us** el cielo; **the flat a. ours** el apartamento que está encima del nuestro; **500 metres a. sea level** 500 metros sobre el nivel del mar; **lift your arms a. your head** levanta los brazos (por encima de la cabeza); **the Ebro a. Zaragoza** el Ebro, antes de llegar a Zaragoza; **there's a mistake in the line a. this one** hay un error en la línea anterior a ésta; **he appears (just) a. me on the list** figura en la lista (justo) antes que yo

(**b**) *(with numbers)* **a. twenty** por encima de veinte; **a. $100** más de 100 dólares; **the temperature didn't rise a. 10° C** la temperatura no pasó de *or* superó los 10°; **store at a. 5° C** guárdese a una temperatura superior a 5°; **children a. the age of eleven** chicos de más de once años; **the food was a. average** la comida era bastante buena; **the temperature was a. average** *or* **normal** la temperatura era superior a la habitual; **children of a. average ability** niños mejor dotados que la media

(**c**) *(in classification, importance, rank)* **he is a. me** está por encima de mí; **they finished a. us in the league** terminaron mejor clasificados que nosotros en la liga; **he was in the year a. me (at school)** iba un año por delante de mí en el colegio; **a general is a. a colonel in the army** el rango de general está por encima del de coronel; **to marry a. oneself** casarse con alguien de clase social superior; **I value happiness a. success** valoro más la felicidad que el éxito; **a. all** por encima de todo, sobre todo; **a. all else, we must avoid defeat** por encima de todo, debemos evitar la derrota

(**d**) *(louder than)* **he tried to make himself heard a. the noise** trató de hacerse oír por encima del ruido; **I couldn't hear her voice a. the music** no la oía por encima de la música

(**e**) *(not subject to)* **to be a. reproach** ser irreprochable; **to be a. suspicion** estar libre de sospecha; **she thinks she's a. criticism** cree que está por encima de las críticas; **even you are not a. failure** ni siquiera tú eres infalible

(**f**) *(superior to)* **he thinks he's a. all that** cree que hacer eso sería humillarse; **she thinks she's a. everyone else** se cree superior a los demás; **he's not a. telling the occasional lie** incluso él se permite mentir de vez en cuando; **to get a. oneself** darse muchos humos

(**g**) *(incomprehensible to)* **his speech was way a. me** *or* **a. my head** no entendí ni la mitad de su discurso

5 *adv* (**a**) *(in general)* arriba; **the sky a.** el cielo; **the flat a.** el apartamento de arriba; **the tenants (of the flat) a.** los inquilinos de arriba; **I heard a shout from a.** oí un grito que venía de arriba; **to have a view from a.** ver desde arriba; **this is the building as seen from a.** este es el edificio visto desde arriba; **imposed from a.** impuesto(a) desde arriba; **orders from a.** órdenes de arriba *or* de los superiores

(**b**) *(in book, document)* **contact the phone number given a.** llame al número de teléfono que aparece más arriba; **the paragraph a.** el párrafo anterior; **in the diagram a.** en el diagrama de arriba; **as noted a....** como se comenta más arriba...; **see a.** ver más arriba

(**c**) *(with numbers)* **women aged eighteen and a.** las mujeres a partir de los dieciocho años; **temperatures of 30° C and a.** temperaturas superiores a los 30°

(**d**) *(in rank)* **officers of the rank of colonel and a.** los coroneles y oficiales de rango superior

(**e**) *Literary (in Heaven)* **the Lord a.** el Señor que está en los Cielos; **a sign from a.** una señal divina

---

above-average [ə'bʌv'ævərɪdʒ] *adj* superior a la media, por encima de la media

above-board [əbʌv'bɔːd] *adj (honest)* honrado(a), sincero(a); **let's keep everything a.** mantengámonos dentro de la legalidad

above-mentioned [əbʌv'menʃənd], **above-named** [əbʌv'neɪmd] **1** *adj* arriba mencionado(a), susodicho(a)

2 *n* **the a.** *(person)* el arriba mencionado, la arriba mencionada

above-the-line [ə'bʌvðə'laɪn] *adj* (**a**) *Fin (expenditure, revenue)* por encima de la línea (**b**) *Com* ***a. advertising*** publicidad *f* pagada

abracadabra [æbrəkə'dæbrə] *exclam* ¡abracadabra!

abrade [ə'breɪd] *vt* (**a**) *Tech* pulir, bruñir (**b**) *(skin)* raspar, excoriar (**c**) *Geol* erosionar

Abraham ['eɪbrəhæm] *pr n* Abraham, Abrahán

abrasion [ə'breɪʒən] *n* (**a**) *Tech* pulido *m*, bruñido *m* (**b**) *(on skin)* abrasión *f* (**c**) *Geol* erosión *f*

abrasive [ə'breɪsɪv] **1** *n (substance)* abrasivo *m*

2 *adj* (**a**) *(surface, substance)* abrasivo(a) (**b**) *(person, manner)* acre, corrosivo(a); *(criticism, wit)* mordaz, incisivo(a)

abrasiveness [ə'breɪsɪvnɪs] *n* (**a**) *(of material)* capacidad *f or* poder *m* de abrasión (**b**) *(of person, manner)* acritud *f*, acrimonia *f*

abreast [ə'brest] *adv* (**a**) *(side by side)* **three/four a.** en fila de a tres/cuatro, de tres/cuatro en fondo; **to come a. of** situarse a la altura de (**b**) *(in touch with)* **to keep a. of sth** mantenerse al tanto de algo

abridge [ə'brɪdʒ] *vt (book)* resumir; *(speech)* resumir, abreviar

abridged [ə'brɪdʒd] *adj* abreviado(a) ►► ***a. edition*** edición *f* abreviada

abridg(e)ment [ə'brɪdʒmənt] *n (of book, speech)* resumen *m*

abroad [ə'brɔːd] *adv* (**a**) *(in another country)* en el extranjero, fuera del país; **to be/live a.** estar/vivir en el extranjero; **to go a.** ir al extranjero

(**b**) *Formal (in public domain)* **to get a.** *(of news)* difundirse; **there are rumours a. about a possible invasion** corre el rumor de una posible invasión

(**c**) *Literary (out of doors)* **not a soul was a. at that early hour** no había ni un alma por las calles a esas horas tempranas; **to venture a.** aventurarse a salir

abrogate ['æbrəgeɪt] *vt Formal* abrogar, derogar

abrupt [ə'brʌpt] *adj* (**a**) *(sudden) (change, movement)* brusco(a), repentino(a); *(departure)* súbito(a), repentino(a); **the evening came to an a. end** la velada terminó bruscamente (**b**) *(curt)* brusco(a), abrupto(a) (**c**) *(steep) (rise, fall, slope)* abrupto(a), escarpado(a)

abruptly [ə'brʌptlɪ] *adv* (**a**) *(suddenly)* bruscamente, repentinamente (**b**) *(curtly)* bruscamente (**c**) *(to rise, fall)* abruptamente, repentinamente

abruptness [ə'brʌptnɪs] *n* (**a**) *(suddenness) (of change, movement)* brusquedad *f*, rapidez *f*; *(of departure)* lo súbito, lo repentino (**b**) *(curtness)* brusquedad *f*, sequedad *f*

ABS [eɪbi:'es] *n Aut* (*abbr* **anti-lock braking system**) ABS *m* ▸▸ ***A. brakes*** frenos *mpl* ABS

abs [æbz] *npl Fam* abdominales *mpl*

abscess ['æbses] *n (general)* absceso *m*; *(in gums)* flemón *m*

abscissa [æb'sɪsə] (*pl* **abscissas** *or* **abscissae** [æb'sɪsi:]) *n Math* abscisa *f*

abscond [əb'skɒnd] *vi Formal* darse a la fuga, huir; *Hum* **he absconded with the money** se esfumó con el dinero

abseil ['æbseɪl] *vi* hacer rappel; **to a. down sth** bajar algo haciendo rappel

abseiling ['æbseɪlɪŋ] *n* rappel *m*; **to go a.** ir a hacer rappel

absence ['æbsəns] *n* (**a**) *(of person)* ausencia *f*; **during** *or* **in my/his/***etc* **a.** durante *or* en mi/su/*etc.* ausencia; **this is her fourth a. this term** es la cuarta vez que se ausenta *or* que falta en lo que va de trimestre; PROV **a. makes the heart grow fonder** la ausencia aviva el cariño

(**b**) *(of thing)* ausencia *f*; *(of evidence, information)* ausencia *f*, falta *f* (**of** de); **in the a. of...** a falta de...

(**c**) *Law* **to be tried/sentenced in one's a.** ser procesado(a)/juzgado(a) en rebeldía

absent 1 *adj* ['æbsənt] (**a**) *(not present, missing)* ausente; **to be a. from school/work** faltar al colegio/al trabajo; *Mil* **a. without leave** ausente sin permiso; **to a. friends!** *(toast)* ¡por los que faltan *or* no están aquí! (**b**) *(lacking)* ausente; **to be conspicuously a.** brillar por su ausencia (**c**) *(distracted)* ausente

2 *vt* [æb'sent] *Formal* **to a. oneself (from)** ausentarse (de)

absentee [æbsən'ti:] *n* ausente *mf* ▸▸ *US* ***a. ballot*** voto *m* por correo; ***a. landlord*** (propietario(a) *m,f*) ausentista *mf or Esp* absentista *mf*

absenteeism [æbsən'ti:ɪzəm] *n* ausentismo *m*, *Esp* absentismo *m*

absently ['æbsəntlɪ] *adv* distraídamente

absent-minded [æbsənt'maɪndɪd] *adj* distraído(a), despistado(a)

absent-mindedly [æbsənt'maɪndɪdlɪ] *adv* distraídamente; **she a. stirred the tea with her pencil** sin darse cuenta, revolvió el té con el lápiz

absent-mindedness [æbsənt'maɪndɪdnɪs] *n* distracción *f*, despiste *m*

absinth(e) ['æbsɪnθ] *n* absenta *f*, ajenjo *m*

absolute ['æbsəlu:t] **1** *n* (**a**) *(rule, value)* principio *m or* valor *m* absoluto (**b**) *Phil* **the a.** lo absoluto

2 *adj* (**a**) *(complete, total)* absoluto(a); **that's the a. truth** es la pura verdad; **she's an a. beginner in French/computing** no sabe absolutamente nada de francés/informática; **it's an a. certainty** es seguro; **the a. maximum/minimum** el máximo/mínimo absoluto ▸▸ ***a. monarch*** monarca *m* absoluto; ***a. power*** poder *m* absoluto

(**b**) *(not relative)* absoluto(a); **in a. terms** en términos absolutos ▸▸ ***a. majority*** mayoría *f* absoluta; *Mus* ***a. pitch*** oído *m* absoluto; *Phys* ***a. zero*** cero *m* absoluto

(**c**) *Law (court order, decree)* firme; **the decree was made a.** concedieron el divorcio por sentencia firme

(**d**) *(as intensifier)* absoluto(a), auténtico(a); **he's an a. fool!** ¡es un completo idiota!; **he's an a. genius!** ¡es un verdadero genio!; **a. rubbish!** ¡no son más que tonterías!; **it's an a. disgrace!** ¡es una auténtica vergüenza!

absolutely [æbsə'lu:tlɪ] *adv* (**a**) *(completely, totally)* absolutamente; **you're a. right** tienes toda la razón; **I'm not a. sure** no estoy completamente seguro; **she a. refuses to do it** se niega rotundamente a hacerlo; **it is a. forbidden** está terminantemente prohibido

(**b**) *(in answer to question)* **it's good, isn't it? – a.** es bueno, ¿verdad? – buenísimo; **are you coming tonight? – a.** ¿vas a venir esta noche? – ¡por supuesto!; **a. not!** ¡en absoluto!

(**c**) *(as intensifier)* absolutamente; **a. disgusting/hilarious** asquerosísimo/divertidísimo

absolution [æbsə'lu:ʃən] *n Rel* absolución *f*; **to grant sb a.** conceder la absolución a alguien

absolutism [æbsə'lu:tɪzəm] *n* absolutismo *m*

absolve [əb'zɒlv] *vt* (**a**) *(from blame, sin)* absolver (**from** *or* **of** de); **to a. sb from** *or* **of all blame** absolver a alguien de toda culpa (**b**) *(from obligation)* eximir (**from** *or* **of** de)

absorb [əb'zɔ:b] *vt* (**a**) *(soak up, take in) (liquid, light, heat)* absorber; **paperwork absorbs too much of my time** paso demasiado tiempo ocupado en papeleos

(**b**) *(shock, sound, impact)* absorber, amortiguar

(**c**) *(cost, losses)* absorber

(**d**) *(incorporate, assimilate) (information, ideas)* asimilar; *(company)* absorber; *(people)* integrar, asimilar; **it's too much to a. all in one day** es demasiado como para asimilarlo en un solo día

(**e**) *(engross)* absorber; **the task completely absorbed our attention** estábamos completamente absortos en la tarea

absorbed [əb'zɔ:bd] *adj (expression)* absorto(a), abstraído(a); **to be a. in sth** estar absorto en algo; **he was utterly a. in the project/his book** el proyecto/libro lo tenía totalmente absorto

absorbency [əb'zɔ:bənsɪ] *n* absorbencia *f*

absorbent [əb'zɔ:bənt] *adj* absorbente ▸▸ *US* ***a. cotton*** algodón *m* hidrófilo

absorbing [əb'zɔ:bɪŋ] *adj (book, work)* absorbente

absorption [əb'zɔ:pʃən] *n* (**a**) *(of liquid, gas, heat, light)* absorción *f*

(**b**) *(of shock, sound, impact)* absorción *f*, amortiguación *f*

(**c**) *(of cost, losses)* absorción *f*

(**d**) *(incorporation, assimilation) (of information, ideas)* asimilación *f*; *(of company)* absorción *f*; *(of people)* integración *f*, asimilación *f*

(**e**) *(being engrossed)* enfrascamiento *m*; **I was struck by her utter a. in the book** me sorprendió verla tan enfrascada *or* inmersa en el libro

abstain [əb'steɪn] *vi* (**a**) *(refrain)* **to a. from doing sth** abstenerse de hacer algo (**b**) *(not vote)* abstenerse (**c**) *(not drink alcohol)* no beber alcohol, *Am* no tomar

abstainer [əb'steɪnə(r)] *n* (**a**) *(person not voting)* abstencionista *mf* (**b**) *(teetotaller)* abstemio(a) *m,f*

abstemious [əb'sti:mɪəs] *adj Formal* frugal, mesurado(a)

abstention [əb'stenʃən] *n* (**a**) *(from action)* abstención *f*; *(from drink, food)* abstinencia *f* (**b**) *(in vote)* abstención *f*

abstinence ['æbstɪnəns] *n (from alcohol, sex)* abstinencia *f* (**from** de)

abstinent ['æbstɪnənt] *adj (lifestyle)* frugal

abstract ['æbstrækt] **1** *n* (**a**) **in the a.** en abstracto (**b**) *(of article)* resumen *m* (**c**) *(work of art)* cuadro *m* abstracto

2 *adj* (**a**) *(theoretical)* abstracto(a) (**b**) *(not concrete)* abstracto(a) ▸▸ ***a. art*** arte *m* abstracto; *Art* ***a. expressionism*** expresionismo *m* abstracto; ***a. noun*** nombre *m* abstracto

3 *vt* [əb'strækt] (**a**) *Formal (remove)* extraer (**from** de) (**b**) *Euph or Hum (steal)* sustraer (**from** de) (**c**) *(summarize)* compendiar, resumir

abstracted [əb'stræktɪd] *adj* abstraído(a), absorto(a)

abstraction [əb'strækʃən] *n* (**a**) *(concept)* abstracción *f*; **he talked in abstractions** empleaba conceptos abstractos al hablar (**b**) *Formal (act of removing)* extracción *f* (**c**) *(absent-mindedness)* distracción *f*; **she wore her customary look of a.** tenía su típica mirada abstraída

abstruse [əb'stru:s] *adj Formal* abstruso(a), impenetrable

absurd [əb'sɜ:d] **1** *adj* absurdo(a); **I look/feel a. in this get-up** parezco/me siento estúpido con esta indumentaria; **don't be a.!** ¡no seas absurdo(a)!

2 *n* **a sense of the a.** un sentido de lo absurdo; **the theatre of the a.** el teatro del absurdo

absurdity [əb'sɜ:dɪtɪ] *n* (**a**) *(irrationality)* irracionalidad *f*; **the a. of paying people to do nothing** lo absurdo de pagar a la gente para que no haga nada (**b**) *(statement, belief)* aberración *f*

absurdly [əb'sɜ:dlɪ] *adv* disparatadamente; **our meal was a. expensive** la comida nos costó un disparate; **we had to get up a. early** nos tuvimos que levantar ridículamente temprano

ABTA ['æbtə] *n* (*abbr* **Association of British Travel Agents**) = asociación británica de agencias de viajes

abundance [ə'bʌndəns] *n* abundancia *f*; **in a.** en abundancia; **she has an a. of talent** tiene talento sobrado; **there is an a. of evidence to suggest this** existen numerosas pruebas que lo sugieren

abundant [ə'bʌndənt] *adj* abundante (**in** en); **he gave a. proof of his loyalty** dio sobradas muestras de su lealtad; **there is a. evidence that...** existen numerosas pruebas que...

abundantly [ə'bʌndəntlɪ] *adv* en abundancia; **we were a. provided for** no nos faltaba de nada; **it is a. clear that...** está clarísimo que...

abuse 1 *n* [ə'bju:s] (**a**) *(misuse)* abuso *m*, mal uso *m*; **alcohol a.** alcoholismo; **drug a.** consumo de drogas; **a. of authority/power** abuso de autoridad/poder; **the scheme is open to a.** este plan es susceptible de abusos

(**b**) *(insults)* insultos *mpl*, improperios *mpl*; **term of a.** insulto, término ofensivo; **to heap** *or* **shower a. on sb** despotricar contra alguien (**c**) *(cruelty)* malos tratos *mpl*; **(sexual) a.** abuso *m* (sexual)

2 *vt* [ə'bjuːz] (**a**) *(misuse) (authority, position, someone's trust)* abusar de (**b**) *(insult)* insultar (**c**) *(ill-treat) (physically)* maltratar; *(sexually)* abusar de

abuser [ə'bjuːzə(r)] *n* (**a**) *(of child)* pederasta *m* (**b**) *(of alcohol)* **(alcohol) a.** alcohólico(a) *m,f* (**c**) *(of drugs)* **(drug) a.** drogodependiente *mf*

abusive [ə'bjuːsɪv] *adj* (**a**) *(person)* grosero(a); *(language)* injurioso(a); **he got quite a.** se puso a soltar improperios (**b**) *(behaviour, treatment)* abusivo(a)

abusively [ə'bjuːsɪvlɪ] *adv* (**a**) *(insultingly)* de manera insultante *or* ofensiva (**b**) *(to behave, treat sb)* abusivamente

abut [ə'bʌt] *(pt & pp* **abutted**) **1** *vt* estar contiguo(a) a
2 *vi* **to a. onto** *or* **against sth** estar adyacente *or* contiguo(a) a algo

abutment [ə'bʌtmənt] *n Archit* estribo *m*, contrafuerte *m*

abuzz [ə'bʌz] *adj* **the office was a. with the news** en la oficina los ánimos estaban exaltados por la noticia; **to be a. with excitement** estar enardecido(a)

ABV (*abbr* **alcohol by volume**) **A. 3.8 percent** 3,8 por ciento Vol.

abysmal [ə'bɪzməl] *adj (stupidity, ignorance)* profundo(a); *(performance, quality)* pésimo(a)

abysmally [ə'bɪzməlɪ] *adv* deplorablemente, lamentablemente; **to fail a.** fracasar estrepitosamente

abyss [ə'bɪs] *n* abismo *m*; IDIOM **to be on the edge of the a.** estar *or* encontrarse al borde del abismo

Abyssinia [æbɪ'sɪnɪə] *n Formerly* Abisinia

Abyssinian [æbɪ'sɪnɪən] *Formerly* **1** *n* abisinio(a) *m,f*
2 *adj* abisinio(a)

AC ['eɪ'siː] *n* (**a**) *Elec* (*abbr* **alternating current**) corriente *f* alterna (**b**) (*abbr* **air-conditioning**) aire *m* acondicionado

a/c (*abbr* **account**) cuenta *f*

acacia [ə'keɪʃə] *n* **a. (tree)** acacia *f*

academe ['ækədiːm] *n Formal or Literary (academic life)* el mundo académico

academia [ækə'diːmɪə] *n* el mundo académico, la universidad

academic [ækə'demɪk] **1** *n (university teacher)* profesor(ora) *m,f* de universidad
2 *adj* (**a**) *(of school, university)* académico(a) ►► ***a. dress*** traje *m* académico *(de toga y birrete)*; ***a. freedom*** libertad *f* de cátedra; ***a. record*** expediente *m* académico; ***the a. staff*** el personal académico; ***a. year*** año *m* académico
(**b**) *(intellectual, scholarly) (study, standards)* académico(a), intelectual; *(person)* intelectual, estudioso(a)
(**c**) *(theoretical, not practical)* teórico(a); **it's entirely a. now** ya carece por completo de relevancia

academically [ækə'demɪklɪ] *adv* académicamente; **to be a. qualified** tener títulos académicos; **to be a. gifted** tener talento para los estudios; **how is she doing a.?** ¿cómo le va en los estudios?

academician [əkædə'mɪʃən] *n* académico(a) *m,f*

academy [ə'kædəmɪ] *n* (**a**) *(society)* academia *f* ►► ***the A. Awards*** los Oscars (**b**) *(school)* academia *f* ►► ***a. of music*** conservatorio *m*

acanthus [ə'kænθəs] *n* acanto *m*

a cappella ['ɑːkə'pelə] *Mus* **1** *adj* a cappella
2 *adv* a cappella

ACAS ['eɪkæs] *n Br* (*abbr* **Advisory, Conciliation and Arbitration Service**) = organismo independiente de arbitraje para conflictos laborales

accede [ək'siːd] *vi Formal* (**a**) *(agree)* **to a. to** acceder a (**b**) *(monarch)* **to a. to the throne** acceder al trono (**c**) *Law* **to a. to a treaty** adherirse a un tratado

accelerate [ək'seləreɪt] **1** *vt (rate, progress, computer)* acelerar ►► *Phys* ***accelerated motion*** movimiento *m* acelerado
2 *vi* (**a**) *(rate, growth)* acelerarse (**b**) *(car, driver)* acelerar

acceleration [əkselə'reɪʃən] *n* aceleración *f*

accelerator [ək'seləreɪtə(r)] *n* (**a**) *(in car)* acelerador *m*; **step on the a.!** ¡acelera! (**b**) *Comptr* acelerador *m* ►► ***a. board*** placa *f* aceleradora; ***a. card*** tarjeta *f* aceleradora

accent ['æksənt] **1** *n* (**a**) *(when speaking)* acento *m*; **she has** *or* **she speaks with a Spanish/southern a.** tiene *or* habla con acento español/del sur (**b**) *(in writing)* acento *m*, tilde *f* (**c**) *(emphasis)* **the a. here is on team work** hacemos especial hincapié en el trabajo en equipo; **to put the a. on sth** *(emphasize)* hacer hincapié en algo (**d**) *(contrasting detail)* relieve *m*, realce *m*
2 *vt (word)* acentuar; **it's accented on the first syllable** se acentúa en la primera sílaba

accented ['æksəntɪd] *adj* **heavily/lightly a.** con un fuerte/ligero acento

accentuate [æk'sentʃʊeɪt] *vt* (**a**) *(word)* acentuar (**b**) *(emphasize) (feature, importance)* acentuar, destacar; *(contrast)* resaltar; **to a. the need for sth** insistir en la necesidad de algo; **to a. the positive** acentuar lo positivo

accentuation [æksentjʊ'eɪʃən] *n (of word)* acentuación *f*

ACCEPT [ək'sept] **1** *vt* (**a**) *(in general)* aceptar; *(reasons)* aceptar, admitir; *(blame)* admitir, reconocer; **to a. sth from sb** *(gift, bribe)* aceptar algo de alguien; **to a. responsibility for sth** asumir la responsabilidad de algo; **the machine won't a. foreign coins** la máquina no funciona con *or* no admite monedas extranjeras; **my novel has been accepted for publication** han aceptado publicar mi novela; **I don't a. that we're to blame** no acepto que nosotros tengamos la culpa; **I just can't a. that she's gone for good** no puedo aceptar que se haya ido para siempre; **it is generally accepted that...** en general, se acepta *or* se reconoce que...; **the accepted procedure** el procedimiento habitual
(**b**) *(person) (into university)* admitir; **to a. sb as a member** admitir a alguien como socio; **I've been accepted for the job** me han aceptado para el trabajo; **to a. sb for what they are** aceptar a alguien tal y como es; **I never really felt accepted there** nunca me sentí aceptado allí
2 *vi* aceptar

---

acceptability [əkseptə'bɪlɪtɪ] *n* aceptabilidad *f*

acceptable [ək'septəbəl] *adj* (**a**) *(satisfactory, tolerable)* aceptable, admisible; **barely/perfectly a.** apenas/totalmente aceptable; **to be a. to sb** venirle bien a alguien; **are these conditions a. to you?** ¿le parecen bien estas condiciones?; **parsley is an a. alternative** se puede sustituir por perejil, el perejil es un sustituto válido ►► *Comptr* ***A. Use Policy*** *(of Internet Service Provider)* = código de conducta definido por un proveedor de acceso a Internet
(**b**) *(welcome)* **that would be most a.** me parece estupendo; **a gift of flowers is always a.** unas flores son siempre un regalo que se agradece

acceptably [ək'septəblɪ] *adv (satisfactorily, tolerably)* aceptablemente; **inflation has remained a. low** la inflación se ha mantenido en un nivel aceptablemente bajo

acceptance [ək'septəns] *n* (**a**) *(of invitation, apology, defeat)* aceptación *f*; **he telephoned his a.** aceptó por teléfono ►► ***a. speech*** discurso *m* de agradecimiento *(al recibir un premio)*
(**b**) *(approval, favour)* acogida *f*, aprobación *f*; **to find a.** tener aceptación; **to meet with general a.** ser bien acogido(a)
(**c**) *(belief)* **there is a general a. that smoking causes cancer** en general hay acuerdo en cuanto a que el tabaco provoca cáncer
(**d**) *Com & Fin (of goods)* aceptación *f*; *(of bill of exchange)* aceptación *f*

access ['ækses] **1** *n* (**a**) *(entry, admission)* acceso *m*; **there is easy a. to the beach** la playa dispone de un cómodo acceso; **the kitchen gives a. to the garage** la cocina da al garaje, por la cocina se entra al garaje; **to gain a. to sth** acceder a algo; **how did the thieves gain a.?** ¿cómo lograron entrar los ladrones?; **to have a. to sth** tener acceso a algo; **a. only** *(sign)* sólo entradas y salidas, vía de paso ►► ***a. road*** (vía *f* de) acceso *m*
(**b**) *(right to contact, use)* acceso *m*; **to have a. to sth/sb** tener acceso a algo/alguien; **to refuse a. to sb** denegar la entrada a alguien
(**c**) *(for divorced parent)* derecho *m* de visita *(a los hijos)*
(**d**) *Br Literary (of emotion)* acceso *m*, arrebato *m*
(**e**) *Comptr* **to have a. to the Internet** tener acceso a Internet ►► ***a. code*** código *m* de acceso; ***a. control*** control *m* de acceso; ***a. level*** nivel *m* de acceso; ***a. number*** *(to Internet Service Provider)* número *m* de acceso; ***a. privileges*** privilegios *mpl* de acceso; ***a. provider*** proveedor *m* de acceso (a Internet); ***a. time*** tiempo *m* de acceso
2 *vt* (**a**) *(information, computer data)* acceder a (**b**) *Formal (building)* acceder a

accessibility [əksesə'bɪlɪtɪ] *n* (**a**) *(of place)* accesibilidad *f* (**b**) *(of explanation, book, movie)* accesibilidad *f* (**c**) *(availability) (of education, health care)* accesibilidad *f*; **we have increased the a. of health care to poor families** hemos mejorado el acceso de los pobres a la sanidad

accessible [ək'sesəbəl] *adj* (**a**) *(place, person)* accesible; **the beach is easily a. on foot** se puede acceder fácilmente a la playa a pie (**b**) *(explanation, book, movie)* accesible (**c**) *(available)* accesible; **to make health care a. to everyone** hacer que todo el mundo tenga acceso a la atención sanitaria

accession [ək'seʃən] *n* (**a**) *(to power, throne)* acceso *m* (**b**) *(library book)* adquisición *f* ▸▸ ***a. number*** signatura *f* (**c**) *Formal (to treaty)* adhesión *f*; **their a. to the European Union** su adhesión a la Unión Europea

accessorize [ək'sesəraɪz] *vt* complementar

accessory [ək'sesərɪ] *n* (**a**) *(for car, camera)* accesorio *m*; **accessories** *(handbag, gloves etc)* complementos *mpl* (**b**) *Law* **a. (to a crime)** cómplice *mf* (de un delito); **a. before the fact** cómplice *(implicado en la preparación)*; **a. after the fact** cómplice encubridor(ora)

accidence ['æksɪdəns] *n Gram* accidentes *mpl*

accident ['æksɪdənt] *n* (**a**) *(unfortunate event)* accidente *m*; **to have an a.** tener *or* sufrir un accidente; *Euph (of small child)* hacerse pipí; **car a.** accidente de coche; **road a.** accidente de tráfico; **their last child was an a.** su último hijo fue un accidente; IDIOM **an a. waiting to happen** un desastre en potencia, una bomba de relojería *or RP* de tiempo; **accidents will happen** le puede pasar a cualquiera ▸▸ ***a. claim form*** *(for car insurance)* parte *m* de accidente; ***a. and emergency unit*** urgencias *fpl*; ***a. insurance*** seguro *m* de accidentes (**b**) *(chance)* **by a.** *(by chance)* por casualidad; *(unintentionally)* sin querer; **that was no a.** eso no fue casualidad; **more by a. than design** más por suerte que por otra cosa

accidental [æksɪ'dentəl] **1** *adj* (**a**) *(chance) (discovery, meeting)* accidental, casual; *(damage, injury)* accidental ▸▸ *Law* ***a. death*** muerte *f* accidental (**b**) *Formal (nonessential)* accidental

2 *n Mus* accidente *m*, accidental *m*

accidentally [æksɪ'dentəlɪ] *adv (unintentionally)* sin querer, accidentalmente; *(by chance)* por casualidad; **a. on purpose** sin querer pero queriendo; **I did it a. on purpose** lo hice sin queriendo

accident-prone ['æksɪdəntprəʊn] *adj* propenso(a) a tener accidentes

acclaim [ə'kleɪm] **1** *n* alabanza *f*, elogios *mpl*; **his play met with great critical a.** su obra fue elogiada por la crítica

2 *vt* (**a**) *(praise, applaud)* alabar, elogiar; **a critically acclaimed novel** una novela elogiada por la crítica (**b**) *(proclaim)* aclamar, proclamar; **Charlemagne was acclaimed emperor** Carlomagno fue aclamado *or* proclamado emperador

acclamation [æklə'meɪʃən] *n* aclamación *f*; **to be elected by a.** salir *or* resultar elegido por aclamación popular

acclimatization [əklaɪmətaɪ'zeɪʃən], *US* **acclimation** [æklɪ'meɪʃən] *n (to climate)* aclimatación *f*; *(to conditions, customs)* adaptación *f*

acclimatize [ə'klaɪmətaɪz], *US* **acclimate** ['æklɪmeɪt] **1** *vt (to climate)* aclimatar (**to** a); *(to conditions, customs)* adaptar (**to** a); **to become acclimatized** *or US* **acclimated to sth** *(to climate)* aclimatarse a algo; *(to conditions, customs)* adaptarse a algo

2 *vi (to climate)* aclimatarse (**to** a); *(to conditions, customs)* adaptarse (**to** a)

accolade ['ækəleɪd] *n (praise)* elogio *m*; *(prize)* galardón *m*

accommodate [ə'kɒmədeɪt] *vt* (**a**) *(provide room for)* alojar, acomodar; **the hotel can a. 300 people** el hotel puede albergar *or* alojar a 300 personas (**b**) *(satisfy)* complacer; *(point of view)* tener en cuenta; **we will do our best to a. you** haremos todo lo posible por complacerle (**c**) *(adapt)* **to a. oneself to sth** adaptarse a algo

accommodating [ə'kɒmədeɪtɪŋ] *adj (helpful)* servicial; *(easy to please)* flexible

accommodation [əkɒmə'deɪʃən] *n* (**a**) *(lodging)* alojamiento *m*; **to look for a.** *(flat to rent)* buscar alojamiento *or* casa *or Esp* piso; *(hotel room)* buscar hospedaje *or* alojamiento *or* habitación; **there is a. in this hotel for fifty people** este hotel alberga a cincuenta personas ▸▸ *Br* ***a. address*** domicilio *m*, señas *fpl*

(**b**) *(space)* **office a.** locales para oficinas; **sleeping a.** sitio, alojamiento; **there is sleeping a. for seven** hay sitio para que duerman siete

(**c**) *Formal (agreement)* **to come to an a.** llegar a un acuerdo satisfactorio

(**d**) *US* **accommodations** *(lodging)* alojamiento *m*; *(on boat, train)* plazas *fpl*

(**e**) *Physiol* acomodación *f*

(**f**) *Com* ***a. bill*** efecto *m* de favor

accompaniment [ə'kʌmpənɪmənt] *n* (**a**) *(generally)* acompañamiento *m*; **he entered to the a. of wild applause** entró envuelto en un enfervorizado aplauso (**b**) *(with food)* complemento *m*, acompañamiento *m* (**c**) *Mus* **guitar/piano a.** acompañamiento de guitarra/piano

accompanist [ə'kʌmpənɪst] *n Mus* acompañante *mf*

accompany [ə'kʌmpənɪ] *vt* (**a**) *(escort)* acompañar; **she was accompanied by her brother** la acompañaba su hermano, iba acompañada de su hermano; **she accompanied me to the door** me acompañó a *or* hasta la puerta

(**b**) *(supplement, join with)* acompañar; **she accompanied her advice with a warning** su consejo iba acompañado de una advertencia; **her photos a. the text** sus fotos ilustraban el texto; **the hot weather is often accompanied by afternoon thunderstorms** el calor viene a menudo acompañado de tormentas vespertinas; **it's an ideal wine to a. seafood** es un vino ideal para acompañar el marisco

(**c**) *Mus* acompañar (**on** a *or* en *or* con)

accompanying [ə'kʌmpənɪɪŋ] *adj* **the a. documents** los documentos adjuntos; **children will not be admitted without an a. adult** no se permite la entrada *or* el acceso a menores sin la compañía de un adulto *or* si no van acompañados de un adulto

accomplice [ə'kʌmplɪs] *n* cómplice *mf* (**in** en)

accomplish [ə'kʌmplɪʃ] *vt (task)* realizar; *(aim)* cumplir, alcanzar; **we didn't a. much** no logramos *or* conseguimos gran cosa; **what have we accomplished after all this effort?** ¿qué hemos logrado *or* conseguido después de tanto esfuerzo?

accomplished [ə'kʌmplɪʃt] *adj (cook, singer, poet)* consumado(a), con talento; *(player of sport, game)* hábil; *(performance)* logrado(a), conseguido(a); **a very a. piece of work** una obra muy lograda *or* conseguida

accomplishment [ə'kʌmplɪʃmənt] *n* (**a**) *(feat)* logro *m*; **it was quite an a. to have finished within budget** fue todo un logro terminar sin salirse del presupuesto (**b**) **accomplishments** *(personal abilities)* talentos *mpl (aprendidos)* (**c**) *(completion)* cumplimiento *m*; **the a. of all their aims** el cumplimiento de todos sus objetivos

accord [ə'kɔːd] **1** *n* (**a**) *(treaty, pact)* acuerdo *m*; **to reach an a. (with)** alcanzar un acuerdo (con) (**b**) *(harmony, conformity)* acuerdo *m*; **to be in a. with** estar de acuerdo con *or* acorde con *or* de conformidad con; **with one a.** unánimemente, al unísono; **of one's own a.** (de) motu propio; **the problem disappeared of its own a.** el problema desapareció por sí solo

2 *vt Formal* conceder (**to** a); **to a. sb great respect** guardar gran respeto por alguien; **to a. sth great significance** atribuir gran relevancia a algo

▸ **accord with** *vt insep Formal* ser acorde con, estar de acuerdo con

accordance [ə'kɔːdəns] *n* **in a. with** de acuerdo con, en conformidad con; **in a. with your instructions, we have burnt the contents of the box** siguiendo sus instrucciones, hemos quemado el contenido de la caja

according [ə'kɔːdɪŋ] **1 according to** *prep* (**a**) *(depending on)* **they are arranged a. to height** están organizados por orden de altura; **a. to whether one is rich or poor** dependiendo de si se es rico o pobre, según se sea rico o pobre; **prices vary a. to how long the job will take** los precios varían en función del tiempo que lleve realizar el trabajo

(**b**) *(in conformity with)* **a. to instructions** según las instrucciones; **everything went a. to plan** todo fue de acuerdo con lo planeado

(**c**) *(citing a source)* **a. to Marx** según Marx; **a. to my watch** según *or* por mi reloj; **the Gospel a. to St Luke** el Evangelio según San Lucas

2 according as *prep* **reward them a. as you see fit** recompénsales como *or* en la medida en que creas conveniente; **the cases are classified a. as to whether they affect national or foreign students only, or both** los casos se clasifican según afecten a los estudiantes nacionales, a los extranjeros o a ambos

accordingly [ə'kɔːdɪŋlɪ] *adv* (**a**) *(appropriately)* como corresponde; **to act a.** actuar en consecuencia; **the budget has been cut by 15 percent, so you should adjust your estimates a.** el presupuesto se ha reducido en un 15 por ciento, por lo que, consecuentemente, deberían modificar sus estimaciones (**b**) *(therefore)* así pues, por consiguiente

accordion [ə'kɔːdɪən] *n* acordeón *m*; **a. player** acordeonista ▸▸ ***a. pleats*** plisado *m*

accordionist [ə'kɔːdɪənɪst] *n* acordeonista *mf*

accost [ə'kɒst] *vt (person)* abordar; **I was accosted by an aggressive beggar** me abordó un mendigo agresivo

ACCOUNT [ə'kaʊnt] **1** *n* (**a**) *(bill, at bank, shop)* cuenta *f*; *Comptr (for Internet)* cuenta *f*; **to have an a. with** tener una cuenta en; **to open an a.** abrir una cuenta; **charge it to** *or* **put it on my a.** cárguelo a *or* póngalo en mi cuenta; **he paid** *or* **settled his a.** pagó sus deudas; *Fin* **accounts payable/receivable** cuentas por pagar/cobrar; IDIOM **to settle (one's) accounts with sb** arreglar cuentas con alguien ▸▸ ***a. number*** número *m* de cuenta

(**b**) *Com* **accounts** *(books, department)* contabilidad; **to do one's accounts** hacer la contabilidad; **she works in accounts** trabaja en (el departamento de) contabilidad ▸▸ ***account(s) book*** libro *m* de contabilidad; ***accounts department*** departamento *m* de contabilidad

(**c**) *(client)* cuenta *f*, cliente *m*; **to win/lose an a.** ganar/perder un cliente ▸▸ ***a. executive*** director(a) *m,f* de cuenta

(**d**) *(credit)* **to buy sth/pay for sth on a.** comprar/pagar algo a crédito

(**e**) *(reckoning)* **by his own a.** *(according to him)* según él mismo; **to keep (an) a. of sth** llevar la cuenta de algo; **to take sth into a., to take a. of sth** tener *or* tomar algo en cuenta; **to take no a. of sth** no tener algo en cuenta; **to call sb to a.** pedir cuentas a alguien; **to hold sb to a. (for sth)** hacer que alguien rinda cuentas (por algo); **the terrorists will be brought to a.** los terroristas tendrán que responder de sus acciones

(**f**) *Formal (importance)* **of no a.** sin importancia; **it's of no** *or* **little a. to me** me trae sin cuidado

(**g**) **on a. of** *(because of)* a causa de; **on a. of her being a minor** por ser menor de edad; **on no a. should you call her, do not call her on any a.** no la llames bajo ningún concepto; **on one's own a.** por cuenta propia; **don't do it on my a.!** ¡no lo hagas por mí!; **don't worry on that a.** no te preocupes por eso

(**h**) *(report)* relato *m*, descripción *f*; **what is your a. of events?** ¿cuál es su versión de los hechos?; **to give an a. of sth** narrar algo; **by** *or* **from all accounts it was a great success** todo apunta a que fue un gran éxito; IDIOM **to give a good a. of oneself** *(in fight, contest)* salir airoso(a), lucirse; IDIOM **to give a poor a. of oneself** *(in fight, contest)* salir mal parado(a)

(**i**) *Formal (use)* **to put** *or* **turn sth to good a.** sacar provecho de algo

2 *vt Formal (consider)* considerar

▸ **account for** *vt insep* (**a**) *(explain, justify)* explicar; **the difference is accounted for by...** ...explica la diferencia; **I can't a. for it** no puedo dar cuenta de ello; **five people have still not been accounted for** todavía no se conoce la suerte de cinco personas; PROV **there's no accounting for taste** sobre gustos no hay nada escrito

(**b**) *(constitute)* **salaries a. for 15 percent of expenditure** los salarios suponen un 15 por ciento de los gastos

(**c**) *(defeat)* derrotar, vencer

---

accountability [əkaʊntə'bɪlɪtɪ] *n* responsabilidad *f* (**to** ante)

accountable [ə'kaʊntəbəl] *adj* **to be a. (to sb/for sth)** ser responsable (ante alguien/de algo); **to hold sb a.** considerar a alguien responsable; **he acts as if he isn't a. to anyone** se comporta como si no tuviera que darle cuentas a nadie; **I can't be held a. for what happens** no puedo hacerme responsable de lo que suceda

accountancy [ə'kaʊntənsɪ] *n* contabilidad *f*; **a degree in a.** un título de *Esp* contable *or Am* contador

accountant [ə'kaʊntənt] *n Esp* contable *mf*, *Am* contador(ora) *m,f*

accounting [ə'kaʊntɪŋ] *n* contabilidad *f* ▸▸ ***a. period*** periodo *m* contable; *Comptr* ***a. program*** programa *m* de contabilidad; ***a. system*** sistema *m* contable; ***a. year*** ejercicio *m* contable

accoutred, *US* **accoutered** [ə'ku:təd] *adj Formal* pertrechado(a), equipado(a); **thus a., we were ready for the blizzard** equipados de este modo *or* de esta guisa, nos encontrábamos preparados para la ventisca

accoutrements [ə'ku:trəmənts], **accouterments** [ə'ku:tərmənts] *npl Formal* pertrechos *mpl*, equipo *m*

Accra [ə'krɑ:] *n* Accra

accredit [ə'kredɪt] *vt* (**a**) *(provide with credentials)* acreditar; **ambassador accredited to Morocco** embajador acreditado en *or* ante Marruecos (**b**) *(recognize as bona fide)* acreditar

accreditation [əkredɪ'teɪʃən] *n* (**a**) *(credentials) (for ambassador, envoy)* credencial *f*, acreditación *f* (**b**) *(recognition) (for school, course)* reconocimiento *m*, homologación *f*

accredited [ə'kredɪtɪd] *adj Formal* acreditado(a); **the country's a. representative to the UN** el representante del país acreditado ante la ONU

accretion [ə'kri:ʃən] *n Formal* (**a**) *(additional item)* aditamento *m* (**b**) *(accumulation)* acumulación *f*

accrue [ə'kru:] **1** *vi Fin (interest)* acumularse; **to a. to sb** *(interest, benefits)* ir a parar a alguien; **accrued benefits** *(under pension scheme)* beneficios acumulados, derechos consolidados; **accrued interest** interés devengado

2 *vt (collect, amass)* acumular, juntar; *(interest)* devengar

acct (*abbr* **account**) cta.

acculturation [əkʌltʃə'reɪʃən] *n* aculturación *f*

accumulate [ə'kju:mjʊleɪt] **1** *vt* acumular

2 *vi* acumularse

accumulation [əkju:mjʊ'leɪʃən] *n* (**a**) *(process)* acumulación *f* (**b**) *(mass)* cúmulo *m* (**c**) *Fin (of capital, interest)* acumulación *f*

accumulator [ə'kju:mjʊleɪtə(r)] *n* (**a**) *Elec (battery)* acumulador *m* (**b**) *Br (in horse-racing)* = apuesta en varias carreras en la que las ganancias de una carrera se apuestan directamente en la siguiente (**c**) *Comptr* acumulador *m*

accuracy ['ækjʊrəsɪ] *n (of calculation, measurement, estimate, prediction)* exacitud *f*, precisión *f*; *(of report, description)* exactitud *f*, minuciosidad *f*; *(of translation, portrayal)* fidelidad *f*; *(of firearm, shot, instrument)* precisión *f*

accurate ['ækjʊrət] *adj (calculation, measurement, estimate, prediction)* exacto(a), preciso(a); *(report, description)* exacto(a), minucioso(a); *(translation, portrayal)* fiel; *(firearm, shot)* certero(a); *(instrument)* preciso(a); **to be a. in one's calculations** acertar uno en sus conjeturas; **to be more a., there were fifteen of them** para ser más exactos, eran quince

accurately ['ækjʊrətlɪ] *adv (to calculate, measure, estimate, predict, remember)* exactamente, con exactitud; *(to describe, report)* detalladamente, minuciosamente; *(to aim)* con precisión; *(to translate, portray)* fielmente

accursed [ə'kɜ:sɪd] *adj* (**a**) *(under a curse)* maldito(a) (**b**) *Fam (expressing frustration, annoyance)* dichoso(a), maldito(a)

accusal [ə'kju:zəl] *n* acusación *f*; **looks of a.** miradas acusatorias

accusation [ækjʊ'zeɪʃən] *n* (**a**) *(allegation, criticism)* acusación *f*; **to make an a. (against sb)** acusar (a alguien); **there was a note of a. in her voice** había un tono acusador en su voz (**b**) *(legal charge)* cargo *m*, acusación *f*; **what are the accusations against him?** ¿de qué está acusado?, ¿qué cargos hay contra él?

accusative [ə'kju:zətɪv] *Gram* **1** *n* acusativo *m*

2 *adj* acusativo(a)

accusatory [ə'kju:zətərɪ] *adj* acusatorio(a)

accuse [ə'kju:z] *vt* acusar; **to a. sb of (doing) sth** acusar a alguien de (hacer) algo; **he is** *or* **he stands accused of tax fraud** se lo acusa *or* está acusado de fraude fiscal; *Ironic* **no one could a. her of being obsessive about punctuality** no se la puede tachar de obsesiva con la puntualidad

accused [ə'kju:zd] *n Law* **the a.** el/la acusado(a)

accuser [ə'kju:zə(r)] *n* acusador(ora) *m,f*

accusing [ə'kju:zɪŋ] *adj (look, stare)* acusador(ora), acusatorio(a)

accusingly [ə'kju:zɪŋlɪ] *adv (to say)* en tono acusador; **he looked at me a.** me lanzó una mirada acusadora

accustom [ə'kʌstəm] *vt* acostumbrar, habituar; **to a. sb to sth** acostumbrar *or* habituar a alguien a algo; **they soon accustomed themselves to the idea** pronto se acostumbraron a la idea

accustomed [ə'kʌstəmd] *adj* (**a**) *(habituated)* **to be a. to (doing) sth** estar acostumbrado(a) a (hacer) algo; **to get** *or* **grow a. to (doing) sth** acostumbrarse a (hacer) algo; **she's not a. to being interrupted** no está acostumbrada *or* habituada a que la interrumpan (**b**) *(usual, expected)* habitual, acostumbrado(a)

AC/DC ['eɪsi:'di:si:] **1** *n Elec* (*abbr* **alternating current/direct current**) corriente *f* alterna/continua

2 *adj Fam (bisexual)* bi, bisexual

ACE [eɪsi:'i:] *n US* (*abbr* **Army Corps of Engineers**) = cuerpo de ingenieros del ejército

ace [eɪs] **1** *n* (**a**) *(in cards)* as *m*; **a. of spades** as de picas; *Fig* **to have an a. up one's sleeve** *or* **an a. in the hole** tener un as en la manga; **to have** *or* **hold all the aces** tener la sartén por el mango; IDIOM **she came within an a. of winning** *(very near to)* estuvo a punto *or* en un tris de ganar (**b**) *(in tennis)* ace *m* (**c**) *Fam (expert)* as *m*; **a flying a.** un as del vuelo (**d**) *(fighter pilot)* as *m* (**e**) *Fam (hole in one)* hoyo *m* en uno

2 *adj* (**a**) *(expert)* **an a. reporter** un as del periodismo (**b**) *Fam (very good)* genial, *Esp* guay, *Andes, CAm, Carib, Méx* chévere, *Méx* padre, *RP* bárbaro(a)

3 *vt US* **to a. an exam** bordar un examen

acerbic [ə'sɜ:bɪk] *adj* (**a**) *(taste)* acerbo(a), acre (**b**) *(person, wit, remark)* acre, mordaz

acerbity [ə'sɜ:bətɪ] *n* (**a**) *(of taste)* acerbidad *f*, acrimonia *f* (**b**) *(of person, wit, remark)* acritud *f*, mordacidad *f*

aces ['eɪsəs] *adj US Fam (excellent)* genial, *Esp* guay, *Andes, CAm, Carib, Méx* chévere, *Méx* padre, *RP* bárbaro(a)

acetate ['æsɪteɪt] *n Chem* acetato *m*

acetic acid [ə'si:tɪk'æsɪd] *n* ácido *m* acético

acetone ['æsɪtəʊn] *n Chem* acetona *f*

acetylene [ə'setəli:n] *n Chem* acetileno *m* ▸▸ ***a. lamp*** lámpara *f* de acetileno; ***a. torch*** soplete *m*

acetylsalicylic acid [ə'si:taɪlsælɪ'sɪlɪk'æsɪd] *n* ácido *m* acetilsalicílico

acey-deucy [ˈeɪsɪˈduːsɪ] *adj US Fam* genial, *Esp* guay, *Andes, CAm, Carib, Méx* chévere, *Méx* padre, *RP* bárbaro(a)

ache [eɪk] **1** *n* dolor *m*; **aches and pains** achaques

2 *vi* **(a)** *(feel pain, be painful)* doler; **my head/tooth aches** me duele la cabeza/la muela, tengo dolor de cabeza/muelas; **I a. all over** me duele todo; **her heart ached to see them so unhappy** se le partía el alma *or* el corazón viéndolos tan desgraciados **(b)** *(feel desire)* ansiar, arder en deseos de; **to be aching to do sth** estar deseando hacer algo

achievable [əˈtʃiːvəbəl] *adj* factible, realizable

achieve [əˈtʃiːv] *vt* conseguir, lograr; **we achieved what we set out to do** conseguimos *or* logramos lo que nos propusimos; **she achieved the impossible** consiguió *or* logró lo imposible; **he'll never a. anything in life** nunca *or* jamás conseguirá *or* logrará nada en la vida; **the demonstration achieved nothing** no se consiguió *or* logró nada con la manifestación; **what will that a.?** ¿qué se conseguirá *or* qué se va a conseguir con eso?

achievement [əˈtʃiːvmənt] *n* **(a)** *(action)* realización *f*, consecución *f* **(b)** *(thing achieved)* logro *m*; **that's quite an a.!** ¡es todo un logro! ►► *Educ* ***a. test*** prueba *f* de rendimiento *or* aprovechamiento **(c)** *(success)* éxito *m*; **I felt a real sense of a.** sentí verdadera satisfacción por el éxito alcanzado

achievement-orient(at)ed [əˈtʃiːvməntˈɔːrɪent(eɪt)ɪd] *adj* **to be a.** estar centrado en *or* orientado hacia la obtención de resultados

achiever [əˈtʃiːvə(r)] *n* triunfador(ora) *m,f*; **a high a.** un triunfador; **he's a low a.** rinde poco

Achilles [əˈkɪliːz] *n Mythol* Aquiles ►► ***A.' heel*** talón *m* de Aquiles; ***A.' tendon*** tendón *m* de Aquiles

aching [ˈeɪkɪŋ] *adj (head, limbs)* dolorido(a); **with an a. heart** con gran dolor; **oh, my a. head!** ¡qué dolor de cabeza!

acid [ˈæsɪd] **1** *n* **(a)** *(chemical)* ácido *m*; IDIOM *Austr* **to put the a. on sb** forzar a alguien (a hacer algo) ►► ***a. rain*** lluvia *f* ácida; *Fig* ***a. test*** prueba *f* de fuego **(b)** *Fam (LSD)* ácido *m*; **to drop a.** tomar *or* meterse ácido **(c)** *Mus* ***a. house*** acid house *m*; ***a. rock*** *(music)* rock *m* psicodélico **(d)** ***a. drop*** *(sweet)* caramelo *m* ácido

2 *adj* **(a)** *(chemical, taste)* ácido(a) **(b)** *(tone, remark)* sarcástico(a)

acid-head [ˈæsɪdhed] *n Fam* **to be an a.** ser un adicto al ácido

acidic [əˈsɪdɪk] *adj* ácido(a)

acidify [əˈsɪdɪfaɪ] *vt* acidificar, acidular

acidity [əˈsɪdɪtɪ] *n* **(a)** *(of chemical, taste)* acidez *f* **(b)** *(of tone, remark)* sarcasmo *m*

acidly [ˈæsɪdlɪ] *adv* con acritud, agriamente

ack-ack [ˈækˈæk] *n Fam Old-fashioned* fuego *m* antiaéreo

acknowledge [əkˈnɒlɪdʒ] *vt* **(a)** *(admit) (mistake, debt, truth)* reconocer, admitir; **we a. that we were wrong** reconocemos que estábamos equivocados; **to a. defeat** admitir una derrota

(b) *(recognize) (person)* saludar; *(achievement, contribution)* reconocer; **she didn't a. me** *or* **my presence** no me saludó; **they acknowledged him as their leader** lo reconocieron como jefe; **it is generally acknowledged that...** es bien sabido que...; **to a. one's sources** hacer referencia *or* citar a las fuentes

(c) *(confirm)* **to a. (receipt of) a letter** acusar recibo de una carta

(d) *(express gratitude for)* dar las gracias por, expresar gratitud por

acknowledged [əkˈnɒlɪdʒd] *adj (expert, authority)* de reconocido prestigio

acknowledg(e)ment [əkˈnɒlɪdʒmənt] *n* **(a)** *(admission) (of mistake, truth)* reconocimiento *m*

(b) *(recognition) (of achievement, contribution)* reconocimiento *m*; **I waved at him, but received no a.** le hice un gesto con la mano pero no respondió a mi saludo *or* no me saludó; **in a. of** en reconocimiento a

(c) *(of letter) & Comptr* acuse *m* de recibo

(d) acknowledg(e)ments *(in book)* menciones *fpl*, agradecimientos *mpl*

ACLU [eɪsiːelˈjuː] *n* (*abbr* **American Civil Liberties Union**) = organización estadounidense para la defensa de las libertades civiles

acme [ˈækmɪ] *n* súmmum *m*, colmo *m*

acne [ˈæknɪ] *n* acné *m*

acolyte [ˈækəlaɪt] *n* acólito *m*

acorn [ˈeɪkɔːn] *n* bellota *f*

acoustic [əˈkuːstɪk] *adj* acústico(a) ►► *Comptr* ***a. coupler*** acoplador *m* acústico; ***a. distortion*** distorsión *f* acústica; ***a. feedback*** acoplamiento *m* acústico; ***a. guitar*** guitarra *f* acústica; ***a. phonetics*** fonética *f* acústica; ***a. tile*** panel *m* acústico *or* de insonorización

acoustics [əˈkuːstɪks] *n* **(a)** *(subject)* acústica *f* **(b)** *(of room, theatre)* acústica *f*; **to have good/bad a.** tener (una) buena/mala acústica

ACP [eɪsiːˈpiː] *n* (*abbr* **American College of Physicians**) = colegio estadounidense de médicos

acquaint [əˈkweɪnt] *vt* **(a)** *(with person)* **to be acquainted with sb** conocer a alguien; **to become** *or* **get acquainted** entablar relación; **she is well acquainted with the mayor** conoce bien al alcalde, tiene una buena relación con el alcalde

(b) *(with facts, situation)* **to be acquainted with sth** conocer algo, estar al corriente de algo; **to a. sb with sth** poner al corriente de algo a alguien; **to a. oneself with sth** familiarizarse con algo; **I'm fully acquainted with the facts** estoy completamente al corriente *or* al tanto de los hechos; **we are well acquainted with his views** conocemos bien sus puntos de vista

acquaintance [əˈkweɪntəns] *n* **(a)** *(person)* conocido(a) *m,f*; **he is an a. (of mine)** es un conocido (mío); **he has a wide circle of acquaintances** tiene un amplio círculo de amistades **(b)** *(familiarity) (with person)* relación *f*; *(with facts)* conocimiento *m* **(with** de); **to make sb's a.** conocer a alguien; **on closer** *or* **further a....** cuando se la trata más..., cuando se la conoce mejor...

acquiesce [ækwɪˈes] *vi* acceder **(in** a)

acquiescence [ækwɪˈesəns] *n Formal* aquiescencia *f*, consentimiento *m*

acquiescent [ækwɪˈesənt] *adj Formal* aquiescente

acquire [əˈkwaɪə(r)] *vt* **(a)** *(property, experience, knowledge, reputation)* adquirir; *(information)* obtener, conseguir; **it took her years to a. fluency in German** le costó años adquirir fluidez en alemán **(b)** *(habit)* adquirir; **to a. a taste for sth** aprender a disfrutar de algo

acquired [əˈkwaɪəd] *adj (characteristic, habit)* adquirido(a); **it's an a. taste** es un placer adquirido con el tiempo ►► ***a. immune deficiency syndrome*** síndrome *m* de inmunodeficiencia adquirida

acquis communautaire [ækiːkəmuːniˈteə(r)] *n EU* acervo *m* comunitario

acquisition [ækwɪˈzɪʃən] *n* **(a)** *(process)* adquisición *f* **(b)** *(thing acquired)* adquisición *f*; **she's the team's latest a.** es la última adquisición del equipo

acquisitive [əˈkwɪzɪtɪv] *adj (person)* **he's very a.** tiene un afán por coleccionar

acquit [əˈkwɪt] (*pt & pp* **acquitted**) *vt* **(a)** *Law* absolver, declarar inocente; **to a. sb of sth** absolver a alguien de algo; **she was acquitted on all charges** quedó absuelta de todos los cargos **(b) to a. oneself well/badly** *(perform)* salir bien/mal parado(a)

acquittal [əˈkwɪtəl] *n* **(a)** *Law* absolución *f*, fallo *m* absolutorio **(b)** *(of duty)* cumplimiento *m*, desempeño *m*

acre [ˈeɪkə(r)] *n* acre *m*, = 4.047 m^2; *Fam* **acres of space** *(lots)* un montón *or Méx* un chorro *or RP* una pila de espacio

acreage [ˈeɪkərɪdʒ] *n* = superficie medida en acres; **how much a. do you have here?** ¿cuánto mide esta finca?, ¿cuántos acres tiene esta finca?

acrid [ˈækrɪd] *adj* **(a)** *(smell, taste, smoke)* acre **(b)** *(language, remark)* acre, mordaz

acrimonious [ækrɪˈməʊnɪəs] *adj (discussion, debate)* agrio(a); *(words, remark)* mordaz, acre

acrimony [ˈækrɪmənɪ] *n* acritud *f*, acrimonia *f*

acrobat [ˈækrəbæt] *n* acróbata *mf*

acrobatic [ækrəˈbætɪk] *adj* acrobático(a)

acrobatics [ækrəˈbætɪks] **1** *n* acrobacias *fpl*

2 *npl* **to do** *or* **perform a.** realizar acrobacias; *Fig* **mental a.** gimnasia mental

acronym [ˈækrənɪm] *n* siglas *fpl*, acrónimo *m*

acrophobia [ækrəˈfəʊbɪə] *n* acrofobia *f*

Acropolis [əˈkrɒpəlɪs] *n* **the A.** la Acrópolis

ACROSS [əˈkrɒs] *prep* **1 (a)** *(from one side to the other of)* a través de; **a trip a. Spain** un viaje por España; **to go a. sth** cruzar algo; **he walked a. the room** cruzó la habitación; **he ran a. the road** cruzó la calle corriendo; **we drove a. the desert** cruzamos el desierto en coche/camión/*etc.*; **she swam a. the river** cruzó el río a nado; **to help sb a. the road** ayudar a alguien a cruzar *or* atravesar la calle; **to travel a. country** viajar a campo traviesa *or* campo través; **she threw it a. the room** lo tiró al otro lado de la habitación; **he stared/shouted a. the table at her** la miró/le gritó desde el otro lado de la mesa; **the bridge a. the river** el puente que cruza el río; **she drew a line a. the page** dibujó una línea horizontal a lo ancho de toda la página; **a grin spread a. her face** una amplia sonrisa se dibujó en su cara; **this jacket is a bit tight a. the shoulders** esta chaqueta queda un poco estrecha de hombros

(b) *(on the other side of)* al otro lado de; **a. the street/border** al otro lado de la calle/frontera; **they live just a. the road** viven justo enfrente; **I saw him a. the room** lo vi en el otro extremo de la sala

(c) *(throughout)* **a. the country** por todo el país; **people came from a. Europe** vino gente de toda Europa; **changes have been introduced a. the syllabus** se han introducido cambios en todo el programa

(d) *(on)* **his coat lay a. the chair** su abrigo estaba sobre la silla; **to hit sb a. the face** cruzarle la cara a alguien

2 *adv* (a) *(from one side to the other)* de un lado a otro; **to run/swim a.** cruzar corriendo/a nado; **we only got halfway a.** cruzamos sólo hasta la mitad; **he walked a. to the door** cruzó la habitación en dirección a la puerta; **she shouted a. to them** les gritó desde el otro lado; **to look a. at sb** *(at table)* mirar a alguien (desde el otro lado de la mesa); *(in room)* mirar a alguien (desde el otro lado de la habitación)

(b) *(with distance)* **it's 10 cm/2 km a.** tiene 10 cm/2 km de ancho

(c) *(opposite)* **a. from me/my house** enfrente; **she was sitting a. from me** estaba sentada enfrente de mí *or* frente a mí

(d) *(in crosswords)* **8 a.** 8 horizontal

---

across-the-board [əˈkrɒsðəˈbɔːd] 1 *adj* generalizado(a); **an a. increase** *(in salary)* un aumento lineal

2 *adv* **there will be changes a.** habrá cambios generalizados; **stock prices have fallen a.** los precios de las acciones han caído de manera generalizada; **this applies a.** se aplica con carácter general

acrostic [əˈkrɒstɪk] *n* acróstico *m*

acrylic [əˈkrɪlɪk] 1 *n* acrílico *m*

2 *adj (fibre, paint, garment)* acrílico(a); *(resin)* sintético(a)

ACT [ækt] 1 *n* (a) *(thing done)* acto *m*; **a criminal a.** un delito; **an a. of aggression** una agresión; **an a. of stupidity** una estupidez; **an a. of terrorism** una acción terrorista; **an a. of war** una acción de guerra; **the sexual a.** el acto sexual; **to be in the a. of doing sth** estar haciendo algo (precisamente); **to catch sb in the a. of doing sth** atrapar a alguien haciendo algo; **to catch sb in the a.** atrapar a alguien in fraganti; IDIOM *Fam* **to get in on the a.** *(get involved)* apuntarse, *Am* anotarse ►► ***a. of faith*** acto *m* de fe; *Law* ***a. of God*** caso *m* fortuito

(b) *(in cabaret, circus) (performance)* número *m*; *(band)* grupo *m*; *Fig* **it's all an a.** es puro teatro *or* pura farsa; IDIOM **to do a vanishing a.** esfumarse, desaparecer, *Am* hacerse humo; IDIOM *Fam* **to get one's a. together** organizarse, ponerse las pilas; IDIOM **he'll be a hard a. to follow** *Esp* su sucesor lo va a tener difícil para emularlo, *Am* a su sucesor se le va a hacer difícil emularlo; IDIOM **to put on an a.** hacer teatro

(c) *(in play)* acto *m*; **A. III** tercer acto

(d) *Law* **a.** (*Br* **of parliament** *or US* **of Congress**) ley *f*

2 *vt* (a) *(of actor)* interpretar; *Fig* **he was acting the part of the caring husband** estaba interpretando *or* haciendo el papel del marido solícito

(b) *(behave like)* IDIOM **to a. the fool** *or* **the goat** hacer el tonto; **to a. the hero** hacerse el héroe; *Fam* **a. your age!** ¡no seas infantil!

3 *vi* (a) *(take action)* actuar; **he was acting on his own** actuaba por iniciativa propia *or Esp* por libre; **the drug acts quickly** la droga actúa rápidamente; **to a. as secretary/chairperson** actuar *or* hacer de secretario(a)/presidente(a), desempeñar *or* ejercer las funciones de secretario(a)/presidente(a); **to a. as a warning/an incentive** servir de advertencia/incentivo; **to a. for sb** *or* **on behalf of sb** *(lawyer)* representar a alguien; **to a. in good faith** actuar de buena fe

(b) *(behave)* actuar, comportarse; **she acted as if she didn't know him** actuó como si no lo conociera

(c) *(pretend)* actuar; **to a. stupid** hacerse el tonto; **to a. all innocent** hacerse el/la inocente

(d) *(actor)* actuar; **which movies has she acted in?** ¿en qué películas ha actuado *or* salido?

► **act on** *vt sep* (a) *(be prompted by)* **to a. on sb's advice** seguir los consejos de alguien; **they were acting on reliable information** actuaban siguiendo información fiable; **to a. on impulse** actuar impulsivamente

(b) *(of drug, chemical)* actuar sobre

► **act out** *vt sep (fantasy)* realizar; *(scene)* representar

► **act up** *vi (child, car, injury)* dar guerra

---

acting [ˈæktɪŋ] 1 *n* (a) *(performance)* interpretación *f*, actuación *f*; **the a. was superb** el trabajo *or* la actuación de los actores era excelente (b) *(profession)* interpretación *f*, profesión *f* de actor/actriz; **I've done a bit of a.** *(theatre)* he hecho un poco de teatro, he interpretado algún papel en el teatro; *(cinema)* he hecho un poco de cine, he interpretado algún papel en el cine

2 *adj (temporary)* en funciones

actinium [ækˈtɪnɪəm] *n Chem* actinio *m*

ACTION [ˈækʃən] 1 *n* (a) *(individual act)* acto *m*, acción *f*; **to be responsible for one's actions** ser responsable de los propios actos; PROV **actions speak louder than words** hechos son amores y no buenas razones, valen más los hechos que las palabras

(b) *(activity)* acción *f*; **the situation calls for immediate a.** la situación requiere una intervención inmediata; **a. and reaction** acción y reacción; **to go into a.** ponerse en acción; **in a.** en acción; **to be out of a.** *(machine)* no funcionar, estar averiado(a); *(person)* estar fuera de combate; **to put sb out of a.** *(of injury, illness)* dejar a alguien fuera de combate; **to put a plan into a.** poner en marcha un plan; **to take a.** actuar; **to take a. against sb** hacer frente a alguien; **I want to see some a. around here!** *(get things moving!)* ¡quiero ver esto en marcha!; IDIOM *Fam* **they were looking for some a.** *(excitement)* estaban buscando acción, *RP* querían un poco de agite; IDIOM *Fam* **Leeds is where the a. is these days** actualmente la movida *or Esp* marcha está en Leeds; IDIOM *Fam* **to want a piece** *or* **slice of the a.** querer un trozo del pastel ►► *Com* ***a. plan*** plan *m* de acción

(c) *Mil* (acción *f* de) combate *m*; **to see a.** entrar en combate; **missing/killed in a.** desaparecido(a)/muerto(a) en combate; *Mil* **a. stations** *(positions)* puestos de combate; *Fam Fig* **a. stations!** *(get ready!)* ¡a sus puestos *or Col, RP* marcas! ►► ***a. movie*** película *f* de acción

(d) *(of movie, novel)* acción *f* ►► *Br TV* ***a. replay*** repetición *f*

(e) *Law* demanda *f*; **to bring an a. against sb (for sth)** demandar a alguien (por algo)

(f) *(effect)* acción *f*, efecto *m* (**on** sobre)

(g) *(mechanism)* mecanismo *m*

2 *vt (decision, point)* poner en acción, poner en práctica

3 *exclam Cin* ¡acción!

---

actionable [ˈækʃənəbəl] *adj Law* susceptible de procesamiento

action-packed [ˈækʃənpækt] *adj (movie, novel)* lleno(a) de acción; *(holiday)* repleto(a) de actividades, movido(a)

activate [ˈæktɪveɪt] *vt* (a) *(alarm, mechanism)* activar (b) *Phys* activar (c) *US (military unit)* movilizar

activated carbon [ˈæktɪveɪtɪdˈkɑːbən] *n* carbón *m* activado

activation [æktɪˈveɪʃən] *n (of alarm, mechanism)* activación *f*

active [ˈæktɪv] 1 *adj* (a) *(lively) (person, imagination, life)* activo(a); *(stock market)* activo(a), agitado(a); **she's still a. at ninety** aún sigue activa a los noventa

(b) *(involved, participating)* activo(a); **to be a. in sth, to take an a. part in sth** participar activamente en algo; **to be politically a.** participar activamente en la política; **to be sexually a.** mantener relaciones sexuales

(c) *(keen, not passive) (interest)* profundo(a), gran, vivo(a); *(dislike)* profundo(a), especial; **to take an a. dislike to sb** tenerle a alguien (una) profunda *or* especial antipatía; **to take an a. interest in sth** interesarse activamente por algo; **you have our a. support** cuenta con nuestro apoyo absoluto *or* incondicional; **the proposal is under a. discussion** la propuesta es objeto de animado debate

(d) *(effective, in operation) (case, file)* abierto(a), pendiente; *(law)* en vigor; *(volcano)* activo(a) ►► *Fin* ***a. account*** cuenta *f* abierta; ***a. ingredient*** principio *m* activo

(e) *Mil* **on a. service** *or US* **duty** en servicio activo; **to be on the a. list** estar en la reserva activa

(f) *Gram* activo(a); **in the a. voice** en voz activa

(g) *Comptr* ***a. file*** fichero *m* activo; ***a. matrix*** matriz *f* activa; ***a. matrix display*** *or* ***screen*** pantalla *f* de matriz activa; ***a. window*** ventana *f* activa

2 *n Gram (voice)* (voz *f*) activa *f*; **in the a.** en activa

actively [ˈæktɪvlɪ] *adv* (a) *(to involve, participate)* activamente; **to be a. involved in sth** estar activamente involucrado en algo (b) *(to disagree, discourage)* radicalmente, enérgicamente; **I a. dislike him** me desagrada profundamente

activism [ˈæktɪvɪsəm] *n* activismo *m*; **political a.** activismo político

activist [ˈæktɪvɪst] *n Pol* activista *mf*

activity [ækˈtɪvɪtɪ] *n* (a) *(liveliness, busyness) (of brain, person)* actividad *f*; *(in place, bank account)* movimiento *m*; **there's been a lot of a. on the Stock Market** ha habido mucho movimiento *or* mucha actividad en la bolsa; **economic/political a.** actividad económica/política

(b) *(action, occupation)* actividad *f*; **business activities** actividades comerciales

(c) *(pastime)* actividad *f*; **activities** *(at holiday camp)* actividades *fpl* ►► ***a. book*** cuaderno *m* de actividades; ***a. holiday*** = vacaciones organizadas en las que se practica algún deporte o actividad similar

actor [ˈæktə(r)] *n* actor(triz) *m,f*

actress ['æktrɪs] *n* actriz *f*; **she's a good a.** es una excelente actriz; IDIOM *Br Fam Hum* **...as the a. said to the bishop** ...y no me malinterpretes

actressy ['æktrɪsɪ] *adj Pej* teatral; **she can be quite a.** a veces le echa mucho teatro

ACTUAL ['æktʃʊəl] *adj* (**a**) *(real)* verdadero(a), real; **the a. result was higher** el resultado real fue superior; **her a. words were...** lo que dijo exactamente fue...; **an a. example** un ejemplo real; **there's no a. rule against it** no existe una norma establecida contra eso; **in a. fact** de hecho, en realidad ►► *Law* ***a. bodily harm*** lesiones *fpl* menos graves, lesiones *fpl* leves; *Com* ***a. cost*** costo *m or Esp* coste *m* efectivo *or* real

(**b**) *(itself)* **although the garden is big, the a. house is small** aunque el jardín es grande, la casa en sí es pequeña; **what happened at the a. moment of the collision?** ¿qué ocurrió en el momento preciso del choque?

> **False friend**: The most common senses of the English adjective **actual** are not translated by the Spanish word **actual**. In Spanish **actual** means "present", "modern" or "topical".

actuality [æktʃʊ'ælɪtɪ] *n Formal* **in a.** en realidad; **the actualities of the situation** la verdad *or* la realidad de la situación

ACTUALLY ['æktʃʊəlɪ] *adv* (**a**) *(really)* en realidad; **what a. happened?** ¿qué ocurrió en realidad?; **what she a. means is...** lo que quiere decir en realidad es...; **did he a. hit you?** ¿de verdad llegó a golpearte?; **I a. spoke to the prime minister himself** de hecho hablé con el primer ministro en persona; **he a. believed me!** ¡me creyó y todo!; **he a. bought me a drink for once!** ¡incluso me invitó a una copa y todo!

(**b**) *(in fact)* **a., I rather like it** la verdad es que me gusta; **a., it** WAS **the right number** de hecho, sí que era el número correcto; **you don't like wine, do you? – I do, a.** no te gusta el vino, ¿verdad? – no, no, sí que me gusta; **did you go? – no, a., I didn't** ¿fuiste? – en realidad *or Esp* pues no, no fui; **I'm not sure, a.** pues no estoy seguro; **the movie was so long, I a. fell asleep halfway through** la película era tan larga que llegué a dormirme a la mitad *or RP* hasta me quedé dormida por la mitad

> **False friend**: The most common senses of the English adverb **actually** are not translated by the Spanish word **actualmente**. In Spanish **actualmente** means "these days" or "at the moment".

actuarial [æktʃʊ'eərɪəl] *adj* actuarial ►► ***a. tables*** tablas *fpl* actuariales

actuary ['æktʃʊərɪ] *n* actuario(a) *m,f* de seguros

actuate ['æktʃʊeɪt] *vt* (**a**) *Formal (motivate)* **her decision was actuated solely by greed** su decisión estaba motivada únicamente por la avaricia (**b**) *Tech* activar

acuity [ə'kju:ɪtɪ] *n (of senses, understanding)* agudeza *f*

acumen ['ækjʊmən] *n* perspicacia *f*, sagacidad *f*; **business a.** perspicacia *f* para los negocios

acupressure ['ækjʊpreʃə(r)] *n* digitopuntura *f*

acupuncture ['ækjʊpʌŋktʃə(r)] *n* acupuntura *f*

acupuncturist ['ækjʊpʌŋktʃərɪst] *n* acupuntor(ora) *m,f*

acute [ə'kju:t] **1** *adj* (**a**) *(serious, intense) (pain)* agudo(a), intenso(a); *(problem, shortage)* acuciante, agudo(a); *(remorse, embarrassment)* intenso(a); **she has an a. awareness of her shortcomings** es plenamente consciente de sus efectos ►► ***a. appendicitis*** apendicitis *f* aguda

(**b**) *(perceptive) (person)* perspicaz; *(mind, eyesight)* agudo(a); *(hearing, sense of smell)* muy fino(a); *(comment)* agudo(a)

(**c**) *Gram* agudo(a); **an "e" a.** una "e" aguda ►► ***a. accent*** acento *m* agudo

(**d**) *Geom* ***a. angle*** ángulo *m* agudo

2 *n (accent)* acento *m* agudo

acute-angled [ə'kju:t'æŋgəld] *adj (triangle)* acutángulo

acutely [ə'kju:tlɪ] *adv* (**a**) *(intensely) (painful, embarrassing)* extremadamente; **to be a. aware** *or* **conscious of sth** ser plenamente consciente de algo (**b**) *(perceptively)* perspicazmente, sutilmente

acuteness [ə'kju:tnɪs] *n* (**a**) *(intensity) (of pain)* agudeza *f*, intensidad *f*; *(of problem, shortage)* gravedad *f* (**b**) *(perceptiveness) (of person, mind)* agudeza *f*, perspicacia *f*; *(of eyesight)* agudeza *f*; *(of hearing, sense of smell)* agudeza *f*, finura *f*; *(of comment, analysis)* agudeza *f*

AD [eɪ'di:] *adv* (*abbr* **Anno Domini**) d. J.C., d.C.

ad [æd] *n Fam (advertisement)* anuncio *m*

adage ['ædɪdʒ] *n* máxima *f*, adagio *m*

adagio [ə'dɑ:dʒɪəʊ] *Mus* **1** *n* (*pl* **adagios**) adagio *m*

2 *adv* adagio

Adam ['ædəm] *pr n* Adán; IDIOM *Fam* **I wouldn't know him from A.** no lo conozco de nada *or RP* para nada ►► ***A.'s apple*** nuez *f*, bocado *m* de Adán

adamant ['ædəmənt] *adj* inflexible; **she is a. that she saw him** insiste en que lo vio; **he is quite a. about it** es bastante inflexible al respecto

adamantine [ædə'mæntaɪn] *adj Literary (will, resistance)* inamovible

adamantly ['ædəməntlɪ] *adv* rotundamente, categóricamente

adapt [ə'dæpt] **1** *vt* (**a**) *(adjust)* adaptar (**for** a); **to a. oneself to sth** adaptarse a algo (**b**) *(book, play)* adaptar; **to a. a novel for the stage** adaptar una novela a la escena

2 *vi* adaptarse (**to** a); **children a. easily** los niños se adaptan a todo fácilmente, los niños tienen una gran capacidad de adaptación

adaptability [ədæptə'bɪlɪtɪ] *n (of person)* adaptabilidad *f*, flexibilidad *f*; *(of product)* adaptabilidad *f*

adaptable [ə'dæptəbəl] *adj* (**a**) *(person)* adaptable; **she's very a.** se adapta a todo (**b**) *(instrument, method)* adaptable; **it's a. to a range of circumstances** puede adaptarse *or* es adaptable a diversas circunstancias

adaptation [ædæp'teɪʃən] *n* (**a**) *(adjustment)* adaptación *f* (**b**) *(of book, play)* adaptación *f*

adaptor, adapter [ə'dæptə(r)] *n* (**a**) *(for several plugs)* ladrón *m*; *(for different socket)* adaptador *m* (**b**) *Comptr* ***a. card*** tarjeta *f* adaptadora

ADC [eɪdi:'si:] *n Mil* (*abbr* **aide-de-camp**) ayudante *m* de campo, edecán *m*

ADD [eɪdi:'di:] *n Med* (*abbr* **attention deficit disorder**) trastorno *m* por déficit de atención

add [æd] **1** *vt* (**a**) *(combine)* añadir (**to** a); **this book adds little to the debate** este libro aporta poco al debate; **it will a. another £100 to the cost** supondrá un incremento del costo de otras 100 libras; **they added 10 percent for service** añadieron un 10 por ciento por el servicio

(**b**) *(say)* añadir; **"and it's far too expensive," he added** "y es demasiado caro", añadió; **I have nothing (further) to a.** no tengo nada más que añadir

(**c**) *Math* sumar; **a. four and** *or* **to five** suma cuatro más cinco

(**d**) *(confer, lend)* **it adds interest/distinction to the occasion** confiere interés/distinción a la ocasión

2 *vi* sumar; **he can't a. properly** no sabe sumar

►**add on** *vt insep* añadir

►**add to** *vt insep* (**a**) *(increase)* aumentar; *(difficulty, crisis)* agravar; **it will only a. to the cost** sólo contribuirá a aumentar *or* incrementar el costo (**b**) *(supplement)* **to a. to what we were saying yesterday...** complementando lo que decíamos ayer... (**c**) *(improve)* **it didn't really a. to the occasion** no contribuyó a mejorar a la ocasión

►**add together** *vt sep* sumar

►**add up 1** *vt sep (figures)* sumar; *(bill)* hacer; **when you a. it all up it was quite cheap** sumándolo todo era *or* resultaba bastante barato

2 *vi* (**a**) *(give correct total)* cuadrar; **these figures don't a. up** estas cifras no cuadran; *Fam (become expensive)* **with five kids, expenses soon a. up** con cinco hijos, los gastos ascienden rápidamente (**b**) *(calculate)* sumar (**c**) *(make sense)* encajar, cuadrar; **it just doesn't a. up** algo no encaja

►**add up to** *vt insep* (**a**) *(of figures)* **it adds up to £126** suma *or* asciende a un total de 126 libras (**b**) *(result in, be equivalent to)* **it all adds up to an enjoyable day out** todo esto da como resultado una agradable excursión; **it adds up to a lot of work for us** supone mucho trabajo para nosotros; **it doesn't a. up to much** no viene a ser gran cosa

added ['ædɪd] *adj* (**a**) *(additional)* adicional; **an a. advantage** *or* **bonus** una ventaja adicional; **no a. sugar** sin azúcar, sin adición de azúcar; **with a. vitamins** con vitaminas añadidas ►► *Econ* ***a. value*** valor *m* añadido *or Am* agregado

(**b**) *(in addition)* **a. to our earlier arguments, this news finally convinced him** esta noticia, sumada a nuestros argumentos anteriores, acabó por convencerlo; **a. to that...** además de eso...

addendum [ə'dendəm] (*pl* **addenda** [ə'dendə]) *n* a(d)denda *f*, adición *f*

adder ['ædə(r)] *n* víbora *f*

addict ['ædɪkt] *n* adicto(a) *m,f*; **(drug) a.** drogadicto(a) *m,f*, toxicómano(a) *m,f*; *Fam* **TV a.** teleadicto(a); *Fam* **I never miss an episode, I'm a complete a.** no me pierdo un episodio, estoy completamente enganchado

addicted [ə'dɪktɪd] *adj* **to be a. to sth** ser adicto(a) a algo; **to become** *or* **get a. to sth** hacerse *or* volverse adicto(a) a algo; *Fam* **she's a. to exercise/hard work** es una adicta al ejercicio físico/al trabajo

addiction [ə'dɪkʃən] *n* adicción *f*; **heroin a.** heroinomanía, adicción a la heroína; **nicotine a.** adicción a la nicotina; **he wants to overcome his a.** quiere superar su adicción

addictive [ə'dɪktɪv] *adj (drug)* adictivo(a); **nicotine is very a.** la nicotina causa gran dependencia; *Fam* **this new series could become a.** esta nueva serie podría crear hábito

adding machine ['ædɪŋməʃi:n] *n* máquina *f* de sumar, sumadora *f*

Addis Ababa ['ædɪs'æbəbə] *n* Addis Abeba

addition [ə'dɪʃən] **1** *n* (**a**) *Math* suma *f* (**b**) *(action)* incorporación *f*, adición *f*; *(thing added)* incorporación *f*, añadido *m*; **an important a. to our collection** una importante incorporación a nuestra colección; **a welcome new a. to our staff/the team** una nueva incorporación a nuestra plantilla/al equipo; **an a. to the family** un nuevo miembro en la familia (**c**) *(to house)* añadido *m*

2 in addition *adv* además; **in a. to** además de

additional [ə'dɪʃənəl] *adj* adicional; **for** *or* **at no a. charge** sin costo adicional ►► *Fin* ***a. voluntary contribution*** contribución *f* complementaria facultativa

additionally [ə'dɪʃənəlɪ] *adv* (**a**) *(further, more)* adicionalmente, de forma *or* manera adicional (**b**) *(moreover)* además

additive ['ædɪtɪv] *n* aditivo *m* ►► *Comptr* ***a. colour*** color *m* aditivo

additive-free ['ædɪtɪv'fri:] *adj* sin aditivos

addle-brained ['ædəlbreɪnd] *adj Fam* atolondrado(a), *Col* apendejado(a)

addled ['ædəld] *adj* (**a**) *(egg)* podrido(a) (**b**) *(mind)* embarullado(a)

add-on ['ædɒn] **1** *n Comptr* extra *m*, suplemento *m*

2 *adj* ***a. fare*** tarifa *f* suplementaria

address [ə'dres] **1** *n* (**a**) *(of person)* dirección *f*, domicilio *m*; *(of letter, package)* dirección *f*, señas *fpl*; **a Baltimore a.** una dirección de Baltimore; **what is your a.?** ¿cuál es tu dirección *or* tus señas?, ¿qué dirección tienes?; **she no longer lives at that a.** ya no vive en esa dirección *or* ese domicilio; **we've changed our a.** hemos cambiado de dirección *or* domicilio; **not known at this a.** *(on returned letter)* destinatario desconocido ►► ***a. book*** agenda *f*, libreta *f* de direcciones; *(in e-mail program)* agenda *f* de direcciones; ***a. label*** etiqueta *f* de dirección

(**b**) *(speech)* alocución *f*, discurso *m*

(**c**) **form of a.** *(when speaking to sb)* tratamiento; **what's the correct form of a. for a bishop?** ¿qué tratamiento recibe un obispo?

(**d**) *Comptr* dirección *f* ►► ***a. bus*** bus *m* de direccionamiento *or* direcciones

2 *vt* (**a**) *(letter, package)* dirigir (**to** a); **the letter was addressed to Tony** la carta iba dirigida a Tony; **the parcel was incorrectly addressed** la dirección (del destinatario) del paquete era incorrecta

(**b**) *(direct) (remarks, criticism)* dirigir (**to** a); **all complaints should be addressed to the manager** todas las reclamaciones deberán ir dirigidas al gerente

(**c**) *(person, crowd)* dirigirse a; **he addressed her as "Your Majesty"** le dio el tratamiento de "Su Majestad"; **a judge should be addressed as "your honour"** un juez recibe el tratamiento de "su señoría"

(**d**) *(question, problem)* abordar; **to a. oneself to sth** abordar algo

(**e**) *(in golf, snooker, pool)* **to a. the ball** golpear la bola

addressee [ædre'si:] *n* destinatario(a) *m,f*

adduce [ə'dju:s] *vt Formal* aducir, alegar

adductor [æ'dʌktə(r)] *n Anat* aductor *m*

Adelaide ['ædəleɪd] *n* Adelaida

adenoidal [ædɪ'nɔɪdəl] *adj* adenoideo(a)

adenoids ['ædɪnɔɪdz] *npl Anat* vegetaciones *fpl* (adenoideas)

adept 1 *n* ['ædept] *Formal* experto(a) *m,f*

2 *adj* [ə'dept] **she is a. at getting her own way** siempre consigue lo que quiere; **he had always been a. at persuading people to support him** siempre se le había dado muy bien conseguir el apoyo de la gente

> **False friend:** The Spanish word **adepto** is not a translation for the English word **adept**. In Spanish **adepto** means "follower" (noun) or "supporting" (adjective).

adequacy ['ædɪkwəsɪ] *n (sufficiency)* idoneidad *f*; **he questioned the a. of the safety measures** cuestionó si las medidas de seguridad serían suficientes; **a solution of only marginal a.** una solución apenas satisfactoria

adequate ['ædɪkwət] *adj* (**a**) *(enough)* suficiente; **to be given a. warning** ser avisado con antelación; **the money we had was more than a.** el dinero del que disponíamos era más que suficiente

(**b**) *(satisfactory, appropriate)* adecuado(a), apropiado(a); **this house is hardly a. for a family of six** en esta casa a duras penas cabe una familia de seis personas; **this one will be quite a.** éste resultará bastante adecuado; **he proved a. to the task** demostró ser la persona adecuada para el trabajo

adequately ['ædɪkwətlɪ] *adv* (**a**) *(sufficiently)* suficientemente (**b**) *(satisfactorily)* satisfactoriamente, adecuadamente; **the engine performs only a. at high speeds** el rendimiento del motor a alta velocidad es apenas satisfactorio

ADHD *n (abbr* **attention deficit hyperactivity disorder**) trastorno *m* por déficit de atención

adhere [əd'hɪə(r)] *vi Formal* (**a**) *(stick)* adherirse (**to** a) (**b**) **to a. to** *(rule)* cumplir, observar; *(belief, plan)* atenerse a

adherence [əd'hɪərəns] *n Formal (to rule)* cumplimiento *m*, observancia *f* (**to** de); *(to belief, plan)* adhesión *f*, apoyo *m* (**to** a)

adherent [əd'hɪərənt] *n* adepto(a) *m,f*

adhesion [əd'hi:ʒən] *n* (**a**) *(stickiness)* adherencia *f* (**b**) *Formal (of person)* adhesión *f* (**to** a) (**c**) *Phys* adhesión *f* (**d**) *Med* adhesión *f*

adhesive [əd'hi:sɪv] **1** *n* adhesivo *m*

2 *adj* adhesivo(a), adherente ►► ***a. tape*** cinta *f* adhesiva

ad hoc [æd'hɒk] **1** *adj* ad hoc; **on an a. basis** ad hoc ►► ***a. committee*** comisión *f* especial

2 *adv* ad hoc; **we deal with these things a.** abordamos estos asuntos ad hoc *or* conforme surgen

ad hominem [æd'hɒmɪnem] **1** *adj* **an a. argument** un argumento ad hominem

2 *adv* ad hominem

adieu [ə'dju:] (*pl* **adieus** *or* **adieux** [ə'dju:z]) *n Archaic or Literary* adiós *m*; **I bid you a.** me despido de usted

ad infinitum ['ædɪnfɪ'naɪtəm] *adv* hasta el infinito, ad infinitum

adipose ['ædɪpəʊs] *adj Anat* adiposo(a) ►► ***a. tissue*** tejido *m* adiposo

adjacent [ə'dʒeɪsənt] *adj (country, territory)* colindante; *(room, building)* contiguo(a), adyacente; **to be a. to** estar al lado de

adjectival [ædʒɪk'taɪvəl] *adj* adjetival; **an a. use** un uso adjetival

adjective ['ædʒɪktɪv] *n* adjetivo *m*

adjoin [ə'dʒɔɪn] *vt (of building, room, land)* lindar con

adjoining [ə'dʒɔɪnɪŋ] *adj (building, room)* contiguo(a); **they wanted a. rooms** querían habitaciones contiguas

adjourn [ə'dʒɜ:n] **1** *vt (meeting, trial)* aplazar, posponer; **the trial was adjourned until the next day** el juicio se aplazó hasta el día siguiente

2 *vi* (**a**) *(end, break off)* **the trial/meeting adjourned** se levantó la sesión *(tras juicio/reunión)* (**b**) *(move elsewhere)* pasar a; **to a. to another room** pasar a otra habitación

adjournment [ə'dʒɜ:nmənt] *n (of meeting, trial)* aplazamiento *m*

adjudge [ə'dʒʌdʒ] *vt* **to a. sb guilty** declarar a alguien culpable; **to a. sb the winner** proclamar a alguien ganador

adjudicate [ə'dʒu:dɪkeɪt] **1** *vt (claim, dispute)* juzgar

2 *vi* actuar como árbitro; **to a. on sth** arbitrar algo, actuar como árbitro en algo

adjudication [ədʒu:dɪ'keɪʃən] *n* (**a**) *(process)* sentencia *f*, resolución *f*; **the matter is up for a.** el asunto está visto para sentencia (**b**) *(decision)* fallo *m*

adjudicator [ə'dʒu:dɪkeɪtə(r)] *n (of dispute)* árbitro *m*; *(of contest)* juez *mf*

adjunct ['ædʒʌŋkt] *n* (**a**) *(addition)* apéndice *m* (**b**) *Gram* complemento *m* circunstancial

adjust [ə'dʒʌst] **1** *vt* (**a**) *(regulate) (heat, volume, speed, pressure)* ajustar, regular; *(lighting, machine)* ajustar, regular; *TV* **do not a. your set** no ajuste los controles de su televisor, = mensaje que indica que el problema de recepción no se debe al televisor

(**b**) *(alter) (plan, method)* ajustar, adaptar; *(length, size)* ajustar; *(salary, wage)* ajustar, modificar; **the government has adjusted prices downwards/upwards** el gobierno ha ajustado los precios a la baja/al alza

(**c**) *(correct)* ajustar, corregir; **the figures have been adjusted to allow for inflation** las cifras se han corregido teniendo en cuenta la inflación

(**d**) *(position of clothing, hat)* arreglar, ajustar; **to a. one's tie** ajustarse la corbata; **please a. your dress before leaving** *(sign)* arréglese la ropa antes de salir

(**e**) *(adapt)* adaptar (**to** a); **to a. oneself to sth** adaptarse a algo

(**f**) *(in insurance)* **to a. a claim** liquidar *or* abonar una reclamación

2 *vi (person)* adaptarse (**to** a); **the cover adjusts to fit all sizes** la funda se adapta a todos los tamaños

adjustable [ə'dʒʌstəbəl] *adj* ajustable, regulable ►► ***a.*** *Br* ***spanner*** *or US* ***wrench*** llave *f* inglesa

adjuster [ə'dʒʌstə(r)] *n US* perito(a) *m,f* tasador(ora) de seguros

adjustment [ə'dʒʌstmənt] *n* (**a**) *(to heat, volume, speed, pressure)* ajuste *m*; *(to lighting, machine)* ajuste *m*; **to make an a. to sth** hacer un ajuste a algo, ajustar algo
(**b**) *(alteration) (to plan, method)* ajuste *m*, cambio *m*; *(to length, size)* ajuste *m*; *(to salary, wage)* modificación *f*
(**c**) *(correction)* ajuste *m*, corrección *f*; **no a. was made for inflation** no se hizo un ajuste que reflejara la inflación
(**d**) *(adaptation)* adaptación *f* (**to** a); **a period of a.** un periodo de adaptación
(**e**) *(of insurance claim)* liquidación *f*, tasación *f*

adjutant ['ædʒətənt] *n Mil* ordenanza *m*

adjutant-general ['ædʒətənt'dʒenərəl] *n Mil* ayudante *mf* general

ad-lib ['æd'lɪb] **1** *n* improvisación *f*
2 *adj* improvisado(a)
3 *adv* improvisadamente
4 *vt* (*pt & pp* **ad-libbed**) improvisar
5 *vi* improvisar

ad-libbing ['æd'lɪbɪŋ] *n* improvisación *f*

adman ['ædmæn] *n Fam* publicista *m*, publicitario *m*

admin ['ædmɪn] *n Fam* (**a**) *(work)* papeleo *m* (**b**) *(department)* administración *f*

administer [əd'mɪnɪstə(r)] *vt* (**a**) *(manage, run) (business, institution)* administrar, dirigir; *(estate, territory, funds)* administrar (**b**) *(give) (punishment)* aplicar; *(blow)* propinar; *(medication)* administrar; **to a. justice** administrar justicia; *Law* **to a. the oath (to sb)** tomar juramento (a alguien)

administrate [əd'mɪnɪstreɪt] *vt (business, institution)* administrar, dirigir

administration [ədmɪnɪ'streɪʃən] *n* (**a**) *(management, running) (of business, institution)* administración *f*; *(of estate, territory, funds)* administración *f* ►► *Law* ***a. order*** mandamiento *m* judicial
(**b**) *(giving) (of punishment, medicine, justice)* administración *f*; *(of oath)* toma *f*
(**c**) *(administrative department)* gestión *f*, administración *f*
(**d**) *US Pol (government)* gobierno *m*, administración *f*; **the Clinton/Bush A.** la administración Clinton/Bush
(**e**) *(receivership)* **to go into a.** ser intervenido(a)

administrative [əd'mɪnɪstrətɪv] *adj* administrativo(a) ►► ***a. assistant*** *(with responsibility)* asistente *mf* de dirección; *(with little responsibility)* auxiliar *mf* administrativo(a); ***a. costs*** costos *mpl or Esp* costes *mpl* administrativos; ***the a. grade*** *(in civil service)* el funcionariado administrativo; ***a. law*** derecho *m* administrativo; ***a. staff*** personal *m* administrativo

administrator [əd'mɪnɪstreɪtə(r)] *n (of business, institution, estate)* administrador(ora) *m,f*

admirable ['ædmɪrəbəl] *adj* admirable

admirably ['ædmɪrəblɪ] *adv* admirablemente; **she coped a.** se las arregló de forma admirable

admiral ['ædmərəl] *n* (**a**) *(in navy)* almirante *m*; *Br* **a. of the fleet,** *US* **fleet a.** almirante de la flota (**b**) *(butterfly)* vanesa *f*

Admiralty ['ædmərəltɪ] *n (in Britain)* **the A.** el Ministerio de Marina, el Almirantazgo

admiration [ædmə'reɪʃən] *n* (**a**) *(feeling)* admiración *f* (**for** por); **to be full of a. for sth/sb** sentir una gran admiración por algo/alguien; **I have nothing but a. for them** no siento más que admiración por ellos; **she was lost in a. of his achievement** se deshizo en elogios por su hazaña (**b**) *(person, thing)* **she was the a. of the entire class** era la admiración de toda la clase

admire [əd'maɪə(r)] *vt* admirar; **I a. her dedication** admiro su dedicación; **I admire him for his honesty** lo admiro por su honradez; **there is much to a. in the movie** es una película digna de admiración; **to a. oneself in the mirror** admirarse en el espejo; **I can't help admiring his cheek** ¡me admira su descaro!

admirer [əd'maɪərə(r)] *n* admirador(ora) *m,f*; *Hum* **I think you have a new a.** creo que tienes un nuevo admirador

admiring [əd'maɪərɪŋ] *adj (look, glance)* de admiración; **he was greeted by a. crowds wherever he went** allá donde iba, era recibido por muchedumbres que lo admiraban

admiringly [əd'maɪərɪŋlɪ] *adv* con admiración

admissible [əd'mɪsɪbəl] *adj* (**a**) *(behaviour, argument)* admisible (**b**) *Law* **to be a. in evidence** ser admisible como prueba ►► ***a. evidence*** prueba *f* admisible

admission [əd'mɪʃən] *n* (**a**) *(entry) (to school, hospital)* ingreso *m* (**to** en); *(to museum, exhibition)* visita *f* (**to** a), entrada *f* (**to** a); **no a. to unaccompanied children** *(sign)* prohibida la entrada a menores no acompañados
(**b**) *(price)* entrada *f*; **a. $3.50/free** entrada 3,50 dólares/gratuita ►► ***a. fee*** entrada *f*
(**c**) *(person admitted) (to school, hospital)* ingreso *m*, *CSur* internación *f*; *(to museum, exhibition)* visita *f*
(**d**) *(acknowledgement) (of guilt, mistake)* confesión *f*; **by** *or* **on his own a.** según él mismo admite

admit [əd'mɪt] (*pt & pp* **admitted**) **1** *vt* (**a**) *(allow to enter)* admitir, dejar pasar; **he was admitted to hospital** ingresó en un hospital; **children not admitted** *(sign)* prohibida la entrada a niños; **a. one** *(on ticket)* individual
(**b**) *(acknowledge) (fact, mistake)* admitir; *(crime, guilt)* confesar; **I a. I was wrong** reconozco *or* admito que estaba equivocado; **I must a. that...** tengo que reconocer *or* debo confesar que...; **I had to a. to myself that...** tuve que reconocer *or* admitir que...; **to a. defeat** darse por vencido(a); **it is generally admitted that women live longer than men** en general, se acepta que las mujeres viven más que los hombres
(**c**) *Formal (allow)* admitir; **the facts a. no other explanation** los hechos no admiten otra explicación
2 *vi* **to a. to** *(mistake)* admitir; *(crime)* confesar; **to a. to doing sth** admitir haber hecho algo

► **admit of** *vt insep Formal* admitir; **her behaviour admits of no excuse** su comportamiento no tiene excusa; **the text admits of only one interpretation** el texto sólo admite una interpretación

admittance [əd'mɪtəns] *n (entry)* acceso *m*, admisión *f*; **to gain a.** ser admitido(a); **to refuse** *or* **deny sb a.** no dejar entrar a alguien; **no a.** *(sign)* prohibido el paso

admittedly [əd'mɪtɪdlɪ] *adv* es cierto que; **a., it was dark when I saw him** es cierto que estaba oscuro cuando lo vi; **an a. serious case** un caso sin duda serio

admixture [æd'mɪkstʃə(r)] *n* (**a**) *Formal (ingredient)* ingrediente *m*, componente *m* (**b**) *Fig (of irony, comedy)* toque *m*, componente *m* (**of** de)

admonish [əd'mɒnɪʃ] *vt Formal (reprimand)* reprender (**for** por)

admonition [ædmə'nɪʃən] *n Formal* (**a**) *(rebuke)* admonición *f*, amonestación *f* (**b**) *(warning)* admonición *f*, advertencia *f*

admonitory [əd'mɒnɪtərɪ] *adj Formal* (**a**) *(rebuking)* admonitorio(a) (**b**) *(warning)* admonitorio(a), de advertencia

ad nauseam [æd'nɔːzɪæm] *adv* hasta la saciedad

adnexa [æd'neksə] *npl Anat* anexos *mpl*

ado [ə'duː] *n Formal* **without more** *or* **further a.** sin más preámbulos, sin más dilación; **much a. about nothing** mucho ruido y pocas nueces

adobe [ə'dəʊbɪ] *n (clay)* adobe *m*

adolescence [ædə'lesəns] *n* adolescencia *f*

adolescent [ædə'lesənt] **1** *n* adolescente *mf*
2 *adj* (**a**) *(boy, girl)* adolescente; **in his adolescent years** en sus años de adolescente (**b**) *(immature)* infantil

Adonis [ə'dəʊnɪs] *n* (**a**) *Mythol* Adonis *m* (**b**) *(handsome youth)* adonis *m*

adopt [ə'dɒpt] *vt* (**a**) *(child)* adoptar (**b**) *(approach, suggestion, habit, tone)* adoptar; **he has adopted a more conciliatory position** ha adoptado una postura más conciliadora (**c**) *Formal (approve) (minutes, report)* aprobar (**d**) *Pol (candidate)* elegir

adopted [ə'dɒptɪd] *adj (country)* adoptivo(a), de adopción; **she didn't know she was a.** no sabía que era adoptada ►► ***a. daughter*** hija *f* adoptiva; ***a. son*** hijo *m* adoptivo

adoption [ə'dɒpʃən] *n* (**a**) *(of child)* adopción *f*; **a. laws/procedure** leyes/procedimiento de adopción; **she's American by a.** es estadounidense de adopción ►► ***a. agency*** agencia *f* de adopciones (**b**) *(of approach, suggestion, habit, tone)* adopción *f* (**c**) *Formal (of minutes, report)* aprobación *f* (**d**) *Pol (of candidate)* elección *f*

adoptive [ə'dɒptɪv] *adj (parent)* adoptivo(a); *(country)* de adopción

adorable [ə'dɔːrəbəl] *adj* encantador(ora); **what an a. little cottage/skirt!** ¡qué casita/faldita tan mona!

adoration [ædə'reɪʃən] *n* adoración *f*; **in a.** con adoración ►► *Rel* ***the A. of the Magi*** la Adoración de los Reyes Magos

adore [ə'dɔː(r)] *vt* (**a**) *(worship)* adorar (**b**) *Fam (like, love)* adorar; **I adored her last movie** me encantó su última película; **they a. their grandchildren** adoran a sus nietos

adoring [ə'dɔːrɪŋ] *adj* devoto(a)

adoringly [ə'dɔːrɪŋlɪ] *adv* apasionadamente, fervorosamente

adorn [ə'dɔːn] *vt* (**a**) *(decorate)* adornar; **she adorned herself with jewels** se adornó con joyas (**b**) *(story)* adornar, embellecer

adornment [ə'dɔːnmənt] *n* (**a**) *(act)* embellecimiento *m* (**b**) *(decorative addition)* adorno *m*, ornamento *m*; **your beauty has no need of a.** tu belleza no necesita de adornos

ADP [eɪdiː'piː] *n* (**a**) *Comptr* (*abbr* **automatic data processing**) proceso *m or* procesamiento *m* automático de datos (**b**) *Biol* (*abbr* **adenosine diphosphate**) ADP *m*

adrenal [ə'driːnəl] *adj Anat* adrenal ▸▸ ***a. gland*** glándula *f* adrenal *or* suprarrenal

adrenalin(e) [ə'drenəlɪn] *n* adrenalina *f*; **to get** *or* **set the a. flowing** provocar una subida de adrenalina

Adriatic [eɪdrɪ'ætɪk] *n* **the A. (Sea)** el (mar) Adriático

adrift [ə'drɪft] *adv* **1** (**a**) **to go a.** *(of boat)* ir a la deriva; **the mutineers set them a. in a lifeboat** los amotinados los dejaron a la deriva en un bote salvavidas (**b**) **to come** *or* **go a.** *(of plan)* irse a pique
2 *adj* (**a**) **to be a.** *(of boat)* ir a la deriva (**b**) **she was (all) a.** *(aimless)* estaba perdida *or* desorientada

adroit [ə'drɔɪt] *adj* diestro(a), hábil; **he was a. at avoiding blame** era muy hábil echando la culpa a los demás

adroitly [ə'drɔɪtlɪ] *adv* hábilmente, con destreza

ADSL [eɪdiːes'el] *n* (*abbr* **asymmetric digital subscriber line**) ADSL *m*

aduki bean [ə'duːkɪbiːn] *n* = tipo de *Esp* judía *or Andes, CAm, Carib, Méx* frijol *or Andes, RP* poroto de color rojo

adulation [ædjʊ'leɪʃən] *n* adulación *f*

adulatory [ædjʊ'leɪtərɪ] *adj Formal* adulatorio(a)

adult ['ædʌlt, ə'dʌlt] **1** *n* adulto(a) *m,f*; **for adults only** sólo para adultos; **let's try and be adults about this, shall we?** abordemos el asunto como adultos, ¿de acuerdo?
2 *adj* (**a**) *(person, animal)* adulto(a) ▸▸ ***a. education*** educación *f* de *or* para adultos; ***a. teeth*** dentición *f* definitiva *or* secundaria (**b**) *(mature) (attitude, behaviour)* adulto(a), maduro(a); **she's very a. for her age** es muy madura para su edad (**c**) *Euph (movie, book)* para adultos ▸▸ ***a. bookstore*** librería *f* para adultos

adulterate [ə'dʌltəreɪt] *vt* adulterar

adulterer [ə'dʌltərə(r)] *n* adúltero(a) *m,f*

adulteress [ə'dʌltrəs] *n* adúltera *f*

adulterous [ə'dʌltərəs] *adj* adúltero(a)

adultery [ə'dʌltərɪ] *n* adulterio *m*; **to commit a.** cometer adulterio

adulthood ['ædʌlthʊd] *n* edad *f* adulta; **to reach a.** alcanzar la edad adulta

adumbrate ['ædʌmbreɪt] *vt Formal* (**a**) *(outline)* esbozar, bosquejar (**b**) *(foreshadow)* presagiar, anunciar

ad valorem ['ædvə'lɔːrəm] *adj (tax)* ad valorem

advance [əd'vɑːns] **1** *n* (**a**) *(forward movement)* avance *m*; *Fig* **he feared the a. of old age** le asustaba envejecer
(**b**) *(progress)* avance *m*, progreso *m*; **the latest advances in medicine** los últimos avances en medicina
(**c**) *(overture)* **to make advances to sb** *(sexual)* insinuarse a alguien; *(in business)* hacer una propuesta inicial a alguien; **she rejected his advances** se resistió a sus insinuaciones
(**d**) *(at auction)* **any a. on £500?** 500 libras, ¿alguien da más?
(**e**) *(loan)* anticipo *m*, adelanto *m*; **an a. on one's salary/against royalties** un anticipo *or* adelanto del sueldo/de los derechos de autor
2 *adj* (**a**) *(prior)* anticipado(a) ▸▸ ***a. booking*** reserva *f* (anticipada); ***a. copy*** *(of book)* ejemplar *m* de anticipo; ***a. notice*** aviso *m* previo; ***a. publicity*** publicidad *f* (previa); ***a. warning*** advertencia *f* previa
(**b**) *(ahead of main body) Mil* ***a. guard*** avanzadilla *f*; *Fig* **the company was the a. guard of capitalism** la empresa era la avanzadilla del capitalismo; *US Pol* ***a. man*** = hombre de confianza de un político que se desplaza al lugar donde se celebrarán mítines o eventos para ultimar su organización; *Mil* ***a. party*** destacamento *m*
3 *vt* (**a**) *(move forward) (chesspiece, troops)* avanzar, adelantar; **the date of the meeting was advanced by one week** adelantaron la fecha de la reunión una semana
(**b**) *(further, improve) (science, knowledge)* hacer avanzar, adelantar; *(career, cause)* hacer avanzar
(**c**) *(propose) (idea, opinion)* presentar; *(theory)* proponer, sugerir; *(suggestion)* plantear
(**d**) *(money)* anticipar, adelantar; **we advanced her £100 on her salary** le anticipamos *or* adelantamos 100 libras de su sueldo
4 *vi* (**a**) *(move forward)* avanzar; **the troops advanced on the city** las tropas avanzaron hacia la ciudad
(**b**) *(make progress) (science, knowledge)* avanzar; **he advanced steadily through the organization** fue ascendiendo a ritmo constante dentro de la organización
(**c**) *(time, evening)* pasar; **as winter advanced food became scarcer** con el paso del invierno la comida fue escaseando; **he mellowed with the advancing years** se hizo más apacible con los años
5 in advance *adv (to pay)* por adelantado; *(to give notice)* con antelación; *(to book, know)* por anticipado, por adelantado; **six weeks in a.** con seis semanas de antelación; **well in a.** mucho antes, con mucha anticipación; **I would like to thank you in a.** quisiera darle las gracias de antemano; **thanking you in a.** *(at close of letter)* agradeciéndole de antemano su atención
6 in advance of *prep (before)* antes que; *(further developed than)* por delante de; **they arrived in a. of their guests** llegaron antes que sus invitados; **their technology is far in a. of ours** su tecnología está muy por delante de la nuestra

advanced [əd'vɑːnst] *adj* (**a**) *(in development) (country, student, technology)* avanzado(a); **she's very a. for her age** está muy adelantada para su edad ▸▸ ***a. gas-cooled reactor*** reactor *m* nuclear refrigerado por gas
(**b**) *(in time)* avanzado(a); **a woman of a. years, a woman a. in years** una mujer de edad avanzada, una mujer entrada en años; **the project was already at an a. stage** el proyecto se encontraba ya en una fase avanzada
(**c**) *(not basic) (course, research)* superior, avanzado(a) ▸▸ *Br* ***A. level*** = examen final o diploma en una asignatura de los estudios preuniversitarios
(**d**) *(progressive)* avanzado(a); **a man of a. ideas** un hombre de ideas avanzadas

advancement [əd'vɑːnsmənt] *n* (**a**) *(promotion)* ascenso *m*; **there is little scope for a.** hay pocas posibilidades de ascenso (**b**) *(improvement)* progreso *m*; **the a. of democracy/the cause** el progreso de la democracia/la causa

advantage [əd'vɑːntɪdʒ] **1** *n* (**a**) *(superiority, better position)* ventaja *f*; **the plan has the a. of being cheap** el plan tiene la ventaja de que es barato; **there's no a. in finishing first** terminar en primer lugar no tiene ninguna ventaja; **to have an a. over** tener ventaja sobre; *Br Formal* **you have the a. of me** parece conocerme mejor que yo a usted
(**b**) *(profit)* **to take a. of** *(person)* aprovecharse de; *(opportunity, occasion)* aprovechar; **they'll only take a.** *(of your generosity, leniency)* van a aprovecharse de ti; **to turn sth to one's a.** sacar provecho de algo; **in the end the changes turned out to our a.** al final los cambios nos beneficiaron *or* favorecieron; **her skills aren't shown to (their) best a.** su talento no brilla todo lo que podría; **the picture may be seen to (its) best a. against a plain wall** donde más gana el cuadro es sobre una pared blanca; **it would be to your a.** te conviene
(**c**) *Sport* **to play a.** aplicar la ley de la ventaja; **a. Sampras** *(in tennis)* ventaja de *or* para Sampras
2 *vt* favorecer, beneficiar

advantaged [əd'vɑːntɪdʒd] *adj* privilegiado(a)

advantageous [ædvən'teɪdʒəs] *adj* ventajoso(a); **to be a. to sb** favorecer *or* beneficiar a alguien

advantageously [ædvən'teɪdʒəslɪ] *adv* **things turned out a. for us** salimos beneficiados *or* favorecidos

advent ['ædvənt] *n* (**a**) *(arrival)* llegada *f*, advenimiento *m* (**b**) *Rel* **A.** Adviento *m* ▸▸ ***A. calendar*** = calendario del Adviento, en el que se abre una ventanita que descubre una imagen o un bombón por cada día que falta hasta Navidad

Adventist ['ædvəntɪst] **1** *n* adventista *mf*
2 *adj* adventista

adventitious [ædvən'tɪʃəs] *adj Formal (accidental)* adventicio(a)

adventure [əd'ventʃə(r)] *n* (**a**) *(experience)* aventura *f*; **to have an a.** correr una aventura; **it was quite an a.** fue toda una aventura ▸▸ *Comptr* ***a. game*** juego *m* de aventuras; ***a. holiday*** viaje *m* de aventura; ***a. holidays*** turismo *m* de aventura; ***a. playground*** parque *m* infantil; ***a. story*** historia *f* de aventuras
(**b**) *(excitement)* aventura *f*; **where's your sense of a.?** ¿dónde está tu espíritu aventurero?

adventurer [əd'ventʃərə(r)] *n* (**a**) *(person fond of adventure)* aventurero(a) *m,f* (**b**) *(dishonest person)* sinvergüenza *mf*

adventuress [əd'ventʃərəs] *n* (**a**) *(person fond of adventure)* aventurera *f* (**b**) *(dishonest person)* sinvergüenza *f*

adventurism [əd'ventʃərɪzəm] *n* temeridad *f*

adventurous [əd'ventʃərəs] *adj (person)* aventurero(a); *(plan, choice)* aventurado(a), arriesgado(a); **be a., try the curry** ¡atrévete, prueba el curry!; **the design of the building is far from a.** el diseño del edificio es todo menos arriesgado *or* atrevido

adventurousness [əd'ventʃərəsnɪs] *n (of person)* audacia *f*, arrojo *m*; *(of plan, choice, design)* audacia *f*

adverb [ˈædvɜːb] *n* adverbio *m* ▸▸ ***a. of degree*** adverbio *m* de cantidad; ***a. of manner*** adverbio *m* de modo; ***a. of place*** adverbio *m* de lugar; ***a. of time*** adverbio *m* de tiempo

adverbial [ədˈvɜːbɪəl] *adj* adverbial; **an a. use** un uso adverbial

adverbially [ədˈvɜːbɪəlɪ] *adv* adverbialmente

adversarial [ædvəˈseərɪəl] *adj* (**a**) *(approach, manner)* de enfrentamiento, de confrontación ▸▸ ***a. politics*** política *f* de enfrentamiento (**b**) *Law* de adversarios, = basado en el enfrentamiento de dos partes

adversary [ˈædvəsərɪ] *n Formal* adversario(a) *m,f*

adversative [ædˈvɜːsətɪv] *adj Gram* adversativo(a) ▸▸ ***a. conjunction*** conjunción *f* adversativa

adverse [ˈædvɜːs] *adj* (**a**) *(negative) (comment, criticism, reaction)* adverso(a), desfavorable (**b**) *(unfavourable) (circumstances)* adverso(a), desfavorable; **the match was cancelled due to a. weather conditions** el partido se canceló debido a las inclemencias del tiempo (**c**) *(wind)* en contra

adversely [ˈædvɜːslɪ] *adv* desfavorablemente, negativamente; **to be a. affected by sth** resultar perjudicado(a) por algo

adversity [ədˈvɜːsɪtɪ] *n* adversidad *f*; **in a.** en la adversidad

advert[1] [ˈædvɜːt] *n Br Fam* anuncio *m*; **the adverts** *(on TV)* los anuncios, la publicidad

advert[2] [ədˈvɜːt] *vi Formal (refer)* **to a. to** referirse a, hacer referencia a

advertise [ˈædvətaɪz] **1** *vt* (**a**) *(product, job)* anunciar; **I saw it advertised in a magazine** lo vi anunciado en una revista; **as advertised on TV** anunciado(a) en televisión

(**b**) *(call attention to)* **don't go advertising the fact that we're thinking of leaving** no vayas por ahí pregonando *or* anunciando que estamos pensando en irnos; **he didn't want to a. his presence** no quería llamar la atención

2 *vi* poner un anuncio (**for sth/sb** pidiendo algo/a alguien); **it pays to a.** hacer publicidad resulta rentable

advertised [ˈædvətaɪzd] *adj* anunciado(a); **the a. time of departure** la hora anunciada de salida; **the a. programme** *(on TV)* el programa anunciado

advertisement [ədˈvɜːtɪsmənt, ædvəˈtaɪzmənt] *n* (**a**) *(on TV, in newspaper)* anuncio *m*; **an a. for toothpaste, a toothpaste a.** un anuncio de pasta de dientes; **to put an a. in the paper** poner un anuncio en el periódico; **I got the job through an a.** encontré el trabajo por un anuncio (**b**) *Fig (example)* **you're not a good a. for your school** no le haces buena publicidad a tu colegio

advertiser [ˈædvətaɪzə(r)] *n* anunciante *mf*

advertising [ˈædvətaɪzɪŋ] *n* publicidad *f*; **it's just an a. gimmick** no es más que un truco publicitario; **he works in a.** trabaja en publicidad ▸▸ ***a. agency*** agencia *f* de publicidad; ***a. campaign*** campaña *f* publicitaria; ***a. revenue*** ingresos *mpl* por publicidad; *Br* ***A. Standards Authority*** = agencia que vela por la calidad y el contenido de la publicidad en televisión

advertorial [ædvəˈtɔːrɪəl] *n* = anuncio de un periódico que tiene la misma presentación que las noticias

advice [ədˈvaɪs] *n* (**a**) *(counsel)* consejo *m*; *(legal, financial)* asesoría *f*; **a piece of a.** un consejo; **that's good a.** es un buen consejo; **my a. (to you) would be to apologize** yo te aconsejaría que pidieras perdón; **when I want your a. I'll ask for it!** ¡cuando quiera un consejo, ya te lo pediré!; **to give sb a.** aconsejar a alguien; **to ask sb's a., to ask sb for a.** pedir consejo a alguien; **to take** *or* **follow sb's a.** seguir el consejo de alguien; **take my a. and say nothing to her** sigue mi consejo y no le digas nada; **to take legal/medical a.** consultar a un abogado/médico ▸▸ ***a. column*** consultorio *m (sentimental, fiscal, etc.)*

(**b**) *(notification)* notificación *f* ▸▸ *Com* ***a. note*** aviso *m* de envío *or* expedición

advisability [ədvaɪzəˈbɪlɪtɪ] *n* conveniencia *f*; **they discussed the a. of performing another operation** discutieron la conveniencia de operar de nuevo

advisable [ədˈvaɪzəbəl] *adj* aconsejable, recomendable; **it is a. to book early** es recomendable reservar con antelación; **I don't think that would be very a.** no creo que sea buena idea

advise [ədˈvaɪz] *vt* (**a**) *(give advice to)* aconsejar; **to a. sb to do sth** aconsejar a alguien hacer *or* que haga algo; **you are strongly advised to...** es muy aconsejable...; **to a. sb against doing sth** aconsejar a alguien que no haga algo; **you'd be well advised to take an umbrella** más vale que lleves un paraguas

(**b**) *(recommend)* **he advised caution** recomendó precaución

(**c**) *(give professional guidance)* asesorar (**on** sobre); **she advises the government on education** es asesora del gobierno en materia de educación, asesora al gobierno en materia de educación

(**d**) *Formal (inform)* **to a. sb that...** informar a alguien de que...; **we are pleased to a. you that...** tenemos el placer de informarle de *or* comunicarle que...; **to a. sb of sth** informar a alguien de algo; **she advised him of the cost** le informó del costo *or Esp* coste; **keep me advised of your progress** mantenme informado de tus progresos

advisedly [ədˈvaɪzɪdlɪ] *adv* a sabiendas, deliberadamente; **I use the term a.** uso la palabra a sabiendas

advisement [ədˈvaɪzmənt] *n US (consultation)* **the matter is still under a.** el asunto está todavía en periodo de consulta

adviser, advisor [ədˈvaɪzə(r)] *n (political)* consejero(a) *m,f*, asesor(ora) *m,f*; *(professional)* asesor(ora) *m,f*

advisory [ədˈvaɪzərɪ] *adj* asesor(ora); **in an a. capacity** en calidad de asesor(ora)

advocaat [ˈædvəkɑː] *n* = licor a base de huevo

advocacy [ˈædvəkəsɪ] *n Formal (support)* defensa *f* (**of** de)

advocate **1** *n* [ˈædvəkət] (**a**) *(of cause, doctrine)* defensor(ora) *m,f* (**of** de) (**b**) *Scot Law* abogado(a) *m,f*; **the Lord A.** el fiscal general

2 *vt* [ˈædvəkeɪt] *(policy, plan)* abogar por, defender; **to a. (doing) sth** abogar por (hacer) algo

adze, *US* **adz** [ædz] *n* azuela *f*

A & E [eɪənˈdiː] *n Br* (*abbr* **Accident and Emergency**) urgencias *fpl*

AEA [eɪiːˈeɪ] *n* (**a**) (*abbr* **Atomic Energy Authority**) = agencia británica para la energía nuclear, *Esp* ≃ CSN *m* (**b**) *US* (*abbr* **Actors' Equity Association**) = sindicato estadounidense al que todos los actores profesionales han de estar afiliados

AEC [eɪiːˈsiː] *n* (*abbr* **Atomic Energy Commission**) = comisión estadounidense para la energía nuclear

Aegean [ɪˈdʒiːən] *n* **the A. (Sea)** el (mar) Egeo; **the A. Islands** las islas del (mar) Egeo

aegis, *US* **egis** [ˈiːdʒɪs] *n Formal* **under the a. of...** bajo los auspicios de...

Aeneas [ɪˈniːəs] *n Mythol* Eneas

aeon, *US* **eon** [ˈiːən] *n* eón *m*; *Fam* **aeons ago** hace siglos

aerate [ˈeəreɪt] *vt* (**a**) *(liquid)* gasificar, carbonatar; *(blood)* oxigenar (**b**) *(soil)* airear

aerated [eəˈreɪtɪd] *adj* (**a**) *(liquid)* carbonatado(a) (**b**) *Br Fam* **to get a. about sth** *(excited, nervous)* ponerse de los nervios por algo; *(annoyed)* coger un berrinche por algo

aerial [ˈeərɪəl] **1** *n (of radio, TV)* antena *f*

2 *adj* aéreo(a) ▸▸ ***a. cartography*** cartografía *f* aérea; ***a. game*** *(in football)* juego *m* aéreo; *US* ***a. ladder*** escalera *f* telescópica *(en camión de bomberos)*; *Art* ***a. perspective*** perspectiva *f* aérea; ***a. photography*** fotografía *f* aérea; *Bot* ***a. root*** raíz *f* aérea; ***a. surveying*** topografía *f* aérea; ***a. view*** vista *f* aérea

aerialist [ˈeərɪəlɪst] *n US* (**a**) *(tightrope walker)* equilibrista *mf*, funámbulo(a) *m,f* (**b**) *(trapeze artist)* trapecista *mf*

aerie *US* = **eyrie**

aero-bars [ˈeərəʊbɑːz] *npl* manillar *m* de triatlón

aerobatic [eərəˈbætɪk] **1** *adj* de acrobacias aéreas

2 *n* **aerobatics** *(movements)* acrobacias *fpl* aéreas

aerobic [eəˈrəʊbɪk] **1** *adj* (**a**) *Biol* aerobio(a) (**b**) *(exercise)* aeróbico(a)

2 *n* **aerobics** *(exercises)* aerobic *m*, aeróbic *m*

aerodrome [ˈeərədrəʊm] *n Br* aeródromo *m*

aerodynamic [eərəʊdaɪˈnæmɪk] **1** *adj* aerodinámico(a)

2 *n* **aerodynamics** aerodinámica *f*

aerodynamically [eərəʊdaɪˈnæmɪklɪ] *adv* aerodinámicamente

aerofoil [ˈeərəʊfɔɪl] *n Br* plano *m* aerodinámico

aerogram(me) [ˈeərəgræm] *n* **a. (form)** aerograma *m*

aeronautical [eərəˈnɔːtɪkəl] *adj* aeronáutico(a) ▸▸ ***a. engineer*** ingeniero(a) *m,f* aeronáutico(a)

aeronautics [eərəˈnɔːtɪks] *n* aeronáutica *f*

aeroplane [ˈeərəpleɪn] *n Br* avión *m*

aerosol [ˈeərəsɒl] *n* (**a**) *(suspension)* aerosol *m* (**b**) *(container)* aerosol *m* ▸▸ ***a. spray*** aerosol *m*

aerospace [ˈeərəspeɪs] **1** *n* espacio *m*

2 *adj* aeroespacial; **the a. industry** la industria aeroespacial

aerostat [ˈeərəʊstæt] *n* aeróstato *m*

aesthete, *US* **esthete** [ˈiːsθiːt] *n* esteta *mf*

aesthetic, *US* **esthetic** [ɪsˈθetɪk] **1** *adj* estético(a)

2 *n* estética *f*

aesthetically, *US* **esthetically** [ɪsˈθetɪklɪ] *adv* estéticamente; **a. pleasing** estéticamente agradable; *Hum* **a. challenged** feo(a), horroroso(a)

aesthetics, *US* **esthetics** [ɪs'θetɪks] *n* estética *f*
aetiology, *US* **etiology** [iːtɪ'ɒlədʒɪ] *n Med* etiología *f*
AF [eɪ'ef] *n US* (*abbr* **Air Force**) = Fuerzas Aéreas estadounidenses
afar [ə'fɑː(r)] *adv Literary* lejos; **from a.** desde lejos
AFC [eɪef'siː] *n US* (*abbr* **American Football Conference**) = una de las conferencias que forman la liga nacional de la NFL
affability [æfə'bɪlɪtɪ] *n* afabilidad *f*, amabilidad *f*
affable ['æfəbəl] *adj* afable, amable
affably ['æfəblɪ] *adv* afablemente, amablemente
affair [ə'feə(r)] *n* (**a**) *(matter, issue)* asunto *m*; **the Watergate a.** el caso Watergate; **the a. in hand** el asunto que nos ocupa; **in the present state of affairs** tal y como están las cosas ►► ***affairs of state*** asuntos *mpl* de Estado
(**b**) *(concern)* asunto *m*; **that's my a.** eso es asunto mío; **it's no a. of his** no es asunto suyo; **she put her affairs in order** puso sus asuntos en orden
(**c**) *(sexual)* aventura *f*, lío *m*; **to have an a. (with sb)** tener una aventura (con alguien); **they're having an a.** tienen un lío *or* una aventura
(**d**) *(event)* acontecimiento *m*; **the wedding was a quiet a.** fue una boda discreta
(**e**) *Fam (thing)* **he was driving one of those sporty affairs** iba en un deportivo de esos; **the house is a three-storey a.** la casa tiene tres pisos de esos; **it was one of those cheese and wine affairs** fue una de esas recepciones en las que sirven queso y vino
affect[1] [ə'fekt] *vt* (**a**) *(have effect on) (person, organ, health)* afectar; *(decision, outcome)* afectar a, influir en; **how will these changes a. you?** ¿cómo te afectarán a ti estos cambios?; **the worst affected areas** las zonas más afectadas (**b**) *(move emotionally)* afectar; **to be deeply affected by sth** estar muy afectado(a) por algo
affect[2] *vt* (**a**) *(indifference, interest, surprise)* afectar, fingir; **to a. an accent** poner un acento; **he affected to like Picasso** fingía que le gustaba Picasso (**b**) *Literary (wear, use)* usar
affect[3] ['æfekt] *n Psy* emociones *fpl*
affectation [æfek'teɪʃən] *n* (**a**) *(in behaviour, manners)* afectación *f*, amaneramiento *m*; **without a.** sin afectación (**b**) *(pretence)* **an a. of interest/boredom** un interés/aburrimiento fingido
affected[1] [ə'fektɪd] *adj* (**a**) *(altered, damaged)* afectado(a); **the worst/least a. areas** las zonas más/menos afectadas (**b**) *(emotionally)* afectado(a), conmovido(a)
affected[2] *adj (unnatural, pretended)* afectado(a), artificial; **her a. interest in opera** su fingido interés por la ópera
affecting [ə'fektɪŋ] *adj* emotivo(a), conmovedor(a)
affection [ə'fekʃən] *n* (**a**) *(liking)* afecto *m*, cariño *m*; **to show sb a.** dar muestras de afecto a alguien; **to feel a. for sb** sentir cariño por alguien; **a rare display of a.** una muestra de afecto poco común; **to hold sb in great a.** tener gran estima a alguien
(**b**) **affections** *(feelings)* sentimientos *mpl*; **to toy** *or* **trifle with sb's affections** jugar con los sentimientos de alguien; **this town has a special place in my affections** esta ciudad ocupa un lugar especial en mi corazón
affectionate [ə'fekʃənət] *adj* afectuoso(a), cariñoso(a) (**towards** con); *Old-fashioned* **your a. niece** *(in letter)* tu sobrina que te quiere
affectionately [ə'fekʃənətlɪ] *adv* cariñosamente; **a. known as "the Terrible Twins"** llamados cariñosamente "los Gemelos Terribles"
affective [ə'fektɪv] *adj Psy* emocional, afectivo(a)
afferent ['æfərənt] *adj Anat* aferente
affidavit [æfɪ'deɪvɪt] *n Law* declaración *f* jurada; **to swear an a.** hacer una declaración jurada
affiliate **1** *n* [ə'fɪlɪət] *(person)* afiliado(a) *m,f*; *(company)* filial *f*
2 *vt* [ə'fɪlɪeɪt] afiliar (**to** *or* **with** a); **affiliated company** (empresa) filial
3 *vi* afiliarse
affiliation [əfɪlɪ'eɪʃən] *n* (**a**) *(link, connection)* conexión *f* (**b**) *(political, religious)* filiación *f*; **his political affiliations** su filiación política (**c**) *Br Law* ***a. order*** = orden de pagar una pensión alimenticia a un hijo ilegítimo
affinity [ə'fɪnɪtɪ] *n* (**a**) *(liking, attraction)* afinidad *f* (**with/between** con/entre); **she felt an a. for such places** sentía atracción por ese tipo de lugares
(**b**) *(relationship, connection)* afinidad *f* (**between/with** entre/con) ►► ***a. card*** = tarjeta de crédito vinculada a una organización humanitaria o de caridad a la que la entidad bancaria transfiere un donativo cada vez que se usa; ***a. marketing*** marketing *m* de afinidad
(**c**) *Chem* afinidad *f* (**for** hacia *or* por)
affirm [ə'fɜːm] **1** *vt* (**a**) *(state)* afirmar, declarar; **"I will be there," he affirmed** "allí estaré", afirmó (**b**) *(confirm) (belief)* ratificar, confirmar; **she affirmed her intention to sell** ratificó su intención de vender
2 *vi Law* prometer *(para evitar jurar sobre la biblia)*
affirmation [æfə'meɪʃən] *n* (**a**) *(statement)* afirmación *f* (**b**) *(confirmation)* ratificación *f*, confirmación *f* (**c**) *Law (declaration)* promesa *f*
affirmative [ə'fɜːmətɪv] **1** *n* (**a**) *Gram* afirmativo *m* (**b**) *(in reply)* **to answer in the a.** responder afirmativamente
2 *adj (answer)* afirmativo(a) ►► *US* ***a. action*** discriminación *f* positiva
3 *exclam* ¡afirmativo!
affirmatively [ə'fɜːmətɪvlɪ] *adv* afirmativamente
affix **1** *n* ['æfɪks] *Ling* afijo *m*
2 *vt* [ə'fɪks] *(notice, poster, stamp)* pegar (**to** a); *(signature)* estampar (**to** en)
afflict [ə'flɪkt] *vt* afligir; **to be afflicted by** *or* **with sth** padecer algo; **the economic problems that a. the nation** los problemas económicos que afligen a la nación
afflicted [ə'flɪktɪd] **1** *adj (parts, area)* afectado(a)
2 *npl* **the a.** las víctimas; *Fam Hum* **don't mock the a.** no te burles de los incapacitados
affliction [ə'flɪkʃən] *n* (**a**) *(suffering)* padecimiento *m* (**b**) *(misfortune)* desgracia *f*
affluence ['æfluːəns] *n* prosperidad *f*, riqueza *f*; **to live in a.** vivir en la abundancia
affluent ['æflʊənt] *adj* acomodado(a); **the a. society** la sociedad opulenta

> **False friend**: The Spanish adjective **afluente** is not a translation for the English word **affluent**. In Spanish **afluente** means "fluent".

afford [ə'fɔːd] *vt* (**a**) *(financially)* permitirse; **can you a. it?** ¿puedes permitírtelo?, ¿puedes pagarlo?; **how much can you a.?** ¿cuánto puedes (llegar a) pagar?; **I can't a. £50!** ¡no puedo pagar 50 libras!; **give what you can a.** da lo que puedas; **to be able to a. sth** poder permitirse algo
(**b**) *(non-financial use)* **I can a. to wait** puedo esperar; **can you a. the time?** ¿tienes tiempo?; **I can't a. not to** no puedo permitirme no hacerlo; **we can't a. another mistake** no podemos permitirnos cometer otro error
(**c**) *Formal (protection, shade)* proporcionar; **the bell tower afforded a panoramic view of the city** el campanario ofrecía una vista panorámica de la ciudad; **to a. sb the opportunity to do sth** proporcionar a alguien la oportunidad de hacer algo
affordable [ə'fɔːdəbəl] *adj (price, purchase)* asequible
afforestation [æfɒrɪ'steɪʃən] *n* forestación *f*
affray [ə'freɪ] *n* (**a**) *Formal* altercado *m*, reyerta *f* (**b**) *Law* altercado *m*, reyerta *f*
affricate ['æfrɪkət] *n Ling* africada *f*
affront [ə'frʌnt] **1** *n* afrenta *f*, ofensa *f*; **it was an a. to her dignity** ofendió su dignidad
2 *vt* afrentar, ofender; **to be/feel affronted** estar/sentirse ofendido(a)
Afghan ['æfgæn] **1** *n* (**a**) *(person)* afgano(a) *m,f* (**b**) *(language)* afgano *m* (**c**) *(dog)* (galgo *m*) afgano *m* (**d**) *US (blanket, shawl)* = manta o chal tejido con diferentes retazos
2 *adj* afgano(a) ►► ***A. coat*** chaquetón *m* afgano, = chaquetón de piel de oveja de ante bordado con rebordes de lana; ***A. hound*** galgo *m* afgano
Afghani [æf'gænɪ] **1** *n* afgano(a) *m,f*
2 *adj* afgano(a)
Afghanistan [æf'gænɪstɑːn] *n* Afganistán
aficionado [əfɪsɪə'nɑːdəʊ] (*pl* **aficionados**) *n* aficionado(a) *m,f*
afield [ə'fiːld] *adv* **to go further a.** ir más allá; **to look further a.** buscar más; **people came from as far a. as Australia** vino gente de lugares tan lejanos como Australia
afire [ə'faɪə(r)] *adj* en llamas; **to set sth a.** prender fuego a algo; **a. with enthusiasm** pletórico de entusiasmo
AFL ['eɪefel] *n* (*abbr* **American Football League**) = la Liga estadounidense de Fútbol Americano
aflame [ə'fleɪm] *adj* **the building was soon a.** el edificio se vio pronto envuelto en llamas; **the evening sky was a. with colour** al atardecer el cielo estaba de un color encendido; **a. with desire/passion** ardiente de deseo/pasión

AFL/CIO [eɪef'elsiːaɪ'əʊ] *n* (*abbr* **American Federation of Labor and Congress of Industrial Organizations**) = federación estadounidense de sindicatos

afloat [ə'fləʊt] *adv* (**a**) *(floating)* a flote; **to stay a.** *(of boat, company)* mantenerse a flote; **to keep sth a.** *(boat, company)* mantener algo a flote (**b**) *(on boat)* en barco; **he had spent most of his life a.** *(at sea)* había pasado la mayor parte de su vida en el mar

aflutter [ə'flʌtə(r)] **1** *adj* **to be (all) a. with excitement** vibrar de emoción; **my heart was all a.** el corazón me palpitaba con fuerza

2 *adv* **she set my heart a.** me hizo palpitar de emoción

afoot [ə'fʊt] *adv* **there is a scheme a. to build a new motorway** hay un proyecto en marcha para construir una nueva autopista; **there's something a.** se está tramando algo; **there was trouble a.** se avecinaban problemas

aforementioned [ə'fɔːmenʃənd], **aforesaid** [ə'fɔːsed] *adj Formal* susodicho(a), mencionado(a); **the a. property** la susodicha propiedad

a fortiori [eɪ'fɔːtɪɔːraɪ] *adv* a fortiori

afoul [ə'faʊl] *adv Literary* **to run a. of sb** tener un conflicto con alguien

afraid [ə'freɪd] *adj* (**a**) *(scared)* **to be a.** tener miedo; **don't be a.** no tengas miedo; **I'm a. of him** me da miedo; **I'm a. of dogs/the dark** le tengo miedo a los perros/a la oscuridad; **I'm a. of making a mistake** tengo miedo de equivocarme; **I was a. of hurting him** no quería hacerle daño; **that's exactly what I was a. of!** ¡eso es precisamente lo que me temía!; **there's nothing to be a. of** no hay nada que temer; **he is a. for his life** teme por su vida; **he isn't a. of hard work** no le asusta el trabajo duro; **I was a. there would be an accident** temía que ocurriera un accidente; IDIOM **he's a. of his own shadow** se asusta hasta de su propia sombra

(**b**) *(sorry)* **I'm a. so/not** me temo que sí/no; **I'm a. she's out** me temo que ha salido; **I'm a. I can't help you** lo siento, no puedo ayudarle; **I'm a. we can't allow that** me temo que eso no está permitido

afresh [ə'freʃ] *adv* de nuevo, otra vez; **to start a.** empezar de nuevo; **to look at a problem a.** dar un nuevo enfoque a la solución de un problema

Africa ['æfrɪkə] *n* África

African ['æfrɪkən] **1** *n* africano(a) *m,f*

2 *adj* africano(a) ►► ***A. elephant*** elefante *m* africano; ***A. Union*** Unión *f* Africana

African-American ['æfrɪkənə'merɪkən] **1** *n* afroamericano(a) *m,f*

2 *adj* afroamericano(a)

Afrikaans [æfrɪ'kɑːnz] *n* afrikaans *m*

Afrikaner [æfrɪ'kɑːnə(r)] **1** *n* afrikáner *mf*

2 *adj* afrikáner

Afro ['æfrəʊ] **1** *n* peinado *m* (a lo) afro

2 *adj* afro

Afro- ['æfrəʊ] *prefix* afro-

Afro-American ['æfrəʊə'merɪkən] **1** *n* afroamericano(a) *m,f*

2 *adj* afroamericano(a)

Afro-Caribbean ['æfrəʊkærɪ'bɪən] **1** *n* afrocaribeño(a) *m,f*

2 *adj* afrocaribeño(a)

aft [ɑːft] *Naut* **1** *adv* a popa; **to go a.** ir a popa

2 *adj (deck)* de popa

AFTER ['ɑːftə(r)] **1** *prep* (**a**) *(with time)* después de; **a. dinner** después de cenar; **what are you going to do a. your studies?** ¿qué vas a hacer cuando termines tus estudios?; **a. a couple of hours he felt much better** al cabo de un par de horas se sentía mucho mejor; **a. years of trying** tras años de intentarlo; **a. a while** al cabo de un rato; **a. today** a partir de hoy; **the day a. tomorrow** pasado mañana; **it's a. five** son más de las cinco; *US* **it's twenty a. six** son las seis y veinte; **a. that, anything seems easy** después de eso, cualquier cosa parece fácil; **I'll never believe her again a. the way she lied to me** nunca volveré a creerle, después de cómo me mintió; **a. all I've done for him!** ¡después de todo lo que he hecho *orAm* hice por él!; **a. all** *(all things considered)* después de todo; **it seems like they're going to do it a. all** parece que al final van a hacerlo

(**b**) *(with motion)* **to run a. sb** correr tras (de) alguien; **to shout a. sb** gritarle a alguien; **to stare a. sb** quedarse mirando a alguien; **to tidy up a. sb** ordenar lo que ha desordenado alguien; **close the door a. you** cierra la puerta al salir; **go a. her and apologize** ve a pedirle perdón

(**c**) *(looking for)* **to be a. sb** buscar a alguien, ir *or* andar detrás de alguien; **the police are a. him** la policía lo busca; **I think she's a. a pay-rise** me parece que anda detrás de *or* va buscando un aumento de sueldo

(**d**) *(expressing order)* **the first crossing a. the traffic lights** el primer cruce después del semáforo; **my name comes a. his on the list** mi nombre viene después del suyo en la lista; **am I a. you (***Br* **in the queue** *or US* **in line)?** ¿voy *or* estoy detrás de usted (en la cola)?; **a. you!** *(you first)* ¡después de usted!; **a. you with the butter** pásame la mantequilla cuando termines; **a. her, he is the best** después de ella, el mejor es él

(**e**) *(expressing repetition)* **day a. day** un día tras otro; **time a. time** una y otra vez; **year a. year** año tras año; **one a. the other** uno tras otro; **page a. page of statistics** páginas y páginas de estadísticas

(**f**) *Br (in honour of)* **to name sth/sb a. sb** ponerle a algo/alguien el nombre de alguien

(**g**) *(in the style of)* **a painting a. Renoir** un cuadro al estilo Renoir

2 *adv* después; **soon/long a.** poco/mucho después; **the day/the week a.** el día/la semana siguiente; **he was angry for some days a.** después de aquello estuvo de mal humor durante unos días

3 *conj* después de que; **shortly a. we had arrived** poco después de llegar; **I came a. he left** llegué cuando él ya se había ido; **a. you've chopped the vegetables, fry them** una vez cortadas las verduras, fríelas; **a. doing sth** después de hacer algo

---

afterbirth ['ɑːftəbɜːθ] *n* placenta *f*, secundinas *fpl*

afterburner ['ɑːftəbɜːnə(r)] *n (of jet engine)* posquemador *m*

aftercare ['ɑːftəkeə(r)] *n (after operation)* atención *f* posoperatoria; *(of convalescent, delinquent)* seguimiento *m*

afterdeck ['ɑːftədek] *n (of ship)* cubierta *f* de popa

after-dinner ['ɑːftədɪnə(r)] *adj (speaker, speech)* de sobremesa

aftereffects ['ɑːftərəfekts] *npl (of accident, crisis)* secuelas *fpl*; *(of drug)* efectos *mpl* secundarios

afterglow ['ɑːftəgləʊ] *n (of sunset)* luz *f* del crepúsculo; *(of pleasant feeling)* regusto *m* placentero

after-hours ['æftər'aʊəz] **1** *adj* **a. drinking** *(after closing time)* = beber en los bares después de la hora legal del cierre; **a. socializing** *(after work)* = salir con los compañeros de trabajo

2 *adv (after closing time)* después de cerrar; *(after work)* después del trabajo

after-image ['ɑːftərɪmɪdʒ] *n* **an a. on the screen/retina** una imagen que persiste en la pantalla/retina

afterlife ['ɑːftəlaɪf] *n* otra vida *f*, vida *f* de ultratumba; **we shall meet in the a.** nos veremos en el más allá

aftermath ['ɑːftəmɑːθ] *n* (**a**) *(period)* periodo *m* posterior; **in the immediate a. (of)** inmediatamente después (de) (**b**) *(result)* secuelas *fpl*, consecuencias *fpl*

afternoon [ɑːftə'nuːn] **1** *n* tarde *f*; **this a.** esta tarde; **tomorrow a.** mañana por la tarde; **yesterday a.** ayer por la tarde; **the next** *or* **following a.** la tarde siguiente; **on the a. of the next day** al día siguiente por la tarde; **the previous a., the a. before** la tarde anterior; **all a.** toda la tarde; **every a.** todas las tardes; **every Friday a.** todas las tardes de los viernes, todos los viernes por la tarde; **in the a.** por la tarde; **at two o'clock in the a.** a las dos de la tarde; **could I have the a. off?** ¿puedo tomarme la tarde libre?; **on Wednesday a.** el miércoles por la tarde; **on the a. of the twelfth** la tarde del doce; **I'm on afternoons this week** esta semana hago turno de tarde; **good a.!**, *Fam* **a.!** ¡buenas (tardes)! ►► ***a. nap*** siesta *f*; ***a. tea*** *(meal)* merienda *f*

2 afternoons *adv esp US* por las tardes

afters ['ɑːftəz] *npl Br Fam* postre *m*

aftersales service ['ɑːftə'seɪlz'sɜːvɪs] *n Com* servicio *m* posventa

after-school ['ɑːftəskuːl] *adj (activities)* extraescolar *(después de las clases)*

aftershave ['ɑːftəʃeɪv] *n (as perfume)* colonia *f* ►► ***a. balm*** *or* ***lotion*** *(to protect skin)* loción *f* para después del afeitado *or Méx* rasurado

aftershock ['ɑːftəʃɒk] *n* réplica *f*

aftertaste ['ɑːftəteɪst] *n also Fig* regusto *m*; **it leaves an unpleasant a.** deja mal sabor de boca

after-tax ['ɑːftətæks] *adj (profits, salary)* después de impuestos

afterthought ['ɑːftəθɔːt] *n* idea *f* tardía; **it was an a.** se me ocurrió después; **the west wing was added as an a.** construir el ala oeste se les ocurrió más tarde

afterward(s) ['ɑːftəwəd(z)] *adv* después; **a. they went home** después *or* luego se fueron a casa; **a long time a.** mucho (tiempo) después; **soon** *or* **shortly a.** poco después; **I only realized a.** no me di cuenta hasta después

afterword ['ɑːftəwɜːd] *n* epílogo *m*

AG *US* (*abbr* **Attorney General**) ≃ ministro(a) *m,f* de Justicia

Aga® ['ɑːgə] *n* = cocina de hierro fundido que se suele tener permanentemente encendida

AGAIN [ə'gen] *adv* (**a**) *(in general)* de nuevo, otra vez; **to do sth a.** hacer algo de nuevo *or* otra vez; **to begin a.** volver a empezar; **don't do it a.!** ¡no lo vuelvas a hacer!; **to say sth a.** volver a decir algo; **he never came back a.** no volvió nunca más; **I'm not going there a.** no pienso volver (allí); **he's finally well a.** por fin se ha recuperado; **what did you say a.?** ¿qué?, ¿cómo has dicho?; **where does he live a.?** ¿dónde dijiste que vivía?; **a. and a.** una y otra vez; **to start all over a.** empezar de nuevo, volver a empezar; **half as much a.** además, añadió la mitad; **I would use twice as much a.** yo usaría el triple; **never a.!** ¡nunca más!; **not a.!** ¿otra vez?; **not you a.!** ¡otra vez tú!; **now and a.** de vez en cuando; **once a.** una vez más; **the same a., please** otra de lo mismo; **yet a.** una vez más

(**b**) *(besides)* además; **(then** *or* **there) a.** *(on the other hand)* por otra parte; **a., I may have imagined it** en fin, *Esp* puede que me lo haya imaginado *or Am* tal vez me lo imaginé

AGAINST [ə'genst] **1** *prep* (**a**) *(in opposition to)* contra, en contra de; **the fight a. crime** la lucha contra el crimen; **to be a. sth/sb** estar en contra de algo/alguien; **to discriminate a. sb** discriminar a alguien; **to have something a. sth/sb** tener algo en contra de algo/alguien; **to have nothing a. sth/sb** no tener nada en contra de algo/alguien; **to play a. sb** jugar contra alguien; **to sail a. the wind** navegar contra el viento; **I won't hear a word said a. her!** ¡no quiero oír ni una palabra contra ella!; **to speak a. sth** hablar en contra de algo; **to swim a. the current** nadar contra corriente; **the odds a. them winning** las posibilidades de que pierdan; **it was a. my principles** iba (en) contra (de) mis principios; **to do sth a. sb's advice** hacer algo desoyendo los consejos de alguien; **a. all probability** contra toda probabilidad; **a. the law** ilegal; **it's a. the rules** va contra las reglas; **a. my will** en contra de mi voluntad; **a. my wishes** contra mis deseos

(**b**) *(as protection from)* contra; **insurance a. fire** seguro contra incendios; **to warn sb a. sth/sb** poner a alguien en guardia contra algo/alguien; **to warn sb a. doing sth** advertir a alguien que no haga algo

(**c**) *(in contact with)* contra; **to lean a. sth** apoyarse en *or Am* contra algo; **she put the ladder a. the wall** puso la escalera contra la pared; **put a tick a. your choice** marque su elección con una señal

(**d**) *(in comparison with)* **the pound rose/fell a. the dollar** la libra subió/bajó frente al dólar; **inflation was 4.1 percent, as a. 3.2 percent last year** hubo una inflación del 4,1 por ciento frente a un 3,2 por ciento el año pasado; **check it a. the list** compruébalo *or Méx* chécalo con la lista; **a. the light** a contraluz

(**e**) *(in relation to)* frente a; **a. a background of rising inflation** en una situación de inflación creciente; **yellow flowers a. a grey wall** flores amarillas sobre un fondo gris

2 *adv* en contra; **there were fourteen votes a.** hubo catorce votos en contra

agape [ə'geɪp] **1** *adj* boquiabierto(a); **mouth a.** boquiabierto(a)
2 *adv* con la boca abierta

agar(-agar) ['eɪgə(r), eɪgər'eɪgə(r)] *n* agar-agar *m*

agaric ['ægərɪk] *n* agárico *m*

agate ['ægət] *n* ágata *f* ►► ***a. type*** (letra *f*) ágata *f*, = letra de 0,180 centímetros usada a veces en los periódicos

agave [ə'geɪvɪ] *n* agave *m*, *Am* maguey *m*

AGE [eɪdʒ] **1** *n* (**a**) *(of person, object)* edad *f*; **to be twenty years of a.** tener veinte años; **what a. is she?, what's her a.?** ¿qué edad tiene?, ¿cuántos años tiene?; **what a. is this church?** ¿cuántos años tiene esta iglesia?; **she's my a.** *or* **the same a. as me** tiene la misma edad que yo; **he's twice my a.** tiene el doble de años que yo; **at the a. of twenty,** *US* **at a. twenty** a los veinte años; **at an early a.** a una edad temprana; **at my a.** a mi edad; **I'm beginning to feel my a.** estoy empezando a sentirme viejo(a); **he doesn't look his a.** no aparenta la edad que tiene; **people of all ages** personas de todas las edades; **you're showing your a.!** ¡estás pregonando tu edad!; **when I was your a.** cuando tenía tu edad, a tu edad; **the fifteen-to-twenty a. bracket** *or* **group** la franja de edad comprendida entre los quince y los veinte años ►► ***a. of consent*** edad *f* núbil; ***a. limit*** límite *m* de edad; ***a. range:*** **people in his a. range** las personas de su edad; **by a. range** *(categorized, sorted)* por edades; ***the a. of reason*** la edad de la razón *or* del juicio

(**b**) **(old) a.** vejez *f*; **photos yellowed with a.** fotos amarillentas por el paso del tiempo; **he has mellowed with a.** se ha suavizado con la edad

(**c**) *(adulthood)* **to be of a.** ser mayor de edad; *also Fig* **to come of a.** alcanzar la mayoría de edad; **to be under a.** ser menor *(para beber, tener relaciones sexuales, etc.)*

(**d**) *(era)* época *f*, edad *f*; **through the ages** a lo largo del tiempo

(**e**) *Fam (long time)* **it's ages since I saw him** hace siglos que no lo veo; **I've been waiting (for) ages** llevo esperando una eternidad; **it took ages (to do it)** llevó siglos hacerlo; **we sat there for what seemed like an a.** estuvimos ahí sentados lo que pareció una eternidad

2 *vt (continuous* **ageing** *or* **aging)** *(person)* envejecer; **aged in oak casks** *(wine)* criado en barriles de roble

3 *vi (person)* envejecer

aged **1** *adj* (**a**) [eɪdʒd] *(of the age of)* **a. twenty** de veinte años (de edad) (**b**) ['eɪdʒɪd] *(old)* anciano(a); **my a. parents** mis ancianos padres
2 *npl* ['eɪdʒɪd] **the a.** los ancianos

ageing, aging ['eɪdʒɪŋ] **1** *n (of person, wine, cheese)* envejecimiento *m* ►► ***a. process*** proceso *m* de envejecimiento
2 *adj (old)* viejo(a); **the problem of Britain's a. population** el problema del envejecimiento de la población británica

ageism ['eɪdʒɪzəm] *n* discriminación *f* por motivos de edad

ageist ['eɪdʒɪst] *adj* discriminatorio(a) por motivos de edad

ageless ['eɪdʒlɪs] *adj* intemporal, atemporal

agency ['eɪdʒənsɪ] *n* (**a**) *Com* agencia *f*; **advertising/travel a.** agencia de publicidad/viajes (**b**) *(of government)* agencia *f*; **international aid agencies** agencias de ayuda internacional (**c**) *Formal* **through the a. of** mediante la intervención de; **by the a. of direct sunlight** por la acción de la luz solar directa

agenda [ə'dʒendə] *n* (**a**) *(of meeting)* orden *m* del día, programa *m*; **to set the a.** *(for meeting)* decidir el orden del día; *Fig* marcar la pauta; *Fig* **the drugs issue is back on the a.** el tema de las drogas vuelve a estar en el candelero; *Fig* **homelessness doesn't come very high on the government's a.** el problema de los sin techo no se encuentra entre las prioridades del gobierno; *Fig* **to be at the top of the a.** ser un asunto prioritario

(**b**) *(set of priorities)* **he has his own a.** tiene sus planes propios; **what is his real a.?** ¿cuáles son sus verdaderas intenciones?

agent ['eɪdʒənt] *n* (**a**) *(representative) (of company)* representante *mf*; *(of writer)* agente *mf*; *(of actor, singer)* representante *mf* (**b**) *(spy)* agente *mf* secreto(a) (**c**) *(instrument)* **to be the a. of** ser la causa de; **an a. of change** un agente del cambio (**d**) *(substance)* agente *m* ►► ***A. Orange*** agente *m* naranja (**e**) *Comptr (software)* agente *m* (**f**) *Gram* complemento *m* agente

agent provocateur ['æʒɒŋprəvɒkə'tɜː(r)] (*pl* **agents provocateurs**) *n* agente *m* provocador

age-old ['eɪdʒəʊld] *adj (custom, problem)* antiguo(a)

agglomerate **1** *vi* [ə'glɒməreɪt] acumularse, aglomerarse
2 *n* [ə'glɒmərət] (**a**) *(mixture)* amalgama *m*, aglomeración *m* (**b**) *Geol* aglomerado *m*

agglutinating [ə'gluːtɪneɪtɪŋ], **agglutinative** [ə'gluːtɪnətɪv] *adj Ling* aglutinante

aggrandizement [ə'grændɪzmənt] *n Pej* engrandecimiento *m*

aggravate ['ægrəveɪt] *vt* (**a**) *(worsen)* agravar; *Law* **aggravated assault/burglary** agresión/robo con agravantes (**b**) *Fam (annoy)* fastidiar, molestar, *RP* hinchar

aggravating ['ægrəveɪtɪŋ] *adj* (**a**) *Law* agravante (**b**) *Fam (annoying)* molesto(a), *RP* hinchón(ona); **it's very a.** fastidia un montón

aggravation [ægrə'veɪʃən] *n* (**a**) *(worsening)* agravamiento *m*, empeoramiento *m* (**b**) *Fam (annoyance)* fastidio *m*, molestia *f*; **he does nothing but cause a.** no hace más que fastidiar

aggregate ['ægrɪgət] **1** *n* (**a**) *(total)* conglomerado *m*; **in the a.** en conjunto (**b**) *Sport* **on a.** en el total de la eliminatoria (**c**) *Constr* árido *m* (de construcción) (**d**) *Geol* agregado *m*, conglomerado *m*
2 *adj* total, conjunto(a) ►► ***a. score*** marcador *m* total

aggression [ə'greʃən] *n* (**a**) *(hostility)* agresividad *f*; **he took out his a. on his family** descargó su agresividad en su familia (**b**) *(attack)* agresión *f*; **an act of a.** una agresión

aggressive [ə'gresɪv] *adj* (**a**) *(hostile)* agresivo(a) (**b**) *(vigorous, dynamic)* enérgico(a), agresivo(a)

aggressively [ə'gresɪvlɪ] *adv* (**a**) *(hostilely)* agresivamente (**b**) *(vigorously)* enérgicamente, agresivamente

aggressiveness [ə'gresɪvnɪs] *n* (**a**) *(hostility)* agresividad *f* (**b**) *(vigour)* acometividad *f*, agresividad *f*

aggressor [ə'gresə(r)] *n* agresor(ora) *m,f*

aggrieved [ə'griːvd] *adj* (**a**) *(hurt, offended)* agraviado(a), ofendido(a); **to be a.** estar ofendido(a); **to feel a. at** *or* **about sth** sentirse agraviado(a) por algo (**b**) *Law* demandante; **the a. party** la parte demandante

aggro ['ægrəʊ] *n Fam* (**a**) *(violence)* camorra *f*, pelea *f*, *Arg* rona *f* (**b**) *(trouble)* líos *mpl*, *Esp* follones *mpl*, *Am* relajo *m*, *Méx* argüende *m*; **people don't complain because they don't want any a.** la gente no se queja porque no quiere meterse en un berenjenal; **my mum's giving me so much a. at the moment** mi madre me está dando mucho la lata últimamente

aghast [ə'gɑːst] *adj* horrorizado(a), espantado(a); **he was a. at the expense** los gastos le horrorizaron *or* espantaron

agile [*Br* 'ædʒaɪl, *US* 'ædʒəl] *adj* ágil

agility [ə'dʒɪlɪtɪ] *n* agilidad *f*

agin [ə'gɪn] *prep Fam Hum* en contra de

aging = **ageing**

agitate ['ædʒɪteɪt] **1** *vt* (**a**) *(liquid)* revolver, agitar (**b**) *(person)* inquietar, agitar

2 *vi* **to a. for/against sth** hacer campaña a favor de/en contra de algo; **they are agitating for better working conditions** están haciendo campaña para mejorar las condiciones laborales

agitated ['ædʒɪteɪtɪd] *adj* inquieto(a), agitado(a); **to be a.** estar inquieto(a) *or* agitado(a); **to become** *or* **get a.** ponerse nervioso(a), agitarse

agitatedly ['ædʒɪteɪtɪdlɪ] *adv* agitadamente

agitation [ædʒɪ'teɪʃən] *n* (**a**) *(of person)* inquietud *f*, agitación *f*; **to be in a state of a.** estar muy agitado(a) *or* inquieto(a) (**b**) *(campaign)* campaña *f*; **there was a lot of a. in favour of nuclear disarmament** se hizo una campaña muy fuerte a favor del desarme nuclear

agitator ['ædʒɪteɪtə(r)] *n* (**a**) *Pol* agitador(ora) *m,f*, activista *mf* (**b**) *(machine)* agitador *m*

agitprop ['ædʒɪtprɒp] *n* agit-prop *f*, = propaganda política normalmente de izquierdas que se da especialmente en las artes escénicas

agleam [ə'gliːm] *adj* resplandeciente, reluciente

aglitter [ə'glɪtə(r)] *adj* destellante

aglow [ə'gləʊ] *adj* **to be a. with** *(colour)* estar encendido(a) de; *(pleasure, excitement)* estar rebosante de

AGM [eɪdʒiː'em] *n* (**a**) *Br Com* (*abbr* **annual general meeting**) asamblea *f* or junta *f* general anual (**b**) (*abbr* **air-to-ground missile**) misil *m* aire-tierra

agnostic [æg'nɒstɪk] **1** *n* agnóstico(a) *m,f*

2 *adj* agnóstico(a); *Fig* **I'm a. on the issue** no tengo opinión formada respecto a ese asunto

agnosticism [æg'nɒstɪsɪzəm] *n* agnosticismo *m*

AGO [ə'gəʊ] *adv* **ten years a.** hace diez años; **a little while a., a short time a.** hace un rato; **a year a. this Friday** hace un año este viernes; **long a., a long time a.** hace mucho (tiempo); **not long a.** no hace mucho (tiempo); **some time a.** hace algún tiempo; **as long a. as 1840** ya en 1840; **how long a. was that?** ¿hace cuánto (tiempo) fue eso?

---

agog [ə'gɒg] *adj* **they watched/listened a.** miraban/escuchaban con avidez e impresionados; **I was a. to discover what had happened** estaba impaciente por descubrir qué había ocurrido; **the scandal set the whole town a.** el escándalo espoleó la curiosidad de toda la ciudad

agonistic [ægə'nɪstɪk] *adj Anat* agonista

agonize ['ægənaɪz] *vi* angustiarse, agobiarse, amargarse (**over** por *or* con); **don't a. over it!** ¡no te angusties *or* agobies (por ello)!; **to a. over how to do sth** sufrir lo indecible para decidir cómo hacer algo

agonized ['ægənaɪzd] *adj* angustiado(a), agobiado(a)

agonizing ['ægənaɪzɪŋ] **1** *adj (pain, death)* atroz; *(silence, wait)* angustioso(a); *(decision, choice, dilemma)* peliagudo(a)

2 *n* congoja *f*, angustia *f*; **why all this a. about something that can't be helped?** ¿para qué angustiarse tanto por algo que no tiene remedio?

agonizingly ['ægənaɪzɪŋlɪ] *adv* angustiosamente; **an a. difficult decision** una decisión dificilísima *or* amarga

agony ['ægənɪ] *n* (**a**) *(physical pain)* dolor *m* intenso, agonía *f*; **to be in a.** morirse de dolor; **to die in a.** morir lenta y dolorosamente; *Fam* **it's a. walking in these shoes** caminar con estos zapatos es un martirio

(**b**) *(anguish)* angustia *f*; **to be in an a. of doubt/remorse** estar angustiado(a) por la duda/el remordimiento; **it was a. just listening to him** el simple hecho de escucharlo era un calvario; *Fam* **to pile** *or* **put on the a.** hacerse el/la mártir ►► *Br* ***a. aunt*** *(in newspaper)* consultor(ora) *m,f* sentimental; ***a. column*** *(in newspaper)* consultorio *m* sentimental

(**c**) *Literary* **in his last** *or* **final a.** *(death throes)* mientras agonizaba

agoraphobia [ægərə'fəʊbɪə] *n* agorafobia *f*

agoraphobic [ægərə'fəʊbɪk] **1** *adj* agorafóbico(a)

2 *n* agorafóbico(a) *m,f*

agouti [ə'guːtɪ] *n* agutí *m*

AGR [eɪdʒiː'ɑː(r)] *n* (*abbr* **advanced gas-cooled reactor**) reactor *m* nuclear de gas

agrarian [ə'greərɪən] *adj* agrario(a) ►► ***a. reform*** reforma *f* agraria

agree [ə'griː] **1** *vt* (**a**) *(reach agreement on) (price, conditions)* acordar, pactar; *(date)* convenir; **we agreed to meet at six** quedamos a las seis; **it was agreed that the money should be invested** se acordó que el dinero debía invertirse; **they couldn't a. what to do next** no conseguían ponerse de acuerdo sobre lo que harían a continuación; **we'll have to a. to differ** *or* **disagree on that** tendremos que aceptar las discrepancias en cuanto a eso

(**b**) *(concur)* **to a. (that)...** estar de acuerdo en que...

(**c**) *(consent)* **to a. to do sth** acordar hacer algo; **he agreed to pay** estuvo de acuerdo en pagar él

(**d**) *(admit)* admitir; **they agreed that they had made a mistake** admitieron que habían cometido un error; **it is generally agreed that...** se suele admitir que...

2 *vi* (**a**) *(be of same opinion, concur)* estar de acuerdo (**about/with** en cuanto a/con); **I think it's too expensive and Peter agrees** yo creo que es demasiado caro y Peter está de acuerdo conmigo; **I quite** *or* **entirely a.** estoy completamente de acuerdo; **I'm afraid I can't a.** lo siento, pero no puedo estar conforme; **I couldn't a. more!** ¡estoy completamente de acuerdo!; **to a. about sth** estar de acuerdo en algo; **at least we a. about that** al menos estamos de acuerdo en eso; **that would be unfortunate, don't you a.?** eso sería una desgracia, ¿no te parece?

(**b**) *(match) (statements, facts, opinions)* coincidir, concordar (**with** con)

(**c**) *(accept)* acceder, consentir

(**d**) *Gram* concordar (**with** con)

> En inglés culto o elevado, y especialmente en inglés americano, **agree** puede ir seguido de **that** más un verbo en subjuntivo (ver el panel SUBJUNCTIVE):
>
> **we agreed that the interview be postponed**
> *acordamos que se aplazara la entrevista*
>
> Lo mismo también podría decirse del siguiente modo:
>
> **we agreed to postpone the interview**
> *acordamos aplazar la entrevista*

► **agree on, agree upon** *vt insep* (**a**) *(be in agreement)* estar de acuerdo en (**b**) *(reach agreement)* ponerse de acuerdo en; **they agreed on Portugal for the honeymoon** acordaron pasar la luna de miel en Portugal; **that was the price we agreed on** ése fue el precio que acordamos

► **agree to** *vt insep* acceder a, aceptar; **he'll never a. to that** nunca accederá a eso; **her parents have agreed to her going abroad** sus padres han decidido dejarla ir al extranjero; **to a. to a condition/a proposal** aceptar una condición/una propuesta; **to a. to sb's request** aceptar la petición de alguien

► **agree with** *vt insep* (**a**) *(approve of)* **I don't a. with all this violence on television** no me parece bien que haya tanta violencia en televisión (**b**) *(of food, climate)* **the climate here agrees with her** este clima le sienta bien; **I must have eaten something that didn't a. with me** he debido comer algo que no me ha sentado bien

agreeable [ə'griːəbəl] *adj* (**a**) *(pleasant)* agradable; *(person)* simpático(a) (**b**) *(willing)* **to be a. to (doing) sth** estar de acuerdo en (hacer) algo; **if you are a.** si estás de acuerdo (**c**) *(acceptable)* **if that is a. to you** si te parece bien

agreeably [ə'grɪəblɪ] *adv* agradablemente; **I was a. surprised (by his performance)** (su actuación) fue una agradable sorpresa

agreed [ə'griːd] *adj* (**a**) *(in agreement)* de acuerdo; **we are a. on** *or* **about the conditions** estamos de acuerdo en lo que respecta a las condiciones; **as a.** según lo acordado; **(are we) a.?** ¿(estamos) de acuerdo? (**b**) *(fixed) (place, price, time)* fijado(a); **an a. statement** *(in the media)* una declaración consensuada

agreement [ə'griːmənt] *n* (**a**) *(assent)* acuerdo *m*; **the proposal met with unanimous a.** la propuesta recibió un apoyo unánime; **there was a. on all sides that...** todas las partes estaban de acuerdo en que...; **to be in a. with sth/sb** estar de acuerdo con algo/alguien

(**b**) *(contract)* contrato *m*, acuerdo *m*; **under the (terms of the) a.** según (las condiciones recogidas en) el acuerdo *or* contrato; **to come to** *or* **reach an a. (with sb)** llegar a un acuerdo (con alguien); **to have an a. with sb** tener un acuerdo *or* un pacto con alguien; **to hold sb to**

an a. hacer que alguien se atenga a un acuerdo; **to break an a.** romper un acuerdo

(**c**) *(of facts, account)* **to be in a. (with)** concordar, coincidir (con) (**d**) *Gram* concordancia *f*

agribusiness ['ægrɪbɪznɪs] *n* industria *f* agropecuaria, agroindustria *f*

agricultural [ægrɪ'kʌltʃərəl] *adj* agrícola ►► ***a. college*** escuela *f* de agricultura; ***a. labourer*** trabajador(ora) *m,f* agrícola; ***a. show*** = muestra de productos agropecuarios

agriculturalist [ægrɪ'kʌltʃərəlɪst], **agriculturist** [ægrɪ'kʌltʃərɪst] *n (expert)* experto(a) *m,f* en agricultura, ingeniero(a) *m,f* agrónomo(a)

agriculture ['ægrɪkʌltʃə(r)] *n* agricultura *f*

agriculturist = **agriculturalist**

agrochemical [ægrəʊ'kemɪkəl] *n* producto *m* agroquímico

agrochemistry [ægrəʊ'kəmɪstrɪ] *n* química *f* agrícola

agronomist [ə'grɒnəmɪst] *n* agrónomo(a) *m,f*

agronomy [ə'grɒnəmɪ] *n* agronomía *f*

aground [ə'graʊnd] *adv* **to run** *or* **go a.** *(of ship)* varar, encallar; *(of project, government)* encallar

ague ['eɪgju:] *n Archaic* fiebres *fpl*

ah [ɑ:] *exclam* ¡ah!

aha [ɑ:'hɑ:] *exclam* ¡ajajá!, ¡ajá!

AHEAD [ə'hed] *adv* (**a**) *(forwards)* adelante; *(in front)* delante, *Am* adelante; **the road a. was clear** no había nadie en la carretera delante *or Am* adelante de nosotros/él/ellos/*etc.*; **to go on a.** adelantarse; **to look (straight) a.** mirar hacia delante *or Am* adelante; **to send sb (on) a.** enviar a alguien por delante, *Am* mandar a alguien adelante; **to send sth on a.** enviar algo por adelantado; **a. of** delante de; **up a.** más adelante

(**b**) *(winning)* **to be a. (of)** *(in race, opinion poll)* ir por delante (de); *(in match)* ir ganando (a); **Liverpool are two goals a.** el Liverpool gana por dos goles; **they are 7 percent a. in the polls** llevan una ventaja del 7 por ciento en los sondeos; **they went a. after twenty minutes** se pusieron por delante en el marcador a los veinte minutos, *RP* en el minuto veinte pasaron a ganar; **to get a.** *(in career)* triunfar; **to get a. of sb** adelantar a alguien

(**c**) *(in time)* **in the years a.** en los años venideros; **the week a. promised to be difficult** la semana siguiente se presentaba difícil; **who knows what lies a.?** ¿quién sabe qué nos espera?; **how far a. should one book?** ¿con cuánta antelación hace falta reservar?; **to plan a.** hacer planes con antelación *or* por adelantado; **to think a.** pensar con *or* tener visión de futuro; **they are an hour a. of us in Colombia** en Colombia están una hora por delante de nosotros *or RP* adelantados con respecto a nosotros; **we have a long day a. of us** nos espera un día muy largo; **they met a. of the summit** se reunieron antes de la cumbre; **the project is a. of schedule** el proyecto va por delante del calendario previsto *or RP* adelantado; **a. of time** antes de tiempo; **he was a. of his time** se adelantó a su tiempo

ahem [ə'hem] *exclam* ¡ejem!

ahoy [ə'hɔɪ] *exclam* **a. there!** ¡ha del barco!; **ship a.!** ¡barco a la vista!

AI [eɪ'aɪ] *n* (**a**) *Comptr* (*abbr* **artificial intelligence**) inteligencia *f* artificial (**b**) *Biol* (*abbr* **artificial insemination**) inseminación *f* artificial

AID [eɪaɪ'di:] *n* (**a**) (*abbr* **artificial insemination by donor**) = inseminación artificial con semen de donante (**b**) (*abbr* **Agency for International Development**) Organismo *m* para el Desarrollo Internacional

aid [eɪd] **1** *n* (**a**) *(help, assistance)* ayuda *f*; **with the a. of** con la ayuda de; **to go/come to sb's a.** acudir en ayuda de alguien; **in a. of** *(fund-raising event)* a beneficio de; IDIOM *Br Fam* **what's (all) this in a. of?** ¿a qué se debe (todo) esto?

(**b**) *(to developing countries, for disaster relief)* ayuda *f*; **overseas** *or* **foreign a.** ayuda exterior ►► ***a. agency*** organismo *m* de cooperación; ***a. worker*** cooperante *mf*

(**c**) *(device)* ayuda *f*; **teaching aids** material didáctico *or* docente

2 *vt* (**a**) *(help, assist) (growth, development)* ayudar a, contribuir a; *(person)* ayudar; **to a. sb with sth** ayudar a alguien con algo; **they aided one another** se ayudaron mutuamente (**b**) *Law* **to a. and abet sb** ser cómplice de alguien; *Fig* **aided and abetted by her sister** con la complicidad *or* cooperación de su hermana

aide [eɪd] *n* asistente *mf*

-aided ['eɪdɪd] *suffix* (**a**) *(assisted)* **computer-a. design** diseño asistido por *Esp* ordenador *or Am* computadora (**b**) *(financially)* **grant-a.** subvencionado(a)

aide-de-camp ['eɪddə'kɒŋ] (*pl* **aides-de-camp**) *n Mil* ayudante *mf* de campo, edecán *m*

aide-mémoire ['eɪdmem'wɑ:(r)] (*pl* **aides-mémoire** ['eɪdzmem'wɑ:(r)]) *n* recordatorio *m*

AIDS [eɪdz] *n* (*abbr* **Acquired Immunodeficiency Syndrome**) sida *m* ►► ***A. clinic*** clínica *f* para enfermos de sida; ***A. sufferer*** enfermo(a) *m,f* de sida; ***A. test*** prueba *f* del sida; ***A. virus*** virus *m* del sida

ail [eɪl] **1** *vt Literary* aquejar; **what ails you?** ¿qué te sucede?

2 *vi* estar delicado(a)

aileron ['eɪlərɒn] *n Av* alerón *m*

ailing ['eɪlɪŋ] *adj* (**a**) *(person)* enfermo(a) (**b**) *(company, economy)* enfermizo(a), débil

ailment ['eɪlmənt] *n* achaque *m*

aim [eɪm] **1** *n* (**a**) *(at target)* puntería *f*; **to take a. at** apuntar a; *Mil* **take a.!** ¡apunten!; **her a. was good** tenía buena puntería (**b**) *(goal)* objetivo *m*, propósito *m*; **with the a. of doing sth** con el propósito de hacer algo; **her a. in going to London was to find a job** se fue a Londres con el propósito de encontrar trabajo

2 *vt (gun)* apuntar (**at** hacia *or* a); *(missile, stone, blow)* dirigir (**at** a); *(camera)* enfocar; *(remark, TV programme)* dirigir (**at** a); **to be aimed at sb** *(of remarks, TV programme)* estar dirigido(a) a alguien; **he aimed his gun at the man's head** apuntó la pistola hacia la cabeza del hombre; **was that remark aimed at me?** ¿iba dirigido a mí ese comentario?; **the announcement was aimed at reassuring the public** el objetivo del anuncio era tranquilizar al público

3 *vi* (**a**) *(with gun)* **to a. at sth/sb** apuntar a *or* hacia algo/alguien; **she aimed at** *or* **for the post, but missed** apuntó hacia el poste, pero falló (**b**) *(intend)* **to a. to do sth** tener la intención de hacer algo; **to a. high** apuntar alto; **he's aiming at** *or* **for quick promotion** su objetivo es conseguir pronto un ascenso

aimless ['eɪmlɪs] *adj (existence)* sin objetivos; *(remark)* vago(a)

aimlessly ['eɪmlɪslɪ] *adv (to wander, walk)* sin rumbo fijo; *(to engage in activity)* baldíamente; **he spent the evening a. shuffling through papers** se pasó la tarde revolviendo papeles sin ningún propósito

aimlessness ['eɪmlɪsnɪs] *n* **the a. of their existence** la falta de rumbo de su existencia

ain't [eɪnt] *Fam* (**a**) = **is not, am not, are not** (**b**) = **has not, have not**

air [eə(r)] **1** *n* (**a**) *(mixture of gases, atmosphere)* aire *m*; **there's a feeling of hope in the a.** hay (un) ambiente de esperanza; **there's a rumour in the a. that they're going to sell** corre el rumor de que van a vender ►► *Aut* ***a. bag*** airbag *m*; ***a. bed*** colchón *m* hinchable *or* neumático; ***a. brake*** *(for vehicle)* freno *m* neumático; *(for plane)* freno *m* aerodinámico; *Br* ***a. brick*** ladrillo *m* ventilador; ***a. cushion*** *(to sit on)* almohadón *m* hinchable; *(of hovercraft)* colchón *m* de aire; ***a. filter*** filtro *m* del aire; ***a. freshener*** ambientador *m*; ***a. intake*** entrada *f* de aire; *Met* ***a. mass*** masa *f* de aire; ***a. mattress*** *(to sleep on)* colchón *m* hinchable; *(for beach, swimming-pool)* colchoneta *f* hinchable; ***a. pistol*** pistola *f* de aire comprimido; ***a. pocket*** bolsa *f* de aire; ***a. pollution*** contaminación *f* atmosférica, polución *f* ambiental; ***a. pressure*** presión *f* atmosférica; ***a. pump*** bomba *f* de aire; ***a. vent*** salida *f* de humos

(**b**) *(sky)* aire *m*; **the smoke rose into the a.** el humo subió hacia el cielo; **to throw sth (up) in the a.** lanzar algo al aire; **to fly through the a.** volar por el aire; **to take to the a.** *(bird)* emprender el vuelo, echar a volar; *(plane)* despegar; **seen from the a....** a vista de pájaro *or* desde el aire...

(**c**) *(relating to flight, aircraft)* **by a.** en avión; **our mail is sent by a.** enviamos el correo por avión *or* por vía aérea ►► ***a. base*** base *f* aérea; *Br* ***a. chief marshal*** general *m* de las fuerzas aéreas; *Br* ***a. commodore*** general *mf* de brigada; ***a. corridor*** corredor *m or* pasillo *m* aéreo; ***a. current*** corriente *f* de aire; ***a. fare*** (precio *m* del) *Esp* billete *m or Am* boleto *m or Am* pasaje *m*; ***the A. Force*** las Fuerzas Aéreas, el Ejército del Aire; ***a. freight*** transporte *m* aéreo; ***a. hostess*** azafata *f* de vuelo, *Am* aeromoza *f*; ***a. lane*** corredor *m or* pasillo *m* aéreo; ***a. letter*** aerograma *m*; ***a. marshal*** teniente *m* general de las fuerzas aéreas; ***a. mile*** milla *f* aérea; ***A. miles:*** **to collect A. miles** juntar millas aéreas; ***a. miss*** conato *m* de colisión aérea; ***a. navigation*** navegación *f* aérea; ***a. power*** capacidad *f* aérea; ***a. rage*** = comportamiento agresivo del pasajero de un avión; ***a. raid*** ataque *m* aéreo; ***a. show*** demostración *f or* exhibición *f* aérea; ***a. shuttle*** *(plane)* puente *m* aéreo; *(bus)* = autobús que realiza los trayectos de la ciudad al aeropuerto y viceversa; ***a. steward*** auxiliar *m* de vuelo; ***a. stewardess*** auxiliar *f* de vuelo, azafata *f*, *Am* aeromoza *f*; ***a. terminal*** terminal *f* de vuelo; ***a. traffic*** tráfico *m* aéreo; ***a. vice-marshal*** general *m* de división

(**d**) *Rad & TV* **to be on (the) a.** *(person, programme)* estar en el aire; **to go on/off (the) a.** *(programme)* empezar/terminar; **I go on (the)**

a. at two o'clock salgo a las dos en punto; **the station goes off (the) a. at midnight** la emisión termina a las doce de la noche; **to take sb off the a.** cortar a alguien; **to take a programme off the a.** *(during transmission)* cortar un programa; *(stop showing)* dejar de emitir un programa
(**e**) *(melody)* melodía *f*, aire *m*
(**f**) *(look, manner)* aire *m*; **he has the a. of somebody who has travelled** tiene aire de haber viajado mucho; **there is an a. of mystery about her** tiene un aire de misterio; **she smiled with a knowing a.** sonrió con aire de complicidad
(**g**) IDIOM **our plans are up in the a.** *(undecided)* nuestros planes están en el aire; **to go up in the a.** *(get angry)* ponerse hecho(a) una furia, subirse por las paredes; **to give oneself airs, to put on airs** *(presume, act affectedly)* darse aires, darse tono
2 *vt* (**a**) *(room)* ventilar, airear (**b**) *(clothing, bedding)* airear, orear (**c**) *(opinions, grievances)* ventilar, airear (**d**) *US Rad & TV* transmitir, emitir
3 *vi US* **the program airs next week** el programa sale al aire la semana que viene

airborne ['eəbɔːn] *adj* (**a**) *(aircraft)* en vuelo; **to be a.** *(aircraft)* estar volando; **once we are a.** cuando estemos volando (**b**) *(seeds, particles)* transportado(a) por el viento (**c**) *(troops)* aerotransportado(a); *(invasion)* aéreo(a)

airbrush ['eəbrʌʃ] **1** *n* aerógrafo *m*
2 *vt (photograph)* retocar *(con aerógrafo)*; *also Fig* **to a. sth/sb out** borrar algo/a alguien

Airbus® ['eəbʌs] *n* Aerobús® *m*, Airbús® *m*

air-conditioned ['eəkən'dɪʃənd] *adj* climatizado(a), con aire acondicionado; **to be a.** *(room)* tener aire acondicionado

air-conditioner ['eəkən'dɪʃənə(r)] *n* aparato *m* de aire acondicionado

air-conditioning ['eəkən'dɪʃənɪŋ] *n* aire *m* acondicionado; **a. system** instalación de aire acondicionado

air-cooled ['eəkuːld] *adj* con refrigeración de aire

aircraft ['eəkrɑːft] (*pl* **aircraft**) *n (aeroplane)* avión *m*; *(any flying vehicle)* aeronave *f* ►► ***a. carrier*** portaaviones *m inv*

aircraftman ['eəkrɑːftmən] *n Br* soldado *m* raso de aviación

aircraftwoman ['eəkrɑːftwʊmən] *n Br* soldado *f* raso de aviación

aircrew ['eəkruː] *n Av* tripulación *f*

airdrome ['eədrəʊm] *n US* aeródromo *m*

airdrop ['eədrɒp] **1** *n* = lanzamiento de un cargamento con paracaídas
2 *vt (supplies)* lanzar con paracaídas

Airedale ['eədeɪl] *n* **A. (terrier)** Airedale terrier *m*

airer ['eərə(r)] *n Br (for clothes)* tendedero *m*

airfield ['eəfiːld] *n* campo *m* de aviación

airflow ['eəfləʊ] *n* corriente *m* de aire

airfoil ['eəfɔɪl] *n US* plano *m* aerodinámico

airframe ['eəfreɪm] *n* armazón *m* del avión

airgun ['eəgʌn] *n (rifle)* escopeta *f* de aire comprimido; *(pistol)* pistola *f* de aire comprimido

airhead ['eəhed] *n Fam* cabeza *mf* de chorlito, simple *mf*

airhole ['eəhəʊl] *n (in container, ice)* respiradero *m*

airing ['eərɪŋ] *n* **to give sth an a.** *(room, opinions, grievances)* ventilar *or* airear algo; *(clothing)* airear *or* orear algo ►► ***a. cupboard*** = ropero en el que se encuentra la caldera del agua caliente, y que se utiliza para orear la ropa, sábanas, etc.

airless ['eəlɪs] *adj (evening, atmosphere)* cargado(a); **an a. room** una habitación en la que falta el aire

airlift ['eəlɪft] **1** *n* puente *m* aéreo
2 *vt (supplies, troops)* transportar mediante un puente aéreo

airline ['eəlaɪn] *n* (**a**) *(company)* línea *f* aérea ►► ***a. pilot*** piloto *mf* comercial (**b**) *(for compressed air)* tubo *m* or conducto *m* del aire

airliner ['eəlaɪnə(r)] *n* avión *m* de pasajeros

airlock ['eəlɒk] *n* (**a**) *(in submarine, spacecraft)* compartimento *m* estanco, esclusa *f* de aire (**b**) *(in pipe)* burbuja *f* de aire

airmail ['eəmeɪl] **1** *n* correo *m* aéreo ►► ***a. letter*** carta *f* por vía aérea
2 *adv* **to send sth a.** enviar algo por vía aérea
3 *vt (letter)* mandar por vía aérea

airman ['eəmən] *n* (**a**) *(pilot)* aviador *m* (**b**) *US Mil* soldado *m* de aviación

airplane ['eəpleɪn] *n US* avión *m*

airplay ['eəpleɪ] *n Rad* **to get a.** ser emitido por la radio

airport ['eəpɔːt] *n* aeropuerto *m* ►► ***a. code*** código *m* de aeropuerto; ***a. tax*** tasas *fpl* de aeropuerto

air-raid ['eəreɪd] *adj* ***a. shelter*** refugio *m* antiaéreo; ***a. warden*** = responsable de operaciones defensivas civiles durante un ataque aéreo; ***a. warning*** alarma *f* antiaérea

air-rifle ['eəraɪfəl] *n* escopeta *f* de aire comprimido

air-sea rescue ['eəsiː'reskjuː] *n* rescate *m* marítimo desde el aire

airship ['eəʃɪp] *n* dirigible *m*

airsick ['eəsɪk] *adj* **to be** *or* **get a.** marearse *(en un avión)*

airsickness ['eəsɪknɪs] *n* mareos *mpl (en un avión)*

airspace ['eəspeɪs] *n* espacio *m* aéreo

airspeed ['eəspiːd] *n* velocidad *f (relativa de vuelo)*

airstrike ['eəstraɪk] *n* ataque *m* aéreo

airstrip ['eəstrɪp] *n* pista *f* de aterrizaje

airtight ['eətaɪt] *adj (container)* hermético(a); *(argument, case)* inatacable

airtime ['eətaɪm] *n Rad & TV* (**a**) *(time allotted)* tiempo *m* de emisión (**b**) *(starting time)* comienzo *m* de la emisión; **five minutes to a.** salimos al aire en cinco minutos

air-to-air ['eətə'eə(r)] *adj (missile)* aire-aire

air-to-ground ['eətə'graʊnd] *adj (missile)* aire-tierra

air-to-surface ['eətə'sɜːfɪs] *adj (missile)* aire-superficie

air-traffic ['eətræfɪk] *adj* ***a. control*** control *m* (del tráfico) aéreo; ***a. controller*** controlador(ora) *m,f* aéreo(a), controlador(ora) *m,f* del tráfico aéreo

airwaves ['eəweɪvz] *npl* **his voice came over the a.** su voz llegó a través de las ondas

airway ['eəweɪ] *n* (**a**) *(of body)* vía *f* respiratoria (**b**) *(for aircraft)* ruta *f* aérea

airwoman ['eəwʊmən] *n* aviadora *f*

airworthiness ['eəwɜːðɪnɪs] *n Av* aptitud *f* de vuelo; **certificate of a.** certificado de aptitud de vuelo, licencia de vuelo

airworthy ['eəwɜːðɪ] *adj Av* **to be a.** estar en condiciones de volar

airy ['eərɪ] *adj* (**a**) *(room, house)* aireado(a) y espacioso(a) (**b**) *(casual) (person, attitude)* ligero(a), despreocupado(a) (**c**) *(fanciful) (plan, idea)* fantasioso(a), poco realista

airy-fairy ['eərɪ'feərɪ] *adj Fam (idea, scheme)* fantasioso(a), poco realista

aisle [aɪl] *n* (**a**) *(between banks of seats, in supermarket)* pasillo *m*; **her father led her up the a.** su padre la acompañó al altar; IDIOM *Fam* **to have them rolling in the aisles** *(of comedian)* hacer que se caigan por los suelos *or RP* se revuelquen por el piso de la risa ►► ***a. seat*** *(in plane)* asiento *m* de pasillo (**b**) *Archit (in church)* nave *f* lateral

aitch [eɪtʃ] *n* **to drop one's aitches** no pronunciar la "h" *(considerado propio del habla poco cuidada)*

Ajaccio [ə'dʒæksɪəʊ] *n* Ajaccio

ajar [ə'dʒɑː(r)] **1** *adj* entornado(a)
2 *adv* entornado(a)

AK (*abbr* **Alaska**) Alaska

aka [eɪkeɪ'eɪ] *adv* (*abbr* **also known as**) alias

akimbo [ə'kɪmbəʊ] *adj* **with arms a.** con los brazos en jarras

akin [ə'kɪn] *adj* **a. to** parecido(a) a; **this is a. to treachery** esto es equiparable *or* semejante a la traición

AL, Ala (*abbr* **Alabama**) Alabama

Alabama [ælə'bæmə] *n* Alabama

alabaster [ælə'bæstə(r)] *n* alabastro *m*; **she had a. skin** tenía la piel transparente *or* de porcelana

à la carte [ælə'kɑːt] **1** *adj* **to have an a. meal** comer a la carta
2 *adv* a la carta

alacrity [ə'lækrɪtɪ] *n Formal* presteza *f*, diligencia *f*

Aladdin [ə'lædɪn] *pr n* Aladino ►► ***A.'s lamp*** la lámpara de Aladino

Alamo ['æləməʊ] *pr n* **the A.** el Álamo

à la mode [ælə'məʊd] **1** *adj* (**a**) *(clothes)* a la moda (**b**) *US (dessert)* con helado
2 *adv* a la moda

alarm [ə'lɑːm] **1** *n* (**a**) *(warning, alert)* alarma *f*; **to raise** *or* **give** *or* **sound the a.** dar la alarma ►► ***a. call*** *(on telephone)* llamada *f* despertador; ***a. call service*** (servicio *m* de) despertador *m* telefónico; ***a. signal*** señal *f* de alarma
(**b**) *(anxiety)* alarma *f*, inquietud *f*; **there's no cause for a.** no hay motivo de alarma; **the government viewed events with increasing a.** el gobierno se fue inquietando cada vez más ante los acontecimientos
(**c**) *(device)* **a. (bell)** timbre *m* de alarma; *Fig* **a. bells started to ring**

when... la señal de alarma saltó cuando...; **a. (clock)** (reloj *m*) despertador *m*; **(fire/burglar) a.** alarma *f* (contra incendios/antirrobo)
2 *vt* **(a)** *(startle)* alarmar; **to be alarmed at sth** estar alarmado(a) por algo **(b)** *(protect with alarm)* **all the doors are alarmed** todas las puertas tienen alarma

alarming [əˈlɑːmɪŋ] *adj* alarmante, inquietante

alarmingly [əˈlɑːmɪŋlɪ] *adv* **the shots were coming a. close** la cercanía de los disparos era alarmante *or* inquietante

alarmism [əˈlɑːmɪzəm] *n* alarmismo *m*

alarmist [əˈlɑːmɪst] **1** *n* alarmista *mf*
2 *adj* alarmista

alas [əˈlæs] **1** *exclam* ¡ay de mí!
2 *adv* desgraciadamente

Alaska [əˈlæskə] *n* Alaska

Alaskan [əˈlæskən] **1** *n* persona *f* de Alaska *(Estados Unidos)*
2 *adj* de Alaska *(Estados Unidos)*

alb [ælb] *n* alba *f*

albacore [ˈælbəkɔː(r)] *n* bonito *m* del norte

Albania [ælˈbeɪnɪə] *n* Albania

Albanian [ælˈbeɪnɪən] **1** *n* **(a)** *(person)* albanés(esa) *m,f* **(b)** *(language)* albanés *m*
2 *adj* albanés(esa)

albatross [ˈælbətrɒs] *n* **(a)** *(bird)* albatros *m inv* **(b)** *(in golf)* albatros *m inv* **(c)** IDIOM **it was (like) an a. round their necks** era un lastre que arrastraban con dificultad

albeit [ɔːlˈbiːɪt] *conj Formal* aunque; **a brilliant, a. uneven, novel** una novela brillante, aunque desigual

albino [ælˈbiːnəʊ] *(pl* **albinos***)* *n* albino(a) *m,f*

album [ˈælbəm] *n* **(a)** *(for photos, stamps)* álbum *m* **(b)** *(for record)* álbum *m*; **a. cover** funda de disco, carátula

albumen [ˈælbjʊmɪn] *n* **(a)** *(in egg)* albumen *m* **(b)** *(in blood)* albúmina *f*

albumin [ˈælbjʊmɪn] *n* albúmina *f*

alchemist [ˈælkəmɪst] *n* alquimista *mf*

alchemy [ˈælkəmɪ] *n* alquimia *f*

alcohol [ˈælkəhɒl] *n* **(a)** *(chemical)* alcohol *m* **(b)** *(drink)* alcohol *m* ▸▸ ***a. abuse*** alcoholismo *m*; ***a. consumption*** consumo *m* de alcohol; ***a. intake*** consumo *m* de alcohol; ***a. problem*** problema *m* con el alcohol

alcohol-free beer [ˈælkəhɒlfriːˈbɪə(r)] *n Br* cerveza *f* sin (alcohol)

alcoholic [ælkəˈhɒlɪk] **1** *n* alcohólico(a) *m,f*
2 *adj* alcohólico(a); **it's very a.** *(of cocktail, punch)* tiene mucho alcohol

alcoholism [ˈælkəhɒlɪzəm] *n* alcoholismo *m*

alcohol-related [ˈælkəhɒlrɪˈleɪtɪd] *adj* **a. illness** *or* **disease** enfermedad relacionada con el alcohol

alcopop [ˈælkəʊpɒp] *n Br* = combinado alcohólico con aspecto de refresco que se comercializa envasado

alcove [ˈælkəʊv] *n* hueco *m*

> **False friend**: The Spanish noun **alcoba** is not a translation for the English word **alcove**. In Spanish **alcoba** means "bedroom".

aldehyde [ˈældəhaɪd] *n Chem* aldehído *m*

al dente [ælˈdenteɪ] *adj* al dente

alder [ˈɔːldə(r)] *n (tree)* aliso *m*

alderman [ˈɔːldəmən] *n* **(a)** *Br Formerly* = concejal de un municipio que ocupaba el puesto inmediatamente inferior al de alcalde **(b)** *US, Can* concejal *m*

alderwoman [ˈɔːldəwʊmən] *n US, Can* concejala *f*

ale [eɪl] *n* = cerveza inglesa de malta

alehouse [ˈeɪlhaʊs] *n Archaic* taberna *f*

alert [əˈlɜːt] **1** *n* alerta *f*; **to be on the a. (for sth)** estar alerta (por si ocurre algo); **the navy has been put on full a.** la marina está en estado de máxima alerta; **they're always on the a. for interesting stories** siempre están al tanto de si escuchan alguna historia interesante ▸▸ *Comptr* ***a. box*** mensaje *m* de alerta
2 *adj (mind)* lúcido(a); **to be a.** *(watchful)* estar alerta *or* vigilante; *(lively)* ser despierto(a) *or* espabilado(a); **to be a. to sth** *(aware of)* ser consciente de algo
3 *vt* alertar, avisar; **he alerted them to the danger** los alertó del peligro

alertness [əˈlɜːtnɪs] *n (watchfulness)* actitud *f* vigilante; *(liveliness)* vivacidad *f*

Aleutian Islands [əˈluːʃənˈaɪləndz] *npl* **the A.** las (Islas) Aleutianas

Alexander [ælɪgˈzɑːndə(r)] *pr n* **A. the Great** Alejandro Magno ▸▸ ***the A. technique*** la técnica de Alexander

Alexandria [ælɪgˈzɑːndrɪə] *n* Alejandría

alexandrine [ælɪgˈzændraɪn] *n Lit* alejandrino *m*, verso *m* alejandrino

alfalfa [ælˈfælfə] *n* alfalfa *f*

alfresco [ælˈfreskəʊ] **1** *adj* al aire libre
2 *adv* al aire libre

algae [ˈældʒiː] *npl* algas *fpl*

algal bloom [ˈælgəlˈbluːm] *n* floración *f or* florecimiento *m* de algas

algebra [ˈældʒɪbrə] *n* álgebra *f*

algebraic [ældʒəˈbreɪɪk] *adj* algebraico(a)

Algeria [ælˈdʒɪərɪə] *n* Argelia

Algerian [ælˈdʒɪərɪən] **1** *n* argelino(a) *m,f*
2 *adj* argelino(a)

Algiers [ælˈdʒɪəz] *n* Argel

ALGOL [ˈælgɒl] *n (abbr* **Algorithmic Oriented Language***)* algol *m*

algorithm [ˈælgərɪðəm] *n Comptr* algoritmo *m*

algorithmic [ælgəˈrɪðmɪk] *adj Comptr* algorítmico(a)

alias [ˈeɪlɪəs] **1** *n* **(a)** *(assumed name)* alias *m inv*; **he has several aliases** tiene varios alias **(b)** *Comptr* alias *m inv*
2 *adv* alias

aliasing [ˈeɪlɪəsɪŋ] *n Comptr* dientes *mpl* de sierra, dentado *m*

alibi [ˈælɪbaɪ] *n Law* coartada *f*; **to produce/establish an a.** preparar/establecer una coartada

Alice band [ˈælɪsbænd] *n* cinta *f* para el cabello

Alice-in-Wonderland [ˈælɪsɪnˈwʌndəlænd] *adj* irreal

alien [ˈeɪlɪən] **1** *n* **(a)** *Formal (foreigner)* extranjero(a) *m,f* **(b)** *(from outer space)* extraterrestre *mf*, alienígena *mf*
2 *adj* **(a)** *(strange)* extraño(a); **it was a. to her nature** era ajeno a su carácter **(b)** *(from outer space)* extraterrestre, alienígena

alienable [ˈeɪlɪənəbəl] *adj Law (property)* enajenable

alienate [ˈeɪlɪəneɪt] *vt* **(a)** *(supporters, readers)* provocar el distanciamiento de; **he has alienated all his former friends** ha conseguido que sus antiguos amigos le diesen la espalda; **this tax will a. car drivers** este impuesto provocará el rechazo de los conductores **(b)** *Law* enajenar

alienated [ˈeɪlɪəneɪtɪd] *adj* rechazado(a); **they feel a. from society** se sienten marginados de la sociedad

alienation [eɪlɪəˈneɪʃən] *n* **(a)** *(of support, friends)* distanciamiento *m* **(b)** *Law* enajenación *f* **(c)** *Theat* ***a. effect*** distanciamiento *m*

alight[1] [əˈlaɪt] **1** *adj (burning)* **to be a.** estar ardiendo *or* en llamas; **his face was a. with happiness** tenía la cara encendida de alegría
2 *adv* **to set sth a.** prender fuego a algo; **to catch a.** prender

alight[2] *vi* **(a)** *Formal (from train, car)* apearse (**at** en) **(b)** *(bird, glance)* posarse (**on** sobre *or* en)

▸ **alight on** *vt insep (fact, solution)* dar con

align [əˈlaɪn] *vt* **(a)** *(place in line)* alinear **(b)** *(politically)* alinear; **to a. oneself with/against sb** alinearse con/contra alguien

alignment [əˈlaɪnmənt] *n* **(a)** *(positioning in line)* alineamiento *m*, alineación *f*; **out of a.** desalineado(a), no alineado(a); **in a.** alineado; **to bring sth into a. with the new regulations** ajustar algo al nuevo reglamento **(b)** *(political)* alineamiento *m*

alike [əˈlaɪk] **1** *adj* igual; **to look a.** parecerse; **no two are a.** no hay dos iguales; **you are all a.!** ¡todos sois iguales!
2 *adv (to treat, dress, think)* igual; **old and young a.** jovenes y viejos por igual; **every day, summer and winter a.** todos los días, ya sea invierno o verano

alimentary [ælɪˈmentərɪ] *adj* alimentario(a) ▸▸ *Anat* ***a. canal*** tracto *m* alimentario, tubo *m* digestivo

alimony [ˈælɪmənɪ] *n Law* pensión *f* (matrimonial) alimenticia

alive [əˈlaɪv] *adj* **(a)** *(living, still existing)* vivo(a); **to be a.** estar vivo(a); **when your father was a.** cuando tu padre vivía; **it's good to be a.** la vida es bella; **he was last seen a. on 21 June** fue visto con vida por última vez el 21 de junio; **no one got out of the building a.** nadie salió con vida del edificio; **no man a. could endure such pain** nadie podría soportar un dolor así; **the oldest man a.** el hombre más viejo del mundo; **to keep sb a.** mantener vivo(a) a alguien; **to keep a memory a.** mantener un recuerdo vivo; **to stay a.** sobrevivir; **to be burnt/buried a.** ser quemado(a)/enterrado(a) vivo(a); **to be a. and well** *(still living)* estar a salvo
(b) *(aware)* **to be a. to sth** ser consciente de algo, darse cuenta de algo
(c) *(full of vitality)* **I've never felt so a.** nunca me he sentido tan lleno de vida; **to come a.** *(place, movie)* animarse; **the district comes**

a. at night el barrio se llena de vida por la noche; **he came a. when someone mentioned food** revivió cuando alguien nombró la comida; IDIOM **to be a. and kicking** estar vivito(a) y coleando

(**d**) *(teeming)* **to be a. with** *(rats, ants)* ser un hervidero de; **the streets were a. with people** las calles eran un hervidero de gente

alkali ['ælkəlaɪ] *n Chem* álcali *m*, base *f*

alkaline ['ælkəlaɪn] *adj Chem* alcalino(a), básico(a)

alkalinity [ælkə'lɪnɪtɪ] *n Chem* alcalinidad *f*, basicidad *f*

alkaloid ['ælkəlɔɪd] *n Chem* alcaloide *m*

alky, alkie ['ælkɪ] *n Fam* (**a**) *(alcoholic)* borrachín(ina) *m,f* (**b**) *US (alcohol)* whisky *m* casero

ALL [ɔ:l] **1** *adj* (**a**) *(every one of)* todos(as); **a. men** todos los hombres; **a. the others** todos los demás; **a. four of them** los cuatro; **a. the books** todos los libros; **they are a. smokers** todos fuman, todos son fumadores; **at a. hours** a todas horas, continuamente ►► ***A. Saints' Day*** día *m* de Todos los Santos; ***A. Souls' Day*** día *m* de los Difuntos

(**b**) *(the whole of)* todo(a); **a. the wine** todo el vino; **a. day** todo el día; **a. week** toda la semana; **he slept a. afternoon** se pasó la tarde durmiendo; **she has lived here a. her life** ha vivido aquí toda la *or* su vida; **a. the time** todo el tiempo; **he leaves the door open a. the time** siempre se deja la puerta abierta; **is that a. the money you're taking?** ¿no te llevas más que ese dinero?

(**c**) *(for emphasis)* **she helped me in a. sorts of ways** me ayudó de mil maneras; **what's a. that noise?** ¿qué es ese escándalo?; **what's a. this about you resigning?** ¿qué es eso de que vas a dimitir?; *Fam* **and a. that** y todo eso; **it's not a. that easy** no es tan fácil; **she wasn't as rude as a. that** tampoco estuvo tan maleducada; **for a. her apparent calm, she was actually very nervous** a pesar de su aparente tranquilidad, estaba realmente muy nerviosa; **you, of a. people, should understand** tú deberías comprenderlo mejor que nadie; **she was playing the sitar, of a. things!** ¡imagínate, estaba tocando nada menos que el sitar!; **of a. the times to phone!** ¡vaya un momento para llamar!

2 *pron* (**a**) *(everyone, each one)* todos(as) *m,fpl*; **a. of them say that..., they a. say that...** todos dicen que...; **a. of us** todos (nosotros); **we a. love him** todos lo queremos; **a. of them are blue, they are a. blue** todos son azules; **a. but the best of us failed** fracasamos todos, salvo los mejores; **a. together** todos juntos

(**b**) *(everything)* *(replacing uncountable noun)* todo(a) *m,f*; *(replacing plural noun)* todos(as) *m,fpl*; **a. was silent** todo estaba en silencio; **I did a. I could** hice todo lo que pude; **he ate it, bones and a.** se lo comió con huesos y todo; **I want a. of it, I want it a.** lo quiero todo; **he has seen/done it a.** está de vuelta de todo; **that says it a.** eso lo dice todo; **it was a. I could do not to laugh** apenas pude aguantar la risa; **best/worst of a....** y lo que es mejor/peor...; **I like this one best of a.** este es el que más me gusta; **most of a.** ante todo; **when I was busiest of a.** cuando estaba más ocupado; **that's a.** eso es todo; **is that a.?** ¿nada más?, ¿eso es todo?; **a. I said was "good morning"** lo único que dije fue "buenos días"; **a. I want is some peace and quiet** lo único que pido es un poco de tranquilidad; **for a. I know** por lo que yo sé; **it's a. the same to me** me da lo mismo; **thirty men in a.** *or* **a. told** treinta hombres en total; **a. in a.** *(to sum up)* en resumen, en suma; *(on balance)* después de todo; **it cost $260, a. in** costó 260 dólares con todo incluido; *Ironic* **it cost a. of £2** costó la increíble suma de 2 libras; IDIOM **when a.'s said and done** a fin de cuentas; PROV **a.'s well that ends well** bien está lo que bien acaba

3 *adv* (**a**) *(entirely)* totalmente, completamente; **he's not a. bad** no es del todo malo; **he was left a. alone** lo dejaron (completamente) solo; **he did it a. on his own** lo hizo él solo; **to be (dressed) a. in black** ir (vestido) todo de negro; **he went a. quiet** enmudeció; **to be a. ears** ser todo oídos; **a. along** desde el principio; **a. along the road** a lo largo de la carretera; **a. around the room** por toda la habitación; **a. at once** *(suddenly)* de repente; *(at the same time)* a la vez; **a. but** *(almost)* casi; **to be a. for sth** ser un(a) gran partidario(a) de algo; **a. over (the place)** por todas partes; *Fam* **at the interview he was a. over the place** *or* **shop** en la entrevista no dio pie con bola *or Esp* una a derechas; *Fam* **she was a. over him at the party** en la fiesta estuvo todo el tiempo encima de él; *Fam Hum* **he was a. over her like a rash** *or* **a cheap suit** se le pegaba como una lapa; **that's him a. over** es típico de él; **a. too soon** demasiado pronto; **it's a. yours** es todo tuyo; IDIOM *Fam* **to be a. in** *(exhausted)* estar hecho(a) polvo *or* una piltrafa, *Col* estar como un chupo, *Méx* estar camotes; IDIOM *Fam* **he's not a. there** está un poco ido

(**b**) *(with comparatives)* **a. the better/worse** tanto mejor/peor; **the noise made it a. the harder to hear them** con el ruido era aún más difícil oírlos

(**c**) *(in games)* **two a.** *(in football)* empate a dos; **four (games) a.** *(in tennis)* empate a cuatro juegos; **fifteen a.** *(in tennis)* quince iguales

4 *n* IDIOM **to give one's a.** darlo todo

all- [ɔ:l] *prefix* **a.-male/female** exclusivamente masculino/femenino; **the first a.-French baseball team** el primer equipo de béisbol integrado exclusivamente por franceses

Allah ['ælə] *n* Alá *m*

all-American ['ɔ:lə'merɪkən] *adj* típico(a) americano(a), típico(a) estadounidense

all-around *US* = **all-round**

allay [ə'leɪ] *vt (doubts, suspicions)* despejar; *(fear, pain)* apaciguar, aplacar

all-clear ['ɔ:l'klɪə(r)] *n* (**a**) *(after air raid)* señal *f* de que pasó el peligro; **to sound the a.** dar la señal que indica el final del bombardeo (**b**) *(for project)* luz *f* verde; **to give sth/sb the a.** dar luz verde a algo/alguien

all-comers ['ɔ:l'kʌməz] *adj* **the British a. 100 m record** el récord de los 100 m en territorio británico

all-conquering ['ɔ:l'kɒŋkərɪŋ] *adj (love, army, team)* arrasador(ora)

all-consuming ['ɔ:lkən'sju:mɪŋ] *adj (passion, thirst for knowledge)* devorador(ora)

all-day ['ɔ:l'deɪ] *adj* de todo el día ►► *Br* ***a. licence:*** **the pub has an a. licence** el pub tiene permiso para servir bebidas alcohólicas a todas horas

allegation [ælɪ'geɪʃən] *n* acusación *f*; **to make an a. (against sb)** acusar (a alguien)

allege [ə'ledʒ] *vt* (**a**) *(claim)* afirmar, declarar; **he alleges that he was beaten up** afirma que le dieron una paliza; **it is alleged that she accepted a bribe** supuestamente aceptó un soborno; **the incident is alleged to have taken place the night before** supuestamente el incidente tuvo lugar la noche anterior (**b**) *Formal (present as evidence)* alegar, aducir

alleged [ə'ledʒd] *adj* presunto(a), supuesto(a)

allegedly [ə'ledʒɪdlɪ] *adv* presuntamente; **they a. broke in and stole $300** presuntamente entraron y robaron 300 dólares; **a. he's the greatest violinist since Paganini** se dice que es el mejor violinista después de Paganini

allegiance [ə'li:dʒəns] *n* lealtad *f*; **to swear a. (to)** jurar lealtad (a); **to switch a.** cambiar de filiación; **to owe a. to sb** deber lealtad a alguien

allegorical [ælɪ'gɒrɪkəl] *adj* alegórico(a)

allegorically [ælɪ'gɒrɪklɪ] *adv* alegóricamente

allegory ['ælɪgərɪ] *n* alegoría *f*

allegretto [ælɪ'gretəʊ] *Mus* **1** *n* (*pl* **allegrettos**) alegreto *m*
2 *adv* alegreto

allegro [ə'legrəʊ] *Mus* **1** *n* (*pl* **allegros**) alegro *m*
2 *adv* alegro

allele [ə'li:l] *n Biol* alelo *m*

alleluia [ælɪ'lu:jə] *exclam* ¡aleluya!

all-embracing ['ɔ:lɪm'breɪsɪŋ] *adj* general, global

Allen key ['ælən'ki:], *US* **Allen wrench** ['ælən'rentʃ] *n* llave *f* allen

allergen ['ælədʒən] *n* alergeno *m*

allergenic [ælə'dʒenɪk] *adj* alergeno(a)

allergic [ə'lɜ:dʒɪk] *adj* alérgico(a) (**to** a); **to be a. to sth** tener alergia a algo, ser alérgico(a) a algo; **(to have) an a. reaction (to sth)** (padecer) una reacción alérgica (a algo); *Hum* **he's a. to hard work** le tiene alergia al trabajo duro

allergist ['ælədʒɪst] *n* alergólogo(a) *m,f*

allergy ['ælədʒɪ] *n* alergia *f*; **to have an a. to sth** tener alergia a algo

alleviate [ə'li:vɪeɪt] *vt (pain, boredom)* aliviar

alleviation [əli:vɪ'eɪʃən] *n* alivio *m*

all-expenses-paid ['ɔ:lɪkspensɪz'peɪd], *US* **all-expense-paid** ['ɔ:lɪkspens'peɪd] *adj* con todos los gastos pagados

alley ['ælɪ] *n* (**a**) *(lane, passage)* callejón *m*, callejuela *f*; IDIOM **that's right up my a.** es lo mío, *Esp* es lo que me va ►► ***a. cat*** gato *m* callejero (**b**) *(in park, garden)* sendero *m*, camino *m* (**c**) *US (on tennis court)* pasillo *m* lateral (**d**) *(for tenpin bowling, skittles)* pista *f*

alleyway ['ælɪweɪ] *n* callejón *m*, callejuela *f*; IDIOM **I wouldn't like to meet him in a dark a.!** ¡no me gustaría encontrarme con él en un callejón oscuro!

all-fired ['ɔ:l'faɪərd] *US Fam* **1** *adj* tremendo(a); **why is he in such an a. rush?** ¿por qué va tan a la carrera *or Esp* tan escopetado?

2 *adv* sumamente; **I wish he wasn't so a. sure of himself** ojalá no estuviera tan sumamente seguro de sí mismo

alliance [ə'laɪəns] *n* (**a**) *(between countries, parties)* alianza *f*; **to enter into** *or* **form an a. (with)** formar una alianza (con), aliarse (con) (**b**) *(by marriage)* alianza *f*

allied ['ælaɪd] *adj* (a) *(countries, forces)* aliado(a); *Hist* **A. forces/losses** fuerzas/pérdidas aliadas (b) *(combined)* asociado(a); **a. to** *or* **with the poor weather, this change was disastrous** este cambio, asociado al mal tiempo, resultó desastroso (c) *(related) (issue, phenomenon)* afín, asociado(a); *(subject, product, industry)* afín

alligator ['ælɪgeɪtə(r)] *n* caimán *m*; **a. shoes/belt** zapatos *mpl*/cinturón *m* de cocodrilo

all-important ['ɔːlɪm'pɔːtənt] *adj* fundamental, esencial

all-in ['ɔːlɪn] *adj* (a) *(price)* con todo incluido (b) *Sport* ***a. wrestling*** lucha *f* libre

all-inclusive ['ɔːlɪn'kluːsɪv] *adj (price, holiday)* con todo incluido

all-in-one ['ɔːlɪn'wʌn] *adj (garment)* de una pieza

alliteration [əlɪtə'reɪʃən] *n* aliteración *f*

alliterative [ə'lɪtərətɪv] *adj* aliterado(a), aliterativo(a); **an a. style** un estilo aliterativo; **a heavily a. passage** un fragmento muy aliterado

all-merciful ['ɔːl'mɜːsɪful] *adj* misericordioso(a)

all-night ['ɔːlnaɪt] *adj (party, session)* de toda la noche; *(shop, diner)* abierto(a) toda la noche

all-nighter ['ɔːl'naɪtə(r)] *n* (a) *(party)* **the party was an a.** la fiesta duró toda la noche (b) *US (study session)* **we pulled an a. for the physics exam** estudiamos toda la noche para el examen de física

allocate ['æləkeɪt] *vt (time, accommodation, task)* asignar (**to** a); *(money, resources)* asignar, destinar (**to** a); **in the time allocated** en el tiempo asignado; **you'll need to a. your time carefully** tienes que repartir tu tiempo con cuidado

allocation [ælə'keɪʃən] *n* (a) *(assignment) (of time, accommodation, tasks)* asignación *f*; *(of money, resources)* asignación *f* (b) *(share)* asignación *f*

allomorph ['æləmɔːf] *n Ling* alomorfo *m*

allopathic [ælə'pæθɪk] *adj Med* alopático(a)

allopathy [æ'lɒpəθɪ] *n Med* alopatía *f*

allophone ['æləfəʊn] *n Ling* alófono *m*

all-or-nothing ['ɔːlə'nʌθɪŋ] *adj* **an a. attitude** una actitud radical

allot [ə'lɒt] (*pt & pp* **allotted**) *vt* (a) *(time, money, duties)* asignar; **in the allotted time, in the time allotted** en el tiempo asignado; **the farmers were allotted a few acres each** se asignaron unos cuantos acres a cada agricultor (b) *St Exch (shares)* distribuir

allotment [ə'lɒtmənt] *n* (a) *Br (plot of land)* huerto *m* de ocio, parcela *f* *(arrendada por el ayuntamiento para cultivo)* (b) *(of time, money, duties)* asignación *f* (c) *St Exch (of shares)* distribución *f*

allotrope ['ælətrəʊp] *n Chem* alótropo *m*

all-out ['ɔːl'aʊt] **1** *adj (effort)* supremo(a); *(opposition, resistance)* total; *(war)* sin cuartel; *(attack)* frontal; **an a. strike** una huelga general

2 *adv* **to go a. to do sth** poner toda la carne en el asador para hacer algo

all-over ['ɔːl'əʊvə(r)] *adj* completo(a); **an a. tan** un bronceado integral

ALLOW [ə'laʊ] *vt* (a) *(permit)* permitir; **to a. sb to do sth** permitir a alguien hacer *or* que haga algo, dejar a alguien hacer algo; **they'll never a. you to do it** nunca te dejarán hacerlo; **I am allowed to do it** tengo permiso para hacerlo; **you are not allowed to walk on the grass** está prohibido pisar el césped; **smoking is not allowed** se prohibe *or* no se permite fumar; **I'd love to, but I'm not allowed** me encantaría, pero no me lo permiten; **we're not allowed sweets** no nos dejan comer caramelos; **the referee allowed the goal** el árbitro dio el gol por válido; **to a. sth to happen** permitir que ocurra algo; **don't a. them to persuade you** no dejes que te convenzan, no te dejes convencer; **a. me!** *(offering help)* ¡permítame!; **I a. myself a glass of whisky now and again** me permito un whisky de vez en cuando; **to a. oneself to be deceived/persuaded** dejarse engañar/convencer

(b) *(allocate, grant)* dar, conceder; **a. an hour to get to the airport** cuenta *or* deja *or* calcula una hora para llegar al aeropuerto; **please a. 28 days for delivery** el envío puede tardar hasta 28 días; **a. two spoonfuls per person** cuenta *or* calcula dos cucharadas por persona; **you are allowed a maximum of two hours to complete this paper** tienen un máximo de dos horas para completar este examen

(c) *Law (evidence)* aceptar

(d) *Formal (admit)* **to a. that...** aceptar que...

▸ **allow for** *vt insep* tener en cuenta; **add another hour to a. for delays** añade una hora más por si hay retraso; **our budget doesn't a. for it** no está incluido en nuestro presupuesto

▸ **allow of** *vt insep Formal* permitir, admitir

allowable [ə'laʊəbəl] *adj (error, delay)* permisible; *(expense)* deducible; **expenses a. against tax** gastos deducibles

allowance [ə'laʊəns] *n* (a) *(government grant)* subsidio *m*

(b) *(supplement to salary or wage) (for housing, food)* suplemento *m*; **travel a.** gastos de viaje, dietas

(c) *(from parents)* asignación *f*; *US (pocket money)* paga *f*

(d) *(entitlement)* **baggage** *or* **luggage a.** = equipaje que se puede facturar sin pagar por sobrepeso; **the ration included a small a. of tobacco** el racionamiento incluía una pequeña asignación de tabaco

(e) *Br (subtracted from taxable income)* = ingresos libres de impuestos

(f) **to make a.** *or* **allowances for sth** *(take into account)* tener algo en cuenta; **you have to make allowances for inflation** tienes que tener en cuenta los efectos de la inflación; **I'm tired of making allowances for his inexperience** estoy harto de hacer concesiones *or* de disculparle por su falta de experiencia

alloy ['ælɔɪ] **1** *n* aleación *f*

2 *vt* alear (**with** con)

all-party ['ɔːl'pɑːtɪ] *adj (committee, initiative)* de todos los partidos

all-pervading ['ɔːlpə'veɪdɪŋ], **all-pervasive** ['ɔːlpə'veɪsɪv] *adj (stench)* penetrante; *(influence)* profundo(a), penetrante

all-points bulletin ['ɔːl'pɔɪnts'bʊlɪtɪn] *n US* = mensaje informativo o aviso urgente enviado a los agentes de policía de una misma zona

all-powerful ['ɔːl'paʊəfʊl] *adj* todopoderoso(a)

all-purpose ['ɔːl'pɜːpəs] *adj* multiuso; **a. cleaner/adhesive** limpiador/adhesivo multiuso

all right, alright [ɔːl'raɪt] **1** *adj* (a) *(adequate)* bueno(a); **the film was a., but nothing special** la película no estaba mal, pero tampoco era nada del otro mundo; **it's a. here** esto no está mal; **the money is a., but it could be better** el sueldo está bien, pero podría estar mejor; **she's a. at dancing/at French** no se le da mal el baile/el francés

(b) *(in good health, safe)* **to be a.** estar bien; **are you a.?** ¿estás bien?; **he was in a car crash but he's a.** tuvo un accidente, pero no le pasó nada; **I hope they'll be a. on their own** espero que se las arreglen bien solos; **do you think the bike will be a. here?** ¿crees que la moto estará bien aquí?; *Br Fam* **an "I'm a., Jack" attitude** una actitud de "ande yo caliente"

(c) *(permissible, satisfactory)* **don't worry, it's a.** no te preocupes, no pasa nada; **is it a. if I smoke?** ¿puedo fumar?; **I'll come later, if that's a. with you** vendré más tarde, si te parece bien; **is everything a., Madam?** *(in shop, restaurant)* ¿está todo bien, señora?; **it's a. by me** por mí, de acuerdo; **it's a. for YOU to laugh!** ¡tú bien puedes reírte!; IDIOM *Br* **it'll be a. on the night** cuando llegue la hora de la verdad todo irá bien

(d) *(sufficiently supplied)* **to be a. for money** tener dinero suficiente; **I'm a. until Monday** puedo aguantar hasta el lunes; **are you a. for food/cigarettes?** ¿tienes suficiente comida/tabaco?

(e) *Fam (very good)* bueno(a); **he's an a. guy** es un buen tipo, *Esp* es un tío legal, *Am* es buena gente; **the boss is a.** el jefe es un buen tipo; *Br* **he's a., is John** *(I like him)* es un buen tipo este John

(f) *Br* **she's a bit of a.!** ¡está buenísima!

2 *adv* (a) *(well)* bien; **the radio is working a.** la radio funciona perfectamente; **did it go a.?** ¿fue bien?; **did you get home a.?** ¿llegaste bien a casa?; **he's doing a. (for himself)** le va bastante bien

(b) *(yes)* de acuerdo, *Esp* vale; **a., so I made a mistake** de acuerdo, cometí un error

(c) *(certainly)* **it's rabies a.** seguro que es rabia; **it was cold a.!** ¡ya lo creo que hacía frío!

(d) *(checking agreement)* **phone me when you get there, a.?** llámame cuando llegues, ¿de acuerdo?

(e) *(expressing irritation)* **a., a.! I'm coming!** ¡ya voy, ya voy!

(f) *(introducing topic)* **a., let's get started** bueno *or Esp* venga, vamos a empezar

3 *exclam Fam* (a) *Br (as greeting)* ¿qué tal? (b) *(in approval)* ¡estupendo!, *Andes, CAm, Carib, Méx* ¡chévere!, *Méx* ¡padre!, *RP* ¡bárbaro!

all-risks ['ɔːl'rɪsks] *adj (insurance)* a todo riesgo

all-round ['ɔːlraʊnd], *US* **all-around** ['ɔːləraʊnd] *adj* (a) *(versatile) (athlete, player)* completo(a); *(ability)* general (b) *(comprehensive) (education, improvement)* general

all-rounder ['ɔːl'raʊndə(r)] *n Br* **he's an a.** todo se le da bien

all-seater ['ɔːlsiːtə(r)] *adj* **a. stadium** = estadio en el que todas las localidades son de asiento

all-singing all-dancing [ɔːl'sɪŋɪŋɔːl'dɑːnsɪŋ] *adj Hum* (a) *(versatile)* multiusos *inv*, todoterreno (b) *(extravagant)* **the conference was an a. affair** el congreso resultó una celebración por todo lo alto

allspice ['ɔːlspaɪs] *n* pimienta *f* inglesa

all-star ['ɔːl'stɑː(r)] *adj* **an a. cast** un reparto de primeras figuras, un reparto estelar ▸▸ *Sport* ***a. game*** partido *m* de las estrellas

all-state ['ɔːl'steɪt] *adj US (player, team)* del estado, estatal

all-terrain [ˈɔːltəˈreɪn] *adj* ***a. bike*** (moto *f*) todoterreno *f*; ***a. vehicle*** todoterreno *m*

all-time [ˈɔːlˈtaɪm] *adj (record)* sin precedentes; *(favourite)* de todos los tiempos; **a. high/low** máximo/mínimo histórico

allude [əˈluːd] *vi* aludir (**to** a); **I wasn't alluding to anybody in particular** no me refería a nadie en particular

allure [əˈlʊə(r)] *n* atractivo *m*, encanto *m*; **it holds no a. for me** no me llama la atención

alluring [əˈlʊərɪŋ] *adj* atractivo(a), seductor(ora)

allusion [əˈluːʒən] *n* alusión *f*; **to make an a. (to)** hacer (una) alusión (a)

allusive [əˈluːsɪv] *adj* alusivo(a)

alluvia *pl of* **alluvium**

alluvial [əˈluːvɪəl] *adj Geog* aluvial; **an a. plain** una llanura aluvial

alluvium [əˈluːvɪəm] (*pl* **alluviums** *or* **alluvia** [əˈluːvɪə]) *n Geog* aluvión *m*

all-weather [ˈɔːlˈweðə(r)] *adj* para cualquier tiempo

ally 1 *n* [ˈælaɪ] aliado(a) *m,f*; **to become allies** hacerse aliados, aliarse; *Hist* **the Allies** los Aliados

2 *vt* [əˈlaɪ] **to a. oneself with...** aliarse con...

alma mater [ˈælməˈmɑːtə(r)] *n* alma mater *f*

almanac [ˈælmənæk] *n (calendar)* almanaque *m*

almighty [ɔːlˈmaɪtɪ] **1** *n* **the A.** el Todopoderoso

2 *adj* (**a**) *(omnipotent)* todopoderoso(a); **A. God, God A.** *(in prayer)* Dios Todopoderoso; **God A.!** *(as oath)* ¡por Dios! (**b**) *Fam (fuss, row)* de mil demonios, *RP* de la gran siete

almond [ˈɑːmənd] *n* almendra *f*; **a. eyes** ojos rasgados ▸▸ ***a. milk*** leche *f* de almendras; ***a. tree*** almendro *m*

almost [ˈɔːlməʊst] *adv* casi; **I can a. reach it** me falta poco para llegar; **he is a. 30** tiene casi 30 años; **it's a. six o'clock** son casi las seis; **we're a. there** *(in journey)* casi hemos llegado; *(in task)* casi hemos acabado; **I a. believed him** estuve a punto de creerle; **he was a. crying with frustration** estaba casi llorando de frustración

alms [ɑːmz] *npl* limosna *f*

almsgiving [ˈɑːmzgɪvɪŋ] *n* **they don't believe in a.** no son partidarios de dar limosna

alms-house [ˈɑːmzhaʊs] *n Br* asilo *m* para pobres

aloe [ˈæləʊ] *n* áloe *m*; **a. vera** áloe vera

aloft [əˈlɒft] *adv* (**a**) *(up, in the air)* por el aire, en vilo; **to hold sth a.** levantar a algo en el aire (**b**) *Naut* **to go a.** subir a un mástil

aloha [əˈləʊhɑː] *exclam US* ¡aloha!

alone [əˈləʊn] **1** *adj* (**a**) *(on one's own)* solo(a); **to be a.** estar solo(a); **to be a. with sb** estar a solas con alguien; **we are not a. in thinking that...** no somos los únicos que pensamos que...; **to leave sth/sb a.** dejar algo/a alguien en paz; **to leave well a.** dejar las cosas como están; **let a....** mucho menos...; **I can't afford a TV, let a. a DVD!** no puedo comprarme un televisor, mucho menos un DVD

(**b**) *(lonely)* solo(a); **she felt very a.** se sentía muy sola

2 *adv* (**a**) *(without others)* **I did it a.** lo hice yo sola; **to live a.** vivir solo(a); **a. among her contemporaries, she criticized the decision** fue la única de sus contemporáneos que criticó la decisión; **to go it a.** ir por libre

(**b**) *(only)* **you a. can help me** tú eres la única que me puede ayudar, sólo tú puedes ayudarme; **my salary a. isn't enough** con mi sueldo sólo no es suficiente; **money a. can't make you happy** el dinero por sí solo no puede darte la felicidad; **with that charm which is his a.** con ese encanto tan suyo

---

ALONG [əˈlɒŋ] **1** *prep* a lo largo de; **to walk a. the shore/a street** caminar por la costa/una calle; **it's the second office a. the corridor** es la segunda oficina del pasillo; **it's halfway a. the road** está en la carretera, a mitad de camino; **there was a table a. one wall** había una mesa a lo largo de una de las paredes; **her skirt trailed a. the floor** arrastraba la falda por el suelo; **somewhere a. the way** en algún punto (del camino); *Fig* en un momento dado

2 *adv* (**a**) *(forwards)* **I was walking a.** iba caminando; **it's a bit further a.** está un poco más adelante; **would you mind going a. to the shop?** ¿te importaría ir a la tienda?; **to move a.** avanzar; **move a., there!** ¡vamos!, *Esp* ¡venga!, *Méx* ¡ándale!, *RP* ¡dale!; **how far a. are you with the project?** ¿cuánto has avanzado con el proyecto?; **he knew all a.** lo sabía desde el principio

(**b**) *(with someone)* **to bring sth/sb a.** traerse a algo/alguien (consigo); **do you want to come a.?** ¿quieres venir?; **to take sth/sb a.** llevar algo/a alguien; **he'll be a. in ten minutes** vendrá en diez minutos; **a. with** *(as well as)* además de, junto con

---

alongside [əˈlɒŋˈsaɪd] **1** *prep* (**a**) *(next to)* junto a; **the taxi drew up a. us** el taxi se detuvo junto a nosotros; *Naut* **to come a. the quay** arrimarse de costado al muelle (**b**) *(together with)* junto con; **I worked a. her for ten years** trabajé con ella (durante) diez años

2 *adv (at side)* **a police motorbike pulled up a.** una motocicleta de la policía se detuvo al lado; *Naut* **to come a.** detenerse al lado

aloof [əˈluːf] **1** *adj (person, manner)* distante

2 *adv* al margen; **to keep** *or* **remain a. (from)** mantenerse al margen (de); **he keeps** *or* **remains a. from his colleagues** no se relaciona con sus compañeros

aloofness [əˈluːfnɪs] *n* actitud *f* distante

alopecia [æləˈpiːʃə] *n Med* alopecia *f*

aloud [əˈlaʊd] *adv* en alto, en voz alta; **I was thinking a.** estaba pensando en voz alta

alpaca [ælˈpækə] *n* (**a**) *(animal)* alpaca *f* (**b**) *(wool)* alpaca *f*

alpenstock [ˈælpənstɒk] *n* alpenstock *m*, = tipo de piolet

alpha [ˈælfə] *n* (**a**) *(Greek letter)* alfa *f* (**b**) *Phys* ***a. particle*** partícula *f* alfa; ***a. radiation*** radiación *f* alfa; ***a. rays*** rayos *mpl* alfa (**c**) *Comptr* ***a. testing*** comprobación *f or* prueba *f* alfa; ***a. version*** versión *f* alfa

alphabet [ˈælfəbet] *n* alfabeto *m* ▸▸ ***a. soup*** sopa *f* de letras; *Fig* **the report was an a. soup of acronyms** el informe era un revoltijo de siglas; *US Fam* ***a. soup agency*** = cualquier departamento u organismo de la administración conocido por sus siglas

alphabetic(al) [ælfəˈbetɪk(əl)] *adj* alfabético(a); **in a. order** en orden alfabético

alphabetically [ælfəˈbetɪklɪ] *adv* alfabéticamente

alphabetize [ˈælfəbətaɪz] *vt* ordenar alfabéticamente

alphanumeric [ˈælfənjuːˈmerɪk] *adj Comptr* ***a. characters*** caracteres *mpl* alfanuméricos; ***a. code*** código *m* alfanumérico; ***a. keypad*** teclado *m* alfanumérico

alphasort [ˈælfəsɔːt] **1** *n* orden *m* alfabético; **to do an a. on sth** ordenar algo alfabéticamente

2 *vt* ordenar alfabéticamente

Alpine [ˈælpaɪn] *adj Geog* alpino(a)

alpine [ˈælpaɪn] *adj (climate, landscape, club, skiing, troops)* alpino(a) ▸▸ ***a. accentor*** acentor *m* alpino; ***a. chough*** chova *f* piquigualda; ***a. swift*** vencejo *m* real

Alps [ælps] *npl* **the A.** los Alpes

already [ɔːlˈredɪ] *adv* ya; **I've a. seen it,** *US* **I a. saw it** ya lo he visto, *Am* ya lo vi; **ten o'clock a.!** ¡ya son las diez!; **things were a. worrying even without this news** la situación ya era preocupante incluso antes de conocer esta noticia

alright = **all right**

Alsace [ælˈsæs] *n* Alsacia; **A.-Lorraine** Alsacia-Lorena

Alsatian [ælˈseɪʃən] **1** *n* (**a**) *(dog)* pastor *m* alemán (**b**) *(person from Alsace)* alsaciano(a) *m,f*

2 *adj (from Alsace)* alsaciano(a)

ALSO [ˈɔːlsəʊ] *adv* también; **my dog is a. called Fido** mi perro también se llama Fido; **a., you can't really afford it anyway** además, de todas formas no te lo puedes permitir; **you can a. tell him he's a liar** además puedes decirle que es un mentiroso, puedes decirle también que es un mentiroso; **not only... but a....** no sólo..., sino también...

---

also-ran [ˈɔːlsəʊræn] *n* (**a**) *(in horse race)* = caballo no clasificado entre los tres primeros (**b**) *(mediocrity)* **he is just an a.** sólo es uno más *or* uno del montón; **the company is an a. in the telecommunications market** es una empresa más *or* del montón en el mercado de las telecomunicaciones

alt [ɔːlt] *n Comptr* ***a. key*** tecla *f* alt

Alta (*abbr* **Alberta**) Alberta

altar [ˈɔːltə(r)] *n* altar *m*; **to lead sb to the a.** llevar a alguien al altar; **to leave sb standing at the a.** dejar plantado(a) a alguien el día de su boda; **to be sacrificed on the a. of success** ser sacrificado en aras del éxito ▸▸ ***a. boy*** monaguillo *m*

altarpiece [ˈɔːltəpiːs] *n* retablo *m*

alter [ˈɔːltə(r)] **1** *vt* (**a**) *(person, design, plan)* cambiar, alterar; **he altered his opinion** cambió de opinión; **that doesn't a. the fact that...** eso no cambia el hecho de que...; **that alters everything** eso lo cambia todo; **to a. course** *(of ship, plane)* cambiar el rumbo (**b**) *(garment)* arreglar (**c**) *US Euph (animal)* operar

2 *vi* cambiar, alterarse

alteration [ɔːltəˈreɪʃən] *n* **(a)** *(to design, plan)* cambio *m*, alteración *f*; *(to timetable)* alteración *f*; **a few minor alterations** unos pequeños retoques; **subject to a.** *(programme, timetable)* susceptible de modificaciones **(b)** *(to garment)* arreglo *m* **(c)** *(to building)* reformas *fpl*; **to have alterations done** hacer reformas

altercation [ɔːltəˈkeɪʃən] *n Formal* altercado *m*; **to have an a. with sb** tener *or* sufrir un altercado con alguien

altered [ˈɔːltəd] *adj* **he is greatly a.** está muy cambiado

alter ego [ˈæltəˈriːgəʊ] (*pl* **alter egos**) *n* álter ego *m*

alternate 1 *n* [ɔːlˈtɜːnət] *US (deputy)* sustituto(a) *m,f*
 2 *adj* **(a)** *(by turns)* alterno(a); **a. spells of good and bad weather** intervalos alternos de buen y mal tiempo **(b)** *(every second)* alterno(a); **on a. days** en días alternos, cada dos días **(c)** *Bot (leaves)* alterno(a) **(d)** *Geom* **a. angles** ángulos alternos **(e)** *US (alternative)* alternativo(a)
 3 *vt* [ˈɔːltəneɪt] alternar
 4 *vi* **(a)** *(happen by turns)* alternar (**with** con) **(b)** *(take turns)* **the two actors alternated in the leading role** los dos actores se alternaban para representar el papel protagonista **(c)** *(vary)* oscilar, fluctuar (**between** entre)

alternately [ɔːlˈtɜːnətlɪ] *adv (by turns)* alternativamente; **the film is a. comic and tragic** la película oscila entre la comedia y la tragedia

alternating [ˈɔːltəneɪtɪŋ] *adj* alterno(a) ►► *Elec* ***a. current*** corriente *f* alterna

alternation [ɔːltəˈneɪʃən] *n* alternancia *f*

alternative [ɔːlˈtɜːnətɪv] **1** *n (choice)* alternativa *f*; **there are alternatives to nuclear power** hay alternativas a la energía nuclear; **there is no a.** no hay alternativa; **what's the a.?** ¿cuál es la alternativa?; **she had no a. but to obey** no tenía más remedio que obedecer; **you leave me with no a.** no me dejas otra alternativa *or* opción
 2 *adj* **(a)** *(different) (plan, route)* alternativo(a); **an a. proposal** una alternativa; **to make a. arrangements** hacer otros planes
 (b) *(not traditional) (press, theatre, music)* alternativo(a) ►► ***a. comedy*** = forma de comedia que surgió en Gran Bretaña en los 80, que rechaza el sexismo y el racismo del humor tradicional; ***a. energy*** energía *f* alternativa; ***a. medicine*** medicina *f* alternativa

alternatively [ɔːlˈtɜːnətɪvlɪ] *adv (on the other hand)* si no; **a., we could go to the beach** si no, podríamos ir a la playa

alternator [ˈɔːltəneɪtə(r)] *n Elec* alternador *m*

although [ɔːlˈðəʊ] *conj* aunque; **a. old, the bike still runs perfectly** a pesar de ser vieja, la moto todavía funciona perfectamente; **I don't think it will work, a. it's worth a try** no creo que funcione, aunque merece la pena probar

altimeter [ˈæltɪmiːtə(r)] *n* altímetro *m*

altitude [ˈæltɪtjuːd] *n* altitud *f*; **at an a. of 8,000 metres** a una altitud de 8.000 metros ►► ***a. sickness*** mal *m* de altura, *Andes* soroche *m*

alto [ˈæltəʊ] *Mus* **1** *n* (*pl* **altos**) contralto *mf*
 2 *adj* contralto ►► ***a. saxophone*** *or Fam* ***sax*** saxo *m* alto

altocumulus [æltəʊˈkjuːmjʊləs] (*pl* **altocumuli** [æltəʊˈkjuːmjʊlaɪ]) *n Met* altocúmulo *m*

altogether [ɔːltəˈgeðə(r)] **1** *adv* **(a)** *(entirely)* completamente, enteramente; **he soon stopped going a.** pronto dejó de ir definitivamente; **it was a. different** era completamente diferente; **I was not a. pleased** no estaba contento del todo **(b)** *(in total)* en total **(c)** *(on the whole)* en general
 2 *n* IDIOM *Fam* **in the a.** *(naked)* como Dios lo trajo al mundo, en cueros, *Chile* pilucho(a), *Col* en bola, *RP* en bolas

altostratus [æltəʊˈstrɑːtəs] (*pl* **altostrati** [æltəʊˈstrɑːtaɪ]) *n Met* altostrato *m*

altruism [ˈæltrʊɪzəm] *n* altruismo *m*

altruist [ˈæltrʊɪst] *n* altruista *mf*

altruistic [æltrʊˈɪstɪk] *adj* altruista

ALU [eɪelˈjuː] *n Comptr* (*abbr* **Arithmetic Logic Unit**) UAL *f*

alum [ˈæləm] *n* alumbre *m*

aluminium [æljʊˈmɪnɪəm], *US* **aluminum** [əˈluːmɪnəm] *n Chem* aluminio *m* ►► ***a. foil*** papel *m* de aluminio *or* plata

alumna [əˈlʌmnə] (*pl* **alumnae** [əˈlʌmniː]) *n US* antigua alumna *f*

alumnus [əˈlʌmnəs] (*pl* **alumni** [əˈlʌmnaɪ]) *n US* antiguo alumno *m*

alveolar [ælvɪˈəʊlə(r)] *adj Anat & Ling* alveolar ►► ***a. ridge*** alveolos *mpl*

alveolus [ælvɪˈəʊləs] (*pl* **alveoli** [ælvɪˈəʊlaɪ]) *n Anat* alveolo *m*

always [ˈɔːlweɪz] *adv* siempre; **I can a. try** siempre puedo intentarlo; **she's a. complaining** siempre se está quejando; **if she won't do it, there's a. Jim** si ella no lo hace, siempre podemos recurrir a Jim

Alzheimer's [ˈæltshaɪməz] *n* **A. (disease)** (enfermedad *f* de) Alzheimer *m* ►► ***A. patient*** enfermo(a) *m,f* de Alzheimer

AM [ˈeɪˈem] *n Rad* (*abbr* **amplitude modulation**) AM, onda *f* media

am [æm] *1st person singular of* **be**

a.m. [ˈeɪˈem] *adv* (*abbr* **ante meridiem**) a.m., de la mañana; **5 a.m.** las 5 de la mañana

AMA [eɪemˈeɪ] *n* **(a)** (*abbr* **American Medical Association**) = colegio de médicos estadounidense **(b)** (*abbr* **American Marketing Association**) = asociación estadounidense de profesionales de márketing y ventas

amalgam [əˈmælgəm] *n* **(a)** *(mixture)* amalgama *f* **(b)** *(for teeth)* amalgama *f*

amalgamate [əˈmælgəmeɪt] **1** *vt* **(a)** *(metals, ideas)* amalgamar **(b)** *(companies)* fusionar
 2 *vi (companies)* unirse, fusionarse

amalgamation [əmælgəˈmeɪʃən] *n* **(a)** *(of ideas)* aglutinación *f* **(b)** *(of companies)* fusión *f*

amanuensis [əmænjʊˈensɪs] (*pl* **amanuenses** [əmænjʊˈensiːz]) *n Formal* amanuense *mf*

amaryllis [æməˈrɪlɪs] *n* amarilis *f*

amass [əˈmæs] *vt (wealth)* amasar; *(objects, information, evidence)* acumular, reunir

amateur [ˈæmətə(r)] **1** *n* **(a)** *(non-professional)* aficionado(a) *m,f*, amateur *mf* **(b)** *Pej* aficionado(a) *m,f*, amateur *mf*
 2 *adj* **(a)** *(painter, musician, sportsperson)* aficionado(a), amateur; *(competition)* de aficionados, amateur; **a. dramatics** teatro aficionado *or* amateur **(b)** *Pej (work, performance)* de aficionado, amateur; **it was a rather a. job** fue un trabajo chapucero *or* de aficionados

amateurish [ˈæməˈtɜːrɪʃ] *adj Pej* chapucero(a)

amateurism [ˈæmətərɪzəm] *n* **(a)** *Sport* amateurismo *m*; **a. prevailed until the 1950s** hasta los años 50, la norma era que los equipos fueran aficionados *or* amateurs **(b)** *Pej (of work, performance)* chapucería *f*

amatory [ˈæmətərɪ] *adj Literary* amatorio(a)

amaze [əˈmeɪz] *vt* asombrar, pasmar; **to be amazed at** *or* **by sth** quedarse atónito(a) *or* pasmado(a) ante algo; **he amazed his colleagues with his resourcefulness** dejó a sus compañeros atónitos *or* asombrados con su inventiva; *Ironic* **go on, a. me!** ¡a ver, sorpréndeme!

amazed [əˈmeɪzd] *adj (expression, look)* de asombro; **he seemed a. to see her** pareció muy asombrado de verla

amazement [əˈmeɪzmənt] *n* asombro *m*, estupefacción *f*; **she watched in a.** miró asombrada; **to our a., he agreed** para sorpresa nuestra, accedió

amazing [əˈmeɪzɪŋ] *adj* **(a)** *(surprising)* asombroso(a), extraordinario(a); **it's a. that no one was hurt** es increíble que nadie resultara herido; **that's a.!** ¡es increíble!, ¡es asombroso! **(b)** *(excellent)* genial, extraordinario(a)

amazingly [əˈmeɪzɪŋlɪ] *adv (extremely)* increíblemente, extraordinariamente; **he's a. patient** tiene una paciencia extraordinaria; **they finished in an a. short time** terminaron increíblemente rápido; **a. (enough)** increíblemente, por extraño que parezca

Amazon [ˈæməzən] *n* **(a) the A.** *(river)* el Amazonas; *(region)* la Amazonia **(b)** *(female warrior, athletic woman)* amazona *f*

Amazonian [æməˈzəʊnɪən] *adj* amazónico(a)

ambassador [æmˈbæsədə(r)] *n* embajador(ora) *m,f*; **the Spanish a. to Morocco** el embajador de España en Marruecos

ambassador-at-large [æmˈbæsədərətˈlɑːdʒ] (*pl* **ambassadors-at-large**) *n US* embajador(ora) *m,f* extraordinario(a)

ambassadorial [æmbæsəˈdɔːrɪəl] *adj* de embajador; **the a. residence** la residencia del embajador

ambassadorship [æmˈbæsədəʃɪp] *n* embajada *f*

amber [ˈæmbə(r)] **1** *n* ámbar *m*
 2 *adj* **(a)** *(necklace, ring)* de ámbar **(b)** *(dress)* ámbar; *(eyes)* ambarino(a) ►► *Br* ***a. light*** semáforo *m* en ámbar

ambergris [ˈæmbəgriːs] *n* ámbar *m* gris

ambiance = **ambience**

ambidextrous [æmbɪˈdekstrəs] *adj* ambidextro(a), ambidiestro(a)

ambience, ambiance [ˈæmbɪəns] *n* ambiente *m*

ambient [ˈæmbɪənt] *adj (temperature)* ambiente, ambiental; *(noise, lighting)* ambiental

ambiguity [æmbɪˈgjuːɪtɪ] *n* ambigüedad *f*; **to avoid any a.** para evitar ambigüedades

ambiguous [æmˈbɪgjʊəs] *adj* ambiguo(a)

ambiguously [æmˈbɪgjʊəslɪ] *adv* ambiguamente, con ambigüedad

ambiguousness [æm'bɪgjʊəsnɪs] *n* ambigüedad *f*

ambit ['æmbɪt] *n Formal* ámbito *m*

ambition [æm'bɪʃən] *n* ambición *f*; **her a. was to become a physicist** su ambición era ser física; **to lack a.** carecer de ambición; **my parents had great ambitions for me** mis padres ambicionaban grandes cosas para mí

ambitious [æm'bɪʃəs] *adj (person, plan)* ambicioso(a); **it's a bit a. for our first attempt** es demasiado ambicioso para un primer intento; **you should try to be more a.** deberías tratar de ser más ambicioso; **they're a. for their children** tienen grandes ambiciones para sus hijos; **our holidays are usually nothing more a. than a week at the beach** nuestras vacaciones suelen consistir en una simple semana en la playa

ambitiously [æm'bɪʃəslɪ] *adv* ambiciosamente; **they started out a.** empezaron con mucha ambición

ambitiousness [æm'bɪʃəsnɪs] *n (of person, plan)* ambición *f*

ambivalence [æm'bɪvələns] *n* ambivalencia *f* (**about** *or* **towards** respecto a)

ambivalent [æm'bɪvələnt] *adj* ambivalente (**about** *or* **towards** respecto a); **to be** *or* **feel a. about sth/sb** no estar muy seguro de lo que se piensa de algo/alguien, ser ambivalente con respecto a algo/alguien

amble ['æmbəl] **1** *n* paseo *m*; **to walk at an a.** caminar despacio *or* sin prisa

2 *vi* (**a**) *(person)* caminar tranquilamente; **she whistled as she ambled along** silbaba mientras caminaba sin prisa; **he just ambles in at 10.15** llega a las diez y cuarto como si tal cosa (**b**) *(horse)* amblar

ambling ['æmblɪŋ] *adj* **with an a. gait** con paso despreocupado

ambrosia [æm'brəʊzɪə] *n* ambrosía *f*

ambulance ['æmbjʊləns] *n* ambulancia *f* ►► *US Pej* ***a. chaser*** = abogado que busca a víctimas de accidentes para poner juicios a los responsables con el objeto de obtener lucrativas indemnizaciones; ***a. man*** hombre *m* de la ambulancia, ambulanciero *m*; ***a. woman*** mujer *f* de la ambulancia, ambulanciera *f*

ambulatory ['æmbjʊlətərɪ] **1** *n Archit* deambulatorio *m*, girola *f*

2 *adj (patient)* ambulatorio(a)

ambush ['æmbʊʃ] **1** *n* emboscada *f*; **to lay** *or* **set an a. for sb** preparar *or* tender una emboscada a alguien; **to lie** *or* **wait in a. for sb** acechar a alguien *(para atacarlo)*

2 *vt* tender una emboscada a; **they were ambushed by the press as they left the airport** la prensa saltó sobre ellos cuando salían del aeropuerto

ameba, amebic *US* = **amoeba, amoebic**

ameliorate [ə'mi:ljəreɪt] *Formal* **1** *vt* mejorar

2 *vi* mejorar

amelioration [əmi:ljə'reɪʃən] *n Formal* mejoramiento *m*, mejora *f*

amen [ɑ:'men] *exclam* (**a**) *Rel* amén (**b**) *Fam* **a. to that!** ¡por supuesto!, *Esp* ¡descarado!

amenable [ə'mi:nəbəl] *adj* (**a**) *(co-operative)* receptivo(a); **to be a. to reason** atender a razones; **to prove a. to a suggestion** acoger bien una sugerencia; **the disease is a. to treatment** la enfermedad responde bien al tratamiento (**b**) *(accountable)* responsable (**to** ante)

amend [ə'mend] *vt* (**a**) *(change) (text, law, constitution)* enmendar, modificar; *(plans, schedule)* modificar (**b**) *(correct) (error)* corregir (**c**) *(improve) (behaviour, habits)* enmendar

amendment [ə'mendmənt] *n* (**a**) *(to text, law, constitution)* enmienda *f* (**to** a), modificación *f* (**to** de); *(to plans, schedule)* modificación *f*; *Pol* **to move an a. (to a bill)** proponer una enmienda (a un proyecto de ley) (**b**) *(of error)* corrección *f* (**c**) *(in behaviour, habits)* enmienda *f*, mejoría *f*

amends [ə'mendz] *npl* **to make a. (for sth)** compensar (algo); **to make a. to sb for sth** resarcir a alguien por *or* de algo

amenity [ə'mi:nɪtɪ] *n (facility, service)* servicio *m*; **amenities** comodidades *fpl*, servicios *mpl*; **the project should cause no loss of a. to local residents** el proyecto no debería causar ningún perjuicio a los residentes

> **False friend**: The Spanish noun **amenidad** is not a translation for the English word **amenity**. In Spanish **amenidad** means "entertaining qualities" or "pleasantness".

amenorrhoea, *US* **amenorrhea** [əmenə'rɪə] *n Med* amenorrea *f*

America [ə'merɪkə] *n* (**a**) *(United States)* Estados Unidos (**b**) *(continent)* América; **the Americas** América ►► ***the A.'s Cup*** *(in sailing)* la Copa del América

American [ə'merɪkən] **1** *n* (**a**) *(from USA)* estadounidense *mf*, americano(a) *m,f* (**b**) *(from continent)* americano(a) *m,f*

2 *adj* (**a**) *(of USA)* estadounidense, americano(a) ►► ***the A. Civil War*** la Guerra Civil *or* de Secesión americana; ***the A. Dream*** el sueño americano; ***A. eagle*** *(bald eagle)* pigargo *m* cabeciblanco, águila *f* cabeciblanca; *(symbol of USA)* águila *f* americana; ***A. football*** fútbol *m* americano; *US* ***A. plan:*** **on the A. plan** a pensión completa

(**b**) *(of continent)* americano(a) ►► ***A. bittern*** avetoro *m* lentiginoso; ***A. coot*** focha *f* americana; ***A. crow*** corneja *f* americana; ***A. golden plover*** chorlito *m* dorado chico; ***A. Indian*** amerindio(a) *m,f*; ***A. kestrel*** cernícalo *m* americano; ***A. redstart*** colirrojo *m* americano; ***A. tree sparrow*** pinzón *m* americano; ***A. wigeon*** ánade *m* silbón americano, pato *m* chalcuán

Americana [əmerɪ'kɑ:nə] *npl* = antiguedades y curiosidades procedentes de Norteamérica, especialmente de la época colonial

Americanism [ə'merɪkənɪzəm] *n* americanismo *m*

Americanization [əmerɪkənaɪ'zeɪʃen] *n* americanización *f*

americium [æmə'rɪsɪəm] *n Chem* americio *m*

Amerindian [æmə'rɪndɪən], **Amerind** ['æmərɪnd] **1** *n* amerindio(a) *m,f*

2 *adj* amerindio(a)

amethyst ['æmɪθɪst] **1** *n* (**a**) *(stone)* amatista *f* (**b**) *(colour)* (color *m*) amatista *m*

2 *adj* (**a**) *(necklace, ring)* de amatistas (**b**) *(eyes)* color amatista

Amex ['æmeks] *n* (**a**) (*abbr* **American Stock Exchange**) Amex *m* (**b**) (*abbr* **American Express**®) = American Express

AM/FM ['eɪem'efem] *n Rad* (*abbr* **amplitude modulation/frequency modulation**) AM/FM

amiability [eɪmɪə'bɪlɪtɪ] *n* afabilidad *f*, amabilidad *f*

amiable ['eɪmɪəbəl] *adj* afable, amable

amiably ['eɪmɪəblɪ] *adv* agradablemente, amablemente

amicable ['æmɪkəbəl] *adj (relationship, agreement)* amistoso(a), amigable; **an a. divorce** un divorcio amistoso; **an a. separation** una separación amistosa; **to settle a dispute in an a. way** resolver una disputa de una manera amistosa

amicably ['æmɪkəblɪ] *adv* amistosamente

amid [ə'mɪd], **amidst** [ə'mɪdst] *prep* entre, en medio de

amide ['æmaɪd] *n Chem* amida *f*

amidships [ə'mɪdʃɪps] *adv* en medio del barco, en mitad del barco

amidst = **amid**

amine ['æmi:n] *n Chem* amina *f*

amino acid [ə'mi:nəʊ'æsɪd] *n Biol* aminoácido *m*

amiss [ə'mɪs] **1** *adj* **there's something a.** algo va mal; **there's something a. with our calculations** algo falla en nuestros cálculos; **have I said something a.?** ¿he dicho algo que no debía?

2 *adv* **to take sth a.** tomarse algo a mal; **a cup of coffee wouldn't go a.** no vendría mal un café

amity ['æmɪtɪ] *n Formal (friendship, good relations)* cordialidad *f*, armonía *f*

ammeter ['æmi:tə(r)] *n Elec* amperímetro *m*

ammo ['æməʊ] *n Fam* munición *f*, municiones *fpl*

ammonia [ə'məʊnɪə] *n* amoniaco *m*

ammonite ['æmənaɪt] *n (mollusc, fossil)* ammonites *m inv*

ammonium [ə'məʊnɪəm] *n* amonio *m* ►► ***a. sulphate*** sulfato *m* amónico

ammunition [æmjʊ'nɪʃən] *n* (**a**) *(for guns)* munición *f* ►► ***a. belt*** *(for machine-gun)* cinta *f* de municiones; *(round waist, over shoulder)* canana *f*; ***a. box*** caja *f* de munición; ***a. dump*** depósito *m* de municiones (**b**) *(in debate, argument)* argumentos *mpl*; **the letter could be used as a. against them** los contenidos de la carta podría usarse como argumento en contra de ellos

amnesia [æm'ni:zɪə] *n Med* amnesia *f*; **to suffer from** *or* **have a.** tener amnesia

amnesiac [æm'ni:zɪæk], **amnesic** [æm'ni:zɪk] **1** *n* amnésico(a) *m,f*

2 *adj* amnésico(a)

amnesty ['æmnəstɪ] *n* amnistía *f*; **to declare an a.** declarar una amnistía; **under an a.** bajo una amnistía

amniocentesis [æmnɪəʊsen'ti:sɪs] *n Med* amniocentesis *f*

amnion ['æmnɪən] *n Anat* amnios *m*

amniotic [æmnɪ'ɒtɪk] *adj* amniótico(a) ►► ***a. fluid*** líquido *m* amniótico; ***a. sac*** bolsa *f* de aguas

amoeba, *US* **ameba** [ə'mi:bə] *n* ameba *f*

amoebic, *US* **amebic** [ə'mi:bɪk] *adj* amebiano(a) ►► ***a. dysentery*** disentería *f* amebiana

amok [ə'mɒk], **amuck** [ə'mʌk] *adv* **the demonstrators ran a. through the town** los manifestantes se descontrolaron y recorrieron la ciudad destrozando todo a su paso; **a gunman ran a.** un hombre perturbado disparó indiscriminadamente contra la multitud

among [ə'mʌŋ], **amongst** [ə'mʌŋst] *prep* (**a**) *(in the midst of)* entre; **it was found a. the rubble** lo encontraron entre los escombros; **we are a. friends** estamos entre amigos; **a. the best** entre los mejores; **several members abstained, myself a. them** varios miembros se abstuvieron y yo fui uno de ellos; **a. other things** entre otras cosas; **they quarrel a. themselves** se pelean entre ellos
(**b**) *(to each of)* entre; **the money was divided a. them** se repartió el dinero entre ellos

amoral [eɪ'mɒrəl] *adj* amoral

amorality [eɪmɒ'rælətɪ] *n* amoralidad *f*

amorous ['æmərəs] *adj* apasionado(a); **to make a. advances (towards sb)** hacer la corte (a alguien); **she was of an a. disposition** era muy apasionada

amorphous [ə'mɔ:fəs] *adj* (**a**) *(formless)* amorfo(a) (**b**) *Chem & Geol* amorfo(a)

amortization [æmɔ:taɪ'zeɪʃən] *n Fin (of debt, asset)* amortización *f*

amortize ['æmɔ:taɪz] *vt Fin (debt, asset)* amortizar

amount [ə'maʊnt] *n* (**a**) *(quantity)* cantidad *f*; **a certain a. of discomfort** una cierta incomodidad; **huge amounts of time and effort** enormes cantidades de tiempo y trabajo; **there are any a. of options** no faltan opciones; **no a. of talking will change the situation** por mucho que hablemos, la situación no va a cambiar; **no a. of money would persuade me to do it** no lo haría ni por todo el oro del mundo
(**b**) *(sum, total)* total *f*; *(of money)* importe *m*, monto *m*; **do you have the exact a.?** ¿tienes la cantidad exacta?; **a cheque to the a. of $100** un cheque de *or* por 100 dólares; **a. due** *(on invoice)* importe debido

► **amount to** *vt insep* (**a**) *(add up to)* ascender a; **her debts a. to £700** sus deudas ascienden a 700 libras; **the savings don't a. to much** los ahorros no son gran cosa
(**b**) *(mean)* **it amounts to the same thing** viene a ser lo mismo, equivale a lo mismo; **what his speech amounts to is an attack on democracy** su discurso viene a ser un ataque a la democracia; **he'll never a. to much** *or* **anything** nunca llegará a nada

amour [ə'mʊə(r)] *n Literary or Hum* affaire *m*

amp [æmp] *n* (**a**) *Elec (unit)* amperio *m*; **a 13-a. plug** un enchufe (con fusible) de 13 amperios (**b**) *Fam (amplifier)* amplificador *m*

amperage ['æmpərɪdʒ] *n* amperaje *m*

ampere ['æmpeə(r)] *n Elec* amperio *m*

ampersand ['æmpəsænd] *n Typ* = signo "&"

amphetamine [æm'fetəmɪn] *n* anfetamina *f*

amphibian [æm'fɪbɪən] **1** *n* (**a**) *(animal)* anfibio *m* (**b**) *(plane)* avión *m* anfibio (**c**) *(vehicle)* vehículo *m* anfibio
2 *adj* anfibio(a)

amphibious [æm'fɪbɪəs] *adj* (**a**) *(animal)* anfibio(a) (**b**) *(plane)* anfibio(a) (**c**) *(vehicle, invasion)* anfibio(a); *Mil* **a. assault** asalto anfibio

amphitheatre, *US* **amphitheater** ['æmfɪθɪətə(r)] *n* anfiteatro *m*

amphora ['æmfərə] (*pl* **amphorae** ['æmfəri:] *or* **amphoras**) *n* ánfora *f*

ample ['æmpəl] *adj* (**a**) *(large) (garment)* amplio(a); *(bosom, proportions)* abundante
(**b**) *(more than sufficient)* de sobra, abundante; **this will be a.** esto será más que suficiente; **you were given a. warning** has tenido tiempo más que suficiente; **we have a. reason to suspect foul play** tenemos razones más que suficientes para sospechar que ha habido juego sucio; **to have a. time/opportunity to do sth** tener tiempo/ocasiones de sobra para hacer algo

amplification [æmplɪfɪ'keɪʃən] *n* (**a**) *(of sound)* amplificación *f* (**b**) *(of remarks, idea)* ampliación *f*

amplifier ['æmplɪfaɪə(r)] *n* amplificador *m*

amplify ['æmplɪfaɪ] *vt* (**a**) *(current, volume)* amplificar (**b**) *(remarks, idea)* ampliar

► **amplify on** *vt insep* ampliar

amplitude ['æmplɪtju:d] *n* (**a**) *Phys (of wave, signal)* amplitud *f* ►► *Rad* ***a. modulation*** modulación *f* de la amplitud (**b**) *Formal (breadth, scope)* amplitud *f*

amply ['æmplɪ] *adv* (**a**) *(on a large scale)* abundantemente; **a. proportioned** *(room, house)* amplio(a); *Euph (person)* de generosas proporciones (**b**) *(more than sufficiently)* ampliamente; **you will be a. rewarded** se te recompensará ampliamente; **as has been a. shown** tal y como ha quedado ampliamente demostrado

ampoule, *US* **ampule** ['æmpu:l] *n* ampolla *f*

amputate ['æmpjʊteɪt] **1** *vt* amputar
2 *vi* amputar

amputation [æmpjʊ'teɪʃən] *n* amputación *f*

amputee [æmpjʊ'ti:] *n* amputado(a) *m,f*

Amsterdam ['æmstədæm] *n* Amsterdam

Amtrak ['æmtræk] *n* = compañía ferroviaria estadounidense

amuck = **amok**

amulet ['æmjʊlɪt] *n* amuleto *m*

amuse [ə'mju:z] *vt* (**a**) *(make laugh, entertain)* divertir (**b**) *(occupy)* distraer, entretener; **to a. oneself by doing sth** distraerse haciendo algo; **you'll have to a. yourself this afternoon** tendrás que entretenerte solo esta tarde

amused [ə'mju:zd] *adj* (**a**) *(delighted, entertained)* divertido(a); **they were a. at** *or* **by his antics** sus payasadas les hicieron gracia; **I was (greatly** *or* **highly) a. to hear that...** me hizo (muchísima) gracia oír que...; **she was not (at all) a.** no le hizo ninguna gracia; *Hum* **we are not a.** no me hace ni pizca de gracia
(**b**) *(occupied)* entretenido(a), distraído(a); **to keep oneself a.** entretenerse, distraerse; **to keep sb a.** entretener a *or* distraer a alguien

amusedly [ə'mju:zɪdlɪ] *adv* **he watched them a.** los miraba divertido

amusement [ə'mju:zmənt] *n* (**a**) *(enjoyment)* diversión *f*; **to watch/smile in a.** mirar/sonreír divertido(a); **much to everyone's a.** para regocijo *or* diversión de todos; **for my own a.** como pasatiempo
(**b**) *(pastime)* distracción *f*, entretenimiento *m*
(**c**) *(at funfair)* atracción *f*; **to go on the amusements** subirse en *or* a las atracciones ►► ***a. arcade*** salón *m* recreativo; ***a. park*** parque *m* de atracciones

amusing [ə'mju:zɪŋ] *adj* divertido(a); **I didn't find it in the least a.** no me hizo ninguna gracia; *Ironic* **very a.!** ¡muy gracioso!

amusingly [ə'mju:zɪŋlɪ] *adv* graciosamente; **a song a. entitled...** una canción con el gracioso título de...

amyl ['æmɪl] *n* amilo *m* ►► ***a. nitrite*** nitrito *m* amílico

an [æn] *see* **a**[2]

Anabaptist [ænə'bæptɪst] **1** *n* anabaptista *mf*
2 *adj* anabaptista

anabolic [ænə'bɒlɪk] *adj* anabólico(a) ►► ***a. steroid*** (esteroide *m*) anabolizante *m*

anachronism [ə'nækrənɪzəm] *n* anacronismo *m*

anachronistic [ənækrə'nɪstɪk] *adj* anacrónico(a)

anaconda [ænə'kɒndə] *n* anaconda *f*

anaemia, *US* **anemia** [ə'ni:mɪə] *n* anemia *f*; **to suffer from a.** tener anemia

anaemic, *US* **anemic** [ə'ni:mɪk] *adj* (**a**) *Med* anémico(a) (**b**) *(weak)* pobre; **an a. voice** una voz débil

anaerobic [ænə'rəʊbɪk] *adj Biol (organism, respiration)* anaerobio(a)

anaesthesia, *US* **anesthesia** [ænəs'θi:zɪə] *n* anestesia *f*

anaesthetic, *US* **anesthetic** [ænəs'θetɪk] *n* anestesia *f*, anestésico *m*; **under a.** bajo (los efectos de la) anestesia; **local/general a.** anestesia local/general

anaesthetist, *US* **anesthetist** [ə'ni:sθətɪst] *n* (**a**) *Br (doctor)* anestesista *mf* (**b**) *US (nurse)* enfermero(a) anestesista

anaesthetize, *US* **anesthetize** [ə'ni:sθətaɪz] *vt* (**a**) *Med* anestesiar (**b**) *(make insensitive)* insensibilizar

anagram ['ænəgræm] *n* anagrama *m*

anal ['eɪnəl] *adj* (**a**) *Anat* anal ►► ***a. fin*** aleta *f* anal (**b**) *Psy (stage)* anal; *(personality)* obsesivo(a) (**c**) *Fam* **he's so a.!** ¡es un maniático *or* quisquilloso!

analgesia [ænəl'dʒi:zɪə] *n* analgesia *f*

analgesic [ænəl'dʒi:zɪk] **1** *n* analgésico *m*
2 *adj* analgésico(a)

analog *US* = **analogue**

analogic(al) [ænə'lɒdʒɪk(əl)] *adj* analógico(a)

analogous [ə'næləgəs] *adj* análogo(a) (**to** *or* **with** a)

analogously [ə'næləgəslɪ] *adv* análogamente

analogue, *US* **analog** ['ænəlɒg] **1** *n* equivalente *m*
2 *adj* analógico(a) ►► ***a. clock*** reloj *m* analógico; ***a. computer*** *Esp* ordenador *m or Am* computador *m* analógico; ***a. watch*** reloj *m* analógico

analogy [ə'nælədʒɪ] *n* analogía *f*; **to draw an a. between two things** establecer una analogía entre dos cosas; **by a. (with)** por analogía (con)

analysable, *US* **analyzable** ['ænəlaɪzəbəl] *adj* analizable; **the sentence is a. in two different ways** la frase se puede analizar de dos maneras distintas

analysand [ə'nælɪsænd] *n Psy* sujeto *m* analizado, sujeto *m* psicoanalizado

analyse, *US* **analyze** ['ænəlaɪz] *vt* **(a)** *(examine, interpret)* analizar **(b)** *Ling (sentence)* analizar **(c)** *Psy* psicoanalizar

analysis [ə'næləsɪs] (*pl* **analyses** [ə'næləsi:z]) *n* **(a)** *(examination, interpretation)* análisis *m inv*; **to subject sth to a.** someter a algo a un análisis; **to hold up under** *or* **withstand a.** sostenerse ante un análisis; **in the final** *or* **last a.** a fin de cuentas **(b)** *Ling (sentence)* análisis *m inv* **(c)** *Psy* psicoanálisis *m inv*; **to be in a.** estar psicoanalizándose

analyst ['ænəlɪst] *n* **(a)** *(specialist)* analista *mf* **(b)** *Psy* psicoanalista *mf*

analytic(al) [ænə'lɪtɪk(əl)] *adj* analítico(a)

analyze *US* = **analyse**

anapaest ['ænəpi:st] *n Lit* anapesto *m*

anaphora [ə'næfərə] *n Ling* anáfora *f*

anaphoric [ænə'fɒrɪk] *adj Ling* anafórico(a)

anaphylactic [ænəfə'læktɪk] *adj Med* anafiláctico(a); **a. shock** shock *or* choque anafiláctico

anarchic [ə'nɑ:kɪk] *adj* anárquico(a)

anarchically [ə'nɑ:kɪklɪ] *adv* anárquicamente

anarchism ['ænəkɪzəm] *n* anarquismo *m*

anarchist ['ænəkɪst] *n* anarquista *mf*

anarchistic [ænə'kɪstɪk] *adj* anarquista

anarcho-syndicalism [æ'nɑ:kəʊ'sɪndɪkəlɪzəm] *n Pol* anarcosindicalismo *m*

anarcho-syndicalist [æ'nɑ:kəʊ'sɪndɪkəlɪst] *Pol* **1** *n* anarcosindicalista *mf*
2 *adj* anarcosindicalista

anarchy ['ænəkɪ] *n* anarquía *f*; **to descend/collapse into a.** caer/hundirse en la anarquía

anathema [ə'næθəmə] *n* **(a)** *(repellent)* **the very idea was a. to her** la sola idea le resultaba repugnante **(b)** *Rel* anatema *m*

anatomical [ænə'tɒmɪkəl] *adj* anatómico(a)

anatomically [ænə'tɒmɪklɪ] *adv* anatómicamente; **a. correct** *(doll, model)* anatómicamente realista

anatomist [ə'nætəmɪst] *n* anatomista *mf*

anatomy [ə'nætəmɪ] *n* **(a)** *(science)* anatomía *f* **(b)** *Hum (body)* anatomía *f*; **every part of his a. hurt** le dolía cada pedacito de su anatomía **(c)** *(analysis) (of crisis, social phenomenon)* análisis *m*

ANC [eɪen'si:] *n* (*abbr* **African National Congress**) ANC *m*, Congreso *m* Nacional Africano

ancestor ['ænsestə(r)] *n* **(a)** *(forefather)* antepasado(a) *m,f* **(b)** *(of computer, system)* antepasado(a) *m,f*

ancestral [æn'sestrəl] *adj* de los antepasados ►► ***a. home*** casa *f* solariega

ancestry ['ænsestrɪ] *n (descent)* linaje *m*, abolengo *m*; **of Spanish/Danish a.** de ascendencia española/danesa, descendiente de españoles/daneses; **to trace one's a.** hacerse el árbol genealógico; **this custom is of more recent a.** esta costumbre es más reciente

anchor ['æŋkə(r)] **1** *n* **(a)** *Naut* ancla *f*; **at a.** fondeado(a), anclado(a); **to drop** *or* **cast a.** echar el ancla, fondear; **to lie** *or* **ride at a.** estar anclado(a); **to weigh a.** levar anclas
(b) *(mainstay, support)* áncora *f* (de salvación); **he needed the a. of family life** necesitaba el áncora de salvación de la vida familiar ►► *US* ***a. store*** tienda *f* ancla, = tienda que atrae a más clientes en un centro comercial
(c) *Sport (in relay team)* último(a) relevista *mf*
(d) *(on radio, TV programme)* presentador(ora) *m,f*, locutor(ora) *m,f*
(e) *Comptr (on web page)* anclaje *m*
2 *vt* **(a)** *Naut* fondear, anclar **(b)** *(fix securely)* sujetar, anclar (**to** a) **(c)** *(radio, TV programme)* presentar
3 *vi Naut* fondear, anclar

anchorage ['æŋkərɪdʒ] *n* **(a)** *(place)* fondeadero *m* **(b)** *(charge)* anclaje *m* **(c)** *(fastening)* anclaje *m*

anchorman ['æŋkəmən] *n* **(a)** *(in radio, TV programme)* presentador *m*, locutor *m* **(b)** *Sport* último relevista *m*

anchorwoman ['æŋkəwʊmən] *n* **(a)** *(in radio, TV programme)* presentadora *f*, locutora *f* **(b)** *Sport* última relevista *f*

anchovy [*Br* 'æntʃəvɪ, *US* æn'tʃəʊvɪ] *n (live, pickled)* boquerón *m*; *(salted)* anchoa *f*

ancient ['eɪnʃənt] **1** *n* **the ancients** los antiguos
2 *adj* **(a)** *(custom, ruins, civilization)* antiguo(a); **in a. times** en la edad antigua, en el pasado remoto ►► ***a. history*** historia *f* antigua; IDIOM **that's a. history** eso pasó a la historia; ***A. Rome*** la antigua Roma **(b)** *Fam (car, clothes)* vetusto(a); **he's forty? that's a.!** ¿cuarenta años? ¡qué carroza!

ancillary [æn'sɪlərɪ] **1** *adj* **(a)** *(staff, workers)* auxiliar **(b)** *(subsidiary) (reason, advantage, cost)* secundario(a); **to be a. to** estar subordinado(a) a
2 *n* **(a)** *(helper)* auxiliar *mf* **(b)** *(of firm)* (empresa *f*) subsidiaria *f*

AND [ænd, *unstressed* ənd, ən] *conj* **(a)** *(in general)* y; *(before "h", "hi")* e; **she can read a. write** sabe leer y escribir; **father a. son** padre e hijo; **my father a. brother** mi padre y mi hermano; **chicken a. chips** pollo con *Esp* patatas *or Am* papas fritas; **rum a. raisin** ron con pasas; **go a. look for it** ve a buscarlo; **come a. see me** ven a verme; **try a. help me** intenta ayudarme; **wait a. see** espera a ver; **nice a. warm** bien calentito(a); **they will receive money a./or food** recibirán dinero o alimentos o ambos, recibirán dinero y/o alimentos; **do that again a. I'll hit you!** como hagas eso otra vez, te pego
(b) *(in numbers)* **two hundred a. two** doscientos dos; **four a. a half** cuatro y medio; **two a. a quarter percent** *(written)* 2,25 por ciento; *(spoken)* dos coma veinticinco por ciento; **an hour a. twenty minutes** una hora y veinte minutos; **four a. five make nine** cuatro y cinco, nueve
(c) *(expressing repetition)* **hours a. hours** horas y horas; **better a. better** cada vez mejor; **she talked a. talked** no paraba de hablar; **you just moan a. moan** no haces más que quejarte
(d) *(introducing a statement or question)* **a. now, the weather** y ahora, el tiempo; **John rang me – a. who's he?** me llamó John – ¿y quién es John?
(e) *Fam (so what?)* **I've read all the works of Shakespeare – a.?** he leído todas las obras de Shakespeare – ¿y?
(f) a. so on (a. so forth) etcétera, etcétera

Andalusia [ændə'lu:sɪə] *n* Andalucía

Andalusian [ændə'lu:sɪən] **1** *n* andaluz(uza) *m,f*
2 *adj* andaluz(uza)

andante [æn'dænteɪ] *Mus* **1** *n* andante *m*
2 *adv* andante

Andean ['ændɪən] *adj* andino(a)

Andes ['ændi:z] *npl* **the A.** los Andes

Andorra [æn'dɔ:rə] *n* Andorra

Andorran [æn'dɔ:rən] **1** *n* andorrano(a) *m,f*
2 *adj* andorrano(a)

Andrew ['ændru:] *pr n* **Saint A.** San Andrés

androgen ['ændrədʒən] *n Physiol* andrógeno *m*

androgynous [æn'drɒdʒɪnəs] *adj* **(a)** *Biol* hermafrodita, andrógino(a) **(b)** *Fig (person, appearance)* andrógino(a)

android ['ændrɔɪd] *n* androide *m*

Andromeda [æn'drɒmɪdə] *n* Andrómeda *f*

anecdotal [ænɪk'dəʊtəl] *adj* anecdótico(a); **a. evidence** pruebas anecdóticas

anecdote ['ænɪkdəʊt] *n* anécdota *f*

anemia, anemic *US* = **anaemia, anaemic**

anemometer [ænə'mɒmɪtə(r)] *n* anemómetro *m*

anemone [ə'nemənɪ] *n* **(a)** *(flower)* anémona *f* **(b)** ***sea a.*** anémona *f* de mar

aneroid ['ænərɔɪd] *n Met* **a. (barometer)** barómetro *m* aneroide

anesthesia, anesthetic *etc US* = **anaesthesia, anaesthetic** *etc*

anesthesiologist [ænəsθi:zɪ'ɒlədʒɪst] *n US* anestesista *mf*

aneurysm, aneurism ['ænjərɪzəm] *n Med* aneurisma *m*

anew [ə'nju:] *adv* de nuevo; **to begin a.** comenzar de nuevo

angel ['eɪndʒəl] *n* **(a)** *Rel* ángel *m*; **an a. of mercy** un ángel misericordioso; **the A. of Darkness** el Ángel de las Tinieblas; IDIOM **to be on the side of the angels** ser de los buenos
(b) *Fam (darling)* **you're an a.!** ¡eres un ángel *or* un sol!; **be an a. and fetch me a glass of water** anda, sé bueno y tráeme un vaso de agua
(c) *Culin US* ***a. (food) cake*** = bizcocho ligero elaborado con claras

de huevo; ***angels on horseback*** = ostras envueltas en tocino y asadas a la parrilla
(**d**) *Fam* ***a. dust*** polvo *m* de ángel

Angeleno [ændʒə'li:nəʊ] (*pl* **Angelenos**) *n* angelino(a) *m,f*

angelfish ['eɪndʒəlfɪʃ] *n* (**a**) *(saltwater fish)* chiribico *m* (**b**) *(freshwater fish)* escalar *m* (**c**) *(shark)* angelote *m*

angelic [æn'dʒelɪk] *adj* angelical; **the children have been a.** los niños se han comportado como angelitos

angelica [æn'dʒelɪkə] *n* (**a**) *(plant)* angélica *f* (**b**) *(for decorating cakes)* = tallos de angélica escarchados que se emplean para decorar pasteles

angelically [æn'dʒelɪklɪ] *adv* angelicalmente; **to behave a.** comportarse como un ángel

angelus ['ændʒələs] *n* (**a**) *(prayer)* ángelus *m* (**b**) *(bell)* ángelus *m*

anger ['æŋgə(r)] **1** *n* ira *f*, *esp Esp* enfado *m*, *esp Am* enojo *m*; **a fit of a.** un ataque de ira; **to speak in a.** hablar con ira
2 *vt esp Esp* enfadar, *esp Am* enojar; **to be easily angered** *esp Esp* enfadarse *or esp Am* enojarse con facilidad
3 *vi* **to be slow to a.** tardar en *esp Esp* enfadarse *or esp Am* enojarse; **to be quick to a., to be easily angered** *esp Esp* enfadarse *or esp Am* enojarse con facilidad

angina [æn'dʒaɪnə] *n Med* **a. (pectoris)** angina *f* (de pecho)

angiosperm ['ændʒɪəʊspɜ:m] *n Bot* angiosperma *f*

Angle ['æŋgəl] *n* anglo(a) *m,f*

angle ['æŋgəl] **1** *n* (**a**) *Math* ángulo *m*; **an a. of 90°, a 90° a.** un ángulo de 90°; **at an a. of...** con un ángulo de...; **she wore her hat at an a.** llevaba el sombrero ladeado; **to cut sth at an a.** cortar algo diagonalmente ▸▸ ***a. of approach*** *(of plane)* ángulo *m* de aproximación
(**b**) *(corner)* ángulo *m*, esquina *f*
(**c**) *Phys* ***a. of incidence*** ángulo *m* de incidencia; ***a. of reflection*** ángulo *m* de reflexión; ***a. of refraction*** ángulo *m* de refracción
(**d**) *(viewpoint)* ángulo *m*, punto *m* de vista; **seen from this a.** visto(a) desde este ángulo; **he examined the issue from all angles** examinó el asunto desde todos los ángulos; **we need a new a. on this story** necesitamos dar un nuevo enfoque a esta historia
(**e**) ***a. bracket*** *(for shelving)* escuadra *f* (en ángulo); *Typ* paréntesis *m* angular
(**f**) *Fam (trick)* **she knows all the angles** se las sabe todas
(**g**) *Fam (motive)* **what's his a. in all this?** ¿qué pretende sacar él de todo esto?
2 *vt* (**a**) *(direct, aim)* orientar; **to a. a shot** *(in tennis)* cruzar un golpe; *(in soccer)* cruzar un tiro *or* chute (**b**) *(slant)* inclinar; **the programme is angled towards the youth market** el programa está dirigido *or* orientado principalmente al público juvenil
3 *vi* (**a**) *(slant)* inclinarse; **the road angles (off) to the right** la carretera se desvía hacia la derecha (**b**) *(fish)* pescar con caña (**c**) *Fam* **to a. for an invitation** ir a la caza *or CSur* la pesca de una invitación

Anglepoise lamp® ['æŋgəlpɔɪz'læmp] *n* lámpara *f* de escritorio articulable, *Esp* flexo *m*

angler ['æŋglə(r)] *n* (**a**) *(person)* pescador(ora) *m,f* (de caña) (**b**) ***a. fish*** rape *m*

Anglican ['æŋglɪkən] *Rel* **1** *n* anglicano(a) *m,f*
2 *adj* anglicano(a); **the A. Church** la iglesia anglicana

Anglicanism ['æŋglɪkənɪzəm] *n* anglicanismo *m*

anglicism ['æŋglɪsɪzəm] *n* anglicismo *m*

anglicize ['æŋglɪsaɪz] *vt* anglicanizar

angling ['æŋglɪŋ] *n* pesca *f* con caña; *(in competitions)* pesca *f* deportiva

Anglo ['æŋgləʊ] (*pl* **Anglos**) *n* (**a**) *US* blanco(a) *m,f (no latino)* (**b**) *Can* anglófono(a) *m,f (en oposición a los francófonos)*

Anglo- ['æŋgləʊ] *prefix* anglo-

Anglo-American ['æŋgləʊə'merɪkən] *adj* angloamericano(a)

Anglo-Irish ['æŋgləʊ'aɪrɪʃ] **1** *adj* angloirlandés(esa)
2 *npl* **the A.** los angloirlandeses

anglophile ['æŋgləfaɪl] *n* anglófilo(a) *m,f*

anglophilia [æŋglə'fɪlɪə] *n* anglofilia *f*

anglophobe ['æŋgləfəʊb] *n* anglófobo(a) *m,f*

anglophobia [æŋglə'fəʊbɪə] *n* anglofobia *f*

anglophone ['æŋgləfəʊn] **1** *n* anglófono(a) *m,f*
2 *adj* anglófono(a)

Anglo-Saxon ['æŋgləʊ'sæksən] **1** *n* (**a**) *(person)* anglosajón(ona) *m,f* (**b**) *(language)* anglosajón *m*
2 *adj* anglosajón(ona)

Angola [æŋ'gəʊlə] *n* Angola

Angolan [æŋ'gəʊlən] **1** *n* angoleño(a) *m,f*
2 *adj* angoleño(a)

angora [æŋ'gɔ:rə] **1** *n* (**a**) *(textile)* angora *f* (**b**) *(animal)* ***a. cat*** gato *m* de angora; ***a. goat*** cabra *f* de angora; ***a. rabbit*** conejo *m* de angora
2 *adj (coat, sweater)* de angora

Angostura bitters® [æŋgə'stjʊərə'bɪtəz] *npl* angostura *f*

angrily ['æŋgrɪlɪ] *adv* airadamente, con *esp Esp* enfado *or esp Am* enojo

angry ['æŋgrɪ] *adj* (**a**) *(person) esp Esp* enfadado(a), *esp Am* enojado(a); *(voice, letter, look, words)* airado(a); *(silence)* lleno de ira; **to be a. (with sb/about sth)** estar *esp Esp* enfadado(a) *or esp Am* enojado(a) (con alguien/por algo); **I'm a. with myself for forgetting** estoy furioso conmigo mismo por haberme olvidado; **to get a. (with sb/about sth)** *esp Esp* enfadarse *or esp Am* enojarse (con alguien/por algo); **to make sb a.** (hacer) *esp Esp* enfadar *or esp Am* enojar a alguien, hacer que alguien se *esp Esp* enfade *or esp Am* enoje; **don't make the dog a.** no enfurezcas al perro; **it makes me a. when I hear that** me pone furioso oír eso
(**b**) *(sea, sky)* tempestuoso(a)
(**c**) *(sore, wound)* irritado(a), inflamado(a)

angst [æŋst] *n* angustia *f*

angst-ridden ['æŋstrɪdən] *adj* lleno(a) de angustia

angstrom ['æŋgstrəm] *n Phys* angstrom *m*

anguish ['æŋgwɪʃ] *n* angustia *f*; **to be in a.** *(worried)* estar preocupadísimo(a); *(in pain)* morirse de dolor; **to cause sb a.** angustiar a alguien; **her indifference caused him great a.** su indiferencia le angustió muchísimo

anguished ['æŋgwɪʃt] *adj* angustiado(a)

angular ['æŋgjʊlə(r)] *adj* (**a**) *(face, features, shape)* anguloso(a) (**b**) *Phys* ***a. acceleration*** aceleración *f* angular; ***a. momentum*** momento *m* angular

anhydride [æn'haɪdraɪd] *n Chem* anhídrido *m*

anhydrous [æn'haɪdrəs] *adj Chem* anhidro(a)

aniline ['ænɪlɪn] *n* anilina *f*

animadversion [ænɪmæd'vɜ:ʃən] *n Formal (criticism)* reconvención *f*, reprobación *f*; **to make animadversions on sth** reprobar *or* censurar algo

animadvert [ænɪmæd'vɜ:t] *vi Formal (criticize)* **a. on** *or* **upon sth/sb** reprobar *or* reconvenir algo/a alguien

animal ['ænɪməl] **1** *n* (**a**) *(creature)* animal *m* ▸▸ *US* ***a. crackers*** = galletas con formas de animales; ***a. fats*** grasas *fpl* animales; ***the a. kingdom*** el reino animal; ***a. life*** fauna *f*; ***a. lover*** amante *mf* de los animales; ***a. rights*** derechos *mpl* de los animales; ***a. shelter*** refugio *m* para animales
(**b**) *(uncivilized person)* **he's an a.** es un animal, es un bestia
(**c**) *(thing)* cosa *f*, cuestión *f*; **Spanish anarchism is a very different a.** el anarquismo español es harina de otro costal; *Fam* **there is no such a.** *(thing)* eso es un cuento chino
2 *adj* (**a**) *(products, behaviour)* animal (**b**) *(desire, needs, instinct)* animal ▸▸ ***a. magnetism*** magnetismo *m* animal

animate **1** *adj* ['ænɪmət] animado(a)
2 *vt* ['ænɪmeɪt] (**a**) *(enliven)* animar, dar vida (**b**) *(motivate)* animar (**c**) *Cin & TV* animar

animated ['ænɪmeɪtɪd] *adj (expression, discussion)* animado(a); **to be a.** estar animado(a); **to become a.** animarse ▸▸ ***a. cartoon*** (película *f* de) dibujos *mpl* animados; *Comptr* ***a. GIF*** GIF *m* animado

animatedly ['ænɪmeɪtɪdlɪ] *adv (to talk, gesture)* animadamente

animation [ænɪ'meɪʃən] *n* (**a**) *(liveliness)* animación *f* (**b**) *Cin & TV* animación *f*

animator ['ænɪmeɪtə(r)] *n Cin* animador(ora) *m,f*

animatronics [ænɪmə'trɒnɪks] *n Cin* animación *f* (asistida) por *Esp* ordenador *or Am* computadora

animism ['ænɪmɪzəm] *n Rel* animismo *m*

animist ['ænɪmɪst] *Rel* **1** *n* animista *mf*
2 *adj* animista

animosity [ænɪ'mɒsɪtɪ] *n* animosidad *f*, hostilidad *f*; **to feel a. towards** *or* **against sb** sentir animosidad hacia *or* contra alguien

animus ['ænɪməs] *n Formal (intense dislike)* animadversión *f*, animosidad *f*

anion ['ænaɪən] *n Phys* anión *m*

anise ['ænɪs] *n* anís *m (planta)*

aniseed ['ænɪsi:d] *n* anís *m* ▸▸ ***a. ball*** bolita *f* de anís

anisette [ænɪ'set] *n* anís *m*

Ankara ['æŋkərə] *n* Ankara

ankle ['æŋkəl] *n* tobillo *m* ►► ***a. boots*** botines *mpl*; ***a. chain*** pulsera *f* para el tobillo; ***a. socks*** calcetines *mpl* cortos, *CSur* zoquetes *mpl*, *Col* medias *fpl* tobilleras

ankle-biter ['æŋkəlbaɪtə(r)] *n Fam* renacuajo(a) *m,f*

ankle-deep ['æŋkəl'di:p] *adj* hasta los tobillos; **she was a. in mud** estaba metida en barro hasta los tobillos

ankle-length ['æŋkəlleŋθ] *adj* **a. sock** calcetín corto *or* tobillero

anklet ['æŋklət] *n* (**a**) *(ankle bracelet)* pulsera *f* para el tobillo (**b**) *US (ankle sock)* calcetín *m* corto *or* tobillero

ankylosis [æŋkɪ'ləʊsɪs] *n Med* anquilosis *f*

annalist ['ænəlɪst] *n* analista *mf*

annals ['ænəlz] *npl Hist & Literary* anales *mpl*

Anne [æn] *pr n* **A. Boleyn** Ana Bolena; **Queen A.** Ana Estuardo; **Saint A.** Santa Ana

annex 1 *vt* [æ'neks] (**a**) *(territory)* anexionar, anexar (**b**) *(document)* anexar, adjuntar
2 *n* ['æneks] *US* = **annexe**

annexation [ænek'seɪʃən] *n (act)* anexión *f*; *(territory)* territorio *m* anexionado

annexe, *US* **annex** ['æneks] *n* (**a**) *(of building)* edificio *m* anejo (**b**) *(of document)* anexo *m*

annihilate [ə'naɪəleɪt] *vt* (**a**) *(destroy)* aniquilar (**b**) *Fam (defeat)* aniquilar

annihilation [ənaɪə'leɪʃən] *n* (**a**) *(destruction)* aniquilación *f* (**b**) *Fam (defeat)* aniquilación *f*

anniversary [ænɪ'vɜ:sərɪ] *n* aniversario *m*; **the first/tenth/fortieth a. of sth** el primer/décimo/cuadragésimo aniversario de algo

anno Domini ['ænəʊ'dɒmɪnaɪ] *adv* después de Cristo

annotate ['ænəteɪt] *vt* anotar

annotated ['ænəteɪtɪd] *adj* anotado(a)

annotation [ænə'teɪʃən] *n* (**a**) *(action)* anotación *f* (**b**) *(note)* anotación *f*

announce [ə'naʊns] 1 *vt* (**a**) *(make known)* anunciar; *(arrival of guest, departure of plane)* anunciar; **we are pleased to a. the birth/marriage of our son** nos complace anunciar el nacimiento/el matrimonio de nuestro hijo; **a whistle announced the departure of the train** un silbato anunció la partida del tren
(**b**) *(declare)* **"I think you're all wrong," she announced** "creo que estáis todos equivocados", declaró *or* anunció
2 *vi US (declare one's candidacy)* **she announced for governor** hizo pública *or* anunció su candidatura al puesto de gobernador

announcement [ə'naʊnsmənt] *n* (**a**) *(of news)* anuncio *m*; **here is a passenger/staff a.** atención: aviso para los pasajeros/los empleados (**b**) *(formal statement)* declaración *f*, anuncio *m*; **I have an important a. to make** tengo algo importante que anunciar

announcer [ə'naʊnsə(r)] *n (on radio, TV programme)* presentador(ora) *m,f*

annoy [ə'nɔɪ] *vt* fastidiar, molestar, *esp Am* enojar; **is this man annoying you?** ¿le está molestando este tipo?; **to get annoyed** molestarse, *esp Esp* enfadarse, *esp Am* enojarse; **to be annoyed with sb** estar molesto(a) *or esp Esp* enfadado(a) *or esp Am* enojado(a) con alguien; **I was annoyed with myself for forgetting** estaba irritado conmigo mismo por haberme olvidado

annoyance [ə'nɔɪəns] *n* (**a**) *(feeling) esp Esp* enfado *m*, *esp Am* enojo *m*; **to my great a.** *or* **much to my a. they had already left** ya se habían marchado, lo que me puso de muy mal humor (**b**) *(annoying thing)* molestia *f*, fastidio *m*

annoying [ə'nɔɪɪŋ] *adj* molesto(a), irritante; **that was him at his most a.** se puso insoportable como nunca; **he has an a. habit of interrupting me** tiene la mala *or* molesta costumbre de interrumpirme; **how a.!** ¡qué fastidio!

annoyingly [ə'nɔɪɪŋlɪ] *adv* irritantemente; **a. enough, I saw the same dress in the sales a month later** ¡qué fastidio!, vi el mismo vestido en las rebajas un mes después

annual ['ænjʊəl] 1 *n* (**a**) *(plant)* planta *f* anual (**b**) *(book)* anuario *m*; *(for children)* = libro grueso de historietas o de una serie televisiva que se publica cada año
2 *adj* anual ►► ***a. general meeting*** asamblea *f or* junta *f* general anual; *Fin* ***a. percentage rate*** *(of interest)* tasa *f* anual equivalente, TAE *m or f*

annualize, annualise ['ænjʊəlaɪz] *vt Fin* anualizar; **an annualized rate of 7 percent** una tasa anualizada del 7 por ciento

annually ['ænjʊəlɪ] *adv* anualmente

annuity [ə'nju:ɪtɪ] *n* anualidad *f*; **to purchase an a.** suscribir *or* contratar una renta vitalicia

annul [ə'nʌl] *(pt & pp* **annulled**) *vt Law (contract, marriage)* anular

annulment [ə'nʌlmənt] *n* anulación *f*

Annunciation [ənʌnsɪ'eɪʃən] *n Rel* **the A.** la Anunciación

anode ['ænəʊd] *n Elec* ánodo *m*

anodized ['ænədaɪzd] *adj* anodizado(a)

anodyne ['ænədaɪn] *adj (bland)* anodino(a), insulso(a)

anoint [ə'nɔɪnt] *vt* ungir (**with** con); **they anointed him king** lo ungieron rey

anomalous [ə'nɒmələs] *adj* anómalo(a)

anomaly [ə'nɒməlɪ] *n* anomalía *f*

anon[1] [ə'nɒn] *adv Literary (soon)* pronto; *Hum* **I'll see you a.** ¡hasta pronto!; **...but more of this a.** ...pero lo dejamos para más adelante

anon[2] (*abbr* **anonymous**) anón.

anonymity [ænə'nɪmɪtɪ] *n* anonimato *m*; **to preserve one's a.** permanecer en el anonimato

anonymous [ə'nɒnɪməs] *adj* (**a**) *(gift, donor, letter)* anónimo(a); **an a. letter** una carta anónima, un anónimo; **to remain a.** permanecer en el anonimato ►► *Comptr* ***a. FTP*** FTP *m* anónimo (**b**) *(impersonal) (organization, suburb)* impersonal

anonymously [ə'nɒnɪməslɪ] *adv* anónimamente

anopheles [ə'nɒfəli:z] *n* **a. (mosquito)** mosquito *m* anófeles

anorak ['ænəræk] *n* (**a**) *(jacket)* anorak *m* (**b**) *Br Fam (person) Esp* maniático(a) *m,f*, *RP* nerd *mf*; **he's a real a. when it comes to films** es un maniático de las minucias del cine

anorexia [ænə'reksɪə] *n Med* anorexia *f* ►► ***a. nervosa*** anorexia *f* nerviosa

anorexic [ænə'reksɪk] *Med* 1 *n* anoréxico(a) *m,f*
2 *adj* anoréxico(a)

A. N. Other [eɪen'ʌðə(r)] *n Br* otra persona *f*; **the group will be you, me and A.** el grupo lo formaremos tú, yo y alguien más

---

ANOTHER [ə'nʌðə(r)] 1 *adj* otro(a); **a. one** otro(a); **a. cup of tea** otra taza de té; **let's do it a. way** vamos a hacerlo de otra manera; **it lasted for a. fifty years** duró otros cincuenta años *or* cincuenta años más; **there are a. two weeks to go** quedan otras dos semanas; **I'll be ready in a. five minutes** estaré listo en cinco minutos más; **don't say a. word** ni una palabra más; **they say he's a. Einstein** dicen que es un nuevo Einstein; **it's just a. day at the office to her** para ella no es más que otro día en la oficina; **that's quite a. matter, that's a. matter** *or* **thing altogether** eso es algo (totalmente) distinto; **a. time, perhaps** *(declining invitation)* quizá en otra ocasión; **he's made yet a. mistake** ha vuelto a equivocarse una vez más
2 *pron* (**a**) *(in general)* otro(a) *m,f*; **give me a.** dame otro; **the government has gone from one scandal to a.** el gobierno ha ido de escándalo en escándalo; **we all have problems of one sort or a.** todos tenemos problemas de algún tipo; **for one thing I don't like her, and for a....** no sólo no me gusta, sino que además...; **what with one thing and a., I forgot** entre unas cosas y otras, se me olvidó, *RP* entre una cosa y otra, me olvidé
(**b**) *(reciprocal)* **they saw one a.** se vieron; **they gave one a. presents** se dieron regalos; **we always help one a.** siempre nos ayudamos el uno al otro; **we like to spend time with one a.** nos gusta pasar tiempo juntos

---

ANSI ['ænsɪ] *n* (*abbr* **American National Standards Institute**) = instituto estadounidense que crea estándares de calidad en el ámbito tecnológico

ANSWER ['ɑ:nsə(r)] 1 *n (to question, letter)* respuesta *f*, contestación *f* (**to** a); *(in exam)* respuesta *f*; *(to problem)* solución *f* (**to** de); **to give sb an a.** dar una respuesta a alguien, contestar a alguien; **she made no a.** no respondió; **I knocked, but there was no a.** llamé a la puerta, pero no hubo respuesta; **there's no a.** *(on telephone)* no contestan; **he has an a. to everything** tiene respuesta para todo; **to know all the answers** saberlo todo; **he was Britain's a. to de Gaulle** fue el de Gaulle británico; **in a. to your comments** para responder a tus comentarios, en respuesta a tus comentarios; *Formal* **in a. to your letter** en respuesta a su carta; *Fig* **that would be the a. to our prayers** eso nos vendría como llovido del cielo
2 *vt* (**a**) *(person, question, letter, advertisement)* responder a, contestar; *(in exam)* responder a; *(problem)* solucionar; **to a. the telephone** contestar *or Esp* coger el teléfono; **to a. the door** abrir la puerta; *Fig* **our prayers were answered** nuestras plegarias fueron atendidas
(**b**) *(respond to) (criticism, accusation)* responder a; **to a. a**

description/need responder a una descripción/una necesidad; *Formal* **I hope this will a. your requirements** espero que esto cumpla sus requisitos; *Law* **to a. a charge** responder a una acusación
3 *vi* (a) *(reply)* responder, contestar; **I knocked, but nobody answered** llamé, pero nadie respondió
(b) *(respond)* **to a. by doing sth** responder haciendo algo
▸ **answer back** *vi* (a) *(be impertinent)* replicar, contestar; **don't a. back!** ¡no me repliques!
(b) *(defend oneself)* **I want the opportunity to a. back** quiero tener la oportunidad de contestar *or* defenderme
▸ **answer for** *vt insep* (a) *(be responsible for)* responder de, ser responsable de; **he has a lot to a. for** tiene mucho que explicar
(b) *(vouch for)* responder por
(c) *(speak for)* hablar por
▸ **answer to** *vt insep* (a) *(be accountable to)* **to a. to sb (for sth)** ser responsable ante alguien (de algo), responder ante alguien (de algo)
(b) *(correspond to) (description)* responder a
(c) *(respond to)* **the dog answers to the name of Rover** el perro responde al nombre de Rover; *Hum* **he answers to the name of Billy Bob** responde al nombre de Billy Bob

---

answerable ['ɑːnsərəbəl] *adj* **to be a. to sb (for sth)** ser responsable ante alguien (de algo), responder ante alguien (de algo); **you will be a. to the company for any damages** será responsable de daños y perjuicios ante la empresa; **I won't be a. for what happens** no me hago responsable de lo que pase; **he acts as if he is a. to no one** se comporta como si no tuviera que responder (de nada) ante nadie

answering ['ɑːnsərɪŋ] *adj* (a) *(echo, call)* **there was no a. voice** no respondió *or* contestó ninguna voz; **the dog waited for an a. bark** el perro esperaba que le devolvieran el ladrido (b) *(for telephone)* ***a. machine*** contestador *m* (automático); ***a. service*** servicio *m* de atención de llamadas *orAm* llamados

answerphone ['ɑːnsəfəʊn] *n Br* contestador *m* (automático)

ant [ænt] *n* hormiga *f*; IDIOM **to have ants in one's pants** *(be constantly moving)* ir acelerado(a), *RP* tener hormigas en la cola; *(be very restless)* estar hecho(a) un manojo de nervios ▸▸ ***a. hill*** hormiguero *m*

antacid [æn'tæsɪd] 1 *n* antiácido *m*
2 *adj* antiácido

antagonism [æn'tægənɪzəm] *n* animadversión *f*, antagonismo *m* (**towards/between** hacia/entre)

antagonist [æn'tægənɪst] *n* (a) *(opponent)* contrincante *mf*, antagonista *mf* (b) *Anat* antagonista *m*

antagonistic [æntægə'nɪstɪk] *adj* hostil; **their initial response was a.** inicialmente reaccionaron con hostilidad; **he's openly a. to the reforms** se opone activamente a las reformas

antagonize [æn'tægənaɪz] *vt* **to a. sb** ganarse la antipatía de alguien; **we can't afford to a. the voters** no podemos permitirnos suscitar la hostilidad de los votantes; **don't a. him!** ¡no te ganes su antipatía!

Antarctic [ænt'ɑːktɪk] 1 *n* **the A.** el Antártico
2 *adj* antártico(a) ▸▸ ***the A. Circle*** el Círculo Polar Antártico; ***the A. Ocean*** el (océano Glacial) Antártico

Antarctica [æn'tɑːktɪkə] *n* la Antártida

ante ['æntɪ] *n* IDIOM *Fam* **to up the a.** *(in gambling, conflict)* elevar la apuesta
▸ **ante up** *Fam US* 1 *vt sep* aflojar, *Esp* apoquinar
2 *vi* aflojar, *Esp* apoquinar

anteater ['æntiːtə(r)] *n* oso *m* hormiguero

antebellum ['æntɪ'beləm] *adj* = anterior a la guerra civil americana

antecede [æntɪ'siːd] *vt* anteceder, preceder

antecedent [æntɪ'siːdənt] 1 *n* (a) **antecedents** *(ancestors)* antepasados *mpl*; *(previous history)* antecedentes *mpl* (b) *Gram* antecedente *m*
2 *adj* (a) *Formal* precedente; **to be a. to sth** preceder a algo (b) *Gram* antecedente

antechamber ['æntɪtʃeɪmbə(r)] *n* antesala *f*

antedate [æntɪ'deɪt] *vt* (a) *(precede in time)* anteceder, preceder; **this fossil antedates all other finds by 10 million years** este fósil es 10 millones de años anterior a cualquier otro hallazgo (b) *(letter, document)* poner fecha anterior a la actual a, antedatar

antediluvian [æntɪdɪ'luːvɪən] *adj Hum* antediluviano(a)

antelope ['æntɪləʊp] (*pl* **antelopes** *or* **antelope**) *n* antílope *m*

antenatal [æntɪ'neɪtəl] *adj* prenatal ▸▸ ***a. clinic*** clínica *f* de obstetricia *or* de preparación al parto; ***a. exercises*** ejercicios *mpl* de preparación al parto

antenna [æn'tenə] *n* (a) (*pl* **antennae** [æn'teniː]) *(of insect, snail)* antena *f* (b) (*pl* **antennas**) *(of radio, TV)* antena *f*

antepenultimate ['æntɪpɪ'nʌltɪmət] *adj* antepenúltimo(a)

anterior [æn'tɪərɪə(r)] *adj* (a) *Formal* anterior, previo(a); **a. to** anterior *or* previo(a) a (b) *Anat & Zool* anterior ▸▸ ***a. cruciate ligament*** ligamento *m* cruzado anterior

anteroom ['æntɪruːm] *n* antesala *f*

anthem ['ænθəm] *n* (a) *(song of loyalty)* himno *m* (b) *Rel & Mus* himno *m*

anther ['ænθə(r)] *n Bot* antera *f*

anthologist [æn'θɒlədʒɪst] *n* autor(ora) *m,f* de una antología

anthologize [æn'θɒlədʒaɪz] *vt* **a much anthologized poem** un poema presente *or* incluido en muchas antologías

anthology [æn'θɒlədʒɪ] *n* antología *f*

Anthony ['æntənɪ] *pr n* **Saint A.** San Antonio; **Saint A. of Padua** San Antonio de Padua

anthracite ['ænθrəsaɪt] *n* antracita *f*

anthrax ['ænθræks] *n Med* carbunco *m*, ántrax *m inv*

anthropocentric ['ænθrəpə'sentrɪk] *adj* antropocéntrico(a)

anthropocentrism ['ænθrəpə'sentrɪzəm] *n* antropocentrismo *m*

anthropoid ['ænθrəpɔɪd] 1 *n* antropoide *m*
2 *adj* antropoide

anthropological ['ænθrəpə'lɒdʒɪkəl] *adj* antropológico(a)

anthropologist ['ænθrə'pɒlədʒɪst] *n* antropólogo(a) *m,f*

anthropology ['ænθrə'pɒlədʒɪ] *n* antropología *f*

anthropomorphic ['ænθrəpə'mɔːfɪk] *adj* antropomórfico(a)

anthropomorphous ['ænθrəpə'mɔːfəs] *adj* antropomórfico(a)

anti ['æntɪ] *Fam* 1 *n* oponente *mf*
2 *adj* **she's rather a.** está bastante en contra; **he's a bit a. all that kind of thing** suele estar en contra de todo ese tipo de cosas

anti- ['æntɪ] *prefix* anti-; **a.American** antiamericano(a)

anti-abortion ['æntɪə'bɔːʃən] *adj* antiabortista; **the a. movement** el movimiento antiabortista

anti-abortionist ['æntɪə'bɔːʃənɪst] *n* antiabortista *mf*

anti-aircraft [æntɪ'eəkrɑːft] *adj* antiaéreo(a)

anti-aliasing [æntɪ'eɪlɪəsɪŋ] *n Comptr* suavizado *m* de contornos

anti-allergenic ['æntɪælə'dʒenɪk] *adj* antialergénico(a)

anti-anxiety ['æntɪæŋ'zaɪətɪ] *adj (drug)* ansiolítico(a)

anti-apartheid ['æntɪə'pɑːtaɪt] *adj* antiapartheid

antiballistic ['æntɪbə'lɪstɪk] *adj* antibalístico, antimisil

antibiotic ['æntɪbaɪ'ɒtɪk] 1 *n* antibiótico *m*
2 *adj* antibiótico(a)

antibody ['æntɪbɒdɪ] *n Med* anticuerpo *m*

Antichrist ['æntɪkraɪst] *n* Anticristo *m*

anticipate [æn'tɪsɪpeɪt] 1 *vt* (a) *(expect)* esperar; *(foresee)* prever; **we don't a. any delays/objections** no esperamos que haya retrasos/objeciones; **he seemed to a. our every move** parecía prever todos nuestros movimientos; **I didn't a. leaving so early** no esperaba marcharme tan pronto; **her eagerly anticipated third novel** su muy esperada tercera novela; **faster/more difficult than anticipated** más rápido/difícil de lo esperado; **as anticipated, there was trouble** como se preveía, hubo problemas
(b) *(foreshadow)* anticipar, anunciar; **her writing anticipated later developments in English fiction** su obra anticipaba la posterior evolución de la narrativa inglesa
(c) *(do or say before)* adelantarse a; **we anticipated our competitors by launching our product first** lanzamos nuestro producto primero y así nos adelantamos a nuestros competidores
2 *vi* adelantarse a los acontecimientos

anticipation [æntɪsɪ'peɪʃən] *n* (a) *(foresight, expectation)* previsión *f*; **in a. of trouble** en previsión de posibles problemas; **to show great a.** *(of tennis, soccer player)* tener mucha visión de juego
(b) *(excitement)* ilusión *f*, expectación *f*; **fans jostled at the gates in eager a.** los fans se apretujaban a la puerta con gran ilusión
(c) *Formal* **yours** *or* **thanking you in a.** *(in letter)* le doy las gracias de antemano

anticipatory [æntɪsɪ'peɪtərɪ] *adj* previsor(ora)

anticlerical ['æntɪ'klerɪkəl] *adj* anticlerical

anticlericalism ['æntɪ'klerɪkəlɪzəm] *n* anticlericalismo *m*

anticlimactic ['æntɪklaɪ'mæktɪk] *adj* decepcionante

anticlimax ['æntɪ'klaɪmæks] *n* gran decepción *f*; **after all the waiting the party came as** *or* **was a bit of an a.** después de toda la espera, la fiesta no fue para tanto; **what an a.!** ¡qué decepción!

anticline ['æntɪklaɪn] *n Geol* anticlinal *m*

anticlockwise ['æntɪ'klɒkwaɪz] *Br* **1** *adj* **in an a. direction** en sentido contrario al de las agujas del reloj
2 *adv* en sentido contrario al de las agujas del reloj

anticoagulant [æntɪkəʊ'ægjʊlənt] **1** *n* anticoagulante *m*
2 *adj* anticoagulante

anticolonialism [æntɪkə'ləʊnɪəlɪzəm] *n* anticolonialismo *m*

anticonvulsant [æntɪkən'vʌlsənt] **1** *n* anticonvulsivo *m*
2 *adj* anticonvulsivo

anticorrosive [æntɪkə'rəʊsɪv] **1** *n* anticorrosivo *m*
2 *adj* anticorrosivo(a)

antics ['æntɪks] *npl* payasadas *fpl*; **he's been up to his usual a.** ha estado haciendo las payasadas de costumbre

anticyclone ['æntɪ'saɪkləʊn] *n Met* anticiclón *m*

anti-dazzle ['æntɪ'dæzəl] *adj Br* antirreflector(ora), antirreflejante; **a. headlights** faros antideslumbrantes

antidepressant [æntɪdɪ'presənt] **1** *n* antidepresivo *m*
2 *adj* antidepresivo(a)

antidote ['æntɪdəʊt] *n also Fig* antídoto *m* (**to** contra)

antidumping ['æntɪ'dʌmpɪŋ] *adj (laws, legislation)* antidumping

anti-establishment ['æntɪɪs'tæblɪʃmənt] *adj* en contra del orden establecido

antifascist ['æntɪ'fæʃɪst] **1** *n* antifascista *mf*
2 *adj* antifascista

antifreeze ['æntɪfri:z] *n* anticongelante *m*

antifungal ['æntɪ'fʌŋgəl] *adj* fungicida

antigen ['æntɪdʒən] *n Biol* antígeno *m*

antiglare ['æntɪ'gleə(r)] *adj* (**a**) *US (mirror, finish)* antirreflector(ora), antirreflejante; **a. headlights** faros antideslumbrantes (**b**) *Comptr* ***a. filter*** filtro *m* de pantalla; ***a. screen*** filtro *m* de pantalla

Antigua and Barbuda [æn'ti:gənbɑ:'bju:də] *n* Antigua y Barbuda

antihero ['æntɪhɪərəʊ] (*pl* **antiheroes**) *n* antihéroe *m*

antiheroine [æntɪ'herəʊɪn] *n* antiheroína *f*

antihistamine ['æntɪ'hɪstəmi:n] **1** *n* antihistamínico *m*
2 *adj* antihistamínico(a) ▸▸ ***a. drug*** antihistamínico *m*

anti-imperialist ['æntɪɪm'pɪərɪəlɪst] **1** *n* antiimperialista *mf*
2 *adj* antiimperialista

anti-inflammatory [æntɪɪn'flæmətərɪ] **1** *n* antiinflamatorio *m*
2 *adj* antiinflamatorio(a) ▸▸ ***a. drug*** antiinflamatorio *m*

anti-inflationary [æntɪɪn'fleɪʃənərɪ] *adj* antiinflacionario(a), antiinflacionista

antiknock ['æntɪ'nɒk] *adj* antidetonante

Antilles [æn'tɪli:z] *npl* **the A.** las Antillas; **the Greater/Lesser A.** las Antillas mayores/menores

anti-lock ['æntɪlɒk] *adj (brakes)* antibloqueo, ABS

antilog ['æntɪlɒg], **antilogarithm** [æntɪ'lɒgərɪðəm] *n Math* antilogaritmo *m*

antimacassar [æntɪmə'kæsə(r)] *n* antimacasar *m*

antimatter ['æntɪmætə(r)] *n Phys* antimateria *f*

antimissile ['æntɪ'mɪsaɪl] *adj* antimisil

antimony ['æntɪmənɪ] *n Chem* antimonio *m*

antinuclear ['æntɪ'nju:klɪə(r)] *adj* antinuclear

antioxidant ['æntɪ'ɒksɪdənt] **1** *n* antioxidante *m*
2 *adj* antioxidante

antipathetic ['æntɪpə'θetɪk] *adj Formal* hostil; **he remains (deeply) a. to the cause** sigue siendo muy hostil a la causa

antipathy [æn'tɪpəθɪ] *n* antipatía *f*; **to feel a. towards sth/sb** sentir antipatía hacia algo/alguien

anti-personnel ['æntɪpɜ:sə'nel] *adj (mine)* antipersona

antiperspirant ['æntɪ'pɜ:spərənt] **1** *n* antitranspirante *m*
2 *adj* antitranspirante; **a. deodorant** desodorante antitranspirante

antiphon ['æntɪfən] *n Mus* antífona *f*

antipodean [æntɪpə'di:ən] **1** *n Hum (Australian, New Zealander)* = australiano o neozelandés
2 *adj* (**a**) *Geog* antípoda, de las antípodas (**b**) *Hum (from Australia, New Zealand)* = de Australia o Nueva Zelanda

antipodes [æn'tɪpədi:z] *npl Geog* antípodas *mpl or fpl*; *Br* **the A.** = Australia y Nueva Zelanda

antipope ['æntɪpəʊp] *n Hist* antipapa *m*

antiprotectionist ['æntiprə'tekʃənist] *Pol & Econ* **1** *n* antiproteccionista *mf*
2 *adj* antiproteccionista

antiquarian [æntɪ'kweərɪən] **1** *n (dealer)* anticuario(a) *m,f*; *(collector)* coleccionista *mf* de antigüedades
2 *adj (book)* antiguo(a) ▸▸ ***a. bookshop*** librería *f* de viejo

antiquary ['æntɪkwərɪ] *n* = **antiquarian**

antiquated ['æntɪkweɪtɪd] *adj* anticuado(a)

antique [æn'ti:k] **1** *n* (**a**) *(object)* antigüedad *f* ▸▸ ***a. dealer*** anticuario(a) *m,f*; ***a. shop*** tienda *f* de antigüedades (**b**) *Hum (person)* carroza *mf*
2 *adj* (**a**) *(old and valuable)* antiguo(a) ▸▸ ***a. furniture*** muebles *mpl* antiguos (**b**) *Hum (person, ideas)* chapado(a) a la antigua

antiquity [æn'tɪkwɪtɪ] *n* (**a**) *(ancient times)* antigüedad *f*; **in the remotest a.** en la más remota antigüedad (**b**) *(age)* antigüedad *f*; **of great a.** muy antiguo(a), de gran antigüedad (**c**) **antiquities** *(buildings, coins, statues)* antigüedades *fpl*

antiracism ['æntɪ'reɪsɪzəm] *n* antirracismo *m*

antiracist ['æntɪ'reɪsɪst] *adj* antirracista

antiriot ['æntɪ'raɪət] *adj* antidisturbios *inv*

anti-roll bar ['æntɪ'rəʊl'bɑ:(r)] *n* barra *f* estabilizadora

antirrhinum [æntɪ'raɪnəm] *n* (boca *f* de) dragón *m*

antisemite ['æntɪ'si:maɪt] *n* antisemita *mf*

antisemitic ['æntɪsɪ'mɪtɪk] *adj (person)* antisemita; *(beliefs, remarks)* antisemítico(a)

antisemitism ['æntɪ'semɪtɪzəm] *n* antisemitismo *m*

antiseptic [æntɪ'septɪk] **1** *n* antiséptico *m*
2 *adj* (**a**) *(antibacterial)* antiséptico(a) (**b**) *Fig (lacking character or warmth)* aséptico(a)

antiserum ['æntɪ'sɪərəm] *n Med* antisuero *m*

antisexism ['æntɪ'seksɪzəm] *n* antisexismo *m*

antisexist ['æntɪ'seksɪst] *adj* antisexista

antisocial ['æntɪ'səʊʃəl] *adj* (**a**) *(disruptive)* incívico(a), antisocial (**b**) *(unsociable)* insociable

antistatic ['æntɪ'stætɪk] *adj* antiestático(a)

antitank ['æntɪ'tæŋk] *adj* anticarro, antitanque

antiterrorist ['æntɪ'terərɪst] *adj* antiterrorista

antitheft ['æntɪ'θeft] *adj* antirrobo

antithesis [æn'tɪθɪsɪs] (*pl* **antitheses** [æn'tɪθɪsi:z]) *n* (**a**) *(exact opposite)* antítesis *f inv*; **he is the a. of a ruthless businessman** es la antítesis del inexorable hombre de negocios (**b**) *Lit* antítesis *f inv* (**c**) *Phil* antítesis *f inv*

antithetic(al) [æntɪ'θetɪk(əl)] *adj* antitético(a)

antitoxin [æntɪ'tɒksɪn] *n Med* antitoxina *f*

antitrades ['æntɪtreɪdz] *npl Geog* vientos *mpl* contraalisios

antitragus [æntɪ'treɪgəs] *n Anat* antitrago *m*

antitrust ['æntɪ'trʌst] *adj US* antimonopolio *inv* ▸▸ ***a. law*** ley *f* antimonopolio

antivirus ['æntɪ'vaɪrəs] *adj Comptr (program, software)* antivirus ▸▸ ***a. program*** (programa *m*) antivirus *m inv*

antivivisectionist ['æntɪvɪvɪ'sekʃənɪst] **1** *n* = persona que se opone a la práctica de experimentos con animales vivos
2 *adj* = contrario a la práctica de experimentos con animales vivos

antler ['æntlə(r)] *n* cuerno *m*; **antlers** cornamenta

antonym ['æntənɪm] *n* antónimo *m*

antsy ['æntsɪ] *adj US Fam* nervioso(a); **I was beginning to get a.** me empezaba a poner de los nervios, *Am* se me empezaban a poner los nervios de punta

Antwerp ['æntwɜ:p] *n* Amberes

anus ['eɪnəs] *n* ano *m*

anvil ['ænvɪl] *n* yunque *m*

anxiety [æŋ'zaɪətɪ] *n* (**a**) *(worry, concern)* preocupación *f*; *(anguish, impatience)* ansiedad *f*; **rising interest rates have caused a. among exporters** la subida de los tipos de interés ha causado preocupación entre los exportadores; **her behaviour has been the cause of great a.** su comportamiento ha causado gran preocupación
(**b**) *(source of worry)* motivo *m* de preocupación; **her son is a great a. to her** su hijo es para ella un gran motivo de preocupación
(**c**) *(eagerness)* ansia *f*, afán *m*; **in her a. not to offend...** en su afán por no ofender...
(**d**) *Med* ansiedad *f*; **an a. attack** un ataque *or* una crisis de ansiedad

anxious ['æŋkʃəs] *adj* (**a**) *(worried)* preocupado(a); *(anguished, impatient)* ansioso(a); **she's a very a. person** es una persona muy inquieta *or* intranquila; **to be a. (for)** estar preocupado(a) (por); **I am a. about his health** me preocupa su salud; **he was a. that all his work might come to nothing** temía que todo su trabajo quedara en nada

(b) *(worrying)* **an a. moment** un momento de preocupación; **it was an a. time for us** en esos momentos estábamos muy preocupados

(c) *(eager)* **to be a. to do sth** estar ansioso(a) *or* impaciente por hacer algo; **he didn't seem at all a. to leave** no parecía tener ninguna prisa por irse; **I was a. that our message should be clear** mi mayor deseo era que nuestro mensaje quedara claro

anxiously ['æŋkʃəslɪ] *adv* (a) *(worriedly)* con preocupación; *(with anguish, impatience)* ansiosamente (b) *(eagerly)* con ansiedad *or* impaciencia

anxiousness ['æŋkʃəsnɪs] *n* (a) *(worry, concern)* preocupación *f*; *(anguish, impatience)* ansiedad *f* (b) *(eagerness)* ansia *f*, afán *m*; **in her a. not to offend...** en su afán por no ofender...

ANY ['enɪ] 1 *pron* (a) *(some)* **have you got a.?** *(with plural nouns)* ¿tienes alguno(a)?; *(with uncountable nouns)* ¿tienes algo?; **I fancy some biscuits, have you got a.?** me comería unas galletas, ¿tienes?; **are there a. left?** ¿queda alguno(a)?; **is there a. left?** ¿queda algo?; **is there a. more?** ¿hay más?; **can a. of them speak English?** ¿alguno (de ellos) habla inglés?

(b) *(in negatives)* ninguno(a) *m,f*; **I haven't got a. and I don't want a.** no tengo y no quiero; **there isn't/aren't a. left** no queda ninguno; **I haven't read a. of her books** no he leído ninguno de sus libros; **there was nothing in a. of the boxes** no había nada en ninguna de las cajas; **few, if a., can read** pocos, o ninguno, saben leer; **I doubt you'll find more than a couple, if a. (at all)** dudo que vayas a encontrar más de dos, como mucho; **she has little, if a., experience** apenas tiene experiencia

(c) *(no particular one)* cualquiera; **a. of us** cualquiera de nosotros; **four dresses, a. of which would have suited her** cuatro vestidos, cualquiera de los cuales le habría quedado bien; **use a. box, use a. one of the boxes** use cualquier caja; **use a. of the boxes** *(only one)* use cualquier caja; *(several)* use las cajas que le parezca

(d) *(every one)* **keep a. you find** quédate con todos los que encuentres

2 *adj* (a) *(some)* **have you a. milk/sugar?** ¿tienes leche/azúcar?; **have you a. apples/cigarettes?** ¿tienes manzanas/cigarrillos?; **is there a. hope?** ¿hay alguna esperanza?; **she has hardly a. experience** apenas tiene experiencia, *Esp* no tiene apenas experiencia; **do you have a. other colours?** ¿tiene algún otro color?; **do you by a. chance know him?** ¿acaso lo conoces?; **I'm not in a. way jealous** no estoy celoso en absoluto *or* ni mucho menos

(b) *(in negatives)* ninguno(a); *(before masculine singular noun)* ningún; **he hasn't got a. money** no tiene dinero; **there weren't a. winners** no hubo ningún ganador; **I didn't win a. prizes** no gané ningún premio; **without a. help** sin ninguna ayuda; **I haven't a. idea** no tengo ni idea; **I can't see a. way of convincing her** no hay manera de convencerla

(c) *(no particular) (before noun)* cualquier; *(after noun)* cualquiera; **you can choose a. two free gifts** puede elegir los dos regalos que prefiera; **come a. day** ven cualquier día, ven un día cualquiera, *RP* vení el día que quieras; **a. one of them could be right** cualquiera de ellos podría tener razón; **a. doctor will tell you the same** cualquier médico te diría lo mismo; *Fig* **a. fool will tell you that** eso lo sabe hasta el más tonto; **a. minute now** de un momento a otro; **a. day now** cualquier día de éstos; **I don't want just a. (old) wine** no quiero un vino cualquiera; **thanks – a. time!** gracias – ¡de nada!; **a. time you need help, let me know** cuando necesites ayuda, dímelo

(d) *(every)* **a. pupil who forgets his books will be punished** los alumnos que olviden sus libros serán castigados; **I'll take a. copies you have** me quedaré con todas las copias que tengas; **a. tension between them has vanished** cualquier tensión que hubiera podido haber entre ellos ha desaparecido; **it can be obtained from a. good bookshop** está a la venta en las mejores librerías; **a. other person would have said yes** cualquier otro hubiera dicho que sí; **at a. rate, in a. case** en cualquier caso

3 *adv* (a) *(with comparative)* **I'm not a. better** no me encuentro mejor, *RP* no me siento nada mejor; **the weather couldn't be a. worse** el tiempo no podía ser peor; **have you a. more milk?** ¿tienes más leche?; **we don't see them a. longer** *or* **more** ya no los vemos; **I don't like her a. more than you do** a mí no me gusta más que a ti; **is that a. easier?** ¿así es más fácil?; **I'm not getting a. younger** los años no pasan en balde, *RP* los años no vienen solos

(b) *Fam (at all)* **that didn't help us a.** eso no nos ayudó para nada; **this printer isn't a. good** esta impresora es bastante mala; **a. old how** de cualquier manera, a la buena de Dios

ANYBODY ['enɪbɒdɪ], **anyone** ['enɪwʌn] *pron* (a) *(indeterminate)* alguien; **would a. like some more coffee?** ¿quiere alguien más café?, ¿alguien quiere más café?; **does a. mind if I close the window?** ¿les importa que cierre la ventana?; **why would a. want to do a thing like that?** ¿por qué iba alguien a querer hacer algo así?, ¿por qué querría alguien hacer algo así?; **if a. asks, I was at home all day** si alguien te pregunta, estuve en casa todo el día; **she'll know, if a. does** si alguien lo sabe es ella

(b) *(in negatives)* nadie; **there isn't a. here** aquí no hay nadie; **there was hardly a. there** no había casi nadie, *Esp* no había apenas nadie; **I've never known a. so intelligent** nunca había conocido a alguien tan inteligente

(c) *(no matter who)* cualquiera; **a. will tell you so** cualquiera te lo diría; **bring along a. you like** trae a quien quieras; **a. holding a US passport, come this way** los que lleven pasaporte estadounidense, vengan por aquí; **I have as much reason as a. to be upset** tengo tanta razón para estar *esp Esp* enfadado *or esp Am* enojado como el que más; **he's no different to a. else** no se diferencia en nada de los demás; **a. else** *or* **a. but her would have refused** cualquier otra se habría negado; **I don't want just a.!** ¡no quiero a cualquiera!

(d) *(person with status)* **he'll never be a.** nunca será nadie, nunca llegará a ser alguien; **a. who's a. in British cinema is going to be there** todo el que es algo en el cine británico estará allí

ANYHOW ['enɪhaʊ] *adv* (a) *(however)* de todas maneras *or* formas, de todos modos; **I was feeling ill, but I decided to go a.** aunque no me encontraba bien decidí ir; **what were you doing in my office, a.?** en cualquier *or* todo caso, ¿que hacías en mi oficina?; **she's really intelligent, well a. that's what I think** es muy inteligente, por lo menos eso me parece a mí; **a., let's get back to what we were saying** bueno, volvamos a lo que estábamos diciendo; **so a., as I was saying...** en todo caso, como iba diciendo...; **a., I really ought to be going** en fin, me tengo que marchar

(b) *Fam (carelessly)* a la buena de Dios, de cualquier manera; **I don't want it done just a.** no quiero que se haga de cualquier manera

any more, *US* **anymore** [enɪ'mɔː(r)] *adv* (a) *(any longer)* **they don't live here a.** ya no viven aquí; **I won't do it a.** no lo haré nunca más, no lo volveré a hacer; **I'll leave if you do that a.** me iré si vuelves a hacerlo (b) *US (now)* ahora; **every time I start the bike a., I remember to check the gas** ahora cuando pongo en marcha la moto, siempre me acuerdo de comprobar la gasolina

anyone = **anybody**

anyplace *US* = **anywhere**

anyroad ['enɪrəʊd] *adv Br Fam* = **anyhow** (a)

anything ['enɪθɪŋ] 1 *pron* (a) *(indeterminate)* algo; **is there a. I can do (to help)?** ¿puedo ayudarte en algo?; **have you a. to write with?** ¿tienes con qué escribir?; **have you a. smaller?** ¿tendría algo más pequeño?; **if a. should happen to me** si me ocurriera algo; **do you notice a. strange about him?** ¿no le notas algo raro?; **think before you say a.** piensa antes de decir *or* de que digas nada; **is (there) a. the matter?** ¿ocurre algo?; **will there be a. else?** *(in shop)* ¿desea algo más?

(b) *(in negatives)* nada; **he doesn't do a.** no hace nada; **hardly a.** casi nada, *Esp* apenas nada; **I can't imagine a. more interesting** no podría imaginarme nada más interesante; **I can't think of a. else** no se me ocurre ninguna otra cosa; **we didn't do a. much** no hicimos gran cosa; **I haven't seen a. of him recently** no le he visto últimamente; **I wouldn't miss it for a. (in the world)** no me lo perdería por nada del mundo

(c) *(no matter what)* cualquier cosa; **he eats a.** come cualquier cosa; **a. you want** lo que quieras; **I love a. French** me gusta todo lo francés; **he would do a. for me** haría cualquier cosa por mí; **I'll do a. I can to help** haré todo lo que pueda por ayudar; **a. is possible** todo es posible; **she could be a. between twenty and thirty-five** podría tener entre veinte y treinta y cinco años; **he was a. but friendly** fue de todo menos amable; **are you angry? – a. but** ¿estás *esp Esp* enfadado(a) *or esp Am* enojado(a)? – ni mucho menos; **all right then, a. for a quiet life!** de acuerdo, ¡lo que sea por un poco de tranquilidad!; **do you agree? – sure, a. you say** ¿estás de acuerdo? – claro, lo que tú digas; **more than a. (else), I want to be a pilot** lo que realmente quiero ser es piloto; *Fam* **as funny as a.** divertidísimo(a); *Fam* **to work like a.** trabajar como loco(a); *Fam* **I miss her like a.** *Esp* la echo muchísimo en falta *or* de menos, *Am* la extraño muchísimo; *Fam* **can I get you a cup of tea or a.?** ¿quieres un té o algo?; *Fam* **it's not that you were wrong or a.** no es que estuvieras equivocado ni nada parecido; *Fam* **don't tell her or a., will you?** no se lo digas, ¿vale *or RP* está bien?, *Méx* ándale, no se lo digas

2 *adv* **is it a. like the last one?** ¿se parece en algo al anterior?; **it**

didn't cost a. like £500 no costó 500 libras ni muchísimo menos; **the food wasn't a. like** *or* **near as bad as they said** la comida no fue en absoluto tan mala como decían

anyway ['enɪweɪ] = **anyhow (a)**

anyways ['enɪweɪz] *adv US* = **anyhow (a)**

ANYWHERE ['enɪweə(r)], *US* **anyplace** ['enɪpleɪs] *adv* **(a)** *(in questions)* **can you see it a.?** ¿lo ves por alguna parte?; **have you found a. to live?** ¿has encontrado un lugar *or* algún sitio para vivir?; **I haven't got a. to sleep tonight** no tengo donde dormir esta noche; **can you recommend a. to stay?** ¿me puedes recomendar algún sitio donde alojarme?; **did you go a. yesterday?** ¿fuiste a alguna parte ayer?; **did you go a. interesting for your holidays?** ¿fuiste a algún lugar interesante de vacaciones?; **did you look a. else?** ¿buscaste en otros sitios?, ¿buscaste en algún otro lado?; **is there a. else we could go?** ¿podríamos ir a algún otro sitio *or* lugar?
(b) *(in negatives)* **I can't find it a.** no lo encuentro por ningún sitio *or* lado; **we never go a. interesting** nunca vamos a ningún sitio *or* lugar interesante; **you won't find them a. else** no los encontrarás en ningún otro lugar; **I wasn't standing a. near you** no estaba cerca de ti ni mucho menos; **he isn't a. near as clever as her** no es ni mucho menos tan listo como ella; **the food wasn't a. near as bad as they said** la comida no fue en absoluto tan mala como decían; **I don't play golf a. near as much as I used to** ya no juego al golf tanto como solía ni mucho menos; *Fig* **we're not getting a.** no estamos consiguiendo nada; *Fig* **this company isn't going a.** esta empresa no va a ninguna parte
(c) *(no matter where)* en cualquier lugar, en cualquier sitio; **put it a.** ponlo en cualquier sitio *or* lado; **sit down a. (you like)** siéntate donde prefieras *or* quieras; **now we can go a.** ahora podemos ir a cualquier parte *or* lado; **I'd know him a.** lo reconocería en cualquier parte *or* lado; **it's miles from a.** está en un lugar muy aislado; **she could be a. between twenty and thirty-five** podría tener entre veinte y treinta y cinco años; **a. else you'd pay twice as much** en cualquier otro lugar pagarías el doble

anywheres ['enɪweəz] *adv US Fam* en cualquier lugar, en cualquier sitio; **they're about the nicest folks you'll meet a.** en ningún lado encontrarás gente más simpática que ésa; **it can take a. from one to two hours** puede tardar entre una y dos horas

anywise ['enɪwaɪz] *adv US* **(a)** *(at all)* en modo alguno **(b)** *Fam (anyhow)* de todos modos, en cualquier caso

Anzac ['ænzæk] *n* (*abbr* **Australia-New Zealand Army Corps**) *(soldier)* = soldado de las fuerzas armadas de Australia y Nueva Zelanda

AO(C)B [eɪəʊ(si:)'bi:] *Br Com* (*abbr* **any other (competent) business**) ruegos *mpl* y preguntas

A-OK [eɪəʊ'keɪ] *US Fam* **1** *adj* de primera, *Esp* fetén *inv*; **everything's A.** todo está de maravilla
2 *adv* **to go A.** ir sobre ruedas *or* de maravilla

aorta [eɪ'ɔ:tə] *n Anat* aorta *f*

apace [ə'peɪs] *adv Literary* raudamente, con celeridad

APART [ə'pɑ:t] *adv* **(a)** *(at a distance)* alejado(a), separado(a); **he was standing a. from the others** se encontraba separado *or* apartado de los demás; **the garage is set a. from the house** el garage no está adosado a la casa; IDIOM **he's a class a. from the rest** es mucho mejor que el resto; **what really sets him a. from his contemporaries...** lo que realmente lo diferencia de sus contemporáneos...
(b) *(separated)* **the two towns are 10 kilometres a.** las dos ciudades están a 10 kilómetros una de la otra; **they're just 3 cm a.** están a sólo 3 cm, hay 3 cm entre ellos; *Fig* **the two sides are still a long way a.** las distancias entre las dos partes son todavía importantes; **with one's legs a.** con las piernas abiertas; **boys and girls were kept a.** los chicos y las chicas estaban separados; **they're never a.** no se separan nunca; **I've grown a. from my sister** me he distanciado de mi hermana; **they've lived a. since 1997** viven separados desde 1997; **they were born two years a.** nacieron con dos años de diferencia; **their birthdays are two days a.** hay dos días entre sus cumpleaños; **it is difficult to tell them a.** es difícil distinguirlos
(c) *(to pieces)* **to blow sth a.** volar algo (en pedazos); **to come** *or* **fall a.** romperse en pedazos; **their marriage has fallen a.** su matrimonio ha fracasado; **to take sth a.** desmontar algo
(d) *(excepting)* **a. from** aparte de; **quite a. from the fact that...** independientemente del hecho de que...; **and that's quite a. from the royalties** y eso sin tener en cuenta los derechos de autor; **such considerations a....** aparte de estas consideraciones...; **joking a.** bromas aparte

apartheid [ə'pɑ:taɪt] *n* apartheid *m*

apartment [ə'pɑ:tmənt] *n* **(a)** *US (dwelling)* apartamento *m*, *Esp* piso *m*, *Arg* departamento *m* ►► ***a. building*** edificio *m* *or* bloque *m* de apartamentos *or Esp* pisos *or Arg* departamentos **(b)** *Br (room)* estancia *f*, habitación *f*; *(bedroom)* dormitorio *m*, alcoba *f*; **the Royal/state apartments** las dependencias *or* estancias reales/oficiales

apathetic [æpə'θetɪk] *adj* apático(a) (**about** respecto a)

apathetically [æpə'θetɪklɪ] *adv* apáticamente, con indiferencia

apathy ['æpəθɪ] *n* apatía *f*; **their a. about** *or* **towards the issue** su apatía *or* total indiferencia hacia el asunto

APB [eɪpi:'bi:] *n US* (*abbr* **all-points bulletin**) = mensaje informativo o aviso urgente enviado a los agentes de policía de una misma zona

APC [eɪpi:'si:] *n* (*abbr* **armoured personnel carrier**) BRM *m*, blindado medio *m* sobre ruedas

ape [eɪp] **1** *n* **(a)** *(animal)* simio *m* **(b)** *Fam (person)* bruto(a) *m,f*, *Esp* patoso(a) *m,f* **(c)** IDIOM *US Fam* **to go a. (over)** *(lose one's temper)* ponerse hecho(a) una furia (por), *RP* calentarse (con *or* por); *(enthuse)* ponerse como loco(a) (por *or* con), *Esp* despendolarse (por *or* con), *RP* coparse (con)
2 *vt (imitate)* imitar, remedar

apeman ['eɪpmæn] *n* hombre *m* mono

Apennines ['æpɪnaɪnz] *npl* **the A.** los Apeninos

aperient [ə'pɪərɪənt] *Med* **1** *n* aperiente *m*, laxante *m*
2 *adj* aperiente, laxante

aperitif [əperɪ'ti:f] *n* aperitivo *m (bebida)*

aperture ['æpətjʊə(r)] *n* **(a)** *(opening)* abertura *f* **(b)** *(of camera)* abertura *f* (del diafragma)

apeshit ['eɪpʃɪt] *adv* IDIOM *US very Fam* **to go a. (over)** *(lose one's temper)* ponerse como un energúmeno (con *or* por), *Esp* agarrarse un buen cabreo (con *or* por), *RP* emputecerse (con *or* por); *(enthuse)* ponerse como loco(a) (con *or* por), *Esp* flipar en colores (con *or* por), *RP* recoparse (con)

APEX ['eɪpeks] *adj* (*abbr* **advance purchase excursion**) ***A. fare*** precio *m* *or* tarifa *f* APEX; ***A. ticket*** *Esp* billete *m* *or Am* boleto *m* *or Am* pasaje *m* (con tarifa) APEX

apex ['eɪpeks] (*pl* **apexes** *or* **apices** ['eɪpɪsi:z]) *n* **(a)** *(of triangle)* vértice *m* **(b)** *(of career)* cima *f*, cumbre *f*

aphasia [ə'feɪzɪə] *n Med* afasia *f*

aphasic [ə'feɪzɪk] *Med* **1** *n* afásico(a) *m,f*
2 *adj* afásico(a)

aphid ['eɪfɪd] *n* pulgón *m*

aphorism ['æfərɪzəm] *n* aforismo *m*

aphoristic [æfə'rɪstɪk] *adj* aforístico(a)

aphrodisiac [æfrə'dɪzɪæk] **1** *n* afrodisíaco *m*
2 *adj* afrodisíaco(a)

Aphrodite [æfrə'daɪtɪ] *n Mythol* Afrodita

apiary ['eɪpɪərɪ] *n* colmenar *m*

apices *pl of* **apex**

apiece [ə'pi:s] *adv* cada uno(a); **they cost £3 a.** cuestan 3 libras cada uno, están a 3 libras

aplenty [ə'plentɪ] *adv* en abundancia; **there was wine a.** corría el vino a raudales

aplomb [ə'plɒm] *n* aplomo *m*; **with great a.** con gran aplomo, con mucha ecuanimidad

apnoea, *US* **apnea** [æp'nɪə] *n Med* apnea *f*

apocalypse [ə'pɒkəlɪps] *n* apocalipsis *m inv*; **the four horsemen of the A.** los cuatro jinetes del Apocalipsis

apocalyptic [əpɒkə'lɪptɪk] *adj* apocalíptico(a)

apocopated [ə'pɒkəpeɪtɪd] *adj Ling* apocopado(a)

apocryphal [ə'pɒkrɪfəl] *adj (story)* apócrifo(a), espurio(a)

apogee ['æpədʒi:] *n* **(a)** *Astron* apogeo *m* **(b)** *(of career)* apogeo *m*, cúspide *f*; **he had reached the a. of his career** había llegado a la cima *or* cúspide de su carrera profesional

apolitical [eɪpə'lɪtɪkəl] *adj* apolítico(a)

Apollo [ə'pɒləʊ] *n Mythol* Apolo

apologetic [əpɒlə'dʒetɪk] *adj (tone, smile)* de disculpa; **she was quite a. about it** lo sentía mucho; **he was most a. when I complained** se deshizo en disculpas cuando me quejé

apologetically [əpɒlə'dʒetɪklɪ] *adv (to smile, shrug)* con aire de disculpa; **"I did try to get here early," he said a.** "hice todo lo que pude por llegar pronto", dijo él disculpándose *or* a modo de disculpa

apologetics [əpɒlə'dʒetɪks] *n* apologética *f*

apologia [æpə'ləʊdʒɪə] *n Formal* apología *f*

apologist [ə'pɒlədʒɪst] *n Formal* apologista *mf*, defensor(ora) *m,f* (**for** de)

apologize [ə'pɒlədʒaɪz] *vi* disculparse (**to sb/for sth** ante alguien/por algo); **I had to a. for you** tuve que pedir disculpas por ti; **there's no need to a.** no hay por qué disculparse; **it's him you should be apologizing to** es a él a quien deberías pedir(le) disculpas; **we a. for any inconvenience this may cause** rogamos disculpen las molestias (causadas); **I can't a. enough** no encuentro palabras para disculparme

apology [ə'pɒlədʒɪ] *n* (**a**) *(expression of regret)* disculpa *f*; **to make/offer an a.** disculparse; **I make no apologies for mentioning this** me siento en la obligación de mencionarlo; **to send one's apologies** *(for not attending meeting)* enviar excusas *or* excusarse por no poder asistir; **I owe you an a.** te debo una disculpa; **they were full of apologies** todo eran disculpas por su parte; **please accept my apologies** le ruego (que) acepte mis disculpas; **I brought them some flowers by way of an a.** les traje flores a modo de disculpa

(**b**) IDIOM *Pej* **an a. for a dinner/football team** una porquería *or Esp* birria de cena/equipo (de fútbol)

(**c**) *Formal (defence)* apología *f*

aponeurosis [æpəʊnjʊə'rəʊsɪs] *n Anat* aponeurosis *f inv*

apoplectic [æpə'plektɪk] *adj* (**a**) *(angry)* **to be a. (with rage)** estar hecho(a) una furia (**b**) *Med* **to be a.** tener apoplejía, ser apoplético(a)

apoplexy ['æpəpleksɪ] *n Med* apoplejía *f*

apostasy [ə'pɒstəsɪ] *n* apostasía *f*

apostate [ə'pɒsteɪt] *n* apóstata *mf*

a posteriori ['eɪpɒsterɪ'ɔːraɪ] *adj* a posteriori

apostle [ə'pɒsəl] *n* apóstol *m*

apostolic(al) [æpɒs'tɒlɪk(əl)] *adj Rel* apostólico(a); **the a. succession** la sucesión apostólica

apostrophe [ə'pɒstrəfɪ] *n* (**a**) *(punctuation mark)* apóstrofo *m* (**b**) *Lit* apóstrofe *m or f*

apostrophize, apostrophise [ə'pɒstrəfaɪz] *vt Lit* apostrofar

apothecary [ə'pɒθəkərɪ] *n Hist* boticario(a) *m,f*

apotheosis [əpɒθɪ'əʊsɪs] (*pl* **apotheoses** [əpɒθɪ'əʊsiːz]) *n* (**a**) *(deification)* deificación *f*, apoteosis *f* (**b**) *(ideal example)* paradigma *m*, quintaesencia *f*

appal, *US* **appall** [ə'pɔːl] (*pt & pp* **appalled**) *vt* horrorizar, espantar; **to be appalled at** *or* **by sth** horrorizarse por algo; **he was appalled at** *or* **by the children's bad language** le horrorizaban las palabrotas que decían los niños; **I'm appalled!** ¡qué horror!, ¡qué espanto!

Appalachia [æpə'leɪtʃɪə] *n* región *f* de los Apalaches

Appalachian [æpə'leɪtʃɪən] **1** *n* **the Appalachians, the A. Mountains** los (montes) Apalaches

2 *adj* de los Apalaches

appall *US* = **appal**

appalling [ə'pɔːlɪŋ] *adj* espantoso(a), horroroso(a); **what an a. prospect/thought!** ¡qué panorama/idea tan terrible!

appallingly [ə'pɔːlɪŋlɪ] *adv* espantosamente, terriblemente; **he speaks French quite a.** habla un francés espantoso; **to treat sb a.** tratar a alguien de manera detestable

apparatchik [æpə'rætʃɪk] *n* (**a**) *(in Communist state)* apparatchik *m*, miembro *m* del aparato (**b**) *Pej (bureaucrat)* burócrata *mf*

apparatus [æpə'reɪtəs] *n* (**a**) *(equipment) (in laboratory, gym)* aparatos *mpl*; **a piece of a.** un aparato (**b**) *Anat* aparato *m*; **the digestive/respiratory a.** el aparato digestivo/respiratorio (**c**) *(of organization)* aparato *m*; **the a. of government** el aparato del gobierno (**d**) *Lit* **critical a.** aparato crítico

apparel [ə'pærəl] **1** *n* (**a**) *Literary (garb)* atuendo *m*, atavío *m* (**b**) *US (clothes)* indumentaria *f*, ropa *f*

2 *vt* (*pt & pp Br* **apparelled**, *US* **appareled**) *Literary (dress, adorn)* ataviar; **brightly/richly apparelled** ataviado(a) con vistosos colores/grandes galas

apparent [ə'pærənt] *adj* (**a**) *(obvious)* evidente; **it was a. to me that...** para mí era evidente *or* estaba claro que...; **to become a.** hacerse patente *or* evidente; **for no a. reason** sin motivo aparente (**b**) *(seeming)* aparente; **with a. ease** con aparente soltura *or* facilidad

apparently [ə'pærəntlɪ] *adv* al parecer, aparentemente; **is she married? – a./a. not** ¿está casada? – eso parece/parece que no; **a. easy/innocent** aparentemente fácil/inocente; **a. he never knew he had a son** según parece *or* por lo visto *or* al parecer nunca supo que tenía un hijo

apparition [æpə'rɪʃən] *n* aparición *f*

appeal [ə'piːl] **1** *n* (**a**) *(call)* llamamiento *m*; **a tearful/heartfelt a.** una emocionada/sentida súplica; **an a. for help/funds** un llamamiento para solicitar ayuda/para recaudar fondos; **an a. for calm** un llamamiento a la calma; **to make an a. for sth** hacer un llamamiento para solicitar algo; **she made an a. on behalf of the victims** hizo un llamamiento en favor de las víctimas *or* los damnificados

(**b**) *(for charity)* = campaña de recaudación de fondos para fines benéficos

(**c**) *Law* recurso *m* de apelación, apelación *f*; **to lodge an a.** presentar una apelación; **on a.** en recurso de apelación, en segunda instancia; **with no right of a.** sin derecho de apelación *or* recurso ▸▸ ***A. Court***

APOSTROPHE "S"

El uso del apóstrofo para indicar posesión puede llevar a confusión y no sólo entre aquellos que están aprendiendo inglés. La regla básica es que se le añade **'s** al sustantivo en singular o al plural irregular que no acaba en **-s** y al plural regular sólo se le añade el apóstrofo.

John's brother-in-law *el hermano político de John*
the scheme's chances of success *las posibilidades de éxito del plan*
the policemen's uniforms *los uniformes de los policías*
the brothers' workplace *el lugar de trabajo de los hermanos*

Si una palabra en singular acaba en **-s**, muchos angloparlantes no saben con seguridad cómo escribir el posesivo y menos aún cómo pronunciarlo. A veces se añade el apóstrofo más **s** (sobre todo en inglés británico) y a veces sólo el apóstrofo (más frecuente en inglés americano y con nombres propios extranjeros):

Wallace Stevens' (*or* **Stevens's) poetry** *la poesía de Wallace Stevens*
Cervantes' plays *las obras de Cervantes*

Al estar el apóstrofo más **s** muy asociado a la idea de posesión, el error más frecuente suele ser escribir el posesivo **its** *(su)* como **it's** (= it is, *es*).
En el uso popular a veces se encuentran apóstrofos incorrectos en plurales normales, en los que no hay idea de posesión:

✗ **tomatoe's 40p per lb** *tomates, 40 peniques la libra*

Otra veces se omiten cuando sería necesario escribirlos. Esto ocurre a menudo en los nombres de las tiendas:

✗ **Jennys Hairdressing Salon** *Salón de peluquería Jenny*

El apóstrofo se puede usar para mostrar el plural de las letras, de fechas y siglas, pero también puede omitirse:

during the 1970's *durante la década de los 70*
there are too many f's in that word *esa palabra tiene demasiadas efes*
I paid all her IOU's *pagué todos su pagarés*

tribunal *m* de apelación; ***a. court judge*** juez *mf* de apelaciones

(**d**) *(attraction)* atractivo *m*, aliciente *m*; **the idea does have a certain a.** la idea resulta un tanto atractiva; **to have** *or* **hold little a. for sb** no atraer mucho a alguien; **to have great a.** ser muy atractivo(a); **their music has a wide a.** su música gusta a gente muy diversa

2 *vt US Law* **to a. a decision** entablar recurso de apelación contra una decisión

3 *vi* (**a**) *(make a plea)* **to a. (to sb) for help/money** solicitar *or* pedir ayuda/dinero (a alguien); **they're appealing for help for the victims** solicitan *or* piden ayuda en favor de las víctimas; **she appealed to me to be patient** me rogó *or* suplicó que tuviera paciencia

(**b**) **to a. to sth** *(invoke)* invocar algo, apelar a algo; **to a. to sb's generosity/sense of justice** apelar a la generosidad/al sentido de (la) justicia de alguien

(**c**) *(attract)* **to a. to sb** atraer a alguien; **the programmes a. most to children** los programas interesan principalmente a los niños; **the book appeals to the reader's imagination** el libro despierta la imaginación del lector; **the idea appealed to me** me atrajo *or* sedujo la idea; **it doesn't a. to me** no me atrae

(**d**) *Law* apelar, recurrir; **to a. against** *(decision, sentence)* interponer recurso de apelación contra, recurrir; **we will a. to the Supreme Court** apelaremos al *or* ante el Tribunal Supremo, interpondremos un recurso de casación (ante el Tribunal Supremo)

appealing [ə'pi:lɪŋ] *adj* (**a**) *(attractive)* atractivo(a), interesante (**b**) *(imploring)* suplicante

---

APPEAR [ə'pɪə(r)] *vi* (**a**) *(come into view)* aparecer; **a head appeared at the window** una cabeza se asomó por la ventana, *Am* una cabeza apareció en la ventana; **where did you a. from?** ¿de dónde has salido?; **he appeared from behind a bush** apareció de detrás *or Am* desde atrás de un seto; **to a. from nowhere** aparecer de repente, surgir de la nada; **his name appears on the list** su nombre figura en la lista; **Hamlet's dead father appeared to him** el difunto padre de Hamlet se le apareció

(**b**) *(actor)* **to a. as Estragon** hacer el papel de Estragón; **she's currently appearing at the National Theatre** actualmente está actuando en el Teatro Nacional; **to a. on TV** salir en televisión; *Fig* **when did your new girlfriend a. on the scene?** ¿desde cuándo sales con tu nueva novia?

(**c**) *Sport* jugar; **he appeared three times for his country** representó tres veces a su país

(**d**) *(publication, movie)* salir, aparecer; **to a. in print** salir publicado, publicarse

(**e**) *Law* **to a. before a court** comparecer ante un tribunal; **to a. on a charge of burglary** comparecer acusado de robo; **to a. for sb** *(of counsel)* representar a alguien

(**f**) *(look, seem)* parecer; **to a. to be lost** parecer perdido(a); **there appears to be a mistake** parece que hay un error; **it appears as if** *or* **though...** parece que...; **it appears not, it would a. not** parece que no; **it appears so, so it would a.** eso parece; **it appears (that)..., it would a. (that)...** parece que...; **it appears to me that...** me parece que...; **everything is not as it appears** las apariencias engañan; **I know how it must a. to you, but...** ya sé lo que debes estar pensando, pero...; **he tried to make it a. as if it had been an accident** intentó hacer parecer que había sido un accidente

---

appearance [ə'pɪərəns] *n* (**a**) *(arrival)* aparición *f*, llegada *f*; **with the a. of fast-food restaurants** con la llegada *or* aparición de los restaurantes de comida rápida; **to make an a. (at)** *(attend)* aparecer (en), presentarse (en); **to put in an a.** hacer acto de presencia

(**b**) *(of actor)* aparición *f*; **she has made a number of television appearances** ha aparecido *or* salido varias veces en televisión; **to make one's first a. on TV** debutar en televisión; **in order of a.** por orden de aparición

(**c**) *Sport* actuación *f*; **it was his last a. for United** fue el último encuentro que disputó con el United

(**d**) *(of publication)* publicación *f*

(**e**) *Law (in court)* comparecencia *f*; **to make an a. before a court** *or* **a judge** comparecer ante un tribunal *or* juez

(**f**) *(looks)* apariencia *f*, aspecto *m*; **to have a good a.** *(person)* tener buena presencia; **he has never bothered much about his a.** nunca se ha preocupado mucho por su aspecto; **unusual/comic in a.** de aspecto insólito/ridículo *or* cómico; **to give every** *or* **the a. of confidence** dar toda la impresión de tener seguridad en sí mismo

(**g**) **appearances** *(outward signs)* apariencias *fpl*; **you shouldn't judge by appearances** no se debe juzgar por las apariencias; **it has all the appearances of a conspiracy** tiene todo el aspecto de ser una conspiración; **appearances can be deceptive** las apariencias engañan; **to keep up appearances** guardar las apariencias; **to** *or* **by all appearances** a juzgar por lo visto; **for appearances' sake** para cubrir *or* guardar las apariencias *or* formas; **contrary to all appearances, against all appearances** en contra de (todo) lo que pudiera parecer, a pesar de las apariencias

appease [ə'pi:z] *vt* (**a**) *(anger)* aplacar, apaciguar; *(person)* calmar, apaciguar (**b**) *Pol* contemporizar con

appeasement [ə'pi:zmənt] *n* (**a**) *(of person, anger)* apaciguamiento *m* (**b**) *Pol* contemporización *f*

appellant [ə'pelənt] *n Law* apelante *mf*, recurrente *mf*

appellate court [ə'pelɪt'kɔ:t] *n US Law* tribunal *m* de apelación

appellation [æpə'leɪʃən] *n Formal* denominación *f*

append [ə'pend] *vt (list, document)* adjuntar (**to** a); *(one's signature)* estampar (**to** en)

appendage [ə'pendɪdʒ] *n* apéndice *m*; **she was tired of being treated as his a.** estaba harta de que se la tratara como si fuera un mero apéndice de él

appendectomy [æpen'dektəmɪ] *n Med* operación *f* de apendicitis, *Spec* apendicectomía *f*

appendices *pl of* **appendix**

appendicitis [əpendɪ'saɪtɪs] *n* apendicitis *f inv*; **to have a.** tener apendicitis

appendix [ə'pendɪks] (*pl* **appendices** [ə'pendɪsi:z]) *n* (**a**) *Anat* apéndice *m*; **to have one's a. (taken) out** operarse de apendicitis (**b**) *(to book, report)* apéndice *m*

appertain [æpə'teɪn] *vi Formal* (**a**) *(belong)* **to a. to** pertenecer a; **the lands appertaining to the Crown** las tierras que son propiedad de la Corona (**b**) *(relate)* **to a. to** ser propio(a) de, guardar relación con

appetite ['æpɪtaɪt] *n* (**a**) *(for food)* apetito *m*; **to have a good a.** tener buen apetito; **to spoil sb's a.** quitarle el apetito a alguien; **to lose one's a.** perder el apetito; **to give sb an a.** abrirle el apetito a alguien; **to work up an a.** abrir *or* despertar el apetito

(**b**) *(for knowledge, adventure)* afán *m*, sed *f*; *(for sex)* deseo *m*, apetito *m* (**for** de); **he has an insatiable a. for work** tiene un insaciable afán de trabajo

appetizer ['æpɪtaɪzə(r)] *n (food, drink)* aperitivo *m*; *Fig* **they showed a few scenes as an a.** proyectaron algunas escenas para abrir *or* hacer boca

appetizing ['æpɪtaɪzɪŋ] *adj (food, smell)* apetitoso(a); *Fig (prospect, suggestion)* sugestivo(a), sugerente

applaud [ə'plɔ:d] **1** *vt* aplaudir; **his efforts are to be applauded** sus esfuerzos son digno de aplauso *or* alabanza; **we a. this decision** aplaudimos esta decisión

2 *vi* aplaudir

applause [ə'plɔ:z] *n (clapping)* aplauso *m*, ovación *f*; *(approval)* aplauso *m*, aprobación *f*; **to win sb's a., to win a. from sb** ganarse el aplauso *or* la aprobación de alguien

apple ['æpəl] *n* (**a**) *(fruit)* manzana *f* ►► ***a. core*** corazón *m* de manzana; ***a. corer*** sacacorazones *m inv* (de manzanas); ***a. dumpling*** bollo *m* relleno de manzana; *US* ***a. jack*** brandy *m or* aguardiente *m* de manzana; ***a. juice*** *Esp* zumo *m or Am* jugo *m* de manzana; ***a. pie*** pastel *m* de manzana; IDIOM **as American as a. pie** típicamente americano(a); ***a. sauce*** compota *f* de manzanas; ***a. slice*** *(covered)* = empanada de hojaldre pequeña rellena de compota de manzana; *(open)* tarta *f* de manzana; ***a. strudel*** = rollito de hojaldre relleno de pasas y manzana; ***a. tart*** tarta *f* de manzana; ***a. tree*** manzano *m*; ***a. turnover*** = especie de empanada de hojaldre rellena de compota de manzana

(**b**) IDIOMS **she was the a. of his eye** era la niña de sus ojos; **to compare apples with oranges** meter en el mismo saco (dos cosas distintas), comparar lo incomparable; **the a. of discord** la manzana de la discordia; PROV **an a. a day keeps the doctor away** medicina extraordinaria es una manzana diaria

applecart ['æpəlkɑ:t] *n* IDIOM **to upset the a.** *(spoil plan)* echar todo por tierra

apple-cheeked ['æpəl'tʃi:kt] *adj* de mejillas sonrosadas

apple-pie ['æpəlpaɪ] *adj Fam* **in a. order** en perfecto orden; **to make sb an a. bed** hacer la petaca a alguien

apple-polisher ['æpəl'pɒlɪʃə(r)] *n US Fam* pelotillero(a) *m,f*, *Esp* pelota *mf*

applet ['æplɪt] *n Comptr* applet *m*

appliance [ə'plaɪəns] *n* (**a**) *(piece of equipment)* aparato *m*; **(electrical** *or* **domestic) a.** electrodoméstico *m* (**b**) *(fire engine)* coche *m* de bomberos (**c**) *(use)* empleo *m*, uso *m*

applicable [ə'plɪkəbəl] *adj* válido(a) (**to** para), aplicable (**to** a); **the rule is not a. in this case** la norma no ha lugar *or* no se aplica en este caso; **delete where not a.** *(on form)* táchese lo que no proceda

applicant ['æplɪkənt] *n (for job, patent, funding)* solicitante *mf*

application [æplɪ'keɪʃən] *n* (**a**) *(request) (for job, patent)* solicitud *f*; **to make an a. for sth** solicitar algo; **further details on a.** se facilitará más información a quien lo solicite ►► ***a. form*** *(for job, shares)* impreso *m* de solicitud

(**b**) *(of theory, technique)* aplicación *f*; **the practical applications of the research** las aplicaciones prácticas de la investigación

(**c**) *(of paint, ointment)* aplicación *f*; **for external a. only** *(medicine)* para uso tópico solamente

(**d**) *(effort)* aplicación *f*, entrega *f*; **he shows real a.** se le ve mucha entrega *or* dedicación, se muestra muy aplicado

(**e**) *Comptr* aplicación *f*, programa *m* ►► ***a. programme*** programa *m* de aplicación

applicator ['æplɪkeɪtə(r)] **1** *n* aplicador *m*

2 *adj* ***a. tampon*** tampón *m* con aplicador

applied [ə'plaɪd] *adj (maths, physics)* aplicado(a) ►► ***a. linguistics*** lingüística *f* aplicada

appliqué [ə'pli:keɪ] *n* aplique *m*, aplicación *f (en costura)*

apply [ə'plaɪ] **1** *vt* (**a**) *(put on)* aplicar; **to a. pressure to** ejercer presión sobre, presionar; **the bank applied pressure on him to repay his loan** el banco le presionó para que liquidara su préstamo; **to a. the brakes** emplear los frenos; **to a. heat to sth** aplicar calor a algo, calentar

(**b**) *(use) (system, theory)* aplicar; **we a. the same rule to all students** aplicamos la misma norma a todos los estudiantes; **he would like to a. his experience in IT to industry** quisiera aplicar su experiencia en informática en el ámbito industrial

(**c**) *(paint, cream, lotion)* aplicar (**to** a, en); **a. the paint using a roller** aplicar la pintura con (un) rodillo

(**d**) *(dedicate)* **to a. one's mind to sth** concentrarse en algo; **to a. oneself to one's work** aplicarse en el trabajo; **he must learn to a. himself** debe aprender a ser más aplicado

2 *vi* (**a**) *(for job, grant)* **to a. (to sb) for sth** solicitar algo (a alguien); **to a. for a job/patent** solicitar un empleo/una patente; **to a. in writing/in person** solicitar por escrito/en persona; **a. within** *(sign)* solicitud, en el interior

(**b**) *(law, rule)* **rule 26b applies in all other cases** la norma 26b se aplicará en todos los demás casos; **this clause no longer applies** esta cláusula ya no está en vigor; **that applies to you too!** ¡esto es válido *or* vale para tí también!

appoint [ə'pɔɪnt] *vt* (**a**) *(nominate) (person, committee)* nombrar, designar; **to a. sb to a post** designar a alguien para un cargo; **she was appointed acting director** la nombraron directora en funciones (**b**) *(place, date, time)* fijar; **let's a. a time for the meeting** fijemos una fecha para la reunión

appointed [ə'pɔɪntɪd] *adj* (**a**) *(nominated) (official, agent)* designado(a) (**b**) *Formal (agreed) (place, date, hour)* fijado(a), convenido(a) (**c**) *Br (furnished, equipped)* **a well a. house** una casa bien equipada *or* acondicionada

appointee [əpɔɪn'ti:] *n* persona *f* nombrada *or* designada

appointment [ə'pɔɪntmənt] *n* (**a**) *(meeting)* cita *f*; **to make an a. with sb** concertar una cita con alguien; **she didn't keep the a.** faltó *or* no acudió a la cita; **I've made/got an a. with the doctor** he pedido/tengo hora con el médico; **do you have an a.?** ¿tiene cita?; **he has a four o'clock a.** tiene cita *or* está citado a las cuatro; **by a. only** con cita previa

(**b**) *(to job, of committee)* nombramiento *m*, designación *f*; **to make an a.** hacer un nombramiento; *Com* **by a. to His/Her Majesty** proveedores de la Casa Real

(**c**) **appointments** *(in newspaper)* ofertas *fpl* de empleo

(**d**) *Formal* **appointments** *(of house)* equipamiento y mobiliario

apportion [ə'pɔ:ʃən] *vt (food, costs, praise)* distribuir, repartir; **to a. blame** repartir la culpa

apportionment [ə'pɔ:ʃənmənt] *n* (**a**) *(of food, costs, praise)* distribución *f*, reparto *m*; *(of blame)* repartición *f*, reparto *m* (**b**) *US Pol* = distribución proporcional entre los estados de los impuestos o del número de representantes en la cámara legislativa

apposite ['æpəzɪt] *adj* apropiado(a), oportuno(a)

apposition [æpə'zɪʃən] *n Gram* **in a. (to)** en aposición (a *or* con)

appraisal [ə'preɪzəl] *n (assessment)* evaluación *f*, valoración *f*; *(valuation)* tasación *f*

appraise [ə'preɪz] *vt (assess)* evaluar, valorar; **to a. the value of** *(property, jewellery)* tasar

appreciable [ə'pri:ʃɪəbəl] *adj (noticeable)* apreciable, sensible; *(significant)* considerable

appreciably [ə'pri:ʃɪəblɪ] *adv (noticeably)* de forma apreciable, sensiblemente; *(significantly)* considerablemente, significativamente

appreciate [ə'pri:ʃɪeɪt] **1** *vt* (**a**) *(be grateful for)* agradecer; **I a. your helping me** te agradezco tu ayuda; **I would a. it if you didn't shout** te agradecería que no gritaras; **we would a. a prompt reply to this letter** le rogamos una pronta respuesta (a la presente); **thanks, I'd really a. that** gracias, le quedaría sumamente agradecido

(**b**) *(grasp, understand)* darse cuenta de; **I fully a. (the fact) that...** me doy perfecta cuenta de que...; **I do a. your concern but...** me hago cargo *or* comprendo su preocupación, pero...; **we a. the risks** somos conscientes de los riesgos; **I hadn't appreciated how difficult it was** no me había dado cuenta de lo difícil que era

(**c**) *(value) (art, wine)* apreciar; *(person, contribution)* valorar; **she has never felt properly appreciated** nunca se ha sentido suficientemente valorada

2 *vi (goods, property, investment)* revalorizarse, apreciarse

appreciation [əpri:ʃɪ'eɪʃən] *n* (**a**) *(gratitude)* gratitud *f*, agradecimiento *m*; **to show one's a. of sth** mostrarse agradecido(a) por algo; **as a sign** *or* **token of our a.** en señal *or* como muestra de agradecimiento; **in a. of** en agradecimiento por

(**b**) *(understanding, awareness)* apreciación *f*, percepción *f*; **he has a thorough a. of the situation** es plenamente consciente de la situación; **she has no a. of what is involved** no se da cuenta de lo que implica

(**c**) *(valuing) (of music, art)* valorización *f*; **an art/music a. course** un curso de introducción *or* aproximación al arte/a la música; **a musical/wine a. society** una asociación de amigos de la música/del vino

(**d**) *(review) (of movie, author's work)* reseña *f*, crítica *f*; *(of person recently deceased)* reseña *f* necrológica

(**e**) *(increase in value)* revalorización *f*, apreciación *f* ►► *Fin* ***a. of assets*** revalorización *f* de activos

appreciative [ə'pri:ʃɪətɪv] *adj* (**a**) *(grateful) (person, response, audience)* agradecido(a); **to be a. of sb's help/efforts** sentirse muy agradecido(a) por la ayuda/los esfuerzos de alguien; **I gave him the present, but he wasn't very a.** le di el regalo, pero no se mostró muy agradecido

(**b**) *(showing understanding, awareness)* **to be a. of sth** ser consciente *or* darse cuenta de algo

(**c**) *(discriminating)* **an a. audience** un público con criterio; **he wrote an a. review of the play** escribió una reseña que valoraba la obra

appreciatively [ə'pri:ʃɪətɪvlɪ] *adv* (**a**) *(gratefully)* con gratitud (**b**) *(with enjoyment, approval)* con aprobación

apprehend [æprɪ'hend] *vt* (**a**) *(arrest)* detener, aprehender (**b**) *Formal (understand)* aprehender, comprender

apprehension [æprɪ'henʃən] *n* (**a**) *(fear)* aprensión *f* (**b**) *Formal (arrest)* detención *f*, aprehensión *f* (**c**) *Formal (understanding)* entendimiento *m*, comprensión *f*

apprehensive [æprɪ'hensɪv] *adj (look, smile)* temeroso(a), receloso(a); **to be a. about (doing) sth** tener miedo de (hacer) algo; **there's nothing to be a. about** no hay nada que temer; **I'm feeling a bit a.** estoy algo intranquilo *or* aprensivo

apprehensively [æprɪ'hensɪvlɪ] *adv* temerosamente, con recelo *or* temor

apprentice [ə'prentɪs] **1** *n* aprendiz(iza) *m,f*; **an a. toolmaker/butcher** un aprendiz de forjador/carnicero(a)

2 *vt* **to a. sb to sb** colocar a alguien de aprendiz(iza) de alguien; **he was apprenticed to a tailor** estaba de aprendiz con un sastre

apprenticeship [ə'prentɪʃɪp] *n also Fig* aprendizaje *m*; **to serve one's a.** hacer el aprendizaje

apprise [ə'praɪz] *vt Formal* poner al corriente, informar (**of** de); **we were not apprised of his arrival** no estábamos informados *or* al corriente de su llegada; **keep me apprised of the situation as it develops** manténgame *or* téngame al corriente de la situación

APPROACH [ə'prəʊtʃ] **1** *n* (**a**) *(coming) (of person, season)* llegada *f*; *(of night)* caída *f*; **I could hear their a.** los oía acercarse; **at the a. of summer** con la llegada del verano; *Av* **we are making our a. into Dallas** estamos efectuando la maniobra de aproximación a Dallas; **to make approaches** *or* **an a. to sb** *(proposal)* hacer una propuesta inicial a alguien

(**b**) *(method)* enfoque *m*, planteamiento *m* (**to** de); *(attitude)* actitud *f*

(**c**) *(route of access)* acceso *m*; **the approaches to a town** los accesos a una ciudad ►► *Aut* ***a. road*** (vía *f* de) acceso *m*

(**d**) **a. (shot)** *(in golf, tennis)* golpe *m* de aproximación

2 *vt* (**a**) *(get nearer to)* acercarse a, aproximarse a; **I'm approaching forty-five** tengo casi cuarenta y cinco años; **the total is approaching 10,000** el total se aproxima a 10.000; **temperatures approaching 50°C** temperaturas que rozan los 50°C; **I felt something approaching joy** sentí algo así como alegría

(**b**) *(go up to)* acercarse a, aproximarse a

(**c**) *(go and talk to)* **to a. sb about a problem** acudir *or* dirigirse a alguien para tratar un problema; **she approached several organizations (for funding)** acudió *or* se dirigió *or* recurrió a varias organizaciones (para pedir fondos); **to be easy/difficult to a.** ser/no ser accesible
(**d**) *(tackle)* abordar, enfocar
3 *vi* acercarse, aproximarse; **the time is approaching when you will have to fend for yourself** se acerca el día en el que tendrás que valerte por ti mismo

approachable [ə'prəʊtʃəbəl] *adj* (**a**) *(place)* accesible; **the house is only a. from the sea** sólo se puede acceder a la casa por el mar (**b**) *(person)* accesible

approaching [ə'prəʊtʃɪŋ] *adj (holiday, season)* próximo(a); **he recognized the a. vehicle** reconoció el vehículo que se aproximaba

approbation [æprə'beɪʃən] *n Formal* aceptación *f*, aprobación *f*

appropriate[1] [ə'prəʊprɪət] *adj (suitable)* adecuado(a), oportuno(a); *(proper)* adecuado(a), pertinente; **the/an a. moment** el/un momento adecuado; **apply using the a. form** solicítese mediante el formulario adecuado; **I am not the most a. person to ask** no soy la persona más indicada para preguntar; **music/remarks a. to the occasion** música apropiada para la ocasión/comentarios apropiados a la ocasión; **take (the) a. action** adoptar (las) medidas oportunas *or* pertinentes; **as a.** según el caso; **delete as a.** táchese según proceda

appropriate[2] [ə'prəʊprɪeɪt] *vt* (**a**) *(take, steal)* apropiarse (de); *Hum* **I seem to have appropriated this pen from somewhere** debo de haberme apropiado (de) esta pluma en alguna parte (**b**) *(set aside) (money, funds)* asignar, destinar (**to** *or* **for a**); **the funds appropriated for** *or* **to the school** los fondos destinados a la escuela

appropriately [ə'prəʊprɪətlɪ] *adv (suitably)* apropiadamente, adecuadamente; *(properly)* con propiedad, como es debido; **the restaurant is a. named "Montezuma's Revenge"** el nombre "Montezuma's Revenge" le viene al restaurante como anillo al dedo *or* que ni pintado

appropriateness [ə'prəʊprɪətnɪs] *n (suitability)* idoneidad *f*, acierto *m*; *(propriety)* corrección *f*, pertinencia *f*

appropriation [əprəʊprɪ'eɪʃən] *n* (**a**) *(taking)* apropiación *f* (**of** de) (**b**) *(setting aside) (of funds)* asignación *f*; **government appropriations** partidas presupuestarias estatales ►► *US* ***Appropriations Committee*** *(of Senate, House)* comité *m* de gastos, comisión *f* de presupuestos

approval [ə'pru:vəl] *n* aprobación *f*; **he gave/withheld his a.** dio/no dio su aprobación; **I've passed it to the director for her a.** se lo he pasado a la directora para que dé el visto bueno; **to meet with sb's a.** recibir *or* merecer la aprobación de alguien; **for (your) a.** *(on document)* para su aprobación *or* visto bueno; *Com* **on a.** a prueba ►► ***a. rating*** *(of product, politician)* índice *m* de aceptación *or* popularidad

approve [ə'pru:v] 1 *vt* aprobar; **the plan must be approved by the committee** el plan debe ser aprobado por el comité; **read and approved** *(on document)* visto y conforme
2 *vi* dar (uno) su aprobación, estar de acuerdo; **do you a.?** ¿está de acuerdo?, ¿le parece bien?; **I can't say I a., but I won't stop you** no puedo decir que me parezca bien, pero no voy a impedírtelo

► **approve of** *vt insep* aprobar; **she doesn't a. of them smoking** no aprueba que fumen; **they didn't a. of me learning to fly** no vieron con buenos ojos que estuviera aprendiendo a volar; **I don't a. of your friends** no me gustan tus amigos

approved [ə'pru:vd] *adj* (**a**) *(method, practice)* establecido(a), válido(a) (**b**) *(authorized)* autorizado(a) (**c**) *Br Formerly* ***a. school*** reformatorio *m*, correccional *m*

approving [ə'pru:vɪŋ] *adj* de aprobación

approvingly [ə'pru:vɪŋlɪ] *adv* con aprobación

approx [ə'prɒks] *adv* (*abbr* **approximately**) aprox., aproximadamente

approximate 1 *adj* [ə'prɒksɪmət] aproximado(a); **an a. answer** una respuesta aproximativa *or* aproximada; **a. to two decimal places** aproximado hasta la segunda cifra decimal
2 *vt* [ə'prɒksɪmeɪt] *(simulate)* reproducir aproximadamente
3 *vi* **to a. to** aproximarse a

approximately [ə'prɒksɪmətlɪ] *adv* aproximadamente; **his income is a. £20,000** sus ingresos rondan *or* están en torno a las 20.000 libras

approximation [əprɒksɪ'meɪʃən] *n* aproximación *f*; **his statement was no more than an a. of the truth** su declaración no fue más que una mera aproximación a la verdad

appurtenances [ə'pɜ:tənənsɪz] *npl Formal* enseres *mpl*, accesorios *mpl*

APR [eɪpi:'ɑ:(r)] *n Fin* (*abbr* **annual percentage rate**) TAE *m or f*

Apr (*abbr* **April**) abril *m*

après-ski ['æpreɪ'ski:] *n* apresquí *m*; **a. clothing/party** vestuario *or* ropa/fiesta de apresquí

apricot ['eɪprɪkɒt] *n* (**a**) *(fruit) Esp* albaricoque *m*, *Andes, RP* damasco *m*, *Méx* chabacano *m* ►► ***a. tree*** *Esp* albaricoquero *m*, *Andes, RP* damasco *m*, *Méx* chabacano *m* (**b**) *(colour)* color *m* melocotón

April ['eɪprɪl] *n* abril *m*; **A. showers** lluvias de abril; PROV **A. showers bring forth May flowers** marzo ventoso y abril lluvioso sacan a mayo florido y hermoso ►► ***A. fool*** *(person)* inocente *mf*; *(practical joke)* inocentada *f*; ***A. Fool's Day*** = 1 de abril, ≃ día *m* de los (Santos) Inocentes; *see also* **May**

a priori [eɪpraɪ'ɔ:raɪ] *adj* a priori

apron ['eɪprən] *n* (**a**) *(clothing) (for washing up)* delantal *m*; *(masonic)* mandil *m*; IDIOM *Fam* **he's still tied to his mother's a. strings** sigue pegado a las faldas de su madre (**b**) *Av* área *f* de estacionamiento (**c**) *Theat* proscenio *m*

apropos [æprə'pəʊ] 1 *adj* oportuno(a), pertinente
2 *prep Formal* **a. (of)** a propósito de; **a. of nothing** sin venir a colación

apse [æps] *n* ábside *m*

apt [æpt] *adj* (**a**) *(appropriate) (word, description)* apropiado(a), acertado(a); **it was very a. that it should end in that way** era lógico *or* (muy) normal que terminara de ese modo, acababa de una forma muy acertada
(**b**) *(likely)* **to be a. to do sth** ser propenso(a) a hacer algo; **I am a. to forget** tiendo a olvidar; **you're a. to offend people if you do that** corres el riesgo de ofender a los demás si haces eso
(**c**) *(quick to learn)* listo(a)

apt. *US* (*abbr* **apartment**) apto. *m*, *Esp* p *m*, *Arg* dpto *m*

aptitude ['æptɪtju:d] *n* aptitud *f*; **to have an a. for** tener aptitudes para; **she shows great a.** demuestra tener grandes aptitudes *or* dotes ►► ***a. test*** prueba *f* de aptitud

aptly ['æptlɪ] *adv* acertadamente; **the a. named "railway of death"** el ferrocarril llamado de la muerte, y no sin razón

aptness ['æptnɪs] *n (of remark, description)* acierto *m*, tino *m*

aqualung ['ækwəlʌŋ] *n* escafandra *f* autónoma

aquamarine ['ækwəmə'ri:n] 1 *n* (**a**) *(gem)* aguamarina *f* (**b**) *(colour)* color *m* aguamarina *or* azul mar
2 *adj (colour)* azul verdoso

aquaplane ['ækwəpleɪn] 1 *n Sport* tabla *f* de esquí náutico *or* acuático
2 *vi* (**a**) *Sport* hacer esquí náutico *or* acuático sobre tabla (**b**) *Br (car)* hacer aquaplaning, patinar

aquarium [ə'kweərɪəm] (*pl* **aquariums** *or* **aquaria** [ə'kweərɪə]) *n* acuario *m*

Aquarius [ə'kweərɪəs] *n (sign of zodiac)* acuario *m*; **to be (an) A.** ser acuario

aquatic [ə'kwætɪk] *adj* acuático(a) ►► ***a. warbler*** carricerín *m* cejudo

aquatint ['ækwətɪnt] *n Art* aguatinta *f*

aqueduct ['ækwɪdʌkt] *n* acueducto *m*

aqueous ['ækwɪəs] *adj Anat* ***a. humour*** humor *m* ácueo *or* acuoso; *Chem* ***a. solution*** disolución *f or* solución *f* acuosa

aquifer ['ækwɪfə(r)] *n Geol* acuífero *m*

aquiline ['ækwɪlaɪn] *adj* aguileño(a), aquilino(a)

Aquitaine ['ækwɪteɪn] *n* Aquitania

aquiver [ə'kwɪvə(r)] *adv* estremeciéndose, temblando; **to go all a.** estremecerse de arriba abajo

AR (*abbr* **Arkansas**) Arkansas

Arab ['ærəb] 1 *n* (**a**) *(person)* árabe *mf* (**b**) *(horse)* caballo *m* árabe
2 *adj* árabe ►► ***the A. League*** la Liga Árabe

arabesque [ærə'besk] *n* (**a**) *Art & Mus* arabesco *m* (**b**) *(in ballet)* arabesco *m*, arabesque *m*

Arabia [ə'reɪbɪə] *n* Arabia

Arabian [ə'reɪbɪən] 1 *n (person)* árabe *mf*
2 *adj* árabe ►► ***the A. Gulf*** el golfo Pérsico; ***the A. Nights*** Las mil y una noches; ***the A. Sea*** el Mar de Arabia *or* de Omán

Arabic ['ærəbɪk] 1 *n (language)* árabe *m*
2 *adj* árabe ►► ***A. numerals*** números *mpl* arábigos

arable ['ærəbəl] *adj* cultivable, arable; **a. land** tierra de cultivo, tierra de labor *or* de labranza

arachnid [ə'ræknɪd] *n Zool* arácnido *m*

arachnophobia [əræknə'fəʊbɪə] *n* aracnofobia *f*

Aragon ['ærəgən] *n* Aragón

Aragonese [ærəgəˈni:z] **1** *n* aragonés(esa) *m,f*
2 *adj* aragonés(esa)

-arama [-əˈrɑ:mə] *suffix Fam Hum* **you should have seen how much we ate ... it was pigarama!** no sabes cómo comimos ... ¡nos salía por las orejas!, *Esp* deberías haber visto cómo nos pusimos de comer... ¡había papeo por un tubo!; **try that new bar ... it's babearama!** tienes que ir a ese nuevo bar ... ¡está lleno de minas buenas! *or Esp* ¡hay mogollón de tías buenas!

Aramaic [ærəˈmeɪɪk] *n* arameo *m*

arbiter [ˈɑ:bɪtə(r)] *n (of taste, fashion)* árbitro *m*

arbitrage [ˈɑ:bɪtrɑ:ʒ] *n St Exch* arbitraje *m*

arbitrarily [ˈɑ:bɪtrərəlɪ, *US* ɑ:rbəˈtrerəlɪ] *adv* arbitrariamente

arbitrary [ˈɑ:bɪtrərɪ] *adj* **(a)** *(random)* arbitrario(a), caprichoso(a) **(b)** *(authoritarian)* tiránico(a), despótico(a)

arbitrate [ˈɑ:bɪtreɪt] **1** *vt* arbitrar
2 *vi* arbitrar (**between** entre)

arbitration [ɑ:bɪˈtreɪʃən] *n* arbitraje *m*; **the dispute went to a.** el conflicto se llevó ante un árbitro ►► ***a. panel*** junta *f* arbitral

arbitrator [ˈɑ:bɪtreɪtə(r)] *n (in dispute)* árbitro *m*, amigable componedor(ora) *m,f*

arbor *US* = **arbour**

arboreal [ɑ:ˈbɔ:rɪəl] *adj (animal)* arborícola

arboretum [ɑ:bəˈri:təm] (*pl* **arboretums** *or* **arboreta** [ɑ:bəˈri:tə]) *n* arboreto *m*

arboriculture [ˈɑ:bərɪkʌltʃə(r)] *n* arboricultura *f*

arborio rice [ɑ:ˈbɒrɪəʊˈraɪs] *n* arroz *m* arborio

arbour, *US* **arbor** [ˈɑ:bə(r)] *n* cenador *m*, pérgola *f*

ARC [ɑ:k] *n* **(a)** *Med* (*abbr* **aids-related complex**) CAS *m*, complejo *m* asociado al sida **(b)** (*abbr* **American Red Cross**) Cruz *f* Roja estadounidense

arc [ɑ:k] **1** *n* **(a)** *(of circle)* arco *m* ►► *Cin* ***a. shot*** plano *m* de arco **(b)** *Elec* arco *m* eléctrico ►► ***a. lamp*** lámpara *f* de arco (voltaico); ***a. welding*** soldadura *f* por arco
2 *vi (move in an arc)* trazar *or* dibujar un arco parábola; **the ball arced into the air** la pelota trazó *or* dibujó un arco *or* una parábola

arcade [ɑ:ˈkeɪd] *n* **(a)** *(for shopping)* galería *f* comercial **(b)** *(amusement arcade)* salón *m or* sala *f* recreativo(a) ►► ***a. game*** videojuego *m (de máquina recreativa)*; ***a. machine*** máquina *f* recreativa **(c)** *Archit* galería *f*

arcane [ɑ:ˈkeɪn] *adj* oscuro(a), misterioso(a)

arch¹ [ɑ:tʃ] **1** *n* **(a)** *Archit* arco *m* **(b)** *(of foot)* puente *m*; **to have fallen arches** tener los pies planos
2 *vt* **to a. one's back** arquear la espalda; **to a. one's eyebrows** enarcar las cejas
3 *vi* hacer un arco (**over** *or* **across** sobre); **the rocket arched into the air** el cohete subió trazando un arco

arch² *adj* **a. enemy** mayor enemigo(a); **a. traitor** gran traidor(ora)

arch³ *adj* **(a)** *(mischievous)* pícaro(a) **(b)** *(superior) (manner)* condescendiente; **they exchanged a. glances** cruzaron miradas de inteligencia *or* complicidad

archaeological, *US* **archeological** [ɑ:kɪəˈlɒdʒɪkəl] *adj* arqueológico(a); **a. site** emplazamiento arqueológico

archaeologist, *US* **archeologist** [ɑ:kɪˈɒlədʒɪst] *n* arqueólogo(a) *m,f*

archaeology, *US* **archeology** [ɑ:kɪˈɒlədʒɪ] *n* arqueología *f*

archaic [ɑ:ˈkeɪɪk] *adj* **(a)** *(ancient)* arcaico(a) **(b)** *Fam (old-fashioned)* arcaico(a), prehistórico(a); **his ideas about sex are pretty a.** sus ideas sobre el sexo son bastante prehistóricas *or* carcas

archaism [ˈɑ:keɪɪzəm] *n* arcaísmo *m*

archangel [ˈɑ:keɪndʒəl] *n* arcángel *m*

archbishop [ɑ:tʃˈbɪʃəp] *n* arzobispo *m*; **the A. of Canterbury** el Arzobispo de Canterbury

archdeacon [ɑ:tʃˈdi:kən] *n* arcediano *m*, archidiácono *m*

archdiocese [ɑ:tʃˈdaɪəsɪs] *n* archidiócesis *f inv*

archduchess [ɑ:tʃˈdʌtʃɪs] *n* archiduquesa *f*

archduchy [ɑ:tʃˈdʌtʃɪ] *n* archiducado *m*

archduke [ɑ:tʃˈdju:k] *n* archiduque *m*

arched [ɑ:tʃt] *adj* **(a)** *(window)* en forma de arco **(b)** *(back)* arqueado(a) **(c)** *(eyebrows)* arqueado(a), enarcado(a)

archeological, archeologist *etc US* = **archaeological, archaeologist** *etc*

archer [ˈɑ:tʃə(r)] *n* arquero(a) *m,f*

archery [ˈɑ:tʃərɪ] *n* tiro *m* con arco

archetypal [ɑ:kɪˈtaɪpəl] *adj* arquetípico(a), típico(a)

archetype [ˈɑ:kɪtaɪp] *n* arquetipo *m*, modelo *m*

Archimedes [ɑ:kɪˈmi:di:z] *pr n* Arquímedes ►► ***A.' principle*** principio *m* de Arquímedes; ***A.' screw*** tornillo *m* de Arquímedes

archipelago [ɑ:kɪˈpeləgəʊ] (*pl* **archipelagoes** *or* **archipelagos**) *n* archipiélago *m*

architect [ˈɑ:kɪtekt] *n* **(a)** *(of building)* arquitecto(a) *m,f* **(b)** *(of scheme)* artífice *mf*; **she was the a. of her own downfall** fue la artífice de su propia perdición

architectural [ɑ:kɪˈtektʃərəl] *adj* arquitectónico(a)

architecturally [ɑ:kɪˈtektʃərəlɪ] *adv* arquitectónicamente

architecture [ˈɑ:kɪtektʃə(r)] *n* **(a)** *(buildings, discipline)* arquitectura *f* **(b)** *Comptr* arquitectura *f*

architrave [ˈɑ:kɪtreɪv] *n Archit* arquitrabe *m*

archive [ˈɑ:kaɪv] *n* **(a)** *(place, collection)* archivo *m* ►► *Cin* ***a. footage*** imágenes *fpl* de archivo **(b)** *Comptr* archivo *m* ►► ***a. file*** fichero *m* de archivo

archivist [ˈɑ:kɪvɪst] *n* archivero(a) *m,f*

archly [ˈɑ:tʃlɪ] *adv* **(a)** *(mischievously)* con picardía, maliciosamente **(b)** *(with superior air)* con aire de superioridad

archway [ˈɑ:tʃweɪ] *n (passage)* arcada *f*; *(entrance)* arco *m*

Arctic [ˈɑ:ktɪk] **1** *n* **the A.** el Ártico
2 *adj* **(a)** *(climate)* ártico(a) ►► ***the A. Circle*** el Círculo Polar Ártico; ***A. fox*** zorro *m* ártico; ***the A. Ocean*** el océano (Glacial) Ártico; ***A. skua*** págalo *m* parásito; ***A. tern*** charrán *m* ártico **(b)** *Fam (very cold)* helado(a), glacial

Ardennes [ɑ:ˈden] *npl* **the A.** las Ardenas

ardent [ˈɑ:dənt] *adj (desire, love)* ardiente, apasionado(a); *(admirer, believer, supporter)* ferviente; **his a. protestations of loyalty convinced no one** sus fervientes manifestaciones de lealtad no convencieron a nadie

ardently [ˈɑ:dəntlɪ] *adv (to desire, love)* apasionadamente; *(to admire, believe, support)* fervientemente

ardour, *US* **ardor** [ˈɑ:də(r)] *n* ardor *m*, fervor *m*

arduous [ˈɑ:djʊəs] *adj* arduo(a), difícil

arduousness [ˈɑ:djʊəsnɪs] *n* arduidad *f*, dificultad *f*

are [ɑ:(r)] *plural and 2nd person singular of* **be**

area [ˈeərɪə] *n* **(a)** *(surface, extent)* área *f*; **it is 500 m² in a., it has** *or* **covers an a. of 500 m²** tiene una extensión *or* abarca una superficie de 500 m²
(b) *(region)* área *f*, zona *f*; *(of town, city)* zona *f*, barrio *m*; **the London a.** la región londinense; **a cotton (growing)/mining a.** una zona algodonera/cuenca minera; **an a. of outstanding natural beauty** una zona de elevado valor paisajístico; **houses were searched over a wide a.** se registraron las viviendas en un extenso radio *or* en una extensa zona; **in the general a.** en los alrededores; **it costs in the a. of $100** cuesta en torno a los 100 dólares ►► ***a. bombing*** bombardeo *m* de área; *US Tel* ***a. code*** prefijo *m*; *Com* ***a. manager*** jefe *m* de zona
(c) *(section) (of brain, lung, skin)* zona *f*, parte *f*; *(of room, building)* zona *f*, parte *f*; **eating a.** comedor; **living a.** zona de estar; **a (no-) smoking a.** un espacio *or* una zona de (no) fumadores
(d) *(of knowledge, topic)* área *f*, ámbito *m*; **it's his main a. of expertise** es su principal especialidad *or* ámbito de conocimientos; **it's a difficult a.** es un tema complicado; **an a. of agreement** un área de acuerdo
(e) *(in front of basement)* patio *m*
(f) *(on soccer pitch)* área *f*

areaway [ˈeərɪəweɪ] *n US (in front of basement)* patio *m*

arena [əˈri:nə] *n* **(a)** *(stadium)* estadio *m* **(b)** *(area of operation) (economic, international)* ruedo *m*; **the political a.** la escena política; **to enter the a.** salir al ruedo, saltar a la palestra

aren't [ɑ:nt] **(a)** = **are not (b) a. I?** = **am I not?**

areola [əˈrɪələ] *n Anat* **(a)** *(of eye)* círculo *m* menor (del iris) **(b)** *(of nipple)* areola *f*, aréola *f*

Argentina [ɑ:dʒənˈti:nə] *n* Argentina

Argentine [ˈɑ:dʒəntaɪn] **1** *n* **(a)** *(person)* argentino(a) *m,f* **(b)** *Old-fashioned* **the A.** *(country)* (la) Argentina
2 *adj* argentino(a)

Argentinian [ɑ:dʒənˈtɪnɪən] **1** *n* argentino(a) *m,f*
2 *adj* argentino(a)

Argie [ˈɑ:dʒɪ] *n Br Fam* = término generalmente ofensivo para referirse a los argentinos acuñado durante la guerra de las Malvinas

argon [ˈɑ:gɒn] *n Chem* argón *m*

Argonaut [ˈɑ:gənɔ:t] *n Mythol* **the Argonauts** los Argonautas

argot ['ɑːgəʊ] *n* jerga *f*, argot *m*

arguable ['ɑːgjʊəbəl] *adj* **(a)** *(questionable)* discutible; **it is a. whether it would have made any difference** cabe la posibilidad de que las cosas hubiesen sido distintas **(b)** *(conceivable)* **it is a. that...** se podría afirmar que...

arguably ['ɑːgjʊəblɪ] *adv* **it's a. the city's best restaurant** es, probablemente, el mejor restaurante de la ciudad; **a., it may have made no difference** probablemente haya dado lo mismo

argue ['ɑːgjuː] **1** *vt* **(a)** *(case, position)* argumentar; **he argued the case for lower taxes** expuso los argumentos para reducir los impuestos; **to a. that...** aducir *or* argumentar que...; **I didn't want to a. the point in detail** no quise discutir a fondo la cuestión
(b) *Formal (indicate)* apuntar hacia, denotar; **such actions a. a complete lack of interest on their part** este tipo de actuaciones denotan una absoluta falta de interés por su parte
2 *vi* **(a)** *(quarrel)* discutir (**with** con); **to a. about sth** discutir sobre algo; **I'm not going to a. about it** *(I refuse to discuss it)* no pienso discutir al respecto; **don't a.!** ¡no discutas!, ¡no protestes!
(b) *(reason)* **to a. for** *(defend)* abogar por; **to a. against** *(oppose)* oponerse a; **we could a. about it all day** podríamos estar discutiéndolo todo el día; **the evidence argues against him** las pruebas hablan *or* están en su contra

▶ **argue out** *vt sep* **I left them to a. it out (between them)** los dejé para que se pusieran de acuerdo

arguing ['ɑːgjuːɪŋ] *n* **that's enough a.** ya basta de discutir, se acabó la discusión; *Fam* **and no a.!** ¡y no hay más que hablar!, ¡y sin rechistar!

argument ['ɑːgjʊmənt] *n* **(a)** *(quarrel)* discusión *f*, pelea *f*; **to have an a. (about sth)** discutir (por algo); **to get into an a.** meterse en una discusión; **and I don't want any arguments!** ¡y punto!; *Hum* **he had an a. with a lamppost** tuvo un percance con una farola
(b) *(debate)* discusión *f*, debate *m*; **it is open to a. whether...** cabe plantearse si...; **you should listen to both sides of the a.** deberías escuchar los dos puntos de vista
(c) *(reason)* argumento *m*; **an a. for/against doing sth** un argumento a favor de/en contra de hacer algo; **there's an a. for doing nothing** hay razones para no hacer nada; **suppose for a.'s sake that...** pongamos por caso que...
(d) *(reasoning)* razonamiento *m*, lógica *f*; **I didn't follow his (line of) a.** no entendí su razonamiento

argumentation [ɑːgjʊmen'teɪʃən] *n* argumentación *f*, razonamiento *m*

argumentative [ɑːgjʊ'mentətɪv] *adj* discutidor(ora), pendenciero(a)

argy-bargy ['ɑːdʒɪ'bɑːdʒɪ] *n Fam* agarrada *f*, trifulca *f*; **I don't want any a. with you** no quiero tenerla contigo

argyle [ɑː'gaɪl] *adj (socks, jumper)* de rombos

aria ['ɑːrɪə] *n Mus* aria *f*

Ariadne [ærɪ'ædnɪ] *n Mythol* Ariadna

Arian ['eərɪən] *n* **to be (an) A.** ser aries

arid ['ærɪd] *adj* **(a)** *(waterless)* árido(a) **(b)** *(argument, style)* árido(a)

aridity [ə'rɪdɪtɪ] *n* **(a)** *(of climate, region)* aridez *f* **(b)** *(of argument, style)* aridez *f*

Aries ['eəriːz] *n (sign of zodiac)* aries *m*; **to be (an) A.** ser aries

aright [ə'raɪt] *adv* correctamente, como es debido

arise [ə'raɪz] (*pt* **arose** [ə'rəʊz], *pp* **arisen** [ə'rɪzən]) *vi* **(a)** *(problem, situation)* surgir; **the question has not yet arisen** todavía no se ha presentado la cuestión; **if complications should a.** si surgieran complicaciones; **should the need a.** si surgiera la necesidad; **a storm arose** se formó una tormenta
(b) *(result)* originarse, arrancar; **a problem that arises from this decision** un problema que tiene su origen en esta decisión; **matters arising from the last meeting** las cuestiones planteadas a raíz *or* como resultado de la última reunión
(c) *Literary (get up)* levantarse; **a., Sir Cedric!** ¡en pie *or* alzaos, Sir Cedric!

aristocracy [ærɪs'tɒkrəsɪ] *n* aristocracia *f*

aristocrat [*Br* 'ærɪstəkræt, *US* ə'rɪstəkræt] *n* aristócrata *mf*

aristocratic [*Br* ærɪstə'krætɪk, *US* ərɪstə'krætɪk] *adj* aristocrático(a)

Aristotle ['ærɪstɒtəl] *pr n* Aristóteles

arithmetic [ə'rɪθmətɪk] *n (calculations)* cálculos *mpl*, aritmética *f*; *(subject)* aritmética *f*; **my a. is absolutely appalling** soy un verdadero desastre para la aritmética; **your a. is spot on** tu cálculo (aritmético) es exacto; **it's a simple question of a.** es una mera *or* simple cuestión de aritmética

arithmetic(al) [ærɪθ'metɪk(əl)] *adj* aritmético(a) ►► *Comptr* ***a. logic unit*** unidad *f* aritmético-lógica; ***a. mean*** media *f* aritmética; ***a. progression*** progresión *f* aritmética

Ariz (*abbr* **Arizona**) Arizona

Arizona [ærɪ'zəʊnə] *n* Arizona

Ark (*abbr* **Arkansas**) Arkansas

ark [ɑːk] *n* arca *f*; IDIOM **like sth out of the a.** antediluviano(a), de los tiempos de Maricastaña *or RP* del Ñaupa *or Chile* del Ñauca ►► ***the A. of the Covenant*** el Arca de la Alianza

Arkansas ['ɑːkənsɔː] *n* Arkansas

ARM [ɑːm] **1** *n* **(a)** *(of person, chair)* brazo *m*; *(of garment)* manga *f*; **to carry sth/sb in one's arms** llevar algo/a alguien en brazos; **she took him in her arms** lo tomó *or Esp* cogió en brazos; **he took my a., he took me by the a.** me tomó *or Esp* cogió del brazo; **to hold the ball at a.'s length** agarrar la pelota con el brazo extendido; **to throw one's arms around sb** abrazar a alguien; **to walk a. in a.** caminar *or* ir del brazo; **he had a young blonde on his a.** iba del brazo de una joven rubia; *Fig* **the long a. of the law** el (largo) brazo de la ley; *Fam Fig* **a list as long as your a.** una lista más larga que un día sin pan; **to receive sb with open arms** *(warmly welcome)* recibir a alguien con los brazos abiertos; IDIOM **to cost an a. and a leg** costar un ojo de la cara *or* un riñón; IDIOM **I'd give my right a. to do it** daría lo que fuera por hacerlo; IDIOM **to keep sb at a.'s length** mantenerse a una distancia prudencial de alguien ►► ***a. wrestling*** los pulsos, *Am* la pulseada
(b) **arms** *(weapons)* armas *fpl*; **to lay down one's arms** deponer las armas; **to take up arms (against)** tomar *or Esp* coger las armas (contra); **under arms** armados y listos para luchar; IDIOM *Fam* **to be up in arms about sth** estar furioso *or RP* caliente por algo ►► ***arms control*** control *m* de armamento; ***arms dealer*** traficante *mf* de armas; ***arms dealing*** compra-venta *f* de armas, tráfico *m* de armas; ***arms race*** carrera *f* armamentista *or* de armamentos; ***arms trafficking*** tráfico *m* de armas
(c) *(in heraldry)* **(coat of) arms** escudo *m* de armas
(d) *(of organization)* sección *f*
(e) *(of spectacles)* patilla *f*; *(of record-player)* brazo *m*
(f) *(of land, water)* brazo *m*
2 *vt (person, country)* armar; **to a. oneself with sth** *(knife, gun)* armarse con algo; *Fig* **to a. oneself with the facts** armarse de datos

armada [ɑː'mɑːdə] *n* **(a)** *Hist* **the (Spanish) A.** la Armada Invencible **(b)** *(any fleet of warships)* armada *f*, flota *f*

armadillo [ɑːmə'dɪləʊ] (*pl* **armadillos**) *n* armadillo *m*

Armageddon [ɑːmə'gedən] *n* apocalipsis *m inv*

Armalite® ['ɑːməlaɪt] *n* Armalite® *f*, = fusil automático muy ligero

armament ['ɑːməmənt] *n (weaponry)* armamento *m*; **armaments** armamento

armature ['ɑːmətʃə(r)] *n* **(a)** *(of motor)* inducido *m* **(b)** *(framework)* armadura *f*; *(for sculpture)* armazón *m or f*, armadura *f*

armband ['ɑːmbænd] *n* **(a)** *(as identification, sign of mourning)* brazalete *m* **(b)** *(for swimming)* manguito *m*, flotador *m*

armchair ['ɑːmtʃeə(r)] *n* sillón *m* ►► ***an a. strategist*** un estratega de salón

Armco® ['ɑːmkəʊ] *n Br (crash barriers)* valla *f* de seguridad

armed [ɑːmd] *adj* armado(a); **to be a.** *(person)* estar armado(a); *(bomb)* estar activado(a); **a. with this new information...** con estos nuevos datos en su poder...; **the suspect is a. and dangerous** el sospechoso va armado y es peligroso; *Fig* **a. only with a map...** provisto únicamente de un mapa...; **a. to the teeth** armado hasta los dientes ►► ***a. conflict*** conflicto *m* armado *or* bélico; ***a. forces*** fuerzas *fpl* armadas; ***a. robbery*** atraco *m* a mano armada

Armenia [ɑː'miːnɪə] *n* Armenia

Armenian [ɑː'miːnɪən] **1** *n* **(a)** *(person)* armenio(a) *m,f* **(b)** *(language)* armenio *m*
2 *adj* armenio(a)

armful ['ɑːmfʊl] *n* brazada *f*; **an a. of papers** un montón de papeles (en los brazos); **in armfuls, by the a.** a brazados *or* brazadas, a montones

armhole ['ɑːmhəʊl] *n* sisa *f*

armistice ['ɑːmɪstɪs] *n* armisticio *m* ►► ***A. Day*** = día en que se conmemora el final de la primera Guerra Mundial

armlock ['ɑːmlɒk] *n (in wrestling)* llave *f* de brazo; **to get sb in(to) an a.** hacerle una llave de brazo a alguien

armor, armored *etc US* = **armour, armoured** *etc*

armorial [ɑː'mɔːrɪəl] *adj (coat of arms)* heráldico(a)

armour, *US* **armor** ['ɑːmə(r)] *n* (a) *(of knight)* armadura *f*; **in full a.** con armadura de pies a cabeza (b) *(of tank, vehicle)* blindaje *m*; **a. plate** *or* **plating** plancha *or* placa blindaje (c) *Mil (tanks)* tanques *mpl*

armour-clad, *US* **armor-clad** [ɑːmə'klæd] *adj (ship, vehicle)* acorazado(a)

armoured, *US* **armored** ['ɑːməd] *adj (vehicle)* blindado(a); *(troops)* blindado(a), acorazado(a) ►► ***a. car*** carro *m* blindado, blindado *m*; ***a. division*** división *f* acorazada; ***a. fighting vehicle*** vehículo *m* de combate acorazado

armourer, *US* **armorer** ['ɑːmərə(r)] *n* (a) *(manufacturer)* armero(a) *m,f* (b) *(in armed forces)* armero(a) *m,f*

armour-piercing, *US* **armor-piercing** ['ɑːmə'pɪəsɪŋ] *adj* perforante

armour-plated, *US* **armor-plated** ['ɑːmə'pleɪtɪd] *adj (vehicle)* blindado(a); *(building)* blindado(a), acorazado(a)

armoury, *US* **armory** ['ɑːmərɪ] *n* (a) *(building, store of weapons)* arsenal *m* (b) *(resources)* armas *fpl*, recursos *mpl*; **such tricks are part of any politician's a.** tales estratagemas forman parte de las armas de cualquier político (c) *US (arms factory)* fábrica *f* de armamento

armpit ['ɑːmpɪt] *n* axila *f*, sobaco *m*; IDIOM *Fam* **it's the a. of the universe** *(place)* es la cloaca del mundo

armrest ['ɑːmrest] *n (of aircraft or train seat)* reposabrazos *m inv*; *(of sofa, armchair)* brazo *m*

arm-twisting ['ɑːm'twɪstɪŋ] *n Fam* **it took a bit of a., but I got him to agree** tuve que apretarle las clavijas un poco, pero logré que cediese

arm-wrestle ['ɑːm'resəl] *vi* **to a. with sb** echar un pulso con alguien

army ['ɑːmɪ] *n* (a) *Mil* ejército *m* (de tierra); **to be in the a.** ser militar; **to go into** *or* **join the a.** alistarse en el ejército; **a. life, life in the a.** vida militar, vida en el ejército ►► *Br* ***A. List*** = relación de oficiales del ejército en activo o en la reserva; ***a. surplus*** excedentes *mpl* del ejército; **a. surplus store** = establecimiento donde se venden ropa y complementos usados del ejército

(b) *(multitude)* batallón *m*, ejército *m*; **an a. of assistants** un ejército *or* batallón de ayudantes

(c) ***a. ant*** hormiga *f* arriera

arnica ['ɑːnɪkə] *n (plant, medicine)* árnica *f*

aroma [ə'rəʊmə] *n* aroma *m*

aromatherapy [ə'rəʊmə'θerəpɪ] *n* aromaterapia *f*

aromatic [ærə'mætɪk] *adj* (a) *(herb, tea, smell)* aromático(a) (b) *Chem* aromático(a); **a. compound** compuesto aromático

arose *pt of* **arise**

AROUND [ə'raʊnd] 1 *prep* (a) *(indicating position)* alrededor de; **a. the table** en torno a la mesa; **to put one's arms a. sb** abrazar a alguien; **he wore a sash a. his waist** llevaba una faja en torno a la cintura; **there were hills all a. the town** la ciudad estaba rodeada de colinas; **she showed no respect for those a. her** no mostraba ningún respeto por la gente que tenía a su alrededor; **I won't be a. the office next week** no estaré en la oficina la próxima semana; **I have a few things to do a. the house** tengo unas cuantas cosas que hacer en casa; **a. here** por aquí (cerca); **all a. the world** por todo el mundo

(b) *(indicating motion)* **they walked a. the lake** dieron la vuelta al lago caminando; **to go a. the corner** dar la vuelta a la esquina; **they skirted a. the town** rodearon la ciudad; **to look a. the room** mirar por toda la habitación; **to show sb a. the house** enseñarle a alguien la casa; **to travel a. the world** viajar por todo el mundo; **to walk a. the town/the streets** caminar por la ciudad/las calles; **you can't go a. the place spreading rumours** no puedes ir por ahí difundiendo rumores

(c) *(based on)* **the team is built a. one player** el equipo está construido en torno a un jugador; **a philosophy centred a. compassion** una filosofía centrada en la compasión

2 *adv* (a) *(surrounding)* alrededor; **a garden with a fence a.** un jardín rodeado por una valla; **there were open fields all a. us** estábamos rodeados de campo por todas partes; **people came from all a.** vino gente de los alrededores; **for miles a.** en millas a la redonda

(b) *(in different directions)* **he looked a. to make sure all was clear** miró a todas partes para asegurarse de que no había peligro; **to run a.** corretear, correr de aquí para allá; **let me show you a.** deja que te enseñe la casa/ciudad/*etc.*; **to travel a.** viajar (por ahí); **to walk a.** pasear (por ahí); **to follow sb a.** seguir a alguien por todas partes; **he has difficulty getting a.** tiene problemas para desplazarse; **she was waving her arms a.** agitaba sus brazos; **he passed the sweets a.** ofreció caramelos a todo el mundo; **I've changed things a. in the living room** he movido algunas cosas en el salón; **there were books lying all a.** había libros por todas partes

(c) *(in opposite direction)* **to look a.** mirar hacia atrás; **to turn a.** *Esp* dar(se) la vuelta, *Am* darse vuelta

(d) *(with circular motion)* **the wheel spun a. and a.** la rueda giraba y giraba

(e) *(in circumference)* de circunferencia; **it's three metres a.** tiene tres metros de circunferencia

(f) *(in the general area)* **is Jack a.?** *(there)* ¿está Jack por ahí?; *(here)* ¿está Jack por aquí?; **he must be a. somewhere** debe estar en alguna parte *or* algún lado; **there was nobody a.** no había nadie (por allí); **I won't be a. next week** no estaré la próxima semana; **there are a lot of tourists a. at the moment** hay muchos turistas por aquí en estos momentos; **there's a virus a.** hay un virus suelto por ahí; **that band has been a. for ages** esa banda lleva siglos tocando; **it's the best printer a.** es la mejor impresora que existe; **there's never a policeman a. when you need one** nunca hay un policía a mano cuando lo necesitas; **to ask a.** preguntar por ahí; **to sit a. doing nothing** estar sin hacer nada; **we're having a few friends a.** hemos invitado a unos cuantos amigos; **see you a.!** ¡nos vemos!; *Fam* **he's been a.** *(is experienced)* ha visto *or* tiene mucho mundo

(g) *(approximately)* **a. thirty** unos treinta; **she's a. thirty** anda por los treinta, tiene unos treinta años; **a. ten years** unos diez años; **at a. one o'clock** alrededor de la una, a eso de la una; **sometime a. November** hacia noviembre; **a. 1990** en torno a 1990; **a. about 200** cerca de 200

---

around-the-clock [ə'raʊndðə'klɒk] 1 *adj* continuo(a), 24 horas al día

2 *adv* (durante) las 24 horas del día

arousal [ə'raʊzəl] *n* (a) *(stimulation) (of interest, suspicion, anger)* despertar *m*, suscitación *f* (b) *(excitement)* excitación *f*; **in a state of a.** *(person, organ)* en estado de excitación

arouse [ə'raʊz] *vt* (a) *(sleeping person)* despertar (b) *(stimulate) (emotion, desire)* despertar, provocar; *(suspicion)* despertar, levantar; *(curiosity, interest)* despertar, suscitar (c) *(sexually)* excitar

arpeggio [ɑː'pedʒɪəʊ] (*pl* **arpeggios**) *n* arpegio *m*

arquebus ['ɑːkwɪbəs] *n* arcabuz *m*

arr *Rail* (*abbr* **arrival**) llegada *f*

arraign [ə'reɪn] *vt Law* hacer comparecer, citar

arraignment [ə'reɪnmənt] *n Law* (a) *(of person)* comparecencia *f* ante el juez *(para el acto de acusación)* (b) *(charges)* acusación *f*

arrange [ə'reɪndʒ] 1 *vt* (a) *(put in order) (books, furniture)* ordenar, colocar; *(hair, flowers)* arreglar; **the chairs were arranged in a circle** las sillas estaban dispuestas en círculo; **a. the books in alphabetical order** ordena los libros por orden alfabético

(b) *(organize) (wedding, meeting)* organizar; *(time, date)* fijar; *(accommodation)* buscar; **to a. to do sth** acordar hacer algo, quedar en hacer algo; **to a. to meet** quedar; **I think I'll a. to be out when he comes** creo que haré lo posible por no estar cuando venga; **to a. what to do** planear qué hacer; **I've arranged things so I have the mornings free** me lo he organizado para tener las mañanas libres; **the meeting is arranged for noon tomorrow** la reunión está fijada para mañana a mediodía; **a. it amongst yourselves** organícenlo entre ustedes; **it was arranged that...** se quedó en que...; **that can be arranged** eso puede arreglarse; **an arranged marriage** un matrimonio concertado

(c) *Mus* arreglar; **arranged for the piano** arreglado para piano

2 *vi* **to a. for sth to be done** disponer que se haga algo; **we've arranged for you to be met at the station** lo hemos preparado para que alguien vaya a buscarle a la estación; **as arranged** según lo acordado

arrangement [ə'reɪndʒmənt] *n* (a) *(order, placing)* disposición *f*

(b) *(plan, preparations)* **to make arrangements** hacer los preparativos; **I'm sorry, I've made other arrangements** lo siento, ya tengo otros planes; **I'll inform you of the travel arrangements later** le informaré sobre los detalles del viaje más tarde

(c) *(agreement)* acuerdo *m*; **the a. was that we would meet outside** habíamos quedado en reunirnos en el exterior; **to come to an a. (with sb)** llegar a un acuerdo (con alguien); **he came to an a. with the bank** llegó a un entendimiento con el banco; **by (prior) a.** con cita previa

(d) *(way of doing things)* arreglo *m*; **it's an odd a., but it seems to work** es un arreglo extraño, pero parece que funciona

(e) *Mus* arreglo *m*

arrant ['ærənt] *adj Formal* cabal, perfecto(a); **it was a. nonsense** fue una cabal *or* perfecta estupidez

array [ə'reɪ] 1 *n* (a) *(arrangement)* despliegue *m* (b) *(variety)* surtido *m*; **they offer a vast a. of dishes** ofrecen un inmenso surtido de platos (c) *(fine clothes)* galas *fpl* (d) *Mil* formación *f*; **in battle a.** en orden de batalla (e) *Comptr & Math* matriz *f*

2 *vt* (a) *(arrange, set out) (troops)* formar, poner en formación; *(dishes)* disponer, colocar (b) *Literary (dress)* ataviar, engalanar

arrears [ə'rɪəz] *npl* atrasos *mpl*; **to be in a. with the rent** ir atrasado(a) en el pago del alquiler *or Méx* de la renta; **they're six months in a.** llevan seis meses de atraso *or* demora (en los pagos), deben seis meses de atrasos; **to get into a.** retrasarse *or Am* demorarse en el pago; **I am paid monthly in a.** me pagan al final de cada mes

arrest [ə'rest] **1** *n* detención *f*, arresto *m*; **to be under a.** estar detenido(a); **you're under a.** queda detenido; **to make an a.** realizar *or* practicar una detención; **they put him under a.** *(police)* lo detuvieron; *(in army)* lo arrestaron ►► ***a. warrant*** orden *f* de arresto, mandamiento *m* de detención

2 *vt* **(a)** *(person)* detener; **he was arrested at the border** lo detuvieron *or* fue detenido en la frontera; *Fig* **my attention was arrested by...** me llamó poderosamente la atención... **(b)** *(development, process)* detener; **a case of arrested development** *(physical)* un caso de atrofia; *(psychological)* un caso de mentalidad infantil

arrestable [ə'restəbəl] *adj (offence)* muy grave

arresting [ə'restɪŋ] *adj* **(a)** *(striking)* arrebatador(ora), fascinante; **an a. image** una imagen impactante **(b)** *Law* **the a. officer** = el agente de policía encargado de practicar la detención

arrhythmia [eɪ'rɪðmɪə] *n Med* arritmia *f*

arrival [ə'raɪvəl] *n* **(a)** *(of person, vehicle)* llegada *f*; **on** *or* **upon a.** al llegar; **the arrivals board/lounge** el tablón/la sala de llegadas ►► ***a. time*** hora *f* de llegada **(b)** *(newcomer)* **a new a.** *(at work, in club)* un(a) recién llegado(a); *(baby)* un(a) recién nacido(a) **(c)** *(advent)* llegada *f*, aparición *f*; **the a. of the motor car** la llegada *or* aparición del automóvil

arrive [ə'raɪv] *vi* **(a)** *(at place)* llegar; **I've just arrived** acabo de llegar; **the first post arrives at eight o'clock** el primer reparto de correspondencia es a las ocho; **the baby arrived three weeks early** el bebé llegó con tres semanas de antelación; **to a. on the scene** aparecer, entrar en escena

(b) *Fam (attain success)* triunfar; **you know you've really arrived when...** te das cuenta de que realmente has conseguido triunfar *or* has alcanzado el éxito cuando...

► **arrive at** *vt insep* **(a)** *(reach)* llegar; **to a. at a decision/solution** llegar a una decisión/solución; **we arrived at the conclusion that...** llegamos a la conclusión de que...; **how did you a. at that figure?** ¿cómo has obtenido esa cifra *or* ese resultado?

(b) *(negotiate) (price)* convenir; **they finally arrived at a mutually acceptable price** finalmente convinieron (en) un precio razonable para ambas partes

arriviste [æri:'vi:st] *n* arribista *mf*

arrogance ['ærəgəns] *n* arrogancia *f*

arrogant ['ærəgənt] *adj* arrogante

arrogantly ['ærəgəntlɪ] *adv* con arrogancia, arrogantemente

arrogate ['ærəgeɪt] *vt Formal (appropriate unjustly)* arrogarse, atribuirse

arrow ['ærəʊ] *n* **(a)** *(missile)* flecha *f* **(b)** *(sign)* flecha *f* ►► *Comptr* ***a. keys*** teclas *fpl* de dirección *or* de movimiento del cursor **(c)** *Br Fam* **arrows** *(darts)* dardos *mpl*

arrowhead ['ærəʊhed] *n* punta *f* de flecha

arrowroot ['ærəʊru:t] *n Culin* arrurruz *m*

arroyo [ə'rɔɪəʊ] *(pl* **arroyos***)* *n US* barranco *m*, arroyada *f*

arse [ɑ:s] *Br Vulg* **1** *n* **(a)** *(buttocks)* culo *m*; **get your a. over here!** ¡ven para acá, *Esp* coño *or Am* carajo!, *Esp* ¡mueve el culo para acá!; **stick** *or* **shove it up your a.!** ¡métetelo en *or* por el culo *or Col* por donde más te duela!

(b) *(stupid person) Esp* gilipollas *mf inv*, *Am* pendejo(a) *m,f*, *RP* boludo(a) *m,f*; **to make an a. of oneself** quedar como *Esp* un(a) gilipollas *or Am* un(a) pendejo(a) *or RP* un(a) boludo(a); **to make an a. of sth** joder algo, *RP* cagar algo

(c) IDIOMS **to get one's a. in gear** ponerse las pilas, *RP* mover las bolas; **to talk out of one's a.** no decir más que *Esp* gilipolleces *or Am* pendejadas *or RP* boludeces; **to work one's a. off** romperse el culo a trabajar, *RP* romperse el culo; **to be out on one's a.: another mistake like that and he'll be out on his a.** *(will be fired)* otro error de esos *Esp* y se va a la puta calle *or Am* y lo echan a patadas en el culo; **to go a. over tit** *or* **tip** *Esp* pegarse una hostia de morros, *Am* romperse el alma; **my a.!** ¡y una mierda!, *Esp* ¡y una polla (como una olla)!, *RP* ¡las pelotas!; **he doesn't know his a. from his elbow** no tiene ni puta idea; **it's my a. that's on the line** soy yo quien tiene el culo al aire

2 *vt* **I can't be arsed (doing it)!** ¡no me da la gana (hacerlo)!, *Esp* ¡no me sale de los huevos (hacerlo)!, *RP* ¡se me cae un huevo (sólo de pensar en hacerlo)!

► **arse about, arse around** *vi Br Vulg (act foolishly) Esp* hacer el gilipollas, *Am* pendejear, *RP* boludear; *(waste time)* tocarse las pelotas *or* los huevos, *RP* rascarse las bolas

► **arse up** *vt sep Br Vulg* **to a. sth up** joder algo

arse-bandit ['ɑ:sbændɪt] *n Br Vulg* maricón *m*, *Esp* bujarrón *m*

arsehole ['ɑ:shəʊl] *n Br Vulg* **(a)** *(anus)* ojete *m*; IDIOM **the a. of the universe** *or* **world** *(place)* la cloaca del mundo **(b)** *(unpleasant person)* hijo(a) *m,f* de puta, cabrón(ona) *m,f*; **don't be such an a.!** ¡no seas tan cabrón!

arseholed ['ɑ:shəʊld] *adj Br Vulg* pedo perdido(a), *Méx* cuete, *RP* en pedo

arse-kisser ['ɑ:skɪsə(r)], **arse-licker** ['ɑ:slɪkə(r)] *n Br Vulg* lameculos *mf inv*

arsenal ['ɑ:sənəl] *n* **(a)** *(building, store of weapons)* arsenal *m* **(b)** *(arms factory)* fábrica *f* de armamento

arsenic ['ɑ:sənɪk] *n Chem* arsénico *m*

arson ['ɑ:sən] *n* incendio *m* provocado *or* doloso; **to commit a.** cometer un delito de incendio provocado *or* doloso

arsonist ['ɑ:sənɪst] *n* incendiario(a) *m,f*, pirómano(a) *m,f*

art[1] [ɑ:t] *n* **(a)** *(in general)* arte *m*; **the arts** las artes; **a. for a.'s sake** el arte por el arte ►► ***a. cinema*** cine *m* de autor; ***the Arts Council*** = institución dependiente de la administración británica que concede ayudas económicas a diferentes organizaciones del mundo de las artes; ***arts and crafts*** *(applied arts)* artes *fpl* decorativas; *(school subject)* trabajos *mpl* manuales; **an arts and crafts fair** una feria de artesanía; *Cin* ***a. director*** director(ora) *m,f* artístico(a); ***a. exhibition*** exposición *f* (artística); ***arts festival*** festival *m* de arte; ***a. form*** manifestación *f* artística; *Ironic* **he has developed idleness into a real a. form** ha hecho de la vagancia un verdadero arte; ***a. gallery*** *(for sale)* galería *f* de arte; *(for exhibition)* museo *m*; ***a. history*** historia *f* del arte; ***a. house cinema*** *(place)* sala *f* de arte y ensayo, = sala donde se proyecta cine de autor; *(film)* cine *m* de autor; ***arts programme*** *(on TV, radio)* programa *m* de arte; ***a. school*** escuela *f* de bellas artes; *US* ***a. theater*** sala *f* de arte y ensayo, = sala donde se proyecta cine de autor; ***a. therapy*** terapia *f* artística

(b) *Univ* **arts** letras *fpl*; **Faculty of Arts, Arts Faculty** facultad de filosofía y letras

(c) *(technique)* arte *m*; **there's an a. to making omelettes** hacer tortillas tiene su arte; **the a. of war/conversation** el arte de la guerra/la conversación; **it's a dying a.** es algo *or* es un arte que se está perdiendo

art[2] *(2nd person singular present of* **be***)* *Archaic & Rel* **thou a. fair** qué bella sois

art deco, Art Deco [ɑ:t'dekəʊ] *n* art decó *m*

artefact, artifact ['ɑ:tɪfækt] *n* objeto *m*

arterial [ɑ:'tɪərɪəl] *adj* **(a)** *Anat* arterial; **a. blood** sangre arterial **(b)** *(road, railway)* principal, arterial

arteriole [ɑ:'tɪərɪəʊl] *n Anat* arteriola *f*

arteriosclerosis [ɑ:'tɪərɪəʊsklə'rəʊsɪs] *n Med* arteriosclerosis *f inv*

artery ['ɑ:tərɪ] *n* **(a)** *Anat* arteria *f* **(b)** *(road)* arteria *f*

artesian well [ɑ:'ti:zɪən'wel] *n* pozo *m* artesiano

Artex® ['ɑ:teks] *n* = pintura densa usada para hacer acabados en relieve en techos y paredes

artful ['ɑ:tfʊl] *adj* **(a)** *(person)* astuto(a), artero(a); **a. dodger** granuja, tunante **(b)** *(solution)* astuto(a), hábil; *(arrangement)* mañoso(a), ingenioso(a)

artfully ['ɑ:tfʊlɪ] *adv (skilfully)* con habilidad *or* maestría, hábilmente; *(craftily)* astutamente

arthritic [ɑ:'θrɪtɪk] *adj* artrítico(a)

arthritis [ɑ:'θraɪtɪs] *n* artritis *f inv*

arthropod ['ɑ:θrəpɒd] *n Zool* artrópodo *m*

arthrosis [ɑ:'θrəʊsɪs] *n Med* artrosis *f inv*

Arthur ['ɑ:θə(r)] *pr n* **King A.** el rey Arturo

artichoke ['ɑ:tɪtʃəʊk] *n* **(a) (globe) a.** alcachofa *f*, *RP* alcaucil *m*; **a. hearts** corazones de alcachofa **(b) (Jerusalem) a.** aguaturma *f*, cotufa *f*

article ['ɑ:tɪkəl] **1** *n* **(a)** *(item)* artículo *m*; **a. of clothing** prenda de vestir; *Fam* **it's the genuine a.!** ¡éste es el auténtico *or* verdadero! ►► ***a. of faith*** dogma *m* de fe **(b)** *(in press)* artículo *m* **(c)** *Gram* **definite/indefinite a.** artículo determinado/indeterminado **(d)** *Br Com* **articles of association** estatutos sociales

2 *vt Law* **to be articled to a firm of solicitors** trabajar en prácticas *or* hacer una pasantía en un bufete de abogados

articled ['ɑ:tɪkəld] *adj* **a. clerk** abogado(a) en prácticas

articulacy [ɑ:'tɪkjʊləsɪ] *n* facilidad *f* de palabra

articulate 1 *adj* [ɑː'tɪkjʊlət] (**a**) *(person)* elocuente; *(description, account)* claro(a), comprensible; **he's not very a.** no sabe expresarse bien (**b**) *(jointed)* articulado(a)
2 *vt* [ɑː'tɪkjʊleɪt] (**a**) *(word, sound)* articular (**b**) *(idea, feeling)* formular, expresar (**c**) *(join)* articular

articulated lorry [ɑː'tɪkjʊleɪtɪd'lɒrɪ] *n* camión *m* articulado

articulately [ɑː'tɪkjʊlətlɪ] *adv (to speak, explain)* claramente; **as you so a. put it** como tú tan bien has expresado

articulation [ɑːtɪkjʊ'leɪʃən] *n* (**a**) *(of words, sound)* articulación *f* (**b**) *(of ideas, feelings)* formulación *f*

articulator [ɑː'tɪkjʊleɪtə(r)] *n Ling* articulador *m*

articulatory [ɑː'tɪkjʊlətrɪ] *adj Ling* articulatorio(a); **a. phonetics** fonética articulatoria

artifact = **artefact**

artifice ['ɑːtɪfɪs] *n* artificio *m*

artificial [ɑːtɪ'fɪʃəl] *adj* (**a**) *(manufactured) (flower, fertilizer, additive, light)* artificial; *(limb)* ortopédico(a); *(hair)* postizo(a) ►► ***a. insemination*** inseminación *f* artificial; *Comptr* ***a. intelligence*** inteligencia *f* artificial; ***a. leather*** *Esp* símil piel *f*, *Esp, Méx* piel *f* sintética, *Andes, Carib, RP* cuero *m* sintético; ***a. respiration*** respiración *f* artificial *or* asistida; ***a. silk*** seda *f* artificial
(**b**) *(contrived) (situation, distinction, conditions)* artificial, ficticio(a); **the scene feels very a.** la escena resulta muy ficticia *or* irreal
(**c**) *(insincere) (manner, smile)* afectado(a), artificial
(**d**) *Astron* ***a. horizon*** horizonte *m* artificial

artificiality [ɑːtɪfɪʃɪ'ælɪtɪ] *n* (**a**) *(of situation, distinction, conditions)* artificialidad *f*, artificiosidad *f* (**b**) *(of manner, smile)* afectación *f*, artificialidad *f*

artificially [ɑːtɪ'fɪʃəlɪ] *adv* artificialmente; **the exchange rate is kept a. high** el tipo de cambio se mantiene artificialmente elevado

artillery [ɑː'tɪlərɪ] *n* artillería *f*; **an a. captain** un capitán de artillería

artilleryman [ɑː'tɪlərɪmən] *n* artillero *m*

artisan [ɑːtɪ'zæn] *n* artesano(a) *m,f*

artist ['ɑːtɪst] *n* artista *mf*; **he is an a.** *(painter, movie director)* es un artista *or* maestro; *(footballer)* es un artista *or* figura; *(chef)* es un artista *or* maestro

artiste [ɑː'tiːst] *n* artista *mf (de espectáculos)*

artistic [ɑː'tɪstɪk] *adj* artístico(a); **she is very a.** tiene mucha sensibilidad artística ►► ***a. director*** director(ora) *m,f* artístico(a); ***a. heritage*** patrimonio *m* histórico-artístico; *Sport* ***a. impression*** impresión *f* artística; ***a. licence*** licencia *f* artística

artistically [ɑː'tɪstɪklɪ] *adv* artísticamente; **to be a. inclined** tener inclinaciones artísticas; **she's very gifted a.** tiene grandes dotes artísticas

artistry ['ɑːtɪstrɪ] *n* arte *m*, destreza *f*

artless ['ɑːtlɪs] *adj* (**a**) *(simple)* inocente, ingenuo(a) (**b**) *(clumsy)* torpe

artlessly ['ɑːtlɪslɪ] *adv* (**a**) *(simply)* abiertamente, ingenuamente (**b**) *(clumsily)* toscamente, torpemente

art nouveau, Art Nouveau ['ɑːtnuː'vəʊ] *n* art nouveau *m*, modernismo *m*

artsy, artsy-crafty *etc US* = **arty, arty-crafty** *etc*

artwork ['ɑːtwɜːk] *n (in book, magazine)* ilustraciones *fpl*

arty ['ɑːtɪ], *US* **artsy** ['ɑːtsɪ] *adj Fam (person)* **the bar attracts an a. crowd** el bar atrae a una clientela bohemia; **the a. decor of the room** la decoración rompedora de la habitación

arty-crafty ['ɑːtɪ'krɑːftɪ], *US* **artsy-crafty** ['ɑːtsɪ'krɑːftɪ] *adj Fam* **the decor is a.** la decoración tiene aspiraciones *or* pretensiones artísticas

arty-farty ['ɑːtɪ'fɑːtɪ], *US* **artsy-fartsy** ['ɑːtsɪ'fɑːtsɪ] *adj Fam* intelectualoide

arum ['eərəm] *n* aro *m*, jaro *m* ►► ***a. lily*** aro *m* de Etiopía, cala *f*

arvo ['ɑːvəʊ] *n Austr Fam (afternoon)* tarde *f*

Aryan ['eərɪən] 1 *n* ario(a) *m,f*
2 *adj* ario(a)

AS [æz, *unstressed* əz] 1 *prep* como; **to be disguised/dressed as a woman** ir disfrazado/vestido de mujer; **to work as an interpreter** trabajar de intérprete; **to work as a team** trabajar en equipo; **to regard sb as a friend** considerar a alguien un amigo; **it doesn't strike me as a good idea** no me parece una buena idea; **it came as no surprise** no sorprendió nada; **to treat sb as a stranger** tratar a alguien como a un extraño; **to act/serve as a protection against sth** actuar/servir de protección contra algo; **she used it as a bandage** lo utilizó a modo de venda; **I'm speaking to you as a lawyer** te estoy hablando en calidad de abogado; **I was unhappy as a child** de niño era muy infeliz; **as a woman, I think that...** como mujer, creo que...; **they applauded as one** aplaudieron al unísono
2 *adv* (**a**) *(with manner)* (tal y) como; **we arrived at eight o'clock, as requested** llegamos a las ocho, tal y como se nos había pedido; **we did exactly as we had been told** hicimos exactamente lo que nos habían dicho; **delete as applicable** táchese lo que corresponda; **he tried as never before** lo intentó como nunca antes; **B as in Birmingham** B de burro
(**b**) *(in comparisons)* **as ... as ...** tan ... como ...; **not as** *or* **so ... as ...** no tan ... como ...; **as tall as me** tan alto como yo; **as white as a sheet** blanco(a) como la nieve; **I pushed/tried as hard as I could** empujé/lo intenté con todas mis fuerzas; **he's as good a player as his father** es tan buen jugador como su padre; **twice as big (as)** el doble de grande (que); **as many as you want** todos los que quieras; **as much as you want** todo lo que quieras; **it costs twice as much (as)** cuesta el doble (que); **he earns five times as much as I do** gana cinco veces más que yo; **she wasn't pleased and she told him as much** no estaba satisfecha y así se lo hizo saber; **there were as few as fifty people there** había tan sólo cincuenta personas allí; **printers from as little as $70** impresoras desde sólo 70 dólares; **I never thought as many as fifty people would come** nunca imaginé que pudieran venir hasta cincuenta personas; **as recently as last week** hace tan sólo una semana; **do it as soon as you can** hazlo en cuanto puedas; **as soon as possible** cuanto antes
(**c**) *(phrases)* **she looked as if** *or* **though she was upset** parecía (como si estuviera) disgustada; **it isn't as if** *or* **though I haven't tried** no será porque no lo he intentado, no es que no lo haya intentado; **it looks as if** *or* **though...** parece que...; *Fam* **as if I'd be interested!** ¡a mí qué me importa!; *Fam (expressing disbelief)* **he reckons he can speak ten languages – as if!** anda *or* va diciendo que habla diez idiomas – ¡qué valor! *or* ¡qué va!; **as for the cost/the food...** en *or* por lo que se refiere al costo/a la comida...; **as for me...** por lo que a mí respecta...; **as from** *or* **of today** a partir de hoy; **she was unsure as to who to invite** no sabía a quién invitar, no estaba segura de a quién invitar; **as well** también; **as well as** así como
3 *conj* (**a**) *(with time) (when)* cuando; *(whilst)* mientras; **he went out as I came in** salió cuando yo entraba; **she talked to me as I worked** me hablaba mientras trabajaba; **as you get older...** a medida que te haces mayor...; **as the years go by** conforme pasan los años; **as necessary** según sea necesario; **we will use this method as and when necessary** utilizaremos este método como y cuando sea necesario; **as always** como siempre
(**b**) *(because)* como; **as he has now left...** como se ha ido..., ahora que se ha ido...; **this scene is important, as it marks a turning point in the plot** esta escena es importante, puesto que *or* ya que marca un punto de inflexión en la trama
(**c**) *(concessive)* **late as it was...** aunque era tarde...; **try as she might...** por mucho que lo intentara...; **unlikely as it might seem...** por improbable que parezca...; **much as I like her...** por mucho que me guste...; **stupid as he is, even he saw the mistake** hasta él, que es tan estúpido, se dio cuenta del error
(**d**) *(with manner)* como; **as I was saying...** como iba diciendo...; **as you know...** como sabes...; **as I remember** si mal no recuerdo; **do as you like** haz lo que quieras; **as I suspected...** (tal y) como sospechaba; **knowing them as I do** conociéndolos como los conozco; **as is often the case..., as often happens...** como suele suceder...; **it's hard enough as it is without this happening!** ¡ya es lo bastante duro como para que ahora pase esto!; **it's far enough as it is!** ¡ya está suficientemente lejos así!; **as it is, there's little we can do** tal y como están las cosas, no podemos hacer mucho; **as it were** por así decirlo; **he's not, as it were, terribly bright** no es muy listo que digamos; **all right, as you wish** de acuerdo, como quieras; **we have no further information as yet** todavía no tenemos más información
(**e**) *(in addition)* **your mother is well, as are the children** tu madre está bien, al igual que los niños
(**f**) *(in comparisons)* **I've got the same bicycle as him** tengo la misma bicicleta que él; **now, as then...** tanto ahora como antes...

ASA [eɪes'eɪ] *n* (**a**) *Br* (*abbr* **Advertising Standards Agency**) = asociación para la vigilancia y control de la publicidad (**b**) *Phot* ***A. number*** sensibilidad *f* (en grados) ASA, número *m* ASA

asafoetida [æsə'fetɪdə] *n* asafétida *f*

asap [eɪeseɪ'piː] *adv* (*abbr* **as soon as possible**) cuanto antes, lo antes posible

asbestos [æs'bestəs] *n* amianto *m*, asbesto *m*

asbestosis [æsbes'təʊsɪs] *n Med* asbestosis *f inv*

ascend [ə'send] 1 *vt* (**a**) *(mountain, steps, ladder)* ascender por, subir (**b**) *(throne)* ascender a, subir a
2 *vi* ascender

ascendancy, ascendency [ə'sendənsɪ] *n* dominio *m*, ascendiente *m* (**over** sobre); **to gain a. (over)** ganar hegemonía (sobre), ganar preponderancia (sobre)

ascendant, ascendent [ə'sendənt] *n* **to be in the a.** ir en ascenso; IDIOM **his star is in the a.** tiene el santo de cara, tiene una buena racha

ascending [ə'sendɪŋ] *adj* (**a**) *(staircase, spiral)* ascendente; **in a. order** *(of priority, size)* en orden ascendente (**b**) *Mus* ascendente

Ascension [ə'senʃən] *n Rel* Ascensión *f* ▸▸ ***A. Day*** día *m* de la Ascensión; ***A. Island*** Ascensión

ascent [ə'sent] *n* (**a**) *(of mountain)* ascensión *f*, subida *f* (**b**) *(rise)* ascenso *m*; **her a. to power** su ascenso al poder

ascertain [æsə'teɪn] *vt (establish)* precisar, determinar; *(find out)* averiguar

ascertainable [æsə'teɪnəbəl] *adj* determinable; **the age of a tree is a. from its cross-section** la edad de un árbol se puede determinar en su corte transversal; **not easily a.** difícil de determinar

ascetic [ə'setɪk] **1** *n* asceta *mf*
2 *adj* ascético(a)

asceticism [ə'setɪsɪzəm] *n* ascetismo *m*

ASCII ['æskɪ] *n Comptr* (*abbr* **American Standard Code for Information Interchange**) ASCII *m* ▸▸ ***A. code*** código *m* ASCII; ***A. text*** texto *m* en formato ASCII; ***A. value*** valor *m* ASCII

ascorbic acid [ə'skɔːbɪk'æsɪd] *n* ácido *m* ascórbico

ascribable [ə'skraɪbəbəl] *adj* atribuible (**to** a)

ascribe [ə'skraɪb] *vt* atribuir (**to** a); **this painting was formerly ascribed to Velazquez** esta obra había sido atribuida anteriormente a Velázquez

ASE [eɪes'iː] *n* (*abbr* **American Stock Exchange**) ASE *m*, = mercado de valores estadounidenses

ASEAN ['æzɪæn] *n* (*abbr* **Association of South-East Asian Nations**) ASEAN *f*

aseptic [eɪ'septɪk] *adj* aséptico(a)

asexual [eɪ'seksjʊəl] *adj* asexual ▸▸ ***a. reproduction*** reproducción *f* asexual

ash[1] [æʃ] *n (tree, wood)* fresno *m*

ash[2] *n* (**a**) *(from fire, cigarette)* ceniza *f*; *Rel* **ashes to ashes, dust to dust** polvo al polvo, cenizas a las cenizas ▸▸ *Rel* ***A. Wednesday*** Miércoles *m inv* de Ceniza (**b**) *(colour)* color *m* ceniza

ashamed [ə'ʃeɪmd] *adj* avergonzado(a), *Andes, CAm, Carib, Méx* apenado(a); **to be a. (of)** estar avergonzado(a) (de); **to feel a.** sentir vergüenza *or Andes, CAm, Carib, Méx* pena; **I'm a. of you!** ¡me das vergüenza *or Andes, CAm, Carib, Méx* pena!; **I am a. to say that...** me avergüenza *or Andes, CAm, Carib, Méx* apena decir que...; **she was a. to show her face in public** se le caía la cara de vergüenza *or* se moría de vergüenza de que la vieran en público; **I'm not a. to admit it** no me avergüenza *or* me da vergüenza reconocerlo; **there is nothing to be a. of** no hay de qué avergonzarse *or Andes, CAm, Carib, Méx* apenarse; **you ought to be a. of yourself!** ¡debería darte vergüenza *or Andes, CAm, Carib, Méx* pena!

ashamedly [ə'ʃeɪmɪdlɪ] *adv* con vergüenza, *Andes, CAm, Carib, Méx* con pena

ash-blond(e) ['æʃblɒnd] **1** *n (colour)* rubio *m* ceniza
2 *adj* rubio(a) ceniza

ashcan ['æʃkæn] *n US* cubo *m* de la basura

ashen ['æʃən] *adj* pálido(a)

ashen-faced ['æʃən'feɪst] *adj* de tez pálida, de cara pálida

Ashkenazi [æʃkə'nɑːzɪ] **1** *n* (*pl* **Ashkenazim** [æʃkə'nɑːzɪm]) askenazí *mf*, asquenazí *mf*
2 *adj* askenazí, asquenazí

ashore [ə'ʃɔː(r)] *adv* en tierra; **to go a.** desembarcar; **he swam a.** nadó hasta la orilla; **to put sb a. (at)** desembarcar a alguien (en); **debris from the wreck was washed a.** las olas arrastraron los restos del naufragio hasta la playa

ashram ['æʃrəm] *n* ashram *m*, = monasterio o lugar de retiro de un gurú hindú

ashtray ['æʃtreɪ] *n* cenicero *m*

Asia ['eɪʒə] *n* Asia ▸▸ ***A. Minor*** Asia Menor

Asian ['eɪʒən] **1** *n* asiático(a) *m,f*; *Br (person from Indian subcontinent)* = persona de la India, Paquistán o Bangladesh
2 *adj* asiático(a); *Br (from Indian subcontinent)* = de la India, Paquistán o Bangladesh ▸▸ *US* ***A. American*** americano(a) *m,f* de origen asiático; ***A. elephant*** elefante *m* asiático

Asiatic [eɪzɪ'ætɪk] **1** *n* asiático(a) *m,f*
2 *adj* asiático(a)

aside [ə'saɪd] **1** *adv* aparte, a un lado; **I stepped a. to let her pass** me aparté *or* me hice a un lado para dejarla pasar; **to put** *or* **set sth a.** apartar *or* reservar algo; **stand a. please!** ¡apártense, por favor!; **to take sb a.** llevarse a alguien aparte; **politics a....** dejando a un lado la política...; **these problems a., we have been very successful** dejando al margen estos problemas, los resultados han sido muy satisfactorios
2 *n* (**a**) *Theat* aparte *m* (**b**) *(digression)* inciso *m*, paréntesis *m inv*
3 aside from *prep* (**a**) *(to the side of)* **it stands a few yards a. from the road** se encuentra a unos metros apartado de la carretera (**b**) *(except for)* aparte de, salvo, exceptuando (**c**) *US (as well as)* aparte de, además de

asinine ['æsɪnaɪn] *adj* cretino(a), majadero(a)

ASK [ɑːsk] **1** *vt* (**a**) *(enquire about)* preguntar; **to a. sb sth** preguntar algo a alguien; **to a. sb about sth** preguntarle a alguien sobre algo; **to a. (sb) a question** hacer una pregunta (a alguien); **to a. sb the time** preguntar la hora a alguien; **to a. sb the way** preguntar a alguien el camino; **may I a. what you think you're doing?** ¿se puede saber qué estás haciendo?; **to a. oneself sth** preguntarse algo; **sometimes I a. myself what would have happened if I'd accepted** a veces me pregunto qué habría ocurrido si hubiera aceptado; **don't a. me!** ¿a mí me lo preguntas?; **if you a. me...** *(in my opinion)* si quieres saber mi opinión...; **I a. you!** *(expressing disapproval)* ¡qué barbaridad!
(**b**) *(request)* pedir; **to a. sb for sth** pedir algo a alguien; **to a. to do sth** *Esp* pedir hacer algo, *Am* pedir para hacer algo; **to a. sb to do sth** pedir a alguien que haga algo; **I asked if I could do it** pedí permiso para hacerlo; *Fig* **she was asking to be criticized** se estaba buscando las críticas; **to a. a favour of sb, to a. sb a favour** pedir un favor a alguien; **to a. sb's advice** pedirle consejo a alguien; **to a. sb's permission to do sth** pedir permiso a alguien para hacer algo; **it's asking a lot of them to win** sería demasiado esperar que ganaran; **if it isn't asking too much** si no es mucho pedir; **we a. that you do not smoke** le rogamos que no fume
(**c**) *(invite)* invitar, convidar; **to a. sb along** invitar a alguien; **to a. sb back (for a drink)** invitar a alguien a casa (a tomar algo); **to a. sb in** invitar a alguien a que pase; **to a. sb over** *or* **round** invitar a alguien; **to a. sb to lunch** convidar a alguien a comer; **he asked me to stay the night** me invitó a pasar la noche
2 *vi* (**a**) *(enquire)* preguntar (**about** por); **she asked about my previous job** me preguntó por mi anterior trabajo; *Formal* **how much do you earn, if you don't mind my asking?** ¿cuánto gana, si no le molesta la indiscreción?; **how did it go? – don't a.!** ¿qué tal fue? – ¡mejor ni hablar!; **why did he do that? – you may well a.!** ¿por qué lo hizo? – ¡buena pregunta!
(**b**) *(request)* **you only have to a.!** ¡no tienes más que pedirlo!

> En inglés culto o elevado, y especialmente en inglés americano, **ask** puede ir seguido de **that** más un verbo en subjuntivo (ver el panel SUBJUNCTIVE):
> **I asked that she forgive my rudeness**
> *rogué que me perdonara mi mala educación*
> Lo mismo también podría decirse del siguiente modo:
> **I asked her to forgive my rudeness**
> *le rogué que me perdonara mi mala educación*

▸**ask after** *vt insep* **to a. after sb** preguntar *or* interesarse por alguien

▸**ask around** *vi (make enquiries)* preguntar por ahí

▸**ask for** *vt insep* (**a**) *(request)* pedir; **I couldn't a. for more** no se puede pedir más; **it's as nice a house as anyone could a. for** no se podría pedir una casa mejor; **he was asking for trouble** se estaba buscando problemas; *Fam* **he was asking for it!** *(deserved it)* ¡se lo estaba buscando!
(**b**) *(want to see)* preguntar por; **there's someone at the door asking for you** hay alguien en la puerta preguntando *or* que pregunta por ti

▸**ask out** *vt sep* (**a**) *(invite)* **to a. sb out for a meal/to the cinema** invitar a alguien a comer/a ir al cine
(**b**) *(as boyfriend, girlfriend)* pedir salir; **have you asked him out yet?** ¿ya le has pedido salir?

---

askance [ə'skæns] *adv (with suspicion)* con recelo; *(with disapproval)* con desdén

askew [ə'skjuː] *adv* **the picture was (hanging) a.** el cuadro estaba torcido; **her dress was a.** llevaba el vestido torcido

asking ['ɑːskɪŋ] *n* **it's yours for the a.** lo tienes a pedir de boca ▸▸ ***a. price*** precio *m* de salida

ASL [eɪes'el] *n* (*abbr* **American Sign Language**) = lenguaje estadounidense de signos para sordos angloparlantes

asleep [ə'sli:p] *adj* (**a**) *(person, animal)* **to be a.** estar dormido(a) *or* durmiendo; **to be fast** *or* **sound a.** estar profundamente dormido(a); **to fall a.** quedarse dormido(a), dormirse; IDIOM **they were a. on their feet** se caían de sueño (**b**) *(numb)* **my arm/foot is a.** tengo un brazo/pie dormido

ASLEF ['æzlef] *n* (*abbr* **Associated Society of Locomotive Engineers and Firemen**) = sindicato británico de maquinistas

asocial [eɪ'səʊʃəl] *adj* asocial

asp [æsp] *n* áspid *m*

asparagus [ə'spærəgəs] *n* (**a**) *(plant)* esparraguera *f* ▸▸ ***a. fern*** esparraguera *f* (**b**) *(vegetable)* espárragos *mpl* ▸▸ ***a. tips*** puntas *fpl* de espárragos

aspartame [*Br* ə'spɑ:teɪm, *US* 'æspərteɪm] *n* aspartamo *m*

ASPCA [eɪespi:si:'eɪ] *n* (*abbr* **American Society for the Prevention of Cruelty to Animals**) = sociedad estadounidense para la prevención de la crueldad contra los animales, ≃ Sociedad *f* Protectora de Animales

aspect ['æspekt] *n* (**a**) *(of problem, subject)* aspecto *m*; **the financial/political aspects (of a plan)** el aspecto *or* lado económico/político (de un plan) (**b**) *(of building)* orientación *f*; **the house has a northern/southern a.** la casa está orientada al norte/sur (**c**) *Literary (appearance)* semblante *m*, apariencia *f* (**d**) *Ling* aspecto *m*

aspen ['æspən] *n* álamo *m* (temblón)

asperity [æ'sperɪtɪ] *n Formal* aspereza *f*

aspersions [əs'pɜ:ʃənz] *npl* **to cast a. (up)on sth** poner en duda algo

asphalt ['æsfælt] *n* asfalto *m*; **an a. road** una carretera asfaltada

asphodel ['æsfədel] *n* asfódelo *m*, gamón *m*

asphyxia [æs'fɪksɪə] *n Med* asfixia *f*

asphyxiate [æs'fɪksɪeɪt] **1** *vt* asfixiar
2 *vi* asfixiarse

asphyxiation [æsfɪksɪ'eɪʃən] *n* asfixia *f*

aspic ['æspɪk] *n Culin* gelatina *f*; *Fig* **it was as if the house had been preserved in a.** parecía que hubieran conservado la casa en alcanfor

aspidistra [æspɪ'dɪstrə] *n* aspidistra *f*

aspirant ['æspɪrənt] **1** *n* aspirante *mf*; **an a. to the title** un aspirante al título
2 *adj* aspirante; **a. politicians** aspirantes a político

aspirate ['æspɪrət] *Ling* **1** *n* sonido *f* aspirado
2 *adj* aspirado(a)
3 *vt* ['æspɪreɪt] aspirar

aspiration [æspɪ'reɪʃən] *n* (**a**) *(ambition)* aspiración *f*; **to have aspirations to greater things/to become a doctor** aspirar a más/a ser médico (**b**) *Ling* aspiración *f*

aspirator ['æspɪreɪtə(r)] *n* succionador *m*, aspirador *m*

aspire [ə'spaɪə(r)] *vi* **to a. to (do) sth** aspirar a (hacer) algo

aspirin ['æsprɪn] *n* aspirina *f*

aspiring [ə'spaɪərɪŋ] *adj* **to be an a. actor** ser un actor en ciernes

ASR [eɪes'ɑ:r] *n US* (*abbr* **air-sea rescue**) rescate *m* aeromarítimo

ass[1] [æs] *n* (**a**) *(animal)* burro *m*, asno *m* (**b**) *Fam (idiot)* borrico(a) *m,f*, tonto(a) *m,f*; IDIOM **to make an a. of oneself** quedar como un tonto

ass[2] *n US Vulg* (**a**) *(buttocks)* culo *m*
(**b**) **she's a nice piece of a.!** *(sexually attractive)* ¡qué buena *or* maciza está!, *Esp* ¡tiene un polvo que no veas!, *Carib* ¡qué jeva más ricota!, *Méx* ¡esa mujer es un cuero!, *RP* ¡qué fuerte que está esa mina!
(**c**) IDIOMS **it's my a. that's on the line** soy yo el que tiene el culo al aire; **you can bet your a. I will!** ¿qué te juegas *or* va a que lo hago?, *RP* ¿a que lo hago?; **to get one's a. in gear** ponerse las pilas, *RP* mover las bolas; **to get one's a. in a sling** estar de mierda hasta el cuello; **to go a. over tit** *Esp* pegarse una hostia de morros, *Am* romperse el alma; **your a. is grass!** ¡la has cagado!

ass-backwards ['æs'bækwədz] *adv US very Fam* **to do sth a.** hacer algo con el culo

ass-wipe ['æswaɪp] *n US Vulg (unpleasant person)* hijo(a) *m,f* de puta, cabrón(ona) *m,f*

assail [ə'seɪl] *vt (attack)* asaltar, agredir (**with** con); **to a. sb with questions** asediar a alguien a preguntas; **assailed by doubt** asaltado por la duda

assailant [ə'seɪlənt] *n Formal* asaltante *mf*, agresor(ora) *m,f*

assassin [ə'sæsɪn] *n* asesino(a) *m,f*

assassinate [ə'sæsɪneɪt] *vt* asesinar

assassination [əsæsɪ'neɪʃən] *n* asesinato *m*; **an a. attempt** un intento de asesinato

assault [ə'sɔ:lt] **1** *n* (**a**) *(attack)* ataque *m*, asalto *m* (**on** a); **they made** *or* **carried out an a. on the camp** atacaron el campamento; *Fig* **the film is an a. on the senses** la película desborda los sentidos ▸▸ *Mil* ***a. course*** pista *f* americana; ***a. rifle*** rifle *m* de asalto; ***a. troops*** tropas *fpl* de asalto
(**b**) *(attempt to overcome)* **his a. on the leadership** su intento de lograr el liderazgo; **their a. on Everest/K2** su intento de escalar el Everest/K2
(**c**) *(verbal attack, criticism)* ataque *m*
(**d**) *Law* agresión *f*; **to commit an a. (on sb)** cometer una agresión (contra alguien) ▸▸ ***a. and battery*** agresión *f* con resultado de lesiones
2 *vt* (**a**) *(attack)* atacar, asaltar; *Fig* **the film assaults the senses** la película desborda los sentidos (**b**) *Law* agredir; **to be assaulted** ser atacado(a) *or* agredido(a); *(sexually)* ser objeto de una agresión sexual

assay [ə'seɪ] **1** *vt (analyse)* ensayar
2 *n (analysis)* ensayo *m*, ensaye *m*

ass-bandit ['æsbændɪt] *n US Vulg* maricón *m*, *Esp* bujarrón *m*

assegai ['æsəgaɪ] *n* azagaya *f*

assemblage [ə'semblɪdʒ] *n* (**a**) *(collection)* conjunto *m*, colección *f* (**b**) *(process)* recolección *f*, reunión *f*; **the a. of the expedition team took many months** llevó muchos meses reunir al equipo para la expedición

assemble [ə'sembəl] **1** *vt* (**a**) *(gather) (people)* reunir, congregar; *(troops)* reunir, agrupar; *(facts, objects)* reunir, recopilar (**b**) *(construct) (machine, furniture)* montar, ensamblar; **the bookcase can be assembled in minutes** la estantería puede montarse *or* ensamblarse en unos minutos
2 *vi (people)* reunirse, congregarse; *(troops)* reunirse

assembled [ə'sembəld] *adj* (**a**) *(gathered together) (people)* congregado(a), reunido(a); *(troops)* reunido(a), agrupado(a) (**b**) *(constructed)* montado(a), ensamblado(a); **factory a.** montado(a) de fábrica

assembler [ə'semblə(r)] *n Comptr* ensamblador *m*

assembly [ə'semblɪ] *n* (**a**) *(gathering) (act)* reunión *f*, asamblea *f*; *(group)* asamblea *f*; **the right of a.** el derecho de reunión *or* asamblea
(**b**) *Sch* = reunión de todos los profesores y los alumnos al principio de la jornada escolar ▸▸ ***a. hall*** *(in school)* salón *m* *or* sala *f* de actos
(**c**) *Pol (legislature)* asamblea *f* legislativa
(**d**) *(of machine, furniture) (process)* montaje *m*, ensamblaje *m*; *(end product)* ensamblado *m* ▸▸ ***a. instructions*** instrucciones *fpl* de montaje; *Ind* ***a. line*** cadena *f* de montaje; ***a. plant*** planta *f* de montaje
(**e**) *Comptr* ***a. language*** lenguaje *m* ensamblador

assemblyman [ə'semblɪmən] *n US* miembro *m* de una asamblea

assemblywoman [ə'semblɪwʊmən] *n US* miembro *f* de una asamblea

assent [ə'sent] **1** *n* asentimiento *m*, consentimiento *m*; **she gave/withheld her a.** dio/no dio su consentimiento
2 *vi* dar el consentimiento (**to** a)

assert [ə'sɜ:t] *vt* (**a**) *(state firmly)* asegurar, afirmar; **to a. that...** asegurar *or* afirmar que... (**b**) *(insist on) (one's rights, point of view)* reafirmar; *(authority)* hacer valer; **to a. oneself** mostrarse firme, imponerse

assertion [ə'sɜ:ʃən] *n* (**a**) *(statement)* afirmación *f*, aseveración *f*; **a highly debatable a.** una afirmación *or* aseveración muy cuestionable (**b**) *(of right, authority)* reafirmación *f*

assertive [ə'sɜ:tɪv] *adj (tone, manner)* categórico(a), enérgico(a); **you should be more a.** deberías mostrar más carácter; **try to sound firm but not too a.** procura parecer firme pero no demasiado inflexible

assertiveness [ə'sɜ:tɪvnɪs] *n (insistence)* carácter *m* enérgico; *(self-confidence)* autoafirmación *f* ▸▸ ***a. training*** cursos *mpl* de afirmación personal

assess [ə'ses] *vt* (**a**) *(estimate) (value)* tasar, valorar; *(damage)* evaluar, valorar; **to a. sb's income** *(for tax purposes)* evaluar la renta de alguien; **the court assessed the damages at $2,000** el tribunal valoró los daños en 2.000 dólares
(**b**) *(analyse)* evaluar; **how do you a. the team's chances?** ¿qué opinas sobre las posibilidades del equipo?
(**c**) *(of teacher, tutor)* evaluar; **students are continuously assessed** los estudiantes siguen una evaluación continua

assessment [ə'sesmənt] *n* (**a**) *(estimate) (of value)* tasación *f*, valoración *f*; *(of damage)* evaluación *f*, valoración *f*; *(for insurance or tax purposes)* tasación *f* (**b**) *(analysis)* evaluación *f*; **what's your a. of the situation?** ¿cómo valora la situación? (**c**) *(by teacher, tutor)* evaluación *f*

assessor [ə'sesə(r)] *n Fin (for insurance, tax)* tasador(ora) *m,f*

asset ['æset] *n* (**a**) *(benefit)* ventaja *f*; **her adaptability is one of her many assets** la capacidad de adaptación es una de sus virtudes *or* ventajas; **she is a great a. to the firm** es una valiosa aportación a la empresa; **knowledge of Russian would be an a.** *(in job advert)* se valorarán conocimientos de ruso

(**b**) *Fin* **assets** activos *mpl*; **assets and liabilities** el activo y el pasivo, las partidas del balance

asset-stripper ['æset'strɪpə(r)] *n* = persona que especula con la compra y liquidación de empresas en quiebra

asset-stripping ['æset'strɪpɪŋ] *n* liquidación *f* (especulativa) de activos

asshole ['æshəʊl] *n US Vulg* (**a**) *(anus)* ojete *m*; IDIOM **the a. of the universe** *or* **world** *(place)* el culo del mundo (**b**) *(unpleasant person)* hijo(a) *m,f* de puta, cabrón(ona) *m,f*; **don't be such an a.!** ¡no seas tan cabrón!

assiduous [ə'sɪdjʊəs] *adj Formal* perseverante

assiduously [ə'sɪdjʊəslɪ] *adv Formal* con perseverancia *or* tesón

assign [ə'saɪn] *vt* (**a**) *(allocate) (task, funds)* asignar (**to** a); **to a. sb to do sth** asignar a alguien la tarea de hacer algo

(**b**) *(designate)* elegir; **the largest room was assigned to be the meeting room** eligieron la sala más grande como sala de reuniones; **a date and place were assigned for the exam** se fijaron la fecha y el lugar del examen

(**c**) *(ascribe) (importance)* atribuir; **the aqueduct has been assigned to the Roman period** el acueducto se atribuye a la época romana

(**d**) *Law* ceder, transferir

assignation [æsɪg'neɪʃən] *n Formal (meeting)* cita *f*, encuentro *m*

assignee [æsaɪ'niː] *n Law* sucesor(ora) *m,f*, concesionario(a) *m,f*

assignment [ə'saɪnmənt] *n* (**a**) *(allocation)* asignación *f* (**b**) *Sch (schoolwork)* tarea *f*, trabajo *m* (**c**) *Journ* encargo *m*, trabajo *m*; **he is on a. in India** está desplazado en la India (**d**) *Mil (mission)* misión *f* (**e**) *Law* cesión *f*, transmisión *f*

assimilate [ə'sɪmɪleɪt] **1** *vt (absorb, integrate) (food, ideas)* asimilar; *(immigrants)* asimilar, integrar

2 *vi* (**a**) *(immigrants)* integrarse (**b**) *(become similar)* **to a. to** *or* **with sth** asimilarse a algo

assimilation [əsɪmɪ'leɪʃən] *n* (**a**) *(absorption, integration) (of food, ideas)* asimilación *f*; *(of immigrants)* integración *f* (**b**) *Ling* asimilación *f*

assist [ə'sɪst] **1** *n Sport* asistencia *f*

2 *vt (person)* ayudar; *(process, development)* colaborar en, contribuir a; **to a. sb in doing** *or* **to do sth** ayudar a alguien a hacer algo; **he assisted her up/down the stairs** le ayudó a subir/bajar las escaleras; **a man is assisting police with their enquiries** la policía esta llevando a cabo el interrogatorio de un sospechoso

3 *vi* (**a**) *(help)* ayudar, colaborar; **she assisted at the operation** asistió *or* ayudó en la operación; **to a. in** *or* **with sth** colaborar en algo (**b**) *Formal (attend)* asistir (**at** a)

assistance [ə'sɪstəns] *n* ayuda *f*, asistencia *f*; **to be of great a.** ser de gran ayuda; **to come to sb's a.** acudir en ayuda de alguien; **can I be of any a.?** ¿puedo ayudar en algo?; **with the a. of sth/sb** con la ayuda de algo/alguien

assistant [ə'sɪstənt] *n* (**a**) *(helper)* ayudante *mf* ►► ***a. manager*** subdirector(ora) *m,f*, director(ora) *m,f* adjunto(a); *US* ***a. professor*** profesor(ora) *m,f* adjunto(a); *Sport* ***a. referee*** árbitro *m* asistente (**b**) *(in shop)* **(shop) a.** dependiente(a) *m,f* (**c**) *Br* **(language) a.** *(in school)* auxiliar *mf* de conversación; *(in university)* lector(ora) *m,f* de lengua extranjera (**d**) *Comptr (software)* asistente *m*

assistantship [ə'sɪstəntʃɪp] *n* (**a**) *US* ayudantía *f*, beca *f (para licenciados universitarios)* (**b**) *Br* **(language) a.** *(in school)* = puesto de auxiliar de conversación; *(in university)* lectorado *m*

assizes [ə'saɪzɪz] *npl Br Law* ≃ audiencia *f* provincial

ass-kisser ['æskɪsə(r)], **ass-licker** ['æslɪkə(r)] *n US Vulg* lameculos *mf inv*

associate **1** *n* [ə'səʊsɪət] (**a**) *(in business)* socio(a) *m,f* (**b**) *(in crime)* cómplice *mf* (**c**) *(of club, institution)* socio(a) *m,f* no numerario(a)

2 *adj (company)* asociado(a) ►► ***a. director*** director(ora) *m,f* adjunto(a); *US* ***a. professor*** profesor(ora) *m,f* adjunto(a) *or* titular

3 *vt* [ə'səʊsɪeɪt] (**a**) *(mentally)* asociar (**with** con); **I don't a. the two things** no relaciono una cosa con la otra *or* lo uno con lo otro (**b**) *(connect)* **to be associated with** estar asociado(a) *or* relacionado(a) con; **I don't want to be associated with it** no quiero tener nada que ver con ello, no quiero que se me relacione con ello

4 *vi* **to a. with sb** frecuentar a *or* tratar con alguien

associated [ə'səʊsɪeɪtɪd] *adj* asociado(a) ►► ***a. company*** empresa *f* asociada

association [əsəʊsɪ'eɪʃən] *n* (**a**) *(group, link)* asociación *f*; **to form an a.** crear una asociación ►► *Phil* ***a. of ideas*** asociación *f* de ideas

(**b**) *(involvement)* vinculación *f*, conexión *f*; **in a. with...** conjuntamente con...; **this programme was made in a. with Belgian television** la televisión belga coprodujo este programa

(**c**) *(connotation)* connotación *f*; **the name has unfortunate associations for her** ese nombre le trae malos recuerdos

(**d**) *Br Sport* ***a. football*** fútbol *m* asociación

assonance ['æsənəns] *n* asonancia *f*

assorted [ə'sɔːtɪd] *adj* (**a**) *(various) (colours, flavours)* diverso(a); *(biscuits, sweets)* surtido(a); **an audience of a. academics and businessmen** una audiencia variopinta formada por académicos y hombres de negocios (**b**) *(matched)* **well-/ill-a.** bien/mal combinado(a) *or* compaginado(a)

assortment [ə'sɔːtmənt] *n (of colours, reasons)* diversidad *f*; *(of biscuits, sweets)* surtido *m*; **she certainly has an odd a. of friends!** no cabe duda de que tiene una extraña colección de amigos

assuage [ə'sweɪdʒ] *vt Formal (anger, person)* apaciguar; *(hunger, thirst)* aplacar; *(grief, pain)* apaciguar, aliviar, paliar

assume [ə'sjuːm] *vt* (**a**) *(suppose)* suponer; **I a. so/not** supongo que sí/no; **he was assumed to be rich** se suponía que era rico; **we can't a. anything** no podemos dar nada por supuesto *or* sentado; **that's assuming a lot** eso es mucho suponer; **assuming (that) you are right...** suponiendo que tengas razón...; **let us a. that...** supongamos que...; **to a. the worst** suponerse *or* imaginarse lo peor

(**b**) *(take over) (duty, power, command)* asumir; *(name)* adoptar; **to a. responsibility for sth** asumir la responsabilidad de algo; **an assumed name** *(false)* un nombre falso

(**c**) *(take on) (appearance, shape)* adquirir, adoptar; *(significance, importance)* cobrar, adquirir

(**d**) *(feign) (indifference, cheerfulness)* adoptar

assumption [ə'sʌmpʃən] *n* (**a**) *(supposition)* suposición *f*; **to work on the a. that...** trabajar sobre la base de que...; **on the a. that the money will be forthcoming, we can go ahead** contando con que dispondremos del dinero, podemos seguir adelante; **this is all based on the a. that...** todo esto partiendo de la base de que...; **that's quite an a.!** ¡eso es mucho suponer!, ¡eso es suponer demasiado!

(**b**) *(of duty, power, responsibility)* asunción *f*; **a. of office** entrada en funciones, toma de posesión del cargo

(**c**) *Rel* **the A.** la Asunción

assurance [ə'ʃʊərəns] *n* (**a**) *(guarantee)* garantía *f*; **to give sb one's a.** dar garantías a alguien; **I can give you an a. that...** puedo garantizarte que... (**b**) *(confidence)* seguridad *f*; **to lack a.** carecer de seguridad; **to answer with a.** responder con seguridad (**c**) *Br (insurance)* seguro *m* ►► ***a. policy*** póliza *f* aseguradora, seguro *m*

assure [ə'ʃʊə(r)] *vt* (**a**) *(guarantee)* asegurar; **to a. sb of sth** asegurar algo a alguien; **her support assured them of success** su respaldo les garantizaba el éxito; **I didn't know, I a. you!** ¡no sabía nada, te lo aseguro *or* garantizo! (**b**) *Br (insure)* asegurar

assured [ə'ʃʊəd] **1** *adj* (**a**) *(certain)* seguro(a); **to be a. of sth** tener algo asegurado(a); **rest a. that...** ten por seguro que... (**b**) *(confident)* seguro(a); **he gave a very a. performance** se mostró muy seguro en su actuación

2 *n (person)* asegurado(a) *m,f*

assuredly [ə'ʃʊərɪdlɪ] *adv (undoubtedly)* sin duda; **when she returns, as she a. will...** cuando regrese, que sin duda lo hará...

Assyria [ə'sɪrɪə] *n* Asiria

Assyrian [ə'sɪrɪən] **1** *n* (**a**) *(person)* asirio(a) *m,f* (**b**) *(language)* asirio *m*

2 *adj* asirio(a)

astatine ['æstətiːn] *n Chem* astato *m*

aster ['æstə(r)] *n* áster *m*

asterisk ['æstərɪsk] **1** *n* asterisco *m*

2 *vt* marcar *or* señalar con un asterisco

astern [ə'stɜːn] *adv* hacia atrás; **to go a.** *(person)* retroceder, ir *or* andar hacia atrás; *(boat)* ciar; **full speed a.!** ¡atrás toda!; **we were a. of the flagship** estabamos situados detrás del buque insignia

asteroid ['æstərɔɪd] *n* asteroide *m* ►► ***a. belt*** cinturón *m* de asteroides

asthma ['æsmə] *n* asma *f*; **to have a.** padecer *or* tener asma; **an a. attack** un ataque de asma *or* disnea respiratoria; **an a. sufferer** un(a) asmático(a)

asthmatic [æs'mætɪk] **1** *n* asmático(a) *m,f*

2 *adj* asmático(a)

astigmatism [ə'stɪgmətɪzəm] *n* astigmatismo *m*

astir [əˈstɜː(r)] *adj Literary* **(a)** *(out of bed)* en planta, en pie **(b)** *(in motion)* bullicioso(a), agitado(a)

astonish [əˈstɒnɪʃ] *vt* asombrar; **to be astonished at** *or* **by** quedarse asombrado(a) por; **I am astonished that...** me asombra que...; **it never fails to a. me that...** no deja de asombrarme que...; *Ironic* **go on, a. me!** a ver, ¡sorpréndeme!

astonished [əˈstɒnɪʃt] *adj (look, reaction)* de asombro, asombrado(a); **she gave him an a. look** ella le miró asombrada

astonishing [əˈstɒnɪʃɪŋ] *adj* asombroso(a), sorprendente; **I find it a. that...** me parece asombroso que...

astonishingly [əˈstɒnɪʃɪŋlɪ] *adv* asombrosamente; **a. enough, she still likes him** aunque parezca mentira, todavía le gusta

astonishment [əˈstɒnɪʃmənt] *n* asombro *m*; **they stared in a.** miraban asombrados; **to my a.** para mi asombro

astound [əˈstaʊnd] *vt* dejar atónito(a), pasmar; **you a. me!** *Formal* me dejas estupefacta *or* atónita; *Ironic* ¡no puede ser!, ¡no me lo puedo creer!

astounded [əˈstaʊndɪd] *adj* atónito(a), pasmado(a); **I was a.** me quedé atónito(a) *or* pasmado(a); **he was a. at** *or* **by her talent** su talento le dejó atónito *or* pasmado

astounding [əˈstaʊndɪŋ] *adj* pasmoso(a), asombroso(a)

astoundingly [əˈstaʊndɪŋlɪ] *adv* increíblemente, asombrosamente; **a. enough, they'd already met** por (muy) increíble que parezca, ya se conocían

astrakhan [ˈæstrəkæn] *n* astracán *m*

astral [ˈæstrəl] *adj* astral ►► ***a. projection*** viaje *m* astral

astray [əˈstreɪ] *adv* **to go a.** *(become lost)* perderse, extraviarse; *(morally)* descarriarse; **to lead sb a.** *(misinform)* desorientar, confundir; *(morally)* descarriar a alguien, llevar a alguien por el mal camino

astride [əˈstraɪd] *prep* **to sit a. sth** sentarse a horcajadas sobre algo; **he stood a. the ditch** estaba con un pie a cada lado de la cuneta

astringent [əˈstrɪndʒənt] **1** *n* loción *f* astringente *m (para contraer tejidos)*
2 *adj* **(a)** *(substance)* astringente *(que contrae tejidos)* **(b)** *(criticism)* áspero(a), agrio(a)

astrodome [ˈæstrədəʊm] *n US (stadium)* estadio *m* cubierto

astrolabe [ˈæstrəleɪb] *n* astrolabio *m*

astrologer [əˈstrɒlədʒə(r)] *n* astrólogo(a) *m,f*

astrological [æstrəˈlɒdʒɪkəl] *adj* astrológico(a) ►► ***a. chart*** carta *f* astral

astrologist [əˈstrɒlədʒɪst] *n* astrólogo(a) *m,f*

astrology [əˈstrɒlədʒɪ] *n* astrología *f*

astronaut [ˈæstrənɔːt] *n* astronauta *mf*

astronomer [əˈstrɒnəmə(r)] *n* astrónomo(a) *m,f*

astronomic(al) [æstrəˈnɒmɪk(əl)] *adj* **(a)** *(research, observation)* astronómico(a) **(b)** *Fam (gigantic)* **the prices are a.!** ¡los precios son astronómicos *or* están por las nubes!

astronomically [æstrəˈnɒmɪklɪ] *adv Fam (to increase)* astronómicamente, desorbitadamente; **it's a. expensive** tiene un precio astronómico

astronomy [əˈstrɒnəmɪ] *n* astronomía *f*

astrophysics [æstrəʊˈfɪzɪks] *n* astrofísica *f*

Astroturf® [ˈæstrəʊtɜːf] *n Sport* (césped *m* de) hierba *f* artificial

Asturian [æˈstʊərɪən] **1** *n* asturiano(a) *m,f*
2 *adj* asturiano(a)

Asturias [æˈstʊərɪəs] *n* Asturias

astute [əˈstjuːt] *adj (person)* astuto(a), sagaz; *(decision, investment)* inteligente, sagaz; *(comment)* agudo(a), perspicaz; **how a. of you!** ¡qué aguda!, ¡qué lista!

astutely [əˈstjuːtlɪ] *adv* astutamente, con sagacidad

astuteness [əˈstjuːtnɪs] *n (of person)* astucia *f*, sagacidad *f*; *(of decision, investment)* inteligencia *f*, sagacidad *f*; *(of comment)* agudeza *f*, perspicacia *f*

asunder [əˈsʌndə(r)] *adv Literary* **to tear sth a.** hacer pedazos algo; **the family had been torn a. by war** la familia había quedado destrozada por la guerra; **to break a.** partirse en dos *or* por la mitad

asylum [əˈsaɪləm] *n* **(a)** *(refuge)* asilo *m*; **to seek a.** buscar asilo; **he was granted/refused a.** se le concedió/se le negó el asilo **(b)** *(institution)* **(mental) a.** manicomio *m*

asymmetric(al) [eɪsɪˈmetrɪk(əl)] *adj* asimétrico(a) ►► *Sport* ***a. bars*** barras *fpl* asimétricas

asymmetry [eɪˈsɪmɪtrɪ] *n* asimetría *f*

asymptotic [æsɪmˈtɒtɪk] *adj Math* asintótico(a)

asynchronous [eɪˈsɪŋkrənəs] *adj Comptr* asíncrono(a) ►► ***a. transfer mode*** modo *m* asíncrono de transferencia

AT [æt, *unstressed* ət] **1** *prep* **(a)** *(with place)* en; **she was sitting at the window** estaba sentada al lado de la ventana; **there's someone at the door** hay alguien en la puerta; **a dog lay at his feet** un perro estaba tumbado a sus pies; **stand at a distance of at least 30 metres** póngase a una distancia de al menos 30 metros; **at the top/bottom** (en la parte de) arriba/abajo; **at the top/bottom of the stairs** en lo alto de/al pie de las escaleras; **at the side** al lado; **at university/the station** en la universidad/la estación; **they live at number 20** viven en el número 20; **I saw him at the hairdresser's** lo vi en la peluquería; **at John's** *(house)* en casa de John; **at home** en casa; IDIOM *Fam* **this club's where it's at** esta disco es lo más in, *RP* este boliche está de lo más de onda; *Fam* **that's not where I'm at** no es mi rollo *or* ambiente

(b) *(with time)* **at six o'clock** a las seis; **at night** *Esp* por la noche, *Am* en la noche, *Arg* a la noche, *Urug* de noche; **at Christmas** en Navidad; **at lunchtime** a la hora de comer; **at a good time** en un momento oportuno; **at a later date** en una fecha posterior; **at the beginning/end** al principio/final; **at the end of the year** al final del año, a finales del año; **at (the age of) twenty** a los veinte años; **at regular intervals** a intervalos regulares

(c) *(with price, rate, level)* a; **at 60 km/h** a 60 km/h; **at top speed** a toda velocidad; **at 50p a kilo** a 50 peniques el kilo; **they sold it at a cheaper price** lo vendieron más barato; **unemployment is at 10 percent** el desempleo está en el 10 por ciento; **I'd put the total at nearer 200** yo diría más bien que un total de cerca de 200; **at 85 metres, it's the town's tallest building** con 85 metros, es el edificio más alto de la ciudad

(d) *(with direction)* a; **to run at sb** abalanzarse sobre alguien; **to point at sb** señalar a alguien; **to throw a stone at sb** tirarle una piedra a alguien; **to grab at sth** tratar de agarrar algo; **stop tugging at my sleeve!** ¡deja de tirarme de la manga!; **to look at sth/sb** mirar algo/a alguien; **to shout at sb** gritar a alguien

(e) *(with cause)* **to be angry at sb** estar *esp Esp* enfadado(a) *or esp Am* enojado(a) con alguien; **to be excited at sth** estar emocionado(a) por algo; **to laugh at a joke** reírse de un chiste; **to be surprised at sth** sorprenderse de algo; **at his command/request** por orden/a petición suya; **at that, he left the room** en ese momento, salió de la habitación; **it's poor quality, and expensive at that** es de mala calidad, y además caro

(f) *(with activity)* **to be at work/play** estar trabajando/jugando; **to be at lunch** estar almorzando; **he's at school at the moment** en estos momentos está en el colegio; **to be at war** estar en guerra; **to be at risk** estar en peligro; **at a gallop** al galope; **I am good at languages** tengo facilidad para los idiomas, *Esp* los idiomas se me dan bien; **he's bad at sport** no tiene habilidad para los deportes, *Esp* se le dan mal los deportes; **she's good at making people feel at home** sabe hacer que la gente se sienta en casa; **he's very experienced at this type of work** tiene mucha experiencia en este tipo de trabajo; *Fam* **have you been at the biscuits again?** ¿ya has vuelto a darle a las galletas?; **she's been at it all weekend** *(working)* ha pasado todo el fin de semana trabajando; **while you're at it, could you buy some sugar?** ya que vas, ¿podrías comprar azúcar?; *Fam* **he's at it again** *(doing the same thing)* ya está otra vez con lo mismo; *very Fam* **they were at it all night** *(having sex)* estuvieron dale que te pego *or RP* dale que te dale toda la noche

(g) *(with superlatives)* **at best/worst** en el mejor/peor de los casos; **at least** al *or* por lo menos; **at (the) most** como mucho; **Scotland is at its best in June** cuando Escocia es más bonita es en junio; **this novel is Faulkner at his best** en esta novela Faulkner está en plena forma; **they didn't play at their best** no jugaron lo mejor que saben

(h) *Comptr (in e-mail address)* arroba *f*; **gwilson at transex, dot, co, dot, uk** gwilson, arroba transex, punto, co, punto, uk ►► ***at sign*** arroba *f*

2 at all *adv* **do you know him at all?** ¿lo conoces de algo?; **can there be any doubt at all that he did it?** ¿no está clarísimo que lo hizo él?; **anything at all** cualquier cosa; **if at all possible** a ser posible; **it affected them very little, if at all** apenas les afectó; **if you are at all dissatisfied** en caso de no estar satisfecho; **if you had any sense at all** si tuvieras el más mínimo sentido común; **we got no credit at all for our work** no se nos reconoció nuestro trabajo en absoluto; **nothing at all** nada en absoluto; **they've done nothing at all** no han hecho nada en absoluto; **not at all** *(not in the slightest)* en absoluto; *(when thanked)* de nada; **I'm not at all astonished** no estoy en absoluto sorprendido; **it's not at all bad** no es nada malo

atavism [ˈætəvɪzəm] *n Biol* atavismo *m*

atavistic [ætəˈvɪstɪk] *adj* atávico(a)

ataxia [əˈtæksɪə] *n Med* ataxia *f*

at-bat [ˈætbæt] *n (in baseball)* turno *m* de bateo

ate *pt of* **eat**

atheism [ˈeɪθɪɪzəm] *n* ateísmo *m*

atheist [ˈeɪθɪɪst] *n* ateo(a) *m,f*

atheistic [eɪθɪˈɪstɪk] *adj* ateo(a)

Athena [əˈθiːnə], **Athene** [əˈθiːnɪ] *n Mythol* Atenea

Athenian [əˈθiːnɪən] **1** *n* ateniense *mf*
2 *adj* ateniense

Athens [ˈæθənz] *n* Atenas

athirst [əˈθɜːst] *adj Literary* sediento(a), con sed

athlete [ˈæθliːt] *n* atleta *mf* ►► *Med* ***a.'s foot*** pie *m* de atleta

athletic [æθˈletɪk] *adj* atlético(a); **she's very a.** es muy atlética *or* deportista ►► ***a. support*** suspensorio *m*

athletics [æθˈletɪks] *npl* (**a**) *Br (track and field)* atletismo *m* ►► ***a. track*** pista *f* de atletismo (**b**) *US* deportes *mpl*

athwart [əˈθwɔːt] *prep (across the path of)* a través de; **the fallen tree lay a. the railway line** el árbol caído quedó atravesado en la vía del tren

atishoo [əˈtɪʃuː] *exclam* ¡achís!

Atlantic [ətˈlæntɪk] **1** *n* **the A.** el Atlántico
2 *adj* atlántico(a); **the A. Ocean** el océano Atlántico ►► *Can* ***the A. Provinces*** las provincias atlánticas

Atlantis [ətˈlæntɪs] *n* la Atlántida

atlas [ˈætləs] *n* (**a**) *(book)* atlas *m inv* (**b**) *Anat* atlas *m inv* (**c**) *Geog* **the A. Mountains** las montañas Atlas, el Atlas

ATM [eɪtiːˈem] *n* (**a**) *Fin* (*abbr* **automated** *or* **automatic teller machine**) cajero *m* automático (**b**) *Comptr* (*abbr* **asynchronous transfer mode**) ATM *m*, modo *m* asíncrono de transferencia

atmosphere [ˈætməsfɪə(r)] *n* (**a**) *(of planet)* atmósfera *f* (**b**) *(feeling, mood)* ambiente *m*, clima *m*; **this place has no a.** este lugar *or* sitio no tiene ambiente; IDIOM **you could have cut the a. with a knife** se respiraba la tensión en el aire; **there's a really bad a. at the office just now** hay un clima crispado en la oficina en estos momentos (**c**) *Phys* atmósfera *f*

atmospheric [ætməsˈferɪk] *adj* (**a**) *(pressure, pollution)* atmosférico(a) ►► ***a. pressure*** presión *f* atmosférica (**b**) *(lighting, movie)* fascinante, envolvente; **the music was very a.** la música era muy envolvente

atmospherics [ætməsˈferɪks] *npl Rad* interferencias *fpl*, ruidos *mpl* atmosféricos

atoll [ˈætɒl] *n Geog* atolón *m*

atom [ˈætəm] *n* (**a**) *Phys* átomo *m* ►► ***a. bomb*** bomba *f* atómica (**b**) IDIOMS **there's not an a. of truth in what you say** no hay ni (una) pizca de verdad en lo que dices; **they haven't an a. of common sense** no tienen ni chispa *or* gota de sentido común

atomic [əˈtɒmɪk] *adj* atómico(a); **the a. age** la era atómica ►► ***a. bomb*** bomba *f* atómica; ***a. clock*** reloj *m* atómico; ***a. energy*** energía *f* atómica *or* nuclear; ***a. explosion*** explosión *f* atómica *or* nuclear; ***a. mass*** masa *f* atómica; ***a. number*** número *m* atómico; ***a. pile*** pila *f* atómica; ***a. weight*** peso *m* atómico

atomize [ˈætəmaɪz] *vt* (**a**) *(annihilate)* aniquilar, pulverizar (**b**) *(liquid)* atomizar, pulverizar

atomizer [ˈætəmaɪzə(r)] *n* atomizador *m*

atonal [eɪˈtəʊnəl] *adj Mus* atonal

atone [əˈtəʊn]

► **atone for** *vt insep (sin, crime)* expiar; *(mistake)* subsanar

atonement [əˈtəʊnmənt] *n (for sin, crime)* expiación *f*; *(for mistake)* subsanación *f*, resarcimiento *m*; **in a. for** como resarcimiento por, en compensación por

atonic [eɪˈtɒnɪk] *adj Ling (syllable)* átono(a)

atop [əˈtɒp] *prep* sobre, encima de

ATP [eɪtiːˈpiː] *n* (**a**) *Sport* (*abbr* **Association of Tennis Professionals**) ATP *f* (**b**) *Biol* (*abbr* **adenosine triphosphate**) ATP *m*

atria *pl of* **atrium**

at-risk [ˈætˈrɪsk] *adj* de riesgo

atrium [ˈeɪtrɪəm] (*pl* **atria** [ˈeɪtrɪə] *or* **atriums**) *n* (**a**) *Archit* atrio *m* (**b**) *Anat* aurícula *f*

atrocious [əˈtrəʊʃəs] *adj* (**a**) *(crime, behaviour)* atroz, cruel (**b**) *Fam (mistake, decision, weather, meal)* penoso(a), atroz; *(pun)* penoso(a), espantoso(a); **his singing is a.** canta de pena, como cantante es malísimo *or* espantoso

atrociously [əˈtrəʊʃəslɪ] *adv* (**a**) *(cruelly)* atrozmente, despiadadamente (**b**) *Fam (very badly)* de pena; **a. bad** malísimo, pésimo

atrocity [əˈtrɒsɪtɪ] *n* atrocidad *f*; **to commit an a.** cometer una atrocidad *or* salvajada

atrophy [ˈætrəfɪ] **1** *n* atrofia *f*
2 *vt* atrofiar
3 *vi* atrofiarse

attaboy [ˈætəbɔɪ] *exclam US Fam* ¡vamos!

attach [əˈtætʃ] **1** *vt* (**a**) *(fasten) (handle, label)* sujetar, fijar (**to** a); *Fig* **to a. oneself to sb** pegarse a alguien
(**b**) *(be part of)* **the research centre is attached to the science department** el centro de investigación está adscrito al departamento de ciencias
(**c**) *(document, cheque)* adjuntar (**to** a); **please find attached...** se adjunta...
(**d**) *(assign) (blame, responsibility, importance)* atribuir (**to** a)
(**e**) *(second)* destinar *or* trasladar temporalmente; **you will be attached to the Ministry of Agriculture** estarás en comisión de servicio en el Ministerio de Agricultura
(**f**) *Law (person)* retener por orden judicial; *(property, salary)* embargar
(**g**) *Comptr* adjuntar (**to** a)
2 *vi Formal* **the benefits that a. to this position are considerable** las ventajas inherentes al puesto son considerables; **no blame attaches to you for what happened** no eres culpable de lo que ocurrió

attaché [əˈtæʃeɪ] *n* agregado(a) *m,f*; **cultural/military a.** agregado(a) cultural/militar

attaché-case [əˈtæʃeɪkeɪs] *n* maletín *m*

attached [əˈtætʃt] *adj* (**a**) *(fastened)* **the refuse receptacle and the a. lid** el receptáculo de desperdicios y la tapa que lleva
(**b**) *(document, cheque)* adjunto(a)
(**c**) *(emotionally)* **to be very a. to sth/sb** tenerle mucho cariño a algo/alguien; **I was very a. to that pen** le tenía mucho apego a esa pluma; **to become/get a. to** tomar cariño a, encariñarse con
(**d**) *Fam* **is he a.?** *(in a relationship)* ¿tiene novia *or* pareja *or* compañera?

attachment [əˈtætʃmənt] *n* (**a**) *(fastening)* fijación *f*, sujeción *f*; **after the a. of the device to the hull, it will send a signal** tras fijar *or* sujetar el dispositivo al casco emitirá una señal
(**b**) *(device)* accesorio *m*
(**c**) *(secondment)* **to be on a. to a department** estar destinado(a) en un departamento; **he's on a. from the university** viene trasladado de la universidad
(**d**) *Comptr (to e-mail)* archivo *m* adjunto, anexo *m*
(**e**) *(fondness)* cariño *m*; **to form an a. to sb** tomar cariño a alguien
(**f**) *Law (of person)* retención *f* por orden judicial; *(of property)* embargo *m*

attack [əˈtæk] **1** *n* (**a**) *(assault) (physical, verbal)* ataque *m*; **the a. on her life failed** el intento de asesinarla fracasó; **to be under a.** estar siendo atacado(a); **she felt as though she were under a.** se sentía como si la estuvieran atacando; **to come under a.** ser atacado(a); **to go on the a.** entrar al ataque; **to leave oneself open to a.** quedarse expuesto al ataque; PROV **a. is the best form of defence** la mejor defensa es el ataque ►► ***a. dog*** perro *m* de ataque
(**b**) *(bout) (of illness)* ataque *m*, acceso *m*; **I had an a. of doubt** me asaltaron las dudas; **an a. of fever** un acceso de fiebre; **an a. of hysteria** un ataque de histeria; **an a. of nerves** un ataque de nervios
2 *vt* (**a**) *(assault) (physically, verbally)* atacar; **he was attacked in the street** lo asaltaron en la calle; **she has been attacked in the press** la prensa ha arremetido contra ella (**b**) *(tackle) (problem, task)* acometer, abordar; *(food)* atacar (**c**) *(of disease)* atacar, afectar; *(of rust)* atacar; **he was attacked by doubts** le invadió la duda
3 *vi (troops, soccer team, animal)* atacar

attacker [əˈtækə(r)] *n* (**a**) *(assailant)* atacante *mf*, agresor(ora) *m,f*; *(soldier)* atacante *mf* (**b**) *(sportsperson)* atacante *mf*

attacking [əˈtækɪŋ] *adj (forces, player)* atacante; *(game, play)* ofensivo(a), agresivo(a)

attagirl [ˈætəgɜːl] *exclam US Fam* ¡vamos!

attain [əˈteɪn] *vt (goal, ambition, greatness)* alcanzar; *(age)* alcanzar, llegar a; *(happiness)* alcanzar, lograr; *(rank)* llegar a

attainable [əˈteɪnəbəl] *adj (goal, ambition)* factible, alcanzable

attainder [əˈteɪndə(r)] *n Law Formerly* muerte *f* civil

attainment [əˈteɪnmənt] *n* (**a**) *(of goal, ambition)* consecución *f*, logro *m*; *(of happiness)* obtención *f*, consecución *f* (**b**) *(skill, achievement)* logro *m*

attempt [ə'tempt] **1** *n (effort)* intento *m*, tentativa *f*; **to make an a. at doing sth** *or* **to do sth** intentar hacer algo; **to make an a. on** *(record)* intentar batir; *(mountain)* intentar escalar; **I made another a. on the paperwork** me puse otra vez manos a la obra con el papeleo; **to make an a. on sb's life** atentar contra la vida de alguien; **they made no a. to help** no trataron de ayudar; **without (making) any a. at concealment** sin ningún disimulo, sin esconder nada; **at the first a.** al primer intento; **it wasn't bad for a first a.** no estuvo mal para ser la primera vez; **I passed the test at my third a.** aprobé (el examen) a la tercera; **he died in the a.** falleció *or* murió en el intento

2 *vt (task, suicide)* intentar, tratar; **to a. to do sth, to a. doing sth** tratar de *or* intentar hacer algo; **to a. a smile** intentar sonreír; **to a. the impossible** intentar lo imposible; **she plans to a. the record again in June** volverá a intentar batir el récord en junio; **to a. an ascent of Everest** intentar escalar el Everest

attempted [ə'temptɪd] *adj* ***a. coup*** intento *m* de golpe de estado, intentona *f* golpista; *Law* ***a. murder*** intento *m* de asesinato; *Law* ***a. robbery*** intento *m* de robo; ***a. suicide*** intento *m* de suicidio

attend [ə'tend] **1** *vt* **(a)** *(meeting)* asistir a, acudir a; *(school, class)* asistir a; **I attended a private school** fui *or* estudié en una escuela privada; **the concert was well attended** al concierto asistió numeroso público

(b) *(patient, customer)* atender; **we were attended by three waiters** nos atendieron tres camareros

(c) *Formal (accompany)* comportar, conllevar; **the mission was attended by great difficulties** la misión entrañaba grandes dificultades; **high inflation is one of the risks which a. this policy** uno de los riesgos que implica *or* conlleva esta política es una elevada tasa de inflación

2 *vi* **(a)** *(be present)* asistir **(b)** *(doctor)* atender, asistir; **the attending physician** el/la médico *(al cargo de un paciente)* **(c)** *(pay attention)* atender, prestar atención; **please a. to what I'm saying** por favor, presta atención *or* atiende a lo que te estoy diciendo

▸ **attend on, attend upon** *vt insep* **(a)** *(of servant)* servir; *(of doctor)* atender, asistir **(b)** *Formal (accompany)* comportar, conllevar; **the many risks and uncertainties which a. upon the project** los numerosos riesgos e incertidumbres que acarrea el proyecto

▸ **attend to** *vt insep* **(a)** *(matter, problem)* ocuparse de; **you should a. to your work** deberías atender a tu trabajo; **I'll a. to it directly, sir** enseguida, señor **(b)** *(patient)* atender, asistir; *(customer)* atender; **are you being attended to, madam?** ¿la están atendiendo *or* la atienden ya, señora?

attendance [ə'tendəns] *n* **(a)** *(presence)* asistencia *f*; **church attendances have fallen** ha disminuido el número de fieles que asisten a misa; **to be in a.** hacer acto de presencia, estar presente; **to be in a. on sb** *(of doctor)* tratar a alguien; *(of servant)* estar a la disposición de alguien; **she arrived with six bodyguards in a.** llegó rodeada de seis guardaespaldas; **his a. has been good/bad, he has a good/bad a. record** su índice de asistencia ha sido bueno/malo ▸▸ *Br* ***a. allowance*** subsidio *m* de asistencia (para minusválidos); ***a. register*** lista *f* de asistencia

(b) *(people present)* asistencia *f*; **there was a good/poor a.** acudió mucha/poca gente; **the class was cancelled because of poor a.** la clase se canceló por falta de asistencia

attendant [ə'tendənt] **1** *n* **(a)** *(in museum)* vigilante *mf*; *(in car park, cloakroom, swimming pool)* encargado(a) *m,f* **(b) attendants** *(of royalty)* séquito

2 *adj Formal* **the difficulties a. on this procedure** las dificultades que este procedimiento conlleva *or* entraña

attention [ə'tenʃən] *n* **(a)** *(concentration, thought)* atención *f*; **to pay a. to sth/sb** *(listen, examine carefully)* prestar atención a algo/alguien; **we paid no a. to the survey** no hicimos caso a *or* de la encuesta; **to pay a. to detail** fijarse en los detalles; **to give sth/sb one's full a.** atender bien algo/a alguien; **she knows how to hold an audience's a.** sabe cómo mantener la atención del público; **to turn** *or* **direct one's a. to sth** dirigir la atención a algo; **your a. please, ladies and gentlemen** atención, señoras y señores ▸▸ *Med* ***a. deficit (hyperactivity) disorder*** trastorno *m* por déficit de atención; ***a. span*** capacidad *f* de concentración

(b) *(notice)* atención *f*; **to attract** *or* **catch sb's a.** llamar la atención de alguien; **the programme drew a. to the suffering of the refugees** el programa llamó la atención sobre el sufrimiento de los refugiados; **I brought the error to the chairman's a.** hice ver el error al presidente; **to draw a. to oneself** llamar la atención; **pay no a. to what he says** no hagas caso de lo que dice, no le prestes atención; **it's just a. seeking** no es más que una forma de llamar la atención; *Formal* **it has come to our a. that...** hemos sido advertidos *or* informados de que...; **for the a. of** *(on hand-delivered letter)* a la atención de

(c) *(care)* cuidados *mpl*, atención *m*; *(repairs)* mantenimiento *m*; **they need medical a.** requieren atención médica; **the engine needs some a.** hay que revisar el motor

(d) *(amorous advances)* **she felt irritated by his unwanted attentions** le molestaban sus galanterías *or* indeseadas atenciones

(e) *Mil* **a.!** ¡firmes!; **to stand at** *or* **to a.** ponerse firme, cuadrarse

attentive [ə'tentɪv] *adj* **(a)** *(paying attention)* atento(a); **a. to detail** pendiente de los detalles, detallista **(b)** *(considerate)* atento(a); **to be a. to sb** estar pendiente de alguien

attentively [ə'tentɪvlɪ] *adv* **(a)** *(with concentration)* atentamente, con atención **(b)** *(considerately)* atentamente

attentiveness [ə'tentɪvnɪs] *n* **(a)** *(concentration)* atención *f* **(b)** *(consideration)* atención *f*, consideración *f*

attenuate [ə'tenjʊeɪt] *vt Formal (weaken)* atenuar, mitigar

attenuating [ə'tenjʊeɪtɪŋ] *adj Law* ***a. circumstances*** (circunstancias *fpl*) atenuantes *fpl*

attest [ə'test] **1** *vt* **(a)** *(affirm, prove)* atestiguar; **this phenomenon/effect is well attested** este fenómeno/efecto está sobradamente comprobado **(b)** *Law (signature)* autenticar

2 *vi* **to a. to** dar testimonio *or* fe de

attestation [æte'steɪʃən] *n Formal* **(a)** *(affirmation)* atestación *f* **(b)** *(proof)* prueba *f*, testimonio *m*; **in a. of sth** como prueba de algo **(c)** *Law (of signature)* autenticación *f*

attested [ə'testɪd] *adj* **(a)** *Law (signature)* autenticado(a) **(b)** *Br (herd, milk)* certificado(a)

Att Gen *(abbr* **Attorney General**) *Br* ≃ fiscal *mf* general del Estado; *US* ≃ ministro(a) *m,f* de Justicia

attic ['ætɪk] *n* **(a)** *(storage space)* desván *m* **(b)** *(room)* ático *m*; **a.** *Br* **flat** *or US* **apartment** ático

attire [ə'taɪə(r)] **1** *n* atuendo *m*, atavío *m*

2 *vt Literary* ataviar, engalanar; **attired in silk** con atuendo de seda

attitude ['ætɪtju:d] *n* **(a)** *(opinion)* actitud *f*; **what's your a. to abortion?** ¿cuál es tu actitud *or* postura ante el aborto?; **to take the a. that...** adoptar la actitud de que...; **happiness is just an a. of mind** la felicidad no es más que un estado de ánimo ▸▸ *Com* ***a. survey*** estudio *m* de actitud

(b) *(manner, behaviour)* actitud *f*; **I don't like your a.** no me gusta tu actitud; **he's got an a. problem** tiene un problema de actitud

(c) *(pose)* pose *f*; **to strike an a.** adoptar una pose

(d) *Fam (self-assurance, assertiveness)* carácter *m*, genio *m*; **to have a.** tener carácter; **a car with a.** un automóvil con carácter *or* garra

attitudinal [ætɪ'tju:dɪnəl] *adj* de actitud

attitudinize [ætɪ'tju:dɪnaɪz] *vi* polemizar

attn *Com* (*abbr* **for the attention of**) a la atención de

attorney [ə'tɜ:nɪ] *n* **(a)** *US (lawyer)* abogado(a) *m,f* **(b)** ***A. General*** *(in England, Wales and Northern Ireland)* ≃ fiscal *mf* general del Estado; *(in United States)* ≃ ministro(a) *m,f* de Justicia

attorney-at-law [ə'tɜ:nɪət'lɔ:] *n US* abogado(a) *m,f*

attract [ə'trækt] **1** *vt* **(a)** *(pull, draw)* atraer; **to a. sb's attention** llamar la atención de alguien; **we hope to a. more young people to the church** confiamos en atraer a más gente joven a la Iglesia

(b) *(give rise to)* **to a. interest/criticism** despertar *or* suscitar interés/críticas; **to a. (sb's) attention** suscitar *or* despertar la atención (de alguien); *Fin* **long-term deposits a. a higher rate of interest** los depósitos a largo plazo devengan un tipo de interés más elevado

(c) *(interest)* atraer; **to be attracted to sth/sb** sentirse atraído(a) por algo/alguien; **the idea doesn't a. me** la idea no me atrae *or* seduce

2 *vi* atraerse; **opposites a.** los polos opuestos se atraen

attraction [ə'trækʃən] *n* **(a)** *(power)* atracción *f*; **the prospect holds little a. for me** la perspectiva no me atrae mucho; **I can't** *or* **don't see the a. of it** no le veo el aliciente *or* atractivo **(b)** *(attractive aspect)* atractivo *m*, aliciente *m*; **it's the city's chief a.** es la principal atracción de la ciudad **(c)** *Phys* atracción *f*

attractive [ə'træktɪv] *adj* **(a)** *(person, smile)* atractivo(a); *(dress)* coqueto(a), interesante; *(picture)* sugerente, atractivo(a); **do you find him a.?** ¿lo encuentras atractivo? **(b)** *(offer, prospect)* atractivo(a); *(price, rate of interest)* interesante, atractivo(a)

attractively [ə'træktɪvlɪ] *adv* **(a)** *(prettily)* con atractivo, con encanto; **the meal was very a. presented** la comida presentaba un aspecto muy apetecible **(b)** *(priced)* **the property was most a. priced** la finca tenía un precio muy interesante

attractiveness [ə'træktɪvnɪs] *n* **(a)** *(of person, smile)* atractivo *m*, encanto *m*; *(of dress, picture)* atractivo *m* **(b)** *(of offer, price)* atractivo *m*, aliciente *m*

attributable [ə'trɪbjʊtəbəl] *adj* **to be a. to** ser atribuible a

attribute 1 *n* ['ætrɪbju:t] atributo *m*
2 *vt* [ə'trɪbju:t] atribuir (**to** a); **to what do you a. your success?** ¿a qué atribuyes tu éxito?

attribution [ætrɪ'bju:ʃən] *n* atribución *f*; **a spurious a.** una imputación falsa; **a debatable a.** una atribución discutible

attributive [ə'trɪbjʊtɪv] *adj Gram* atributivo(a)

attributively [ə'trɪbjʊtɪvlɪ] *adv Ling* como atributo

attrition [ə'trɪʃən] *n* (**a**) *(wearing down)* desgaste *m*; **war of a.** guerra de desgaste (**b**) *Ind* amortización *f* de puestos de trabajo por jubilación

attune [ə'tju:n] *vt* **to a. oneself** *or* **become attuned to sth** adaptarse *or* amoldarse a algo; **he's attuned to their way of thinking** sintoniza muy bien con su manera de pensar

atypical [eɪ'tɪpɪkəl] *adj* atípico(a)

atypically [eɪ'tɪpɪklɪ] *adv* atípicamente, de manera atípica *or* anormal

AU [eɪ'ju:] *n* (*abbr* **African Union**) UA *f*

aubergine ['əʊbəʒi:n] *n Br* berenjena *f*

auburn ['ɔ:bən] *adj (hair)* (color) caoba

auction ['ɔ:kʃən] 1 *n* subasta *f*; **sold at** *or* **by a.** vendido(a) en pública subasta; **to put sth up for a.** sacar algo a subasta ►► ***a. bridge*** bridge *m* de subasta; ***a. room*** sala *f* de subastas
2 *vt* subastar

► **auction off** *vt sep* liquidar mediante subasta, subastar

auctioneer [ɔ:kʃə'nɪə(r)] *n* subastador(ora) *m,f*

audacious [ɔ:'deɪʃəs] *adj* (**a**) *(daring)* audaz, osado(a) (**b**) *(impudent)* insolente, descarado(a)

audaciously [ɔ:'deɪʃəslɪ] *adv* (**a**) *(boldly)* audazmente, osadamente (**b**) *(impudently)* insolentemente, descaradamente

audacity [ɔ:'dæsɪtɪ], **audaciousness** [ɔ:'deɪʃəsnɪs] *n* (**a**) *(daring)* audacia *f*, osadía *f* (**b**) *(impudence)* insolencia *f*, descaro *m*; **he had the a. to ask for a pay rise** tuvo la osadía de pedir un aumento de sueldo

audibility [ɔ:dɪ'bɪlɪtɪ] *n* audibilidad *f*

audible ['ɔ:dɪbəl] *adj* audible; **the music was barely a.** apenas podía oírse la música

audibly ['ɔ:dɪblɪ] *adv* de manera audible

audience ['ɔ:dɪəns] *n* (**a**) *(spectators) (at film, play)* espectadores *mpl*, público *m*; *(at concert, lecture)* auditorio *m*, público *m*; *(of TV programme)* espectadores *mpl*, audiencia *f*; *(of radio programme)* oyentes *mpl*; **the studio a.** *(of TV or radio programme)* el público; **is there much of an a. for this sort of thing?** ¿hay algún tipo de público al que le interese algo así?; **his books appeal to a wide a.** sus libros interesan a un público muy extenso ►► ***a. participation*** participación *f* del público; ***a. share*** índice *f* de audiencia
(**b**) *(meeting with monarch, Pope)* audiencia *f*; **to grant sb an a.** conceder una audiencia a alguien

audio ['ɔ:dɪəʊ] *adj* ***a. book*** audiolibro *m*; ***a. cassette*** cinta *f* de audio; ***a. conference*** audioconferencia *f*; ***a. equipment*** equipo *m* de sonido; ***a. frequency*** audiofrecuencia *f*; ***a. tape*** cinta *f* de audio

audio-typist ['ɔ:dɪəʊtaɪpɪst] *n* mecanógrafo(a) *m,f* con dictáfono

audiovisual [ɔ:dɪəʊ'vɪzjʊəl] 1 *adj* audiovisual
2 *n* **audiovisuals** medios *mpl* audiovisuales

audit ['ɔ:dɪt] 1 *n Fin* auditoría *f*
2 *vt* (**a**) *Fin* auditar (**b**) *US (class, lecture)* asistir de oyente a

audition [ɔ:'dɪʃən] *Theat* 1 *n* prueba *f*, audición *f*; **to hold auditions for a play** realizar pruebas a actores para una obra de teatro; **to do an a.** hacer una prueba *or* audición
2 *vt (of director)* hacer una prueba *or* audición a
3 *vi (actor)* hacer una prueba *or* audición

auditor ['ɔ:dɪtə(r)] *n* (**a**) *Fin* auditor(ora) *m,f* (**b**) *US (student)* oyente *mf*

auditorium [ɔ:dɪ'tɔ:rɪəm] (*pl* **auditoriums** *or* **auditoria** [ɔ:dɪ'tɔ:rɪə]) *n* auditorio *m*

auditory ['ɔ:dɪtrɪ] *adj* auditivo(a) ►► *Anat* ***a. nerve*** nervio *m* auditivo; ***a. phonetics*** fonética *f* auditiva

au fait [əʊ'feɪ] *adj* **to be a. with sth** estar al día de algo

Aug (*abbr* **August**) ago.

auger ['ɔ:gə(r)] *n* barrena *f*, taladro *m*

aught [ɔ:t] *pron Literary* **for a. I know** por lo que yo alcanzo a comprender; **for a. I care** por lo que a mí respecta

augment [ɔ:g'ment] *vt* incrementar, aumentar

augmented [ɔ:g'mentɪd] *adj Mus* aumentado(a)

au gratin [əʊ'grætæn] *adj* gratinado(a), al gratén

augur ['ɔ:gə(r)] 1 *vt* **it augurs no good** no augura nada bueno
2 *vi* **to a. well/ill** ser un buen/mal augurio

augury ['ɔ:gjʊrɪ] *n* (**a**) *(omen)* augurio *m*, presagio *m* (**b**) *(divination)* adivinación *f*

August ['ɔ:gəst] *n* agosto *m*; *see also* **May**

august [ɔ:'gʌst] *adj Literary (distinguished)* augusto(a)

Augustan [ɔ:'gʌstən] *adj* (**a**) *(classical)* augustal (**b**) *(post-classical)* neoclásico(a)

Augustine [ɔ:'gʌstɪn, *US* 'ɔ:gəsti:n] *pr n* **Saint A.** San Augustín

Augustinian [ɔ:gə'stɪnɪən] 1 *n* (**a**) *(monk)* agustino(a) *m,f* (**b**) *(follower)* agustino(a) *m,f*
2 *adj* agustiniano(a), agustino(a)

Augustus [ɔ:'gʌstəs] *pr n* **A. (Caesar)** César Augusto

auk [ɔ:k] *n* alca *f*

au naturel [əʊnætjʊ'rel] *adj* (**a**) *(food, method of cooking)* al natural, en crudo (**b**) *(person)* en cueros, desnudo(a)

aunt [ɑ:nt] *n* tía *f* ►► *Br* ***A. Sally*** *(at fairground)* blanco *m* (de feria); *(target of abuse)* objeto *m* de burlas *or* mofas

auntie, aunty ['ɑ:ntɪ] *n Fam* (**a**) tita *f*, tiíta *f* (**b**) *Br* **A. (Beeb)** la BBC

AUP [eɪju:'pi:] *n Comptr* (*abbr* **acceptable use policy**) política *f* aceptable de uso

au pair [əʊ'peə(r)] 1 *n* au pair *mf*
2 *vi* trabajar de au pair

aura ['ɔ:rə] *n* (**a**) *(atmosphere)* aura *f* (**b**) *(surrounding body)* aura *f*

aural ['ɔ:rəl] *adj* auditivo(a); **a. comprehension/skills** comprensión/capacidad auditiva

aurally ['ɔ:rəlɪ] *adv* auditivamente; **a. handicapped** disminuido(a) *or* discapacitado(a) auditivo(a)

au revoir [əʊrə'vwɑ:(r)] *exclam* ¡adiós!, ¡chao!

auricle ['ɔ:rɪkəl] *n Anat* (**a**) *(of heart)* aurícula *f* (**b**) *(of ear)* pabellón *m* de la oreja

aurora [ə'rɔ:rə] (*pl* **auroras** *or* **aurorae** [ə'rɔ:ri:]) *n Astron* aurora *f* ►► ***a. australis*** aurora *f* austral; ***a. borealis*** aurora *f* boreal

auspices ['ɔ:spɪsɪz] *npl* **under the a. of** bajo los auspicios de

auspicious [ɔ:'spɪʃəs] *adj* prometedor(a), halagüeño(a); **we made an a. beginning** comenzamos con buen pie; **on this a. occasion** en esta feliz *or* jubilosa ocasión

auspiciously [ɔ:'spɪʃəslɪ] *adv* de manera halagüeña

Aussie ['ɒzɪ] *Fam* 1 *n* australiano(a) *m,f*
2 *adj* australiano(a)

austere [ɒ'stɪə(r)] *adj* austero(a)

austerity [ɒ'sterɪtɪ] *n* (**a**) *(simplicity)* austeridad *f*, sobriedad *f* (**b**) *(hardship)* austeridad *f*, estrechez *f*; **a. measures** medidas de austeridad; **the austerities of life at boarding school** la austeridad de la vida en un internado

Australasia [ɒstrə'leɪʒə] *n* Australasia

Australasian [ɒstrə'leɪʒən] *adj* de Australasia

Australia [ɒ'streɪlɪə] *n* Australia

Australian [ɒ'streɪlɪən] *n* 1 australiano(a) *m,f*
2 *adj* australiano(a) ►► ***A. rules football*** fútbol *m* australiano

Austria ['ɒstrɪə] *n* Austria

Austrian ['ɒstrɪən] 1 *n* austriaco(a) *m,f*
2 *adj* austriaco(a)

Austro-Hungarian ['ɒstrəʊhʌŋ'geərɪən] *adj Hist* austrohúngaro; **the A. Empire** el Imperio Austrohúngaro

AUT [eɪju:'ti:] *n* (*abbr* **Association of University Teachers**) = sindicato británico de profesores universitarios

autarchy ['ɔ:tɑ:kɪ] *n Pol* autarquía *f*

autarky ['ɔ:tɑ:kɪ] *n Econ* autarquía *f*

authentic [ɔ:'θentɪk] *adj* (**a**) *(artefact)* auténtico(a), genuino(a) (**b**) *(atmosphere, recreation)* auténtico(a), fidedigno(a)

authentically [ɔ:'θentɪklɪ] *adv (to recreate)* fielmente; **the food is a. Chinese** la comida es genuinamente china

authenticate [ɔ:'θentɪkeɪt] *vt* autentificar, autenticar

authentication [ɔ:θentɪ'keɪʃən] *n* (**a**) *(of painting, document, signature)* autentificación *f*, autenticación *f* (**b**) *Comptr* autentificación *f*, autenticación *f*

authenticity [ɔ:θen'tɪsɪtɪ] *n* (**a**) *(of artefact)* autenticidad *f* (**b**) *(of atmosphere, recreation)* autenticidad *f*, verosimilitud *f*

author ['ɔːθə(r)] **1** *n* (**a**) *(writer) (by profession)* escritor(ora) *m,f*; *(of a book)* autor(ora) *m,f* (**b**) *(cause, creator)* autor(ora) *m,f*; **she was the a. of her own downfall** ella fue la causante de su propia ruina
2 *vt* crear, ser el autor/la autora de

authoress ['ɔːθərɪs] *n Old-fashioned (writer)* escritora *f*, autora *f*

authoring ['ɔːθərɪŋ] *adj Comptr* ***a. language*** lenguaje *m* de autor; ***a. system*** sistema *m* de autor; ***a. tool*** herramienta *f* de autor

authoritarian [ɔːθɒrɪ'teərɪən] **1** *n* autoritario(a) *m,f*
2 *adj* autoritario(a)

authoritarianism [ɔːθɒrɪ'teərɪənɪzəm] *n* autoritarismo *m*

authoritative [ɔː'θɒrɪtətɪv] *adj* (**a**) *(manner, voice, person)* autoritario(a) (**b**) *(study, source)* autorizado(a)

authoritatively [ɔː'θɒrɪtətɪvlɪ] *adv (reliably)* con autoridad, con dominio

authority [ɔː'θɒrɪtɪ] *n* (**a**) *(power)* autoridad *f*; **I'd like to speak to someone in a.** quisiera hablar con el responsable; **to have an air of a.** mostrar seguridad *or* aplomo
(**b**) *(forcefulness, confidence)* autoridad *f*, seguridad *f*; **her conviction gave a. to her argument** su propia convicción confería peso a su razonamiento; **his opinions carry a lot of a.** su opinión goza de gran autoridad
(**c**) *(authorization)* autorización *f*; **to give sb a. to do sth** autorizar a alguien a hacer algo; **they have no a. to stop him** no tienen poder para detenerlo; **on whose a. did they search the house?** ¿quién les dio autorización para que registraran la casa?; **he did it on his own a.** lo hizo bajo su responsabilidad; **without a.** sin autorización
(**d**) *(people in command)* autoridad *f*; **the authorities** las autoridades; **the proper authorities** el/los organismo(s) competente(s); *Br* **the local education/housing a.** la autoridad local competente en materia de enseñanza/vivienda; **we'll go to the highest a. in the land** acudiremos a la más alta autoridad *or* instancia del país
(**e**) *(expert, source)* autoridad *f*; **I have it on his own a. that she was there** él mismo me ha dicho que ella estuvo allí; **to be an a. on sth** ser una autoridad en algo; IDIOM **to have it on good a.** saberlo de buena tinta *or RP* fuente

authorization [ɔːθəraɪ'zeɪʃən] *n (act, permission)* autorización *f*

authorize ['ɔːθəraɪz] *vt* autorizar; **to a. sb to do sth** autorizar a alguien a hacer algo; **to a. a loan** autorizar un préstamo; **she is authorized to act for her father** esta autorizada para obrar en nombre de su padre

authorized ['ɔːθəraɪzd] *adj* autorizado(a), oficial; **(entry to) a. persons only** *(sign)* prohibido el paso a toda persona no autorizada ▸▸ ***a. dealer*** distribuidor *m* autorizado; ***the A. Version*** *(of Bible)* = versión oficial de la Biblia protestante en inglés

authorship ['ɔːθəʃɪp] *n (author's identity)* autoría *f*; **a work of unknown a.** una obra de autor desconocido

autism ['ɔːtɪzəm] *n* autismo *m*

autistic [ɔː'tɪstɪk] *adj* autista

auto ['ɔːtəʊ] (*pl* **autos**) *n US* automóvil *m*, *Esp* coche *m*, *Am* carro *m*, *RP* auto *m* ▸▸ ***a. accident*** accidente *m* automovilístico; ***a. industry*** industria *f* automovilística *or* del automóvil; ***a. parts*** repuestos *mpl or* recambios *mpl* de automóvil

auto- ['ɔːtəʊ] *prefix* auto-

autobiographical [ɔːtəbaɪə'græfɪkəl] *adj* autobiográfico(a)

autobiography [ɔːtəbaɪ'ɒgrəfɪ] *n* autobiografía *f*

autocorrect [ɔːtəʊkə'rekt] *vt Comptr* corregir automáticamente

autocracy [ɔː'tɒkrəsɪ] *n* autocracia *f*

autocrat ['ɔːtəkræt] *n* autócrata *mf*

autocratic [ɔːtə'krætɪk] *adj* autocrático(a)

Autocue® ['ɔːtəʊkjuː] *n Br TV* teleapuntador *m*

auto-da-fé ['ɔːtəʊdə'feɪ] (*pl* **autos-da-fé** ['ɔːtəʊzdə'feɪ]) *n Hist* auto *m* de fe

autodestruct ['ɔːtəʊdɪ'strʌkt] **1** *vi* autodestruirse
2 *adj* autodestructivo(a)

autodialler ['ɔːtəʊdaɪələ(r)] *n* (dispositivo *m* de) marcación *f* automática

autodidact ['ɔːtəʊ'daɪdækt] *n* autodidacta *mf*

autoerotic ['ɔːtəʊɪ'rɒtɪk] *adj* autoerótico(a)

autoeroticism ['ɔːtəʊɪ'rɒtɪsɪzəm] *n* autoerotismo *m*

autoflow ['ɔːtəʊfləʊ] *n Comptr* salto *m* automático de línea

autofocus ['ɔːtəʊfəʊkəs] *n* autofocus *m*, autofoco *m*

autogenous [ɔː'tɒdʒənəs] *adj* autógeno(a)

autogiro, autogyro ['ɔːtəʊ'dʒaɪərəʊ] *n* autogiro *m*

autograph ['ɔːtəgrɑːf] **1** *n* autógrafo *m* ▸▸ ***a. album*** *or* ***book*** álbum *m* de autógrafos; ***a. hunter*** cazador(ora) *m,f* de autógrafos
2 *adj (manuscript, letter)* autógrafo(a)
3 *vt* autografiar

autogyro = **autogiro**

autoimmune [ɔːtəʊɪ'mjuːn] *adj* **a. disease** enfermedad autoinmune

autoimmunity [ɔːtəʊɪ'mjuːnɪtɪ] *n* autoinmunidad *f*

automaker ['ɔːtəʊmeɪkə(r)] *n US* fabricante *m* de automóviles

automat ['ɔːtəmæt] *n US* = restaurante en el que la comida se obtiene de máquinas expendedoras

automata *pl of* **automaton**

automate ['ɔːtəmeɪt] *vt* automatizar

automated telling machine ['ɔːtəmeɪtɪd'telɪŋməʃiːn], **automatic telling machine** [ɔːtə'mætɪk'telɪŋməʃiːn] *n* cajero *m* automático

automatic [ɔːtə'mætɪk] **1** *n* (**a**) *(car)* coche *m or* automóvil *m or Am* carro *m or RP* auto *m* (con cambio) automático (**b**) *(pistol)* pistola *f* automática (**c**) *(washing machine)* lavadora *f* (automática), *RP* lavarropas *m* (automático)
2 *adj* (**a**) *(machine, mechanism)* automático(a) ▸▸ ***a. brake*** freno *m* automático; *Comptr* ***a. data processing*** proceso *m or* procesamiento *m* automático de datos; ***a. dialling*** marcado *m* automático; *Comptr* ***a. feed*** avance *m* automático; ***a. focusing*** enfoque *m* automático; *Av* ***a. pilot*** piloto *m* automático; *Fig* **to be on a. pilot** tener puesto el piloto automático; *Aut* ***a. transmission*** transmisión *f* automática
(**b**) *(car)* automático(a), con cambio automático
(**c**) *(pistol)* automático(a)
(**d**) *(unreflecting, instantaneous)* automático(a), inmediato(a) ▸▸ ***a. writing*** escritura *f* automática

automatically [ɔːtə'mætɪklɪ] *adv* automáticamente; **I just a. assumed he was right** di automáticamente por sentado que tenía razón

automation [ɔːtə'meɪʃən] *n* automatización *f*

automaton [ɔː'tɒmətən] (*pl* **automata** [ɔː'tɒmətə]) *n* autómata *m*

automobile ['ɔːtəməʊbiːl] *n* automóvil *m*, *Am* carro *m*, *RP* auto *m*; **an a. manufacturer** un fabricante de automóviles ▸▸ ***the a. industry*** la industria automovilística *or* del automóvil; ***a. workers*** trabajadores *mpl* del sector del automóvil

automotive [ɔːtə'məʊtɪv] *adj (engineering, industry)* automotor(ora)

autonomous [ɔː'tɒnəməs] *adj* autónomo(a)

autonomy [ɔː'tɒnəmɪ] *n* autonomía *f*

autopilot ['ɔːtəʊpaɪlət] *n (in vehicle)* piloto *m* automático; **on a.** *(vehicle)* con el piloto automático; **to be on a.** *(person)* tener puesto el piloto automático

autopsy ['ɔːtɒpsɪ] *n* autopsia *f*; **to carry out an a.** practicar *or* efectuar una autopsia

auto-reverse [ɔːtəʊrɪ'vɜːs] *n (on cassette recorder)* autorreverse *m*, cambio *m* automático de dirección de cinta

auto-save ['ɔːtəʊseɪv] *Comptr* **1** *n* autoguardado *m*
2 *vt* guardar automáticamente

autostart ['ɔːtəʊstɑːt] *n Comptr* arranque *m* automático

auto-suggestion ['ɔːtəʊsə'dʒestʃən] *n Psy* autosugestión *f*

autotimer ['ɔːtəʊ'taɪmə(r)] *n* temporizador *m* automático

autowinder ['ɔːtəʊ'waɪndə(r)] *n (for camera)* rebobinador *m* automático

autumn ['ɔːtəm] *n* otoño *m*; **a. leaves** hojas otoñales; **in (the) a.** en otoño; IDIOM **in the a. of his years** en el otoño de su vida

autumnal [ɔː'tʌmnəl] *adj* otoñal ▸▸ ***a. equinox*** equinoccio *m* de otoño

auxiliary [ɔːg'zɪl(ɪ)ərɪ] **1** *n* (**a**) *(assistant)* auxiliar *mf* (**b**) *(soldier)* soldado *m* auxiliar (**c**) *Gram* **a. (verb)** (verbo *m*) auxiliar *m*
2 *adj* auxiliar

AV (**a**) (*abbr* **Authorized Version**) = traducción oficial de la Biblia protestante en inglés publicada en 1611 (**b**) (*abbr* **audiovisual**) audiovisual

avail [ə'veɪl] *Literary* **1** *n* **of no a.** baldío, vano; **it would be of no a. to complain** quejarse sería un ejercicio baldío; **to no a.** en vano; **to little a.** sin grandes resultados, sin mucho éxito; **to be of little a.** ser poco útil *or* provechoso; **to what a.?** ¿con qué fin?, ¿para qué?
2 *vt* **to a. oneself of sth** aprovechar algo

availability [əveɪlə'bɪlɪtɪ] *n* disponibilidad *f*; **check on the a. of tickets** comprueba si quedan *or* hay billetes; **offer subject to a.** oferta válida hasta agotar existencias

available [ə'veɪləbəl] *adj* (**a**) *(information, services, products)* disponible; **the best/first a.** el mejor/primero que hay *or* de que se dispone; **not easily a.** difícil de conseguir; **tickets are still a.** todavía quedan entradas *or Méx* boletos; **they're a. in three sizes** vienen en tres tamaños diferentes; **money is a. for...** hay dinero para...; **they used the time a. to evacuate the area** emplearon el tiempo de que disponían en desalojar la zona; **we tried every a. means** lo intentamos por todos los medios posibles; **legal aid should be a. to everyone** todo el mundo debería poder contar con un abogado de oficio; **a. only on prescription** (dispensable) sólo con receta médica; **these drugs are readily a. on the street** estas drogas son fácilmente asequibles en la calle; *Comptr* **a. to download from our website** puede ser descargado desde nuestro sitio web; **a. on DVD, a. in DVD format** disponible en DVD ▸▸ *Fin* ***a. balance*** saldo *m* disponible; *Phot* ***a. light*** iluminación *f* disponible

(**b**) *(person)* disponible, libre; **to be a.** *(free)* estar disponible *or* libre; *Euph* no tener compromiso; **the minister was not a. for comment** el ministro no se prestó a hacer comentarios; **to make oneself a. (to sb)** ponerse a disposición (de alguien)

avalanche ['ævəlɑːntʃ] *n also Fig* alud *m*, avalancha *f*

avant-garde [ævɒŋ'gɑːd] **1** *n* vanguardia *f*

2 *adj* vanguardista, de vanguardia

avarice ['ævərɪs] *n* avaricia *f*

avaricious [ævə'rɪʃəs] *adj* avaricioso(a)

avatar ['ævətɑː(r)] *n Comptr* avatar *m*

AVC [eɪviː'siː] *n Br Fin* (*abbr* **additional voluntary contributions**) = aportaciones realizadas al plan de pensiones personal complementario

Ave (*abbr* **Avenue**) avda. *f*

avenge [ə'vendʒ] *vt (person, crime)* vengar; **to a. oneself on sb** vengarse de alguien

avenger [ə'vendʒə(r)] *n* vengador(ora) *m,f*

avenging [ə'vendʒɪŋ] *adj* vengador(ora); **an a. angel** un ángel vengador

avenue ['ævɪnjuː] *n* (**a**) *(street)* avenida *f* (**b**) *(in park, garden)* paseo *m* (**c**) *(approach)* **an a. to success/fame** un camino hacia el éxito/la fama; **a new a. of enquiry** una nueva vía de investigación

aver [ə'vɜː(r)] (*pt & pp* **averred**) *vt Formal* aseverar

average ['ævərɪdʒ] **1** *n* promedio *m*, media *f*; **to work out the a.** calcular la media *or* el promedio; **on a.** de media, como promedio; **above/below a.** por encima/debajo del promedio *or* de la media

2 *adj* (**a**) *(mean, typical)* medio(a); **of a. size** de tamaño mediano; **the a. Englishman** el inglés medio; **in an a. week** en una semana normal; **that's about a. for this time of year** eso es lo normal para esta época del año (**b**) *(unexceptional)* regular; **how was your day? – a.** ¿qué tal se te ha dado el día? – normal; **a very a. singer** un cantante muy mediocre *or* del montón

3 *vt* (**a**) *Math* calcular la media *or* el promedio de (**b**) *(typically reach, number)* alcanzar una media *or* un promedio de; **to a. eight hours work a day** trabajar un promedio de ocho horas diarias

▸ **average out** *vi* **my expenses a. out at £400 per month** tengo una media de gastos de 400 libras al mes; **things a. out in the long run** a la larga todo se termina equilibrando

averse [ə'vɜːs] *adj* reacio(a) (**to** a); **to be a. to (doing) sth** ser reacio a (hacer) algo; **he's not a. to making money out of the crisis** no tiene reparo en especular con la crisis; **he is not a. to the occasional glass of wine** no le hace ascos a un vino de vez en cuando

aversion [ə'vɜːʃən] *n* (**a**) *(feeling)* aversión *f*; **to have an a. to sth/sb** sentir aversión por algo/alguien ▸▸ ***a. therapy*** terapia *f* de aversión (**b**) *(thing disliked)* fobia *f*; **rap music is my a.** no soporto el rap

avert [ə'vɜːt] *vt* (**a**) *(turn away) (eyes, thoughts)* apartar, desviar (**b**) *(prevent) (misfortune, accident)* evitar, impedir

aviary ['eɪvɪərɪ] *n* pajarera *f*

aviation [eɪvɪ'eɪʃən] *n* aviación *f* ▸▸ ***a. fuel*** combustible *m* de aviación

aviator ['eɪvɪeɪtə(r)] *n Old-fashioned* aviador(ora) *m,f* ▸▸ ***a. glasses*** gafas *fpl* de aviador

avid ['ævɪd] *adj* ávido(a) (**for** de); **an a. reader of thrillers** un ávido lector de novelas de intriga

avidly ['ævɪdlɪ] *adv* ávidamente

Avignon ['ævɪnjɒn] *n* Aviñón

avionics [eɪvɪ'ɒnɪks] **1** *n (science)* aviónica *f*

2 *npl (instruments, equipment)* equipo *m* de aviónica

avocado [ævə'kɑːdəʊ] (*pl* **avocados**) *n* (**a**) *(fruit)* **a. (pear)** aguacate *m*, *Andes, RP* palta *f* (**b**) *(colour)* verde *m* aguacate

avocet ['ævəʊset] *n* avoceta *f*

avoid [ə'vɔɪd] *vt (person, thing)* evitar; *(punishment, danger, question)* evitar, eludir; **to a. doing sth** evitar hacer algo; **try to a. giving them too much information** procura no facilitarles demasiada información; **to a. paying taxes** *(legally)* evitar *or* eludir el pago de impuestos; *(illegally)* evadir impuestos; **you've been avoiding me** has estado esquivándome; IDIOM **to a. sth/sb like the plague** huir de algo/alguien como de la peste; **don't a. the issue** no eludas la cuestión; **she avoided my eyes** esquivaba mi mirada

avoidable [ə'vɔɪdəbəl] *adj* evitable

avoidance [ə'vɔɪdəns] *n* **to ensure the a. of stress...** para evitar el estrés...; **his a. of the real issue annoyed me** el hecho de que evitara el asunto clave me molestó

avoirdupois [ævədə'pɔɪz, ævwaːdjʊ'pwaː] *n* (**a**) *(system)* = sistema británico de medidas de peso que tiene como unidad la libra (**b**) *US Fam Hum (of person)* sobrepeso *m*, gordura *f*; **people were beginning to comment on his a.** se empezaba a comentar que estaba de buen año

avow [ə'vaʊ] *vt Formal* confesar, reconocer; **to a. oneself beaten** darse por vencido(a), admitir la derrota; **he openly avowed himself (to be) a communist** reconoció públicamente que era comunista

avowal [ə'vaʊəl] *n* confesión *f*

avowed [ə'vaʊd] *adj* declarado(a)

avowedly [ə'vaʊɪdlɪ] *adv* abiertamente, claramente

avuncular [ə'vʌŋkjʊlə(r)] *adj* paternalista

aw [ɔː] *exclam* ¡oh!

await [ə'weɪt] *vt* (**a**) *(wait for)* esperar, *Esp* aguardar; **a long-awaited holiday** unas ansiadas vacaciones; **we a. your instructions** quedamos en espera de sus instrucciones; **to be awaiting trial** *(prisoner)* estar en espera de juicio

(**b**) *(be in store for)* esperar, *Esp* aguardar; **a nasty surprise awaited her** le esperaba una desagradable sorpresa; **who knows what may await us** quién sabe lo que nos deparará el futuro *or* destino

awake [ə'weɪk] **1** *adj* (**a**) *(not sleeping)* **to be a.** estar despierto(a); **to stay a.** quedarse despierto(a); **he lay a. for hours** permaneció despierto en la cama durante horas; **the coffee kept her a.** el café la mantuvo despierta; **the noise kept me a.** el ruido me mantuvo en vela; **he was wide a.** estaba completamente *or* totalmente despierto

(**b**) *(aware)* consciente (**to** de); **we're all a. to the dangers** todos somos conscientes del peligro *or* riesgo

2 *vt* (*pt* **awoke** [ə'wəʊk], *pp* **awoken** [ə'wəʊkən]) (**a**) *(from sleep)* despertar (**b**) *(curiosity, suspicions)* despertar, levantar; *(memories)* reavivar

3 *vi* (**a**) *(emerge from sleep)* despertarse; **I awoke from a deep sleep** desperté de un profundo sueño; **to a. from a trance/coma** salir de un trance/coma (**b**) *(become aware)* percatarse, darse cuenta; **to a. to a danger** percatarse *or* tomar conciencia de un peligro; **he suddenly awoke to the fact that he was no longer young** de repente se dio cuenta *or* se apercibió de que ya no era joven

awaken [ə'weɪkən] (*pt* **awakened** *or* **awoke** [ə'wəʊk], *pp* **awakened** *or* **awoken** [ə'wəʊkən]) **1** *vt* = **awake**

2 *vi* = **awake**

awakening [ə'weɪkənɪŋ] *n* despertar *m*; **it was a rude a.** fue una cruel desilusión *or* una amarga decepción

award [ə'wɔːd] **1** *n* (**a**) *(prize)* premio *m*, distinción *f*; **to make/be given an a.** conceder/recibir un premio *or* galardón; **an a. for bravery** una distinción al valor; **the annual awards ceremony** la ceremonia anual de entrega de premios (**b**) *Law* indemnización *f* (**c**) *Austr (minimum wage)* **a. (wage)** salario *m* mínimo

2 *vt* (**a**) *(prize, contract)* otorgar, conceder; *(medal)* imponer, otorgar; **to a. sth to sb** otorgar *or* conceder algo a alguien; **she was awarded first prize** le concedieron *or* otorgaron el primer premio (**b**) *Law (damages)* otorgar, conceder (**c**) *Sport (penalty)* conceder

award-winner [ə'wɔːd'wɪnə(r)] *n (person)* galardonado(a) *m,f*; *(film, book)* obra *f* galardonada *or* premiada

award-winning [ə'wɔːd'wɪnɪŋ] *adj* premiado(a), galardonado(a)

aware [ə'weə(r)] *adj* (**a**) *(conscious)* **to be a. of** ser consciente de; **he's well a. of the risks** es plenamente consciente de los riesgos; **I wasn't a. of his presence** no advertí su presencia; **I wasn't a. there was a problem about it** no sabía que esto presentase ningún problema; **are you a. of the trouble you've caused?** ¿te das cuenta del trastorno que has ocasionado?; **to be a. that...** ser consciente de que...; **to become a. of** darse cuenta de; **not that I am a. of** no, que yo sepa; **as far as I'm a.** por lo que yo sé

(**b**) *(informed, concerned)* concienciado(a); **environmentally/politically a.** preocupado(a) por el medio ambiente/la política

awareness [ə'weənɪs] *n* conciencia *f* (**of** de); **he has little a. of the situation** no es muy consciente de la situación; **a heightened a. of colour** una intensificación del color; **to increase a. of an issue** aumentar el nivel de concienciación sobre un tema

awash [ə'wɒʃ] *adj* (**a**) *(flooded)* **to be a. (with)** estar inundado(a) (de) (**b**) *(full)* **to be a. (with)** estar inundado(a) (de)

AWAY [ə'weɪ] 1 *adv* (a) *(with distance)* **a long way a., far a.** muy lejos; **it's 10 kilometres a.** está a 10 kilómetros; **it's miles a.** está lejísimos; **how far a. is Dallas?** ¿a cúantos kilómetros está Dallas?; **I like living a. from the centre** me gusta vivir lejos del centro; **to keep** *or* **stay a. from sth/sb** mantenerse alejado(a) de algo/alguien; **she sat a. from the rest of the group** se sentó aparte del resto del grupo; **to stand a. from sth** mantenerse alejado(a) de algo

(b) *(with direction)* **the bus drove a.** el autobús partió; **to go a.** marcharse, irse; **go a.!** ¡vete!; **to move a. from sth/sb** apartarse de algo/alguien; **to turn a.** apartar *or* desviar la mirada; **the police were facing a. from the crowd** los policías daban la espalda a la multitud

(c) *(not present)* **to be a.** *(not at work)* estar fuera; **Billy's a. today** *(not at school)* Billy no ha venido hoy; **I was a. sick three days last week** falté tres días por enfermedad la semana pasada; **she was a. with a cold** estaba en casa con un resfriado; IDIOM *Fam* **to be a. with the fairies** *(senile)* estar chocho(a); *(eccentric)* estar tocado(a) del ala; *(daydreaming)* estar en Babia *or* en las nubes; **he's a. on holiday/business** está de vacaciones/en viaje de negocios

(d) *(with time)* **right a.** inmediatamente; **Christmas is only two weeks a.** sólo quedan dos semanas para las Navidades; **Christmas is still a long way a.** todavía falta mucho para Navidad; **we live two minutes a. from the centre** vivimos a dos minutos del centro

(e) *(indicating removal)* **to take sth a. from sb** quitarle algo a alguien; **he peeled a. the top layer** levantó la capa superficial; **to carry sb a.** llevarse a alguien; **she wiped her tears a.** se secó las lágrimas; **to give sth a.** regalar algo

(f) *(indicating disappearance)* **the snow has all melted a.** la nieve se ha derretido; **the noise faded a.** el ruido se desvaneció; **they partied the night a.** estuvieron de fiesta toda la noche

(g) *(in the correct place)* **to put sth a.** recoger algo; **to file sth a.** archivar algo

(h) *(indicating continuous action)* **I was working a., when suddenly...** estaba concentrado trabajando, cuando de repente...; **the two girls were chattering a. at the back** las dos niñas estaban charlando en la parte de atrás

(i) *(indicating escape)* **to get a. from sb** escaparse de alguien; **to get a. from it all** desconectarse de todo

(j) *Sport* **to play/win a. (from home)** jugar/ganar fuera (de casa)

2 *adj Sport (team, captain)* visitante; **they won the a. leg against Liverpool** ganaron el partido de ida en el campo del Liverpool; **an a. game** un partido fuera de casa; **an a. goal** un gol marcado fuera de casa; **they won on a. goals** ganaron gracias al valor doble de los goles marcados fuera de casa; **the a. strip** el equipaje *or* la indumentaria reserva; **an a. win** una victoria visitante *or* a domicilio

---

awe [ɔː] 1 *n* sobrecogimiento *m*, temor *m*; **to be** *or* **stand in a. of sth/sb** estar intimidado(a) ante algo/alguien; **I stared at her in a.** la miré anonadado

2 *vt* sobrecoger, impresionar; **they were awed by the cathedral** se quedaron impresionados con la catedral; **the music awed them into silence** sobrecogidos por la música guardaron silencio

awed [ɔːd] *adj* **she spoke in an a. whisper** susurró estremecida

awe-inspiring ['ɔːnspaɪərɪŋ] *adj* sobrecogedor(ora)

awesome ['ɔːsəm] *adj* (a) *(tremendous)* sobrecogedor(ora) (b) *US Fam (wonderful)* alucinante, *Andes, RP* macanudo(a), *Méx* padrísimo

awestruck ['ɔːstrʌk] *adj* sobrecogido(a), impresionado(a)

awful ['ɔːfʊl] 1 *adj* (a) *(crime, death, vengeance)* horrible, espantoso(a)

(b) *Fam (very bad) (weather, experience)* horroroso(a), horrendo(a); *(person)* asqueroso(a), repugnante; **she was simply a. to him** lo trataba como un trapo; **I feel a.** *(ill, ashamed)* me siento muy mal *or Esp* fatal; **she looks a.** *(ill)* tiene muy mal aspecto; *(badly dressed)* tiene una pinta *or* facha horrenda; **to smell/taste a.** oler/saber muy mal *or Esp* fatal; **how a. for you!** ¡pobrecito!; **I've just had an a. thought** se me acaba de ocurrir una espantosa idea

(c) *Fam (outrageous)* **you are a.!** ¡eres tremendo!

(d) *Fam (as intensifier)* **an a. lot** muchísimo, un montón; **an a. lot of people** un montón de gente, *Andes, CAm, Carib, Méx* harta gente; **what an a. bore!** *(person)* ¡qué muermazo!; *(task)* ¡qué tostonazo!; **he's an a. fool** es un perfecto imbécil; **they took an a. chance** corrieron un riesgo enorme

2 *adv US Fam* **it was a. nice of them to come** fue estupendo que vinieran; **I'm a. busy right now** estoy ocupadísimo *or* superocupado en este momento

awfully ['ɔːfəlɪ] *adv* (a) *(very badly)* espantosamente, *Esp* fatal

(b) *Fam (very)* tremendamente; **a. funny/nice** divertidísimo(a)/superbonito(a); **I'm a. sorry/glad** lo siento/me alegro muchísimo; **she's an a. good player** es una jugadora buenísima

(c) *Br Fam Old-fashioned* **thanks a.** muchísimas gracias

awfulness ['ɔːfʊlnɪs] *n* (a) *(of weather, experience, person)* lo horroroso, lo espantoso (b) *(of crime, death, vengeance)* atrocidad *f*

awhile [ə'waɪl] *adv* **wait a.** espere un poco; **not yet a.** por el momento no

awkward ['ɔːkwəd] *adj* (a) *(clumsy)* torpe

(b) *(inconvenient) (moment, time)* inoportuno(a); *(location)* difícil; **you've come at an a. time** has venido en un mal momento; **the switch is in an a. place** el interruptor está en un lugar de difícil acceso; **their house is a. to get to** es complicado *or* difícil llegar hasta su casa; **it's a. to use** es difícil *or* complicado de usar

(c) *(embarrassed, uneasy) (silence, situation)* incómodo(a), embarazoso(a); **she felt a. about going** la incomodaba *or* desagradaba la idea de ir; **an a. moment** un momento delicado *or* violento

(d) *(difficult to deal with) (problem, person)* difícil; *Fam* **he's an a. customer** es un tipo difícil; **to make things a. for sb** hacerle la vida imposible a alguien; **they could make things a. for her if you don't cooperate** podrían amargarle *or* complicarle la vida si no colaboras; **he's at an a. age** está en la edad del pavo; **he's just being a.** no está por la labor, está poniendo pegas

awkwardly ['ɔːkwədlɪ] *adv* (a) *(clumsily)* torpemente; **to put sth a.** expresar algo con torpeza; **he fell a.** cayó mal (b) *(inconveniently)* **the lever is a. placed** la palanca está mal situada; **their house is a. situated** su casa tiene mala ubicación (c) *(with embarrassment, unease)* embarazosamente, incómodamente; **she grinned a.** sonrió de mala gana

awkwardness ['ɔːkwədnɪs] *n* (a) *(clumsiness)* torpeza *f* (b) *(inconvenience)* inconveniencia *f*, incomodidad *f* (c) *(embarrassment, unease)* incomodidad *f*, lo embarazoso; **the a. of the situation** lo violento *or* embarazoso de la situación (d) *(lack of co-operation)* falta *f* de cooperación *or* colaboración

awl [ɔːl] *n* lezna *f*

awning ['ɔːnɪŋ] *n (of shop, over window)* toldo *m*; *(at door of hotel, theatre)* marquesina *f*; *(on ship's deck)* toldos *mpl*

awoke *pt of* **awake**

awoken *pp of* **awake, awaken**

AWOL ['eɪwɒl] *adj Mil* (*abbr* **absent without leave**) **to be A.** estar ausente sin permiso; *Fig* **to go A.** desaparecer así como así

awry [ə'raɪ] 1 *adj* torcido(a), ladeado(a); **his hair was all a.** iba totalmente despeinado; **his tie was a.** tenía la corbata torcida *or* ladeada

2 *adv* **to go a.** salir mal

axe, *US* **ax** [æks] 1 *n* (a) *(tool)* hacha *f* (b) *Fam (guitar)* guitarra *f*, *RP* viola *f* (c) IDIOMS **to have an a. to grind** tratar de barrer para adentro; *Fam* **to get the a.** *(person)* ser puesto(a) de patitas en la calle; *(programme, plan)* ser machacado(a) *or* pulverizado(a)

2 *vt Fam (jobs, project)* suprimir; *(spending)* recortar a saco

axes *pl of* **axis**

axiom ['æksɪəm] *n* axioma *m*

axiomatic [æksɪə'mætɪk] *adj* axiomático(a), incontrovertible

axis ['æksɪs] (*pl* **axes** ['æksiːz]) *n* (a) *Math* eje *m* ▸▸ ***a. of revolution*** eje *m* de rotación; ***a. of symmetry*** eje *m* de simetría (b) *Hist* **the A.** el Eje; **the A. powers** las potencias del Eje (c) *Anat* axis *m inv*

axle ['æksəl] *n* eje *m*; **front/rear a.** eje delantero/trasero

axon ['æksɒn] *n Anat* axón *m*

ayatollah [aɪə'tɒlə] *n* ayatola *m*, ayatolá *m*

aye[1] [aɪ] *n Literary (ever)* **for a.** para siempre, por siempre (jamás)

aye[2] 1 *n Pol* sí *m*, voto *m* a favor; **ayes and noes** votos a favor y en contra; **the ayes have it** gana el sí

2 *adv Scot, Irish* sí

3 *exclam* (a) *Naut* **a., a. sir!** ¡sí *or* a la orden, señor! (b) *Fam* **a. a., what's all this then?** ¡pero...bueno!, ¿qué significa *or* es esto?

AYH [eɪwaɪ'eɪtʃ] (*abbr* **American Youth Hostels**) = organización estadounidense de albergues juveniles

AZ (*abbr* **Arizona**) Arizona

azalea [ə'zeɪlɪə] *n* azalea *f*

Azerbaijan [æzəbaɪ'dʒɑːn] *n* Azerbaiyán

Azerbaijani [æzəbaɪ'dʒɑːnɪ], **Azeri** [ə'zeərɪ] 1 *n* azerbaiyano(a) *m,f*

2 *adj* azerbaiyano(a)

azimuth ['æzɪməθ] *n* acimut *m*

Azores [ə'zɔːz] *npl* **the A.** las Azores

AZT [eɪzed'tiː] *n Pharm* (*abbr* **azidothymidine**) AZT *m*

Aztec ['æztek] 1 *n* azteca *mf*

2 *adj* azteca

azure ['eɪʒə(r), 'æʒʊə(r)] *Literary* 1 *n* azur *m*, azul *m* celeste

2 *adj* azur, azul celeste

B, b

B, b [biː] *n (letter)* B, b

B [biː] *n* **(a)** *(secondary)* ***B-movie*** película *f* de serie B; *Br* ***B-road*** carretera *f* secundaria; ***B-side*** *(of single record)* cara *f* B **(b)** *Mus* si *m* **(c)** *Sch (grade)* notable *m*; **to get a B** sacar un notable

b (*abbr* **born**) **b 1972** nacido(a) en 1972

BA [biː'eɪ] *n Univ* (*abbr* **Bachelor of Arts**) **(a)** *(qualification)* ≃ licenciatura *f* en Humanidades **(b)** *(person)* ≃ licenciado(a) *m,f* en Humanidades

BAA [biːeɪ'eɪ] *n* (*abbr* **British Airports Authority**) = organismo aeroportuario británico, *Esp* ≃ Aena *f*

baa [bɑː] **1** *n* balido *m*
2 *vi* (*pt & pp* **baaed** *or* **baa'd** [bɑːd]) balar

babble ['bæbəl] **1** *n* **(a)** *(of voices)* parloteo *m*; *(of baby)* balbuceo *m* **(b)** *(of stream)* murmullo *m*, susurro *m*
2 *vt (say quickly)* farfullar, barbullar; *(say foolishly)* parlotear sobre
3 *vi* **(a)** *(baby)* balbucear; *(adult)* farfullar; **to b. away** *or* **on (about sth)** parlotear (sobre algo); **what are you babbling about?** ¿qué estás barbullando *or* farfullando? **(b)** *(water)* murmurar; **a babbling stream** un arroyo murmurante

babbling ['bæblɪŋ] *adj (stream)* murmurante, susurrante

babe [beɪb] *n* **(a)** *Literary (child)* bebé *m*, *Andes* guagua *mf*, *RP* nene(a) *m,f*; **a b. in arms** un niño de pecho; IDIOM **they were like babes in the wood** eran como corderitos **(b)** *Fam (woman)* nena *f* **(c)** *Fam (term of address)* cariño *m*, cielo *m* **(d)** *US Fam (attractive man) Esp* tío *m* bueno, *Am* tipo *m* bueno

babel ['beɪbəl] *n* **(a)** *(noise, confusion)* jaleo *m*; **a b. of voices** un guirigay, una algarabía de voces **(b)** ***the tower of B.*** la torre de Babel

baboon [bə'buːn] *n* babuino *m*, papión *m*

baby ['beɪbɪ] **1** *n* **(a)** *(infant)* bebé *m*, *Andes* guagua *mf*, *RP* nene(a) *m,f*; **to have a b.** tener un hijo *or* niño ▸▸ *Fam* ***b. batterer*** = persona que maltrata a un bebé; *Fam* ***b. blues*** depre *f (posparto)*; ***b. boom*** explosión *f* demográfica; ***b. boomer*** = persona nacida durante el periodo de explosión demográfica que siguió a la Segunda Guerra Mundial; ***b. bouncer*** = columpio elástico para bebés; *Br* ***B. Buggy***® sillita *f* de paseo *or* de niño; *US* ***b. buggy*** *or* ***carriage*** cochecito *m* de niño; ***b. doll*** *(toy)* muñeca *f*; ***b. food*** alimentos *mpl* infantiles; ***b. grand*** *(piano)* piano *m* de media cola; ***the B. Jesus*** el niño Jesús; ***b. jumper*** = columpio elástico para bebés; *Br* ***b. milk*** leche *f* maternizada; ***b. seat*** *(in car)* silla *f* de seguridad para bebés; *US* ***b. shower*** = pequeña fiesta en la que se llevan regalos para el futuro bebé; ***b. snatcher*** *(woman)* ladrona *f* de bebés; ***b. talk*** habla *f* infantil; ***b. tooth*** diente *m* de leche; ***b. wipes*** toallitas *fpl* húmedas
(b) *US Fam (young woman)* chavala *f*, *Esp* tía *f*; **she's my b.** es mi chavala
(c) *US Fam (term of endearment)* cariño *m*, cielo *m*
(d) *US Fam (person)* chaval(ala) *m,f*, *Esp* tío(a) *m,f*; **he's one tough b.** es un tipo duro *or* de mucho cuidado
(e) IDIOMS **the project was his b.** él era el padre de la criatura; **to sleep like a b.** dormir como un lirón; **we have to avoid throwing the b. out with the bathwater** tenemos que evitar dañar lo bueno al eliminar lo malo; **to leave sb holding the b.** endilgar el muerto a alguien
2 *adj* **(a)** *(boy, girl)* **they had a b. boy/girl** tuvieron un niño/una niña; **b. brother** hermanito; **b. sister** hermanita **(b)** *(animal)* **a b. tiger/panda** un cachorro de tigre/de oso panda; **a b. elephant** una cría de elefante **(c)** *(carrot, sweetcorn)* de tamaño pequeño
3 *vt* mimar, tratar como a un bebé

baby-blue ['beɪbɪ'bluː] *adj (eyes)* azul celeste

baby-changing ['beɪbɪ'tʃeɪndʒɪŋ] *adj* **b. room/area** sala/zona para cambiar pañales

baby-doll ['beɪbɪdɒl] *adj* ***b. nightie*** picardías *m inv*; ***b. pyjamas*** picardías *m inv*

baby-faced ['beɪbɪfeɪst] *adj* con cara de niño

Babygro® ['beɪbɪgrəʊ] (*pl* **Babygros**) *n Br* pelele *m*

babyhood ['beɪbɪhʊd] *n* primera infancia *f*

babyish ['beɪbɪɪʃ] *adj Pej* infantil

Babylon ['bæbɪlɒn] *n* Babilonia

Babylonian [bæbɪ'ləʊnɪən] **1** *n* **(a)** *(person)* babilonio(a) *m,f* **(b)** *(language)* babilonio *m*
2 *adj* babilónico(a)

baby-minder ['beɪbɪmaɪndə(r)] *n* niñera *f*

baby-sit ['beɪbɪsɪt] (*pt & pp* **baby-sat** ['beɪbɪsæt]) **1** *vt (child)* cuidar de
2 *vi* cuidar a niños, hacer de *Esp* canguro *or Am* babysitter; **to b. for sb** cuidar a los niños de alguien

baby-sitter ['beɪbɪsɪtə(r)] *n Esp* canguro *mf*, *Am* babysitter *mf*

baby-walker ['beɪbɪwɔːkə(r)] *n Br* andador *m*, tacataca *m*

baccalaureate [bækə'lɔːrɪət] *n (at school)* bachillerato *m*

baccarat ['bækərɑː] *n* bacarrá *m*

bacchanalia [bækə'neɪlɪə] *npl* bacanales *fpl*

Bacchus ['bækəs] *n Mythol* Baco

baccy ['bækɪ] *n Br Fam* tabaco *m*

bachelor ['bætʃələ(r)] *n* **(a)** *(single man)* soltero *m* ▸▸ ***b. flat*** apartamento *m or Esp* piso *m or Arg* departamento *m* de soltero; *Old-fashioned* ***b. girl*** soltera *f*; *Fam* ***b. pad*** picadero *m*, *RP* bulín *m*; *US* ***b. party*** despedida *f* de soltero
(b) *Univ* ***B. of Arts*** *(qualification)* licenciatura *f* (en Humanidades); *(person)* licenciado(a) *m,f* (en Humanidades); *Univ* ***B. of Science*** *(qualification)* licenciatura *f* (en Ciencias); *(person)* licenciado(a) *m,f* (en Ciencias)

bacillus [bə'sɪləs] (*pl* **bacilli** [bə'sɪlaɪ]) *n Biol* bacilo *m*

BACK [bæk] **1** *n* **(a)** *(of person)* espalda *f*; *(of animal)* lomo *m*; **to carry sth on one's b.** llevar algo a cuestas; **to fall on one's b.** caerse de espaldas; **to lie on one's b.** estar acostado(a) de espaldas; **I only saw her from the b.** sólo la vi de espaldas; **to sit/stand with one's b. to sth/sb** dar la espalda a algo/alguien; *also Fig* **to turn one's b. on sb** volver la espalda a alguien; **b. pain** dolor de espalda; **to have b. problems** tener problemas de espalda
(b) *(of page, hand, book, envelope)* dorso *m*; *(of chair)* respaldo *m*; *(of computer, TV, watch)* parte *f* trasera *or* de atrás; *(of dress, jacket)* espalda *f*; *(of spoon, fork)* parte *f* de atrás; *(of queue)* final *m*; *(of house, car)* parte *f* trasera *or* de atrás; *(of room)* fondo *m*; **he banged the b. of his head** se golpeó la parte posterior de la cabeza; **the b. of the neck** la nuca, *Esp* el cogote; **at the b. (of)** *(behind)* en la parte de atrás (de), detrás (de); *(to the rear of)* al fondo (de); **the dress fastens at the b.** el vestido se abrocha por detrás; **at the b. of the bus/cinema** al fondo del autobús/cine; **at the b. of the book** al final del libro; *US* **in b. (of)** *(behind)* en la parte de atrás (de), detrás (de); *(to the rear of)* al fondo (de); *Br* **in the b.,** *US* **in b.** *(of car)* atrás, en el asiento trasero; **put it in the b. of the van** ponlo en la parte de atrás de la furgoneta; **to have sth at** *or* **in the b. of one's mind** tener algo en la cabeza; *Br* **out** *or* **round the b.,** *US* **out b.** *(of house)* en la parte de atrás; **b. to front** *Esp* del revés *(con lo de detrás hacia delante)*, *Am* de atrás para adelante; **your jumper's on b. to front** *Esp* llevas el jersey al *or* del revés, *Am* tienes puesto el pulóver de atrás para adelante; *Fig* **to get sth b. to front** *(misunderstand)* entender algo al revés; *Fig* **to know sth b. to front** saberse algo de pe a pa *or* al dedillo; **he knows London like the b. of his hand** conoce Londres como la palma de la mano; *Fam* **in the b. of beyond** en el quinto infierno *or Esp* pino, *Chile* en la punta del cerro, *Col* en la Patagonia, *RP* donde el diablo perdió el poncho
(c) *(in rugby)* = cualquiera de los jugadores del número 9 al 15; *(in soccer)* defensa *mf*; **right/left b.** *(in soccer)* defensa lateral derecho/izquierdo
(d) IDIOMS **to do sth behind sb's b., to go behind sb's b. and do sth** hacer algo a espaldas de alguien; **he did it while my b. was turned** lo hizo a mis espaldas; **to be glad to see the b. of sb** alegrarse de perder a alguien de vista; **to break the b. of the work** hacer la parte más dura del trabajo; **to have one's b. to the wall** estar contra las cuerdas; **put**

your b. into it! ¡ponte a hacerlo en serio!; *Fam* **to put** *or* **get sb's b. up** jorobar a alguien, *Esp* hinchar las narices a alguien; *Fam* **get off my b.!** ¡déjame en paz!, *Esp* ¡deja de fastidiarme!, *RP* ¡no hinches!; *Fam* **the boss was on my b. all day** el jefe estaba todo el día encima de mí; **on the b. of: he was selected on the b. of his recent good performances** fue seleccionado a raíz de sus buenas actuaciones recientes

2 *adj* (a) *(in space) (part, wheel, leg)* trasero(a), de atrás; *Br* **the b. end of the year** el final del año; **to go in the b. way** entrar por la puerta de atrás; IDIOM **to put sth on the b. burner** dejar algo para más tarde, *Esp* aparcar algo; IDIOM **to be on the b. foot** estar a la defensiva ►► *Br Parl* ***the b. benches*** = escaños ocupados por diputados que no desempeñan cargos ni en el gobierno ni en la oposición; *US* ***the b. country*** el monte remoto; ***b. door*** puerta *f* trasera *or* de atrás; *also Fig* **he got in through the b. door** entró por la puerta de atrás; *Fig* **the government has been accused of trying to bring the legislation in through the b. door** han acusado al gobierno de intentar implantar sus medidas a través de una legislación paralela; ***the b. four*** *(in soccer)* = los dos defensas laterales y los dos centrales; ***b. garden*** jardín *m (en la parte de atrás de una casa)*; *US* ***b. haul*** trayecto *m* de vuelta; ***b. heel*** *(in soccer)* taconazo *m*; ***b. marker*** *(in race)* rezagado(a) *m,f*; ***the b. nine*** *(in golf)* los últimos nueve hoyos; ***b. office*** *(of shop)* trastienda *f*; *(of business)* despacho *m (en la parte trasera)*; ***the b. page*** *(of newspaper)* la contraportada *or Perú, RP* contratapa; ***b. pass*** *(in soccer)* cesión *f* (al portero); *Euph* ***b. passage*** *(rectum)* recto *m*; *Cin* ***b. projection*** transparencia *f*; ***b. road*** carretera *f* secundaria; ***b. room*** cuarto *m* del fondo, habitación *f* trasera; ***the b. row*** *(at theatre, cinema)* la última fila; ***b. seat*** *(of car)* asiento *m* de atrás; *Fig* **to take a b. seat** quedarse en segundo plano; ***b. straight*** *(of athletics track)* recta *f* final

(b) *(in time)* ***b. catalogue*** *(of musician)* discografía *f*; ***b. issue*** número *m* atrasado; ***b. number*** número *m* atrasado; ***b. pay*** atrasos *mpl*, salario *m* atrasado; ***b. rent*** alquiler *m or Méx* renta *f* pendiente de pago, atrasos *mpl*

3 *adv* (a) *(in space)* atrás; **3 kilometres b.** 3 kilómetros atrás; **a few pages b.** unas cuantas páginas atrás; **to look b.** mirar hacia atrás; **she pushed her chair b.** empujó su silla hacia atrás; **sit b. and relax** ponte cómodo y relájate; **stand b.!** ¡atrás!; **to step b.** dar un paso atrás; **he peeled the wrapper b.** abrió el envoltorio; **to tie one's hair b.** recogerse el pelo atrás; **b. and forth** de un lado a otro, para acá y para allá; **I spent hours going b. and forth between the two offices** me pasé horas yendo y viniendo de una oficina a la otra; **b. here/there** aquí/ahí atrás; **he's b. in tenth place** está en el décimo lugar

(b) *(in return, retaliation)* **to call sb b.** llamar más tarde a alguien; **to fight b.** defenderse; **to get one's own b. (on sb)** tomarse la revancha (contra alguien), desquitarse (de alguien); **to get b. at sb, to get sb b.** vengarse de alguien; **to smile b. at sb** devolver a alguien la sonrisa; **to write b.** contestar, responder *(por carta)*; **if you kick me I'll kick you b.** si me pegas una patada, te la devuelvo

(c) *(to original starting point, owner)* **to arrive b.** volver, llegar; **when will she be b.?** ¿cuándo vuelve?, *Esp* ¿cuándo estará de vuelta?; **things are b. to normal** las cosas han vuelto a la normalidad; **it's b. to work this week** volvemos al trabajo esta semana; **b. in an hour** *(on note, sign)* vuelvo en una hora; **to bring sth b.** traer algo; **to come/go b.** volver, *Andes, CAm, Carib, Méx* regresarse; **to get b.** volver; **I couldn't get b. to sleep** no pude volver a dormirme; **to give sth b. to sb** devolverle algo a alguien; **to put sth b.** poner algo en su sitio; **shall we walk b.?** ¿volvemos caminando?; **I don't want it b.** no me lo devuelvas; **on the way b.** *(whilst returning)* en el camino de vuelta, a la vuelta; **b. in Britain** en Gran Bretaña; **b. home** *(in one's home country)* en mi país; *Fig* **miniskirts are b. this year** las minifaldas se han vuelto a poner de moda este año; *Fig* **he may have lost, but he'll be b.** puede que haya perdido *or* habrá perdido, pero volverá

(d) *(in time)* **a few years b.** hace unos cuantos años; **b. when...** cuando..., en el tiempo en que...; **b. in 1982** allá por 1982; **b. in January** allá en enero; **as far b. as 1914** ya en 1914

(e) *(again)* **he stuck his head b. out of the window** volvió a asomar la cabeza por la ventana; **do you want me to go b. over the instructions?** ¿quieres que vuelva a explicarte las instrucciones?; **she played the tape b.** puso *or* reprodujo la cinta

4 *vt* (a) *(support)* respaldar, apoyar; *(financially)* financiar, dar respaldo financiero a

(b) *(bet on)* apostar por

(c) *(move backwards)* mover hacia atrás; **to b. one's car into the garage** entrar en el garaje marcha atrás; **he backed his car into a lamppost** dio marcha atrás y chocó contra una farola

(d) *(strengthen) (with material, card)* **to b. sth with sth** reforzar algo con algo *(por la parte de atrás)*

5 *vi (move backwards)* retroceder, ir hacia atrás; *(car, driver)* recular, ir marcha atrás; **to b. round a corner** *(in car)* hacer marcha atrás alrededor de una esquina

► **back away** *vi* alejarse (retrocediendo); *Fig* **to b. away from a commitment/policy** echarse atrás en un compromiso/una política

► **back down** *vi* echarse atrás; **to b. down from sth** echarse atrás en algo; **they backed down from raising interest rates** se echaron atrás a la hora de subir los tipos de interés

► **back off** *vi (move back)* echarse atrás; *Fig* **to b. off from a commitment/policy** echarse atrás en un compromiso/una política; *Fig* **b. off!** *(leave me alone)* ¡déjame en paz!

► **back on to** *vt insep* dar por la parte de atrás a

► **back out** *vi* (a) *(move backwards)* salir de espaldas; *(in car)* salir marcha atrás; **he backed out of the room** salió de la habitación caminando hacia atrás

(b) *(withdraw)* echarse atrás; **to b. out of an agreement** retirarse de un acuerdo

► **back up** 1 *vt sep* (a) *(support)* respaldar; **will you b. me up?** *(corroborate my story)* ¿me apoyarás?

(b) *Comptr (file)* hacer una copia de seguridad de

(c) *(move backwards)* **to b. one's car up** dar marcha atrás

2 *vi* (a) *(move backwards)* retroceder; *(in car)* dar marcha atrás; **b. up a bit, will you?** *(person)* échate un poco para atrás

(b) *(traffic)* **cars were backed up for miles** había millas de atasco

(c) *Comptr* hacer copias de seguridad

---

backache ['bækeɪk] *n* dolor *m* de espalda; **to have b.** tener dolor de espalda

backbeat ['bækbiːt] *n Mus* tiempo *m* débil

backbench [bæk'bentʃ] *n Br Parl* **the backbenches** = escaños ocupados por los diputados sin cargo en el gobierno o la oposición ►► ***b. MP*** diputado(a) *m,f* ordinario(a) *(sin cargo en el gobierno o la oposición)*; ***b. revolt*** indisciplina *f* de voto en el parlamento

backbencher ['bæk'bentʃə(r)] *n Br Parl* diputado(a) *m,f* ordinario(a) *(sin cargo en el gobierno o la oposición)*

backbite ['bækbaɪt] *vi Fam* chismorrear

backbiting ['bækbaɪtɪŋ] *n Fam* chismorreo *m*, murmuración *f*, *RP* chusmerío *m*

backblocks ['bækblɒks] *npl Austr Fam* **the b.** el quinto infierno *or Esp* pino, *Andes, RP* donde el diablo perdió el poncho, *Chile* la punta del cerro, *Col* la Patagonia

backboard ['bækbɔːd] *n (in basketball)* tablero *m*, tabla *f*

backbone ['bækbəʊn] *n* (a) *(spine)* columna *f* vertebral, espina *f* dorsal; IDIOM **he's got no b.** no tiene agallas (b) *(mainstay)* columna *f* vertebral, pilar *m*; **tourism is the b. of the economy** el turismo es el principal soporte de la economía (c) *Comptr* red *f* troncal

backbreaking ['bækbreɪkɪŋ] *adj (work)* extenuante, agotador(ora)

backchat ['bæktʃæt] *n Br Fam* impertinencias *fpl*, insolencias *fpl*; **and I want none of your b.!** ¡y no me repliques!, ¡y no quiero ni que rechistes!

backcloth ['bækklɒθ] *n Theat* telón *m* de fondo

backcomb ['bækkəʊm] *vt* cardar

backcourt ['bækkɔːt] *n* (a) *(in tennis)* fondo *m* de la pista (b) *(in basketball)* lado *m* propio de la cancha ►► ***b. violation*** campo atrás *m*

backdate ['bækdeɪt] *vt* (a) *(cheque, document)* poner fecha anterior (b) *(pay increase)* **the increase will be backdated to 1 July** el aumento tendrá efecto retroactivo a partir del uno de julio

backdoor [bæk'dɔː(r)] *adj (methods)* subrepticio(a)

backdrop ['bækdrɒp] *n* (a) *Theat* telón *m* de fondo (b) *(background)* **against a b. of continuing violence** con la violencia como constante telón de fondo

-backed [bækt] *suffix* (a) *(with back)* **a high-b. chair** una silla de respaldo alto; **a broad-b. man** un hombre ancho de hombros *or* de espaldas anchas (b) *(supported by)* **US-b. rebels** rebeldes apoyados por Estados Unidos

backer ['bækə(r)] *n* (a) *(of political party, project)* fuente *f* de financiación (b) *(person betting)* apostador(ora) *m,f*, apostante *mf*

backfield ['bækfiːld] *n (in American football) (players)* defensa *f*, zaga *f*; *(area)* zona *f* defensiva

backfill ['bækfɪl] *Constr* 1 *n (material)* relleno *m*, terraplén *m*

2 *vt (foundation, excavation)* rellenar

backfire [bæk'faɪə(r)] 1 *n (of car)* petardeo *m*, explosiones *fpl*

2 *vi* (a) *(car)* petardear (b) *(plan)* **it backfired on them** les salió el tiro por la culata

back-formation ['bækfɔːmeɪʃən] *n Ling* derivación *f* regresiva

backgammon ['bækgæmən] *n* backgammon *m*

background ['bækgraʊnd] *n* (**a**) *(in scene, painting, view)* fondo *m*; **yellow flowers on a green b.** flores amarillas sobre un fondo verde; **in the b.** al fondo, en el fondo; *Fig* **to stay** *or* **remain in the b.** quedarse en segundo plano; *Fig* **to push sb into the b.** relegar a alguien a un segundo plano ►► ***b. music*** música *f* ambiental *or* de fondo; ***b. noise*** ruido *m* de fondo; *Astron & Phys* ***b. radiation*** radiación *f* de fondo
(**b**) *(of person) (social)* origen *m*, extracción *f*; *(educational)* formación *f*; *(professional)* experiencia *f*; **he comes from a disadvantaged b.** procede de un entorno desfavorecido; **we need someone with a b. in computers** necesitamos a alguien que tenga experiencia en informática
(**c**) *(circumstances)* antecedentes *mpl*; **the b. to the present crisis** los antecedentes de la crisis actual; **against a b. of unrest** en un contexto de disturbios; **give me some b.** *(information)* ponme en contexto ►► ***b. information*** información *f*, antecedentes *mpl*; ***b. reading:* to do some b. reading on a topic** documentarse en una materia
(**d**) *Comptr* **the program works in the b.** el programa se ejecuta en segundo plano ►► ***b. printing*** impresión *f* subordinada; ***b. processing*** procesamiento *m* subordinado

backhand ['bækhænd] **1** *n (in tennis)* revés *m*; **keep serving to his b.** continúa sirviéndole al revés
2 *adj (stroke, volley)* de revés

backhanded [bæk'hændɪd] *adj* (**a**) *(blow)* de revés; **she gave him a b. slap** le soltó *or* dio un revés (**b**) **a b. compliment** un cumplido con doble sentido

backhander ['bækhændə(r)] *n Br Fam (bribe)* soborno *m*, *Andes, RP* coima *f*, *CAm, Méx* mordida *f*

back-heel [bæk'hiːl] *vt* **to b. the ball** dar un taconazo al balón

backhoe ['bækhəʊ] *n US* excavadora *f*

backing ['bækɪŋ] *n* (**a**) *(support)* apoyo *m*, respaldo *m*; **financial b.** respaldo financiero (**b**) *(material)* relleno *m*, refuerzo *m* (**c**) *Mus (accompaniment)* acompañamiento *m* ►► ***b. vocals*** coros *mpl*

backlash ['bæklæʃ] *n (reaction)* reacción *f* violenta; **a right-wing b.** un contraataque súbito de la derecha

backless ['bæklɪs] *adj* ***b. dress*** vestido *m* con la espalda al aire; ***b. shoes*** zapatos *mpl* sin talón

backlight ['bæklaɪt] *n Comptr (of screen)* retroiluminación *f*

backlist ['bæklɪst] *n (of publisher)* catálogo *m* (de publicaciones)

backlit ['bæklɪt] *adj Comptr* retroiluminado(a)

backlog ['bæklɒg] *n* acumulación *f*; **to clear a b.** ponerse al día con el trabajo; **a b. of work** trabajo atrasado *or* acumulado; **a b. of correspondence/orders** correspondencia atrasada *or* pendiente/pedidos atrasados *or* pendientes

backpack ['bækpæk] **1** *n* mochila *f*
2 *vi* viajar con la mochila al hombro; **she backpacked around Europe** recorrió Europa con la mochila al hombro

backpacker ['bækpækə(r)] *n* mochilero(a) *m,f*

backpacking ['bækpækɪŋ] *n* **to go b.** viajar con mochila

back-pedal ['bæk'pedəl] *vi* (**a**) *(on bicycle)* pedalear hacia atrás (**b**) *(change mind)* dar marcha atrás, echarse atrás; **to b. on a promise** retirar una promesa

backrest ['bækrest] *n* respaldo *m*

backroom ['bækruːm] *adj Fam* **the b. boys** los rostros anónimos, = la gente que hace el trabajo técnico en la sombra

back-scratching ['bækskrætʃɪŋ] *n Fam* intercambio *m* de favores, *Esp* compadreo *m*; **in the world of finance, b. plays a role in many transactions** en el mundo de las finanzas la política del "hoy por ti, mañana por mí" interviene en muchas operaciones

back-seat driver ['bæksiːt'draɪvə(r)] *n Fam* = pasajero que molesta constantemente al conductor con sus consejos

backside [bæk'saɪd] *n Fam* trasero *m*; **to get off one's b.** mover el culo

backslapping ['bækslæpɪŋ] **1** *n (joviality)* efusividad *f*, felicitaciones *fpl* efusivas
2 *adj* efusivo(a), cordial

backslash ['bækslæʃ] *n Comptr* barra *f* invertida

backsliding ['bækslaɪdɪŋ] *n Fam* recaída *f*, reincidencia *f*

backspace ['bækspeɪs] **1** *n Comptr* **b. (key)** (tecla *f* de) retroceso *m*
2 *vi* retroceder, pulsar la tecla de retroceso

backspin ['bækspɪn] *n Sport (in snooker, billiards)* efecto *m* picado *or* bajo; *(in tennis)* efecto *m* cortado; **he put b. on when potting the black** picó la bola al meter la negra

back-stabbing ['bækstæbɪŋ] **1** *n* puñaladas *fpl* por la espalda, zancadillas *fpl*
2 *adj* con mala idea, traicionero(a)

backstage [bæk'steɪdʒ] **1** *n* bastidores *mpl*
2 *adv also Fig* entre bastidores; **to go b. after the performance** ir a los camerinos después de la representación

backstairs [bæk'steəz] *n* escalera *f* de servicio ►► ***b. gossip*** chismorreo *m* subrepticio

backstitch ['bækstɪtʃ] **1** *n (in sewing)* pespunte *m*
2 *vt* pespuntear
3 *vi* hacer pespuntes

backstop ['bækstɒp] *n Sport* (**a**) *(barrier)* valla *f* de fondo *(para retener la pelota)* (**b**) *(in baseball, rounders)* cátcher *mf*, receptor(ora) *m,f*

backstory ['bækstɔːrɪ] *n* **this conversation fills us in on the b.** la conversación nos remite a los sucesos anteriores a la trama

backstreet ['bækstriːt] *n* callejuela *f*; **the backstreets** *(of city)* las zonas deprimidas ►► ***b. abortion*** aborto *m* clandestino

backstroke ['bækstrəʊk] *n (in swimming)* espalda *f*; **to do** *or* **swim (the) b.** nadar a espalda

backstroker ['bækstrəʊkə(r)] *n* espaldista *mf*

backswing ['bækswɪŋ] *n Sport* swing *m* de retroceso

backtalk ['bæktɔːk] *n US Fam* impertinencias *fpl*, insolencias *fpl*

back-to-back ['bæktə'bæk] **1** *n (house)* casa *f* adosada *(característica de zonas industriales)*
2 *adj (in time)* **b. meetings** reuniones seguidas
3 *adv* (**a**) *(physically)* espalda con espalda (**b**) *(consecutively)* sucesivamente; **to watch two films b.** ver dos películas seguidas

backtrack ['bæktræk] *vi* (**a**) *(retrace one's steps)* volver atrás, retroceder; **we backtracked to the main road** recorrimos el camino de vuelta hasta la carretera principal (**b**) *(renege)* retractarse, volverse atrás; **to b. on a promise** incumplir una promesa; **to b. on a decision** retractarse de una decisión

backup ['bækʌp] *n* (**a**) *(support)* apoyo *m*, respaldo *m*; **to call for b.** pedir refuerzos; **the expedition had no technical b.** la expedición no contaba con medios técnicos ►► ***b. system*** sistema *m* de apoyo; ***b. team*** equipo *m* técnico
(**b**) *Comptr* copia *f* de seguridad; **to do the b.** hacer la copia de seguridad ►► ***b. copy*** copia *f* de seguridad; ***b. disk*** disquete *m* con la copia de seguridad; ***b. file*** copia *f* de seguridad; ***b. system*** *(for doing the backup)* sistema *m* de copia de seguridad; *(auxiliary system)* sistema *m* auxiliar
(**c**) *US Aut* caravana *f* ►► ***b. light*** luz *f* de marcha atrás

backward ['bækwəd] **1** *adj* (**a**) *(direction)* hacia atrás; **she left without a b. glance** partió sin mirar atrás; *Fig* **a b. step** un paso atrás (**b**) *(retarded) (country)* atrasado(a); *(child)* retrasado(a); IDIOM *Br Fam* **he isn't b. in coming forward** no se deja intimidar, *Esp* no se corta (**c**) *Comptr* **b. compatible** compatible con versiones anteriores
2 *adv* = **backwards**

backward-looking ['bækwəd'lʊkɪŋ] *adj* **a b. culture** una cultura anclada en el pasado

backwardness ['bækwədnɪs] *n (of child, country)* atraso *m*

backward(s) ['bækwəd(z)] *adv* (**a**) *(to rear)* hacia atrás; **to fall b.** caerse hacia atrás; **to walk b.** caminar de espaldas; **to walk b. and forwards** caminar de un lado para otro; **she goes b. and forwards between London and Paris** va y viene de Londres a París; *also Fig* **a step b.** un paso atrás; IDIOM **to bend** *or* **lean over b. to help** hacer todo lo posible por ayudar
(**b**) *(towards the past)* hacia el pasado, hacia atrás; **to look b.** mirar hacia atrás *or* al pasado, volver la vista atrás
(**c**) *(the wrong way round)* **you've got your cap on b.** llevas la gorra del revés; *Fig* **to do sth b.** hacer algo al revés
(**d**) *(thoroughly)* **to know sth b.** conocer algo de pe a pa

backwash ['bækwɒʃ] *n* (**a**) *(of boat)* estela *f* (**b**) *(repercussions)* repercusiones *fpl*

backwater ['bækwɔːtə(r)] *n* (**a**) *(of river)* remanso *m*, aguas *fpl* estancadas (**b**) *(isolated place)* zona *f* estancada, lugar *m* atrasado; **Jibrovia is a cultural b.** Jibrovia está muy atrasado culturalmente

backwoods ['bækwʊdz] *npl* (**a**) *(forest)* bosque *m*, monte *m* (**b**) *(remote area)* lugar *m* apartado, zona *f* aislada

backwoodsman ['bækwʊdzmən] *n* (**a**) *(inhabitant)* = persona que vive apartada de la civilización (**b**) *(uncouth person)* palurdo(a) *m,f*

backyard ['bæk'jɑːd] *n* (**a**) *Br (enclosed area)* patio *m* trasero; *Fig* **a "not in my b." attitude** = la actitud típica de la persona a la que le parece bien que exista algo mientras no le afecte (**b**) *US (garden)* jardín *m* trasero; *Fig* **we can't let this happen in our own b.** no podemos permitir que esto ocurra a dos puertas de nuestra casa

bacon ['beɪkən] *n* (**a**) *(meat)* panceta *f*, *Méx* tocino *m*, *Esp* bacon *m*, *Esp* beicon *m* ►► ***b. burger*** hamburguesa *f* con beicon; ***b. slicer*** máquina *f* de cortar fiambre (**b**) IDIOMS *Fam* **to save sb's b.** salvarle el pellejo a alguien; *Fam* **to bring home the b.** *(succeed)* triunfar; *(earn wages)* ganar el pan

BACS [bæks] *n* (*abbr* **bankers' automated clearing services**) = sistema informatizado que permite a una entidad bancaria realizar pagos a los clientes de otra entidad

bacteria [bæk'tɪərɪə] *npl* bacterias *fpl*

bacterial [bæk'tɪərɪəl] *adj* bacteriano(a)

bacteriological [bæktɪərɪə'lɒdʒɪkəl] *adj* bacteriológico(a)

bacteriologist [bæktɪərɪ'ɒlədʒɪst] *n* bacteriólogo(a) *m,f*

bacteriology [bæktɪərɪ'ɒlədʒɪ] *n* bacteriología *f*

bacterium [bæk'tɪərɪəm] (*pl* **bacteria** [bæk'tɪərɪə]) *n Biol* bacteria *f*

Bactrian camel ['bæktrɪən'kæməl] *n* camello *m* (bactriano)

BAD [bæd] (*comparative* **worse** [wɜːs], *superlative* **worst** [wɜːst]) **1** *adj* (**a**) *(of poor quality)* malo(a), mal *(before singular masculine noun)*; **b. weather** mal tiempo; **the light is b.** no hay suficiente luz; **b. light stopped play** la falta de luz obligó a suspender el encuentro; **the pay is b.** el sueldo es malo; **it's not b.** *(fair)* no está mal; *(good)* no está nada mal; **how are you? – not (so** *or* **too) b.** ¿cómo estás? – no me va mal; **he's not a b. tennis player** no juega mal a tenis; *Br Fam* **this cake isn't half b.** *(it's good)* este pastel está de rechupete *or Méx* padrísimo; **they're paying £200 – that can't be b.** pagan 200 libras – no está nada mal; **I've been b. about writing** no he escrito tanto como debiera; **he's b. at English** tiene dificultades con el inglés, se le da mal el inglés, *Am* el inglés se le hace difícil; **I'm really b. at cooking** soy un desastre cocinando; **I'm b. at remembering birthdays** soy un desastre para acordarme de los cumpleaños; **she's b. at keeping secrets** no sabe guardar un secreto; **things are going from b. to worse** las cosas van de mal en peor; **things are looking b. (for them)** las cosas (les) van mal; **it was a b. time to leave** era un mal momento para irse; **to have a b. time** pasarlo mal; **in b. faith** de mala fe; *Br Old-fashioned* **it's b. form to be late for work** no se llega tarde al trabajo; **it was a b. idea to invite them** no fue una buena idea invitarlos; IDIOM **to give sth up as a b. job** dejar algo por imposible; **he made a b. job of painting the kitchen** pintó la cocina muy mal; **to be a b. loser** ser un mal perdedor; **I had a b. night** *(didn't sleep)* he pasado una mala noche; *Fam* **I'm having a b. hair day** *(my hair's a mess)* tengo el pelo hecho un desastre; *(I'm having a bad day)* hoy tengo un mal día ►► ***b. cheque*** cheque *m* sin fondos; *Fin* ***b. debts*** impagados *mpl*; ***b. luck*** mala suerte *f*; *Comptr* ***b. sector*** sector *m* dañado

(**b**) *(unpleasant)* malo(a); **to have a b. effect on sth** perjudicar algo; **I have a b. feeling about this interview** esta entrevista me da mala espina; **it's really b. the way you have to wait so long for an appointment** está muy mal que haya que esperar tanto tiempo para ser citado; IDIOM **to get into sb's b. books** entrar en la lista negra de alguien; *Fig* **she's b. news** es una tipa de cuidado, no te traerá más que problemas ►► ***b. blood*** *(mutual resentment)* mala sangre *f*; **there's b. blood between them** existe una gran hostilidad entre ellos; ***b. dream*** pesadilla *f*; ***b. feeling*** *(resentment)* animadversión *f*; ***b. habit*** mala costumbre *f*; ***b. joke*** broma *f* de mal gusto; ***b. language:*** **to use b. language** decir palabrotas, ser malhablado(a); ***b. manners*** mala educación *f*, malos modales *mpl*; **it's b. manners to...** es de mala educación...; ***b. mood:*** **to be in a b. mood** estar de mal humor; *Fam* ***b. trip*** *(on LSD)* mal viaje *m*; ***b. word*** palabrota *f*; IDIOM **nobody has a b. word to say about her** nadie habla mal de ella

(**c**) *(unfortunate)* **it's (really) too b.!, that's too b.!** *(a shame)* ¡es una (verdadera) pena *or* lástima!; **it's too b. we couldn't come!** ¡qué pena *or* lástima que no pudiéramos ir!; **too b.!** *(bad luck)* ¡qué se le va a hacer!; *(that's your problem)* ¡mala suerte!; **it's b. enough having to climb all these stairs without being made to wait for ages too** ya es bastante tener que subir todas estas escaleras, para que encima me hagan esperar durante horas; **he'll come to a b. end** terminará mal

(**d**) *(not healthy)* enfermo(a); **he's got a b. back/heart** está mal de la espalda/del corazón; **is your b. leg any better?** ¿va mejor tu pierna mala?; **smoking/alcohol is b. for you** fumar/el alcohol es perjudicial para la salud; **it's b. for a young child to be so isolated** no es bueno que un niño pequeño esté tan aislado; **to be in a b. way** estar muy mal

(**e**) *(wicked) (person, behaviour)* malo(a); **(you) b. girl/boy!** ¡malo/mala!; **to be a b. influence on sb** ejercer una mala influencia sobre alguien; **it would look b. if we didn't invite them** quedaríamos bastante mal si no los invitáramos; **the b. guys** *(in movie)* los malos; IDIOM **he's a b. lot** es un elemento de cuidado

(**f**) *(serious) (mistake, illness, accident)* grave; *(pain, headache)* fuerte; **I've got a b. cough** tengo una tos terrible

(**g**) *(rotten)* malo(a), podrido(a); **to be b.** estar malo(a) *or* podrido(a); **to go b.** estropearse, echarse a perder; *Fig* **a b. apple** una manzana podrida

(**h**) *(guilty)* **to feel b. about sth** sentirse mal por algo

(**i**) *Fam (excellent)* genial; **this music's so b.** esta música está genial *or Méx* padrísima

2 *n Fam* **I'm £50 to the b.** he salido perdiendo 50 libras; *Fig* **to go to the b.** echarse a perder; **to take the b. with the good** estar a las duras y a las maduras, *RP* estar en las buenas y en las malas

3 *adv US (badly)* **I need it real b.** lo necesito desesperadamente; **she's hurt b.** está malherida; **he treats me b.** me trata muy mal; *Fam* **he's got it b. (for her)** *(he's in love)* está enamoradísimo (de ella), *Esp* está coladito (por ella), *RP* tiene un metejón (con ella)

badass ['bædæs] *US very Fam* **1** *n (person)* matón(ona) *m,f*, *Esp* chulo(a) *m,f*

2 *adj* (**a**) *(intimidating, tough)* matón(ona), *Esp* macarra (**b**) *(excellent)* genial, *Esp* molón(ona), *Andes, CAm, Carib, Méx* chévere, *Méx* padrísimo(a), *RP* bárbaro(a)

baddie, baddy ['bædɪ] *n Fam (in movie)* **the b.** el malo (de la película); **the goodies and the baddies** *(in conflict, war)* los buenos y los malos

bade *pt of* **bid**[2]

badge [bædʒ] **1** *n* (**a**) *(bearing coat of arms, logo)* insignia *f*; *(round, made of metal)* chapa *f*; *(pin)* pin *m* (**b**) *(distinguishing mark, symbol)* insignia *f*

2 *vt US* proveer de una insignia

badger ['bædʒə(r)] **1** *n (animal)* tejón *m*

2 *vt* acosar, importunar; **to b. sb into doing sth** dar la lata a alguien para que haga algo; **she's always badgering me with questions** siempre me está acosando con preguntas

badinage ['bædɪnɑːʒ] *n* chanza *f*

badlands ['bædlændz] *npl Geog* = zona yerma con formaciones rocosas que han sufrido gran erosión

bad-looking [bæd'lʊkɪŋ] *adj* **he's not b.** es bastante *Esp* guapo *or Am* lindo

badly ['bædlɪ] *adv* (*comparative* **worse** [wɜːs], *superlative* **worst** [wɜːst]) (**a**) *(not well)* mal; **to do b.** hacerlo mal; **he didn't do b.** *(in contest)* le fue (bastante) bien; **his business is doing b.** le va mal el negocio; **to go b.** ir mal; **he took it very b.** se lo tomó muy mal; **to be b. off** *(poor)* estar *or* andar mal de dinero; *(in bad situation)* estar mal; **we are b. off for money/time** nos falta dinero/tiempo; **to get on b. (with sb)** llevarse mal (con alguien); **I feel very b. about it** me siento muy mal *or Esp* fatal al respecto; **b. dressed** mal vestido(a)

(**b**) *(critically, negatively)* mal; **don't think b. of him for what he did** no lo juzgues mal por lo que hizo; **the play/novel was b. received** la obra/novela tuvo una mala acogida

(**c**) *(seriously)* gravemente; **to be b. beaten** *(lose, be injured)* recibir *or* llevarse una tremenda paliza; **b. damaged** gravemente dañado(a); **to go b. wrong** salir rematadamente mal

(**d**) *(greatly)* mucho; **to want sth b.** desear algo mucho; **to be b. in need of sth, to b. need sth** necesitar algo urgentemente

bad-mannered [bæd'mænəd] *adj* maleducado(a)

badminton ['bædmɪntən] *n* bádminton *m*; **b. racket/court** raqueta/cancha *or* pista de bádminton

badmouth ['bædmaʊθ] *vt US Fam* hablar mal de

badness ['bædnɪs] *n* (**a**) *(poor quality)* mala calidad *f* (**b**) *(wickedness)* maldad *f*

bad-tempered [bæd'tempəd] *adj (remark)* malhumorado(a); **to be b.** *(person) (by nature)* tener mal carácter; *(temporarily)* estar de mal humor; **he made a b. apology** se excusó malhumorado

BAE [biːeɪ'iː] *n US* (*abbr* **Bachelor of Arts in Education**) (**a**) *(qualification)* ≃ licenciatura *f* en Magisterio (**b**) *(person)* ≃ licenciado(a) *m,f* en Magisterio

BAF [biːeɪ'ef] *n Br* (*abbr* **British Athletics Federation**) = federación británica de atletismo

baffle[1] ['bæfəl] *vt* (**a**) *(confuse)* desconcertar; **to be baffled** estar desconcertado(a) *or* atónito(a); **I'm baffled as to why she did it** no logro entender por qué lo hizo (**b**) *(frustrate)* frustrar, malograr

baffle[2] *n Tech (for sound)* pantalla *f* (acústica), bafle *m*; *(for light)* deflector *m*

bafflement ['bæfəlmənt] *n* desconcierto *m*

baffling ['bæflɪŋ] *adj* desconcertante, incomprensible

BAFTA ['bæftə] *n* (*abbr* **British Academy of Film and Television Arts**) = organización británica que anualmente concede premios a personalidades del cine y de la televisión

bag [bæg] **1** *n* (**a**) *(of paper, plastic)* bolsa *f* ►► *Fam* ***b. lady*** vagabunda *f*, = mujer sin hogar que se desplaza llevando todas sus pertenencias en bolsas de plástico; *Fam* ***b. of tricks*** repertorio *m* (de recursos), *Esp* truquillos *mpl*

(**b**) *(handbag) Esp* bolso *m*, *Andes, RP* cartera *f*, *Méx* bolsa *f*; *(holdall)* bolsa *f (de viaje o de deporte)*; *(suitcase)* maleta *f*, *Méx* petaca *f*, *RP* valija *f* ►► ***b. snatcher*** tironero(a) *m,f*

(**c**) *Fam (quantity of drugs)* dose *f*

(**d**) *(in hunting)* cacería *f*

(**e**) *Fam* **bags of** *(lots)* un montón de; **there's bags of room** hay muchísimo sitio

(**f**) *Br very Fam Pej (woman)* **old b.** bruja

(**g**) *Fam (interest)* historia *f*, rollo *m*; **it's not my b.** no me interesa *or Esp* va (ese rollo)

(**h**) IDIOMS **to have bags under one's eyes** tener ojeras, tener bolsas debajo de los ojos; *Fam* **to be a b. of bones** estar esquelético(a) *or Esp* en los huesos; **it's in the b.** *(deal, victory)* lo tenemos en el bote; **he let the secret out of the b.** descubrió el secreto; *Fam* **to pull sth out of the b.** sacarse algo de la manga, *RP* sacar algo de la galera

2 *vt* (*pt & pp* **bagged**) (**a**) *(put in bag)* guardar en una bolsa, embolsar (**b**) *(in hunting)* cobrar (**c**) *Br Fam (claim)* pedirse, *Esp* pillar; **she always bags the best seat** siempre consigue *or Esp* coge el mejor asiento

bagatelle [bægə'tel] *n* (**a**) *(board game)* billar *m* romano (**b**) *(triviality)* bagatela *f*; **a mere b.** una simple bagatela, una nimiedad (**c**) *Mus* bagatela *f*

bagel ['beɪgəl] *n* = tipo de rosca de pan compacto de origen judío

bagful ['bægfʊl] *n* bolsa *f (llena)*

baggage ['bægɪdʒ] *n* (**a**) *(luggage)* equipaje *m*; *Fig* **he's carrying a lot of b. from his first marriage** arrastra una gran carga de su primer matrimonio ►► ***b. allowance*** equipaje *m* permitido; *US* ***b. car*** *(on train)* furgón *m* de equipajes; ***b. handler*** mozo(a) *m,f* de equipajes; ***b. reclaim*** recogida *f* de equipajes; *US* ***b. room*** consigna *f*

(**b**) *Hist* ***b. train*** *(of army)* convoy *m* de bagaje

(**c**) *Fam Hum* **you cheeky b.!** ¡mala pécora!

baggy ['bægɪ] *adj (garment)* suelto(a), holgado(a)

Baghdad [bæg'dæd] *n* Bagdad

bagman ['bægmən] *n Fam US (racketeer)* = persona que cobra, transporta y reparte dinero bajo las órdenes de un mafioso

bagpiper ['bægpaɪpə(r)] *n* gaitero(a) *m,f*

bagpipes ['bægpaɪps] *npl* gaita *f*

bags [bægz] *vt Br Fam* **b. I go first!** ¡prímer!, ¡yo primero!; **b. I have that seat!** ¡me pido ese asiento!

baguette [bæ'get] *n* baguette *f*, barra *f* de pan

bah [bɑː] *exclam* ¡bah!

Baha'i [bə'hɑːɪ] **1** *n* bahai *mf*

2 *adj* bahai

Baha'ism [bə'hɑːɪzəm] *n* bahaísmo *m*

Bahamas [bə'hɑːməz] *npl* **the B.** las Bahamas

Bahamian [bə'heɪmɪən] **1** *n* bahamés(esa) *m,f*

2 *adj* bahamés(esa)

Bahrain [bɑː'reɪn] *n* Bahrein

Bahraini [bɑː'reɪnɪ] **1** *n* bahriní *mf*

2 *adj* bahriní

bail [beɪl] *n Law (guarantee)* fianza *f*; **on b.** en libertal provisional; **to release sb on b.** poner a alguien en libertad provisional; **to grant b.** conceder la libertad provisional; **to stand** *or US* **post b. for sb** pagar la fianza de alguien; **to forfeit** *or Fam* **jump b.** violar la libertad provisional ►► *US* ***b. bond*** escritura *f* de afianzamiento *or* caución; *US* ***b. bondsman*** fiador(ora) *m,f*, garante *m,f*

► **bail out** **1** *vt sep Law* **to b. sb out** pagar la fianza de alguien

2 *US* = **bale out**

bailey ['beɪlɪ] *n (of castle) (wall)* muralla *f*; *(courtyard)* patio *m* interior, plaza *f* fortificada

Bailey bridge ['beɪlɪbrɪdʒ] *n* puente *m* Bailey

bailiff ['beɪlɪf] *n* (**a**) *Law* alguacil *mf* (**b**) *(on estate)* administrador(ora) *m,f*

bailiwick ['beɪlɪwɪk] *n* (**a**) *Law* bailía *f*, alguacilazgo *m* (**b**) IDIOM *Hum* **it's not my b.** *(area of expertise)* no es mi especialidad

bailout ['beɪlaʊt] *n (of company)* = rescate de una empresa en apuros

bain-marie ['bænmə'riː] *n* olla *f* para baño María

bairn [beərn] *n Scot* niño(a) *m,f*

bait [beɪt] **1** *n (for fish)* cebo *m*; *Fig* cebo *m*, anzuelo *m*; *Fig* **to rise to the b.** morder el anzuelo; *Fig* **to swallow** *or* **take the b.** morder el anzuelo, picar

2 *vt* (**a**) *(attach bait to)* cebar (**b**) *(torment)* hostigar, atormentar

baize [beɪz] *n* tapete *m*

Bajan ['beɪdʒən] *Fam* **1** *n* barbadense *mf*

2 *adj* barbadense

bake [beɪk] **1** *vt* (**a**) *(bread, cake)* cocer (al horno), hornear; *(potatoes)* asar (**b**) *(dry, harden)* resecar; **the land had been baked dry** el campo se había resecado

2 *vi* (**a**) *(food)* cocerse (**b**) *(person)* hacer cosas en el horno (**c**) *(dry, harden)* resecarse

3 *n (dish)* plato *m* cocinado al horno

baked [beɪkt] *adj* ***b. beans*** alubias *fpl* con tomate *or Méx* jitomate; ***b. potato*** = patata asada con piel que se suele comer con un relleno

Bakelite® ['beɪkəlaɪt] *n* baquelita *f*

baker ['beɪkə(r)] *n* panadero(a) *m,f*; **b.'s (shop)** panadería *f* ►► ***b.'s dozen*** docena *f* de fraile *(trece)*; ***b.'s yeast*** levadura *f* de panadero

bakery ['beɪkərɪ] *n* panadería *f*

Bakewell tart ['beɪkwel'tɑːt] *n Br* = tarta con base de hojaldre, una capa de mermelada y bizcocho con sabor a almendras

baking ['beɪkɪŋ] **1** *n* **to do the b.** *(bread)* cocer el pan; *(cakes)* hacer pasteles ►► ***b. powder*** levadura *f* (en polvo); ***b. sheet*** placa *f* de hornear; ***b. soda*** bicarbonato *m* sódico; ***b. tin*** molde *m* para hornear; ***b. tray*** bandeja *f* de hornear

2 *adj Fam* **it's b. (hot)** hace un calor achicharrante *or RP* calcinante; **I'm b. (hot)** ¡me estoy asando!, ¡estoy asado(a)!

baklava ['bækləvə] *n* baclava *m*, = pastel de hojaldre, miel y frutos secos

baksheesh [bæk'ʃiːʃ] *n Old-fashioned or Hum* gratificación *f*

balaclava [bælə'klɑːvə] *n* **b. (helmet)** pasamontañas *m inv*

balalaika [bælə'laɪkə] *n* balalaika *f*, balalaica *f*

balance ['bæləns] **1** *n* (**a**) *(equilibrium)* equilibrio *m*; **to keep/lose one's b.** mantener/perder el equilibrio; **to throw sb off b.** hacer que alguien pierda el equilibrio; *Fig* desconcertar a alguien; **the b. of power** el equilibrio *or* la correlación de fuerzas; **to hold the b. of power** *(political party)* tener la llave de la gobernabilidad, ser el partido bisagra; **the b. of evidence is against him** las pruebas hablan en su contra; **on b.** en conjunto; IDIOM **to catch sb off b.** *Esp* pillar *or Esp* coger *or Am* agarrar a alguien desprevenido(a); IDIOM **to strike a b.** establecer un equilibrio ►► ***b. beam*** *(in gymnastics)* barra *f* de equilibrio; ***b. bridge*** puente *m* basculante

(**b**) *(counterweight)* contrapeso *m*

(**c**) *(of account)* saldo *m* ►► ***b. available*** saldo *m* disponible; ***b. brought forward*** saldo *m* anterior; ***b. carried forward*** saldo *m* a cuenta nueva; *Econ* ***b. of payments*** balanza *f* de pagos; ***b. sheet*** balance *m*; *Econ* ***b. of trade*** balanza *f* comercial

(**d**) *(remaining amount)* resto *m*, diferencia *f*; **I'll pay the b. later** el resto lo pagaré más adelante

(**e**) *(for weighing)* balanza *f*; IDIOM **to hang** *or* **lie** *or* **be in the b.** *(decision, result)* estar en el aire

(**f**) *(on hi-fi system)* balance *m*

2 *vt* (**a**) *(object)* poner en equilibrio; **she balanced the basket on her head** se puso la cesta en equilibrio sobre la cabeza; *Fig* **he sought to b. the claims of the two parties** trató de buscar el equilibrio entre las reivindicaciones de ambos bandos

(**b**) *(act as a counterweight to)* contrarrestar, contrapesar

(**c**) *Aut* **to b. the wheels** hacer un equilibrado de ruedas

(**d**) *(consider)* **to b. sth against sth** contraponer algo a algo, sopesar algo frente a algo

(**e**) *Fin* **to b. the books** hacer que cuadren las cuentas; **to b. the budget** hacer que cuadre *or* ajustar el presupuesto

3 *vi* (**a**) *(physically)* estar *or* mantenerse en equilibrio; **the scales b.** la balanza está equilibrada (**b**) *Fin* cuadrar; **she couldn't get the accounts to b.** no consiguió que le cuadraran las cuentas

► **balance out** *vi* compensarse, equilibrarse; **it will all b. out in the end** al final una cosa compensará a la otra, al final será lo comido por lo servido

balanced ['bælənst] *adj (person)* equilibrado(a); *(view, account)* objetivo(a), imparcial; *(diet)* equilibrado(a)

balancing act ['bælənsɪŋ'ækt] *n* **to do** *or* **perform a political b.** hacer malabarismos en política

balcony ['bælkənɪ] *n* (**a**) *(on building) (small)* balcón *m*; *(larger)* terraza *f* (**b**) *(in theatre)* anfiteatro *m*

bald [bɔːld] *adj* **(a)** *(person)* calvo(a); **to go b.** quedarse calvo(a); IDIOM *Fam* **as b. as a coot** *or* **an egg** con la cabeza monda y lironda, como una bola de billar, *RP* con la cabeza como una bocha ►► ***b. eagle*** pigargo *m* cabeciblanco, águila *f* cabeciblanca; ***b. patch*** calva *f*, claro *m*
(b) *(tyre)* desgastado(a); *(mountainside)* pelado(a), desnudo(a)
(c) *(truth)* simple, llano(a); **the report contained a b. statement of the facts** el informe *or CAm, Méx* reporte contenía una mera descripción de los hechos

balderdash [ˈbɔːldədæʃ] *n Fam* bobadas *fpl*, tonterías *fpl*; **b.!** ¡bobadas!

bald-faced [ˈbɔːldfeɪst] *adj US (lie, liar)* descarado(a)

bald-headed [ˈbɔːldˈhedɪd] **1** *adj* calvo(a)
2 *adv Fam* **to go at sth b.** arremeter ciegamente contra algo

balding [ˈbɔːldɪŋ] *adj* medio calvo(a)

baldly [ˈbɔːldlɪ] *adv* francamente, llanamente; **put b. like that it sounds quite unpleasant** dicho con esa franqueza, suena muy desagradable

baldness [ˈbɔːldnɪs] *n* **(a)** *(of person)* calvicie *f* **(b)** *(of tyre)* lisura *f*, desgaste *m*; *(of mountainside)* desnudez *f* **(c)** *(of statement, demand)* franqueza *f*

bale [beɪl] **1** *n (of cloth)* fardo *m*, bala *f*; *(of hay)* paca *f*, bala *f*
2 *vt (hay, cotton)* enfardar, empacar

► **bale out,** *US* **bail out 1** *vt sep* **(a)** *(boat)* achicar **(b)** *(rescue)* sacar de apuros; **your parents won't always be there to b. you out!** ¡tus padres no van a estar siempre ahí para sacarte las castañas del fuego!; **to b. a company out** sacar a una empresa del apuro
2 *vi* **(a)** *(pilot)* tirarse *or* lanzarse en paracaídas **(b)** *(from difficult situation)* desentenderse, lavarse las manos **(c)** *(in boat)* achicar agua

Balearic [bælɪˈærɪk] **1** *npl* **the Balearics** las Baleares
2 *adj* **the B. Islands** las (Islas) Baleares

baleen [bəˈliːn] *n* barbas *fpl* de ballena ►► ***b. whale*** ballena *f (suborden)*

baleful [ˈbeɪlfʊl] *adj* maligno(a); **she gave me a b. stare** me lanzó una mirada asesina

balefully [ˈbeɪlfʊlɪ] *adv* con malignidad

baler [ˈbeɪlə(r)] *n (machine)* empacadora *f*

Bali [ˈbɑːlɪ] *n* Bali

Balinese [bælɪˈniːz] **1** *n* **(a)** *(person)* balinés(esa) *m,f* **(b)** *(language)* lengua *f* balinesa
2 *adj* balinés(esa)

balk = **baulk**

Balkan [ˈbɔːlkən] **1** *npl* **the Balkans** los Balcanes
2 *adj* balcánico(a), de los Balcanes

Balkanization, balkanization [bɔːlkənaɪˈzeɪʃən] *n* balcanización *f*, fragmentación *f* en estados

ball[1] [bɔːl] **1** *n* **(a)** *(for tennis, golf, cricket, baseball)* pelota *f*; *(of clay, of dough, for billiards)* bola *f*; *(for rugby, basketball, soccer)* balón *m*, pelota *f*; **to roll sth (up) into a b.** hacer una bola con algo; **a b. of wool** un ovillo de lana ►► ***b. boy*** *(in tennis)* recogepelotas *m inv*; ***b. game*** *(in general)* juego *m* de pelota; *US (baseball match)* partido *m* de béisbol; IDIOM **that's a whole new b. game** ése es otro cantar; ***b. girl*** *(in tennis)* recogepelotas *f inv*
(b) *(in soccer) (pass)* pase *m*; **a through b.** una apertura; **good b.!** ¡buen pase!
(c) *(in baseball) (foul throw)* bola *f*
(d) *(of foot)* eminencia *f* metatársica; *(of thumb)* pulpejo *m*, eminencia *f* tenar; **to stand on the balls of one's feet** estar de puntillas
(e) *Tech* ***b. joint*** junta *f* esférica
(f) *Vulg* **balls** *(testicles)* huevos *mpl*, cojones *mpl*; *(nonsense) Esp* gilipolleces *fpl*, *Am* pendejadas *fpl*, *RP* boludeces *fpl*; *(courage)* huevos *mpl*, cojones *mpl*; **to have the balls to do sth** tener huevos *or* cojones para hacer algo; *Fig* **to have sb by the balls** tener a alguien agarrado *or Esp* cogido por los huevos *or Esp* cojones; IDIOM *US* **to break** *or* **bust sb's balls** romperle los huevos *or* las pelotas a alguien; **what a load of balls!** ¡qué montón de gilipolleces!; **balls to them!** ¡que se vayan a la puta mierda!
(g) IDIOMS **to be on the b.** *(alert)* estar despierto(a); *(knowledgeable)* estar muy enterado(a); **to play b. (with sb)** *(co-operate)* cooperar (con alguien); **to start/keep the b. rolling** poner/mantener las cosas en marcha; **to have the b. at one's feet** tener una oportunidad de oro; **the b. is in your court** te toca dar el siguiente paso, la pelota está en tu tejado
2 *vt* **(a)** *(form into ball) (wool)* ovillar; *(fists)* cerrar, apretar **(b)** *US Vulg (have sex with) Esp* follarse a, *Am* cogerse a, *Méx* chingarse a
3 *vi US Vulg (have sex)* joder, *Esp* follar, *Am* coger, *Méx* chingar

► **balls up,** *US* **ball up** *vt sep very Fam* **he ballsed** *or US* **balled up the accounts** armó un cacao *or RP* despelote con las cuentas; **you've ballsed** *or US* **balled everything up!** ¡la has cagado bien cagada!, ¡la cagaste de lo lindo!

ball[2] *n (party)* baile *m*; IDIOM *Fam* **to have a b.** pasárselo en grande ►► ***b. dress*** traje *m* de fiesta; ***b. gown*** traje *m* de fiesta

ballad [ˈbæləd] *n (poem, song)* balada *f*

ball-and-socket joint [bɔːləndˈsɒkɪtˈdʒɔɪnt] *n* **(a)** *Tech* junta *f* articulada **(b)** *Med* enartrosis *f inv*

ballast [ˈbæləst] **1** *n* **(a)** *Naut* lastre *m*; *Fig* **the more experienced players give the team a bit of b.** los jugadores más experimentados dan cierto peso al equipo **(b)** *Rail* balasto *m*
2 *vt (balloon, ship)* lastrar

ball-bearing [ˈbɔːlˈbeərɪŋ] *n* **(a)** *(ring)* rodamiento *m or* cojinete *m* de bolas **(b)** *(single ball)* bola *f* metálica

ball-breaker [ˈbɔːlbreɪkə(r)], **ball-buster** [ˈbɔːlbʌstə(r)] *n US Vulg* **(a)** *(woman)* déspota *f* con los hombres *or Esp* tíos **(b)** *(problem, situation)* asunto *m* jodido, *Esp* jodienda *f*

ballcock [ˈbɔːlkɒk] *n* flotador *m*

ballerina [bæləˈriːnə] *n* bailarina *f*

ballet [ˈbæleɪ] *n* ballet *m* ►► ***b. dancer*** bailarín(ina) *m,f*; ***b. shoe*** zapatilla *f* de ballet

ballistic [bəˈlɪstɪk] *adj* **(a)** *(missile)* balístico(a) **(b)** IDIOM *Fam* **to go b.** ponerse hecho(a) una furia, *RP* calentarse

ballistics [bəˈlɪstɪks] *n* balística *f*

ballocks = **bollocks**

balloon [bəˈluːn] **1** *n* **(a)** *(for party)* globo *m* **(b)** *(for travel)* **(hot-air) b.** globo *m* (aerostático); IDIOM *Fam* **when the b. goes up** cuando se arme la gorda **(c)** *(in cartoon)* bocadillo *m* **(d)** *Comptr* ***b. help*** globos *mpl* de ayuda **(e)** *(for brandy)* **b. (glass)** copa *f* de coñac **(f)** *Culin* ***b. whisk*** batidor *m*
2 *vi* **(a)** *(swell)* hincharse como un globo; **to b. (out)** *(sail)* hincharse, inflarse **(b)** *(grow dramatically)* dispararse

ballooning [bəˈluːnɪŋ] *n* **to go b.** montar en globo

balloonist [bəˈluːnɪst] *n* piloto *mf* de globo aerostático

ballot [ˈbælət] **1** *n (process)* votación *f*; *(paper)* voto *m*; **to hold a b.** celebrar una votación; **to put sth to a b.** someter algo a votación ►► ***b. box*** urna *f*; **this matter should be decided at** *or* **by the b. box** este asunto habrá que decidirlo en las urnas; ***b. paper*** papeleta *f* (de voto), voto *m*, *Col* tarjetón *m*, *Méx, RP* boleta *f*
2 *vt Pol (membership)* consultar por votación
3 *vi* **to b. for sth** votar por algo

ballot-rigging [ˈbælətrɪgɪŋ] *n* fraude *m* electoral, pucherazo *m*

ballpark [ˈbɔːlpɑːk] *US* **1** *n* campo *m* de béisbol; IDIOM *Fam* **to be in the right b.** no estar *or* andar muy descaminado(a) *or* desencaminado(a)
2 *adj* **a b. figure** una cifra aproximada

ballplayer [ˈbɔːlpleɪə(r)] *n US Sport (basketball)* jugador(ora) *m,f* de baloncesto, baloncestista *mf*; *(football)* jugador(ora) *m,f* de fútbol, futbolista *mf*; *(baseball)* jugador(ora) *m,f* de béisbol, beisbolista *mf*

ballpoint [ˈbɔːlpɔɪnt] *n* **b. (pen)** bolígrafo *m*, *Carib* pluma *f*, *Col, Ecuad* esferográfico *m*, *CSur* lapicera *f*, *Méx* pluma *f* (atómica)

ballroom [ˈbɔːlruːm] *n* salón *m* de baile ►► ***b. dancing*** bailes *mpl* de salón *(clásicos)*

balls-up [ˈbɔːlzʌp], *US* **ball-up** [ˈbɔːlʌp] *n Br very Fam* **he made a total b. of the timetable** armó un cacao *or RP* despelote con el horario; **the course was a complete b.** el curso fue una cagada total

ballsy [ˈbɔːlzɪ] *adj very Fam* con (muchos) huevos

ball-up *n US* = **balls-up**

bally [ˈbælɪ] *adj Br Fam Old-fashioned* condenado(a); **the b. idiot/fool** el condenado idiota/imbécil

ballyhoo [bælɪˈhuː] *Fam* **1** *n* lío *m*, *Esp* escandalera *f*, *RP* batifondo *m*; **what's all the b. about?** ¿a qué viene tanto lío?
2 *vt US (book, show)* dar (mucho) bombo

balm [bɑːm] *n* **(a)** *(ointment)* bálsamo *m* **(b)** *(plant)* melisa *f*

balmy [ˈbɑːmɪ] *adj (weather)* cálido(a), suave

baloney, boloney [bəˈləʊnɪ] *n* **1 (a)** *Fam (nonsense)* tonterías *fpl*, bobadas *fpl* **(b)** *US (sausage)* = embutido ahumado de gran tamaño y elaborado con distintos tipos de carne
2 *exclam* ¡tonterías!, ¡bobadas!

balsa [ˈbɔːlsə] *n* **b. (wood)** madera *f* de balsa

balsam [ˈbɔːlsəm] *n* **(a)** *(ointment)* bálsamo *m* **(b)** *(plant)* balsamina *f* ►► ***b. poplar*** chopo *m* de agua, álamo *m* balsámico; ***b. spruce*** picea *f* azul *or* de Engelmann

balsamic vinegar [bɔːl'sæmɪk 'vɪnɪgə(r)] *n* vinagre *m* (balsámico) de Módena

balsawood ['bɒlsəwʊd] *n* madera *f* de balsa

balti ['bɔːltɪ] *n Br Culin* = plato hindú que se come en la misma cazuela en que se prepara

Baltic ['bɔːltɪk] **1** *n* **the B.** el (mar) Báltico
2 *adj* báltico(a); **the B. Sea** el mar Báltico; **the B. States** los países bálticos

balustrade [bælə'streɪd] *n* balaustrada *f*

bamboo [bæm'buː] *n* bambú *m*; **b. screen/table** biombo/mesa de bambú; **b. shoots** brotes de bambú

bamboozle [bæm'buːzəl] *vt Fam (confuse, trick)* enredar, liar; **to b. sb into doing sth** liar *or* enredar a alguien para que haga algo

ban [bæn] **1** *n* prohibición *f*; **to put** *or* **impose a b. on sth** prohibir algo; **to lift the b. on sth** levantar la prohibición de algo; **a nuclear test b.** una prohibición de pruebas *or* ensayos nucleares
2 *vt* (*pt & pp* **banned**) prohibir; **to b. sb from doing sth** prohibir a alguien hacer algo; **to b. sb from the premises** prohibirle a alguien la entrada al local; **b. the bomb!** ¡no a la bomba (atómica)!

banal [bə'næl] *adj* banal

banality [bə'nælɪtɪ] *n* banalidad *f*

banana [bə'nɑːnə] *n* (**a**) *(fruit)* plátano *m*, *CAm, Col* banano *m*, *RP* banana *f*, *Ven* cambur *m* ►► ***b. fritter*** plátano *m* rebozado y frito; ***b. republic*** república *f* bananera; ***b. skin*** *(of fruit)* piel *f* de plátano *or CAm, Col* banano *or RP* banana *or Ven* cambur; *Fig* trampa *f* potencial; ***b. split*** banana split *m*; ***b. tree*** platanero *m*, *Am* bananero *m*
(**b**) IDIOMS *Fam* **to be bananas** *(mad)* estar como una cabra *or Méx* destrompado *or RP* de la nuca; **to go bananas** *(angry)* ponerse hecho(a) un basilisco, *CSur* rayarse

band[1] [bænd] *n* (**a**) *(strip) (of metal, cloth, leather)* banda *f*, tira *f*; *(on hat)* cinta *f* (**b**) *(stripe) (of colour, light)* raya *f*, franja *f* (**c**) *(ring)* anillo *m*; **wedding b.** alianza (**d**) *(on cigar)* vitola *f* (**e**) *Rad* banda *f* (**f**) *(of age, ability)* franja *f*, banda *f*

band[2] *n* (**a**) *(group)* grupo *m*; *(of friends)* pandilla *f*, grupo *m*; *(of robbers)* banda *f*, grupo *m* (**b**) *Mus (pop group)* grupo *m* (de música); *(jazz, brass)* banda *f*

►**band together** *vi* unirse

bandage ['bændɪdʒ] **1** *n* (**a**) *(fabric)* venda *f* (**b**) *(on wound, broken arm)* vendaje *m*, venda *f*
2 *vt* vendar; **the nurse bandaged his arm** la enfermera le vendó el brazo

►**bandage up** *vt sep* vendar

Band-aid® ['bændeɪd] *n US Esp* tirita® *f*, *Am* curita *f*; IDIOM *Fam* **a B. solution** un parche

bandan(n)a [bæn'dænə] *n* fular *m or* pañuelo *m* de colores

bandbox ['bændbɒks] *n (for hats)* caja *f* de sombreros, sombrerera *f*

bandicoot ['bændɪkuːt] *n* bandicut *m*

banding ['bændɪŋ] *n* (**a**) *Br Educ* = agrupamiento de alumnos según su capacidad o aptitud (**b**) *Fin* asignación *f* a una franja *or* horquilla

bandit ['bændɪt] *n* bandolero *m*, bandido *m*

bandleader ['bændliːdə(r)] *n* líder *mf (de un grupo musical)*

bandmaster ['bændmɑːstə(r)] *n* director *m (de una banda de música)*

bandolier, bandoleer [bændə'lɪə(r)] *n* bandolera *f*

band-saw ['bændsɔː] *n* sierra *f* (mecánica) de cinta

bandsman ['bændzmən] *n Mus* músico *m (de banda)*

bandstand ['bændstænd] *n* quiosco *m* de música

bandwagon ['bændwægən] *n Fam* **to jump** *or* **climb on the b.** subirse al carro

bandwidth ['bændwɪdθ] *n Comptr & Rad* ancho *m* de banda

bandy[1] ['bændɪ] *adj (legs)* arqueado(a) *(hacia afuera)*

bandy[2] *vt (words, insults)* intercambiar, cambiar; **don't b. words with me!** ¡a mí no me replica *or* replique usted!

►**bandy about, bandy around** *vt sep (expression, story)* **his name is being bandied about** suena *or* se oye mucho su nombre; **all sorts of figures are being bandied about in the press** en la prensa se barajan toda clase de cifras

bandy-legged ['bændɪ'leg(ɪ)d] *adj* estevado(a)

bane [beɪn] *n* cruz *f*, perdición *f*; **he's the b. of my life** es mi cruz, es mi ruina; **this tax has become the b. of local government** este impuesto ha sido la perdición de la administración local

baneful ['beɪnfʊl] *adj Literary* pernicioso(a), funesto(a)

bang [bæŋ] **1** *n* (**a**) *(noise)* golpe *m*; *(explosion)* explosión *f*; **the door shut with a b.** la puerta se cerró de un portazo; **to shut the door with a b.** cerrar dando un portazo; **there was a loud b.** se oyó un fuerte zambombazo; IDIOM **to go (***Br* **off** *or US* **over** *or US* **out) with a b.** *(party, event)* salir redondo(a); IDIOM *US Fam* **to get a b. out of sth/sb** disfrutar de lo lindo con algo/alguien
(**b**) *(blow)* golpe *m*; **to get a b. on the head** darse un golpe en la cabeza
(**c**) *Vulg (sexual intercourse)* **to have a b.** echar un polvo *or Cuba* palo, *Andes, CAm, Carib, RP* coger, *Méx* chingar
2 *adv* (**a**) **to go b.** *(explode)* explotar ruidosamente; *Br Fam* **b. went my hopes of a quiet weekend** a paseo se fue la ilusión de un fin de semana tranquilo; *Br Fam* **b. goes that idea** pues habrá que pensar otra cosa; **b. go my chances of winning!** ¡adiós a la posibilidad de ganar!
(**b**) *Fam (exactly)* **b. in the middle** justo en medio; **his house is b. in the middle** *or* **centre of town** su casa está en todo el centro *or Méx* en el mero centro de la ciudad; **to be b. on, to get it b. on** *(guess, answer)* acertar de lleno, dar justo en el clavo; **I walked b. into him** me di de narices *or* bruces con él; **the missile was b. on target** el misil dio de lleno en el blanco; **b. on time** justo a tiempo; IDIOM *Fam* **you've got me b. to rights** me has pillado *or Am* pescado in fraganti *or* con las manos en la masa; **b. up-to-date** totalmente al día
3 *exclam (sound of gun)* ¡pum!; *(explosion)* ¡bum!; *(blow, slam)* ¡pum!
4 *vt* (**a**) *(hit)* golpear; **to b. one's head (against** *or* **on sth)** golpearse la cabeza (contra *or* con algo); **he banged his fist on the table** dio un puñetazo en la mesa; IDIOM **I could have banged their heads together!** me entraron *or* dieron ganas de hacerles chocar las cabezas
(**b**) *(slam) (door, window)* cerrar de golpe; **she banged the door shut** cerró de un portazo
(**c**) *Vulg (have sex with)* echar un polvo *or Cuba* palo con, *Andes, CAm, Carib, RP* coger, *Méx* chingar
5 *vi* (**a**) *(hit)* **to b. at** *or* **on the door** aporrear la puerta; **to b. on the table with one's fist** golpear la mesa con el puño; **to b. into sth/sb** darse de bruces con algo/alguien
(**b**) *(door, window)* batir, dar golpes; **the door banged shut** la puerta se cerró de un portazo; **the door was banging all night** la puerta estuvo toda la noche dando golpes *or* portazos
(**c**) *Vulg (have sex)* echar un *Esp* polvo *or Cuba* palo, *Andes, CAm, Carib, RP* coger, *Méx* chingar

►**bang about, bang around** *vi (make noise)* armar jaleo

►**bang away** *vi* (**a**) *(with gun)* **the robbers were banging away at the police** los ladrones tiroteaban a la policía; **the artillery kept banging away at the enemy positions** la artillería bombardeaba sin cesar las posiciones enemigas (**b**) *(keep working)* **he was banging away on his typewriter** no cesaba de aporrear la máquina de escribir

►**bang down** *vt sep* dejar caer de golpe *or* bruscamente; **he banged the receiver down** colgó de golpe

►**bang on** *vi Br Fam* **to b. on about sth** dar la lata *or* la murga con algo, jorobar con algo

►**bang out** *vt sep Fam* **someone was banging out a tune on the piano** alguien aporreaba el piano

►**bang up** *vt sep very Fam* (**a**) *Br (imprison)* meter en *Esp* chirona *or Andes, RP* cana *or Méx* bote (**b**) *Br (make pregnant)* hacer un bombo *or* una barriga a, dejar preñada (**c**) *US (damage)* jorobar, dejar hecho(a) polvo

banger ['bæŋə(r)] *n* (**a**) *Br Fam (sausage)* salchicha *f*; **bangers and mash** salchichas con puré de patatas *or Am* papas (**b**) *Br (firework)* petardo *m* (**c**) *Fam (car)* **old b.** cacharro viejo, carraca

Bangkok [bæŋ'kɒk] *n* Bangkok

Bangladesh [bæŋglə'deʃ] *n* Bangladesh

Bangladeshi [bæŋglə'deʃɪ] **1** *n* bangladesí *mf*
2 *adj* bangladesí

bangle ['bæŋgəl] *n* brazalete *m*, pulsera *f*

bangs [bæŋz] *npl US* flequillo *m*, *Am* cerquillo *m (corto)*

bang-up ['bæŋʌp] *adj US Fam* de primera, de fábula

banish ['bænɪʃ] *vt* (**a**) *(exile)* desterrar; **he was banished from Rome** fue desterrado de Roma (**b**) *(thought)* alejar, apartar; **he banished all thought of her from his mind** se la quitó por completo de la cabeza

banishment ['bænɪʃmənt] *n* destierro *m*

banister, bannister ['bænɪstə(r)] *n* pasamanos *m inv*, *Esp* barandilla *f*; **to slide down the banister(s)** bajar deslizándose por el pasamanos

banjo ['bændʒəʊ] (*pl* **banjos**) *n* banjo *m*

bank[1] [bæŋk] **1** *n* **(a)** *(of river, canal)* orilla *f*, margen *f*; **the banks of Lake Como** la ribera del lago de Como; **the river has overflowed** *or* **burst its banks** el río se ha desbordado *or* salido de madre
(b) *(slope)* terraplén *m*
(c) *(mass) (of earth)* terraplén *m*; *(of snow)* montículo *m*; *(of clouds, fog)* banco *m*; **banks of flowers** tapices de flores
(d) *(of lights, switches)* batería *f*, tablero *m*; **banks of seats** gradas con asientos
(e) *(on racetrack, road)* peralte *m*
2 *vt* **(a)** *(border)* flanquear; **the road is banked by trees** la carretera se halla flanqueada por dos filas de árboles **(b)** *(heap up) (earth, snow)* amontonar **(c)** *(plane)* inclinar, ladear **(d)** *(racetrack, road)* peraltar
3 *vi* **(a)** *(clouds, mist)* formar(se) bancos; *(snow)* acumularse **(b)** *(plane)* ladearse, escorarse **(c)** *(racetrack, road)* formar un peralte

▸ **bank up** **1** *vt sep (earth, snow)* amontonar; *(fire)* **she banked up the fire** añadió más carbón al fuego haciendo un montón
2 *vi (cloud)* formarse bancos

bank[2] **1** *n* **(a)** *(financial institution)* banco *m*, entidad *f* bancaria ▸▸ ***b. account*** cuenta *f* bancaria; ***b. balance*** saldo *m* bancario, haberes *mpl* bancarios; ***b. book*** cartilla *f*, libreta *f*; ***b. card*** tarjeta *f* bancaria; ***b. charges*** comisión *f* bancaria, gastos *mpl* bancarios; ***b. clearing*** compensación *f* bancaria; ***b. clerk*** empleado(a) *m,f* de banca; ***b. details*** datos *mpl* bancarios; ***b. draft*** efecto *m* interbancario; *US* ***b. examiner*** auditor(ora) *m,f* público(a); *Br* ***b. holiday*** día *m* festivo; ***b. loan*** préstamo *m or* crédito *m* bancario; ***b. manager*** director(ora) *m,f* de banco; *Fin* ***b. rate*** tipo *m or Am* tasa *f* de interés bancario; ***b. robber*** atracador(ora) *m,f or* ladrón(ona) *m,f* de bancos; ***b. statement*** extracto *m or* balance *m* de cuenta; ***b. transfer*** transferencia *f* bancaria
(b) *(in gambling)* banca *f*; **to break the b.** hacer saltar la banca; IDIOM **it won't break the b.** no vas a arruinarte por eso
(c) *(store)* **blood/data b.** banco de sangre/datos
2 *vt (money, cheque)* depositar, *Esp* ingresar
3 *vi* **to b. with** tener una cuenta en; **where do you b.?, who do you b. with?** *(individual)* ¿cuál es tu banco?, ¿en qué banco tienes cuenta?; *(company)* ¿con qué banco trabajas?

▸ **bank on** *vt insep (outcome, success)* contar con

bankable ['bæŋkəbəl] *adj (actor, actress)* taquillero(a), de éxito

banker ['bæŋkə(r)] *n* **(a)** *Fin* banquero *m* ▸▸ ***b.'s card*** tarjeta *f* bancaria; ***b.'s draft*** giro *m* bancario; ***b.'s order*** domiciliación *f* (bancaria); ***b.'s reference*** aval *m* bancario **(b)** *(in betting, game)* banca *f*

banking ['bæŋkɪŋ] *n (occupation)* banca *f*, sector *m* bancario; *(activity)* operaciones *fpl* bancarias ▸▸ ***b. confidentiality*** secreto *m* bancario; ***b. hours*** horario *m* de los bancos; **what are the b. hours in Ecuador?** ¿qué horario hacen *or* tienen los bancos en Ecuador?; ***b. house*** casa *f* de banca

banknote ['bæŋknəʊt] *n* billete *m* (de banco)

bankroll ['bæŋkrəʊl] *US Fam* **1** *n* **(a)** *(cash)* fajo *m* de billetes **(b)** *(funds)* fondos *mpl*, capital *m*
2 *vt (finance)* financiar

bankrupt ['bæŋkrʌpt] **1** *n Fin* quebrado(a) *m,f*
2 *adj* **(a)** *Fin* en quiebra, en bancarrota; **to be b.** estar en quiebra; **to go b.** quebrar, ir a la quiebra **(b)** *(totally lacking)* **to be morally b.** estar en quiebra moral; **to be b. of ideas** carecer de ideas
3 *vt* **(a)** *Fin (company, person)* conducir a la quiebra, llevar a la ruina **(b)** *Fam (person)* arruinar, dejar en la ruina

bankruptcy ['bæŋkrʌptsɪ] *n* **(a)** *Law* quiebra *f*, bancarrota *f*; **to present** *or* **file one's petition for b.** presentar una petición *or* solicitud de declaración de quiebra **(b)** *Fam (poverty)* ruina *f*; **moral b.** quiebra moral

banner ['bænə(r)] **1** *n* **(a)** *(flag)* bandera *f*; *(of trade union, regiment, club)* estandarte *m*; *(at demonstration)* pancarta *f* ▸▸ ***b. headlines*** *(in newspaper)* grandes titulares *mpl* **(b)** *Comptr* pancarta *f* (publicitaria), banner *m*
2 *adj US (outstanding)* extraordinario(a), fabuloso(a)

bannister = **banister**

banns [bænz] *npl* amonestaciones *fpl*; **to publish the b.** correr las amonestaciones

banoffee pie [bə'nɒfɪ'paɪ] *n* tarta *f* de plátanos y caramelo

banquet ['bæŋkwɪt] **1** *n* banquete *m*
2 *vi* **(a)** *(hold a formal dinner)* celebrar un banquete **(b)** *(dine lavishly)* darse un banquete

banquette [bæŋ'ket] *n (seat)* banco *m* acolchado

banshee ['bænʃiː] *n* = espíritu femenino de la mitología irlandesa cuyos gemidos auguran la muerte; IDIOM **to wail like a b.** llorar como un alma en pena *or* como una Magdalena

bantam ['bæntəm] *n* gallina *f* de Bantam

bantamweight ['bæntəmweɪt] *n (in boxing)* peso *m* gallo

banter ['bæntə(r)] **1** *n* bromas *fpl*, chanzas *fpl*
2 *vi* bromear (**with** con)

bantering ['bæntərɪŋ] *adj* jocoso(a); **b. tone** tono jocoso

Bantu ['bæntuː] **1** *n* **(a)** *(person)* bantú *mf* **(b)** *(language)* bantú *m*
2 *adj* bantú

banyan ['bænjæn] *n* **b. (tree)** baniano *m*, higuera *f* de Bengala

baobab ['beɪəʊbæb] *n* **b. (tree)** baobab *m*

bap [bæp] *n Br* = panecillo blando redondo

baptism ['bæptɪzəm] *n* bautismo *m*; *Fig* **a b. of fire** un bautismo de fuego

baptismal [bæp'tɪzməl] *adj* ***b. certificate*** partida *f* de bautismo; ***b. font*** pila *f* bautismal

Baptist ['bæptɪst] *n* baptista *mf*, bautista *mf*

baptist(e)ry ['bæptɪstrɪ] *n (part of church)* baptisterio *m*

baptize [bæp'taɪz, *US* 'bæptaɪz] *vt* bautizar; **he was baptized Richard Henry, but everyone calls him George** su nombre de pila es Richard Henry, pero todos le llaman George

bar [bɑː(r)] **1** *n* **(a)** *(of metal)* barra *f*; *(on window, of cage)* barrote *m*; IDIOM **to be behind bars** estar entre rejas; **they put him behind bars** lo metieron entre rejas; **push b. to open** *(sign on exit doors)* accione la palanca para abrir ▸▸ ***b. ends*** *(of bicycle)* cuernos *mpl*
(b) *(block) (of soap)* pastilla *f*; *(of chocolate)* tableta *f*; **gold bars** lingotes de oro, oro en barras
(c) *(of electric fire)* resistencia *f*; **a three-b. fire** una estufa (eléctrica) de tres resistencias
(d) *(stripe) (of colour, light)* franja *f* ▸▸ ***b. chart*** gráfico *m* de barras; *Comptr* ***b. code*** código *m* de barras
(e) *(obstacle)* barrera *f*; *(ban)* prohibición *f*; **to be a b. to sth** constituir una barrera para algo; **to impose a b. on sth** prohibir algo
(f) *Law* **the B.** *Br (barristers)* = conjunto de los abogados que ejercen en tribunales superiores; *US (lawyers in general)* la abogacía; *Br* **to be called to the B.** obtener el título de abogado(a), ingresar en la abogacía; **the prisoner at the b.** el/la acusado(a); *US* **to be at b.** *(case)* estar en manos de los tribunales ▸▸ *US* ***b. association*** colegio *m* de abogados; *US* ***b. exam*** = examen que habilita para ejercer la profesión de abogado; *Br* ***B. Finals*** = examen de habilita para ejercer la profesión de "barrister"
(g) *(pub, in hotel)* bar *m*; *(pub counter)* barra *f*; **to sit/stand at the b.** sentarse/estar en la barra ▸▸ ***b. billiards*** billar *m* romano; *US* ***b. girl*** *(barmaid)* camarera *f*, chica *f* de la barra; ***b. snack*** aperitivo *m*, tentempié *m*; ***b. staff*** camareros(as) *mpl,fpl*, *Am* meseros(as) *mpl,fpl*, *RP* mozos(as) *mpl,fpl*; ***b. stool*** taburete *m*
(h) *Comptr (of menu)* barra *f*
(i) *Mus* compás *m*
(j) *(in river, bay)* bajío *m*, barra *f*
(k) *(unit of atmospheric pressure)* bar *m*
(l) *US Mil* insignia *f*
(m) *Br Mil (on decoration)* = insignia que indica que se ha recibido la misma condecoración por segunda vez
2 *vt* (*pt & pp* **barred**) **(a)** *(fasten with bar)* **to b. the door (against sb)** atrancar la puerta (para impedir el paso a alguien)
(b) *(obstruct)* obstruir; **to b. sb's way** obstruir el camino *or* impedir el paso a alguien
(c) *(ban)* **to b. sb from a place** prohibir la entrada de alguien a un lugar; **to b. sb from doing sth** prohibir a alguien hacer algo
3 *prep* salvo, excepto; **b. none** sin excepción; IDIOM **it's all over b. the shouting** la suerte está echada

barb [bɑːb] *n* **(a)** *(on hook, arrow)* lengüeta *f*; *(on barbed wire)* pincho *m*, púa *f* **(b)** *(on feather)* barba *f* **(c)** *(remark)* dardo *m*

Barbadian [bɑː'beɪdɪən] **1** *n* persona *f* de Barbados
2 *adj* de Barbados

Barbados [bɑː'beɪdɒs] *n* Barbados

barbarian [bɑː'beərɪən] **1** *n* bárbaro(a) *m,f*
2 *adj* bárbaro(a)

barbaric [bɑː'bærɪk] *adj* **(a)** *(uncivilized)* bárbaro(a), salvaje **(b)** *(cruel)* bárbaro(a), cruel; **a 4 am start? that's b.!** ¿empezar a las cuatro de la mañana? ¡qué barbaridad!

barbarically [bɑː'bærɪklɪ] *adv* salvajemente

barbarism ['bɑːbərɪzəm] *n* **(a)** *(uncivilized state)* barbarie *f* **(b)** *(in language)* barbarismo *m*, solecismo *m*

barbarity [bɑː'bærɪtɪ] *n* **(a)** *(act)* barbaridad *f*, atrocidad *f* **(b)** *(cruelty)* barbarie *f*

barbarous ['bɑːbərəs] *adj (act, behaviour)* bárbaro(a)

Barbary ['bɑːbərɪ] *n* ***B. ape*** macaco *m* (de Gibraltar)

barbecue ['bɑːbɪkjuː] **1** *n* barbacoa *f, Andes, RP* asado *m*; **to have a b.** hacer una barbacoa *or Andes, RP* un asado ►► ***b. sauce*** salsa *f* (para) barbacoa
2 *vt* asar en la barbacoa

barbed [bɑːbd] *adj* (**a**) *(arrow, hook)* con lengüeta(s) ►► ***b. wire*** alambre *m* de espino *or* de púas; ***b. wire fence*** alambrada *f* (**b**) *(remark, comment)* afilado(a), mordaz

barbel ['bɑːbəl] *n* (**a**) *(fish)* barbo *m* (**b**) *(spine on fish)* barbilla *f*

barbell ['bɑːbel] *n* barra *f* de pesas, haltera *f*

barber ['bɑːbə(r)] *n* barbero *m*; **to go to the b.'s** ir a la peluquería

barbershop ['bɑːbəʃɒp] *n US* barbería *f* ►► ***b. quartet*** cuarteto *m* de voces masculinas

barbican ['bɑːbɪkən] *n* (**a**) *(wall, tower)* barbacana *f* (**b**) **the B.** = gran centro cultural londinense

barbie ['bɑːbɪ] *n Austr Fam* barbacoa *f, Andes, RP* asado *m*

Barbie doll® ['bɑːbiːdɒl] *n* muñeca *f* Barbie

barbiturate [bɑː'bɪtjʊreɪt] *n* barbitúrico *m*

barbwire ['bɑːrbwaɪər] *n US* alambre *m* de espino *or* de púas

Barcelona [bɑːsə'ləʊnə] *n* Barcelona

bar-code scanner ['bɑːkəʊd'skænə(r)] *n* lector *m* de código de barras

bard [bɑːd] *n* (**a**) *Literary (poet)* bardo *m*; **the B.** = Shakespeare (**b**) *Hist (Celtic)* bardo *m* (**c**) *(Welsh)* bardo *m*

bardolatry [bɑː'dɒlətrɪ] *n Hum* = admiración excesiva hacia Shakespeare y su obra

bare [beə(r)] **1** *adj* (**a**) *(naked) (body)* desnudo(a); **his head was b.** tenía la cabeza descubierta; **they were b. to the waist** estaban desnudos de cintura para arriba; **to fight with one's b. hands** luchar sin armas; **he killed a tiger with his b. hands** mató a un tigre con sus propias manos; **in one's b. feet** descalzo(a)
(**b**) *(not covered, unadorned) (tree, branch)* desnudo(a), sin hojas; *(wire)* pelado(a); *(wood)* al natural, sin tratar; *(wall)* vacío(a); *(floorboards)* sin alfombrar; *(ground)* sin vegetación; **a b. earth floor** un piso *or* suelo de tierra; **the tree was b. of leaves** el árbol no tenía hojas; **to strip a house b.** *(thieves)* llevarse absolutamente todo de una casa; **to lay sth b.** poner algo de manifiesto, descubrir algo; **to lay b. one's heart (to sb)** abrir el corazón (a alguien)
(**c**) *(empty) (room)* vacío(a); *(hillside, landscape)* pelado(a); **the cupboard was b.** el armario estaba vacío; **the room was b. of furniture** la habitación no tenía muebles
(**d**) *(simple, plain)* mero(a), simple; **I just told him the b. facts** le expliqué los simples hechos
(**e**) *(just sufficient)* **a b. majority** una mayoría por los pelos; **the b. minimum** lo imprescindible, lo indispensable; **I took the barest minimum of cash** me llevé solamente el dinero imprescindible; **a b. pass** *(in exam)* un aprobado raspado *or* por los pelos; **the b. bones of the case are...** lo esencial del caso es...; **the b. necessities (of life)** lo indispensable (para vivir); **they manage to scrape a b. living from the land** a duras penas sobreviven de la tierra
2 *vt* (**a**) *(part of body)* descubrir, dejar al descubierto; **to b. one's head** descubrirse (la cabeza); **to b. one's teeth** enseñar los dientes; **she refused to b. her breasts for the camera** se negó a enseñar los pechos a la cámara; **he bared his heart** *or* **soul to me** me abrió su corazón *or* alma
(**b**) *(wire)* pelar
(**c**) *(dagger, sword)* desenvainar, desenfundar

bareassed ['beəræst] *adj US Fam* en pelotas

bareback ['beəbæk] **1** *adj* ***b. rider*** jinete *m*/amazona *f* que monta a pelo
2 *adv* **to ride b.** *(on horse)* montar a pelo; *Fam (have unprotected sex)* hacerlo a pelo *or* al natural

barechested [beə'tʃestɪd] *adj* con el pecho al aire, desnudo(a) de cintura para arriba

barefaced ['beəfeɪst] *adj (lie, liar)* descarado(a); **what b. cheek!** ¡pero qué cara más dura!

barefoot ['beəfʊt], **barefooted** [beə'fʊtɪd] **1** *adj* descalzo(a)
2 *adv* descalzo(a)

bare-handed [beə'hændɪd] **1** *adj (unarmed)* desarmado(a)
2 *adv (fight)* a puño limpio, sin armas

bareheaded [beə'hedɪd] **1** *adj* sin sombrero
2 *adv* sin sombrero

bareknuckle ['beənʌkəl] *adj (fight)* sin guantes, a puñetazo limpio; *Fig* **a b. encounter** *(debate, argument)* un enfrentamiento violento ►► ***b. fighter*** = púgil que pelea sin guantes

barelegged [beə'leg(ɪ)d] **1** *adj* con las piernas desnudas
2 *adv* con las piernas desnudas

barely ['beəlɪ] *adv* (**a**) *(scarcely)* apenas; **I had b. arrived when I heard the news** acababa de llegar cuando oí la noticia (**b**) *(sparsely)* **b. furnished** amueblado(a) con lo indispensable

bareness ['beənɪs] *n* (**a**) *(nakedness)* desnudez *f* (**b**) *(lack of covering or adornment) (of tree, branch)* desnudez *f*; *(of wall)* vacío *m*, desnudez *f* (**c**) *(emptiness) (of room)* vacío *m*; *(of hillside, landscape)* desnudez *f*, despoblación *f*

Barents ['beərənts] *n* **the B. Sea** el Mar de Barents

barf [bɑːf] *vi Fam* echar la papa, potar ►► *Hum* ***b. bag*** bolsa *f* para potar

barfly ['bɑːflaɪ] *n US Fam* borrachuzo(a) *m,f, Am* borrachón(ona) *m,f*

bargain ['bɑːgɪn] **1** *n* (**a**) *(agreement)* pacto *m*, trato *m*; **to make** *or* **strike a b.** hacer un pacto; **you haven't kept your side** *or* **part of the b.** no has cumplido tu parte del trato; **he drives a hard b.** es bueno regateando; **into the b.** *(what's more)* encima, además
(**b**) *(good buy)* ganga *f, Esp* chollo *m*; **it's a real** *or* **what a b.!** ¡es una auténtica ganga!, *Esp* ¡es un verdadero chollo! ►► ***b. basement*** sección *f* de oportunidades; ***b. break*** = vacaciones cortas de precio económico; ***b. counter*** mostrador *m* de saldos *or* oportunidades; ***b. hunter*** buscador(ora) *m,f* de gangas; ***b. hunting*** caza *f* de gangas; ***b. price*** precio *m* de saldo; ***b. store*** comercio *m* de saldos
2 *vi* (**a**) *(haggle)* regatear; **we bargained over the price** regateamos el precio; **I won't b. with you** no voy a discutir el precio con usted (**b**) *(negotiate)* negociar; **the unions are bargaining with management for an 8 percent pay rise** los sindicatos están negociando con la patronal una mejora de sueldo del 8 por ciento

▸ **bargain away** *vt sep (rights, privileges)* malvender, malbaratar

▸ **bargain for** *vt insep* **I hadn't bargained for that** no contaba con eso; **he got more than he bargained for** se encontró con más de lo que esperaba

▸ **bargain on** *vt insep* **I didn't b. on that** no contaba con eso

bargaining ['bɑːgɪnɪŋ] *n* (**a**) *(haggling)* regateo *m* (**b**) *(negotiating)* negociación *f*; **we are in a strong b. position** nos encontramos en una sólida posición para negociar ►► ***b. chip:*** **to use sth/sb as a b. chip** utilizar algo/a alguien como baza de negociación; ***b. power*** poder *m* de negociación; ***the b. table*** la mesa de negociaciones

barge [bɑːdʒ] **1** *n* (**a**) *(boat)* barcaza *f* (**b**) *(for parties, river cruises)* = barco para fiestas o pequeñas travesías turísticas; **the royal b.** la falúa real
2 *vi* **to b. into sb** darse un topetazo contra alguien, chocar con alguien; **to b. into a conversation** meterse *or* entrometerse en una conversación; **he barged through the crowd** se abrió paso a empujones *or* empellones entre el gentío
3 *vt (goalkeeper, player)* **to b. sb out of the way** quitar a alguien de en medio de un empujón; **to b. one's way** abrirse paso a empujones

▸ **barge in** *vi* (**a**) *(enter)* irrumpir (**b**) *(interrupt)* interrumpir, entrometerse

▸ **barge past** *vi* abrirse paso a empujones

bargee [bɑː'dʒiː], *US* **bargeman** ['bɑːdʒmən] *n* gabarrero(a) *m,f*

bargepole ['bɑːdʒpəʊl] *n Br* pértiga *f*; IDIOM **I wouldn't touch it with a b.** no lo tocaría ni con pinzas

barhop ['bɑːhɒp] *vi US* ir de copas *or* de bares

baritone ['bærɪtəʊn] **1** *n* (**a**) *(singer)* barítono *m* (**b**) *(voice)* (voz *f* de) barítono *m*
2 *adj (part, voice)* baritonal, de barítono

barium ['beərɪəm] *n Chem* bario *m* ►► *Med* ***b. meal*** (papilla *f* de) sulfato *m* de bario

bark[1] [bɑːk] **1** *n (of tree)* corteza *f*; **to strip** *or* **take the b. off a tree** descortezar un árbol
2 *vt* **to b. one's shins (against sth)** arañarse *or* rasguñarse las espinillas (con algo)

bark[2] **1** *n (of dog, seal, fox)* ladrido *m*; IDIOM **his b. is worse than his bite** perro ladrador, poco mordedor, *RP* perro que ladra no muerde
2 *vt (order)* gritar
3 *vi* (**a**) *(dog, seal, fox)* ladrar; IDIOM *Fam* **you're barking up the wrong tree** estás muy equivocado *or* confundido (**b**) *(person)* gritar; **to b. out an order** dar una orden a gritos *or* vociferando

barkeep ['bɑːkiːp], **barkeeper** ['bɑːkiːpə(r)] *n US* camarero(a) *m,f, Am* mesero(a) *m,f, RP* mozo(a) *m,f*

barker ['bɑːkə(r)] *n (in circus)* vocero(a) *m,f or* voceador(ora) *m,f* de feria

barking ['bɑːkɪŋ] *adj Br Fam* **b. (mad)** como una cabra, loco(a) de remate, *Méx* zafado(a)

barley ['bɑːlɪ] *n* cebada *f* ▸▸ ***b. sugar*** azúcar *m or f* cande; ***b. water*** hordiate *m*, agua *f* de cebada; *Br* ***b. wine*** = cerveza de alta graduación

barmaid ['bɑːmeɪd] *n esp Br* camarera *f*, *Am* mesera *f*, *RP* moza *f*

barman ['bɑːmən] *n* camarero *m*, *Am* mesero *m*, *RP* mozo *m*

bar mitzvah [bɑː'mɪtsvə] *n* Bar Mitzvah *m*, = ceremonia de confirmación religiosa de un niño judío a los trece años

barmy ['bɑːmɪ] *adj Br Fam* chiflado(a); **to be b.** estar chiflado(a)

barn [bɑːn] *n* (**a**) *(for grain)* granero *m*; *(for hay)* pajar *m*; *(for cattle)* establo *m* ▸▸ ***b. dance*** baile *m* campestre; ***b. owl*** lechuza *f*
(**b**) *US (for railroad trucks)* cochera *f* de ferrocarril
(**c**) IDIOMS **their house is a great b. of a place** su casa es un inmenso caserón; **were you born in a b.?** ¿no te han enseñado a cerrar la puerta?, *Esp* pareces de Madrid, *RP* ¿tenés cola?; **he couldn't hit a b. door** tiene una pésima puntería

barnacle ['bɑːnəkəl] *n* (**a**) *(shellfish)* bálano *m* (**b**) ***b. goose*** barnacla *f* cariblanca

barney ['bɑːnɪ] *n Br Fam* **to have a b. (with sb)** tener una pelotera *or* agarrada (con alguien)

barnstorm ['bɑːnstɔːm] *vi* (**a**) *Theat* hacer una gira por provincias (**b**) *US Pol* hacer campaña (electoral) por los pueblos

barnstorming ['bɑːnstɔːmɪŋ] *adj (speech, performance)* apoteósico(a)

barnyard ['bɑːnjɑːd] *n* corral *m* ▸▸ ***b. humour*** humor *m* vulgar *or* grosero

barometer [bə'rɒmɪtə(r)] *n* barómetro *m*

barometric [bærə'metrɪk] *adj* barométrico(a) ▸▸ ***b. pressure*** presión *f* barométrica

baron ['bærən] *n* (**a**) *(noble)* barón *m* (**b**) *(tycoon)* **oil/press b.** magnate del petróleo/de la prensa (**c**) *Culin* **a b. of beef** solomillo

baroness ['bærənes] *n* baronesa *f*

baronet ['bærənet] *n* baronet *m (título inglés)*

baronetcy ['bærənətsɪ] *n (rank, title)* título *m* de baronet

baronial [bə'rəʊnɪəl] *adj* baronal

barony ['bærənɪ] *n (rank, land)* baronía *f*

baroque [bə'rɒk] **1** *n* barroco *m*
2 *adj* barroco(a)

barrack ['bærək] *vt* (**a**) *(soldiers)* acuartelar (**b**) *Br (heckle)* abuchear

barracking ['bærəkɪŋ] *n Br (jeering, shouting)* abucheo *m*

barrack-room ['bærəkruːm] *adj Br (humour, language)* tabernario(a) ▸▸ ***b. lawyer*** abogado(a) *m,f* de secano *(que de todo dice saber)*

barracks ['bærəks] *npl* cuartel *m*

barracuda [bærə'kuːdə] *n* barracuda *f*

barrage ['bærɑːʒ] **1** *n* (**a**) *Mil (of artillery fire)* batería *f* de fuego ▸▸ ***b. balloon*** globo *m* cautivo *or* de barrera (**b**) *(of questions, complaints, insults)* lluvia *f*, aluvión *m* (**c**) *(dam)* presa *f*
2 *vt* **to b. sb with questions** acribillar a alguien a preguntas

barre [bɑː(r)] *n (in ballet)* barra *f* (fija)

barred [bɑːd] *adj (window)* enrejado(a)

barrel ['bærəl] **1** *n* (**a**) *(container)* barril *m*, tonel *m*; *(of oil)* barril *m*; IDIOM *Fam* **to have sb over a b.** tener a alguien en un puño; *Fam* **the party wasn't exactly a b. of fun** *or* **laughs** la fiesta no fue la más divertida del mundo; IDIOM *US* **it was more fun than a b. of monkeys** fue divertidísimo ▸▸ ***b. organ*** organillo *m*; *Archit* ***b. vault*** bóveda *f* de cañón
(**b**) *(of gun)* cañón *m*
(**c**) *(of pen)* cañón *m*
(**d**) *(of lock)* cañón *m*
2 *vt* (*pt & pp* **barrelled**, *US* **barreled**) *(beer, oil)* embarrilar
3 *vi* **to b. along** ir disparado(a) *or* a toda mecha; **to b. past** pasar disparado(a) *or* a toda mecha

barrel-chested ['bærəl'tʃestɪd] *adj (person)* robusto(a)

barrelful ['bærəlfʊl] *n* barril *m*

barren ['bærən] *adj* (**a**) *(infertile) (land)* yermo(a); *(landscape)* árido(a) (**b**) *Archaic & Literary (woman)* yermo(a)

barrenness ['bærənnɪs] *n (of land)* aridez *f*, esterilidad *f*

barrette [bə'ret] *n US* pasador *m*

barricade ['bærɪkeɪd] **1** *n* barricada *f*
2 *vt (door, street)* poner barricadas en; **she had barricaded herself into the room** se había atrincherado en su habitación

▸**barricade off** *vt sep (street)* bloquear con barricadas

barrier ['bærɪə(r)] *n* (**a**) *(fence, gate)* barrera *f*; *Br (at railway station)* barrera *f*
(**b**) *(obstacle, impediment)* barrera *f*; **a b. to economic growth** un impedimento para el crecimiento económico ▸▸ ***b. cream*** *(for skin)* crema *f* protectora *or* barrera; ***b. method*** *(of contraception)* (método *m*) anticonceptivo *m* de barrera; *Med* ***b. nursing*** atención *f* sanitaria en régimen de aislamiento; ***b. reef*** arrecife *m* barrera

barring ['bɑːrɪŋ] *prep* salvo, excepto; **b. accidents** salvo imprevistos; **b. a miracle** a menos que ocurra un milagro; **b. rain the concert will take place tomorrow** salvo que la lluvia lo impida, el concierto se celebrará mañana

barrio ['bærɪəʊ] (*pl* **barrios**) *n US* barrio *m* hispano

barrister ['bærɪstə(r)] *n Br Law* abogado(a) *m,f (que ejerce en tribunales superiores)*

bar-room ['bɑːruːm] *US* **1** *n* bar *m*
2 *adj* **b. brawl** riña *or* gresca de bar

barrow ['bærəʊ] *n* (**a**) *(wheelbarrow)* carretilla *f* (**b**) *Br (in market)* carreta *f* ▸▸ ***b. boy*** vendedor *m* ambulante *(con tenderete)* (**c**) *(burial mound)* túmulo *m*

Bart (*abbr* **Baronet**) baronet *m*

bartender ['bɑːtendə(r)] *n US* camarero(a) *m,f*, *Am* mesero(a) *m,f*, *RP* mozo(a) *m,f*

barter ['bɑːtə(r)] **1** *n* trueque *m*
2 *vt* trocar, intercambiar (**for** por)
3 *vi* hacer trueques, practicar el trueque

▸**barter away** *vt sep (rights, privileges)* malvender, malbaratar

Bartholomew [bɑː'θɒləmjuː] *pr n* **Saint B.** San Bartolomé

baryon ['bærɪɒn] *n Phys* barión *m*

basal ['beɪsəl] *adj* basal

basalt ['bæsɔːlt] *n* basalto *m*

bascule bridge ['bæskjuːl'brɪdʒ] *n* puente *m* basculante

base [beɪs] **1** *n* (**a**) *(bottom)* base *f*; *(of column)* base *f*, *Spec* basa *f*; *(of tree, triangle)* base *f* ▸▸ *Fin* ***b. (lending) rate*** tipo *m or Am* tasa *f* de interés básico; *US* ***b. pay*** salario *m or* sueldo *m* mínimo; *US* ***b. salary*** salario *m or* sueldo *m* mínimo
(**b**) *(support, stand)* base *f*, soporte *m*
(**c**) *(centre of activities) (for explorers, military forces)* base *f*; *(of company)* sede *f* central; **Glasgow is a good b. from which to explore the Highlands** Glasgow es un buen punto de partida para explorar las Tierras Altas ▸▸ ***b. camp*** *(for climbers, explorers)* campamento *m* base
(**d**) *(of food, paint)* base *f*; **dishes with a rice/pasta b.** platos a base de arroz/pasta
(**e**) *(in baseball)* base *f*; IDIOM **to be off b.** estar muy equivocado(a); IDIOM **to touch b. with sb** mantener contacto con alguien; IDIOM **she didn't get past first b.** no llegó a superar la primera etapa ▸▸ ***b. hit*** hit *m*
(**f**) *Sport* ***b. jumping*** salto *m* base
(**g**) *Chem* base *f*
(**h**) *Math* base *f*
2 *adj* (**a**) *Formal (motive, conduct)* vil, bajo(a)
(**b**) ***b. metals*** *(non-precious)* metales *mpl* comunes *or* no preciosos
3 *vt* (**a**) *(found)* basar (**on** en); **to be based on** estar basado(a) en, basarse en (**b**) *(locate)* **to be based in Bath** *(job, operation)* desarrollarse en Bath; *(person)* residir *or* vivir en Bath; *(troops, company)* estar radicado(a) en Bath

baseball ['beɪsbɔːl] *n (game)* béisbol *m*, *Cuba, Méx* beisbol *m*; *(ball)* pelota *f or* bola *f* de béisbol *or Cuba, Méx* beisbol ▸▸ ***b. cap*** gorra *f* de visera; ***b. diamond*** diamante *m* de béisbol; ***b. game*** partido *m* de béisbol *or Cuba, Méx* beisbol; ***b. player*** jugador(ora) *m,f* de béisbol, *Am* pelotero(a) *m,f*; ***b. team*** equipo *m* de béisbol *or Cuba, Méx* beisbol

baseboard ['beɪsbɔːd] *n US (along base of wall)* zócalo *m*, rodapié *m*

-based [beɪst] *suffix* (**a**) *(located)* **the company is Tokyo-b.** la empresa tiene su sede en Tokio (**b**) *(centred)* **a science-b. curriculum** un plan de estudios enfocado hacia las ciencias; **an oil-b. economy** una economía basada en el petróleo; **an interview-b. study** un estudio basado en entrevistas (**c**) *(composed)* **a water-b. paint** una pintura al agua *or* a base de agua

Basel ['bɑːzəl] *n* Basilea

baseless ['beɪslɪs] *adj* infundado(a), sin fundamento; **to be b.** *(rumour, accusation)* carecer de fundamento

baseline ['beɪslaɪn] *n* (**a**) *(in tennis)* línea *f* de saque *or* de fondo (**b**) *(standard for comparison)* base *f* de comparación, referencia *f* (**c**) *Comptr* línea *f* de base

baseliner ['beɪslaɪnə(r)] *n (in tennis)* jugador(ora) *m,f* de fondo

basely ['beɪslɪ] *adv Formal* vilmente

baseman ['beɪsmæn] *n* **first/second/third b.** *(in baseball)* (jugador(ora) de) primera/segunda/tercera base

basement ['beɪsmənt] *n* sótano *m*, *Andes, RP* subsuelo *m* ►► ***b. flat*** (apartamento *m* or *Esp* piso *m* or *Arg* departamento *m* del) sótano *m*

baseness ['beɪsnɪs] *n Formal* vileza *f*, bajeza *f*

bases *pl of* **basis**

bash [bæʃ] *Fam* **1** *n* (**a**) *(blow)* porrazo *m*, castañazo *m* (**b**) *(dent) (in wood, metal)* bollo *m* (**c**) *(party)* juerga *f*, fiesta *f* (**d**) *Br (attempt)* **to have a b. at (doing) sth** intentar (hacer) algo; **I'll give it a b.** voy a probar *or* a intentarlo

2 *vt* (**a**) *(hit)* golpear; **to b. one's head** darse un castañazo en la cabeza (**b**) *(dent)* **it got a bit bashed** se abolló un poco (**c**) *(criticize)* despotricar contra, decir pestes de; **they're always bashing the unions** están siempre despotricando contra los sindicatos

► **bash about, bash around** *vt sep Fam* (**a**) *(beat) (person)* sacudir, zurrar (**b**) *(handle roughly) (package, toy)* tratar a patadas

► **bash down** *vt sep Br Fam (door)* echar abajo

► **bash in** *vt sep Br Fam (door)* echar abajo; **I'll b. your face in!** ¡te parto la cara!

► **bash into** *vt insep* darse (un porrazo) contra

► **bash on** *vi Br Fam (with journey, task)* seguir

► **bash up** *vt sep Br Fam (person)* dar una paliza a; *(car)* abollar

bashful ['bæʃfʊl] *adj* tímido(a)

bashfully ['bæʃfʊlɪ] *adv* con timidez

bashfulness ['bæʃfʊlnɪs] *n* timidez *f*

bashing ['bæʃɪŋ] *n Fam (physical)* paliza *f*, tunda *f*; *(verbal)* varapalo *m*; **to get a b.** llevarse una paliza *or* tunda

-bashing ['bæʃɪŋ] *suffix Fam* **union-b.** ataque a los sindicatos

BASIC ['beɪsɪk] *n Comptr* (*abbr* **Beginners' All-purpose Symbolic Instruction Code**) (lenguaje *m*) BASIC *m*

basic ['beɪsɪk] **1** *n* **the basics** *(fundamental aspects)* lo esencial; *(of language, science)* los fundamentos; **they learned to cook with just the basics** aprendieron a cocinar con lo básico; **let's get down to basics** centrémonos en lo esencial; **to go** *or* **get back to basics** poner más énfasis en lo esencial, recuperar los valores fundamentales

2 *adj* (**a**) *(fundamental)* básico(a), fundamental; **to be b. to sth** ser básico(a) *or* fundamental para algo

(**b**) *(elementary, essential)* básico(a); **I get the b. idea** me hago una idea; **take a few b. precautions** toma las precauciones básicas ►► ***b. commodity*** artículo *m* de primera necesidad; ***b. training*** *(for job)* formación *f* básica; *(in army)* formación *f* elemental

(**c**) *(primitive)* sencillo(a), simple; **the accommodation was pretty b.** el alojamiento era de lo más modesto *or* sencillo

(**d**) *(before additions, subtractions)* ***b. pay*** sueldo *m* base; ***b. rate*** *(of income tax)* tipo *m* mínimo *or* básico, *Am* tasa *f* mínima *or* básica; *Br* ***b. salary*** sueldo *m* base; ***b. wage*** salario *m* base *or* básico

basically ['beɪsɪklɪ] *adv* (**a**) *(fundamentally)* básicamente, fundamentalmente; **they are both b. the same** vienen a ser lo mismo; **she's b. a very shy person** es fundamentalmente tímida

(**b**) *(in short)* en una palabra, en definitiva; **what happened? – b., we got thrashed** ¿que pasó? – pues, en una palabra, que nos dieron un palizón; **b., I think he is wrong** en el fondo, creo que está equivocado

basil [*Br* 'bæzəl, *US* 'beɪzəl] *n* albahaca *f*

basilica [bə'zɪlɪkə] *n* basílica *f*

basilisk ['bæzɪlɪsk] *n* (**a**) *(mythological creature)* basilisco *m* ►► ***b. stare*** mirada *f* asesina (**b**) *Zool* basilisco *m*

basin ['beɪsən] *n* (**a**) *(for cooking)* recipiente *m*, bol *m*; *(plastic, for washing up)* palangana *f*, *Esp* barreño *m* (**b**) *(for washing hands)* lavabo *m*, *Am* lavamanos *m inv* (**c**) *Geog* cuenca *f* (**d**) *(in harbour)* dársena *f*

basinful ['beɪsənfʊl] *n Br Fam* **to have had a b. (of sth)** estar hasta la (mismísima) coronilla

basis ['beɪsɪs] (*pl* **bases** ['beɪsi:z]) *n* (**a**) *(foundation)* base *f*; **on the b. of this information** de acuerdo con *or* según esta información; **we are proceeding on that b.** procederemos partiendo de esa base; **that's no b. for a happy marriage** ésa no es una base sólida para un matrimonio feliz; **the b. for assessing income tax** la base para calcular el impuesto sobre la renta

(**b**) *(reason, grounds)* base *f*, fundamento *m*; **the accusations have no b. in fact** las acusaciones no se basan en los hechos

(**c**) *(system, arrangement)* **on a weekly b.** semanalmente; **on a monthly b.** mensualmente; **on a national b.** a escala nacional; **on an informal b.** informalmente; **I will be taking part on an unofficial b.** participaré con carácter extraoficial

bask [bɑ:sk] *vi* **he was basking in the sun** disfrutaba del sol tumbado; **to b. in sb's favour** gozar del favor de alguien; **he was basking in all the unexpected publicity** se regocijaba con toda aquella inesperada publicidad

basket ['bɑ:skɪt] *n* (**a**) *(container)* cesta *f*; *(for waste paper)* papelera *f*; IDIOM *Fam* **to be a b. case** *(person)* ser un caso perdido ►► ***b. chair*** silla *f* de mimbre; ***b. making*** cestería *f*; ***b. weaving*** cestería *f* (**b**) *Econ* ***b. of currencies*** cesta *f* de monedas *or* divisas (**c**) *(in basketball)* canasta *f*; **to score a b.** encestar ►► ***b. average*** básquet average *m*

basketball ['bɑ:skɪtbɔ:l] *n (game)* baloncesto *m*, *Am* básquetbol *m*; *(ball)* pelota *f or* balón *m* de baloncesto ►► ***b. court*** cancha *f or* pista *f* de baloncesto, *Am* cancha *f* de básquetbol; ***b. game*** partido *m* de baloncesto; ***b. player*** jugador(ora) *m,f* de baloncesto, baloncestista *mf*, *Am* basquetbolista *mf*

basketful ['bɑ:skɪtfʊl] *n* cesta *f*

basketwork ['bɑ:skɪtwɜ:k] *n (art)* cestería *f*

basking shark ['bɑ:skɪŋ'ʃɑ:k] *n* tiburón *m* peregrino, marrajo *m* gigante

Basle [bɑ:l] *n* Basilea

basmati rice [bæz'mætɪ'raɪs] *n* arroz *m* basmati, = variedad de arroz de grano largo de origen indio

Basque [bɑ:sk] **1** *n* (**a**) *(person)* vasco(a) *m,f* (**b**) *(language)* vasco *m*, vascuence *m*

2 *adj* vasco(a); **the B. Country** el País Vasco, Euskadi

basque [bɑ:sk] *n (woman's garment)* corpiño *m*

bas-relief ['bɑ:rɪ'li:f] *n Art* bajorrelieve *m*, bajo relieve *m*

bass[1] [bæs] *n (seawater)* lubina *f*, róbalo *m*; *(freshwater)* perca *f*

bass[2] [beɪs] *Mus* **1** *n* (**a**) *(voice, singer)* bajo *m*; *(on amplifier)* graves *mpl* (**b**) *(guitar)* bajo *m* ►► ***b. player*** bajista *mf* (**c**) *(double-bass)* contrabajo *m*

2 *adj (in music)* bajo(a) ►► ***b. clef*** clave *f* de fa; ***b. drum*** bombo *m*; ***b. guitar*** bajo *m*

basset ['bæsɪt] *n* **b. (hound)** basset *m*

bassinet ['bæsɪnet] *n (cot)* moisés *m inv*, cuco *m*; *(carriage)* cochecito *m*

bassist ['beɪsɪst] *n Mus* bajista *mf*

bassoon [bə'su:n] *n* fagot *m*

bassoonist [bə'su:nɪst] *n* fagot *mf*

bastard ['bɑ:stəd] **1** *n* (**a**) *(illegitimate child)* hijo(a) *m,f* ilegítimo(a), (hijo(a) *m,f*) bastardo(a) *m,f*

(**b**) *very Fam (unpleasant person)* hijo(a) *m,f* de puta, cabrón(ona) *m,f*

(**c**) *very Fam (person, fellow)* **you lucky b.!** ¡qué suerte tienes, desgraciado(a) *or* cabrón(ona)!; **poor b.!** ¡pobre desgraciado(a)!

(**d**) *very Fam (unpleasant thing, task)* **a b. of a job** un trabajo muy jodido; **this oven is a b. to clean** este horno es jodido de limpiar

2 *adj (child)* bastardo(a)

bastardize ['bɑ:stədaɪz] *vt (corrupt)* degradar

baste [beɪst] *vt* (**a**) *(meat)* regar con grasa (**b**) *(sew)* hilvanar (**c**) *(beat)* dar *or* propinar una paliza

bastion ['bæstɪən] *n* (**a**) *(of fortress)* bastión *m*, baluarte *m* (**b**) *(stronghold)* bastión *m*, baluarte *m*; **the last b. of Stalinism** el último bastión del estalinismo

bat[1] [bæt] *n* (**a**) *(animal)* murciélago *m*; IDIOM *Fam* **like a b. out of hell** como alma que lleva el diablo; IDIOM *Hum* **to have bats in the belfry** estar tocado(a) del ala *or* mal de la azotea (**b**) *Fam Pej (woman)* **old b.** bruja (**c**) *US Fam (drinking spree)* **to be on a b.** irse de parranda *or* de borrachera

bat[2] **1** *n* (**a**) *(for cricket, baseball)* bate *m*; *(for table tennis)* pala *f*; **to be at b.** *(in baseball)* estar de bateando, batear ►► *US* ***b. boy*** *(in baseball)* cargabates *mf inv* (**b**) IDIOMS *Br Fam* **to do sth off one's own b.** hacer algo por cuenta propia; *US Fam* **right off the b.** a bote pronto, de buenas a primeras; *US Fam* **to go to b. for sb** dar la cara por alguien

2 *vt* (*pt & pp* **batted**) (**a**) *(hit)* golpear, dar golpes a; **she batted the flies away with her fan** espantó las moscas con el abanico (**b**) *(blink)* **she batted her eyelashes at him** lo coqueteó con la mirada; IDIOM **he didn't b. an eye(lid)** ni se inmutó, ni pestañeó; **she did it without batting an eyelid** lo hizo sin pestañear

3 *vi (in cricket, baseball)* batear

► **bat around** *vt sep US Fam (idea)* intercambiar opiniones sobre

batch [bætʃ] *n* (**a**) *(of goods, material)* lote *m*, partida *f*; *(of recruits)* tanda *f*; *(of bread)* hornada *f* (**b**) *Comptr* ***b. file*** fichero *m* por lotes; ***b. processing*** proceso *m* por lotes

bated ['beɪtɪd] *adj* **with b. breath** con el alma en vilo

BATF [bi:eɪti:'ef] *n US* (*abbr* **Bureau of Alcohol, Tobacco and Firearms**) = organismo que controla el alcohol, el tabaco y las armas de fuego

bath [bɑ:θ] **1** *n* (**a**) *(action)* baño *m*; **to take** *or* **have a b.** tomar *or* darse un baño, bañarse; IDIOM **to take a b.** *(lose heavily)* experimentar grandes pérdidas; **to give sb a b.** bañar a alguien; **to run** *or Formal* **draw a b.** llenar la bañera (de agua)
(**b**) *(bathtub)* bañera *f*, *Am* tina *f*, *Arg* bañadera *m*; **she's in the b.** está en el baño *or* dándose un baño ►► ***B. chair*** silla *f* de ruedas *(con capota)*; ***b. mat*** alfombrilla *f* de baño; ***b. salts*** sales *fpl* de baño; ***b. towel*** toalla *f* de baño
(**c**) *Br* **(swimming) baths** piscina *f*, *Méx* alberca *f*, *RP* pileta *f*
(**d**) *(for chemicals, dye, in photography)* baño *m*
2 *vt* bañar
3 *vi* bañarse

bathcube ['bɑ:θkju:b] *n Br* = cubito soluble con esencias aromáticas para el agua de baño

bathe [beɪð] **1** *n Old-fashioned* **to go for a b.** ir a bañarse
2 *vt* (**a**) *(wound)* lavar (**b**) *(cover)* **she was bathed in sweat** estaba empapada en *or* de sudor; **her face was bathed in tears** tenía la cara bañada en lágrimas; **the hills were bathed in light** las colinas estaban inundadas de luz
3 *vi* (**a**) *Old-fashioned (swim)* bañarse (**b**) *US (take a bath)* bañarse

bather ['beɪðə(r)] *n* (**a**) *(swimmer)* bañista *mf* (**b**) *Austr* **bathers** *(costume)* traje *m* de baño, *Esp* bañador *m*

bathetic [bə'θetɪk] *adj Formal* = que pasa de lo sublime a lo común o banal

bathhouse ['bɑ:θhaʊs] *n* baños *mpl* públicos

bathing ['beɪðɪŋ] *n* **b. is prohibited** *(sign)* prohibido bañarse ►► ***b. cap*** gorro *m* de baño; ***b. costume*** traje *m* de baño, *Esp* bañador *m*, *Col* vestido *m* de baño, *RP* malla *f*; ***b. hut*** caseta *f* de baño; ***b. suit*** traje *m* de baño, *Esp* bañador *m*, *Col* vestido *m* de baño, *RP* malla *f*; ***b. trunks*** bañador *m* (de hombre)

bathos ['beɪθɒs] *n* = paso de lo sublime a lo común

bathrobe ['bɑ:θrəʊb] *n* albornoz *m*, *Am* salida *f*

bathroom ['bɑ:θru:m] *n* (**a**) *(with bath)* cuarto *m* de baño ►► ***b. furniture*** muebles *mpl* de baño; ***b. scales*** báscula *f* de baño; ***b. suite*** = conjunto de bañera, lavabo e inodoro (**b**) *(toilet)* baño *m*, *Esp* servicio *m*, *CSur* toilette *m*; **to go to** *or* **use the b.** ir al baño

bathtub ['bɑ:θtʌb] *n* bañera *f*, *Am* tina *f*, *Arg* bañadera *m*

bathyscaphe ['bæθɪskeɪf] *n* batiscafo *m*

bathysphere ['bæθɪsfɪə(r)] *n* batisfera *f*

batik [bə'ti:k] *n* batik *m*

batman ['bætmən] *n Br Mil* ordenanza *m*

baton ['bætən] *n* (**a**) *(in relay race)* testigo *m*; *also Fig* **to pass the b. to sb** pasar(le) el testigo a alguien (**b**) *(of conductor)* batuta *f* (**c**) *Br (of policeman)* porra *f* ►► ***b. charge*** carga *f* con porras; ***b. round*** *(plastic bullet)* bala *f* de plástico

bats [bæts] *adj Fam* **to be b.** estar tocado(a) del ala *or* mal de la azotea

batsman ['bætsmən] *n (in cricket)* bateador *m*

battalion [bə'tæljən] *n* batallón *m*

batten ['bætən] *n* (**a**) *(supporting strip of wood)* listón *m* (**b**) *Naut (for sail)* sable *m*; *(for closing hatch)* palanca *f* de cierre

► **batten down** *vt insep* **to b. down the hatches** *(on ship)* cerrar las escotillas; *Fig (before crisis)* atarse *or* apretarse los machos

► **batten on, batten upon** *vt insep Br* **they b. on the weak and impressionable** se aprovechan de los débiles y los crédulos

batter¹ ['bætə(r)] *n (in baseball)* bateador(ora) *m,f*

batter² **1** *n* (**a**) *(to coat food for frying)* pasta *f* para rebozar (**b**) *(for pancakes)* masa *f* (**c**) *US (for cakes)* mezcla *f* pastelera
2 *vt (fish, vegetables)* rebozar y freír

batter³ **1** *vt (beat) (door)* aporrear; *(person)* pegar, maltratar; **the ship was battered by the waves** el barco fue sacudido por las olas
2 *vi (hammer)* **to b. at** *or* **on the door** aporrear la puerta; **the waves battered against the coast** las olas batían contra la costa

► **batter about** *vt sep* (**a**) *(person)* vapulear (**b**) *(ship)* azotar

► **batter down** *vt sep* **to b. the door down** echar la puerta abajo

► **batter in** *vt sep (skull)* aplastar *or* partir a golpes; *(door)* abatir *or* derribar a golpes

battered ['bætəd] *adj* (**a**) *(person)* maltratado(a); **a refuge for b. wives** un hogar para mujeres maltratadas (**b**) *(furniture)* desvencijado(a); *(briefcase, suitcase)* deslucido(a), deteriorado(a); *(hat)* ajado(a); *(car)* abollado(a) (**c**) *(food)* rebozado(a)

battering ['bætərɪŋ] *n (beating)* paliza *f*; *Fig (in games, sports)* paliza *f*; *(from critics)* varapalo *m*; **the building took a b.** el edificio sufrió estragos; **the team took a bad b.** el equipo se llevó una buena paliza; **his confidence took a b.** su confianza recibió un varapalo ►► ***b. ram*** ariete *m*

battery ['bætərɪ] *n* (**a**) *(of radio, clock)* pila *f*; *(of car, video camera, laptop)* batería *f*; **to be b. operated** *or* **powered** funcionar a *or* con pilas; **batteries not included** pilas no incluidas ►► ***b. charger*** cargador *m* de pilas/baterías
(**b**) *Mil (of guns)* batería *f*; *Fig* **a b. of criticism** un aluvión de críticas; *Psy* **a b. of tests** una batería de pruebas
(**c**) *Agr* ***b. farm*** granja *f* avícola intensiva; ***b. farming*** avicultura *f* intensiva; ***b. hen*** gallina *f* de granja avícola intensiva
(**d**) *Law* lesiones *fpl*

batting ['bætɪŋ] *n (in cricket, baseball)* bateo *m* ►► ***b. average*** media *f* or promedio *m* de bateo; ***b. order*** orden *m* de bateo

battle ['bætəl] **1** *n* (**a**) *(fight)* batalla *f*; **to fight a b.** librar una batalla; **he died** *or* **was killed in b.** murió en combate; **to do** *or* **join b.** entrar en combate; **to give b.** presentar batalla; **to do b. with sb** librar una batalla contra alguien ►► ***b. cry*** grito *m* de guerra; ***b. fatigue*** fatiga *f* de combate; ***b. plan*** plan *m* de batalla; ***b. royal*** batalla *f* campal
(**b**) *(struggle)* lucha *f*; **the b. for freedom** la lucha por *or* en favor de la libertad; **the b. against poverty** la lucha contra la pobreza; **to do b. for/against** *or* **with** luchar por *or* en favor de/contra; **b. of wills** enfrentamiento *or* conflicto personal; **a b. of wits** un duelo de ingenio
(**c**) IDIOMS **we're fighting the same b.** estamos en el mismo bando *or* *RP* barco; **don't fight his battles for him** deja que se defienda él solo; **getting started is half the b.** lo más difícil es empezar
2 *vi* (**a**) *(fight)* batallar, luchar (**for/against** por/contra); **they battled for control of the government** luchaban por (hacerse con) el control del gobierno (**b**) *(struggle)* luchar; **surgeons battled to save his life** los cirujanos hicieron lo indecible por salvarle la vida; **to b. on** seguir luchando
3 *vt US (fight against)* luchar contra

battle-axe, *US* **battle-ax** ['bætəlæks] *n* (**a**) *(weapon)* hacha *f* de guerra (**b**) *Fam Pej (woman)* arpía *f*, bruja *f*

battle-cruiser ['bætəlkru:zə(r)] *n* crucero *m*

battledress ['bætəldres] *n* uniforme *m (de campaña)*

battlefield ['bætəlfi:ld], **battleground** ['bætəlgraʊnd] *n also Fig* campo *m* de batalla

battlefront ['bætəlfrʌnt] *n* frente *m* de batalla

battleground = **battlefield**

battle-hardened ['bætəl'hɑ:dənd] *adj* curtido(a)

battlements ['bætəlmənts] *npl* almenas *fpl*

battler ['bætlə(r)] *n Fam* luchador(ora) *m,f*

battle-scarred ['bætəlskɑ:d] *adj (place)* minado(a) por la guerra *or* la batalla; **b. soldiers** soldados marcados por la guerra

battleship ['bætəlʃɪp] *n* acorazado *m*

batty ['bætɪ] *adj Fam* pirado(a), chiflado(a); **to be b.** *(person)* estar chiflado(a) *or* pirado(a); *(idea)* ser peregrino(a)

batwing ['bætwɪŋ] *adj* ***b. sleeve*** manga *f* japonesa

bauble ['bɔ:bəl] *n* (**a**) *(cheap ornament)* chuchería *f* (**b**) *(Christmas decoration)* bola *f* de Navidad

baud [bɔ:d] *n Comptr* baudio *m* ►► ***b. rate*** velocidad *f* de transmisión

baulk, balk [bɔ:(l)k] **1** *n (in snooker, billiards)* cabaña *f* de salida, cuadro *m*
2 *vt (frustrate, defeat)* frustrar, hacer fracasar
3 *vi* **to b. at sth** *(person)* mostrarse reticente *or* echarse atrás ante algo; **he baulked at paying such a price** se mostraba reticente a pagar un precio tan alto

bauxite ['bɔ:ksaɪt] *n* bauxita *f*

Bavaria [bə'veərɪə] *n* Baviera

Bavarian [bə'veərɪən] **1** *n* bávaro(a) *m,f*
2 *adj* bávaro(a)

bawd [bɔ:d] *n Archaic (prostitute)* bordiona *f*, buscona *f*

bawdiness ['bɔ:dɪnɪs] *n* obscenidad *f*

bawdy ['bɔ:dɪ] *adj (remark, humour)* picante, verde ►► *Archaic* ***b. house*** *(brothel)* mancebía *f*, casa *f* de lenocinio

bawl [bɔ:l] **1** *vt (order)* gritar; *(insult)* proferir
2 *vi* (**a**) *(shout)* gritar, vociferar (**b**) *(cry) (baby, child)* berrear; *Fam* **the baby was bawling his head off** el bebé berreaba como un descosido

► **bawl out** *vt sep* (**a**) *(shout)* **to b. out an order** gritar una orden (**b**) *Fam (reprimand)* **to b. sb out** reñir *or* regañar a alguien

bawling out ['bɔ:lɪŋ'aʊt] *n Fam (reprimand)* **to give sb a b.** echar un rapapolvo *or Esp* una bronca a alguien; **to get a b.** llevarse un rapapolvo *or Esp* una bronca

bay[1] [beɪ] *n (shrub)* laurel *m* ▸▸ ***b. leaf*** (hoja *f* de) laurel *m*

bay[2] *n* (**a**) *(on coastline)* bahía *f* ▸▸ ***the B. of Bengal*** el Golfo de Bengala; ***the B. of Biscay*** el Golfo de Vizcaya

(**b**) *Archit* entrante *m*, hueco *m* ▸▸ ***b. window*** ventana *f* salediza

(**c**) *Br (area)* **(parking) b.** área *f* de estacionamiento

(**d**) *Comptr* hueco *m*, bahía *f*

(**e**) *(in hunting)* **to be at b.** estar acorralado(a); **to hold** *or* **keep sth/sb at b.** *(keep at a distance)* tener a raya algo/a alguien; **I'm managing to keep my cold at b.** estoy consiguiendo frenar mi resfriado; **to keep** *or* **hold hunger at b.** contener el hambre

(**f**) *(horse)* alazán *m*, caballo *m* alazán

bay[3] *vi (dog, wolf)* aullar; IDIOM **to b. for sb's blood** pedir el pellejo *or* la cabeza de alguien

bayonet ['beɪənɪt] **1** *n* bayoneta *f*; **at b. point** a punta de bayoneta ▸▸ ***b. fitting*** (cierre *m* de) bayoneta *f*; ***b. socket*** enchufe *m* de bayoneta

2 *vt* **he was bayoneted several times, but survived** aunque le asestaron varios bayonetazos logró sobrevivir; **to b. sb to death** matar a alguien a bayonetazos

bayou ['baɪu:] *n* afluente *m* pantanoso

bazaar [bə'zɑ:(r)] *n* (**a**) *(in Middle East)* bazar *m* (**b**) *(for charity)* mercadillo *m*

bazooka [bə'zu:kə] *n* bazuca *m*, bazooka *m*

B & B [bi:ən'bi:] *n* (*abbr* **bed and breakfast**) *(hotel)* = hostal familiar en el que el desayuno está incluido en el precio de la habitación; *(service)* habitación *f* y desayuno

B2B [bi:tu:'bi:] (*abbr* **business to business**) empresa a empresa

BBB [bi:bi:'bi:] *n US* (*abbr* **Better Business Bureau**) = oficina de ética comercial

BBC [bi:bi:'si:] *n* (*abbr* **British Broadcasting Corporation**) BBC *f*

BB gun ['bi:bi:'gʌn] *n US* escopeta *f* de aire comprimido

BBQ ['bɑ:bɪkju:] *n Fam* (*abbr* **barbecue**) barbacoa *f*, *Andes, RP* asado *m*; **B. sauce** salsa *f* (para) barbacoa; **B. chicken** pollo *m* a la brasa

BBS [bi:bi:'es] *n Comptr* (*abbr* **Bulletin Board Service**) BBS *f*

BC [bi:'si:] **1** *adv* (*abbr* **before Christ**) a.C.

2 (*abbr* **British Columbia**) Columbia Británica

Bcc [bi:si:'si:] *Comptr* (*abbr* **blind carbon copy**) Cco

B-cell ['bi:sel] *n Med* célula *f* B

BCG [bi:si:'dʒi:] *n Med* (*abbr* **bacillus Calmette-Guérin**) BCG *m*, = vacuna contra la tuberculosis

BD [bi:'di:] (*abbr* **Bachelor of Divinity**) *(qualification)* licenciatura *f* en teología; *(person)* licenciado(a) *m,f* en teología

BDA [bi:di:'eɪ] (*abbr* **British Dental Association**) = asociación de dentistas británicos

BDS [bi:di:'es] (*abbr* **Bachelor of Dental Surgery**) *(qualification)* licenciatura *f* en odontología; *(person)* licenciado(a) *m,f* en odontología

BE [bi:]

En el inglés hablado, y en el escrito en estilo coloquial, el verbo **be** se contrae de forma que **I am** se transforma en **I'm**, **he/she/it is** se transforman en **he's/she's/it's** y **you/we/they are** se transforman en **you're/we're/they're**. Las formas negativas **is not**, **are not**, **was not** y **were not** se transforman en **isn't**, **aren't**, **wasn't** y **weren't**.

1 *vi* (*present* **I am, you/we/they are, he/she/it is**; *pt* **were** [wɜ:(r)]; *1st and 3rd person singular* **was** [wɒz]; *pp* **been** [bi:n]) (**a**) *(indicating permanent quality, condition)* ser; **sugar is sweet** el azúcar es dulce; **veal is very tasty** la ternera es muy sabrosa; **he's always very smart** siempre va muy elegante; **she's irritable by nature** es irritable por naturaleza; **she's English** es inglesa; **he's clever** es inteligente; **she's dead** está muerta; **I'm a doctor** soy médico; **he's a good doctor** es un buen médico; **it's real silk/leather** es pura seda/de cuero auténtico; **it's 2 metres wide** tiene 2 metros de ancho; **three and two are five** tres y dos (son) cinco; **is it that you don't like me?** ¿es que no te gusto?; **just be yourself** compórtate con naturalidad; **I'm not myself today** hoy no estoy muy allá; **we're very happy together** somos muy felices

(**b**) *(indicating temporary state)* estar; **I'm tired** estoy cansado(a); **the bottle is empty/full** la botella está vacía/llena; **this veal is very tasty** esta ternera está muy sabrosa; **you're very smart today** hoy vas muy elegante; **she's rather irritable this morning** está bastante irritable esta mañana; **to be wet/dry** estar mojado(a)/seco(a); **to be cold/hot** *(person)* tener frío/calor; *(thing)* estar frío(a)/caliente; **it's cold/hot** *(weather)* hace frío/calor; **my feet are cold** tengo los pies fríos; **it's cloudy** está nublado; **to be hungry/thirsty** tener hambre/sed; **don't be long** no tardes mucho; **to be right** tener razón; **to be wrong** estar equivocado(a); **he was Hamlet in the play** hacía de Hamlet en la obra; **to be twenty (years old)** tener veinte años; **I was twenty last week** cumplí veinte años la semana pasada; **I'm very happy because I've had a pay rise** estoy muy feliz porque me han subido el sueldo

(**c**) *(expressing identity)* ser; **hello, I'm Paul** hola, soy Paul; **it's me/Paul** *(on phone)* soy yo/Paul; **this is my friend Ann** *(when introducing)* ésta es mi amiga Ann; **is that Ann?** *(when asking who's there)* ¿eres Ann?; **this is Martin Bell, in Sarajevo** Martin Bell, desde Sarajevo

(**d**) *(with time, date)* ser; **it's six o'clock** son las seis (en punto); **when is the concert?** ¿cuándo es el concierto?; **today is the tenth** hoy estamos a diez; **what day is it today?** ¿qué día es hoy?; **it's Monday** es lunes; **it's a year since I saw her** hace un año que no la veo

(**e**) *(with location)* estar; **where is the station?** ¿dónde está la estación?; **is this where you work?** ¿es aquí donde trabajas?; **it's 25 miles to Seattle** quedan 25 millas a Seattle; **to be at home** estar en casa; **where was I?** *(after digression)* ¿por dónde iba?

(**f**) *(with cost)* ser, costar; **how much are the shoes?** ¿cuánto son *or* cuestan los zapatos?; **how much is it?** ¿cuánto es?; **how much is a kilo of apples?** ¿a cuánto está el kilo de manzanas?; **that will be** *or* **that's £25, please** son 25 libras

(**g**) *(with health)* estar; **how are you?** ¿cómo estás?; **I'm fine** estoy bien; **he's better** está mejor

(**h**) *(with imperatives)* **be good!** ¡sé bueno!; **be still!** ¡estate quieto!; **be careful!** ¡ten cuidado!; **don't be stupid!** ¡no seas tonto!; **let's be reasonable** seamos razonables

(**i**) *(exist)* **there is/are...** hay...; **are there any beaches there?** ¿hay alguna playa allí?; **to be or not to be** ser o no ser; **this famous company is no longer** esta famosa compañía ha dejado de existir; **the best band that ever was** el mejor grupo que ha existido jamás; **let him be!** ¡déjale en paz!; **we've decided to let it be** hemos decidido dejarlo; **how can this be?** ¡no es posible!; **they had high hopes of winning, but it was not to be** tenían muchas esperanzas de lograr la victoria, pero no ocurrió así; **be that as it may** así y todo

(**j**) *(with question tags)* **she's clever, isn't she?** es inteligente ¿verdad?; **they're big, aren't they?** son grandes ¿verdad?; **you aren't from around here, are you?** tú no eres de aquí ¿no?

(**k**) *(in ellipses)* **is this the right answer? – yes it is/no it isn't** ¿es ésta la respuesta correcta? – sí/no; **it's good, isn't it? – I suppose it is** es bueno, ¿a qué sí? – supongo; **are you happy? – yes I am/no I am not** ¿estás contento? – sí/no

(**l**) *(as past participle of* **go***)* **I have been to London** he estado en Londres

2 *v aux* (**a**) *(in continuous tenses)* estar; **to be doing sth** estar haciendo algo; **she is/was laughing** se está/estaba riendo; **I'm leaving tomorrow** me voy mañana; **I'll be returning next week** volveré la próxima semana; **I've been waiting for hours** llevo horas esperando; **it's raining** está lloviendo, llueve

(**b**) *(in passives)* ser; **six employees were made redundant** fueron despedidos seis empleados; **they have been seen in London** han sido vistos *or* se les ha visto en Londres; **I haven't been invited** no me han invitado; **he was tortured and killed** lo torturaron y lo asesinaron; **he was killed in an accident** murió en un accidente; **she is respected by all** todos la respetan; **measures are being taken to control inflation** se están tomando medidas para controlar la inflación; **the decision to free the prisoners has been taken** se ha tomado la decisión de soltar a los presos; **the building is being renovated** están restaurando el edificio; **passengers are requested not to smoke** se ruega a los pasajeros que no fumen; **I should have been told earlier** me lo debían haber dicho antes; **the solution was heated to boiling point** se calentó la solución hasta el punto de ebullición

(**c**) *(indicating future)* **the house is to be sold** la casa se va a vender; **we are to leave on Tuesday** saldremos el martes; **he was never to see them again** nunca volvería a verlos; **we were to have got married, but...** íbamos a casarnos, pero...

(**d**) *(indicating conditional)* **if he were to sell the house...** si vendiera la casa...; **were I to tell you a secret, could you keep it?** si te contara un secreto, ¿lo sabrías guardar?

(**e**) *(indicating possibility, uncertainty)* **what are we to do?** ¿qué vamos a hacer?; **how was I to know?** ¿cómo lo iba a saber?; **what's to stop me from telling her?** ¿qué me impide contárselo?; **who is to say which is better?** ¿quién sabe cuál es el mejor?; **he was nowhere to be seen** no se le veía por ninguna parte

(**f**) *(indicating order, obligation)* **you are not to mention this to anyone** no debes decir esto a nadie; **you are to stay there** debes quedarte allí; **he is to be pitied** hay que sentir lástima por él

beach [biːtʃ] 1 *n* playa *f* ▸▸ ***b. bag*** bolsa *f* de playa; ***b. buggy*** buggy *m* (de playa); *Fam* ***b. bum*** vago(a) *m,f* de playa; *Fam* ***b. bunny*** = amiga de los surfistas; ***b. hut*** caseta *f*; *US* ***b. soccer*** fútbol *m* playa; ***b. thick-knee*** *(bird)* alcaraván *m* playero; ***b. volleyball*** voley *m* playa

2 *vt (boat, ship)* varar; **the whale beached itself on the shore** la ballena se quedó varada en la playa; IDIOM **like a beached whale** tumbado(a) y espatarrado(a)

beach-ball ['biːtʃ'bɔːl] *n* balón *m or* pelota *f* de playa

beachcomber ['biːtʃkəʊmə(r)] *n* (**a**) *(person)* = persona que se dedica a recoger objetos y materiales que encuentra en la playa (**b**) *(wave)* ola *f* encrespada *or* rompiente

beachfront ['biːtʃfrʌnt] *n* primera línea *f* de playa; **a b. hotel/property** un hotel/inmueble en primera línea de playa

beachhead ['biːtʃhed] *n Mil* cabeza *f* de playa

beachwear ['biːtʃweə(r)] *n* ropa *f* de playa *or* playera

beacon ['biːkən] *n* (**a**) *(for plane, ship)* baliza *f* (**b**) *(lighthouse)* faro *m* (**c**) *(bonfire)* fuego *m*, hoguera *f*; *Fig* **a b. of hope** un rayo de esperanza

bead [biːd] 1 *n* (**a**) *(of glass)* cuenta *f*; **a string of beads** unas cuentas ensartadas; *Archaic* **to tell one's beads** rezar el rosario (**b**) *(of dew, sweat)* gota *f*, perla *f* (**c**) *(on gun)* punto *m* de mira; **to draw a b. on sb** apuntar a alguien

2 *vt (decorate)* adornar con abalorios

beaded ['biːdɪd] *adj* (**a**) *(decorated)* adornado(a) con abalorios *or* cuentecillas (**b**) *(with moisture)* rociado(a), salpicado(a); **b. with sweat** cubierto(a) de gotas de sudor

beading ['biːdɪŋ] *n* (**a**) *(on furniture, walls)* moldura *f* (**b**) *(on garment)* adorno *m* de cuentas

beadle ['biːdəl] *n Br* (**a**) *(in university)* bedel(ela) *m,f* (**b**) *Hist (in church)* = ayudante del párroco en la iglesia anglicana, ≃ pertiguero(a) *m,f*

beady ['biːdɪ] *adj* **he had his b. eyes on it** lo miraba intensamente; **his b. eyes never left the money** no quitaba ojo al dinero

beady-eyed ['biːdɪ'aɪd] *adj (observant)* atento(a), vigilante

beagle ['biːgəl] *n* beagle *m*

beagling ['biːglɪŋ] *n* **to go b.** ir de cacería *(con perros de raza beagle)*

beak [biːk] *n* (**a**) *(of bird, turtle, octopus)* pico *m* (**b**) *Fam (nose)* napias *fpl* (**c**) *Br Fam (magistrate)* juez *m*

beaker ['biːkə(r)] *n* (**a**) *(cup)* vaso *m (generalmente de plástico)* (**b**) *Chem* vaso *m* de precipitados

be-all and end-all ['biːɔːlən'endɔːl] *n Fam* **the b.** lo más importante del mundo; **it's not the b. of life** no lo es todo en la vida

beam [biːm] 1 *n* (**a**) *(in building)* viga *f*; *(in gymnastics)* barra *f* de equilibrio

(**b**) *(of light)* rayo *m*; *Phys* haz *m*; **the headlights were on full** *or US* **high b.** llevaba puestas las luces largas *or* de carretera

(**c**) *(of ship)* manga *f*, anchura *f* máxima; **on the port/starboard b.** a babor/estribor; *Fam Fig* **broad** *or* **wide in the b.** *(of person)* ancho(a) de caderas

(**d**) *(smile)* sonrisa *f* luminosa *or* radiante

(**e**) IDIOMS *Fam* **you're way off b.** te equivocas de medio a medio; *Fam* **to be on (the) b.** estar *or* ir bien encaminado(a)

2 *vt* (**a**) *(programme)* emitir; *(information)* mandar, enviar; **the pictures were beamed all over the world** las imágenes se emitieron a todo el mundo (**b**) *(show with a smile)* **she beamed her thanks** mostró su agradecimiento con una sonrisa (**c**) IDIOM *Hum* **b. me up Scotty!** ¡tierra trágame!

3 *vi* (**a**) *(shine) (sun, moon)* brillar (**b**) *(smile)* **to b. with pride/pleasure** sonreír con orgullo/de placer

beam-ends ['biːm'endz] *npl* (**a**) *Naut* **on her b.** *(of ship)* muy escorado(a) (**b**) *Br Fam* **to be on one's b.** estar en las últimas, estar sin blanca

beaming ['biːmɪŋ] *adj* **a b. smile** una sonrisa radiante

bean [biːn] 1 *n* (**a**) *(vegetable) Esp* alubia *f*, *Esp* judía *f*, *Andes, CAm, Carib, Méx* frijol *m*, *Andes, RP* poroto *m*; **(green) b.** *Esp* judía *f* verde, *Bol, RP* chaucha *f*, *Chile* poroto *m* verde, *Carib, Col* habichuela *f*, *Méx* ejote *m*, *Ven* vainita *f* ▸▸ *US Fam* ***b. counter*** contable *mf* chupatintas; ***b. curd*** tofu *m*

(**b**) *(of coffee)* grano *m*

(**c**) *Br Old-fashioned or Hum (form of address)* **hello, old b.!** ¡qué tal, viejo!

(**d**) ***b. goose*** ánsar *m* campestre

(**e**) IDIOMS *Fam* **to be full of beans** *(energy)* estar lleno(a) de vitalidad, *RP* estar con todas las pilas; *US (nonsense)* tener la cabeza llena de pájaros, ser un cabeza hueca; **it didn't cost a b.** no costó un centavo *or Esp* duro *or Méx, RP* peso; **it isn't worth a b.** no vale un pimiento *or Am* pepino; **he hasn't a b.** no tiene (ni) un centavo *or Esp* duro *or Méx, RP* peso; *US* **he doesn't know beans about it** no tiene ni la más remota idea

2 *vt US* **to b. sb** dar a alguien un golpe (en la cabeza)

beanbag ['biːnbæg] *n* (**a**) *(for juggling)* bola *f* de malabares (**b**) *(for sitting on)* puf *m* relleno de bolitas

beanfeast ['biːnfiːst] *n Br Hum* francachela *f*

beanie ['biːnɪ] *n* **b. (hat)** casquete *m*

beano ['biːnəʊ] (*pl* **beanos**) *n Br Old-fashioned & Hum (party)* juerga *f*

beanpole ['biːnpəʊl] *n* (**a**) *(stick)* guía *f*, rodrigón *m* (**b**) *Fam (tall, thin person)* fideo *m*, larguirucho(a) *m,f*

beanshoots ['biːnʃuːts], **beansprouts** ['biːnspraʊts] *npl* = brotes de judía germinada utilizados en la comida oriental

beanstalk ['biːnstɔːk] *n* tallo *m* de *Esp* judía *or Andes, CAm, Carib, Méx* frijol *or Andes, RP* poroto

bear[1] [beə(r)] *n* (**a**) *(animal)* oso(a) *m,f* ▸▸ ***b. cub*** osezno *m*

(**b**) *(person)* energúmeno(a) *m,f*, ogro *m*

(**c**) *St Exch* ***b. market*** mercado *m* bajista *or* a la baja

(**d**) IDIOMS **to give sb a b. hug** dar un fuerte abrazo a alguien; **to be like a b. with a sore head** estar de un humor de perros; **the place was like a b. garden** el lugar parecía una jaula de fieras; *very Fam Hum* **do bears shit in the woods?** ¿y a ti qué te parece? ¡pues claro!

BEAR[2] (*pt* **bore** [bɔː(r)], *pp* **borne** [bɔːn]) 1 *vt* (**a**) *(carry)* llevar; *(bring)* traer, portar; *(weight, load)* soportar; **to b. sth away** llevarse algo; *Literary* **the sound of guns was borne along on the air** el sonido de los cañones fue arrastrado por el aire; *Hum* **I come bearing gifts** mira qué maravillas te traigo; *Formal* **to b. oneself with dignity** comportarse con dignidad; **to b. sth in mind** tener algo presente *or* en cuenta; **we will b. the costs** nos haremos cargo de los costos *or Esp* costes; **to b. the blame for sth** asumir la responsabilidad de algo; **to b. the responsibility for sth** cargar con la responsabilidad de algo

(**b**) *(endure)* soportar, aguantar; **I can't b. him** no puedo soportarlo, no lo soporto; **I could b. it no longer** no podía aguantar más; **I can't b. to see you unhappy** no soporto verte triste; **it was more than I could b. to see his smug expression** su expresión de engreimiento fue ya demasiado; **this theory doesn't b. closer examination** esta teoría no resiste un análisis detallado; **it doesn't b. thinking about** no quiero ni pensarlo

(**c**) *(produce)* **she bore him three children** le dio tres hijos; **we filmed the lioness bearing its young** filmamos a la leona pariendo (a sus crías); **to b. interest** *(investment)* devengar intereses; **to b. fruit** *(tree)* dar fruto, fructificar; *(effort, plan)* dar fruto(s), ser fructífero(a)

(**d**) *Formal (have)* **to b. a resemblance to** guardar cierto parecido con; **it bears no relation to...** no tiene nada que ver con...; **a poster bearing his name** un póster con su nombre; **his face bears a scar** tiene una cicatriz en la cara; *Fig* **she bears the scars of an unhappy childhood** está marcada por una infancia infeliz

(**e**) *Formal (feel)* **he bears them no ill will** no les desea ningún mal

2 *vi* (**a**) *(move)* **to b. (to the) right/left** echarse hacia la derecha/izquierda; **the road then bears south** la carretera tuerce después hacia el sur

(**b**) *(have effect)* **to bring pressure to b. on sb** ejercer presión sobre alguien; **he brought his considerable expertise to b. on the project** aportó su notable experiencia al proyecto

▸ **bear down (up)on** *vt insep* (**a**) *(approach threateningly)* abalanzarse sobre; **the enemy tanks were bearing down (up)on us** los tanques enemigos se nos echaban encima

(**b**) *(press down on)* aplastar

▸ **bear on, bear upon** *vt insep Formal (have connection with)* afectar a

▸ **bear out** *vt sep (theory)* corroborar; **I can b. her out** puedo corroborar lo que dice

▸ **bear up** *vi* resistir; **b. up!** ¡ánimo!; **how are you bearing up?** ¿cómo lo llevas?

▸ **bear upon** = **bear on**

▸ **bear with** *vt insep* tener paciencia con; **if you could b. with me a minute...** si no le importa esperar un momento...

bearable ['beərəbəl] *adj* soportable

bear-baiting ['beəbeɪtɪŋ] *n Hist* = espectáculo que consiste en atar a un oso y atacarle con perros y pinchos

beard [bɪəd] 1 *n* (**a**) *(on person)* barba *f*; **to grow/have a b.** dejarse/tener barba; **two-day's growth of b.** una barba de dos días (**b**) *(on goat, fish, oyster, plant)* barba *f*

2 *vt Literary (confront)* arrostrar; **to b. the lion in his den** meterse en la boca del lobo

bearded ['bɪədɪd] *adj* con barba ►► ***b. tit*** bigotudo *m*; ***b. vulture*** quebrantahuesos *m*

beardless ['bɪədlɪs] *adj* imberbe, sin barba; **a b. youth** un joven imberbe *or* barbilampiño

bearer ['beərə(r)] *n* (**a**) *(of news)* portador(ora) *m,f*; **a b. of good tidings/bad news** un(a) portador(ora) de buenas/malas noticias (**b**) *(of cheque)* portador(ora) *m,f*; *(of passport)* titular *mf* ►► *Fin* ***b. bond*** bono *m or* título *m* al portador (**c**) *(servant)* mozo(a) *m,f* de carga

bearing ['beərɪŋ] *n* (**a**) *(of person)* porte *m*; **a man of distinguished b.** un hombre de porte distinguido

(**b**) *(in mechanism, engine)* cojinete *m*, rodamiento *m*

(**c**) *(endurance)* **it's beyond** *or* **past all b.** no hay quien lo aguante

(**d**) *Naut (orientation)* rumbo *m*, demora *f*; **to take a (compass) b. on sth** medir (con brújula) la demora de algo; IDIOM **to find** *or* **get one's bearings** orientarse; IDIOM **to lose one's bearings** desorientarse

(**e**) *(relevance)* relación *f* (**on** con); **it has no b. on the matter** es ajeno al asunto; **his comments have some** *or* **a b. on the present situation** sus comentarios guardan cierta relación con la situación actual; **the event had no b. on the outcome of the war** el acontecimiento no tuvo nada que ver con el desenlace de la guerra

bearish ['beərɪʃ] *adj Fin (market)* bajista

bearnaise [beɪə'neɪz] *adj* **b. sauce** salsa bearnesa

bearskin ['beəskɪn] *n* (**a**) *(rug)* alfombra *f* (de piel) de oso (**b**) *(hat)* birretina *f*, = casco alto de piel utilizado en algunos regimientos británicos

beast [bi:st] *n* (**a**) *(animal)* bestia *f*, animal *m* ►► ***b. of burden*** bestia *f or* animal *m* de carga; ***b. of prey*** animal *m* de presa (**b**) *Fam (unpleasant person)* bestia *mf*; **a b. of a job** un trabajo de chinos *or Am* negros (**c**) *US Fam (ugly woman)* coco *m*, *Esp* feto *m* (malayo), *Am* bagre *m*

beastliness ['bi:stlɪnɪs] *n Fam (of person, behaviour)* mala idea *f*, saña *f*

beastly ['bi:stlɪ] *Fam* **1** *adj (smell, taste)* horroroso(a), asqueroso(a); **to be b. to sb** portarse como un(a) canalla con alguien; **a b. job** *(task)* una tarea asquerosa; **what b. weather!** ¡qué tiempo tan horrible!

2 *adv* bestialmente, horriblemente; **it's b. cold!** ¡hace un frío bárbaro!

BEAT [bi:t] **1** *n* (**a**) *(of heart)* latido *m*; **a single b. of the drum** un golpe del tambor; **the b. of the drums** el redoble de los tambores

(**b**) *(in music) (rhythm)* ritmo *m*; *(in bar)* tiempo *m*; **on the b.** a tiempo ►► ***b. box*** *(drum machine)* caja *f* de ritmos; *Fam (radio)* radiocasete *m or Esp* loro *m* grande *(portátil)*

(**c**) *Br (of policeman)* ronda *f*; **on the b.** de ronda; **we need more policemen on the b.** hacen falta más policías en las calles

2 *adj Fam* (**a**) *(exhausted)* **to be (dead) b.** estar hecho(a) polvo *or* una piltrafa

(**b**) *(defeated)* derrotado(a); **we knew they had us b. when...** supimos que nos iban a ganar cuando...; **you've got me b. there!** ¡ahí me has pillado!

3 *vt* (*pt* **beat**, *pp* **beaten** ['bi:tən]) (**a**) *(hit) (object)* golpear (repetidamente); *(person)* pegar; *(carpet, rug)* sacudir; *(eggs)* batir; **to b. a drum** tocar el tambor; **he beats his wife** pega a su mujer; **the naughty boy was soundly beaten** el niño travieso se llevó una buena paliza; **the victim had been severely beaten** la víctima había sido golpeada brutalmente; **to b. sb black and blue** darle a alguien una paliza tremenda; **to b. sb to death** matar a alguien a golpes; **he b. her senseless** la dejó sin sentido de una paliza; *Fam* **I'll b. your brains out!** ¡te voy a partir la cara!; IDIOM *Fam* **to b. one's brains out over sth** comerse el coco por algo; *Fig* **to b. one's breast** darse golpes de pecho; *Vulg* **to b. one's meat** *(masturbate)* hacerse una paja; **to b. the retreat** batirse en retirada; IDIOM **I b. a hasty retreat** salí corriendo; **to b. a path through the crowd** abrirse camino entre la multitud; IDIOM **to b. a path to sb's door** pelearse *or Esp* darse de bofetadas por alguien; *Fam* **to b. it**, *US* **to b. feet** *(go away)* largarse, *RP* borrarse; *Fam* **b. it!** ¡largo!, ¡esfúmate!, *RP* ¡borrate!

(**b**) *(flap)* **the bird b. its wings** el pájaro batió las alas

(**c**) *Mus* **to b. time** llevar el compás

(**d**) *(defeat)* ganar a, derrotar a; *(record)* batir; *(score, problem)* superar; *(illness)* vencer, superar; **we b. them easily** les ganamos sin dificultad; **they b. us 2–0** nos ganaron *or* derrotaron (por) 2-0; *Fig* **to b. sb hollow** dar una paliza a alguien; **he b. me into third place** me dejó en tercer puesto, me superó en la lucha por el segundo puesto; **to b. the goalkeeper** *(in soccer)* batir al portero *or Am* arquero; **we intend to b. unemployment** queremos acabar con el desempleo *or Am* la desocupación; **to b. sb at sth** ganar *or* derrotar a alguien a algo; IDIOM **to b. sb at their own game** derrotar a alguien con sus propias armas; *US Fam* **to b. the rap** librarse; *Fig* **to b. the system** derrotar al sistema; *Fam* **it beats me why he did it** no tengo ni idea de por qué lo hizo; PROV **if you can't b. them, join them** si no puedes vencer al enemigo, únete a él

(**e**) *(be better than)* **it beats having to go to the office every day** es mucho mejor que ir a la oficina todos los días; *Fam* **it beats the hell out of going on foot** es mucho mejor *or Esp* mola mucho más que ir a pie, *RP* es mucho más copante que caminar; **that will take some beating** eso va a ser difícil de mejorar; **nobody can b. our prices** nuestros precios son imbatibles; **you can't b. a good book** no hay nada mejor que un buen libro; **if you like sandy beaches, Fuerteventura is hard to b.** si te gustan las playas de arena, no hay nada mejor que Fuerteventura; *Fam* **can you b. that!** *(expressing annoyance)* ¡te lo puedes creer!, ¿no es increíble?; *Fam* **that beats everything!** ¡es lo mejor que he oído en mi vida!

(**f**) *(arrive before)* **I b. her to the bathroom** llegué al baño antes que ella; **he b. me to it** se me adelantó; **let's see if you can b. the clock and do it in less than ten seconds** a ver si puedes hacerlo en menos de diez segundos; **they b. the deadline by five hours** lo acabaron cinco horas antes del final del plazo establecido; **buy now and b. the rush!** ¡compre ahora y evite las colas!; **I got up early to b. the traffic** me levanté temprano para adelantarme a la hora *Esp* punta *or Am* pico

(**g**) *(metal, panels)* batir

4 *vi* (**a**) *(heart)* latir; *(drums)* redoblar

(**b**) *(hit)* **to b. against/on sth** golpear contra/en algo

(**c**) *(wings)* batir

(**d**) IDIOM **to b. about** *or* **around the bush** andarse *or* irse por las ramas

(**e**) *Naut* **to b. (to windward)** barloventear

► **beat back** *vt sep* rechazar

► **beat down 1** *vt sep (price)* conseguir una rebaja en; **I b. him down to £40 for the dress** conseguí que me dejara el vestido en 40 libras

2 *vi (rain)* caer con fuerza; *(sun)* caer a plomo

► **beat off 1** *vt sep* (**a**) *(dogs, enemy)* rechazar

(**b**) *(competition, rivals)* superar a

2 *vi US Vulg (masturbate)* hacerse una paja

► **beat out** *vt sep (fire, flames)* apagar

► **beat up** *vt sep Fam* dar una paliza a

► **beat up on** *vt insep US Fam* dar una paliza a; **stop beating up on yourself** no lo pases mal por eso

---

beat-'em-up ['bi:təmʌp] *n Fam (video game)* juego *m* de lucha

beaten ['bi:tən] **1** *adj (gold)* batido(a); **b. earth** tierra batida; IDIOM **off the b. track** *(difficult to reach)* retirado(a); *(not crowded with tourists)* fuera del circuito turístico

2 *pp of* **beat**

beaten-up ['bi:tənʌp] *adj Fam (vehicle)* desvencijado(a), destartalado(a)

beater ['bi:tə(r)] *n* (**a**) *(in cookery)* batidora *f*, batidor *m* (**b**) *(in hunting)* ojeador(ora) *m,f*

beatific [bɪə'tɪfɪk] *adj Literary* beatífico(a); **b. smile** sonrisa beatífica

beatification [bi:ætɪfɪ'keɪʃən] *n Rel* beatificación *f*

beatify [bɪ'ætɪfaɪ] *vt* beatificar

beating ['bi:tɪŋ] *n (assault, defeat)* paliza *f*; **to give sb a b.** dar una paliza a alguien; **to take** *or* **get a b.** *(person, team)* recibir una paliza; *(belief, faith)* quedar maltrecho(a); **the ship took a real b. in the storm** la tormenta dejó el barco bastante maltrecho; **that performance will take some/a lot of b.** será difícil/muy difícil superar su actuación

beatitude [bi:'ætɪtju:d] *n Rel* beatitud *f*; **the Beatitudes** *(in the Bible)* las Bienaventuranzas

beatnik ['bi:tnɪk] *n* beatnik *mf*, miembro *m* de la generación beat

beat-up ['bi:tʌp] *adj Fam (vehicle)* desvencijado(a), destartalado(a)

beau [bəʊ] (*pl* **beaux** [bəʊz]) *n Old-fashioned or Hum (suitor)* galán *m*, dandi *m*

Beaufort scale ['bəʊfətskeɪl] *n Met* escala *f* de Beaufort

beaut [bju:t] *Fam* **1** *n* **what a b.!** ¡qué preciosidad *or Am* preciosura!; **he's going to have a b. of a black eye** le van a poner el ojo la mar de morado

2 *adj Austr* sensacional, fantástico(a)

beauteous ['bju:tɪəs] *adj Literary* bello(a), hermoso(a)

beautician [bju:'tɪʃən] *n* esteticista *mf*

beautiful ['bju:tɪfʊl] *adj* **(a)** *(attractive) (woman)* bonita, *esp Esp* guapa; *(child, animal)* bonito(a), precioso(a); *(music, dress, landscape)* hermoso(a), precioso(a) ►► ***the b. people*** la gente guapa, la beautiful people **(b)** *(splendid) (weather, meal)* espléndido(a), magnífico(a); *(smell, taste)* delicioso(a); **what a b. goal!** ¡qué golazo!

beautifully ['bju:tɪfʊlɪ] *adv* **(a)** *(to sing, dress)* de maravilla **(b)** *(splendidly)* de maravilla; **they behaved b.** se portaron de maravilla; **you put that b.!** ¡yo no lo habría dicho *or* expresado mejor!, ¡muy bien dicho!

beautify ['bju:tɪfaɪ] *vt* embellecer

beauty ['bju:tɪ] **1** *n* **(a)** *(attribute)* belleza *f*; PROV **b. is in the eye of the beholder** sobre gustos no hay nada escrito; PROV **b. is only skin deep** la belleza no es más que algo superficial ►► ***b. contest*** concurso *m* de belleza; ***b. parlour*** salón *m* de belleza; ***b. queen*** miss *f*; ***b. salon*** *or US* ***shop*** salón *m* de belleza; *Hum* ***b. sleep*** dosis *f inv* de sueño; **I need my b. sleep** necesito una cura de sueño, necesito dormir para estar como una rosa; ***b. spot*** *(on face)* lunar *m*; *(in country)* paraje *m* de gran belleza

(b) *(person)* belleza *f*

(c) *(object)* preciosidad *f*; **his new hi-fi's a b.** su nuevo equipo de alta fidelidad es una preciosidad *or* una monada; *Fam* **that was a b. of a goal!** ¡qué golazo más precioso!; *Fam* **he's got a b. of a black eye** tiene un ojo la mar de morado

(d) that's the b. of it eso es lo mejor; **the b. of the system is its simplicity** lo bueno *or* lo mejor del sistema es su simplicidad

2 *exclam Br Fam* **(you) b.!** ¡vaya maravilla!

beaux *pl of* **beau**

beaver ['bi:və(r)] *n* **(a)** *(animal)* castor *m*; IDIOM *Fam* **to work like a b.** trabajar como una hormiguita **(b)** *(fur)* (piel *f* de) castor *m* **(c)** *Vulg (woman's genitals) Esp* coño *m*, *Esp* conejo *m*, *Andes, RP* concha *f*, *Méx* panocha *f*

► **beaver away** *vi* afanarse *or* aplicarse (**at** en)

bebop ['bi:bɒp] *n Mus* bebop *m*

becalmed [bɪ'kɑ:md] *adj* **the ship lay b.** el barco estaba al pairo

became *pt of* **become**

because [bɪ'kɒz] **1** *conj* porque; **b. it's short, he thinks it's easy** como es corto se cree que es fácil; **it was all the more difficult b. he was sick** resultó aún más difícil porque estaba enfermo; **why? – just b.** ¿por qué? – porque sí; **why can't I go? – b. you can't!** ¿por qué no puedo ir? – porque no; **just b. you're my sister, it doesn't mean you can boss me about** el hecho de que seas mi hermana no significa que puedas darme órdenes

2 because of *prep* debido a, a causa de; **we couldn't move b. of the snow** no podíamos movernos a causa de la nieve; **I couldn't go to work b. of the subway strike** no pude ir a trabajar debido a la huelga de metro; **he's ineligible b. of his age** no tiene posibilidades de ser elegido por razones de edad; **we lost, and all b. of you!** hemos perdido, ¡y todo por tu culpa!; **it was all b. of a silly misunderstanding** todo se debió a un absurdo malentendido

béchamel [beɪʃə'mel] *n* **b. (sauce)** besamel *f*, bechamel *f*, *Col, CSur* salsa *f* blanca

beck [bek] *n* **to be at sb's b. and call** estar a (la entera) disposición de alguien; **she has him at her b. and call** lo tiene a su entera disposición

beckon ['bekən] **1** *vt* **to b. sb in** hacer a alguien una seña para que entre; **I beckoned them over** les hice señas para que se me acercaran; **he beckoned me to follow him** me hizo señas para que lo siguiera

2 *vi* **(a)** *(signal)* **to b. to sb** hacer una seña a alguien **(b)** *(attract, call)* **I can't stay, work beckons** no puedo quedarme, el trabajo me reclama; **the beach beckoned** la playa era una gran tentación; **the bright lights of the city beckoned** las luces de la ciudad atraían con su resplandor; **fame beckoned** la fama llamó a mi/su/*etc.* puerta

BECOME [bɪ'kʌm] (*pt* **became** [bɪ'keɪm], *pp* **become**) **1** *vi (boring, jealous, suspicious)* volverse; *(old, difficult, stronger)* hacerse; *(happy, sad, thin)* ponerse; **to b. angry** *esp Esp* enfadarse, *esp Am* enojarse; **to b. interested** interesarse; **to b. famous** hacerse famoso; **he became convinced of her innocence** se convenció de su inocencia; **it's becoming colder** *(weather)* está haciendo más frío; **it's becoming harder and harder** es *or* se hace cada vez más difícil; **to b. a teacher/doctor/member** hacerse profesor/médico/miembro; **he's going to b. a father** va a ser padre; **the firm became a part of our group fifteen years ago** la compañía entró a formar parte de *or* se incorporó a nuestro grupo hace quince años; **we became friends** nos hicimos amigos; **she became Britain's number one in 1999** se convirtió en el número uno británico en 1999; **to b. king** convertirse en rey; **it became clear that she had no intention of co-operating** quedó claro que no pensaba cooperar; **his motives only became known later** sus motivos sólo se supieron más tarde; **this is becoming a bit of a habit** esto se está convirtiendo en un hábito

2 *vt Formal (of clothes, colour)* sentar bien a; **such behaviour doesn't b. you** ese comportamiento no es propio *or* digno de ti

► **become of** *vt insep* **what will b. of him?** ¿qué va a ser de él?; **I don't know what has b. of her** no sé qué ha sido de ella

---

becoming [bɪ'kʌmɪŋ] *adj* **(a)** *(behaviour)* apropiado(a) **(b)** *(attractive)* **green looks very b. on her** le sienta muy bien el verde

becquerel ['bekərel] *n Phys* becquerel *m*

BEd [bi:'ed] *n Univ* (*abbr* **Bachelor of Education**) **(a)** *(qualification)* licenciatura *f* en ciencias de la educación **(b)** *(person)* licenciado(a) *m,f* en ciencias de la educación

bed [bed] **1** *n* **(a)** *(for sleeping)* cama *f*; **to be in b.** estar en la cama; **he was in b. by midnight** se había acostado antes de la medianoche; **he's in b. with (the) flu** está en cama con gripe; *Fam Fig* **to be in b. with sb** estar del lado de alguien; **to be good in b.** ser bueno(a) en la cama, portarse bien en la cama; **to get into b.** meterse en la cama, acostarse; **to get out of b.** levantarse; **did I get you out of b.?** ¿te he despertado?; IDIOM *Fam* **to have got out of b. on the wrong side** haberse levantado con el pie izquierdo; **to go to b.** irse a la cama, ir a acostarse; **to go to b. with sb** irse a la cama *or* acostarse con alguien; **to put** *or* **get the children to b.** acostar a los niños; **to make the b.** hacer la cama; **they made me up a b.** me prepararon una cama; IDIOM *Fam* **you've made your b., now you'll have to lie in it** el que siembra vientos recoge tempestades; **she took to her b. with flu** cayó en la cama con gripe ►► ***b. and board*** pensión *f* completa; ***b. and breakfast*** *(hotel)* = hostal familiar en el que el desayuno está incluido en el precio de la habitación; *(service)* habitación y desayuno; ***b. linen*** ropa *f* de cama

(b) *(bottom) (of river)* lecho *m*, cauce *m*; *(of lake, sea, ocean)* lecho *m*, fondo *m*

(c) *(of flowers)* macizo *m*; PROV **life is not a b. of roses** la vida no es un *Esp* lecho *or Am* mar de rosas

(d) *Geol* estrato *m*

(e) *Culin (of rice, lettuce)* base *f*, lecho *m*

(f) *Tech (of machine)* bancada *f*

(g) *Typ (of printing press)* patina *f*; *Br* **to put a newspaper to b.** cerrar la edición de un periódico

2 *vt* (*pt & pp* **bedded**) **(a)** *(embed)* asentar, fijar **(b)** *Fam (have sex with)* llevarse a la cama a

► **bed down** **1** *vt sep (children)* acostar, meter en la cama a

2 *vi* **to b. down (for the night)** acostarse

► **bed out** *vt sep (plants)* plantar *(en el exterior o al aire libre)*

bedazzle [bɪ'dæzəl] *vt (impress)* deslumbrar, impresionar

bedbath ['bedbɑ:θ] *n* = lavado que se practica a un enfermo postrado en cama

bedbug ['bedbʌg] *n* chinche *f*

bedchamber ['bedtʃeɪmbə(r)] *n Archaic* cámara *f*

bedclothes ['bedkləʊðz] *npl* ropa *f* de cama

bedcover ['bedkʌvə(r)] *n* colcha *f*

beddable ['bedəbəl] *adj Fam & Hum (attractive person)* **to be b.** estar bueno(a) *or Esp* macizo(a) *or RP* para el crimen

-bedded [bedɪd] *suffix* **single/twin-b. room** habitación individual/doble con dos camas

bedding ['bedɪŋ] *n* **(a)** *(sheets, blankets)* ropa *f* de cama **(b)** ***b. plant*** *(in gardening)* planta *f* de jardín

beddy-byes ['bedɪbaɪz] *n Fam* cama *f*; **come on kids, (time for) b.!** ¡vamos niños, un beso y a la cama!

bedeck [bɪ'dek] *vt Literary* engalanar (**with** con); **the balcony was bedecked with flowers** el balcón estaba engalanado con flores

bedevil [bɪ'devəl] (*pt & pp* **bedevilled**, *US* **bedeviled**) *vt* **to be bedevilled by problems** tener muchos problemas; **this is the kind of problem which has bedevilled the project from the start** éste es el tipo de problema que ha dificultado el proyecto desde el principio; **to be bedevilled by bad luck** tener la negra, estar maldito(a)

bedfellow ['bedfeləʊ] *n* IDIOM **they make strange bedfellows** forman una extraña pareja

bed-jacket ['beddʒækɪt] *n* mañanita *f (prenda)*

bedlam ['bedləm] *n* olla *f* de grillos, alboroto *m*; **it's absolute b. in town today!** la ciudad es hoy una auténtica olla de grillos

bedmate ['bedmeɪt] *n* compañero(a) *m,f* de cama

Bedouin ['bedʊɪn] **1** *n* beduino(a) *m,f*

2 *adj* beduino(a)

bedpan ['bedpæn] *n* cuña *f*

bedpost ['bedpəʊst] *n* pilar *m* de la cama; **between you, me and the b.** entre tú y yo, que quede entre nosotros

bedraggled [bɪ'dræɡəld] *adj* desaliñado(a) y empapado(a)

bed-rest ['bedrest] *n* reposo *m* en cama

bedridden ['bedrɪdən] *adj* **to be b.** estar postrado(a) en la cama

bedrock ['bedrɒk] *n* (**a**) *Geol* lecho *m* rocoso (**b**) *(of beliefs, faith)* base *f*, fondo *m*

bedroll ['bedrəʊl] *n* petate *m*

bedroom ['bedru:m] *n* (**a**) *(in house)* dormitorio *m*, habitación *f*, *Am* cuarto *m*, *CAm, Col, Méx* recámara *f* ►► *Fam Hum* ***b. eyes*** mirada *f* lasciva; ***b. farce*** *(play)* farsa *f* or comedia *f* de alcoba; ***b. suite*** *(furniture)* dormitorio *m* (**b**) *(in hotel)* habitación *f*, *Am* cuarto *m*, *CAm, Col, Méx* recámara *f*

-bedroomed ['bedru:md] *suffix* **two/three-b. house** casa de dos/tres dormitorios

Beds (*abbr* **Bedfordshire**) Bedfordshire

bedside ['bedsaɪd] *n* **at sb's b.** al lado de *or* junto a la cama de alguien ►► ***b. book*** libro *m* de cabecera; ***b. lamp*** lamparita *f* de noche; ***b. manner*** *(of doctor)* actitud *f* ante el paciente; ***b. table*** mesilla *f or* mesita *f* (de noche), *Andes* velador *m*, *Méx* buró *m*, *RP* mesa *f* de luz

bedsit ['bedsɪt], **bedsitter** ['bedsɪtə(r)] *n Br* cuarto *m* de alquiler ►► ***b. land*** = zona con muchos cuartos de alquiler

bedsitting-room [bed'sɪtɪŋru:m] *n Br Formal* cuarto *m* de alquiler

bedsock ['bedsɒk] *n* calcetín *m* para dormir

bedsore ['bedsɔ:(r)] *n* úlcera *f* de decúbito

bedspread ['bedspred] *n* colcha *f*

bedsprings ['bedsprɪŋz] *npl* somier *m (de muelles)*

bedstead ['bedsted] *n* (armazón *m or f* de la) cama *f*

bedtime ['bedtaɪm] *n* **it's b.!** ¡es hora de irse a la cama!; **what's your usual b.?** ¿a qué hora te sueles acostar?; **it's past my b.** ya debería estar acostado ►► ***b. story*** cuento *m (contado antes de acostarse)*

bed-wetting ['bedwetɪŋ] *n* = problema infantil de orinarse en la cama por las noches, *Spec* enuresis *f inv* (nocturna)

bee [bi:] *n* (**a**) *(insect)* abeja *f* ►► ***b. sting*** *(wound)* picadura *f* de abeja (**b**) *US (social event)* círculo *m* (social); **quilting/sewing b.** club *or* círculo de colchadura/costura

(**c**) IDIOMS *Fam* **you've been a busy (little) b.!** ¡has trabajado como una hormiguita!, *RP* ¡has trabajado de lo lindo!; *Fam* **to have a b. in one's bonnet about sth** estar obsesionado(a) con algo; *Br Fam* **he thinks he's the b.'s knees** se cree el rey del mambo

Beeb [bi:b] *n Br Fam Hum* **the B.** la BBC

beech [bi:tʃ] *n (wood)* (madera *f* de) haya *f*; **b. (tree)** haya *f* ►► ***b. grove*** hayal *m*, hayedo *m*; ***b. mast*** hayucos *mpl (que han caído del árbol)*

beechnut ['bi:tʃnʌt] *n* hayuco *m*

bee-eater ['bi:i:tə(r)] *n* abejaruco *m*

beef [bi:f] **1** *n* (**a**) *(meat)* (carne *f* de) vaca *f or Am* res *f* ►► *Br* ***b. olive*** = picadillo enrollado en un filete fino; ***b. stew*** guiso *m* de vaca; ***b. stroganoff*** ternera *f* strogonoff; *Br* ***b. tea*** consomé *m or* caldo *m* de carne; *Br* ***b. tomato*** tomate *m* grande, *Méx* jitomate *m* bola

(**b**) *Fam (strength)* **to have plenty of b.** ser fornido(a), *Esp* estar cachas; **give it some b.!** ¡un poco más de esfuerzo!

(**c**) *Fam (complaint)* queja *f*; **what's your b.?** ¿de qué te quejas?; **my b. is with him** mi problema es con él

2 *vi Fam (complain)* quejarse (**about** de)

► **beef up** *vt sep Fam (forces, resources)* reforzar; *(legislation)* fortalecer; **I'm going to b. up the report with some statistics** voy a darle más fuerza al informe con algunas estadísticas

beefburger ['bi:fbɜ:ɡə(r)] *n* hamburguesa *f*

beefcake ['bi:fkeɪk] *n Fam* tipos *mpl* musculosos *or Esp* cachas

Beefeater ['bi:fi:tə(r)] *n* = guardia de la Torre de Londres

beefsteak ['bi:fsteɪk] *n* filete *m*, bistec *m*, *RP* bife *m* ►► *US* ***b. tomato*** tomate *m or Méx* jitomate *m* grande

beefy ['bi:fɪ] *adj Fam (muscular)* fornido(a), *Esp* muy cachas

beehive ['bi:haɪv] *n* (**a**) *(for bees)* colmena *f* (**b**) **b. (hairdo)** moño *m* italiano

beekeeper ['bi:ki:pə(r)] *n* apicultor(ora) *m,f*, colmenero(a) *m,f*

beekeeping ['bi:ki:pɪŋ] *n* apicultura *f*

beeline ['bi:laɪn] *n* IDIOM *Fam* **to make a b. for sb/sth** ir directamente hacia alguien/algo

Beelzebub [bɪ'elzɪbʌb] *pr n* Belcebú

beemer ['bi:mə(r)] *n Fam (BMW car)* BMW *m*

been *pp of* **be**

beep [bi:p] **1** *n (sound)* pitido *m*

2 *vt* (**a**) *(sound)* **to b. the** *or* **one's horn** tocar la bocina *or* el claxon, pitar (**b**) *(page)* **to b. sb** llamar a alguien al buscapersonas *or Esp* busca *or Méx* localizador *or RP* radiomensaje

3 *vi* pitar

beeper ['bi:pə(r)] *n (pager)* buscapersonas *m inv*, *Esp* busca *m*, *Méx* localizador *m*, *RP* radiomensaje *m*

beer [bɪə(r)] *n* cerveza *f*; **to go for a b.** ir a tomar una cerveza; IDIOM **it's not all b. and skittles** no todo es de color de rosa ►► *US Fam* ***b. bash*** fiesta *f* (a base) de cerveza, *Esp* botellón *m*; *Fam* ***b. belly*** barrigón *m*, panza *f (de beber cerveza)*; *US Fam* ***b. bust*** fiesta *f* (a base) de cerveza, *Esp* botellón *m*; ***b. garden*** terraza *f* (interior) de un bar; ***b. glass*** jarra *f* de cerveza; *Fam* ***b. gut*** barrigón *m*, panza *f (de beber cerveza)*; ***b. mat*** posavasos *m inv* (de cartón); ***b. tent*** = carpa abierta con establecimiento de bebidas

beery ['bɪərɪ] *adj (smell, breath, taste)* a cerveza

beeswax ['bi:zwæks] *n* cera *f* (de abeja); *US Fam* **it's none of your b.!** ¡a ti nadie te ha dado vela en este entierro!, ¡a ti qué te importa!

beet [bi:t] *n* (**a**) *(sugar beet)* remolacha *f* (azucarera) ►► ***b. sugar*** azúcar *m or f* de remolacha (**b**) *US (beetroot)* remolacha *f*, *Méx* betabel *m*

beetle[1] ['bi:təl] **1** *n* (**a**) *(insect)* escarabajo *m* (**b**) **(Volkswagen) B.** (Volkswagen) Escarabajo *m*

2 *vi Fam* escarabajear, pulular; **to b. off** salir pitando, largarse

beetle[2] *vi (cliff)* colgar, descollar

beetle-browed ['bi:təlbraʊd] *adj (with bushy eyebrows)* cejudo(a); *(scowling)* ceñudo(a)

beetroot ['bi:tru:t] *n Br* remolacha *f*, *Méx* betabel *m*; IDIOM *Fam* **to go** *or* **turn b.** ponerse colorado(a) *or* rojo(a) como un tomate

beezer ['bi:zə(r)] *n Fam (nose)* napias *fpl*

befall [bɪ'fɔ:l] (*pt* **befell** [bɪ'fel], *pp* **befallen** [bɪ'fɔ:lən]) *Literary* **1** *vt* sobrevenir a; **no harm will b. her** no le sobrevendrá ningún mal, no le acontecerá mal alguno

2 *vi* sobrevenir, acontecer; **whatever may b.** lo que pueda acontecer

befit [bɪ'fɪt] (*pt & pp* **befitted**) *vt* **such behaviour hardly befits a man of the cloth** esa conducta no se corresponde con la de un ministro del Señor; **as befits a king** como corresponde a un rey; **in a manner befitting a statesman** de manera acorde con la dignidad de un estadista

befitting [bɪ'fɪtɪŋ] *adj* digno(a); **with b. modesty** con la debida modestia

befog [bɪ'fɒg] (*pt & pp* **befogged**) *vt (confuse)* ofuscar

BEFORE [bɪ'fɔ:(r)] **1** *prep* (**a**) *(with time)* antes de; **b. Christmas** antes de Navidad; **I got here b. you** he llegado antes que tú; **shut the door b. leaving** cierra la puerta antes de salir; **the day b. the battle** la víspera de la batalla; **b. that,...** antes (de eso)...; **we have a lot of work b. us** tenemos un montón de trabajo delante de nosotros; **he was old b. his time** envejeció prematuramente; **b. long** dentro de poco; **you ought to have finished b. now** ya tendrías que haber acabado

(**b**) *(with place)* ante, delante de; **b. my very eyes** ante mis propios ojos; **this lady is b. me (in the queue)** esta señora va delante de mí; **the school is a mile b. the crossroads** el colegio está una milla antes del cruce; **the road stretched out b. them** la carretera se extendía ante ellos; **to appear b. the judge** comparecer ante el juez; **the question b. us is whether or not she is guilty** la cuestión que nos ocupa es su culpabilidad o su inocencia; **A comes b. B** A va antes *or* delante de B

(**c**) *(in importance)* **she puts her family b. everything else** para ella su familia es lo primero; **profit comes b. all else for this firm** esta empresa antepone los beneficios a cualquier otra cosa

2 *adv* (**a**) *(with time)* antes; **two days b.** dos días antes; **the day/year b.** el día/año anterior; **the evening b.** la tarde anterior; **I have seen him b.** lo he visto antes; **I've told you b.** ya te lo he dicho (otras veces); **I told him to stop singing, but he just carried on as b.** le dije que parara de cantar, pero él siguió haciéndolo

(**b**) *(in space)* **this page and the one b.** esta página y la anterior

3 *conj* antes de que; **come and see me b. you leave** ven a verme antes de marcharte; **b. I forget, will you...?** antes de que se me olvide, ¿podrías...?; **give it to her b. she cries** dáselo antes de que empiece a llorar; **it was ages b. they finally left** tardaron *or Am* se demoraron siglos en marcharse; **shut up b. I call your father!** ¡cállate o llamaré a tu padre!; **I will die b. I let you have my job** antes morirme que dejarte mi trabajo; **b. you know it, he'll be telling** US **what to do!** ¡cualquier día de éstos empezará a darnos órdenes!

beforehand [bɪ'fɔ:hænd] *adv (in advance)* de antemano, con antelación; **two hours b.** con dos horas de antelación, dos horas antes; **I must tell you b. that...** debo prevenirte de que...

before-tax [bɪ'fɔːtæks] *adj (income)* bruto(a); **b. income** renta bruta

befriend [bɪ'frend] *vt* hacerse amigo(a) de, trabar amistad con; **I was befriended by a stray dog** un perro callejero se hizo amigo mío

befuddled [bɪ'fʌdəld] *adj (confused)* aturdido(a); **to be b. (with)** estar aturdido(a) (por); **his mind was b. with drink** su mente estaba trastornada por la bebida

beg [beg] *(pt & pp* **begged**) **1** *vt* (**a**) *(solicit as charity)* mendigar, pedir; **she begged money from the passers-by** pedía limosna a los transeúntes; IDIOM **to b., borrow or steal sth** conseguir algo a cualquier precio *or* cueste lo que cueste

(**b**) *(ask for, plead with)* **to b. sb to do sth** rogar *or* suplicar a alguien que haga algo; **to b. a favour of sb** pedir un favor a alguien; **to b. forgiveness** pedir *or* implorar perdón; *Formal* **please, I b. you!** ¡por favor, se lo ruego!; **I b. your pardon** *(I apologize)* perdón; *(what did you say?)* ¿cómo dice?

(**c**) *Formal (request politely)* **I b. to differ** me veo obligado a discrepar, discrepo

(**d**) IDIOM **to b. the question: his proposal begs the question of whether we need any change at all** habría que preguntarse si realmente hace falta el cambio que lleva implícito su propuesta; **her definition of mental illness begs the question of what normal behaviour is** su definición de enfermedad mental nos llevaría a preguntarnos qué es en realidad el comportamiento normal

2 *vi* (**a**) *(solicit charity)* **to b. (for sth)** *(money, food)* mendigar (algo); **they live by begging** viven de la mendicidad *or* de las limosnas

(**b**) *(ask, plead)* **to b. (for sth)** *(for help, a chance)* pedir *or* rogar (algo); **to b. for mercy/forgiveness** implorar clemencia/perdón

(**c**) IDIOMS *Fam* **there's a piece of cake going begging** queda un trozo de tarta más solo que la una, *RP* hay un pedazo de torta muriéndose de frío; *Fam* **these jobs are going begging** estos trabajos los hay a patadas

▸ **beg off** *vi* disculparse *or* excusarse por no ir

> En inglés culto o elevado, y especialmente en inglés americano, **beg** puede ir seguido de **that** más un verbo en subjuntivo (ver el panel SUBJUNCTIVE):
> **we begged that they give us more time**
> *pedimos que les dieran más tiempo*
> Lo mismo también podría decirse de las siguientes formas:
> **we begged to be given more time**
> **we begged them to give us more time**

began *pt of* **begin**

beget [bɪ'get] *(pt* **begot** [bɪ'gɒt], *pp* **begotten** [bɪ'gɒtən]) *vt Formal* (**a**) *(father)* engendrar (**b**) *(cause)* generar, engendrar; **poverty begets crime** la pobreza genera delincuencia

beggar ['begə(r)] **1** *n* (**a**) *(person who begs)* mendigo(a) *m,f*; PROV **beggars can't be choosers** a falta de pan, buenas son (las) tortas (**b**) *Br Fam (person, fellow)* **poor b.!** ¡pobre diablo!; **lucky b.!** ¡qué suertudo(a)!

2 *vt* **to b. belief** ser difícil de creer; **to b. description** *(be impossible to describe)* resultar indescriptible; *(of something bad)* no tener nombre

beggarly ['begəlɪ] *adj* mísero(a)

beggar-my-neighbour ['begəmaɪ'neɪbə(r)] *n (card game)* = juego de naipes consistente en quedarse con todas las cartas, ≃ guerrilla *f*; *Fig* **b. policies/competition** política/competencia para arruinar al rival

beggary ['begərɪ] *n* mendicidad *f*, miseria *f*

begging ['begɪŋ] *n* mendicidad *f* ▸▸ ***b. bowl*** platillo *m* de las limosnas; *Fig* **many companies have had to approach the government with a b. bowl** muchas empresas se han visto obligadas a mendigar subvenciones al gobierno; ***b. letter*** carta *f* de súplica *(pidiendo dinero)*

BEGIN [bɪ'gɪn] *(pt* **began** [bɪ'gæn], *pp* **begun** [bɪ'gʌn]) **1** *vt* empezar, comenzar; **to b. a new job** empezar en un trabajo nuevo; **to b. to do sth, to b. doing sth** empezar *or* comenzar a hacer algo; **it's beginning to look like we won't finish on time** cada vez más parece que no acabaremos a tiempo; **I couldn't (even) b. to describe...** no sé ni cómo empezar a describir...; **you can't (even) b. to imagine how hard it was** no te puedes ni imaginar remotamente lo difícil que fue

2 *vi* empezar, comenzar; **there's so much to tell you, I don't know where to b.** tengo tantas cosas que contarte, que no sé por dónde empezar; **the hottest June since records began** el junio más caluroso desde que se efectúan mediciones; **to b. again** comenzar de nuevo, volver a empezar; **he began as a stagehand** empezó como tramoyista; **it began as a joke, but ended in tragedy** comenzó siendo una broma, pero acabó en tragedia; **let's b. at the beginning** comencemos por el principio; **to b. by doing sth** empezar por hacer algo; **he was nice enough to b. with, but...** al principio era bastante simpático, pero...; **it was broken to b. with** estaba roto desde el principio; **to b. with,...** *(firstly)* para empezar,...

beginner [bɪ'gɪnə(r)] *n* principiante *mf*; **a b.'s course** un curso de *or* para principiantes ▸▸ ***b.'s luck*** la suerte del principiante

beginning [bɪ'gɪnɪŋ] *n* (**a**) *(in time)* principio *m*, comienzo *m*; **in** *or* **at the b.** al principio; **at the b. of the year/month** a principios de año/mes; **from the b.** desde el principio; **from b. to end** de principio a fin; **the b. of the end** el principio del fin

(**b**) *(early part, stage)* principio *m*, comienzo *m*; **I enjoyed the b. of the movie/book** me gustó el principio de la película/del libro; **the b. of the world** el principio *or* comienzo del mundo; **I have the beginnings of a cold** tengo un principio de resfriado

(**c**) *(origin)* **the first beginnings of civilization** los orígenes de la civilización; **the problem has its beginnings in...** el problema tiene su origen en...

begone [bɪ'gɒn] *exclam Literary or Hum* ¡fuera (de aquí)!

begonia [bɪ'gəʊnɪə] *n* begonia *f*

begot *pt of* **beget**

begotten *pp of* **beget**

begrudge [bɪ'grʌdʒ] *vt* (**a**) *(resent)* **I don't b. him the money** no me duele dejarle el dinero; **he begrudges every minute spent away from his family** le pesa cada minuto que no ha pasado al lado de su familia; **I b. spending so much** me duele gastar tanto (**b**) *(envy)* **I don't b. him his success** no le envidio su éxito

begrudgingly [bɪ'grʌdʒɪŋlɪ] *adv (unwillingly)* a regañadientes

beguile [bɪ'gaɪl] *vt* (**a**) *(enchant)* seducir (**b**) *(deceive)* engañar; **to b. sb into doing sth** engatusar a alguien para que haga algo; **to b. sb with promises** encandilar a alguien con promesas (**c**) *(pass pleasantly)* **to b. (away) the hours** dejar pasar las horas plácidamente

beguiling [bɪ'gaɪlɪŋ] *adj* seductor(ora)

beguine [bɪ'giːn] *n* beguine *m*

begun *pp of* **begin**

behalf [bɪ'hɑːf] *n* **on** *or US* **in b. of sb, on** *or US* **in sb's b.** en nombre de alguien; **I'm here on b. of the president** estoy aquí en representación del presidente; **she accepted the award on his b.** aceptó el galardón en su nombre; **your lawyer acts on your b.** tu abogado te representa; **I'm ringing on b. of a friend** llamo de parte de un amigo; **on b. of all of us, I'd like to say...** en nombre de todos, me gustaría decir que...; **don't worry on my b.** no te preocupes por mí

behave [bɪ'heɪv] **1** *vi* (**a**) *(act) (person)* portarse, comportarse; **why are you behaving like this?** ¿por qué te portas así?; **to know how to b.** saber comportarse; **to b. well/badly** portarse bien/mal; **to b. oddly/suspiciously** comportarse *or* actuar de forma extraña/sospechosa; **what a way to b.!** ¡menudo comportamiento!

(**b**) *(act properly)* portarse bien, comportarse; **will you b.!** ¡compórtate!

(**c**) *(function) (car, machine)* funcionar

2 *vt* **to b. oneself** comportarse, portarse bien; **b. yourself!** ¡compórtate (como es debido)!

behaviour, *US* **behavior** [bɪ'heɪvjə(r)] *n* (**a**) *(of person, animal)* comportamiento *m*, conducta *f*; **their b. was disgraceful** tuvieron un comportamiento penoso; **her b. towards her mother was unforgivable** su comportamiento con su madre era imperdonable; **to be on one's best b.** portarse *or* comportarse muy bien

(**b**) *(of atom, chemical, light)* comportamiento *m*

behavioural, *US* **behavioral** [bɪ'heɪvjərəl] *adj* del comportamiento, de la conducta ▸▸ ***b. psychology*** psicología *f* conductual

behaviourism, *US* **behaviorism** [bɪ'heɪvjərɪzəm] *n Psy* conductismo *m*

behaviourist, *US* **behaviorist** [bɪ'heɪvjərɪst] *Psy* **1** *n* conductista *mf*, behaviorista *mf*

2 *adj* conductista, behaviorista

behead [bɪ'hed] *vt* decapitar

beheading [bɪ'hedɪŋ] *n* decapitación *f*

beheld *pt & pp of* **behold**

behest [bɪ'hest] *n Formal* orden *f*, mandato *m*; **at sb's b., at the b. of sb** por orden *or* a instancias de alguien

BEHIND [bɪ'haɪnd] **1** *prep* detrás de, tras; **to be b. sb** *(situated)* estar detrás de alguien; *(less advanced)* ir por detrás de alguien; *(support)* respaldar a alguien; **close the door b. you** cierra la puerta cuando salgas *or* al salir; **to follow close b. sb** seguir de cerca a alguien; **look b. you** mira detrás de ti; **I have five years' experience as a teacher b. me** tengo cinco años de experiencia como profesora a mis espaldas; **to be b. schedule** ir atrasado(a); **she's been able to put her divorce b. her** ha conseguido dejar atrás su divorcio; **let's put it all b. us** olvidemos todo esto; **she's ten minutes b. the leaders** *(in race)* está a diez minutos de la cabeza de la carrera; **Brazil are a goal b. Italy with a minute to go** Brasil pierde por un gol ante Italia cuando queda un minuto; **to be b. the times** no andar con los tiempos; **the reasons b. sth** los motivos de algo; **the woman b. their success** la mujer detrás de su éxito; **what's b. all this?** ¿qué hay detrás de todo esto?

2 *adv* detrás; **to look b.** mirar hacia atrás; **from b.** *(to attack)* por la espalda; **the German wasn't far b.** el alemán no iba mucho más atrás; **to be b. with one's work/with the rent** estar atrasado(a) en el trabajo/en el pago del alquiler; **they are only three points b.** *(in contest)* están a sólo tres puntos; **they went a goal b. after ten minutes** encajaron el 1 a 0 a los diez minutos; **the rest of us followed on b.** el resto seguimos detrás; **to leave sth b.** dejarse algo; *Fig* **I used to be an alcoholic, but I've left all that b.** era un alcohólico, pero todo eso ha quedado ya atrás; **to stay** *or* **remain b.** quedarse; **you go ahead, I'll walk b.** adelántate, yo te seguiré

3 *n Fam (buttocks)* trasero *m*

behindhand [bɪ'haɪndhænd] *adv* **to be b. with one's work/with the rent** estar atrasado(a) en el trabajo/en el pago del alquiler

behind-the-scenes [bɪ'haɪndðə'si:nz] *adj* entre bastidores, oculto(a); **a b. look at politics/the world of newspapers** una mirada a la cara desconocida *or* oculta de la política/del mundo de la prensa

behold [bɪ'həʊld] *(pt & pp* **beheld** [bɪ'held]) *Literary* **1** *vt* contemplar; **he was a sight to b.** era digno de ver

2 *vi* **b.!** ¡atención!, ¡mira!; **lo and b.!** ¡héteme aquí!, ¡mira por dónde!

beholden [bɪ'həʊldən] *adj Formal* **to be b. to sb** estar en deuda con alguien; **I don't want to be b. to anyone** no quiero tener obligaciones con nadie

beholder [bɪ'həʊldə(r)] *n* observador(ora) *m,f*

behove [bɪ'həʊv], *US* **behoove** [bɪ'hu:v] *vt Formal or Old-fashioned* **it behoves you to be respectful to your elders** es tu deber *or* has de respetar a tus mayores; **it ill behoves her to criticize** más le conviene no criticar

beige [beɪʒ] **1** *n* beige *m inv*, *Esp* beis *m inv*

2 *adj* beige, *Esp* beis

Beijing [beɪ'ʒɪŋ] *n* Pekín

being ['bi:ɪŋ] *n* **(a)** *(creature)* ser *m* **(b)** *(existence)* **to bring sth into b.** crear algo, hacer que algo vea la luz; **to come into b.** nacer; **the company is no longer in b.** la empresa ya no existe **(c)** *(essential nature)* ser *m*; **her whole b. rebelled at the thought** todo su ser se rebelaba contra la mera idea; **with all my b.** con todo mi corazón

Beirut [beɪ'ru:t] *n* Beirut

bejewelled [bɪ'dʒu:əld] *adj* enjoyado(a)

belabour, *US* **belabor** [bɪ'leɪbə(r)] *vt* **(a)** *(beat)* apalear **(b)** *(criticize)* vapulear, poner como un trapo; **to b. sb with insults** poner verde a alguien

Belarus [belə'ru:s], **Belorussia** [beləʊ'rʌʃə], **Byelorussia** [bɪeləʊ'rʌʃə] *n* Bielorrusia

belated [bɪ'leɪtɪd] *adj* tardío(a); **wishing you a b. happy birthday** deseándote, con retraso *or Am* demora, un feliz cumpleaños

belatedly [bɪ'leɪtɪdlɪ] *adv* tardíamente, con retraso *or Am* demora

belay [bɪ'leɪ] **1** *n (in mountaineering) (rope attached to rock)* amarre *m* de seguridad

2 *vi (in mountaineering)* **we belayed across the mountain** cruzamos la montaña con la cuerda asegurada a la pared

belaying pin [bɪ'leɪɪŋ'pɪn] *n Naut* cabilla *f* de amarre

belch [beltʃ] **1** *n (burp)* eructo *m*; **to give a b.** eructar

2 *vt (smoke, flames)* escupir

3 *vi (person)* eructar

▸**belch forth, belch out 1** *vt sep (smoke, flames)* escupir

2 *vi* salir despedido(a)

beleaguer [bɪ'li:gə(r)] *vt (harass)* asediar, acosar

beleaguered [bɪ'li:gəd] *adj (city, army)* sitiado(a), asediado(a); *(government)* acosado(a); *(project)* bloqueado(a); *(person)* atormentado(a)

Belfast ['belfa:st] *n* Belfast

belfry ['belfrɪ] *n* campanario *m*

Belgian ['beldʒən] **1** *n* belga *mf*

2 *adj* belga

Belgium ['beldʒəm] *n* Bélgica

Belgrade [bel'greɪd] *n* Belgrado

belie [bɪ'laɪ] *vt* **(a)** *(contradict)* contradecir **(b)** *(give false idea of)* **his experience is belied by his youthful looks** su experiencia queda enmascarada por su apariencia juvenil; **her youthful figure belied her age** su figura juvenil no reflejaba su edad

belief [bɪ'li:f] *n* **(a)** *(conviction)* creencia *f*; **in the b. that...** en el convencimiento de que...; **in the mistaken b. that...** creyendo equivocadamente que...; **it is my b. that...** estoy convencido(a) de que...; **it is beyond b.** es imposible de creer

(b) *(confidence)* confianza *f*, fe *f*; **to have b. in oneself** tener confianza en uno(a) mismo(a)

(c) *(religious faith)* creencias *fpl*, fe *f*; **b. in God** fe en Dios; **people of all beliefs and of none** personas de variadas creencias (religiosas) y sin ellas

believable [bɪ'li:vəbəl] *adj* verosímil, creíble

BELIEVE [bɪ'li:v] **1** *vt* creer; **I b. (that) I am right** creo no equivocarme; **her name's Joan, I b.** creo que su nombre es Joan; **I b. him to be alive** creo que está vivo; **he believes himself to be right** se cree que tiene razón; **she is believed to be here** se cree que está aquí; **if the opinion polls are to be believed...** si hacemos caso a las encuestas...; **I don't b. a word of it** no me creo (ni) una palabra; **you won't** *or* **you'll never b. who phoned last night** ¿a que no te imaginas quién llamó anoche?; **I could never b. such a thing of him** no me creo que pueda ser capaz de eso; **the remaining passengers are missing, believed dead** el resto de los pasajeros continúan desaparecidos, temiéndose por sus vidas; **if you b. that, you'll b. anything!** ¡hace falta ser ingenuo para creerse eso!, ¡cualquiera se lo cree!; **I'll b. it when I see it** ¡eso tengo que verlo con mis propios ojos!; IDIOM **I'll b. you (though thousands wouldn't)** si tú lo dices; **I b. not** creo que no; **I b. so** así lo creo, creo que sí; **b. it or not** aunque no te lo creas; **b. you me!** ¡créeme!; **you'd better b. it!** ¡ya lo creo que sí!; **I don't b. it!** ¡no me lo puedo creer!; **don't you b. it!** ¡no te lo creas!; **I can well b. it** no me extrañaría nada; **I couldn't b. my luck** ¡qué suerte más increíble tuve!; **I could scarcely b. my eyes/ears** no podía creer lo que veían mis ojos/lo que estaba oyendo; **would you b. it** *or* **who would have believed it, she's joined the Communist Party** aunque parezca increíble, se ha afiliado al Partido Comunista; **let's make b. (that) we're on a desert island** hagamos como que estamos en una isla desierta

2 *vi* **(a)** *(have faith)* creer; **to b. in sth** creer en algo; **to b. in God** creer en Dios; **to b. in sb** *(have confidence)* creer en alguien, tener fe en alguien; **to b. in oneself** tener confianza en uno(a) mismo(a)

(b) *(be in favour)* **to b. in sth** ser partidario(a) de algo; **I don't b. in making promises** no soy partidario de las promesas

believer [bɪ'li:və(r)] *n* **(a)** *(religious person)* creyente *mf* **(b)** *(supporter)* **to be a great b. in sth** ser un(a) gran partidario(a) de algo

Belisha beacon [bə'li:ʃə'bi:kən] *n Br* = farola intermitente junto a un paso de peatones

belittle [bɪ'lɪtəl] *vt* menospreciar, restar importancia a; **to b. oneself** restarse importancia

belittling [bɪ'lɪtlɪŋ] *adj* desdeñoso(a), despectivo(a)

Belize [be'li:z] *n* Belice

Belizean [be'li:zɪən] **1** *n* beliceño(a) *m,f*

2 *adj* beliceño(a)

bell [bel] **1** *n* **(a)** *(of church)* campana *f*; *(handbell)* campanilla *f*; *(on door, bicycle)* timbre *m*; *(on cat, hat)* cascabel *m*; *(on cow)* cencerro *m*; **to ring the b.** *(on door)* llamar al timbre ▸▸ ***b. buoy*** boya *f* de campana; ***b. jar*** campana *f* de vidrio *or Esp* cristal; ***b. pull*** tirador *m* (de la campanilla); ***b. push*** (botón *m* del) timbre *m*; ***b. tent*** tienda *f* (de campaña) cónica *or* redonda, *Am* carpa *f* cónica *or* redonda; ***b. tower*** (torre *f* del) campanario *m*

(b) *Br Fam (telephone call)* **to give sb a b.** dar un telefonazo *or Méx* echar un fonazo a alguien

(c) *US* ***b. pepper*** pimiento *m* (morrón)

(d) *Naut* **it sounded four/eight bells** dio cuatro/ocho campanadas

(e) IDIOMS **saved by the b.** salvado por la campana *or* por los pelos; *Fam* **and the same to you with bells on** y tú más, *Esp* me rebota (y en tu culo explota); **a model with bells and whistles** un modelo de lo más completo

2 *vt* IDIOM **to b. the cat** ponerle el cascabel al gato

3 *vi (stag)* bramar

belladonna [belə'dɒnə] *n* (a) *(plant)* belladona *f* (b) *(poison)* atropina *f*

bell-bottomed ['bel'bɒtəmd] *adj (trousers)* acampanado(a), de campana

bell-bottoms ['belbɒtəmz] *npl* pantalones *mpl* de campana; **a pair of b.** unos pantalones de campana

bellboy ['belbɔɪ] *n* botones *m inv*

belle [bel] *n* bella *f*, belleza *f*; **the b. of the ball** la reina de la fiesta

belles-lettres [bel'letrə] *npl* (bellas) letras *fpl*, literatura *f*

bell-flower ['belflaʊə(r)] *n* campanilla *f*, campánula *f*

bellhop ['belhɒp] *n US* botones *m inv*

bellicose ['belɪkəʊs] *adj* belicoso(a)

belligerence [bə'lɪdʒərəns] *n* beligerancia *f*

belligerent [bə'lɪdʒərənt] 1 *n* contendiente *m*

2 *adj* (a) *(aggressive)* belicoso(a), agresivo(a) (b) *(at war)* beligerante

belligerently [bə'lɪdʒərəntlɪ] *adv* con tono beligerante, agresivamente

bellow ['beləʊ] 1 *n (of bull)* mugido *m*, bramido *m*; *(of elephant)* barrito *m*, bramido *m*; *(of person)* bramido *m*, rugido *m*, berrido *m*

2 *vt* **to b. (out) sth** *(order)* ordenar algo vociferando *or* a gritos; *(song)* cantar algo a voz en grito

3 *vi* bramar; **to b. at sb** *(with rage)* gritarle *or* vociferarle a alguien; **he bellowed with pain** gritaba de dolor; **the crowd bellowed with laughter** la multitud lanzaba sonoras carcajadas

bellows ['beləʊz] *npl* (a) *(for fire, furnace)* fuelle *m*; **a pair of b.** un fuelle (b) *(for accordion, organ)* fuelles *mpl* (c) *(on camera)* fuelle *m*

bellringer ['belrɪŋə(r)] *n* campanero(a) *m,f*

bellringing ['belrɪŋɪŋ] *n (hobby)* campanología *f*

bellwether ['belweθə(r)] *n* (a) *(sheep)* = carnero con cencerro que guía al rebaño (b) *(leader)* cabecilla *mf*; **the b. of the recovering economy** la punta de lanza *or* el motor de la recuperación económica

belly ['belɪ] *n* (a) *(stomach)* vientre *m*, barriga *f*, *Chile* guata *f*; **to have a full/an empty b.** tener la barriga llena/vacía; IDIOM *Fam* **to go b. up** *(company)* irse a pique ►► *Fam* ***b. button*** ombligo *m*; ***b. dance*** danza *f* del vientre; ***b. flop:*** **to do a b. flop** darse un panzazo *or* planchazo; ***b. landing*** *(in plane)* aterrizaje *m* de panza *or* sin el tren; ***b. laugh*** sonora carcajada *f*

(b) *Culin* ***b. pork*** falda *f* de cerdo

(c) *(of plane, ship)* panza *f*; *(of sail)* seno *m*

► **belly out** *vi* hinchar, inflar

bellyache ['belɪeɪk] *Fam* 1 *n* dolor *m* de barriga

2 *vi (complain)* rezongar, quejarse, *Méx* repelar (**about** de)

belly-dance ['belɪdɑːns] *vi* bailar la danza del vientre

belly-flop ['belɪflɒp] (*pt & pp* **belly-flopped**) *vi* darse un panzazo *or* planchazo

bellyful ['belɪfʊl] *n* IDIOM *Fam* **to have had a b. (of sth)** estar hasta la coronilla (de algo)

belong [bɪ'lɒŋ] *vi* (a) **to b. to** *(be property of)* pertenecer a; **that book belongs to me** este libro es mío *or* me pertenece; **that book belongs to Jane** ese libro pertenece a Jane *or* es de Jane; **who does this pullover b. to?** ¿de quién es este suéter?; **to b. to the Crown** *(land)* pertenecer a *or* ser propiedad de la corona

(b) *(be member)* **to b. to** *(club)* pertenecer a, ser socio(a) de; *(party)* pertenecer a, estar afiliado(a) a; *(union)* estar afiliado(a) a, formar parte de; **it belongs to the cod family** pertenece a la familia del bacalao

(c) *(have a proper place)* ir; **to put sth back where it belongs** devolver algo a su sitio; **go back home where you b.** vuelve al lugar del que procedes *or* vienes; **the saucepans don't b. in that cupboard** las ollas no van en esa alacena; **these gloves b. together** estos guantes van juntos; **she belongs in another era** es de otra época; **these issues b. in a court of law** estos asuntos le corresponden a un tribunal de justicia

(d) *(fit in)* **I feel I b. here** siento que éste es mi sitio; **to feel that one doesn't b.** sentirse un(a) extraño(a); **he belongs in teaching** lo suyo es la enseñanza *or* docencia

belonging [bɪ'lɒŋɪŋ] *n* **to have a sense of b.** sentirse (como) en casa

belongings [bɪ'lɒŋɪŋz] *npl* pertenencias *fpl*; **personal b.** efectos personales

Belorussia = **Belarus**

Belorussian [beləʊ'rʌʃən], **Byelorussian** [bɪeləʊ'rʌʃən] 1 *n* (a) *(person)* bielorruso(a) *m,f* (b) *(language)* bielorruso *m*

2 *adj* bielorruso(a)

beloved [bɪ'lʌvɪd] 1 *n Literary* amado(a) *m,f*; **dearly b., we are gathered here today...** queridísimos hermanos, nos hemos reunido hoy aquí...

2 *adj* (a) *(person)* amado(a), querido(a); *(thing)* adorado(a); **my b. father** mi querido padre (b) [bɪ'lʌvd] **he was b. by** *or* **of all his friends** lo querían todos sus amigos

BELOW [bɪ'ləʊ] 1 *prep* (a) *(physically)* debajo de; **they tunnelled b. the fence** hicieron un túnel por debajo de la valla; **the houses b. us seemed small** las casas allá abajo se veían pequeñas; **the sun disappeared b. the horizon** el sol desapareció por el horizonte; **he appears b. me on the list** está por debajo de mí en la lista; **b. (the) ground** bajo tierra; **b. the knee** por debajo de la rodilla; **b. sea level** por debajo del nivel del mar; **b. the surface** bajo la superficie

(b) *(with numbers)* por debajo de; **unemployment is b. 10 percent** el desempleo está por debajo del 10 por ciento; **a score b. 50 is poor** un resultado de menos de 50 es insuficiente; **children b. the age of ten** niños menores de diez años; **to be b. average** estar por debajo de la media; **children of b. average ability** niños de un nivel de aptitud inferior; **10 (degrees) b. zero** 10 (grados) bajo cero

(c) *(in classification, importance, rank)* **they finished b. us in the league** acabaron por detrás de nosotros en la liga; **he was in the year b. me (at school)** iba al curso posterior al mío; **I am b. him in rank** estoy por debajo suyo en rango

2 *adv* (a) *(physically)* abajo; **the houses b. seemed small** las casas allá abajo se veían pequeñas; **on the floor b.** en el piso de abajo; **ring the number b.** llame al número que aparece abajo; **to go down b.** *(on ship)* bajar *(a una cubierta inferior)*; **see b.** *(on document)* ver más abajo *or* adelante

(b) *(with numbers)* **children aged ten and b.** niños de diez años para abajo; **a score of 50 or b. is poor** un resultado de menos de 50 es insuficiente; **it's 10 degrees b.** hace 10 grados bajo cero

below-the-line [bɪ'ləʊðə'laɪn] *adj* (a) *Fin (expenditure, revenue)* por debajo de la línea (b) *(advertising, promotion) Com* ***b. advertising*** publicidad *f* directa

belt [belt] 1 *n* (a) *(for trousers)* cinturón *m*, correa *f*; IDIOM **to tighten one's b.** apretarse el cinturón; *Fig* **now that I've got some experience under my b.** ahora que tengo algo de experiencia a mis espaldas; **to hit sb below the b.** *(in boxing)* dar un golpe bajo a alguien; *Fig* **that was a bit below the b.!** *(remark, criticism)* ¡eso ha sido un golpe bajo! ►► ***b. buckle*** hebilla *f*; ***b. loop*** trabilla *f*, *RP* presilla *f*

(b) *(in martial arts)* cinturón *m*; **to be a brown/black b.** ser cinturón marrón/negro

(c) *(of machine)* correa *f* ►► ***b. drive*** transmisión *f* por correa

(d) *(area) (of land)* franja *f*, cinturón *m*; *(of cloud)* franja *f*, capa *f*; **the coal-mining b.** la cuenca carbonífera

(e) *Fam (blow)* golpetazo *m*; **to give sb a b.** dar un golpetazo a alguien; **he gave the ball a terrific b.** le dio un tremendo golpetazo a la pelota; **I'll give you a b. in the mouth** te voy a partir la boca

(f) *Fam (of spirits)* lingotazo *m*

2 *vt* (a) *(dress, trousers)* abrochar *(con un cinturón)*; **he belted the gun round his waist** se ajustó el cinturón que portaba el revólver; **a belted raincoat** una gabardina con cinturón (b) *Fam (hit)* dar un golpetazo a; *(with belt)* dar correazos a; *(ball)* pegar un cañonazo a

3 *vi Fam (move quickly)* **to b. along** ir a toda pastilla *or RP* máquina; **she belted down the stairs** bajó las escaleras a toda pastilla *or RP* máquina

► **belt down** *vi Br Fam (rain)* llover a cántaros, caer chuzos de punta

► **belt out** *vt sep Fam (sing loudly)* cantar a grito pelado

► **belt up** *vi Br* (a) *Fam (be silent)* cerrar el pico, cortar el rollo; **b. up!** ¡cierra el pico! (b) *(fasten seat belt)* abrocharse el cinturón (de seguridad)

belt-and-braces ['beltən'breɪsɪz] *adj Fam (policy, decision)* extremadamente cuidadoso(a)

belter ['beltə(r)] *n Br Fam* **that goal was a real b.** fue un gol de antología *or Méx* padrísimo *or RP* de morirse; **it's a b. of a song** esa canción *Esp* es la leche *or Méx* está padre *or RP* está que mata

belting ['beltɪŋ] *n Fam* **to give sb a b.** *(as punishment)* azotar a alguien; *(in fight)* dar una soba *or* paliza a alguien; *(in match, competition)* darle una paliza a alguien

belt-tightening ['belttaɪtənɪŋ] *n* restricción *f* del gasto, medidas *fpl* de austeridad

beltway ['beltweɪ] *n US* carretera *f* de circunvalación, ronda *f* (de circunvalación); *Pol* **inside the b.** = en los círculos oficiales de Washington

bemoan [bɪ'məʊn] *vt* lamentar, lamentarse de; **to b. one's fate** quejarse uno(a) de su suerte

bemuse [bɪ'mju:z] *vt* desconcertar, confundir

bemused [bɪ'mju:zd] *adj* perplejo(a), desconcertado(a); **to be b.** estar perplejo(a) *or* desconcertado(a)

bench [bentʃ] **1** *n* **(a)** *(seat)* banco *m* ►► ***b. press*** *(equipment)* = aparato para levantar pesas con los brazos tumbado sobre un banco
(b) *(work table)* banco *m*
(c) *Br Law* **the B.** la magistratura; **address your remarks to the B.** dirija sus observaciones al juez; **she has been raised to the B.** ha sido nombrada juez; **to sit on the B.** ser juez, pertenecer a la judicatura
(d) *Parl* **the opposition benches** los escaños de la oposición
(e) *Sport* banquillo *m*; **to be on the b.** estar en el banquillo
2 *vt US Sport* mandar *or* enviar al banquillo

benchmark ['bentʃmɑ:k] *n (for comparison)* punto *m* de referencia ►► *Comptr* ***b. test*** prueba *f* comparativa

benchmarking ['bentʃmɑ:kɪŋ] *n Com* evaluación *f* comparativa

bench-press ['bentʃpres] *vt* **I b. a hundred** levanto cien kilos *(tumbado en un banco)*

bend [bend] **1** *n* **(a)** *(of road, river)* curva *f*; *(of pipe, arm)* codo *m*; IDIOM **to be round the b.** estar *Esp* majara *or Am* zafado(a) *or RP* piantado(a); IDIOM **to go round the b.** volverse loco *or Esp* majara, *CSur* rayarse, *Méx* zafarse; IDIOM **to drive sb round the b.** sacar a alguien de sus casillas, poner a alguien a cien
(b) the bends *(decompression sickness)* enfermedad *f* de los buzos; *Med* aeroembolismo *m*
2 *vt (pt & pp* **bent** [bent]) **(a)** *(part of body)* doblar; **to b. one's arm/back** doblar el brazo/la espalda; **they bent their heads over their books** inclinaron *or* doblaron la cabeza sobre los libros; **on bended knee** de rodillas; **to go down on bended knee (to sb)** ponerse de rodillas (ante alguien); *Fam Hum* **to b. one's** *or* **the elbow** *(drink alcohol)* empinar el codo; IDIOM *Br Fam* **he bent my ear** *(told me his problems)* me contó sus penas
(b) *(change shape of) (pipe, wire)* doblar; **do not b.** *(on envelope)* no doblar; IDIOM **to b. the rules** ser flexible en la interpretación de las reglas; IDIOM **to b. sb to one's will** doblegar a alguien
(c) *Sport* **to b. the ball** pegar a la pelota con efecto *or* de rosca, dar efecto a la pelota
(d) *Literary (direct, turn)* **they bent their steps towards home** encaminaron sus pasos hacia su casa; **we b. all our efforts to fighting racism** encauzamos todos nuestros esfuerzos hacia la lucha contra el racismo; **they bent themselves to the task** se entregaron a la labor
3 *vi* **(a)** *(person)* inclinarse; **to b. backwards/forwards** inclinarse hacia atrás/hacia adelante
(b) *(road, river)* hacer una curva, girar; *(branch, tree)* doblarse, vencerse; **the road bends to the left** la carretera gira *or* hace una curva a la izquierda; **to b. under the strain of sth** ceder bajo la presión de algo
(c) *(submit)* ceder (**to** a *or* ante); **the government bent to pressure from the union** el gobierno cedió ante la presión de los sindicatos

► **bend down** *vi* agacharse

► **bend over** *vi* agacharse; IDIOM **to b. over backwards for sb/to do sth** desvivirse por alguien/por hacer algo

bender ['bendə(r)] *n Fam* **(a)** *(drinking session)* juerga *f*, parranda *f*, *Am* rumba *f*; **to go on a b.** irse de juerga *or* de copas **(b)** *Br (homosexual)* marica *m*

bendy ['bendɪ] *adj* **(a)** *(curvy)* serpenteante **(b)** *(flexible)* flexible, maleable; **a b. toy** un juguete flexible

---

BENEATH [bɪ'ni:θ] **1** *prep* **(a)** *(physically)* debajo de; **they tunnelled b. the fence** hicieron un túnel por debajo de la valla; **the houses b. us seemed small** las casas allá abajo se veían pequeñas; **the shelf was straining b. the weight of the books** la estantería cedía bajo el peso de los libros; **b. that self-confident exterior, she's really very insecure** bajo esa apariencia de confianza hay mucha inseguridad; *Fig* **b. the surface he was a bundle of nerves** por dentro era un manojo de nervios
(b) *(in classification, importance)* **they finished b. us in the league** quedaron por detrás nuestro en la liga; **he was in the year b. me** *(at school)* iba al curso posterior al mío; **I am b. him in rank** estoy por debajo suyo en rango
(c) *(unworthy of)* **to marry b. oneself** casarse con alguien de clase social inferior; **she thinks it's b. her to work** cree que trabajar supondría rebajarse; **b. contempt** (completamente) despreciable
2 *adv* abajo; **from b.** desde abajo

Benedictine [benɪ'dɪktɪn] *Rel* **1** *n* **(a)** *(monk, nun)* benedictino(a) *m,f* **(b)** *(drink)* (licor *m*) benedictino *m*
2 *adj* benedictino(a)

benediction [benɪ'dɪkʃən] *n Rel* **(a)** *(blessing)* bendición *f* **(b)** *(service)* bendición *f* (sacramental)

benefactor ['benɪfæktə(r)] *n* benefactor(ora) *m,f*

benefactress ['benɪfæktrɪs] *n* benefactora *f*

benefice ['benɪfɪs] *n* beneficio *m* (eclesiástico)

beneficence [bɪ'nefɪsəns] *n Literary (kindness)* beneficiencia *f*

beneficent [bɪ'nefɪsənt] *adj Formal* benéfico(a)

beneficial [benɪ'fɪʃəl] *adj* **(a)** *(helpful, favourable)* beneficioso(a), provechoso(a) (**to** para); **the legislation is particularly b. to the self-employed** la legislación favorece especialmente a los trabajadores autónomos; **the information proved highly b.** la información resultó muy provechosa **(b)** *Law* usufructuario(a) ►► ***b. interest*** usufructo *m*

beneficiary [benɪ'fɪʃərɪ] *n* beneficiario(a) *m,f*

benefit ['benɪfɪt] **1** *n* **(a)** *(advantages)* beneficio *m*, provecho *m*; *(individual advantage)* ventaja *f*; **the benefits of a good education** las ventajas de una buena educación; **she is starting to feel the benefits of the treatment** está empezando a notar los efectos beneficiosos del tratamiento; **for sb's b., for the b. of sb** en atención a alguien; **that remark was for your b.** ese comentario iba dirigido a ti; **for the b. of those who arrived late...** para los que llegaron tarde...; **the holiday wasn't of much b. to him** las vacaciones no le resultaron demasiado provechosas; **to have the b. of sth** contar con algo; **to derive b. from** sacar provecho de; **to offer sb the b. of one's experience** aportarle a alguien el beneficio de la experiencia propia; **to give sb the b. of the doubt** dar a alguien el beneficio de la duda
(b) *(state payment)* prestación *f*, subsidio *m*; **to be on b.** cobrar un subsidio; **social security benefits** prestaciones sociales ►► *Br* ***the Benefits Agency*** la oficina de prestaciones; *US* ***b. society*** mutua *f*, mutualidad *f*
(c) benefits (package) *(to employee)* paquete *m* de prestaciones
(d) *(charity event)* acto *m* benéfico ►► ***b. concert*** concierto *m* benéfico; ***b. gala*** gala *f* benéfica; *Sport* ***b. match*** partido *m* de homenaje; ***b. performance*** función *f* benéfica
2 *vt* beneficiar, favorecer
3 *vi* **to b. by** *or* **from** beneficiarse de, sacar provecho de; **no one is likely to b. by** *or* **from the closures** no parece que los cierres vayan a beneficiar a nadie; **everyone will b. in the end** todo el mundo saldrá ganando *or* beneficiado al final; **who benefits most from his death?** ¿quién saca más provecho de su muerte?

Benelux ['benɪlʌks] *n* (el) Benelux; **the B. countries** los países del Benelux

benevolence [bɪ'nevələns] *n* benevolencia *f*

benevolent [bɪ'nevələnt] *adj* benévolo(a) ►► ***b. society*** cofradía *f* benéfica

benevolently [bɪ'nevələntlɪ] *adv* benévolamente, con benevolencia

BEng, *US* **BEngr** [bi:'eŋ] *n* (*abbr* **Bachelor of Engineering**) **(a)** *(qualification)* licenciatura *f* en ingeniería **(b)** *(person)* licenciado(a) *m,f* en ingeniería

Bengal [beŋ'gɔ:l] *n* Bengala ►► ***B. tiger*** tigre *m* de Bengala

Bengali [beŋ'gɔ:lɪ] **1** *n* **(a)** *(person)* bengalí *mf* **(b)** *(language)* bengalí *m*
2 *adj* bengalí

BEngr *US* = **BEng**

benighted [bɪ'naɪtɪd] *adj Literary (person)* ignaro(a), lego(a); *(country)* ignaro(a)

benign [bɪ'naɪn] *adj* **(a)** *(attitude, look)* bondadoso(a) **(b)** *(climate)* benigno(a) **(c)** *Med (tumour)* benigno(a)

benignly [bɪ'naɪnlɪ] *adv* **(a)** *(kindly)* bondadosamente **(b)** *(not harshly)* de forma benigna

Benin [be'ni:n] *n* Benín

Beninese [benɪ'ni:z] **1** *n* beninés(esa) *m,f*
2 *adj* beninés(esa)

benny ['benɪ] *n Fam (drug)* anfeta *f*

bent [bent] **1** *n (inclination)* inclinación *f*; **to have a natural b. for music** tener una inclinación natural por la música; **he followed his (natural) b. (and went into the theatre)** siguió su inclinación (natural) (y se metió a hacer teatro)
2 *adj* **(a)** *(curved)* torcido(a), curvado(a) **(b)** *(determined)* **to be b. on (doing) sth** estar empeñado(a) en hacer algo **(c)** *Br Fam (dishonest)* corrupto(a); **a b. copper** un policía corrupto **(d)** *Br very Fam (homosexual)* maricón(ona); *Br* IDIOM **to be as b. as a nine bob note** *or* **as a three pound note** ser marica perdido, ser de la otra acera *or* de la acera de enfrente **(e)** IDIOM *US Fam* **b. out of shape** *(angry, upset)* hecho(a) una fiera, *Méx* como agua para chocolate **(f)** *US Fam* **get b.!** ¡vete al cuerno!, *Esp* ¡que te den!
3 *pt & pp of* **bend**

bentwood ['bentwʊd] *n* madera *f* curvada

benumbed [bɪ'nʌmd] *adj Literary* (**a**) *(made insensitive)* entumecido(a); **b. by the** *or* **with cold** entumecido(a) *or* agarrotado(a) por el frío (**b**) *(stupefied)* paralizado(a); **b. with fear** paralizado(a) *or* aturdido(a) por el miedo

benzene ['benzi:n] *n Chem* benceno *m* ▸▸ ***b. ring*** anillo *m* bencénico *or* de benceno

benzin(e) ['benzi:n] *n Chem* bencina *f*

benzocaine ['benzəʊkeɪn] *n Med* benzocaína *f*

benzoic acid [ben'zəʊɪk'æsɪd] *n Chem* ácido *m* benzoico

bequeath [bɪ'kwi:ð] *vt Formal* **to b. sth (to sb)** legar algo (a alguien)

bequest [bɪ'kwest] *n Law* legado *m*

berate [bɪ'reɪt] *vt Formal* **to b. sb (for sth)** reconvenir *or* reñir a alguien (por algo)

Berber ['bɜ:bə(r)] **1** *n* (**a**) *(person)* bereber *mf* (**b**) *(language)* bereber *m*
2 *adj* bereber

bereaved [bɪ'ri:vd] **1** *npl* **the b.** los allegados del (de la) difunto(a)
2 *adj* privado(a) de un ser querido; **a b. mother** una madre que ha perdido a un hijo; **he's recently b.** ha perdido recientemente a un ser querido

bereavement [bɪ'ri:vmənt] *n* pérdida *f* (de un ser querido); **owing to a recent b.** por el reciente fallecimiento de un familiar ▸▸ ***b. counselling*** = atención psicológica prestada a personas que sufren por la pérdida de un ser querido

bereft [bɪ'reft] *adj* **to be b. of** carecer de; **a manifesto b. of new ideas** un manifiesto carente de ideas nuevas; **to feel b.** sentirse desolado(a) *or* desconsolado(a)

beret ['bereɪ] *n* boina *f*

berg [bɜ:g] *n (iceberg)* iceberg *m*

bergamot ['bɜ:gəmɒt] *n* bergamota *f*

beribboned [bɪ'rɪbənd] *adj (hair)* adornado(a) con cintas

beriberi ['berɪ'berɪ] *n Med* beriberi *m*

Bering ['berɪŋ] *n* **the B. Sea** el mar de Bering; **the B. Strait** el estrecho de Bering

berk [bɜ:k] *n Br Fam* idiota *mf*

berkelium [bɜ:'ki:lɪəm] *n Chem* berquelio *m*

Berks (*abbr* **Berkshire**) (condado *m* de) Berkshire

Berlin [bɜ:'lɪn] *n* Berlín ▸▸ *Hist* ***the B. Wall*** el Muro de Berlín

Berliner [bɜ:'lɪnə(r)] *n* berlinés(esa) *m,f*

Bermuda [bə'mju:də] *n* (las) Bermudas ▸▸ ***B. shorts*** bermudas *fpl*; ***B. Triangle*** triángulo *m* de las Bermudas

Bermudan [bə'mju:dən] **1** *n* bermudeño(a) *m,f*
2 *adj* bermudeño(a)

Bern(e) [bɜ:n] *n* Berna

berry ['berɪ] *n* baya *f*

berserk [bə'zɜ:k] *adj Fam* **to go b.** volverse loco(a)

berth [bɜ:θ] **1** *n* (**a**) *(on train, ship)* litera *f* (**b**) *(in harbour)* amarradero *m*; IDIOM **to give sb a wide b.** evitar a alguien
2 *vt Naut* atracar
3 *vi Naut* atracar

beryl ['berəl] *n Geol* berilo *m*

beryllium [be'rɪlɪəm] *n Chem* berilio *m*

beseech [bɪ'si:tʃ] (*pt & pp* **besought** [bɪ'sɔ:t] *or* **beseeched**) *vt Literary* implorar, suplicar; **to b. sb to do sth** rogar *or* suplicar a alguien que haga algo; **I b. you, have mercy!** ¡se lo suplico, tenga compasión *or* piedad!

beseeching [bɪ'si:tʃɪŋ] *adj* suplicante, implorante

beseechingly [bɪ'si:tʃɪŋlɪ] *adv* con aire suplicante *or* de súplica

beset [bɪ'set] (*pt & pp* **beset**) *vt* (**a**) *(assail)* acosar; **b. with dangers/difficulties** plagado(a) de peligros/dificultades; **she was b. by doubts** le asaltaron las dudas (**b**) *(surround)* asediar

besetting [bɪ'setɪŋ] *adj Formal* **his b. sin was greed** su principal defecto era la glotonería

beside [bɪ'saɪd] *prep* (**a**) *(next to)* al lado de; **seated b. me** sentado(a) a mi lado; **a house b. the lake** una casa a la orilla del *or* junto al lago; IDIOM **that's b. the point** eso no viene al caso; IDIOM **he was b. himself with joy** no cabía en sí de gozo; IDIOM **he was b. himself with anger** estaba fuera de sí (de ira)
(**b**) *(compared to)* al lado de; **b. him, everyone else appears slow** a su lado todos parecen lentos; **the results don't look very brilliant b. last year's** los resultados no parecen muy brillantes si se comparan con los del año pasado

besides [bɪ'saɪdz] **1** *prep* (**a**) *(in addition to)* además de; **b. being old, she's also extremely deaf** además de vieja, está sorda como una tapia; **...b. which, she was unwell** ...además de lo cual, no se encontraba bien
(**b**) *(apart from)* además de, aparte de; **nobody knew b. me** nadie lo sabía excepto yo
2 *adv* (**a**) *(in addition)* además; **many more b.** muchos(as) otros(as); **he owns two apartments and a house in the country b.** tiene dos apartamentos y, además, una casa en el campo; **he knows the rudiments but little else b.** tiene unas nociones elementales, pero poco más
(**b**) *(furthermore)* además, es más; **it's an excellent play and, b., the tickets aren't expensive** es una obra excelente y, además *or* es más, las entradas no son caras; **b., I don't even like the circus** además *or* es más, ni siquiera me gusta el circo

besiege [bɪ'si:dʒ] *vt* (**a**) *(castle, town)* sitiar, asediar; *Fig* **their house was besieged by journalists** su casa estaba sitiada por periodistas (**b**) *(harass)* **he was besieged by doubt** le asaltó la duda; **to b. sb with complaints/requests** asediar a alguien con quejas/peticiones

besieger [bɪ'si:dʒə(r)] *n* sitiador(ora) *m,f*, asediador(ora) *m,f*

besmear [bɪ'smɪə(r)] *n* **to b. sth/sb with sth** embadurnar algo/a alguien con *or* de algo

besmirch [bɪ'smɜ:tʃ] *vt Literary (face)* manchar; *(reputation)* mancillar

besom ['bi:zəm, 'bɪzəm] *n* (**a**) *(broom)* escoba *f* (**b**) *Scot Fam (woman)* **she's a cheeky b.!** ¡es una descarada *or Esp* fresca!

besotted [bɪ'sɒtɪd] *adj* (**a**) *(infatuated)* **to be b. with sth/sb** estar embobado(a) con algo/alguien (**b**) *(confused)* **b. with drink** aturdido(a) *or* trastornado(a) por la bebida

besought *pt & pp of* **beseech**

bespatter [bɪ'spætə(r)] *vt* salpicar (**with** de)

bespeak [bɪ'spi:k] (*pt* **bespoke** [bɪ'spəʊk], *pp* **bespoken** [bɪ'spəʊkən]) *vt Literary (indicate)* denotar, revelar

bespectacled [bɪ'spektəkəld] *adj* con gafas

bespoke [bɪ'spəʊk] **1** *adj (made to measure)* a medida ▸▸ ***b. tailor*** sastre *m (que hace trajes a medida)*
2 *pt of* **bespeak**

bespoken [bɪ'spəʊkən] *pp of* **bespeak**

Bessarabia [besə'reɪbɪə] *n* Besarabia

Bessemer ['besɪmə(r)] *n Tech* ***B. converter*** (convertidor *m*) bessemer *m*; ***B. process*** proceso *m* bessemer

BEST [best] (*superlative of* **good, well**) **1** *n* (**a**) *(in general)* **the b.** el/la/lo mejor; **the Russians are (simply) the b.** los rusos son los mejores; **it's the b. I can do** no lo puedo hacer mejor; **she will accept nothing but the b.** sólo acepta lo mejor; **we'll provide you with the b. of service** le daremos el mejor servicio posible; **this novel is his b.** ésta es su mejor novela; **I did my b. – well, your b. just isn't good enough** hice todo lo que pude – pues parece que no ha sido suficiente; **at b.** en el mejor de los casos; **it was average at b.** era, como mucho, regular; **he was at his b.** estaba en plena forma; **this is French cuisine at its b.** éste es un ejemplo de lo mejor de la cocina francesa; **it's hard enough at the b. of times** incluso en el mejor de los casos ya resulta bastante difícil; **the b. of it is...** lo mejor del caso es que...; **we are the b. of friends** somos muy buenos amigos; **I am in the b. of health** estoy pletórico(a) de salud; **it happened for the b.** fue para bien; **to bring out the b. in sb** poner de manifiesto lo mejor de alguien; **she did her (level) b.** hizo todo lo que pudo; **to get the b. of the bargain** salir ganando en un trato; **to get the b. of sb** *(defeat)* superar a alguien; **to get the b. out of sth** sacar el máximo provecho de algo; **we've had the b. of the good weather** el mejor tiempo ya ha pasado; **he wants to have the b. of both worlds** él quiere tenerlo todo; **this camcorder offers you the b. of both worlds** esta videocámara le permite ganar por partida doble; **to hope for the b.** esperar que todo vaya bien; **a draw is the b. we can hope for** un empate es lo máximo a lo que podemos aspirar; **I'll want to look my b.** tendré que arreglarme lo mejor posible; **we will have to make the b. of it** nos las tendremos que arreglar *or Esp* apañar; *Sport* **to play the b. of three** jugar al mejor de tres; **I want the b. for you** te deseo lo mejor; **to the b. of my belief** *or* **knowledge** por lo que yo sé; **I will do it to the b. of my ability** lo haré lo mejor que pueda; **he can sing with the b. of them** canta como el mejor; *Fam* **all the b.!** ¡te deseo lo mejor!; *(at end of letter)* un saludo, *RP* cariños; **b. of all...** y lo mejor de todo es que...; **(the) b. of luck!** ¡que tengas mucha suerte!
(**b**) *Sport (performance)* plusmarca *f*; **personal b.** plusmarca personal
(**c**) *Br (beer)* = "bitter" de calidad superior

2 *adj* mejor; **my b. dress** mi mejor vestido; **she is b. at French** *(of group of people)* es la mejor en francés; *(French is her best subject)* lo que mejor se le da es el francés; **it is b. to...** lo mejor es...; **the b. thing to do would be to phone her** lo mejor sería que la llamáramos; **it took the b. part of a year** llevó casi todo un año; **to know what is b. for sb** saber lo que le conviene a alguien; **to want what is b. for sb** querer lo mejor para alguien; *Com* **b. before...** consumir preferentemente antes de...; **this is a b. case scenario** esto es lo que ocurriría en el mejor de los casos; **may the b. man win** *(in contest)* que gane el mejor; **Doug and I are b. friends** Doug es mi mejor amigo; IDIOM **to put one's b. foot forward** *(hurry)* ir a toda marcha; *(do one's best)* dar lo mejor de sí mismo(a) ►► *Cin & TV* ***b. boy*** ayudante *m* del electricista; ***b. man*** *(at wedding)* = amigo del novio encargado de ayudar en la boda; *Com* ***b. practice*** las mejores iniciativas prácticas; ***b. wishes*** *(on card, letter)* un saludo cordial *or* afectuoso; **give her my b. wishes** envíale saludos *or CAm, Col, Ecuad* saludes (de mi parte)

3 *adv* mejor; **which do you like b.?** ¿cuál te gusta más?; **I like fish b.** lo que más me gusta es el pescado; **I comforted her as b. I could** la consolé lo mejor que pude; **this area is b. avoided** es mejor evitar esta área; **she came off b.** ella fue la que salió mejor parada; **our team did b.** nuestro equipo fue el mejor; **you had b. not mention it** más vale que no lo menciones; **we'd b. be going** tenemos que irnos ya; **you know b.** tú sabrás; **you always think you know b.** siempre te crees que sabes más que nadie; **to make the b. use of sth** aprovechar algo al máximo; **do as you think b.** haz lo que te parezca mejor; **he is b. known for his sculptures** se le conoce sobre todo por sus esculturas; **the b. dressed man** el hombre mejor vestido; **they are the b. off** *(in good situation)* son los que mejor están; *(richest)* son los que más dinero tienen

4 *vt Formal (in contest, argument)* superar

bestial ['bestɪəl] *adj* brutal, bestial

bestiality [bestɪ'ælɪtɪ] *n* **(a)** *(cruelty)* brutalidad *f*, bestialidad *f* **(b)** *(sexual practice)* bestialismo *m*, zoofilia *f*

bestiary ['bestɪərɪ] *n* bestiario *m*

bestir [bɪ'stɜː(r)] *(pt & pp* **bestirred**) *vt Formal* **to b. oneself** espabilarse, poner manos a la obra

bestow [bɪ'stəʊ] *vt (title, award)* conceder **(on** a); *(honour)* conferir **(on** a); **we shouldn't b. too much importance on these remarks** no deberíamos conceder demasiada importancia a tales comentarios

bestrewn [bɪ'struːn] *adj Literary* sembrado(a) **(with** de)

bestride [bɪ'straɪd] *(pt* **bestrode** [bɪ'strəʊd], *pp* **bestridden** [bɪ'strɪdən]) *vt Formal (horse)* montar; *(chair, fence)* sentarse a horcajadas sobre

bestseller [best'selə(r)] *n* **(a)** *(book)* éxito *m* editorial *or* de ventas, best-séller *m* **(b)** *(author)* autor(ora) *m,f* de best-séllers, best-séller *mf*

bestselling [best'selɪŋ] *adj* **b. novel/author** novela/escritor(ora) de éxito

bet [bet] **1** *n* **(a)** *(gamble)* apuesta *f*; **to make** *or* **place a b.** hacer una apuesta; **to win/to lose a b.** ganar/perder una apuesta; **they're taking bets** aceptan apuestas; IDIOM **all bets are off** todo está en el aire

(b) *(guess, option)* **my b. is that he'll come** personalmente, creo que vendrá; **your best b. would be to...** lo mejor que puedes hacer es...; **it's a safe b.** es casi seguro; **Cyrano's is a good b. if you like French food** Cyrano's es una buena elección si te gusta la comida francesa

2 *vt* (*pt & pp* **bet** *or* **betted**) **(a)** *(gamble)* apostar; **I'll b. you £10 (that he won't come)** te apuesto 10 libras (a que no vendrá)

(b) *Fam (expressing conviction)* **it took me ages to do it – I b. it did!** tardé un montón en hacerlo – ¡no me extraña! *or* ¡no hace falta que lo jures!; **I b. you don't/can't!** ¡a que no!; **I b. you she'll win** te apuesto que gana ella, qué te apuestas a que gana ella; **I b. you anything (you like) he won't manage it** te apuesto lo que quieras a que no lo consigue; **you can b. your life** *or* **your bottom dollar they'll say no** me juego la cabeza *or* lo que quieras a que dicen que no

3 *vi* **(a)** *(gamble)* **to b. on a horse/a race** apostar a un caballo/en una carrera; **I'm betting on him winning** apuesto a que gana; IDIOM **if I were a betting man,...** si tuviera que apostar,...

(b) *Fam (expressing conviction)* **(do you) wanna b.?** ¿qué te juegas?; **don't b. on it** no te fíes ni un pelo, yo no me jugaría nada; **I wouldn't b. on it** yo no me apostaría nada; **you b.!** ¡ya lo creo!, ¡por supuesto!; **John says he's sorry – I b. (he does)!** John dice que lo siente – ¡ya lo creo! *or Esp* ¡hombre, claro!; *Ironic* **he says he'll pay you tomorrow – I b.!** dice que te pagará mañana – ¡ya, claro! *or* ¡sí, seguro!

beta ['biːtə] *n* **(a)** *(Greek letter)* beta *f* **(b)** *Phys* ***b. particle*** partícula *f* beta; ***b. radiation*** radiación *f* beta; ***b. rays*** rayos *mpl* beta **(c)** *Comptr* ***b. testing*** pruebas *fpl* beta; ***b. version*** versión *f* beta **(d)** *Physiol* ***b. wave*** onda *f* beta

beta-blocker ['biːtəblɒkə(r)] *n Pharm* betabloqueante *m*

betake [bɪ'teɪk] *(pt* **betook** [bɪ'tʊk], *pp* **betaken** [bɪ'teɪkən]) *vt Formal* **to b. oneself** trasladarse

betel ['biːtəl] *n* betel *m* ►► ***b. nut*** areca *f*

bête noire [bet'nwɑː(r)] *(pl* **bêtes noires** [bet'nwɑːz]) *n* bestia *f* negra; **her real b. is unpunctuality** lo que verdaderamente hace que se la lleven los demonios es la falta de puntualidad

Bethlehem ['beθlɪhem] *n* Belén

betide [bɪ'taɪd] *vt Literary* **our thoughts are with them, whatever may b. them** nuestros pensamientos los acompañan, sea cual fuere lo que pudiera acontecerles; **woe b. him/you** pobre de él/ti

betoken [bɪ'təʊkən] *vt Formal* **(a)** *(symbolize)* señalar, ser una señal de **(b)** *(be sign of, presage)* augurar, presagiar

betook *pt of* **betake**

betray [bɪ'treɪ] *vt* **(a)** *(person, country)* traicionar; *(spouse)* engañar, ser infiel a; **to b. sb's trust** abusar de la confianza de alguien; **he betrayed the rebels to the police** delató a los rebeldes ante la policía **(b)** *(secret, fact)* revelar; **to b. a confidence** revelar un secreto *or* una confidencia; **his tone betrayed a lack of conviction** su tono revelaba falta de convicción

betrayal [bɪ'treɪəl] *n* **(a)** *(of person, country)* traición *f*; **an act of b.** una traición; **a b. of trust** un abuso de confianza **(b)** *(of secret, fact)* muestra *f*, indicio *m*; **her expression gave no b. of her true feelings** su expresión no permitía adivinar sus verdaderos sentimientos

betrothal [bɪ'trəʊðəl] *n Literary* compromiso *m*

betrothed [bɪ'trəʊðd] *Formal* **1** *n* prometido(a) *m,f*; **his/her b.** su prometido(a)

2 *adj* prometido(a); **she was b. to the prince** estaba prometida al príncipe

BETTER ['betə(r)] *(comparative of* **good, well**) **1** *n* **which is the b. (of the two)?** ¿cuál es el mejor (de los dos)?; **it's not bad, but I've seen b.** no está mal, pero los he visto mejores; **she deserves b.** se merece *or Am* amerita algo mejor; **I expected b. of you** esperaba más de ti; **you should respect your (elders and) betters** deberías guardar respeto a tus mayores; **I'm all the b. for a rest** este descanso me ha hecho mucho bien; **to change for the b.** cambiar para mejor; **to get the b. of sb** poder con alguien; **his shyness got the b. of him** pudo más su timidez; **the faster/sooner the b.** cuanto más rápido/antes, mejor

2 *adj* **(a)** *(of higher quality, more suitable)* mejor; **to be b. (than)** *(be superior)* ser mejor (que); **to be b.** *(feel well again)* estar mejor; **he's b. at tennis than his brother** juega al tenis mejor que su hermano; **she's b. at chemistry than him** se le da mejor la química que a él; **it was b. than expected** fue mejor de lo esperado; **it's b. than nothing** es mejor que nada; **it's one of his b. novels** está entre sus mejores novelas; **it would be b. for you to go** más vale que te vayas; **what could be b. than...?** ¿podría haber algo mejor que...?; **they're no** *or* **little b. than criminals** no son más que criminales; **that's b.** ¡así está mejor!; **it could hardly have come at a b. time** no podría haber llegado más oportunamente; **to get b.** mejorar; **this athlete just gets b. (and b.)** este atleta cada vez es mejor

(b) IDIOMS **to go one b.** hacerlo mejor; *Ironic* **b. late than never** más vale tarde que nunca; **b. safe than sorry** más vale prevenir que curar; **b. luck next time!** ¡a ver si hay más suerte la próxima vez!; **it took the b. part of a week** llevó casi toda una semana; **the carpet's seen b. days** la *Esp* moqueta *or Am* alfombra está para que la jubilen; **I did it against my b. judgement** lo hice a pesar de no estar convencido(a); *Br Fam Hum* **my b. half** mi media naranja; **to appeal to sb's b. nature** apelar a la bondad de alguien

3 *adv* mejor; **our team did b.** nuestro equipo lo hizo mejor; **you'd do b. not to listen to him** más vale que no le escuches; **I am feeling b.** me siento mejor; **you'll feel b. for a cup of tea** un té te hará sentirte mejor; **to get to know sb b.** ir conociendo mejor a alguien; **you had b. not stay** más vale que no te quedes; **we'd b. be going** tenemos que irnos ya; **you'd b. not be lying!** ¡más vale que no estés mintiendo!; IDIOM **you'd b. believe it!** ¡ya lo creo que sí!; **you always think you know b.** siempre te crees que sabes más que nadie; **I know b. than to tell her my secrets** la conozco demasiado bien como para contarle mis secretos; **you should know b. than to ask him for money!** ¡para qué le pides dinero si ya sabes cómo es!; **I like this one b.** éste me gusta más; **there's nothing I like b. than to...** nada me gusta más que...; **to think b. of it** cambiar de idea, pensárselo mejor; **to think b. of sb (for doing sth)** tener mejor concepto de alguien (por haber hecho algo); **b. and b.** cada vez mejor; **b. still...** incluso mejor...; **so much the b., all the b.** tanto mejor; **for b. or worse** para bien o para mal; **the b. equipped of the two** el mejor equipado de los dos; **those problems are b. avoided** más vale evitar esos problemas; **he's b.**

known for his sculptures se le conoce más bien por sus esculturas; **to be b. off** *(at an advantage)* estar mejor; *(financially)* tener más dinero
4 *vt (improve)* superar; *(surpass)* mejorar; **she wants to b. herself** quiere mejorar su situación

---

betterment ['betəmənt] *n* (a) *(improvement)* mejora *f* (b) *Law (of property)* mejora *f*

better-off [betər'ɒf] 1 *npl* **the b.** los más acomodados, los más favorecidos (económicamente)
2 *adj* más acomodado(a), de mejor posición económica

betting ['betɪŋ] *n* juego *m*, apuestas *fpl*; IDIOM *Fam* **the b. is that...** lo más probable es que...; IDIOM **what's the b. he doesn't come back?** ¿qué te apuestas a que no vuelve? ▸▸ *Br* ***b. shop*** casa *f* de apuestas; ***b. slip*** boleto *m* de apuestas

bettor ['betə(r)] *n US* apostante *mf*, apostador(ora) *m,f*

BETWEEN [bɪ'twi:n] 1 *prep* entre; **b. eight and nine o'clock** entre (las) ocho y (las) nueve; **b. Boston and London** entre Boston y Londres; **the final will be b. the Blue Jays and the Red Sox** la final la disputarán los Blue Jays y los Red Sox; **b. them they managed to move the table** entre todos consiguieron mover la mesa; **we bought it b. us** lo compramos entre todos; **you must choose b. them** tienes que elegir entre ellos; **I hope this won't come b. us** espero que esto no se interponga entre nosotros; **one man stands b. him and the title** entre él y el título sólo hay un hombre; **I did the course in b. getting married and having a baby** hice el curso entre la boda y el nacimiento del bebé; **it's something b. a duck and an ostrich** es una especie de mezcla de pato y avestruz; **I'm b. jobs just now** en estos momentos no estoy trabajando; **this is strictly b. you and me** esto debe quedar entre tú y yo
2 *adv* **(in) b.** en medio; **the trees in b.** los árboles que están en medio; **showers, with sunny spells in b.** chubascos, con intervalos soleados; **there were terrible storms, but it was beautiful in b. times** hubo terribles tormentas, pero entremedias hizo un tiempo magnífico

---

betweentimes [bɪ'twi:ntaɪmz] *adv* entremedias

betwixt [bɪ'twɪkst] *Old-fashioned & Literary* 1 *prep* entre
2 *adv* **b. and between** entre dos aguas, *Esp* entre Pinto y Valdemoro

bevel ['bevəl] 1 *n (on wood, glass)* bisel *m* ▸▸ ***b. square*** escuadra *f* falsa
2 *vt (pt & pp* **bevelled**, *US* **beveled**) *(wood, glass)* biselar

bevelled, *US* **beveled** ['bevəld] *adj* biselado(a)

beverage ['bevərɪdʒ] *n* bebida *f*

bevvied ['bevɪd] *adj Br Fam* bebido(a), borracho(a)

bevvy ['bevɪ] *n Br Fam* (a) *(alcoholic drink)* **to go for** *or* **have a b.** tomarse una copa *or* copichuela (b) *(drinking session)* **to go on the b.** agarrarse un pedo *or Méx* una pea

bevy ['bevɪ] *n (group)* nube *f*

bewail [bɪ'weɪl] *vt* lamentar

beware [bɪ'weə(r)] 1 *vi* tener cuidado (**of** con); **b.!** ¡cuidado!; **b. of the dog** *(sign)* cuidado con el perro; **b. of pickpockets** *(sign)* atención a los carteristas; **b. of cheap imitations** no acepte burdas imitaciones
2 *vt* **b. what you say to her** ten cuidado con lo que le dices

Bewick's swan ['bju:ɪks'swɒn] *n* cisne *m* chico

bewilder [bɪ'wɪldə(r)] *vt* desconcertar

bewildered [bɪ'wɪldəd] *adj* desconcertado(a); **I was b. by their lack of interest** me dejó atónito su falta de interés

bewildering [bɪ'wɪldərɪŋ] *adj* desconcertante; **in b. detail** con sorprendente minuciosidad

bewilderingly [bɪ'wɪldərɪŋlɪ] *adv* desconcertantemente; **the issue is b. complex** el asunto es increíblemente *or* extraordinariamente complicado

bewilderment [bɪ'wɪldəmənt] *n* desconcierto *m*; **"why?" she asked in b.** "¿por qué?", preguntó desconcertada; **to my complete b., he refused** para mi mayor asombro, dijo que no

bewitch [bɪ'wɪtʃ] *vt* (a) *(cast spell over)* hechizar, embrujar (b) *(fascinate)* embrujar, cautivar

bewitching [bɪ'wɪtʃɪŋ] *adj (smile, beauty)* cautivador(ora)

BEYOND [bɪ'jɒnd] 1 *prep* (a) *(in space)* más allá de; **the house is b. the church** la casa está pasada la iglesia; *Fig* **they can't see b. short-term success** no ven más allá del éxito inmediato
(b) *(in time)* **it continued b. midnight** siguió hasta más allá de la medianoche; **b. a certain date** después de *or* pasada una fecha determinada
(c) *(exceeding)* **that is b. the scope of this study** eso queda fuera del ámbito de este estudio; **unemployment has gone b. 10 percent** el desempleo ha sobrepasado el 10 por ciento; **my responsibilities go b. purely administrative work** mis responsabilidades van más allá del trabajo meramente administrativo; **to live b. the age of ninety** superar los noventa años; IDIOM **he lived b. his means** vivió por encima de sus posibilidades; IDIOM **it's b. me (how) they can do it** no comprendo cómo lo hacen; **due to circumstances b. our control** por circunstancias ajenas a nuestra voluntad; **to be b. belief** ser difícil de creer; **he's lazy b. belief** es perezoso *or* vago a más no poder; IDIOM **I am b. caring** ya me trae sin cuidado; **it's b. doubt/question (that...)** es indudable/incuestionable (que...); **b. a shadow of a doubt** sin sombra de duda; *Law* **this proves his innocence b. (a) reasonable doubt** esto disipa cualquier duda razonable en torno a su inocencia; IDIOM **it's b. a joke** esto ya pasa de castaño oscuro; **b. reach** inalcanzable; **he has changed b. recognition** está irreconocible; **b. repair** irreparable; **it was b. our wildest dreams** superaba nuestros sueños más optimistas
(d) *(except)* aparte de, además de; **I have nothing to say b. observing that...** únicamente quisiera hacer notar que...
2 *adv* más allá; **we could see the river and the hills b.** podíamos ver el río y detrás las colinas; **up to the year 2010 and b.** hasta el año 2010 y después de esa fecha
3 *n Literary* **the (great) b.** el más allá

---

bezel ['bezəl] *n (edge of chisel)* bisel *m*

Bézier curve ['bezɪekɜ:v] *n* curva *f* de Bezier

BFA [bi:ef'eɪ] *n US* (*abbr* **Bachelor of Fine Arts**) (a) *(qualification)* ≃ licenciatura *f* en Bellas Artes (b) *(person)* ≃ licenciado(a) *m,f* en Bellas Artes

B-girl ['bi:gɜ:l] *n US* chica *f* de alterne

bhajee, bhaji ['bɑ:dʒi:] *n Br Culin* = aperitivo indio a base de verdura especiada, rebozada y frita

bhangra ['bæŋgrə] *n Mus* bhangra *m*

bhp [bi:eɪtʃ'pi:] *n* (*abbr* **brake horsepower**) caballos *mpl* de vapor de potencia (al freno)

Bhutan [bu:'tɑ:n] *n* Bután

bi [baɪ] *adj Fam* (*abbr* **bisexual**) bisexual, bi

bi- [baɪ] *prefix* bi-

BIA [bi:aɪ'eɪ] *n US* (*abbr* **Bureau of Indian Affairs**) = oficina para asuntos relacionados con los indios nativos

biannual [baɪ'ænjʊəl] *adj* bianual

biannually [baɪ'ænjʊəlɪ] *adv* bianualmente

bias ['baɪəs] 1 *n* (a) *(prejudice)* prejuicio *m*; **to have a b. against** tener prejuicios contra, estar predispuesto(a) en contra de; **there is still considerable b. against women candidates** todavía existen muchos prejuicios en contra de las candidaturas femeninas; **the right/left-wing b. of the paper** la tendencia de derechas/de izquierda del periódico; **to be without b.** ser imparcial
(b) *(inclination)* inclinación *f*; **to have a b. towards** sentir inclinación por; **the curriculum has a scientific b.** el plan de estudios tiene un enfoque científico
(c) *(in sewing)* bies *m*, sesgo *m*; **cut on the b.** cortado al bies *or* al sesgo ▸▸ ***b. binding*** ribete *m* cortado al bies
(d) *(in statistics, sampling)* margen *m* de error
2 *vt (pt & pp* **biased** *or* **biassed**) influir en; **to b. sb against/for sth** predisponer a alguien en contra/a favor de algo

bias(s)ed ['baɪəst] *adj* (a) *(prejudiced)* parcial, sesgado(a); **b. reporting** cobertura sesgada *or* parcial; **to be b. against sth/sb** tener prejuicios contra algo/alguien; **you're b. in her favour** estás predispuesto a favor de ella; **try not to be b.** intenta ser imparcial (b) *(weighted)* **the course is b. towards the arts** el curso está enfocado hacia el campo de las letras

biathlon [baɪ'æθlɒn] *n* biatlón *m*

biathlete [baɪ'æθli:t] *n* atleta *mf* de biatlón, biatleta *mf*

bib [bɪb] *n* (a) *(for baby)* babero *m* (b) *(of apron, dungarees)* peto *m*; IDIOM *Fam* **in one's best b. and tucker** de punta en blanco (c) *Sport* camiseta *f*

bible ['baɪbəl] *n* biblia *f*; **the B.** la Biblia; *Fig* **this dictionary is his b.** este diccionario es su biblia; **the fisherman's b.** la biblia del pescador *or* de los pescadores ▸▸ *Br Fam Pej* ***b. basher*** proselitista *mf* fanático(a); *US* ***the B. Belt*** = zona integrista protestante en el sur de los Estados Unidos; ***b. paper*** papel *m* biblia; *Fam Pej* ***b. thumper*** proselitista *mf* fanático(a)

biblical ['bɪblɪkəl] *adj* bíblico(a); *Hum* **he had known her in the b. sense** se la había llevado al huerto ▸▸ ***b. history*** historia *f* sagrada

bibliographer [bɪblɪ'ɒgrəfə(r)] *n* bibliógrafo(a) *m,f*

bibliographical [bɪblɪə'græfɪkəl] *adj* bibliográfico(a)

bibliography [bɪblɪ'ɒgrəfɪ] *n* bibliografía *f*

bibliomania [bɪblɪə'meɪnɪə] *n* bibliomanía *f*

bibliophile ['bɪblɪəfaɪl] *n* bibliófilo(a) *m,f*

bibulous ['bɪbjʊləs] *adj Hum (person)* beodo(a); *(evening)* de alcohol

bicameral [baɪ'kæmərəl] *adj Pol* bicameral

bicarb [baɪ'kɑːb] *n Fam* bicarbonato *m*

bicarbonate [baɪ'kɑːbəneɪt] *n* bicarbonato *m* ▸▸ ***b. of soda*** bicarbonato *m* sódico

biccy, bickie ['bɪkɪ] *n Fam Br (biscuit)* galletita *f*

bicentenary [baɪsen'tiːnərɪ], *US* **bicentennial** [baɪsen'tenɪəl] **1** *n* bicentenario *m*

2 *adj* bicentenario(a)

biceps ['baɪseps] *npl Anat* bíceps *m inv*

bicker ['bɪkə(r)] *vi* reñir, pelearse (**about** *or* **over** por)

bickering ['bɪkərɪŋ] *n* riñas *fpl*, peleas *fpl*; **stop your b.!** ¡ya basta de peleas!

bickie = **biccy**

bicoastal [baɪ'kəʊstəl] *adj US* **a b. company** una compañía implantada en ambas costas

bicultural [baɪ'kʌltʃərəl] *adj* con dos culturas

bicuspid [baɪ'kʌspɪd] **1** *n* premolar *m*

2 *adj (tooth)* premolar, *Spec* bicúspide

bicycle ['baɪsɪkəl] **1** *n* bicicleta *f*; **to ride a b.** montar en bicicleta ▸▸ ***b. chain*** cadena *f* de bicicleta; ***b. clips*** = pinzas que ciñen los pantalones a las pantorrillas para montar en bicicleta; ***b. kick*** *(in soccer)* tijereta *f*, chilena *f*; ***b. pump*** bomba *f* de bicicleta; ***b. rack*** *(on pavement)* soporte *m* para estacionar bicicletas; *(on car)* baca *f* para bicicletas

2 *vi* ir en bicicleta; **she bicycles to work** va en bicicleta a trabajar

bicyclist ['baɪsɪklɪst] *n* ciclista *mf*

bid[1] [bɪd] **1** *n* **(a)** *(offer)* oferta *f*; *(at auction)* puja *f*, oferta *f*; **to put in a b. for** *(house)* hacer una oferta por; *(contract)* licitar por, hacer una oferta de licitación por ▸▸ *St Exch* ***b. price*** precio *m* comprador

(b) *(attempt)* tentativa *f*, intento *m*; **a rescue/suicide b.** un intento de rescate/suicidio; **to make a b. for freedom** hacer un intento de escapar; **to make a b. for power** intentar conseguir el poder; **Birmingham fails in b. for next Olympics** *(in headlines)* Birmingham fracasa en la puja por la sede de las próximas olimpiadas

(c) *(in cards)* declaración *f*; **no b.** paso

2 *vt* (*pt & pp* **bid**) **(a)** *(offer)* ofrecer; *(at auction)* pujar (**for** por); **he b. £2,000 for the painting** ofreció *or* pujó 2.000 libras por el cuadro; **what am I b. for this table?** ¿qué ofrecen por esta mesa?

(b) *(in cards)* declarar

3 *vi* **(a)** *(at auction)* pujar (**for** por); *(for contract)* licitar (**for** por), hacer una oferta de licitación (**for** por); **they're bidding against us** están pujando por lo mismo que nosotros

(b) *(make attempt)* **he's bidding for the presidency** se presenta (como candidato) a la presidencia

▸ **bid in** *vi (in auction)* = pujar por un artículo del lote propio para mantenerlo

▸ **bid up** *vt sep (price)* hacer aumentar *(por medio de pujas artificiales)*

bid[2] (*pt* **bade** [bæd, beɪd] *or* **bid**; *pp* **bidden** ['bɪdən] *or* **bid**) *vt Literary* **(a)** *(greet)* **to b. sb welcome** dar la bienvenida a alguien; **to b. sb goodbye** despedir a alguien

(b) *(ask, order)* **to b. sb enter** hacer pasar a alguien, invitar a entrar a alguien; **to b. sb be silent** ordenar callar a alguien; **do as you are bidden** haz lo que se te ordena

(c) **to b. fair to do sth** *(show promise)* prometer hacer algo

biddable ['bɪdəbəl] *adj (docile)* dócil; **he wasn't very b. on changing the closing date** no cedió un ápice para cambiar la fecha de entrega

bidden *pp of* **bid**[2]

bidder ['bɪdə(r)] *n* **(a)** *(at auction)* postor(ora) *m,f*; *(for contract)* licitador(ora) *m,f*; **the highest b.** el mejor postor **(b)** *(in cards)* apostante *mf*

bidding[1] ['bɪdɪŋ] *n (at auction)* puja *f*; **to start the b. at £5,000** comenzar la puja con 5.000 libras; **b. was brisk** la puja ascendía rápidamente, la puja estaba animada

bidding[2] *n Literary (command)* **to do sb's b.** llevar a cabo las órdenes de alguien

biddy ['bɪdɪ] *n Fam Pej* **old b.** vieja *f*, abuela *f*

bide [baɪd] *vt* **to b. one's time** esperar el momento oportuno

bidet ['biːdeɪ] *n* bidé *m*

bidirectional ['baɪdaɪ'rekʃənəl] *adj Comptr* bidireccional

biennial [baɪ'enɪəl] **1** *n* **(a)** *Bot* planta *f* bienal **(b)** *(event)* bienal *f*

2 *adj* **(a)** *(plant)* bienal **(b)** *(event)* bienal

biennially [baɪ'enɪəlɪ] *adv* bienalmente

bier [bɪə(r)] *n (for carrying coffin)* andas *fpl*

biff [bɪf] *Fam* **1** *n* mamporro *m*

2 *vt* dar un mamporro a

bifocal [baɪ'fəʊkəl] **1** *n* **bifocals** gafas *fpl or Am* anteojos *mpl* bifocales; **a pair of bifocals** unas gafas *or Am* unos anteojos bifocales

2 *adj* bifocal

BIFU ['bɪfuː] *n* (*abbr* **Banking, Insurance and Finance Union**) = sindicato británico de empleados del sector financiero

bifurcate ['baɪfəkeɪt] *vi Formal (road)* bifurcarse

bifurcation [baɪfə'keɪʃən] *n Formal* bifurcación *f*

BIG [bɪg] **1** *adj* **(a)** *(large, tall)* grande; *(before singular nouns)* gran; **a b. problem** un problema grande, un gran problema; **a b. increase** un gran *or* importante incremento; **a b. mistake** un gran *or* grave error; **how b. is it?** ¿cómo es de grande?; **to grow big(ger)** crecer; **the bigger the better** cuanto(s) más, mejor; *Fam* **it's written with a b. "P"** se escribe con una "P" grande; *Fam* **he always uses such b. words** siempre utiliza palabras muy complicadas; *Fam* **you b. bully!** ¡pedazo de matón!; *Fam* **you b. baby!** ¡mariquita!; *Literary* **she was b. with child** se le notaba la gravidez; **he's a b. eater** come un montón; **she's into jazz in a b. way** le va mucho el jazz; **he's fallen for her in a b. way** está completamente loco por ella; **they contributed to our success in a b. way** ellos contribuyeron en gran medida a nuestro éxito; IDIOM *Ironic* **that's b. of you!** ¡qué generoso(a)!; *Fam Ironic* **b. deal!** ¡vaya cosa!, *RP* ¡gran cosa!; *Fam* **it's no b. deal** ¡no es nada!, ¡no es para tanto!; *Fam* **there's no need to make a b. deal (out) of it** no es para tanto; IDIOM **to be a b. fish in a small pond** ser el que manda, pero en un ámbito reducido; IDIOM **he's getting too b. for his boots** *or* **breeches** *or US* **britches** está empezando a darse humos, se lo tiene muy creído; **a b. hand for our guest!** ¡un gran aplauso para nuestro invitado!; *Fig* **to have a b. mouth** *(be indiscreet)* ser un/una bocazas; *Fam Fig* **why did you have to open your b. mouth?** ¿por qué has tenido que ser tan bocazas *or RP* barriga resfriada?; IDIOM **to wield the b. stick** amenazar con castigos duros ▸▸ *Fam* ***the B. Apple*** *(New York)* Nueva York; ***b. band*** *(group)* big band *f*, = banda de música original de los años 40 dominada por instrumentos de viento; *(music)* big band *f*, = música interpretada por una big band; ***the B. Bang*** el big bang, la gran explosión; ***the B. Bang theory*** la teoría del big bang; ***B. Ben*** el Big Ben; *US Fam* ***the B. Board*** = la Bolsa de Nueva York; ***b. business*** los grandes negocios; **microchips are b. business at the moment** los microchips son un gran negocio en estos momentos; *Fam* ***the B. C*** el cáncer; ***b. cat*** felino *m* mayor; ***the b. city*** la gran ciudad; *US Fam* ***B. Daddy*** el jefazo, el mandamás; ***b. dipper*** *(roller coaster)* montaña *f* rusa; *US Astron* ***the B. Dipper*** la Osa Mayor; *Br Aut* ***b. end*** cabeza *f* de biela; ***b. game*** *(in hunting)* caza *f* mayor; *US* ***B. Government*** = forma de gobierno en la que se recaudan elevados impuestos para crear una sociedad de bienestar; *Fam* ***b. hair*** cabello *m* voluminoso; ***b. hand*** *(of clock)* manecilla *f* de los minutos; *US Fam* ***b. house*** *(prison)* cárcel *f*, *Esp* chirona *f*, *Andes, RP* cana *f*, *Méx* bote *m*; **in the b. house** en la cárcel *or Esp* la chirona *or Andes, RP* la cana *or Méx* el bote; ***the b. picture*** la visión global; ***the b. screen*** la pantalla grande; *Br Fam* ***the B. Smoke*** la gran ciudad *(especialmente Londres)*; ***b. spender:*** **to be a b. spender** gastar mucho; ***b. toe*** dedo *m* gordo del pie; ***b. top*** *(of circus)* carpa *f*; ***b. wheel*** *(at fair) Esp* noria *f*, *Andes* rueda *f* de Chicago, *Arg* vuelta *f* al mundo, *Chile, Urug* rueda *f* gigante, *Méx* rueda *f* de la fortuna; *Fam (powerful person)* pez *m* gordo

(b) *(important)* importante; **this week's b. story** la noticia de la semana; **to have b. ideas** tener grandes ideas; **they're still looking for the b. idea** aún están buscando la fórmula del éxito; IDIOM *Fam* **hey, what's the b. idea?** ¡eh!, ¿qué está pasando aquí?; **I've got b. plans for you** tengo grandes planes para ti; **the boss is very b. on punctuality** el jefe le da mucha importancia a la puntualidad; *Fam* **our small company can't compete with the b. boys** nuestra pequeña compañía no puede competir con los grandes (del sector); **it's her b. day tomorrow** mañana es su gran día; **today's a b. day for us** hoy es un día muy importante para nosotros; **when's the b. day?** *(wedding date)* ¿cuándo es la boda?; **b. league companies** compañías de primera línea; **to earn b. money** *or US Fam* **bucks** ganar millones ▸▸ *Fam* ***b. cheese*** mandamás *m*, pez *m* gordo; *Fam* ***b. fish*** *(important person)* pez *m* gordo; *Fam* ***the b. guns*** *(important people)* los pesos pesados; ***a b. name*** una gran figura; *Fam* ***b. noise*** mandamás *m*, pez *m* gordo; *Fam* ***b. shot*** mandamás *m*, pez *m* gordo; *Fam* ***b. talk*** palabrería *f*

(c) *(successful, popular)* famoso(a), popular; **it was b. last year**

(music, fashion) hizo furor el año pasado; **they're b. in the States** tienen mucho éxito en los Estados Unidos; **to make it b.** triunfar; **to make** *or* **hit the b. time** conseguir el éxito

(**d**) *(grown-up, older)* **my b. brother/sister** mi hermano/hermana mayor; **you're a b. girl now** ya eres mayorcita ►► ***B. Brother*** *(police state)* el Gran Hermano

2 *adv* **it went over b. with them** *(go down well)* les sentó muy bien; **he always talks b.** se le va siempre la fuerza por la boca; **to think b.** pensar a lo grande

---

bigamist ['bɪgəmɪst] *n* bígamo(a) *m,f*

bigamous ['bɪgəməs] *adj* bígamo(a)

bigamy ['bɪgəmɪ] *n* bigamia *f*

big-boned ['bɪg'bəʊnd] *adj* huesudo(a)

big-budget ['bɪg'bʌdʒɪt] *adj* de gran presupuesto

biggie, biggy ['bɪgɪ] *n Fam* **it's going to be a b.!** *(new movie, CD)* ¡va a ser un exitazo!; **I think this storm's going to be a b.** me parece que ésta va a ser una tormenta de las gordas

biggish ['bɪgɪʃ] *adj* grandecito(a), más bien grande

biggy = **biggie**

bighead ['bɪghed] *n Fam* (**a**) *(person)* creído(a) *m,f* (**b**) *US (conceit)* engreimiento *m*

bigheaded [bɪg'hedɪd] *adj Fam* creído(a), engreído(a); **we don't want him getting b.** no queremos que se vuelva un creído

big-hearted [bɪg'hɑːtɪd] *adj* **to be b.** tener gran corazón

bight [baɪt] *n (of coastline)* ensenada *f*

bigmouth ['bɪgmaʊθ] *n Fam* bocazas *mf inv*, *Am* bocón(ona) *m,f*

big-name ['bɪg'neɪm] *adj Fam* renombrado(a), de renombre

bigot ['bɪgət] *n* fanático(a) *m,f*, intolerante *mf*

bigoted ['bɪgətɪd] *adj* fanático(a), intolerante

bigotry ['bɪgətrɪ] *n* fanatismo *m*, intolerancia *f*

big-shot ['bɪgʃɒt] *adj Fam* de altos vuelos

big-ticket ['bɪgtɪkɪt] *adj US Fam* caro(a)

big-time ['bɪgtaɪm] *Fam* 1 *adj* de altos vuelos; **a b. politician** un pez gordo de la política, un político de alto nivel *or* de altos vuelos

2 *adv* a lo grande, *Esp* a base de bien; **to be into sth b.** estar supermetido(a) en algo; **he's screwed up b.** ¡la ha fastidiado bien!, ¡buena la ha hecho!

bigwig ['bɪgwɪg] *n Fam* pez *m* gordo

bijou ['biːʒuː] *adj Br (house, café)* muy cuco(a), muy mono(a); *(area, party)* finolis

bike [baɪk] 1 *n* (**a**) *Fam (bicycle)* bici *f*; *Br* **on your b.!** *(go away)* ¡largo!, ¡piérdete!; *(don't talk nonsense)* ¡no digas *Esp* chorradas *or Am* pendejadas *or RP* pavadas! ►► ***b. shed*** cobertizo *m* para bicicletas (**b**) *Fam (motorcycle)* moto *f* (**c**) *very Fam* **she's the town b.** *(promiscuous)* es el putón verbenero *or* la pelandusca del pueblo

2 *vi Fam* (**a**) *(by bicycle)* ir en bici; **we biked into town** fuimos al pueblo en bici (**b**) *(on motorcycle)* ir en moto

biker ['baɪkə(r)] *n Fam (motorcyclist)* motero(a) *m,f*

bikeway ['baɪkweɪ] *n US* carril-bici *m*

biking ['baɪkɪŋ] *n* ciclismo *m*; **b. is one of his favourite pastimes** montar en bici es uno de sus pasatiempos preferidos

bikini [bɪ'kiːnɪ] *n* biquini *m* ►► ***b. bottom*** parte *f* de abajo del biquini; ***b. line:*** **to have one's b. line done** depilarse las ingles; ***b. top*** parte *f* de arriba del biquini

bilabial [baɪ'leɪbɪəl] *Ling* 1 *n* bilabial *f*

2 *adj* bilabial

bilateral [baɪ'lætərəl] *adj* bilateral

bilberry ['bɪlbərɪ] *n* arándano *m*

bile [baɪl] 1 *n* (**a**) *Physiol* bilis *f inv*, hiel *f* ►► ***b. duct*** conducto *m* biliar (**b**) *Literary (irritability)* bilis *f inv*, hiel *f*

2 *adj Anat* biliar

bi-level ['baɪ'levəl] *adj US (house)* a dos niveles

bilge [bɪldʒ] *n* (**a**) *Naut* pantoque *m*; **the bilges** la sentina; **b. (water)** agua *f* de sentinas (**b**) *Fam (nonsense)* tonterías *fpl*, *Esp* chorradas *fpl*, *Am* pendejadas *fpl*; **to talk (a lot of) b.** no decir más que tonterías *or Esp* chorradas *or Am* pendejadas

bilharzia [bɪl'hɑːzɪə] *n Med* bilharziosis *f inv*, esquistosomiasis *f inv*

bilingual [baɪ'lɪŋgwəl] *adj* bilingüe; **he's b. in French and Russian** es bilingüe en francés y ruso

bilingualism [baɪ'lɪŋgwəlɪzəm] *n* bilingüismo *m*

bilious ['bɪlɪəs] *adj* (**a**) *Med* bilioso(a) ►► ***b. attack*** cólico *m* bilioso (**b**) *(bad-tempered)* bilioso(a), atrabiliario(a) (**c**) *(revolting)* **b. green** de un color verde amarillento nauseabundo

biliousness ['bɪlɪəsnɪs] *n* (**a**) *Med* bilis *f inv* (**b**) *(bad temper)* bilis *f inv*

bilk [bɪlk] *vt (cheat)* engañar, estafar; **they bilked her out of her fortune** le estafaron y se quedaron con toda su fortuna

Bill [bɪl] *n Br Fam* **the (Old) B.** *(the police) Esp* la pasma, *Andes* los pacos, *Col* los tombos, *Méx* los cuicos, *RP* la cana

bill[1] [bɪl] 1 *n (of bird)* pico *m*

2 *vi* **to b. and coo** *(birds)* arrullarse; *Fam (lovers)* hacerse mimos *or* arrumacos

bill[2] 1 *n* (**a**) *(in restaurant, hotel)* cuenta *f*; *(for goods, services)* factura *f*; *(for lighting, electricity)* recibo *m*, factura *f*; **put it on my b.** póngalo en mi cuenta ►► ***bills payable*** efectos *mpl* a pagar; ***bills receivable*** efectos *mpl* a cobrar

(**b**) *US (banknote)* billete *m*

(**c**) *(notice)* cartel *m*; **(stick) no bills** *(sign)* prohibido fijar carteles; **to fit** *or* **fill the b.** venir como anillo al dedo

(**d**) *Theat* **to head** *or* **top the b.** estar en cabecera de cartel

(**e**) *(list, document)* **the doctor gave me a clean b. of health** el médico me dio el visto bueno; IDIOM *US Fam* **to sell sb a b. of goods** dar a alguien gato por liebre ►► *Fin* ***b. of exchange*** letra *f* de cambio; ***b. of fare*** menú *m*, carta *f*; *Law* ***b. of indictment*** acta *f* de acusación; *Naut* ***b. of lading*** conocimiento *m* de embarque; *Com* ***b. of sale*** escritura *f or* contrato *m* de compraventa

(**f**) *Pol (proposed law)* proyecto *m* de ley

(**g**) *US* ***the B. of Rights*** = las diez primeras enmiendas a la constitución estadounidense, relacionadas con la garantía de las libertades individuales

2 *vt* (**a**) *(send invoice to)* enviar la factura a, facturar (**b**) *(publicize)* anunciar; **it was billed as the debate of the decade** fue anunciado como el debate del decenio

billboard ['bɪlbɔːd] *n* valla *f* publicitaria

billet ['bɪlɪt] 1 *n Mil* acantonamiento *m*

2 *vt* acantonar

billet-doux ['bɪleɪ'duː] (*pl* **billets-doux** ['bɪleɪ'duːz]) *n Hum or Literary* misiva *f* de amor

billfold ['bɪlfəʊld] *n US* cartera *f*, billetera *f*

billhook ['bɪlhʊk] *n* podadera *f*, navaja *f* jardinera

billiard ['bɪljəd] *n* **billiards** billar *(con agujeros)*; **to play billiards** jugar al billar ►► ***b. ball*** bola *f* de billar; ***b. cue*** taco *m* de billar; ***b. table*** mesa *f* de billar

billing ['bɪlɪŋ] *n Theat* puesto *m* en el reparto *(por orden de importancia)*; **to get top b.** ser cabeza de cartel, encabezar el reparto

billion ['bɪljən] *n* (**a**) *(thousand million)* mil millones *mpl*, millardo *m* (**b**) *Br Old-fashioned (million million)* billón *m* (**c**) *Fam* **I've got billions of things to do!** ¡tengo miles de cosas que hacer!

billionaire [bɪljə'neə(r)] *n* multimillonario(a) *m,f*

billionairess [bɪljəneə'res] *n* multimillonaria *f*

billionth ['bɪljənθ] 1 *n* milmillonésima *f*

2 *adj* milmillonésimo(a); *Fam* enésimo(a)

billow ['bɪləʊ] 1 *n* (**a**) *(of smoke)* nube *f* (**b**) *(wave)* ola *f* grande, oleada *f*

2 *vi* ondear; **smoke billowed out of the chimney** salían nubes de humo de la chimenea

► **billow out** *vi* hincharse

billowing ['bɪləʊɪŋ] *adj* hinchado(a)

billowy ['bɪləʊɪ] *adj (dress, sail)* ondeante; *(clouds)* ondulante

billposter ['bɪlpəʊstə(r)] *n* **billposters will be prosecuted** *(sign)* prohibido fijar carteles (responsable el anunciante)

billy ['bɪlɪ] *n* (**a**) *Br, Austr (container)* cazo *m* (**b**) *US* **b. (club)** porra *f* (**c**) **b. (goat)** macho *m* cabrío

billycan ['bɪlɪkæn] *n Br, Austr* olla *f*

billy-o(h) ['bɪlɪəʊ] *n Br Fam* **to run like b.** correr como alma que lleva el diablo

bimbo ['bɪmbəʊ] (*pl* **bimbos**) *n Fam Pej* = mujer atractiva y de pocas luces

bimetallic [baɪmɪ'tælɪk] *adj Tech* ***b. strip*** banda *f or* lámina *f* bimetálica

bimonthly [baɪ'mʌnθlɪ] 1 *adj* (**a**) *(every two months)* bimestral (**b**) *(twice monthly)* bimensual

2 *adv* (**a**) *(every two months)* bimestralmente (**b**) *(twice monthly)* bimensualmente, dos veces al mes

bin [bɪn] **1** *n* **(a)** *Br (domestic)* balde *m*, *Esp* cubo *m*; *(very large)* contenedor *m*; *(for waste paper, on lamppost)* papelera *f*, *Arg, Méx* cesto *m*, *Carib* zafacón *m*, *Chile* papelero *m*, *Col* caneca *f*, *Méx* bote *m*; **to put sth in the b.** tirar algo a la basura
(b) *(for coal)* carbonera *f*; *(for grain)* granero *m*; *Br (for bread)* panera *f*
(c) *Br (for wine)* botellero *m* ▸▸ ***b. end*** resto *m* *(de botellas de vino)*
(d) *Br Fam (psychiatric hospital)* loquero *m*
2 *vt* (*pt & pp* **binned**) **(a)** *(store)* almacenar **(b)** *Br Fam (discard)* tirar (a la papelera)

binary ['baɪnərɪ] *adj* **(a)** *Math & Comptr* binario(a) ▸▸ ***b. code*** código *m* binario; ***b. digit*** dígito *m* binario; ***b. file*** archivo *m* binario; ***b. notation*** numeración *f* binaria; ***b. number*** número *m* binario; ***b. search*** búsqueda *f* binaria; ***b. system*** sistema *m* binario **(b)** *Mil* ***b. weapon*** arma *f* química de agente binario **(c)** *Astron* ***b. star*** estrella *f* binaria *or* doble; ***b. system*** sistema *m* binario

bin-bag ['bɪnbæg] *n Br* bolsa *f* de basura

bind [baɪnd] **1** *n Fam* **(a)** *(awkward situation)* **to be in a b.** estar en un apuro
(b) *Br (inconvenience)* **it's a real b. to have to...** es un verdadero fastidio tener que..., es una verdadera lata tener que...
2 *vt* (*pt & pp* **bound** [baʊnd]) **(a)** *(tie)* atar; **to b. sb hand and foot** atar a alguien de pies y manos; *Fig* **they are bound together by ties of friendship** les unen lazos *or* vínculos de amistad
(b) *(bandage)* vendar
(c) *(book)* encuadernar; **bound in leather** encuadernado en cuero *or Esp, Méx* piel
(d) *(garment)* atar
(e) *(cause to stick)* unir, ligar; **b. the mixture with egg** ligar la mezcla con huevo
(f) *(oblige)* **she bound me to secrecy** me hizo prometer que guardaría el secreto
3 *vi (sauce)* ligarse

▸ **bind over** *vt sep Law* **to b. sb over** obligar judicialmente a alguien; *Br* **they were bound over to keep the peace** les fue impuesta una caución de buen comportamiento; *US* **he was bound over to the grand jury** estaba obligado (por ley) a comparecer ante el jurado de acusación

▸ **bind up** *vt sep* **(a)** *(cut, wound)* vendar **(b)** **to be bound up with sth** *(involved)* estar íntimamente relacionado(a) con algo

binder ['baɪndə(r)] *n* **(a)** *(for papers)* carpeta *f* **(b)** *(bookbinder)* encuadernador(ora) *m,f*; *(company)* empresa *f* de encuadernación **(c)** *(farm machinery)* empacadora *f* **(d)** *(glue, for sauce)* aglutinante *m*

binding ['baɪndɪŋ] **1** *n* **(a)** *(of book)* cubierta *f*, tapa *f* **(b)** *(on skis)* fijación *f*
2 *adj (agreement, commitment)* vinculante; **the agreement is b. on all parties** el acuerdo es vinculante para todas las partes

bindweed ['baɪndwiːd] *n* enredadera *f*

binge [bɪndʒ] *Fam* **1** *n (drinking spree)* borrachera *f*; **to go on a b.** ir de juerga *or Esp* marcha; **to go on a shopping b.** ir de compras y traerse media tienda; **a chocolate b.** un atracón de chocolate
2 *vi* **to b. on sth** darse un atracón de algo; **a cycle of bingeing and dieting** un ciclo de atracones y dietas

bingo ['bɪŋgəʊ] **1** *n* bingo *m* ▸▸ ***b. caller*** locutor(ora) *m,f* de bingo; ***b. hall*** (sala *f* de) bingo *m*
2 *exclam* ¡olé!, ¡bravo!

bin-liner ['bɪnlaɪnə(r)] *n Br* bolsa *f* de basura

binman ['bɪnmæn] *n Br* basurero *m*

binnacle ['bɪnəkəl] *n Naut* bitácora *f*

binocular [bɪ'nɒkjʊlə(r)] *adj* binocular; **b. vision** visión binocular

binoculars [bɪ'nɒkjʊləz] *npl* prismáticos *mpl*

binomial [baɪ'nəʊmɪəl] *Math* **1** *n (algebra)* binomio *m*
2 *adj* ***b. distribution*** distribución *f* binomial; ***b. theorem*** binomio *m* de Newton

bint [bɪnt] *n Br very Fam Pej* tipa *f*, *Esp* tía *f*

bioassay [baɪəʊə'seɪ] *n* bioensayo *m*

biochemic(al) [baɪəʊ'kemɪk(əl)] *adj* bioquímico(a)

biochemist [baɪəʊ'kemɪst] *n* bioquímico(a) *m,f*

biochemistry [baɪəʊ'kemɪstrɪ] *n* bioquímica *f*

biodata ['baɪəʊdeɪtə] *n* datos *mpl* biográficos

biodegradable [baɪəʊdɪ'greɪdəbəl] *adj* biodegradable

biodiversity [baɪəʊdaɪ'vɜːsɪtɪ] *n* biodiversidad *f*

bioengineering ['baɪəʊendʒɪ'nɪərɪŋ], **biological engineering** [baɪə'lɒdʒɪkəlendʒɪ'nɪərɪŋ] *n* **(a)** *Med* ingeniería *f* biomédica **(b)** *Biol* bioingeniería *f*

biofeedback [baɪəʊ'fiːdbæk] *n Psy* biorreacción *f*

biogas ['baɪəʊgæs] *n* biogás *m*

biographer [baɪ'ɒgrəfə(r)] *n* biógrafo(a) *m,f*

biographic(al) [baɪə'græfɪk(əl)] *adj* biográfico(a)

biography [baɪ'ɒgrəfɪ] *n* biografía *f*

biological [baɪə'lɒdʒɪkəl] *adj* biológico(a) ▸▸ ***b. clock*** reloj *m* biológico; ***b. diversity*** diversidad *f* biológica; ***b. niche*** nicho *m* biológico; ***b. warfare*** guerra *f* bacteriológica; ***b. washing powder*** detergente *m* de *or* con acción biológica

biological engineering = **bioengineering**

biologist [baɪ'ɒlədʒɪst] *n* biólogo(a) *m,f*

biology [baɪ'ɒlədʒɪ] *n* biología *f*

biomass ['baɪəʊmæs] *n* biomasa *f*

biometrics [baɪəʊ'metrɪks] *n* biometría *f*

bionic [baɪ'ɒnɪk] *adj* biónico(a)

bionics [baɪ'ɒnɪks] *n* biónica *f*

biophysicist [baɪəʊ'fɪzɪsɪst] *n* biofísico(a) *m,f*

biophysics [baɪəʊ'fɪzɪks] *n* biofísica *f*

biopic ['baɪəʊpɪk] *n Fam (movie)* película *f* biográfica

biopiracy [baɪəʊ'paɪrəsɪ] *n* biopiratería *f*

biopsy ['baɪɒpsɪ] *n Med* biopsia *f*

biorhythm ['baɪəʊrɪðəm] *n* biorritmo *m*

BIOS ['baɪɒs] *n Comptr* (*abbr* **Basic Input/Output System**) BIOS *m or f*

bioscope ['baɪəʊskəʊp] *n SAfr* cine *m*

biosphere ['baɪəʊsfɪə(r)] *n* biosfera *f*

biosynthesis [baɪəʊ'sɪnθɪsɪs] *n* biosíntesis *f inv*

biotech ['baɪəʊtek] **1** *n* biotecnología *f*
2 *adj (industry, company)* de biotecnología

biotechnology [baɪəʊtek'nɒlədʒɪ] *n* biotecnología *f*

bioterrorism ['baɪəʊ'terərɪzəm] *n* bioterrorismo *m*

bioterrorist ['baɪəʊ'terərɪst] *n* bioterrorista *mf*

bipartisan [baɪ'pɑːtɪzæn] *adj Pol* bipartito(a)

bipartite [baɪ'pɑːtaɪt] *adj* **(a)** *(in two parts)* con dos partes, *Spec* bipartido(a) **(b)** *(agreement, talks)* bipartito(a), bilateral

biped ['baɪped] **1** *n* bípedo(a) *m,f*
2 *adj* bípedo(a)

biplane ['baɪpleɪn] *n* biplano *m*

bipolar [baɪ'pəʊlə(r)] *adj Elec (transistor)* bipolar

biracial [baɪ'reɪʃəl] *adj* **a b. area** una zona en la que conviven gentes de dos razas

birch [bɜːtʃ] **1** *n* **(a)** *(tree, wood)* abedul *m* **(b)** *Br (rod for whipping)* vara *f*; **to give sb the b.** azotar a alguien
2 *vt (beat)* azotar

Bircher ['bɜːtʃə(r)] *n US Pol* = miembro de la John Birch Society, asociación estadounidense anticomunista y ultraconservadora

bird [bɜːd] *n* **(a)** *(gen)* pájaro *m*; *(as opposed to mammals, reptiles etc)* ave *f* ▸▸ ***b. of ill omen*** pájaro *m* de mal agüero; ***b.'s nest soup*** sopa *f* de nido de golondrina; ***b. of paradise*** ave *f* del paraíso; ***b. of paradise flower*** flor *m* del paraíso; ***b. of passage*** *(bird)* ave *f* migratoria *or* de paso; *(person)* ave *f* de paso; ***b. of prey*** (ave *f*) rapaz *f*, ave *f* de presa; ***b. sanctuary*** refugio *m* de aves; *Av* ***b. strike*** colisión *f* con un ave; ***b. table*** comedero *m* de pájaros
(b) *Br Fam (woman)* nena *f*, *Arg* piba *f*
(c) *Fam (man)* tipo *m*; **he's a strange** *or* **odd** *or* **queer b.** es un tipo raro
(d) *Br Fam (imprisonment)* **to do b.** pasar una temporada a la sombra
(e) IDIOMS **she eats like a b.** come como un pajarito; **the b. has flown** el pájaro ha volado; **a little b. told me** me lo dijo un pajarito; **it's (strictly) for the birds** es cosa de bobos, es del género tonto; *Br* **to give sb the b.** *(boo, shout at)* abroncar *or* abuchear a alguien; *US* **to give** *or* **flip sb the b.** = hacer un gesto grosero a alguien con el dedo medio hacia arriba, ≃ hacer un corte de mangas a alguien; **to kill two birds with one stone** matar dos pájaros de un tiro; *Euph* **to tell sb about the birds and the bees** explicar a alguien de dónde vienen los niños; PROV **a b. in the hand is worth two in the bush** más vale pájaro en mano que ciento volando; PROV **birds of a feather flock together** Dios los cría y ellos se juntan; **he and his father are birds of a feather** él y su padre son de tal palo, tal astilla

birdbath ['bɜːdbɑːθ] *n* = especie de pila con agua que se coloca en el jardín para que los pájaros se refresquen

birdbrain ['bɜːdbreɪn] *n Fam* cabeza *mf* de chorlito

bird-brained ['bɜ:dbreɪnd] *adj Fam* **to be b.** ser un(a) majadero(a); **a b. idea** una majadería

birdcage ['bɜ:dkeɪdʒ] *n* jaula *f*

birdcall ['bɜ:dkɔ:l] *n* canto *m*

bird-dog ['bɜ:ddɒg] *US* **1** *n* perro *m* cobrador
2 *vt (watch)* vigilar de cerca, estar encima de

birder ['bɜ:də(r)] *n Fam* aficionado(a) *m,f* a la observación de aves

bird-fancier ['bɜ:dfænsɪə(r)] *n Br* criador(ora) *m,f* de pájaros

birdhouse ['bɜ:dhaʊs] *n US* **(a)** *(box)* caja *f* nido **(b)** *(aviary)* pajarera *f*

birdie ['bɜ:dɪ] **1** *n* **(a)** *Fam (bird)* pajarito *m*; *Br* **watch the b.!** *(photographer to children)* ¡mira el pajarito! **(b)** *(in golf)* uno *m* bajo par, birdie *m*; **a b. 3** un birdie en un par cuatro
2 *vt (in golf)* **to b. a hole** hacer uno bajo par *or* birdie en un hoyo

birding ['bɜ:dɪŋ] *n Fam* observación *f* de aves; **to go b.** ir a observar aves

birdlike ['bɜ:dlaɪk] *adj (appetite, movements)* de pajarito

bird-lime ['bɜ:dlaɪm] *n* liga *f*

birdseed ['bɜ:dsi:d] *n* alpiste *m*

bird's-eye view ['bɜ:dzaɪ'vju:] *n* **to have a b.** *(of place)* tener una vista panorámica *(desde arriba)*; *(of situation)* tener una visión de conjunto

birdshot ['bɜ:dʃɒt] *n* perdigones *mpl*

birdsong ['bɜ:dsɒŋ] *n* canto *m* de los pájaros *or* las aves

birdwatcher ['bɜ:dwɒtʃə(r)] *n* aficionado(a) *m,f* a la observación de aves, observador(ora) *m,f* de aves

birdwatching ['bɜ:dwɒtʃɪŋ] *n* observación *f* de aves; **to go b.** ir a observar aves

biretta [bɪ'retə] *n Rel* birreta *f*

biriani, biryani [bɪrɪ'ɑ:nɪ] *n Culin* = plato indio a base de arroz especiado, con azafrán y carne o pescado

Birmingham ['bɜ:mɪŋəm] *n* Birmingham

Biro® ['baɪrəʊ] *(pl* **Biros***)* *n Br* **B. (pen)** bolígrafo *m*, *Carib* pluma *f*, *Col, Ecuad* esferográfico *m*, *CSur* lapicera *f*, *Méx* pluma *f* (atómica)

birth [bɜ:θ] *n also Fig* nacimiento *m*; *(delivery)* parto *m*; **to give b. (to sb)** dar a luz (a alguien); **at b.** al nacer; **from b.** de nacimiento; **Irish by b.** irlandés(esa) de nacimiento; **of noble/low b.** de noble/baja cuna ►► ***b. certificate*** partida *f* de nacimiento; ***b. control*** control *m* de (la) natalidad; ***b. control methods*** métodos *mpl* anticonceptivos; ***b. mother*** madre *f* biológica; *also Fig* ***b. pangs*** dolores *mpl* del parto; ***b. parent*** *(father)* padre *m* biológico; *(mother)* madre *f* biológica; ***b. rate*** tasa *f or* índice *m* de natalidad; ***b. sign*** signo *m* del zodiaco

birthday ['bɜ:θdeɪ] *n* cumpleaños *m inv*; **on her twenty-first b.** el día que cumplió veintiún años; **she was forty-two on her last b.** tiene cuarenta y dos años cumplidos; **let me buy the b. girl/boy a drink** te invito a una copa por estar de cumpleaños; IDIOM *Fam* **she was in her b. suit** estaba como su madre la trajo al mundo ►► ***b. cake*** tarta *f* de cumpleaños; ***b. card*** (tarjeta *f* de) felicitación *f* de cumpleaños; *Br* ***b. honours*** = títulos honorarios concedidos el día del cumpleaños del monarca británico; ***b. party*** fiesta *f* de cumpleaños; ***b. present*** regalo *m* de cumpleaños

birthing pool ['bɜ:θɪŋpu:l] *n Br* = bañera portátil para partos en el agua

birthmark ['bɜ:θmɑ:k] *n* antojo *m*, marca *f* de nacimiento

birthplace ['bɜ:θpleɪs] *n* lugar *m* de nacimiento

birthright ['bɜ:θraɪt] *n* derecho *m* natural

biryani = **biriani**

Biscay ['bɪskeɪ] *n* **the Bay of B.** el Golfo de Vizcaya

biscuit ['bɪskɪt] **1** *n* **(a)** *Br (sweet, salted)* galleta *f*; IDIOM *Fam* **that really takes the b.!** ¡esto es el colmo! **(b)** *US (muffin)* tortita *f*, bollo *m* **(c)** *(colour)* beige *m inv*, *Esp* beis *m inv* **(d)** *(ceramics)* bizcocho *m*, biscuit *m*
2 *adj (colour)* beige *inv*, *Esp* beis *inv*

bisect [baɪ'sekt] *vt* **(a)** *Math* bisecar **(b)** *(of road) (town, area)* dividir por la mitad

bisexual [baɪ'seksjʊəl] **1** *n* bisexual *mf*
2 *adj* bisexual

bisexuality [baɪseksjʊ'ælɪtɪ] *n* bisexualidad *f*

bishop ['bɪʃəp] *n* **(a)** *Rel* obispo *m* ►► ***bishops' conference*** conferencia *f* episcopal **(b)** *(in chess)* alfil *m*

bishopric ['bɪʃəprɪk] *n* **(a)** *(office)* obispado *m* **(b)** *(diocese)* obispado *m*

bismuth ['bɪzməθ] *n Chem* bismuto *m*

bison ['baɪsən] *n* bisonte *m*

bisque [bɪsk] *n* **(a)** *Culin* crema *f* de mariscos, bisqué *m* ►► ***lobster b.*** crema *f* de langosta **(b)** *(unglazed china)* bizcocho *m*

bistro ['bi:strəʊ] *(pl* **bistros***)* *n* restaurante *m* pequeño

bisulphate, *US* **bisulfate** [baɪ'sʌlfeɪt] *n Chem* bisulfato *m*

bisync [baɪ'sɪŋk], **bisynchronous** [baɪ'sɪŋkrənəs] *adj Comptr* bisíncrono(a)

bit[1] [bɪt] *n* **(a)** *(in horseriding)* bocado *m*; IDIOM **to have the b. between one's teeth** haber tomado *or Esp* cogido carrerilla **(b)** *(for drill)* broca *f*

BIT[2] *n* **(a)** *(piece)* trozo *m*; **would you like a b. of cake?** ¿quieres un trozo de pastel?; **he has eaten every b.** se ha comido hasta el último bocado; **to blow sth to bits** volar algo en pedazos; **to come** *or* **fall to bits** romperse en pedazos; *Fig* **this house is falling to bits!** ¡esta casa se cae en pedazos!; **to take sth to bits** desarmar *or* desmontar algo; **to tear/smash sth to bits** hacer añicos algo; **I'm doing it a b. at a time** lo estoy haciendo poco a poco; **b. by b.** poco a poco; *Fam* **I'm not into the whole marriage b.** el rollo del matrimonio no va conmigo; **bits and pieces** *or* **bobs** *(personal belongings)* cosas, trastos; IDIOM *Fam* **to have a b. on the side** tener un rollo, *RP* tener una historia; IDIOM *Fam* **she's my b. on the side** tengo un rollo *or RP* una historia con ella

(b) *(part)* parte *f*; **this is the easy b.** ésta es la parte fácil; **the best b. was when...** lo mejor fue cuando...; **I have done my b.** yo he cumplido con mi parte; **I try to do my b. for charity** intento poner mi granito de arena por las organizaciones benéficas

(c) *(expressing amount)* **a b. of** *(some)* un poco de; **a b. of advice** un consejo; **we had a b. of difficulty in finding him** nos costó un poco encontrarlo; **do a b. of exercise every day** haz algo de ejercicio todos los días; **with a b. of luck** con un poco de suerte; **a b. of news** una noticia; **would you like some more coffee? – just a b., please** ¿quieres más café? – sólo un poquito; **he's a b. of an idiot** es bastante idiota; **I've got a b. of a sore throat** me duele un poco la garganta; **this could become a b. of a problem** puede que esto dé problemas; **he views himself as a b. of an authority on the subject** se cree toda una autoridad en el tema; **that'll take a b. of doing** no será nada fácil hacerlo; **it takes a b. of getting used to** se tarda algo en acostumbrarse; **that must have cost a b.!** ¡debe de haber costado una fortuna *or* un dineral!; IDIOM *Fam* **she's a b. of all right** está muy buena, no está nada mal; IDIOM *Br Fam* **a b. of fluff** *or* **stuff** *or* **skirt** un bombón

(d) *(expressing degree)* **a b. late/heavy/tired** un poco tarde/pesado(a)/cansado(a); **a b. more/less** un poco más/menos; **could you turn the fire up a b.?** ¿podrías subir el fuego un poco?; **it's a b. like a Picasso** se parece algo a un Picasso; **it's a b. too small** es un poco pequeño; **I'm a b. cold, actually** la verdad es que tengo algo de frío; **it's a b. annoying** es bastante molesto; **this curry's a b. on the hot side** este curry está muy picante; **I'm every b. as good as him** no tengo nada que envidiarle; **a good b. older** bastante más viejo(a); **he wasn't the least b. nervous** no estaba nervioso en absoluto; **a little b. worried/tired** algo preocupado(a)/cansado(a); **you haven't changed a b.** no has cambiado lo más mínimo; **he's not a b. like his father** no se parece en nada a su padre; IDIOM **not a b. (of it)!** ¡en absoluto!; **it's quite a b. warmer today** hace bastante más calor hoy; **we saved quite a b. of time** ahorramos bastante tiempo; IDIOM *Fam* **that's a b. much!** ¡eso es pasarse!; *Fam* **it was a b. much of them to expect us to help** ¡fue un poco fuerte esperar que les ayudáramos!

(e) *(with time)* rato *m*, momento *m*; **I'm popping out for a b.** voy a salir un rato *or* momento; **I'll be back in a b.** vuelvo en un momento; **wait a b.!** ¡espera un poco!

(f) *Comptr* bit *m*; **bits per second** bits por segundo; **a 16-b. computer** *Esp* un ordenador *or Am* una computadora de 16 bits ►► ***b. chain*** cadena *f* de bits; ***b. command*** comando *m* binario

(g) *Fam (coin)* moneda *f*; *US* **two bits** 25 centavos

(h) *US Fam (term of imprisonment)* **he did a b. in Fort Worth** estuvo *Esp* enchironado *or Méx* en el bote *or RP* en cana en Fort Worth

---

bit[3] *pt of* **bite**

bitch [bɪtʃ] **1** *n* **(a)** *(female dog)* perra *f*; *(female wolf)* loba *f*
(b) *very Fam Pej (unpleasant woman)* bruja *f*, zorra *f*
(c) *Br Fam (person)* **the poor b.** la pobre desgraciada; **the lucky b.** la muy suertuda
(d) *Fam (awkward thing, task)* fastidio *m*, *Esp* jodienda *f*; **her place is a b. to find without a map** no hay Dios que encuentre su casa sin un mapa; **I've had a b. of a day** he tenido un día bien jodido; IDIOM **life's a b.!** ¡qué vida más perra!
(e) *Fam (complaint)* queja *f*; **what's their latest b.?** ¿de qué se quejan ahora?
2 *vi Fam* **(a)** *(complain)* quejarse, *Esp* dar la tabarra
(b) *(say malicious things about)* chismorrear; **he's always bitching**

about his colleagues siempre está poniendo a parir *or RP* sacándole el cuero a sus compañeros

3 *vt US Fam (spoil)* jorobar

▸ **bitch up** *vt sep US Fam* jorobar

bitchin ['bɪtʃɪn] *adj US very Fam* cojonudo(a), *Méx* chingón(ona), *RP* macanudo(a)

bitchiness ['bɪtʃɪnɪs] *n Fam* mala idea *f*, mala uva *f*

bitchy ['bɪtʃɪ] *adj Fam* malicioso(a), *Esp* puñetero(a); **she was very b. to the new girl** fue muy puñetera con la chica nueva

bite [baɪt] 1 *n* (a) *(of person, dog)* mordisco *m*; *(of insect)* picadura *f*; *(of snake)* mordedura *f*, picadura *f*

(b) *(mouthful)* bocado *m*; **he took a b. out of the apple** dio un bocado a la manzana; **I haven't had a b. to eat all day** no he probado bocado en todo el día

(c) *(in fishing)* **I haven't had a b. all day** no han picado en todo el día

(d) *(sharpness, fierceness) (of speech, article)* chispa *f*; **this mustard has a bit of a b.** esta mostaza está fuertecilla

(e) *(in dentistry)* mordida *f*

(f) IDIOMS *Fam* **to put the b. on sb** hacer chantaje a alguien; *Br* **to get another** *or* **a second b. at the cherry** tener una segunda oportunidad

2 *vt* (*pt* **bit** [bɪt], *pp* **bitten** ['bɪtən]) (a) *(of person, dog)* morder; *(of insect, snake)* picar; **the dog bit him in** *or* **on the leg** el perro le mordió en la pierna; **the dog bit the rope in two** el perro rompió la cuerda de un mordisco; **to b. one's lip** *(accidentally)* morderse un labio; *(not cry out in pain)* morderse la lengua; *also Fig* **to b. one's tongue** morderse la lengua; **to b. one's nails** morderse las uñas

(b) *Fam (bother)* **what's biting him?** ¿qué mosca le ha picado?

(c) IDIOMS *Fam* **to b. the bullet** agarrar el toro por los cuernos *or RP* las astas; *Fam* **to b. the dust** *(scheme, plan)* irse a pique *or* al garete *or RP* al cuerno; **to b. the hand that feeds you** morder la mano que nos da de comer; PROV **once bitten twice shy** gato escaldado del agua fría huye, *RP* el que se quemó con leche, ve una vaca y llora; *US Fam* **b. me!**, *very Fam* **b. my ass!** *Esp* ¡vete a tomar por culo!, *Méx* ¡vete a la chingada!, *RP* ¡andá a cagar!

3 *vi* (a) *(person, dog)* morder; *(insect, snake)* picar; **to b. into sth** dar un mordisco a algo; **he bit through the cord** rompió la cuerda de un mordisco

(b) *(penetrate) (screw, drill)* penetrar; **the cost bit into our savings** los gastos supusieron una merma en nuestros ahorros; **the acid bit into the metal** el ácido corroyó el metal; **the rope bit into his wrists** la cuerda se le clavaba en las muñecas

(c) *(be felt) (cuts, recession)* hacerse notar; **the law is beginning to b.** la ley comienza a hacerse notar

(d) *(take bait)* picar, morder el anzuelo

(e) *US Fam (be bad)* ser una mierda

▸ **bite back** *vt sep* contener

▸ **bite off** *vt sep* arrancar de un mordisco; IDIOM **to b. off more than one can chew** querer abarcar demasiado; *Fam* **there's no need to b. my head off!** ¡no hace falta que me contestes así!

biter ['baɪtə(r)] *n Br* IDIOM **it's a case of the b. bit** es como el cazador cazado

bite-sized ['baɪtsaɪzd], **bitesize** ['baɪtsaɪz] *adj* del tamaño de un bocado

biting ['baɪtɪŋ] *adj* (a) *(wind, cold)* penetrante (b) *(satire, wit, sarcasm)* penetrante

bitingly ['baɪtɪŋlɪ] *adj* **a b. cold wind** un viento helador

bitmap ['bɪtmæp] *Comptr* 1 *adj* en mapa de bits

2 *n* mapa *m* de bits

bit-mapped ['bɪtmæpt] *adj Comptr* en mapa de bits

bit-part ['bɪtpɑːt] *n (in play, movie)* papel *m* secundario

bitten *pp of* **bite**

bitter ['bɪtə(r)] 1 *n Br (beer)* = cerveza sin burbujas y de tono castaño

2 *adj* (a) *(taste)* amargo(a); IDIOM **it was a b. pill to swallow** costó mucho tragar (con) aquello ▸▸ ***b. almond*** almendra *f* amarga; ***b. lemon*** *(drink)* refresco *m* de limón

(b) *(wind, cold, weather)* recio(a)

(c) *(resentful) (person)* amargado(a), resentido(a); **to be b. about sth** estar resentido(a) por algo

(d) *(extremely unpleasant) (argument, words)* agrio(a); *(tears)* de amargura; *(blow)* duro(a); *(experience, memories, disappointment)* amargo(a)

(e) *(persistent) (opposition)* recio(a); *(struggle)* encarnizado(a); **to go on/resist to the b. end** seguir/resistir hasta el final

bitterly ['bɪtəlɪ] *adv* (a) **it was b. cold** hacía un frío horrible (b) *(resentfully)* **to complain b.** quejarse amargamente (c) *(extremely)* enormemente, terriblemente; **we were b. disappointed** nos llevamos una decepción tremenda; **I b. regretted telling them** me arrepentí enormemente de habérselo dicho

bittern ['bɪtən] *n* avetoro *m*

bitterness ['bɪtənɪs] *n* (a) *(taste)* amargor *m* (b) *(of cold, wind, weather)* crudeza *f*, inclemencia *f* (c) *(resentment)* amargura *f*, amargor *m*; **there was no b. in his voice** no había rastro de amargura en su voz (d) *(of opposition, struggle)* crudeza *f*

bitters ['bɪtəz] *npl (flavour for drinks)* bíter *m*, = aromatizante o tónico amargo del estilo de la angostura

bittersweet ['bɪtəswiːt] *adj (taste)* agridulce; **b. memories** recuerdos entre dulces y amargos

bitty ['bɪtɪ] *adj Fam* (a) *(incomplete, disconnected)* deshilvanado(a) (b) *US (small)* **a little b. town** una ciudad chiquitita

bitumen ['bɪtjʊmɪn] *n* betún *m*

bituminous [bɪ'tjuːmɪnəs] *adj* bituminoso(a) ▸▸ ***b. coal*** hulla *f*

bivalent [baɪ'veɪlənt] *adj Chem* bivalente

bivalve ['baɪvælv] *n Zool* (molusco *m*) bivalvo *m*

bivariate [baɪ'veərɪət] *adj Math* bivariante

bivouac ['bɪvʊæk] 1 *n* vivac *m*, vivaque *m*

2 *vi* (*pt & pp* **bivouacked**) vivaquear

bivvy ['bɪvɪ] *n Fam* vivac *m*, vivaque *m* ▸▸ ***b. bag*** saco *m* de vivac

bi-weekly [baɪ'wiːklɪ] 1 *adj* (a) *(fortnightly)* quincenal (b) *(twice weekly)* bisemanal

2 *adv* (a) *(fortnightly)* quincenalmente (b) *(twice weekly)* dos veces por semana

3 *n* (a) *(fortnightly publication)* publicación *f* quincenal (b) *(twice weekly publication)* publicación *f* bisemanal

biz [bɪz] *n* negocio *m*; *Br Fam* **it's the b.!** ¡es demasié *or Esp* la bomba!

bizarre [bɪ'zɑː(r)] *adj* extraño(a), raro(a)

bizarrely [bɪ'zɑːlɪ] *adv* extrañamente, de una forma extraña *or* rara

bk (a) (*abbr* **book**) l. (b) (*abbr* **bank**) bco.

blab [blæb] (*pt & pp* **blabbed**) *Fam* 1 *vt* soltar

2 *vi* (a) *(tell secret)* cantar; **someone has blabbed to the newspapers** alguien se lo ha soplado a los periódicos (b) *(chatter)* parlotear, *Esp* largar, *Méx* platicar, *RP* chusmear

blabber ['blæbə(r)] *vi Fam (chatter)* parlotear, *Esp* largar, *Méx* platicar, *RP* chusmear

blabbermouth ['blæbəmaʊθ] *n Fam* cotorra *f*, bocazas *mf inv*, *Am* bocón(ona) *m,f*

black [blæk] 1 *n* (a) *(colour)* negro *m*; **to be dressed in b.** ir vestido(a) de negro

(b) *(person)* negro(a) *m,f*

(c) *(darkness)* oscuridad *f*

(d) *(in chess)* **B. wins in three moves** las negras ganan en tres movimientos

(e) IDIOMS **to be in the b.** *(financially)* tener saldo positivo; **it says here in b. and white...** aquí *Esp* pone *or Am* dice claramente que...; **to see everything in b. and white** tener una actitud maniquea; **he'd swear b. is white** es capaz de vender a su madre

2 *adj* (a) *(colour)* negro(a); **b. and blue** *(bruised)* amoratado(a); **they beat him b. and blue** la paliza lo dejó amoratado; IDIOM **as b. as tar** *or Br* **pitch** oscuro como la boca del lobo ▸▸ ***b. bass*** perca *f* americana; ***b. bean*** *(haricot, fermented) Esp* judía *f* negra, *Andes, CAm, Carib, Méx* frijol *m* negro, *Andes, RP* poroto *m* negro; ***b. bear*** oso *m* negro; ***b. belt*** *(in martial arts)* cinturón *m* negro; **to be a b. belt** ser cinturón negro; *Av* ***b. box*** caja *f* negra; ***b. bread*** pan *m* moreno *or* negro (de centeno); ***b. cab*** = típico taxi negro británico; ***b. duck*** ánade *m* sombrío; ***b. eye*** ojo *m* morado; **to give sb a b. eye** ponerle un ojo morado a alguien; ***b. grouse*** gallo *m* lira; ***b. guillemot*** arao *m* aliblanco; *Astron* ***b. hole*** agujero *m* negro; ***b. ice*** placas *fpl* de hielo; ***b. kite*** milano *m* negro; ***b. light*** luz *f* negra; ***b. lung (disease)*** neumoconiosis *f*; ***b. nightshade*** hierba *f* mora; ***b. olive*** aceituna *f* negra; ***b. panther*** pantera *f* negra; ***b. pepper*** pimienta *f* negra; *esp Br* ***b. pudding*** morcilla *f*; ***b. rat*** rata *f* campestre; ***b. redstart*** colirrojo *m* tizón; *Fig* ***b. sheep*** oveja *f* negra; ***b. stork*** cigüeña *f* negra; ***b. tern*** fumarel *m*; ***b. tie*** *Esp* pajarita *f* negra, *Chile* humita *f* negra, *Col* corbatín *m* negro, *Méx* corbata *f* de moño negra, *RP* moñito *m* negro, *Ven* corbata *f* de lacito negra; *(on invitation)* se ruega ir de etiqueta; *Br* ***b. treacle*** melaza *f* oscura; ***b. vulture*** buitre *m* monje; ***b. wheatear*** collalba *f* negra; ***b. widow (spider)*** viuda *f* negra

(b) *(race)* negro(a); **a b. man** un negro; **a b. woman** una negra; **the b. vote** el voto negro, el voto de los negros ▸▸ ***B. Africa*** el África negra; ***B. Consciousness*** (el movimiento de) la conciencia negra; ***B.***

Muslims musulmanes *mpl* negros, negros *mpl* musulmanes; ***the B. Panthers*** los Panteras Negras; ***B. Power*** el poder negro; ***B. Studies*** = estudios de lo relacionado con la raza negra
(c) *(coffee)* solo(a), *RP* negro(a); *(tea)* solo(a)
(d) *(evil, unfavourable)* **to give sb a b. look** lanzar a alguien una mirada asesina; **the future is looking b.** el futuro se presenta muy negro; **he's not as b. as he's painted** no es tan malo como lo pintan; **it's a b. day for Britain** es un día negro *or* aciago para Gran Bretaña; **to be in sb's b. books** haber caído en desgracia con alguien, estar en la lista negra de alguien; **that earned him a b. mark** aquello supuso un borrón en su historial; **a b. mark against sb** un punto en contra de alguien ►► ***the b. arts*** las artes de encantamiento, la brujería; ***b. magic*** magia *f* negra; ***b. mass*** misa *f* negra; ***b. spot*** *(for accidents)* punto *m* negro
(e) *(macabre)* ***b. comedy*** *(play, movie)* comedia *f* de humor negro; ***b. humour*** humor *m* negro
(f) *(unofficial)* ***b. economy*** economía *f* sumergida; ***b. market*** mercado *m* negro; ***b. marketeer*** estraperlista *mf*
(g) *(in proper names)* ***the B. Country*** = la región industrial de las Midlands de Inglaterra; ***the B. Death*** la peste negra; ***the B. Forest*** la Selva Negra; ***B. Forest gateau*** = tarta de chocolate y guindas; ***B. Friar*** dominico *m*; ***the B. Hole of Calcutta:*** IDIOM **it's like the B. Hole of Calcutta in there** es como una lata de sardinas; *Br Fam* ***B. Maria*** *(police van)* furgón *m* celular *or* policial; *Parl* ***B. Rod*** = ujier de la cámara de los lores británica encargado de convocar a los comunes cuando se abre el periodo de sesiones; ***the B. Sea*** el Mar Negro; *Hist* ***the B. and Tans*** = fuerza armada de policía que Gran Bretaña envió en 1920 a Irlanda para combatir el levantamiento independentista; ***the B. Watch*** = regimiento del ejército británico que cuenta con la falda escocesa como parte de su uniforme
3 *vt* (a) *(blacken)* ennegrecer, pintar de negro; *(shoes)* embetunar; **to b. sb's eye** ponerle un ojo morado a alguien (b) *Br (boycott) (company)* boicotear

► **black out** 1 *vt sep* (a) *(censor) (piece of writing)* borrar, tachar; *(person in photo)* suprimir (b) *(city)* dejar a oscuras (c) *Rad & TV* **industrial action has blacked out this evening's programmes** la huelga ha obligado a suspender los programas de esta noche
2 *vi (faint)* desmayarse

► **black up** *vi Theat* = pintarse la cara para interpretar el papel de un negro

black-and-white ['blækən'waɪt] *adj (movie, TV, illustration)* en blanco y negro

blackball ['blækbɔːl] *vt* vetar, votar en contra de

blackberry ['blækbərɪ] 1 *n* (a) *(bush)* zarzamora *f* (b) *(berry)* mora *f*
2 *vi* **to go blackberrying** ir a buscar moras

blackbird ['blækbɜːd] *n* mirlo *m*

blackboard ['blækbɔːd] *n* pizarra *f*, encerado *m*, *Am* pizarrón *m* ►► ***the b. jungle*** = la escuela como lugar de enfrentamiento violento entre alumnos y profesores

blackcap ['blækkæp] *n* curruca *f* capirotada

blackcurrant ['blækkʌrənt] *n* (a) *(berry)* grosella *f* negra (b) *(bush)* grosellero *m* (negro)

blacken ['blækən] 1 *vt* (a) *(make black)* ennegrecer; **he blackened his face** se pintó la cara de negro; **clouds blackened the sky** las nubes oscurecían el cielo (b) *(make dirty)* manchar; **smoke-blackened buildings** edificios ennegrecidos por el humo (c) *Fig (name, reputation)* manchar
2 *vi (cloud, sky)* ennegrecerse, oscurecerse

black-eyed ['blækaɪd] *adj* ***b. bean*** alubia *f* carilla; ***b. pea*** alubia *f* carilla; ***b. Susan*** *(flower)* rubeckia *f*

blackface ['blækfeɪs] *n Old-fashioned* **in b.** con la cara pintada de negro

blackguard ['blægɑːd] *n Old-fashioned* villano *m*, bellaco *m*

blackhead ['blækhed] *n* punto *m* negro, barrillo *m*

blacking ['blækɪŋ] *n (for shoes)* betún *m*

blackjack ['blækdʒæk] *n* (a) *(card game)* veintiuna *f* (b) *US (truncheon)* porra *f*

blackleg ['blækleg] *Fam* 1 *n (strikebreaker)* esquirol(ola) *m,f*
2 *vi* romper la huelga

blacklist ['blæklɪst] 1 *n* lista *f* negra
2 *vt* poner en la lista negra

blackly ['blæklɪ] *adv (angrily)* enfurecidamente

blackmail ['blækmeɪl] 1 *n* chantaje *m*
2 *vt* hacer chantaje a, chantajear; **to b. sb into doing sth** chantajear a alguien para que haga algo

blackmailer ['blækmeɪlə(r)] *n* chantajista *mf*

blackness ['blæknɪs] *n* (a) *(dirtiness)* negrura *f* (b) *(darkness)* oscuridad *f*

blackout ['blækaʊt] *n* (a) *(during air raid)* apagón *m* (b) *(power failure)* apagón *m* (c) *(fainting fit)* desmayo *m*; **to have a b.** sufrir un desmayo, desmayarse (d) *Rad & TV* **to impose a news b.** prohibir la cobertura informativa

Blackshirt ['blækʃɜːt] *n Hist* camisa *mf* negra

blacksmith ['blæksmɪθ] *n* herrero *m*

blackstrap ['blækstræp] *n US* **b. (molasses)** melaza *f* oscura

blackthorn ['blækθɔːn] *n* endrino *m*

black-tie ['blæk'taɪ] *adj* de etiqueta

blacktop ['blæktɒp] *n US* (a) *(substance)* asfalto *m* (b) *(road)* carretera *f*

bladder ['blædə(r)] *n* (a) *Anat* vejiga *f* (b) *(of football)* cámara *f* (de aire)

bladderwrack ['blædəræk] *n* fuco *m*

blade [bleɪd] *n* (a) *(of knife, sword, razor)* hoja *f*; *(of ice skate)* cuchilla *f* (b) *(of propeller, oar, fan)* pala *f* (c) *(of grass)* brizna *f*, hoja *f* (d) *(of tongue)* cara *f* superior (e) *US Fam (knife)* navaja *f* (f) *Archaic or Literary (young man)* mozo *m*

blag [blæg] (*pt & pp* **blagged**) *vt Br Fam* (a) *(steal)* robar (b) *(scrounge)* **to b. oneself sth** agenciarse algo; **to b. one's way in** colarse

blah [blɑː] *Fam* 1 *n* (a) *(meaningless remarks, nonsense)* sandeces *fpl*, *Esp* chorradas *fpl*, *Am* pendejadas *fpl*, *RP* pavadas *fpl* (b) **b., b., b.** *(to avoid repetition)* y tal y cual, patatín patatán (c) *US* **to have the blahs** *(feel depressed)* estar depre
2 *adj (dull)* soso(a), *Esp* peñazo

blame [bleɪm] 1 *n* (a) *(responsibility)* culpa *f*; **where does the b. lie?** ¿quién tiene la culpa?; **to put** *or* **lay the b. (for sth) on sb** culpar a alguien (de algo), echar la culpa a alguien (de algo); **to take** *or* **bear the b. (for sth)** asumir la culpa (de algo); **to shift the b. onto someone else** quitarse el muerto de encima; **I get the b. for everything!** ¡siempre me echan la culpa de todo!
(b) *(reproof)* tacha *f*; **her conduct has been without b.** su conducta ha sido irreprochable *or* intachable
2 *vt* (a) *(consider responsible)* culpar, echar la culpa a; **to b. sb for sth, to b. sth on sb** echar la culpa a alguien de algo; **I b. the parents!** ¡la culpa la tienen los padres!; **don't b. me for it!** ¡a mí no me eches la culpa!; **don't b. me if you're late** ¡si llegas tarde, yo no tengo la culpa!; **he blames himself for what happened** se echa la culpa de lo que pasó; **she has nobody to b. but herself, she has only herself to b.** ella, y sólo ella, tiene la culpa; **to be to b. (for)** tener la culpa (de); **the bad weather was to b.** el mal tiempo tuvo la culpa
(b) *(reproach)* culpar; **I don't b. you for wanting to leave** no me extraña que quieras marcharte; **she's left him – well, can you b. her?** ella le ha dejado – ¡a ver!, ¡y con razón!

blameless ['bleɪmlɪs] *adj (person)* inocente; *(conduct, life)* intachable

blamelessly ['bleɪmlɪslɪ] *adv* de manera intachable

blameworthy ['bleɪmwɜːðɪ] *adj (person)* culpable; *(conduct)* reprobable

blanch [blɑːntʃ] 1 *vt Culin* escaldar
2 *vi (go pale)* palidecer, ponerse pálido(a)

blancmange [blə'mɒnʒ] *n* = budín dulce de aspecto gelatinoso a base de leche y maicena

bland [blænd] *adj* (a) *(flavour, food)* soso(a), insulso(a); *(diet)* suave (b) *(person)* insulso(a), anodino(a); **b. assurances** promesas tibias

> **False friend:** The Spanish adjective **blando** is not a translation for the English word **bland**. In Spanish **blando** means "soft", "tender", "weak" or "lenient".

blandishments ['blændɪʃmənts] *npl Formal* halagos *mpl*, lisonjas *fpl*

blandly ['blændlɪ] *adv (to reply, smile)* tibiamente, con tibieza

blandness ['blændnɪs] *adj* (a) *(of flavour, food)* sosería *f*, insulsez *f* (b) *(of person)* insulsez *f*

blank [blæŋk] 1 *n* (a) *(space)* espacio *m* en blanco; **fill in the blanks** rellene los espacios en blanco; **my mind is a b.** no recuerdo absolutamente nada; IDIOM **to draw a b.** *(inquiry)* no sacar nada en claro *or* en limpio
(b) *(gun cartridge)* cartucho *m* de fogueo; **to fire** *or* **shoot blanks** disparar tiros de fogueo; *Fam (be infertile)* ser estéril
(c) *(form)* formulario *m* *or* impreso *m* (sin rellenar)
(d) *(unfinished piece of metal) (for cutting key)* llave *f* ciega; *(for minting coin)* moneda *f* sin acuñar
2 *adj* (a) *(unwritten on) (paper)* en blanco; *(cassette, disk)* virgen; **leave this line b.** no escribir en esta línea ►► ***b. cheque*** cheque *m* en blanco; IDIOM **to give sb a b. cheque to do sth** dar carta blanca a

alguien para hacer algo; *Comptr* ***b. unformatted disk*** disquete *m* sin formatear

(b) *(empty) (screen)* en blanco; **my mind went b.** se me quedó la mente en blanco ►► ***b. cartridge*** *(for gun)* cartucho *m* de fogueo

(c) *(expressionless) (face, look)* vacío(a), inexpresivo(a); **he looked b. when I mentioned your name** no dio muestras de reconocer tu nombre cuando lo mencioné

(d) *(absolute) (refusal, rejection)* rotundo(a)

(e) ***b. verse*** *(in poetry)* verso *m* blanco, verso *m* suelto

3 *vt Br (deliberately ignore)* **he blanked me** hizo como que no me veía

►**blank out** 1 *vt sep (erase) (text, memory)* borrar

2 *vi (lose consciousness)* perder la conciencia *or* el conocimiento

blanket ['blæŋkɪt] 1 *n* (a) *(for bed)* manta *f*, *Am* cobija *f*, *Am* frazada *f*; IDIOM *Br* **to be born on the wrong side of the b.** ser hijo(a) ilegítimo(a) (b) *(of fog, cloud)* manto *m*

2 *adj (agreement, ban)* general, total; **the government imposed a b. ban on demonstrations** el gobierno prohibió todas las manifestaciones ►► ***b. bath*** = lavado que se practica a un paciente postrado en cama; *Rad & TV* ***b. coverage*** *(of event)* cobertura *f or* emisión *f* ininterrumpida; ***b. stitch*** punto *m* de festón; ***b. term (for)*** término *m* genérico (para referirse a)

3 *vt (cover)* cubrir (**with** *or* **in** de)

►**blanket out** *vt sep* oscurecer, eclipsar

blankety-blank ['blæŋkətɪ'blæŋk] *Fam Euph* 1 *adj* maldito(a), *Esp* puñetero(a)

2 *exclam* **what the b. are you doing here?** ¿qué porras haces tú aquí?

blankly ['blæŋklɪ] *adv* (a) *(to look, stare) (without expression)* inexpresivamente; *(without understanding)* sin comprender; **she stared b. into the distance** tenía la mirada perdida en la distancia (b) *(to refuse)* de plano, rotundamente

blare [bleə(r)] 1 *n* estruendo *m*

2 *vi (radio, music, trumpet)* tronar

►**blare out** 1 *vt sep* dar a todo volumen

2 *vi (radio, music, trumpet)* tronar

blarney ['blɑ:nɪ] *n Fam* coba *f*, labia *f*; IDIOM **he's kissed the B. Stone** tiene un pico de oro

blasé [*Br* 'blɑ:zeɪ, *US* blɑ:'zeɪ] *adj* **she was very b. about the accident** no le dio mayor importancia al accidente

blaspheme [blæs'fi:m] *vi* blasfemar (**against** contra)

blasphemer [blæs'fi:mə(r)] *n* blasfemo(a) *m,f*

blasphemous ['blæsfəməs] *adj* blasfemo(a)

blasphemy ['blæsfəmɪ] *n* blasfemia *f*

blast [blɑ:st] 1 *n* (a) *(of wind)* ráfaga *f*; *(of heat, steam)* bocanada *f*; **at full b.** *(of machines)* a toda máquina ►► ***b. furnace*** alto horno *m*

(b) *(sound) (of whistle, horn)* pitido *m*; *Fam* **the radio was on full b.** la radio estaba a todo volumen

(c) *(explosion)* explosión *f*; *(shock wave)* onda *f* expansiva; IDIOM *Fam* **meeting him was a real b. from the past!** ¡encontrarme con él fue como volver de repente al pasado! ►► ***b. wave*** onda *f* de choque

(d) *US Fam (good time)* **it was a b.** lo pasamos genial, *Esp* fue una pasada; **we had a b.** lo pasamos bomba; **he gets a b. out of teasing her** le encanta tomarle el pelo

2 *vt* (a) *(with explosives) (hole, tunnel)* abrir (con la ayuda de explosivos); **the rocket was blasted into space** el cohete fue lanzado al espacio; **the building had been blasted by a bomb** una bomba había volado el edificio

(b) *(with gun)* **to b. sb's head off** volarle la cabeza a alguien

(c) *Fam (criticize)* machacar, atacar

(d) *Formal (destroy) (crops)* arrasar, asolar; **to b. sb's hopes** dar al traste con las esperanzas de alguien

(e) *Br Fam* **b. (it)!** ¡maldita sea!; **b. that train!** ¡maldito tren!

3 *vi (radio, television, music)* tronar, sonar estruendosamente

►**blast off** *vi (space rocket)* despegar

blasted ['blɑ:stɪd] 1 *adj* (a) *Formal (plant)* arruinado(a), destruido(a); **a b. oak** un roble partido por un rayo (b) *Fam (for emphasis)* dichoso(a), *Esp* puñetero(a); **it's a b. nuisance!** ¡es una pesadez *or* lata! (c) *Fam (drunk)* trompa; *(on drugs)* colocado(a)

2 *adv Fam (for emphasis)* **don't go so b. fast!** ¡no hace falta que vayas a toda velocidad!

blast-off ['blɑ:stɒf] *n (of space rocket)* despegue *m*, lanzamiento *m*

blatant ['bleɪtənt] *adj* manifiesto(a); **must you be so b. about it?** no hace falta que se entere todo el mundo; **a b. lie** una mentira evidente

blatantly ['bleɪtəntlɪ] *adv* ostensiblemente, manifiestamente; **it's b. obvious** es más que evidente

blather ['blæðə(r)] *US Fam* 1 *n Esp* paridas *fpl*, *Am* pendejadas *fpl*, *RP* pavadas *fpl*

2 *vi* desbarrar, decir *Esp* paridas *or Am* pendejadas *or RP* pavadas

blaze [bleɪz] 1 *n* (a) *(fire) (in hearth)* fuego *m*, hoguera *f*; *(uncontrolled)* fuego *m*, incendio *m*; **five die in b.** *(in headline)* cinco muertos en un incendio

(b) *(of colour, light)* explosión *f*; **they died in a b. of gunfire** murieron acribillados en un tiroteo; **in a b. of anger** en un ataque de ira; **in a b. of publicity** acompañado(a) de una gran campaña publicitaria; **to go out in a b. of glory** marcharse de forma apoteósica

(c) *(mark) (on tree)* marca *f*, señal *f*; *(on horse)* mancha *f (de color claro)*

(d) *Fam* **to run/work like blazes** correr/trabajar como una bala *or* a toda mecha; *Fam* **what the blazes does he want?** ¿qué diablo *or* diantre(s) quiere?; **who/why the blazes...?** ¿quién/por qué demonios *or* diantres...?; *Fam* **go** *or Br* **get to blazes!** ¡váyase usted a la porra!

2 *vt* (a) *(proclaim, publish)* proclamar; **the news was blazed across the front page** la noticia apareció en portada en grandes caracteres (b) *(lead)* abrir, dirigir; IDIOM **to b. a trail** abrir nuevos caminos

3 *vi* (a) *(fire)* arder; *(sun)* abrasar (b) *(light)* estar encendido(a) *or Am* prendido(a); *(eyes, gem)* brillar; **to b. with anger** estar encendido(a) de ira (c) *(gun)* disparar ininterrumpidamente

►**blaze away** *vi (with gun)* disparar continuamente

blazer ['bleɪzə(r)] *n* (chaqueta *f*) blazer *m*

blazing ['bleɪzɪŋ] *adj* (a) *(sun, heat)* abrasador(ora), achicharrante; **a b. hot day** un día achicharrante (b) *(building)* en llamas (c) *(furious)* iracundo(a), fuera de sí; **a b. row** una discusión violenta

blazon ['bleɪzən] *vt* (a) *(decorate)* ornar (**with** con) (b) *(broadcast)* proclamar *or* pregonar a los cuatro vientos; **his name was blazoned all over the news** su nombre sonaba en todos los noticiarios

bldg (*abbr* **building**) ed., edificio *m*

bleach [bli:tʃ] 1 *n* lejía *f*, *Arg* lavandina *f*, *CAm, Chile, Méx, Ven* cloro *m*, *Col* decol *m*, *Urug* jane *f*

2 *vt (cloth)* desteñir; **hair bleached by the sun** cabellos descoloridos por el sol

3 *vi* **to b. in the sun** *(hair)* decolorarse con el sol; **do not b.** *(washing instruction)* no poner en lejía

bleachers ['bli:tʃəz] *npl US* gradas *fpl* descubiertas

bleaching powder ['bli:tʃɪŋ'paʊdə(r)] *n* cloruro *m* de cal, polvos *mpl* de blanqueo

bleak [bli:k] *adj* (a) *(landscape, mountain)* desolado(a) (b) *(weather)* desapacible (c) *(grim) (situation, existence, outlook)* desolador(ora); **the future looks b.** el futuro se presenta desolador

bleakly ['bli:klɪ] *adv* sombríamente

bleakness ['bli:knɪs] *n* (a) *(of landscape)* desolación *f* (b) *(of weather)* desapacibilidad *f* (c) *(hopelessness)* carácter *m* desolador

blearily ['blɪərɪlɪ] *adv* con ojos de sueño

bleary ['blɪərɪ] *adj (eyes)* de sueño

bleary-eyed ['blɪərɪ'aɪd] *adj* **to be b.** tener ojos de sueño

bleat [bli:t] 1 *n* (a) *(of lamb, goat, calf)* balido *m* (b) *(of person)* lamento *m*

2 *vi* (a) *(lamb, goat, calf)* balar (b) *Pej (complain)* quejarse, lamentarse (**about** de); **stop bleating!** ¡no seas quejica!

bleating ['bli:tɪŋ] 1 *adj (of lamb, goat, calf)* balador(ora)

2 *n* (a) *(of lamb, goat, calf)* balidos *mpl* (b) *Pej (complaining)* lamento *m*

bleed [bli:d] (*pt & pp* **bled** [bled]) 1 *vt* (a) *Med* sangrar; IDIOM **to b. sb dry** chupar la sangre a alguien (b) *(radiator)* purgar

2 *vi* (a) *(person)* sangrar; **his nose is bleeding** le sangra la nariz; **to b. to death** morir desangrado(a) (b) *(colour)* correrse (c) *Typ* sangrar

3 *n Typ* sangrado *m*

bleeder ['bli:də(r)] *n Br Fam* imbécil *mf*, soplagaitas *mf inv*; **poor b.** pobre diablo; **you lucky b.!** ¡qué suerte (tienes), cabrón!

bleeding ['bli:dɪŋ] 1 *n* hemorragia *f*; **has the b. stopped?** ¿te ha dejado de salir sangre?

2 *adj* (a) *(wound)* sangrante ►► *Fam Pej* ***b. heart*** *(person)* abogado(a) *m,f* de causas perdidas, blandengue *mf* (b) *Br Fam (for emphasis)* **you b. liar!** ¡pedazo de *or Méx* pinche mentiroso!; **you b. idiot!** ¡maldito *or Méx* pinche imbécil!

3 *adv Br Fam (for emphasis)* **it's b. cold/expensive** hace un frío/es caro de la leche; **that was b. stupid!** ¡qué estupidez!; **you're b. (well) coming with me!** ¡mecachis en la mar, tú te vienes conmigo!

bleep [bli:p] 1 *n* pitido *m*

2 *vt (page)* **to b. sb** llamar a alguien al buscapersonas *or Esp* busca *or Méx* localizador *or RP* radiomensaje

3 *vi* pitar

▸ **bleep out** *vt sep Fam TV* censurar con un pitido

bleeper ['bli:pə(r)] *n Br (pager)* buscapersonas *m inv*, *Esp* busca *m*, *Méx* localizador *m*, *RP* radiomensaje *m*

blemish ['blemɪʃ] **1** *n* **(a)** *(mark)* mancha *f*, marca *f*; *(on fruit)* maca *f* **(b)** *(on reputation)* mancha *f*, mácula *f*; **her reputation is without b.** su reputación es intachable
2 *vt Fig (spoil)* manchar, perjudicar

blench [blentʃ] *vi* **(a)** *(flinch)* inmutarse **(b)** *(turn pale)* palidecer, ponerse pálido(a)

blend [blend] **1** *n* **(a)** *(mixture)* mezcla *f* **(b)** *Ling* palabra *f* compuesta *(formada por parte de dos sustantivos)* **(c)** *Comptr* degradado *m*
2 *vt* **(a)** *(styles, ideas)* conjugar (**with** con) **(b)** *Culin* mezclar; *(in blender)* batir; **b. the butter and sugar (together), b. the sugar into the butter** mezclar el azúcar y la mantequilla
3 *vi* **(a)** *(mix together)* mezclarse; **their voices blended into one** sus voces sonaron al unísono **(b)** *(merge)* fundirse **(c) to b. into** *(surroundings)* confundirse con; **to b. into the background** *(go unnoticed)* pasar desapercibido(a)

▸ **blend in** *vi (with surroundings)* armonizar (**with** con)

blended ['blendɪd] *adj* **b. tea/tobacco** mezcla de tés/tabacos; **b. whisky** whisky de mezcla

blender ['blendə(r)] *n Esp* batidora *f*, *Am* licuadora *f*

blenny ['blenɪ] *n* blenio *m*, cangüeso *m*

bless [bles] (*pt & pp* **blessed** [blest]) *vt* **(a)** *(say blessing for)* bendecir; **God b. America** Dios bendiga a América; **I b. the day I learnt to swim** bendito sea el día en que aprendí a nadar
(b) *(in exclamations)* **God b. you!** ¡(que) Dios te bendiga!; **b. you!** *(when someone sneezes)* ¡salud!, *Esp* ¡jesús!; *(in thanks)* ¡gracias!; *Old-fashioned* **b. my soul!** ¡válgame Dios!; **b. me if I hadn't left the keys at home!** ¡pues no me había dejado las llaves en casa!
(c) *(gift)* **he is blessed with quick wits/good health** tiene la suerte de ser muy espabilado/tener muy buena salud; **they have been blessed with two fine children** han tenido dos hermosos hijos

blessed ['blesɪd] *adj* **(a)** *(holy)* sagrado(a), santo(a); **b. are the peacemakers** bienaventurados son los que buscan la paz ►► ***the B. Sacrament*** el Santísimo Sacramento
(b) *(in Roman Catholic church)* **the B. Edith Stein** la beata Edith Stein
(c) *Fam (for emphasis)* dichoso(a); **every b. day** todos los santos días; **a b. nuisance** una pesadez; **I can't see a b. thing!** ¡no veo ni jota *or* un pepino!

blessing ['blesɪŋ] *n* **(a)** *(religious)* bendición *f*; **the priest said the b.** el cura dio la bendición
(b) *(approval)* aprobación *f*; **with the b. of his parents** con el consentimiento de sus padres; **the chairman gave the plan his b.** el presidente dio su aprobación *or* visto bueno al proyecto
(c) *(benefit, advantage)* bendición *f*, bondad *f*; **it was a b. that no one was hurt** fue una bendición que nadie saliera herido; IDIOM **it turned out to be a b. in disguise** pese a las apariencias, resultó ser una bendición; IDIOM **to count one's blessings** dar gracias (a Dios) por lo que se tiene

blether ['bleðə(r)] *vi Fam* **(a)** *(talk)* charlar **(b)** *(talk rubbish)* desbarrar, decir *Esp* paridas *or Am* pendejadas *or RP* pavadas

blew *pt of* **blow**

blight [blaɪt] **1** *n* **(a)** *(crop disease)* mildiu *m* **(b)** *(destructive influence)* plaga *f*; **to cast a b. on sth** enturbiar algo
2 *vt* **(a)** *(crop)* infestar, arruinar **(b)** *(spoil, ruin)* arruinar, socavar; **a region blighted by poverty and epidemic** una región asolada por la pobreza y la enfermedad; **to b. sb's hopes** truncar las esperanzas de alguien

blighter ['blaɪtə(r)] *n Br Fam Old-fashioned (fellow)* tipo *m*, *Esp* gachó *m*; **lucky b.** suertudo(a); **poor b.** pobre diablo

Blighty ['blaɪtɪ] *n Br Fam Old-fashioned* Inglaterra

blimey ['blaɪmɪ] *exclam Br Fam* ¡miércoles!, ¡caramba!, *Méx* ¡ay güey!

blimp [blɪmp] *n* **(a)** *(airship, balloon)* dirigible *m* **(b)** *Br Fam Pej* **a (Colonel) B.** un reaccionario, un carca

blimpish ['blɪmpɪʃ] *adj Br* reaccionario(a)

blind[1] [blaɪnd] **1** *npl* **the b.** los ciegos, los invidentes; IDIOM **it's like the b. leading the b.** es como un ciego guiando a otro ciego ►► ***b. school*** escuela *f* para ciegos
2 *adj* **(a)** *(unable to see) & Fig* ciego(a); **a b. man** un ciego; **a b. woman** una ciega; **to be b.** ser *or* estar ciego(a); **to go b.** quedarse ciego(a); *Fig* **to be b. to sth** no ver algo; **she was b. to the consequences** no era capaz de ver las consecuencias; **to be b. in one eye** ser tuerto(a); *Fam* **I'm b. without my glasses** sin *Esp* gafas *or Am* anteojos no veo nada; IDIOM **to be as b. as a bat** ser cegato(a) perdido(a); IDIOM **to turn a b. eye (to sth)** hacer la vista gorda (con algo); IDIOM **to be b. with fury** estar ciego(a) de ira ►► ***b. alley*** callejón *m* sin salida; ***b. date*** cita *f* a ciegas; ***b. man's buff*** la gallinita ciega; ***b. side*** *(for driver)* ángulo *m* muerto; *(of person)* zona *f* que queda fuera del ángulo de visión; ***b. spot*** *(for driver)* ángulo *m* muerto; *(in eye)* punto *m* ciego; *Fig (problem of understanding)* punto *m* flaco; ***b. test*** test *m* ciego; *US Fin* ***b. trust*** = gestión de las inversiones de un personaje importante por la que él desconoce los detalles para evitar un posible conflicto de intereses
(b) *(unthinking) (loyalty, trust)* ciego(a); **he flew into a b. rage** le entró una rabia ciega; **b. with anger** ciego(a) de ira ►► ***b. faith*** fe *f* ciega
(c) *(hidden from sight) (entrance, turning)* sin visibilidad
(d) *(without opening) (wall)* ciego(a)
(e) *Fam (as intensifier)* **he didn't take a b. bit of notice** maldito el caso que hizo; **it didn't make a b. bit of difference** no importó lo más mínimo
3 *adv* **(a)** *(without seeing)* **to buy sth b.** comprar algo a ciegas; **to fly b.** volar a ciegas
(b) *Culin* **to bake b.** hornear *(sin el relleno)*
(c) *(as intensifier)* **to be b. drunk** estar borracho(a) perdido(a); **I would swear b. it was him** juraría por mi madre que era él
4 *vt (deprive of sight, dazzle)* cegar; **he was blinded** se quedó ciego; *Fig* **love blinded her to his faults** el amor le impedía ver sus defectos; IDIOM **to b. sb with science** confundir a alguien utilizando términos muy técnicos

blind[2] *n* **(a)** *(deception, decoy)* tapadera *f*; **it's just a b.** no es más que una tapadera **(b)** *(for window)* persiana *f*; *(roller type)* persiana *f* (de tela) enrollable; *(Venetian)* persiana *f* veneciana *or* de lamas **(c)** *US (for hunters, birdwatchers)* puesto *m* de observación

blinder ['blaɪndə(r)] *n Br Fam* **(a)** *(drinking session)* borrachera *f* **(b)** *(excellent example)* **a b. of a goal** un golazo; **a b. of a shot** un tiro increíble; **the keeper played a b.** el portero *or Am* arquero hizo un paradón

blinders ['blaɪndəz] *npl US (for horse)* anteojeras *fpl*

blindfold ['blaɪndfəʊld] **1** *n* venda *f*
2 *vt* vendar los ojos a
3 *adv* IDIOM **I could do the job b.** podría hacer el trabajo con los ojos vendados *or* cerrados

blinding ['blaɪndɪŋ] *adj* **(a)** *(light, flash)* cegador(ora); *(pain)* agudísimo(a); *(intensity)* tremendo(a) **(b)** *Br Fam (excellent)* fenomenal, *Esp* muy guay, *Andes, CAm, Carib, Méx* chévere, *Méx* padre, *RP* bárbaro(a)

blindingly ['blaɪndɪŋlɪ] *adv* **it was b. obvious** estaba clarísimo, saltaba a la vista

blindly ['blaɪndlɪ] *adv* **(a)** *(to grope, hit out)* a ciegas **(b)** *(to obey, follow)* ciegamente

blindness ['blaɪndnɪs] *n also Fig* ceguera *f*

blindworm ['blaɪndwɜ:m] *n* lución *m*

blink [blɪŋk] **1** *n* **(a)** *(of eyes)* parpadeo *m*, pestañeo *m* **(b)** *Comptr* ***b. rate*** velocidad *f* de parpadeo **(c)** IDIOMS **in the b. of an eye** en un abrir y cerrar de ojos; *Fam* **the TV is on the b. again** *(malfunctioning)* ya se ha vuelto a escacharrar la tele
2 *vt* **(a) to b. one's eyes** parpadear, pestañear **(b)** *US* **to b. one's lights** dar *or* echar las luces
3 *vi* **(a)** *(person)* parpadear, pestañear **(b)** *(lights, cursor)* parpadear

▸ **blink at** *vt insep (ignore)* no hacer caso de, hacer caso omiso de

▸ **blink away, blink back** *vt insep* **to b. away** *or* **back one's tears** contener las lágrimas

blinker ['blɪŋkə(r)] **1** *n Aut* **b. (light)** *(turn signal)* intermitente *m*; *(warning light)* luz *f* intermitente
2 *vt (horse)* poner anteojeras a; *Fig* **their affection for her had blinkered them to her faults** el cariño que sentían por ella les impedía ver sus defectos

blinkered ['blɪnkəd] *adj (approach, attitude)* estrecho(a) de miras, cerrado(a)

blinkers ['blɪŋkəz] *npl* **(a)** *(for horse)* anteojeras *fpl*; *Fig* **to be wearing b.** ser estrecho(a) de miras **(b)** *Fam (indicators)* intermitentes *mpl*

blinking ['blɪŋkɪŋ] **1** *adj* **(a)** *(light)* intermitente **(b)** *Br Fam (for emphasis)* condenado(a), dichoso(a); **the b. thing won't work!** ¡este condenado *or* dichoso cacharro no funciona!; **what a b. nuisance!** ¡vaya lata *or RP* embole!
2 *adv Fam (for emphasis)* **it's b. cold/expensive** hace un frío/es caro de narices; **you're so b. stubborn!** ¡mira que eres tozudo!

blip [blɪp] *n* **(a)** *(sound)* pitido *m* **(b)** *(on radar screen)* parpadeo *m* **(c)** *Fam (temporary problem)* pequeño problema *m*

bliss [blɪs] *n* (**a**) *(happiness)* éxtasis *m inv*; **breakfast in bed, what b.!** el desayuno en la cama, ¡qué maravilla! (**b**) *Rel* dicha *f*, gloria *f*

blissful ['blɪsfʊl] *adj* maravilloso(a), feliz; **we had a b. time in France** en Francia lo pasamos maravillosamente; **to be in b. ignorance** ser felizmente ignorante

blissfully ['blɪsfʊlɪ] *adv* felizmente; **b. happy** completamente feliz; **b. ignorant** felizmente ignorante

B-list ['bi:lɪst] *adj (actor, celebrity)* de segunda (fila)

blister ['blɪstə(r)] **1** *n* (**a**) *(on feet, skin)* ampolla *f*; *(on paint)* burbuja *f* (**b**) *Com* ***b. pack*** blister *m*

2 *vt (feet, skin)* levantar ampollas en, ampollar; *(paint)* hacer que salgan burbujas en

3 *vi (feet, skin)* ampollarse; *(paint)* hacer burbujas

blistering ['blɪstərɪŋ] *adj* (**a**) *(sun, heat)* abrasador(ora), achicharrante (**b**) *(criticism, attack)* feroz, despiadado(a) (**c**) *(fast)* **she's setting a b. pace** está imponiendo un ritmo vertiginoso

blithe [blaɪð] *adj* (**a**) *(cheerful)* alegre (**b**) *(thoughtless)* despreocupado(a)

blithely ['blaɪðlɪ] *adv* (**a**) *(cheerfully)* alegremente (**b**) *(thoughtlessly)* despreocupadamente

blithering ['blɪðərɪŋ] *adj Fam* **a b. idiot** un verdadero idiota

BLitt [bi:'lɪt] *n Br* (*abbr* **Bachelor of Letters**) (**a**) *(qualification)* licenciatura *f* en filología *(rama de literatura)* (**b**) *(person)* licenciado(a) *m,f* en filología *(rama de literatura)*

blitz [blɪts] **1** *n* (**a**) *(air bombardment)* bombardeo *m* aéreo; *Hist* **The B.** = bombardeo alemán de ciudades británicas en 1940-41 (**b**) *Fam Fig* **let's have a b. on that paperwork** vamos a quitarnos de encima estos papeles

2 *vt* bombardear desde el aire

blitzed [blɪtst] *adj Fam* (**a**) *(on alcohol)* trompa *inv*; **to get b.** agarrarse un pedo (**b**) *(on drugs)* colocado(a), *RP* falopeado(a); **to get b.** colocarse, *RP* falopearse

blizzard ['blɪzəd] *n* ventisca *f*, tormenta *f* de nieve

bloated ['bləʊtɪd] *adj* (**a**) *(stomach, limb)* hinchado(a); **to feel b.** notarse *or* estar hinchado(a) (**b**) *(ego)* exagerado(a); **b. with self-importance** henchido(a) de presunción (**c**) *(budget)* hinchado(a)

bloater ['bləʊtə(r)] *n* arenque *m* ahumado

blob [blɒb] *n* (**a**) *(drop) (of cream, jam)* pegote *m*; *(of paint)* goterón *m*; *(of ink)* gota *f* (**b**) *(shapeless mass)* **a b. on the horizon** una mancha en el horizonte; **if he goes on eating like that he'll just be a b.** como siga comiendo así se va a poner como un globo

bloc [blɒk] *n Pol* bloque *m*

block [blɒk] **1** *n* (**a**) *(of ice, wood, stone)* bloque *m*; *(of butcher, for execution)* tajo *m*; IDIOM **I'm putting my head on the b. for you** me estoy jugando el pellejo por ti; **(building) blocks** *(toy)* bloques (de construcción); *US* **on the (auctioneer's) b.** a subasta ►► ***b. capitals*** (letras *fpl*) mayúsculas *fpl*; ***b. diagram*** *(flowchart)* diagrama *m* (de flujo *or* bloques); ***b. and tackle*** *(for lifting)* polipasto *m*, sistema *m* de poleas

(**b**) *(building)* bloque *m*; *(in prison, hospital)* pabellón *m* ►► *Br* ***b. of flats*** bloque *m* de apartamentos *or Esp* pisos

(**c**) *(group of buildings)* manzana *f*, *Am* cuadra *f*; **we walked round the b.** dimos la vuelta a la manzana; *US* **the school is five blocks away** el colegio está a cinco *Esp* manzanas *or Am* cuadras

(**d**) *(group) (of shares)* paquete *m*; *(of seats, tickets)* grupo *m*, conjunto *m*; *Comptr* **a b. of text** un bloque de texto ►► ***b. booking*** reserva *f* de grupo; *Br* ***b. grant*** *(to local government)* subvención *f* (del gobierno central); *Br* ***b. release*** *(for study)* = periodo de permiso para estudiar; ***b. vote*** voto *m* por delegación

(**e**) *(of paper)* bloc *m*

(**f**) *(in race)* **(starting) blocks** tacos *mpl* de salida; **to be first off the blocks** hacer la salida más rápida

(**g**) *Fam (head)* **I'll knock your b. off!** ¡te rompo la crisma!

(**h**) *(obstruction) (in pipe)* bloqueo *m*; **to put a b. on sth** *(cheque, account, imports)* bloquear algo; **we've put blocks on all the roads** hemos bloqueado *or* cortado todas las carreteras; **to have a (mental) b. about sth** tener un bloqueo mental con algo; **I have a (mental) b. about mathematics** las matemáticas no me entran en la cabeza

(**i**) *(in basketball, volleyball)* bloqueo *m*

(**j**) *Med (anaesthetic)* anestesia *f*

2 *vt* (**a**) *(obstruct) (pipe, road)* bloquear; *(toilet, sink)* atascar; *(artery, exit, stairs)* obstruir; **my nose is blocked** tengo la nariz taponada; **to b. sb's way** cerrar el paso a alguien; **to b. sb's view** no dejar ver a alguien

(**b**) *(hinder) (proposal)* bloquear; *(traffic)* obstruir, bloquear; *(progress)* dificultar; *Fin* **to b. a cheque** anular un cheque

(**c**) *(in basketball, volleyball)* bloquear

(**d**) *Typ (on book cover)* estampar

(**e**) *Comptr* **to b. text** seleccionar un bloque de texto; **to b. and copy** seleccionar y copiar

(**f**) *Theat (moves, scene)* = establecer los movimientos y las posiciones de los actores en escena

► **block in** *vt sep* (**a**) *(sketch out)* esbozar (**b**) *(prevent free movement of)* tapar la salida a, cerrar el paso a

► **block off** *vt sep (road, exit)* cortar, bloquear

► **block out** *vt sep* (**a**) *(light)* impedir el paso de; *(memory)* enterrar; **she wears earplugs to b. out the music** se pone tapones en los oídos para no oír la música (**b**) *(sketch out)* esbozar

► **block up** *vt sep (door, window)* atrancar; *(hole, entrance)* tapar; **my nose is blocked up** tengo la nariz congestionada

blockade [blɒ'keɪd] **1** *n* bloqueo *m*; **to impose a b. on** imponer un bloqueo; **to lift** *or* **raise a b.** levantar un bloqueo; **to be under b.** sufrir un bloqueo; **to run a b.** eludir un embargo

2 *vt* bloquear

blockage ['blɒkɪdʒ] *n (in pipe, on road, in intestine)* obstrucción *f*

blockboard ['blɒkbɔ:d] *n* contrachapado *m or* panel *m* de listones

blockbuster ['blɒkbʌstə(r)] *n Fam* (**a**) *(book, movie)* bombazo *m*, gran éxito *m* (**b**) *(bomb)* bomba *f* de demolición

blocked [blɒkt] *adj Fin (account)* congelado(a); *(cheque)* bloqueado(a)

blocked-up ['blɒkt'ʌp] *adj* **to have a b. nose** tener la nariz taponada

blockhead ['blɒkhed] *n Fam* zoquete *m*, tarugo *m*

blockhouse ['blɒkhaʊs] *n Mil* blocao *m*

bloke [bləʊk] *n Br Fam* tipo *m*, *Esp* tío *m*; **she's got a new b.** tiene un nuevo novio *or Esp* ligue

blokeish ['bləʊkɪʃ] *adj Br Fam (attitude)* típico(a) de machitos *or Esp* de tíos

blond [blɒnd] **1** *n (man)* rubio *m*, *Méx* güero *m*, *CAm* chele *m*, *Carib* catire *m*, *Col* mono *m*

2 *adj* rubio(a), *Méx* güero(a), *CAm* chele(a), *Carib* catire(a), *Col* mono(a)

blonde [blɒnd] **1** *n (man, woman)* rubio(a) *m,f*, *Méx* güero(a) *m,f*, *CAm* chele(a) *m,f*, *Carib* catire(a) *m,f*, *Col* mono(a) *m,f*

2 *adj* rubio(a), *Méx* güero(a), *CAm* chele(a), *Carib* catire(a), *Col* mono(a)

blood [blʌd] **1** *n* (**a**) *(body fluid)* sangre *f*; **to give** *or* **donate b.** donar sangre ►► ***b. bank*** banco *m* de sangre; ***b. cell*** glóbulo *m*; ***b. clot*** coágulo *m*; ***b. count*** recuento *m* de células sanguíneas, hemograma *m*; ***b. donor*** donante *mf* de sangre; ***b. group*** grupo *m* sanguíneo; ***b. heat*** temperatura *f* (normal) del cuerpo; ***b. money*** *(for committing murder)* = dinero pagado para que se cometa un asesinato; *(compensation)* indemnización *f* por fallecimiento *(en delito de sangre)*; ***b. orange*** (naranja *f*) sanguina *f*; ***b. plasma*** plasma *m* sanguíneo; ***b. poisoning*** septicemia *f*; ***b. pressure*** tensión *f* (arterial), presión *f* arterial; **to have high/low b. pressure** tener la tensión alta/baja; *Fig* **her b. pressure goes up every time she talks politics** cada vez que habla de política le sube la adrenalina; ***b. products*** productos *mpl* sanguíneos; *US* ***b. pudding*** morcilla *f*; *US* ***b. sausage*** morcilla *f*; ***b. serum*** suero *m* sanguíneo; ***b. sports*** = deportes sangrientos como la caza o las peleas de gallos; ***b. sugar*** (nivel *m* de) azúcar *m or f* en la sangre; ***b. test*** análisis *m inv* de sangre; ***b. transfusion*** transfusión *f* sanguínea; ***b. type*** grupo *m* sanguíneo; ***b. vessel*** vaso *m* sanguíneo

(**b**) *(breeding, kinship)* **of noble/Italian b.** de sangre noble/italiana ►► ***b. brother*** hermano *m* de sangre; ***b. relation*** *or* ***relative:*** **they are b. relations** *or* **relatives** les unen lazos de sangre

(**c**) *Br Archaic or Literary (young man)* **a young b.** un doncel

(**d**) IDIOMS **travelling/the theatre runs in her b.** lleva el viajar/el teatro en la sangre; **to have b. on one's hands** tener las manos manchadas de sangre; **he's after your b.** te tiene ojeriza; *also Fig* **they're out for b.** tienen sed de sangre; **his b. is up** tiene los ánimos encendidos; **the b. rushed to his head** se puso hecho una furia; **fresh** *or* **new** *or* **young b.** savia nueva; **in cold b.** a sangre fría; **it makes my b. run cold** me hiela la sangre; **it makes my b. boil when...** me hierve la sangre cuando...; **b., sweat and tears** sangre, sudor y lágrimas; **it's like trying to get b. out of a stone** es como intentar sacar agua de una piedra; PROV **b. is thicker than water** la sangre tira

2 *vt (initiate) (soldier, politician)* dar el bautismo de fuego a

blood-and-thunder ['blʌdən'θʌndə(r)] *adj (book, movie)* de acción y violencia

bloodbath ['blʌdbɑ:θ] *n* baño *m* de sangre

bloodcurdling ['blʌdkɜ:dlɪŋ] *adj* aterrador(ora), horripilante

bloodhound ['blʌdhaʊnd] *n* sabueso *m*

bloodily ['blʌdɪlɪ] *adv* de manera sangrienta

bloodless ['blʌdlɪs] *adj* (**a**) *(without bloodshed)* incruento(a), sin derramamiento de sangre; **a b. coup** *(in country)* un golpe incruento; *Fig (in company, political party)* un golpe de mano (**b**) *(pale)* pálido(a) (**c**) *(lacking energy, emotion)* sin chispa

bloodletting ['blʌdletɪŋ] *n* (**a**) *Med* sangría *f* (**b**) *(slaughter)* sangría *f*, matanza *f*; *Fig (internal feuding)* luchas *fpl* intestinas

bloodline ['blʌdlaɪn] *n* (**a**) *(of people)* genealogía *f*, linaje *m* (**b**) *(of animal)* pedigrí *m*

bloodlust ['blʌdlʌst] *n* ansias *fpl* de sangre

blood-red ['blʌd'red] *adj* de un rojo intenso

bloodshed ['blʌdʃed] *n* derramamiento *m* de sangre

bloodshot ['blʌdʃɒt] *adj (eyes)* inyectado(a) de sangre

bloodstain ['blʌdsteɪn] *n* mancha *f* de sangre

bloodstained ['blʌdsteɪnd] *adj* manchado(a) de sangre

bloodstock ['blʌdstɒk] *n (horses)* caballos *mpl* de carreras, purasangres *mpl*

bloodstone ['blʌdstəʊn] *n Geol* heliotropo *m (gema)*

bloodstream ['blʌdstriːm] *n* torrente *m or* flujo *m* sanguíneo

bloodsucker ['blʌdsʌkə(r)] *n* (**a**) *(mosquito, leech)* chupador(ora) *m,f* de sangre (**b**) *Fam (person)* sanguijuela *f*, parásito(a) *m,f*

bloodthirsty ['blʌdθɜːstɪ] *adj* (**a**) *(person)* sanguinario(a) (**b**) *(film, story)* sangriento(a)

bloody ['blʌdɪ] **1** *adj* (**a**) *(bleeding)* sanguinolento(a), sangriento(a); *(bloodstained)* ensangrentado(a); *(battle, revolution)* sangriento(a); **to give sb a b. nose** hacer sangrar la nariz a alguien; *Fig* dar un escarmiento a alguien, infligir una herida a alguien ►► ***B. Mary*** *(drink)* bloody mary *m*

(**b**) *Br, Austr very Fam (for emphasis)* maldito(a), *Esp* puñetero(a), *Méx* pinche; **a b. liar** un mentiroso de mierda; **you b. idiot!** ¡tonto del culo!; **where's my b. wallet?** ¿dónde he puesto la maldita *or Esp* puñetera cartera?; **it's a b. shame she didn't come** fue una putadilla que no viniera; **b. hell!** ¡me cago en la mar!, ¡mierda!, *Méx* ¡en la madre!

(**c**) *Br Fam Old-fashioned (unpleasant)* fastidioso(a); **he's been perfectly b. about it** ha estado de lo más desagradable al respecto

2 *adv Br, Austr very Fam (for emphasis)* **it's b. hot!** ¡hace un calor del carajo *or Esp* de la leche *or RP* de mierda!; **not b. likely!** ¡ni de coña *or RP* en pedo!, *Méx* ¡no mames!; **he can b. well do it himself!** ¡que lo haga él, carajo *or Esp* joder!; **it was b. awful!** ¡fue horroroso!; **it was b. brilliant!** ¡fue brutal!, *Esp* ¡fue cojonudo *or* la hostia!, *Méx* ¡fue de poca madre!, *RP* ¡fue para alquilar balcones!; *Ironic* **that's just b. marvellous!** ¡genial!, *Esp* ¡me parece cojonudo!, *RP* ¡ahora sí estamos bárbaro!

3 *vt* ensangrentar; **to b. someone's nose** ensangrentar la nariz a alguien; *Fig* dar un escarmiento a alguien, infligir una herida a alguien

bloody-minded [blʌdɪ'maɪndɪd] *adj Br* terco(a), difícil; **he's just being b.** tiene ganas de fastidiar

bloody-mindedness [blʌdɪ'maɪndɪdnɪs] *n Br* terquedad *f*; **he did it out of sheer b.** lo hizo puramente por fastidiar

bloom [bluːm] **1** *n* (**a**) *(flower)* flor *f*; (**b**) *(state)* **to come into b.** florecer; **in (full) b.** en flor, florecido(a); *Fig* en su apogeo; **in the b. of youth** en la flor de la edad (**c**) *(on fruit, leaves)* vello *m*, pelusa *f*; IDIOM **to take the b. off sth** empañar algo

2 *vi* (**a**) *(garden, flower)* florecer; *Fig* **to b. with health** estar rebosante de salud (**b**) *(talent, the arts)* florecer

bloomer ['bluːmə(r)] *n* (**a**) *(plant)* **a night b.** una planta que florece de noche (**b**) *Fam (mistake)* metedura *f* de pata (**c**) *Br (bread)* hogaza *f*

bloomers ['bluːməz] *npl* pololos *mpl*

blooming ['bluːmɪŋ] **1** *adj* (**a**) *(healthy)* **b. (with health)** rebosante de salud (**b**) *Br Fam (for emphasis)* condenado(a); **you b. idiot!** ¡pedazo de idiota!; **I've lost my b. keys!** ¡he perdido las malditas llaves!

2 *adv Br Fam* **b. awful** pésimo, *Esp* fatal; **he's b. useless!** ¡es un inútil!; **you can b. well do it yourself!** ¡puedes hacerlo tú mismo, guapo!

blooper ['bluːpə(r)] *n US Fam Hum* metedura *f* de pata

blossom ['blɒsəm] **1** *n* flor *f*; **to be in b.** estar en flor

2 *vi* (**a**) *(flower, bush)* florecer (**b**) *(person, relationship, the arts)* florecer; **a blossoming friendship/interest** una amistad/un interés floreciente; **to b. into sth** transformarse en algo

blot [blɒt] **1** *n (of ink)* borrón *m*, mancha *f*; *Fig* tacha *f*, mácula *f*; IDIOM **to be a b. on the landscape** estropear el paisaje

2 *vt (pt & pp* **blotted**) (**a**) *(stain)* emborronar, manchar; IDIOM **he had blotted his copybook** había manchado su reputación (**b**) *(with blotting paper)* secar

► **blot out** *vt sep (sun, light)* impedir el paso de; *(memory)* enterrar

blotch [blɒtʃ] **1** *n* (**a**) *(of colour, ink)* mancha *f* (**b**) *(on skin)* mancha *f*, enrojecimiento *m*; **he came out in blotches** le salieron manchas

2 *vt (clothing, paper)* manchar

blotchy ['blɒtʃɪ] *adj (skin)* con manchas

blotter ['blɒtə(r)] *n* (**a**) *(blotting pad)* hoja *f* de papel secante (**b**) *US (log book)* registro *m* de incidencias

blotting paper ['blɒtɪŋpeɪpə(r)] *n* papel *m* secante

blotto ['blɒtəʊ] *adj Fam (drunk)* **to be b.** estar *Esp, RP* mamado(a) *or Méx* cuete

blouse [blaʊz] *n* (**a**) *(for woman)* blusa *f*; IDIOM *Br Fam Hum* **a big girl's b.** un mariquita, un gallina (**b**) *(for soldier)* guerrera *f*; *(for sailor)* marinera *f*, blusa *f* de marinero (**c**) *(for farmer, worker)* guardapolvo *m*

blouson ['bluːzɒn] *n* (**a**) *Br (jacket)* cazadora *f* (**b**) *US (dress, blouse)* blusón *m (con cinturón)*

blow[1] [bləʊ] *n* (**a**) *(hit)* golpe *m*; *(with axe)* hachazo *m*; **to come to blows (over sth)** llegar a las manos (por algo); *Fig* **to soften** *or* **cushion the b.** suavizar el golpe; IDIOM **to strike a b. for sth** romper una lanza por algo; **without striking a b.** sin tener que batirse, sin llegar a las manos; **at one b.** de un golpe

(**b**) *(setback)* duro golpe *m*; **this news came as** *or* **was a b. to us** la noticia fue un duro golpe para nosotros; **it was a b. to her pride** hirió su orgullo

BLOW[2] *(pt* **blew** [bluː], *pp* **blown** [bləʊn]) **1** *vt* (**a**) *(of wind)* **the wind blew the fence down** *or* **over** el viento derribó la valla; **the wind blew the door open** el viento abrió la puerta; **we were blown off course** el viento nos hizo perder el rumbo; IDIOM **it really blew the cobwebs away** me despejó por completo

(**b**) *(of person) (flute, whistle, horn)* tocar; **to b. the dust off sth** soplar el polvo que hay en algo; *Fig (plan, scheme)* desenterrar algo; **she blew smoke in his face** le echó humo a la cara; **to b. bubbles** hacer pompas de jabón; **to b. glass** soplar vidrio; **to b. sb a kiss** lanzar un beso a alguien; **to b. one's nose** sonarse la nariz; IDIOM **to b. one's own trumpet** *or* **horn** echarse flores, *RP* batirse el parche; IDIOM **to b. the whistle on sth/sb** dar la alarma sobre algo/alguien

(**c**) *Elec* **the hairdryer has blown a fuse** ha saltado un fusible en el secador; IDIOM *Fam* **to b. a fuse** *or* **gasket** *(person)* ponerse hecho(a) una furia, *RP* rayarse

(**d**) *(cause to explode)* **to b. sth to pieces** volar algo; **the ship was blown right out of the water** el barco salió volando por los aires; **we've blown a tyre** se nos ha pinchado una rueda; *Fam* **to b. sb's brains out** saltarle a alguien la tapa de los sesos; IDIOM **to b. sb's cover** desvelar la verdadera identidad de alguien; IDIOM *Br Fam* **to b. the gaff on sb** descubrir a alguien; IDIOM **to b. the lid off sth** *(reveal)* sacar algo a la luz; IDIOM *Fam* **to b. one's lid** *or* **stack** *or* **top** ponerse hecho(a) un basilisco, *RP* rayarse; *Fam* **the Grand Canyon blew my mind** el Gran Cañón me dejó patidifuso(a); *Fig* **this discovery blows their theory sky-high** este descubrimiento echa por tierra su teoría

(**e**) *Fam (waste) (chance, opportunity)* echar a perder, mandar al garete; **that's blown it!** ¡lo ha estropeado todo!

(**f**) *Fam (spend) (money)* fundir, *RP* fumar; **he blew all his savings on a holiday** se fundió *or RP* fumó todos sus ahorros en unas vacaciones

(**g**) *US Fam (leave)* **to b. town** largarse de la ciudad

(**h**) *Fam (in exclamations)* **b. it!** *(expressing annoyance)* ¡ostras!; *Br* **b. me,** *US* **b. me down!, well I'll be blowed!** *(expressing surprise)* ¡no fastidies!; *Br* **b. me if he didn't tell her anyway** ¡y no te fastidia, va y se lo cuenta!; **b. the cost!** ¡a paseo con el costo!; **I'm blowed if I'm going to help her** ya puede esperar sentada si cree que le voy a ayudar; *Old-fashioned* **well, I'll be blowed!** ¡cáspita!, ¡demontre!

(**i**) *Vulg (fellate)* **to b. sb** chupársela *or Esp* comérsela a alguien; **b. me!** ¡chúpame *or Esp* cómeme la polla!

2 *vi* (**a**) *(wind, person)* soplar; **the fence blew down** *or* **over** el viento derribó la valla; **the door blew open/shut** el viento abrió/cerró la puerta; **my papers blew out of the window** mis papeles salieron volando por la ventana; **his scarf was blowing in the wind** el viento agitaba su bufanda; **dust blew in her eyes** se le llenaron los ojos de polvo; **to b. on one's fingers** calentarse los dedos soplando; **to b. on one's soup** soplar en la sopa; IDIOM **he's always blowing hot and cold** está cambiando constantemente de opinión

(b) *(whistle, horn)* sonar; **the whistle had blown before the goal** el pitido sonó antes del gol
(c) *Elec (fuse)* fundirse
(d) *(tyre)* reventarse
(e) *(breathe hard)* resoplar
3 *n* **(a)** *(of person)* soplido *m*; **she gave her nose a b.** se sonó la nariz
(b) *Br (walk)* **to go (out) for a b.** salir a dar una vuelta, salir a tomar el aire
(c) *Br Fam (cannabis)* chocolate *m*, *Méx* mota *f*, *RP* yerba *f*
(d) *US Fam (cocaine)* coca *f*, *Esp* perico *m*, *CSur* merca *f*, *Col* perica *f*

▸**blow away** **1** *vt sep* **(a)** *(of wind)* **the wind blew the newspaper away** el viento se llevó el periódico volando
(b) *Fam (shoot dead)* **to b. sb away** dejar seco(a) a alguien de un disparo; **they blew away the opposition** barrieron a la oposición; *Fig* **his latest film blew me away** su última película me dejó alucinado
2 *vi (paper, hat)* salir volando

▸**blow in** *vi Fam (arrive)* aterrizar

▸**blow off** **1** *vt sep* **the wind blew her hat off** el viento le quitó el sombrero; *Fam* **to b. sb's head off** *(with gun)* volarle la cabeza a alguien
2 *vi (hat)* salir volando

▸**blow out** **1** *vt sep (extinguish)* apagar; **the storm blew itself out** la tormenta se extinguió
2 *vi* **(a)** *(be extinguished)* apagarse
(b) *(tyre)* reventarse

▸**blow over** *vi (storm)* amainar; *(scandal)* calmarse

▸**blow up** **1** *vt sep* **(a)** *(inflate) (balloon, tyre)* inflar, hinchar
(b) *(cause to explode)* explosionar, (hacer) explotar; **they blew up the embassy** volaron la embajada
(c) *Phot (enlarge)* ampliar; *Fig* **the press blew the incident up** la prensa exageró el incidente; *Fig* **it had been blown up out of all proportion** se sacaron las cosas de quicio
2 *vi* **(a)** *(bomb)* explotar, hacer explosión; *Fig (lose one's temper)* ponerse hecho(a) una furia; **the van blew up** la furgoneta saltó por los aires
(b) *(begin)* **there's a storm blowing up** se está formando una tormenta
(c) *Fam (athlete, cyclist)* desfallecer

---

blow-by-blow ['bləʊbaɪ'bləʊ] *adj (account)* detallado(a), con todo lujo de detalles

blow-dry ['bləʊdraɪ] **1** *n* secado *m*
2 *vt* secar con secador de mano

blower ['bləʊə(r)] *n* **(a)** *(device)* ventilador *m* **(b)** *Br Fam (telephone)* teléfono *m*; **to get on the b. to sb** dar un telefonazo a alguien

blowfly ['bləʊflaɪ] *n* moscardón *m*, moscarda *f*

blowgun ['bləʊgʌn] *n US* cerbatana *f*

blowhard ['bləʊhɑːd] *n US Fam* fanfarrón(ona) *m,f*, *Esp* fantasma *mf*

blowhole ['bləʊhəʊl] *n* **(a)** *(of whale)* espiráculo *m* **(b)** *(in ice)* respiradero *m*

blowjob ['bləʊdʒɒb] *n Vulg* chupada *f*, *Esp* mamada *f*; **to give sb a b.** chupársela *or Esp* comérsela a alguien

blowlamp ['bləʊlæmp] *n Br* soplete *m*

blown *pp of* **blow**

blow-out ['bləʊaʊt] *n* **(a)** *(of tyre)* reventón *m*, *Am* ponchadura *f* **(b)** *Fam (big meal)* comilona *f*, *Esp* cuchipanda *f* **(c)** *(of fuse)* **there's been a b.** se han fundido los plomos **(d)** *(of oil or gas well)* erupción *f*

blowpipe ['bləʊpaɪp] *n (weapon)* cerbatana *f*

blowsy = **blowzy**

blowtorch ['bləʊtɔːtʃ] *n* soplete *m*

blow-up ['bləʊʌp] *n* **(a)** *(photograph)* ampliación *f* **(b)** *Fam (of temper)* estallido *m* de ira

blowy ['bləʊɪ] *adj* ventoso(a), de mucho viento

blowzy, blowsy ['blaʊzɪ] *adj (woman)* desaseada y gorda

BLT [biːel'tiː] *n (abbr* **bacon, lettuce and tomato***)* sándwich *m* de lechuga, tomate y tocino *or Esp* beicon

blub [blʌb] *(pt & pp* **blubbed***) vi Br Fam (cry)* lloriquear

blubber ['blʌbə(r)] **1** *n* **(a)** *(of whale)* grasa *f* de ballena **(b)** *Fam (fat)* grasa *f* **(b)** *Fam (cry)* **to have a b.** llorar como una Magdalena
2 *vi Fam (cry)* lloriquear

blubbery ['blʌbərɪ] *adj Fam* **(a)** *(fat)* fofo(a) **(b)** *(tearful)* lloroso(a); **she gets all b. at weddings** siempre le da la llorera en las bodas

bludge [blʌdʒ] *Austr Fam* **1** *n* ganga *f*, *Esp* chollo *m*
2 *vt* gorrear, *Esp, Méx* gorronear, *RP* garronear

bludgeon ['blʌdʒən] **1** *n (club)* palo *m*, cachiporra *f*
2 *vt* **(a)** *(beat)* apalear; **he was bludgeoned to death** lo mataron a palos **(b)** *(force)* **to b. sb into doing sth** forzar a alguien a que haga algo

bludger ['blʌdʒə(r)] *n Austr Fam* gorrón(ona) *m,f*, *RP* garronero(a) *m,f*

blue [bluː] **1** *n* **(a)** *(colour)* azul *m*
(b) *(sky)* cielo *m*; **the plane rose into the b.** el avión se perdió en la distancia; IDIOM **out of the b.** inesperadamente
(c) **the blues** *(music)* el blues; **to sing the blues** cantar blues
(d) *Fam* **to have the blues** *(be depressed)* estar muy depre
(e) *Br Sport* = persona que ha sido elegida para representar a Oxford o Cambridge en un deporte
2 *adj* **(a)** *(colour)* azul; **to go** *or* **turn b.** ponerse amoratado(a); **b. with cold** amoratado(a) de frío ▸▸ *Fam* **b. baby** niño(a) *m,f* cianótico(a); ***b. berets*** cascos *mpl* azules; ***b. blood*** sangre *f* azul; ***b. book*** *Br* informe *m* de una comisión parlamentaria; *US (social register)* lista *f* de famosos; ***b. cheese*** queso *m* azul; ***b. flag*** *(clean beach award)* bandera *f* azul, = distintivo de playa limpia en la Europa comunitaria; ***b. fox*** zorro *m* azul; ***b. jay*** arrendajo *m* azul; ***b. jeans*** (pantalones *mpl*) vaqueros *mpl*; ***b. line*** *(in ice hockey)* línea *f* azul; *Mus* ***b. note*** = tercera o séptima sostenida, nota muy usada en el "blues"; ***b. pencil:*** **to take a b. pencil to sth** censurar algo; *US* ***b. plate (special)*** plato *m* del día; ***b. ribbon*** *(first prize)* primer premio *m*; ***b. rinse*** *(hair colouring)* tinte *m* azulado; ***b. tit*** herrerillo *m*; ***b. whale*** ballena *f* azul
(b) *Fam (sad)* **to feel b.** estar depre *or* triste
(c) *Fam (indecent) (joke)* verde; **to tell b. stories** contar chistes verdes; **a b. film** *or* **movie** una película porno
(d) IDIOMS *Fam* **she can complain until she's b. in the face** puede quejarse todo lo que quiera; *Vulg* **to have b. balls** tener dolor de huevos *(por no haber satisfecho la excitación sexual)*; *Fam* **to be in a b. funk** estar muerto(a) de miedo; **once in a b. moon** de uvas a peras, *RP* cada muerte de obispo; *Fam* **to scream** *or* **shout b. murder** poner el grito en el cielo; **to turn the air b.** decir palabrotas

blue-arsed fly ['bluːɑːst'flaɪ] *n* IDIOM *Br very Fam* **to run about** *or* **around like a b.** *Esp* andar más liado(a) que la pata de un romano, *Méx* andar reacelerado(a), *RP* andar como maleta de loco

bluebell ['bluːbel] *n* campanilla *f*

blueberry ['bluːbərɪ] *n US* arándano *m*

bluebird ['bluːbɜːd] *n* azulejo *m*

blue-black ['bluː'blæk] *adj* azul oscuro(a)

blue-blooded ['bluː'blʌdɪd] *adj* de sangre azul

bluebottle ['bluːbɒtəl] *n* moscarda *f*, mosca *f* azul

blue-chip ['bluːtʃɪp] *adj Fin (shares, company)* de gran liquidez, puntero(a)

blue-collar ['bluː'kɒlə(r)] *adj (union, background)* obrero(a); *(job)* manual ▸▸ ***b. worker*** obrero(a) *m,f*, trabajador(ora) *m,f* manual

blue-eyed ['bluːaɪd] *adj* de ojos azules; IDIOM *Br Fam* **his mother's b. boy** el niño bonito de mamá; IDIOM *Br Fam* **the boss's b. boy** el favorito del jefe

bluegrass ['bluːgrɑːs] *n* **(a)** *(plant)* espiguilla *f*, hierba *f* de punta *(americana)* **(b)** *Mus* bluegrass *m*, = estilo de música country propio del sur de Estados Unidos

blue-green algae ['bluːgriːn'ældʒiː] *npl* algas *fpl* verdeazuladas

bluenose ['bluːnəʊz] *n US Fam (prig)* puritano(a) *m,f*, mojigato(a) *m,f*

blue-pencil [bluː'pensəl] *vt (censor)* censurar

blueprint ['bluːprɪnt] *n* **(a)** *Archit & Ind* cianotipo *m*, plano *m* **(b)** *(plan)* proyecto *m*; **a b. for success** la fórmula del éxito

blue-ribbon ['bluː'rɪbən] *adj US* **(a)** *(prestigious)* distinguido(a), selecto(a) **(b)** *Law* **b. jury** jurado *m* especial

blue-sky ['bluːskaɪ] *adj US* **(a)** *(research)* puramente teórico(a) *or* especulativo(a) **(b)** *(stocks, shares)* fraudulento(a)

bluestocking ['bluːstɒkɪŋ] *n Pej Old-fashioned* marisabidilla *f*

bluesy ['bluːzɪ] *adj (music)* con aire de blues

bluethroat ['bluːθrəʊt] *n* pechiazul *m*

bluewater ['bluːwɔːtə(r)] *adj* en mar abierto

bluff[1] [blʌf] **1** *n (pretence)* farol *m*; **to call sb's b.** *(at cards)* ver a alguien un farol; *(in negotiation)* retar a alguien a que cumpla sus fanfarronadas
2 *vt* **to b. sb into believing sth** hacerle creer algo a alguien; **she bluffed her way out of the problem** se escabulló del apuro a base de engaños; **we'll just have to b. it out** tendremos que marcarnos un farol
3 *vi (pretend)* fingir, simular; *(in cards)* tirarse un farol

bluff[2] *n (cliff)* despeñadero *m*

bluff[3] *adj (manner)* abrupto(a)

bluffer ['blʌfə(r)] *n* farolero(a) *m,f*

bluish ['blu:ɪʃ] *adj* azulado(a), tirando a azul

blunder ['blʌndə(r)] 1 *n (mistake)* metedura *f or Am* metida *f* de pata; *(more serious)* error *m* (de bulto)
2 *vi* (**a**) *(make mistake)* meter la pata; *(more seriously)* cometer un error (de bulto) (**b**) *(move clumsily)* **to b. about** *or* **around** dar tropezones aquí y allá; **to b. along** avanzar dando tumbos; **to b. into sth/sb** tropezar con algo/alguien; **he blundered through the interview** durante la entrevista fue de tropiezo en tropiezo

blunderbuss ['blʌndəbʌs] *n* trabuco *m*

blundering ['blʌndərɪŋ] *adj* torpe; *Fam* **he's a b. idiot!** ¡es un metepatas!

blunt [blʌnt] 1 *adj* (**a**) *(blade)* romo(a), desafilado(a); *(pencil)* desafilado(a); **a b. instrument** *(weapon)* un instrumento contundente; **it's rather a b. instrument for solving the problem** es un método bastante burdo para resolver el problema (**b**) *(frank) (manner, statement, person)* franco(a); *(refusal)* contundente; **to be b.,...** para ser francos,...
2 *vt* (**a**) *(blade, pencil, scissors)* desafilar (**b**) *(dull) (anger, enthusiasm)* atenuar, templar

bluntly ['blʌntlɪ] *adv (frankly)* sin rodeos, claramente; **to put it b.,...** para decirlo sin rodeos,...

bluntness ['blʌntnɪs] *n* (**a**) *(of blade)* embotadura *f* (**b**) *(of manner, statement, person)* franqueza *f*, llaneza *f*

blur [blɜ:(r)] 1 *n (vague shape)* imagen *f* borrosa; *(unclear memory)* vago recuerdo *m*; **without my glasses, everything is a b.** sin *Esp* las gafas *or Am* los anteojos lo veo todo borroso; **my childhood is all a b. to me now** recuerdo mi infancia muy vagamente; **to go by in a b.** *(time)* pasar sin sentir *or* en un suspiro
2 *vt (pt & pp* **blurred**) *(writing, image, outline)* desdibujar, difuminar; *(memory)* desdibujar, difuminar; **tears blurred my eyes** las lágrimas me empañaban los ojos; **this definition blurs the distinction between right and wrong** esta definición no aclara la distinción entre lo correcto y lo incorrecto
3 *vi (writing, image, outline)* desdibujarse, difuminarse; *(memory)* desdibujarse, difuminarse

blurb [blɜ:b] *n Fam (on book cover)* notas y citas *fpl* promocionales

blurred [blɜ:d], **blurry** ['blɜ:rɪ] *adj* borroso(a)

blurt [blɜ:t] *vt sep* **to b. (out)** soltar

blush [blʌʃ] 1 *n* (**a**) *(of embarrassment)* rubor *m*, sonrojo *m*; **to spare sb's blushes** salvar a alguien del bochorno; *Fig* **the first b. of dawn** el primer albor (**b**) ***b. wine*** = vino rosado de color pálido (**c**) IDIOM **at first b.** a primera vista
2 *vi* ruborizarse, sonrojarse; **to b. with shame** ponerse colorado(a) de vergüenza *or Am* pena; **I b. to admit it** me da vergüenza *or Am* pena confesarlo

blusher ['blʌʃə(r)] *n (rouge)* colorete *m*

blushing ['blʌʃɪŋ] *adj* ruborizado(a), sonrojado(a); **b. bride** (novia) afortunada

bluster ['blʌstə(r)] 1 *n (protests, threats)* bravuconadas *fpl*, fanfarronadas *fpl*
2 *vt* **"how dare you!" he blustered** "¿cómo te atreves?" gritó jactanciosamente; **he tried to b. his way out of the situation** trató de salir del paso con bravuconadas
3 *vi* (**a**) *(wind)* soplar racheado (**b**) *(protest, threaten)* echar bravatas

blustering ['blʌstərɪŋ] 1 *n (protests, threats)* bravuconadas *fpl*, fanfarronadas *fpl*
2 *adj* bravucón(ona)

blustery ['blʌstərɪ] *adj* **a b. day** un día de viento fuerte y racheado

blvd (*abbr* **boulevard**) bulevar *m*, paseo *m*

B-lymphocyte ['bi:lɪmfəsaɪt] *n* célula *f* B

BM (*abbr* **Bachelor of Medicine**) *(qualification)* licenciatura *f* en medicina; *(person)* licenciado(a) *m,f* en medicina

BMA [bi:em'eɪ] *n* (*abbr* **British Medical Association**) = colegio británico de médicos

BMus [bi:'mʌz] (*abbr* **Bachelor of Music**) *(qualification)* licenciatura *f* en música; *(person)* licenciado(a) *m,f* en música

BMX [bi:em'eks] (*abbr* **Bicycle Motocross**) *n* ciclocross *m*; **B. bike** bicicleta de ciclocross

bn (*abbr* **billion**) mil millones *mpl*, millardo *m*

BO [bi:'əʊ] *n Fam* (**a**) (*abbr* **body odour**) sobaquina *f*, olor *m* a sudor (**b**) (*abbr* **box office**) taquilla *f*

boa ['bəʊə] *n* (**a**) *(snake)* **b. (constrictor)** boa *f* (constrictor) (**b**) *(clothing)* **feather b.** boa

boar ['bɔ:(r)] *n* (**a**) *(male pig)* verraco *m* (**b**) *(wild pig)* jabalí *m*

board [bɔ:d] 1 *n* (**a**) *(of wood)* tabla *f*, tablón *m*; *(for notices)* tablón *m*; *(for chess, draughts)* tablero *m*; *(blackboard)* pizarra *f*, encerado *m*, *Am* pizarrón *m*; IDIOM **to go by the b.** *(be abandoned, ignored)* irse a pique; **across the b.** de manera global *or* general ►► ***b. game*** juego *m* de mesa
(**b**) *(material)* cartón *m* madera
(**c**) *(group of people)* **b. (of directors)** consejo *m* de administración, junta *f* directiva; **to be on the b.** ser miembro del consejo de administración *or* de la junta directiva ►► *US* ***b. of education*** = organismo encargado de la educación pública en el ámbito local; ***b. of enquiry*** comisión *f* investigadora; *Educ* ***b. of examiners*** tribunal *m* (de examinadores); *Br* ***b. of governors*** *(of school)* consejo *m* escolar; ***b. meeting*** reunión *f* del consejo, junta *f*; *US* ***b. of regents*** junta *f* rectora; *Br* ***B. of Trade*** = departamento ministerial responsable de la supervisión del comercio y de la promoción de las exportaciones; *US* ***b. of trade*** cámara *f* de comercio; ***b. of trustees*** junta *f* de síndicos
(**d**) *(meals)* **half b.** media pensión; **full b.** pensión completa; **b. and lodging** *or US* **room** alojamiento y comida
(**e**) **on b.** *(ship, plane, train)* a bordo; **to go on b.** subir a bordo; IDIOM *Br* **to take an idea/a proposal on b.** aceptar una idea/una propuesta
(**f**) *Comptr* placa *f*; **on b.** instalado(a)
(**g**) *US Fin* bolsa *f*
2 *vt* (**a**) *(ship, plane)* embarcar en; *(train, bus)* subir a, montar en (**b**) *(attack) (ship)* abordar (**c**) *(provide lodging)* alojar
3 *vi* (**a**) *(lodge)* alojarse (**with** en casa de); *(at school)* estar interno(a) (**b**) *(get on) (ship, plane)* embarcar; *(train, bus)* subir, montar (**c**) *Av* **flight 123 is now boarding** el vuelo 123 está en estos momentos procediendo al embarque

► **board out** *vt sep* alojar

► **board up** *vt sep (house, window)* cubrir con tablas, entablar

boarder ['bɔ:də(r)] *n* (**a**) *(lodger)* huésped *mf* (**b**) *(at school)* interno(a) *m,f*

boarding ['bɔ:dɪŋ] *n* (**a**) *Av* ***b. card*** tarjeta *f* de embarque; *Naut* ***b. party*** pelotón *m* de abordaje; *Av* ***b. pass*** tarjeta *f* de embarque (**b**) *(lodging)* ***b. house*** pensión *f*; ***b. school*** internado *m*

boardroom ['bɔ:dru:m] *n* sala *f* de juntas; **the decision was taken at b. level** la junta directiva tomó la decisión

boardwalk ['bɔ:dwɔ:k] *n US* paseo *m* marítimo entarimado

boast [bəʊst] 1 *n* jactancia *f*, alarde *m*; **it's his proud b. that he has never lost a game** alardea *or* se jacta de no haber perdido nunca un partido
2 *vt* (**a**) *(brag)* jactarse de, alardear de; **he boasted that he could beat me** se jactó de que podía ganarme (**b**) *(possess)* poseer; **the school boasts a fine library** el colegio posee una excelente biblioteca
3 *vi* alardear (**about** de); **it's nothing to b. about!** ¡no es como para estar orgulloso!

boaster ['bəʊstə(r)] *n* jactancioso(a) *m,f*, fanfarrón(ona) *m,f*

boastful ['bəʊstfʊl] *adj* jactancioso(a), presuntuoso(a)

boastfully ['bəʊstfʊlɪ] *adv* con (mucha) jactancia *or* presunción

boastfulness ['bəʊstfʊlnɪs] *n* jactancia *f*, presunción *f*

boasting ['bəʊstɪŋ] *n* jactancia *f*, alardeo *m*

boat [bəʊt] *n (in general)* barco *m*; *(small)* barca *f*, bote *m*; *(large)* buque *m*; **I came by b.** vine en barco; **to take to the boats** meterse en las lanchas salvavidas; IDIOM **we're all in the same b.** estamos todos en el mismo barco; IDIOM **to push the b. out** *(celebrate lavishly)* tirar la casa por la ventana ►► ***b. deck*** cubierta *f*; ***b. people*** *(refugees)* boat people *mpl inv*, = personas que huyen por mar buscando asilo político; *(in Caribbean)* balseros *mpl*; ***b. train*** = ferrocarril que enlaza con una línea marítima

boat-builder ['bəʊtbɪldə(r)] *n* constructor(ora) *m,f* de barcos

boater ['bəʊtə(r)] *n (straw hat)* canotier *m*

boathook ['bəʊthʊk] *n* bichero *m*

boathouse ['bəʊthaʊs] *n* cobertizo *m* para barcas

boating ['bəʊtɪŋ] *n* paseo *m* en barca; **b. accident** accidente en barco; **to go b.** ir a pasear en barca

boatload ['bəʊtləʊd] *n (of cargo, tourists)* cargamento *m*; *Fig* **by the b.** a espuertas

boatman ['bəʊtmən] *n* barquero *m*

boatswain ['bəʊsən] *n Naut* contramaestre *m*

boatyard ['bəʊtjɑ:d] *n* astillero *m*

Bob [bɒb] *n Br Fam* **...and B.'s your uncle!** ...¡y ya está!, ...¡y a vivir!

bob[1] [bɒb] 1 *n* (**a**) *(abrupt movement) (curtsy)* ligera genuflexión *f (a modo de saludo)*, reverencia *f*; **he signalled his agreement with a b. of his head** mostró su conformidad asintiendo (con la cabeza) (**b**) *(hairstyle)* corte *m* estilo paje (**c**) *(bobsleigh)* bobsleigh *m*, bob *m* (**d**) *(weight) (on pendulum)* pesa *f*; *(on plumbline)* plomada *f*

2 *vt* (*pt & pp* **bobbed**) (**a**) **to b. one's head** *(signalling assent)* hacer un gesto con la cabeza; **she bobbed a curtsy** hizo una reverencia (**b**) **to have one's hair bobbed** *(cut short)* cortarse el pelo a lo paje

3 *vi* (**a**) *(move)* **to b. up and down** moverse arriba y abajo; **to b. about** *(on water)* mecerse; **to b. in/out** entrar/salir (**b**) *(curtsy)* hacer una reverencia (**c**) **to b. for apples** *(party game)* = juego consistente en atrapar con la boca las manzanas que flotan en un recipiente de agua

▸ **bob up** *vi* aparecer, presentarse

bob[2] (*pl* **bob**) *n Br Fam (shilling)* chelín *m*; **that must have cost a few b.** debe haber costado buena *Esp* pasta *or Am* plata *or Méx* lana; **she's not short of a b. or two** le sobra la *Esp* pasta *or Am* plata *or Méx* lana

bobbin [ˈbɒbɪn] *n (on machine)* canilla *f*, bobina *f*; *(for thread)* carrete *m*, bobina *f* ▸▸ ***b. lace*** encaje *m* de bolillos

bobble [ˈbɒbəl] 1 *n* (**a**) *(on hat)* borla *f*, pompón *m* (**b**) *US Fam (mistake)* pifia *f*; *(in American football)* = pérdida del balón al caérsele a un jugador de las manos; *(in baseball)* = recepción torpe de la pelota

2 *vt US Fam (ball)* manejar torpemente

bobble-hat [ˈbɒbəlhæt] *n Br* gorro *m* con borla *or* pompón

bobby [ˈbɒbɪ] *n Br Fam (policeman)* poli *mf*

bobby-dazzler [bɒbɪˈdæzlə(r)] *n Br Fam* pimpollo *m*, bombón *m*

bobby-pin [ˈbɒbɪpɪn] *n US (for hair)* horquilla *f*

bobby socks, bobby sox [ˈbɒbɪsɒks] *npl US (for girls)* calcetines *mpl* cortos *or* de colegiala, *CSur* zoquetes *mpl*, *Col* medias *fpl* tobilleras

bobby-soxer [ˈbɒbɪsɒksə(r)] *n US Fam* quinceañera *f*

bobcat [ˈbɒbkæt] *n* lince *m* rojo

bobolink [ˈbɒbəlɪŋk] *n* charlatán *m*

bobsled [ˈbɒbsled], **bobsleigh** [ˈbɒbsleɪ] 1 *n* bobsleigh *m*, bob *m*

2 *vi* hacer bobsleigh, hacer bob

bobtail [ˈbɒbteɪl] *n* (**a**) *(animal)* animal *m* rabicorto (**b**) *(tail)* cola *f* cortada

bobwhite [ˈbɒbwaɪt] *n* (**northern**) **b.** colín *m* de Virginia

Boche [bɒʃ] *n Old-fashioned Pej* **the B.** los cabezas cuadradas

bock [bɒk] *n US (dark beer)* = cerveza oscura con mucho cuerpo

bod [bɒd] *n Fam* (**a**) *Br (person)* tipo(a) *m,f*, *Esp* tío(a) *m,f*; **he's an odd b.** es un bicho raro (**b**) *(body)* cuerpo *m*; **he's got a nice b.** tiene un cuerpazo

bodacious [bəʊˈdeɪʃəs] *adj US Fam* tremendo(a), *Esp* de (agárrate y) no te menees

bode [bəʊd] 1 *vt* presagiar, augurar; **this bodes nothing good (for)** esto no hace presagiar nada bueno (para)

2 *vi* **this bodes well/ill for the future** es un buen/mal presagio para el futuro

bodge [bɒdʒ] *Br Fam* 1 *n* **b. (job)** chapuza *f*

2 *vt* hacer una chapuza con

bodger [ˈbɒdʒə(r)] *n Br Fam* chapuzas *mf inv*, chapucero(a) *m,f*

bodice [ˈbɒdɪs] *n* (**a**) *(part of dress)* cuerpo *m* (**b**) *(undergarment)* corpiño *m*

bodice-ripper [ˈbɒdɪsrɪpə(r)] *n Fam (book, movie)* = novela o película romántica de tono truculento y ambientación histórica

bodily [ˈbɒdɪlɪ] 1 *adj* corporal; **b. functions** funciones fisiológicas; **b. needs** necesidades físicas

2 *adv* en volandas; **he was carried b. to the door** lo llevaron en volandas hasta la puerta

bodkin [ˈbɒdkɪn] *n (needle)* aguja *f* de enjaretar

body [ˈbɒdɪ] *n* (**a**) *(of person, animal)* cuerpo *m*; *Fig* **to have enough to keep b. and soul together** tener lo justo para vivir ▸▸ ***b. armour*** protección *f* corporal antibalas; *(in sports)* protecciones *fpl*; *Fig* ***a b. blow*** *(severe setback)* un duro golpe; ***b. clock*** reloj *m* biológico; *Cin* ***b. double*** doble *mf* de cuerpo; ***b. fascism*** dictadura *m* del cuerpo; ***b. fluids*** fluido *m* corporal; ***b. hair*** vello *m* corporal; ***b. heat*** calor *m* animal; ***b. image*** imagen *f* corporal; ***b. language*** lenguaje *m* corporal; ***b. milk*** body milk *m*, leche *f* corporal; ***b. odour*** olor *m* corporal; ***b. paint*** maquillaje *m* de cuerpo; ***b. piercing*** perforaciones *fpl* en el cuerpo, piercing *m*; ***b. popping*** *(dancing)* = manera de bailar propia de los años ochenta, moviendo el cuerpo como un robot; *Med* ***b. scan*** escáner *m* (del cuerpo); *Med* ***b. scanner*** escáner *m* (de cuerpo); ***b. search*** registro *m*, cacheo *m*; ***b. stocking*** body *m*; ***b. warmer*** chaleco *m* acolchado

(**b**) *(dead)* cadáver *m*; IDIOM **over my dead b.!** ¡por encima de mi cadáver! ▸▸ ***b. bag*** bolsa *f* para cadáveres; *Mil* ***b. count*** *(of casualties)* número *m* de bajas; *Hist* ***b. snatcher*** profanador(ora) *m,f* de tumbas

(**c**) *(of hair, wine)* cuerpo *m*

(**d**) *(group)* grupo *m*, conjunto *m*; *(organization)* entidad *f*; **public b.** organismo público; **a large b. of people** un nutrido grupo de gente; **they left/rose in a b.** se marcharon/se levantaron a la vez ▸▸ *Law* ***b. corporate*** persona *f* jurídica; ***the b. politic*** el Estado, la nación

(**e**) *(mass)* **a b. of evidence** un conjunto de pruebas; **b. of water** masa de agua; **there is a large b. of support for the policy** la política cuenta con un gran apoyo

(**f**) *(main part) (of car)* carrocería *f*; *(of plane)* fuselaje *m*; *(of camera, stringed instrument)* cuerpo *m*; *(of dress)* cuerpo *m*; *(of hall, church)* parte *f* central ▸▸ ***b. shop*** taller *m* de chapa y pintura

(**g**) *(of letter, e-mail)* cuerpo *m*, texto *m*; *(of argument)* núcleo *m*

(**h**) *(garment)* body *m* ▸▸ ***b. stocking*** *(leotard)* malla *f*; *(women's undergarment)* body *m*

(**i**) *Fam Old-fashioned* gachó *m*, gachí *f*

(**j**) *Phys* cuerpo *m*

bodybuilder [ˈbɒdɪbɪldə(r)] *n* culturista *mf*

body-building [ˈbɒdɪbɪldɪŋ] *n* culturismo *m*

bodycheck [ˈbɒdɪtʃek] *Sport* 1 *n* blocaje *m*

2 *vt* blocar

bodyguard [ˈbɒdɪgɑːd] *n (person)* guardaespaldas *mf inv*, escolta *mf*; *(group)* escolta *f*

bodysurf [ˈbɒdɪsɜːf] *vi* hacer surf sin tabla

bodywork [ˈbɒdɪwɜːk] *n (of car)* carrocería *f*

Boer [bɔː(r)] *n* bóer *mf* ▸▸ ***the B. War*** la guerra anglo-bóer

boff [bɒf] *vt US Fam (have sex with)* echar un casquete con

boffin [ˈbɒfɪn] *n Br Fam Hum (scientist)* sabio *m*, lumbrera *f*

bog [bɒg] *n* (**a**) *(marsh)* pantano *m*, ciénaga *f* (**b**) *Br Fam (toilet)* baño *m*, *Esp* tigre *m* ▸▸ ***b. paper*** papel *m* higiénico *or* de baño; ***b. roll*** papel *m* higiénico *or* de baño

▸ **bog down** *vt sep* **to get bogged down** *(in mud, details)* quedarse atascado(a)

▸ **bog off** *vi Br very Fam* **b. off!** *(go away) Esp* ¡vete a tomar por saco!, *Méx* ¡vete a la chingada!, *RP* ¡andate a la mierda!; *(expressing contempt, disagreement)* ¡ni de coña!, *Méx* ¡no mames!, *RP* ¡ni soñando!

bogey [ˈbəʊgɪ] 1 *n* (**a**) *(cause of fear)* pesadilla *f* (**b**) *Br Fam (snot)* moco *m* (**c**) *(in golf)* uno *m* sobre par, bogey *m*; **a b. 5** un bogey en un par cuatro

2 *vt (in golf)* **to b. a hole** hacer uno sobre par, hacer bogey en un hoyo

bogeyman [ˈbəʊgɪmæn] *n* **the b.** el coco, el hombre del saco

boggle [ˈbɒgəl] *vi Fam* **he boggled at the thought of her reaction** le horripilaba pensar cómo reaccionaría ella; **she boggled at paying such a price** se quedó pasmada de tener que pagar un precio tan alto; IDIOM **the mind boggles!** ¡no me lo puedo ni imaginar!

boggy [ˈbɒgɪ] *adj (land)* cenagoso(a)

bogie [ˈbəʊgɪ] *n Br Rail* (**a**) *(wheel unit)* bogie *m* (**b**) *(truck)* vagoneta *f*

Bogota [bɒgəˈtɑː] *n* Bogotá

bog-standard [ˈbɒgˈstændəd] *adj Br Fam* del montón, corrientucho(a)

bogus [ˈbəʊgəs] *adj* (**a**) *(false)* falso(a); *Fam* **he's completely b.** es un farsante (**b**) *US Fam (unpleasant)* de lo más pesado, latoso(a); *(unfashionable)* carca

Bohemian [bəʊˈhiːmɪən] 1 *n* (**a**) *(from Bohemia)* bohemio(a) *m,f* (**b**) *(unconventional)* bohemio(a) *m,f*

2 *adj* bohemio(a)

bohunk [ˈbəʊhʌŋk] *n US Fam* (**a**) *(Eastern European immigrant)* = término ofensivo para referirse a los inmigrantes de la Europa del Este (**b**) *(country bumpkin)* palurdo(a) *m,f*, *Esp* paleto(a) *m,f*, *RP* pajuerano(a) *m,f*

boil[1] [bɔɪl] *n Med* forúnculo *m*, pústula *f*

boil[2] 1 *n* **to come to the b.** empezar *or* romper a hervir; **to bring sth to the b.** hacer que algo hierva; **to be on the b.** *(kettle, water)* estar hirviendo; *Fig (situation)* estar cociéndose *or* fraguándose; **to go off the b.** dejar de hervir; *Fig (movie, career)* flaquear

2 *vt (liquid)* hervir; *(eggs, meat, vegetables)* hervir, cocer; **to b. the kettle** poner el agua a hervir; *Fig* **he can't even b. an egg!** ¡no sabe ni freír un huevo!

3 *vi* (**a**) *(liquid)* hervir; **the kettle's boiling** el agua está hirviendo; **the kettle boiled dry** el hervidor se quedó sin agua; IDIOM *Fam* **to keep the pot boiling** mantener el asunto vivo (**b**) *(person)* estar furioso(a); **to b. with rage** montar en cólera (**c**) *(ocean)* bullir

▸ **boil away** *vi* (**a**) *(continue boiling)* hervir (**b**) *(evaporate)* consumirse

▸**boil down** *vt sep (reduce)* reducir

▸**boil down to** *vt insep Fam* **it all boils down to...** todo se reduce a...; **it boils down to the same thing** a fin de cuentas, todo es lo mismo

▸**boil over** *vi* **(a)** *(milk, soup)* salirse, rebosar **(b)** *(situation)* estallar; **the unrest boiled over into violence** el malestar estalló en demostraciones de violencia

▸**boil up 1** *vt sep (water, kettle)* poner a hervir
2 *vi (emotion)* **frustration was boiling up inside her** por dentro sentía el resquemor de la frustración

boiled [bɔɪld] *adj* **(a)** *(cooked)* hervido(a), cocido(a); **a b. egg** *(soft)* un huevo pasado por agua; *(hard)* un huevo duro; **b. potatoes** *Esp* patatas *or Am* papas cocidas *or* hervidas ▸▸ ***b. ham*** jamón *m* (de) York, jamón *m* dulce; ***b. rice*** arroz *m* blanco; *Br* ***b. sweet*** caramelo *m* **(b)** *Fam* **b. shirt** camisa de pechera rígida

boiler ['bɔɪlə(r)] *n* **(a)** *(water heater, in engine)* caldera *f* ▸▸ ***b. room*** (sala *f* de) calderas *fpl* **(b)** *(chicken)* gallina *f*, pollo *m* viejo **(c)** *Fam Pej* **(old) b.** vejestorio *m*, (vieja) foca *f*

boilermaker ['bɔɪləmeɪkə(r)] *n* **(a)** *(metalworker)* calderero *m* **(b)** *US Fam* = un whisky seguido de una cerveza

boilerplate ['bɔɪləpleɪt] **1** *n* texto *m* estándar
2 *adj* estándar; **b. contract** modelo de contrato

boilersuit ['bɔɪləsu:t] *n Br* mono *m* (de trabajo), *Am* overol *m*, *CSur, Cuba* mameluco *m*, *Ven* braga *f*

boiling ['bɔɪlɪŋ] **1** *adj* hirviente; *Fam* **I'm b.!** ¡me estoy asando! ▸▸ ***b. point*** punto *m* de ebullición; IDIOM **the situation has reached b. point** la situación está al rojo vivo
2 *adv* **it's b. hot** hace un calor abrasador

boiling-water reactor ['bɔɪlɪŋ'wɔ:tərɪ'æktə(r)] *n* reactor *m* de agua en ebullición

boil-in-the-bag ['bɔɪlɪnðə'bæg] *adj (food)* para hervir en bolsa

boisterous ['bɔɪstərəs] *adj* **(a)** *(person)* alborotador(ora), bullicioso(a); **to be in a b. mood** estar alborotado(a) **(b)** *(sea)* embravecido(a), bravo(a); *(wind)* tempestuoso(a)

boisterously ['bɔɪstərəslɪ] *adv (to behave)* ruidosamente, escandalosamente

boisterousness ['bɔɪstərəsnɪs] *n (of person)* actitud *f* alborotadora, actitud *f* bulliciosa

bold [bəʊld] **1** *adj* **(a)** *(brave)* audaz; **he put a b. face on it, he put on a b. front** mantuvo el tipo
(b) *(shameless, impudent)* caradura, osado(a); IDIOM **to be as b. as brass** ser un(a) caradura, *Esp* tener más cara que espalda; *Formal* **who might you be, if I may make so b.?** ¿quién es usted?, si me permite el atrevimiento
(c) *(striking)* marcado(a), acentuado(a); **in b. relief** en relieve
(d) *Typ* **b. (type** *or* **face)** (letra *f*) negrita *f*; **b. italics** letra cursiva en negrita
2 *n Typ* **in b.** en negrita

boldface ['bəʊldfeɪs] **1** *n* negrita *f*
2 *adj* en negrita

boldly ['bəʊldlɪ] *adv* **(a)** *(bravely)* audazmente, con audacia **(b)** *(shamelessly, impudently)* con descaro *or* osadía, descaradamente **(c)** *(strikingly)* llamativamente, marcadamente; **b. designed** de diseño atrevido

boldness ['bəʊldnɪs] *n* **(a)** *(courage)* audacia *f* **(b)** *(shamelessness, impudence)* descaro *m*, osadía *f* **(c)** *(force)* viveza *f*

bole [bəʊl] *n (of tree)* tronco *m*

bolero [bə'leərəʊ] *(pl* **boleros***)* *n* **(a)** *(music, dance)* bolero *m* **(b)** *(jacket)* bolero *m*, torera *f*

Bolivia [bə'lɪvɪə] *n* Bolivia

Bolivian [bə'lɪvɪən] **1** *n* boliviano(a) *m,f*
2 *adj* boliviano(a)

boll [bəʊl] *n Bot* cápsula *f* ▸▸ ***b. weevil*** gorgojo *m* del algodón

bollard ['bɒləd] *n* **(a)** *Naut* bolardo *m*, noray *m* **(b)** *Br (traffic barrier)* bolardo *m*

bollix ['bɒlɪks] *very Fam* **1** *n Irish* pesado(a) *m,f*, *Esp* coñazo *mf*, *RP* rompebolas *mf*
2 *vt US* **to b. sth (up)** joder algo

bollock ['bɒlək] *Br very Fam* **1** *adv* **b. naked** en bolas, *Esp* en pelota picada
2 *vt* **to b. sb** poner a alguien como un trapo *or Méx* como camote, *Esp* echar una bronca que te cagas a alguien

bollocking ['bɒləkɪŋ] *n Br very Fam* **to give sb a b.** poner a alguien como un trapo *or Méx* como camote, *Esp* echar una bronca que te cagas a alguien; **he got a b. from the boss** el jefe le puso como un trapo *or Méx* como camote, *Esp* se llevó una bronca que te cagas del jefe

bollocks, ballocks ['bɒləks] *Br Vulg* **1** *npl* **(a)** *(testicles)* cojones *mpl*, huevos *mpl* **(b)** *(nonsense)* **(that's) b.!** eso son *Esp* gilipolleces *or Am* pendejadas!; **the film was a load of b.** la película era una *Esp* gilipollez *or Am* pendejada
2 *exclam* ¡mierda!, *Esp* ¡joder!

▸**bollocks up** *vt sep Br Vulg* **to b. sth up** cagarla con algo

Bollywood ['bɒlɪwʊd] *n* = la industria cinematográfica de la India

Bologna [bə'lɒnjə] *n* Bolonia

bologna [bə'ləʊnɪ] *n US (sausage)* = embutido ahumado de gran tamaño y elaborado con distintos tipos de carne

Bolognese [bɒlə'neɪz] **1** *n (person)* boloñés(esa) *m,f*
2 *adj* **(a)** *(from Bologna)* boloñés(esa) **(b)** ***B. sauce*** (salsa *f*) boloñesa *f*

boloney = **baloney**

Bolshevik ['bɒlʃəvɪk], **Bolshevist** ['bɒlʃəvɪst] **1** *n* bolchevique *mf*
2 *adj* bolchevique

Bolshevism ['bɒlʃəvɪzəm] *n* bolchevismo *m*

Bolshevist = **Bolshevik**

bolshie, bolshy ['bɒlʃɪ] *adj Br Fam* respondón(ona); **she's in a b. mood** está muy respondona

bolster ['bəʊlstə(r)] **1** *n* almohada *f* cilíndrica
2 *vt (confidence, pride)* reforzar, fortalecer

▸**bolster up** *vt sep (regime, theory)* reforzar; **bolstered up by recent successes** reforado(a) por los recientes logros; *Fin* **to b. up the dollar** reforzar *or* fortalecer el dólar

bolt [bəʊlt] **1** *n* **(a)** *(on door)* cerrojo *m*, pestillo *m*; IDIOM *Fam* **he has shot his b.** ha quemado sus últimos cartuchos
(b) *(metal fastening)* perno *m*
(c) *(of rifle)* cerrojo *m*
(d) *(of crossbow)* flecha *f*
(e) *(dash)* **she made a b. for the door** se precipitó hacia la puerta; **he made a b. for it** salió disparado ▸▸ ***b. hole*** refugio *m*
(f) *(of lightning)* rayo *m*; IDIOM **to come like a b. from the blue** ocurrir de sopetón, pillar *or Am* agarrar a todo el mundo por sorpresa
(g) *(of cloth)* rollo *m*
2 *adv* **b. upright** erguido(a)
3 *vt* **(a)** *(lock)* **to b. the door/window** cerrar la puerta/ventana con pestillo **(b)** *(attach with bolts)* atornillar **(c)** *(eat)* engullir **(d)** *(sift)* tamizar
4 *vi* **(a)** *(move quickly)* **a rabbit bolted across the field** un conejo cruzó el prado como un rayo **(b)** *(escape)* *(horse)* salir de estampida; *(person)* salir huyendo **(c)** *(plants)* retoñar prematuramente

▸**bolt down** *vt sep* **(a)** *(eat quickly)* **to b. sth down** engullir *or* zamparse algo **(b)** *(fasten)* atornillar; IDIOM **the burglars stole everything that wasn't bolted down** los ladrones dejaron la casa limpio

bomb [bɒm] **1** *n* **(a)** *(explosive device)* bomba *f*; **the b.** la bomba atómica; **to drop/plant a b.** arrojar/colocar una bomba; IDIOM *Fam* **this place looks as if a b. has hit it** parece como si aquí hubiera caído una bomba; IDIOM *Br Fam* **to go like a b.** *(go quickly)* ir como una bala; *(be successful)* salir a pedir de boca; IDIOM *Br Fam* **to go down a b. (with sb): their proposals went down a b. with the chairman** al presidente le encantaron sus propuestas ▸▸ ***b. disposal*** desactivación *f* de bombas; ***b. disposal expert*** (experto *m*) artificiero *m*; ***b. disposal squad*** brigada *f* de artificieros, brigada *f* de desactivación de bombas; ***b. scare*** amenaza *f* de bomba; ***b. shelter*** refugio *m* antiaéreo; ***the b. squad*** la brigada de explosivos; ***b. warning*** aviso *m* de bomba
(b) *Br Fam (fortune)* **it cost a b.** costó un ojo de la cara; **to make a b.** forrarse
(c) *US Fam (failure)* fiasco *m*, desastre *m*
(d) *(into swimming-pool)* **to do a b.** tirarse en bomba, hacer la bomba
2 *vt* **(a)** *(from air)* bombardear **(b)** *(put bomb in)* colocar una bomba en
3 *vi Fam* **(a)** *US (fail)* fracasar estrepitosamente **(b)** *Br (go quickly)* **he bombed down the road** pasó disparado por la calle

▸**bomb along** *vi Br Fam (go quickly)* ir a toda máquina *or Esp* pastilla

▸**bomb out 1** *vt sep* **(a) he was bombed out (of his house)** *(in air raid)* el bombardeo lo dejó sin casa; *(by terrorists)* la bomba lo dejó sin casa **(b)** *Br Fam* **to b. sb out** *(let down)* dejar a alguien en la estacada
2 *vi Fam (be eliminated)* **to b. out of sth** quedar apeado(a) *or* eliminado(a) de algo

bombard [bɒm'bɑːd] *vt* bombardear; *Fig* **to b. sb with questions** bombardear a alguien con preguntas

bombardier [bɒmbə'dɪə(r)] *n* (**a**) *Br (army rank)* ≃ cabo *m* primero de artillería (**b**) *(in aircraft)* bombardero(a) *m,f*

bombardment [bɒm'bɑːdmənt] *n* bombardeo *m*

bombast ['bɒmbæst] *n* ampulosidad *f*, altisonancia *f*

bombastic [bɒm'bæstɪk] *adj* ampuloso(a), altisonante

Bombay [bɒm'beɪ] *n* Bombay ►► ***B. duck*** = pescado en salazón utilizado como condimento en la cocina hindú; ***B. mix*** = aperitivo picante compuesto por fídeos secos, lentejas y cacahuetes

bombe [bɔm] *n Culin* = postre consistente en una gran bola de helado rellena, por ejemplo, de natillas, bizcocho o nueces

bombed (out) ['bɒmd('aʊt)] *adj very Fam (drunk) Esp* bolinga, *Méx* cuete, *RP* en pedo; *(on drugs)* flipado(a), colocado(a), *RP* falopeado(a)

bomber ['bɒmə(r)] *n* (**a**) *(aircraft)* bombardero *m* ►► ***b. jacket*** cazadora *f or CSur* campera *f or Méx* chamarra *f* de aviador (**b**) *(person)* terrorista *mf (que coloca bombas)*

bombing ['bɒmɪŋ] *n* (**a**) *(aerial)* bombardeo *m* ►► ***b. range*** campo *m* de tiro; ***b. run*** incursión *f* aérea, misión *f* de bombardeo (**b**) *(by terrorist)* atentado *m* con bomba

bombshell ['bɒmʃel] *n* (**a**) *Old-fashioned (shell)* obús *m* (**b**) IDIOMS **to drop a b.** dejar caer una bomba; *Fam* **a blonde b.** una rubia *or Méx* güera *or CAm* catira despampanante *or* explosiva

bombsight ['bɒmsaɪt] *n* visor *m* de bombardeo

bombsite ['bɒmsaɪt] *n* lugar *m* arrasado por un bombardeo; *Br Fig* **your bedroom is a b.!** ¡tu cuarto está hecho una leonera!

bona fide ['bəʊnə'faɪdɪ] *adj* auténtico(a), genuino(a)

bona fides ['bəʊnə'faɪdiːz] *npl* **to check sb's b.** comprobar las credenciales de alguien

bonanza [bə'nænzə] *n* (**a**) *(record profit, winnings)* filón *m*; **a b. year** un año de grandes beneficios *or* de bonanza; **she had a real b. at the sales** encontró muchas gangas en las rebajas (**b**) *US (in mine)* bonanza *f*

bonbon ['bɒnbɒn] *n* caramelo *m*

bonce [bɒns] *n Br Fam (head)* coco *m*, *Esp* tarro *m*

bond [bɒnd] **1** *n* (**a**) *(between materials)* unión *f*

(**b**) *(between people)* vínculo *m*; **to feel a b. with sb** sentir un vínculo de unión con alguien; **marriage/family bonds** vínculos matrimoniales/familiares

(**c**) *Literary* **bonds** *(ropes, chains)* ataduras *fpl*

(**d**) *Chem* enlace *m*

(**e**) *Fin* bono *m* ►► ***b. issue*** emisión *f* de bonos; ***b. market*** mercado *m* de obligaciones de renta fija

(**f**) *Law* fianza *f*; *Formal* **my word is my b.** siempre cumplo mi palabra

(**g**) *Com* **to be in b.** estar en depósito aduanero

(**h**) **b. (paper)** papel *m* de carta

2 *vt* (**a**) *(stick)* pegar, adherir (**b**) *Fig (unite)* **to b. together** unir (**c**) *Com (goods)* poner en depósito aduanero

3 *vi* (**a**) *(stick)* pegar, adherirse (**b**) *Fig (form attachment)* unirse (**with** a)

bondage ['bɒndɪdʒ] *n* (**a**) *Literary (slavery)* esclavitud *f*, servidumbre *f*; **to be in b. to** estar sometido(a) a, ser esclavo(a) de (**b**) *(sexual practice)* bondage *m*, = práctica sexual en la que se ata a uno de los participantes ►► ***b. gear*** = prendas y adornos de bondage

bonded ['bɒndɪd] *adj (company)* con responsabilidad legal ►► ***b. warehouse*** depósito *m* franco

bondholder ['bɒndhəʊldə(r)] *n* obligacionista *mf*, poseedor(ora) *m,f* de bonos

bonding ['bɒndɪŋ] *n* (lazos *mpl* de) unión *f*

bondservant ['bɒndsɜːvənt] *n Hist* siervo(a) *m,f*

bondsman ['bɒndzmən] *n* (**a**) *Hist (serf)* siervo *m* (**b**) *US (for insurance)* avalista *mf*

bond(s)woman ['bɔnd(z)wʊmən] *n Hist (serf)* sierva *f*

bondswoman ['bɒndzwʊmən] *n* avalista *f*

bone [bəʊn] **1** *n* (**a**) *(of person, animal)* hueso *m*; *(of fish)* espina *f*; **made from b.** (hecho) de hueso; **her finger was cut to the b.** se cortó el dedo hasta el hueso ►► ***b. china*** porcelana *f* fina; ***b. marrow*** *Anat* médula *f* (ósea); *Culin* tuétano *m*; ***b. meal*** harina *f* de hueso; ***b. structure:* she has good b. structure** tiene las facciones delicadas

(**b**) **bones** *(remains)* restos *mpl*

(**c**) *US Fam* **bones** *(dice)* dados *mpl*

(**d**) IDIOMS **b. of contention** manzana de la discordia, caballo de batalla; **chilled** *or* **frozen to the b.** helado hasta la médula; **close to** *or* **near the b.** *(tactless, risqué)* fuera de tono; **to cut spending down to the b.** recortar el gasto al máximo; **to be b. idle** *or* **lazy** ser más vago(a) que la chaqueta de un guardia, *RP* ser un(a) vagoneta; *Fam* **to have a b. to pick with sb** tener que arreglar *or* ajustar cuentas con alguien; **to work one's fingers to the b.** matarse a trabajar *or RP* trabajando; **to make no bones about doing sth** no tener reparos *or* ningún reparo en hacer algo; **he made no bones about it** no trató de disimularlo; **I (can) feel it in my bones** tengo una corazonada, lo presiento

2 *vt* (**a**) *(fillet) (chicken)* deshuesar; *(fish)* quitar las espinas a (**b**) *US Vulg (have sex with) Esp* follarse *or* tirarse a, *Am* cogerse a, *Méx* chingarse a

3 *vi US Vulg (have sex) Esp* follar, *Am* coger, *Méx* chingar

►**bone up on** *vt insep Fam* empollarse

boned [bəʊnd] *adj (meat)* deshuesado(a); *(fish)* sin espinas, en filetes

bone-dry ['bəʊn'draɪ] *adj* completamente seco(a)

bonehead ['bəʊnhed] *US Fam* **1** *n* estúpido(a) *m,f*, *Esp* berzotas *mf inv*

2 *adj* estúpido(a)

boneless ['bəʊnlɪs] *adj (meat)* sin hueso, deshuesado(a); *(fish)* sin espinas, desespinado(a)

boner ['bəʊnə(r)] *n* (**a**) *Vulg (erection)* **to have a b.** *Esp* estar empalmado, *Am* tenerla parada

(**b**) *US Fam (mistake)* metedura *f* de pata; **to pull a b.** meter la pata

boneshaker ['bəʊnʃeɪkə(r)] *n Fam (car)* tartana *f*, cafetera *f*

bonfire ['bɒnfaɪə(r)] *n* hoguera *f*, fogata *f* ►► *Br* ***B. Night*** = fiesta de la noche del 5 de noviembre en que se hacen hogueras y hay fuegos artificiales

bong [bɒŋ] **1** *n* (**a**) *(sound)* retumbo *m* (**b**) *(for smoking drugs)* narguile *m*, pipa *f* de agua

2 *vi* retumbar

bongo ['bɒŋgəʊ] *n Mus* **b. drums, bongos** bongós *mpl*

bonhomie ['bɒnəmiː] *n* camaradería *f*

bonk[1] [bɒŋk] *Fam* **1** *n (blow)* tortazo *m*, viaje *m*

2 *vt (hit)* pegar

bonk[2] *Br very Fam* **1** *n (sex)* **to have a b.** *Esp* echar un casquete

2 *vt (have sex with)* echar un casquete con

3 *vi (have sex)* echar un casquete

bonkers ['bɒŋkəz] *adj Br Fam (mad)* **to be b.** estar chiflado(a) *or Esp* majareta; **to go b.** volverse majareta

bon mot [bɒn'məʊ] *n* salida *f* ingeniosa, agudeza *f*

Bonn [bɒn] *n* Bonn

bonnet ['bɒnɪt] *n* (**a**) *(hat)* capota *f*, cofia *f* (**b**) *Br (of car)* capó *m*, *CAm, Méx* cofre *m*; **let's have a look under the b.** vamos a echar un vistazo al motor

bonny ['bɒnɪ] *adj Scot* bonito(a), precioso(a)

bonsai ['bɒnsaɪ] *n* bonsai *m*

bonus ['bəʊnəs] *n* (**a**) *(for productivity, seniority)* plus *m*; **Christmas b.** aguinaldo *(dinero)* ►► ***b. number*** *(in lottery)* ≃ (número *m*) complementario *m*; ***b. scheme*** sistema *m* de primas

(**b**) *(in insurance, for investment)* prima *f* ►► *Br Com* ***b. issue*** emisión *f* gratuita de acciones

(**c**) *(advantage)* ventaja *f* adicional; **it's a real b. living so near the shops** es una verdadera suerte tener las tiendas tan a la mano

bon viveur ['bɒnviː'vɜː(r)], **bon vivant** ['bɒnviː'vɒnt] *n* **he's a b.** le gusta vivir bien, es un sibarita

bon voyage ['bɒnvɔɪ'ɑːʒ] *n* buen viaje *m*

bony ['bəʊnɪ] *adj* (**a**) *(person, limb)* huesudo(a) (**b**) *(fish)* con muchas espinas

bonzer ['bɒnzə(r)] *adj Austr Fam* genial, *Esp* guay, *RP* bárbaro(a)

bonzo ['bɒnzəʊ] *adj US Fam* pirado(a), grillado(a)

boo [buː] **1** *n* (*pl* **boos**) abucheo *m*

2 *vt* abuchear; **he was booed off the stage** salió de escena entre los abucheos del público

3 *vi* **they started to b.** se comenzaron a oír abucheos

4 *exclam (of audience, crowd)* ¡buu!, ¡fuera!; *(to frighten sb)* ¡uuh!; IDIOM **he wouldn't say b. to a goose** es muy tímido, *Esp* es un cortado

boob [buːb] *Fam* **1** *n* (**a**) *Br (mistake)* metedura *f or Am* metida *f* de pata; **to make a b.** meter la pata, *Méx* segarla (**b**) *Br* **boobs** *(breasts)* tetas; **to have a b. job** operarse del pecho ►► ***b. tube*** = top ajustado sin mangas ni tirantes (**c**) *US (person)* lelo(a) *m,f*, bobalicón(ona) *m,f* ►► ***b. tube*** *(television)* caja *f* tonta

2 *vi Br (make mistake)* meter la pata

boo-boo ['bu:bu:] *n Fam* (**a**) *(blunder)* metedura *f or Am* metida *f* de pata; **to make a b.** meter la pata (**b**) *US (injury)* pupa *f*

booby ['bu:bɪ] *n* (**a**) *(bird)* alcatraz *m*, piquero *m* (**b**) *Fam (fool)* bobalicón(ona) *m,f*, *Esp* memo(a) *m,f* ►► *US* ***b. hatch*** loquero *m*; ***b. prize*** premio *m* para el farolillo rojo; ***b. trap*** *(explosive device)* bomba *f* trampa *or* camuflada; *(practical joke)* trampa *f*

booby-trap ['bu:bɪtræp] *(pt & pp* **booby-trapped***)* *vt (with explosive device)* colocar una bomba trampa en; *(as practical joke)* colocar una trampa en

booger ['bu:gə(r)] *n US Fam* (**a**) *(nasal mucus)* moco *m* (**b**) *(person)* pillastre *mf* (**c**) *(thing)* chisme *m*, cacharro *m*

boogie ['bu:gɪ] *Fam* **1** *n* (**a**) *(dance)* **to have a b.** echarse un bailecito, menear el esqueleto (**b**) *US very Fam* = término generalmente ofensivo para referirse a un negro, *RP* grone *m*

2 *vi* (**a**) *(dance)* echarse un bailecito, menear el esqueleto (**b**) *US (leave)* largarse, *Esp* darse el piro

boogie-woogie ['bu:gɪ'wu:gɪ] *n* bugui-bugui *m*

boo-hoo ['bu:'hu:] *exclam* ¡buaaah!

booing ['bu:ɪŋ] *n* abucheo *m*

book [bʊk] **1** *n* (**a**) *(printed volume)* libro *m*; **I'm in the b.** *(telephone directory)* mi número está en la guía, estoy en la guía ►► ***b. club*** círculo *m* de lectores; ***b. end*** sujetalibros *m inv*; ***b. fair*** feria *f* del libro; ***b. lover*** amante *mf* de la lectura, lector(ora) *m,f* apasionado(a) *or* ávido(a); ***b. review*** reseña *f* literaria; ***b. token*** vale *m* para comprar libros

(**b**) *(small bound set) (of stamps)* librillo *m*; *(of matches)* caja *f* (de solapa); *(of tickets)* talonario *m*

(**c**) *Fin* **the books** *(of company)* la contabilidad; **to do the books** llevar la contabilidad ►► ***b. entry*** anotación *f* contable, asiento *m* contable; ***b. price*** valor *m* contable; ***b. value*** valor *m* contable

(**d**) *(of club, association)* **to be on the books** ser socio(a)

(**e**) *(betting)* **to open/keep a b. on sth** hacer/tener una apuesta sobre algo

(**f**) *(of opera, musical)* libreto *m*

(**g**) IDIOMS **to bring sb to b. for sth** obligar a alguien a rendir cuentas por algo; **physics is a closed b. to me** la física es un misterio para mí; **to be an open b.** *(person)* ser (como) un libro abierto; **to talk** *or* **speak like a b.** hablar como un libro; **I can read her like a b.** no tiene secretos para mí, la conozco como la palma de mi mano; **in my b....** a mi modo de ver...; **to be in sb's good/bad books** estar a buenas/malas con alguien, *RP* estar en buenos/malos términos con alguien; **to do sth by** *or* **according to the b.** hacer algo según las normas; *Fam* **that's one for the books!** ¡qué milagro!, ¡esto va a hacer historia!; *Fam* **that suits my b.** por mí, estupendo; **to throw the b. at sb** castigar a alguien con la máxima severidad

2 *vt* (**a**) *(reserve)* reservar; *(performer)* contratar; **to b. sb on a flight** reservarle (plaza en) un vuelo a alguien; **to be fully booked** *(theatre, flight)* estar completo(a); *(person)* tener la agenda completa

(**b**) *(record details of) (police suspect)* fichar; *(traffic offender)* multar

(**c**) *Br (soccer player)* mostrar una tarjeta amarilla a

(**d**) *US Fam* **to b. it** *(leave)* largarse, *Esp* darse el piro

3 *vi* (**a**) *(make reservation)* reservar, hacer reserva (**b**) *US Fam (leave)* largarse, *Esp* darse el piro (**c**) *US Fam (move quickly)* ir a toda mecha

► **book in 1** *vt sep* **to b. sb in** hacer una reserva para alguien

2 *vi (take a room)* tomar una habitación; *Br (register)* registrarse

► **book into** *vt insep (hotel)* tomar una habitación en, registrarse en

► **book up 1** *vt sep* **the hotel is fully booked up** el hotel está al completo; **I'm booked up for this evening** ya he quedado para esta noche

2 *vi* **that show books up quickly** las entradas para ese espectáculo se agotan pronto

bookable ['bʊkəbəl] *adj* (**a**) *(seat, flight)* que se puede reservar con antelación (**b**) *(offence)* (merecedor(ora)) de tarjeta

bookbinder ['bʊkbaɪndə(r)] *n* encuadernador(ora) *m,f*

bookbinding ['bʊkbaɪndɪŋ] *n* encuadernación *f*

bookcase ['bʊkkeɪs] *n* librería *f*, estantería *f*

bookie ['bʊkɪ] *n Fam (in betting)* corredor(ora) *m,f* de apuestas

booking ['bʊkɪŋ] *n* (**a**) *(reservation)* reserva *f*; **to make a b.** hacer una reserva ►► ***b. fee*** suplemento *m or* recargo *m* por reserva; ***b. office*** taquilla *f*, *Am* boletería *f* (**b**) *(of comedian, singer)* compromiso *m* (**c**) *(in soccer)* tarjeta *f* amarilla; **to receive a b.** recibir una tarjeta amarilla

bookish ['bʊkɪʃ] *adj* (**a**) *(person)* estudioso(a) (**b**) *Pej (approach, style)* académico(a), sesudo(a)

bookkeeper ['bʊkki:pə(r)] *n Fin* tenedor(ora) *m,f* de libros

bookkeeping ['bʊkki:pɪŋ] *n Fin* contabilidad *f*

book-learning ['bʊklɜ:nɪŋ] *n* **he doesn't have much b.** no tiene muchos estudios

booklet ['bʊklɪt] *n* folleto *m*

booklist ['bʊklɪst] *n (reading list)* bibliografía *f*

bookmaker ['bʊkmeɪkə(r)] *n (in betting)* corredor(ora) *m,f* de apuestas

bookmark ['bʊkmɑ:k] **1** *n* (**a**) *(for book)* marcapáginas *m inv* (**b**) *Comptr* marcador *m*, favorito *m*

2 *vt Comptr (Web page)* añadir a la lista de marcadores *or* favoritos

bookmobile ['bʊkməbi:l] *n US* bibliobús *m*, biblioteca *f* móvil *or* ambulante

bookplate ['bʊkpleɪt] *n* ex libris *m inv*

bookrest ['bʊkrest] *n* atril *m* (de pie)

bookseller ['bʊkselə(r)] *n* librero(a) *m,f*

bookshelf ['bʊkʃelf] *n (single shelf)* estante *m*; **bookshelves** *(set of shelves)* estantería *f*

bookshop ['bʊkʃɒp] *n* librería *f*

bookstall ['bʊkstɔ:l] *n* (**a**) *(in street)* puesto *m* de libros (**b**) *Br (in railway station)* quiosco *m* de prensa

bookstand ['bʊkstænd] *n* (**a**) *(in bookstore, library)* expositor *m* de libros (**b**) *(for supporting book)* atril *m* (de pie) (**c**) *(in railway station)* quiosco *m* de prensa

bookstore ['bʊkstɔ:(r)] *n US* librería *f*

bookworm ['bʊkwɜ:m] *n* (**a**) *Fam (avid reader)* ratón *m* de biblioteca (**b**) *(insect)* piojo *m* de los libros

Boolean ['bu:lɪən] *adj Comptr (logic, operator)* booleano(a) ►► ***B. algebra*** álgebra *f* de Boole; ***B. search*** búsqueda *f* booleana

boom[1] [bu:m] *n* (**a**) *Naut (for sail)* botavara *f* (**b**) *(barrier across river, harbour)* barrera *f* (**c**) *Cin & TV* jirafa *f*

boom[2] **1** *n (economic)* auge *m*, boom *m*; **b. and bust** auge y crisis; **b. town** ciudad en auge

2 *vi (business, trade)* estar en auge, dispararse; **sales are booming** las ventas se han disparado

boom[3] **1** *n (sound)* estruendo *m*, retumbo *m* ►► *Fam* ***b. box*** radiocasete *m or Esp* loro *m* grande *(portátil)*

2 *vt (say loudly)* aullar, bramar; **"nonsense!" she boomed** "¡tonterías!" bramó

3 *vi (thunder, gun, voice)* retumbar; *(waves)* bramar

► **boom out 1** *vt sep (say)* decir vociferando

2 *vi (gun, voice)* retumbar

boomerang ['bu:məræŋ] **1** *n* bumerán *m*; **b. effect** efecto bumerán

2 *vi Fam* **to b. on sb** volverse contra alguien

booming ['bu:mɪŋ] *adj* (**a**) *(voice)* estruendoso(a), atronador(ora) (**b**) *(business, industry)* en auge

boon [bu:n] *n* bendición *f*; **this service is a b. for the elderly** este servicio es una bendición para los ancianos; **a b. companion** *(person)* un amigo íntimo; **the book will be a b. companion to the backpacker** el libro será un compañero de viaje imprescindible para los mochileros

boondocks ['bu:ndɒks] *npl US Fam* **in the b.** en el quinto infierno *or Esp* pino, *Andes, RP* donde el diablo perdió el poncho, *Chile* en la punta del cerro, *Col* en la Patagonia

boondoggle ['bu:ndɒgəl] *vi US Fam* pérdida *f* de tiempo

boor [bʊə(r)] *n* grosero(a) *m,f*, cafre *mf*

boorish ['bʊərɪʃ] *adj (person, behaviour)* grosero(a), ordinario(a)

boorishly ['bʊərɪʃlɪ] *adv* groseramente, con ordinariez

boost [bu:st] **1** *n* (**a**) *(of rocket)* propulsión *f*; *(of economy)* impulso *m*; **a b. in sales** un rápido incremento en las ventas; **to give sth/sb a b.** dar un impulso a algo/alguien (**b**) *(upward push)* **to give sb a b.** impulsar *or* dar impulso a alguien hacia arriba

2 *vt* (**a**) *(rocket)* propulsar; *Tel (signal)* amplificar; *(economy, sales, productivity)* impulsar, estimular; *(hopes)* alimentar; *(morale)* levantar; **this success will really b. his confidence** este éxito le dará más seguridad en sí mismo (**b**) *(promote) (product, candidate)* impulsar (**c**) *US Fam (steal)* afanar, *Esp* sisar

3 *vi US Fam (shoplift)* afanar, *Esp* sisar *(en comercios)*

booster ['bu:stə(r)] *n* (**a**) *(on missile, spacecraft)* **b. (rocket)** (cohete *m*) propulsor *m* (**b**) *Elec* elevador *m* de tensión ►► *US* ***b. cables*** pinzas *fpl or* cables *mpl* (de arranque) de batería (**c**) *Med* **b. (shot)** revacunación *f* (**d**) *US Fam (supporter)* **he's a great b. for his home town** le entusiasma ir cantando las maravillas de su ciudad natal (**e**) *US Fam (shoplifter)* ratero(a) *m,f (en comercios)*

boot [bu:t] **1** *n* (**a**) *(footwear)* bota *f*; *(ankle-length)* botín *m*; **football/rugby b.** bota de fútbol/rugby ►► *US Mil* ***b. camp*** campamento *m* de reclutas; ***b. polish*** betún *m*; ***b. scraper*** limpiabarros *m inv* (**b**) *Fam (kick)* **to give sth a b.** darle a algo una patada *or* un puntapié; **he needs a b. up the backside** ése lo que necesita es una buena patada en el trasero

(**c**) *Br (of car)* maletero *m*, *CAm*, *Méx* cajuela *f*, *RP* baúl *m*

(**d**) *Comptr* ***b. disk*** disco *m* de arranque; ***b. sector*** sector *m* de arranque

(**e**) *Br Fam Pej (ugly woman)* coco *m*, *Esp* feto *m* (malayo), *Am* bagre *m*

(**f**) *Fam (dismissal)* **to give sb the b.** dar la patada a alguien, poner a alguien de patitas en la calle; **to get the b.** *(from work)* ser despedido(a); **his girlfriend gave him the b.** su novia le dio calabazas

(**g**) **to b.** *(as well)* además, por añadidura

(**h**) IDIOMS **the b. is on the other foot** se ha dado la vuelta a la tortilla; *Br Fam* **to put** *or* **stick the b. in** *(beat severely, criticize)* ensañarse; **to die with one's boots on** morir con las botas puestas

2 *vt* (**a**) *Fam (kick)* dar una patada a (**b**) *Comptr* arrancar

3 *vi Comptr* **to b. (up)** arrancar

▸ **boot in** *vt sep Fam* **to b. a door in** abrir una puerta a patada limpia

▸ **boot out** *vt sep Fam* **to b. sb out** poner a alguien en la calle, echar a alguien

▸ **boot up** 1 *vt sep (computer)* arrancar

2 *vi (computer, person)* arrancar

bootable ['bu:təbəl] *adj Comptr (disk)* de arranque

bootblack ['bu:tblæk] *n US* limpiabotas *mf inv*

booted ['bu:tɪd] *adj* con botas ▸▸ ***b. warbler*** zarcero *m* escita

bootee [bu:'ti:] *n (child's shoe)* patuco *m*

booth [bu:ð] *n* (**a**) *(for telephone, in voting)* cabina *f* (**b**) *(at fair)* barraca *f or* caseta *f* (de feria); *(at trade fair)* stand *m* (**c**) *(in restaurant)* mesa *f (rodeada de asientos corridos fijados al suelo)*

boot-jack ['bu:tdʒæk] *n* sacabotas *m inv*

bootlace ['bu:tleɪs] *n* cordón *m* ▸▸ ***b. tie*** lazo *m*

bootleg ['bu:tleg] 1 *vt* (*pt & pp* **bootlegged**) (**a**) *(alcohol) (make)* elaborar clandestinamente; *(sell)* contrabandear; **he made a fortune by bootlegging rum** hizo una fortuna con el contrabando *or* estraperlo de ron (**b**) *(copy illegally) (recording, cassette)* piratear; **these "Rolexes" were bootlegged in South Korea** estos Rolex falsos son de fabricación coreana

2 *adj* (**a**) *(alcohol)* de estraperlo, de contrabando (**b**) *(recording, cassette)* pirata; *(watch, jeans)* falso(a)

bootlegger ['bu:tlegə(r)] *n* (**a**) *(of alcohol)* contrabandista *mf*, estraperlista *mf* (**b**) *(of recordings)* pirateador(ora) *m,f*; *(of watches, jeans)* = persona que fabrica productos de marca falsos

bootless ['bu:tlɪs] *adj Literary (fruitless)* infructuoso(a)

bootlicker ['bu:tlɪkə(r)] *n Fam* lameculos *mf inv*, *Esp* pelota *mf*, *Méx* arrastrado(a) *m,f*, *RP* chupamedias *mf inv*

bootmaker ['bu:tmeɪkə(r)] *n* botero(a) *m,f*

boots ['bu:ts] *n Br (in hotel)* limpiabotas *m inv*

bootstrap ['bu:tstræp] *n* (**a**) IDIOM **he pulled himself up by his bootstraps** logró salir adelante por su propio esfuerzo (**b**) *Comptr* arranque *m* ▸▸ ***b. routine*** secuencia *f* de arranque

booty ['bu:tɪ] *n* (**a**) *(loot)* botín *m* (**b**) *US Fam (buttocks)* culo *m*, *Am* cola *f* (**c**) *US Fam (sexual intercourse)* **to get some b.** mojar el *Esp* churro *or RP* bizcocho, *Méx* echarse un caldito

booze [bu:z] *Fam* 1 *n* bebida *f*, *Esp* priva *f*, *RP* chupi *m*; **to be on the b.** empinar el codo, darle a la bebida *or Esp* a la priva *or RP* al chupi; **she's off the b.** ha dejado la bebida *or Esp* priva, *RP* dejó el chupi

2 *vi* empinar el codo, *RP* chupar

boozehound ['bu:zhaʊnd] *n US Fam* borrachuzo(a) *m,f*

boozer ['bu:zə(r)] *n Fam* (**a**) *(person)* bebedor(ora) *m,f*, esponja *f*, *Am* tomador(ora) *m,f* (**b**) *Br (pub)* bar *m*, *Esp* bareto *m*

booze-up ['bu:zʌp] *n Br Fam* juerga *f*; **to have a b.** agarrarse una curda

boozy ['bu:zɪ] *adj Fam (person)* borrachín(ina); *(occasion)* lleno(a) de alcohol; *(voice, breath)* de borracho(a)

bop[1] [bɒp] 1 *n* (**a**) *(music)* bebop *m* (**b**) *Br Fam (dance)* baile *m*

2 *vi* (*pt & pp* **bopped**) *Br Fam (dance)* bailotear

bop[2] *Fam* 1 *n (blow)* golpecito *m*

2 *vt* (*pt & pp* **bopped**) *(hit)* dar un golpecito a; **she bopped him on the head** le dio un coscorrón

boracic [bə'ræsɪk] *adj Chem* bórico(a) ▸▸ ***b. acid*** ácido *m* bórico

borage ['bɒrɪdʒ] *n* borraja *f*

borax ['bɔ:ræks] *n* bórax *m inv*

Bordeaux [bɔ:'dəʊ] *n* (**a**) *(city)* Burdeos (**b**) *(wine)* burdeos *m inv*

bordello [bɔ:'deləʊ] (*pl* **bordellos**) *n* burdel *m*, lupanar *m*

border ['bɔ:də(r)] 1 *n* (**a**) *(edge)* borde *m*; *(on clothes)* ribete *m*

(**b**) *(frontier)* frontera *f*; **to cross the b.** cruzar la frontera ▸▸ ***b. crossing*** paso *m* fronterizo; ***b. guard*** guardia *m* fronterizo; ***b. incident*** incidente *m* fronterizo; ***b. town*** ciudad *f* fronteriza

(**c**) *(in garden)* arriate *m*

(**d**) *(proper names)* **the Borders** los Borders, = región en el sureste de Escocia limítrofe con Inglaterra ▸▸ ***B. collie*** Border collie *m*; ***B. terrier*** Border terrier *m*

2 *vt* (**a**) *(line edges of)* bordear (**b**) *(be adjacent to)* lindar con (**c**) *(country)* limitar con; **Mexico borders Texas** México tiene frontera con Tejas

▸ **border on** *vt insep* (**a**) *(of country)* limitar con; **Italy and Austria b. on each other** Italia y Austria tienen frontera común, Italia y Austria son limítrofes (**b**) *(be close to)* rayar en, bordear; **to b. on insanity/the ridiculous** rayar en *or* bordear la locura/lo ridículo

borderland ['bɔ:dəlænd] *n* frontera *f*, zona *f* fronteriza

borderline ['bɔ:dəlaɪn] 1 *n* frontera *f*, límite *m*; **to be on the b.** estar en el límite, estar en la frontera

2 *adj* **a b. case** un caso dudoso; **a b. pass** un aprobado raspado

bore[1] [bɔ:(r)] 1 *n (person)* pelma *mf*, pelmazo(a) *m,f*; *(thing)* fastidio *m*, lata *f*; **what a b.!** ¡qué fastidio *or* lata!; **visiting them is such a b.!** ¡visitarlos es un fastidio *or* una lata!

2 *vt* aburrir; **I won't b. you with the details** no te voy a aburrir con los detalles; IDIOM *Fam Hum* **to b. the pants off sb** aburrir como una ostra *or RP* un perro a alguien; IDIOM **housework bores me stiff** *or* **rigid** *or* **to tears** *or* **to death** las tareas de la casa me fastidian un montón *or Esp* me amuerman cantidad

bore[2] 1 *n* (**a**) *(calibre)* calibre *m*; *(of pipe)* diámetro *m* interior; **a 12 b. shotgun** una escopeta del calibre 12 (**b**) *(drilled hole)* agujero *m*, perforación *f*; **a test b.** una perforación de prospección

2 *vt (with drill)* perforar, taladrar; **to b. a hole/tunnel/well** abrir un agujero/un túnel/un pozo; **to b. a hole in sth** taladrar algo

3 *vi* **to b. for water/minerals** hacer perforaciones *or* prospecciones en búsqueda *or* busca de agua/minerales; **to b. through sth** perforar *or* taladrar algo; **I felt his eyes boring into me** noté que me taladraba con la mirada

bore[3] *n (of river)* macareo *m*

bore[4] *pt of* **bear**[2]

bored [bɔ:d] *adj* aburrido(a); **to be b. (with)** estar aburrido(a) (de); **I'm b. with my job** mi trabajo me aburre; *Fam* **I was b. stiff** *or* **rigid** *or* **to tears** *or* **to death** me aburrí como una ostra *or RP* un perro

boredom ['bɔ:dəm] *n* aburrimiento *m*

borehole ['bɔ:həʊl] *n* perforación *f*

borer ['bɔ:rə(r)] *n* (**a**) *(tool) (for wood, metal)* barrena *f*; *(for mine, well)* perforadora *f* (**b**) *(insect)* carcoma *f*

boric ['bɔ:rɪk] *adj Chem* ***b. acid*** ácido *m* bórico

boring ['bɔ:rɪŋ] *adj* aburrido(a); **to be b.** ser aburrido(a)

boringly ['bɔ:rɪŋlɪ] *adv* de la manera más aburrida

born [bɔ:n] 1 *adj* **he's a b. story-teller/leader** es un narrador/líder nato; **he's a b. loser** es un perdedor nato; *Fam* **in all my b. days** en toda mi santa vida

2 (*pp of* **bear** *used to form passive*) (**a**) **to be b.** nacer; **I was b. in London/in 1975** nací en Londres/en 1975; **I was b. for this** *(it's my destiny)* he nacido para esto; **she was b. blind** nació ciega, es ciega de nacimiento; **she was b. lucky** nació con estrella; **she was b. Elizabeth Hughes, but writes as E.R. Johnson** su nombre verdadero es Elizabeth Hughes, pero escribe con el seudónimo E.R. Johnson; **she was b. and bred in London, she's a Londoner, b. and bred** nació y se crió en Londres; **to be b. into the world** venir al mundo; **she was b. into a poor family** nació en una familia humilde; **he was b. of an American father and a Greek mother** es hijo de padre estadounidense y madre griega; **a cynicism b. of experience** un escepticismo producto de la experiencia

(**b**) IDIOMS *Fam* **I wasn't b. yesterday** no me chupo el dedo; *Fam* **there's one b. every minute** hace falta ser bobo(a); **to be b. under a lucky star** haber nacido con (buena) estrella, *RP* haber nacido bajo una estrella; **to be b. with a silver spoon in one's mouth** nacer con un *or* el pan debajo del brazo

-born [bɔ:n] *suffix* **he's New York-b.** es neoyorquino de nacimiento, nació en Nueva York; **she's English-b.** es inglesa de nacimiento, nació en Inglaterra

born-again Christian ['bɔ:nəgen'krɪstʃən] *n Rel* = cristiano convertido a un culto evangélico

borne *pp of* **bear**[2]

Borneo ['bɔ:nɪəʊ] *n* Borneo

boron ['bɔ:rɒn] *n Chem* boro *m*

borough ['bʌrə] *n* (**a**) *Br* = división administrativa y electoral que comprende un municipio o un distrito urbano ►► ***b. council*** *(of town)* municipio *m*; *(within city)* sede *f* de distrito (**b**) *US (municipality)* municipio *m*; *(in Alaska)* condado *m*

borrow ['bɒrəʊ] **1** *vt* (**a**) *(take on loan)* tomar prestado(a); **to b. sth from sb** pedir algo prestado a alguien; **can I b. your book?** ¿me prestas *or Esp* dejas tu libro?; **I borrowed his bicycle without him knowing** le tomé la bicicleta prestada sin que lo supiera; **to b. a book from the library** tomar prestado un libro de la biblioteca; **to b. money from the bank** pedir un crédito al banco; IDIOM **to be living on borrowed time** *(ill person, government)* tener los días contados; *US* **to b. trouble** buscarse problemas

(**b**) *(appropriate) (idea)* sacar; *(word)* tomar; **a word borrowed from Russian** un préstamo del ruso, una palabra de origen ruso

(**c**) *(in subtracting figures)* llevarse

(**d**) *(in golf)* = golpear la bola desviada para que la irregularidad del terreno la guíe hacia el hoyo

2 *vi* **she's always borrowing from other people** siempre está pidiendo cosas prestadas a los demás; **to b. against one's salary** pedir un adelanto del sueldo; **to b. against one's property** pedir un préstamo utilizando una propiedad como garantía

3 *n (in golf)* inclinación *f*, irregularidad *f*

borrower ['bɒrəʊə(r)] *n (from bank)* prestatario(a) *m,f*; *(from library)* usuario(a) *m,f*; PROV **neither a b. nor a lender be** ni prestes ni pidas prestado

borrowing ['bɒrəʊɪŋ] *n* (**a**) *(of money, word)* préstamo *m*, *Méx* prestamiento *m* (**b**) *Fin* **government b.** (nivel de) endeudamiento del Estado ►► ***b. rate*** tipo *m* de interés de los empréstitos

borscht [bɔːʃt] *n* = sopa a base de remolacha

borstal ['bɔːstəl] *n Br Formerly* correccional *m*, reformatorio *m*

borzoi ['bɔːzɔɪ] *n* galgo *m* ruso, borzoi *m*

Bosch [bɒʃ] *pr n* **(Hieronymus) B.** el Bosco

bosh [bɒʃ] *Fam Old-fashioned* **1** *n* tonterías *fpl*, *Am* pendejadas *fpl*, *RP* pavadas *fpl*

2 *exclam* ¡pamplinas!

Bosnia ['bɒznɪə] *n* Bosnia

Bosnia-Herzegovina ['bɒznɪəhɜːtsəgə'viːnə] *n* Bosnia y Hercegovina

Bosnian ['bɒznɪən] **1** *n* bosnio(a) *m,f*

2 *adj* bosnio(a); **B. Croat** croata de Bosnia; **B. Muslim** musulmán(ana) de Bosnia; **B. Serb** serbio(a) de Bosnia

bosom ['bʊzəm] **1** *n* (**a**) *(breast, chest)* pecho *m*; **her ample b.** sus abundantes senos *or* pechos; **he clutched her/the book to his b.** la estrechó/estrechó el libro contra su pecho; **he harboured a great hatred in his b.** albergaba un intenso odio en sus entrañas (**b**) *(heart, centre)* seno *m*; **in the b. of one's family** en el seno de la familia (**c**) *(of dress)* pechera *f*

2 *adj* **b. friend** amigo(a) del alma; *Fam* **b. buddy** amiguete(a) de toda la vida

-bosomed ['bʊzəmd] *suffix* **big/small-b.** con mucho/poco pecho

bosomy ['bʊzəmɪ] *adj* pechugona

Bosphorus ['bɒsfərəs] *n* **the B.** el Bósforo

boss[1] [bɒs] *n* (**a**) *(on shield)* tachón *m* (**b**) *(on wheel hub)* cubo *m* (**c**) *Archit* clave *f*

boss[2] **1** *n* (**a**) *Fam (at work)* jefe(a) *m,f*; **he's his own b.** trabaja por cuenta propia; **ok, you're the b.** bueno *or Esp* vale, lo que tú digas; IDIOM **to show sb who's b.** enseñar a alguien quién manda (**b**) *Fam (of union, party)* líder *mf*

2 *vt Fam* **to b. sb (about** *or* **around)** dar órdenes a alguien (a diestro y siniestro)

3 *adj Fam (excellent)* genial, *Esp* guay, *RP* bárbaro(a); **you're looking b.!** ¡estás guapísimo!

boss-eyed ['bɒsaɪd] *adj Br Fam* bizco(a)

bossily ['bɒsɪlɪ] *adv* de manera autoritaria

bossiness ['bɒsɪnɪs] *n Fam* **I can't stand b.** no soporto a la gente mandona

bossy ['bɒsɪ] *adj* mandón(ona)

bossy-boots ['bɒsɪ'buːts] *n Fam* marimandón(ona) *m,f*

Boston ['bɒstən] *n* Boston ►► ***the B. Tea Party*** el motín del Té de Boston

Bostonian [bɒ'stəʊnɪən] **1** *n* bostoniano(a) *m,f*

2 *adj* bostoniano(a)

bosun ['bəʊsən] *n Naut* contramaestre *m*

botanic(al) [bə'tænɪk(əl)] *adj* botánico(a) ►► ***b. garden(s)*** jardín *m* botánico

botanist ['bɒtənɪst] *n* botánico(a) *m,f*

botany ['bɒtənɪ] *n* botánica *f*

botch [bɒtʃ] *Fam* **1** *n* chapuza *f*; **to make a b. of a job/an interview** hacer una chapuza de trabajo/entrevista

2 *vt* **to b. (up) a job/an interview** hacer una chapuza de trabajo/entrevista

botched [bɒtʃt] *adj Fam* chapucero(a); **a b. attempt at suicide** un intento de suidicio chapucero; **his b. apology only made matters worse** sus torpes disculpas no hicieron más que empeorar las cosas

BOTH [bəʊθ] **1** *pron* ambos(as), los/las dos; **b. of my brothers** mis dos hermanos; **my sister's a doctor – so are b. of mine!** mi hermana es médica – ¡mis dos hermanas también!; **b. (of them) are dead, they are b. dead** los dos *or* ambos están muertos; **b. of these printers are faulty, these printers are b. faulty** estas dos impresoras son defectuosas; **b. of us agree, we b. agree** los dos estamos de acuerdo; **I'll tell them b. later** se lo diré (a los dos) más tarde; **two teams, b. of which are unbeaten** dos equipos, los dos imbatidos; **my sisters, b. of whom are married** mis dos hermanas, que están casadas

2 *adj* ambos(as), los/las dos; **b. (the) brothers** ambos hermanos, los dos hermanos; **b. my brothers** mis dos hermanos; **my sister's a doctor – b. mine are too!** mi hermana es médica – ¡mis dos hermanas también!; **to hold sth in b. hands** sostener algo con las dos manos; **on b. sides** a ambos lados; **on b. sides of the Atlantic** a ambos lados del Atlántico; **to look b. ways** mirar a uno y otro lado; IDIOM **you can't have it b. ways** o una cosa o la otra, no puedes tenerlo todo

3 *adv* **b. you and I** tanto tú como yo; **she is b. intelligent and beautiful** es inteligente y, además, hermosa; **I speak b. German and Spanish** hablo alemán y español

BOTHER ['bɒðə(r)] **1** *n* (**a**) *(trouble)* problemas *mpl*, dificultades *fpl*; *(inconvenience)* molestia *f*; **thanks a lot – it was no b.** muchas gracias – no hay de qué; **if it's not too much b.** si no te es mucha molestia; **it wasn't worth the b.** no valió la pena; **to get into b. with the law** meterse en problemas con la justicia; **to go to the b. of doing sth** tomarse la molestia de hacer algo; *Br Fam* **I've been having a bit** *or* **a spot of b. with my back** he estado bastante fastidiado *or RP* embromado de la espalda últimamente; *Br Fam* **there was a spot of b. outside the pub** *(fighting)* hubo bronca a la salida del pub

(**b**) *Br (person)* **sorry to be such a b.** siento dar tanto mal

2 *vt* (**a**) *(annoy)* molestar (**about** por); **my back's still bothering me** todavía me molesta la espalda; **I hate to** *or* **I'm sorry to b. you but...** siento tener que molestarte pero...

(**b**) *(concern, worry)* preocupar; **to be bothered about sth** estar preocupado(a) por algo; **heights don't b. me** las alturas no me dan miedo; **don't b. yourself** *or* **your head about that** no te preocupes por eso

(**c**) *Fam (care about)* **I can't be bothered** no tengo ganas, paso; **I can't be bothered doing it** *or* **to do it** paso de hacerlo; **I'm not bothered** me da igual

3 *vi* (**a**) *(care)* preocuparse (**about** por)

(**b**) *(take the trouble)* **he didn't even b. to apologize** ni siquiera se molestó en pedir disculpas; **you'd know what I'd said if you'd bothered to listen** si te hubieras molestado en escucharme, te habrías enterado; **I didn't b. with breakfast today** hoy no he desayunado; **don't b.!** ¡no te molestes!; **I don't know why I b.!** ¡no sé ni por qué me molesto!; **thanks, but you needn't have bothered** gracias, pero no debías haberte molestado; **there's nothing to be gained, so why b. going?** si no vamos a sacar ningún partido, ¿para qué ir?; **he left without bothering to say thank you** se marchó sin ni siquiera dar las gracias

4 *exclam Br* ¡caramba!

botheration [bɒðə'reɪʃən] *exclam Fam* ¡caramba!, ¡vaya por Dios!

bothersome ['bɒðəsəm] *adj* incordiante, molesto(a)

Botswana [bɒt'swɑːnə] *n* Botsuana

bottle ['bɒtəl] **1** *n* (**a**) *(container)* botella *f*; *(of medicine)* frasco *m*; *(for baby)* biberón *m*; **he drank (straight) from the b.** bebió directamente de la botella, bebió a morro ►► ***b. bank*** contenedor *m* de vidrio; *Fam* ***b. blonde*** rubia *f or Méx* güera *f* teñida; ***b. green*** verde *m* botella; ***b. rack*** botellero *m*; *Fam* ***b. tan*** bronceado *m or* moreno *m* artificial

(**b**) *(alcohol) Fam* **he was too fond of the b.** era demasiado aficionado a la bebida *or* a empinar el codo; **bring your own b.** *(on invitation)* trae una botella de algo; *(on advert, menu)* = aviso de un restaurante que indica que es posible consumir bebidas alcohólicas traídas de fuera; *Fam* **to be on the b.** beber mucho; *Fam* **to take to** *or* **hit the b.** darse a la bebida; *Fam* **she's been off the b. for six**

months lleva seis meses sin beber ►► ***b. party*** fiesta *f (a la que cada invitado lleva una botella)*
(**c**) *Br Fam (courage)* **to have a lot of b.** tener muchas agallas; **to lose one's b.** acobardarse
2 *vt* (**a**) *(wine)* embotellar (**b**) *(fruit)* envasar, poner en conserva
► **bottle out** *vi Br Fam* rajarse; **he bottled out of telling her the truth** se rajó y no le dijo la verdad
► **bottle up** *vt sep* (**a**) *(emotions, anger)* reprimir, contener (**b**) *(military unit)* contener
bottlebrush ['bɒtəlbrʌʃ] *n* escobilla *f* para limpiar botellas
bottled ['bɒtəld] *adj* embotellado(a) ►► ***b. gas*** gas *m* butano, gas *m* de bombona; ***b. water*** agua *f* embotellada
bottle-feed ['bɒtəlfi:d] (*pt & pp* **bottle-fed**) *vt* dar el biberón a
bottle-feeding ['bɒtəlfi:dɪŋ] *n* lactancia *f* artificial
bottleful ['bɒtəlfʊl] *n* botella *f*; **they drink sherry by the b.** se beben el jerez por botellas
bottleneck ['bɒtəlnek] **1** *n* (**a**) *(in road, traffic)* embotellamiento *m*, estrechamiento *m* (**b**) *(in production)* atasco *m*
2 *vt US* obstaculizar, entorpecer
bottlenose(d) dolphin ['bɒtəlnəʊz'dɒlfɪn] *n* delfín *m* mular
bottle-opener ['bɒtələʊpənə(r)] *n* abrebotellas *m inv*
bottling plant ['bɒtəlɪŋ'plɑ:nt] *n* embotelladora *f*

BOTTOM ['bɒtəm] **1** *n* (**a**) *(lowest part) (of well, sea, swimming-pool)* fondo *m*; *(of stairs, mountain, page, ladder)* pie *m*; *(of list)* final *m*; **it's in the b. of the cup** está en el fondo de la taza; **at the b. of** *(well, sea)* en el fondo de; *(stairs, mountain, page)* al pie de; **he's at the b. of the class** es el último de la clase; **my team are at the b. of the league** mi equipo está en la cola de la liga; **I'll wait for you at the b.** *(of hill)* te esperaré abajo; **I started at the b. and worked my way up** *(in job)* comencé desde abajo y fui ascendiendo a base de trabajo; **from the b. of one's heart** de todo corazón; **the b. has fallen out of the market** la demanda ha caído en *Esp* picado *or Am* picada; **at the b. of the fifth (inning)** *(in baseball)* en la segunda parte del quinto turno de bateo; *also Fig* **to touch b.** tocar fondo
(**b**) *(underside) (of cup, box)* parte *f* de abajo; *(of shoe)* suela *f*; *(of ship)* casco *m*; **there's a sticker on the b. of the box** hay una etiqueta en la parte de abajo de la caja
(**c**) *(furthest end) (of table)* final *m*; *(of bed)* pie *m*; *(of corridor)* fondo *m*; **at the b. of the garden** al fondo del jardín; **at the b. of the street** al final de la calle
(**d**) *(of clothing)* **bikini b.** parte de abajo del bikini; **pyjama bottoms** pantalones del pijama *or Am* piyama; **the b. of my trousers has a hole in it** mis pantalones tienen un agujero en la parte del trasero
(**e**) *Fam (buttocks)* trasero *m*, culo *m*
(**f**) IDIOMS **at b.** *(fundamentally)* en el fondo; **to be at the b. of sth** *(be the reason for)* ser el motivo de algo; *(person)* estar detrás de algo; **to be at the b. of the heap** *or* **pile** estar en lo más bajo de la escala; **to get to the b. of sth** llegar hasta el fondo de algo; *Fam* **bottoms up!** ¡salud!
2 *adj* inferior; **the b. layer/drawer** la capa/el cajón de abajo del todo; **the b. 20 percent of schoolchildren** el 20 por ciento de los escolares con peores resultados; **the b. score was 23** el peor resultado fue un 23; **the b. team in the league** el (equipo) colista; *Fam* **you can bet your b. dollar that...** puedes apostar lo que quieras a que...; *Br* **b. drawer** *(of bride-to-be)* ajuar; **b. floor** planta baja; **in b. gear** en primera (velocidad); *Sport* **the b. half of the draw** la parte de abajo de los cruces; **the b. line** *(financially)* el saldo final; **£500 is my b. line** no voy a bajar de 500 libras; **the b. line is that he is unsuited to the job** la realidad es que no resulta adecuado para el trabajo; **b. sheet** sábana bajera
3 *adv (in last place)* **to come** *or* **finish b.** llegar *or* finalizar el último
► **bottom out** *vi (recession, unemployment)* tocar fondo

bottomless ['bɒtəmlɪs] *adj (abyss)* sin fondo; *(reserve)* inagotable; *Fig* **a b. pit** *(costly project)* un pozo *or Am* barril sin fondo; *(very hungry person)* una persona con mucho saque
bottommost ['bɒtəmməʊst] *adj* de más abajo; **the b. layers of society** los estratos más bajos de la sociedad
bottom-up ['bɒtəm'ʌp] *adj (approach, method)* de lo general a lo particular; **b. processing** = procesamiento que parte de lo particular para crear un marco general
botulin ['bɒtjʊlɪn] *n* toxina *f* botulínica
botulism ['bɒtjʊlɪzəm] *n* botulismo *m*
Boudicca = **Boadicea**
boudoir ['bu:dwɑ:(r)] *n* tocador *m*
bouffant ['bu:fɒŋ] *adj* ahuecado(a)
bougainvillea [bu:gən'vɪlɪə] *n* buganvilla *f*
bough [baʊ] *n* rama *f*
bought *pt & pp of* **buy**
bouillon ['bu:jɒn] *n Culin* caldo *m* ►► *US* ***b. cube*** pastilla *f or* cubito *m* de caldo (concentrado)
boulder ['bəʊldə(r)] *n* roca *f* (redondeada) ►► *Geol* ***b. clay*** = depósito glaciar compuesto por arcilla y rocas
boulevard ['bu:ləvɑ:d] *n* bulevar *m*, paseo *m*
bounce [baʊns] **1** *n* (**a**) *(of ball) (action)* rebote *m*, bote *m*; **to catch a ball on the b.** agarrar una bola a bote pronto ►► ***b. pass*** *(in basketball)* pase *m* de pique *or* picado
(**b**) *(spring)* **there isn't much b. in this ball** esta pelota no bota mucho
(**c**) *(energy)* vitalidad *f*, chispa *f*
(**d**) *(of hair)* vigor *m*, vitalidad *f*
(**e**) *US Fam (dismissal)* **to give sb the b.** echar a alguien, poner a alguien de patitas en la calle; **he got the b.** lo echaron, lo pusieron de patitas en la calle
(**f**) *Comptr* ***b. message*** mensaje *m* rebotado
(**g**) IDIOM *Fam* **on the b.: three games on the b.** tres partidos seguidos
2 *vt* (**a**) *(cause to spring)* botar; **he bounced the baby on his knee** movía al niño arriba y abajo sobre la rodilla; *Fig* **to b. an idea off sb** preguntar a alguien su opinión acerca de una idea; IDIOM **to b. sb into doing sth** presionar a alguien para que haga algo
(**b**) *Fam (cheque)* **the bank bounced my cheque** el banco me rechazó el cheque
(**c**) *US Fam (dismiss, eject)* echar, poner en la calle
3 *vi* (**a**) *(object)* botar, rebotar; **the ball bounced down the steps** la pelota cayó botando por las escaleras; **to b. off the wall** *(ball)* rebotar en la pared; *Fig* **criticism bounces off him** las críticas le resbalan
(**b**) *(person)* **he bounced up and down on the bed** daba saltos en la cama; **to b. into/out of a room** entrar a/salir de una habitación con energía
(**c**) *Fam (cheque)* ser rechazado(a)
(**d**) *Comptr* rebotar
► **bounce back** *vi (after illness, disappointment)* recuperarse, reponerse; **the pound has bounced back against the dollar** la libra se ha recuperado frente al dólar
bouncer ['baʊnsə(r)] *n Fam (doorman)* gorila *m*, matón *m*
bouncing ['baʊnsɪŋ] *adj (baby)* robusto(a)
bouncy ['baʊnsɪ] *adj* (**a**) *(ball)* que bota bien; *(mattress)* elástico(a); *(hair)* flexible ►► ***b. castle*** castillo *m* hinchable (**b**) *(lively)* **to be b.** *(person)* tener mucha vitalidad
bound[1] [baʊnd] **1** *n* (**a**) *(leap)* salto *m*; **at one b.** de un salto (**b**) *(limit)* límite *m*
2 *vi* (**a**) *(leap)* saltar; **to come bounding up to sb** ir hacia alguien dando saltos *or* brincos; **the children bounded into/out of the classroom** los niños entraban y salían de la clase dando saltos (**b**) *(beat fast)* **my heart bounded within me when I saw her** cuando la ví me empezo a palpitar el corazón a toda velocidad
bound[2] *adj* (**a**) *(destined)* **b. for** con destino a; **b. for great/better things** destinado(a) a hacer grandes/mejores cosas; **where are you b. for?** ¿hacia dónde se dirige?
(**b**) *(certain)* **he's b. to come** seguro que viene; **it was b. to happen** tenía que suceder; **it's b. to be painful at first** al principio seguro que va a ser doloroso; *Old-fashioned* **she's up to no good, I'll be b.** estoy seguro de que anda tramando algo
(**c**) *(obliged)* **you are b. to report any change in your income** tienes obligación de notificar cualquier cambio en tus ingresos; **to be b. by an oath/a contract/a treaty** estar obligado(a) por un juramento/un contrato/un tratado; **to be (legally) b. to do sth** tener la obligación legal *or* estar obligado(a) por ley a hacer algo; **the teacher felt b. to report the incident** el profesor se sintió obligado a dar cuenta del incidente; *Formal* **I feel** *or* **am b. to say (that)...** he de decir que...
(**d**) *(tied)* **b. hand and foot** atado(a) de pies y manos
(**e**) *(book)* encuadernado(a); **b. in boards/leather** encuadernado(a) en cartoné/en piel
bound[3] *vt (border)* **the region is bounded to the north by a mountain range** la región limita al norte con una cordillera montañosa
bound[4] *pt & pp of* **bind**
-bound [baʊnd] *suffix (heading towards)* **a south-b. train** un tren (que va) hacia el sur; **city-b. traffic** tráfico entrante, tráfico que se dirige hacia la ciudad

boundary ['baʊndərɪ] *n* **(a)** *(limit, border)* frontera *f*, límite *m*; **b. line** *(of parish, property)* límite, línea divisoria, linde; **the b. (line) between fact and fiction** la frontera *or* el límite entre la realidad y la ficción

(b) *Sport* **b. (line)** *(in cricket)* línea *f* de fuera, límites *mpl*; *(in basketball)* línea *f* de fondo; **to hit** *or* **to score a b.** *(in cricket)* = anotarse cuatro carreras con un golpe que saca la bola fuera del campo de juego (o seis si la bola no llega a tocar el suelo)

bounden ['baʊndən] *adj Formal* **b. duty** deber ineludible

bounder ['baʊndə(r)] *n Old-fashioned Fam* sinvergüenza *m*

boundless ['baʊndlɪs] *adj* ilimitado(a), sin límites

bounds [baʊndz] *npl (limit)* límites *mpl*; **to be out of b.** estar vedado(a); **the castle gardens are out of b. to visitors** no se permite la entrada de los visitantes a los jardines del castillo; **the ball went out of b.** *(in golf)* la pelota salió fuera de límites; **it is (not) beyond the b. of possibility** (no) es del todo imposible; **within the b. of possibility** dentro de lo posible; **to know no b.** *(anger, ambition, grief)* no conocer límites; **within b.** dentro de un orden *or* límite

bounteous ['baʊntɪəs] *adj Literary* **(a)** *(person)* munificente, próvido(a) **(b)** *(plentiful)* copioso(a), abundante

bountiful ['baʊntɪfʊl] *adj* **(a)** *(person)* magnánimo(a), generoso(a) **(b)** *(plentiful)* abundante, copioso(a); **in b. supply** abundante, copioso(a)

bounty ['baʊntɪ] *n* **(a)** *(reward)* recompensa *f* ▸▸ ***b. hunter*** cazarrecompensas *mf inv* **(b)** *Literary (generosity)* generosidad *f*, exuberancia *f* **(c)** *Literary (gift)* regalo *m*, obsequio *m*

bouquet [bu:'keɪ] *n* **(a)** *(of flowers)* ramo *m*; *Fig* **he won many bouquets for his Othello** su Otelo fue muy elogiado **(b)** *(of wine)* buqué *m* **(c)** *Culin* ***b. garni*** ramillete *m* de hierbas aromáticas

bourbon ['bɜ:bən] *n* **(a)** *US (whiskey)* whisky *m* americano, bourbon *m* **(b)** *Hist* **the Bourbons** la casa de Borbón, los Borbones **(c)** *Br* **B. biscuit** = galleta de chocolate rellena de crema de chocolate

bourgeois ['bʊəʒwɑ:] **1** *n (pl* **bourgeois***)* burgués(esa) *m,f*

2 *adj also Pej* burgués(esa), aburguesado(a)

bourgeoisie [bʊəʒwɑ:'zi:] *n* burguesía *f*

bout [baʊt] *n* **(a)** *(of work, activity)* periodo *m*; **a b. of drinking** una borrachera de varios días **(b)** *(of illness, depression)* ataque *m*; **she's prone to frequent bouts of illness** sufre frecuentes episodios de enfermedad **(c)** *(boxing, wrestling match)* combate *m*

boutique [bu:'ti:k] *n* **(a)** *(fashion shop)* boutique *f* **(b)** *(within larger store)* boutique *f*

bouzouki [bʊ'zu:kɪ] *n* bouzouki *m*, buzuki *m*

bovine ['bəʊvaɪn] *adj* **(a)** *(of cattle)* bovino(a) ▸▸ ***b. spongiform encephalopathy*** encefalopatía *f* espongiforme bovina **(b)** *Pej (stupid)* tonto(a), embobado(a)

Bovril® ['bɒvrɪl] *n Br* Bovril® *m*, = concentrado de carne

bovver ['bɒvə(r)] *n Br Fam* camorra *f*, *Esp* follón *m* ▸▸ ***b. boots*** botas *fpl* militares *or* de tachuelas; ***b. boy*** camorrista *m*, *RP* camorrero *m*

bow[1] [bəʊ] **1** *n* **(a)** *(weapon)* arco *m*; **a b. and arrow** un arco y flechas **(b)** *(for violin, cello)* arco *m* **(c)** *(in hair, on dress)* lazo *m*; **to tie sth in a b.** atar algo con un lazo ▸▸ ***b. tie*** *Esp* pajarita *f*, *Arg* moñito *m*, *CAm, Carib, Col* corbatín *m*, *Chile* humita *f*, *Méx* corbata *f* de moño, *Urug* moñita *f*, *Ven* corbata *f* de lacito **(d)** ***b. window*** mirador *m*, ventanal *m* curvo **(e)** ***b. legs*** piernas *fpl* estevadas

2 *vi* **(a)** *(bend)* combarse **(b)** *Mus* manejar el arco

bow[2] [baʊ] *n (of ship)* proa *f*

bow[3] [baʊ] **1** *n (with head)* inclinación *f* de cabeza; *(with upper body)* reverencia *f*; **to take a b.** *(performer)* salir a saludar; *Fig* **this is splendid work, take a b.!** ¡es un trabajo magnífico, mi más sincera enhorabuena!

2 *vt* **to b. one's head** inclinar la cabeza

3 *vi* **(a)** *(as greeting, sign of respect)* inclinar la cabeza; *Fig* **to b. and scrape (to)** *(act servilely)* ser empalagoso(a) (con), mostrarse servil (ante *or* hacia) **(b)** *(yield)* **to b. to sth/sb** rendirse ante algo/alguien; **to b. to the inevitable** rendirse ante lo inevitable; **I b. to your superior knowledge** me descubro ante tus conocimientos

▸ **bow down 1** *vt sep (weigh down)* **he was bowed down with worry** las preocupaciones lo habían doblegado

2 *vi* inclinarse (**to** *or* **before** ante); **to b. down before sb** inclinarse ante alguien

▸ **bow out 1** *vt sep (of servant, usher)* despedir con una reverencia

2 *vi (resign)* retirarse

bowdlerize ['baʊdləraɪz] *vt (text, account)* expurgar, censurar

bowed [baʊd] *adj* **with b. head** con la cabeza inclinada; **b. with age** encorvado(a) por la edad

bowel ['baʊəl] *n* **(a)** *Anat* intestino *m*; **bowels** entrañas *fpl* ▸▸ ***b. complaint*** afección *f or* trastorno *m* intestinal; ***b. movement*** evacuación *f*, deposición *f*; **to have a b. movement** hacer de vientre **(b)** *Literary* **the bowels of the earth** las entrañas de la Tierra

bower ['baʊə(r)] *n* **(a)** *(arbour)* rincón *m* umbrío **(b)** *Literary (boudoir)* boudoir *m*, tocador *m*

bowerbird ['baʊəbɜ:d] *n* tilonorrinco *m*

bowfin ['bəʊfɪn] *n (fish)* amia *f*

bowhead ['bəʊhed] *n (whale)* ballena *f* franca *or* de Groenlandia

bowie knife ['bəʊɪ'naɪf] *n* machete *m*

bowing[1] ['baʊɪŋ] *n* **b. and scraping** obsequiosidad

bowing[2] ['bəʊɪŋ] *n Mus* manejo *m* del arco

bowl[1] [bəʊl] *n* **(a)** *(dish)* cuenco *m*, bol *m*; *(for washing up)* palangana *f*, *Esp* barreño *m*; **a b. of soup, please** un plato de sopa, por favor; **fruit b.** frutero; **salad b.** ensaladera; **soup b.** plato sopero **(b)** *(of toilet)* taza *f* **(c)** *(of pipe)* cazoleta *f* **(d)** *(of spoon)* cuenco *m* **(e)** *(arena)* estadio *m*

bowl[2] **1** *vt* **(a)** *(in bowling) (ball)* lanzar; **I bowled 160** anoté 160 puntos **(b)** *(in cricket) (ball)* lanzar; **he bowled (out) the batsman** su lanzamiento descalificó al bateador

2 *vi* **(a)** *(in cricket, bowling alley)* lanzar la bola; *(on grass)* lanzar la bocha **(b)** *(move quickly)* **they came bowling down the street** *(on bicycles, in car)* pasaron por la calle volando

▸ **bowl along** *vi* **we were bowling along** íbamos volando

▸ **bowl over** *vt sep* **(a)** *(knock down)* derribar **(b)** *Fam (amaze)* dejar pasmado(a), dejar atónito(a); **she was bowled over by the news** la noticia la dejó pasmada

bow-legged [bəʊ'legɪd] *adj* con las piernas arqueadas, estevado(a)

bowler ['bəʊlə(r)] *n* **(a)** *(hat)* **b. (hat)** sombrero *m* hongo, bombín *m* **(b)** *(in cricket)* lanzador(ora) *m,f* **(c)** *(in bowling) (on grass)* jugador(ora) *m,f (de bochas inglesas)*; *(in bowling alley)* jugador(ora) *m,f (de bolos)*

bowlful ['bəʊlfʊl] *n* cuenco *m*, bol *m*

bowline ['bəʊlɪn] *n Naut* bolina *f* ▸▸ ***b. knot*** as *m* de guía

bowling ['bəʊlɪŋ] *n* **(a)** *(on grass)* **to go b.** ir a jugar a las bochas ▸▸ ***b. green*** cancha *f* de bochas (inglesas) **(b)** *(in bowling alley)* (juego *m* de) bolos *mpl*; **to go b.** ir a jugar a los bolos ▸▸ ***b. alley*** pista *f* de bolos; *(building)* bolera *f*; ***b. ball*** bola *f* (de bolos)

bowls ['bəʊlz] *n (game)* bochas *fpl inv* (inglesas), = juego parecido a la petanca que se juega sobre césped, y en el que las bolas se lanzan a ras de suelo

bowman ['bəʊmən] *n* arquero *m*

bowser ['baʊzə(r)] *n* **(a)** *Av* camión *m* cisterna **(b)** *Austr (petrol pump)* surtidor *m* de gasolina *or RP* nafta

bowsprit ['bəʊsprɪt] *n Naut* bauprés *m*

bowstring ['bəʊstrɪŋ] *n* cuerda *f* de arco

bow-wow 1 *n* ['baʊwaʊ] *(dog)* gua-gua *m*, guau-guau *m*

2 *exclam* [baʊ'waʊ] ¡guau! ¡guau!

box [bɒks] **1** *n* **(a)** *(container)* caja *f*; **a b. of chocolates** una caja de bombones; IDIOM **in a pine** *or* **wooden b.** *(coffin)* con los pies por delante ▸▸ ***b. camera*** cámara *f* de cajón; *US* ***b. canyon*** = cañón de paredes verticales; *Constr* ***b. girder*** viga *f* hueca; *Aut* ***b. junction*** cruce *m* con parrilla *or* cuadrícula *(de líneas amarillas)*; ***b. kite*** cometa *f or CAm, Méx* papalote *m or RP* barrilete *m* de caja; *US* ***b. lunch*** = almuerzo que se compra listo para comer y que viene en una caja; ***b. pleat*** tabla *f (en falda)*; *Br* ***b. spanner*** llave *m* de tubo; ***b. spring*** muelle *m*; *US* ***b. wrench*** llave *f* de tubo

(b) *(in theatre)* palco *m* ▸▸ ***b. seat*** localidad *f* de palco; IDIOM **to be in the b. seat** estar en una situación privilegiada

(c) *Cin & Theat* ***b. office*** taquilla *f*, *Am* boletería *f*; **it was a success at the b. office, it did good b. office** fue un éxito de taquilla

(d) *(vaulting horse)* plinto *m*

(e) *(in cricket, hockey)* protector *m* genital

(f) *(printed, drawn)* recuadro *m*; **tick the b.** ponga una cruz en la casilla

(g) *Comptr (for graphics)* caja *f*

(h) *(postal)* apartado *m* de correos, *Am* casilla *f* postal, *Andes, RP* casilla *f* de correos, *Col* apartado *m* aéreo; **b. number 12** apartado de correos número 12

(i) *(in soccer)* **(penalty) b.** área *f* (de castigo)

(j) *(blow)* **a b. round** *or* **on the ears** un cachete

(k) *(tree)* boj *m*

(l) *Br Fam (television)* **the b.** la tele; **what's on the b. tonight?** ¿qué echan en la tele esta noche?

(m) IDIOM *Fam* **to be out of one's b.** *(drunk)* estar borracho(a) como una cuba, estar totalmente *Méx* cuete *or RP* en pedo

(n) *Vulg (woman's genitals)* *Esp* coño *m*, *Esp* conejo *m*, *Col* cuca *f*,

Méx paloma *f*, *RP* concha *f*, *Ven* cuchara *f*
2 *vt* (**a**) *(place in box)* **to b. sth (up)** colocar algo en una caja (**b**) *(fight)* pelear con, boxear con (**c**) *(hit)* **to b. sb's ears, to b. sb round the ears** darle un cachete a alguien (**d**) *Naut* **to b. the compass** cuartear la aguja
3 *vi (fight)* boxear; IDIOM **to b. clever** actuar con astucia

▸ **box in** *vt sep* (**a**) *(pipes, meter)* tapar, cubrir; *(bath, washbasin)* = cubrir con madera la parte inferior de algo (**b**) *(in race)* encajonar, encerrar; *Fig* **to feel boxed in** sentirse encerrado(a) *or* encajonado(a)

boxcar ['bɒkskɑ:(r)], **box-wagon** ['bɒkswægən] *n US* vagón *m* de mercancías, furgón *m* (de mercancías)

boxed [bɒkst] *adj* en estuche; **a b. set** *(of CDs, videos, books)* un (juego en) estuche

boxer ['bɒksə(r)] *n* (**a**) *(fighter)* boxeador *m* (**b**) **boxers, b. shorts** *(underwear)* calzoncillos *mpl*, boxers *mpl* (**c**) *(dog)* bóxer *m*

boxercise ['bɒksəsaɪz] *n* = forma de ejercicio que incorpora elementos de boxeo

boxing ['bɒksɪŋ] *n* boxeo *m*, *CAm, Méx* box *m* ▸▸ ***b. glove*** guante *m* de boxeo; ***b. match*** combate *m* de boxeo; ***b. ring*** ring *m*

Boxing Day ['bɒksɪŋ'deɪ] *n Br* = San Esteban, el 26 de diciembre, fiesta nacional en Inglaterra y Gales

box-office ['bɒksɒfɪs] *adj* **a b. hit** *or* **success** un éxito de taquilla *or Am* boletería; **b. receipts** *or* **takings** ingresos de taquilla

boxroom ['bɒksru:m] *n Br* = en una vivienda, cuarto pequeño sin ventana que se suele usar como trastero

box-wagon = **boxcar**

boxwood ['bɒkswʊd] *n* (madera *f* de) boj *m*

boxy ['bɒksɪ] *adj* cuadrado(a), achaparrado(a)

boy [bɔɪ] 1 *n* (**a**) *(male child)* chico *m*; *(baby)* niño *m*; **I'd known him since we were boys** lo conocía desde que éramos niños ▸▸ ***b. band*** = grupo de música formado por chicos jóvenes; ***Boys' Brigade*** = organización protestante británica de escultismo para chicos; *Br Fam* ***b. racer*** niñato *m* al volante; ***B. Scout*** boy scout *m*, escultista *m*; *US Fam Hum* ***b. toy*** amiguito *m*, = amante muy joven; ***b. wonder*** joven *m* prodigio
(**b**) *(son)* chico *m*, niño *m*; **they have three boys** tienen tres niños *or* chicos; **the Smiths' b.** el hijo *or* chico de los Smith
(**c**) *(male adult)* **one of the boys** uno del grupo, uno más; **a night out with the boys** una noche de parranda con los amigos
(**d**) *Fam (term of address)* **my dear b.** querido muchacho; *Br* **how are you, old b.?** ¿cómo estás, caballero?
(**e**) *Old-fashioned (native servant)* criado *m (de las colonias)*
(**f**) *(addressing dog, horse)* **down, b.!** ¡quieto!
(**g**) IDIOMS **he's just a b. when it comes to women** es muy inocentón para los asuntos de mujeres; *Br Fam* **the boys in blue** la policía, la poli; **you shouldn't send a b. to do a man's job** hay cosas que requieren un hombre hecho y derecho; *Fam* **he threatened to send the boys round** amenazó con enviar a los matones; *Fam* **to play with the big boys** jugar *or* ir en serio
2 *exclam Fam* **oh b.!** ¡vaya!; **b. was he angry!** ¡anda que no estaba furioso!

boycott ['bɔɪkɒt] 1 *n* boicot *m*; **to place under a b.** boicotear
2 *vt* boicotear

boyf [bɔɪf] *n Br Fam* noviete *m*, *Esp* maromo *m*

boyfriend ['bɔɪfrend] *n* novio *m*

boyhood ['bɔɪhʊd] *n* niñez *f*

boyish ['bɔɪɪʃ] *adj* (**a**) *(of man) (looks, grin)* infantil (**b**) *(of woman) (looks, behaviour)* varonil

boy-meets-girl ['bɔɪmi:ts'gɜ:l] *adj* **a b. story** una típica historia de amor

boyo ['bɔɪəʊ] (*pl* **boyos**) *n Fam (in Welsh and Irish dialect)* chico *m*, chaval *m*, *Méx* chavo *m*, *Arg* pibe *m*

bozo ['bəʊzəʊ] (*pl* **bozos**) *n US Fam* zoquete *m*, tarugo *m*

BP [bi:'pi:] *n* (*abbr* **blood pressure**) tensión *f* (arterial), presión *f* sanguínea

Bp (*abbr* **Bishop**) obispo *m*

bpd (*abbr* **barrels per day**) barriles *mpl* diarios

BPhil [bi:'fɪl] (*abbr* **Bachelor of Philosophy**) (**a**) *(qualification)* licenciatura *f* en filosofía (**b**) *(person)* licenciado(a) *m,f* en filosofía

bpi [bi:pi:'aɪ] *n Comptr* (**a**) (*abbr* **bits per inch**) bpp (**b**) (*abbr* **bytes per inch**) bpp

BPR [bi:pi:'ɑ:(r)] *n* (*abbr* **business process reengineering**) BPR *m or f*

bps [bi:pi:'es] *n Comptr* (*abbr* **bits per second**) bps

Bq (*abbr* **becquerel**) Bq

BR [bi:'ɑ:(r)] *n Br Formerly* (*abbr* **British Rail**) = compañía británica estatal de ferrocarril

Br (*abbr* **brother**) **B. Anselm** hermano Anselm

bra [brɑ:] *n* sostén *m*, *Esp* sujetador *m*, *Carib, Col, Méx* brasier *m*, *RP* corpiño *m*

brace [breɪs] 1 *n* (**a**) *(reinforcement, support)* abrazadera *f*, refuerzo *m*
(**b**) *(on teeth)* **a b., braces** aparato *m* (corrector)
(**c**) *Med* **neck/back b.** collarín *m*
(**d**) *Br* **braces** *(for trousers)* tirantes *mpl*; **a pair of braces** unos tirantes
(**e**) (*pl* **brace**) *(of birds, pistols)* par *m*
(**f**) *(tool)* ***b. and bit*** berbiquí *m*
(**g**) *Mus & Typ (bracket)* llave *f*
2 *vt* (**a**) *(reinforce)* reforzar (**b**) *(steady, prepare)* **he braced his body/himself for the impact** se preparó para el impacto; **to b. oneself (for)** *(shock, surprise)* prepararse *or Chile, Méx, Ven* alistarse (para)
3 *vi US (prepare)* prepararse

▸ **brace up** *vi US (take heart)* armarse de valor

bracelet ['breɪslɪt] *n* (**a**) *(jewellery)* pulsera *f* (**b**) *Fam* **bracelets** *(handcuffs)* esposas *fpl*

bracer ['breɪsə(r)] *n Fam (drink)* reconstituyente *m*, tónico *m*

brachial ['breɪkɪəl] *adj Anat* braquial

brachiocephalic ['brækɪəʊsə'fælɪk] *adj Anat* braquiocefálico(a)

brachiosaurus [brækɪə'sɔ:rəs] *n* braquiosaurio *m*

brachycephalic ['brækɪsə'fælɪk] *adj Anat* braquicéfalo(a)

brachycephalism ['brækɪ'sefəlɪzəm] *n Anat* braquicefalia *f*

bracing ['breɪsɪŋ] *adj (wind, weather)* vigorizante

bracken ['brækən] *n* helechos *mpl*

bracket ['brækɪt] 1 *n* (**a**) *(for shelves)* escuadra *f*, soporte *m*
(**b**) *(in writing)* paréntesis *m inv*; *(round)* paréntesis *m inv*; *(square)* corchete *m*; *(curly)* llave *f*; *(angle)* paréntesis *m inv* angular; **in brackets** entre paréntesis; **open/close brackets** *(in dictation)* abrir/cerrar paréntesis
(**c**) *(group)* banda *f*, grupo *m*; **age/income b.** banda de edad/de renta
2 *vt* (**a**) *(word, phrase, symbol) (in round brackets)* poner *or* encerrar entre paréntesis; *(in square brackets)* poner *or* encerrar entre corchetes (**b**) *(link vertically with curly bracket)* unir con una llave (**c**) *(classify)* asociar (**with** con); **they resented being bracketed together** lamentaron que los pusieran en el mismo saco

brackish ['brækɪʃ] *adj (water)* ligeramente salobre *or* salado(a)

brad [bræd] *n* clavo *m*

bradawl ['brædɔ:l] *n* lezna *f*

brae [breɪ] *n Scot* (**a**) *(hillside)* ladera *f* (**b**) *(slope)* cuesta *f*

brag [bræg] (*pt & pp* **bragged**) 1 *vt* jactarse de
2 *vi* jactarse (**about** de); **it's nothing to b. about** no es como para estar orgulloso, no es como para jactarse
3 *n* (**a**) *(boast)* alarde *m*, pavoneo *f* (**b**) *(card game)* = juego de cartas predecesor del póker

braggadocio [brægə'dəʊtʃɪəʊ] *n Literary* baladronada *f*, bravata *f*

braggart ['brægət] *n* fanfarrón(ona) *m,f*

Brahma ['brɑ:mə] *n Rel* Brahma

Brahman ['brɑ:mən], **Brahmin** ['brɑ:mɪn] *n (person)* brahmán *m*, bramán *m*

Brahmaputra [brɑ:mə'pu:trə] *n* **the B.** el Brahmaputra

Brahmin ['brɑ:mɪn] *n* (**a**) = **Brahman** (**b**) *US Fam* = miembro de la aristocracia social e intelectual

braid [breɪd] 1 *n* (**a**) *(of hair)* trenza *f*; **she wears her hair in braids** lleva trenzas (**b**) *(of thread)* galón *m*
2 *vt* (**a**) *(hair, thread)* trenzar (**b**) *(decorate)* **the uniform is braided with gold** el uniforme lleva ribetes dorados

Braille [breɪl] *n* braille *m*; **to read/learn B.** leer/aprender braille ▸▸ ***B. alphabet*** alfabeto *m* braille

brain [breɪn] 1 *n* (**a**) *(organ)* cerebro *m*; **brains** *(as food)* sesos *mpl*; **to suffer b. damage** sufrir una lesión cerebral ▸▸ *Med* ***b. death*** muerte *f* cerebral; ***b. scan*** escáner *m* cerebral; *Anat* ***b. stem*** tronco *m* del encéfalo; ***b. surgeon*** neurocirujano(a) *m,f*; ***b. tumour*** tumor *m* cerebral
(**b**) *Fam (clever person)* **he's a real b.** es un verdadero cerebro *or* cerebrito
(**c**) *(intelligence, mind) Fam* **to have brains** tener cerebro; **I don't have the brains to become a doctor** no tengo el coco necesario para ser médico; **anyone with half a b.** cualquiera que tenga dos dedos de frente; *Fam* **she's the brains of the business** ella es el cerebro del

negocio; IDIOM *Fam* **to have money/sex on the b.** estar obsesionado(a) con el dinero/sexo ►► ***the b. drain*** la fuga de cerebros; *US* ***b. trust*** *(advisers)* comité *m* de asesores expertos; ***brains trust*** *(on TV, radio)* panel *m* de expertos

2 *vt Fam (hit)* descalabrar

brainbox ['breɪnbɒks] *n Br Fam (intelligent person)* cerebro *m*

brainchild ['breɪntʃaɪld] *n (idea, project)* idea *f*

brain-dead ['breɪnded] *adj* (a) *Med* clínicamente muerto(a) (b) *Pej* subnormal

brainless ['breɪnlɪs] *adj* insensato(a)

brainpower ['breɪnpaʊə(r)] *n* capacidad *f* intelectual, intelecto *m*

brainstorm ['breɪnstɔːm] 1 *n Fam* (a) *(mental confusion)* cruce *m* de cables (b) *US (brilliant idea)* idea *f* genial

2 *vi* hacer una lluvia *or* tormenta de ideas

brainstorming ['breɪnstɔːmɪŋ] *n* **b. session** tormenta de ideas, sesión de reflexión creativa

brainteaser ['breɪntiːzə(r)] *n Fam* rompecabezas *m inv*

brainwash ['breɪnwɒʃ] *vt* lavar el cerebro a; **to b. sb into doing sth** lavar el cerebro a alguien para que haga algo

brainwave ['breɪnweɪv] *n* (a) *Physiol* onda *f* cerebral (b) *Fam* **to have a b.** tener una idea genial *or* una brillante idea

brainwork ['breɪnwɜːk] *n* trabajo *m* intelectual

brainy ['breɪnɪ] *adj Fam* **to be b.** tener mucho coco

braise [breɪz] *vt* estofar, *Andes, Méx* ahogar

brake[1] [breɪk] 1 *n* freno *m*; **to put on** *or* **apply the brake(s)** frenar; *Fig* **to put the brakes on a project** frenar un proyecto ►► ***b. block*** portazapata *m* del freno; ***b. fluid*** líquido *m* de frenos; ***b. horsepower*** potencia *f* al freno; ***b. lights*** luces *fpl* de freno, luces *fpl* de frenado; ***b. lining*** forro *m or* revestimiento *m* del freno; ***b. pad*** pastilla *f* del freno; ***b. pedal*** (pedal *m* del) freno *m*; ***b. shoe*** zapata *f* (del freno); *Br* ***b. van*** *(on train)* furgón *m* de cola, furgón-freno *m*

2 *vi* frenar

brake[2] *n (land)* matorral *m*

brake[3] *n* (a) *(carriage)* break *m* (b) *Br (car)* ranchera *f*

brakeman ['breɪkmən] *n* (a) *US RAIL* guardafrenos *mf inv* (b) *(for bobsleigh)* frenador *m*

brakesman ['breɪksmən] *n Rail* guardafrenos *mf inv*

braking distance ['breɪkɪŋ'dɪstəns] *n* distancia *f* de frenado *or* de seguridad

bramble ['bræmbəl] 1 *n (plant)* zarza *f*

2 *vi* **to go brambling** ir a recoger moras

brambling ['bræmblɪŋ] *n (bird)* pinzón *m* real

bran [bræn] *n* salvado *m* ►► *Br* ***b. tub*** = juego de feria en que se extraen regalos de un recipiente lleno de salvado

branch [brɑːntʃ] 1 *n* (a) *(of tree)* rama *f*

(b) *(division) (of family, subject)* rama *f*; *(of government, organization)* división *f*, departamento *m*; *(of river)* afluente *m*; *(of road, railway)* ramal *m*, derivación *f* ►► ***b. line*** *(of railway)* línea *f* secundaria, ramal *m*

(c) *(of bank)* sucursal *f*; *(of shop)* establecimiento *m* ►► ***b. manager*** director(ora) *m,f* de sucursal; ***b. office*** sucursal *f*

(d) *(of organization, union) (department)* división *f*, sección *f*; *(local group, office)* delegación *f*

(e) *US (stream)* arroyo *m*

(f) *Comptr* ramificación *f*, bifurcación *f*

2 *vi* bifurcarse

► **branch off** *vi* (a) *(road)* desviarse, bifurcarse (**from** de); *(driver)* desviarse (**from** de) (b) *(discussion)* desviarse

► **branch out** *vi* ampliar horizontes, diversificarse; **the company has branched out into electronics** la compañía ha ampliado su oferta a productos de electrónica; **I've decided to b. out on my own** *(become self-employed)* he decidido establecerme por mi cuenta

brand [brænd] 1 *n* (a) *Com (of product)* marca *f*; *Fig* **she has her own b. of humour** tiene un humor muy suyo ►► ***b. image*** imagen *f* de marca; ***b. leader*** marca *f* líder (en el mercado); ***b. loyalty*** lealtad *f or* fidelidad *f* a la marca; ***b. name*** marca *f* de fábrica, nombre *m* comercial; ***b. recognition*** reconocimiento *m* de marca

(b) *(on cattle)* marca *f*, hierro *m*

(c) *(branding-iron)* marca *f*, hierro *m*

(d) *(burning wood)* tea *f*

(e) *Literary (torch)* tea *f*, antorcha *f*

2 *vt* (a) *(cattle)* marcar (con el hierro); *Fig* **the image was branded on her memory** la imagen se le quedó grabada en la memoria

(b) *(label)* **to b. sb (as) a liar/coward** tildar a alguien de mentiroso(a)/cobarde

(c) *Com (product)* dar nombre comercial a; **the product is branded differently in our three main markets** el producto lleva tres marcas diferentes en nuestros tres mercados principales

branding-iron ['brændɪŋaɪən] *n* hierro *m* (de marcar)

brandish ['brændɪʃ] *vt* blandir

brand-new ['brænd'njuː] *adj* flamante, completamente nuevo(a)

brandy ['brændɪ] *n (cognac)* brandy *m*, coñac *m*, *RP* cognac *m*; *(more generally)* aguardiente *m*; **cherry/plum b.** aguardiente de cerezas/ciruelas ►► *Br* ***b. butter*** = crema a base de mantequilla, azúcar y coñac para aderezar postres; ***b. glass*** copa *f* de coñac; *Br* ***b. snap*** barquillo *m* (relleno) de crema

brash [bræʃ] *adj* desparpajado(a); **I find his b. manner annoying** me molesta su desparpajo

brashly ['bræʃlɪ] *adv* con desparpajo, con brusquedad

brashness ['bræʃnɪs] *n* desparpajo *m*, brusquedad *f*

brass [brɑːs] *n* (a) *(metal)* latón *m*; IDIOM *Br Fam* **it's not worth a b. farthing** no vale un pepino *or* pimiento; IDIOM *Br very Fam* **it's b. monkey weather!** ¡hace un frío que pela *or Am* de la masita!; IDIOM *Fam* **to get down to b. tacks** ir al grano ►► *US* ***b. knuckles*** puño *m* americano

(b) *(objects)* **brass(es)** piezas *fpl* de latón; **the b. is cleaned once a week** las piezas de latón se limpian una vez a la semana

(c) *(memorial plaque)* placa *f* (conmemorativa) ►► ***b. rubbing*** *(technique)* = técnica de reproducción de placas frotando el papel sobre una superficie de latón

(d) *Mus (brass instruments)* metales *mpl* ►► ***b. band*** banda *f*

(e) *Mil Fam* **the (top) b., the b. hats** *(in army)* la plana mayor, los peces gordos

(f) *Br Fam (money) Esp* pasta *f*, *Esp, RP* guita *f*, *Am* plata *f*, *Méx* lana *f*

(g) *Br Fam (cheek, nerve)* cara *f*, caradura *f*; IDIOM **to have a b. neck** tener más cara que espalda, *RP* ser un(a) caradura; **to have the b. (neck) to do sth** tener la caradura de hacer algo

► **brass off** *vt sep Br Fam* poner histérico(a), poner de los nervios; **to be brassed off (with)** estar hasta la coronilla (de)

brasserie ['bræsərɪ] *n* restaurante *m*, casa *f* de comidas

brassière [brə'zɪə(r)] *n* sostén *m*, *Esp* sujetador *m*, *Carib, Col, Méx* brasier *m*, *RP* corpiño *m*

brass-necked [brɑːs'nekt] *adj Br Fam* caradura

brasswork ['brɑːswɜːk] *n* latón *m*

brassy ['brɑːsɪ] *adj* (a) *(colour)* del color del latón, color latón (b) *(sound)* estridente (c) *Fam (woman)* escandalosa

brat [bræt] *n Pej* niñato(a) *m,f* ►► *Fam* ***b. pack*** camada *f or* hornada *f* de jóvenes promesas

Bratislava [brætɪ'slɑːvə] *n* Bratislava

bravado [brə'vɑːdəʊ] *n* fanfarronería *f*, bravuconería *f*; **these words were sheer b.** eran sólo palabras vanas

brave [breɪv] 1 *n* (a) *(native American)* guerrero *m* indio (b) *Literary* **the b.** los valientes; **the bravest of the b.** los más valientes

2 *adj* (a) *(courageous)* valiente, valeroso(a); **a b. effort** un intento encomiable; **you'll have to be b. and tell him** tendrás que armarte de valor y decírselo; IDIOM **to put a b. face on it, to put on a b. front** poner al mal tiempo buena cara (b) *Literary (splendid)* magnífico(a), espléndido(a); **a b. new world** un mundo nuevo y espléndido

3 *vt (danger, weather)* encarar, afrontar

► **brave out** *vt sep* **to b. it out** aguantar, plantar cara; **he had to b. out the crisis alone** tuvo que lidiar con la crisis él solo

bravely ['breɪvlɪ] *adv* valientemente, valerosamente

bravery ['breɪvərɪ] *n* valentía *f*, valor *m*

bravo [brɑː'vəʊ] *exclam* ¡bravo!

bravura [brə'vjʊrə] *n (spirit, zest)* brío *m*, entrega *f*; *Mus* virtuosismo *m*; **a b. performance** *Mus* una virtuosa interpretación; *Fig* una brillante actuación

brawl [brɔːl] 1 *n* trifulca *f*, refriega *f*

2 *vi* pelearse

brawler ['brɔːlə(r)] *n* camorrista *m*, pendenciero *m*

brawn [brɔːn] *n* (a) *Fam (strength)* fuerza *f*, músculo *m*; **he's got more b. than brains** tiene más músculo que seso (b) *Br Culin* queso *m* de cerdo, *Esp* cabeza *f* de jabalí

brawny ['brɔːnɪ] *adj* musculoso(a)

bray [breɪ] 1 *n* (a) *(of donkey)* rebuzno *m* (b) *(laugh)* risotada *f*

2 *vi* (a) *(donkey)* rebuznar (b) *(laugh)* carcajearse

brazen ['breɪzən] *adj* (a) *(shameless)* descarado(a); *Old-fashioned or Hum* **a b. hussy** una pelandusca (b) *Literary (made of brass)* de latón; *(brass-coloured)* color latón (c) *Literary (in sound)* metálico(a)

▸**brazen out** *vt sep* **to b. it out** echarle mucha cara al asunto

brazen-faced ['breɪzənfeɪst] *adj* desvergonzado(a), descarado(a)

brazenly ['breɪzənlɪ] *adv* con el mayor descaro

brazier ['breɪzɪə(r)] *n* brasero *m*

Brazil [brə'zɪl] *n* Brasil

brazil [brə'zɪl] *n* **b. (nut)** coquito *m* del Brasil

Brazilian [brə'zɪlɪən] **1** *n* brasileño(a) *m,f*
2 *adj* brasileño(a)

breach [bri:tʃ] **1** *n* **(a)** *(in wall)* brecha *f*; IDIOM **to step into the b.** *(in emergency)* echar un cable, cubrir el vacío
(b) *(of agreement, rules)* violación *f*, incumplimiento *m*; *(of trust)* abuso *m*; **in b. of sth** en contra de algo; **in b. of the law** infringiendo la ley ▸▸ ***b. of confidence*** abuso *m* de confianza; ***b. of contract*** incumplimiento *m* de contrato; ***b. of discipline*** incumplimiento *m* de las normas; *Law* ***b. of the peace*** alteración *f* del orden público; *Br Pol* ***b. of privilege*** abuso *m* de la inmunidad parlamentaria; *Old-fashioned* ***b. of promise*** incumplimiento *m* de compromiso matrimonial
(c) *(in friendship)* ruptura *f*
2 *vt* **(a)** *(defences)* atravesar, abrir brecha en **(b)** *(contract, agreement)* violar, incumplir
3 *vi (whale)* saltar *(fuera del agua)*

bread [bred] **1** *n* **(a)** *(food)* pan *m*; **a loaf of b.** un pan; **b. and butter** pan con mantequilla; **they put the prisoner on b. and water** pusieron al prisionero a pan y agua ▸▸ *Br* ***b. bin,*** *US* ***b. box*** panera *f*; ***b. knife*** cuchillo *m* del pan; ***b. pudding*** budín *m* de pan; ***b. sauce*** = salsa hecha con leche, miga de pan y condimentos
(b) *Fam (money) Esp* pasta *f*, *Esp, RP* guita *f*, *Am* plata *f*, *Méx* lana *f*
(c) IDIOMS **to put b. on the table** ganar el pan, *RP* parar la olla; **very nice, but it won't put b. on the table** muy bonito, pero eso no te va a dar de comer; **to take the b. out of sb's mouth** quitarle el pan de la boca a alguien; **the customers are our b. and butter** lo que nos da de comer son los clientes; **he knows which side his b. is buttered on** él sabe lo que le conviene; **his b. always falls butter side down** siempre le salen las cosas mal; *Br Fam* **it's the best thing since sliced b.** es lo más *or Esp* el no va más *or Esp* la bomba *or Am* lo máximo
2 *vt (fish, cutlet)* empanar

bread-and-butter ['bredən'bʌtə(r)] *adj Fam* **b. issues** asuntos básicos ▸▸ ***b. pudding*** = postre elaborado a base de rebanadas de pan y mantequilla con pasas

breadbasket ['bredbɑ:skɪt] *n* **(a)** *(basket)* cesta *f* del pan **(b)** *Geog* granero *m* **(c)** *Fam (stomach)* panza *f*

breadboard ['bredbɔ:d] *n* tabla *f* de cortar el pan

breadcrumb ['bredkrʌm] **1** *n* miga *f*; **breadcrumbs** *(in recipe)* pan rallado; **fried in breadcrumbs** empanado(a)
2 *vt (fish, cutlet)* empanar

breaded ['bredɪd] *adj* empanado(a)

breadfruit ['bredfru:t] *n* fruto *m* del árbol del pan ▸▸ ***b. tree*** árbol *m* del pan

breadline ['bredlaɪn] *n (queue)* = cola de gente que espera su ración de alimentos gratuitos; IDIOM **on the b.** en la indigencia; **we're not on the b. yet** todavía no tenemos que salir a pedir

breadstick ['bredstɪk] *n* colín *m*

breadth [bredθ] *n* **(a)** *(width)* ancho *m*, anchura *f*; **the stage is 60 metres in b.** el escenario tiene 60 metros de ancho **(b)** *(of outlook, understanding)* amplitud *f*

breadthways ['bredθweɪz], **breadthwise** ['bredθwaɪz] *adj* a lo ancho

breadwinner ['bredwɪnə(r)] *n* **the b.** el/la que mantiene a la familia

BREAK [breɪk] **1** *n* **(a)** *(gap, opening) (in wall, fence)* abertura *f*, hueco *m*; *(in clouds)* claro *m*; *(in electric circuit)* corte *m*; **at b. of day** al despuntar el día ▸▸ *Comptr* ***b. key*** tecla *f* de interrupción; *Elec* ***b. switch*** interruptor *m*
(b) *(interval, pause)* descanso *m*, pausa *f*; *(at theatre)* entreacto *m*, descanso *m*; *(in conversation)* pausa *f*; *(holiday)* vacaciones *fpl*; *Br* **b. (time)** *(at school)* recreo *m*; **(commercial) b.** *(on TV, radio)* pausa *f* publicitaria, anuncios *mpl*; **to take a b.** *(rest)* descansar; **to work/talk without a b.** trabajar/hablar sin pausa *or* sin descanso; *Fam* **give me a b.!** *(leave me alone)* ¡déjame en paz!; *(I don't believe you)* ¡no digas tonterías!
(c) *(change) (in routine)* cambio *m*; **there's been a b. in the deadlock** se ha desbloqueado la situación; **a b. in the weather** un paréntesis de buen tiempo; **a b. with tradition** una ruptura con la tradición; **I've decided to make a clean b.** he decidido hacer borrón y cuenta nueva; **she's wanted to leave him for years but only recently decided to make the b.** lleva años queriendo dejarle pero sólo recientemente ha decidido romper con él
(d) *(in bone)* fractura *f*, rotura *f*
(e) *Fam (escape)* fuga *f*; **he made a b. for the door** se abalanzó hacia la puerta; **to make a b. for it** intentar escaparse
(f) *Fam (chance)* oportunidad *f*, *Am* chance *m*; **to give sb a b.** *(give opportunity)* dar una oportunidad *or Am* un chance a alguien; **big b.** gran oportunidad; **a lucky b.** un golpe de suerte
(g) *(in tennis)* **b. (of serve)** ruptura *f* (del servicio) ▸▸ ***b. point*** punto *m* de break *or* ruptura
(h) *(in snooker, billiards) (points)* tacada *f*
(i) *(in cycling)* escapada *f*; **he made a b.** *(in soccer, rugby)* se escapó de sus adversarios
(j) *(in song)* **an instrumental b.** una parte instrumental
(k) *(in golf)* caída *f*
(l) *(carriage)* break *m*
2 *vt* (*pt* **broke** [brəʊk], *pp* **broken** ['brəʊkən]) **(a)** *(in general)* romper; *(machine)* romper, estropear; **I've broken my bicycle** se me ha roto la bicicleta; **to b. one's arm/leg** romperse *or* partirse un brazo/una pierna; IDIOM **b. a leg!** *(good luck!)* ¡buena suerte!; **to b. sth into pieces** romper algo en pedazos; **she broke the roll in two** partió el panecillo en dos; **the river broke its banks** el río se desbordó; *Fig* **to b. one's back doing sth** deslomarse *or* desriñonarse haciendo algo; **to b. bread** *(take communion)* comulgar; *also Fig* **to b. camp** levantar el campamento; *also Fig* **to b. cover** ponerse al descubierto; **to b. sb's hold** *(escape)* escaparse de alguien; IDIOM **to b. the ice** romper el hielo; *US Fig* **to b. jail** evadirse; *Fig* **to b. the mould** romper moldes; *Fig* **I nearly broke my neck!** ¡casi me abro la cabeza!; *Fig* **I'll b. her neck if she does it again** como lo vuelva a hacer le partiré la cara; *Fig* **this product breaks new ground** este producto es muy innovador; **to b. ranks** romper filas; **without breaking sweat** sin derramar una gota de sudor; *Fig* sin despeinarse; **to b. wind** soltar una ventosidad
(b) *(surpass)* **to b. a record** batir un récord; **to b. the sound barrier** superar la barrera del sonido
(c) *(interrupt)* **to b. one's journey/holiday** interrumpir el viaje/las vacaciones; **it broke my concentration** me desconcentró; **to b. the monotony** romper la monotonía
(d) *(end) (links, relations)* romper; **to b. the deadlock** desbloquear la situación; **to b. a habit** romper con una mala costumbre; **to b. the silence/tension** romper el silencio/la tensión; **he broke his silence** rompió su silencio; **to b. a strike** reventar una huelga; IDIOM *Fam Hum* **why b. the habit of a lifetime?** ¿y por qué cambiar ahora?
(e) *(cushion, soften) (blow)* amortiguar; **the tree broke his fall** el árbol amortiguó su caída
(f) *(destroy) (person, health, resistance)* acabar con, arruinar; **to b. sb's heart** romper el corazón de alguien; **to b. sb's spirit** minar la moral a alguien; **to b. the bank** *(in games)* hacer saltar la banca; **it's only $5, so it won't exactly b. the bank!** sólo cuesta 5 dólares, ¡no me voy a arruinar!
(g) *(violate) (agreement, promise)* romper; *(law, rules)* violar; **you broke your word** no cumpliste tu palabra
(h) *(reveal) (story)* descubrir, revelar (**to** a); **to b. the news of sth to sb** dar la noticia de algo a alguien; **try to b. it to her gently** intenta decírselo con mucho tacto
(i) *(decipher) (code)* descifrar
(j) *(horse)* domar
(k) *(in tennis)* **to b. sb's serve** romper el servicio a alguien
3 *vi* **(a)** *(glass, bone)* romperse; *(machine)* romperse, estropearse; **my bracelet broke** se me rompió la pulsera; **to b. into pieces** romperse en pedazos; **to b. in two** romperse *or* partirse en dos; **the sea broke against the rocks** el mar rompía contra las rocas
(b) *(health)* sucumbir; *(resistance)* desmoronarse; **he broke under torture** se desmoronó con la tortura
(c) *(begin) (storm)* estallar, desatarse; **dawn broke** amaneció; **day was beginning to b.** despuntaba el día
(d) *(news, story)* saltar, estallar
(e) *(voice) (at puberty)* cambiar; **her voice broke with emotion** se quedó con la voz quebrada por la emoción
(f) *(change) (weather)* abrirse
(g) *(escape)* **to b. free (from)** escaparse (de); **to b. free** *or* **loose** soltarse
(h) *(have pause, rest)* hacer una pausa; **let's b. for coffee** paremos para tomar un café
(i) *(in tennis)* romper el servicio
(j) *(in snooker, billiards)* romper

▸**break away** *vi* **(a)** *(escape)* escapar (**from** de) **(b)** *(from party, country)* separarse (**from** de)

▸**break down** **1** *vt sep* **(a)** *(destroy) (door)* echar abajo; *(resistance)* vencer; **they were unable to b. down the opposition's defence** no consiguieron superar la defensa del equipo contrario; **saliva breaks down food** la saliva descompone la comida; *Fig* **we need to b. down the barriers between the two sides** necesitamos derribar las barreras entre las dos partes

(**b**) *(analyse) (argument)* dividir; *(figures)* desglosar

2 *vi* (**a**) *(machine)* estropearse; *(car)* averiarse, estropearse; *(talks)* romperse; *(argument)* fallar, desmoronarse (**b**) *(person) (under pressure, physically)* derrumbarse; **to b. down (in tears)** romper a llorar

▸ **break even** *vi* cubrir gastos, no tener pérdidas

▸ **break in 1** *vt sep (horse, new shoes)* domar; *(new recruit)* amoldar

2 *vi* (**a**) *(burglar)* entrar *(en una casa)* (**b**) *(interrupt)* interrumpir

▸ **break into** *vt insep* (**a**) *(of burglar) (house)* entrar en; **somebody broke into the vehicle through the window** alguien entró en el vehículo rompiendo la ventana

(**b**) *(begin suddenly)* **to b. into laughter/a song/a run** echarse a reír/cantar/correr; **to b. into a sweat** ponerse a sudar

(**c**) *(gain presence in) (market)* penetrar en, introducirse en

(**d**) *(use) (money)* **I'll have to b. into my savings** tendré que echar mano de mis ahorros

▸ **break off 1** *vt sep* (**a**) *(detach) (twig, handle)* partir, desprender; **he broke off a piece of chocolate** partió una porción de chocolate

(**b**) *(terminate) (relations, engagement)* romper

(**c**) *(interrupt) (journey, holiday, speech)* interrumpir

2 *vi* (**a**) *(become detached)* partirse, desprenderse

(**b**) *(stop talking)* interrumpirse; **to b. off to do sth** parar para hacer algo

▸ **break open 1** *vt sep* (**a**) *(lock, safe)* forzar; *(door) (kick down)* echar abajo (**b**) *(melon, coconut)* abrir

2 *vi (burst)* romperse, partirse

▸ **break out** *vi* (**a**) *(escape)* escaparse (**of** de)

(**b**) *(start) (disease, argument)* desatarse; *(war)* estallar; *(fire)* comenzar; **he broke out in a sweat** le entraron sudores; **she broke out in a rash** le salió un sarpullido

▸ **break through 1** *vt insep (wall, barrier)* atravesar; *Fig (sb's reserve, shyness)* superar

2 *vi (sun)* salir

▸ **break up 1** *vt sep* (**a**) *(machine, company)* desmantelar; *(ship)* desguazar

(**b**) *(ground, soil)* mullir

(**c**) *(fight, quarrel)* poner fin a; *(demonstration)* disolver; *Fam* **b. it up!** *(stop fighting)* ¡basta ya (de pelear)!

(**d**) *US Fam (cause to laugh)* **it broke me up** me hizo morirme de risa *or* desternillarme

2 *vi* (**a**) *(disintegrate)* hacerse pedazos; *(family, group)* separarse; *(crowd)* dispersarse

(**b**) *(end) (meeting, school term)* terminar; *(marriage, relationship)* romperse, terminar; **to b. up with sb** romper con alguien

(**c**) *US Fam (laugh)* desternillarse de risa

▸ **break with** *vt insep* romper con

---

breakable ['breɪkəbəl] **1** *n* **breakables** objetos *mpl* frágiles

2 *adj* frágil, rompible

breakage ['breɪkɪdʒ] *n* **all breakages must be paid for** *(sign)* el cliente deberá abonar cualquier artículo que resulte roto

breakaway ['breɪkəweɪ] **1** *n (in cycling)* escapada *f*; **to establish a b.** organizar *or* montar una escapada

2 *adj* **a b. group** *(from party, organization)* un grupo escindido *(del principal)*; *(in cycling)* un grupo de escapados; **a b. republic** una república secesionada

breakdance ['breɪkdɑːns] **1** *n* breakdance *m*

2 *vi* hacer breakdance, bailar breakdance

breakdancing ['breɪkdɑːnsɪŋ] *n* break *m*, breakdance *m*

breakdown ['breɪkdaʊn] *n* (**a**) *(of car, machine)* avería *f*; **to have a b.** tener *or* sufrir una avería ▸▸ ***b. service*** asistencia *f* en carretera, ayuda *f* en carretera; *Br* ***b. truck*** grúa *f*; *Br* ***b. van*** grúa *f*

(**b**) *(failure) (of talks)* ruptura *f*; *(of communication, system) Esp* fallo *m*, *Am* falla *f*; *(of service)* interrupción *f*; *(of tradition)* desmoronamiento *m*, desintegración *f*; *(of marriage, relationship)* ruptura *f*

(**c**) *(mental collapse)* **he had a (nervous) b.** le dio una depresión *or* una crisis nerviosa

(**d**) *(analysis) (of figures, costs)* desglose *m*; **a b. of the population by age and occupation** un desglose de la población por edad y ocupación

breaker ['breɪkə(r)] *n* (**a**) *(wave)* ola *f* grande (**b**) *Br (scrap merchant)* **the ship was sent to the breakers** enviaron el barco al desguace ▸▸ ***breaker's yard*** *(for cars, boats)* desguace *m* (**c**) *Fam (CB operator)* radioaficionado(a) *m,f*

break-even point [breɪk'iːvənpɔɪnt] *n Fin* punto *m* de equilibrio, umbral *m* de rentabilidad

breakfast ['brekfəst] **1** *n* desayuno *m*; **to have b.** desayunar; **to have sth for b.** desayunar algo, tomar algo para desayunar; IDIOM **to have** *or* **eat sb for b.** merendarse a alguien ▸▸ ***b. cereal*** cereales *mpl* (de desayuno); ***b. television*** programación *f* matinal

2 *vi* **to b. (on sth)** desayunar (algo)

break-in ['breɪkɪn] *n (burglary)* robo *m (en el interior de una casa o edificio)*

breaking ['breɪkɪŋ] *n* (**a**) *Law* ***b. and entering*** allanamiento *m* de morada (**b**) ***b. point*** *(of person, patience)* límite *m*; **the situation has reached b. point** se ha llegado a una situación límite

breakneck ['breɪknek] *adj* **at b. speed** a una velocidad de vértigo

break-out ['breɪkaʊt] *n (from prison)* evasión *f*

breakthrough ['breɪkθruː] *n* (**a**) *(major advance, discovery)* avance *m*, adelanto *m*; **to make a b.** *(in talks)* dar un gran paso adelante; **the b. came when...** el gran avance se produjo cuando... (**b**) *Mil (in enemy lines)* penetración *f*

break-up ['breɪkʌp] *n* (**a**) *(disintegration) (of relationship)* ruptura *f*; *(of country, empire, organization)* desintegración *f*, desmembración *f* (**b**) *(of ship)* desguace *m* (**c**) *(of ice)* ruptura *f*

breakwater ['breɪkwɔːtə(r)] *n* rompeolas *m inv*

bream [briːm] *n* (**a**) *(freshwater)* = tipo de carpa (**b**) *(saltwater)* **(sea) b.** besugo *m*

breast [brest] **1** *n* (**a**) *(of woman)* pecho *m*, seno *m*; **a child at the b.** un niño que mama ▸▸ ***b. cancer*** cáncer *m* de mama; ***b. pump*** sacaleches *m inv*

(**b**) *Literary (of man, woman)* pecho *m*; **he held her to his b.** la abrazó contra su pecho; IDIOM **to make a clean b. of it** confesarlo todo

(**c**) *(of chicken)* pechuga *f*

(**d**) *(of garment)* pechera *f* ▸▸ ***b. pocket*** bolsillo *m or CAm, Méx, Perú* bolsa *f* superior

2 *vt* (**a**) *(face) (waves, storm)* encarar (**b**) *(reach summit of)* coronar (**c**) *Sport* **the runner breasted the tape** el corredor alcanzó la cinta de meta

breast-beating ['brestbiːtɪŋ] *n* lamentos *mpl*, lamentaciones *fpl*

breastbone ['brestbəʊn] *n* esternón *m*

breastfed ['brestfed] *adj* amamantado(a)

breastfeed ['brestfiːd] *(pt & pp* **breastfed** ['brestfed]) **1** *vt* dar el pecho a, amamantar

2 *vi* dar el pecho

breastfeeding ['brestfiːdɪŋ] *n* lactancia *f* materna

breastplate ['brestpleɪt] *n (of armour)* peto *m (de armadura)*

breaststroke ['breststrəʊk] *n* braza *f*; **to do** *or* **swim the b.** *Esp* nadar a braza, *Am* nadar pecho

breaststroker ['breststrəʊkə(r)] *n* bracista *mf*

breastwork ['brestwɜːk] *n Mil* parapeto *m*

breath [breθ] *n* (**a**) *(respiration)* respiración *f*; *(air inhaled)* inspiración *f*; *(air exhaled)* espiración *f*; **he took huge breaths** inspiró grandes bocanadas de aire; **to take a deep b.** inspirar profundamente; **bad b.** mal aliento; *Fam* **coffee b.** aliento a café; **fries b.** aliento a *Esp* patatas *or Am* papas fritas; **out of b.** sin aliento, sin respiración; **to pause** *or* **stop for b.** pararse para tomar aliento; **to get one's b. back** recuperar la respiración; **to go out for a b. of fresh air** salir a tomar el aire; IDIOM **she's a real b. of fresh air** es una verdadera bocanada de aire fresco; *also Fig* **to hold one's b.** contener la respiración; IDIOM *Fam* **don't hold your b.!** ¡ya puedes esperar sentado(a)!; *Fig* **to take sb's b. away** quitar la respiración a alguien; **to waste one's b.** malgastar saliva ▸▸ ***b. freshener*** spray *m* bucal; ***b. test*** prueba *f* de alcoholemia

(**b**) *(while speaking)* **he said it all in one b.** lo dijo todo de un tirón; **with her dying b.** con su último aliento; **in the same b.** a la vez, al mismo tiempo; **they are not to be mentioned in the same b.** no tienen punto de comparación; **in the next b.** al momento siguiente; **under one's b.** en voz baja, en un susurro

(**c**) *(gust)* ráfaga *f*; **a b. of wind** una brisa

(**d**) *(hint)* **the first b. of spring** el primer indicio de la primavera; **the faintest b. of scandal** el mínimo indicio de escándalo

breathable ['briːðəbəl] *adj* (**a**) *(atmosphere)* respirable (**b**) *(fabric)* transpirable, que transpira

breathalyse, *US* **breathalyze** ['breθəlaɪz] *vt (driver)* hacer la prueba de la alcoholemia a

Breathalyser®, *US* **Breathalyzer®** ['breθəlaɪzə(r)] *n* alcoholímetro *m* ▸▸ ***B. test*** prueba *f* del alcohol *or* de (la) alcoholemia

breathe [bri:ð] **1** *vt* (**a**) *(inhale)* respirar, inspirar; *(exhale)* espirar, exhalar; **he breathed alcohol over her** le echó el aliento (con olor) a alcohol
(**b**) IDIOMS **to b. fire** *(in anger)* echar chispas; *Literary* **to b. one's last** exhalar el último suspiro; **to b. new life into sth** *(project, scheme)* dar vida a algo; **to b. a sigh of relief** dar un suspiro de alivio; **don't b. a word (of it)!** ¡no digas una palabra!
2 *vi* (**a**) *(person)* respirar; **to b. heavily** *or* **deeply** *(after exertion)* respirar profundamente *or* entrecortadamente; *(during illness)* respirar con dificultad; *Fig* **to b. easily** *or* **freely (again)** volver a respirar tranquilo(a); **I need room to b.** *(in relationship)* necesito espacio vital; IDIOM **to b. down sb's neck** *(pursue)* pisar los talones a alguien; *(supervise closely)* estar constantemente encima de alguien
(**b**) *(wine)* respirar, airearse
(**c**) *(fabric)* transpirar
▸**breathe in** **1** *vt sep* inspirar, aspirar
2 *vi* inspirar, aspirar
▸**breathe out** **1** *vt sep* espirar
2 *vi* espirar
breathed [bri:ðd] *adj Ling (unvoiced)* sordo(a)
breather ['bri:ðə(r)] *n Fam (rest)* respiro *m*; **to have** *or* **take a b.** tomarse un respiro
breathing ['bri:ðɪŋ] *n* respiración *f* ▸▸ ***b. apparatus*** respirador *m*; *Fig* ***b. space*** respiro *m*
breathless ['breθlɪs] *adj* (**a**) *(person)* jadeante; **we waited in b. excitement** esperamos con ansiosa emoción (**b**) *(calm, silence)* completo(a)
breathlessly ['breθlɪslɪ] *adv* **"it was a disaster!" he said b.** "fue un desastre", dijo sin aliento; **we waited b. for the result** esperamos el resultado ansiosamente
breathlessness ['breθlɪsnɪs] *n* dificultades *fpl* respiratorias
breathtaking ['breθteɪkɪŋ] *adj* (**a**) *(view, beauty)* impresionante, asombroso(a) (**b**) *(cynicism, stupidity)* impresionante, asombroso(a); **with a b. lack of tact** con una falta de tacto asombrosa
breathtakingly ['breθteɪkɪŋlɪ] *adv* asombrosamente; **b. beautiful** de una belleza arrebatadora
breathy ['breθɪ] *adj* **to have a b. voice** tener la voz jadeante
Brechtian ['brektɪən] *adj* brechtiano(a)
bred *pt & pp of* **breed**
breech [bri:tʃ] *n* (**a**) *Med* ***b. birth*** parto *m* de nalgas; *Med* ***b. delivery*** parto *m* de nalgas (**b**) *(of gun)* recámara *f* ▸▸ ***b. loader*** arma *f* de retrocarga
breechblock ['bri:tʃblɒk] *n* cubrechimenea *m*, bloque *m* de cierre
breeches ['brɪtʃɪz] *npl* (pantalones *mpl*) bombachos *mpl*; **a pair of b.** unos (pantalones) bombachos ▸▸ ***b. buoy*** boya *f* de salvamento del andarivel
breech-loading ['bri:tʃləʊdɪŋ] *adj* de retrocarga
breed [bri:d] **1** *n* (**a**) *(of animal)* raza *f* (**b**) *(kind)* raza *f*; *Fig* **a dying b.** una especie en (vías de) extinción; **she is one of the new b. of executives** pertenece al nuevo género de ejecutivos
2 *vt* (*pt & pp* **bred** [bred]) (**a**) *(animals)* criar; **they're specially bred for racing** los crían especialmente para las carreras (**b**) *(create) (discontent, violence)* crear, producir; **dirt breeds disease** la suciedad genera enfermedades
3 *vi* reproducirse; **to b. like rabbits** reproducirse como conejos
breeder ['bri:də(r)] *n* (**a**) *(of animals)* criador(ora) *m,f* (**b**) *(animal)* reproductor(ora) *m,f* (**c**) *Phys* ***b. reactor*** reactor *m* nuclear reproductor
breeding ['bri:dɪŋ] *n* (**a**) *(of animals)* cría *f*; **the b. season** *(for animals)* la época de cría ▸▸ ***b. ground*** criadero *m*; *Fig (of discontent, revolution)* caldo *m* de cultivo (**b**) *(of person)* **(good) b.** (buena) educación *f*; **to lack b.** no tener educación
breeze [bri:z] **1** *n* (**a**) *(light wind)* brisa *f*; **there's quite a b.** hace una fuerte brisa (**b**) *Fam* **it was a b.** fue pan comido *or* coser y cantar
2 *vi* **to b. along** pasar con aire despreocupado; **to b. in/out** *(casually)* entrar/salir despreocupadamente
▸**breeze through** *vt insep (test, interview)* despachar con facilidad; **she breezed through her finals** pasó los exámenes finales sin problemas
breezeblock ['bri:zblɒk] *n Br* bloque *m* de cemento ligero
breezily ['bri:zɪlɪ] *adv (casually)* con aire despreocupado; *(cheerfully)* alegremente
breezy ['bri:zɪ] *adj* (**a**) *(weather)* **it's b.** hace aire (**b**) *(person, attitude) (casual)* despreocupado(a); *(cheerful)* alegre
Bren gun ['brengʌn] *n* ametralladora *f* Bren
brent goose ['brent'gu:s] *n* barnacla *f* carinegra
brethren ['breðrɪn] *npl Rel* hermanos *mpl*
Breton ['bretɒn] **1** *n* (**a**) *(person)* bretón(ona) *m,f* (**b**) *(language)* bretón *m*
2 *adj* bretón(ona)
breve [bri:v] *n Mus* breve *f*
breviary ['bri:vɪərɪ] *n Rel* breviario *m*
brevity ['brevɪtɪ] *n* (**a**) *(shortness)* brevedad *f* (**b**) *(succinctness)* brevedad *f*; PROV **b. is the soul of wit** lo bueno, si breve, dos veces bueno
brew [bru:] **1** *n* (**a**) *(beer)* cerveza *f* (**b**) *US Fam (drink of beer)* birra *f*, *Méx* cheve *f*; **we had a few brews** nos tomamos unas cuantas birras (**c**) *(strange mixture)* brebaje *m*; **a heady b. of sex, politics and murder** una embriagadora combinación de sexo, política y asesinatos
2 *vt* (**a**) *(beer)* elaborar, fabricar (**b**) *(tea)* preparar (**c**) *(plot, scheme)* urdir, tramar
3 *vi* (**a**) *(make beer)* fabricar *or* elaborar cerveza (**b**) *(tea)* hacerse (**c**) *(approach)* **there's a storm brewing** se está preparando *or* se avecina una tormenta; **there's trouble brewing** se está fraguando *or* cociendo algo
▸**brew up** *vi* (**a**) *(storm, trouble)* fraguarse, prepararse (**b**) *Br Fam (make tea)* preparar el té
brewer ['bru:ə(r)] *n (firm)* fabricante *mf* de cerveza; IDIOM *Br Fam Hum* **to have b.'s droop** no poder empalmarse por culpa del alcohol; ▸▸ ***b.'s yeast*** levadura *f* de cerveza
brewery ['brʊərɪ] *n* fábrica *f* de cerveza, cervecera *f*
brewing ['bru:ɪŋ] *n (business)* fabricación *f* de cerveza
brewski ['bru:skɪ] *n US Fam* birra *f*, *Méx* cheve *f*
brew-up ['bru:ʌp] *n Br Fam* **to have a b.** hacer té, preparar té
briar, brier ['braɪə(r)] *n* (**a**) *(plant)* brezo *m* ▸▸ ***b. rose*** escaramujo *m* (**b**) *(pipe)* pipa *f* (de madera) de brezo
bribe [braɪb] **1** *n* soborno *m*; **to take bribes** aceptar sobornos; **she won't take bribes** es insobornable, no acepta sobornos; **he was accused of offering bribes** lo acusaron de ofrecer sobornos
2 *vt* sobornar; **to b. sb into doing sth** sobornar a alguien para que haga algo
bribery ['braɪbərɪ] *n* soborno *m*; **to be open to b.** dejarse sobornar, aceptar sobornos
bric-à-brac ['brɪkəbræk] *n* baratijas *fpl*, chucherías *fpl*
brick [brɪk] **1** *n* (**a**) *(building block)* ladrillo *m*; **bricks and mortar** *(building materials)* ladrillos y mortero; *(property)* bienes inmuebles ▸▸ ***b. red*** color *m* teja
(**b**) *(material)* ladrillo *m*; **b. wall/house** muro/casa de ladrillo(s); **it's made of b.** está hecho de ladrillo
(**c**) *(for children)* **(toy) bricks** piezas *fpl* de construcción *(de juguete)*
(**d**) *(of ice cream)* barra *f*, bloque *m*
(**e**) *Br Fam Old-fashioned* **he's a b.** es un gran tipo
(**f**) IDIOMS **it's like talking to a b. wall** es como hablarle a la pared; **you're banging your head against a b. wall** te estás esforzando para nada; *Fam* **to drop a b.** meter la pata; *Vulg* **to be built like a b. shithouse** ser un camión, *Esp* estar cachas; PROV **you can't make bricks without straw** no se puede trabajar sin materia prima
2 *vi Br Fam* **I was bricking it** estaba muerto de miedo, *Esp* los tenía de corbata
▸**brick in, brick up** *vt sep (window, doorway)* tapiar
brickbat ['brɪkbæt] *n (insult)* pulla *f*, detracción *f*
brickie ['brɪkɪ] *n Br Fam* albañil *m*
bricklayer ['brɪkleɪə(r)] *n* albañil *mf*
bricklaying ['brɪkleɪɪŋ] *n* albañilería *f*
brick-red ['brɪk'red] *adj* (de) color teja
brickwork ['brɪkwɜ:k] *n* (obra *f* de) ladrillos *mpl*, enladrillado *m*
brickworks ['brɪkwɜ:ks] *n* fábrica *f* de ladrillos, ladrillar *m*
brickyard ['brɪkjɑ:d] *n* fábrica *f* de ladrillos, ladrillar *m*
bridal ['braɪdəl] *adj* nupcial ▸▸ ***b. dress*** traje *m* de novia; ***b. gown*** traje *m* de novia; ***b. shop*** boutique *f* de novia; ***b. suite*** suite *f* nupcial
bride [braɪd] *n* novia *f (en boda)*; **the b. and groom** los novios; **his b. of four months killed herself** su esposa se suicidó cuatro meses después de la boda
bridegroom ['braɪdgru:m] *n* novio *m*
bridesmaid ['braɪdzmeɪd] *n* dama *f* de honor; IDIOM **always the b., never the bride** siempre le toca ser el segundón/la segundona
bride-to-be ['braɪdtə'bi:] *n* futura esposa *f*
bridge[1] [brɪdʒ] **1** *n* (**a**) *(over river, road, valley)* puente *m*; IDIOM **we'll cross that b. when we come to it** no nos adelantemos a los acontecimientos; *Fig* **a b. building effort** un esfuerzo por tender un puente

(**b**) *(on ship)* puente *m* (de mando)
(**c**) *(on teeth)* puente *m*
(**d**) *(of violin)* puente *m*
(**e**) *(of nose)* caballete *m*; *(of glasses)* puente *m*
(**f**) *(in billiards, snooker)* caballete *m*
(**g**) *Comptr (between networks)* puente *m*
(**h**) *US Fin* ***b. loan*** crédito *m* de puente
(**i**) *(in song)* puente *m*
2 *vt* (**a**) *(river, gorge)* tender un puente sobre (**b**) *(differences)* **to b. a gap** llenar un vacío; **to b. the gap between rich and poor** acortar la distancia entre ricos y pobres; **we need to b. the gap between theory and practice** tenemos que aunar la teoría y la práctica

bridge[2] *n (card game)* bridge *m*

bridgehead ['brɪdʒhed] *n Mil* cabeza *f* de puente

bridgework ['brɪdʒwɜːk] *n (in dentistry)* puente *m*

bridging loan ['brɪdʒɪŋləʊn] *n Br Fin* crédito *m* provisional *or* de puente

bridle ['braɪdəl] **1** *n* brida *f* ►► ***b. path*** camino *m* de herradura; ***b. way*** camino *m* de herradura
2 *vt* embridar, poner la brida a; IDIOM **to b. one's tongue: he'll have to learn to b. his tongue** tendrá que aprender a medir sus palabras
3 *vi (with anger)* indignarse (**at** por)

brie [briː] *n* (queso *m*) brie *m*

brief [briːf] **1** *n* (**a**) *Law* escrito *m*; **he accepted the b.** aceptó el caso (**b**) *(instructions)* **our b. was to design a functional office space** teníamos instrucciones de crear un espacio de trabajo funcional; *Fig* **that goes beyond our b.** eso no entra en el ámbito de nuestras competencias; *Fig* **I hold no b. for...** estoy en contra *or* no soy partidario(a) de...
(**c**) *Br Fam (lawyer)* abogado(a) *m,f*
(**d**) **in b.** *(briefly)* en suma
2 *adj* (**a**) *(short in duration)* breve; **a b. interval** un breve intervalo (**b**) *(succinct)* breve; **to be b.** *(when talking)* ser breve; **to be b...., in b....** en pocas palabras... (**c**) *(short in length)* corto(a); **a very b. pair of shorts** unos pantalones muy cortos
3 *vt* (**a**) *(inform)* informar (**on** sobre, acerca de); *(before meeting)* poner al corriente (**on** sobre, acerca de); *(before a mission)* dar instrucciones a (**on** sobre, acerca de) (**b**) *Law* pasar la instrucción del caso a
4 *vi* **to b. against sb** dar informes negativos sobre alguien

briefcase ['briːfkeɪs] *n* maletín *m*, portafolios *m inv*

briefing ['briːfɪŋ] *n* (**a**) *(meeting)* sesión *f* informativa (**b**) *(information)* información *f*; *(written)* informe *m*

briefly ['briːflɪ] *adv* (**a**) *(for a short time)* brevemente (**b**) *(succinctly)* en pocas palabras; **(put) b....** en pocas palabras...

briefness ['briːfnɪs] *n* (**a**) *(in duration)* brevedad *f* (**b**) *(succinctness)* brevedad *f* (**c**) *(in length)* lo corto

briefs [briːfs] *npl (underwear) (woman's) Esp* bragas *fpl*, *Esp* braga *f*, *Col* blúmers *mpl*, *Ecuad* follones *mpl*, *RP* bombacha *f*; *(man's)* calzoncillos *mpl*

brier = **briar**

Brig (*abbr* **Brigadier**) gral. de brigada

brig [brɪg] *n* (**a**) *(ship)* bergantín *m* (**b**) *(prison on ship)* calabozo *m* (**c**) *US Fam (prison) Esp* chirona *f*, *Andes, RP* cana *f*, *Méx* bote *m*

brigade [brɪ'geɪd] *n* (**a**) *Mil* brigada *f* (**b**) *Fam Pej (group)* brigada *f*

brigadier [brɪgə'dɪə(r)] *n Br* general *m* de brigada ►► *US* ***b. general*** general *m* de brigada

brigand ['brɪgənd] *n Literary* malhechor *m*, bandido *m*

bright [braɪt] **1** *adj* (**a**) *(sun, light)* brillante; *(day)* claro(a), luminoso(a); *(weather)* despejado(a); *(room)* luminoso(a); *(colour)* vivo(a); **a b. red/blue umbrella** un paraguas de color rojo/azul vivo; **cloudy with b. intervals** nublado con intervalos despejados; *Fig* **the b. lights** la gran ciudad; **b. red** rojo vivo; **to go b. red** *(blush)* ruborizarse
(**b**) *(shining) (diamond, metal, eyes)* brillante
(**c**) *(optimistic) (future, situation)* prometedor(ora); **it was the only b. spot in the day** fue el único momento bueno del día; **to look on the b. side (of things)** fijarse en el lado bueno (de las cosas)
(**d**) *(cheerful)* alegre; **he's always so b. and breezy** siempre está de lo más alegre
(**e**) *(clever) (person)* inteligente; *(idea, suggestion)* brillante, genial; *Ironic* **whose b. idea was that?** ¿quién tuvo la genial *or* brillante idea?; **he's b. at physics** se le da bien la física; IDIOM **to be as b. as a button** *or* **a new penny** *(clever)* ser la mar de espabilado(a), *Esp* ser más listo(a) que el hambre; *(fresh, awake)* estar como una rosa, estar fresco(a) como una lechuga; **b. spark** *(person)* listo(a), listillo(a)
2 *adv (to burn)* vivamente; *(to shine)* radiantemente, brillantemente; **b. and early** tempranito

brighten ['braɪtən] **1** *vt* (**a**) *(room)* alegrar, avivar (**b**) *(mood)* alegrar, animar
2 *vi* (**a**) *(weather, sky)* aclararse (**b**) *(face, eyes, mood)* alegrarse, animarse (**c**) *(prospects)* mejorar

► **brighten up** **1** *vt sep (room, mood)* alegrar
2 *vi* (**a**) *(weather, sky)* despejarse (**b**) *(person, face)* animarse

bright-eyed ['braɪt'aɪd] *adj* con los ojos brillantes; *Fig (enthusiastic)* vivo(a); IDIOM *Fam* **b. and bushy-tailed** alegre y contento(a)

brightly ['braɪtlɪ] *adv* (**a**) *(to shine)* radiantemente, brillantemente; *(to burn)* vivamente; **b. coloured** de vivos colores; **b. polished** resplandeciente (**b**) *(to say, smile)* alegremente

brightness ['braɪtnɪs] *n* (**a**) *(of light, sun)* luminosidad *f*, brillo *m*; *(of colour)* viveza *f*; **b. (control)** *(on TV)* (mando *m* del) brillo *m* (**b**) *(cheerfulness)* alegría *f* (**c**) *(cleverness)* inteligencia *f*

brights [braɪts] *npl US (headlights)* **to put the b. on** dar *or* poner las largas

brill[1] [brɪl] *n (fish)* remol *m*, rombo *m*

brill[2] *adj Br Fam* genial, *Esp* guay

brilliance ['brɪljəns] *n* (**a**) *(of light, colour, smile)* resplandor *m*, brillo *m* (**b**) *(of person, idea)* genialidad *f* (**c**) *(of performance)* genialidad *f*

brilliant ['brɪljənt] **1** *adj* (**a**) *(bright, intense) (light, sun, smile)* radiante, resplandeciente; *(colour)* brillante (**b**) *(intelligent) (person, mind, idea)* genial (**c**) *(outstanding) (musician, performance, future, career)* brillante; *(success)* clamoroso(a) (**d**) *Br Fam (excellent)* genial, *Andes CAm, Carib, Méx* chévere, *Andes, CSur* macanudo(a), *Méx* padre, *RP* bárbaro(a)
2 *n (diamond)* brillante *m*

brilliantine ['brɪljəntiːn] *n* brillantina *f*

brilliantly ['brɪljəntlɪ] *adv* (**a**) *(to shine)* radiantemente; **b. coloured** de vivos colores; **b. lit** muy iluminado(a) (**b**) *(to act, play, perform)* magníficamente

Brillo pad® ['brɪləʊ'pæd] *n* = estropajo hecho de fibra de acero embebida en jabón

brim [brɪm] **1** *n* (**a**) *(of cup, glass)* borde *m*; **full to the b.** lleno hasta el borde (**b**) *(of hat)* ala *f*
2 *vi* (*pt & pp* **brimmed**) *(with liquid, enthusiasm)* **to be brimming with** rebosar de; **her eyes brimmed with tears** tenía los ojos anegados de lágrimas

► **brim over** *vi* rebosar, desbordarse; *Fig* **to be brimming over with health/ideas** estar rebosante de salud/ideas

brimful ['brɪmfʊl] *adj* hasta el borde; *Fig* **b. of health/ideas** pletórico(a) de salud/ideas

brimstone ['brɪmstəʊn] *n Literary* azufre *m*; **fire and b.** fuego del infierno

brindled ['brɪndəld] *adj* pardo(a) con manchas

brine [braɪn] *n* (**a**) *(for preserving)* salmuera *f* (**b**) *(seawater)* agua *f* del mar

BRING [brɪŋ] (*pt & pp* **brought** [brɔːt]) *vt* (**a**) *(take)* traer; **b. me a chair, would you?** ¿me podrías traer una silla, por favor?; **b. a bottle (with you)** trae una botella; **the sound of sirens brought people onto the streets** las sirenas hicieron que la gente saliera a la calle; **to b. sth out of one's pocket** sacar algo del bolsillo; **the path brought us to a lake** el camino nos llevó a un lago; **what brings you to London?** ¿qué te trae por Londres?; **to b. sth to sb's attention** llamar la atención de alguien sobre algo; **that brings us to my final point...** esto nos lleva al último punto...; **he brings a wealth of technical expertise to the job** aporta a su trabajo sus grandes conocimientos técnicos; **to b. a child into the world** traer al mundo a un niño; *Law* **to b. an action against sb** interponer una demanda *or* entablar un pleito contra alguien; *Law* **to b. charges against sb** presentar cargos contra alguien; *Law* **to b. sb to trial** llevar a alguien a juicio; *Fig* **the pictures brought home to us the full horror of the war** las imágenes nos hicieron sentir en carne propia el tremendo horror de la guerra
(**b**) *(lead to, cause)* traer; **it has brought me great happiness** me ha causado gran alegría; **the announcement brought an angry reaction** el anuncio produjo una reacción airada; **the change brought new problems with it** el cambio trajo *or* acarreó nuevos problemas; **to b. sb (good) luck/bad luck** traer (buena) suerte/mala suerte a alguien; **to b. new hope to sb** infundir nuevas esperanzas a alguien; **to b. tears to sb's eyes** hacerle llorar a alguien
(**c**) *(cause to come to a particular condition)* **the latest death brings the total to seventy** la última muerte pone el total en setenta; **to b. oneself into an upright position** incorporarse; **to b. sth to the boil** hacer que algo hierva; **to b. sb to the brink of ruin** dejar a alguien al borde de la ruina; **to b. sth into disrepute** perjudicar la reputación de

algo, desprestigiar algo; **it brought me into conflict with the authorities** me enfrentó con las autoridades; **to b. sth to an end** poner fin a algo; **the earthquake brought the building to the ground** el terremoto derrumbó el edificio; **she brought the bus to a halt** detuvo el autobús; **to b. sth to light** sacar algo a la luz; **to b. sth to mind** traer a la memoria algo; **to b. sth into question** poner en duda algo; **to b. sb up short** detener a alguien; **to b. oneself to do sth** resolverse a hacer algo; **I couldn't b. myself to tell her** no pude decírselo

(**d**) *(be sold for)* **the house won't b. very much** la casa no reportará mucho dinero

▸**bring about** *vt sep (cause)* provocar, ocasionar

▸**bring along** *vt sep* traer

▸**bring around** = **bring round**

▸**bring back** *vt sep* (**a**) *(return with)* traer; **b. me back a loaf of bread from the shop** tráeme una barra de pan de la tienda

(**b**) *(return) (purchase)* devolver; *(person)* traer de vuelta; **to b. sb back to life/health** devolver la vida/la salud a alguien; **that brings us back to the issue of human rights** esto nos trae de vuelta *or* de nuevo al tema de los derechos humanos

(**c**) *(cause to remember)* recordar; **to b. back memories of sth to sb** traer a alguien recuerdos de algo

(**d**) *(reintroduce) (law, punishment)* reinstaurar; **they're going to b. back trams** van a volver a poner tranvías

▸**bring down** *vt sep* (**a**) *(from shelf, attic)* bajar

(**b**) *(cause to fall) (soldier, plane, footballer)* derribar; *(government)* derrocar; IDIOM *Fam* **her performance brought the house down** su actuación enfervorizó al público

(**c**) *(lower) (price, temperature)* bajar; *(inflation)* reducir

(**d**) *(land) (aircraft)* aterrizar

▸**bring forth** *vt sep Formal (cause)* producir, generar

▸**bring forward** *vt sep* (**a**) *(proposal, plan)* presentar; *(witness)* hacer comparecer (**b**) *(advance time of)* adelantar (**c**) *Com* pasar a cuenta nueva; **brought forward** saldo anterior

▸**bring in** *vt sep* (**a**) *(consult) (expert, consultant)* contratar los servicios de; **we're going to have to b. the police in** vamos a tener que recurrir a la policía; **could I just b. in Mr Lamont on that point?** ¿podría el Sr. Lamont decirnos lo que piensa al respecto?

(**b**) *(take to police station)* **the police brought him in for questioning** la policía lo llevó a comisaría para interrogarlo

(**c**) *(earn) (of person)* ganar; *(of sale, investment)* generar

(**d**) *(law, bill)* introducir

(**e**) *Law (verdict)* pronunciar

(**f**) *(attract)* **this should b. the crowds in** esto debería atraer a las masas

(**g**) *(washing)* entrar

▸**bring off** *vt sep* (**a**) *(accomplish)* conseguir; *(plan, deal)* llevar a cabo (**b**) *Sport (player)* sacar, sustituir (**c**) *Vulg (masturbate)* hacer *Esp* correrse *or Am* venirse *or RP* irse a; **to b. oneself off** provocarse un orgasmo

▸**bring on** *vt sep* (**a**) *(cause)* provocar; **you've brought it on yourself** tú te lo has buscado; **she brought shame on her entire family** deshonró a toda su familia

(**b**) *Sport (substitute)* sacar (al campo), hacer entrar a

(**c**) *(cause to flower)* **the good weather has brought on the daffodils** el buen tiempo ha hecho florecer antes los narcisos

▸**bring out** *vt sep* (**a**) *(new product)* sacar

(**b**) *(provoke, elicit)* **to b. out the best/worst in sb** sacar lo mejor/peor de alguien; **to b. out the flavour in sth** realzar el sabor de algo; **strawberries b. her out in a rash** las fresas le provocan un sarpullido; **to b. sb out (of his/her shell)** sacar a alguien de su concha

(**c**) *(cause to strike)* poner en huelga

▸**bring round, bring around** *vt sep* (**a**) *(take)* traer (**b**) *(revive)* hacer volver en sí, reanimar (**c**) *(persuade)* convencer; **she brought him round to her point of view** le convenció (**d**) *(direct)* **he brought the conversation round to the subject of...** sacó a colación el tema de...

▸**bring through** *vt sep (help to overcome)* **to b. sb through sth** ayudar a alguien a superar algo

▸**bring together** *vt sep* (**a**) *(cause to meet)* reunir (**b**) *(make closer)* acercar, unir

▸**bring up** *vt sep* (**a**) *(subject)* sacar a colación

(**b**) *(child)* educar; **she brought up ten children** crió a diez hijos; **I was brought up in Spain** fui criado(a) en España; **I was brought up (as) a Christian** me dieron una educación cristiana; **I was brought up to show respect for my elders** me enseñaron a respetar a mis mayores, me educaron en el respeto a mis mayores; **they're very well/badly brought up** están muy bien/mal educados

(**c**) *(vomit)* vomitar

(**d**) *(charge)* **he's been brought up on a charge of assault** ha sido acusado de agresión

---

bring-and-buy ['brɪŋən'baɪ] *adj Br* **b. (sale)** = mercadillo benéfico de compra y venta

brink [brɪŋk] *n also Fig* borde *m*; **on the b. of** *(tears, disaster, success, death)* al borde de; *Fig* **to be on the b. of doing sth** estar a punto de hacer algo

brink(s)manship ['brɪŋk(s)mənʃɪp] *n (in politics, diplomacy)* = política consistente en arriesgarse hasta el límite para obtener concesiones de la parte contraria

briny ['braɪnɪ] **1** *n Fam* **the b.** el mar

2 *adj* salobre

brio ['bri:əʊ] *n* brío *m*

brioche [bri:'ɒʃ] *n* brioche *m*

briquet(te) [brɪ'ket] *n* briqueta *f*

brisk [brɪsk] *adj* (**a**) *(weather, wind)* fresco(a), vigorizante (**b**) *(efficient) (person, manner)* enérgico(a) (**c**) *(rude)* brusco(a) (**d**) *(rapid)* rápido(a); **at a b. pace** a paso ligero (**e**) *Com* **business is b.** el negocio va muy bien; **to do a b. trade in sth** hacer el agosto con algo

brisket ['brɪskɪt] *n* falda *f* de ternera

briskly ['brɪsklɪ] *adv* (**a**) *(efficiently)* enérgicamente (**b**) *(rudely)* bruscamente (**c**) *(rapidly)* rápidamente (**d**) *Com* **currency futures are trading b.** el mercado de futuros de divisas está muy activo

briskness ['brɪsknɪs] *n* (**a**) *(of manner, tone of voice)* brío *m*, energía *f* (**b**) *(of pace)* rapidez *f*

bristle ['brɪsəl] **1** *n (on face)* pelo *m* de la barba; *(of animal, brush)* cerda *f*; *(of plant)* pelo *m*

2 *vi* (**a**) *(animal's fur)* erizarse (**b**) *(show anger)* **to b. (with anger)** enfurecerse; **they bristled at any suggestion of bias** se enfurecieron ante la insinuación de que había existido parcialidad (**c**) *(be full)* **the hall was bristling with security men** la sala estaba repleta de agentes de seguridad; **the situation was bristling with difficulties** la situación estaba erizada de dificultades

bristling ['brɪslɪŋ] *adj (beard, moustache)* hirsuto(a)

bristly ['brɪslɪ] *adj (chin)* con barba de tres días; *(beard)* erizado(a), pinchudo(a)

bristols ['brɪstəlz] *npl Br very Fam* domingas *fpl*, tetamen *m*, *Méx* chichis *mpl*, *RP* lolas *fpl*

Brit [brɪt] *n Fam* británico(a) *m,f*

Britain ['brɪtən] *n* Gran Bretaña

Britannia [brɪ'tænɪə] *n* = personificación de Gran Bretaña en forma de una mujer guerrera que lleva tridente y casco

Britannic [brɪ'tænɪk] *adj Formal* **His** *or* **Her B. Majesty** Su Majestad Británica

britches ['brɪtʃɪz] *npl US* (pantalones *mpl*) bombachos *mpl*

Briticism ['brɪtɪsɪzəm] *n* término *m* (del inglés) británico

British ['brɪtɪʃ] **1** *npl* **the B.** los británicos

2 *adj* británico(a) ▸▸ ***B. Columbia*** la Columbia británica; ***the B. Council*** el British Council, = organismo encargado de promover la lengua y cultura británicas en el extranjero; ***the B. Isles*** las Islas Británicas; ***B. Legion*** = organismo que presta servicios y apoya a los militares británicos retirados; ***the B. Library*** la biblioteca nacional británica; ***the B. Museum*** el museo británico; ***B. Summer Time*** = hora oficial de verano en Gran Bretaña; ***B. thermal unit*** unidad *f* térmica británica *(= 1.055 julios)*

Britisher ['brɪtɪʃə(r)] *n US* británico(a) *m,f*

Briton ['brɪtən] *n* (**a**) *(British citizen)* británico(a) *m,f* (**b**) *Hist* britano(a) *m,f*

Britpop ['brɪtpɒp] *n* Britpop *m*, = música pop británica de los noventa compuesta por grupos con influencias de los sesenta

Brittany ['brɪtənɪ] *n* Bretaña

brittle ['brɪtəl] **1** *adj* (**a**) *(fragile) (glass, bones, peace, relationship)* frágil; *(paper, branches)* quebradizo(a) ▸▸ ***b. bone disease*** = osteopatía hereditaria que provoca una fragilidad anormal en los huesos (**b**) *(forced) (laughter)* crispado(a); *(smile)* forzado(a) (**c**) *(irritable)* **to be b.** *(permanent quality)* ser susceptible; *(temporarily)* estar susceptible

2 *n (sweet)* = dulce hecho a base de caramelo y frutos secos

bro [brəʊ] *n Fam* (**a**) *(brother)* hermano *m* (**b**) *US (male friend)* compadre *m*, *Esp* colega *m*, *CAm, Méx* mano *m*; **yo, b.!** ¿qué pasa colega *or Esp* tronco?

broach [brəʊtʃ] *vt* (**a**) *(subject, question)* sacar a colación, abordar (**b**) *(barrel)* espitar

broad[1] [brɔːd] 1 *adj* (a) *(wide)* ancho(a); *(smile, sense)* amplio(a); **to be 5 metres b.** medir *or* tener 5 metros de ancho; **to have b. shoulders** ser ancho(a) de espaldas; *Fig (be resilient)* aguantar carros y carretas *or* lo que te/le/*etc.* echen; IDIOM *Fam* **it's as b. as it's long** lo mismo me da que me da lo mismo ►► ***b. bean*** haba *f*
(b) *(extensive)* amplio(a), extenso(a); **a b. syllabus** un programa de estudios amplio *or* extenso; **a b. range of products** una amplia *or* extensa gama de productos
(c) *(general) (sense, consensus, support)* amplio(a), mayoritario(a); **he gave a b. outline of the scheme** expuso el plan en líneas generales; **to be in b. agreement** estar de acuerdo en líneas generales; *Fig* **the movement was a b. church** el movimiento admitía miembros de diversas tendencias
(d) *(obvious, marked) (accent)* marcado(a); **to drop a b. hint** lanzar *or* soltar una clara indirecta; **in b. daylight** en pleno día
(e) *(humour)* basto(a)
(f) *(liberal) (mind)* abierto(a); **b. views** actitud abierta
2 *n (widest part)* **the b. of the back** la parte más ancha de la espalda

broad[2] *n US Fam* tipa *f*, *Esp* tía *f*

broadband ['brɔːdbænd] *Tel* 1 *n* banda *f* ancha
2 *adj* de banda ancha

broad-based ['brɔːdbeɪst] *adj* de amplio espectro

broad-brimmed ['brɔːd'brɪmd] *adj (hat)* de ala ancha

broadcast ['brɔːdkɑːst] 1 *n (programme)* emisión *f*
2 *vt (pt & pp* **broadcast)** (a) *(programme, news)* transmitir, emitir; **the match will be b. live** el partido se emitirá en directo; *Fam* **don't b. it!** ¡no lo pregones! (b) *(seed)* sembrar al voleo
3 *vi (station)* emitir

broadcaster ['brɔːdkɑːstə(r)] *n (person)* presentador(ora) *m,f*

broadcasting ['brɔːdkɑːstɪŋ] *n (programmes)* emisiones *fpl*, programas *mpl*; **he works in b.** trabaja en la televisión/radio ►► ***b. rights*** derechos *mpl* de emisión (por televisión); ***b. station*** emisora *f*

broadcloth ['brɔːdklɒθ] *n* = tejido de acabado satinado

broaden ['brɔːdən] 1 *vt (road)* ensanchar; **to b. sb's horizons** ampliar los horizontes de alguien; **reading broadens the mind** leer amplía los horizontes culturales
2 *vi* **to b. (out)** ensancharse, ampliarse

broadly ['brɔːdlɪ] *adv* (a) *(widely)* **to smile b.** esbozar una amplia sonrisa (b) *(generally)* en general; **b. speaking** en términos generales

broad-minded [brɔːd'maɪndɪd] *adj* tolerante, de mentalidad abierta

broad-mindedness [brɔːd'maɪndɪdnɪs] *n* tolerancia *f*, mentalidad *f* abierta

Broads [brɔːdz] *npl* **the (Norfolk) B.** = parque nacional de marismas situado en el este de Inglaterra en el que proliferan lagos y canales

broadsheet ['brɔːdʃiːt] *n (newspaper)* periódico *m* de formato grande *(característico de la prensa británica seria)*

broad-shouldered [brɔːd'ʃəʊldəd] *adj* ancho(a) de espaldas

broadside ['brɔːdsaɪd] 1 *n also Fig* **to fire a b.** soltar una andanada
2 *adv* **b. (on)** lateralmente, de lado

broad-spectrum ['brɔːd'spektrəm] *adj* de amplio espectro

broadsword ['brɔːdsɔːd] *n* sable *m*

Broadway ['brɔːdweɪ] *n* Broadway

brocade [brə'keɪd] *n (cloth)* brocado *m*

broccoli ['brɒkəlɪ] *n* brécol *m*, brócoli *m*

brochure ['brəʊʃə(r)] *n* folleto *m*

brogue[1] [brəʊg] *n (shoe)* zapato *m* de vestir *(de cuero calado)*

brogue[2] *n (accent)* acento *m (especialmente el irlandés)*

broil [brɔɪl] *US* 1 *vt (grill)* asar a la parrilla
2 *vi* abrasarse, achicharrarse; **broiling sun** sol abrasador

broiler ['brɔɪlə(r)] *n* (a) *(chicken)* pollo *m* (tomatero) (b) *US (grill)* grill *m* (c) *US Fam (hot day)* día *m* achicharrante

broke [brəʊk] 1 *adj Fam* (a) **to be b.** *(penniless)* estar sin un centavo *or Méx* sin un peso *or Esp* sin blanca; **to go b.** arruinarse; IDIOM **to go for b.** jugarse el todo por el todo (b) *(broken)* estropeado(a); PROV **if it ain't b. don't fix it** si no está roto, no lo arregles
2 *pt of* **break**

broken ['brəʊkən] 1 *adj* (a) *(smashed, fractured) (object, bone)* roto(a)
(b) *(not working)* estropeado(a)
(c) *(ruined) (person, heart)* destrozado(a); **he's a b. man** está destrozado; **to come from a b. home** provenir de un hogar deshecho *or* roto
(d) *(promise, agreement)* roto(a)
(e) *(uneven) (ground, surface)* accidentado(a); *(sleep)* discontinuo(a); **b. cloud** nubes y claros
(f) *(line)* discontinuo(a)
(g) *(speech)* inconexo(a); **in a b. voice** con la voz quebrada; **to speak b. English** chapurrear inglés
2 *pp of* **break**

broken-down ['brəʊkən'daʊn] *adj* (a) *(not working)* averiado(a) (b) *(in poor condition) (car)* destartalado(a); *(person)* enfermo(a)

broken-hearted ['brəʊkən'hɑːtɪd] *adj* **to be b.** estar desolado(a) *or* desconsolado(a); **she was b. when she found out** se le partió el alma cuando se enteró

brokenly ['brəʊkənlɪ] *adv (to speak)* de manera inconexa

broker ['brəʊkə(r)] 1 *n Fin* agente *mf*, corredor(ora) *m,f*
2 *vt* **to b. an agreement** preparar un acuerdo

brokerage ['brəʊkərɪdʒ] *n Fin* (a) *(fee)* corretaje *m*, correduría *f* (b) *(office)* correduría *f*

brolly ['brɒlɪ] *n Br Fam* paraguas *m inv*

bromide ['brəʊmaɪd] *n* (a) *Chem* bromuro *m* ►► ***b. paper*** papel *m* de bromuro de plata (b) *(platitude)* fórmula *f* caduca

bromine ['brəʊmiːn] *n Chem* bromo *m*

bronchi *pl of* **bronchus**

bronchial ['brɒŋkɪəl] *adj Anat* bronquial; **the b. tubes** los bronquios

bronchiole ['brɒŋkɪəʊl] *n Anat* bronquiolo *m*

bronchitic [brɒŋ'kɪtɪk] *adj Med* bronquítico(a)

bronchitis [brɒŋ'kaɪtɪs] *n* bronquitis *f inv*

bronchodilator ['brɒŋkəʊdaɪ'leɪtə(r)] *n Pharm* broncodilatador *m*

bronchus ['brɒŋkəs] *(pl* **bronchi** ['brɒŋkaɪ]) *n Anat* bronquio *m*

bronco ['brɒŋkəʊ] *(pl* **broncos)** *n* potro *m* salvaje

brontosaurus [brɒntə'sɔːrəs] *n* brontosaurio *m*

Bronx cheer ['brɒŋks'tʃɪə(r)] *n US Fam* pedorreta *f*

bronze [brɒnz] 1 *n* (a) *(metal)* bronce *m* ►► ***the B. Age*** la Edad de(l) Bronce (b) **b. (medal)** medalla *f* de bronce (c) *(sculpture)* bronce *m*
2 *adj* (a) *(material)* de bronce (b) *(colour)* color (de) bronce

bronzed [brɒnzd] *adj (tanned)* bronceado(a)

brooch [brəʊtʃ] *n* broche *m*

brood [bruːd] 1 *n* (a) *(of birds)* nidada *f*; *(of animals)* camada *f* ►► ***b. mare*** yegua *f* de cría (b) *Hum (of children)* prole *f*, progenie *f* (c) *Pej (group, kind)* secuaces *mpl*
2 *vi* (a) *(bird)* empollar (b) *(person)* dar vueltas (**about** *or* **over** *or* **on** a); **to b. over one's mistakes** rumiar los propios errores; **it's no use brooding on** *or* **over the past** lo pasado, pasado está (c) *(loom)* cernerse; **the monument broods over the town's main square** el monumento se cierne sobre la plaza principal de la ciudad

brooding ['bruːdɪŋ] *adj (atmosphere)* desasosegante, amenazador(ora); *(expression, presence)* pesaroso(a)

broody ['bruːdɪ] *adj* (a) *(hen)* clueca (b) *Br (woman)* **in springtime, I get b.** en primavera me surge el instinto maternal (c) *(moody)* apesadumbrado(a)

brook[1] [brʊk] *n (stream)* arroyo *m*, riachuelo *m* ►► *US* ***b. trout*** trucha *f* de arroyo

brook[2] *vt Formal (tolerate)* tolerar, consentir; **he will b. no opposition** no admitirá oposición

broom [bruːm] *n* (a) *(plant)* retama *f*, escoba *f* (b) *(for cleaning)* escoba *f*; *Fig* **a new b.** = jefe recién llegado que quiere cambiar radicalmente las cosas; PROV **a new b. sweeps clean** escoba nueva barre bien

broomstick ['bruːmstɪk] *n* palo *m* de escoba

Bros *npl Com (abbr* **Brothers) Riley B.** Hnos. Riley

broth [brɒθ] *n (soup) (thin)* sopa *f*, caldo *m*; *(thick)* potaje *m*, sopa *f*

brothel ['brɒθəl] *n* burdel *m* ►► *Fam* ***b. creepers*** = zapatos de ante de suela gruesa

brother ['brʌðə(r)] *n* (a) *(family member)* hermano *m* (b) *(fellow member) (of trade union)* compañero *m*; **brothers in arms** compañeros de lucha; **his b. officers** sus compañeros (c) *(monk)* hermano *m* (d) *US Fam (fellow black male)* hermano *m*

brotherhood ['brʌðəhʊd] *n* (a) *(feeling)* fraternidad *f* (b) *(group)* hermandad *f*; **the b. of man** la humanidad (c) *Rel* hermandad *f*

brother-in-law ['brʌðərɪnlɔː] *(pl* **brothers-in-law)** *n* cuñado *m*

brotherly ['brʌðəlɪ] *adj* fraternal, fraterno(a)

brougham ['bruːəm] *n (carriage)* berlina *f*, cupé *m*

brought *pt & pp of* **bring**

brouhaha ['bruːhɑːhɑː] *n Fam* revuelo *m*, jaleo *m*

brow [braʊ] *n* (a) *(forehead)* frente *f* (b) *(eyebrow)* ceja *f* (c) *(of hill)* cima *f*, cumbre *f*

browbeat ['braʊbiːt] *(pt* **browbeat**, *pp* **browbeaten** ['braʊbiːtən]) *vt* intimidar; **to b. sb into doing sth** intimidar a alguien para que haga algo

brown [braʊn] **1** *n* marrón *m*, *Am* color *m* café
2 *adj* marrón, *Am* café; *(hair, eyes)* castaño(a); *(skin) (tanned)* bronceado(a); *(natural)* moreno(a); IDIOM **as b. as a berry** muy moreno(a), *RP* negro(a) como un carbón; IDIOM **to be (lost) in a b. study** estar totalmente absorto(a) *or* ensimismado(a) ▸▸ ***b. ale*** cerveza *f* tostada; ***b. bear*** oso *m* pardo; ***b. booby*** alcatraz *m* pardo; ***b. bread*** pan *m* integral; ***b. coal*** lignito *m*; ***b. fish owl*** búho *m* pescador; *Com* ***b. goods*** equipamiento *m* audiovisual; ***b. owl*** cárabo *m*; ***b. paper*** papel *m* de estraza; ***b. rat*** rata *f* de alcantarilla; ***b. rice*** arroz *m* integral; *Br* ***b. sauce*** = salsa oscura a base de fruta, vinagre y especias; ***b. sugar*** azúcar *m or f* moreno(a)
3 *vt* **(a)** *(in cooking)* dorar **(b)** *(tan)* poner moreno, broncear
4 *vi* **(a)** *(in cooking)* dorarse **(b)** *(tan)* ponerse moreno, broncearse

brownbag ['braʊn'bæg] *vt US Fam* **to b. it** *(drink)* = beber de una botella de licor sin sacarla de su bolsa de papel; *(food)*= llevar la comida al trabajo en una bolsa de papel

browned-off ['braʊnd'ɒf] *adj Br Fam* **to be b. (with sth/sb)** estar hasta las narices (de algo/alguien)

brownfield ['braʊnfi:ld] *n* **(a)** *US* **b. (site)** = antigua área industrial contaminada **(b)** *Br* **b. site** = terreno urbanizable en el que previamente había edificios que han sido demolidos

Brownie ['braʊnɪ] *n* **B. (Guide)** *(member of girls' organization)* escultista *f*; IDIOM **to win** *or* **get B. points** anotarse tantos *or RP* porotos

brownie ['braʊnɪ] *n US (cake)* bizcocho *m* de chocolate y nueces

browning ['braʊnɪŋ] *n Br Culin* colorante *m* (marrón)

brownish ['braʊnɪʃ] *adj* parduzco(a)

brown-nose ['braʊnnəʊz] *very Fam* **1** *n* lameculos *mf inv*
2 *vt* lamer el culo a
3 *vi* lamer culos, ser un/una lameculos

Brownshirt ['braunʃɜ:t] *n Hist* camisa *mf* parda

brownstone ['braʊnstəʊn] *n US* **(a)** *(house)* casa *f* de piedra arenisca rojiza **(b)** *(stone)* piedra *f* arenisca rojiza

browse [braʊz] **1** *n* **to have a b.** echar una ojeada ▸▸ *Comptr* ***b. mode*** modo *m* de consulta
2 *vt Comptr* **to b. the Web** navegar por la Web
3 *vi* **(a)** *(in bookshop, magazine)* echar una ojeada; **to b. through sth** *(book, magazine)* hojear algo **(b)** *(animal)* **to b. on sth** pacer algo

browser ['braʊzə(r)] *n Comptr* navegador *m*

browsing ['braʊzɪŋ] *n Comptr* navegación *f*; **fast/secure b.** navegación rápida/segura

brucellosis [bru:sə'ləʊsɪs] *n Med* brucelosis *f inv*

bruise [bru:z] **1** *n* **(a)** *(on body)* cardenal *m*, moradura *f* **(b)** *(on fruit)* maca *f*, magulladura *f*
2 *vt* **(a)** *(person, sb's arm)* magullar; **to b. one's arm** hacerse un cardenal en el brazo; **his ego was bruised** su ego quedó algo magullado **(b)** *(feelings)* herir
3 *vi* **to b. easily** *(fruit)* macarse con facilidad; **he bruises easily** le salen cardenales con facilidad

bruised [bru:zd] *adj* **(a)** *(body)* magullado(a), lleno(a) de cardenales **(b)** *(fruit)* con macas, magullado(a) **(c)** *(feelings)* herido(a)

bruiser ['bru:zə(r)] *n Fam* matón *m*

bruising ['bru:zɪŋ] **1** *n (bruises)* moratones *mpl*, moraduras *fpl*
2 *adj (encounter, impact)* duro(a), violento(a)

bruit [bru:t] *vt Literary* **to b. sth about** *or* **around** divulgar algo, hacer correr el rumor de algo

Brum [brʌm] *n Br Fam* Birmingham

Brummie ['brʌmɪ] *Br Fam* **1** *n* persona *f* de Birmingham *(Inglaterra)*
2 *adj* de Birmingham *(Inglaterra)*

brunch [brʌntʃ] **1** *n* desayuno-comida *m*
2 *vi* tomar un desayuno-comida

Brunei [bru:'naɪ] *n* Brunei

brunette [bru:'net] *n* morena *f*

brunt [brʌnt] *n* **she bore the b. of the criticism** recibió la mayor parte de las críticas; **the north of the city bore the b. of the attack** el norte de la ciudad fue la parte más afectada por el ataque

bruschetta [brʊs'ketə] *n* = tostada con tomate, albahaca y aceite de oliva

brush [brʌʃ] **1** *n* **(a)** *(for clothes, hair, teeth)* cepillo *m*; *(for sweeping)* cepillo *m*, escoba *f*; *(for scrubbing)* cepillo *m*; *(for painting pictures)* pincel *m*; *(for house-painting, shaving)* brocha *f*
(b) *(action) (to clothes, hair, teeth, horse)* cepillado *m*; **to give one's hair a b.** cepillarse el pelo; **to give the floor a b.** barrer el suelo
(c) *(light touch)* roce *m*; **she felt the b. of his lips on her neck** notó en el cuello el roce de sus labios
(d) *(encounter, skirmish)* roce *m*; *Fam* **to have a b. with the law** tener un problemilla con la ley; **to have a b. with death** encontrarse cara a cara con la muerte
(e) *(of fox)* cola *f*
(f) *(in motor, generator)* escobilla *m*
(g) *(undergrowth)* maleza *f*, matorrales *mpl* ▸▸ ***b. fire*** incendio *m* de matorrales; *Fig* ***b. fire war*** (pequeño) enfrentamiento *m or* conflicto *m* bélico
2 *vt* **(a)** *(clean)* cepillar; *(floor)* barrer; **to b. one's hair** cepillarse el pelo; **to b. one's teeth** lavarse *or* cepillarse los dientes
(b) *(move)* **she brushed her hair back from her face** se retiró *or* apartó el pelo de la cara
(c) *(touch lightly)* rozar
3 *vi* **to b. against sth/sb** rozar algo/a alguien; **to brush past sth/sb** pasar rozando algo/a alguien

▸**brush aside** *vt sep* **(a)** *(move aside)* apartar **(b)** *(ignore) (objection, criticism)* hacer caso omiso de; *(opponent)* ningunear

▸**brush away** *vt sep* **(a)** *(remove) (tears)* enjugar; *(insect)* espantar **(b)** *(person, difficulty)* deshacerse de

▸**brush down** *vt sep (clothing, horse)* cepillar

▸**brush off** **1** *vt sep* **(a)** *(dust, dirt)* sacudir **(b)** *Fam (dismiss)* no hacer caso a, pasar de
2 *vi (dirt)* salir, irse; **it will b. off easily** saldrá *or* se irá fácilmente

▸**brush on** *vt sep (apply)* aplicar

▸**brush up** *vt sep* **(a)** *(leaves, crumbs)* barrer **(b)** *Fam (subject, language)* **to b. up (on)** pulir, dar un repaso a

brushed [brʌʃt] *adj (cotton, nylon)* afelpado(a)

brush-off ['brʌʃɒf] *n Fam* **to give sb the b.** no hacer ni caso a alguien; **I got the b.** no me hicieron ni caso, pasaron de mí

brushstroke ['brʌʃstrəʊk] *n Art* pincelada *f*; *(in house-painting)* brochazo *m*

brush-up ['brʌʃʌp] *n* **(a)** *Br (clean-up)* **to have a wash and b.** arreglarse **(b)** *Fam (revision)* repaso *m*, puesta *f* al día

brushwood ['brʌʃwʊd] *n* **(a)** *(as fuel)* leña *f*, broza *f* **(b)** *(undergrowth)* maleza *f*, broza *f*

brushwork ['brʌʃwɜ:k] *n Art* pincelada *f*, técnica *f* del pincel

brusque [bru:sk] *adj* brusco(a)

brusquely ['bru:sklɪ] *adv* bruscamente

brusqueness ['bru:sknɪs] *n* brusquedad *m*

Brussels ['brʌsəlz] *n* Bruselas ▸▸ ***B. sprouts*** coles *fpl* de Bruselas

brutal ['bru:təl] *adj* **(a)** *(cruel)* brutal **(b)** *(uncompromising) (honesty)* brutal, crudo(a); **with b. frankness** con una franqueza brutal **(c)** *(severe) (climate, cold)* abominable, crudo(a)

brutality [bru:'tælɪtɪ] *n* brutalidad *f*; **police b.** la brutalidad de la policía

brutalize ['bru:təlaɪz] *vt* **(a)** *(make cruel)* embrutecer; *(make insensitive)* insensibilizar **(b)** *(ill-treat)* tratar con brutalidad

brutalizing ['bru:təlaɪzɪŋ] *adj (making cruel)* embrutecedor(ora); *(making insensitive)* insensibilizante

brutally ['bru:təlɪ] *adv* **(a)** *(cruelly)* brutalmente **(b)** *(uncompromisingly)* **he was b. frank about our prospects** fue de una sinceridad aplastante al hablar de nuestras posibilidades

brute [bru:t] **1** *n* **(a)** *(animal)* bestia *mf* **(b)** *(person)* bestia *mf*
2 *adj* **(a)** *(purely physical)* **b. force** *or* **strength** fuerza bruta **(b)** *(mindless)* inconsciente, salvaje; **an act of b. stupidity** una salvajada

brutish ['bru:tɪʃ] *adj* **(a)** *(animal-like) (behaviour)* de troglodita; *(appearance)* de animal **(b)** *(cruel)* brutal

Brutus ['bru:təs] *pr n* Bruto

Brylcreem® ['brɪlkri:m] **1** *n* gomina *f*
2 *vt* engominar

bryony ['braɪənɪ] *n* nueza *f*, brionia *f*

BS [bi:'es] **(a)** (*abbr* **British Standard(s)**) normativa *f* británica **(b)** *US* (*abbr* **Bachelor of Surgery**) *(qualification)* licenciatura *f* en Cirugía; *(person)* licenciado(a) *m,f* en Cirugía **(c)** *US Fam* (*abbr* **bullshit**) *Esp* gilipolleces *fpl*, *Am* pendejadas *fpl*, *RP* boludeces *fpl*

BSc [bi:es'si:] *n Univ* (*abbr* **Bachelor of Science**) *(qualification)* licenciatura *f* (en Ciencias); *(person)* licenciado(a) *m,f* (en Ciencias)

BSE [bi:es'i:] *n* (*abbr* **bovine spongiform encephalopathy**) EEB *f (enfermedad de las vacas locas)*

BSI [bi:es'aɪ] *n Br* (*abbr* **British Standards Institution**) = asociación británica de normalización, *Esp* ≃ AENOR *f*

BST [bi:es'ti:] *n Br* (*abbr* **British Summer Time**) = horario británico de verano

BT [bi:'ti:] *n* (*abbr* **British Telecom**) BT, = compañía telefónica británica

BTA [bi:ti:'eɪ] *n* (*abbr* **British Tourist Authority**) = departamento británico de turismo

BTEC ['bi:tek] *n Br* (*abbr* **Business and Technician Education Council**) = organismo británico encargado de la formación profesional

BTU [bi:ti:'ju:] *n* (*abbr* **British thermal unit**) BTU *f*

BTW, btw (*abbr* **by the way**) *(in e-mail messages)* a propósito, por cierto

bubba ['bʌbə] *n US Fam* (**a**) *(brother)* hermano *m* (**b**) *(southern male)* = hombre inculto y campechano del sur de los Estados Unidos

bubble ['bʌbəl] **1** *n* (**a**) *(in liquid)* burbuja *f*; *(of soap)* pompa *f*; **to blow bubbles** hacer pompas de jabón ►► ***b. bath*** *(liquid)* espuma *f* de baño; *(bath)* baño *m* de espuma; *Phys* ***b. chamber*** cámara *f* de burbujas; ***b. gum*** chicle *m (para hacer globos)*, *Urug* chicle *m* globero; *Comptr* ***b. memory*** memoria *f* de burbuja; ***b. wrap*** plástico *m* de embalar de burbujas

(**b**) *Com* ***b. pack*** blister *m*

(**c**) *(illusion)* **the b. has burst** la buena racha ha terminado

(**d**) *Br Culin* ***b. and squeak*** = refrito de patata y repollo hervidos

2 *vi* (**a**) *(form bubbles)* burbujear, borbotar; **the gas bubbled to the surface** el gas salía burbujeando a la superficie

(**b**) *(gurgle)* borbollar; **then soup was bubbling away on the stove** la sopa borbollaba en el fuego

(**c**) *(brim)* **the children were bubbling with excitement** los niños estaban rebosantes de entusiasmo

► **bubble over** *vi (soup, milk)* salirse, desbordarse; *Fig* **to b. over with joy** rebosar alegría

bubble-jet ['bʌbəldʒet] *n Comptr* **b. (printer)** impresora *f* de inyección

bubbly ['bʌblɪ] **1** *n Fam (champagne)* champán *m*

2 *adj* (**a**) *(liquid)* espumoso(a) (**b**) *(person, personality)* alegre, jovial

bubonic plague [bju:'bɒnɪk'pleɪg] *n* peste *f* bubónica

buccaneer [bʌkə'nɪə(r)] *n* bucanero *m*

buccaneering [bʌkə'nɪərɪŋ] *adj* desaprensivo(a)

Bucharest ['bʊkərest] *n* Bucarest

buck [bʌk] **1** *n* (**a**) *(deer)* ciervo *m* (macho); *(rabbit)* conejo *m* (macho) (**b**) *US, Austr Fam (dollar)* dólar *m*; **to make a fast** *or* **quick b.** hacer dinero fácil (**c**) *Fam (responsibility)* **to pass the b.** escurrir el bulto; **the b. stops here** aquí recae la responsabilidad última (**d**) *(jump)* sacudida *f* (**e**) *Fam Archaic or Literary (young man)* pollo *m*

2 *adv US Fam* **b. naked** en cueros, *Chile* pilucho(a), *Col* en bola

3 *vt* (**a**) *(of horse)* **the horse bucked its rider** el caballo dio un salto y tiró al jinete (**b**) *Fam (resist)* **to b. the odds** desafiar las leyes de la probabilidad; **to b. the system** oponerse al sistema; **to b. a trend** invertir una tendencia

4 *vi* (**a**) *(horse)* corcovear (**b**) *US (car)* avanzar a sacudidas (**c**) *US Fam (resist)* **to b. against change** plantarse ante los cambios

(**d**) *US Fam (strive)* **he's bucking for promotion** se está dejando la piel para conseguir el ascenso

► **buck up** *Fam* **1** *vt sep* (**a**) *(encourage)* animar, entonar (**b**) *(improve)* **to b. up one's ideas** espabilarse

2 *vi* (**a**) *(cheer up)* animarse (**b**) *(hurry)* espabilarse, aligerar

buckboard ['bʌkbɔ:d] *n US* = carruaje abierto de cuatro ruedas

bucked [bʌkt] *adj Br Fam* animado(a), contento(a); **I was really b. to hear the fantastic news** esas noticias tan buenas me dieron muchos ánimos

bucket ['bʌkɪt] **1** *n* (**a**) *(container)* balde *m*, *Esp* cubo *m*; **a b. of water** un balde *or Esp* cubo de agua ►► ***b. seat*** asiento *m* envolvente; *Fam* ***b. shop*** *Br (for air tickets)* agencia *f* de viajes barata; *(for shares)* = agencia de cambio y bolsa fraudulenta

(**b**) *(of dredger, grain elevator, waterwheel)* cangilón *m*; *(of mechanical digger)* cuchara *f*, cazo *m*

(**c**) IDIOMS *Br Fam* **it's raining buckets** está lloviendo a cántaros *or RP* a baldes; *Fam* **to cry** *or* **weep buckets** llorar a mares

2 *vi Fam* (**a**) *Br (rain)* **it's bucketing (down)** está lloviendo a cántaros (**b**) *(move hurriedly)* **we were bucketing along** íbamos a todo correr *or Esp* toda pastilla

bucketful ['bʌkɪtfʊl] *n* balde *m or Esp* cubo *m* (lleno)

Buck House ['bʌk'haʊs] *n Fam* palacio *m* de Buckingham

bucking bronco ['bʌkɪŋ'brɒŋkəʊ] *n* toro *m* mecánico

Buckingham Palace ['bʌkɪŋəm'pælɪs] *n* palacio *m* de Buckingham

buckle ['bʌkəl] **1** *n* (**a**) *(on belt, dress)* hebilla *f* (**b**) *(in wheel)* abolladura *f*; *(in girder, structure)* torcedura *f*

2 *vt* (**a**) *(fasten)* abrochar (**b**) *(deform) (girder, structure)* torcer; *(wheel)* abollar

3 *vi* (**a**) *(fasten)* abrocharse (**b**) *(deform) (girder, structure)* torcerse; *(wheel)* abollarse; **the bridge buckled under the weight of traffic** el puente se combó por el peso del tráfico (**c**) *(knees)* doblarse; **he buckled at the knees** se le doblaron las rodillas

► **buckle down** *vi* poner manos a la obra; **to b. down to a task** ponerse a hacer una tarea

► **buckle to** *vi Fam* poner manos a la obra

► **buckle up** *vi US* abrocharse el cinturón

buckler ['bʌklə(r)] *n (shield)* rodela *f*

buckram ['bʌkrəm] *n* bucarán *m*

Bucks [bʌks] (*abbr* **Buckinghamshire**) (condado *m* de) Buckinghamshire

bucksaw ['bʌksɔ:] *n* segueta *f*

Buck's fizz [bʌks'fɪz] *n Br* = cóctel a base de champán y jugo de naranja; *Esp* ≃ agua *f* de Valencia

buckshee [bʌk'ʃi:] *Br Fam* **1** *adj* gratis *inv*

2 *adv* gratis

buckshot ['bʌkʃɒt] *n* perdigones *mpl*

buckskin ['bʌkskɪn] *n* piel *f (de ciervo o cabra)*

buckteeth *pl of* **bucktooth**

buckthorn ['bʌkθɔ:n] *n* espino *m* negro

bucktooth ['bʌktu:θ] (*pl* **buckteeth** ['bʌkti:θ]) *n* diente *m* de conejo; **to have buckteeth** tener dientes de conejo

bucktoothed [bʌk'tu:θt] *adj* con dientes de conejo

buckwheat ['bʌkwi:t] *n* alforfón *m*

bucolic [bju:'kɒlɪk] *adj Literary* bucólico(a)

bud [bʌd] **1** *n* (**a**) *(of leaf, branch)* brote *m*; *(of flower)* capullo *m*; **the trees are in b.** los árboles están cubiertos de brotes (**b**) *US Fam (term of address)* **hey, b.!** *(to stranger)* ¡oye!; *(to friend)* ¡qué hay, *Esp* colega *or Am* compadre!

2 *vi* (*pt & pp* **budded**) (**a**) *(plant)* brotar, salir (**b**) *(talent)* brotar, nacer

Budapest ['bu:dəpest] *n* Budapest

Buddha ['bʊdə] *n* Buda *m*

Buddhism ['bʊdɪzəm] *n* budismo *m*

Buddhist ['bʊdɪst] **1** *n* budista *mf*

2 *adj* budista

budding ['bʌdɪŋ] *adj (genius, actor)* en ciernes, incipiente

buddleia ['bʌdlɪə] *n* budleya *f*

buddy ['bʌdɪ] *n Fam* (**a**) *US (friend) Esp* colega *m*, *Am* hermano *m*, *Am* compadre *m*, *Méx* cuate *m* ►► *Cin* ***b. movie*** = película que narra las peripecias de dos amigos; ***b. system*** sistema *m* de compañerismo

(**b**) *US (term of address)* **thanks, b.!** *(to friend, stranger)* ¡gracias, colega *or Am* hermano *or Am* compadre *or Méx* manito!; **hey, b.!** ¡oye, colega!, *Am* ¡eh, compañero!

(**c**) *(friend of AIDS sufferer)* = voluntario que ayuda a un enfermo del sida

► **buddy up** *vi Fam US* **to b. up to sb** hacer la *Esp* pelota *or Méx* barba a alguien, *CSur* chupar las medias a alguien

buddy-buddy ['bʌdɪ'bʌdɪ] *adj US Fam* muy amiguete(a); **to be b. with sb** ser muy amiguete(a) de alguien

budge [bʌdʒ] **1** *vt* (**a**) *(move)* mover; *(stain)* quitar, *Am* sacar (**b**) **I couldn't b. him** *(change his mind)* no conseguí hacerle cambiar de opinión

2 *vi* (**a**) *(move)* moverse; *(stain)* irse, quitarse (**b**) *(yield)* ceder; **he won't b. an inch** no dará su brazo a torcer, no cederá un ápice

budgerigar ['bʌdʒərɪgɑ:(r)] *n* periquito *m* (australiano)

budget ['bʌdʒɪt] **1** *n* presupuesto *m*; *Br Pol* **the B.** ≃ los Presupuestos Generales del Estado; **to go over b.** salirse del presupuesto; **we are within b.** no nos hemos salido del presupuesto; **on a b.** con un presupuesto limitado, por poco dinero ►► ***b. account*** *(with a shop)* cuenta *f* de cliente; *(with a bank)* cuenta *f* para domiciliaciones; ***b. cut*** recorte *m* presupuestario; *Br Pol* ***B. Day*** = día en que se anuncian los Presupuestos Generales del Estado; ***b. deficit*** déficit *m* presupuestario; ***b. flights*** vuelos *mpl* a precios reducidos; ***b. holidays*** vacaciones *fpl* económicas; ***b. surplus*** superávit *m* presupuestario

2 *vt (time, money)* calcular; **how much has been budgeted for advertising?** ¿cuánto dinero se ha presupuestado para publicidad?

3 *vi* administrar(se) el dinero; **to b. for** *(include in budget)* contemplar en el presupuesto; **we hadn't budgeted for these expenses** *(hadn't foreseen)* no contábamos con estos gastos

budgetary ['bʌdʒɪtərɪ] *adj Fin* presupuestario(a)

budgie ['bʌdʒɪ] *n Br Fam* periquito *m* (australiano)

Buenos Aires ['bwenəˈsaɪrɪz] *n* Buenos Aires

buff [bʌf] **1** *n* (**a**) *(colour)* marrón *m* claro (**b**) *(leather)* gamuza *f* (**c**) *(polishing cloth)* gamuza *f*; *(disc)* disco *m* pulidor (**d**) *(enthusiast)* **film** *or* **movie b.** cinéfilo(a); **opera b.** entendido(a) en ópera (**e**) *Fam* **in the b.** *(naked)* en cueros

2 *adj* (**a**) *(in colour)* marrón claro(a) (**b**) *(jacket, coat)* de gamuza

3 *vt (polish)* sacar brillo a

▸ **buff up** *vt sep* **to b. sth up** sacar brillo a algo

buffalo ['bʌfələʊ] *(pl* **buffalo** *or* **buffaloes**) **1** *n* (**a**) *(African, Indian)* búfalo *m* ▸▸ ***b. mozzarella*** mozzarella *f* de búfala (**b**) *(American bison)* búfalo *m*, bisonte *m* (**c**) *US* ***b. wings*** alitas *fpl* de pollo fritas

2 *vt US Fam (confuse, intimidate)* apabullar

buffer[1] ['bʌfə(r)] *n* (**a**) *Rail (on train, at end of track)* tope *m*; **to act as a b. (against)** amortiguar ▸▸ ***b. state*** estado *m* barrera; ***b. zone*** zona *f* de protección (**b**) *US (on car)* parachoques *m inv*, *Méx* defensas *fpl*, *RP* paragolpes *m inv* (**c**) *Comptr* búfer *m*, buffer *m*, memoria *f* intermedia (**d**) *(for polishing)* gamuza *f* (**e**) *Chem* tampón *m* ▸▸ ***b. solution*** solución *f* tampón

buffer[2] *n Br Fam* **old b.** vejete *m*

buffet[1] ['bʌfɪt] **1** *vt (of wind)* zarandear, azotar; *Fig* **he was buffeted by the crowds** le arrolló *or* zarandeó la multitud; *Fig* **to be buffeted by events** verse sacudido(a) por el remolino de los acontecimientos

2 *n (blow)* golpe *m*; *Fig* **the buffets of fate** *or* **fortune** los reveses *or* golpes del destino *or* de la fortuna

buffet[2] ['bʊfeɪ] *n* (**a**) *(sideboard)* mostrador *m* de comidas, bufé *m* (**b**) *(meal)* bufé *m* ▸▸ ***b. lunch*** (almuerzo *m* tipo) bufé *m* (**c**) *(at station)* cafetería *f* ▸▸ ***b. car*** vagón *m* restaurante, bar *m*

buffeting ['bʌfɪtɪŋ] *n* **to take a b.** *(ship)* ser zarandeado(a); *Fig (person)* recibir un repaso

buffoon [bə'fu:n] *n* payaso *m*, bufón *m*; **to act** *or* **to play the b.** hacer el payaso

buffoonery [bə'fu:nərɪ] *n* majaderías *fpl*, payasadas *fpl*

bug [bʌg] **1** *n* (**a**) *(biting insect)* bicho *m (que pica)*; *US (any insect)* bicho *m*, insecto *m*

(**b**) *Fam (illness)* infección *f*; **there's a b. going round** hay un virus rondando por ahí; **I've got a stomach b.** tengo el estómago revuelto

(**c**) *Fam (craze)* gusanillo *m*; **the travel b.** el gusanillo de viajar

(**d**) *Comptr (fault) (in machine, software, system)* error *m*; **there are still a few bugs to be ironed out** todavía quedan por solucionar algunos errores

(**e**) *(listening device)* micrófono *m* oculto

2 *vt (pt & pp* **bugged**) (**a**) *(telephone)* pinchar, intervenir; *(room)* poner micrófonos en (**b**) *Fam (annoy)* molestar, fastidiar; **stop bugging me about it!** ¡deja de darme la lata con eso!; **there's something about him that really bugs me!** ¡tiene algo que me fastidia!

3 *vi US Fam (eyes)* **his eyes bugged** se le salieron los ojos de las órbitas

▸ **bug off** *vi US Fam (leave)* largarse, *Esp* pirarse; **b. off!** ¡fuera!, ¡lárgate!

▸ **bug out** *vi US Fam* (**a**) *(leave)* largarse, *Esp* pirarse (**b**) *(go mad)* tener una venada (**c**) *(eyes)* **his eyes bugged out** se le salieron los ojos de las órbitas

bugaboo ['bʌgəbu:] *n US Fam* coco *m*

bugbear ['bʌgbeə(r)] *n Fam* tormento *m*, pesadilla *f*

bug-eyed ['bʌgaɪd] *adj* **to be b.** *(permanently)* tener ojos saltones; **she was b. in amazement** se le salían los ojos de las órbitas de asombro; *Hum* **a b. monster** un monstruo con ojos de besugo *or Am* de pescado

bug-free [bʌg'fri:] *adj Comptr* sin errores

bugger ['bʌgə(r)] **1** *n* (**a**) *very Fam (unpleasant person)* hijo(a) *m,f* de puta, cabrón(ona) *m,f*; **you silly b.!** ¡qué tonto(a) eres!; **the poor b.!** ¡pobre desgraciado!; **to play silly buggers** hacer el *Esp* gilipollas, hacerse *Méx* el pendejo *or RP* el pavo

(**b**) *Br very Fam (unpleasant thing)* **a b. of a job** una putada de trabajo; **her house is a b. to find** es bastante jodido encontrar su casa

(**c**) *Br very Fam (for emphasis)* **he knows b. all about it** no tiene ni puta idea; **there's b. all left in the fridge** carajo *or Esp* joder, no queda nada en la nevera; **I don't** *or* **couldn't give a b.!** ¡me importa un carajo!, *Esp* ¡me la trae floja!

(**d**) *(electronic eavesdropper)* = persona que se dedica a instalar micrófonos ocultos

(**e**) *Old-fashioned (sodomite)* sodomita *m*

2 *vt* (**a**) *(sodomize)* sodomizar

(**b**) *Br very Fam (exhaust)* dejar hecho(a) polvo

(**c**) *Br very Fam (ruin, break)* joder, cargarse, *Méx* chingar; **that's really buggered it!** ¡lo ha jodido todo bien!

(**d**) *Br very Fam (for emphasis)* **b. it!** ¡carajo!, *Esp* ¡joder!, *RP* ¡la puta (digo)!; **b. me!** ¡carajo!, *Esp* ¡la hostia!, *RP* ¡la puta (digo)!; **I'll be buggered if I'm going to pay for it!** ¡no lo voy a pagar ni loco *or Esp* ni de coña *or RP* ni en joda!; **b. the expense, let's buy it!** ¡al carajo con el precio, vamos a comprarlo!

3 *exclam* ¡carajo!, *Esp* ¡joder!, *RP* ¡la puta (digo)!

▸ **bugger about, bugger around** *Br very Fam* **1** *vt sep* **stop buggering me about** *or* **around!** *Esp* ¡deja de marearme, joder!, *Méx* ¡deja de chingarme!, *RP* ¡puta, dejá de volverme loco!

2 *vi Esp* hacer el gilipollas, *Am* pendejear

▸ **bugger off** *vi Br very Fam* abrirse, *Esp, RP* pirarse; **b. off!** ¡vete a la mierda!

▸ **bugger up** *vt sep Br very Fam* joder

buggered ['bʌgəd] *adj Br very Fam* (**a**) *(exhausted)* hecho(a) polvo, *Col* como un chupo, *Méx* camotes *inv*

(**b**) *(broken)* jodido(a)

(**c**) *(in trouble)* **if we don't get the money soon, we're b.** si no conseguimos el dinero pronto, la hemos cagado

(**d**) *(for emphasis)* **well, I'm b.!** *(in surprise)* ¡carajo!, *Esp* ¡joder!; **I'm b. if I'll do anything to help** *(in annoyance)* no pienso ayudar ni de coña; **(I'm) b. if I know** no tengo ni puta idea

buggery ['bʌgərɪ] **1** *n* (**a**) *Law* sodomía *f* (**b**) *Br very Fam* **to run like b.** correr *Esp* a toda hostia *or RP* a los pedos, *Méx* ir hecho la raya; **is he a good cook? – is he b.!** ¿cocina bien? – ¡qué va a cocinar bien ni qué carajo *or Esp* ni qué hostias *or RP* ni en pedo!

2 *exclam Br very Fam* ¡carajo!, *Esp* ¡joder!, *RP* ¡la puta (digo)!

bugging device ['bʌgɪŋdɪ'vaɪs] *n (in room)* micrófono *m* oculto; *(in telephone)* = aparato para intervenir llamadas

buggy ['bʌgɪ] *n* (**a**) *Br (pushchair)* sillita *f* (de niño) (**b**) *US (pram)* cochecito *m* (de niño) (**c**) *(carriage)* calesa *f*

bughouse ['bʌghaʊs] *US Fam* **1** *n* loquero *m*, frenopático *m*

2 *adj* loco(a), pirado(a)

bugle ['bju:gəl] *n* corneta *f*, clarín *m*

bugler ['bju:glə(r)] *n* corneta *mf*, clarín *mf*

bugloss ['bju:glɒs] *n* lengua *f* de buey

bug-ridden ['bʌgrɪdən] *adj Comptr* lleno(a) de errores

build [bɪld] **1** *n* (**a**) *(physique)* complexión *f*, constitución *f*; **a man of slight/heavy b.** un hombre menudo/corpulento; **he has the b. of a rugby player** tiene la complexión de un jugador de rugby

(**b**) *(construction work)* construcción *m*; **the b. took four months** su construcción llevó cuatro meses

2 *vt (pt & pp* **built** [bɪlt]) (**a**) *(construct) (wall, ship, bridge, nest, road)* construir; *(house)* construir, edificar; *(barrier, structure)* levantar; *(car)* fabricar; **this furniture was built to last** estos muebles están fabricados para que duren mucho tiempo

(**b**) *(found, develop) (empire)* construir, levantar; *(career, reputation)* forjarse, labrarse

(**c**) *Com* **to b. the business** ampliar el negocio; **to b. one's market share** incrementar la cuota de mercado

3 *vi* (**a**) *(construct)* construir, edificar (**b**) *(increase) (excitement, tension)* crecer, aumentar

▸ **build in** *vt sep* (**a**) *Constr* empotrar (**b**) *Fig (safeguard)* incorporar

▸ **build into** *vt sep* (**a**) *Constr* empotrar en (**b**) *Fig (safeguard)* incorporar en

▸ **build on** *vt sep* (**a**) *(add)* añadir (**b**) *(use as foundation)* **she built on their achievements** siguió avanzando a partir de sus logros; **he had built all his hopes on passing the exam** todas sus esperanzas se cimentaban en que aprobaría el examen

▸ **build up** **1** *vt sep* (**a**) *(increase) (expectations)* alimentar; *(resources)* aumentar; **to b. up speed** tomar *or Esp* coger velocidad; **to b. sb's hopes up** dar esperanzas a alguien; *Hum* **don't b. your hopes up!** ¡no te hagas ilusiones!

(**b**) *(develop) (business)* ampliar; *(reputation)* forjarse; *(strength, fortune)* acumular; **he built up the business from scratch** creó su negocio desde cero; **you need to b. up your strength again** tienes que recobrar fuerzas; **to b. up an immunity (to sth)** hacerse inmune (a algo); **this success built up her confidence** aquel éxito le hizo ganar seguridad en sí misma

(**c**) *(hype)* **the press built her up as a future champion** la prensa construyó su imagen de futura campeona; **it wasn't as good as it was built up to be** no fue tan bueno como se había hecho creer

2 *vi* (**a**) *(accumulate) (work, debts, dust)* acumularse

(**b**) *(clouds)* formarse

(**c**) *(tension, pressure)* incrementarse, aumentar; **traffic is building up** el tráfico está aumentando; **the film builds up to an incredible climax** la tensión de la película aumenta hasta llegar a un final apoteósico

builder ['bɪldə(r)] *n* (**a**) *(worker)* albañil *m* ▸▸ *Br Fam Hum* ***b.'s bum*** culo *m* de obrero, = parte superior del trasero que asoma cuando alguien lleva los pantalones caídos (**b**) *(small businessman)* contratista *mf* de obras ▸▸ ***b.'s merchant*** comerciante *mf* de materiales para la construcción

building ['bɪldɪŋ] *n* (**a**) *(structure)* edificio *m* ▸▸ ***buildings insurance*** seguro *m* de hogar *or* de la casa
(**b**) *(trade)* construcción *f*; *(activity)* obras *fpl*; **b. is due to start on Monday** las obras empiezan el lunes ▸▸ ***b. block*** *(toy)* pieza *f* (de construcción); *Fig* unidad *f* básica; ***b. contractor*** contratista *mf* de obras; ***the b. industry*** el sector de la construcción; ***b. materials*** material *m* de construcción; ***b. permit*** licencia *f* de obras; ***b. site*** obra *f*; *Br* ***b. society*** ≃ caja *f* de ahorros

build-up ['bɪldʌp] *n* (**a**) *(of tension, forces)* incremento *m*, aumento *m*; *(of troops)* concentración *f*; **b. of traffic, traffic b.** atasco
(**b**) *(before election, public event)* **in the b. to the game** conforme se acerca el día del partido; **the long b. to the elections** la larga precampaña electoral
(**c**) *(publicity)* **they gave the product a big b.** el producto vino precedido de una gran campaña publicitaria; **after all the b....** después de toda la expectación creada...

built [bɪlt] **1** *pt & pp of* **build**
2 *adj* (**a**) *(building)* **b. (out) of sth** hecho(a) de algo; **British b.** de construcción británica, construido en Gran Bretaña (**b**) *(person)* **to be powerfully b.** tener una complexión imponente; **he was slightly b.** era de escasa corpulencia

built-in ['bɪlt'ɪn] *adj* (**a**) *(in structure) (cupboard)* empotrado(a); *(in car, computer)* incorporado(a); **it has a b. timer** lleva un temporizador incorporado (**b**) *(safeguard, obsolescence)* inherente

built-to-order ['bɪlttuː'ɔːdə(r)] *adj Comptr* construido(a) a medida

built-up ['bɪlt'ʌp] *adj* (**a**) *(area)* urbanizado(a) (**b**) *(heel, shoe)* con alza

bulb [bʌlb] *n* (**a**) *(of plant)* bulbo *m* (**b**) *(light bulb) Esp* bombilla *f*, *Andes, Méx* foco *m*, *CAm, Carib* bombillo *m*, *RP* lamparita *f* (**c**) *(of thermometer)* cubeta *f*

bulbous ['bʌlbəs] *adj* bulboso(a), en forma de bulbo

Bulgaria [bʌl'geərɪə] *n* Bulgaria

Bulgarian [bʌl'geərɪən] **1** *n* (**a**) *(person)* búlgaro(a) *m,f* (**b**) *(language)* búlgaro *m*
2 *adj* búlgaro(a)

bulge [bʌldʒ] **1** *n* (**a**) *(lump, swelling)* bulto *m*, abultamiento *m* (**b**) *(increase)* crecimiento *m or* aumento *m* repentino
2 *vi* (**a**) *(be full)* estar repleto(a) (**with** de) (**b**) *(swell)* abombarse; *Fig* **her eyes bulged at the sight of all the food** al ver tanta comida parecía que se le iban a salir los ojos de las órbitas; **to b. out** sobresalir

bulghur ['bʌlgə(r)] *n* **b. (wheat)** trigo *m* bulgur

bulging ['bʌldʒɪŋ] *adj (bag, pocket, wallet)* abultado(a); *(stomach)* hinchado(a); **b. eyes** ojos saltones

bulimia [bʊ'liːmɪə] *n* bulimia *f*

bulimic [bʊ'liːmɪk] **1** *n* bulímico(a) *m,f*
2 *adj* bulímico(a)

bulk [bʌlk] **1** *n* (**a**) *(mass)* masa *f*, volumen *m*; *(of person)* mole *f*, corpachón *m*; **a man of enormous b.** un hombre grandullón, una mole de hombre
(**b**) *(main part)* **the b. (of sth)** el grueso (de algo); **the b. of the estate was woodland** la mayor parte de la finca era bosque
(**c**) *Com* **in b.** a granel; **to buy/sell in b.** comprar/vender al por mayor; **a b. order** un pedido al por mayor ▸▸ ***b. buying*** compra *f* al por mayor; ***b. carrier*** carguero *m* (de mercancía) a granel; ***b. mail*** envío *m* (postal) masivo; ***b. purchase*** compra *f* al por mayor; ***b. rate*** *(for postage)* = tarifa reducida para envíos masivos
(**d**) *(dietary fibre)* fibra *f*
2 *vt* **to b. sth out** *or* **up** abultar algo
3 *vi* **to b. large** *(problem)* tener relieve; **the prospect of defeat bulked large in their minds** no se les quitaba de la cabeza la posibilidad de salir derrotados

bulk-buy ['bʌlk'baɪ] **1** *vt* comprar al por mayor
2 *vi* comprar al por mayor

bulkhead ['bʌlkhed] *n* mamparo *m*

bulkiness ['bʌlkɪnɪs] *n (of thing)* voluminosidad *f*; *(of person)* corpulencia *f*

bulky ['bʌlkɪ] *adj* (**a**) *(large) (thing)* grande, voluminoso(a); *(person)* corpulento(a) (**b**) *US (sweater)* de tejido flojo(a) *or* suelto(a)

bull[1] [bʊl] **1** *n* (**a**) *(male animal) (cow)* toro *m*; *(whale)* ballena *f* (macho) ▸▸ *Br Fam* ***b. bars*** *(on car)* defensa *f* delantera, = barra o pantalla protectora de metal para casos de choque con animales; ***b. elephant*** elefante *m* (macho); ***b. terrier*** bulterrier *m*
(**b**) *St Exch* ***b. market*** mercado *m* alcista
(**c**) *Fam (nonsense)* **to talk b.** decir sandeces *or* idioteces
(**d**) *(centre of target)* diana *f*; **to hit the b.** dar en el blanco
(**e**) *US* ***b. session*** *(discussion)* charla *f* informal *(especialmente entre hombres)*
(**f**) IDIOM **like a b. in a china shop** como un elefante en una cacharrería; **to take the b. by the horns** agarrar *or Esp* coger el toro por los cuernos
2 *exclam very Fam* ¡y un cuerno!

bull[2] *n Rel* bula *f*

bulldog ['bʊldɒg] *n* bulldog *m* ▸▸ *Br* ***B.®*** ***clip*** pinza *f* sujetapapeles

bulldoze ['bʊldəʊz] *vt* (**a**) *(flatten) (area, land)* allanar, nivelar; *(building)* demoler; *(remove)* derribar (**b**) *(push, force)* **to b. sb into doing sth** forzar *or* obligar a alguien a hacer algo; **she bulldozed her way to the top** se abrió paso a empellones hasta la cima; **they bulldozed the legislation through parliament** consiguieron que se aprobara la ley de mala manera

bulldozer ['bʊldəʊzə(r)] *n* bulldozer *m*

bulldyke ['bʊldaɪk] *n very Fam* marimacho *f*

bullet ['bʊlɪt] *n* (**a**) *(for gun)* bala *f*, proyectil *m*; IDIOM *Br Fam* **he got the b.** lo pusieron de patitas en la calle, le dieron la patada ▸▸ ***b. hole*** agujero *m* de bala; ***b. wound*** herida *f* de bala (**b**) *Comptr & Typ* topo *m* (**c**) *Rail* ***b. train*** tren *m* de alta velocidad

bulleted ['bʊlɪtɪd] *adj Comptr & Typ* **b. list** lista con topos

bullet-headed ['bʊlɪt'hedɪd] *adj* (**a**) *(round headed)* de cabeza apepinada (**b**) *US (obstinate)* terco(a), obstinado(a)

bulletin ['bʊlɪtɪn] *n* boletín *m* ▸▸ *US Comptr* ***b. board*** tablón *m* de anuncios; *Comptr* ***b. board service*** tablón *m* de anuncios electrónico

bullet-proof ['bʊlɪtpruːf] **1** *adj* antibalas *inv*, a prueba de balas ▸▸ ***b. vest*** chaleco *m* antibalas
2 *vt (door, vehicle)* blindar

bullfight ['bʊlfaɪt] *n* corrida *f* de toros

bullfighter ['bʊlfaɪtə(r)] *n* torero(a) *m,f*

bullfighting ['bʊlfaɪtɪŋ] *n* toreo *m*

bullfinch ['bʊlfɪntʃ] *n* camachuelo *m*

bullfrog ['bʊlfrɒg] *n* rana *f* toro

bull-headed ['bʊl'hedɪd] *adj Fam (obstinate)* cabezón(ona), terco(a)

bullhorn ['bʊlhɔːn] *n US* megáfono *m*

bullion ['bʊljən] *n* **gold/silver b.** oro/plata en lingotes *or* barras

bullish ['bʊlɪʃ] *adj* (**a**) *Fin (market)* al alza (**b**) *Fam (optimistic)* optimista

bull-mastiff ['bʊl'mæstɪf] *n* bullmastiff *m*

bull-necked ['bʊl'nekt] *adj (person)* cuellicorto(a)

bullock ['bʊlək] *n* buey *m*

bullpen ['bʊlpen] *n US* (**a**) *(cell)* calabozo *m*, celda *f* (**b**) *(in baseball)* = área de calentamiento para los pitchers

bullring ['bʊlrɪŋ] *n (building)* plaza *f* de toros; *(arena)* ruedo *m*

bullrush = **bulrush**

bull's-eye ['bʊlzaɪ] **1** *n* (**a**) *(of target)* diana *f*, blanco *m*; *also Fig* **to hit the b.** dar en el blanco (**b**) *(sweet)* = caramelo de menta duro
2 *exclam (in darts)* ¡blanco!; *(celebrating success)* ¡bingo!

bullshit ['bʊlʃɪt] *Vulg* **1** *n (nonsense) Esp* gilipolleces *fpl*, *Am* pendejadas *fpl*, *RP* boludeces *fpl*
2 *exclam* ¡y una mierda!, *RP* ¡las bolas!
3 *vt (pt & pp* **bullshitted**) **don't b. me, I want the truth!** ¡no me jodas *or Méx* chingues, dime la verdad!; **she bullshitted her way into the job** consiguió el trabajo dándoselas
4 *vi (talk nonsense)* decir *Esp* gilipolleces *or Am* pendejadas *or RP* boludeces

bullshitter ['bʊlʃɪtə(r)] *n Vulg (smooth talker)* fantasma *mf*; **he's a b.** *(talks nonsense)* no me dice más que *Esp* gilipolleces *or Am* pendejadas *or RP* boludeces

bullwhip ['bʊlwɪp] **1** *n* látigo *m (de cuero trenzado)*
2 *vt* dar latigazos a, azotar con un látigo a

bully ['bʊlɪ] **1** *n* (**a**) *(thug)* matón(ona) *m,f*; *(at school) Esp* abusón(ona) *m,f*, *Am* abusador(ora) *m,f* (**b**) *(in field hockey)* bully *m*
2 *exclam Fam* **b. for you!** ¡bravo!; *Ironic* ¡enhorabuena!
3 *vt* intimidar; **to b. sb into doing sth** intimidar a alguien para que haga algo

▸**bully off** *vi (in field hockey)* comenzar el juego con un bully *or* saque neutral

bully beef ['bʊlɪbiːf] *n Br Fam* fiambre *m* de vaca en conserva

bully-boy ['bʊlɪbɔɪ] *n* matón *m*; **b. tactics** tácticas de intimidación

bullying ['bʊlɪɪŋ] **1** *n* intimidación *f*
2 *adj* intimidatorio(a), amenazador(ora)

bully-off ['bʊlɪɒf] *n (in field hockey)* bully *m* (inicial)

bulrush, bullrush ['bʊlrʌʃ] *n* (**a**) *Br (reed mace)* anea *f*, espadaña *f* (**b**) *US (soft rush)* junco *m*

bulwark ['bʊlwək] *n* (**a**) *(wall)* bastión *m* (**against** contra) (**b**) *(breakwater)* rompeolas *m inv*, malecón *m* (**c**) **bulwarks** *(of ship)* borda *f* (**d**) *Fig (protection)* bastión *m* (**against** contra)

bum [bʌm] *Fam* **1** *n* (**a**) *Br (buttocks)* trasero *m*, culo *m*, *Am* cola *f* ►► *Br* ***b. bag*** riñonera *f*, *Méx* cangurera *f*; *Vulg* ***b. boy*** puto *m*, chapero *m*; ***b. fluff*** *(beard)* pelusilla *f*, primera barba *f*
(**b**) *US (tramp)* vagabundo(a) *m,f*; **on the b.** *(scrounging)* a la sopa boba; *(as a vagrant)* de vagabundo(a)
(**c**) *(worthless person)* cero *m* a la izquierda; IDIOM **to give sb the b.'s rush** *(dismiss, eject)* poner a alguien de patitas en la calle; IDIOM **to give sth the b.'s rush** *(idea, suggestion)* mandar algo a hacer gárgaras
(**d**) *(enthusiast)* fanático(a) *m,f*, *Esp* forofo(a) *m,f*; **a ski b.** un fanático *or Esp* forofo del esquí; **to be a beach b.** pasarse la vida en la playa
2 *adj (of poor quality)* malo(a), *Esp* cutre, *RP* berreta; **she got a b. deal** la trataron a patadas; **a b. rap** *(false charge)* una acusación falsa; **b. steer** engañifa
3 *vt (pt & pp* **bummed**) **to b. sth from** *or* **off sb** *Esp* gorronear *or Méx* gorrear *or RP* garronear algo a alguien; **can I b. a lift** *or* **a ride to the station?** ¿me llevas a la estación?

►**bum around** *Fam* **1** *vt insep* **to b. around Australia/the country** vagabundear por Australia/el país; **to b. around the house** haraganear por casa
2 *vi (be idle)* holgazanear, gandulear; *(travel)* vagabundear

bumble ['bʌmbəl] *vi* (**a**) *(move clumsily)* **to b. about** *or* **along** *or* **around** ir a trompicones (**b**) *(talk confusedly)* **to b. on (about sth)** farfullar (algo)

bumble-bee ['bʌmbəlbi:] *n* abejorro *m*

bumbling ['bʌmblɪŋ] *adj* **b. fool** *or* **idiot** tonto(a), inútil

bumf, bumph [bʌmf] *n Br Fam* papelotes *mpl*

bummed [bʌmd] *adj US Fam* **to be b.** estar con la moral por los suelos

bummer ['bʌmə(r)] *n Fam (annoying thing)* lata *f*, *RP* embole *m*, *Ven* lava *f*; **what a b.!** ¡qué lata!; **it was a real b. being stuck at home all day** fue una pesadez *or Esp* un latazo tener que quedarse en casa todo el día

bump [bʌmp] **1** *n* (**a**) *(jolt)* golpe *m*, sacudida *f*; *Fig* **to come (back) down to earth with a b.** volver a la dura realidad; IDIOM *Br* **to give sb the bumps** *(on birthday)* = lanzar a alguien por el aire, tantas veces como años cumpla, sujetándole varias personas por las extremidades para después dejar que caiga al suelo ►► ***b. start*** *(for car)* = método de arranque de un coche empujándolo mientras se mete la marcha conforme se pone en movimiento
(**b**) *(lump) (on head)* chichón *m*; *(in surface)* bollo *m*; *(on road)* bache *m*
2 *vt* (**a**) *(hit)* **to b. one's head against sth** golpearse en la cabeza con algo (**b**) *(air passenger)* dejar en tierra (por overbooking) (**c**) *US Fam (remove)* cargarse
3 *vi* (**a**) *(move with jerks)* traquetear, dar sacudidas; **the old bus bumped along the country roads** el viejo autobús iba dando tumbos por las carreteras rurales del país
(**b**) *(collide)* darse un topetazo, chocar; **the boat bumped against the pier** la embarcación topó *or* chocó contra el muelle
(**c**) *Fam* **to b. and grind** *(stripper, dancer)* bailar de forma provocativa *(moviendo la pelvis)*
4 *adv* **the driver went b. into the car in front** el conductor se dio un topetazo *or* golpe con el coche de delante; *Hum* **things that go b. in the night** cosas que emiten misteriosos ruidos durante la noche

►**bump into** *vt insep* (**a**) *(collide with)* chocar con (**b**) *Fam (meet by chance)* encontrarse con, toparse con

►**bump off** *vt sep Fam (kill)* liquidar, cargarse a

►**bump up** *vt sep Fam (price)* subir

bumper ['bʌmpə(r)] **1** *n* (**a**) *(of car)* parachoques *m inv*, *Méx* defensas *fpl*, *RP* paragolpes *m inv* ►► ***b. sticker*** adhesivo *m* para parachoques *or Méx* defensas *fpl or RP* paragolpes *m inv* (**b**) ***b. car*** *(at fairground)* auto *m or* coche *m* de choque, *Méx* carrito *m* chocón, *RP* autito *m* chocador (**c**) *(full glass)* vaso *m* a rebosar
2 *adj* abundante, excepcional ►► ***b. crop*** cosecha *f* excepcional; *Br* ***b. issue*** número *m* especial

bumper-to-bumper ['bʌmpətə'bʌmpə(r)] *adj* **there was b. traffic** había caravana

bumph = **bumf**

bumpkin ['bʌmpkɪn] *n* **(country) b.** palurdo(a) *m,f*, *Esp* paleto(a) *m,f*

bump-start ['bʌmpstɑ:t] *vt* **to b. a car** arrancar un coche empujando

bumptious ['bʌmpʃəs] *adj* presuntuoso(a), engreído(a)

bumpy ['bʌmpɪ] *adj* (**a**) *(road, surface)* lleno(a) de baches, accidentado(a) (**b**) *(journey, flight)* incómodo(a), agitado(a); *Fam Fig* **to have a b. ride** encontrar muchos obstáculos

bun [bʌn] *n* (**a**) *(sweetened roll)* bollo *m*; *(sponge-cake)* bizcocho *m*; *(for beefburger)* panecillo *m* (redondo); IDIOM *Br Euph & Hum* **to have a b. in the oven** estar esperando a la cigüeña, estar con bombo ►► *Br Fam Hum* ***b. fight*** *Esp* merendola *f*, *Am* té *m* (multitudinario)
(**b**) *(hair)* moño *m*, *Méx* chongo *m*; **to wear one's hair in a b.** llevar el pelo recogido en un moño
(**c**) *US Fam* **buns** *(buttocks)* trasero, culo

bunch [bʌntʃ] *n* (**a**) *(of flowers)* ramo *m*, ramillete *m*; *(of bananas, grapes)* racimo *m*; *(of carrots)* manojo *m*; **the best** *or* **the pick of the b.** el mejor de todo el lote; **the best of a bad b.** lo único que se salva; IDIOM *Br Old-fashioned & Hum* **to give sb a b. of fives** darle un mamporro *or* puñetazo a alguien
(**b**) *(of keys)* manojo *m*
(**c**) *(of people)* grupo *m*; *(of friends)* pandilla *f*; *(of cyclists)* pelotón *m*
(**d**) *(of hair)* **to wear one's hair in bunches** peinarse con *or* llevar coletas
(**e**) *Fam (lot)* **to have a whole b. of things to do** tener un montón de cosas que hacer; *Ironic* **thanks a b.!** ¡gracias, generoso(a)!

►**bunch together** *vi (people)* apiñarse

►**bunch up** *vi* (**a**) *(group of people)* apelotonarse, apiñarse (**b**) *(clothing)* arrugarse, hacerse arrugas en

bundle ['bʌndəl] **1** *n* (**a**) *(of papers)* manojo *m*; *(of banknotes)* fajo *m*; *(of straw, sticks)* haz *m*, gavilla *f*; *(of clothes)* fardo *m*, hato *m*; *(of fibres, wires)* haz *m*; *Fam* **she's a b. of nerves** es un manojo de nervios; *Fam Ironic* **he's a real b. of fun** *or* **laughs** es un tipo aburridísimo, *Esp* es un muermo de tío, *RP* es un tipo embolante; *Fam Ironic* **thanks a b.!** ¡muy amable por tu parte!, ¡es todo un detalle!
(**b**) *Com* paquete *m*, kit *m*
(**c**) *Fam (large sum of money)* **to cost a b.** costar un dineral; **to make a b.** forrarse
(**d**) *Br Fam* **to go a b. on sth/sb** *(be enthusiastic about)* volverse loco(a) por algo/alguien, pirrarse por *or RP* coparse con algo/alguien; **I don't go a b. on horror films** no me vuelven loco las películas de terror
2 *vt* (**a**) *(make into a bundle)* liar, juntar; **they bundled the straw into sheaves** hicieron haces con la paja; **the notes were bundled in $10,000 packets** los billetes venían en fajos de 10.000 dólares
(**b**) *(move quickly)* **to b. sb out of the door** sacar a alguien a empujones por la puerta; **to b. sb into a taxi** meter a alguien a empujones en un taxi
(**c**) *Comptr* **it comes bundled with over $2,000 worth of software** viene acompañado de software por valor de más de 2.000 dólares

►**bundle off** *vt sep (send)* despachar

►**bundle up** *vt sep* (**a**) *(tie up)* liar, envolver; **he bundled his clothes up in a sheet** se sirvió de una sábana para hacer un hatillo con la ropa (**b**) *(dress warmly)* arropar, envolver

bung [bʌŋ] **1** *n* (**a**) *(of barrel)* tapón *m* (**b**) *Br Fam (bribe)* soborno *m*, *Andes, RP* coima *f*, *CAm, Méx* mordida *f*
2 *vt* (**a**) *(pipe, hole)* atascar, taponar (**b**) *Fam (put, throw)* echar, *Am* botar; **b. it there** échalo *or Am* bótalo ahí; **b. it on the bill** ponlo *or* mételo en la cuenta; **we'll b. in a few extras** añadiremos algunos suplementos

►**bung up** *vt sep Fam (pipe, hole)* atascar, taponar; **my nose is bunged up** tengo la nariz taponada

bungalow ['bʌŋgələʊ] *n* (**a**) *(single-storey house)* bungaló *m* (**b**) *(in tropics, at beach)* bungaló *m*

bungee jumping ['bʌndʒi:'dʒʌmpɪŋ] *n* puenting *m*

bunghole ['bʌŋhəʊl] *n* agujero *m* de barril

bungle ['bʌŋgəl] **1** *vt (job, task)* echar a perder, hacer mal; **they bungled their attempt to escape** fastidiaron su intento de fuga
2 *vi* hacer chapuzas
3 *n Br* **to make a b. of sth** hacer un estropicio *or* chapuza con algo

bungler ['bʌŋglə(r)] *n* chapucero(a) *m,f*, chapuzas *mf inv*

bungling ['bʌŋglɪŋ] **1** *n* estropicio *m*, chapuza *f*
2 *adj* chapucero(a)

bunion ['bʌnjən] *n (on foot)* juanete *m*

bunk[1] [bʌŋk] *n (bed)* litera *f* ►► ***b. bed*** litera *f*

bunk[2] *n Fam* (a) *(nonsense)* estupidez *f*, idiotez *f*; **that's a load of b.** eso es una sarta de estupideces (b) *Br* **to do a b.** *(run away) Esp* darse el piro, *Esp* pirarse, *Méx* rajarse, *RP* tomarse el buque; *(from prison)* fugarse

▸ **bunk down** *vi* acostarse, echarse a dormir

▸ **bunk off** *Br Fam* 1 *vt insep* **to b. off school** *Esp* hacer novillos, *Col* capar colegio, *Méx* irse de pinta, *RP* hacerse la rabona; **we bunked off geography** nos fumamos la clase de geografía
2 *vi Esp* hacer novillos, *Col* capar colegio, *Méx* irse de pinta, *RP* hacerse la rabona

bunker ['bʌŋkə(r)] *n* (a) *(for coal)* carbonera *f* (b) *Mil* búnker *m* (c) *Br (on golf course)* búnker *m*

bunkhouse ['bʌŋkhaʊs] *n US* barracón *m (para trabajadores)*

bunkum ['bʌŋkəm] *n Fam* palabrería *f*, tonterías *fpl*

bunk-up ['bʌŋkʌp] *n Br Fam* **to give sb a b.** aupar a alguien

bunny ['bʌnɪ] *n Fam* **b. (rabbit)** conejito *m* ▸▸ ***b. girl*** conejita *f* (de club nocturno)

Bunsen burner ['bʌnsən'bɜːnə(r)] *n* mechero *m* Bunsen

bunt [bʌnt] 1 *n (in baseball)* toque *m*
2 *vi* golpear ligeramente

bunting[1] ['bʌntɪŋ] *n* (a) *(decorations)* banderines *mpl* (b) *(fabric)* lanilla *f*

bunting[2] *n (bird)* escribano *m*

buoy [bɔɪ] *n* boya *f*

▸ **buoy up** *vt sep* (a) *(keep afloat)* mantener a flote (b) *(person, spirits)* animar, alentar (c) *(economy, prices, currency)* mantener al alza

buoyancy ['bɔɪənsɪ] *n* (a) *(in water)* flotabilidad *f* (b) *(of person)* optimismo *m* (c) *(of economy, prices, currency)* firmeza *f*

buoyant ['bɔɪənt] *adj* (a) *(in water)* flotante (b) *(person, mood)* optimista, vital (c) *(economy, prices, currency)* boyante

BUPA ['buːpə] *n* (*abbr* **British United Provident Association**) = seguro médico privado británico

buppie ['bʌpɪ] *n US Fam* yuppie *m* negro

burble ['bɜːbəl] 1 *vt (say)* farfullar
2 *vi* (a) *(stream)* borbotar (b) *(person)* mascullar; **to b. on about** parlotear sobre

burbot ['bɜːbət] *n* lota *f*

burbs [bɜːbz] *npl US Fam* barrios *mpl* del extrarradio; **to live in the b.** vivir en el extrarradio

burden ['bɜːdən] 1 *n* (a) *Formal (heavy load)* carga *f*
(b) *(heavy responsibility, strain)* carga *f*; **to be a b. (to sb)** ser una carga (para alguien); *Law* **the b. of proof** la carga de la prueba; **the b. of responsibility** el peso de la responsabilidad
(c) *(chorus, refrain)* estribillo *m*
(d) *(theme, central idea)* hilo *m* conductor, idea *f* principal; **what is the main b. of her argument?** ¿cuál es la idea principal de su razonamiento?
2 *vt* (a) *(weigh down)* cargar, sobrecargar (**with** con *or* de) (b) *(trouble)* molestar, agobiar; **I don't want to b. you with my problems** no quiero que mis problemas supongan una carga para ti; **she was burdened with guilt** el sentimiento de culpa la agobiaba; **to b. sb with taxes** ahogar a alguien con impuestos

burdensome ['bɜːdənsəm] *adj* pesado(a), molesto(a)

burdock ['bɜːdɒk] *n* bardana *f*

bureau ['bjʊərəʊ] (*pl* **bureaux** ['bjʊərəʊz]) *n* (a) *Br (desk)* secreter *m*, escritorio *m* (b) *US (chest of drawers)* cómoda *f* (c) *(office)* oficina *f*, departamento *m* ▸▸ ***b. de change*** oficina *f* de cambio (de moneda) (d) *US (government department)* departamento *m*

bureaucracy [bjʊə'rɒkrəsɪ] *n* burocracia *f*

bureaucrat ['bjʊərəkræt] *n* burócrata *mf*

bureaucratic [bjʊərə'krætɪk] *adj* burocrático(a)

bureaucratize [bjʊə'rɒkrətaɪz] *vt* burocratizar

bureaux *pl of* **bureau**

burette, *US* **buret** [bjʊ'ret] *n* bureta *f*

burg [bɜːg] *n US Fam (city, town)* ciudad *f*

burgee ['bɜːdʒiː] *n US* banderín *m*

burgeon ['bɜːdʒən] *vi* (a) *(trade, relationship)* florecer; **a burgeoning talent** un talento incipiente (b) *(plant)* brotar

burger ['bɜːgə(r)] *n Fam (hamburger)* hamburguesa *f* ▸▸ ***b. bar*** hamburguesería *f*, búrger *m*

burgher ['bɜːgə(r)] *n Hist or Hum* burgués(esa) *m,f*

burglar ['bɜːglə(r)] *n* ladrón(ona) *m,f* ▸▸ ***b. alarm*** alarma *f* antirrobo *(en casa, edificio)*

burglarize ['bɜːgləraɪz] *vt US* robar, desvalijar

burglar-proof ['bɜːgləpruːf] *adj* a prueba de ladrones

burglary ['bɜːglərɪ] *n* robo *m (en una casa o edificio)*

burgle ['bɜːgəl] *vt* robar, desvalijar

burgomaster ['bɜːgəmɑːstə(r)] *n* burgomaestre *m*

Burgundian [bɜː'gʌndɪən] 1 *n* borgoñés(esa) *m,f*, borgoñón(ona) *m,f*
2 *adj* borgoñés(esa), borgoñón(ona)

Burgundy ['bɜːgəndɪ] *n* Borgoña

burgundy ['bɜːgəndɪ] *adj* (a) *(colour)* burdeos *inv* (b) *(wine)* de Borgoña

burial ['berɪəl] *n* entierro *m*; **to give sb a decent/Christian b.** enterrar a alguien de forma digna/cristiana ▸▸ ***b. chamber*** cámara *f* mortuoria; ***b. mound*** túmulo *m*

burial-ground ['berɪəl'graʊnd] *n* cementerio *m*

Burkina-Faso [bɜː'kiːnə'fæsəʊ] *n* Burkina Faso

burlap ['bɜːlæp] *n US* arpillera *f*

burlesque [bɜː'lesk] 1 *n* (a) *(parody)* parodia *f* (b) *US Theat* espectáculo *m* de variedades, revista *f*
2 *adj* burlesco(a), paródico(a)
3 *vt* parodiar

burly ['bɜːlɪ] *adj* (a) *(strong, robust)* fornido(a), corpulento(a) (b) *US (direct)* directo(a), franco(a)

Burma ['bɜːmə] *n* Birmania

Burmese [bɜː'miːz] 1 *npl (people)* **the B.** los birmanos
2 *n* (a) *(language)* birmano *m* (b) **B. (cat)** gato(a) *m,f* birmano(a), gato(a) *m,f* sagrado(a) de Birmania
3 *adj* birmano(a)

burn[1] [bɜːn] 1 *n* (a) *(wound)* quemadura *f* (b) *(scorch mark)* quemadura *f* (c) *Fam* **to go for the b.** *(when exercising)* continuar hasta que duelan los músculos
2 *vt* (*pt & pp* **burnt** [bɜːnt] *or* **burned**) (a) *(fuel, building)* quemar; *(waste, rubbish)* quemar, incinerar; **the stove burns wood/coal** la cocina funciona con leña/carbón; **did you b. yourself?** ¿te has quemado?; **I've burnt the dinner** se me ha quemado la cena; **to b. one's hand/finger** quemarse la mano/el dedo; **to b. one's tongue/mouth** *(with hot food, drink)* escaldarse *or* quemarse la lengua/boca; **to b. a hole in sth** hacer un agujero a algo quemándolo; *Fig* **to b. a hole in sb's pocket** *(money)* quemarle a alguien en las manos; **he burnt his initials into the wood** grabó sus iniciales a fuego en la madera; **to be burnt alive** ser quemado(a) vivo(a); **to be burnt to death** morir abrasado(a); **the house was burnt to the ground** la casa quedó reducida a cenizas
(b) *US Fam (swindle)* timar, dar gato por liebre a; **they were badly burned in the stockmarket crash** la crisis de la bolsa les hizo perder mucha *Esp* pasta *or Am* plata
(c) *US Fam (anger)* poner negro(a)
(d) *Comptr (CD-ROM)* estampar
(e) IDIOMS **to have money to b.** *(rich person)* tener dinero de sobra; **she's just got paid so she's got money to b.** le acaban de pagar y tiene dinero para gastar; **to b. one's boats** *or* **one's bridges** quemar las naves; **to b. the candle at both ends** forzar la máquina, *RP* andar a mil, = intentar hacer demasiadas cosas al mismo tiempo y no dormir lo suficiente; **to b. the midnight oil** quedarse hasta muy tarde *(estudiando o trabajando)*, *Andes* trasnocharse
3 *vi* (a) *(fire, fuel, building)* arder; *(food)* quemarse; **I can smell something burning** (algo) huele a quemado; **this wood won't b.** esta madera no arderá bien; **the fire is burning low** el fuego está bajo; **the church burned to the ground** la iglesia quedó arrasada por el fuego
(b) *(light)* estar encendido(a) *or Am* prendido(a)
(c) *(with desire, anger, enthusiasm)* arder (**with** de); **my face was burning** *(with embarrassment)* me puse como un tomate; **to be burning to do sth** estar deseando hacer algo
(d) *(sting, smart)* escocer; **the wind made her face b.** el viento le cortaba la cara
(e) *(get sunburnt)* quemarse

▸ **burn down** 1 *vt sep* incendiar, quemar
2 *vi* quemarse; **the candle has burned down** la vela se ha consumido

▸ **burn off** *vt sep* (a) *(vegetation)* quemar (b) *(gas)* quemar (c) *(paint)* retirar, quitar *(aplicando una llama)* (d) *(calories)* quemar

▸ **burn out** 1 *vt sep* (a) **to b. itself out** *(fire)* consumirse, agotarse (b) **to b. oneself out** *(become exhausted)* agotarse
2 *vi* (a) *(fire)* consumirse (b) *(person)* quemarse (c) *(bulb, fuse)* fundirse (d) *Aut* **the clutch had burnt out** se había quemado el embrague

▸ **burn up** 1 *vt sep* (a) *(consume) (energy)* consumir, gastar; *(fuel)* consumir, gastar; *(calories)* quemar; **the desire for revenge was burning him up** ardía en deseos de vengarse; IDIOM **to b. up the miles**

correr como el viento (**b**) *US Fam* **to b. sb up** poner negro(a) *or* a cien a alguien
2 *vi (rocket, meteorite)* entrar en combustión

burn² *n Scot (stream)* arroyo *m*

burner ['bɜːnə(r)] *n* (**a**) *(on a stove)* quemador *m* (**b**) *Comptr* tostadora *f*, grabadora *f*; **a CD b.** una tostadora *or* grabadora de CDs

burning ['bɜːnɪŋ] *adj* (**a**) *(on fire)* en llamas; **the b. bush** *(in bible)* la zarza ardiente (**b**) *(very hot) (heat, sun)* abrasador(ora); **to be b. hot** abrasar; **I had a b. sensation in my stomach** tuve una sensación de quemazón en el estomago (**c**) *(intense) (passion)* abrasador(ora); *(ambition)* irrefrenable (**d**) *(urgent, topical)* **a b. issue** un asunto candente; **the b. question** la pregunta candente *or* clave

burnish ['bɜːnɪʃ] *vt (polish)* bruñir; **her hair was like burnished gold** su pelo relumbraba como el oro

burn-out ['bɜːnaʊt] *n* (**a**) **I had a b.** *(of engine)* se me quemó; **what caused the b.?** *(in electrical system)* ¿por qué se fundió? (**b**) *Fam (exhaustion)* agotamiento *m*

burnt [bɜːnt] **1** *adj* quemado(a); **to be b.** estar quemado(a); **a b. offering** *Rel* un holocausto; *Hum* un trozo quemado (de comida) ►► ***b. sienna*** siena *m* tostado; ***b. umber*** ocre *m* pardo
2 *pt & pp of* **burn**

burnt-out ['bɜːnt'aʊt] *adj* (**a**) *(building)* calcinado(a), carbonizado(a) (**b**) *(fuse)* fundido(a); *(engine)* gripado(a) (**c**) *Fam (person)* quemado(a); **she was b. by thirty** a los treinta ya estaba quemada

burp [bɜːp] **1** *n* eructo *m*
2 *vi* eructar
3 *vt* **to b. a baby** sacar el aire a un bebé, *RP* hacer a un bebé hacer provecho

burr [bɜː(r)] *n* (**a**) *(rough edge)* rebaba *f* (**b**) *(of plant)* erizo *m* (**c**) *(noise)* ronroneo *m* (**d**) *(in accent)* **to speak with a b.** hablar arrastrando la "r"

burrow ['bʌrəʊ] **1** *n (of animal)* madriguera *f*
2 *vt* (**a**) *(hole) (of person)* excavar; *(of animal, insect)* excavar; **he burrowed his way underneath the prison wall** salió de la prisión excavando un túnel (**b**) *(nestle)* acomodar; **the cat burrowed its head into my shoulder** el gato se acurrucó en mi hombro
3 *vi* (**a**) *(dig) (person, animal)* excavar (**b**) *(search)* rebuscar; **he burrowed around in his desk** rebuscó en su escritorio (**c**) *(nestle)* acurrucarse, hacerse un ovillo

bursa ['bɜːsə] (*pl* **bursae** ['bɜːsiː] *or* **bursas** ['bɜːsəz]) *n Anat* bolsa *f*

bursar ['bɜːsə(r)] *n Univ* tesorero(a) *m,f*

bursary ['bɜːsərɪ] *n* (**a**) *(office)* tesorería *f (de una facultad)* (**b**) *Br (scholarship)* beca *f*

bursitis [bɜː'saɪtɪs] *n Med* bursitis *f inv*

burst [bɜːst] **1** *n* (**a**) *(in pipe, tyre)* reventón *m*
(**b**) *(sudden eruption) (of applause)* salva *f*; *(of activity, enthusiasm)* arranque *m*; **a b. of energy** un arrebato de energía; **a b. of gunfire** una ráfaga de disparos; **a b. of laughter** una carcajada; **a b. of speed** un acelerón; **to work in bursts** trabajar a rachas
2 *vt* (*pt & pp* **burst**) (**a**) *(balloon, bubble, pipe, tyre)* reventar
(**b**) **to b. its banks** *(river)* desbordarse
(**c**) *Fam* **he almost b. a blood vessel** casi le da un síncope
3 *vi* (**a**) *(explode, break open)* reventar; *Fig* **to b. onto the scene** saltar a la palestra; **he b. onto the political scene in the early 1980s** irrumpió en el mundo de la política a principios de los ochenta
(**b**) *(be full)* **to be bursting at the seams** *(room, bus)* estar hasta los topes; **the town was bursting with refugees** la ciudad estaba a reventar de refugiados; *Fam* **to be fit to b.** *(full of food)* estar a punto de reventar; *Fam* **I'm bursting (for the toilet)** (estoy que) me meo
(**c**) *(enter, move suddenly)* **she b. through the door** cruzó la puerta como una exhalación; **the front door b. open** la puerta delantera se abrió súbitamente *or* de golpe; **the sun suddenly b. through the clouds** el sol salió súbitamente *or* abrió paso entre las nubes
(**d**) *(be eager, enthusiastic)* **to be bursting with pride/joy** reventar de orgullo/alegría; **to be bursting to do sth** morirse de ganas de hacer algo

► **burst in** *vi (enter)* irrumpir; **to b. in on sth/sb** interrumpir algo/a alguien

► **burst into** *vt insep* (**a**) *(enter)* irrumpir en (**b**) *(suddenly start)* **to b. into flames** inflamarse; **to b. into song** ponerse a cantar; **to b. into laughter/tears** echarse a reír/llorar

► **burst open** *vi (door, suitcase)* abrirse de golpe; *(plastic bag)* reventar

► **burst out** **1** *vi* (**a**) *(leave suddenly)* salir de estampida; **two men suddenly b. out of the room** de pronto, dos hombres abandonaron la sala precipitadamente (**b**) *(start suddenly)* **to b. out laughing** soltar una carcajada; **to b. out crying** echarse *or* romper a llorar
2 *vt insep (exclaim)* exclamar, espetar

bursting ['bɜːstɪŋ] *n* **b. point** lleno absoluto; **full to b.** lleno hasta los topes, lleno a reventar; **I'm full to b.** estoy que reviento

Burton ['bɜːtən] *n* IDIOM *Br Fam* **it's gone for a B.** *(machine, appliance)* se ha estropeado *or Esp* cascado; *(chance)* se ha ido al garete; **he's gone for a B.** estiró la pata, *Esp* la ha cascado, *CAm, Méx* lió el petate

Burundi [bə'rʊndɪ] *n* Burundi

bury ['berɪ] *vt* (**a**) *(body, treasure)* enterrar; **to be buried alive** ser enterrado(a) vivo(a); **he was buried at sea** arrojaron sus restos mortales al mar; **buried treasure** tesoro oculto *or* enterrado; **she has already buried two husbands** ha sobrevivido a dos maridos; IDIOM **to b. the hatchet** *(end quarrel)* enterrar el hacha de guerra; IDIOM **to b. one's head in the sand** esconder la cabeza bajo el ala, adoptar la política del avestruz; IDIOM **we agreed to b. our differences** acordamos hacer borrón y cuenta nueva
(**b**) *(of avalanche, mudslide)* sepultar
(**c**) *(thrust, plunge)* **he buried his hands in his pockets** metió las manos hasta el fondo de los bolsillos; **she buried the knife in his back** le clavó el cuchillo en la espalda; **the bullet buried itself in the wall** la bala se incrustó en la pared
(**d**) *(hide)* **to b. oneself in sth** *(work, book)* enfrascarse en algo; **he always has his nose buried in a book** está siempre enfrascado *or* sumido en la lectura; **to b. oneself in the country** retirarse al campo; **to b. one's face in one's hands** esconder la cara en las manos
(**e**) *Fam (defeat)* machacar

bus [bʌs] **1** *n* (**a**) *(vehicle)* autobús *m*, *Andes* buseta *f*, *Bol, Arg* colectivo *m*, *CAm, Méx* camión *m*, *CAm, Carib* guagua *f*, *Urug* ómnibus *m*, *Ven* microbusete *m*; **by b.** en autobús ►► ***b. conductor*** cobrador(ora) *m,f* de autobús; ***b. driver*** conductor(ora) *m,f* de autobús; ***b. lane*** carril *m* bus; ***b. route*** línea *f* de autobús; ***b. shelter*** marquesina *f*; ***b. station*** estación *f* de autobuses, *CAm, Méx* central *f* camionera; ***b. stop*** parada *f* de autobús
(**b**) *Br Fam (car)* cacharro *m*, tartana *f*
(**c**) *Comptr* bus *m* ►► ***b. controller*** controlador(ora) *m,f* del bus; ***b. error*** error *m* de bus; ***b. width*** anchura *f* del bus
2 *vt* (*pt & pp* **bused** *or* **bussed**) (**a**) *(transport)* transportar en autobús (**b**) *Fam (travel by bus)* **to b. it** ir en autobús (**c**) *US* **to b. tables** *(in restaurant)* recoger mesas
3 *vi* ir en autobús

► **bus in** *vt sep* llevar/traer en autobús

bus-boy ['bʌsbɔɪ] *n US* ayudante *m* de camarero

busby ['bʌzbɪ] *n* birretina *f*, = casco alto de piel

bus-girl ['bʌsgɜːl] *n US* ayudanta *f* de camarero

bush [bʊʃ] *n* (**a**) *(plant)* arbusto *m*, mata *f*; **we hid in the bushes** nos escondimos entre los matorrales *or* matojos; *Fig* **a b. of black hair** una mata de pelo moreno
(**b**) **the b.** *(in Africa, Australia)* = parte no cultivada del país, fuera de las ciudades ►► ***b. jacket*** sahariana *f*; *US* ***b. league*** = liga profesional estadounidense de béisbol de menor importancia que la liga nacional; *Fam* ***b. telegraph*** *Esp* radio *f* macuto, *Cuba, CRica, Pan* radio *f* bemba; **I heard it on the b. telegraph** me lo contó un pajarito, me enteré por radio *Esp* macuto *or Cuba, CRica, Pan* bemba
(**c**) *Br (metal sleeve)* cojinete *m*
(**d**) *Vulg (woman's pubic hair)* felpudo *m*

bush-baby ['bʊʃbeɪbɪ] *n* gálago *m*, lémur *m*

bushed [bʊʃt] *adj Fam (exhausted)* **to be b.** estar molido(a) *or* reventado(a)

bushel ['bʊʃəl] *n* = medida de áridos *(GB = 36,35 litros; US = 35,23 litros)*; *Fig* **don't hide your light under a b.** no ocultes tus buenas cualidades

bushfire ['bʊʃfaɪə(r)] *n* incendio *m* de matorral

bushing ['bʊʃɪŋ] *n US (metal sleeve)* cojinete *m*

bush-league ['bʊʃliːg] *adj US Pej* de tres al cuarto

Bushman ['bʊʃmən] *n* bosquimano(a) *m,f*

bushman ['bʊʃmən] *n Austr* = persona que vive o viaja por zonas apartadas de la civilización

bushmaster ['bʊʃmɑːstə(r)] *n (snake)* cascabel *f* muda, *Ven* cuaima *f*

bushranger ['bʊʃreɪndʒə(r)] *n* (**a**) *Austr (fugitive)* = fugitivo que vive en zonas desiertas (**b**) *US (backwoodsman)* = persona que vive apartada de la civilización

bushwhack ['bʊʃwæk] **1** *vt US Fam (ambush)* tender una emboscada a
2 *vi US, Austr* = vivir o viajar por zonas apartadas de la civilización

bushy ['bʊʃɪ] *adj* (**a**) *(area)* de matorrales (**b**) *(tree)* frondoso(a); *(beard, eyebrows, hair)* espeso(a)

busily ['bɪzɪlɪ] *adv* activamente, diligentemente; **she is b. collecting material for her next book** está recopilando laboriosamente información para su próximo libro

BUSINESS ['bɪznɪs] *n* (**a**) *(individual company)* empresa *f*, negocio *m*; **she has her own b.** tiene su propia empresa *o* propio negocio ►► ***b. administration*** administración *f* de empresas; ***b. to b.*** empresa a empresa; ***b. management*** gestión *f or* administración *f* de empresas; ***b. premises*** local *m* comercial

(**b**) *(commercial activity)* negocios *mpl*; **b. as usual** *(on sign)* seguimos abiertos durante las reformas; *Fig* **it was b. as usual as the Raiders won again** los Raiders volvieron a ganar como de costumbre; **the music b.** la industria de la música; **I'm learning b. Spanish** estoy aprendiendo español comercial; **it's bad b. to be rude to customers** no es rentable tratar mal a los clientes; **to be in b.** dedicarse a los negocios; *Fig* **now we're back in b.** ya estamos otra vez en marcha; **to be in the computing b.** *(person)* trabajar en el sector de la informática; **I'm not in the b. of making concessions** no estoy por hacer concesiones; **he's the best centre forward in the b.** es el mejor delantero centro del mundo; **to do b. (with)** hacer negocios (con); **we do a lot of b. with Germany** tenemos un gran volumen de negocios con Alemania; **it was a pleasure to do b. with you** ha sido un placer tratar con usted; **souvenir shops are doing good b. this year** las tiendas de recuerdos están teniendo un buen año; IDIOM **he's a man you can do b. with** es un hombre con el que se puede tratar; **to go into b. (with)** montar un negocio (con); **to go out of b.** quebrar; **how's b.?** ¿cómo van los negocios?; **b. is good/bad at the moment** en estos momentos el negocio va bien/mal; **it's good/bad for b.** es bueno/malo para los negocios; **to lose b. (to sb)** perder clientes *or* clientela (a manos de alguien); **to go to London on b.** ir a Londres en viaje de negocios; **I'm here on b.** estoy aquí por cuestiones de negocios; **we open for b. at nine** abrimos al público a las nueve; **to put sb out of b.** obligar a alguien a cerrar; **to talk b.** hablar de negocios; *Fam* **the b. end of a gun** la boca de un cañón/rifle/*etc.* ►► *Fin* ***b. account*** cuenta *f* comercial; ***b. appointment*** cita *f* de negocios; ***b. card*** tarjeta *f* de visita; *Av* ***b. class*** clase *f* ejecutiva; ***the b. community*** la comunidad empresarial; ***b. computing*** informática *f* de gestión; ***b. graphics*** gráficos *mpl* para presentaciones; ***b. hours*** *(of company)* horario *m* de trabajo; *(of shop)* horario *m* comercial; ***b. incubator*** vivero *m* de empresas; ***b. loan*** crédito *m* comercial; ***b. lunch*** comida *f* de trabajo; ***b. park*** parque *m* empresarial; ***b. plan*** plan *m* económico; ***b. process reengineering*** reingeniería *f* de procesos; ***b. school*** escuela *f* de comercio; ***b. studies*** (ciencias *fpl*) empresariales *fpl*; ***b. suit*** traje *m* de calle; ***b. trip*** viaje *m* de negocios

(**c**) *(matters to be dealt with)* **we have a lot of b. to get through in this meeting** tenemos que tratar muchos asuntos en esta reunión; **to get down to b.** ir a lo esencial, ir a lo importante; IDIOM **to mean b.** ir en serio; **what's your b. here?** ¿qué te trae por aquí?; *Fam* **he was working like nobody's b.** estaba trabajando de lo lindo; *Br very Fam* **to do the b.** *(have sex)* echar un polvete; *Br Fam* **it's the b.!** *(excellent)* ¡es fantástico *or* genial!; **any other b.** *(on agenda)* ruegos y preguntas

(**d**) *(affair, matter)* asunto *m*; **it's a sad** *or* **sorry b.** es un asunto lamentable *or* triste; **I'm sick of the whole b.** estoy harto de todo este asunto; **what a b.!** ¡menudo lío!; **what's all that b. about you not getting paid?** ¿qué es eso de que no te han pagado?

(**e**) *(proper concern, responsibility)* asunto *m*; **that's your/my b.** es asunto tuyo/mío; **it's none of your b.** no es asunto tuyo; **it's not my b. to...** no me corresponde a mí...; **I was just going about my b.** yo simplemente iba a lo mío; **you had no b. telling her that** no tenías ningún derecho a decírselo; **to make it one's b. to do sth** proponerse algo; **mind your own b.** métete en tus asuntos; **I was sitting there minding my own b....** estaba sentado ocupado en mis cosas...

(**f**) *Fam Hum (excrement)* **the dog did its b.** el perro hizo sus necesidades

businesslike ['bɪznɪslaɪk] *adj (manner)* eficiente; *(meeting, conversation)* formal

businessman ['bɪznɪsmæn] *n (executive, manager)* hombre *m* de negocios, ejecutivo *m*; *(owner of business)* empresario *m*; **to be a good b.** tener cabeza para los negocios

businesswoman ['bɪznɪswʊmən] *n (executive, manager)* mujer *f* de negocios, ejecutiva *f*; *(owner of business)* empresaria *f*; **to be a good b.** tener cabeza para los negocios

busing *US* = **bussing**

busk [bʌsk] *vi Br (street musician)* actuar en la calle

busker ['bʌskə(r)] *n Br (street musician)* músico(a) *m,f* ambulante

busload ['bʌsləʊd] *n* **a b. of workers** un autobús repleto de trabajadores; **the tourists arrived by the b.** *or* **in busloads** los turistas iban llegando por tandas en autobús

busman ['bʌsmən] *n* IDIOM *Fam* **a b.'s holiday** = tiempo libre que se ocupa con una actividad similar a la del trabajo habitual

bus(s)ing ['bʌsɪŋ] *n US* = transporte de estudiantes a colegios alejados para favorecer el equilibrio racial

bust[1] [bʌst] *n* (**a**) *(of woman)* busto *m*; **b. measurement** medida de busto (**b**) *(statue)* busto *m*

bust[2] *Fam* **1** *n* (**a**) *(police raid)* redada *f*; **drug(s) b.** operación *or* redada antidroga (**b**) *US (failure)* quiebra *f*

2 *adj* (**a**) *(broken)* **to be b.** estar estropeado(a) *or Esp* escacharrado(a) (**b**) *(having no money)* arruinado(a); **to go b.** *(bankrupt)* quebrar; **victory/the championship or b.!** ¡la victoria/el campeonato o nada! (**c**) *(in pontoon)* **(I'm) b.** me pasé

3 *vt* (*pt & pp* **bust** *or* **busted**) (**a**) *(break)* escacharrar; *Fig* **to b. a gut** *or* **a blood vessel (doing sth)** dejarse la piel (haciendo algo), *RP* romperse el alma (haciendo algo); *US very Fam* **to b. one's ass (doing sth)** dejarse las pelotas *or* la piel (haciendo algo)

(**b**) *(arrest)* trincar (**for** por)

(**c**) *(raid)* hacer una redada en

(**d**) *US Mil (demote)* degradar; **he got busted to sergeant** lo degradaron a sargento

(**e**) *US (horse)* domar

► **bust out** *vi Fam (escape)* fugarse, largarse

► **bust up** *Fam* **1** *vt sep* (**a**) *(disrupt) (event)* reventar; *(friendship, relationship)* romper (**b**) *(damage, destroy) (bar, flat)* destrozar, arrasar

2 *vi* (**a**) *(boyfriend, girlfriend)* cortar, romper; **he has b. up with his girlfriend** ha cortado con su novia (**b**) *US (laugh)* romper a reír

bustard ['bʌstəd] *n* **(great) b.** avutarda *f* ►► ***houbara b.*** hubara *f*

busted ['bʌstɪd] *adj Fam (arm, leg)* roto(a); *(appliance)* estropeado(a), *Esp* escacharrado(a)

buster ['bʌstə(r)] *n US Fam (term of address) Esp* tío *m*, *Esp* tronco *m*, *Méx* cuate *m*, *RP* boludo *m*; **who are you looking at, b.?** ¿tú qué miras, *Esp* tronco *or Méx* cuate *or RP* boludo?

bustier ['buːstiːeɪ] *n (garment)* bustier *m*

bustle ['bʌsəl] **1** *n* (**a**) *(activity)* bullicio *m*, trajín *m* (**b**) *(on dress)* polisón *m*

2 *vi* (**a**) *(move busily)* **to b. (about** *or* **around)** trajinar; **he bustled about** *or* **around (in) the kitchen** iba de un lado para otro en la cocina (**b**) *(be excited)* **to b. with sth** bullir de algo, ser un hervidero de algo

bustling ['bʌsəlɪŋ] *adj (city, street, shop)* bullicioso(a)

bust-up ['bʌstʌp] *n Fam* (**a**) *Br (quarrel)* bronca *f*; **to have a b.** tener una bronca (**b**) *(of relationship)* ruptura *f*

busty ['bʌstɪ] *adj Fam* pechugona, tetona

busy ['bɪzɪ] **1** *adj* (**a**) *(person)* ocupado(a); **to be b.** *(person)* estar ocupado(a); **he was too b. to notice** estaba demasiado atareado como para darse cuenta; **I'm afraid I'm b. tomorrow** me temo que tengo compromisos que atender mañana; *Fam* **to be a b. bee** estar *or* andar siempre liado(a) *or* haciendo algo; **to be b. doing sth** estar haciendo algo; **to keep sb b.** dar que hacer a alguien; **he likes to keep b.** le gusta tener algo que hacer; **make sure they're kept b.** asegúrate de que no se quedan sin hacer nada

(**b**) *(port, street)* transitado(a), de mucho tránsito; *(office)* ajetreado(a); *(shop)* concurrido(a); *(day, week)* ajetreado(a); *(schedule)* apretado(a); **to be b.** *(day, week)* ser ajetreado(a); **I've had a b. day** he tenido un día muy ajetreado; **the train was very b.** el tren iba muy lleno; **a b. road** una carretera con mucho tráfico; **this is our busiest period** *(business, shop)* éste es el periodo en que tenemos más movimiento *or* ajetreo

(**c**) *US (telephone line)* ocupado(a); **the line is b.** (el teléfono) da ocupado, *Esp* (el teléfono) está comunicando

(**d**) *(overelaborate)* recargado(a), barroco(a)

(**e**) *Br* ***b. Lizzie*** alegría *f* de la casa

2 *vt* **to b. oneself with sth** entretenerse con algo

busybody ['bɪzɪbɒdɪ] *n Fam* entrometido(a) *m,f*, metomentodo *mf*

BUT [bʌt] **1** *conj* (**a**) *(in general)* pero; **small b. strong** pequeño, pero fuerte; **I told her to do it b. she refused** le dije que lo hiciera, pero se negó; **I had no choice b. to tell him** no tuve otra opción que decírselo; **it's all right to be angry, b. to resort to violence...!** ¡está bien *esp Esp* enfadarse *or esp Am* enojarse, pero recurrir a la violencia...!; **he defended her, b. then he is her father** la defendió, pero claro, es su padre; **you could go by train, b. then it is more expensive** podrías ir en tren, aunque claro, es más caro

(**b**) *(direct contrast)* sino; **not once b. twice** no una vez sino dos; **we**

shouldn't tell them, b. keep it secret no se lo deberíamos decir, sino mantenerlo en secreto

(c) *(introducing statement)* **...b. let us turn to the subject of human rights** ...pero pasemos al tema de los derechos humanos; **b. I tell you I saw it!** ¡te aseguro que lo vi!; **b. that's fantastic!** ¡qué genial *or* estupendo!

2 *prep (except)* salvo, excepto; **all b. one of them passed** aprobaron todos menos uno; **any day b. tomorrow** cualquier día salvo mañana; **she is anything b. stupid** es todo menos tonta; **it's nothing b. prejudice** no son más que prejuicios; **you've done nothing b. complain** no has hecho más que quejarte; **what could I do b. invite him?** ¿qué otra cosa podía hacer más que invitarlo?; **you cannot b. wonder at her self-confidence** su confianza en sí misma es increíble; **I couldn't help b. notice** no pude evitar darme cuenta; **who b. John could solve this problem?** ¿quién sino John podría resolver este problema?; **b. for you/him** *(had it not been for)* de no ser por ti/él, si no es por ti/él; **the room was empty b. for a table and a chair** no había más que una mesa y una silla en la habitación; **the last b. one** el/la penúltimo(a); **the next b. one** el próximo no, el otro

3 *adv* (a) *Formal (only)* **he is b. a child** no es más que un niño; **had I b. known!** ¡si lo hubiera sabido!; **this is b. one of the possible explanations** ésta no es sino una de las posibles explicaciones; **he has b. recently lost his job** acaba de perder su trabajo; **one can b. try** por lo menos lo podemos intentar

(b) *(for emphasis)* **she wrote to me every day, b. every single day** me escribió todos los días, sin faltar uno solo

4 *n* **no buts!** ¡no hay peros que valgan!

---

butane ['bju:teɪn] *n* butano *m*; **b. (gas)** gas *m* butano

butch [bʊtʃ] 1 *n Fam (masculine lesbian)* marimacho *m*

2 *adj Fam* (a) *(woman)* marimacho; **she looks rather b.** tiene pinta de marimacho (b) *(man)* muy macho *or* machote

butcher ['bʊtʃə(r)] 1 *n* (a) *(meat salesman)* carnicero(a) *m,f*; **the b.'s (shop)** la carnicería ►► ***b.'s block*** tajo *m* (b) *(murderer)* carnicero(a) *m,f* (c) IDIOM *Br Fam* **to have a b.'s (at sth/sb)** echar un vistazo *or* una ojeada (a algo/alguien) (d) ***b. bird*** *(shrike)* alcaudón *m*

2 *vt* (a) *(animal)* matar, sacrificar (b) *(massacre)* masacrar (c) *(ruin)* hacer una escabechina con; **the censors butchered the movie** los censores masacraron la película

butchery ['bʊtʃərɪ] *n* carnicería *f*; *Fig* carnicería *f*, matanza *f*

butler ['bʌtlə(r)] *n* mayordomo *m*

butt [bʌt] 1 *n* (a) *(blow with head) (by animal)* embestida *f*; *(by person)* testarazo *m*, cabezazo *m*

(b) *(end) (of rifle)* culata *f*; *(of cigarette)* colilla *f*

(c) *US Fam (cigarette)* pito *m*

(d) *US Fam (buttocks)* trasero *m*; **don't just sit around on your b. all day!** ¡no te pases el día entero apoltronado!; **move your b.!** ¡mueve el culo!

(e) *(in archery, shooting) (target)* blanco *m*; *(mound behind target)* = montículo protector detrás del blanco

(f) *(for grouse shooting)* = montículo tras el que se ocultan los cazadores

(g) *(person)* **to be the b. of a joke** ser el blanco de una broma

(h) *(barrel)* tonel *m*, cuba *f*

(i) *(in carpentry)* ***b. joint*** junta *f*

2 *vt (hit with head) (of animal)* embestir; *(of person)* dar *or* arrear un cabezazo a

► **butt in** *vi (interrupt)* inmiscuirse, entrometerse

► **butt out** *vi US Fam* dejar de entrometerse; **b. out!** ¡no te metas donde no te llaman!

butte [bju:t] *n US* otero *m*, cerro *m*

butter ['bʌtə(r)] 1 *n* mantequilla *f*, *RP* manteca *f*; IDIOM **she looks as if b. wouldn't melt in her mouth** parece incapaz de matar una mosca, *Esp* parece como si no hubiera roto un plato en su vida ►► ***b. bean*** = tipo de judía blanca; ***b. cream*** = crema para pasteles hecha de azúcar glas y mantequilla; ***b. dish*** mantequera *f*; ***b. icing*** = crema para pasteles hecha de azúcar glas y mantequilla; ***b. knife*** cuchillo *m* de mantequilla *or RP* manteca

2 *vt* untar de mantequilla *or RP* manteca

► **butter up** *vt sep Fam (flatter)* hacer la rosca a

butterball ['bʌtəbɔ:l] *n US Fam* gordinflón(ona) *m,f*

buttercup ['bʌtəkʌp] *n* ranúnculo *m*, botón *m* de oro

butterfat ['bʌtəfæt] *n* grasa *f* de la leche

butter-fingered ['bʌtəfɪŋgəd] *adj Fam* torpe, manazas *inv*

butterfingers ['bʌtəfɪŋgəz] *n Fam (clumsy person)* torpe *mf*, manazas *mf inv*

butterfly ['bʌtəflaɪ] *n* (a) *(insect)* mariposa *f* ►► ***b. effect*** efecto *m* mariposa; *Br* ***b. kiss*** beso *m* de mariposa *(caricia con las pestañas)*; ***b. net*** cazamariposas *m inv*; ***b. nut*** palomilla *f*, tuerca *f* de mariposa *f*; ***B. Pillow®*** mariposa *f* cervical; ***b. valve*** válvula *f* de mariposa

(b) *(in swimming)* **b. (stroke)** (estilo *m*) mariposa *f*; **to do *or* swim (the) b.** nadar a mariposa

(c) IDIOM **I had butterflies (in my stomach)** me temblaban las rodillas; **she gets butterflies (in her stomach) before a performance** le entra un hormigueo (en el estómago) antes de cada actuación

buttermilk ['bʌtəmɪlk] *n* (a) *(by-product from butter making)* suero *m* (de leche) (b) *US (curdled milk)* leche *f* cuajada *or* batida *(para beber)*

butterscotch ['bʌtəskɒtʃ] *n* = dulce de mantequilla y azúcar

buttery ['bʌtərɪ] 1 *n Br (in Oxford or Cambridge college)* cantina *f*, cafetería *f*

2 *adj* mantecoso(a); **a b. taste** un sabor a mantequilla

butthead ['bʌthed] *n US Fam* zoquete *mf*, zopenco(a) *m,f*

buttinski [bʌ'tɪnskɪ] *n US Fam* metomentodo *mf*

buttock ['bʌtək] *n* nalga *f*

button ['bʌtən] 1 *n* (a) *(on clothes)* botón *m* ►► ***b. lift*** *(in skiing)* telesquí *m*; ***b. mushroom*** champiñón *m* pequeño (b) *(on machine)* botón *m*; *Comptr (on mouse, screen)* botón *m* (c) *US (badge)* chapa *f* (d) **(little) b. quail** torillo *m* (e) IDIOMS *Fam* **on the b.** *(punctual)* en punto, a la hora; **to be right on the b.** *(accurate)* dar en el clavo

2 *vt* (a) *(shirt)* abotonar; **to b. one's shirt** abotonarse la camisa (b) *Fam* **b. it *or* your lip *or* your mouth!** ¡cierra el pico!

3 *vi* cerrarse, abrocharse; **the blouse buttons at the back** la blusa se abrocha en la espalda *or* por detrás

► **button up** *vt sep (shirt, dress)* abotonar; **to b. up one's shirt** abotonarse la camisa

button-down ['bʌtəndaʊn] *adj* (a) *(collar)* abrochado(a); *(shirt)* de cuello abrochado (b) *US (conventional)* convencional

buttonhole ['bʌtənhəʊl] 1 *n* (a) *(in clothing)* ojal *m* ►► ***b. stitch*** *(sewing)* puntada *f* de refuerzo, punto *m* de ojal (b) *Br (flower)* ojal *m*

2 *vt (detain)* **to b. sb** agarrar a alguien para hablar

button-nosed ['bʌtənnəʊzd] *adj* de nariz pequeña

button-through ['bʌtənθru:] *adj* abotonado(a) de arriba a abajo

buttress ['bʌtrɪs] 1 *n* (a) *Archit* contrafuerte *m* (b) *(support)* apoyo *m*, pilar *m*

2 *vt* (a) *Archit* reforzar con contrafuertes (b) *(support) (argument, system)* respaldar

butty ['bʌtɪ] *n Br Fam Esp* bocadillo *m*, *Esp* bocata *m*, *Am* sándwich *m*

buxom ['bʌksəm] *adj* (a) *(full-bosomed)* de amplios senos (b) *(plump)* de carnes generosas

buy [baɪ] 1 *n* compra *f*; **a good/bad b.** una buena/mala compra

2 *vt (pt & pp* **bought** [bɔ:t]) (a) *(purchase)* comprar; **to b. sth new/second-hand/on credit** adquirir algo nuevo/de segunda mano/a crédito *or* plazos; **to b. sb sth, to b. sth for sb** comprar algo a *or* para alguien; **to b. sth from** *or Fam* **off sb** comprarle algo a alguien; **she bought herself a pair of skis** se compró un par de esquís; **they bought it for £100** lo compraron por 100 libras; **$20 won't b. you very much these days** 20 dólares no te dan para mucho hoy en día; **let me b. you a drink** te invito a tomar algo

(b) *(gain, obtain)* **money can't b. you love/happiness** el dinero no atrae el amor/no da la felicidad

(c) *(bribe)* comprar, sobornar; **he can't be bought** no se deja comprar *or* sobornar

(d) *Fam (believe)* tragarse; **she won't b. that** *(won't believe)* no se lo tragará; **OK, I'll b. that!** bueno, me lo creo

(e) IDIOMS **to b. time** ganar tiempo; *Fam* **he bought it** *or US* **the farm** *(has died)* estiró la pata, *Esp* la ha palmado

3 *vi* comprar (**from** a); **b. now, pay later** compre ahora y pague después

► **buy back** *vt sep* recomprar (**from** a); **can I b. my bicycle back from you?** ¿me vendes la bici que me compraste?

► **buy in** *vt sep (supplies)* aprovisionarse de

► **buy into** *vt insep (company, scheme)* adquirir una parte *or* acciones de; *(theory, idea)* identificarse con

► **buy off** *vt sep Fam (opponent)* comprar

► **buy out** *vt sep* (a) *Com* comprar la parte de; **he was bought out for $50,000** le compraron su parte por 50.000 dólares (b) *Mil* **to b. oneself out** pagar para salir del ejército

► **buy up** *vt sep* acaparar, comprar la totalidad de

buy-back ['baɪbæk] *n Com* recompra *f*

buyer ['baɪə(r)] *n* (a) *(customer)* comprador(ora) *m,f*; **a b.'s market** un mercado favorable al comprador (b) *(for store, company)* representante *mf* del departamento de compras

buy-out ['baɪaʊt] *n Com* adquisición *f* (de todas las acciones)

buzz [bʌz] 1 *n* (a) *(noise) (of conversation)* rumor *m*; *(of machine, insects)* zumbido *m*; **the announcement caused a b. of excitement** el anuncio levantó un cuchicheo *or* murmullo de emoción ►► *Fam Hist* ***b. bomb*** bomba *f* volante *(en la Segunda Guerra Mundial)*; *US* ***b. saw*** sierra *f* circular; *Fam* ***b. word*** palabra *f* de moda

(b) *Fam (phone call)* **to give sb a b.** dar a alguien un toque *or* un telefonazo, *Méx* echar un fonazo a alguien

(c) *Fam (gossip)* **what's the b.?** ¿qué se comenta?

(d) *Fam (thrill)* **to give sb a b.** volver loco(a) *or* dar mucho gusto a alguien; **to get a b. out of sth** volverse loco(a) con algo; *US* **he got a b. on** le dio un subidón *or RP* acelere

2 *vt Fam* (a) *(on intercom)* llamar por el portero electrónico; *(on pager)* llamar a través del *Esp* busca *or Méx* localizador *or RP* radiomensaje

(b) *US (telephone)* dar un telefonazo *or Méx* echar un fonazo a

(c) *(in aircraft) (building, town)* sobrevolar casi rozando; *(other aircraft)* volar muy cerca de *(para darle un aviso)*

3 *vi* (a) *(make noise)* zumbar; **my ears were buzzing** me zumbaban los oídos

(b) *(with buzzer)* **he buzzed for his secretary** llamó a su secretaria por el interfono

(c) *Fam (be lively)* **the whole town was buzzing with excitement** toda la ciudad hervía de animación; **my head was buzzing with ideas** las ideas me bullían en la cabeza

(d) *Fam US (leave)* largarse, pirarse

► **buzz off** *vi Br Fam* largarse, *Esp, RP* pirarse; **b. off!** ¡lárgate!, ¡fuera!

buzzard ['bʌzəd] *n* (a) *(hawk)* ratonero *m* común (b) *US (vulture)* buitre *m*

buzzer ['bʌzə(r)] *n (electric bell)* timbre *m*; **the b. downstairs is broken** se ha estropeado el portero electrónico

buzzing ['bʌzɪŋ] *n* zumbido *m*

Bvd *US* (*abbr* **Boulevard**) bulevar *m*

b & w, b/w *Phot & Cin* (*abbr* **black and white**) b/n, blanco y negro

BY [baɪ] 1 *prep* (a) *(expressing agent)* por; **he was arrested by the police** fue detenido por la policía; **made by hand** hecho a mano; **the song was written by Lennon** la canción fue escrita por Lennon, Lennon escribió la canción; **a play by Shakespeare** una obra de Shakespeare

(b) *(close to)* junto a; **by the fire** junto al fuego; **by the side of the road** al borde de la carretera; **the dog sat by her side** el perro se sentó a su lado

(c) *(via)* por; **enter by the back door** entra por la puerta de atrás; **to go by the same route** ir por la misma ruta; **by land/sea** por tierra/mar

(d) *(with manner, means)* **by rail** en tren; **by car/plane** en coche/avión; **to make a reservation by phone** reservar algo por teléfono; **to send sth by courier** enviar algo por mensajero; **to pay by credit card** pagar con tarjeta de crédito; **by moonlight** a la luz de la luna; **what do you mean by that?** ¿qué quieres decir con eso?; **to call sb by their first name** llamar a alguien por su nombre (de pila); **to take sb by the hand/arm** tomar *or Esp* coger a alguien de la mano/del brazo; **he took the sword by the hilt** agarró la espada por la empuñadura; **to know sb by sight** conocer a alguien de vista; **he had two children by his first wife** tuvo dos hijos de su primera esposa; **to earn one's living by teaching** ganarse la vida enseñando; **the machine is activated by pressing this button** la máquina se enciende apretando este botón; **he achieved fame by becoming the first man to set foot on the Moon** se hizo famoso por ser el primer hombre en la Luna

(e) *(past)* **he walked right by me without stopping** pasó por mi lado sin detenerse; **we drove by the school on the way here** pasamos delante del colegio camino de aquí

(f) *(at or before)* **he should be here by now** debería estar ya aquí; **by then it was too late** para entonces ya era demasiado tarde; **by tomorrow** para mañana; **by 1995 they were all dead** en 1995 ya estaban todos muertos; **by the time I arrived, she had already gone** para cuando llegué, ya se había marchado

(g) *(during)* **by day** de día; **by night** de noche, por la noche

(h) *(with measurements, quantities, numbers)* **to divide by three** dividir entre tres; **to multiply by three** multiplicar por tres; **to sell sth by weight/the kilo** vender algo al peso/por kilos; **3 metres by 2** 3 por 2 metros, 3 metros por 2; **to increase by 50 percent** aumentar en un 50 por ciento; **the price has gone up by $5** el precio ha subido 5 dólares; **you were exceeding the speed limit by 30 km/h** ibas 30 km/h por encima del límite de velocidad; **we are paid by the hour** nos pagan por horas; **they came by the thousand** vinieron a miles

(i) *(according to)* **I'm Swedish by birth** soy sueco de nacimiento; **by law** por ley; **that's all right by me** a mí me parece bien; **she's a teacher by profession** es profesora; **to go by appearances...** a juzgar por las apariencias...; **I will not live by their standards** me niego a vivir siguiendo sus criterios

(j) *(with reflexive pronouns) see* **myself, himself, yourself** *etc*

(k) *(as a result of)* **by chance/mistake** por casualidad/error; **I was surprised by what she said** me sorprendió lo que dijo

(l) *(indicating process)* **day by day** día a día; **little by little** poco a poco; **one by one** uno(a) a uno(a); **step by step** paso a paso; **two by two** de dos en dos

(m) **come by my house some time** *(visit)* pásate por mi casa algún día de éstos

2 *adv* (a) **by and by** *(gradually)* poco a poco; *(soon)* dentro de poco; **by and large** en general, por lo general; **by the way..., by the by** *or* **bye...** a propósito...

(b) *(past)* **to pass by** *(person)* pasar; *(time)* transcurrir, pasar; **to drive by** pasar sin detenerse *(en coche)*

(c) **you must come by some time** *(visit)* tienes que visitarnos un día de éstos

(d) *(in reserve)* **I've been putting some money by for Christmas** he apartado algo de dinero para las Navidades

bye [baɪ] 1 *n Sport* **to get a b.** *(into next round)* = pasar a la fase siguiente en una competición sin necesidad de enfrentarse a un contrincante

2 *exclam Fam* ¡adiós!, ¡hasta luego!, *Am* ¡bye!, *Am* ¡chau!

bye-bye ['baɪ'baɪ] *exclam Fam* ¡adiós!, ¡hasta luego!, *Am* ¡bye!, *Am* ¡chau!

bye-byes ['baɪ'baɪz] *n Fam* **go (to) b. now** a la camita ahora mismo

by(e)-law ['baɪlɔː] *n* (a) *Br (made by local government)* ordenanza *f* municipal (b) *(made by company, association)* estatutos *mpl*

by-election ['baɪɪlekʃən] *n Br Pol* = elección parcial en una sola circunscripción para cubrir un escaño dejado vacante

Byelorussia = **Belarus**

Byelorussian = **Belorussian**

bygone ['baɪgɒn] 1 *n* IDIOM **let bygones be bygones** lo pasado, pasado está, *Am* lo pasado, pisado

2 *adj* pasado(a), pretérito(a); **in b. days** en otros tiempos

by-law = **bye-law**

byline ['baɪlaɪn] *n Journ* pie *m* de autor

BYOB (*abbr* **bring your own bottle**) = sigla que indica bien que se lleven bebidas, en el caso de una fiesta, o bien que se pueden consumir bebidas alcohólicas traídas de fuera, en el caso de un restaurante

bypass ['baɪpɑːs] 1 *n* (a) *(road)* (carretera *f* de) circunvalación *f* (b) *(heart operation)* bypass *m*

2 *vt* (a) *(of road)* circunvalar; *(of traveller)* bordear, no atravesar (b) *(circumvent) (difficulty)* evitar, esquivar; *(superior)* rehuir; **I bypassed the personnel officer and spoke directly to the boss** me salté al responsable de personal y me dirigí directamente al director

by-play ['baɪpleɪ] *n Theat* acción *f* secundaria

by-product ['baɪprɒdʌkt] *n* (a) *(of industrial process)* subproducto *m* (b) *(consequence)* consecuencia *f*

byre ['baɪə(r)] *n Br* establo *m*

byroad ['baɪrəʊd] *n* carretera *f* secundaria

bystander ['baɪstændə(r)] *n* espectador(ora) *m,f*, transeúnte *mf*

byte [baɪt] *n Comptr* byte *m*

byway ['baɪweɪ] *n (road)* carretera *f* secundaria

byword ['baɪwɜːd] *n* **to be a b. for...** ser sinónimo de...

by-your-leave ['baɪjɔː'liːv] *n* IDIOM **without so much as a b.** sin (ni) siquiera pedir permiso

Byzantine [bɪ'zæntaɪn, 'bɪzəntiːn] 1 *n Hist* bizantino(a) *m,f*

2 *adj* (a) *Hist* bizantino(a) (b) *(intricate, complex)* bizantino(a)

Byzantium [bɪ'zæntɪəm] *n* Bizancio

C, c

C, c [siː] *n (letter)* C

C [siː] *n* **(a)** *Mus* do *m* **(b)** *Sch (grade)* aprobado *m*; **to get a C.** *(in exam, essay)* sacar un aprobado **(c)** (*abbr* **Celsius** *or* **centigrade**) C **(d)** (*abbr* **century**) s.; **C. 16** s. XVI **(e)** *Fam* **the big C.** el cáncer **(f)** *(Roman numeral)* C **(g)** *US Fam* **C. note** billete de cien dólares

c (*abbr* **cent(s)**) *(of dollar)* centavo *m*; *(of euro)* céntimo *m*

c, ca (*abbr* **circa**) *(with dates)* h., hacia; *(with figures, amounts)* aprox.; **c. 820 AD** hacia el año 820 d.C.

C++ [ˈsiːplʌsˈplʌs] *n Comptr* C++ *m*

CA **(a)** (*abbr* **California**) California **(b)** *Br* (*abbr* **chartered accountant**) censor(ora) *m,f* jurado(a) de cuentas, contador(ora) *m,f* público(a) **(c)** (*abbr* **Consumers' Association**) asociación *f* de consumidores **(d)** (*abbr* **Central America**) América Central, Centroamérica

C/A, c/a *Fin* (*abbr Br* **current** *or* **cheque** *or US* **checking account**) c/c

CAA [siːeɪˈeɪ] *n* (*abbr* **Civil Aviation Authority**) = organismo regulador de la aviación civil en Gran Bretaña

CAB [siːeɪˈbiː] *n Br* (*abbr* **Citizen's Advice Bureau**) = oficina de asesoría para los ciudadanos, *Esp* ≃ OCU *f*

cab [kæb] *n* **(a)** *(taxi)* taxi *m* ▸▸ ***c. driver*** taxista *mf*; ***c. rank*** parada *f* de taxis **(b)** *(of lorry, train, crane)* cabina *f* **(c)** *(horse-drawn)* coche *m* de caballos

cabal [kəˈbɑːl] *n Pej* camarilla *f*

cabaret [ˈkæbəreɪ] *n* **(a)** *(show)* cabaré *m*, cabaret *m* ▸▸ ***c. artist*** *(female)* cabaretera *f*; *(male or female)* artista *mf* de variedades **(b)** *(nightclub)* cabaré *m*, cabaret *m*

cabbage [ˈkæbɪdʒ] *n* **(a)** *(vegetable)* col *f*, repollo *m* ▸▸ ***c. lettuce*** lechuga *f* repollada; ***c. patch*** huerto *m* de coles; ***c. rose*** rosa *f* de cien hojas *or* de Castilla; ***c. white*** *(butterfly)* mariposa *f* de la col **(b)** *Br Fam (brain-damaged person)* vegetal *m* **(c)** *Br Fam (dull person)* pasmarote *m*, pasmado(a) *m,f*, *Méx* pendejo(a) *m,f*, *RP* papanatas *mf inv* **(d)** *US Fam (money)* *Esp* pasta *f*, *Am* plata *f*

cabbala [kəˈbɑːlə] *n* cábala *f*

cabbalist [ˈkæbəlɪst] *n* cabalista *mf*

cabbalistic [kæbəˈlɪstɪk] *adj* cabalístico(a)

cabbie, cabby [ˈkæbɪ] *n Fam* taxista *mf*, *RP* tachero(a) *m,f*

caber [ˈkeɪbə(r)] *n (in Scotland)* tronco *m*; **tossing the c.** = prueba típica de los "Highland Games" consistente en llevar erguido un largo tronco y luego lanzarlo

cabin [ˈkæbɪn] *n* **(a)** *(hut)* cabaña *f* **(b)** *(of ship)* camarote *m* ▸▸ ***c. boy*** grumete *m*; ***c. class*** clase *f* cabina; ***c. cruiser*** yate *m* (de motor) **(c)** *(of plane)* cabina *f* ▸▸ ***c. attendant*** auxiliar *mf* de vuelo; ***c. staff*** personal *m* de cabina, tripulación *f* de cabina de pasajeros **(d)** *Br (signal box)* sala *f* de agujas, puesto *m* de señales **(e)** *Br (of lorry, train)* cabina *f*

cabinet [ˈkæbɪnɪt] *n* **(a)** *(piece of furniture)* armario *m*; *(with glass front)* vitrina *f* **(b)** *Pol* gabinete *m*; **to form a c.** formar un gabinete; **they took the decision in c.** tomaron la decisión en un consejo de ministros ▸▸ ***c. crisis*** crisis *f* ministerial; ***c. meeting*** (reunión *f* del) consejo *m* de ministros; ***c. minister*** ministro(a) *m,f* (con cartera); ***c. reshuffle*** remodelación *f* del gabinete

cabinet-maker [ˈkæbɪnɪtmeɪkə(r)] *n* ebanista *mf*; **c.'s (shop)** ebanistería *f*

cabinet-making [ˈkæbɪnɪtmeɪkɪŋ] *n* ebanistería *f*

cable [ˈkeɪbəl] **1** *n* **(a)** *(electrical)* cable *m*
(b) *(rope, wire)* cable *m* ▸▸ ***c. car*** teleférico *m*, funicular *m (por aire)*; ***c. railway*** funicular *m*; ***c. release*** *(for camera)* disparador *m* de cable
(c) *(fibre-optic)* cable *m*; *TV* **c. (television)** televisión *f* por cable, cablevisión *f*; **only available on c.** disponible sólo a través de televisión por cable ▸▸ ***c. company*** operador(ora) *m,f* de cable, cableoperador(ora) *m,f*; ***c. distribution*** distribución *f* por cable; *Comptr* ***c. modem*** módem *m* cable; ***c. operator*** operador(ora) *m,f* de cable, cableoperador(ora) *m,f*
(d) *(in knitting)* ***c. stitch*** punto *m* de ochos *or* de trenzas
(e) *(telegram)* cable(grama) *m* ▸▸ ***c. transfer*** *(of money)* giro *m or* transferencia *f* telegráfica
(f) *Naut (measurement)* cable *m (120 brazas en Estados Unidos y 100 en el Reino Unido)*
2 *vt (message)* cablegrafiar; **I cabled them to say I needed more money** les mandé un cable *or* les cablegrafié para decirles que necesitaba más dinero

cablegram [ˈkeɪbəlgræm] *n* cable *m*, cablegrama *m*

cableway [ˈkeɪbəlweɪ] *n* transportador *m* aéreo

cabling [ˈkeɪbəlɪŋ] *n* cables *mpl*

caboodle [kəˈbuːdəl] *n* IDIOM *Fam* **the whole (kit and) c.** todo, *Esp* toda la pesca

caboose [kəˈbuːs] *n* **(a)** *US (on train)* furgón *m* de cola **(b)** *Naut* bodega *f* **(c)** *US Fam (buttocks)* trasero *m*

cabrilla [kəˈbrɪlə] *n* cabrilla *f*

cabriolet [ˈkæbrɪəleɪ] *n Aut* cabriolé *m*, descapotable *m*, *Am* convertible *m*

cacao [kəˈkɑːəʊ] *n* **(a)** *(plant)* cacao *m* **(b)** *(bean)* (semilla *f* de) cacao *m*

cache [kæʃ] **1** *n* **(a)** *(of drugs, arms)* alijo *m* **(b)** *Comptr* caché *f* ▸▸ ***c. card*** tarjeta *f* caché; ***c. memory*** memoria *f* caché; ***c. RAM*** RAM *f* caché
2 *vt* **(a)** *(hide)* esconder **(b)** *Comptr (data)* meter en la memoria caché

cachet [ˈkæʃeɪ] *n (distinction)* caché *m*, cachet *m*, distinción *f*

cack [kæk] *Br Fam* **1** *n* **(a)** *(excrement)* caca *f* **(b)** *(nonsense)* bobadas *fpl*, tonterías *fpl*, *Esp* chorradas *fpl*; **don't talk c.!** ¡no digas bobadas! **(c)** *(worthless things)* porquerías *fpl*; **the film was a load of c.** la película era una porquería
2 *adj (bad)* *Esp* chungo(a), *Am* feo(a); **her dress sense is c.** tiene un gusto nefasto para vestirse
3 *vt* **he was cacking himself** *(scared)* estaba cagado (de miedo)

cack-handed [ˈkækˈhændɪd] *adj Fam* torpe, *Esp* patoso(a)

cackle [ˈkækəl] **1** *n* **(a)** *(of hen)* cacareo *m*, cloqueo *m* **(b)** *Fam (talking)* parloteo *m*; *(laughter)* carcajeo *m*; **she gave a loud c.** soltó una risotada; **cut the c.!** ¡corta el rollo!, *RP* ¡parála!
2 *vt* **"you're trapped!" cackled the old witch** "estás atrapado", dijo con una risotada la vieja bruja
3 *vi* **(a)** *(hen)* cacarear, cloquear **(b)** *Fam (laugh)* carcajearse

cacophonous [kəˈkɒfənəs] *adj* discordante, cacofónico(a)

cacophony [kəˈkɒfənɪ] *n* **(a)** *(harsh sounds)* estrépito *m*; **a c. of voices** un griterío *or* una bulla enorme **(b)** *Ling* cacofonía *f*

cactus [ˈkæktəs] (*pl* **cacti** [ˈkæktaɪ]) *n* cactus *m inv*, cacto *m* ▸▸ ***c. wren*** chochín *m* de los cactos

CAD [siːeɪˈdiː] *n Comptr* (*abbr* **computer-aided** *or* **-assisted design**) CAD *m*

cad [kæd] *n Fam Old-fashioned* canalla *m*

cadaver [kəˈdævə(r)] *n* cadáver *m*

cadaverous [kəˈdævərəs] *adj* cadavérico(a)

CAD/CAM [ˈkædˈkæm] *n Comptr* (*abbr* **computer-aided design/computer-assisted manufacture**) CAD/CAM *m*

caddie, caddy [ˈkædɪ] **1** *n (in golf)* caddy *mf*, cadi *mf* ▸▸ ***c. car*** carrito *m* de golf; ***c. cart*** carrito *m* de golf
2 *vi* **to c. for sb** hacer de caddy para alguien

caddis fly [ˈkædɪsflaɪ] *n* frigánea *f*

caddish [ˈkædɪʃ] *adj Br Fam Old-fashioned (behaviour)* canallesco(a); *(person)* canalla; **that was a c. thing to do** eso fue una canallada

caddy [ˈkædɪ] *n* **(a)** *(container)* **(tea) c.** caja *f* para el té **(b)** *US (cart)* carrito *m* **(c)** = **caddie**

cadence [ˈkeɪdəns] *n* cadencia *f*

cadenza [kəˈdenzə] *n Mus* cadencia *f (pasaje para solista)*

cadet [kə'det] *n* (**a**) *Mil* cadete *m* ►► ***c. corps*** = organismo que, en algunas escuelas, enseña disciplina militar (**b**) *Br (police)* = alumno de una academia de policía

cadge [kædʒ] *Fam* **1** *vt* gorrear, *Esp, Méx* gorronear, *RP* garronear (**from** *or* **off** a); **he cadged a meal from** *or* **off his aunt** le gorreó *or Esp, Méx* gorroneó *or RP* garroneó una comida a su tía; **can I c. a lift from you?** ¿me puedes llevar *or CAm, Méx, Perú* dar aventón?

2 *vi* **she's always cadging off** *or* **from her friends** siempre está gorreando *or Esp, Méx* gorroneando *or RP* garroneando de sus amigos

3 *n Br Esp* gorrón(ona) *m,f*; **to be on the c.** estar gorreando *or Esp, Méx* gorroneando *or RP* garroneando

cadger ['kædʒə(r)] *n Fam* gorrero(a) *m,f, Esp, Méx* gorrón(ona) *m,f, RP* garronero(a) *m,f*

cadmium ['kædmɪəm] *n Chem* cadmio *m* ►► ***c. yellow*** amarillo *m* cadmio

cadre ['kɑːdrə] *n Mil & Pol* cuadro *m*

CAE [siːeɪ'iː] *n Comptr* (*abbr* **computer-aided** *or* **-assisted engineering**) ingeniería *f* asistida por *Esp* ordenador *or Am* computadora

caecum, *US* **cecum** ['siːkəm] (*pl* **caeca**, *US* **ceca** ['siːkə]) *n Anat* (intestino *m*) ciego *m*

Caesar ['siːzə(r)] *pr n* César ►► ***C. salad*** ensalada *f* César, = ensalada de lechuga, huevo pasado por agua, ajo, queso rallado y picatostes

caesarean, *US* **cesarean** [sɪ'zeərɪən] **1** *n* cesárea *f*; **it was a c.** *(delivery)* fue un nacimiento por *or* mediante cesárea; **to be a c.** *(baby)* nacer por *or* mediante cesárea; **she has to have a c.** tienen que hacerle una *or* la cesárea; **the baby was born by c.** nació por *or* mediante cesárea

2 *adj* ***c. section*** operación *f* de cesárea; **to be born** *or* **delivered by c. section** nacer mediante una operación de cesárea

caesium, *US* **cesium** ['siːzɪəm] *n Chem* cesio *m*

caesura, *US* **cesura** [sɪ'zjʊərə] (*pl* **caesuras, cesuras** *or* **caesurae, cesurae** [sɪ'zjʊəriː]) *n Lit* cesura *f*

café, cafe ['kæfeɪ] *n* (**a**) *(coffee shop)* café *m*, cafetería *f* ►► ***c. au lait*** café *m* con leche; ***c. society*** = el mundillo de los cafés y restaurantes de moda (**b**) *(cheap restaurant)* cafetería *f*, restaurante *m* barato

cafeteria [kæfə'tɪərɪə] *n* (**a**) *(in school, hospital, museum)* cafetería *f*, comedor *m* (**b**) *(cheap restaurant)* cafetería *f*, restaurante *m* barato

cafetière [kæfə'tjeə(r)] *n Br* cafetera *f* (de émbolo)

caff [kæf] *n Br Fam* = cafetería barata

caffeine ['kæfiːn] *n* cafeína *f*

caffeine-free ['kæfiːn'friː] *adj* sin cafeína

caftan ['kæftæn] *n* caftán *m*

cage [keɪdʒ] **1** *n* (**a**) *(for bird or animal)* jaula *f* (**b**) *(of elevator)* cabina *f*; *(in coal mine)* jaula *f* (**c**) *Sport (for discus, hammer)* jaula *f* (de protección); *(of ice-hockey goal)* portería *f*

2 *vt* enjaular; **to feel caged in** sentirse enjaulado(a)

caged [keɪdʒd] *adj* enjaulado(a); **he was like a c. animal** era como un animal enjaulado

cagey, *US* **cagy** ['keɪdʒɪ] *adj* **to be c. (about sth)** *(cautious)* ir *or Esp* andar con tiento (con algo); *(evasive)* salirse por la tangente (en cuanto a algo); **he was being c. about his qualifications** no quería dar demasiados detalles sobre su titulación

cagily ['keɪdʒɪlɪ] *adv* con tiento, cautelosamente; **to answer c.** *(deliberately vaguely)* dar una respuesta vaga

caginess ['keɪdʒɪnɪs] *n* tiento *m*, cautela *f*

cagoule [kə'guːl] *n Br* chubasquero *m*

cagy *US* = **cagey**

cahoots [kə'huːts] *npl* IDIOM *Fam* **to be in c. (with sb)** estar conchabado(a) (con alguien), *RP* estar metido(a) (con alguien)

CAI [siːeɪ'aɪ] *n Comptr* (*abbr* **computer-aided instruction**) enseñanza *f* asistida por *Esp* ordenador *or Am* computadora

caiman = **cayman**

Cain [keɪn] *pr n* Caín; IDIOM *Fam* **to raise C.** armar la gorda *or Esp* la marimorena

cairn ['keən] *n* hito *m* de piedras ►► ***c. terrier*** terrier *m* cairn

Cairo ['kaɪrəʊ] *n* El Cairo

caisson ['keɪsən] *n Tech* (**a**) *(watertight chamber)* cajón *m* (estanco), campana *f* neumática ►► ***c. disease*** enfermedad *f* de los cajones *or* de los buzos (**b**) *(for raising sunken ships)* camello *m* (**c**) *(for dock)* compuerta *f* flotante (**d**) *(for ammunition)* cajón *m* de municiones

cajole [kə'dʒəʊl] *vt* engatusar; **to c. sb into doing sth** engatusar a alguien para que haga algo; **they eventually cajoled the information out of him** lo engatusaron para sacarle la información

cajolery [kə'dʒəʊlərɪ] *n* engatusamiento *m*

cajoling [kə'dʒəʊlɪŋ] **1** *n* engatusamiento *m*

2 *adj* engatusador(ora)

Cajun ['keɪdʒən] **1** *n* (**a**) *(person)* cajún *mf*, = persona de Luisiana descendiente de inmigrantes franceses (**b**) *(language)* = lengua derivada del francés hablado en Luisiana

2 *adj* cajún, = característico de los habitantes de Luisiana descendiente de inmigrantes franceses

cake [keɪk] **1** *n* (**a**) *(food)* pastel *m*, *Esp* tarta *f*, *Col, CSur* torta *f*, *Col* ponqué *m*; *(small)* pastel *m*; **a chocolate c.** un pastel *or Esp* una tarta de chocolate; **to make** *or* **bake a c.** *(small)* hacer *or* cocinar un pastel; *(big)* hacer *or* cocinar un pastel *or Esp* una tarta ►► ***c. shop*** pastelería *f*; ***c. stand*** = mueble para servir pasteles formado por varios platos superpuestos y sujetados por un armazón; *Br* ***c. tin*** molde *m* de pastel

(**b**) *(block) (of soap, chocolate, paint, shoe polish)* pastilla *f*

(**c**) IDIOMS **it's a piece of c.** es facilísimo, está tirado, *RP* es un boleto; **that takes the c.!** ¡esto es el colmo!; PROV **you can't have your c. and eat it** no se puede estar en misa y repicando, *RP* no se puede chiflar y comer gofio

2 *vt* **her shoes were caked with mud** tenía los zapatos llenos de barro

3 *vi* endurecerse; **the mud had caked on his boots** el barro se le había secado en las botas

cakehole ['keɪkhəʊl] *n Br Fam* **shut your c.!** ¡cierra el pico!

cakewalk ['keɪkwɔːk] *n* IDIOM *US Fam* **it was a c.** *(easy task)* fue pan comido, fue un paseo

CAL [kæl] *n Comptr* (*abbr* **computer-aided** *or* **-assisted learning**) enseñanza *f* asistida por *Esp* ordenador *or Am* computadora

cal. (**a**) (*abbr* **calorie**) cal. (**b**) (*abbr* **calibre**) calibre *m*

calabash ['kæləbæʃ] *n* (**a**) *(fruit)* calabaza *f*, *Am* güira *f*, *Andes, RP* zapallo *m*, *Carib* ahuyama *f* (**b**) *(tree)* calabacero *m*, *Am* güiro *m*, *Andes, RP* zapallo *m*, *Col, Ven* totumo *m*

calaboose ['kæləbuːs] *n US Fam* calabozo *m*; **in the c.** en la cárcel *or Esp* en chirona *or Andes, RP* en la cana *or Méx* en el bote

calamari [kælə'mɑːrɪ] *npl Culin* calamares *mpl*

calami *pl of* **calamus**

calamine ['kæləmaɪn] *n* calamina *f* ►► ***c. lotion*** loción *f* de calamina

calamitous [kə'læmɪtəs] *adj* calamitoso(a), desastroso(a)

calamity [kə'læmɪtɪ] *n* calamidad *f*, desastre *m*

calamus ['kæləməs] (*pl* **calami** ['kæləmaɪ]) *n* cálamo *m*, ácoro *m*

calandra lark [kə'lændrə'lɑːk] *n* calandria *f*

calcareous [kæl'keərɪəs] *adj Chem* calcáreo(a)

calcic ['kælsɪk] *adj Chem* cálcico(a)

calcification [kælsɪfɪ'keɪʃən] *n* calcificación *f*

calcify ['kælsɪfaɪ] **1** *vt* calcificar

2 *vi* calcificarse

calcination [kælsɪ'neɪʃən] *n* calcinación *f*

calcine ['kælsaɪn] **1** *vt* calcinar

2 *vi* calcinarse

calcite ['kælsaɪt] *n Geol* calcita *f*

calcium ['kælsɪəm] *n Chem* calcio *m* ►► ***c. carbonate*** carbonato *m* cálcico; ***c. hydrate*** hidrato *m* de calcio; ***c. hydroxide*** hidróxido *m* de calcio; ***c. phosphate*** fosfato *m* cálcico

calculable ['kælkjʊləbəl] *adj* calculable

calculate ['kælkjʊleɪt] **1** *vt* (**a**) *(reckon) (mathematically)* calcular; *(estimate, evaluate)* calcular, estimar; **he calculated that his chances of success were reasonably good** calculó *or* estimó que tenía bastante buenas posibilidades de tener éxito

(**b**) *(design, intend)* **his remark was calculated to shock** pretendió impresionar con el comentario; **his comments were scarcely calculated to inspire confidence** sus comentarios no inspiraron demasiado optimismo que digamos

2 *vi* **to c. on (doing) sth** contar con (hacer) algo

calculated ['kælkjʊleɪtɪd] *adj* (**a**) *(considered)* calculado(a); **a c. risk** un riesgo calculado (**b**) *(intentional)* deliberado(a); **a c. insult** un insulto intencionado

calculating ['kælkjʊleɪtɪŋ] *adj* (**a**) *(scheming)* calculador(ora) (**b**) *(adding)* ***c. machine*** calculadora *f*

calculation [kælkjʊ'leɪʃən] *n* (**a**) *(mathematical)* cálculo *m*; **to make a c.** hacer *or* efectuar un cálculo; **to be out in one's calculations** equivocarse en el cálculo *or* en los cálculos

(**b**) *(estimate)* **to upset sb's calculations** desbaratar los cálculos de alguien; **by my calculations we should be there soon** según mis cálculos deberíamos llegar allí pronto

(c) *(self-interested forethought)* **his action was more the result of c. than principle** su acción obedecía más a un cálculo premeditado que a una cuestión de principios

calculator ['kælkjʊleɪtə(r)] *n* (**a**) *(electronic)* calculadora *f* (**b**) *(table)* tabla *f*

calculus ['kælkjʊləs] (*pl* **calculuses** *or* **calculi** ['kælkjʊlaɪ, 'kælkjʊli:]) *n* (**a**) *Math* cálculo *m* (infinitesimal) (**b**) *Med* cálculo *m*

Calcutta [kæl'kʌtə] *n* Calcuta

caldera [kæl'deərə] *n Geol* caldera *f*

Caledonia [kælɪ'dəʊnɪə] *n* Caledonia

Caledonian [kælɪ'dəʊnɪən] **1** *n* caledonio(a) *m,f*

2 *adj* caledonio(a)

calendar ['kælɪndə(r)] **1** *n* (**a**) *(system)* calendario *m* (**b**) *(list of days and dates)* calendario *m* ►► ***c. month*** mes *m* natural; ***c. year*** año *m* natural, *Am* año *m* calendario (**c**) *(list of events)* calendario *m*; **a key date in the legal/sporting c.** una fecha clave en el calendario jurídico/deportivo

2 *vt* **it has been calendared for 16 June** la fecha ha sido fijada para el 16 de junio

calendarize ['kælɪndəraɪz] *vt Fin* desglosar en el calendario

calender ['kælɪndə(r)] *n (machine)* calandria *f*

calendula [kæ'lendjʊlə] *n* caléndula *f*, maravilla *f*

calf[1] [kɑ:f] (*pl* **calves** [kɑ:vz]) *n* (**a**) *(young cow, bull)* becerro(a) *m,f*, ternero(a) *m,f*; **the cow is in** *or* **with c.** la vaca está preñada; IDIOM **to kill the fatted c.** tirar la casa por la ventana ►► ***c. love*** amor *m* de adolescente (**b**) *(skin)* piel *f* de becerro (**c**) *(young elephant, giraffe, buffalo)* cría *f*; *(young whale)* ballenato *m*

calf[2] (*pl* **calves** [kɑ:vz]) *n (of leg)* pantorrilla *f* ►► ***c. muscle*** gemelo *m*

calfskin ['kɑ:fskɪn] *n* piel *f* de becerro

caliber *US* = **calibre**

calibrate ['kælɪbreɪt] *vt (instrument)* calibrar

calibration [kælɪ'breɪʃən] *n (of instrument)* calibrado *m*, calibración *f*

calibre, *US* **caliber** ['kælɪbə(r)] *n* (**a**) *(of firearm)* calibre *m* (**b**) *(of person)* calibre *m*, categoría *f*; **the work is of the highest c.** es un trabajo de gran categoría; **the two applicants are not of the same c.** los dos aspirantes no son del mismo calibre *or* de la misma categoría

calico ['kælɪkəʊ] (*pl* **calicoes**) **1** *n* (**a**) *Br (white fabric)* percal *m*, calicó *m* (**b**) *US (printed fabric)* percal *m*, calicó *m*

2 *adj US* **a c. cat** = gato de tres colores, normalmente blanco con manchas negras y rojizas

Calif (*abbr* **California**) California

California [kælɪ'fɔ:nɪə] *n* California ►► ***C. condor*** cóndor *m* de California; ***C. quail*** codorniz *f* de California

Californian [kælɪ'fɔ:nɪən] **1** *n* californiano(a) *m,f*

2 *adj* californiano(a) ►► ***C. privet*** aligustre *m* de California

californium [kælɪ'fɔ:nɪəm] *n Chem* californio *m*

calipers *US* = **callipers**

caliph ['keɪlɪf] *n* califa *m*

caliphate ['kælɪfeɪt] *n* califato *m*

calisthenics *US* = **callisthenics**

CALL [kɑ:l] *n Comptr* (*abbr* **computer-assisted language learning**) enseñanza *f* de idiomas asistida por *Esp* ordenador *or Am* computadora

CALL [kɔ:l] **1** *n* (**a**) *(cry) (of person)* llamada *f*, grito *m*, *Am* llamado *m*; *(of animal)* grito *m*; *(of bird)* reclamo *m*; *(of horn, bugle)* toque *m*

(**b**) *(alert, summons) (at airport)* aviso *m*, llamada *f*, *Am* llamado *m*; *(in theatre)* aviso *m*; **would you like a c. in the morning?** ¿quiere que lo despertemos *Esp* por *or Am* en la mañana?

(**c**) *(appeal)* llamamiento *m*, llamada *f*, *Am* llamado *m*; **there were calls for a strike** hubo llamamientos a la huelga; **there were calls for her resignation** pidieron su dimisión; **a c. for unity/compassion** un llamamiento a la unidad/la compasión; *Com* **a c. for tenders** una convocatoria a la licitación; **a c. to arms** una llamada a (tomar) las armas; **a c. to order** una llamada al orden ►► ***c. alarm*** alarma *f (para anciano o discapacitado)*

(**d**) *(on phone)* llamada *f*, *Am* llamado *m*; *(long-distance)* llamada *f* interurbana, *Esp* conferencia *f*, llamada *f or Am* llamado *m* larga distancia; **to get** *or* **receive a c.** recibir una llamada *or Am* un llamado; **to give sb a c.** llamar a alguien; **to make a c.** hacer una llamada *or Am* un llamado; **to put a c. through (to sb)** pasar una llamada *or Am* un llamado (a alguien); **to return sb's c.** devolverle la llamada *or Am* el llamado a alguien; **you have a c. from Canada** tienes una llamada *or Am* un llamado de *or* desde Canadá, te llaman de *or* desde Canadá; **there's a c. for you** tienes una llamada *or Am* un llamado, te llaman; **he's on a c.** está hablando por teléfono, está con una llamada *or Am* un llamado; **will you accept the c.?** *(when charges are reversed)* ¿acepta la llamada *or Am* el llamado?; **I'll take the c. in my office** pásame la llamada *or Am* el llamado a mi oficina ►► ***c. barring*** bloqueo *m or* prohibición *f* de llamadas *or Am* llamados; ***c. box*** *Br* cabina *f* telefónica *or* de teléfono; *US* teléfono *m* de emergencia; ***c. centre*** centro *m* de atención telefónica; ***c. diversion*** desvío *m* de llamada *or Am* llamado; ***c. forwarding*** desvío *m* de llamada *or Am* llamado; ***c. girl*** prostituta *f (que concierta sus citas por teléfono)*; *US* ***c. letters*** *(of radio station)* código *m* de identificación; ***c. sign*** *(of radio station)* código *m* de identificación; ***c. transfer*** desvío *m* de llamada *or Am* llamado; ***c. waiting*** llamada *f or Am* llamado *m* en espera

(**e**) *(visit)* visita *f*; **to pay a c. on sb, to pay sb a c.** hacer una visita a alguien

(**f**) *(demand)* demanda *f* (**for** de); **there are a lot of calls on my time** tengo muchos compromisos; **there's not much c. for it** no tiene mucha demanda, no hay mucha demanda de ello; **there's no c. for rudeness!** no hace falta ser grosero; **to be on c.** *(doctor)* estar de guardia; **he showed bravery beyond the c. of duty** mostró un valor excepcional; *Hum* **I need to answer a c. of nature** necesito hacer mis necesidades ►► ***c. number*** *(for library book)* signatura *f*; *US* ***c. slip*** *(for library book)* ficha *f*

(**g**) *(decision)* decisión *f*; **it's a hard c.** es una decisión difícil; **it's your c.** *(when tossing coin)* tú eliges

(**h**) *(in basketball, baseball, tennis)* decisión *f*

(**i**) *Literary (attraction)* llamada *f*, *Am* llamado *m*; **the c. of the wild** la llamada *or Am* el llamado de la naturaleza

(**j**) *(option)* **you'll have first c.** serás el primero al que consultemos

(**k**) *St Exch (claim)* requerimiento *m* de pago ►► ***c. option*** opción *f* de compra

(**l**) *Fin* ***c. money*** dinero *m* a la vista, préstamo *m* al cliente

(**m**) *(in bridge)* canto *m*

2 *vt* (**a**) *(summon) (person)* llamar; **the headmaster called me into his study** el director me llamó a su despacho; **he called me over to show me something** me llamó para enseñarme *or* mostrarme una cosa; **he felt called to be a priest** sintió la llamada *or Am* el llamado del Señor; *Law* **to c. sb to give evidence** llamar a alguien a prestar declaración; *Law* **to c. sb as a witness** llamar a alguien a testificar; **to c. sb's attention to sth** llamar la atención de alguien sobre algo; **it calls to mind when...** me hace recordar *or Am* acordar cuando...; **to c. sb to order** llamar a alguien al orden; **to c. sth into play** poner algo en juego; **to c. sth into question** poner algo en tela de juicio

(**b**) *(announce) (meeting, strike, election)* convocar; *(flight)* anunciar

(**c**) *(on phone)* llamar, telefonear; **I'm going to c. the police** voy a llamar a la policía; **we called his house** llamamos a su casa; IDIOM *Hum* **don't c. us, we'll c. you** ya lo(a) llamaremos

(**d**) *(name)* llamar; **we called him Spot** le pusimos Spot; **she is called Teresa** se llama Teresa; **what's he/it called?** ¿cómo se llama?; **c. me by my first name** llámame por mi nombre (de pila); **to c. sb names** insultar a alguien; **to c. sb all the names** *or* **every name under the sun** poner a alguien de vuelta y media

(**e**) *(describe as)* llamar; **to c. sb a liar/a thief** llamar a alguien mentiroso/ladrón; **are you calling me a thief?** ¿me estás llamando ladrón?; **she calls herself a consultant** dice que es una asesora; *Ironic* **c. yourself a mechanic!** ¡vaya un experto en mecánica (que estás tú hecho)!

(**f**) *(consider)* **I wouldn't c. her a friend** no es exactamente una amiga; **do you c. that clean?** ¿llamas limpio a esto?; **we'll c. it $10** dejémoslo en *or* digamos 10 dólares; **let's c. it a day** ya está bien por hoy; **let's c. it a draw** dejémoslo en empate; **I want a place I can c. my own** quiero tener mi propia casa

(**g**) *(shout)* **to c. sb's name** llamar a alguien por su nombre

(**h**) *Fin* **to c. a loan** exigir el pago *or* la amortización de un préstamo

(**i**) *Sport (declare, judge)* **the umpire called the shot out** el juez de silla dijo que la bola había sido mala *or* que la bola había salido

(**j**) *(in poker)* ver; **I called him for $50** vi sus 50 dólares

3 *vi* (**a**) *(person, bird, animal)* llamar; *(horn, bugle)* sonar; **to c. for help** pedir ayuda a gritos; **he called to his companions** llamó a sus compañeros

(**b**) *(on phone)* llamar; **did anyone c. while I was out?** ¿me llamó alguien mientras no estaba?; **(may I ask) who's calling?** ¿de parte de quién?

(**c**) *(visit) (person)* venir, pasarse

(**d**) *(when tossing coin)* **you c.!** ¡tú eliges!

►**call aside** *vt sep* llamar aparte

►**call at** *vt insep* (**a**) *(visit) (of person)* pasarse por; **to c. at the baker's** pasarse por la panadería; **I called (round) at Steve's** me pasé por casa de Steve

(**b**) *(stop)* **the ship called at several ports** el barco hizo escala en varios puertos; **this train will c. at York and Peterborough** este tren efectúa parada en York y Peterborough

▸ **call away** *vt sep* **she was called away from the office** tuvo que salir de la oficina; **she's been called away on business** ha tenido que marcharse por un asunto de negocios

▸ **call back 1** *vt sep* **(a)** *(summon again)* hacer volver; **as I was leaving he called me back** me llamó cuando ya me iba
(b) *(on phone)* volver a llamar; **could you c. me back later?** ¿podría llamarme más tarde?
2 *vi* **(a)** *(on phone)* volver a llamar
(b) *(return)* volver (a pasar)

▸ **call by** *vi Br (visit)* pasarse

▸ **call down** *vt sep* **(a)** *Literary* **to c. sth down on** *or* **upon sb** invocar algo sobre alguien
(b) *US Fam (reprimand)* llamar la atención a, dar un toque a

▸ **call for** *vt insep* **(a)** *(require)* requerir, necesitar; **this calls for a celebration!** ¡esto hay que celebrarlo!; **that wasn't called for!** ¡eso no era necesario!, ¡no había necesidad de eso!
(b) *(demand)* exigir; **the opposition called for an official statement** la oposición exigió una declaración oficial
(c) *Br (come to collect)* **a young man called for you** un joven vino a verte; **I'll c. for you/it at twelve** pasaré a recogerte/recogerlo a las doce

▸ **call forth** *vt insep* **(a)** *Formal (provoke)* provocar
(b) *Literary (summon)* convocar

▸ **call in 1** *vt sep* **(a)** *(doctor, police)* llamar; *(into room)* hacer pasar
(b) *(recall) (defective goods)* retirar del mercado; *(banknotes)* retirar de la circulación; *(library books)* reclamar
(c) *(loan)* pedir la devolución *or* el pago de; *(favour)* pedir la devolución de
2 *vi* **(a)** *(visit)* **to c. in on sb** ir a *or* pasarse por casa de alguien
(b) *(phone)* llamar

▸ **call off** *vt sep* **(a)** *(cancel) (meeting, match, trip, search)* suspender; *(strike)* desconvocar; *(deal)* cancelar, suspender
(b) *(dog)* llamar; **I want you to c. off your thugs** quiero que retires a tus matones

▸ **call on, call upon** *vt insep* **(a)** *(request, invite)* **to c. on sb to do sth** invitar a alguien a que haga algo; **I now c. on the mayor to open this conference** y cedo al alcalde el honor de inaugurar este congreso
(b) *(require)* **she may be called on to give evidence** puede que la hagan comparecer como testigo
(c) *(visit)* visitar; **the sales reps c. on their clients monthly** los representantes van a ver *or* visitan a los clientes todos los meses
(d) *(make use of)* recurrir a; **he had to c. on every ounce of concentration** tuvo que concentrarse al máximo

▸ **call out 1** *vt sep* **(a)** *(troops)* convocar; *(doctor)* llamar; **the workers were called out on strike** se convocó a los trabajadores a la huelga
(b) *(shout)* gritar; *(numbers in bingo, lottery)* cantar
2 *vi (shout out)* gritar

▸ **call round** *vi Br* **I'll c. round this afternoon** pasaré a verte *or* visitarte esta tarde

▸ **call up** *vt sep* **(a)** *(reinforcements)* pedir
(b) *(on phone)* llamar
(c) *Mil (draft)* llamar a filas, reclutar
(d) *(select for team)* convocar
(e) *Comptr (data, information)* visualizar
(f) *(spirit)* invocar

▸ **call upon** *vt insep* = **call on**

---

callboy ['kɔːlbɔɪ] *n* **(a)** *Theat* traspunte *m* **(b)** *US (bellboy)* botones *m inv*

caller ['kɔːlə(r)] *n* **(a)** *(visitor)* visita *f* **(b)** *(on phone)* persona *f* que llama; **many of our callers have been asking about the cost of the scheme** muchos de nuestros oyentes han llamado preguntando cuánto costaría el proyecto **(c)** *(in bingo)* = persona que canta los números

calligrapher [kə'lɪgrəfə(r)] *n* calígrafo(a) *m,f*

calligraphy [kə'lɪgrəfɪ] *n* caligrafía *f*

call-in ['kɔːlɪn] *n US Rad & TV* **c. show** = programa con llamadas de los televidentes/oyentes

calling ['kɔːlɪŋ] *n* **(a)** *(vocation)* vocación *f*; **that's very good work, I think you might have missed your c.!** ese trabajo está muy bien, ¡te deberías haber dedicado a esto! **(b)** *Formal (profession)* profesión *f* ▸▸ *US* ***c. card*** tarjeta *f* de visita; *Fig* sello *m* inconfundible; *Fam Hum* **Lassie left her c. card on the carpet** Lassie dejó un regalito en la alfombra

callipers, *US* **calipers** ['kælɪpəz] *npl* **(a)** *(for legs)* aparato *m* ortopédico **(b)** *(measuring device)* calibrador *m*, calibre *m*

callisthenics, *US* **calisthenics** [kælɪs'θenɪks] *n* gimnasia *f* sueca, calistenia *f*

callous ['kæləs] *adj* cruel, desalmado(a); **to make sb c.** encallecer a alguien; **to become c.** encallecerse

calloused ['kæləst] *adj* calloso(a), encallecido(a); **to become c.** *(hands, feet)* encallecerse

callously ['kæləslɪ] *adv* cruelmente, despiadadamente

callousness ['kæləsnɪs] *n* crueldad *f*, inhumanidad *f*

call-out ['kɔːlaʊt] *n Br (by maintenance man)* desplazamiento *m* ▸▸ ***c. charge*** tarifa *f* por desplazamiento

callow ['kæləʊ] *adj* inmaduro(a); **a c. youth** un joven bisoño *or* inexperto

call-up ['kɔːlʌp] *n Mil* llamada *f or Am* llamado *m* a filas, reclutamiento *m*; **to get one's c. papers** recibir la orden de reclutamiento, ser llamado(a) a filas

callus ['kæləs] *n* **(a)** *(on skin)* callo *m*, callosidad *f* **(b)** *Med (on broken bone)* callo *m*

calm [kɑːm] **1** *n* calma *f*, tranquilidad *f*; *also Fig* **the c. before the storm** la calma que precede a la tormenta
2 *adj* **(a)** *(person)* tranquilo(a), reposado(a); **to stay c.** mantener la calma; **to become** *or* **grow calmer** calmarse; **to be c. and collected** mantenerse sereno(a) **(b)** *(sea)* tranquilo(a), en calma; *(weather)* apacible
3 *vt* calmar, tranquilizar; **this will c. your nerves** esto te calmará *or* tranquilizará

▸ **calm down 1** *vt sep (person)* calmar, tranquilizar
2 *vi (person)* calmarse, tranquilizarse; *(situation)* calmarse; **c. down!** ¡cálmate!, ¡tranquilízate!

calming ['kɑːmɪŋ] *adj (influence, effect)* tranquilizador(ora), tranquilizante; **her words had a c. effect on him** sus palabras consiguieron tranquilizarlo

calmly ['kɑːmlɪ] *adv* serenamente, tranquilamente; **she took the news very c.** se tomó la noticia con mucha calma

calmness ['kɑːmnɪs] *n (of person)* calma *f*, tranquilidad *f*; *(of voice, sea)* calma *f*

Calor gas® ['kæləgæs] *n Br* butano *m*

caloric [kə'lɒrɪk] *adj* calórico(a)

calorie ['kælərɪ] *n* caloría *f*; *Fam* **to watch** *or* **count the calories** cuidar la línea ▸▸ ***c. content*** contenido *m or* aporte *m* calórico

calorie-controlled ['kælərɪkən'trəʊld] *adj (diet)* bajo(a) en calorías

calorific [kælə'rɪfɪk] *adj* calorífico(a) ▸▸ ***c. value*** *(of fuel)* poder *m* calorífico; *(of food)* valor *m* calórico

calorimeter [kælə'rɪmɪtə(r)] *n Chem* calorímetro *m*

calque [kælk] *n Ling* calco *m*

calumniate [kə'lʌmnɪeɪt] *vt Formal* calumniar

calumnious [kə'lʌmnɪəs] *adj Formal* calumnioso(a)

calumny ['kæləmnɪ] *n* calumnia *f*

Calvados ['kælvədɒs] *n* calvados *m inv*

Calvary ['kælvərɪ] *n Rel* calvario *m*

calve [kɑːv] *vi (cow)* parir

calves *pl of* **calf**

Calvin ['kælvɪn] *pr n* **John C.** Juan Calvino

Calvinism ['kælvɪnɪzəm] *n* calvinismo *m*

Calvinist ['kælvɪnɪst] **1** *n* calvinista *mf*
2 *adj* calvinista

calypso [kə'lɪpsəʊ] (*pl* **calypsos**) *n* calipso *m*

calyx ['keɪlɪks] (*pl* **calyxes** *or* **calyces** ['keɪlɪsiːz]) *n Bot* cáliz *m*

CAM [siːeɪ'em] *n Comptr* (*abbr* **computer-aided** *or* **-assisted manufacture**) CAM *f*, fabricación *f* asistida por *Esp* ordenador *or Am* computadora

cam [kæm] *n Tech* leva *f*

camaraderie [kæmə'rɑːdərɪ] *n* camaradería *f*, compañerismo *m*

camber ['kæmbə(r)] *n* **(a)** *(curve) (of road)* caída *f*, peralte *m*; *(of ship deck)* brusca *f*; *(of aircraft wing)* curvatura *f* **(b)** *(of car wheels)* inclinación *f*

cambered ['kæmbəd] *adj (road)* peraltado(a); *(ship's deck)* con brusca

Cambodia [kæm'bəʊdɪə] *n* Camboya

Cambodian [kæm'bəʊdɪən] **1** *n* camboyano(a) *m,f*
2 *adj* camboyano(a)

Cambrian ['kæmbrɪən] *Geol* **1** *n* **the C.** el cámbrico
2 *adj (period)* cámbrico(a)

cambric ['kæmbrɪk] *n* batista *f*

Cambridge ['keɪmbrɪdʒ] *n* Cambridge

Cambs (*abbr* **Cambridgeshire**) (condado *m* de) Cambridgeshire

camcorder ['kæmkɔːdə(r)] *n* videocámara *f* (portátil)

came *pt of* **come**

camel ['kæməl] **1** *n* (**a**) *(animal)* camello *m* ▸▸ ***c. driver*** camellero(a) *m,f; US Fam Pej* ***c. jockey*** *Esp* moro(a) *m,f, Andes, CSur, Ven* turco(a) *m,f;* ***c. racing*** carreras *fpl* de camellos (**b**) *(colour)* beige *m inv, Esp* beis *m inv*

2 *adj (coat, jacket) (of camelhair)* de pelo de camello; *(coloured)* beige *inv, Esp* beis *inv*

camelhair ['kæməlheə(r)] *n* pelo *m* de camello ▸▸ ***c. coat*** abrigo *m* de pelo de camello

camellia [kə'miːlɪə] *n* camelia *f*

Camembert ['kæməmbeə(r)] *n* (queso *m*) camembert *m*

cameo ['kæmɪəʊ] (*pl* **cameos**) *n* (**a**) *(stone)* **c. (brooch)** camafeo *m* (**b**) *Cin* aparición *f* breve *(de un actor famoso)*; **he has a c. role in...** aparece brevemente en...

camera ['kæmərə] *n* (**a**) *(photographic)* cámara *f* (fotográfica), máquina *f* de fotos *or* fotográfica; *(for TV, cinema)* cámara *f*; *TV* **off c.** fuera de imagen; *TV* **on c.** delante de la cámara; **the c. never lies** la cámara nunca miente ▸▸ ***c. crew*** equipo *m* de filmación; ***c. lens*** objetivo *m* (**b**) *Law* **in c.** a puerta cerrada (**c**) ***c. obscura*** cámara *f* oscura

cameraman ['kæmərəmæn] *n* cámara *m*, operador *m*

camera-ready copy ['kæmərəredɪ'kɒpɪ] *n Typ* copia *f* lista para ser filmada

camera-shy ['kæmərəʃaɪ] *adj* **she's extremely c.** le da muchísima vergüenza *or Am* pena que le hagan fotos/que le filmen

camerawoman ['kæmərəwʊmən] *n* cámara *f*, operadora *f*

camerawork ['kæmərəwɜːk] *n* fotografía *f*

Cameroon [kæmə'ruːn] *n* Camerún

Cameroonian [kæmə'ruːnɪən] **1** *n* camerunés(esa) *m,f*

2 *adj* camerunés(esa)

camiknickers ['kæmɪnɪkəz] *npl* picardías *m inv*

camisole ['kæmɪsəʊl] *n* combinación *f*

camomile, chamomile ['kæməmaɪl] *n* manzanilla *f*, camomila *f* ▸▸ ***c. tea*** (infusión *f* de) manzanilla *f*

camouflage ['kæməflɑːʒ] **1** *n also Fig* camuflaje *m*

2 *vt also Fig* camuflar

camp[1] [kæmp] **1** *n* (**a**) *(place)* campamento *m*; **to make** *or* **pitch** *or* **set up c.** acampar; **to break c.** levantar el campamento ▸▸ ***c. bed*** cama *f* plegable, catre *m* (**b**) *US* **(summer) c.** colonia *f*, campamento *m* de verano (**c**) *(group)* bando *m*; **the conservative c.** el bando conservador; **to go over to the other c.** pasarse al otro bando

2 *vi* **to c. (out)** acampar

camp[2] *Fam* **1** *adj* (**a**) *(behaviour, manner)* amariposado(a), amanerado(a) (**b**) *(style, taste)* amanerado(a), *Esp* hortera, *Col* lobo(a), *Méx* corriente, *RP* groncho(a)

2 *n* amaneramiento *m*, pluma *f*

▸**camp up** *vt sep* afeminar, amanerar; **to c. it up** remedar a las mujeres *(en gestos, la voz)*

campaign [kæm'peɪn] **1** *n* (**a**) *(military)* campaña *f* (**b**) *(electoral, marketing)* campaña *f*; **a c. against drugs** una campaña contra las drogas; **a c. for a shorter working week** una campaña para conseguir la reducción de la semana laboral ▸▸ ***c. manager*** *(in election)* director(ora) *m,f or* jefe(a) *m,f* de campaña; ***c. worker*** = persona que trabaja en una campaña electoral

2 *vi* **to c. for/against** hacer campaña a favor de/en contra de

campaigner [kæm'peɪnə(r)] *n* defensor(ora) *m,f*; **to be a c. for/against** hacer campaña a favor de/en contra de

campanile [kæmpə'niːlɪ] *n* campanil *m*, campanario *m (torre independiente)*

campanology [kæmpə'nɒlədʒɪ] *n* campanología *f*

campanula [kæm'pænjʊlə] *n Bot* campanilla *f*, campánula *f*

Camp David [kæmp'deɪvɪd] *n* = residencia campestre del presidente estadounidense

camper ['kæmpə(r)] *n* (**a**) *(person)* campista *mf* (**b**) *(vehicle)* **c. (van)** autocaravana *f*

campfire ['kæmpfaɪə(r)] *n* fuego *m or* hoguera *f* (de campamento)

camp-follower ['kæmp'fɒləʊə(r)] *n* (**a**) *Hist* = vendedor, prostituta, etc. que se desplaza con un ejército (**b**) *(politician)* político(a) *m,f* oportunista

campground ['kæmpgraʊnd] *n US* camping *m*

camphor ['kæmfə(r)] *n* alcanfor *m* ▸▸ ***c. tree*** alcanforero *m*

camphorated ['kæmfəreɪtɪd] *adj* alcanforado(a)

camping ['kæmpɪŋ] *n* acampada *f*; *(on commercial campsite)* camping *m*; **to go c.** ir de acampada; *(on commercial campsite)* ir de camping ▸▸ ***c. mat*** aislante *m (colchoneta)*; ***c. site*** lugar *m* de acampada; *(commercial)* camping *m*; ***c. stove*** hornillo *m*

campion ['kæmpɪən] *n (red)* coronaria *f*; *(white)* colleja *f*

campsite ['kæmpsaɪt] *n* lugar *m* de acampada; *(commercial)* camping *m*

campus ['kæmpəs] *n* campus *m inv*; **to live on/off c.** vivir en el campus/fuera del campus ▸▸ *Br* ***c. university*** universidad *f* en torno a un campus

camshaft ['kæmʃɑːft] *n Tech* árbol *m* de levas

can[1] [kæn] **1** *n* (**a**) *(container) (for food, drink)* lata *f*; *(for hairspray, polish)* bote *m*; *(for petrol)* bidón *m*; *US (for rubbish)* balde *m*, cubo *m*; **it's in the c.** *(movie)* está rodado; *Fam Fig* **the project's in the c.** el proyecto sale adelante seguro, *Esp* tenemos el proyecto en el bote; IDIOM **to open a c. of worms** sacar a la luz un asunto espinoso; IDIOM **it's a real c. of worms** es un asunto espinoso

(**b**) *US Fam (toilet)* baño *m*, *Esp* tigre *m*

(**c**) *US Fam (prison)* cárcel *f*, *Esp* chirona *f*, *Andes, RP* cana *f*, *Méx* bote *m*; **in the c.** en la cárcel *or Esp* en chirona *or Andes, RP* en la cana *or Méx* en el bote

(**d**) *US Fam (buttocks)* trasero *m*; **to kick sb in the c.** dar a alguien una patada en el culo *or* trasero

2 *vt* (*pt & pp* **canned**) (**a**) *(fruit, meat)* enlatar (**b**) *US Fam* **c. it!** *(keep quiet)* ¡cállate la boca! (**c**) *US Fam (dismiss)* poner de patitas en la calle

CAN[2] [*stressed* kæn, *unstressed* kən] *modal aux v*

El verbo **can** carece de infinitivo, de gerundio y de participio. En infinitivo o en participio, se empleará la forma correspondiente de **be able to**, por ejemplo: **he wanted to be able to speak English**; **she has always been able to swim**. En el inglés hablado, y en el escrito en estilo coloquial, la forma negativa **cannot** se transforma en **can't**.

(**a**) *(be able to)* poder; **I c. go** puedo ir; **c. you help me?** ¿puedes ayudarme?, ¿me ayudas?; **we cannot possibly do it** no podemos hacerlo de ninguna manera; **I will come as soon as I c.** vendré lo antes posible; **he was very disappointed – c. you blame him?** se quedó muy desilusionado – ¡no me extraña!; **he will do what** *or* **all he c.** hará lo que pueda; **it can't be done** es imposible, no se puede hacer; **we c. but try** por lo menos lo podemos intentar; **I can't but dispute that claim** no puedo por menos que estar en desacuerdo con esa afirmación; *US* **c. do** *(yes, I will)* lo haré; *US* **no c. do** *(no, I won't)* no puedo hacerlo

(**b**) *(know how to)* saber; **I c. swim** sé nadar; **she c. play the violin** sabe tocar el violín; **I c. speak Spanish** hablo español

(**c**) *(indicating possibility)* poder; **adult animals c. grow to 6 metres** los ejemplares adultos pueden llegar a los 6 metros; **a full description c. be found on page 56** en la página 56 hay *or* se encuentra una descripción completa; **you c. be really stupid sometimes** a veces eres bien estúpido; **she can't have realized what was going on** seguro que no se daba cuenta de lo que pasaba; **there c. be no doubt that...** no cabe duda de que...; **c. it be true?** ¡no puede ser!; **you CAN'T be serious!** ¡no lo dirás en serio!; **you CAN'T be tired already!** ¡no me digas que ya estás cansado!; **what CAN he want now?** ¿pero qué es lo que quiere ahora?

(**d**) *(indicating permission)* poder; **c. I ask you something?** ¿te puedo hacer una pregunta?; **c. I borrow a pencil? – no, you can't/yes you c.** ¿me prestas un lápiz? – no/sí; **you can't smoke in here** aquí está prohibido fumar; **you can't play a jack after a king** no se puede echar una jota después de un rey; **we can't phone home from work** no nos dejan llamar a casa desde el trabajo

(**e**) *(indicating request)* **c. you tell those kids to shut up?** ¿quieres decirles a esos niños que se callen?; **can't you be a bit quieter?** ¿podrías hacer *or* armar menos ruido?; **mummy, c. I have an ice cream, please?** mamá, ¿me compras un helado?; **c. I have the chicken, please?** para mí pollo, por favor

(**f**) *(indicating order)* **you c. leave this room at once!** ¡sal de la habitación ahora mismo!; *Fam* **and you c. shut up and all!** ¡y tú cierra el pico también!

(**g**) *(with verbs indicating senses or mental processes: not translated)* **I c. see/hear them** los veo/oigo; **you c. taste the pepper in it** se nota la pimienta; **I c. see you don't believe me** ya veo que no me crees; **how c. you tell?** ¿cómo lo sabes?; **I can't remember/understand** no recuerdo/entiendo

Cana ['keɪnə] *n* Caná; **the wedding feast at C.** las bodas de Caná

Canaan ['keɪnən] *n* Canaán

Canaanite ['keɪnənaɪt] *n* cananeo(a) *m,f*

Canada ['kænədə] *n* (el) Canadá ►► ***C. goose*** barnacla *f* canadiense

Canadian [kə'neɪdɪən] **1** *n* canadiense *mf*
2 *adj* canadiense ►► ***C. canoe*** canoa *f* canadiense

canal [kə'næl] *n* (**a**) *(waterway)* canal *m* ►► ***c. boat*** gabarra *f*; ***the C. Zone*** *(in Panama)* la zona del Canal (**b**) *Anat* canal *m*

canalize ['kænəlaɪz] *vt* (**a**) *(region)* construir canales en; *(river)* canalizar, encauzar (**b**) *(efforts, funds)* canalizar

canapé ['kænəpeɪ] *n* canapé *m*

canard ['kænɑːd] *n (false report) Esp* bulo *m*, patraña *f*

Canary [kə'neərɪ] *n* **the C. Islands, the Canaries** las Islas Canarias, las Canarias; **C. Islander** canario(a)

canary [kə'neərɪ] *n* (**a**) *(bird)* canario *m* (**b**) *(colour)* **c. (yellow)** amarillo *m* canario ►► ***c. grass*** alpiste *m*

canasta [kə'næstə] *n* canasta *f (en naipes)*

Canberra ['kænbərə] *n* Canberra

cancan ['kæn'kæn] *n* cancán *m*

cancel ['kænsəl] (*pt & pp* **cancelled**, *US* **canceled**) **1** *vt* (**a**) *(call off) (meeting, match, trip)* suspender; *(huelga, manifestación)* desconvocar; *(flight, train)* suspender, cancelar
(**b**) *(revoke) (contract)* rescindir; *(agreement)* cancelar; *(order, subscription, reservation)* anular, cancelar; *(cheque)* anular, invalidar; *(debt)* saldar, amortizar
(**c**) *(ticket) (by stamping)* matasellar; *(by punching)* perforar
(**d**) *(cross out)* tachar
(**e**) *Math* eliminar
(**f**) *Comptr* cancelar ►► ***c. button*** botón *m* de cancelar
2 *vi* **he called to c.** llamó para cancelarlo; **they were supposed to be playing tonight, but they've cancelled** iban a tocar hoy, pero lo han suspendido

►**cancel out** *vt sep* (**a**) *(benefit)* neutralizar, anular; *(debt)* enjugar; **to c. each other out** *(effects, forces)* anularse, contrarrestarse (**b**) *Math* anular

cancellation [kænsə'leɪʃən] *n* (**a**) *(calling off) (of match, meeting, trip)* suspensión *f*; *(of flight, train)* suspensión *f*, cancelación *f*
(**b**) *(revocation) (of agreement)* cancelación *f*; *(of contract)* rescisión *f*; *(of order, subscription, reservation)* anulación *f*, cancelación *f*; *(of cheque)* anulación *f*, invalidación *f*; *(of debt)* amortización *f*, liquidación *f* ►► ***c. charge*** tarifa *f* de cancelación de reserva; ***c. fee*** tarifa *f* de cancelación de reserva
(**c**) *(on postage stamp)* matasellos *m inv*

Cancer ['kænsə(r)] *n (sign of zodiac)* Cáncer *m*; **to be (a) C.** ser Cáncer

cancer ['kænsə(r)] *n (disease)* cáncer *m*; **lung/skin c.** cáncer de pulmón/de piel; **to die of c.** morir de cáncer; *Fig* **we must remove the c. of militarism** hay que eliminar el cáncer del militarismo ►► ***c. drug*** fármaco *m* contra el cáncer; ***c. patient*** enfermo(a) *m,f* de cáncer; ***c. research*** investigación *f* del cáncer; ***c. specialist*** cancerólogo(a) *m,f*; *Fam* ***c. stick*** pitillo *m*, *Am* pucho *m*

cancer-causing ['kænsəkɔːzɪŋ] *adj* cancerígeno(a)

Cancerian [kæn'sɪərɪən] *n (person)* Cáncer *mf inv*

cancerous ['kænsərəs] *adj Med* canceroso(a); **c. tumour** tumor canceroso

candela [kæn'delə] *n Phys* candela *f*

candelabra [kændɪ'lɑːbrə] (*pl* **candelabras** *or* **candelabra**) *n* candelabro *m*

C and F (*abbr* **cost and freight**) C. & F., CAF, costo *m or Esp* coste *m* y flete

C and I (*abbr* **cost and insurance**) C. & I., costo *m or Esp* coste *m* y seguro

candid ['kændɪd] *adj (person, smile, report)* sincero(a), franco(a); **I'd like your c. opinion** me gustaría que me dijeras lo que piensas sinceramente; **to be quite c.,...** para ser sincero *or* franco,... ►► *TV* ***c. camera*** cámara *f* oculta

> **False friend**: The Spanish adjective **cándido** is not a translation for the English word **candid**. In Spanish **cándido** means "ingenuous, naive".

candida ['kændɪdə] *n Med* Candida *m* albicans *(hongo que causa la candidiasis)*

candidacy ['kændɪdəsɪ], **candidature** ['kændɪdətʃə(r)] *n* candidatura *f*

candidate ['kændɪdeɪt] *n* (**a**) *(for job, in election)* candidato(a) *m,f*; **to stand as a c. (for)** presentarse como candidato (a); *Fig* **he's a c. for the sack if ever there was one** es el candidato número uno para ser despedido (**b**) *(in exam)* examinando(a) *m,f*, candidato(a) *m,f*

candidature = **candidacy**

candidiasis [kændɪ'daɪəsɪs] *n Med* candidiasis *f inv*

candidly ['kændɪdlɪ] *adv* sinceramente, francamente

candidness ['kændɪdnɪs] *n* sinceridad *f*, franqueza *f*

candied ['kændɪd] *adj* escarchado(a), confitado(a), *Col, Méx* cristalizado(a), *RP* abrillantado(a) ►► ***c. peel*** piel *f* de naranja/limón escarchada

candle ['kændəl] *n* (**a**) *(domestic)* vela *f*; *(in church)* vela *f*, cirio *m* ►► ***c. grease*** sebo *m* (**b**) *Phys* candela *f* (**c**) IDIOMS **he can't hold a c. to you** no te llega ni a la suela del zapato; **it's not worth the c.** no vale *or Esp* merece la pena

candlelight ['kændəllaɪt] *n* luz *f* de las velas; **by c.** a la luz de las velas

candlelit ['kændəllɪt] *adj (room)* iluminado(a) con velas; **a c. dinner** una cena a la luz de las velas

Candlemas ['kændəlməs] *n Rel* la Candelaria

candlestick ['kændəlstɪk] *n* palmatoria *f*, candelero *m*

candlewick ['kændəlwɪk] *n* chenile *f*

can-do ['kæn'duː] *adj* **I admire her c. spirit** admiro su espíritu decidido

candour, *US* **candor** ['kændə(r)] *n* sinceridad *f*, franqueza *f*

> **False friend**: The Spanish noun **candor** is not a translation for the English word **candour**. In Spanish **candor** means "innocence, naivety".

C and W (*abbr* **country and western**) música *f* country

candy ['kændɪ] *n US (sweet)* caramelo *m*; *(sweets)* dulces *mpl*, golosinas *fpl* ►► ***c. apple*** manzana *f* acaramelada; ***c. bar*** barra *f* de chocolate, chocolatina *f*; ***c. store*** confitería *f*

candyfloss ['kændɪflɒs] *n Br* algodón *m* dulce

candy-striped ['kændɪstraɪpt] *adj* de rayas

cane [keɪn] **1** *n* (**a**) *(of sugar, bamboo)* caña *f*; *(for furniture, baskets)* mimbre *m* ►► ***c. furniture*** muebles *mpl* de mimbre; ***c. spirit*** aguardiente *m* de caña; ***c. sugar*** azúcar *f* de caña (**b**) *(rod) (walking-stick)* bastón *m*; *(for punishment)* vara *f*, palmeta *f*; *(for supporting plant)* rodrigón *m*; **to get the c.** ser castigado(a) con la vara
2 *vt* (**a**) *(beat)* pegar con la vara *or* palmeta (**b**) *Fam (defeat)* dar una paliza *or Esp* un palizón a

canine ['keɪnaɪn] **1** *n* (**a**) *Zool* can *m* (**b**) *Anat* **c. (tooth)** colmillo *m*, (diente *m*) canino *m*
2 *adj* canino(a)

caning ['keɪnɪŋ] *n* (**a**) *(beating)* castigo *m* con la vara *or* palmeta (**b**) *Fam (defeat)* paliza *f*, *Esp* palizón *m*

canister ['kænɪstə(r)] *n* (**a**) *(for flour, sugar, film, oil)* lata *f* (**b**) *(for tear gas, smoke)* bote *m*

canker ['kæŋkə(r)] *n* (**a**) *Med* ulceración *f* (**b**) *Bot* cancro *m* (**c**) *(evil influence)* cáncer *m*

cannabis ['kænəbɪs] *n (plant)* cáñamo *m*, cannabis *m*; *(drug)* hachís *m*, cannabis *m* ►► ***c. resin*** resina *f* (de cannabis)

canned [kænd] *adj* (**a**) *(food)* enlatado(a), en lata ►► *Fig* ***c. laughter*** risas *fpl* de fondo, risas *fpl* grabadas; *Fig* ***c. music*** música *f* de supermercado (**b**) *Fam (drunk) Esp* ciego(a), *Méx* cuete, *RP* en pedo; **to get c.** agarrarse una borrachera *or Esp* una buena curda *or Méx* un cuete

cannellini bean [kænə'liːnɪbiːn] *n* alubia *f* blanca

cannelloni [kænə'ləʊnɪ] *n* canelones *mpl*

canner ['kænə(r)] *n (business)* empresa *f* de conservas

cannery ['kænərɪ] *n* fábrica *f* de conservas

cannibal ['kænɪbəl] *n* caníbal *mf*, antropófago(a) *m,f*

cannibalism ['kænɪbəlɪzəm] *n* canibalismo *m*, antropofagia *f*

cannibalistic [kænɪbə'lɪstɪk] *adj* caníbal, antropófago(a)

cannibalization [kænɪbəlaɪ'zeɪʃən] *n Mktg* canibalismo *m*, canibalización *f (de productos)*

cannibalize ['kænɪbəlaɪz] *vt* (**a**) *(machinery, car)* desguazar *(para aprovechar las piezas)* (**b**) *Mktg* canibalizar *(productos)*

cannily ['kænɪlɪ] *adv* hábilmente, con astucia

canning ['kænɪŋ] *n* enlatado *m*, envasado *m* ►► ***c. plant*** planta *f* de enlatado *or* envasado

cannon ['kænən] **1** *n* (**a**) *(gun)* cañón *m* ►► ***c. fodder*** carne *f* de cañón (**b**) *Br (in billiards, snooker)* carambola *f*
2 *vi* (**a**) *(bump)* **to c. into sth/sb** chocar contra algo/alguien (**b**) *Br (in billiards, snooker)* **to c. into** hacer carambola con

cannonball ['kænənbɔːl] *n* bala *f* de cañón

cannot ['kænɒt] = **can not**

cannula ['kænjʊlə] (*pl* **cannulas** *or* **cannulae** ['kænjʊliː]) *n Med* cánula *f*

canny ['kænɪ] *adj (choice, remark)* astuto(a); **he's very c. with his money** es muy cuidadoso con su dinero

canoe [kə'nu:] **1** *n* (**a**) *(eskimo)* kayak *m*; *(native American)* canoa *f* (**b**) *(sporting)* piragua *f*, kayak *m* ►► *Sport* ***c. polo*** kayak *m* polo

2 *vi* recorrer en canoa; **we canoed down the Orinoco** descendimos el Orinoco en canoa

canoeing [kə'nu:ɪŋ] *n* piragüismo *m*; **to go c.** ir a hacer piragüismo

canoeist [kə'nu:ɪst] *n* piragüista *mf*

canon ['kænən] *n* (**a**) *(religious decree)* canon *m*; *Fig* **canons of good taste** cánones del buen gusto ►► ***c. law*** derecho *m* canónico

(**b**) *(priest)* canónigo *m*

(**c**) *(accepted body of works) (of writer)* = obras de un autor aceptadas como suyas; *(of religion)* canon *m*; **most women writers have usually been excluded from the c.** la mayoría de las mujeres escritoras no han sido consideradas tradicionalmente como dignas de ser estudiadas

(**d**) *Mus* canon *m*

canonical [kə'nɒnɪkəl] *adj* (**a**) *Rel (text)* canónico(a) (**b**) *(accepted)* canónico(a)

canonization [kænənaɪ'zeɪʃən] *n* canonización *f*

canonize ['kænənaɪz] *vt Rel* canonizar

canoodle [kə'nu:dəl] *vi Hum* besuquearse, *Esp* darse el lote

can-opener ['kænəʊpənə(r)] *n* abrelatas *m inv*

canopy ['kænəpɪ] *n* (**a**) *(above bed)* dosel *m*; *(outside shop)* toldo *m* (**b**) *(of trees)* copas *fpl* de los árboles (**c**) *(of parachute)* tela *f*, casquete *m*

cant [kænt] **1** *n* (**a**) *(insincere talk)* hipocresías *fpl*, falsedades *fpl*; *(clichés)* tópicos *mpl* (**b**) *(jargon)* jerga *f* (**c**) *(slope)* inclinación *f*, pendiente *f*; *(oblique surface)* superficie *f* inclinada

2 *vt (tilt)* inclinar

3 *vi* (**a**) *(tilt)* inclinarse (**b**) *(slope)* estar inclinado(a)

can't [kɑ:nt] = **can not**

Cantab (*abbr* **Cantabrigiensis**) *(in degree titles)* = abreviatura que indica que un título fue obtenido en la universidad de Cambridge

Cantabria [kæn'tæbrɪə] *n* Cantabria

Cantabrian [kæn'tæbrɪən] *n* **1** *(person)* cántabro(a) *m,f*

2 *adj* cántabro(a) ►► ***the C. Mountains*** la Cordillera Cantábrica; ***the C. Sea*** el (Mar) Cantábrico

cantaloup(e) ['kæntəlu:p] *n* melón *m* francés *or* cantaloup

cantankerous [kæn'tæŋkərəs] *adj* cascarrabias, refunfuñón(ona)

cantata [kæn'tɑ:tə] *n Mus* cantata *f*

canteen [kæn'ti:n] *n* (**a**) *(in factory, office)* cantina *f*, comedor *m*; *(in school)* comedor *m* (**b**) *(on military base)* cantina *f (tienda)* (**c**) *(water bottle)* cantimplora *f* (**d**) *Br (set)* **a c. of cutlery** una cubertería (**e**) *Mil (mess tin)* plato *m* de campaña *or* del rancho

canter ['kæntə(r)] **1** *n (on horse)* medio galope *m*; **the horse won at a c.** el caballo ganó la carrera cruzando la línea de meta a medio galope; *Fig* **they won at a c.** ganaron sin dificultad

2 *vi (horse)* ir a medio galope; *Fig* **to c. through an exam** pasar un examen con facilidad

Canterbury bell ['kæntəbrɪ'bel] *n* farolillo *m*

canticle ['kæntɪkəl] *n Mus* cántico *m*

cantilever ['kæntɪli:və(r)] **1** *n (in engineering)* voladizo *m*, viga *f* voladiza ►► ***c. bridge*** puente *m* voladizo

2 *vt* **the stand had a roof that was cantilevered over the seats** la grada tenía una cubierta en voladizo sobre los asientos

canting ['kæntɪŋ] *adj (hypocritical)* hipócrita

canto ['kæntəʊ] (*pl* **cantos**) *n (section of poem)* canto *m*

Canton [kæn'tɒn] *n* Cantón

canton ['kæntɒn] *n* cantón *m*

cantonal ['kæntənəl] *adj* cantonal

Cantonese [kæntə'ni:z] **1** *n* (**a**) *(person)* cantonés(esa) *m,f* (**b**) *(language)* cantonés *m*

2 *adj* cantonés(esa)

cantonment [kən'tu:nmənt] *n Mil* acantonamiento *m*

cantor ['kæntɔ:(r)] *n Rel* (**a**) *(Jewish)* = en una sinagoga, persona que dirige los cantos (**b**) *(Christian)* chantre *m*, sochantre *m*

Canuck [kə'nʌk] *n US Fam* (**a**) *(Canadian)* = término a veces peyorativo para referirse a los canadienses (**b**) *(French Canadian)* = término a veces peyorativo para referirse a los francocanadienses

Canute [kə'nju:t] *pr n* Canuto

canvas ['kænvəs] *n* (**a**) *(cloth)* lona *f*; **under c.** *(in tent)* en una tienda de campaña *or Am* carpa; *(on sailing ship)* a vela ►► ***c. shoes*** zapatillas *fpl* de lona, playeras *fpl* (**b**) *(for painting)* lienzo *m*, tela *f*; *(for embroidery)* cañamazo *m* (**c**) *(painting)* cuadro *m*, lienzo *m* (**d**) *(of boxing ring)* lona *f* (**e**) *(in rowing)* = la parte delantera de un bote de remos

canvasback ['kænvəsbæk] *n* porrón *m* coacoxtle

canvass ['kænvəs] **1** *vt* (**a**) *Pol* **to c. a street/an area** visitar las casas de una calle/una zona haciendo campaña electoral (**b**) *US Pol* **to c. votes** *(scrutinize)* escrutar los votos (**c**) *Com (consumers, customers)* encuestar (**d**) *(seek opinions)* **to c. opinion** hacer un sondeo de opinión informal

2 *vi* (**a**) *Pol* = hacer campaña electoral hablando directamente con los electores por las casas o en la calle (**b**) *Com* **to c. for customers** tratar de captar clientes

3 *n (for votes)* = recorrido por las casas o en la calle haciendo campaña electoral hablando directamente con los electores ►► ***c. returns*** = resultados de los sondeos informales realizados por los activistas que hacen campaña electoral en la calle

canvasser ['kænvəsə(r)] *n* (**a**) *Pol* = persona que va de casa en casa tratando de captar votos para un partido (**b**) *US (scrutineer)* escrutador(ora) *m,f* (**c**) *Com (salesman)* representante *mf*; *(door-to-door)* vendedor(ora) *m,f* a domicilio; **no canvassers** *(notice on door)* prohibida la venta a domicilio

canvassing ['kænvəsɪŋ] *n* (**a**) *Pol* captación *f* de votos; **all parties have intensified their c. in the last few days** todos los partidos han intensificado sus esfuerzos por captar votos en los últimos días (**b**) *Com (for orders)* captación *f* de pedidos; *(for custom)* captación *f* de clientes

canyon ['kænjən] *n* cañón *m*

canyoning ['kænjənɪŋ] *n Sport* barranquismo *m*

CAP [si:eɪ'pi:] *n EU* (*abbr* **Common Agricultural Policy**) PAC *f*

cap [kæp] **1** *n* (**a**) *(headgear) (without peak)* gorro *m*; *(with peak)* gorra *f*; *(of nurse, waitress)* cofia *f*; IDIOM **to go c. in hand to sb** acudir a alguien en actitud humilde; IDIOM **to set one's c. at sb** poner los ojos en alguien; PROV **if the c. fits, wear it** quien se pica, ajos come ►► ***c. and bells*** gorro *m* de campanillas; ***c. and gown*** gorra *f* y bonete *m*

(**b**) *(cover) (of bottle)* tapón *m*; *(metal)* chapa *f*; *(of pen)* capucha *f*, capuchón *m*; *(for tooth)* funda *f*; *(of mushroom)* sombrero *m*, sombrerillo *m* ►► *Tech* ***c. screw*** tornillo *m* de capuchón

(**c**) *(for toy gun)* fulminante *m*

(**d**) *(limit)* **to put a c. on sth** poner un tope a algo

(**e**) *Br Sport* **to win a c.** entrar en la selección nacional; **he won his first international c.** debutó con la selección nacional

(**f**) *(contraceptive device)* diafragma *m*

(**g**) *US Fam (bullet)* plomo *m*, bala *f*

2 *vt* (*pt & pp* **capped**) (**a**) *(cover)* **to be capped with** estar cubierto(a) de *or* por

(**b**) *(surpass, do better than)* superar; **that caps the lot!** ¡es el colmo!; **to c. it all,...** para colmo,...

(**c**) *(limit) (spending, taxation)* poner un tope a; *(local authority)* limitar las competencias fiscales de

(**d**) *Br Sport* **he was capped for England** fue internacional *or* jugó con la selección inglesa; **the manager decided to c. two new players** el seleccionador decidió que debutaran dos nuevos jugadores

(**e**) *(tooth)* poner una funda a

(**f**) *US Fam (shoot)* llenar de plomo, *Am* balear, *Am* abalear, *Méx* balacear

cap. (**a**) (*abbr* **capacity**) capacidad *f* (**b**) (*abbr* **capital**) cap.

capability [keɪpə'bɪlɪtɪ] *n* (**a**) *(ability, capacity)* capacidad *f* (**to do sth** para hacer algo); **it is beyond our capabilities** no entra dentro de nuestras posibilidades (**b**) *Mil* capacidad *f*; **nuclear c.** capacidad nuclear

capable ['keɪpəbəl] *adj* (**a**) *(able)* **to be c. of doing sth** *(be able to do)* ser capaz de hacer algo; **that man's c. of anything** ese hombre es capaz de cualquier cosa (**b**) *(competent)* capaz, competente; **the project is now in the c. hands of Mr Simpson** el proyecto queda ahora a cargo del muy competente señor Simpson

capably ['keɪpəblɪ] *adv* competentemente; **c. assisted by...** con la inestimable colaboración de...

capacious [kə'peɪʃəs] *adj (room, container)* espacioso(a); *(clothes)* amplio(a)

capacitance [kə'pæsɪtəns] *n Elec* capacitancia *f*, capacidad *f* eléctrica (de un condensador)

capacitor [kə'pæsɪtə(r)] *n Elec* condensador *m*

capacity [kə'pæsɪtɪ] *n* (**a**) *(of container, bus)* capacidad *f*; *(of hall, theatre, stadium)* capacidad *f*, aforo *m*; **the stadium has a c. of 40,000** el estadio tiene capacidad para 40.000 espectadores, el estadio

tiene un aforo de 40.000 espectadores; **a c. crowd** *(in hall, stadium)* un lleno (absoluto); **full to c.** *(hall, theatre, stadium)* lleno hasta la bandera
(**b**) *(of engine)* cilindrada *f*
(**c**) *(aptitude)* capacidad *f*; **to have a c. for sth** tener capacidad para algo; **beyond/within my c.** fuera de/dentro de mis posibilidades
(**d**) *(role)* calidad *f*, condición *f*; **in my c. as...** en mi calidad de...; **to act in one's official c.** actuar *or* intervenir oficialmente *or* de manera oficial; **he's acting in an advisory c.** actúa *or* interviene en calidad de asesor
(**e**) *(output)* capacidad *f* productiva, rendimiento *m* (máximo); **to work at full c.** trabajar a pleno rendimiento; **the factory has not yet reached c.** la fábrica aún no ha alcanzado su capacidad productiva

caparison [kəˈpærɪsən] *n (for horse)* gualdrapa *f*

cape[1] [keɪp] *n (cloak)* capa *f*; *(of bullfighter)* capote *m*

cape[2] *n Geog* cabo *m* ►► ***C. Canaveral*** Cabo *m* Cañaveral; ***the C. of Good Hope*** el Cabo de Buena Esperanza; ***C. Horn*** (el) Cabo de Hornos; ***C. Town*** Ciudad del Cabo

Cape Verde [ˈkeɪpˈvɜːd] *n* Cabo Verde

Cape Verdean [ˈkeɪpˈvɜːdɪən] **1** *n* caboverdiano(a) *m,f*
2 *adj* caboverdiano(a)

caper[1] [ˈkeɪpə(r)] *n (plant, food)* alcaparra *f*

caper[2] **1** *n* (**a**) *(nonsense)* **I'm getting too old for this sort of c.** me estoy haciendo mayor para este tipo de tonterías; **he was up to his old capers again** ya estaba haciendo otra vez de las suyas; **what a c.!** *(fuss)* ¡qué *Esp* follón *or* lío! (**b**) *US Fam (illegal activity)* chanchullo *m*
2 *vi* **to c. (about)** retozar

capercaillie [kæpəˈkeɪlɪ] *n* urogallo *m*

capful [ˈkæpfʊl] *n (of liquid)* tapón *m (lleno)*; **add two capfuls to a hot bath** añada dos tapones a una bañera llena de agua caliente

capi *pl of* **capo**[2]

capillarity [kæpɪˈlærɪtɪ] *n Phys* capilaridad *f*

capillary [kəˈpɪlərɪ] **1** *n* capilar *m*; **capillaries** *mpl* vasos capilares ►► ***c. action*** capilaridad *f*; ***c. tube*** tubo *m* capilar
2 *adj* capilar

capital [ˈkæpɪtəl] **1** *n* (**a**) *(letter)* mayúscula *f*; **write in capitals** escriba con mayúsculas
(**b**) *(city)* capital *f*; **the financial c. of the world** la capital financiera del mundo
(**c**) *Archit* capitel *m*
(**d**) *Fin* capital *m*; *(assets)* patrimonio *m*, capital *m*; **c. and labour** el capital y los trabajadores; **to raise c.** reunir capital; **to live off one's c.** vivir del capital que se posee *(sin invertirlo)*; *Fig* **to make c. out of sth** sacar partido de algo ►► ***c. assets*** activo *m* fijo, bienes *mpl* de capital; ***c. equipment*** bienes *mpl* de equipo *or* de producción; ***c. expenditure*** inversión *f* en activo fijo; ***c. flight*** evasión *f* de capitales *or* divisas; ***c. gains*** plusvalías *fpl or* ganancias *fpl* de capital ***c. gains tax*** impuesto *m* sobre (las) plusvalías; ***c. goods*** bienes *mpl* de capital; ***c. injection*** inyección *f or* aportación *f* de capital; ***c. investment*** inversión *f* (de capital); ***c. market*** mercado *m* de capitales; *US* ***c. stock*** capital *m* escriturado; ***c. tax*** impuesto *m* sobre el capital; ***c. yield*** rendimiento *m or* renta *f* del capital
2 *adj* (**a**) *(principal)* ***c. city*** capital *f*
(**b**) *(important)* capital; **of c. importance** de capital importancia ►► ***c. ship*** = cualquiera de los barcos más grandes e importantes de una marina de guerra
(**c**) *(letter)* mayúscula; **c. T** T mayúscula; **in c. letters** en mayúsculas; *Fam* **he's arrogant with a c. A** es terriblemente arrogante, *Esp* es un arrogante de tomo y lomo, *RP* es rearrogante
(**d**) *Law* ***c. crime*** delito *m* capital; ***c. offence*** delito *m* capital; ***c. punishment*** pena *f* capital *or* de muerte
(**e**) *Br Old-fashioned (splendid)* excelente

capital-intensive [ˈkæpɪtəlɪnˈtensɪv] *adj* con grandes necesidades de capital

capitalism [ˈkæpɪtəlɪzəm] *n* capitalismo *m*

capitalist [ˈkæpɪtəlɪst] **1** *n* capitalista *mf*
2 *adj* capitalista

capitalistic [ˈkæpɪtəlɪstɪk] *adj* capitalista

capitalization [kæpɪtəlaɪˈzeɪʃən] *n Fin* capitalización *f*

capitalize [ˈkæpɪtəlaɪz] *vt* (**a**) *(provide with capital)* financiar, capitalizar (**b**) *Fin (convert into capital)* capitalizar, convertir en capital; **capitalized expense** gasto amortizable (**c**) *(word, letter)* escribir con mayúscula

► **capitalize on** *vt insep* aprovechar, aprovecharse de, capitalizar

capitation [kæpɪˈteɪʃən] *n Fin* **c. (tax)** impuesto *m* por cabeza, capitación *f*

Capitol [ˈkæpɪtəl] *n* (**a**) *(in Rome)* **the C.** el Capitolio (**b**) *(in US)* **the C.** *(national)* el Capitolio; **the (state) C.** el Capitolio (del Estado) ►► ***C. Hill*** el Capitolio

capitula *pl of* **capitulum**

capitulate [kəˈpɪtjʊleɪt] *vi* capitular (**to** ante)

capitulation [kəpɪtjʊˈleɪʃən] *n* capitulación *f*, rendición *f* (**to** ante)

capitulum [kəˈpɪtjʊləm] (*pl* **capitula** kəˈpɪtjʊlə]) *n Bot* cabezuela *f*

caplet [ˈkæplɪt] *n US* comprimido *m*, pastilla *f (de forma ovalada)*

capo[1] [ˈkæpəʊ] (*pl* **capos**) *n (for guitar)* cejilla *f*, ceja *f*

capo[2] (*pl* **capos** *or* **capi** [ˈkæpiː]) *n (mafia boss)* capo *m*

capon [ˈkeɪpɒn] *n Culin* capón *m*

capper [ˈkæpə(r)] *n US Fam* **that was the c.** aquello fue el colmo

cappuccino [kæpəˈtʃiːnəʊ] (*pl* **cappuccinos**) *n* (café *m*) capuchino *m*

caprice [kəˈpriːs] *n* capricho *m*

capricious [kəˈprɪʃəs] *adj (person, horse, fate)* caprichoso(a); *(weather)* cambiante

capriciously [kəˈprɪʃəslɪ] *adv* caprichosamente

capriciousness [kəˈprɪʃəsnɪs] *n* carácter *m* caprichoso

Capricorn [ˈkæprɪkɔːn] *n (sign of zodiac)* Capricornio *m*; **to be (a) C.** ser Capricornio

capriole [ˈkæprɪəʊl] *n* cabriola *f*

caps [kæps] *npl Comptr & Typ* (*abbr* **capital letters**) (letras *fpl*) mayúsculas *fpl* ►► ***c. lock*** mayúsculas *fpl* fijas; ***c. lock key*** tecla *f* de mayúsculas fijas

capsicum [ˈkæpsɪkəm] *n* pimiento *m*

capsize [kæpˈsaɪz] **1** *vt* hacer volcar
2 *vi* volcar

capstan [ˈkæpstən] *n Naut* cabrestante *m*

capsular [ˈkæpsjʊlə(r)] *adj* capsular

capsule [ˈkæpsjuːl] *n* (**a**) *(container)* cápsula *f* (**b**) *(pill)* cápsula *f* (**c**) **(space) c.** cápsula *f* espacial (**d**) *Bot* cápsula *f* (**e**) *Anat* cápsula *f*

Capt *Mil* (*abbr* **Captain**) Capitán(ana) *m,f*

captain [ˈkæptɪn] **1** *n* (**a**) *(of boat)* capitán(ana) *m,f*; *(of aircraft)* comandante *mf*; **this is your c. speaking** les habla el comandante; **captains of industry** industriales poderosos, magnates de la industria (**b**) *(of team)* capitán(ana) *m,f* (**c**) *(in army, air force)* capitán(ana) *m,f*; **c. Carruthers** el capitán Carruthers (**d**) *US (in police)* comisario(a) *m,f* (**e**) *US (head waiter)* maître *m*; *(of bellboys)* jefe *m* de botones
2 *vt Sport* capitanear; **he captained his side to victory** condujo a su equipo a la victoria con él de capitán

captaincy [ˈkæptɪnsɪ] *n Sport* capitanía *f*; **under his c. they won the league** ganaron la liga con él de capitán

caption [ˈkæpʃən] **1** *n* (**a**) *(under picture)* pie *m* de foto; *(under cartoon)* texto *m* (**b**) *(heading)* titular *m*, encabezamiento *m*, *Méx, RP* encabezado *m* (**c**) *Cin (subtitle)* subtítulo *m*
2 *vt* (**a**) *(picture)* añadir un pie de foto a (**b**) *Cin* subtitular

captious [ˈkæpʃəs] *adj Formal (person)* puntilloso(a), criticón(ona); *(remark, attitude)* crítico(a)

captivate [ˈkæptɪveɪt] *vt* cautivar, embelesar

captivating [ˈkæptɪveɪtɪŋ] *adj (smile, manner)* cautivador(ora), arrebatador(ora)

captive [ˈkæptɪv] **1** *n* cautivo(a) *m,f*, prisionero(a) *m,f*
2 *adj* cautivo(a); **he was taken c.** fue hecho prisionero; **they were held c. for four days** los tuvieron prisioneros durante cuatro días; **he knew he had a c. audience** sabía que su público no tenía elección ►► *Mktg* ***c. market*** mercado *m* cautivo

captivity [kæpˈtɪvɪtɪ] *n* cautividad *f*, cautiverio *m*; **in c.** en cautividad *or* cautiverio

captor [ˈkæptə(r)] *n* captor(ora) *m,f*

capture [ˈkæptʃə(r)] **1** *vt* (**a**) *(take prisoner) (person)* capturar, apresar; *(wild animal)* capturar; *(town)* tomar; *(in chess, draughts)* comer
(**b**) *(gain control of) (attention, interest)* captar; *Com (market)* acaparar, hacerse con; **this exciting prospect captured our imagination** esta apasionante posibilidad atrajo *or* despertó nuestro interés
(**c**) *(succeed in representing) (mood)* reflejar, reproducir; **this photograph captures the moment perfectly** esta fotografía refleja *or* reproduce el momento perfectamente; **they captured the event on film** filmaron el acontecimiento
(**d**) *Comptr (data)* meter, introducir
2 *n* (**a**) *(of person)* captura *f*, apresamiento *m*; *(of wild animal)* captura *f*; *(of town)* toma *f* (**b**) *Comptr (of data)* captura *f*

Capuchin [ˈkæpʊtʃɪn] **1** *n (monk)* capuchino *m*
2 *adj* capuchino *m*

capuchin ['kæpʊtʃɪn] *n* **c. (monkey)** (mono *m*) capuchino *m*

CAR [siːeɪ'ɑː(r)] *n* (*abbr* **Central African Republic**) República *f* Centroafricana

car [kɑː(r)] *n* (**a**) *(automobile)* coche *m*, *Am* carro *m*, *CSur* auto *m*; **by c.** en coche *or Am* carro *or CSur* auto ►► ***c. bomb*** coche *m* bomba; *Br* ***c. boot sale*** = mercadillo en el que los particulares venden objetos que traen el maletero del coche; ***c. coat*** tres cuartos *m inv*; ***c. crash*** accidente *m* de coche *or* de automóvil *or* automovilístico; ***c. dealer*** *(in general)* vendedor(ora) *m,f* de coches; *(of particular make)* concesionario *m* de automóviles; ***c. door*** puerta *f* (del coche); ***c. ferry*** transbordador *m* de vehículos, ferry *m* para vehículos; *Br* ***c. hire*** alquiler *m* de coches, *Méx* renta *f* de carros; ***c. industry*** industria *f* automovilística; ***c. insurance*** seguro *m* del automóvil; ***c. lot*** = terreno al aire libre en el que están expuestos los coches en venta; *Br* ***c. park*** parking *m*, estacionamiento *m*, *Esp* aparcamiento *m*, *Col, Pan* parqueadero *m*; ***c. phone*** teléfono *m* de coche; ***c. pool*** *(of company, organization)* flota *f* de vehículos; *(car-sharing scheme)* = acuerdo para compatir un coche entre varias personas para ir a trabajar, llevar a los niños al colegio, etc.; ***c. radio*** radio *f* (del coche), autorradio *m o f*; *US* ***c. rental*** alquiler *m* de coches, *Méx* renta *f* de carros; ***c. show*** feria *f* del automóvil; ***c. wash*** tren *m or* túnel *m* de lavado

(**b**) *US (train, subway carriage)* vagón *m*, coche *m*

(**c**) *US (tram)* tranvía *f*

(**d**) *US (of lift)* cabina *f*

(**e**) *(of balloon)* barquilla *f*; *(of airship)* góndola *f*

carabiner [kærə'biːnə(r)] *n (in mountaineering)* mosquetón *m*

Caracas [kə'rækəs] *n* Caracas

caracole ['kærəkəʊl] *n* escarceo *m*

carafe [kə'ræf] *n* jarra *f*

carambola [kærəm'bəʊlə] *n* (**a**) *(tree)* carambolo *m* (**b**) *(fruit)* carambola *f*

caramel ['kærəməl] *n* (**a**) *(burnt sugar)* caramelo *m* ►► ***c. flavouring*** aromatizante *m* con sabor a caramelo (**b**) *(toffee)* caramelo *m*

caramelize ['kærəməlaɪz] **1** *vt* caramelizar, poner a punto de caramelo

2 *vi* caramelizarse, ponerse a punto de caramelo

carapace ['kærəpeɪs] *n Zool* caparazón *m*

carat ['kærət] *n* (**a**) *(of gold)* quilate *m*; **18-c. gold** oro de 18 quilates (**b**) *(for diamonds)* quilate *m*

caravan ['kærəvæn] *n* (**a**) *Br (pulled by car)* caravana *f*, rulot *f* ►► ***c. holiday*** vacaciones *fpl* en caravana; ***c. site*** camping *m* para caravanas (**b**) *(of gypsy)* carromato *m* (**c**) *(in desert)* caravana *f*

caravanette [kærəvə'net] *n Br* autocaravana *f*

caravanning ['kærəvænɪŋ] *n Br* caravaning *m*; **to go c.** ir de vacaciones en caravana, ir de caravaning

caravel(le) ['kærəvel] *n* carabela *f*

caraway ['kærəweɪ] *n (plant)* alcaravea *f*; **c. seeds** carvis

carbide ['kɑːbaɪd] *n Chem* carburo *m*

carbine ['kɑːbaɪn] *n* carabina *f*

carbohydrate [kɑːbəʊ'haɪdreɪt] *n* (**a**) *Chem* hidrato *m* de carbono, carbohidrato *m* (**b**) *(foodstuff)* hidrato *m* de carbono, carbohidrato *m*

carbolic [kɑː'bɒlɪk] *adj Chem* ***c. acid*** fenol *m*, ácido *m* fénico *or* carbólico; ***c. soap*** jabón *m* (desinfectante) de brea

carbon ['kɑːbən] *n* (**a**) *Chem* carbono *m* ►► *Biol* ***c. cycle*** ciclo *m* del carbono; ***c. (14) dating*** prueba *f* del *or* datación *f* por carbono 14; ***c. dioxide*** dióxido *m or* bióxido *m* de carbono, anhídrido *m* carbónico; ***c. fibre*** fibra *f* de carbono; ***c. monoxide*** monóxido *m* de carbono; ***c. steel*** acero *m* al carbono (**b**) *(for copying)* **c. (paper)** papel *m* carbón *or* de calco ►► ***c. copy*** copia *f* en papel carbón; *Fig* calco *m*, copia *f* exacta

carbonaceous [kɑːbə'neɪʃəs] *adj* carbonoso(a)

carbonate ['kɑːbəneɪt] **1** *n Chem* carbonato *m*

2 *vt (drink)* gasificar

carbonated ['kɑːbəneɪtɪd] *adj* carbónico(a), con gas ►► ***c. drink*** bebida *f* carbónica; ***c. water*** agua *f* con gas

carbonic [kɑː'bɒnɪk] *adj Chem* carbónico(a) ►► ***c. acid*** ácido *m* carbónico

carboniferous [kɑːbə'nɪfərəs] **1** *n* **the C.** el carbonífero

2 *adj (period)* carbonífero(a)

carbonization [kɑːbənaɪ'zeɪʃən] *n* carbonización *f*

carbonize ['kɑːbənaɪz] *vt* convertir en carbono

carborundum® [kɑːbə'rʌndəm] *n* carborundo *m*

carboy ['kɑːbɔɪ] *n* bombona *f*, garrafón *m*

carbuncle ['kɑːbʌŋkəl] *n* (**a**) *Med* = acumulación de forúnculos (**b**) *Geol* carbunclo *m*, carbúnculo *m*

carburation [kæbjʊ'reɪʃən] *n* carburación *f*

carburettor, *US* **carburetor** [kɑːbjʊ'retə(r)] *n* carburador *m*

carcass ['kɑːkəs] *n* (**a**) *(of animal)* animal *m* muerto; *(at butcher's)* res *f* muerta; **(chicken) c.** huesos *mpl or* restos *mpl* (de pollo) (**b**) *Fam Hum (of person)* **move your c.!** ¡mueve el culo! (**c**) *(of building, ship, car)* armazón *m*

carcinogen [kɑː'sɪnədʒen] *n Med* agente *m* carcinógeno *or* cancerígeno

carcinogenic [kɑːsɪnə'dʒenɪk] *adj Med* carcinógeno(a), cancerígeno(a)

carcinoma [kɑːsɪ'nəʊmə] *n Med* carcinoma *m*

card[1] [kɑːd] **1** *n* (**a**) *(for game)* carta *f*, naipe *m*; **to play cards** jugar a las cartas ►► ***c. game*** juego *m* de cartas *or* naipes; ***c. table*** mesa *f* de juego *(para cartas)*; ***c. trick*** truco *m or* juego *m* de cartas

(**b**) *(with printed information)* tarjeta *f*; *(for index)* ficha *f* ►► ***c. catalogue*** fichero *m* (de tarjetas); ***c. file*** fichero *m* de tarjetas; ***c. index*** fichero *m* (de tarjetas)

(**c**) *(for identification) (for club, library)* carné *m*, carnet *m*, *CSur, Méx* credencial *m*; *(for business)* tarjeta *f* (de visita) ►► ***c. key*** tarjeta *f*; *Pol* ***c. vote*** votación *f* por delegación

(**d**) *(greetings card)* tarjeta *f*; *(postcard)* (tarjeta *f*) postal *f*

(**e**) *(thin cardboard)* cartulina *f* ►► ***c. mount*** *(for print, photograph)* paspartú *m*

(**f**) *Comptr* tarjeta *f* ►► ***c. punch*** perforadora *f*

(**g**) *(in golf)* tarjeta *f* (de recorrido)

(**h**) *(of race meeting)* programa *m* (de carreras)

(**i**) *Fam Old-fashioned* **he's a real c.!** ¡es todo un personaje!

(**j**) IDIOMS **play your cards right and you could get promoted** si juegas bien tus cartas, puedes conseguir un ascenso; **the cards are stacked against him** lleva las de perder; **to have** *or* **hold all the cards** tener la sartén por el mango; **to play** *or* **keep one's cards close to one's chest** no dar ninguna pista, *RP* no mostrar el juego; **to play one's best** *or* **strongest** *or* **trump c.** jugarse la mejor carta; **to put one's cards on the table** poner las cartas sobre la mesa, *RP* mostrar el juego; **to have a c. up one's sleeve** tener un as en la manga; **it is** *Br* **on** *or US* **in the cards that...** es más que probable que...; *Br Fam* **to get one's cards** ser despedido(a)

2 *vt* (**a**) *(in golf)* entregar una tarjeta (con un recorrido) de (**b**) *US (ask for identity card)* pedir el carné a

card[2] *Tex* **1** *n* carda *f*

2 *vt* cardar

cardamom ['kɑːdəməm] *n* cardamomo *m*, grana *f* del Paraíso

cardan joint ['kɑːdəndʒɔɪnt] *n* cardán *m*

cardboard ['kɑːdbɔːd] **1** *n* cartón *m* ►► ***c. box*** caja *f* de cartón; ***c. city*** = lugar donde duermen los vagabundos

2 *adj* (**a**) *(container, partition)* de cartón; **a c. cut-out** una figura de cartón (**b**) *Fig (insubstantial)* vacío(a)

card-carrying ['kɑːdkærɪɪŋ] *adj* **c. member** miembro *or* socio(a) (de pleno derecho); **a c. Communist** un miembro del partido comunista

cardholder ['kɑːdhəʊldə(r)] *n* titular *mf* (de una tarjeta)

cardiac ['kɑːdɪæk] *adj* cardíaco(a) ►► ***c. arrest*** paro *m* cardíaco; ***c. massage*** masaje *m* cardíaco

cardie ['kɑːdɪ] *n Br Fam* cárdigan *m*, chaqueta *f* (de punto)

cardigan ['kɑːdɪgən] *n* cárdigan *m*, chaqueta *f* (de punto)

cardinal ['kɑːdɪnəl] **1** *n* (**a**) *Rel* cardenal *m* (**b**) *(bird)* cardenal *m* ►► ***northern c.*** cardenal *m* de Virginia

2 *adj (importance, significance)* capital, cardinal ►► ***c. number*** número *m* cardinal; ***c. point*** punto *m* cardinal; ***c. sins*** pecados *mpl* capitales; ***c. virtues*** virtudes *fpl* cardinales

cardiogram ['kɑːdɪəgræm] *n* cardiograma *m*

cardiograph ['kɑːdɪəgrɑːf] *n* cardiógrafo *m*

cardiography [kɑːdɪ'ɒgrəfɪ] *n* cardiografía *f*

cardiologist [kɑːdɪ'ɒlədʒɪst] *n* cardiólogo(a) *m,f*

cardiology [kɑːdɪ'ɒlədʒɪ] *n* cardiología *f*

cardiopulmonary [kɑːdɪəʊ'pʌlmənərɪ] *adj Med* cardiorrespiratorio(a)

cardiovascular [kɑːdɪəʊ'væskjʊlə(r)] *adj Med* cardiovascular ►► ***c. system*** sistema *m* cardiovascular

carditis [kɑː'daɪtɪs] *n Med* carditis *f*

cardphone ['kɑːdfəʊn] *n Br* teléfono *m* que funciona con tarjetas

card-sharp(er) ['kɑːdʃɑːp(ə(r))] *n Pej* tahúr(ura) *m,f*, fullero(a) *m,f*

CARE [keə(r)] *n* (*abbr* **Co-operative for American Relief to Everywhere**) = organización estadounidense de ayuda humanitaria ►► ***C. package*** = paquete conteniendo ayuda humanitaria

---

CARE [keə(r)] **1** *n* **(a)** *(worry)* preocupación *f*, inquietud *f*; *(problem)* preocupación *f*; **she doesn't have a c. in the world** no tiene ni una sola preocupación

(b) *(attention, effort)* cuidado *m*, atención *f*; **to do sth with great c.** hacer algo con mucho cuidado; **to drive with c.** conducir *or Am* manejar con precaución *or* prudencia; **he was charged with driving without due c. and attention** fue acusado de conducción temeraria; **to take c. to do sth** procurar hacer algo; **take c. not to spill** *or* **that you don't spill any ink** ten cuidado de no derramar tinta; **take c. on the roads** conduce *or Am* maneja con prudencia; **I've taken a lot of c. over this piece of work** he puesto mucho cuidado en este trabajo; **take more c. with your handwriting** pon más atención en tu caligrafía

(c) *(looking after)* cuidado *m*; **(medical) c.** asistencia *f* médica; *Br* **to put a child in c.** poner a un niño bajo la tutela del Estado; *Br* **she was taken into c.** fue puesto bajo tutela; **to be in** *or* **under sb's c.** estar al cuidado de alguien; **write to me c. of Mrs Wallace** escríbeme a la dirección de la Sra Wallace; **to take c. of** *(look after) (person)* cuidar de; *(animal, machine)* cuidar; *(deal with)* ocuparse de; **to take c. of oneself** cuidarse; **it will take c. of itself** se resolverá por sí solo; **take good c. of him, won't you?** cuídalo bien, ¿de acuerdo?; **that has all been taken c. of by our lawyers** nuestros abogados ya se han ocupado de todo eso; **that takes c. of the financial side of things** y con eso ya hemos terminado con el aspecto financiero; **I'll take c. of the bill** yo pago la cuenta; *Fam* **take c. (of yourself)** *(goodbye)* ¡cuídate!, *CAm, Méx* ¡que estés bien! ►► *Br* ***c. in the community*** = política que aboga que el cuidado de discapacitados o ancianos no dependa de instituciones como hospitales o asilos, sino de sus familias y la comunidad en general; ***c. label*** *(on garment)* etiqueta *f* con las instrucciones de lavado

2 *vt* **(a)** *(mind)* **I don't c. what he says** no me importa lo que diga; **what do I c.?** ¿y a mí que me importa?; **who cares what they think?** ¿a quién le importa lo que piensen ellos?; **I don't c. whether he likes it or not** me da lo mismo que le guste o no

(b) *Formal (like)* **would you c. to come with me?** ¿podría *or* le gustaría acompañarme?; **would you c. to try some of this wine?** ¿quiere probar este vino?; **I wouldn't c. to find out what he's like when he's angry** no quiero ni imaginarme cómo es cuando se *esp Esp* enfada *or esp Am* enoja; **I was more nervous than I cared to admit** estaba más nervioso de lo que quería admitir

(c) *(be willing to)* **he'll tell anyone who cares to listen** va por ahí contándoselo a todo el mundo

3 *vi* **(a)** *(be concerned)* preocuparse **(about** por); **no one seems to c.** no parece importarle a nadie, nadie parece preocuparse; **that's all he cares about** eso es lo único que le preocupa; **he said she'd be angry, as if I cared** dijo que se *esp Esp* enfadaría *or esp Am* enojaría, como si me importara; **you can go ahead and tell her for all I c.** me trae sin cuidado que se lo digas, *RP* por mí, decíselo; **I could be dead for all they c.** por ellos, como si me muero, *Am* por ellos, podría morirme; **I couldn't** *or US Fam* **could c. less!** ¡me trae sin cuidado!, ¡me importa un pepino!; **I don't c.!** ¡me da igual!, ¡no me importa!; **see if I c.!** ¡me trae sin cuidado!, ¡me importa un pepino!; **who cares?** ¿qué más da?

(b) *(feel affection)* **I really c. about you** me importas mucho

►**care for** *vt insep* **(a)** *(look after) (person)* cuidar (de); *(animal, machine)* cuidar; **well cared for** bien cuidado(a)

(b) *Formal (like)* **I don't c. for this music** no me gusta esta música; **would you c. for some tea?** ¿quiere un té?, ¿le *Esp* apetece *or Carib, Col, Méx* provoca *or Méx* antoja un té?

(c) *(feel affection towards)* **I c. for you deeply** me importas muchísimo

---

careen [kə'ri:n] **1** *vt (ship)* inclinar para carenar

2 *vi (rush)* ir a toda velocidad; **the train careened from side to side** el tren se bamboleaba de un lado a otro

career [kə'rɪə(r)] **1** *n (working life, profession)* carrera *f*; **a c. in banking/engineering** (una) carrera en el sector de la banca/ingeniería; **to make a c. for oneself** labrarse un futuro, hacer carrera; **her university c.** su paso por la universidad; **it was a good/bad c. move** fue bueno/malo para mi/tu/*etc.* carrera; **a job with c. prospects** un trabajo con buenas perspectivas profesionales ►► ***careers advice*** orientación *f* profesional *or* vocacional; ***careers adviser*** asesor(ora) *m,f* de orientación profesional; ***c. break*** interrupción *f* de la carrera profesional; ***c. diplomat*** diplomático(a) *m,f* de carrera; *Br* ***c. girl*** = joven ambiciosa que da mucha importancia a su carrera; ***careers guidance*** orientación *f* profesional *or* vocacional; ***careers officer*** asesor(ora) *m,f* de orientación profesional; ***c. path*** trayectoria *f* profesional; ***careers service*** servicio *m* de orientación profesional; ***c. woman*** = mujer ambiciosa que da mucha importancia a su carrera

2 *vi* **to c. (along)** ir a toda velocidad; **he careered right into me** se me echó encima

careerism [kə'rɪərɪzəm] *n Pej* arribismo *m*

careerist [kə'rɪərɪst] *n Pej* arribista *mf*

carefree ['keəfri:] *adj* despreocupado(a)

careful ['keəfʊl] *adj* **(a)** *(taking care)* cuidadoso(a); *(prudent)* cauto(a), prudente; **(be) c.!** ¡(ten) cuidado!; **to be c. to do sth** tener cuidado de *or* procurar hacer algo; **to be c. with money** ser ahorrador(ora); **be c. with that vase!** ¡(ten) cuidado con ese jarrón!; **be c. not to drop it** procura que no se te caiga; **be c. crossing the road** ten cuidado al cruzar *or* cuando cruces la calle; **be c. what you say** cuidado con lo que dices; **she was c. not to mention this** tuvo cuidado de *or* procuró no mencionar esto; **you can't be too c. these days** en estos tiempos que corren toda precaución es poca

(b) *(thorough) (work, inspection, person)* cuidadoso(a), detallado(a); **they made a c. examination of the evidence** examinaron las pruebas cuidadosamente; **after c. consideration** tras mucho reflexionar

carefully ['keəfʊlɪ] *adv* **(a)** *(cautiously, with attention)* cuidadosamente; *(to drive)* con cuidado, con precaución; *(to think, choose)* con cuidado; *(to listen, watch)* atentamente, detenidamente; **she chose her words c.** eligió sus palabras cuidadosamente **(b)** *(thoroughly)* cuidadosamente

carefulness ['keəfʊlnɪs] *n* **(a)** *(caution)* cuidado *m*, prudencia *f* **(b)** *(thoroughness)* cuidado *m*, meticulosidad *f*

careless ['keəlɪs] *adj* **(a)** *(negligent)* descuidado(a); **to be c. (about sth)** descuidar (algo); **to be c. with money** tener muy poco cuidado con el dinero; **he's c. about his appearance** descuida mucho su aspecto; **a c. act** una imprudencia; **a c. mistake** un descuido; **a c. remark** una observación inoportuna ►► ***c. driving*** conducción *f* temeraria

(b) **c. of** *(indifferent to)* sin preocuparse por, indiferente a

(c) *(carefree) (person)* despreocupado(a); *(look, smile)* natural; **she danced with c. grace** bailaba con gracia natural

carelessly ['keəlɪslɪ] *adv* **(a)** *(negligently)* descuidadamente **(b)** *(casually)* con aire despreocupado

carelessness ['keəlɪsnɪs] *n* **(a)** *(negligence)* descuido *m*, negligencia *f* **(b)** *(casualness)* despreocupación *f*

carer ['keərə(r)] *n* = persona que cuida de un familiar enfermo o anciano, sin que necesariamente reciba compensación económica por ello

caress [kə'res] **1** *n* caricia *f*

2 *vt* acariciar

caret ['kærət] *n Typ* signo *m* de intercalación

caretaker ['keəteɪkə(r)] *n* **(a)** *Br (of building)* conserje *m*, portero(a) *m,f*; *(of school)* conserje *m* ►► ***c. government*** gobierno *m* provisional; ***c.'s lodge*** portería *f*; ***c.'s office*** portería *f* **(b)** *(carer)* **he's his grandmother's c.** se encarga de cuidar de su abuela

careworn ['keəwɔ:n] *adj* agobiado(a); **to be c.** estar agobiado(a)

carfare ['kɑ:feə(r)] *n US* (precio *m* del) *Esp* billete *m or Am* boleto *m or Am* pasaje *m*

cargo ['kɑ:gəʊ] (*pl* **cargoes**) *n* cargamento *m* ►► ***c. boat*** barco *m* de carga, carguero *m*; ***c. plane*** avión *m* de carga; ***c. ship*** barco *m* de carga, carguero *m*; ***c. trousers*** pantalones *mpl* tipo cargo; ***c. winch*** maquinilla *f* de carga

carhop ['kɑ:hɒp] *n US Fam (serving food)* camarero(a) *m,f (que acerca la comida al coche de los clientes)*

Carib ['kærɪb] *n* **(a)** *(person)* caribe *mf* **(b)** *(language)* caribe *m*

Caribbean [kærɪ'bi:ən, *US* kə'rɪbɪən] **1** *n* **the C.** *(region)* las Antillas, el Caribe; *(sea)* el Caribe

2 *adj* caribeño(a), antillano(a); **the C. islands** las Antillas; **the C. Sea** el (mar) Caribe

caribou ['kærɪbu:] *n* caribú *m*

caricature ['kærɪkətʃʊə(r)] **1** *n* caricatura *f*, *Am* caricato *m*

2 *vt* caricaturizar

caricaturist ['kærɪkətʃʊərɪst] *n* caricaturista *mf*

Caricom ['kærɪkɒm] *n* (*abbr* **Caribbean Community**) Caricom *m o f*

caries ['keəri:z] (*pl* **caries**) *n Med* caries *f inv*

carillon [kə'rɪljən] *n* carillón *m*

caring ['keərɪŋ] *adj (person)* afectuoso(a), solícito(a); *(society)* solidario(a); **a c. environment** un entorno con calor humano ▸▸ ***the c. professions*** = las profesiones relacionadas con la salud y la asistencia social

carjack ['kɑ:dʒæk] *Fam* **1** *n* secuestro *m* de coche *or Am* carro *or CSur* auto
2 *vt* **they were carjacked** se los llevaron secuestrados en el coche *or Am* carro *or CSur* auto

carjacking ['kɑ:dʒækɪŋ] *n Fam* secuestro *m* de un coche *or Am* carro *or CSur* auto

carless ['kɑ:lɪs] *adj* sin coche *or Am* carro *or CSur* auto; **we were c. for two weeks** estuvimos dos semanas sin coche *or Am* carro *or CSur* auto

carload ['kɑ:ləʊd] *n* **(a)** *(in car)* **we got them home in three carloads** los llevamos a casa en tres viajes; **volunteers arrived by the c.** llegaban coches y coches *or Am* carros y carros *or CSur* autos y autos con voluntarios **(b)** *US (by rail)* vagón *m (lleno)*

carmaker ['kɑ:meɪkə(r)] *n US* fabricante *m* de automóviles

carman ['kɑ:mən] *n US* conductor *m*

Carmelite ['kɑ:məlaɪt] **1** *n (monk)* (monje *m*) carmelita *m*; *(nun)* (monja *f*) carmelita *f*
2 *adj* carmelita

carmine ['kɑ:maɪn] **1** *n (colour)* carmín *m*
2 *adj* (color) carmín *inv*

carnage ['kɑ:nɪdʒ] *n* matanza *f*

carnal ['kɑ:nəl] *adj* carnal; *Formal* **to have c. knowledge of sb** haber mantenido relaciones íntimas *or* sexuales con alguien ▸▸ *US* ***c. abuse*** agresión *f* sexual a menores

carnality [kɑ:'nælɪtɪ] *n Literary* carnalidad *f*, sensualidad *f*

carnally ['kɑ:nəlɪ] *adv* carnalmente

carnation [kɑ:'neɪʃən] *n* **(a)** *(flower)* clavel *m* **(b)** *(colour)* rosa *m*

carnelian [kə'ni:ljən] *n* cornalina *f*

carnival ['kɑ:nɪvəl] *n* **(a)** *(traditional festival)* carnaval *m*; **there was a c. atmosphere in the town** había un ambiente carnavalesco *or* de carnaval en la ciudad **(b)** *(funfair)* feria *f*

carnivore ['kɑ:nɪvɔ:(r)] *n* carnívoro *m*

carnivorous [kɑ:'nɪvərəs] *adj* carnívoro(a)

carob ['kærəb] *n* **(a)** *(substance)* extracto *m* de algarroba *(sucedáneo de chocolate)* **(b)** *(tree)* algarrobo *m* ▸▸ ***c. bean*** algarroba *f*

carol ['kærəl] **1** *n* **(Christmas) c.** villancico *m* ▸▸ ***c. singer*** = persona que forma parte de un coro que canta villancicos en lugares públicos
2 *vt* (*pt & pp* **carolled**, *US* **caroled**) **(a)** *(of bird)* cantar **(b)** *(of person) (sing)* cantar con alegría; **"I'm home again!" she carolled** "¡he vuelto a casa!", dijo con una voz cantarina **(c)** *(praise)* alabar
3 *vi* **(a)** *(baby, bird)* cantar **(b)** *(person)* cantar con alegría; **to go carolling** ir a cantar villancicos

Caroline ['kærəlaɪn] *adj* **the C. Islands** las (islas) Carolinas

carom ['kærəm] *US* **1** *n (in billiards, pool)* carambola *f*
2 *vi* **(a)** *(in billiards, pool)* **to c. into** hacer carambola con **(b)** **to c. into sth/sb** chocar contra algo/alguien

carotene ['kærəti:n] *n* caroteno *m*

carotid [kə'rɒtɪd] *n Anat* **c. (artery)** (arteria *f*) carótida *f*

carouse [kə'raʊz] *vi* estar de parranda

carousel [kærə'sel] *n* **(a)** *US (at fair)* tiovivo *m*, carrusel *m*, *RP* calesita *f* **(b)** *(at airport)* cinta *f* transportadora de equipajes **(c)** *(for slides)* carro *m*

carp[1] [kɑ:p] (*pl* **carp**) *n (fish)* carpa *f*

carp[2] *vi* quejarse (sin motivo) (**at** de); **he's always carping on about having too much work** siempre se está quejando de que tiene demasiado trabajo

carpal ['kɑ:pəl] **1** *n Anat* hueso *m* carpiano
2 *adj Anat* carpiano(a) ▸▸ *Med* ***c. tunnel syndrome*** síndrome *m or* estrechamiento *m* del túnel carpiano

Carpathians [kɑ:'peɪθɪənz] *npl* **the C.** los Cárpatos

carpel ['kɑ:pəl] *n Bot* carpelo *m*

carper ['kɑ:rpə(r)] *n (complainer)* quejica *mf*; *(fault-finder)* criticón(ona) *m,f*

carpenter ['kɑ:pɪntə(r)] **1** *n* carpintero(a) *m,f*; **c.'s (shop)** carpintería *f*
2 *vt (wood, joint)* **the parts were carefully carpentered to fit together** las piezas habían sido fabricadas para encajar perfectamente

carpentry ['kɑ:pɪntrɪ] *n* carpintería *f*

carpet ['kɑ:pɪt] **1** *n* **(a)** *(rug)* alfombra *f*, *Am* tapete *m*; *(fitted) Esp* moqueta *f*, *Am* alfombra *f*, *RP* moquette *m*; *Fig* **a c. of flowers** una alfombra de flores ▸▸ ***c. slippers*** zapatillas *fpl* de casa; ***c. tile*** trozo *m* cuadrado de *Esp* moqueta *or Am* alfombra *or RP* moquette
(b) IDIOMS **to pull the c. out from under sb** retirarle el apoyo a alguien repentinamente; *Br Fam* **to be on the c.** *(in trouble)* llevarse una buena regañina *or Esp* bronca; *Br Fam* **to put sb on the c.** *(reprimand)* echar una regañina *or Esp* bronca a alguien ▸▸ ***c. bombing*** bombardeo *m* de saturación
2 *vt* **(a)** *(floor) Esp* enmoquetar, *Am* alfombrar, *RP* moquetear; **the ground was carpeted with flowers** el suelo estaba cubierto por una alfombra de flores **(b)** *Br Fam* **to c. sb** echar una regañina *or Esp* bronca a alguien

> **False friend:** The Spanish noun **carpeta** is not a translation for the English word **carpet**. In Spanish **carpeta** means "file, folder".

carpet-bag ['kɑ:pɪtbæg] *n* maleta *f or RP* valija *f* tapizada

carpetbagger ['kɑ:pɪtbægə(r)] *n Pol (opportunist)* candidato(a) *m,f* cunero(a)

carpeted ['kɑ:pɪtɪd] *adj Esp* enmoquetado(a), *Am* alfombrado(a)

carpeting ['kɑ:pɪtɪŋ] *n (fabric)* tejido *m* de alfombra; *(carpets)* alfombrado *m*

carpet-sweeper ['kɑ:pɪtswi:pə(r)] *n* cepillo *m* mecánico (para alfombras)

carpi *pl of* **carpus**

carping ['kɑ:pɪŋ] **1** *n* critiqueo *m*
2 *adj (complaining)* quejica; *(fault-finding)* criticón(ona); **c. criticism(s)** critiqueo

carport ['kɑ:pɔ:t] *n Aut* plaza *f* de estacionamiento *or Esp* aparcamiento techado *(al lado de una casa)*

carpus ['kɑ:pəs] (*pl* **carpi** ['kɑ:paɪ, 'kɑ:pi:]) *n Anat* carpo *m*

carrag(h)een ['kærəgi:n] *n Culin* carragena *f*, alga *f* roja de Irlanda

carrel ['kærəl] *n (in library)* cubículo *m or* pupitre *m* (de estudio)

carriage ['kærɪdʒ] *n* **(a)** *(vehicle)* carroza *f*, carruaje *m* ▸▸ ***c. clock*** reloj *m* de mesa (con asa); *Sport* ***c. driving*** trotones *mpl*, = carreras de carros en torno a un circuito al aire libre
(b) *Br (of train)* vagón *m*, coche *m*
(c) *(of typewriter)* carro *m* ▸▸ ***c. return*** retorno *m* de carro
(d) *(of gun)* cureña *f*
(e) *Com (transport)* transporte *m*, porte *m*; *(cost)* portes *mpl*; **c. forward** porte debido; **c. free** franco(a) de porte; **c. paid** porte pagado
(f) *(bearing) (of person)* porte *m*

carriageway ['kærɪdʒweɪ] *n Aut* calzada *f*; **the northbound c.** la calzada en dirección norte

carrier ['kærɪə(r)] *n* **(a)** *(of disease, infection)* portador(ora) *m,f* **(b)** *Com (company)* transportista *m*; *(airline)* línea *f* aérea **(c)** *(container) (on bicycle)* portaequipaje *m*, transportín *m*; **c. (bag)** bolsa *f* (de plástico) **(d)** *Comptr & Tel* portadora *f* ▸▸ ***c. signal*** señal *f* de portadora; ***c. tone*** tono *m* de portadora **(e)** ***c. pigeon*** *(bird)* paloma *f* mensajera

carrier-based ['kærɪə'beɪst], **carrier-borne** ['kærɪəbɔ:n] *adj Mil* **c. bombers** bombarderos desplazados en portaaviones

carrion ['kærɪən] *n* carroña *f* ▸▸ ***c. crow*** corneja *f* negra

carrion-eating ['kærɪən'i:tɪŋ] *adj (animal)* carroñero(a)

carrot ['kærət] *n* **(a)** *(plant, vegetable)* zanahoria *f* ▸▸ ***c. cake*** pastel *m* de zanahoria; ***c. juice*** *Esp* zumo *m or Am* jugo *m* de zanahoria **(b)** *Fig (incentive)* **to hold out a c.** mostrar un señuelo; IDIOM **to use the c. and stick approach** utilizar una táctica de incentivos y amenazas

carroty ['kærətɪ] *adj (hair)* cobrizo(a), pelirrojo(a)

CARRY ['kærɪ] **1** *vt* **(a)** *(transport, convey)* llevar; *(goods, passengers)* transportar; *(disease)* ser portador(ora) de; *(electricity)* conducir; **a bus carrying schoolchildren** un autobús con escolares; **this plane can c. 59 passengers** este avión tiene cabida *or* capacidad para 59 pasajeros; **I've been carrying this note around for ages** llevo siglos cargando con esta nota, hace siglos que ando dando vueltas con esta nota; **to c. sth away** *or* **off** llevarse algo; **the boat was carried away by the tide** la marea arrastró el barco; **the injured player was carried off the pitch on a stretcher** sacaron al jugador lesionado del campo en camilla; **she carried him up to the first floor** lo subió en brazos *or Am* cargó hasta el primer piso; **to be carrying a child** *(be pregnant)* estar embarazada; IDIOM *Fam* **to c. the can** pagar el pato *or* los platos rotos; **she carries herself like a queen** tiene el porte de una reina; **to c. oneself well** tener buen porte
(b) *(have on one's person) (gun, money)* llevar (encima), *Méx* cargar
(c) *(support, bear)* sostener, aguantar; **will it c. the weight of those**

books? ¿aguantará el peso de esos libros?; **his legs wouldn't c. him any further** sus piernas no lo aguantaban más; **you're carrying too much weight** *(are overweight)* estás demasiado gordo; *Fig* **to c. the cost of sth** correr con el costo de algo

(**d**) *(contain, have)* **this product carries a warning/a guarantee** este producto viene con un aviso/una garantía; **to c. an advertisement/article** *(of newspaper)* publicar un anuncio/artículo; **the news carried an item on Somalia** el telediario *or Am* noticiero incluyó un reportaje sobre Somalia; **to c. authority** tener autoridad; **to c. conviction** ser convincente; **to c. weight** tener peso

(**e**) *(involve) (fine, penalty, risk, consequences)* conllevar; **the post carries a lot of responsibility** el puesto conlleva una gran responsabilidad

(**f**) *(take, extend)* **to c. sth too far/to extremes** llevar algo demasiado lejos/ hasta los extremos; **to c. an argument to its logical conclusion** llevar un argumento hasta las últimas consecuencias

(**g**) *(capture, win)* **he carried all before him** arrolló, tuvo un éxito arrollador; *US* **Clinton carried the state** Clinton triunfó electoralmente en el estado; **his argument carried the day** su argumentación consiguió la victoria

(**h**) *(convince)* **we need to c. the party members with us** necesitamos convencer a los afiliados del partido; **her speech carried the meeting** su discurso convenció a los reunidos

(**i**) *(proposal, motion)* aprobar; **the motion was carried unanimously** la moción se aprobó por unanimidad; *Pol* **the bill was carried (by 30 votes)** se aprobó el proyecto de ley (por 30 votos)

(**j**) *Com (keep in stock)* tener (en almacén)

(**k**) *(compensate for)* **the team cannot afford to c. players who are not good enough** el equipo no puede permitirse tener jugadores mediocres

(**l**) *(help)* **their determination carried them to victory** su determinación los llevó a la victoria

(**m**) *Math* llevar(se); **3, c. 2** 3, (me) llevo 2

(**n**) *(sing correctly) (tune)* cantar bien

2 *vi* (**a**) *(reach destination) (sound)* oírse; **your voice isn't carrying to the back of the room** su voz no llega al fondo de la sala; **her voice carries well** tiene una voz potente; **the ball didn't c. to the fielder** la bola botó *or Am* picó antes de llegar al defensor

(**b**) *Fam (carry a gun)* **he could be carrying** puede que vaya armado

3 *n Comptr & Math* acarreo *m*

▸ **carry away** *vt sep* **to get carried away (by sth)** *(excited)* emocionarse (por *or* con algo); *(overenthusiastic)* entusiasmarse (por *or* con algo); **I got a bit carried away with the garlic** se me ha ido la mano con el ajo; **I got carried away and said something I didn't mean** me exalté y dije algo que no quería decir; **don't get too carried away!** ¡no te emociones demasiado!

▸ **carry back** *vt sep* **the song carried me back to the days of my youth** la canción me hizo recordar mi juventud

▸ **carry forward** *vt sep Fin* pasar a nueva columna; **carried forward** *(at foot of page)* suma y sigue

▸ **carry off** *vt sep* (**a**) *(take away) (object, hostage)* llevarse; **to c. off a prize** *(win)* llevarse un premio

(**b**) *(do successfully)* **she carried it off (well)** salió airosa; **he carried off the role brilliantly** representó el papel brillantemente; **she carries off that short dress wonderfully** a ella sí que le queda bien ese vestido corto

(**c**) *Euph (kill) (by disease)* llevarse; **hundreds were carried off by the epidemic** la epidemia se llevó cientos de vidas

▸ **carry on 1** *vt sep* (**a**) *(continue) (tradition)* seguir; *(discussion)* continuar

(**b**) *(undertake) (business, trade)* dirigir, gestionar; *(correspondence, conversation)* mantener

2 *vi* (**a**) *(continue)* continuar, seguir; **c. on!** ¡sigue!, ¡adelante!; **to c. on doing sth** seguir haciendo algo; **we're trying to c. on as normal** intentamos seguir como si no hubiera pasado nada; **she just carried on regardless** siguió como si nada; **c. on with what you were doing** continúa con lo que estabas haciendo

(**b**) *Fam (behave badly)* hacer trastadas; **I don't like the way she carries on** no me gusta su forma de comportarse

(**c**) *Fam (have an affair)* tener un lío *or Méx* una movida *or RP* un asunto (**with** con)

(**d**) *Fam (argue)* **they were carrying on at each other** estaban tirándose los trastos a la cabeza

▸ **carry out** *vt sep* (**a**) *(perform) (work, experiment, research)* llevar a cabo, efectuar, realizar

(**b**) *(fulfil) (promise, threat, order)* cumplir; *(plan)* llevar a cabo; *(instructions)* cumplir, seguir

▸ **carry over** *vt sep* (**a**) *(postpone)* aplazar; **this match has been carried over from last week** este es el partido aplazado la semana pasada; **that will have to be carried over to the next meeting** eso tendremos que dejarlo para la siguiente reunión; **you may c. over your holiday entitlement to the following year** puedes trasladar las vacaciones que te corresponden al año siguiente

(**b**) *(retain)* **a practice carried over from the previous regime** una práctica heredada del antiguo régimen

(**c**) *Acct (balance)* trasladar al siguiente ejercicio; **to c. over a loss to the following year** trasladar una pérdida *or* un rendimiento negativo al siguiente ejercicio, repercutir una pérdida *or* un rendimiento negativo en el ejercicio siguiente

(**d**) = **carry forward**

▸ **carry through** *vt sep* (**a**) *(help to succeed)* **her determination carried her through** su determinación la sostuvo

(**b**) *(implement)* llevar a cabo; **they are determined to c. through the reforms** están decididos a llevar a cabo las reformas

---

carryall [ˈkærɪɔːl] *n US* bolsa *f (de viaje o de deporte)*

carry-back [ˈkærɪˈbæk] *n Fin* pérdida *f* trasladada al ejercicio anterior, compensación *f* con ejercicios anteriores

carrycot [ˈkærɪkɒt] *n Br* moisés *m*, capazo *m*

carrying [ˈkærɪɪŋ] *n* (**a**) ***c. charges*** *(for transport)* gastos *mpl* de transporte; *(for goods stored)* gastos *mpl* de almacenamiento, costo *m or Esp* coste *m* de mantenimiento (**b**) *US* ***c. charge*** *(on credit purchase)* recargo *m*, comisión *f*

carrying-on [ˈkærɪɪŋˈɒn] *(pl* **carryings-on**) *n Fam* (**a**) *(fuss, commotion)* jaleo *m*, *Esp* follón *m* (**b**) *(improper behaviour)* líos *mpl*

carry-on[1] [ˈkærɪˈɒn] *n Br Fam* bronca *f*, *Esp* follón *m*; **what a c.!** ¡menuda bronca!

carry-on[2] *adj* **c. baggage** *or* **luggage** equipaje de mano

carry-out [ˈkærɪˈaʊt] *n* (**a**) *US, Scot (food)* = comida preparada para llevar (**b**) *Scot (drink)* = bebidas alcohólicas que se compran para llevar (**c**) *US & Scot (restaurant)* = restaurante donde se vende comida para llevar

carry-over [ˈkærɪˈəʊvə(r)] *n* (**a**) *(habit, influence, trace)* remanente *m* (**b**) *Fin (amount)* pérdida *f* trasladada al ejercicio siguiente

car-sick [ˈkɑːsɪk] *adj* **to be c.** estar mareado(a) *(en el coche)*; **to get c.** marearse *(en el coche)*

car-sickness [ˈkɑːsɪknɪs] *n* mareo *m (en el coche)*; **he suffers from c.** se marea en el coche *or Am* carro *or CSur* auto

cart[1] [kɑːt] **1** *n* (**a**) *(drawn by horse)* carro *m*, carreta *f*; IDIOM **to put the c. before the horse** empezar la casa por el tejado ▸▸ ***c. track*** pista *f* (**b**) *(pushed by hand)* carretilla *f* (**c**) *(golf cart)* carrito *m* de golf (**d**) *US (in supermarket)* carrito *m*

2 *vt Fam (carry)* cargar con; **I've been carting this around all afternoon** llevo cargando con esto toda la tarde

▸ **cart away** *vt sep* llevarse

▸ **cart off** *vt sep Fam* **to c. sb off** llevarse a alguien (a la fuerza)

cart[2] *n Fam* (*abbr* **cartridge**) *(for video game)* cartucho *m*

carte blanche [ˈkɑːtˈblɑːnʃ] *n* **to give sb c. (to do sth)** dar a alguien carta blanca (para hacer algo)

cartel [kɑːˈtel] *n Econ* cartel *m*, cártel *m*; **to form a c.** formar un cartel *or* cártel; **an oil/steel c.** un cartel *or* cártel petrolero/siderúrgico

Cartesian [kɑːˈtiːʒən] *adj* (**a**) *Phil* cartesiano(a) (**b**) *Math* ***C. coordinates*** coordenadas *fpl* cartesianas

Carthage [ˈkɑːθɪdʒ] *n Hist* Cartago

Carthaginian [kɑːθəˈdʒɪnɪən] *Hist* **1** *n* cartaginense *mf*

2 *adj* cartaginense

carthorse [ˈkɑːthɔːs] *n* caballo *m* de tiro

Carthusian [kɑːˈθjuːzɪən] *Rel* **1** *n* cartujo *m*

2 *adj* cartujo(a)

cartilage [ˈkɑːtɪlɪdʒ] *n* cartílago *m*

cartilaginous [kɑːtɪˈlædʒɪnəs] *adj Anat* cartilaginoso(a)

cartload [ˈkɑːtləʊd] *n* carretada *f*

cartographer [kɑːˈtɒgrəfə(r)] *n* cartógrafo(a) *m,f*

cartographic [kɑːtəˈgræfɪk] *adj* cartográfico(a)

cartography [kɑːˈtɒgrəfɪ] *n* cartografía *f*

carton [ˈkɑːtən] *n* (**a**) *(cardboard box)* caja *f* (de cartón) (**b**) *(for yoghurt, cream)* envase *m*; *(for milk, juice)* cartón *m*, tetrabrik® *m* (**c**) **a c. of cigarettes** un cartón de cigarrillos

cartoon [kɑːˈtuːn] *n* (**a**) *(drawing) (in newspaper)* chiste *m*, viñeta *f* ▸▸ ***c. strip*** tira *f* cómica (**b**) *(movie) (feature length)* película *f* de dibujos animados; **they showed some cartoons before the movie** pasaron dibujos animados antes de la película (**c**) *Art* cartón *m*

cartoonist [kɑːˈtuːnɪst] *n* (**a**) *(for newspaper)* humorista *mf* gráfico(a), dibujante *mf* de humor *or* de chistes; *(of comic strip)* humorista *mf* gráfico(a), *Méx* monero(a) *m,f* (**b**) *(for cartoon film)* animador(ora) *m,f*

cartridge [ˈkɑːtrɪdʒ] *n* (**a**) *(for firearm)* cartucho *m* ►► ***c. belt*** canana *f*, cartuchera *f*; ***c. case*** casquillo *m* de bala (**b**) *(refill) (of film)* cartucho *m*; *(for pen)* recambio *m* (**c**) *(for tape deck)* cartucho *m* (**d**) *(for record-player)* cartucho *m* (**e**) *Art* ***c. paper*** papel *m* de dibujo (**f**) *Comptr (disk)* cartucho *m*; **ink/toner c.** cartucho de tinta/tóner

cartwheel [ˈkɑːtwiːl] **1** *n* (**a**) *(wheel)* rueda *f* de carro (**b**) *(in gymnastics)* voltereta *f* lateral; **to turn cartwheels** hacer la voltereta lateral

2 *vi* dar vueltas de campana laterales; **the vehicle went cartwheeling across the track** el vehículo dio varias vueltas de campana sobre la pista

cartwright [ˈkɑːtraɪt] *n* carretero(a) *m,f*

carve [kɑːv] *vt* (**a**) *(wood, stone)* tallar, esculpir, labrar; *(name, inscription)* grabar, tallar; **it was carved from a single block of wood** fue tallado *or* esculpido a partir de un solo bloque de madera; **he carved his name on the desk** grabó su nombre en el pupitre (**b**) *(meat)* trinchar

► **carve out** *vt sep* **to c. out a career for oneself** forjarse *or* labrarse una carrera

► **carve up** *vt sep* (**a**) *(meat)* trinchar; *(carcass)* descuartizar; *Andes, RP* despostar; *Fig (territory)* repartir, dividir (**b**) *Fam* **to c. sb up** *(attack with knife)* apuñalar *or* rajar a alguien (**c**) *Br Fam* **to c. sb up** *(in car)* = adelantar a alguien y reincorporarse al carril cruzándose bruscamente por delante del vehículo adelantado

carved [kɑːvd] *adj (wood, stone)* tallado(a), esculpido(a), labrado(a)

carver [ˈkɑːvə(r)] *n* (**a**) *(knife)* cuchillo *m* de trinchar (**b**) **carvers** cubiertos *mpl* de trinchar

carvery [ˈkɑːvərɪ] *n Br* = restaurante que ofrece carne trinchada en el momento

carving [ˈkɑːvɪŋ] *n* (**a**) *(object)* talla *f* (**b**) *(decoration) (in wood, stone)* labrado *m*, tallado *m* (**c**) *(of meat)* ***c. board*** trinchero *m*

carving-fork [ˈkɑːvɪŋfɔːk] *n (for meat)* tenedor *m* de trinchar

carving-knife [ˈkɑːvɪŋnaɪf] *n (for meat)* cuchillo *m* de trinchar

caryatid [kærɪˈætɪd] *n Archit* cariátide *f*

Casanova [kæsəˈnəʊvə] *pr n* Casanova; **he's a C.** es un donjuán *or* un casanova

casbah [ˈkæzbɑː] *n* kasba(h) *f*

cascade [kæsˈkeɪd] **1** *n* (**a**) *(waterfall)* cascada *f* (**b**) *(of hair, sparks)* cascada *f*

2 *vi* (**a**) *(water)* caer formando una cascada (**b**) *(hair, sparks)* caer en cascada

CASE [keɪs] *n Comptr* (*abbr* **computer-aided software engineering**) ingeniería *f* de sistemas asistida por *Esp* ordenador *or Am* computadora

CASE¹ [keɪs] **1** *n* (**a**) *(instance, situation)* caso *m*; **it's a c. of not having any choice** la cuestión es que no tenemos alternativa; **it was a c. of signing or being fired** era cuestión de firmar o ser despedido; **a c. in point** un buen ejemplo, un caso claro; **in c. of emergency/accident** en caso de urgencia/accidente; **in any c.** en cualquier caso; **in my/his c.** en mi/su caso; **in no c. should you...** en ningún caso deberías...; **in that c.** en ese caso; **in this c.** en este caso; **in which c.** en cuyo caso ►► ***c. study*** estudio *m* de caso (real)

(**b**) *(actual state of affairs)* **that is not the c. in Great Britain** en Gran Bretaña no es así; **that is/isn't the c.** es/no es así; **if that's the c....** si es así...; **as** *or* **whatever the c. may be** según el caso; **as is often/usually the c.** como suele ocurrir

(**c**) *(investigation)* caso *m*; **we have ten detectives on the c.** tenemos diez detectives en el caso; **a murder/fraud c.** un caso de asesinato/de fraude; **the c. is closed** el caso ha sido cerrado; *Fam Fig* **don't worry, I'm on the c.** no te preocupes que yo me encargo del tema; IDIOM *US Fam* **to have a c. on sb** estar colgado(a) *or* prendado(a) de alguien, *RP* tener un metejón con alguien; IDIOM *Fam* **he's always on my c.** siempre me está agobiando; *Fam* **the teacher has been on my c. ever since I arrived** el profesor ha estado encima de mí desde que llegué; IDIOM *Fam* **get off my c.!** ¡déjame en paz!, *RP* ¡cortála!

(**d**) *Law* causa *f*, caso *m*; **the c. for the defence** la defensa; **the c. for the prosecution** la acusación; **to bring a c. for sth against sb** entablar un pleito por algo contra alguien; **we don't have a c.** no tenemos nada en lo que basar el caso; **to win/lose one's c.** ganar/perder el caso; **the c. continues** el juicio continúa ►► ***c. law*** jurisprudencia *f*; ***c. load:*** **the courts simply cannot cope with the c. load** los tribunales no dan abasto con un número tan grande de casos

(**e**) *Med* caso *m*; **all burns cases are treated here** todos los casos de quemaduras son atendidos aquí ►► *Med* ***c. history*** historia *f* médica, historial *m* médico; ***c. load:*** **the c. loads of young doctors** el número de casos que tienen que atender los doctores jóvenes

(**f**) *(argument)* **the c. for/against sth** los argumentos a favor de/en contra de algo; **she argued her c. very convincingly** defendió su postura muy convincentemente; **to have a (good) c.** estar respaldado(a) por buenos argumentos; **to make (out) a c. for/against sth** exponer los argumentos a favor de/en contra de algo; **there's a c. for doing nothing** se podría argumentar que es mejor no hacer nada

(**g**) *Fam (eccentric person)* caso *m*; **he's a real c.!** ¡es todo un caso!

2 in case *adv* **just in c.** por si acaso; **I'll take my umbrella (just) in c.** llevaré el paraguas por si acaso

3 in case *conj* por si; **in c. he isn't there** por si no está allí; **bring an umbrella in c. it rains** trae un paraguas por si llueve; **in c. you were wondering, she's my sister** por si te lo estás preguntando, es mi hermana; **I'm trying to work, in c. you hadn't noticed** estoy intentando trabajar, por si no te habías dado cuenta

case² **1** *n* (**a**) *(container) (for spectacles)* funda *f*; *(for jewellery)* estuche *m*; **a cigarette c.** una pitillera; **(packing) c.** cajón *m*; **(display** *or* **glass) c.** vitrina *f*; **a c. of wine** una caja de vino ►► ***c. discount*** *(on wine)* = descuento por compra de cajas enteras; ***c. knife*** cuchillo *m* de monte (**b**) *(suitcase)* maleta *f*, *RP* valija *f*; *(briefcase)* maletín *m*, cartera *f* (**c**) *(of bullet, shell)* casquillo *m* (**d**) *Typ* **lower/upper c.** caja *f* baja/alta; *Comptr* **this e-mail address is c. sensitive** hay que respetar las mayúsculas y las minúsculas en esta dirección de correo electrónico, esta dirección de correo electrónico distingue entre mayúsculas y minúsculas (**e**) *Gram* caso *m*

2 *vt (enclose)* **the containers are cased in concrete** los contenedores están revestidos de cemento

case³ *vt Fam* **to c. the joint** echar una ojeada al lugar *(antes de cometer un delito)*

casebook [ˈkeɪsbʊk] *n* (**a**) *(medical, legal)* registro *m* (**b**) *(study aid)* colección *f* de estudios

case-hardened [ˈkeɪsˈhɑːdənd] *adj* (**a**) *(steel)* de cementación (**b**) *(insensitive)* **even c. policemen wept** hasta los policías más insensibilizados lloraron

casein [ˈkeɪsiːn] *n* caseína *f*

casement [ˈkeɪsmənt] *n* (**a**) *(window)* **c. (window)** ventana *f* (batiente) (**b**) *(window frame)* marco *m*

casework [ˈkeɪswɜːk] *n* asistencia *f* social en casos individuales

caseworker [ˈkeɪswɜːkə(r)] *n* asistente *mf* social

cash [kæʃ] **1** *n* (**a**) *(coins, banknotes)* (dinero *m* en) efectivo *m*; **to pay (in) c.** pagar en efectivo; **c. on delivery** entrega contrarreembolso; **c. in hand** al contado ►► ***c. account*** cuenta *f* de caja; ***c. advance*** adelanto *m or* anticipo *m* en metálico; ***c. balance*** *(status)* estado *m* de cuenta; *(amount remaining)* saldo *m* de caja; ***c. bar*** = en un acontecimiento social, bar en el que se paga por las consumiciones; ***c. book*** registro *m or* libro *m* de caja; ***c. box*** caja *f* (para el dinero); ***c. card*** tarjeta *f (del cajero automático)*; ***c. and carry*** *(shop)* almacén *m* (de venta) al por mayor; *Fam* ***c. cow*** fuente *f* de ingresos, mina *f*; ***c. crop*** cultivo *m* comercial; *Fin* ***c. deposit*** depósito *m or Esp* ingreso *m* en efectivo; *Br* ***c. desk*** (mostrador *m* de) caja *f*; ***c. discount*** descuento *m or* rebaja *f* por pronto pago; ***c. dispenser*** cajero *m* automático; *Fin* ***c. flow*** flujo *m* de caja, cash-flow *m*; **to have c. flow problems** tener problemas de tesorería *or* liquidez; *Hum* no ir muy bien de dinero; *Acct* ***c. flow statement*** estado *m* de flujo de caja; ***c. machine*** cajero *m* automático; ***c. payment*** pago *m* en efectivo; *Br* ***c. point*** cajero *m* automático; ***c. price*** precio *m* al contado; ***c. prize*** premio *m* en efectivo *or* metálico; ***c. purchase*** compra *f* al contado; *Fin* ***c. ratio*** coeficiente *m* de caja; *Acct* ***c. received*** *(balance sheet item)* efectivo *m*, cobros *mpl* por caja; ***c. register*** caja *f* registradora; ***c. sale*** venta *f* al contado; *Acct* ***c. statement*** estado *m* de caja, cuenta *f* de tesorería; ***c. terms*** condiciones *fpl* de pago al contado; ***c. withdrawal*** reintegro *m* (en efectivo)

(**b**) *Fam (money in general)* dinero *m*, *Am* plata *f*, *Méx* lana *f*; **to be short of c.** ir un poco mal de dinero; **I ran out of c.** me quedé sin dinero

2 *vt (cheque, postal order)* hacer efectivo(a), cobrar; **could you c. this cheque for me?** *(in bank)* ¿podría cobrar *or* hacer efectivo este cheque?

► **cash in** **1** *vt sep (insurance policy)* hacer efectivo(a), cobrar; *(bond, savings certificate)* hacer efectivo(a), canjear (en dinero); *(gambling chips)* cambiar; IDIOM *US Fam* **to c. in one's chips** *(die)* estirar la pata, *Esp* diñarla, *CAm, Méx* liar el petate

2 *vi Fam* (**a**) **to c. in on** *(profit from)* aprovechar, sacar provecho de (**b**) *US (die)* estirar la pata, *Esp* diñarla, *CAm, Méx* liar el petate

► **cash up** *vi Br* hacer la caja

cashback [ˈkæʃbæk] *n Br* = servicio que ofrece la posibilidad de sacar dinero de una cuenta en el momento de pagar con tarjeta de débito una compra en un supermercado; **would you like any c.?** ¿quiere sacar dinero de la cuenta?

cashew [ˈkæʃuː] *n* **c. (nut)** anacardo *m*

cashier[1] [kæˈʃɪə(r)] *n* cajero(a) *m,f* ►► ***c.'s cheque*** talón *m* bancario; *Br* ***c.'s desk*** caja *f*

cashier[2] *vt Mil* destituir

cashing up [ˈkæʃɪŋˈʌp] *n Com* arqueo *m*

cashless [ˈkæʃlɪs] *adj (transaction)* sin dinero en efectivo; *(economy)* en la que no se maneja dinero en efectivo

cashmere [ˈkæʃmɪə(r)] *n* cachemir *m*; **a c. sweater** un suéter de cachemir

casing [ˈkeɪsɪŋ] *n* (**a**) *Tech (of machine)* cubierta *f*, carcasa *f* (**b**) *(of tyre)* cubierta *f* (**c**) *(of wire, shaft)* revestimiento *m* (**d**) *(of sausage)* piel *f*

casino [kəˈsiːnəʊ] (*pl* **casinos**) *n* casino *m*

cask [kɑːsk] *n* tonel *m*, barril *m*

casket [ˈkɑːskɪt] *n* (**a**) *(for jewellery)* cofre *m*, arqueta *f* (**b**) *US (coffin)* ataúd *m*

> **False friend:** The Spanish noun **casquete** is not a translation for the English word **casket**. In Spanish **casquete** means "skullcap".

CASM [ˈkæzəm] *n Comptr* (*abbr* **computer-aided sales and marketing**) ventas *fpl* y márketing asistidos por *Esp* ordenador *or Am* computadora

Caspar [ˈkæspə(r)] *pr n* Gaspar

Caspian [ˈkæspɪən] **1** *n* **the C.** el Caspio
2 *adj* ***the C. Sea*** el mar Caspio; ***C. tern*** pagaza *f* piquirroja

Cassandra [kəˈsændrə] *n* (**a**) *Mythol* Casandra (**b**) *Fig* = persona cuyas profecías son desoídas

cassava [kəˈsɑːvə] *n* (**a**) *(plant)* mandioca *f* (**b**) *(food)* tapioca *f*

casserole [ˈkæsərəʊl] **1** *n* (**a**) *(cooking vessel)* cazuela *f*, cacerola *f* (**b**) *(food)* cazuela *f*, guisado *m*; **chicken c.** pollo a la cazuela, guisado de pollo
2 *vt* guisar en cazuela

cassette [kəˈset] *n* (**a**) *(audio, video)* cinta *f*, casete *f* ►► ***c. deck*** platina *f*, pletina *f*; ***c. head cleaner*** cinta *f or* casete *f* limpiadora; ***c. player*** casete *m*, magnetófono *m*; ***c. recorder*** casete *m*, magnetófono *m*; ***c. single*** cinta *f* de single, single *m* en (formato de) cinta; ***c. storage rack*** mueble *m* para guardar cintas (**b**) *(for still camera)* cartucho *m*

cassia [ˈkæsɪə] *n* cañafístula *f*

Cassiopeia [kæsɪəˈpɪə] *n* Casiopea

cassis [kæˈsiːs] *n* casis *m*

cassiterite [kəˈsɪtəraɪt] *n Geol* casiterita *f*

cassock [ˈkæsək] *n* sotana *f*

cassowary [ˈkæsəweərɪ] *n* **(southern) c.** casuario *m*

cast [kɑːst] **1** *n* (**a**) *(of play, movie)* reparto *m* ►► ***c. list*** reparto *m*
(**b**) *(reproduction)* reproducción *f*; *(mould)* molde *m*
(**c**) ***c. iron*** hierro *m* fundido *or* colado
(**d**) *Med* **(plaster) c.** escayola *f*, *esp Am* yeso *m*; **she had her arm in a c.** tenía el brazo escayolado *or esp Am* enyesado
(**e**) *(type, form)* **the delicate c. of her features** la delicadeza de sus rasgos; **a very liberal c. of mind** una mentalidad muy liberal
(**f**) *(colour, shade)* matiz *m*, toque *m*; **white with a pinkish c.** blanco con un matiz *or* toque rosa
(**g**) *(of fishing line)* lanzamiento *m*; *(of net)* redada *f*
(**h**) *(squint)* bizquera *f*; **he has a c. in his eye** es bizco
2 *vt* (*pt & pp* **cast**) (**a**) *(throw) (stone)* tirar, lanzar; *(line)* lanzar; *(net)* lanzar, echar; **to c. a spell over sb** hechizar *or* encantar a alguien; **to c. lots (for sth)** sortear (algo), echar (algo) a suertes; *Literary* **the tyrant c. his enemies into prison** el tirano envió a sus enemigos a la cárcel; **the editor has c. his net wide** el editor ha aplicado criterios muy amplios en su selección
(**b**) *(direct) (shadow)* proyectar, hacer; **the accident c. a shadow over their lives** el accidente ensombreció sus vidas; **she c. a desperate glance at her mother** lanzó una mirada desesperada hacia su madre; *Fig* **to c. a cloud over sth** ensombrecer algo; **to c. doubt on sth** poner en duda algo; **to c. one's eyes over sth** echar una ojeada a algo; *also Fig* **to c. light on sth** arrojar luz sobre algo; **to c. one's mind back to sth** remontarse a algo; **the evidence c. suspicion on him** las pruebas lo señalan como sospechoso
(**c**) *(shed, throw off)* **the horse c. a shoe** al caballo se le cayó una herradura; **to c. its skin** *(reptile)* mudar de piel *or* camisa; **c. all fear from your mind** no tengas ningún miedo
(**d**) *(vote)* emitir; **to c. one's vote (for sb)** emitir el voto (por alguien), votar (por alguien); **the number of votes c.** el número de votos emitidos
(**e**) *Theat & Cin* **to c. a movie/play** seleccionar a los actores para una película/obra; **she was c. as** *or* **in the role of Desdemona** la eligieron para el papel de Desdémona; **he was c. against type** le dieron un papel opuesto al que acostumbra a representar
(**f**) *(metal)* fundir; *(statue)* fundir, vaciar; **it was c. in bronze** fue fundido en bronce; *Fig* **they are all c. in the same mould** están todos cortados por el mismo patrón
(**g**) *(horoscope)* preparar
3 *vi (in fishing) (with rod)* lanzar la caña; *(with net)* lanzar la red

►**cast about, cast around** *vi* **to c. about** *or* **around for sth** intentar encontrar algo

►**cast aside** *vt sep* (**a**) *(book, clothes)* deshacerse de (**b**) *(idea, prejudice)* abandonar

►**cast away** *vt sep (sailor)* **to be c. away** ser un/una náufrago(a)

►**cast down** *vt sep* **to be c. down** estar deprimido(a) *or* abatido(a)

►**cast off 1** *vt sep (clothes, chains, traditions)* deshacerse de; **c. off all your cares!** ¡olvida tus preocupaciones!
2 *vi* (**a**) *Naut* soltar amarras (**b**) *(in knitting)* rematar una vuelta

►**cast on** *vi (in knitting)* engarzar una vuelta

►**cast out** *vt sep Literary* expulsar

►**cast up** *vt sep (of sea, tide, waves)* arrojar a la costa

castanets [kæstəˈnets] *npl* castañuelas *fpl*

castaway [ˈkɑːstəweɪ] *n* náufrago(a) *m,f*

caste [kɑːst] *n (social rank)* casta *f*

castellated [ˈkæstəleɪtɪd] *adj Archit* acastillado(a), almenado(a)

caster [ˈkɑːstə(r)] *n* (**a**) *(for sugar)* espolvoreador *m* ►► *Br* ***c. sugar*** azúcar *m or f* extrafino(a), azúcar *m o f* molido(a) (**b**) *(wheel)* ruedecita *f*

castigate [ˈkæstɪgeɪt] *vt Formal (criticize)* reprender

Castile [kæˈstiːl] *n* Castilla

Castilian [kæsˈtɪlɪən] **1** *n* (**a**) *(person)* castellano(a) *m,f* (**b**) *(language)* castellano *m*
2 *adj* castellano(a); **C. Spanish** castellano

casting [ˈkɑːstɪŋ] **1** *n* (**a**) *Theat & Cin* reparto *m* ►► ***the c. couch:*** **she denied having got the part on the c. couch** negó haberse acostado con alguien para obtener el papel; ***c. director*** director(ora) *m,f* de reparto (**b**) *(metal piece)* pieza *f* fundida (**c**) *(of sculpture)* vaciado *m*
2 *adj* ***c. vote*** voto *m* de calidad

cast-iron [ˈkɑːstˈaɪən] *adj* (**a**) *(stove, gate)* de hierro fundido; **a c. pot** una olla de hierro fundido (**b**) *(solid, unbreakable)* **c. alibi/guarantee** coartada/garantía irrefutable; *Hum* **he has a c. stomach** tiene un estómago a prueba de bombas

castle [ˈkɑːsəl] **1** *n* (**a**) *(building)* castillo *m*; IDIOM **to build castles in the air** *or* **in Spain** construir castillos en el aire (**b**) *(in chess)* torre *f*
2 *vi (in chess)* enrocarse

castling [ˈkɑːsəlɪŋ] *n (in chess)* enroque *m*

cast-off [ˈkɑːstɒf] **1** *n* (**a**) *(garment)* prenda *f* vieja *or* usada (**b**) *Fam (person)* persona *f* rechazada
2 *adj* **c. clothing** ropa vieja *or* usada

castor [ˈkɑːstə(r)] *n (on furniture)* ruedecita *f*

castor oil [kɑːstəˈrɔɪl] *n* aceite *m* de ricino ►► ***c. plant*** ricino *m*

castrate [kæsˈtreɪt] *vt (animal)* castrar, capar; *(person)* castrar

castrated [kæsˈtreɪtɪd] *adj (animal)* castrado(a), capado(a); *(person)* castrado(a)

castrati *pl of* **castrato**

castration [kæsˈtreɪʃən] *n* castración *f* ►► ***c. complex*** complejo *m* de castración

castrato [kæˈstrɑːtəʊ] (*pl* **castratos** *or* **castrati** [kæˈstrɑːtiː]) *n* castrado *m*

Castroist [ˈkæstrəʊɪst] **1** *n* castrista *mf*
2 *adj* castrista

casual [ˈkæʒjʊəl] **1** *adj* (**a**) *(relaxed, informal)* informal; **c. clothes** ropa informal *or* de sport
(**b**) *(superficial)* **to make c. conversation** hablar de cosas insustanciales; **even a c. glance would reveal that...** incluso una mirada superficial revelaría...; **it was just a c. suggestion** no era más que una sugerencia de pasada ►► ***c. sex*** relaciones *fpl* sexuales ocasionales
(**c**) *(unconcerned)* despreocupado(a), tranquilo(a); *(careless)* descuidado(a); *(remark, glance)* de pasada, casual; **they were very c. about it** parecía no importarles la cosa
(**d**) *(employment, worker)* eventual; **to employ sb on a c. basis** dar

empleo a alguien de manera eventual
(**e**) *(chance) (meeting)* casual; *(reader)* ocasional
(**f**) ***c. water*** *(in golf)* agua *f* accidental *or* ocasional
2 *n Br Fam (soccer hooligan)* = aficionado al fútbol de extracción modesta pero que gasta bastante dinero en ropa y que siempre va en grupo

casualization [kæʒjʊəlaɪ'zeɪʃən] *n Econ* **c. of labour** precarización del mercado de trabajo

casually ['kæʒjʊəlɪ] *adv* (**a**) *(unconcernedly)* **she remarked quite c. that...** comentó de pasada que...; **he treated the issue rather c.** se tomó el asunto bastante a la ligera (**b**) *(informally) (to talk)* en tono informal; **to dress c.** vestirse de manera informal, vestirse de sport

casualty ['kæʒjʊəltɪ] *n* (**a**) *(in accident, earthquake)* víctima *f*; *(in war)* baja *f*; *Br* **fortunately, there were no casualties** no hubo que lamentar desgracias personales ►► ***c. list*** *(in accident)* lista *f* de víctimas; *(in war)* lista *f* de bajas (**b**) *Br* **c. (department)** (servicio *m* de) urgencias *fpl*

> **False friend**: The Spanish noun **casualidad** is not a translation for the English word **casualty**. In Spanish **casualidad** means "coincidence".

casuistic(al) [kæʒjʊ'ɪstɪk(əl)] *adj Pej (argument)* hábil pero basado en falsedades

casuistry ['kæʒjʊɪstrɪ] *n Pej* **he made his case with his usual c.** expuso su caso argumentándolo hábilmente con falsedades

casus belli ['kɑːzəs'beliː] (*pl* **casus belli**) *n Literary* casus belli *m inv*

CAT [kæt] *n Med* (*abbr* **Computerized Axial Tomography**) TAC *f* ►► ***C. scan*** escáner *m* (TAC)

cat [kæt] *n* (**a**) *(animal) (domestic)* gato(a) *m,f*; *(lion, tiger)* felino *m*, félido *m*; **the big cats** los grandes felinos ►► ***c. burglar*** ladrón(ona) *m,f (que entra en las casas escalando)*; ***c.'s cradle*** = juego consistente en formar diferentes figuras utilizando los dedos y un cordel; ***c. door*** gatera *f*; ***c. flap*** gatera *f*; ***c. food*** comida *f* para gatos; ***c. litter*** arena *f* para gatos; ***c.'s paw*** instrumento *m*; **he's just a c.'s paw for the government** no es más que un mero instrumento del gobierno
(**b**) *US Fam Old-fashioned (man)* tipo *m*, *Esp* tío *m*
(**c**) *Fam (whip)* azote *m* (de nueve cuerdas)
(**d**) IDIOMS **a c. may look at a king** con mirar no hago daño a nadie; *Fam* **has the c. got your tongue?** *Esp* ¿(se) te ha comido la lengua el gato?, *Am* ¿te comieron la lengua los ratones?; *Fam* **I don't have** *or* **stand a c. in hell's chance** no tengo la más mínima posibilidad *or Am* chance; *Fam* **who's "she"? the c.'s mother?** ¿qué es eso de "ella"? ella tiene un nombre; **to fight like c. and dog** *Esp* llevarse como el perro y el gato, *Am* pelear como perro y gato; **look what the c.'s dragged in** mira quién amanece *or Am* anda por aquí; **you look like something the c. brought in** ¿tú has visto la facha que llevas?; **to look like the c. that got the cream** estar más ancho(a) que largo(a), *RP* estar redondo(a); *Br* **to wait to see which way the c. will jump** ver de qué lado sopla el viento; PROV **when the c.'s away, the mice will play** cuando el gato duerme bailan los ratones; **to play a c.-and-mouse game with sb** jugar al ratón y al gato con alguien; *Fam* **to be like a c. on a hot tin roof** *or* **on hot bricks** estar histérico(a); **to let the c. out of the bag** revelar el secreto, *Esp* descubrir el pastel; **to set the c. among the pigeons** meter al lobo en el redil; *Fam* **there isn't enough room to swing a c.** no se puede uno ni mover; *Fam* **he thinks he's the c.'s whiskers** *or* **pyjamas** se lo tiene muy creído, se cree el no va más *or RP* el súmum, *Méx* se cree que es la única Coca-Cola® en el desierto

catabolism [kə'tæbəlɪzəm] *n Biochem* catabolismo *m*

cataclysm ['kætəklɪzəm] *n* cataclismo *m*

cataclysmic [kætə'klɪzmɪk] *adj* catastrófico(a)

catacombs ['kætəkuːmz] *npl* catacumbas *fpl*

catafalque ['kætəfælk] *n* catafalco *m*

Catalan ['kætəlæn] 1 *n* (**a**) *(person)* catalán(ana) *m,f* (**b**) *(language)* catalán *m*
2 *adj* catalán(ana)

catalepsy ['kætəlepsɪ] *n Med* catalepsia *f*

cataleptic [kætə'leptɪk] *adj Med* cataléptico(a)

catalogue, *US* **catalog** ['kætəlɒg] 1 *n* catálogo *m*; *Fig* **a c. of complaints** una retahíla de quejas; **a c. of disasters** una serie *or* cadena de desastres ►► ***c. number*** *(in library)* signatura *f*
2 *vt* catalogar

Catalonia [kætə'ləʊnɪə] *n* Cataluña

Catalonian [kætə'ləʊnɪən] *adj* catalán(ana)

catalpa [kə'tælpə] *n* catalpa *f*

catalyse, *US* **catalyze** ['kætəlaɪz] *vt Chem* catalizar

catalysis [kə'tælɪsɪs] *n Chem* catálisis *f*

catalyst ['kætəlɪst] *n also Fig* catalizador *m*

catalytic [kætə'lɪtɪk] *adj Chem* catalizador(ora), catalítico(a) ►► *Aut* ***c. converter*** catalizador *m*

catalyze *US* = **catalyse**

catamaran [kætəmə'ræn] *n* catamarán *m*

cataphora [kə'tæfərə] *n Ling* catáfora *f*

cataphoric [kætə'fɒrɪk] *adj Ling* catafórico(a)

catapult ['kætəpʌlt] 1 *n* (**a**) *Br (hand-held)* tirachinas *m inv* (**b**) *(mediaeval siege weapon)* catapulta *f* (**c**) *(on aircraft carrier)* catapulta *f*
2 *vt* catapultar; **to be catapulted into the air** salir despedido(a) por los aires; **to c. sb to stardom** lanzar *or* catapultar a alguien al estrellato

cataract ['kætərækt] *n* (**a**) *(in river)* catarata *f*; *Fig* **the rain was falling in cataracts** llovía a cántaros (**b**) *Med* catarata *f*; **she's got cataracts** tiene cataratas

catarrh [kə'tɑː(r)] *n* catarro *m*

catarrhal [kə'tɑːrəl] *adj* catarral

catastrophe [kə'tæstrəfɪ] *n* catástrofe *f* ►► *Math* ***c. theory*** teoría *f* de las catástrofes

catastrophic [kætə'strɒfɪk] *adj* catastrófico(a)

catastrophically [kætə'strɒfɪkəlɪ] *adv* catastróficamente

catatonic [kætə'tɒnɪk] *adj Med* catatónico(a)

catbird ['kætbɜːd] *n* (**a**) *(bird)* pájaro *m* gato (**b**) *US Fam* **to be in the c. seat** estar bien situado(a)

catcall ['kætkɔːl] 1 *n* silbido *m*; **the actors were greeted with catcalls** los actores fueron recibidos con silbidos *or* abucheos
2 *vi* silbar, abuchear

CATCH [kætʃ] 1 *n* (**a**) *(act) (of ball)* parada *f (sin que la pelota toque el suelo)*; **to play c.** *(ball game)* jugar a (que no caiga) la pelota; *(chasing game)* jugar al corre-corre-que-te-pillo, *RP* jugar a la mancha
(**b**) *(thing caught) (in fishing)* pesca *f*, captura *f*; *Fam* **her new boyfriend's a real c.** su nuevo novio es un buen partido
(**c**) *(fastening) (on door)* pestillo *m*; *(on box, jewellery, window)* cierre *m*
(**d**) *(disadvantage)* trampa *f*; **there must be a c. in it somewhere** tiene que haber alguna trampa, aquí hay gato encerrado; **where's the c.?** ¿dónde está la trampa?; IDIOM **a catch-22 situation** un callejón sin salida
(**e**) *(in voice)* **there was a c. in her voice** tenía la voz entrecortada
(**f**) *Mus* canon *m*
(**g**) *Agr* ***c. crop*** cultivo *m* intermedio *or* intercalado
2 *vt* (*pt & pp* **caught** [kɔːt]) (**a**) *(thrown object, falling object)* atrapar, *Esp* coger, *Am* agarrar; **c. (it)!** *(when throwing something)* ¡agárralo!, *Esp* ¡cógelo!; **she caught him before he hit the ground** lo agarró antes de que se cayera al suelo; **we put the bucket there to c. the dripping water** pusimos el balde ahí para que el agua de la gotera cayera dentro; *US* **shall we c. a bite to eat?** *Am* ¿comemos algo?, *Esp* ¿tomamos algo (de comer)?; **to c. one's breath** *(after exercise)* recobrar el aliento; *(in surprise)* quedarse sin aliento; **a sudden noise made her c. her breath** un ruido repentino hizo que se le cortara la respiración; **to c. hold of sth** agarrarse a algo; **to c. a few rays** tomar un poco el sol; **my room catches the sun** a mi habitación le da el sol; **you look as if you've caught the sun** parece que te ha pegado el sol
(**b**) *(capture) (prey, mouse, thief)* atrapar, capturar; *(fish)* pescar; **he caught her by the arm** la agarró del brazo; **this photo catches the atmosphere of the match** esta fotografía refleja la atmósfera del partido
(**c**) *(surprise, discover) Esp* pillar, *Esp* coger, *Am* pescar; **to c. sb doing sth** *Esp* coger *or Am* pescar a alguien haciendo algo; **we got caught in a shower** nos agarró *or Esp* cogió un chubasco; **we were caught without any matches** nos vimos sin fósforos *or Esp* cerillas; *Fam* **you won't c. me doing that!** ¡no haría eso ni borracho *or* loco!; *Fam* **you won't c. me doing that again!** ¡no pienso volver a hacerlo!; **you won't c. my husband dancing** a mi marido no lo verás bailar ni borracho *or RP* loco; **to c. oneself doing sth** sorprenderse haciendo algo; *Fam* **to c. sb napping** agarrar *or Esp* coger a alguien desprevenido; IDIOM **to c. sb red-handed** *or Fam* **at it** agarrar *or Esp* coger a alguien con las manos en la masa, *Esp* coger *or Am* agarrar *or Am* pescar a alguien in fraganti; IDIOM *Fam* **to c. sb with their pants** *or Br* **trousers down** pescar a alguien desprevenido, *Esp* pillar a alguien en bragas, *RP* agarrar a alguien en bolas; IDIOM **he was caught short** le entraron unas ganas repentinas de ir al baño
(**d**) *(take) (bus, train, taxi)* tomar, *Esp* coger
(**e**) *(be in time for) (bus, train)* alcanzar, llegar a; **I must leave, I've**

got a train to c. me marcho, tengo que tomar *or Esp* coger un tren; **to c. the post** llegar a tiempo a la recogida del correo; **you need to c. the disease in its early stages** *(start treating)* hay que actuar contra la enfermedad en su fase inicial

(**f**) *(manage to see) (programme, movie, play)* ver, alcanzar a ver; **to c. a glimpse of sth** vislumbrar algo; **to c. sight of sth** ver algo

(**g**) *(manage to find) Esp* pillar, *Esp* coger, *Am* agarrar; **you've caught me at a bad time** me *Esp* pillas *or Am* agarras en un mal momento; **I'll c. you later!** luego te veo

(**h**) *(notice) (see)* ver; *(hear)* (alcanzar a) oír; *(smell)* percibir; **did you c. the irony in her voice?** ¿has captado el tono irónico de su voz?; **I didn't c. what he said** no oí *or Esp* cogí lo que dijo

(**i**) *(trap, entangle)* **I caught my dress on a nail, my dress got caught on a nail** me enganché el vestido en un clavo; **don't c. your fingers in the door** no te *Esp* pilles *or Am* agarres los dedos con la puerta; **to c. sb's attention** *or* **eye** llamar la atención de alguien; **to c. sb's imagination** capturar la imaginación de alguien

(**j**) *(become infected with)* agarrar, *Esp* coger, *Am* pescar; **to c. a cold** resfriarse, *Esp* coger *or Méx* pescar un resfriado, *Andes, RP* agarrarse *or* pescarse un resfrío; **to c. the flu** *Esp* coger la gripe, *Am* pescar una gripe; **I caught this cold from** *or* **off you** tú me pegaste este *Esp, Méx* resfriado *or Andes, RP* resfrío; **you'll c. your death (of cold) out there!** ¡vas a agarrar *or Esp* coger *or Méx* pescar un resfriado de muerte ahí fuera!, *Andes, RP* ¡te vas a agarrar un resfrío mortal ahí afuera!; **he's caught the habit from his sister** se le ha pegado la costumbre de su hermana

(**k**) *(hit)* **he caught me (a blow) on the chest** me dio un golpe en el pecho; **the stone caught her on the arm** la piedra le dio en el brazo; **he caught his knee on the table** se dio con la rodilla en la mesa; *Fam* **you'll c. it!** *(get into trouble)* ¡te la vas a *Esp* cargar *or Esp* ganar *or Méx, RP* ligar!

(**l**) **to c. fire** *or* **light** *(go on fire)* prenderse

3 *vi* (**a**) *(fire)* prender

(**b**) *(in door)* quedarse pillado(a); *(on nail)* quedarse enganchado(a); **my skirt caught on a nail** se me enganchó la falda en un clavo

(**c**) *(person)* **to c. at sth** tratar de agarrar *or Esp* coger algo

(**d**) *(voice)* **her voice caught** su voz se entrecortó

▸ **catch on** *vi* (**a**) *(fashion)* cuajar

(**b**) *Fam (understand)* darse cuenta (**to** de), enterarse (**to** de)

▸ **catch out** *vt sep* **to c. sb out** *(discover, trick) Esp* pillar *or Am* agarrar a alguien; **I got caught out by the weather** me sorprendió *or Esp* cogió el mal tiempo

▸ **catch up 1** *vi (close gap, get closer)* **to c. up with sb** alcanzar a alguien; **we have a long way to go before we c. up with our competitors** todavía nos queda mucho para ponernos a la altura de nuestros competidores; **I'm going to c. up on some sleep** voy a recuperar algo de sueño; **we must c. up with each other some time** *(meet up)* tenemos que quedar para ponernos al día de lo que pasa por nuestras vidas; **to c. up with one's work** ponerse al día en el trabajo; **his past has caught up with him** ha salido a relucir su pasado; **the police will c. up with you eventually** la policía acabará atrapándote *or Esp* cogiéndote

2 *vt sep* (**a**) *(reach)* **to c. sb up** alcanzar a alguien

(**b**) **to get caught up in sth** *(become entangled)* verse envuelto(a) *or* enredarse en algo; *Fig (become involved)* ensimismarse en algo; *Fig* **he was totally caught up in his book** estaba totalmente absorto en su libro

---

catch-all ['kætʃɔːl] *adj Fam* **a c. term** un término muy general *or* que vale para todo

catch-as-catch-can ['kætʃəzkætʃ'kæn] **1** *n (wrestling)* catch *m*, = variedad de lucha libre

2 *adj US* de cualquier manera, a la buena de Dios; **there's no strict order, it's c.** no hay ningún orden fijo, se hace de cualquier manera *or* a la buena de Dios

catcher ['kætʃə(r)] *n (in baseball)* cácher *mf*, catcher *mf*, receptor(ora) *m,f*

catching ['kætʃɪŋ] *adj (disease, habit)* contagioso(a)

catchline ['kætʃlaɪn] *n (in advertising campaign)* eslogan *m*

catchment area ['kætʃmənt'eərɪə] *n* (**a**) *(drainage area)* cuenca *f* (**b**) *(of school, hospital)* área *f* de cobertura

catchpenny ['kætʃpenɪ] *adj* **this novel is a c. affair** esta novela no está escrita más que para vender

catchphrase ['kætʃfreɪz] *n* coletilla *f*, latiguillo *m*

catchword ['kætʃwɜːd] *n* (**a**) *(catchphrase)* coletilla *f*, latiguillo *m* (**b**) *Typ* reclamo *m*

catchy ['kætʃɪ] *adj (tune, slogan)* pegadizo(a)

cat-claw vine ['kætklɔː'vaɪn] *n* uña *f* de gato

catechism ['kætəkɪzəm] *n* catecismo *m*

catechize ['kætəkaɪz] *vt* (**a**) *Rel* catequizar (**b**) *(examine)* interrogar, cuestionar

categoric(al) [kætɪ'gɒrɪk(əl)] *adj (denial)* categórico(a), terminante; *(refusal)* rotundo(a); **he was quite c. in his denial** lo negó rotundamente

categorically [kætɪ'gɒrɪkəlɪ] *adv* categóricamente

categorization [kætəgəraɪ'zeɪʃən] *n* clasificación *f*

categorize ['kætəgəraɪz] *vt* clasificar (**as** como)

category ['kætəgərɪ] *n* categoría *f* ▸▸ ***c. climb*** *(in cycling)* puerto *m* puntuable; **first c. climb** *(in cycling)* puerto de primera; *Phil* ***c. mistake*** error *m* categórico

cater ['keɪtə(r)] **1** *vi* (**a**) *(provide food) (at weddings)* dar *or* organizar banquetes; *(for company, airline)* dar servicio de comidas *or* catering; **we c. for groups of up to 50** *(in restaurant)* servimos a grupos de hasta 50 personas; **parties catered for** *(sign in restaurant)* se organizan banquetes

(**b**) **to c. for** *(needs, requirements)* tener en cuenta; **to c. for all tastes** atender a todos los gustos; **to c. to sth** *(indulge)* complacer; **does the building c. for disabled staff?** ¿tiene el edificio accesibilidad para personal discapacitado?

2 *vt US (party, event)* dar el servicio de comida y bebida de, hacer el catering de

cater-cornered ['keɪtəkɔːnəd] *US Fam* **1** *adj* diagonal

2 *adv* en diagonal, diagonalmente

caterer ['keɪtərə(r)] *n (company)* empresa *f* de hostelería; *(person)* hostelero(a) *m,f*

catering ['keɪtərɪŋ] *n (trade)* catering *m*, hostelería *f*; **to do the c.** *(at party)* dar el servicio de comida y bebida ▸▸ ***c. manager*** responsable *mf* del catering; ***c. school*** escuela *f* de hostelería

caterpillar ['kætəpɪlə(r)] *n* oruga *f* ▸▸ ***c. track*** *(on tank, tractor)* oruga *f*; ***c. tractor*** (tractor *m*) oruga *f*

caterwaul ['kætəwɔːl] *vi (cat)* maullar; *(person)* chillar

caterwauling ['kætəwɔːlɪŋ] *n (of cat)* maullidos *mpl*; *(of person)* aullidos *mpl*

catfight ['kætfaɪt] *n* (**a**) *(between cats)* pelea *f* entre gatos (**b**) *Fam* pelea *f* entre mujeres

catfish ['kætfɪʃ] *n* (**a**) *(freshwater)* siluro *m*, bagre *m* (**b**) *(saltwater)* perro *m* del norte

catfoot ['kætfʊt] *vi US* deslizarse como un gato

catgut ['kætgʌt] *n* (**a**) *(for rackets, stringed instruments)* cuerda *f* de tripa (**b**) *(in surgery)* catgut *m*, hilo *m* de sutura

catharsis [kə'θɑːsɪs] (*pl* **catharses** [kə'θɑːsiːz]) *n* catarsis *f inv*

cathartic [kə'θɑːtɪk] *adj* catártico(a)

cathedra *see* **ex cathedra**

cathedral [kə'θiːdrəl] *n* catedral *f* ▸▸ ***c. city*** ciudad *f* catedralicia; ***c. town*** ciudad *f* catedralicia

Catherine ['kæθrɪn] *pr n* **C. the Great** Catalina la Grande; **C. of Aragon** Catalina de Aragón ▸▸ ***C. wheel*** *(firework)* girándula *f*

catheter ['kæθɪtə(r)] *n Med* catéter *m*

catheterize ['kæθɪtəraɪz] *vt Med* introducir un catéter en, practicar un cateterismo a

cathode ['kæθəʊd] *n Elec* cátodo *m* ▸▸ ***c. rays*** rayos *mpl* catódicos; ***c. ray tube*** tubo *m* de rayos catódicos

Catholic ['kæθəlɪk] **1** *n* católico(a) *m,f*

2 *adj* ▸▸ ***the C. church*** la iglesia católica

catholic ['kæθəlɪk] *adj (wide-ranging)* ecléctico(a); **to be c. in one's tastes** tener unos gustos muy eclécticos

Catholicism [kə'θɒlɪsɪzəm] *n* catolicismo *m*

cathouse ['kæthaʊs] *n US Fam* burdel *m*

cation ['kætaɪən] *n Phys* catión *m*

catkin ['kætkɪn] *n (on bush, tree)* amento *m*, candelilla *f*

catlike ['kætlaɪk] *adj* gatuno(a)

catmint ['kætmɪnt], **catnip** ['kætnɪp] *n* menta *f* de gato

catnap ['kætnæp] *Fam* **1** *n* siestecilla *f*, *Am* siestita *f*; **to have a c.** echarse una siestecilla *or Am* siestita, dar una cabezada

2 *vi* echarse una siestecilla *or Am* siestita, dar una cabezada

catnip = **catmint**

cat-o'-nine-tails [kætə'naɪnteɪlz] *n* azote *m* (de nueve cuerdas)

Catseye®, cat's eye ['kætsaɪ] *n (on road)* captafaro *m*, = baliza reflectante en la calzada

catsuit ['kætsuːt] *n Br* mallas *fpl*

catsup ['kætsʌp] *n US* ketchup *m*, catchup *m*
cattail ['kætteɪl] *n US* espadaña *f (planta)*
cattery ['kætərɪ] *n* residencia *f* para gatos
cattle ['kætəl] *npl* ganado *m* (vacuno) ►► ***c. breeder*** ganadero(a) *m,f*; ***c. breeding*** cría *f* de ganado vacuno; ***c. cake*** = especie de pienso concentrado para el ganado; ***c. egret*** garcilla *f* bueyera; ***c. fair*** feria *f* de ganado; ***c. farmer*** ganadero(a) *m,f (de vacuno)*; *Br* ***c. grid*** paso *m* canadiense, reja *f (que impide el paso del ganado)*; ***c. market*** feria *f* de ganado; *Br Fam (nightclub)* discoteca *f* para ligar *or Esp* de ligue *or RP* para el levante; ***c. prod*** picana *f*; ***c. ranch*** rancho *m* ganadero, *RP* estancia *f*; ***c. rustler*** cuatrero(a) *m,f*, ladrón(ona) *m,f* de ganado; ***c. shed*** establo *m*; ***c. show*** feria *f* de ganado; ***c. track*** cañada *f*; ***c. truck*** vagón *m* de ganado
cattleman ['kætəlmən] *n* ganadero *m*
catty ['kætɪ] *adj Fam* malicioso(a), malintencionado(a)
catty-cornered ['kætɪkɔːnəd] *US Fam* **1** *adj* diagonal
2 *adv* en diagonal, diagonalmente
CATV [siːeɪtiː'viː] *n US* (*abbr* **community antenna television**) *(cable TV)* televisión *f* por cable; *(via shared aerial)* antena *f* (colectiva) comunitaria
catwalk ['kætwɔːk] *n* pasarela *f*
Caucasian [kɔː'keɪʒən] **1** *n* (**a**) *(in anthropology)* caucásico(a) *m,f* (**b**) *US (white person)* blanco(a) *m,f* (**c**) *(person from the Caucasus)* caucasiano(a) *m,f* (**d**) *Ling* caucásico *m*
2 *adj* (**a**) *(in anthropology)* caucásico(a) (**b**) *US (white)* blanco(a) (**c**) *(from the Caucasus)* caucasiano(a) (**d**) *Ling* caucásico(a)
Caucasus ['kɔːkəsəs] *n* **the C.** el Cáucaso
caucus ['kɔːkəs] *n Pol* (**a**) *(group within party)* = dentro de un partido político, grupo que actúa en bloque a la hora de coordinar tácticas y proponer candidatos
(**b**) *US (before elections)* = reunión de activistas locales para elegir al candidato presidencial de cada uno de los partidos políticos
(**c**) *US (within legislative body)* grupo *m*; **the Democratic c.** el grupo demócrata; **c. (meeting)** = reunión de los miembros de un partido político
(**d**) *Austr* = reunión de los miembros del Partido Laborista en el Parlamento Federal
caudal ['kɔːdəl] *adj* (**a**) *Anat* caudal (**b**) *Zool* caudal ►► ***c. fin*** caleta *f* caudal
caught *pt & pp of* **catch**
caul [kɔːl] *n Anat* amnios *m*
cauldron ['kɔːldrən] *n* caldero *m*
cauli ['kɒlɪ] *n Br Fam* coliflor *f*
cauliflower ['kɒlɪflaʊə(r)] *n* coliflor *f* ►► ***c. cheese*** = coliflor con besamel de queso; ***c. ear*** *(swollen ear)* oreja *f* hinchada por los golpes
caulk [kɔːlk] *vt Naut* calafatear
caulking ['kɔːlkɪŋ] *n Naut* calafateo *m*
causal ['kɔːzəl] *adj* causal; **a c. link (between)** una relación causa-efecto *or* de causalidad (entre)
causality [kɔː'zælɪtɪ] *n Formal* causalidad *f*
causally ['kɔːzəlɪ] *adv* causalmente; **the two events are c. linked** los dos hechos tienen la misma causa
causation [kɔː'zeɪʃən] *n Formal* causalidad *f*
causative ['kɔːzətɪv] **1** *n Gram (verb)* verbo *m* factitivo *or* causativo
2 *adj* (**a**) *Formal* causante (**b**) *Gram (verb)* factitivo(a), causativo(a)
cause [kɔːz] **1** *n* (**a**) *(origin)* causa *f*; **the c. of the disease is not yet known** se desconoce *or* todavía no se conoce la causa de la enfermedad; **she is the c. of his being in prison** está en prisión por culpa de ella; **c. and effect** causa y efecto
(**b**) *(reason)* motivo *m*, razón *f*; **with (good) c.** con razón; **without good c.** sin razón alguna; **his condition is giving c. for concern** su estado es preocupante; **to have good c. for doing sth** tener un buen motivo para hacer algo; **I have no c. for complaint** no tengo motivo de queja *or* motivos para quejarme; **there's no c. to be concerned** no hay por qué preocuparse
(**c**) *(purpose, mission)* causa *f*; **in the c. of justice** en defensa de la justicia; **her devotion to the c.** su dedicación a la causa; **it's a lost c.** es una causa perdida; **it's all in a good c.** es por una buena causa; **to make common c. (with sb)** hacer causa común (con alguien)
2 *vt* causar; **smoking causes cancer** el tabaco provoca cáncer; **I didn't mean to c. offence** no pretendía ofender a nadie; **he was accused of deliberately causing a fire** lo acusaron de provocar deliberadamente un incendio; **to c. trouble** crear problemas; **to c. sb to do sth** hacer que alguien haga algo; **what caused him to change his mind?** ¿qué hizo que cambiara de opinión?
cause célèbre ['kɔːzsə'lebrə] (*pl* **causes célèbres**) *n (legal case)* caso *m* célebre
causeway ['kɔːzweɪ] *n* paso *m* elevado *(sobre agua)*
caustic ['kɔːstɪk] *adj* (**a**) *Chem* cáustico(a) ►► ***c. soda*** sosa *f* cáustica (**b**) *(biting, sarcastic)* cáustico(a), mordaz
caustically ['kɔːstɪkəlɪ] *adv* cáusticamente, con un tono cáustico
cauterize ['kɔːtəraɪz] *vt Med* cauterizar
caution ['kɔːʃən] **1** *n* (**a**) *(prudence)* prudencia *f*, cautela *f*; **to exercise c.** actuar con precaución; **to proceed with c.** *(generally)* proceder con cautela; *(in car)* ser prudente; **to throw c. to the wind(s)** olvidarse de la prudencia (**b**) *(warning)* advertencia *f*; **to be given a c.** *Law* recibir una advertencia; *Sport* ser amonestado(a) (**c**) *Br Fam Old-fashioned* **you are a (proper) c.!** ¡eres la repera!
2 *vt* (**a**) *(warn)* advertir; **he cautioned them to be careful** les advirtió que tuvieran cuidado; **to c. sb against sth** prevenir a alguien contra algo (**b**) *Law (on arrest)* leer los derechos a; *(instead of prosecuting)* amonestar (**for** por) (**c**) *Sport* amonestar (**for** por)
cautionary ['kɔːʃənərɪ] *adj* **a c. tale** un cuento ejemplar
cautious ['kɔːʃəs] *adj* cauto(a), prudente; **she's c. about making predictions** es muy cauta *or* prudente a la hora de efectuar predicciones
cautiously ['kɔːʃəslɪ] *adv* cautelosamente, con prudencia
cautiousness ['kɔːʃəsnɪs] *n* cautela *f*, prudencia *f*
cavalcade [kævəl'keɪd] *n* cabalgata *f*
cavalier [kævə'lɪə(r)] **1** *n Hist* **C.** = seguidor de Carlos I en la guerra civil inglesa del siglo XVII
2 *adj* demasiado despreocupado(a); **to be c. about sth, to have a c. attitude towards sth** tomarse algo a la ligera
cavalry ['kævəlrɪ] *n* caballería *f* ►► ***c. charge*** carga *f* de la caballería; ***c. twill*** = tipo de tejido resistente utilizado para pantalones, etc.
cavalryman ['kævəlrɪmæn] *n* soldado *m* de caballería
cave [keɪv] *n* cueva *f*, caverna *f* ►► ***c. dweller*** cavernícola *mf*, troglodita *mf*, hombre *m* de las cavernas; ***c. painting*** pintura *f* rupestre
► **cave in** *vi (ground, structure)* hundirse, ceder; *Fig (stop resisting)* rendirse, darse por vencido(a)
caveat ['kævɪæt] *n* (**a**) *Law* = demanda de notificación previa ante un tribunal (**b**) *Formal (warning)* salvedad *f*, reserva *f*; **with the c. that...** con la salvedad de que...; **it was a case of c. emptor** era un caso en el que la responsabilidad caía por cuenta y riesgo del consumidor
cave-in ['keɪvɪn] *n* (**a**) *(of ground, structure)* hundimiento *m*, derrumbamiento *m* (**b**) *(surrender)* rendición *f*
caveman ['keɪvmæn] *n* cavernícola *m*, troglodita *m*
caver ['keɪvə(r)] *n* espeleólogo(a) *m,f*
cavern ['kævən] *n* caverna *f*
cavernous ['kævənəs] *adj (room, pit, building)* tenebroso(a); *(voice)* cavernoso(a); *(eyes)* hundido(a)
cavewoman ['keɪvwʊmən] *n* cavernícola *f*, troglodita *f*
caviar(e) ['kævɪɑː(r)] *n* caviar *m*
cavil ['kævɪl] (*pt & pp* **cavilled**, *US* **caviled**) *vi Literary* poner reparos (**at** a)
caving ['keɪvɪŋ] *n* espeleología *f*; **to go c.** hacer espeleología
cavity ['kævɪtɪ] *n* (**a**) *(hole)* cavidad *f* ►► ***c. wall insulation*** aislamiento *m* de doble pared (**b**) *(of tooth)* caries *f inv* (**c**) *Anat (nasal)* fosa *f*; **the stomach/cranial c.** la cavidad estomacal/craneal
cavort [kə'vɔːt] *vi* retozar, brincar
cavy ['keɪvɪ] *n (animal)* cobaya *f*, conejillo *m* de Indias
caw [kɔː] **1** *n (of bird)* graznido *m*
2 *vi* graznar
cawing ['kɔːɪŋ] *n (of bird)* graznido *m*
cay [kiː] *n* cayo *m*
Cayenne [keɪ'en] *n* Cayena
cayenne [keɪ'en] *n (spice)* **c. (pepper)** cayena *f*
cayman, caiman ['keɪmən] *n* caimán *m*
Cayman Islands ['keɪmənaɪləndz] *n* **the C.** las Islas Caimán
CB [siː'biː] *n (abbr* **Citizens' Band**) banda *f* ciudadana *or* de radioaficionados
CBC [siːbiː'siː] *n* (*abbr* **Canadian Broadcasting Corporation**) cadena *f* CBC *(de radio y televisión canadiense)*
CBD [siːbiː'diː] *n US* (*abbr* **cash before delivery**) pago *m* antes de la entrega
CBer [siː'biːə(r)] *n US Fam* cebeísta *mf*, radioaficionado(a) *m,f*

CBI [si:bi:ˈaɪ] *n* (*abbr* **Confederation of British Industry**) = organización empresarial británica, ≃ *Esp* CEOE *f*

CBS [si:bi:ˈes] *n* (*abbr* **Columbia Broadcasting System**) CBS *f*

cc [si:ˈsi:] **1** (**a**) (*abbr* **cubic centimetre**) c.c. (**b**) (*abbr* **carbon copy**) cc, copias a
2 *vt Com* **make sure you cc that letter to the chairman** asegúrate de enviar una copia de esa carta al presidente

CCTV [si:si:ti:ˈvi:] *n* (*abbr* **closed-circuit television**) circuito *m* cerrado de televisión

CD [si:ˈdi:] *n* (**a**) (*abbr* **compact disc**) *(for music)* CD *m*, (disco *m*) compacto *m*; *(for software)* CD *m* ▸▸ ***CD burner*** estampadora *f* de CD; ***CD drive*** unidad *f or* lector *m* de CD, lector *m* de CD; ***CD player*** (lector *m or* reproductor *m* de) CD *m*; ***CD rack*** mueble *m* para CDs; ***CD reader*** lector *m* de CD; ***CD recorder*** grabadora *f* de CD; ***CD single*** CD *m* sencillo; ***CD tower*** torre *f* de almacenamiento de CDs; ***CD writer*** estampadora *f or* grabadora *f* de CD
(**b**) (*abbr* **Corps Diplomatique**) CD
(**c**) (*abbr* **certificate of deposit**) certificado *m* de depósito

cd/fwd *Acct* (*abbr* **carried forward**) suma y sigue

CD-i, CDI [si:di:ˈaɪ] *n Comptr* (*abbr* **compact disc interactive**) CD-I *m*

CD-R [si:di:ˈɑ:(r)] *n Comptr* (**a**) (*abbr* **compact disc recorder**) grabadora *f* de CD-ROM (**b**) (*abbr* **compact disc recordable**) disco *m* compacto regrabable

Cdr *Mil* (*abbr* **Commander**) Comandante *mf*

Cdre *Naut* (*abbr* **Commodore**) Comodoro *m*

CD-ROM [si:di:ˈrɒm] *n Comptr* (*abbr* **compact disc read-only memory**) CD-ROM *m* ▸▸ ***C. burner*** estampadora *f* de CD-ROM; ***C. drive*** unidad *f or* lector *m* de CD-ROM, lector *m* de CD-ROM; ***C. reader*** lector *m* de CD-ROM; ***C. recorder*** grabadora *f* de CD-ROM; ***C. writer*** estampadora *f* de CD-ROM

CDT [si:di:ˈti:] *n US* (*abbr* **Central Daylight Time**) = hora en el huso horario del centro de los Estados Unidos y Canadá

CDW [si:di:ˈdʌbəlju:] *n* (*abbr* **collision damage waiver**) CDW *m*, cobertura *f* parcial de daños por colisión

CE (**a**) (*abbr* **Council of Europe**) CE *m* (**b**) (*abbr* **Church of England**) Iglesia *f* anglicana (**c**) (*abbr* **Civil Engineer**) ingeniero(a) *m,f* civil (**d**) (*abbr* **Common** *or* **Christian Era**) **1492 CE** 1492 d. J.C.

cease [si:s] **1** *vt* abandonar, suspender; **to c. firing** dejar de disparar; **c. fire!** ¡alto el fuego!; *Com* **to c. trading** *(as company)* cerrar el negocio, suspender la actividad comercial; *(on Stock Exchange)* suspender la cotización
2 *vi* cesar; **to c. doing** *or* **to do sth** dejar de hacer algo; **the organization ceased to exist in 1974** la organización dejó de existir en 1974; **she never ceased in her efforts to free him** nunca cejó en sus esfuerzos por conseguir su liberación; **it never ceases to amaze me (that...)** no deja de sorprenderme (que...)
3 *n Formal* **without c.** sin cesar

ceasefire [ˈsi:sfaɪə(r)] *n* alto *m* el fuego, tregua *f*

ceaseless [ˈsi:slɪs] *adj* incesante

ceaselessly [ˈsi:slɪslɪ] *adv* incesantemente, sin parar

cecum *US* = **caecum**

cedar [ˈsi:də(r)] *n* (**a**) *(tree)* cedro *m* ▸▸ ***c. of Lebanon*** cedro *m* del Líbano (**b**) *(wood)* cedro *m*

cedarwood [ˈsi:dəwʊd] *n* madera *f* de cedro

cede [si:d] *vt Law (territory, property)* ceder

cedilla [səˈdɪlə] *n* cedilla *f*

CEEB [si:i:i:ˈbi:] *n US* (*abbr* **College Entrance Examination Board**) = institución sin ánimo de lucro que gestiona exámenes como el de acceso a la universidad y asesora sobre ayudas financieras y becas

Ceefax® [ˈsi:fæks] *n Br* = teletexto de la BBC

ceilidh [ˈkeɪlɪ] *n* = en Escocia e Irlanda, fiesta en la que se bailan danzas tradicionales

ceiling [ˈsi:lɪŋ] *n* (**a**) *(of room)* techo *m* ▸▸ ***c. rose*** rosetón *m* (de techo) (**b**) *(limit)* techo *m*, tope *m*; **to reach a c.** tocar techo; **the government has set a 3 percent c. on wage rises** el gobierno ha marcado un techo *or* tope del 3 por ciento para los incrementos salariales ▸▸ ***c. price*** precio *m* máximo autorizado (**c**) *Av* techo *m*, altura *f* máxima

celandine [ˈseləndaɪn] *n Bot* celidonia *f*

celeb [səˈleb] *n Fam* famoso(a) *m,f*

celebrant [ˈselɪbrənt] *n Rel* celebrante *mf*

celebrate [ˈselɪbreɪt] **1** *vt* (**a**) *(birthday, Christmas)* celebrar; *(event, victory)* celebrar, festejar; **this month he celebrates fifty years as an actor** este mes cumple cincuenta años como actor (**b**) *(praise) (person, sb's beauty)* celebrar; **to c. sb's achievements** celebrar los logros de alguien; **to c. the memory of sth/sb** celebrar la memoria de algo/alguien (**c**) *Rel* **to c. mass** celebrar *or* decir misa
2 *vi* **let's c.!** ¡vamos a celebrarlo!

celebrated [ˈselɪbreɪtɪd] *adj* célebre

celebration [selɪˈbreɪʃən] *n* (**a**) *(commemoration) (of birthday, Christmas)* celebración *f*; **celebrations** *(of anniversary, victory)* actos *mpl* conmemorativos; **to join in the celebrations** unirse a las celebraciones; **in c.** en celebración; **in c. of Christmas/forty years of peace** para celebrar la Navidad/cuarenta años de paz; **this calls for a c.!** ¡esto hay que celebrarlo!; **a c. of sb's achievements** una celebración de los logros de alguien
(**b**) *(praise)* celebración *f*; **he wrote the poem in c. of her beauty** escribió el poema para celebrar su belleza
(**c**) *Rel* celebración *f*

celebratory [seləˈbreɪtərɪ] *adj (atmosphere, mood)* festivo(a), de celebración; **we had a c. drink after the game** después del partido tomamos unas bebidas de celebración

celebrity [sɪˈlebrɪtɪ] *n* (**a**) *(person)* celebridad *f*, famoso(a) *m,f* (**b**) *(fame)* celebridad *f*, fama *f*

celebutante [sɪˈlebjʊtɑ:nt] *n US* nuevo(a) famoso(a) *m,f*

celeriac [səˈleərɪæk] *n* apio *m* nabo

celerity [sɪˈlerətɪ] *n Literary* celeridad *f*

celery [ˈselərɪ] *n* apio *m*; **a c. stick, a stick of c.** una rama de apio ▸▸ ***c. salt*** sal *f* de apio

celestial [sɪˈlestɪəl] *adj Astron* celeste; *Literary* celestial ▸▸ ***c. body*** cuerpo *m* celeste; ***c. coordinates*** coordenadas *fpl* celestes; ***c. map*** mapa *m* celeste; ***c. meridian*** meridiano *m* celeste; ***c. navigation*** navegación *f* celeste; ***c. pole*** polo *m* celeste; ***c. sphere*** esfera *f* celeste

celiac *US* = **coeliac**

celibacy [ˈselɪbəsɪ] *n* celibato *m*

celibate [ˈselɪbət] *adj* célibe

cell [sel] *n* (**a**) *(in prison)* celda *f*, calabozo *m*; *(in monastery)* celda *f* ▸▸ ***c. block*** bloque *m* de celdas (**b**) *(of honeycomb)* celda *f* (**c**) *Elec (photoelectric)* célula *f*; *(battery)* pila *f* (**d**) *Biol* célula *f* ▸▸ ***c. culture*** cultivo *m* celular; ***c. division*** división *f* celular; ***c. line*** línea *f* celular; ***c. nucleus*** núcleo *m* celular; ***c. theory*** teoría *f* celular; ***c. wall*** pared *f* celular (**e**) *(underground group)* célula *f* (**f**) *Comptr (in spreadsheet)* celda *f*

cellar [ˈselə(r)] *n* (**a**) *(basement)* sótano *m* (**b**) *(for wine)* bodega *f*; **he keeps a good c.** tiene una buena bodega

cellist [ˈtʃelɪst] *n* violonchelista *mf*

cello [ˈtʃeləʊ] (*pl* **cellos**) *n* violonchelo *m*, violoncelo *m*, chelo *m*

Cellophane® [ˈseləfeɪn] *n Br* celofán *m*

cellphone [ˈselfəʊn] *n* teléfono *m* móvil *or Am* celular

cellular [ˈseljʊlə(r)] *adj* (**a**) *Biol* celular (**b**) *(blanket)* celular (**c**) ***c. phone*** teléfono *m* móvil *or Am* celular

cellulite [ˈseljʊlaɪt] *n* celulitis *f inv (acumulación de grasa)*

cellulitis [seljʊˈlaɪtɪs] *n Med* celulitis *f inv (inflamación)*

celluloid® [ˈseljʊlɔɪd] *n* celuloide *m*; **the true story: now on c.** la historia real, ahora en la pantalla grande

cellulose [ˈseljʊləʊs] *n* celulosa *f*

Celsius [ˈselsɪəs] *adj* centígrado(a); **10 degrees C.** 10 grados centígrados ▸▸ ***C. degree*** grado *m* Celsius; ***C. scale*** escala *f* Celsius; ***C. thermometer*** termómetro *m* centígrado

Celt [kelt] *n* celta *mf*

Celtiberian [keltɪˈbɪərɪən] **1** *n* celtíbero(a) *m,f*
2 *adj* celtíbero(a)

Celtic [ˈkeltɪk] **1** *n (language)* celta *m*
2 *adj* celta, céltico(a) ▸▸ ***C. cross*** cruz *f* celta

cement [sɪˈment] **1** *n* (**a**) *(in building)* cemento *m* ▸▸ ***c. mixer*** hormigonera *f* (**b**) *(glue)* cola *f* (**c**) *(in dentistry) (for filling cavities)* empaste *m*; *(for attaching crowns)* cemento *m*
2 *vt* (**a**) *(cover with cement)* cubrir de cemento (**b**) *(fix together) (with glue)* encolar, pegar; *(bricks)* juntar con cemento; **they cemented the plaque to the wall** pegaron la placa a la pared con cemento (**c**) *(make firm) (friendship)* consolidar, cimentar

cemetery [ˈsemətrɪ] *n* cementerio *m*

cenotaph [ˈsenətɑ:f] *n* cenotafio *m*; **the C.** = monumento en Londres a los caídos en las dos Guerras Mundiales

Cenozoic [si:nəʊˈzəʊɪk] *Geol* **1** *n* **the C.** el cenozoico
2 *adj (era)* cenozoico(a)

censer [ˈsensə(r)] *n (in church)* incensario *m*

censor ['sensə(r)] **1** *n* **(a)** *(of books, films)* censor(ora) *m,f*; **it'll never get past the censors** no pasará la censura **(b)** *Hist (in ancient Rome)* censor *m*
2 *vt* censurar

censorious [sen'sɔ:rɪəs] *adj (person)* censurador(ora); *(look)* reprobatorio(a); **to be c. of** censurar

censorship ['sensəʃɪp] *n* censura *f*

censurable ['senʃərəbəl] *adj Formal* censurable

censure ['senʃə(r)] **1** *n* censura *f*, crítica *f*; **even he is not above c.** hasta a él se le puede censurar; *Pol* **vote of c.** moción de censura
2 *vt* censurar, criticar

census ['sensəs] *n* censo *m*; **to take a c. of** censar

cent [sent] *n (of dollar)* centavo *m*; *(of euro)* céntimo *m*; *US Fam* **I haven't got a c.** no tengo ni un centavo *or Esp* duro *or Méx* peso; IDIOM *US Fam* **to put one's two cents (worth) in** *Esp* meter baza, *Am* meterse

centaur ['sentɔ:(r)] *n* centauro *m*

centenarian [sentɪ'neərɪən] *n* centenario(a) *m,f*

centenary [sen'ti:nərɪ] **1** *n* centenario *m*
2 *adj* centenario(a)

centennial [sen'tenɪəl] *US* **1** *n* centenario *m*
2 *adj* centenario(a)

center, centerboard *etc US* = **centre, centreboard** *etc*

centesimal [sen'tesɪməl] *adj* centesimal

centigrade ['sentɪgreɪd] *adj* centígrado(a); **10 degrees c.** 10 grados centígrados

centigram(me) ['sentɪgræm] *n* centigramo *m*

centilitre, *US* **centiliter** ['sentɪli:tə(r)] *n* centilitro *m*

centimetre, *US* **centimeter** ['sentɪmi:tə(r)] *n* centímetro *m*

centipede ['sentɪpi:d] *n* ciempiés *m inv*

central ['sentrəl] *adj* **(a)** *(in location)* central; **c. Miami** el centro de Miami ▸▸ ***the C. African Republic*** la República Centroafricana; ***C. America*** Centroamérica, América Central; ***C. American*** centroamericano(a); *Sport* ***c. defender*** defensa *mf* central, central *mf*; ***C. Europe*** Europa Central; ***C. European*** centroeuropeo(a); ***C. European Time*** hora *f* de Europa central; ***c. midfielder*** *(in soccer)* centrocampista *mf*; *Br* ***c. reservation*** *(on motorway)* mediana *f*, *Col, Méx* camellón *m*; *US* ***C. Standard Time*** hora *f* oficial del meridiano 90°
(b) *(in convenient location)* céntrico(a); **our hotel is quite c.** nuestro hotel es bastante céntrico
(c) *(in importance)* central, primordial; **it is c. to our plans** es el eje sobre el que giran nuestros planes; **exports played a c. part in our recovery** las exportaciones han desempeñado un papel central *or* primordial en nuestra recuperación ▸▸ ***c. character*** *(in book, movie)* personaje *m* central, protagonista *mf*
(d) *(at heart of network)* central ▸▸ ***c. bank*** banco *m* central; *Cin* ***c. casting*** = el departamento de un estudio de cine encargado de los repartos; *Hum* **he looked like a gangster from c. casting** parecía un gángster de película; ***c. computer*** *Esp* ordenador *m* central, *Am* computadora *f* central; ***C. European Bank*** Banco *m* Central Europeo; ***c. government*** gobierno *m* central; ***c. heating*** calefacción *f* central; ***C. Intelligence Agency*** Agencia *f* Central de Inteligencia; *Aut* ***c. locking*** cierre *m* centralizado; ***c. nervous system*** sistema *m* nervioso central; *Comptr* ***c. processing unit*** unidad *f* central de proceso
(e) *Ling* **c. vowel** vocal central

centralism ['sentrəlɪzəm] *n Pol* centralismo *m*

centralist ['sentrəlɪst] *Pol* **1** *n* centralista *mf*
2 *adj* centralista

centrality [sen'trælətɪ] *n* **(a)** *(of location)* situación *f* céntrica **(b)** *(of argument, idea)* carácter *m* esencial

centralization [sentrəlaɪ'zeɪʃən] *n* centralización *f*

centralize ['sentrəlaɪz] *vt* centralizar

centralized ['sentrəlaɪzd] *adj* centralizado(a)

centrally ['sentrəlɪ] *adv* **(a)** *(located)* **we live quite c.** vivimos en una zona muy céntrica **(b)** *(organized)* **c. controlled** de control *or Am* monitoreo centralizado; **c. funded** de financiación *or Am* financiamiento central; **the house is c. heated** la casa tiene calefacción central; *Econ* **a c. planned economy** una economía de planificación centralizada

centre, *US* **center** ['sentə(r)] **1** *n* **(a)** *(of object, shape)* centro *m*; **in the c.** en el centro ▸▸ ***c. of gravity*** centro *m* de gravedad; *Phys* ***c. of mass*** centro *m* de masa; ***c. punch*** punzón *m*; ***c. spread*** *(in newspaper)* página *f* central; *(in magazine)* póster *m* central
(b) *(of town)* centro *m*; **urban c.** centro urbano, ciudad; **she lives in the city c.** *or* **the c. of town** vive en el centro de la ciudad
(c) *(building)* centro *m*; **a sports/health c.** un centro deportivo/de salud
(d) *(in politics)* centro *m*; **left of c.** de izquierdas; **right of c.** de derechas; **a party of the c. left/right** un partido de centroizquierda/centroderecha
(e) *(focus, location) (of commerce, finance)* centro *m*; *(of unrest)* foco *m*; **c. of attention** centro de atención; **c. of interest** centro de interés; **c. of population** centro demográfico
(f) *Theat* ***c. stage*** parte *f* central del escenario; IDIOM **to take c. stage** centrar la atención
(g) *Sport (position) (in basketball)* pívot *mf*; *(in American football)* central *mf*; **(inside/outside) c.** *(in rugby)* centro *mf* (izquierdo/derecho) ▸▸ ***c. back*** *(in soccer)* defensa *mf* central, central *mf*; ***c. circle*** círculo *m* central; ***c. court*** pista *f* central; ***c. field*** *(in baseball)* jardín *m* central, campo *m* exterior central; ***c. fielder*** *(in baseball)* jugador(ora) *m,f* exterior central; ***c. forward*** *(in soccer)* delantero *m* centro; ***c. half*** *(in soccer)* medio *mf* centro
(h) *Sport (pass)* centro *m*
2 *vt* **(a)** *(focus) (attack, bombing)* centrar, concentrar (**on** sobre); *(attention, interest)* centrar, concentrar (**on** en) **(b)** *Typ (text)* centrar **(c)** *Sport (ball)* centrar

▸ **centre around** *vt insep* **(a)** *(located)* **the village is centred around the church** el pueblo se extiende en torno a la iglesia **(b)** *(have as focus)* centrarse en torno a; **the debate has centred around his personality** el debate se ha centrado en torno a su personalidad

▸ **centre on** *vt insep (concentrate)* centrarse en; **all their attention was centred on the World Cup** toda su atención estaba centrada en el Mundial; **the conversation centred on politics** la conversación giró en torno a la política

▸ **centre round** *vt insep* = **centre around**

centreboard, *US* **centerboard** ['sentəbɔ:d] *n Naut* orza *f* de la quilla

centred, *US* **centered** ['sentəd] *adj* **(a)** *(situated in the centre)* centrado(a) **(b)** *(mentally focused)* centrado(a)

centrefold, *US* **centerfold** ['sentəfəʊld] *n (in magazine)* póster *m* central

centreline, *US* **centerline** ['sentəlaɪn] *n* **(a)** *(of tennis court, road)* línea *f* central **(b)** *(of geometrical figure, aeroplane)* eje *m*; *(of yacht)* crujía *f*

centrepiece, *US* **centerpiece** ['sentəpi:s] *n* **(a)** *(on table)* centro *m* de mesa **(b)** *(main element)* núcleo *m*, eje *m*

centrifugal [sentrɪ'fju:gəl] *adj Phys* centrífugo(a) ▸▸ ***c. force*** fuerza *f* centrífuga; ***c. pump*** bomba *f* centrífuga

centrifuge ['sentrɪfju:dʒ] *n (for separating liquids)* centrifugadora *f*, separador *m* centrífugo

centring, *US* **centering** ['sentərɪŋ] *n* **(a)** *(on position)* centrado *m* **(b)** *Typ (of text)* centrado *m*

centripetal [sen'trɪpɪtəl] *adj Phys* centrípeto(a) ▸▸ ***c. acceleration*** aceleración *f* centrípeta; ***c. force*** fuerza *f* centrípeta

centrist ['sentrɪst] *n* centrista *mf*

centuries-old ['sentʃəri:z'əʊld] *adj (custom, tradition)* secular, ancestral; *(building)* centenario(a)

centurion [sen'tʃʊərɪən] *n Hist* centurión *m*

century ['sentʃərɪ] *n* **(a)** *(a hundred years)* siglo *m*; **the 2nd c.** *(written)* el siglo II; *(spoken)* el siglo dos *or* segundo; **in the 20th c.** en el siglo XX **(b)** *(in cricket)* = cien (o más de cien) carreras **(c)** *Hist (in ancient Rome)* centuria *f*

century-old ['sentʃərɪ'əʊld] *adj (institution, building)* centenario(a)

CEO [si:i:'əʊ] *n Com* (*abbr* **chief executive officer**) director(ora) *m,f* gerente, consejero(a) *m,f* delegado(a)

cep [sep] *n* boleto *m* comestible *or* calabaza

cephalic [sə'fælɪk] *adj Anat* cefálico(a)

cephalopod ['sefələpɒd] *n Zool* cefalópodo *m*

ceramic [sə'ræmɪk] **1** *n (vase, figure)* cerámica *f*
2 *adj* de cerámica; **c. tile** *(on floor)* baldosa; *(on wall)* azulejo ▸▸ ***c. hob*** placa *f* de vitrocerámica

ceramics [sə'ræmɪks] *n (art)* cerámica *f*

cereal ['sɪərɪəl] *n* **(a)** *(plant, grain)* cereal *m* ▸▸ ***c. crops*** cosechas *fpl* de cereal **(b)** *(food)* **(breakfast) c.** cereales *mpl* (de desayuno)

cerebellum [serɪ'beləm] (*pl* **cerebella** [serɪ'belə]) *n Anat* cerebelo *m*

cerebra *pl of* **cerebrum**

cerebral ['serɪbrəl] *adj* **(a)** *Anat* cerebral ▸▸ ***c. cortex*** córtex *m inv or* corteza *f* cerebral; ***c. hemisphere*** hemisferio *m* cerebral; *Med* ***c. palsy*** parálisis *f inv* cerebral **(b)** *(intellectual)* cerebral

cerebration [serɪ'breɪʃən] *n* reflexión *f*, meditación *f*

cerebrospinal [serəbrəʊ'spaɪnəl] *adj Anat (fluid)* cefalorraquídeo(a)

cerebrum ['serɪbrəm] (*pl* **cerebrums** *or* **cerebra** ['serɪbrə]) *n Anat* cerebro *m*

ceremonial [serɪ'məʊnɪəl] 1 *n* ceremonial *m*; **ceremonials** ceremoniales
2 *adj* ceremonial

ceremonially [serɪ'məʊnɪəlɪ] *adv* de manera ceremonial

ceremonious [serɪ'məʊnɪəs] *adj* ceremonioso(a)

ceremoniously [serɪ'məʊnɪəslɪ] *adv* ceremoniosamente

ceremony ['serɪmənɪ] *n* (**a**) *(formality)* ceremonia *f*; **with/without c.** con/sin ceremonia; *Fig* **he was sacked without c.** lo despidieron sin ningún miramiento; **there's no need to stand on c.** no hace falta cumplir con formalidades (**b**) *(occasion, rite)* ceremonia *f*; **the marriage c.** la ceremonia nupcial

Ceres ['sɪəri:z] *n Mythol* Ceres

cerise [sə'ri:z] 1 *n* color *m* cereza
2 *adj* de color cereza

cerium ['sɪərɪəm] *n* cerio *m*

cert [sɜ:t] *n Fam* **it's a (dead) c. to win** no cabe ninguna duda de que ganará; **he's a c. for the job** conseguirá el trabajo con toda seguridad

cert. (*abbr* **certificate**) certificado *m*

certain ['sɜ:tən] 1 *adj* (**a**) *(sure)* seguro(a); **to be c. about sth** estar seguro(a) de algo; **she was quite c. about the identity of the killer** no tenía la menor duda acerca de la identidad del asesino; **to be c. of sth** estar seguro(a) de algo; **to be c. of doing sth** ir a hacer algo seguro; **she's c. of finishing in the top three** seguro que queda entre las tres primeras; **it now seems c. she is guilty** ahora parece claro *or* seguro que es culpable; **she's c. to win** seguro que va a ganar; **he is c. to come** vendrá con toda seguridad; **his promotion is c. to cause a scandal** su ascenso provocará sin lugar a dudas un escándalo; **to make c. of sth** asegurarse de algo; **he made c. that all the doors were locked** se aseguró de que todas las puertas estuvieran cerradas; **one thing at least is c.,...** por lo menos una cosa es segura *or* está clara,...; **for c.** con certeza; **I don't know for c.** no lo sé con certeza; **I'll have it tomorrow for c.** lo tendré para mañana seguro; **he won't do that again, that's for c.!** no lo volverá a hacer, ¡puedes estar seguro de ello!
(**b**) *(inevitable)* **defeat seemed c.** la derrota parecía inevitable; **the soldiers faced c. death** los soldados iban a una muerte segura
(**c**) *(particular)* cierto(a), determinado(a); **for c. reasons** por ciertos motivos; **a c. person** cierta persona; **a c. Richard Sanders** un tal Richard Sanders; **in a c. sense he's right** en cierta manera tiene razón; **I suppose he has a c. charm** supongo que tiene un cierto encanto *or* un no sé qué
(**d**) *(some)* **there's been a c. amount of confusion over this** ha habido cierta confusión sobre esto; **to a c. extent** *or* **degree** hasta cierto punto, en cierta medida; **c. people** algunas personas
2 *pron Formal* **c. of us/them** algunos de nosotros/ellos

certainly ['sɜ:tənlɪ] *adv* (**a**) *(undoubtedly)* sin duda, ciertamente; **she's c. very clever, but...** sin duda es muy lista, pero...
(**b**) *(definitely)* por supuesto; **we will c. be there** por supuesto *or* seguro que estaremos allí
(**c**) *(for emphasis)* desde luego; **that was c. some goal!** ¡menudo golazo!; **I c. won't be recommending that movie!** ¡no pienso recomendar esa película ni en broma!; **can you help me? – c.!** ¿me puedes ayudar? – ¡desde luego *or* por supuesto!; **are you angry? – I most c. am!** ¿estás *esp Esp* enfadado *or esp Am* enojado? – ¡claro *or* ya lo creo que sí!; **c. not!** ¡ni hablar!

certainty ['sɜ:təntɪ] *n* (**a**) *(conviction)* certeza *f*, certidumbre *f*; **she said it with some c.** lo dijo con certidumbre
(**b**) *(inevitability)* **there is no c. that we will win** no es seguro que ganemos
(**c**) *(fact)* **there are no certainties any more** ya no se puede dar nada por seguro; **they had lost faith in the old certainties** habían perdido la fe en las cosas seguras de antaño; **to know sth for a c.** saber algo a ciencia cierta; **it's a c. that they will win** es seguro *or* cosa segura que ganarán, van a ganar seguro

CertEd [sɜ:t'ed] *n Br* (*abbr* **Certificate in Education**) = título que permite ejercer de profesor en centros de enseñanza secundaria

certifiable ['sɜ:tɪfaɪəbəl] *adj* (**a**) *(attested)* que se puede certificar (**b**) *(mad)* **to be c.** estar como para que lo/la encierren

certificate 1 *n* [sə'tɪfɪkət] (**a**) *(official confirmation)* certificado *m*; **marriage/death c.** certificado *or* partida de matrimonio/defunción ►► *Av* ***c. of airworthiness*** certificado *m* de aeronavegabilidad; *Com* ***c. of incorporation*** = certificado de constitución de una sociedad; ***c. of origin*** certificado *m* de origen; ***c. of registration*** *(of ship)* patente *f* de navegación (**b**) *(in education)* título *m*
2 *vt* [sɜ:'tɪfɪkeɪt] certificar

certificated [sɜ:'tɪfɪkeɪtɪd] *adj* certificado(a)

certification [sɜ:tɪfɪ'keɪʃən] *n* (**a**) *(act)* certificación *f* (**b**) *(document)* certificado *m*

certified ['sɜ:tɪfaɪd] *adj (qualified)* diplomado(a); *(document)* certificado(a) ►► *US* ***c. check*** cheque *m* conformado; *US* ***c. mail*** correo *m* certificado; *US* ***c. milk*** leche *f* con certificado sanitario; *US* ***c. public accountant*** *Esp* censor(ora) *m,f* jurado(a) de cuentas, *Am* contador(ora) *m,f* público(a); *Law* ***c. true copy*** *(document)* copia *f* auténtica compulsada; *(appearing on document)* es fiel copia del original

certify ['sɜ:tɪfaɪ] 1 *vt* (**a**) *(confirm)* certificar; **this document certifies that he is a qualified doctor** este documento acredita que tiene la titulación de médico; **to c. that sth is true** dar fe de que algo es verdad; **this is to c. that...** por la presente certifico que...
(**b**) *(declare)* **to c. sb insane** declarar demente a alguien; **she was certified dead at 6.43 am** se certificó su muerte a las 6.43 de la mañana; *Fam* **he ought to be certified!** ¡está chalado!, ¡está mal de la azotea!
(**c**) *US* **to c. a cheque** conformar un cheque
2 *vi* **the bruises certified to the truth of her story** las magulladuras probaban la veracidad de su historia

certitude ['sɜ:tɪtju:d] *n Formal* certidumbre *f*

cerulean [sɪ'ru:lɪən] *adj Literary* cerúleo(a)

Cervantine [sɜ:'væntaɪn] *adj* cervantino(a)

cervical ['sɜ:vɪkəl] *adj Anat* (**a**) *(of the cervix)* cervical ►► ***c. cancer*** cáncer *m* cervical; ***c. smear*** frotis *m inv* cervical, citología *f* (cervical) (**b**) *(of the neck)* cervical ►► ***c. collar*** collarín *m*; ***c. vertebra*** vértebra *f* cervical

cervix ['sɜ:vɪks] (*pl* **cervices** ['sɜ:vɪsi:z]) *n Anat* cuello *m* del útero

cesarean *US* = **caesarean**

cesium *US* = **caesium**

cessation [se'seɪʃən] *n Formal* cese *m*; **c. of hostilities** cese de hostilidades

cession ['seʃən] *n Formal* cesión *f*

cesspit ['sespɪt], **cesspool** ['sespu:l] *n* pozo *m* negro; *Fig* sentina *f*, cloaca *f*

cesura *US* = **caesura**

CET [si:i:'ti:] *n* (**a**) (*abbr* **Central European Time**) hora *f* de Europa central (**b**) *EU* (*abbr* **common external tariff**) AEC *m*

cetacean [sɪ'teɪʃən] *Zool* 1 *n* cetáceo *m*
2 *adj* cetáceo(a)

cetane ['si:teɪn] *n Chem* cetano *m* ►► ***c. number*** índice *m or* número *m* de cetano

Ceylon [sɪ'lɒn] *n Formerly* Ceilán

CF [si:'ef] *n* (*abbr* **cost and freight**) CF *m*, costo *m or Esp* coste *m* y flete

cf [si:'ef] (*abbr* **confer, compare**) cf., cfr.

CFC [si:ef'si:] *n Chem* (*abbr* **chlorofluorocarbon**) CFC *m*

CFO [si:ef'əʊ] *n US* (*abbr* **chief financial officer**) director(ora) *m,f* financiero(a)

CFR [si:ef'ɑ:(r)] *n* (*abbr* **Code of Federal Regulations**) = código de normas que cubre las áreas de competencia del gobierno federal estadounidense

CFTC [si:efti:'si:] *n* (*abbr* **Commodity Futures Trading Commission**) = comisión creada en 1973 con el fin de controlar las transacciones comerciales en los mercados de futuros estadounidenses

cg (*abbr* **centigramme(s)**) cg

CGA [si:dʒi:'eɪ] *n Comptr* (*abbr* **colour graphics adaptor**) CGA *m*

CGI [si:dʒi:'aɪ] *n Comptr* (**a**) (*abbr* **common gateway interface**) interfaz *f* común de pasarela (**b**) (*abbr* **computer-generated images**) imágenes *fpl* generadas por *Esp* ordenador *or Am* computadora

CGS system [si:dʒi:'es'sɪstəm] *n Phys* (*abbr* **centimetre-gramme-second system**) sistema *m* cegesimal

CH (**a**) *Br* (*abbr* **Companion of Honour**) = condecoración que se entrega al ciudadano que ha prestado algún servicio destacado al Estado (**b**) (*abbr* **central heating**) calefacción *f* central (**c**) (*abbr* **clearing house**) cámara *f* de compensación

ch (*abbr* **chapter**) cap.

cha-cha-cha [tʃɑ:tʃɑ:'tʃɑ:], **cha-cha** ['tʃɑ:tʃɑ:] *n* chachachá *m*

Chad [tʃæd] *n* Chad

Chadian ['tʃædɪən] 1 *n* chadiano(a) *m,f*
2 *adj* chadiano(a)

chador ['tʃʌdə(r)] *n* chador *m*

chafe [tʃeɪf] **1** *vt (rub)* rozar, hacer rozadura en; **his shirt collar chafed his neck** el cuello de la camisa le rozaba *or* le hacía rozadura en el cuello

2 *vi* (**a**) *(rub)* rozar, hacer rozadura (**b**) *(resent)* **to c. at** *or* **against sth** sentirse irritado(a) por algo

chaff [tʃæf] **1** *n* (**a**) *(of grain)* granzas *fpl*, barcia *f* (**b**) *(worthless material)* paja *f*

2 *vt (tease)* tomar el pelo a

chaffinch ['tʃæfɪntʃ] *n* pinzón *m* (vulgar)

chafing ['tʃeɪfɪŋ] *n* (**a**) *(of skin)* irritación *f*, rozadura *f* (**b**) *(warming)* ***c. dish*** = aparato para mantener la comida caliente en la mesa

chagrin ['ʃægrɪn] *n* disgusto *m*, desazón *f*; **much to my/her c.** muy a mi/su pesar

chain [tʃeɪn] **1** *n* (**a**) *(metal)* cadena *f*; *Aut* **(snow) chains** cadenas *fpl* (para el hielo); **we keep the dog on a c.** tenemos al perro encadenado; **in chains** encadenado(a); *Fig* **to form a human c.** formar una cadena humana; **to pull the c.** *(in toilet)* tirar de la cadena; IDIOM **to pull** *or* **yank sb's c.** fastidiar *or* mosquear a alguien ►► *Tech* ***c. drive*** transmisión *f* por cadena; ***c. gang*** cadena *f* de presidiarios; ***c. guard*** *(on bicycle)* protector *m* de cadena, cubrecadena *f*; ***c. mail*** cota *f* de malla; ***c. of office*** *(of mayor)* collar *m* de mando; ***c. stitch*** *(in knitting)* punto *m* de cadeneta; ***c. wheel*** *(de bicicleta)* plato *m*

(**b**) *(of mountains, islands)* **a c. of mountains** una cadena montañosa, una cordillera; **a c. of islands, an island c.** una cadena de islas

(**c**) *(of shops)* cadena *f*; **c. of stores** cadena de tiendas ►► ***c. store*** tienda *f (perteneciente a una cadena)*

(**d**) *(series) (of ideas)* serie *f* encadenada; **a c. of events** una concatenación de sucesos ►► ***c. of command*** estructura *f* de mando; ***c. letter*** = carta en la que se pide al destinatario que envíe copias de la misma a otras personas; *US* ***c. lightning*** relámpagos *mpl* en zigzag; ***c. reaction*** reacción *f* en cadena

(**e**) *(measure of length)* = medida equivalente a 22 yardas o 20,10 metros

2 *vt* encadenar; **to c. sth/sb to sth** encadenar algo/a alguien a algo; **they chained themselves to the railings in protest** se encadenaron a la verja como forma de protesta; IDIOM **to be chained to one's desk** estar todo el día en el trabajo

► **chain up** *vt sep* encadenar

chain-link fence ['tʃeɪnlɪŋk'fens] *n* verja *f* de eslabón de cadena *or* de tela metálica

chainsaw ['tʃeɪnsɔː] *n* motosierra *f*, sierra *f* mecánica

chain-smoke ['tʃeɪnsməʊk] *vi* fumar un cigarrillo tras otro

chain-smoker ['tʃeɪn'sməʊkə(r)] *n* fumador(ora) *m,f* empedernido(a)

chair [tʃeə(r)] **1** *n* (**a**) *(seat)* silla *f*; *(armchair)* sillón *m*

(**b**) *(chairperson) (of meeting)* presidente(a) *m,f*; *(of debate)* moderador(ora) *m,f*; **to be in the c.** ocupar la presidencia; **to address the c.** dirigirse a la presidencia, dirigirse al presidente/a la presidenta; **to take the c.** ocupar la presidencia, presidir

(**c**) *Univ (of professor)* cátedra *f*; **she holds the c. of Physics** ocupa la cátedra de Física

(**d**) *US Fam (electric chair)* **the c.** la silla eléctrica; **to go to** *or* **get** *or* **be sent to the c.** ser enviado a la silla eléctrica

(**e**) *(on railway line)* cojinete *m*

2 *vt* (**a**) *(meeting)* presidir; *(debate)* moderar (**b**) *Br (hero, victor)* llevar a hombros; **they chaired him out of the hall** lo sacaron a hombros del salón de actos

chairbound ['tʃeəbaʊnd] *adj* inválido(a) *(en silla de ruedas)*

chairlift ['tʃeəlɪft] *n* telesilla *m*

chairman ['tʃeəmən] *n* (**a**) *(of meeting, debate)* moderador *m*; **to act as c.** hacer de moderador; **Mister C.** Señor Presidente; **Madam C.** Señora Presidenta

(**b**) *(of company)* presidente *m* (del consejo de administración); **to act as c.** ocupar la presidencia; **c. and managing director** presidente y consejero delegado, presidente y máximo responsable ejecutivo ►► ***C. of the Board*** presidente *m* del consejo de administración

(**c**) *Pol* **C. Mao** Mao

chairmanship ['tʃeəmənʃɪp] *n* presidencia *f*; **under the c. of Mr Greene** bajo *or* durante la presidencia del Señor Greene

chairperson ['tʃeəpɜːsən] *n (of meeting, debate)* moderador(ora) *m,f*

chairwoman ['tʃeəwʊmən] *n* (**a**) *(of meeting, debate)* moderadora *f*; **to act as c.** hacer de moderadora; **Madam C.** Señora Presidenta (**b**) *(of company)* presidenta *f* (del consejo de administración); **to act as c.** ocupar la presidencia; **c. and managing director** presidenta y consejera delegada, presidenta y máxima responsable ejecutiva ►► ***C. of the Board*** presidenta *f* del consejo de administración

chaise [ʃeɪz] *n (carriage)* tílburi *m*

chaise longue [ʃeɪz'lɒŋ] (*pl* **chaises longues** [ʃeɪz'lɒŋ]) *n* chaise longue *f*

chalcedony [kæl'sedənɪ] *n Geol* calcedonia *f*

chalcopyrite [kælkə'paɪraɪt] *n Geol* calcopirita *f*

chalet ['ʃæleɪ] *n* (**a**) *(in mountains)* chalé *m* (**b**) *(in holiday camp)* cabaña *f*

chalice ['tʃælɪs] *n Rel* cáliz *m*

chalk [tʃɔːk] **1** *n* (**a**) *(mineral)* creta *f*

(**b**) *(for blackboard)* tiza *f*, *Méx* gis *m*; *(for cue)* tiza *f* ►► ***c. dust*** polvo *m* de tiza; *Br* ***c. and talk*** = método de enseñanza tradicional centrado en las explicaciones del profesor y la utilización de la pizarra; *US* ***c. talk*** conferencia *f (utilizando una pizarra)*

(**c**) IDIOMS *Br* **they are as different as c. and cheese** no se parecen para nada *or* ni en el blanco de los ojos, son como el día y la noche; *Br Fam* **by a long c.: not by a long c.** ni de lejos; **she was the best candidate by a long c.** era, de lejos, la mejor candidata

2 *vt* (**a**) *(mark)* trazar *or* marcar con tiza; *(write)* escribir con tiza (**b**) *(cue)* dar tiza a

► **chalk up** *vt sep* (**a**) *(victory)* apuntarse (**b**) *(charge, credit)* **to c. sth up to sb** apuntarle algo en la cuenta a alguien; **to c. sth up to experience** asumir algo como una experiencia positiva

chalkboard ['tʃɔːkbɔːd] *n US* pizarra *f*, encerado *m*, *Am* pizarrón *m*

chalkface ['tʃɔːkfeɪs] *n Br Hum* **the people at the c.** los profesores

chalkpit ['tʃɔːkpɪt] *n* cantera *f* de creta

chalky ['tʃɔːkɪ] *adj* (**a**) *(containing chalk) (soil)* calizo(a); *(water)* calcáreo(a) (**b**) *(like chalk)* terroso(a) (**c**) *(hands, face)* lleno(a) de tiza *or Méx* de gis

challenge ['tʃælɪndʒ] **1** *n* (**a**) *(invitation to contest, duel)* desafío *m*; **to issue/accept a c.** lanzar/aceptar un desafío

(**b**) *(exacting task)* desafío *m*, reto *m*; **to enjoy a c.** disfrutar con las tareas difíciles; **to rise to the c.** estar a la altura de las circunstancias; **the job presents a real c.** el trabajo constituye un auténtico reto; **are you up to the c.?** ¿te sientes capacitado?; **where's the c. in that?** ¿y eso qué tiene de difícil?

(**c**) *(to authority)* **this was a direct c. to my authority** esto fue un ataque directo a mi autoridad

(**d**) *(competition)* **they present no real c. to his leadership** no suponen una amenaza seria a su liderazgo

(**e**) *(to potential juror)* recusación *f*

(**f**) *Mil (demand for identity, password)* (orden *f* de) alto *m*; **they failed to respond to the policeman's c.** no se detuvieron cuando el policía les dio el alto

2 *vt* (**a**) *(to a contest, fight)* desafiar, retar; **to c. sb to do sth** desafiar *or* retar a alguien a hacer algo; **to c. sb to a duel** desafiar *or* retar a alguien a un duelo; **to c. sb to a game of tennis** retar a alguien a un partido de tenis

(**b**) *(make demands on)* **you need a job that will c. you** necesitas un trabajo que represente un reto para ti

(**c**) *(dispute) (statement, authority)* cuestionar, poner en duda; **she challenged his right to decide** puso en duda que él tuviera derecho a decidir; **when challenged on this point, he was evasive** cuando se le discutió este punto, respondió con evasivas

(**d**) *(juror)* recusar

(**e**) *Mil (demand identity, password from)* dar el alto a; **when challenged by a policeman, he ran away** cuando un policía le dio el alto, se echó a correr

challenged ['tʃælɪndʒd] *adj* **physically c.** discapacitado(a) físico(a); *Hum* **to be vertically c.** ser muy bajito(a) *or* un retaco

challenger ['tʃælɪndʒə(r)] *n* (**a**) *(in race, election)* aspirante *mf* (**b**) *Mktg* competidor *m*

challenging ['tʃælɪndʒɪŋ] *adj* (**a**) *(defiant)* desafiante (**b**) *(demanding) (ideas, theory)* estimulante, provocador(ora); *(job, task)* estimulante

chamber ['tʃeɪmbə(r)] *n* (**a**) *(hall)* sala *f*; *Pol* **Lower/Upper C.** cámara *f* baja/alta ►► ***C. of Commerce*** cámara *f* de comercio; ***c. of horrors*** *(at funfair)* casa *f* del terror; **the troops discovered a real c. of horrors in the town** las tropas descubrieron auténticas atrocidades en la ciudad; ***c. music*** música *f* de cámara; ***c. orchestra*** orquesta *f* de cámara

(**b**) *(of heart)* cavidad *f* (cardíaca)

(**c**) *(of revolver)* recámara *f*

(**d**) *Law* **chambers** *(of barrister, judge)* despacho *m*; **the case was heard in chambers** el caso se vio a puerta cerrada

(**e**) *Archaic (room)* aposento *m*

chamberlain ['tʃeɪmbəlɪn] *n* chambelán *m*

chambermaid ['tʃeɪmbəmeɪd] *n* camarera *f* (de hotel)

chamberperson ['tʃeɪmbəpɜːsən] *n (woman)* camarera *f* (de hotel); *(man)* camarero *m* de hotel

chamberpot ['tʃeɪmbəpɒt] *n* orinal *m*, *Am* bacinica *f*

chameleon [kə'miːlɪən] *n* (**a**) *(reptile)* camaleón *m* (**b**) *(person)* camaleón *m*

chamfer ['tʃæmfə(r)] **1** *n* bisel *m*
2 *vt* biselar

chamois (*pl* **chamois**) *n* (**a**) ['ʃæmwɑː] *(animal)* rebeco *m*, gamuza *f* (**b**) ['ʃæmɪ] **c. (leather)** *(material)* ante *m*; *(cloth)* gamuza *f*

chamomile = **camomile**

champ[1] [tʃæmp] *n Fam* campeón(ona) *m,f*

champ[2] *vi (munch)* mascar; **to c. at the bit** *(horse)* morder *or* tascar el freno; *(person)* hervir de impaciencia

champagne [ʃæm'peɪn] **1** *n* champán *m*, champaña *m o f* ▸▸ ***c. bottle*** botella *f* de champán; ***c. glass*** copa *f* de champán; *Hum* ***c. socialist*** = persona de ideas progresistas y con un estilo de vida lujoso
2 *adj (colour)* champán *inv*

champers ['ʃæmpəz] *n Br Fam* champán *m*

champion ['tʃæmpɪən] **1** *n* (**a**) *(in sport)* campeón(ona) *m,f*; **world/European c.** campeón(ona) mundial/de Europa ▸▸ ***the Champions League*** *(in soccer)* la Liga de Campeones (**b**) *(of cause)* abanderado(a) *m,f*, defensor(ora) *m,f*; **a c. of the poor** un defensor de los pobres
2 *vt* defender, abanderar; **she championed the cause of birth control** abanderó la causa del control de la natalidad
3 *adj* (**a**) *(in sport, competition)* triunfador(ora) (**b**) *Br Fam (very good)* súper *inv*

championship ['tʃæmpɪənʃɪp] *n* (**a**) *Sport* campeonato *m*; **the c.-winning team** el equipo campeón (**b**) *(support)* defensa *f*

chance [tʃɑːns] **1** *n* (**a**) *(luck)* casualidad *f*, suerte *f*; **by c.** por casualidad; **have you got a lighter by any c.?** ¿no tendrás por casualidad un encendedor?; **to leave things to c.** dejar las cosas al azar; **to leave nothing to c.** no dejar nada a la improvisación; **it was pure c. that I found it** lo encontré por pura casualidad; IDIOM *Fam* **c. would be a fine thing!** ¡qué más quisiera yo!; **it was a c. in a million** *(flukish)* había una posibilidad entre un millón
(**b**) *(opportunity)* oportunidad *f*, *Am* chance *f*; **to give sb a c.** darle una oportunidad a alguien; **now's your c.!** ¡ésta es la tuya!, ¡ésta es tu oportunidad!; **it's your last c.** es tu última oportunidad; **when I get the c.** en cuanto tenga ocasión *or* oportunidad; **some children simply don't get a c. in life** algunos niños nunca reciben una oportunidad en sus vidas; **he never had** *or* **stood a c.** nunca recibió una oportunidad; **give her a c. to defend herself** dale la oportunidad de que se defienda ella misma; **give me a c., I'm trying to explain!** ¡déjame, que estoy intentando explicarme!; **given half a c.** a la mínima (oportunidad), como te descuides; **given the c., he could prove to be an excellent player** si le dieran la oportunidad, podría demostrar que es un excelente jugador; **to be in with a c.** tener posibilidades; **it's the c. of a lifetime** es una oportunidad única en la vida, es una oportunidad de oro
(**c**) *(likelihood)* posibilidad *f* (**of** de); **to have** *or* **stand a c.** tener posibilidades; **is there any c. of seeing you again?** ¿nos podríamos volver a ver de nuevo?; **there's no c. of that happening** es imposible que suceda; *Fam* **(the) chances are (that)...** lo más seguro es que...; **what are her chances of making a full recovery?** ¿qué posibilidades hay de que se recupere por completo?; *Fam* **no c.!** *Esp* ¡qué va!, *Am* ¡para nada!, *Méx* ¡ni modo!; **it's a c. in a million** *(unlikely)* es altamente improbable, hay muy pocas posibilidades
(**d**) *(risk)* riesgo *m*; **to take a c.** correr el riesgo; **it's a c. we'll have to take** es un riesgo que habrá que correr; **I'm taking no chances** no pienso correr riesgos; **I'll take my chances** correré el riesgo
2 *adj* **a c. discovery/meeting** un descubrimiento/encuentro casual
3 *vt (risk)* **to c. doing sth** arriesgarse a hacer algo; **I can't c. her finding out about it** no me puedo arriesgar a que lo descubra; *Fam* **to c. it, to c. one's arm** arriesgarse, jugársela; **let's c. it** *or* **our luck** arriesguémonos, juguémonosla
4 *vi (happen)* **to c. to do sth** hacer algo por casualidad; **I chanced to be staying at the same hotel** estaba en el mismo hotel por casualidad

▸**chance on, chance upon** *vt insep* encontrar por casualidad

chancel ['tʃɑːnsəl] *n* presbiterio *m*

chancellery ['tʃɑːnsələrɪ] *n* (**a**) *Br (in embassy)* cancillería *f* (**b**) *US (diplomatic staff)* personal *m* diplomático (**c**) *(in Austria, Germany)* cancillería *f*

chancellor ['tʃɑːnsələ(r)] *n* (**a**) *(of university) Br* rector(ora) *m,f* honorario(a); *US* rector(ora) *m,f* (**b**) *(of Austria, Germany)* canciller *m* (**c**) *Br Pol* **C. (of the Exchequer)** ≃ ministro(a) *m,f* de (Economía y) Hacienda (**d**) *Br (of embassy)* canciller *m* (**e**) *US (judge)* = juez que preside un "chancery"

chancellorship ['tʃɑːnsələʃɪp] *n* (**a**) *(of university) Br* rectorado *m* honorario; *US* rectorado *m* (**b**) *(of Austria, Germany)* cancillería *f* (**c**) *Br (of Exchequer)* **the economy had done extremely well under Mr Smith's c.** la economía marchó excelentemente cuando el Sr. Smith estuvo al frente del ministerio de Hacienda

chancer ['tʃɑːnsə(r)] *n Br Fam Pej* oportunista *mf*

chancery ['tʃɑːnsərɪ] *n* (**a**) *Br Law* **C. Division** = en la sección de lo civil del tribunal supremo, división que trata casos de derecho hipotecario, derecho de sociedades, fideicomisos y patentes (**b**) *US Law* = tribunal que trata casos fuera del ámbito del derecho consuetudinario (**c**) *Br (in embassy)* cancillería *f*

chancre ['ʃæŋkə(r)] *n Med* chancro *m*

chancy ['tʃɑːnsɪ] *adj Fam (risky)* arriesgado(a)

chandelier [ʃændə'lɪə(r)] *n* araña *f (lámpara)*

chandler ['tʃɑːndlə(r)] *n* (**a**) *Naut* abastecedor(ora) *m,f* de buques (**b**) *Old-fashioned (candle maker)* cerero(a) *m,f*, fabricante *mf* de velas

CHANGE [tʃeɪndʒ] **1** *n* (**a**) *(alteration)* cambio *m* (**in/to** en/a); **we live in a time of great c.** vivimos en una época de grandes cambios; **she dislikes c. of any kind** los cambios le desagradan; **a c. for the better/worse** un cambio a *or* para mejor/peor; **there has been no c. in the situation** la situación no ha cambiado; **a c. in the weather** un cambio de tiempo; **a c. of address** un cambio de domicilio; **please notify us of any c. of address** por favor, comuníquenos cualquier cambio de domicilio; **a c. of course** *(for ship)* un cambio de dirección; *(for government)* un golpe de timón; *Fig* **a c. of direction** un giro, un viraje; **to have a c. of heart** cambiar de parecer; **he had a c. of mind** cambió de idea; **several changes of mind later...** después de cambiar de idea varias veces...; **a c. of scene** un cambio de aires; **a c. of venue** *(for sports match)* un cambio de estadio; *(for meeting)* un cambio de lugar; *(for concert)* un cambio de local *or* de sala; **for a c.** para variar; **to make changes to sth** hacer cambios en algo, cambiar algo; **living in the country will be a big c. for us** la vida en el campo nos va a suponer todo un cambio; **that makes a c.** es toda una novedad; **walking to work makes a pleasant c. from driving** no está nada mal caminar al trabajo de vez en cuando en vez de conducir; **this rice is a welcome c. from pasta** qué alegría comer arroz por una vez en lugar de pasta; PROV **a c. is as good as a rest** un cambio de actividad es casi tan bueno como un descanso
(**b**) *(fresh set or supply)* **a c. of clothes** una muda (de ropa); **a c. of underwear** una muda
(**c**) *(in journey)* transbordo *m*; **if you go by bus you'll have to make two changes** si vas en autobús tendrás que hacer dos transbordos; **you can get there by train with a c. at Bristol** puedes llegar hasta ahí en tren haciendo transbordo en Bristol
(**d**) *(money)* cambio *m*, *Esp* vueltas *fpl*, *Andes, CAm, Méx* sencillo *m*, *Carib, Col* devuelta *f*, *RP* vuelto *m*; **small** *or* **loose c.** (dinero *m*) suelto *m*; **the machine doesn't give c.** la máquina no da *or* devuelve cambio; **have you got c. for a $10 bill?** ¿tienes cambio de 10 dólares?; **I have a dollar in c.** tengo un dólar en monedas; **keep the c.** quédese con el cambio; **you've given me the wrong c.** me ha dado el cambio equivocado; **you won't get much c. out of £300** te costará por lo menos 300 libras; *Fam Fig* **don't bother asking him, you won't get any c. out of him** ni te molestes en pedírselo, con ése no cuentes ▸▸ ***c. machine*** máquina *f* de cambiar monedas
(**e**) *Euph* **the c. (of life)** *(menopause)* la menopausia
2 *vt* (**a**) *(alter, transform)* cambiar; **to c. sth into sth** transformar algo en algo; **the prince was changed into a frog** el príncipe fue transformado en rana; **there's no point in trying to c. him** no vale la pena intentar cambiarlo; **she wants to c. the world** quiere cambiar el mundo; **the illness completely changed his personality** la enfermedad cambió su personalidad por completo; **let's c. the living-room around** cambiemos las cosas de sitio en el salón; **I'm going to c. my image** voy a cambiar mi imagen; **to c. colour** *(of object, animal, person)* cambiar de color; **to c. direction** *(of vehicle)* cambiar de dirección; *(of process, historical events)* cambiar de curso; *Br Aut* **to c. gear** cambiar de marcha; **to c. one's mind** cambiar de opinión; **he's changed his mind about moving to New York** ha cambiado de opinión sobre su traslado a Nueva York; **to c. one's name** cambiarse de nombre; **he changed his name to Wilson** se puso de nombre Wilson; **to c. the subject** cambiar de tema; *Fig* **to c. tack** *(try different approach)* cambiar de táctica; IDIOM **you've certainly changed your tune!** ¡vaya, parece que has cambiado de opinión!; *Fig* **to c. one's**

ways cambiar de comportamiento

(**b**) *(exchange)* cambiar (**for** por); **to c. one thing for another** cambiar una cosa por otra; *Sport* **to c. ends** cambiar de lado; **they c. the guard at eleven o'clock** *(in prison)* el cambio de los guardias se produce a las once; **to c. hands** *(of money, car)* cambiar de manos; **I've decided to c. jobs** he decidido cambiar de trabajo; **to c. places with sb** *(in room)* cambiar el sitio *or* de lugar con alguien; *(in job)* ponerse en el lugar de alguien, cambiar de tareas con alguien; IDIOM **I wouldn't like to c. places with him** no me gustaría estar en su lugar; **to c. sides** cambiar de lado; **to c. trains** hacer transbordo

(**c**) *(replace)* cambiar; **if the shoes are too small we'll c. them for you** si los zapatos le van muy pequeños los puede cambiar; **to c. a fuse** cambiar un fusible

(**d**) *(with clothing, linen)* **to get changed** cambiarse (de ropa); **to c. one's clothes/shirt** cambiarse de ropa/camisa; **to c. the bedsheets** cambiar las sábanas; **to c. a** *Br* **nappy** *or US* **diaper** cambiar los pañales; **to c. the baby** cambiar al bebé *orAndes* a la guagua *or RP* al nene

(**e**) *(money)* cambiar; **could you c. a $20 bill for two tens?** ¿me podrías cambiar un billete de 20 dólares en *or* por dos de diez?; **to c. dollars into euros** cambiar dólares por euros

3 *vi* (**a**) *(alter)* cambiar; **the wind changed** el viento cambió; **to c. for the better/worse** cambiar a *or* para mejor/peor; **nothing will make him c.** nada lo hará cambiar; **he has changed in appearance** su apariencia ha cambiado; **we waited for the lights to c.** esperamos a que cambiara el semáforo; **winter changed to spring** la primavera siguió al invierno; *Br Aut* **to c. into first gear** cambiar a primera; **nothing changes!** ¡siempre lo mismo!

(**b**) *(be transformed)* **to c. into sth** transformarse en algo

(**c**) *(put on other clothes)* cambiarse; **to c. into sth more comfortable** ponerse algo más cómodo; **why don't you c. out of your suit and put on something more comfortable?** ¿por qué no te quitas *orAm* sacas el traje y te pones algo más cómodo?

(**d**) *(passenger)* hacer transbordo; **c. at Preston for all stations to Liverpool** todos los pasajeros en dirección a Liverpool deben hacer transbordo en Preston; **all c.!** ¡fin de trayecto!

▸ **change down** *vi Br Aut* reducir (de marcha); **he changed down into third** redujo a tercera

▸ **change off** *vi US (alternate)* turnarse, hacer turnos (**with** con)

▸ **change over** *vi* cambiarse; **to c. over from sth to sth** cambiar de algo a algo; **to c. over from dictatorship to democracy** pasar de la dictadura a la democracia; **to c. over to another channel** cambiar de canal

▸ **change up** *vi Br Aut* cambiar a una marcha más larga; **he changed up into third** puso la tercera

---

changeability [tʃeɪndʒə'bɪlɪtɪ] *n* (**a**) *(of weather)* variabilidad *f* (**b**) *(of moods)* variabilidad *f*

changeable ['tʃeɪndʒəbəl] *adj* (**a**) *(weather)* variable, cambiante (**b**) *(person)* variable

changed [tʃeɪndʒd] *adj* alterado(a); **I'm a c. man** he cambiado completamente; **these are c. days** los tiempos han cambiado

changeless ['tʃeɪndʒlɪs] *adj* invariable

changeling ['tʃeɪndʒlɪŋ] *n (in folklore)* = niño que las hadas reemplazan por otro al nacer

changemaker ['tʃeɪndʒmeɪkə(r)] *n US (machine)* máquina *f* de cambios

change-over ['tʃeɪndʒəʊvə(r)] *n* (**a**) *(switch)* transición *f* (**to** a); **the c. to gas went smoothly** el cambio a la utilización de gas transcurrió sin contratiempos (**b**) *Br Sport* relevo *m*

changing ['tʃeɪndʒɪŋ] 1 *n* ***c. of the guard*** cambio *m* de guardia; ***c. mat*** *(for baby)* cambiador *m*

2 *adj* cambiante; **we live in a c. world** vivimos en un mundo en constante cambio

changing-room ['tʃeɪndʒɪŋru:m] *n* (**a**) *(for sport, in theatre)* vestuario *m*, vestuarios *mpl* (**b**) *(in shop)* probador *m*

channel ['tʃænəl] 1 *n* (**a**) *(broad strait)* canal *m*; **the (English) C.** el Canal de la Mancha; **a C.** *or* **cross-C. ferry** un ferry que atraviesa el Canal de la Mancha ▸▸ ***C. Islander*** habitante *mf* de las islas del Canal de la Mancha; ***the C. Islands*** las islas Anglonormandas *or* del Canal de la Mancha; ***the C. Tunnel*** el Eurotúnel, el túnel del Canal (de la Mancha)

(**b**) *(riverbed)* cauce *m*; *(navigable course)* canal *m*

(**c**) *(furrow, groove)* ranura *f*; *(on a column)* acanaladura *f*

(**d**) *(means, conduit)* cauce *m*; **all enquiries must go through the proper channels** todas las consultas han de seguir los trámites *or* cauces apropiados; **they tried to obtain his release through diplomatic channels** intentaron obtener su liberación a través de los cauces diplomáticos; **to keep open the channels of communication** mantener abiertos los canales de de comunicación ▸▸ ***c. of distribution*** canal *m* de distribución

(**e**) *TV* canal *m*; **the movie is on another c.** la película la ponen en otro canal ▸▸ *Br* ***c. hopping*** zapping *m*, zapeo *m*; *US* ***c. surfing*** zapping *m*, zapeo *m*

(**f**) *Rad (frequency band)* banda *f*

(**g**) *Comptr (for IRC)* canal *m*

2 *vt* (*pt & pp* **channelled**, *US* **channeled**) (**a**) *(liquid)* canalizar, encauzar (**b**) *(resources, effort)* canalizar

channel-hop ['tʃænəlhɒp], *US* **channel-surf** ['tʃænəlsɜ:f] *vi Fam* zapear, hacer zapping

channelling ['tʃænəlɪŋ] *n (of resources, efforts)* canalización *f*

chant [tʃɑ:nt] 1 *n* (**a**) *(of demonstrators, crowd)* consigna *f*; *(at sports matches)* cántico *m* (**b**) *Rel* canto *m*

2 *vt* (**a**) *(of demonstrators, crowd)* corear (**b**) *Rel* salmodiar

3 *vi* (**a**) *(demonstrators, crowd)* corear (**b**) *Rel* salmodiar

chanterelle [tʃæntə'rel] *n* rebozuelo *m*

chant(e)y *US* = **shanty**

chanting ['tʃɑ:ntɪŋ] 1 *n* (**a**) *(of demonstrators, crowd)* consignas *fpl*; *(at sports matches)* cánticos *mpl* (**b**) *Rel* canto *m*

2 *adj (demonstrators, crowd)* **there were thousands of c. demonstrators in the streets** había miles de manifestantes en las calles coreando consignas

chaos ['keɪɒs] *n* caos *m inv*; **there has been c. on the roads today** hoy el tráfico en las carreteras ha sido un caos *or* caótico ▸▸ *Phys* ***c. theory*** (la) teoría *f* del caos

chaotic [keɪ'ɒtɪk] *adj* caótico(a)

chaotically [keɪ'ɒtɪklɪ] *adv* de forma caótica, caóticamente

chap [tʃæp] 1 *n* (**a**) *Fam (man)* tipo *m*, *Esp* tío *m*, *RP* flaco *m*; **he's a good c.** es un buen tipo *or Esp* tío *or RP* flaco; **be a good c. and tell him I'm not in** pórtate y dile que no estoy; *Old-fashioned* **how are you, old c.?** ¿cómo va todo, viejo amigo? (**b**) *(sore)* llaga *f*, grieta *f*

2 *vt (lips, skin)* agrietar, cortar

3 *vi (lips, skin)* agrietarse, cortarse

chaparral [tʃæpə'ræl] *n* chaparral *m*

chapat(t)i [tʃə'pætɪ] *n* chapati *m*, = pan sin levadura aplanado típico de la India

chapel ['tʃæpəl] *n* (**a**) *(in church, school)* capilla *f* ▸▸ ***c. of ease*** capilla *f* sufragánea; ***c. of rest*** = capilla en la que descansa el féretro antes del funeral (**b**) *Br (Nonconformist church)* templo *m* (**c**) *Irish, Scot (Catholic church)* iglesia *f* (católica) (**d**) *Br (of trade unionists)* = rama de un sindicato dentro de una empresa del sector de las artes gráficas, la edición o el periodismo

chaperone ['ʃæpərəʊn] 1 *n* (**a**) *(for young unmarried woman)* señora *f* de compañía, *Esp* carabina *f*, *Am* chaperona *f* (**b**) *(for group)* acompañante *mf*

2 *vt* **to c. sb** *Esp* acompañar a alguien como carabina, *Am* ir de chaperona de alguien

chaplain ['tʃæplɪn] *n* capellán *m*

chaplaincy ['tʃæplɪnsɪ] *n* capellanía *f*

chaplet ['tʃæplɪt] *n* (**a**) *(wreath)* corona *f* (de flores) (**b**) *Rel* rosario *m*

chapped [tʃæpt] *adj (lips, skin)* cortado(a), agrietado(a)

chappie, chappy ['tʃæpɪ] *n Br Fam* tipo *m*, *Esp* tío *m*, *RP* flaco *m*

chaps [tʃæps] *npl (worn by cowboy)* zahones *mpl*, *Col, Ven* zamarros *mpl*, *Méx* chaparreras *fpl*

chapstick® ['tʃæpstɪk] *n* protector *m* labial, *Esp* barra *f* de cacao de labios

chapter ['tʃæptə(r)] *n* (**a**) *(of book)* capítulo *m*; **c. eight** capítulo ocho; **the holiday was a c. of accidents** las vacaciones consistieron en una sucesión de accidentes; **this closed a particularly violent c. in our history** esto cerró un capítulo particularmente violento de nuestra historia; IDIOM **to quote** *or* **give c. and verse** dar pelos y señales

(**b**) *(of organization)* sección *f*; *(of religious organization)* capítulo *m* ▸▸ *US* ***c. house*** *(of fraternity, sorority)* = lugar de reunión de una asociación de universitarios

(**c**) *(of cathedral)* cabildo *m* ▸▸ ***c. house*** sala *f* capitular

char[1] [tʃɑ:(r)] (*pt & pp* **charred**) 1 *vt (scorch)* carbonizar, quemar

2 *vi* carbonizarse

char[2] *Br Fam* 1 *n (cleaning lady)* señora *f* de la limpieza

2 *vi* (*pt & pp* **charred**) *(clean)* **to c. for sb** trabajar como señora de la limpieza para alguien

char[3] *n Br Fam (tea)* té *m*

char[4] (*pl* **char** *or* **chars**) *n (fish)* salvelino *m*

charabanc ['ʃærəbæŋ] *n Br Old-fashioned* autobús *m or Esp* autocar *m* turístico

character ['kærɪktə(r)] *n* (**a**) *(in novel, play)* personaje *m* ▸▸ ***c. actor*** actor *m* de carácter, = actor especializado en personajes poco convencionales; ***c. part*** papel *m* de carácter; ***c. sketch*** descripción *f* de un personaje, semblanza *f*

(**b**) *(unusual person)* personaje *m*; **the place attracts all sorts of characters** el lugar atrae a todo tipo de personajes; **he's quite a c.!** *(eccentric, entertaining)* es todo un personaje

(**c**) *Pej (person)* tipo(a) *m,f*; **some c. in a uniform told us to leave** un tipo de uniforme nos dijo que nos marcháramos

(**d**) *(nature, personality)* carácter *m*; **the war completely changed his c.** la guerra cambió su personalidad por completo; **is there such a thing as national c.?** ¿existe la noción de carácter nacional?; **such rudeness is entirely in c. for him** esa grosería es típica de él; **it was out of c. for her to be so unhelpful** no era típico de ella ser tan poco servicial

(**e**) *(reputation)* **a person of good c.** una persona íntegra ▸▸ ***c. assassination*** campaña *f* de desprestigio; *Br* ***c. reference*** *(when applying for job)* referencias *fpl*; *Law* ***c. witness*** = testigo que declara en favor del buen carácter del acusado

(**f**) *(aspect, quality)* carácter *m*; **it was the vindictive c. of the punishment she objected to** a lo que se oponía era al carácter vengativo del castigo

(**g**) *(determination, integrity)* carácter *m*; **she's a woman of great c.** es una mujer con mucho carácter; **to have/lack c.** tener/no tener carácter

(**h**) *(distinction, originality)* carácter *m*; **the house had (great) c.** la casa tenía mucho carácter

(**i**) *Typ* carácter *m*

(**j**) *Comptr* carácter *m*; **characters per inch** caracteres por pulgada; **characters per second** caracteres por segundo ▸▸ ***c. code*** código *m* de carácter; ***c. map*** mapa *m* de caracteres; ***c. mode*** modo *m* carácter; ***c. recognition*** reconocimiento *m* de caracteres; ***c. set*** juego *m* de caracteres; ***c. string*** cadena *f* de caracteres

character-building ['kærɪktə'bɪldɪŋ], **character-forming** ['kærɪktə'fɔːmɪŋ] *adj Br* que imprime carácter; **it's c.** imprime carácter

characterful ['kærɪktəful] *adj* lleno(a) de carácter

characteristic [kærɪktə'rɪstɪk] **1** *n* característica *f*

2 *adj* característico(a); **she refused all honours with c. humility** rechazó los honores con la humildad que le caracteriza

characteristically [kærəktə'rɪstɪklɪ] *adv* **he was c. modest about his victory** reaccionó ante su victoria con la modestia que lo caracteriza; **c., she put her family first** como es característico en ella, su familia era lo primero

characterization [kærɪktəraɪ'zeɪʃən] *n* (**a**) *Formal (description)* caracterización *f* (**b**) *(in novel, play)* caracterización *f*; **he's very poor at c.** *(writer)* no se le da nada bien la caracterización de personajes; *(actor)* no tiene talento para la interpretación

characterize ['kærɪktəraɪz] *vt* (**a**) *(be typical of)* caracterizar; **his music is characterized by a sense of joy** su música se caracteriza por una impresión de alegría (**b**) *(describe)* definir; **I would hardly c. him as naive!** ¡yo no lo definiría como ingenuo, ni mucho menos!

characterless ['kærɪktəlɪs] *adj* anodino(a), sin carácter

charade [ʃə'rɑːd] *n* (**a**) *(farce)* farsa *f* (**b**) **charades** *(party game)* charada *f*

charbroil ['tʃɑːbrɔɪl] *vt US* asar a la parrilla

charcoal ['tʃɑːkəʊl] **1** *n* (**a**) *(fuel)* carbón *m* (vegetal) (**b**) *(for drawing)* carboncillo *m* ▸▸ ***c. burner*** carbonero(a) *m,f*; ***c. drawing*** dibujo *m* al carboncillo; ***c. grey*** gris *m* marengo

2 *adj (colour)* gris marengo

chard [tʃɑːd] *n* acelgas *fpl*

CHARGE [tʃɑːdʒ] **1** *n* (**a**) *(cost)* precio *m*, tarifa *f*; *(to an account)* adeudo *m*, cargo *m*; **to make a c. for sth** cobrar por algo; **there's a c. of one pound for use of the locker** hay que pagar una libra para utilizar la taquilla; **what's the c. for delivery?** ¿cuánto cuesta el envío?; **there is no c. for admission** la entrada es gratuita; **at no extra c.** sin cargo adicional; **free of c.** gratis; **what's the c.?** ¿cuánto cuesta?, ¿cuánto (te) cobran?; *US* **will that be cash or c.?** ¿pagará en efectivo o con tarjeta? ▸▸ ***c. account*** cuenta *f* de crédito; ***c. card*** tarjeta *f* de compra

(**b**) *Law* cargo *m*; **he was arrested on a c. of...** fue arrestado acusado de...; **to bring a c. against sb** presentar cargos contra alguien; **to drop the charges** retirar los cargos; **they will have to answer** *or* **face charges of fraud** tendrán que responder a acusaciones de fraude; **you are under arrest – on what c.?** queda arrestado – ¿de qué se me acusa? ▸▸ *Br* ***c. sheet*** pliego *m* de acusaciones

(**c**) *(accusation)* acusación *f*; **the government rejected charges that it was mismanaging the economy** el gobierno rechazó las acusaciones de que estaba gestionando mal la economía; **she laid herself open to charges of dishonesty** se expuso a que la acusaran de falta de honradez

(**d**) *(responsibility)* **he had a dozen salesmen under his c.** tiene a una docena de vendedores a su cargo; **to be in c. (of)** estar a cargo (de), ser el/la encargado(a) (de); **to be in** *or* **have c. of doing sth** estar a cargo de hacer algo; **she's in c. of public relations** está a cargo *or* se encarga de las relaciones públicas; **to be in sb's c.** estar a cargo *or* al cuidado de alguien; **to put sb in c. (of)** poner a alguien a cargo (de); **who's in c. here?** ¿quién manda aquí?; **I demand to see the person in c.** exijo ver al encargado; **can I leave you in c. of the kids for a few minutes?** ¿te puedes encargar de los niños durante un rato?; **to take c. (of)** hacerse cargo (de)

(**e**) *(person in one's care)* **the nanny took her charges to the zoo** la niñera llevó a los niños a su cargo al zoo ▸▸ *Br* ***c. hand*** encargado(a) *m,f*; ***c. nurse*** enfermero(a) *m,f* jefe

(**f**) *(of explosive)* carga *f*

(**g**) *Elec* carga *f*; **put the battery on c. overnight** pon la batería a cargar por la noche

(**h**) *(attack) (by troops, police)* carga *f*; *(by bull)* embestida *f*

(**i**) *Fam (thrill)* **to get a c. out of sth/doing sth** disfrutar como un enano haciendo algo

2 *vt* (**a**) *(price)* cobrar; **how much** *or* **what do you c. for this service?** ¿cuánto cobran por este servicio?; **you will be charged for postage** los gastos de envío correrán a tu cargo; **they didn't c. us for the coffee** no nos cobraron el café

(**b**) *(pay for by credit)* **c. it to my account** cárguelo a mi cuenta; **c. it to the company** póngalo en la cuenta de la compañía; *US* **I'll c. it** *(pay by credit card)* lo pagaré con tarjeta de crédito

(**c**) *Law* acusar; **to c. sb with a crime** acusar a alguien de un delito; **he was charged with assaulting a policeman** lo acusaron de atacar a un policía

(**d**) *(accuse)* **to c. sb with having done sth** acusar a alguien de haber hecho algo

(**e**) *Formal (give responsibility)* **to c. sb to do sth, to c. sb with doing sth** encomendarle a alguien que haga algo; **she was charged with the task of interviewing applicants** se le encomendó la tarea de entrevistar candidatos

(**f**) *(gun)* cargar

(**g**) *Elec* cargar

(**h**) *(attack) (of troops, police)* cargar contra; *(of bull)* embestir; **the police charged the crowd** la policía cargó contra la multitud

(**i**) *Formal (fill)* **please c. your glasses** por favor llenen los vasos

3 *vi* (**a**) *(rush)* cargar; **the rhino suddenly charged** el rinoceronte cargó de repente; **to c. about** *or* **around** corretear alocadamente; **he charged in** entró apresuradamente; *Fig* **you can't just c. in and start telling everybody what to do** no puedes llegar y empezar a decirle a todo el mundo lo que tiene que hacer

(**b**) *(attack) (troops, police, bull)* cargar; **to c. at sb** cargar contra alguien; **c.!** ¡a la carga!

(**c**) *(ask money)* **we don't c. for this service** no cobramos por este servicio

(**d**) *Elec* cargarse

▸ **charge off** *vt insep US* calificar como incobrable

▸ **charge up** *vt sep* (**a**) *(battery)* cargar

(**b**) *(expenses)* cargar en cuenta

---

chargeable ['tʃɑːdʒəbəl] *adj* (**a**) *(of cost)* imputable; **travelling expenses are c. to the employer** los gastos de desplazamiento corren a cargo del empresario (**b**) *(taxable)* gravable (**c**) *Law* **a c. offence** un delito

charged [tʃɑːdʒd] *adj* (**a**) *(situation, atmosphere)* **he spoke in a voice c. with emotion** hablaba embargado por la emoción; **an emotionally c. issue** un tema con una fuerte carga emotiva; **a highly c. atmosphere** un ambiente muy tenso (**b**) *Elec* cargado(a); **positively/negatively c.** con carga positiva/negativa

chargé d'affaires ['ʃɑːʒeɪdæ'feəz] (*pl* **chargés d'affaires**) *n* encargado(a) *m,f* de negocios

charger ['tʃɑːdʒə(r)] *n* (**a**) *Elec* cargador *m* (de pilas/baterías) (**b**) *Literary (horse)* caballo *m* de batalla (**c**) *(dish)* fuente *f*, bandeja *m*

chariot ['tʃærɪət] *n (in battles)* carro *m (de caballos)*; *(in ancient Rome)* cuadriga *f*; *Hum* **your c. awaits!** ¡su carruaje está listo!

charioteer [tʃærɪə'tɪə(r)] *n* auriga *m*

charisma [kə'rɪzmə] *n* carisma *m*

charismatic [kærɪz'mætɪk] *adj* carismático(a) ▸▸ *Rel* ***the C. movement*** el movimiento carismático

charitable ['tʃærɪtəbəl] *adj* (a) *(giving) (person, action)* caritativo(a) (b) *(kind) (person)* amable, generoso(a); **it would be c. to call him misguided** decir que va *or Esp* anda descaminado sería demasiado generoso
(c) *(organization, work)* benéfico(a), de caridad ►► ***c. donations*** donaciones *fpl* benéficas, donativos *mpl* benéficos; ***c. institution*** institución *f* benéfica; ***c. organization*** entidad *f* benéfica; ***c. trust*** fundación *f* benéfica

charitably ['tʃærɪtəblɪ] *adv (kindly)* con generosidad; **he spoke very c. of his former opponent** habló con mucha generosidad de su antiguo rival

charity ['tʃærɪtɪ] *n* (a) *(kindness, generosity)* caridad *f*; **he bought the painting out of c.** compró el cuadro por caridad
(b) *(help to the needy)* caridad *f*; **they're too proud to accept c.** son demasiado orgullosos para aceptar caridad; **they raised £10,000 for c.** reunieron 10.000 libras para obras benéficas PROV **c. begins at home** *Esp* la caridad bien entendida empieza por uno mismo, *Am* la caridad empieza por casa
(c) *(organization)* entidad *f or* organización *f* benéfica; **all proceeds will go to c.** toda la recaudación se dedicará a obras de beneficencia; **she does a lot of c. work** trabaja mucho para entidades benéficas ►► ***c. raffle*** rifa *f* benéfica; *Br* ***c. shop*** = tienda perteneciente a una entidad benéfica en la que normalmente se venden artículos de segunda mano

charlady ['tʃɑːleɪdɪ] *n Br* señora *f* de la limpieza

charlatan ['ʃɑːlətən] *n* charlatán(ana) *m,f*, embaucador(ora) *m,f*

Charlemagne ['ʃɑːləmeɪn] *pr n* Carlomagno

Charles ['tʃɑːlz] *pr n* **C. I/II** Carlos I/II

Charleston ['tʃɑːlstən] *n* charlestón *m*

charley horse ['tʃɑːlɪhɔːs] *n US Fam* calambre *m*

charlie ['tʃɑːlɪ] *n Fam* (a) *Br (fool)* **to look/feel a right** *or* **proper C.** parecer/sentirse tonto(a) (b) *(cocaine)* coca *f* (c) *US Mil (Vietcong)* **Charlie** el Vietcong

Charlie Chaplin ['tʃɑːlɪ'tʃæplɪn] *pr n (film character)* Charlot

charlotte ['ʃɑːlət] *n* (a) *(baked)* **apple c.** = postre elaborado con manzanas, azúcar, mantequilla y pan (b) *(cold)* **c. (russe)** carlota *f* (rusa)

charm [tʃɑːm] **1** *n* (a) *(attractiveness, attractive quality)* encanto *m*, atractivo *m*; **he has great c.** tiene mucho encanto; **the charms of the big city** los encantos *or* atractivos de la gran ciudad; **to turn on the c.** ponerse encantador(ora) ►► *Fam* ***c. offensive*** campaña *f* de imagen; *US* ***c. school*** = escuela privada de etiqueta para señoritas
(b) *(spell)* hechizo *m*; **to be under a c.** estar hechizado(a); **it worked like a c.** funcionó a las mil maravillas
(c) *(talisman)* **a lucky c.** un amuleto (de la suerte) ►► ***c. bracelet*** pulsera *f* de dijes
2 *vt* hechizar, encantar; **they charmed the money out of her** la sedujeron para sacarle el dinero; **he charmed his way to the top** se sirvió de sus encantos para encumbrarse a lo más alto

charmed [tʃɑːmd] *adj* (a) *(delighted)* encantado(a); **she sang to a c. audience** cantó delante de un público entregado; **pleased to meet you – c., I'm sure** *(in introduction)* encantado(a) de conocerlo(a) – lo mismo digo (b) *(by magic)* encantado(a); **to lead a c. life** tener buena estrella

charmer ['tʃɑːmə(r)] *n* **to be a real c.** ser encantador(ora)

charming ['tʃɑːmɪŋ] *adj* encantador(ora); *Ironic* **(that's) c.!** ¡qué simpático(a)!

charmingly ['tʃɑːmɪŋlɪ] *adv* de forma encantadora; **he seemed c. naive** tenía una inocencia encantadora

charmless ['tʃɑːmlɪs] *adj (person)* desangelado(a)

charnel house ['tʃɑːnəlhaʊs] *n Hist* osario *m*; *Fig* **the country has been turned into a c.** el país se ha convertido en un cementerio

charred [tʃɑːd] *adj (wood, body)* carbonizado(a)

chart [tʃɑːt] **1** *n* (a) *(map)* carta *f* (b) *(graph)* gráfico *m*; *(of hospital patient)* gráficas *fpl* de evolución *or* de constantes (c) **the charts** *(pop music)* las listas (de éxitos); **she's in the charts** está en las listas de éxitos; **she's got a record in the charts** tiene un disco en las listas de éxitos
2 *vt* (a) *(on map)* hacer un mapa de (b) *(on table, graph)* representar gráficamente; **this graph charts sales over the last ten years** este gráfico representa *or* refleja las ventas de los últimos diez años (c) *(trace, describe)* describir; **the book charts the rise of fascism** el libro describe el auge del fascismo

charter ['tʃɑːtə(r)] **1** *n* (a) *(of town)* fuero *m*; *(of university, organization)* estatutos *mpl*; *(of company)* escritura *f* de constitución, carta *f* fundacional; **the UN C.** la Carta de las Naciones Unidas (b) *(lease, licence)* fletamiento *m*; *(charter flight)* chárter *m* ►► ***c. flight*** vuelo *m* chárter; *Naut* ***c. party*** carta *f* de fletamento; ***c. plane*** avión *m* chárter
2 *vt* (a) *(company)* constituir, otorgar carta fundacional a (b) *(plane, ship)* fletar

chartered ['tʃɑːtəd] *adj (qualified)* colegiado(a) ►► *Br* ***c. accountant*** censor(ora) *m,f* jurado(a) de cuentas; ***c. surveyor*** tasador(ora) *m,f* de la propiedad

charterhouse ['tʃɑːtəhaʊs] *n (monastery)* cartuja *f*

chartreuse [ʃɑː'trɜːz] *n* chartreuse *m*

chart-topping ['tʃɑːt'tɒpɪŋ] *adj Br* en el número de uno de las listas de éxitos

charwoman ['tʃɑːwʊmən] *n* señora *f* de la limpieza

chary ['tʃeərɪ] *adj (cautious)* cauteloso(a); **to be c. of doing sth** mostrarse reacio(a) a la hora de hacer algo

Charybdis [kə'rɪbdɪs] *n Mythol* **Scylla and C.** Escila y Caribdis

chase [tʃeɪs] **1** *n* (a) *(pursuit)* persecución *f*; **to give c. to sb** perseguir a alguien (b) *(in cycling)* persecución *f*, caza *f* (c) **the c.** *(hunting)* la caza
2 *vt* (a) *(pursue)* perseguir; **he's always chasing young women** siempre va detrás de chicas jóvenes; **to c. rainbows** hacer castillos en el aire (b) *(expel)* **he chased them off his land** los expulsó de sus tierras; **the reporters were chased from** *or* **out of the house** los periodistas fueron expulsados de la casa (c) *(metal)* cincelar
3 *vi* **to c. after sb** perseguir a alguien; **to c. after women** ir detrás de las chicas, andar detrás de las *Méx* faldas *or RP* polleras; **she chased all round London to find that dress** dio vueltas por todo Londres para encontrar ese vestido

► **chase away** *vt sep* ahuyentar

► **chase down** *vt sep (runner, cyclist)* perseguir

► **chase up** *vt sep (report, information)* hacerse con; *(debt)* reclamar; **I'll c. them up about it** les llamaré para recordárselo; **can you c. up the manager for me?** ¿podría localizarme al encargado?

chaser ['tʃeɪsə(r)] *n* (a) *(drink)* = vasito de licor que se toma después de la cerveza (b) *(horse)* caballo *m* de carreras

chasm ['kæzəm] *n (deep fissure)* abismo *m*, sima *f*; *Fig* abismo *m*

chassis ['ʃæsɪ] (*pl* **chassis** ['ʃæsɪz]) *n* (a) *(of car)* chasis *m inv*, bastidor *m* (b) *(of radio, TV)* bastidor *m* (c) *Fam (woman's body)* cuerpazo *m*, percha *f*; *Hum* **she's got a classy c.** tiene un cuerpazo tremendo, tiene buena percha

chaste [tʃeɪst] *adj* casto(a)

chastely ['tʃeɪstlɪ] *adv* castamente

chasten ['tʃeɪsən] *vt* (a) *(subdue, humble)* escarmentar (b) *(punish, reprimand)* castigar

chastened ['tʃeɪsənd] *adj (subdued, humbled)* escarmentado(a)

chasteness ['tʃeɪstnɪs] *n* castidad *f*

chastening ['tʃeɪsənɪŋ] *adj* **prison had a c. effect on him** su encarcelamiento tuvo un efecto aleccionador; **it's a c. thought** es una idea que da que pensar

chastise [tʃæs'taɪz] *vt Formal* (a) *(reprimand)* reprender (b) *(beat)* castigar

chastisement [tʃæs'taɪzmənt] *n Formal* castigo *m*

chastity ['tʃæstɪtɪ] *n* castidad *f* ►► ***c. belt*** cinturón *m* de castidad

chasuble ['tʃæzjʊbəl] *n Rel* casulla *f*

chat [tʃæt] **1** *n* (a) *(informal conversation)* charla *f*, *CAm, Méx* plática *f*; **to have a c.** charlar; **there's too much c. and not enough work going on here!** ¡mucho hablar y poco trabajar hay aquí! ►► ***c. line*** *(on telephone)* línea *f* compartida, party line *f*; *(erotic)* teléfono *m* erótico; *Br* ***c. show*** *(on TV)* tertulia *f* televisiva; *Br* ***c. show host*** presentador(ora) *m,f* de tertulia televisiva
(b) *Comptr* charla *f*, chat *m* ►► ***c. room*** sala *f* de conversación
2 *vi* (*pt & pp* **chatted**) (a) *(talk informally)* charlar, *CAm, Méx* platicar (**to** *or* **with** con) (b) *Comptr* charlar, chatear (**to** *or* **with** con)

► **chat up** *vt sep Br Fam* **to c. sb up** intentar ligar con alguien *or* ligarse a alguien, *RP* intentar levantar a alguien

château ['ʃætəʊ] (*pl* **châteaus** *or* **châteaux** ['ʃætəʊz]) *n* castillo *m*

château-bottled ['ʃætəʊ'bɒtəld] *adj* embotellado(a) por el productor

chattel ['tʃætəl] *n Law* **goods and chattels** bienes (muebles) ►► *US* ***c. mortgage*** hipoteca *f* sobre bienes muebles

chatter ['tʃætə(r)] **1** *n* (a) *(of people)* cháchara *f*, parloteo *m*; *(of birds)* parloteo *m*; *(of monkeys)* chillido *m* (b) *(of machines)* tecleo *m*, traqueteo *m* (c) *(of teeth)* castañeteo *m*
2 *vi* (a) *(person)* parlotear; *(bird)* parlotear; *(monkey)* chillar; **she sat quietly while Maria chattered away** se sentó tranquilamente

mientras Maria parloteaba; *Br Pej* **the chattering classes** los intelectualoides (**b**) *(machine)* traquetear (**c**) *(teeth)* **my teeth were chattering (with cold/fear)** me castañeteaban los dientes (de frío/miedo)

chatterbox ['tʃætəbɒks] *n Fam* cotorra *f*, parlanchín(ina) *m,f*

chattiness ['tʃætɪnɪs] *n* locuacidad *f*; **she was irritated by his c.** le irritaba su constante parloteo

chatty ['tʃætɪ] *adj (person)* hablador(ora); *(letter)* desenfadado(a)

chat-up line ['tʃætʌplaɪn] *n Br Fam* frase *f* típica para ligar

Chaucerian [tʃɔː'sɪərɪən] **1** *n* (**a**) *(poet)* = poeta imitador de Chaucer (**b**) *(scholar)* experto(a) *m,f* en Chaucer
 2 *adj* chauceriano(a)

chauffeur ['ʃəʊfə(r)] **1** *n Esp* chófer *m*, *Am* chofer *m*
 2 *vt* **we were chauffeured to the airport** el *Esp* chófer *or Am* chofer nos llevó al aeropuerto

chauffeur-driven ['ʃəʊfə'drɪvən] *adj* con *Esp* chófer *or Am* chofer

chauvinism ['ʃəʊvɪnɪzəm] *n* (**a**) *(sexism)* machismo *m* (**b**) *(nationalism)* chovinismo *m*, patrioterismo *m*

chauvinist ['ʃəʊvɪnɪst] *n* (**a**) *(sexist)* machista *m* (**b**) *(nationalist)* chovinista *mf*, patriotero(a) *m,f*

chauvinistic [ʃəʊvɪ'nɪstɪk] *adj* (**a**) *(sexist)* machista (**b**) *(nationalist)* chovinista, patriotero(a)

chaw [tʃɔː] *Fam* **1** *n (of tobacco)* = porción de tabaco de mascar
 2 *vt* = **chew**
 3 *vi* = **chew**

cheap [tʃiːp] **1** *n* **to do sth on the c.** hacer algo en plan barato *or* mirando el dinero
 2 *adj* (**a**) *(inexpensive)* barato(a); **c. at (half) the price** tirado(a) de precio; **it's c. to run** *(car)* gasta muy poco; **c. and cheerful** *(wine)* bueno pero sin pretensiones; **a c. and cheerful way to brighten up a room** una manera sencilla y económica de alegrar una habitación ►► ***c. rate*** tarifa *f* reducida *or* económica
 (**b**) *(of little value)* barato(a); **human life is c. in many countries** en muchos países la vida humana vale muy poco; **c. and nasty** de chichinabo, de chicha y nabo
 (**c**) *(of poor quality)* barato(a)
 (**d**) *(low, despicable)* **I feel c.!** ¡qué bajo he caído!; **the way he treated her made her feel c.** la trató de tal manera que la hizo sentirse despreciable
 (**e**) *(tasteless, mean)* burdo(a), rastrero(a); **a c. joke/remark** un chiste/comentario de mal gusto; **that was a c. shot** eso ha sido un golpe bajo; **a c. trick** un truco sucio
 (**f**) *US (stingy)* mezquino(a)
 3 *adv* **to buy sth c.** comprar algo barato; **it's cheaper to buy 10 kilos** sale más barato *or* económico comprar 10 kilos; **clothes of that quality don't come c.** la ropa de esta calidad no es barata; *Fam* **the bicycle was going c.** la bicicleta estaba tirada de precio *or* estaba regalado

cheapen ['tʃiːpən] *vt* (**a**) *(lower, debase)* degradar, rebajar; **to c. oneself** rebajarse (**b**) *(reduce the price of)* abaratar

cheapie ['tʃiːpɪ] *n Fam* **a c. will do just as well as an expensive one** uno baratucho servirá lo mismo que uno caro

cheapjack ['tʃiːpdʒæk] *Fam* **1** *n* comerciante *mf* de trastos baratos
 2 *adj (shoddy)* chapucero(a)

cheaply ['tʃiːplɪ] *adv (to buy, sell)* barato; **they can manufacture more c. than we can** pueden fabricar con un costo *or Esp* coste más bajo que el nuestro; **to live c.** vivir con poco dinero

cheapness ['tʃiːpnɪs] *n* (**a**) *(low price)* bajo precio *m* (**b**) *(low value)* poco valor *m* (**c**) *(tastelessness)* vulgaridad *f*; *(meanness, nastiness)* bajeza *f*, vileza *f*

cheapo ['tʃiːpəʊ] *adj Fam (of low quality)* barato(a), *Esp* cutre, *RP* berreta

cheapskate ['tʃiːpskeɪt] *n Fam* roñica *mf*, roñoso(a) *m,f*

cheat [tʃiːt] **1** *n* (**a**) *(dishonest person)* tramposo(a) *m,f*; *(in exam)* copión(ona) *m,f* (**b**) *(deception, trick)* trampa *f*; **that's a c.** eso es trampa ►► ***c. sheet*** *Esp, Ven* chuleta *f*, *Arg* machete *m*, *Méx* acordeón *m*, *Urug* trencito *m* (**c**) *(for computer game)* truco *m (clave)*
 2 *vt* (**a**) *(defraud, swindle)* engañar, timar; **he cheated her out of the money** le estafó el dinero; **to feel cheated** sentirse engañado *or* timado (**b**) *Literary (avoid)* **to c. death** burlar a la muerte
 3 *vi* (**a**) *(in game)* hacer trampa; **he always cheats at cards** siempre hace trampas jugando a las cartas (**b**) *(in exam)* copiar

►**cheat on** *vt insep* (**a**) *(falsify)* **he cheated on his income tax** hizo trampas en la declaración de la renta (**b**) *(be unfaithful to)* **he cheats on his wife** engaña a su mujer

cheating ['tʃiːtɪŋ] **1** *n* (**a**) *(in game)* trampas *fpl*; **that's c.!** ¡eso es trampa! (**b**) *(in exam)* **c. is severely punished** el copiar se castiga con severidad
 2 *adj* (**a**) *(dishonest)* poco honrado(a) (**b**) *(unfaithful)* **she was sick of her c. husband** estaba harta de que su marido la engañara

Chechen ['tʃetʃen] **1** *n* checheno(a) *m,f*
 2 *adj* checheno(a)

Chechnya ['tʃetʃenɪə] *n* Chechenia

check[1] [tʃek] **1** *n* (**a**) *(inspection)* control *m*, inspección *f*; **the airline ordered checks on all their planes** la línea aérea ordenó que se efectuaran inspecciones en todos sus aviones
 (**b**) *(inquiry, investigation)* **the police ran a c. on her** la policía investigó sus antecedentes; **to keep a c. on sth/sb** controlar algo/a alguien
 (**c**) *(restraint)* freno *m*; **the courts act as a c. upon the president** los tribunales ejercen de contrapeso frente al presidente; **to put a c. on sth** poner freno a algo; **to keep sth/sb in c.** mantener algo/a alguien a raya *or* bajo control; **he kept** *or* **held his anger in c.** controló su rabia ►► *Pol* ***checks and balances*** = sistema de controles entre el poder ejecutivo, el legislativo y el judicial para evitar una acumulación de poderes
 (**d**) *(in chess)* jaque *m*; **to put sb in c.** poner en jaque a alguien; **c.!** ¡jaque!
 (**e**) *US (cheque)* cheque *m*; **to make out** *or* **write a c. (to sb)** extender un cheque *or* talón (a alguien); **a c. for $50** un cheque de 50 dólares
 (**f**) *US (in restaurant)* cuenta *f*; *(ticket for coat, luggage)* resguardo *m*; **c. please!** ¡la cuenta, por favor!
 (**g**) *US (tick)* marca *f*, señal *f* de visto bueno
 (**h**) *Comptr* ***c. box*** caja *f* de verificación, casilla *f* de verificación
 2 *vt* (**a**) *(verify, examine) (information)* comprobar, *Guat, Méx* checar; *(passport, ticket)* revisar; *(machine)* inspeccionar; **she didn't c. her facts before writing the article** no comprobó los datos antes de escribir el artículo; **the doctor checked my blood pressure** el doctor me comprobó la presión sanguínea; **to c. (that)...** comprobar que...; **to c. sth against sth** *(compare)* confrontar *or* cotejar algo con algo; **all quotations were checked against the original sources** todas las citas fueron contrastadas *or* cotejadas con las fuentes originales; **to c. sth for errors** comprobar algo en búsqueda *or Esp* busca de fallos *or Am* fallas, comprobar algo por si hubiera fallos *or Am* fallas; **I'll c. my diary** voy a mirar mi agenda; **I need to c. my e-mail** tengo que mirar mi correo electrónico
 (**b**) *(restrain) (inflation, enemy advance)* frenar; *(emotion, impulse)* contener, reprimir; **to c. oneself** contenerse
 (**c**) *(in chess)* dar jaque
 (**d**) *US (coat, hat)* dejar en el guardarropa; *(baggage)* dejar en consigna
 (**e**) *US (tick)* marcar (como comprobado)
 3 *vi (verify)* comprobar, *Méx* checar; **to c. with sb** preguntar a alguien
 4 *exclam (yes)* ¡sí!; *(to superior)* ¡sí, señor!

►**check in** **1** *vt sep* (**a**) *(baggage)* facturar, *Am* despachar; *(passenger)* registrar (**b**) *US (library book)* devolver
 2 *vi* (**a**) *(at hotel)* registrarse (**b**) *(at airport)* facturar (**c**) *US (phone)* **it's a little late, I'd better c. in with my parents** es un poco tarde, será mejor que les regunte a mis padres por teléfono

►**check into** *vt insep* **to c. into a hotel** registrarse en un hotel

►**check off** *vt sep (item on list)* marcar (como comprobado)

►**check on** *vt insep* (**a**) *(facts)* **to c. on sth** comprobar algo (**b**) *(person)* **to c. on sb** controlar *or* vigilar a alguien; **the doctor checked on two patients before leaving** el doctor comprobó cómo estaban dos pacientes antes de marcharse

►**check out** **1** *vt sep* (**a**) *(investigate) (person)* investigar; *(information)* comprobar, verificar, *Am* chequear, *Méx* checar; *Fam* **we could c. out the new pub** podíamos ir a ver qué tal está el nuevo bar (**b**) *Fam (look at)* mirar, echar un ojo a; **c. it/her out!** ¡fíjate!, ¡no te lo pierdas! (**c**) *US (library book)* sacar
 2 *vi* (**a**) *(leave hotel)* dejar el hotel *(tras pagar)* (**b**) *(prove to be correct) (story)* cuadrar (**c**) *Fam (die)* estirar la pata, *Esp* diñarla

►**check over** *vt sep (goods)* revisar

►**check up** *vi* **I'm not sure of the exact figure, but I can c. up for you** no sé cuál es la cifra exacta, pero la puedo buscar; **to c. up on sb** *(investigate)* hacer averiguaciones sobre alguien; **he's always checking up on me** siempre está controlándome; **to c. up on sth** enterarse de algo

check[2] **1** *n (pattern)* cuadros *mpl*; **a suit in broad c.** un traje a cuadros grandes
 2 *adj* a cuadros

checkbook *US* = **chequebook**

checked [tʃekt] *adj* a cuadros

checker ['tʃekə(r)] *n US* (**a**) *(piece)* dama *f*; **checkers** *(game)* damas *fpl* (**b**) *(in supermarket)* cajero(a) *m,f* (**c**) *(in left-luggage office, cloakroom)* encargado(a) *m,f*

checkerboard ['tʃekəbɔːd] *n US* tablero *m* de damas *or* de ajedrez

checkered *US* = **chequered**

check-in ['tʃekɪn] *n Av* facturación *f*; **c. (desk)** mostrador *m* de facturación ►► ***c. time*** = hora a la que hay que facturar; **c. time is thirty minutes prior to departure** la facturación podrá realizarse treinta minutos antes de la salida

checking ['tʃekɪŋ] *n* (**a**) *(verification, examination)* control *m*; *(more detailed)* examen *m*, inspección *f* (**b**) *US* ***c. account*** cuenta *f* corriente

checklist ['tʃeklɪst] *n* lista *f* de comprobaciones *or* de control

checkmark ['tʃekmɑːk] *n US* marca *f*, señal *f* de visto bueno

checkmate ['tʃekmeɪt] **1** *n (in chess)* jaque *m* mate
2 *vt* (**a**) *(in chess)* dar jaque mate a (**b**) *(opponent)* frustrar

checkout ['tʃekaʊt] *n* (**a**) *(in supermarket)* (mostrador *m* de) caja *f* ►► ***c. assistant*** cajero(a) *m,f*; ***c. display*** pantalla *f* de la caja registradora; ***c. girl*** cajera *f* (**b**) *(in hotel)* **c. time is at twelve noon** la habitación debe dejarse libre a las doce del mediodía

checkpoint ['tʃekpɔɪnt] *n* control *m*

checkroom ['tʃekruːm, 'tʃekrʊm] *n US* (**a**) *(for coats, hats)* guardarropa *f* (**b**) *(for luggage)* consigna *f*

checksum ['tʃeksʌm] *n Comptr* suma *f* de comprobación *or* control

check-up ['tʃekʌp] *n* (**a**) *(for person) (at doctor's)* revisión *f* (médica), chequeo *m* médico, reconocimiento *m* médico; *(at dentist's)* revisión *f* (**b**) *US (for car)* revisión *f*

Cheddar ['tʃedə(r)] *n* queso *m* Cheddar

cheek [tʃiːk] **1** *n* (**a**) *(of face)* mejilla *f*; **to dance c. to c.** bailar muy agarrados; **c. by jowl (with sb)** hombro con hombro (con alguien); IDIOM **to turn the other c.** poner la otra mejilla ►► ***c. pouch*** abazón *m* (**b**) *(buttock)* nalga *f* (**c**) *Fam (impudence)* cara *f*, caradura *f*, frescura *f*; **I've never heard such c.!** ¡pero qué cara más dura!; **he's got a c.!** ¡qué caradura!, *Esp* ¡vaya morro!; **what (a) c.!, of all the c.!** ¡qué caradura!
2 *vt Br Fam (be impudent to)* ser descarado(a) con

cheekbone ['tʃiːkbəʊn] *n* pómulo *m*

cheekily ['tʃiːkɪlɪ] *adv* con mucho descaro, descaradamente

cheekiness ['tʃiːkɪnɪs] *n* descaro *m*

cheeky ['tʃiːkɪ] *adj Fam* descarado(a), fresco(a), caradura; *Hum* **c. devil** descarado(a), *Esp* carota; *Hum* **c. monkey** desvergonzado(a), *Esp* faltón(ona)

cheep [tʃiːp] **1** *n (of bird)* piada *f*; *Fam Fig* **I don't want to hear a c. from you!** ¡no quiero oírte decir ni pío!
2 *vi (bird)* piar

cheer [tʃɪə(r)] **1** *n* (**a**) *(shout) (of crowd)* ovación *f*; *(of single person)* grito *m* de entusiasmo; **three cheers for Gemma!** ¡tres hurras por Gemma! (**b**) *Fam* **cheers!** *(when drinking)* ¡salud!; *Br (goodbye)* ¡chao!, *Am* ¡chau!; *Br (thanks)* ¡gracias! (**c**) *Literary (mood)* **to be of good c.** estar de buen humor; **there's little c. in this quarter's sales figures** las cifras del último trimestre no son como para estar de celebración
2 *vt* (**a**) *(applaud)* aclamar, vitorear (**b**) *(make happier)* animar
3 *vi (shout) (crowd)* lanzar vítores, gritar de entusiasmo; *(single person)* gritar de entusiasmo

► **cheer on** *vt sep (support)* animar, vitorear, jalear

► **cheer up** **1** *vt sep (person)* animar; *(room)* alegrar
2 *vi* animarse; **c. up!** ¡anímate!

cheerful ['tʃɪəfʊl] *adj (person, atmosphere, mood)* alegre, animado(a); *(colour, smile, news)* alegre

cheerfully ['tʃɪəfʊlɪ] *adv* alegremente; *Fam* **I could c. strangle him!** ¡lo estrangularía con mucho *or* sumo gusto!

cheerfulness ['tʃɪəfʊlnɪs] *n* alegría *f*

cheerily ['tʃɪərɪlɪ] *adv* jovialmente

cheeriness ['tʃɪərɪnɪs] *n* alegría *f*

cheering ['tʃɪərɪŋ] **1** *n (of crowd)* gritos *mpl* de ánimo
2 *adj (comforting)* alentador(ora)

cheerio [tʃɪərɪ'əʊ] *exclam Br* (**a**) *(goodbye)* ¡chao!, *Am* ¡chau! (**b**) *Old-fashioned (when drinking)* ¡salud!

cheerleader ['tʃɪəliːdə(r)] *n* animadora *f*

cheerless ['tʃɪəlɪs] *adj* triste, sombrío(a)

cheery ['tʃɪərɪ] *adj* jovial, alegre

cheese [tʃiːz] *n* queso *m*; **c. sandwich/omelette** sandwich *m*/tortilla *f* de queso; *Fam* **(say) c.!** *(for photograph)* ¡sonríe!, *Esp* ¡(di) patata!, *Méx* ¡(di) rojo!, *RP* ¡decí (whisky)!; *Br Fam* **hard c.!** ¡qué le vamos a hacer!, ¡mala suerte! ►► ***c. dish*** quesera *f*; ***c. fondue*** fondue *f* de queso; ***c. grater*** rallador *m* de queso; ***c. maker*** *(person)* quesero(a) *m,f*; ***c. plant*** costilla *f* de hombre; ***c. portion*** quesito *m*; ***c. shop*** quesería *f*; ***c. spread*** queso *m* para untar; ***c. straw*** colín *m* de queso; ***c. triangle*** quesito *m*; ***c. and wine*** *(party, reception)* = fiesta o recepción en la que se sirve un aperitivo consistente normalmente en vino y queso

► **cheese off** *vt sep Br Fam (annoy, irritate)* **to c. sb off** jorobar a alguien, *Méx, RP* poner como loco a alguien; **to be cheesed off (with)** estar hasta las narices *or* la coronilla (de)

cheeseboard ['tʃiːzbɔːd] *n* (**a**) *(board)* tabla *f* para el queso (**b**) *(selection)* tabla *f* de quesos

cheeseburger ['tʃiːzbɜːgə(r)] *n* hamburguesa *f* de *or* con queso

cheesecake ['tʃiːzkeɪk] *n* (**a**) *(dessert)* tarta *f* de queso (**b**) *Fam (pictures of attractive women)* **the walls were covered with c.** las paredes estaban llenas de fotos de chicas

cheesecloth ['tʃiːzklɒθ] *n* estopilla *f*

cheesemonger ['tʃiːzmʌŋgə(r)] *n Br* quesero(a) *m,f*

cheeseparing ['tʃiːzpeərɪŋ] **1** *n* tacañería *f*
2 *adj* tacaño(a)

cheesy ['tʃiːzɪ] *adj* (**a**) *(flavour, smell)* a queso; *(sauce, dish)* con sabor a queso (**b**) *Fam Pej (inferior)* de tres al cuarto, *Esp* cutre, *RP* de cuarta (**c**) *(grin)* de oreja a oreja

cheetah ['tʃiːtə] *n* guepardo *m*

chef [ʃef] *n* chef *m*, jefe(a) *m,f* de cocina ►► *US* ***c.'s salad*** = ensalada con lechuga, queso, huevos duros y trozos de carne

chemical ['kemɪkəl] **1** *n* producto *m* químico, sustancia *f* química
2 *adj* químico(a) ►► ***c. analysis*** análisis *m inv* químico; ***c. bond*** enlace *m* químico; ***c. compound*** compuesto *m* químico(a); ***c. element*** elemento *m* químico; ***c. engineer*** ingeniero(a) *m,f* químico(a); ***c. engineering*** ingeniería *f* química; ***c. equilibrium*** equilibrio *m* químico; ***c. fertilizer*** abono *m* químico; ***c. formula*** fórmula *f* química; *Fam* ***the c. generation*** = la generación del bakalao y las pastillas; ***c. reaction*** reacción *f* química; ***c. symbol*** símbolo *m* químico; ***c. toilet*** inodoro *m* (de desecho) químico; ***c. valency*** valencia *f* química; ***c. warfare*** guerra *f* química; ***c. weapons*** armas *fpl* químicas

chemically ['kemɪkəlɪ] *adv* químicamente

chemise [ʃə'miːz] *n* (**a**) *(dress)* vestido *m* camisero (**b**) *(undergarment)* combinación *f*

chemist ['kemɪst] *n* (**a**) *(scientist)* químico(a) *m,f* (**b**) *Br (pharmacist)* farmacéutico(a) *m,f*; **c.'s (shop)** farmacia *f*

chemistry ['kemɪstrɪ] *n* (**a**) *(science)* química *f*; *(properties)* composición *f* química ►► ***c. set*** juego *m* de química (**b**) *(interaction)* sintonía *f*; **there was a certain c. between them** entre ellos había una cierta sintonía *or* un cierto entendimiento

chemotherapy ['kiːməʊ'θerəpɪ] *n Med* quimioterapia *f*

chenille [ʃə'niːl] *n Tex* felpilla *f*

cheque, *US* **check** [tʃek] *n* cheque *m*, talón *m*; **a c. for $50** un cheque de 50 dólares; **to make out a c. (to sb), to write (sb) a c.** extender un cheque *or* talón (a alguien); **to cash a c.** hacer efectivo un cheque *or* talón; **to pay by c.** pagar con cheque *or* talón; **to stop a c.** suspender el pago de un cheque *or* talón; **will you take a c.?** ¿le puedo extender un cheque *or* pagar con cheque? ►► ***c. account*** cuenta *f* corriente; *Br* ***c. card*** = tarjeta que avala los cheques; ***c. number*** número *m* de cheque; ***c. stub*** talón *m* *or* matriz *f* *or* resguardo *m* de cheque

chequebook, *US* **checkbook** ['tʃekbʊk] *n* talonario *m* (de cheques), chequera *f* ►► ***c. journalism*** periodismo *m* de exclusivas (a golpe de talonario)

chequered, *US* **checkered** ['tʃekəd] *adj* (**a**) *(pattern)* a cuadros ►► *Sport* ***c. flag*** bandera *f* de llegada, bandera *f* a cuadros (**b**) *(varied)* **she's had a somewhat c. career** su trayectoria ha estado llena de altibajos

Chequers ['tʃekəz] *n* = la segunda residencia oficial del primer ministro británico, en el medio de la campiña británica

cherish ['tʃerɪʃ] *vt (person)* querer, tener mucho cariño a; *(possessions)* apreciar; *(hope, illusion)* albergar, abrigar; *(memory)* conservar

cherished ['tʃerɪʃt] *adj* preciado(a)

cheroot [ʃə'ruːt] *n* = cigarro puro cortado por ambos extremos

cherry ['tʃerɪ] 1 *n* (a) *(fruit)* cereza *f*; **c. (tree)** cerezo *m*; **c. (wood)** (madera *f* de) cerezo *m* ►► ***c. blossom*** flor *f* de cerezo; ***c. brandy*** brandy *m* de cereza; ***c. orchard*** cerezal *m* (b) *(colour)* **c. (red)** color *m* cereza (c) ***c. plum*** mirobolano *m* (d) ***c. tomato*** tomate *m* cereza (e) *Fam (virginity)* virginidad *f*; **to lose one's c.** perder la virginidad
2 *adj US Fam (in perfect condition)* inmaculado(a), impecable

cherry-pick ['tʃerɪpɪk] *Fam* 1 *vt* seleccionar sólo lo mejor de
2 *vi* seleccionar sólo lo mejor

cherry-red ['tʃerɪ'red] *adj* rojo cereza; **c. lips** labios rojizos

cherub ['tʃerəb] (*pl* **cherubs** *or* **cherubim** ['tʃerəbɪm]) *n* (a) *(angel)* querubín *m* (b) *Fam (child)* angelito(a) *m,f*

cherubic [tʃə'ru:bɪk] *adj* angelical

cherubim *pl of* **cherub**

chervil ['tʃɜ:vɪl] *n* perifollo *m*

Ches (*abbr* **Cheshire**) (condado *m* de) Cheshire

Cheshire ['tʃeʃə(r)] *n* IDIOM **to grin like a C. cat** sonreír de oreja a oreja

chess [tʃes] *n* ajedrez *m*; **a game of c.** una partida de ajedrez ►► ***c. player*** ajedrecista *mf*, jugador(ora) *m,f* de ajedrez; ***c. tournament*** torneo *m* de ajedrez

chessboard ['tʃesbɔ:d] *n* tablero *m* de ajedrez

chessman ['tʃesmæn], **chesspiece** ['tʃespi:s] *n* pieza *f* (de ajedrez)

chest [tʃest] 1 *n* (a) *(of person)* pecho *m*; *(breasts)* pechos *mpl*; IDIOM **I needed to get it off my c.** necesitaba desahogarme ►► ***c. cold*** catarro *m* *or Esp, Méx* resfriado *m* *or Andes, RP* resfrío *m* de pecho; ***c. expander*** extensor *m*; ***c. infection*** infección *f* de las vías respiratorias; ***c. pains*** dolores *mpl* de pecho; ***c. pass*** *(in basketball)* pase *m* de pecho; ***c. protector*** *(in baseball)* peto *m*; ***c. X-ray*** radiografía *f* de los pulmones
(b) *(box) (for clothes)* baúl *m*; *(for treasure)* cofre *m* ►► ***c. of drawers*** cómoda *f*; ***c. freezer*** arcón *m* congelador
2 *vt* **to c. the ball down** *(in soccer)* parar y bajar la pelota con el pecho

chesterfield ['tʃestəfi:ld] *n (sofa)* = tipo de sofá en el que los brazos son de la misma altura que el respaldo

chestnut ['tʃesnʌt] 1 *n* (a) *(nut)* castaña *f*; *(wood)* castaño *m*; **c. (tree)** castaño *m* ►► ***c. purée*** crema *f* de castaña; ***c. stuffing*** relleno *m* de castaña (b) *(colour)* color *m* castaño (c) *(horse)* alazán(ana) *m,f* (d) IDIOM *Fam* **an old c.** *(joke)* un chiste viejísimo
2 *adj (hair)* castaño(a); *(horse)* castaño(a), zaino(a)

chesty ['tʃestɪ] *adj* (a) *(cough)* de pecho (b) *Fam (woman)* pechugona, tetona, *Méx* chichona

chevron ['ʃevrən] *n* (a) *(on uniform)* galón *m* (b) *(on road)* = marca indicadora de curva con flechas en la dirección de la curva

chew [tʃu:] 1 *n* (a) *(confectionery)* caramelo *m* (b) *(of tobacco)* = porción de tabaco de mascar (c) *(for dog)* juguete *m* *(para masticar)*
2 *vt* masticar, mascar; **to c. one's nails** morderse las uñas; **to c. a bone** roer un hueso; IDIOM *Fam* **to c. the fat** *or* **the rag** estar de charla *or Esp* palique *or Méx* plática (con alguien)
3 *vi* masticar; **to c. at** *or* **on sth** *(bone, stick)* mordisquear algo

► **chew out** *vt sep US Fam (reprimand)* echar una regañina *or Esp* bronca a; **to get chewed out** llevarse una regañina *or Esp* bronca

► **chew over** *vt sep Fam* rumiar

► **chew up** *vt sep (food)* masticar; *(slippers, carpet)* mordisquear; *Fig* **that machine chewed up my favourite cassette** el casete destrozó mi cinta favorita

chewing ['tʃu:ɪŋ] *n* masticación *f* ►► ***c. tobacco*** tabaco *m* de mascar

chewing-gum ['tʃu:ɪŋ'gʌm] *n* chicle *m*, goma *f* de mascar

chewy ['tʃu:ɪ] *adj (meat, bread)* correoso(a); *(confectionery)* gomoso(a), correoso(a)

chiaroscuro [kɪɑ:rə'skʊərəʊ] (*pl* **chiaroscuros**) *n Art* claroscuro *m*

chic [ʃi:k] *adj* chic, elegante

Chicago [ʃɪ'kɑ:gəʊ] *n* Chicago

Chicana [tʃɪ'kɑ:nə] *n US* chicana *f*

chicane [ʃɪ'keɪn] *n Sport* chicane *f*

chicanery [ʃɪ'keɪnərɪ] *n (trickery)* supercherías *fpl*

Chicano [tʃɪ'kɑ:nəʊ] *n US* chicano *m*

chichi ['ʃi:ʃi:] *adj Fam Pej* pintoresco(a) y cursi

chick [tʃɪk] *n* (a) *(young bird)* polluelo *m*; *(young chicken)* pollito *m* (b) *Fam (woman)* nena *f*, *Arg* piba *f*, *Méx* chava *f*

chickadee ['tʃɪkədi:] *n* **black-capped c.** carbonero capirotado

chicken ['tʃɪkɪn] 1 *n* (a) *(bird)* gallina *f*; *(meat)* pollo *m*; IDIOM **it's a c. and egg situation** en esta situación no se sabe quién fue primero, la gallina o el huevo; IDIOM **his chickens have come home to roost** ahora está sufriendo las consecuencias de sus actos; PROV **don't count your chickens (before they're hatched)** no cantes victoria antes de tiempo ►► ***c. breast*** pechuga *f* de pollo; ***c. farmer*** avicultor(ora) *m,f*; ***c. leg*** pata *f* de pollo; ***c. livers*** higadillos *mpl* de pollo; ***c. run*** corral *m*; ***c. soup*** sopa *f* de pollo; ***c. wire*** tela *f* metálica, red *f* de alambre
(b) *Fam (coward)* gallina *mf*, *Esp* miedica *mf*
(c) *Fam (game)* **to play c.** jugar a ver quién se acobarda antes
2 *adj Fam (cowardly)* **to be c.** ser un/una gallina

► **chicken out** *vi Fam* acobardarse, *Méx* ciscarse, *RP* achicarse; **he chickened out of telling her the truth** no se atrevió a decirle la verdad; **he chickened out at the last minute** en el último minuto se acobardó

chickenfeed ['tʃɪkɪnfi:d] *n* (a) *(food)* grano *m* (b) *Fam (insignificant sum)* calderilla *f*

chicken-hearted ['tʃɪkɪn'hɑ:tɪd], **chicken-livered** ['tʃɪkɪn'lɪvəd] *adj Fam* gallina, cobarde

chickenpox ['tʃɪkɪnpɒks] *n* varicela *f*

chickenshit ['tʃɪkənʃɪt] *adj very Fam US* gallina, cobarde

chickpea ['tʃɪkpi:] *n* garbanzo *m*

chickweed ['tʃɪkwi:d] *n* pamplina *f*, álsine *f*

chicory ['tʃɪkərɪ] *n* (a) *(salad vegetable)* achicoria *f* (b) *(coffee additive, substitute)* achicoria *f*

chide [tʃaɪd] (*pt* **chided** *or* **chid** [tʃɪd], *pp* **chided** *or* **chidden** ['tʃɪdən]) *vt* reprender, regañar

chief [tʃi:f] 1 *n* (a) *(of tribe)* jefe(a) *m,f*; IDIOM **there are too many chiefs and not enough Indians here** aquí hay demasiados mandos y poca tropa, *Am* acá hay más caciques que indios (b) *(head) Fam* **the c.** el/la jefe(a) ►► ***c. of police*** jefe(a) *m,f* de policía; ***c. of staff*** *Mil* jefe(a) *m,f* del Estado Mayor; *US (of president, governor)* jefe(a) *m,f* de gabinete
2 *adj* (a) *(most important)* principal
(b) *(head) Br* ***c. accountant*** jefe(a) *m,f* de contabilidad; *US* ***c. canvasser*** *(in elections)* presidente(a) *m,f* de mesa; *Br* ***c. constable*** jefe(a) *m,f* de policía; *Com* ***c. executive,*** *US* ***c. executive officer*** consejero(a) *m,f* delegado(a), director(ora) *m,f* gerente; *US* ***c. financial officer*** director(ora) *m,f* financiero(ra); *Br* ***c. inspector*** inspector(ora) *m,f* jefe; *Law* ***c. justice*** *(in USA)* = presidente del Tribunal Supremo; ***c. librarian*** bibliotecario(a) *m,f* jefe; *Naut* ***c. petty officer*** suboficial *mf* mayor de marina; *Br Parl* ***C. Whip*** = persona al frente del grupo de encargados de mantener la disciplina de un partido político en el parlamento

chiefly ['tʃi:flɪ] *adv* principalmente

chieftain ['tʃi:ftən] *n (of clan)* jefe *m* (del clan)

chiffchaff ['tʃɪftʃæf] *n* mosquitero *m*

chiffon ['ʃɪfɒn] *n* gasa *f*; **a c. scarf** un fular

chiffonade [ʃɪfə'neɪd] *n US* = verdura picada servida como guarnición

chiffon(n)ier [ʃɪfə'nɪə(r)] *n* = cómoda alta y estrecha

chigger ['tʃɪgə(r)] *n* (a) *(sand flea)* nigua *f* (b) *US (parasitic larva)* = parásito que causa un intenso picor en la piel humana

chignon ['ʃi:njɒn] *n* moño *m*, *Méx* chongo *m*

chihuahua [tʃɪ'wɑ:wɑ:] *n* (perro *m*) chihuahua *m*

chilblain ['tʃɪlbleɪn] *n* sabañón *m*

child [tʃaɪld] (*pl* **children** ['tʃɪldrən]) *n* niño(a) *m,f*; *(son)* hijo *m*; *(daughter)* hija *f*; **they have three children** tienen tres hijos; **children's literature** literatura infantil; **children's boutique** boutique infantil; **children's hospital** hospital infantil; **he's a c. of the 60s** es un producto de los años 60; **don't be such a c.!** ¡no seas niño *or Esp* crío!; **it's c.'s play** es un juego de niños; *Old-fashioned* **to be with c.** estar encinta; *Old-fashioned* **to get a woman with c.** dejar a una mujer encinta; PROV **the c. is father to** *or* **of the man** las experiencias de la infancia marcan el carácter para siempre ►► ***c. abuse*** = malos tratos y/o agresión sexual a menores; *Br* ***c. benefit*** ayuda *f* familiar por hijos; ***children's home*** hospicio *m*; ***c. labour*** trabajo *m* de menores; ***c. lock*** cierre *m* de seguridad a prueba de niños; ***c. molester*** corruptor(ora) *m,f* de menores; ***c. pornography*** pornografía *f* infantil; ***c. prodigy*** niño(a) *m,f* prodigio; ***c. psychiatrist*** especialista *mf* en psiquiatría infantil; ***C. Support Agency*** = agencia estatal británica que vela por el cumplimiento de la ley en materia de pensiones alimenticias

child-bearing ['tʃaɪldbeərɪŋ] *n* maternidad *f*; **of c. age** en edad de tener hijos

childbirth ['tʃaɪldbɜːθ] *n* parto *m*; **to die in c.** morir al dar a luz, morir en el parto

childcare ['tʃaɪldkeə(r)] *n* cuidado *m* de menores *or* niños, puericultura *f*

child-friendly ['tʃaɪld'frendlɪ] *adj* **a c. restaurant** un restaurante en el que están bienvenidos los niños

childhood ['tʃaɪldhʊd] *n* niñez *f*, infancia *f*; **his c. home** la casa de su niñez *or* infancia

childish ['tʃaɪldɪʃ] *adj Pej* pueril, infantil; **don't be c.** no seas niño *or* crío

childishness ['tʃaɪldɪʃnɪs] *n Pej* puerilidad *f*, infantilismo *m*; **that's just c.!** ¡son cosas de niños!

childless ['tʃaɪldlɪs] *adj* **to be c.** no tener hijos; **a c. couple** una pareja sin hijos

childlike ['tʃaɪldlaɪk] *adj (innocence)* infantil; *(appearance)* aniñado(a)

childminder ['tʃaɪldmaɪndə(r)] *n Br* niñero(a) *m,f*, *Esp* canguro *mf*

childproof ['tʃaɪldpruːf] *adj* **c. bottle** = botella que los niños no pueden abrir; **c. lock** *(in car)* cierre de seguridad a prueba de niños

children *pl of* **child**

Chile ['tʃɪlɪ] *n* Chile

Chilean ['tʃɪlɪən] **1** *n* chileno(a) *m,f*
 2 *adj* chileno(a)

chili = **chilli**

chill [tʃɪl] **1** *n* **(a)** *(illness)* resfriado *m*; **to catch a c.** resfriarse, agarrar *or Esp* coger *or Méx* pescar un resfriado, *Andes, RP* agarrarse *or* pescarse un resfrío
 (b) *(coldness)* **there's a c. in the air** hace bastante fresco; **to take the c. off sth** templar algo; **his remark cast a c. over the meeting** su comentario enfrió la reunión; **I sensed a certain c. in his welcome** noté cierta frialdad en su bienvenida ▸▸ ***c. factor*** índice *m* de enfriamiento (del aire)
 (c) *(feeling of fear)* escalofrío *m*; **a c. ran down my spine** sentí un escalofrío; **a c. of fear** un escalofrío de temor
 2 *adj (wind)* frío(a)
 3 *vt (wine, food)* poner a enfriar

▸ **chill out** *vi Fam* relajarse; **he likes chilling out at home** le encanta estar tranqui *or* relajarse en casa; **I wish he'd c. out a bit** ojalá se tomara las cosas con más calma; **c. (out)!** ¡calma!, ¡tranqui!

chilled [tʃɪld] *adj* **(a)** *(cold)* frío(a); **c. white wine** vino blanco frío; **serve c.** *(on product)* sírvase frío; **to be c. to the bone/the marrow** estar muerto(a) de frío **(b)** *Fam (relaxed)* **c. (out)** relajado(a), *Esp* tranqui

chiller ['tʃɪlə(r)] *n Fam (book)* libro *m* de miedo; *(movie)* película *f* de miedo

chil(l)i ['tʃɪlɪ] *n* **c. (pepper)** chile *m*, *Esp* guindilla *f*, *Andes, RP* ají *m*; **c. (con carne)** = guiso picante de carne picada y alubias rojas ▸▸ *US* ***c. dog*** perrito *m* caliente *or Col, Méx* perro *m* caliente *or RP* pancho *m* con chile; ***c. powder*** chile *m or Esp* guindilla *f* en polvo

chillin ['tʃɪlɪn] *adj US Fam* genial

chilliness ['tʃɪlɪnɪs] *n* **(a)** *(of air, wind)* frío *m* **(b)** *(of greeting, manner)* frialdad *f*

chilling ['tʃɪlɪŋ] *adj (frightening)* escalofriante

chillout room ['tʃɪlaʊtruːm] *n Fam (in nightclub)* chill out *m*, = habitación o espacio apartado en una discoteca en los que la gente puede descansar y escuchar música ambiental

chilly ['tʃɪlɪ] *adj* **(a)** *(cold)* frío(a); **it's a bit c. out** hace bastante fresco fuera **(b)** *(unfriendly)* frío(a)

chime [tʃaɪm] **1** *n (of bells)* repique *m*; *(of clock)* campanada *f*; *(of doorbell)* campanilleo *m*; **chimes** *(for door)* carillón *m*
 2 *vt* **the clock chimed nine o'clock** el reloj dio las nueve
 3 *vi* **(a)** *(bells)* repicar; *(clock)* dar la hora; *(doorbell)* sonar (con ruido de campanilla) **(b)** *(agree)* **his view chimes with mine** su opinión coincide con la mía

▸ **chime in** *vi* **(a)** *Fam (in conversation)* meter baza *or Méx, RP* la cuchara; **they all chimed in at once** se pusieron todos a hablar a la vez **(b)** *(agree)* **his explanation chimes in with the facts** su explicación concuerda con los hechos

chimera [kaɪ'mɪərə] *n (unrealistic idea)* quimera *f*

chimeric(al) [kaɪ'merɪk(əl)] *adj* quimérico(a)

chimney ['tʃɪmnɪ] *n* **(a)** *(of house, factory, engine)* chimenea *f* ▸▸ ***c. breast*** campana *f* (de la chimenea); ***c. stack*** chimenea *f (parte que sobresale)*; ***c. swift*** vencejo *m* espinoso de las chimeneas **(b)** *(of lamp)* tubo *m* **(c)** *(in rock face)* chimenea *f*

chimneypiece ['tʃɪmnɪpiːs] *n Br* repisa *f* (de la chimenea)

chimneypot ['tʃɪmnɪpɒt] *n* (cañón *m* exterior de) chimenea *f*

chimney-sweep ['tʃɪmnɪswiːp] *n* deshollinador(ora) *m,f*

chimpanzee [tʃɪmpæn'ziː], *Fam* **chimp** [tʃɪmp] *n* chimpancé *m*

chin [tʃɪn] *n* mentón *m*, barbilla *f*; IDIOM **to keep one's c. up** mantener los ánimos; IDIOM **to take it on the c.** aguantarlo sin rechistar

China ['tʃaɪnə] *n* China ▸▸ ***the C. Sea*** el mar de China

china ['tʃaɪnə] *n* **(a)** *(material)* loza *f*; *(porcelain)* porcelana *f* ▸▸ ***c. clay*** caolín *m*; ***c. doll*** muñeca *f* de porcelana **(b)** *(plates, cups)* vajilla *f* de loza; *(porcelain)* vajilla *f* de porcelana ▸▸ ***c. cabinet*** chinero *m*

> **False friend**: The Spanish noun **china** is not a translation for the English word **china**. In Spanish **china** means Chinese woman or "small stone, pebble", and in Latin America it can also mean an Indian woman or servant.

Chinaman ['tʃaɪnəmən] *n Old-fashioned or Pej* chino *m*

Chinatown ['tʃaɪnətaʊn] *n* barrio *m* chino *(de la comunidad china)*

chinaware ['tʃaɪnəweə(r)] *n* **(a)** *(porcelain objects)* porcelana *f* **(b)** *(plates, cups)* vajilla *f* de loza; *(porcelain)* vajilla *f* de porcelana

chinchilla [tʃɪn'tʃɪlə] *n* **(a)** *(animal)* chinchilla *f* **(b)** *(fur)* (piel *f* de) chinchilla *f*

chin-chin ['tʃɪn'tʃɪn] *exclam Br Fam Old-fashioned* **(a)** *(when drinking)* ¡chin chin! **(b)** *(hello, goodbye)* ¡salud!

Chinese [tʃaɪ'niːz] **1** *n* **(a)** *(person)* chino(a) *m,f* **(b)** *(language)* chino *m* **(c)** *Fam (meal)* comida *f* china; *(restaurant)* chino *m*
 2 *npl* **the C.** los chinos
 3 *adj* chino(a) ▸▸ *Br* ***C. burn:* to give sb a C. burn** = agarrar el antebrazo de una persona con las dos manos y girarlas en dirección contraria produciendo gran dolor, *RP* hacer una tortura china a alguien; ***C. cabbage*** col *f* china, repollo *m* chino; ***C. checkers*** damas *fpl* chinas; ***C. gooseberry*** kiwi *m*; ***C. lantern*** lámpara *f* china *or* de papel; *Br* ***C. leaves*** col *f* china, repollo *m* chino; ***C. New Year*** el Año Nuevo chino; *Fig* ***a C. puzzle*** un rompecabezas; ***C. restaurant*** restaurante *m* chino; ***C. takeaway*** *(shop)* tienda *f* de comida china para llevar; *(meal)* comida *f* china para llevar; ***C. tea*** té *m* chino; *Fin & St Exch* ***C. walls*** murallas *fpl* chinas, = separación de departamentos dentro de una entidad financiera para evitar el conflicto de intereses

Chink [tʃɪŋk] *n Fam* = término generalmente ofensivo para referirse a los chinos

chink[1] [tʃɪŋk] *n (gap)* resquicio *m*; *(in rock, wall)* grieta *f*; IDIOM **to find a c. in sb's armour** encontrar el punto flaco de alguien

chink[2] **1** *n (sound)* tintineo *m*
 2 *vt (glasses)* entrechocar
 3 *vi* tintinear

Chinkie, Chinky ['tʃɪŋkɪ] *n Fam* **(a)** *(person)* = término generalmente ofensivo para referirse a los chinos **(b)** *Br (meal)* comida *f* china; *(restaurant)* (restaurante *m*) chino *m*

chinless wonder ['tʃɪnlɪs'wʌndə(r)] *n Br Fam* niño *m* bien *or* de papá, *Esp* niñato *m*, *RP* nene *m* bien *or* de papá

chinos ['tʃiːnəʊz] *npl* (pantalones *mpl*) chinos *mpl*

chinstrap ['tʃɪnstræp] *n* barboquejo *m*

chintz [tʃɪnts] *n (textile)* cretona *f* satinada

chintzy ['tʃɪntsɪ] *adj* **(a)** *(fabric, sofa)* de cretona satinada con estampado **(b)** *US (cheap, poor-quality)* barato(a), ordinario(a) **(c)** *US Fam (miserly)* roñoso(a), tacaño(a), *CSur* amarrete(a), *Méx* codo(a)

chin-up ['tʃɪnʌp] *n (exercise)* flexión *f (colgando de una barra con los brazos)*

chinwag ['tʃɪnwæg] *Fam* **1** *n* **to have a c. (with sb)** charlar (con alguien), *CAm, Méx* platicar (con alguien)
 2 *vi* charlar, estar de cháchara, *CAm, Méx* platicar

chip [tʃɪp] **1** *n* **(a)** *(of wood)* viruta *f*; *(of marble)* lasca *f*; *(out of plate, cup)* mella *f*, desportilladura *f*; **this glass has a c. (in it)** este vaso está desportillado; **chocolate chips** trozos de chocolate
 (b) *Br* **chips** *(French fries) Esp* patatas *fpl or Am* papas *fpl* fritas ▸▸ ***c. pan*** freidora *f*; ***c. shop*** = tienda que vende comida para llevar, especialmente pescado frito con *Esp* patatas *or Am* papas fritas; ***c. van*** = furgoneta en la que se vende comida similar a la de una "chip shop"
 (c) *US* **(potato) chips** *(crisps) Esp* patatas *fpl or Am* papas *fpl* fritas *(de bolsa)*
 (d) *(in gambling, card games)* ficha *f*
 (e) *Comptr* chip *m*, pastilla *f*
 (f) *(in soccer, rugby)* vaselina *f*, globo *m*; **c. (shot)** *(in golf)* chip *m*, golpe *m* corto
 (g) IDIOMS **he's a c. off the old block** de tal palo, tal astilla; **to have a c. on one's shoulder (about sth)** tener complejo (por algo); *Fam* **when the chips are down** en los momentos difíciles; *Br Fam* **he's had**

his chips *(has failed) Esp* ya ha tenido su oportunidad, *Am* perdió su chance; *(has died)* la ha palmado, *Am* estiró la pata, *CAm, Méx* lió el petate, *RP* la quedó

2 *vt* (*pt & pp* **chipped**) (**a**) *(shape by cutting)* tallar (**b**) *(damage) (plate, cup)* mellar, desportillar; *(paint)* desconchar; *(furniture)* astillar; **to c. one's tooth** mellarse un diente (**c**) *Culin* cortar (**d**) *(ball) (in soccer, rugby)* picar; *(in golf)* dar un golpe corto con la cucharilla a; **to c. the goalkeeper** *(in soccer)* hacerle una vaselina al portero

3 *vi (plate, cup)* mellarse, desportillarse; *(paint)* desconcharse; *(furniture)* astillarse

▸**chip away** *vt sep (plaster, paint)* desconchar

▸**chip away at** *vt insep* (**a**) *(wood, stone)* dar golpes a (**b**) *(confidence, reputation)* erosionar, socavar

▸**chip in** *Fam* **1** *vt insep* (**a**) *(contribute)* poner; **we all chipped in $5** todos pusimos *or* contribuimos con 5 dólares (**b**) *(say)* **"I think he's right," chipped in Johnny** "creo que tiene razón", saltó Johnny

2 *vi* (**a**) *(in collection of money)* poner algo (de dinero); **they all chipped in to buy her a present** todos pusieron algo para comprarle un regalo (**b**) *(in discussion)* meter baza *or Méx, RP* la cuchara, terciar; **to c. in with a suggestion** aportar alguna sugerencia

▸**chip off** **1** *vt sep (break off)* arrancar

2 *vi (plaster, paint)* desconcharse

chipboard ['tʃɪpbɔːd] *n* aglomerado *m*

chipmunk ['tʃɪpmʌŋk] *n* ardilla *f* listada *or* estriada

chipolata [tʃɪpə'lɑːtə] *n Br* salchichilla *f*

chipped [tʃɪpt] *adj* (**a**) *(damaged) (plate, cup)* mellado(a), desportillado(a); *(paint)* desconchado(a); *(furniture)* astillado(a) (**b**) *(sliced, cut) US* ***c. beef*** = carne de vaca ahumada cortada en filetes finos; *Br* ***c. potatoes*** *Esp* patatas *fpl* fritas, *Am* papas *fpl* fritas

Chippendale ['tʃɪpəndeɪl] *n* **a C. table/sideboard** una mesa/un aparador estilo chippendale *(estilo de mobiliario inglés del siglo XVIII)*

chipper ['tʃɪpə(r)] *adj Fam* (**a**) *(lively)* animado(a), alegre; **I'm feeling very c.** estoy muy animado (**b**) *(smartly dressed)* elegante, chic

chippings ['tʃɪpɪŋz] *npl* (**a**) *(of wood)* virutas *fpl* (**b**) *(in roadwork)* gravilla *f*; **slow, loose c.** *(sign)* precaución, gravilla suelta

chippy ['tʃɪpɪ] **1** *n Fam* (**a**) *Br (fish and chip shop)* = tienda que vende comida para llevar, especialmente pescado frito con *Esp* patatas *or Am* papas fritas (**b**) *Br (carpenter)* carpintero(a) *m,f* (**c**) *US Pej (woman)* mujer *m* alegre

2 *adj (aggressive)* irritable

chiromancy [kaɪrə'mænsɪ] *n* quiromancia *f*

chiropodist [kɪ'rɒpədɪst] *n* podólogo(a) *m,f*, *Am* podiatra *mf*

chiropody [kɪ'rɒpədɪ] *n* podología *f*

chiropractic [kaɪrə'præktɪk] *n* quiropráctica *f*

chiropractor ['kaɪrəpræktə(r)] *n* quiropráctico(a) *m,f*

chirp [tʃɜːp], **chirrup** ['tʃɪrəp] **1** *n* (**a**) *(of birds)* trino *m* (**b**) *(of grasshopper)* chirrido *m*

2 *vi* (**a**) *(bird)* trinar (**b**) *(grasshopper)* chirriar

chirpy ['tʃɜːpɪ] *adj Fam* alegre, animado(a)

chirrup = **chirp**

chisel ['tʃɪzəl] **1** *n (for wood)* formón *m*; *(for stone)* cincel *m*

2 *vt* (*pt & pp* **chiselled**, *US* **chiseled**) (**a**) *(in woodwork, sculpture)* tallar; **to c. sth from** *or* **in** *or* **out of marble** tallar algo en mármol; *Fig* **chiselled features** rasgos muy dibujados (**b**) *Fam (cheat)* **to c. sb out of sth** timarle algo a alguien; **to c. sb out of his money** estafar a alguien

chiseller, *US* **chiseler** ['tʃɪzələ(r)] *n Fam (cheat)* timador(ora) *m,f*

chit [tʃɪt] *n* (**a**) *(note)* nota *f* (**b**) *(voucher)* vale *m* (**c**) *(receipt)* recibo *m* (**d**) *Fam Old-fashioned (girl)* moza *f*, muchacha *f*

chitchat ['tʃɪttʃæt] *n Fam* charla *f*, cháchara *f*, *CAm, Méx* plática *f*

chitterlings ['tʃɪtəlɪŋz], **chitlins** ['tʃɪtlɪnz] *npl* mondongo *m*, callos *mpl*

chitty ['tʃɪtɪ] *n Br* (**a**) *(voucher)* vale *m* (**b**) *(receipt)* recibo *m*

chiv [ʃɪv] *n Fam* pincho *m*, cuchillo *m*

chivalric ['ʃɪvəlrɪk] *adj (literature)* caballeresco(a)

chivalrous ['ʃɪvəlrəs] *adj* caballeroso(a), caballeresco(a)

chivalrously ['ʃɪvəlrəslɪ] *adv* caballerosamente

chivalrousness ['ʃɪvəlrəsnɪs] *n (courteous behaviour)* caballerosidad *f*

chivalry ['ʃɪvəlrɪ] *n* (**a**) *(courteous behaviour)* caballerosidad *f*; *Hum* **c. is not dead** todavía quedan caballeros (**b**) *Hist* caballería *f*

chives [tʃaɪvz] *npl* cebollinos *mpl*

chiv(v)y ['tʃɪvɪ] *vt Br Fam* **to c. sb into doing sth** dar la lata *or RP* hinchar a alguien para que haga algo; **to c. sb along** *or* **up** meter prisa *or Am* apurar a alguien

chlamydia [klə'mɪdɪə] *n Med* linfogranuloma *m* venéreo

chloral ['klɔːrəl] *n Chem* cloral *m* ▸▸ ***c. hydrate*** hidrato *m* de cloral

chlorate ['klɔːreɪt] *n Chem* clorato *m*

chloric ['klɒrɪk] *adj Chem* clórico(a) ▸▸ ***c. acid*** ácido *m* clórico

chloride ['klɔːraɪd] *n Chem* cloruro *m*

chlorinate ['klɒrɪneɪt] *vt* clorar

chlorinated ['klɒrɪneɪtɪd] *adj* clorado(a)

chlorination [klɒrɪ'neɪʃən] *n* cloración *f*

chlorine ['klɔːriːn] *n Chem* cloro *m*

chlorite ['klɔːraɪt] *n Geol* clorita *f*

chlorofluorocarbon [klɔːrəʊflʊərəʊ'kɑːbən] *n Chem* clorofluorocarbono *m*

chloroform ['klɒrəfɔːm] **1** *n Chem* cloroformo *m*

2 *vt* cloroformar

chlorophyll, *US* **chlorophyl** ['klɒrəfɪl] *n Biol* clorofila *f*

chloroplast ['klɒrəplæst] *n Bot* cloroplasto *m*

choc [tʃɒk], **choccy** ['tʃɒkɪ] *n Br Fam* chocolate *m*

chocaholic [tʃɒkə'hɒlɪk] *n Fam Hum* adicto(a) *m,f* al chocolate, chocolatero(a) *m,f*

choc-ice ['tʃɒkaɪs] *n Br* bombón *m* helado *(sin palo)*

chock [tʃɒk] *n (for wheel of car, plane)* calzo *m*

chock-a-block ['tʃɒkə'blɒk], *Br* **chocka** ['tʃɒkə] *adj Fam* abarrotado(a) (**with** de)

chock-full [tʃɒk'fʊl] *adj Fam* abarrotado(a) (**of** de)

chocolate ['tʃɒklət] **1** *n* (**a**) *(solid, liquid)* chocolate *m*; **a c. ice cream/milkshake** un helado/un batido de chocolate ▸▸ ***c. bar*** chocolatina *f*; ***c. biscuit*** galleta *f* de chocolate; ***c. cake*** tarta *f or* pastel *m or Col, CSur* torta *f* de chocolate; ***c. chip cookie*** galleta *f* con trozos de chocolate; ***c. finger*** = galleta alargada cubierta de chocolate; ***c. milk*** cacao *m*; ***c. sauce*** chocolate *m* líquido

(**b**) *(drink)* chocolate *m*; **(hot** *or* **drinking) c.** chocolate *m* a la taza *or* caliente

(**c**) *(sweet, candy)* bombón *m*; **a box of chocolates** una caja de bombones

(**d**) *(colour)* marrón *m* oscuro, color *m* chocolate

2 *adj* (**a**) *(made of chocolate)* de chocolate (**b**) *(in colour)* **c. (coloured)** marrón oscuro, color chocolate

chocolate-box ['tʃɒklətbɒks] *adj Fam* **a c. landscape** un paisaje de tarjeta postal

CHOICE [tʃɔɪs] **1** *n* (**a**) *(act)* elección *f*; **that's an excellent c., sir** excelente elección, señor; **the c. is yours, it's your c.** la decisión es suya; **to make** *or* **take one's c.** elegir, escoger; **to have first c.** poder elegir el primero; **by** *or* **from c.** por (propia) elección; **cake with the ice cream of your c.** pastel con helado a elegir; **the drink of your c.** la bebida que prefieras; **it has become the drug of c. for doctors treating this illness** se ha convertido en la droga preferida por los doctores que tratan esta enfermedad

(**b**) *(thing chosen)* elección *f*; **he was a surprise c. as party leader** fue una elección sorpresa como líder del partido; **my first c. would be...** mi primera opción sería...; **the c. of venue was rather controversial** la elección del lugar fue bastante polémica

(**c**) *(alternative)* alternativa *f*, opción *f*; **you give me no c. but to dismiss you** no me dejas otra alternativa que despedirte; **you have the c. of staying or coming with us** puedes elegir entre quedarte o venir con nosotros; **they were given a c. between tennis and soccer** les dieron a elegir entre tenis y fútbol; **you have no c. in the matter** no tienes otra opción; **we had no c. but to do it** no tuvimos más remedio que hacerlo

(**d**) *(selection)* selección *f*, surtido *m*; **there isn't much c.** no hay mucho donde elegir; **available in a wide c. of colours** disponible en una amplia gama de colores; **you have a c. of three starters** puedes elegir entre tres primeros platos

2 *adj* (**a**) *(well chosen)* escogido(a); **she used some c. language** *(offensive)* soltó unas cuantas lindezas

(**b**) *(food, wine)* selecto(a); *(meat)* de calidad

choir ['kwaɪə(r)] *n* (**a**) *(group of singers)* coro *m* ▸▸ ***c. practice*** ensayo *m* del coro; ***c. school*** escuela *f* de canto; ***c. stalls*** sillería *f* del coro (**b**) *(part of church)* coro *m*

choirboy ['kwaɪəbɔɪ] *n* niño *m* de coro

choirmaster ['kwaɪəmɑːstə(r)] *n* director *m* de coro

choirmistress ['kwaɪəmɪstrɪs] *n* directora *f* de coro

choke [tʃəʊk] **1** *n* (**a**) *Aut* estárter *m* (**b**) ***c. chain*** *(for dog)* = collar corredizo que aprisiona el cuello si el perro tira de él (**c**) *(of artichoke)* barba *f*

2 *vt* (**a**) *(strangle)* ahogar, estrangular; **to c. sb to death** estrangular a alguien (**b**) *(block)* atascar; **the roads were choked with traffic** las carreteras estaban atascadas *or* colapsadas de tráfico; **the garden was choked with weeds** el jardín estaba inundado de malas hierbas

3 *vi* (**a**) *(asphyxiate)* ahogarse; **she choked on a fish bone** se atragantó con una espina; **he choked on his own vomit** se ahogó en su propio vómito; *Fig* **to c. with anger** ponerse rojo(a) de ira; *Fig* **to c. with laughter** morirse de risa (**b**) *Sport Fam* venirse abajo por los nervios

▸**choke back** *vt sep (tears, words, anger)* contener

▸**choke off** *vt sep* (**a**) *(discussion)* cortar; **his screams were choked off** sus gritos se acallaron (**b**) *(supply, investment)* cortar

▸**choke up** *vt sep* (**a**) *(drain)* atascar (**b**) *Fam (emotionally)* conmover

choked ['tʃəʊkt] *adj Fam (emotional)* conmovido(a), emocionado(a); **I was really choked at the wedding** me emocioné mucho en la boda

choker ['tʃəʊkə(r)] *n* (**a**) *(necklace)* gargantilla *f* (**b**) *(cloth band)* tirilla *f*

choler ['kɒlə(r)] *n Literary (anger)* cólera *f*

cholera ['kɒlərə] *n* cólera *m*

choleric ['kɒlərɪk] *adj Literary* colérico(a)

cholesterol [kɒ'lestərɒl] *n* colesterol *m* ▸▸ ***c. level*** nivel *m* de colesterol

chomp [tʃɒmp] **1** *vt* masticar, mascar

2 *vi* masticar, mascar; **the cow was chomping away at a tuft of grass** la vaca estaba mascando *or* masticando una mata de hierba

Chomskyan ['tʃɒmskɪən] *adj* de Chomsky

choo-choo ['tʃu:tʃu:] *n (in children's language)* (tren *m*) chú-chú *m*

CHOOSE [tʃu:z] (*pt* **chose** [tʃəʊz], *pp* **chosen** ['tʃəʊzən]) **1** *vt* (**a**) *(select)* elegir, escoger; **to c. sb sth, to c. sth for sb** elegir algo a *or* para alguien; **there's not much** *or* **a lot to c. between them** no es fácil escoger entre los dos; **c. your words carefully** piensa bien lo que dices

(**b**) *(elect)* elegir; **they chose her as** *or* **to be party leader** la eligieron como líder del partido

(**c**) *(decide)* decidir; **to c. to do sth** decidir hacer algo; **they chose to ignore his rudeness** decidieron no hacer caso de su grosería; **I didn't c. to invite her** *(I had no alternative)* la invité porque no tenía otra alternativa

2 *vi* (**a**) *(make choice)* elegir, escoger; **c. for yourself** elige tú mismo; **there's a wide range to c. from** hay una amplia gama donde elegir; **there's not a lot to c. from** no hay mucho donde elegir

(**b**) *(please, want)* **I'll do as I c.** haré lo que me parezca; **if you c., you can receive cash instead** si lo prefiere, se lo podemos abonar en efectivo

▸**choose up** *US* **1** *vt* seleccionar

2 *vi* seleccionar los jugadores

chooser ['tʃu:zə(r)] *n Comptr* selector *m*

choosy ['tʃu:zɪ] *adj Fam* exigente (**about** con); **I can't afford to be (too) c.** no me puedo permitir ser muy exigente

chop [tʃɒp] **1** *n* (**a**) *(with axe)* hachazo *m*; *(with side of hand)* manotazo *m*, cate *m* (**b**) *Br Fam (dismissal, cancellation)* **she got the c.** *(was sacked)* la pusieron de patitas en la calle; **to be for the c.** *(plan, scheme, organization)* ser lo próximo en desaparecer; **I hear Sammy's for the c.** he oído decir que van a poner de patitas en la calle a Sammy (**c**) *(of lamb, pork)* chuleta *f*

2 *vt* (*pt & pp* **chopped**) (**a**) *(wood)* cortar; *(meat)* trocear; *(vegetables)* picar (**b**) *Fam (budget, funding)* reducir; *(project)* eliminar

3 *vi* (**a**) *(hit)* **to c. at** *(with axe, sword)* golpear (**b**) *Br* IDIOM **to c. and change** cambiar de idea continuamente

▸**chop down** *vt sep (tree)* derribar, talar

▸**chop off** *vt sep* cortar; **to c. sb's head off** cortarle a alguien la cabeza

▸**chop up** *vt sep (wood)* cortar; *(meat)* trocear; *(vegetables)* picar

chop-chop ['tʃɒp'tʃɒp] *exclam Fam* ¡venga, vamos!; **get to work, c.!** ¡bueno, vamos, a trabajar!, *Esp* ¡hala, venga, a trabajar!

chopper ['tʃɒpə(r)] *n* (**a**) *(for meat)* tajadera *f* (**b**) *Br (axe)* hacha *f* pequeña (**c**) *Fam (helicopter)* helicóptero *m* (**d**) *Fam (bicycle)* bicicleta *f*; *(motorbike)* chóper *f*, = moto de gran cilindrada con un gran manillar (**e**) *Br Vulg (penis) Esp* polla *f*, *Am* verga *f*

choppers ['tʃɒpəz] *npl Fam* (**a**) *(false teeth)* dentadura *f* postiza (**b**) *(teeth)* dientes *mpl*, *Esp* piños *mpl*

chopping ['tʃɒpɪŋ] *n* ***c. block*** *(butcher's)* tajo *m*, tajadera *f*; ***c. board*** tabla *f* de cocina (para cortar)

choppy ['tʃɒpɪ] *adj* (**a**) *(sea, lake)* picado(a); **to be c.** estar picado(a) (**b**) *(narrative, style)* tosco(a), sin pulir

chops [tʃɒps] *npl Fam (of person, animal) Esp* morros *mpl*, *Am* trompa *f*; *Fam Fig* **to lick one's c.** *(to relish)* relamerse (de gusto)

chopsticks ['tʃɒpstɪks] *npl* palillos *mpl (chinos)*

chop suey [tʃɒp'su:ɪ] *n* chop suey *m*, = plato de la cocina china con verduras y carne servido con arroz

choral ['kɔ:rəl] *adj Mus* coral ▸▸ ***c. society*** orfeón *m*, coral *f*

chorale [kɒ'rɑ:l] *n* (**a**) *(hymn)* coral *m* (**b**) *US (choir)* coral *f*, orfeón *m*

chord [kɔ:d] *n* (**a**) *Mus* acorde *m*; **to touch a c. (in sb)** tocar la fibra sensible (de alguien); **her speech struck a c. with the electorate** su discurso caló hondo en el electorado (**b**) *Math (of arc)* cuerda *f*

chordate ['kɔ:deɪt] *Zool* **1** *n* cordado *m*

2 *adj* cordado

chore [tʃɔ:(r)] *n* (**a**) *(domestic task)* tarea *f* doméstica; **ironing is one c. I don't mind doing** el planchado es una de las tareas domésticas que no me importa hacer; **to do the chores** hacer las tareas (**b**) *Fam (unpleasant, tedious task)* fastidio *m*, *Esp* lata *f*, *RP* embole *m*; *Fam* **what a c.!** ¡vaya fastidio!

chorea [kə'rɪə] *n Med* corea *f*

choreograph ['kɒrɪəgrɑ:f] *vt* coreografiar

choreographer [kɒrɪ'ɒgrəfə(r)] *n* coreógrafo(a) *m,f*

choreographic [kɒrɪə'græfɪk] *adj* coreográfico(a)

choreography [kɒrɪ'ɒgrəfɪ] *n* coreografía *f*

chorister ['kɒrɪstə(r)] *n* orfeonista *mf*, miembro *m* de un coro

choroid ['kɔ:rɔɪd] *n Anat* coroides *f*

chortle ['tʃɔ:təl] **1** *n* risa *f* placentera

2 *vi* reírse con placer; **to c. with delight at** *or* **over sth** reírse con placer de algo

chorus ['kɔ:rəs] **1** *n* (**a**) *(of song)* estribillo *m*; *(in opera, cantata)* coro *m*; **we all joined in (on) the c.** cantamos el estribillo todos juntos (**b**) *(group of singers)* coro *m* (**c**) *Theat (dancers, singers)* coro *m* ▸▸ ***c. girl*** corista *f*; ***c. line*** coro *m* de revista (**d**) *(in classical Greek drama)* coro *m* (**e**) *(of complaints, groans)* coro *m*; **in c.** a coro; **a c. of protest** un coro de protestas

2 *vt* corear, decir a coro

chorusmaster ['kɔ:rəsmɑ:stə(r)] *n* director *m* de coro

chose *pt of* **choose**

chosen ['tʃəʊzən] **1** *adj* escogido(a), elegido(a); **the c. few** los elegidos ▸▸ ***the c. people*** el pueblo elegido

2 *pp of* **choose**

chough [tʃʌf] *n* chova *f* piquirroja

choux pastry ['ʃu:'peɪstrɪ] *n* pasta *f* brisa

chow[1] [tʃaʊ], **chow-chow** ['tʃaʊ'tʃaʊ] *n (dog)* chow-chow *m*

chow[2] *n Fam (food)* papeo *m*, *Esp* manduca *f*, *Méx* itacate *m*, *RP* morfi *m*

▸**chow down** *vi US Fam* liarse a comer *or Esp, Ven* papear *or RP* morfar

chowder ['tʃaʊdə(r)] *n* = crema de pescado o de mariscos

chowderhead ['tʃaʊdəhed] *n US Fam* cenutrio(a) *m,f*, *RP* lenteja *mf*

chow mein [tʃaʊ'meɪn] *n* chow mein *m*, = plato de la cocina china con verduras y carne o pescado servido con fideos chinos

Christ [kraɪst] *n* (**a**) *(Jesus)* Cristo *m*; **the C. child** el niño Jesús (**b**) *Fam (as oath)* **C. (Almighty)!** ¡Dios!; **for C.'s sake!** ¡por (el amor de) Dios!; **C. (alone) knows** *(I have no idea)* sabe Dios, (sólo) Dios sabe

christen ['krɪsən] *vt* (**a**) *(baptize)* bautizar; *(nickname)* bautizar; **he was christened "Bigears"** le pusieron de apodo "Bigears" (**b**) *Fam (use for first time)* estrenar

Christendom ['krɪsəndəm] *n Old-fashioned (people, countries)* la cristiandad; **the most beautiful princess in C.** la princesa más bella de la cristiandad

christening ['krɪsənɪŋ] *n (baptism)* bautizo *m*

Christian ['krɪstʃən, 'krɪstɪən] **1** *n* cristiano(a) *m,f*

2 *adj* cristiano(a); *Old-fashioned* **that was a very C. thing to do** ha/has sido muy amable *or* generoso ▸▸ ***C. democrat*** democratacristiano(a) *m,f*, democristiano(a) *m,f*; ***the C. era*** la era cristiana; ***C. name*** nombre *m* de pila; ***C. Science*** Ciencia *f* Cristiana; ***C. Scientist*** = miembro de la Ciencia Cristiana

Christianity [krɪstɪ'ænɪtɪ] *n* cristianismo *m*, cristiandad *f*

Christianize ['krɪstʃənaɪz] *vt* cristianizar

Christlike ['kraɪstlaɪk] *adj* **his C. features** sus rasgos, tan parecidos a los de Cristo; **a C. sacrifice** un sacrificio como el de Cristo

Christmas ['krɪsməs] *n* Navidad *f*, Navidades *fpl*; **I'm staying with my parents over C.** voy a pasar la Navidad *or* las Navidades con mis padres; **at C.** en Navidad; **I gave her a new bike for C.** le compré una moto nueva como regalo de Navidad; **Merry** *or* **Happy C.!** ¡Feliz Navidad! ▸▸ *Br* ***C. box*** *(money)* aguinaldo *m*; ***C. cactus*** cactus *m inv* de Navidad; ***C. cake*** = pastel de Navidad a base de frutas; ***C. card*** tarjeta *f* de Navidad, *Esp* crismas *m inv*; ***C. carol*** villancico *m*; ***C. club*** = en una tienda, cuenta en la que los clientes van poniendo regularmente contribuciones como forma de ahorrar para hacer las compras navideñas; ***C. cracker*** = cilindro de papel que produce un pequeño estallido al abrirlo estirándolo por los extremos y contiene un regalito de Navidad; ***C. Day*** día *m* de Navidad; ***C. dinner*** comida *f* de Navidad; ***C. Eve*** Nochebuena *f*; ***C. flower*** flor *m* de Pascua; ***C. hamper*** cesta *f* de Navidad; ***C. Island*** Isla *f* de Navidad; ***C. present*** regalo *m* de Navidad; ***C. pudding*** = pudin con pasas y otras frutas típico de Navidad; ***C. shoppers*** gente *f* que hace las compras navideñas; ***C. stocking*** = calcetín que los niños cuelgan de la chimenea para que Papá Noel meta en él los regalos; ***C. tree*** árbol *m* de Navidad

Christmassy ['krɪsməsɪ] *adj Fam* navideño(a)

Christmastide ['krɪsməstaɪd] *n Literary* Pascua *f*, Navidad *f*; **at C.** en Pascua *or* Navidad

Christopher ['krɪstəfə(r)] *pr n* **Saint C.** San Cristóbal; **C. Columbus** Cristóbal Colón

chromatic [krəʊ'mætɪk] *adj* cromático(a) ▸▸ *Mus* ***c. scale*** escala *f* cromática

chromatography [krəʊmə'tɒgrəfɪ] *n Chem* cromatografía *f*

chrome [krəʊm] **1** *n* cromo *m* ▸▸ ***c. yellow*** amarillo *m* cromo

2 *adj* cromado(a)

3 *vt* cromar

chromium ['krəʊmɪəm] **1** *n Chem* cromo *m* ▸▸ ***c. dioxide*** dióxido *m* de cromo; ***c. steel*** acero *m* al cromo

2 *adj* de cromo

chromium-plated ['krəʊmɪəm'pleɪtɪd] *adj* cromado(a)

chromosomal [krəʊmə'səʊməl] *adj Biol* cromosómico(a)

chromosome ['krəʊməsəʊm] *n Biol* cromosoma *m*

chromosphere ['krəʊməsfɪə(r)] *n Astron* cromosfera *f*

chronic ['krɒnɪk] *adj* **(a)** *(invalid, ill-health)* crónico(a); **c. unemployment** desempleo crónico, *Esp* paro estructural, *Am* desocupación crónica ▸▸ *Med* ***c. fatigue syndrome*** encefalomielitis *f inv* miálgica **(b)** *(habitual) (smoker, gambler)* empedernido(a) **(c)** *Br Fam (very bad)* desastroso(a)

chronically ['krɒnɪkəlɪ] *adv* **(a)** *(ill)* **to be c. ill** ser un/una enfermo(a) crónico(a) **(b)** *Fam (very badly)* desastrosamente, *Esp* fatal

chronicle ['krɒnɪkəl] **1** *n* crónica *f*

2 *vt* relatar, escribir la crónica de

chronicler ['krɒnɪklə(r)] *n* cronista *mf*

chronological [krɒnə'lɒdʒɪkəl] *adj* cronológico(a); **in c. order** por orden cronológico

chronologically [krɒnə'lɒdʒɪkəlɪ] *adv* cronológicamente

chronology [krə'nɒlədʒɪ] *n* cronología *f*

chronometer [krə'nɒmɪtə(r)] *n* cronómetro *m*

chrysalis ['krɪsəlɪs], **chrysalid** ['krɪsəlɪd] (*pl* **chrysalides** [krɪ'sælɪdiːz]) *n Zool* pupa *f*, crisálida *f*

chrysanthemum [krɪ'zænθəməm] *n* crisantemo *m*

chub [tʃʌb] *n* cacho *m (pez)*

chubbiness ['tʃʌbɪnɪs] *n* gordura *f*

chubby ['tʃʌbɪ] *adj Fam* rechoncho(a), regordete, rollizo(a)

chubby-cheeked [tʃʌbɪ'tʃiːkt] *adj Fam* mofletudo(a)

chuck[1] [tʃʌk] **1** *n* **(a)** *(tap)* golpecito *m*; **he gave her a c. under the chin** le dio un golpecito en la barbilla **(b)** *(meat)* **c. (steak)** aguja *f* (de ternera) ▸▸ ***c. wagon*** = cantina ambulante en un carromato **(c)** IDIOM *Br Fam* **to give sb the c.** cortar con alguien, *Andes, CAm, Carib* botar a alguien

2 *vt* **(a)** *(tap)* dar un golpecito a; **to c. sb under the chin** darle un golpecito a alguien en la barbilla **(b)** *Fam (throw, throw away)* tirar, *Am* botar; **c. it in the bin** tíralo *or* bótalo a la papelera; **they chucked him off the bus** lo echaron del autobús **(c)** *Fam (finish relationship with)* cortar con, *Andes, CAm, Carib* botar a

▸ **chuck away** *vt sep Fam* tirar (a la basura), *Am* botar; *Fig (opportunity)* desperdiciar

▸ **chuck down** *vt sep Br Fam* **it's chucking it down** *(raining)* está lloviendo a cántaros, *Esp* están cayendo chuzos de punta

▸ **chuck in** *vt sep Br Fam (job, studies)* dejar, mandar al diablo *or* a paseo; **sometimes I feel like chucking it all in** a veces me dan ganas de mandarlo todo al diablo *or* a paseo; **to c. one's hand in** *(at cards)* dejar una mano; *Fig (admit defeat)* tirar la toalla

▸ **chuck out** *vt sep Fam* **(a)** *(throw away)* tirar *or Am* botar **(b)** *(eject from pub, house)* echar

▸ **chuck up** *vi Fam (vomit)* devolver, *Esp* echar la papilla

chuck[2] *n Tech (of drill)* mandril *m*, portabrocas *m inv*

chucker-out [tʃʌkər'aʊt] *n Br Fam (in pub, club)* gorila *m*, matón *m*

chucking-out time ['tʃʌkɪŋ'aʊttaɪm] *n Br Fam (in pub)* hora *f* de cierre

chuckle ['tʃʌkəl] **1** *n* risita *f*; **they had a good c. about** *or* **over it** se echaron unas risitas comentando el tema

2 *vi* reírse por lo bajo; **to c. to oneself** reír entre dientes

chucklehead ['tʃʌkəlhed] *n Fam* zoquete *m*, *Esp* tarugo *m*

chuff [tʃʌf] *vi* **the train chuffed up the hill** el tren subió la colina resoplando

chuffed [tʃʌft] *adj Br Fam* **to be c. about sth** estar encantado(a) con algo; **I was c. to bits** estaba contentísimo *or* loco de contento

chug [tʃʌg] **1** *vi* (*pt & pp* **chugged**) **(a)** *(move slowly and steadily)* **the train chugged up the hill** el tren resollaba cuesta arriba; *Fam* **he's still chugging along in the same job** sigue tirando con el mismo trabajo **(b)** *Br very Fam (masturbate)* hacerse una *or Am* la paja

2 *vt Fam (drink quickly)* engullir, tragar

3 *n* **(a)** *(noise)* resoplido *m* **(b)** *Br very Fam* **to have a c.** *(masturbate)* hacerse una *or Am* la paja

▸ **chug down** *vt sep Fam (drink quickly)* engullir, tragar

chug-a-lug ['tʃʌgə'lʌg] *vt US Fam (drink quickly)* engullir, tragar

chukka ['tʃʌkə], **chukker** ['tʃʌkə(r)] *n Sport (in polo)* tiempo *m*, periodo *m*

chum[1] [tʃʌm] *n Fam* amiguete(a) *m,f*; **listen, c., you'd better watch it!** ¡eh, amigo *or Esp* tío, ya puedes andarte con cuidado!

▸ **chum up** *vi Fam* hacerse amiguetes; **to c. up with sb** hacerse amiguete de alguien

chum[2] *n US (bait)* carnada *f*

chummy ['tʃʌmɪ] *adj Fam* **to be c. with sb** ir de amiguete(a) con alguien; **to get c. with sb** hacerse muy amiguete de alguien

chump [tʃʌmp] *n Fam* **(a)** *(foolish person)* zoquete *mf* **(b)** *Br* **to be off one's c.** *(mad)* faltarle un tornillo a alguien, *Esp* estar mal de la chaveta *or* azotea, *RP* estar del tomate; **to go off one's c.** perder la chaveta, volverse majara **(c)** *US Fam* ***c. change*** *(small amount of money)* unas monedillas, algo de dinerillo **(d)** *Br* ***c. chop*** chuleta *f (con hueso)*

chunder ['tʃʌndə(r)] *vi Br & Austr Fam* devolver, *Esp* echar la papilla

chunk [tʃʌŋk] *n (of wood, bread, stone)* trozo *m*, pedazo *m*; *(of time, money)* cantidad *f*; **a whole c. of the budget went on equipment** toda una parte del presupuesto se fue en comprar equipo

chunky ['tʃʌŋkɪ] *adj* **(a)** *Fam (person) (stocky)* fortachón(ona), *Esp* cuadrado(a); *(chubby)* rechoncho(a), regordete **(b)** *(food, stew)* con trozos sólidos **(c)** *Br (clothing)* **a c. pullover** un suéter *or Esp* jersey *or RP* pulóver grueso *or* gordo **(d)** *(jewellery)* grueso(a) y pesado(a)

Chunnel ['tʃʌnəl] *n Fam* **the C.** el Eurotúnel

chunter ['tʃʌntə(r)] *vi Br Fam* murmurar; **what's he chuntering about now?** ¿y ahora qué murmura?, *Esp* ¿y ahora sobre qué está cascando?

church [tʃɜːtʃ] *n* **(a)** *(building)* iglesia *f* ▸▸ ***c. architecture*** arquitectura *f* religiosa; ***c. hall*** = sala para actividades parroquiales

(b) *(as place of worship)* **to go to c.** *(Catholic)* ir a misa; *(Protestant)* ir al oficio ▸▸ ***c. service*** oficio *m* religioso

(c) *(institution)* **the C.** la Iglesia; **C. and State** la Iglesia y el Estado; **to enter the C.** *(as priest)* ser ordenado sacerdote; *(as nun)* meterse a monja ▸▸ ***the c. calendar*** el calendario eclesiástico; ***the C. of England*** la Iglesia anglicana; ***the C. Fathers*** los Padres de la Iglesia; ***the C. of Rome*** la Iglesia de Roma; ***the C. of Scotland*** la Iglesia de Escocia *(presbiteriana)*; ***C. year*** año *m* eclesiástico

churchgoer ['tʃɜːtʃgəʊə(r)] *n* **to be a c.** ser cristiano(a) practicante

churchgoing ['tʃɜːtʃgəʊɪŋ] *Rel* **1** *adj* practicante; **the c. public** la gente que va a la iglesia

2 *n* **there has been a decline in c.** ha habido un descenso en el número de personas que acuden a la iglesia

Churchillian [tʃɜː'tʃɪlɪən] *adj* típico(a) de Churchill

churchman ['tʃɜːtʃmən] *n* **(a)** *(clergyman)* clérigo *m* **(b)** *(layman)* laico *m*, lego *m*

churchwarden ['tʃɜːtʃ'wɔːdən] *n (in Church of England)* ≃ sacristán *m*

churchwoman ['tʃɜːtʃwʊmən] *n* (**a**) *(clergywoman)* mujer *f* sacerdote (**b**) *(laywoman)* laica *f*, lega *f*

churchyard ['tʃɜːtʃjɑːd] *n* cementerio *m* *(de iglesia)*, camposanto *m* *(de iglesia)*

churl [tʃɜːl] *n Literary* **don't be such a c.!** ¡no seas tan grosero!

churlish ['tʃɜːlɪʃ] *adj* grosero(a); **it would be c. not to acknowledge the invitation** sería una grosería no aceptar la invitación

churlishly ['tʃɜːlɪʃlɪ] *adv* groseramente

churlishness ['tʃɜːlɪʃnɪs] *n* grosería *f*

churn [tʃɜːn] **1** *n* (**a**) *(for making butter)* mantequera *f* (**b**) *Br (for milk)* lechera *f*
2 *vt* (**a**) *(butter)* batir (**b**) *(water)* agitar; *(mud)* remover
3 *vi* **my stomach's churning** *(because of nervousness)* tengo un nudo en el estómago

▸ **churn out** *vt sep Fam* (**a**) *(produce rapidly)* producir como churros; **he churns out novel after novel** escribe novelas como churros (**b**) *(produce mechanically)* producir como churros

▸ **churn up** *vt sep (water)* agitar; *(mud)* remover; **the propeller churned up the water** la hélice agitaba el agua

chute [ʃuːt] *n* (**a**) *(for parcels, coal)* rampa *f*; (*Br* **rubbish** *or US* **garbage**) **c.** colector *m* de basuras (**b**) *(in swimming pool, playground)* tobogán *m* ▸▸ *US* ***chutes and ladders*** ≃ el juego de la oca (**c**) *Fam (parachute)* paracaídas *m inv* (**d**) IDIOM *US* **out of the c.** desde el principio

chutney ['tʃʌtnɪ] *n* = salsa agridulce y picante a base de fruta

chutzpah ['hʊtspə] *n Fam* descaro *m*, frescura *f*

CI [siː'aɪ] *n* (*abbr* **counter-intelligence**) contraespionaje *m*

CIA [siːaɪ'eɪ] *n* (*abbr* **Central Intelligence Agency**) CIA *f*

ciao [tʃaʊ] *exclam* ¡chao!, *Am* ¡chau!

ciborium [sɪ'bɔːrɪəm] (*pl* **ciboria** [sɪ'bɔːrɪə]) *n Rel (vessel)* copón *m*

cicada [sɪ'kɑːdə] *n (insect)* cigarra *f*, chicharra *f*

cicatrice ['sɪkətrɪs], **cicatrix** ['sɪkətrɪks] (*pl* **cicatrices** [sɪkə'traɪsiːz]) *n* cicatriz *f*

Cicero ['sɪsərəʊ] *pr n* Cicerón

cicerone [sɪsə'rəʊnɪ] (*pl* **cicerones** *or* **ciceroni** [sɪsə'rəʊniː]) *n* cicerone *mf*

Ciceronian [sɪsə'rəʊnɪən] *adj* ciceroniano(a)

CID [siːaɪ'diː] *n* (*abbr* **Criminal Investigation Department**) = policía judicial británica

cider ['saɪdə(r)] *n* (**a**) *(alcoholic)* sidra *f* ▸▸ ***c. apple*** manzana *f* sidrera; ***c. press*** lagar *m*; ***c. vinegar*** vinagre *m* de sidra (**b**) *US (non-alcoholic) Esp* zumo *or Am* jugo *m* de manzana

CIF, cif [siːaɪ'ef] *n* (*abbr* **cost, insurance and freight**) CIF *m*, costo *m or Esp* coste *m*, seguro y flete

cig [sɪg] *n Br Fam* pitillo *m*, *Am* pucho *m*

cigar [sɪ'gɑː(r)] *n* (cigarro *m*) puro *m*; IDIOM *US Fam* **close, but no c.!** ¡casi, casi, pero no! ▸▸ ***c. band*** vitola *f*; ***c. butt*** colilla *f* de puro, *CAm* yegua *f*, *CAm, Ven* chinga *f*; ***c. case*** cigarrera *f*; ***c. cutter*** cortacigarros *m inv*, cortapuros *m inv*; *US* ***c. store*** ≃ estanco *m*

cigarette [sɪgə'ret] *n* cigarrillo *m*; **have you got any cigarretes?** ¿tienes cigarrillos *or* tabaco? ▸▸ ***c. ash*** ceniza *f* (de cigarrillo); ***c. butt*** colilla *f*, *Am* pucho *m*; ***c. card*** = pequeño cromo que solía venir en algunos paquetes de cigarrillos; ***c. case*** pitillera *f*, petaca *f*; ***c. end*** colilla *f*, *Am* pucho *m*; ***c. holder*** boquilla *f*; ***c. lighter*** encendedor *m*, *Esp* mechero *m*; ***c. machine*** *(vending machine)* máquina *f* (expendedora) de tabaco; *(for rolling cigarettes)* máquina *f* de liar tabaco; ***c. pack*** *or* ***packet*** paquete *m* de cigarrillos *or* de tabaco, *RP* atado *m*; ***c. paper*** papel *m* de fumar, *Andes* mortaja *f*; ***c. stub*** colilla *f*, *Am* pucho *m*

cigarillo [sɪgə'rɪləʊ] (*pl* **cigarillos**) *n* purito *m*

ciggy ['sɪgɪ] *n Br Fam* pitillo *m*, *Am* pucho *m*

ciguatera [sɪgwə'terə] *n US* = intoxicación alimentaria producida por el consumo de pescado coralino en el que se ha acumulado una sustancia tóxica

cilantro [sɪ'læntrəʊ] *n US* cilantro *m*

C-in-C [siːɪn'siː] *n Mil* (*abbr* **Commander-in-Chief**) comandante *m* en jefe

cinch [sɪntʃ] **1** *n* (**a**) *Fam* **it's a c.** *(easy task)* es pan comido; *(certain)* es cosa hecha *or* segura, es fijo (**b**) *US (for saddle)* cincha *f*
2 *vt* (**a**) *Fam (win easily)* llevarse algo de calle (**b**) *US (horse)* cinchar

cinchona [sɪŋ'kəʊnə] *n (tree)* quino *m*

cinder ['sɪndə(r)] *n* **cinders** *(from fire, volcano)* cenizas *fpl*; *(from furnace)* escoria *f*; IDIOM **burnt to a c.** completamente carbonizado(a) ▸▸ ***c. track*** pista *f* de ceniza

cinderblock ['sɪndəblɒk] *n US* bloque *m* de cemento ligero

Cinderella [sɪndə'relə], *Fam* **Cinders** ['sɪndəz] *n* Cenicienta *f*

cine ['sɪnɪ] *n Br* ***c. camera*** *(professional)* cámara *f* cinematográfica *or* de cine; *(amateur)* tomavistas *m inv*; ***c. film*** película *f*; ***c. projector*** proyector *m* de cine

cineaste ['sɪnɪæst] *n* cinéfilo(a) *m,f*

cinema ['sɪnəmə] *n* (**a**) *Br (building)* cine *m*; **to go to the c.** ir al cine; **there's nothing on at the c.** no ponen nada en el cine; **at a c. near you from Friday** en todos los cines desde el viernes ▸▸ ***c. screen*** pantalla *f* de cine (**b**) *(art)* cine *m*; **Spanish c.** el cine español

cinema-goer ['sɪnəməgəʊə(r)] *n Br* **these scenes shocked many cinema-goers** estas escenas sacudieron a muchos espectadores; **as regular cinema-goers will know...** como los asiduos *or* aficionados al cine ya sabrán...; **she's not a regular c.** no va al cine con regularidad

cinema-going ['sɪnəməgəʊɪŋ] *Br* **1** *adj* **the c. public** los cinéfilos
2 *n* **there has been an increase in c.** ha aumentado la asistencia a los cines

Cinemascope® ['sɪnəməskəʊp] *n* cinemascope® *m*

cinematic [sɪnɪ'mætɪk] *adj* cinematográfico(a)

cinematographer [sɪnəmə'tɒgrəfə(r)] *n* director(ora) *m,f* de fotografía, operador(ora) *m,f* de cine

cinematography [sɪnəmə'tɒgrəfɪ] *n* fotografía *f*

cinephile ['sɪnɪfaɪl] *n* cinéfilo(a) *m,f*

Cinerama® [sɪnə'rɑːmə] *n* cinerama® *m*

cinnabar ['sɪnəbɑː(r)] *n* cinabrio *m*

cinnamon ['sɪnəmən] *n* (**a**) *(spice)* canela *f*; **a c. bun** un bollo con canela ▸▸ ***c. stick*** palito *m* de canela en rama (**b**) *(tree)* canelo *m*

cipher, cypher ['saɪfə(r)] *n* (**a**) *(code)* clave *f*, cifra *f*; **written in c.** cifrado(a), codificado(a) ▸▸ ***c. text*** texto *m* cifrado (**b**) *(monogram)* cifra *f*, monograma *m* (**c**) *(nonentity)* **he's a mere c.** es un don nadie

circa ['sɜːkə] *prep* hacia; **c. 820 AD** hacia el año 820 d.C.

circadian [sɜː'keɪdɪən] *adj Biol* circadiano(a) ▸▸ ***c. rhythm*** ritmo *m* circadiano

Circe ['sɜːsɪ] *n Mythol* Circe

circle ['sɜːkəl] **1** *n* (**a**) *(shape)* círculo *m*; **to sit in a c.** sentarse en círculo; **we stood in a c. around him** nos pusimos en círculo alrededor suyo; IDIOM **we're going round in circles** estamos dándole vueltas a lo mismo; IDIOM **to come full c.** volver al punto de partida
(**b**) *(under eyes)* ojera *f*; **she had dark circles under her eyes** tenía ojeras
(**c**) *(in theatre)* anfiteatro *m*; **lower/upper c.** primer/segundo anfiteatro
(**d**) *(group)* círculo *m*; **c. of friends** círculo de amistades; **in artistic/political circles** en los círculos artísticos/políticos; **in certain circles** en determinados círculos
(**e**) *(in discus, shot, hammer)* área *f or* círculo *m* de lanzamiento
2 *vt* (**a**) *(draw circle round)* rodear con un círculo (**b**) *(go round)* girar en torno de (**c**) *(surround)* rodear (**d**) IDIOM *US* **to c. the wagons** preparar la defensa
3 *vi (plane, birds)* volar en círculo, hacer círculos; **the plane circled overhead** el avión sobrevolaba en círculo

circlet ['sɜːklɪt] *n (on head)* diadema *f (corona)*

circuit ['sɜːkɪt] *n* (**a**) *(electric)* circuito *m* ▸▸ ***c. board*** placa *f* de circuito; ***c. breaker*** cortacircuitos *m inv*
(**b**) *(journey around)* circuito *m*; **we made a c. of the grounds** hicimos un recorrido por los terrenos; **the Earth's c. around the Sun** la órbita de la Tierra alrededor del Sol; **he did two circuits of the track** dio dos vueltas a la pista
(**c**) *(series of venues) (for comedian, singer, sportsperson)* circuito *m*; **she's been on the c. for a long time** lleva mucho tiempo en el circuito ▸▸ ***c. judge*** juez *mf* de distrito, ≃ juez *mf* de la audiencia provincial
(**d**) *(motor-racing track)* circuito *m* ▸▸ ***c. training*** circuitos *mpl* (de entrenamiento)

circuitous [sə'kjuːɪtəs] *adj* (**a**) *(route)* **we got there by a c. route** dimos muchos rodeos para llegar (**b**) *(argument, reasoning)* enrevesado(a)

circuitry ['sɜːkɪtrɪ] *n* (**a**) *Comptr* circuitería *f* (**b**) *Elec* sistema *m* de circuitos

circular ['sɜːkjʊlə(r)] **1** *n (letter, advertisement)* circular *f*
2 *adj* (**a**) *(movement, shape)* circular ▸▸ *Comptr* ***c. reference*** referencia *f* circular; ***c. saw*** sierra *f* circular (**b**) *(for general distribution)* **a c. letter** *or* **memo** una circular (**c**) *(argument, reasoning)* circular

circularity [sɜːkjʊ'lærətɪ] *n* (**a**) *(of movement, shape)* forma *f* circular (**b**) *(of argument, reasoning)* carácter *m* circular

circularize ['sɜ:kjʊləraɪz] *vt* mandar circulares a; **all our branches have been circularized with the information** se han enviado circulares con la información a todas nuestras delegaciones

circulate ['sɜ:kjʊleɪt] **1** *vt (document)* hacer circular; **please c. the minutes of this morning's meeting** por favor pasen una circular con *or* distribuyan copias de las actas de la reunión de esta mañana
2 *vi* (**a**) *(blood, traffic)* circular; *(money)* circular (**b**) *(at party)* alternar

circulating library ['sɜ:kjʊleɪtɪŋ'laɪbrərɪ] *n US* biblioteca *f (de la que se pueden sacar libros)*

circulation [sɜ:kjʊ'leɪʃən] *n* (**a**) *(of air, blood, money)* circulación *f*; **for internal c. only** *(on document)* para uso interno solamente; **to be in c.** *(money)* estar en circulación; *Fig* **to be out of c.** *(person)* estar fuera de la circulación; **notes in c.** papel moneda en circulación
(**b**) *Med* circulación *f*, riego *m* sanguíneo; **to have good/poor c.** tener buena/mala circulación
(**c**) *(of newspaper, magazine)* tirada *f*; **it has a c. of about 20,000** tiene una tirada de aproximadamente 20.000 ejemplares

circulatory [sɜ:kjʊ'leɪtərɪ] *adj Anat* circulatorio(a) ►► ***c. system*** sistema *m* circulatorio

circumcise ['sɜ:kəmsaɪz] *vt* circuncidar

circumcised ['sɜ:kəmsaɪzd] *adj* circunciso(a)

circumcision [sɜ:kəm'sɪʒən] *n* circuncisión *f*; **female c.** ablación del clítoris

circumference [sə'kʌmfərəns] *n* circunferencia *f*

circumflex ['sɜ:kəmfleks] **1** *n* acento *m* circunflejo
2 *adj* ***c. accent*** acento *m* circunflejo

circumlocution [sɜ:kəmlə'kju:ʃən] *n Formal* circunlocución *f*, circunloquio *m*

circumlocutory [sɜ:kəm'lɒkju:tərɪ] *adj Formal* lleno(a) de circunlocuciones *or* circunloquios

circumnavigate [sɜ:kəm'nævɪgeɪt] *vt* circunnavegar

circumnavigation [sɜ:kəmnævɪ'geɪʃən] *n* circunnavegación *f*

circumscribe ['sɜ:kəmskraɪb] *vt* (**a**) *(limit)* restringir, circunscribir (**b**) *Geom* circunscribir

circumspect ['sɜ:kəmspekt] *adj Formal* circunspecto(a), *Esp* comedido(a)

circumspection [sɜ:kəm'spekʃən] *n Formal* circunspección *f*

circumstance ['sɜ:kəmstæns] *n* (**a**) *(situation)* circunstancia *f*; **you have to take into account the circumstances they lived in** hay que tener en cuenta las circunstancias en las que vivían; **in** *or* **under the circumstances** dadas las circunstancias; **in** *or* **under normal circumstances** en circunstancias normales; **in** *or* **under no circumstances** en ningún caso; **due to circumstances beyond our control** debido a circunstancias ajenas a nuestra voluntad
(**b**) *(fate)* las circunstancias; **she was a victim of c.** fue víctima de las circunstancias
(**c**) *Formal (financial situation)* **circumstances** situación *f* económica, posición *f*; **to live in reduced circumstances** haber venido a menos

circumstantial [sɜ:kəm'stænʃəl] *adj* (**a**) *Law* **c. evidence** pruebas indiciarias *or* de indicios (**b**) *Formal (description, report)* detallado(a)

circumstantiate [sɜ:kəm'stænʃɪeɪt] *vt Formal* corroborar (con datos)

circumvent [sɜ:kəm'vent] *vt Formal (law, rule)* burlar

circumvention [sɜ:kəm'venʃən] *n Formal (of law, rule)* **the c. of a rule** el burlar una norma

circus ['sɜ:kəs] *n* (**a**) *(show)* circo *m*; **a c. clown/performer** un payaso/un artista de circo (**b**) *Br (roundabout)* rotonda *f*, *Esp* glorieta *f*

cirrhosis [sɪ'rəʊsɪs] *n Med* cirrosis *f inv*; **c. of the liver** cirrosis hepática

cirri *pl of* **cirrus**

cirrocumulus [sɪrəʊ'kju:mjʊləs] (*pl* **cirrocumuli** [sɪrəʊ'kju:mjʊlaɪ]) *n Met* cirrocúmulo *m*

cirrostratus [sɪrəʊ'strɑ:təs] (*pl* **cirrostrati** [sɪrəʊ'strɑ:taɪ]) *n Met* cirroestrato *m*

cirrus ['sɪrəs] (*pl* **cirri** ['sɪraɪ]) *n Met* cirro *m*

CIS [si:aɪ'es] *n* (*abbr* **Commonwealth of Independent States**) CEI *f*

cissy ['sɪsɪ] *n Br Fam (weak male)* blandengue *m*, llorica *m*; *(effeminate male)* mariquita *m*

Cistercian [sɪ'stɜ:ʃən] **1** *n* cisterciense *mf*
2 *adj* cisterciense

cistern ['sɪstən] *n (water tank)* cisterna *f*; *(for lavatory)* cisterna *f*

citadel ['sɪtədel] *n* ciudadela *f*

citation [saɪ'teɪʃən] *n* (**a**) *(from author)* cita *f* (**b**) *Mil* mención *f* (de honor)

cite [saɪt] *vt* (**a**) *(quote)* citar; **he cited it as an example** lo citó como ejemplo (**b**) *(commend)* **she was cited for bravery** fue elogiada por su valor (**c**) *Law* citar; **they were cited to appear as witnesses** fueron citados para comparecer como testigos

citizen ['sɪtɪzən] *n* (**a**) *(of nation, state)* ciudadano(a) *m,f*; **to become a Spanish c.** obtener la nacionalidad española; **a c. of the world** un ciudadano del mundo ►► *Br* ***Citizen's Advice Bureau*** = oficina de asesoría para los ciudadanos, *Esp* ≃ OCU *f*; *Br* ***Citizens' Charter*** = iniciativa gubernamental introducida en 1991 para garantizar servicios públicos de una mínima calidad
(**b**) *(of town)* ciudadano(a) *m,f*; **the citizens of the town** los habitantes de la ciudad
(**c**) *(civilian)* civil *mf* ►► ***c.'s arrest*** = detención realizada por un civil; ***Citizens' Band (Radio)*** (radio *f* de) banda *f* ciudadana *or* de radioaficionados

citizenry ['sɪtɪzənrɪ] *n (of town, nation)* ciudadanía *f*, ciudadanos *mpl*

citizenship ['sɪtɪzənʃɪp] *n* ciudadanía *f*

citrate ['sɪtreɪt] *n Chem* citrato *m*

citric acid ['sɪtrɪk'æsɪd] *n Chem* ácido *m* cítrico

citril finch ['sɪtrɪl'fɪntʃ] *n* verderón *m* serrano

citron ['sɪtrən] *n* (**a**) *(fruit)* cidra *f* (**b**) *(tree)* cidro *m*

citrus fruit ['sɪtrəs'fru:t] *n* cítrico *m*; **they grow c.** cultivan cítricos

city ['sɪtɪ] *n* (**a**) *(large town)* ciudad *f*; **life in the c., c. life** la vida en la ciudad; *US Fam* **a c. cop** un poli urbano ►► ***c. bus*** autobús *m* urbano; ***c. break*** *(holiday)* = vacaciones de corta duración para visitar una ciudad; ***c. centre*** centro *m* de la ciudad; *Journ* ***c. desk*** sección *f* de economía; *Journ* ***c. editor*** *Br* redactor(ora) *m,f* jefe(a) de economía; *US* redactor(ora) *m,f* de local; ***c. fathers*** *(council)* gobierno *m* municipal, consistorio *m*; *US* ***c. hall*** ayuntamiento *m*; *US* ***c. manager*** = gestor contratado por un ayuntamiento para encargarse de la gestión municipal; ***c. planner*** urbanista *mf*; ***c. planning*** urbanismo *m*; *Pej* ***c. slicker*** urbanita *mf* presuntuoso(a); *Br* ***c. technology college*** = centro de formación profesional ubicado normalmente en una zona deprimida de la ciudad y con financiación empresarial
(**b**) *Br* **the C.** la City (de Londres), = el barrio financiero y bursátil de Londres
(**c**) *US Fam* **you should see the people at the gym – it's fat c.!** tendrías que ver la gente que va al gimnasio, ¡es el país de los gordos *or* es gordilandia!; **try the park, it's dope c.!** pásate por el parque, ¡es el paraíso de las drogas!

city-dweller ['sɪtɪdwelə(r)] *n* habitante *mf* de ciudad, urbanita *mf*

cityscape ['sɪtɪskeɪp] *n* paisaje *m* urbano

city-state ['sɪtɪ'steɪt] *n* ciudad-estado *f*

civet ['sɪvət] *n* (**a**) *(animal)* **c. (cat)** civeta *f* (**b**) *(secretion)* civeto *m*

civic ['sɪvɪk] *adj* cívico(a); **to do one's c. duty** cumplir con la obligación de uno como ciudadano ►► ***c. centre*** = area o complejo que acoge las oficinas administrativas de la ciudad

civics ['sɪvɪks] *n (subject)* educación *f* cívica

civil ['sɪvəl] *adj* (**a**) *(of society)* civil ►► ***c. aviation*** aviación *f* civil; ***c. defence*** protección *f* civil; ***c. disobedience*** desobediencia *f* civil; ***c. disturbance*** desorden *m* público; ***c. engineer*** ingeniero(a) *m,f* civil, ingeniero(a) *m,f* de caminos, canales y puertos; ***c. engineering*** ingeniería *f* civil; ***c. law*** derecho *m* civil; *Law* ***c. liability*** responsabilidad *f* civil; ***c. liberty*** libertad *f* individual *or* civil; ***c. list*** = presupuesto anual concedido por el parlamento a la corona británica; *Law* ***c. marriage*** matrimonio *m* civil; *Law* ***c. rights*** derechos *mpl* civiles; ***c. servant*** funcionario(a) *m,f*; ***the c. service*** la administración (pública), el funcionariado; ***c. society*** la sociedad civil; ***c. war*** guerra *f* civil; ***the C. War*** *(American)* la Guerra de Secesión (americana); *(Spanish)* la Guerra Civil (española)
(**b**) *(polite)* cortés; **that's very c. of you!** ¡qué amable de tu parte!; **keep a c. tongue in your head!** ¡ten cuidado con el lenguaje que utilizas!

civilian [sɪ'vɪljən] **1** *n* civil *mf*
2 *adj* civil; **in** *or* **wearing c. clothes** de paisano

civility [sɪ'vɪlɪtɪ] *n* (**a**) *(quality)* cortesía *f* (**b**) *(act)* cumplido *m*

civilization [sɪvɪlaɪ'zeɪʃən] *n* civilización *f*

civilize ['sɪvɪlaɪz] *vt* civilizar

civilized ['sɪvɪlaɪzd] *adj (society, behaviour)* civilizado(a); **they have real coffee in their office – very c.!** tienen café auténtico en la oficina – ¡qué refinados!

civilly ['sɪvəlɪ] *adv* con civilidad *or* cortesía

civvy ['sɪvɪ] *n Fam* **civvies** *(clothes)* ropa *f* de paisano ►► *Br* ***c. street*** vida *f* de civil *or* de paisano

CJD [si:dʒeɪ'di:] *n* (*abbr* **Creutzfeldt-Jakob disease**) enfermedad *f* de Creutzfeldt-Jakob

cl (*abbr* **centilitre(s)**) cl

clack [klæk] **1** *n (sound)* golpeteo *m*
2 *vi* golpetear; **their friendship set tongues clacking** su amistad dio mucho que hablar

clad [klæd] **1** *adj* ataviado(a) (**in** de); **c. in rags** andrajoso(a)
2 *pt & pp of* **clothe**
3 *vt Tech (building)* revestir

cladding ['klædɪŋ] *n Tech (on building)* revestimiento *m*

claim [kleɪm] **1** *n* (**a**) *(for damages, compensation)* reclamación *f* (**for** de); **to make** *or* **put in a c.** hacer *or* presentar una reclamación; **to lay c. to sth** reivindicar (la posesión de) algo; **I have many claims on my time** estoy muy ocupado; **he has a c. to the throne of France** tiene derechos sobre el trono de Francia; **his only c. to fame** su único título de gloria
(**b**) *(in insurance)* reclamación *f*; **to make a c. on insurance** dar parte al seguro; **the company pays 65 percent of all claims** la empresa paga el 65 por ciento de las reclamaciones ►► ***claims assessor*** perito(a) *m,f* tasador(ora) de seguros; ***c. form*** *(for insurance) (after theft, fire, holiday cancellation)* formulario *f* de reclamación; *(after car accident)* parte *m* de accidente
(**c**) *(assertion)* afirmación *f*; **she makes no c. to originality** no pretende ser original; **c. and counter-claim** réplica y contrarréplica
(**d**) *(piece of land)* terreno *m*, explotación *f*
2 *vt* (**a**) *(as a right)* reclamar; **to c. compensation/damages (from sb)** reclamar (a alguien) una compensación/daños y perjuicios; **he claimed all the credit** reivindicó todo el mérito; **these images instantly c. our attention** estas imágenes nos llamaron la atención inmediatamente; **to c. a prize** hacerse con un premio; **to c. responsibility for sth** atribuirse la responsabilidad de algo
(**b**) *(assert)* **to c. that...** afirmar que...; **it is claimed that...** dicen que...; **he claims to be an expert** asegura ser un experto; **I can't c. to be a close friend** no puedo pretender que soy un amigo íntimo
(**c**) *(assert ownership of) (baggage)* recoger; *(lost property)* reclamar; **the epidemic claimed thousands of lives** la epidemia segó miles de vidas
3 *vi* **to c. for** *or* **on sth** *(insurance)* reclamar algo

►**claim back** *vt sep (expenses, cost)* reclamar; **c. the money back if they don't agree to change it** si no te lo quieren cambiar pide que te devuelvan el dinero

claimant ['kleɪmənt] *n* (**a**) *(to throne)* aspirante *mf*, pretendiente *mf* (**b**) *(for social security)* solicitante *mf*; *(for insurance)* reclamante *mf*

clairvoyance [kleə'vɔɪəns] *n* clarividencia *f*

clairvoyant [kleə'vɔɪənt] **1** *n* vidente *mf*
2 *adj* **to be c.** ser clarividente

clam [klæm] *n* (**a**) *(shellfish)* almeja *f*; IDIOM **to shut up like a c.** no decir esta boca es mía ►► ***c. chowder*** sopa *f* de almejas (**b**) *US Fam (dollar)* dólar *m*

►**clam up** (*pt & pp* **clammed**) *vi Fam* no decir esta boca es mía *or* ni mú

clambake ['klæmbeɪk] *n US* (**a**) *(picnic)* = picnic en la playa en el que se preparan almejas (**b**) *(party)* fiesta *f*

clamber ['klæmbə(r)] *vi* trepar (**up** *or* **over** por)

clammy ['klæmɪ] *adj (weather, walls)* húmedo(a); **his hands were c.** tenía las manos húmedas y frías

clamor *US* = **clamour**

clamorous ['klæmərəs] *adj* (**a**) *(crowd)* vociferante (**b**) *(protest, complaint)* vehemente

clamour, *US* **clamor** ['klæmə(r)] **1** *n* (**a**) *(noise)* griterío *m*, clamor *m* (**b**) *(demands)* demandas *fpl* (**for** de); *(protest)* protestas *fpl*; **a c. of protest** una oleada de protestas
2 *vi (make noise)* clamar; **to c. for sth** *(demand)* clamar por algo; **the children clamoured to go out** los niños pedían salir a gritos

clamp [klæmp] **1** *n* (**a**) *(of vice)* mordaza *f*, abrazadera *f* (**b**) *Med* pinza *f* quirúrgica, clamp *m* (**c**) **(wheel) c.** *(for car)* cepo *m* (**d**) *Br (for potatoes)* = montón formado por patatas cultivadas y cubierto con paja y tierra para protegerlo de los rigores del invierno
2 *vt* (**a**) *(fasten)* sujetar (**to** a) (**b**) *(car)* poner un cepo a (**c**) *(curfew, restrictions)* imponer; **the authorities clamped a curfew on the town** las autoridades impusieron el toque de queda en la ciudad

►**clamp down on** *vt insep Fam (people, tax evasion, violence)* tomar medidas contundentes contra; **to c. down on inflation** tomar medidas contundentes contra la inflación, poner coto a la inflación

clampdown ['klæmpdaʊn] *n Fam* medidas *fpl* contundentes (**on** contra); **there has been a c. on credit** ha habido una reducción drástica de los créditos

clamworm ['klæmwɜ:m] *n US* = gusano utilizado como cebo

clan [klæn] *n* clan *m*

clandestine [klæn'destɪn] *adj* clandestino(a)

clandestinely [klæn'destɪnlɪ] *adv* clandestinamente, de forma clandestina

clang [klæŋ] **1** *n* ruido *m* metálico, estrépito *m*
2 *vi (bell)* repicar; **the gate clanged shut** la verja se cerró con gran estrépito

clanger ['klæŋə(r)] *n Br Fam* metedura *f or Am* metida *f* de pata, patinazo *m*; IDIOM **to drop a c.** meter la pata

clangour, *US* **clangor** ['klæŋgə(r)] *n Formal* ruido *m* metálico; **the c. of the bells was driving him mad** el repicar de las campanas lo estaba volviendo loco

clank ['klæŋk] **1** *n* sonido *m* metálico
2 *vt* hacer ruido con
3 *vi* **the chains clanked** las cadenas produjeron un sonido metálico

clannish ['klænɪʃ] *adj Pej (group, person)* exclusivista, cerrado(a)

clansman ['klænzmən] *n* miembro *m* de un clan

clanswoman ['klænzwʊmən] *n* miembra *f* de un clan

clap [klæp] **1** *n* (**a**) *(with hands)* aplauso *m*; **to give sb a c.** *(applaud)* aplaudir a alguien (**b**) *(pat)* palmada *f* (**c**) *(noise)* **a c. of thunder** el estampido de un trueno (**d**) *very Fam (venereal disease)* **the c.** gonorrea; **to have (a dose of) the c.** haber agarrado *or Esp* pillado la gonorrea
2 *vt* (*pt & pp* **clapped**) (**a**) *(applaud)* aplaudir; **to c. one's hands** *(to applaud)* aplaudir; *(to get attention, mark rhythm)* dar palmadas
(**b**) *(pat, slap)* **to c. sb on the back** dar a alguien una palmada en la espalda
(**c**) *(put)* **he clapped his hat on** se encasquetó el sombrero; *Fam* **to c. sb in prison** *Esp* enchironar a alguien, meter *Méx* en el bote *or RP* en cana a alguien; *Fam* **to c. eyes on sth/sb** ver algo/a alguien; **the minute she clapped eyes on him** en el momento en que lo vio *or* le echó el ojo
3 *vi (applaud)* aplaudir; *(to get attention, to mark rhythm)* dar palmadas

clapboard ['klæpbɔ:d] *n* tablón *m* (de madera); **a c. house** una casa de tablones de madera

Clapham ['klæpəm] *n* IDIOM *Br* **the man on the C. omnibus** el hombre de la calle

clapometer [klæ'pɒmɪtə(r)] *n* = aparato utilizado en concursos televisivos para medir la intensidad de los aplausos de la audiencia

clapped-out [klæpt'aʊt] *adj Br Fam (person)* rendido(a), hecho(a) polvo; *(car, machine)* destartalado(a), *Esp* cascado(a), *Méx* jodido(a); **to be c.** estar destartalado(a) *or Esp* cascado(a) *or Méx* jodido(a)

clapper ['klæpə(r)] *n* (**a**) *(of bell)* badajo *m* (**b**) *Br Fam* **to run/work like the clappers** correr/trabajar como un condenado(a)

clapperboard ['klæpəbɔ:d] *n Cin* claqueta *f*

clapping ['klæpɪŋ] *n (applause)* aplausos *mpl*

claptrap ['klæptræp] *n Fam* majaderías *fpl*, *Am* huevadas *fpl*, *Am* pendejadas *fpl*

claque [klæk] *n* (**a**) *Theat (for applause)* claque *m* (**b**) *(group of admirers)* claque *m*

claret ['klærət] **1** *n (wine, colour)* burdeos *m inv*
2 *adj (colour)* burdeos

clarification [klærɪfɪ'keɪʃən] *n (explanation)* aclaración *f*; **to ask for c.** pedir una aclaración

clarify ['klærɪfaɪ] **1** *vt* (**a**) *(explain)* aclarar; **to c. sb's mind on sth** aclarar algo a alguien (**b**) *(butter)* clarificar
2 *vi* (**a**) *(matter, situation)* aclararse (**b**) *(butter)* clarificarse

clarinet [klærɪ'net] *n* clarinete *m*

clarinettist [klærɪ'netɪst] *n* clarinetista *mf*

clarion ['klærɪən] *n Hist* clarín *m*; *Fig* **a c. call** una llamada inequívoca

clarity ['klærɪtɪ] *n* (**a**) *(of explanation, text, style)* claridad *f*; **c. of mind** claridad de ideas (**b**) *(of liquid)* claridad *f* (**c**) *(of sound, image)* claridad *f*

clash [klæʃ] **1** *n* (**a**) *(conflict) (of interests)* conflicto *m*; *(of opinions)* discrepancia *f*; *(of ideas)* confrontación *f*; **he was wearing green trousers and a pink sweater – what a terrible c.!** llevaba pantalones verdes y un suéter rosa – ¡qué combinación tan horrible!
(**b**) *(between people, troops)* enfrentamiento *m*, choque *m*; **there have been clashes in the streets** ha habido enfrentamientos callejeros

(c) *(of events, appointments)* coincidencia *f*; **there's a c. in my diary on Friday, could we move our meeting to Monday?** el viernes tengo algo a la misma hora, ¿podríamos cambiar la reunión al lunes?

(d) *(of metal objects)* **the c. of swords/cymbals** el sonido del choque de las espadas/los platillos

(e) *Sport (between teams)* choque *m*

2 *vi* (a) *(be incompatible) (evidence, explanations)* contradecirse; *(interests)* entrar en conflicto; *(colours, designs)* no pegar, desentonar; **the wallpaper clashes with the carpet** el papel no pega con la *Esp* moqueta *or Am* alfombra; **that shirt clashes with your trousers** esa camisa desentona *or* no pega con los pantalones

(b) *(come into conflict)* enfrentarse (**with** con *or* a); **police clashed with protesters** la policía se enfrentó con *or* a los manifestantes, hubo enfrentamientos entre la policía y los manifestantes

(c) *(appointments, events)* **to c. with** coincidir con

(d) *(metal objects)* entrechocarse

3 *vt (metallic objects)* entrechocar

clasp [klɑːsp] 1 *n* (a) *(on necklace, handbag)* broche *m*, cierre *m* ►► ***c. knife*** navaja *f* (b) *(hold)* **a hand c.** un apretón de manos

2 *vt (grip)* agarrar; *(embrace)* estrechar; **to c. sb in one's arms** estrechar a alguien entre los brazos; **to clasp sth to one's breast** estrechar algo contra el pecho; **to c. sb's hand** agarrar a alguien de la mano

class [klɑːs] 1 *n* (a) *(social group)* clase *f* ►► ***c. struggle*** lucha *f* de clases; ***c. system*** sistema *m* de clases; ***c. war*** guerra *f* de clase

(b) *(lesson)* clase *f*; **I've got a history c. now** ahora tengo clase de historia; **she's taking classes in mathematics** está haciendo un curso de matemáticas; **before/after c.** antes/después de clase

(c) *(group of students)* clase *f*; **she's in my c. for French** está en mi clase de francés; **the c. of '91** la promoción del '91

(d) *(category)* clase *f*; *Fig* **to be in a c. of one's own** constituir una clase aparte

(e) *(in transport)* clase *f*; **first/second c.** primera/segunda clase

(f) *(stylishness)* clase *f*; **to have a lot of c.** tener mucha clase

(g) *US Law* **c. action (suit)** = acción civil ejercida conjuntamente por varios afectados en representación propia y de terceros

2 *vt (classify)* catalogar (**as** como)

3 *adj Fam (excellent)* **a c. hi-fi** un equipo de alta fidelidad de categoría; **to be a c. act** *(person)* tener un toque de distinción

class-conscious [ˈklɑːsˈkɒnʃəs] *adj Pej* clasista

class-consciousness [ˈklɑːsˈkɒnʃəsnɪs] *n* conciencia *f* de clase

classic [ˈklæsɪk] 1 *n* (a) *(book, movie)* clásico *m* (b) *Sch & Univ* **classics** (lenguas *fpl*) clásicas *fpl* (c) *Fam* **it was a c.!** *Esp* ¡fue la pera *or* la monda!, *Méx* ¡estuvo padrísimo!, *RP* ¡fue de lo mejor! (d) *Sport* (prueba *f*) clásica *f*

2 *adj* (a) *(outstanding)* clásico(a) (b) *(typical, representative)* **a c. example** un ejemplo típico (c) *(traditional)* clásico(a) ►► ***c. car*** automóvil *m* de época *(especialmente de entre 1925 y 1942)* (d) *Fam* **it was c.!** *Esp* ¡fue la pera *or* la monda!, *Méx* ¡estuvo padrísimo!, *RP* ¡fue de lo mejor!

classical [ˈklæsɪkəl] *adj* (a) *(traditional)* clásico(a) ►► ***c. ballet*** danza *f* clásica; ***c. music*** música *f* clásica (b) *(of ancient Greece, Rome)* clásico(a); **C. Latin/Greek** latín/griego clásico; **in c. times** en tiempos de los clásicos

classically [ˈklæsɪkəlɪ] *adv (trained, educated)* a la manera clásica; **she's not c. beautiful, but she's very attractive** no es bella a la manera clásica, pero es muy atractiva

classicism [ˈklæsɪsɪzəm] *n* clasicismo *m*

classicist [ˈklæsɪsɪst] *n* estudiante *mf* de clásicas

classifiable [ˈklæsɪfaɪəbəl] *adj* **most of her work is c. as fiction** la mayor parte de su obra se puede clasificar como ficción; **his work is not easily c.** su obra es difícil de clasificar

classification [klæsɪfɪˈkeɪʃən] *n* (a) *(action)* clasificación *f* (b) *(category)* clasificación *f* (c) *Br (of movies)* clasificación *f*

classified [ˈklæsɪfaɪd] 1 *adj* (a) ***c. advertisements*** *or* ***ads*** *(in newspaper)* anuncios *mpl* por palabras, anuncios *mpl* breves (b) *(secret)* reservado(a), confidencial

2 *n* **the classifieds** *(in newspaper)* los anuncios por palabras, los anuncios breves

classify [ˈklæsɪfaɪ] *vt* (a) *(categorize)* clasificar (b) *(documents, information)* clasificar como secreto (c) *Br (movie)* clasificar

classless [ˈklɑːslɪs] *adj (society)* sin clases, sin barreras sociales; *(accent)* desclasado(a)

classmate [ˈklɑːsmeɪt] *n* compañero(a) *m,f* de clase

classroom [ˈklɑːsruːm, ˈklɑːsrʊm] *n* aula *f*, clase *f*

classwork [ˈklɑːswɜːk] *n* trabajo *m* de clase

classy [ˈklɑːsɪ] *adj Fam* con clase, elegante

clatter [ˈklætə(r)] 1 *n* ruido *m*, estrépito *m*; **he sat down with a c.** se sentó con gran estrépito

2 *vt* **they clattered the bins noisily as they emptied them** armaron un gran estrépito con las papeleras mientras las vaciaban

3 *vi (typewriter)* repiquetear; **the bin clattered down the stairs** el balde rodó escaleras abajo con estrépito; **he clattered up the stairs** subió las escaleras con estrépito; **to c. about** *(person)* trastear, trapalear

Claudius [ˈklɔːdɪəs] *pr n (emperor)* Claudio

clausal [ˈklɔːzəl] *adj Gram* oracional

clause [klɔːz] *n* (a) *(of contract, treaty, law)* cláusula *f* (b) *(of sentence)* oración *f* (simple), cláusula *f*

claustrophobia [klɔːstrəˈfəʊbɪə] *n* claustrofobia *f*

claustrophobic [klɔːstrəˈfəʊbɪk] *adj* claustrofóbico(a)

clavichord [ˈklævɪkɔːd] *n Mus* clavicordio *m*

clavicle [ˈklævɪkəl] *n Anat* clavícula *f*

claw [klɔː] 1 *n* (a) *(of animal, bird)* garra *f*; *(of crab, lobster)* pinza *f*; *also Fig* **to show one's claws** mostrar las garras; IDIOM *Fam* **to get one's claws into sb** echarle el guante a alguien, *Am* pescar a alguien (b) *(of hammer)* oreja *f* ►► ***c. hammer*** martillo *m* de carpintero *or* de oreja

2 *vt (scratch)* arañar; *Fig* **to c. one's way to the top** lograr abrirse paso hasta la cima del éxito

3 *vi* **to c. at sth/sb** arañar algo/a alguien

►**claw back** *vt sep* (a) *(money)* recobrar, recuperar (b) *(regain)* **she clawed her way back into the lead** recuperó el liderato

clawback [ˈklɔːbæk] *n (sum)* reembolso *m*, devolución *f*

clay [kleɪ] *n* (a) *(material)* arcilla *f* ►► ***c. pipe*** pipa *f* de cerámica (b) *Sport* **on c.** en tierra batida ►► ***c. court*** *(for tennis)* pista *f* de tierra batida; ***c. pigeon*** plato *m*; ***c. pigeon shooting*** tiro *m* al plato

clayey [ˈkleɪɪ] *adj* arcilloso(a)

claymation [kleɪˈmeɪʃən] *n Cin & TV* animación *f* con plastilina

CLEAN [kliːn] 1 *adj* (a) *(not dirty)* limpio(a); *(air)* puro(a); **are your hands c.?** ¿tienes las manos limpias?; **wipe the bath c.** limpia la bañera; **he keeps his home very c.** tiene su casa muy limpia; **c. drinking water** agua potable; **a c. fuel/technology** *(non-polluting)* un combustible/una tecnología no contaminante

(b) *(unmarked)* **a c. piece of paper** una hoja (de papel) en blanco; **he was given a c. bill of health** lo declararon sano; *Fig* **the inspectors gave the building a c. bill of health** los inspectores dieron el visto bueno al edificio; **to have a c.** *Br* **driving** *or US* **driver's licence** no tener puntos de penalización en *Esp* el carné de conducir *or Am* la licencia para conducir; **to start with a c. sheet** *or* **slate** hacer borrón y cuenta nueva, empezar de cero otra vez; **he kept a c. sheet** *(in soccer)* no le metieron ni un gol

(c) *(morally pure) (humour, joke)* sano(a); **good c. fun** diversión sana; **keep it c., we don't want to offend anybody** sin groserías, no queremos que se ofenda nadie; **a c. game** un juego limpio; **c. living** vida sana

(d) *(clear) (shape, outline)* nítido(a); *(cut)* limpio(a); *(flavour)* bien definido(a); **the building has c. lines** el edificio tiene líneas bien definidas; **a c. break** *(of bone)* una fractura limpia; *Fig* **it would be better for us to make a c. break** *(end relationship)* sería mejor que lo dejáramos, *RP* sería mejor que dejáramos; *Fig* **to make a c. break with the past** romper radicalmente con el pasado; *Fig* **to make a c. getaway** escaparse sin ser seguido; IDIOM **he showed his pursuers a c. pair of heels** puso tierra de por medio entre él y sus perseguidores; *Fig* **to make a c. sweep** *(of prizes, in election)* arrasar; *(replace staff)* renovar a todo el personal

(e) *Fam (not in possession of gun)* desarmado(a); **they arrested him, but he was c.** *(not in possession of drugs)* lo detuvieron, pero no llevaba *or Am* tenía drogas encima; **I've been c. for six months now** *(no longer on drugs)* no me he metido nada en los últimos seis meses

(f) *Fam* **to be c.** *(innocent)* estar limpio(a)

2 *adv* (a) *(completely)* **to cut c. through sth** cortar algo limpiamente; **they got c. away** se escaparon sin que nadie los siguiera; *Fam* **I c. forgot** me olvidé completamente; **the bullet went c. through his chest** la bala le perforó el pecho

(b) *Fam* **to come c. (about sth)** *(admit the truth)* decir la verdad *or* sincerarse (acerca de algo)

3 *vt* (a) *(remove dirt from)* limpiar; **to c. one's hands** limpiarse las manos; **to c. one's teeth** limpiarse *or* cepillarse los dientes; **c. the dirt off the mantelpiece** limpia la repisa; **I cleaned the mud from my shoes** me limpié el barro de los zapatos; **to c. one's plate** *(eat all one's food)* limpiar el plato; *US Fam* **to c. sb's clock** *(attack)* partir la cara a

alguien; *(defeat)* dar una paliza a alguien
(**b**) *(chicken, fish)* limpiar
4 *vi* (**a**) *(do housework)* limpiar
(**b**) **it doesn't c. very well** *(detergent)* no limpia muy bien; *(carpet, oven)* es difícil de limpiar
5 *n* (**a**) *(wash)* **to give sth a c.** limpiar algo; **the bathroom needs a c.** hay que limpiar el baño
(**b**) ***c. and jerk*** *(in weightlifting)* arrancada *f* en dos tiempos
▸ **clean down** *vt sep (wall, work surface, table)* limpiar
▸ **clean off** 1 *vt sep* (**a**) *(mud, stain)* quitar
(**b**) *(sofa, table)* limpiar
2 *vi (mud, stain)* irse, desaparecer
▸ **clean out** *vt sep* (**a**) *(cupboard, room)* limpiar de arriba abajo
(**b**) *Fam (rob)* desplumar; *(leave without money)* dejar *Esp* sin blanca *or Am* sin un centavo; **we're completely cleaned out** estamos *Esp* sin blanca *or Am* sin un centavo
▸ **clean up** 1 *vt sep* (**a**) *(place, person)* limpiar; **to c. oneself up** limpiarse; **to c. up the seas/air** reducir la contaminación de los mares/del aire; *Fig* **the police intend to c. up the city** la policía pretende limpiar la ciudad
(**b**) IDIOMS **we need to c. up our image** tenemos que limpiar nuestra imagen; *Fam* **to c. up one's act** empezar a portarse como Dios manda, *Esp* ponerse las pilas; *Fam* **the company has been told that unless it cleans up its act it will be fined** le han dicho a la empresa que si no rectifica su comportamiento será multada; *Fam* **you've got to c. up your act!** *(give up drugs, alcohol)* ¡tienes que limpiarte!
2 *vi* (**a**) *(tidy up)* ordenar; *(wash oneself)* lavarse; **to c. up after sb** limpiar lo que ha ensuciado alguien
(**b**) *Fam (make large profits)* forrarse; *(win all prizes, medals)* arrasar

---

clean-cut ['kli:n'kʌt] *adj* (**a**) *(features, outline)* nítido(a) (**b**) *(person, image)* sano(a)

cleaner ['kli:nə(r)] *n* (**a**) *(person)* limpiador(ora) *m,f* (**b**) *(substance)* producto *m* de limpieza (**c**) **c.'s** *(dry cleaner's)* tintorería *f*; IDIOM *Fam* **to take sb to the cleaners** *(defeat)* darle un buen baño a alguien

cleaning ['kli:nɪŋ] *n* limpieza *f*; **to do the c.** hacer la limpieza, limpiar; **I've got a lot of c. to do** tengo que limpiar mucho; **c. materials** productos de limpieza ▸▸ ***c. lady*** mujer *f or* señora *f* de la limpieza

clean-limbed ['kli:n'lɪmd] *adj* alto(a) y fornido(a)

cleanliness ['klenlɪnɪs] *n (of place)* limpieza *f*; *(of person)* higiene *f*; PROV **c. is next to godliness** la limpieza ante todo

clean-living ['kli:n'lɪvɪŋ] *adj* sano(a), sin vicios

cleanly[1] ['kli:nlɪ] *adv* (**a**) *(to fight)* limpiamente (**b**) *(to break, cut)* limpiamente

cleanly[2] ['klenlɪ] *adj Literary* **a young boy should be c. in thought** un joven debería tener pensamientos limpios

cleanness ['kli:nnɪs] *n* (**a**) *(lack of dirt) (of hands, habits)* limpieza *f*; *(of water, air, fuel)* pureza *f* (**b**) *(of shape, outline)* nitidez *f*

clean-out ['kli:naʊt] *n* buena limpieza *f*, limpieza *f* a fondo

cleanse [klenz] *vt* (**a**) *(clean) (skin, blood, wound)* limpiar (**b**) *(purify)* purificar; **he was cleansed of his sins** quedó limpio de sus pecados

cleanser ['klenzə(r)] *n* (**a**) *(for household use)* producto *m* de limpieza (**b**) *(for skin)* loción *f* limpiadora

clean-shaven ['kli:n'ʃeɪvən] *adj (man, face)* (bien) afeitado(a); **to be c.** *(just shaved)* estar bien afeitado(a); *(have no beard)* no tener barba ni bigote

cleansing ['klenzɪŋ] *adj* (**a**) *(lotion, power)* limpiador(ora) ▸▸ ***c. milk*** leche *f* limpiadora; ***c. solution*** *(for contact lenses)* solución *f* limpiadora (**b**) *Br* ***c. department*** servicio *m* municipal de limpieza

clean-up ['kli:nʌp] *n* limpieza *f*; **to give sth a c.** limpiar algo

---

CLEAR [klɪə(r)] 1 *adj* (**a**) *(transparent) (liquid)* claro(a); *(glass, gel)* transparente; **c. honey** miel líquida; **a c. soup** un caldo; *Fig* **to have a c. conscience** tener la conciencia tranquila
(**b**) *(cloudless) (sky, weather)* despejado(a); **to be c.** *(sky)* estar despejado(a); **on a c. day** en un día despejado
(**c**) *(unobstructed) (road)* despejado(a); *(floor, table)* limpio(a); **the roads are c. of snow** no hay nieve en las carreteras; **make sure the corridor is c. of obstacles** asegúrate de que no haya obstáculos en el pasillo; **to have a c. view of sth** ver algo claramente; **to be c.** *(road)* estar despejado(a); **all c.!** ¡no hay peligro!
(**d**) *(not dull) (colour)* claro(a); *(complexion, skin)* limpio(a); **c. blue** azul claro
(**e**) *(distinct) (sound, image)* nítido(a); IDIOM **as c. as a bell** *(voice, sound)* perfectamente audible
(**f**) *(not confused)* **c. thinking is needed in a crisis** en un momento de crisis hay que mantener la mente despejada; **to have/keep a c. head** tener/mantener la mente despejada
(**g**) *(easy to understand) (instructions, report)* claro(a); **to be c.** *(explanation)* ser claro(a); **to be a c. speaker** hablar con claridad; **to make it c. (to sb) that...** dejar bien claro (a alguien) que...; **to make oneself c.** expresarse con claridad *or* claramente; **let's get this c.** que quede esto claro; **do I make myself c.?** ¿queda claro?
(**h**) *(obvious, evident)* claro(a); **it is c. that...** es evidente que..., está claro que...; **it is becoming c. to me that you don't care** me estoy dando cuenta de que no te importa; **it's far from c. who will win the election** no está nada claro quién va a ganar las elecciones; IDIOM **it's (as) c. as day** está más claro que el agua; IDIOM *Fam Hum* **it's (as) c. as mud** de claro no tiene nada
(**i**) *(sure)* **I wasn't c. what she meant** no me quedó claro lo que quería decir; **are you c. on** *or* **about that?** ¿lo tienes claro?; **he is quite c. about what has to be done** tiene muy claro lo que hay que hacer; **I want to be c. in my mind about it** lo quiero tener muy claro
(**j**) *(unqualified) (victory, improvement)* claro(a); **a c. majority** una amplia mayoría; **a c. profit** un beneficio neto; **a c. winner** un claro vencedor
(**k**) *(free)* **c. of** *(not touching)* despegado(a) de; *(at safe distance)* alejado(a) de; **when the plane is c. of the ground** cuando el avión haya despegado; **once you are c. of the area** una vez que estés a una distancia prudencial; **I have two c. weeks at the end of May** tengo dos semanas libres a final de mayo; **they are six points c. of their nearest rivals** les sacan seis puntos a sus inmediatos perseguidores
(**l**) ***c. round*** *(in showjumping)* ronda *f* sin penalizaciones
(**m**) *(net) (money, wages)* neto(a); **he brings home $2,000 c.** trae a casa 2.000 dólares netos; **a c. profit** un beneficio neto
2 *adv* (**a**) *(distinctly)* **reading you loud and c.** te oigo alto y claro
(**b**) *(out of the way)* **make sure the curtains hang c. of the floor** asegúrate de que las cortinas no tocan el suelo; **he pulled her c. of the wreckage** la sacó de entre los restos del accidente; **when we got c. of the town** cuando ya habíamos dejado la ciudad atrás; **stay c. of the edge of the cliff!** ¡no te acerques al acantilado!; **I'd stay c. of him if I were you** yo de ti no me acercaría a él; **to steer c. of sth/sb** evitar algo/a alguien; **stand c. of the doors!** ¡apártense de las puertas!
(**c**) *(all the way)* **the thieves got c. away** los ladrones consiguieron escapar; **you can see c. to the hills** la vista alcanza hasta las colinas
3 *vt* (**a**) *(remove)* quitar, sacar; *Comptr (data)* borrar; **could you c. those books off the table?** ¿podrías quitar *or* sacar esos libros de la mesa?; **he cleared the backlog of work** actualizó *or* puso al día el trabajo atrasado; **to c. a debt** saldar una deuda
(**b**) *(remove obstructions from) (road, area, blocked nose)* despejar; *(forest)* talar; *(pipe) Esp* desatascar, *Am* destapar; **to c. one's desk** ordenar la mesa; **to c. the table** recoger *or* quitar la mesa; **to c. one's head** despejar la mente; **to c. one's throat** carraspear; **he cleared a space for the plates** hizo un hueco *or* espacio para los platos, *Andes* hizo campo para los platos; **the police cleared the square of demonstrators** la policía despejó la plaza de manifestantes; **the judge cleared the court** el juez mandó desalojar la sala; **to c. a path through the crowd** abrirse camino entre la multitud; IDIOM **to c. the decks** ponerse al día y finalizar los asuntos pendientes; *also Fig* **to c. the ground (for)** abrir el camino (a); *also Fig* **to c. the way (for sth)** abrir el camino (a algo)
(**c**) *(exonerate)* eximir; *Law* absolver; **to c. sb of blame** eximir de culpa a alguien; **give him a chance to c. himself** dale una oportunidad para que limpie su nombre; **they campaigned to c. his name** hicieron una campaña para limpiar su nombre; **he tried to c. his name** trató de limpiar su nombre
(**d**) *(purify) (wine, beer)* encolar
(**e**) *(refresh)* **to c. the air** *(of storm)* refrescar el ambiente; **his apology cleared the air** sus disculpas distendieron el ambiente; **I went for a walk to c. my head** *(from hangover)* me fui a dar una vuelta para despejarme; *(from confusion)* me fui a dar una vuelta para aclarar las ideas
(**f**) *(pass)* **to c. customs** pasar la aduana; **the bill cleared the Senate** el proyecto de ley fue aprobado por el Senado
(**g**) *(not touch)* **to c. a fence** *(of horseman)* sortear una valla; **the horse cleared the fence with ease** el caballo salvó la valla con facilidad; **the plane barely cleared the trees** el avión no rozó los árboles por muy poco; **make sure it clears the ground** asegúrate de que no toca el suelo
(**h**) *(authorize) (plan, proposal)* aprobar; *(cheque)* compensar, dar por bueno; **we've been cleared for take-off** nos han dado permiso para el despegue *or Am* decolaje; **I'll need to c. it with the boss** necesito el visto bueno del jefe
(**i**) *(solve)* **to c. a case** resolver un caso
(**j**) *(make profit of)* **she clears $45,000 a year** gana 45.000 dólares limpios al año; **she cleared 10 percent on the deal** se llevó un 10 por ciento en el acuerdo

(**k**) **to c. the ball** *(in soccer, rugby, hockey)* despejar la pelota
(**l**) *Com (old stock)* liquidar
4 *vi* (**a**) *(weather, sky)* despejarse; *(fog)* levantarse; **the water eventually cleared** el agua acabó por aclararse
(**b**) *(expression)* **her face cleared** su cara cambió *or* se alegró
(**c**) *(cheque)* **the cheque hasn't cleared yet** el cheque no ha sido compensado todavía
(**d**) *Com* **reduced to c.** *(on sign)* liquidación
5 *n* (**a**) **to be in the c.** *(not under suspicion)* estar fuera de sospecha; *(out of danger)* estar fuera de peligro
(**b**) *Sport* **to be in the c.** estar solo(a)

▸ **clear away 1** *vt sep (remove)* quitar (de en medio); *(tidy up)* ordenar; *(dishes)* recoger
2 *vi (clouds)* despejarse; *(fog)* levantarse

▸ **clear off 1** *vt sep (debt)* liquidar
2 *vi Br Fam (leave)* largarse; **c. off!** ¡largo!, ¡fuera!

▸ **clear out 1** *vt sep* (**a**) *(empty)* vaciar, ordenar
(**b**) *(get rid of)* deshacerse de; **they cleared everyone out of the room** desalojaron a todo el mundo de la habitación
(**c**) *Fam (leave without money)* dejar *Esp* sin blanca a *or Am* sin un centavo a; **that last game cleared me out** la última partida me ha dejado *Esp* sin blanca *or Am* sin un centavo
2 *vi Fam (leave)* largarse

▸ **clear up 1** *vt sep* (**a**) *(tidy)* ordenar; *(toys)* recoger
(**b**) *(doubt, misunderstanding, problem)* aclarar; *(mystery)* resolver
2 *vi* (**a**) *(tidy up)* ordenar; **to c. up after sb** limpiar lo que ha ensuciado alguien
(**b**) *(weather)* despejarse
(**c**) *(cold, infection)* desaparecer

---

clearance ['klɪərəns] *n* (**a**) *(removal)* eliminación *f*
(**b**) *Com* **reduced for c.** rebajado(a) por liquidación (de existencias) ▸▸ ***c. sale*** liquidación *f* (de existencias)
(**c**) *(authorization)* autorización *f*; *(of cheque)* compensación *f*; *(from customs)* despacho *m* de aduanas; **to get c. to do sth** obtener autorización para hacer algo; **the plane was given c. to land** el avión recibió permiso para aterrizar
(**d**) *(gap)* margen *m*, espacio *m*; **there was less than a metre c. between the roof of the bus and the bridge** quedaba menos de un metro de espacio entre el techo del autobús y el puente ▸▸ *US* ***c. lights*** *(on truck)* luces *fpl* de gálibo
(**e**) *(in soccer, rugby, hockey)* despeje *m*
(**f**) *(in high jump, pole vault)* salto *m* válido
(**g**) *(in snooker, pool)* tacada *f* final *(metiendo todas las bolas)*

clear-cut ['klɪə'kʌt] *adj (line, shape)* claro(a), bien definido(a); *(issue, division)* claro(a), inequívoco(a); **it isn't as c. as you think** no está tan claro como piensas

clear-eyed ['klɪər'aɪd] *adj* (**a**) *(sharp-sighted)* observador(ora) (**b**) *(perceptive)* perspicaz

clear-headed ['klɪə'hedɪd] *adj* lúcido(a)

clearing ['klɪərɪŋ] *n* (**a**) *(in forest)* claro *m* (**b**) *Fin (of cheque)* compensación *f* ▸▸ *Br* ***c. bank*** banco *m* compensador *or* de compensación; ***c. house*** *Fin* cámara *f* de compensación; *(for information, materials)* centro *m* coordinador

clearly ['klɪəlɪ] *adv* (**a**) *(to see, hear, explain, describe, think, write)* claramente, con claridad (**b**) *(obviously)* claramente; **he is c. wrong** está claramente equivocado; **they c. didn't expect us** está claro que no nos esperaban; **c.!** ¡sin duda!; **c. not!** ¡en absoluto!

clearness ['klɪənɪs] *n* (**a**) *(of explanation, text, style)* claridad *f* (**b**) *(of liquid)* claridad *f* (**c**) *(of sound, image)* claridad *f* (**d**) *(of victory)* amplitud *f*

clear-out ['klɪəraʊt] *n* **I need to give my desk a c.** tengo que limpiar *or* ordenar mi escritorio

clear-sighted [klɪə'saɪtɪd] *adj (perceptive)* lúcido(a), clarividente

clearway ['klɪəweɪ] *n Br* = trecho de calle o carretera en donde está prohibido detenerse

cleat [kli:t] *n* (**a**) *(on shoe)* taco *m* (**b**) *Naut* cornamusa *f*

cleavage ['kli:vɪdʒ] *n* (**a**) *(of woman)* escote *m*; **to show a lot of c.** *(of woman)* llevar un escote muy amplio; *(of dress)* enseñar mucho escote (**b**) *Biol (of cell)* división *f* (**c**) *Geol* exfoliación *f*

cleave [kli:v] (*pt* **cleaved** *or* **cleft** [kleft] *or* **clove** [kləʊv], *pp* **cleaved** *or* **cleft** *or* **cloven** ['kləʊvən]) *vt Literary* hendir, partir en dos

▸ **cleave through** *vt insep (slice)* penetrar, atravesar; **the police cleaved through the crowd** la policía se abrió camino a través de la multitud; **to c. through the waves** surcar las olas

▸ **cleave to** (*pt & pp* **cleaved**) *vt insep Formal* aferrarse a

cleaver ['kli:və(r)] *n* cuchillo *m* de carnicero, tajadera *f*

clef [klef] *n Mus* clave *f*

cleft [kleft] **1** *n* grieta *f*, hendidura *f*
2 *adj* hendido(a); **to have a c. chin** tener la barbilla hundida; **to have a c. palate** tener fisura de paladar; IDIOM **to be (caught) in a c. stick** *(in awkward situation)* estar entre la espada y la pared
3 *pt & pp of* **cleave**

clematis ['klemətɪs, klə'meɪtɪs] *n* clemátide *f*

clemency ['klemənsɪ] *n* (**a**) *(mercy)* clemencia *f* (**b**) *(of weather)* benignidad *f*

clement ['klemənt] *adj* (**a**) *(person)* clemente (**b**) *(weather)* bonancible, benigno(a)

clementine ['klemənti:n, 'keləntaɪn] *n Br* clementina *f*

clench [klentʃ] *vt (fist, jaw, buttocks)* apretar; *(grasp firmly)* agarrar; **to speak through clenched teeth** hablar rechinando los dientes; **he gave a clenched fist salute** saludó con el puño cerrado *or* alzado

Cleopatra [kli:ə'pætrə] *pr n* Cleopatra

clerestory ['klɪəstɔ:rɪ] *n Archit* triforio *m*

clergy ['klɜ:dʒɪ] *n* clero *m*

clergyman ['klɜ:dʒɪmən] *n* clérigo *m*

clergywoman ['klɜ:dʒɪwʊmən] *n* mujer *f* sacerdote

cleric ['klerɪk] *n* clérigo *m*

clerical ['klerɪkəl] *adj* (**a**) *(administrative)* administrativo(a) ▸▸ ***c. assistant*** auxiliar *mf* administrativo(a); ***c. error*** error *m* administrativo; ***c. work*** trabajo *m* de oficina (**b**) *Rel* clerical ▸▸ ***c. collar*** alzacuello *m*

clericalism ['klerɪkəlɪzəm] *n* clericalismo *m*

clerihew ['klerɪhju:] *n Lit* = poema humorístico formado por dos pareados y que contiene el nombre de una persona famosa

clerk [klɑ:k, *US* klɜ:rk] **1** *n* (**a**) *(in office)* oficinista *mf* (**b**) *(in court)* oficial(ala) *m,f*, secretario(a) *m,f* (**c**) *US (in store)* dependiente(a) *m,f* (**d**) *Br Constr* ***c. of works*** maestro(a) *m,f* de obras (**e**) ***c. of the course*** *(in horse-racing)* = persona responsable del funcionamiento de un hipódromo
2 *vi US* (**a**) *(as assistant)* **to c. for sb** trabajar de ayudante de alguien (**b**) *(work in store)* trabajar de dependiente

clever ['klevə(r)] *adj* (**a**) *(intelligent) (person, animal)* listo(a); **she's very c. at mathematics** se le dan muy bien las matemáticas; *Ironic* **oh, very c.!** *(in response to stupid act)* ¡qué hábil!; *(in response to joke)* ¡qué gracioso!
(**b**) *(cunning)* astuto(a); **he was too c. for us** fue más astuto que nosotros; IDIOM *Fam* **she's too c. by half** se pasa de lista *or RP* viva ▸▸ *Br Fam Pej* ***c. clogs*** *or* ***dick*** sabelotodo *mf*, *Esp* listillo(a) *m,f*
(**c**) *(skilful)* habilidoso(a), hábil; **it was very c. the way he persuaded her** fue una manera muy habilidosa *or* hábil de convencerla; **to be c. with one's hands** ser muy habilidoso(a), *Esp* ser un(a) manitas
(**d**) *(ingenious) (book, movie, story, plan, idea)* ingenioso(a)

clever-clever ['klevə'klevə(r)] *adj Br Fam* **a c. remark** un comentario de sabiondo *or* enterado; **all very c., but does it tell us anything new?** todo muy ingenioso, pero nos dice algo que no supiéramos ya

cleverly ['klevəlɪ] *adv* (**a**) *(intelligently)* inteligentemente (**b**) *(cunningly)* astutamente (**c**) *(skilfully)* habilidosamente, hábilmente (**d**) *(ingeniously)* ingeniosamente

cleverness ['klevənɪs] *n (of person, plan)* inteligencia *f*

clew ['klu:] *n Naut* puño *m* de la escota

cliché ['kli:ʃeɪ] *n (idea, phrase)* tópico *m*, lugar *m* común, cliché *m*

clichéd ['kli:ʃeɪd] *adj* tópico(a); **the characters are very c.** los personajes están muy esterotipados; **a c. comment** *or* **remark** un tópico, un lugar común, un cliché

cliché-ridden ['kli:ʃeɪ'rɪdən] *adj* lleno(a) de tópicos *or* lugares comunes *or* clichés

click ['klɪk] **1** *n* (**a**) *(of fingers, tongue)* chasquido *m* (**b**) *(of button)* clic *m* (**c**) *Comptr* clic *m* (**d**) ***c. beetle*** baticabeza *m*
2 *vt* **to c. one's fingers** chasquear los dedos; **to c. one's heels** dar un taconazo; **to c. one's tongue** chasquear la lengua
3 *vi* (**a**) *(make a sound)* hacer clic (**b**) *Comptr* hacer clic (**on** en); **c.-and-drag** hacer clic y arrastrar (**c**) *Fam (become clear)* **suddenly it clicked** de pronto caí en la cuenta (**d**) *Fam (get on well)* **they clicked at once** se entendieron desde el primer momento (**e**) *Fam (be a success)* **to c. with the public** *(play, movie)* conectar con el público

clickable ['klɪkəbəl] *adj Comptr* ▸▸ ***c. image*** imagen *f* interactiva; ***c. image map*** mapa *m* interactivo

clickety-click ['klɪkətɪ'klɪk] *n* traqueteo *m*

client ['klaɪənt] *n* (**a**) *(customer)* cliente(a) *m,f* ▸▸ ***c. base*** base *f* de clientes; ***c. state*** estado *m* satélite (**b**) *Comptr* cliente *m* ▸▸ ***c./server model*** modelo *m* cliente/servidor

clientele [kli:ɒn'tel] *n* clientela *f*

cliff [klɪf] *n* acantilado *m* ▸▸ ***c. face*** ladera *f* del acantilado

cliffhanger ['klɪfhæŋə(r)] *n* **the movie was a real c.** la película tenía mucho *Esp* suspense *or Am* suspenso; **the election was a real c.** no se supo quién ganaría las elecciones hasta el último momento

climacteric [klaɪ'mæktərɪk] *n* (**a**) *(critical period)* momento *m* crítico (**b**) *(menopause)* climaterio *m*

climactic [klaɪ'mæktɪk] *adj* culminante

climate ['klaɪmət] *n* clima *m*; *Fig* **in the current c.** en las actuales circunstancias ▸▸ ***c. change*** cambio *m* climático; *Aut* ***c. control*** climatizador *m*; ***c. range*** régimen *m* climático

climatic [klaɪ'mætɪk] *adj* climático(a) ▸▸ ***c. zone*** zona *f* climática

climatological ['klaɪmətə'lɒdʒɪkəl] *adj* climatológico(a)

climatology [klaɪmə'tɒlədʒɪ] *n* climatología *f*

climax ['klaɪmæks] **1** *n* (**a**) *(peak)* clímax *m inv*, momento *m* culminante (**b**) *(sexual)* orgasmo *m*

2 *vt* culminar (**with** con)

3 *vi* (**a**) *(film, story)* culminar (**with** con) (**b**) *(reach orgasm)* llegar al orgasmo

climb [klaɪm] **1** *n* (**a**) *(on foot) (up hill)* ascensión *f*, subida *f*; *(of mountaineer)* escalada *f*; **it's quite a c.** hay una buena subida; **it's a steep c.** es una cuesta *or* subida muy empinada (**b**) *(in car, on bicycle)* subida *f*, ascenso *m* (**c**) *(of aircraft)* subida *f*, ascenso *m*

2 *vt (tree)* subir a, trepar a; *(hill, ladder)* subir; *(rope)* subir por, trepar por; *(mountain, cliff)* escalar; **to c. the stairs** subir las escaleras; *Fig* **to c. the walls** subirse por las paredes

3 *vi* (**a**) *(person)* ascender, subir; *(mountaineer)* escalar; *(sun)* subir; **to c. into bed** meterse en la cama; **to c. over a wall** trepar por un muro; **he climbed out of the hole/through an opening** salió del agujero trepando/por una abertura; **to c. to power** ascender al poder

(**b**) *(road)* subir

(**c**) *(car, cyclist)* subir, ascender

(**d**) *(aircraft)* subir, ascender

(**e**) *(prices, figures)* subir

(**f**) **to c. (socially** *or* **in the world)** ascender socialmente

▸ **climb down 1** *vt insep (descend)* bajar de

2 *vi* (**a**) *(descend)* descender, bajar (**b**) *Fig (in argument, conflict)* echarse atrás, dar marcha atrás

▸ **climb up 1** *vt insep (tree)* subir a, trepar a; *(hill, ladder)* subir; *(rope)* subir por, trepar por; *(mountain, cliff)* escalar

2 *vi* subir

climb-down ['klaɪmdaʊn] *n* marcha *f* atrás

climber ['klaɪmə(r)] *n* (**a**) *(mountain climber)* alpinista *mf*, *Am* andinista *mf*; *(rock climber)* escalador(ora) *m,f* (**b**) *(plant)* (planta *f*) trepadora *f* (**c**) *(cyclist)* escalador(ora) *m,f*

climbing ['klaɪmɪŋ] *n (mountain climbing)* alpinismo *m*, *Am* andinismo *m*; *(rock climbing)* escalada *f*; **to go c.** hacer alpinismo, ir de escalada ▸▸ ***c. boots*** botas *fpl* de montaña; ***c. frame*** = en los parques, estructura de hierro o madera para que trepen los niños; ***c. iron*** trepador *m*, garfio *m* para trepar; ***c. plant*** planta *f* trepadora; ***c. stalk*** tallo *m* trepador; ***c. wall*** pared *f (en un rocódromo)*

climes [klaɪmz] *npl Literary or Hum* latitudes *fpl*, tierras *fpl*; **foreign c.** tierras foráneas

clinch [klɪntʃ] **1** *n* (**a**) *(of boxers)* abrazo *m* (**b**) *(of lovers)* abrazo *m*; **they were in a c.** estaban abrazados

2 *vt* (**a**) *(settle) (deal)* cerrar; *(argument)* zanjar; **that clinches it!** ¡eso lo resuelve del todo! (**b**) *Constr (nail)* remachar

3 *vi (boxers)* abrazarse

clincher ['klɪntʃə(r)] *n Fam* **cost was the c. in deciding which method to use** el costo fue el elemento decisivo a la hora de elegir el método; **the c. came two minutes from full time** el gol decisivo llegó a dos minutos del final

cline [klaɪn] *n* curva *f*

cling [klɪŋ] (*pt & pp* **clung** [klʌŋ]) *vi* (**a**) *(hold on tightly)* **to c. to** *(rope, person)* aferrarse a; *Fig* **to c. to an opinion** aferrarse a una idea (**b**) *(stick)* pegarse; **a dress that clings to the body** un vestido que se pega *or* ciñe al cuerpo (**c**) *(smell)* pegarse, adherirse; **the smell of smoke clings to your clothes for days** el olor del tabaco impregna la ropa durante días

▸ **cling together** *vi* (**a**) *(people)* **they clung together for warmth** se abrazaron unos a otros para mantener el calor; **new immigrants often c. together for security** los inmigrantes recién llegados suelen formar una piña para preservar su seguridad

(**b**) *(things)* **newly washed and spin-dried sheets c. together** las sábanas recién lavadas y centrifugadas se quedan pegadas; **the leaves clung together in clumps** las hojas se apelmazan en montones

clingfilm ['klɪŋfɪlm], **clingwrap** ['klɪŋræp] *n Br* plástico *m* transparente *(para envolver alimentos)*

clingy ['klɪŋɪ] *adj* (**a**) *(child)* mimoso(a), pegajoso(a); *(boyfriend, girlfriend)* pegajoso(a), empalagoso(a) (**b**) *(clothes)* ceñido(a), ajustado(a); **clothes get very c. in this humidity** la ropa se pega mucho con tanta humedad

clinic ['klɪnɪk] *n* (**a**) *(hospital)* clínica *f* (**b**) *(department, session)* consulta *f* (**c**) *Br (private hospital)* clínica *f* privada (**d**) *(consultant's teaching session)* clase *f* práctica; *Sport* clínic *m*

clinical ['klɪnɪkəl] *adj* (**a**) *Med* clínico(a) ▸▸ ***c. linguistics*** lingüística *f* aplicada a los trastornos del lenguaje; ***c. psychology*** psicología *f* clínica; ***c. thermometer*** termómetro *m* clínico; ***c. trials*** ensayos *mpl* clínicos (**b**) *(unemotional)* aséptico(a)

clinically ['klɪnɪkəlɪ] *adv* (**a**) *Med* clínicamente; **c. dead** clínicamente muerto(a); **c. depressed** con un cuadro clínico de depresión (**b**) *(unemotionally)* asépticamente

clinician [klɪ'nɪʃən] *n* facultativo(a) *m,f*, clínico(a) *m,f*

clink[1] [klɪŋk] **1** *n (sound)* tintineo *m*

2 *vt* hacer tintinear; **to c. glasses (with sb)** brindar (con alguien)

3 *vi (glasses)* tintinear

clink[2] *n Fam (prison) Esp* trena *f*, *Esp* trullo *m*, *Andes, RP* cana *f*, *Méx* bote *m*

clinker ['klɪŋkə(r)] *n* (**a**) *(ash)* escoria *f* (**b**) *US Fam (mistake, gaffe)* metedura *f or Am* metida *f* de pata (**c**) *US Fam (movie, play)* fracaso *m*

clinker-built ['klɪŋkə'bɪlt] *adj (boat)* de tingladillo

clip[1] [klɪp] **1** *n* (**a**) *(for paper)* clip *m*, sujetapapeles *m inv* (**b**) *(brooch)* broche *m*; *(for hair)* clip *m* para el pelo, horquilla *f*; *(for tie)* alfiler *m* (**c**) *(for bullets)* cargador *m*

2 *vt* (*pt & pp* **clipped**) *(attach)* sujetar (con un clip)

3 *vi* **the two pieces c. together** las dos piezas se acoplan

clip[2] **1** *n* (**a**) *Br Fam (blow)* **to give sb a c. on** *or* **round the ear** darle a alguien un *Esp* cachete *or Am* una cachetada en la oreja (**b**) *(of movie)* fragmento *m*; *(of programme)* avance *m* (**c**) *US (from newspaper)* recorte *m* (**d**) *Fam (speed)* **at a (good) c.** a toda marcha *or Esp* pastilla (**e**) *US Fam Pej* ***c. joint*** garito *m or RP* boliche *m* carero (**f**) *Comptr* ***c. art*** clip art *m*, dibujos *mpl* artísticos

2 *vt* (*pt & pp* **clipped**) (**a**) *(cut) (hair)* cortar; *(hedge)* podar; *(ticket)* picar; **c. the coupon out of the magazine** recorte el cupón de la revista; **he clipped five seconds off the record** rebajó el récord cinco segundos; IDIOM **to c. sb's wings** cortar las alas a alguien (**b**) *(hit)* dar un golpe a; *Br Fam* **to c. sb round the ear** dar un sopapo a alguien

▸ **clip on** *vi* sujetarse

clipboard ['klɪpbɔ:d] *n* (**a**) *(writing board)* carpeta *f* con sujetapapeles (**b**) *Comptr* portapapeles *m inv*

clip-clop ['klɪpklɒp] **1** *n* **we heard the c. of horses' hooves** oímos el cabalgar de los caballos

2 *vi* (*pt & pp* **clip-clopped**) **the horse clip-clopped away** se oyó el cabalgar del caballo conforme se marchaba

clip-on ['klɪpɒn] *adj* ***c. bow tie*** *Esp* pajarita *f* (de broche), *Méx* corbata *f* de moño (de broche), *RP* moñito *m* (de broche); ***c. earrings*** pendientes *mpl or Am* aretes *mpl* de clip; ***c. microphone*** micrófono *m* de solapa; ***c. sunglasses*** suplemento *m* (de sol), = gafas de sol para ponerse sobre las gafas graduadas

clipped [klɪpt] *adj (accent, tone)* entrecortado(a)

clipper ['klɪpə(r)] *n (ship)* clíper *m*

clippers ['klɪpəz] *npl (for hair)* maquinilla *f (para cortar el pelo)*; *(for nails)* cortaúñas *m inv*; *(for hedge)* podadera *f*, tijeras *fpl* de podar

clippie ['klɪpɪ] *n Br Fam Old-fashioned* cobrador(ora) *m,f*

clipping ['klɪpɪŋ] *n* (**a**) *(from newspaper)* recorte *m* (**b**) **clippings** *(from nails)* pedazos *mpl*; *(from hair)* recortes *mpl*; *(from hedge)* trozos *mpl*; **grass clippings** hierba cortada

clique [kli:k] *n* camarilla *f*, círculo *m*

cliquey ['kli:kɪ] *adj* exclusivista; **students tend to be rather c.** los estudiantes tienden a formar grupos muy cerrados

clit [klɪt] *n Vulg* pepita *f*, clítoris *m inv*

clitoral ['klɪtərəl] *adj* del clítoris ▸▸ ***c. circumcision*** ablación *f* del clítoris

clitoridectomy [klɪtərɪ'dektəmɪ] *n* clitoridectomía *f*

clitoris ['klɪtərɪs] *n* clítoris *m inv*

Cllr *Br* (*abbr* **Councillor**) concejal(ala) *m,f*

cloaca [kləʊ'ɑːkə] *n Biol* cloaca *f*

cloak [kləʊk] **1** *n* capa *f*; *Fig* **under the c. of darkness** bajo el manto de la oscuridad; *Fig* **the business was a c. for his illegal activities** la empresa era una tapadera para sus actividades ilegales
2 *vt Fig* **cloaked in darkness** envuelto(a) en la oscuridad; *Fig* **cloaked in secrecy** rodeado(a) de secreto

cloak-and-dagger ['kləʊkən'dægə(r)] *adj (movie, book)* de intriga; **a c. affair** un asunto lleno de intrigas

cloakroom ['kləʊkruːm, 'kləʊkrʊm] *n* (**a**) *(for coats, bags)* guardarropa *m* ►► ***c. attendant*** guardarropa *mf*; ***c. ticket*** vale *m* del guardarropa (**b**) *Br Euph (toilet)* servicio *m*

clobber[1] ['klɒbə(r)] *n Br Fam* (**a**) *(clothes)* trapos *mpl*, ropa *f* (**b**) *(belongings)* trastos *mpl*

clobber[2] *vt Fam* (**a**) *(hit)* sacudir (**b**) *(defeat)* dar una paliza a (**c**) *(penalize)* castigar

cloche [klɒʃ] *n* (**a**) *(for plants)* campana *f* protectora (**b**) ***c. hat*** sombrero *m* de campana

clock [klɒk] **1** *n* (**a**) *(for telling the time)* reloj *m (grande o de pared)*; **to work round the c.** trabajar día y noche; **a race against the c.** una carrera contrarreloj; **they worked against the c.** trabajaron a contrarreloj *or* contra reloj; **to put the clocks forward/back** adelantar/atrasar los relojes; IDIOM **to turn the c. back** retroceder en el tiempo; **to watch the c.** = estar siempre pendiente de la hora de finalización de la jornada laboral ►► ***c. face*** esfera *f* (del reloj); ***c. radio*** radio *f* despertador; ***c. tower*** torre *f* del reloj
(**b**) *Fam (mileometer)* ≃ cuentakilómetros *m inv*; **it's got 30,000 miles on the c.** ha hecho 30.000 millas
(**c**) *(taximeter)* taxímetro *m*
(**d**) *Comptr* reloj *m* ►► ***c. speed*** velocidad *f* de reloj
(**e**) ***c. golf*** = juego en el que hay que golpear la pelota de golf con el putter desde diferentes posiciones de un perímetro circular
2 *vt* (**a**) *(measure speed of)* medir la velocidad de; *(reach speed of)* alcanzar; *(achieve time of)* registrar un tiempo de (**b**) *Fam (hit) Esp* cascar, endiñar (**c**) *Fam (notice) (person, thing)* echar el ojo a; *(situation)* captar, cazar, coscarse de

► **clock in** *vi (at work)* fichar (a la entrada), *Am* marcar tarjeta (a la entrada)

► **clock off** *vi (at work)* fichar (a la salida), *Am* marcar tarjeta (a la salida)

► **clock on** = **clock in**

► **clock out** = **clock off**

► **clock up** *vt sep (votes, profits)* registrar; **he clocked up another ten points** anotó otros diez puntos; **I've clocked up ten hours overtime** he hecho diez horas extras; **this car has clocked up 10,000 miles** este coche *or Am* carro *or CSur* auto marca 10.000 millas

clockmaker ['klɒkmeɪkə(r)] *n* relojero(a) *m,f*

clock-watcher ['klɒkwɒtʃə(r)] *n Fam* = trabajador que está siempre pendiente de que dé la hora para irse

clockwise ['klɒkwaɪz] **1** *adj* **in a c. direction** en el sentido de las agujas del reloj
2 *adv* en el sentido de las agujas del reloj

clockwork ['klɒkwɜːk] **1** *n* **to go** *or* **run like c.** marchar a la perfección
2 *adj (toy)* mecánico(a)

clod [klɒd] *n* (**a**) *(of earth)* terrón *m* (**b**) *Fam (idiot)* lerdo(a) *m,f*, tarugo(a) *m,f*

clodhopper ['klɒdhɒpə(r)] *n Fam* (**a**) *(person)* ganso(a) *m,f*, *Esp* patoso(a) *m,f* (**b**) *(shoe)* zapatón *m*

clodhopping ['klɒdhɒpɪŋ] *adj Fam* torpe, *Esp* patoso(a)

clog [klɒg] **1** *n (shoe)* zueco *m*
2 *vt (pt & pp* **clogged***) (pipe, filter)* bloquear, atascar; *(system)* bloquear
3 *vi* bloquearse, atascarse

► **clog up** **1** *vt sep (pipe, filter)* bloquear, atascar; *(system)* bloquear; **the roads were clogged up** las carreteras estaban colapsadas
2 *vi* bloquearse, atascarse

clog-dance ['klɒgdɑːns] *n* = baile con zuecos

cloisonné ['klwæzəneɪ] **1** *n* esmalte *m* tabicado, cloisonné *m*
2 *adj* de esmalte tabicado *or* cloisonné

cloister ['klɔɪstə(r)] **1** *n* claustro *m*
2 *vt (seclude)* **to c. oneself away** enclaustrarse

cloistered ['klɔɪstəd] *adj* **to lead a c. life** no tener mucha relación con el mundo exterior

clone [kləʊn] **1** *n* (**a**) *Biol* clon *m* (**b**) *Comptr* clónico *m* (**c**) *Fam (imitator)* clon *m*, copia *f* (**d**) *Fam (homosexual)* marica *m*, mariposón *m*
2 *vt Biol* clonar

cloning ['kləʊnɪŋ] *n Biol* clonación *f*

clonk = **clunk**

CLOSE[1] [kləʊs] **1** *adj* (**a**) *(in distance, time)* cercano(a), próximo(a); **to be c. to** *(near)* estar cerca de; **we are c. to an agreement** estamos a punto de alcanzar un acuerdo; **to be c. to tears/victory** estar a punto de llorar/vencer; **they are very c. in age** se llevan muy pocos años; **to be c. on fifty** estar cerca de los cincuenta; **it's c. on nine o'clock** son cerca de las nueve; **that was c., she nearly saw me** me he librado por poco, casi me ve; **we won, but it was a c. (run) thing** ganamos por un pelo; IDIOM **he keeps things c. to his chest** es muy callado, no suelta prenda; **c. combat** combate cuerpo a cuerpo; **in c. proximity to** muy cerca de; **at c. quarters** de cerca; **he was shot at c. range** le dispararon *or Am* lo balearon a quemarropa; **this razor gives a very c. shave** con esta maquinilla se obtiene un afeitado al ras *or Esp* un afeitado muy apurado; IDIOM **I had a c. call** *or* **shave when I nearly missed my flight** me faltó un pelo para perder el avión, *Am* por un pelito no perdí el avión
(**b**) *(in relationship) (contact, co-operation, relationship)* estrecho(a); *(community)* unido(a); **there's a c. connection between the two things** las dos cosas están íntimamente relacionadas; **to be c. to sb** *(friends)* tener mucha confianza con alguien; *(relatives)* estar muy unido(a) a alguien; **a c. friend** un amigo íntimo; **a c. relative** un pariente cercano *or* próximo; **sources c. to the Prime Minister** fuentes cercanas al primer ministro; **a subject c. to my heart** un tema por el que tengo un especial interés; **to be in c. contact with sb** tener mucho contacto con alguien; **c. to home** *(remark, criticism)* personal; **an example from closer to home** un ejemplo que nos será más familiar
(**c**) *(roughly similar)* **is his name Tim? – you're c., it's Tom** ¿se llama Tim? – casi, se llama Tom; **his version of events was c. to the truth** su versión de los acontecimientos era bastante fiel a la realidad; **he bears a very c. resemblance to his father** se parece mucho a su padre; **they are very c. in ideology** tienen unas ideas muy parecidas; **it's the closest thing we've got to an operating theatre** es lo más parecido que tenemos a un quirófano
(**d**) *(thorough) (examination, attention)* cuidadoso(a); *(observer)* atento(a); **to keep a c. eye** *or* **watch on sth/sb** vigilar de cerca algo/a alguien; **to take a c. look at sth** mirar algo detenidamente; **in c. confinement** aislado(a)
(**e**) *(weather)* bochornoso(a); *(room)* cargado(a); **it's terribly close today** hoy hace un bochorno increíble; **it's very close in here** el ambiente está muy cargado, el aire está viciado
(**f**) *(contest, election, race)* reñido(a); **she came a c. second** llegó segunda muy cerca de la primera; **the result is too c. to call** es imposible saber quién va a ganar
(**g**) *(secretive)* reservado(a); **to be c. about sth** ser reservado con algo
(**h**) *Fam (miserly)* tacaño(a), *Esp* rácano(a), *Carib, Col, Méx* amarrado(a)
(**i**) *Br* **the c. season** *(for hunting)* la veda; *(in sport)* la temporada de descanso *(al final de la liga)*
(**j**) *Com & Fin Br* **c. company** = tipo de sociedad anónima controlada por un máximo de cinco socios; *US* **c. corporation** = tipo de sociedad anónima controlada por un número pequeño de socios
(**k**) *(compact) (weave, print)* apretado(a); *(grain)* fino(a), cerrado(a); *Mil* **in c. formation** en formación cerrada
(**l**) *Ling (vowel)* cerrado(a)
(**m**) *Mus* ***c. harmony*** armonía *f* cerrada
2 *n* (**a**) *(cul-de-sac)* callejón *m*
(**b**) *Br (of cathedral)* = recinto en torno a una catedral
(**c**) *Scot (of tenement)* = pasadizo cubierto que conecta la calle y las escaleras de un bloque de viviendas
3 *adv* (**a**) *(near)* cerca; **c. to** cerca de; **to come c. to death** estar a punto de morir; **to come c. to doing sth** estar a punto de hacer algo; **did they win? – no, they didn't even come c.** ¿ganaron? – no, ni de lejos; **don't get too c. to the edge** no te acerques demasiado al borde; **he lives c. to here** *or* **c. by** vive cerca de aquí; **to follow c. behind sb** seguir de cerca a alguien; **they were sitting c. together** estaban sentados muy juntos; **c. at hand** a mano; **look at it c. to** *or* **up** míralo de cerca
(**b**) *(tight)* **to hold sb c.** abrazar a alguien fuerte

CLOSE[2] [kləʊz] **1** *n* (**a**) *(end)* final *m*; **to bring sth to a c.** poner término a algo, dar por terminado(a) algo; **to come** *or* **draw to a c.** tocar *or* llegar a su fin; **we must draw the meeting to a c.** debemos concluir la reunión; **towards the c. of the century** hacia el final del siglo; **at c. of play** *(in cricket)* al final del día

(**b**) *Com* **at c. of business** al cierre del negocio ▸▸ *St Exch* ***c. of trading*** cierre *m* de la sesión
(**c**) *Comptr* ***c. box*** cuadro *m* de cierre
2 *vt* (**a**) *(shut) (door, eyes, shop)* cerrar; *(curtains)* cerrar, correr; *Fig* **to c. one's eyes to sth** *(ignore)* no querer ver algo; **to c. one's mind to sth** cerrarse a algo; *Fig* **to c. ranks (around sb)** cerrar filas (en torno a alguien)
(**b**) *(shut down) (factory, business)* cerrar; **fog has closed the airport** la niebla ha obligado a cerrar el aeropuerto
(**c**) *(end) (meeting, debate)* terminar; *(conference)* clausurar; *(case)* cerrar
(**d**) *(reduce) (distance, gap)* reducir
(**e**) *(bank account)* cancelar
(**f**) *(electrical circuit)* cerrar
(**g**) **to c. a deal (with sb)** cerrar un trato (con alguien)
3 *vi* (**a**) *(shut) (shop, business)* cerrar; *(door, window)* cerrarse; **the bakery closes on Fridays** la panadería está cerrada los viernes
(**b**) *(end) (meeting, movie, book, speaker)* terminar, finalizar
(**c**) *(wound, opening)* cerrarse; **the gap between them was closing fast** la distancia que los separaba se iba reduciendo rápidamente
(**d**) *(cover, surround)* **the waves closed over him** las olas se le echaron encima; **my fingers closed around the gun** empuñé la pistola
(**e**) *Fin* **the pound closed at $1.65** la libra cerró a 1.65 dólares; **the shares closed up/down** al cierre de la sesión las acciones habían subido/bajado con respecto al precio de salida

▸ **close down** **1** *vt sep (business, factory)* cerrar
2 *vi* (**a**) *(business, factory)* cerrar
(**b**) *Br Rad & TV* finalizar la emisión

▸ **close in** *vi* (**a**) *(night)* acercarse; *(fog)* espesarse
(**b**) **to c. in on sb** ir cercando a alguien; **to c. in for the kill** *(lion, tiger)* acercarse para matar; **the days are closing in** los días se están acortando

▸ **close off** *vt sep (area, building)* cerrar

▸ **close on** *vt insep (prey, target)* acercarse a

▸ **close out** *vt sep US (goods)* liquidar

▸ **close up** **1** *vt sep (hole, shop, wound)* cerrar
2 *vi* (**a**) *(wound, hole)* cerrarse
(**b**) *(shopkeeper)* cerrar
(**c**) *(hide emotions)* cerrarse

▸ **close with** *vt sep* (**a**) *(settle deal with)* cerrar el trato con
(**b**) *Literary (enemy)* enzarzarse con

---

close-cropped ['kləʊs'krɒpt] *adj (hair)* al rape; *(grass)* muy corto(a)

closed [kləʊzd] *adj* (**a**) *(shut)* cerrado(a); **behind c. doors** a puerta cerrada; *Fig* **he's a c. book** es un tipo misterioso; **computing is a c. book to me** la informática para mí es un verdadero misterio; **to have a c. mind** tener una mentalidad cerrada
(**b**) *(restricted) Math* **a c. set** un conjunto cerrado; *Cin* **to film on a c. set** rodar a puerta cerrada; **a c. society** una sociedad cerrada ▸▸ *Br* ***c. season*** *(for hunting)* veda *f*; *Ind* ***c. shop*** = centro de trabajo que emplea exclusivamente a trabajadores de un sindicato en particular
(**c**) *Ling (sound, syllable)* cerrado(a)
(**d**) *Elec (circuit, switch)* cerrado(a) ▸▸ ***c.-circuit television*** circuito *m* cerrado de televisión

closed-door ['kləʊz'dɔː(r)] *adj US (meeting)* a puerta cerrada; **they held a c. meeting** se reunieron a puerta cerrada

close-down ['kləʊzdaʊn] *n* (**a**) *(of shop, business)* cierre *m* (por cese de negocio) (**b**) *Br TV & Rad* cierre *m* (de emisión)

close-fisted [kləʊs'fɪstɪd] *adj Fam* agarrado(a), roñoso(a), *Am* amarrado(a)

close-fitting ['kləʊs'fɪtɪŋ] *adj* ajustado(a)

close-grained ['kləʊs'greɪnd] *adj (wood)* de grano fino *or* cerrado

close-knit ['kləʊs'nɪt] *adj (community, group)* muy unido(a)

closely ['kləʊslɪ] *adv* (**a**) *(not distantly) (to follow)* de cerca; **to c. resemble sb** parecerse mucho a alguien; **c. related/connected** íntimamente relacionado(a)/conectado(a) (**b**) *(tightly)* con fuerza (**c**) *(attentively) (to examine, watch, follow)* de cerca; **to listen c.** escuchar atentamente (**d**) *(evenly)* **c. contested** muy reñido(a) (**e**) *(densely) (populated)* densamente; **c. packed** apiñado(a)

closeness ['kləʊsnɪs] *n* (**a**) *(physical nearness)* proximidad *f*, cercanía *f* (**b**) *(of relationship, contact)* intimidad *f* (**c**) *(similarity) (of copy, translation)* parecido *m* (**d**) *(thoroughness) (of examination)* minuciosidad *f* (**e**) *Fam (stinginess)* tacañería *f* (**f**) *(compactness) (of weave)* lo tupido; *(of print)* lo apretado

closeout ['kləʊzaʊt] *n US* liquidación *f*

close-run ['kləʊs'rʌn] *adj (election, race)* reñido(a)

close-set ['kləʊs'set] *adj* **to have c. eyes** tener los ojos muy juntos

close-shaven [kləʊs'ʃeɪvən] *adj* **he was c.** se había dado un afeitado al ras *or Esp* un afeitado apurado

closet ['klɒzɪt] **1** *n* (**a**) *(cupboard)* armario *m*; IDIOM *Fam* **to come out of the c.** *(as homosexual)* salir del armario, declararse homosexual públicamente; *Hum* **many economists are coming out of the c. as Keynesians** muchos economistas están confesando sin pudor su keynesianismo (**b**) *Old-fashioned (small room)* habitación *f* pequeña (**c**) *Old-fashioned* **(water) c.** váter *m*, excusado *m*
2 *adj Fam* **c. communist/alcoholic** comunista/alcohólico(a) encubierto(a); **c. gay** homosexual no declarado(a); **she's a c. Julio Iglesias fan** le encanta Julio Iglesias, pero nunca lo confesaría
3 *vt* **to be closeted with sb** *(in meeting)* estar encerrado(a) con alguien

closetful ['klɒzɪtfʊl] *n* **a c. of dresses** un armario lleno de vestidos

close-up ['kləʊsʌp] *n* primer plano *m*; **in c.** en primer plano

closing ['kləʊzɪŋ] *n (shutting)* cierre *m* ▸▸ ***c. ceremony*** ceremonia *f* de clausura; ***c. date*** fecha *f* límite; ***c. headlines*** *(in news programme)* titulares *fpl (al final del programa)*; *Fin* ***c. price*** cotización *f* al cierre; ***c. speech*** discurso *m* de clausura; ***c. time*** *(of pub)* hora *f* de cierre

closure ['kləʊʒə(r)] *n* (**a**) *(of company, shop)* cierre *m* (**b**) *(of meeting)* conclusión *f*, finalización *f*; **to move the c.** *(of debate)* pedir la conclusión *or* finalización (**c**) *(for container)* cierre *m* (**d**) *(feeling of completion)* **the bereaved families need some sort of c.** los familiares de las víctimas necesitan llegar a un desenlace satisfactorio (**e**) *Ling* oclusión *f*

clot [klɒt] **1** *n* (**a**) *(of blood)* coágulo *m* (**b**) *Fam (stupid person)* lelo(a) *m,f*, *Esp* memo(a) *m,f*
2 *vi* (*pt & pp* **clotted**) *(blood)* coagularse

cloth [klɒθ] *n* (**a**) *(material)* tela *f*, tejido *m*; IDIOM **to be cut from the same c.** estar cortados(as) por el mismo patrón, ser tal para cual ▸▸ ***c. binding*** encuadernación *f* en tela; ***c. cap*** gorra *f* de tela *or* paño; ***the c. cap vote*** el voto de la clase trabajadora *or* obrera (**b**) *(individual piece) (for cleaning)* trapo *m*; *(tablecloth)* mantel *m* (**c**) **a man of the c.** *(clergyman)* un ministro de Dios

cloth-bound ['klɒθbaʊnd] *adj (book)* encuadernado(a) en tela

clothe [kləʊð] (*pt & pp* **clad** [klæd] *or* **clothed**) *vt* vestir; *Fig* **the countryside was clothed in snow** el campo estaba cubierto de nieve; *Fig* **the hills were clothed in mist** las colinas estaban envueltas de niebla

cloth-eared ['klɒθɪəd] *adj Br Fam Hum* duro(a) de oído

cloth-ears ['klɒθɪəz] *n Fam Hum* sorderas *mf inv*

clothes [kləʊðz] *npl* (**a**) *(garments)* ropa *f*; **to put one's c. on** vestirse, ponerse la ropa; **to take one's c. off** quitarse *or Am* sacarse la ropa, desvestirse; **to have no c. on** estar desnudo(a); **in one's best c.** con las mejores ropas ▸▸ ***c. basket*** cesto *m* de la ropa (sucia); ***c. brush*** cepillo *m* para la ropa; ***c. hanger*** percha *f*; ***c. horse*** tendedero *m* (plegable); *Fam Pej (person)* pijo(a) *m,f*, presumido(a) *m,f* con la ropa; ***c. moth*** polilla *f*; *Br* ***c. peg*** pinza *f* (de la ropa); *US* ***c. pin*** pinza *f* (de la ropa); ***c. pole*** palo *m* del tendedero; ***c. prop*** = palo utilizado para elevar la cuerda del tendedero; ***c. shop*** tienda *f* de ropa *or* de modas
(**b**) *Br (bedclothes)* ropa *f* de cama

clothesline ['kləʊðzlaɪn] *n* cuerda *f* de tender la ropa

clothier ['kləʊðɪə(r)] *n (clothes seller)* vendedor(ora) *m,f* de ropa

clothing ['kləʊðɪŋ] *n (clothes)* ropa *f*; **an article of c.** una prenda de vestir; **the c. industry** la industria del vestido *or* del textil y la confección; **c. manufacturers** fabricantes de ropa ▸▸ ***c. allowance*** asignación *f* para ropa

clotted cream ['klɒtɪd'kriːm] *n* = *Esp* nata *or Am* crema de leche muy espesa típica del suroeste de Inglaterra

cloture ['kləʊtʃə(r)] *US Pol* **1** *n* = adelanto de la finalización de un debate solicitando una votación
2 *vt* = adelantar la finalización de un debate solicitando una votación

cloud [klaʊd] **1** *n* (**a**) *(in sky)* nube *f*; **there's a lot of c. today** hoy está muy nublado ▸▸ *Met* ***c. base*** parte *f* inferior del manto nuboso; *Phys* ***c. chamber*** cámara *f* de niebla; *Met* ***c. cover*** cielo *m* nuboso, nubosidad *f*
(**b**) *(of dust, smoke, gas, insects)* nube *f*
(**c**) *(haze) (on mirror)* vaho *m*; *(in liquid)* nube *f*
(**d**) IDIOMS **to be under a c.** *(in disgrace)* haber caído en desgracia; **he left under a c.** se marchó bajo sospecha, salió por la puerta falsa *or* de atrás; **to have one's head in the clouds** estar en las nubes; PROV **every c. has a silver lining** no hay mal que por bien no venga; *Fam* **she is on c. nine** está más contenta que un chico con zapatos nuevos *or Esp* que unas castañuelas

2 *vt* (**a**) *(mirror)* empañar; *(liquid)* enturbiar (**b**) *(obscure)* nublar; **to c. the issue** embrollar las cosas; **his judgement was clouded** no podía pensar con claridad, estaba ofuscado (**c**) *(spoil)* empañar; **the news clouded their happiness** las noticias empañaron su alegría
3 *vi* (**a**) *(liquid)* enturbiarse (**b**) *(face)* entristecerse

▸**cloud over** *vi (sky)* nublarse

cloudburst ['klaʊdbɜːst] *n* chaparrón *m*

cloud-capped ['klaʊdkæpt] *adj* cubierto(a) de nubes

cloud-cuckoo-land ['klaʊd'kʊkuːlænd] *n Br Fam* **to be (living) in c.** estar en Babia *or* la luna

cloudiness ['klaʊdɪnɪs] *n* (**a**) *(of sky, day)* nubosidad *f* (**b**) *(of liquid)* aspecto *m* turbio

cloudless ['klaʊdlɪs] *adj (sky)* despejado(a), sin nubes; *(future)* despejado(a)

cloudy ['klaʊdɪ] *adj* (**a**) *(sky, day)* nublado(a) (**b**) *(liquid)* turbio(a) (**c**) *(confused)* confuso(a)

clout [klaʊt] *Fam* **1** *n* (**a**) *(blow)* tortazo *m*, sopapo *m*; **to give sth/sb a c.** dar algo/a alguien un tortazo *or* sopapo (**b**) *(power, influence)* poder *m*, influencia *f*; **to have** *or* **carry a lot of c.** ser muy influyente
2 *vt (hit)* sacudir, *Esp* atizar, *RP* mandar

clove[1] [kləʊv] *n (of garlic)* diente *m*

clove[2] *n (spice)* clavo *m*

clove[3] *pt of* **cleave**

cloven ['kləʊvən] **1** *adj* **c. hoof** pezuña *or* pata hendida
2 *pp of* **cleave**

cloven-hooved ['kləʊvən'huːvd] *adj* con la pezuña *or* pata hendida

clover ['kləʊvə(r)] *n (plant)* trébol *m*; IDIOM **to be in c.** vivir a cuerpo de rey

cloverleaf ['kləʊvəliːf] *n* hoja *f* de trébol ▸▸ ***c. junction*** (cruce *m or* nudo *m* de) trébol *m*

clown [klaʊn] **1** *n* (**a**) *(in circus)* payaso *m*; **to act the c.** hacer el payaso; **to make a c. of oneself** hacer el payaso (**b**) *Theat (in Shakespearean drama)* payaso *m*, bufón *m*
2 *vi* **to c. (about** *or* **around)** hacer el payaso

cloy [klɔɪ] *vi* empalagar

cloying ['klɔɪɪŋ] *adj* empalagoso(a)

cloze test ['kləʊztest] *n* = prueba de comprensión en la que el lector tiene que reemplazar los espacios en blanco en un texto con las palabras que faltan

club [klʌb] **1** *n* (**a**) *(society, in sport)* club *m*; **soccer/tennis c.** club de fútbol/tenis; IDIOM *Fam* **join the c.!** ¡ya eres uno más!, ¡bienvenido al club!; IDIOM *Br Fam Hum* **to be in the (pudding) c.** *(pregnant) Esp* estar con bombo, *Esp* estar preñada, *Am* estar de encargo, *Am* estar esperando a la cigüeña ▸▸ ***c. chair*** = butaca tapizada; ***c. class*** clase *f* preferente *or* club; ***c. sandwich*** sándwich *m* club; *US* ***c. soda*** soda *f*
(**b**) *(nightclub)* discoteca *f*, sala *f* (de fiestas); **the c. scene** el mundo de las discotecas
(**c**) *(gentlemen's club)* club *m* de caballeros
(**d**) *(weapon)* palo *m*, garrote *m*
(**e**) **(Indian) c.** *(for exercise)* maza *f*
(**f**) *(in golf)* palo *m*
(**g**) *(in cards)* trébol *m*; **clubs** *(suit)* tréboles *mpl*; **ace/nine of clubs** as/nueve de tréboles
(**h**) ***c. foot*** *(congenitally deformed)* pie *m* deforme
(**i**) *US* ***c. car*** coche *m* restaurante
2 *vt (pt & pp* **clubbed)** *(hit)* apalear; **he was clubbed to death** murió apaleado

▸**club together** *vi* **to c. together (to buy sth)** poner dinero entre todos (para comprar algo)

clubbable ['klʌbəbəl] *adj Br Old-fashioned* sociable

clubber ['klʌbə(r)] *n Fam* discotequero(a) *m,f*

clubbing ['klʌbɪŋ] *n* **to go c.** ir de discotecas

clubhead ['klʌbhed] *n* cabeza *f (de un palo de golf)*

clubhouse ['klʌbhaʊs] *n* = en unas instalaciones deportivas, edificio en el que se encuentran los vestuarios y el bar

clubland ['klʌblənd] *n Br* (**a**) *(nightclub area)* zona *f* de discotecas (**b**) *(area of gentlemen's clubs)* = zona del centro de Londres en la que se encuentran la mayor parte de los clubes de caballeros de Londres

clubmoss ['klʌbmɒs] *n* pie *m* de lobo

clubroom ['klʌbruːm, 'klʌbrʊm] *n* sala *f* de reuniones

cluck [klʌk] **1** *n* (**a**) *(of hen)* cacareo *m*; *(of person)* chasquido *m* (**b**) *Fam (fool)* **you dumb c.!** ¡tonto del bote!
2 *vi (hen)* cacarear; *(person)* chasquear la lengua

clue [kluː] *n* (**a**) *(in crime, mystery)* pista *f*; **her hat provides a c. to her profession** el sombrero ofrece una pista sobre su profesión; **to give sb a c.** dar una pista a alguien; **where's John? – I haven't a c.!** ¿dónde está John? – ¡no tengo ni idea!; *Fam* **he hasn't got a c.** no tiene ni idea (**b**) *(in crossword)* definición *f*, pregunta *f*

▸**clue in** *vt sep Fam (person)* informar, poner al día

▸**clue up** *vt sep Fam (person)* informar, poner al día

clued-up [kluːd'ʌp] *adj Fam* **to be c. (on** *or* **about sth)** estar muy puesto(a) (en algo)

clueless ['kluːlɪs] *adj Fam* **he's c. (about)** es un *Esp* negado *or Méx* desmadre *or RP* queso (para)

clump [klʌmp] **1** *n* (**a**) *(of bushes)* mata *f*; *(of people, trees)* grupo *m* (**b**) *(of weeds)* matojo *m*; *(of earth)* terrón *m* (**c**) *(of hair)* mechón *m* (**d**) *(sound)* **the c. of her footsteps** el ruido de sus pisotones
2 *vt (group)* amontonar
3 *vi* **to c. about** dar pisotones

▸**clump together 1** *vt* amontonar
2 *vi (trees)* agruparse; **traffic tends to c. together even outside peak times** el tráfico tiende a ser muy pesado incluso fuera de las horas punta

clumpy ['klʌmpɪ] *adj Fam* **c. shoes** zapatones

clumsily ['klʌmzɪlɪ] *adv* (**a**) *(awkwardly)* con torpeza, torpemente (**b**) *(crudely, ineptly)* burdamente, toscamente

clumsiness ['klʌmzɪnɪs] *n* (**a**) *(awkwardness) (of person, movement)* torpeza *f* (**b**) *(crudeness, ineptness)* tosquedad *f*

clumsy ['klʌmzɪ] *adj* (**a**) *(ungainly, awkward) (person, movement)* torpe (**b**) *(crude, inept) (attempt, burglary)* burdo(a), tosco(a)

clung *pt & pp of* **cling**

clunk [klʌŋk], **clonk** [klɒŋk] **1** *n* estrépito *m*
2 *vi* golpear estrepitosamente

clunker ['klʌŋkə(r)] *n US Fam* (**a**) *(car)* cafetera *f*, carraca *f* (**b**) *(failure)* fracaso *m*

clunky ['klʌŋkɪ] *adj (shoes, furniture)* basto(a)

cluster ['klʌstə(r)] **1** *n* (**a**) *(group) (of flowers)* ramo *m*; *(of grapes)* racimo *m*; *(of people, islands, stars)* grupo *m*; *(of cases of an illness)* conjunto *m*, serie *f* ▸▸ ***c. bomb*** bomba *f* de dispersión *or* fragmentación (**b**) ***c. analysis*** *(in statistics)* análisis *m inv* de conglomerados (**c**) *Comptr* cluster *m*, bloque *m*
2 *vt* **to be clustered together** *(houses)* estar apiñado(a); *(cases of an illness)* estar concentrado(a)
3 *vi* **to c. round sth/sb** apiñarse en torno a algo/alguien; **to c. together** apiñarse

clutch[1] [klʌtʃ] **1** *n* (**a**) *(grasp)* **he had us in his clutches** nos tenía en sus garras; **she had fallen into his clutches** había caído en sus garras ▸▸ ***c. bag*** *Esp* bolso *m or Andes, RP* cartera *f or Méx* bolsa *f (sin asas)*
(**b**) *Aut* embrague *m*; **to let the c. in** pisar el embrague, embragar; **to let the c. out** soltar el embrague, desembragar ▸▸ ***c. cable*** cable *m* de embrague; ***c. pedal*** (pedal *m* de) embrague *m*
(**c**) *US Fam (crisis)* **when the c. comes** a la hora de la verdad
2 *vt* (**a**) *(hold tightly)* agarrar firmemente; **she clutched her coat to her chest** apretaba el abrigo contra su pecho (**b**) *(seize)* **to c. hold of sth** agarrar algo
3 *vi* **to c. at sth** agarrarse a algo; IDIOM **to c. at straws** agarrarse a un clavo ardiendo

clutch[2] *n* (**a**) *(of eggs, chicks)* nidada *f* (**b**) *(of people)* grupo *m*; *(of things)* montón *m*

clutter ['klʌtə(r)] **1** *n* desbarajuste *m*; **in a c.** revuelto(a); **among the c. on her desk** entre el desbarajuste de su mesa
2 *vt* **to be cluttered (up) with sth** estar abarrotado(a) de algo; **his mind was cluttered with useless facts** tenía la cabeza llena de información inútil

cluttered ['klʌtəd] *adj* revuelto(a)

cm (*abbr* **centimetre(s)**) cm

Cmdr (*abbr* **commander**) comandante *mf*

CMYK ['siːemwaɪ'keɪ] *Typ* (*abbr* **cyan magenta yellow black**) CMYK

CNAA [siːeneɪ'eɪ] *n Univ* (*abbr* **Council for National Academic Awards**) = organismo británico que expide los títulos universitarios

CND [siːen'diː] *n* (*abbr* **Campaign for Nuclear Disarmament**) = organización británica en favor del desarme nuclear

CNN [siːen'en] *n TV* (*abbr* **Cable News Network**) CNN *f*

C-note ['siːnəʊt] *n US Fam* billete *m* de cien dólares

CO[1] [siː'əʊ] (*pl* **COs**) *n* (**a**) *Mil* (*abbr* **Commanding Officer**) oficial *m* al mando (**b**) (*abbr* **conscientious objector**) objetor(ora) *m,f* de conciencia

CO² (*abbr* **Colorado**) Colorado

Co, co [kəʊ] *n* (**a**) *Com* (*abbr* **company**) cía; *Fig* **Jane and co** Jane y compañía (**b**) (*abbr* **county**) condado *m*

c/o [siː'əʊ] (*abbr* **care of**) en el domicilio de

coach [kəʊtʃ] **1** *n* (**a**) *esp Br (bus)* autobús *m*, *Esp* autocar *m* ►► ***c. driver*** conductor(ora) *m,f* de autobús; ***c. party*** grupo *m* de viajeros en autobús; ***c. station*** estación *f* de autobuses; ***c. tour*** gira *f* en autobús; ***c. trip*** excursión *f* en autobús
(**b**) *(horse-drawn carriage)* coche *m* de caballos, diligencia *f*; IDIOM **to drive a c. and horses through sth** saltarse algo a la torera ►► ***c. house*** *(for keeping carriage)* cochera *f*
(**c**) *(section of train)* vagón *m*
(**d**) *US Av* **to travel c.** viajar en clase turista ►► ***c. class*** clase *f* turista
(**e**) *(of athlete, team)* entrenador(ora) *m,f*; *(of pupil)* profesor(ora) *m,f* particular
2 *vt* (**a**) *(athlete, team)* entrenar (**b**) *(pupil)* dar clases particulares a; **to c. sb for an exam** ayudar a alguien a preparar un examen (**c**) *(witness)* **the police coached the witness** la policía preparó la declaración del testigo; **he had been carefully coached in what to say** le habían indicado lo que tenía que decir

coachbuilder ['kəʊtʃbɪldə(r)] *n Aut* carrocero(a) *m,f*

coaching ['kəʊtʃɪŋ] *n* (**a**) *(of athlete, team)* entrenamiento *m* (**b**) *(of pupil)* clases *fpl* particulares (**c**) *Hist* ***c. inn*** taberna *f* de posta

coachload ['kəʊtʃləʊd] *n* **a c. of tourists** un autobús (lleno) de turistas

coachman ['kəʊtʃmən] *n* cochero *m*

coachwork ['kəʊtʃwɜːk] *n Aut* carrocería *f*

coagulant [kəʊ'ægjʊlənt] *n Med* coagulante *m*

coagulate [kəʊ'ægjʊleɪt] *vi* coagularse

coagulation [kəʊægjʊ'leɪʃən] *n* coagulación *f*

coal [kəʊl] **1** *n* (**a**) *(fuel)* carbón *m*; **a lump of c.** un trozo de carbón ►► ***c. bunker*** carbonera *f*; ***c. cellar*** carbonera *f*; ***c. dust*** polvo *m* de carbón; ***c. fire*** hoguera *f* *or* lumbre *f* de carbón; ***c. gas*** gas *m* de carbón *or* de hulla; ***c. industry*** industria *f* del carbón; ***c. merchant*** carbonero(a) *m,f*; ***c. mine*** mina *f* de carbón; ***c. miner*** minero(a) *m,f* (del carbón); ***c. mining*** minería *f* del carbón; *US* ***c. oil*** petróleo *m*; ***c. tar*** alquitrán *m* mineral *or* de hulla
(**b**) ***c. tit*** carbonero *m* garrapinos
(**c**) IDIOMS **to carry coals to Newcastle** ir a vendimiar y llevar uvas de postre; **to haul sb over the coals** echar una regañina *or Esp* bronca a alguien
2 *vi Naut* repostar carbón

coal-burning ['kəʊlbɜːnɪŋ] *adj* de carbón

coalesce [kəʊə'les] *vi (views, interests)* fundirse; *(movements, groups)* coaligarse

coalface ['kəʊlfeɪs] *n* cabeza *f* *or* frente *m* de mina

coalfield ['kəʊlfiːld] *n* yacimiento *m* de carbón; *(large region)* cuenca *f* carbonífera

coal-fired ['kəʊlfaɪəd] *adj* de carbón

coalfish ['kəʊlfɪʃ] *n* carbonero *m*

coaling station ['kəʊlɪŋsteɪʃən] *n* = puerto en el que los barcos se pueden aprovisionar de carbón

coalition [kəʊə'lɪʃən] *n* coalición *f*; **to form a c.** formar una coalición ►► ***c. government*** gobierno *m* de coalición

coalman ['kəʊlmæn] *n* carbonero *m*

coalshed ['kəʊlʃed] *n* cobertizo *m* para el carbón

coarse [kɔːs] *adj* (**a**) *(person, language)* grosero(a), basto(a); *(laugh)* grosero(a) (**b**) *(not refined) (features)* grosero(a), basto(a); *(accent)* vulgar, común (**c**) *(in texture) (surface)* áspero(a); *(sand)* grueso(a); *(salt)* gordo(a); *(fabric)* basto(a), grosero(a); **to have c. hair** tener el pelo basto (**d**) *Sport* ***c. fishing*** pesca *f* de río *(salvo trucha y salmón)*

coarse-featured ['kɔːs'fiːtjəd] *adj* de rasgos bastos

coarse-grained ['kɔːsgreɪnd] *adj* (**a**) *(rock, salt, wood, leather)* de grano grueso (**b**) *(person)* grosero(a), basto(a)

coarsely ['kɔːslɪ] *adv* (**a**) *(vulgarly)* groseramente (**b**) *(roughly)* **c. chopped** cortado(a) en trozos grandes; **c. ground** molido(a) grueso(a)

coarsen ['kɔːsən] **1** *vt* (**a**) *(texture, appearance)* volver áspero(a) (**b**) *(person, speech)* embrutecer, volver grosero(a) *or* basto(a)
2 *vi* (**a**) *(texture, appearance)* volverse áspero(a); *(features)* volverse grosero(a) *or* basto(a) (**b**) *(person, speech)* embrutecer, volverse grosero(a) *or* basto(a)

coarseness ['kɔːsnɪs] *n* (**a**) *(of person, language)* grosería *f* (**b**) *(of surface, texture)* aspereza *f*

coast [kəʊst] **1** *n* (**a**) *(of country)* costa *f*; **she lives on the c.** vive en la costa; **it's a small island just off the c.** es una isla pequeña a poca distancia de la costa; **it was broadcast c. to c.** fue retransmitido de costa a costa en todo el país; IDIOM **the c. is clear** no hay moros en la costa ►► ***c. road*** carretera *f* costera *or* litoral
(**b**) *(act of coasting)* **a gentle c. downhill** *(in car)* una sencilla bajada en punto muerto; *(on bicycle)* una sencilla bajada sin pedalear
2 *vi* (**a**) *(freewheel) (in car)* rodar en punto muerto; *(on bicycle)* rodar sin pedalear (**b**) *(progress without effort)* **she coasted through her exams** pasó sus exámenes con toda facilidad; **he's coasting** *(not working hard)* está viviendo de las rentas (**c**) *Naut* recorrer la costa

coastal ['kəʊstəl] *adj* costero(a) ►► ***c. fishing*** pesca *f* de bajura; ***c. vessel*** buque *m* de cabotaje; ***c. waters*** aguas *fpl* costeras

coaster ['kəʊstə(r)] *n* (**a**) *(ship)* buque *m* de cabotaje (**b**) *(for glass)* posavasos *m inv*

coastguard ['kəʊstgɑːd] *n* (**a**) *(organization)* servicio *m* de guardacostas (**b**) *esp Br (person)* guardacostas *mf inv*

coastguardsman ['kəʊstgɑːdzmən] *n US* guardacostas *m inv*

coastline ['kəʊstlaɪn] *n* costa *f*, litoral *m*

coast-to-coast ['kəʊsttə'kəʊst] *adj* de costa a costa

coat [kəʊt] **1** *n* (**a**) *(overcoat)* abrigo *m*; *(jacket)* chaqueta *f*, *Méx* chamarra *f*, *RP* campera *f* ►► ***c. hook*** colgador *m* (**b**) *(of dog, horse)* pelaje *m* (**c**) *(covering) (of snow, paint, dust)* capa *f*; **give it a c. of paint/varnish** dale una mano de pintura/barniz (**d**) ***c. of arms*** escudo *m* de armas (**e**) *Hist* ***c. of mail*** cota *f* de malla(s)
2 *vt* (**a**) *(cover)* cubrir (**with** de); **coated with mud** cubierto(a) de barro, embarrado(a) (**b**) *(in cookery)* cubrir (**with** de); **to c. sth in breadcrumbs** empanar *or* rebozar algo; **hazelnuts coated with chocolate** avellanas recubiertas de *or* bañadas en chocolate

coated ['kəʊtɪd] *adj* (**a**) *(tongue)* sucio(a) (**b**) *(paper)* couché, cuché

coat-hanger ['kəʊthæŋə(r)] *n* percha *f*

coati [kəʊ'ɑːtɪ] *n* coatí *m*

coating ['kəʊtɪŋ] *n (of paint, dust)* capa *f*

coatrack ['kəʊtræk] *n* perchero *m*

coatstand ['kəʊtstænd] *n* perchero *m*

coat-tails ['kəʊtteɪlz] *npl* frac *m*; *Fig* **on sb's c.** a la sombra de alguien

coauthor [kəʊ'ɔːθə(r)] **1** *n* coautor(ora) *m,f*
2 *vt* **to c. a book with sb** escribir un libro conjuntamente con alguien

coax [kəʊks] *vt* persuadir; **to c. sb into doing sth** persuadir a alguien para que haga algo; **to c. sth out of sb** sonsacar algo a alguien; **he coaxed the box open with a screwdriver** abrió la caja forzándola con un destornillador

coaxial [kəʊ'æksɪəl] *adj Comptr* coaxial ►► ***c. cable*** cable *m* coaxial

coaxing ['kəʊksɪŋ] **1** *n* persuasión *m*; **no amount of c. would get him to agree** no fue posible persuadirle para que aceptara
2 *adj* persuasivo(a)

cob [kɒb] *n* (**a**) *(horse)* jaca *f* (**b**) *(male swan)* cisne *m* macho (**c**) *(of maize)* mazorca *f* (**d**) *Br (bread)* pan *m* de hogaza, pan *m* redondo

cobalt ['kəʊbɔːlt] *n Chem* cobalto *m* ►► ***c. blue*** azul *m* (de) cobalto

cobber ['kɒbə(r)] *n Austr Fam* amigo *m*, *Esp* colega *m*, *Esp* tío *m*, *Andes, CAm, Carib, Méx* mano *m*, *RP* flaco *m*

cobble ['kɒbəl] **1** *n* adoquín *m*
2 *vt* adoquinar

►**cobble together** *vt sep Fam (make hastily)* improvisar, *Esp* apañar

cobbled ['kɒbəld] *adj (path, street)* adoquinado(a)

cobbler¹ ['kɒblə(r)] *n (shoe repairer)* zapatero(a) *m,f* (remendón(ona)); *(shoemaker)* zapatero(a) *m,f (fabricante)*

cobbler² *n* (**a**) *US (dessert)* = postre caliente compuesto por una fruta cubierta por masa quebrada (**b**) *(drink)* = refresco con jugo de frutas, vino u otra bebida alcohólica y hielo

cobblers ['kɒbləz] *Br* **1** *npl* (**a**) *very Fam (nonsense) Esp* paridas *fpl*, *Am* pendejadas *fpl*, *RP* pelotudeces *fpl* (**b**) *Vulg (testicles)* huevos *mpl*, *Esp* cojones *mpl*
2 *exclam very Fam* ¡menuda *Esp* parida *or Am* pendejada *or RP* pelotudez!

cobblestone ['kɒbəlstəʊn] *n* adoquín *m*

cobnut ['kɒbnʌt] *n* avellana *f*

COBOL ['kəʊbɒl] *n Comptr* (*abbr* **Common Business-Oriented Language**) (lenguaje *m*) COBOL *m*

cobra ['kəʊbrə] *n* cobra *f*

cobweb ['kɒbweb] *n* telaraña *f*, tela *f* de araña; *Fig* **to brush the cobwebs off sth** desempolvar algo; IDIOM **to clear away the cobwebs, to blow the cobwebs away** despejarse

coca ['kəʊkə] *n (bush, substance)* coca *f*; **c. leaves** cocas *fpl*, hojas *fpl* de coca

Coca-Cola® [kəʊkə'kəʊlə] *n* Coca-Cola® *f*

cocaine [kə'keɪn, kəʊ'keɪn] *n* cocaína *f*; **c. addict** cocainómano(a)

coccyx ['kɒksɪks] (*pl* **coccyges** [kɒk'saɪdʒi:z]) *n Anat* coxis *m inv*

cochineal ['kɒtʃɪni:l, kɒtʃɪ'ni:l] *n* (**a**) *(insect)* cochinilla *f* (**b**) *(colouring)* carmín *m*, cochinilla *f*

cochlea ['kɒklɪə] (*pl* **cochleae** ['kɒklɪi:]) *n Anat* caracol *m* (del oído)

cock [kɒk] **1** *n* (**a**) *(male fowl)* gallo *m*; *(male bird)* macho *m*; IDIOM *Fam* **he thinks he's c. of the walk** *Esp* se cree que es el amo del cotarro, *Am* se cree el patrón de la vereda ►► ***c. sparrow*** gorrión *m* macho
(**b**) *(tilt)* **a c. of the head** una inclinación de la cabeza
(**c**) *(tap)* llave *f* de paso
(**d**) *Vulg (penis) Esp* polla *f*, *Am* verga *f*, *Chile* pico *m*, *Chile* penca *f*, *Méx* pito *m*, *RP* pija *f*, *Ven* pinga *f*
(**e**) *Br Fam (term of address)* macho *m*, *Esp* colega *m*; **all right, me old c.!** ¡qué pasa, macho!
(**f**) *Br very Fam (nonsense) Esp* gilipolleces *fpl*, *Am* pendejadas *fpl*, *RP* boludeces *fpl*
(**g**) *(of hay)* montón *m*
2 *vt* (**a**) *(lift up)* **the dog/horse cocked its ears** el perro/caballo levantó las orejas; **the dog cocked its leg** el perro levantó la pata; IDIOM **to c. a snook at sb** hacer burla a alguien (**b**) *(tilt)* inclinar (**c**) *(gun)* montar, amartillar

► **cock up** **1** *vt sep Br very Fam* **to c. sth up** cagar *or Esp* joder *or Méx* madrear algo
2 *vi* **he's cocked up again** ha vuelto a cagarla *or Esp* joderla *or Méx* madrearla

cockade [kɒ'keɪd] *n* escarapela *f*

cock-a-doodle-doo ['kɒkədu:dəl'du:] *exclam* ¡quiquiriquí!

cock-a-hoop ['kɒkə'hu:p] *adj* **he was c. about the result** estaba encantado con el resultado

cock-a-leekie [kɒkə'li:kɪ] *n* = sopa escocesa de pollo y puerros

cockamamie ['kɒkəmeɪmɪ] *adj US Fam* demencial

cock-and-bull story ['kɒkən'bʊlstɔ:rɪ] *n Fam* cuento *m* chino

cockatoo [kɒkə'tu:] (*pl* **cockatoos**) *n* cacatúa *f*

cockatrice [kɒkə'tri:s] *n Mythol* = monstruo con la cabeza, patas y alas de un gallo y el cuerpo y la cola de una serpiente

cockchafer ['kɒktʃeɪfə(r)] *n* melolonta *f*

cock-crow ['kɒkkrəʊ] *n Literary* **at c.** al amanecer

cocked [kɒkt] *adj* IDIOM **to knock sth/sb into a c. hat** *(outclass)* dar mil *or* cien vueltas a algo/alguien

cockerel ['kɒkərəl] *n* gallo *m* joven

cocker spaniel ['kɒkə'spænjəl] *n* cocker *mf*

cock-eyed ['kɒkaɪd] *adj Fam* (**a**) *(person)* bisojo(a) (**b**) *(decision, plan)* disparatado(a) (**c**) *(crooked)* torcido(a)

cockfight ['kɒkfaɪt] *n* pelea *f* de gallos

cockfighting ['kɒkfaɪtɪŋ] *n* peleas *fpl* de gallos

cockiness ['kɒkɪnɪs] *n* descaro *m*, engreimiento *m*, *Esp* chulería *f*

cockle ['kɒkəl] *n* (**a**) *(shellfish)* berberecho *m* (**b**) IDIOM *Fam* **it warmed the cockles of his heart** le alegró el corazón

cockleshell ['kɒkəlʃel] *n* (**a**) *(shell)* concha *f* de berberecho (**b**) *(boat)* cascarón *m*

Cockney ['kɒknɪ] **1** *n* (**a**) *(person)* = habitante de los barrios obreros del este de Londres (**b**) *(dialect)* = habla de los barrios obreros del este de Londres
2 *adj* = de los barrios obreros del este de Londres

cockpit ['kɒkpɪt] *n* (**a**) *(of passenger plane)* cabina *f*; *(of fighter plane)* carlinga *f* (**b**) *(of racing car)* cabina *f*, habitáculo *m* (**c**) *(of boat)* puente *m* de mando (**d**) *(for cockfights)* reñidero *m*, *Col* gallera *f*, *Cuba* gallería *f*, *Méx* palenque *m*

cockroach ['kɒkrəʊtʃ] *n* cucaracha *f*

cockscomb ['kɒkskəʊm] *n* (**a**) *(on cockerel)* cresta *f* (**b**) *(plant)* cresta *f* de gallo (**c**) *Old-fashioned (upstart)* mocosa *f*

cocksucker ['kɒksʌkər] *n Vulg* hijo(a) *m,f* de puta

cocksure ['kɒkʃʊə(r)] *adj* arrogante

cocktail ['kɒkteɪl] *n also Fig* cóctel *m*; **a lethal c. of drugs** un cóctel letal de drogas ►► ***c. bar*** coctelería *f*, bar *m* de cócteles; ***c. cabinet*** mueble *m* bar; ***c. dress*** vestido *m* de noche; ***c. lounge*** bar *m* *(de hotel)*; ***c. onion*** cebolla *f* pequeña *(servida como aperitivo)*; ***c. party*** cóctel *m*; ***c. sausage*** salchicha *f* pequeña *(servida como aperitivo)*; ***c. shaker*** coctelera *f*; ***c. stick*** palillo *m*; ***c. waitress*** camarera *f or Méx* mesera *f or RP* moza *f* de bar

cocktease(r) ['kɒkti:z(ə(r))] *n Vulg* calientabraguetas *f inv*, *Esp* calientapollas *f inv*, *Col, Ven* calientahuevos *f inv*, *RP* calientapija *f*

cock-up ['kɒkʌp] *n Br very Fam* cagada *f*; **to make a c. of sth** cagarla con algo; **it was a c., not a conspiracy** fue un error, no una conspiración

cocky ['kɒkɪ] *adj Fam* gallito(a), engreído(a), *Esp* chulo(a); **don't get c.!** ¡no seas gallito!, *Esp* ¡no te pongas chulo!

coco ['kəʊkəʊ] *n Br Fam* **I should c.!** ¡y tanto que sí!, ¡ya lo creo!

cocoa ['kəʊkəʊ] *n (powder)* cacao *m*; **a cup of c.** una taza de leche con cacao ►► ***c. bean*** semilla *f or* grano *m* de cacao; ***c. butter*** manteca *f* de cacao; ***c. powder*** cacao *m* en polvo

coconut ['kəʊkənʌt] *n (fruit)* coco *m*; **c. (tree)** cocotero *m* ►► ***c. ice*** cocada *f*; ***c. matting*** estera *f* de fibra de coco; ***c. milk*** leche *f or* agua *f* de coco; ***c. oil*** aceite *m* de coco; ***c. palm*** cocotero *m*; ***c. shy*** = juego de feria que consiste en derribar cocos con una pelota

cocoon [kə'ku:n] **1** *n (of insect)* capullo *m*
2 *vt* **to be cocooned from the outside world** estar sobreprotegido(a) del mundo exterior

COD [si:əʊ'di:] *Com* (*abbr* **cash on delivery**) **1** *n* entrega *f* contra reembolso
2 *adv* contra reembolso

cod[1] [kɒd] (*pl* **cod**) *n* bacalao *m* ►► ***c. roe*** huevas *fpl* de bacalao; ***the C. War*** = enfrentamiento diplomático entre el Reino Unido e Islandia por la pesca del bacalao en aguas islandesas entre 1972 y 1976

cod[2] *Br Fam* **1** *n (hoax)* engaño *m*
2 *adj (bogus)* falso(a)

coda ['kəʊdə] *n* (**a**) *Mus* coda *f* (**b**) *(in book)* colofón *m*

coddle ['kɒdəl] *vt* (**a**) *(child)* mimar (**b**) *(egg)* **coddled eggs** = huevos cocidos a fuego lento

code [kəʊd] **1** *n* (**a**) *(cipher)* código *m*, clave *f*; **in c.** cifrado(a) ►► ***c. book*** libro *m* de códigos; ***c. name*** nombre *m* en clave; ***c. word*** contraseña *f* (**b**) *(used to identify)* código *m* ►► ***c. number*** código *m* (**c**) *(rules)* código *m*; **c. of conduct** código de conducta; **c. of practice** código de conducta (**d**) *Comptr* código *m* (**e**) *(for telephone number)* prefijo *m* (**f**) *Ling* ***c. switching*** cambio *m* de código
2 *vt* (**a**) *(message)* codificar, cifrar (**b**) *(identify)* codificar (**c**) *Comptr* codificar

coded ['kəʊdɪd] *adj* en código

codeine ['kəʊdi:n] *n* codeína *f*

co-dependant [kəʊdɪ'pendənt] *n* codependiente *mf*

co-dependency [kəʊdɪ'pendənsɪ] *n* codependencia *f*, dependencia *f* mutua

codfish ['kɒdfɪʃ] (*pl* **codfish** *or* **codfishes**) *n* bacalao *m*

codger ['kɒdʒə(r)] *n Fam* **old c.** vejete, abuelo

codicil ['kəʊdɪsɪl] *n Law* codicilo *m*

codification [kəʊdɪfɪ'keɪʃən] *n* codificación *f*

codify ['kəʊdɪfaɪ] *vt* codificar

coding ['kəʊdɪŋ] *n* (**a**) *(of message)* codificación *f*, cifrado *m* (**b**) *Comptr* codificación *f* ►► ***c. error*** error *m* de codificación

cod-liver oil ['kɒdlɪvə'rɔɪl] *n* aceite *m* de hígado de bacalao

codpiece ['kɒdpi:s] *n Hist* = pieza de vestuario que se colocaba encima de la bragueta

co-driver ['kəʊdraɪvə(r)] *n* copiloto *mf*

codswallop ['kɒdzwɒləp] *n Br Fam* majaderías *fpl*, sandeces *fpl*, *Am* pendejadas *fpl*; **a load of c.** una sarta de majaderías

co-ed [kəʊ'ed] **1** *n* (**a**) *(school)* colegio *m* mixto (**b**) *US (female student)* alumna *f* de escuela mixta
2 *adj* mixto(a)

coeducation ['kəʊedjʊ'keɪʃən] *n* educación *f or* enseñanza *f* mixta

coeducational ['kəʊedjʊ'keɪʃənəl] *adj (school)* mixto(a)

coefficient [kəʊɪ'fɪʃənt] *n Math* coeficiente *m* ►► *Phys* ***c. of expansion*** coeficiente *m* de dilatación

coelacanth ['si:ləkænθ] *n* celacanto *m*

coeliac, *US* **celiac** ['si:lɪæk] *adj Anat* abdominal, celiaco(a) ►► *Med* ***c. disease*** enfermedad *f* celiaca

co-enzyme [kəʊ'enzaɪm] *n Biol* coenzima *f*

coequal [kəʊ'i:kwəl] **1** *n* **they were, in theory, coequals** en teoría tenían el mismo nivel
2 *adj* del mismo nivel

coerce [kəʊ'ɜːs] *vt* coaccionar; **to c. sb into doing sth** coaccionar a alguien para que haga algo

coercion [kəʊ'ɜːʃən] *n* coacción *f*

coercive [kəʊ'ɜːsɪv] *adj* coactivo(a), coercitivo(a)

coeval [kəʊ'iːvəl] *Formal* **1** *n* coetáneo(a) *m,f*, contemporáneo(a) *m,f*
2 *adj* coetáneo(a), contemporáneo(a)

co-exist ['kəʊɪg'zɪst] *vi* convivir, coexistir

co-existence ['kəʊɪg'zɪstəns] *n* convivencia *f*, coexistencia *f*

co-extensive [kəʊɪk'stensɪv] *adj* **c. with** *(in space)* con la misma extensión que; *(in time)* con la misma duración que

C of E [siːəv'iː] *adj Br* (*abbr* **Church of England**) anglicano(a)

coffee ['kɒfɪ] *n* café *m*; **two coffees, please!** ¡dos cafés, por favor!; **black c.** café *Esp* solo *or Am* negro; **white c.** café con leche ►► ***c. bar*** café *m*, cafetería *f*; ***c. bean*** grano *m* de café; ***c. break*** descanso *m* para el café; ***c. cake*** *Br* tarta *f or* pastel *m or Col, CSur* torta *f* de moka; *US* = pan dulce con frutos secos; ***c. cup*** taza *f* de café; ***c. grinder*** molinillo *m* de café; ***c. grounds*** posos *mpl* del café; ***c. house*** café *m*; *US* ***c. klatsch*** = tertulia informal en la que se sirve café; ***c. machine*** *(in café)* cafetera *f*; *(vending machine)* máquina *f* de café; ***c. mill*** molinillo *m* de café; *Br* ***c. morning*** = reunión matinal que a veces tiene fines benéficos; ***c. mug*** taza *f* (alta) de café; ***c. pot*** cafetera *f*; ***c. shop*** cafetería *f*; ***c. spoon*** cucharilla *f* de café; ***c. table*** mesita *f* baja, mesa *f* de centro, *RP* mesa *f* ratona; ***c.-table book*** libro *m* ilustrado de gran formato

coffee-coloured ['kɒfɪkʌləd] *adj* color café *inv*

coffer ['kɒfə(r)] *n (chest)* cofre *m*; *Fig* **the company's coffers** las arcas de la empresa

cofferdam ['kɒfədæm] *n* ataguía *f*, compartimento *m* estanco

coffered ['kɒfəd] *adj Archit* artesonado(a); **a c. ceiling** un (techo) artesonado

coffin ['kɒfɪn] *n* ataúd *m*, féretro *m* ►► *Fam* ***c. nail*** *(cigarette)* pitillo *m*, *Am* pucho *m*

cog [kɒg] *n (tooth)* diente *m (en engranaje)*; *(wheel)* rueda *f* dentada; *Fig* **I'm only a c. in the machine** no soy más que una pieza del engranaje ►► ***c. railway*** tren *m* de cremallera

cogency ['kəʊdʒənsɪ] *n Formal* poder *m*, convicción *f*

cogent ['kəʊdʒənt] *adj Formal* poderoso(a), convincente

cogently ['kəʊdʒəntlɪ] *adv Formal* con poder *or* convicción, convincentemente

cogitate ['kɒdʒɪteɪt] *vi Formal* meditar, reflexionar (**about** *or* **on** sobre)

cogitation [kɒdʒɪ'teɪʃən] *n Formal* meditación *f*, reflexión *f*

cognac ['kɒnjæk] *n* coñá *m*, coñac *m*

cognate ['kɒgneɪt] *Ling* **1** *n* término *m* emparentado, cognado *m*
2 *adj* emparentado(a)

cognition [kɒg'nɪʃən] *n* cognición *f*, conocimiento *m*

cognitive ['kɒgnɪtɪv] *adj* cognitivo(a), cognoscitivo(a) ►► *Psy* ***c. dissonance*** disonancia *f* cognitiva; ***c. psychology*** psicología *f* cognitiva; ***c. science*** ciencia *f* del conocimiento; ***c. therapy*** terapia *f* cognitiva

cognizance ['kɒgnɪzəns] *n Formal* (**a**) *(knowledge)* **to take c. of** tener en cuenta (**b**) *Law* **within the c. of this court** bajo la jurisdicción *or* competencia de este tribunal

cognizant ['kɒgnɪzənt] *adj Formal* **to be c. of sth** tener conocimiento de algo

cognomen [kɒg'nəʊmen] (*pl* **cognomens** *or* **cognomina** [kɒg'nəʊmɪnə]) *n Formal (nickname)* cognomen *m*

cognoscenti [kɒgnə'sentiː] *npl* entendidos *mpl*

cogwheel ['kɒgwiːl] *n* rueda *f* dentada

cohabit [kəʊ'hæbɪt] *vi* cohabitar, convivir (**with** con)

cohabitation [kəʊhæbɪ'teɪʃən] *n* cohabitación *f*, convivencia *f*

coheir ['kəʊ'eə(r)] *n* coheredero(a) *m,f*

coheiress ['kəʊ'eərɪs] *n* coheredera *f*

cohere [kəʊ'hɪə(r)] *vi* (**a**) *(stick together)* pegarse; **his vague memories of the event started to c.** sus vagos recuerdos del acontecimiento empezaban a cobrar sentido (**b**) *(be logically consistent)* ser coherente, tener cohesión *or* coherencia

coherence [kəʊ'hɪərəns] *n* (**a**) *(cohesion)* cohesión *f* (**b**) *(logical consistency)* coherencia *f*

coherent [kəʊ'hɪərənt] *adj* coherente; *Fam* **the man wasn't c.** era incoherente, no conseguía expresarse

coherently [kəʊ'hɪərəntlɪ] *adv* coherentemente, con coherencia

cohesion [kəʊ'hiːʒən] *n* cohesión *f* ►► *EU* ***c. fund*** fondo *m* de cohesión

cohesive [kəʊ'hiːsɪv] *adj* (**a**) *(united)* cohesionado(a) (**b**) *Phys (force)* cohesivo(a)

cohort ['kəʊhɔːt] *n* (**a**) *Pej (associate, companion)* acólito(a) *m,f*, secuaz *mf* (**b**) *(group)* cohorte *f* (**c**) *(in statistics)* cohorte *f* (**d**) *Hist* cohorte *f*

coif [kɔɪf] *n (skullcap)* cofia *f*

coiffure [kwɑː'fjʊə(r)] **1** *n* peinado *m*
2 *vt* peinar; **she was elegantly coiffured, as ever** iba tan elegantemente peinada como de costumbre

coil [kɔɪl] **1** *n* (**a**) *(of rope, wire)* rollo *m* (**b**) *(single loop)* bucle *m*, vuelta *f*; *(of smoke)* círculo *m*; **the snake's coils** los anillos de la serpiente (**c**) *(electrical)* bobina *f* (**d**) *Br (contraceptive device)* DIU *m*, espiral *f*
2 *vt* enrollar (**round** alrededor de)
3 *vi* (**a**) *(river, smoke)* **the river coiled through the valley** el río bajaba zigzagueando por el valle; **the smoke coiled into the air** el humo ascendía formando volutas (**b**) *(snake)* **the python coiled around its prey** la pitón se enroscó en torno a su presa

► **coil up 1** *vt sep (rope, hose)* enrollar; **the snake coiled itself up** la serpiente se enroscó *or* enrolló
2 *vi (snake)* enroscarse, enrollarse

coiled [kɔɪld] *adj* enrollado(a); *Fig* **like a c. spring** en tensión

coin [kɔɪn] **1** *n* (**a**) *(single item)* moneda *f*; **a 10p c.** una moneda de 10 peniques; IDIOM **the other side of the c.** la otra cara de la moneda ►► ***c. box*** *(of telephone, vending machine)* depósito *m* de monedas; *(in church)* cepillo *m* (**b**) *(metal currency)* moneda *f*; IDIOM **to pay sb back in his own c.** pagar a alguien con *or* en la misma moneda
2 *vt* (**a**) *(mint)* **to c. money** acuñar moneda; *Fam* **he's simply coining it** se está forrando, *Méx* se está pudriendo en dinero (**b**) *(new word, phrase)* acuñar; **to c. a phrase...** por así decirlo..., valga la expresión...

coinage ['kɔɪnɪdʒ] *n* (**a**) *(coins)* monedas *fpl* (**b**) *(new word, phrase)* **a recent c.** una expresión de nuevo cuño (**c**) *(creation) (of money)* acuñación *f* (**d**) *(creation) (of word)* acuñación *f*

coincide [kəʊɪn'saɪd] *vi* (**a**) *(in space, time)* coincidir (**with** con) (**b**) *(correspond)* coincidir

coincidence [kəʊ'ɪnsɪdəns] *n* (**a**) *(accident)* coincidencia *f*; **by c.** por casualidad; **what a c.!** ¡qué coincidencia! (**b**) *(correspondence)* coincidencia *f*

coincidental [kəʊɪnsɪ'dentəl] *adj* casual, accidental; **there was nothing c. about this** esto no tenía nada de accidental *or* fortuito

coincidentally [kəʊɪnsɪ'dentəlɪ] *adv* casualmente

coin-operated ['kɔɪnɒpəreɪtɪd] *adj* **c. machine** máquina de monedas

coir [kɔɪə(r)] *n* fibra *f* de coco

coital ['kɔɪtəl] *adj* del coito

coitus ['kɔɪtəs] *n Formal* coito *m* ►► ***c. interruptus*** coitus *m inv* interruptus

Coke® [kəʊk] *n* Coca-Cola® *f*

coke [kəʊk] **1** *n* (**a**) *(fuel)* coque *m* (**b**) *Fam (cocaine)* coca *f*
2 *vt (coal)* coquizar

coked-up [kəʊkt'ʌp] *adj Fam* **to be c.** estar hasta arriba de coca

cokehead ['kəʊkhed] *n Fam* cocainómano(a) *m,f*

Col *Mil* (*abbr* **Colonel**) coronel *m*

col[1] (*abbr* **column**) col.

col[2] [kɒl] *n (of mountain)* puerto *m*, paso *m*

cola ['kəʊlə] *n* (**a**) *(drink)* (refresco *m* de) cola *f* (**b**) *(tree)* cola *f* ►► ***c. nut*** nuez *f* de cola

colander ['kɒləndə(r)] *n* escurridor *m*

COLD [kəʊld] **1** *n* (**a**) *(low temperature)* frío *m*; **he doesn't seem to feel the c.** parece que no siente el frío; **come in out of the c.** entra aquí, que hace frío
(**b**) *(illness)* catarro *m*, *Esp, Méx* resfriado *m*, *Andes, RP* resfrío *m*; **to have a c.** estar acatarrado(a), tener un *Esp, Méx* resfriado *or Andes, RP* resfrío; **to catch a c.** agarrar *or Esp* coger *or Méx* pescar un resfriado, *Andes, RP* agarrarse *or* pescarse un resfrío; **a c. in the chest** un catarro *or Esp, Méx* resfriado *or Andes, RP* resfrío de pecho; **a c. in the head** un catarro
(**c**) IDIOMS **to come in from the c.** salir del ostracismo; **to be left out in the c.** ser dejado(a) de lado
2 *adj* (**a**) *(in temperature)* frío(a); **to be c.** *(person)* tener frío; *(thing)* estar frío(a); **my feet are c.** tengo los pies fríos; **it's c.** *(weather)* hace frío; **to get c.** enfriarse; **to be in a c. sweat** tener sudores fríos; **the thought made him break out in a c. sweat** sólo de pensarlo le entraban escalofríos *or* sudores fríos; *Fam* **a c. one** *(beer)* una cervecita,

una birra, *Méx* una chela ▸▸ ***c. buffet*** buffet *m* frío; ***c. calling*** *(in marketing)* contacto *m* en frío *or* sin previo aviso; ***c. chisel*** cortafrío *m, RP* cortafierro *m*; ***c. cream*** crema *f* de belleza; *US* ***c. cuts*** fiambres *mpl* y embutidos; ***c. frame*** *(in garden)* = cajonera para proteger a las plantas; *Met* ***c. front*** frente *m* frío; *Phys* ***c. fusion*** fusión *f* fría *or* en frío; ***c. meats*** fiambres *mpl* y embutidos; ***c. snap*** ola *f* de frío; ***c. sore*** herpes *m inv* labial, *Esp* calentura *f*, *Méx* fuego *m*; ***c. spell*** ola *f* de frío; ***c. start*** *(of car)* arranque *m* en frío; ***c. steel:*** **they attacked with c. steel** atacaron con la bayoneta calada; ***c. storage*** *(of food)* conservación *f* en cámara frigorífica; *Fig* **to put sth into c. storage** dejar algo para más tarde, *Esp* aparcar algo; ***c. store*** *(room)* cámara *f* frigorífica; *Fam* ***c. turkey*** *(withdrawal symptoms)* síndrome *m* de abstinencia, *Esp* mono *m*; **to go c. turkey** cortar por lo sano con las drogas; ***c. war*** guerra *f* fría; ***c. warrior*** partidario(a) *m,f* de la guerra fría

(**b**) *(person, manner, welcome)* frío(a); **to be c. towards sb** ser frío con alguien, tratar a alguien con frialdad; **to have a c. heart** no tener corazón; **in the c. light of day** a la fría luz del día

(**c**) *(colour)* frío(a)

(**d**) *(in children's game)* **is it over here? – no, you're getting colder** ¿está por ahí? – frío, frío

(**e**) *Comptr* ***c. boot*** reinicio *m* en frío, reinicio *m Esp* del ordenador *or Am* de la computadora *(tras haberlo/a apagado/a por completo)*

(**f**) IDIOMS **c. as charity** frío(a) como el hielo; **c. as ice** frío(a) como el hielo; *Fam* **it leaves me c.** *(doesn't interest or impress me)* ni me va ni me viene, *Esp* me deja frío(a), *RP* no me mueve un pelo; **their trail was c.** se había perdido su rastro; **in c. blood** a sangre fría; **it was a c. comfort to know...** no servía de mucho consuelo saber...; **that's c. comfort** eso no es un consuelo; **to get c. feet** echarse atrás; *Fam* **he's a c. fish** es un grosero *or Esp* borde; **to give sb the c. shoulder** tratar a alguien con frialdad; **to put sth into c. storage** postergar *or Esp* aparcar algo indefinidamente; **to pour** *or* **throw c. water on sth** echar un jarro *or RP* balde de agua fría sobre algo

3 *adv* (**a**) *(without preparation)* **to do sth c.** hacer algo en frío

(**b**) *Fam* **to be out c.** *(unconscious)* estar inconsciente; **he knocked him (out) c.** lo dejó inconsciente de un golpe

(**c**) *US Fam (absolutely)* **she turned me down c.** me rechazó de plano; **he knows his subject c.** sabe un montón del tema

cold-blooded ['kəʊld'blʌdɪd] *adj* (**a**) *(animal)* de sangre fría (**b**) *(unfeeling) (act)* desalmado(a); **to be c.** *(animal)* tener la sangre fría; *(person)* ser desalmado(a); **c. murder** asesinato a sangre fría

cold-bloodedly ['kəʊld'blʌdɪdlɪ] *adv* a sangre fría; **he went about the business quite c.** abordó el asunto con bastante sangre fría

coldcock ['kəʊld'kɒk] *vt US Fam* dejar K.O. *or* sin sentido

cold-filtered ['kəʊld'fɪltəd] *adj (beer)* filtrado(a) en frío

cold-hearted [kəʊld'hɑːtɪd] *adj (person, decision)* insensible

coldly ['kəʊldlɪ] *adv* fríamente, con frialdad

coldness ['kəʊldnɪs] *n* (**a**) *(of weather)* frialdad *f* (**b**) *(of manner)* frialdad *f*; **there is a c. between them** hay frialdad entre ellos

cold-pressed ['kəʊldprest] *adj (olive oil)* prensado(a) en frío

cold-shoulder ['kəʊld'ʃəʊldə(r)] *vt* tratar con frialdad a

coleslaw ['kəʊlslɔː] *n* = ensalada de repollo, zanahoria y cebolla con mayonesa

coley ['kəʊlɪ] *n* carbonero *m*

colic ['kɒlɪk] *n* cólico *m*

colicky ['kɒlɪkɪ] *adj* **a c. baby** un bebé con cólico

coliseum, colosseum [kɒlə'sɪəm] *n* coliseo *m*

colitis [kɒ'laɪtɪs] *n Med* colitis *f inv*

collaborate [kə'læbəreɪt] *vi* (**a**) *(on project)* colaborar (**on** en) (**b**) *Pej (during occupation)* colaborar (**with** con)

collaboration [kəlæbə'reɪʃən] *n* (**a**) *(on project)* colaboración *f* (**with** con); **in c. with** en colaboración con (**b**) *Pej (with occupying enemy)* colaboracionismo *m* (**with** con)

collaborative [kə'læbərətɪv] *adj* colectivo(a), en colaboración

collaborator [kə'læbəreɪtə(r)] *n* (**a**) *(on project)* colaborador(ora) *m,f* (**b**) *Pej (with the enemy)* colaboracionista *mf*

collage ['kɒlɑːʒ] *n (art)* collage *m*

collagen ['kɒlədʒən] *n Biol* colágeno *m*

collapse [kə'læps] **1** *n* (**a**) *(of building, bridge, wall)* hundimiento *m*, desplome *m* (**b**) *(of person)* colapso *m*; *(of health)* deterioro *m*; *(of lung)* colapso *m* (**c**) *(of prices, currency, economy)* desplome *m*, hundimiento *m*; *(of defences, resistance)* desplome *m*, hundimiento *m*; *(of government)* caída *f*, hundimiento *m*; *(of business)* hundimiento *m*

2 *vt* (**a**) *(fold up) (table, chair)* plegar (**b**) *(merge) (paragraphs, entries)* integrar, juntar; *Comptr (subdirectories)* contraer

3 *vi* (**a**) *(fall down) (building, bridge, wall)* desplomarse, hundirse (**b**) *(person)* sufrir un colapso, desplomarse; *(health)* deteriorarse; *(lung)* colapsar; **he collapsed and died** tuvo un colapso y se murió; **to c. with laughter** desternillarse de risa; **I collapsed from the heat** sufrí un colapso por el calor (**c**) *(prices, resistance, currency, economy)* desplomarse, hundirse; *(government)* caer, hundirse; *(business)* hundirse (**d**) *(fold up)* plegarse

collapsed [kə'læpst] *adj (lung)* colapsado(a)

collapsible [kə'læpsəbəl] *adj (table, bed, boat)* plegable; *(steering column)* desarmable

collar ['kɒlə(r)] **1** *n* (**a**) *(of garment)* cuello *m* ▸▸ ***c. stud*** = cierre automático para cuellos de quita y pon (**b**) *(for dog)* collar *m*; *(for horse)* collera *f* (**c**) *(marking on bird, animal)* collar *m* (**d**) *Tech* abrazadera *f* (**e**) *Culin (of bacon)* cuello *m*

2 *vt Fam* (**a**) *(seize, capture)* cazar, agarrar (**b**) *(appropriate)* agarrar, pescar

collarbone ['kɒləbəʊn] *n* clavícula *f*

collard greens ['kɒlɑːd'griːnz] *npl US* col *f* rizada, *RP* repollo *m* rizado

collared dove ['kɒləd'dʌv] *n* tórtola *f* turca

collarless ['kɒləlɪs] *n* ***c. shirt*** camisa *f* sin cuello

collate [kɒ'leɪt] *vt* (**a**) *(assemble) (information, texts)* recopilar; *Typ (sheets, signatures)* ordenar (**b**) *(compare) (text)* cotejar, comparar (**with** con)

collateral [kə'lætərəl] **1** *n Fin* garantía *f* (prendaria)

2 *adj* (**a**) *Fin* ***c. loan*** préstamo *m* pignoraticio *or* con garantía prendaria; *Fin* ***c. security*** garantía *f* (prendaria) (**b**) *Mil* ***c. damage*** daños *mpl* colaterales, bajas *fpl* civiles *(en un bombardeo)* (**c**) *(branch, family, artery)* colateral

collation [kə'leɪʃən] *n* (**a**) *(of information, texts)* recopilación *f*; *Typ (of sheets, signatures)* ordenación *f* (**b**) *(comparison) (of texts)* cotejo *m*, comparación *f* (**c**) *Formal (light meal)* colación *f*, refrigerio *m*

colleague ['kɒliːg] *n* compañero(a) *m,f*, colega *mf*

collect[1] [kə'lekt] **1** *vt* (**a**) *(gather) (supporters, belongings)* reunir, juntar; *(data, evidence, news)* recoger, reunir; *(taxes)* recaudar; *(fine, debt, rent)* recaudar; **they're collecting money for charity** recogen dinero para una organización benéfica

(**b**) *(accumulate)* **to c. dust** acumular polvo; **solar panels c. the heat** el calor es acumulado por paneles solares

(**c**) *(pick up)* recoger, pasar a buscar; **I'll c. you at midday** te recogeré *or* pasaré a buscar al mediodía

(**d**) *(take away)* recoger; **the council collects the rubbish** el ayuntamiento se encarga de la recogida de basuras; **when is the mail collected?** ¿cuándo es la recogida del correo?

(**e**) *(as hobby) (stamps, books)* coleccionar

(**f**) *(compose)* **she collected her thoughts** puso en orden sus ideas; **to c. oneself** concentrarse

2 *vi* (**a**) *(people)* reunirse; *(things, dust, water)* acumularse (**b**) *(gather money)* recoger dinero, hacer una colecta (**for** para) (**c**) *US* **c. on delivery** entrega contra reembolso

3 *adj US* ***c. call*** llamada *f or Am* llamado *m* a cobro revertido

4 *adv US* **to call sb c.** llamar a alguien a cobro revertido; **to send a parcel c.** enviar un paquete a gastos debidos

▸**collect up** *vt sep* recoger

collect[2] ['kɒlekt] *n (prayer)* colecta *f*

collectable [kə'lektəbəl] **1** *n* **collectables** piezas *fpl* coleccionables *or* de coleccionista

2 *adj (desirable)* codiciado(a)

collected [kə'lektɪd] *adj* (**a**) *(calm)* sereno(a), entero(a) (**b**) **the c. works of...** las obras completas de...

collecting [kə'lektɪŋ] *n* ***c. agency*** agencia *f* especializada en el cobro de deudas; ***c. bank*** banco *m* especializado en el cobro de deudas; ***c. tin*** lata *f (utilizada como hucha o alcancía)*

collection [kə'lekʃən] *n* (**a**) *(group) (of objects)* montón *m*; *(of people)* grupo *m*

(**b**) *(things collected) (of stamps, paintings)* colección *f*; *(of poems, essays)* recopilación *f*

(**c**) *(of fashion designer)* colección *f*; **Porto's new winter c.** la nueva colección de invierno de Porto

(**d**) *(act of collecting) (of money)* cobro *m*; *(of rubbish, letters)* recogida *f*; *(of taxes)* recaudación *f*; **your order is ready for c.** puede pasar a recoger su pedido; **c. times are 8. 45 and 17. 30** *(from letter box)* la recogida de cartas es a las 8.45 y a las 17.30

(**e**) **to make** *or* **take a c.** *(for charity)* hacer una colecta ▸▸ ***c. plate*** *(in church)* platillo *m* para las limosnas

collective [kə'lektɪv] **1** *n (group)* colectivo *m*; *(farm)* (granja *f*) cooperativa *f*
2 *adj* colectivo(a) ►► ***c. agreement*** convenio *m* colectivo; ***c. bargaining*** negociación *f* colectiva; *Gram* ***c. noun*** sustantivo *m or* nombre *m* colectivo; ***c. security*** seguridad *f* colectiva; ***c. unconscious*** inconsciente *m or* subconsciente *m* colectivo

collectively [kə'lektɪvlɪ] *adv* colectivamente; **they are c. known as...** se los conoce como...

collectivism [kə'lektɪvɪzəm] *n Pol* colectivismo *m*

collectivist [kə'lektɪvɪst] *adj* colectivista

collectivization [kəlektɪvaɪ'zeɪʃən] *n* colectivización *f*

collectivize [kə'lektɪvaɪz] *vt* colectivizar

collector [kə'lektə(r)] *n* **(a)** *(of paintings, stamps)* coleccionista *mf* ►► ***c.'s item*** pieza *f* de coleccionista **(b)** *(of money) (of taxes)* recaudador(ora) *m,f*; *(of debts)* cobrador(ora) *m,f*; **our collectors will be on the streets over Christmas** *(for charity)* nuestros voluntarios irán recaudando dinero por las calles durante las Navidades

colleen ['kɒliːn, kɒ'liːn] *n Irish* chica *f*, muchacha *f*

college ['kɒlɪdʒ] *n* **(a)** *(for adult or further education)* escuela *f* ►► *Br* ***c. of further education*** = centro de enseñanza donde se pueden cursar estudios de formación profesional y bachillerato
(b) *(for vocational training)* instituto *m*, escuela *f* ►► *Br* ***c. of education*** escuela *f* de pedagogía *or* magisterio
(c) *US (university)* universidad *f*; **to be at c.** estar en la universidad; **a c. student** un(a) universitario(a); IDIOM *US* **to give it the old c. try** ir a por todas
(d) *Br (part of university)* colegio *m* universitario
(e) *(professional organization)* colegio *m* (profesional)
(f) *(electoral body)* colegio *m*; **the C. of Cardinals** el colegio cardenalicio

collegiate [kə'liːdʒɪət] *adj* **(a)** *(university)* = formado por varios colegios universitarios **(b)** *US (life, atmosphere)* universitario(a) **(c)** *Rel* ***c. church*** colegiata *f*

collide [kə'laɪd] *vi* **(a)** *(crash)* colisionar, chocar (**with** con *or* contra) **(b)** *(clash)* enfrentarse; **I can see that we are going to c. on this issue** ya veo que nos vamos a enfrentar por este tema

collie ['kɒlɪ] *n* collie *m*

collier ['kɒlɪə(r)] *n* **(a)** *(miner)* minero(a) *m,f* del carbón **(b)** *(ship)* barco *m* carbonero

colliery ['kɒlɪərɪ] *n* mina *f* de carbón

collision [kə'lɪʒən] *n* **(a)** *(crash)* colisión *f*, choque *m*; **to be in c. (with)** chocar *or* colisionar (con), entrar en colisión (con); **to be on a c. course** *(aeroplanes, ships)* estar a punto de chocar *or* colisionar ►► *Aut* ***c. damage waiver*** cobertura *f* parcial de daños por colisión **(b)** *Fig (clash)* enfrentamiento *m*; **they are on a c. course** terminarán enfrentándose

collocate ['kɒləkeɪt] *Ling* **1** *n* colocador *m*, colocación *f*
2 *vi* ser colocador típico *or* colocación típica (**with** de)

collocation [kɒlə'keɪʃən] *n Ling* colocación *f* (típica), enlace *m* típico

colloid ['kɒlɔɪd] *n Chem* coloide *m*

colloidal [kə'lɔɪdəl] *adj Chem* coloidal ►► ***c. suspension*** suspensión *f or* sistema *m* coloidal

colloquia *pl of* **colloquium**

colloquial [kə'ləʊkwɪəl] *adj* coloquial

colloquialism [kə'ləʊkwɪəlɪzəm] *n* voz *f or* término *m* coloquial

colloquially [kə'ləʊkwɪəlɪ] *adv* coloquialmente; **known c. as...** conocido(a) coloquialmente como...

colloquium [kə'ləʊkwɪəm] (*pl* **colloquia** [kə'ləʊkwɪə] *or* **colloquiums**) *n Formal* coloquio *m*

colloquy ['kɒləkwɪ] (*pl* **colloquies**) *n Formal* coloquio *m*

collude [kə'luːd] *vi* conspirar, confabularse; **to c. with sb in sth** conspirar con alguien en algo, actuar en connivencia con alguien en algo

collusion [kə'luːʒən] *n* connivencia *f*; **to be in c. with sb** estar en connivencia con alguien

collywobbles ['kɒlɪwɒbəlz] *npl Fam* **to have the c.** *(be nervous)* tener *Esp* canguelo *or Méx* mello *or RP* chuchi

Colo (*abbr* **Colorado**) Colorado

Cologne [kə'ləʊn] *n* Colonia

cologne [kə'ləʊn] *n* **(eau de) c.** (agua *f* de) colonia *f*

Colombia [kə'lʌmbɪə] *n* Colombia

Colombian [kə'lʌmbɪən] **1** *n* colombiano(a) *m,f*
2 *adj* colombiano(a)

Colombo [kə'lʌmbəʊ] *n* Colombo

colon ['kəʊlɒn, 'kəʊlən] *n* **(a)** *Anat* colon *m* **(b)** *(punctuation mark)* dos puntos *mpl*

colonel ['kɜːnəl] *n* coronel *m*

colonial [kə'ləʊnɪəl] **1** *n* **(a)** *(colonist)* colono *m* **(b)** *Br Old-fashioned or Hum* = persona de una antigua colonia británica
2 *adj* **(a)** *(power, life)* colonial; *Pej (attitude)* colonialista **(b)** *US (architecture)* = de estilo colonial estadounidense **(c)** *Br Formerly (troops, customs)* = de las antiguas colonias británicas

colonialism [kə'ləʊnɪəlɪzəm] *n* colonialismo *m*

colonic [kə'lɒnɪk] *adj* de colon ►► *Med* ***c. irrigation*** irrigación *f* de colon

colonist ['kɒlənɪst] *n* colonizador(ora) *m,f*, colono *m*

colonization [kɒlənaɪ'zeɪʃən] *n* colonización *f*

colonize ['kɒlənaɪz] *vt* colonizar

colonizer ['kɒlənaɪzə(r)] *n* colonizador(ora) *m,f*

colonnade [kɒlə'neɪd] *n* columnata *f*

colony ['kɒlənɪ] *n* **(a)** *(of people)* colonia *f*; *Fig* **the English c. in Paris** la colonia inglesa en París **(b)** *(of animals)* colonia *f* **(c)** *Hist* **the Colonies** *Br* las colonias, *US* = las trece colonias

colophon ['kəʊləfɒn, 'kɒləfən] *n Typ* **(a)** *(ornament)* logotipo *m*, símbolo *m* **(b)** *(identifying publisher)* colofón *m*

color, colored *etc US* = **colour, coloured** *etc*

Colorado [kɒlə'rɑːdəʊ] *n* Colorado ►► ***C. beetle*** escarabajo *m* de la *Esp* patata *or Am* papa

colorant ['kʌlərənt] *n* **(a)** *(for food)* colorante *m* **(b)** *(for hair)* tinte *m*

coloration [kʌlə'reɪʃən] *n* coloración *f*

coloratura [kɒlərə'tʊərə] *n Mus* **(a)** *(passage, style)* coloratura *f* **(b)** *(singer)* **c. (soprano)** soprano *f* coloratura

colossal [kə'lɒsəl] *adj* colosal

colosseum = **coliseum**

colossus [kə'lɒsəs] (*pl* **colossi** [kə'lɒsaɪ] *or* **colossuses**) *n* **(a)** *(statue)* coloso *m* **(b)** *(person)* coloso(a) *m,f*, gigante *mf*

colostomy [kə'lɒstəmɪ] *n Med* colostomía *f* ►► ***c. bag*** = bolsa de evacuación para una colostomía

colour, *US* **color** ['kʌlə(r)] **1** *n* **(a)** *(hue)* color *m*; **what c. is it?** ¿de qué color es?; **it's blue in c.** es de color azul; **he painted the room in bright/dark colours** pintó la habitación de colores brillantes/oscuros; **c. photograph/film** fotografía/película en color; **in c.** *(film)* en color; *(magazine)* a color ►► *Phot* ***c. balance*** equilibrio *m* de colores; ***c. code*** código *m* de colores; *Typ* ***c. correction*** calibración *f or* corrección *f* de color; *Comptr* ***c. display*** monitor *m* en color; *Phot* ***c. filter*** filtro *m* de color; *Comptr* ***c. monitor*** monitor *m* en color; *Comptr* ***c. printer*** impresora *f* en color; *Comptr* ***c. printing*** impresión *m* en color; ***c. scheme*** combinación *f* de colores; *Typ* ***c. separation*** separación *f* de colores; ***c. supplement*** *(of newspaper)* suplemento *m* en color; ***c. television*** televisión *f* en color; *Phys* ***c. temperature*** temperatura *f* del color; ***c. therapy*** cromoterapia *f*
(b) *(complexion)* color *m*; **her c. isn't good** tiene mala cara; **to lose one's c.** palidecer, perder los colores; **to get one's c. back** recuperar los colores; **to bring the c. back to sb's cheeks** hacer que alguien recupere los colores
(c) *(skin colour)* color *m* de la piel; **c. isn't an issue here** no se trata de una cuestión del color de la piel; *US* **person of c.** persona de color ►► ***c. bar*** discriminación *f* racial; **to operate a c. bar** discriminar racialmente; ***c. prejudice*** prejuicios *mpl* raciales
(d) *(aspect)* **the political c. of a newspaper** el color (político) de un periódico; **under the c. of patriotism** bajo el pretexto del patriotismo; **the matter took on a different c.** el asunto tomó un cariz diferente
(e) *(liveliness, interest)* colorido *m*; **to give c. to a story** dar colorido a una historia
(f) *(paint, dye)* **the colours have run** ha desteñido; **a box of colours** *(watercolour paints)* una caja de acuarelas
(g) *Mil* ***c. party*** = grupo de soldados que portan el estandarte del regimiento
(h) *(snooker ball)* bola *f* de color
(i) IDIOMS **to be off c.** *(person) Esp* estar pocho(a), *Am* estar de capa caída; *(joke)* estar fuera de tono; **let's see the c. of your money** veamos primero el dinero
2 *vt* **(a)** *(change colour of)* colorear; **to c. sth blue** *(in picture)* pintar *or* colorear algo de azul; *(with dye)* teñir algo de azul; **to c. one's hair** teñirse el pelo **(b)** *(affect) (judgement, view)* influir en
3 *vi (blush)* ruborizarse

►**colour in,** *US* **color in** *vt sep* colorear

►**colour up** *vi (blush)* ruborizarse, sonrojarse

colour-blind, *US* **color-blind** ['kʌləblaɪnd] *adj* daltónico(a)

colour-blindness, *US* **color-blindness** ['kʌləblaɪndnɪs] *n* daltonismo *m*

colour-coded, *US* **color-coded** ['kʌlə'kəʊdɪd] *adj* **the wires are c.** los cables están coloreados de acuerdo con un código

coloured, *US* **colored** ['kʌləd] **1** *n* (**a**) *(person)* = término para referirse a una persona de color, a veces considerado ofensivo o anticuado (**b**) *SAfr* **Coloured** mestizo(a) *m,f* (**c**) **coloureds** *(clothes)* ropa *f* de color

2 *adj* (**a**) *(illustration)* coloreado(a); **brightly c.** de colores vivos; **c. pencils** lápices de colores (**b**) *(person)* = término para describir a una persona de color, hoy en día considerado ofensivo o anticuado (**c**) *SAfr* **Coloured** mestizo(a) (**d**) *(exaggerated)* **a highly c. narrative** una narrativa llena de colorido

> **False friend**: The Spanish word **colorado** is not a translation for the English word **coloured**. In Spanish **colorado** means "red".

colour-fast, *US* **color-fast** ['kʌləfɑːst] *adj (fabric)* que no destiñe

colourful, *US* **colorful** ['kʌləfʊl] *adj* (**a**) *(having bright colours)* de colores vivos *or* brillantes (**b**) *(interesting, exciting)* lleno(a) de colorido; **a c. character** un personaje pintoresco; **he has a c. past** tiene un pasado pintoresco (**c**) *(vivid) (language, description)* expresivo(a), vívido(a); *Euph* **they used some rather c. language** utilizaron un lenguage muy subido de tono

colourfully, *US* **colorfully** ['kʌləfʊlɪ] *adv* (**a**) *(with bright colours)* con colores vivos *or* brillantes (**b**) *(vividly)* expresivamente, vívidamente; *Euph* **he expresses himself rather c.** utiliza un lenguage muy subido de tono

colouring, *US* **coloring** ['kʌlərɪŋ] *n* (**a**) *(in food)* colorante *m* (**b**) *(complexion)* tez *f*; **to have dark/fair c.** ser de tez morena/clara (**c**) *(of animal)* colorido *m* (**d**) *(act)* **go and do some c.** vete a colorear ►► ***c. book*** libro *m* para colorear

colouring-in, *US* **coloring-in** ['kʌlərɪŋ'ɪn] *n* **go and do some c.** vete a colorear ►► ***c. book*** libro *m* para colorear

colourize, *US* **colorise** ['kʌləraɪz] *vt Cin* colorear, transformar por coloreado

colourless, *US* **colorless** ['kʌləlɪs] *adj* (**a**) *(clear)* incoloro(a) (**b**) *Fig (dull)* insulso(a), inexpresivo(a)

colours, *US* **colors** ['kʌləz] *npl* (**a**) *(of sports team)* colores *mpl*, camiseta *f*; *(in horse-racing)* colores *mpl*; **to wear the school c.** llevar los colores del colegio (**b**) *Mil (flag)* bandera *f*, enseña *f*; **to be called to the c.** ser llamado(a) a filas (**c**) IDIOMS **to pass with flying c.** aprobar con todos los honores; **to sail under false c.** navegar bajo falso pabellón; **to show oneself in one's true c.** quitarse la máscara

Colt® [kəʊlt] *n (revolver)* Colt® *m*

colt [kəʊlt] *n* (**a**) *(horse)* potro *m* (**b**) *Sport* benjamín(ina) *m,f*

coltsfoot ['kəʊltsfʊt] *(pl* **coltsfoot** *or* **coltsfoots***) n* tusilago *m*, fárfara *f*

columbine ['kɒləmbaɪn] *n* aguileña *f*

Columbus [kə'lʌmbəs] *n* **Christopher C.** Cristóbal Colón ►► *US* ***C. Day*** = festividad que conmemora la llegada de Colón a América, *Esp* ≃ el día de la Hispanidad, *Am* ≃ el día de la Raza

column ['kɒləm] *n* (**a**) *(of building)* columna *f* (**b**) *(in newspaper)* columna *f*; **she has a c. in "The Times"** tiene una columna en "The Times", es columnista de "The Times"; **the story got a lot of c. inches** *(good coverage)* la prensa se hizo amplio eco de la noticia (**c**) *(of troops)* columna *f*; **a supply/relief c.** un convoy de aprovisionamiento/de ayuda humanitaria (**d**) *(on screen, in table)* columna *f* ►► *Comptr* ***c. graph*** gráfico *m* en columnas

columnist ['kɒləmɪst] *n* columnista *mf*

coma ['kəʊmə] *n* coma *m*; **in a c.** en estado de coma; **to go into/be in a c.** entrar en/estar en coma

comatose ['kəʊmətəʊs] *adj* (**a**) *Med* comatoso(a) (**b**) *Fam (exhausted)* hecho(a) polvo; *(asleep)* frito(a), *Esp* sobado(a)

comb [kəʊm] **1** *n* (**a**) *(for hair)* peine *m*; *(worn in hair)* peineta *f*; **to run a c. through one's hair, to give one's hair a c.** peinarse (**b**) *(for horses)* peine *m* (**c**) *Tex (for cotton, wool)* peine *m* (**d**) *(of cock)* cresta *f* (**e**) *(honeycomb)* panel *m* (**f**) ***c. binding*** *(plastic)* encuadernación *f* en canutillo

2 *vt* (**a**) *(hair)* **I combed the girl's hair** peiné a la chica; **to c. one's hair** peinarse (**b**) *(horse)* peinar (**c**) *Tex (cotton, wool)* peinar; **combed cotton** algodón peinado (**d**) *(area, town)* peinar, rastrear minuciosamente; **she combed the book for references to the crisis** buscó por todo el libro referencias a la crisis

combat ['kɒmbæt] **1** *n* combate *m*; **to die in c.** caer *or* morir en combate; **women are now used in a c. role** las mujeres son utilizadas ahora como combatientes ►► ***c. fatigue*** fatiga *f* de combate; ***c. fatigues*** traje *m* de combate; ***c. jacket*** guerrera *f*; ***c. trousers*** pantalones *mpl* de combate; ***c. unit*** unidad *f* de combate; ***c. zone*** área *f* de combate

2 *vt (disease, prejudice, crime)* combatir

combatant ['kɒmbətənt] **1** *n* combatiente *mf*

2 *adj* combatiente

combative ['kɒmbətɪv] *adj* combativo(a), beligerante

combatively ['kɒmbətɪvlɪ] *adv* con combatividad *or* beligerancia

combination [kɒmbɪ'neɪʃən] *n* (**a**) *(mixture)* combinación *f*; **a c. of circumstances** un cúmulo de circunstancias ►► ***c. therapy*** *(for HIV)* terapia *f* combinada

(**b**) *(association, team)* **together they formed a winning c.** juntos forman una combinación ganadora

(**c**) *(code) (for lock, safe)* combinación *f* ►► ***c. lock*** cierre *m* de combinación

(**d**) *Math* combinación *f*

(**e**) *(in showjumping)* = obstáculo de dos o más partes

(**f**) *Br (motorbike and sidecar)* moto *f* con sidecar

(**g**) *Br* **combinations** *(underclothing)* calzoncillos *mpl* largos

combine **1** *n* ['kɒmbaɪn] (**a**) *Agr* **c. (harvester)** cosechadora *f* (**b**) *Econ* grupo *m* empresarial

2 *vt* [kəm'baɪn] combinar; **to c. business with pleasure** combinar los negocios con el placer; **to c. forces** aunar esfuerzos; **the event was organized by all the groups combined** el acontecimiento fue organizado por una combinación de todos los grupos; **this, combined with her other problems, made her ill** esto, en combinación *or* junto con sus otros problemas, hizo que enfermara

3 *vi* [kəm'baɪn] *(merge)* unirse, combinarse; *(people)* unirse; *(chemical elements)* combinarse

combined [kəm'baɪnd] **1** *adj* conjunto(a); **our c. efforts** todos nuestros esfuerzos ►► *Sport* ***c. event*** clasificación *f* combinada; *Mil* ***c. forces*** fuerzas *fpl* conjuntas

2 *n Sport* combinada *f*

combining form [kəm'baɪnɪŋfɔːm] *n Gram* afijo *m*

combo ['kɒmbəʊ] *(pl* **combos***) n* (**a**) *Mus* conjunto *m* (**b**) *Fam (combination)* combinación *f*

combustible [kəm'bʌstɪbəl] *adj* combustible

combustion [kəm'bʌstʃən] *n* combustión *f* ►► ***c. chamber*** cámara *f* de combustión; ***c. engine*** motor *m* de combustión

COME [kʌm] *(pt* **came** [keɪm], *pp* **come)** **1** *vi* (**a**) *(in general)* venir (**from** de); *(arrive)* venir, llegar; **here c. the children** ya llegan *or* ahí vienen los niños; **c. (over) here!** ¡ven aquí!; **c. and have a look** ven a ver; **I'll c. and help** iré a ayudar; **coming!** ¡ya voy!; **she came running towards us** vino corriendo hacia nosotros; **the rain came pouring down** se puso a llover a cántaros; **can I c. to the park with you?** ¿puedo ir al parque contigo?; **someone is coming to fix the VCR tomorrow** mañana vendrá alguien a arreglar el *Esp* vídeo *or Am* video; **why don't you c. to dinner some time?** ¿por qué no vienes a cenar un día de éstos?; **she always comes to me for help** siempre acude a mí en búsqueda de ayuda; **to c. to sb's rescue** acudir al rescate de alguien; **to c. first/last** *(in race, competition)* llegar *or* terminar primero/último; *Fig* **my family comes first** mi familia es lo primero; **c. away from there, it's dangerous** sal *or Esp* quítate de ahí, que es peligroso; **my name comes before hers on the list** mi nombre está *or* va antes que el de ella en la lista; **to c. for sth/sb** *(pick up)* venir en búsqueda *or Esp* busca de algo/alguien; **they came from three-nil down to win** remontaron el tres (a) cero y ganaron; **the pain comes and goes** el dolor es intermitente; **you can't just c. and go as you please** no puedes entrar y salir como te dé la gana; **the deadline came and went** el plazo pasó; IDIOM *Fam* **I don't know whether I'm coming or going!** ¡no sé dónde tengo la cabeza!; *Fam* **c., c.!** ¡bueno, bueno!, *Esp* ¡venga ya!; *Fam* **c. again?** ¿cómo (dices)?; **lying comes naturally to her** mentir es algo natural en ella; **now that I c. to think of it** ahora que lo pienso; **c. to that, she never told me either** ahora que lo mencionas, a mí tampoco me lo dijo

(**b**) *(in time)* venir; **Christmas is coming** llega la Navidad; **summer has c. early this year** el verano se ha adelantado este año; **what comes next?** ¿qué viene a continuación?; **a chance like that won't c. again** una oportunidad *or Am* chance como esa no se volverá a presentar; **the time has c. to...** ha llegado el momento de...; **she will be ten c. January** cumple diez años en enero; **the weather should be better c. Sunday** el tiempo debería mejorar el domingo; **she's got a nasty shock coming** se va a llevar una sorpresa desagradable; **to take things as they c.** tomarse las cosas como vienen; **it came as a relief to me** fue un gran alivio para mí; **to c. as a surprise** ser una sorpresa, resultar sorprendente; **it comes as no surprise that...** no es de extrañar que...; **c. what may** suceda lo que suceda; **in the days/years to c.** en días/

años venideros; IDIOM *Fam* **he had it coming (to him)** se lo estaba buscando

(c) *(be available)* **it comes in three sizes** viene en tres tallas *or RP* talles; **the computer comes with a free modem** *Esp* el ordenador *or Am* la computadora viene con un módem de regalo; **work of that quality doesn't c. cheap** un trabajo de esa calidad no sale barato; **do you want milk or sugar in your coffee? – I'll have it as it comes** ¿quieres el café con leche o con azúcar? – me da igual, como sea; *Fam* **he's as tough as they c.** es duro como el que más, *RP* es más duro que la miércoles; **it's as good as they c.** es de lo mejor que hay

(d) *(become)* **to c. of age** hacerse mayor de edad; **how did the door c. to be open?** ¿cómo es que estaba la puerta abierta?; **he has c. to be regarded as the greatest novelist of his time** ha llegado a ser considerado el novelista más grande de su época; *Literary* **it came to pass that...** aconteció que...; **he had a poor start to the season but he came good eventually** comenzó mal la temporada pero con el tiempo se puso a la altura de lo que se esperaba de él; **to c. loose** aflojarse; **to c. open** abrirse; **to c. true** cumplirse, hacerse realidad; **to c. unstuck** fracasar

(e) *very Fam (have orgasm) Esp* correrse, *Am* venirse, *RP* irse

2 *vt* (a) *(travel)* **we've c. a long way to be here** hemos venido desde lejos para estar aquí; *Fig* **she has c. a long way since then** ha progresado mucho desde entonces

(b) *Br Fam (pretend to be)* **don't c. the innocent with me!** ¡no te hagas el inocente conmigo!; *Fam* **don't c. it with me!** *(don't lie to me)* ¡no me vengas con ésas!; *(don't be cheeky) Esp* ¡no te pongas chulo(a) conmigo!, *Am* ¡no te hagas el vivo conmigo!

3 *n very Fam (semen)* leche *f*

▸**come about** *vi* (a) *(happen)* ocurrir, suceder; **how did it c. about that...?** ¿cómo fue que...?; **the discovery came about quite by accident** el descubrimiento ocurrió de forma bastante accidental

(b) *(boat, wind)* cambiar de dirección *or* rumbo

▸**come across** 1 *vt insep (find)* encontrar, encontrarse con; **I've never c. across that expression before** es la primera vez que encuentro esa expresión

2 *vi (make an impression)* **to c. across well/badly** quedar bien/mal, dar buena/mala impresión; **she comes across as (being) a bit arrogant** da la impresión de que es un poco arrogante

▸**come across with** *vt insep Fam (provide)* **he came across with the money he owed me** me dio el dinero que me debía; **the crook came across with the names of his accomplices** el granuja reveló los nombres de sus cómplices

▸**come after** *vt insep (chase)* perseguir

▸**come along** *vi* (a) *(accompany)* **why don't you c. along?** ¿por qué no te vienes?; **she asked me to c. along (with them)** me pidió que les acompañara

(b) *(occur)* venir; **don't just accept the first job that comes along** no aceptes el primer trabajo que encuentres; **chances like this don't c. along very often** oportunidades como ésta no se presentan todos los días

(c) *(as exhortation)* **c. along!** ¡vamos!, *Esp* ¡venga!

(d) *(project, work)* marchar, progresar; **the patient is coming along well** el paciente está mejorando; **how's the project coming along?** ¿qué tal marcha el proyecto?; **his Spanish is coming along well** su español va mejorando

▸**come apart** *vi* deshacerse; **to c. apart at the seams** descoserse; *Fig* **under pressure he came apart** se derrumbó ante la presión

▸**come at** *vt insep (attack)* atacar, *Esp* ir a por; **he came at me with a knife** me atacó *or Esp* fue a por mí con un cuchillo; **questions were coming at me from all sides** me llovían preguntas por todas partes

▸**come away** *vi* (a) *(become detached)* soltarse; **to c. away from sth** desprenderse de algo

(b) *(leave)* **c. away from that door!** ¡apártate de esa puerta!; **I came away from the meeting feeling cheated** salí de la reunión sintiéndome engañado

▸**come back** *vi* (a) *(return)* volver, regresar, *Col, Méx* regresarse; **to c. back to what I was saying,...** volviendo a lo que decía antes,...

(b) *(to memory)* **it's all coming back to me** ahora me acuerdo de todo

(c) *(reply)* responder; *US (retort)* replicar; **they came back with an argument in favour of the project** respondieron con un argumento a favor del proyecto

(d) *(recover)* recuperarse; **the Pistons came back strongly in the final quarter** los Pistons remontaron en el último cuarto

(e) *(become fashionable again)* ponerse de moda otra vez

▸**come before** *vt insep* (a) *(court, judge)* comparecer ante; *(parliament)* presentarse ante

(b) *(be more important than)* anteponerse a

▸**come between** *vt insep* **she won't let anything c. between her and her work** no permite que nada interfiera con su trabajo; **let's not let this disagreement c. between us** no dejemos que este desacuerdo se interponga entre nosotros

▸**come by** 1 *vt insep (acquire)* conseguir; **jobs are hard to c. by** es difícil conseguir un trabajo; **how did she c. by all that money?** ¿de dónde sacó todo ese dinero?

2 *vi (visit)* pasarse; **I'll c. by tomorrow** me pasaré mañana (por tu casa)

▸**come down** 1 *vt insep (descend) (ladder, stairs, mountain)* bajar por

2 *vi* (a) *(descend)* bajar; *(rain)* caer; **c. down from that tree!** ¡bájate de ese árbol!; **the plane came down in a field/the sea** el avión tuvo que aterrizar en un campo/cayó al mar; **he's coming down from Scotland** viene desde Escocia; IDIOM **you've c. down in my estimation** ahora te tengo en menos estima; IDIOM **to c. down in the world** venir a menos

(b) *(reach)* **her hair comes down to her waist** el pelo le llega hasta la cintura

(c) *(collapse)* venirse abajo, hundirse; **the ceiling came down** el techo se vino abajo *or* se hundió

(d) *(decrease) (temperature, prices)* bajar, descender; **he's ready to c. down 10 percent on the price** está dispuesto a bajar el precio un 10 por ciento

(e) *(be demolished)* demoler, derribar; **these shacks will soon c. down** pronto demolerán *or* derribarán estas chozas

(f) *(decide)* **to c. down in favour of** decantarse a favor de

(g) *(be passed down)* **a few fragmentary ballads are all that have come down to us** todo lo que nos ha llegado son los trozos de unas cuantas baladas; **this custom comes down from the Romans** esta costumbre se ha heredado *or* viene de los romanos

(h) *Br (from university)* licenciarse, *Am* egresar

(i) *Fam (from drug)* **it took me ages to c. down** los efectos me duraron una eternidad

▸**come down on** *vt insep (reprimand)* regañar

▸**come down to** *vt insep (be a matter of)* reducirse a, tratarse de; **when it comes down to it...** a la hora de la verdad...

▸**come down with** *vt insep (become ill) Esp* pillar, *Am* agarrarse; **he came down with a cold** *Esp* pilló un resfriado, *Am* se agarró un resfrío

▸**come forward** *vi (as candidate)* presentarse; **no witnesses have yet c. forward** todavía no han aparecido testigos

▸**come from** *vt insep* (a) *(originate from)* **to c. from France** *(person)* ser francés(esa); **to c. from Chicago** ser de Chicago; **to c. from a middle-class background** proceder de un entorno de clase media; **where is the money going to c. from?** ¿de dónde va a salir el dinero?; **this word comes from the Greek** esta palabra viene del griego; **that's surprising coming from him** viniendo de él, es sorprendente; *Fam Fig* **I can see where you're coming from, but...** entiendo tus razones, pero...

(b) *(result from)* **that's what comes from telling lies** eso es lo que pasa por contar mentiras

▸**come in** *vi* (a) *(enter) (person)* entrar; **c. in!** ¡adelante!, ¡pase!; **I won't be coming in (to work) tomorrow** no vendré (a trabajar) mañana

(b) *(arrive) (train, flight)* llegar; **to c. in first/second** llegar en primer/segundo lugar; **reports are coming in of a major accident** nos llegan noticias de un grave accidente; **it's nice to have some money coming in** está bien tener ingresos

(c) *(have a role)* entrar; *Fam* **that's where you c. in** ahí es cuando entras tú

(d) *(prove to be)* **to c. in handy** *or* **useful** resultar útil, venir bien

(e) *(comment)* intervenir; **can I c. in on that last point?** ¿podría hacer un comentario sobre ese último punto?

(f) *(on radio)* **c. in unit number one, over** adelante unidad uno, cambio

(g) *(be introduced)* entrar en vigor; **when do the new rules c. in?** ¿cuándo entran en vigor las nuevas normas?

(h) *(government)* llegar al poder

(i) *(become seasonable)* **when do strawberries c. in?** ¿cuándo es la temporada de las fresas?

(j) *(become fashionable)* ponerse de moda

(k) *(tide)* subir

▸**come in for** *vt insep* **to c. in for praise/criticism** recibir alabanzas/críticas

▸**come into** *vt insep* (a) *(enter) (room, city)* entrar en; **he came into my life five years ago** entró en mi vida hace cinco años; **luck didn't c.**

into it la suerte no tuvo nada que ver; **to c. into existence** nacer, surgir; **to c. into fashion** ponerse de moda; **to c. into force** *or* **effect** *(of law, ruling)* entrar en vigor; **this bike really comes into its own on rough terrain** es en terrenos accidentados donde esta moto rinde de verdad; **to c. into the world** venir al mundo

(**b**) *(inherit)* heredar

▶ **come of** *vt insep (result from)* **no good will c. of it** no saldrá nada bueno de esto; **everyone was keen on the idea, but nothing ever came of it** a todo el mundo le interesaba la idea, pero no se llegó a materializar; **that's what comes of being too ambitious** eso es lo que pasa por ser demasiado ambicioso

▶ **come off** 1 *vt insep* (**a**) *(fall from) (horse, bicycle)* caerse de

(**b**) *(be removed from) (of button)* caerse; *(of label)* despegarse; *(of paint)* desconcharse; **the handle has c. off this cup** se ha soltado el asa de esta taza

(**c**) *(stop taking) (medicine, drugs)* dejar de tomar

(**d**) *(have completed)* **the team is coming off a run of defeats** el equipo ha tenido una racha de derrotas

(**e**) *Fam* **c. off it!** *(don't be ridiculous)* ¡anda ya!

2 *vi* (**a**) *(be removed) (button)* caerse; *(label)* despegarse; *(paint)* levantarse; **the handle came off in my hand** se me quedó el asa en la mano

(**b**) *(fall)* caerse

(**c**) *(leave football field)* retirarse

(**d**) *(succeed) (plan)* salir; *(joke)* funcionar; **my trip to China didn't c. off** al final no me fui de viaje a China

(**e**) *(fare, manage)* **to c. off well/badly** *(in contest)* quedar bien/mal; **she came off worst again** ha vuelto a salir la peor parada

(**f**) *very Fam (reach orgasm)* correrse, *RP, Ven* acabar

▶ **come on** 1 *vi* (**a**) *(as exhortation)* **c. on!** *(hurry up, try harder)* ¡vamos!, *Esp* ¡venga!; *(expressing disbelief)* ¡anda ya!; **c. on in!** ¡entra!, ¡pasa!; **why don't you c. on over to our place?** ¿por qué no te vienes a (nuestra) casa?

(**b**) *(make progress)* marchar, progresar; **how's the project coming on?** ¿qué tal marcha el proyecto?; **his Spanish is coming on well** su español va mejorando

(**c**) *(appear) (on stage, in movie)* salir, aparecer; *(substitute)* salir

(**d**) *Fam (behave, act)* **don't c. on all macho with me!** ¡a mí no te me pongas macho!; **you came on a bit strong** te pasaste un pelo

(**e**) *(start) (heating, lights)* encenderse, *Am* prenderse; *(TV programme)* empezar; **I feel a cold coming on** me estoy resfriando *or* acatarrando; **as night came on** conforme se hacía de noche

(**f**) *Br Fam (start menstruating)* **she had come on that morning** le había venido la regla esa mañana

2 *vt insep (find) (person, object)* encontrar, encontrarse con

▶ **come on to** *vt insep* (**a**) *(proceed to consider)* **we now c. on to the next point on the agenda** pasamos ahora al siguiente punto del orden del día

(**b**) *Fam (flirt)* intentar seducir a, *Esp* tirar los tejos a, *Méx* echarle los perros a, *RP* cargar a

▶ **come out** *vi* (**a**) *(person, sun)* salir; *(flower)* salir; *Comptr* **to c. out of a document** salir de un documento; **that didn't c. out the way I meant it** no he querido decir eso

(**b**) *(magazine, book)* salir; *(movie)* estrenarse

(**c**) *(tooth, screw, hair)* caerse; *(stain)* salir, quitarse

(**d**) *(become known)* **it came out that...** se descubrió que...; **the truth will c. out in the end** al final se sabrá la verdad

(**e**) *(declare oneself publicly)* **to c. out in favour of/against sth** declararse a favor de/en contra de algo; **to c. out on strike** declararse en huelga; *Fam* **to c. out (of the closet)** *(homosexual)* salir del armario, declararse homosexual públicamente; *Hum* **he finally came out as a country and western fan** acabó declarándose abiertamente un fan de la música country

(**f**) *(emerge, finish up)* salir; **everything will c. out fine** todo saldrá bien

(**g**) *(in competition, exam)* **I came out top in maths** fui el primero en matemáticas; **to c. out on top** *(win)* ganar

(**h**) *Old-fashioned (into society)* debutar

(**i**) *(photographs)* salir; **the photos have c. out well** las fotos han salido bien

▶ **come out at** *vt insep (amount to)* **the total comes out at 450** el total asciende a 450

▶ **come out in** *vt insep* **I came out in a rash** me salió un sarpullido; **I came out in spots** me salieron granos

▶ **come out of** *vt insep (result from)* **the only good thing to c. out of it was...** lo único positivo del asunto fue...; **to c. out of an affair well/badly** salir bien/mal parado(a) de un asunto

▶ **come out with** *vt insep* **to c. out with an opinion** expresar una opinión; **she comes out with some really stupid comments** mira que dice tonterías a veces; **he finally came out with it** al final lo consiguió

▶ **come over** 1 *vt insep (affect)* sobrevenir; **a strange feeling came over me** me sobrevino una extraña sensación; **what's c. over you?** ¿qué te ha pasado?

2 *vi* (**a**) *(move, travel in direction of speaker)* **at the party she came over to talk to me** se acercó a hablar conmigo en la fiesta; **his family came over with the early settlers** su familia llegó con los primeros colonos; **I met him in the plane coming over** me lo encontré en el vuelo que me traía aquí

(**b**) *(make impression)* **to c. over well/badly** quedar bien/mal; **she comes over (as) a bit arrogant** da la impresión de que es un poco arrogante

(**c**) *(feel)* **to c. over all funny** sentirse raro(a); **to c. over all dizzy** marearse

(**d**) *(visit)* pasarse; **I'll c. over tomorrow** me pasaré mañana (por tu casa)

(**e**) *(change sides)* **they came over to our side** se pasaron a nuestro bando; **he finally came over to their way of thinking** al final acabó por compartir su punto de vista

▶ **come round** *vi* (**a**) *(visit)* pasarse; **c. round and see me one day** pásate a verme un día

(**b**) *(regain consciousness)* volver en sí

(**c**) *(accept)* **to c. round to sb's way of thinking** terminar aceptando la opinión de alguien

(**d**) *(change to better mood)* **don't worry, she'll soon c. round** no te preocupes, ya se le pasará

(**e**) *(recur)* **my birthday has c. round again** otra vez es mi cumpleaños; **the summer holidays will soon be coming round again** pronto llegarán otra vez las vacaciones de verano

▶ **come through** 1 *vt insep* (**a**) *(penetrate)* penetrar, entrar (**b**) *(survive) (war, crisis, illness)* sobrevivir a

2 *vi* (**a**) *(message, news)* llegar; **you're coming through loud and clear** se te recibe alto y claro

(**b**) *(show)* **the fear came through in his voice** el temor se revelaba en su voz; **her enthusiasm comes through in her letters** su entusiasmo se refleja en sus cartas

(**c**) *(survive)* sobrevivir

(**d**) *(enter)* pasar; **c. through into my office** pase a mi oficina

(**e**) *(be granted, approved)* **my request for a transfer finally came through** al final fue aprobada mi solicitud de traslado

(**f**) *US Fam (do what is expected)* **he came through in the end** al final hizo lo que tenía que hacer; **they came through with the money** pusieron el dinero

▶ **come to** 1 *vt insep* (**a**) *(amount to)* sumar, alcanzar; **how much does it c. to?** ¿a cuánto asciende?; **the scheme never came to anything, the scheme came to nothing** el plan se quedó en nada

(**b**) *(reach) (place, decision, conclusion)* llegar a; **to c. to the end (of sth)** llegar al final (de algo); **to c. to harm** sufrir daño; **to c. to the point** ir al grano; **to c. to rest** detenerse; **what is the world coming to?** ¿adónde vamos a ir a parar?; **when it comes to...** en cuestión de...; **if it comes to that, you're not exactly a genius either** si nos fijamos en eso, no es que tú seas tampoco un genio; IDIOM **he got what was coming to him** se la estaba buscando

(**c**) *(occur to)* **the answer came to him all of a sudden** la respuesta se le ocurrió de repente; **it will c. to me later** ya me saldrá

2 *vi (regain consciousness)* volver en sí

▶ **come together** *vi* (**a**) *(gather)* reunirse

(**b**) *(begin to go well)* **things are really starting to c. together for us** las cosas nos están comenzando a salir bien

▶ **come under** *vt insep* (**a**) *(be classified under) (heading)* ir bajo

(**b**) *(be responsibility of)* **that doesn't c. under our department** no es responsabilidad de nuestro departamento

(**c**) *(be subjected to) (pressure, scrutiny)* ser sometido(a) a; **his motives have c. under suspicion** sus motivos han sido puestos en duda; **the measures have c. under heavy criticism** las medidas han sido duramente criticadas; **to c. under attack** ser atacado(a)

▶ **come up** 1 *vt insep (stairs, hill)* subir

2 *vi* (**a**) *(sun, plant)* salir, crecer; **my carrots are coming up nicely** la zanahorias están saliendo *or* creciendo muy bien

(**b**) *(reach)* **the mud came up to our knees** el barro nos llegaba a las rodillas

(**c**) *(arise) (opportunity, problem)* surgir, presentarse; *(issue, name)* surgir; *(job)* salir; **there are some interesting films coming up on television** van a poner algunas películas interesantes en la televisión; **I'll let you know if anything comes up** te avisaré si surge algo; **two glasses of wine, please – coming up!** dos vasos de vino, por favor –

¡marchando!; **a nice house has c. up for sale** ha salido a la venta una casa bonita

(**d**) *(happen unexpectedly)* **she's ready for anything that might c. up** está preparada para cualquier imprevisto; **I can't make it, something has c. up** no voy a poder ir, me ha surgido algo

(**e**) *(happen in due course)* **Christmas is coming up** llega la Navidad

(**f**) *Law* **to c. up before the judge** *or* **the court** *(accused)* comparecer delante del juez *or* del tribunal; *(case)* verse delante del juez *or* del tribunal; **the case comes up for trial tomorrow** el caso se verá mañana

(**g**) *(travel)* venir; **we've got some friends coming up to visit us** van a venir a visitarnos unos amigos

(**h**) *(approach)* **to c. up behind sb** acercarse a alguien por atrás

(**i**) *(go up)* subir; IDIOM **to c. up in the world** ascender socialmente

(**j**) *(turn out)* **that old sideboard has c. up beautifully** *(after cleaning)* ese aparador antiguo ha quedado estupendamente; IDIOM **to c. up smelling of roses** salir airoso(a)

(**k**) *(turn on)* **when the lights came up at the interval** cuando se encendieron las luces en el intermedio

(**l**) *Br (to university)* empezar los estudios

► **come up against** *vt insep* **to c. up against opposition/a problem** encontrarse con oposición/un problema

► **come up for** *vt insep* **the agreement is coming up for review** el acuerdo va a ser revisado; **the chairperson is coming up for re-election** se va a volver a elegir presidente

► **come upon** *vt insep (find) (person, object)* encontrar, encontrarse con

► **come up to** *vt insep* (**a**) *(approach)* acercarse a; **a man came up to me and started talking** un hombre se me acercó y comenzó a hablarme; **we're coming up to Christmas** se acerca la Navidad; **it's coming up to nine o'clock** ya son casi las nueve

(**b**) *(reach, equal)* llegar a (la altura de); **the water came up to her chin** el agua le llegaba a la (altura de la) barbilla; **the movie didn't c. up to my expectations** la película no fue tan buena como yo esperaba

► **come up with** *vt insep* (**a**) *(find) (money)* encontrar

(**b**) *(think of)* **they came up with a wonderful idea** se les ocurrió una idea maravillosa; **what will she c. up with next?** ¿qué será lo próximo que se le ocurra?

---

comeback ['kʌmbæk] *n* (**a**) *(of sportsperson)* vuelta *f* a la competición *or Am* competencia; *(of actor)* regreso *m*; **to make a c.** *(of fashion)* volver; *(of actor)* volver a actuar; *(of sportsperson)* volver a la competición *or Am* competencia (**b**) *(opportunity for retaliation)* posibilidad *f* de reclamar; **I've got no c.** no hay nada que pueda hacer, sólo me queda el recurso del pataleo (**c**) *(retort)* réplica *f*

comedian [kə'mi:dɪən] *n* (**a**) *(comic)* humorista *mf*; *Fig (funny person)* payaso(a) *m,f* (**b**) *Theat (comic actor)* actor *m* cómico

comedienne [kəmi:dɪ'en] *n* (**a**) *(comic)* humorista *f* (**b**) *Theat (comic actress)* actriz *f* cómica

comedown ['kʌmdaʊn] *n Fam* degradación *f*

comedy ['kɒmədɪ] *n* (**a**) *(play, movie)* comedia *f*; *(TV series)* serie *f* cómica *or* de humor; IDIOM **it was a c. of errors from start to finish** fue una payasada de principio a fin ►► *Lit* ***c. of manners*** comedia *f* de costumbres (**b**) *(humorous entertainment)* humor *m*, humorismo *m* ►► ***c. show*** *(on TV)* programa *m* de humor (**c**) *(humorousness)* gracia *f*, comicidad *f*

come-hither ['kʌm'hɪðə(r)] *adj Fam* **c. look** mirada seductora

comely ['kʌmlɪ] *adj Literary* hermoso(a), bello(a)

come-on ['kʌmɒn] *n Fam* **to give sb the c.** *(sexually)* intentar seducir a alguien, *Esp* tirar los tejos a alguien, *Méx* echarle los perros a alguien, *RP* cargar a alguien; **it was a c. to get buyers interested** era un señuelo para atraer a los compradores

comer ['kʌmə(r)] *n* (**a**) *(arrival)* **open to all comers** abierto(a) para todo el mundo; **he was willing to take on all comers** estaba dispuesto a enfrentarse a cualquier rival (**b**) *US Fam (potential success)* **she's a real c.!** ¡tiene mucho potencial!, ¡promete mucho!

comestibles [kə'mestɪbəlz] *npl Formal* comestibles *mpl*

comet ['kɒmɪt] *n* cometa *m*

come-uppance [kʌm'ʌpəns] *n Fam* **he'll get his c.** ya tendrá su merecido

comfort ['kʌmfət] **1** *n* (**a**) *(ease)* comodidad *f*; **to live in c.** vivir confortablemente; **in the c. of one's own home** en el calor del hogar; **the bullets were too close for c.** las balas pasaban peligrosamente cerca ►► ***c. food*** = comida sencilla y que llena; *US* ***c. station*** servicio *m*, *Esp* aseos *mpl*, *Am* baños *mpl*, *Am* lavatorios *mpl*

(**b**) *(amenities)* **every modern c.** todas las comodidades modernas; **I like my c.** *or* **comforts** me gustan las comodidades

(**c**) *(consolation)* consuelo *m*; **it's a c. to know the children are safe** consuela saber que los niños están a salvo; **if it's any c.,...** si te sirve de consuelo,...; **to take c. from** *or* **in sth** consolarse con algo; **I took c. from** *or* **in the knowledge that it would soon be over** me consoló saber que pronto acabaría; *Ironic* **some c. you are/that is!** ¡menudo consuelo!

2 *vt (console)* consolar, confortar

comfortable ['kʌmfətəbəl] *adj* (**a**) *(bed, chair, clothes, shoes)* cómodo(a); *(room)* cómodo(a), confortable; **to be c.** *(person)* estar cómodo(a); **to make oneself c.** ponerse cómodo(a); **to feel c.** sentirse a gusto, sentirse cómodo(a); **I wouldn't feel c. accepting that money** no me sentiría bien si aceptara ese dinero

(**b**) *(income)* holgado(a); *(life)* cómodo(a); **to be in c. circumstances** estar en una situación holgada *or* desahogada

(**c**) *(patient)* estable; **the patient is c.** el paciente no sufre demasiados dolores; **he had a c. night** pasó una noche relajada

(**d**) *(majority, lead, win)* holgado(a); **we're leading by a c. margin** vamos ganando por un holgado margen

comfortably ['kʌmfətəblɪ] *adv* (**a**) *(to sit)* cómodamente (**b**) *(without difficulty)* holgadamente, cómodamente; **to live c.** vivir sin apuros; **to win c.** ganar holgadamente; **we should manage it c. in two hours** deberíamos poder hacerlo con toda comodidad en dos horas (**c**) *(in financial comfort)* holgadamente, desahogadamente; **to be c. off** estar en una situación holgada *or* desahogada

comforter ['kʌmfətə(r)] *n* (**a**) *US (quilt)* edredón *m* (**b**) *(for baby)* chupete *m* (**c**) *Old-fashioned (scarf)* bufanda *f*

comforting ['kʌmfətɪŋ] *adj* reconfortante

comfrey ['kʌmfrɪ] *n* consuelda *f*

comfy ['kʌmfɪ] *adj Fam (bed, chair)* cómodo(a); **to be c.** *(person)* estar cómodo(a)

comic ['kɒmɪk] **1** *n* (**a**) *(performer)* cómico(a) *m,f*, humorista *mf* (**b**) *(magazine)* **c. (book)** *(for children) Esp* tebeo *m*, *Am* revista *f* de historietas, *CSur* revista *f* de chistes; *(for adults)* cómic *m* (**c**) *US* **comics** *(in newspaper, magazine)* tiras *fpl* cómicas

2 *adj* cómico(a); **to provide some c. relief** aliviar la situación con un toque de humor ►► ***c. opera*** ópera *f* cómica *or* bufa; ***c. strip*** tira *f* cómica

comical ['kɒmɪkəl] *adj* cómico(a)

coming ['kʌmɪŋ] **1** *n* (**a**) *(of person)* venida *f*, llegada *f*; *(of night)* caída *f*; **there was a lot of c. and going next door** había muchas idas y venidas en la puerta de al lado; **I've lost track of all the comings and goings in this company** he perdido la cuenta de la gente que llega y se va de esta empresa (**b**) **c. of age** *(reaching adulthood)* mayoría de edad; **the c. of age of Icelandic cinema** la mayoría de edad del cine islandés (**c**) *Old-fashioned* **c. out** *(in society)* debut, presentación

2 *adj* (**a**) *(approaching) (year, week)* próximo(a); **this c. weekend** la semana próxima *or* que viene (**b**) *Fam (promising)* **he's the c. man** es un tipo con una gran proyección de futuro

Comintern ['kɒmɪntɜ:n] *n Hist* (*abbr* **Communist International**) Comintern *f*, Komintern *f*

comma ['kɒmə] *n* coma *f*

command [kə'mɑ:nd] **1** *n* (**a**) *(order)* orden *f*; **to give a c.** dar una orden; **to do sth at sb's c.** hacer algo por orden de alguien; **they are at your c.** están a sus órdenes ►► *Theat & TV* ***c. performance*** gala *f* real

(**b**) *(authority, control) (of army, expedition)* mando *m*; **to be in c. (of)** estar al mando (de); **to be in c. of a situation** dominar una situación; **to be at sb's c.** estar a las órdenes de alguien; **he took c. of the situation** tomó el mando de la situación ►► *Mil* ***c. and control*** centro *m* de mando; *Econ* ***c. economy*** economía *f* dirigida; *Astron* ***c. module*** módulo *m* de mando; ***c. post*** puesto *m* de mando

(**c**) *(mastery)* dominio *m*; **c. of the seas** dominio de los mares; **she has a good c. of English** tiene un buen dominio del inglés; **he has many resources at his c.** tiene muchos recursos a su disposición

(**d**) *Mil* **Northern/Southern c.** *(area)* el comando Norte/Sur

(**e**) *Comptr* comando *m*, instrucción *f* ►► ***c. interpreter*** intérprete *m* de comandos; ***c. key*** tecla *f* de comando; ***c. language*** lenguaje *m* comando, lenguaje *m* de comandos; ***c. line*** línea *f* de comando; ***c. processor*** intérprete *m* de procesos

2 *vt* (**a**) *(order)* mandar, ordenar; **to c. sb to do sth** mandar a alguien que haga algo; **she commanded that we leave immediately** nos ordenó que nos marcharamos de inmediato

(**b**) *(ship, regiment)* estar al mando de, mandar

(**c**) *(have at one's disposal)* disponer de; **with all the skill he could c.** con toda la habilidad de que disponía

(**d**) *(inspire) (respect, admiration)* infundir, inspirar; *(attention)*

obtener; **to c. a high price** alcanzar un precio elevado; **she can c. a high salary** puede pedir *or* exigir un buen sueldo
(**e**) *(of building, statue)* **the statue/building commands a view of the entire city** desde la estatua/el edificio se ve toda la ciudad

> En inglés culto o elevado, y especialmente en inglés americano, **command** puede ir seguido de **that** más un verbo en subjuntivo (ver el panel SUBJUNCTIVE):
> **she commanded that a list of names be drawn up**
> *ordenó que se elaborara una lista de nombres*
> Lo mismo también podría decirse del siguiente modo:
> **she commanded that a list of names should be drawn up**

commandant ['kɒməndænt, kɒmən'dænt] *n Mil* comandante *mf*

commandeer [kɒmən'dɪə(r)] *vt* (**a**) *Mil* requisar (**b**) *(take for one's own use)* apropiarse de

commander [kə'mɑːndə(r)] *n* (**a**) *(person in charge) (of garrison, camp, unit)* comandante *mf* (**b**) *Br Naut* capitán(ana) *m,f* de fragata (**c**) *(of police)* = oficial de policía de alta graduación a cargo de un distrito de Londres

commander-in-chief [kə'mɑːndərɪn'tʃiːf] *n Mil* comandante *mf* en jefe

commanding [kə'mɑːndɪŋ] *adj* (**a**) *Mil* ***c. officer*** oficial *m* (al mando) (**b**) *(dominant) (position)* dominante; *(lead)* abrumador(ora) (**c**) *(tone, appearance)* autoritario(a)

commandment [kə'mɑːndmənt] *n Rel* mandamiento *m*; **to keep the commandments** cumplir los mandamientos

commando [kə'mɑːndəʊ] (*pl* **commandos**) *n Mil (soldier, unit)* comando *m*; **a c. raid** una incursión de comandos; **a c. unit** una unidad de comandos

commemorate [kə'meməreɪt] *vt* conmemorar

commemoration [kəmemə'reɪʃən] *n* conmemoración *f*; **in c. of** en conmemoración de

commemorative [kə'memərətɪv] *adj* conmemorativo(a)

commence [kə'mens] *Formal* **1** *vt* comenzar; **to c. doing sth** comenzar a hacer algo; *Law* **to c. proceedings against sb** entablar un pleito contra alguien
2 *vi* comenzar

commencement [kə'mensmənt] *n* (**a**) *Formal (beginning)* comienzo *m*, inicio *m* (**b**) *US Univ* ceremonia *f* de graduación

commend [kə'mend] *vt* (**a**) *(praise)* encomiar, elogiar; **to c. sb for bravery** elogiar la valentía de alguien; **highly commended** accésit, mención
(**b**) *(recommend)* **he commended the proposal to the committee** encomendó la propuesta a la comisión; **the train journey has little to c. it** el viaje en tren tiene poco de recomendable
(**c**) *(entrust)* encomendar (**to** a); *Rel* **we commended our souls to God** encomendamos nuestras almas a Dios

commendable [kə'mendəbəl] *adj* encomiable

commendably [kə'mendəblɪ] *adv* **his speech was c. brief** su discurso fue de una brevedad digna de encomio

commendation [kɒmen'deɪʃən] *n* (**a**) *(praise)* encomio *m*; **worthy of c.** digno(a) de encomio *or* mención (**b**) *(award in competition)* accésit *m*, mención *f*; **to receive a c.** recibir un accésit *or* una mención

commensurate [kə'menʃərət] *adj Formal* acorde (**with** con), proporcional (**with** a); **you will receive a salary c. with the position** percibirá un salario adecuado a su puesto; **of c. value** de un valor similar

comment ['kɒment] **1** *n* (**a**) *(remark)* comentario *m*; **to make a c. on sth** hacer un comentario acerca de algo; **she let it pass without c.** lo dejó pasar sin hacer ningún comentario; **(it's a) fair c.** no te/le/*etc.* falta razón
(**b**) *(reaction)* impresiones *fpl*, valoraciones *fpl*; **no one was available for c.** nadie quiso hacer declaraciones *or* valorar el asunto; **no c.** sin comentarios
(**c**) *(gossip, criticism)* **the decision provoked much c.** la decisión suscitó muchos comentarios
(**d**) *(note)* comentario *m*
2 *vt* **to c. that...** comentar que...; **"how interesting," he commented** "qué interesante", comentó
3 *vi* hacer comentarios; **to c. on sth** comentar algo

commentary ['kɒməntərɪ] *n* (**a**) *(on TV, radio)* comentarios *mpl* ►► *Sport* ***c. box*** cabina *f* de comentaristas (**b**) *(on text)* comentario *m*

commentate ['kɒmənteɪt] *vi (for TV, radio)* hacer de comentarista; **to c. on a match** ser el/la comentarista de un partido

commentator ['kɒmənteɪtə(r)] *n (on TV, radio)* comentarista *mf*; **a political c.** un(a) comentarista político(a)

commerce ['kɒmɜːs] *n* (**a**) *(trade)* comercio *m* (**b**) *Formal (of ideas, opinions)* intercambio *m* (**c**) *(government department)* el Ministerio de Comercio; *US* **Secretary of C.** Ministro(a) de Comercio

commercial [kə'mɜːʃəl] **1** *adj* (**a**) *(relating to business)* comercial ►► ***c. artist*** diseñador(ora) *m,f* gráfico(a) de publicidad; *Fin* ***c. bank*** banco *m* comercial; *TV & Rad* ***c. break*** pausa *f* publicitaria; ***c. college*** escuela *f* de secretariado administración; ***c. contract*** contrato *m* mercantil; ***c. department*** departamento *m* comercial; ***c. law*** derecho *m* mercantil; ***c. paper*** efecto *m* de comercio; ***c. photography*** fotografía *f* publicitaria; ***c. traveller*** viajante *mf* de comercio; ***c. value*** valor *m* comercial; ***c. vehicle*** vehículo *m* de transporte de mercancías
(**b**) *(profitable)* rentable; **it's not a c. proposition** no es rentable
(**c**) *Pej (profit-seeking)* comercial; **their motives are purely c.** sus motivos son estrictamente comerciales
(**d**) *(television, radio)* comercial
2 *n (TV, radio advertisement)* anuncio *m* (publicitario)

commercialism [kə'mɜːʃəlɪzəm] *n Pej* comercialismo *m*

commercialize [kə'mɜːʃəlaɪz] *vt* comercializar

commercially [kə'mɜːʃəlɪ] *adv* comercialmente; **to be c. successful** *(product)* ser un éxito de ventas; *(movie, play)* ser un éxito de taquilla *orAm* boletería; **c. viable** rentable, viable desde el punto de vista económico

commie ['kɒmɪ] *Fam Pej* **1** *n (communist)* rojo(a) *m,f*
2 *adj* rojo(a)

commis ['kɒmɪ] *n (waiter)* ayudante *mf* de camarero; **c. (chef)** ayudante *mf* de cocina

commiserate [kə'mɪzəreɪt] *vi* **he commiserated with me** me dijo cuánto lo sentía

commiseration [kəmɪzə'reɪʃən] *n* **he offered his commiserations** dijo cuánto lo sentía; **(you have) my commiserations** te compadezco, cuánto lo siento

commissar [kɒmɪ'sɑː(r)] *n Pol* comisario(a) *m,f* político(a)

commissariat [kɒmɪ'seərɪət, kɒmɪ'sɑːrɪət] *n* (**a**) *Mil (department)* intendencia *f* (**b**) *Mil (food supplies)* provisiones *fpl*

commissary ['kɒmɪsərɪ] *n US* (**a**) *Mil (shop)* economato *m* (**b**) *Mil (officer)* intendente *mf* (**c**) *(cafeteria)* cafetería *f (en estudio cinematográfico)*

commission [kə'mɪʃən] **1** *n* (**a**) *Com (payment)* comisión *f*; **to charge c.** cobrar comisión; **to work on a c. basis** trabajar a comisión; **I get (a) 5 percent c.** me llevo el 5 por ciento de comisión
(**b**) *(order)* encargo *m*; **to give a c. to an artist** encargar algo a un artista
(**c**) *(body)* comisión *f*, comité *m*; **c. of inquiry, fact-finding c.** comisión de investigación ►► ***C. for Racial Equality*** = organismo británico subvencionado por el gobierno que lucha contra el racismo
(**d**) *(service)* **out of/in c.** *(ship)* fuera de/en servicio; *(machine, car)* averiado(a)/en funcionamiento; **you'll be out of c. for six weeks** *(to athlete)* estarás alejado de las pistas durante seis semanas
(**e**) *Mil* nombramiento *m*; **to resign one's c.** renunciar al rango de oficial
(**f**) *Formal (of deed, crime)* comisión *f*, perpetración *f*; **sins of c. and omission** pecados de obra y omisión
2 *vt* (**a**) *(order) (new building, work of art, book)* encargar; **to c. sb to do sth** encargar a alguien hacer algo *or* que haga algo (**b**) *Mil* **to be commissioned** ser nombrado(a) (**c**) *(ship)* poner en servicio

commissionaire [kəmɪʃə'neə(r)] *n Br (at hotel, cinema)* portero *m* de librea

commissioner [kə'mɪʃənə(r)] *n* (**a**) *(member of commission)* comisionado(a) *m,f*; *EU* comisario(a) *m,f* (**b**) ***c. of police*** comisario(a) *m,f* de policía (**c**) *Law* ***c. for oaths*** ≃ notario(a) *m,f*, *CRica, Ecuad, RP* ≃ escribano(a) *m,f*

commissioning [kə'mɪʃənɪŋ] *n (in publishing)* = encargo de trabajos ►► ***c. editor*** = director editorial responsable de encargar trabajos externos

commit [kə'mɪt] **1** *vt* (**a**) *(error, crime)* cometer; **to c. suicide** suicidarse
(**b**) **to c. oneself** *(promise)* comprometerse; **to c. oneself to (doing) sth** comprometerse a (hacer) algo; **he refused to c. himself** rechazó comprometerse
(**c**) *(oblige)* obligar; **to c. sb to doing sth** obligar a alguien a hacer algo
(**d**) *(entrust)* confiar, encomendar; **to c. sth to writing** *or* **paper** poner algo por escrito; **to c. sth to memory** memorizar algo
(**e**) *(send)* **to c. sb to prison** encarcelar a alguien; **he was committed** *(to mental institution)* fue ingresado en un psiquiátrico; **to c. troops to a battle** asignar tropas para una batalla

(**f**) *Law* **to c. sb for trial** enviar a alguien a un tribunal superior para ser juzgado
(**g**) *Pol (legislative bill)* enviar a una comisión
2 *vi (emotionally)* comprometerse

commitment [kə'mɪtmənt] *n* (**a**) *(obligation)* compromiso *m*; **I'm afraid I have other commitments** me temo que tengo otros compromisos; **family commitments** compromisos familiares; **my present financial commitments mean I am unable to help** mis compromisos financieros actuales me impiden ayudar; *Com* **free home trial with no c. to buy** prueba en casa gratuita sin obligación de compra
(**b**) *(promise)* compromiso *m*; **to make a c. (to sth/sb)** comprometerse (con algo/alguien)
(**c**) *(dedication)* entrega *f* (**to** a), compromiso *m* (**to** con); **his c. to the cause of legal reform** su entrega a *or* su compromiso con la causa de la reforma legal; **she lacks c.** no se entrega *or* compromete lo suficiente
(**d**) *(emotional engagement)* **so many men avoid c. in relationships** hay tantos hombres que evitan comprometerse en las relaciones
(**e**) *Pol (of legislative bill)* envío *m* a una comisión

committal [kə'mɪtəl] *n* (**a**) *(to mental hospital, prison)* reclusión *f*, ingreso *m* (**to** en) ▸▸ *Law* ***c. proceedings*** auto *m* de prisión, orden *f* de encarcelamiento (**b**) *(of coffin to ground)* enterramiento *m*, sepultura *f*

committed [kə'mɪtɪd] *adj* (**a**) *(dedicated) (writer, artist)* comprometido(a); **a c. Socialist/Christian** un(a) socialista/cristiano(a) comprometido(a); **he didn't seem very c.** no parecía muy entregado; **to be c. to an idea** estar comprometido(a) con una idea (**b**) *(under obligation)* comprometido(a); **you're not c. to paying a fixed sum** no está obligado *or* no se compromete a pagar una suma fija

committee [kə'mɪtɪ] *n* comité *m*, comisión *f*; **to sit** *or* **be on a c.** ser miembro de un comité ▸▸ ***c. of inquiry*** comisión *f* investigadora; ***c. meeting*** reunión *f* del comité; ***c. member*** miembro *mf* del comité; *EU* ***C. of the Regions*** comité *m* de las Regiones; *Br Parl* ***c. stage*** *(of bill)* = fase de aprobación de una ley en la que la estudia una comisión de diputados

committeeman [kə'mɪtɪmən] *n* miembro *m* de un comité *or* una comisión

committeeperson [kə'mɪtɪpɜːsən] *n* miembro *mf* de un comité *or* una comisión

committeewoman [kə'mɪtɪwʊmən] *n* miembro *f* de un comité *or* una comisión

commode [kə'məʊd] *n* (**a**) *(chest of drawers)* cómoda *f* (**b**) *(for chamberpot)* silla *f* con orinal, silla *f* (de) servicio

commodious [kə'məʊdɪəs] *adj Formal* amplio(a), espacioso(a)

> **False friend**: The Spanish adjective **cómodo** is not a translation for the English word **commodious**. In Spanish **cómodo** means "comfortable", "convenient", "easy" or "lazy".

commodity [kə'mɒdɪtɪ] *n* (**a**) *(product)* bien *m* de consumo; *Fig* **a rare c.** un bien muy escaso (**b**) *St Exch* materia *f* prima ▸▸ ***c. exchange*** bolsa *f* de materias primas; ***c. futures*** futuros *mpl* sobre materias primas; ***the c.*** *or* ***commodities market*** el mercado de materias primas

> **False friend**: The Spanish noun **comodidad** is not a translation for the English word **commodity**. In Spanish **comodidad** means "comfort" or "convenience".

commodore ['kɒmədɔː(r)] *n* (**a**) *(in navy)* comodoro *m* (**b**) *(of merchant ships)* = capitán al mando de un convoy de buques (**c**) *(of shipping line)* = capitán al mando de una flota de buques (**d**) *(of yacht club)* presidente(a) *m,f*

common ['kɒmən] **1** *n* (**a**) **to have sth in c. (with sb)** tener algo en común (con alguien); **they have certain ideas in c.** tienen algunas ideas en común; **in c. with you,...** al igual que tú,... (**b**) *(land)* = campo municipal para uso del común, ≃ ejido *m*
2 *adj* (**a**) *(frequent, widespread)* común, frecuente; **it's quite c. for people to find the experience upsetting** es bastante común *or* frecuente que la experiencia resulte traumática; **a c. occurrence** un suceso común *or* frecuente; **it was a c. sight in my youth** era bastante común cuando era joven; **the c. belief of the period that...** entonces se creía que...; **it's c. practice nowadays** es común hoy en día; **in c. use** de uso corriente
(**b**) *(shared)* común (**to** a); *Br* **to make c. cause with sb** hacer causa común con alguien; **it is by c. consent the best** está considerado por todos como el mejor; **it's c. knowledge** es de(l) dominio público ▸▸ *EU* ***C. Agricultural Policy*** Política *f* Agrícola Común; *Math & Fig* ***c. denominator*** denominador *m* común; *Br Sch* ***C. Entrance*** = examen de ingreso a un colegio privado, que se realiza normalmente a los trece años; *EU* ***c. external tariff*** arancel *m* externo común, tarifa *f* exterior común; *Math & Fig* ***c. factor*** factor *m* común; *EU* ***C. Fisheries Policy*** Política *f* Pesquera Común; *Comptr* ***c. gateway interface*** interfaz *f* común de pasarela; ***the c. good*** el bien común; ***c. grave*** fosa *f* común; *Fig* ***c. ground*** puntos *mpl* en común; ***c. land*** terreno *m* comunal; ***c. law*** derecho *m* consuetudinario; *Formerly* ***the C. Market*** el Mercado Común; ***c. ownership*** propiedad *f* colectiva; ***c. property*** bienes *mpl* comunales; ***c. room*** *(in institution)* sala *f* de estar, salón *m*; *(for pupils)* sala *f* de alumnos; *(for teachers)* sala *f* de profesores
(**c**) *(average, ordinary)* común, corriente; **it's only c. courtesy to reply** lo cortés en estos casos es responder ▸▸ ***c. carrier*** transportista *mf*; ***the c. cold*** el *Esp, Méx* resfriado *or Andes, RP* resfrío común; ***c. criminal*** delincuente *mf* común; ***the c. man*** el ciudadano medio; ***c. name*** *(of plant)* nombre *m* común; ***the c. people*** la gente corriente; ***c. sense*** sentido *m* común; *US St Exch* ***c. stock*** acciones *fpl* ordinarias; ***the c. touch*** el don de gentes
(**d**) *(vulgar)* ordinario(a); IDIOM *Fam* **as c. as muck** más basto(a) que la lija, vulgarote(a), *RP* regroncho(a)
(**e**) *Gram (gender)* común ▸▸ ***c. noun*** nombre *m or* sustantivo *m* común
(**f**) *Mus* **c. time** *or* **measure** cuatro por cuatro

commonality [kɒmən'ælɪtɪ] *n Formal* (**a**) *(shared area)* **there is a c. of interest between the two groups** hay cierta comunidad de intereses entre los dos grupos (**b**) *(common people)* **the c.** la plebe

commonalty ['kɒmənəltɪ] *n Formal (common people)* **the c.** la plebe

commoner ['kɒmənə(r)] *n* (**a**) *(not noble)* plebeyo(a) *m,f* (**b**) *Br Univ* = estudiante que no disfruta de una de las becas que concede su universidad

common-law ['kɒmənlɔː] *adj* ***c. husband*** esposo *m* de hecho; ***c. marriage*** matrimonio *m or* unión *f* de hecho; ***c. wife*** esposa *f* de hecho

commonly ['kɒmənlɪ] *adv* (**a**) *(usually, generally)* comúnmente; **c. known as...** comúnmente conocido como... (**b**) *(vulgarly)* ordinariamente

common-or-garden [kɒmənɔː'gɑːdən] *adj Br Fam* corriente y moliente, común y corriente

commonplace ['kɒmənpleɪs] **1** *n* tópico *m*, lugar *m* común
2 *adj* común, habitual; **mobile phones have become c.** los teléfonos móviles se han convertido en algo muy común *or* habitual

Commons ['kɒmənz] *npl Br, Can* **the (House of) C.** la Cámara de los Comunes

commons ['kɒmənz] *npl* (**a**) *Archaic or Literary* **the c.** *(common people)* la plebe (**b**) *Old-fashioned or Hum (food)* **we'll be on short c. till the end of the month** tendremos que ponernos a dieta hasta final de mes

common-sense ['kɒmənsens], **commonsensical** [kɒmən'sensɪkəl] *adj (attitude, approach, decision)* con sentido común

commonweal ['kɒmənwiːl] *n Literary (common good)* bien *m* común

Commonwealth ['kɒmənwelθ] *n* (**a**) *(of nations)* **the (British) C.** la Commonwealth, la Comunidad Británica de Naciones ▸▸ ***the C. Games*** los Juegos de la Commonwealth
(**b**) *(in state names)* **the C. of Australia** la Commonwealth de Australia; **the C. of Massachusetts/Pennsylvania** el Estado de Massachusetts/Pensilvania ▸▸ ***the C. of Independent States*** la Confederación de Estados Independientes
(**c**) *Hist* **the C.** la República, = en Inglaterra, el periodo transcurrido entre la ejecución de Carlos I en 1649 y la Restauración de 1660

commotion [kə'məʊʃən] *n* (**a**) *(noise)* alboroto *m*; **what's all the c. (about)?** ¿a qué viene todo este alboroto? (**b**) *(uproar)* alboroto *m*, tumulto *m*; **to cause a c.** causar un alboroto

comms [kɒmz] *n Comptr* comunicaciones *fpl* ▸▸ ***c. package*** software *m* de comunicaciones; ***c. port*** puerto *m* de comunicaciones

communal ['kɒmjʊnəl] *adj* (**a**) *(shared) (bathroom, changing room)* comunal, compartido(a) (**b**) *(of community)* comunitario(a); **a c. activity** una actividad comunitaria; **c. life** vida en comunidad (**c**) *(between social groups)* **c. violence** violencia entre comunidades

communally ['kɒmjʊnəlɪ] *adv* en comunidad; **c. owned** de propiedad comunitaria

commune **1** *n* ['kɒmjuːn] (**a**) *(collective)* comuna *f* (**b**) *(administrative unit)* municipio *m*, *Am* comuna *f* (**c**) *Hist* **the (Paris) C.** la Comuna de París
2 *vi* [kə'mjuːn] estar en comunión (**with** con); **to c. with nature** estar en comunión con la naturaleza

communicable [kə'mju:nɪkəbəl] *adj* (a) *(information, ideas)* que se puede comunicar (b) *(disease)* contagioso(a)

communicant [kə'mju:nɪkənt] *n Rel* comulgante *mf*

communicate [kə'mju:nɪkeɪt] 1 *vt (information, idea, feelings)* comunicar (**to** a)

2 *vi* (a) *(person)* comunicarse (**with** con); **they c. with each other by phone** se comunican por teléfono; **we can't seem to c. any more** ya no nos comunicamos como antes (b) *(rooms)* comunicarse (**with** con)

communicating [kə'mju:nɪkeɪtɪŋ] *adj (rooms)* que se comunican; **c. door** puerta de comunicación ▸▸ ***c. vessels*** vasos *mpl* comunicantes

communication [kəmju:nɪ'keɪʃən] *n* (a) *(contact)* comunicación *f*; **to be in c. (with sb)** estar en contacto (con alguien); **he broke off all c. with us when he resigned** cortó las relaciones con nosotros tras su dimisión; **radio c.** comunicación por radio ▸▸ ***c. cord:*** **to pull the c. cord** accionar la alarma *(en los trenes)*; ***c. skills*** dotes *fpl or* aptitud *f* para la comunicación (b) *Formal (message)* comunicado *m*

communications [kəmju:nɪ'keɪʃənz] *npl* (a) *(means of contact, transport)* comunicaciones *fpl*; **c. are very poor in this region** las comunicaciones son muy malas en esta región

(b) *Tel* ***c. centre*** centro *m or* nudo *m* de comunicaciones; ***c. satellite*** satélite *m* de telecomunicaciones; ***c. technology*** tecnología *f* de las telecomunicaciones

(c) *Comptr* ***c. protocol*** protocolo *m* de comunicaciones; ***c. software*** software *m* de comunicaciones

communicative [kə'mju:nɪkətɪv] *adj* comunicativo(a) ▸▸ *Ling* ***c. competence*** competencia *f* comunicativa

communicator [kə'mju:nɪkeɪtə(r)] *n* comunicador(ora) *m,f*

communion [kə'mju:njən] *n* (a) *Rel (sacrament)* comunión *f*; **to take** *or* **receive C.** comulgar ▸▸ ***c. bread*** pan *m* bendito; ***c. cup*** cáliz *m*; ***c. wine*** vino *m* de comunión (b) *(denomination)* confesión *f* (c) *Formal (communication)* comunión *f*; **they sought to live in c. with nature** buscaban vivir en comunión con la naturaleza

communiqué [kə'mju:nɪkeɪ] *n* comunicado *m*

communism ['kɒmjʊnɪzəm] *n* comunismo *m*

communist ['kɒmjʊnɪst] 1 *n* comunista *mf*

2 *adj* comunista ▸▸ ***the C. Manifesto*** el Manifiesto Comunista

community [kə'mju:nɪtɪ] *n* (a) *(group of people)* comunidad *f*; *(group of animals)* colonia *f*; **the Jewish c.** la comunidad judía; **the business c.** el sector empresarial, los empresarios; **a sense of c.** un espíritu de comunidad; **to improve c. relations** mejorar las relaciones entre las comunidades ▸▸ ***c. care*** asistencia *f* social domiciliaria; ***c. centre*** ≃ centro *m* cívico *or* social; *Br Formerly* ***c. charge*** ≃ contribución *f* urbana; *US* ***c. chest*** = fondo comunitario para actividades de beneficiencia a nivel local; *US* ***c. college*** = centro docente que ofrece cursos de enseñanza superior de dos años de duración; ***c. medicine*** medicina *f* social; ***c. policeman*** policía *m* de barrio, *Esp* policía *m* de proximidad; ***c. policing*** policía *f* de barrio, *Esp* policía *f* de proximidad; *Br* ***c. school*** = colegio que ofrece cursos extracurriculares a la comunidad y que suele servir de centro comunitario; ***c. service*** servicios *mpl* a la comunidad *(impuestos como pena sustitutiva de cárcel)*; ***c. singing*** = canto en grupo en el que todo el mundo toma parte; ***c. spirit*** espíritu *m* comunitario; ***c. work*** trabajo *m or* asistencia *f* social de zona

(b) *(locality)* comunidad *f*; **a small mining c.** una pequeña comunidad minera

(c) *Rel* comunidad *f*

(d) *Formal (sharing)* comunidad *f*; **c. of goods/interests** comunidad de bienes/intereses

(e) **the (European) C.** la Comunidad (Europea) ▸▸ *EU* ***C. directive*** directiva *f* comunitaria

commutable [kə'mju:təbəl] *adj* (a) *(journey)* suficientemente corto(a) para hacerlo en el día (b) *Law (sentence)* conmutable

commutation [kɒmju:'teɪʃən] *n* (a) *Law (of sentence)* conmutación *f* (b) *US (commuting)* = viaje diario al lugar de trabajo ▸▸ ***c. ticket*** abono *m*

commute [kə'mju:t] 1 *vt* (a) *Law* conmutar (**to** por) (b) *Fin* **to c. an annuity into a lump sum** conmutar una anualidad por un pago único

2 *vi* **to c. (to work)** viajar diariamente al lugar de trabajo

commuter [kə'mju:tə(r)] *n* = persona que viaja diariamente al trabajo ▸▸ ***c. town*** ciudad *f* dormitorio; ***c. train*** = tren de cercanías que las personas utilizan para desplazarse diariamente al lugar de trabajo

Comoros ['kɒmərəʊz] *n* **the C. (Islands)** las (Islas) Comores

compact 1 *n* ['kɒmpækt] (a) *(for powder)* polvera *f* (b) *(treaty)* pacto *m* (c) *US (car)* utilitario *m*

2 *adj* [kəm'pækt] (a) *(small)* compacto(a) (b) *(dense)* compacto(a) (c) *(concise)* conciso(a)

3 *vt* [kəm'pækt] compactar, comprimir

compact disc ['kɒmpækt'dɪsk] *n* (disco *m*) compacto *m* ▸▸ ***c. player*** reproductor *m* de discos compactos

compacting [kəm'pæktɪŋ] *n Comptr (of file)* compresión *f*

compactly [kəm'pæktlɪ] *adv (made)* de manera compacta; **c. designed** diseñado(a) de manera compacta

compactness [kəm'pæktnɪs] *n* (a) *(smallness)* **the c. of the design** lo compacto del diseño (b) *(denseness)* **the c. of the soil** lo compacto del suelo (c) *(conciseness)* **the c. of his style** lo conciso de su estilo

companion [kəm'pænjən] *n* (a) *(friend)* compañero(a) *m,f*; **a drinking/travelling c.** un compañero de borrachera/viaje

(b) *Old-fashioned (employee)* dama *f* de compañía

(c) *(one of pair)* pareja *f*; **the c. volume** el volumen que lo acompaña

(d) *(guidebook)* guía *f*, manual *m* (**to** de)

(e) *(in titles)* = en algunas órdenes de caballería, miembro con el grado más bajo ▸▸ ***C. of Honour*** = miembro de una orden fundada por George V en 1917

companionable [kəm'pænjənəbəl] *adj* sociable

companionship [kəm'pænjənʃɪp] *n (company)* compañía *f*; *(camaraderie)* compañerismo *m*

companionway [kəm'pænjənweɪ] *n Naut* escalera *f* de cámara

company ['kʌmpənɪ] *n* (a) *(companionship)* compañía *f*; **to be good c.** ser buena compañía; **to keep sb c.** hacer compañía a alguien; **in sb's c.** en compañía de alguien; **I like** *or* **am fond of my own c.** me gusta estar solo(a); **in c. with others** junto con otros; **we request the pleasure of your c. at dinner** tenemos el honor de invitarlo a cenar; **to part c. (with sb)** separarse (de alguien); PROV **two's c., three's a crowd** dos es compañía, tres es multitud

(b) *(companions)* compañía *f*; **to get into bad c.** mezclarse con malas compañías; **if I'm wrong, I'm in good c.** si me equivoco, no soy el único; **I don't like the c. he keeps** no me gustan las compañías con las que anda; PROV **a man is known by the c. he keeps** dime con quién andas y te diré quién eres

(c) *(people present)* **you shouldn't pick your nose in c.** no se debe uno meter el dedo en la nariz delante de (la) gente

(d) *(guests)* **we're expecting c.** tenemos invitados; *Fam* **we've got c.!** *(there's someone else here, we're being followed)* ¡tenemos compañía!

(e) *Com* empresa *f*, compañía *f*; **to form** *or* **incorporate a c.** constituir (en sociedad) una empresa; **Jones & C.** Jones y Compañía; **he's a real c. man** es un auténtico hombre de empresa; **on** *or* **in c. time** *(make telephone call etc)* en horas de trabajo ▸▸ ***c. car*** coche *m or Am* carro *m or RP* auto *m* de empresa; ***c. director*** director(ora) *m,f* de empresa; *Br* ***c. law*** derecho *m* de sociedades; ***c. policy*** política *f* de empresa; *Com* ***c. secretary*** jefe(a) *m,f* de administración

(f) *(army unit)* compañía *f*

(g) *(theatre group)* compañía *f*

(h) *Naut* **the ship's c.** la tripulación (del barco)

(i) *US Fam* **the C.** la CIA

comparable ['kɒmpərəbəl] *adj* comparable (**to** *or* **with** a *or* con); **the two cases are not c.** no se pueden comparar los dos casos

comparably ['kɒmpərəblɪ] *adv* de forma similar

comparative [kəm'pærətɪv] 1 *n Gram* comparativo *m*

2 *adj* (a) *(cost, comfort, wealth)* relativo(a); **she's a c. stranger to me** casi no la conozco (b) *(study, research, linguistics)* comparado(a) ▸▸ ***c. grammar*** gramática *f* comparada; ***c. literature*** literatura *f* comparada

comparatively [kəm'pærətɪvlɪ] *adv (quite)* relativamente

compare [kəm'peə(r)] 1 *n Literary* **beyond c.** incomparable

2 *vt* (a) *(contrast)* comparar (**with** *or* **to** con); **compared with** *or* **to...** comparado(a) con..., en comparación con...; *Fig* **to c. notes (with sb)** intercambiar pareceres *or* opiniones (con alguien); **to c. like with like** comparar dos iguales

(b) *(liken)* comparar; **to compare sth to sth** comparar algo con algo; **he has been compared to Kerouac** se le ha comparado con Kerouac

(c) *Gram* formar el comparativo de

3 *vi* compararse (**with** con *or* a); **they just don't c.** no tienen ni punto de comparación; **how do our results c. with those of our competitors?** ¿cómo son nuestros resultados en comparación con los de nuestros competidores?; **how do they c. in (terms of) price?** ¿cuál es la relación en cuestión de precio?; **to c. favourably** *or* **well with sth** resultar ser mejor que algo

comparison [kəm'pærɪsən] *n* (**a**) *(generally)* comparación *f*; **in** *or* **by c.** en comparación; **there is no c.** no hay punto de comparación; **this book stands** *or* **bears c. with the classics** este libro puede compararse con los clásicos; **to draw** *or* **make a c. between** establecer un paralelismo entre (**b**) *Gram* comparación *f*; **degrees of c.** grados de comparación

compartment [kəm'pɑːtmənt] *n* (**a**) *(section)* compartimento *m* (**b**) *(on train)* compartimento *m*

compartmentalize [kɒmpɑːt'mentəlaɪz] *vt also Fig* dividir en compartimentos, compartimentar

compass ['kʌmpəs] *n* (**a**) *(for finding direction)* brújula *f* ►► ***c. card*** brújula *f* giroscópica; ***c. needle*** aguja *f* magnética; ***c. rose*** rosa *f* de los vientos (**b**) *Math* **compasses** compás *m*; **a pair of compasses** un compás (**c**) *Formal (range)* ámbito *m*, alcance *m*; **beyond the c. of the human mind** más allá de lo que la mente humana llega a imaginar

compassion [kəm'pæʃən] *n* compasión *f*; **to arouse c.** despertar compasión; **to show c.** mostrar compasión; **you have no c.** no tienes compasión ►► ***c. fatigue*** insensibilización *f*

compassionate [kəm'pæʃənət] *adj (person, attitude)* compasivo(a); **to be c. towards sb** ser compasivo(a) con alguien; **on c. grounds** por compasión ►► ***c. leave*** = permiso por enfermedad grave o muerte de un familiar

compatibility [kəmpætə'bɪlɪtɪ] *n* compatibilidad *f*

compatible [kəm'pætəbəl] *adj* compatible (**with** con); **IBM-c.** compatible IBM ►► *Comptr* ***c. computer*** *Esp* ordenador *m* *orAm* computadora *f* compatible

compatriot [kəm'pætrɪət] *n* compatriota *mf*

compel [kəm'pel] (*pt & pp* **compelled**) *vt* (**a**) *(force)* obligar; **to c. sb to do sth** obligar a alguien a hacer algo; **I feel compelled to admit to a certain envy** me siento obligado a admitir que siento algo de envidia

(**b**) *(elicit, demand)* **to c. admiration** inspirar admiración; **to c. respect** inspirar *or* imponer respeto; **a tone of voice that compels attention** un tono de voz que llama la atención

compelling [kəm'pelɪŋ] *adj* (**a**) *(argument, reason)* poderoso(a), convincente; *(urgency)* apremiante (**b**) *(movie, performance)* absorbente; **the report makes c. reading** el informe es fascinante

compendia *pl of* **compendium**

compendious [kəm'pendɪəs] *adj Formal* condensado(a) y completo(a)

compendium [kəm'pendɪəm] (*pl* **compendiums** *or* **compendia** [kəm'pendɪə]) *n Br* (**a**) *(book)* compendio *m* (**b**) **a c. of games** *(board games)* unos juegos reunidos

compensable [kəm'pensəbəl] *adj* compensable

compensate ['kɒmpənseɪt] **1** *vt (make amends to)* compensar, indemnizar (**for** por)

2 *vi* (**a**) *(make up)* **to c. for sth** compensar algo; *(with money)* compensar algo (**b**) *Psy* compensar (**for** por)

compensation [kɒmpən'seɪʃən] *n* (**a**) *(reparation)* compensación *f*; *(money)* indemnización *f*; **the job has its compensations** el trabajo tiene sus ventajas; **in c. for** en compensación por ►► *Br Law* ***c. order*** orden *m* de pago de compensación; ***c. package*** *Br (for redundancy)* indemnización *f* por despido; *US (when starting new job)* ayuda *f* por traslado (**b**) *Psy* compensación *f*

compensatory [kɒmpen'seɪtərɪ] *adj* compensatorio(a)

compere, compère ['kɒmpeə(r)] **1** *n* presentador(ora) *m,f*

2 *vt (programme, show)* presentar

compete [kəm'piːt] *vi* (**a**) *(vie)* competir (**with/for** con *or* contra/por); **to c. for a prize** competir por un premio; **her cooking can't c. with yours** su comida no se puede comparar con la tuya; **children here aren't encouraged to c.** aquí no se fomenta la competitividad entre los niños

(**b**) *(commercially)* competir; **we have to c. on an international level** tenemos que competir a nivel internacional

(**c**) *(in sporting event)* competir; **to c. against sb for sth** competir contra alguien por algo; **there are only three teams competing** sólo compiten tres equipos

competence ['kɒmpɪtəns] *n* (**a**) *(ability)* capacidad *f*, cualidades *fpl*; **they questioned his c. to hold the post** pusieron en entredicho su capacidad *or* sus cualidades para desempeñar el cargo; **it's beyond my c. to assess the quality of his work** no estoy capacitado para evaluar la calidad de su trabajo (**b**) *Law* competencia *f* (**c**) *Ling* competencia *f*

competent ['kɒmpɪtənt] *adj* (**a**) *(capable)* competente; **is she c. to handle the accounts?** ¿está capacitada para encargarse de la contabilidad?; **he's quite c. at French** habla francés bastante bien; **a c. piece of work** un trabajo bien realizado (**b**) *Law (witness)* competente, capacitado(a)

competently ['kɒmpɪtəntlɪ] *adv* competentemente

competing [kəm'piːtɪŋ] *adj* (**a**) *(rival)* **there are many c. claims on our budget** nuestro presupuesto tiene que repartirse entre muchas necesidades (**b**) *(in sporting event)* participante; **all c. teams must report to the stewards** todos los equipos participantes deben presentarse ante los jueces

competition [kɒmpə'tɪʃən] *n* (**a**) *(contest)* concurso *m*; *(in sport)* competición *f* *orAm* competencia *f*; **to enter a c.** inscribirse en una competición *or Am* competencia (**b**) *(rivalry)* competencia *f*; **c. for the position is fierce** la competencia por el puesto es feroz; **to be in c. with sb** competir con alguien (**c**) *(opposition)* **the c.** la competencia; **you're up against some tough c.** te vas a enfrentar a una competencia muy dura

competitive [kəm'petɪtɪv] *adj* (**a**) *(involving competition)* competitivo(a); **to be chosen by c. examination** ser elegido(a) en una oposición ►► ***c. sports*** deportes *mpl* de competición *orAm* competencia; *Com* ***c. tendering*** adjudicación *f* por concurso público

(**b**) *(person, environment)* competitivo(a)

(**c**) *Com (product, price, company)* competitivo(a); **we have to stay c.** tenemos que seguir siendo competitivos ►► ***c. advantage*** ventaja *f* competitiva

competitively [kəm'petɪtɪvlɪ] *adv* (**a**) *(in contest)* competitivamente; **to play c.** *(in competitions)* jugar en competiciones; *(intent on winning)* ser muy competitivo en el juego (**b**) *Com* **c. priced goods** productos a precios muy competitivos

competitiveness [kəm'petɪtɪvnɪs] *n* (**a**) *(of person)* competitividad *f* (**b**) *Com (of product, price, company)* competitividad *f*

competitor [kəm'petɪtə(r)] *n* (**a**) *(in contest)* competidor(ora) *m,f* (**b**) *Com* competidor(ora) *m,f*

compilation [kɒmpɪ'leɪʃən] *n* recopilación *f*, compilación *f* ►► ***c. album*** (álbum *m*) recopilatorio *m*

compile [kəm'paɪl] *vt* (**a**) *(gather) (facts, material)* recopilar, compilar (**b**) *(compose) (list)* elaborar; *(dictionary)* redactar (**c**) *Comptr* compilar

compiler [kəm'paɪlə(r)] *n* (**a**) *(of facts, material)* recopilador(ora) *m,f*, compilador(ora) *m,f* (**b**) *(of dictionary)* redactor(ora) *m,f* (**c**) *Comptr* compilador *m*

complacency [kəm'pleɪsənsɪ] *n* autocomplacencia *f*; **to shake sb out of their c.** sacar a alguien de su autocomplacencia

> **False friend**: The Spanish noun **complacencia** is not a translation for the English word **complacency**. In Spanish **complacencia** means "pleasure, satisfaction" or "indulgence".

complacent [kəm'pleɪsənt] *adj* autocomplaciente; **to be c. about sth** ser demasiado relajado(a) respecto a algo; **to become** *or* **get c.** volverse autocomplaciente

complacently [kəm'pleɪsəntlɪ] *adv* con autocomplaciencia

complain [kəm'pleɪn] **1** *vi* (**a**) *(grumble, protest)* quejarse (**about** de); **I complained to the manager** me quejé al encargado; **I can't c. about the service** no tengo queja alguna del servicio; **how are things? – I can't c.** ¿cómo van las cosas? – no me puedo quejar; **stop complaining!** ¡deja de quejarte *or* de protestar! (**b**) **to c. of** *(symptoms)* estar aquejado(a) de

2 *vt* **to c. that...** quejarse de que...; **she complained that he was always late** se quejó de que siempre llegaba tarde

complainant [kəm'pleɪnənt] *n Law* reclamante *mf*

complaining [kəm'pleɪnɪŋ] *n* quejas *fpl*

complaint [kəm'pleɪnt] *n* (**a**) *(grievance)* queja *f*; **to have cause** *or* **grounds for c.** tener motivos de queja; **to lodge** *or* **make a c. (against sb)** presentar una queja (contra alguien)

(**b**) *(formal protest)* queja *f*, reclamación *f*, *Am* reclamo *m* ►► ***complaints book*** libro *m* de reclamaciones *or Am* reclamos; ***complaints department*** departamento *f* de reclamaciones *orAm* reclamos; ***complaints office*** oficina *f* de reclamaciones *orAm* reclamos

(**c**) *(illness)* afección *f*, dolencia *f*; **she suffers from a skin c.** tiene un problema de piel

complement ['kɒmplɪmənt] **1** *n* (**a**) *(supplement)* complemento *m* (**b**) *Gram* complemento *m* (**c**) *Math* complemento *m* (**d**) *Naut* **the full c.** la dotación, la tripulación; *Fig* **I still have my full c. of**

teeth todavía conservo toda mi dentadura
2 *vt* complementar; **they c. each other well** *(of two people, flavours, colours)* se complementan muy bien

complementary [kɒmplɪ'mentərɪ] *adj* complementario(a) ►► *Math* ***c. angle*** ángulo *m* complementario; ***c. colours*** colores *mpl* complementarios; ***c. medicine*** medicina *f* alternativa

complete [kəm'pli:t] 1 *adj* (a) *(lacking nothing)* completo(a); **Christmas wouldn't be c. without a turkey** las Navidades no estarían completas sin un pavo; **my happiness is c.** soy completamente feliz; **the c. works of...** las obras completas de...; **c. with fitted plug** con el enchufe incluido
(b) *(finished)* terminado(a), acabado(a); **the work is now c.** el trabajo ya está terminado
(c) *(total, thorough)* total, absoluto(a); **a c. turnaround in the situation** un vuelco total de la situación; **it came as a c. surprise** fue una sorpresa absoluta; **a c. (and utter) failure** un fracaso total; **she is a c. fool** es tonta de remate; **he's a c. stranger** es un completo desconocido
2 *vt* (a) *(make whole)* completar; **I just need one more card to c. my collection** sólo me falta una postal para completar la colección; *Com* **to c. an order** completar un pedido (b) *(finish)* terminar (c) *(fill in)* **to c. a form** rellenar un impreso

completely [kəm'pli:tlɪ] *adv* completamente, totalmente

completeness [kəm'pli:tnɪs] *n* (a) *(wholeness)* **there's a c. to the movie/novel** es una película/novela muy redonda; **they added a final volume to the series for c.** añadieron un último volumen para redondear la colección (b) *(thoroughness)* **the c. of their victory/defeat** lo categórico de su victoria/derrota

completion [kəm'pli:ʃən] *n* (a) *(of work)* finalización *f*, terminación *f*; **the bridge is due for c. in January** la finalización del puente está prevista para enero; **in the process of c.** a punto de ser completado; **on c.** al terminar; **to be nearing c.** estar próximo a concluir ►► ***c. date*** fecha *f* de finalización (b) *Law (of sale)* consumación *f*

completist [kəm'pli:tɪst] *n Fam* **this album is strictly for Dylan completists** este álbum es únicamente para los que coleccionan todo lo de Dylan

complex ['kɒmpleks] 1 *n* (a) *(of buildings)* complejo *m*; **shopping/industrial c.** un complejo comercial/industrial (b) *Psy* complejo *m*; **to have a c. about one's weight** tener complejo de gordo(a); *Fam* **you'll give her a c.** le va a entrar complejo
2 *adj* complejo(a), complicado(a); **this is where things start to get a bit c.** aquí es donde se complican las cosas; **it's a c. issue** es un tema complejo *or* complicado ►► ***c. number*** número *m* complejo; ***c. sentence*** oración *f* compuesta

complexion [kəm'plekʃən] *n* (a) *(of face)* tez *f*; **to have a dark/fair c.** tener la tez oscura/clara; **to have a good** *or* **clear c.** tener un buen cutis (b) *(aspect)* cariz *m*; **that puts a different c. on it** eso le da otro cariz diferente

> **False friend**: The Spanish noun **complexión** is not a translation for the English word **complexion**. In Spanish **complexión** means "build".

complexity [kəm'pleksɪtɪ] *n* complejidad *f*

compliance [kəm'plaɪəns] *n* (a) *(conformity)* cumplimiento *m* (**with** de); **to enforce c.** hacer cumplir las normas; **in c. with your wishes** en cumplimiento de sus deseos (b) *(submission)* docilidad *f*, sumisión *f*

compliant [kəm'plaɪənt] *adj* (a) *(obedient, submissive)* dócil, sumiso(a) (b) *(with legislation, norm)* **all procedures must be c. with the new legislation** todos los procedimientos deben estar en conformidad con la nueva legislación

complicate ['kɒmplɪkeɪt] *vt* complicar; **the issue is complicated by the fact that...** el asunto se complica aún más debido al hecho de que...; **that complicates matters** eso complica el asunto

complicated ['kɒmplɪkeɪtɪd] *adj* complicado(a); **to become** *or* **to get c.** complicarse

complication [kɒmplɪ'keɪʃən] *n* complicación *f*; **complications** *(in patient's condition)* complicaciones; **you're always causing complications!** ¡siempre estás complicando las cosas!

complicity [kəm'plɪsɪtɪ] *n* complicidad *f* (**in** en)

compliment ['kɒmplɪmənt] 1 *n* cumplido *m*; **to pay sb a c.** hacer un cumplido a alguien; *also Ironic* **to return the c.** devolver el cumplido; **with compliments** con mis mejores deseos; **to send one's compliments to sb** enviar saludos *or CAm, Col, Ecuad* saludes a alguien; *Formal* **compliments of the season** Felices Fiestas ►► ***compliments slip*** nota *f* de cortesía
2 *vt* **to c. sb on sth** felicitar a alguien por algo

complimentary [kɒmplɪ'mentərɪ] *adj* (a) *(praising)* elogioso(a); **they weren't very c. about my paintings** no hablaron muy bien de mis cuadros (b) *(free)* de regalo, gratuito(a) ►► ***c. copy*** *(of book)* ejemplar *m* de regalo *or* gratuito; ***c. ticket*** invitación *f*

compline ['kɒmplɪn] *n Rel* completas *fpl*

comply [kəm'plaɪ] *vi* **to c. with** *(rule)* cumplir, ajustarse a; *(order)* cumplir; *(request)* someterse a; **I will c. with your wishes** obedeceré tus deseos; **cars must c. with existing regulations** los coches deben cumplir el reglamento existente

component [kəm'pəʊnənt] 1 *n* (a) *(element)* pieza *f* (b) *Comptr & Elec* componente *m*
2 *adj* ***c. part*** pieza *f*

comport [kəm'pɔ:t] *vt Formal* **to c. oneself** conducirse, comportarse

comportment [kəm'pɔ:tmənt] *n Formal* conducta *f*, comportamiento *m*

compose [kəm'pəʊz] 1 *vt* (a) *(make up, constitute)* **to be composed of** estar compuesto(a) de (b) *(music, poetry)* componer; *(letter, e-mail)* redactar (c) *Typ (set)* componer (d) *(calm)* **to c. oneself** serenarse; **she composed her features** se serenó; **I need to c. my thoughts** necesito poner en orden mis ideas
2 *vi (create music)* componer

composed [kəm'pəʊzd] *adj* sereno(a)

composer [kəm'pəʊzə(r)] *n* compositor(ora) *m,f*

composite ['kɒmpəzɪt] 1 *adj* (a) *(compound)* compuesto(a) ►► ***c. photograph*** fotografía *f* de superposición, = fotografía formada a partir de la superposición de dos o más fotografías (b) *Bot* de las compuestas (c) *Math* compuesto(a), no primo
2 *n* (a) *(compound)* combinación *f* (b) *Bot* compuesta *f* (c) *Pol (conference motion)* = moción resultante de la amalgama de propuestas elaboradas a nivel local para su discusión a nivel nacional

composition [kɒmpə'zɪʃən] *n* (a) *(constitution)* composición *f*; **the chemical c. of water** la composición química del agua (b) *(piece of music)* composición *f* (c) *(essay)* redacción *f* (d) *(act of composing music)* composición *f* (e) *Typ* composición *f* (f) *Law (agreement with creditors)* acuerdo *m*

compositor [kəm'pɒzɪtə(r)] *n Typ* cajista *mf*

> **False friend**: The Spanish noun **compositor** is not a translation for the English word **compositor**. In Spanish **compositor** means "composer".

compos mentis ['kɒmpəs'mentɪs] *adj Law* en pleno uso de sus facultades mentales; *Hum* **I'm never c. before midday** yo no soy persona *or* no valgo para nada antes del mediodía

compost ['kɒmpɒst] 1 *n* compost *m*, mantillo *m* ►► ***c. heap*** montón *m* de compost *or* mantillo
2 *vt* (a) *(treat with compost)* tratar con compost *or* mantillo (b) *(convert into compost)* convertir en compost *or* mantillo

composure [kəm'pəʊʒə(r)] *n* compostura *f*; **to lose/recover one's c.** perder/recobrar la compostura

compote ['kɒmpɒt] *n* (a) *Culin* compota *f* (b) *US (dish)* compotera *f*

compound[1] 1 *n* ['kɒmpaʊnd] (a) *Chem* compuesto *m* (b) *Gram* compuesto *m*
2 *adj* ['kɒmpaʊnd] (a) *(of several parts)* compuesto(a) ►► *Biol* ***c. eye*** ojo *m* compuesto; *Med* ***c. fracture*** fractura *f* abierta *or* expuesta (b) *Gram (sentence)* compuesto(a) ►► ***c. tense*** tiempo *m* compuesto; ***c. verb*** perífrasis *f inv* verbal (c) *Math (number)* compuesto(a) ►► ***c. fraction*** fracción *f* mixta (d) *Fin* ***c. interest*** interés *m* compuesto
3 *vt* [kəm'paʊnd] (a) *(make up)* **to be compounded of sth** estar compuesto(a) de algo (b) *(make worse) (problem)* complicar, empeorar; *(error)* agravar, exacerbar (c) *Law (settle)* **to c. a debt** liquidar una deuda pagando sólo una parte
4 *vi* [kəm'paʊnd] *Law* **to c. with sb** *(over debt)* llegar a un acuerdo con alguien

compound[2] ['kɒmpaʊnd] *n (enclosure)* recinto *m*

comprehend [kɒmprɪ'hend] *vt* (a) *(understand)* comprender (b) *Formal (include)* comprender, abarcar

comprehensibility [kɒmprɪhensə'bɪlɪtɪ] *n* **despite the increase in volume there is little loss in c.** a pesar del aumento de tamaño se sigue comprendiendo bien

comprehensible [kɒmprɪ'hensəbəl] *adj* comprensible

comprehension [kɒmprɪ'henʃən] *n* (**a**) *(understanding)* comprensión *f*; **it is beyond my c.** me resulta incomprensible (**b**) *Sch (exercise)* ejercicio *m* de comprensión; **a reading/listening c.** un ejercicio de comprensión escrita/oral

comprehensive [kɒmprɪ'hensɪv] *adj* **1** (**a**) *(thorough, complete) (answer, study, view)* detallado(a), completo(a); *(defeat, victory)* rotundo(a) ►► *Fin* ***c. insurance*** seguro *m* a todo riesgo (**b**) *Br* ***c. school*** ≃ instituto *m* (de enseñanza secundaria)

2 *n Br* ≃ instituto *m* (de enseñanza secundaria)

> **False friend**: The Spanish adjective **comprensivo** is not a translation for the English word **comprehensive**. In Spanish **comprensivo** means "understanding".

comprehensively [kɒmprɪ'hensɪvlɪ] *adv* (**a**) *(thoroughly)* **the book deals with these issues c.** el libro aborda estos asuntos con todo detalle; **they were c. defeated** sufrieron una derrota aplastante (**b**) *Br* **he was educated c.** = estudió en una "comprehensive school"

compress 1 *n* ['kɒmpres] *Med* compresa *f*, apósito *m*

2 *vt* [kəm'pres] (**a**) *(gas)* comprimir; **compressed air** aire comprimido (**b**) *(text)* condensar; **three centuries are compressed into two chapters** en dos capítulos se condensan tres siglos (**c**) *Comptr* comprimir

compressed [kəm'prest] *adj Comptr* comprimido(a)

compression [kəm'preʃən] *n* compresión *f* ►► ***c. ratio*** *Comptr* índice *m* de compresión; *(of engine)* relación *f* de compresión; ***c. stroke*** *(of engine)* carrera *f* de compresión; *Comptr* ***c. utility*** utilidad *f* de compresión, compresor *m*

compressor [kəm'presə(r)] *n* (**a**) *Comptr* compresor *m* (**b**) *Tech* compresor *m*

comprise [kəm'praɪz] *vt* (**a**) *(consist of)* comprender, incluir; **to be comprised of** constar de (**b**) *(constitute)* constituir; **women c. 60 percent of the population** las mujeres constituyen el 60 por ciento de la población

compromise ['kɒmprəmaɪz] **1** *n* solución *f* negociada *or* intermedia; **to reach a c.** alcanzar una solución intermedia; **there must be no c.** no estamos dispuestos a negociar

2 *vt* (**a**) *(principles)* traicionar (**b**) *(jeopardize)* poner en peligro; **to c. oneself** ponerse en un compromiso

3 *vi* (**a**) *(make concessions)* transigir, hacer concesiones; **to c. with sb (on sth)** transigir (con alguien) en algo, hacer concesiones (a alguien) en algo (**b**) *(be lax)* **we'll never c. on safety** nunca comprometeremos la seguridad

> **False friend**: The Spanish noun **compromiso** is not a translation for the English word **compromise**. In Spanish **compromiso** means "commitment", "agreement" or "engagement".

compromising ['kɒmprəmaɪzɪŋ] *adj* comprometedor(ora)

comptroller [kən'trəʊlə(r)] *n Fin* interventor(ora) *m,f* ►► *US* ***C. General*** Interventor(ora) *m,f* General

compulsion [kəm'pʌlʃən] *n* (**a**) *(obligation)* obligación *f*; **under c.** bajo coacción; **to be under no c. to do sth** no estar obligado(a) a hacer algo (**b**) *(urge)* impulso *m*

compulsive [kəm'pʌlsɪv] *adj* (**a**) *(obsessive)* compulsivo(a); **he's a c. liar** miente por compulsión ►► *Med* ***c. eating*** ingesta *f* compulsiva (**b**) *(absorbing)* **the programme was c. viewing** el programa fue absorbente *or* fascinante

compulsorily [kəm'pʌlsərəlɪ] *adv* obligatoriamente

compulsory [kəm'pʌlsərɪ] *adj* obligatorio(a); **military service is c.** hay servicio militar obligatorio; **Latin is c.** el latín es obligatorio ►► ***c. education*** educación *f* obligatoria; ***c. figures*** *(in figure skating)* programa *m* obligatorio; *Br* ***c. purchase*** expropiación *f* forzosa; *Br* ***c. purchase order*** expropiación *f* forzosa; ***c. redundancy*** despido *m* forzoso

compunction [kəm'pʌŋkʃən] *n* reparo *m*; **he has no c. about stealing** no tiene ningún reparo en robar; **without c.** sin reparos

computation [kɒmpjʊ'teɪʃən] *n* cálculo *m*

computational [kɒmpjʊ'teɪʃənəl] *adj* computacional ►► ***c. linguistics*** lingüística *f* computacional

compute [kəm'pjuːt] **1** *vt* calcular

2 *vi* calcular; *Fam Hum* **does not c.!** no cuadra

computer [kəm'pjuːtə(r)] *n Esp* ordenador *m*, *Am* computadora *f*, *Am* computador *m*; **he's good at computers** se le dan muy bien *Esp* los ordenadores *or Am* las computadoras, sabe mucho de informática; **he works in computers** es informático; **to have sth on c.** tener algo en *Esp* el ordenador *or Am* la computadora ►► ***c. animation*** animación *f* por *Esp* ordenador *or Am* computadora; *US* ***c. camp*** = colonia de verano en la que se aprende informática; ***c. centre*** centro *m* de cálculo; ***c. dating*** sistema *m* informatizado de emparejamiento *(de agencia matrimonial)*; ***c. department*** departamento *m* informático; ***c. engineer*** ingeniero(a) *m,f* informático(a); ***c. equipment*** equipo *m* informático; ***c. expert*** experto(a) *m,f* en informática; ***c. fair*** salón *m or* feria *f* de la informática; ***c. game*** juego *m* de *Esp* ordenador *or Am* computadora; *Fam* ***c. geek*** monstruo *m* de la informática; ***c. graphics*** infografía *f*; ***c. literacy*** conocimientos *mpl* de informática; ***c. network*** red *f* informática; ***c. operator*** operador(ora) *m,f* de *Esp* ordenadores *or Am* computadoras; ***c. printout*** listado *m*, copia *f* impresa; ***c. program*** programa *m* informático; ***c. programmer*** programador(ora) *m,f*; ***c. programming*** programación *f* (de *Esp* ordenadores *or Am* computadoras); ***c. science*** informática *f*; ***c. scientist*** informático(a) *m,f*; ***c. simulation*** simulación *f* por *Esp* ordenador *or Am* computadora; ***c. system*** sistema *m* informático; ***c. technician*** técnico(a) *m,f* informático(a); ***c. terminal*** terminal *m* de *Esp* ordenador *or Am* computadora; ***c. virus*** virus *m inv* informático

computer-aided [kəm'pjuːtəreɪdɪd], **computer-assisted** [kəm'pjuːtərə'sɪstɪd] *adj* ►► ***c. design*** diseño *m* asistido por *Esp* ordenador *or Am* computadora; ***c. engineering*** ingeniería *f* asistida por *Esp* ordenador *or Am* computadora; ***c. learning*** enseñanza *f* asistida por *Esp* ordenador *or Am* computadora; ***c. manufacture*** fabricación *f* asistida por *Esp* ordenador *or Am* computadora

computer-enhanced [kəm'pjuːtərən'hɑːnst] *adj* retocado(a) *or* procesado(a) por *Esp* ordenador *or Am* computadora

computer-generated [kəm'pjuːtə'dʒenəreɪtɪd] *adj* generado(a) por *Esp* ordenador *or Am* computadora

computerization [kəmpjuːtəraɪ'zeɪʃən] *n* informatización *f*, *Am* computarización *f*, *Am* computadorización *f*

computerize [kəm'pjuːtəraɪz] *vt* informatizar, *Am* computarizar, *Am* computadorizar

computerized [kəm'pjuːtəraɪzd] *adj* informatizado(a), *Am* computarizado(a), *Am* computadorizado(a) ►► ***c. axial tomography*** tomografía *f* axial computerizada

computer-literate [kəm'pjuːtə'lɪtərɪt] *adj* **to be c.** tener conocimientos de informática

computing [kəm'pjuːtɪŋ] *n* informática *f*, *Am* computación *f* ►► ***c. course*** curso *m* de informática; ***c. skills*** conocimientos *mpl* de informática

comrade ['kɒmreɪd] *n* camarada *mf*, compañero(a) *m,f*

comrade-in-arms ['kɒmreɪdɪn'ɑːmz] *n* compañero(a) *m,f* de armas

comradeship ['kɒmrədʃɪp] *n* camaradería *f*

comsat ['kɒmsæt] *n* (*abbr* **communications satellite**) satélite *m* de telecomunicaciones

Con *Br Pol* (*abbr* **Conservative**) conservador(ora)

con[1] [kɒn] *Fam* **1** *n (swindle)* timo *m*, *Andes, RP* truchada *f*; **what a c.!** ¡menudo timo!, *Andes, RP* ¡qué truchada! ►► ***c. man*** timador *m*, *Andes, RP* cagador *m*; ***c. trick*** timo *m*, *RP* truchada *f*

2 *vt* (*pt & pp* **conned**) (**a**) *(swindle)* timar, *RP* cagar; **to c. sth out of sb, to c. sb out of sth** timarle *or* estafarle algo a alguien; **to c. sb into doing sth** embaucar a alguien para que haga algo (**b**) *Old-fashioned (study)* estudiar; *(learn by heart)* memorizar

con[2] *n Fam (prisoner)* recluso(a) *m,f*, preso(a) *m,f*

con[3] *n (disadvantage)* **the pros and cons** los pros y los contras

concatenated [kɒn'kætəneɪtɪd] *adj Comptr* concadenado(a)

concatenation [kənkætə'neɪʃən] *n* (**a**) *Formal (series)* concatenación *f* (**b**) *Comptr* concatenación *f*

concave ['kɒnkeɪv] *adj* cóncavo(a)

concavity [kɒn'kævətɪ] *n* concavidad *f*

conceal [kən'siːl] *vt (object)* ocultar, esconder (**from** de); *(fact)* ocultar (**from** a); **to c. oneself** esconderse, ocultarse

concealed [kən'siːld] *adj (lighting)* indirecto(a); *(driveway, entrance)* oculto(a); **danger! c. entrance** *(sign)* ¡peligro, entrada/salida sin visibilidad!; **he spoke with barely c. fury** habló sin apenas poder contener su *esp Esp* enfado *or esp Am* enojo

concealer [kən'siːlə(r)] *n (cosmetics)* corrector *m*; *(for use under eyes)* antiojeras *m inv*

concealment [kən'siːlmənt] *n* (**a**) *(act of hiding)* **the pattern on the animal's skin aids c.** el dibujo de la piel del animal le ayuda a camuflarse (**b**) *Law* ocultación *f* de pruebas

concede [kən'siːd] **1** *vt* (**a**) *(admit)* reconocer, admitir; **to c. defeat** admitir la derrota; **she was forced to c. that he was right** se vio obligada a reconocer que él tenía razón (**b**) *(give up)* ceder; **he refused to**

c. any further ground se negó a ceder más terreno (**c**) *(grant, allow)* conceder (**d**) *Sport* **to c. a goal** encajar un gol

2 *vi* ceder

conceit [kən'siːt] *n* (**a**) *(vanity)* engreimiento *m*, presuntuosidad *f* (**b**) *Lit (witty idea)* idea *f* ingeniosa

conceited [kən'siːtɪd] *adj* engreído(a), presuntuoso(a)

conceivable [kən'siːvəbəl] *adj* concebible, posible; **it is c. that...** es posible que...; **they tried every c. means of persuading him** intentaron convencerle por todos los medios posibles; **what c. reason could I have for lying?** ¿y por qué razón iba yo a mentir?

conceivably [kən'siːvəblɪ] *adv* posiblemente; **she could c. have done it** es posible que lo haya hecho ella

conceive [kən'siːv] 1 *vt* (**a**) *(idea, plan)* concebir; **it's impossible to c. such a thing** es imposible imaginar algo así; **I can't c. why they did it** no me cabe en la cabeza por qué lo hizo (**b**) *(child)* concebir (**c**) *(form, develop)* **she conceived a passion for jazz** le entró pasión por el jazz

2 *vi* (**a**) *(think, imagine)* **to c. of** imaginar, concebir (**b**) *(become pregnant)* concebir

concentrate ['kɒnsəntreɪt] 1 *vt* (**a**) *(focus)* concentrar; **we must c. our attention on this problem** debemos concentrar nuestra atención en este problema; **the threat helped to c. their minds** la amenaza les hizo aplicarse (**b**) *(bring together)* concentrar; **our support is concentrated in the South** nuestro apoyo está concentrado en el Sur

2 *vi* (**a**) *(pay attention)* concentrarse (**on** en); **I can't c. with all that noise** con todo ese ruido no me puedo concentrar

(**b**) *(focus)* concentrarse; **the government should c. on improving the economy** el gobierno debería concentrarse en mejorar la economía; **her talk concentrated on economic issues** su discurso se centró en temas económicos

(**c**) *(gather)* concentrarse; **the population tends to c. in cities** la población tiende a concentrarse en las ciudades

3 *n* concentrado *m*

concentrated ['kɒnsəntreɪtɪd] *adj* (**a**) *(liquid)* concentrado(a) (**b**) *(effort)* intenso(a), consciente

concentration [kɒnsən'treɪʃən] *n* (**a**) *(mental)* concentración *f*; **she has remarkable powers of c.** tiene una capacidad de concentración extraordinaria ►► ***c. span*** capacidad *f* de concentración; **he has a c. span of about three seconds** no es capaz de concentrarse más de tres segundos (**b**) *(focusing)* concentración *f* (**c**) *(grouping)* concentración *f* ►► ***c. camp*** campo *m* de concentración (**d**) *Chem* concentración *f*

concentric [kən'sentrɪk] *adj Math* concéntrico(a)

concept ['kɒnsept] *n* concepto *m*

conception [kən'sepʃən] *n* (**a**) *(of child)* concepción *f* (**b**) *(of idea)* concepción *f* (**c**) *(understanding)* idea *f*; **to have no c. of sth** no tener ni idea de algo

conceptual [kən'septjʊəl] *adj* conceptual ►► ***c. art*** arte *m* conceptual

conceptualize [kən'septjʊəlaɪz] *vt* formarse un concepto de

concern [kən'sɜːn] 1 *n* (**a**) *(interest, affair)* interés *m*; **that's my c.** eso es asunto mío; **it's no c. of mine/yours, it's none of my/your c.** no es de mi/tu incumbencia; **it's of no c. to me whether you go or not** me da igual que vayas o no; **of public c.** de interés público

(**b**) *(worry, compassion)* preocupación *f*; **their main c. is to avoid defeat** lo más importante para ellos es evitar la derrota; **my one c. is that...** lo único que me preocupa es que...; **there is growing c. that...** preocupa cada vez más a la gente que...; **this is a matter of some c. to us** nos preocupa bastante este asunto; **I did it out of c. for you** lo hice por ti; **to give cause for c.** dar motivos de preocupación; **there is no cause for c.** no hay motivo de preocupación; **to show c.** mostrar preocupación; **he showed no c. for their safety** dejó claro que su seguridad no le importaba

(**c**) *(company)* empresa *f*

2 *vt* (**a**) *(affect)* concernir, incumbir; **this matter does not c. you** este asunto no te concierne *or* incumbe; **those concerned will be informed in writing** se informará por escrito a los interesados; **as far as I'm concerned...** por lo que a mí respecta...; **as far as your salary is concerned...** en cuanto a *or* por lo que se refiere a tu salario...; **I'm useless where figures are concerned** soy inútil para los números; **to whom it may c.** *(in letter)* a quien corresponda

(**b**) *(worry)* preocupar; **it concerns me that...** me preocupa que...

(**c**) *(occupy)* **to c. oneself with** *or* **about sth** preocuparse de algo; **so far, I have concerned myself only with the causes of the problem** hasta ahora, sólo me he ocupado de las causas del problema

(**d**) *(be about)* **the article concerns revelations regarding the president** el artículo trata de revelaciones sobre el presidente; **it concerns your request for a transfer** tiene que ver con tu petición de traslado

concerned [kən'sɜːnd] *adj* (**a**) *(worried)* preocupado(a) (**about** *or* **for** por); **I don't feel at all c.** no estoy nada preocupado; **a c. expression** una expresión de preocupación; **a group of c. citizens** un grupo de ciudadanos preocupados (**b**) *(involved)* implicado(a), competente; **pass this request on to the department c.** remítase la solicitud al departamento competente; **the people c.** las personas afectadas

concerning [kən'sɜːnɪŋ] *prep* en relación con *or* a, respecto a; **I wrote to her c. the lease** le escribí con referencia al arrendamiento

concert ['kɒnsət] *n* (**a**) *(musical)* concierto *m*; **in c.** en concierto ►► ***c. grand*** piano *m* de cola *or* de concierto; ***c. hall*** sala *f* de conciertos; ***c. party*** *(entertainment)* compañía *f* de artistas de revista; *Fam St Exch* = grupo de inversores que planea la adquisición mayoritaria de las acciones de una empresa para desbancar a la directiva; ***c. pianist*** concertista *mf* de piano; *Mus* ***c. pitch*** diapasón *m* normal; ***c. venue*** *(indoors)* sala *f* de conciertos; *(outdoors)* recinto *m* para conciertos

(**b**) *Formal (co-operation)* **in c. with** en colaboración con

concerted [kən'sɜːtɪd] *adj* conjunto(a), concertado(a); **a c. effort** un esfuerzo conjunto; **c. action** una acción *or* actuación concertada

concertina [kɒnsə'tiːnə] *n* 1 *(musical instrument)* concertina *f*

2 *vi (collapse) (car)* arrugarse como un acordeón

concertmaster ['kɒnsətmɑːstə(r)] *n US* primer violín *m*

concerto [kən'tʃɜːtəʊ] (*pl* **concertos**) *n Mus* concierto *m*; **piano/violin c.** concierto para piano/violín

concession [kən'seʃən] *n* (**a**) *(compromise)* concesión *f*; **to make concessions** hacer concesiones; **the only c. the film makes to reality is...** la única concesión que la película hace a la realidad es..., el único aspecto en que la película se acerca a la realidad es...

(**b**) *Br (discount)* descuento *m*; **price: £4.50 (concessions £3)** precio: 4,50 libras (estudiantes, jubilados, etc. 3 libras)

(**c**) *Com (within store)* concesión *f*

(**d**) *(mining, drilling rights)* concesión *f*, derechos *mpl* de explotación

concessionaire [kənseʃə'neə(r)] *n* concesionario(a) *m,f*

concessionary [kən'seʃənərɪ] *adj* con descuento ►► *Br* ***c. ticket*** *Esp* billete *m or Am* boleto *m or Am* pasaje *m* con descuento *(para niños, estudiantes, parados o jubilados)*

conch [kɒntʃ] *n* caracola *f*

conchy, conchie ['kɒnʃɪ] *n Fam Pej Old-fashioned* objetor(ora) *m,f* de conciencia

concierge ['kɒnsɪeʒ] *n* (**a**) *(in apartment block)* portero(a) *m,f* (**b**) *US (in hotel)* conserje *mf*

conciliate [kən'sɪlɪeɪt] 1 *vt* (**a**) *(appease)* apaciguar (**b**) *(reconcile)* conciliar

2 *vi Formal* **to c. between two people/countries** mediar entre dos personas/países

conciliation [kənsɪlɪ'eɪʃən] *n* (**a**) *(appeasement)* conciliación *f* (**b**) *(reconciliation)* arbitraje *m*, conciliación *f* (**c**) *(in dispute)* conciliación *f*; **the dispute went to c.** el conflicto controversia se sometió a conciliación ►► ***c. service*** órgano *m* de conciliación

conciliator [kən'sɪlɪeɪtə(r)] *n* (**a**) *(appeaser)* conciliador(ora) *m,f* (**b**) *Ind (in dispute)* conciliador(ora) *m,f*

conciliatory [kən'sɪlɪətərɪ] *adj* conciliador(ora); **she was at her most c.** se mostró de lo más conciliadora, mostró su vena más conciliatoria

concise [kən'saɪs] *adj* (**a**) *(succinct)* conciso(a), sucinto(a); **to be c.** ser conciso *or* breve (**b**) *(dictionary)* abreviado(a)

concisely [kən'saɪslɪ] *adv* con concisión, concisamente

conciseness [kən'saɪsnɪs], **concision** [kən'sɪʒən] *n* concisión *f*

conclave ['kɒnkleɪv] *n* (**a**) *(private meeting)* cónclave *m*, conciliábulo *m* (**b**) *Rel* cónclave *m*; **in c.** en cónclave

conclude [kən'kluːd] 1 *vt* (**a**) *(finish)* concluir; **to be concluded...** continuará... (**b**) *(settle) (deal)* cerrar, firmar; **to c. a treaty** firmar un tratado (**c**) *(deduce)* **to c. that...** concluir que...

2 *vi (finish)* concluir; **to c., I would just like to say...** para concluir, me gustaría decir...

concluding [kən'kluːdɪŋ] *adj* final

conclusion [kən'kluːʒən] *n* (**a**) *(inference)* conclusión *f*; **to draw a c.** sacar una conclusión; **it's up to you to draw your own conclusions** puedes sacar tus propias conclusiones; **to come to** *or* **reach a c.** llegar a una conclusión; **this leads me to the c. that...** esto me lleva a la conclusión de que...; IDIOM **to jump to conclusions** sacar conclusiones precipitadas

(**b**) *(end)* conclusión *f*; **to bring sth to a c.** concluir algo; **in c.** en conclusión, concluyendo

(**c**) *(of deal, treaty)* firma *f*

conclusive [kən'kluːsɪv] *adj* concluyente; **the evidence is still not c.** las pruebas todavía no son concluyentes

conclusively [kən'klu:sɪvlɪ] *adv (to prove, argue, show)* de manera concluyente

concoct [kən'kɒkt] *vt* (**a**) *(dish, drink)* preparar, confeccionar (**b**) *(plan, excuse)* tramar, fraguar

concoction [kən'kɒkʃən] *n* (**a**) *(drink)* poción *f*, brebaje *m*; *(dish)* mejunje *m* (**b**) *(invention)* invención *f*

concomitant [kən'kɒmɪtənt] *Formal* **1** *n* concomitancia *f*, hecho *m* concomitante

2 *adj* concomitante (**with** con); **the snow and the c. delays** la nieve y los consiguientes retrasos

concord ['kɒŋkɔ:d] *n* (**a**) *Formal (harmony)* armonía *f*, concordia *f* (**b**) *Gram* concordancia *f* (**c**) *Mus* concordancia *f*

concordance [kən'kɔ:dəns] *n* (**a**) *(agreement)* consonancia *f*, acuerdo *m*; **to be in c. with...** estar en consonancia con... (**b**) *(of Bible, author's works)* concordancia *f* (**to** con)

concordat [kɒn'kɔ:dæt] *n* concordato *m*

Concorde ['kɒŋkɔ:d] *n Av* Concorde *m*

concourse ['kɒŋkɔ:s] *n* (**a**) *(in railway station, airport)* vestíbulo *m* (**b**) *(crowd, gathering)* concurrencia *f*

> **False friend:** The Spanish noun **concurso** is not a translation for the English word **concourse**. In Spanish **concurso** means "competition".

concrete ['kɒŋkri:t] **1** *n* hormigón *m*, *Am* concreto *m* ▸▸ ***c. jungle*** jungla *f* de(l) asfalto; ***c. mixer*** hormigonera *f*

2 *adj (definite)* concreto(a); **we need c. proof** necesitamos pruebas concretas ▸▸ *Gram* ***c. noun*** sustantivo *m* concreto; ***c. poetry*** poesía *f* concreta

3 *vt* pavimentar con hormigón *or Am* concreto

▸ **concrete over** *vt sep (yard, field)* pavimentar con hormigón *or Am* concreto

concubine ['kɒŋkjʊbaɪn] *n* concubina *f*

concupiscence [kən'kju:pɪsəns] *n Formal* concupiscencia *f*

concur [kən'kɜ:(r)] (*pt & pp* **concurred**) *vi* (**a**) *(agree)* coincidir, estar de acuerdo (**with** con); **the experts' opinions c.** los expertos coinciden en sus opiniones (**b**) *(occur together)* concurrir, coincidir

concurrence [kən'kʌrəns] *n* (**a**) *(agreement)* coincidencia *f* (**b**) *(simultaneous occurrence)* concurrencia *f*, coincidencia *f*

concurrent [kən'kʌrənt] *adj* (**a**) *(event)* simultáneo(a) (**b**) *Law* **two c. sentences** dos condenas concurrentes *or* simultáneas

concurrently [kən'kʌrəntlɪ] *adv* simultáneamente; *Law* **the two sentences to run c.** las dos condenas se cumplirán concurrentemente *or* simultáneamente

concuss [kən'kʌs] *vt* conmocionar

concussed [kən'kʌst] *adj* conmocionado(a)

concussion [kən'kʌʃən] *n* conmoción *f* cerebral

condemn [kən'dem] *vt* (**a**) *Law (sentence)* condenar (**to** a); **to c. sb to death** condenar a alguien a muerte (**b**) *(censure)* condenar (**c**) *(force, doom)* **they are condemned to live in poverty** están condenados a vivir en la miseria (**d**) *(declare unsafe) (building)* declarar en ruina; *(meat)* declarar no apto para el consumo (**e**) *US (property)* expropiar

condemnation [kɒndem'neɪʃən] *n* (**a**) *(sentence)* condena *f* (**b**) *(criticism)* condena *f*; **I have nothing but c. for such actions** acciones así sólo merecen mi más absoluta repulsa (**c**) *(of building)* declaración *m* de estado ruinoso; *(of meat)* declaración *f* de no apto(a) para el consumo (**d**) *US (of property)* expropiación *f*

condemnatory [kən'demnətərɪ] *adj* condenatorio(a)

condemned [kən'demd] *adj* (**a**) *(sentenced)* condenado(a); **the c. cell** la celda de los condenados a muerte (**b**) *(declared unfit) (building)* declarado(a) en ruina; *(meat)* declarado(a) no apto(a) para el consumo

condensation [kɒnden'seɪʃən] *n* (**a**) *(of gas, liquid, vapour)* condensación *f* (**b**) *(on glass)* vaho *m*; *(on walls)* condensación *f*, vapor *m* condensado (**c**) *(abridgement)* condensación *f* (**d**) *Phys (of beam)* condensación *f*

condense [kən'dens] **1** *vt* (**a**) *(gas, liquid)* condensar (**b**) *(text)* condensar (**c**) *Phys (beam)* condensar

2 *vi* condensarse

condensed [kən'denst] *adj* (**a**) *(abridged)* resumido(a), condensado(a); **a c. book** un libro condensado (**b**) *(concentrated)* concentrado(a), condensado(a) ▸▸ ***c. milk*** leche *f* condensada; ***c. soup*** sopa *f* concentrada (**c**) *Typ (font, print)* condensado(a)

condenser [kən'densə(r)] *n Tech* condensador *m*

condescend [kɒndɪ'send] *vi* (**a**) *(behave patronizingly)* **to c. towards sb** tratar a alguien con aires de superioridad (**b**) *(lower oneself)* **to c. to do sth** dignarse a *or* tener a bien hacer algo

condescending [kɒndɪ'sendɪŋ] *adj* altivo(a), condescendiente

condescendingly [kɒndɪ'sendɪŋlɪ] *adv* altivamente, con altivez

condescension [kɒndɪ'senʃən] *n* altivez *f*, condescendencia *f*

condign [kən'daɪn] *adj Formal (appropriate)* merecido(a)

condiment ['kɒndɪmənt] *n* condimento *m*

condition [kən'dɪʃən] **1** *n* (**a**) *(state)* condiciones *fpl*, estado *m*; **in good/bad c.** en buenas/malas condiciones, en buen/mal estado; **the patient is in a stable c.** el paciente está estable; **in a critical c.** en estado crítico; **you're in no c. to drive** no estás en condiciones de conducir *or Am* manejar; **to be out of c.** *(person)* no estar en forma; **to be in (good) c.** *(person)* estar en (buena) forma; **in your c.** *(to pregnant woman)* en tu estado; **the human c.** la condición humana

(**b**) **conditions** *(circumstances)* circunstancias *fpl*; **working conditions** condiciones laborales; **driving conditions** estado de las carreteras; **living conditions** condiciones de vida; **weather conditions** condiciones meteorológicas, estado del tiempo

(**c**) **conditions** *(of contract, offer)* términos *mpl*, condiciones *fpl* ▸▸ *Law* ***conditions of employment*** términos *mpl* del contrato; ***conditions of sale*** condiciones *fpl* de venta

(**d**) *(requirement)* condición *f*; **on (the) c. that...** con la condición *or* a condición de que...; **on no c.** bajo ningún concepto; **on one c.** con una condición

(**e**) *Med* enfermedad *f*, afección *f*; **heart c.** afección cardíaca

(**f**) *Formal (social status)* condición *f*

2 *vt* (**a**) *(influence)* condicionar; **we have been conditioned to believe that...** nos han programado para creer que...; *Psy* **a conditioned reflex** *or* **response** un reflejo condicionado (**b**) *(hair)* suavizar, acondicionar; *(fabric)* suavizar; *(muscles)* tonificar

conditional [kən'dɪʃənəl] **1** *n Gram* condicional *m*, potencial *m*

2 *adj* (**a**) *(dependent on other factors)* condicional; **to be c. on** *or* **upon sth** depender de algo, tener algo como condición ▸▸ *Law* ***c. discharge*** remisión *f* condicional de la pena (**b**) *Gram* condicional

conditionally [kən'dɪʃənəlɪ] *adv* condicionalmente

conditioner [kən'dɪʃənə(r)] *n (for hair)* suavizante *m*, acondicionador *m*; *(for fabric)* suavizante *m*

conditioning [kən'dɪʃənɪŋ] **1** *n* (**a**) *(psychological)* condicionamiento *m* (**b**) *(of hair, fabric)* suavizamiento *m*, acondicionamiento *m*

2 *adj (shampoo)* suavizante, acondicionador(ora)

condo ['kɒndəʊ] (*pl* **condos**) *n US* (**a**) *(apartment)* apartamento *m*, *Esp* piso *m*, *Arg* departamento *m (en propiedad)* (**b**) *(building)* = bloque de apartamentos poseídos por diferentes propietarios

condolence [kən'dəʊləns] *n* pésame *m*; **a letter of c.** una carta de pésame *or* condolencia; **to offer sb one's condolences** dar el pésame a alguien

condom ['kɒndɒm] *n* preservativo *m*, condón *m*

condominium [kɒndə'mɪnɪəm] *n* (**a**) *US (apartment)* apartamento *m*, *Esp* piso *m*, *Arg* departamento *m (en propiedad)* (**b**) *US (building)* = bloque de apartamentos poseídos por diferentes propietarios (**c**) *(joint sovereignty)* condominio *m*

condone [kən'dəʊn] *vt* justificar; **I cannot c. such behaviour** no puedo justificar ese tipo de comportamiento; **I'm not condoning what they've done** no estoy justificando lo que han hecho

condor ['kɒndɔ:(r)] *n* cóndor *m*

conducive [kən'dju:sɪv] *adj* **to be c. to** ser favorable para, facilitar; **these conditions are not c. to economic growth** estas condiciones no son favorables para el crecimiento de la economía; **this weather is not c. to study** con este tiempo no apetece estudiar, con este tiempo no dan ganas de estudiar

conduct 1 *n* ['kɒndʌkt] (**a**) *(behaviour)* conducta *f*; **bad/good c.** mala/buena conducta (**b**) *(management)* **his c. of the war** la manera en que condujo la guerra

2 *vt* [kən'dʌkt] (**a**) *(business, operations)* gestionar, hacer; *(campaign, experiment, inquiry)* realizar, hacer; *(religious service)* oficiar; *Law* **she conducted her own case** se encargó de su propia defensa (**b**) *(guide)* **we were conducted round the factory** nos llevaron por toda la fábrica; **a conducted tour** una visita guiada (**c**) *Mus (orchestra)* dirigir (**d**) *(heat, electricity)* conducir (**e**) **to c. oneself** *(behave)* comportarse, conducirse

3 *vi* [kən'dʌkt] *Mus* dirigir

conductance [kən'dʌktəns] *n Phys* conductancia *f*

conduction [kən'dʌkʃən] *n Phys* conducción *f*

conductive [kən'dʌktɪv] *adj Phys* conductor(ora); **c. material** conductor

conductivity [kɒndʌk'tɪvɪtɪ] *n Phys* conductividad *f*

conductor [kən'dʌktə(r)] *n* (**a**) *Br (on bus)* cobrador(ora) *m,f, RP* guarda *mf* (**b**) *US (on train)* revisor *m* (**c**) *(of orchestra)* director(ora) *m,f* de orquesta (**d**) *(of heat, electricity)* conductor *m*

conductress [kən'dʌktrɪs] *n* (**a**) *Br (on bus)* cobradora *f, RP* guarda *f* (**b**) *US (on train)* revisora *f*

conduit ['kɒndjʊɪt] *n* conducto *m*

condyle ['kɒndɪl] *n Anat* cóndilo *m*

cone [kəʊn] *n* (**a**) *(shape)* cono *m* (**b**) **(traffic) c.** cono *m (de tráfico)* (**c**) *(for ice cream)* cucurucho *m* (**d**) *(in retina)* cono *m* (**e**) *(of pine, fir)* piña *f*

► **cone off** *vt sep Br* delimitar con conos

conehead ['kəʊnhed] *n US Fam* (**a**) *(intellectual)* cerebrito *m* (**b**) *(idiot)* cabeza *m* de chorlito; **you c.!** ¡cabeza de chorlito!

cone-shaped ['kəʊnʃeɪpt] *adj* cónico(a)

confab ['kɒnfæb] *n Fam (discussion)* deliberación *f*; **to have a c. about sth** deliberar sobre algo

confection [kən'fekʃən] *n Formal* (**a**) *(sweet, cake)* dulce *m* (**b**) *(creation)* creación *f*

> **False friend:** The Spanish noun **confección** is not a translation for the English word **confection**. In Spanish **confección** means "tailoring, dressmaking" or "preparation, making".

confectioner [kən'fekʃənə(r)] *n (cake maker)* pastelero(a) *m,f*; *(sweet maker)* confitero(a) *m,f*; **c.'s (shop)** *(cake shop)* pastelería *f*; *(sweet shop)* confitería *f* ►► *Culin* ***c.'s custard*** crema *f* pastelera; *US* ***c.'s sugar*** azúcar *m Esp, Méx* glas *or Esp* de lustre *or Chile* flor *or Col* pulverizado *or RP* impalpable

confectionery [kən'fekʃənərɪ] *n* dulces *mpl*

confederacy [kən'fedərəsɪ] *n* (**a**) *(alliance)* confederación *f* (**b**) *(conspiracy)* conspiración *f* (**c**) *Hist* **the C.** *(in American Civil War)* la Confederación

confederate [kən'fedərət] **1** *n* (**a**) *(member of confederacy)* confederado(a) *m,f* (**b**) *(accomplice)* compinche *mf*, cómplice *mf* (**c**) *Hist* confederado(a) *m,f*
2 *adj* (**a**) *(allied)* confederado(a) (**b**) *Hist* **C.** confederado(a); **the C. States** los Estados Confederados
3 *vt (ally, unite)* confederar
4 *vi* confederarse

confederation [kənfedə'reɪʃən] *n* confederación *f*

confer [kən'fɜː(r)] *(pt & pp* **conferred***)* **1** *vt (title, rank, powers)* conferir, otorgar (**on** a); *(degree, diploma)* conceder, otorgar (**on** a)
2 *vi (discuss)* deliberar (**with** con); **contestants are not allowed to c.** a los concursantes no se les permite hablar entre ellos

conference ['kɒnfərəns] *n* (**a**) *(meeting)* reunión *f*; **to be in c.** estar reunido(a); **we hope to get management to the c. table** esperamos que la dirección se siente en la mesa de negociaciones ►► *Tel* ***c. call*** multiconferencia *f*; ***c. room*** sala *f* de juntas *or* reuniones
(**b**) *(congress)* congreso *m*; **the Labour Party c.** el congreso del Partido Laborista ►► ***c. centre*** palacio *m* de congresos; ***c. delegate*** delegado(a) *m,f* de un congreso; ***c. hostess*** azafata *f* de exposiciones y congresos, azafata *f* de ferias y congresos; ***c. pack*** carpeta *f* con el material del congreso
(**c**) *US Sport* conferencia *f*

conferment [kən'fɜːmənt], **conferral** [kən'fɜːrəl] *n* otorgamiento *m*, concesión *f*

confess [kən'fes] **1** *vt* (**a**) *(admit) (fault, crime)* confesar, admitir; **to c. that...** confesar que...; **I must c. I was baffled, too** debo admitir que yo también me quedé perplejo(a) (**b**) *Rel (sins, sinner)* confesar
2 *vi* (**a**) *(admit)* confesar; **to c. to a crime** confesar haber cometido un delito; **to c. to sth** confesarse culpable de algo, confesar algo; **I c. to being shocked** confieso que estoy impactado; **I must** *or* **I have to c.,...** tengo que *or* debo confesar que... (**b**) *Rel* confesarse

confessed [kən'fest] *adj* confeso(a), declarado(a)

confession [kən'feʃən] *n* (**a**) *(of guilt)* confesión *f*; **to make a c.** confesar, hacer una confesión; **I have a c. to make** tengo que hacer una confesión (**b**) *Rel (sacrament)* confesión *f*; **the priest heard our c.** el sacerdote nos confesó, el sacerdote nos oyó en confesión; **to go to c.** confesarse (**c**) *(declaration)* **a c. of faith** una profesión de fe (**d**) *(religious body)* confesión *f*; **the Anglican c.** la confesión anglicana

confessional [kən'feʃənəl] **1** *n Rel* confesionario *m*, confesonario *m*
2 *adj* **the c. tone of the memoir** el tono íntimo de la biografía; **she was in a c. mood** estaba dispuesta a hacer revelaciones íntimas

confessor [kən'fesə(r)] *n Rel* confesor *m*

confetti [kən'fetɪ] *n* confeti *m*

confidant ['kɒnfɪdænt] *n* confidente *m*

confidante [kɒnfɪ'dænt] *n* confidente *f*

confide [kən'faɪd] **1** *vt* (**a**) *(reveal)* confiar; **to c. sth to sb** confiarle algo a alguien; **to c. a secret to sb** confiarle un secreto a alguien; **she confided her fear to them** les confió que tenía miedo (**b**) *(entrust)* confiar; **to c. sth to sb's care** confiar a alguien el cuidado de algo
2 *vi* **to c. in sb** confiarse a *or* confesarse con alguien; **there's nobody I can c. in** no puedo confiar en nadie

confidence ['kɒnfɪdəns] *n* (**a**) *(trust)* confianza *f*; **to have c. in sb** fiarse de alguien, tener confianza en alguien; **we have c. in her ability** tenemos confianza en su capacidad; **to have every c. that...** estar completamente seguro(a) de que...; **they have put all their c. in him** han depositado toda su confianza en él; **she put her c. in the doctors' skill** confía en el saber hacer de los médicos; **to take sb into one's c.** confiarse a alguien ►► ***c. trick*** timo *m*, estafa *f*; ***c. trickster*** embaucador(ora) *m,f*, timador(ora) *m,f*
(**b**) *(self-assurance)* confianza *f* (en uno mismo); **she's full of c.** tiene mucha confianza en sí misma
(**c**) *(secrecy)* **in c.** confidencialmente; **she told me in the strictest c.** me lo contó con la más absoluta reserva
(**d**) *(secret)* **to exchange confidences** intercambiar confidencias
(**e**) *Math* ***c. interval*** intervalo *m* de confianza

confidence-building ['kɒnfɪdəns'bɪldɪŋ] *adj (exercise, activity)* para incrementar la confianza

confident ['kɒnfɪdənt] *adj* (**a**) *(certain)* seguro(a); **to be c. of** *(success, outcome)* estar seguro(a) de; **to be c. that...** estar seguro(a) de que... (**b**) *(self-assured) (person)* seguro(a) de sí mismo(a); *(performance)* lleno(a) de seguridad; **in a c. tone** con un tono de seguridad

confidential [kɒnfɪ'denʃəl] *adj* (**a**) *(private)* confidencial, secreto(a); *(on envelope)* confidencial; **I would like you to treat this conversation as c.** me gustaría que consideraras esta conversación como confidencial (**b**) *(attached to one person)* de confianza ►► ***c. secretary*** secretario(a) *m,f* de confianza (**c**) *(tone, manner)* confiado(a)

confidentiality [kɒnfɪdenʃɪ'ælətɪ] *n* confidencialidad *f*, reserva *f*; **all inquiries are treated with complete c.** todas las consultas son confidenciales

confidentially [kɒnfɪ'denʃəlɪ] *adv* confidencialmente; **c., I don't trust him** entre tú y yo, no confío en él

confidently ['kɒnfɪdəntlɪ] *adv* con seguridad, con confianza; **I c. predict (that)...** pronostico con seguridad (que)...

confiding [kən'faɪdɪŋ] *adj* confiado(a)

configurable [kən'fɪg(j)ərəbəl] *adj* configurable

configuration [kənfɪg(j)ə'reɪʃən] *n* configuración *f*

configure [kən'fɪg(j)ə(r)] *vt* configurar

confine [kən'faɪn] *vt* (**a**) *(imprison)* confinar, recluir
(**b**) *(restrict movement of)* **to be confined to bed** tener que guardar cama; **to be confined to barracks** quedarse acuartelado
(**c**) *(limit)* **to c. oneself to sth** limitarse a algo; **we confined ourselves to (discussing) the financial arrangements** nos limitamos a discutir los aspectos financieros; **damage was confined to the centre** los destrozos se localizaron en el centro; **please c. your remarks to the subject under consideration** le rogamos se ciña al tema en cuestión
(**d**) *(a fire)* aislar

confined [kən'faɪnd] *adj (area, atmosphere)* limitado(a), reducido(a); **in a c. space** en un espacio limitado

confinement [kən'faɪnmənt] *n* (**a**) *(in prison)* reclusión *f*, encierro *m*; *Mil* **c. to barracks** acuartelamiento (**b**) *Old-fashioned (birth)* parto *m*

confines ['kɒnfaɪnz] *npl* límites *mpl*, confines *mpl*; **within/beyond the c. of** dentro/más allá de los límites *or* confines de; **within the c. of the home** en el ámbito del hogar

confirm [kən'fɜːm] *vt* (**a**) *(verify)* confirmar, corroborar; **I can c. that story** puedo confirmar esa historia; **to c. that...** confirmar que...
(**b**) *(arrangement, reservation)* confirmar; **to be confirmed** *(on poster, programme)* por confirmar
(**c**) *(strengthen) (belief, doubts, resolve)* confirmar, reafirmar; **my suspicions were confirmed** mis sospechas se vieron confirmadas
(**d**) *(ratify) (treaty)* ratificar; *(result, nomination)* confirmar
(**e**) *Rel* confirmar

confirmation [kɒnfə'meɪʃən] *n* (**a**) *(verification)* confirmación *f*
(**b**) *(of arrangement, reservation)* confirmación *f*; **on c. of your booking** cuando confirme la reserva
(**c**) *(strengthening) (of belief, doubts, resolve)* confirmación *f*, reafirmación *f*
(**d**) *(ratification) (of treaty)* ratificación *f*; *(of result, nomination)*

confirmación *f* ►► *US* ***c. hearing*** = reunión de senadores para dar el visto bueno a un alto cargo nombrado por el presidente
(e) *Rel* confirmación *f*

confirmed [kən'fɜ:md] *adj (smoker, liar)* empedernido(a); **he's a c. bachelor** es un solterón empedernido; *Euph* es de la otra acera

confiscate ['kɒnfɪskeɪt] *vt* confiscar; **to c. sth from sb** confiscar algo a alguien

confiscation [kɒnfɪs'keɪʃən] *n* confiscación *f*; **their property is liable to c.** sus propiedades son susceptibles de ser confiscadas, sus propiedades están sujetas a confiscación

conflagration [kɒnflə'greɪʃən] *n Formal* incendio *m*

conflate [kən'fleɪt] *vt Formal* aunar

conflation [kən'fleɪʃən] *n Formal* refundición *f*

conflict 1 *n* ['kɒnflɪkt] conflicto *m*; **to be in c. (with)** estar en conflicto (con); **to come into c. with** entrar en conflicto con; **our differing beliefs brought us into c.** nuestra disparidad de opiniones nos hizo entrar en conflicto; **a c. of interests** un conflicto de intereses
2 *vi* [kən'flɪkt] *(evidence, reports)* chocar (**with** con)

conflicting [kən'flɪktɪŋ] *adj (opinions)* encontrado(a); *(reports, evidence)* contradictorio(a); *(interests)* opuesto(a), encontrado(a)

confluence ['kɒnflʊəns] *n* confluencia *f*

conform [kən'fɔ:m] *vi* (**a**) *(be in keeping with) (laws, standards)* ajustarse (**to** a); *(expectations)* ajustarse, responder (**with** a); **to c. to type: the supporters conformed to type and wrecked the bar** los hinchas hicieron honor a su fama y destrozaron el bar
(**b**) *(behave conventionally)* ser conformista, actuar como todo el mundo; **there's tremendous pressure to c.** existe una enorme presión para que uno se comporte como los demás
(**c**) *Rel* seguir los preceptos de la iglesia

conformism [kən'fɔ:mɪzəm] *n* conformismo *m*

conformist [kən'fɔ:mɪst] 1 *n* conformista *mf*
2 *adj* conformista

conformity [kən'fɔ:mətɪ] *n* conformidad *f*; **in c. with...** de conformidad con..., conforme a...

confound [kən'faʊnd] *vt* (**a**) *(frustrate)* frustrar (**b**) *(surprise)* desconcertar, sorprender; **he confounded his critics** desconcertó *or* sorprendió a sus críticos (**c**) *Formal (mix up)* confundir (**d**) *Fam Old-fashioned* **c. it/him!** ¡maldita sea!

confounded [kən'faʊndɪd] *adj Fam Old-fashioned* condenado(a), dichoso(a), *RP, Méx* maldito(a); **it's a c. nuisance!** ¡es una maldita pesadez!

confront [kən'frʌnt] *vt* (**a**) *(meet face to face)* enfrentarse a; **the two groups of demonstrators confronted each other** los dos grupos de manifestantes se enfrentaron; **to be confronted by a problem** enfrentarse a un problema
(**b**) *(face up to)* enfrentarse a, hacer frente a; **to c. sb (about sth)** hablar cara a cara con alguien (acerca de algo); **to c. a problem** encarar un problema
(**c**) *(present)* **they confronted him with evidence of his crimes** le presentaron pruebas de sus crímenes

confrontation [kɒnfrʌn'teɪʃən] *n* (**a**) *(conflict)* confrontación *f*, enfrentamiento *m* (**b**) *(encounter)* confrontación *f*, enfrentamiento *m*

confrontational [kɒnfrʌn'teɪʃənəl] *adj* polémico(a), controvertido(a)

Confucian [kən'fju:ʃən] 1 *n* confuciano(a) *m,f*
2 *adj* confuciano(a)

Confucius [kən'fju:ʃəs] *pr n* Confucio

confuse [kən'fju:z] *vt* (**a**) *(bewilder)* desconcertar, confundir; **don't c. me!** ¡no me confundas!; **to c. the issue, to c. matters** complicar el asunto *or* las cosas (**b**) *(mix up)* confundir (**with** con); **you're confusing me with my brother** confundes con mi hermano; **don't c. the two issues** no confundas los dos asuntos

confused [kən'fju:zd] *adj* (**a**) *(bewildered) (person)* confundido(a), desorientado(a); **to get c.** desorientarse; **I'm a bit c. about what's happening** estoy un poco confundido con lo que ha ocurrido (**b**) *(mixed up) (mind, ideas, situation)* confuso(a)

confusedly [kən'fju:zɪdlɪ] *adv* confusamente, de manera confusa

confusing [kən'fju:zɪŋ] *adj* confuso(a); **Mexican history is very c.** la historia de México es muy complicada; **I hope my explanation wasn't too c.** espero que mi explicación no fuera demasiado confusa; **the plot gets a bit c.** la trama se complica un poco

confusingly [kən'fju:zɪŋlɪ] *adv* confusamente; **c., both twins do exactly the same courses at university** para mayor confusión, ambos gemelos cursan la misma carrera universitaria

confusion [kən'fju:ʒən] *n* (**a**) *(perplexity)* desconcierto *m*; **this only added to my c.** eso sólo aumentó mi desconcierto
(**b**) *(embarrassment)* turbación *f*, aturdimiento *m*; **I was thrown into c.** me quedé turbado *or* aturdido
(**c**) *(mixing up)* confusión *f*
(**d**) *(uncertainty)* **there is some c. as to who won** existe cierta confusión acerca de quién ganó; **to avoid c., I will number the cases** para evitar confusión, le asignaré un número a cada caso
(**e**) *(disorder)* confusión *f*; **to throw sth into c.** *(country, party)* sumir a algo en el desconcierto; *(plans)* trastocar algo por completo

confute [kən'fju:t] *vt Formal (person)* rebatir los argumentos de; *(theory)* rebatir, refutar

conga ['kɒŋgə] 1 *n (dance)* conga *f*
2 *vi* bailar la conga

congeal [kən'dʒi:l] *vi (blood)* coagularse; *(fat, lava, paint)* solidificarse; *(food)* cuajarse

congenial [kən'dʒi:nɪəl] *adj (person)* simpático(a); *(atmosphere)* agradable

congenital [kən'dʒenɪtəl] *adj (disease, deformity)* congénito(a); *Fig* **c. liar** mentiroso(a) patológico(a)

conger ['kɒŋgə(r)] *n* **c. (eel)** congrio *m*

congested [kən'dʒestɪd] *adj* (**a**) *(street)* congestionado(a); **the streets were c. with traffic** el tráfico colapsaba las calles (**b**) *(lungs)* congestionado(a) (**with** por); **to become c. (with blood)** congestionarse (por una acumulación de sangre)

congestion [kən'dʒestʃən] *n* (**a**) *(of traffic)* congestión *f* (**b**) *(of lungs)* congestión *f*

conglomerate [kən'glɒmərət] 1 *n* (**a**) *Com* conglomerado *m* de empresas (**b**) *Geol* conglomerado *m*
2 *adj (composed of various things)* conglomerado(a)
3 *vi* [kən'glɒməreɪt] aglomerarse; **the revellers tend to c. in the city centre** los juerguistas suelen aglomerarse *or* darse cita en el centro de la ciudad

conglomeration [kənglɒmə'reɪʃən] *n* conglomerado *m*

Congo ['kɒŋgəʊ] *n* (**a**) **the C.** *(country)* el Congo; **the Democratic Republic of C.** la República Democrática del Congo (**b**) *(river)* **the C.** el Congo

Congolese [kɒŋgə'li:z] 1 *n* congoleño(a) *m,f*
2 *adj* congoleño(a)

congrats [kən'græts] *exclam Fam* ¡felicidades!, ¡enhorabuena!

congratulate [kən'grætjʊleɪt] *vt* felicitar (**on** por); **I c. you** le felicito; **to c. oneself on (having done) sth** felicitarse por (haber hecho) algo

congratulations [kəngrætjʊ'leɪʃənz] *npl* enhorabuena *f*, felicitaciones *fpl*; **c. on the new job/your engagement/passing your exams** enhorabuena por tu nuevo trabajo/tu compromiso/haber aprobado tus exámenes; **to give** *or* **offer one's c. to sb** dar la enhorabuena a alguien; **c.!** ¡felicidades!; **I hear c. are in order** he oído que hay que darle la enhorabuena a alguien

congratulatory [kən'grætjʊlətərɪ] *adj* de felicitación

congregate ['kɒŋgrɪgeɪt] *vi* congregarse

congregation [kɒŋgrɪ'geɪʃən] *n (of church)* fieles *mpl*, feligreses *mpl*; **St Albans has a large c.** St Alban tiene una nutrida comunidad de fieles *or* feligreses

congregational [kɒŋgrɪ'geɪʃənəl] *adj* (**a**) *(relating to a congregation)* de la congregación (**b**) **the C. Church** la iglesia congregacionalista

congress ['kɒŋgres] *n* (**a**) *(conference)* congreso *m* (**b**) *US Pol* **C.** el Congreso *(de los Estados Unidos)*

congressional [kən'greʃənəl] *adj US Pol (leaders, report, committee)* del Congreso; *(election)* al Congreso ►► ***c. district*** circunscripción *f* electoral (del Congreso); ***c. elections*** ≃ elecciones *fpl* legislativas; ***c. immunity*** inmunidad *f* parlamentaria; ***C. Medal of Honor*** = máxima condecoración militar en EE.UU. otorgada por el Congreso como reconocimiento al valor demostrado en acto de servicio; ***C. privilege*** inmunidad *f* parlamentaria; ***C. Record*** actas *fpl* del Congreso de los EE.UU.

Congressman ['kɒŋgresmæn] *n US Pol* congresista *m*, *Am* congresal *m*

Congresswoman ['kɒŋgreswʊmən] *n US Pol* congresista *f*, *Am* congresal *f*

congruence ['kɒŋgrʊəns], **congruency** ['kɒŋgrʊənsɪ] *n* (**a**) *Formal (correspondence)* congruencia *f* (**b**) *Geom* congruencia *f*

congruent ['kɒŋgrʊənt] *adj* (**a**) *Formal (correspondent)* acorde (**with** con) (**b**) *Geom* congruente

conic ['kɒnɪk] *adj Geom* cónico(a) ►► ***c. section*** sección *f* cónica

conical ['kɒnɪkəl] *adj* cónico(a) ►► ***c. projection (in mapmaking)*** proyección *f* cónica

conifer ['kɒnɪfə(r)] *n* conífera *f*

coniferous [kə'nɪfərəs] *adj* conífero(a); **a c. forest** un bosque de coníferas

conjectural [kən'dʒektʃərəl] *adj* basado en conjeturas

conjecture [kən'dʒektʃə(r)] **1** *n* conjetura *f*; **whether he knew or not is a matter for c.** sólo se pueden hacer conjeturas sobre si lo sabía o no; **it's sheer c.** no son más que conjeturas
2 *vt* conjeturar
3 *vi* hacer conjeturas

conjointly ['kɒndʒɔɪntlɪ] *adv Formal* conjuntamente

conjugal ['kɒndʒəgəl] *adj* conyugal; **he demanded his c. rights** pidió a su esposa que cumpliera sus deberes conyugales

conjugate ['kɒndʒəgeɪt] *Gram* **1** *vt* conjugar
2 *vi* conjugarse

conjugation [kɒndʒə'geɪʃən] *n Gram* conjugación *f*

conjunction [kən'dʒʌŋkʃən] *n* **(a)** *(combination)* conjunción *f*; **in c. with** junto con **(b)** *Gram* conjunción *f* **(c)** *(of planets)* conjunción *f*

conjunctiva [kɒndʒʌŋk'taɪvə] (*pl* **conjunctivas** *or* **conjunctivae** [kɒndʒʌŋk'taɪvi:]) *n Anat* conjuntiva *f*

conjunctivitis [kəndʒʌŋktɪ'vaɪtɪs] *n Med* conjuntivitis *f inv*

conjuncture [kən'dʒʌŋktʃə(r)] *n Formal* coyuntura *f*

conjure ['kʌndʒə(r)] **1** *vt* **(a)** *(produce)* **to c. a rabbit from a hat** hacer aparecer un conejo de un sombrero; **they conjured a bottle of wine out of nowhere** *or* **thin air** hicieron aparecer una botella de vino como por arte de magia **(b)** *Archaic (appeal to)* conminar, conjurar
2 *vi (do magic)* hacer juegos de manos; IDIOM *Br* **his is a name to c. with** es un personaje de muchas campanillas

► **conjure up** *vt sep* **(a)** *(produce)* hacer aparecer; **she conjured up a meal** preparó una comida prácticamente con nada **(b)** *(call to mind)* evocar

conjurer, conjuror ['kʌndʒərə(r)] *n* mago(a) *m,f*, prestidigitador(ora) *m,f*

conjuring ['kʌndʒərɪŋ] *n* magia *f*, prestidigitación *f* ►► ***c. trick*** juego *m* de manos

conjuror = **conjurer**

conk [kɒŋk] *Fam* **1** *n* **(a)** *(blow)* mamporro *m*; **he gave me a c. on the nose** me dio un mamporro en la nariz **(b)** *Br (nose)* napia *f*, *Esp* napias *fpl*
2 *vt (hit)* dar un mamporro

► **conk out** *vi Fam* **(a)** *(stop working) (car, TV) Esp* escacharrarse, *Am* descomponerse, *Méx* desconchinflarse **(b)** *(fall asleep)* quedarse frito(a) *or Esp* roque *or Méx* súpito(a) **(c)** *US (die)* estirar la pata, palmarla

conker ['kɒŋkə(r)] *n Fam* **(a)** *(chestnut)* castaña *f* **(b)** *Br* **conkers** *(game)* = juego con castañas ensartadas en cordeles cuyo objetivo es romper la castaña del contricante

Conn (*abbr* **Connecticut**) Connecticut

connect [kə'nekt] **1** *vt* **(a)** *(pipes, wires, gas)* conectar, empalmar (**to** con *or* a); **to be connected to sth** estar conectado(a) *or* enchufado(a) a algo; **to c. sth to the mains** enchufar algo, conectar algo a la red; **to get connected** *(to telephone system, Internet)* conectarse
(b) *(link)* conectar; **to c. sth with** *or* **to** conectar algo a; **a corridor connects the room to the library** un pasillo comunica la habitación con la biblioteca
(c) *(associate) (person, problem)* relacionar (**with** con), vincular (**with** con *or* a); **to be connected with...** estar relacionado(a) con...; **are they connected?** ¿existe algún vínculo *or* alguna relación entre ellos?; **the two issues are not connected** los dos asuntos no están relacionados; **there is nothing to c. the two crimes** no hay nada que relacione los dos delitos; **I'd never connected the two things before** nunca había asociado las dos cosas hasta ahora; **to be well connected** *(socially)* estar bien relacionado(a), tener buenos contactos
(d) *Tel* poner, pasar; **could you c. me with Lost Property, please?** ¿me pasa *or Esp* pone con el departamento de objetos perdidos, por favor?; **I'm trying to c. you** estoy intentando pasarle
2 *vi* **(a)** *(wires, roads, pipes)* conectarse, empalmarse; **the living-room connects with the kitchen** el salón da a la cocina; **this road connects with the motorway** esta carretera va a parar a la autopista *or* enlaza con la autopista
(b) *(train, plane)* enlazar (**with** con)
(c) *(blow)* dar en el blanco; **my fist connected with his chin** le di un puñetazo en la barbilla; **he connected with a right to the jaw** le encajó un derechazo en la mandíbula
(d) *(people) (emotionally)* entenderse, conectar
(e) *Comptr (to the Internet)* conectarse ►► ***c. time*** tiempo *m* de conexión

► **connect up 1** *vt sep (pipes, wires)* conectar
2 *vi* **(a)** *(pipes, wires)* ensamblarse, conectarse **(b)** *Comptr (to the Internet)* conectarse

Connecticut [kə'netɪkət] *n* Connecticut

connecting [kə'nektɪŋ] *adj (rooms)* que se comunican ►► ***c. door*** puerta *f* que comunica; ***c. flight*** vuelo *m* de enlace *or* conexión; *Tech* ***c. rod*** biela *f*

connection [kə'nekʃən] *n* **(a)** *(of pipes, wires)* conexión *f*, empalme *m*; *(electrical)* conexión *f*
(b) *Tel* conexión *f*; **a bad c.** una mala conexión
(c) *Comptr (to Internet)* conexión *f*; **to establish a c.** conectarse; **to have a fast/slow c.** tener una conexión rápida/lenta ►► ***c. kit*** kit *m* de conexión
(d) *(link, association)* conexión *f*, vínculo *m*; **to make a c. between X and Y** relacionar X con Y; **does this have any c. with what happened yesterday?** ¿tiene esto algo que ver con lo que pasó ayer?; **he has CIA connections** tiene vínculos con la CIA; **that was when I made the c.** entonces lo relacioné; **in c. with** en relación con; **in this c.** a este respecto
(e) *(acquaintance, contact)* **she has important connections** está bien relacionada; **he used his connections to get the job** utilizó sus contactos para conseguir el trabajo; **she has some useful connections in the publishing world** tiene algunos contactos útiles en el mundo editorial
(f) *(family relationship)* familiares *mpl*, parientes *mpl*; **her family has Scottish connections** su familia tiene parientes escoceses
(g) *(train, plane)* enlace *m*, conexión *f*; **I missed my c.** perdí el enlace *or* la conexión
(h) *US Fam (drug dealer)* camello *m*, *Méx* narco *mf*

connective [kə'nektɪv] **1** *n Gram* nexo *m*
2 *adj Anat* ***c. tissue*** tejido *m* conjuntivo

connectivity [kɒnek'tɪvɪtɪ] *n Comptr* conectividad *f*

connector [kə'nektə(r)] *n* **(a)** *(for wire, piping)* conector *m*, junta *f* **(b)** *Comptr* conector *m*

conning tower ['kɒnɪŋ'taʊə(r)] *n* **(a)** *(on submarine)* falsa torre *f* **(b)** *(on warship)* torre *f* de mando

conniption [kə'nɪpʃn] *n US Fam* **to have conniptions** *or* **a c. fit** agarrar *or Esp* coger una rabieta

connivance [kə'naɪvəns] *n* connivencia *f*, complicidad *f*; **to be in c. with sb** estar en connivencia con alguien; **to do sth with the c. of** *or* **in c. with** hacer algo con la complicidad de *or* en connivencia con; **it would have been impossible without the c. of the authorities** habría sido imposible sin la connivencia *or* la complicidad de las autoridades

connive [kə'naɪv] *vi* **(a)** *(conspire)* **to c. (with)** confabularse (con) **(b)** *(work towards)* **to c. at** contribuir a

conniving [kə'naɪvɪŋ] *adj* confabulador(ora)

connoisseur [kɒnə'sɜ:(r)] *n* entendido(a) *m,f* (**of** en)

connotation [kɒnə'teɪʃən] *n* **(a)** *(association)* connotación *f* **(b)** *Ling & Phil* connotación *f*

connote [kə'nəʊt] *vt* **(a)** *(imply)* tener connotaciones de, connotar **(b)** *Ling & Phil* connotar

connubial [kə'nju:bɪəl] *adj Formal* conyugal

conquer ['kɒŋkə(r)] *vt* **(a)** *(defeat) (country, sb's heart)* conquistar **(b)** *(overcome) (difficulty, one's shyness, fears)* vencer; **Everest was conquered in 1953** el Everest fue conquistado en 1953 **(c)** *(market, market share)* conquistar

conquering ['kɒŋkərɪŋ] *adj* vencedor(ora)

conqueror ['kɒŋkərə(r)] *n* conquistador(ora) *m,f*; *Hist* **(William) the C.** (Guillermo) el Conquistador

conquest ['kɒŋkwest] *n* **(a)** *(of land, person)* conquista *f*; **the c. of space** la conquista del espacio **(b)** *(land, person conquered)* conquista *f*; **to make a c. of sb** conquistar a alguien; **he would boast of his conquests** se jactaba de sus conquistas **(c)** *Hist* **the (Norman) C.** la conquista normanda

Cons *Br Pol* (*abbr* **Conservative**) conservador(ora)

consanguinity [kɒnsæŋ'gwɪnɪtɪ] *n* consanguinidad *f*

conscience ['kɒnʃəns] *n* conciencia *f*; **to have a clear** *or* **an easy c.** tener la conciencia tranquila; **my c. is clear** tengo la conciencia tranquila; **he has a guilty c.** le remuerde la conciencia; **she had three**

deaths on her c. sobre su conciencia pesaban tres muertes; **in all c.** en conciencia ►► *Law* ***c. clause*** cláusula *f* de conciencia; ***c. money*** = dinero que se da para descargar la conciencia

conscience-stricken ['kɒnʃəns'strɪkən] *adj* lleno(a) de remordimientos

conscientious [kɒnʃɪ'enʃəs] *adj (worker)* concienzudo(a); **she's c. about wiping her feet before entering the house** nunca deja de limpiarse los zapatos antes de entrar en casa ►► ***c. objector*** objetor(ora) *m,f* de conciencia

conscientiously [kɒnʃɪ'enʃəslɪ] *adv* concienzudamente

conscientiousness [kɒnʃɪ'enʃəsnɪs] *n* escrupulosidad *f*, esmero *m*

conscious ['kɒnʃəs] *adj* **(a)** *(awake)* **to be c.** estar consciente; **to become c.** volver en sí, recobrar la con(s)ciencia
(b) *(aware)* **to be c. of** ser consciente de; **to become c. of** cobrar conciencia de, darse cuenta de; **I wasn't c. of having annoyed you** no me di cuenta de que te estaba molestando; **to be c. that...** ser consciente de que...; *Psy* **the c. mind** la con(s)ciencia, el consciente
(c) *(intentional)* consciente, deliberado(a); **to make a c. effort to do sth** hacer un esfuerzo consciente para hacer algo; **to make a c. decision to do sth** tomar conscientemente la decisión de hacer algo

-conscious ['kɒnʃəs] *suffix* **fashion-c.** que sigue la moda; **health-c.** preocupado(a) por la salud

consciously ['kɒnʃəslɪ] *adv (deliberately)* conscientemente, adrede

consciousness ['kɒnʃəsnɪs] *n* **(a)** *(state of being awake)* con(s)ciencia *f*, conocimiento *m*; **to lose c.** quedar inconsciente, perder el conocimiento; **to regain c.** volver en sí, recobrar el conocimiento **(b)** *(awareness)* conciencia *f*, concienciación *f*; **to raise sb's c. of sth** concienciar a alguien de algo ►► ***c. raising*** concienciación *f* **(c)** *(mentality)* conciencia *f*; **the national c.** la conciencia nacional **(d)** *Psy* conciencia *f*

conscript **1** *vt* [kən'skrɪpt] reclutar *(forzosamente)*; **he was conscripted into the army** le llamaron a filas *or* a cumplir el servicio militar; *Hum* **I've been conscripted to do the dishes** me han reclutado para fregar los platos
2 *n* ['kɒnskrɪpt] recluta *mf (forzoso)*
3 *adj* ['kɒnskrɪpt] *(army)* de reclutas

conscription [kən'skrɪpʃən] *n* reclutamiento *m* obligatorio

consecrate ['kɒnsɪkreɪt] *vt* **(a)** *Rel (church)* consagrar (**to** a); *(bread and wine)* consagrar **(b)** *(dedicate)* consagrar (**to** a)

consecrated ['kɒnsɪkreɪtɪd] *adj Rel (church, bread)* consagrado(a); **in c. ground** en tierra consagrada

consecration [kɒnsɪ'kreɪʃən] *n* **(a)** *Rel (of church)* consagración *f*; **the C.** la Consagración **(b)** *(dedication)* consagración *f*

consecutive [kən'sekjʊtɪv] *adj* **(a)** *(successive)* consecutivo(a); **on three c. days** en tres días consecutivos; **they have had five c. home wins** llevan cinco victorias seguidas en casa **(b)** *Gram (clause)* consecutivo(a)

consecutively [kən'sekjʊtɪvlɪ] *adv* consecutivamente; **three times c.** tres veces consecutivas *or* seguidas; *Law* **the sentences to be served c.** las condenas se cumplirán de forma sucesiva *or* sucesivamente

consensual [kən'sensjʊəl] *adj* **(a)** *(approach, politics)* consensuado(a) **(b)** *(sexual activity)* consentido(a) **(c)** *Law (contract)* consensual

consensus [kən'sensəs] *n* consenso *m*; **to reach a c.** alcanzar un consenso; **the c. of opinion** el parecer de la mayoría; **the general c. was that...** la opinión generalizada era que...; **there was no c. about what to do** no hubo consenso sobre qué hacer ►► ***c. politics*** política *f* de consenso

consent [kən'sent] **1** *n* consentimiento *m*; **to give/withhold one's c. to sth** dar/negar el consentimiento a algo; **we got married without my parents' c.** nos casamos sin el permiso *or* consentimiento de mis padres; **by mutual c.** de común acuerdo
2 *vi* **to c. to (do) sth** consentir (en hacer) algo; **they consented to my request** accedieron a mi solicitud

consenting [kən'sentɪŋ] *adj* puestos(as) de acuerdo ►► *Law* ***c. adult*** mayor *mf* de edad (que actúa de motu proprio)

consequence ['kɒnsɪkwəns] *n* **(a)** *(result)* consecuencia *f*; **the policy had terrible consequences** esa política tuvo terribles consecuencias; **as a c. (of)** como consecuencia (de); **in c.** en consecuencia; **to take** *or* **suffer the consequences** sufrir las consecuencias; **regardless of the consequences** independientemente de las consecuencias
(b) *(importance)* **it is of some c. to me** para mí tiene bastante importancia; **of little c.** de poca relevancia; **of no c.** irrelevante; **a person of no** *or* **little c.** una persona de ninguna *or* escasa importancia
(c) consequences *(game)* = juego consistente en componer un cuento con fragmentos que cada participante escribe por separado y pasa al siguiente

consequent ['kɒnsɪkwənt] *adj Formal* consiguiente; **a glut and the c. drop in prices** un exceso de oferta con la consiguiente *or* subsiguiente caída de precios; **c. upon sth** resultante de algo

consequential [kɒnsɪ'kwenʃəl] *adj Formal* **(a)** *(resultant)* consiguiente, resultante **(b)** *(significant)* trascendente, relevante

consequently ['kɒnsɪkwəntlɪ] *adv* por consiguiente, en consecuencia

conservancy [kən'sɜːvənsɪ] *n* **(a)** *Br (commission)* junta *f* rectora **(b)** *(protected area)* área *f* protegida

conservation [kɒnsə'veɪʃən] *n* **(a)** *(of the environment) n* conservación *f or* protección *f* del medio ambiente; *(of energy, resources)* conservación *f* ►► ***c. area*** *(of town, city)* zona *f* arquitectónica protegida; *(nature reserve)* zona *f* protegida **(b)** *(of works of art)* conservación *f* **(c)** *Phys* conservación *f*

conservationist [kɒnsə'veɪʃənɪst] *n* ecologista *mf*

conservatism [kən'sɜːvətɪzəm] *n* **(a)** *(in habits, politics)* conservadurismo *m* **(b)** *Br Pol* **C.** conservadurismo *m*

Conservative [kən'sɜːvətɪv] *Br Pol* **1** *n* conservador(ora) *m,f*; **the Conservatives** los conservadores
2 *adj* conservador(ora); **the C. Party** el Partido Conservador

conservative [kən'sɜːvətɪv] *adj* **(a)** *(traditional)* conservador(ora) **(b)** *(cautious)* prudente, cauto(a); **a c. estimate** un cálculo moderado

conservatively [kən'sɜːvətɪvlɪ] *adv* **(a)** *(to dress)* de forma conservadora, con un estilo conservador **(b)** *(cautiously)* **it was c. estimated at £5,000** se calculó en 5.000 libras como mínimo

conservatoire [kən'sɜːvətwɑː(r)] *n Mus* conservatorio *m*

conservatory [kən'sɜːvətrɪ] *n* **(a)** *(greenhouse)* invernadero *m (adosado a una casa)* **(b)** *(extension to house)* = habitación acristalada adosada a una casa **(c)** *Mus* conservatorio *m*

conserve **1** *vt* [kən'sɜːv] **(a)** *(protect) (monument, countryside, wildlife)* conservar, preservar **(b)** *(save) (water, energy)* conservar; **to c. one's strength** ahorrar energías
2 *n* ['kɒnsɜːv] *(jam)* compota *f*

consider [kən'sɪdə(r)] **1** *vt* **(a)** *(think over)* considerar; **I'll c. it** lo consideraré; **to c. doing sth** considerar hacer algo; **to c. whether to do sth** contemplar la posibilidad de hacer algo; **the jury retired to c. its verdict** el jurado se retiró a deliberar; **to c. sb for a job** tener en cuenta a alguien para un puesto
(b) *(take into account)* tener en cuenta; **he has a wife and family to c.** tiene que pensar en su mujer y en sus hijos; **she never considers anybody but herself** sólo piensa en sí misma; **if you c. what might have happened...** teniendo en cuenta lo que podría haber sucedido...; **all things considered** mirándolo bien, bien mirado
(c) *(regard)* considerar; **we c. it likely that...** consideramos que lo más probable es...; **to c. oneself happy** considerarse feliz; **I c. him a friend** yo lo considero un amigo; **I would c. it an honour** lo consideraría todo un honor; **it is considered to be the best treatment available** está considerado como *or* se le considera como el mejor tratamiento disponible; **we can c. ourselves lucky** podemos considerarnos afortunados; **c. it done!** ¡considéralo hecho!, ¡dalo por hecho!; **c. yourself dismissed!** ¡date por despedido!
(d) *Formal (look at)* observar
2 *vi (think)* reflexionar; **I need time to c.** necesito tiempo para reflexionar

considerable [kən'sɪdərəbəl] *adj* considerable; **a c. number (of)** un considerable número (de); **with c. difficulty** con grandes dificultades; **to a c. extent** en buena *or* gran medida

considerably [kən'sɪdərəblɪ] *adv* considerablemente

considerate [kən'sɪdərət] *adj* considerado(a) (**towards** *or* **to** con); **that's very c. of you** es todo un detalle por tu parte

considerately [kən'sɪdərətlɪ] *adv* con consideración

considerateness [kən'sɪdərətnɪs] *n* consideración *f*

consideration [kənsɪdə'reɪʃən] *n* **(a)** *(deliberation)* **the matter needs careful c.** es necesario considerar el asunto con detenimiento; **different possibilities are under c.** se están estudiando varias posibilidades; **after due c.** tras las debidas deliberaciones; **to give a proposal some c.** considerar una propuesta; **to take sth into c.** tomar algo en consideración; *Formal* **in c. of** *(because of)* en consideración *or* atención a
(b) *(factor)* factor *m*; **it's an important c. in reaching a decision** es un factor a tener muy en cuenta a la hora de tomar una decisión; **money is always the first c.** el dinero es siempre el primer factor que se tiene en cuenta
(c) *(respect)* consideración *f*; **have you no c. for other people?** ¿es que no tienes respeto por los demás?; **show some c.!** ¡ten un poco de consideración!; **out of c. for** por consideración hacia

(**d**) *(importance)* **of no c.** de ninguna importancia *or* trascendencia (**e**) *Formal (payment)* **for a small c.** a cambio de una pequeña retribución

considered [kən'sɪdəd] *adj* **a c. response** una respuesta pensada detenidamente; **it is my c. opinion that...** tras pensarlo muy detenidamente, creo que...

considering [kən'sɪdərɪŋ] **1** *prep* considerando, teniendo en cuenta; **c. (that) she'd never played the part before, she did very well** considerando *or* teniendo en cuenta que nunca había representado ese papel, lo hizo muy bien

2 *conj* considerando que, teniendo en cuenta que; **c. (that) he is so young** teniendo en cuenta su juventud

3 *adv* **it's not so bad, c.** no está tan mal, después de todo

consign [kən'saɪn] *vt* (**a**) *(entrust)* confiar (**to** a) (**b**) *(send)* consignar, enviar (**to** a) (**c**) *(relegate)* **I consigned his last letter to the rubbish bin** tiré su última carta a la basura

consignee [kɒnsaɪ'niː] *n Com* consignatario(a) *m,f*

consigner, consignor [kən'saɪnə(r)] *n Com* consignador(ora) *m,f*

consignment [kən'saɪnmənt] *n* (**a**) *(dispatch)* envío *m*; **goods for c.** mercancías listas para ser enviadas ►► ***c. note*** aviso *m or Esp* albarán *m* de envío (**b**) *(batch of goods)* envío *m*, remesa *f*

consignor = **consigner**

consist [kən'sɪst]

► **consist in** *vt insep* consistir en; **the book's charm consists largely in its simplicity** el encanto *or* atractivo del libro radica en buena medida en su simplicidad

► **consist of** *vt insep* consistir en, constar de; **the book consists solely of amusing anecdotes** el libro consta exclusivamente de anécdotas divertidas

consistency [kən'sɪstənsɪ] *n* (**a**) *(of substance, liquid)* consistencia *f* (**b**) *(of actions, arguments)* coherencia *f*, congruencia *f*; **to lack c.** ser incongruente (**c**) *(of performance, work)* regularidad *f*, constancia *f*

consistent [kən'sɪstənt] *adj* (**a**) *(coherent) (reasoning, behaviour)* coherente, congruente; **c. with** *(theory, principles)* coherente con (**b**) *(unvarying) (quality, standard)* invariable, constante; *(performance)* constante, regular; *(refusal, failure)* constante, continuo(a); **I try to be c.** trato de ser consecuente; **she was c. in her choice of partners** fue consecuente a la hora de elegir compañeros

> **False friend**: The Spanish adjective **consistente** is not a translation for the English word **consistent**. In Spanish **consistente** means "solid" or "sound, convincing".

consistently [kən'sɪstəntlɪ] *adv* (**a**) *(coherently) (to argue, behave)* coherentemente, congruentemente (**b**) *(without variation) (to perform)* con un nivel constante de calidad; *(to fail, deny, oppose)* constantemente

consolation [kɒnsə'leɪʃən] *n* consuelo *m*; **that's one c.** es un consuelo; **if it's any c.** si te sirve de consuelo ►► ***c. prize*** premio *m* de consolación

consolatory [kən'sɒlətərɪ] *adj (message, words)* de consuelo, consolador(ora)

console[1] ['kɒnsəʊl] *n* (**a**) *(control panel)* consola *f* (**b**) *(cabinet)* consola *f* (**c**) *Mus (on organ)* consola *f* (**d**) ***c. table*** consola *f*

console[2] [kən'səʊl] *vt* consolar; **c. yourself with the thought that it was cheap** consuélate pensando que, al menos, fue barato

consolidate [kən'sɒlɪdeɪt] **1** *vt* (**a**) *(reinforce)* consolidar (**b**) *Com (companies)* fusionar; *(debts)* consolidar

2 *vi* consolidarse

consolidated [kən'sɒlɪdeɪtɪd] *adj* consolidado(a) ►► *Fin* ***c. accounts*** cuentas *fpl* consolidadas; *Fin* ***c. balance sheet*** balance *m* consolidado

consolidation [kənsɒlɪ'deɪʃən] *n* (**a**) *(reinforcement)* consolidación *f* (**b**) *Com (of companies)* fusión *f*; *(of debts)* consolidación *f*

consoling [kən'səʊlɪŋ] *adj (idea, thought)* de consuelo, consolador(ora)

consols ['kɒnsəlz] *npl Br Fin* valores *mpl* consolidados

consommé [*Br* kən'sɒmeɪ, *US* 'kɒnsəmeɪ] *n* consomé *m*

consonant ['kɒnsənənt] **1** *n* consonante *f* ►► *Ling* ***c. cluster*** grupo *m* consonántico

2 *adj Formal* **c. with** en consonancia con

consonantal [kɒnsə'næntəl] *adj* consonántico(a)

consort ['kɒnsɔːt] *n (spouse of monarch)* consorte *mf*

► **consort with** [kən'sɔːt] *vt insep* asociarse con

consortium [kən'sɔːtɪəm] (*pl* **consortia** [kən'sɔːtɪə] *or* **consortiums**) *n Com* consorcio *m*

conspectus [kən'spektəs] *n Formal* (**a**) *(overview)* visión *f* general (**b**) *(summary)* resumen *m*

conspicuous [kən'spɪkjʊəs] *adj (person)* visible; *(colour)* llamativo(a); *(bravery, intelligence)* notable; *(failure, lack)* manifiesto(a); **to look c.** resaltar, llamar la atención; **to feel c.** tener la sensación de que se está llamando la atención; **to make oneself c.** hacerse notar; **in a c. position** en un lugar bien visible; **to be c. by one's/its absence** brillar por su ausencia ►► ***c. consumption*** ostentación *f* en el consumo

conspicuously [kən'spɪkjʊəslɪ] *adv (dressed)* de forma llamativa; **the publicity campaign was c. successful** la campaña de publicidad fue un éxito evidente

conspiracy [kən'spɪrəsɪ] *n* (**a**) *(plot)* conspiración *f*, conjura *f*; **c. of silence** pacto de silencio ►► ***c. theory*** = teoría que sostiene la existencia de una conspiración, generalmente imaginaria (**b**) *(plotting)* conspiración *f*; *Law* **he's been charged with c.** se le ha acusado de conspiración

conspirator [kən'spɪrətə(r)] *n* conspirador(ora) *m,f*

conspiratorial [kənspɪrə'tɔːrɪəl] *adj* conspirador(ora), de conspiración

conspire [kən'spaɪə(r)] *vi* (**a**) *(plot)* conspirar (**against/with** contra/con); **to c. (with sb) to do sth** conspirar (con alguien) para hacer algo (**b**) *(combine) (events)* obrar (**against** contra); **circumstances conspired against me** las circunstancias obraban en mi contra; **everything conspired to make him late** todo se confabuló para que llegara tarde

constable ['kʌnstəbəl, 'kɒnstəbəl] *n Br* policía *mf*; **C. Jenkins** agente Jenkins

constabulary [kən'stæbjʊlərɪ] *n Br* (cuerpo *m* de) policía *f*

Constance ['kɒnstəns] *n* **Lake C.** lago Constanza

constancy ['kɒnstənsɪ] *n Literary (loyalty)* lealtad *f*, fidelidad *f*; *(of feelings)* constancia *f*

constant ['kɒnstənt] **1** *adj* (**a**) *(unchanging) (price, temperature)* constante (**b**) *(continuous) (attention, questions)* continuo(a), constante; *(interruptions, noise)* constante; **it's a c. worry to me** me preocupa constantemente; **the machinery is in c. use** la maquinaria se usa constantemente (**c**) *Literary (loyal)* leal

2 *n* constante *f*

Constantinople [kɒnstæntɪ'nəʊpəl] *n Formerly* Constantinopla

constantly ['kɒnstəntlɪ] *adv* constantemente; **c. diminishing returns** rendimientos en constante descenso

constellation [kɒnstə'leɪʃən] *n* (**a**) *(of stars)* constelación *f* (**b**) *(of celebrities)* pléyade *f*

consternation [kɒnstə'neɪʃən] *n* consternación *f*; **I watched in c. as he carried out his threat** observé consternado cómo cumplió con sus amenazas; **the prospect filled me with c.** el panorama me llenó de consternación

constipate ['kɒnstɪpeɪt] *vt* estreñir

constipated ['kɒnstɪpeɪtɪd] *adj* estreñido(a)

> **False friend**: The Spanish word **constipado** is not a translation for the English word **constipated**. In Spanish **constipado** means "suffering from a cold".

constipation [kɒnstɪ'peɪʃən] *n* estreñimiento *m*

constituency [kən'stɪtjʊənsɪ] *n Pol* (**a**) *(district)* distrito *m* electoral (**b**) *(electors)* electores *mpl* potenciales ►► *Br* ***c. party*** sección *f* local del partido *(en una circunscripción electoral)*

constituent [kən'stɪtjʊənt] **1** *n* (**a**) *Pol* elector(ora) *m,f* (**b**) *(part)* elemento *m* (constitutivo)

2 *adj* constitutivo(a) ►► ***c. assembly*** asamblea *f* constituyente

constitute ['kɒnstɪtjuːt] *vt* (**a**) *(represent)* constituir; **it constitutes a major change in policy** constituye un importante cambio de política (**b**) *(make up)* constituir, formar (**c**) *(set up) (committee)* constituir, fundar

constitution [kɒnstɪ'tjuːʃən] *n* (**a**) *(of state, organization)* constitución *f* (**b**) *(of person)* constitución *f*; **to have a strong c.** ser de constitución robusta; **to have the c. of an ox** estar hecho(a) un roble, estar fuerte como un toro

constitutional [kɒnstɪ'tjuːʃənəl] **1** *n Old fashioned or Hum (walk)* paseo *m*

2 *adj (reform, decision)* constitucional ►► ***c. court*** tribunal *m* constitucional; ***c. law*** derecho *m* constitucional; ***c. monarchy*** monarquía *f* constitucional; ***c. rights*** garantías *fpl* constitucionales

constitutionality [kɒnstɪtju:ʃə'nælətɪ] *n Formal* constitucionalidad *f*

constitutionally [kɒnstɪ'tju:ʃənəlɪ] *adv* constitucionalmente

constrain [kən'streɪn] *vt Formal* restringir, constreñir; **to feel constrained to do sth** sentirse obligado(a) a hacer algo

constraint [kən'streɪnt] *n (restriction)* limitación *f*, restricción *f*; **to place constraints (up)on sth/sb** imponer restricciones a algo/alguien; **to do sth under c.** hacer algo bajo coacción; **to speak without c.** hablar abiertamente; **financial constraints** restricciones económicas; **social constraints** limitaciones sociales

constrict [kən'strɪkt] *vt* **(a)** *(make narrow) (blood vessels, intestine)* constreñir, contraer **(b)** *(restrict) (flow, breathing)* dificultar; *(person, economy)* constreñir; **to feel constricted (by sth)** sentirse constreñido(a) (por algo)

constricted [kən'strɪktɪd] *adj* **(a)** *(narrowed) (blood vessel, intestine)* constreñido(a) **(b)** *(restricted) (breathing, movement)* inhibido(a), coartado(a)

constriction [kən'strɪkʃən] *n* **(a)** *(in chest, throat)* constricción *f*; **c. of the blood vessels** vasoconstricción **(b)** *(restriction) (of person, economy)* constricción *f*

constrictor [kən'strɪktə(r)] *n* **(a)** *Anat* músculo *m* constrictor **(b)** *(snake)* serpiente *f* constrictora

construct 1 *vt* [kən'strʌkt] **(a)** *(build)* construir; **to c. sth out of sth** construir algo con algo **(b)** *(formulate) (sentence)* construir; *(system, theory)* construir, elaborar; **a beautifully constructed play** una obra muy bien montada

2 *n* ['kɒnstrʌkt] *(idea)* concepto *m*

construction [kən'strʌkʃən] *n* **(a)** *(act of building, thing built)* construcción *f*; **under c.** en construcción ►► ***the c. industry*** (el sector de) la construcción; ***c. set*** *(toy)* juego *m* de construcción; ***c. site*** obra *f*; ***c. workers*** obreros *mpl* de la construcción

(b) *(thing built)* construcción *f*

(c) *(formulation) (of sentence)* construcción *f*; *(of system, theory)* construcción *f*, elaboración *f*

(d) *(interpretation)* **to put a favourable/unfavourable c. on sb's words** darle un sentido bueno/malo a las palabras de alguien

(e) *Gram* construcción *f*

constructive [kən'strʌktɪv] *adj* **(a)** *(comment, proposal)* constructivo(a); **c. criticism** críticas constructivas **(b)** *Br Law* ***c. dismissal*** = despido forzado por presiones del empresario

constructively [kən'strʌktɪvlɪ] *adv* constructivamente, de manera constructiva

constructor [kən'strʌktə(r)] *n* constructor(ora) *m,f* ►► ***constructors' championship*** *(in motor racing)* mundial *m* de constructores

construe [kən'stru:] *vt* **(a)** *(interpret)* interpretar; **it could hardly be construed as a compliment** difícilmente podría interpretarse como un cumplido **(b)** *(parse)* analizar sintácticamente **(c)** *Old-fashioned (translate)* traducir literalmente

> **False friend**: The Spanish verb **construir** is not a translation for the English word **construe**. In Spanish **construir** means "to build", "to manufacture" or "to construct".

consubstantiation ['kɒnsəbstænsɪ'eɪʃən] *n Rel* consustanciación *f*

consul ['kɒnsəl] *n* **(a)** *(diplomat)* cónsul *mf* ►► ***c. general*** cónsul *mf* general **(b)** *(Roman)* cónsul *m*

consular ['kɒnsjʊlə(r)] *adj* consular

consulate ['kɒnsjʊlət] *n* consulado *m*

consulship ['kɒnsəlʃɪp] *n* consulado *m*

consult [kən'sʌlt] 1 *vt* **(a)** *(ask) (doctor, expert)* consultar; **to c. sb about sth** consultar algo a alguien; **I wasn't consulted** no se me consultó **(b)** *(refer to) (book, map, watch)* consultar

2 *vi* consultar; **I'll have to c. with head office about this** tendré que consultarlo con la central; **they consulted together over what steps to take next** debatieron qué medidas tomar a continuación

consultancy [kən'sʌltənsɪ] *n* **(a)** *(of medical specialist)* = plaza de especialista hospitalario **(b)** *Com* asesoría *f*, consultoría *f*; **to do c. work** desarrollar tareas de asesoría *or* consultoría ►► ***c. fees*** honorarios *mpl* de asesoría *or* consultoría

consultant [kən'sʌltənt] *n* **(a)** *(medical specialist)* médico(a) *m,f* especialista *(en hospital)* **(b)** *(contracted adviser)* asesor(ora) *m,f*, consultor(ora) *m,f*

consultation [kɒnsəl'teɪʃən] *n* **(a)** *(with doctor)* consulta *f* **(b)** *(discussion)* consulta *f*; **there was no c. about the decision** la decisión no fue consultada; **to hold a c. (with)** consultar (con); **in c. with sb** con la asesoría de alguien **(c)** *(reference)* consulta *f*; **the dictionary is designed for easy c.** el diseño del diccionario favorece su fácil consulta

consultative [kən'sʌltətɪv] *adj* consultivo(a); **in a c. capacity** a título consultivo

consulting [kən'sʌltɪŋ] *adj* asesor(ora) ►► ***c. room*** *(of doctor)* consulta *f*, consultorio *m*

consumables [kən'sju:məbəlz] *npl* **(a)** *(goods)* bienes *mpl* consumibles **(b)** *Comptr* consumibles *mpl*

consume [kən'sju:m] *vt* **(a)** *(eat, drink)* consumir **(b)** *(use up) (energy, fuel, time)* consumir **(c)** *(burn up) (of fire, flames)* reducir a cenizas; **fire consumed the building** las llamas arrasaron el edificio; *Fig* **to be consumed with jealousy/desire** estar consumido(a) por los celos/el deseo

consumer [kən'sju:mə(r)] *n (of product)* consumidor(ora) *m,f* ►► ***c. association*** asociación *f* de consumidores; ***c. credit*** crédito *m* al consumo; ***c. demand*** demanda *f* de consumo; ***c. durables*** bienes *mpl* de consumo duraderos; ***c. goods*** bienes *mpl* de consumo; ***c. organization*** organización *f* de consumidores; *US Econ* ***c. price index*** índice *m* de precios al consumo, IPC *m*; ***c. protection*** protección *f* del consumidor; ***the c. society*** la sociedad de consumo; ***c. spending*** consumo *m* privado; ***c. terrorism*** terrorismo *m* contra la cadena de consumo

consumerism [kən'sju:mərɪzəm] *n* **(a)** *(consumer protection)* protección *f* al consumidor **(b)** *Pej (consumption)* consumismo *m*

consuming [kən'sju:mɪŋ] *adj (passion)* arrebatado(a), arrollador(ora); *(interest)* ferviente, absorbente

consummate 1 *adj* ['kɒnsjʊmət] **(a)** *(supreme)* consumado(a); **with c. skill** con una habilidad consumada **(b)** *(utter) (fool, liar)* completo(a), perfecto(a)

2 *vt* ['kɒnsəmeɪt] *(marriage, relationship)* consumar

consummation [kɒnsə'meɪʃən] *n* **(a)** *(of marriage, relationship)* consumación *f* **(b)** *(of life's work)* consumación *f*

consumption [kən'sʌmpʃən] *n* **(a)** *(of food, fuel, resources)* consumo *m*; **unfit for human c.** no apto(a) para el consumo humano **(b)** *(purchasing)* consumo *m* **(c)** *Old-fashioned (tuberculosis)* tisis *f inv*

consumptive [kən'sʌmptɪv] *Old-fashioned* 1 *n* tísico(a) *m,f*

2 *adj* tísico(a)

cont **(a)** (*abbr* **contents**) contenidos *mpl* **(b)** (*abbr* **continued**) sigue

contact ['kɒntækt] 1 *n* **(a)** *(communication)* contacto *m*; **we don't have much c. with our neighbours** no tenemos demasiado contacto con nuestros vecinos; **to be in/come into c. with sb** estar/ponerse en contacto con alguien; **to make c. with sb** contactar con alguien, ponerse en contacto con alguien; **to lose c. with sb** perder el contacto con alguien; **c. address/number** dirección/número de contacto

(b) *(touch)* contacto *m*; **to be in/come into c. with** estar/ponerse en contacto con; **physical c.** contacto físico ►► ***c. allergy*** alergia *f* de contacto; *Phot* ***c. print*** copia *f* de contacto; ***c. sport*** deporte *m* de contacto

(c) *(person)* contacto *m*; **he has lots of contacts** tiene muchos contactos

(d) *Elec* contacto *m*; **to make/break (the) c.** hacer/interrumpir (el) contacto

(e) *(lens)* ***c. lens*** lente *f* de contacto, *Esp* lentilla *f*, *Méx* pupilente *f*; **she wears c. lenses** *or Fam* **contacts** lleva lentes de contacto

2 *vt* contactar con, ponerse en contacto con; **we'll c. you later on this week** nos pondremos en contacto con usted a finales de esta semana

contactable [kən'tæktəbəl] *adj* localizable; **I'm c. at this number** estoy localizable en este número

contagion [kən'teɪdʒən] *n* **(a)** *(infection)* contagio *m* **(b)** *Literary (harmful influence)* peste *f*

contagious [kən'teɪdʒəs] *adj* **(a)** *(disease)* contagioso(a); **he's no longer c.** ya no es contagioso **(b)** *(laughter)* contagioso(a)

contain [kən'teɪn] *vt* **(a)** *(hold)* contener **(b)** *(include)* contener **(c)** *(restrain)* contener; **I could scarcely c. my indignation** apenas podía contener la indignación; **to c. oneself** contenerse, aguantarse **(d)** *(hold back) (enemy, inflation, fire, epidemic)* contener

container [kən'teɪnə(r)] *n* **(a)** *(for storage)* recipiente *m* **(b)** *(for transport)* contenedor *m*; **c. lorry/ship** camión/buque de transporte de contenedores ►► ***c. terminal*** terminal *f* de contenedores

containerize [kən'teɪnəraɪz] *vt (cargo)* meter en contenedores

containment [kən'teɪnmənt] *n (of political power, problem)* contención *f*

contaminate [kən'tæmɪneɪt] *vt also Fig* contaminar

contamination [kəntæmɪ'neɪʃən] *n* contaminación *f*

contd (*abbr* **continued**) cont.; **c. on page 14** sigue en la página 14

contemplate ['kɒntəmpleɪt] *vt* (**a**) *(consider)* contemplar; **to c. marriage/suicide** considerar el matrimonio/suicidio, pensar en casarse/suicidarse; **to c. doing sth** contemplar (la posibilidad de) hacer algo; **it's too awful to c.** no quiero ni contemplarlo (**b**) *(look at)* contemplar (**c**) *(foresee)* prever; **I didn't c. delays of this sort** no preví que fuera a haber retrasos de este tipo

contemplation [kɒntəm'pleɪʃən] *n* (**a**) *(thought)* contemplación *f*; **deep in c.** reflexionando profundamente (**b**) *(observation)* contemplación *f* (**c**) *(meditation)* meditación *f*; **a life of c.** una vida contemplativa

contemplative [kən'templətɪv] *adj* (**a**) *(look, mood)* contemplativo(a), meditabundo(a) (**b**) *Rel (order, prayer)* contemplativo(a)

contemplatively [kən'templətɪvlɪ] *adv* pensativamente

contemporaneous [kəntempə'reɪnɪəs] *adj Formal* simultáneo(a); **to be c. (with sth)** ocurrir a la par (que algo), coincidir en el tiempo (con algo)

contemporaneously [kəntempə'reɪnɪəslɪ] *adv Formal (to exist, live)* en *or* durante la misma época

contemporary [kən'tempərərɪ] **1** *n* contemporáneo(a) *m,f*; **he was a c. of mine at university** era de mi misma promoción universitaria

2 *adj* (**a**) *(modern)* contemporáneo(a); **a study of c. Britain** un estudio de la Gran Bretaña actual *or* contemporánea ►► ***c. dance*** ballet *m* moderno, danza *f* moderna (**b**) *(of the same period)* contemporáneo(a), coetáneo(a) (**with** de)

contempt [kən'tempt] *n* (**a**) *(scorn)* desprecio *m*, menosprecio *m*; **to hold sth/sb in c.** sentir desprecio por algo/alguien; **to treat sth/sb with c.** tratar algo/a alguien con desprecio; **I feel nothing but c. for him** lo único que siento por él es desprecio (**b**) *Law* **c. (of court)** desacato *m* (al tribunal); **to charge sb with c. (of court)** acusar a alguien de desacato

contemptible [kən'temptəbəl] *adj* despreciable

contemptuous [kən'temptjʊəs] *adj* despreciativo(a), despectivo(a); **to be c. of** mostrar desprecio hacia

contemptuously [kən'temptʃʊəslɪ] *adv (to laugh, reject, smile)* con desprecio

contend [kən'tend] **1** *vt Formal (maintain, argue)* **to c. that...** afirmar *or* alegar que...

2 *vi* (**a**) *(deal)* enfrentarse (**with** a *or* con); **the difficulties I have to c. with** las dificultades a las que me tengo que enfrentar; **they still had the guards to c. with** todavía les quedaba enfrentarse con los guardias (**b**) *(compete)* **to c. (with sb) for sth** disputarse algo (con alguien), competir (contra alguien) por algo

contender [kən'tendə(r)] *n* contendiente *mf* (**for** a); **an Oscar c.** un aspirante al Oscar; **a strong c. (for)** un serio aspirante (a)

contending [kən'tendɪŋ] *adj (views, interests)* encontrados(as), enfrentados(as)

content[1] ['kɒntent] *n* (**a**) *(amount contained)* contenido *m*; **high protein/fibre c.** alto contenido en proteínas/fibra

(**b**) **contents** *(of pockets, drawer, letter)* contenido *m*; *(table in book)* índice *m*; **the contents of the house were auctioned off separately** subastaron el mobiliario de la casa por separado ►► ***contents insurance*** seguro *m* del contenido

(**c**) *(substance)* contenido *m*; **all style and no c.** bien presentado pero sin sustancia ►► *Ling* ***c. word*** palabra *f* con contenido semántico

(**d**) *Comptr* ***c. provider*** proveedor *m* de contenidos

content[2] [kən'tent] **1** *adj* **to be c. with sth** estar satisfecho(a) con *or* de algo; **not c. with having ruined our evening,...** no contento con habernos estropeado la velada,...; **he's quite c. to let others do all the work** se complace en dejar a los demás hacer todo el trabajo; **she wasn't c. just to know what had happened, she wanted to know why** no le satisfacía saber simplemente qué ocurrió, quería saber el porqué

2 *vt* **to c. oneself with (doing) sth** contentarse con (hacer) algo; **my reply seemed to c. them** al parecer, se quedaron contentos con mi respuesta

3 *n* **to one's heart's c.** a placer, a discreción

contented [kən'tentɪd] *adj (person, smile)* satisfecho(a) (**with** con *or* de); **to be c. (with)** estar satisfecho(a) (con *or* de)

contentedly [kən'tentɪdlɪ] *adv* con satisfacción; **she sighed c.** suspiró satisfecha

contention [kən'tenʃən] *n* (**a**) *(dispute)* disputa *f*; **his morals are not in c.** nadie pone en tela de juicio sus principios morales (**b**) *(competition)* **to be in c. (for sth)** tener posibilidades (de ganar algo); **to be out of c.** no tener ninguna posibilidad; **the teams in c. for the title** los equipos que compiten por el título (**c**) *Formal (opinion)* argumento *m*; **my c. is that...** sostengo que...

contentious [kən'tenʃəs] *adj* (**a**) *(issue, views)* polémico(a) (**b**) *(person)* que siempre se mete en discusiones

contentment [kən'tentmənt] *n* satisfacción *f*; **a look of c.** una mirada de satisfacción

contest **1** *n* ['kɒntest] (**a**) *(competition)* concurso *m*; *(in boxing)* combate *m* (**b**) *(struggle)* contienda *f*, pugna *f*; **a c. for/between** una contienda *or* lucha por/entre (**c**) *US Law* **no c.** nolo contendere, no quiero litigar

2 *vt* [kən'test] (**a**) *(dispute) (statement, right, decision)* impugnar, rebatir; **to c. a will** impugnar un testamento (**b**) *(in election)* **to c. a seat** disputar un escaño; *Pol* **a fiercely contested election** unas elecciones muy reñidas

contestant [kən'testənt] *n (in competition, game)* concursante *mf*; *(in sporting competition)* competidor(ora) *m,f*

context ['kɒntekst] *n* contexto *m*; **in/out of c.** en/fuera de contexto; **to quote sth out of c.** citar algo fuera de contexto; **to put sth into c.** poner algo en contexto; **the wider social c.** el contexto social más amplio

context-dependent ['kɒntekstdɪ'pendənt] *adj* **to be c.** depender del contexto

context-sensitive help ['kɒntekst'sensɪtɪvhelp] *n Comptr* ayuda *f* contextual

contextual [kɒn'tekstjʊəl] *adj* contextual, relativo(a) al contexto

contextualize [kɒn'tekstjʊəlaɪz] *vt* contextualizar

contiguity [kɒntɪ'gju:ɪtɪ] *n Formal* contigüedad *f*

contiguous [kən'tɪgjʊəs] *adj Formal* contiguo(a) (**with** con)

continence ['kɒntɪnəns] *n* (**a**) *Med* control *m* de los esfínteres (**b**) *(self-restraint)* continencia *f*

continent[1] ['kɒntɪnənt] *n* (**a**) *(land mass)* continente *m* (**b**) *Br (Europe)* **(on) the C.** (en) Europa continental

continent[2] *adj* (**a**) *Med* continente (**b**) *(restrained)* continente

continental [kɒntɪ'nentəl] **1** *adj* (**a**) *(in geography)* continental ►► ***c. drift*** deriva *f* continental; ***c. shelf*** plataforma *f* continental; ***c. slope*** talud *m* continental (**b**) *Br (European)* de la Europa continental ►► ***c. breakfast*** desayuno *m* continental; ***c. quilt*** edredón *m* (**c**) *US* **the c. United States** *(mainland)* tierra firme estadounidense; *Hist* las colonias confederadas

2 *n Br Old-fashioned* europeo(a) *m,f (de la Europa continental)*

contingency [kən'tɪndʒənsɪ] *n* (**a**) *(possibility)* contingencia *f*, eventualidad *f*; **to allow for contingencies** tomar precauciones ante cualquier eventualidad ►► *Law* ***c. fee*** honorarios *mpl* condicionales; ***c. fund*** fondo *m* de emergencia; ***c. plan*** plan *m* de emergencia (**b**) *(chance, uncertainty)* contingencia *f*, eventualidad *f*

contingent [kən'tɪndʒənt] **1** *n (group)* contingente *m*

2 *adj Formal* (**a**) *(dependent)* contingente; **to be c. on sth** depender de algo (**b**) *Phil (truth)* contingente

continua *pl of* **continuum**

continual [kən'tɪnjʊəl] *adj* (**a**) *(continuous, uninterrupted)* continuo(a) (**b**) *(repeated)* continuo(a)

continually [kən'tɪnjʊəlɪ] *adv (ceaselessly, repeatedly)* continuamente, constantemente; **I c. have to remind him it's my house** tengo que recordarle constantemente que se trata de mi casa

continuance [kən'tɪnjʊəns] *n* (**a**) *(prolongation)* mantenimiento *m* (**b**) *US Law* aplazamiento *m*

continuant [kən'tɪnjʊənt] *n Ling* sonido *m* continuo

continuation [kəntɪnjʊ'eɪʃən] *n* (**a**) *(extension) (of story)* continuación *f*; *(of road)* continuación *f*, prolongación *f* (**b**) *(prolongation)* continuación *f*, prolongación *f* (**c**) *(resumption)* continuación *f*, reanudación *f*

continue [kən'tɪnju:] **1** *vt* (**a**) *(carry on)* continuar, seguir; **to c. doing** *or* **to do sth** continuar *or* seguir haciendo algo (**b**) *(after interruption)* reanudar; **to be continued** continuará; **continued on page 30** sigue en la página 30; **"furthermore," he continued...** "además", prosiguió...

2 *vi* (**a**) *(carry on)* continuar, seguir; **the rain continued for three days** no paró de llover en tres días, siguió lloviendo durante tres días; **to c. with sth** seguir con algo; **it's not something I want to c. with** no es algo que quiera seguir haciendo; **if you c. with this appalling behaviour,...** si sigues portándote así de mal,...; **we continued along the road for an hour** seguimos *or* continuamos por la carretera durante una hora; **he continued on his way** reanudó su camino; **the situation cannot c.** esto no puede continuar *or* seguir así

(**b**) *(resume)* continuar, proseguir; **the talks will c. today** las conversaciones se reanudarán hoy

(**c**) *(remain)* seguir; **she will c. as director until December** seguirá

ocupando el puesto de director hasta diciembre
(d) *(extend)* prolongarse; **the path continues on down to the river** el camino se prolonga hasta el río

continued [kən'tɪnjuːd] *adj (support, interest)* constante

continuing [kən'tɪnjuːɪŋ] *adj (conflict, involvement)* continuado(a) ►► *Br* ***c. education*** formación *f* continua

continuity [kɒntɪ'njuːɪtɪ] *n* **(a)** *(cohesion)* continuidad *f* **(b)** *(on radio, TV)* continuidad *f* ►► ***c. announcer*** locutor(ora) *m,f* de continuidad **(c)** *Cin* continuidad *f* ►► ***c. girl*** script *f*, anotadora *f*

continuo [kən'tɪnjʊəʊ] (*pl* **continuos**) *n Mus* bajo *m* continuo

continuous [kən'tɪnjʊəs] **1** *adj* **(a)** *(uninterrupted, unbroken)* continuo(a) ►► *Sch & Univ* ***c. assessment*** evaluación *f* continua; *St Exch* ***c. market*** mercado *m* continuo; *Comptr* ***c. mode*** modo *m* continuo; *Comptr* ***c. paper*** papel *m* continuo; *Cin* ***c. performance*** sesión *f* continua; *Comptr* ***c. stationery*** papel *m* continuo; *Comptr & Typ* ***c. tone*** tono *m* continuo **(b)** *Gram (tense, aspect)* continuo(a)
2 *n Gram* continuo *m*

continuously [kən'tɪnjʊəslɪ] *adv* continuamente, ininterrumpidamente

continuum [kən'tɪnjʊəm] (*pl* **continua** [kən'tɪnjʊə] *or* **continuums**) *n* continuo *m*

contort [kən'tɔːt] **1** *vt (body, features)* contorsionar
2 *vi* contorsionarse; **his face contorted in pain** tenía el rostro contraído de dolor

contorted [kən'tɔːtɪd] *adj* **(a)** *(face)* crispado(a), contorsionado(a); *(body)* contorsionado(a) **(b)** *(logic, argument)* tergiversado(a)

contortion [kən'tɔːʃən] *n (of body, features)* contorsión *f*; *Fig* **he went through all sorts of contortions to justify this decision** recurrió a toda clase de argumentos enrevesados para justificar la decisión

contortionist [kən'tɔːʃənɪst] *n* contorsionista *mf*

contour ['kɒntʊə(r)] **1** *n* **(a)** *(shape, outline)* contorno *m*, perfil *m*; **the contours of the hill** el contorno de la colina **(b)** **c. (line)** *(on map)* curva *f* de nivel ►► ***c. map*** mapa *m* topográfico
2 *vt* **(a)** *(map)* acotar **(b)** *(shape)* moldear

contraband ['kɒntrəbænd] *n* **(a)** *(smuggling)* contrabando *m* **(b)** *(smuggled goods)* **c. (goods)** mercancía *f* de contrabando

contrabassoon [kɒntrəbə'suːn] *n Mus* contrafagot *m*

contraception [kɒntrə'sepʃən] *n* anticoncepción *f*

contraceptive [kɒntrə'septɪv] **1** *n* anticonceptivo *m*
2 *adj* anticonceptivo(a) ►► ***c. method*** método *m* anticonceptivo; ***c. pill*** píldora *f* anticonceptiva; ***c. sponge*** esponja *f* vaginal

contract **1** *n* ['kɒntrækt] **(a)** *(agreement, document)* contrato *m*; **to break one's c.** incumplir el contrato; **to be under c.** estar contratado(a); **to enter into a c.** firmar un contrato ►► ***c. of employment*** contrato *m* de trabajo; ***c. law*** derecho *m* contractual; ***c. of sale*** contrato *m or* escritura *f* de compraventa; ***c. staff*** personal *m* contratado
(b) *(won by tender)* contrata *f*; **to put work out to c.** subcontratar un trabajo, otorgar la contrata de un trabajo
(c) *Fam* **to take out a c. on sb** *(hire assassin)* contratar a un asesino para matar a alguien ►► ***c. killer*** asesino(a) *m,f* a sueldo
(d) *(in bridge)* contrato *m* ►► ***c. bridge*** (bridge *m*) contrato *m*
2 *vt* [kən'trækt] **(a)** *(illness)* contraer; **to c. debts** contraer deudas **(b)** *(hire)* **to c. sb (to do sth)** contratar a alguien (para hacer algo) **(c)** *(muscle)* contraer **(d)** *Gram* contraer; **a contracted form** una forma contracta
3 *vi* [kən'trækt] **(a)** *(make agreement)* **to c. to do sth** firmar un contrato para hacer algo **(b)** *(shrink)* contraerse

►**contract in** *vi Br* suscribirse

►**contract out** *Com* **1** *vt sep* **the cleaning service was contracted out** el servicio de limpieza lo lleva una contrata
2 *vi Br* excluirse, optar por salirse (**of** de)

contracting [kən'træktɪŋ] *adj* **(a)** *(involved in contract)* contratante; **the c. parties** las partes contratantes **(b)** ***c. company*** *(subcontractor)* empresa *f* contratante, contratista *mf*

contraction [kən'trækʃən] *n* **(a)** *(of metal, pupil)* contracción *f* **(b)** *Med* contracción *f*; **contractions have begun** *(before childbirth)* han empezado las contracciones **(c)** *Gram* contracción *f*

contractor [kən'træktə(r)] *n (sub-contractor)* contratista *mf*; **building c.** contratista de obras; **haulage c.** transportista

contractual [kən'træktjʊəl] *adj* contractual

contractually [kən'træktjʊəlɪ] *adv* contractualmente; **c. bound/obliged to do sth** vinculado(a)/obligado(a) por contrato a hacer algo

contradict [kɒntrə'dɪkt] *vt* **(a)** *(disagree with)* contradecir; **she hates being contradicted** no soporta que la contradigan; **to c. oneself** contradecirse **(b)** *(conflict with)* contradecirse con; **their statements c. each other** sus declaraciones se contradicen **(c)** *(deny)* desmentir

contradiction [kɒntrə'dɪkʃən] *n* contradicción *f*; **he's full of contradictions** está lleno de contradicciones; **it's a c. in terms** es una contradicción en sí misma

contradictory [kɒntrə'dɪktərɪ] *adj* contradictorio(a)

contradistinction [kɒntrədɪ'stɪŋkʃən] *n Formal* **in c. to** en contraposición a

contraflow ['kɒntrəfləʊ] *n Br* **c. (system)** habilitación *f* del carril contrario

contraindication [kɒntrəɪndɪ'keɪʃən] *n Med* contraindicación *f*

contralto [kən'træltəʊ] (*pl* **contraltos**) *n Mus* contralto *f*

contraption [kən'træpʃən] *n Fam* cachivache *m*, artilugio *m*

contrapuntal [kɒntrə'pʌntəl] *adj Mus* de contrapunto

contrarily [kən'treərɪlɪ] *adv* caprichosamente

contrariness [kən'treərɪnɪs] *n* espíritu *m* de contradicción; **with his usual c....** con sus habituales ganas de llevar la contraria...

contrary ['kɒntrərɪ] **1** *n* **the c.** lo contrario; **on the c.** por el *or* al contrario; **unless you hear to the c.** salvo que te digan lo contrario *or* otra cosa; **quite the c.!** ¡todo lo contrario!
2 *adj* **(a)** *(opposite)* contrario(a); **c. to** contrario(a) a; **c. to my expectations** al contrario de lo que esperaba; **c. to popular belief,...** en contra de lo que vulgarmente se cree,... **(b)** *(wind)* en contra, de cara **(c)** [kən'treərɪ] *(awkward)* caprichoso(a)

contrast **1** *n* ['kɒntrɑːst] **(a)** *(difference)* contraste *m*; **to be a c. (to sth)** ser un contraste (con algo); **in c. with** *or* **to** en contraste con; **by c.** por el contrario; **for c.** para contrastar **(b)** *TV & Phot* contraste *m*; **turn up the c.** sube el contraste ►► ***c. button*** botón *m* de contraste
2 *vt* [kən'trɑːst] **to c. sth with sth** contrastar *or* comparar algo con algo *or* algo y algo
3 *vi* [kən'trɑːst] contrastar (**with** con)

contrasting [kən'trɑːstɪŋ] *adj* opuesto(a)

contrastive [kən'trɑːstɪv] *adj* opuesto(a), antagónico(a) ►► *Ling* ***c. stress*** acento *m* contrastivo

contravene [kɒntrə'viːn] *vt* contravenir

contravention [kɒntrə'venʃən] *n* contravención *f*; **in c. of...** contraviniendo...

contretemps ['kɒntrətɒm] (*pl* **contretemps**) *n (disagreement)* roce *m*, discusión *f*

contribute [kən'trɪbjuːt] **1** *vt* **(a)** *(money)* contribuir con, aportar **(b)** *(ideas, enthusiasm)* contribuir con, aportar; **what can they c. to the project?** ¿que pueden aportar al proyecto? **(c)** *(article, poem)* contribuir con, aportar; **to c. an article to a newspaper** escribir una colaboración para un periódico
2 *vi* **(a)** *(donate money)* contribuir; **to c. to a charity** realizar un donativo a una organización benéfica **(b)** *(give, add)* **she still has a lot to c.** todavía tiene mucho que aportar; **he rarely contributes to discussions** rara vez interviene en las discusiones; **to c. to the success of sth** contribuir al éxito de algo **(c)** *(journalist, author)* **to c. to a newspaper/magazine** escribir para un periódico/una revista **(d)** *(to pension scheme)* cotizar

contributing [kən'trɪbjuːtɪŋ] *adj* **a c. factor** un factor determinante

contribution [kɒntrɪ'bjuːʃən] *n* **(a)** *(to project, activity)* contribución *f*, aportación *f*; *(to discussion)* intervención *f*; **to make a c. to** contribuir a; **he made some interesting contributions to the discussion** nizo algunas aportaciones interesantes a la discusión; **the soufflé was Tim's c.** Tim trajo el suflé **(b)** *(payment) (to charity)* donación *f*; *(to pension scheme)* cotización *f*; **social security contributions** cotizaciones a la seguridad social **(c)** *(to newspaper)* colaboración *f*

contributor [kən'trɪbjʊtə(r)] *n* **(a)** *(to charity)* donante *mf* **(b)** *(to newspaper)* colaborador(ora) *m,f*

contributory [kən'trɪbjʊtərɪ] *adj* **(a)** *(cause, factor)* determinante ►► *Law* ***c. negligence*** imprudencia *f or* negligencia *f* (culposa), culpa *f* concurrente **(b)** *Fin* ***c. pension scheme*** plan *m* de pensiones contributivo

contrite [kən'traɪt] *adj* arrepentido(a); **to be c.** estar arrepentido(a)

contrition [kən'trɪʃən] *n* arrepentimiento *m*, contrición *f* ►► *Rel* **an act of c.** un acto de contrición

contrivance [kən'traɪvəns] *n* **(a)** *(device)* aparato *m* **(b)** *(scheme, plan)* estratagema *f*

contrive [kən'traɪv] *vt* (**a**) *(device, scheme)* idear, inventar (**b**) *(manage)* **to c. to do sth** arreglárselas *or* ingeniárselas para hacer algo; **she contrived to confuse matters still further** se las ingenió para complicar el asunto todavía más

contrived [kən'traɪvd] *adj (words, compliment)* estudiado(a), forzado(a); *(ending, plot)* artificioso(a)

control [kən'trəʊl] **1** *n* (**a**) *(power, command)* control *m*; **to take c.** ponerse al mando, tomar el control; **to gain c. of sth** hacerse con el control de algo; **to have c. of** *or* **over** controlar; **to be in c. of** *(in charge of)* estar al cargo de; **to be back in c.** *(of situation)* volver a controlar la situación; **to get out of c.** descontrolarse; **under c.** bajo control; **to keep sth under c.** mantener algo bajo control; **to bring a fire under c.** controlar un incendio; **under British/government c.** bajo control británico/del gobierno; **due to circumstances beyond** *or* **outside our c.** debido a circunstancias ajenas a nuestra voluntad; **out of c.** fuera de control; **the fire was out of c.** el fuego estaba fuera de control; **her children are completely out of c.** sus hijos están totalmente descontrolados; **to lose/regain c.** perder/recuperar el control; **he lost c. (of himself)** perdió el control; **she likes to feel in c.** le gusta notar que lleva las riendas ►► ***c. centre*** centro *m* de control; *Fam* ***c. freak*** maniático(a) *m,f* del control y del orden; ***c. tower*** *(at airport)* torre *f* de control

(**b**) *(of device)* mando *m*; **volume/brightness c.** mando del volumen/brillo; **the controls** los mandos; **to be at the controls** estar a los mandos; **to take over the controls** tomar los mandos ►► ***c. column*** palanca *f* de mando; ***c. panel*** *(of vehicle, machine)* tablero *m or* cuadro *m* de mandos; *Comptr* ***c. unit*** unidad *f* de control

(**c**) *(of ball)* control *m*; **he showed good c.** mostró un buen control

(**d**) *(restraint)* control *m* (**on** sobre); **to place controls on sth** controlar algo

(**e**) *(experiment)* prueba *f* de control ►► ***c. group*** grupo *m* de control

(**f**) *(checkpoint)* control *m*

(**g**) *(base)* (centro *m* de) control *m*; **to call c.** llamar al centro de control

(**h**) *Comptr* (tecla *f* de) control *m* ►► ***c. key*** tecla *f* de control; ***c. panel*** panel *m* de control

2 *vt* (*pt & pp* **controlled**) (**a**) *(be in charge of) (company, country)* controlar, dominar

(**b**) *(regulate) (production, expenditure, flow)* controlar, regular

(**c**) *(child, pupils)* controlar, dominar; *(vehicle)* manejar, controlar; *(ball)* controlar; **to c. the traffic** dirigir el tráfico

(**d**) *(restrict) (disease, inflation, fire)* controlar; **to c. oneself** controlarse, dominarse; **she was unable to c. her anger** fue incapaz de dominar su ira

(**e**) *(verify) (accounts)* controlar, verificar; *(experiment)* comprobar, controlar

controllable [kən'trəʊləbəl] *adj* controlable; **it's no longer c.** está fuera de control

controlled [kən'trəʊld] *adj* (**a**) *(person)* controlado(a), contenido(a); *(emotions, voice)* contenido(a), sereno(a) (**b**) *(regulated)* controlado(a), regulado(a) ►► *Econ* ***c. economy*** economía *f* dirigida; ***c. explosion*** explosión *f* controlada (**c**) *(experiment)* controlado(a)

controller [kən'trəʊlə(r)] *n* (**a**) *(person in charge)* director(ora) *m,f*; *(financial)* interventor(ora) *m,f* (**b**) *Comptr* controlador(ora) *m,f*

controlling [kən'treʊlɪŋ] *adj Fin* **to have a c. interest (in)** tener el control accionarial (sobre), tener una participación mayoritaria (en)

controversial [kɒntrə'vɜːʃəl] *adj* polémico(a), controvertido(a); **he's trying to be c.** está tratando de ser polémico, está intentando crear polémica

controversially [kɒntrə'vɜːʃəlɪ] *adv* con gran polémica

controversy ['kɒntrəvɜːsɪ, kən'trɒvəsɪ] *n* polémica *f*, controversia *f*; **to cause** *or* **give rise to c.** causar *or* crear polémica *or* controversia

controvert ['kɒntrəvɜːt] *vt Formal (dispute, deny)* controvertir

contumacious [kɒntjuː'meɪʃəs] *adj* (**a**) *Formal (disobedient)* contumaz (**b**) *Law* contumaz

contumacy ['kɒntjʊməsɪ] *n* (**a**) *Formal (disobedience)* contumacia *f* (**b**) *Law* contumacia *f*

contumely ['kɒntjuːmlɪ] *n Formal (scorn)* contumelia *f*

contusion [kən'tjuːʒən] *n Med* contusión *f*

conundrum [kə'nʌndrəm] *n* (**a**) *(riddle)* adivinanza *f*, acertijo *m* (**b**) *(problem)* enigma *m*

conurbation [kɒnə'beɪʃən] *n* conurbación *f*

convalesce [kɒnvə'les] *vi* convalecer; **she's convalescing from** *or* **after a bad bout of flu** está convaleciente de una gripe seria

convalescence [kɒnvə'lesəns] *n* convalecencia *f*

convalescent [kɒnvə'lesənt] *n (patient)* convaleciente *mf* ►► ***c. home*** clínica *f* de reposo

convection [kən'vekʃən] *n* convección *f* ►► ***c. current*** corriente *f* de convección; ***c. heater*** calentador *m* de aire, convector *m*

convector [kən'vektə(r)] *n* **c. (heater)** calentador *m* de aire, convector *m*

convene [kən'viːn] **1** *vt (meeting)* convocar

2 *vi (committee, meeting)* reunirse

convener, convenor [kən'viːnə(r)] *n* (**a**) *(of meeting)* convocante *mf* (**b**) *Br (in trade union)* representante *mf* sindical

convenience [kən'viːnɪəns] *n* (**a**) *(ease, benefit)* conveniencia *f*; **we can now offer the c. of phone booking** ahora podemos ofrecerle la comodidad de reservar por teléfono; **for c., for c.'s sake** por comodidad; **at your c.** a su conveniencia, como mejor le convenga; *Formal* **at your earliest c.** en cuanto le sea posible ►► ***c. food*** comida *f* preparada; ***c. store*** tienda *f* de ultramarinos, *Col, Méx* tienda *f*, *CSur* almacén *m*, *Cuba* bodega *f* de barrio

(**b**) *(facility)* **the house has every modern c.** la casa está dotada de todas las comodidades modernas

(**c**) *Br* **(public) c.** *(toilet)* servicio *m* público, *Esp* aseos *mpl* públicos, *Am* baños *mpl* públicos

convenient [kən'viːnɪənt] *adj* (**a**) *(suitable) (arrangement)* conveniente, adecuado(a); *(time, place)* oportuno(a); **if it is c. for you** si te viene bien; **it's not very c. for me** no me viene muy bien; **would one o'clock be c.?** ¿le viene bien a la una?

(**b**) *(handy) (place)* bien situado(a); *(method)* práctico(a), cómodo(a); **c. for** próximo(a) a; **the house is very c. for local shops and schools** la casa está muy cerca de las tiendas y los colegios; **how c.!** ¡que ni pintado!; *Ironic* **he says he's left his wallet at home – well how c.!** dice que se ha dejado la cartera en casa – ¡qué casualidad!

conveniently [kən'viːnɪəntlɪ] *adv* convenientemente; **c. located** bien situado(a), (en un sitio) muy a mano; *Ironic* **she had c. left her purse at home** se había dejado el monedero en casa, lo cual le vino muy bien

convenor = **convener**

convent ['kɒnvənt] *n Rel* convento *m*; **to enter a c.** ingresar en un convento ►► ***c. education*** educación *f* religiosa; **she had a c. education** fue a un colegio de monjas; ***c. school*** colegio *m* de monjas

convention [kən'venʃən] *n* (**a**) *(conference)* congreso *m*; *US Pol* convención *f*; **medical/scientific c.** congreso médico/científico ►► ***c. centre*** palacio *m* de congresos

(**b**) *(agreement)* convención *f*, convenio *m* (**on** sobre)

(**c**) *(established practice)* convencionalismo *m*, convención *f*; **to go against c.** ir contra las convenciones; **to defy c.** actuar en contra de las convenciones; **the c. is that...** según la costumbre...

conventional [kən'venʃənəl] *adj* (**a**) *(customary, traditional)* convencional; **he's terribly c.** es sumamente convencional; **the c. wisdom is that...** la opinión tradicional es que... (**b**) *(non-nuclear)* ***c. warfare*** guerra *f* convencional; ***c. weapons*** armas *fpl* convencionales (**c**) *Comptr* ***c. memory*** memoria *f* convencional

conventionally [kən'venʃənəlɪ] *adv (to dress, behave)* de manera convencional; **c., this is regarded as a fault** convencionalmente, esto se considera una falta

converge [kən'vɜːdʒ] *vi* (**a**) *(lines, people)* converger, convergir (**on** con) (**b**) *(economies)* converger, convergir

convergence [kən'vɜːdʒəns] *n* (**a**) *(of ideas, opinions)* convergencia *f* (**b**) *(economic)* convergencia *f* ►► ***c. criteria*** criterios *mpl* de convergencia

convergent [kən'vɜːdʒənt] *adj* (**a**) *(ideas, opinions)* convergente (**b**) *(economies)* convergente (**c**) *Psy (thinking)* convergente

converging lens [kən'vɜːdʒɪŋ'lenz] *n Phys* lente *f* convergente

conversant [kən'vɜːsənt] *adj* **to be c. with sth** estar familiarizado(a) con algo

conversation [kɒnvə'seɪʃən] *n* conversación *f*; **to have a c. (with sb)** mantener una conversación (con alguien); **to get into c. with sb** entablar conversación con alguien; **to make c. (with)** dar conversación (a); **to be (deep) in c. with sb** estar en plena conversación con alguien; **they had run out of c.** se les acabó la conversación; **the art of c.** el arte de hablar *or* conversar *or CAm, Méx* platicar; **it was a bit of a c. killer** *or* **stopper** nos dejó sin habla ►► ***c. class*** clase *f* de conversación; ***c. piece*** tema *m* de conversación

conversational [kɒnvə'seɪʃənəl] *adj* (**a**) *(tone, style)* coloquial (**b**) *Comptr (mode)* conversacional

conversationalist [kɒnvə'seɪʃənəlɪst] *n* conversador(ora) *m,f*; **to be a good c.** ser buen conversador

conversationally [kɒnvə'seɪʃənəlɪ] *adv* **he mentioned, quite c., that he had got a new job** como quien no quiere la cosa, mencionó que tenía un empleo nuevo

converse[1] [kən'vɜːs] *vi (talk)* conversar (**about** *or* **on** sobre)

converse[2] ['kɒnvɜːs] **1** *n (opposite)* **the c.** lo contrario, lo opuesto
2 *adj (opinion, statement)* contrario(a), opuesto(a)

conversely [kən'vɜːslɪ] *adv* por el contrario, a la inversa

conversion [kən'vɜːʃən] *n* (**a**) *(in religion, political beliefs)* conversión *f* (**b**) *(alteration)* conversión *f*, transformación *f* ►► *Fin* ***c. issue*** emisión *f* convertible; ***c. table*** *(for measurements)* tabla *f* de conversión *or* de equivalencias (**c**) *(in American football, rugby)* transformación *f* (**d**) *Comptr* conversión *f* ►► ***c. program*** programa *f* de conversión

convert **1** *n* ['kɒnvɜːt] *(in religion, political beliefs)* converso(a) *m,f* (**to** a); **to become a c. to sth** convertirse a algo
2 *vt* [kən'vɜːt] (**a**) *(in religion, political beliefs)* convertir (**to** a); **to c. sb to sth** convertir a alguien a algo
(**b**) *(alter, adapt)* transformar, convertir (**into** en)
(**c**) **to c. a try** *(in rugby)* transformar un ensayo, realizar la transformación; **to c. a pass** *(in American football)* transformar un pase
(**d**) *Law* apropiarse indebidamente de; **to c. funds to another purpose** malversar fondos
(**e**) *Fin (bonds, securities, loan stock)* convertir
(**f**) *Comptr* convertir (**to/into** en)
3 *vi* [kən'vɜːt] (**a**) *(in religion, political beliefs)* convertirse (**to** a) (**b**) *(transform)* convertirse (**into** en); **the settee converts into a bed** el sofá se convierte en cama

converted [kən'vɜːtɪd] *adj (building)* reformado(a)

converter [kən'vɜːtə(r)] *n* (**a**) *Rad & Elec* convertidor *m* (**b**) *(for steel)* convertidor *m*

convertibility [kənvɜːtə'bɪlətɪ] *n* (**a**) *(of currency)* convertibilidad *f* (**b**) *(of building, car, machine)* convertibilidad *f*

convertible [kən'vɜːtəbəl] **1** *adj* (**a**) *(settee)* convertible; *(car)* descapotable, *Am* convertible (**b**) *Fin (bonds, securities)* convertible ►► ***c. currency*** moneda *f or* divisa *f* convertible
2 *n (car)* descapotable *m*, *Am* convertible *m*

convex ['kɒnveks] *adj* convexo(a)

convexity [kɒn'veksɪtɪ] *n* convexidad *f*

convey [kən'veɪ] *vt* (**a**) *(communicate)* transmitir; **I tried to c. the seriousness of the situation to him** intenté transmitirle la gravedad de la situación; **it's impossible to c. in words** *(feeling, sight)* es imposible expresarlo con palabras; *Formal* **please c. my appreciation to the host** por favor, hágale llegar *or* transmítale mis saludos *or CAm, Col, Ecuad* saludes al anfitrión
(**b**) *(transport) (people, goods)* transportar; *(electricity)* conducir, llevar
(**c**) *Law (property)* traspasar, transferir

conveyance [kən'veɪəns] *n* (**a**) *(of goods)* transporte *m*
(**b**) *Formal (vehicle)* vehículo *m*
(**c**) *Law (transfer of property)* traspaso *m*, transmisión *f*; *(document)* escritura *f* de traspaso

conveyancing [kən'veɪənsɪŋ] *n Law* contratación *f* inmobiliaria

conveyor [kən'veɪə(r)] *n* (**a**) **c. (belt)** cinta *f* transportadora (**b**) *Formal (person)* mensajero(a) *m,f*, portador(ora) *m,f*

convict **1** *n* ['kɒnvɪkt] convicto(a) *m,f*
2 *vt* [kən'vɪkt] **to c. sb (of a crime)** declarar a alguien culpable (de un delito), condenar a alguien (por un delito); **to be convicted of sth** ser condenado(a) por algo
3 *vi* [kən'vɪkt] condenar

convicted [kən'vɪktɪd] *adj Law (murderer, rapist)* convicto(a); **you stand c. by your own words** tus propias palabras te incriminan

conviction [kən'vɪkʃən] *n* (**a**) *Law* condena *f* (**for** por); **to have no previous convictions** no tener condenas anteriores (**b**) *(belief, certainty)* convicción *f*; **a person of strong convictions** una persona de profundas convicciones; **her voice lacked c.** le faltaba convicción en la voz; **to carry c.** ser convincente; **he acted from** *or* **in the c. that...** actuó convencido de que...

convince [kən'vɪns] **1** *vt* convencer; **to c. sb to do sth** convencer a alguien para hacer algo *or* para que haga algo; **to c. sb of sth** convencer a alguien de algo
2 *vi* convencer

convinced [kən'vɪnst] *adj (pacifist, Christian)* convencido(a); **he was c. he was right** estaba convencido de que tenía razón; **I'm still to be c.** sigo sin convencerme; **to be convinced of sth** estar convencido de algo

convincing [kən'vɪnsɪŋ] *adj* convincente; **she wasn't very c. as Juliet** no estaba muy convincente en el papel de Julieta

convincingly [kən'vɪnsɪŋlɪ] *adv* convincentemente

convivial [kən'vɪvɪəl] *adj (person)* sociable; *(atmosphere)* agradable

conviviality [kənvɪvɪ'ælɪtɪ] *n (of person)* cordialidad *f*; *(of atmosphere)* amenidad *f*

convocation [kɒnvə'keɪʃən] *n* (**a**) *Formal (summoning)* convocación *f*, convocatoria *f* (**b**) *Br Rel* asamblea *f* (**c**) *Br Univ* asamblea *f*

convoke [kən'vəʊk] *vt* convocar

convoluted ['kɒnvəluːtɪd] *adj* (**a**) *(argument, explanation)* intrincado(a), enrevesado(a) (**b**) *(shape)* enrollado(a)

convolution [kɒnvə'luːʃən] *n Formal* (**a**) *(of argument, explanation)* enrevesamiento *m* (**b**) *Anat (of brain)* circunvolución *f*

convolvulus [kən'vɒlvjʊləs] (*pl* **convolvuluses** *or* **convolvuli** [kən'vɒlvjʊlaɪ]) *n Bot* convolvulácea *f*

convoy ['kɒnvɔɪ] **1** *n (of ships, lorries)* convoy *m*; **to travel in c.** viajar en convoy
2 *vt (escort)* escoltar

convulse [kən'vʌls] **1** *vt* (**a**) *(person)* convulsionar; **to be convulsed with laughter** desternillarse de risa; **to be convulsed with pain** retorcerse de dolor (**b**) *(disrupt)* sacudir
2 *vi (face)* **his face convulsed with** *or* **in pain** hizo una mueca de dolor

convulsions [kən'vʌlʃənz] *npl Med* convulsiones *fpl*; **to go into** *or* **have c.** tener convulsiones; **to be in c.** *(of laughter)* desternillarse de risa

convulsive [kən'vʌlsɪv] *adj* convulsivo(a); **c. laughter/sobs** risas/sollozos incontenibles *or* irreprimibles

convulsively [kən'vʌlsɪvlɪ] *adv* de forma convulsiva

coo [kuː] **1** *n (of dove, pigeon)* arrullo *m*
2 *vi (dove, pigeon)* arrullar; **the neighbours came to c. over the baby** los vecinos vinieron a hacer monerías al bebé
3 *vt (endearments, sweet nothings)* susurrar
4 *exclam Fam* ¡vaya!

cooee ['kuːiː] *exclam* ¡yuju!

cook [kʊk] **1** *n* cocinero(a) *m,f*; **he's a very good c.** es muy buen cocinero, cocina muy bien; IDIOM *Fam Hum* **as usual, I was chief c. and bottlewasher** como siempre, yo me encargué de todo; PROV **too many cooks spoil the broth** = es difícil obtener un buen resultado cuando hay demasiadas personas trabajando en lo mismo
2 *vt* (**a**) *(prepare) (meal, dish)* preparar; *(boil, bake, fry)* guisar, cocinar (**b**) IDIOMS *Fam* **to c. the books** falsificar las cuentas; *Fam* **to c. sb's goose** hundir a alguien
3 *vi* (**a**) *(person)* cocinar; *(food)* cocinarse, hacerse (**b**) IDIOMS *Fam* **now we're cooking with gas!** ahora sí (que sí), ahora la cosa marcha; *Fam* **what's cooking?** *(what's happening?)* ¿qué se cuece por aquí?, *Am* ¿qué andan tramando por acá?

► **cook up** **1** *vt insep* (**a**) *(food)* preparar, cocinar; *Fam Fig* **to c. up an excuse/a story** inventarse una excusa/un cuento (**b**) *Fam (heroin)* cocinarse, calentarse
2 *vi Fam (heat heroin)* cocinarse *or* calentarse un pico

cookbook ['kʊkbʊk] *n* libro *m* de cocina

cook-chill ['kʊk'tʃɪl] *adj* congelado(a) precocinado(a)

cooked [kʊkt] *adj (food)* cocinado(a); *(meal)* caliente; *(pasta, vegetables)* cocido(a); **this meat isn't c.** esta carne no está bien hecha; **is it c. through?** ¿está bien hecho? ►► ***c. breakfast*** desayuno *m* caliente; ***c. meats*** fiambres *mpl*

cooker ['kʊkə(r)] *n* (**a**) *(stove)* cocina *f*, *Col, Méx, Ven* estufa *f* (**b**) *Br Fam (apple)* manzana *f* para asar

cookery ['kʊkərɪ] *n* cocina *f* ►► ***c. book*** libro *m* de cocina; ***c. programme*** programa *m* de cocina

cookhouse ['kʊkhaʊs] *n* cocina *f (de campaña)*

cookie ['kʊkɪ] *n* (**a**) *US (biscuit)* galleta *f* ►► ***c. cutter*** molde *m* de galletas
(**b**) *Fam (person)* **a smart c.** un(a) espabilado(a), *Méx* un(a) listo(a), *RP* un(a) avivado(a); **a tough c.** un(a) *Esp* tío(a) *or Am* tipo(a) duro(a) de pelar
(**c**) *Comptr* cookie *m*
(**d**) IDIOMS *Fam* **that's the way the c. crumbles!** ¡qué se le va a hacer!; **he was caught with his hand in the c. jar** lo pillaron con las manos en la masa; *Fam* **to toss** *or US* **shoot one's cookies** *(vomit) Esp* echar la pota, *Am* arrojar

cooking ['kʊkɪŋ] *n* cocina *f*; **to do the c.** cocinar; **I prefer good home c.** yo prefiero la buena comida casera ►► ***c. apple*** manzana *f* para asar; ***c. chocolate*** chocolate *m* fondant; ***c. foil*** papel *m* (de) aluminio; ***c. salt*** sal *f* común *or* de cocina, sal *f* gorda; ***c. time*** tiempo *m* de cocción; ***c. utensils*** utensilios *mpl* de cocina

cook-off ['kʊkɒf] *n US* concurso *m* de cocina

cookout ['kʊkaʊt] *n US* comida *f* al aire libre

cookware ['kʊkweə(r)] *n* utensilios *mpl* de cocina

cool [ku:l] **1** *n* **(a)** *(coldness)* fresco *m*; **in the c. of the evening** al fresco de la tarde **(b)** *(calm)* **to keep/lose one's c.** mantener/perder la calma
2 *adj* **(a)** *(wind, weather, liquid) (cold)* fresco(a); *(lukewarm)* tibio(a); **it's c.** hace fresco; **don't let your soup get c.** no dejes que se te enfríe la sopa; **keep in a c. place** conservar en un lugar fresco ►► ***c. bag*** nevera *f or CSur* heladera *f or Méx* refrigerador *m* portátil; ***c. box*** nevera *f or CSur* heladera *f or Méx* refrigerador *m* portátil
(b) *(calm)* sereno(a); **keep c.!** *(stay calm)* ¡mantén la calma!; **to keep a c. head** mantener la cabeza fría; **he's a c. customer!** ¡qué sangre fría tiene!; IDIOM **as c. as a cucumber** imperturbable, impasible, *RP* fresco(a) como una lechuga
(c) *(not friendly)* frío(a); **to be c. to** *or* **towards sb** mostrarse frío(a) con alguien; **they seemed rather c. towards the suggestion** recibieron la sugerencia con frialdad
(d) *Fam (of sum of money)* **he lost a c. thousand (dollars)** *(money)* perdió la friolera de mil dólares
(e) *Fam (fashionable)* genial, *Esp* guay, *Andes, CAm, Carib, Méx* chévere, *Méx* padre, *RP* copado(a); **he still thinks it's c. to smoke** todavía cree que se lleva fumar, *Esp* todavía cree que mola fumar
(f) *Fam (excellent)* genial, *Esp* guay, *Andes, CAm, Carib, Méx* chévere, *Andes, RP* macanudo(a), *Méx* padre; **we had a really c. weekend** pasamos un fin de semana genial
(g) *Fam (allowed, acceptable)* **is it c. to smoke in here?** ¿se puede fumar aquí dentro?; **everything's c.!** *(there's nothing to worry about)* ¡todo está *Esp* guay *or Am* OK!
(h) *Fam (accepting, not upset)* conforme; **are you c. with that?** *Esp* ¿vale?, *Andes, RP* ¿listo?, *Méx* ¿OK?; **I thought she'd be angry, but she was really c. about it** pensé que se mosquearía, pero se lo tomó superbién *or Am* rebién
3 *exclam Fam* ¡qué genial!, *Esp* ¡qué guay!, *Andes, CAm, Carib, Méx* ¡qué chévere!, *Andes, RP* ¡qué bueno!, *Méx* ¡qué padre!
4 *adv Fam* **to play it c.** aparentar calma; **play it c.!** ¡tómatelo con calma!
5 *vt (make cold)* enfriar; *(make less warm) (air, one's feet)* refrescar; *(food, drink)* enfriar (un poco); **c. it!** ¡tranquilo!, *Esp* ¡tranqui!; *Fam* **to c. one's heels** esperar, hacer antesala
6 *vi* **(a)** *(become cold)* enfriarse **(b)** *(become less warm) (air)* refrescarse; *(food, drink)* enfriarse (un poco); *(ardour, enthusiasm)* apagarse; **his anger soon cooled** pronto se le pasó el *esp Esp* enfado *or esp Am* enojo

► **cool down 1** *vt sep* **(a)** *(liquid, food)* enfriar (un poco); *(machine)* enfriar **(b) this will c. you down** *(cold drink)* esto te refrescará
2 *vi* **(a)** *(weather)* refrescar; *(liquid, food)* enfriarse (un poco); *(machine)* enfriarse **(b)** *(become calm)* calmarse, tranquilizarse

► **cool off** *vi* **(a)** *(become cooler)* **he had a shower to c. off** se dio una ducha para refrescarse **(b)** *(affection, enthusiasm)* enfriarse; *(angry person)* calmarse, tranquilizarse

coolant ['ku:lənt] *n* refrigerante *m*

cooler ['ku:lə(r)] *n* **(a)** *(for drinks)* nevera *f or CSur* heladera *f or Méx* refrigerador *m* portátil **(b)** *Fam (prison) Esp* chirona *f*, *Andes, RP* cana *f*, *Méx* bote *m*; **in the c.** en *Esp* chirona *or Andes, RP* cana *or Méx* bote **(c)** *(drink)* **(wine) c.** = refresco a base de vino y jugo de frutas

cool-headed ['ku:l'hedɪd] *adj* **to be c.** tener la cabeza fría, tener serenidad

coolie ['ku:lɪ] *n* culi *m*

cooling ['ku:lɪŋ] *adj* refrescante ►► ***c. tower*** torre *f* de refrigeración

cooling-off period ['ku:lɪŋ'ɒfpɪərɪəd] *n* **(a)** *Ind (in dispute)* periodo *m* de reflexión **(b)** *(after signing agreement)* periodo *m* de reflexión

coolly ['ku:llɪ] *adv* **(a)** *(calmly)* tranquilamente, con serenidad **(b)** *(without enthusiasm)* friamente, con frialdad

coolness ['ku:lnɪs] *n* **(a)** *(in temperature)* frescor *m* **(b)** *(calmness)* serenidad *f*, tranquilidad *f* **(c)** *(lack of friendliness, enthusiasm)* frialdad *f*; **I sensed a certain c. in his welcome** sentí una cierta frialdad en su bienvenida

coon [ku:n] *n* **(a)** *US Fam (raccoon)* mapache *m* **(b)** *Fam (black person)* = término generalmente ofensivo para referirse a los negros

coop [ku:p] *n* corral *m*

► **coop up** *vt sep* encerrar

co-op ['kəʊɒp] *n* cooperativa *f*; *Br* **the C.** = cadena de supermercados británica propiedad de una cooperativa

cooper ['ku:pə(r)] *n* tonelero(a) *m,f*

co-operate [kəʊ'ɒpəreɪt] *vi* cooperar (**with** con)

co-operation [kəʊɒpə'reɪʃən] *n* cooperación *f*; **we didn't get much c. from them** no cooperaron demasiado con nosotros; **in c. with, with the c. of** en cooperación con, con la cooperación de

co-operative [kəʊ'ɒpərətɪv] **1** *n* cooperativa *f*
2 *adj* **(a)** *(helpful)* cooperativo(a); **he has been most c.** ha cooperado muchísimo **(b)** *(joint, collective)* conjunto(a); **it was a c. effort** fue un esfuerzo conjunto ►► ***c. society*** cooperativa *f*

co-operatively [kəʊ'ɒpərətɪvlɪ] *adv* de forma cooperativa

co-opt [kəʊ'ɒpt] *vt* **to c. sb onto a committee** nombrar a alguien miembro de una comisión; **to c. sb to do sth** elegir a alguien para que haga algo

co-ordinate 1 *n* [kəʊ'ɔ:dɪnət] **(a)** *Math* coordenada *f* ►► ***c. geometry*** geometría *f* analítica **(b) co-ordinates** *(clothes)* conjuntos *mpl*
2 *adj Gram (clause)* coordinado(a)
3 *vt* [kəʊ'ɔ:dɪneɪt] coordinar

co-ordinated [kəʊ'ɔ:dɪneɪtɪd] *adj* **(a)** *(physically)* coordinado(a); **he's not very c.** no coordina muy bien, no tiene mucha coordinación **(b)** *(concerted)* coordinado(a) ►► *Phys* ***C. Universal Time*** tiempo *m* universal coordinado

co-ordinating [kəʊ'ɔ:dɪneɪtɪŋ] *adj* **(a)** *(body, officer)* coordinador(ora) **(b)** *Gram* **c. conjunction** conjunción coordinada

co-ordination [kəʊɔ:dɪ'neɪʃən] *n* **(a)** *(ease of movement)* coordinación *f* **(b)** *(of efforts)* coordinación *f*

co-ordinator [kəʊ'ɔ:dɪneɪtə(r)] *n* coordinador(ora) *m,f*

coot [ku:t] *n* **(a)** *(bird)* focha *f* **(b)** *Fam Old-fashioned (idiot)* merluzo(a) *m,f*, *RP* tontuelo(a) *m,f*

cootie ['ku:tɪ] *n US Fam* piojo *m*

co-owner ['kəʊ'əʊnə(r)] *n* copropietario(a) *m,f*

co-ownership ['kəʊ'əʊnəʃɪp] *n* copropiedad *f*

cop [kɒp] *Fam* **1** *n* **(a)** *(police officer)* poli *mf*; **the cops** la poli; **to play cops and robbers** jugar a polis y cacos ►► ***c. shop*** *(police station)* comisaría *f* **(b)** *Br Old-fashioned (arrest)* **it's a fair c.!** ¡me han *Esp* pillado *or Am* agarrado con todo el equipo! **(c)** *Br* **it's not much c.** *(not very good)* no es nada del otro mundo
2 *vt* **(a)** *(catch)* **to c. sb** pescar *or Esp* pillar *or Am* agarrar a alguien; **to c. hold of sth** pillar algo; **c. (a load of) this!** *(listen)* ¡oye esto!; *(look)* ¡mira!, ¡no te lo pierdas!, *Esp* ¡al loro!
(b) *Br* **to c. it** *(be punished)* cargársela; *(die)* estirar la pata, *Esp* palmarla, *Méx* petaleársela
(c) *US Fam* **to c. some zees** echar una cabezadita *or* un sueñecito
(d) *Fam* **to c. a plea** = declararse culpable de un delito menor para evitar ser acusado de otro más grave

► **cop out** *vi Fam* zafarse, *Esp* escaquearse, *RP* zafar; **he copped out of telling her** se zafó *or Esp* escaqueó de decírselo, *RP* zafó de decírselo

copartner [kəʊ'pɑ:tnə(r)] *n* socio(a) *m,f*

copartnership [kəʊ'pɑ:tnəʃɪp] *n* sociedad *f*

cope [kəʊp] **1** *vi* arreglárselas; **to c. with** hacer frente a, poder con; **I can't c. with her when she gets angry** no puedo con ella cuando se enfada; **the system can't c. with this volume of work** el sistema no puede con tal cantidad de trabajo; **he can't c. with his job** no puede con su trabajo; **I couldn't c. without her** no sé qué haría sin ella; **I just can't c.!** ¡es demasiado para mí!, ¡no puedo con ello!
2 *vt* **(a)** *(provide with coping)* poner una albardilla a **(b)** *(join timbers)* acoplar
3 *n Rel* capa *f* pluvial

Copenhagen [kəʊpən'hɑ:gən] *n* Copenhague

Copernican [kə'pɜ:nɪkən] *adj* copernicano(a)

Copernicus [kə'pɜ:nɪkəs] *pr n* Copérnico

copestone ['kəʊpstəʊn] *n (coping-stone)* (piedra *f* de) albardilla *f*

copier ['kɒpɪə(r)] *n (photocopying machine)* fotocopiadora *f*

co-pilot ['kəʊpaɪlət] *n* copiloto *mf*

coping ['kəʊpɪŋ] *n (on wall)* albardilla *f* ►► ***c. saw*** sierra *f* de marquetería

coping-stone ['kəʊpɪŋstəʊn] *n* (piedra *f* de) albardilla *f*

copious ['kəʊpɪəs] *adj* abundante, copioso(a); **he took c. notes** tomó numerosas notas

copiously ['kəʊpɪəslɪ] *adv* abundantemente, copiosamente

cop-out ['kɒpaʊt] *n Fam* **to be a c.** ser una forma de zafarse *or Esp* escaquearse *or RP* zafar

copper ['kɒpə(r)] **1** *n* **(a)** *(metal)* cobre *m* ►► ***c. sulphate*** sulfato *m* de cobre **(b)** *Fam* **coppers** *(coins)* calderilla *f*, *RP* chirolas *fpl*, *Méx* morralla *f (sólo monedas de uno y dos peniques)* **(c)** *(colour)* color *m*

cobrizo (**d**) *Fam (police officer)* poli *mf* (**e**) *(container)* caldero *m*
2 *adj* (**a**) *(made from copper)* de cobre (**b**) *(copper-coloured)* cobrizo(a)

copper-bottomed [kɒpə'bɒtəmd] *adj* (**a**) *(pot)* con fondo de cobre (**b**) *(guarantee, commitment)* sólido(a)

copperhead ['kɒpəhed] *n (snake) (American)* serpiente *f* cabeza de cobre; *(Australian)* = serpiente venenosa australiana

copperplate ['kɒpəpleɪt] *n (writing)* letra *f* inglesa

coppery ['kɒpərɪ] *adj* cobrizo(a)

coppice ['kɒpɪs] *n* arboleda *f*, soto *m*

copra ['kɒprə] *n* copra *f*

coprocessor [kəʊ'prəʊsesə(r)] *n Comptr* coprocesador *m*

coproduction [kəʊprə'dʌkʃən] *n Cin* coproducción *f*

coprolalia [kɒprə'leɪlɪə] *n Psy* coprolalia *f*

copse [kɒps] *n* arboleda *f*, soto *m*

Copt [kɒpt] *n* copto(a) *m,f*

copter ['kɒptə(r)] *n Fam* helicóptero *m*

Coptic ['kɒptɪk] 1 *adj* copto(a)
2 *n (language)* copto *m*

copula ['kɒpjʊlə] (*pl* **copulas** *or* **copulae** ['kɒpjʊli:]) *n Gram* cópula *f*

copulate ['kɒpjʊleɪt] *vi* copular

copulation [kɒpjʊ'leɪʃən] *n* cópula *f*

copulative ['kɒpjʊlətɪv] *adj Gram* copulativo(a) ►► ***c. conjunction*** conjunción *f* copulativa

copy ['kɒpɪ] 1 *n* (**a**) *(reproduction)* copia *f*; **to make a c. of sth** hacer una copia de algo ►► *Comptr* ***c. protection*** protección *f* contra copia
(**b**) *(of letter, document)* copia *f* ►► ***c. typist*** mecanógrafo(a) *m,f*
(**c**) *(of book, newspaper)* ejemplar *m*
(**d**) *Journ* **advertising c.** textos publicitarios; **the story made good c.** la noticia dio mucho de sí ►► ***c. deadline*** fecha *f* límite de edición; ***c. editor*** corrector(ora) *m,f* de estilo
2 *vt* (**a**) *(reproduce)* copiar
(**b**) *(imitate, emulate)* copiar, imitar
(**c**) *(in order to cheat)* copiar (**from** de); **he copied the answer from me** se copió de mí; **he copied the answer from a book** copió la respuesta de un libro
(**d**) *(photocopy)* fotocopiar
(**e**) *Comptr (text, file)* copiar; **to c. sth to disk** copiar algo a un disco; **to c. and paste sth** copiar y pegar algo
(**f**) *(send copy to)* enviar una copia a; **to c. sb with sth** enviar una copia de algo a alguien
3 *vi* (**a**) *(cheat)* copiarse (**from** de) (**b**) *Comptr* **to c. and paste** copiar y pegar (**c**) *US Tel (hear)* **do you c.?** ¿me oyes *or* recibes?

► **copy down, copy out** *vt sep* copiar; **to c. out a passage from a book** copiar un pasaje de un libro; **I copied it down wrong** lo copié mal

copybook ['kɒpɪbʊk] 1 *n* cuaderno *m* de caligrafía; IDIOM **to blot one's c.** empañar (uno) su prestigio
2 *adj (perfect)* de libro ►► ***a c. example*** un ejemplo perfecto

copycat ['kɒpɪkæt] 1 *n Fam* copión(ona) *m,f*
2 *adj* **c. crime** = delito inspirado en otro similar

copy-edit ['kɒpɪedɪt] 1 *vt (article, book)* corregir el estilo de
2 *vi* corregir el estilo

copyist ['kɒpɪɪst] *n* copista *mf*

copy-protected ['kɒpɪprə'tektɪd] *adj Comptr* protegido(a) contra copia

copyread ['kɒpɪri:d] *US* 1 *vt* corregir el estilo de
2 *vi* corregir el estilo

copyreader ['kɒpɪri:də(r)] *n US* corrector(ora) *m,f* de estilo

copyright ['kɒpɪraɪt] 1 *n* copyright *m*, derechos *mpl* de autor, propiedad *f* intelectual; **she has (the) c. on the book** tiene el copyright *or* los derechos de autor del libro; **this book is out of c.** los derechos de autor sobre este libro han vencido ►► ***c. (deposit) library*** = cada una de las seis bibliotecas que tiene derecho a recibir gratis una copia de cada libro que se publica en el Reino Unido; ***c. law*** leyes *fpl* de la propiedad intelectual
2 *vt* registrar como propiedad intelectual
3 *adj* = protegido por las leyes de la propiedad intelectual

copywriter ['kɒpɪraɪtə(r)] *n* redactor(ora) *m,f* creativo(a) *or* de publicidad

coquetry ['kɒkɪtrɪ] *n* coquetería *f*

coquette [kɒ'ket] *n* (mujer *f*) coqueta *f*

coquettish [kɒ'ketɪʃ] *adj* coqueto(a)

cor [kɔ:(r)] *exclam Br Fam* ¡caramba!, *Esp* ¡jolines!; **c. blimey!** ¡demonios!, ¡caramba!

coracle ['kɒrəkəl] *n* = barco de remos hecho de mimbre con revestimiento impermeable

coral ['kɒrəl] 1 *n* coral *m* ►► ***c. island*** isla *f* coralina; ***c. reef*** arrecife *m* de coral; ***the C. Sea*** el Mar del Coral; ***c. snake*** serpiente *f* de coral, *Am* coralillo *m o f*
2 *adj* coralino(a)

cor anglais ['kɔ:rɒŋ'gleɪ] (*pl* **cors anglais** ['kɔ:zɒŋ'gleɪ]) *n Mus* corno *m* inglés

corbel ['kɔ:bəl] *n Archit* ménsula *f*

cord [kɔ:d] *n* (**a**) *(string)* cuerda *f*, cordel *m*; *(for curtains, pyjamas)* cordón *m* (**b**) *Elec* cable *m*, cordón *m* (**c**) *(corduroy)* pana *f*; **a c. jacket/skirt** una chaqueta *or Méx* chamarra *or RP* campera/falda *or RP* pollera de pana; **cords** pantalones de pana

cordial ['kɔ:dɪəl] 1 *n (drink)* refresco *m*
2 *adj* (**a**) *(friendly)* cordial (**b**) *(deeply felt)* profundo(a)

cordiality [kɔ:dɪ'ælɪtɪ] *n* cordialidad *f*

cordially ['kɔ:dɪəlɪ] *adv* (**a**) *(warmly)* cordialmente; *US* **c. yours** *(at end of letter)* un cordial saludo (**b**) *(completely) (to hate, detest)* completamente

cordite ['kɔ:daɪt] *n* cordita *f*

cordless ['kɔ:dlɪs] *adj* ***c. kettle*** = hervidor eléctrico con soporte independiente enchufado a la red; ***c. microphone*** micrófono *m* inalámbrico; ***c. phone*** teléfono *m* inalámbrico

cordon ['kɔ:dən] *n* cordón *m*; **a police c.** un cordón policial

► **cordon off** *vt sep* acordonar

cordon bleu ['kɔ:dɒn'blɜ:] *adj* **a c. cook** un(a) cocinero(a) cordon bleu *or* de primera categoría

cordon sanitaire [kɔ:'dɒnsænɪ'tɜ:(r)] *n* cordón *m* sanitario

corduroy ['kɔ:dərɔɪ] *n* pana *f*; **a c. jacket/skirt** una chaqueta *or Méx* chamarra *or RP* campera/falda *or RP* pollera de pana; **c. trousers, corduroys** pantalones de pana

CORE [kɔ:(r)] (*abbr* **Congress of Racial Equality**) *n* = organización estadounidense contra el racismo

core [kɔ:(r)] 1 *n* (**a**) *(of apple, pear)* corazón *m*; *(of earth)* núcleo *m*, endosfera *f*; *(of nuclear reactor)* núcleo *m*; **he's rotten to the c.** está corrompido hasta la médula; **it shook me to the c.** me afectó profundamente
(**b**) *(of problem)* meollo *m*; **a hard c. of support** un núcleo sólido de apoyo ►► *Sch* ***c. curriculum*** asignaturas *fpl* troncales; *Com* ***c. market:*** **the c. market for the product is among 18–30 year-olds** el sector del mercado al que va dirigido fundamentalmente el producto es el comprendido entre los 18–30 años; ***c. time*** *(in flexitime)* tiempo *m* mínimo
(**c**) *Elec (of cable)* alma *f*
2 *vt (apple, pear)* quitar *or* sacar el corazón a

coreligionist [kəʊrɪ'lɪdʒənɪst] *n* correligionario(a) *m,f*

corer ['kɔ:rə(r)] *n* sacacorazones *m inv* (de manzanas)

co-respondent [kəʊrɪ'spɒndənt] *n Law (in divorce suit)* codemandado(a) *m,f*

Corfu [kɔ:'fu:] *n* Corfú

corgi ['kɔ:gɪ] *n* corgi *mf*

coriander [kɒrɪ'ændə(r)] *n* cilantro *m*

Corinth ['kɒrɪnθ] *n* Corinto

Corinthian [kə'rɪnθɪən] 1 *n (from Corinth)* corintio(a) *m,f*
2 *adj* (**a**) *(from Corinth)* corintio(a) (**b**) *Archit* corintio(a)

cork [kɔ:k] 1 *n* (**a**) *(material)* corcho *m* ►► ***c. oak*** *or* ***tree*** alcornoque *m* (**b**) *(stopper)* (tapón *m* de) corcho *m*; IDIOM *Fam* **put a c. in it!** ¡cierra el pico!, *RP* ¡cortála!
2 *vt (bottle)* encorchar

corkage ['kɔ:kɪdʒ] *n* = recargo que se cobra en un restaurante por el consumo de bebidas traídas de fuera

corkboard ['kɔ:kbɔ:d] *n* tablero *m* de corcho

corked [kɔ:kt] *adj (wine)* agrio(a) *(por entrada de aire al descomponerse el corcho)*

corker ['kɔ:kə(r)] *n Fam Old-fashioned* **she's a real c.** *(good-looking)* está buenísima; **a c. of a joke** un chiste tronchante *or Am* cómico; **a c. of a fib** una trola *or RP* un boleto como una casa, *Méx* un chisme enorme

corking ['kɔ:kɪŋ] *adj Fam Old-fashioned* excelente, estupendo(a)

corkscrew ['kɔ:kskru:] 1 *n* sacacorchos *m inv*
2 *vi (staircase)* ascender/descender en espiral; **the plane corkscrewed out of the sky** el avión cayó trazando una espiral

corm [kɔːm] *n Bot* bulbo *m*

cormorant ['kɔːmərənt] *n* cormorán *m*

Corn (*abbr* **Cornwall**) (condado *m* de) Cornwall *or* Cornualles

corn[1] [kɔːn] *n* (**a**) *Br (wheat)* trigo *m* ►► ***c. circle*** = franja aplastada y circular de terreno cultivado, que aparece por causas supuestamente paranormales; ***c. exchange*** = edificio donde se solía comerciar en trigo

(**b**) *(maize)* maíz *m*, *Andes, RP* choclo *m* ►► ***c. bread*** pan *m* de maíz *or Andes, RP* choclo; ***c. on the cob*** mazorca *f* de maíz *or Andes, RP* choclo, *Méx* elote *m*; ***c. meal*** harina *f* de maíz; ***c. oil*** aceite *m* de maíz; ***c. syrup*** almíbar *m* de maíz

(**c**) ***c. bunting*** triguero *m*

(**d**) *Fam (sentimentality)* sensiblería *f*, cursilería *f*; **the book is pure c.** el libro es una auténtica cursilada

corn[2] *n (on foot)* callo *m*; IDIOM *Br Fam* **to tread on sb's corns** *(upset)* ponerle a alguien el dedo en la llaga, darle a alguien donde le duele ►► ***c. plaster*** parche *m* para callos

cornball ['kɔːnbɔːl] *US Fam* **1** *n* tarugo(a) *m,f*

2 *adj (sentimental)* sensiblero(a), cursi

corncob ['kɔːnkɒb] *n* mazorca *f*; **c. pipe** = pipa de fumar hecha de una mazorca seca

corncrake ['kɔːnkreɪk] *n* rey *m or* guión *m* de codornices

cornea ['kɔːnɪə] *n Anat* córnea *f*

corneal ['kɔːnɪəl] *adj Med* de la córnea; **c. graft** injerto de córnea

corned beef ['kɔːnd'biːf] *n* = fiambre de carne de vaca prensado y enlatado

cornelian [kɔː'niːlɪən] *n* cornalina *f*

corner ['kɔːnə(r)] **1** *n* (**a**) *(of page, screen)* esquina *f*; *(of room)* rincón *m*; *(of mouth, eye)* comisura *f*; **out of the c. of one's eye** con el rabillo del ojo; **a forgotten c. of the world** un rincón perdido del globo; IDIOM **from the four corners** *or* **every c. of the earth** desde todos los rincones de la tierra

(**b**) *(of street)* esquina *f*; **I'll meet you at** *or* **on the c.** quedamos en la esquina; **it's at** *or* **on the c. of Washington Avenue and Main Street** está en la esquina de Washington Avenue y *or* con Main Street; **the house on** *or* **at the c.** la casa de la esquina; *also Fig* **it's just round the c.** está a la vuelta de la esquina; **to turn the c.** doblar la esquina; *Fig (economy, company)* empezar a mejorar ►► ***c.*** *Br* ***shop*** *or US* ***store*** = tienda pequeña de barrio que vende productos alimenticios, de limpieza, golosinas, etc.

(**c**) *(bend in road)* curva *f* (cerrada)

(**d**) *(difficult situation)* **to be in a (tight) c.** estar en un apuro *or* aprieto

(**e**) *(in soccer, hockey)* saque *m* de esquina, córner *m* ►► ***c. flag*** banderín *m* de córner; ***c. kick*** *(in soccer)* saque *m* de esquina, córner *m*

(**f**) *(in boxing)* rincón *m*, esquina *f* ►► ***c. man*** ayudante *m* del preparador

2 *vt* (**a**) *(person, animal)* acorralar, arrinconar (**b**) *(market)* monopolizar, acaparar; **to c. the market in sth** monopolizar el mercado de algo

3 *vi (car)* girar, torcer

cornered ['kɔːnəd] *adj (animal, prey)* acorralado(a), arrinconado(a); **we've got him c.** lo tenemos acorralado

cornering ['kɔːnərɪŋ] *n Br (of driver, car)* **his c. is poor** no sabe girar muy bien; **this model has improved c. performance** este modelo ha mejorado la forma de tomar las curvas

cornerstone ['kɔːnəstəʊn] *n also Fig* piedra *f* angular

cornet [*Br* 'kɔːnɪt, *US* kɔː'net] *n* (**a**) *(musical instrument)* corneta *f* (**b**) *Br (for ice cream)* cucurucho *m*

cornet(t)ist [kɔː'netɪst] *n Mus* corneta *mf*

corn-fed ['kɔːnfed] *adj (chicken)* alimentado(a) a base de trigo

cornfield ['kɔːnfiːld] *n* (**a**) *Br (of wheat)* trigal *m* (**b**) *US (of maize)* maizal *m*

cornflakes ['kɔːnfleɪks] *npl* copos *mpl* de maíz *or Andes, RP* choclo

cornflour ['kɔːnflaʊə(r)] *n Br* harina *f* de maíz *or Andes, RP* choclo, maicena® *f*

cornflower ['kɔːnflaʊə(r)] *n* aciano *m* ►► ***c. blue*** azul *m* violáceo

cornice ['kɔːnɪs] *n* (**a**) *Archit* cornisa *f* (**b**) *(ledge of snow)* cornisa *f*

Cornish ['kɔːnɪʃ] **1** *npl (people)* **the C.** la gente de Cornualles

2 *n (language)* córnico *m*

3 *adj* de Cornualles ►► *Br* ***C. pasty*** empanada *f* de carne y *Esp* patatas *or Am* papas

cornstarch ['kɔːnstɑːtʃ] *n US* harina *f* de maíz *or Andes, RP* choclo, maicena® *f*

cornucopia [kɔːnjʊ'kəʊpɪə] *n* (**a**) *Art* cornucopia *f*, cuerno *m* de la abundancia (**b**) *(abundant source)* fuente *f* inagotable

Cornwall ['kɔːnwəl] *n* Cornualles

corny ['kɔːnɪ] *adj Fam* (**a**) *(joke)* viejo(a), trillado(a) (**b**) *(movie, novel)* sensiblero(a), cursi

corolla [kə'rɒlə] *n Bot* corola *f*

corollary [kə'rɒlərɪ] *n* corolario *m*

corona [kə'rəʊnə] *n* (**a**) *Astron* corona *f* (**b**) *Phys* **c. (discharge)** descarga *f* de corona (**c**) *Bot* corona *f*

coronary ['kɒrənərɪ] **1** *n* **he had a c.** le dio un infarto (de miocardio)

2 *adj Med* coronario(a) ►► ***c. artery*** arteria *f* coronaria; ***c. bypass*** bypass *m* coronario; ***c. heart disease*** cardiopatía *f* coronaria; ***c. thrombosis*** trombosis *f* coronaria

coronation [kɒrə'neɪʃən] *n* coronación *f* ►► ***c. chicken*** = pollo con mayonesa aromatizada con curry

coroner ['kɒrənə(r)] *n Law* = persona que preside una investigación sobre un caso de muerte sospechosa

coronet ['kɒrənɪt] *n (small crown)* corona *f* pequeña

Corp (**a**) *Com* (*abbr* **corporation**) ≃ S.A. (**b**) *Mil* (*abbr* **corporal**) cabo *mf*

corpora *pl of* **corpus**

corporal[1] ['kɔːpərəl] *adj* corporal ►► ***c. punishment*** castigo *m* corporal

corporal[2] *n Mil* cabo *mf*

corporate ['kɔːpərət] *adj* (**a**) *(collective) (decision, responsibility)* colectivo(a) ►► *Pol* ***c. state*** estado *m* corporativo

(**b**) *Com (of company)* de empresa, corporativo(a) ►► ***c. culture*** cultura *f* empresarial; ***c. event*** acto *m* de empresa; ***c. hospitality*** actos *mpl* sociales de la empresa; ***c. identity*** identidad *f* corporativa; ***c. image*** imagen *f* corporativa *or* de empresa; ***c. interests*** los intereses de los empresarios *or* del capital; ***c. lawyer*** abogado(a) *m,f* de empresa; *Fin* ***c. raider*** tiburón *m*; ***c. sponsorship*** patrocinio *m* corporativo; ***c. strategy*** estrategia *f* empresarial

(**c**) *(incorporated)* constituido(a), incorporado(a)

corporation [kɔːpə'reɪʃən] *n* (**a**) *Com* sociedad *f* anónima ►► *Br* ***c. tax*** impuesto *m* de sociedades (**b**) *(council)* consistorio *m*, ayuntamiento *m*; *Br* **a c. bus** un autobús del ayuntamiento (**c**) *Fam (paunch)* panza *f*, barriga *f*

corporatism ['kɔːpərətɪzəm] *n Pol* corporativismo *m*

corporeal [kɔː'pɔːrɪəl] *adj Formal* corpóreo(a)

corps [kɔː(r)] (*pl* **corps** [kɔːz]) *n* (**a**) *Mil* cuerpo *m* (**b**) *(trained team of people)* cuerpo *m*; **the diplomatic c.** el cuerpo diplomático (**c**) *Theat* **corps de ballet** cuerpo de ballet

corpse [kɔːps] **1** *n* cadáver *m*

2 *vi Fam (actor)* reírse

corpulence ['kɔːpjʊləns] *n* obesidad *f*

corpulent ['kɔːpjʊlənt] *adj* obeso(a)

corpus ['kɔːpəs] (*pl* **corpuses** *or* **corpora** ['kɔːpərə]) *n* (**a**) *(works of author)* recopilación *f*, corpus *m inv* (**b**) *(for analysis)* corpus *m inv* ►► ***c. linguistics*** lingüística *f* de corpus

corpuscle ['kɔːpʌsəl] *n Anat* glóbulo *m*; **red/white (blood) c.** glóbulo rojo/blanco

corral [kə'rɑːl] **1** *n US* corral *m*, cercado *m*

2 *vt (cattle, horses)* encorralar, acorralar; *Fig (people)* acorralar; *Fam* **to c. sb into doing sth** acorralar a alguien para que haga algo

correct [kə'rekt] **1** *adj* (**a**) *(exact) (amount, figure)* exacto(a); *(information, use, spelling)* correcto(a); **do you have the c. time?** ¿sabes qué hora es exactamente?; **he is c.** tiene razón; **that is c.** (eso es) correcto; **am I c. in thinking that...?** ¿tengo razón al pensar que...?, ¿estoy en lo cierto al pensar que...?; **to prove c.** resultar (ser) correcto(a); *Math* **c. to four decimal places** redondeado(a) hasta el cuarto decimal

(**b**) *(person, behaviour)* correcto(a); **the c. procedure** lo correcto; **as is only c.** como es debido *or* procede

2 *vt* (**a**) *(rectify)* corregir; **to c. a mistake/misunderstanding** corregir un error/un malentendido (**b**) *(exam, proofs, homework)* corregir (**c**) *(person)* corregir; **c. me if I'm wrong, but...** corríjame si me equivoco, pero...; **I stand corrected** reconozco mi error

correcting fluid [kə'rektɪŋfluːɪd] *n* líquido *m* corrector

correction [kə'rekʃən] *n* (**a**) *(of exam, proofs, homework)* corrección *f* (**b**) *(alteration, rectification) (of error)* corrección *f*; **to make corrections (to sth)** corregir (algo) (**c**) *Old-fashioned (punishment)* **house of c.** correccional

correctional [kə'rekʃənəl] *adj US* ***c. facility*** *or* ***institution*** correccional *m*

corrective [kə'rektɪv] **1** *n* enmienda *f*; **to serve as a c. to sth** enmendar algo
2 *adj* corrector(ora), correctivo(a); **to take c. action to rectify a problem** poner remedio a un problema ►► *Med* ***c. surgery*** cirugía *f* correctiva

correctly [kə'rektlɪ] *adv* **(a)** *(exactly)* correctamente; **I'm not sure I heard you c.** no estoy seguro de haberte oído bien **(b)** *(properly)* correctamente, apropiadamente

correlate ['kɒrɪleɪt] **1** *vt* relacionar (**with** con)
2 *vi* presentar una correlación (**with** con); **these two trends are closely correlated** estas dos tendencias guardan una estrecha relación

correlation [kɒrɪ'leɪʃən] *n* correlación *f*

correlative [kə'relətɪv] *Gram* **1** *n* correlativo *m*
2 *adj* correlativo(a)

correspond [kɒrɪs'pɒnd] *vi* **(a)** *(be in accordance)* corresponderse (**with** con) **(b)** *(be equivalent)* corresponder (**with** *or* **to** con *or* a), corresponderse (**with** *or* **to** con); **the festival corresponds to our New Year** el festival corresponde a nuestro Año Nuevo **(c)** *(write letters)* mantener correspondencia (**with** con)

correspondence [kɒrɪs'pɒndəns] *n* **(a)** *(relationship)* correspondencia *f*, relación *f* (**between** entre)
(b) *(letter writing)* correspondencia *f*; **they kept up a regular c.** se carteaban de forma habitual, mantenían una correspondencia habitual; **to be in c. with sb** mantener correspondencia con alguien ►► ***c. course*** curso *m* por correspondencia
(c) *(letters)* correspondencia *f* ►► ***c. column*** *(in newspaper)* cartas *f* al director

correspondent [kɒrɪs'pɒndənt] *n* **(a)** *(of newspaper, radio)* corresponsal *mf*; **our Middle East c.** nuestro corresponsal en Oriente Medio **(b)** *(letter writer)* **he's a good c.** escribe cartas con regularidad; **he's a bad c.** se le da muy mal escribir cartas

corresponding [kɒrɪ'spɒndɪŋ] *adj* **(a)** *(equivalent)* correspondiente **(b)** ***c. member*** *(of society, club)* miembro *mf* correspondiente

correspondingly [kɒrɪ'spɒndɪŋlɪ] *adv* proporcionalmente

corridor ['kɒrɪdɔː(r)] *n* **(a)** *(in building, train)* pasillo *m*; **the corridors of power** las altas esferas **(b)** *(for air traffic)* corredor *m*, pasillo *m* aéreo **(c)** *(strip of territory)* corredor *m*

corroborate [kə'rɒbəreɪt] *vt* corroborar

corroborating [kə'rɒbəreɪtɪŋ], **corroborative** [kə'rɒbərətɪv] *adj (evidence, statement)* corroborativo(a)

corroboration [kərɒbə'reɪʃən] *n* corroboración *f*; **to provide c. of sth** corroborar algo

corrode [kə'rəʊd] **1** *vt also Fig* corroer
2 *vi* corroerse

corrosion [kə'rəʊʒən] *n* corrosión *f*

corrosive [kə'rəʊsɪv] **1** *n* corrosivo *m*
2 *adj* corrosivo(a)

corrugated ['kɒrəgeɪtɪd] *adj* ondulado(a) ►► ***c. iron*** chapa *f* ondulada; ***c. paper*** papel *m* ondulado

corrugation [kɒrə'geɪʃən] *n* ondulación *f*

corrupt [kə'rʌpt] **1** *adj* **(a)** *(dishonest)* corrupto(a); **c. practices** corrupción **(b)** *(depraved, immoral)* corrompido(a) **(c)** *(text, manuscript)* alterado(a) **(d)** *Comptr* corrompido(a)
2 *vt* **(a)** *(make dishonest)* corromper **(b)** *(deprave, debase)* corromper; **to c. sb's morals** pervertir a alguien **(c)** *(text, manuscript)* alterar **(d)** *Comptr* corromper

corruptible [kə'rʌptəbəl] *adj* corruptible

corruption [kə'rʌpʃən] *n* **(a)** *(of official, politician)* corrupción *f* **(b)** *(depravity, debasement)* corrupción *f*; **a c. of the truth** una tergiversación *or* deformación de la verdad ►► ***c. of minors*** corrupción *f* de menores **(c)** *(of text, manuscript)* alteración *f* **(d)** *Comptr* corrupción *f*

corruptly [kə'rʌptlɪ] *adv* **(a)** *(dishonestly)* corruptamente, de forma deshonesta **(b)** *(in a depraved way)* corrompidamente, de forma corrompida

corsage [kɔː'sɑːʒ] *n* **(a)** *(flowers)* ramillete *m* **(b)** *(bodice)* cuerpo *m*

corsair [kɔː'seə(r)] *n Old-fashioned* **(a)** *(pirate)* corsario *m* **(b)** *(ship)* buque *m* corsario

corset ['kɔːsɪt] *n* corsé *m*

Corsica ['kɔːsɪkə] *n* Córcega

Corsican ['kɔːsɪkən] **1** *n* corso(a) *m,f*
2 *adj* corso(a)

cortege, cortège [kɔː'teʒ] *n* cortejo *m* (fúnebre)

Cortes ['kɔːtez] *pr n* Hernán Cortes

cortex ['kɔːteks] (*pl* **cortices** ['kɔːtɪsiːz]) *n* **(a)** *Anat* corteza *f* **(b)** *Bot* corteza *f*

Cortez ['kɔːtez] *pr n* Hernán Cortes

cortisone ['kɔːtɪzəʊn] *n* cortisona *f*

corundum [kə'rʌndəm] *n Geol* corindón *m*

coruscate ['kɒrəskeɪt] *vi* chispear

coruscating ['kɒrəskeɪtɪŋ] *adj (wit)* chispeante, ocurrente

corvette [kɔː'vet] *n* corbeta *f*

cos[1] [kɒz] *n Math* (*abbr* **cosine**) cos

cos[2] *conj Fam (because)* porque

cos[3] [kɒs] *n* **c. (lettuce)** lechuga *f* romana

cosh [kɒʃ] *Br* **1** *n* porra *f*
2 *vt* golpear con una porra

cosignatory [kəʊ'sɪgnətrɪ] *n Formal* firmante *mf* conjunto(a) (**to** *or* **of** de)

cosily, *US* **cozily** ['kəʊzɪlɪ] *adv* **(a)** *(warmly, comfortably)* cómodamente, confortablemente; *(furnished, decorated)* acogedoramente **(b)** *(in a friendly way)* amigablemente

cosine ['kəʊsaɪn] *n Math* coseno *m*

cosiness, *US* **coziness** ['kəʊzɪnɪs] *n* **(a)** *(warmth, comfort)* comodidad *f*, confort *m* **(b)** *(of relationship)* intimidad *f*

cosmetic [kɒz'metɪk] **1** *n* cosmético *m*; **cosmetics** cosméticos *mpl*, maquillaje *m*
2 *adj* **(a)** *(for beautifying)* cosmético(a) ►► ***c. surgery*** cirugía *f* estética; ***c. surgery clinic*** clínica *f* de cirugía estética **(b)** *(superficial)* cosmético(a); **the changes were only c.** eran unos cambios superficiales *or* puramente decorativos

cosmetician [kɒzmə'tɪʃən] *n (specialist)* cosmetólogo(a) *m,f*

cosmic ['kɒzmɪk] *adj* **(a)** *(relating to the universe)* cósmico(a) ►► *Astron* ***c. radiation*** radiación *f* cósmica; ***c. rays*** rayos *mpl* cósmicos **(b)** *(large, significant)* astronómico(a); **of c. proportions** de dimensiones astronómicas

cosmography [kɒz'mɒgrəfɪ] *n* cosmografía *f*

cosmology [kɒz'mɒlədʒɪ] *n* cosmología *f*

cosmonaut ['kɒzmənɔːt] *n* cosmonauta *mf*

cosmopolitan [kɒzmə'pɒlɪtən] **1** *n* cosmopolita *mf*
2 *adj* cosmopolita

cosmos ['kɒzmɒs] *n* **the c.** el cosmos

Cossack ['kɒsæk] **1** *adj* cosaco(a)
2 *n* cosaco(a) *m,f*

cosset ['kɒsɪt] *vt* mimar

cossie ['kɒzɪ] *n Br & Austr Fam* traje *m* de baño, *Esp* bañador *m*, *RP* malla *f*

cost [kɒst] **1** *n* **(a)** *(price)* costo *m*, *Esp* coste *m*; **maintenance costs** costos de mantenimiento; **the radio was repaired at a c. of £50** la reparación de la radio costó 50 libras; **the c. in human terms** *(of unemployment, closure)* el costo humano; **think of the c. (involved)!** ¡piensa lo que costará!; **at little c.** a bajo precio; **at no extra c.** sin costo adicional; **at great c.** *(financial)* por un precio alto; *Fig* a un alto precio; *Fig* **at the c. of...** a costa de...; *Com* **at c. (price)** a precio de costo *or Esp* coste ►► *Fin* ***c. accounting*** contabilidad *f* de costos *or Esp* costes; ***c. cutting*** reducción *f* de gastos; *Econ* ***c. of living*** costo *m or Esp* coste *m* de la vida; ***c. of living index*** índice *m* del costo *or Esp* coste de la vida; *Com* ***c. of production*** costo *m* de producción
(b) *Law* **costs** costas *fpl* (judiciales); **he was awarded costs** le concedieron la indemnización de las costas judiciales; **he was ordered to pay costs** le ordenaron el pago de las costas judiciales
(c) IDIOMS **to count the c. of sth** ver las consecuencias de algo; **at any c.** a toda costa, cueste lo que cueste; **at all costs** a toda costa, a cualquier precio; **he'll do it whatever the c. to his health** lo hará aunque le cueste la salud; **as I found out to my c.** como pude comprobar para mi desgracia
2 *vt* **(a)** (*pt & pp* **cost**) costar; **how much** *or* **what does it c.?** ¿cuánto cuesta?; **it costs $25** cuesta 25 dólares; **it costs nothing to join** hacerse socio no cuesta nada; **it doesn't c. anything to be polite** no cuesta nada ser educado; **whatever it costs** cueste lo que cueste; *Fam* **it'll c. you!** ¡te saldrá caro!; *Fam* **to c. a fortune** *or* **the earth** *or* **an arm and a leg** costar una fortuna *or* un ojo de la cara; **it c. her a lot of time and effort** le costó mucho tiempo y trabajo; **to c. sb dear** costarle caro a alguien; **the attempt c. him his life** el intento le costó la vida
(b) (*pt & pp* **costed**) *Com (budget)* calcular el costo de; **a carefully costed budget** un presupuesto con los costos muy estudiados
3 *vi Fam* **it's going to c.** va a salir por un pico, va a salir carillo

co-star ['kəʊstɑː(r)] **1** *n* coprotagonista *mf*
2 *vt* (*pt & pp* **co-starred**) **co-starring...** coprotagonizado(a) por...
3 *vi* ser el coprotagonista

Costa Rica ['kɒstə'riːkə] *n* Costa Rica

Costa Rican ['kɒstə'riːkən] **1** *n* costarricense *mf*
2 *adj* costarricense

cost-benefit ['kɒst'benɪfɪt] *adj Econ* ***c. analysis*** análisis *m inv* de costo-beneficio *or Esp* coste-beneficio

cost-conscious ['kɒst'kɒnʃəs] *adj* **to be c.** ser consciente de los costos *or Esp* costes

cost-cutting ['kɒst'kʌtɪŋ] **1** *n* reducción *f* de costos *or Esp* costes
2 *adj (drive, campaign)* de reducción de costos *or Esp* costes

cost-effective ['kɒstɪ'fektɪv] *adj* rentable

costermonger ['kɒstəmʌŋgə(r)] *n Br Old-fashioned* vendedor(ora) *m,f* de fruta ambulante

costing ['kɒstɪŋ] *n Com* cálculo *m* de costos *or Esp* costes

costive ['kɒstɪv] *adj* estreñido(a)

costly ['kɒstlɪ] *adj* caro(a); **a c. error** *or* **mistake** un error muy caro

costume ['kɒstjuːm] *n* (**a**) *(in play, film)* traje *m*; *(fancy dress)* disfraz *m*; **are you going to the party in c.?** ¿vas a ir disfrazado a la fiesta?; **costumes by...** *(in credits)* vestuario... ▸▸ ***c. designer*** diseñador(ora) *m,f* de vestuario, figurinista *mf*; ***c. drama*** *(TV series)* serie *f* de época; *(movie)* película *f* de época; ***c. hire*** *(fancy dress)* alquiler *m* de disfraces; *(for play, wedding)* alquiler *m* de trajes y vestidos; ***c. jewellery*** bisutería *f*
(**b**) *(traditional dress)* **national c.** traje típico
(**c**) **(swimming) c.** traje *m* de baño, *Esp* bañador *m*, *RP* malla *f*
(**d**) *Br Old-fashioned (woman's suit)* traje *m* de chaqueta

costumier [kɒ'stjuːmɪə(r)] *n* diseñador(ora) *m,f* de vestuario, figurinista *mf*

cosy, *US* **cozy** ['kəʊzɪ] **1** *adj* (**a**) *(warm, snug)* acogedor(ora); **it's c. here** se está bien aquí; **to feel c.** sentirse a gusto (**b**) *(intimate)* **a c. relationship** una relación demasiado estrecha *or* amistosa; **he's a bit too c. with the boss** tiene una relación demasiado amistosa con el jefe
2 *n (for tea-pot)* cubreteteras *m inv*; *(for egg)* cubrehuevos *m inv*

▸**cosy up** *vi* **to c. up to sb** *(snuggle up)* acurrucarse contra alguien; *Fig (ingratiate oneself)* adular a alguien, tratar de ganarse el favor de alguien

cot [kɒt] *n* (**a**) *Br (for child)* cuna *f* ▸▸ ***c. death*** (síndrome *m* de la) muerte *f* súbita infantil (**b**) *US (folding bed)* catre *m*, cama *f* plegable

cotangent ['kəʊ'tændʒənt] *n Math* cotangente *f*

coterie ['kəʊtəriː] *n* camarilla *f*

coterminous [kəʊ'tɜːmɪnəs] *adj Formal* colindante, limítrofe (**with** con)

cottage ['kɒtɪdʒ] *n* (**a**) *(home in country)* casa *f* de campo, chalé *m* ▸▸ ***c. cheese*** queso *m* fresco; ***c. hospital*** hospital *m* rural; ***c. industry*** industria *f* artesanal; ***c. loaf*** pan *m* payés, hogaza *f*; ***c. pie*** = pastel de carne picada y puré de patata (**b**) *Br Fam (public toilet) Esp* servicios *mpl or Am* baños *mpl (utilizados como lugar de encuentro por homosexuales)*

cottaging ['kɒtədʒɪŋ] *n Br Fam* = encuentros homosexuales en baños públicos

cotter ['kɒtə(r)] *n Tech (wedge)* chaveta *f*; **c. (pin)** chaveta *f*

cotton ['kɒtən] *n* (**a**) *(material, plant)* algodón *m*, *Am* cotón *m*; **a c. shirt** una camisa de algodón ▸▸ *US* ***the C. belt*** el cinturón de algodón, = la región algodonera al sudeste de Estados Unidos; ***c. bud*** bastoncillo *m* (de algodón); *US* ***c. candy*** algodón *m* dulce; ***c. gin*** almarrá *f*; ***c. mill*** fábrica *f* de algodón; ***c. picker*** *(person)* recolector(ora) *m,f* de algodón; *(machine)* recolectora *f* de algodón; ***c. thistle*** cardo *m* borriquero, espina *f* blanca; *Br* ***c. wool*** algodón *m* (hidrófilo *or* en rama); IDIOM **to wrap sb in c. wool** criar a alguien entre algodones
(**b**) *Br (thread)* hilo *m* (de algodón)

▸**cotton on** *vi Fam* enterarse, *Esp* coscarse, *RP* captar; **I didn't c. on to what she meant at first** al principio no me enteraba de lo que quería decir

▸**cotton to** *vt insep US Fam* (**a**) *(take a liking to)* **I didn't c. to her at first** al principio no me cayó bien (**b**) *(approve of)* aprobar

cottonmouth ['kɒtənmaʊθ] *n* mocasín *m* de agua

cotton-pickin' ['kɒtənpɪkɪn] *adj US Fam* maldito(a)

cottonseed ['kɒtənsiːd] *n* semilla *f* de algodón

cottontail ['kɒtənteɪl] *n* tapetí *m*

cotyledon [kɒtɪ'liːdən] *n Bot* cotiledón *m*

couch [kaʊtʃ] **1** *n* sofá *m*; *Fam Fig* **to be on the c.** *(in psychoanalysis)* estar en el psicoanalista ▸▸ ***c. grass*** grama *f* del norte, cerrillo *m*; *Fam* ***c. potato*** = persona perezosa que se pasa todo el día viendo la tele
2 *vt (express)* expresar, formular (**in** en)

couchette [kuː'ʃet] *n* litera *f*

cougar ['kuːgə(r)] *n* puma *m*

cough [kɒf] **1** *n* tos *f*; **to have a c.** tener tos; **I can't get rid of this c.** no consigo curarme esta tos ▸▸ ***c. drop*** pastilla *f* para la tos; ***c. mixture*** jarabe *m* para la tos; ***c. sweet*** caramelo *m* para la tos; ***c. syrup*** jarabe *m* para la tos
2 *vi* toser; **a coughing fit** un ataque de tos
3 *vt (blood)* expectorar

▸**cough up 1** *vt sep* (**a**) *(phlegm, blood)* toser (**b**) *Fam (money)* poner, *Esp* apoquinar, *RP* garpar
2 *vi Fam (pay up)* poner dinero, *Esp* apoquinar, *RP* garpar

could [kʊd] *modal aux v*

> En el inglés hablado, y en el escrito en estilo coloquial, la forma negativa **could not** se transforma en **couldn't**.

(**a**) *(was able to: past of* **can***)* **I c. hear them talking** los oía hablar; **I c. have tried harder** podía haberme esforzado más; **they couldn't very well refuse** les resultaba imposible negarse; **he couldn't have been kinder** fue de lo más amable; **he was as happy as c. be** estaba en la gloria; **(it) c. be** podría ser; **how COULD you!** ¡cómo has podido!; **I c. have hit him!** *(I was so angry)* ¡me dieron ganas de pegarle!; **you c. have warned me!** ¡me podías haber avisado!, ¡haberme avisado!
(**b**) *(indicating ability or skill)* **I c. swim well at that age** a esa edad nadaba muy bien; **she c. speak three languages** hablaba tres idiomas
(**c**) *(in requests)* **c. you get me some water?** ¿me puedes traer un poco de agua?; **c. you be quiet please?** ¿te podrías callar, por favor?; **c. I borrow your newspaper?** ¿me prestas el periódico?
(**d**) *(indicating supposition or speculation)* **it c. break at any time** podría partirse en cualquier momento; **you c. well be right** es muy posible que tengas razón; **they c. have changed their plans (for all we know)** podrían haber cambiado de planes; **what c. I have done with the keys?** ¿qué habré hecho yo con las llaves?
(**e**) *(in conditional)* **if I had more money, I c. buy a new guitar** si tuviera más dinero podría comprarme una guitarra nueva
(**f**) *(in suggestions)* **we c. always telephone** siempre podríamos llamar *or Am* hablar por teléfono; **you c. go to the beach** podrías ir a la playa; **couldn't we at least talk about it?** ¿no podríamos hablar del tema?

couldn't ['kʊdənt] = **could not**

couldn't-care-less ['kʊdəntkeə'les] *adj* pasota; **c. attitude** actitud pasota

coulis ['kuːliː] *n Culin* = puré de pescado, ave, fruta o verdura

coulomb ['kuːlɒm] *n Elec* culombio *m*

council ['kaʊnsəl] *n* (**a**) *(organization, body)* consejo *m* ▸▸ ***C. of Europe*** Consejo *m* de Europa; *EU* ***C. of Ministers*** Consejo *m* de Ministros
(**b**) *(local government) (of town)* ayuntamiento *m*, concejo *m*; *(of region, county)* autoridades *fpl* regionales, ≃ diputación *f* provincial; **to be on the c.** ser concejal(ala) ▸▸ *Br* ***c. estate*** urbanización de viviendas de protección oficial; *Br* ***c. house*** vivienda *f* pública de alquiler; *Br* ***c. tax*** ≃ contribución *f* urbana
(**c**) *(meeting)* consejo *m*; **to hold a c. of war** *(in wartime)* celebrar un consejo de guerra; *Fig (in emergency)* celebrar una reunión de emergencia
(**d**) *Rel* concilio *m*

councillor, *US* **councilor** ['kaʊnsɪlə(r)] *n Pol* concejal(ala) *m,f*

councilman ['kaʊnsəlmən] *n US* concejal *m*

councilwoman ['kaʊnsəlwʊmən] *n US* concejala *f*

counsel ['kaʊnsəl] **1** *n* (**a**) *(advice)* consejo *m*; **to take c. with sb (about sth)** pedir consejo a alguien (sobre algo); **he's someone who keeps his own c.** siempre se reserva su opinión (**b**) *Law* abogado(a) *m,f*; **if c. would approach the bench** ruego a la defensa y la acusación que se acerquen al estrado ▸▸ ***c. for the defence*** abogado(a) *m,f* defensor(ora); ***c. for the prosecution*** fiscal *mf*
2 *vt* (*pt & pp* **counselled,** *US* **counseled**) (**a**) *(advise)* aconsejar; **to c. sb to do sth** aconsejar a alguien que haga algo; **to c. caution** aconsejar prudencia (**b**) *(give psychological help to)* proporcionar apoyo psicológico a
3 *vi* **I would c. against accepting the offer** yo no aconsejaría aceptar la oferta

counselling ['kaʊnsəlɪŋ] *n* apoyo *m* psicológico, ayuda *f* psicológica; **you need c.** necesitas apoyo psicológico *or* ayuda psicológica; **to seek c.** solicitar apoyo psicológico *or* ayuda psicológica

counsellor ['kaʊnsələ(r)] *n* **(a)** *(adviser)* consejero(a) *m,f*, asesor(ora) *m,f*; *(therapist)* psicólogo(a) *m,f* **(b)** *US Law* abogado(a) *m,f*

count[1] [kaʊnt] *n (nobleman)* conde *m*

count[2] **1** *n* **(a)** *(calculation)* cuenta *f*; *(of votes)* recuento *m*; **at the last c.** según las cifras más recientes; **we had ten bottles left, at the last c.** en el último recuento nos quedaban diez botellas; **to keep/lose c. of** llevar/perder la cuenta de; **I've lost c. of the number of times...** he perdido la cuenta de cuántas veces...; **on the c. of three** a la (voz) de tres ►► *Gram* ***c. noun*** nombre *m* contable

(b) *(total, number)* (número *m*) total *m*; **the casualty c. has risen to 34** el número *or* la cifra total de víctimas se eleva ya a 34

(c) *(in boxing)* cuenta *f* (hasta diez); IDIOM **to be out for the c.** *(boxer)* estar fuera de combate; *Fig (fast asleep) Esp* estar roque

(d) *Law* cargo *m*, acusación *f*; **guilty on both counts** culpable de los dos cargos; *Fig* **she said it would be quick and painless, but she was wrong on both counts** dijo que sería rápido y sin dolor, pero se equivocaba en ambas cosas; *Fig* **on a number of counts** en una serie de puntos

2 *vt* **(a)** *(enumerate)* contar; **I counted ten people in the room** conté a diez personas en la habitación; **I'm counting the days until I leave the company** cuento los días que faltan para poder marcharme de la empresa; *Fig* **you can c. them on the fingers of one hand** se pueden contar con los dedos de una mano; **to c. sheep** *(in order to fall asleep)* contar ovejitas

(b) *(include)* contar; **have you counted yourself?** ¿te has contado?; **counting the dog, there were four of us** éramos cuatro, contando al perro; **there were four of us, not counting the dog** eramos cuatro sin contar al perro

(c) *(consider)* considerar; **I c. him as a friend** lo considero un amigo; **I c. him among my friends** lo incluyo entre mis amigos; **c. yourself lucky you weren't killed** considérate afortunado(a) por haber salido con vida

3 *vi* **(a)** *(by numbers)* contar; **to c. (up) to ten** contar hasta diez; **to c. on one's fingers** contar con los dedos; **counting from tomorrow** contando a partir de mañana

(b) *(be valid)* contar, valer; **two children c. as one adult** dos niños cuentan como un adulto; **that one doesn't c.** ese no cuenta; **it counts as one of my worst holidays** fue una de mis peores vacaciones; **his record counted in his favour** su historial contaba en su favor; **to c. for nothing** no contar para nada

(c) *(be important)* contar; **every vote counts** todos los votos cuentan *or* son importantes; **experience counts more than qualifications** la experiencia cuenta más que los títulos; **we have to make this opportunity c.** tenemos que hacer valer esta ocasión

► **count against** *vt insep* ir en contra de, perjudicar

► **count down** *vi* hacer la cuenta atrás; *Fig* **the whole nation is counting down to the elections** toda la nación espera *or Esp* aguarda con interés el día de las elecciones

► **count for** *vt insep* **their opinion doesn't c. for much** su opinión no cuenta gran cosa

► **count in** *vt sep* contar con; **c. me in!** ¡cuenta conmigo!

► **count on** *vt insep* **(a)** *(rely on)* contar con; **we're counting on you** contamos contigo; **to c. on sb to do sth** contar con que alguien haga algo; **don't c. on it** no cuentes con ello

(b) *(expect)* contar con; **I'm counting on getting away by five o'clock** cuento con salir *or* con que saldré antes de las cinco; **I wasn't counting on my husband being here** no contaba con que mi marido estuviera aquí

► **count out** *vt sep* **(a)** *(money)* contar **(b)** *(exclude)* dejar fuera, excluir; **c. me out!** ¡no cuentes conmigo! **(c)** *(in boxing)* **to be counted out** quedar fuera de combate (tras la cuenta hasta diez)

► **count towards** *vt insep (contribute to)* contar para, valer para

► **count up** *vt sep* contar, hacer la cuenta de

► **count upon** *vt insep* = **count on**

countable ['kaʊntəbəl] *adj Gram* contable

countdown ['kaʊntdaʊn] *n* cuenta *f* atrás; **to start the c.** comenzar la cuenta atrás; **the c. to the wedding/Christmas has begun** ha comenzado la cuenta atrás de la boda/las Navidades

countenance ['kaʊntɪnəns] *Formal* **1** *n* **(a)** *(face)* semblante *m*; **to keep one's c.** guardar la compostura; **to lose c.** *(person, government)* perder la compostura **(b)** *(support)* **to give** *or* **lend c. to sth** dar respaldo a algo

2 *vt* respaldar; **I would never c. such a thing!** ¡nunca respaldaría *or* apoyaría semejante cosa!

counter[1] ['kaʊntə(r)] *n* **(a)** *(in shop)* mostrador *m*; *(in pub)* barra *f*; *(in bank)* ventanilla *f*; **it's available over the c.** *(of medicine)* se vende sin receta; *Fin* **to buy shares over the c.** comprar acciones sin cotización oficial; **under the c.** bajo cuerda ►► *US* ***c. check*** cheque *m* de ventanilla; ***c. staff*** *(in bank, post office)* personal *m* de ventanilla

(b) *(in kitchen)* encimera *f*

(c) *(token)* ficha *f*

(d) *(counting device)* contador *m*

counter[2] **1** *n* **(a)** *(counterbalance)* contrapeso *m*; **to act as a c. to** servir de contrapeso a **(b)** *(in boxing)* contraataque *m*, respuesta *f*

2 *adv* **c. to** en contra de; **to act c. to sb's advice/wishes** actuar en contra de los consejos/deseos de alguien; **to go** *or* **run c. to** estar en contra de

3 *vt* **(a)** *(argument, assertion)* responder a; **to c. that...** replicar que... **(b) to c. a blow** *(in boxing)* responder a un golpe

4 *vi* **(a) to c. by doing sth** reaccionar haciendo algo **(b)** *(in boxing)* contraatacar, responder

counteract [kaʊntə'rækt] *vt* contrarrestar

counterargument ['kaʊntərɑːgjʊmənt] *n* argumento *m* contrario

counter-attack ['kaʊntərətæk] **1** *n* contraataque *m*

2 *vt* contraatacar

3 *vi* contraatacar

counter-attraction ['kaʊntərə'trækʃən] *n* rival *m*

counterbalance ['kaʊntə'bæləns] **1** *n* contrapeso *m*; *Fig* **to act as a c. (to sth)** contrarrestar (algo)

2 *vt* contrarrestar

counterbid ['kaʊntəbɪd] *n Fin (during takeover)* contraoferta *f*

counterblast ['kaʊntəblɑːst] *n* dura réplica *f*

countercharge ['kaʊntətʃɑːdʒ] **1** *n Law* contradenuncia *f*

2 *vi* contraatacar

3 *vt* **to c. that...** contraatacar diciendo que...

counter-claim ['kaʊntəkleɪm] *n* contrarréplica *f*, contrademanda *f*

counter-clockwise ['kaʊntə'klɒkwaɪz] *US* **1** *adj* **in a c. direction** en sentido opuesto al de las agujas del reloj

2 *adv* en sentido opuesto al de las agujas del reloj

counter-culture ['kaʊntəkʌltʃə(r)] *n* contracultura *f*

counterdemonstration ['kaʊntədemən'streɪʃən] *n* manifestación *f* contraria, contramanifestación *f*

counterespionage [kaʊntər'espɪənɑːʒ] *n* contraespionaje *m*

counterfeit ['kaʊntəfɪt] **1** *n* falsificación *f*

2 *adj (banknote, passport, document)* falso(a); *Fig (sympathy, affection)* falso(a), fingido(a)

3 *vt (banknote, passport, document)* falsificar; *Fig (sympathy, affection)* fingir

counterfeiter ['kaʊntəfɪtə(r)] *n (of banknote, passport, document)* falsificador(ora) *m,f*

counterfoil ['kaʊntəfɔɪl] *n* matriz *f*

counter-insurgency [kaʊntərɪn'sɜːdʒənsɪ] *n Mil* medidas *fpl* para sofocar una revuelta

counterintelligence ['kaʊntərɪn'telɪdʒəns] *n* contraespionaje *m*

counterintuitive ['kaʊntəɪn'tjuːɪtɪv] *adj* contraintuitivo(a)

countermand [kaʊntə'mɑːnd] *vt* revocar

countermeasure ['kaʊntəmeʒə(r)] *n* medida *f* en sentido contrario

counteroffensive ['kaʊntərə'fensɪv] *n* contraofensiva *f*

counteroffer ['kaʊntər'ɒfə(r)] *n* contraoferta *f*

counterpane ['kaʊntəpeɪn] *n* colcha *f*

counterpart ['kaʊntəpɑːt] *n* homólogo(a) *m,f*; **there is no c. in our system** no hay un equivalente en nuestro sistema

counterpoint ['kaʊntəpɔɪnt] *n Mus* contrapunto *m*

counterpoise ['kaʊntəpɔɪz] **1** *n* contrapeso *m*; **to be in c.** servir de contrapeso

2 *vt* contrapesar

counterproductive ['kaʊntəprə'dʌktɪv] *adj* contraproducente

counterproposal ['kaʊntəprə'pəʊzəl] *n* contrapropuesta *f*

counterpunch ['kaʊntəpʌntʃ] **1** *n (in boxing)* devolución *f* de un golpe

2 *vi* devolver un golpe

counter-revolution ['kaʊntərevə'luːʃən] *n* contrarrevolución *f*

counter-revolutionary ['kaʊntərevə'luːʃənərɪ] **1** *n* contrarrevolucionario(a) *m,f*

2 *adj* contrarrevolucionario(a)

countersign ['kaʊntəsaɪn] *vt* refrendar

countersignature ['kaʊntə'sɪgnətʃə(r)] *n* refrendo *m*

countersink ['kaʊntəsɪŋk] *Tech* **1** *n* **(a)** *(hole)* avellanado *m* **(b)** *(tool)* avellanador *m*
2 *vt* **(a)** *(hole)* avellanar **(b)** *(screw)* atornillar

counter-tenor ['kaʊntə'tenə(r)] *n Mus* contratenor *m*, contralto *mf*

counterterrorism [kaʊntə'terərɪzəm] *n* contraterrorismo *m*

countervailing ['kaʊntəveɪlɪŋ] *adj* compensatorio(a)

counterweight ['kaʊntəweɪt] *n* contrapeso *m*; **to act as a c. (to sth)** servir de contrapeso (a algo), contrarrestar (algo)

countess ['kaʊntəs] *n* condesa *f*

countless ['kaʊntlɪs] *adj* innumerables, incontables; **on c. occasions** en innumerables ocasiones; **I've told you c. times not to do that** te he dicho miles de veces que no hagas eso

countrified ['kʌntrɪfaɪd] *adj* rústico(a)

country ['kʌntrɪ] *n* **(a)** *(state, people)* país *m*; **the whole c. was saddened by the news** la noticia entristeció a todo el país; **up and down the c.** por todo el país; **they were ready to fight/die for their c.** estaban dispuestos a luchar/morir por la patria; *Br Pol* **to go to the c.** *(call elections)* convocar elecciones; **the old c.** mi tierra, el terruño
(b) *(as opposed to town)* campo *m*; **in the c.** en el campo; **c. people** la gente del campo; **c. lifestyle** modo de vida rural *or* campestre; **to travel across c.** *(in car, on bike, on foot)* ir campo a través ►► *Fam Pej* ***c. bumpkin*** *Esp* paleto(a) *m,f*, *Esp* palurdo(a) *m,f*, *Méx* pelado(a) *m,f*, *RP* pajuerano(a) *m,f*; ***c. club*** club *m* de campo; ***c. cousin*** palurdo(a) *m,f*, pueblerino(a) *m,f*; ***c. dancing*** bailes *mpl* regionales *or* tradicionales; ***c. house*** casa *f* solariega *or* de campo; ***c. life*** vida *f* campestre; ***c. seat*** casa *f* solariega, quinta *f*
(c) *(area)* terreno *m*, tierras *fpl*; **this is good farming c.** estas tierras son buenas para la agricultura y la ganadería; **Wordsworth/Faulkner c.** la tierra de Wordsworth/Faulkner
(d) *(music)* **c. (and western)** música *f* country

countryman ['kʌntrɪmən] *n* **(a)** *(compatriot)* compatriota *m*, paisano *m*; **a fellow c.** un compatriota **(b)** *(who lives in the country)* campesino *m*

countryside ['kʌntrɪsaɪd] *n* campo *m*; **in the c.** en el campo

countrywide [kʌntrɪ'waɪd] *adj* a escala nacional

countrywoman ['kʌntrɪwʊmən] *n* **(a)** *(compatriot)* compatriota *f*, paisana *f*; **a fellow c.** una compatriota **(b)** *(who lives in the country)* campesina *f*

county ['kaʊntɪ] *n* **(a)** *(in UK)* condado *m* ►► ***c. council*** = órgano de gobierno de un condado; *Law* ***c. court*** = tribunal de justicia de un condado, *Esp* ≃ audiencia *f* provincial; ***c. town*** capital *f* de condado
(b) *(in USA)* condado *m* ►► *Law* ***c. court*** = tribunal de justicia de un condado, *Esp* ≃ audiencia *f* provincial; ***c. fair*** feria *f* rural anual; ***the c. line*** el límite del condado; ***c. seat*** capital *f* de condado

coup [ku:] (*pl* **coups** [ku:z]) *n* **(a)** *(surprising achievement)* golpe *m* de efecto; **to pull off a c.** dar un golpe de efecto; **it was quite a c.** fue todo un golpe de efecto ►► ***c. de grâce*** golpe *m* de gracia, tiro *m* de gracia **(b)** *Pol* **c. (d'état)** golpe *m* de Estado

coupé ['ku:peɪ] *n (car)* cupé *m*

couple ['kʌpəl] **1** *n* **(a)** *(of things)* par *m*; **a c. of** un par de; **were there many mistakes? – only a c.** ¿había muchas faltas? – sólo un par; *US Fam* **he's a c. years older** es un par de años mayor **(b)** *(people)* pareja *f*; **they make a lovely c.** hacen una pareja encantadora **(c)** *Phys* par *m* de fuerzas
2 *vt* **(a)** *(associate)* relacionar, asociar (**with** con); **her name has been coupled with his** *(romantically)* su nombre se ha relacionado *or* asociado con el de él **(b)** *(combine)* conjugar, combinar; **coupled with** junto con **(c)** *Rail* enganchar, acoplar
3 *vi (have sexual intercourse) (people)* copular; *(animals)* aparearse

coupler ['kʌplə(r)] *n* **(a)** *Elec* acoplador *m* **(b)** *US Rail* enganche *m*

couplet ['kʌplɪt] *n Lit* pareado *m*

> **False friend:** The Spanish noun **cuplé** is not a translation for the English word **couplet**. In Spanish **cuplé** means "saucy popular song".

coupling ['kʌplɪŋ] *n* **(a)** *(linking)* combinación *f*; *(of ideas, names)* asociación *f*, emparejamiento *m* **(b)** *Elec* acoplamiento *m* **(c)** *Br Rail* enganche *m* **(d)** *(sexual intercourse) (between people)* cópula *f*; *(between animals)* apareamiento *m*

coupon ['ku:pɒn] *n* **(a)** *(for discount, special offer)* cupón *m*, vale *m*; *(for rationing)* cupón *m* **(b)** *Fin* cupón *m* **(c)** *Br* **football** *or* **pools c.** boleto (de las quinielas)

courage ['kʌrɪdʒ] *n* valor *m*, coraje *m*; **to have the c. to do sth** tener valor para hacer algo; **to take one's c. in both hands** armarse de valor; **to pluck up** *or* **screw up the c. (to do sth)** armarse de valor (para hacer algo); **he didn't have the c. of his convictions** no tuvo coraje para defender sus convicciones; **he took c. from the news** aquella noticia le animó *or* le dio ánimos

courageous [kə'reɪdʒəs] *adj* valiente

courageously [kə'reɪdʒəslɪ] *adv* valientemente

courgette [kʊə'ʒet] *n Br* calabacín *m*, *CSur* zapallito *m*, *Méx* calabacita *f*

courier ['kʊrɪə(r)] *n* **(a)** *(messenger)* mensajero(a) *m,f* ►► ***c. service*** servicio *m* de mensajería **(b)** *(in tourism)* guía *mf* **(c)** *(drug smuggler)* correo *m*, enlace *m*

COURSE [kɔ:s] **1** *n* **(a)** *(direction, bearing) (of river)* curso *m*; **to be on c.** *(ship)* seguir el rumbo; **to be on c. for** *(likely to achieve)* ir camino de; **to be off c.** haber perdido el rumbo; **the boat was blown off c.** el viento desvió el barco de su rumbo; *also Fig* **to change c.** cambiar de rumbo; **to set c. for** poner rumbo a; **to steer a c. between recklessness and excessive caution** encontrar un término medio entre la imprudencia y una cautela excesiva
(b) *(progression) (of time, events)* transcurso *m*, curso *m*; *(of illness)* curso *m*; **during** *or* **in the c. of the campaign** durante el transcurso de la campaña; **in the c. of my investigations** en el curso de mis investigaciones; **I'll find out in the c. of the next few months** me enteraré a lo largo de los próximos meses; **in the c. of time** con el tiempo; **in the normal** *or* **ordinary c. of events** normalmente; **to be in the c. of doing sth** estar haciendo algo; **to let things take** *or* **run their c.** dejar que las cosas sigan su curso; **the flu has run its c.** el proceso gripal ha completado su evolución; **throughout the c. of history** durante el transcurso de la historia
(c) *(approach)* **a c. of action** una táctica (a seguir); **it is the only c. left open to us** es la única posibilidad *or* opción que nos queda
(d) *Educ (self-contained)* curso *m*; *(as part of degree)* asignatura *f*; **to do** *or* **take a c. in sth** hacer un curso de algo; **to go on a (training) c.** acudir a un curso (de formación); **(degree) c.** carrera; **a c. of lectures** un ciclo de conferencias
(e) *Med* **a c. of treatment** un tratamiento; **the doctor put me on a c. of antibiotics/injections** el doctor me recetó antibióticos/inyecciones
(f) *(of meal)* plato *m*; **first c.** primer plato; **main c.** plato principal; **what would you like for your first c.?** ¿qué van a comer de primer plato?, *Esp* ¿qué tomarán de primero?; **a three-c. meal** una comida con primer y segundo platos, y postre
(g) *(for race)* circuito *m*; *(for golf) Esp* campo *m*, *Am* cancha *f*; *(for showjumping)* recorrido *m*; *also Fig* **to stay the c.** aguantar hasta el final
(h) *(of bricks)* hilada *f*, *RP* hilera *f*
2 of course *adv (expressing agreement)* claro; *(clearly, unsurprisingly)* naturalmente; **of c. you can come!** ¡pues claro que puedes venir!; **can I have a go? – of c. (you can)** ¿puedo intentarlo? – claro (que sí); **ah, of c., that's why he wouldn't tell me** ah, claro, por eso no me lo quería decir; **he is, of c., very experienced in this area** tiene, naturalmente, una gran experiencia en este área; **of c., you can't expect them to accept it immediately** por supuesto, no se puede esperar que lo acepten de inmediato; **of c. not!** ¡claro *or* por supuesto que no!; **did you tell her? – of c. I didn't!** ¿se lo dijiste? – ¡claro *or* por supuesto que no!
3 *vt (hunt)* **to c. hares** cazar liebres con perros
4 *vi (liquid)* correr; **tears coursed down her cheeks** las lágrimas caían por sus mejillas; **the blood coursed through his veins** la sangre le corría por las venas

---

coursebook ['kɔ:sbʊk] *n* manual *m*, libro *m* de texto

courser ['kɔ:sə(r)] *n* **(a)** *Literary (horse)* corcel *m* **(b)** *(bird)* corredor *m*

courseware ['kɔ:sweə(r)] *n Comptr* software *m* didáctico

coursework ['kɔ:swɜ:k] *n* trabajo *m* realizado durante el curso

court [kɔ:t] **1** *n* **(a)** *Law* tribunal *m*; *(room)* sala *f*; **the c. rose** los asistentes se pusieron de pie; **to appear in c.** *(accused, witness)* comparecer ante un tribunal; **to go to c.** ir a los tribunales *or* a juicio; **to take sb to c.** llevar a alguien a juicio *or* a los tribunales; **to settle a case out of c.** arreglar una disputa sin acudir a los tribunales; **are you prepared to say that in c.?** ¿está dispuesto a decir eso delante de un tribunal?; **I'll see you in c. then!** ¡pues nos veremos en los tribunales!; IDIOM **to be laughed out of c.** *(idea)* ser ridiculizado(a); IDIOM **I was laughed out of c.** se rieron de mí; IDIOM **to rule sth out of c.** rechazar algo de plano ►► ***c. of appeal*** tribunal *m* de apelación; ***c. appearance*** *(of defendant)* comparecencia *f* en un juicio; ***c. case*** caso *m* judicial, proceso *m*; ***c. of inquiry*** comisión *f* de investigación; ***c. of law*** tribunal *m*; ***c. order*** orden *f* judicial
(b) *(for tennis, basketball)* pista *f*, cancha *f*; *(for squash)* pista *f*; **he**

was on c. for three hours pasó tres horas en la pista ►► *US* ***c. tennis*** = versión primitiva del tenis que se juega en una pista con paredes

(**c**) *(royal)* corte *f*; *Fig* **she held c. in the hotel bar, surrounded by a posse of journalists** entretuvo a un grupo de periodistas en el bar del hotel ►► ***c. card*** figura *f (naipe)*; ***c. circular*** boletín *m* de la corte; ***c. correspondent*** corresponsal *mf* en la corte; ***c. jester*** bufón *m* de la corte; *Br* ***c. shoe*** zapato *m* de salón

(**d**) *(courtyard)* patio *m*

(**e**) *Old-fashioned* **to pay c. to** *(woo)* hacer la corte a

2 *vt* (**a**) *Old-fashioned (woo)* cortejar (**b**) *(seek) (sb's friendship, favour)* intentar ganarse; *(failure)* exponerse a; *(death)* jugar con; **to c. disaster** jugársela, buscarse problemas

3 *vi Old-fashioned* **to be courting** *(couple)* cortejarse

court-appointed ['kɜːtə'pɔɪntɪd] *adj* nombrado(a) por un tribunal ►► ***c. defence lawyer*** abogado(a) *m,f* de oficio

courteous ['kɜːtɪəs] *adj* cortés (**to** *or* **towards** con)

courteously ['kɜːtɪəslɪ] *adv* cortésmente

courtesan ['kɔːtɪzæn] *n Literary* cortesana *f*

courtesy ['kɜːtəsɪ] *n* (**a**) *(politeness)* cortesía *f*; **at least have the c. to apologize** por lo menos tenga la cortesía *or* la gentileza de pedir disculpas; **by c. of...** por cortesía de... ►► ***c. call*** visita *f* de cortesía *or* cumplido; ***c. car*** coche *m* de cortesía; ***c. light*** *(in car)* luz *f* interior; ***c. title*** título *m* de cortesía; ***c. visit*** visita *f* de cortesía *or* cumplido

(**b**) *(polite action, remark)* cortesía *f*; **do me the c. of listening** ten la cortesía de escucharme; **to exchange courtesies** intercambiar cumplidos

courthouse ['kɔːthaʊs] *n US Law* palacio *m* de justicia

courtier ['kɔːtɪə(r)] *n* cortesano(a) *m,f*

courtly ['kɔːtlɪ] *adj Literary* refinado(a), distinguido(a) ►► ***c. love*** amor *m* cortés

court-martial ['kɔːt'mɑːʃəl] *Mil* **1** *n* (*pl* **courts-martial**) consejo *m* de guerra; **to be tried by c.** ser sometido(a) a un consejo de guerra

2 *vt* (*pt & pp* **court-martialled**, *US* **court-martialed**) someter a un consejo de guerra a; **he was court-martialled** le sometieron a un consejo de guerra

courtroom ['kɔːtruːm] *n Law* sala *f* de juicios ►► *Cin & Theat* ***c. drama*** = película u obra de teatro cuyo argumento gira en torno a un juicio

courtship ['kɔːtʃɪp] *n* (**a**) *Old-fashioned (wooing)* cortejo *m* (**b**) *(attempts to attract)* **his c. of the youth vote** sus intentos de ganarse el voto juvenil (**c**) *(of animals, birds)* cortejo *m*; **c. dance** baile de cortejo; **c. display** parada nupcial

courtside ['kɔːtsaɪd] **1** *n* **at c.** a pie de pista

2 *adj* ***c. seat*** *(at basketball match)* silla *f* de pista

courtyard ['kɔːtjɑːd] *n* patio *m*

couscous ['kuːskuːs] *n* cuscús *m*

cousin ['kʌzən] *n* primo(a) *m,f*; **a distant c.** un(a) primo(a) lejano(a); **it's a distant c. of the sparrow** es un pariente lejano del gorrión; **our British/American cousins** nuestros primos británicos/estadounidenses

couture [kuː'tʊə(r)] *n* alta costura *f*

couturier [kuː'tʊərɪeɪ] *n* modisto *m*

covalent bond ['kəʊveɪlənt'bɒnd] *n Chem* enlace *m* covalente

covariance [kəʊ'veərɪəns] *n Math* covarianza *f*

cove[1] [kəʊv] *n (small bay)* cala *f*, ensenada *f*

cove[2] *n Br Fam Old-fashioned (person)* tipo *m*, *Esp* gachó *m*

coven ['kʌvən] *n* aquelarre *m*

covenant ['kʌvənənt] **1** *n* (**a**) *(agreement)* pacto *m*, convenio *m* (**b**) *Br (to charity)* = acuerdo para realizar regularmente una donación a una entidad benéfica la cual, además, recibe los impuestos con que haya sido gravada la cantidad donada (**c**) *Rel* **the C.** la Alianza

2 *vt (money)* = donar por el sistema de "covenant"

Coventry ['kɒvəntrɪ] *n* IDIOM **to send sb to C.** hacer el vacío a alguien

COVER ['kʌvə(r)] **1** *n* (**a**) *(lid)* tapa *f*

(**b**) *(soft covering)* funda *f*; *(for cushion, typewriter)* funda *f*; **covers** *(of bed)* mantas *fpl* (y sábanas); **under the covers** debajo de las sábanas

(**c**) *(of book)* tapa *f*; *(of magazine)* portada *f*, tapa *f*; **front c.** portada; **back c.** contraportada, *Perú, RP* contratapa; **to read a book from c. to c.** leerse un libro de principio a fin ►► ***c. girl*** chica *f* de portada *or RP* tapa; ***c. page*** *(of fax)* página *f* de portada; ***c. price*** precio *m*; ***c. sheet*** *(of fax)* página *f* de portada; ***c. story*** tema *m* de portada

(**d**) *(shelter)* protección *f*; **the soldiers looked for c.** los soldados buscaron un lugar en el que protegerse; **we'll give you c.** *(by shooting)* te cubriremos; **to break c.** ponerse al descubierto; **to run for c.** correr a ponerse a cubierto; **to take c.** ponerse a cubierto; **to take c. from sth** protegerse *or* resguardarse de algo; **under c. of darkness** al amparo de la oscuridad

(**e**) *(disguise, front)* tapadera *f*; **my c. has been blown** me han desenmascarado; **they use the business as a c. for money laundering activities** utilizan el negocio como tapadera *or* pantalla para sus operaciones de blanqueo *or* lavado de dinero ►► ***c. story*** tapadera *f*

(**f**) *Fin (in insurance)* cobertura *f*; **full c.** cobertura máxima; **to take out c. against sth** protegerse *or* asegurarse contra algo ►► *Br* ***c. note*** póliza *f* provisional

(**g**) *Fin (in banking)* garantía *f*

(**h**) *(temporary replacement)* **to provide c. for sb** reemplazar a alguien; **there is no c. available for her when she's ill** no hay nadie que la reemplace cuando se pone enferma

(**i**) *(song)* **c. (version)** versión *f (de una canción original)*

(**j**) *(in restaurant)* **they have 200 covers** tienen capacidad para 200 comensales ►► ***c. charge*** cubierto *m*

(**k**) *Com (envelope)* **to send sth under plain c.** enviar algo en un sobre sin la dirección del remitente; **to send sth under separate c.** enviar algo por separado *or* aparte

(**l**) *US* ***c. letter*** *(for job application)* carta *f* de presentación

2 *vt* (**a**) *(person, object)* cubrir; *(with a lid)* tapar; *(hole, gap)* tapar; *(seat, sofa)* tapizar; *(book)* forrar; **to be covered in sth** estar cubierto(a) de algo; **to c. one's eyes** taparse los ojos; **to c. one's face** taparse la cara; **to c. a wall with paint** recubrir de pintura una pared; **the ground was covered with snow** el suelo estaba cubierto de nieve; **his face was covered in spots** tenía la cara llena de granos; **to c. oneself with glory** cubrirse de gloria; **I was covered in** *or* **with shame** me moría de vergüenza; IDIOM **to c. oneself** *or Br* **one's back** *or US very Fam* **one's ass** cubrirse las espaldas

(**b**) *(hide) (one's embarrassment, confusion)* ocultar; **to c. one's tracks** no dejar rastro

(**c**) *(travel over)* cubrir, recorrer; **we covered 100 km** cubrimos *or* recorrimos 100 kms

(**d**) *(extend over)* cubrir; **water covers most of the earth's surface** el agua cubre la mayor parte de la corteza terrestre; **to c. a lot of ground** *(in book, discussion)* abarcar mucho

(**e**) *(include, deal with)* cubrir; **the law covers the whole of the banking sector** la ley abarca a todo el sector bancario; **I think that covers everything** creo que con eso que ya he tocado todos los puntos; IDIOM **I've got it covered** me estoy ocupando de ello

(**f**) *(of journalist)* cubrir; **to c. a story** cubrir una noticia

(**g**) *(be sufficient for)* cubrir; **to c. one's costs** cubrir gastos; **$20 should c. it** 20 dólares deberían bastar *or* ser suficientes

(**h**) *(insure)* cubrir, asegurar (**against** contra); **are we covered against flooding?** ¿estamos asegurados contra inundaciones?

(**i**) *(with gun)* cubrir; **you c. me while I cross the street** cúbreme mientras cruzo la calle; **we've got the door covered** estamos apuntando a la puerta

(**j**) *(of musician, band)* **to c. a song** hacer una versión de una canción

(**k**) *(of animal)* cubrir

► **cover for** *vt insep* (**a**) *(replace temporarily)* reemplazar *or* sustituir temporalmente (**b**) *(provide excuses for)* excusar

► **cover up 1** *vt sep* (**a**) *(conceal)* ocultar (**b**) *(person, object)* cubrir; *(with a lid)* tapar; **to c. oneself up** *(with clothing)* taparse

2 *vi* (**a**) *(conceal the truth)* encubrir (**for sb** a alguien) (**b**) *(put on clothes) (to keep warm)* abrigarse; *(as protection from the sun)* protegerse

coverage ['kʌvərɪdʒ] *n (on TV, in newspapers)* cobertura *f* informativa; **radio/television c. of the game** cobertura televisiva/radiofónica del partido

coveralls ['kʌvərɔːlz] *npl US* mono *m* (de trabajo), *Am* overol *m*

covered ['kʌvəd] *adj (walkway, market)* cubierto(a) ►► ***c. swimming pool*** piscina *f* cubierta; ***c. wagon*** carreta *f*

covering ['kʌvərɪŋ] **1** *n* (**a**) *(of snow, dust, chocolate)* capa *f* (**b**) *(protective) (on furniture)* funda *f*

2 *adj* (**a**) *Mil* ***c. fire*** fuego *m* de cobertura (**b**) *Br* ***c. letter*** carta *f* de presentación

coverlet ['kʌvəlɪt] *n* colcha *f*

covert 1 *adj* ['kəʊvɜːt] *(secret)* encubierto(a) ►► ***c. operations*** operaciones *fpl* clandestinas *or* secretas

2 *n* ['kʌvət] *(hiding place for animals)* matorral *m*

covertly ['kəʊvɜːtlɪ] *adv* a escondidas, de manera encubierta

cover-up ['kʌvərʌp] *n* encubrimiento *m*; **there has been a c.** han intentado encubrir el asunto; **the government denied there was any c.** el gobierno negó que hubiera habido encubrimiento alguno

covet ['kʌvɪt] *vt* codiciar; *Rel* **thou shalt not c....** no codiciarás...; **the much-coveted Pulitzer Prize** el codiciadísimo premio Pulitzer

covetous ['kʌvɪtəs] *adj* codicioso(a); **to be c. of** codiciar

covetousness ['kʌvɪtəsnɪs] *n* codicia *f*

covey ['kʌvɪ] *n (of partridge, grouse)* nidada *f*

cow[1] [kaʊ] *n* (**a**) *(farm animal)* vaca *f*; IDIOM **till the cows come home** hasta que las ranas críen pelo ►► ***c. parsley*** perifollo *m* silvestre (**b**) *(female elephant, seal, whale)* hembra *f* (**c**) *very Fam Pej (woman)* bruja *f*, pécora *f*; **poor c.** pobre infeliz *or* desgraciada; **lucky c.** *Esp* tía *or Am* tipa suertuda; **you silly c.!** ¡boba!

cow[2] *vt* acobardar, intimidar; **to c. sb into submission** reducir a alguien a la obediencia; **to look cowed** parecer intimidado(a); **a cowed look** una mirada acobardada or intimidada

coward ['kaʊəd] *n* cobarde *mf*

cowardice ['kaʊədɪs] *n* cobardía *f*; **moral c.** cobardía moral

cowardliness ['kaʊədlɪnɪs] *n* cobardía *f*

cowardly ['kaʊədlɪ] *adj* cobarde; **what a c. thing to do!** ¡eso es de cobardes!

cowbell ['kaʊbel] *n* cencerro *m*

cowboy ['kaʊbɔɪ] *n* (**a**) *(in American West)* vaquero *m*; **to play cowboys and indians** jugar a indios y vaqueros; **a c. film** *or* **movie** una película de vaqueros *or* del oeste ►► ***c. boots*** (botas *fpl*) camperas *fpl* (**b**) *Br Fam Pej (careless or dishonest workman)* jeta *m*, sinvergüenza *m*; **a c. company** una empresa de sinvergüenzas; **some c. builder/electrician** un sinvergüenza de albañil/electricista

cowcatcher ['kaʊkætʃə(r)] *n US* quitapiedras *m inv*

cower ['kaʊə(r)] *vi* acoquinarse, amilanarse; **the dog was cowering in a corner** el perro estaba encogido en una esquina; **he stood cowering before the boss** se quedó de pie acoquinado *or* amilanado ante el jefe

cowgirl ['kaʊgɜːl] *n* vaquera *f*

cowhand ['kaʊhænd] *n* vaquero *m*

cowherd ['kaʊhɜːd] *n* vaquero *m*

cowhide ['kaʊhaɪd] *n* cuero *m*

cowl [kaʊl] *n* (**a**) *(monk's hood)* capucha *f* (**b**) *(on chimney)* sombrerete *m* (**c**) *(on sweater, dress)* **c. neck** *or* **neckline** cuello vuelto

cowlick ['kaʊlɪk] *n* mechón *m*

cowling ['kaʊlɪŋ] *n* capó *m*

cowman ['kaʊmən] *n* (**a**) *Br (cowherd)* vaquero *m* (**b**) *US (ranch owner)* ganadero *m*

cowmuck ['kaʊmʌk] *n* estiércol *m* de vaca

co-worker [kəʊ'wɜːkə(r)] *n US* compañero(a) *m,f* de trabajo

cowpat ['kaʊpæt] *n Fam* boñiga *f* (de vaca), *Méx* caca *f*, *Col, RP* mierda *f*

cowpea ['kaʊpiː] *n* alubia *f* carilla

cowpoke ['kaʊpəʊk] *n US Fam* vaquero *m*

cowpox ['kaʊpɒks] *n* vacuna *f*

cowpuncher ['kaʊpʌntʃə(r)] *n US Fam Old-fashioned* vaquero *m*

cowrie, cowry ['kaʊrɪ] *n (mollusc, shell)* cauri *m*

cowshed ['kaʊʃed] *n* establo *m*

cowshit ['kaʊʃɪt] *n Vulg* mierda *f* de vaca

cowslip ['kaʊslɪp] *n* prímula *f*

cox [kɒks] **1** *n* timonel *mf*

2 *vt* llevar el timón de; **he coxed them to victory** los condujo a la victoria

3 *vi* hacer de timonel

coxcomb = **cockscomb**

coxed [kɒkst] *adj* ***c. fours*** cuatro *m* con (timonel); ***c. pairs*** dos *m inv* con (timonel)

coxless ['kɒkslɪs] *adj* ***c. fours*** cuatro *m* sin (timonel); ***c. pairs*** dos *m inv* sin (timonel)

coxswain ['kɒksən, 'kɒksweɪn] *n* timonel *mf*

coy [kɔɪ] *adj* (**a**) *(shy)* timorato(a); **she gave him a c. look** lo miró con timidez (**b**) *(evasive)* evasivo(a); **to be c. about sth** mostrarse evasivo(a) en relación con algo

coyly ['kɔɪlɪ] *adv* (**a**) *(shyly)* con estudiada timidez (**b**) *(evasively)* de manera evasiva

coyness ['kɔɪnɪs] *n* (**a**) *(shyness)* timidez *f* (**b**) *(evasiveness)* evasión *f*

coyote [kɔɪ'jəʊtɪ] *n* coyote *m*

coypu ['kɔɪpuː] (*pl* **coypus** *or* **coypu**) *n* coipo *m*

cozy, cozily *etc US* = **cosy, cosily** *etc*

CP [siː'piː] *n* (*abbr* **Communist Party**) PC *m*

CPA [siːpiː'eɪ] *n US* (*abbr* **certified public accountant**) *Esp* contable *mf* diplomado(a), *Am* contador(ora) *m,f* público(a)

CPI [siːpiː'aɪ] *n US Econ* (*abbr* **consumer price index**) IPC *m*, Índice *m* de Precios al Consumo

cpi [siːpiː'aɪ] *n Comptr* (*abbr* **characters per inch**) cpp

Cpl *Mil* (*abbr* **Corporal**) cabo *m*

CPR [siːpiː'ɑː(r)] *n Med* (*abbr* **cardiopulmonary resuscitation**) masaje *m* cardiaco

CPS [siːpiː'es] *n* (*abbr* **Crown Prosecution Service**) ≃ Fiscalía *f* General del Estado

cps [siːpiː'es] *n Comptr* (*abbr* **characters per second**) cps

CPU [siːpiː'juː] *n Comptr* (*abbr* **central processing unit**) CPU *f*

Cr (*abbr* **Crescent**) = calle en forma de media luna

crab [kræb] **1** *n* (**a**) *(crustacean)* cangrejo *m*, *Am* jaiba *f* ►► ***c. stick*** palito *m* de cangrejo

(**b**) *Astron* **the C.** el Cangrejo

(**c**) *Fam (irritable person)* quejica *mf*

(**d**) *Fam (pubic louse)* ladilla *f*; **to have crabs** tener ladillas

(**e**) *(gymnastic position)* puente *m*

(**f**) *(in rowing)* **he caught a c.** erró *or* falló con el remo

(**g**) ***c. apple*** *(fruit)* manzana *f* silvestre; *(tree)* manzano *m* silvestre

(**h**) ***c. plover*** *(bird)* chorlito *m* cangrejero

2 *vi (grumble)* rezongar

crabbed [kræbd] *adj* **c. writing** letra apretada y difícil de leer

crabby ['kræbɪ] *adj Fam* gruñón(ona)

crack [kræk] **1** *n* (**a**) *(in glass, porcelain)* raja *f*; *(in skin, wood, wall, ground, ice)* grieta *f*; *Fig* **cracks have started to appear in his alibi** su coartada está empezando a hacer agua

(**b**) *(gap)* rendija *f*; **the door was open a c.** la puerta estaba entreabierta

(**c**) *(sound) (of whip)* chasquido *m*; *(of twig, bone)* crujido *m*; *(of gun)* disparo *m*; **a c. of thunder** un trueno; IDIOM **she wasn't given a fair c. of the whip** no le dieron ninguna oportunidad

(**d**) *(blow)* **a c. on the head** un porrazo en la cabeza

(**e**) *Fam (attempt)* intento *m*; **to have a c. at (doing) sth** intentar (hacer) algo

(**f**) *Fam (joke, insult)* chiste *m*

(**g**) *(first moment)* **to get up at the c. of dawn** levantarse al amanacer

(**h**) *Comptr (software)* = programa utilizado para desproteger otro programa

(**i**) *(drug)* **c. (cocaine)** crack *m*

(**j**) *Vulg (woman's genitals)* coño *m*, *Col* cuca *f*, *Méx* paloma *f*, *RP* concha *f*

(**k**) *Vulg (anus)* ojete *m*, culo *m*

2 *adj Fam* de primera; **she's a c. shot** es una tiradora de primera; **c. troops** tropas de élite

3 *vt* (**a**) *(fracture) (cup, glass)* rajar; *(skin, wood, wall, ground, ice)* agrietar; *(bone)* fisurarse; **he cracked his head open** se abrió la cabeza

(**b**) *(make sound with) (whip)* chasquear; *(fingers, knuckles)* hacer crujir; *Fig* **to c. the whip** usar la mano dura

(**c**) *(hit)* **to c. sb over the head** dar a alguien un porrazo en la cabeza; **he cracked his head against the wall** se dio con la cabeza contra la pared

(**d**) *(solve) (problem)* resolver; *(code)* descifrar; **the police think they have cracked the case** la policía cree haber resuelto el caso; *Fam* **I think we've cracked it!** ¡creo que lo hemos resuelto!

(**e**) *(break open) (nut, egg)* cascar; *(safe)* forzar; *US Fam* **I didn't c. a book all term** no toqué un libro en todo el trimestre; *Fam* **to c. (open) a bottle** abrir una botella; *Fam* **she didn't c. a smile all evening** no se le escapó una sonrisa en toda la noche

(**f**) *Comptr (protection)* descifrar, saltarse; *(program)* desproteger

(**g**) *(market)* colapsar

(**h**) *Fam (joke)* soltar, contar

(**i**) *Chem* descomponer

4 *vi* (**a**) *(cup, glass)* rajarse; *(skin, wood, wall, ground, ice)* agrietarse; *(bone)* fisurarse

(**b**) *(voice) (with emotion)* quebrarse

(**c**) *(person) (under pressure)* venirse abajo, derrumbarse; **his nerve cracked** perdió los nervios; **their marriage cracked under the strain** su matrimonio se vino abajo por la presión

(**d**) *(make noise) (twig, bone)* crujir; *(whip)* chasquear; **I heard a rifle c.** oí el disparo de un rifle

(**e**) *Fam* **to get cracking** ponerse en marcha *or* manos a la obra; **get cracking!** ¡manos a la obra!

► **crack down** *vi* **to c. down on sth** adoptar medidas severas contra algo

► **crack up** *Fam* **1** *vt sep* (**a**) *(repute)* **it's not all it's cracked up to be** no es tan bueno como lo pintan (**b**) *(cause to laugh)* **to c. sb up** hacer que alguien se parta *or* se muera *or Esp* se tronche *or Méx* se ataque *or RP* se descostille de risa

2 *vi* (**a**) *(ice, ground)* agrietarse (**b**) *Fam (laugh)* partirse *or* morirse *or Esp* troncharse *or RP* descostillarse *or Méx* atacarse de risa (**c**) *Fam (have nervous breakdown)* tener un ataque de nervios *or* una crisis nerviosa; **I must be cracking up** *(going mad)* me estoy volviendo loco *or Esp* majareta

crackbrained ['krækbreɪnd] *adj Fam* descabellado(a)

crackdown ['krækdaʊn] *n* medidas *fpl* severas; **a c. on drugs/tax evasion** medidas severas contra las drogas/la evasión fiscal

cracked [krækt] *adj* (**a**) *(cup, glass)* rajado(a); *(skin, wood, wall, ground, ice)* agrietado(a); *(bone)* fisurado(a) (**b**) *(voice)* quebrado(a) (**c**) *Fam (crazy)* **to be c.** estar chiflado(a) *or Esp* majareta

cracker ['krækə(r)] *n* (**a**) *(biscuit)* galleta *f* salada, cracker *f*

(**b**) *(firework)* petardo *m*

(**c**) *Br Fam (excellent thing, person)* **the first goal was an absolute c.** el primer gol fue de antología; **she's a c.** *(very attractive)* está muy buena, *Esp* está como un tren, *RP* está que mata

(**d**) (**Christmas**) **c.** = cilindro de papel que produce un pequeño estallido al abrirlo estirándolo por los extremos y contiene un regalito de Navidad

(**e**) *Comptr* cracker *mf*, pirata *mf* informático(a)

(**f**) *US Fam (poor white)* = término que se usa peyorativamente para referise a un blanco pobre en el Sur de Estados Unidos

cracker-barrel ['krækəbærəl] *adj US Fam (wisdom, philosophy)* simplón(ona)

crackerjack ['krækədʒæk] *US Fam* **1** *n (excellent person)* figura *mf*, fuera de serie *mf*; *(excellent thing)* cosa *f* genial *or* fuera de serie

2 *adj (excellent)* genial, fuera de serie

crackers ['krækəz] *adj Br Fam (mad)* **to be c.** estar como una cabra; **to go c.** volverse majareta, *RP* pirarse

crackhead ['krækhed] *n Fam* adicto(a) *m,f* al crack

crackhouse ['krækhaʊs] *n Fam* = lugar de reunión de adictos al crack

cracking ['krækɪŋ] **1** *adj Br Fam* (**a**) *(very good)* genial, fuera de serie (**b**) *(very fast)* rapidísimo(a); **at a c. pace** a toda mecha *or* pastilla, *Méx* hecho(a) la raya, *RP* a los piques

2 *n* (**a**) *Chem* craqueo *m* (**b**) *Comptr* pirateo *m*

crackle ['krækəl] **1** *n (of twigs, paper)* crujido *m*; *(of fire)* crepitación *f*; *(of radio)* ruido *m* de fondo, interferencias *fpl*; *(of gunfire)* chasquido *m*

2 *vi (twigs, paper)* crujir; *(fire)* crepitar; *(radio)* tener ruido de fondo *or* interferencias; *Fig* **to c. with energy** *(film, performance)* rebosar energía

crackling ['kræklɪŋ] *n* (**a**) *(on roast pork)* piel *f* tostada (**b**) *US* **cracklings** cortezas *fpl* de cerdo, *Am* chicharrones *mpl*

crackly ['kræklɪ] *adj* (**a**) *(paper)* crujiente (**b**) *(sound)* **it's a bit c.** *(radio)* hay interferencias; *(record)* tiene ruidos de fondo; **the phone line was a bit c.** había interferencias en la línea telefónica

crackpot ['krækpɒt] *Fam* **1** *n* pirado(a) *m,f*, *Esp* majareta *mf*, *Méx* zafado(a) *m,f*

2 *adj* descabellado(a)

crack-up ['krækʌp] *n Fam (of person)* hundimiento *m*, derrumbe *m*

Cracow ['krækaʊ] *n* Cracovia

cradle ['kreɪdəl] **1** *n* (**a**) *(for child, of civilization)* cuna *f*; **the c. of democracy/civilization** la cuna de la democracia/civilización; IDIOM **from the c. to the grave** de la cuna a la sepultura ►► ***c. cap*** = especie de costra que sale en la cabeza de un bebé, producida por una infección (**b**) *(for cleaning windows, painting)* andamio *m* colgante (**c**) *(for telephone receiver)* soporte *m*

2 *vt* acunar; **the village was cradled in a valley** el pueblo estaba situado en el seno de un valle

cradle-snatcher ['kreɪdəlsnætʃə(r)], *US* **cradle-robber** ['kreɪdəlrɒbə(r)] *n Fam Hum* asaltacunas *mf inv*, = persona que mantiene relaciones con otra persona muy joven

craft¹ [krɑːft] **1** *n* (**a**) *(trade)* oficio *m*; *(skill)* arte *m* ►► ***c. union*** sindicato *m* gremial (**b**) **crafts** *(handcrafts)* artesanía *f* ►► ***c. fair*** feria *f* de artesanía; ***c. knife*** cúter *m*, cuchilla *f*; ***c. studio*** taller *m* de artesanía (**c**) *(cunning)* artimañas *fpl*; **to obtain sth by c.** obtener algo por medio de artimañas

2 *vt (fashion)* elaborar; **crafted by hand** hecho(a) a mano; **a beautifully crafted film** una película bellamente elaborada *or* realizada

craft² (*pl* **craft**) *n (boat)* embarcación *f*; *(aircraft)* avión *m*, nave *f*; *(spacecraft)* nave *f* espacial

craftily ['krɑːftɪlɪ] *adv* muy ladinamente; **c. worded** muy hábilmente *or* astutamente expresado

craftiness ['krɑːftɪnɪs] *n* astucia *f*, maña *f*

craftsman ['krɑːftsmən] *n* artesano *m*

craftsmanship ['krɑːftsmənʃɪp] *n* (**a**) *(skill)* destreza *f*, maestría *f* (**b**) *(workmanship)* trabajo *m*

craftswoman ['krɑːftswʊmən] *n* artesana *f*

craftwork ['krɑːftwɜːk] *n* trabajos *mpl* manuales, manualidades *fpl*

crafty ['krɑːftɪ] *adj* astuto(a), mañoso(a); **you c. old devil!** ¡qué pillo eres!

crag [kræg] *n* peñasco *m*, risco *m*

craggy ['krægɪ] *adj (rocky)* escarpado(a); *(features)* marcado(a)

cram [kræm] (*pt & pp* **crammed**) **1** *vt (things)* embutir (**into** en); *(people)* apiñar (**into** en); **he crammed the clothes into the suitcase** llenó la maleta *or RP* valija de ropa hasta los topes; **there were ten of us crammed into a tiny office** éramos diez personas apiñadas en una oficina pequeñísima; **to be crammed with sth** estar repleto(a) de algo; **to c. food into one's mouth** llenarse la boca de comida; **they crammed as much sightseeing as possible into their three days** no pararon de ver monumentos y sitios en los tres días que tenían; **we crammed a lot into one day** hicimos un montón de cosas en un día

2 *vi* (**a**) *(squeeze)* **we all crammed into the taxi** nos apiñamos todos en el taxi (**b**) *Fam (study)* matarse estudiando, *Esp* empollar, *RP* tragar; **to c. for an exam** matarse estudiando *or Esp* empollar *or RP* tragar para un examen

cram-full [kræm'fʊl] *adj Fam* atestado(a), abarrotado(a)

crammer ['kræmə(r)] *n Br (school)* academia *f* de preparación intensiva

cramp [kræmp] **1** *n* (**a**) *(muscle pain)* calambre *m*; **to have c.** *or US* **a c.** tener calambres; **to have stomach c.,** *US* **to have cramps** tener retortijones (**b**) *(in carpentry)* abrazadera *f* (**c**) *Constr* **c.(-iron)** grapa *f*

2 *vt* (**a**) *(restrict)* limitar, coartar; IDIOM *Fam* **to c. sb's style** ser un estorbo para alguien, coartar a alguien (**b**) *(secure with a cramp)* grapar, poner una grapa a

cramped [kræmpt] *adj* (**a**) *(room)* estrecho(a); **to be c. for space** tener muy poco espacio; **they live in very c. conditions** vivir muy apretados (**b**) *(handwriting)* apretado(a)

crampon ['kræmpɒn] *n* crampón *m*

cranberry ['krænbərɪ] *n* arándano *m* agrio ►► ***c. juice*** *Esp* zumo *m or Am* jugo *m* de arándanos; ***c. sauce*** salsa *f* de arándanos

crane [kreɪn] **1** *n* (**a**) *(for lifting)* grúa *f* ►► *Cin* ***c. shot*** plano *m* desde la grúa (**b**) *(bird)* grulla *f*

2 *vt* **to c. one's neck** estirar el cuello

3 *vi* **to c. forward** inclinarse hacia delante (estirando el cuello)

cranefly ['kreɪnflaɪ] *n* típula *f*

crania *pl of* **cranium**

cranial ['kreɪnɪəl] *adj Anat* craneal ►► ***c. nerve*** nervio *m* craneal

cranium ['kreɪnɪəm] (*pl* **crania** ['kreɪnɪə]) *n Anat* cráneo *m*

crank¹ [kræŋk] *n (gear mechanism)* cigüeñal *m* ►► ***c. handle*** manivela *f*

► **crank out** *vt sep US Fam* **she cranks out a new novel every year** cada año saca su novela de rigor

► **crank up** *vt sep (engine)* poner en marcha con manivela; *(volume)* subir a tope; *Fam Fig* **to c. oneself up** ponerse las pilas, ponerse a funcionar

crank² *n Fam* (**a**) *(eccentric)* rarito(a) *m,f*, maniático(a) *m,f* (**b**) *US Fam (grumpy person)* cascarrabias *mf inv*, gruñón(ona) *m,f*

crankcase ['kræŋkkeɪs] *n* cárter *m*

crankiness ['kræŋkɪnɪs] *n Fam* (**a**) *(eccentricity)* rarezas *fpl* (**b**) *US (bad temper)* malas pulgas *fpl*

crankshaft ['kræŋkʃɑːft] *n Aut* cigüeñal *m*

cranky ['kræŋkɪ] *adj Fam* (**a**) *(eccentric)* rarito(a), maniático(a) (**b**) *US (grumpy)* cascarrabias, gruñón(ona)

cranny ['krænɪ] *n* rendija *f*

crap [kræp] *very Fam* **1** *n* (**a**) *(excrement)* mierda *f*; **to have** *or* **take a c.** cagar, *Esp* echar una cagada, *Col, RP* embarrarla, *Méx* chingarla

(**b**) *(dirt, disgusting substance)* porquería *f*, mierda *f*

(**c**) *(worthless things)* mierda *f*, porquerías *fpl*; **the movie/book was a load of c.** la película/el libro era una mierda; **clear all your c. off the bed** quita toda tu mierda *or* todas tus porquerías de la cama; **he eats nothing but c.** no come más que porquerías *or Esp* guarrerías

(**d**) *(nonsense) Esp* gilipolleces *fpl*, *Esp* paridas *fpl*, *Col, Méx* pendejadas *fpl*, *RP* pelotudeces *fpl*; **he's full of c.** no dice más que *Esp* gilipolleces *or Col, Méx* pendejadas *or RP* pelotudeces (**e**) *(unfair treatment, interference)* **I'm not taking that c. from you!** ¡a mí no me vengas con esas!; **I don't need this c.!** *(I'm sick of this)* ¡estoy hasta los huevos!

(**f**) *US (dice game)* sevenleven *m*, = juego de apuestas con dos dados; **c. game** partida de sevenleven

2 *adj Br* (**a**) *(of poor quality) Esp* fatal, *Esp* de puta pena, *Am* pésimo; **it's c.!** ¡es una mierda!; **he's a c. teacher** es una mierda de profesor

(**b**) *(unpleasant)* de pena, de mierda; **I had a c. time at my parents'** lo pasé *Esp* fatal *or Esp* de puta pena *or Am* pésimo en casa de mis padres; **that was a c. thing to say to her!** ¡fue una putada decirle eso!

(**c**) **to feel c.** *(ill)* estar hecho(a) una mierda, *Esp* sentirse fatal, *Méx* estar jodido(a), *RP* sentirse para la mierda; **I felt c. about having let them down** *(guilty)* me sentí fatal *or Méx* una mierda *or RP* para la mierda por haberles fallado

3 *vt* (*pt & pp* **crapped**) **he was crapping himself** *(scared)* estaba cagado (de miedo)

4 *vi (defecate)* cagar

▸ **crap out** *vi very Fam* cagarse, rajarse; **to c. out of sth** cagarse y no poder con algo; **to c. out of doing sth** cagarse y no hacer algo

crapper ['kræpə(r)] *n very Fam (toilet)* cagódromo *m*

crappy ['kræpɪ] *adj* = **crap**

craps [kræps] *n US (game)* sevenleven *m*, = juego de apuestas con dos dados; **to shoot c.** jugar al sevenleven

crapshoot ['kræpʃuːt] *n US Fam (risky venture)* jugada *f* dudosa

crapulous ['kræpjʊləs], **crapulent** ['kræpjʊlənt] *adj Formal* ebrio(a)

crash [kræʃ] 1 *n* (**a**) *(noise)* estruendo *m*; **a c. of thunder** un trueno; **there was a loud c. from the kitchen** se oyó un estruendo que venía de la cocina; **with a c.** con gran estrépito

(**b**) *(accident)* choque *m*, colisión *f*; **car/train/plane c.** accidente de coche/tren/avión; **to have a c.** tener un accidente; **to be (involved) in a c.** *(person)* verse involucrado(a) en un accidente ▸▸ *Aut* ***c. barrier*** quitamiedos *m inv*; ***c. dive*** *(of plane)* caída *f* en *Esp* picado *or Am* picada; *(of submarine)* inmersión *f* a toda máquina; ***c. helmet*** casco *m* (protector)

(**c**) *(financial)* quiebra *f* (financiera), crack *m*

(**d**) *Comptr* bloqueo *m*

2 *adj* ***c. course*** curso *m* intensivo; ***c. diet*** dieta *f* drástica

3 *adv* **he ran c. into a wall** se estrelló contra un muro; **something went c. in the attic** algo se cayó con gran estrépito en el desván

4 *exclam* ¡pum!, ¡zas!

5 *vt* (**a**) *(plane)* estrellar; **she crashed the car** se estrelló con el coche *or Am* carro *or CSur* auto; **to c. a car into a wall/tree** estrellar un coche *or Am* carro *or CSur* auto contra una pared/un árbol (**b**) *(bang together)* **he crashed the cymbals together** entrechocó los platillos (**c**) *Fam* **to c. a party** colarse en una fiesta

6 *vi* (**a**) *(make noise) (waves)* romper; *(cymbals, thunder)* sonar; **the bookcase crashed to the ground** la estantería cayó con estruendo

(**b**) *(car, train)* chocar, estrellarse (**into** contra); *(plane)* estrellarse (**into** contra); **to c. into sth/sb** *(person)* chocar *or* estrellarse contra algo/alguien

(**c**) *(fall)* **the tree came crashing down** el árbol se vino abajo

(**d**) *(business, economy, stock market)* quebrar; **share prices crashed** el precio de las acciones cayó estrepitosamente

(**e**) *Comptr* bloquearse, colgarse

(**f**) *Fam (sleep)* dormir, *Esp* sobar; **can I c. at your place?** ¿puedo quedarme a dormir *or Esp* sobar *or RP* roncar en tu casa? ▸▸ ***c. pad:*** **he lets me use his place as a c. pad** me deja dormir *or Esp* sobar en su casa

▸ **crash out** *vi Fam (go to sleep)* quedarse frito(a) *or Esp* sopa; **he had crashed out on the sofa** se quedó frito *or Esp* sopa en el sofá

crash-dive ['kræʃdaɪv] *vi (submarine)* realizar una inmersión de emergencia

crashing ['kræʃɪŋ] *adj* **a c. bore** un tostón

crash-land ['kræʃ'lænd] 1 *vi (aircraft, pilot)* realizar un aterrizaje forzoso

2 *vt (aircraft)* hacer aterrizar en una emergencia

crash-landing ['kræʃ'lændɪŋ] *n* aterrizaje *m* forzoso *or* de emergencia

crass [kræs] *adj (person, remark)* zafio(a); **c. ignorance/stupidity** ignorancia/estupidez supina

crate [kreɪt] 1 *n* (**a**) *(box)* cajón *m*; *(for bottles)* caja *f* (**b**) *Fam (aircraft)* cafetera *f*; *(car)* cacharro *m*, cafetera *f*

2 *vt (goods)* poner en cajones, embalar

crater ['kreɪtə(r)] *n* cráter *m*

cratered ['kreɪtəd] *adj* lleno(a) de cráteres

cravat [krə'væt] *n* pañuelo *m*, fular *m*

crave [kreɪv] 1 *vt* (**a**) *(affection, tobacco)* ansiar (**b**) *Formal (beg)* suplicar, implorar; **to c. sb's pardon** suplicar *or* implorar el perdón de alguien

2 *vi* **to c. for** *(affection, tobacco)* ansiar

craven ['kreɪvən] *adj Literary* cobarde

craving ['kreɪvɪŋ] *n (in general)* ansia *f* (**for** de); *(of pregnant woman)* antojo *m*; **to have a c. for sth** *(in general)* desear vehementemente algo, ansiar algo; **I used to have cravings for anchovies** *(of pregnant woman)* me entraban antojos de comer anchoas

craw [krɔː] *n Fam* **having to apologize stuck in my c.** se me hizo muy cuesta arriba tener que disculparme; **his arrogant attitude really sticks in my c.** no puedo tragar su arrogancia

crawfish *US* = **crayfish**

crawl [krɔːl] 1 *n* (**a**) *(slow pace)* paso *m* lento; **the traffic was moving at a c.** el tráfico avanzaba lentamente; **to slow to a c.** *(traffic, pace)* casi paralizarse (**b**) *(swimming stroke)* (estilo *m*) crol *m*; **to do** *or* **swim the c.** nadar a crol (**c**) ***c. space*** *(under suspended floor)* = espacio entre las plantas de un edificio que permite el acceso a las cañerías e instalación eléctrica

2 *vi* (**a**) *(person)* arrastrarse; *(baby)* gatear; **he crawled into bed** se fue arrastrando hasta meterse en la cama

(**b**) *(move slowly) (car, traffic)* avanzar lentamente; *(insect)* trepar

(**c**) *Fam (be infested)* **the house was crawling with cockroaches** la casa estaba infestada de cucarachas; **the streets were crawling with police** las calles estaban plagadas de policía

(**d**) *(come out in goose pimples)* **it makes my skin** *or* **flesh c.** me pone la carne de gallina

(**e**) *Fam (be obsequious)* **to c. to sb** arrastrarse ante alguien; **he'll come crawling back** ya volverá arrastrándose

crawler ['krɔːlə(r)] *n* (**a**) *Fam (obsequious person)* adulador(ora) *m,f*, *Esp* pelota *mf*, *Am* arrastrado(a) *m,f*, *Méx* lambiscón(ona) *m,f*, *RP* chupamedias *mf inv* (**b**) *Br* ***c. lane*** carril *m* (adicional) para tráfico lento (**c**) *Comptr* rastreador *m*

crayfish ['kreɪfɪʃ], *US* **crawfish** ['krɔːfɪʃ] *n* (**a**) *(freshwater)* cangrejo *m* de río (**b**) *(saltwater)* langosta *f*

crayon ['kreɪɒn] 1 *n (wax)* (barra *f* de) cera *f*; *(pastel)* (barra *f* de) pastel *m*; *(pencil)* lápiz *m* de color

2 *vt* pintar con ceras

3 *vi* pintar con ceras

craze [kreɪz] 1 *n* locura *f*, moda *f* (**for** de); **it's becoming a c.** se está poniendo de moda

2 *vt (send mad)* volver loco(a)

crazed [kreɪzd] *adj* (**a**) *(mad)* demente, delirante; **c. with fear** muerto(a) de miedo; **c. with grief** loco(a) de dolor (**b**) *(ceramics)* agrietado

crazily ['kreɪzɪlɪ] *adv* (**a**) *(to behave)* alocadamente (**b**) *(crookedly)* empinadamente

craziness ['kreɪzɪnɪs] *n* locura *f*

crazy ['kreɪzɪ] 1 *adj* (**a**) *(mad)* loco(a); **to be c.** estar loco(a); **to go c.** volverse loco(a); **to drive** *or* **send sb c.** volver loco(a) a alguien; **like c.** *(to run, work)* como un loco; **this is c.!** ¡esto es una locura! ▸▸ *US* ***c. bone*** hueso *m* de la risa; ***c. golf*** minigolf *m*; *US* ***c. quilt*** colcha *f* de patchwork

(**b**) *Fam (very keen)* **she's c. about motorbikes** las motos la vuelven loca; **to be c. about sb** estar loco(a) por alguien; **I'm not c. about the idea** la idea no me entusiasma

(**c**) *(crooked)* **at a c. angle** formando un ángulo grotesco ▸▸ *Br* ***c. paving*** pavimento *m* de formas irregulares

2 *n US (person)* loco(a) *m,f*

CRE [siːɑːr'iː] *n* (*abbr* **Commission for Racial Equality**) = órgano oficial británico contra el racismo

creak [kriːk] 1 *n (of hinge)* chirrido *m*; *(of timber, shoes)* crujido *m*, rechinar *m*; *(of person's joints)* chirrido *m*, crujido *m*

2 *vi* (**a**) *(make noise) (hinge)* chirriar, rechinar; *(timber, shoes, person's joints)* crujir (**b**) *(plot, dialogue)* chirriar, flaquear

creaky ['kriːkɪ] *adj* (**a**) *(chair, floorboard, person's joints)* que cruje; *(door hinge)* que chirría, chirriante (**b**) *(unconvincing)* **the dialogue is a bit c.** los diálogos chirrían un poco

cream [kriːm] 1 *n* (**a**) *(of milk) Esp* nata *f*, *Am* crema *f* (de leche); **c. of tomato/chicken (soup)** crema de tomate *or Méx* jitomate/pollo ▸▸ ***c. bun*** pastel *m* de *Esp* nata *or Am* crema; ***c. cake*** pastel *m* de *Esp* nata *or Am* crema; ***c. cheese*** queso *m* blanco para untar; *Br* ***c. cracker*** galleta *f* salada, cracker *f*; ***c. puff*** *(pastry)* pastel *m* de *Esp* nata *or Am* crema; *Fam (weakling)* enclenque *m,f*; ***c. soda*** refresco *m or* gaseosa *f* de vainilla; *Br* ***c. tea*** = merienda a base de té, bollos con *Esp* nata *or Am* crema y mermelada

(**b**) *Fig* **the c.** *(best part)* la flor y nata

(**c**) *(filling for cookies, chocolates)* crema *f*
(**d**) *(lotion)* crema *f*; **face/hand c.** crema facial/de manos
(**e**) *(colour)* (color *m*) crema *m*
(**f**) ***c. of tartar*** crémor *m* tártaro
2 *adj* **c.(-coloured)** (color) crema ►► ***c.-coloured courser*** corredor *m* sahariano
3 *vt* (**a**) *(skim)* quitar la *Esp* nata *orAm* crema a (**b**) *Culin (beat)* batir ►► ***creamed coconut*** crema *f* de coco; ***creamed potatoes*** puré *m* de patatas; ***creamed rice*** arroz *m* con leche (**c**) *Fam (defeat)* hacer tortilla *or* papilla; *US (beat up)* hacer papilla *or* puré (**d**) *Vulg* **to c. one's jeans** correrse
4 *vi Vulg* (**a**) *(become sexually aroused) (woman)* ponerse caliente (**b**) *(ejaculate)* correrse

►**cream off** *vt sep* seleccionar, quedarse con; **to c. off the best students** seleccionar a *or* quedarse con los mejores estudiantes

creamer ['kri:mə(r)] *n* (**a**) *(milk substitute)* leche *f* en polvo (**b**) *US (jug)* jarrita *f* para la *Esp* nata *orAm* crema (**c**) *(machine)* desnatadora *f*

creamery ['kri:mərɪ] *n* (**a**) *(shop)* lechería *f* (**b**) *(factory)* central *f* lechera, fábrica *f* de productos lácteos

creaminess ['kri:mɪnɪs] *n (in taste, texture)* cremosidad *f*

creamy ['kri:mɪ] *adj* (**a**) *(containing cream)* con *Esp* nata *orAm* crema (**b**) *(in texture) (liquid)* cremoso(a); *(skin)* de porcelana (**c**) *(in colour)* **c. white** crema

crease [kri:s] **1** *n* (**a**) *(in skin, paper, crumpled fabric)* arruga *f*; *(in ironed trousers)* raya *f*; **to put a c. in a pair of trousers** hacerle la raya a unos pantalones (**b**) *(in cricket)* = línea que delimita la posición del bateador o del lanzador
2 *vt* (**a**) *(clothes)* arrugar (**b**) *(furrow)* **to c. one's brow** fruncir el ceño; **the bullet creased his scalp** la bala le rozó el cuero cabelludo
3 *vi (become creased)* arrugarse

►**crease up** *Br Fam* **1** *vt sep* **to c. sb up** *(make laugh)* hacer que alguien se parta *or RP* se descostille *or Méx* se ataque de risa
2 *vi (laugh)* partirse *or RP* descostillarse *or Méx* atacarse de risa

create [krɪ'eɪt] **1** *vt* (**a**) *(bring into being)* crear (**b**) *(cause) (employment, problems)* crear; **to c. a sensation** causar sensación (**c**) *(appoint)* **he was created (a) baron** le nombraron barón
2 *vi Br Fam (get angry, cause fuss)* ponerse hecho(a) una furia

creation [krɪ'eɪʃən] *n* (**a**) *(process)* creación *f*; *Rel* **the C.** la creación; *Fam* **where in c. did you get that hat!** ¡de dónde demonios sacaste ese sombrero! (**b**) *(something created)* creación *f*; **the latest creations** *(fashions)* las últimas creaciones

creationism [krɪ'eɪʃənɪzəm] *n* creacionismo *m*

creationist [krɪ'eɪʃənɪst] *n* creacionista *mf*

creative [krɪ'eɪtɪv] *adj* creativo(a); **the c. process** el proceso creativo; **we need some c. thinking** necesitamos pensar creativamente ►► *Fin* ***c. accounting*** maquillaje *m* de cuentas, artificios *mpl* contables; ***c. writing*** creación *f* literaria

creatively [kri:'eɪtɪvlɪ] *adv* creativamente, de forma creativa

creativity [krɪə'tɪvɪtɪ] *n* creatividad *f*

creator [krɪ'eɪtə(r)] *n* creador(ora) *m,f*; *Rel* **the C.** el Creador

creature ['kri:tʃə(r)] *n* (**a**) *(living being, animal)* criatura *f*; **we are all God's creatures** todos somos criaturas del Señor; **creatures from outer space** criaturas del espacio exterior ►► ***c. comforts*** (pequeños) placeres *mpl* de la vida
(**b**) *(person)* criatura *f*; **poor creature!** ¡pobrecito!; **he's a c. of habit** es un animal de costumbres
(**c**) *Pej (instrument)* **the chairman is a c. of the government** el presidente es un títere del Gobierno

crèche [kreʃ] *n* (**a**) *Br (nursery)* guardería *f* (infantil); **will there be a c. at the conference?** ¿habrá servicio de guardería en el congreso? (**b**) *US (Nativity scene)* belén *m*, pesebre *m* (**c**) *US (orphanage)* orfanato *m*

cred [kred] *n Br Fam* **he lost his (street) c.** ya no lo tienen por un tipo legal

credence ['kri:dəns] *n* **to give** *or* **lend c. to sth** dar crédito a algo

credentials [krɪ'denʃəlz] *npl* (**a**) *(references, proof of ability)* referencias *fpl*; **he quickly established his c.** pronto demostró su valía (**b**) *(of ambassador)* credenciales *fpl*

credibility [kredɪ'bɪlɪtɪ] *n* credibilidad *f*; **the party has lost c. with the electorate** el partido ha perdido credibilidad con los votantes ►► ***c. gap*** vacío *m or* falta *f* de credibilidad

credible ['kredɪbəl] *adj* creíble; **a c. alternative** una alternativa creíble

credibly ['kredəblɪ] *adv* de forma creíble

credit ['kredɪt] **1** *n* (**a**) *(with bank)* crédito *m*; **to be in c.** *(person, account)* tener saldo positivo; **to give sb c.** *(of bank)* conceder un crédito a alguien; **he has £50 to his c.** tiene un saldo de 50 libras; **on the c. side** *(in accounts)* en el haber; *Fig* **on the credit side, the changes will cut costs** en el lado positivo, los cambios recortarán costos; *Fig* **on the c. side, he's a good cook** tiene en su haber ser un buen cocinero ►► ***c. account*** cuenta *f* abierta *or* a crédito; ***c. balance*** saldo *m* acreedor; ***c. broker*** intermediario(a) *m,f* financiero(a); ***c. card*** tarjeta *f* de crédito; *Econ* ***c. control*** control *m* crediticio *or* de crédito; ***c. limit*** límite *m* de descubierto *or* de crédito; *US* ***c. line*** línea *f* de crédito, descubierto *m* permitido; ***c. rating*** clasificación *f or* grado *m* de solvencia; *Econ* ***c. squeeze*** restricción *f* de crédito; ***c. transfer*** transferencia *f* bancaria; ***c. union*** cooperativa *f* de crédito
(**b**) *(in shop)* **to buy/sell on c.** comprar/vender a crédito; **to give sb c.** fiar a alguien ►► ***c. note*** vale *m* de compra; ***c. sale*** venta *f* a crédito
(**c**) *(belief)* crédito *m*; **to give c. to sth** dar crédito a algo; **to gain c.** *(of theory)* ganar aceptación
(**d**) *(recognition, honour)* reconocimiento *m*; **you'll have to give her c. for that** se lo tendrás que reconocer; **you're smarter than I gave you c. for** eres más lista de lo que yo creía; **to take the c. for sth** apuntarse el mérito de algo; **to her c., she refused** se negó, lo cual dice mucho en su favor; **she has five novels to her c.** tiene cinco novelas a sus espaldas; **it does you c.** puedes estar orgulloso de ello; **you're a c. to the school** eres motivo de orgullo para la escuela; **all c. to them** se merecen todo el reconocimiento; IDIOM **c. where c.'s due, Joe did most of the work** en justicia, hay que reconocer que Joe hizo la mayor parte del trabajo
(**e**) *(of movie)* **credits** títulos *mpl* de crédito
(**f**) *Sch & Univ (in modular course)* crédito *m*
(**g**) *Sch & Univ* **(pass with) c.** notable *m*
2 *vt* (**a**) *(money)* abonar; **to c. an account with $200, to c. $200 to an account** abonar 200 dólares en una cuenta
(**b**) *(attribute)* **to c. sb with sth** atribuir algo a alguien; **I credited you with more sense** te consideraba más sensato; **c. me with a bit more intelligence!** ¡deja de tomarme por tonto!; **she's credited with being the first woman to sail round the world** a ella se le atribuye el mérito de ser la primera mujer en dar la vuelta al mundo en velero
(**c**) *(believe)* creer; **would you c. it?** ¿te lo quieres creer?

creditable ['kredɪtəbəl] *adj* encomiable, digno(a) de encomio

creditably ['kredɪtəblɪ] *adv* encomiablemente; **we managed to come out of it quite c.** conseguimos salir con la cabeza alta

creditor ['kredɪtə(r)] *n Fin* acreedor(ora) *m,f*

creditworthy ['kredɪtwɜ:ðɪ] *adj* solvente

credo ['kri:dəʊ] (*pl* **credos**) *n* (**a**) *Rel* credo *m* (**b**) *Fig* credo *m*

credulity [krɪ'dju:lɪtɪ] *n* credulidad *f*

credulous ['kredjʊləs] *adj* crédulo(a)

creed [kri:d] *n* (**a**) *Rel* credo *m* (**b**) *(set of beliefs)* credo *m*; **people of every colour and c.** gente de todas las razas y credos

creek [kri:k] *n* (**a**) *Br (small bay)* cala *f* (**b**) *US, Austr (stream)* riachuelo *m* (**c**) IDIOM *Fam* **to be up the c. (without a paddle)** tenerlo claro, *Esp* ir de culo

creel [kri:l] *n* nasa *f*

creep [kri:p] **1** *n Fam* (**a**) *(unpleasant person)* asqueroso(a) *m,f*
(**b**) *Br (obsequious person) Esp* pelota *mf*, *Am* arrastrado(a) *m,f*, *Méx* lambiscón(ona) *m,f*, *RP* chupamedias *mf inv*
(**c**) IDIOMS **he/it gives me the creeps** *(makes me uneasy)* me pone la piel de gallina; *(disgusts me)* me da asco; **I always get the creeps when I'm alone in the house** *(get frightened)* siempre me da escalofríos quedarme solo en casa, siempre que me quedo solo en casa me entra el *Esp* canguelo *orArg* cuiqui *or Col* culillo *or Méx* mello
2 *vi* (*pt & pp* **crept** [krept]) (**a**) *(move stealthily) (animal, person)* moverse sigilosamente, deslizarse; **to c. in** colarse; **to c. out** escapar (sigilosamente)
(**b**) *(move slowly)* **the minutes c. by** los minutos transcurrían lentamente; **inflation continues to c. towards 10 percent** la inflación se sigue acercando al 10 por ciento
(**c**) *(appear gradually, unnoticed)* aparecer *or* surgir poco a poco; **a mistake has crept into our calculations** se nos ha colado un error en los cálculos
(**d**) IDIOM *Fam* **it makes my flesh c.** me pone la carne de gallina
(**e**) *(plants)* trepar

►**creep up** *vi* (**a**) *(approach stealthily)* acercarse con sigilo; **she crept up behind me** se me acercó por detrás sin que me diese cuenta (**b**) *(inflation, prices)* aumentar progresivamente *or* gradualmente

►**creep up on** *vt insep* (**a**) *(in order to attack, surprise)* **they crept up on him from behind** se acercaron a él por detrás sigilosamente; **old age has crept up on me** los años se me han echado encima (**b**) *(catch up with)* alcanzar gradualmente; **the deadline is creeping up on us** la fecha límite se nos está echando encima

creeper ['kri:pə(r)] *n (plant)* enredadera *f*; *(in wild)* liana *f*

creeping ['kri:pɪŋ] *adj* (**a**) *(gradual)* paulatino(a); **c. privatization** privatización gradual subrepticia (**b**) ***c. stalk*** *(of plant)* tallo *m* rastrero (**c**) *Fam (obsequious)* adulador(ora); **a c. Jesus** un chupacirios

creepy ['kri:pɪ] *adj Fam* (**a**) *(unpleasant)* repugnante, repelente (**b**) *(frightening)* espeluznante

creepy-crawly ['kri:pɪ'krɔ:lɪ] *n Fam* bicho *m*, bicharraco *m*

cremate [krɪ'meɪt] *vt* incinerar

cremation [krɪ'meɪʃən] *n* incineración *f*, cremación *f*

crematorium [kremə'tɔ:rɪəm] (*pl* **crematoria** [kremə'tɔ:rɪə]) *n* (**a**) *(oven)* (horno *m*) crematorio *m* (**b**) *(establishment)* crematorio *m*

crematory ['kremətrɪ] *n US* crematorio *m*

crème [krem] *n* ***c. brulée*** = natillas cubiertas con una capa de azúcar quemado, ≃ crema *f* catalana; ***c. caramel*** flan *m*; IDIOM ***the c. de la c.*** *(the best)* la flor y nata; ***c. fraîche*** *Esp* nata *f or Am* crema *f* fresca fermentada; ***c. de menthe*** pipermín *m*, licor *m* de menta

crenellated, *US* **crenelated** ['krenəleɪtɪd] *adj* almenado(a)

crenellation, *US* **crenelation** [krenə'leɪʃən] *n* almenaje *m*, almenas *fpl*

creole ['kri:əʊl] **1** *n* (**a**) *(person)* criollo(a) *m,f* (**b**) *Ling* criollo *m*
 2 *adj* criollo(a)

creosote ['krɪəsəʊt] **1** *n* creosota *f*
 2 *vt* creosotar

crêpe [kreɪp] *n* (**a**) *(textile)* crepé *m*, crespón *m*, crêpe *m* ▸▸ ***c. bandage*** venda *f*; ***c. de Chine*** crepé *m or* crespón *m or* crêpe *m* de la China (**b**) **c. (rubber)** goma *f*, crepé *m* ▸▸ ***c.(-rubber) soles*** zapatos *mpl* de suela de goma *or* de crepé (**c**) **c. (paper)** papel *m* crespón *or* pinocho (**d**) [krep] *(pancake)* crepe *f*, crêpe *f*

crept *pt & pp of* **creep**

crepuscular [krɪ'pʌskjʊlə(r)] *adj Literary* crepuscular

Cres (*abbr* **Crescent**) = calle en forma de medialuna

crescendo [krɪ'ʃendəʊ] (*pl* **crescendos**) *n* (**a**) *Mus* crescendo *m*; **to rise to a c.** alcanzar el punto culminante (**b**) *Fig* crescendo *m*; **to rise to a c.** *(complaints)* alcanzar el punto culminante

crescent ['kresənt] **1** *n* (**a**) *(shape)* medialuna *f* (**b**) *(street)* = calle en forma de medialuna
 2 *adj* **c.(-shaped)** en forma de medialuna ▸▸ ***c. moon*** cuarto *m* creciente; *(when waning)* luna *f* menguante; *(when waxing)* luna *f* creciente

cress [kres] *n* berro *m*

crest [krest] **1** *n* (**a**) *(of bird)* cresta *f*; *(of helmet)* penacho *m* (**b**) *(of wave)* cresta *f*; IDIOM **on the c. of a wave** en la cresta de la ola (**c**) *(of hill)* cima *f* (**d**) *(coat of arms)* escudo *m*
 2 *vt (hill, rise)* coronar, llegar a la cumbre de

crested ['krestɪd] *adj* (**a**) *(animal, bird)* con cresta ▸▸ ***c. lark*** cogujada *f*; ***c. tit*** herrerillo *m* capuchino (**b**) *(notepaper)* con membrete

crestfallen ['krestfɔ:lən] *adj* abatido(a)

Cretaceous [krɪ'teɪʃəs] *Geol* **1** *n* **the C.** el cretácico *or* cretáceo
 2 *adj (period)* cretácico(a), cretáceo(a)

Cretan ['kri:tən] **1** *n* cretense *mf*
 2 *adj* cretense

Crete [kri:t] *n* Creta

cretin ['kretɪn] *n* (**a**) *Fam Pej (idiot)* cretino(a) *m,f* (**b**) *Med* cretino(a) *m,f*, enfermo(a) *m,f* de cretinismo

cretinism ['kretɪnɪzəm] *n Med* cretinismo *m*

cretinous ['kretɪnəs] *adj* estúpido(a), cretino(a)

cretonne ['kretɒn] *n* cretona *f*

Creutzfeldt-Jakob disease ['krɔɪtsfelt'ja:kɒbdɪ'zi:z] *n* enfermedad *f* de Creutzfeld(t)-Jakob

crevasse [krə'væs] *n* (**a**) *(in glacier)* grieta *f* (**b**) *US (in riverbank)* quiebra *f*

crevice ['krevɪs] *n* grieta *f*

crew[1] [kru:] **1** *n* (**a**) *(of ship, plane)* tripulación *f*; *(of tank)* dotación *f*, personal *m*; *(of ambulance)* personal *m* ▸▸ ***c. cut*** rapado *m*; ***c. neck*** cuello *m* redondo (**b**) *(team of workers)* equipo *m* (**c**) *Cin* equipo *m* (de rodaje) (**d**) *Fam (gang, group)* pandilla *f*, *Méx* bola *f*, *RP* barra *f*
 2 *vt (ship, plane)* tripular
 3 *vi (sailor)* **to c. for sb** formar parte de la tripulación de alguien

crew[2] *pt of* **crow**

crib [krɪb] **1** *n* (**a**) *US (cradle)* cuna *f* ▸▸ ***c. death*** (síndrome *m* de la) muerte *f* súbita infantil (**b**) *(Nativity scene)* belén *m*, pesebre *m* (**c**) *(for cattle) (stall)* establo *m*, cuadra *f*; *(manger)* pesebre *m* (**d**) *Fam (at school) (translation)* traducción *f (que permite entender el original)*; *(in exam) Esp, Ven* chuleta *f*, *Arg* machete *m*, *Chile* torpedo *m*, *Col, Méx* acordeón *m*, *Perú* comprimido *m*, *Urug* trencito *m*
 2 *vt* (*pt & pp* **cribbed**) *Fam (at school)* copiar (**from** *or* **off** de); **the scene was cribbed from Rabelais** la escena era un plagio de Rabelais
 3 *vi Fam* copiar (**from** *or* **off** de)

cribbage ['krɪbɪdʒ] *n* = juego de naipes en el que los puntos se van anotando con clavijas en un tablero

crick [krɪk] **1** *n (in neck)* **to have/get a c. in one's neck** tener tortícolis
 2 *vt* **to c. one's neck** hacerse daño en el cuello

cricket[1] ['krɪkɪt] *n (insect)* grillo *m*

cricket[2] *n (sport)* críquet *m*; IDIOM *Br* **that's not c.!** ¡eso es juego sucio! ▸▸ ***c. ball*** pelota *f* de críquet; ***c. bat*** bate *m* de críquet; ***c. pitch*** campo *m* de críquet

cricketer ['krɪkɪtə(r)] *n* jugador(ora) *m,f* de críquet

cricketing ['krɪkɪtɪŋ] *adj* **the c. nations of the world** los países del mundo en los que se juega al críquet

crikey ['kraɪkɪ] *exclam Fam Old-fashioned* ¡caramba!

crime [kraɪm] *n* (**a**) *(act) (serious)* crimen *m*; *(less serious)* delito *m*; **a c. against humanity** un crimen contra la humanidad; **a c. of passion** un crimen pasional; **to commit a c.** cometer un delito, delinquir; *Fig* **it's a c.** *(outrageous)* es un crimen; *Fig* **it's not a c. to...** no es ningún crimen...
 (**b**) *(illegality)* delincuencia *f*; **c. is on the increase** está aumentando la delincuencia; PROV **c. doesn't pay** delinquir no vale la pena ▸▸ ***c. prevention*** prevención *f* de la delincuencia; ***c. wave*** ola *f* de delincuencia; ***c. writer*** escritor(ora) *m,f* de novela negra

Crimea [kraɪ'mɪə] *n* Crimea

Crimean [kraɪ'mɪən] *adj* de Crimea; *Hist* **the C. War** la guerra de Crimea

criminal ['krɪmɪnəl] **1** *n (in general)* delincuente *mf*; *(serious)* criminal *mf*
 2 *adj* (**a**) *(illegal)* delictivo(a), criminal ▸▸ ***c. liability*** responsabilidad *f* penal; ***c. negligence*** negligencia *f* criminal; ***c. offence*** delito *m* (penal)
 (**b**) *(relating to crime)* criminal; **a c. investigation** una investigación criminal; **to instigate c. proceedings against sb** demandar a alguien ante un juzgado de lo penal ▸▸ ***c. court*** juzgado *m* de lo penal; ***C. Investigation Department*** = policía judicial británica; ***c. law*** derecho *m* penal; ***c. lawyer*** abogado(a) *m,f* criminalista, penalista *mf*; ***c. record*** antecedentes *mpl* penales
 (**c**) *Fam (outrageous)* escandaloso(a); **a c. waste of money** un despilfarro disparatado; **it's c. what they've done to the rainforest** es un crimen lo que han hecho con las selvas tropicales

criminality [krɪmɪ'nælɪtɪ] *n (in general)* delincuencia *f*; *(serious)* criminalidad *f*

criminalization [krɪmɪnəlaɪ'zeɪʃən] *n* penalización *f*

criminalize ['krɪmɪnəlaɪz] *vt* penalizar

criminally ['krɪmɪnəlɪ] *adv* (**a**) *(for legal purposes)* a efectos penales, penalmente; **the c. insane** los (delincuentes) psicópatas; **he was c. negligent** cometió un delito de negligencia (**b**) *(outrageously)* escandalosamente

criminologist [krɪmɪ'nɒlədʒɪst] *n* criminólogo(a) *m,f*

criminology [krɪmɪ'nɒlədʒɪ] *n* criminología *f*

crimp [krɪmp] **1** *vt* (**a**) *(for decoration) (hair)* rizar (con tenacillas); *(cloth)* plisar; *(pie crust)* hacer un reborde a (**b**) *(to seal)* sellar *(mediante presión)* (**c**) *US Fam (hinder)* obstaculizar
 2 *n* (**a**) *(wave in hair)* rizo *m*, bucle *m*; *(in cloth)* pliegue *m* (**b**) *US Fam (obstacle)* estorbo *m*; **to put a c. into sth** obstaculizar algo

crimpers ['krɪmpəz], **crimping irons** ['krɪmpɪŋaɪənz] *npl* planchas *fpl* de pelo

Crimplene® ['krɪmpli:n] *n* = tejido de poliéster antiarrugas

crimson ['krɪmzən] **1** *n* carmesí *m*; **to turn c.** ponerse colorado(a), sonrojarse
 2 *adj* carmesí
 3 *vi (face)* ponerse colorado(a), sonrojarse; *(sky)* ponerse rojo, teñirse de rojo

cringe [krɪndʒ] *vi* (**a**) *(show fear)* encogerse; **to c. in terror** encogerse de terror *or* aterrorizado(a) (**b**) *(be embarrassed)* tener vergüenza ajena, abochornarse; **it makes me c.** me produce vergüenza ajena; **I c. at the very thought** me sonrojo sólo de pensarlo (**c**) *(be servile)* rebajarse (**before/to** ante)

cringe-making ['krɪndʒmeɪkɪŋ] *adj Br Hum* que da vergüenza ajena

cringing ['krɪndʒɪŋ] *adj* (**a**) *(afraid)* atemorizado(a) (**b**) *(servile)* servil

crinkle ['krɪŋkəl] 1 vt (paper) arrugar; to c. one's nose arrugar la nariz
2 vi arrugarse; his nose crinkled at the smell se le arrugó la nariz del olor
3 n (a) (wrinkle) arruga f (b) (noise) crujido m

crinkle-cut ['krɪŋkəlkʌt] adj (chips, crisps) ondulado(a)

crinkly ['krɪŋklɪ] adj (paper) arrugado(a); (hair) rizado(a), crespo(a)

crinoline ['krɪnəlɪn] n crinolina f

cripes [kraɪps] exclam Br Fam Old-fashioned ¡caramba!, ¡cáspita!

cripple ['krɪpəl] 1 n inválido(a) m,f; an emotional c. un inválido emocional
2 vt (a) (person) dejar inválido(a), lisiar (b) (industry, system) deteriorar, arruinar; (ship, plane, tank) inutilizar

crippled ['krɪpəld] adj (a) (person) lisiado(a); to be c. with rheumatism estar incapacitado(a) por el reumatismo (b) (industry, system) deteriorado(a), arruinado(a); (plane, ship, tank) inutilizado(a); the country is c. with debt el país está asfixiado por la deuda

crippling ['krɪplɪŋ] adj (a) (illness) incapacitante (b) (taxes, strike) pernicioso(a); (debt) asfixiante

crisis ['kraɪsɪs] (pl crises ['kraɪsi:z]) n crisis f inv; an energy c. una crisis energética; in c. en crisis; to go through a c. atravesar una crisis; to settle or to resolve a c. resolver una crisis; to have a c. of confidence pasar una etapa de inseguridad, tener una crisis de confianza; the situation has reached c. point la situación ha llegado a un punto crítico ►► c. management gestión f de crisis

crisp [krɪsp] 1 n Br crisps Esp patatas fpl or Am papas fpl fritas (de bolsa); burnt to a c. achicharrado(a)
2 adj (a) (crunchy) (apple, lettuce) fresco(a); (pastry, bacon) crujiente, RP crocante; (snow) crujiente (b) (fresh, neat) (clothing, linen) fresco(a); (image, outline) nítido(a); a c. five pound note un billete de cinco libras nuevecito (c) (air, breeze) fresco(a) (d) (concise) (style) conciso(a) (e) (brisk) (tone, manner) seco(a)
3 vt tostar
4 vi tostarse

crispbread ['krɪspbred] n = galleta crujiente de trigo o centeno empleada como sustituto adelgazante del pan

crisply ['krɪsplɪ] adv (to say) secamente

crispness ['krɪspnɪs] n (a) (of apple, lettuce) frescor m, frescura f; (of pastry, bacon) lo crujiente, RP lo crocante; (of snow) lo crujiente (b) (of clothing, linen) frescor m, frescura f; (of image, outline) nitidez f (c) (of air, breeze) frescor m, frescura f (d) (of style) concisión f (e) (of tone, manner) sequedad f

crispy ['krɪspɪ] adj (bacon, batter) crujiente, RP crocante

criss-cross ['krɪskrɒs] 1 vt entrecruzar
2 vi entrecruzarse
3 adj entrecruzado(a); in a c. pattern con un diseño entrecruzado
4 adv the poles lay c. on the floor los postes estaban entrecruzados en el suelo

crit [krɪt] n Fam (review) crítica f

criterion [kraɪ'tɪərɪən] (pl criteria [kraɪ'tɪərɪə]) n criterio m ►► Educ c. referencing evaluación f por criterios

criterium [kraɪ'tɪərɪəm] n Sport criterium m

critic ['krɪtɪk] n (a) (reviewer) crítico(a) m,f; movie/art/theatre c. crítico cinematográfico/de arte/teatral (b) (fault-finder) criticón(ona) m,f; she has her critics tiene sus detractores

critical ['krɪtɪkəl] adj (a) (negative) crítico(a); to be c. of criticar; don't be so c.! ¡no seas tan crítico!
(b) (analytical) crítico(a); to look at sth with a c. eye mirar algo con un ojo crítico
(c) (essay, study) crítico(a); it was a c. success fue un éxito de crítica or entre la crítica ►► c. edition edición f crítica
(d) (decisive) crítico(a), decisivo(a); this is a c. time for them es un momento crítico para ellos; it's c. that we get a decision by Monday se hace del todo imprescindible que para el lunes hayamos tomado una decisión; she was in a c. condition or on the c. list (of patient) se encontraba en estado crítico
(e) Phys to go c. (of reactor) alcanzar el punto crítico ►► c. angle ángulo m crítico; c. mass masa f crítica; c. temperature temperatura f crítica
(f) Com c. path analysis análisis m inv del camino crítico, análisis m inv de ruta crítica

critically ['krɪtɪklɪ] adv (a) (disparagingly) en or con tono crítico (b) (crucially) it is c. important (that...) es de vital importancia (que...) (c) (seriously) seriamente; c. ill en estado crítico (d) (by critics) c. acclaimed elogiado(a) por la crítica

criticism ['krɪtɪsɪzəm] n (a) (negative comment) crítica f; this isn't meant as a c. but... esto no es una crítica, pero... (b) (of movie, novel) crítica f, reseña f

criticize ['krɪtɪsaɪz] 1 vt (a) (comment negatively on) criticar; to c. sb for (doing) sth criticar a alguien por (hacer) algo (b) (of movie, novel) hacer la crítica de, reseñar
2 vi all you ever do is c. no haces más que criticar

critique [krɪ'ti:k] 1 n crítica f
2 vt analizar, evaluar

critter ['krɪtə(r)] n US Fam bicho m

croak [krəʊk] 1 n (of frog) croar m; (of raven) graznido m; (of person) gruñido m
2 vt (a) (utter) mascullar (b) very Fam (kill) cepillarse
3 vi (a) (frog) croar; (raven) graznar; (person) gruñir (b) very Fam (die) palmar, espicharla

Croat ['krəʊæt], **Croatian** [krəʊ'eɪʃən] 1 n (a) (person) croata mf (b) (language) croata m
2 adj croata

Croatia [krəʊ'eɪʃə] n Croacia

Croatian = Croat

crochet ['krəʊʃeɪ] 1 n ganchillo m, Col, CSur crochet m, Méx gancho m ►► c. hook aguja f de ganchillo or Col, CSur crochet or Méx gancho
2 vt to c. sth hacer algo a ganchillo or Col, CSur crochet or Méx gancho
3 vi hacer ganchillo or Col, CSur crochet or Méx gancho m

crock [krɒk] n (a) (pot) vasija f de barro (b) Fam old c. (person) viejo(a) chocho(a); (car) cacharro, Esp tartana (c) Vulg it's a c. of shit es una cagada or Méx una pendejada or RP una boludez

crockery ['krɒkərɪ] n vajilla f

crocodile ['krɒkədaɪl] n (a) (animal) cocodrilo m ►► Elec c. clip pinza f cocodrilo; c. tears lágrimas fpl de cocodrilo (b) (material) c. (skin) piel f de cocodrilo; c. shoes zapatos de piel de cocodrilo (c) (line of pupils) fila f; to walk in a c. caminar en fila de a dos

crocus ['krəʊkəs] n azafrán m

Croesus ['kri:səs] pr n Creso; IDIOM to be as rich as C. Esp ser un Creso or un Onassis, Am ser Rockefeller

croft [krɒft] n Scot granja f pequeña

crofter ['krɒftə(r)] n Scot granjero(a) m,f

croissant ['krwæsɒŋ] n croisant m

crone [krəʊn] n Pej old c. bruja

crony ['krəʊnɪ] n amigote m, amiguete(a) m,f

cronyism ['krəʊnɪɪzəm] n Pej amiguismo m, enchufismo m

crook [krʊk] 1 n (a) (criminal) granuja mf, bribón(ona) m,f (b) (shepherd's staff) cayado m; (bishop's) báculo m (c) (curve) recodo m; to hold sth in the c. of one's arm llevar algo en brazos or en el brazo
2 vt (finger, arm) doblar; IDIOM all she has to do is c. her little finger and he comes running no tiene más que chasquear los dedos y él viene corriendo
3 adj Austr Fam (ill) malo(a), pachucho(a)

crooked ['krʊkɪd] adj (a) (not straight) torcido(a); (lane, path) tortuoso(a); his hat was on c. llevaba el sombrero ladeado; to give a c. smile sonreír socarronamente (b) Fam (dishonest, illegal) (deal) sucio(a); (person) corrupto(a)

crookedly ['krʊkɪdlɪ] adv (a) (to walk, stand) de manera encorvada or ladeada (b) (to smile) con socarronería

crookery ['krʊkərɪ] n corruptelas fpl

croon [kru:n] 1 vt canturrear
2 vi canturrear

crooner ['kru:nə(r)] n cantante mf melódico(a)

crop [krɒp] 1 n (a) (harvest) cosecha f; to get in or to harvest the crops cosechar, recoger la cosecha; a poor/good c. una mala/buena cosecha; Fig this year's c. of films la cosecha de películas de este año
(b) (variety) cultivo m ►► c. circle = franja aplastada y circular de terreno cultivado, que aparece por causas supuestamente paranormales; Agr c. rotation rotación f de cultivos; c. spraying fumigación f de cultivos
(c) (whip) (riding) c. fusta f
(d) (of bird) buche m
(e) (haircut) corte m al rape
(f) Typ c. mark marca f de (re)corte
2 vt (pt & pp cropped) (a) (cut) (hair, tail) cortar; (photograph) recortar (b) (of cattle) (grass) pacer (c) (harvest) cosechar
3 vi (land) to c. well ser fértil

► **crop up** vi (arise) surgir; his name cropped up in the conversation su nombre surgió en la conversación; **sorry I was late, something cropped up** siento haber llegado tarde, me surgió un imprevisto

cropper ['krɒpə(r)] *n* IDIOM *Fam* **to come a c.** *(fall)* darse un porrazo *or Esp* batacazo *or Méx* madrazo; *(fail)* pinchar

croquet ['krəʊkeɪ] *n* croquet *m*

croquette [krɒ'ket] *n* croqueta *f*

crosier, crozier ['krəʊzɪə(r)] *n* báculo *m*

cross [krɒs] **1** *n* **(a)** *(religious symbol)* cruz *f*; **to make the sign of the c.** *(blessing self)* santiguarse; *(blessing others)* dar la bendición; IDIOM **it's a heavy c. to bear** es una cruz, es una pesada carga; **we all have our crosses to bear** todos tenemos alguna *or* nuestra cruz
(b) *(sign, shape)* cruz *f*; **he signed with a c.** firmó con una equis
(c) *(hybrid) (of animals)* cruce *m*, híbrido *m*, *Am* cruza *f*; *Fig* **to be a c. between A and B** ser una mezcla de A y B
(d) *(in soccer)* centro *m*; *(in boxing)* (golpe *m*) directo *m*
(e) *Tex* **cut on the c.** *(material)* cortado(a) al bies *or* al sesgo
2 *adj* **(a)** *(annoyed) esp Esp* enfadado(a), *esp Am* enojado(a) (**about/with** por/con); **to be c. (with)** estar *esp Esp* enfadado(a) *or esp Am* enojado(a) (con); **to get c. (with sb)** *esp Esp* enfadarse *or esp Am* enojarse (con alguien); **it makes me c.** me da mucha rabia; **we've never exchanged a c. word** nunca nos hemos levantado la voz, nunca nos hemos dicho una palabra más alta que otra
(b) c. hairs *or* **wires** *(of gunsight, telescope)* punto de mira
3 *vt* **(a)** *(go across) (river, road)* cruzar; *(room, sea)* cruzar, atravesar; **to c. sb's path** cruzarse en el camino de alguien; **it crossed my mind (that...)** se me ocurrió (que...); IDIOM **we'll c. that bridge when we come to it** *Esp* no adelantemos acontecimientos, *Am* no nos adelantemos a los acontecimientos; IDIOM **to c. the Rubicon** cruzar el Rubicón
(b) *(span) (of bridge)* atravesar, cruzar
(c) *(place across)* cruzar; **to c. one's legs/arms** cruzar las piernas/los brazos; **to c. one's eyes** poner los ojos bizcos; IDIOM **to keep one's fingers crossed** cruzar los dedos; IDIOM *Br Parl* **to c. the floor (of the House)** cambiar de partido; IDIOM **to c. sb's palm with silver** *(bribe)* sobornar a alguien, *Esp* soltarle parné a alguien; IDIOM **to c. swords (with)** verse las caras *or* habérselas (con); IDIOM **we must have got our wires crossed** parece que no nos hemos entendido bien
(d) *(write line across)* **to c. one's t's** ponerle el palito a la te
(e) *(oppose)* oponerse a, contrariar; **he had been crossed in love** había sido desafortunado en amores
(f) *(animals, plants)* cruzar (**with** con)
(g) *Sport (ball, puck)* centrar
(h) *Br (cheque)* **to c. a cheque** cruzar un cheque
(i) *Rel* **to c. oneself** santiguarse; IDIOM *Fam* **c. my heart (and hope to die)!** ¡te lo juro!, ¡que me caiga aquí mismo si no es cierto!
4 *vi* **(a)** *(roads, lines)* cruzarse; **our letters crossed in the post** nuestras cartas se cruzaron en el correo **(b)** *(pass over)* cruzar; **she crossed to the other side of the road** cruzó (al otro lado de) la carretera; **they crossed from Dover to Boulogne** cruzaron de Dover a Boulogne

▸**cross off** *vt sep* tachar; **c. his name off the list** tacha su nombre de la lista

▸**cross out** *vt sep* tachar

▸**cross over** *vi* **(a)** *(go across)* cruzar **(b)** *(pop band)* cambiar de estilo; **to c. over into the mainstream** *(band, actor)* darse a conocer al gran público; **to c. over into everyday use** *(technical term)* pasar al lenguaje cotidiano

crossbar ['krɒsbɑ:(r)] *n* **(a)** *(on bike)* barra *f (de la bicicleta)* **(b)** *(of goalposts)* larguero *m*

crossbeam ['krɒsbi:m] *n* viga *f* (transversal)

crossbencher [krɒs'bentʃə(r)] *n Br Parl* = miembro de la Cámara de los Lores que no pertenece a ningún partido

crossbill ['krɒsbɪl] *n* piquituerto *m*

crossbones ['krɒsbəʊnz] *npl* **the skull and c.** la calavera y las tibias

cross-border ['krɒs'bɔ:də(r)] *adj (trade, co-operation)* entre países fronterizos; *(attack)* fronterizo(a) ▸▸ ***c. pollution*** contaminación *f* transfronteriza *or* transfrontera

crossbow ['krɒsbəʊ] *n* ballesta *f*

crossbred ['krɒsbred] *adj* cruzado(a)

crossbreed ['krɒsbri:d] **1** *n (animal, plant)* híbrido *m*, cruce *m*, *Am* cruza *f*
2 *vt (animals, plants)* cruzar

cross-Channel ['krɒs'tʃænəl] *adj* ***c. ferry*** = transbordador que cruza el Canal de la Mancha; ***c. trade*** = comercio entre Gran Bretaña y el resto de Europa

crosscheck ['krɒstʃek] **1** *n* comprobación *f*, verificación *f* (**against** con); **they ran a c. on the two sets of medical records** cotejaron los dos grupos de historiales médicos
2 *vt* comprobar, verificar (**against** con)
3 *vi* hacer una verificación (**against** con); **make sure the information crosschecks against our records** asegúrate de que la información coincide con la de nuestro registro

cross-country ['krɒs'kʌntrɪ] **1** *adj (vehicle)* todoterreno ▸▸ ***c. runner*** corredor(ora) *m,f* de cross; ***c. running*** campo *m* a través, cross *m*; ***c. skiing*** esquí *m* de fondo; ***c. skis*** esquís *mpl* de fondo
2 *adv (travel)* a campo a través

crosscourt ['krɒskɔ:t] *adj Sport* cruzado(a)

cross-cultural [krɒs'kʌltʃərəl] *adj* intercultural, entre culturas

cross-current ['krɒskʌrənt] *n (in sea)* contracorriente *f*; *(of opinion)* tendencia *f* a contracorriente

cross-cut saw ['krɒskʌt'sɔ:] *n* (sierra *f*) tronzadera *f*, tronzador *m*

cross-dressing [krɒs'dresɪŋ] *n* travestismo *m*

crossed [krɒst] *adj* ***c. cheque*** cheque *m* cruzado *or* barrado, talón *m* cruzado; ***c. line*** *(on telephone)* cruce *m* de líneas

cross-examination ['krɒsɪgzæmɪ'neɪʃən] *n* interrogatorio *m*; **to admit sth under c.** confesar algo durante un interrogatorio

cross-examine ['krɒsɪg'zæmɪn] *vt* interrogar

cross-eyed ['krɒsaɪd] *adj* bizco(a)

cross-fertilization ['krɒsfɜ:tɪlaɪ'zeɪʃən] *n* **(a)** *(between plants)* polinización *f* cruzada **(b)** *(cultural)* mestizaje *m* (cultural); *(of ideas)* intercambio *m*

cross-fertilize [krɒs'fɜ:tɪlaɪz] *vt* **(a)** *(plants)* polinizar con fecundación cruzada **(b)** *Fig* favorecer el mestizaje (cultural) entre

cross-field ['krɒsfi:ld] *adj Sport* ***c. ball*** cruce *m*; ***c. pass*** cruce *m*

crossfire ['krɒsfaɪə(r)] *n also Fig* fuego *m* cruzado; **they were caught in the c.** el fuego cruzado los pilló *or Esp* cogió *or Am* agarró en medio

cross-grained ['krɒsgreɪnd] *adj* **(a)** *(wood)* nudoso(a), con nudos **(b)** *(person)* difícil

crosshatch ['krɒshætʃ] *vt* sombrear, rayar

crosshatching ['krɒshætʃɪŋ] *n* sombreado *m*

crossing ['krɒsɪŋ] *n* **(a)** *(of sea)* travesía *f*; **we had a good c.** tuvimos una buena travesía **(b)** *(across street)* paso *m* de peatones ▸▸ ***US c. guard*** = persona encargada de ayudar a cruzar la calle a los colegiales

cross-legged [krɒs'leg(ɪ)d] *adv* **to sit c.** sentarse con las piernas cruzadas

crossly ['krɒslɪ] *adv* con *esp Esp* enfado *or esp Am* enojo

cross-over ['krɒsəʊvə(r)] **1** *n (of career)* salto *m*, cambio *m*
2 *adj Mus (style)* híbrido(a), de fusión

crosspatch ['krɒspætʃ] *n Fam* cascarrabias *mf inv*

crosspiece ['krɒspi:s] *n* travesaño *m*

cross-platform ['krɒs'plætfɔ:m] *adj Comptr* multiplataforma *inv*

cross-ply ['krɒsplaɪ] *adj (tyre)* (de cubierta) diagonal

cross-pollination ['krɒspɒlɪ'neɪʃən] *n Bot* polinización *f* cruzada

cross-post ['krɒspəʊst] *vt Comptr* hacer un envío masivo de

cross-posting [krɒs'pəʊstɪŋ] *n Comptr* = envío masivo de mensajes por correo electrónico a diferentes grupos de noticias

cross-purposes [krɒs'pɜ:pəsɪz] *npl* **they were (talking) at c. with each other** sin darse cuenta, estaban hablando de cosas distintas

cross-question [krɒs'kwestʃən] *vt* interrogar

cross-refer ['krɒsrɪ'fɜ:(r)] *vt* remitir (**to** a)

cross-reference [krɒs'refərəns] **1** *n* referencia *f*, remisión *f*
2 *vt* remitir (**to** a)

crossroad ['krɒsrəʊd] *n US (across a road)* cruce *m*, intersección *f*; *(between main roads)* carretera *f* secundaria *(que comunica dos carreteras principales)*

crossroads ['krɒsrəʊdz] *n* encrucijada *f*; **to be at a c.** *(person, process)* estar en una encrucijada

cross-section ['krɒs'sekʃən] *n* **(a)** *(cut, diagram)* sección *f* transversal **(b)** *(sample)* muestra *f* (representativa)

cross-stitch ['krɒsstɪtʃ] *n* punto *m* de cruz

crosstalk ['krɒstɔ:k] *n* **(a)** *Rad & Tel* interferencia *f* **(b)** *Br (witty exchange)* intercambio *m* de comentarios agudos

crosstown ['krɒstaʊn] *adj US (bus, train)* que cruza la ciudad

cross-training ['krɒs'treɪnɪŋ] *n Sport* ejercicios *mpl* combinados (de suelo y aparatos)

crosstree ['krɒstri:] *n Naut* cruceta *f*

crosswalk ['krɒswɔ:k] *n US* paso *m* de peatones

crossways = **crosswise**

crosswind ['krɒswɪnd] *n* viento *m* lateral

crosswise ['krɒswaɪz], **crossways** ['krɒsweɪz] **1** *adj* diagonal, transversal

2 *adv* en diagonal, transversalmente

crossword ['krɒswɜ:d] *n* **c. (puzzle)** crucigrama *m*

crotch [krɒtʃ] *n (of person, trousers)* entrepierna *f*

crotchet ['krɒtʃɪt] *n* **(a)** *Br Mus* negra *f* **(b)** *US (eccentric habit)* manía *f* **(c)** *US (trick, device)* truco *m*

crotchety ['krɒtʃətɪ] *adj Fam (irritable)* gruñón(ona)

crouch [kraʊtʃ] *vi* **to c. (down)** *(animal)* agazaparse; *(person)* agacharse

croup [kru:p] *n* **(a)** *Med* garrotillo *m*, crup *m* **(b)** *(of animal)* grupa *f*

croupier ['kru:pɪə(r)] *n* crupier *m*

crouton ['kru:tɒn] *n* picatoste *m (en forma de dado)*

crow [krəʊ] **1** *n* **(a)** *(bird)* corneja *f*; **as the c. flies** en línea recta; IDIOM *US Fam* **to eat c.** tragarse (uno) sus palabras ►► ***c.'s feet*** *(facial lines)* patas *fpl* de gallo; ***c.'s nest*** *(on ship)* cofa *f* **(b)** *(sound) (of cock)* cacareo *m*; *(of baby)* balbuceo *m*; **he gave a c. of triumph** dio un grito de alegría

2 *vi* (*pt* **crowed** *or* **crew** [kru:], *pp* **crowed**) **(a)** *(cock)* cacarear **(b)** *(baby)* balbucear **(c)** *(boast, rejoice)* pavonearse, alardear (**about** de); **it's nothing to c. about!** ¡no es como para estar orgulloso!; **to c. over sth** *(own triumph)* pavonearse *or* alardear de algo; *(other's misfortune)* mofarse de algo

3 *vt* alardear

crowbar ['krəʊbɑ:(r)] *n* palanqueta *f*

crowd [kraʊd] **1** *n* **(a)** *(large number of people)* muchedumbre *f*, multitud *f*; *(at sports match)* público *m*; **a c. of noisy children** una multitud de niños revoltosos; **there was quite a c.** había bastante gente; **there were crowds of people in town** había un montón de gente en el centro; **the concert drew a good c.** el concierto congregó a mucha gente *or* mucho público; **to be a c. puller** atraer a las masas; **don't get lost in the c.** no te pierdas entre la muchedumbre ►► ***c. scene*** *(in movie)* escena *f* de masas

(b) *Fam (group)* pandilla *f*, *Méx* bola *f*, *RP* barra *f*; **the usual c. were there** estaba la gente de siempre, estaban los de siempre; **to be in with the wrong c.** andar con malas compañías; **they stick to their own c.** siempre van con su gente

(c) *(majority)* **to go with** *or* **follow the c.** seguir a la mayoría; **she doesn't like to be one of the c.** no le gusta ser una más; IDIOM **to stand out from the c.** destacar, sobresalir

2 *vt* **(a)** *(fill, cram)* atestar, abarrotar; **people crowded the streets/the shops** las calles/tiendas estaban abarrotadas (de gente); **the park was crowded with sunbathers** el parque estaba lleno de gente tomando el sol; **the tables are crowded together** las mesas están apelotonadas

(b) *Fam (jostle, pressurize)* **I was crowded off the bus** me sacaron del autobús a empujones; **stop crowding me!** ¡deja de acosarme!

(c) *US* **to c. the plate** *(in baseball)* estar muy cerca de la base

(d) *Naut* **to c. on sail** hacer fuerza de vela

3 *vi* **to c. (together)** apiñarse, amontonarse; **to c. round sth/sb** apiñarse en torno de algo/a alguien; **they crowded round to read the poster** se apiñaron en torno al póster para leerlo; **we crowded into the room** nos apretujamos en la habitación; **they came crowding through the door** entraron en tropel por la puerta

► **crowd in** *vi* **(a)** *(enter)* entrar en tropel **(b)** *(thoughts)* agolparse; **gloomy thoughts kept crowding in on me** los pensamientos sombríos se agolpaban dentro de mí

► **crowd out** *vt sep* **(a)** *(fill)* atestar, llenar hasta los topes **(b)** *(exclude)* **to c. sb out of a deal/the market** excluir a alguien de un acuerdo/del mercado; **small shops are being crowded out by bigger stores** las grandes tiendas están dejando al pequeño comerciante fuera del mercado

crowded ['kraʊdɪd] *adj* **(a)** *(busy)* abarrotado(a), atestado(a) (**with** de); **to be c. (with)** estar abarrotado(a) *or* atestado(a) de; **he has a c. schedule** tiene una agenda muy apretada **(b)** *(overpopulated)* superpoblado(a); **c. inner-city areas** las zonas deprimidas y superpobladas del centro de la ciudad

crown [kraʊn] **1** *n* **(a)** *(of monarch)* corona *f*; **the C.** *(institution)* la Corona ►► *Br Law* ***c. court*** = tribunal superior de lo penal; ***the c. jewels*** las joyas de la corona; *Fam Hum (man's genitals) Esp* el paquete *m*, *Méx* la cosa *f*, *RP* el bulto *m*; ***c. land*** *(in UK)* = tierras que pertenecen a la corona; ***c. prince*** príncipe *m* heredero; ***c. princess*** princesa *f* heredera; *Law* ***C. Prosecution Service*** ≃ Fiscalía *f* General del Estado; ***c. of thorns*** corona *f* de espinas

(b) *(top) (of head)* coronilla *f*; *(of hat)* copa *f*; *(of hill)* cima *f*; *(of road)* centro *m*; *(on tooth)* corona *f*, funda *f*

(c) *(currency)* corona *f*

(d) *(outstanding achievement)* cima *f*, cumbre *f*; **it was the c. of his career** fue la cima *or* cumbre de su carrera

(e) *(paper size)* = tamaño de papel de 385 x 505 mm

2 *vt* **(a)** *(as monarch)* coronar; **to c. sb king** coronar rey a alguien **(b)** *(sit on top of)* **the woods that c. the hill** los bosques que coronan la cima de la colina

(c) *(finish off, make perfect)* **her election success crowned her career** su victoria en las elecciones fue la cima *or* cumbre de su carrera; IDIOM *Ironic* **to c. it all...** para colmo..., para remate *or RP* rematar...

(d) to c. a tooth ponerle una corona a una muela

(e) *(in draughts, checkers)* **to c. a piece** coronar un peón

(f) *Fam (hit on the head)* **I'll c. you!** ¡te voy a dar una!, *Esp* ¡te voy a sacudir!

3 *vi US (in checkers)* coronar

crowned [kraʊnd] *adj* **the c. heads of Europe** las testas coronadas de Europa

crowning ['kraʊnɪŋ] *adj (achievement)* supremo(a); **c. glory** *(finest act, thing)* gloria suprema; **the red hair that was her c. glory** el pelo rojo que era el remate de su belleza

crozier = **crosier**

CRT [si:ɑ:'ti:] *n Tech* (*abbr* **cathode ray tube**) TRC *m*

crucial ['kru:ʃəl] *adj* **(a)** *(very important, decisive)* crucial; **there's a c. difference** hay una diferencia crucial; **c. seconds were ticking away** se estaban perdiendo unos segundos vitales; **improving exports has never been more c.** nunca fue tan importante como ahora incrementar las importaciones **(b)** *Br Fam (very good)* genial, *Esp* guay, *Andes, CAm, Carib, Méx* chévere, *Andes, RP* macanudo(a), *Méx* padre

crucially ['kru:ʃəlɪ] *adv* de manera crucial; **it is c. important** es de una importancia crucial *or* vital

crucible ['kru:sɪbəl] *n also Fig* crisol *m*

crucifix ['kru:sɪfɪks] *n* crucifijo *m*

crucifixion [kru:sɪ'fɪkʃən] *n* crucifixión *f*

cruciform ['kru:sɪfɔ:m] *adj Formal* cruciforme

crucify ['kru:sɪfaɪ] *vt* **(a)** *(execute)* crucificar **(b)** *Fam (defeat, criticize)* **the minister was crucified in the press** la prensa crucificó al ministro; **they were crucified by the Dodgers** los Dodgers les dieron una paliza; **my mum will c. us if she finds out!** ¡si mamá se entera nos mata!

crud [krʌd] *n Fam* **(a)** *(dirt)* porquería *f*, mugre *f* **(b)** *(nonsense)* bobadas *fpl*, sandeces *fpl*, *Am* huevadas *fpl* **(c)** *US (dirty, untidy person)* cerdo(a) *m,f*, *Esp* guarro(a) *m,f*

cruddy ['krʌdɪ] *adj Fam* **(a)** *(dirty)* mugriento(a), *Esp* guarro(a) **(b)** *(bad)* asqueroso(a), *Esp* cutre, *RP* groncho(a) **(c)** *(unwell)* **I feel c.** no me encuentro bien, *Esp* me encuentro chungo

crude [kru:d] **1** *adj* **(a)** *(unsophisticated)* tosco(a); **a c. but effective method** un método tosco pero efectivo **(b)** *(rude, vulgar)* ordinario(a), grosero(a) **(c)** *(oil)* crudo(a)

2 *n (oil)* crudo *m*

crudely ['kru:dlɪ] *adv* **(a)** *(simply)* toscamente **(b)** *(vulgarly)* de forma ordinaria, groseramente; **to gesture c.** hacer gestos groseros

crudeness ['kru:dnɪs], **crudity** ['kru:dɪtɪ] *n* **(a)** *(simplicity)* tosquedad *f* **(b)** *(vulgarity)* ordinariez *f*, grosería *f*

crudités ['kru:dɪteɪz] *npl Culin* crudités *fpl*

cruel ['krʊəl] *adj* cruel (**to** con); *(fate)* aciago(a), *Esp* fatal; **it was c. luck** fue muy mala suerte, fue tremendamente injusto; **it was a c. disappointment** fue una tremenda decepción; **a c. wind** un viento inclemente; PROV **you have to be c. to be kind** quien bien te quiere te hará llorar

cruelly ['krʊəlɪ] *adv* cruelmente, con crueldad; **they were c. mistaken in thinking him a friend** estaban completamente engañados al pensar que era su amigo

cruelty ['krʊəltɪ] *n* **(a)** *(ill-treatment)* crueldad *f* (**to** con); **divorce on the grounds of c.** divorcio por motivos de crueldad *or* ensañamiento **(b)** *(cruel act)* crueldad *f*; **he had to suffer the cruelties of his classmates** tuvo que soportar las humillaciones de sus compañeros de clase

cruelty-free ['krʊəltɪ'fri:] *adj (cosmetics)* = elaborado y probado sin el uso de animales

cruet ['krʊɪt] *n* **(a)** *Culin* **c. (stand** *or* **set)** vinagreras *fpl* **(b)** *Rel* vinajeras *fpl*

cruise [kruːz] **1** *n (on ship)* crucero *m*; **to go on a c.** ir de crucero ►► *Aut* ***c. control*** control *m* (automático) de velocidad; ***c. missile*** misil *m* de crucero
2 *vi* (**a**) *(ship)* navegar tranquilamente; *(warship)* patrullar; *(passengers)* hacer un crucero; *(car, plane)* ir a velocidad de crucero; **it was cruising at 25 knots** *(ship)* navegaba a 25 nudos; **cruising speed** *(of ship, plane)* velocidad de crucero
(**b**) *(achieve easily)* **I cruised through the exam** para mí el examen fue un paseo; **the Rovers cruised to a 3-0 victory** los Rovers obtuvieron una cómoda victoria por 3-0
(**c**) *Fam (look for sexual partner)* tratar de ligar, *Esp* buscar ligue
(**d**) *US Fam (leave)* irse, marcharse, *Méx* rajarse; **ready to c.?** ¿nos piramos *or* abrimos ya?, *Méx* ¡ándale, vámonos!, *RP* ¿vamos yendo?
(**e**) *Hum* **you're cruising for a bruising!** tú sigue así y te ganarás un soplamocos
3 *vt* (**a**) *(ocean) (liner)* navegar por; *(warship)* navegar por, patrullar (**b**) *Fam (person)* intentar ligar con *or Méx* a, *RP* intentar enganchar con; *(place)* ir a ligar por, ir de *Esp* ligue *or RP* levante por

cruiser ['kruːzə(r)] *n* (**a**) *(warship)* crucero *m* (**b**) *(pleasure boat)* **(cabin) c.** yate *m* (de motor) (**c**) *US (police patrol car)* coche *m* patrulla, *CSur* patrullero *m*

cruiserweight ['kruːzəweɪt] **1** *adj (in boxing)* del peso semipesado
2 *n (in boxing)* peso *m* semipesado

cruller ['krʌlə(r)] *n US* rosquilla *f*

crumb [krʌm] **1** *n* (**a**) *(of bread)* miga *f*; **my only c. of comfort is...** lo único que me consuela es...; *Fig* **he was left with the crumbs** no le dejaron más que las migajas; *Fig* **they make the profit and we get the crumbs from the table** ellos se embolsan los beneficios y a nosotros sólo nos quedan las migajas (**b**) *Fam Pej (person)* mamarracho(a) *m,f*, mequetrefe *mf*
2 *vi (cover in breadcrumbs)* empanar

crumble ['krʌmbəl] **1** *vt (bread, stock cube)* desmigajar, desmenuzar
2 *vi (stone, plaster)* desmenuzarse; *(bread)* desmigajarse; *(building)* desmoronarse, derrumbarse; *(empire, resistance)* desmoronarse, venirse abajo; *Fig* **his world was crumbling around him** se le caía el mundo encima
3 *n (dessert)* = postre al horno a base de compota con masa quebrada dulce por encima

crumbly ['krʌmblɪ] **1** *adj* **it's very c.** se desmenuza muy fácilmente
2 *n Br Fam (old person)* ancianito(a) *m,f*, viejecito(a) *m,f*

crumbs [krʌmz] *exclam Fam* ¡vaya por Dios!

crummy ['krʌmɪ] *adj Fam* (**a**) *(bad)* malo(a), *Esp* cutre, *Col* corroncho(a), *RP* groncho(a) (**b**) *(unwell)* **I feel c.** estoy hecho polvo, *Esp* me siento fatal

crumpet ['krʌmpɪt] *n* (**a**) *(teacake)* = torta pequeña que se come con mantequilla (**b**) *Br Fam (women) Esp* titis *fpl*, *Esp* tías *fpl*, *Méx* viejas *fpl*, *RP* minas *fpl*; **a bit of c.** *Esp* una tía maciza, *Am* una tipa bien buena

crumple ['krʌmpəl] **1** *vt (material, dress)* arrugar; **to c. sth into a ball** hacer una pelota con algo
2 *vi* (**a**) *(crease)* arrugarse (**b**) *(collapse) (structure)* desmoronarse; *(person)* desplomarse; *(resistance)* sucumbir; **his face crumpled and tears came to his eyes** se le descompuso el rostro y sus ojos se llenaron de lágrimas ►► *Aut* ***c. zone*** zona *f* de absorción (de golpes)

crunch [krʌntʃ] **1** *n (sound)* crujido *m*; IDIOM **when it comes to the c.** a la hora de la verdad
2 *adj Fam (crucial)* crucial, transcendental; **a c. game** un partido decisivo
3 *vt* (**a**) *(with teeth)* ronzar, machacar con los dientes (**b**) *(numbers, data)* devorar
4 *vi* (**a**) *(with teeth)* ronzar; **to c. on sth** ronzar algo (**b**) *(make sound)* crujir; **the snow/gravel crunched beneath my feet** la nieve/grava crujía a mi paso

► **crunch up** *vt sep* arrugar; **he crunched the letter up and threw it in the bin** hizo una pelota con la carta y la tiró a la papelera

crunchy ['krʌntʃɪ] *adj* crujiente, *RP* crocante

crupper ['krʌpə(r)] *n* (**a**) *(on saddle)* baticola *f* (**b**) *(of horse)* grupa *f*, ancas *fpl*

crusade [kruː'seɪd] **1** *n* (**a**) *Hist* **the Crusades** las Cruzadas (**b**) *(campaign)* cruzada *f*; **a c. for/against sth** una cruzada *or* campaña a favor de/en contra de algo
2 *vi* **to c. for/against** emprender una cruzada a favor de/en contra de

crusader [kruː'seɪdə(r)] *n* (**a**) *Hist* cruzado *m* (**b**) *(campaigner)* paladín *m*, defensor(ora) *m,f*; **a c. against injustice** un paladín de la justicia

crush [krʌʃ] **1** *n* (**a**) *(crowd)* muchedumbre *f*, aglomeración *f*; **there was a terrible c.** había un gentío horrible; **we lost each other in the c.** nos separamos entre el gentío ►► *Theat* ***c. bar*** = bar de un teatro donde se sirven bebidas en los descansos de una representación; ***c. barrier*** barrera *f or* valla *f* de seguridad
(**b**) *(drink)* **orange c.** naranjada
(**c**) *Fam (infatuation)* **to have a c. on sb** estar embobado(a) con alguien, *Esp* estar colado(a) por *or* encaprichado(a) de alguien
2 *vt* (**a**) *(squash, smash) (person, thing)* estrujar, aplastar; *(grapes, garlic)* prensar, aplastar; *(ice)* picar; **they were crushed to death** murieron aplastados
(**b**) *(squeeze, press)* apretujar; **to be crushed together** estar apretujados(as); **too many things had been crushed into the box** habían metido a presión demasiadas cosas en la caja
(**c**) *(crease)* arrugar; **crushed velvet** terciopelo arrugado *or* aplastado
(**d**) *(defeat, repress) (opponent, revolt)* aplastar, destrozar; **to c. sb's hopes** echar por tierra las esperanzas de alguien; **she felt crushed by the news** la noticia la dejó desolada
3 *vi* (**a**) *(squeeze)* **we crushed into the taxi** nos estrujamos para entrar en el taxi (**b**) *(crease)* arrugarse

crushing ['krʌʃɪŋ] *adj (blow, defeat)* demoledor(ora), aplastante; *(remark)* hiriente, humillante; **he can be terribly c. when he wants to be** puede ser tremendamente hiriente cuando se lo propone

crush-resistant ['krʌʃrɪzɪstənt] *adj (fabric)* inarrugable

crust [krʌst] **1** *n* (**a**) *(of bread, pie)* corteza *f*; **to cut the crusts off sandwiches** cortar los bordes de los sándwiches; **a c. of bread** un mendrugo; IDIOM *Br Fam* **to earn a** *or* **one's c.** ganarse el pan (**b**) **the earth's c.** la corteza terrestre
2 *vi* **to c. (over)** *(become covered with a crust)* cubrirse con una costra; *(wound)* encostrarse

crustacean [krʌs'teɪʃən] *n Zool* crustáceo *m*

crusty ['krʌstɪ] **1** *adj* (**a**) *(bread, roll)* crujiente, *RP* crocante (**b**) *Br (person)* malhumorado(a), gruñón(ona)
2 *n Br Fam* zarrapastroso(a) *m,f*, desaliñado(a) *m,f*

crutch [krʌtʃ] *n* (**a**) *(for walking)* muleta *f*; **to be on crutches** ir con muletas (**b**) *(support)* apoyo *m*, sostén *m*; **he uses notes as a mental c.** utiliza notas como apoyo (**c**) *(of trousers, person)* entrepierna *f*

crux [krʌks] *n* **the c. of the matter** el quid de la cuestión

cruzado [kruː'sɑːdəʊ] (*pl* **cruzados**) *n Formerly (Brazilian currency)* cruzado *m*

cry [kraɪ] **1** *n* (**a**) *(call) (of person)* grito *m*; *(in demonstration)* consigna *f*; **to give** *or* **utter a c.** dar un grito; **there were cries of "down with the king!"** se oían gritos de "¡abajo el rey!"; **"democracy now!" was the c.** la consigna era "¡democracia ya!"; **a c. of pain** un grito de dolor; **he heard a c. for help** oyó un grito de socorro; *Fig* **a c. for help** un grito de auxilio; **it's a far c. from what we expected** dista mucho de lo que esperábamos
(**b**) *(of birds, animals)* chillido *m*; *(of hounds)* aullido *m*; **to be in full c.** *(of hounds)* ir detrás como fieras; *Fig* **the opposition is in full c. after the government** la oposición está criticando al gobierno a voz en grito
(**c**) *(weeping)* **to have a good c.** llorar abundantemente
2 *vt* (*pt & pp* **cried** [kraɪd]) (**a**) *(exclaim)* exclamar; **"look!," she cried** "fíjate", exclamó; *Old-fashioned* **the peddler was crying his wares** el vendedor ambulante iba pregonando sus mercancías (**b**) *(weep)* **she cried herself to sleep** lloró hasta quedarse dormida; **he cried tears of joy** lloraba de alegría
3 *vi* (**a**) *(weep)* llorar; **to c. over sth** llorar por algo; **she cried in** *or* **with frustration** lloraba de impotencia; **we laughed until we cried** nos reímos hasta que se nos saltaron las lágrimas; IDIOM **to c. on sb's shoulder** tomar *or* agarrar a alguien de paño de lágrimas; PROV **there's no point in crying over spilt milk** a lo hecho, pecho
(**b**) *(shout, call)* gritar; **to c. for help** gritar pidiendo ayuda
(**c**) *(bird, animal)* chillar; *(hounds)* aullar

► **cry down** *vt sep* menospreciar, quitar mérito a

► **cry off** *vi* echarse atrás; **he cried off, saying he had a cold** se echó atrás diciendo que estaba enfriado; **I had to c. off at the last minute** tuve que echarme atrás en el último momento

► **cry out** **1** *vt sep* (**a**) *(shout)* gritar (**b**) *(weep)* **to c. one's eyes** *or* **heart out** llorar a lágrima viva
2 *vi (shout)* gritar; *Fam* **for crying out loud!** ¡por el amor de Dios!; *Fam* **that wall is crying out for a coat of paint** esa pared está pidiendo a gritos una mano de pintura

► **cry up** *vt sep* ensalzar, alabar; **to c. up sb's chances of winning** exagerar las posibilidades de ganar de alguien

crybaby ['kraɪbeɪbɪ] *n Fam* llorica *mf*

crying ['kraɪɪŋ] **1** *n (weeping)* llanto *m*
2 *adj (need)* acuciante, apremiante; **it's a c. shame that...** es una auténtica vergüenza que...; **there is a c. need for more teachers** existe una necesidad apremiante de contar con más profesores

cryogenics [kraɪəʊ'dʒenɪks] *n* criogenia *f*

cryonic [kraɪ'ɒnɪk] *adj* criónico(a), criogénico(a) ►► ***c. suspension*** suspensión *f* criónica *or* criogénica

cryonics [kraɪ'ɒnɪks] *n* crionización *f*, criogenización *f*

cryosurgery [kraɪəʊ'sɜːdʒərɪ] *n* criocirugía *f*

crypt [krɪpt] *n* cripta *f*

cryptanalysis [krɪptə'næləsɪs] *n* criptoanálisis *m inv*

cryptic ['krɪptɪk] *adj (remark, hint)* críptico(a) ►► ***c. crossword*** crucigrama *m* críptico

crypto- ['krɪptəʊ] *prefix* cripto-; **c.-fascist** criptofascista

cryptogram ['krɪptəgræm] *n* criptograma *m*

cryptographer [krɪp'tɒgrəfə(r)] *n* criptógrafo(a) *m,f*

cryptography [krɪp'tɒgrəfɪ] *n* criptografía *f*

crystal ['krɪstəl] **1** *n* **(a)** *(glass)* cristal *m* **(b)** *(mineral)* cristal *m*; **salt/sugar crystals** cristales de sal/azúcar ►► ***c. healing*** curación *f* con cristales; *Phys* ***c. lattice*** estructura *f or* malla *f* cristalina; *Rad* ***c. set*** receptor *m* de (radio de) galena **(c)** *(of watch, clock)* cristal *m*, vidrio *m*
2 *adj* **(a)** *(clear)* transparente, claro(a); IDIOM **to be c. clear** *(of issue)* ser de una claridad meridiana; **to make sth c. clear** dejar algo muy claro **(b)** *(made of glass)* de cristal ►► ***c. ball*** bola *f* de vidrio *or Esp* cristal

crystal-clear ['krɪstəl'klɪə(r)] *adj (water)* cristalino(a); *(explanation)* clarísimo(a), más claro(a) que el agua

crystalline ['krɪstəlaɪn] *adj* **(a)** *Chem* cristalino(a) **(b)** *(clear)* cristalino(a)

crystallization [krɪstəlaɪ'zeɪʃən] *n* **(a)** *Chem* cristalización *f* **(b)** *(of plan, idea)* cristalización *f*

crystallize ['krɪstəlaɪz] **1** *vt* **(a)** *Chem* cristalizar **(b)** *Culin* **crystallized fruits** frutas escarchadas *or Col, Méx* cristalizadas *or RP* abrillantadas
2 *vi* **(a)** *Chem* cristalizar **(b)** *(plan, idea)* cristalizar

crystallography [krɪstə'lɒgrəfɪ] *n* cristalografía *f*

CSA [siːes'eɪ] *n* (*abbr* **Child Support Agency**) = agencia estatal británica que vela por el cumplimiento de la ley en materia de pensiones alimenticias

CS gas [siːes'gæs] *n* gas *m* lacrimógeno

CST [siːes'tiː] *n US* (*abbr* **Central Standard Time**) = hora oficial en el centro de los Estados Unidos

CT[1] (*abbr* **Connecticut**) Connecticut

CT[2] [siː'tiː] *n US Med* (*abbr* **Computerized Tomography**) TAC *f* ►► ***CT scan*** escáner *m* (TAC)

Ctrl *Comptr* (*abbr* **control**) Ctrl ►► ***C. key*** tecla *f* Ctrl

cu (*abbr* **cubic**) cúbico

cub [kʌb] *n* **(a)** *(of fox, lion)* cachorro *m*; *(of bear)* osezno *m*; *(of wolf)* lobezno *m*, lobato *m* **(b)** *Fam (youngster)* **young c.** jovencito(a) **(c)** *(in youth organization)* **C. (Scout)** lobato *m*, niño *m* explorador **(d)** *(novice)* ***c. reporter*** periodista *mf* novato(a)

Cuba ['kjuːbə] *n* Cuba

Cuban ['kjuːbən] **1** *n* cubano(a) *m,f*
2 *adj* cubano(a) ►► ***C. heels*** tacones *mpl* cubanos; *Hist* ***the C. missile crisis*** la crisis de los misiles (cubanos)

cubbyhole ['kʌbɪhəʊl] *n (cupboard)* armario *m* empotrado; *(room)* cuartito *m*

cube [kjuːb] **1** *n (shape)* cubo *m*; *(of sugar)* terrón *m* ►► *Math* ***c. root*** raíz *f* cúbica
2 *vt* **(a)** *(cut into cubes)* cortar en daditos **(b)** *Math* elevar al cubo

cubic ['kjuːbɪk] *adj* cúbico(a) ►► ***c. capacity*** capacidad *f*, volumen *m*; ***c. metre*** metro *m* cúbico

cubicle ['kjuːbɪkəl] *n (in hospital, dormitory, public toilet)* cubículo *m*; *(in swimming pool)* cabina *f*, vestuario *m*

cubism ['kjuːbɪzəm] *n Art* cubismo *m*

cubist ['kjuːbɪst] *Art* **1** *n* cubista *mf*
2 *adj* cubista

cubit ['kjuːbɪt] *n (measurement)* codo *m*

cuboid ['kjuːbɔɪd] *Math* **1** *n* paralelepípedo *m* rectángulo
2 *adj* cúbico(a)

cuckold ['kʌkəld] **1** *n* cornudo *m*
2 *vt* poner los cuernos a

cuckoo ['kʊkuː] **1** *n* (*pl* **cuckoos**) cuco *m*; **great spotted c.** críalo ►► ***c. clock*** reloj *m* de cuco, *RP* reloj *m* cucú; ***c. spit*** espumilla *f* del cércopo
2 *adj Fam (mad)* **to be c.** estar pirado(a), *Méx* estar zafado(a)

cucumber ['kjuːkʌmbə(r)] *n* pepino *m*

cud [kʌd] *n* **to chew the c.** *(of cow)* rumiar; *(of person)* rumiárselo

cuddle ['kʌdəl] **1** *n* abrazo *m*; **they were having a c.** se estaban haciendo arrumacos; **to give sb a c.** dar un abrazo a alguien
2 *vt* abrazar
3 *vi* arrimarse; **to c. up to sb** arrimarse a alguien

cuddly ['kʌdlɪ] *adj Fam (child, animal)* tierno(a) ►► ***c. toy*** muñeco *m* de peluche

cudgel ['kʌdʒəl] **1** *n* porra *f*, palo *m*; IDIOM **to take up the cudgels on sb's behalf** salir en defensa de alguien, *Am* quebrar una lanza por alguien
2 *vt* (*pt & pp* **cudgelled**, *US* **cudgeled**) IDIOM **to c. one's brains** estrujarse el cerebro, devanarse los sesos

cue[1] [kjuː] **1** *n (of actor)* entrada *f*, pie *m*; **to miss one's c.** no oír la entrada *or* el pie; **to give sb their c.** dar el pie a alguien; *Fig* **to take one's c. from sb** tomar ejemplo de alguien; **as if on c.** en ese preciso instante; **her yawn was our c. to leave** su bostezo fue lo que nos dio pie para irnos ►► ***c. card*** *(for public speaker)* tarjeta *f (en la que están anotados los puntos más importantes)*
2 *vt* **(a)** *(actor)* dar la entrada a **(b)** *(track on CD)* buscar

► **cue in** *vt sep (actor)* dar el pie a; *(musician)* dar la entrada a

cue[2] **1** *n (in billiards, pool)* taco *m* ►► ***c. ball*** bola *f* jugadora; ***c. rack*** taquera *f*
2 *vt* embocar

cuff[1] [kʌf] **1** *n* **(a)** *(of shirt)* puño *m* ►► ***c. links*** gemelos *mpl* **(b)** *US (of trousers)* vuelta *f* **(c)** *Fam* **cuffs** *(handcuffs)* esposas *fpl* **(d)** IDIOMS *Fam* **off the c.** improvisadamente; **I can't tell you off the c.** así a bote pronto *or RP* de la nada no te lo puedo decir; *US* **he bought it on the c.** *(on credit)* le fiaron lo que compró
2 *vt Fam (put handcuffs on)* esposar

cuff[2] *Fam* **1** *n (blow)* cachete *m*, cate *m*; **I got a c. round** *or* **on the ear** me gané un bofetón
2 *vt (hit)* dar un sopapo *or Am* una cachetada a; **to c. sb round the ear** dar un sopapo a alguien

cuirass [kwɪ'ræs] *n* coraza *f*

cuisine [kwɪ'ziːn] *n* cocina *f*

cul-de-sac ['kʌldəsæk] (*pl* **culs-de-sac** ['kʌldəsæk] *or* **cul-de-sacs**) *n* callejón *m* sin salida

culinary ['kʌlɪnərɪ] *adj* culinario(a)

cull [kʌl] **1** *n (of seals, deer)* sacrificio *m (selectivo)*
2 *vt* **(a)** *(animals)* sacrificar *(selectivamente)* **(b)** *(select)* extraer, recoger (**from** de); **recipes culled from the world's cuisines** recetas seleccionadas de entre las cocinas de todo el mundo

culminate ['kʌlmɪneɪt] *vi* **(a)** *(climax)* **to c. in** culminar en **(b)** *Astron* culminar

culmination [kʌlmɪ'neɪʃən] *n* **(a)** *(peak, climax)* culminación *f* **(b)** *Astron* culminación *f*

culottes [kjuː'lɒts] *npl* falda *f or Am* pollera *f* pantalón; **a pair of c.** una falda *or Am* pollera pantalón

culpability [kʌlpə'bɪlətɪ] *n Formal* culpabilidad *f*

culpable ['kʌlpəbəl] *adj* culpable ►► *Scot Law* ***c. homicide*** homicidio *m* involuntario

culprit ['kʌlprɪt] *n* culpable *mf*; **poor housing is the main c. for high infant mortality** la precariedad de la vivienda es el principal responsable *or* la causa principal del elevado índice de mortalidad infantil

cult [kʌlt] *n* **(a)** *(belief)* culto *m* **(b)** *(sect)* secta *f* **(c)** *(craze, minority fashion)* culto *m*; **he became a c. figure** se convirtió en objeto de culto; **c. movie/novel** película/novela de culto

cultist ['kʌltɪst] *n* adepto(a) *m,f or* miembro *mf* de una secta

cultivate ['kʌltɪveɪt] *vt* **(a)** *(land, crop)* cultivar **(b)** *(idea, person, friendship)* cultivar; **to c. the mind** cultivar la mente

cultivated ['kʌltɪveɪtɪd] *adj* **(a)** *(land, plant)* cultivado(a) **(b)** *(educated)* culto(a)

cultivation [kʌltɪ'veɪʃən] *n* **(a)** *(of land, crop)* cultivo *m*; **fields under c.** tierras en cultivo **(b)** *(of taste)* cultivo *m*; *(of relations)* cultivo *m*, fomento *m*

cultivator ['kʌltɪveɪtə(r)] *n* **(a)** *(machine)* cultivadora *f* **(b)** *(person)* cultivador(ora) *m,f*; **a c. of useful contacts** una persona que cultiva los contactos útiles

cultural ['kʌltʃərəl] *adj* cultural; **it's a c. desert** es un desierto cultural ▸▸ ***c. anthropology*** antropología *f* cultural; ***c. attaché*** agregado *m* cultural; ***c. heritage*** acervo *m* cultural; *Hist* ***the C. Revolution*** la Revolución Cultural

culturally ['kʌltʃərəlɪ] *adv* culturalmente

culture ['kʌltʃə(r)] **1** *n* (**a**) *(artistic activity, refinement)* cultura *f*; **a man of c.** un hombre culto *or* con cultura; **to have no c.** no tener cultura, ser inculto(a) ▸▸ *Hum* ***c. vulture*** devorador(ora) *m,f* de cultura
(**b**) *(society)* cultura *f*; **a c. of violence/nepotism** una cultura de violencia/nepotismo; **popular/youth c.** cultura popular/juvenil ▸▸ ***c. shock*** choque *m* cultural
(**c**) *Biol* cultivo *m* ▸▸ ***c. medium*** caldo *m* de cultivo
(**d**) *Agr (of land, crops)* cultivo *m*; *(of animals, poultry)* cría *f*
2 *vt Biol* cultivar

cultured ['kʌltʃəd] *adj* (**a**) *(educated)* culto(a) (**b**) *(pearl)* cultivado(a)

culvert ['kʌlvət] *n* (**a**) *(for water)* alcantarilla *f* (**b**) *(for cable)* conducto *m* subterráneo

cum[1] [kʌm] *prep* **kitchen-c.-dining room** cocina-comedor; **he's a joiner-c.-gardener** es carpintero y jardinero

cum[2] *n Vulg (semen)* leche *f*, *Esp* lefa *f*

cumbersome ['kʌmbəsəm] *adj (bulky)* engorroso(a); *(baggage)* voluminoso(a); *(process, system, style)* pesado(a); **a c. way to do** *or* **of doing sth** una manera muy farragosa de hacer algo

cumin ['kʌmɪn] *n* comino *m*

cum laude [kʊm'laʊdeɪ] *adv US Univ* cum laude

cummerbund ['kʌməbʌnd] *n* fajín *m* (de esmoquin)

cumulative ['kju:mjʊlətɪv] *adj* acumulativo(a) ▸▸ ***c. interest*** interés *m* acumulable

cumuli *pl of* **cumulus**

cumulonimbus [kju:mjʊləʊ'nɪmbəs] (*pl* **cumulonimbi** [kju:mjʊləʊ'nɪmbaɪ]) *n Met* cumulonimbo *m*

cumulus ['kju:mjʊləs] (*pl* **cumuli** ['kju:mjʊlaɪ]) *n Met* cúmulo *m*

cuneiform ['kju:nɪfɔ:m] *adj* cuneiforme

cunnilingus [kʌnɪ'lɪŋgəs] *n* cunilinguo *m*, cunnilingus *m inv*

cunning ['kʌnɪŋ] **1** *n* astucia *f*
2 *adj* (**a**) *(devious)* astuto(a), artero(a); IDIOM **to be as c. as a fox** tener la astucia de un zorro (**b**) *(ingenious)* ingenioso(a) (**c**) *US (cute)* mono(a), *Esp* majo(a), *Am* lindo(a)

cunningly ['kʌnɪŋlɪ] *adv* (**a**) *(deviously)* astutamente (**b**) *(ingeniously)* ingeniosamente

cunt [kʌnt] *n Vulg* (**a**) *(vagina)* coño *m*, *Col* cuca *f*, *Méx* paloma *f*, *RP* concha *f* (**b**) *(as insult)* hijo(a) *m,f* de puta, cabrón(ona) *m,f*

cup [kʌp] **1** *n* (**a**) *(for drinking)* taza *f*; **c. of coffee/tea** (taza de) café/té; **would you like another c.?** ¿te *Esp* apetece *or Carib, Col, Méx* provoca otra taza?, ¿quieres *or CSur* querés otra taza?
(**b**) *Culin (measurement)* taza *f*; **add two cups of sugar** añada dos tazas de azúcar
(**c**) *(trophy)* copa *f*; **the (European) C. Winners C.** *(in soccer)* la Recopa (de Europa) ▸▸ ***c. final*** final *f* de (la) copa; ***c. tie*** *(in soccer)* eliminatoria *f* de copa
(**d**) *(punch)* ponche *m (con vino)*; **champagne c.** sorbete de champán
(**e**) *(of bra)* copa *f* ▸▸ ***c. size*** talla *f* de copa
(**f**) *(in golf)* hoyo *m*
(**g**) IDIOMS *Fam* **it's not my c. of tea** no es santo de mi devoción, *Esp* no me va mucho; *Fam* **it's not everyone's c. of tea** no (le) gusta a todo el mundo; *Fam Old-fashioned* **he was in his cups** llevaba unas copitas de más; *Literary* **he drained the c. of sorrow** apuró el cáliz de la amargura; *Literary* **my c. runneth over!** ¡no quepo en mí de gozo!
2 *vt* (*pt & pp* **cupped**) **to c. one's hands** *(to hold liquid)* ahuecar las manos; **to c. one's hands round one's mouth** poner las manos en la boca a modo de bocina; **he cupped her breasts in his hands** cubrió sus pechos con las manos; **she cupped a hand to her ear** se llevó la mano a la oreja para oír mejor

cupboard ['kʌbəd] *n* armario *m*; **the c. was bare** la despensa estaba vacía, no quedaba nada que llevarse a la boca; IDIOM *Br Fam* **it was c. love** era un amor interesado ▸▸ ***c. space*** armarios *mpl*

cupcake ['kʌpkeɪk] *n* (**a**) *(cake)* ≃ magdalena *f* (**b**) *Fam (eccentric person)* bicho *m* raro (**c**) *US Fam (homosexual)* mariquita *m*

cupful ['kʌpfʊl] *n* taza *f*

Cupid ['kju:pɪd] *n* Cupido; **to play C.** hacer de celestino(a)

cupid ['kju:pɪd] *n Art* cupido *m*, querubín *m*

cupidity [kju:'pɪdɪtɪ] *n Formal* codicia *f*

cupola ['kju:pələ] *n* (**a**) *Archit (ceiling, roof)* cúpula *f*; *(turret)* linterna *f* (**b**) *(gun turret)* torreta *f*

cuppa ['kʌpə] *n Br Fam* (taza *f* de) té *m*

cupric ['kju:prɪk] *adj Chem* cúprico(a)

cupro-nickel ['kju:prəʊ'nɪkəl] *n* cuproníquel *m*

cur [kɜ:(r)] *n Old-fashioned* (**a**) *(dog)* chucho *m* (**b**) *(person)* perro(a) *m,f*, granuja *mf*

curable ['kjʊərəbəl] *adj* curable

Curaçao [kjʊərə'səʊ] *n* Curasao *m*

curaçao [kjʊərə'səʊ] *n* curasao *m*

curassow [kjʊərə'səʊ] *n* hoco *m*, guaco *m*

curate[1] ['kjʊərət] *n Rel* coadjutor *m*; IDIOM *Br* **it's a c.'s egg** tiene alguna que otra cosa buena

curate[2] [kjʊə'reɪt] *vt (exhibition)* **the exhibition was curated by Horace Watkins** Horace Watkins era el director de la exposición

curative ['kjʊərətɪv] **1** *n* remedio *m* curativo
2 *adj* curativo(a)

curator [kjʊə'reɪtə(r)] *n (of museum)* conservador(ora) *m,f* (de museos); *(of exhibition)* comisario(a) *m,f*, director(ora) *m,f*

curb [kɜ:b] **1** *n* (**a**) *(limit)* freno *m*; **to put a c. on sth** poner freno a algo; **she kept a c. on her anger** dominó *or* controló su ira (**b**) *US (at roadside)* bordillo *m* (de la acera), *Chile* solera *f*, *Col, Perú* sardinel *m*, *CSur* cordón *m* (de la vereda), *Méx* borde *m* (de la banqueta) (**c**) *(on harness)* **c. (bit)** freno *m*; **c. (chain)** barbada *f*
2 *vt* (**a**) *(restrain) (spending)* frenar, contener; *(emotions)* refrenar (**b**) *(horse)* poner la barbada a (**c**) *US* **c. your dog** *(sign)* controle a su perro

curbstone *US* = **kerbstone**

curd [kɜ:d] *n (from milk)* **curd(s)** cuajada *f*; **curds and whey** cuajada y suero (de la leche) ▸▸ ***c. cheese*** queso *m* blanco

curdle ['kɜ:dəl] **1** *vt* (**a**) *(milk, sauce)* cortar; **the heat has curdled the milk** la leche se ha cortado por el calor, el calor ha cortado la leche (**b**) IDIOMS *Fam* **he has a face that would c. milk** tiene la cara avinagrada; **the thought was enough to c. my blood** sólo de pensarlo se me helaba la sangre
2 *vi* (**a**) *(milk, sauce)* cortarse; **if the mayonnaise curdles, start again** si se corta la mayonesa, empieza otra vez (**b**) IDIOM **his screams made my blood c.** sus gritos me helaron la sangre

cure ['kjʊə(r)] **1** *n* (**a**) *(remedy)* cura *f* (**for** para); **to take** *or* **follow a c.** *(at health spa)* tomar las aguas; **there is no known c.** no se conoce ninguna cura (**b**) *(recovery)* curación *f*; **to be beyond** *or* **past c.** *(person)* no tener curación, ser incurable; *Fig (problem, situation)* no tener remedio (**c**) *Rel* **the c. of souls** la cura de almas
2 *vt* (**a**) *(person) (of illness)* curar, sanar; *Fig (of bad habit)* quitar, curar; **to c. sb of sth** curar a alguien de algo (**b**) *(preserve) (meat, fish)* curar; *(hides)* curtir; *(tobacco)* curar

cure-all ['kjʊərɔ:l] *n* panacea *f*

curettage [kjʊ'retɪdʒ] *n Med* raspado *m*, legrado *m*

curfew ['kɜ:fju:] *n (restriction, time)* toque *m* de queda; **to impose/lift a c.** decretar/levantar un toque de queda; *US* **to be under c.** *(teenager)* estar castigado(a) sin salir

curia ['kjʊərɪə] *n Rel* **the (papal) c.** la curia pontificia *or* romana

curie ['kjʊərɪ] *n Phys* curio *m*, curie *m*

curio ['kjʊərɪəʊ] (*pl* **curios**) *n* curiosidad *f*, rareza *f*

curiosity [kjʊərɪ'ɒsɪtɪ] *n* (**a**) *(interest)* curiosidad *f*; **out of c.** por curiosidad; PROV **c. killed the cat** por querer saber la zorra perdió la cola, mejor no te metas donde no te llaman (**b**) *(novelty)* curiosidad *f*; **I was something of a c.** era un bicho raro

curious ['kjʊərɪəs] *adj* (**a**) *(inquisitive)* curioso(a); **to be c. to see/know** tener curiosidad por ver/saber; **I'm c. as to what happened next** tengo curiosidad por *or* me intriga saber qué ocurrió después (**b**) *(strange)* curioso(a); **the c. thing (about it) is...** lo curioso (del caso) es que...

curiously ['kjʊərɪəslɪ] *adv* (**a**) *(inquisitively)* con curiosidad, con extrañeza (**b**) *(strangely)* curiosamente; **c. enough** por raro que parezca, aunque parezca mentira

curium ['kjʊərɪəm] *n Chem* curio *m*

curl [kɜ:l] **1** *n* (**a**) *(of hair)* rizo *m*, *Andes, RP* rulo *m*; **her hair hung in curls** tenía cabellos con tirabuzones (**b**) *(of smoke)* voluta *f*; **with a c. of the lip** con una mueca
2 *vt* (**a**) *(hair)* rizar (**b**) *(roll, twist)* **to c. one's lip** hacer un gesto de desprecio; **to c. oneself into a ball** enroscarse, hacerse un ovillo; **to c. the ball** *(in soccer)* dar al balón con efecto *or* de rosca
3 *vi* (**a**) *(hair)* rizarse (**b**) *(paper)* abarquillarse; *(leaf)* rizarse; **her lip curled in contempt** hizo una mueca de desprecio con el labio (**c**) *(smoke)* formar volutas

▸ **curl up** *vi* (**a**) *(settle down) (in bed, on sofa)* acurrucarse (**b**) *(hedgehog, person)* enroscarse, hacerse un ovillo; **she curled up in front of the fire with a book** se hizo un ovillito frente a la chimenea con un libro; *Fam* **when I saw him at the party, I just wanted to c. up and die** cuando lo vi en la fiesta pensé "tierra trágame" (**c**) *(leaves)* rizarse; *(paper)* abarquillarse (**d**) *(smoke)* subir formando volutas

curler ['kɜːlə(r)] *n* (**a**) *(for hair)* rulo *m*, *Chile* tubo *m*, *RP* rulero *m*, *Ven* rollo *m* (**b**) *(player)* jugador(ora) *m,f* de curling

curlew ['kɜːljuː] *n* zarapito *m* ▸▸ ***c. sandpiper*** correlimos *m inv* zarapitín

curlicue ['kɜːlɪkjuː] *n* floritura *f*

curling ['kɜːlɪŋ] *n* (**a**) *(sport)* curling *m*, = deporte consistente en el deslizamiento sobre hielo de piedras pulidas lo más cerca posible de una meta ▸▸ ***c. stone*** piedra *f* de curling (**b**) ***c. tongs*** *(for hair)* tenacillas *fpl*

curly ['kɜːlɪ] **1** *adj (hair)* rizado(a), *Chile, Col* crespo(a), *Méx* quebrado(a), *RP* enrulado(a) ▸▸ *Typ* ***c. brackets*** llaves *fpl*; ***c. endive*** escarola *f*; *Comptr* ***c. quotes*** comillas *fpl* tipográficas

2 *n Fam (person with curly hair)* **hi there, c.** hola, ricitos

curmudgeon [kə'mʌdʒən] *n Old-fashioned* cascarrabias *mf inv*

currant ['kʌrənt] *n* (**a**) *(dried fruit)* pasa *f* (de Corinto) ▸▸ ***c. bun*** bollo *m* de pasas (**b**) *(berry)* grosella *f* ▸▸ ***c. bush*** grosellero *m*

currency ['kʌrənsɪ] *n* (**a**) *Fin* moneda *f*; **to buy c.** comprar divisas; **foreign c.** divisas ▸▸ ***c. market*** mercado *m* de divisas; ***c. swap*** permuta *f* de divisas; ***c. unit*** unidad *f* monetaria (**b**) *(acceptance, credence)* **to give c. to a rumour** extender un rumor; **to gain c.** *(of idea, belief)* extenderse

current ['kʌrənt] **1** *n* (**a**) *(of water, opinion)* corriente *f*; **to swim against the c.** nadar contra corriente; *Fig* **to swim** *or* **go against the c.** ir a *or* nadar contra corriente (**b**) *(of electricity)* corriente *f* ▸▸ ***c. limiter*** limitador *m* de corriente

2 *adj* (**a**) *(existing, present)* actual; *(year, month)* en curso; **his c. whereabouts are unknown** se desconoce su paradero actual; **in c. use** de uso corriente ▸▸ ***c. affairs*** (temas *mpl* de) actualidad *f*

(**b**) *(presently valid) (price)* vigente; *(licence)* válido(a), vigente ▸▸ ***c. issue*** *(of magazine)* (último) número *m*

(**c**) *Br Fin* ***c. account*** cuenta *f* corriente; ***c. assets*** activo *m* circulante; ***c. expenditure*** gasto *m* corriente *or* ordinario; ***c. liabilities*** pasivo *m* corriente, obligaciones *fpl* a corto plazo

currently ['kʌrəntlɪ] *adv* actualmente, en este momento; **c. showing** *(at cinema)* en cartelera

curriculum [kə'rɪkjʊləm] (*pl* **curricula** [kə'rɪkjʊlə]) *n Sch* plan *m* de estudios, currículo *m*; **the maths c.** los contenidos del programa de matemáticas; **across the c.** en todas las asignaturas del plan de estudios ▸▸ *esp Br* ***c. vitae*** currículum *m* (vitae)

curry[1] ['kʌrɪ] *Culin* **1** *n* curry *m*; **chicken/lamb c.** pollo/cordero al curry ▸▸ *Br* ***c. house*** restaurante *m* de comida india; ***c. powder*** curry *m (especia)*; ***c. sauce*** salsa *f* de curry

2 *vt* **curried chicken/lamb** pollo/cordero al curry

curry[2] *vt (horse)* almohazar; IDIOM **to c. favour with sb** ganarse el favor de alguien con zalamerías

currycomb ['kʌrɪkəʊm] *n* almohaza *f*

curse [kɜːs] **1** *n* (**a**) *(jinx, affliction)* maldición *f*; **to call down** *or* **put a c. on sb** echar una maldición a alguien; **a c. on...!** ¡maldito(a) sea...! (**b**) *(swearword)* maldición *f*, juramento *m*; *Fam* **curses!** ¡caramba!, ¡maldición! (**c**) *Fig (bane)* lacra *f*, pesadilla *f*; **the c. of unemployment** la lacra del desempleo (**d**) *Fam Old-fashioned* **the c.** *(period)* el mes, la regla

2 *vt* (**a**) *(damn)* maldecir; **I c. the day I met him!** ¡maldito sea el día en que lo conocí!; **c. it!** ¡maldito sea! (**b**) *(swear at)* insultar (**c**) *(afflict)* **to be cursed with sth** *(person)* estar aquejado(a) de algo, padecer de algo; **the region is cursed with high winds** la región es azotada por fuertes vientos; **he is cursed with a violent temper** tiene la desgracia de tener mal genio

3 *vi* maldecir

cursed [kɜːst, 'kɜːsɪd] *adj* maldito(a)

cursive ['kɜːsɪv] **1** *n* cursiva *f*

2 *adj* cursivo(a)

cursor ['kɜːsə(r)] *n* (**a**) *Comptr* cursor *m* ▸▸ ***c. blink rate*** velocidad *f* de parpadeo del cursor; ***c. keys*** teclas *fpl* de cursor (**b**) *(of slide rule)* cursor *m*

cursorily ['kɜːsərəlɪ] *adv* someramente, por encima

cursory ['kɜːsərɪ] *adj* somero(a); **a c. glance** un vistazo superficial

curt [kɜːt] *adj* brusco(a), seco(a); **with a c. nod** con un gesto brusco *or* seco

curtail [kɜː'teɪl] *vt* (**a**) *(shorten)* acortar (**b**) *(reduce, limit)* restringir, limitar

curtailment [kɜː'teɪlmənt] *n* (**a**) *(shortening)* acortamiento *m* (**b**) *(reduction, limitation)* restricción *f*, limitación *f*

curtain ['kɜːtən] *n* (**a**) *(for window)* cortina *f*; *Fig* **a c. of smoke/rain** una cortina de humo/lluvia ▸▸ ***c. hook*** gancho *m* de cortina; ***c. rail*** riel *m*; ***c. ring*** aro *m* de cortina; ***c. rod*** barra *f* de cortina

(**b**) *(in theatre)* telón *m*; IDIOM **to bring down the c. on sth** dar por finalizado algo; IDIOM *Fam* **it's curtains for him** es su final ▸▸ *Theat* ***c. call*** saludo *m*; **she took four c. calls** salió cuatro veces a saludar

(**c**) *Constr* ***c. wall*** muro *m or* pared *f* de cerramiento

▸ **curtain off** *vt sep* separar con una cortina

curtain-raiser ['kɜːtənreɪzə(r)] *n Theat* número *m* introductorio; *Fig* prólogo *m*

curtly ['kɜːtlɪ] *adv* secamente, con brusquedad

curtness ['kɜːtnɪs] *n* brusquedad *f*; **the c. of his tone** la brusquedad de su tono

curts(e)y ['kɜːtsɪ] **1** *n* reverencia *f*; **to make** *or* **give a c.** hacer una reverencia

2 *vi* hacer una reverencia (**to** a *or* ante)

curvaceous [kɜː'veɪʃəs] *adj* escultural

curvature ['kɜːvətʃə(r)] *n* curvatura *f*; *Med* **c. of the spine** desviación de columna

curve [kɜːv] **1** *n* (**a**) *(line, shape, in road)* curva *f*; **the c. of the bay** la curva de la bahía (**b**) *Fam (of woman)* **she was all curves** era todo curvas, tenía un cuerpo escultural (**c**) *Math* curva *f* (**d**) *US* ***c. ball*** *(in baseball)* bola *f* con mucho efecto; IDIOM **to throw sb a c. ball** poner a alguien en un aprieto

2 *vi (line, surface)* curvarse; *(road, river)* hacer una curva; **to c. (to the) left/right** curvarse a la izquierda/derecha

3 *vt (ball)* lanzar con mucho efecto

curved [kɜːvd] *adj* curvo(a), curvado(a)

curvilinear [kɜːvɪ'lɪnɪə(r)] *adj* curvilíneo(a)

curvy ['kɜːvɪ] *adj* (**a**) *(line, road)* sinuoso(a) (**b**) *Fam (woman)* escultural

Cusco = **Cuzco**

cushion ['kʊʃən] **1** *n* (**a**) *(on chair)* cojín *m*, almohadón *m*; *(of air)* colchón *m* (**b**) *(on billiard table)* banda *f* (**c**) *(protection)* amortiguador *m* (**against** para)

2 *vt* (**a**) *(blow, impact)* amortiguar (**b**) *(protect)* **to c. sb against sth** proteger a alguien de algo

cushy ['kʊʃɪ] *adj Fam* fácil; **a c. number** una ganga, *Esp* un chollo, *Méx* pan comido

cusp [kʌsp] *n* (**a**) *Astron* cuerno *m* (de la luna); **on the c. (of)** en el borde (de) (**b**) *(of tooth)* corona *f*

cuspidor ['kʌspɪdɔː(r)] *n US* escupidera *f*

cuss [kʌs] *Fam* **1** *n* (**a**) *(curse)* maldición *f*, juramento *m* ▸▸ *US* ***c. word*** palabrota *f*, *Esp* taco *m* (**b**) *(person)* maldito(a) *m,f*, *Esp* puñetero(a) *m,f*

2 *vt US* **to c. sb (out)** poner a alguien de vuelta y media

3 *vi* maldecir, jurar

cussed ['kʌsɪd] *adj US Fam* (**a**) *(stubborn)* tozudo(a), *Esp* puñetero(a) (**b**) *(cursed)* maldito(a), *Esp* puñetero(a)

cussedness ['kʌsɪdnɪs] *n Fam* **out of sheer c.** por pura tozudez

custard ['kʌstəd] *n* (**a**) *(sweet sauce)* natillas *fpl* ▸▸ ***c. powder*** polvos *mpl* para hacer natillas (**b**) *(baked)* crema *f* ▸▸ ***c. tart*** tarta *f* de crema (**c**) ***c. pie*** *(in slapstick comedy)* pastel *m or Esp* tarta *f* de crema (**d**) ***c. apple*** chirimoya *f*

custodial [kʌ'stəʊdɪəl] *adj Law* ***c. sentence*** pena *f* de reclusión *or* de cárcel

custodian [kʌs'təʊdɪən] *n* (**a**) *(of building, library)* conservador(ora) *m,f* (**b**) *(of principles, morals)* guardián(ana) *m,f*

custody ['kʌstədɪ] *n* (**a**) *(of children)* custodia *f*; **to have c. of sb** tener la custodia de alguien; **he was given** *or* **awarded c. (of the child)** le otorgaron *or* concedieron la custodia (del niño) ▸▸ ***c. battle*** batalla *f* legal por la custodia (**b**) *(detention)* **to be in (police) c.** estar detenido(a); **to take sb into c.** detener a alguien (**c**) *Formal (keeping)* custodia *f*; **in safe c.** bien custodiado(a)

custom ['kʌstəm] *n* (**a**) *(tradition, practice)* costumbre *f*; **it was his c. to rise early** tenía la costumbre de levantarse temprano; **the c. is to leave a small tip** es costumbre dejar una pequeña propina; **according to c.** según la costumbre

(**b**) *Com* **we value your c.** apreciamos la confianza que deposita en nosotros; **to lose sb's c.** perder a alguien como cliente; **to take one's c. elsewhere** comprar en otra parte

(**c**) *Fin* ***c. house*** aduana *f*

customarily ['kʌstəmərɪlɪ] *adv* por lo común, normalmente

customary ['kʌstəmərɪ] *adj* (**a**) *(traditional)* acostumbrado(a), de costumbre; **it is c. to...** es costumbre... (**b**) *(usual)* habitual; **with his c. good humour** con su buen humor habitual

custom-built ['kʌstəm'bɪlt] *adj* hecho(a) de encargo

customer ['kʌstəmə(r)] *n* (**a**) *(in shop, of business)* cliente(a) *m,f*; **the c. is always right** el cliente siempre tiene la razón ►► *Com* ***c. base*** clientela *f* fija, clientes *mpl* fijos; *Com* ***c. care*** atención *f* al cliente; *Com* ***c. loyalty*** fidelidad *f* del cliente; *Com* ***c. services (department)*** (departamento *m* de) atención *f* al cliente

(**b**) *Fam (character)* **an awkward c.** un tipo quisquilloso; **he's a queer** *or* **an odd c.** es un tipo raro

customer-centred, *US* **customer-centered** ['kʌstəmə'sentəd] *adj Com (approach, company)* centrado(a) en el cliente

customer-driven ['kʌstəmə'drɪvən], **customer-focused** ['kʌstəmə'fəʊkəst] *adj Com (company)* centrado(a) en el cliente

customizable ['kʌstəmaɪzəbəl] *adj Comptr (program, menu)* personalizable

customize ['kʌstəmaɪz] *vt* (**a**) *(modify)* adaptar al gusto del cliente (**b**) *Comptr (program, menu)* personalizar

custom-made ['kʌstəm'meɪd] *adj (equipment)* personalizado(a); *(clothes)* hecho(a) a medida; *(musical instrument)* de encargo

customs ['kʌstəmz] *npl* (**a**) *(authorities, checkpoint)* aduana *f*; **to go through c.** pasar la aduana ►► ***c. agent*** agente *mf* de aduanas; ***c. allowance*** cantidad *f* libre de impuestos; ***c. declaration*** declaración *f* en la aduana; ***c. duties*** derechos *mpl* arancelarios; ***c. officer*** inspector(ora) *m,f or* agente *mf* de aduanas; ***c. official*** inspector(ora) *m,f or* agente *mf* de aduanas; ***c. union*** unión *f* aduanera

(**b**) *(duty)* derechos *mpl* arancelarios *or* de aduana

CUT [kʌt] **1** *n* (**a**) *(in flesh, wood, cloth)* corte *m*; **to make a c. in sth** *(with knife, scissors)* hacer un corte en algo; IDIOM **to be a c. above sth/sb** ser mejor que *or* estar por encima de algo/alguien

(**b**) *(reduction) (in wages, prices)* recorte *m* (**in** de); **to make cuts to** *(budget)* recortar; **to take a pay c.** *or* **a c. in pay** aceptar un recorte salarial

(**c**) *(deletion)* corte *m*; **to make cuts to** *(text, movie)* cortar; **a ten-second c.** un corte de diez segundos

(**d**) *(blow) (with knife)* navajazo *m*; *(with sword)* estocada *f*; *Fig* **his treachery was the unkindest c. of all** su traición fue el golpe más bajo de todos; *Fig* **the c. and thrust of parliamentary debate** el toma y daca del debate parlamentario

(**e**) *Fam (portion, share)* parte *f*, tajada *f*; **a c. of the profits** una tajada de los beneficios

(**f**) *(of meat)* corte *m*; **a c. of meat** un corte de carne

(**g**) *(style) (of clothes, hair)* corte *m*

(**h**) *(trim) (of hair)* corte *m*; **a c. and blow-dry** cortar y marcar

(**i**) *(in golf)* corte *m*; **to make/miss the c.** meterse/no meterse en el corte

(**j**) *(in cards)* corte *m*

(**k**) *Cin (edit)* versión *f*; *(transition)* corte *m* (**from/to** de/a)

(**l**) *Sport (backspin)* efecto *m* cortado

(**m**) *Br (canal)* canal *m*

2 *adj* (**a**) ***c. flowers*** flores *fpl* cortadas; ***c. glass*** vidrio *m or Esp* cristal *m* tallado; *Fam* ***a c. glass accent*** un acento muy afectado; *Comptr* ***c. sheet feeder*** alimentador *m* hoja a hoja

(**b**) *Fig* **c. and dried** *(problem, situation)* claro(a), nítido(a); *(solution, result)* preestablecido(a)

3 *vt* (*pt & pp* **cut**) (**a**) *(with knife, scissors)* cortar; **c. me/yourself a slice of cake** córtame/córtate un trozo de pastel; **to c. a hole in sth** hacer un agujero en algo *(cortando)*; **to c. oneself (on sth)** cortarse (con algo); **to c. one's finger/knee** hacerse un corte en un dedo/una rodilla; *also Fig* **to c. one's throat** cortarse el cuello; **to c. one's wrists** cortarse las muñecas; **to c. sb loose** *or* **free** soltar a alguien; **to c. sth to pieces** cortar algo en pedazos; *Fig (criticize)* poner algo por los suelos; **to c. a swathe through sth** hacer estragos en algo

(**b**) *(divide into parts)* partir; *(in slices)* rebanar; **to c. sth in two** *or* **in half** cortar algo en dos *or* por la mitad; **to c. sth into quarters** cortar algo en cuatro; **to c. sth into slices** cortar algo en rodajas; **to c. sth open** *(bag, melon)* abrir algo *(cortando)*; **to c. one's head open** abrirse la cabeza

(**c**) *(trim) (grass, lawn)* cortar; **to have one's hair c.** (ir a) cortarse el pelo; **to c. sb's hair** cortarle el pelo a alguien; **to c. one's nails** cortarse las uñas

(**d**) *(shape) (diamond, glass, stone)* tallar; *(key)* hacer; **a well c. suit** un traje bien cortado

(**e**) *(dig) (tunnel)* abrir, excavar; **steps had been c. in the rock** habían excavado escalones en la roca

(**f**) *(reduce) (wages, prices)* recortar; **the firm c. its costs by 30 percent** la empresa redujo sus costos en un 30 por ciento; **we have to c. our workforce to 300** tenemos que reducir nuestra plantilla a 300

(**g**) *(shorten) (movie, text)* acortar; **to c. a speech/a visit short** abreviar un discurso/una visita; **to c. a long story short...** en resumidas cuentas...

(**h**) *(interrupt)* **to c. sb short** cortar a alguien; **they c. the enemy's supply line** cortaron la línea de suministro del enemigo

(**i**) *(eliminate, suppress)* eliminar; **the scene was c. from the movie** eliminaron la escena de la película; *very Fam* **c. the crap!** *Esp* ¡corta el rollo de una puñetera vez!, *Esp* ¡déjate de gilipolleces!, *Andes* ¡déjate de joder!, *Méx* ¡ya no me jodas!, *RP* ¡dejá de romper los huevos!

(**j**) *(switch off) (engine)* parar; **c. the lights!** ¡apague las luces!, ¡fuera luces!

(**k**) *Cin (edit)* montar

(**l**) *Comptr* **to c. and paste sth** cortar y pegar algo

(**m**) *(cross, intersect)* cortar; **where the path cuts the road** donde el camino se cruza con la carretera; **to c. a corner** *(in car)* tomar una esquina

(**n**) *(upset)* herir; **to c. sb to the quick** herir a alguien en lo más profundo

(**o**) *Fam (ignore, snub)* desdeñar, despreciar; **to c. sb dead** no hacer ni caso a alguien

(**p**) *Fam (drug)* cortar (**with** con)

(**q**) *(cards)* cortar; **to c. the cards** *or* **deck** cortar la baraja

(**r**) *(tooth)* echar, *RP* cortar; **the baby is cutting his first tooth** al bebé le está saliendo su primer diente, el bebé está echando *or RP* cortando su primer diente; *Fig* **to c. one's teeth on sth** iniciarse con *or* en algo

(**s**) *Old-fashioned* **to c. a record** *or* **disc** *(make recording)* grabar un disco

(**t**) IDIOMS *US* **to c. class** *or* **school** faltar a clase, *Esp* hacer novillos, *Col* capar clase, *Méx* irse de pinta, *RP* hacerse la rabona, *Ven* hacer la cimarra; **to c. one's coat according to one's cloth** adaptarse (uno) a sus posibilidades; **to c. corners** hacer las cosas chapuceramente; **to c. a fine figure** *or Br* **a dash** tener un aspecto elegante; **that's cutting it** *or* **things (a bit) fine** eso es ir muy justo; **the atmosphere was so tense you could c. it with a knife** había tanta tensión en el ambiente que se podía cortar con un cuchillo; **that cuts no ice with me** eso me deja frío, *RP* eso no me mueve un pelo; **to c. one's losses** cortar por lo sano

4 *vi* (**a**) *(with knife, scissors)* cortar; **it cuts easily** *(meat, fabric)* se corta fácilmente; **it will c. into six pieces** saldrán seis trozos

(**b**) *Cin* **c.!** ¡corten!; **to c. to another scene** saltar a otra escena

(**c**) *Comptr* **to c. and paste** cortar y pegar

(**d**) *(in cards)* cortar

(**e**) IDIOMS **that's an argument that cuts both ways** es un arma de doble filo; **to c. to the chase** ir al grano; **to c. loose** *(become independent)* romper las ataduras; *(in sport)* abrir brecha; *Fam* **to c. and run** escabullirse, *Esp* escaquearse, *RP* picárselas

►**cut across** *vt insep* (**a**) *(take short cut through)* atajar por (**b**) *(transcend)* transcender; **this issue cuts across party lines** este tema está por encima de las diferencias entre partidos

►**cut back 1** *vt sep* (**a**) *(reduce)* reducir, recortar (**b**) *(bush, tree)* podar

2 *vi* (**a**) *(double back)* volver sobre sus pasos (**b**) *Cin* volver (**to** a)

►**cut back on** *vt insep (expenses, production)* reducir, recortar; **to c. back on smoking** fumar menos; **to c. back on drinking** beber *or Am* tomar menos

►**cut down** *vt sep* (**a**) *(tree)* talar, cortar; **they were c. down by machine-gun fire** los abatió una ráfaga de ametralladora; IDIOM **to c. sb down to size** bajarle los humos a alguien (**b**) *(shorten, reduce) (speech, text)* reducir; *(spending, time)* recortar, reducir

►**cut down on** *vt insep* reducir; **he has c. down on smoking** fuma menos; **try to c. down on carbohydrates** intenta reducir el consumo de hidratos de carbono *or* carbohidratos

►**cut in 1** *vi* (**a**) *(interrupt conversation)* interrumpir; **to c. in on sb/sb's conversation** interrumpir a alguien/la conversación de alguien (**b**) *(start working)* **the thermostat cuts in automatically** el termostato se pone en funcionamiento automáticamente (**c**) *(car, athlete)* **a van c. in in front of me** se me metió delante una camioneta

2 *vt sep (include)* **we should c. him in on the deal** deberíamos permitir que participara en el negocio

►**cut into** *vt insep (with knife)* cortar; **the rope was cutting into his wrists** la cuerda se le hincaba en las muñecas; **the work was cutting into her free time** el trabajo estaba interfiriendo en su tiempo libre

►**cut off** *vt sep* (**a**) *(remove)* cortar; **to c. off sb's head** cortarle la cabeza a alguien; **to c. off sb's arm** cortarle *or* amputarle el brazo a

alguien; IDIOM **to c. off one's nose to spite one's face** tirar piedras contra el propio tejado
(**b**) *(disconnect)* cortar; **I've been c. off** *(had electricity, water etc disconnected)* me han cortado la luz/el agua/*etc.*; *(during phone conversation)* se ha cortado la comunicación
(**c**) *(disinherit)* **her family c. her off without a penny** su familia no le dejó ni un centavo
(**d**) *(interrupt)* interrumpir; **to c. sb off in mid-sentence** interrumpir a alguien a mitad de frase; **the enemy c. off our supplies** el enemigo nos cortó los suministros
(**e**) *(isolate)* aislar; **we're c. off from the rest of the country here** aquí estamos aislados del resto del país; **to c. oneself off (from)** desconectarse (de)
(**f**) *(intercept)* **they c. off the enemy's retreat** le cortaron la retirada al enemigo

▶ **cut out** 1 *vt sep* (**a**) *(picture)* recortar; *(tumour)* extirpar; *(from text, movie)* eliminar
(**b**) *(stop, eliminate)* **to c. out cigarettes/chocolate** dejar de fumar/de comer chocolate; **c. out the stupid remarks!** ¡déjate de comentarios estúpidos!; *Fam* **c. it out!** ¡basta ya!
(**c**) *(light, sound)* apagar
(**d**) *(exclude)* **to c. sb out of a deal** excluir a alguien de un trato; **to c. sb out of one's will** desheredar a alguien
(**e**) IDIOMS **to be c. out for sth** *(suited)* estar hecho(a) para algo; *Fam* **I've really got my work c. out** lo tengo verdaderamente difícil, me las estoy viendo negras *or RP* en figurillas
2 *vi* (**a**) *(stop working) (thermostat)* desconectarse; *(engine)* calarse (**b**) *US Fam (leave)* largarse

▶ **cut through** *vt insep* (**a**) *(slice)* **the knife c. clean through the rope** el cuchillo cortó limpiamente la cuerda; *Fig* **she c. through all the waffle and got straight to the point** se dejó de rodeos y fue al grano (**b**) *(take short cut via)* atajar por

▶ **cut up** 1 *vt sep* (**a**) *(meat, vegetables)* cortar, trocear; *(paper)* recortar (**b**) *(attack with razor, knife)* **the robbers c. him up** los ladrones le hicieron varios cortes en la cara (**c**) *Fam* **to be very c. up (about sth)** *(upset)* estar muy afectado(a) (por algo) (**d**) *(when driving)* cruzarse por delante de
2 *vi Fam* (**a**) *Br* **to c. up rough** *(person)* ponerse hecho(a) una fiera, hacerse el *Méx* pendejo *or RP* pavo (**b**) *US (misbehave)* hacer el ganso

---

cutaneous [kjʊ'teɪnɪəs] *adj Med* cutáneo(a)

cutaway ['kʌtəweɪ] 1 *n* (**a**) *Cin* cambio *m* de plano (**to** a) (**b**) *(coat)* chaqué *m*
2 *adj (diagram, model)* con un corte interno

cutback ['kʌtbæk] *n* (**a**) *(reduction)* reducción *f*, recorte *m* (**b**) *US Cin* flashback *m*

cute [kju:t] *adj* (**a**) *(sweet)* bonito(a), mono(a) (**b**) *(good-looking) Esp* guapo(a), *Am* buen(ena) mozo(a), *RP* pintón(ona) (**c**) *US (clever)* listo(a); **don't get c. with me** no te hagas el listo conmigo

cuticle ['kju:tɪkəl] *n* cutícula *f*

cutie ['kju:tɪ] *n Fam (child, woman)* preciosidad *f*, monada *f*

cutie-pie ['kju:tɪpaɪ] *n Fam* bomboncito *m*, monín(ina) *m,f*

cutlass ['kʌtləs] *n* alfanje *m*

cutler ['kʌtlə(r)] *n* cuchillero *m*

cutlery ['kʌtlərɪ] *n* cubiertos *mpl*, cubertería *f*

cutlet ['kʌtlɪt] *n* (**a**) *(of meat)* chuleta *f* (**b**) *(croquette)* ≃ croqueta *f*; **vegetable cutlets** = especie de croquetas de verdura

cutoff ['kʌtɒf] *n* (**a**) *(limit)* ***c. date*** fecha *f* tope; ***c. point*** límite *m*, tope *m* (**b**) *(in flow, supply)* corte *m* (**c**) *US (shortcut)* atajo *m*

cut-offs ['kʌtɒfs] *npl Fam* vaqueros *mpl* recortados, *Chile* bluyíns *mpl* recortados, *Méx* pantalones *mpl* de mezclilla recortados

cutout ['kʌtaʊt] *n* (**a**) *(shape)* figura *f* recortada (**b**) *Elec* cortacircuitos *m inv*

cut-price ['kʌt'praɪs] *adj* rebajado(a); **c. travel/fashions** viaje/modas a precios rebajados

cutter ['kʌtə(r)] *n* (**a**) *(person) (of clothes)* cortador(ora) *m,f*; *(of jewels)* cortador(ora) *m,f*; *(of film)* montador(ora) *m,f* (**b**) *(ship)* cúter *m*; *(ship's boat)* bote *m*; *(of coastguard)* guardacostas *m inv*

cut-throat ['kʌtθrəʊt] 1 *n* matón *m*, asesino(a) *m,f*
2 *adj* **c. competition** competencia salvaje *or* sin escrúpulos ▸▸ ***c. razor*** navaja *f* barbera

cutting ['kʌtɪŋ] 1 *n* (**a**) *(of plant)* esqueje *m* (**b**) **(newspaper) c.** recorte *m* (de periódico) (**c**) *(for railway, road)* desmonte *m* (**d**) *Cin* ***c. room*** sala *f* de montaje; *Fig* **the scenes ended up on the c. room floor** las escenas fueron eliminadas en el montaje
2 *adj (wind)* cortante; *(remark)* hiriente, cortante ▸▸ ***c. edge*** filo *m* cortante; *Fig* **to be at the c. edge of** estar a la vanguardia de

cuttlebone ['kʌtəlbəʊn] *n* jibión *m*

cuttlefish ['kʌtəlfɪʃ] *n* sepia *f*, jibia *f*

Cuzco, Cusco ['ku:skəʊ] *n* Cuzco

CV [si:'vi:] *n* (*abbr* **curriculum vitae**) CV, currículum *m* vitae

cwt (*abbr* **hundredweight**) (**a**) *(metric)* 50 kg (**b**) *(imperial) Br (112 lb)* = 50,8 kg; *US (100 lb)* = 45,36 kg

cyan ['saɪæn] 1 *n* cián *m*
2 *adj* cián

cyanide ['saɪənaɪd] *n Chem* cianuro *m*

cyberbanking ['saɪbəbæŋkɪŋ] *n Comptr* banca *f* electrónica

cybercafe ['saɪbəkæfeɪ] *n Comptr* cibercafé *m*

cybercrime ['saɪbəkraɪm] *n Comptr* cibercrimen *m*

cyberculture ['saɪbəkʌltʃə(r)] *n Comptr* cibercultura *f*

cybernaut ['saɪbənaʊt] *n Comptr* cibernauta *mf*

cybernetic [saɪbə'netɪk] *adj Comptr* cibernético(a) ▸▸ ***c. organism*** organismo *m* cibernético, ciborg *m*

cybernetics [saɪbə'netɪks] *n Comptr* cibernética *f*

cyberpunk ['saɪbəpʌŋk] *n Comptr (science fiction)* ciberpunk *m*

cybersex ['saɪbəseks] *n Comptr* cibersexo *m*

cyberspace ['saɪbəspeɪs] *n Comptr* ciberespacio *m*; **in c.** en el ciberespacio

cybersquatter ['saɪbəskwɒtə(r)] *n Comptr* ciberokupa *mf*

cyberterrorism ['saɪbəterərɪzəm] *n Comptr* ciberterrorismo *m*

cyborg ['saɪbɔ:g] *n Comptr* ciborg *m*

Cyclades ['sɪklədi:z] *n* **the C.** las Cícladas

cyclamen ['sɪkləmən] *n* ciclamen *m*, pamporcino *m*

cycle ['saɪkəl] 1 *n* (**a**) *(pattern)* ciclo *m*; **the c. of the seasons** el ciclo de las estaciones
(**b**) *(bicycle)* bicicleta *f* ▸▸ *Br* ***c. lane*** carril-bici *m*; ***c. path*** *(through park, town)* carril *m* para bicicletas; *(through countryside)* sendero *m* para bicicletas; ***c. racing*** carreras *fpl* ciclistas; ***c. rack*** *(on pavement)* soporte *m* para bicicletas; *(on car)* baca *f* para bicicletas
(**c**) *Comptr & Elec* ciclo *m*
(**d**) *(of songs, plays)* ciclo *m*
2 *vi* ir en bicicleta; **she cycles into town every day** va al centro en bicicleta todos los días

cycleway ['saɪkəlweɪ] *n (through park, town)* carril *m* para bicicletas; *(through countryside)* sendero *m* para bicicletas

cyclic(al) ['sɪklɪk(əl)] *adj* cíclico(a)

cycling ['saɪklɪŋ] *n* ciclismo *m*; **to go c.** salir en bicicleta; **I'd never gone cycling before** nunca había montado en bicicleta; **to go on a c. holiday** hacer cicloturismo ▸▸ ***c. shorts*** culotte *m*, culottes *mpl*; ***c. track*** pista *f* de ciclismo

cyclist ['saɪklɪst] *n* ciclista *mf*

cyclo-cross ['saɪkləkrɒs] *n* ciclocross *m*

cyclometer [saɪ'klɒmətə(r)] *n* cuentakilómetros *m inv*

cyclone ['saɪkləʊn] *n Met* ciclón *m*

cyclonic [saɪ'klɒnɪk] *adj Met* ciclónico(a)

Cyclops ['saɪklɒps] *n Mythol* Cíclope *m*

cyclorama [saɪklə'rɑ:mə] *n Theat* ciclorama *m*

cyclotron ['saɪklətrɒn] *n Phys* ciclotrón *m*

cygnet ['sɪgnɪt] *n* cisne *m* joven

cylinder ['sɪlɪndə(r)] *n* (**a**) *(shape)* cilindro *m* (**b**) *(in engine)* cilindro *m*; IDIOM **to be firing on all cylinders** funcionar a pleno rendimiento ▸▸ ***c. block*** bloque *m* (de cilindros); ***c. head*** culata *f* (**c**) *(gas container)* bombona *f* (**d**) *(of revolver)* cilindro *m*

cylindrical [sɪ'lɪndrɪkəl] *adj* cilíndrico(a)

cymbal ['sɪmbəl] *n* platillo *m*

cynic ['sɪnɪk] *n* descreído(a) *m,f*, suspicaz *mf*; **cynics will say she married for money** los más suspicaces dirán que se casó por dinero; **you're such a c.!** ¡siempre estás pensando lo peor!

cynical ['sɪnɪkəl] *adj* (**a**) *(sceptical)* descreído(a), suspicaz; **to be c. about sth** ser escéptico(a) respecto a algo; **you're so c.!** ¡cómo puedes pensar siempre lo peor! (**b**) *(unscrupulous)* desaprensivo(a), sin escrúpulos

cynically ['sɪnɪklɪ] *adv* (**a**) *(sceptically)* descreídamente, con suspicacia (**b**) *(unscrupulously)* desaprensivamente, sin escrúpulos

cynicism ['sɪnɪsɪzəm] *n (scepticism)* descreimiento *m*, suspicacia *f*

cypher = **cipher**

cypress ['saɪprəs] *n* ciprés *m*
Cypriot ['sɪprɪət] **1** *n* chipriota *mf*
2 *adj* chipriota
Cyprus ['saɪprəs] *n* Chipre
Cyrillic [sɪ'rɪlɪk] **1** *adj* cirílico(a)
2 *n* cirílico *m*
cyst [sɪst] *n Med* quiste *m*
cystic fibrosis ['sɪstɪkfaɪ'brəʊsɪs] *n Med* fibrosis *f inv* cística *or* quística
cystitis [sɪs'taɪtɪs] *n Med* cistitis *f inv*
cytology [saɪ'tɒlədʒɪ] *n Biol* citología *f*
cytoplasm ['saɪtəplæzəm] *n Biol* citoplasma *m*
czar [zɑː(r)] *n* zar *m*
Czech [tʃek] **1** *n* (**a**) *(person)* checo(a) *m,f* (**b**) *(language)* checo *m*
2 *adj* checo(a) ►► ***the C. Republic*** la República Checa
Czechoslovak = **Czechoslovakian**
Czechoslovakia [tʃekəslə'vækɪə] *n Formerly* Checoslovaquia
Czechoslovakian [tʃekəslə'vækɪən], **Czechoslovak** [tʃekə'sləʊvæk] *Formerly* **1** *n* checoslovaco(a) *m,f*
2 *adj* checoslovaco(a)

D, d

D, d [diː] *n (letter)* D, d

D [diː] *n* (**a**) *Mus* re *m* (**b**) *Sch* **to get a D** *(in exam, essay) (pass)* sacar un aprobado *or* suficiente bajo; *(fail) Esp* suspender, *Am* reprobar (**c**) *US Pol* (*abbr* **Democratic**) demócrata *mf* (**d**) **the D** *(in soccer)* el semicírculo, la medialuna *(del área)*; *(in snooker)* la medialuna *(de la cabaña)*

d (**a**) (*abbr* **died**) **d 1913** fallecido(a) en 1913 (**b**) *Br Formerly* (*abbr* **penny**) penique *m*

DA [diː'eɪ] *n* (**a**) *US Law* (*abbr* **district attorney**) fiscal *mf* (del distrito) ▸▸ ***the DA's office*** la oficina del fiscal (del distrito) (**b**) *Fam* (*abbr* **duck's** *Br* **arse** *or US* **ass**) = estilo de peinado masculino popular en los años cincuenta consistente en llevar el pelo corto peinado hacia atrás

D/A [diː'eɪ] *Com* (*abbr* **documents against acceptance**) documentos contra aceptación

da [dɑː] *n Fam Irish* papá *m*

dab [dæb] **1** *n* (**a**) *(of paint, glue, perfume)* pizca *f*, toque *m*; *Br Fam* **dabs** *(fingerprints)* huellas *fpl* dactilares *or* digitales; *esp Br Fam* **she's a d. hand at drawing** dibuja que es un alucine (**b**) *(fish)* limanda *f*

2 *vt* (*pt & pp* **dabbed**) *(paint, glue, perfume)* aplicar, poner; **she dabbed her eyes with a handkerchief** se secó los ojos delicadamente con un pañuelo

▸**dab at** *vt insep* **he dabbed at the stain with a sponge** dio unas pasaditas a la mancha con una esponja; **she dabbed at his tears with a handkerchief** le secó las lágrimas con un pañuelo

▸**dab off** *vt sep* **d. off any excess oil on the fish with a paper towel** quite con cuidado el exceso de aceite del pescado con una servilleta de papel

▸**dab on** *vt sep* **d. on the paint with a brush** aplique la pintura con pinceladas cortas; **d. antiseptic on the wound** pon con cuidado un poco de antiséptico en la herida

dabble ['dæbəl] **1** *vt* **they dabbled their feet in the water** chapoteaban en el agua

2 *vi* **he dabbles in politics** se entretiene con la política; **to d. on the Stock Market** jugar a la bolsa

dabbler ['dæblə(r)] *n* aficionado(a) *m,f*, diletante *mf*

dabchick ['dæbtʃɪk] *n* zampullín *m* chico

Dacca ['dækə] *n Formerly* Dacca

dace [deɪs] (*pl* **dace** *or* **daces**) *n* cacho *m (pez)*

dacha ['dætʃə] *n* dacha *f*

dachshund ['dækshʊnd] *n* perro *m* salchicha, dachshund *m*

Dacron® ['dækrɒn] *n* dacrón® *m*

dactyl ['dæktɪl] *n Lit* dáctilo *m*

dactylic [dæk'tɪlɪk] *adj Lit* dactílico(a)

dad [dæd] *n Fam* (**a**) *(father) (said by child)* papá *m*; *(said by adult) Esp* padre *m*, *Am* papá *m* (**b**) *(old man)* abuelo *m*

Dada ['dɑːdɑː] *Art* **1** *n* Dadá *m*

2 *adj* dadaísta

Dadaism ['dɑːdɑːɪzəm] *n Art* dadaísmo *m*

Dadaist ['dɑːdɑːɪst] *Art* **1** *n* dadaísta *mf*

2 *adj* dadaísta

daddy ['dædɪ] *n Fam* papi *m*, papaíto *m*; **the d. bear/elephant** el papá oso/elefante; IDIOM **the d. of them all** el que se lleva la palma

daddy-longlegs ['dædɪ'lɒŋlegz] *n Fam* (**a**) *Br (cranefly)* típula *f* (**b**) *US (harvestman)* segador *m*

dado ['deɪdəʊ] *n* (**a**) *(of wall)* friso *m* ▸▸ ***d. rail*** zócalo *m*, friso *m* (**b**) *Archit (of column, pedestal)* dado *m*

Daedalus ['diːdələs] *n Mythol* Dédalo

daemon ['diːmən] *n* (**a**) *(demigod)* semidiós *m inv* (**b**) = **demon**

daff [dæf] *n Br Fam* narciso *m*

daffodil ['dæfədɪl] *n* narciso *m (de los prados)*

daffy ['dæfɪ] *adj Fam* chiflado(a), chalado(a)

daft [dɑːft] **1** *adj Br Fam* tonto(a), *Am* sonso(a), *Am* zonzo(a); **it was a d. thing to do/say** hacer/decir esto fue una tontería; **to be d. about sth/sb** estar loco por algo/alguien

2 *adv* **don't talk d.** no digas tonterías

dag [dæg] *n Austr Fam* (**a**) *(unfashionable person) Esp* hortera *mf*, *Chile* cuico(a) *m,f*, *Méx* naco(a) *m,f*, *RP* terraja *mf* (**b**) *(untidy person)* zarrapastroso(a) *m,f*

dagger ['dægə(r)] *n* (**a**) *(weapon)* daga *f*, puñal *m* (**b**) *Typ* cruz *f*, obelisco *m* (**c**) IDIOM **to be at daggers drawn (with sb)** estar a matar (con alguien); **to look** *or US* **shoot daggers at sb** fulminar a alguien con la mirada

dago ['deɪgəʊ] (*pl* **dagos**) *n very Fam* = término generalmente ofensivo para referirse a españoles, italianos, portugueses o latinoamericanos

daguerreotype [də'gerətaɪp] *n* daguerrotipo *m*

dahl, d(h)al [dɑːl] *n* = potaje hindú muy especiado a base de legumbres

dahlia ['deɪlɪə] *n* dalia *f*

Dáil (Éireann) ['dɔɪl('eərən)] *n* = cámara baja del parlamento de la República de Irlanda

daily ['deɪlɪ] **1** *n* (**a**) *(newspaper)* diario *m*, periódico *m* (**b**) *Br Fam* señora *f* de la limpieza

2 *adj* diario(a); **on a d. basis** a diario; **our d. bread** el pan nuestro de cada día; *Fam* **the d. grind** la rutina diaria; **the d. round** la ronda diaria ▸▸ *Fam Old-fashioned* ***d. dozen*** ejercicios *mpl* (de gimnasia) diarios; *Br* ***d. help*** señora *f* de la limpieza; ***d. paper*** diario *m*, periódico *m*

3 *adv* diariamente; **twice d.** dos veces al día

daintily ['deɪntɪlɪ] *adv* (**a**) *(to eat, hold)* con finura, con delicadeza; *(to walk)* con gracia y donaire (**b**) *(to dress)* con gusto, con refinamiento

dainty ['deɪntɪ] **1** *adj* (**a**) *(features, lace, ornament)* delicado(a), fino(a) (**b**) *(movement)* grácil; **to walk with d. steps** caminar con paso grácil (**c**) *(tasty)* **d. morsels** delicias suculentas (**d**) *(fussy)* **she's a d. eater** es muy quisquillosa con la comida

2 *n* **dainties** *(cakes)* exquisiteces *mpl*; *(sweets)* confites *mpl*, golosinas *fpl*

daiquiri ['dækərɪ] *n* daiquiri *m*, *Am* daiquirí *m*

dairy ['deərɪ] *n* (**a**) *(on farm)* vaquería *f* ▸▸ ***d. cattle*** vacas *fpl* lecheras, rebaño *m* lechero; ***d. cow*** vaca *f* lechera; ***d. farm*** vaquería *f*; ***d. farming*** la industria lechera (**b**) *(factory)* central *f* lechera ▸▸ ***d. produce*** productos *mpl* lácteos (**c**) *(shop)* lechería *f*

dairymaid ['deərɪmeɪd] *n Old-fashioned* lechera *f*

dairyman ['deərɪmən] *n* lechero *m*

dais ['deɪɪs] *n* tarima *f*

daisy ['deɪzɪ] *n* margarita *f*; IDIOM *Fam* **he's pushing up the daisies** está criando malvas ▸▸ ***d. chain*** guirnalda *f* de margaritas

daisy-chain ['deɪzɪtʃeɪn] *vt Comptr* conectar en bucle

daisy-cutter ['deɪzɪkʌtə(r)] *n Fam (bomb)* bomba *f* BLU 82 "corta margaritas"

daisy-wheel ['deɪzɪwiːl] *n Comptr* margarita *f* ▸▸ ***d. printer*** impresora *f* de margarita

Dakar ['dækɑː(r)] *n* Dakar

Dakota [də'kəʊtə] *n* **the Dakotas** la Dakota del Norte y la del Sur

dal = **dahl**

Dalai Lama ['dælaɪ'lɑːmə] *n* **the D.** el Dalai-lama

dale [deɪl] *n* valle *m*

dalesman ['deɪlzmən] *n Br* = habitante de los valles del norte de Inglaterra, especialmente de Yorkshire

dalliance ['dælɪəns] *n Formal* flirteo *m*, coqueteo *m*

dally ['dælɪ] *vi* (**a**) *(dawdle)* perder el tiempo; **to d. over a decision** demorarse en tomar una decisión (**b**) *Old-fashioned (flirt)* **to d. with sb** coquetear con alguien

Dalmatian [dæl'meɪʃən] *n (dog)* dálmata *m*

dam [dæm] **1** *n* (**a**) *(barrier)* dique *m*, presa *f* (**b**) *(reservoir)* embalse *m* (**c**) *(animal)* madre *f*
2 *vt (pt & pp* **dammed**) *(valley)* construir una presa en; *(river, lake)* embalsar

▸ **dam up** *vt sep* (**a**) = **dam** (**b**) *(one's feelings)* reprimir

damage ['dæmɪdʒ] **1** *n* (**a**) *(to machine, building)* daños *mpl*; *(to health, reputation)* perjuicio *m*, daño *m*; **to do** *or* **cause d. to sth** ocasionar daños a algo, perjudicar a algo; **the storm did a lot of d.** la tormenta ocasionó grandes daños; **the d. is done** el daño ya está hecho; IDIOM *Fam* **what's the d.?** ¿qué se debe? ▸▸ ***d. limitation*** limitación *f* de daños; **it was a d. limitation exercise** se trató de una acción para minimizar los daños
(**b**) *Law* **damages** daños *mpl* y perjuicios; **to award damages to sb (for sth)** conceder a alguien una indemnización por daños y perjuicios (por algo)
2 *vt (machine, building)* dañar; *(health, reputation)* perjudicar, dañar

damaged ['dæmɪdʒd] *adj* dañado(a); **d. goods** *(stock)* mercancías dañadas; *Old-fashioned (person)* persona con un pasado oscuro

damaging ['dæmɪdʒɪŋ] *adj* perjudicial; **it was a d. admission** fue una confesión perjudicial; **it's a d. blow to his election chances/career** es un duro golpe a sus posibilidades de salir elegido/su carrera

Damascus [də'mæskəs] *n* Damasco

damask ['dæməsk] *n* (**a**) *(silk, linen)* damasco *m* (**b**) ***d. rose*** rosa *f* de Jericó

dame [deɪm] *n* (**a**) *US Fam (woman)* tipa *f*, *Esp* gachí *f*, *CSur* mina *f*, *Méx* vieja *f* (**b**) *Br (in pantomime)* = personaje femenino de una vieja interpretado por un actor (**c**) *Br (title)* = título nobiliario concedido a una mujer

damfool ['dæmfu:l] *adj Fam* estúpido(a), ridículo(a)

dammit ['dæmɪt] *exclam Fam* ¡maldita sea!; IDIOM *Br* **or as near as d.** o casi casi

damn [dæm] **1** *n Fam* **I don't give a d.** me importa un bledo *or* comino; **I don't give a d. about what they say** me importa un bledo *or* comino lo que digan; **it's not worth a d.** no vale un pimiento
2 *adj Fam* maldito(a); **you d. fool!** ¡maldito idiota!; **it's a d. nuisance!** ¡qué fastidio!; **it's one d. thing after another** es que es una cosa *or CAm, Carib, Col* vaina detrás de la otra
3 *adv Fam* (**a**) *(as intensifier)* **d. good** genial, buenísimo(a); **it's a d. shame** es una auténtica pena; **he's so d. slow** ¡mira que es lento!, es lento como él sólo; **you know d. well what I mean!** ¡sabes de sobra lo que quiero decir!
(**b**) *Br* **d. all** *(absolutely nothing)* nada de nada; **d. all money/help** nada de dinero/ayuda; **he knows d. all about politics** no tiene ni la más remota idea *or Esp* ni puñetera idea de política
4 *vt* (**a**) *(criticize severely)* vapulear, criticar duramente; IDIOM **to d. sb with faint praise** criticar veladamente a alguien con falsos elogios; **you're damned if you do and damned if you don't** si lo haces, mal, y si no lo haces, también mal
(**b**) *Rel* condenar
(**c**) *Fam* **d. it!** ¡maldita sea!; **d. you!** ¡maldito seas!; **he lied to me, d. him!** el muy maldito me mintió; **d. the expense/the consequences!** ¡a la porra con los gastos/las consecuencias!; **well I'll be damned!** ¡que me aspen!, ¡madre mía!; **I'm** *or* **I'll be damned if I'm going to apologize** no tengo la menor intención de disculparme; **I'm damned if I'm going to help him!** ¡va listo *or* lo lleva claro si piensa que voy a ayudarle!; **I'm damned if I understand** no entiendo nada de nada
5 *exclam Fam* ¡maldita sea!

damnable ['dæmnəbəl] *adj Old-fashioned* horrible, detestable

damnably ['dæmnəblɪ] *adv Old-fashioned* terriblemente, sumamente

damnation [dæm'neɪʃən] *n* **1** *Rel* condenación *f*
2 *exclam Fam* ¡maldición!

damned [dæmd] **1** *adj* (**a**) *Rel (soul)* condenado(a) (**b**) *Fam* = **damn**
2 *adv Fam* **d. good** genial, buenísimo(a)
3 *n Rel* **the d.** los condenados

damnedest ['dæmdəst] *Fam* **1** *n* **to do one's d. (to do sth)** hacer todo lo posible (por hacer algo)
2 *adj US* **it was the d. thing!** ¡fue de lo más raro!, ¡fue una cosa rarísima!

damning ['dæmɪŋ] *adj (admission, revelation)* condenatorio(a); **d. evidence** pruebas condenatorias; **the report was a damning indictment of the government** el informe ponía en seria tela de juicio al gobierno

damp [dæmp] **1** *n* humedad *f* ▸▸ *Constr* ***d. course*** aislante *m* hidrófugo *or* antihumedad
2 *adj* húmedo(a); **a d. patch** una mancha de humedad; *Fig* **a d. squib** un chasco
3 *vt* (**a**) *(with water)* humedecer, mojar (**b**) *(sound, vibration)* amortiguar; *Fig* **to d. sb's spirits** *or* **enthusiasm** desanimar a alguien

▸ **damp down** *vt sep* (**a**) *(fire)* sofocar (**b**) *(enthusiasm, ardour)* apagar, enfriar

dampen ['dæmpən] *vt* (**a**) *(make wet)* humedecer (**b**) *(enthusiasm, ardour)* apagar; **to d. sb's spirits** desanimar a alguien

damper ['dæmpə(r)] *n* (**a**) *Mus* sordina *f*, apagador *m* (**b**) *(in furnace, chimney)* regulador *m* de tiro (**c**) *Elec & Tech* amortiguador *f* (**d**) IDIOM **to put a d. on sth** ensombrecer algo; **his arrival put a d. on proceedings** su llegada ensombreció el acto

dampness ['dæmpnɪs] *n* humedad *f*

damp-proof ['dæmppru:f] **1** *vt* aislar de la humedad
2 *n Constr* ***d. course*** aislante *m* hidrófugo *or* antihumedad

damsel ['dæmzəl] *n Literary* doncella *f*, damisela *f*; *Hum* **a d. in distress** una doncella en apuros

damson ['dæmzən] *n* (**a**) *(fruit)* ciruela *f* damascena (**b**) *(tree)* ciruelo *m* damasceno

dan [dæn] *n (in martial arts)* dan *m*

dance [dɑ:ns] **1** *n* (**a**) *(action)* baile *m*; **may I have the next d.?** ¿me concede el próximo baile?; **traditional dances** danzas *or* bailes tradicionales; IDIOM *Fam* **to lead sb a (merry) d.** traer a alguien al retortero *or* a mal traer, *RP* sacar canas verdes a alguien ▸▸ ***the d. of the seven veils*** la danza de los siete velos
(**b**) *(piece of music)* baile *m*
(**c**) *(art)* danza *f*; **to study d.** estudiar danza ▸▸ ***d. company*** compañía *f* de danza; ***d. school*** academia *f* de baile
(**d**) *(social occasion)* baile *m*; **to hold a d.** celebrar un baile ▸▸ ***d. band*** orquesta *f* de baile; ***d. floor*** pista *f* de baile; ***d. hall*** salón *m* de baile; ***d. music*** música *f* de baile
2 *vt (waltz, polka)* bailar; **to d. the night away** bailar durante toda la noche; **she danced the baby on her knee** puso al bebé a bailar sobre sus rodillas; IDIOM **to d. attendance on sb** atender servilmente a alguien
3 *vi* (**a**) *(person)* bailar; **they danced down the road** bajaron la calle dando brincos; **to d. for joy** dar saltos de alegría; IDIOM **to d. to sb's tune** *(obey)* bailar al son que toca alguien (**b**) *Literary (leaves)* mecerse; *(light, eyes)* bailar

dancer ['dɑ:nsə(r)] *n* bailarín(ina) *m,f*

dancing ['dɑ:nsɪŋ] *n* baile *m*; **to go d.** ir a bailar ▸▸ ***d. partner*** pareja *f* de baile; ***d. shoes*** zapatos *mpl* de baile

D and C [di:ən'si:] *n Med* (*abbr* **dilatation and curettage**) operación *f* de legrado

dandelion ['dændɪlaɪən] *n* diente *m* de león ▸▸ ***d. clock*** vilano *m* del diente de león

dander ['dændə(r)] *n* IDIOM *Fam* **to get sb's d. up** *(annoy)* sacar de quicio a alguien

dandified ['dændɪfaɪd] *adj (appearance)* de petimetre, de dandi; **a d. young man** un petimetre

dandle ['dændəl] *vt* montar a caballito (en las rodillas)

dandruff ['dændrʌf] *n* caspa *f* ▸▸ ***d. shampoo*** champú *m* anticaspa

dandy ['dændɪ] **1** *n* petimetre *m*, dandi *m*
2 *adj Fam* genial; **everything's just (fine and) d.** está todo fenómeno

Dane [deɪn] *n* danés(esa) *m,f*

dang [dæŋ] *exclam US Fam* ¡maldita sea!

danger ['deɪndʒə(r)] *n* peligro *m*; **d., keep out!** *(sign)* peligro, prohibido el paso; **in/out of d.** en/fuera de peligro; **to be in d. of doing sth** correr el peligro de hacer algo; **to be a d. to sth/sb** ser un peligro para algo/alguien; **to put sth/sb in d.** poner algo/a alguien en peligro; **there is no d. that...** no hay peligro de que...; **to be on the d. list** *(patient)* estar muy grave; **to be off the d. list** *(patient)* estar fuera de peligro ▸▸ ***d. money*** prima *f or* plus *m* de peligrosidad; *Fig* ***d. sign*** señal *f* de peligro

dangerous ['deɪndʒərəs] *adj* peligroso(a); IDIOM **to be** *or* **tread on d. ground** pisar *or* meterse en un terreno peligroso ▸▸ ***d. driving*** conducción *f* temeraria; ***d. play*** juego *m* peligroso

dangerously ['deɪndʒərəslɪ] *adv* peligrosamente; **they came d. close to losing** estuvieron en un tris de caer derrotados; **to live d.** vivir al límite

dangle ['dæŋgəl] **1** *vt* balancear, hacer oscilar; *Fig* **the company dangled a bonus in front of its workers** la empresa ofreció una paga extra a sus trabajadores como incentivo
2 *vi* colgar; **he was dangling at the end of the rope** colgaba del extremo de la cuerda; IDIOM **to keep sb dangling** tener a alguien pendiente

Danish ['deɪnɪʃ] **1** *n* (**a**) *(language)* danés *m* (**b**) *US (pastry)* = pastel dulce de hojaldre
2 *adj* danés(esa) ►► ***D. blue (cheese)*** queso *m* azul danés; ***D. pastry*** = pastel dulce de hojaldre

dank [dæŋk] *adj (weather, dungeon)* frío(a) y húmedo(a)

Dantean ['dæntɪən], **Dantesque** [dæn'tesk] *adj* dantesco(a)

Danube ['dænju:b] *n* **the D.** el Danubio

Daphne ['dæfnɪ] *n Mythol* Dafne

dapper ['dæpə(r)] *adj* pulcro(a), atildado(a)

dapple ['dæpəl] *vt* motear

dappled ['dæpəld] *adj (horse)* rodado(a); **the d. light on the forest floor** el lecho del bosque, salpicado de luces y sombras

dapple-grey, *US* **dapple-gray** ['dæpəlgreɪ] **1** *adj* tordillo(a)
2 *n (horse)* tordillo *m*

Darby and Joan ['dɑ:bɪən'dʒəʊn] *n* = matrimonio ideal de ancianos que siguen llevando una vida en común totalmente feliz ►► ***D. club*** = club para personas de la tercera edad

dare [deə(r)] **1** *n* reto *m*, desafío *m*; **he would do anything for a d.** es capaz de hacer cualquier cosa si le desafían a ello; **they did it for a d.** lo hicieron para demostrar que podían
2 *vt* (**a**) *(be sufficiently brave)* **to d. to do sth** atreverse a hacer algo; **I lay there hardly daring to breathe** estaba ahí sin apenas atreverme a respirar
(**b**) *(challenge)* **to d. sb to do sth** retar a alguien a que haga algo; **I d. you to tell her!** ¿a que no se lo dices?, ¿a que no eres capaz de decírselo?
(**c**) *Literary (risk)* **he was willing to d. death for fame and glory** estaba dispuesto a arriesgar la vida a cambio de la fama y la gloria; **few would d. the tyrant's displeasure** pocos osarían provocar las iras del tirano
3 *modal aux v* **to d. do sth** atreverse a hacer algo; **I d. not** *or* **daren't ask him** no me atrevo a preguntarle; **don't you d. tell her!** ¡ni se te ocurra decírselo!; **how d. you!** ¡cómo te atreves!; **just you d.!** ¡atrévete!; **d. I say it...** casi no me atrevo a decirlo...; **I d. say** probablemente; **I d. say she's right** me atrevería a decir que tiene razón; *Ironic* **he was most apologetic – I d. say!** lo sentía muchísimo – ¡no era para menos!

dare-devil ['deədevəl] **1** *n* temerario(a) *m,f*
2 *adj* temerario(a), osado(a)

daring ['deərɪŋ] **1** *n* atrevimiento *m*, osadía *f*
2 *adj* (**a**) *(courageous)* audaz, atrevido(a) (**b**) *(provocative)* atrevido(a)

daringly ['deərɪŋlɪ] *adv* (**a**) *(courageously)* con audacia *or* atravemiento (**b**) *(provocatively)* con atrevimiento; **a d. low neckline** un escote muy atrevido

dark [dɑ:k] **1** *n* (**a**) *(darkness)* oscuridad *f*; **to be afraid of the d.** tener miedo a la oscuridad; **before/after d.** antes/después del anochecer; **in the d.** en la oscuridad; **to see in the d.** ver en la oscuridad
(**b**) IDIOMS **to be in the d. (about sth)** *Am* no tener idea (sobre algo), *Esp* estar in albis (sobre algo); **to keep sb in the d. (about sth)** mantener a alguien en la ignorancia (acerca de algo); **his answer left us completely in the d.** su respuesta no nos aclaró nada
2 *adj* (**a**) *(not illuminated)* oscuro(a); **it's d. by six o'clock** a las seis ya es de noche; **it's getting d.** está oscureciendo *or* anocheciendo; **the d. side of the moon** la cara oculta de la luna
(**b**) *(colour, dress, suit)* oscuro(a); **d. blue/brown** azul/marrón oscuro ►► ***d. chocolate*** chocolate *m* negro; ***d. glasses*** gafas *fpl* oscuras; *Astron* ***d. matter*** materia *f* oscura; ***d. meat*** *(of poultry)* carne *f* (oscura) del muslo
(**c**) *(skin, hair)* oscuro(a), moreno(a); **to have d. hair** ser moreno(a)
(**d**) *(gloomy) (thought, mood)* sombrío(a)
(**e**) *(sinister) (look)* siniestro(a); **d. powers** las fuerzas del mal, una mano negra; **there's a d. side to her** tiene una cara oculta *or* siniestra; **a d. chapter in the country's history** un capítulo oscuro *or* sombrío de la historia del país
(**f**) *(mysterious)* oscuro(a); **in darkest Africa** en el corazón de África, en lo más recóndito del continente africano; IDIOM **to be a d. horse** *(in competition)* ser quien puede dar la campanada; *(in politics)* ser el/la candidato(a) sorpresa; *(secretive person)* ser un enigma ►► *Old-fashioned* ***the D. Continent*** el continente negro
(**g**) *Hist* **the D. Ages** la Edad Media *(antes del año mil)*; *Fig* **to be in the D. Ages** estar en la prehistoria
(**h**) *Ling* velar

darken ['dɑ:kən] **1** *vt (sky, colour)* oscurecer; **a darkened room** una habitación ensombrecida; IDIOM **never d. my door again!** ¡no vuelvas a pisar el umbral de mi casa!, ¡no quiero verte nunca más!
2 *vi* (**a**) *(sky, colour)* oscurecerse (**b**) *(thoughts, mood)* ensombrecerse

darkie = **darky**

darkish ['dɑ:kɪʃ] *adj* tirando a oscuro(a); **d. hair** pelo tirando a moreno

darkly ['dɑ:klɪ] *adv (to say, hint)* con tono siniestro

darkness ['dɑ:knɪs] *n* (**a**) *(of night, room)* oscuridad *f*; **d. had fallen** había caído la noche; **in d.** a oscuras, en tinieblas (**b**) *(of skin, hair)* lo moreno (**c**) *(of colour)* tonalidad *f* oscura

darkroom ['dɑ:kru:m] *n Phot* cuarto *m* oscuro

dark-skinned ['dɑ:k'skɪnd] *adj* moreno(a)

darky, darkie ['dɑ:kɪ] *n Br Fam Pej* moreno(a) *m,f*, negro(a) *m,f*

darling ['dɑ:lɪŋ] **1** *n* (**a**) *(term of affection)* encanto *m*; **d.!** ¡querido(a)!; **he was an absolute d. about it** fue un encanto; **be a d. and...** sé bueno(a) y... (**b**) *(favourite)* niño(a) *m,f* mimado(a); **she's the d. of the press** es la niña mimada de la prensa
2 *adj* (**a**) *(beloved)* querido(a), queridísimo(a) (**b**) *Fam (delightful)* mono(a), precioso(a)

darn[1] [dɑ:n] **1** *vt (mend)* zurcir
2 *n* zurcido *m*

darn[2] *Fam* **1** *adj* maldito(a); **it's a d. nuisance!** ¡es un verdadero fastidio!; **you're a d. fool** ¡eres más tonto que Abundio!
2 *adv* condenadamente; **we were d. lucky** tuvimos una suerte loca; **you know d. well what I mean!** sabes de sobra lo que quiero decir
3 *vt* **d. it!** ¡mecachis!, ¡caray!; **he's late, d. him!** ¡maldito sea, ya llega tarde!; **well, I'll be darned!** ¡qué increíble!, ¡yo alucino!
4 *exclam* ¡caramba!

darned [dɑ:nd] **1** *adj* = **darn**[2]
2 *adv* = **darn**[2]

darning ['dɑ:nɪŋ] *n* (**a**) *(action)* zurcido *m* ►► ***d. needle*** aguja *f* de zurcir (**b**) *(items to be darned)* ropa *f* para zurcir

dart [dɑ:t] **1** *n* (**a**) *(missile)* dardo *m*; **darts** *(game)* dardos; **to play darts** jugar a los dardos (**b**) *(movement)* **to make a d. for sth** salir disparado(a) hacia algo (**c**) *(in clothes)* pinza *f*
2 *vt* **to d. a glance at sb** lanzar una mirada a alguien
3 *vi (move quickly)* precipitarse; **to d. away** *or* **off** salir disparado(a); **to d. in/out** entrar/salir precipitadamente; **her eyes darted from one face to another** sus ojos saltaban de una cara a otra

dartboard ['dɑ:tbɔ:d] *n* diana *f*

Dartford warbler ['dɑ:tfəd'wɔ:blə(r)] *n* curruca *f* rabilarga

Darwinian [dɑ:'wɪnɪən] **1** *n* darviniano(a) *m,f*, darvinista *mf*
2 *adj* darviniano(a)

Darwinism ['dɑ:wɪnɪzəm] *n* darvinismo *m*

dash [dæʃ] **1** *n* (**a**) *(of liquid)* chorrito *m*; *Fig (of humour, colour)* toque *m*, pizca *f*
(**b**) *(hyphen)* guión *m*; *(in Morse)* raya *f*; *Typ* **em-d.** guión, raya; *Typ* **en-d.** guión
(**c**) *(run)* carrera *f*; **to make a d. for the exit** salir disparado hacia la salida; **to make a d. for it** *(rush)* echar a correr; *(escape)* huir precipitadamente
(**d**) *Sport* **the 60 metres d.** los 60 metros lisos
(**e**) *(style)* dinamismo *m*, brío *m*; **to cut a d.** tener un aspecto elegante
(**f**) *Fam (in car)* cuadro *m* de mandos, *Esp* salpicadero *m*
2 *vt* (**a**) *(throw)* arrojar; **to d. sth to the ground** arrojar algo al suelo; **to d. sth to pieces** hacer trizas *or* añicos algo; **several boats were dashed against the cliffs** varios barcos se estrellaron contra los acantilados (**b**) *(destroy)* **to d. sb's hopes** truncar las esperanzas de alguien (**c**) *Fam (damn)* **d. (it)!** ¡caramba!
3 *vi* (**a**) *(move quickly)* correr, ir apresuradamente; **the dog dashed across the road** el perro atravesó la carretera como una exhalación; **to d. in/out** entrar/salir apresuradamente; **I'm just dashing out to the shops** salgo disparado a las tiendas; **to d. about** *or* **around** correr de acá para allá; *Fam* **I must d.** tengo que salir pitando (**b**) *(waves)* romper

► **dash off** **1** *vt sep* **to d. off a letter** escribir a toda prisa *or Am* a todo apuro una carta
2 *vi* salir corriendo

Dash
En inglés británico hoy se tiende más al uso del signo menos (-) separado del texto por un espacio a ambos lados en lugar de la raya:
she came – running – to the door
pero en inglés americano se conserva más el uso de la raya (—) sin espacios a ambos lados
she came—running—to the door
También se utilizan en inglés para introducir una clarificación o recapitulación (especialmente en contextos más coloquiales), a diferencia del español, en que preferimos usar los dos puntos:
I knew all the key people attending the meeting – authors, editors and translators
La raya inglesa puede indicar la omisión de una palabra o de parte de ella. En español solemos usar los puntos suspensivos con este fin:
Mr B— won't turn up

dashboard ['dæʃbɔːd] *n* tablero *m* de mandos, *Esp* salpicadero *m*

dashed [dæʃt] *adj Fam Old-fashioned* dichoso(a), maldito(a)

dashing ['dæʃɪŋ] *adj* (**a**) *(lively)* imponente; **a d. young man** un joven apuesto (**b**) *(smart, stylish)* deslumbrante; **you look very d. in that hat** estás muy elegante con ese sombrero

dastardly ['dæstədlɪ] *adj Old-fashioned (act, person)* ruin, malvado(a)

DAT [diːeɪ'tiː] *n* (*abbr* **digital audio tape**) cinta *f* digital de audio, DAT ►► *Comptr* ***D. cartridge*** cartucho *m* DAT; ***D. drive*** unidad *f* DAT

data ['deɪtə] *n* (**a**) *(information)* datos *mpl*; **an item** *or* **piece of d.** un dato; **we have very little d. on that** disponemos de escasos datos al respecto
(**b**) *Comptr* datos *mpl* ►► ***d. acquisition*** recogida *f* de datos; ***d. analysis*** análisis *m* de datos; ***d. bank*** banco *m* de datos; ***d. bus*** bus *m* de datos; ***d. capture*** recogida *f* de datos; ***d. communications*** transmisión *f* (electrónica) de datos; ***d. compression*** compresión *f* de datos; ***d. conversion*** conversión *f* de datos; ***d. encryption*** encriptación *f* de datos; ***d. entry*** proceso *m or* entrada *f* de datos; ***d. input*** entrada *f* de datos; ***d. link*** enlace *m* para transmisión de datos; ***d. loss*** pérdida *f* de datos; ***d. management*** gestión *m* de datos; ***d. privacy*** confidencialidad *f* de los datos; ***d. processing*** proceso *m or* procesamiento *m* de datos; ***d. protection*** protección *f* de datos; ***d. recorder*** *(on aircraft)* caja *f* negra; ***d. recovery*** recuperación *f* de datos; ***d. traffic*** tráfico *m* de datos; ***d. transfer rate*** velocidad *f* de transferencia de datos

database ['deɪtəbeɪs] *Comptr* **1** *n* base *f* de datos ►► ***d. management*** gestión *f* de bases de datos; ***d. management system*** sistema *m* de gestión de bases de datos
2 *vt* introducir en una base de datos

datacomms ['deɪtəkɒmz] *n Comptr* transmisión *f* de datos

dataglove ['deɪtəglʌv] *n Comptr* guante *m* de datos

datagram ['deɪtəgræm] *n Comptr* datagrama *m*

date[1] [deɪt] *n (fruit)* dátil *m* ►► ***d. palm*** palmera *f* datilera

date[2] **1** *n* (**a**) *(day)* fecha *f*; **what's the d. (today)?, what's today's d.?** ¿a qué (fecha) estamos hoy?, ¿qué fecha es hoy?, *Am* ¿a cómo estamos?; **to fix** *or* **set a d. (for sth)** fijar una fecha (para algo); **to d.** hasta la fecha; **up to d.** al día; **to bring sb up to d. on sth** poner a alguien al día de algo; **out of d.** anticuado(a), pasado(a) de moda; **at a later** *or* **some future d.** en una fecha futura; **d. as postmark** con la fecha del matasellos ►► ***d. of birth*** fecha *f* de nacimiento; ***d. of issue*** fecha *f* de expedición; ***d. stamp*** sello *m* con la fecha
(**b**) *(period)* **of an earlier/a later d.** de una fecha anterior/posterior; **to put a d. to sth** *(remember when it happened)* recordar en qué fecha ocurrió algo; *(estimate when built, established)* fechar *or* datar algo
(**c**) *(meeting)* cita *f*; **let's make it a d.** vamos a quedar de fijo; **to have a d. with sb** haber quedado *or* tener una cita con alguien ►► ***d. rape*** = violación por una persona con quien se sale o con quien se tiene una relación
(**d**) *US (girlfriend, boyfriend)* pareja *f*; **can I bring a d.?** ¿puedo venir acompañado?, ¿puedo venir con pareja?
(**e**) *(performance)* actuación *f*
2 *vt* (**a**) *(letter, ticket)* fechar; **it's dated last Sunday** *(letter)* tiene fecha del domingo pasado (**b**) *(fix date of) (antique, remains)* datar, fechar; *Fig* **that dates you** eso demuestra lo viejo que eres (**c**) *US (go out with)* salir con
3 *vi* (**a**) **to d. from** *or* **back to** *(custom, practice)* remontarse a; *(building)* datar de (**b**) *(go out of fashion)* pasar de moda (**c**) *US (go out with boyfriend, girlfriend)* **how long have they been dating?** ¿cuánto tiempo llevan saliendo?; **he hasn't started dating yet** aún no ha empezado a salir con chicas

dated ['deɪtɪd] *adj (clothes, style)* anticuado(a), pasado(a) de moda; *(word)* desusado(a)

dateline ['deɪtlaɪn] *n* (**a**) *Geog* meridiano *m* de cambio de fecha (**b**) *Journ* **d. Tel Aviv** fechado(a) en Tel Aviv

date-stamp ['deɪtstæmp] **1** *n* (**a**) *(instrument)* fechador *m* (**b**) *(mark)* fecha *f*
2 *vt (book, letter)* fechar, poner fecha a

dating agency ['deɪtɪŋ'eɪdʒənsɪ] *n* agencia *f* de contactos

dative ['deɪtɪv] *Gram* **1** *n* dativo *m*
2 *adj* dativo(a)

datum ['deɪtəm] (*pl* **data** ['deɪtə]) *n Phil* dato *m*

daub [dɔːb] **1** *n* (**a**) *(of paint)* mancha *f*, pintarrajo *m* (**b**) *Fam Pej (painting)* mamarracho *m*
2 *vt (with mud, paint)* embadurnar (**with** de); **the walls were daubed with slogans** las paredes estaban pintarrajeadas de eslóganes; **to d. paint on sth** embadurnar algo de pintura

daughter ['dɔːtə(r)] *n* hija *f*

daughter-in-law ['dɔːtərɪnlɔː] *n* nuera *f*

daughterly ['dɔːtəlɪ] *adj* filial; **to behave in a d. way** comportarse como una hija

daunt [dɔːnt] *vt* intimidar, acobardar; *Formal* **nothing daunted** sin dejarse arredrar

daunting ['dɔːntɪŋ] *adj* desalentador(ora), desmoralizante; **a d. task** una tarea ingente

dauntless ['dɔːntlɪs] *adj* impávido(a), imperturbable

dauntlessly ['dɔːntlɪslɪ] *adv* impávidamente, imperturbablemente

dauphin ['dəʊfɪn] *n Hist* delfín *m*

davenport ['dævənpɔːt] *n* (**a**) *Br (desk)* escritorio *m* davenport (**b**) *US (sofa)* sofá *m* grande

David ['deɪvɪd] *pr n* **King D.** el rey David

Davis Cup ['deɪvɪs'kʌp] *n* **the D.** la Copa Davis

davit ['dævɪt] *n Naut* pescante *m*

Davy Jones' locker ['deɪvɪdʒəʊnz'lɒkə(r)] *n* el fondo del mar

Davy lamp ['deɪvɪlæmp] *n* lámpara *f* de seguridad

dawdle ['dɔːdəl] *vi* perder el tiempo (**over** con)

► **dawdle away** *vt sep* **to d. away the entire morning** perder *or* desperdiciar toda la mañana

dawdler ['dɔːdlə(r)] *n* lento(a) *m,f*

dawn [dɔːn] **1** *n* (**a**) *(daybreak)* amanecer *m*, alba *f*; **at d.** al alba; **from d. to dusk** de sol a sol ►► ***the d. chorus*** el canto de los pájaros al amanecer; ***d. raid*** *Mil* ataque *m* sorpresa al amanecer; *Fin* ataque *m* sorpresa (especulativo) (**b**) *(of life, civilization)* albores *mpl*, despertar *m*; **since the d. of time** desde el principio de los tiempos
2 *vi* (**a**) *(day)* amanecer; **the day dawned bright and clear** el día amaneció claro y despejado (**b**) *Fig (life, civilization)* despertar

► **dawn on** *vt insep* **the truth finally dawned on him** finalmente vio la verdad; **it dawned on me that...** caí en la cuenta de que...

DAY [deɪ] *n* (**a**) *(period of 24 hours)* día *m*; **once/twice a d.** una vez/dos veces al día; **the d. after tomorrow** pasado mañana; **the d. before yesterday** anteayer; **we had a d. out at the seaside** fuimos a pasar el día a la playa; **any d. now** cualquier día de estos; **d. after d.** día tras día; **d. by d.** día a día; **d. in d. out** día tras día; **every d.** todos los días; **every other d.** cada dos días, un día sí y otro no, *Am* día por medio; **we've been searching for them for days** llevamos días buscándolos; **we're going to the beach for the d.** vamos a pasar el día a la playa; **from d. one** desde el primer día; **from d. to d.** de un día para otro; **from one d. to the next** de un día para otro; **from that d. on** desde aquel día; **in a few days' time** en unos pocos días; **soup of the d.** sopa del día; **one d., one of these days, some d.** un *or* cualquier día (de éstos); **the other d.** el otro día; **a year ago to the d.** hace exactamente un año; **to this d.** hasta el día de hoy; *Fam* **it's not every d. (that) you get promoted** no te ascienden todos los días; **I had a bad d. today** hoy ha sido un mal día; *US* **have a nice d.!** ¡que tenga un buen día!; **to have an off d.** tener un mal día; *Fam* **hurry up, we haven't got all d.!** ¡date prisa *or Andes, RP* apúrate, no tenemos todo el día! ►► *Rel* ***d. of abstinence*** día *m* de vigilia; *Rel* ***D. of Atonement*** Día *f* de la Expiación; *Fin* ***d. book*** diario *m* de entradas y salidas; *Com* ***days of grace*** periodo *m* de gracia; ***D. of Judgement*** Día *m* del Juicio Final; ***d. of reckoning*** hora *f* de pagar las culpas; ***d. of rest*** día *m* de descanso; *Br* ***d. return*** *(train ticket) Esp* billete *m or Am* boleto *m or Am* pasaje *m* de ida y vuelta en el día; ***d. trip*** excursión *f* de un día
(**b**) *(hours of daylight)* día *m*; **all d. (long)** todo el día; **by d., during the d.** durante el día; **to sleep by d.** dormir por el día; **to work d. and night** trabajar día y noche ►► ***d. bed*** diván *m*; ***d. care*** *(for children)*

servicio *m* de guardería (infantil); *(for elderly people)* = servicio de atención domiciliaria a los ancianos; ***d. care centre*** *(for children)* guardería *f* (infantil); ***d. cream*** crema *f* de día; *Cin* ***d. for night*** noche *f* americana; ***d. nursery*** guardería *f*; ***d. patient*** paciente *mf* ambulatorio(a); ***d. pupil*** alumno(a) *m,f* externo(a); ***d. room*** *(in hospital)* = sala de estar en la que los pacientes ven la televisión, charlan, etc.; ***d. school*** colegio *m* sin internado

(c) *(period of work)* jornada *f*; **to work a seven-hour d.** hacer *or* trabajar una jornada de siete horas; *Fam* **I'm on days this week** *(working day shift)* esta semana voy de días, *Am* esta semana trabajo de día; **to be paid by the d.** cobrar por día trabajado; **to take** *or* **have a d. off** tomarse un día libre; **to work days** trabajar el turno de día *or* diurno; **did you have a good d. at work?** ¿qué tal te ha ido hoy en el trabajo? ►► *Br* ***d. of action*** día *m* de huelga; ***d. labourer*** jornalero(a) *m,f*; ***d. release*** = sistema que permite a un trabajador realizar cursos de formación continua un día a la semana; ***d. shift*** *(in factory)* turno *m* de día *or* diurno

(d) *(era)* **in my d.** en mis tiempos; **in my university days** en mis tiempos de universitario; **he was a great player in his d.** en su tiempo fue un gran jugador; **in the days before electricity** antes de que hubiera electricidad; **in the days of...** en tiempos de...; **in days to come** más adelante, en el futuro; **in days gone by** antaño; **in this d. and age** en los tiempos que corren; **in those days** en aquellos tiempos; **she was the greatest actress of her d.** fue la actriz más grande de su tiempo; **the good old days** los buenos tiempos; **the best days of their lives** los mejores días de sus vidas; **these days** hoy (en) día; **those were the days!** ¡aquellos sí que eran buenos tiempos!; **he began/ended his days in poverty** comenzó/terminó sus días en la pobreza; **your d. will come** tu día llegará; **the d. will come when...** llegará el día en el que...; **communism has had its d.** el comunismo ha pasado a la historia

(e) IDIOMS *Fam* **he's sixty if he's a d.** tiene como mínimo sesenta años; **in all my (born) days** en toda mi vida; **it's all in a d.'s work** son los gajes del oficio; **it's been one of those days!** ¡ha sido un día loco!; *US Fam* **a d. at the beach** algo facilísimo, un paseo; **the game was a d. at the beach for the Dodgers** el partido fue facilísimo *or* un paseo para los Dodgers; *Fam* **I don't have any time for word processors, give me a typewriter any d.** donde esté *or* haya una máquina de escribir que se quiten los procesadores de textos; *Fam* **when it comes to holidays, give me the beach any d.** en cuanto a las vacaciones, donde esté la playa, que se quite lo demás; *Fam* **that'll be the d.!** ¡no lo verán tus ojos!, ¡cuando las ranas críen pelo!, *RP* ¡el día del golero *or* arquero!; **it's my lucky d.!** ¡es mi día (de suerte)!; **this isn't my d.!** ¡hoy no es mi día!; **it's rather late in the d. to start worrying about that** ya es un poco tarde como para preocuparse por eso; **his/its days are numbered** sus días están contados, tiene los días contados; *Fam* **let's call it a d.** dejémoslo por hoy; **to carry** *or* **win the d.** *(win battle)* conseguir la victoria; *Fam Hum* **don't give up the d. job!** mira, mejor dedícate a otra cosa; **we decided to make a d. of it** decidimos aprovechar para pasar el día; *Fam* **to make sb's d.** alegrarle el día a alguien; **to name the d.** *(of wedding)* fijar la fecha de la boda

---

day-boy ['deɪbɔɪ] *n Br* alumno *m* externo

daybreak ['deɪbreɪk] *n* amanecer *m*, alba *f*; **at d.** al alba

daydream ['deɪdriːm] **1** *n* fantasía *f*

2 *vi* fantasear, soñar despierto(a); **to d. about sth** fantasear sobre algo

day-girl ['deɪgɜːl] *n Br* alumna *f* externa

Day-Glo® ['deɪgləʊ] *adj* fosforescente, fosforito(a)

daylight ['deɪlaɪt] *n* **(a)** *(dawn)* amanecer *m*; **before d.** antes de que amanezca

(b) *(light of day)* (luz *f* del) día *m*; **it was still d.** todavía era de día; **in d.** de día; **in broad d.** a plena luz del día; **d. hours** horas de luz ►► *US* ***d. saving time*** horario *m* oficial de verano

(c) IDIOMS **to begin to see d.** *(approach end of task)* vislumbrarse el final; *(begin to understand)* empezar a ver algo claro; **to scare the living daylights out of sb** dar un susto de muerte a alguien; **it's d. robbery!** ¡es un atraco a mano armada!

daylong ['deɪlɒŋ] *adj* de un día

daytime ['deɪtaɪm] *n* día *m*; **in the d.** durante el día ►► ***d. TV*** programación *f* diurna *or* de día

day-to-day ['deɪtə'deɪ] *adj* diario(a), cotidiano(a); **on a d. basis** día a día

day-tripper ['deɪ'trɪpə(r)] *n* dominguero(a) *m,f*; **the town was full of day-trippers** el pueblo estaba lleno de gente que había venido a pasar el día

daze [deɪz] **1** *n* aturdimiento *m*; **to be in a d.** estar aturdido(a)

2 *vt* aturdir; **I was dazed by the impact** el golpe me dejó aturdida

dazed [deɪzd] *adj* aturdido(a)

dazzle ['dæzəl] **1** *n* **(a)** *(of headlights)* resplandor *m*, brillo *m* **(b)** *(of publicity)* hechizo *m*

2 *vt* **(a)** *(of light)* deslumbrar **(b)** *(of beauty, skill)* deslumbrar, encandilar

dazzling ['dæzlɪŋ] *adj* **(a)** *(light, intensity)* deslumbrante **(b)** *(beauty, skill)* deslumbrante, que encandila

dazzlingly ['dæzlɪŋlɪ] *adv* **(a)** *(bright, intense)* deslumbrantemente **(b)** *(beautiful, skilful)* deslumbrantemente

dB (*abbr* **decibel(s)**) dB

dbase ['diːbeɪs] *n Comptr* (*abbr* **database**) base *f* de datos

DBMS [diːbiːem'es] *n Comptr* (*abbr* **database management system**) sistema *m* de gestión de bases de datos

DC [diː'siː] *n* **(a)** *Elec* (*abbr* **direct current**) corriente *f* continua **(b)** (*abbr* **District of Columbia**) DC, Distrito de Columbia

DCL (*abbr* **Doctor of Civil Law**) doctor(ora) *m,f* en derecho civil

DD [diː'diː] **(a)** (*abbr* **Doctor of Divinity**) Doctor(ora) *m,f* en Teología **(b)** *Comptr* (*abbr* **double density**) doble densidad *f*

D/D (*abbr* **direct debit**) domiciliación *f* bancaria *or* de pago, *Am* débito *m* bancario

D-Day ['diː'deɪ] *n* **(a)** *Mil* el día D ►► *Hist* ***the D. landings*** el Desembarco de Normandía **(b)** *Fig* el día D

DDT [diːdiː'tiː] *n* (*abbr* **dichlorodiphenyltrichloroethane**) DDT *m*

DE (*abbr* **Delaware**) Delaware

DEA [diːiː'eɪ] *n* (*abbr* **Drug Enforcement Administration**) = departamento estadounidense de lucha contra la droga

deacon ['diːkən] *n Rel* diácono *m*

deaconess ['diːkənes] *n Rel* diaconisa *f*

deactivate [diː'æktɪveɪt] *vt* desactivar

DEAD [ded] **1** *adj* **(a)** *(not alive)* muerto(a); **a d. man** un muerto; **a d. woman** una muerta; **a d. body** un cádaver; *Fam* **over my d. body!** ¡por encima de mi cadáver!; **to be d.** estar muerto(a); **he was d. on arrival** cuando llegó al hospital ya había muerto, *Esp* ingresó cadáver; **to give sb up for d.** dar a alguien por muerto; **to shoot sb d.** matar a alguien a tiros; *Fig* **half d. with fright** medio muerto(a) de miedo; **wanted d. or alive** se busca vivo(a) o muerto(a); *Fig* **they were more d. than alive** estaban más muertos que vivos; *Fam Fig* **if dad finds out, you're d.** si papá se entera, te mata; IDIOM **to step into** *or* **fill d. men's shoes** pasar a ocupar el puesto de uno que ha muerto, *RP* ocupar el lugar del muerto; IDIOM *Fam* **to be d. from the neck up** tener la cabeza llena de serrín *or Am* aserrín; IDIOM **to be d. to the world** *(asleep)* estar como un tronco; *(drunk)* estar K.O., estar inconsciente; IDIOM *Fam* **as d. as a doornail** *or* **a dodo** muerto(a) y bien muerto(a); *Fam* **I wouldn't be seen** *or* **caught d. in that dress!** ¡no me pondría ese vestido ni borracha *or* loca!; IDIOM **to leave sth d. in the water** condenar algo al fracaso; IDIOM **to flog** *or US* **beat a d. horse** esforzarse inútilmente; IDIOM *Fam* **he's d. meat** se puede dar por muerto; PROV **d. men tell no tales** los muertos no hablan ►► *US* ***d. bolt*** cerradura *f* embutida *or* de pestillo; *Fam Fig* ***d. duck:*** **the project proved to be a d. duck** el proyecto estaba condenado al fracaso desde el principio; *also Fig* ***d. end*** callejón *m* sin salida; **to come to a d. end** meterse en un callejón sin salida; ***d. man's handle*** = control de seguridad que tiene que estar accionado para que el aparato funcione; *Mus* ***d. march*** marcha *f* fúnebre; *Fam* ***d. men*** *(empty bottles)* cascos *mpl*, botellas *fpl* vacías; ***the D. Sea*** el mar Muerto; ***the D. Sea Scrolls*** los Manuscritos del Mar Muerto

(b) *(numb)* dormido(a); **my leg went d.** se me durmió la pierna; *Fam* **to give sb a d. leg** = golpear a alguien en cierto músculo de manera que se le quede la pierna floja durante unos instantes

(c) *(not working) (battery)* gastado(a), agotado(a); **the engine's d.** no funciona el motor; **the phone/line is d.** no hay línea, *RP* da muerto; **the battery has gone d.** se ha gastado *or* agotado la batería; **the phone/line went d.** se cortó la línea

(d) *(not alight) (fire, match, cigarette)* extinguido(a)

(e) *(no longer continuing)* **the deal still isn't d.** todavía hay esperanzas de alcanzar un acuerdo; *Fig* **d. and buried** finiquitado(a) ►► ***d. letter*** *(undelivered letter)* = carta que no se puede repartir ni devolver; *(law)* letra *f* muerta

(f) *(language)* muerto(a)

(g) *(lacking energy) (voice, eyes, performance, colour)* apagado(a); *(sound)* sordo(a); **this place is d. in winter** este lugar está muerto en invierno; *Fig* **he's a d. weight** es un peso muerto

(h) *(absolute) (silence)* absoluto(a), completo(a); **to hit a target d. centre** alcanzar el objetivo en pleno centro; IDIOM *Fam* **it/he was a d. loss** resultó ser un desastre total; IDIOM *Fam* **to be a d. ringer for sb** ser idéntico(a) a alguien ►► ***d. calm*** calma *f* chicha; *Fam* ***d. cert***

ganador(ora) *m,f* seguro(a); ***d. halt:*** **to come to a d. halt** detenerse por completo; ***d. heat*** *(in race)* empate *m*; *Naut* ***d. reckoning*** estima *f*

(i) *Fam (tired)* **to be d.** estar muerto(a); **I'm d. on my feet** estoy que me muero *or* que me caigo

(j) *Sport (out of play)* muerto(a); **the ball went d.** *(in rugby)* la pelota acabó en balón muerto ►► ***d. ball situation*** *(in football)* jugada *f* a balón parado

(k) *Fam* **are these glasses d.?** *(said by bar staff)* ¿me puedo llevar los vasos?

2 *adv* (a) *(completely) (certain, wrong)* totalmente, completamente; *Fam* **d. beat** *or* **tired** hecho(a) polvo, molido(a); *Fam* **you're d. right** tienes toda la razón del mundo; **to be d. (set) against sth** oponerse rotundamente a algo; **to be d. set on doing sth** estar completamente decidido(a) a hacer algo; **d. slow** *(sign)* muy despacio; **they arrived d. on time** llegaron puntualísimos; *Fam* **to be d. wrong** equivocarse de medio a medio; **to stop d.** pararse en seco; **to stop sb d. in their tracks** hacer que alguien se pare en seco

(b) *Fam (very)* **you were d. lucky** fuiste muy suertudo; **the movie was d. boring** la película fue aburridísima *or Esp* un tostón *or RP* un embole; **the exam was d. easy** el examen fue facilísimo, *Esp* el examen estuvo chupado *or* tirado, *RP* el examen fue un boleto; **these meatballs are d. good** estas albóndigas están de morirse *or RP* del otro mundo

(c) *(exactly)* **d. on six o'clock** a las seis en punto; **you're d. on** *(exactly right)* exactamente; **it hit the target d. centre** dio de lleno en el blanco; **to stare d. ahead** mirar fijamente hacia delante

3 *n* **at d. of night** a altas horas de la noche; **in the d. of winter** en pleno invierno

4 *npl* **the d.** los muertos; *Fig* **to come back from the d.** resucitar; **to rise from the d.** resucitar (de entre los muertos)

---

dead-and-alive ['dedəndə'laɪv] *adj Br (place)* de mala muerte

dead-ball line [ded'bɔːllaɪn] *n (in rugby)* línea *f* de balón muerto

deadbeat ['dedbiːt] *n Fam* (a) *(lazy person)* vago(a) *m,f*, holgazán(ana) *m,f* (b) *(tramp)* indigente *mf* (c) *(parasite)* gorrero(a) *m,f*, *Esp, Méx* gorrón(ona) *m,f*, *RP* garronero(a) *m,f*

deaden ['dedən] *vt (blow, sound, pain)* amortiguar, atenuar; **to become deadened to sth** volverse insensible a algo

deadhead ['dedhed] 1 *n* (a) *US Fam (lazy person)* vago(a) *m,f*, holgazán(ana) *m,f* (b) *US (user of free ticket for theatre)* espectador(ora) *m,f* con invitación; *(user of free ticket for bus, train)* viajero(a) *m,f* con *Esp* billete *or Am* boleto *or Am* pasaje gratuito (c) *Br (of plant)* flor *f* marchita

2 *vt (plant)* cortar las flores marchitas a

dead-letter box [ded'letə(r)bɒks], **dead-letter drop** [ded'letə(r)drɒp] *n* = escondrijo donde los espías dejan y recogen cartas

deadline ['dedlaɪn] *n (day)* fecha *f* límite; *(time)* plazo *m*; **to meet a d.** cumplir un plazo; **to miss a d.** no cumplir con un plazo; **to work to a d.** trabajar con un plazo

deadlock ['dedlɒk] 1 *n* (a) *(stalemate)* punto *m* muerto; **to reach (a) d.** llegar a un punto muerto; **to break the d.** salir del impasse (b) *(on door)* candado *m*

2 *vt* **to be deadlocked** *(of talks, negotiations)* estar en un punto muerto

deadly ['dedlɪ] 1 *adj* (a) *(mortal) (poison, blow, enemy)* mortal, mortífero(a); *(sin)* capital; *(weapon)* mortífero(a); *(pallor)* cadavérico(a); **to d. effect** con efectos devastadores ►► ***d. nightshade*** belladona *f* (b) *(complete) (silence)* sepulcral; *(accuracy)* certero(a), infalible; **in d. earnest** *(say)* muy en serio, totalmente en serio (c) *Fam (boring)* aburridísimo(a)

2 *adv (very)* **d. accurate** tremendamente exacto(a); **d. boring** mortalmente aburrido(a); **to be d. serious about sth** decir algo completamente en serio

deadness ['dednɪs] *n* (a) *(of voice, eyes, performance)* falta *f* de vida; *(of colour)* lo apagado; *(of sound)* debilidad *f* (b) *(of place)* falta *f* de animación

dead-on ['ded'ɒn] *adj Fam* atinado(a)

deadpan ['dedpæn] 1 *adj (expression)* inexpresivo(a); *(humour)* socarrón(ona)

2 *adv* de manera inexpresiva

deadwood ['dedwʊd] *n* (a) *(of tree)* ramas *fpl* secas (b) *(in company)* **there is too much d. in this office** en esta oficina sobra mucha gente *or* hay mucha gente que está de más

deaf [def] 1 *adj* sordo(a); **a d. man** un sordo; **a d. woman** una sorda; **to be d.** ser *or* estar sordo(a); **d. and dumb** sordomudo(a); **to go d.** quedarse sordo(a); **to be d. in one ear** ser sordo(a) de un oído; IDIOM **as d. as a post** sordo(a) como una tapia; **to turn a d. ear to sb** hacer caso omiso de alguien; **the appeal fell on d. ears** el llamamiento cayó en saco roto; *Fig* **she was d. to his appeals** hizo oídos sordos a sus requerimientos; *Fam* **are you d.? I said "no"!** ¿estás sordo o qué? ¡he dicho que no!

2 *npl* **the d.** los sordos

deaf-aid ['defeɪd] *n* audífono *m*

deafen ['defən] *vt* ensordecer; *Fam* **that noise is deafening me!** ese ruido me está dejando sorda

deafening ['defənɪŋ] *adj* ensordecedor(ora); *Hum* **the silence was d.** había un silencio abrumador

deaf-mute [def'mjuːt] *n Old-fashioned* sordomudo(a) *m,f*

deafness ['defnɪs] *n* sordera *f*

deal[1] [diːl] *n (wood)* madera *f* de conífera, madera *f* blanda

deal[2] 1 *n* (a) *(agreement)* acuerdo *m*; *(in business)* trato *m*; **to do** *or* **make a d. (with sb)** hacer un trato (con alguien); **it's a d.!** ¡trato hecho!; **the union got a good d. for its members** el sindicato logró un buen acuerdo para sus afiliados; **the d. is off** se ha roto el acuerdo; IDIOM *US Fam* **what's the d.?** *(what happened?)* ¿qué pasó?, ¿qué ha pasado?

(b) *(bargain)* oferta *f*; **I got a good d. on this video** este *Esp* vídeo *or Am* video me salió muy barato

(c) *(treatment)* **to give sb a fair d.** dar un trato justo a alguien; **the president promised a new** *or* **better d. for teachers** el presidente prometió una renovación de la situación de los maestros; **to get a good/bad d.** recibir un buen/mal trato

(d) *(amount)* **a good** *or* **great d.**, *Old-fashioned* **a d.** *(a lot)* mucho; **not a great d.** no mucho; **there's not a great d. I can do to help** no puedo hacer mucho para ayudar; **they haven't had a great d. of luck** no han tenido demasiada suerte, han tenido muy poca suerte; **to have a great d. to do** tener mucho que hacer; **a good** *or* **great d. of my time** gran parte de mi tiempo; **a good/great d. faster** mucho/bastante más rápido; **I didn't enjoy it a great d.** no me gustó demasiado

(e) *(in cards)* **(it's) your d.** te toca repartir *or* dar; **whose d. is it?** ¿quién da *or* reparte?

2 *vt* (*pt & pp* **dealt** [delt]) (a) *(cards)* repartir, dar; **he dealt me a king** me dio *or* repartió un rey; **to d. sb in** repartir *or* dar cartas a alguien; *Fig* **d. me in** cuenta conmigo (b) *(blow)* **to d. sth/sb a blow** dar un golpe a algo/alguien; *Fig* **our hopes have been dealt a severe blow** nuestras ilusiones han sufrido un serio revés (c) *(sell)* **to d. drugs** traficar con droga, pasar droga

3 *vi* (a) *(trade)* **to d. in leather/shares** comerciar con pieles/acciones; **to d. in drugs** traficar con droga, pasar droga; *Fig* **to d. in death/human misery** hacer negocio con la muerte/la miseria humana (b) *(in drugs)* traficar con droga, pasar droga (c) *(in cards)* repartir, dar

►**deal out** *vt sep (cards, justice)* repartir; **she dealt out a heavy sentence to them** les infligió una severa condena; **d. me out (this hand)** no me repartas cartas (esta mano), (esta mano) no voy

►**deal with** *vt insep* (a) *(subject)* tratar; **the book deals with her rise to power** el libro trata sobre su ascenso al poder

(b) *(tackle, cope with) (complaint)* ocuparse de; *(situation, criticism)* hacer frente a, afrontar; **the switchboard deals with over 1,000 calls a day** desde la centralita se gestionan más de 1.000 llamadas diarias; **the problem is being dealt with** nos estamos ocupando del problema; **we're dealing with a very difficult problem here** aquí nos enfrentamos a un serio problema; **I know how to d. with him** sé cómo tratarlo; **how is she dealing with his death?** ¿qué tal lleva lo de su muerte?; **I'll d. with it** *(problem, situation)* yo me ocuparé del asunto; **that's that dealt with** eso ya está listo

(c) *(have dealings with)* tener tratos con; **I usually d. with the boss** normalmente hablo *or* negocio con el jefe; **to d. with a company** tener relaciones *or* tratos con una empresa; **she's not an easy woman to d. with** no es una mujer de trato fácil

(d) *(punish)* **she dealt severely with them** les impuso un severo castigo; **I'll d. with you later** ya hablaremos tú y yo después

dealer ['diːlə(r)] *n* (a) *(in card game)* = jugador que reparte (b) *Com* comerciante *mf* (**in** de); **(art) d.** marchante *mf* (de arte); **(car) d.** *(in general)* vendedor(ora) *m,f* (de coches *or Am* carros *or RP* autos); **a Ford/Toyota d.** un concesionario Ford/Toyota (c) *(in drugs)* traficante *mf*

dealership ['diːləʃɪp] *n Aut* (a) *(showroom)* concesionario *m* (b) *(franchise)* concesión *f*

dealing ['diːlɪŋ] *n* (a) *Br (on stock exchange)* contratación *f* ►► ***d. room*** sala *f* de cambios (b) *(in drugs)* tráfico *m*

dealings ['diːlɪŋz] *npl* tratos *mpl*; **to have d. with sb** estar en tratos con alguien

dealt *pt & pp of* **deal**

dean [diːn] *n* (**a**) *Rel* deán *m* (**b**) *Univ* decano(a) *m,f* ►► *US* ***Dean's List*** = lista de los alumnos considerados más sobresalientes por el decano de una universidad

deanery ['diːnərɪ] *n Rel (residence)* residencia *f* del deán

dear [dɪə(r)] **1** *adj* (**a**) *(loved)* querido(a); **Margaret dearest** queridísima Margaret; **to hold sth/sb d.** apreciar mucho algo/a alguien; **all that I hold d. (in life)** todo lo que tiene un significado especial para mí (en la vida); **he's a d. friend (of mine)** es un amigo muy querido; **my dearest wish is that...** mi mayor deseo es que...; **a place d. to the hearts of...** un lugar muy querido para...; IDIOM *Fam* **to run for d. life** correr desesperadamente

(**b**) *(in spoken form of address)* **my d. fellow** querido *or* mi estimado colega; **my d. girl** jovencita; **my d. Mrs Stevens** mi querida Sra. Stevens

(**c**) *(in letter)* **D. Sir** Muy Sr. mío; **D. Madam** Muy Sra. mía; **D. Sir or Madam, D. Sir/Madam** Muy Sres. míos; **D. Mr Thomas** Estimado Sr. Thomas; **D. Andrew** Querido Andrew; **My dearest Gertrude** Queridísima Gertrude; IDIOM **a D. John letter** = una carta para poner fin a una relación amorosa

(**d**) *(delightful)* mono(a), precioso(a); **she's such a d. girl** es una chica tan encantadora; **what a d. little child/cottage/frock!** ¡qué monada de criatura/chalé/vestido!

(**e**) *(expensive)* caro(a); **things are getting dearer** todo está cada vez más caro

2 *exclam* **d. me!, d., d.!, oh d.!** *(in shock, disapproval)* ¡madre mía!; **oh d.!** *(expressing worry)* ¡vaya por Dios!

3 *n* **poor d.** pobrecito(a); **my d.** cariño mío, mi amor; **my dearest** querido(a); **she's such a d.** ¡es un cielo!; **be a d. and...** sé bueno y...; *Fam* **an old d.** una viejecita; **will that be all, d.?** *(said by shop assistant, waitress)* ¿algo más, cielo?

4 *adv (to buy, sell)* caro; *Fig* **it cost me d.** me costó muy caro

dearly ['dɪəlɪ] *adv* (**a**) *(very much)* **I love him d.** lo quiero muchísimo; **I would d. love to know** me encantaría saberlo; *Rel* **d. beloved** queridos hermanos y hermanas; **d. beloved son of...** *(on gravestone)* el hijo amado de... (**b**) *(at high cost)* **she paid d. for her mistake** pagó muy caro su error

dearth [dɜːθ] *n* escasez *f* (**of** de)

deary ['dɪərɪ] *n Fam* cariño *m*, corazón *m*; **d. me!** ¡madre mía!

death [deθ] *n* (**a**) *(end of life)* muerte *f*; **at the time of his d.** cuando falleció, en el momento de su muerte; **to put sb to d.** ejecutar a alguien; **he fell to his d.** se mató de una caída; **he was beaten/stabbed to d.** lo mataron a golpes/a puñaladas; **he was burnt to d.** murió abrasado; **a fight to the d.** una lucha a muerte; **there's been a d. in the family** ha fallecido alguien de la familia; **d. to traitors!** ¡muerte a *or* mueran los traidores!; **till d. do us part** hasta que la muerte nos separe ►► ***d. camp*** campo *m* de exterminio; ***d. certificate*** certificado *m or* partida *f or* acta *f* de defunción; *Br Formerly* ***d. duties*** impuesto *m* de sucesiones; ***d. knell*** toque *m* de difuntos; *Fig* **to sound the d. knell for sth** asestar el golpe de gracia a algo *or* anunciar el final de algo; ***d. mask*** mascarilla *f*; ***d. penalty*** pena *f* de muerte; ***d. rate*** tasa *f* de mortalidad; ***d. rattle*** último estertor *m*; *US* ***d. row*** galería *f* de los condenados a muerte; ***d. sentence*** pena *f* de muerte; *Fin* ***d. in service (benefit)*** indemnización *f* por fallecimiento del trabajador; ***d. squad*** escuadrón *m* de la muerte; *US* ***d. tax*** impuesto *m* de sucesiones; ***d. threat*** amenaza *f* de muerte; *also Fig* ***d. throes*** últimos estertores *mpl*, agonía *f*; **to be in one's d. throes** estar agonizando; *Fig* **to be in its d. throes** *(project, business)* estar en las últimas; ***d. toll*** número *m or* saldo *m* de víctimas mortales; ***d. warrant*** orden *f* de ejecución; IDIOM **to sign one's own d. warrant** firmar la propia sentencia de muerte; ***d. wish*** ganas *fpl* de morir

(**b**) IDIOMS **to be sick to d. of sth** estar hasta la coronilla de algo; **to be scared to d.** estar muerto(a) de miedo; **to be in at the d.** ver el final; *Fam* **to do sth to d.** repetir algo hasta la saciedad *orAm* el hartazgo; **it's been done to d.** *(play, subject for novel)* eso está muy visto; *Fam* **you'll be the d. of me** *(with amusement)* vas a acabar conmigo, *RP* me vas a sacar canas verdes; *(with irritation)* me vas a matar (a disgustos); **you'll catch your d. (of cold)!** ¡vas a agarrar *orEsp* coger un resfriado de muerte!, *RP* ¡te vas a agarrar un resfrío fenomenal!; **to be at d.'s door** estar a las puertas de la muerte; **to look like d. warmed** *Br* **up** *or US* **over** tener una pinta horrorosa

deathbed ['deθbed] *n* lecho *m* de muerte; **a d. confession** una confesión en artículo mortis

deathblow ['deθbləʊ] *n Fig* golpe *m* mortal; **to deal a d. to sth** asestarle un golpe mortal a algo

deathly ['deθlɪ] **1** *adj (pallor)* cadavérico(a); *(silence)* sepulcral

2 *adv* **d. pale** lívido(a), pálido(a); **d. cold** muerto(a) de frío

death's-head ['deθshed] *n* calavera *f* ►► *US* ***d. hawkmoth*** mariposa *f* de la muerte; ***d. moth*** mariposa *f* de la muerte

deathtrap ['deθtræp] *n* **it's a d.** *(house, car)* es un auténtico peligro

deathwatch beetle ['deθwɒtʃ'biːtəl] *n* carcoma *f*

deb [deb] *n Fam* debutante *f*

debacle [deɪ'bɑːkəl] *n* desastre *m*, debacle *f*

debag [diː'bæg] (*pt & pp* **debagged**) *vt Fam* quitar *orAm* sacar los pantalones a

debar [diː'bɑː(r)] (*pt & pp* **debarred**) *vt (from club, pub)* prohibir la entrada (**from** en); **to d. sb from doing sth** prohibirle a alguien hacer algo

debark[1] [diː'bɑːk] **1** *vt* desembarcar

2 *vi* desembarcar

debark[2] *vt (tree)* quitar la corteza a

debase [dɪ'beɪs] *vt* (**a**) *(degrade) (person, sport, ideal)* degradar; **to d. oneself** degradarse (**b**) *(coinage)* = depreciar una moneda rebajando su contenido metálico

debasement [dɪ'beɪsmənt] *n* (**a**) *(of person, sport, ideal)* degradación *f* (**b**) *(of coinage)* = reducción del valor por rebaja en el contenido metálico

debatable [dɪ'beɪtəbəl] *adj* discutible; **it is d. whether...** es discutible que...

debate [dɪ'beɪt] **1** *n* debate *m*; **after much** *or* **lengthy d. they decided to buy it** tras mucho debatir decidieron comprarlo; **after much d., he chose the Ferrari** después de darle muchas vueltas se decantó por el Ferrari; **to be open to d.** ser discutible

2 *vt (issue)* debatir, discutir; **a much/hotly debated question** una cuestión muy/acaloradamente debatida; **he debated (with himself) whether to go** se debatía entre ir y no ir

3 *vi* debatir (**with/on** con/sobre)

debater [dɪ'beɪtə(r)] *n* polemista *mf*, persona *f* que participa en debates

debating [dɪ'beɪtɪŋ] *n* = debates y discusiones organizados por una institución o asociación ►► ***d. society*** = asociación que organiza debates en una universidad o instituto

debauched [dɪ'bɔːtʃt] *adj* depravado(a), degenerado(a)

debauch [dɪ'bɔːtʃ] *Literary* **1** *n* orgía *f*

2 *vt (person)* corromper, pervertir

debauched [dɪ'bɔːtʃt] *adj* vicioso(a), libertino(a)

debauchee [dɪbɔː'tʃiː] *n Literary* vicioso(a) *m,f*, libertino(a) *m,f*

debauchery [dɪ'bɔːtʃərɪ] *n* libertinaje *m*, depravación *f*

debenture [dɪ'bentʃə(r)] *n Fin* obligación *f* ►► ***d. bond*** obligación *f* hipotecaria; ***debentures issue*** emisión *f* de obligaciones

debilitate [dɪ'bɪlɪteɪt] *vt* debilitar

debilitating [dɪ'bɪlɪteɪtɪŋ] *adj* debilitador(ora), debilitante; **it has a d. effect on her concentration** ejerce un efecto debilitante *or* debilitador en su capacidad de concentración

debility [dɪ'bɪlɪtɪ] *n* debilidad *f*

debit ['debɪt] *Fin* **1** *n* cargo *m*, adeudo *m*; *Br* **your account is in d.** el saldo de su cuenta es negativo ►► ***d. balance*** saldo *m* deudor; ***d. card*** tarjeta *f* de débito; ***d. entry*** asiento *m* de adeudo *or* de cargo; ***d. note*** nota *f* de adeudo *or* de cargo; ***d. side*** debe *m*, columna *f* de la izquierda; *Fig* **on the d. side** en el lado negativo

2 *vt (account, person)* adeudar, debitar; **to d. sb's account with $50, to d. $50 from sb's account** adeudar *or* debitar 50 dólares en la cuenta de alguien

debonair [debə'neə(r)] *adj (person)* gallardo(a); *(smile, charm)* jovial, alegre

debouch [dɪ'baʊtʃ] *vi* (**a**) *(river)* desembocar (**b**) *Mil (troops)* emerger, surgir

debrief [diː'briːf] *vt* **to d. sb on a mission** pedir a alguien que rinda cuentas sobre una misión

debriefing [diː'briːfɪŋ] *n* interrogatorio *m (tras una misión)*

debris ['debriː, *US* də'briː] *n* (**a**) *(of building)* escombros *mpl*; *(of plane, car)* restos *mpl*; *Fig* **he wanted to salvage something from the d. of his marriage** quería rescatar algo de un matrimonio hecho pedazos (**b**) *Geol* ***d. cone*** cono *m* de deyección

debt [det] *n* (**a**) *(moral obligation)* deuda *f*; **I shall always be in your d.** siempre estaré en deuda contigo; **he has paid his d. to society** ha saldado su deuda con la sociedad; **to owe sb a d. of gratitude** tener una deuda de gratitud con alguien; **d. of honour** deuda de honor

(**b**) *(financial obligation, sum owed)* deuda *f*; **bad d.** deuda incobrable; **to get** *or* **run into d.** endeudarse; **to be in d. (to)** estar endeudado(a) (con); **to get out of d.** salir del endeudamiento; **he always paid his debts** siempre saldaba sus cuentas ►► ***d. collector*** cobrador(ora) *m,f* de morosos; ***d. rescheduling*** reprogramación *f* de la deuda; ***d. restructuring*** reprogramación *f* de la deuda; ***d. servicing*** servicio *m* de la deuda; *Fin* ***d. swap*** intercambio *m* de la deuda

debtor ['detə(r)] *n* deudor(ora) *m,f* ►► ***d. nation*** nación *f* deudora *or* endeudada

debt-ridden ['detrɪdən] *adj* agobiado(a) *or* abrumado(a) por las deudas

debug [diː'bʌg] (*pt & pp* **debugged**) *vt* (**a**) *Comptr* depurar, eliminar errores en (**b**) *(remove hidden microphones from)* limpiar de micrófonos

debugger [diː'bʌgə(r)] *n Comptr* depurador *m*

debugging [diː'bʌgɪŋ] *n* (**a**) *Comptr* depuración *f* (**b**) *(removal of microphones)* eliminación *f* de micrófonos

debunk [diː'bʌŋk] *vt Fam* echar por tierra

debut ['deɪbjuː] **1** *n* debut *m*; **to make one's d.** debutar; **her d. performance** su primera actuación, su debut

2 *vi* debutar (**as** como)

débutante, debutante ['debjʊtɑːnt] *n* debutante *f*

Dec (*abbr* **December**) dic. *m*

decade ['dekeɪd] *n* decenio *m*, década *f*

decadence ['dekədəns] *n* decadencia *f*

decadent ['dekədənt] *adj* decadente; *Hum* **how d.!** ¡qué decadente!

decaf(f) ['diːkæf] *n Fam* descafeinado *m*

decaffeinated [diː'kæfɪneɪtɪd] *adj* descafeinado(a)

decagon ['dekəgən] *n Geom* decágono *m*

decahedron [dekə'hiːdrən] *n Geom* decaedro *m*

decal ['diːkæl] *n US* calcomanía *f*

decalcify [diː'kælsɪfaɪ] *vt Physiol* descalcificar

decalitre ['dekəliːtə(r)] *n* decalitro *m*

Decalogue ['dekəlɒg] *n* **the D.** el Decálogo, las Tablas de la Ley

decamp [dɪ'kæmp] *vi* (**a**) *Mil* levantar el campamento (**b**) *Fam (abscond)* esfumarse, *Esp* darse el piro; **to d. to another room** largarse a otra habitación

decant [dɪ'kænt] *vt* (**a**) *(wine)* decantar (**b**) *(people)* conducir

decanter [dɪ'kæntə(r)] *n* licorera *f*

decapitate [dɪ'kæpɪteɪt] *vt* decapitar

decapitation [dɪkæpɪ'teɪʃən] *n* decapitación *f*

decapod ['dekəpɒd] *n* (**a**) *(crustacean)* decápodo *m* (**b**) *(mollusc)* decápodo *m*

decarbonize [diː'kɑːbənaɪz] *vt Aut* descarburar

decathlete [dɪ'kæθliːt] *n* decatleta *mf*

decathlon [dɪ'kæθlɒn] *n* decatlón *m*

decay [dɪ'keɪ] **1** *n* (**a**) *(of wood, stone, food, corpse)* putrefacción *f*, descomposición *f*; *(of teeth)* caries *f inv* (**b**) *(of civilization)* declive *m*, decadencia *f*; *(of building)* ruina *f*; *also Fig* **to fall into d.** alcanzar un estado ruinoso, deteriorarse; **it's a custom which has fallen into d.** es una costumbre que ha caído en desuso (**c**) *Phys* descomposición *f*, desintegración *f*

2 *vi* (**a**) *(wood, stone, food, corpse)* pudrirse, descomponerse; *(teeth)* picarse, cariarse (**b**) *(decline)* declinar (**c**) *Phys* descomponerse, desintegrarse

3 *vt (wood, stone, food, corpse)* pudrir, descomponer; *(tooth)* cariar

decaying [dɪ'keɪɪŋ] *adj (wood, stone, food, corpse)* podrido(a), en descomposición; *(teeth)* cariado(a); **d. inner-city slums** zonas en deterioro del centro de la ciudad

decease [dɪ'siːs] *n Formal* fallecimiento *m*

deceased [dɪ'siːst] *Formal* **1** *adj* difunto(a); **James Porton, d.** el difunto James Porton

2 *n* **the d.** el/la difunto(a)

decedent [dɪ'siːdənt] *n US Law* finado(a) *m,f*, difunto(a) *m,f*

deceit [dɪ'siːt] *n* engaño *m*; **by d.** valiéndose de engaños

deceitful [dɪ'siːtfʊl] *adj (person)* falso(a); *(behaviour)* engañoso(a); **to be d.** ser un(a) falso(a)

deceitfully [dɪ'siːtfʊlɪ] *adv* **to obtain sth d.** conseguir algo con engaños

deceitfulness [dɪ'siːtfʊlnɪs] *n* falsedad *f*

deceive [dɪ'siːv] **1** *vt* engañar; **to be deceived by appearances** dejarse engañar por las apariencias; **to d. oneself** engañarse; **to d. sb into thinking sth** hacer creer algo a alguien; **don't be deceived** no te engañes; **I thought my eyes were deceiving me** no daba crédito a lo que estaba viendo

2 *vi* engañar; **it was not done with intent to d.** no se hizo con intención de engañar

deceiver [dɪ'siːvə(r)] *n* impostor(ora) *m,f*, embustero(a) *m,f*

decelerate [diː'seləreɪt] *vi* decelerar, desacelerar

deceleration [diːselə'reɪʃən] *n* deceleración *f*, desaceleración *f*

December [dɪ'sembə(r)] *n* diciembre *m*; *see also* **May**

decency ['diːsənsɪ] *n* (**a**) *(of dress, behaviour)* decencia *f*, decoro *m*; **common d.** (mínima) decencia; **he didn't even have the d. to tell us first** ni siquiera tuvo la delicadeza de decírnoslo primero (**b**) *Formal* **the decencies** *(conventional standards)* las convenciones sociales; **to observe the decencies** guardar las formas

decent ['diːsənt] *adj* (**a**) *(respectable)* decente, decoroso(a); **d., church-going folk** gente de bien, que va a misa; *Old-fashioned* **to do the d. thing** *(marry woman one has made pregnant)* hacer lo que es decente y casarse; *Hum* **are you d.?** *(dressed)* ¿estás visible *or* presentable?; **she remarried after a d. interval** volvió a casarse tras un decoroso periodo de tiempo

(**b**) *(of acceptable quality, size)* decente; **I earn a d. wage** gano un sueldo decente; **a d. meal** una comida decente; **a d. night's sleep** una buena noche de descanso; **he speaks d. Spanish** habla un español aceptable (**c**) *Fam (kind)* **a d. chap** un buen tipo; **it's very d. of you** es muy amable de tu parte

decently ['diːsəntlɪ] *adv* (**a**) *(respectably)* con decencia, decentemente; **to treat people d.** tratar a los demás con decencia (**b**) *(reasonably)* **they pay quite d.** pagan un sueldo bastante decente (**c**) *Fam (kindly)* con amabilidad

decentralization [diːsentrəlaɪ'zeɪʃən] *n* descentralización *f*

decentralize [diː'sentrəlaɪz] **1** *vt* descentralizar

2 *vi* descentralizarse

deception [dɪ'sepʃən] *n* engaño *m*; **by d.** valiéndose de engaños

> **False friend**: The Spanish noun **decepción** is not a translation for the English word **deception**. In Spanish **decepción** means "disappointment".

deceptive [dɪ'septɪv] *adj* engañoso(a); **appearances can be d.** las apariencias engañan

deceptively [dɪ'septɪvlɪ] *adv* engañosamente; **d. worded/written** formulado/escrito engañosamente; **it looks d. easy** a primera vista parece muy fácil

decibel ['desɪbel] *n* decibelio *m*

decide [dɪ'saɪd] **1** *vt* (**a**) *(choose, resolve)* decidir; **to d. to do sth** decidir hacer algo; **what have you decided?** ¿qué has decidido?; **it was decided to wait for her reply** se decidió esperar su respuesta; **nothing has been decided** no hay nada decidido; **to d. one's own future** decidir *or* determinar (uno) su propio porvenir; **the weather hasn't decided what it's doing yet** el tiempo no termina de aclararse

(**b**) *(determine) (outcome, sb's fate)* decidir; **that was what decided me** eso fue lo que me hizo decidirme

(**c**) *(settle) (debate, war)* resolver; **that decides the matter** eso resuelve la cuestión; **the issue will be decided at our next meeting** el asunto se resolverá en nuestra próxima reunión

2 *vi* (**a**) *(make up one's mind)* decidir; **what shall we do? – you d.** ¿qué hacemos? – tú decides; **she couldn't d. between the two** no se decidía entre los dos; **you'll have to d. for yourself** tendrás que decidirte tú solo; **I can't d. whether to go or not** no sé si ir o no; **to d. in favour of/against sb** *(judge, jury)* fallar a favor de/en contra de alguien; **to d. against doing sth** decidir no hacer algo; **to d. in favour of doing sth** decidir hacer algo

(**b**) *(determine)* **he planned to become a doctor but circumstances decided otherwise** quería ser médico pero el destino no quiso que así fuera

►**decide on** *vt insep* decidirse por; **have you decided on a date/a name?** ¿has escogido una fecha/un nombre?; **I've decided on Greece for my holiday** he elegido Grecia para pasar mis vacaciones

decided [dɪ'saɪdɪd] *adj* (**a**) *(person, manner)* decidido(a), resuelto(a); *(opinion)* tajante (**b**) *(difference, preference, improvement)* claro(a), marcado(a)

decidedly [dɪ'saɪdɪdlɪ] *adv* (**a**) *(to answer, say)* categóricamente (**b**) *(very)* decididamente; **he was d. unhelpful** no ayudó en lo más mínimo; **I feel d. unwell today** decididamente, no me encuentro bien hoy

decider [dɪ'saɪdə(r)] *n* **the d.** *(goal, match etc)* el gol/partido/*etc.* decisivo

deciding [dɪ'saɪdɪŋ] *adj* decisivo(a); **the d. factor** el factor decisivo

deciduous [dɪ'sɪdjʊəs] *adj Bot* de hoja caduca, caducifolio(a)

decilitre, *US* **deciliter** ['desɪliːtə(r)] *n* decilitro *m*

decimal ['desɪməl] **1** *n* número *m* decimal
2 *adj (number)* decimal ►► ***d. currency*** moneda *f* (de sistema) decimal; ***d. place:*** **correct to five d. places** correcto(a) hasta la quinta cifra decimal; ***d. point*** coma *f* (decimal); ***d. system*** sistema *m* decimal

decimalization [desɪməlaɪ'zeɪʃən] *n* conversión *f* al sistema decimal

decimalize ['desɪməlaɪz] **1** *vt* decimalizar, convertir al sistema decimal
2 *vi* convertirse al sistema decimal

decimate ['desɪmeɪt] *vt* **(a)** *(inflict heavy losses on)* diezmar **(b)** *(in Roman army)* diezmar

decipher [dɪ'saɪfə(r)] *vt* descifrar

decision [dɪ'sɪʒən] *n* **(a)** *(choice, judgement)* decisión *f*; **to come to** *or* **arrive at** *or* **reach a d.** llegar a una decisión; **to make** *or* **take a d.** tomar una decisión; **it's your d.** es tu decisión; **the referee's d. is final** la decisión del juez es final **(b)** *Formal (decisiveness)* decisión *f*, determinación *f*; **to act/speak with d.** actuar/hablar con decisión

decision-making [dɪ'sɪʒənmeɪkɪŋ] *n* toma *f* de decisiones; **the d. process** el proceso para la toma de decisiones

decisive [dɪ'saɪsɪv] *adj* **(a)** *(battle, argument, factor, influence)* decisivo(a) **(b)** *(manner, person, tone)* decidido(a); **be d.!** ¡sé más resuelto!

decisively [dɪ'saɪsɪvlɪ] *adv* **(a)** *(conclusively)* contundentemente; **they were d. defeated** fueron derrotados claramente *or* contundentemente **(b)** *(firmly, with decision)* con decisión, decididamente

decisiveness [dɪ'saɪsɪvnɪs] *n* **(a)** *(of factor, battle, argument, question)* contundencia *f* **(b)** *(of manner, person, tone)* firmeza *f*, decisión *f*

deck [dek] **1** *n* **(a)** *(of ship)* cubierta *f*; **on d.** en cubierta; **to go (up) on d.** salir a cubierta; **below d.** bajo cubierta; IDIOM **to clear the decks** ponerse al día y finalizar los asuntos pendientes ►► ***d. chair*** tumbona *f*, hamaca *f*; ***d. chair attendant*** = persona que se ocupa del alquiler de tumbonas en playas y piscinas; ***d. hand*** marinero *m*; ***d. house*** camareta *f* alta; ***d. tennis*** = modalidad de tenis para jugar sobre la cubierta de un barco
(b) top *or* **upper/bottom d.** *(of bus)* piso de arriba/abajo
(c) *(outside house)* terraza *f* entarimada
(d) *(of cards)* **d. (of cards)** baraja *f*; IDIOM **he's not playing with a full d.** le falta un tornillo
(e) *Fam (ground)* **to hit the d.** *(fall)* caer de bruces; *(lie down)* echar cuerpo a tierra; *(get out of bed)* levantarse
(f) cassette d. pletina *f*; **tape d.** pletina *f*
2 *vt* **(a)** *(decorate)* **to d. oneself out in sth** engalanarse con algo; **the town centre was decked out for the parade** el centro vistió sus mejores galas para el desfile **(b)** *Fam (knock to ground)* tumbar, noquear

-decker ['dekə(r)] *suffix* **double-d. bus** autobús de dos pisos; **triple-d. sandwich** sándwich de tres pisos

deckle-edged ['dekəl'edʒd] *adj (paper)* de barba

declaim [dɪ'kleɪm] **1** *vt* proclamar, pregonar
2 *vi* pregonar; **to d. against sth** declamar en contra de algo

declamatory [dɪ'klæmətərɪ] *adj* declamatorio(a)

declaration [deklə'reɪʃən] *n* **(a)** *(statement)* declaración *f*; **d. of love/war** declaración de amor/guerra ►► *also Fig* ***d. of faith*** profesión *f* de fe; *Hist* ***the D. of Independence*** la declaración de independencia de los Estados Unidos; ***d. of intent*** declaración *f* de intenciones **(b)** *(in cards)* declaración *f*

declarative [dɪ'klærətɪv] *adj* declaratorio(a)

declare [dɪ'kleə(r)] **1** *vt* **(a)** *(proclaim, announce)* declarar; **to d. war (on)** declarar la guerra (a); **to d. sb guilty/innocent** declarar a alguien culpable/inocente; **to d. sb bankrupt** declarar a alguien en quiebra; *Fin* **to d. a dividend of 10 percent** fijar un dividendo del 10 por ciento; **to d. oneself** *(proclaim one's love)* declararse; **to d. oneself for/against sth** declararse *or* pronunciarse a favor de/en contra de algo
(b) have you anything to d.? *(at customs)* ¿(tiene) algo que declarar?
(c) *(trumps, suit)* declarar
2 *vi* **(a) to d. for/against sth** declararse a favor de/en contra de algo; *Old-fashioned* **I do d.!** ¡demontre! **(b)** *(in cards)* declarar

declared [dɪ'kleəd] *adj (intention, opponent)* declarado(a) ►► *Fin* ***d. capital*** capital *m* declarado *or* escriturado

declassify [di:'klæsɪfaɪ] *vt* desclasificar; **the information/file has been declassified** se ha desclasificado la información/el archivo

declension [dɪ'klenʃən] *n Gram* declinación *f*

declination [deklɪ'neɪʃən] *n* **(a)** *Astron* declinación *f* **(b)** *US (refusal)* rechazo *m*

decline [dɪ'klaɪn] **1** *n* **(a)** *(decrease, reduction) (in prices, standards, crime, profits)* descenso *m*, disminución *f*; **there has been a d. in child mortality** se ha producido un descenso de la mortalidad infantil; **to be on the d.** ir en descenso
(b) *(process of deterioration) (of person, empire)* declive *m*; **to go into d.** decaer, debilitarse; **to be in d.** estar en declive; **to fall into d.** entrar en decadencia; *Old-fashioned* **to fall into a d.** *(person)* entrar en decadencia
2 *vt* **(a)** *(offer, invitation)* declinar; **to d. to do sth** declinar hacer algo **(b)** *Gram* declinar
3 *vi* **(a)** *(refuse)* rehusar **(b)** *(health, influence, empire, industry)* declinar; *(standards)* decaer, bajar; *(numbers)* disminuir, reducirse; **to d. in importance/value** perder importancia/valor **(c)** *(slope downwards)* descender, inclinarse **(d)** *Gram* declinar

declining [dɪ'klaɪnɪŋ] *adj* **(a)** *(decreasing)* decreciente **(b)** *(deteriorating)* en declive, en decadencia; **he is in d. health** su salud está empeorando *or* deteriorándose; **in my d. years** en mis últimos años

declivity [dɪ'klɪvətɪ] *n Formal (slope)* declive *m*

declutch [di:'klʌtʃ] *vi* desembragar

decode [di:'kəʊd] *vt* descodificar, descifrar

decoder [di:'kəʊdə(r)] *n* descodificador *m*

decoding [di:'kəʊdɪŋ] *n* descodificación *f*

décolletage [deɪkɒl'tɑ:ʒ] *n* escote *m*

decolonization [di:kɒlənaɪ'zeɪʃən] *n* descolonización *f*

decolonize [di:'kɒlənaɪz] *vt* descolonizar

decommission [di:kə'mɪʃən] *vt* **(a)** *(of nuclear reactor)* desmantelar **(b)** *(of warship)* retirar de servicio **(c)** *(of weapons)* entregar

decompose [di:kəm'pəʊz] **1** *vi* **(a)** *(rot)* descomponerse **(b)** *(break down)* desintegrarse
2 *vt Chem* descomponer

decomposing [di:kəm'pəʊzɪŋ] *adj (corpse)* en descomposición

decomposition [di:kɒmpə'zɪʃən] *n* descomposición *f*

decompress [di:kəm'pres] *vt Comptr (file)* descomprimir

decompression [di:kəm'preʃən] *n* descompresión *f* ►► ***d. chamber*** cámara *f* de descompresión; ***d. sickness*** aeroembolismo *m*

decongestant [di:kən'dʒestənt] **1** *n Med* descongestionante *m*
2 *adj* descongestionante, anticongestivo(a)

deconsecrate [di:'kɒnsɪkreɪt] *vt* secularizar

deconstruct [di:kən'strʌkt] *vt Lit* deconstruir

deconstruction [di:kən'strʌkʃən] *n Lit* teoría *f* desconstructiva, desconstruccionismo *m*

decontaminate [di:kən'tæmɪneɪt] *vt* descontaminar

decontamination [di:kəntæmɪ'neɪʃən] *n* descontaminación *f*

decontrol [di:kən'trəʊl] *vt (trade, prices)* desregularizar, liberalizar

décor ['deɪkɔ:(r)] *n (in house, on stage)* decoración *f*

decorate ['dekəreɪt] **1** *vt* **(a)** *(cake, room, tree) (with decorations)* decorar, adornar (**with** con) **(b)** *(house, room) (with paint)* pintar; *(with wallpaper)* empapelar **(c)** *(with medal)* condecorar; **to be decorated for bravery** ser condecorado por haber dado muestras de valor
2 *vi (with paint)* pintar; *(with wallpaper)* empapelar

decorating ['dekəreɪtɪŋ] *n (of house, room)* **he did all the d. in the new house himself** pintó y empapeló la casa nueva él solo

decoration [dekə'reɪʃən] *n* **(a)** *(on cake, for party)* decoración *f*; **she's just there for d.** sólo está allí de adorno; **decorations** adornos *mpl* **(b)** *(of room) (with paint)* pintado *m*; *(with wallpaper)* empapelado *m* **(c)** *(medal)* condecoración *f*

decorative ['dekərətɪv] *adj* **(a)** *(ornamental)* decorativo(a) ►► ***the d. arts*** las artes decorativas **(b)** *Br* **the house is in excellent d. order** el interior de la casa se encuentra en excelente estado

decorator ['dekəreɪtə(r)] *n* **(painter and) d.** pintor(ora) *m,f (que también empapela)*

decorous ['dekərəs] *adj Formal (person, behaviour)* decoroso(a)

decorum [dɪ'kɔ:rəm] *n* decoro *m*; **to behave with d.** comportarse con decoro

decoy **1** *n* ['di:kɔɪ] **(a)** *(bird)* señuelo *m* **(b)** *(person, object)* señuelo *m*; **to act as a d.** hacer *or* servir de señuelo
2 *vt* [dɪ'kɔɪ] atraer con un señuelo; **to d. sb into doing sth** lograr que alguien haga algo utilizando un señuelo

decrease **1** *n* ['di:kri:s] *(in size, popularity, price)* reducción *f*, disminución *f* (**in** de); **a d. in the number of applications** un descenso en el número de solicitudes; **to be on the d.** estar disminuyendo, decrecer
2 *vt* [dɪ'kri:s] disminuir, reducir
3 *vi* [dɪ'kri:s] disminuir; **the price has decreased** ha bajado el precio

decreasing [dɪ'kri:sɪŋ] *adj* decreciente; **a d. number of visitors** un número de visitantes cada vez menor

decreasingly [dɪ'kri:sɪŋlɪ] *adv* cada vez menos

decree [dɪ'kri:] 1 *n* decreto *m*; **to issue a d.** promulgar un decreto; **by royal d.** por real decreto ►► *Law* ***d. absolute*** sentencia *f* definitiva de divorcio; *Law* ***d. nisi*** sentencia *f* provisional de divorcio
2 *vt* decretar; **fate decreed that...** estaba escrito que..., el destino quiso que...

> En inglés culto o elevado, y especialmente en inglés americano, **decree** puede ir seguido de **that** más un verbo en subjuntivo (ver el panel SUBJUNCTIVE):
> **the new regulation decreed that no one take more than ten days holiday in any one month**
> *la nueva norma decretaba que nadie tomara más de diez días de vacaciones al mes*
> Lo mismo también podría decirse de las formas siguientes:
> **the new regulation decreed that no one should take more than ten days holiday in any one month**
> **the new regulation decreed that no one was to take more than ten days holiday in any one month**

decrepit [dɪ'krepɪt] *adj* (**a**) *(person)* decrépito(a) (**b**) *(thing)* ruinoso(a)

decrepitude [dɪ'krepɪtju:d] *n Formal* (**a**) *(of person)* decrepitud *f* (**b**) *(of thing)* ruina *f*, deterioro *m*

decriminalization [di:krɪmɪnəlaɪ'zeɪʃən] *n* despenalización *f*

decriminalize [di:'krɪmɪnəlaɪz] *vt* despenalizar

decry [dɪ'kraɪ] *vt* censurar, condenar; **the union has decried the suggested increase as an insult** el sindicato ha condenado el aumento propuesto por considerarlo un insulto

decrypt [di:'krɪpt] *vt Comptr* descifrar

decryption [di:'krɪpʃən] *n Comptr* descifrado *m*

DEd [di:'ed] *n* (*abbr* **Doctor of Education**) doctor(ora) *m,f* en pedagogía

dedicate ['dedɪkeɪt] *vt* (**a**) *(devote)* dedicar; **to d. oneself to sb/sth** consagrarse a alguien/algo; **she dedicated her life to helping the poor** consagró *or* dedicó su vida a ayudar a los pobres (**b**) *(book, record)* dedicar (**to** a) (**c**) *(consecrate) (church, shrine)* consagrar (**d**) *US (open for public use)* inaugurar

dedicated ['dedɪkeɪtɪd] *adj* (**a**) *(committed)* entregado(a), dedicado(a); **a d. teacher/doctor** un profesor/médico entregado por completo a su trabajo; **to be d. to sth** estar consagrado(a) a algo (**b**) *Comptr* dedicado(a), especializado(a) ►► *Comptr* ***d. line*** línea *f* dedicada; ***d. word processor*** procesador *m* de textos *(ordenador, computadora)*

dedicatee [dedɪkə'ti:] *n* destinatario(a) *m,f* de una dedicatoria

dedication [dedɪ'keɪʃən] *n* (**a**) *(devotion)* dedicación *f*, entrega *f* (**to** a); **a life of d.** una vida de entrega (**b**) *(of book)* dedicatoria *f*

dedicatory [dedɪ'keɪtərɪ] *adj* dedicatorio(a)

deduce [dɪ'dju:s] *vt* deducir (**from** de); **what do you d. from that?** ¿qué deduces de eso?; **I deduced that she was lying** deduje que estaba mintiendo

deducible [dɪ'dju:sɪbəl] *adj* deducible (**from** de)

deduct [dɪ'dʌkt] *vt* descontar, deducir (**from** de); **tax is deducted at source** la deducción la realiza el pagador; **after deducting expenses** después de descontar los gastos

deductible [dɪ'dʌktɪbəl] *adj* deducible; *Fin* **d. for tax purposes** desgravable

deduction [dɪ'dʌkʃən] *n* (**a**) *(subtraction)* deducción *f*; **after deductions** *(from pay, salary)* después de (hacer las) deducciones; **I take home £200 a week after deductions** me llevo a casa 200 libras netas por semana (**b**) *(conclusion)* deducción *f*; **by (a process of) d.** por deducción

deductive [dɪ'dʌktɪv] *adj* deductivo(a)

deed [di:d] 1 *n* (**a**) *(action)* acción *f*, obra *f*; **a brave d.** una actuación valiente; **we want deeds not words** queremos hechos, no palabras; IDIOM **to do one's good d. for the day** hacer la buena acción *or* obra del día; **in word and d.** de palabra y obra
(**b**) *Law (document)* escritura *f*, título *m* de propiedad ►► ***d. of covenant*** = escritura que formaliza el pago de una donación periódica a una entidad, generalmente benéfica, o a un individuo; ***d. of partnership*** escritura *f* de constitución de sociedad; ***d. poll:*** **to change one's name by d. poll** cambiarse legalmente el nombre
2 *vt US Law (transfer)* ceder, donar

deejay ['di:dʒeɪ] *Fam* 1 *n* pincha *mf*, disc-jockey *mf inv*
2 *vi* pinchar (música)

deem [di:m] *vt Formal* considerar, estimar; **it was deemed necessary to call an enquiry** se consideró necesario solicitar una investigación; **she was deemed (to be) the rightful owner** fue considerada la propietaria legítima

de-emphasize [di:'emfəsaɪz] *vt (need, claim, feature)* quitar énfasis *or* importancia a

deep [di:p] 1 *n Literary* (**a**) *(ocean)* **the d.** las profundidades del mar (**b**) *(depth)* **in the d. of winter** en lo más duro del invierno
2 *adj* (**a**) *(vertically) (water, hole, snow, wound)* profundo(a); *(dish)* hondo(a); **to be 10 metres d.** tener 10 metros de profundidad; **to give a d. sigh** dar un profundo *or* hondo suspiro, suspirar profundamente; **take a d. breath** respire hondo; **the d. blue sea** los mares insondables; IDIOM **to be in/get into d. water** estar/meterse en un lío ►► ***d. end*** *(of swimming pool)* parte *f* profunda; IDIOM **to go off (at) the d. end (at sb)** ponerse hecho(a) un basilisco (con alguien); IDIOM **she was thrown in at the d. end** la hicieron empezar de golpe *or* sin preparación; *Ling* ***d. structure*** estructura *f* profunda
(**b**) *(horizontally) (forest, cupboard, serve)* profundo(a); **the cupboard is a metre d.** el armario tiene un metro de fondo; **the crowd stood 15 d.** la multitud formaba filas de 15 en fondo; **d. in the forest** en el corazón del bosque; *Hum* **d. in Virginia, in deepest Virginia** en el Virginia ►► ***the D. South*** *(of USA)* la América profunda de los estados del sur; ***d. space*** espacio *m* interplanetario *or* intergaláctico
(**c**) *(strong, intense) (feelings)* profundo(a), intenso(a); *(sleep)* profundo(a); **in deepest sympathy** *(on card)* con mi más sincero pésame; **they were d. in conversation** estaban enfrascados en la conversación *or CAm, Méx* plática; **d. in debt** endeudado(a) hasta el cuello; **to be in d. mourning** estar de riguroso luto; *Vulg* **to be in d. shit** estar metido(a) en un lío de cojones; **d. in thought** ensimismado(a); **to be in d. trouble** estar en un serio aprieto
(**d**) *(profound) (thinker, book, thought, remark)* profundo(a); **he's a d. one** *(mysterious)* es enigmático; **(it's) too d. for me!** es demasiado profundo para mí
(**e**) *(colour)* intenso(a); **a d. blue** un azul intenso
(**f**) *(sound, voice)* grave
3 *adv* profundamente; **she thrust her hand d. into the bag** metió la mano hasta el fondo de la bolsa; **the crowd lining the road was four d.** la gente se agolpaba en cuatro filas a lo largo de la calle; **the snow lay d. on the ground** una gran capa de nieve cubría el suelo; **to look d. into sb's eyes** mirar a alguien fijamente a los ojos; **to walk d. into the forest** internarse en el bosque; **to work d. into the night** trabajar hasta bien entrada la noche; **d. down he's very kind** en el fondo, es muy amable; **mistrust between the two families runs d.** la desconfianza entre las dos familias está profundamente arraigada; **don't get in too d.** *(involved)* no te impliques demasiado; *Fam* **she's in it pretty d.** está metida hasta el cuello

deepen ['di:pən] 1 *vt* (**a**) *(well, ditch)* profundizar, ahondar (**b**) *(sorrow, interest)* acentuar, agudizar; *(knowledge)* profundizar en; *(crisis)* profundizar, agudizar, *(mystery)* crecer, aumentar; *(love, friendship)* estrechar; **to d. one's understanding of sth** ahondar en el conocimiento de algo (**c**) *(sound, voice)* hacer más grave; *(colour)* intensificar
2 *vi* (**a**) *(river)* hacerse más profundo(a) (**b**) *(silence, mystery, knowledge)* hacerse más profundo(a); *(crisis)* ahondarse, acentuarse; *(love, friendship)* estrecharse; *(conviction, belief)* afianzarse; *(sorrow, interest)* acentuarse, agudizarse (**c**) *(colour)* intensificarse; *(sound, voice)* hacerse más grave

deep-dish ['di:pdɪʃ] *adj US Culin* **d. pie** = pastel que se cuece en un recipiente hondo y que sólo tiene una costra por encima

deepening ['di:pənɪŋ] *adj (silence, shadows, emotion)* cada vez más profundo(a), creciente; *(crisis)* cada vez más acentuado(a), cada vez mayor

deep-freeze ['di:p'fri:z] 1 *n* congelador *m*
2 *vt* congelar

deep-fry ['di:p'fraɪ] *vt* freír (en aceite muy abundante)

deep-fryer ['di:p'fraɪə(r)] *n* freidora *f*

deeply ['di:plɪ] *adv* (**a**) *(to breathe, sigh, sleep)* profundamente; *(to think, study)* a fondo (**b**) *(touched, offended)* profundamente; *(relieved, grateful)* profundamente, sumamente; **to care d. about sth/sb** preocuparse profundamente por algo/alguien

deepness ['di:pnɪs] *n* (**a**) *(vertical distance) (of water, hole, snow, wound)* profundidad *f* (**b**) *(horizontal distance) (of shelf, cupboard)* profundidad *f*, hondura *f* (**c**) *(strength, intensity) (of feeling, sleep)* profundidad *f* (**d**) *(of thought, remark)* profundidad *f* (**e**) *(of colour)* intensidad *f* (**f**) *(of sound, voice)* gravedad *f*

deep-pan ['di:ppæn] *adj Culin* ***d. pizza*** pizza *f* gruesa

deep-rooted ['di:pru:tɪd] *adj (prejudice, fear)* muy arraigado(a)

deep-sea ['di:p'si:] *adj (exploration)* de las profundidades marinas; *(creatures)* abisal ►► ***d. diver*** buceador(ora) *m,f or* buzo *m* de profundidad; ***d. fishing*** pesca *f* de altura

deep-seated ['diːp'siːtɪd] *adj (distrust, belief, prejudice)* muy arraigado(a)
deep-set ['diːpset] *adj (eyes)* hundido(a)
deep-six ['diːp'sɪks] *vt US Fam* (**a**) *(throw away)* tirar (**b**) *(rule out)* rechazar
deep-throated ['diːp'θrəʊtɪd] *adj (cough, laugh)* bronco(a)
deepwater ['diːpwɔːtə(r)] *adj (port, fish)* de aguas profundas
deer ['dɪə(r)] (*pl* **deer**) *n* ciervo *m*, venado *m*
deerskin ['dɪəskɪn] *n* piel *f* de ciervo
deerstalker ['dɪəstɔːkə(r)] *n (hat)* gorro *m* de cazador (con orejeras)
de-escalate [diː'eskəleɪt] **1** *vt (crisis)* desacelerar
2 *vi (crisis)* remitir
de-escalation [diːeskə'leɪʃən] *n (of crisis)* desaceleración *f*
def [def] *adj Fam* genial, *Esp* guay, *Esp* dabuten
deface [dɪ'feɪs] *vt (statue, painting, poster)* desfigurar, afear; *(book)* pintarrajear
de facto [deɪ'fæktəʊ] **1** *adj* de hecho
2 *adv* de hecho
defamation [defə'meɪʃən] *n* difamación *f*; **d. of character** difamación
defamatory [dɪ'fæmətərɪ] *adj* difamatorio(a)
defame [dɪ'feɪm] *vt* difamar
default [dɪ'fɔːlt] **1** *n* (**a**) *Law & Sport (failure to appear)* incomparecencia *f*; **to win sth by d.** ganar algo por incomparecencia (del contrario)
(**b**) *(lack of alternative)* **he became the boss by d.** a falta de otra persona, él terminó por convertirse en el jefe
(**c**) *Comptr* ***d. drive*** unidad *f* (de disco) por defecto *or* omisión; *Comptr* ***d. settings*** valores *mpl or* configuración *f* por defecto *or* omisión
(**d**) *Fin* mora *f* ►► ***d. interest*** interés *m* de mora *or* moratorio
2 *vi* (**a**) *Law* **to d. on payments** *(of debt, alimony)* incumplir los pagos (**b**) *Comptr* **to d. to sth** seleccionar algo por defecto
defaulter [dɪ'fɔːltə(r)] *n Fin* moroso(a) *m,f*
defeat [dɪ'fiːt] **1** *n* (**a**) *(of army, team, government)* derrota *f*; **our d. of the enemy** la derrota que infligimos al enemigo; **to admit d.** admitir la derrota; **to suffer (a) d.** sufrir una derrota (**b**) *(of project, bill)* rechazo *m*; *Parl (of measure)* rechazo *m*
2 *vt* (**a**) *(army, government, opponent)* derrotar, vencer; **that rather defeats the object of the exercise** eso se contradice con la finalidad de la operación; **we were defeated by the weather** el mal tiempo pudo con nosotros; **it defeats me** *(I don't understand)* no alcanzo a comprenderlo (**b**) *(proposal, bill, motion)* rechazar
defeatism [dɪ'fiːtɪzəm] *n* derrotismo *m*
defeatist [dɪ'fiːtɪst] **1** *n* derrotista *mf*
2 *adj* derrotista
defecate ['defəkeɪt] *vi Formal* defecar
defecation [defə'keɪʃən] *n Formal* defecación *f*
defect **1** *n* ['diːfekt] defecto *m*; **hearing/speech d.** defecto auditivo/en el habla; **a character d.** un defecto de carácter
2 *vi* [dɪ'fekt] *(to enemy country)* desertar (**from** de); **to d. to another party** pasarse a otro partido; **she defected to our main competitor** se pasó a nuestro principal competidor
defection [dɪ'fekʃən] *n (to enemy country)* deserción *f*; *(to another party)* cambio *m* de partido
defective [dɪ'fektɪv] *adj* (**a**) *(flawed) (machine, hearing, sight)* defectuoso(a); *(reasoning)* erróneo(a) (**b**) *Gram* defectivo(a)
defector [dɪ'fektə(r)] *n (to enemy country)* desertor(ora) *m,f*; *(to another party)* tránsfuga *mf*
defence, *US* **defense** [dɪ'fens] *n* (**a**) *(of country)* defensa *f*; **how much is spent on d.?** ¿cuánto se gasta en defensa?; *Br* **the Ministry of D.,** *US* **the Department of Defense** el Ministerio de Defensa; *Br* **D. Minister** ministro(a) de Defensa; *US* **Secretary of Defense** secretario(a) de Defensa ►► ***d. contract*** contrato *m* de defensa; ***d. industry*** industria *f* de defensa; ***d. spending*** gasto *m* de defensa
(**b**) *(of person, cause)* defensa *f*; **to come to sb's d.** salir en defensa de alguien; **to speak in sb's d.** *(in support of)* hablar en defensa de alguien; *(following attack)* salir en defensa de alguien; **to act in d. of sth** *(in support of)* actuar en defensa de algo; *(following attack)* salir en defensa de algo ►► ***d. mechanism*** mecanismo *m* de defensa
(**c**) *(thing providing protection, argument)* defensa *f*, protección *f*; **to use sth as a d. against sth** utilizar algo como defensa *or* protección contra algo; **to put up a stubborn d.** plantear una férrea defensa; **defences** *(of country)* defensas *fpl*; **the body's natural defences against infection** las defensas naturales del cuerpo contra la infección; *Fig* **my defences were down** había bajado la guardia; **he had no d. against her charms** estaba indefenso ante sus encantos
(**d**) *Law* defensa *f*; **the d.** *(lawyers)* la defensa; **to appear for the d.** comparecer por la defensa; **she conducted her own d.** se encargó de su propia defensa ►► ***d. counsel*** abogado(a) *m,f* defensor(ora); ***d. witness*** testigo *mf* de descargo
(**e**) *Sport* defensa *f*; **they're weak in d.** tienen una defensa débil, son débiles en defensa
defenceless, *US* **defenseless** [dɪ'fenslɪs] *adj* indefenso(a)
defencelessness, *US* **defenselessness** [dɪ'fenslɪsnɪs] *n* indefensión *f*
defenceman [dɪ'fensmæn] *n (in ice hockey)* defensa *mf*
defend [dɪ'fend] **1** *vt* (**a**) *(protect)* defender (**from** de); **to d. sth/sb from** *or* **against attack** defender algo/a alguien de un ataque; **to d. oneself** defenderse (**b**) *(justify) (opinion, argument)* defender; **do you have anything to say to d. yourself?** ¿tiene algo que decir en su defensa? (**c**) *(goalmouth, title)* defender (**d**) *Law* defender
2 *vi* (**a**) *Law* defender, actuar por la defensa (**b**) *Sport* defender
defendant [dɪ'fendənt] *n Law (in civil court)* demandado(a) *m,f*; *(in criminal court)* acusado(a) *m,f*
defender [dɪ'fendə(r)] *n* (**a**) *(of country, belief)* defensor(ora) *m,f* (**b**) *Sport* defensa *mf*
defending [dɪ'fendɪŋ] *adj* (**a**) *(in sport)* **the d. champion** el defensor del título, el actual campeón (**b**) *Law* **d. counsel** abogado(a) defensor(ora)
defense, defenseless *etc US* = **defence, defenceless** *etc*
defensible [dɪ'fensəbəl] *adj* (**a**) *(idea, opinion)* justificable, defendible (**b**) *(against military attack)* defendible
defensive [dɪ'fensɪv] **1** *n* **to be on the d.** estar a la defensiva
2 *adj* defensivo(a); **to get d.** ponerse a la defensiva; **there's no need to be** *or* **get so d.!** no hace falta que te pongas *or* que estés tan a la defensiva ►► ***d. end*** *(in American football)* defensive end *m*; ***d. line*** *(in American football)* línea *f* de defensa; ***d. rebound*** *(in basketball)* rebote *m* defensivo
defensively [dɪ'fensɪvlɪ] *adv* a la defensiva; **she answered d.** respondió en actitud defensiva
defensiveness [dɪ'fensɪvnɪs] *n* actitud *f* defensiva; **I was suspicious when she spoke with such d.** me hizo sospechar que hablara tan a la defensiva
defer [dɪ'fɜː(r)] (*pt & pp* **deferred**) **1** *vt* (**a**) *(delay, postpone)* aplazar, posponer; **to d. sth to a later date** aplazar algo para una fecha posterior; **to d. doing sth** postergar algo; *Law* **to d. sentencing** diferir *or* aplazar una sentencia (**b**) *(from military service)* conceder una prórroga a; **to d. sb on medical grounds** conceder una prórroga a alguien por motivos de salud
2 *vi* **to d. to** *(person, knowledge)* ceder ante, deferir a
deference ['defərəns] *n* deferencia *f*; **to treat sb with d., to pay** *or* **to show d. to sb** tratar a alguien con deferencia, demostrar deferencia hacia alguien; **in** *or* **out of d. to...** por deferencia hacia...
deferential [defə'renʃəl] *adj* deferente; **to be d. to sb** mostrar deferencia hacia alguien
deferentially [defə'renʃəlɪ] *adv* con deferencia, deferentemente
deferment [dɪ'fɜːmənt] *n* (**a**) *(of payment, decision)* aplazamiento *m* (**b**) *US (of military service)* prórroga *f*
deferral [dɪ'fɜːrəl] *n (of payment, decision, sentence)* aplazamiento *m*
deferred [dɪ'fɜːd] *adj* aplazado(a) ►► *Fin* ***d. liabilities*** pasivo *m* diferido, pasivo *m* exigible a largo plazo; *St Exch* ***d. ordinary shares*** acciones *fpl* ordinarias de dividendo diferido
defiance [dɪ'faɪəns] *n* desafío *m*; **I will not tolerate any further d.** no toleraré nuevos actos de rebeldía; **a gesture of d.** un gesto desafiante; **in d. of the law/my instructions** desafiando la ley/mis instrucciones
defiant [dɪ'faɪənt] *adj (look, gesture, remark)* desafiante; *(person)* insolente
defiantly [dɪ'faɪəntlɪ] *adv (to act)* de manera desafiante; *(to look, gesture, remark)* con aire desafiante
defibrillation [diːfɪbrɪ'leɪʃən] *n Med* desfibrilación *f*
defibrillator [diː'fɪbrɪleɪtə(r)] *n Med* desfibrilador *m*
deficiency [dɪ'fɪʃənsɪ] *n* (**a**) *(lack) (of resources)* escasez *f*; *(of vitamins, minerals)* carencia *f*, deficiencia *f*; **a d. in calcium, a calcium d.** carencia de calcio ►► *Med* ***d. disease*** enfermedad *f* carencial (**b**) *(flaw, defect)* deficiencia *f*, defecto *m* (**c**) *(deficit)* déficit *m*
deficient [dɪ'fɪʃənt] *adj* deficiente; **he is d. in vitamin C** le falta *or Esp* anda bajo de vitamina C; **their diet is d. in calcium** su dieta es pobre en calcio; **to be mentally d.** ser deficiente mental; **he is somewhat d. in imagination** le falta algo de imaginación

deficit ['defɪsɪt] *n Fin* déficit *m*; **to be in d.** tener déficit; **to make up the d.** enjugar el déficit; **the balance of payments shows a d. of £800 million** la balanza de pagos arroja un déficit de 800 millones de libras ▸▸ *Econ* ***d. financing*** financiación *f* mediante déficit

defile[1] [dɪ'faɪl] *vt* (**a**) *(sacred place, tomb)* profanar (**b**) *Literary (memory)* profanar, mancillar

defile[2] ['di:faɪl] *n* desfiladero *m*

defilement [dɪ'faɪlmənt] *n* (**a**) *(of sacred place, tomb)* profanación *f* (**b**) *Literary (of memory)* profanación *f*, mancillamiento *m*

definable [dɪ'faɪnəbəl] *adj* definible (**as** como)

define [dɪ'faɪn] *vt* (**a**) *(give meaning of) (term, word)* definir; **he defines politics as the art of the possible** define la política como el arte de lo posible (**b**) *(delimit, identify) (boundary, extent, powers)* delimitar, distinguir; *(objectives)* definir (**c**) *(object, shape)* definir; **the figures in the painting are not clearly defined** las figuras del cuadro no están claramente definidas

defining [dɪ'faɪnɪŋ] *adj* (**a**) *(decisive)* decisivo(a) (**b**) *(distinctive)* definidor(ora), distintivo(a)

definite ['defɪnɪt] *adj* (**a**) *(precise) (plan, date, answer, decision)* claro(a), definitivo(a); *(views)* concluyente; **he has very d. ideas on the subject** tiene unas ideas muy claras al respecto
(**b**) *(noticeable) (change, advantage, improvement)* claro(a), indudable
(**c**) *(sure, certain)* seguro(a); **I've heard rumours, but nothing d.** he oído rumores, pero nada en firme; **are you d. about it?** ¿estás seguro (de ello)?, ¿lo tienes claro?; **it's not d. yet** todavía no está claro
(**d**) *Gram* ***d. article*** artículo *m* determinado

definitely ['defɪnɪtlɪ] *adv* (**a**) *(precisely) (to fix, arrange)* en concreto, de forma definitiva; **he told me very d. that he didn't want to come** me dijo definitivamente que no quería venir
(**b**) *(noticeably) (improved, superior)* claramente, sin duda
(**c**) *(certainly)* con certeza; **that's d. the man I saw** no me queda ninguna duda de que ése fue el hombre que vi; **she's d. leaving, but I don't know when** se va seguro, pero no sé cuándo; **I'll d. be there** seguro que estaré allí; **are you going? – d.!** ¿vas a ir? – ¡claro!; **d. not!** ¡desde luego que no!

definition [defɪ'nɪʃən] *n* (**a**) *(of word, term)* definición *f*; **my d. of happiness would be...** por felicidad yo entiendo...; **by d.** por definición (**b**) *(statement) (of boundary, extent, powers)* delimitación *f*; *(of objectives)* definición *f* (**c**) *(of TV, binoculars)* definición *f*; *(of photograph, sound)* nitidez *f*, claridad *f*

definitive [dɪ'fɪnɪtɪv] *adj* (**a**) *(conclusive) (battle, result, answer)* definitivo(a), concluyente (**b**) *(authoritative) (biography, edition)* definitivo(a); **his is the d. study on the subject** el suyo es el estudio más autorizado sobre la materia

definitively [dɪ'fɪnɪtɪvlɪ] *adv* definitivamente

deflate [di:'fleɪt] **1** *vt* (**a**) *(ball, tyre)* deshinchar, desinflar (**b**) *(economy)* producir una deflación en (**c**) *(person)* desanimar; **to d. sb's ego** bajarle los humos a alguien
2 *vi* (**a**) *(ball, tyre)* deshincharse, desinflarse (**b**) *(economy)* sufrir una deflación

deflated [di:'fleɪtɪd] *adj* (**a**) *(ball, tyre)* deshinchado(a) (**b**) *(person)* desilusionado(a), abatido(a)

deflation [di:'fleɪʃən] *n* (**a**) *(of ball, tyre)* desinflamiento *m* (**b**) *(of economy)* deflación *f*

deflationary [di:'fleɪʃənərɪ] *adj* deflacionario(a)

deflect [dɪ'flekt] **1** *vt (ball, bullet, light, sound)* desviar; *(person)* distraer, desviar (**from** de); **the ball was deflected into the net** la pelota fue desviada a la red; **to d. criticism** distraer la atención de los críticos
2 *vi (projectile, light)* desviarse (**off** de)

deflection [dɪ'flekʃən] *n (of ball, bullet, light, sound, magnetic needle)* desviación *f*; **it was a lucky d. off the post** fue un afortunado desvío del poste

deflower [di:'flaʊə(r)] *vt Old-fashioned or Literary (woman)* desflorar, desvirgar

defog [di:'fɒg] *vt US Aut* desempañar

defoliant [di:'fəʊlɪənt] *n* defoliante *m*

defoliate [di:'fəʊlɪeɪt] *vt* defoliar

defoliation [di:fəʊlɪ'eɪʃən] *n* defoliación *f*

deforest [di:'fɒrɪst] *vt* deforestar

deforestation [di:fɒrɪs'teɪʃən] *n* de(s)forestación *f*

deform [dɪ'fɔ:m] *vt* deformar

deformation [di:fɔ:'meɪʃən] *n* deformación *f*

deformed [dɪ'fɔ:md] *adj (person, limb)* deforme; **the baby was born d.** el bebé nació con una malformación

deformity [dɪ'fɔ:mɪtɪ] *n* deformidad *f*; *(in baby, unborn child)* malformación *f* congénita

DEFRA ['defrə] *n* (*abbr* **Department of the Environment, Food and Rural Affairs**) = departamento del gobierno británico de medio ambiente, alimentación y asuntos rurales

defragment [di:fræg'ment] *vt Comptr* desfragmentar

defragmentation [di:frægmen'teɪʃən] *n Comptr* desfragmentación *f*

defraud [dɪ'frɔ:d] *vt* defraudar, estafar; **to d. sb of sth** defraudar algo a alguien

defray [dɪ'freɪ] *vt Formal (cost, expenses)* sufragar, costear

defrock [di:'frɒk] *vt* expulsar del sacerdocio

defrost [di:'frɒst] **1** *vt* (**a**) *(food)* descongelar; *(refrigerator)* deshelar, descongelar (**b**) *US (windshield)* desempañar
2 *vi (food)* descongelarse; *(refrigerator)* deshelarse, descongelarse

defroster [di:'frɒstə(r)] *n US (for windshield)* luneta *f* térmica, dispositivo *m* antivaho

deft [deft] *adj* diestro(a), hábil; **to be d. at (doing) sth** ser muy habilidoso(a) con algo

deftly ['deftlɪ] *adv* con destreza, hábilmente

deftness ['deftnɪs] *n* destreza *f*, habilidad *f*

defunct [dɪ'fʌŋkt] *adj* (**a**) *(person)* difunto(a) (**b**) *(company, scheme)* ya desaparecido(a); *(theory)* trasnochado(a)

defuse [di:'fju:z] *vt* (**a**) *(bomb)* desactivar (**b**) *(situation)* calmar, apaciguar

defy [dɪ'faɪ] *vt* (**a**) *(disobey)* desobedecer; *(law, rule)* desacatar; **many defied the curfew to be there** muchos no respetaron el toque de queda para estar allí
(**b**) *(elude)* desafiar; **to d. description** ser indescriptible; **his behaviour defies logic** su comportamiento va en contra de toda lógica
(**c**) *Formal (challenge)* desafiar; **to d. sb to do sth** desafiar a alguien a hacer *or* a que haga algo

degaussing [di:'gaʊsɪŋ] *n Comptr* desmagnetización *f*

degeneracy [dɪ'dʒenərəsɪ] *n (process, state)* degeneración *f*

degenerate **1** *n* [dɪ'dʒenərət] *(person)* degenerado(a) *m,f*
2 *adj* [dɪ'dʒenərət] degenerado(a)
3 *vi* [dɪ'dʒenəreɪt] degenerar (**into** en); **his health was degenerating** su salud se estaba deteriorando; **the discussion degenerated into an argument** la conversación degeneró en discusión

degeneration [dɪdʒenə'reɪʃən] *n* degeneración *f*

degenerative [dɪ'dʒenərətɪv] *adj* degenerativo(a) ▸▸ *Med* ***d. disease*** enfermedad *f* degenerativa

degradation [degrə'deɪʃən] *n* (**a**) *(corruption, debasement)* degradación *f* (**b**) *(poverty)* degradación *f*

degrade [dɪ'greɪd] *vt* (**a**) *(debase)* rebajar, degradar; **I won't d. myself by answering that** no me rebajaré a contestar a eso (**b**) *Mil (officer)* degradar (**c**) *Mil (enemy defences)* deteriorar

degrading [dɪ'greɪdɪŋ] *adj* degradante

degrease [di:'gri:s] *vt* desengrasar

degree [dɪ'gri:] *n* (**a**) *(extent, level)* grado *m*; **there are varying degrees of opposition to the new law** existen diversos grados *or* niveles de oposición a la nueva ley; **there was a certain d. of mistrust between them** había un cierto grado de desconfianza entre ellos; **an honour of the highest d.** un honor del más alto grado; **a d. of precision never before thought possible** un grado de precisión nunca antes imaginable; **a d. of risk** un cierto riesgo, un elemento de riesgo; **a d. of truth** cierto grado de verdad, algo de cierto *or* de verdad; **to a d.** *(somewhat)* hasta cierto punto; *(exceedingly)* en grado sumo; **to such a d. that...** hasta tal punto que...; **by degrees** poco a poco, gradualmente ▸▸ *Gram* ***d. of comparison*** grado *m* de comparación
(**b**) *(of temperature, in geometry, geography)* grado *m*; **it's 25 degrees** *(of temperature)* hace 25 grados; **ten degrees below zero** diez grados bajo cero; **it's two degrees east of Greenwich** está situado a dos grados al este de Greenwich; **a 90-d. angle** un ángulo de noventa grados ▸▸ ***d. centigrade*** grado *m* centígrado
(**c**) *(at university) (title)* título *m* universitario, licenciatura *f*; *(course)* carrera *f*; **postgraduate d.** título/curso de posgrado; **to take** *or* **do a d.** hacer *or* estudiar una carrera; **to have a d. in physics** ser licenciado(a) en física ▸▸ ***d. ceremony*** ceremonia *f* de graduación
(**d**) *Archaic or Literary (rank, status)* **of high/low degree** de alto/bajo rango, de alta/baja condición social

dehumanization [di:hju:mənaɪ'zeɪʃən] *n* deshumanización *f*

dehumanize [di:'hju:mənaɪz] *vt* deshumanizar

dehumidifier [di:hju:'mɪdɪfaɪə(r)] *n* deshumidificador *m*

dehydrate [diːhaɪ'dreɪt] **1** *vt (person, food)* deshidratar
2 *vi (person)* deshidratarse

dehydrated [diːhaɪ'dreɪtɪd] *adj (person, food)* deshidratado(a); **to be d.** estar deshidratado(a); **to become d.** deshidratarse

dehydration [diːhaɪ'dreɪʃən] *n* deshidratación *f*

dehydrogenate [diːhaɪ'drɒdʒəneɪt] *vt Chem* deshidrogenar

de-ice [diː'aɪs] *vt* quitar el hielo de

de-icer [diː'aɪsə(r)] *n (for car)* descongelador *m* (de parabrisas); *(on plane)* dispositivo *m* de descongelación

deictic ['daɪktɪk] *adj Ling* deíctico(a)

deification [deɪɪfɪ'keɪʃən] *n* deificación *f*, divinización *f*

deify ['deɪɪfaɪ] *vt* deificar, divinizar

deign [deɪn] *vt* **to d. to do sth** dignarse a hacer algo

deindustrialization [diːɪndʌstrɪəlaɪ'zeɪʃən] *n* desindustrialización *f*

deinstall [diːɪn'stɔːl] *vt Comptr* desinstalar

deinstaller [diːɪn'stɔːlə(r)] *n Comptr* desinstalador *m*

deionize [diː'aɪənaɪz] *vt Chem* desionizar; **deionized water** agua desionizada

deism ['deɪɪzəm] *n* deísmo *m*

deist ['deɪɪst] *n* deísta *mf*

deity ['deɪɪtɪ] *n (god)* deidad *f*, divinidad *f*; **the D.** Dios

deixis ['daɪksɪs] *n Ling* deixis *f*

déjà vu ['deɪʒɑː'vuː] *n* déjà vu *m*; **when I went in, I experienced a strange feeling of d.** cuando entré, sentí como si ya hubiera estado allí antes

dejected [dɪ'dʒektɪd] *adj* abatido(a); **to be d.** estar abatido(a)

dejectedly [dɪ'dʒektɪdlɪ] *adv* con abatimiento

dejection [dɪ'dʒekʃən] *n* abatimiento *m*

> **False friend:** The Spanish noun **deyección** is not a translation for the English word **dejection**. In Spanish **deyección** means "debris" or "excretion".

de jure [deɪ'dʒʊəreɪ] **1** *adj* de jure
2 *adv* de jure

dekko ['dekəʊ] *n Br Fam* **to have** *or* **take a d. at sth/sb** echar un vistazo *or* una ojeada a algo/alguien

Del (*abbr* **Delaware**) Delaware

del key ['delkiː] *n* tecla *f* de borrado

Delaware ['deləweə(r)] *n* Delaware

delay [dɪ'leɪ] **1** *n* retraso *m*, *Am* demora *f*; **without d.** sin dilación *or* demora; **there's no time for d.** no hay tiempo que perder; **an hour's d., a d. of an hour** un retraso *or Am* una demora de una hora; **all flights are subject to d.** todos los vuelos llevan retraso *or Am* demora; **there has been a d. in processing your application** se ha producido un retraso *or Am* una demora en la tramitación de su solicitud; **the defence lawyer requested a d. in the hearing** el abogado de la defensa solicitó un aplazamiento de la vista
2 *vt* **(a)** *(cause to be late) (project, person)* retrasar; *(traffic)* retener, demorar; **to be delayed** *(train)* llevar retraso; *(person)* llegar tarde, retrasarse, *Am* demorarse; **I don't want to d. you** no te quiero entretener; **delaying tactics** tácticas dilatorias
(b) *(postpone, defer) (decision, departure)* retrasar, demorar; **she d. leaving until the last possible moment** retrasó *or* demoró su marcha hasta el último momento
3 *vi* retrasarse, demorarse; **don't d.!** ¡no deje pasar más tiempo!

delayed [dɪ'leɪd] *adj (effect, reaction)* retardado(a); **she's suffering from d. shock** está sufriendo un shock retardado

delayed-action [dɪ'leɪd'ækʃən] *adj (fuse, drug)* de efecto retardado

delectable [dɪ'lektəbəl] *adj* delicioso(a)

delectation [dɪlek'teɪʃən] *n Formal or Hum* deleite *m*; **for your d.** para mayor deleite suyo

delegate **1** *n* ['delɪgət] **(a)** *(at meeting, conference)* delegado(a) *m,f* **(b)** *US (in House of Representatives)* = representante de un territorio que aún no ha adquirido la categoría de estado
2 *vt* ['delɪgeɪt] *(power, responsibility)* delegar (**to** en); **to d. sb to do sth** delegar en alguien para hacer algo
3 *vi* ['delɪgeɪt] delegar responsabilidades; **she's not very good at delegating** no se le da bien delegar responsabilidades

delegation [delɪ'geɪʃən] *n* **(a)** *(group of delegates)* delegación *f* **(b)** *(of work, power)* delegación *f*

delete [dɪ'liːt] **1** *vt* **(a)** *(erase)* borrar, suprimir; *(cross out)* tachar; **d. where inapplicable** táchese lo que no corresponda ►► *Comptr* ***d. key*** tecla *f* de borrado **(b)** *Com (from stock, catalogue)* retirar; **to d. sth from stock** descatalogar algo
2 *vi* borrar, suprimir

deleterious [delɪ'tɪərɪəs] *adj Formal* nocivo(a), perjudicial (**to** para)

deletion [dɪ'liːʃən] *n* **(a)** *(action)* supresión *f*, borrado *m* **(b)** *(passage, word deleted)* supresión *f*

Delhi ['delɪ] *n* Delhi; *Hum* **D. belly** = diarrea sufrida por extranjeros en los países tropicales

deli ['delɪ] *n Fam (shop)* = tienda de ultramarinos *or Am* enlatados de calidad ►► ***d. counter*** *(in supermarket)* mostrador *m* de delicatessen

deliberate **1** *adj* [dɪ'lɪbərət] **(a)** *(intentional)* deliberado(a), intencionado(a); **it wasn't d.** fue sin querer; **it was quite d.!** ¡fue a propósito *or* adrede! **(b)** *(unhurried)* pausado(a) **(c)** *(careful, studied)* reflexivo(a); **her speech was slow and d.** hablaba de modo pausado y articulaba las palabras claramente
2 *vi* [dɪ'lɪbəreɪt] *(think)* reflexionar (**on** *or* **upon** sobre); *(discuss)* deliberar (**on** *or* **upon** sobre)
3 *vt* [dɪ'lɪbəreɪt] deliberar sobre; **they deliberated what to do next** deliberaron sobre qué hacer a continuación

deliberately [dɪ'lɪbərətlɪ] *adv* **(a)** *(intentionally)* a propósito, deliberadamente; **I d. didn't invite her** no la invité adrede *or* a propósito **(b)** *(unhurriedly)* pausadamente

deliberation [dɪlɪbə'reɪʃən] *n* **(a)** *(thought)* reflexión *f*; **after much d.** tras largas deliberaciones **(b)** *(discussion)* deliberación *f*; **there were endless deliberations about what to do** hubo interminables deliberaciones acerca de qué hacer **(c)** *(unhurriedness)* pausa *f*; **to do sth with d.** hacer algo pausadamente

deliberative [dɪ'lɪbərətɪv] *adj (assembly, process)* deliberativo(a)

delicacy ['delɪkəsɪ] *n* **(a)** *(fineness) (of lace, features)* delicadeza *f* **(b)** *(subtlety) (of smell, colour, flavour)* suavidad *f*, finura *f* **(c)** *(fragility) (of person, health)* fragilidad *f* **(d)** *(gentleness) (of touch)* suavidad *f*, lo delicado *m* **(e)** *(sensitivity) (of mechanism, situation)* lo delicado; **it's a matter of some d.** es un tema algo delicado **(f)** *(tact, sensitivity)* delicadeza *f*, tacto *m* **(g)** *(food)* exquisitez *f*

delicate ['delɪkət] **1** *adj* **(a)** *(fine) (lace, features)* delicado(a) **(b)** *(subtle) (smell, colour, flavour)* suave **(c)** *(fragile) (health)* frágil, delicado(a); *(child)* enfermizo(a) **(d)** *(gentle) (touch)* suave, delicado(a) **(e)** *(sensitive) (mechanism, situation)* delicado(a); **a d. international situation** una situación internacional delicada
2 delicates *npl (clothes)* prendas *fpl* delicadas

delicately ['delɪkətlɪ] *adv* **(a)** *(finely)* **d. carved** primorosamente tallado(a) **(b)** *(subtly) (scented, coloured, flavoured)* suavemente, finamente **(c)** *(gently) (to touch)* con suavidad, con delicadeza **(d)** *(tactfully, sensitively)* con delicadeza; **the mechanism is very d. balanced** el equilibrio del mecanismo es muy delicado

delicatessen [delɪkə'tesən] *n (shop)* = tienda de ultramarinos *or Am* enlatados de calidad ►► ***d. counter*** mostrador *m* de delicatessen

delicious [dɪ'lɪʃəs] *adj* **(a)** *(tasty)* delicioso(a); **to look/taste d.** tener un aspecto/sabor delicioso **(b)** *(very enjoyable)* divino(a), delicioso(a)

deliciously [dɪ'lɪʃəslɪ] *adv* **(a)** *(tastily)* deliciosamente **(b)** *(very enjoyably)* divinamente, deliciosamente

delight [dɪ'laɪt] **1** *n* **(a)** *(pleasure)* gusto *m*, placer *m*; **she listened with d.** escuchó con deleite; **to my/her d.** para mi/su deleite; **he took d. in her failure** se alegró de su fracaso; **to take d. in doing sth** disfrutar haciendo algo
(b) *(source of pleasure)* placer *m*, encanto *m*; **the delights of Blackpool** los encantos *or* placeres de Blackpool; **they're a d. to teach** es una delicia darles clases
2 *vt* deleitar, encantar; **to d. the ear/eye** deleitar el oído/la vista; **her show has delighted audiences everywhere** su show ha hecho las delicias del público en todo el mundo
3 *vi* **she delights in her grandchildren** disfruta con sus nietos; **to d. in doing sth** disfrutar haciendo algo; **she delights in irritating people** disfruta sacando de quicio a la gente

delighted [dɪ'laɪtɪd] *adj* encantado(a); **a d. smile** una sonrisa encantadora; **to be d. (with sth)** estar encantado(a) (con algo); **I was d. at the news** la noticia me llenó de alegría; **I'm d. to see you** me alegro mucho de verte; **I'm d. that you can come** me alegra mucho que puedas venir; **I would be d. to attend** me encantaría poder asistir; **could you come to dinner on Saturday? – I'd be d. (to)** ¿querrías venir a cenar el sábado? – me encantaría

delightedly [dɪ'laɪtɪdlɪ] *adv* con alegría

delightful [dɪˈlaɪtfʊl] *adj (person, smile)* encantador(ora); *(meal, evening)* delicioso(a); **she looked d. in her new dress** estaba preciosa con su vestido nuevo

delightfully [dɪˈlaɪtfʊlɪ] *adv (to dance, sing)* maravillosamente; **the evenings were d. cool** hacía un frescor por las tardes delicioso; **he was d. unpretentious** tenía una modestia que era una delicia

delimit [diːˈlɪmɪt] *vt* delimitar

delimiter [diːˈlɪmɪtə(r)] *n Comptr* delimitador *m*

delineate [dɪˈlɪnɪeɪt] *vt Formal* (**a**) *(sketch)* delinear, trazar; **the outline of the town was delineated against the sunset** el contorno de la ciudad se dibujaba sobre la puesta de sol (**b**) *(plan, proposal)* detallar, especificar; *(character in novel)* definir, dibujar

delineation [dɪlɪnɪˈeɪʃən] *n Formal* (**a**) *(outline, sketch)* descripción *f* (**b**) *(of plan, proposal)* descripción *f*; *(of character in novel)* descripción *f*

delinquency [dɪˈlɪŋkwənsɪ] *n* (**a**) *(criminal behaviour)* delincuencia *f* (**b**) *Fin* morosidad *f*, impago *m*

delinquent [dɪˈlɪŋkwənt] **1** *n* delincuente *mf*
2 *adj* (**a**) *(law-breaking)* delincuente (**b**) *Fin (person, account)* moroso(a)

delirious [dɪˈlɪrɪəs] *adj* (**a**) *(raving)* delirante; **to be d.** delirar (**b**) *(excited, wild)* loco(a) de contento; **to be d. about sth** estar como loco(a) con algo; **I'm not exactly d. at the prospect** no estoy lo que se dice loca de alegría ante esa perspectiva

deliriously [dɪˈlɪrɪəslɪ] *adv* **to be d. happy** estar loco(a) de alegría

delirium [dɪˈlɪrɪəm] *n* (**a**) *Med* delirio *m* ►► ***d. tremens*** delírium *m* tremens (**b**) *(state of excitement)* delirio *m*, desvarío *m*; **to be in a d. of joy** estar loco(a) de alegría, delirar de alegría

delist [diːˈlɪst] *vt Com (product)* descatalogar

deliver [dɪˈlɪvə(r)] **1** *vt* (**a**) *(to person, home) (letter, parcel, goods)* entregar (**to** a); *(newspaper, milk)* repartir; **the train delivered us safely home** el tren nos trajo sanos y salvos a casa; IDIOM **to d. the goods** estar a la altura de las circunstancias
(**b**) *(achieve) (result, victory, deal)* alcanzar, lograr
(**c**) *(blow)* propinar
(**d**) *(produce) (speech, verdict)* pronunciar; **to d. a service** prestar un servicio; *Formal* **to d. oneself of an opinion** emitir una opinión
(**e**) *Med* **to d. a baby** traer al mundo a un niño; **the baby was delivered at 6.08 this morning** el niño nació a las 6.08 de esta mañana; *Formal or Literary* **she was delivered of a daughter** dio a luz a una niña
(**f**) *Literary (free, rescue)* **to d. sb from sth** *(from evil, temptation)* librar a alguien de algo; *(from prison, captivity)* liberar a alguien de algo; **d. us from evil** líbranos del mal
(**g**) *US Pol* **can he d. the Black vote?** ¿sabrá arrastrar (con él) el voto de la comunidad negra?
(**h**) *(of rocket)* liberar
(**i**) **to d. a pass** *(in soccer)* hacer un pase
2 *vi* (**a**) *Com* repartir; **we d.** repartimos a domicilio (**b**) *(fulfil promise)* **their proposal is impressive, but can they d.?** la propuesta es impresionante, pero ¿podrán llevarla a la práctica?

►**deliver over** *vt sep* **he delivered himself over to the police** se entregó a la policía

►**deliver up** *vt sep (fugitive, town)* entregar

deliverance [dɪˈlɪvərəns] *n Literary* liberación *f*

deliverer [dɪˈlɪvərə(r)] *n* (**a**) *Formal or Literary (saviour)* libertador(ora) *m,f* (**b**) *Com (of goods)* repartidor(ora) *m,f*

delivery [dɪˈlɪvərɪ] *n* (**a**) *(to person, home) (of letter, parcel)* entrega *f*; *(consignment)* envío *m*, entrega *f*; **there are deliveries every other day** se realizan entregas en días alternos; **to take d. of sth** recibir algo; **allow two weeks for d.** *(on order form)* la entrega se realizará en un plazo de dos semanas; **payment on d.** pago contra entrega; **to pay on d.** pagar en el momento de la entrega ►► ***d. charges*** gastos *mpl* de envío *or* transporte; ***d. date*** fecha *f* de entrega; ***d. man*** repartidor *m*; ***d. note*** nota *f* de entrega, *Esp* albarán *m*; ***d. time*** plazo *m* de entrega; ***d. van*** furgoneta *f* de reparto
(**b**) *(style of speaking)* discurso *m*, oratoria *f*
(**c**) *Med (of baby)* parto *m* ►► ***d. room*** sala *f* de partos, paritorio *m*
(**d**) *Literary (saving)* liberación *f*
(**e**) *(in cricket)* lanzamiento *m*

dell [del] *n Literary* nava *f*, vallejo *m*

delouse [diːˈlaʊs] *vt* despiojar

Delphic [ˈdelfɪk] *adj* (**a**) *Hist* délfico(a) ►► ***the D. oracle*** el oráculo de Delfos (**b**) *Literary (obscure)* ambiguo(a), oscuro(a)

delphinium [delˈfɪnɪəm] *n* espuela *f* de caballero

delta [ˈdeltə] *n* (**a**) *(Greek letter)* delta *f* (**b**) *(of river)* delta *m* (**c**) *Av* ***d. wing*** ala *f* en delta

deltoid [ˈdeltɔɪd] *Anat* **1** *n* deltoides *m inv*
2 *adj* **d. muscle** deltoides

delude [dɪˈluːd] *vt* engañar; **he deluded them into thinking that he was a millionaire** les engañó haciéndoles creer que era millonario; **to d. oneself** engañarse; **let's not d. ourselves about his motives** no nos engañemos acerca de sus motivos

deluded [dɪˈluːdɪd] *adj (mistaken, foolish)* engañado(a); **a poor d. young man** un pobre joven iluso

deluge [ˈdeljuːdʒ] **1** *n* (**a**) *(downpour)* diluvio *m* (**b**) *(flood)* inundación *f* (**c**) *(of letters, questions)* avalancha *f*, lluvia *f*
2 *vt* (**a**) *(flood)* inundar (**b**) *(overwhelm)* inundar (**with** de); **we have been deluged with requests for/offers of help** estamos desbordados con tantas solicitudes/ofertas de ayuda

delusion [dɪˈluːʒən] *n* (**a**) *(illusion, mistaken idea)* engaño *m*, ilusión *f*; **to be under a d.** estar engañado(a); **delusions of grandeur** delirios de grandeza (**b**) *Psy* idea *f* delirante; **to suffer from delusions** tener delirios

delusive [dɪˈluːsɪv], **delusory** [dɪˈluːsərɪ] *adj Formal* ilusorio(a), engañoso(a)

deluxe [dɪˈlʌks] *adj* de lujo

delve [delv] *vi* (**a**) *(investigate)* rebuscar, ahondar; **to d. into the past** hurgar en el pasado (**b**) *(search, rummage)* rebuscar; **to d. into a bag** rebuscar en una bolsa (**c**) *(dig, burrow)* hurgar, escarbar

Dem (*abbr* **Democrat**) demócrata *mf*

demagnetize [diːˈmægnətaɪz] *vt Tech* desimantar, desmagnetizar

demagog *US* = **demagogue**

demagogic [deməˈgɒgɪk] *adj* demagógico(a)

demagogue, *US* **demagog** [ˈdeməgɒg] *n* demagogo(a) *m,f*

demagoguery [deməˈgɒgərɪ], **demagogy** [ˈdeməgɒgɪ] *n* demagogia *f*

demand [dɪˈmɑːnd] **1** *n* (**a**) *(request)* exigencia *f*; *(for pay rise)* demanda *f or* reivindicación *f* salarial; **there have been many demands for the minister's resignation** muchos han exigido *or* pedido la dimisión del ministro; **to make demands on sb** exigir mucho de alguien; **I have a lot of demands on my time** estoy *or Esp* ando siempre muy ocupado; **payable on d.** exigible a la vista, pagadero(a) a su presentación; **feeding on d.** = alimentación a un bebé cuando lo pide y no a horas preestablecidas; **by popular d.** a petición popular
(**b**) *(for goods)* demanda *f* (**for** de); **to be in (great) d.** estar muy solicitado(a); **there isn't much d. for that model** ese modelo no tiene mucha demanda; **science teachers are in increasing d.** hay una demanda cada vez mayor de profesores de ciencias ►► *Fin* ***d. deposit*** depósito *m* a la vista, depósito *m* disponible; ***d. note*** pagaré *m* a la vista
2 *vt* (**a**) *(insist on)* exigir; **I d. to see the manager** exijo ver al jefe; **to d. an apology/explanation** exigir una disculpa/explicación; **they're demanding payment** demandan *or* exigen el pago; **to d. to do sth** exigir *or* querer hacer algo; **to d. (that) sb do sth** exigir a alguien que haga algo; **to d. sth of** *or* **from sb** exigir algo a alguien
(**b**) *(require)* requerir, exigir; **the task demands a lot of care and attention** la tarea requiere mucho cuidado y atención

> En inglés culto o elevado, y especialmente en inglés americano, **demand** puede ir seguido de **that** más un verbo en subjuntivo (ver el panel SUBJUNCTIVE):
> **I demand that our arguments be heard**
> *exijo que se escuchen nuestros argumentos*
> Lo mismo también podría decirse del siguiente modo:
> **I demand that our arguments should be heard**

demanding [dɪˈmɑːndɪŋ] *adj (person)* exigente; **to be d.** *(job)* exigir mucho (esfuerzo); **he's a d. child** es un niño que da mucho trabajo

demand-led [dɪˈmɑːndˈled] *adj Econ* arrastrado(a) por la demanda

demarcate [ˈdiːmɑːkeɪt] *vt Formal* delimitar, demarcar

demarcation [diːmɑːˈkeɪʃən] *n* (**a**) *(boundary, border)* demarcación *f* ►► ***d. line*** línea *f* de demarcación (**b**) *Ind* delimitación *f* de atribuciones ►► ***d. dispute*** = enfrentamiento entre grupos sindicales y la patronal sobre la delimitación de las tareas que sus miembros deben realizar en el trabajo

dematerialize [diːməˈtɪərɪəlaɪz] *vi* desvanecerse (en el aire)

demean [dɪˈmiːn] *vt* degradar; **to d. oneself** rebajarse; **your behaviour demeans the office you hold** su comportamiento desmerece el cargo que ocupa

demeaning [dɪˈmiːnɪŋ] *adj* degradante

demeanour, *US* **demeanor** [dɪ'mi:nə(r)] *n* (**a**) *(behaviour)* comportamiento *m*, conducta *f* (**b**) *(manner, bearing)* porte *m*; **he had the d. of a gentleman** tenía el porte de un caballero

demented [dɪ'mentɪd] *adj* (**a**) *(insane)* demente; **I couldn't make sense of his d. ravings** no conseguía entender su locura (**b**) *Fam (half mad)* trastornado(a), perturbado(a); **to be d. with grief** estar trastornado(a) por el dolor; **to drive sb d.** volver loco(a) a alguien

dementedly [dɪ'mentɪdlɪ] *adv* de forma demencial

dementia [dɪ'menʃə] *n Med* demencia *f*

demerara [demə'reərə] *n* **d. (sugar)** azúcar *m* moreno de caña

demerger [di:'mɜ:dʒə(r)] *n Br Com* separación *f*, disolución *f*

demerit [di:'merɪt] *n* (**a**) *Formal (fault, flaw)* demérito *m*, deficiencia *f* (**b**) *US (in school or military record)* falta *f (en el historial)*

demesne [dɪ'meɪn] *n Hist (land)* tierras *fpl* solariegas

demigod ['demɪgɒd] *n* semidiós *m*

demijohn ['demɪdʒɒn] *n* damajuana *f*

demilitarization [di:mɪlɪtəraɪ'zeɪʃən] *n* desmilitarización *f*

demilitarize [di:'mɪlɪtəraɪz] *vt* desmilitarizar

demilitarized zone [di:'mɪlɪtəraɪzd'zəʊn] *n* zona *f* desmilitarizada

demi-monde ['demɪmɒnd] *n* bajos *mpl* fondos

demise [dɪ'maɪz] **1** *n* (**a**) *Formal (of person)* fallecimiento *m*, deceso *m*; *(of newspaper, empire)* cierre *m*, desaparición *f* (**b**) *Law (transfer)* transferencia *f* en arrendamiento

2 *vt Law (lease)* transferir en arrendamiento; *(bequeath)* transmitir por sucesión

demisemiquaver [demɪ'semɪkweɪvə(r)] *n Mus* fusa *f*

demist [di:'mɪst] *vt Br Aut* desempañar

demister [di:'mɪstə(r)] *n Br Aut* luneta *f* térmica, dispositivo *m* antivaho

demitasse ['demɪtæs] *n (cup)* taza *f* pequeña, tacita *f*

demo ['deməʊ] (*pl* **demos**) *n Fam* (**a**) *(protest)* mani *f* (**b**) *(musical)* maqueta *f* ▸▸ ***d. tape*** maqueta *f (cinta)* (**c**) *Comptr* demo *f* ▸▸ ***d. disk*** disco *m* de demostración

demob [di:'mɒb] (*pt & pp* **demobbed**) *Br Fam* **1** *vt (troops)* licenciar, desmovilizar

2 *n (demobilization)* licencia *f* (absoluta), desmovilización *f*; **d. suit** = traje que se les daba a los soldados cuando se licenciaban

demobilization [di:məʊbɪlaɪ'zeɪʃən] *n* licencia *f* (absoluta), desmovilización *f*

demobilize [di:'məʊbɪlaɪz] *vt* licenciar, desmovilizar

democracy [dɪ'mɒkrəsɪ] *n* (**a**) *(system)* democracia *f* (**b**) *(state)* democracia *f*

Democrat ['deməkræt] *n US (politician, voter)* demócrata *mf*; **the Democrats** los demócratas, el partido demócrata

democrat ['deməkræt] *n* demócrata *mf*

Democratic [demə'krætɪk] *adj US Pol* demócrata

democratic [demə'krætɪk] *adj* (**a**) *(country, organization, election)* democrático(a) ▸▸ ***the D. People's Republic of Korea*** la República Popular de Corea; ***the d. process*** el proceso de democratización; ***the D. Republic of Congo*** la República Democrática del Congo

(**b**) *(person, attitude)* democrático(a); **he's very d. about how he runs things** es muy democrático a la hora de dirigir las cosas

democratically [demə'krætɪklɪ] *adv* democráticamente

democratization [dɪmɒkrətaɪ'zeɪʃən] *n* democratización *f*

democratize [dɪ'mɒkrətaɪz] *vt* democratizar

demodulate [di:'mɒdjʊleɪt] *vt Rad* producir la desmodulación de

demodulator [di:'mɒdjʊleɪtə(r)] *n* demodulador *m*

demographer [dɪ'mɒgrəfə(r)] *n* demógrafo(a) *m,f*

demographic [demə'græfɪk] **1** *adj* demográfico(a)

2 *n* **demographics** *(statistics)* datos *mpl* demográficos, estadísticas *fpl* demográficas

demography [dɪ'mɒgrəfɪ] *n* demografía *f*

demolish [dɪ'mɒlɪʃ] *vt* (**a**) *(building)* demoler, derribar (**b**) *(theory)* desbaratar; *(opponent)* aplastar (**c**) *Fam (food)* engullir, zamparse

demolition [demə'lɪʃən] *n* (**a**) *(of building)* demolición *f*, derribo *m* ▸▸ ***d. charge*** carga *f* de voladura; ***d. squad*** equipo *m* de demolición

(**b**) *(of theory)* desmantelamiento *m*, destrucción *f*; *(of opponent)* destrucción *f*

(**c**) *Sport* ***d. derby*** = concurso en el que varios vehículos viejos chocan entre sí hasta que sólo queda uno en funcionamiento

(**d**) *Mil* **demolitions** *(explosives)* explosivos *mpl*; **demolitions expert** experto en explosivos

demon ['di:mən] *n* (**a**) *(devil, evil spirit)* demonio *m* (**b**) IDIOMS **that child's a little d.** ese niño es un diablillo; *Fam* **he's a d. tennis player** es un fiera jugando al tenis; *Hum* **the d. drink** el demonio de la bebida

demonetarize [di:'mʌnətəraɪz], **demonetize** [di:'mʌnətaɪz] *vt Fin (currency)* desmonetizar

demoniacal [di:mə'naɪəkəl] *adj* demoníaco(a), diabólico(a)

demonic [dɪ'mɒnɪk] *adj* demoníaco(a) ▸▸ ***d. possession*** posesión *f* demoníaca *or* del demonio

demonology [di:mə'nɒlədʒɪ] *n* demonología *f*

demonstrable [dɪ'mɒnstrəbəl] *adj* demostrable

demonstrably [dɪ'mɒnstrəblɪ] *adv* **a theory that is d. untrue** una teoría cuya falsedad es fácilmente demostrable

demonstrate ['demənstreɪt] **1** *vt* (**a**) *(fact, theory)* demostrar; **to d. how sth works** hacer una demostración de cómo funciona algo (**b**) *(appliance, machine)* hacer una demostración de (**c**) *(ability, quality)* demostrar; **she demonstrated great musical ability** demostró tener una gran aptitud para la música

2 *vi (politically)* manifestarse (**for/against** a favor de/en contra de)

demonstration [demən'streɪʃən] *n* (**a**) *(of fact, theory, skills)* demostración *f* (**b**) *(of appliance, machine)* demostración *f* ▸▸ ***d. model*** modelo *m* de muestra (**c**) *(political)* manifestación *f*; **to go on a d.** participar en una manifestación; **to hold** *or* **stage a d.** celebrar *or* organizar una manifestación

demonstrative [dɪ'mɒnstrətɪv] **1** *adj* (**a**) *(person)* efusivo(a), extravertido(a) (**b**) *Gram* demostrativo(a)

2 *n Gram* demostrativo *m*

demonstratively [dɪ'mɒnstrətɪvlɪ] *adv (effusively)* efusivamente, afectuosamente

demonstrator ['demənstreɪtə(r)] *n* (**a**) *(of product)* demostrador(ora) *m,f* comercial (**b**) *(political)* manifestante *mf* (**c**) *Br Univ* asistente *mf* *or* auxiliar *mf* del profesor

demoralization [dɪmɒrəlaɪ'zeɪʃən] *n* desmoralización *f*

demoralize [dɪ'mɒrəlaɪz] *vt* desmoralizar

demoralizing [dɪ'mɒrəlaɪzɪŋ] *adj* desmoralizador(ora)

demote [dɪ'məʊt] *vt* (**a**) *(in army, organization)* degradar, relegar (a un puesto más bajo) (**b**) *Sport* **two teams were demoted** dos equipos fueron descendidos de categoría

demotic [dɪ'mɒtɪk] *adj* (**a**) *Formal (popular)* popular (**b**) *Ling* popular, coloquial; **d. Greek** (griego) demótico

demotion [dɪ'məʊʃən] *n* (**a**) *(of person)* degradación *f* (**b**) *Sport* descenso *m* de categoría

demotivate [di:'məʊtɪveɪt] *vt* desmotivar

demur [dɪ'mɜ:(r)] (*pt & pp* **demurred**) **1** *vi* objetar; **to d. at a suggestion** poner objeciones a una sugerencia

2 *n* **without d.** sin poner objeciones *or* reparos

demure [dɪ'mjʊə(r)] *adj (modest)* recatado(a)

demurely [dɪ'mjʊəlɪ] *adv* recatadamente, con recato

demurrage [dɪ'mʌrɪdʒ] *n Com* sobrestadía *f*

demystify [di:'mɪstɪfaɪ] *vt* aclarar, clarificar

demythologize [di:mɪ'θɒlədʒaɪz] *vt* desmitificar

den [den] *n* (**a**) *(of animal)* guarida *f* (**b**) *(haunt)* **a d. of thieves** una cueva de ladrones; **a d. of iniquity** un antro de depravación (**c**) *(room)* cuarto *m* privado, madriguera *f*

denationalization [di:næʃənəlaɪ'zeɪʃən] *n* desnacionalización *f*

denationalize [di:'næʃənəlaɪz] *vt* desnacionalizar

denature [di:'neɪtʃə(r)] *vt* desnaturalizar; **denatured alcohol** alcohol desnaturalizado

denazification [di:nɑ:tsɪfɪ'keɪʃən] *n Hist* = proceso de erradicación ideológica del nazismo en Alemania por parte de los aliados tras la Segunda Guerra Mundial

dendrite ['dendraɪt] *n Anat* dendrita *f*

dendrochronology [dendrəʊkrə'nɒlədʒɪ] *n* dendrocronología *f*

dendron ['dendrɒn] *n Anat* dendrita *f*

dengue ['deŋgeɪ] *n Med* dengue *m*

deniable [dɪ'naɪəbəl] *adj* refutable, negable

denial [dɪ'naɪəl] *n* (**a**) *(of accusation, guilt)* negación *f*; **to issue a d.** emitir un desmentido; **no one believed his denials** nadie creyó sus desmentidos

(**b**) *(of right, request)* denegación *f*; *Law* **d. of justice** denegación de justicia

(**c**) *(disavowal, repudiation)* negación *f*, rechazo *m*; **it's a d. of everything we stand for** supone una negación de todo lo que representamos

(**d**) *(abstinence)* renuncia *f*, abnegación *f*

(**e**) *Psy* **to be in d.** atravesar una fase de negación *or* rechazo

denier ['denɪə(r)] *n* denier *m*; **20 d. tights** medias de un denier 20

denigrate ['denɪgreɪt] *vt* (**a**) *(person)* denigrar (**b**) *(ability, achievement)* despreciar, menospreciar

denigration [denɪ'greɪʃən] *n* (**a**) *(of person)* trato *m* denigrante (**of** a) (**b**) *(of sb's ability, achievement)* desprecio *m*, menosprecio *m*

denim ['denɪm] *n* tela *f* vaquera; **denims** *(jeans)* vaqueros *mpl, Chile* bluyíns *mpl, Méx* pantalones *mpl* de mezclilla; **d. jacket** cazadora *or CSur* campera *or Méx* chamarra vaquera; **d. shirt** camisa vaquera

denizen ['denɪzən] *n* (**a**) *Literary or Hum (dweller)* morador(ora) *m,f* (**b**) *Bot & Biol* = planta o animal que se ha adaptado a un entorno donde no es autóctono

Denmark ['denmɑːk] *n* Dinamarca

denominate [dɪ'nɒmɪneɪt] *vt Formal (name)* denominar

denomination [dɪnɒmɪ'neɪʃən] *n* (**a**) *Rel* confesión *f* (**b**) *Fin* valor *m* (nominal) (**c**) *Formal (designation, specification)* denominación *f*, categoría *f*

denominational [dɪnɒmɪ'neɪʃənəl] *adj Rel* confesional

denominator [dɪ'nɒmɪneɪtə(r)] *n Math* denominador *m*

denotation [diːnəʊ'teɪʃən] *n Phil & Ling* denotación *f*

denote [dɪ'nəʊt] *vt* (**a**) *Formal (signify)* denotar (**b**) *Phil* denotar

denouement [deɪ'nuːmɒŋ] *n* desenlace *m*

denounce [dɪ'naʊns] *vt* (**a**) *(inform against)* denunciar; **to d. sb to the authorities** denunciar a alguien ante las autoridades; **to d. sb as an impostor** denunciar a alguien por impostor (**b**) *(criticize publicly)* denunciar, condenar

dense [dens] *adj* (**a**) *(smoke, fog, traffic, population)* denso(a); *(jungle, undergrowth)* tupido(a); *(crowd)* nutrido(a) (**b**) *(text, article)* denso(a) (**c**) *Phys* denso(a) (**d**) *Fam (stupid)* corto(a)

densely ['densli] *adv* densamente; **d. packed** muy apretado(a); **d. populated** densamente poblado(a)

denseness ['densnɪs] *n* (**a**) *Fam (stupidity)* falta *f* de luces (**b**) *(of smoke, fog, population)* densidad *f*; *(of jungle, undergrowth)* densidad *f*, espesura *f* (**c**) *(of prose)* densidad *f*

density ['densɪtɪ] *n* (**a**) *(of smoke, fog, population)* densidad *f*; *(of jungle, undergrowth)* densidad *f*, espesura *f* (**b**) *(of prose)* densidad *f* (**c**) *Phys* densidad *f*

dent [dent] **1** *n (in metal, wall)* abolladura *f*; **to make a d. in sth** abollar algo, hacer una abolladura *or* marca en algo; *Fig* **the wedding made a d. in his savings** la boda le costó una buena parte de sus ahorros; IDIOM **this defeat made a d. in his self-confidence** esa derrota minó su seguridad en sí mismo

2 *vt* (**a**) *(car, metal)* abollar (**b**) *(confidence, pride)* minar

3 *vi (metal)* abollarse

dental ['dentəl] **1** *adj* (**a**) *Med (treatment, hygiene)* dental ►► ***d. appointment*** cita *f* con el dentista; ***d. floss*** hilo *m or* seda *f* dental; ***d. hygienist*** higienista *mf* dental; ***d. nurse*** enfermera *f* de dentista; ***d. practice*** clínica *f* dental, consulta *f* de dentista; ***d. surgeon*** odontólogo(a) *m,f*; ***d. surgery*** *(activity)* odontología *f*; *Br (office)* clínica *f* dental; ***d. technician*** mecánico(a) *m,f* dentista, protésico(a) *m,f* dental

(**b**) *Ling* dental

2 *n Ling* dental *f*

dentifrice ['dentɪfrɪs] *n (paste, powder)* dentífrico *m*

dentine ['dentiːn], *US* **dentin** ['dentɪn] *n* dentina *f*

dentist ['dentɪst] *n* dentista *mf*; **to go to the d.('s)** ir al dentista; **the d.'s** *Br* **surgery** *or US* **office** la consulta del dentista

dentistry ['dentɪstrɪ] *n (subject)* odontología *f*

dentition [den'tɪʃən] *n Anat* dentición *f*

denture ['dentʃə(r)] *n (artificial tooth)* prótesis *f inv* dental; **(set of) dentures** dentadura *f* postiza

denude [dɪ'njuːd] *vt* **to be denuded of** estar desprovisto(a) de; **a landscape denuded of trees** un paisaje despojado *or* desprovisto de árboles

denunciation [dɪnʌnsɪ'eɪʃən] *n* (**a**) *(accusation)* denuncia *f* (**b**) *(criticism)* denuncia *f*, condena *f*

Denver boot ['denvə'buːt] *n Aut Fam* cepo *m*

deny [dɪ'naɪ] *vt* (**a**) *(accusation, fact)* negar; *(rumour)* desmentir; **I can't** *or* **won't** *or* **don't d. I found it amusing, but...** no niego que lo encontré divertido, pero...; **to d. doing sth, to d. having done sth** negar haber hecho algo; **there's no denying that...** es innegable que...; **to d. all knowledge of sth** negar tener conocimiento de algo

(**b**) *(right, request)* denegar; **to d. sb sth** *or* **sth to sb** denegar algo a alguien; **she was denied access to the information/room** le denegaron el acceso a la información/sala; **to d. sb his rights** denegar *or* negar a alguien sus derechos

(**c**) *(deprive)* **to d. oneself sth** privarse de algo; **she denied herself to feed her children** se privó de comer para alimentar a sus hijos, sufrió privaciones para poder alimentar a sus hijos

(**d**) *Literary (disavow, repudiate)* renegar de; **thou shalt d. me thrice** me negarás tres veces

deodorant [diː'əʊdərənt] *n* desodorante *m*; **d. stick/spray** desodorante de barra/de spray

deodorize [diː'əʊdəraɪz] *vt* desodorizar, eliminar el mal olor de

deoxidize [diː'ɒksɪdaɪz] *vt Chem* desoxidar

deoxygenate [diː'ɒksɪdʒəneɪt] *vt Chem* desoxigenar

deoxyribonucleic acid [diː'ɒksɪraɪbəʊnjuː'kleɪɪk'æsɪd] *n Biochem* ácido *m* desoxirribonucleico

dep *Rail* (*abbr* **departure**) salida *f*

depart [dɪ'pɑːt] **1** *vi Formal* (**a**) *(leave)* salir (**from** de); **the Baltimore train will d. from platform 6** el tren con destino a Baltimore efectuará su salida por la vía 6; **they departed for Canada from Portsmouth** salieron de Portsmouth para Canadá (**b**) *(deviate, vary)* **to d. from** *(tradition, subject, truth)* desviarse de

2 *vt Literary* **to d. this life** dejar este mundo, pasar a mejor vida

> **False friend**: The Spanish verb **departir** is not a translation for the English word **depart**. In Spanish **departir** means "to talk, to converse".

departed [dɪ'pɑːtɪd] **1** *n* **the d.** los difuntos

2 *adj (dead)* difunto(a); **his dear d.** su difunta esposa, su esposa que en paz descanse

department [dɪ'pɑːtmənt] *n* (**a**) *(in company, shop)* departamento *m*; **the toy/clothing d.** la sección de juguetería/confección ►► ***d. store*** grandes almacenes *mpl*

(**b**) *(in university, school)* departamento *m*; **the French d.** el departamento de francés

(**c**) *(of government)* ministerio *m* ►► *US* ***D. of Agriculture*** Ministerio *m* de Agricultura; *US* ***D. of Commerce*** Ministerio *m* de Comercio; *US* ***D. of the Interior*** Ministerio *m* del Interior; *US* ***D. of Labor*** Ministerio *m* de Trabajo; *US* ***D. of State, State D.*** Departamento *m* de Estado, = Ministerio de Asuntos Exteriores estadounidense; *Br* ***D. of Trade and Industry*** Ministerio *m* de Industria y Comercio

(**d**) *(field, responsibility)* **recruiting staff is not my d.** la contratación de personal no es competencia mía; *Fig* **cooking's not really my d.** realmente, cocinar no es mi fuerte

(**e**) *(administrative area)* departamento *m*

departmental [diːpɑːt'mentəl] *adj* de departamento; **at a d. level** a nivel departamental *or* de departamento ►► ***d. head*** jefe(a) *m,f* de departamento

departmentalize [diːpɑːt'mentəlaɪz] *vt (organization)* dividir en departamentos, compartimentar

departure [dɪ'pɑːtʃə(r)] *n* (**a**) *(of plane, train)* salida *f* ►► ***d. gate*** puerta *f* de embarque; ***d. lounge*** *(in airport)* sala *f* de embarque; ***d. time*** hora *f* de salida

(**b**) *(of person) (from place)* partida *f*; *(from competition)* salida *f*; **her unexpected d. from politics** su inesperada marcha de la política; *Formal* **to take one's d.** retirarse

(**c**) *(from tradition, subject, truth)* alejamiento *m*; **a d. from company policy** un cambio en la política de la compañía; **a d. from his usual habits** un cambio en sus hábitos; **a new d.** un camino distinto, una innovación

depend [dɪ'pend] *vi* depender; **that/it depends** depende

►**depend on, depend upon** *vt sep* (**a**) *(be determined by)* **that depends on you** eso depende de ti; **it depends on how much money I have** depende de cuánto dinero tenga; **our future may d. on it** nuestro futuro podría depender de eso; **it takes up to three hours, depending on the route you take** dependiendo de la ruta que se tome, se tarda más de tres horas

(**b**) *(rely on)* **to d. on sth/sb (for sth)** depender de algo/alguien (para algo); **we d. on oil for our prosperity** nuestra prosperidad depende del petróleo

(**c**) *(trust, be sure of)* confiar en alguien; **we need somebody who can be depended on to be discreet** necesitamos a alguien en cuya discreción podamos confiar; *Ironic* **you can d. on him to be late** puedes estar seguro(a) de que llegará tarde; **you can d. on it!** ¡cuenta con ello!, ¡tenlo por seguro!

dependability [dɪpendə'bɪlɪtɪ] *n (of person)* formalidad *f*; *(of car)* fiabilidad *f*

dependable [dɪ'pendəbəl] *adj (person)* formal; *(friend)* leal; *(car)* fiable, *Am* confiable

dependant [dɪ'pendənt] *n* **his/her dependants** las personas a su cargo; **do you have any dependants?** ¿tiene personas a su cargo?

dependence [dɪ'pendəns] *n* (**a**) *(reliance)* dependencia *f* (**on** de) (**b**) *(trust)* dependencia *f*, confianza *f* (**on** en) (**c**) *(addiction)* **morphine/heroin d.** adición a la morfina/heroína

dependency [dɪ'pendənsɪ] *n* (**a**) *(territory)* dependencia *f* (**b**) *(reliance)* dependencia *f*, confianza *f* ▸▸ ***d. culture*** cultura *f* de la dependencia del Estado

dependent [dɪ'pendənt] *adj* (**a**) *(reliant)* dependiente; **to be d. on sth/sb** depender de algo/alguien; **to be d. on drugs** ser drogodependiente(a); **to be d. on heroin** ser heroinómano(a); *Formal* **he has two d. children** tiene dos hijos a su cargo
(**b**) *(contingent)* **to be d. on sth** depender de algo, estar supeditado(a) a algo; **their prosperity was d. on the continuation of the war** su prosperidad dependía de *or* estaba supeditada a la continuación de la guerra
(**c**) *Gram (clause)* subordinado(a)
(**d**) *Math (variable)* dependiente

depersonalize [di:'pɜ:sənəlaɪz] *vt* (**a**) *(person, organization)* despersonalizar, deshumanizar (**b**) *(issue, argument)* **we should d. the issue and deal with the facts** tenemos que dejar a un lado el plano personal del asunto y centrarnos en los hechos

depict [dɪ'pɪkt] *vt* (**a**) *(of painting)* retratar, plasmar (**b**) *(of book, piece of writing)* describir

depiction [dɪ'pɪkʃən] *n* (**a**) *(picture)* representación *f* (**b**) *(description)* descripción *f*

depilate ['depɪleɪt] *vt* depilar

depilatory [dɪ'pɪlətərɪ] *adj* depilatorio(a); **d. cream** crema depilatoria

deplane [di:'pleɪn] *vi US* desembarcar del avión, abandonar el avión

deplete [dɪ'pli:t] *vt* mermar; **the illness depleted her strength** la enfermedad consumió *or* mermó sus fuerzas; **the soil has been depleted of nutrients** los nutrientes del suelo se han agotado; **to be seriously depleted** *(strength, stocks)* haber disminuido mucho ▸▸ *Chem* ***depleted uranium*** uranio *m* empobrecido

depletion [dɪ'pli:ʃən] *n (reduction)* disminuición *f*, merma *f*; *(of soil)* agotamiento *m*; **the d. of the ozone layer** la degradación de la capa de ozono

deplorable [dɪ'plɔ:rəbəl] *adj* deplorable; **in a d. condition** en un estado deplorable

deplorably [dɪ'plɔ:rəblɪ] *adv* deplorablemente

deplore [dɪ'plɔ:(r)] *vt* (**a**) *(regret)* deplorar; **we all d. the loss of life involved** todos lamentamos la pérdida de vidas humanas que lleva consigo (**b**) *(condemn, disapprove of)* condenar, rechazar; **everyone deplores violence against unarmed civilians** todo el mundo condena los ataques contra la población civil desarmada

deploy [dɪ'plɔɪ] **1** *vt* (**a**) *(troops)* desplegar (**b**) *(argument, charm)* hacer uso de, utilizar
2 *vi (troops)* desplegarse

deployment [dɪ'plɔɪmənt] *n* (**a**) *(of troops)* despliegue *m* (**b**) *(of argument, charm)* utilización *f*

depolarize [di:'pəʊləraɪz] *vt* despolarizar

depoliticize [di:pə'lɪtɪsaɪz] *vt* despolitizar

deponent [dɪ'pəʊnənt] **1** *n Law* declarante *mf*
2 *adj Gram (verb)* deponente

depopulate [di:'pɒpjʊleɪt] *vt* despoblar

depopulated [di:'pɒpjʊleɪtɪd] *adj* despoblado(a); **to become d.** despoblarse

depopulation [di:pɒpjʊ'leɪʃən] *n* despoblación *f*

deport [dɪ'pɔ:t] *vt* (**a**) *(expel)* deportar (**b**) *Formal (behave)* **to d. oneself** comportarse, conducirse

deportation [di:pɔ:'teɪʃən] *n* deportación *f* ▸▸ ***d. order*** orden *f* de deportación

deportee [di:pɔ:'ti:] *n* deportado(a) *m,f*

deportment [dɪ'pɔ:tmənt] *n Formal* (**a**) *(behaviour)* comportamiento *m*, conducta *f* (**b**) *(carriage, posture)* porte *m*

depose [dɪ'pəʊz] *vt* (**a**) *(remove)* deponer (**b**) *Law* declarar, deponer

deposit [dɪ'pɒzɪt] **1** *n* (**a**) *(in bank account)* depósito *m*; **to make a d.** hacer *or* realizar un depósito *or Esp* ingreso; **on d.** en una cuenta de ahorros, en depósito ▸▸ *Br* ***d. account*** cuenta *f or* depósito *m* a plazo fijo; *Fin* ***d. guarantee fund*** fondo *m* de garantía de depósito; ***d. slip*** resguardo *m or* comprobante *m* de depósito *or Esp* ingreso
(**b**) *(returnable)* señal *f*, fianza *f*; *(first payment)* entrega *f* inicial, *Esp* entrada *f*; **to put down a d. (on sth)** pagar la entrega inicial *or Esp* entrada (de algo); **a d. for a stereo** una señal para una cadena de música; **is there a d. on the bottle?** ¿cobran el envase *or* el casco?; *Br Pol* **to lose one's d.** = perder el dinero depositado al presentarse como candidato por no haber sacado suficientes votos
(**c**) *(of oil, minerals)* yacimiento *m*
(**d**) *(sediment, silt)* depósito *m*; *(in wine)* poso *m*
2 *vt* (**a**) *(put down, leave)* depositar; **the bus deposited me in front of my house** el autobús me dejó delante de mi casa; **I have deposited the papers with my lawyer** he entregado la documentación a mi abogado
(**b**) *(in bank account) Esp* ingresar, *Am* depositar; *Fin* **to d. sth as security** depositar algo como garantía, hacer un depósito como garantía
(**c**) *(of liquid, river)* depositar

depositary [dɪ'pɒzɪtərɪ] *n Formal* depositario(a) *m,f*

deposition [di:pə'zɪʃən] *n* (**a**) *Law* declaración *f* (**b**) *(removal of leader)* destitución *f*, deposición *f* (**c**) *Geol* sedimentación *f*

depositor [dɪ'pɒzɪtə(r)] *n Fin* depositante *mf*

depository [dɪ'pɒzɪtərɪ] *n (store)* depósito *m*, almacén *m*; *(for furniture)* guardamuebles *m inv*

depot [*Br* 'depəʊ, *US* 'di:pəʊ] *n* (**a**) *Mil* depósito *m*; *Com* almacén *m* (**b**) *Br (for keeping and repairing buses)* cochera *f* (**c**) *US (bus station)* estación *f* de autobuses, *CAm, Méx* central *f* camionera; *(railway station)* estación *f* de tren *or* de ferrocarril

depravation [deprə'veɪʃən] *n* depravación *f*

deprave [dɪ'preɪv] *vt* pervertir, depravar

depraved [dɪ'preɪvd] *adj* depravado(a)

depravity [dɪ'prævɪtɪ] *n* (**a**) *(corruption)* depravación *f* (**b**) *(act)* acto *m* depravado

deprecate ['deprɪkeɪt] *vt Formal* (**a**) *(disapprove of, deplore)* censurar (**b**) *(denigrate, disparage)* menospreciar, infravalorar; **to d. sb's efforts** restar importancia *or* mérito a los esfuerzos de alguien

deprecating ['deprɪkeɪtɪŋ], **deprecatory** ['deprɪkeɪtərɪ] *adj* (**a**) *(disapproving)* de desaprobación; **to be d. about sth/sb** mostrar desaprobación por algo/alguien (**b**) *(disparaging)* despreciativo(a), despectivo(a)

depreciate [dɪ'pri:ʃɪeɪt] **1** *vt* (**a**) *Com (value of sth)* depreciar, amortizar; *(currency)* depreciar, devaluar (**b**) *Formal (denigrate)* menospreciar, denigrar
2 *vi (property, prices, currency)* depreciarse; *(equipment)* perder valor, bajar de precio; **the pound has depreciated against the dollar** la libra se ha depreciado *or* devaluado con respecto al dólar

depreciation [dɪpri:ʃɪ'eɪʃən] *n* (**a**) *(of property, prices, currency)* depreciación *f*; *(of equipment)* pérdida *f* de valor (**b**) *Formal (disparagement)* menosprecio *m*

depredation [deprə'deɪʃən] *n Formal* **depredations** *(of war, time)* estragos *mpl*; **environmental d.** estragos en el medio ambiente

depress [dɪ'pres] *vt* (**a**) *(person)* deprimir; **it depressed her to talk about it** la deprimía hablar de ello (**b**) *(prices)* hacer bajar; *(economy)* deprimir (**c**) *Formal (push down) (button)* pulsar; *(clutch)* presionar

depressant [dɪ'presənt] *Med* **1** *n (sedative)* depresor *m*
2 *adj* depresor(ora)

depressed [dɪ'prest] *adj* (**a**) *(person)* deprimido(a); **to be d.** estar deprimido(a); *Med* **to be (clinically) d.** tener un cuadro clínico de depresión; **to make sb d.** deprimir a alguien (**b**) *(economically) (area, industry)* deprimido(a); *(prices, wages)* reducido(a), disminuido(a); *St Exch* **the market is d.** el mercado experimenta una recesión, el mercado se encuentra deprimido

depressing [dɪ'presɪŋ] *adj* deprimente; **these figures make for d. reading** estas cifras son deprimentes

depressingly [dɪ'presɪŋlɪ] *adv* **d. slow** de una lentitud deprimente; **his lack of interest was d. clear** su clara falta de interés era deprimente

depression [dɪ'preʃən] *n* (**a**) *(of person)* depresión *f*; *Med* **(clinical) d.** depresión (clínica) (**b**) *(of economy)* depresión *f*; *Hist* **the (Great) D.** la Gran Depresión (**c**) *(hollow, indentation)* depresión *f*, hoyo *m* (**d**) *Met* depresión *f* atmosférica, zona *f* de bajas presiones

depressive [dɪ'presɪv] *Med* **1** *n (person)* depresivo(a) *m,f*
2 *adj* depresivo(a); **he had a tendency to be d.** tendía a deprimirse *or* a la depresión ▸▸ ***d. disorder*** trastorno *m* depresivo

depressor [dɪ'presə(r)] *n* (**a**) *Anat (muscle)* depresor *m* (**b**) *(instrument)* **a tongue d.** un depresor (para la garganta)

depressurize [di:'preʃəraɪz] *vt* despresurizar

deprivation [deprɪ'veɪʃən] *n* (**a**) *(lack)* falta *f* (**b**) *(poverty)* privación *f*; **a life of d.** una vida llena de privaciones *or* penurias; **emotional d.** falta de cariño

deprive [dɪ'praɪv] *vt* **to d. sb of sth** privar a alguien de algo; **they were deprived of food** no se les dio de comer; **he was deprived of his inheritance** fue despojado de su herencia, fue desheredado; **I won't d. you of the pleasure of telling him** no seré yo quien te prive del placer de contárselo; **he deprives himself so his children can eat** pasa privaciones para que sus hijos puedan comer

deprived [dɪ'praɪvd] *adj (background, area)* desfavorecido(a); **the boy is emotionally d.** el chico tiene carencias afectivas

deprogram [di:'prəʊgræm] *vt (cult member)* desprogramar

deprogrammer [di:'prəʊgræmə(r)] *n* desprogramador(ora) *m,f*

dept (*abbr* **department**) dpto.

depth [depθ] *n* (**a**) *(vertical distance) (of water, hole, snow, wound)* profundidad *f*; **the wreck was located at a d. of 200 metres** los restos del naufragio se encontraban a doscientos metros de profundidad; **to be out of one's d.** *(in water)* no hacer pie; *Fig* **she was out of her d. in her new job/in the competition** el nuevo trabajo/el campeonato le venía grande ►► *Mil* ***d. charge*** carga *f* de profundidad
(**b**) *(horizontal distance) (of shelf, cupboard)* profundidad *f*, fondo *m*
(**c**) *(strength, intensity) (of feeling, sleep)* profundidad *f*; **in d.** *(investigate, discuss)* a fondo, en profundidad
(**d**) *(of knowledge, thought)* profundidad *f*
(**e**) *(of colour)* intensidad *f*
(**f**) *(of sound, voice)* gravedad *f*, tono *m* grave
(**g**) *Phot* ***d. of field*** profundidad *f* de campo
(**h**) **the depths** *(of ocean)* las profundidades (marinas); **the depths of despair** la más absoluta desesperación; **in the depths of the forest** en la espesura del bosque; **in the depths of winter** en pleno invierno

deputation [depjʊ'teɪʃən] *n* delegación *f*

depute [dɪ'pju:t] *vt* **to d. sb to do sth** delegar en alguien para que haga algo; **she deputed the running of the business to her eldest son** encomendó a su hijo mayor la gestión del negocio, delegó en su hijo mayor para que dirigiera el negocio

deputize ['depjʊtaɪz] **1** *vt (make a deputy)* **to d. sb** nombrar a alguien como sustituto
2 *vi* **to d. for sb** suplir a alguien

deputy ['depjʊtɪ] *n* (**a**) *(substitute)* sustituto(a) *m,f*; *(second-in-command)* asistente *mf*, lugarteniente *mf*; **to act as sb's d.** sustituir a alguien ►► ***d. director*** director(ora) *m,f* adjunto(a); ***d. manager*** director(ora) *m,f* adjunto(a); ***d. mayor*** teniente *mf* (de) alcalde; ***d. prime minister*** vicepresidente(a) *m,f* del Gobierno
(**b**) *(political representative)* diputado(a) *m,f*
(**c**) *US (policeman)* **d. (sheriff)** ayudante *mf* del sheriff

derail [di:'reɪl] **1** *vt* **to be derailed** *(train)* descarrilar; *(project, negotiations)* desbaratarse
2 *vi (train)* descarrilar

derailleur [dɪ'reɪlɪə(r)] *n* cambio *m* de marchas

derailment [dɪ'reɪlmənt] *n* descarrilamiento *m*

derange [dɪ'reɪndʒ] *vt* (**a**) *(drive insane)* volver loco(a), desquiciar (**b**) *(disarrange, disorder)* trastornar, desorganizar

deranged [dɪ'reɪndʒd] *adj* perturbado(a); **to be d.** estar perturbado(a)

derangement [dɪ'reɪndʒmənt] *n* (**a**) *(mental illness)* perturbación *f or* trastorno *m* mental (**b**) *(disorder, disarray)* trastorno *m*, desorganización *f*

derby *n* [*Br* 'dɑ:bɪ, *US* 'dɜ:rbɪ] (**a**) *Sport* derby *m*; *Br* **the D.** el Derby, = carrera de caballos celebrada en Epsom Downs, Inglaterra, desde 1780; *US* **the Kentucky D.** = carrera de caballos anual que se celebra en Louisville, Kentucky, desde 1875 (**b**) *US (hat)* bombín *m*, sombrero *m* hongo

derecognize [di:'rekəgnaɪz] *vt (country, trade union)* retirar el reconocimiento oficial a

deregulate [di:'regjʊleɪt] *vt Com & Econ* liberalizar, desregular

deregulation [di:regjʊ'leɪʃən] *n Com & Econ* liberalización *f*, desregulación *f*

derelict ['derəlɪkt] **1** *adj* (**a**) *(abandoned)* ruinoso(a), en ruinas (**b**) *Formal (negligent, neglectful)* negligente
2 *n* (**a**) *(person)* indigente *mf* (**b**) *Naut* derrelicto *m*

dereliction [derɪ'lɪkʃən] *n* (**a**) *(abandonment)* ruina *f* (**b**) *(neglect)* ***d. of duty*** incumplimiento *m* del deber

deride [dɪ'raɪd] *vt* ridiculizar, burlarse de

de rigueur [dərɪ'gɜ:(r)] *adj* de rigor

derision [dɪ'rɪʒən] *n* burla *f*, escarnio *m*; **to be an object of d.** ser objeto de burla

derisive [dɪ'raɪsɪv] *adj* burlón(ona)

derisively [dɪ'raɪsɪvlɪ] *adv (to say, speak)* con sorna, con burla

derisory [dɪ'raɪsərɪ] *adj (amount)* irrisorio(a)

derivable [dɪ'raɪvəbəl] *adj* deducible (**from** de)

derivation [derɪ'veɪʃən] *n* (**a**) *(of word)* origen *m*; **what is the d. of...?** ¿cuál es el origen de...?, ¿de dónde procede *or* deriva...? (**b**) *Math* derivación *f*

derivative [dɪ'rɪvətɪv] **1** *n* (**a**) *(word)* derivado *m* (**b**) *Math* derivada *f* (**c**) *St Exch* derivado *m*, producto *m* financiero derivado
2 *adj Pej (novel, idea, writer)* poco original

derive [dɪ'raɪv] **1** *vt (pleasure, satisfaction)* encontrar (**from** en); *(courage, hope, inspiration)* proceder, derivar (**from** de); *(benefit, profit)* obtener (**from** de); **to be derived from** *(name, behaviour)* derivar *or* provenir de; **it's derived from oil** se deriva del petróleo, se obtiene a partir del petróleo
2 *vi* **to d. from** derivar *or* provenir de; **the word originally derives from Turkish** la palabra se deriva *or* procede originariamente del turco

dermal ['dɜ:məl] *adj Med* dérmico(a)

dermatitis [dɜ:mə'taɪtɪs] *n Med* dermatitis *f inv*

dermatological [dɜ:mətə'lɒdʒɪkəl] *adj Med* dermatológico(a)

dermatologist [dɜ:mə'tɒlədʒɪst] *n Med* dermatólogo(a) *m,f*

dermatology [dɜ:mə'tɒlədʒɪ] *n Med* dermatología *f*

dermis ['dɜ:mɪs] *n Anat* dermis *f inv*

derogate ['derəgeɪt]

► **derogate from** *vi Formal* (**a**) *(detract from)* quitar mérito a (**b**) *(authority, law)* menoscabar, restringir; **this change in no way derogates from her existing rights** este cambio no restringe de ningún modo sus actuales derechos

derogatory [dɪ'rɒgətərɪ] *adj* despectivo(a); **she was quite d. about my efforts** mostró un gran desprecio por *or* hacia mis esfuerzos

> **False friend**: The Spanish adjective **derogatorio** is not a translation for the English word **derogatory**. In Spanish **derogatorio** means "repealing" or "rescinding".

derrick ['derɪk] *n* (**a**) *(crane)* grúa *f* (**b**) *(over oil well)* torre *f* de perforación

derrière [derɪ'eə(r)] *n Euph or Hum* trasero *m*

derring-do ['derɪŋ'du:] *n Hum* hazañas *fpl*, proezas *fpl*; **tales of d.** cuentos épicos

derringer ['derɪndʒə(r)] *n US* = pistola corta y de gran calibre

derv [dɜ:v] *n Br (fuel)* gasóleo *m*, gasoil *m*

dervish ['dɜ:vɪʃ] *n* derviche *m*; IDIOM **like a dancing** *or* **whirling d.** como un descosido(a)

desalinate [di:'sælɪneɪt] *vt* desalar, desalinizar

desalination [di:sælɪ'neɪʃən] *n* desalinización *f* ►► ***d. plant*** planta *f* desalinizadora

descale [di:'skeɪl] *vt* quitar la cal *or* el sarro a

descant ['deskænt] **1** *n Mus* contrapunto *m* ►► ***d. recorder*** flautín *m*
2 *vi Literary* **to d. on** *or* **upon sth** *(comment, ramble)* disertar sobre algo largo y tendido

descend [dɪ'send] **1** *vi* (**a**) *(go down) (person, path, plane)* descender
(**b**) *(fall)* **darkness descended** cayó la noche; **silence descended on the battlefield** el campo de batalla quedó sumido en el silencio; **a mood of despair descended upon the country** el país quedó sumido en un sentimiento de desesperación
(**c**) *(sink, stoop)* **I never thought she would d. to malicious gossip** nunca pensé que fuera a caer tan bajo como para chismorrear con tanta malicia, *RP* nunca pensé que llegaría a ese nivel subterráneo de chismerío; **to d. to sb's level** rebajarse al nivel de alguien
(**d**) **to d. from sb** *(be related to)* descender de alguien; **dogs and wolves probably d. from a common ancestor** probablemente, los perros y los lobos descienden de un antepasado común
(**e**) *(be passed down)* **Lord Grey's title descended to his grandson** el título de Lord Grey recayó en *or* pasó a su nieto; **the expression has descended to us from the Romans** hemos heredado esa expresión de los romanos
2 *vt* (**a**) *(hill, stairs)* descender por, bajar (**b**) *(be related to)* **to be descended from sb** descender de alguien

► **descend on** *vt insep (attack) (group of people)* abalanzarse sobre, invadir; *(village, town)* caer sobre; **every summer tourists d. on the city** todos los veranos los turistas invaden la ciudad; **the children descended on the table of goodies** los niños se abalanzaron *or* lanzaron sobre la mesa de golosinas; **we can't all d. on him without warning** *(visit en masse)* no podemos presentarnos allí todos sin avisar

descendant [dɪ'sendənt] *n* descendiente *m*

descending [dɪ'sendɪŋ] *adj* (**a**) *(staircase, spiral)* descendente; **in d. order** *(of priority, size)* en orden descendente *or* decreciente (**b**) *Mus* descendente

descent [dɪ'sent] *n* (**a**) *(downward movement) (of plane, from mountain)* descenso *m*; **the stream makes a gentle d.** el arroyo describe una suave pendiente; *Literary* **a d. into hell** un descenso a los infiernos (**b**) *(slope)* bajada *f*, pendiente *f* (cuesta abajo) (**c**) *(ancestry)* ascendencia *f*; **of Mexican d.** de ascendencia mexicana (**d**) *(transmission)* transmisión *f* (**e**) *(invasion)* invasión *f*, incursión *f*

descramble [di:'skræmbəl] *vt* descodificar

describe [dɪs'kraɪb] *vt* (**a**) *(depict verbally)* describir; **witnesses described the man as tall and dark-haired** la descripción de los testigos correspondía a la de un hombre alto y moreno; **the book describes how they escaped** el libro describe *or* cuenta cómo escaparon

(**b**) *(characterize)* definir; **she describes herself as an artist** se define a sí misma como artista; **his methods have been described as unorthodox** sus métodos han sido calificados de poco ortodoxos; **I wouldn't d. it as a complete failure** yo no lo definiría como un fracaso rotundo

(**c**) *Formal (draw, follow) (circle, line)* describir, trazar; **the severed head described an elegant arc in the air** la cabeza cortada describió un elegante arco en el aire

description [dɪs'krɪpʃən] *n* (**a**) *(account, representation)* descripción *f*; **to give a d. (of)** dar *or* hacer una descripción (de); **to answer** *or* **fit the d.** responder a la descripción; **I don't know anyone of that d.** no conozco a nadie con esa descripción; **beyond d.** indescriptible

(**b**) *(kind)* tipo *m*, clase *f*; **birds of all descriptions** todo tipo de aves; **she's a journalist of some d.** es periodista, no sé de qué tipo exactamente; **we were unable to find a vehicle of any d.** no pudimos encontrar ningún vehículo de ninguna clase

descriptive [dɪs'krɪptɪv] *adj (name, expression)* descriptivo(a); *(adjective)* calificativo(a); **he has great d. powers** tiene una gran habilidad para las descripciones ►► ***d. linguistics*** lingüística *f* descriptiva

descriptor [dɪs'krɪptə(r)] *n Comptr* descriptor *m*

descry [dɪ'skraɪ] *vt Literary* divisar

desecrate ['desɪkreɪt] *vt* profanar

desecration [desɪ'kreɪʃən] *n* profanación *f*

desegregate [di:'segrɪgeɪt] *vt* terminar con la segregación racial en

desegregation [di:segrɪ'geɪʃən] *n* eliminación *f* de la segregación racial (**of** en)

deselect [di:sɪ'lekt] *vt* (**a**) *Br Pol* no reelegir como candidato(a) (**b**) *Comptr* deseleccionar

desensitize [di:'sensɪtaɪz] *vt (emotionally)* insensibilizar; **children have become desensitized to violence** los niños se han hecho insensibles a la violencia

desert[1] ['dezət] *n* desierto *m*; **d. region** región desértica; **d. storm** tormenta del desierto ►► ***d. boots*** botas *fpl* de ante *(con cordones)*; ***d. island*** isla *f* desierta; ***d. rat*** rata *f* del desierto; ***d. rose*** rosa *f* del desierto

desert[2] [dɪ'zɜ:t] **1** *vt (place, family)* abandonar; *(organization, principle)* abandonar, desertar de; *Mil* **to d. one's post** abandonar el puesto; *Fig* **his courage deserted him** el valor le abandonó

2 *vi (from army)* desertar (**from** de); **one of the officers deserted to the enemy** uno de los oficiales desertó para pasarse al enemigo

deserted [dɪ'zɜ:tɪd] *adj* desierto(a); **the streets were d.** las calles estaban desiertas

deserter [dɪ'zɜ:tə(r)] *n* desertor(ora) *m,f*

desertification [dɪzɜ:tɪfɪ'keɪʃən] *n* desertización *f*

desertion [dɪ'zɜ:ʃən] *n* (**a**) *Law* abandono *m* del hogar (**b**) *Mil* deserción *f* (**c**) *(of cause, organization)* deserción *f*

deserts [dɪ'zɜ:ts] *npl* IDIOM **he got his just d.** recibió su merecido

deserve [dɪ'zɜ:v] **1** *vt* merecer, merecerse, *Am* ameritar; **to d. (to do) sth** merecer *or Am* ameritar (hacer) algo; **the case deserves serious consideration** el caso merece *or Am* amerita toda nuestra atención; **they d. each other** están hechos el uno para el otro; **she got what she deserved** recibió su merecido; **to d. whatever** *or* **everything one gets** merecérselo; **they d. better than this** se merecen algo mejor que esto

2 *vi Formal* **to d. well of sb** merecer el reconocimiento de alguien

deservedly [dɪ'zɜ:vɪdlɪ] *adv* merecidamente; **she was d. reprimanded** fue reprendida, y con razón

deserving [dɪ'zɜ:vɪŋ] *adj (cause, organization)* meritorio(a); **(to be) d. of sth** (ser) digno(a) *or* merecedor(ora) de algo; **a d. case** un caso merecedor de ayuda; *Old-fashioned* **the d. poor** los pobres dignos *or* merecedores de ayuda

déshabille [deɪzə'bi:, dɪsə'bi:l] *n* **in d.** en deshabillé *or* salto de cama

desiccant ['desɪkənt] *n Chem* desecante *m*

desiccated ['desɪkeɪtɪd] *adj* (**a**) *(dried)* seco(a), desecado(a) ►► ***d. coconut*** coco *m* rallado y seco (**b**) *Fig (person)* seco(a), rancio(a)

desideratum [dɪzɪdə'rɑ:təm] (*pl* **desiderata** [dɪzɪdə'rɑ:tə]) *n Formal* desiderátum *m inv*

design [dɪ'zaɪn] **1** *n* (**a**) *(decorative pattern)* dibujo *m*, motivo *m*

(**b**) *(style, composition) (of car, furniture, clothes)* modelo *m*, diseño *m*; **our latest d.** nuestro último modelo; **the problems were due to poor d.** los problemas se debieron a un mal diseño *or* a un diseño defectuoso; **d. fault** defecto de diseño

(**c**) *(drawing) (of building, machine)* diseño *m*

(**d**) *(subject)* diseño *m*

(**e**) *(planning) (of product, machine)* diseño *m*; **it's still at the d. stage** todavía se halla en fase de diseño

(**f**) *(intention)* propósito *m*; **by d.** a propósito; **to have designs on sth/sb** tener las miras puestas en algo/alguien

2 *vt* (**a**) *(plan) (building, vehicle, clothes)* diseñar; *(syllabus, course)* estructurar; **she designs jewellery** es diseñadora de joyas

(**b**) *(intend)* **the book is designed for children** el libro está pensado *or* concebido para los niños; **it's specially designed for very low temperatures** está especialmente concebido para bajas temperaturas; **the system is designed to favour the landowners** el sistema está pensado para favorecer a los terratenientes; **his remarks were designed to shock** sus comentarios pretendían escandalizar

designate ['dezɪgneɪt] **1** *vt* (**a**) *(appoint, assign)* designar; **to d. sb to do sth** designar a alguien para hacer algo; **he designated her as his successor** la nombró su sucesora; **this area has been designated a national park** esta zona ha sido declarada parque nacional

(**b**) *Formal (indicate, signify)* indicar, señalar; **the flags on the map d. enemy positions** las banderas del mapa indican posiciones enemigas

(**c**) *Formal (name)* nombrar, designar; **we've been designated the "Co-ordinating Committee"** se nos ha nombrado "Comité de Coordinación"

2 *adj* designado(a), nombrado(a)

designated ['dezɪgneɪtɪd] *adj* (**a**) *(in baseball)* ***d. hitter*** bateador(ora) *m,f* designado(a) (**b**) *esp US* ***d. driver*** = persona que accede a no beber alcohol durante una salida nocturna para llevar a los demás en coche a casa al final de la misma

designation [dezɪg'neɪʃən] *n* (**a**) *(appointment)* nombramiento *m* (**b**) *(title)* denominación *f* (**c**) *Com* **d. of origin** denominación de origen

designedly [dɪ'zaɪnɪdlɪ] *adv* a propósito

designer [dɪ'zaɪnə(r)] *n* diseñador(ora) *m,f*; **(set) d.** *Theat* escenógrafo(a) *m,f*; *Cin* decorador(ora) *m,f* ►► ***d. clothes*** ropa *f* de diseño; ***d. drugs*** drogas *fpl* de diseño; ***d. label*** marca *f* de moda (exclusiva); *Hum* ***d. stubble*** barba *f* de tres días

designing [dɪ'zaɪnɪŋ] *adj* intrigante, maquinador(ora)

desirability [dɪzaɪərə'bɪlɪtɪ] *n* (**a**) *(of outcome)* conveniencia *f*; **no one questions the d. of the measure** nadie cuestiona la conveniencia de la medida (**b**) *(of person)* atractivo *m*

desirable [dɪ'zaɪərəbəl] *adj* (**a**) *(attractive)* apetecible; *(sexually)* deseable; **d. residence** *(in advert)* propiedad impecable (**b**) *(advisable)* deseable; **a knowledge of French is d.** *(in job advert)* se valorarán los conocimientos de francés

desire [dɪ'zaɪə(r)] **1** *n* (**a**) *(wish)* deseo *m*; **I feel no d. to go** no me *Esp* apetece *or Carib, Col, Méx* provoca nada ir, *CSur* no tengo nada de ganas de ir; **I have no d. to hurt anyone's feelings, but...** no pretendo herir los sentimientos de nadie, pero...; **my one d. is that you should be happy** mi único deseo es que seas feliz (**b**) *(sexual)* deseo *m*; **to feel d. for sb** desear a alguien

2 *vt* (**a**) *(want, wish)* desear; **to d. (to do) sth** desear (hacer) algo; **if you so d.** si así lo desea; **it leaves a lot to be desired** deja mucho que desear (**b**) *(sexually)* desear (**c**) *Formal (request)* **your presence is desired at the palace** se solicita su presencia en palacio

desired [dɪ'zaɪəd] *adj* **his words had the d. effect** sus palabras tuvieron el efecto deseado *or* pretendido; **measure out the quantity d.** mida *or* pese la cantidad deseada

desirous [dɪ'zaɪərəs] *adj Formal* deseoso(a) (**of** de); **he was d. of re-establishing friendly relations** estaba deseoso de reestablecer relaciones de amistad; **he seemed d. to assist us** parecía estar deseoso de ayudarnos

desist [dɪ'sɪst] *vi Formal* desistir (**from** de)

desk [desk] *n* (**a**) *(in school)* pupitre *m*; *(in office)* mesa *f*, escritorio *m* ▸▸ ***d. diary*** agenda *f*; ***a d. job*** un trabajo de oficina; ***d. lamp*** lámpara *f* de mesa *or* de escritorio; ***d. research*** trabajo *m* de documentación; ***d. tidy*** organizador *m* de escritorio
(**b**) *(in hotel)* recepción *f* ▸▸ *US* ***d. clerk*** recepcionista *mf*
(**c**) *Journ* sección *f*; **the foreign/sports d.** la sección de noticias internacionales/de información deportiva
(**d**) *(in foreign ministry, intelligence organization)* oficina *f* regional; **the Central America d.** la Oficina regional para Centroamérica

desk-bound ['deskbaʊnd] *adj* **a d. job** un trabajo de oficina; **he doesn't like being d.** no le gusta tener que trabajar en la oficina

deskilling [diː'skɪlɪŋ] *n* = pérdida de la aportación humana en un trabajo como resultado de la introducción de una nueva tecnología

desktop ['desktɒp] *n Comptr* escritorio *m* ▸▸ ***d. computer*** *Esp* ordenador *m or Am* computadora *f* de sobremesa; ***d. publishing*** autoedición *f*; ***d. publishing operator*** autoeditor(ora) *m,f*

desolate ['desələt] **1** *adj* (**a**) *(deserted) (place, landscape)* desolado(a) (**b**) *(cheerless) (person, look)* desolado(a), afligido(a); *(future, prospect)* desolador(ora)
2 *vt* (**a**) *(area, place)* desolar, devastar; *(depopulate)* despoblar (**b**) *(person)* desolar, asolar; **he was desolated at** *or* **by the news** la noticia lo dejó desolado

desolation [desə'leɪʃən] *n* (**a**) *(of place, defeated country)* desolación *f* (**b**) *(of person)* desolación *f*

despair [dɪs'peə(r)] **1** *n* (**a**) *(hopelessness)* desesperación *f*; **to be in d. (at** *or* **over sth)** estar desesperado(a) (por *or* a causa de algo); **to drive sb to d.** llevar a alguien a la desesperación (**b**) *(cause of distress)* **William was the d. of his teachers** William llevaba a sus profesores por la calle de la amargura, William traía locos a sus profesores
2 *vi* desesperarse; **to d. of doing sth** perder la esperanza de hacer algo; **don't d., help is on the way** no desesperen, la ayuda está en camino; **I d. of you** contigo me desespero, no sé qué voy a hacer contigo

despairing [dɪ'speərɪŋ] *adj (cry, look)* de desesperación; *(person)* desesperado(a)

despairingly [dɪ'speərɪŋlɪ] *adv* con desesperación, desesperadamente

despatch = **dispatch**

desperado [despə'rɑːdəʊ] (*pl* **desperados**) *n* forajido(a) *m,f*

> **False friend:** The Spanish word **desesperado** is not a translation for the English word **desperado**. In Spanish **desesperado** means "desperate".

desperate ['despərət] *adj* (**a**) *(hopeless, despairing) (person, situation)* desesperado(a); **we heard d. screams** oímos gritos de desesperación; **to be d.** estar desesperado(a)
(**b**) *(extreme)* desesperado(a); **to be in d. need of sth** necesitar algo desesperadamente; **d. measures are required** es necesario adoptar medidas urgentes, se impone adoptar medidas a la desesperada; **these are d. times** corren tiempos muy difíciles
(**c**) *(reckless)* **a d. criminal** un delincuente capaz de cualquier cosa; **a d. attempt to escape** un intento de huida a la desesperada, un intento desesperado de escapar; **I'm afraid she'll do something d.** temo que cometa cualquier locura
(**d**) *(intent, eager)* **to be d. for money** necesitar dinero urgentemente; **to be d. to do sth** morirse de ganas de hacer algo; *Fam* **I'm d. for a cigarette** me muero por un cigarrillo

desperately ['despərətlɪ] *adv* (**a**) *(hopelessly) (in love)* perdidamente; **d. ill** gravísimamente enfermo(a); **they are d. poor** son extremadamente pobres
(**b**) *(recklessly) (to fight, plead)* desesperadamente
(**c**) *(as intensifier)* **to be d. sorry about sth** lamentar algo muchísimo; **to d. need sth** necesitar algo desesperadamente; **we're d. busy at the moment** estamos sumamente ocupados en este momento; **do you want to go? – not d.** ¿quieres ir? – no me muero de ganas *or* no estoy desesperado por ir

desperation [despə'reɪʃən] *n* desesperación *f*; **in d.** preso(a) de la desesperación; **she did it in d.** lo hizo por desesperación *or* a la desesperada

despicable [dɪ'spɪkəbəl] *adj (person, action)* despreciable; **you're d.!** ¡eres un ser despreciable *or* detestable!; **it was a d. thing to do** fue despreciable hacer eso

despise [dɪ'spaɪz] *vt* despreciar; **he despised himself for his cowardice** se despreciaba a sí mismo por ser un cobarde; **such simple pleasures are not to be despised** no hay que despreciar esos pequeños placeres

despite [dɪ'spaɪt] *prep* a pesar de, pese a; **he laughed d. himself** muy a su pesar se río; **d. the fact that...** a pesar de que...

despoil [dɪ'spɔɪl] *vt Literary* expoliar, saquear; **the cathedral was despoiled of its treasures** despojaron la catedral de todos sus tesoros

despondence [dɪ'spɒndəns], **despondency** [dɪ'spɒndənsɪ] *n* desánimo *m*, abatimiento *m*

despondent [dɪ'spɒndənt] *adj* desanimado(a), abatido(a); **to be d.** estar desanimado(a) *or* abatido(a); **to become d.** desanimarse, abatirse

despondently [dɪ'spɒndəntlɪ] *adv* con desánimo, con aire abatido

despot ['despɒt] *n* déspota *mf*

despotic [dɪs'pɒtɪk] *adj* despótico(a)

despotically [dɪ'spɒtɪklɪ] *adv* despóticamente

despotism ['despətɪzəm] *n* despotismo *m*

des res ['dez'rez] *n Br* (*abbr* **desirable residence**) *(in advert)* propiedad *f* impecable; *Fam Hum* pisito *m*

dessert [dɪ'zɜːt] *n* postre *m*; **what's for d.?** ¿qué hay de postre? ▸▸ ***d. pear*** pera *f* de agua; ***d. plate*** plato *m* de postre; ***d. trolley*** carrito *m* de los postres; ***d. wine*** vino *m* dulce

dessertspoon [dɪ'zɜːtspuːn] *n* cuchara *f or Ven* cucharilla *f* de postre; *(as measurement)* cucharada *f* de las de postre

dessertspoonful [dɪ'zɜːtspuːnfʊl] *n* cucharada *f* de las de postre

destabilization [diːsteɪbɪlaɪ'zeɪʃən] *n* desestabilización *f*

destabilize [diː'steɪbəlaɪz] *vt* desestabilizar

destination [destɪ'neɪʃən] *n* (lugar *m* de) destino *m*; **to reach one's d.** llegar uno a su destino ▸▸ *Comptr* ***d. disk*** disco *m* de destino; ***d. drive*** unidad *f* (de disco) de destino

destine ['destɪn] *vt Literary* destinar

destined ['destɪnd] *adj* (**a**) *(intended, fated)* destinado(a); **to be d. to do sth** estar destinado a hacer algo; **their plan was d. to fail** su plan estaba abocado al fracaso; **he was d. never to see her again** su destino era no volver a verla jamás; **they were d. for an early grave** su destino era morir a una corta edad; **the equipment was d. for civilian use** el equipo estaba destinado a ser utilizado por la población civil
(**b**) *(of plane, ship)* **d. for** con destino *or* rumbo a

destiny ['destɪnɪ] *n* destino *m*, sino *m*; **she felt it was her d. to become a writer** sentía que su destino era convertirse en escritora

destitute ['destɪtjuːt] **1** *adj* (**a**) *(extremely poor)* indigente; **to be utterly d.** estar en la miseria (**b**) *Formal (lacking)* **to be d. of** carecer de, estar desprovisto(a) de
2 *npl* **the d.** los desposeídos, los desheredados

destitution [destɪ'tjuːʃən] *n* indigencia *f*; **to live in d.** vivir en la indigencia

> **False friend:** The Spanish noun **destitución** is not a translation for the English word **destitution**. In Spanish **destitución** means "dismissal".

destroy [dɪ'strɔɪ] *vt* (**a**) *(demolish, wreck)* destruir, acabar con; **they threaten to d. our democratic way of life** amenazan con destruir nuestro estilo democrático de vida; **the experience destroyed his faith in humanity** la experiencia acabó con su fe en la humanidad
(**b**) *(damage, ruin)* destruir; *(health, career, reputation)* acabar con, destruir; *(friendship, marriage)* destruir, destrozar; **he was destroyed by his wife's death** la muerte de su esposa le dejó deshecho *or* destrozado
(**c**) *(kill) (sick or unwanted animal)* sacrificar; *(vermin)* acabar con, destruir
(**d**) *Fam (defeat)* arrasar, aplastar

destroyer [dɪ'strɔɪə(r)] *n Naut* destructor *m*

destruct [dɪ'strʌkt] *US* **1** *vt (missile, rocket)* destruir
2 *vi* destruirse
3 *adj (button, mechanism)* de destrucción

destruction [dɪ'strʌkʃən] *n* (**a**) *(demolition, devastation) (of building, town, forest)* destrucción *f*; *(of career, reputation)* ruina *f*, destrucción *f* (**b**) *(damage)* destrozos *mpl*; **the d. caused by the fire/storm** los destrozos ocasionados por el fuego/la tormenta (**c**) *(cause of ruin)* perdición *f*, ruina *f*; **drink proved to be his d.** la bebida resultó ser su perdición

destructive [dɪ'strʌktɪv] *adj* (**a**) *(weapon)* destructivo(a); **the d. power of a bomb** el poder destructor *or* destructivo de una bomba (**b**) **a d. child** un niño destrozón

destructiveness [dɪ'strʌktɪvnɪs] *n* (**a**) *(of bomb, weapon)* capacidad *f* destructora *or* destructiva (**b**) *(of person)* tendencia *f* destructiva *or* destructora

desuetude [dɪ'sju:ɪtju:d] *n Literary* desuso *m*; **to fall into d.** *(custom, law)* caer en desuso

desultorily ['desəltərɪlɪ] *adv (to converse)* sin ganas *or* entusiasmo, con desgana; *(to inspect, browse)* sin propósito fijo

desultory ['desəltərɪ] *adj (attempt, manner)* sin convicción, desganado(a); **to have a d. conversation** mantener a desgana una conversación *or CAm, Méx* plática; **in a d. manner** *or* **fashion** de una forma *or* manera desganada

detach [dɪ'tætʃ] **1** *vt* **(a)** *(separate)* separar (**from** de); **to d. oneself from sth** *(to gain objectivity)* distanciarse de algo; **she managed to d. herself from the rest of the group** se las arregló para distanciarse del resto del grupo **(b)** *(troops)* destacar

2 *vi* retirarse, quitarse

detachable [dɪ'tætʃəbəl] *adj (cover, handle)* extraíble; *(accessories)* desmontable; *(hood, lining)* de quita y pon

detached [dɪ'tætʃt] *adj* **(a)** *(separate)* separado(a); **to become** *or* **get d. from sth** alejarse *or* separarse de algo; **to become d. from reality** perder el contacto con la realidad ►► *esp Br* ***d. house*** casa *f or* chalé *m* individual; *Med* ***d. retina*** desprendimiento *m* de retina **(b) to be d.** *(objective)* ser imparcial; *(cold, distant)* ser despegado(a) *or* distante

detachment [dɪ'tætʃmənt] *n* **(a)** *(separation)* separación *f*, desprendimiento *m* **(b)** *(objectivity)* imparcialidad *f*; *(coldness)* despego *m*, desapego *m*; **with an air of d.** con (aire de) despego *or* desapego **(c)** *(military unit)* destacamento *m*

detail [*Br* 'di:teɪl, *US* dɪ'teɪl] **1** *n* **(a)** *(item of information, of painting, photograph)* detalle *m*; **to pay attention to d.** prestar atención a los pequeños detalles; **to go into detail(s)** entrar en detalles; **it's not important, it's just a d.** es sólo un detalle sin importancia; **in d.** en *or* con detalle; **in great d.** con todos los detalles; **minor details** detalles sin importancia

(b) details *(information)* detalles *mpl*; *(address and phone number)* datos *mpl* (personales); **for further details please contact...** para obtener información más detallada, se ruega contactar con...; **let me take down your details** permítame que anote sus datos

(c) *(intricacy)* **the d. of the carving** la complejidad *or* minuciosidad de la talla

(d) *Mil (group of soldiers)* piquete *m*, cuadrilla *f*

2 *vt* **(a)** *(describe, enumerate)* detallar **(b)** *Mil (assign)* destacar; **to d. sb to do sth** encomendar a alguien hacer algo

detailed ['di:teɪld] *adj* detallado(a); **a d. description** una descripción detallada *or* pormenorizada; **a d. account** una cuenta detallada

detain [dɪ'teɪn] *vt* **(a)** *Formal (delay)* entretener; **I won't d. you any longer** no le quitaré más tiempo; **I'm afraid I've been detained** *(when cancelling appointment)* me temo que me he entretenido demasiado; **such details need not d. us** no deberíamos entretenernos en estos detalles

(b) *(suspect)* detener; **to d. sb for questioning** detener a alguien para interrogarlo

(c) *Sch (pupil)* dejar castigado(a), castigar a quedarse después de clase

detainee [di:teɪ'ni:] *n* detenido(a) *m,f*

detect [dɪ'tekt] *vt (of person)* percibir; *(of machine)* detectar; *(source of a problem)* identificar, hallar; **do I d. a certain lack of enthusiasm on your part?** ¿noto una cierta falta de entusiasmo por tu parte?; **without being detected** sin ser descubierto

detectable [dɪ'tektəbəl] *adj (by person)* perceptible; *(by machine, device)* detectable

detection [dɪ'tekʃən] *n (discovery) (of mines, planes)* detección *f*; *(by detective)* investigación *f*; **to escape d.** *(mistake, theft)* no ser detectado(a)

detective [dɪ'tektɪv] *n (on police force, private)* detective *mf* ►► ***d. agency*** agencia *f* de detectives; ***d. bureau*** agencia *f* de detectives; ***d. story*** relato *m* policiaco; ***d. work*** investigación *f*

detector [dɪ'tektə(r)] *n (device)* detector *m* ►► *Br* ***d. van*** = furgoneta que detecta a los usuarios de televisión que no han pagado la licencia para recibir el servicio

détente [deɪ'tɒnt] *n* distensión *f (entre países)*

detention [dɪ'tenʃən] *n* **(a)** *Law* detención *f*, arresto *m*; **in d.** bajo arresto ►► ***d. centre*** centro *m* de internamiento *or* reclusión; ***d. order*** orden *f* de arresto **(b)** *Sch* **to get** *or* **be given d.** = ser castigado a quedarse en el colegio después de terminadas las clases; **the entire class was given an hour's d.** toda la clase se quedó castigada una hora después de clase

deter [dɪ'tɜ:(r)] *(pt & pp* **deterred**) *vt* **(a)** *(discourage)* disuadir (**from** de); **to d. sb from doing sth** disuadir a alguien de que haga algo **(b)** *(prevent) (war, attack)* impedir

detergent [dɪ'tɜ:dʒənt] **1** *n* detergente *m*

2 *adj* detergente

deteriorate [dɪ'tɪərɪəreɪt] *vi (situation, health, relations, sight, hearing)* deteriorarse; *(weather, work)* empeorar; **this quarrel might d. into something worse** esta discusión podría degenerar en algo mucho peor

deterioration [dɪtɪərɪə'reɪʃən] *n (of situation, health, relations, sight, hearing)* deterioro *m*; *(of weather)* empeoramiento *m*

determinable [dɪ'tɜ:mɪnəbəl] *adj* concretable, determinable

determinant [dɪ'tɜ:mɪnənt] **1** *n Formal* factor *m* determinante

2 *adj* determinante

determination [dɪtɜ:mɪ'neɪʃən] *n* **(a)** *(resoluteness)* decisión *f*, determinación *f*; **she showed real d.** demostró ser una persona muy resuelta *or* decidida **(b)** *(establishment, fixing)* determinación *f*, establecimiento *m*

determine [dɪ'tɜ:mɪn] *vt* **(a)** *(govern, influence)* determinar, condicionar **(b)** *Formal (decide)* decidir, resolver; **to d. to do sth** tomar la determinación de hacer algo **(c)** *(identify) (cause, origin)* determinar **(d)** *(settle)* fijar, determinar

determined [dɪ'tɜ:mɪnd] *adj* decidido(a), resuelto(a); **a d. effort** un esfuerzo denodado; **he's a very d. young man** es un joven muy decidido; **to be d. to do sth** estar decidido(a) a hacer algo; **I'm d. that this will not happen again** estoy empeñado en que esto no vuelva a suceder

determinedly [dɪ'tɜ:mɪndlɪ] *adv* decididamente, con determinación

determiner [dɪ'tɜ:mɪnə(r)] *n Gram* determinante *m*

determining [dɪ'tɜ:mɪnɪŋ] *adj (factor, influence)* determinante, decisivo(a)

determinism [dɪ'tɜ:mɪnɪzəm] *n Phil* determinismo *m*

determinist [dɪ'tɜ:mɪnɪst] *Phil* **1** *n* determinista *mf*

2 *adj* determinista

deterrence [dɪ'terəns] *n* disuasión *f*

deterrent [dɪ'terənt] **1** *n* elemento *m* de disuasión; **to act as a d.** tener un efecto disuasorio; **a nuclear d.** un arma nuclear como elemento de disuasión

2 *adj* disuasivo(a), disuasorio(a) ►► ***d. force*** fuerza *f* disuasoria *or* de disuasión

detest [dɪ'test] *vt* detestar; **she detests having to make small talk** detesta tener que hablar sobre temas triviales

detestable [dɪ'testəbəl] *adj* detestable, odioso(a)

detestation [di:tes'teɪʃən] *n Formal* odio *m*, aborrecimiento *m* (**of** a)

dethrone [di:'θrəʊn] *vt* destronar

detonate ['detəneɪt] **1** *vt* explosionar, hacer explotar

2 *vi* detonar, explotar

detonation [detə'neɪʃən] *n* detonación *f*

detonator ['detəneɪtə(r)] *n* detonador *m*

detour ['di:tʊə(r)] **1** *n* desvío *m*; **to make a d.** dar un rodeo

2 *vi* desviarse, dar un rodeo

detoxicate [di:'tɒksɪkeɪt] *vt* **(a)** *(person)* desintoxicar **(b)** *(poison)* eliminar la toxicidad de

detoxification [di:tɒksɪfɪ'keɪʃən], *Fam* **detox** ['di:tɒks] *n* desintoxicación *f* ►► ***d. centre*** centro *m* de desintoxicación; ***d. programme*** programa *m* de desintoxicación

detoxify [di:'tɒksɪfaɪ] *vt* **(a)** *(person)* desintoxicar **(b)** *(substance)* purificar, eliminar la toxicidad de

detract [dɪ'trækt]

► **detract from** *vt insep* disminuir, mermar; *(achievement, contribution)* restar importancia *or* valor a; **the oil refinery detracts from the beauty of the place** la refinería de petróleo resta belleza al lugar

detraction [dɪ'trækʃən] *n* detracción *f*

detractor [dɪ'træktə(r)] *n* detractor(ora) *m,f*

detrain [di:'treɪn] *US* **1** *vi* apearse, bajar del tren

2 *vt (troops)* desembarcar; *(supplies)* descargar

detriment ['detrɪmənt] *n Formal* **to the d. of...** en detrimento de...; **without d. to...** sin perjuicio para...

detrimental [detrɪ'mentəl] *adj Formal* perjudicial (**to** para); **to have a d. effect on** perjudicar

detrimentally [detrɪ'mentəlɪ] *adv Formal* perjudicialmente

detritus [dɪ'traɪtəs] *n* **(a)** *Formal (debris)* detrito *m* **(b)** *Geol* detrito *m*, detritus *m inv*

de trop [də'trəʊ] *adj* **I felt a little d.** me sentí como que sobraba

detumescence [di:tju:'mesəns] *n* desinflamación *f*, detumescencia *f*

deuce [djuːs] *n* (**a**) *(in tennis)* deuce *m* (**b**) *(in cards, dice)* dos *m* (**c**) *Fam Old-fashioned (as expletive)* **where the d. is it?** ¿dónde diantre está?; **how the d. should I know?** ¿cómo diantre iba yo a saberlo?

deus ex machina [ˈdeɪəseksˈmækɪnə] *n* deus ex machina *m*

deuterium [dʒuːˈtɪərɪəm] *n Chem* deuterio *m*

Deutschmark [ˈdɔɪtʃmɑːk] *n Formerly* marco *m* alemán

devaluation [diːvæljʊˈeɪʃən] *n* devaluación *f*

devalue [diːˈvæljuː] *vt* (**a**) *(currency)* devaluar (**b**) *(person, achievements, efforts)* restar mérito a

devastate [ˈdevəsteɪt] *vt* (**a**) *(crops, village)* devastar (**b**) *(overwhelm)* destrozar, desolar; **I was devastated by the news** la noticia me dejó destrozado *or* desolado

devastated [ˈdevəsteɪtɪd] *adj* (**a**) *(crops, village)* devastado(a) (**b**) *(person)* destrozado(a), desolado(a)

devastating [ˈdevəsteɪtɪŋ] *adj* (**a**) *(storm, bombardment)* devastador(ora); *(news, discovery)* desolador(ora), terrible; *(argument, criticism)* demoledor(ora); **to d. effect** con un efecto demoledor (**b**) *(charm, beauty)* arrollador(ora); **he has a d. wit** tiene un ingenio pasmoso *or* apabullante

devastatingly [ˈdevəsteɪtɪŋlɪ] *adv* **d. effective** de efectos devastadores; **d. frank/direct** terriblemente *or* tremendamente franco/directo; **d. beautiful/handsome** de una belleza arrolladora

devastation [devəsˈteɪʃən] *n* desolación *f*, devastación *f*; **scenes of utter d.** escenas de completa devastación *or* desolación

develop [dɪˈveləp] **1** *vt* (**a**) *(body, region)* desarrollar; *(site, land)* urbanizar

(**b**) *(expand, elaborate) (theory, argument)* desarrollar; *(business, market)* ampliar, expandir

(**c**) *(improve) (product, method, design)* desarrollar; *(skills)* perfeccionar

(**d**) *(acquire) (infection)* contraer; *(symptom)* empezar a presentar; *(habit)* adquirir; **to d. a temperature** *or* **a fever** empezar a tener fiebre; **to d. a fault** *(machine)* empezar a fallar; **to d. a liking for sth** tomar afición a algo; **to d. a taste for sth** agarrarle *or Esp* cogerle el gusto a algo

(**e**) *Phot* revelar

2 *vi* (**a**) *(body, region, plot)* desarrollarse; **let's see how things d.** vamos a ver cómo evolucionan las cosas; **to d. into sth** transformarse *or* convertirse en algo; **as the story developed...** a medida que la historia se iba desarrollando... (**b**) *(become apparent) (problem, difficulty)* surgir, aparecer; *(talent, trend)* desarrollarse

developed [dɪˈveləpt] *adj* (**a**) *(country)* desarrollado(a); *(land)* urbanizado(a); **he has a highly d. sense of irony** posee un finísimo sentido de la ironía (**b**) *(film)* revelado(a)

developer [dɪˈveləpə(r)] *n* (**a**) *(of land)* promotor(ora) *m,f* inmobiliario(a) (**b**) *(person)* **a slow d.** una persona lenta en su desarrollo (**c**) *Phot* revelador *m*, líquido *m* de revelado (**d**) *Comptr* desarrollador(ora) *m,f*

developing [dɪˈveləpɪŋ] **1** *n Phot* revelado *m*; **d. bath/tank** baño/cubeta de revelado

2 *adj (region, country)* en (vías de) desarrollo; *(crisis)* creciente; **a d. interest in...** un creciente interés en...

development [dɪˈveləpmənt] *n* (**a**) *(growth) (of body, region)* desarrollo *m*; *(of site, land)* urbanización *f* ►► ***d. agency*** agencia *f* de cooperación; ***d. aid*** ayuda *f* al desarrollo; *Br* ***d. area*** = área deprimida en la que el gobierno fomenta la creación de nuevas industrias; *Econ* ***d. potential*** potencial *m* de explotación

(**b**) *(expansion, elaboration) (of argument, theory)* desarrollo *m*

(**c**) *(improvement) (of product, method, design)* desarrollo *m*; **it's still at the d. stage** se encuentra todavía en la fase de desarrollo

(**d**) *(progress, change)* cambio *m*, variación *f*; **recent developments in the industry** la evolución reciente de la industria; **there have been some interesting developments** se han dado novedades interesantes; **to await further developments** esperar a ver cómo se desarrolla la situación; **the latest developments in medical research** los últimos avances de la investigación médica

(**e**) *(housing project)* urbanización *f*

developmental [dɪveləpˈmentəl] *adj* de desarrollo ►► ***d. psychology*** psicología *f* del desarrollo

deviance [ˈdiːvɪəns], **deviancy** [ˈdiːvɪənsɪ] *n* (**a**) *(variation, difference)* desviación *f*; **d. from the norm** desviación *or* apartamiento de la norma (**b**) *Psy* desviación *f*

deviant [ˈdiːvɪənt] **1** *adj (behaviour, growth)* desviado(a), anómalo(a)

2 *n (social, sexual)* pervertido(a) *m,f*, persona *f* de conducta desviada

deviate [ˈdiːvɪeɪt] *vi (in behaviour, from course)* desviarse (**from** de); **to d. from the norm** desviarse *or* apartarse de la norma

deviation [diːvɪˈeɪʃən] *n* (**a**) *(in behaviour, from course)* desviación *f* (**from** de) (**b**) *(in statistics)* desviación *f*

deviationism [diːvɪˈeɪʃənɪzəm] *n Pol* desviacionismo *m*

deviationist [diːvɪˈeɪʃənɪst] *Pol* **1** *n* desviacionista *f*

2 *adj* desviacionista

device [dɪˈvaɪs] *n* (**a**) *(for measuring, processing, cutting)* aparato *m*; *(for safety, security)* dispositivo *m*; **an explosive d.** un artefacto explosivo; **a nuclear d.** un dispositivo nuclear

(**b**) *(method, scheme)* estratagema *f*; IDIOM **to leave sb to his own devices** dejar a alguien que se las arregle solo

(**c**) *Comptr* dispositivo *m*, periférico *m* ►► ***d. driver*** controlador *m* de dispositivos *or* periféricos

(**d**) *(in heraldry)* divisa *f*

devil [ˈdevəl] **1** *n* (**a**) *(evil being)* diablo *m*, demonio *m*; **the D.** el diablo *or* demonio; *Old-fashioned* **the d. take him!** ¡que el diablo se lo lleve!; *Old-fashioned* **go to the d.!** ¡vete al infierno!, ¡al diablo contigo!

(**b**) *Fam (person)* **poor d.!** ¡pobre diablo!; **you little d.!** *(to child)* ¡granujilla!; **you lucky d.!** ¡qué suerte tienes!; **he's a bit of a d.** *(daring, reckless)* no se corta un pelo; **go on, be a d.!** ¡vamos, date el gusto!

(**c**) *Fam (for emphasis)* **what the d. are you doing?** ¿qué diablos *or* demonios estás haciendo?; **how the d....?** ¿cómo diablos *or* demonios...?; **how the d. should I know?** ¿y yo cómo diablos *or* demonios voy a saberlo?; **he has a d. of a temper** tiene un carácter endiablado; **we had a d. of a job moving it** sudamos tinta para moverlo

(**d**) *(trainee barrister)* aprendiz *mf* de abogado

(**e**) *US* ***d.'s food cake*** = pastel de chocolate; ***devils on horseback*** *Br (with prunes)* = ciruelas pasas envueltas en bacon y asadas a la parrilla; *US (with oysters)* = ostras envueltas en bacon y asadas a la parrilla

(**f**) IDIOMS **to be (caught) between the d. and the deep blue sea** estar entre la espada y la pared; **talk of the d....** hablando del rey de Roma...; **to give the d. his due...** hay que reconocer que...; **there'll be the d. to pay** se va a armar la gorda *or* la de San Quintín; **to work like the d.** trabajar como un(a) negro(a) *or Am* como loco(a); **(to play) d.'s advocate** (hacer de) abogado del diablo; **d. take the hindmost!** ¡sálvese quien pueda!; PROV **better the d. you know (than the d. you don't)** más vale lo malo conocido (que lo bueno por conocer); PROV **the d. makes** *or* **finds work for idle hands** el ocio es la madre de todos los vicios

2 *vt Culin* preparar con picante y especias; **devilled eggs** = huevos duros preparados con salsa picante

3 *vi Br* **to d. for sb** *(lawyer)* trabajar de pasante para alguien; *(author)* trabajar de ayudante para alguien

devilish [ˈdevəlɪʃ] **1** *adj* (**a**) *(fiendish, mischievous)* diabólico(a) (**b**) *Fam Old-fashioned (extreme)* endemoniado(a), infernal

2 *adv Fam Old-fashioned* **it's d. cold** hace un frío que pela; **this work is d. hard** este trabajo es la mar de difícil

devilishly [ˈdevəlɪʃlɪ] *adv* (**a**) *(fiendishly, mischievously)* endemoniadamente (**b**) *Fam Old-fashioned (as intensifier)* endemoniadamente; **it's d. hot in there** allí hace un calor endemoniado

devil-may-care [ˈdevəlmeɪˈkeə(r)] *adj* despreocupado(a)

devilment [ˈdevəlmənt] *n (mischief)* malicia *f*, diabluras *fpl*; **out of d.** por malicia

devilry [ˈdevəlrɪ] *n* (**a**) *(mischief)* malicia *f*, diabluras *fpl*; **out of d.** por malicia (**b**) *(black magic)* brujería *f*, magia *f* negra

devious [ˈdiːvɪəs] *adj* (**a**) *(person, mind)* retorcido(a); *(means, method)* intrincado(a), enrevesado(a); **that's a bit d. of you!** ¡qué maquiavélico eres! (**b**) *(route)* sinuoso(a)

deviously [ˈdiːvɪəslɪ] *adv* maquiavélicamente

deviousness [ˈdiːvɪəsnɪs] *n* (**a**) *(of person, mind)* zorrería *f*, artería *f*; *(of means, method)* carácter *m* maquiavélico (**b**) *(of route)* sinuosidad *f*

devise [dɪˈvaɪz] *vt* (**a**) *(plan, plot)* idear; *(method, scheme)* concebir, elaborar (**b**) *Law (property)* legar

devising [dɪˈvaɪzɪŋ] *n* **a system of his own d.** un sistema de elaboración propia

devoice [diːˈvɔɪs] *vt Ling* desonorizar

devoid [dɪˈvɔɪd] *adj* desprovisto(a) (**of** de); **d. of interest** carente de interés

devolution [diːvəˈluːʃən] *n* (**a**) *(of duty, responsibility)* delegación *f* (**b**) *Pol* transferencia *f* de poder político, traspaso *m* de competencias; **they want d.** quieren la autonomía (política) (**c**) *Law (of property)* cesión *f*, traspaso *m*

devolve [dɪ'vɒlv] **1** *vt (functions, powers)* transferir, traspasar (**to** a)
2 *vi* (**a**) *(responsibility, power)* recaer (**on** *or* **upon** en); **it devolves on** *or* **upon me to decide** me corresponde a mí decidir (**b**) *Law (estate)* pasar (**on** a); **the property devolves on** *or* **upon the son** el patrimonio pasa al hijo *or* recae en el hijo

> **False friend**: The Spanish verb **devolver** is not a translation for the English word **devolve**. In Spanish the main meaning of **devolver** is "to give back, to return" or "to throw up".

devolved [dɪ'vɒlvd] *adj (parliament, power)* delegado(a)

Devonian [dɪ'vəʊnɪən] *Geol* **1** *n* **the D.** el devónico
2 *adj (period)* devónico(a)

devote [dɪ'vəʊt] *vt (time, money, energy)* dedicar (**to** a); **to d. oneself to** consagrarse a; **she devotes all her energies to writing** dedica todas sus energías a la escritura; **the whole meeting was devoted to a discussion of the sales figures** toda la reunión estuvo dedicada a discutir las cifras de ventas

devoted [dɪ'vəʊtɪd] *adj (parent, husband, wife)* devoto(a); *(admirer, follower)* devoto(a), ferviente; **to be d. to sb** tener auténtica devoción por alguien, tener un enorme cariño a alguien; **they are d. to each other** están muy unidos; **after years of d. service** tras años de abnegada dedicación

devotedly [dɪ'vəʊtɪdlɪ] *adv* con devoción, con fervor

devotee [devəʊ'tiː] *n* (**a**) *(of person, idea)* adepto(a) *m,f*; *(of sport, music)* fanático(a) *m,f*, entusiasta *mf* (**of** de) (**b**) *(of god, religion)* devoto(a) *m,f*

devotion [dɪ'vəʊʃən] *n* (**a**) *(to friend, family)* devoción *f*; *(to cause, leader)* dedicación *f*, entrega *f*; *(of time, money, energy)* dedicación *f*; **he showed great d. to duty** demostró su gran entrega *or* lealtad al deber (**b**) *(to god, saint)* devoción *f*; **devotions** *(prayers)* oraciones *fpl*

devotional [dɪ'vəʊʃənəl] *adj Rel (pictures, objects)* de devoción, de culto; *(literature, manual)* litúrgico(a)

devour [dɪ'vaʊə(r)] *vt* (**a**) *(consume) (food)* devorar; *(book)* devorar, leer con avidez; **he devoured her with his eyes** la devoraba con la mirada (**b**) *(of fire)* devorar, destruir; *Fig* **he was devoured by jealousy** los celos lo devoraban

devout [dɪ'vaʊt] *adj* (**a**) *(person)* devoto(a); **a d. Catholic/Muslim** un católico/musulmán devoto (**b**) *Formal (wish, hope)* sincero(a)

devoutly [dɪ'vaʊtlɪ] *adv* (**a**) *(to pray)* con devoción (**b**) *Formal (earnestly)* fervientemente, con fervor

dew [djuː] *n* rocío *m*

dewberry ['djuːbərɪ] *n* = tipo de zarzamora

dewclaw ['djuːklɔː] *n* espolón *m*

dewdrop ['djuːdrɒp] *n* (**a**) *(on plant, window)* gota *f* de rocío (**b**) *Br Fam (on nose)* moco *m* colgando

dewlap ['djuːlæp] *n* papada *f*

dewy ['djuːɪ] *adj* cubierto(a) de rocío

dewy-eyed [djuːɪ'aɪd] *adj* (**a**) *(naive)* ingenuo(a), candoroso(a) (**b**) *(loving, sentimental)* cándido(a), inocente, sentimental

dexedrine ['deksədriːn] *n* dexedrina *f*

dexterity [deks'terɪtɪ] *n (mental, physical)* destreza *f*

dexterous, dextrous ['dekstrəs] *adj* (**a**) *(physically)* diestro(a), hábil (**b**) *(skilful)* hábil

dexterously ['dekstrəslɪ] *adv* con destreza, hábilmente

dextrin(e) ['dekstrɪn] *n Chem* dextrina *f*

dextrose ['dekstrəʊs] *n* dextrosa *f*

dextrous = **dexterous**

dexy ['deksɪ] *n Fam* dexedrina *f*

DfE [diːef'iː] *n* (*abbr* **Department for Education**) = ministerio británico de educación

DG [diː'dʒiː] *n* (*abbr* **director-general**) director(ora) *m,f* general

Dhaka ['dækə] *n* Dacca

dhal = **dahl**

dhoti ['dəʊtɪ] *n* taparrabos *m inv (hindú)*

diabetes [daɪə'biːtiːz] *n* diabetes *f inv*; **to have d.** padecer *or* tener diabetes ▸▸ *Med* ***d. insipidus*** diabetes *f* insípida; *Med* ***d. mellitus*** diabetes *f* mellitus

diabetic [daɪə'betɪk] **1** *n* diabético(a) *m,f*; **d. chocolate/jam** chocolate/mermelada para diabéticos ▸▸ *Med* ***d. coma*** coma *m* diabético
2 *adj* diabético(a)

diabolic [daɪə'bɒlɪk] *adj (evil)* diabólico(a), demoníaco(a)

diabolical [daɪə'bɒlɪkəl] *adj* (**a**) *(evil)* diabólico(a), demoníaco(a) (**b**) *Br Fam (very bad)* espantoso(a) (**c**) *Br Fam (as intensifier)* **what a d. liberty!** ¡qué *or* menudo descaro!

diabolically [daɪə'bɒlɪklɪ] *adv* (**a**) *(fiendishly)* diabólicamente, endemoniadamente (**b**) *Br Fam (very badly)* espantosamente, pésimamente; **they played d.** jugaron pésimamente *or Esp* de pena (**c**) *Br Fam (as intensifier)* terriblemente; **the results were d. bad** los resultados fueron espantosos; **he's d. incompetent** es un inútil total

diabolism [daɪ'æbəlɪzəm] *n* diabolismo *m*, culto *m* al diablo

diachronic [daɪə'krɒnɪk] *adj Ling* diacrónico(a)

diacritic [daɪə'krɪtɪk] *n Ling* signo *m* diacrítico

diadem ['daɪədem] *n* diadema *f*

diaeresis, *US* **dieresis** [daɪ'erəsɪs] *n Ling* diéresis *f inv*

diagnose ['daɪəgnəʊz] *vt* (**a**) *(illness)* diagnosticar; **the illness was wrongly diagnosed** se le dio un diagnóstico erróneo a la enfermedad; **he was diagnosed as having eczema** le diagnosticaron un eccema (**b**) *(fault, problem)* determinar

diagnosis [daɪəg'nəʊsɪs] (*pl* **diagnoses** [daɪəg'nəʊsiːz]) *n* (**a**) *(of illness)* diagnóstico *m*; **to make** *or* **give a d.** emitir un diagnóstico (**b**) *(of situation)* diagnóstico *m*

diagnostic [daɪəg'nɒstɪk] **1** *adj* diagnóstico(a) ▸▸ *Comptr* ***d. program*** programa *m* de diagnóstico; *Educ* ***d. test*** prueba *f* diagnóstico
2 *n (symptom)* síntoma *m*, indicador *m*

diagonal [daɪ'ægənəl] **1** *n* diagonal *f*; **on the d.** al bies, al sesgo
2 *adj* diagonal

diagonally [daɪ'ægənəlɪ] *adv* en diagonal, diagonalmente; **d. opposite (from)** diagonalmente opuesto (a)

diagram ['daɪəgræm] **1** *n* diagrama *m*
2 *vt* (*pt & pp* **diagrammed**) hacer un diagrama de

diagrammatic [daɪəgrə'mætɪk] *adj* gráfico(a), esquemático(a); **in d. form** en forma de diagrama

dial ['daɪəl] **1** *n* (**a**) *(of clock)* esfera *f*; *(of radio)* dial *m*; *(of phone)* disco *m*; *(on instrument panel)* cuadrante *m* ▸▸ *US* ***d. code*** prefijo *m* (telefónico); *US* ***d. tone*** tono *m (de marcar)* (**b**) *Br Fam Old-fashioned (face)* jeta *f*, cara *f*
2 *vt* (*pt & pp* **dialled**, *US* **dialed**) *(phone number)* marcar, *Andes, RP* discar; **to d. Spain direct** llamar a España directamente; **to d.** *Br* **999** *or US* **911** ≃ llamar al teléfono de emergencia; **the number you have dialled has not been recognized** el número marcado no existe
3 *vi* marcar, *Andes, RP* discar

dialect ['daɪəlekt] *n* dialecto *m*

dialectal [daɪə'lektəl] *adj* dialectal

dialectic [daɪə'lektɪk] **1** *n* dialéctica *f*
2 *adj* dialéctico(a)

dialectical [daɪə'lektɪkəl] *adj* dialéctico(a) ▸▸ ***d. materialism*** materialismo *m* dialéctico

dialectics [daɪə'lektɪks] *n* dialéctica *f*

dialectologist [daɪəlek'tɒlədʒɪst] *n* dialectólogo(a) *m,f*

dialectology [daɪəlek'tɒlədʒɪ] *n* dialectología *f*

dialling ['daɪəlɪŋ] *n Br* ***d. code*** prefijo *m* (telefónico); *Br* ***d. tone*** tono *m (de marcar)*

dialogue, *US* **dialog** ['daɪəlɒg] *n (conversation)* diálogo *m*; *(in novel, movie)* diálogo *m*; *Pol* **to enter into a d. (with)** establecer un diálogo (con) ▸▸ *Comptr* ***d. box*** cuadro *m* de diálogo; *Comptr* ***d. mode*** modo *m* (de) diálogo

dial-up ['daɪlʌp] *n Comptr* conexión *f* telefónica *or Spec* por línea conmutada ▸▸ ***d. access*** acceso *m* telefónico *or Spec* por línea conmutada; ***d. account*** cuenta *f* con acceso telefónico *or Spec* por línea conmutada

dialysis [daɪ'ælɪsɪs] *n Med* diálisis *f inv* ▸▸ ***d. machine*** aparato *m* de diálisis

diamanté [dɪə'mɒnteɪ] *n (fabric, dress)* strass *m*

diameter [daɪ'æmɪtə(r)] *n* diámetro *m*; **the wheel is 60 cm in d.** la rueda tiene 60 cms de diámetro

diametric(al) [daɪə'metrɪk(əl)] *adj* (**a**) *Geom* diametral (**b**) *(complete)* **in d. opposition to** diametralmente opuesto(a) a; **she's the d. opposite of her sister** es diametralmente opuesta a su hermana

diametrically [daɪə'metrɪklɪ] *adv* **to be d. opposed to** ser diametralmente opuesto(a) a

diamond ['daɪəmənd] *n* (**a**) *(gem)* diamante *m*; IDIOM *US* **she is a d. in the rough** vale mucho, aunque no tenga muchos modales ▸▸ ***d. anniversary*** bodas *fpl* de diamante; ***d. jubilee*** (celebración *f* del) sexagésimo aniversario *m*; ***d. necklace*** collar *m* de diamantes; ***d. ring***

sortija *f* de diamantes; *(effect during eclipse)* anillo *m* de diamante(s); *Br* ***d. wedding*** bodas *fpl* de diamante
(**b**) *(shape)* rombo *m*
(**c**) *(in cards)* diamante *m*; **diamonds** diamantes *mpl*; **ace/nine of diamonds** as/nueve de diamantes
(**d**) *(in baseball)* diamante *m*

diamondback ['daɪəməndbæk] *n* (**a**) *(snake)* serpiente *f* de cascabel *(con manchas en forma de diamante)* (**b**) *(turtle)* tortuga *f* diamante

diamorphine [daɪə'mɔːfiːn] *n Pharm* diacetilmorfina *f*

Diana [daɪ'ænə] *n Mythol* Diana

diaper ['daɪəpə(r)] *n US* pañal *m* ►► ***d. rash*** escoceduras *fpl or* eritema *m* del pañal

diaphanous [daɪ'æfənəs] *adj Literary* diáfano(a)

diaphragm ['daɪəfræm] *n* (**a**) *Anat* diafragma *m* (**b**) *Phot* diafragma *m* (**c**) *(contraceptive)* diafragma *m*

diarist ['daɪərɪst] *n (in newspaper)* cronista *mf*; *(private)* escritor(ora) *m,f* de diarios

diarize, dairise ['daɪəraɪz] *vt* poner en el diario

diarrhoea, *US* **diarrhea** [daɪə'rɪə] *n* diarrea *f*

diary ['daɪərɪ] *n* (**a**) *(as personal record)* diario *m*; **to keep a d.** llevar un diario (**b**) *(for appointments)* agenda *f* (**c**) *Br (in newspaper)* = columna de sucesos de actualidad

Diaspora [daɪ'æspərə] *n* **the D.** la diáspora

diastole [daɪ'æstəlɪ] *n Physiol* diástole *f*

diatom ['daɪətɒm] *n Biol* diatomea *f*

diatomic [daɪə'tɒmɪk] *adj Chem* diatómico(a)

diatonic [daɪə'tɒnɪk] *adj Mus* diatónico(a) ►► ***d. scale*** escala *f* diatónica

diatribe ['daɪətraɪb] *n* diatriba *f* (**against** contra *or* en contra de)

diazepam [daɪ'æzəpæm] *n Pharm* diazepán *m*

dibble ['dɪbəl] *n (gardening tool)* plantador *m*

dibs [dɪbz] *n* IDIOM *Fam* **to have first d. (of sth)** tener la primicia (de algo)

dice [daɪs] **1** *n* (*pl* **dice**) *(in game)* dado *m*; **to shoot** *or Br* **play d.** jugar a los dados; IDIOM *Fam* **no d.!** ¡no ha habido suerte!
2 *vt (meat, potatoes)* cortar en dados
3 *vi* IDIOM **to d. with death** jugarse la piel *or Am* la vida

dicey ['daɪsɪ] *adj Fam* arriesgado(a)

dichotomy [daɪ'kɒtəmɪ] *n* dicotomía *f*

dick [dɪk] **1** *n* (**a**) *US Fam (detective)* sabueso(a) *m,f* (**b**) *Vulg (penis) Esp* polla *f*, *esp Am* verga *f*, *Chile* pico *m*, *Méx* pito *m*, *RP* pija *f*, *Ven* pinga *f* (**c**) *Vulg (idiot) Esp* gilipollas *mf inv*, *Am* pendejo(a) *m,f*, *RP* pelotudo(a) *m,f* (**d**) *US Vulg (nothing)* **he didn't do d.** no hizo una puta mierda; **you don't know d.** no tienes ni puta idea
2 *vt US Vulg Esp* follarse, *Am* coger; **his best friend was dicking his wife** su mejor amigo se estaba tirando a su mujer

dickens ['dɪkɪnz] *n* **what the d.?** ¿qué diablos?; **we had a d. of a job getting a Hungarian translator** nos costó Dios y ayuda encontrar un traductor húngaro

Dickensian [dɪ'kenzɪən] *adj* (**a**) *(typical of Dickens)* dickensiano(a) (**b**) *(celebration, Christmas)* jovial y acogedor(ora) (**c**) *(conditions, squalor)* de la época victoriana, dickensiano(a)

dicker ['dɪkə(r)] *vi* **to d. with sb (for sth)** regatear con alguien (por algo)

dickey = **dickie**

dickhead ['dɪkhed] *n Vulg Esp* gilipollas *mf inv*, *Am* pendejo(a) *m,f*, *RP* boludo(a) *m,f*

dickie, dickey ['dɪkɪ] *n Fam* (**a**) *(shirt front)* pechera *f* (**b**) **d. (bow)** *Esp* pajarita *f*, *CAm, Carib, Col* corbatín *m*, *Chile* humita *f*, *Méx* corbata *f* de moño, *RP* moñito *m*, *Ven* corbata *f* de lacito

dicky ['dɪkɪ] *adj Br Fam* **to have a d. heart** no estar muy bien del corazón

dicky-bird ['dɪkɪbɜːd] *n* (**a**) *(in children's language)* pío pío *m*, pajarito *m* (**b**) *Br Fam* **not a d.** ni pío

dicotyledon [daɪkɒtɪ'liːdən] *n Bot* dicotiledónea *f*

dicta *pl of* **dictum**

Dictaphone® ['dɪktəfəʊn] *n* dictáfono *m*

dictate **1** *n* ['dɪkteɪt] **she followed the dictates of her conscience** siguió los dictados de su conciencia
2 *vt* [dɪk'teɪt] (**a**) *(letter, passage)* dictar (**to** a) (**b**) *(determine) (choice)* imponer, dictar; *(conditions)* imponer; **circumstances d. that we postpone the meeting** las circunstancias (nos) obligan a aplazar la reunión; **common sense dictates that we should leave early** el sentido común dicta *or* nos dice que nos marchemos temprano
3 *vi* [dɪk'teɪt] (**a**) *(dictate text)* dictar (**b**) *(give orders)* **to d. to sb** dar órdenes a alguien; **I won't be dictated to!** ¡no voy a permitir que me den órdenes!

dictation [dɪk'teɪʃən] *n* (**a**) *(of letter, story)* dictado *m*; **to take d.** escribir al dictado; **at d. speed** a velocidad de dictado (**b**) *Sch* dictado *m*; **to do (a) d.** hacer un dictado

dictator [dɪk'teɪtə(r)] *n* dictador(ora) *m,f*

dictatorial [dɪktə'tɔːrɪəl] *adj (power, manner)* dictatorial

dictatorially [dɪktə'tɔːrɪəlɪ] *adv* de manera dictatorial

dictatorship [dɪk'teɪtəʃɪp] *n* dictadura *f* ►► ***d. of the proletariat*** dictadura *f* del proletariado

diction ['dɪkʃən] *n* (**a**) *(enunciation)* dicción *f*; **to have good d.** tener una buena dicción (**b**) *(choice of words)* lenguaje *m*

DIALOGUE

Uso de las comillas
La forma más frecuente de indicar el diálogo en textos en inglés es mediante el uso de comillas dobles (“ ”) o sencillas (‘ ’).

Si una cita acaba antes de que lo haga la oración, se incluye en la cita el signo de puntuación, bien una coma o un signo de interrogación o de exclamación:

"Are you serious?" he asked. *—¿Hablas en serio? —preguntó.*
"That's outrageous!" she exclaimed. *—¡Eso es un escándalo! —exclamó.*
"I suppose he thinks that's funny," she muttered. *—Imagino que creerá que tiene gracia —murmuró.*

Cuando uno de los hablantes continúa su intervención durante más de un párrafo, cada uno de estos comienza con nuevas comillas, pero sólo se cierran las comillas en el último párrafo. En inglés americano se prefieren las comillas dobles y en inglés británico las sencillas, aunque se usan también las dobles. Cuando aparece una cita dentro de otra cita más larga, la cita breve usa un tipo de comillas y la otra otro distinto:

"It says here he was 'absolutely delighted'," said Philip.
'It says here he was "absolutely delighted",' said Philip.
—Dice aquí que estaba «totalmente encantado» —dijo Philip.

Otra diferencia notable entre el inglés americano y el británico es que en el primero la coma o el punto al final de la oración se incluyen siempre antes de cerrar las comillas y en el segundo se añaden después, a no ser que sean parte de la cita. En inglés británico se escribe normalmente:

He said I was "a promising young talent".

Y en inglés americano:

He said I was "a promising young talent."

dictionary [ˈdɪkʃənərɪ] *n* diccionario *m*

dictum [ˈdɪktəm] (*pl* **dicta** [ˈdɪktə] *or* **dictums**) *n Formal* (**a**) *(statement)* sentencia *f*, aforismo *m* (**b**) *(maxim)* máxima *f* (**c**) *Law* dictamen *m*

did *pt of* **do**

didactic [dɪˈdæktɪk] *adj* (**a**) *(intended to instruct)* didáctico(a) (**b**) *Pej (excessively concerned with message)* doctrinario(a)

didactics [dɪˈdæktɪks] *n* didáctica *f*

diddle [ˈdɪdəl] *vt* (**a**) *Fam (swindle)* tangar, timar; **they diddled him out of the money** le engatusaron para sacarle el dinero (**b**) *US very Fam (have sex with)* tirarse a

diddly [ˈdɪdəlɪ] *n US Fam* **that's not worth d.** no vale un pimiento

diddly-squat [ˈdɪdəlɪˈskwɒt] *n US Fam* cero *m* pelotero

diddlyshit [ˈdɪdəlɪˈʃɪt] *n US Vulg* **I don't give a d.** me importa un carajo *or* una mierda

diddums [ˈdɪdəmz] *exclam Fam* ¡nanay!

diddy [ˈdɪdɪ] *Fam* **1** *n* (**a**) *(breast)* teta *f* (**b**) *(idiot)* bobito(a) *m,f*, zoquete *m*

2 *adj* pequeñito(a), enanísimo(a)

didgeridoo [dɪdʒərɪˈduː] *n* = instrumento de viento originario de Australia, hecho con caña de bambú

didn't [ˈdɪdənt] = **did not**

die[1] [daɪ] *n* (**a**) (*pl* **dice** [daɪs]) *(in game)* dado *m*; IDIOM **the d. is cast** la suerte está echada (**b**) (*pl* **dies** [daɪz]) *(punch)* troquel *m* ►► ***d. casting*** vaciado *m*

die[2] **1** *vi* (**a**) *(stop living)* morir; **she is dying** se está muriendo; **to d. young/a hero** morir (de) joven/como un héroe; **she died of cancer/AIDS** murió de cáncer/sida; **to d. from** *or* **of one's wounds** morir de las heridas recibidas; **she died in her bed** *(of natural causes)* murió de muerte natural; *Literary* **he died by his own hand** murió por su propia mano, se dio muerte a sí mismo; *Fam* **I'd rather d.!** ¡ni borracho!; *Fam* **I nearly died (laughing/of shame)** casi me muero (de risa/de vergüenza *or CAm, Carib, Col, Méx* pena); IDIOM *Fam* **never say d.!** ¡nunca te des por vencido!

(**b**) *(fire, light)* extinguirse, apagarse; *(memory, image)* morir, borrarse; **their love died** su amor se extinguió; **her secret died with her** se llevó el secreto a la tumba; **to d. hard** *(habit, rumour)* ser difícil de eliminar; **the engine died on me** se me estropeó el motor

(**c**) *Fam (want very much)* **to be dying to do sth** morirse de ganas de hacer algo; **I'm dying for a cigarette** me muero de ganas de fumar un cigarrillo; **it was a house to d. for** la casa era para caerse de espaldas *or* de agárrate y no te menees; **she's dying to see him** se muere de ganas de verlo

2 *vt* **to d. a natural/violent death** morir de muerte natural/violenta; IDIOM **to d. the death** quedarse en nada

►**die away** *vi (sound, voice)* desvanecerse

►**die back** *vi (plant)* secarse

►**die down** *vi* (**a**) *(fire)* remitir; *(wind)* calmarse; *(sound)* atenuarse; *(applause)* irse apagando (**b**) *(excitement, scandal)* apaciguarse

►**die off** *vi* morirse; **to be dying off** ir muriéndose

►**die out** *vi* (**a**) *(family, species, tradition)* extinguirse, desaparecer (**b**) *(fire)* extinguirse, apagarse

die-cast [ˈdaɪkɑːst] **1** *vt* vaciar

2 *adj* fundido(a) a presión *or* a troquel, troquelado(a)

diehard [ˈdaɪhɑːd] **1** *n* intransigente *mf*

2 *adj* intransigente

dieresis *US* = **diaeresis**

diesel [ˈdiːzəl] **1** *n* (**a**) *(fuel)* gasoil *m*, gasóleo *m* (**b**) *(railway engine)* locomotora *f* diesel (**c**) *(car)* coche *m or Am* carro *m or RP* auto *m* (de motor) diesel

2 *adj* diesel ►► *very Fam* ***d. dyke*** marimacho *m*; ***d. engine*** motor *m* diesel; ***d. fuel*** gasoil *m*, gasóleo *m*; ***d. oil*** gasoil *m*, gasóleo *m*

diet [ˈdaɪət] **1** *n* (**a**) *(habitual food)* dieta *f*; **a balanced/poor d.** una dieta equilibrada/pobre; **you should reduce the fat in your d.** deberías reducir la cantidad de grasas en tus comidas *or* en tu dieta; **they live on a d. of root vegetables** se alimentan *or* llevan una dieta a base de tubérculos

(**b**) *(restricted food)* dieta *f*, régimen *m*; **to be/go on a d.** estar/ponerse a dieta *or* régimen

(**c**) *(assembly)* dieta *f*

2 *vi* hacer dieta *or* régimen

3 *adj (low-calorie)* light, bajo(a) en calorías

dietary [ˈdaɪətərɪ] *adj* dietético(a) ►► ***d. fibre*** fibra *f* alimenticia; ***d. laws*** leyes *fpl* dietéticas

dietetic [daɪəˈtetɪk] *adj* dietético(a)

dietetics [daɪəˈtetɪks] *n* dietética *f*

dietician [daɪəˈtɪʃən] *n* especialista *mf* en dietética, *Am* dietista *mf*

differ [ˈdɪfə(r)] *vi* (**a**) *(be different)* ser distinto(a) *or* diferente (**from** de); **how does this model d. from yours?** ¿en qué se diferencia este modelo del tuyo?; **to d. in size/colour** diferenciarse por el tamaño/color; **they d. from each other in one respect** se diferencian *or* se distinguen en un aspecto

(**b**) *(disagree)* discrepar (**with sb/about sth** de alguien/en algo); *Formal* **I beg to d.** me veo obligado a discrepar; IDIOM **to agree to d.** reconocer mutuamente las discrepancias

difference [ˈdɪfərəns] *n* (**a**) *(disparity)* diferencia *f* (**between** entre); **there's a big d. between liking someone and loving them** hay una gran diferencia de que te guste alguien a quererlo; **to notice a (big) d. in sth/sb** percibir una (gran) diferencia en algo/alguien; **that makes no** *or* **doesn't make any d.** eso no cambia nada; **would it make any d. to you if we left earlier?** ¿te importa si nos vamos antes?; **it makes no d. (to me)** (me) da igual *or* lo mismo; **it made a big d. to him** para él supuso mucho; **that makes all the d.** eso cambia mucho las cosas; *Fam* **tell her, then, for all the d. it will make** pues díselo, total, para lo que va a servir; **I just want to make a d.** tan sólo quiero aportar algo al mundo; **a product with a d.** un producto distinto a los demás; **to be able to tell the d. between two things** ser capaz de distinguir entre dos cosas

(**b**) *(disagreement)* diferencia *f*, discrepancia *f*; **we've had our differences in the past** en el pasado ha habido sus más y sus menos entre nosotros; **we have to settle our differences** tenemos que resolver nuestras diferencias; **a d. of opinion** una diferencia de opiniones; **to have a d. of opinion with sb** discrepar en algo con alguien

(**c**) *(in numbers, quantity)* diferencia *f*; **to pay the d.** pagar la diferencia; *Fam* **(it's the) same d.** igual da, lo mismo me da

different [ˈdɪfərənt] **1** *adj* (**a**) *(not the same)* diferente, distinto(a); **that's quite a d. matter** eso es una cuestión aparte; **I'm working for a d. firm now** ahora trabajo para otra empresa; **you look d.** se te ve distinta, tienes otro aspecto; **to be d. from** *or* **to** *or US* **than** ser diferente *or* distinto(a) de; **she feels a d. person** se siente otra (persona); **he just wants to be d.** sólo busca ser diferente; **she always has to be d.** le gusta destacar

(**b**) *(various)* diferentes, distintos(as); **I spoke to d. people about it** hablé de ello con varias personas

(**c**) *(unusual)* **it's certainly d.** sin duda es original *or* poco común

2 *adv Fam* **she thinks he's a saint but I know d.** ella piensa que es un santo pero sé que no es así; **they won't know any d.** no lo van a notar, no se van a dar cuenta

differential [dɪfəˈrenʃəl] **1** *n* diferencial *m*; **wage** *or* **pay differentials** diferencias salariales

2 *adj* diferencial ►► *Math* ***d. calculus*** cálculo *m* diferencial; ***d. equation*** ecuación *f* diferencial; *Aut* ***d. gear*** diferencial *m*

differentiate [dɪfəˈrenʃɪeɪt] **1** *vt* (**a**) *(distinguish)* diferenciar, distinguir (**from** de); **we should d. between morality and religion** deberíamos distinguir entre moral y religión (**b**) *Math* diferenciar

2 *vi* diferenciar, distinguir (**between** entre)

differentiation [dɪfərenʃɪˈeɪʃən] *n* (**a**) *(difference)* diferencia *f*, diferenciación *f* (**b**) *Math* diferenciación *f*

differently [ˈdɪfərəntlɪ] *adv* de forma diferente; **if things had turned out d.** si las cosas hubieran salido de otra forma; **she acts d. from** *or US* **than us** su comportamiento es diferente al nuestro; *Euph* **d. abled** discapacitado(a)

difficult [ˈdɪfɪkəlt] *adj* (**a**) *(hard) (task, problem)* difícil; *(book, question)* complejo(a), difícil; **he's had a d. life** ha tenido una vida difícil; **I found it d. to get established** me resultó difícil *or* me costó establecerme

(**b**) *(awkward)* difícil; **you're just being d.** no estás siendo razonable; **he's d. to get on with** no es fácil llevarse bien con él; **to make life d. for sb** complicarle la vida a alguien; **to make things d. for sb** poner las cosas difíciles a alguien; **she's at a d. age** está en una edad difícil

difficulty [ˈdɪfɪkəltɪ] *n* (**a**) *(trouble)* dificultad *f*; **to have d. (in) doing sth** tener dificultad en hacer algo; **to be in d.** *or* **difficulties** estar en dificultades; **to get into d.** *or* **difficulties** verse en apuros, encontrar problemas; **with/without d.** con/sin dificultad

(**b**) *(obstacle, problem)* dificultad *f*, problema *m*; **the main d. is getting there** el mayor problema *or* la mayor dificultad es llegar hasta allí; **to make difficulties (for sb)** crear dificultades (a alguien)

diffidence [ˈdɪfɪdəns] *n* pudor *m*, retraimiento *m*

diffident [ˈdɪfɪdənt] *adj* pudoroso(a), retraído(a)

diffidently [ˈdɪfɪdəntlɪ] *adv (to smile)* tímidamente; *(to express oneself, say sth)* con poca seguridad en sí mismo

diffract [dɪˈfrækt] *vt Phys* difractar

diffraction [dɪ'frækʃən] *n Phys* difracción *f* ►► ***d. grating*** red *f or* rejilla *f* de difracción

diffuse 1 *adj* [dɪ'fju:s] *(light)* difuso(a); *(literary style)* difuso(a), prolijo(a); *(sense of unease)* vago(a), difuso(a)
2 *vt* [dɪ'fju:z] difundir
3 *vi* [dɪ'fju:z] difundirse

diffused [dɪ'fju:zd] *adj* **d. lighting** iluminación difusa *or* difuminada

diffuseness [dɪ'fju:snɪs] *n (of style)* prolijidad *f*

diffuser [dɪ'fju:zə(r)] *n* difusor *m*

diffusion [dɪ'fju:ʒən] *n* **(a)** *(of light, news)* difusión *f* **(b)** *Phys* difusión *f*

dig [dɪg] 1 *n* **(a)** *(in archeology)* excavación *f*; **to go on a d.** ir de excavaciones **(b)** *(poke)* golpe *m*; **a d. in the ribs** *(with elbow)* un codazo en las costillas **(c)** *(remark)* pulla *f*; **to have a d. at sb, to get a d. in at sb** lanzar una pulla a alguien
2 *vt* (*pt & pp* **dug** [dʌg]) **(a)** *(hole, grave)* cavar; *(garden)* cavar en; *(well)* excavar; **the dog dug a hole by the tree** el perro escarbó *or* hizo un agujero junto al árbol; **to d. potatoes** sacar *or* arrancar *Esp* patatas *or Am* papas; IDIOM **she is digging her own grave** está cavando su propia tumba
(b) *(thrust, jab)* **she dug me in the ribs (with her elbow)** me dio un codazo en las costillas, me clavó el codo en las costillas
(c) *Fam (like)* **she really digs that kind of music** ese tipo de música le gusta un montón
(d) *Fam (look at)* fijarse en; **d. that guy over there** ¡fíjate en ese tipo!, ¡no te pierdas a ese tipo!
(e) *Fam (understand)* captar, pillar
3 *vi* **(a)** *(person)* cavar; *(animal)* escarbar; *(in archeology)* excavar; **to d. for gold** realizar prospecciones en búsqueda de oro; **d. deep (into your pockets)** sean generosos **(b)** *(search, investigate)* **he spends hours digging about in old junk shops** se pasa horas rebuscando en tiendas de objetos usados; **if you d. a bit deeper** si ahondas un poco más **(c)** *Fam (understand)* **you d.?** ¿lo pillas?

► **dig in** 1 *vt sep* **(a) to d. oneself in** *(soldiers)* atrincherarse **(b)** IDIOM **to d. one's heels in** emperrarse
2 *vi* **(a)** *Fam (start eating)* ponerse a comer; **d. in!** ¡a comer! **(b)** *(soldiers)* atrincherarse

► **dig into** *vt insep* **(a)** IDIOM **to d. oneself into a hole** empeorar las cosas, meterse en una situación difícil, complicarse la vida **(b)** *(delve into)* echar mano de; **they had to d. into their savings** tuvieron que echar mano de sus ahorros **(c)** *(jab)* **to d. sth into sth** clavar algo en algo; **your elbow is digging into me** me estás clavando el codo

► **dig out** *vt sep* **(a)** *(bullet, splinter)* extraer; *(person) (from ruins, snow drift)* rescatar **(b)** *Fam (find) (information)* encontrar; *(object)* rescatar

► **dig up** *vt sep* **(a)** *(plant)* arrancar, desarraigar; *(treasure, body)* desenterrar **(b)** *(road)* levantar **(c)** *Fam (find) (information)* desenterrar, sacar a la luz; *(person)* sacar

digest 1 *n* ['daɪdʒest] **(a)** *(of book, facts)* resumen *m*; **in d. form** de forma resumida **(b)** *(journal)* boletín *m*, revista *f* **(c)** *Law* repertorio *m* de jurisprudencia, digesto *m*
2 *vt* [dɪ'dʒest] **(a)** *(food)* digerir **(b)** *(idea, information)* digerir **(c)** *Formal (summarize)* compendiar

digestible [dɪ'dʒestəbəl] *adj* **(a)** *(food)* digerible, fácil de digerir; **to be easily d.** digerirse fácilmente **(b)** *(facts, information)* digerible, fácil de digerir

digestion [dɪ'dʒestʃən] *n* digestión *f*

digestive [dɪ'dʒestɪv] *adj* digestivo(a); *Br* **d. (biscuit)** galleta *f* integral ►► ***d. system*** aparato *m* digestivo; ***d. tract*** tubo *m or* tracto *m* digestivo

digger ['dɪgə(r)] *n* **(a)** *(machine)* excavadora *f* **(b)** *Fam (Australian)* australiano(a) *m,f*; *(New Zealander)* neozelandés(esa) *m,f*

digicash ['dɪdʒɪkæʃ] *n Comptr* dinero *m* electrónico

digit ['dɪdʒɪt] *n* **(a)** *(finger)* dedo *m* **(b)** *(number)* dígito *m*; **a three-d. number** un número de tres dígitos

digital ['dɪdʒɪtəl] *adj* **(a)** *(of fingers)* digital, dactilar
(b) *(watch, computer)* digital ►► *Comptr* ***d. audio tape*** cinta *f* digital (de audio); ***d. camera*** cámara *f* digital; ***d. recording*** grabación *f* digital; *Comptr* ***d. signal*** señal *f* digital; *Comptr* ***d. signature*** firma *f* electrónica; ***d. tape*** cinta *f* digital; ***d. television*** televisión *f* digital; ***d. versatile disk*** disco *m* versátil digital; ***d. video*** *Esp* vídeo *m or Am* video *m* digital; ***d. video camera*** cámara *f* de *Esp* vídeo *or Am* video digital

digital/analog converter ['dɪdʒɪtəl'ænəlɒgkən'vɜ:tə(r)] *n Comptr* conversor *m* digital analógico, analogizador *m*

digitalin [dɪdʒɪ'teɪlɪn] *n Pharm* digitalina *f*

digitalis [dɪdʒɪ'teɪlɪs] *n* **(a)** *Bot* digital *f* **(b)** *Med* digitalina *f*

digitize ['dɪdʒɪtaɪz] *Comptr* 1 *vt* digitalizar, escanear
2 *vi* digitalizar, escanear

digitizer ['dɪdʒɪtaɪzə(r)] *n Comptr* digitalizador *m*

diglossia [daɪ'glɒsɪə] *n Ling* diglosia *f*

dignified ['dɪgnɪfaɪd] *adj* **(a)** *(person, silence)* digno(a) **(b)** *(stately)* majestuoso(a), señorial; **he made a d. exit** realizó una salida llena de solemnidad, salió de forma majestuosa

dignify ['dɪgnɪfaɪ] *vt (give prestige to)* dignificar; **I won't d. that remark with a reply** un comentario así no merece *or Am* amerita siquiera una contestación

dignitary ['dɪgnɪtərɪ] *n Formal* dignatario(a) *m,f*

dignity ['dɪgnɪtɪ] *n* **(a)** *(status)* dignidad *f*; **she considered it beneath her d. to respond** le pareció que responder supondría una degradación; **to stand on one's d.** ponerse muy digno(a) **(b)** *(poise)* dignidad *f*; **with d.** con dignidad **(c)** *(rank, title)* dignidad *f*, categoría *f*

digraph ['daɪgrɑ:f] *n Ling* dígrafo *m*

digress [daɪ'gres] *vi* divagar; **you're digressing from the subject** se está apartando del tema; **..., but I d.** ..., pero me estoy alejando del tema

digression [daɪ'greʃən] *n* digresión *f*; **if I might be permitted a d....** si me permite hacer una disgresión *or* un inciso...

digressive [daɪ'gresɪv] *adj (style, passage)* lleno(a) de digresiones

digs [dɪgz] *npl Br* **to live in d.** vivir en una habitación *or* un cuarto de alquiler

dihedral [daɪ'hi:drəl] *Geom* 1 *n* diedro *m*
2 *adj* diedro

dike = **dyke**

diktat ['dɪktæt] *n* decreto *m*; **to govern by d.** gobernar por decreto

dilapidated [dɪ'læpɪdeɪtɪd] *adj (building)* derruido(a); *(car)* destartalado(a); **to be d.** *(building)* estar derruido(a); *(car)* estar destartalado(a)

dilapidation [dɪlæpɪ'deɪʃən] *n* **(a)** *(of building)* ruina *f*, grave deterioro *m*; **in a state of d.** en estado ruinoso **(b)** *Br Law* = cantidad cobrada a un inquilino por las reparaciones que sean necesarias cuando acaba el contrato de alquiler

dilatation and curettage [daɪlə'teɪʃənənkjʊ'retɪdʒ] *n Med* operación *f* de legrado

dilate [daɪ'leɪt] 1 *vt* dilatar
2 *vi* **(a)** *(eyes)* dilatarse **(b)** *Formal (talk, write)* **to d. on** *or* **upon a topic** extenderse *or* explayarse sobre un tema

dilation [daɪ'leɪʃən] *n* dilatación *f*

dilator [daɪ'leɪtə(r)] *n* **(a)** *(instrument)* dilatador *m* **(b)** *(muscle)* dilatador *m*

dilatory ['dɪlətərɪ] *adj Formal (person, action, tactics)* dilatorio(a); **to be d. in doing sth** hacer algo con dilación

dildo ['dɪldəʊ] (*pl* **dildos**) *n* **(a)** *(sex aid)* consolador *m* **(b)** *very Fam (person)* gil *mf*, soplagaitas *mf inv*

dilemma [daɪ'lemə] *n* dilema *m*, disyuntiva *f*; **to be in a d.** estar en un dilema; **this leaves me in something of a d.** esto me pone en un cierto dilema

dilettante [dɪlɪ'tæntɪ] *n* diletante *mf*

dilettantish [dɪlɪ'tæntɪʃ] *adj* diletante

diligence ['dɪlɪdʒəns] *n* diligencia *f*

diligent ['dɪlɪdʒənt] *adj (person)* diligente; *(work)* concienciudo(a), minucioso(a); **he is very d. in his work** *or* **carrying out his work** se esmera mucho en la realización de su trabajo

diligently ['dɪlɪdʒəntlɪ] *adv* con diligencia, diligentemente

dill[1] [dɪl] *n* eneldo *m* ►► ***d. pickle*** pepinillo *m* en vinagre (al eneldo)

dill[2] *n Austr Fam (fool)* bobo(a) *m,f*, memo(a) *m,f*

dilly ['dɪlɪ] *n US Fam Old-fashioned* **a d. of a joke** un chiste sensacional; **a d. of a storm** *Esp* una tormenta de aúpa, *Am* una señora tormenta

dilly-dally ['dɪlɪ'dælɪ] *vi Fam* **(a)** *(loiter)* entretenerse **(b)** *(hesitate)* titubear, vacilar

dilute [daɪ'lu:t] 1 *adj* diluido(a)
2 *vt* **(a)** *(wine, acid)* diluir; **d. to taste** diluir al gusto de cada uno **(b)** *(policy, proposal)* debilitar, restar eficacia a

dilution [daɪ'lu:ʃən] *n* **(a)** *(of wine, acid)* dilución *f* **(b)** *(of policy, proposal)* debilitamiento *m*

dim [dɪm] 1 *adj* **(a)** *(light)* tenue; *(room)* poco iluminado(a), oscuro(a)
(b) *(indistinct) (shape, outline)* tenue; *(memory)* vago(a); *(eyesight)* débil; **her eyes grew d. with tears** sus ojos fueron empañándose

or nublándose por las lágrimas; IDIOM **in the d. and distant past** en un pasado lejano *or* remoto

(c) *(chance, hope)* remoto(a), lejano(a)

(d) IDIOM **to take a d. view of sth** *(regard unfavourably)* desaprobar algo

(e) *Fam (stupid)* tonto(a), corto(a) de alcances, *Am* sonso(a), *Am* zonzo(a)

2 *vt* (*pt & pp* **dimmed**) (a) *(light)* atenuar; *Aut* **to d. one's headlights** poner las luces de cruce (b) *(memory)* ir borrando; *(mind, senses)* ir debilitando; **his eyes were dimmed with tears** las lágrimas le empañaban *or* nublaban los ojos

3 *vi* (a) *(light)* atenuarse (b) *(memory)* ir borrándose; *(sight)* ir debilitándose

► **dim out** *vt sep US* ir oscureciendo

dime [daɪm] *n US* moneda *f* de diez centavos; *Fam* **it's not worth a d.** no vale un centavo *or Esp* un duro; IDIOM *Fam* **they're a d. a dozen** los hay a patadas; IDIOM **it can turn on a d.** *(of car)* da la vuelta en una baldosa, tiene un ángulo de giro muy pequeño ►► ***d. store*** (tienda *f* de) baratillo *m*, *Esp* (tienda *f* de) todo a cien *m*

dimension [daɪ'menʃən] *n* (a) *(measurement)* dimensión *f* (b) *(scope)* alcance *m*, magnitud *f*; **a problem of these dimensions** un problema de estas dimensiones *or* proporciones (c) *(aspect)* dimensión *f*; **the book adds a whole new d. to the subject** el libro aporta toda una nueva dimensión al asunto

diminish [dɪ'mɪnɪʃ] 1 *vt* (a) *(number)* reducir; *(effect, power)* disminuir; *(value)* disminuir (b) *(person)* infravalorar, menospreciar

2 *vi* disminuir; **to d. in number/size** disminuir en número/de talla; **the euro has diminished in value over the past few months** el euro ha disminuido de valor *or* se ha depreciado en los últimos meses

diminished [dɪ'mɪnɪʃt] *adj* (a) *Mus* disminuido(a) (b) *Law* ***d. responsibility*** responsabilidad *f* atenuada

diminishing [dɪ'mɪnɪʃɪŋ] *adj (number, effect, influence)* decreciente; *(value)* cada vez menor, cada vez más reducido(a); **the law of d. returns** la ley de los rendimientos decrecientes

diminuendo [dɪmɪnjʊ'endəʊ] *Mus* 1 *n* (*pl* **diminuendos**) diminuendo *m*

2 *adv* diminuendo

diminution [dɪmɪ'nju:ʃən] *n Formal (number, effect, influence, value)* disminución *f*; **there has been no d. in his powers as a novelist** sus grandes facultades como novelista no se han visto mermadas

diminutive [dɪ'mɪnjʊtɪv] 1 *n Gram* diminutivo *m*

2 *adj* (a) *(small)* diminuto(a), minúsculo(a) (b) *Gram* diminutivo(a)

dimly ['dɪmlɪ] *adv (to remember)* vagamente; *(to see)* con dificultad; **d. lit** en penumbra, con luz tenue

dimmer ['dɪmə(r)] *n* (a) *(for lamp)* **d. (switch)** regulador *m* de intensidad (b) *US Aut* **dimmers** *(headlights)* luces cortas *or* de cruce; *(parking lights)* luces de estacionamiento ►► ***d. switch*** conmutador *m or* palanca *f* de luces

dimness ['dɪmnɪs] *n* (a) *(of light)* lo tenue; *(of room)* penumbra *f* (b) *(of memory)* lo vago; *(of shape)* lo tenue (c) *Fam (stupidity)* torpeza *f*, cortedad *f*

dimout ['dɪmaʊt] *n US* reducción *f* de las luces

dimple ['dɪmpəl] 1 *n* (a) *(in cheek, chin)* hoyuelo *m* (b) *(in surface of ground, water)* rizo *m*, remolino *m*

2 *vt* (a) *(of smile)* **the grin dimpled her cheeks** la sonrisa le hizo hoyuelos en las mejillas (b) *(of wind) (surface of water)* formar remolinos en, rizar

3 *vi* (a) *(cheek)* **her cheeks dimpled when she smiled** se le hicieron hoyuelos en las mejillas al sonreír (b) *(surface of ground, water)* rizarse, ondularse

dimpled ['dɪmpəld] *adj* (a) *(cheek, chin)* con hoyuelos (b) *(surface)* con ondulaciones

dim sum ['dɪm'sʌm] *n Culin* = selección de entrantes de comida china hechos al vapor o fritos

dimwit ['dɪmwɪt] *n Fam* estúpido(a) *m,f*, idiota *mf*

dim-witted [dɪm'wɪtɪd] *adj Fam* estúpido(a), idiota

din [dɪn] 1 *n (of traffic, machinery)* estrépito *m*; *(of people)* jaleo *m*, alboroto *m*

2 *vt Fam* **to d. sth into sb** meterle en la cabeza algo a alguien

dinar ['di:nɑ:(r)] *n* dinar *m*

din-dins ['dɪndɪnz] *n (in children's language)* comidita *f*

dine [daɪn] *Formal* 1 *vt* **to wine and d. sb** llevar a alguien a cenar

2 *vi* cenar; **to d. off** *or* **on sth** cenar algo, tomar algo para cenar

► **dine out** *vi* cenar fuera; *Fig* **he'll be able to d. out on that story for months** esa historia le dará tema de conversación para varios meses

diner ['daɪnə(r)] *n* (a) *(person)* comensal *mf* (b) *US (restaurant)* restaurante *m* barato (c) *US (on train)* vagón *m* restaurante

dinette [daɪ'net] *n* área *f* de comedor

ding [dɪŋ] 1 *vi* sonar

2 *vt (bell)* hacer sonar, tocar

3 *n* **I heard the d. of the bell from the kitchen** oí el talán talán de la campana desde la cocina

ding-a-ling ['dɪŋəlɪŋ] *n* (a) *(ring)* tilín *m* (b) *US Fam (fool)* bobo(a) *m,f*, *Esp* memo(a) *m,f*

dingbat ['dɪŋbæt] *n* (a) *US Fam (fool)* chalado(a) *m,f* (b) *US Fam (thing)* chisme *m*, trasto *m* (c) *Typ* (carácter *m*) dingbat *m*

ding-dong ['dɪŋ'dɒŋ] 1 *n* (a) *(sound)* din don *m*; **to go d.** hacer din don (b) *Fam (fight)* trifulca *f*

2 *adj (argument, contest)* reñido(a)

dinghy ['dɪŋ(g)ɪ] *n* (a) **(rubber) d.** lancha *f* neumática (b) **(sailing) d.** bote *m* de vela

dinginess ['dɪndʒɪnɪs] *n* (a) *(of room, street)* sordidez *f* (b) *(of colour)* lo sucio, lo deslustrado

dingle ['dɪŋgəl] *n* hondonada *f* frondosa

dingo ['dɪŋgəʊ] (*pl* **dingoes**) *n* dingo *m*

dingus ['dɪŋʌs] *n US Fam* chisme *m*, cacharro *m*

dingy ['dɪndʒɪ] *adj* (a) *(room, street)* sórdido(a) (b) *(colour)* sucio(a), deslustrado(a)

dining ['daɪnɪŋ] *n* ***d. car*** *(on train)* vagón *m* restaurante; ***d. club*** sociedad *f* gastronómica; ***d. hall*** *(in school)* comedor *m*; ***d. room*** comedor *m*; ***d. table*** mesa *f* de comedor

dink [dɪŋk] *n* (a) *(in tennis, volleyball)* dejada *f* (b) *US very Fam* = término ofensivo para referirse a un vietnamita

dinkum ['dɪŋkəm] *adj Austr Fam (person, thing)* auténtico(a); **fair d.** está bien, *Esp* vale

Dinky ['dɪŋkɪ] *n Hum Fam* (*abbr* **double income no kids yet**) = pareja joven que trabaja y no tiene hijos

dinky ['dɪŋkɪ] *adj* (a) *Br Fam (small and charming)* lindo(a), chiquitín(ina); **look at that d. little chair!** ¡mira qué sillita tan mona *or* cuca! (b) *US Pej (insignificant)* vulgar, del montón; **a d. little house/hotel room** una casucha/un cuartucho de hotel

dinner ['dɪnə(r)] *n* (a) *(evening meal)* cena *f*; **to have d.** cenar; **what's for d.?** ¿qué hay de cena?; **to ask sb round for d.** invitar a alguien a cenar; **they went out to d.** salieron a cenar ►► ***d. plate*** plato *m* llano; ***d. service*** vajilla *f*; ***d. table*** mesa *f*; ***d. time*** hora *f* de cenar

(b) *(midday meal)* comida *f*, almuerzo *m*; **to have d.** comer, almorzar; **what's for d.?** ¿qué hay de comida?; IDIOM *Fam* **he's seen more movies than I've had hot dinners** ese ha visto más películas que pelos tiene en la cabeza, *Esp* ese ha visto películas a porrillo ►► ***d. hour*** *(at school)* hora *f* de comer; ***d. lady*** camarera *f*, *Am* mesera *f*, *RP* moza *f (en un comedor escolar)*; ***d. time*** hora *f* de comer

(c) *(formal occasion)* cena *f* de gala ►► ***d. dance*** cena *f* con baile; ***d. jacket*** esmoquin *m*; ***d. party*** cena *f (en casa con invitados)*

dinnerware ['dɪnəweə(r)] *n US* vajilla *f*

dinosaur ['daɪnəsɔ:(r)] *n* (a) *(animal)* dinosaurio *m* (b) *Fam (outdated person)* dinosaurio *m*; *(outdated thing)* reliquia *f*

DIN plug ['dɪnplʌg] *n Elec* conector *m* DIN

dint [dɪnt] *n* (a) **by d. of** *(by means of)* a fuerza de (b) *US (dent)* abolladura *f*

diocesan [daɪ'ɒsɪzən] *adj Rel* diocesano(a)

diocese ['daɪəsɪs] *n Rel* diócesis *f inv*

diode ['daɪəʊd] *n Elec* diodo *m*

Dionysiac [daɪə'nɪzɪæk], **Dionysian** [daɪə'nɪzɪən] *adj Literary* dionisíaco(a), dionisiaco(a)

Dionysus [daɪə'naɪsɪs] *pr n* Dionisio

dioptre, *US* **diopter** [daɪ'ɒptə(r)] *n* dioptría *f*

diorama [daɪə'rɑ:mə] *n* diorama *m*

dioxide [daɪ'ɒksaɪd] *n Chem* dióxido *m*

dioxin [daɪ'ɒksɪn] *n Chem* dioxina *f*

dip [dɪp] 1 *n* (a) *(in road, land) (hollow)* hondonada *f*; *(slope)* pendiente *f* (b) *(drop) (in prices, temperature)* caída *f*, descenso *m* (c) *Fam (swim)* chapuzón *m*, baño *m*; **to go for a d.** ir a darse un chapuzón (d) *(sauce)* salsa *f* fría *(para mojar aperitivos)* (e) *(for sheep)* baño *m* desinfectante (f) *Fam (pickpocket)* carterista *mf* (g) *US Fam (idiot)* imbécil *mf*

2 *vt* (*pt & pp* **dipped**) (a) *(immerse)* meter (**in(to)** en); *(food)* mojar (**in(to)** en); **d. the fish in the beaten egg** pase el pescado por el huevo batido

(b) *(put in)* meter; **he dipped his hand in his pocket** se metió la mano en el bolsillo

(c) *(lower)* bajar; *Br* **to d. one's headlights** poner las luces de cruce; **the plane dipped its wings** el avión se alabeó
(d) *(sheep)* dar un baño desinfectante a
3 *vi* (a) *(road, land)* bajar *or* descender un poco; **the road dips sharply** la carretera desciende describiendo una pendiente pronunciada
(b) *(prices, temperature)* caer, descender; **shares dipped on the London Stock Market yesterday** las acciones experimentaron ayer una caída en la bolsa londinense
(c) *(move down)* bajar; **she dipped down behind the wall** se agachó tras el muro; **the sun dipped below the horizon** el sol se hundió en el horizonte

▸ **dip into** *vt insep* (a) *(draw upon) (savings, capital)* recurrir a, echar mano de (b) *(dabble in) (book, subject)* echar un vistazo a

DipEd [dɪp'ed] *n Br Educ* (*abbr* **Diploma in Education**) = diploma de capacitación para la enseñanza

diphtheria [dɪf'θɪərɪə] *n Med* difteria *f*

diphthong ['dɪfθɒŋ] *n Ling* diptongo *m*

diplodocus [dɪ'plɒdəkəs] *n* diplodocus *m inv*, diplodoco *m*

diploid ['dɪplɔɪd] *adj Biol* diploide

diploma [dɪ'pləʊmə] *n* diploma *m*, título *m*; **postgraduate d.** título de posgrado; **to take** *or* **do a d.** sacarse un diploma *or* título, diplomarse; **to have a d. in physics** estar diplomado en física, tener el título de físico

diplomacy [dɪ'pləʊməsɪ] *n* (a) *(between nations)* diplomacia *f* (b) *(tact)* diplomacia *f*

diplomat ['dɪpləmæt], **diplomatist** [dɪ'pləʊmətɪst] *n* (a) *(official)* diplomático(a) *m,f* (b) *(tactful person)* persona *f* diplomática; **he's a real d.** es muy diplomático

diplomatic [dɪplə'mætɪk] *adj* (a) *(official)* diplomático(a) ▸▸ ***d. bag*** valija *f* diplomática; ***d. corps*** cuerpo *m* diplomático; ***d. immunity*** inmunidad *f* diplomática; ***d. incident*** incidente *m* diplomático; ***d. passport*** pasaporte *m* diplomático; ***d. relations*** relaciones *fpl* diplomáticas; ***d. service*** diplomacia *f*, cuerpo *m* diplomático
(b) *(tactful)* diplomático(a); **that wasn't very d.** eso no fue muy diplomático

diplomatist = **diplomat**

dipole ['daɪpəʊl] *n Elec* dipolo *m*

dipped [dɪpt] *adj Br* **d. headlights** luces de cruce *or* cortas

dipper ['dɪpə(r)] *n* (a) *US (ladle)* cucharón *m*, cazo *m* (b) *(bird)* mirlo *m* acuático

dippy ['dɪpɪ] *adj Fam (mad)* locuelo(a), chiflado(a); **she's d. about him** se muere por sus huesitos, está colada por él

dipshit ['dɪpʃɪt] *n US Vulg* soplagaitas *mf inv*, *Esp* gilipollas *mf inv*

dipso ['dɪpsəʊ] (*pl* **dipsos**) *n Fam* borracho(a) *m,f*

dipsomania [dɪpsə'meɪnɪə] *n* dipsomanía *f*

dipsomaniac [dɪpsə'meɪnɪæk] *n* dipsómano(a) *m,f*, dipsomaníaco(a) *m,f*

dipstick ['dɪpstɪk] *n* (a) *Aut* varilla *f* del aceite (b) *Fam (idiot)* idiota *mf*, imbécil *mf*

DIP switch ['dɪpswɪtʃ] *n Comptr* interruptor *m* DIP

dipswitch ['dɪpswɪtʃ] *n Br Aut* conmutador *m or* palanca *f* de luces

diptych ['dɪptɪk] *n Art* díptico *m*

dir [dɜ:(r)] *n Comptr* (*abbr* **directory**) directorio *m*

dire ['daɪə(r)] *adj* (a) *(ominous) (warning)* nefasto(a), siniestro(a)
(b) *(serious, extreme) (situation, poverty)* alarmante, angustioso(a); *(consequences)* terrible; **to be in d. need of sth** tener una necesidad acuciante de algo; **to be in d. straits** estar en un serio apuro; **out of d. necessity** por tener una necesidad perentoria
(c) *Fam (bad)* pésimo(a); **the film was pretty d.** la película era infumable

direct [dɪ'rekt, daɪ'rekt] **1** *adj* (a) *(without deviation or interruption)* directo(a); **to be a d. descendant of sb** ser descendiente directo(a) de alguien; **keep out of d. sunlight** *(on label)* mantener fuera de la exposición directa al sol *or* a los rayos solares ▸▸ ***d. flight*** vuelo *m* directo *or* sin escalas; ***d. free kick*** *(in soccer)* tiro *m* libre directo; ***d. free kick offence*** falta *f* libre directa
(b) *(without intermediary)* directo(a); **to have a d. influence on sth** influir directamente en algo ▸▸ *Pol* ***d. action*** acción *f* directa; *Fin* ***d. debit*** domiciliación *f* bancaria *or* de pago, *Am* débito *m* bancario; ***d. dialling*** llamada *f* directa, *Am* llamado *m* directo; ***d. line*** línea *f* directa; *Com* ***d. mail*** correo *m* directo, correo *m* comercial; *Com* ***d. mailing*** publicidad *f* directa; *Pol* ***d. rule*** gobierno *m* directo; *Com* ***d. selling*** venta *f* directa
(c) *(exact)* exacto(a); **a d. quotation** una cita literal; **the d. opposite** justamente lo contrario; **to score a d. hit** dar en el blanco, hacer diana
(d) *(frank) (person, question, answer)* directo(a), franco(a); **he was always very d. with us** fue siempre muy directo con nosotros, nos habló siempre con toda franqueza
(e) *Elec* ***d. current*** corriente *f* continua
(f) *Gram* ***d. object*** complemento *m or* objeto *m* directo; ***d. question*** pregunta *f* directa *or* en estilo directo; ***d. speech*** estilo *m* directo
2 *adv (to travel, write)* directamente; *(to broadcast)* en directo; **to dial d.** hacer una llamada directa *or Am* un llamado directo
3 *vt* (a) *(remark, gaze, effort)* dirigir (**at** a); **their criticism was directed against the manager** sus críticas iban dirigidas contra el encargado; **he directed my attention to the map** hizo que dirigiera mi atención al mapa, me hizo fijarme en el mapa; **I directed my steps homewards** dirigí mis pasos hacia casa
(b) *(show the way)* **can you d. me to the station?** ¿podría indicarme cómo llegar a la estación?
(c) *(company, traffic)* dirigir
(d) *(instruct)* **to d. sb to do sth** mandar *or* indicar a alguien que haga algo; **as directed** según las instrucciones
(e) *Cin (movie, scene)* dirigir
(f) *Law* **to d. the jury: the judge directed the jury to bring in a verdict of guilty** el juez ordenó al jurado que emitiera un veredicto de culpabilidad
4 *vi Cin* dirigir

> En inglés culto o elevado, y especialmente en inglés americano, **direct** puede ir seguido de **that** más un verbo en subjuntivo (ver el panel SUBJUNCTIVE):
> **he directed that no further action be taken**
> *ordenó que no se tomaran otras medidas*
> Lo mismo también podría decirse de la siguiente forma:
> **he directed that no further action should be taken**

direct-grant school [dɪ'rektgrɑ:nt'sku:l] *n Br Formerly* = escuela privada financiada parcialmente por el Estado, a condición de que sea admitido un porcentaje de alumnos exentos de pago

direction [dɪ'rekʃən, daɪ'rekʃən] *n* (a) *(way)* dirección *f*; **in the d. of...** en dirección a...; **in the right/wrong d.** en la dirección correcta/equivocada; **in every d., in all directions** en todas direcciones ▸▸ ***d. finder*** radiogoniómetro *m*
(b) *(of movie, play, project)* dirección *f*; **under the d. of...** dirigido(a) por...
(c) *(instruction)* dirección *f*, supervisión *f*; **they worked under my d.** trabajaban bajo mi supervisión; **read the directions on the label** lea las indicaciones *or* instrucciones en la etiqueta
(d) *(purpose)* **he has no d. in his life** no tiene un norte *or* un rumbo en la vida
(e) **directions** *(to place)* indicaciones *fpl*; **he asked me for directions to the station** me preguntó cómo se llegaba a la estación

directional [dɪ'rekʃənəl, daɪ'rekʃənəl] *adj* direccional, de dirección ▸▸ *Rad* ***d. aerial*** antena *f* direccional *or Spec* directiva; ***d. coupler*** acoplador *m* direccional

directive [dɪ'rektɪv, daɪ'rektɪv] *n* directiva *f*; **an EU d.** una directiva de la UE

directly [dɪ'rektlɪ, daɪ'rektlɪ] **1** *adv* (a) *(without deviation or interruption) (to go)* directamente; **to be d. descended from sb** ser descendiente directo(a) de alguien; **to come d. to the point** ir directo al grano
(b) *(without intermediary) (to write)* directamente; **the affair concerns me d.** el asunto me afecta directamente *or* de lleno; **he reports d. to me** él me rinde cuentas directamente a mí, yo soy su inmediato superior
(c) *(exactly) (opposite, above)* justo, directamente
(d) *(frankly) (to answer, speak)* directamente, abiertamente
(e) *(immediately)* pronto, en breve; **d. before/after lunch** justo antes/después de comer; **I'm coming d.** voy ahora mismo
2 *conj* **I'll come d. I've finished** vendré en cuanto acabe

directness [dɪ'rektnɪs, daɪ'rektnɪs] *n* franqueza *f*

director [dɪ'rektə(r), daɪ'rektə(r)] *n* (a) *(of company)* director(ora) *m,f* ▸▸ *Sport* ***d. of football*** director(ora) *m,f* técnico(a); *Br Law* ***d. of public prosecutions*** ≃ Fiscal *mf* General del Estado; *Educ* ***d. of studies*** jefe(a) *m,f* de estudios
(b) *(of movie, play)* director(ora) *m,f* ▸▸ ***d.'s chair*** silla *f* plegable de tela, silla *f* de director; **it was his first time in the d.'s chair** era la primera vez que dirigía una película; ***d. of photography*** director(ora) *m,f* de fotografía
(c) *(of orchestra)* director(ora) *m,f* de orquesta

directorate [dɪ'rektərət, daɪ'rektərət] *n* (a) *(post)* dirección *f* (b) *(board)* consejo *m* de administración

director-general [dɪ'rektə'dʒenərəl, daɪ'rektə'dʒenərəl] *n* director(ora) *m,f* general

directorial [dɪrek'tɔːrɪəl, daɪrek'tɔːrɪəl] *adj Theat & Cin (career, debut)* como director(ora); *(work)* de director(ora)

directorship [dɪ'rektəʃɪp, daɪ'rektəʃɪp] *n* dirección *f*, puesto *m* de director(ora)

directory [dɪ'rektərɪ, daɪ'rektərɪ] *n* (a) *(of phone numbers)* guía *f* (telefónica), listín *m* (de teléfonos), *Am* directorio *m* de teléfonos; **(street) d.** callejero *m* ▸▸ *Br* ***d. enquiries,*** *US* ***d. assistance*** (servicio *m* de) información *f* telefónica (b) *Comptr* directorio *m*

dirge [dɜːdʒ] *n* (a) *Rel* canto *m* fúnebre (b) *Fam (depressing tune)* = canción sombría y aburrida

dirigible [dɪ'rɪdʒəbəl] *n* dirigible *m*

dirk [dɜːk] *n Scot* daga *f*, puñal *m*

dirndl ['dɜːndəl] *n* dirndl *m*, = traje de corpiño entallado y falda de vuelo

dirt [dɜːt] *n* (a) *(mud, dust)* suciedad *f*; **don't tread d. into the carpet** no ensucies la *Esp* moqueta *orAm* alfombra con la suciedad del zapato; IDIOM **to treat sb like d.** tratar a alguien como a un trapo; **dog d.** excremento de perro
(b) *(soil)* tierra *f* ▸▸ *US* ***d. farmer*** = agricultor que labra su propia tierra; ***d. road*** camino *m* de tierra; ***d. track*** pista *f* de tierra; ***d. track racing*** carreras *fpl* sobre pistas de tierra
(c) *(obscenity)* **that movie is nothing but d.** esa película es una cochinada
(d) *Fam (scandal)* **to dig for d. on sb** buscar material comprometedor acerca de alguien

dirtbag ['dɜːtbæg] *n US Fam (person)* cerdo(a) *m,f*

dirtbox ['dɜːtbɒks] *n Br Vulg* culo *m*, ojete *m*

dirt-cheap ['dɜːt'tʃiːp] *Fam* 1 *adj* tirado(a) de precio
2 *adv* tirado(a) de precio

dirtily ['dɜːtɪlɪ] *adv* (a) *(to eat)* como un cerdo (b) *(to play, fight)* sucio (c) *(to laugh)* lascivamente

dirt-poor ['dɜːtpʊə(r)] *adj Fam* **to be d.** ser más pobre que las ratas

dirty ['dɜːtɪ] 1 *adj* (a) *(unclean)* sucio(a); **to get d.** *(person, object)* ensuciarse, mancharse; *also Fig* **to get one's hands d.** mancharse las manos; *Fam* **the d. mac brigade** la pandilla de los viejos verdes; IDIOM **the party is washing its d. linen in public** el partido está sacando sus propios trapos sucios a la luz pública, *RP* el partido está sacando los trapitos al sol
(b) *(unprincipled, ruthless)* sucio(a); **a d. player** un deportista que juega sucio; **it's a d. business** es un asunto sucio; **to give sb a d. look** fulminar a alguien con la mirada; *Fam* **it's a d. (rotten) shame** es una injusticia asquerosa ▸▸ *Fam* ***d. dog*** canalla *mf*, perro(a) *m,f*; ***d. money*** dinero *m* sucio; ***d. play*** juego *m* subterráneo; *US Fam* ***d. pool*** juego *m* sucio; *Br Hum* ***d. stop-out*** parrandero(a) *m,f*, juerguista *mf*; ***d. trick*** jugarreta *f*, mala pasada *f*; ***d. tricks campaign*** campaña *f* de descrédito *or* difamación; ***d. war*** guerra *f* sucia; *also Fig* ***d. work*** trabajo *m* sucio; **I'm not doing his d. work for him** no voy a hacerle el trabajo sucio
(c) *(obscene) (movie)* pornográfico(a); *(book, language)* obsceno(a), lascivo(a); **to have a d. mind** tener una mente calenturienta; **to have a d. laugh** *(salacious)* tener una risa lasciva; *(earthy)* tener una risa pícara ▸▸ ***d. joke*** chiste *m* verde; ***d. old man*** viejo *m* verde; *Fam Hum* ***d. weekend*** escapada *f* (romántica) de fin de semana; ***d. word*** palabrota *f*; *Fam* **"middle class" is a d. word around here** la palabra "clase media" no está muy bien vista aquí
(d) *(weather)* horroroso(a)
(e) *(colour)* desvaído(a); **a d. brown colour** un color marronáceo
2 *adv* (a) *(to fight, play)* sucio (b) *(obscenely)* **to talk d.** decir obscenidades (c) *Br Fam (for emphasis)* **a d. big hole** un pedazo de agujero
3 *vt (soil) (hands, clothes)* ensuciar, manchar; *(reputation)* manchar; *Fig* **I wouldn't d. my hands with it** yo no me mancharía las manos en ese asunto; *Euph* **to d. oneself** ensuciarse
4 *vi* **to d. easily** *(material, car etc)* ensuciarse con facilidad
5 *n* IDIOM *Br Fam* **to do the d. on sb** jugársela a alguien

dis = **diss**

disability [dɪsə'bɪlɪtɪ] *n* (a) *(handicap)* discapacidad *f*, minusvalía *f* ▸▸ ***d. allowance*** subsidio *m* por discapacidad *or* invalidez; ***d. benefit*** seguro *m* de incapacidad *or* de invalidez (b) *Law* incapacidad *f*, invalidez *f*

disable [dɪ'seɪbəl] *vt* (a) *(person)* discapacitar, incapacitar; **a disabling disease** una enfermedad que provoca una incapacidad (b) *(tank, ship)* inutilizar; *(alarm system)* desactivar (c) *Comptr (option)* desactivar (d) *Law* incapacitar

disabled [dɪ'seɪbəld] 1 *adj* (a) *(handicapped)* discapacitado(a), minusválido(a); **a d. man** un discapacitado *or* minusválido; **a d. woman** una discapacitada *or* minusválida; **d. ex-servicemen** inválidos de guerra ▸▸ ***d. access*** acceso *m* para minusválidos; ***d. parking space*** estacionamiento *m* para minusválidos; ***d. toilet*** servicio *m orAm* baño *m orAm* lavatorio *m* para minusválidos
(b) *(tank, ship)* inutilizado(a)
(c) *Comptr (option)* desactivado(a)
2 *npl* **the d.** los discapacitados *or* minusválidos

disablement [dɪs'eɪbəlmənt] *n* (a) *(handicap)* discapacidad *f*, invalidez *f* (b) *(of tank, ship)* inutilización *f*

disabuse [dɪsə'bjuːz] *vt Formal* desengañar (**of** de); **you'll just have to d. yourself of that notion** intenta desengañarte de esa idea

disadvantage [dɪsəd'vɑːntɪdʒ] 1 *n* desventaja *f*, inconveniente *m*; **to be at a d.** estar en desventaja; **it's to her d. that...** va en detrimento suyo que..., supone una desventaja para ella que...; **the situation works** *or* **is to his d.** la situación lo perjudica, la situación le es desfavorable; **to put sb at a d.** poner a alguien en desventaja
2 *vt* perjudicar

disadvantaged [dɪsəd'vɑːntɪdʒd] 1 *adj (family, background)* desfavorecido(a)
2 *npl* **the d.** los desfavorecidos

disadvantageous [dɪsædvæn'teɪdʒəs] *adj* desventajoso(a), desfavorable; **to be d. to sb** ser desfavorable para alguien, no resultar ventajoso para alguien; **in a d. position** en una posición nada ventajosa

disadvantageously [dɪsædvæn'teɪdʒəslɪ] *adv* desfavorablemente

disaffected [dɪsə'fektɪd] *adj* descontento(a); **d. youth** juventud descontenta *or* desencantada

disaffection [dɪsə'fekʃən] *n* descontento *m*, desapego *m*

disaffiliate [dɪsə'fɪlɪeɪt] *vi* darse de baja (**from** de)

disagree [dɪsə'griː] *vi* (a) *(have different opinion)* no estar de acuerdo (**with** con); **I have to d.** discrepo, no estoy de acuerdo; **we d. on everything** no estamos de acuerdo en nada; **I can't say I d. with her** no puedo decir que no esté de acuerdo con ella
(b) *Euph (quarrel)* tener una discusión, discutir (**with** con)
(c) *(not correspond) (reports, figures)* no cuadrar, no coincidir
(d) *(climate, food)* **to d. with sb** sentarle mal a alguien

disagreeable [dɪsə'griːəbəl] *adj (person, remark, weather)* desagradable; **don't be so d.!** ¡no seas tan desagradable *or* antipática!

disagreeably [dɪsə'griːəblɪ] *adv (to behave)* de forma desagradable

disagreement [dɪsə'griːmənt] *n* (a) *(failure to agree)* desacuerdo *m*; **to be in d. with sb** estar en desacuerdo con alguien; **there was a lot of d. as to what to do** nadie se ponía de acuerdo sobre qué hacer (b) *Euph (quarrel)* discusión *f*; **to have a d. with sb (about** *or* **over sth)** discutir con alguien (por *or* acerca de algo) (c) *(discrepancy)* discrepancia *f*

disallow [dɪsə'laʊ] *vt Formal* (a) *(objection)* rechazar (b) *(goal)* anular

disambiguate [dɪsæm'bɪgjʊeɪt] *vt* clarificar, eliminar ambigüedades de

disappear [dɪsə'pɪə(r)] *vi* (a) *(vanish) (person, object, snow)* desaparecer; **she disappeared from sight** la perdimos de vista; **he disappeared into the crowd** se esfumó entre la multitud; **he keeps disappearing whenever you need him** siempre desaparece cuando más falta hace; **where did you d. to?** ¿dónde te habías metido?; **to d. over the horizon** desaparecer por el horizonte; **to make sth d.** hacer desaparecer algo, hacer que algo desaparezca
(b) *(cease to exist) (pain, problem)* desaparecer; **the species is fast disappearing in the wild** la especie está en vías de extinción en estado salvaje

disappearance [dɪsə'pɪərəns] *n* desaparición *f*

disappearing act [dɪsə'pɪərɪŋækt] *n* **to do a d.** *(conjurer)* hacer una desaparición; *Fam (sneak away)* hacer mutis (por el foro); *Fam* **the scissors have done a d.** las tijeras se las ha tragado la tierra

disappoint [dɪsə'pɔɪnt] 1 *vt* (a) *(person)* decepcionar, desilusionar; **he was once again disappointed in his attempt to reach the summit** quedó nuevamente decepcionado al no conseguir coronar la cumbre (b) *(hope, ambition)* frustrar, dar al traste con
2 *vi* defraudar, decepcionar

disappointed [dɪsə'pɔɪntɪd] *adj* (a) *(person)* decepcionado(a), desilusionado(a); **to be d.** estar decepcionado(a) *or* desilusionado(a); **are you d. at** *or* **with the results?** ¿estás decepcionado con los resultados?, ¿te han decepcionado los resultados?; **she was d. with the book** el libro le decepcionó; **to be d. in sb** llevarse una decepción *or*

desilusión con alguien; **to be d. in love** sufrir *or* llevarse un desengaño amoroso
(**b**) *(hope, ambition)* frustrado(a)

disappointing [dɪsəˈpɔɪntɪŋ] *adj* decepcionante; **how d.!** ¡qué decepción!, ¡qué desilusión!

disappointingly [dɪsəˈpɔɪntɪŋlɪ] *adv* de manera decepcionante; **she got d. low grades** sacó unas notas decepcionantes

disappointment [dɪsəˈpɔɪntmənt] *n* (**a**) *(feeling)* decepción *f*, desilusión *f*; **to her great d. she failed** para su gran desilusión, suspendió; **book early to avoid d.** reserve ahora para evitar desilusiones
(**b**) *(experience)* decepción *f*, chasco *m*; **to be a d.** *(person, movie)* ser decepcionante; **she has suffered many disappointments** ha sufrido *or* se ha llevado muchos desengaños *or* decepciones

disapprobation [dɪsæprəˈbeɪʃən] *n Formal* desaprobación *f*

disapproval [dɪsəˈpruːvəl] *n* desaprobación *f*, disconformidad *f*; **a look of d.** una mirada de desaprobación *or* disconformidad; **she showed/expressed her d. of the decision** mostró/expresó su disconformidad *or* desaprobación con la decisión; **he shook his head in d.** hizo un gesto de desaprobación con la cabeza

disapprove [dɪsəˈpruːv] **1** *vi* estar en contra, mostrar desaprobación; **to d. of sth** desaprobar algo; **to d. of sb** no ver con buenos ojos a alguien, no tener buena opinión de alguien; **to d. of doing sth** no estimar correcto hacer algo; **I d. of parents who smack their children** no me parece bien que los padres peguen a sus hijos
2 *vt* no aprobar, rechazar

disapproving [dɪsəˈpruːvɪŋ] *adj (tone, look)* desaprobatorio(a); **to be d. of sth** desaprobar algo

disapprovingly [dɪsəˈpruːvɪŋlɪ] *adv* con desaprobación

disarm [dɪsˈɑːm] **1** *vt* (**a**) *(country, enemy)* desarmar; *(bomb)* desactivar (**b**) *(charm)* desarmar
2 *vi* desarmarse

disarmament [dɪsˈɑːməmənt] *n* desarme *m* ►► ***d. talks*** conversaciones *fpl* para el desarme

disarming [dɪsˈɑːmɪŋ] *adj (smile)* arrebatador(ora), irresistible

disarmingly [dɪsˈɑːmɪŋlɪ] *adv* **she's d. honest/friendly** su honradez/amabilidad te desarma

disarranged [dɪsəˈreɪndʒd] *adj Formal (hair, clothes)* desarreglado(a)

disarray [dɪsəˈreɪ] *n (of person, room, clothing)* desorden *m*; **in d.** *(untidy)* en desorden; *(confused)* sumido(a) en el caos; **the army retreated in d.** el ejército se batía en retirada desordenadamente; **the company was thrown into d.** la empresa quedó sumida en el caos *or* en la confusión

disassemble [dɪsəˈsembəl] **1** *vt (machine, furniture)* desmontar, desarmar
2 *vi* desmontarse, desarmarse

disassociate [dɪsəˈsəʊsɪeɪt] *vt* disociar; **to d. oneself from sth/sb** desmarcarse de algo/alguien

disassociation [dɪsəsəʊsɪˈeɪʃən] *n* (**a**) *(act)* disociación *f*, separación *f* (**b**) *Psy* disociación *f*

disaster [dɪˈzɑːstə(r)] *n* (**a**) *(natural, man-made)* desastre *m*, catástrofe *f*; **the holiday was one d. after another** las vacaciones fueron un catálogo de desastres ►► ***d. area*** zona *f* catastrófica; *Fam (untidy place)* leonera *f*, cuadra *f*; *Fam* **he's a (walking) d. area** *(person)* es un desastre ambulante; **my desk is just a d. area** tengo la mesa hecha un desastre; ***d. fund*** fondo *m* de ayuda para los damnificados; *Cin* ***d. movie*** película *f* de catástrofes
(**b**) *(complete failure)* desastre *m*; **the project is heading for d.** el proyecto está abocado al fracaso; **as a manager, he's a d.!** como director es un desastre *or* una calamidad; **to end in d.** terminar en desastre
(**c**) *(very bad luck)* **d. struck** se produjo un desastre *or* una catástrofe

disastrous [dɪˈzɑːstrəs] *adj* desastroso(a), catastrófico(a); **...with d. results** ...con consecuencias desastrosas

disastrously [dɪˈzɑːstrəslɪ] *adv* desastrosamente; **to go d. wrong** salir desastrosamente

disavow [dɪsəˈvaʊ] *vt Formal* (**a**) *(knowledge, responsibility, statement)* negar, desmentir (**b**) *(child)* renegar de, rechazar

disavowal [dɪsəˈvaʊəl] *n Formal* (**a**) *(of knowledge, responsibility, statement)* desmentido *m*, mentís *m* (**b**) *(of child)* rechazo *m*, repudio *m*

disband [dɪsˈbænd] **1** *vt (army, club, organization)* disolver
2 *vi* disolverse

disbar [dɪsˈbɑː(r)] *vt Law* expulsar de la abogacía, inhabilitar como abogado(a)

disbelief [dɪsbɪˈliːf] *n* incredulidad *f*; **in d.** con incredulidad

disbelieve [dɪsbɪˈliːv] *vt (person, story)* no creer, dudar de; **it's not that I d. you, but...** no es que dude de ti, pero..., no es que no te crea, pero...

disbelieving [dɪsbɪˈliːvɪŋ] *adj (stare, frown)* incrédulo(a), de duda

disburse [dɪsˈbɜːs] *vt Formal* desembolsar

disbursement [dɪsˈbɜːsmənt] *n Formal* (**a**) *(payment)* desembolso *m* (**b**) *(action)* desembolso *m*

disc, *US* **disk** [dɪsk] *n* (**a**) *(flat circular object)* disco *m* ►► ***d. brake*** freno *m* de disco; ***d. wheel*** *(of bicycle)* rueda *f* lenticular (**b**) *(record)* disco *m* ►► ***d. jockey*** pinchadiscos *mf inv* (**c**) *Anat* disco *m*

discard [dɪsˈkɑːd] **1** *vt* (**a**) *(get rid of) (thing, person)* desechar; *(plan, proposal, possibility)* descartar; **to d. one's clothes** desembarazarse de la ropa (**b**) *(in cards)* descartarse
2 *vi (in cards)* descartarse

discarded [dɪˈskɑːdɪd] *adj* desechado(a), descartado(a)

discern [dɪˈsɜːn] *vt* distinguir, apreciar; **I could d. no difference between them** no pude percibir ninguna diferencia entre ellos

discernible [dɪˈsɜːnɪbəl] *adj* perceptible; **there is no d. difference** no hay una diferencia apreciable

discerning [dɪˈsɜːnɪŋ] *adj (audience, customer)* entendido(a); *(taste)* cultivado(a)

discernment [dɪˈsɜːnmənt] *n* discernimiento *m*, criterio *m*

discharge **1** *n* [ˈdɪstʃɑːdʒ] (**a**) *(of patient)* alta *f*; *(of prisoner)* puesta *f* en libertad; *(of employee)* despido *m*; *(of soldier)* licencia *f* (**b**) *(of firearm)* descarga *f*, disparo *m* (**c**) *(of gas, chemical)* emisión *f*; *(of electricity)* descarga *f*; *(of pus, fluid)* supuración *f*; *(vaginal)* flujo *m* (vaginal) (**d**) *(of duty)* cumplimiento *m*; *(of debt)* liquidación *f*; *(of fine)* abono *m*
2 *vt* [dɪsˈtʃɑːdʒ] (**a**) *(patient)* dar el alta a; *(prisoner)* poner en libertad; *(employee)* despedir; *(soldier)* licenciar; **she discharged herself from hospital** se dio de alta del hospital; **a discharged bankrupt** una rehabilitación del quebrado
(**b**) *(unload) (cargo)* descargar, desembarcar; *(passengers)* desembarcar
(**c**) *(firearm)* descargar, disparar
(**d**) *(gas, chemical)* emitir; *(electricity)* descargar; *(pus, fluid)* supurar
(**e**) *(duty)* cumplir; *(debt)* saldar, liquidar; *(fine)* abonar
3 *vi* [dɪsˈtʃɑːdʒ] (**a**) *(ship)* descargar (**b**) *(wound)* supurar (**c**) *(river, sewer)* desembocar, ir a parar a (**d**) *Elec* descargarse

disciple [dɪˈsaɪpəl] *n* (**a**) *Rel* discípulo(a) *m,f* (**b**) *(follower)* discípulo(a) *m,f*

disciplinarian [dɪsɪplɪˈneərɪən] *n* **he's such a strict d.** le gusta llevar una severa disciplina

disciplinary [ˈdɪsɪplɪnərɪ] *adj* disciplinario(a); **to take d. action against sb** abrirle a alguien un expediente disciplinario; *Sport* **he has a poor d. record** tiene un abultado historial de sanciones ►► *Sport* ***d. committee*** comité *m* de competición

discipline [ˈdɪsɪplɪn] **1** *n* (**a**) *(control)* disciplina *f*; **to keep** *or* **maintain d.** guardar la disciplina (**b**) *(academic subject)* disciplina *f*
2 *vt* (**a**) *(punish)* castigar (**b**) *(train)* disciplinar; **to d. oneself** disciplinarse; **she had disciplined herself to show no emotion** se había impuesto la disciplina de no mostrar sentimientos

disciplined [ˈdɪsɪplɪnd] *adj* disciplinado(a)

disclaim [dɪsˈkleɪm] *vt* (**a**) *(deny)* negar; **she disclaimed all knowledge of the matter** negó saber nada del asunto; **he tried to d. responsibility for the accident** intentó declinar cualquier responsabilidad en el accidente (**b**) *(renounce)* renunciar a

disclaimer [dɪsˈkleɪmə(r)] *n* negación *f* de responsabilidad; **to issue a d.** hacer público un comunicado negando toda responsabilidad

disclose [dɪsˈkləʊz] *vt* (**a**) *(reveal) (secret, feelings)* revelar; **they refused to d. his whereabouts** rehusaron desvelar su paradero (**b**) *(uncover)* descubrir

disclosure [dɪsˈkləʊʒə(r)] *n* (**a**) *(act)* revelación *f* (**b**) *(fact revealed)* revelación *f*

disco [ˈdɪskəʊ] (*pl* **discos**) *n* discoteca *f* ►► ***d. dancer*** bailarín(ina) *m,f* de música disco; ***d. music*** música *f* disco

discography [dɪsˈkɒgrəfɪ] *n* discografía *f*

discolour, *US* **discolor** [dɪsˈkʌlə(r)] **1** *vt (fade)* decolorar; *(stain)* teñir, manchar
2 *vi (fade)* ponerse descolorido(a); *(stain)* dejar mancha, manchar

discolouration, *US* **discoloration** [dɪskʌləˈreɪʃən] *n* mancha *f* descolorida

discombobulate [dɪskəmˈbɒbjʊleɪt] *vt US Fam Hum* trastornar, despendolar

discomfit [dɪsˈkʌmfɪt] *vt Formal* **(a)** *(confuse, embarrass)* turbar, desconcertar; **to feel discomfited** sentirse turbado(a) *or* desconcertado(a) **(b)** *(thwart) (plan, project)* frustrar, desbaratar

discomfiture [dɪsˈkʌmfɪtʃə(r)] *n Formal* turbación *f*, desconcierto *m*

discomfort [dɪsˈkʌmfət] **1** *n (lack of comfort)* incomodidad *f*; *(pain)* molestia *f*, dolor *m*; **to be in d.** sufrir, pasarlo mal; **to the great d. of their friends** para gran incomodo de sus amigos

2 *vt* incomodar, molestar

discomposure [dɪskəmˈpəʊʒə(r)] *n Formal* desconcierto *m*, aturdimiento *m*

disconcert [dɪskənˈsɜːt] *vt* **(a)** *(fluster)* desconcertar **(b)** *(upset)* preocupar

disconcerting [dɪskənˈsɜːtɪŋ] *adj* **(a)** *(causing confusion, embarrassment)* desconcertante **(b)** *(upsetting)* preocupante

disconcertingly [dɪskənˈsɜːtɪŋlɪ] *adv* de manera desconcertante

disconnect [dɪskəˈnekt] *vt (gas, electricity, phone)* cortar, desconectar; *(machine, appliance)* desenchufar, desconectar; **we've been disconnected** nos han cortado el gas/la electricidad/el teléfono

disconnected [dɪskəˈnektɪd] *adj* **(a)** *(events, account)* inconexo(a) **(b)** *(wire, plug)* desconectado(a), desenchufado(a); *(telephone)* desconectado(a)

disconnection, disconnexion [dɪskəˈnekʃən] *n (of phone, gas, water)* desconexión *f*

disconsolate [dɪsˈkɒnsələt] *adj* desconsolado(a) (**at** por); **to be d. (at)** estar desconsolado(a) (por)

disconsolately [dɪsˈkɒnsələtlɪ] *adv* desconsoladamente

discontent [dɪskənˈtent] *n* **(a)** *(dissatisfaction)* descontento *m* **(b)** *(person)* persona *f* descontenta

discontented [dɪskənˈtentɪd] *adj* descontento(a); **to be d. (with)** estar descontento(a) (con)

discontinuation [dɪskəntɪnjʊˈeɪʃən] *n (of product, model)* desaparición *f*; *(of practice, production, treatment)* suspensión *f*; **this design flaw led to the product's d.** este defecto en el diseño hizo que el producto se dejara de fabricar

discontinue [dɪskənˈtɪnjuː] *vt* **(a)** *(practice, production, treatment)* suspender, interrumpir; *Com* **it's a discontinued line** ese modelo ya no se fabrica **(b)** *Law (action, suit)* sobreseer, suspender

discontinuity [dɪskɒntɪˈnjuːətɪ] *n* **(a)** *(of process, sequence)* interrupción *f*, suspensión *f* **(b)** *Math (of function, curve)* discontinuidad *f* **(c)** *Geol* discontinuidad *f*

discontinuous [dɪskənˈtɪnjʊəs] *adj* **(a)** *(line)* discontinuo(a); *(process, run of events)* intermitente **(b)** *Math (function, curve)* discontinuo(a)

discord [ˈdɪskɔːd] *n* **(a)** *(conflict)* discordia *f* **(b)** *Mus (unpleasant sound)* sonido *m* discordante; *(lack of harmony)* discordancia *f*

discordant [dɪsˈkɔːdənt] *adj* **(a)** *(opinions)* discordante, discorde **(b)** *(music)* discordante, discorde

discotheque [ˈdɪskətek] *n* sala *f* de fiestas

discount [ˈdɪskaʊnt] **1** *n* descuento *m*, rebaja *f*; **there's a 5 percent d. on radios** las radios tienen un 5 por ciento de descuento *or* rebaja; **she got a (10 percent) d.** le hicieron un (10 por ciento de) descuento; **at a d.** *(sale)* con descuento; *St Exch (shares)* al descuento, a un precio reducido; **politeness is at a d. these days** hoy en día la educación no es un valor en alza ►► ***d. house*** *Br Fin* sociedad *f* mediadora del mercado de dinero, casa *f* de descuento; *US (store)* tienda *f* de saldos; *Fin* ***d. rate*** tipo *m* *or Am* tasa *f* de descuento; ***d. store*** tienda *f* de saldos

2 *vt* **(a)** *(price, goods)* rebajar **(b)** *Fin (sum of money, bill, banknote)* descontar **(c)** [dɪsˈkaʊnt] *(suggestion, possibility)* descartar; **you have to d. half of what she says as exaggeration** la mitad de lo que dice es una exageración, en la mitad de lo que dice está exagerando; **it's not something you can d.** no es algo que puedas descartar

discountenance [dɪsˈkaʊntənəns] *vt* **(a)** *(disapprove of)* repudiar, desaprobar **(b)** *(embarrass)* avergonzar

discourage [dɪsˈkʌrɪdʒ] *vt* **(a)** *(dishearten)* desalentar, desanimar; **to become discouraged** desalentarse, desanimarse

(b) *(dissuade) (burglars, visitors)* disuadir, ahuyentar; *(crime)* poner trabas a, impedir; **we are trying to d. smoking** estamos tratando de animar a que la gente deje de fumar, estamos tratando de evitar que se fume; **it's a practice which should be discouraged** es una práctica que debería desaconsejarse; **all these strikes are discouraging investors** todas estas huelgas están disuadiendo a los inversores; **to d. sb from doing sth** tratar de disuadir a alguien de que haga algo

discouragement [dɪsˈkʌrɪdʒmənt] *n* **(a)** *(loss of enthusiasm)* desaliento *m*, desánimo *m* **(b)** *(attempt to discourage)* **my suggestions met with d.** mis sugerencias se toparon con reticencias **(c)** *(deterrent)* **it serves as a d. to burglars** actúa de freno contra los ladrones; **to act as a d.** frenar

discouraging [dɪsˈkʌrɪdʒɪŋ] *adj* desalentador(ora); **the response to the appeal was d.** la respuesta al llamamiento fue desalentadora

discourse [ˈdɪskɔːs] **1** *n* **(a)** *Formal (speech)* discurso *m*; *(essay)* disertación *f*, tratado *m* **(b)** *Ling* discurso *m* ►► ***d. analysis*** análisis *m inv* del discurso **(c)** *Literary (conversation)* conversación *f*; **to engage in d. with sb** enfrascarse en una conversación con alguien

2 *vi* **to d. (up)on a subject** disertar sobre un tema

discourteous [dɪsˈkɜːtɪəs] *adj* descortés (**to** *or* **towards** con)

discourteously [dɪsˈkɜːtjəslɪ] *adv* de forma descortés, con descortesía

discourtesy [dɪsˈkɜːtəsɪ] *n* descortesía *f*; **I meant no d.** no pretendía ser descortés

discover [dɪsˈkʌvə(r)] *vt* **(a)** *(country, answer, reason)* descubrir; **we soon discovered what was wrong** enseguida descubrimos lo que andaba mal, nos dimos cuenta enseguida de lo que andaba mal; **I finally discovered my glasses in my desk** al final encontré mis gafas en mi mesa

(b) *(realize)* darse cuenta, notar; **when did you d. that your wallet had been stolen?** ¿cuándo se dio cuenta de *or* notó que le habían sustraído la cartera?

(c) *(actor, singer)* descubrir

discoverer [dɪsˈkʌvərə(r)] *n* descubridor(ora) *m,f*

discovery [dɪsˈkʌvərɪ] *n* **(a)** *(act, event)* descubrimiento *m*; **to make a d.** realizar un descubrimiento; **a voyage of d.** un viaje lleno de descubrimientos **(b)** *(actor, singer, place, thing)* descubrimiento *m*, hallazgo *m*; **he's quite a d.** *(new actor, soccer player)* es todo un descubrimiento **(c)** *Law (of documents)* revelación *f*

discredit [dɪsˈkredɪt] **1** *n* descrédito *m*; **to bring d. on** *or* **upon** desacreditar *or* desprestigiar a; **to be a d. to sth/sb** desacreditar algo/a alguien; **to his great d., he lied** para su gran descrédito, mintió

2 *vt* **(a)** *(person)* desacreditar **(b)** *(report, theory)* poner en entredicho, cuestionar

discreditable [dɪsˈkredɪtəbəl] *adj (person, practice)* vergonzoso(a), ignominioso(a)

discredited [dɪsˈkredɪtɪd] *adj (person, theory)* desacreditado(a)

discreet [dɪsˈkriːt] *adj* **(a)** *(tactful)* discreto(a); **you can trust him to be d.** puedes confiar en su discreción **(b)** *(inconspicuous)* discreto(a); **at a d. distance** a una distancia prudencial

discreetly [dɪsˈkriːtlɪ] *adv* discretamente, con discreción; **it is d. concealed** está oculto con discreción

discrepancy [dɪsˈkrepənsɪ] *n* discrepancia *f* (**between** entre); **there's a d. in the accounts** existe una discrepancia en las cuentas

discrete [dɪsˈkriːt] *adj* **(a)** *(distinct)* diferenciado(a), independiente **(b)** *Math & Phys* discreto(a)

discretion [dɪsˈkreʃən] *n* **(a)** *(tact)* discreción *f* **(b)** *(judgement)* criterio *m*; **at your d.** a discreción, a voluntad; **at the judges' d.** a discreción de los jueces; **use your (own) d.** sigue tu propio criterio; **I'll leave it to your d.** lo dejo a tu criterio; **the age of d.** la madurez; PROV **d. is the better part of valour** la prudencia es la madre de la ciencia

discretionary [dɪsˈkreʃənərɪ] *adj* discrecional

discriminate [dɪsˈkrɪmɪneɪt] **1** *vt* discriminar, distinguir (**from** de)

2 *vi* **(a)** *(distinguish)* **to d. between** discriminar *or* distinguir entre **(b)** *(act with bias)* **to d. against sb** discriminar a alguien; **she felt she was being discriminated against** sentía que la estaban discriminando; **to d. in favour of** discriminar a favor de

discriminating [dɪsˈkrɪmɪneɪtɪŋ] *adj (audience, customer)* entendido(a); *(taste)* cultivado(a); **he is not very d. in his choice of friends** no es muy selectivo *or* exigente a la hora de elegir a sus amistades

discrimination [dɪskrɪmɪˈneɪʃən] *n* **(a)** *(bias)* discriminación *f*; **racial/sexual/religious d.** discriminación racial/sexual/religiosa **(b)** *(taste)* buen gusto *m*, refinamiento *m*; *(judgement)* criterio *m*, sensatez *f* **(c)** *(differentiation)* distinción *f*, diferenciación *f*

discriminatory [dɪsˈkrɪmɪnətərɪ] *adj* discriminatorio(a)

discursive [dɪsˈkɜːsɪv] *adj* dilatado(a), con muchas digresiones *or* divagaciones

discus [ˈdɪskəs] *n* **(a)** *(object)* disco *m* *(para lanzamientos)* ►► ***d. thrower*** lanzador(ora) *m,f* de disco **(b)** *(event)* **he was second in the d.** quedó segundo en el lanzamiento de disco

discuss [dɪs'kʌs] *vt* (a) *(talk about) (problem, price, subject)* discutir, hablar de; *(person)* hablar de; *(debate)* debatir; **I want to d. it with my lawyer** quiero consultarlo con mi abogado; **I don't want to d. it** no quiero hablar de ello (b) *(examine) (of author, report)* estudiar, analizar; **d.** *(in exam questions)* analizar

discussion [dɪs'kʌʃən] *n* (a) *(talk)* discusión *f*; *(debate)* debate *m*; **there has been no d. about this** esto no se ha discutido; **the matter is under d.** el asunto está siendo discutido; **to come up for d.** *(in meeting)* discutirse; **after much d.** después de largas deliberaciones ▸▸ ***d. group*** coloquio *m*; *Comptr* grupo *m* de discusión, coloquio *m*; *Comptr* ***d. list*** lista *f* de discusión; ***d. programme*** *(on TV, radio)* programa *f* debate, coloquio *m*
(b) *(examination) (by author, in report)* análisis *m inv*

disdain [dɪs'deɪn] 1 *n* desdén *m*, desprecio *m* (**for** por); **a look of d.** una mirada de desprecio; **with** *or* **in d.** con desdén *or* desprecio
2 *vt* desdeñar, despreciar; **to d. to do sth** no dignarse a hacer algo

disdainful [dɪs'deɪnfʊl] *adj* desdeñoso(a); **she was d. of my chances in the race** desdeñó mis posibilidades de ganar la carrera

disease [dɪ'zi:z] *n* (a) *(illness)* enfermedad *f*; **to fight d.** luchar contra las enfermedades (b) *(vice, evil)* mal *m*, enfermedad *f*

diseased [dɪ'zi:zd] *adj* (a) *(plant, limb)* enfermo(a); **to be d.** estar afectado(a) por una enfermedad (b) *(evil, corrupt) (mind, imagination)* enfermizo(a)

disembark [dɪsɪm'bɑ:k] 1 *vt* desembarcar
2 *vi* desembarcar (**from** de)

disembodied [dɪsɪm'bɒdɪd] *adj (voice, presence)* inmaterial, incorpóreo(a)

disembowel [dɪsɪm'baʊəl] (*pt & pp* **disembowelled**, *US* **disemboweled**) *vt* destripar

disenchant [dɪsɪn'tʃɑ:nt] *vt* desencantar, desilusionar; **a disenchanting experience** una experiencia desilusionante *or* decepcionante

disenchanted [dɪsɪn'tʃɑ:ntɪd] *adj* desencantado(a) (**with** con)

disenchantment [dɪsɪn'tʃɑ:ntmənt] *n* desencanto *m* (**with** con)

disenfranchise [dɪsɪn'fræntʃaɪz], **disfranchise** [dɪs'fræntʃaɪz] *vt* privar del derecho de voto a

disengage [dɪsɪn'geɪdʒ] 1 *vt* (a) *(separate)* soltar; **I tried to d. my hand from his** intenté soltarme de su mano; **to d. oneself from sth** desasirse de algo (b) *(gear)* quitar; **to d. the clutch** desembragar (c) *(troops)* retirar
2 *vi* (a) *(separate)* desasirse, soltarse (**from** de) (b) *(gears)* desconectarse (c) *(troops)* retirarse

disengagement [dɪsɪn'geɪdʒmənt] *n* (a) *(from political group, organization)* desvinculación *f* (b) *(of troops)* retirada *f*

disentangle [dɪsɪn'tæŋgəl] *vt* (a) *(untangle) (string, hair)* desenredar (b) *(free)* **I tried to d. my dog from the net** traté de soltar a mi perro de la red; **to d. oneself from a difficult situation** desembarazarse de una situación complicada (c) *(plot, mystery)* desenredar, desentrañar

disequilibrium [dɪsekwɪ'lɪbrɪəm] *n Formal* desequilibrio *m*

disestablish [dɪsɪ'stæblɪʃ] *vt (church)* separar del Estado

disfavour, *US* **disfavor** [dɪs'feɪvə(r)] *n* **to be in d. (with)** no ser visto(a) con buenos ojos (por); **to fall into d.** caer en desgracia; **to regard sth/sb with d.** no ver con buenos ojos algo/a alguien

disfigure [dɪs'fɪgə(r)] *vt (person, statue)* desfigurar; *(landscape)* deteriorar, afear; **a disfiguring disease** una enfermedad que deja a una persona desfigurada

disfigurement [dɪs'fɪgəmənt] *n (of person, statue)* desfiguración *f*; *(of landscape)* deterioro *m*, afeamiento *m*

disfranchise = **disenfranchise**

disgorge [dɪs'gɔ:dʒ] 1 *vt* (a) *(liquid, sewage)* expulsar; *(people)* derramar; **his bag burst, disgorging its contents onto the floor** se le rompió la bolsa y su contenido se desparramó por el suelo (b) *(give unwillingly) (information)* desembuchar
2 *vi (river)* desembocar

disgrace [dɪs'greɪs] 1 *n* (a) *(shame)* vergüenza *f*; **it will bring d. on** *or* **to the family** traerá la deshonra a la familia; **to resign in d.** dimitir a causa de un escándalo; **there's no d. in being poor** ser pobre no es ninguna deshonra
(b) *(disfavour)* **he is in d. with the party** el partido está muy disgustado con él
(c) *(shameful example or thing)* escándalo *m*, vergüenza *f*; **it's a d.!** ¡es un escándalo *or* una vergüenza!; **he is a d. to his family/country** es una vergüenza *or* deshonra para su familia/país; **look at you, your hair's a d.!** mírate, tienes el pelo hecho una birria
2 *vt* (a) *(bring shame on) (person)* avergonzar; *(family, country)* deshonrar; **to d. oneself** caer en la deshonra (b) *(discredit)* **a disgraced politician** un político desacreditado

disgraceful [dɪs'greɪsfʊl] *adj (behaviour, appearance)* vergonzoso(a), indignante; **it's d.!** ¡es una vergüenza!

disgracefully [dɪs'greɪsfʊlɪ] *adv* vergonzosamente; **she was d. late** fue vergonzoso lo tarde que llegó

disgruntled [dɪs'grʌntəld] *adj* contrariado(a), descontento(a); **to be d.** estar contrariado(a) *or* descontento(a)

disguise [dɪs'gaɪz] 1 *n (costume)* disfraz *m*; **to put on** *or* **wear a d.** ponerse *or* llevar un disfraz; **in d.** disfrazado(a)
2 *vt* (a) *(person)* disfrazar (**as** de); *(object)* ocultar, camuflar; **to d. oneself** disfrazarse (b) *(one's feelings, the truth)* ocultar, disfrazar; **there is no disguising the fact that...** no se puede ocultar el hecho de que...

disgust [dɪs'gʌst] 1 *n* asco *m*, repugnancia *f*; **to fill sb with d.** dar asco a alguien; **she left in d.** se marchó indignada *or* asqueada; **much to my d.** para mi gran indignación
2 *vt* repugnar; **I was disgusted by their behaviour** me dio asco su comportamiento

> **False friend**: The Spanish words **disgusto** and **disgustar** are not translations for the English word **disgust**. In Spanish **disgusto** means "annoyance" or "disappointment" and **disgustar** means "to upset".

disgusted [dɪs'gʌstɪd] *adj* indignado(a), asqueado(a); **to be d. with** *or* **by sth/sb** estar indignado(a) con *or* por algo/alguien; **he was** *or* **felt d. with himself** sentía asco de sí mismo, estaba indignado consigo mismo

disgustedly [dɪs'gʌstɪdlɪ] *adv* con indignación, con asco

disgusting [dɪs'gʌstɪŋ] *adj* (a) *(revolting) (person, behaviour, smell)* asqueroso(a), repugnante; *(habit, language)* indecente, vergonzoso(a) (b) *(disgraceful)* vergonzoso(a)

disgustingly [dɪs'gʌstɪŋlɪ] *adv* (a) *(sickeningly)* **a d. bad meal** una comida asquerosa (b) *Fam* **to be d. rich** estar podrido(a) de millones

dish [dɪʃ] 1 *n* (a) *(bowl) (for serving)* fuente *f*; *(for cooking)* cazuela *f*; **dishes** *(crockery)* platos *mpl*; **to do** *or* **wash the dishes** lavar los platos, fregar los cacharros ▸▸ ***d. mop*** estropajo *m*; *US* ***d. soap*** lavavajillas *m inv (detergente)*
(b) *(food)* plato *m* ▸▸ ***d. of the day*** plato *m* del día
(c) *(of radio telescope)* reflector *m*; **d.** (*Br* **aerial** *or US* **antenna**) *(for TV)* antena *f* parabólica
(d) *Fam Old-fashioned (good-looking man or woman)* bombón *m*
2 *vt* (a) *Br (chances, hopes)* truncar, arruinar (b) *US (criticize)* **to d. sb** criticar a alguien (c) IDIOM *Fam* **to d. the dirt (on sb)** sacar los trapos sucios (de alguien), *RP* sacar los trapitos al sol (de alguien)

▸ **dish out** *vt sep* (a) *(food)* repartir, servir (b) *(distribute) (money, leaflets)* repartir; *(advice)* dar; IDIOM **you can d. it out but you can't take it** repartes golpes a diestro y siniestro, pero contigo que no se metan

▸ **dish up** 1 *vt sep* (a) *(meal)* servir (b) *Fam (arguments, excuses)* ofrecer, presentar
2 *vi insep (serve food)* servir

disharmony [dɪs'hɑ:mənɪ] *n* discordia *f*

dishcloth ['dɪʃklɒθ] *n (for washing)* bayeta *f*; *(for drying)* paño *m* (de cocina), *CAm* secador *m*, *Chile* paño *m* de loza, *Col* limpión *m*, *Méx* trapón *m*, *RP* repasador *m*

dishearten [dɪs'hɑ:tən] *vt* descorazonar, desalentar; **don't get disheartened** trata de no desanimarte

disheartening [dɪs'hɑ:tənɪŋ] *adj* descorazonador(ora)

dishevelled, *US* **disheveled** [dɪ'ʃevəld] *adj (hair)* desaliñado(a), despeinado(a); *(clothes)* desastrado(a), desarreglado(a); *(person, appearance)* desaliñado(a), descuidado(a); **to be d.** estar desaliñado(a)

dishonest [dɪs'ɒnɪst] *adj* deshonesto(a), poco honrado(a); **by d. means** por medios fraudulentos *or* deshonestos

dishonestly [dɪs'ɒnɪstlɪ] *adv (to act, obtain)* de forma poco honrada; *(to answer, speak)* con engaños

dishonesty [dɪs'ɒnɪstɪ] *n* deshonestidad *f*, falta *f* de honradez

dishonour, *US* **dishonor** [dɪs'ɒnə(r)] 1 *n* deshonra *f*; **to bring d. on sb** deshonrar a alguien, llevar la deshonra a alguien
2 *vt* (a) *(family, country, profession)* deshonrar (b) *Fin (cheque)* no pagar, devolver

dishonourable, *US* **dishonorable** [dɪs'ɒnərəbəl] *adj* deshonroso(a) ▸▸ *Mil* ***d. discharge*** expulsión *f* por conducta deshonrosa

dishonourably, *US* **dishonorably** [dɪs'ɒnərəblɪ] *adv (to behave)* de manera deshonrosa; *Mil* **to be d. discharged** ser expulsado(a) por conducta deshonrosa

dishpan ['dɪʃpæn] *n US* balde *m*, palangana *f (para fregar los platos)*; **to have d. hands** tener manos de fregona

dishrag ['dɪʃræg] *n US* bayeta *f*

dishtowel ['dɪʃtaʊəl] *n* paño *m* (de cocina), *CAm* secador *m*, *Chile* paño *m* de loza, *Col* limpión *m*, *Méx* trapón *m*, *RP* repasador *m*

dishwasher ['dɪʃwɒʃə(r)] *n* (**a**) *(person)* lavaplatos *mf inv*, friegaplatos *mf inv* (**b**) *(machine)* lavavajillas *m inv*; **d. safe** *(glass, plate)* que se puede meter en el lavavajillas

dishwater ['dɪʃwɔːtə(r)] *n* agua *f* de fregar (los platos); *Fig* **this coffee is like d.!** ¡este café es puro aguachirle!, *RP* ¡este café parece caldo de medias!

dishy ['dɪʃɪ] *adj Br Fam* de buen ver, *Esp* majo(a)

disillusion [dɪsɪ'luːʒən] **1** *vt* desilusionar; **I hate to d. you, but...** siento desilusionarte, pero...; **he has been disillusioned by his experiences** sus experiencias lo han acabado por desilusionar

2 *n* = **disillusionment**

disillusioned [dɪsɪ'luːʒənd] *adj* desencantado(a), desilusionado(a); **to be d. (with)** estar desencantado(a) (con)

disillusionment [dɪsɪ'luːʒənmənt] *n* desencanto *m*, desilusión *f* (**with** con); **the electorate's increasing d. with the government** el creciente desencanto del electorado con el gobierno

disincentive [dɪsɪn'sentɪv] *n* traba *f*; **it acts as a d. to creativity** constituye una traba para la creatividad

disinclination [dɪsɪnklɪ'neɪʃən] *n* falta *f* de interés (**to do sth** en hacer algo); **her d. to believe him** su poca disposición a creerle; **the West's d. to go on lending** la actitud reacia de Occidente a seguir realizando préstamos

disinclined [dɪsɪn'klaɪnd] *adj* **to be d. to do sth** no tener ganas de *or* interés por hacer algo; **I felt d. to help** no tenía ganas de ayudar, no me apetecía ayudar

disinfect [dɪsɪn'fekt] *vt* desinfectar

disinfectant [dɪsɪn'fektənt] *n* desinfectante *m*

disinflation [dɪsɪn'fleɪʃən] *n Econ* desinflación *f*

disinformation [dɪsɪnfə'meɪʃən] *n* desinformación *f*

disingenuous [dɪsɪn'dʒenjʊəs] *adj* falso(a), poco sincero(a)

disingenuousness [dɪsɪn'dʒenjʊəsnɪs] *n* falsedad *f*, falta *f* de sinceridad

disinherit [dɪsɪn'herɪt] *vt* desheredar

disintegrate [dɪs'ɪntɪgreɪt] *vi* (**a**) *(break into pieces) (stone, wet paper)* desintegrarse, deshacerse; *(plane, rocket)* desintegrarse (**b**) *(break down) (coalition, empire, the family)* desintegrarse; *(calm, confidence)* disiparse, volatilizarse; *(health)* hundirse (**c**) *Phys* desintegrarse

disintegration [dɪsɪntɪ'greɪʃən] *n* desintegración *f*

disinter [dɪsɪn'tɜː(r)] (*pt & pp* **disinterred**) *vt* (**a**) *(body)* desenterrar (**b**) *(fact, information, scandal)* desenterrar, desempolvar

disinterest [dɪs'ɪntrɪst], **disinterestedness** [dɪs'ɪntrɪstɪdnɪs] *n* (**a**) *(objectivity)* imparcialidad *f* (**b**) *(lack of interest)* desinterés *m*

disinterested [dɪs'ɪntrɪstɪd] *adj* (**a**) *(objective)* desinteresado(a), imparcial (**b**) *(uninterested)* **he was d. in the movie** no le interesaba la película

disinterestedly [dɪs'ɪntrɪstɪdlɪ] *adv* (**a**) *(objectively)* desinteresadamente, con imparcialidad (**b**) *(with a lack of interest)* sin interés

disinterestedness = **disinterest**

disinvest [dɪsɪn'vest] *vi Fin* retirar el capital invertido

disinvestment [dɪsɪn'vestmənt] *n Fin* desinversión *f*

disjointed [dɪs'dʒɔɪntɪd] *adj (conversation, film, speech)* deshilvanado(a), inconexo(a)

disjointedly [dɪs'dʒɔɪntɪdlɪ] *adv* de forma deshilvanada *or* inconexa

disjunctive [dɪs'dʒʌŋktɪv] *adj Gram* disyuntivo(a) ▸▸ ***d. conjunction*** conjunción *f* disyuntiva

disk [dɪsk] *n* (**a**) *Comptr* disco *m*; **on d.** en disquete *or* disco ▸▸ ***d. controller*** controlador *m* del disco; ***d. drive*** unidad *f* de disco, disquetera *f*; ***d. driver*** controlador *m* de disco; ***d. mailer*** sobre *m* para el envío de discos; ***d. operating system*** sistema *m* operativo de disco; ***d. space*** espacio *m* en disco (**b**) *US* = **disc**

diskette [dɪs'ket] *n Comptr* disquete *m*

dislikable [dɪs'laɪkəbəl] *adj* desagradable, antipático(a)

dislike [dɪs'laɪk] **1** *n (of things)* aversión *f* (**of** por); *(of people)* antipatía *f* (**of** hacia); **to have a d. for** *or* **of sth** tener aversión a algo; **my likes and dislikes** las cosas que me gustan y las que me disgustan; **to take a d. to sb** tomar *or Esp* coger antipatía a alguien

2 *vt* **I d. him/it** no me gusta; **I don't d. him/it** no me disgusta; **I d. them** no me gustan; **I don't d. them** no me disgustan; **I d. getting up early** no me gusta madrugar; **he is much disliked** cae muy mal, se le tiene mucha antipatía

dislocate ['dɪsləkeɪt] *vt* (**a**) *(shoulder, hip)* dislocar; **the fall dislocated his shoulder** se cayó y se dislocó el hombro; **to d. one's shoulder** dislocarse el hombro (**b**) *(plan, timetable)* trastocar

dislocation [dɪslə'keɪʃən] *n* (**a**) *(of shoulder, hip)* dislocación *f* (**b**) *(of plan)* desbaratamiento *m*

dislodge [dɪs'lɒdʒ] *vt* (**a**) *(brick, tile)* soltar (**b**) *(something stuck)* sacar (**from** de) (**c**) *(opponent)* desplazar, desalojar; **nothing would d. him from his position on arms control** nada lo haría abandonar su postura respecto al control armamentístico

disloyal [dɪs'lɔɪəl] *adj* desleal; **to be d. to sth/sb** ser desleal a *or* con algo/alguien

disloyally [dɪs'lɔɪəlɪ] *adv* de forma desleal, con deslealtad

disloyalty [dɪs'lɔɪəltɪ] *n* deslealtad *f* (**to** a *or* con); **an act of d.** un acto desleal *or* de deslealtad

dismal ['dɪzməl] *adj* (**a**) *(gloomy) (place)* sombrío(a), tétrico(a); *(face, person)* triste; *(song)* triste, deprimente; *(day, weather)* muy triste; *(future)* negro(a) (**b**) *(extremely poor) (performance)* nefasto(a), *Esp* fatal; *(failure)* estrepitoso(a), rotundo(a); *Hum* **the d. science** = la economía

dismally ['dɪzməlɪ] *adv (to perform)* rematadamente mal, *Esp* fatal; *(to fail)* estrepitosamente

dismantle [dɪs'mæntəl] **1** *vt* (**a**) *(object, scenery, exhibition)* desmontar (**b**) *(system, arrangement)* desmantelar

2 *vi* desmontarse

dismast [dɪs'mɑːst] *vt (ship)* desarbolar

dismay [dɪs'meɪ] **1** *n* consternación *f*; **in** *or* **with d.** con consternación; **to be filled with d. by sth** estar profundamente consternado(a) por algo; **(much) to my d.** para mi consternación

2 *vt* consternar; **there's no need to be dismayed** no hay por qué consternarse

dismayed [dɪs'meɪd] *adj* consternado(a); **don't look so d.** no tengas ese aire tan consternado *or* abatido

dismember [dɪs'membə(r)] *vt* (**a**) *(body)* descuartizar (**b**) *(country, company)* desmembrar

dismiss [dɪs'mɪs] *vt* (**a**) *(from job) (employee)* despedir; *(magistrate, official)* destituir, cesar; *Mil* **to d. sb from the service** separar del servicio a alguien, dar de baja a alguien

(**b**) *(send away) (school class)* dejar marcharse; **to d. sb** dar a alguien permiso para retirarse; **d. him from your thoughts!** sácatelo *or* quítatelo de la cabeza; *Sch* **class dismissed!** ¡esto es todo por hoy!; *Mil* **d.!** ¡rompan filas!

(**c**) *(not take seriously) (thought, theory)* descartar; *(proposal, suggestion)* rechazar; *(threat, danger)* no hacer caso de; **the suggestion was dismissed as being irrelevant** la sugerencia fue rechazada por no venir al caso; **he was long dismissed as a crank** durante mucho tiempo se le calificó de maniático

(**d**) *Law (case)* sobreseer; *(appeal)* desestimar

(**e**) *(in cricket)* vencer

dismissal [dɪs'mɪsəl] *n* (**a**) *(of employee)* despido *m*; *(of magistrate, official)* destitución *f*, cese *m* (**b**) *(of thought, theory, proposal, suggestion)* rechazo *m*; **we were worried by his d. of the danger** estábamos preocupados por cómo desestimaba el peligro (**c**) *Law (of case)* sobreseimiento *m*; *(of appeal)* desestimación *f*

dismissive [dɪs'mɪsɪv] *adj (tone of voice, gesture)* desdeñoso(a), despectivo(a); **to be d. of sth/sb** ser despectivo(a) con algo/alguien; **he was very d. of my chances** se mostró escéptico en cuanto a mis posibilidades

dismount **1** *vt* [dɪs'maʊnt] (**a**) *(cause to fall) (from horse)* desmontar (**b**) *(gun, device)* desmontar, desarmar (**c**) *Comptr* desmontar

2 *vi* [dɪs'maʊnt] *(from horse, bicycle)* desmontar, bajarse (**from** de)

3 *n* ['dɪsmaʊnt] *(in gymnastics)* salida *f*

disobedience [dɪsə'biːdɪəns] *n* desobediencia *f*; **an act of d.** un acto de desobediencia

disobedient [dɪsə'biːdɪənt] *adj* desobediente; **to be d. to sb** desobedecer a alguien; **that was very d. of you** eso fue una muestra de gran desobediencia por tu parte

disobey [dɪsə'beɪ] *vt (person, rule, order)* desobedecer

disobliging [dɪsə'blaɪdʒɪŋ] *adj Formal (unhelpful)* poco servicial, poco atento(a)

disorder [dɪs'ɔ:də(r)] **1** *n* **(a)** *(confusion, untidiness)* desorden *m*; **in d.** en desorden; **the meeting broke up in d.** la reunión se disolvió en medio de una gran confusión; **the army retreated in d.** el ejército se retiró en desbandada

(b) *(unrest)* desorden *m*; **serious disorders have broken out** se han producido graves disturbios

(c) *Med* dolencia *f*; **a nervous d.** un trastorno nervioso; **a blood d.** una disfunción vascular

2 *vt (make untidy) (files, papers)* desordenar, desorganizar

disordered [dɪs'ɔ:dəd] *adj* **(a)** *(confused, untidy) (room, files)* desordenado(a) **(b)** *(mind)* desordenado(a); *Br* **to be mentally d.** sufrir un trastorno mental

disorderly [dɪs'ɔ:dəlɪ] *adj* **(a)** *(untidy) (room, house, files)* desordenado(a) **(b)** *(unruly) (mob)* alborotado(a); *(person, conduct)* indisciplinado(a); **to lead a d. life** llevar una vida desordenada ▸▸ *Law* ***d. conduct*** escándalo *m* público; *Law* ***d. house*** casa *f* de prostitución

disorganization [dɪsɔ:gənaɪ'zeɪʃən] *n* desorganización *f*

disorganize [dɪs'ɔ:gənaɪz] *vt (plans, schedule)* desorganizar, trastocar

disorganized [dɪs'ɔ:gənaɪzd] *adj (person, ideas, system)* desorganizado(a)

disorientate [dɪs'ɔ:rɪənteɪt], **disorient** [dɪs'ɔ:rɪənt] *vt* desorientar; **to become disorientated** *or* **disoriented** desorientarse

disorientation [dɪsɔ:rɪən'teɪʃən] *n* desorientación *f*

disown [dɪs'əʊn] *vt (wife, child)* repudiar; *(country)* renegar de; *(statement)* no reconocer como propio(a)

disparage [dɪs'pærɪdʒ] *vt* desdeñar, menospreciar

disparaging [dɪs'pærɪdʒɪŋ] *adj* desdeñoso(a), menospreciativo(a); **to be d. about sth/sb** desdeñar or menospreciar algo/a alguien

disparagingly [dɪs'pærɪdʒɪŋlɪ] *adv* con desdén, desdeñosamente

disparate ['dɪspərɪt] *adj Formal* dispar

disparity [dɪs'pærɪtɪ] *n* **(a)** *(inequality) (in ages, wealth, status)* disparidad *f* **(b)** *(inconsistency) (in report, statement)* discrepancia *f*, divergencia *f*

dispassionate [dɪs'pæʃənət] *adj* **(a)** *(calm)* desapasionado(a) **(b)** *(impartial)* ecuánime, imparcial; **to take a d. view of things** ver las cosas de manera ecuánime *or* imparcial

dispassionately [dɪs'pæʃənətlɪ] *adv* **(a)** *(calmly)* desapasionadamente, sin apasionamiento **(b)** *(impartially)* ecuánimemente, imparcialmente

dispatch, despatch [dɪs'pætʃ] **1** *n* **(a)** *(of letter, parcel, merchandise)* envío *m*, expedición *f*; *(of messenger, troops)* envío *m*

(b) *(message)* despacho *m*; *Mil* **he was mentioned in dispatches** aparecía mencionado en partes de guerra ▸▸ ***d. box*** *(for papers)* valija *f* oficial; *Br* **at the d. box** *(in Parliament)* en la tribuna de oradores; *US* ***d. case*** *(for papers)* valija *f* oficial; *Com* ***d. note*** nota *f* de envío; *Mil* ***d. rider*** *(on motorbike)* mensajero(a) *m,f* motorizado(a); *(on horse)* emisario *m*, correo *m*

(c) *Formal (promptness)* **with d.** con celeridad *or* prontitud

2 *vt* **(a)** *(send) (letter, parcel, merchandise)* enviar, despachar; *(messenger, troops)* enviar **(b)** *(kill)* dar muerte a **(c)** *Formal (task)* dar cuenta de, despachar **(d)** *Fam (food)* despacharse

dispel [dɪs'pel] *(pt & pp* **dispelled***)* *vt* **(a)** *(doubt, fear)* disipar **(b)** *(clouds, mist)* disipar

dispensable [dɪs'pensəbəl] *adj* prescindible

dispensary [dɪs'pensərɪ] *n Med* dispensario *m*, botiquín *m*

dispensation [dɪspen'seɪʃən] *n* **(a)** *(administration) (of charity, justice)* administración *f*

(b) *(handing out)* dispensación *f*, despacho *m*

(c) *(exemption)* dispensa *f* **(from** de**)**; **to receive d. from military service** quedar exento(a) de realizar el servicio militar; **as a special d. the prisoner was allowed to attend the funeral** como gracia *or* dispensa especial, se permitió al prisionero asistir al funeral

(d) *Pol & Rel (system)* sistema *f*, régimen *m*

dispense [dɪs'pens] *vt* **(a)** *(administer) (charity, justice)* administrar **(b)** *(hand out) (medication, prescription)* administrar; *(advice)* repartir **(c)** *(of vending machine)* expedir **(d)** *Formal (exempt)* **to d. sb from (doing) sth** dispensar a alguien de (hacer) algo

▸ **dispense with** *vt insep (do without, get rid of)* prescindir de; **to d. with the formalities** prescindir de las formalidades

dispenser [dɪs'pensə(r)] *n* **(a)** *(machine)* máquina *f* expendedora; **coffee d.** máquina automática de café; **soap d.** dispositivo dosificador de jabón **(b)** *(pharmacist)* farmacéutico(a) *m,f*

dispensing chemist [dɪs'pensɪŋ'kemɪst] *n* farmacéutico(a) *m,f*

dispersal [dɪs'pɜ:səl], **dispersion** [dɪs'pɜ:ʃən] *n* **(a)** *(of crowd, seeds)* dispersión *f* **(b)** *(of gas)* dispersión *f* **(c)** *(of light by prism)* descomposición *f*

disperse [dɪs'pɜ:s] **1** *vt* **(a)** *(crowd, seeds)* dispersar; *(knowledge, information)* difundir **(b)** *(gas)* dispersar **(c)** *(light) (of prism)* descomponer

2 *vi* **(a)** *(crowd)* dispersarse **(b)** *(darkness, clouds)* disiparse

dispersion = **dispersal**

dispirit [dɪ'spɪrɪt] *vt* desanimar, desalentar

dispirited [dɪs'pɪrɪtɪd] *adj* desanimado(a), desalentado(a); **to be d.** estar desanimado(a) *or* desalentado(a)

dispiritedly [dɪ'spɪrɪtɪdlɪ] *adv* con desánimo, con desaliento

dispiriting [dɪ'spɪrɪtɪŋ] *adj* desalentador(ora), descorazonador(ora)

displace [dɪs'pleɪs] *vt* **(a)** *(shift) (object, refugees, population)* desplazar **(b)** *(supplant)* sustituir **(c)** *Phys (water, air)* desplazar **(d)** *Med* **to d. a bone** dislocar un hueso

displaced [dɪs'pleɪst] *adj* desplazado(a) ▸▸ ***d. persons*** desplazados *mpl*

displacement [dɪs'pleɪsmənt] *n* **(a)** *(of refugees, population)* desplazamiento *m* **(b)** *(of water, ship)* desplazamiento *m* **(c)** *(substitution)* **d. (of A by B)** sustitución *f* (de A por B) **(d)** *Psy* ***d. activity*** actividad *f* sublimadora

display [dɪs'pleɪ] **1** *n* **(a)** *(of goods)* muestra *f*; *(of handicrafts, paintings)* exposición *f*; **on d.** expuesto(a); **to put sth on d.** exponer algo ▸▸ ***d. cabinet*** vitrina *f*; ***d. copy*** *(of book)* ejemplar *m* de muestra; ***d. stand*** expositor *m*; ***d. window*** escaparate *m*, *Am* vidriera *f*, *Chile, Col, Méx* vitrina *f*

(b) *(of affection, interest, anger)* demostración *f*, muestra *f*; *(of courage, determination, ignorance)* manifestación *f*, despliegue *m*; *(of sport)* exhibición *f*; **a d. of force** un despliegue de fuerza; **to make a great d. of sth** hacer gran ostentación *or* exhibición de algo, exteriorizar mucho algo

(c) *Comptr* pantalla *f* ▸▸ ***d. area*** área *f* de visualización; ***d. menu*** menú *m* de visualización; ***d. unit*** monitor *m*

(d) ***d. advertising*** *(in newspaper)* publicidad *f* visual

2 *vt* **(a)** *(goods)* disponer; *(on sign)* mostrar **(b)** *(affection, interest, anger)* demostrar, mostrar; *(courage, determination, ignorance)* manifestar, desplegar **(c)** *Comptr (image, data)* visualizar

3 *vi (bird, animal)* realizar la parada nupcial

displease [dɪs'pli:z] *vt* disgustar, desagradar; **to be displeased with sb** estar disgustado(a) con alguien; **to be displeased with** *or* **at sth** estar disgustado(a) con *or* por algo

displeasing [dɪs'pli:zɪŋ] *adj* desagradable; **the exam results were d. to your parents** los resultados de los exámenes disgustaron a tus padres

displeasure [dɪs'pleʒə(r)] *n* disgusto *m*, desagrado *m*; **to incur sb's d.** provocar el enojo de alguien

disport [dɪ'spɔ:t] *vt Formal* **to d. oneself** divertirse; **they published photos of him disporting himself on the beach** publicaron fotos de él divirtiéndose en la playa

disposable [dɪs'pəʊzəbəl] *adj* **1** **(a)** *(camera, pen, lighter)* desechable ▸▸ *US* ***d. diaper*** pañal *m* desechable, *Esp* braga-pañal *m*; *Com* ***d. goods*** productos *mpl* desechables, productos *mpl* de usar y tirar; *Br* ***d. nappy*** pañal *m* desechable, *Esp* braga-pañal *m* **(b)** *(funds)* disponible ▸▸ ***d. income*** poder *m* adquisitivo

2 *n* **(a)** *(nappy)* pañal *m* desechable **(b)** *(lighter)* encendedor *m* *or* *Esp* mechero *m* no recargable

disposal [dɪs'pəʊzəl] *n* **(a)** *(of rubbish, evidence, body)* eliminación *f*; **waste** *or* **refuse d.** eliminación de desechos *or* residuos

(b) *US (disposal unit)* trituradora *f* de basuras

(c) *(of property)* venta *f*

(d) *(availability)* **to have sth at one's d.** disponer de algo; **to put sth/sb at sb's d.** poner algo/a alguien a disposición de alguien; **I am entirely at your d.** estoy a su entera disposición; **in the time at our d.** en el tiempo del que disponemos

(e) *Formal (arrangement)* disposición *f*, colocación *f*; *(of troops)* despliegue *m*

dispose [dɪs'pəʊz] **1** *vt Formal* **(a)** *(arrange) (ornaments, books)* disponer, colocar; *(troops, forces)* desplegar **(b)** *(incline, persuade)* predisponer; **his moving testimonial disposed the jury to leniency** su conmovedor testimonio predispuso al jurado a adoptar una postura indulgente

2 *vi* PROV **man proposes, God disposes** el hombre propone y Dios dispone

▸ **dispose of** *vt insep* **(a)** *(get rid of) (rubbish, evidence, body)* eliminar **(b)** *(sell) (property)* vender **(c)** *(deal with) (problem, question,* *task)* acabar con; **to d. of an argument** echar por tierra un argumento (**d**) *Formal (have at one's disposal)* disponer de (**e**) *Euph (kill)* eliminar (**f**) *Hum (eat)* dar buena cuenta de, merendarse

disposed [dɪs'pəʊzd] *adj (willing)* **to be d. to do sth** estar dispuesto(a) a hacer algo; **I am d. to be lenient** estoy dispuesto a ser indulgente; **to be well/ill d. towards sb** estar predispuesto(a) a favor/en contra de alguien

disposition [dɪspə'zɪʃən] *n* (**a**) *(temperament)* carácter *m*; **a man of a placid d.** un hombre de carácter plácido (**b**) *(inclination)* **to have a d. to do sth** tener tendencia a hacer algo (**c**) *Formal (arrangement) (of buildings, ornaments)* disposición *f*, colocación *f*; *(of troops)* despliegue *m* (**d**) *Law* traspaso *m*, enajenación *f*

dispossess [dɪspə'zes] *vt* desposeer (**of** de)

dispossessed [dɪspə'zest] **1** *npl* **the d.** los desposeídos
2 *adj* desposeído(a)

dispossession [dɪspə'zeʃən] *n* desposeimiento *m*

disproof [dɪs'pru:f] *n* (**a**) *(action)* refutación *f* (**b**) *(evidence, fact)* refutación *f*

disproportion [dɪsprə'pɔ:ʃən] *n* desproporción *f*; **to be in d. to sth** ser desproporcionado(a) en relación con algo, no guardar proporción con algo

disproportionate [dɪsprə'pɔ:ʃənət] *adj (excessive)* desproporcionado(a); **to be d. to sth** ser desproporcionado(a) respecto a algo; **a d. amount of time/money** una cantidad de tiempo/dinero desmesurada; **the police response was entirely d.** la respuesta de la policía fue completamente desproporcionada

disproportionately [dɪsprə'pɔ:ʃənətlɪ] *adv* desproporcionadamente; **a d. large sum of money** una cantidad enorme *or* desmesurada de dinero

disprove [dɪs'pru:v] (*pp* **disproved**, *Law* **disproven** [dɪs'prəʊvən]) *vt* refutar

disputable [dɪs'pju:təbəl] *adj* discutible

disputant [dɪs'pju:tənt] *n Formal* debatiente *mf*

disputation [dɪspju:'teɪʃən] *n Formal* (**a**) *(debate)* debate *m* (**b**) *(argument)* polémica *f*, controversia *f*

disputatious [dɪspju:'teɪʃəs] *adj Formal* disputador(ora)

dispute [dɪs'pju:t] **1** *n* (**a**) *(debate)* discusión *f*, debate *m*; **there's some d. about the matter** existe un cierto debate en torno a la cuestión; **it's open to d.** es cuestionable; **it's beyond d.** es indiscutible
(**b**) *(argument, contention)* pelea *f*, disputa *f*; **to be in d.** *(proposals, territory, ownership)* estar en litigio; **the matter in d.** la cuestión debatida; **a border d.** un conflicto fronterizo
(**c**) *Ind* **(industrial) d.** conflicto *m* laboral; **to be in d. with management (over sth)** estar en conflicto con la dirección (por algo)
2 *vt* (**a**) *(subject, claim, statement)* debatir, discutir; **I'm not disputing that** eso no lo discuto; **her courage can hardly be disputed** nadie puede poner en duda su valentía (**b**) *(decision)* cuestionar; *Law (will)* impugnar (**c**) *(contest, final)* disputar; **two teams are currently disputing the leadership** dos equipos se disputan actualmente el liderazgo
3 *vi* discutir (**about** *or* **over** sobre)

disputed [dɪs'pju:tɪd] *adj* (**a**) *(decision, fact, claim)* discutido(a), polémico(a) (**b**) *(fought over)* **this is a much d. territory** este territorio es objeto de un fuerte litigio

disqualification [dɪskwɒlɪfɪ'keɪʃən] *n* (**a**) *(from competition, exam)* descalificación *f*; *(from standing for election)* inhabilitación *f* (**b**) *(disqualifying factor)* impedimento *m* (**for** para); **it's not necessarily a d.** no constituye necesariamente un impedimento (**c**) *Br Law* **a year's d. from driving** un año de suspensión *Esp* del permiso de conducir *or Am* de la licencia para conducir

disqualify [dɪs'kwɒlɪfaɪ] *vt* (**a**) *(from competition, exam)* descalificar; *(from standing for election)* inhabilitar; **to d. sb from doing sth** incapacitar a alguien para hacer algo; **her youth disqualifies her from participating** no puede participar por razón de su juventud, su juventud le impide participar; **being a woman doesn't d. me from expressing an opinion** el hecho de ser mujer no me quita el derecho a expresar mi opinión
(**b**) *Br Law* **to d. sb from driving** retirar a alguien *Esp* el permiso de conducir *or Am* la licencia para conducir

disquiet [dɪs'kwaɪət] *Formal* **1** *n* inquietud *f*, desasosiego *m*
2 *vt* inquietar, desasosegar

disquieting [dɪs'kwaɪətɪŋ] *adj Formal* inquietante

disquisition [dɪskwɪ'zɪʃən] *n Formal* disquisición *f* (**on** acerca de)

disregard [dɪsrɪ'gɑ:d] **1** *n* indiferencia *f*, menosprecio *m* (**for** por); **with complete d. for her own safety** sin preocuparse en lo más mínimo por su propia seguridad
2 *vt (warning, fact, feelings)* no tener en cuenta; *(order)* desacatar; *(instructions)* hacer caso omiso a, desoír; *(danger)* despreciar; **I'll d. what you just said** voy a hacer caso omiso de lo que acabas de decir, voy a hacer como si no hubiera oído lo que acabas de decir

disrepair [dɪsrɪ'peə(r)] *n* **in (a state of) d.** deteriorado(a); **to fall into d.** deteriorarse

disreputable [dɪs'repjʊtəbəl] *adj* (**a**) *(dishonourable) (person, behaviour)* poco respetable; *(action, methods)* vergonzoso(a) (**b**) *(not respectable, shady) (neighbourhood, pub)* de mala reputación

disreputably [dɪs'repjʊtəblɪ] *adv (to behave)* de forma poco respetable

disrepute [dɪsrɪ'pju:t] *n* **to bring sth into d.** desprestigiar algo; **to fall into d.** caer en descrédito

disrespect [dɪsrɪ'spekt] *n* irreverencia *f*, falta *f* de respeto; **to treat sth/sb with d.** tratar a algo/alguien irrespetuosamente; **she has a healthy d. for authority** tiene una sana falta de respeto por la autoridad; **I meant no d.** no pretendía faltar al respeto

disrespectful [dɪsrɪ'spektfʊl] *adj* irrespetuoso(a); **to be d. to sb** ser irrespetuoso(a) con alguien, faltarle el respeto a alguien; **it would be d. not to go to the funeral** sería una falta de respeto no asistir al funeral

disrobe [dɪs'rəʊb] **1** *vt* (**a**) *Formal (judge, priest, monarch)* despojar de sus vestiduras a (**b**) *Hum (undress)* desvestir, dejar en cueros
2 *vi* (**a**) *Formal (judge, priest, monarch)* despojarse de las vestiduras (**b**) *Hum (undress)* desvestirse, ponerse en cueros

disrupt [dɪs'rʌpt] *vt (traffic)* entorpecer, trastornar; *(plan)* trastornar, trastocar; *(meeting, lesson)* interrumpir, alterar el desarrollo de; *(life, routine)* alterar

disruption [dɪs'rʌpʃən] *n (of traffic)* entorpecimiento *m*, trastorno *m* (**to** de); *(of plan)* desbaratamiento *m* (**to** de); *(of meeting)* interrupción *f* (**of** de); *(of life, routine)* alteración *f* (**to** de); **we apologize to viewers for the d. to this evening's programmes** pedimos disculpas a los telespectadores por los cambios que está sufriendo la programación de esta noche

disruptive [dɪs'rʌptɪv] *adj (person, behaviour, factor)* alborotador(ora), revoltoso(a); **to be d.** ocasionar trastornos; **to have a d. influence on sb** tener una influencia perjudicial sobre alguien

dis(s) [dɪs] *vt US Fam* faltar (al respeto) a

dissatisfaction [dɪsætɪs'fækʃən] *n* insatisfacción *f* (**with** con); **there is growing d. with his policies** existe una creciente insatisfacción con sus políticas

dissatisfied [dɪ'sætɪsfaɪd] *adj* insatisfecho(a) (**with** con); **to be d. (with)** estar insatisfecho(a) (con); **the meal/explanation left me d.** la comida/explicación no me satisfizo

dissect [dɪ'sekt] *vt* (**a**) *(animal, plant)* diseccionar (**b**) *(argument, theory, book)* diseccionar

dissecting [dɪ'sektɪŋ] *adj (table, room)* de disección ▸▸ ***d. microscope*** microscopio *m* de disección

dissection [dɪ'sekʃən] *n* (**a**) *(of animal, plant)* disección *f* (**b**) *(of argument, theory, book)* disección *f*

dissemble [dɪ'sembəl] *Formal* **1** *vt (feelings, motives)* ocultar, disimular
2 *vi* disimular

disseminate [dɪ'semɪneɪt] *Formal* **1** *vt (knowledge, idea, information)* propagar, difundir
2 *vi* propagarse, difundirse

disseminated [dɪ'semɪneɪtɪd] *adj Med* ***d. sclerosis*** esclerosis *m inv* múltiple

dissemination [dɪsemɪ'neɪʃən] *n Formal (of knowledge, idea, information)* difusión *f*, propagación *f*

dissension [dɪ'senʃən] *n Formal* disensión *f*, discordia *f*; **there is d. in the ranks** *(in army)* existen desavenencias en el seno de las tropas; *(in political party)* existen disensiones entre las filas del partido

dissent [dɪ'sent] **1** *n* (**a**) *(disagreement)* discrepancia *f*, disconformidad *f*; **to voice** *or* **to express one's d.** manifestar *or* expresar alguien su disentimiento; *Sport* **he was booked for d.** fue amonestado por protestar (**b**) *Rel* disidencia *f* (**c**) *US Law* voto *m* particular
2 *vi* (**a**) *(not conform)* disentir (**from** de); **two members of the inquiry dissented from the findings** dos miembros de la investigación discreparon en cuanto a sus resultados (**b**) *Rel* disidir

dissenter [dɪ'sentə(r)] *n* (**a**) *(generally)* disidente *mf* (**b**) *Rel* disidente *mf*

dissenting [dɪ'sentɪŋ] *adj* discrepante; **a d. voice** una voz discordante

dissertation [dɪsə'teɪʃən] *n* (**a**) *Univ Br (for higher degree)* tesina *f*; *US (doctoral)* tesis *f* (**b**) *Formal (essay, speech)* disertación *f*

disservice [dɪ'sɜːvɪs] *n* **to do sb a d.** perjudicar a alguien; **to do oneself a d.** perjudicarse a sí mismo, hacerse un flaco favor

dissidence ['dɪsɪdəns] *n Pol* disidencia *f*

dissident ['dɪsɪdənt] **1** *n* disidente *mf*
2 *adj* disidente

dissimilar [dɪ'sɪmɪlə(r)] *adj* distinto(a) (**to** de); **the cases are too d. to compare** los casos son demasiado distintos como para compararlos; **they are not d.** no son distintos; **it's not d. to what was happening twenty years ago** no es diferente de lo que ocurría hace veinte años

dissimilarity [dɪssɪmɪ'lærɪtɪ] *n* desigualdad *f*, disimilitud *f* (**between** entre)

dissimulate [dɪ'sɪmjʊleɪt] *Formal* **1** *vt (feelings)* disimular
2 *vi* disimular

dissimulation [dɪsɪmjʊ'leɪʃən] *n Formal* disimulo *m*

dissipate ['dɪsɪpeɪt] **1** *vt* (**a**) *(disperse) (fears, doubts)* disipar (**b**) *(waste) (fortune, one's energy)* derrochar (**c**) *Phys (heat, energy)* disipar
2 *vi (mist, doubts)* disiparse

dissipated ['dɪsɪpeɪtɪd] *adj (lifestyle, adolescence)* disipado(a), disoluto(a)

dissipation [dɪsɪ'peɪʃən] *n* (**a**) *(dispersal) (of fears, doubts)* disipación *f* (**b**) *(wasting) (of fortune, energy)* derroche *m* (**c**) *Phys (of heat, energy)* disipación *f* (**d**) *(loose living)* disipación *f*; **to lead** *or* **live a life of d.** llevar *or* vivir una vida disoluta

dissociate [dɪ'səʊsɪeɪt] **1** *vt* disociar; **to d. oneself from sth/sb** desmarcarse de algo/alguien
2 *vi Chem* disociarse

dissociation [dɪsəʊsɪ'eɪʃən] *n* (**a**) *(act)* disociación *f*, separación *f* (**b**) *Chem* disociación *f* (**c**) *Psy* disociación *f*

dissociated [dɪ'səʊsɪeɪtɪd] *adj Psy* disociado(a) ►► ***d. personality*** personalidad *f* disociada

dissoluble [dɪ'sɒljʊbəl] *adj* disoluble

dissolute ['dɪsəluːt] *adj (person, life)* disoluto(a)

dissolution [dɪsə'luːʃən] *n* (**a**) *(of assembly, parliament)* disolución *f* (**b**) *(of marriage, alliance, empire)* disolución *f*

dissolve [dɪ'zɒlv] **1** *vt* (**a**) *(in liquid)* disolver (**b**) *(empire, marriage, parliament)* disolver
2 *vi* (**a**) *(salt, sugar)* disolverse; **it dissolves in water** es soluble en agua (**b**) *(assembly, parliament)* disolverse (**c**) *(marriage, alliance, empire)* disolverse (**d**) *(fear, hopes)* desvanecerse (**e**) **to d. into tears** deshacerse en lágrimas; **to d. into laughter** partirse de risa (**f**) *Cin & TV* fundirse
3 *n Cin & TV* fundido *m* encadenado

dissonance ['dɪsənəns] *n* (**a**) *Mus* disonancia *f* (**b**) *(disagreement)* discordancia *f*

dissonant ['dɪsənənt] *adj* (**a**) *Mus* disonante (**b**) *(clashing) (opinions, colours)* discordante

dissuade [dɪ'sweɪd] *vt (person)* disuadir; **she was not to be dissuaded** nadie la iba a disuadir; **to d. sb from doing sth** disuadir a alguien de hacer algo

dissuasion [dɪ'sweɪʒən] *n* disuasión *f*

dissuasive [dɪ'sweɪsɪv] *adj (person, effect)* disuasivo(a), disuasorio(a); **it had a powerful d. effect on them** ejerció un poderoso efecto disuasorio sobre ellos

dissyllabic = **disyllabic**

dissyllable = **disyllable**

distaff ['dɪstɑːf] *n* (**a**) *(in spinning)* rueca *f* (**b**) *Literary* **on the d. side** en la rama femenina de la familia

distal ['dɪstəl] *adj Anat* distal

distance ['dɪstəns] **1** *n* (**a**) *(between two places)* distancia *f*; **a short d. away** bastante cerca; **some d. away** bastante lejos; **it's some** *or* **quite a** *or* **a good d. from here** está bastante lejos de aquí; **it's no d. (at all)** está cerquísimo; **at a d. of...** a una distancia de...; **you can't see it from** *or* **at this d.** desde tan lejos no se ve; **it is within walking/cycling d. of the station** se puede ir andando/en bicicleta desde la estación; **to keep sb at a d.** guardar las distancias con alguien; **to keep one's d. (from)** mantener las distancias ►► ***d. education*** educación *f* a distancia, enseñanza *f* a distancia; ***d. learning*** educación *f* a distancia
(**b**) *(distant point, place)* **from a d.** desde lejos; **in the d.** en la lejanía, a lo lejos; **to admire sb from** *or* **at a d.** admirar a alguien desde lejos
(**c**) *(separation in time)* **at this d. in time...** después de tanto tiempo...; **at a d. of two hundred years, it's very difficult to know** después de doscientos años es muy difícil saberlo
(**d**) *Sport* **to go the d.** *(in boxing)* aguantar todos los asaltos; *(of racehorse)* acabar la carrera; *Fig* resistir hasta el final ►► ***d. race*** carrera *f* de fondo; ***d. runner*** corredor(ora) *m,f* de fondo; ***d. running*** fondo *m*
2 *vt* **she soon distanced herself from the other runners** no tardó en distanciarse de los demás corredores; **to d. oneself from sth/sb** *(dissociate oneself)* distanciarse de algo/alguien

distant ['dɪstənt] *adj* (**a**) *(in space)* distante, lejano(a); **three kilometres d.** a tres kilómetros de distancia
(**b**) *(in time)* lejano(a); **in the d. past/future** en el pasado/un futuro lejano; **the time is not far d. when...** no falta mucho para que...
(**c**) *(tenuous) (resemblance)* vago(a); **a d. relative** un pariente lejano
(**d**) *(reserved, aloof)* distante; **to have a d. manner** ser distante
(**e**) *(distracted)* distraído(a); **she had a d. look** tenía la mirada distante *or* perdida

distantly ['dɪstəntlɪ] *adv* (**a**) *(not closely) (to resemble)* vagamente; **d. related** *(people)* lejanamente emparentado(a); *(ideas, concepts)* vagamente relacionado(a) (**b**) *(reservedly)* distantemente, con frialdad (**c**) *(distractedly) (to answer, smile)* distraídamente

distaste [dɪs'teɪst] *n* desagrado *m* (**for** por); **to feel d. for sth** sentir aversión hacia algo; **he'll have to overcome his d. for hard work** tendrá que vencer su aversión hacia el trabajo duro

distasteful [dɪs'teɪstfʊl] *adj* (**a**) *(unpleasant) (task, thought)* desagradable; **I find it extremely d.** me parece deplorable (**b**) *(in bad taste) (joke, remark)* de mal gusto

distemper[1] [dɪs'tempə(r)] *n (disease)* moquillo *m*

distemper[2] **1** *n (paint)* (pintura *f* al) temple *m*
2 *vt* pintar con (pintura al) temple

distend [dɪs'tend] **1** *vt* hinchar
2 *vi* hincharse

distended [dɪs'tendɪd] *adj* hinchado(a)

distil [dɪs'tɪl] (*pt & pp* **distilled**) *vt* (**a**) *(water, whisky)* destilar (**b**) *(information)* condensar

► **distil off, distil out** *vt sep Chem* extraer (mediante destilación)

distillate ['dɪstɪlət] *n Chem* destilado *m*

distillation [dɪstɪ'leɪʃən] *n* (**a**) *(of water, whisky)* destilación *f* (**b**) *(distillate)* destilado *m* (**c**) *(of information)* condensación *f*, compendio *m*

distilled water [dɪs'tɪld'wɔːtə(r)] *n* agua *f* destilada

distiller [dɪs'tɪlə(r)] *n* (**a**) *(person)* destilador(ora) *m,f* (**b**) *(business)* destilería *f*

distillery [dɪs'tɪlərɪ] *n* destilería *f*

distinct [dɪs'tɪŋkt] *adj* (**a**) *(different)* distinto(a); **to be d. from** ser distinto(a) de; **the two issues are quite d. from each other** se trata de dos asuntos completamente distintos; **as d. from** a diferencia de
(**b**) *(clear) (change, idea, preference, voice)* claro(a); *(memory)* vívido(a)
(**c**) *(real) (possibility, feeling, advantage, improvement)* claro(a); **it is a d. possibility** *(in answer to question)* es una opción muy posible; **I have the d. impression she's trying to avoid me** tengo la clara impresión de que está tratando de evitarme; **there's a d. smell of smoke in here** aquí huele claramente a humo

distinction [dɪs'tɪŋkʃən] *n* (**a**) *(difference)* distinción *f*; **to make** *or* **draw a d. between** establecer una distinción entre; **they made no d. between enemy soldiers and civilians** no hicieron distinciones entre los soldados enemigos y los civiles
(**b**) *(honour, recognition)* honor *m*; **to win** *or* **gain d. (as)** adquirir mucho prestigio (como), destacarse (como); *Ironic* **I had the d. of coming last** me correspondió el honor de ser el último
(**c**) *(excellence)* **a writer/scientist of d.** un escritor/científico destacado; **with d.** *(perform, serve)* de manera sobresaliente
(**d**) *Sch & Univ* ≃ matrícula *f* de honor; **he got a d. in maths** ≃ sacó matrícula de honor en matemáticas

distinctive [dɪs'tɪŋktɪv] *adj* (**a**) *(characteristic)* característico(a), distintivo(a) (**of** de) (**b**) *Ling* ***d. feature*** rasgo *m* distintivo

distinctively [dɪs'tɪŋktɪvlɪ] *adv* de manera característica

distinctly [dɪs'tɪŋktlɪ] *adv* (**a**) *(clearly) (to speak, hear)* claramente, con claridad; **I d. remember telling you** recuerdo con toda claridad habértelo dicho (**b**) *(decidedly) (better, easier)* claramente; *(stupid, ill-mannered)* verdaderamente; **by then the weather was d. cold** para entonces el tiempo era claramente frío

distinguish [dɪs'tɪŋgwɪʃ] **1** *vt* (**a**) *(recognize)* distinguir (**b**) *(characterize, differentiate)* distinguir (**from** de) (**c**) *(earn praise, honour)* **to d. oneself by...** distinguirse por...; **I didn't exactly d. myself on the football field** yo no sobresalía precisamente por jugar bien al fútbol
2 *vi* **to d. between** distinguir entre

distinguishable [dɪs'tɪŋgwɪʃəbəl] *adj* (a) *(visible)* visible; **the horizon was hardly d. in the fog** el horizonte apenas se distinguía entre la niebla (b) *(recognizable)* distinguible; **to be d.** distinguirse (c) *(differentiable)* diferenciable (**from** de); **the two species are not easily d. from a distance** las dos especies son difíciles de diferenciar *or* distinguir desde lejos

distinguished [dɪs'tɪŋgwɪʃt] *adj (person, performance, career)* destacado(a); *(air)* distinguido(a); **to look d.** tener aire distinguido

distinguishing [dɪs'tɪŋgwɪʃɪŋ] *adj (mark, characteristic)* característico(a), distintivo(a); **d. feature** rasgo físico característico

distort [dɪs'tɔːt] *vt* (a) *(shape, face)* deformar; *(sound)* distorsionar (b) *(meaning, facts)* distorsionar, tergiversar; *(judgement)* distorsionar; **his upbringing distorted his view of the world** su educación distorsionó su percepción del mundo (c) *Elec, Rad & TV* distorsionar

distorted [dɪs'tɔːtɪd] *adj* (a) *(shape, face)* deformado(a); *(sound)* distorsionado(a) (b) *(account)* distorsionado(a), tergiversado(a)

distortion [dɪs'tɔːʃən] *n* (a) *(of shape, face)* deformación *f*; *(of sound)* distorsión *f* (b) *(of meaning, facts)* distorsión *f*, tergiversación *f* (c) *Elec, Rad & TV* distorsión *f*

distract [dɪs'trækt] *vt* (a) *(break concentration of)* distraer (**from** de); **to d. sb's attention** distraer a alguien; **d. her for a couple of minutes** distráela un par de minutos; **this is distracting us from our main purpose** esto nos está alejando de nuestro objetivo principal; **she is easily distracted** se distrae con facilidad (b) *(amuse)* distraer

distracted [dɪs'træktɪd] *adj* (a) *(confused) (person, look)* abstraído(a), ausente (b) *(upset)* desazonado(a); **d. with worry** alterado(a) por la preocupación

distractedly [dɪs'træktɪdlɪ] *adv* (a) *(with thoughts elsewhere)* distraídamente (b) *(anxiously)* desazonadamente; **she was sobbing d.** lloraba desconsoladamente

distracting [dɪs'træktɪŋ] *adj (disruptive)* **that noise is very d.** ese ruido distrae mucho; **it's very d. having so many people in the office** es fácil distraerse con tanta gente en la oficina

distraction [dɪs'trækʃən] *n* (a) *(distracting thing)* distracción *f*; **it would be an unwelcome d.** supondría una distracción muy molesta; **I need a place where I can work without d.** necesito un lugar donde poder trabajar sin que nada me distraiga
(b) *(amusement)* entretenimiento *m*, distracción *f*
(c) *(madness)* **to drive sb to d.** sacar a alguien de quicio; **to love sb to d.** amar a alguien con locura

distrain [dɪ'streɪn] *vi Law* **to d. on sb's goods** embargar los bienes de alguien

distraint [dɪ'streɪnt] *n Law* embargo *m*

distraught [dɪs'trɔːt] *adj* desconsolado(a), consternado(a) (**over** por); **to be d. (with grief)** estar desconsolado(a) *or* consternado(a)

distress [dɪs'tres] **1** *n* (a) *(suffering) (mental)* sufrimiento *m*, angustia *f*; *(physical)* sufrimiento *m*; **to cause sb d.** hacer sufrir a alguien; **to be in d.** *(person)* estar sufriendo mucho; *(ship, plane)* estar en situación de peligro ►► ***d. flare*** bengala *f* (de socorro); ***d. signal*** señal *f* de socorro (b) *(hardship)* dificultades *fpl*; **to be in financial d.** tener dificultades financieras
2 *vt* (a) *(upset)* afligir, angustiar; **he was distressed by the animal's suffering** lo angustiaba el sufrimiento del animal (b) *(furniture, clothing)* envejecer

distressed [dɪs'trest] *adj* (a) *(person)* angustiado(a), afligido(a); **to be d.** estar angustiado(a) *or* afligido(a); **there's no need to get d.** no hay necesidad de angustiarse (b) *Euph (financially)* **to be in d. circumstances** encontrarse en una situación difícil (c) *(wood, paintwork)* envejecido(a)

distressing [dɪs'tresɪŋ] *adj (upsetting)* angustioso(a); *(worrying)* preocupante

distressingly [dɪs'tresɪŋlɪ] *adv* **we have d. few options** tenemos tan pocas opciones que es angustiante

distribute [dɪs'trɪbjuːt] **1** *vt* (a) *(hand out) (money, leaflets, gifts)* distribuir (b) *(share out, allocate) (wealth, weight)* distribuir, repartir (c) *(spread) (paint)* extender; **make sure the glue is evenly distributed** extienda bien la cola (d) *Fin (dividend)* repartir (e) *Com & Cin (supply)* distribuir
2 *vi Com* realizar la distribución

distribution [dɪstrɪ'bjuːʃən] *n* (a) *(of money, leaflets, gifts)* distribución *f*
(b) *(sharing out)* reparto *m*; **d. of wealth** reparto de la riqueza
(c) *(spread) (of paint, load, population)* distribución *f*
(d) *Com & Cin (supply)* distribución *f*; **to have a wide d.** *(movie, product)* tener (una) buena distribución ►► *Econ* ***d. channel*** canal *m* de comercialización; ***d. cost*** costo *m* de distribución; ***d. list*** *(of memo)* lista *f* de distribución; ***d. network*** red *f* de distribución
(e) *Math (in statistics)* distribución *f*

distributive [dɪs'trɪbjʊtɪv] *adj* (a) *Com* de la distribución; **the d. trades** el sector de la distribución (b) *Gram* distributivo(a)

distributor [dɪs'trɪbjʊtə(r)] *n* (a) *(person, company)* distribuidor(ora) *m,f*; *(of movie)* distribuidora *f* (b) *Aut* distribuidor *m*, *Esp* delco® *m* ►► ***d. cap*** tapa *f* del distribuidor *or Esp* delco®

distributorship [dɪs'trɪbjʊtəʃɪp] *n Com* **to have the d. for...** ser el distribuidor exclusivo de...

district ['dɪstrɪkt] *n* (a) *(of country) (administrative area)* comarca *f*; *(more generally)* zona *f*, región *f*; **the D. of Columbia** el Distrito de Columbia ►► *US* ***d. attorney*** fiscal *mf* del distrito; *Br Formerly* ***d. council*** junta *f* municipal; ***d. court*** tribunal *m* federal; *Br* ***d. nurse*** = enfermera que visita a los pacientes en sus casas (b) *(of town, city)* barrio *m*

distrust [dɪs'trʌst] **1** *n* desconfianza *f*; **my d. of her** mi falta de confianza en ella; **to have a deep d. of sth/sb** desconfiar mucho de algo/alguien
2 *vt* desconfiar de

distrustful [dɪs'trʌstfʊl] *adj* desconfiado(a); **to be d. of** desconfiar de

distrustfully [dɪs'trʌstfʊlɪ] *adv* con desconfianza

disturb [dɪs'tɜːb] *vt* (a) *(annoy, interrupt) (person)* molestar; *(sleep, concentration)* perturbar; **the police disturbed the burglar as he was breaking in** la policía sorprendió al ladrón cuando penetraba en el inmueble; **"do not d."** *(sign)* "se ruega no molesten *or* no molestar"; *Law* **to d. the peace** alterar el orden público
(b) *(worry)* preocupar
(c) *(disarrange) (papers, room)* desordenar; *(water surface)* agitar

disturbance [dɪs'tɜːbəns] *n* (a) *(interruption, disruption)* interrupción *f* (b) *(nuisance, noise)* molestia *f*; **to cause a d.** molestar (c) *(atmospheric, emotional)* perturbación *f* (d) *(fight, riot)* altercado *m*; **disturbances** *(unrest)* altercados, disturbios; **to cause** *or* **create a d.** provocar altercados

disturbed [dɪs'tɜːbd] *adj* (a) *(distressed, upset) (mentally, emotionally)* trastornado(a), perturbado(a); **to be d.** *(mentally, emotionally)* estar trastornado(a) *or* perturbado(a) (b) *(concerned, worried)* inquieto(a), preocupado(a); **I was d. by this turn of events** me inquietó el cariz que estaban tomando los acontecimientos (c) *(interrupted) (night, sleep)* agitado(a)

disturbing [dɪs'tɜːbɪŋ] *adj* (a) *(worrying)* preocupante (b) *(upsetting)* perturbador(ora); **some viewers may find these scenes d.** estas escenas pueden herir la sensibilidad de algunos espectadores

disturbingly [dɪs'tɜːbɪŋlɪ] *adv* **the level of pollution is d. high** el (alto) nivel de contaminación es preocupante; **the crime rate has risen d. fast** el número de delitos está creciendo de manera preocupante

disulphide, *US* **disulfide** [daɪ'sʌlfaɪd] *n Chem* disulfuro *m*

disunite [dɪsjuː'naɪt] *vt* desunir, separar

disunited [dɪsjuː'naɪtɪd] *adj* desunido(a)

disunity [dɪs'juːnɪtɪ] *n* desunión *f*

disuse [dɪs'juːs] *n* falta *f* de uso; **the machine rusted from d.** la máquina se oxidó por falta de uso; **to fall into d.** caer en desuso

disused [dɪs'juːzd] *adj (machine)* en desuso; *(public building)* vacío(a); *(mine, well, railway line)* abandonado(a)

disyllabic, dissyllabic [dɪsɪ'læbɪk] *adj* bisílabo(a)

disyllable, dissyllable [dɪ'sɪləbəl] *n* palabra *f* bisílaba

ditch [dɪtʃ] **1** *n* zanja *f*; *(at roadside)* cuneta *f*; *(as defence)* foso *m*
2 *vt* (a) *Fam (get rid of) (car, useless object)* deshacerse de; *(girlfriend, boyfriend)* plantar; *(plan, idea)* descartar (b) *Av* **to d. a plane** amerizar, hacer un amerizaje forzoso
3 *vi Fam (plane)* amerizar

dither ['dɪðə(r)] *Fam* **1** *n* **to be all of a d., to be in a d.** aturrullarse
2 *vi (be indecisive)* vacilar (**about** *or* **over** acerca de); **stop dithering (about)!** *(decide)* ¡decídete ya!; *(make a start)* ¡deja de vacilar!

ditherer ['dɪðərə(r)] *n Fam* **he's such a terrible d.** es superindeciso

ditransitive [daɪ'trænsɪtɪv] *adj Gram* ditransitivo(a), doble transitivo(a)

ditto ['dɪtəʊ] *adv* ídem; *Fam* **I'm hungry – d.** tengo hambre – ídem (de ídem) ►► ***d. marks*** comillas *fpl* de repetición

ditty ['dɪtɪ] *n Fam* tonadilla *f*

diuretic [daɪjʊ'retɪk] **1** *n* diurético *m*
2 *adj* diurético(a)

diurnal [daɪ'ɜːnəl] *adj* (a) *Literary (daily)* diario(a) (b) *Zool (animal)* diurno(a)

div [dɪv] *n Br Fam* estúpido(a) *m,f*

diva ['di:və] *n* diva *f*

divan [dɪ'væn] *n* (**a**) *(sofa)* diván *m* (**b**) ***d. bed*** cama *f* turca

dive [daɪv] **1** *n* (**a**) *(from poolside, diving board)* salto *m* de cabeza; *(of diver, submarine)* inmersión *f*
(**b**) *(of plane, bird) Esp* picado *m, Am* picada *f*; **the plane went into a d.** el avión se lanzó en *Esp* picado *orAm* picada
(**c**) *Fam (sudden movement)* **to make a d. for sth** lanzarse hacia algo; **to make a d. for the exit** salir corriendo hacia la salida; **I made a d. for the vase** *(to stop it breaking)* me lancé a recoger el jarrón
(**d**) *Fam Pej (place)* antro *m*
(**e**) *(in soccer) (by goalkeeper)* estirada *f*; **it was a blatant d.** *(to gain penalty)* se tiró descaradamente
(**f**) *Fam (in boxing)* **to take a d.** dejarse ganar
2 *vi* (*pt US* **dove** [dəʊv]) (**a**) *(from poolside, diving board)* tirarse de cabeza; *(scuba-diver)* bucear; *(deep-sea diver, submarine)* sumergirse; **to d. for clams/pearls** recoger almejas/perlas buceando
(**b**) *(aircraft, bird)* lanzarse en *Esp* picado *orAm* picada
(**c**) *(move quickly)* lanzarse; **the rabbit dived down its hole** el conejo se metió disparado en su madriguera; **she dived under the bed** se metió a toda prisa debajo de la cama; **to d. for cover** ponerse a cubierto; **she dived out of sight** salió disparada a esconderse; **he dived under the covers and shut his eyes** se metió corriendo bajo las mantas y cerró los ojos
(**d**) *(reach for quickly)* **he dived for his camera** se lanzó a por su cámara; **he dived into his pocket** se apresuró a meter la mano en el bolsillo
(**e**) *(in soccer) (goalkeeper)* hacer *or* realizar una estirada; *(to gain penalty)* tirarse (a la piscina)

► **dive in** *vi* (**a**) *(swimmer)* tirarse de cabeza (**b**) *Fam* **d. in!** *(eat)* ¡empieza! (**c**) *Fam (start immediately)* lanzarse

dive-bomb ['daɪvbɒm] *vt* bombardear (cayendo) en *Esp* picado *or Am* picada

dive-bomber ['daɪvbɒmə(r)] *n* bombardero *m (tipo Stuka)*

diver ['daɪvə(r)] *n* (**a**) *(person) (from diving board)* saltador(ora) *m,f* de trampolín; *(with scuba apparatus)* submarinista *mf*, buzo *m*; *(deep-sea)* buzo *m*; **pearl/clam d.** pescador de perlas/almejas (**b**) *(bird)* colimbo *m*; **black-throated d.** colimbo ártico; **great northern d.** colimbo grande; **red-throated d.** colimbo chico

diverge [daɪ'vɜ:dʒ] *vi* (**a**) *(rays, lines)* divergir; *(roads)* bifurcarse; **our paths diverged** *(in life)* nuestros caminos se separaron (**b**) *(opinions, persons)* discrepar, divergir (**from** de); **to d. from the truth** *(story, account)* alejarse de la verdad

divergence [daɪ'vɜ:dʒəns] *n* (**a**) *(of roads, rays, lines)* divergencia *f* (**from** de) (**b**) *(of people, opinions)* discrepancia *f*, divergencia *f*

divergent [daɪ'vɜ:dgənt] *adj* (**a**) *(paths, lines)* divergente (**b**) *(accounts)* discrepante (**c**) *Psy (thinking)* divergente

diverging [daɪ'vɜ:dʒɪŋ] *adj* (**a**) *(paths, lines)* divergente (**b**) *(accounts)* discrepante

divers ['daɪvəz] *adj Archaic or Literary (several)* diversos(as), varios(as)

diverse [daɪ'vɜ:s] *adj* (**a**) *(different from each other)* distinto(a); **they are very d. in their approach** tienen enfoques muy distintos (**b**) *(varied)* diverso(a)

diversification [daɪvɜ:sɪfɪ'keɪʃən] *n Com* diversificación *f* (**into** hacia)

diversify [daɪ'vɜ:sɪfaɪ] *Com* **1** *vt* diversificar
2 *vi* diversificarse; **to d. into software/banking** ampliar el campo de actividades al software/a la banca

diversion [daɪ'vɜ:ʃən] *n* (**a**) *(of traffic, funds)* desvío *m*; *(of river)* desviación *f* (**b**) *(distraction)* distracción *f*; **to create a d.** distraer la atención (**c**) *(amusement)* distracción *f*; **to seek d. from sth** (tratar de) distraerse con algo

diversionary [daɪ'vɜ:ʃənərɪ] *adj (remark, proposal)* para distraer la atención; **to use d. tactics** utilizar una táctica de despiste

diversity [daɪ'vɜ:sɪtɪ] *n* diversidad *f*

divert [daɪ'vɜ:t, dɪ'vɜ:t] *vt* (**a**) *(traffic, river)* desviar (**from** de); **the train was diverted via Birmingham** desviaron el tren por Birmingham; **the plane was diverted to Newark** desviaron el avión a Newark (**b**) *(attention)* desviar (**from** de) (**c**) *Formal (amuse)* **to d. oneself** distraerse

diverting [daɪ'vɜ:tɪŋ] *adj* entretenido(a), distraído(a)

divest [daɪ'vest] *vt Formal* (**a**) *(take away from)* **to d. sb of sth** despojar a alguien de algo (**b**) **to d. oneself of** *(coat, clothes)* despojarse de

divestiture [daɪ'vestɪtʃə(r)], **divestment** [daɪ'vestmənt] *n US Fin* desinversión *f*; **d. of assets** desinversión de activos

divide [dɪ'vaɪd] **1** *n* (**a**) *(gulf)* división *f*, separación *f*; IDIOM *Euph* **to cross the Great D.** *(die)* pasar a mejor vida (**b**) *US Geog (watershed)* línea *f* divisoria de aguas; **the Great** *or* **Continental D.** la Divisoria Continental
2 *vt* (**a**) *(split up) (property, kingdom, land)* dividir (**between** *or* **among** entre); **to d. sth in two/three** dividir algo en dos/tres partes
(**b**) *Math* dividir; **to d. 346 by 17** dividir 346 entre 17
(**c**) *(share)* repartir (**between** *or* **among** entre); **he divides his time between the office and home** divide su tiempo entre la oficina y su casa
(**d**) *(separate)* separar (**from** de); IDIOM **d. and rule** divide y vencerás
(**e**) *(disunite) (family, party, country)* dividir
(**f**) *Br Pol* **to d. the House on an issue** someter un asunto a votación parlamentaria
3 *vi* (**a**) *(road)* bifurcarse (**b**) *(group, cells)* dividirse; **the class divided into groups** la clase se dividió en grupos (**c**) *Math* dividir; **10 divides by 2** 10 es divisible por 2 (**d**) *Br (parliament)* votar; **the House divided on the issue** el parlamento votó sobre la cuestión

► **divide off** *vt sep* separar (**from** de)

► **divide out** *vt sep* repartir (**between** *or* **among** entre)

► **divide up 1** *vt sep* repartir; **they divided the area/work up between them** se repartieron el área/el trabajo entre ellos
2 *vi (group)* dividirse

divided [dɪ'vaɪdɪd] *adj* (**a**) *Bot* seccionado(a) (**b**) *(disunited) (family, party)* dividido(a); **to be d.** estar dividido(a); **a family d. against itself** una familia dividida; **I feel d. (in my mind)** *or* **my mind is d. on the issue** estoy indeciso(a) respecto a ese asunto ►► *US* ***d. highway*** autovía *f*; ***d. skirt*** falda *f* pantalón

dividend ['dɪvɪdend] *n* (**a**) *(from investment)* dividendo *m*; IDIOM **to pay dividends** resultar beneficioso(a) (**b**) *Math* dividendo *m*

divider [dɪ'vaɪdə(r)] *n* (**a**) *(in room) (thin wall)* tabique *m*; *(screen)* mampara *f* (**b**) *(for files)* separador *m* (**c**) *Math* **(a pair of) dividers** (un) compás *m* de puntas

dividing [dɪ'vaɪdɪŋ] *adj* ***d. line*** línea *f* divisoria; **the d. line between confidence and arrogance** la línea que separa la seguridad en uno mismo y la arrogancia; ***d. wall*** muro *m* divisorio

divination [dɪvɪ'neɪʃən] *n* adivinación *f*

divine [dɪ'vaɪn] **1** *adj* (**a**) *(judgement, worship, intervention)* divino(a); **d. right** derecho divino (**b**) *Fam (wonderful)* precioso(a), divino(a); **you look d. in that dress** estás divina con ese vestido
2 *vt* (**a**) *Literary (conjecture, guess)* adivinar (**b**) *(locate) (water)* descubrir
3 *n Literary (member of clergy)* eclesiástico *m*

divinely [dɪ'vaɪnlɪ] *adv* (**a**) *(by God)* **d. inspired** de inspiración divina (**b**) *Fam (wonderfully)* divinamente

diving ['daɪvɪŋ] *n* (**a**) *(into water) (from poolside, diving board)* salto *m* (de cabeza); *(sporting event)* saltos *mpl* de trampolín; *(scuba diving)* submarinismo *m*, buceo *m*; *(deep sea)* buceo *m* en alta mar; **to go d.** hacer submarinismo ►► ***d. bell*** campana *f* de buzo; ***d. board*** trampolín *m*; ***d. mask*** gafas *fpl* submarinas; ***d. suit*** traje *m* de buceo *or* de hombre rana
(**b**) ***d. header*** *(in soccer)* cabezazo *m* en plancha

divining rod [dɪ'vaɪnɪŋrɒd], **dowsing rod** ['daʊzɪŋrɒd] *n* varilla *f* de zahorí

divinity [dɪ'vɪnɪtɪ] *n* (**a**) *(divine nature, god)* divinidad *f* (**b**) *(subject)* teología *f*

divisible [dɪ'vɪzɪbəl] *adj* divisible (**by** por *or* entre)

division [dɪ'vɪʒən] *n* (**a**) *(separation, in maths)* división *f*; **religious/class divisions** divisiones religiosas/de clase ►► *Math* ***d. sign*** signo *m* de división *or* dividir
(**b**) *(distribution)* reparto *m* ►► ***d. of labour*** división *f* del trabajo
(**c**) *(discord)* discordia *f*; **a d. of opinion** división de opiniones
(**d**) *(unit) (of army, company)* división *f*
(**e**) *(in sports league)* **first/second d.** primera/segunda división
(**f**) *Br Parl* votación *f* ►► ***d. bell*** = campana o timbre que llama a los parlamentarios a la cámara cuando se va a realizar una votación; ***d. lobby*** = cada uno de los dos pasillos que se utilizan para votar en la Cámara de los Comunes

divisive [dɪ'vaɪsɪv] *adj (policy, issue)* disgregador(ora)

divisor [dɪ'vaɪzə(r)] *n Math* divisor *m*

divorce [dɪ'vɔ:s] **1** *n* divorcio *m*; **to file** *or* **to sue for (a) d.** poner una demanda de divorcio; **to get** *or* **to obtain a d.** obtener el divorcio; **to start d. proceedings (against sb)** emprender los trámites de divorcio (contra alguien) ►► ***d. court*** = tribunal especializado en divorcios y anulaciones; ***d. lawyer*** (abogado(a) *m,f*) matrimonialista *mf*; ***d. settlement*** acuerdo *m* de divorcio

2 *vt* (a) *(spouse)* divorciarse de; **you should d. him** deberías divorciarte de él (b) *(separate)* separar (**from** de)

3 *vi (husband and wife)* divorciarse

divorced [dɪ'vɔːst] *adj* (a) *(person)* divorciado(a); **a d. woman** una (mujer) divorciada; **to get d. (from sb)** divorciarse (de alguien) (b) *(separated)* **to be d. from reality** *(person)* haber perdido el contacto con la realidad; *(suggestion, plan)* ser descabellado(a)

divorcee [dɪvɔː'siː] *n* divorciado(a) *m,f*

divorcée [dɪvɔː'seɪ] *n* divorciada *f*

divot ['dɪvət] *n* chuleta *f*, = trozo de tierra y hierba arrancado al jugar al golf

divulge [daɪ'vʌldʒ] *vt* divulgar, dar a conocer

divvy ['dɪvɪ] *n Fam* (a) *(share)* tajada *f*, parte *f* (b) *Br (idiot)* imbécil *mf*, merluzo(a) *m,f*

▶ **divvy up** *vt sep Fam* repartirse

Diwali [diː'wɑːlɪ] *n Rel* = fiesta religiosa hindú celebrada en torno a octubre o noviembre en honor de Lakshmi, la diosa de la fortuna

Dixie ['dɪksɪ] *n US Fam* = el sudeste de Estados Unidos

dixie ['dɪksɪ] *n Br Fam Mil* olla *f*, puchero *m*

Dixieland ['dɪksɪlænd] *Mus* 1 *n* Dixieland *m*

2 *adj* **D. jazz** Dixieland *m*

DIY [diːaɪ'waɪ] (*abbr* **do-it-yourself**) bricolaje *m*; **a D. enthusiast** un amante del bricolaje; **D. store** tienda *or* almacén de bricolaje

dizzily ['dɪzɪlɪ] *adv* (a) *(to rise) (cliffs, prices)* vertiginosamente (b) *Fam (to behave, laugh)* atolondradamente

dizziness ['dɪzɪnɪs] *n* mareos *mpl*; **a spell of d.** un mareo

dizzy ['dɪzɪ] 1 *adj* (a) *(giddy, unsteady) (because of illness)* mareado(a); *(feeling vertigo)* con vértigo; **to be d.** *(because of illness)* estar mareado(a); *(feeling vertigo)* tener *or* sentir vértigo; **you'll make yourself d.** te vas a marear; **just watching them makes me (feel) d.** sólo con mirarlos me mareo ▸▸ ***d. spell*** mareo *m*

(b) *(height, speed)* de vértigo; **to reach the d. heights of government** alcanzar las altas esferas del gobierno

(c) *Fam (foolish)* lelo(a), atontado(a); **a d. blonde** una rubia *or Méx* güera locuela

2 *vt (person)* marear

DJ ['diːdʒeɪ] 1 *n* (a) (*abbr* **disc jockey**) pinchadiscos *mf inv*, disc-jockey *mf* (b) *Fam* (*abbr* **dinner jacket**) esmoquin *m*

2 *vi* pinchar (música)

Djakarta = **Jakarta**

Djibouti [dʒɪ'buːtɪ] *n* Yibuti

djinn [dʒɪn] *n* genio *m*

dl (*abbr* **decilitre(s)**) dl

DLitt [diː'lɪt] *n* (*abbr* **Doctor of Letters**) doctor(ora) *m,f* en filología *(rama de literatura)*

DMs [diː'emz] *npl Br Fam* (*abbr* **Dr Martens**) (botas *fpl*) Dr. Martens *fpl*

DMus [diː'mʌs] *n* (*abbr* **Doctor of Music**) doctor(ora) *m,f* en música

DMZ (*abbr* **demilitarized zone**) zona *f* desmilitarizada

DNA [diːen'eɪ] *n Chem* (*abbr* **deoxyribonucleic acid**) ADN *m* ▸▸ ***D. fingerprinting*** pruebas *fpl* de(l) ADN, pruebas *fpl* de identificación genética; ***D. profile*** perfil *m* de ADN; ***D. test*** prueba *f* del ADN

Dnieper ['niːpə(r)] *n* **the D.** el Dniéper

D-notice ['diːnəʊtɪs] *n Br Pol* = escrito en el que el gobierno pide a un medio de comunicación que no publique una noticia por razones de seguridad

DNS *Comptr* (*abbr* **Domain Name System**) DNS *m*

do[1] [dəʊ] *n Mus* do *m*

DO[2] [duː] 1 *v aux*

> En el inglés hablado, y en el escrito en estilo coloquial, las formas negativas **do not**, **does not** y **did not** se transforman en **don't**, **doesn't** y **didn't**

(*3rd person singular* **does** [dʌz], *pt* **did** [dɪd], *pp* **done** [dʌn]) (a) *(not translated in negatives and questions)* **I don't speak Spanish** no hablo español; **I didn't see him** no lo vi; **don't be so stupid!** ¡no seas tan estúpido(a)!; **don't let's fall out over it** no nos vayamos a pelear por esto; **do you speak Spanish?** ¿hablas español?; **did you see him?** ¿lo viste?; **don't you speak Spanish?** ¿no hablas español?; **didn't you see him?** ¿no lo viste?; **doesn't she look lovely?** ¿verdad que está preciosa?; **doesn't it (just) make you mad the way they get paid double what we do?** es para ponerse hecho una furia que ellos cobren el doble que nosotros; **where did she go?** ¿adónde fue?; **why don't we have a drink?** ¿por qué no nos tomamos una copa?

(b) *(for emphasis)* **she DOES speak Spanish!** ¡sí que habla español!; **I DIDN'T see him!** ¡te digo que no lo vi!; **DO be careful!** ¡ten mucho cuidado, por favor!; *Fam* **DO shut up!** ¡haz el favor de callarte!; **so you DO know her after all** así que después de todo sí que la conoces; **if you DO decide to come...** si finalmente decides venir...; **we do stock them normally, but we're out of them at the moment** normalmente sí tenemos, pero en este momento se nos han agotado; **I did warn you** yo ya te avisé; **you DO say some silly things!** ¡mira que llegas a decir tonterías!, *RP* ¡mirá que decís cada cosa!; **well you did kick him first** fuiste tú la que le dio la patada en primer lugar; **I do believe she lied to me** tengo la sospecha de que me mintió; *Fam* **do I love that song!** ¡pero cómo me gusta esa canción!; *Fam* **boy, did he get angry!** ¡uf!, se puso furioso, *Esp* jo, ¡y cómo se enfadó!, *RP* pa, ¡se requete enojó!

(c) *(substituting main verb)* **she writes better than I do** escribe mejor que yo; **he has always loved her and still does** siempre la ha querido y todavía la quiere; **if you want to speak to him, do it now** si quieres hablar con él, hazlo ahora; **who said that? – I did** ¿quién dijo eso? – yo; **you don't have to worry about that, but I do** tú no tienes por qué preocuparte de eso, pero yo sí; **they wanted to stop, but we didn't** querían parar, pero nosotros no; **I speak Spanish – do you?** hablo español – ¿de verdad?; *Ironic* **I want a bike for Christmas – do you now** *or* **indeed?** para Navidad quiero una bici – ¡no me digas!; **I think it's great, don't you?** me parece genial, ¿y a ti? *or Esp* ¿a que sí? *or RP* ¿no es verdad?; **you look better than you did** ahora tienes mejor aspecto que antes; **I feel concerned for my son, as do most parents** me preocupa mi hijo, como a la mayoría de (los) padres; **switch the light off – I have done** apaga la luz – ya lo he hecho; **why do you feel that way? – I just do!** ¿por qué te sientes así? – ¡no lo sé!; **will they come? – they may do** ¿vendrán? – *Esp* puede que *or Am* talvez sí; **can I have some more tea? – please do** ¿podría tomar más té? – por favor; **do you speak Spanish? – no I don't** ¿hablas español? – no; **you hid my book! – no I didn't** ¡has escondido mi libro! – ¡no!; **did you see him? – (yes) I did** ¿lo viste? – sí; *Fam* **you didn't clean your room – I did so!** no has limpiado tu habitación – ¡claro que la limpié! *or Esp* ¡que sí que la he limpiado!; **I don't like them – nor** *or* **neither do I** no me gustan – a mí tampoco; **I like them – so do I** me gustan – a mí también; **you forgot your keys – so I did** te olvidaste las llaves – es verdad; **I liked her – you didn't!** *(surprised)* me cayó bien – ¿de verdad? *or* ¿en serio?; **I wear a toupee – you do?** *(astonished)* llevo peluquín – ¿en serio?; **oh no you don't!** *(don't do that)* ¡ni se te ocurra!

(d) *(in tag questions)* **you speak Spanish, don't you?** tú hablas español, ¿no?; **John lives near here, doesn't he?** John vive cerca de aquí, ¿verdad?; **you do like her, don't you?** sí que te gusta, ¿no?; **they said they'd come early, didn't they?** dijeron que vendrían temprano, ¿no?; **you didn't see him, did you?** tú no lo viste, ¿verdad?; **you didn't believe her, did you?** no le creíste, ¿a que no? *or* ¿no?; **so you finally passed, did you?** así que finalmente aprobaste, ¿no?; **so you think you can play chess, do you?** ¿así que crees que sabes jugar al ajedrez?

(e) *(in sentences beginning with adverbial phrase)* **not only did you lie...** no sólo mentiste...; **little did I realize...** ni me di cuenta de...

2 *vt*

> **Do**, unido a muchos nombres, expresa actividades, como **to do the gardening**, **to do the ironing** y **to do the shopping**. En este diccionario, estas estructuras se encuentran bajo los nombres respectivos.

(a) *(in general)* hacer; **what are you doing?** ¿qué haces?, ¿qué estás haciendo?; **what do you do (for a living)?** *(what's your job?)* ¿a qué te dedicas?, ¿en qué trabajas?; **to do sth to sb** hacer algo a alguien; **I hate what your job is doing to you** me parece terrible cómo te está afectando el trabajo; **to do sb good** sentar bien a alguien; **to do sb harm** hacer daño *or* mal a alguien; **it just isn't done!** *(is not acceptable behaviour)* ¡eso no se hace!, ¡eso no está bien!; **he's done it!** *(managed it)* ¡lo ha conseguido!; **that does it!** *(expressing annoyance)* ¡esto ya es demasiado!; **we need to do something about this problem** tenemos que hacer algo sobre *or* respecto a este problema; **there's not much we can do (about it)** ¿qué le vamos a hacer?; **what are you doing for New Year?** ¿qué vas a hacer para fin de año?; **what are we going to do for food?** ¿y qué vamos a comer?; **to do sth for sb** hacer algo por alguien; **what can I do for you?** ¿qué desea?, ¿puedo ayudarle en algo?; **that hairstyle does nothing for her** ese peinado no le favorece nada; *Fam* **this music doesn't do anything for me** esta música no me dice nada; *Fam* **she really does something for me** me vuelve loco, me pone a cien; **what do you do with yourself in the evenings?** ¿qué haces por las tardes?; **I was so embarrassed I didn't know what to do with myself** estaba tan avergonzada *or Andes, CAm, Carib, Méx* apenada que no sabía dónde meterme; **he does nothing but sleep, all he does is sleep** no hace más que dormir; PROV **what's done is done** lo hecho, hecho está (**b**) *(carry out) (task, work)* hacer; **you'll have to do it again** tendrás que hacerlo otra vez; **what do I do to start the machine?** ¿qué hago para poner en marcha la máquina?; **it can't be done any quicker** no se puede hacer más rápidamente; **what a foolish thing to do!** ¡que tontería!; **to do the housework** hacer las tareas *or* labores de la casa; **to do the washing-up** lavar *or* fregar (los platos); **I'll do the talking** déjame hablar a mí; *Hum* **don't do anything I wouldn't do** no hagas nada que yo no haría

(**c**) *(clean, wash, brush)* **to do the bathroom** limpiar el baño; **to do the dishes** lavar *or* fregar (los platos); **to do one's hair** peinarse, arreglarse el pelo; **to do one's nails** arreglarse las uñas; **to do one's teeth** lavarse los dientes

(**d**) *(fix, mend)* reparar, arreglar; **I've come to do the roof** he venido a reparar *or* arreglar el tejado

(**e**) *(make, prepare, give, sell)* **they do good food here** aquí hacen muy bien de comer; **do you do carpets?** ¿venden *or* tienen alfombras?; **do you do day trips to France?** *(to travel agent)* ¿organizan visitas de un día a Francia?; **I can do you a ham sandwich** te puedo preparar un *Esp* bocadillo *or Am* sandwich de jamón; *Br* **the pub does a good lunch** en el pub se almuerza bien; **I'll do you a deal on this sale** te voy a hacer un trato *or* precio especial en éste; **do a few copies of this page for me** hazme *or* sácame unas copias de esta página

(**f**) *(study)* hacer, estudiar; *Br (course)* hacer; **to do French/physics** *(at school, university)* estudiar francés/física; **we're doing Cervantes** estamos estudiando *or* dando Cervantes

(**g**) *(solve) (sums, crossword, equation)* hacer

(**h**) *Cin, Theat & TV* **he did Hamlet last year** *(produced, directed)* el año pasado hizo Hamlet; *(played part of)* el año pasado hizo de Hamlet

(**i**) *(finish)* **well that's that done, thank goodness** bueno, ya hemos terminado, menos mal; **have** *or* **are you done complaining?** ¿has terminado ya de quejarte?, ¿ya terminaste de quejarte?; **it will never be done in time** no va a estar terminado a tiempo; **done!** *(in bargain)* ¡trato hecho!

(**j**) *(cook)* hacer; **to do sth in the oven/under the grill** hacer algo al horno/grill; **how would you like your steak done?** ¿cómo quiere el filete *or Andes, RP* bife?; **to be done** *(food)* estar hecho(a)

(**k**) *(speed, distance)* **the motorbike was/we were doing 150 km per hour** la moto iba/íbamos a 150 kms por hora; **this vehicle can do 150 km per hour** este vehículo alcanza los 150 kms por hora; **it does 41 miles to the gallon** *Esp* $\simeq$ consume 7 litros a los cien (kilómetros), *Am* $\simeq$ hace 14,5 kilómetros por litro; **we did the trip in under two hours** hicimos el viaje en menos de dos horas

(**l**) *(serve, attend to)* servir, atender; **I'll just do this gentleman first** serviré *or* atenderé primero a este caballero; *Fam* **they do you very well in this hotel** en este hotel te tratan muy bien

(**m**) *Fam (visit)* hacerse; **to do London** ver Londres; **to do the sights** visitar los lugares de interés; **we did Europe in a week** nos hicimos Europa en una semana

(**n**) *(with time)* **I did a year in China** pasé un año en China; *Fam* **he did ten years for robbery** estuvo diez años en *Esp* chirona *or Andes, RP* cana *or Méx* bote por robo

(**o**) *Fam (impersonate)* **she does a very good Roseanne** imita muy bien a Roseanne; **she did a McEnroe** *(acted like)* se comportó como McEnroe

(**p**) *Fam (take)* **to do drugs** tomar drogas; **let's do lunch** tenemos que quedar para comer

(**q**) *Br Fam (punish, prosecute)* **he was done for fraud** lo juzgaron *or Esp* empapelaron por fraude; **I got done by my dad for smoking** mi padre me regañó *or Esp* echó la bronca *or RP* rezongó por fumar

(**r**) *Br Fam (beat up)* **I'm going to do you!** vas a recibir tu merecido, *Esp* ¡te voy a dar un repaso!, *RP* ¡te la vas a ligar!

(**s**) *Fam (kill)* cargarse a

(**t**) *Fam (cheat)* **I've been done!** ¡me han timado!; **they did me for £100** me timaron 100 libras

(**u**) *Fam (spoil)* **you've really done it now!** ¡ahora sí que la has hecho!; **that's done it, we'll never win now!** ¡la has/hemos *Esp* fastidiado *or Andes, Méx, Ven* fregado, ahora sí que no ganamos!, *RP* ¡ya está, ahora sí que no ganamos más!

(**v**) *Fam (be sufficient or suitable for)* **will that/$20 do you?** ¿te basta *or* alcanza con eso/con 20 dólares?; **those shoes will have to do the children for another year** esos zapatos les tendrán que valer *or* servir a los niños hasta el año que viene; **there, that should do it** bueno *or Esp* venga, con eso ya está

(**w**) *Fam (rob, burgle)* hacer, limpiar

(**x**) *Fam* **to do it (with sb)** *(have sex)* hacerlo (con alguien)

3 *vi* (**a**) *(in general)* hacer; **do as I do** haz lo mismo que yo; **do as your father says** haz lo que dice tu padre; *Fam* **do as I say, not as I do** sigue mi consejo y no hagas lo que yo, *RP* hacé lo que yo digo y no lo que yo hago; **you'd do well to take her advice** harías bien en seguir su consejo; **to do well by sb** comportarse bien con alguien; **they've done well by their daughter** han mirado por el bien de su hija; PROV **do as you would be done by** trata al prójimo como quisieras que te trataran a ti

(**b**) *(perform, get on)* **she did well/badly** le fue bien/mal; **he is doing well/badly at school** le va bien/mal en el colegio; **how am I doing?** ¿qué tal lo estoy haciendo?; **how are you doing?** ¿qué tal te va?, ¿cómo te va?; **how are we doing with the corrections?** *(checking progress)* ¿qué tal van las correcciones?; **how are we doing for time?** ¿qué tal vamos de tiempo?; *Formal* **how do you do?** encantado(a) de conocerlo(la); **how did you do in the interview?** ¿qué tal te salió la entrevista?, *RP* ¿cómo te fue en la entrevista?; **the tomatoes are doing well this year** los tomates están creciendo hermosos este año; **he has done very well for himself** ha prosperado mucho; **well done!** ¡muy bien!

(**c**) *(referring to health)* **the patient is doing well** el paciente se está recuperando; **how is she doing, doctor?** ¿qué tal va, doctor?; **mother and baby are both doing well** la madre y el niño se encuentran bien

(**d**) *(suffice, be acceptable)* **a kilo should/won't do** un kilo será/no será suficiente; **will £20 do?** ¿será suficiente *or Esp* llegará con 20 libras?; **will this room do?** ¿qué tal le parece esta habitación?; **you may not like it, but it'll just have to do** puede que no te guste, pero tendrás que conformarte; **I've only got a red one – that'll do** sólo tengo uno rojo – ése servirá *or* valdrá; **that'll do nicely** eso vendrá de maravilla; **that'll do!** *(expressing annoyance)* ¡ya basta *or Esp* vale!; **this will never do!** ¡esto es intolerable!; **it doesn't do to insult your boss** no conviene insultar a tu jefe; **it wouldn't do to be late** quedaría mal llegar tarde; **to make do** arreglárselas, apañárselas

(**e**) *(finish)* **hasn't she done yet?** ¿no ha terminado aún?; **I haven't** *or* **I'm not done with you yet** todavía no terminamos, todavía no he acabado contigo

(**f**) *Fam (happen)* **there was nothing doing down at the club** no pasaba nada en el club, *Esp* no había nada de marcha en el club; **nothing doing!** ¡nada de eso!, ¡de eso nada!

4 *n* (**a**) **do's and don'ts** *(rules)* reglas *fpl* básicas

(**b**) *Fam (party, celebration)* fiesta *f*; **he's having a do to celebrate his promotion** va a hacer una fiesta para celebrar su ascenso

(**c**) *Fam (excrement)* **dog** *or* **doggie do** caca *f* de perro

> Debido a la variedad de funciones de **do** como verbo modal, en una conversación en inglés puede muy bien repetirse el verbo con distintas funciones, en oraciones totalmente naturales aunque al hispano hablante le parezcan extrañas. Por ejemplo:
>
> **I think he's quite wrong – oh you do, do you?**
> *creo que no tiene nada de razón – ah sí, ¿eh?*
> **I did think about doing it the way you suggested – well *do* do it that way next time!**
> *sí pensé hacerlo como tú sugeriste – pues la próxima vez sí lo haces así*

▸**do away with** *vt insep* (**a**) *(abolish) (institution, rule, restriction)* suprimir, eliminar (**b**) *Fam (kill)* acabar con; **to do away with oneself** quitarse de en medio

▸**do down** *vt sep Br* (**a**) *(criticize, disparage)* desacreditar, menospreciar; **to do oneself down** minusvalorarse, infravalorarse (**b**) *Fam (cheat)* timar a

▸**do for** *vt insep Fam* (**a**) *(finish off) (person, plan, company)* acabar con; **he's done for** *(he's had it)* está perdido, lo tiene crudo *or* claro (**b**) *Br (exhaust)* agotar; **shopping always does for me** ir de compras siempre me deja agotado(a); **I'm done for!** *(exhausted)* ¡estoy hecho(a) polvo!

▸**do in** *vt sep Fam* (**a**) *(kill)* cargarse, cepillarse; *(beat up)* dar un repaso; **he did himself in** se mató (**b**) *esp Br (exhaust)* **I'm absolutely done in** estoy hecho(a) migas (**c**) *Br (damage)* **to do one's back/knee in** fastidiarse la espalda/rodilla

▸**do out** *vt sep* (**a**) *(decorate)* decorar; **the room was done out in blue** la habitación estaba decorada de azul (**b**) *Br Fam (clean)* limpiar

▸**do out of** *vt sep Fam* **to do sb out of sth** *(deprive)* privar a alguien de algo; *(cheat)* tangar *or* estafar algo a alguien

▸**do over** *vt sep* (**a**) *Br Fam (beat up)* **to do sb over** dar una tunda a alguien (**b**) *Br Fam (rob, burgle)* hacer (**c**) *(redecorate)* **the whole house needs doing over** la casa entera necesita reformas (**d**) *US (repeat)* volver a hacer

▸**do up 1** *vt sep* (**a**) *(fasten)* abrochar; **to do one's buttons up** abrocharse los botones; **do your coat up** abróchate el abrigo; **to do one's shoes** *or* **laces up** atarse los zapatos *or* cordones; **to do one's tie up** hacerse el nudo de la corbata; **do me up, will you?** abróchame, ¿quieres?

(**b**) *(wrap)* envolver

(c) *(improve appearance of)* remozar, renovar; **to do oneself up** *(dress smartly)* arreglarse, *Esp* ponerse guapo(a); **she was all done up** iba toda arreglada; **the house needs a bit of doing up** hay que arreglar un poco la casa

2 *vi (clothes)* abrocharse; **it does up at the side** se abrocha por el costado

▸ **do with** *vt insep* **(a)** *(benefit from)* **I could do with a cup of tea** no me vendría mal una taza de té; **this room could do with being painted** a esta habitación le hace falta *or* no le vendría mal una capa de pintura; **I could have done with some help** no me hubiera venido mal una ayuda

(b) *(expressing involvement)* **it's to do with your husband** tiene que ver con tu marido; **what has that got to do with it?** ¿y qué tiene que ver (con ello)?; **I want nothing to do with him** no quiero tener nada que ver con él; **I had nothing to do with it** no tuve nada que ver con eso; **it has** *or* **it's nothing to do with you** *(not your business)* no es asunto tuyo; **we don't have much to do with the people next door** no tenemos mucha relación con los vecinos de al lado; **we have nothing to do with them any more** ya no tenemos nada que ver con ellos; **he is** *or* **has something to do with the railways** hace algo relacionado con los trenes

(c) *(finish)* **to have done with sth** terminar con algo; **have you done with the scissors yet?** ¿has terminado con las tijeras?; **I'm done with men for ever** no quiero volver a ver a un hombre en mi vida; **I've done with making excuses for her** ya no voy a inventarle más excusas; **let's have done with it!** ¡acabemos de una vez!

(d) *Br Fam (tolerate)* **I can't be doing with people like that** paso de esa clase de gente; **I can't do with** *or* **be doing with you complaining all the time** ya estoy harto(a) de que te quejes todo el rato

▸ **do without** **1** *vt insep (manage without)* pasar sin; **I couldn't do without a computer** no podría pasar sin *Esp* ordenador *or Am* computadora; **I could do without your snide remarks** me sobran *or* puedes ahorrarte tus comentarios sarcásticos; **I could do without having to travel an hour to work** si no tuviera que viajar una hora hasta el trabajo no pasaría nada

2 *vi* **we haven't got any left, so you'll just have to do without** no nos queda ninguno, tendrás que arreglártelas sin él/ellos

---

DOA [di:əʊ'eɪ] *adj Med* (*abbr* **dead on arrival**) **he was D.** cuando llegó al hospital ya había muerto, *Esp* ingresó cadáver

doable ['du:əbəl] *adj Fam* realizable, factible; **is it d. in the time available?** ¿es posible hacerlo en el tiempo que tenemos?

DOB (*abbr* **date of birth**) = fecha de nacimiento

dob [dɒb]

▸ **dob in** [dɒb] *vt sep Austr Fam* delatar, *Esp* chivarse de

Dobermann ['dəʊbəmən] *n* **D. (pinscher)** dobermann *m inv*

doc [dɒk] *n Fam* doctor(ora) *m,f*

docile ['dəʊsaɪl] *adj* dócil

docilely ['dəʊsaɪlɪ] *adv* dócilmente

docility [də'sɪlətɪ] *n* docilidad *f*

dock[1] [dɒk] **1** *n (for ships)* muelle *m*; **to be in d.** *(ship)* estar atracado(a); **the docks** el puerto ▸▸ ***d. strike*** huelga *f* de estibadores; ***d. worker*** estibador *m*

2 *vi* **(a)** *(ship)* atracar **(b)** *(two spacecraft)* acoplarse

dock[2] *n Law* banquillo *m* (de los acusados); *Fig* **to be in the d.** *(government, public figure)* estar en el banquillo

dock[3] *vt* **(a)** *(tail)* recortar **(b)** *(wages)* recortar

dock[4] *n (plant)* acederón *m*, acedera *f*

docker ['dɒkə(r)] *n* estibador *m*

docket ['dɒkɪt] **1** *n* **(a)** *(on parcel) (indicating contents)* etiqueta *f*; *(delivery note)* nota *f* de entrega, *Esp* albarán *m* **(b)** *Br (customs document)* certificado *m* de aduana **(c)** *Br Law (summary)* sumario *m*, expediente *m* **(d)** *US Law (agenda)* orden *m* del día

2 *vt (parcel)* etiquetar

docking ['dɒkɪŋ] *n* **(a)** *(in space)* acoplamiento *m* **(b)** *Comptr* ***d. station*** estación *f* base

dockland ['dɒklænd] *n* barrio *m* portuario; **Docklands** *(in London)* = zona de Londres en la que se concentran grandes empresas, sobre todo de índole financiera

dockside ['dɒksaɪd] *n* **on the d.** en el muelle

dockyard ['dɒkjɑ:d] *n* astillero *m*

Doc Martens [dɒk'mɑ:tənz] *npl Fam* (botas *fpl*) Dr. Martens *fpl*

doctor ['dɒktə(r)] **1** *n* **(a)** *(medical)* médico(a) *m,f*; **good morning, d.** buenos días, doctor; **dear D. Cameron** *(in letter)* Estimado Dr. Cameron; **to go to the d.('s)** ir al médico; **d.'s line** *or* **note** justificante *m* del médico; IDIOM *Fam* **that's just what the d. ordered** me/le/*etc.* viene como anillo al dedo **(b)** *Univ* doctor(ora) *m,f* (**of** en)

2 *vt* **(a)** *Fam (tamper with) (accounts, evidence, text)* amañar; *(photograph)* trucar; *(food wine)* adulterar **(b)** *Br (cat)* castrar, capar

doctoral ['dɒktərəl] *adj Univ* doctoral; **d. candidate** doctorando(a) ▸▸ ***d. thesis*** tesis *f* doctoral

doctorate ['dɒktərɪt] *n Univ* doctorado *m*; **to have/to do a d. in sth** tener/hacer un doctorado en algo

doctoring ['dɒktərɪŋ] *n Fam (profession)* medicina *f*

doctrinaire [dɒktrɪ'neə(r)] *adj* doctrinario(a)

doctrinal [dɒk'traɪnəl] *adj* doctrinal

doctrine ['dɒktrɪn] *n* **(a)** *(religious dogma)* doctrina *f* **(b)** *US (political principle)* doctrina *f*

docudrama ['dɒkjʊdrɑ:mə] *n* docudrama *m*

document **1** *n* ['dɒkjʊmənt] documento *m*; **to draw up a d.** redactar un documento; *Law* **the documents in the case** el dossier (del caso) ▸▸ ***d. holder*** *(for keyboarder)* atril *m*; *Comptr* ***d. reader*** digitalizador *m*, lector *m* de documentos; ***d. shredder*** máquina *f* destructora de documentos; ***d. wallet*** *(of card, plastic)* carpeta *f*

2 *vt* ['dɒkjʊment] **(a)** *(write about, record)* documentar; **it is well documented** está bien documentado; **the first documented case** el primer caso registrado *or* documentado **(b)** *(support with evidence)* documentar

documentarist [dɒkjʊ'mentərɪst] *n Cin & TV* documentalista *mf*

documentary [dɒkjʊ'mentərɪ] **1** *n* documental *m* ▸▸ *Com* ***d. bill*** letra *f* documentaria; ***d. database*** base *f* de datos documental; ***d. evidence*** pruebas *fpl* instrumentales; *Com* ***d. letter of credit*** carta *f* de crédito documentaria

2 *adj* documental

documentation [dɒkjʊmen'teɪʃən] *n* documentación *f*

DOD [di:əʊ'di:] *n* (*abbr* **Department of Defense**) = ministerio de defensa de los Estados Unidos

dodder ['dɒdə(r)] *vi* renquear, caminar *or Esp* andar con paso vacilante

doddering ['dɒdərɪŋ] *adj (walk)* renqueante, vacilante; **d. old fool** viejo chocho

doddery ['dɒdərɪ] *adj* renqueante; **a d. old man** un viejo chocho

doddle ['dɒdəl] *n Br Fam* **it's a d.** es pan comido

dodecagon [dəʊ'dekəgən] *n Geom* dodecágono *m*

dodecahedron [dəʊdekə'hi:drən] *n Geom* dodecaedro *m*

Dodecanese [dəʊdekə'ni:z] *n* **the D.** el Dodecaneso

dodge [dɒdʒ] *n* **1** **(a)** *(movement)* regate *m*, quiebro *m* **(b)** *Fam (trick)* truco *m*; **tax d.** trampa para engañar a Hacienda

2 *vt* **(a)** *(blow, person, bullets, falling rock, ball)* esquivar **(b)** *(responsibility, question)* eludir; *(tax)* evadir; **to d. the issue** eludir *or* esquivar el asunto; **to d. school** faltar a clase, *Esp* hacer novillos, *Col* capar clase, *Méx* irse de pinta, *RP* hacerse la rabona

3 *vi* apartarse bruscamente

Dodgems® ['dɒdgəmz] *npl Br* autos *mpl or* coches *mpl* de choque, *Méx* carritos *mpl* chocones, *RP* autitos *mpl* chocadores; **to have a ride** *or Fam* **go on the D.** montar en los autos de choque

dodger ['dɒdʒə(r)] *n* **he's a bit of a d.** no hace más que zafarse *or Esp* escaquearse

dodgy ['dɒdʒɪ] *adj Br Fam* **(a)** *(dangerous, risky) (area, situation)* peligroso(a), *Esp* chungo(a)

(b) *(untrustworthy, barely legal) (person)* dudoso(a); **a d. business deal** un chanchullo

(c) *(not working properly, unstable) (brakes, weather)* **the engine sounds a bit d.** el motor no suena nada bien; **the ceiling looks a bit d.** el techo tiene toda la pinta de ir a caerse; **my stomach's been a bit d. recently** tengo el estómago hecho una pena últimamente, *Esp* tengo el estómago un poco chungo últimamente

dodo ['dəʊdəʊ] (*pl* **dodos** *or* **dodoes**) *n* dodo *m*; IDIOM **(as) dead as a d.** muerto(a) y bien muerto(a)

DOE [di:əʊ'i:] *n* **(a)** *Formerly* (*abbr* **Department of the Environment**) = ministerio británico del medio ambiente **(b)** (*abbr* **Department of Energy**) = ministerio británico de energía

doe [dəʊ] *n* **(a)** *(deer)* cierva *f* **(b)** *(rabbit)* coneja *f*; *(hare)* liebre *f (hembra)*

doe-eyed ['dəʊaɪd] *adj* de mirada tierna

doer ['du:ə(r)] *n (dynamic person)* persona *f* muy activa; **she is more (of) a d. than a talker** es de las que hablan poco pero hacen mucho

does [dʌz] *3rd person singular of* **do**

doeskin ['dəʊskɪn] *n* cabritilla *f*; **d. gloves** guantes de cabritilla

doesn't ['dʌzənt] = **does not**

doff [dɒf] *vt also Fig* **to d. one's cap to sb** descubrirse ante alguien

dog [dɒg] **1** *n* **(a)** *(animal)* perro(a) *m,f*; *(male fox, wolf)* macho *m* ▸▸ ***d. biscuit*** galleta *f* para perros; ***d. breeder*** criador(ora) *m,f* de perros; ***d. collar*** *(of dog)* collar *m* de perro; *Fam (of cleric)* alzacuello *m*; ***the d. days*** la canícula; ***d. food*** comida *f* para perros; ***d. handler*** adiestrador(ora) *m,f* de perros; ***d. Latin*** latín *m* de cocina, latín *m* macarrónico; ***d. licence*** licencia *f* del perro; ***d. paddle*** *(swimming stroke)* estilo *m* perrito; ***d. racing,*** *Br Fam* ***the dogs*** carreras *fpl* de galgos; ***d. rose*** escaramujo *m*; ***d. sitter*** = persona que cuida del perro de otra que está de viaje; ***d. show*** concurso *m* canino; ***D. Star*** Sirio; ***d. tag*** *(of dog, soldier)* placa *f* de identificación
(b) *Fam (person)* **you lucky d.!** ¡qué potra tienes!; **dirty d.** canalla, perro(a) asqueroso(a)
(c) *Fam Pej (ugly woman)* coco *m*, *Esp* cardo *m*, *Andes, RP* bagre *m*
(d) *US Fam (useless thing)* desastre *m*
(e) IDIOMS **give a d. a bad name (and hang him)** no es fácil desprenderse de la mala reputación; *Br Vulg Hum* **to be the d.'s bollocks** estar de puta madre; *Fam* **to make a d.'s breakfast** *or* **dinner of sth** hacer de algo un desastre, hacer una chapuza con algo; *Fam* **he doesn't have** *or* **stand a d.'s chance** no tiene ni la más remota posibilidad; *Br Fam* **he was dressed up like a d.'s dinner** estaba vestido muy ordinario, *Esp* iba muy hortera, *RP* estaba muy terraja; *Fam* **it's a d.-eat-d. world** es un mundo de fieras; *Fam* **to go to the dogs** irse a pique, hundirse; *Fam* **this country's going to the dogs** el país se está yendo a pique; *Fam* **to lead a d.'s life** llevar una vida de perros; *Fam* **to be a d. in the manger** ser como el perro del hortelano, que ni come ni deja comer; **to work like a d.** trabajar como un(a) condenado(a); *Fam Hum* **I'm going to see a man about a d.** *(going to the toilet)* voy a mudarle el agua al canario *or* a los garbanzos; *(going somewhere unspecified)* voy a dar una vuelta *or Esp* un voltio; PROV **you can't teach an old d. new tricks** a perro viejo no hay tus tus; PROV **every d. has his day** todos tenemos nuestro momento de gloria
2 *vt* (*pt & pp* **dogged**) **(a)** *(follow)* perseguir, seguir; **to d. sb's footsteps** seguir los pasos de alguien **(b)** *(plague)* **she was dogged by misfortune** le perseguía la mala suerte

dogcart ['dɒgkɑːt] *n* = coche de caballos de dos ruedas

doge [dəʊdʒ] *n Hist* dux *m inv*, dogo *m*

dog-ear ['dɒgɪə(r)] **1** *n* doblez *m (en la esquina de una página)*
2 *vt (page)* doblar la esquina de

dog-eared ['dɒgɪəd] *adj* ajado(a), con las esquinas dobladas

dog-end ['dɒgend] *n Br Fam* colilla *f*

dogfight ['dɒgfaɪt] *n* **(a)** *(between dogs)* pelea *f* de perros **(b)** *(between planes)* combate *m* aéreo **(c)** *(between people)* lucha *f* encarnizada

dogfish ['dɒgfɪʃ] *n* lija *f*, pintarroja *f*

dogged ['dɒgɪd] *adj* tenaz, perseverante

doggedly ['dɒgɪdlɪ] *adv* tenazmente, con tenacidad

doggedness ['dɒgɪdnɪs] *n* tenacidad *f*

doggie = **doggy**

doggerel ['dɒgərəl] *n (comical)* poesía *f* burlesca; *(bad)* ripios *mpl*

doggo ['dɒgəʊ] *adv Br Fam* **to lie d.** permanecer escondido(a)

doggone ['dɒgɒn] *exclam US Fam* **d. (it)!** ¡maldita sea!, ¡mecachis en la mar!

doggone(d) ['dɒgɒn(d)] *US Fam* **1** *adj* maldito(a), *Esp* puñetero(a); **I've lost the d. keys** ya he perdido las malditas *or Esp* puñeteras llaves
2 *adv* **it's so d. hot!** ¡vaya un calorazo que hace!

doggy, doggie ['dɒgɪ] **1** *n Fam (in children's language)* perrito *m* ▸▸ ***d. bag*** bolsa *f* para las sobras de la comida
2 *adj* **(a)** *(smell)* a perro **(b)** *(liking dogs)* **he's a d. person** le gustan los perros

doggy-paddle ['dɒgɪpædəl] **1** *n* estilo *m* perrito
2 *vi* nadar al estilo perrito

doghouse ['dɒghaʊs] *n* **(a)** *US (kennel)* perrera *f* **(b)** IDIOM *Fam* **to be in the d.** haber caído en desgracia

dogleg ['dɒgleg] **1** *n* **(a)** *(in corridor)* esquina *f*, ángulo *m*; *(in road)* curva *f* cerrada **(b)** *(golf hole)* hoyo *m* en ángulo
2 *vi (road, corridor)* = hacer una curva muy cerrada; **the hole doglegs to the left** el hoyo hace un ángulo hacia la izquierda

doglike ['dɒglaɪk] *adj (devotion)* perruno(a)

dogma ['dɒgmə] *n* dogma *m*

dogmatic [dɒg'mætɪk] *adj* dogmático(a)

dogmatically [dɒg'mætɪklɪ] *adv* dogmáticamente

dogmatism ['dɒgmətɪzəm] *n* dogmatismo *m*

do-gooder ['duː'gʊdə(r)] *n Fam Pej* = persona idealista que intenta siempre ayudar a los demás, incluso cuando no lo necesitan

dogsbody ['dɒgzbɒdɪ] *n Br Fam* burro *m* de carga; **I'm not your d.** no soy tu criado

dog-tired ['dɒg'taɪəd] *adj Fam* molido(a), hecho(a) polvo *or* puré

dogtooth ['dɒgtuːθ] *n* **(a)** *(pattern)* pata *f* de gallo; **in a d. check** de pata de gallo **(b)** ***d. violet*** *(plant)* diente *m* de perro

dogwood ['dɒgwʊd] *n* cornejo *m*, cerezo *m* silvestre

doh [dəʊ] *n Mus* do *m*

doily, doyly ['dɔɪlɪ] *n* blonda *f*, *RP* carpeta *f*

doing ['duːɪŋ] *n* **(a)** *(work)* **this is his d.** esto es obra suya; **it was none of my d.** yo no he tenido nada que ver; **that takes some d.** eso tiene su trabajo *or* no es ninguna tontería **(b)** **doings** *(activities)* actividades *fpl*

do-it-yourself ['duːɪtjə'self] *n* bricolaje *m*; **a d. enthusiast** un amante del bricolaje

Dolby® ['dɒlbɪ] *n* dolby® *m inv*; **in D. stereo** en estéreo Dolby

doldrums ['dɒldrəmz] *npl* **(a)** *Geog* **the D.** *(zone)* los doldrums, = la zona de las calmas ecuatoriales **(b)** IDIOM **to be in the d.** *(person)* estar con la moral baja, *Am* estar con el ánimo por el piso; *(trade, economy)* estar estancado(a)

dole [dəʊl] *n Br Fam* subsidio *m* de desempleo, *Esp* paro *m*; **to be on the d.** cobrar el subsidio de desempleo *or Esp* paro; **to go on the d.** apuntarse para cobrar el desempleo, *Esp* apuntarse al paro; **to join the d. queue** pasar a engrosar las filas del desempleo *or Esp* paro

▸ **dole out** *vt sep Fam* repartir; *(in small amounts)* repartir con cuentagotas

doleful ['dəʊlfʊl] *adj* triste

dolefully ['dəʊlfʊlɪ] *adv* apesadumbradamente, con tristeza

doll [dɒl] *n* **(a)** *(toy)* muñeca *f*; **to play with dolls** jugar con muñecas ▸▸ *Br* ***d.'s house*** casa *f* de muñecas **(b)** *Fam (attractive woman)* muñeca *f* **(c)** *US Fam (kind person)* encanto *m*

▸ **doll up** *vt sep Fam* **to d. oneself up, to get dolled up** emperifollarse

dollar ['dɒlə(r)] *n* dólar *m*; **to look like a million dollars** ir con una pinta que quita el hipo, ir despampanante; IDIOM *Fam Hum* **the sixty-four-thousand d. question** la pregunta del millón; IDIOM *US* **(it's) dollars to doughnuts that he'll be there** puedes apostar lo que quieras a que estará allí ▸▸ ***d. area*** área *f* del dólar; ***d. bill*** billete *m* de un dólar; *Fam* ***d. diplomacy*** diplomacia *f* del dólar; ***d. sign*** signo *m* del dólar; IDIOM *Fam Hum* **to have d. signs in one's eyes** pensar sólo en el dinero

dollarization [dɒləraɪ'zeɪʃən] *n* dolarización *f*

dolled up [dɒld'ʌp] *adj Fam* **to get d.** emperifollarse

dollhouse ['dɒlhaʊs] *n US* casa *f* de muñecas

dollop ['dɒləp] *Fam* **1** *n (serving)* cucharada *f*
2 *vt* **to d. food out onto plates** servir grandes cucharadas de comida en los platos

dolly ['dɒlɪ] **1** *n* **(a)** *Fam (toy)* muñequita *f* **(b)** *Br Fam Old-fashioned* **d. bird** *(woman)* muñeca *f* **(c)** *Br* ***d. mixtures*** *(sweets)* pastillas *fpl* de goma, *Esp* gominolas *fpl* **(d)** *Cin & TV* plataforma *f* móvil, dolly *f* ▸▸ ***d. shot*** travelling *m*
2 *vi Cin & TV* **to d. in/out** avanzar/retroceder con la plataforma móvil *or* la dolly

dolmen ['dɒlmən] *n (prehistoric monument)* dolmen *m*

dolomite ['dɒləmaɪt] *n* **(a)** *(mineral)* dolomita *f* **(b)** *(rock)* dolomita *f*

Dolomites ['dɒləmaɪts] *n* **the D.** los Dolomitas

dolorous ['dɒlərəs] *adj Literary* doloroso(a), penoso(a)

dolphin ['dɒlfɪn] *n* delfín *m*

dolphinarium [dɒlfɪ'neərɪəm] *n* delfinario *m*

dolphin-watching ['dɒlfɪnwɒtʃɪŋ] *n* observación *f* de delfines; **to go d.** ir a observar delfines

dolt [dəʊlt] *n* estúpido(a) *m,f*, idiota *mf*

domain [də'meɪn] *n* **(a)** *(lands)* dominios *mpl* **(b)** *(area of influence, expertise)* ámbito *m*, campo *m*; **that is outside my d.** eso queda fuera de mi campo **(c)** *Comptr* dominio *m* ▸▸ ***d. name*** nombre *m* de dominio; ***D. Name System*** Sistema *m* de Nombres de Dominio

dome [dəʊm] *n* **(a)** *(on building)* cúpula *f* **(b)** *Literary (of heavens, sky)* bóveda *f*; **the d. of his bald head** su cráneo calvo **(c)** *Fam (head)* coco *m*, *Esp* chola *f*

domed [dəʊmd] *adj* **(a)** *(building)* con cúpula **(b)** *(shaped like a dome) (roof)* abovedado(a); *(forehead)* abombado(a)

Domesday Book ['du:mzdeıbʊk] *n Hist* **the D.** = catastro de Inglaterra realizado por encargo de Guillermo el Conquistador en 1086

domestic [də'mestık] **1** *n* (**a**) *Fam (argument)* riña *f* familiar (**b**) *(servant)* criado(a) *m,f*
2 *adj* (**a**) *(of the home, family)* doméstico(a); **he's a d. sort of person** es muy hogareño(a); **to be in d. service** trabajar en el servicio doméstico ►► ***d. bliss*** felicidad *f* hogareña; ***d. help*** servicio *m* doméstico; *Br* ***d. science*** *(school subject)* economía *f* doméstica; ***d. servant*** criado(a) *m,f*; ***d. violence*** violencia *f* doméstica *or* en el hogar
(**b**) *(animal, pet)* doméstico(a); **d. fowl** aves domésticas
(**c**) *(not foreign) (policy, market, trade)* interior; *(flight, economy)* nacional; **d. sales** ventas domésticas, ventas internas

domesticate [də'mestıkeıt] *vt* (**a**) *(animal)* domesticar (**b**) *Hum (person)* domesticar

domesticated [də'mestıkeıtıd] *adj* (**a**) *(animal)* domesticado(a) (**b**) *Hum* **to be d.** *(person)* estar muy bien enseñado(a)

domestication [dəmestı'keıʃən] *n (of animal)* domesticación *f*

domesticity [dɒmes'tısıtı] *n* vida *f* hogareña *or* doméstica; **the cosy d. of their life** su agradable vida hogareña

domestique [dɒmes'ti:k] *n (in cycling)* doméstico(a) *m,f*

domicile ['dɒmısaıl] *n* (**a**) *Formal (house)* domicilio *m* (**b**) *Law* domicilio *m*

domiciled ['dɒmısaıld] *adj* **to be d. in** estar domiciliado(a) en

domiciliary [dɒmı'sılıərı] *adj Formal (visit)* a domicilio; *(care, services)* domiciliario(a)

dominance ['dɒmınəns] *n* (**a**) *(pre-eminence)* predominio *m*; **the d. of the sport by European athletes** el dominio ejercido en este deporte por atletas europeos (**b**) *Biol (of gene, species)* dominancia *f*

dominant ['dɒmınənt] **1** *adj* (**a**) *(most important) (team, person)* dominante (**b**) *(building, geographical feature)* dominante (**c**) *Biol (species)* dominante; **the d. male/female** el macho/la hembra dominante ►► ***d. gene*** gen *m* dominante (**d**) *Mus* dominante
2 *n* (**a**) *Biol (gene)* gen *m* dominante; *(species)* especie *f* dominante (**b**) *Mus (note)* dominante *f*

dominate ['dɒmıneıt] **1** *vt* (**a**) *(control, be preeminent in)* dominar; **to d. a match** *or* **game** *(of player, team)* dominar un partido; **financial matters dominated the discussion** los asuntos financieros predominaron en la discusión (**b**) *(of mountain, building)* dominar
2 *vi* dominar

dominating ['dɒmıneıtıŋ] *adj (feature, colour)* dominante, predominante; *(personality)* dominante

domination [dɒmı'neıʃən] *n* dominio *m*; **Spain was under Roman d. at the time** en aquella época España se encontraba bajo el dominio de los romanos

domineer [dɒmı'nıə(r)] *vi* dominar; **to d. over sb** someter a alguien

domineering [dɒmı'nıərıŋ] *adj* dominante

Dominica [də'mınıkə] *n* Dominica

Dominican [də'mınıkən] **1** *n* (**a**) *(person from Dominican Republic)* dominicano(a) *m,f* (**b**) *(person from Dominica)* dominicano(a) *m,f* (**c**) *(monk, nun)* dominico(a) *m,f*
2 *adj* (**a**) *(of Dominican Republic)* dominicano(a) ►► ***the D. Republic*** la República Dominicana (**b**) *(of Dominica)* dominicano(a) (**c**) *(monk, nun, order)* dominico(a)

dominion [də'mınjən] *n* (**a**) *Literary (rule, authority)* dominio *m*; **to have** *or* **exercise d. over sb** tener a alguien bajo el dominio de uno (**b**) *(territory)* dominio *m* (**c**) *Formerly (in British Commonwealth)* dominio *m*

domino ['dɒmınəʊ] (*pl* **dominoes**) *n* (**a**) *(for game)* ficha *f* de dominó; **dominoes** *(game)* dominó *m* ►► *Pol* ***the d. effect*** el efecto dominó (**b**) *(cloak, mask)* dominó *m*

Don [dɒn] *n* **the (River) D.** el Don

don[1] [dɒn] *n Br Univ* profesor(ora) *m,f (especialmente de Oxford o Cambridge)*

don[2] (*pt & pp* **donned**) *vt Formal (hat, clothes)* enfundarse, ponerse

donate [də'neıt] *vt* donar; **to d. blood** donar sangre

donation [də'neıʃən] *n* (**a**) *(action)* donación *f* (**b**) *(money, goods or blood given)* donativo *m*, donación *f*; **to make a d.** hacer un donativo

done [dʌn] **1** *pp of* **do**
2 *adj* (**a**) *(finished)* **to get sth d.** hacer algo; IDIOM **d. and dusted: everything should be d. and dusted by the end of the month** todo tiene que estar completamente acabado para fin de mes (**b**) *(fitting)* **the d. thing** lo correcto; **it's not the d. thing** no se hace

doner kebab ['dəʊnəkə'bæb] *n* kebab *m*, = pan de pitta relleno de carne de cordero asada

dong [dɒŋ] *n* (**a**) *(sound of bell)* tolón tolón *m*, (sonido *m* de la) campanada *f* (**b**) *very Fam (penis)* verga *f*, *Esp* polla *f*, *Esp* cipote *m*

dongle ['dɒŋgəl] *n Comptr* llave *f* de hardware, mochila *f*

donjon ['dɒndʒən] *n* torre *f* del homenaje

Don Juan [dɒn'hwɑ:n] *n* donjuán *m*

donkey ['dɒŋkı] *n* (**a**) *(animal)* burro *m*; IDIOM *Fam* **I haven't seen him for d.'s years** hace siglos que no lo veo ►► ***d. jacket*** chaqueta *f or Méx* chamarra *f or RP* campera *f* gruesa de trabajo (**b**) *(person)* burro(a) *m,f* (**c**) *Br Fam (clumsy player)* armario *m*

donkey-work ['dɒŋkıwɜ:k] *n Fam* **to do the d.** *(drudgery)* hacer el trabajo más pesado; *(difficult part)* hacer lo más difícil

donnish ['dɒnıʃ] *adj Br (person, manner, humour)* académico(a), = típico de los profesores universitarios de Oxford y Cambridge

donor ['dəʊnə(r)] *n* (**a**) *(to charity)* donante *mf* (**b**) *(of blood, organ)* donante *mf* ►► ***d. card*** carné *m* de donante; ***d. insemination*** = inseminación artificial con semen procedente de un donante (**c**) *Art* donante *m*

don't [dəʊnt] = **do not**

dontcha, dontcher ['dəʊntʃə] *Br Fam* = **don't you**

don't know ['dəʊnt'nəʊ] *n* (**a**) *(answer)* no sé *m* (**b**) *(person)* = persona que no sabe o no contesta en un cuestionario

donut ['dəʊnʌt] *n US* dónut *m*

doobie ['du:bı] *n Fam* porro *m*

doodah ['du:dɑ:], *US* **doodad** ['du:dæd] *n Fam* chisme *m*, *CAm, Carib, Col* vaina *f*, *RP* coso *m*

doo-doo ['du:'du:] *n US Fam (in children's language)* caca *f*; **to be in deep d.** *(trouble)* estar metido(a) en un lío

doodle ['du:dəl] *Fam* **1** *n* garabato *m*
2 *vt* garabatear
3 *vi* garabatear

doodlebug ['du:dəlbʌg] *n* (**a**) *US (insect)* larva *f* de la hormiga león (**b**) *Br Fam Hist (flying bomb)* bomba *f* volante

doofus ['du:fəs] *n US Fam* idiota *mf*

doohickey ['du:'hıkı] *n US Fam* chisme *m*

doolally [du:'lælı] *adj Br Fam* chiflado(a), *Esp* majara

doom [du:m] **1** *n* (**a**) *(terrible fate, ruin)* fatalidad *f*; **it's not all d. and gloom** no todo es tan terrible (**b**) *Literary (death)* **he fell to his d.** se despeñó y se mató; **thousands were sent to their d.** miles de personas fueron enviadas a la muerte
2 *vt* **to be doomed** *(unlucky)* tener mala estrella; *(about to die)* ir hacia una muerte segura; *(of plan, marriage, expedition)* estar condenado(a) al fracaso; **to be doomed to do sth** estar fatalmente predestinado(a) a hacer algo; **they were doomed to a life of poverty** estaban condenados a vivir una vida de miseria

doom-laden ['du:mleıdən] *adj* funesto(a)

doomsday ['du:mzdeı] *n* día *m* del Juicio Final; **till d.** hasta el día del Juicio Final; **the d. scenario** la más catástrofica de las situaciones

door [dɔ:(r)] *n* (**a**) *(of building, room, vehicle, wardrobe)* puerta *f*; **front d.** *(of house, building)* puerta principal; *(of block of flats)* portal; **back/side d.** puerta trasera/lateral; **there's someone at the d.** están llamando a la puerta; **answer the d.** ve a ver quién llama; **to see sb to the d.** acompañar a alguien a la puerta *or* a la salida; **to show sb the d.** *(ask to leave)* echar a alguien; **to shut the d. in sb's face** dar a alguien con la puerta en las narices; **out of doors** al aire libre; **behind closed doors** *(meet, take decision)* a puerta cerrada; **she lives two doors away** vive a dos portales de aquí; *Theat* **tickets available at the d.** *(sign)* venta de entradas en la puerta ►► ***d. chain*** cadena *f* del cerrojo; ***d. handle*** tirador *m*; ***d. viewer*** mirilla *f*
(**b**) IDIOMS **to lay sth at sb's d.** achacar algo a alguien; PROV **when one d. shuts another opens** cuando una puerta se cierra, se abre otra; **the agreement leaves the d. open for further discussion** el acuerdo deja una puerta abierta a ulteriores negociaciones; **the discovery opens the d. to medical advances** el descubrimiento abre una puerta a nuevos avances en medicina

doorbell ['dɔ:bel] *n* timbre *m*

do-or-die ['du:ɔ:'daı] *adj* **he has a d. approach to any challenge** ante cualquier reto va a por todas

doorframe ['dɔ:freım] *n* marco *m* de la puerta

doorjamb ['dɔ:dʒæm] *n* jamba *f*, montante *m*

doorkeeper ['dɔ:ki:pə(r)] *n* portero(a) *m,f*

doorknob ['dɔ:nɒb] *n* pomo *m*

doorknocker ['dɔ:nɒkə(r)] *n* aldaba *f*, llamador *m*

doorman ['dɔ:mən] *n* portero *m*

doormat ['dɔːmæt] *n* felpudo *m*; IDIOM **to treat sb like a d.** tratar como un trapo *or* pisotear a alguien

doorpost ['dɔːpəʊst] *n* jamba *f*

doorsill ['dɔːsɪl] *n* umbral *m*

doorstep ['dɔːstep] **1** *n* **(a)** *(step)* escalón *m* de entrada; **he stood on the d.** se quedó en el umbral; *Fig* **on one's d.** *(very near)* en la misma puerta; **they're building a huge factory practically on my d.** están construyendo una fábrica enorme prácticamente delante de mi puerta **(b)** *Br Fam (slice of bread)* rebanada *f* gruesa de pan
2 *vt Br* **(a)** *(of canvasser) (district)* = ir haciendo campaña de puerta en puerta en **(b)** *(of journalist)* **he was doorstepped by journalists** había periodistas esperándolo a la puerta de su casa
3 *vi Br (canvasser)* = ir haciendo campaña de puerta en puerta

doorstop ['dɔːstɒp] *n (fixed)* tope *m*; *(wedge)* cuña *f*

door-to-door ['dɔːtə'dɔː(r)] **1** *adj Pol* ***d. canvassing*** = campaña electoral en la que los representantes de los partidos van de casa en casa; ***d. enquiries*** investigación *f* de casa en casa; *Com* ***d. salesman*** vendedor *m* a domicilio; ***d. selling*** venta *f* a domicilio
2 *adv* **(a)** *(to sell)* **to sell sth d.** vender algo a domicilio **(b)** *(to travel)* **the journey takes twenty-five minutes d.** el viaje dura veinticinco minutos de puerta a puerta

doorway ['dɔːweɪ] *n* puerta *f*, entrada *f*; **in the d.** a *or* en la puerta

dopamine ['dəʊpəmiːn] *n Biochem* dopamina *f*

doozy ['duːzɪ] *n US Fam* **a d. of a movie** una película bestial *or Méx* padrísima *or RP* genial; **they had a real d. of an argument** tuvieron una pelotera colosal *or* bárbara

dope [dəʊp] **1** *n* **(a)** *Fam (hashish, cannabis)* costo *m*; *(marijuana)* maría *f* ▸▸ ***d. dealer*** camello *m*
(b) *(for horse, athlete)* droga *f* ▸▸ ***d. test*** *(for athlete)* control *m or* prueba *f* antidoping
(c) *Fam (idiot)* tonto(a) *m,f*, bobo(a) *m,f*, *Am* sonso(a) *m,f*, *Am* zonzo(a) *m,f*
(d) *Fam (news, information)* información *f*; **to give sb the d. on sth** contarle algo a alguien; **have you got any d. on the murder?** ¿sabes algo acerca del asesinato?
(e) *(varnish)* barniz *m*
2 *vt (person, horse)* drogar; *(food, drink)* echar droga en
3 *adj US Fam (excellent)* genial, *Esp* guay, *Andes, CAm, Carib, Méx* chévere, *Méx* padre

▸**dope out** *vt sep US Fam (work out, understand)* entender

dopehead ['dəʊphed] *n Fam* porrero(a) *m,f*, fumeta *mf*

dopey, dopy ['dəʊpɪ] *adj Fam* **(a)** *(stupid)* tonto(a), bobo(a), *Am* sonso(a), *Am* zonzo(a) **(b)** *(not alert)* **I was a bit d.** estaba un poco zombi

doppelgänger ['dɒpəlgæŋə(r)] *n* doble *mf*

Doppler ['dɒplə(r)] *n Phys* ***the D. effect*** el efecto Doppler; ***D. shift*** desplazamiento *m* Doppler

dopy = **dopey**

Dordogne [dɔː'dɔɪn] *n* **the D.** la Dordoña

do-re-mi [dəʊreɪ'miː] *n US Fam (money)* pasta *f*

Doric ['dɒrɪk] **1** *adj Archit* dórico(a)
2 *n Scot* **the D.** = dialecto rural escocés

dork [dɔːk] *n US Fam* petardo(a) *m,f*

dorky ['dɔːkɪ] *adj US Fam (person)* petardo(a); *(clothes)* fuera de onda

dorm [dɔːm] *n Fam* dormitorio *m (colectivo)*

dormancy ['dɔːmənsɪ] *n Formal* **(a)** *(of seed, spore)* vida *f* latente **(b)** *(of volcano)* inactividad *f*

dormant ['dɔːmənt] **1** *adj* **(a)** *(seed, spore)* en estado de latencia **(b)** *(volcano)* inactivo(a) **(c)** *(emotions, ideas)* latente
2 *adv* **to lie d.** permanecer latente

dormer ['dɔːmə(r)] *n* **d. (window)** claraboya *f*

dormice *pl of* **dormouse**

dormie ['dɔːmɪ] *adj (in golf)* **to be d. three** llevar tres golpes de ventaja *(cuando quedan tres hoyos)*

dormitory ['dɔːmɪtərɪ] *n* **(a)** *(in school, institution)* dormitorio *m (colectivo)* ▸▸ ***d. town*** ciudad *f* dormitorio **(b)** *US Univ* ≃ colegio *m* mayor

Dormobile® ['dɔːməbiːl] *n* combi *f*

dormouse ['dɔːmaʊs] (*pl* **dormice** ['dɔːmaɪs]) *n* lirón *m*

dorsal ['dɔːsəl] *adj* dorsal

DOS [dɒs] *n Comptr* (*abbr* **disk operating system**) DOS *m* ▸▸ ***D. prompt*** indicador *m or* señal *f* de DOS

dosage ['dəʊsɪdʒ] *n (amount)* dosis *f inv*; *(directions on bottle)* posología *f*; **to increase the d.** aumentar la dosis

dose [dəʊs] *n* **1** **(a)** *(amount)* dosis *f inv*; *Fig* **in small doses** en pequeñas dosis; **children are fine... in small doses** los niños están bien... para un rato; **with a strong d. of humour** con una buena dosis de humor; IDIOM *Br* **to go through sth like a d. of salts** hacer algo a toda velocidad *or* en dos patadas
(b) *(of illness)* **a d. of flu** una gripe *or Am* gripa
(c) *Fam* **to catch a d.** *(venereal disease)* agarrar una enfermedad venérea
2 *vt Fam* tomar; **to d. oneself (up) with pills** tomarse una fuerte dosis de pastillas

dosh [dɒʃ] *n Br Fam (money) Esp* pasta *f*, *Am* plata *f*, *Méx* lana *f*, *RP* guita *f*

doss [dɒs] *Br Fam* **1** *n* **(a)** *(sleep)* **to have a d.** echarse a dormir *or Esp* sobar **(b)** **it was a d.** *(easy)* fue pan comido, fue coser y cantar
2 *vi* **to d. in a park** dormir *or Esp* sobar en un parque

▸**doss about, doss around** *vi Br Fam* gandulear

▸**doss down** *vi Br Fam* echarse a dormir *or Esp* sobar

dosser ['dɒsə(r)] *n Br Fam* **(a)** *(tramp)* vagabundo(a) *m,f* **(b)** *(lazy person)* vago(a) *m,f* perdido(a) *or Esp* del copón

doss-house ['dɒshaʊs] *n Br Fam* pensión *f* de mala muerte

dossier ['dɒsɪeɪ] *n* dossier *m*, expediente *m*; **to keep a d. on sb** tener a alguien fichado

dot [dɒt] **1** *n* punto *m*; **dots and dashes** *(Morse code)* puntos y rayas; **d., d., d.** *(in punctuation)* puntos *mpl* suspensivos; **on the d.** *(exactly)* en punto; IDIOM *Br Fam* **since the year d.** desde el año catapún *or RP* de ñaupa *or Chile* de ñauca ▸▸ ***d. com (company)*** empresa *f* punto com; *Comptr* ***d. matrix printer*** impresora *f* matricial *or* de agujas
2 *vt* (*pt & pp* **dotted**) **(a)** *(mark with dot)* **to d. an "i"** poner el punto sobre una "i"; IDIOM **to d. the i's (and cross the t's)** dar los últimos toques
(b) *(spot, fleck)* salpicar; **dotted with** salpicado(a) de; **the lake was dotted with boats** el lago estaba salpicado de barcas; **the islands are dotted all round the coast** las islas se hallan esparcidas por toda la costa
(c) *Mus (note)* poner un puntillo a
(d) *Fam* **to d. sb one** *(hit)* darle a alguien

dotage ['dəʊtɪdʒ] *n* **to be in one's d.** estar chocho(a), chochear

dotard ['dəʊtəd] *n* viejo(a) *m,f* chocho(a)

dote [dəʊt]

▸**dote on, dote upon** *vt insep* mimar, adorar

doth [*stressed* dʌθ, *unstressed* dəθ] *Literary or Rel 3rd pers sing of* **do**

doting ['dəʊtɪŋ] *adj (parents, grandparents)* **he has a d. mother** su madre lo adora

dotted line ['dɒtɪd'laɪn] *n* línea *f* punteada *or* de puntos; **to sign on the d.** *(on form)* estampar *or* firmar en la línea punteada *or* de puntos; *Fig* estampar la firma; **tear along the d.** rasgar por la línea punteada *or* de puntos

dotterel ['dɒtərəl] *n* chorlito *m* carambolo

dotty ['dɒtɪ] *adj Fam (person)* chalado(a); **a d. idea** una chaladura; **to be d.** estar chalado(a); **he's d. about her** se le cae la baba con ella

double ['dʌbəl] **1** *n* **(a)** *(of person)* doble *mf*
(b) *Cin & TV (stand-in)* doble *mf*
(c) *(hotel room)* habitación *f* doble
(d) *(drink)* doble *m*
(e) **doubles** *(in tennis)* dobles *mpl*; **a doubles match** un partido de dobles
(f) *Sport* **the d.** *(two titles)* el doblete
(g) *(in snooker, pool)* doblete *m*
(h) *(in baseball)* doble *m*, = bateo que permite llegar a la segunda base
(i) *(in darts)* (tiro *m* al) doble *m*
(j) *(in bridge)* doble *m*
(k) *(in betting)* **d. or quits** doble o nada
(l) **at** *or* **on the d.** *(quickly)* a toda velocidad, corriendo
2 *adj* **(a)** *(twice as much or many)* doble; **it's d. the price/size** tiene el doble de precio/tamaño, cuesta/mide el doble; **her wages are d. mine** gana el doble que yo, tiene el doble de sueldo que yo; **a d. gin/whisky** una ginebra/un whisky doble ▸▸ *Br* ***d. cream*** *Esp* nata *f* para montar, *Am* crema *f* líquida enriquecida, *RP* crema *f* doble; ***d. knitting*** punto *m* doble; ***d. spacing*** doble espacio *m*; ***d. time*** *(pay)* paga *f* doble; **in d. time** *(march)* a paso ligero; *(play music)* a doble tiempo
(b) *(in pair)* **d. three, nine, four, d. two** *(phone number)* treinta y tres, noventa y cuatro, veintidós; **d. m** *(when spelling)* doble eme, dos emes ▸▸ ***d. act*** *(two entertainers)* pareja *f* de humoristas; ***d. bill*** *(at cinema)* programa *m or* sesión *f* doble; *US* ***d. boiler*** olla *f* para

baño María; ***d. booking*** *(in hotel, on plane)* doble reserva *f*; ***d. chin*** papada *f*; ***d. date*** cita *f* de dos parejas; ***d. doors*** puerta *f* doble; *Fin* ***d. entry*** doble entrada *f*; *US Cin* ***d. feature*** *(at cinema)* sesión *f* doble; ***d. figures*** números *mpl* de dos cifras; **inflation is now in d. figures** la inflación ha superado la barrera del 10 por ciento; *Br Univ* ***d. first*** = licenciatura en dos especialidades con las calificaciones más altas; ***d. helix*** doble hélice *f*; *US Fin* ***d. indemnity*** = seguro de vida en el que se paga el doble del capital cuando el asegurado muere por accidente; *US Law* ***d. jeopardy*** = principio de no ser juzgado dos veces por el mismo delito; *Gram* ***d. negative*** doble negación *f*; ***d. parking*** estacionamiento *m or Esp* aparcamiento *m* en doble fila; *Med* ***d. pneumonia*** pulmonía *f* doble; *Br* ***d. saucepan*** olla *f* para baño María; *Fam* ***d. whammy*** mazazo *m* por partida doble; *US* ***d. whole note*** breve *f*; *Br* ***d. yellow line*** = línea doble continua de color amarillo próxima al bordillo que indica prohibición total de estacionamiento

(**c**) *(for, of two people)* doble ►► ***d. bed*** cama *f* de matrimonio, cama *f* doble; ***d. occupancy*** = ocupación de una habitación por dos personas; ***d. room*** habitación *f* doble

(**d**) *(dual) (purpose, advantage)* doble; **to lead a d. life** llevar una doble vida ►► ***d. agent*** agente *mf* doble; ***d. bind:* to be in a d. bind** estar en un dilema; ***d. bluff*** supuesto farol *m*; ***d. cross*** timo *m*; *Br Fam* ***d. Dutch:* to talk d. Dutch** hablar en chino; ***d. exposure*** *(of photograph)* doble exposición *f*; ***d. meaning*** doble sentido *m*; ***d. standard*** doble moral *f*; ***d. take:* to do a d. take** reaccionar un instante más tarde; ***d. vision*** visión *f* doble

(**e**) *Sport* ***d. bogey*** *(in golf)* doble bogey *m*; ***d. dribble*** *(in basketball)* dobles *mpl*; ***d. fault*** *(in tennis)* doble falta *f*; ***d. pump*** *(in basketball)* rectificación *f* en el aire; ***d. salko*** *(in figure skating)* doble salko *m*; ***d. team*** *(in basketball)* dos *m* contra uno

(**f**) ***d. bass*** contrabajo *m*

3 *adv* (**a**) *(twice as much)* el doble; **to charge sb d.** cobrar a alguien el doble; **it costs d. what it did last year** cuesta el doble de lo que costaba el año pasado; **they pay him d. if he works at night** si trabaja por la noche le pagan el doble; **to see d.** ver doble

(**b**) *(in two)* **to fold sth d.** doblar algo por la mitad; **to be bent d.** estar doblado(a) *or* agachado(a)

4 *vt* (**a**) *(multiply by 2)* duplicar; **he doubled my salary** me duplicó el sueldo

(**b**) *(fold)* doblar por la mitad

(**c**) *(in betting, bridge)* doblar; **to d. the stakes** doblar la apuesta

(**d**) *Cin & TV* ser el doble de

(**e**) *Theat* **the cast doubles several of the parts** varios actores hacen más de un papel cada uno

5 *vi* (**a**) *(increase)* duplicarse

(**b**) **to d. as** *(person)* hacer también de; *(thing)* funcionar también como

(**c**) *Cin & TV (stand in)* hacer de doble (**for** de)

(**d**) *Theat (play two roles)* hacer dos papeles; **he doubles as the priest and the servant** hace de cura y de criado

►**double back** *vi (person, animal, vehicle)* volver sobre sus pasos; **the path doubles back on itself** el camino vuelve hacia atrás

►**double up** *vi* (**a**) *(bend)* doblarse; **to d. up with** *or* **in pain** retorcerse de dolor; **to d. up with laughter** troncharse de risa

(**b**) **to d. up as** *(person)* hacer también de; *(thing)* funcionar también como

(**c**) *(share)* compartir

(**d**) *(in betting)* = utilizar el premio de una apuesta para volver a apostar

double-barrelled ['dʌbəl'bærəld] *adj* (**a**) *(shotgun)* de dos cañones (**b**) *(surname)* compuesto(a)

double-blind ['dʌbəl'blaɪnd] *adj (experiment)* a doble ciego

double-book ['dʌbəl'bʊk] *vt (seat, room)* reservar por partida doble; **I've double-booked myself for next Friday** *(doing two things)* he quedado en hacer dos cosas a la vez el viernes que viene

double-breasted ['dʌbəl'brestɪd] *adj (suit, jacket)* cruzado(a)

double-check ['dʌbəl'tʃek] **1** *vt* comprobar de nuevo; **make sure you d. everything** comprueba todo dos veces

2 *vi* comprobar de nuevo

double-click ['dʌbəl'klɪk] *Comptr* **1** *n* doble click *m*

2 *vt* hacer doble click en

3 *vi* hacer doble click (**on** en)

double-clutch ['dʌbəl'klʌtʃ] *vi US Aut* = cambiar de marcha con la técnica del doble embrague

double-cross ['dʌbəl'krɒs] *vt* engañar, traicionar

double-dealer ['dʌbəl'di:lə(r)] *n* tramposo(a) *m,f*

double-dealing ['dʌbəl'di:lɪŋ] *n* doblez *f*, duplicidad *f*

double-decker ['dʌbəl'dekə(r)] **1** *n Br* autobús *m* de dos pisos

2 *adj* (**a**) *Br (bus)* de dos pisos (**b**) *Fam (sandwich)* de dos pisos

double-declutch ['dʌbəldi:'klʌtʃ] *vi Br Aut* = cambiar de marcha con la técnica del doble embrague

double-density disk ['dʌbəl'densɪtɪ'dɪsk] *n* disco *m* de doble densidad

double-edged ['dʌbəl'edʒd] *adj (blade, remark)* de doble filo; IDIOM **to be a d. sword** ser un arma de doble filo, ser una espada de dos filos

double entendre ['du:blɒn'tɒndrə] *n* doble sentido *m*, equívoco *m*

double-entry ['dʌbəl'entrɪ] *n Fin* doble entrada *f*; **d. bookkeeping** contabilidad *f* por partida doble

double-fault [dʌbəl'fɔ:lt] *n (in tennis)* doble falta *f*

double-glazed ['dʌbəl'gleɪzd] *adj* con doble acristalamiento

double-glazing ['dʌbəl'gleɪzɪŋ] *n* doble acristalamiento *m*

double-headed [dʌbəl'hedɪd] *adj* (**a**) *(eagle)* bicéfalo(a) (**b**) *(coin)* de dos caras

doubleheader [dʌbəl'hedə(r)] *n US Sport* dos encuentros *mpl* consecutivos

double-jointed ['dʌbəl'dʒɔɪntɪd] *adj* **to be d.** = tener las articulaciones más flexibles de lo normal de modo que se doblan hacia atrás

double-lock ['dʌbəl'lɒk] *vt* cerrar con dos vueltas (de llave)

double-park ['dʌbəl'pɑ:k] **1** *vt* estacionar *or Esp* aparcar en doble fila

2 *vi* estacionarse *or Esp* aparcar en doble fila

double-quick ['dʌbəl'kwɪk] **1** *adj* **in d. time** *(to move, finish, work)* a toda velocidad

2 *adv* rapidísimamente

double-space [dʌbəl'speɪs] *vt* escribir a doble espacio

double-speak = **double-talk**

doublet ['dʌblɪt] *n Hist* jubón *m*; **d. and hose** calzas y jubón

double-talk ['dʌbəltɔ:k], **double-speak** ['dʌbəlspi:k] *n* equívocos *mpl*, ambigüedades *fpl*; **we asked for a raise and he gave us a lot of d. about bonuses** le pedimos un aumento de sueldo y nos soltó un rollo acerca de primas

doublethink ['dʌbəlθɪŋk] *n* (asunción *f* de) ideas *fpl* contradictorias

doubloon [dʌ'blu:n] *n* doblón *m*

doubly ['dʌblɪ] *adv* (**a**) *(twice as much)* doblemente, por partida doble; **it's d. important that...** es doblemente importante que...; **she's d. careful now** ahora tiene el doble de cuidado (**b**) *(in two ways)* por partida doble; **he's d. wrong, then** en ese caso, se equivoca por partida doble

doubt [daʊt] **1** *n* duda *f*; **to have doubts about sth** tener dudas sobre algo; **I have my doubts** yo tengo mis dudas (al respecto); **to be in d.** *(person)* tener dudas; *(outcome)* ser incierto(a); **we are in no d. as to his competence** no tenemos dudas en cuanto a su competencia; **your ability is not open to** *or* **in d.** no se cuestiona *or* no se pone en duda tu capacidad; **if** *or* **when in d.** en caso de duda; **beyond d.** sin lugar a dudas; *Law* **to prove sth beyond reasonable d.** demostrar algo más allá de toda duda fundada; **no d.** sin duda; **he's very witty – no d.** es muy ingenioso – lo no dudo; **he'll no d. be late** seguro que llega tarde; **there is no d. that...** no cabe duda de que...; **there is no d. about her guilt** no hay duda alguna acerca de su culpabilidad; **I have no d.** *or* **doubts about it** no tengo la menor duda; **I have no d. (that) she's telling the truth** no me cabe la menor duda de que dice la verdad; **there is some d. about her guilt** se tienen dudas acerca de su culpabilidad; **there is now considerable d. about the convictions** ahora se tienen grandes dudas acerca de las condenas; **there is room for d.** caben dudas; **there is room for d. about his honesty** cabe dudar de su honradez; **without (a) d.** sin duda alguna, sin lugar a dudas; **to cast d. on sth** poner en tela de juicio algo, cuestionar algo; **to raise doubts about sth** poner algo en duda; **to raise doubts in sb's mind** hacer dudar a alguien

2 *vt* (**a**) *(think unlikely)* dudar; **I d. it** lo dudo; **I don't d. it** no lo dudo; **I d. (that) he's telling the truth** dudo que diga la verdad; **I d. whether that is the case** dudo que sea así; **I d. if it makes him happy** dudo que le haga feliz

(**b**) *(mistrust)* dudar de; **do you d. me?** ¿acaso dudas de mí?; **I don't d. his honesty** no dudo de su honradez; **she began to d. the evidence of her own eyes** empezó a dudar de lo que había visto con sus propios ojos

3 *vi (have doubts)* tener dudas, dudar

doubter ['daʊtə(r)] *n* escéptico(a) *m,f*

doubtful ['daʊtfʊl] *adj* (**a**) *(uncertain) (person)* dubitativo(a); *(outcome)* incierto(a); **to be d. about sth** tener dudas acerca de algo; **I'm d. about his chances** no estoy seguro de que tenga muchas posibilidades; **it is d.**

whether he will succeed es dudoso que tenga éxito; **she looked d.** se mostró indecisa

(**b**) *(questionable)* dudoso(a); **a joke in d. taste** un chiste de gusto dudoso; **she has rather d. dress sense** su gusto a la hora de vestir es más que dudoso

(**c**) *Fin* ***d. debt*** deuda *f* de cobro dudoso

doubtfully ['daʊtfʊlɪ] *adv* con aire dubitativo, sin demasiada convicción

doubting ['daʊtɪŋ] *adj* escéptico(a), incrédulo(a); **a d. Thomas** un(a) escéptico(a) *or* incrédulo(a)

doubtless ['daʊtlɪs], **doubtlessly** ['daʊtlɪslɪ] *adv* sin duda, indudablemente; **d. he will have something to say about it** seguro que *or* sin duda tendrá algo que decir a todo esto; **Jean will be there, I suppose – d.** me imagino que Jean estará allí – seguro

douche [du:ʃ] **1** *n* (**a**) *(jet of water) (vaginal)* irrigación *f* vaginal; *(rectal)* irrigación *f* rectal (**b**) *(instrument) (vaginal)* irrigador *m* vaginal; *(rectal)* irrigador *m* rectal

2 *vt* irrigar

douche-bag ['du:ʃbæg] *n* (**a**) *(device) (vaginal)* irrigador *m* vaginal; *(rectal)* irrigador *m* rectal (**b**) *US Fam (person)* mal nacido(a) *m,f*, desgraciado(a) *m,f*

dough [dəʊ] *n* (**a**) *(for bread)* masa *f* (**b**) *Fam (money) Esp* pasta *f*, *Esp, RP* guita *f*, *Am* plata *f*, *Méx* lana *f*

doughnut ['dəʊnʌt] **1** *n (with hole)* dónut *m*; *(without hole)* buñuelo *m*

2 *vi (surround speaker)* = en el Parlamento, rodear varios diputados a un orador de su mismo partido para que en televisión parezca que la sala está llena

doughty ['daʊtɪ] *adj Literary* corajudo(a), valiente

doughy ['dəʊɪ] *adj* (**a**) *(in consistency)* pastoso(a), blando(a) (**b**) *(complexion)* pálido(a)

dour [dʊə(r)] *adj* severo(a), adusto(a)

Douro ['daʊrəʊ] *n* **the D.** el Duero

douse, dowse [daʊs] *vt* (**a**) *(soak)* empapar, mojar; **he doused himself with** *or* **in aftershave** se empapó de colonia (**b**) *(extinguish)* apagar

dove[1] [dʌv] *n* (**a**) *(bird)* paloma *f*; **the d. of peace** la paloma de la paz ▸▸ ***d. grey*** gris *m* perla (**b**) *Pol* partidario(a) *m,f* de la negociación *(en política exterior)*

dove[2] *US pt of* **dive**

dovecot(e) ['dʌvkɒt] *n* palomar *m*

dove-grey, *US* **dove-gray** ['dʌvgreɪ] *adj* gris perla *inv*

Dover sole ['dəʊvə'səʊl] *n* lenguado *m*

dovetail ['dʌvteɪl] **1** *vt* (**a**) *(joint)* ensamblar a *or* con cola de milano (**b**) *(combine)* **he managed to d. his plans with hers** consiguió hacer encajar sus planes con los de ella

2 *vi (fit closely)* encajar (**with** *or* **into** en *or* con); **the two projects d. nicely** los dos proyectos se complementan muy bien

3 *n* cola *f* de milano ▸▸ ***d. joint*** (ensambladura *f* de *or* con) cola *f* de milano

dovish ['dʌvɪʃ] *adj Pol (person, speech)* conciliador(ora)

dowager ['daʊədʒə(r)] *n* (**a**) *(noblewoman)* viuda *f (de un noble)* ▸▸ ***d. duchess*** duquesa *f* viuda (**b**) *(grand-looking woman)* señorona *f*, matrona *f* ▸▸ *Fam* ***d.'s hump*** cifosis *f inv*

dowdy ['daʊdɪ] *adj (woman, dress)* soso(a)

dowel ['daʊəl] *n* **d. (pin)** espiga *f*, tubillón *m*

Dow-Jones ['daʊ'dʒəʊnz] *n* **the D. (average** *or* **index)** el índice Dow-Jones

DOWN[1] [daʊn] **1** *prep* (**a**) *(moving from top to bottom)* **to fall d. the stairs** caerse por las escaleras (abajo); **pour it d. the sink** échalo por el *Esp, Méx* fregadero *or Chile, Col, Ven* lavaplatos *or RP* pileta; **to go d. the plughole** colarse por el desagüe; **the rabbit disappeared d. its hole** el conejo desapareció en su madriguera; **she ran her finger d. the page** recorrió hacia abajo la página con su dedo; **we walked d. the hill** bajamos la colina; **she spilled ketchup d. her blouse** se manchó la blusa de ketchup; **tears streamed d. her cheeks** ríos de lágrimas bajaban por sus mejillas

(**b**) *(at the bottom of)* **the kitchen is d. the stairs** la cocina está escaleras abajo

(**c**) *(along)* **it's just d. the road** está a la vuelta de la esquina; **d. the line** *(in tennis)* cerca de la línea de saque; **to go d. the street** ir por la calle; **to look d. the corridor** mirar por el pasillo; **go d. the corridor and turn right** ve hasta el fondo del pasillo y gira a la derecha; **it's halfway d. the corridor** está a mitad de pasillo; **they sailed d. the river** navegaron río abajo; **to work d. a mine** trabajar en una mina; **we don't get many visitors d. our way** no vienen muchos visitantes por aquí; IDIOM **three years d. the line** *or* **road** de aquí a tres años

(**d**) *Br Fam (to, in)* **we're going d. the disco** nos vamos a acercar a la disco, vamos hasta la discoteca; **I've got to go d. the town** tengo que bajar al centro; **he'll be d. the pub** estará en el bar

(**e**) *Fam (inside)* **get this whisky d. you** métete este whisky en el cuerpo

(**f**) *(relating to time)* **d. the years** a través de los años; **d. (through) the ages** a través de los siglos

2 *adv* (**a**) *(with motion)* abajo; **I'll be d. in a minute** bajo enseguida; **come d. here** ven aquí abajo; **the book had fallen d. behind the sofa** el libro se había caído detrás del sofá; **go d. to the basement** baja al sótano; **my trousers keep slipping d.** se me caen los pantalones; **put your bags d. on the floor** deja *or* pon las bolsas en el suelo; **everything was perfect, d. to the last detail** todo estuvo perfecto, hasta el último detalle; **d.!** *(to dog)* ¡tumbado!; **d. with traitors!** ¡abajo *or* fuera los traidores!; *Br Fam* **d. under** en/a Australia y Nueva Zelanda

(**b**) *(with position)* abajo; **it's another 50 metres d.** está 50 metros más abajo; **we're halfway d.** estamos a mitad de descenso; **d. at the bottom of the mountain/page** al pie de la montaña/la página; **d. below** abajo; **d. here/there** aquí/ahí abajo; **further d.** más abajo; **it's on the third shelf d.** está en el tercer estante empezando por encima *or Am* empezando de arriba; **she lives three floors d.** vive tres pisos más abajo; **his office is three doors d. on the left** *(along passage)* su oficina es la tercera puerta a la izquierda; **from the waist d.** de (la) cintura para abajo; **we'll be d. at the mall** estaremos en el centro comercial

(**c**) *(to or at lower level)* **the blinds are d.** las persianas están cerradas *or Esp* echadas *or RP* bajadas; **the price is d.** ha bajado el precio; **all our televisions are d. this month** *(in price)* este mes tenemos rebajados todos los televisores; **inflation is d. on last year** la inflación ha bajado con respecto al año pasado; **interest rates are d. to 5 percent** los tipos *or RP* las tasas de interés han bajado al 5 por ciento; *Fin* **the pound is d. two cents against the dollar** la libra ha bajado dos centavos frente al dólar; **I'm trying to keep my weight d.** estoy intentando no engordar; **could you turn the music d.?** ¿podrías bajar la música?; **everyone from the boss d.** todos, desde el jefe hacia *or* para abajo; **d. to the smallest details** hasta el mínimo detalle

(**d**) *(facing downwards)* hacia abajo; **smooth side d.** con la parte lisa hacia abajo

(**e**) *(on floor, ground)* **you need to put newspaper d.** tienes que poner papel de periódico *or* diario en el suelo; **he was d. for a count of eight** *(boxer)* se levantó cuando ya habían contado hasta ocho

(**f**) *(from city, the north)* **she came d. from Berlin** bajó de Berlín; **she's from d. South** es del Sur; **we drove d. to New Orleans** bajamos en coche *or Am* carro *or CSur* auto hasta Nueva Orleans; *US* **to go d. East** = ir hacia la parte noreste de Estado Unidos, ir hacia el este; *Br Univ* **she went d. from Oxford** *(on vacation)* salió de Oxford *(durante las vacaciones)*; *(graduated)* se licenció por la universidad de Oxford

(**g**) *(downstairs)* **I'll be d. in a minute** bajo en un minuto; **they aren't d. yet** todavía no han bajado

(**h**) *(reduced to)* **I'm d. to my last cigarette** sólo me queda un cigarrillo; **the team was d. to 10 men** el equipo se había quedado con 10 jugadores

(**i**) *(behind, less)* **they are a goal d.** pierden por un gol; **the cashier is £10 d.** al cajero le faltan 10 libras; **he's three minutes d. on the leader** va a tres minutos del líder

(**j**) *(in writing)* **get it d. in writing** *or* **on paper** apúntalo, escríbelo; **I'm not d. on the list** no estoy (apuntado) en la lista; **you're d. to go last** estás apuntado para salir el último; **they've got me d. for the 200 m hurdles** me han apuntado para los 200 metros vallas

(**k**) *(as deposit)* **we paid $100 d.** pagamos un depósito de 100 dólares

(**l**) *(underinflated)* **one of my tyres is d.** tengo una rueda desinflada *or* deshinchada

(**m**) *(indicating responsibility)* **it's d. to her** *(her decision)* ella decide; *(her achievement)* es gracias a ella; **it's d. to you to make the plan succeed** de ti depende que el plan tenga éxito; **our failure is d. to a lack of effort** nuestro fracaso se debe a una falta de esfuerzo

3 *adj* (**a**) *(depressed)* **to be/feel d.** estar/encontrarse deprimido(a)

(**b**) *(not working)* **to be d.** *(computer)* no funcionar; **the network is d.** se ha caído la red; **the lines are d.** no hay línea

(**c**) *(finished)* **one d., two to go!** ¡uno menos, ya sólo quedan dos!

(**d**) *(ill)* **he's d. with the flu** está con gripe *or Col, Méx* gripa

(**e**) *Comptr* ***d. arrow*** flecha *f* abajo; ***d. arrow key*** tecla *f* de flecha abajo

(**f**) *(elevator, escalator)* que baja

(**g**) *(as deposit)* ***d. payment*** desembolso *m or Am* cuota *f* inicial

(**h**) *Fam* IDIOMS **to be d. on sth/sb** haber agarrado *or Esp* cogido manía a algo/alguien, *RP* habérselas agarrado con algo/alguien; **to be**

d. on one's luck no estar de suerte

4 *vt* (a) *(put down)* **to d. tools** *(workers)* dejar de trabajar

(b) *(aircraft, opponent)* derribar

(c) *(drink)* **he downed his beer and left** se terminó la cerveza de un trago y se fue; **he can d. a pint in thirty seconds** se bebe *or* toma una pinta en treinta segundos

5 *n* (a) **downs** *(hills)* colinas *fpl*

(b) *(in American football)* down *m*, = cada uno de los cuatro intentos de avance que tiene el equipo atacante; **first d.** primer down

(c) IDIOM *Fam* **to have a d. on sb** haber agarrado *or Esp* cogido manía a alguien, *RP* habérselas agarrado con alguien

---

down² *n* (a) *(feathers)* plumón *m* (b) *(fine hair on skin)* pelusa *f* (c) *(on plant, fruit)* pelusa *f*

down-and-out ['daʊnən'aʊt] *Fam* 1 *n (tramp)* vagabundo(a) *m,f*, indigente *mf*

2 *adj* **to be d.** ser indigente

down-at-heel ['daʊnət'hi:l] *adj* (a) *(person, appearance)* desastrado(a); *(bar)* destartalado(a); *(district)* pobre, ruinoso(a) (b) *(shoe)* desgastado(a)

downbeat ['daʊnbi:t] 1 *n Mus* primer tiempo *m* del compás

2 *adj* (a) *(gloomy, pessimistic)* triste, pesimista (b) *(restrained)* **to be d. about sth** minimizar algo

downcast ['daʊnkɑ:st] *adj* (a) *(eyes, gaze)* bajo(a) (b) *(person)* deprimido(a), abatido(a); **to be d.** estar deprimido(a) *or* abatido(a)

downer ['daʊnə(r)] *n Fam* (a) *(drug)* calmante *m*, depresor *m* (b) **what a d.!** *(how depressing)* ¡qué palo!; **to be on a d.** estar con la depre; **it was a real d.** fue un buen palo; **the film's a complete d.** la película te deja totalmente hecho polvo

downfall ['daʊnfɔ:l] *n (of government)* caída *f*; *(of person)* perdición *f*; **drink was his d.** la bebida fue su perdición

downfield [daʊn'fi:ld] 1 *adj* hacia adelante

2 *adv* hacia adelante

downgrade ['daʊngreɪd] *vt* (a) *(job)* rebajar de categoría; **he was downgraded to area manager** lo rebajaron de categoría a director de zona (b) *(belittle)* denigrar

downhearted [daʊn'hɑ:tɪd] *adj* desanimado(a), abatido(a); **don't be d.!** ¡no te desanimes!

downhill [daʊn'hɪl] 1 *adj (road)* cuesta abajo ►► ***d. skiing*** (esquí *m* de) descenso *m*

2 *adv also Fig* **to go d.** ir cuesta abajo; IDIOM **it was d. all the way** *(unproblematic)* fue coser y cantar, *RP* fue con viento a favor; *(in continual decline)* fue cuesta abajo

3 *n Sport* (prueba *f* de) descenso *m*

down-home ['daʊn'həʊm] *adj US Fam* hogareño(a)

Downing Street ['daʊnɪŋstri:t] *n* Downing Street

down-in-the-mouth ['daʊnɪnðə'maʊθ] *adj* **to be/look d.** estar/parecer deprimido(a) *or* tristón(ona)

download ['daʊn'ləʊd] *Comptr* 1 *n* descarga *f*

2 *vt* bajar, descargar

3 *vi* descargarse

downloadable [daʊn'ləʊdəbəl] *adj Comptr* descargable ►► ***d. font*** fuente *f* cargable

down-market [daʊn'mɑ:kɪt] 1 *adj* popular, barato(a); **it's a rather d. area** no es una zona elegante

2 *adv* **to move d.** dirigirse a un público más popular

downpipe ['daʊnpaɪp] *n Br* canalón *m*

downplay ['daʊnpleɪ] *vt (significance, importance of sth)* restar importancia a

downpour ['daʊnpɔ:(r)] *n* aguacero *m*, tromba *f* de agua

downright ['daʊnraɪt] 1 *adj* (a) *(utter, complete) (stupidity, dishonesty)* absoluto(a), completo(a); **it's a d. lie!** ¡es completamente falso! (b) *(blunt, frank)* rudo(a)

2 *adv (stupid, untrue)* absolutamente, completamente; **the sales assistant was d. rude** la dependienta estuvo increíblemente maleducada; **it would be d. suicidal!** ¡eso sería completamente suicida!

downriver ['daʊn'rɪvə(r)] *adv (to travel, live)* río abajo

downshift ['daʊnʃɪft] *vi* (a) *US (change gear)* reducir (b) *(change lifestyle)* relajar el ritmo de vida

downside ['daʊnsaɪd] *n* (a) *(underside)* parte *f* de abajo; *US* **d. up** boca abajo (b) *(disadvantage)* inconveniente *m*, aspecto *m* negativo; **on the d., we'll have to sleep in the train** lo malo es que tendremos que dormir en el tren

downsize ['daʊnsaɪz] *Com* 1 *vt (of company)* hacer reajuste de plantilla en, reducir plantilla en

2 *vi* hacer reajuste de plantilla, reducir plantilla

downsizing ['daʊnsaɪzɪŋ] *n Com* reajuste *m* de plantilla

downslope ['daʊnsləʊp] *n* cuesta *f* abajo

Down's Syndrome ['daʊnz'sɪndrəʊm] *n* síndrome *m* de Down

downstage [daʊn'steɪdʒ] *adv Theat* en la parte delantera del escenario; **d. from her** delante de ella; **to stand d. of sb** estar más cerca del público que alguien

downstairs 1 *adj* ['daʊnsteəz] de abajo; **the d. apartment/bathroom** el apartamento/cuarto de baño de abajo

2 *adv* [daʊn'steəz] (a) *(descending stairs)* abajo; **to come/go d.** bajar (la escalera); **she ran/fell d.** corrió/cayó escaleras abajo (b) *(on lower floor)* **he lives d.** vive en el apartamento *or Esp* piso de abajo; **the family d.** la familia que vive en el piso de abajo (c) *Old-fashioned (among the servants)* **what will they think of this d.?** ¿qué va a pensar el servicio?

3 *n* [daʊn'steəz] (a) *(of house)* piso *m* de abajo (b) *Old-fashioned (servants)* el servicio

downstate ['daʊnsteɪt] *US* 1 *adj* del sur del estado; **d. New York** el sur del estado de Nueva York

2 *adv* al sur del estado

downstream [daʊn'stri:m] 1 *adv* (a) *(to live, travel)* aguas abajo (**from** de) (b) *Ind (in production process)* en una fase posterior, aguas abajo

2 *adj (on river)* **the d. villages** los pueblos río abajo

downstroke ['daʊnstrəʊk] *n* (a) *(in engine)* movimiento *m* descendente, *Spec* carrera *f* descendente (b) *(in writing)* trazo *m* hacia abajo

downswing ['daʊnswɪŋ] *n* (a) *Econ* (fase *f* de) contracción *f*, bajón *m* (b) *(in golf)* swing *m* hacia abajo

downtime ['daʊntaɪm] *n Comptr & Ind* paro *m* técnico

down-to-earth ['daʊntə'ɜ:θ] *adj* práctico(a), realista

downtown ['daʊn'taʊn] *US* 1 *n* centro *m* (urbano)

2 *adj* del centro; **d. theatres** teatros del centro; **d. New York** el centro de Nueva York

3 *adv* **he gave me a lift d.** me llevó *or CAm, Méx, Perú* me dio aventón al centro; **to live d.** vivir en el centro

downtrodden ['daʊntrɒdən] *adj* (a) *(oppressed)* oprimido(a) (b) *(grass)* pisoteado(a)

downturn ['daʊntɜ:n] *n Econ* (fase *f* de) contracción *f*, bajón *m*

downward ['daʊnwəd] 1 *adj (movement, path, trend)* descendente; **to take a d. glance** *or* **look at sth** dirigir la mirada hacia abajo para ver algo

2 *adv* = **downwards**

downward-compatible ['daʊnwədkəm'pætəbəl] *adj Comptr* compatible con versiones anteriores

downward(s) ['daʊnwəd(z)] *adv* hacia abajo; **to look d.** mirar hacia abajo; **we will have to revise our estimates d.** tendremos que revisar nuestros cálculos a la baja; **everyone from the president d.** todo el mundo, empezando por el presidente

downwind [daʊn'wɪnd] *adv* en la dirección del viento; **they lived d. from the brewery** el viento solía llevar el olor de la fábrica de cerveza hasta donde vivían

downy ['daʊnɪ] *adj* (a) *(fluffy) (feathers, hair)* sedoso(a); *(chick)* suave (b) *(surface) (leaf, skin)* aterciopelado(a)

dowry ['daʊrɪ] *n* dote *f*

dowse [daʊz] 1 *vi* **to d. for water** buscar agua con varilla de zahorí

2 *vt* = **douse**

dowsing rod = **divining rod**

doyen ['dɔɪən] *n* decano *m*, más veterano *m*

doyenne [dɔɪ'en] *n* decana *f*, más veterana *f*

doyly = **doily**

doz (*abbr* **dozen**) docena *f*

doze [dəʊz] 1 *n* cabezada *f*, sueñecito *m*; **to have a d.** echar una cabezada

2 *vi* dormitar

► **doze off** *vi* quedarse traspuesto(a)

dozen ['dʌzən] *n* docena *f*; **a d. eggs** una docena de huevos; **half a d. eggs** media docena de huevos; **86 cents a d.** 86 centavos la docena; **they're sold by the d.** se venden por docenas; **have some more, there are dozens of them** toma unos cuantos más, tenemos docenas; *Fam* **dozens of times/people** montones de veces/personas

dozenth ['dʌzənθ] *adj* duodécimo(a); *Fam* **for the d. time** por enésima vez

dozy ['dəʊzɪ] *adj Fam* (**a**) *(sleepy)* amodorrado(a) (**b**) *(stupid)* bobo(a), idiota

DP ['di:'pi:] *n* (**a**) (*abbr* **data processing**) proceso *m* de datos (**b**) (*abbr* **displaced person**) desplazado(a) *m,f*

DPhil [di:'fɪl] *n Br* (*abbr* **Doctor of Philosophy**) doctor(ora) *m,f* en filosofía

dpi [di:pi:'aɪ] *n Comptr* (*abbr* **dots per inch**) ppp

DPP [di:pi:'pi:] *n Br* (*abbr* **Director of Public Prosecutions**) ≃ Fiscal *mf* General del Estado

Dr (*abbr* **doctor**) Dr., Dra.; **Dr Jones** *(on envelope)* Dr. Jones; **Dear Dr Jones** *(in letter)* Estimado Dr. Jones

drab [dræb] *adj (colours, clothes)* soso(a), insulso(a); *(person)* gris, soso(a); *(surroundings, atmosphere)* anodino(a)

drabness ['dræbnɪs] *n (of colour, clothes)* sosería *f*; *(of surroundings, atmosphere)* sosería *f*, insulsez *f*

drachma ['drækmə] *n Formerly* dracma *m or f*

draconian [drə'kəʊnɪən] *adj* draconiano(a)

Dracula ['drækjʊlə] *pr n* **(Count) D.** (el conde) Dracula

draft [drɑ:ft] **1** *n* (**a**) *(of letter, proposal, novel)* borrador *m*; **this is only the first d.** esto no es más que el primer borrador ►► *Pol* ***d. bill*** anteproyecto *m* de ley; *Comptr* ***d. mode*** modo *m* borrador; *Comptr* ***d. quality*** calidad *f* borrador; ***d. treaty*** borrador *m* del tratado
(**b**) *Fin* letra *f* de cambio, giro *m*
(**c**) *Mil (detachment) (of troops)* destacamento *m*
(**d**) *US (conscription)* llamada *f* or *Am* llamado *m* a filas, reclutamiento *m* ►► ***d. board*** oficina *f* de reclutamiento; ***d. card*** cartilla *f* de reclutamiento; ***d. dodger*** = persona que se libra de tener que alistarse en el ejército mediante subterfugios
(**e**) *US* = **draught**
(**f**) *US Sport* draft *m*, selección *f* de jugadores; **first round d. pick** *(player)* = jugador escogido en la primera ronda de selección de los drafts
2 *vt* (**a**) *(letter, proposal)* hacer un borrador de; **to d. a bill** redactar un anteproyecto de ley
(**b**) *US Mil* llamar a filas a, reclutar; **he was drafted into the army** lo llamaron a filas

► **draft in** *vt sep (troops, supporters)* movilizar; **I was drafted in to do the washing-up** me encargaron lavar los platos

draft-proof, draftsman *etc US* = **draught-proof, draughtsman** *etc*

drag [dræg] **1** *n* (**a**) *(air resistance)* resistencia *f* del aire
(**b**) *(handicap, hindrance)* carga *f*, lastre *m*; **unemployment is a d. on the economy** el desempleo representa un lastre para la economía
(**c**) *Fam (boring person)* plomo *m*, pelma *mf*; *(boring task)* rollo *m*, lata *f*; **the party was a real d.** la fiesta fue un rollazo; **what a d.!** ¡qué lata!, ¡vaya rollo!
(**d**) *Fam (on cigarette)* chupada *f*, *Esp* calada *f*, *Am* pitada *f*; **to take a d. on a cigarette** dar una chupada a un cigarrillo
(**e**) *(women's clothing)* **he was in d.** iba vestido de mujer ►► ***d. act*** número *m* de transformismo; ***d. artist*** transformista *m*, travestí *m (que viste espectacularmente)*; ***d. queen*** transformista *m*, travestí *m (que viste espectacularmente)*
(**f**) ***d. racing*** = carreras de aceleración en coches preparados; ***d. strip*** = pista para carreras de aceleración en coches preparados
(**g**) *US Fam* **the main d.** la calle mayor *or* principal
(**h**) *US Fam (influence) Esp* enchufe *m*, *Chile* pituto *m*, *Col, Méx, RP, Ven* palanca *f*, *RP* acomodo *m*
2 *vt* (*pt & pp* **dragged**) (**a**) *(pull along ground)* arrastrar; **to d. sth on** *or* **along the ground** arrastrar a alguien por el suelo; IDIOM **they dragged their feet over the decision** se anduvieron con muchos rodeos hasta tomar la decisión; IDIOM **to d. sb's name through the mud** *or* **mire** arrastrar el nombre de alguien por el lodo
(**b**) *Fam (move with difficulty)* **he dragged me to a concert** me llevó a rastras a un concierto; **we eventually dragged ourselves away from the party** finalmente y a regañadientes nos fuimos de la fiesta; **I had to d. the truth out of her** tuve que arrancarle la verdad; **don't d. me into this!** ¡no me metas en esto!; IDIOM **to d. sb through the courts** llevar a alguien a juicio
(**c**) *(trawl) (pond, canal)* dragar; **they dragged the lake for the body** dragaron el lago en busca del cadáver
(**d**) *Comptr* arrastrar; **d. and drop** arrastrar y soltar
(**e**) **to d. the ball back** *(in soccer)* pasar la pelota hacia atrás
3 *vi* (**a**) *(coat, scarf)* arrastrar, ir arrastrando
(**b**) *(movie, conversation)* resultar pesado(a); **the meeting dragged to a close** la reunión terminó por fin; **the minutes dragged by** los minutos transcurrían de manera interminable

► **drag down** *vt sep Fig* **don't let him d. you down with him** no te dejes arrastrar por él

► **drag in** *vt sep* sacar a colación

► **drag on** *vi (meeting, movie)* durar eternamente; **don't let the matter d. on** no dejes que el tema se eternice; **the day dragged on** el día parecía eternizarse

► **drag out** *vt sep (meeting, speech)* alargar innecesariamente

► **drag up** *vt* (**a**) *(refer to)* sacar a relucir
(**b**) *Br Fam Hum* **where were you dragged up?** ¿dónde has aprendido esos modales?

dragnet ['drægnet] *n (in deep-sea fishing)* red *f* de arrastre *or* barredera; *Fig (to catch criminals)* emboscada *f*

dragon ['drægən] *n* (**a**) *(mythological creature)* dragón *m* (**b**) *Fam (fearsome woman)* ogro *m*, bruja *f* (**c**) IDIOMS *Fam* **to chase the d.** *(smoke heroin)* hacerse *or* fumarse un cigarrillo de heroína *or Esp* chino (de caballo)

dragonfly ['drægənflaɪ] *n* libélula *f*, caballito *m* del diablo

dragoon [drə'gu:n] **1** *n Mil* dragón *m*
2 *vt* **to d. sb into doing sth** obligar a alguien a hacer algo

dragster ['drægstə(r)] *n* dragster *m*, = automóvil preparado o modificado para participar en carreras de aceleración en distancias cortas

drain [dreɪn] **1** *n* (**a**) *(for water)* desagüe *m*; *(for sewage)* alcantarilla *f*; *(grating)* sumidero *m*; IDIOM **to go down the d.** *(money, time)* echarse a perder; *(work)* irse al traste; IDIOM **to laugh like a d.** reírse a carcajadas
(**b**) *Med* drenaje *m*
(**c**) *(on strength, resources)* merma *f*, mengua *f* (**on** de); **the space programme is a d. on the country's resources** el programa espacial se lleva muchos de los recursos del país; **all that travelling was a terrible d. on him** tanto viajar lo dejó exhausto
2 *vt* (**a**) *(liquid)* vaciar, quitar (**from** de); *(pond)* desaguar; *(swamp)* drenar; *(oil tank, sink)* vaciar; *(dishes, pasta, vegetables)* escurrir
(**b**) **to d. one's glass** *(drink up)* apurar el vaso
(**c**) *Med* drenar
(**d**) *(strength, resources)* mermar, menguar; **to d. sb of his/her strength** extenuar a alguien; *Fig* **to d. wealth from a country** debilitar la economía de un país; *Fig* **to feel drained** estar extenuado(a)
3 *vi* (**a**) *(liquid)* irse; **the colour drained from her face** se puso pálida, empalideció repentinamente
(**b**) *(sink, river)* desaguar; *(washed dishes, vegetables)* escurrir

► **drain away** *vi (liquid)* irse; *(strength, enthusiasm)* diluirse, agotarse; *(fear, tension)* disiparse

► **drain off 1** *vt sep* (**a**) *(liquid)* quitar, escurrir; *(dishes, vegetables)* escurrir
(**b**) *Med* drenar
2 *vi* escurrirse

drainage ['dreɪnɪdʒ] *n* (**a**) *(on land)* drenaje *m*; **soil with good d.** un suelo con buen drenaje ►► ***d. ditch*** acequia *f* de drenaje (**b**) *(system) (in house)* sistema *m* de desagüe; *(in town)* alcantarillado *m*

drainboard *US* = **drainer**

drained [dreɪnd] *adj Fig (person)* exhausto(a)

drainer ['dreɪnə(r)], **draining board** ['dreɪnɪŋbɔ:d], *US* **drainboard** ['dreɪnbɔ:d] *n* escurridero *m*, escurreplatos *m inv*

drainpipe ['dreɪnpaɪp] *n* tubo *m* de desagüe ►► ***d. trousers, drainpipes*** pantalones *mpl* de pitillo

drake [dreɪk] *n* pato *m*

DRAM ['di:ræm] *n Comptr* (*abbr* **dynamic random access memory**) (memoria *f*) RAM *f* dinámica

dram [dræm] *n* (**a**) *Pharm* = 1,8 gramos (**b**) *Fam (of whisky)* chupito *m*

drama ['drɑ:mə] *n* (**a**) *(art form)* teatro *m*, arte *m* dramático; **Spanish d.** el teatro español ►► ***d. documentary*** documental *m* dramatizado; ***d. school*** escuela *f* de arte dramático
(**b**) *(play)* obra *f* de teatro, drama *m*; *Fig* **to make a d. out of sth** hacer una tragedia de algo
(**c**) *(excitement, tension)* dramatismo *m*; **a moment of high d.** un momento de gran dramatismo; **full of d.** *(film, story)* muy dramático; *Fam Pej* **she's such a d. queen!** ¡es muy teatrera!

dramatherapy ['drɑ:məθerəpɪ] *n Psy* (técnica *f* del) psicodrama *m*

dramatic [drə'mætɪk] *adj* (**a**) *(actor, work)* dramático(a) ►► ***d. irony*** = en una obra de teatro, situación en la que el espectador sabe más que los personajes (**b**) *(change, reduction)* drástico(a); *(increase, rise, event, scenery)* espectacular; *(effect)* dramático(a); **there's no need to be so d. about it** no hay por qué ponerse tan dramático

dramatically [drə'mætɪklɪ] *adv* (**a**) *(suddenly, markedly) (to change, reduce)* drásticamente; *(to increase, rise, improve)* espectacularmente; **d. different** radicalmente distinto (**b**) **to be d. effective** *(scene, entrance)* tener un efecto dramático

dramatics [drə'mætɪks] *npl* (**a**) *Theat* arte *m* dramático, teatro *m* (**b**) *(behaviour)* histrionismo *m*, dramatismo *m* exagerado; *Fam* **OK, cut the d. and calm down** *Esp* vale *or Arg* dale *or Méx* órale, deja de echarle tanto teatro y tranquilízate

dramatis personae ['drɑːmətɪspɜː'səʊnaɪ] *npl Lit* dramatis personae *mpl*, personajes *mpl*

dramatist ['dræmətɪst] *n* dramaturgo(a) *m,f*

dramatization [dræmətaɪ'zeɪʃən] *n* (**a**) *(for theatre, radio, television)* dramatización *f* (**b**) *(exaggeration)* dramatización *f*, exageración *f*

dramatize ['dræmətaɪz] **1** *vt* (**a**) *(novel) (for theatre, radio, television)* dramatizar; **dramatized for radio/TV by...** adaptado para la radio/televisión por... (**b**) *(exaggerate)* **to d. a situation** dramatizar una situación
  2 *vi* dramatizar

dramaturge ['dræmətɜːdʒ], **dramaturgist** ['dræmətɜːdʒɪst] *n Lit* dramaturgo(a) *m,f*

dramaturgy ['dræmətɜːdʒɪ] *n Lit* dramática *f*, dramaturgia *f*

drank *pt of* **drink**

drape [dreɪp] **1** *vt* (**a**) *(adorn) (table, coffin)* cubrir (**with** con); *(room)* adornar (**with** *or* **in** con); **the stage was draped with** *or* **in black** el escenario estaba decorado con telas negras colgadas; **they draped the flag over the coffin** cubrieron el ataúd con la bandera
  (**b**) *(hang)* colgar; **she draped a leg over the chair arm** colgó la pierna por encima del brazo del sillón; **he draped himself over the sofa** se asomó por detrás del sofá con el cuerpo colgando sobre el respaldo
  2 *n US* **drapes** cortinas *fpl*

draper ['dreɪpə(r)] *n Br* mercero(a) *m,f*; **d.'s (shop)** mercería *f*, tienda *f* de confección

drapery ['dreɪpərɪ] *n Br* (**a**) *(goods)* artículos *mpl* de confección, tejidos *mpl* (**b**) *(shop)* mercería *f*, tienda *f* de confección (**c**) *Art (in sculpture, painting)* paños *mpl*

drastic ['dræstɪk] *adj (measure, remedy, effect, decline, rise)* drástico(a), radical

drastically ['dræstɪklɪ] *adv* drásticamente

drat [dræt] *exclam Fam* **d. (it)!** ¡caramba!

dratted ['drætɪd] *adj Fam* dichoso(a), condenado(a); **where's that d. brother of mine?** ¿dónde se ha metido el bobo de mi hermano?

draught, *US* **draft** [drɑːft] *n* (**a**) *(wind)* corriente *f* (de aire); **I can feel a d.** noto una corriente de aire; **there's a terrific d. in here** aquí hay *or* hace una corriente terrible ▸▸ ***d. excluder*** burlete *m* (**b**) *(in fireplace)* tiro *m* (**c**) *(drink)* trago *m*; **on d.** *(beer)* de barril ▸▸ ***d. beer*** cerveza *f* de barril (**d**) *(of medicine)* dosis *f* (**e**) *(of ship)* calado *m* (**f**) ***d. animal*** animal *m* de tiro

draughtboard ['drɑːftbɔːd] *n Br* tablero *m* de damas

draught-proof, *US* **draft-proof** ['drɑːftpruːf] **1** *vt* hacer hermético(a)
  2 *adj* hermético(a)

draughts ['drɑːfts] *n Br (game)* damas *fpl*; **to play d.** jugar a las damas

draughtsman, *US* **draftsman** ['drɑːftsmən] *n* (**a**) *(artist)* delineante *mf* (**b**) *Br (in games)* ficha *f* de damas

draughtsmanship, *US* **draftsmanship** ['drɑːftsmənʃɪp] *n (in artistic drawing)* dibujo *m* (artístico); *(in technical drawing)* dibujo *m* lineal, delineación *f*

draughty, *US* **drafty** ['drɑːftɪ] *adj* **this room/house is a bit d.** en este cuarto/esta casa hay *or* hace bastante corriente

DRAW [drɔː] **1** *n* (**a**) *(in game, argument)* empate *m*; *(in chess)* tablas *fpl*; **the game ended in a d.** el partido acabó en empate
  (**b**) *(for lottery, sporting competition)* sorteo *m*; **the d. will take place tonight** el sorteo se celebrará esta noche; **they are in the top half of the d.** han quedado sorteados en la parte de arriba de los cruces
  (**c**) *(of playing card)* **it's your d.** te toca robar
  (**d**) *(attraction)* atracción *f*; **she's a big d.** tiene mucho gancho
  (**e**) *(of gun)* **to be quick on the d.** desenfundar rápido *or* con rapidez; **to beat sb to the d.** desenfundar más rápido que alguien
  (**f**) *(on cigarette, pipe)* chupada *f*, *Esp* calada *f*, *RP* pitada *f*
  (**g**) *US (gully)* barranco *m*
  (**h**) *(golf shot)* golpe *m* con efecto lateral
  2 *vt* (*pt* **drew** [druː], *pp* **drawn** [drɔːn]) (**a**) *(scene, diagram, map)* dibujar; *(line)* trazar; **to d. a picture of sth** hacer un dibujo de algo; **to d. sb's picture** hacer el retrato de alguien; *Fig* **she drew a vivid picture of events** pintó un vivo retrato de los acontecimientos; **the author has drawn his characters well** el escritor ha retratado bien a sus personajes; *Hum* **do you want me to d. you a map?** ¿te tengo que hacer un esquema?; *Fig* **I d. the line at sharing my bed with him** lo que no pienso hacer es compartir la cama con él; *Fig* **he doesn't know where to d. the line** se pasa de la raya; *Fig* **the agreement draws a line under the dispute** el acuerdo pone fin a la disputa
  (**b**) *(pull, lead) (cart)* tirar de; *(person)* llevar (**towards** hacia); **a carriage drawn by two horses** un carro tirado por dos caballos; **she drew me towards the door** me llevó hacia la puerta; **he drew her towards him in a passionate embrace** la atrajo hacia él, abrazándola apasionadamente; **she drew the shawl around her shoulders** envolvió sus hombros con el chal; **he drew his hand wearily across his forehead** se pasó la mano por la frente con gesto cansado; *Fig* **I won't be drawn into your argument** no pienso meterme en su discusión; *Fig* **let's not get drawn into that argument** no empecemos con esta discusión; *Fig* **to be drawn into a life of crime** verse arrastrado(a) a una vida delictiva; **he barely had time to d. breath** apenas tuvo tiempo de respirar; **to d. a meeting to a close** poner fin a una reunión; **to d. a bow** *(in archery)* tensar un arco; **to d. the blinds** bajar la persiana; **to d. the curtains** *(open)* correr *or* descorrer las cortinas; *(close)* correr *or Esp* echar *or RP* cerrar las cortinas
  (**c**) *(extract) (cork, tooth, nail)* sacar (**from** de); *(pistol, gun)* desenfundar; *(sword)* desenvainar; *Fig (strength, comfort, inspiration)* hallar (**from** en); **he drew a knife on me** me sacó un cuchillo; **to d. water from a well** sacar agua de un pozo; **to d. money from the bank** sacar dinero del banco; **to d. blood** hacer sangre; **his remark had clearly drawn blood** evidentemente su comentario ha hecho mucho daño; **our members are drawn from all walks of life** nuestros socios proceden de diferentes profesiones; *Fig* **she refused to be drawn on the issue** eludió dar detalles sobre el asunto
  (**d**) *(attract)* atraer; **the programme drew attention to the suffering of the refugees** el programa llamó la atención sobre el sufrimiento de los refugiados; **I drew the error to the chairman's attention** hice ver el error al presidente; **to d. attention to oneself** llamar la atención; **to d. a crowd** atraer a una multitud; **my eyes were drawn to his hat** su sombrero me llamó la atención; **to feel drawn to sth/sb** sentirse atraído(a) hacia algo/alguien; **to d. the enemy's fire** atraer el fuego del enemigo; IDIOM **to d. sb's fire** suscitar las críticas *or* iras de alguien
  (**e**) *(tie)* **to d. a game with sb** empatar con alguien
  (**f**) *(choose at random) (card)* tomar, extraer; **I drew the winning ticket** saqué el boleto ganador; **to d. lots** echar a suertes; **they were drawn against** *or* **they drew the champions** les tocó enfrentarse a los campeones; IDIOM **I drew the short straw** me tocó la peor parte, *Am* me tocó bailar con la más fea
  (**g**) *(receive) (salary, pension, benefit)* percibir
  (**h**) *(establish)* **to d. a comparison with sth** establecer una comparación con algo; **to d. a conclusion from sth** sacar una conclusión de algo
  (**i**) *(provoke) (reaction, comment, criticism, laughter)* provocar; *(applause)* arrancar; **the trick drew a gasp of astonishment from the crowd** el truco provocó un grito de sorpresa entre el público; **his confession drew tears from his mother** su confesión hizo brotar lágrimas de los ojos de su madre
  (**j**) *Fin* **to d. a cheque (on)** librar *or* girar un cheque (a cargo de)
  (**k**) **to d. the ball** *(in golf)* golpear la pelota con efecto *(intencionalmente)*
  (**l**) *(disembowel)* destripar
  (**m**) *Tech (wire, rod)* tirar; *(metal, glass sheet)* laminar
  (**n**) *Naut* **the ocean liner draws 8 metres** el transatlántico tiene 8 metros de calado
  3 *vi* (**a**) *(illustrate)* dibujar
  (**b**) *(in game)* empatar (**with** *or* **against** con); **they drew two-two** *or* **two all** empataron a dos
  (**c**) *(move)* **to d. ahead of** *or* **past sb** adelantar a alguien; **they drew alongside us** se pusieron a nuestra altura; **the train drew into the station** el tren entró en *or Am* a la estación; **the crowd drew to one side** la multitud se hizo a un lado; **to d. level with sb** ponerse a la altura de alguien; **the campaign is drawing to an end** *or* **a close** la campaña llega *or* toca a su fin; **to d. to a halt** detenerse, *Am* parar; **to d. near** *or* **close** acercarse, aproximarse
  (**d**) *(choose card, straw)* echar a suertes; **they drew for partners** se echaron a suertes quién iba con quién
  (**e**) *(take out gun)* desenfundar
  (**f**) *(fire, chimney)* tirar
  (**g**) *(tea)* reposar

▸ **draw apart** *vi (separate)* separarse (**from** de)

▸ **draw aside** **1** *vi* apartarse; **I drew aside to let them pass** me aparté para dejarlos pasar
  2 *vt sep (person)* apartar; *(curtain)* descorrer, apartar

▸ **draw away** *vi* (**a**) *(move away) (person, vehicle)* alejarse (**from** de) (**b**) *(move ahead)* adelantarse

▸ **draw back** 1 *vt sep (sheet, veil, hand)* retirar
2 *vi* echarse atrás (**from** de); **the child drew back in fear** el niño retrocedió asustado; *Fig* **to d. back from doing sth** echarse atrás a la hora de hacer algo

▸ **draw down** *vt sep* (**a**) *(blinds)* bajar
(**b**) *(provoke)* provocar; **their policy drew down a storm of protest** su política provocó una ola de protestas

▸ **draw in** 1 *vt sep* (**a**) *(make picture of)* **I'm going to d. the head in next** ahora voy a dibujar la cabeza
(**b**) *(claws)* esconder
(**c**) *(attract)* atraer
(**d**) *(inhale)* aspirar; **to d. in a deep breath** inspirar *or* aspirar profundamente
2 *vi* (**a**) *(move)* **the bus drew in to the kerb** el autobús se detuvo junto a la acera; **the train drew in (to the station)** el tren llegó (a la estación)
(**b**) *(day)* hacerse más corto; **the nights are drawing in** las noches se están alargando, los días se están haciendo más cortos

▸ **draw off** *vt sep* (**a**) *Br (clothing, gloves)* quitarse
(**b**) *(liquid)* extraer
(**c**) *(pursuers, critics)* distraer

▸ **draw on** 1 *vt insep* (**a**) *(resources, savings, experience)* recurrir a
(**b**) *(cigarette, pipe)* dar una chupada *or Esp* calada a
(**c**) *(put on)* ponerse; **he drew on a pair of trousers** se puso unos pantalones
2 *vt sep (entice, encourage)* alentar, espolear
3 *vi* **evening was drawing on** caía la tarde; **winter is drawing on** se está acercando el invierno

▸ **draw out** 1 *vt sep* (**a**) *(remove)* sacar; **the police managed to d. the names out of him** la policía consiguió sacarle los nombres
(**b**) *(money from bank)* sacar
(**c**) *(prolong)* alargar, prolongar
(**d**) *(encourage to talk)* **to d. sb out (on sth)** hacer que alguien suelte a hablar (de algo)
2 *vi* (**a**) *(vehicle)* partir; **the train drew out (of the station)** el tren partió (de la estación)
(**b**) *(days)* hacerse más largo

▸ **draw together** 1 *vt sep (people, objects)* unir; **the child's illness had drawn them together** la enfermedad del niño los había unido
2 *vi (unite)* aunarse

▸ **draw up** 1 *vt sep* (**a**) *(pull)* **to d. up a chair** acercar una silla; **she drew herself up to her full height** se levantó cuan larga era
(**b**) *(will)* redactar; *(plan, itinerary)* diseñar; *(list)* elaborar, confeccionar
(**c**) *(position)* **the troops were drawn up on the hill** las tropas estaban colocadas *or* situadas en la colina
2 *vi (vehicle)* parar, detenerse; **the other boat drew up alongside us** el otro barco se detuvo a nuestro lado

▸ **draw upon** *vt insep (resources, savings, experience)* recurrir a

---

drawback ['drɔːbæk] *n* inconveniente *m*

drawbridge ['drɔːbrɪdʒ] *n* puente *m* levadizo

drawee ['drɔːiː] *n Fin (of cheque)* librado(a) *m,f*

drawer [drɔː(r)] *n* (**a**) *(in furniture)* cajón *m* (**b**) *Fin (of cheque)* librador(ora) *m,f* (**c**) *(sketcher)* dibujante *mf*

drawers [drɔːz] *npl Old-fashioned (for women) Esp* bragas *fpl*, *Esp* braga *f*, *CAm, Carib, Méx* blúmer *m*, *CAm* calzón *m*, *Méx* pantaleta *f*, *RP* bombacha *f*; *(for men)* calzoncillos *mpl*, *Chile* fundillos *mpl*, *Col* pantaloncillos *mpl*, *Méx* calzones *mpl*

drawing ['drɔːɪŋ] *n* (**a**) *(illustration)* dibujo *m*; **to make a d. of sth** hacer un dibujo de algo ▸▸ ***d. board*** tablero *m* de dibujo; IDIOM **it's still on the d. board** *(plan, project)* está todavía en fase de proyecto; IDIOM **back to the d. board!** ¡hay que volver a empezar desde cero *or* el principio!; ***d. paper*** papel *m* de dibujo; *Br* ***d. pin*** *Esp* chincheta *f*, *Am* chinche *f*
(**b**) ***d. room*** *(in house)* sala *f* de estar, salón *m*
(**c**) ***d. power*** *(attractive capacity)* poder *m* de convocatoria
(**d**) *Fin US* ***d. account*** cuenta *f* de depósitos a la vista; ***d. rights*** derechos *mpl* de giro

drawl [drɔːl] 1 *n* acento *m* cansino; **he spoke with a Texan d.** hablaba con un típico acento tejano
2 *vt* arrastrar
3 *vi* arrastrar los sonidos al hablar

drawn [drɔːn] 1 *adj* (**a**) *(face, features)* demacrado(a); **to look d.** tener aspecto demacrado; **d. features** facciones demacradas (**b**) *(game)* empatado(a)
2 *pp of* **draw**

drawn-out ['drɔːn'aʊt] *adj* interminable, sempiterno(a); **a long d. dispute** una disputa sempiterna

drawstring ['drɔːstrɪŋ] *n* cordón *m*; **d. hood/trousers** capucha/pantalón que se ata con un cordón

dray [dreɪ] *n (cart)* carreta *f*, carretón *m*

dread [dred] 1 *n* pavor *m*, terror *m*; **she has a terrible d. of heights** le tiene un pavor tremendo a las alturas; **she lives in d. of her ex-husband** vive aterrorizada por su ex-marido; **he waited in d. for the phone to ring** esperó aterrado a que sonara el teléfono
2 *vt* **she dreaded telling him** la idea de decírselo le aterraba; **she's dreading the journey** la idea del viaje le aterra; **I d. to think!** ¡me da pavor pensarlo!
3 *adj Literary* sobrecogedor(ora)

dreaded ['dredɪd] *adj* temido(a), temible; *Hum* **they brought out the d. holiday slides** sacaron las temidas diapositivas de sus vacaciones

dreadful ['dredfʊl] *adj* (**a**) *(terrible)* espantoso(a), horroroso(a); **to feel d.** *(ill, embarrassed)* sentirse muy mal *or Esp* fatal; **to look d.** tener un aspecto terrible; **how d.!** ¡qué horror! (**b**) *Fam (for emphasis)* **it's a d. bore!** ¡es un aburrimiento total!; **it's a d. shame!** ¡es una vergüenza absoluta!

dreadfully ['dredfʊlɪ] *adv Fam* (**a**) *(very badly)* espantosamente, *Esp* fatal; **the children behaved d.** los niños se portaron muy mal *or Esp* fatal (**b**) *(very)* terriblemente; **I'm d. sorry** lo siento muchísimo

dreadlocks ['dredlɒks], *Fam* **dreads** [dredz] *npl* trenzas *fpl* rastafari

dreadnought ['drednɔːt] *n Hist* acorazado *m*

dreads = **dreadlocks**

dream [driːm] 1 *n* (**a**) *(during sleep)* sueño *m*; **to have a d. (about)** soñar (con); **to have bad dreams** tener pesadillas; **sweet** *or* **pleasant dreams!** ¡que sueñes con los angelitos! ▸▸ ***d. sequence*** *(in movie)* sueño *m*; ***the d. time*** *(Aboriginal)* = mítico periodo en el que, según la tradición aborigen australiana, se formó la tierra y sus pobladores; ***d. world*** mundo *m* de ensueño
(**b**) *(wish, fantasy, ideal)* sueño *m*; **her d. was to become a pilot** su sueño era ser piloto; **the woman of his dreams** la mujer de sus sueños; **my d. house/job** la casa/el trabajo de mis sueños, la casa/el trabajo que siempre soñé; **even in her wildest dreams she never thought she'd win first prize** nunca en la vida hubiera imaginado que iba a ganar el primer premio ▸▸ *Pol* ***a d. ticket*** *(candidates)* un equipo ganador
(**c**) *(daydream)* ensoñación *f*; **he's always in a d.** siempre está con la cabeza en las nubes, siempre está soñando despierto
(**d**) IDIOMS **a d. come true** un sueño hecho realidad; **it worked like a d.** salió a la perfección; **my interview went like a d.** la entrevista me salió a las mil maravillas; *Fam* **a d. of a house** una casa de ensueño; *Fam* **she's a real d.!** ¡es un encanto!, ¡es un sol!; *Fam* **in your dreams!** ¡ya te gustaría a ti!, ¡eso quisieras tú!
2 *vt (pt & pp* **dreamt** [dremt] *or* **dreamed**) (**a**) *(in sleep)* **to d. that...** soñar que...; **she dreamt she was flying** soñó que volaba; **you must have dreamt it** lo debes de haber soñado
(**b**) *(daydream)* soñar, imaginar; **to d. idle dreams** perder el tiempo con fantasías
(**c**) *(imagine)* imaginar, soñar; **I never dreamt (that) you would take me seriously** nunca imaginé que me tomarías en serio
3 *vi* (**a**) *(in sleep)* soñar (**of** *or* **about** con); **I must be dreaming!** ¡debo de estar soñando!
(**b**) *(daydream)* soñar despierto(a); **stop dreaming and get on with your work!** ¡deja de pensar en las musarañas y ponte a trabajar!; **for years she'd dreamt of having a cottage in the country** durante años soñó con tener una casita en el campo; IDIOM *Fam* **d. on!** *(that'll never happen)* ¡ya puedes esperar sentado(a)!; *(that's not the case)* ¡qué va!
(**c**) *Fam (imagine, consider)* **I wouldn't d. of it!** ¡jamás se me ocurriría!; **she'd never d. of complaining** nunca se le pasaría por la cabeza la idea de quejarse

▸ **dream away** *vt sep* **she would d. away the hours watching the clouds float by** se pasaba las horas soñando, mirando pasar las nubes

▸ **dream up** *vt* idear, inventarse; **it's some new scheme the government has dreamt up** es un nuevo plan que se ha sacado de la manga el gobierno; **where did you d. that one up?** ¿de dónde te has sacado eso?

dreamboat ['driːmbəʊt] *n Fam* bombón *m*

dreamer ['driːmə(r)] *n* (**a**) *(idealist, visionary)* visionario(a) *m,f* (**b**) *(daydreamer)* soñador(ora) *m,f*

dreamily ['dri:mɪlɪ] *adv (to act, move, speak)* como en sueños

dreamless ['dri:mlɪs] *adj (sleep)* sin sueños

dreamlike ['dri:mlaɪk] *adj* onírico(a)

dreamt *pt & pp of* **dream**

dreamy ['dri:mɪ] *adj* **(a)** *(dreamlike)* soñador(ora); **the d. look in her eye** su mirada soñadora **(b)** *Fam (wonderful)* de ensueño

dreary ['drɪərɪ] *adj* **(a)** *(bleak) (surroundings, weather)* deprimente **(b)** *(dull) (life, job)* triste, deprimente; *(person)* sombrío(a)

dreck [drek] *n US Fam* **(a)** *(rubbish)* porquería *f*, mierda *f* **(b)** *(excrement)* mierda *f*

dredge [dredʒ] **1** *vt* **(a)** *(river)* dragar; *Fig* **she dredged her memory** rebuscó en su memoria **(b)** *(with flour, sugar)* espolvorear

2 *n (net)* red *f* de arrastre

▸**dredge up** *vt* **(a)** *(from river, canal)* sacar del agua al dragar **(b)** *(scandal, memory)* sacar a relucir

dredger ['dredʒə(r)] *n* **(a)** *(ship)* dragador *m* **(b)** *(for flour, sugar)* tamiz *m*

dregs [dregz] *npl (of drink)* posos *mpl*; **she drank the tea down to the d.** se bebió el té sin dejar ni una gota; *Fig* **the d. of society** la escoria de la sociedad

drench [drentʃ] *vt* empapar (**with** *or* **in** con *or* en); **drenched to the skin** calado(a) hasta los huesos; **to be drenched with sweat** estar empapado(a) de sudor

Dresden ['drezdən] *n* Dresde ▸▸ ***D. china*** porcelana *f* de Dresde

dress [dres] **1** *n* **(a)** *(for woman)* vestido *m*

(b) *(clothing)* traje *m*; **national d.** traje típico (del país); **formal d.** traje formal; **informal d.** vestido informal; **to have good/no d. sense** saber/no saber vestirse, tener/no tener estilo para vestir ▸▸ ***d. circle*** *(in theatre)* piso *m* principal, palco *m* de platea; ***d. code*** normas *fpl* en el vestir, código *m* vestimentario; ***d. rehearsal*** *(of play)* ensayo *m* general; ***d. shirt*** camisa *f* de vestir; ***a d. suit*** un traje de gala; ***d. uniform*** uniforme *m* de gala

2 *vt* **(a)** *(person)* vestir; **to d. oneself, to get dressed** vestirse; **to be dressed in black** ir vestido(a) de negro; **dressed in rags** andrajoso(a), harapiento(a); **dressed as a man** vestida *or* disfrazada de hombre; **dressed as a clown/a witch** *(for a party)* disfrazado(a) de payaso/de bruja; **well/badly dressed** bien/mal vestido(a); IDIOM **she was dressed to kill** iba imponente

(b) *(wound)* vendar

(c) *(salad)* aderezar, *Esp* aliñar; **dressed crab** changurro

(d) *(finish) (stone, timber)* acabar

(e) *Agr (field)* abonar

(f) *(neuter) (animal)* castrar

(g) *Mil* **to d. ranks** alinear a los soldados

3 *vi* **(a)** *(get dressed, wear clothes)* vestirse; **to d. well/badly** vestir(se) bien/mal; **to d. in white** ir vestido(a) de blanco, vestir de blanco

(b) *(dress formally)* **to d. for dinner** ponerse elegante *or* vestirse para la cena

▸**dress down 1** *vt sep (scold)* regañar, *Esp* echar un rapapolvo a

2 *vi (wear casual clothes)* ir vestido(a) con ropa informal

▸**dress up 1** *vt sep* **(a)** *(put on best clothes)* arreglar, vestir de etiqueta; **she was all dressed up, she was dressed up to the nines** llevaba puestas sus mejores galas; IDIOM *Fam Hum* **all dressed up and nowhere to go** compuesta y sin novio

(b) *(disguise)* disfrazar (**as** de *or* como); **it's the same old clichés dressed up as new ideas** son los mismos tópicos de siempre disfrazados de ideas nuevas

(c) *(smarten)* arreglar

2 *vi* **(a)** *(elegantly)* arreglarse, vestirse de etiqueta

(b) *(in fancy dress)* disfrazarse (**as** de)

dressage ['dresɑ:ʒ] *n* doma *f* de caballos

dresser ['dresə(r)] *n* **(a)** *(person)* **a smart/sloppy d.** una persona elegante/descuidada vistiendo, una persona elegante/descuidada en el vestir **(b)** *(in kitchen)* aparador *m* **(c)** *US (in bedroom)* cómoda *f* **(d)** *Theat* ayudante *mf* de camerino

dressing ['dresɪŋ] *n* **(a)** *(putting clothes on)* ***d. gown*** bata *f*; ***d. room*** *Theat* camerino *m*; *Sport* vestuario *m*; ***d. table*** tocador *m* **(b)** *(for wound)* vendaje *m*, gasa *f* ▸▸ *Mil* ***d. station*** puesto *m* de socorro, enfermería *f* **(c)** *(for salad)* aderezo *m*, *Esp* aliño *m* **(d)** *US (stuffing)* relleno *m* **(e)** *Agr (fertilizer)* abono *m*

dressing-down ['dresɪŋ'daʊn] *n* **to give sb a d.** regañar a alguien, *Esp* echar un rapapolvo a alguien

dressmaker ['dresmeɪkə(r)] *n* modisto(a) *m,f*; **d.'s (shop)** taller *m* de costura *or* confección

dressmaking ['dresmeɪkɪŋ] *n* corte *m* y confección

dressy [dresɪ] *adj Fam (clothes, person)* elegante, puesto(a); *(event)* elegante

drew *pt of* **draw**

dribble ['drɪbəl] **1** *n* **(a)** *(saliva)* baba *f* **(b)** *(of blood, oil)* reguero *m* **(c)** *Sport* regate *m*, dribbling *m*

2 *vi* **(a)** *(person, baby)* babear **(b)** *(liquid)* gotear; *Fig* **to d. in/out** *(people)* entrar/salir poco a poco **(c)** *Sport* avanzar con el balón controlado; **to d. past a defender** regatear *or* driblar a un defensa

3 *vt* **(a)** *(trickle)* **he was dribbling milk from his mouth** le salía un hilo de leche de la boca; **be careful with that jug, you're dribbling water everywhere!** ¡cuidado con la jarra, que estás derramando agua por todas partes! **(b)** *Sport (in football)* regatear, driblar

dribbling ['drɪblɪŋ] *n Sport* dribbling *m*

dribs [drɪbz] *npl* **in d. and drabs** poco a poco, con cuentagotas

dried [draɪd] *adj (meat, fish)* desecado(a), en salazón; *(milk, eggs)* en polvo ▸▸ ***d. flowers*** flores *fpl* secas; ***d. fruit*** fruta *f* pasa

drier, dryer ['draɪə(r)] *n* **(a)** *(for hair)* secador *m* **(b)** *(for clothes) (machine)* secadora *f*; *(rack)* tendedero *m*

drift [drɪft] **1** *n* **(a)** *(of current)* movimiento *m*, arrastre *m*; *(of business, conversation)* tendencia *f*; *(of events)* curso *m* ▸▸ ***d. ice*** masa *f* de hielo flotante; ***d. net*** *(for fishing)* red *f* de deriva

(b) *(deviation from course) (of plane, ship)* desviación *f*; **the d. towards war** el inexorable rumbo hacia la guerra

(c) *(meaning) (of person's words)* sentido *m*, idea *f*; *Fam* **I get the d.** ya veo cuál es la idea; *Fam* **if you catch** *or* **get my d.** tú ya me entiendes, tú ya sabes por donde voy

(d) *(of snow)* ventisquero *m*

(e) *Ling* evolución *f*

2 *vi* **(a)** *(boat)* ir a la deriva; **to d. off course** desviarse del rumbo; **to d. onto the rocks** ir a la deriva hacia las rocas

(b) *(move without fixed aim) (economy)* ir a la deriva; *(conversation)* derivar; *(events)* discurrir; *(person)* vagar, errar; **to let things d.** dejar que las cosas vayan a la deriva; **people drifted in and out during the speech** durante el discurso, la gente entraba y salía; **the conversation drifted from one topic to another** la conversación divagaba, saltando de un tema a otro; **to d. apart** irse separando poco a poco; **to d. into war/crime** ir derivando hacia la guerra/la delincuencia

(c) *(sand, snow)* amontonarse

▸**drift off** *vi (fall asleep)* quedarse dormido(a)

drifter ['drɪftə(r)] *n* **(a)** *(person)* alma *f* errante **(b)** *(boat)* trainera *f*

driftwood ['drɪftwʊd] *n* madera *f* flotante

drill [drɪl] **1** *n* **(a)** *(electric tool)* taladradora *f*; *(manual tool)* taladro *m* (manual); *(of dentist)* torno *m*; *(pneumatic)* martillo *m* neumático ▸▸ ***d. hole*** *(in wood, brick)* taladro *m*; *(for oil well)* perforación *f*

(b) *(bit)* **d. (bit)** broca *f*

(c) *(training, exercises)* ejercicio *m* ▸▸ ***d. sergeant*** *(in army)* sargento(a) *m,f* de instrucción

(d) *Br Fam (routine, method)* **I know the d.** ya conozco el procedimiento; **what's the d.?** *(what do you want me to do?)* ¿qué tengo que hacer?; *(what's the system or method?)* ¿cómo se hace?

(e) *(material)* dril *m*

(f) *Agr (machine)* sembradora *f*

(g) *Agr (furrow)* surco *m*

2 *vt* **(a)** *(well, road)* perforar; **to d. a hole in sth** taladrar un agujero en algo; **to d. a tooth** hacer un agujero en un diente con el torno

(b) *(train) (soldiers)* entrenar; **to d. pupils in pronunciation** hacer practicar la pronunciación a los alumnos; *Fam* **to d. sth into sb** meterle algo en la cabeza a alguien

3 *vi* **(a)** *(in ground)* **to d. for oil** hacer perforaciones en búsqueda *or Esp* busca de petróleo

(b) *(troops)* entrenar, practicar

drilling ['drɪlɪŋ] *n* ***d. platform*** plataforma *f* de perforación (petrolífera); ***d. rig*** torre *f* de perforación (petrolífera)

drily, dryly ['draɪlɪ] *adv (to comment)* lacónicamente

drink [drɪŋk] **1** *n* **(a)** *(in general)* bebida *f*; **a d. of water/milk** un vaso de agua/leche; **hot/cold drinks** bebidas calientes/frías; **give the children a d.** dale algo de beber a los niños; **there's plenty of food and d.** hay comida y bebida de sobra ▸▸ ***drinks machine*** máquina *f* (expendedora) de bebidas

(b) *(alcoholic)* copa *f*; **to have a d.** tomar una copa; **to go for a d.** ir a tomar una copa; **to be the worse for d.** haber tomado una copa de más; **to take to d.** darse a la bebida; **to have a d. problem** tener un problema con la bebida

(c) *Fam* **the d.** *(the sea)* el mar

2 *vt* (*pt* **drank** [dræŋk], *pp* **drunk** [drʌŋk]) beber, tomar; **would you like something to d.?** ¿quieres tomar algo?; **to d. sb's health** brindar a la salud de alguien; **to d. sb under the table** aguantar bebiendo *or*

Am tomando más que alguien; **to d. oneself to death** morir alcoholizado(a) *or* por el alcohol; **he drank himself into a stupor** se emborrachó tanto que quedó totalmente aturdido
3 *vi* (a) *(generally)* beber; **she drank out of** *or* **from the bottle** bebió directamente de la botella
(b) *(drink alcohol)* beber, *Am* tomar; **I don't d.** no bebo, *Am* no tomo; **don't d. and drive** si bebes no conduzcas, *Am* si tomas no manejes; **to d. to sb/sth** brindar por alguien/algo; IDIOM *Fam* **to d. like a fish** beber como un cosaco

▸ **drink in** *vt sep (fresh air)* respirar; *(words)* absorber; *(applause)* regodearse con; *(view)* admirar embelesado(a); **to d. in the atmosphere** empaparse del ambiente

▸ **drink up** 1 *vt sep* beberse todo
2 *vi* **d. up!** *(in pub)* ¡vayan terminando!

drinkable ['drɪŋkəbəl] *adj (water)* potable; *(wine, beer)* pasable, aceptable

drink-driver ['drɪŋk'draɪvə(r)] *n Br* conductor(ora) *m,f* en estado de embriaguez

drink-driving ['drɪŋk'draɪvɪŋ] *n Br* **he was arrested for d.** lo detuvieron por conducir *or Am* manejar en estado de embriaguez

drinker ['drɪŋkə(r)] *n* bebedor(ora) *m,f*; **I'm not a coffee d.** no suelo tomar café; **he's a heavy d.** es un bebedor empedernido

drinking ['drɪŋkɪŋ] *n* **heavy d. is bad for you** beber *or Am* tomar mucho es malo; **his d. is becoming a problem** está empezando a beber demasiado; **it was her d. that destroyed the marriage** la afición de ella a la bebida destruyó el matrimonio; **his d. companions** sus compañeros de borracheras; **I'm not a d. man** no suelo beber *or Am* tomar; **d. and driving** conducción en estado de embriaguez ▸▸ ***d. chocolate*** chocolate *m* a la taza *(poco espeso)*; ***d. fountain*** fuente *f* (de agua potable); ***d. song*** canción *f* de taberna; ***d. straw*** pajita *f*, *Col, Ven* pitillo *m*, *Méx* popote *m*; ***d. water*** agua *f* potable; **the village's d. water is contaminated** el agua del pueblo no es apta para su consumo

drinking-up time ['drɪŋkɪŋ'ʌptaɪm] *n Br* = tiempo que tienen los clientes de un bar para acabarse las bebidas después de la hora oficial de cierre

drip [drɪp] 1 *n* (a) *(drop)* gota *f*; *(sound)* goteo *m*; **I caught the drips in a bucket** puse un balde para recoger las gotas que caían
(b) *(in hospital)* gota a gota *m inv*; **she's on a d.** le han puesto suero
(c) *Fam (weak person)* sosaina *mf*
2 *vt (pt & pp* **dripped**) gotear; **you're dripping water all over the floor** estás derramando agua por todo el suelo; **his words dripped venom** sus palabras destilaban veneno
3 *vi* (a) *(liquid)* gotear; **the rain is dripping down my neck** me entra la lluvia por el cuello; **sweat dripped from his brow** le caían gotas de sudor de la frente
(b) *(tap, nose, washing, hair, trees)* gotear; *(walls)* estar empapado(a); **to be dripping with sweat/blood** estar empapado(a) en sudor/sangre
(c) *(have to excess)* **to be dripping with jewels** ir cargado(a) de joyas; **dripping with sentimentality** preñado(a) de sentimentalismo

drip-dry ['drɪp'draɪ] 1 *adj* que no necesita plancha
2 *vt* colgar a secar en una percha
3 *vi* secarse en una percha

drip-feed ['drɪpfi:d] 1 *n (device)* gota a gota *m*, goteo *m*; *(solution)* suero *m* (intravenoso)
2 *vt* poner el gota a gota a, alimentar con suero intravenoso a

dripping ['drɪpɪŋ] 1 *n* grasa *f*
2 *adj* **a d. tap** *Esp* un grifo *or Chile, Col, Méx* una llave *or RP* una canilla que gotea
3 *adv* **to be d. wet** estar empapado(a)

drip-proof ['drɪp'pru:f] *adj (paint, varnish)* que no gotea

drippy ['drɪpɪ] *adj* (a) *Fam Pej (person)* blandengue (b) *(tap, nose)* que gotea

DRIVE [draɪv] 1 *n* (a) *(trip)* viaje *m* (en coche *or Am* carro *or CSur* auto); **it's an hour's d. away** está a una hora en coche *or Am* carro *or CSur* auto; **to go for** *or* **take a d.** dar una vuelta en coche *or Am* carro *or CSur* auto
(b) *Aut (of car)* tracción *f*; **four-wheel d.** *(car)* cuatro por cuatro, vehículo con tracción a *or Am* en las cuatro ruedas; *(system)* tracción a *or Am* en las cuatro ruedas; **left-hand d.** *(car)* vehículo con el volante al *or Am* del lado izquierdo ▸▸ ***d. belt*** correa *f* de transmisión; ***d. shaft*** (eje *m* de) transmisión *f*
(c) *Comptr* unidad *f* de disco
(d) *Mil* ofensiva *f*
(e) *Sport (in golf)* golpe *m* largo, drive *m*; *(in tennis)* golpe *m* natural, drive *m*; *(in soccer)* disparo *m* fuerte; *(in American football)* avance *m* ofensivo, ataque *m*
(f) *(of house)* camino *m* de entrada
(g) *(street)* calle *f*
(h) *(initiative, energy)* brío *m*, empuje *m*; **to have plenty of d.** tener mucho brío *or* empuje; **he lacks d.** le falta brío *or* empuje
(i) *(strong need)* instinto *m*
(j) *(campaign)* **sales/membership d.** campaña de ventas/para captar socios; **we're on an economy d.** estamos en una campaña de ahorro
(k) *(of cattle)* = traslado de ganado vacuno en manadas
(l) *(competition) (of whist, bridge)* competición *f*, *Am* competencia *f*
2 *vt (pt* **drove** [drəʊv], *pp* **driven** ['drɪvən]) (a) *(car, train)* conducir, *Am* manejar; *(racing car, motor boat)* pilotar; **to d. sb to school** llevar a alguien al colegio en coche *or Am* carro *or CSur* auto; **could you d. me home/into town?** ¿me puedes llevar (en coche *or Am* carro *or CSur* auto) a casa/al centro?; **she drove the car into a tree** empotró el coche *or Am* carro *or CSur* auto contra un árbol; **she drives a BMW** tiene un BMW; **I d. a truck** soy camionero
(b) *(cover) (distance)* cubrir; **we drove 400 miles in a day** cubrimos 400 millas en un día
(c) *(direct, guide, force) (cattle, people)* conducir, guiar; **to d. sb to do sth** empujar a alguien a que haga algo; **to d. prices up/down** hacer que los precios suban/bajen; **we were driven off course by the wind** el viento nos apartó de nuestro rumbo; **they have driven us into a corner** nos han arrinconado; **the movement was driven underground** el movimiento se vio forzado a pasar a la clandestinidad; **he was driven to it** se vio forzado a ello; **driven by jealousy, he killed her** guiado por los celos, la mató; **the situation is driving me to despair/distraction** la situación me está desesperando/sacando de quicio; **to d. sb to drink** hacer que alguien se dé a la bebida; *Fam* **it's enough to d. you to drink!** ¡es como para volverse loco(a)!; **to d. sb mad** *or* **crazy** volver loco(a) a alguien; IDIOM *Fam* **to d. sb round the bend** *or* **twist** agotar la paciencia a alguien, *Esp* hacer que alguien acabe hasta el gorro, *RP* inflar a alguien; *Fam* **it drives me wild** *(I love it)* me vuelve loco; **to d. oneself too hard** *(at work)* matarse a trabajar; **to d. a hard bargain** ser un(a) duro(a) negociador(ora), no regalar nada a nadie
(d) *(hammer)* **to d. a nail home** clavar un clavo; IDIOM **to d. a point home: she used shocking examples to d. her point home** usó ejemplos impactantes para dejarlo bien claro
(e) *(bore) (hole)* hacer; *(shaft, tunnel)* abrir
(f) *(machine)* impulsar, hacer funcionar; **to be driven by electricity** funcionar con electricidad; *Fig* **he is driven by a desire for revenge** lo motiva *or* impulsa un deseo de venganza
(g) *(expel)* **they were driven from the country/their homes** fueron forzados a abandonar su país/sus hogares; **he was driven out of office** fue obligado a abandonar el cargo
(h) *(hit hard) (in soccer)* lanzar con fuerza; **she drove the ball past her opponent** *(in tennis)* superó a su rival con un drive; **he drove the ball 250 yards** *(in golf)* hizo un drive de 250 yardas; **to d. a post into the ground** clavar un poste en el suelo; *Fig* **he really drove the message home** dejó bien claro su mensaje
3 *vi* (a) *(in car)* conducir, *Am* manejar; **can you d.?** ¿sabes conducir *or Am* manejar?; **I've decided to d. rather than take the train** he decidido ir en coche *or Am* carro *or CSur* auto en vez de en tren; **to d. at 100 km/h** ir a 100 km/h.; **to d. to work** ir al trabajo en coche *or Am* carro *or CSur* auto; **we drove home/down to the coast** fuimos en coche *or Am* carro *or CSur* auto a casa/a la costa; **they drove all night** viajaron toda la noche; **they d. on the left** circulan por la izquierda
(b) *(car)* responder; *Fam* **it drives like a dream** responde de maravilla
(c) *(army, herd of cattle)* avanzar; **they drove towards the coast** avanzaron hacia la costa
(d) *(dash)* golpear, azotar; **rain was driving against the window** la lluvia golpeaba la ventana
(e) *(in American football)* **they drove upfield** avanzaron hacia *Esp* la portería contraria *or Am* el arco contrario

▸ **drive against** *vt insep (of rain, hail)* golpear con fuerza

▸ **drive at** *vi* **what are you driving at?** ¿qué estás insinuando?

▸ **drive away** 1 *vt sep* (a) *(car)* **you can d. the car away today** se puede llevar el automóvil hoy mismo; **to d. sb away** llevarse a alguien en un coche *or Am* carro *or CSur* auto (b) *(cause to leave) (person)* expulsar; *(animal)* ahuyentar; *Fig* **to d. sb away** *(alienate)* ahuyentar a alguien
2 *vi (in car)* irse, marcharse *(en vehículo)*

▸ **drive back** *vt sep (enemy, opposition)* hacer retroceder

▸ **drive by** *vi* **they waved to us as they drove by** nos saludaron cuando pasaron por delante de nosotros; **they drove by without stopping** pasaron de largo

▸ **drive in** *vt sep (nail, stake)* clavar

▸ **drive into** *vt insep (crash into)* chocar contra

▸ **drive off** 1 *vt sep (repel)* repeler
2 *vi* (a) *(in car)* irse (b) *(in golf)* salir

▸ **drive on** 1 *vi (in car)* seguir adelante
2 *vt sep (push)* empujar

▸ **drive out** *vt sep (person)* expulsar; *(thought)* alejar; **to d. out evil spirits** *(from a place, person)* alejar los malos espíritus

▸ **drive over** *vi* ir en coche *or Am* carro *or CSur* auto

▸ **drive past** 1 *vt insep (in car)* **we drove past a castle** pasamos por delante de un castillo
2 *vi (in car)* pasar de largo

▸ **drive up** *vi (person)* llegar *(en vehículo)*; *(car)* llegar

drive-by ['draɪv'baɪ] *adj* **d. shooting** *or* **killing** tiroteo *or* asesinato desde un vehículo

drive-in ['draɪvɪn] *n* **d. (cinema)** autocine *m*; **d. (restaurant)** = establecimiento de comida rápida que atiende a los clientes sin que éstos necesiten salir de su vehículo

drivel ['drɪvəl] 1 *n Fam Esp* chorradas *fpl, CAm, Méx* babosadas *fpl, Chile* leseras *fpl, CSur, Perú, Ven* macanas *fpl*; **to talk d.** decir chorradas
2 *vi* (a) *(speak foolishly)* decir *Esp* chorradas *or CAm, Méx* babosadas *or Chile* leseras *or CSur, Perú, Ven* macanas; **what's he drivelling on about?** ¿qué chorradas está contando? (b) *(dribble)* babear

drivelling, *US* **driveling** ['drɪvəlɪŋ] *adj Fam* charlatán(ana), *CSur* macaneador(ora); **you d. idiot!** ¡vaya tonterías que dices!

driven ['drɪvən] 1 *pp of* **drive**
2 *adj* (a) *(ambitious)* ambicioso(a) (b) *(snow)* arrastrado(a) por el viento

-driven ['drɪvən] *suffix* (a) *(fuelled by)* **steam-d.** de vapor (b) *(led by)* **market/consumer-d.** impulsado(a) por el mercado/por los consumidores

driver ['draɪvə(r)] *n* (a) *(of car, bus)* conductor(ora) *m,f*; *(of lorry)* camionero(a) *m,f*; *(of taxi)* taxista *mf*; *(of train)* maquinista *mf*; *(of racing car, motor boat, bobsleigh)* piloto *mf*; *(of horse-drawn vehicle)* cochero(a) *m,f*; **he's a good/bad d.** es un buen/mal conductor ▸▸ ***drivers' championship*** *(in motor racing)* campeonato *m* de pilotos; *US* ***d.'s license*** *Esp* carné *m or* permiso *m* de conducir, *Bol, Ecuad, Perú* brevet *m*, *Carib* licencia *f* de conducir, *Méx* licencia *f* de manejar *or* para conducir, *RP* permiso *m* de conductor, *Urug* libreta *f* de manejar; ***d.'s seat*** asiento *m* del conductor; IDIOM **to be in the d.'s seat** estar al mando
(b) *(golf club)* driver *m*, madera *f* uno
(c) *Comptr* controlador *m*
(d) *(determining factor)* factor *m* crucial

drive-through ['draɪvθru:] *n* = establecimiento que atiende a sus clientes a través de una ventana sin que tengan que salir del automóvil

drive-time ['draɪvtaɪm] *n* = la hora punta durante la cual aumenta el número de oyentes radiofónicos; *Rad* **d. programme** = programa dirigido a los conductores (durante la hora punta)

driveway ['draɪvweɪ] *n* camino *m* de entrada

driving ['draɪvɪŋ] 1 *n* (a) *(in car)* conducción *f*, *Am* manejo *m*; **I like d.** me gusta conducir *or Am* manejar; **his d. is awful** conduce *or Am* maneja muy mal; *Law* **he was charged with d.** *Br* **under the influence** *or US* **while intoxicated** lo acusaron de conducir *or Am* manejar en estado de embriaguez; IDIOM **to be in the d. seat** estar al mando ▸▸ ***d. conditions*** condiciones *fpl* de conducción *or Am* manejo; ***d. instructor*** profesor(ora) *m,f* de autoescuela; ***d. lessons*** clases *fpl* de conducir *or Am* manejar; *Br* ***d. licence*** *Esp* carné *m or* permiso *m* de conducir, *Bol, Ecuad, Perú* brevet *m*, *Carib* licencia *f* de conducir, *Méx* licencia *f* de manejar *or* para conducir, *RP* permiso *m* de conductor, *Urug* libreta *f* de manejar; ***d. mirror*** espejo *m* retrovisor; ***d. school*** autoescuela *f*; ***d. test*** examen *m* de conducir; **to pass one's d. test** aprobar el examen de conducir
(b) *(in golf)* ***d. range*** campo *m* de tiro *or* prácticas (para golf)
2 *adj* (a) *(rain)* torrencial; **we could hardly see because of the d. snow** apenas había visibilidad debido a la ventisca de nieve
(b) *(motivating) (ambition)* **her d. ambition spurred her on** la ambición era lo que la espoleaba a seguir; **the d. force (behind sth)** la fuerza motriz (detrás de algo)
(c) *Tech (powered) (shaft, belt)* motor(triz) ▸▸ ***d. wheel*** rueda *f* motriz

drizzle ['drɪzəl] 1 *n* llovizna *f*, *Andes, RP* garúa *f*
2 *vi* lloviznar, chispear, *Andes, RP* garuar; **it's drizzling** está lloviznando *or Andes, RP* garuando

drizzly ['drɪzlɪ] *adj* **a d. day** un día de llovizna *or Andes, RP* garúa

droll [drəʊl] *adj* (a) *(comical)* gracioso(a); *Ironic* **oh, very d.!** ¡muy gracioso! (b) *(odd, quaint)* singular, curioso(a)

drollery ['drəʊlərɪ] *n (joking)* bromas *fpl*, chistes *mpl*

dromedary ['drɒmədərɪ] *n* dromedario *m*

drone [drəʊn] 1 *n* (a) *(bee)* zángano *m* (b) *Pej (person)* zángano(a) *m,f* (c) *(noise) (of bee, engine, aircraft)* zumbido *m*; **the d. of his voice** el zumbido de su voz (d) *Mus (of bagpipe) (pipe)* roncón *m* (e) *(plane)* avión *m* teledirigido
2 *vi (bee, engine, aircraft)* zumbar

▸ **drone on** *vi* **to d. on about sth** soltar una perorata sobre algo; **he was still droning on an hour late** una hora más tarde todavía seguía con su cantinela

drongo ['drɒŋgəʊ] (*pl* **drongoes** *or* **drongos**) *n Austr Fam* imbécil *mf*, inútil *mf*

drool [dru:l] 1 *n US* (a) *(saliva)* baba *f* (b) *(nonsense) Esp* chorradas *fpl*, *Am* disparates *mpl*, *CAm, Méx* babosadas *fpl*, *Chile* leseras *fpl*, *CSur, Perú, Ven* macanas *fpl*
2 *vi* babear; *Fig* **she was drooling at the idea** se le caía la baba con sólo pensarlo; *Fig* **she was drooling over him** se le caía la baba con él

droop [dru:p] 1 *n* **he could tell she was tired from the d. of her shoulders** sabía que estaba cansada porque encorvaba los hombros
2 *vi* (a) *(bow, slope) (head)* inclinarse; *(shoulders)* encorvarse (b) *(bend, collapse) (flower)* marchitarse; *Fig (person)* desanimarse

drooping ['dru:pɪŋ] *adj* (a) *(eyelids, shoulders)* caído(a); *(moustache)* lacio(a) (b) *(flagging)* **to revive sb's d. spirits** levantar el ánimo de alguien

droopy ['dru:pɪ] *adj (ears, eyelids, shoulders)* caído(a); *(moustache)* lacio(a); **we were all feeling pretty d.** estábamos todos bastante cansados

DROP [drɒp] 1 *n* (a) *(of liquid)* gota *f*; **there hasn't been a d. of rain for weeks** no ha caído una gota de agua desde hace semanas; **would you like a d. of wine?** ¿quieres un poco de vino?, *Esp* ¿te apetece un poco de vino?; **could I have a d. more coffee?** ¿me podrías poner un poquitín *or* poquitito más de café?; **you've had a d. too much** *(to drink) Esp* llevas una copa de más, *Am* tienes unas copas de más; **I haven't touched a d. since** desde entonces no he bebido *or Am* tomado ni una gota; IDIOM **it's only a d. in the ocean** no es más que un grano de arena en el desierto
(b) **drops** *(for eyes, nose)* gotas *fpl*
(c) *(decrease) (in price, temperature, voltage)* caída *f*, descenso *m* (in de); **a d. in our wages** una reducción de nuestros sueldos
(d) *(fall)* caída *f*, descenso *m*; *(in parachuting)* salto *m*; **a d. of 10 metres** una caída de 10 metros; **a sudden d. in the ground level** una caída repentina del terreno; IDIOM **I'd go there at the d. of a hat** iría allí sin pensarlo *or Esp* pensármelo dos veces; IDIOM **we have to be ready to change our strategy at the d. of a hat** tenemos que estar preparados para cambiar nuestra estrategia de un momento a otro *or* de la noche a la mañana; IDIOM *US Fam* **to have the d. on sb** sacar ventaja a alguien ▸▸ ***d. tank*** *(on aircraft)* depósito *m* lanzable
(e) *(of supplies) (by parachute)* suministro *m* aéreo; **to make a d.** lanzar suministros ▸▸ ***d. zone*** = zona sobre la que se lanzan suministros
(f) *Sport (in golf)* drop *m*; **to take a d.** dropar ▸▸ ***d. ball*** *(in soccer)* saque *m* neutral; ***d. goal*** *(in rugby)* gol *m* de botepronto; ***d. handlebars*** manillar *m* de cuerno de cabra; ***d. kick*** *(in rugby)* (puntapié *m* de) botepronto *m*; ***d. shot*** *(in tennis, badminton)* dejada *f*
(g) *(sweet)* caramelo *m*; **lemon/fruit d.** caramelo de limón/frutas
(h) *(earring) Esp* pendiente *m*, *Am* arete *m* *(en forma de lágrima)*; *(on chandelier)* lágrima *f*
(i) *(collection point)* punto *m* de recogida
(j) *Theat (trapdoor)* trampilla *f*, escotillón *m*; **d. (curtain)** telón *m*
(k) *Typ* ***d. cap*** letra *f* capitular
(l) *Tech* ***d. forge*** *or* ***hammer*** *(in foundry)* martinete *m*
2 *vt* (*pt & pp* **dropped**) (a) *(allow to fall) (accidentally)* dejar caer; *(deliberately)* tirar, dejar caer, *Andes, CAm, Carib, Méx* botar; *(bomb)* lanzar, tirar; **I've dropped my watch** se me ha caído el reloj; **he dropped the catch** *(in cricket, baseball)* se le cayó la pelota en la recepción; **d. it!** *(to dog)* ¡déjalo!, ¡suelta!; **they dropped food by parachute** lanzaron alimentos mediante paracaídas; **I'll d. it in the post** *or* **mail** lo mandaré por correo; **to d. a curtsy** hacer una reverencia; **to d. anchor** echar el ancla; **to d. one's trousers** bajarse los pantalones; IDIOM **to d. sb in it** meter a alguien en un lío
(b) *(lower) (prices)* bajar; *(hem)* bajar; **she dropped her eyes/voice** bajó los ojos/la voz; **d. your speed** reduzca la velocidad
(c) *(person from car)* dejar; **I'll d. you at the station** te dejaré en la estación
(d) *(deliver)* dejar; **we dropped the parcel at John's on the way**

home de camino a casa dejamos el paquete en casa de John

(e) *(abandon) (idea, plan)* abandonar; *(subject, boyfriend)* dejar; **we dropped everything and ran outside** dejamos todo y salimos corriendo; **I can't d. everything just because you're here** no puedo dejarlo todo sólo porque estés aquí; **to d. sb** *(as friend)* abandonar *or* dejar a alguien; **to d. maths/French** dejar las matemáticas/el francés; **let's d. the subject** dejemos el tema; *Fam* **just d. it, will you!** *(change subject)* ¡basta ya, por favor!, *Esp* déjalo ya, ¿te parece?; *Law* **to d. the charges** retirar los cargos

(f) *(omit) (letter, syllable)* saltarse, omitir; *(not pronounce)* no pronunciar; *(story, article)* no publicar; **to d. sb from a team** excluir a alguien de un equipo; **he drops his h's** *or* **aitches** no pronuncia la hache; **I've dropped a stitch** se me ha salido un punto; **you can d. the "doctor"** no hace falta que me llames "doctor"; **let's d. the formalities, shall we?** dejemos las formalidades a un lado, ¿de acuerdo?

(g) *(lose) (points, set)* perder; **he dropped $50 on the deal** perdió 50 dólares en el trato

(h) *(give)* **to d. sb a line/a card** mandar unas líneas/una postal a alguien

(i) *(utter)* **to d. (sb) a hint** lanzar una indirecta (a alguien); **she let (it) d. that she had been there** *(accidentally)* se le escapó que había estado allí; *(deliberately)* dejó caer que había estado allí; IDIOM **to d. names** dárselas de conocer a muchos famosos

(j) *(in rugby)* **to d. a goal** marcar un gol de botepronto

(k) *(in golf)* **to d. a shot** hacer un bogey

(l) *Fam (knock down)* tumbar

(m) *Am Fam (spend)* pulirse

(n) *(of animal) (give birth)* tener

(o) *Fam* **to d. acid** tomarse *or* meterse un ácido

3 *vi* (a) *(object, liquid)* caer, caerse; *(ground)* caer; **it dropped onto the floor** se cayó al suelo; **it dropped out of my pocket** se me cayó del bolsillo; **to d. into sb's lap** *(opportunity)* llegarle a alguien como venido(a) *or* llovido(a) del cielo; **the road drops into the valley** la carretera desciende hacia el valle; *Theat* **the curtain dropped** cayó el telón

(b) *(sink down, collapse, sag)* caer; **she dropped into an armchair** se dejó caer en un sillón; **he dropped to the ground** se echó al suelo; **she dropped to her knees** cayó de rodillas; **my jaw dropped** me quedé boquiabierto; *Fam* **I'm ready** *or* **fit to d.** estoy hecho polvo, *Esp* estoy para el arrastre; *Fam* **we danced until we dropped** bailamos hasta más no poder *or* hasta caer rendidos; **he'll work until he drops** trabajará hasta caer rendido; **to d. dead** caerse muerto(a); *Fam* **d. dead!** ¡muérete!, *RP* ¡morite!; IDIOM *Fam* **people are dropping like flies** la gente está cayendo como moscas

(c) *(prices, temperature, demand)* caer, bajar; *(voice)* bajar; *(wind)* amainar; *(speed)* disminuir; **inflation has dropped below 3 percent** la inflación ha caído por debajo del 3 por ciento; **the temperature dropped below zero** las temperaturas descendieron por debajo de los cero grados; **shares dropped a point** las acciones cayeron un entero; **the pound dropped three points against the dollar** la libra bajó tres enteros frente al dólar; **the Stealers have dropped to seventh in the league** los Stealers han descendido al séptimo puesto de la liga

(d) *(subject)* **we have decided to let the matter d.** hemos decidido pasar por alto el asunto; *Fam* **let it d.!** ¡basta ya!, *Esp* ¡déjalo ya!, *RP* ¡acabala!

(e) *(animal) (give birth)* parir

▶ **drop away** *vi* (a) *(ground)* descender (b) *(interest, membership, attendance)* disminuir

▶ **drop back** *vi (intentionally)* retrasarse, *Am* demorarse; **he's dropped back from third to fifth place** ha pasado del tercer al quinto puesto

▶ **drop behind** 1 *vt insep* **she has dropped behind the rest of the class** ha quedado rezagada respecto al resto de la clase

2 *vi (athlete)* rezagarse; **you've been dropping behind with your schoolwork** te has ido retrasando con tus estudios

▶ **drop by** 1 *vt insep* **why don't you d. by our house some time?** ¿por qué no te pasas por nuestra casa un rato de éstos?

2 *vi* **I thought I'd d. by for a chat** se me ocurrió pasarme a charlar *or CAm, Méx* platicar un rato

▶ **drop down** *vi (person)* agacharse; *(table leaf)* abatirse

▶ **drop in** 1 *vt sep (deliver)* **I'll d. it in on my way to work** pasaré a dejarlo de camino al trabajo

2 *vi* **he dropped in yesterday** se pasó por aquí ayer; **to d. in on sb** pasar a visitar a alguien

▶ **drop off** 1 *vt sep (person from car)* dejar; **he called round to d. some work off for me** se acercó para traerme algo de trabajo

2 *vi* (a) *(fall)* caerse (b) **to d. off (to sleep)** quedarse dormido(a)

(c) *(interest, membership, attendance)* bajar, disminuir

▶ **drop out** *vi* (a) *(from a contest)* retirarse (b) *(from society)* marginarse (c) **to d. out of school/university** dejar la escuela/la universidad

▶ **drop round** 1 *vt sep (deliver)* entregar, llevar; **I'll d. it round at your place tomorrow** lo dejaré en tu casa mañana

2 *vi (visit)* pasarse

---

drop-dead gorgeous ['drɒpded'gɔːdʒəs] *adj Fam* guapísimo(a); **to be/look d.** estar como un tren *or* para parar un tren

drop-down menu ['drɒpdaʊn'menjuː] *n Comptr* menú *m* desplegable

drop-forge ['drɒp'fɔːdʒ] *vt Tech* forjar con el martinete

drophead coupé ['drɒphedkuː'peɪ] *n Br* cupé *m* descapotable

drop-in centre ['drɒp'ɪnsentə(r)] *n Br* = centro asistencial en el que no se necesita cita previa

drop-kick ['drɒpkɪk] *vt (ball)* golpear con un puntapié de botepronto; *(goal)* marcar de botepronto

drop-leaf table ['drɒpliːf'teɪbəl] *n* mesa *f* de alas

droplet ['drɒplɪt] *n* gotita *f*

drop-off ['drɒpɒf] *n* (a) *(decrease)* descenso *m* (b) *US (descent)* descenso *m*

dropout ['drɒpaʊt] *n Fam* (a) *(from society)* marginado(a) *m,f* (b) *(from school, university)* = persona que ha abandonado los estudios ▸▸ ***d. rate*** *(from university)* índice *m* de abandono de los estudios

drop-out ['drɒpaʊt] *n (in rugby)* saque *m* de 22

dropper ['drɒpə(r)] *n (for medicine)* cuentagotas *m inv*

dropping-off ['drɒpɪŋ'ɒf] *n (decrease)* descenso *m*

droppings ['drɒpɪŋz] *npl* excrementos *mpl*

drop-scone ['drɒpskɒn] *n Br* = tortita gruesa y esponjosa

dropsy ['drɒpsɪ] *n Med* hidropesía *f*

dross [drɒs] *n* (a) *(waste coal)* escoria *f* (b) *Fam (rubbish)* porquería *f*, basura *f*; **the movie was a load of d.** la película era una auténtica basura *or* porquería

drought [draʊt] *n* sequía *f*

drove [drəʊv] 1 *n (of animals)* manada *f*; *(of people)* horda *f*, legión *f*; **in droves** en manadas; *Hum* **people stayed away in droves** asistieron cuatro gatos

2 *pt of* **drive**

drover ['drəʊvə(r)] *n* conductor *m* de ganado, *RP* tropero *m*

drown [draʊn] 1 *vt* (a) *(kill by drowning)* ahogar; **to be drowned** morir ahogado(a); **to d. oneself** ahogarse; IDIOM **to d. one's sorrows (in drink)** ahogar las penas (en alcohol)

(b) *(flood) (field, village)* inundar; **he drowned his food in ketchup** inundó de ketchup la comida; **don't d. it!** *(my drink)* ¡no me lo vayas a aguar!

(c) *(make inaudible)* ahogar; **his voice was drowned (out) by the music** la música ahogaba su voz

2 *vi (die by drowning)* ahogarse

▶ **drown out** *vt sep* ahogar

drowned [draʊnd] *adj* ahogado(a); IDIOM **to look like a d. rat** ir calado(a) hasta los huesos

drowning ['draʊnɪŋ] 1 *n (death)* **there have been four drownings** *or* **cases of d. this year** se han ahogado cuatro personas este año; **to save sb from d.** salvar a alguien de morir ahogado(a)

2 *adj* **a d. man** un hombre que se está ahogando; **the last thoughts of the d. man were of his family** la familia ocupó los últimos pensamientos del hombre que se ahogaba; PROV **a d. man will clutch at a straw** = en una situación desesperada uno se agarra a un clavo ardiendo

drowse [draʊz] *vi* dormitar

drowsiness ['draʊzɪnɪs] *n* somnolencia *f*, sueño *m*; **may cause d.** *(on label)* puede causar somnolencia

drowsy ['draʊzɪ] *adj (person)* somnoliento(a), soñoliento(a); *(afternoon)* soporífero(a); **to be d.** estar somnoliento(a); **to make sb (feel) d.** *(atmosphere, drug)* amodorrar

drub [drʌb] *(pt & pp* **drubbed**) *vt (defeat thoroughly)* aplastar, hundir

drubbing ['drʌbɪŋ] *n Fam (thorough defeat)* paliza *f*; **to give sb a real d.** dar una buena paliza a alguien; **to get a good d.** ser vapuleado

drudge [drʌdʒ] 1 *n* = persona que tiene un trabajo pesado y aburrido

2 *vi* trajinar

drudgery ['drʌdʒərɪ] *n* trabajo *m* (duro y) rutinario; **the sheer d. of it!** ¡qué lata de trabajo!

drug [drʌg] **1** *n* **(a)** *(medicine)* medicamento *m*; **he was put on drugs by the doctor** el médico le recetó varios medicamentos
(b) *(illegal)* droga *f*; **hard/soft drugs** drogas duras/blandas; **to be on drugs** *(as a habit)* drogarse, tomar drogas; *(at particular time)* estar drogado(a); **to take** *or* **do drugs** drogarse, tomar drogas; **I don't do drugs** no tomo drogas; IDIOM **music is (like) a d. for him** para él, la música es (como) una droga ►► ***d. abuse*** drogadicción *f*; ***d. addict*** drogadicto(a) *m,f*, toxicómano(a) *m,f*; ***d. addiction*** drogadicción *f*; ***d. baron*** capo *m* de la droga, gran narco *m*; ***d. czar*** jefe(a) *m,f* de la lucha contra la droga; ***d. dealer*** *(large-scale)* narcotraficante *mf*, traficante *mf* de drogas; *(small-scale)* traficante *mf* de drogas; ***d. dealing*** tráfico *m* de estupefacientes *or* drogas; ***D. Enforcement Administration*** = departamento estadounidense de lucha contra la droga; *Fam* ***d. peddler*** camello *mf*; ***d. pusher*** camello *mf*; ***d. squad*** brigada *f* antidroga *or* de estupefacientes; ***drugs test*** prueba *f* antidoping *or* antidopaje, control *m* antidoping; ***d. trafficking*** tráfico *m* de estupefacientes *or* drogas
2 *vt* (*pt & pp* **drugged**) drogar; **they had drugged his wine/food** le echaron una droga en el vino/la comida; **to d. oneself up** *(with medicine)* atiborrarse de medicamentos; *(with illegal drugs)* atiborrarse de drogas; **she was drugged up to the eyeballs** *(after operation)* estaba hasta arriba de narcóticos

drugget [ˈdrʌgɪt] *n* alpujarra *f*, droguete *m*

druggie, druggy [ˈdrʌgɪ] *n Fam* drogata *mf*

druggist [ˈdrʌgɪst] *n US* farmacéutico(a) *m,f*

druggy = **druggie**

drugstore [ˈdrʌgstɔː(r)] *n US* = tienda que vende cosméticos, periódicos, medicamentos, etc.

drug-taking [ˈdrʌgˈteɪkɪŋ] *n* consumo *m* de drogas

druid [ˈdruːɪd] *n* druida *m*

druidic(al) [druːˈɪdɪk(əl)] *adj* druídico(a)

drum [drʌm] **1** *n* **(a)** *(musical instrument)* tambor *m*; **to beat** *or* **bang a d.** golpear *or* tocar un tambor; **to play (the) drums** tocar la batería; **Keith Wilson on drums** a la batería, Keith Wilson; IDIOM **to beat** *or* **bang the d. for sth/sb** anunciar algo/a alguien a bombo y platillo, dar mucho bombo a algo/alguien ►► ***d. and bass*** drum and bass *m*; ***d. kit*** batería *f*; ***d. machine*** caja *f* de ritmos; *Mil* ***d. major*** tambor *m* mayor; ***d. majorette*** majorette *f (que encabeza el desfile)*; ***d. roll*** redoble *m* de tambor
(b) *(container)* barril *m*; *(for oil)* bidón *m*; *(for rope, cable)* tambor *m*
(c) *(of machine)* tambor *m* ►► *Aut* ***d. brake*** freno *m* de tambor; *Comptr* ***d. scanner*** escáner *m* de tambor
(d) *Archit* tambor *m*
2 *vt* (*pt & pp* **drummed**) **she was drumming her fingers on the table** estaba tamborileando en la mesa con los dedos; **to d. one's heels on the floor** golpear repetidamente en el suelo con el talón
3 *vi* **(a)** *(play drums in pop band)* tocar la batería; *(play single drum)* tocar el tambor
(b) *(beat)* **the rain was drumming on the window panes** la lluvia golpeaba en los cristales

►**drum into** *vt sep* **to d. sth into sb** meterle algo en la cabeza a alguien a fuerza de repetirlo; **we had it drummed into us that...** nos repitieron hasta la saciedad que...

►**drum out** *vt sep* **he was drummed out of the club/the army** lo expulsaron del club/del ejército

►**drum up** *vt (support, enthusiasm)* reunir; *(customers)* reclutar, reunir

drumbeat [ˈdrʌmbiːt] *n* toque *m* de tambor

drumhead [ˈdrʌmhed] *n* **(a)** *(of drum)* parche *m* **(b)** *Mil* **d. court-martial** = consejo de guerra que se celebra en el campo de batalla

drumlin [ˈdrʌmlɪn] *n Geol* montículo *m* ovalado

drummer [ˈdrʌmə(r)] *n* **(a)** *(in pop band)* batería *mf*, *Am* baterista *mf*; *(on single drum)* tambor *mf* **(b)** *(in military band)* tamborilero(a) *m,f*, tambor *mf* ►► ***d. boy*** tamborilero *m*

drumstick [ˈdrʌmstɪk] *n* **(a)** *(for playing drums)* baqueta *f* **(b)** *(chicken leg)* muslo *m*

drunk [drʌŋk] **1** *n* **(a)** *(person)* borracho(a) *m,f* ►► *US Fam* ***d. tank*** celda *f* para los borrachos
(b) *Fam (binge)* borrachera *f*
2 *adj* **(a)** *(on alcohol)* borracho(a); **to be d.** estar borracho(a); **to get d.** emborracharse; **to get sb d.** emborrachar a alguien; *Law* **d. and disorderly behaviour** estado de embriaguez con conducta violenta; *Law* **d. and incapable** incapacitado(a) por los efectos del alcohol; IDIOM **d. as a lord** borracho(a) como una cuba
(b) *(intoxicated, overwhelmed)* **d. with power/success** ebrio(a) de poder/por el éxito
3 *pp of* **drink**

drunkard [ˈdrʌŋkəd] *n* borracho(a) *m,f*

drunk-driver [ˈdrʌŋkˈdraɪvə(r)] *n US* conductor(ora) *m,f* en estado de embriaguez

drunk-driving [ˈdrʌŋkˈdraɪvɪŋ] *n US* **he was arrested for d.** lo detuvieron por conducir *or Am* manejar en estado de embriaguez

drunken [ˈdrʌŋkən] *adj (person)* borracho(a); *(party, argument)* acalorado(a) por el alcohol; **d. brawl** trifulca de borrachos; **in a d. stupor** aturdido(a) por el alcohol

drunkenly [ˈdrʌŋkənlɪ] *adv* **there were people singing d. in the street** había borrachos cantando en la calle; **he slumped d. into an armchair** cayó borracho en un sillón; **he staggered d. down the street/the stairs** iba calle/escaleras abajo tambaleándose por la borrachera

drunkenness [ˈdrʌŋkənnɪs] *n (state)* embriaguez *f*, borrachera *f*; *(habit)* alcoholismo *m*

drunkometer [drʌŋˈkɒmɪtə(r)] *n US Fam* alcoholímetro *m*

drupe [druːp] *n Bot* drupa *f*

druthers [ˈdrʌðəz] *npl US Fam* **if I had my d.** si pudiera hacer lo que me diera la gana

Druze, Druse [druːz] **1** *n* druso(a) *m,f*; **the D.** los drusos
2 *adj* druso(a)

dry [draɪ] **1** *adj* **(a)** *(not wet, lacking moisture) (climate, clothing, skin, bread)* seco(a); **to be d.** *(thirsty)* estar seco(a); *(cow)* no dar leche; **the weekend will be d.** el tiempo será seco *or* no habrá precipitaciones durante el fin de semana; **my mouth/throat is d.** tengo la boca/garganta seca; **to run** *or* **go d.** *(well, river)* secarse; **for d. hair** *(shampoo)* para cabello seco; **to be kept d.** *(sign on container)* no mojar; IDIOM **as d. as a bone** reseco(a); IDIOM **there wasn't a d. eye in the house** la sala entera lloraba a lágrima viva *or* a moco tendido ►► *Phys* ***d. battery*** pila *f* (seca); *Phys* ***d. cell*** pila *f* (seca); ***a d. cough*** una tos seca; *Naut* ***d. dock*** dique *m* seco; ***d. fly*** *(in angling)* mosca *f* artificial; ***d. goods*** *Br (grain, pulses, tea, coffee)* alimentos *mpl* no perecederos *(no enlatados)*; *US (drapery)* artículos *mpl* de confección; *US* ***d. goods store*** mercería *f*, tienda *f* de confección; ***d. ice*** nieve *f* carbónica, hielo *m* seco; ***d. land*** tierra *f* firme; ***d. measure*** medida *f* para áridos; ***d. riser*** = cañería para subir agua a los pisos de un edificio en caso de incendio; ***d. rot*** putrefacción *f* de la madera; ***d. run*** ensayo *m*; ***d. season*** estación *f* seca; ***d. skiing*** esquí *m* en pista artificial; ***d. ski slope*** pista *f* de esquí artificial
(b) *(boring)* aburrido(a), árido(a); IDIOM **to be (as) d. as dust** ser un aburrimiento *or Esp* tostón
(c) *(humour)* lacónico(a)
(d) *(wine, champagne)* seco(a) ►► ***d. martini*** dry martini *m*, ginebra *f* con martini seco; ***d. sherry*** jerez *m* fino
(e) *(state, town)* que prohibe la venta de alcohol
(f) *Br Fam (hardline)* duro(a)
2 *vt (clothes, dishes, fruit)* secar; **to d. one's eyes** *or* **tears** secarse los ojos *or* las lágrimas; **to d. oneself** secarse; **to d. one's hair/hands** secarse el pelo/las manos
3 *vi (clothes, hair, fruit, leaves)* secarse; **you wash, I'll d.** friega tú y yo seco
4 *n* **(a)** *Br Fam (hardliner)* duro(a) *m,f*
(b) *Austr Fam (dry season)* estación *f* seca
(c) *(dry place)* **come into the d.** entra aquí, que está seco
(d) *(with towel, cloth)* **give your hair a d.** sécate el pelo con la toalla

►**dry off** **1** *vt* secar; **to d. oneself off** secarse
2 *vi* secarse

►**dry out** **1** *vt sep* **(a)** *(skin, hair)* resecar
(b) *(alcoholic)* desintoxicar
2 *vi* **(a)** *(moisture, wet thing)* secarse **(b)** *(alcoholic)* desintoxicarse

►**dry up** **1** *vt sep* **(a)** *(well, pool)* secar **(b)** *(dishes)* secar
2 *vi* **(a)** *(well, pool, river)* secarse **(b)** *(funds, conversation, inspiration)* agotarse **(c)** *(actor, public speaker)* quedarse en blanco **(d)** *Fam* **d. up!** *(shut up)* ¡cierra el pico! **(e)** *Br (do drying-up)* secar (los platos)

dryad [ˈdraɪæd] *n Mythol* dríada *f*

dry-clean [draɪˈkliːn] *vt* limpiar *or* lavar en seco; **to have sth dry-cleaned** *(at laundry)* llevar algo a la tintorería; *(in hotel)* mandar algo al servicio de tintorería; **d. only** *(on label)* lavado en seco

dry-cleaner's [draɪˈkliːnəz] *n* tintorería *f*; **to be in** *or* **at the d.** *(garment)* estar en la tintorería

dry-cleaning [draɪˈkliːnɪŋ] *n* **(a)** *(process)* limpieza *f* or lavado *m* en seco **(b)** *(clothes)* **to collect the d.** recoger la ropa de la tintorería

dryer = **drier**

dry-eyed ['draɪ'aɪd] *adj* **I remained d. throughout the film** no lloré en toda la película

dry-fly fishing ['draɪflaɪ'fɪʃɪŋ] *n* pesca *f* con mosca artificial

drying ['draɪɪŋ] *n* **I'll do the d.** yo seco ►► ***d. cupboard*** *(for clothes)* = armario o cuartito donde se tiende la ropa; ***d. rack*** *(for dishes)* escurreplatos *m inv*; ***d. room*** *(for clothes)* = habitación donde se tiende la ropa

drying-up [draɪɪŋ'ʌp] *n Br* **to do the d.** secar (los platos) ►► ***d. cloth*** trapo *m* de secar los platos

dryly = **drily**

dryness ['draɪnɪs] *n* **(a)** *(of weather, skin, wine)* sequedad *f* **(b)** *(of prose style)* aridez *f* **(c)** *(of humour)* laconismo *m*

dry-roasted ['draɪrəʊstɪd] *adj (peanuts)* tostado(a)

dry-stone wall ['draɪstəʊn'wɔ:l] *n* muro *m* de piedra (sin argamasa)

DSC [di:es'si:] *n Br Mil* (*abbr* **Distinguished Service Cross**) ≃ cruz *f* al mérito militar

DSc [di:es'si:] *n* (*abbr* **Doctor of Science**) doctor(ora) *m,f* en ciencias

DSL [di:es'el] *n Comptr* (*abbr* **Digital Subscriber Line**) línea *f* digital por suscripción

DSO [di:es'əʊ] *n Br Mil* (*abbr* **Distinguished Service Order**) ≃ medalla *f* al mérito militar

DST [di:es'ti:] *n* (*abbr* **daylight saving time**) horario *m* oficial de verano

DTI [di:ti:'aɪ] *n Br* (*abbr* **Department of Trade and Industry**) ≃ Ministerio *m* de Industria

DTLR [di:ti:el'ɑ:(r)] *n* (*abbr* **Department for Transport, Local Government and the Regions**) = departamento del gobierno británico de transporte, administraciones locales y las regiones

DTP [di:ti:'pi:] *n Comptr* (*abbr* **desktop publishing**) autoedición *f* ►► ***D. operator*** autoeditor(a) *m,f*

DTs [di:'ti:z] *npl* (*abbr* **delirium tremens**) delírium tremens *m inv*; **to have the D.** tener un delírium tremens

dual ['djʊəl] *adj (purpose, function)* doble; **with the d. aim of reducing inflation and stimulating demand** con el doble propósito de reducir la inflación y estimular la demanda ►► *Br* ***d. carriageway*** *(road)* (tramo *m* de) autovía *f*; ***d. controls*** *(in car)* doble juego *m* de pedales; *(in plane)* doble juego *m* de mandos; ***d. nationality:* to have d. nationality** tener doble nacionalidad; ***d. ownership*** copropiedad *f*; ***d. personality*** doble personalidad *f*

dual-control ['djʊəlkən'trəʊl] *adj (car)* con doble juego de pedales; *(plane)* con doble juego de mandos

dualism ['djʊəlɪzəm] *n Phil* dualismo *m*

duality [djʊ'ælɪtɪ] *n* dualidad *f*

dual-purpose ['djʊəl'pɜ:pəs] *adj* de doble uso

dub [dʌb] **1** *n (music)* dub *m*
2 *vt* (*pt & pp* **dubbed**) **(a)** *(movie)* doblar; **dubbed into Spanish** doblado(a) al español **(b)** *(call)* apodar **(c)** *(make a knight)* armar caballero

dubbin ['dʌbɪn] *n* grasa *f* de cuero, ≃ grasa *f* de caballo

dubbing ['dʌbɪŋ] *n Cin* doblaje *m*

dubiety [dju:'baɪətɪ] *n Formal* dudas *fpl*

dubious ['dju:bɪəs] *adj* **(a)** *(uncertain)* dudoso(a), inseguro(a); *(outcome, value)* dudoso(a); **to be d. (about sth)** no estar convencido(a) (de algo); **to look d.** *(person)* parecer dubitativo(a) **(b)** *(questionable) (distinction, honour, reputation, decision, origin)* dudoso(a); **a d. character** un tipo sospechoso; **those mussels look a bit d.** esos mejillones tienen una pinta sospechosa

dubiously ['dju:bɪəslɪ] *adv* **(a)** *(doubtfully)* dudosamente, dubitativamente **(b)** *(in suspect manner)* sospechosamente

Dublin ['dʌblɪn] *n* Dublín ►► ***D. Bay prawn*** langostino *m*

Dubliner ['dʌblɪnə(r)] *n* dublinés(esa) *m,f*

ducat ['dʌkət] *n* **(a)** *Hist* ducado *m* **(b)** *US Fam* **ducats** *(money) Esp* pasta *f*, *Esp, RP* guita *f*, *Am* plata *f*, *Méx* lana *f*

ducal ['dju:kəl] *adj* ducal

duchess ['dʌtʃɪs] *n* duquesa *f*

duchy ['dʌtʃɪ] *n* ducado *m*

duck [dʌk] **1** *n* **(a)** pato *m*; IDIOM **to take to sth like a d. to water** sentirse en algo como pez en el agua; IDIOM **criticism runs off him like water off a d.'s back** le resbalan las críticas ►► ***ducks and drakes:* to play ducks and drakes** *(game)* hacer cabrillas *or* hacer la rana en el agua; IDIOM **to play ducks and drakes with sth** *(money)* despilfarrar algo; *(facts)* tratar algo caprichosamente; ***d. pond*** estanque *m* de patos
(b) *(in cricket)* **to be out for a d.** = ser eliminado sin haber hecho ninguna carrera; *Fig* **to break one's d.** romper la mala racha
(c) *very Fam* ***d.'s*** *Br* ***arse*** *or US* ***ass*** *(hairstyle)* = estilo de peinado masculino popular en los años cincuenta consistente en llevar el pelo corto peinado hacia atrás
(d) *US Fam* **it's d. soup** *(something easily done)* es coser y cantar
(e) *Br Fam (form of address)* **what do you want, ducks?** ¿qué quieres, artista?
(f) *(material)* lona *f*
(g) **ducks** *(trousers)* pantalones *mpl* de lona
2 *vt* **(a)** *(one's head)* agachar; **to d. sb** *(under water)* hacer una ahogadilla a alguien **(b)** *(avoid)* **to d. the issue** eludir el tema
3 *vi (to avoid being hit)* agacharse; *(under water)* zambullirse; **d.!** ¡adentro!; **to d. behind a hedge** agacharse detrás de un seto

► **duck down** *vi* agacharse

► **duck out of** *vt insep* **to d. out of sth/doing sth** zafarse de algo/hacer algo

duck-billed platypus ['dʌkbɪld'plætɪpəs] *n* ornitorrinco *m*

duckboard ['dʌkbɔ:d] *n* tablón *m*; **they laid duckboards over the mud** tendieron un paso de tablones sobre el barro

duck-egg blue ['dʌkeg'blu:] **1** *n* azul *m* verdoso claro
2 *adj* azul verdoso(a) claro(a)

duckie = **ducky**

ducking ['dʌkɪŋ] *n* **he got** *or* **took a d. (thrown into water)** le dieron un chapuzón; *(head pushed under water)* le hicieron una aguadilla *or* ahogadilla; **d. and diving** *(shady dealings)* trapicheos; *(when under attack)* fintas y amagos

duckling ['dʌklɪŋ] *n* patito *m*

duckweed ['dʌkwi:d] *n* lenteja *f* de agua

ducky, duckie ['dʌkɪ] *n Fam* cielo *m*, corazón *m*

duct [dʌkt] *n* **(a)** *(for fuel, air)* conducto *m* **(b)** *Anat* conducto *m*; **tear/hepatic d.** conducto lacrimal/hepático

ductile ['dʌktaɪl] *adj* **(a)** *Tech (metal, plastic)* dúctil **(b)** *(person)* dúctil

dud [dʌd] *Fam* **1** *n* **(a)** *(person)* **to be a d. at maths/sport** ser un desastre para las matemáticas/el deporte **(b)** *(useless thing)* **most of these batteries are duds** la mayoría de estas pilas no van **(c)** *(shell)* proyectil *m* que no estalla
2 *adj* **(a)** *(useless)* defectuoso(a) **(b)** *(banknote)* falso(a); *(cheque)* sin fondos **(c)** *(shell, bomb)* que no estalla

dude [dju:d, du:d] *n US Fam* **(a)** *(man)* tipo *m*, *Esp* tío *m* ►► ***d. ranch*** = rancho acondicionado para el turista urbanita **(b)** *(term of address) Esp* colega *m*, *Esp* tío *m*, *Andes, CAm, Carib, Méx* mano *m*, *RP* flaco *m* **(c)** *(dandy) Esp* pijo(a) *m,f*, *Méx* popis *m inv*, *RP* pituco(a) *m,f*, *Ven* pitoco(a) *m,f*

dudgeon ['dʌdʒən] *n* **in high d.** encolerizado(a)

duds [dʌdz] *npl Fam (clothes)* trapos *mpl*

due [dju:] **1** *adj* **(a)** *(owed)* pagadero(a); **to become** *or* **fall d.** ser pagadero(a); **are you d. any money from him?** ¿te debe dinero?; **you're d. an apology** mereces *or Am* ameritas una disculpa; **I think we're d. a bit of luck/some good weather** creo que ya nos toca tener un poco de suerte/buen tiempo; **I'm d. (for) a rise** *(I will receive one)* me van a subir el sueldo; *(I deserve one)* me deberían subir el sueldo; **d. to...** *(because of, as result of)* debido a...
(b) *(merited, proper)* debido(a); **after d. consideration** tras la debida consideración; **to fail to exercise d. care and attention** ser culpable de negligencia; **to give sb d. warning** poner a alguien sobre aviso; *Law* **d. process (of law)** garantías legales; **with all d. respect,...** con el debido respeto,...; **in d. course** *(when appropriate)* a su debido tiempo; *(eventually)* al final
(c) *(expected)* **the train/he is d. (to arrive) at two o'clock** el tren/él tiene la llegada prevista a las dos; **when is he d.?** ¿cuándo llega?; **to be d. to do sth: he's d. to take up the post next month** está previsto que empiece a trabajar el mes que viene; **she's d. back any minute** volverá en cualquier momento; **when is their baby d.?** ¿para cuándo esperan el niño?; **the movie/book is d. out soon** la película/el libro está a punto de aparecer ►► *Fin* ***d. date*** (fecha *f* de) vencimiento *m*; **when's the d. date?** *(of baby)* ¿cuándo sales de cuentas?; *Fin* ***d. date reminder*** aviso *m* de vencimiento
2 *n* **(a)** *(right)* **to give him his d., he did apologize** para ser justos con él, hay que decir que se disculpó
(b) **dues** *(for membership)* cuota *f*; *Fig* **to pay one's dues** saldar (uno) sus cuentas
3 *adv* **d. north** justo al *or* hacia el norte; **to head d. south** dirigirse derecho al *or* hacia el sur

duel ['djʊəl] **1** *n* (**a**) *(over matter of honour)* duelo *m*; **to fight a d.** batirse en duelo (**b**) *(contest, conflict)* contienda *f*, conflicto *m*
2 *vi* (*pt & pp* **duelled**, *US* **dueled**) (**a**) *(over matter of honour)* batirse en duelo (**with** con) (**b**) *(in contest, conflict)* discutirse, pelearse (**with** con)

duelling, *US* **dueling** ['dju:əlɪŋ] *n* duelos *mpl*; **d. was illegal** era ilegal batirse en duelo ►► ***d. pistols*** pistolas *fpl* de duelo

duellist, *US* **duelist** ['dju:əlɪst] *n* duelista *m*

duet [dju:'et] *n Mus* dúo *m*; **to sing/play a d.** cantar/tocar un dúo; **piano/violin d.** dúo para piano/violín

duff [dʌf] *Fam* **1** *n* (**a**) *(pudding)* pudin *m* de frutas (**b**) IDIOM *Br* **to be up the d.** *(pregnant)* estar preñada; **to get sb up the d.** dejar preñada a alguien (**c**) *US (buttocks)* trasero *m*, culo *m*; **get up off your d.!** ¡mueve el culo!
2 *adj (bad, useless)* malísimo(a); **he's d. at darts** es malísimo jugando a los dardos

►**duff up** *vt sep Br Fam* dar una paliza a

duffel = **duffle**

duffer ['dʌfə(r)] *n Fam* (**a**) *(incompetent person)* ceporro(a) *m,f*, nulidad *f*; **to be a d. at history/French** ser una nulidad en historia/francés (**b**) *(old man)* **old d.** viejales *m inv*, abuelo *m*, *Esp* pureta *m*

duffle, duffel ['dʌfəl] *n* **d. (coat)** trenca *f* ►► ***d. bag*** talega *f* de lona

dug[1] *pt & pp of* **dig**

dug[2] [dʌg] *n* (**a**) *(of animal)* teta *f* (**b**) *Fam (of human)* teta *f*

dugout ['dʌgaʊt] *n* (**a**) *(canoe)* piragua *f*, canoa *f (hecha con un tronco vaciado)* (**b**) *(shelter)* refugio *m* subterráneo (**c**) *Sport* banquillo *m (en foso)*

DUI [di:ju:'aɪ] *n US* (*abbr* **driving under the influence**) **he was charged with D.** le acusaron de conducir *or Am* manejar bajo los efectos del alcohol

duke [dju:k] *n* (**a**) *(nobleman)* duque *m*; **the D. of York** el duque de York (**b**) *Fam (fist)* puño *m*; **put up your dukes!** ¡en guardia!

►**duke out** *vt sep US Old-fashioned* **to d. it out (with sb)** pelear a puñetazos (con alguien)

dukedom ['dju:kdəm] *n (territory, title)* ducado *m*

dulcet ['dʌlsɪt] *adj Literary* dulce, melodioso(a); *Ironic* **her d. tones** su dulce voz

dulcimer ['dʌlsɪmə(r)] *n Mus* salterio *m*, dulcémele *m*

dull [dʌl] **1** *adj* (**a**) *(boring) (book, movie, person)* aburrido(a); *(job, life, party)* insulso(a), soso(a); **it's deadly d. here** esto es un aburrimiento; **there's never a d. moment with him around** cuando estás con él no tienes un momento de aburrimiento; IDIOM **to be as d. as ditchwater** ser más soso(a) que la calabaza
(**b**) *(not intelligent)* tonto(a), torpe, *Am* sonso(a), *Am* zonzo(a)
(**c**) *(listless)* apático(a)
(**d**) *(not sharp) (tool, blade)* romo(a); *(sound, pain)* sordo(a)
(**e**) *(not bright) (colour, surface)* mate, apagado(a); *(light)* tenue, velado(a); *(eyes)* apagado(a); *(weather, sky)* gris, triste
(**f**) *Com & Fin (market)* flojo(a)
2 *vt* (**a**) *(reduce intensity of) (pleasure)* enturbiar; *(the senses)* embotar; *(pain)* mitigar, atenuar; *(sound)* apagar
(**b**) *(make less bright) (colours, eyes)* apagar
(**c**) *(make blunt) (blade)* desafilar, embotar
3 *vi* (**a**) *(become less acute) (pleasure)* atenuar, mermar; *(pain)* paliar, mitigar; *(mind)* embotar (**b**) *(become less bright) (colour)* apagarse; *(eyes)* perder el brillo

dullard ['dʌləd] *n Literary* pavisoso(a) *m,f*, sosaina *mf*

dullness ['dʌlnɪs] *n* (**a**) *(tedium)* **the d. of the book/speech** lo aburrido que era el libro/discurso (**b**) *(lack of intelligence)* necedad *f*, torpeza *f* (**c**) *(listlessness)* apatía *f* (**d**) *(of tool, blade)* embotamiento *m*; *(of sound, pain)* lo amortiguado (**e**) *(of colour, surface, light, eyes)* falta *f* de brillo; **the d. of the sky/weather depressed him** el cielo/tiempo gris lo deprimía

dullsville ['dʌlzvɪl] *n Fam (boring place)* **it's d. round here** este lugar es aburridísimo *or Esp* es un muermo

dully ['dʌllɪ] *adv* (**a**) *(boringly)* pesadamente (**b**) *(not brightly)* pálidamente, sin brillo (**c**) *(listlessly)* apáticamente, con apatía; **..., she said d.** ..., dijo con apatía

duly ['dju:lɪ] *adv* (**a**) *(properly)* como corresponde, debidamente; **d. appointed/elected** nombrado(a)/elegido(a) como corresponde; **we were d. worried** estábamos preocupados con razón (**b**) *(as expected)* **he said he'd be punctual and he d. arrived on the stroke of eight** dijo que llegaría puntual y confirmando las previsiones, llegó a las ocho en punto

dumb [dʌm] *adj* (**a**) *(mute)* mudo(a); **to be struck d. with astonishment** quedarse mudo(a) de asombro; **d. animals** los animales indefensos; **d. insolence** actitud insolente; **in d. show** sin palabras
(**b**) *US Fam (stupid) (person, action)* bobo(a), estúpido(a); **that was a d. thing to do/say** fue una estupidez hacer/decir eso; **to play** *or* **act d.** hacerse el tonto; **d. blonde** rubia *or Méx* güera sin cerebro
(**c**) **d. waiter** *(between floors)* montaplatos; *(stand)* mesita auxiliar

►**dumb down** *vt sep (population, youth, electorate)* reducir el nivel cultural de; *(newspaper, programme)* empobrecer los contenidos de

dumbass ['dʌmæs] *US very Fam* **1** *n* gil *mf*, lerdo(a) *m,f*, *Esp* gilipuertas *mf inv*
2 *adj* lerdo(a), *Esp* gilipollesco(a)

dumbbell ['dʌmbel] *n* (**a**) *(for weightlifting)* pesa *f* (**b**) *Fam (person)* colgado(a) *m,f*

dumbfound [dʌm'faʊnd] *vt* dejar boquiabierto(a), dejar pasmado(a); **we were dumbfounded by the news** la noticia nos dejó boquiabiertos *or* pasmados

dumbfuck ['dʌmfʌk] *n Vulg* cabrón(ona) *m,f*

dumbing (down) ['dʌmɪŋ(daʊn)] *n (of population, youth, electorate)* reducción *f* del nivel cultural; *(of newspaper, programme)* empobrecimiento *m* de contenidos

dumbly ['dʌmlɪ] *adv* sin decir palabra

dumbo ['dʌmbəʊ] *n Fam* idiota *mf*, imbécil *mf*

dumbstruck ['dʌmstrʌk] *adj* boquiabierto(a), pasmado(a)

dumdum bullet ['dʌmdʌm'bʊlɪt] *n* (bala *f*) dumdum *f*

dummy ['dʌmɪ] **1** *n* (**a**) *(in shop window)* maniquí *m*; *(of ventriloquist)* muñeco *m*
(**b**) *(fake object for display)* **to be a d.** ser de pega; **all the bottles are dummies** todas las botellas son de pega
(**c**) *Br (for baby)* chupete *m*
(**d**) *Fam (idiot)* idiota *mf*, imbécil *mf*
(**e**) *Pej (mute)* mudo(a) *m,f*
(**f**) *(in soccer, rugby)* amago *m*; **to sell sb a d.** hacerle un amago a alguien
(**g**) *(in bridge)* mano *f* del muerto
(**h**) *Fin (representative)* hombre *m* de paja
2 *vt (in soccer, rugby)* **to d. sb** hacerle un amago a alguien
3 *adj (fake)* falso(a) ►► *Fin* ***d. buyer*** comprador(ora) *m,f* ficticio(a); ***d. issue*** *(of newspaper, magazine)* ejemplar *m* de prueba; ***d. run*** prueba *f*

►**dummy up** *vi US Fam (remain quiet)* no decir ni mu

dump [dʌmp] **1** *n* (**a**) *(for refuse)* vertedero *m*, basurero *m* ►► ***d. truck*** volquete *m*
(**b**) *Fam (town)* ciudad *f* de mala muerte; *(village)* pueblo *m* de mala muerte; *(messy room, flat)* pocilga *f*; **what a d.!** ¡qué asco de sitio!, *Esp* ¡qué sitio más cutre!, *RP* ¡qué lugar más terraja!
(**c**) *Mil (store)* depósito *m*
(**d**) *Comptr* **(memory** *or* **storage) d.** volcado *m* de memoria
(**e**) *very Fam* **to** *Br* **have** *or US* **take a d.** *(defecate)* jiñar, poner una piedra
2 *vt* (**a**) *(put down)* soltar, dejar; *(unload)* descargar; **just d. your bags over there** pon *or* deja tus bolsas ahí; **I'm just going home to d. my things** voy a casa a dejar mis cosas
(**b**) *(dispose of) (rubbish, old car)* tirar, *Am* botar; *(nuclear, toxic waste)* verter; *Fam (lover, boyfriend, girlfriend)* dejar, dar calabazas a; **he just dumped me off at the motorway exit** me dejó tirado a la salida de la autopista; *Fam* **to d. sth on sb** encasquetar algo a alguien; **she's dumped the kids on me for the weekend** me ha encasquetado (a) los niños durante el fin de semana
(**c**) *Econ* inundar el mercado con, hacer dumping con
(**d**) *Comptr (memory)* volcar

►**dump on** *vt insep US Fam (criticize) (person)* poner verde a; *(project, suggestion)* dejar por los suelos, *Esp* poner a parir *or* como un trapo, *Méx* viborear

dumpbin ['dʌmpbɪn] *n Com* expositor *m*

dumper ['dʌmpə(r)] *n* **d. (truck)** volquete *m*

dumping ['dʌmpɪŋ] *n* (**a**) **no d.** *(sign)* prohibido arrojar basuras ►► ***d. ground*** vertedero *m* (**b**) *Econ* dumping *m*

dumpling ['dʌmplɪŋ] *n* (**a**) *(in stew)* = bola de masa hervida (**b**) *(sweet)* **apple d.** bollo relleno de manzana (**c**) *Fam (fat man, woman)* gordo(a) *m,f*

dumps [dʌmps] *npl* IDIOM *Fam* **to be down in the d.** estar con la moral por los suelos, *Am* estar con el ánimo por el piso

Dumpster® ['dʌmpstə(r)] *n US* contenedor *m* (de escombros)

dumpy ['dʌmpɪ] *adj Fam* rechoncho(a), achaparrado(a)

dun[1] [dʌn] 1 *n* (a) *(colour)* pardo *m* (b) *(horse)* caballo *m* pardo
2 *adj (colour)* pardo(a)

dun[2] *(pt & pp* **dunned**) *vt* **to d. sb for payment** apremiar a alguien para que pague; **a dunning letter** una carta en la que se pide que se pague una deuda

dunce [dʌns] *n* burro(a) *m,f;* **to be a d. at sth** ser muy burro(a) para algo ►► ***d.'s*** *or* ***d. cap*** ≃ orejas *fpl* de burro

dunderhead ['dʌndəhed] *n Fam* tonto(a) *m,f* del bote

dune [dju:n] *n* **(sand) d.** duna *f* ►► ***d. buggy*** buggy *m*

dung [dʌŋ] *n* (a) *(excrement)* excremento *m* (b) *(manure)* estiércol *m*

dungarees [dʌŋgə'ri:z] *npl* (a) *(with bib)* (pantalón *m* de) peto *m;* **a pair of d.** unos pantalones de peto (b) *US (trousers)* vaqueros *mpl, Chile* bluyíns *mpl, Méx* pantalones *mpl* de mezclilla

dung-beetle ['dʌŋbi:təl] *n* escarabajo *m* pelotero

dungeon ['dʌndʒən] *n* mazmorra *f*

dungheap ['dʌŋhi:p], **dunghill** ['dʌŋhɪl] *n* estercolero *m*

dunk [dʌŋk] 1 *n (in basketball)* mate *m*
2 *vt* (a) *(in liquid) (dip)* mojar; *(submerge)* sumergir, hundir (b) *(in basketball)* machacar

Dunkirk [dʌn'kɜ:k] *n* Dunkerque

dunlin ['dʌnlɪn] *n* correlimos *m inv*

dunno [də'nəʊ] *Fam* = **don't know**

dunnock ['dʌnək] *n* acentor *m*

duo ['dju:əʊ] *(pl* **duos**) *n* dúo *m*

duodecimal [dju:əʊ'desɪməl] *adj* duodecimal

duodenal [dju:əʊ'di:nəl] *adj Anat* duodenal

duodenum [dju:əʊ'di:nəm] *n Anat* duodeno *m*

duopoly [dju:'ɒpəlɪ] *n Com* duopolio *m*

DUP [di:ju:'pi:] *n* (*abbr* **Democratic Unionist Party**) = Partido Unionista Democrático, que apoya la permanencia de Irlanda del Norte en el Reino Unido

dupe [dju:p] 1 *n* ingenuo(a) *m,f,* primo(a) *m,f*
2 *vt* engañar; **to d. sb into doing sth** engañar a alguien para que haga algo; **she duped him into believing that...** le hizo creer que...

duplex ['dju:pleks] 1 *n US (apartment)* dúplex *m*
2 *adj* (a) *US* ***d. apartment*** dúplex *m;* ***d. house*** chalet *m* adosado (b) *Comptr* dúplex *m*

duplicate ['dju:plɪkət] 1 *n (copy)* duplicado *m,* copia *f;* **in d.** por duplicado
2 *adj (key, document)* duplicado(a); *(receipt, certificate)* por duplicado; **d. copy** *(of key, receipt, certificate)* duplicado, copia
3 *vt* ['dju:plɪkeɪt] (a) *(document)* duplicar, hacer un duplicado de; *(key)* copiar, hacer un duplicado de (b) *(result, conditions)* repetir; **we're duplicating work unnecessarily** estamos duplicando el trabajo innecesariamente

duplicating machine ['dju:plɪkeɪtɪŋmə'ʃi:n] *n* copiadora *f*

duplication [dju:plɪ'keɪʃən] *n* (a) *(copying)* duplicación *f* (b) *(repetition)* repetición *f;* **to avoid d. of effort** para evitar la duplicación del trabajo

duplicator ['dju:plɪkeɪtə(r)] *n (machine)* mimeógrafo *m,* multicopista *f*

duplicitous [dju:'plɪsɪtəs] *adj Formal* falso(a), artero(a)

duplicity [dju:'plɪsɪtɪ] *n Formal* duplicidad *f*

durability [djʊərə'bɪlɪtɪ] *n* (a) *(of construction, fabric)* durabilidad *f* (b) *(of relationship, peace)* durabilidad *f; (of politician, athlete)* resistencia *f*

durable ['djʊərəbəl] 1 *adj* (a) *(construction, fabric)* duradero(a) (b) *(friendship, peace)* duradero(a); *(politician, athlete)* resistente (c) *Com* **d. goods** bienes duraderos
2 *n* **(consumer) durables** bienes *mpl* de consumo duraderos

duration [djʊ'reɪʃən] *n* duración *f;* **to be of short/long d.** ser de corta/larga duración, durar poco/mucho; **for the d. of** durante todo(a); **for the d.** hasta el final

duress [djʊ'res] *n* **under d.** bajo coacción

> **False friend:** The Spanish noun **dureza** is not a translation for the English word **duress**. In Spanish **dureza** means "hardness", "harshness" or "strength".

durex® ['dju:reks] *n* (a) *Br Fam (condom)* condón *m,* preservativo *m* (b) *Austr (adhesive tape)* cinta *f* adhesiva, *Esp* papel *m* celo

durian ['djʊərɪən] *n* durián *m*

during ['djʊərɪŋ] *prep* (a) *(in the course of)* durante; **they met d. the war** se conocieron durante la guerra; **d. the investigation it emerged that...** durante la investigación salió a la luz que... (b) *(throughout)* durante; **d. the war it was used as a hospital** durante la guerra se utilizó como hospital

durst [dɜ:st] *Archaic or Literary pt of* **dare**

durum ['dʌrəm] *n* **d. (wheat)** trigo *m* duro

dusk [dʌsk] *n* crepúsculo *m,* anochecer *m;* **at d.** al anochecer

duskiness ['dʌskɪnɪs] *n* **the d. of his complexion** su tez morena

dusky ['dʌskɪ] *adj* (a) *(dark) (room, colour)* oscuro(a) (b) *(complexion)* moreno(a), oscuro(a); *Hum* **a d. maiden** una doncella de tez morena

dust [dʌst] 1 *n* (a) *(dirt, powder)* polvo *m* ►► ***d. bag*** *(for vacuum cleaner)* bolsa *f;* ***d. bowl*** zona *f* semidesértica; ***d. cloth*** trapo *m or* bayeta *f* del polvo; ***d. cloud*** polvareda *f,* nube *f* de polvo; ***d. cover*** *(for book)* sobrecubierta *f; (for furniture) (fitted)* funda *f; (loose)* sábana *f (para proteger del polvo);* ***d. devil*** remolino *m;* ***d. jacket*** *(for book)* sobrecubierta *f;* ***d. sheet*** sábana *f (para proteger del polvo);* ***d. storm*** tormenta *f* de polvo
(b) *(action)* **to give sth a d.** quitar *or* sacar el polvo a algo
(c) *Literary (earthly remains)* polvo *m*
(d) IDIOMS **to let the d. settle** dejar que las aguas vuelvan a su cauce; **once the d. has settled** *(when the fuss is over)* cuando haya pasado la tormenta; *Fam* **you won't see me for d.!** pondré pies en polvorosa
2 *vt* (a) *(clean) (room, furniture)* limpiar el polvo de; IDIOM **done and dusted: we thought the deal was done and dusted** creíamos que el acuerdo estaba atado y bien atado (b) *(sprinkle) (with flour, sugar)* espolvorear (**with** con)

► **dust down** *vt sep* (a) *(clothes, furniture)* quitar *or* sacar el polvo a; **he dusted himself down** se sacudió el polvo (b) *(reprimand)* reprender

► **dust off** *vt sep* (a) *(clothes, furniture)* quitar *or* sacar el polvo a; *(crumbs, dandruff)* sacudir; **he dusted himself off** se sacudió el polvo (b) *Fig (legislation, one's French)* desempolvar

dust-bath ['dʌstbɑ:θ] *n* **to take a d.** *(bird)* revolcarse en el polvo

dustbin ['dʌstbɪn] *n Br* cubo *m or Am* bote *m* de la basura ►► ***d. lid*** tapa *f* del cubo *or Am* bote de la basura; ***d. liner*** bolsa *f* de basura; ***d. man*** basurero *m*

dustcart ['dʌstkɑ:t] *n Br* camión *m* de la basura

dustcloth ['dʌstklɒθ] *n US* trapo *m or* bayeta *f* del polvo

duster ['dʌstə(r)] *n* (a) *Br (cloth)* trapo *m or* bayeta *f* del polvo; *(for blackboard)* borrador *m* (b) *US (housecoat)* guardapolvo *m* (c) *US (coat)* guardapolvo *m*

dust-free ['dʌst'fri:] *adj (environment)* sin polvo

dustheap ['dʌsthi:p] *n US (rubbish heap)* basura *f,* basurero *m;* IDIOM **to be consigned to the d.** *(idea, plan)* quedar descartado(a); **if you don't update your skills you'll end up on the d.** como no te recicles nadie te va a querer contratar

dusting ['dʌstɪŋ] *n* (a) *(of room, furniture)* **to do the d.** limpiar *or* quitar el polvo (b) *(with sugar)* **give the cake a d. of cocoa** espolvorear el pastel con cacao

dustman ['dʌstmən] *n Br* basurero *m*

dustpan ['dʌstpæn] *n* recogedor *m* ►► ***d. and brush*** cepillo *m* y recogedor

dust-up ['dʌstʌp] *n Fam (brawl)* bronca *f,* trifulca *f;* **to have a d. (with sb)** tener una bronca (con alguien)

dusty ['dʌstɪ] *adj* (a) *(room, furniture, road)* polvoriento(a); **to get d.** llenarse de polvo (b) *(colour)* apagado(a) (c) IDIOM *Br Fam* **to get a d. answer** ser respondido(a) con evasivas

Dutch [dʌtʃ] 1 *npl (people)* **the D.** los holandeses
2 *n* (a) *(language)* neerlandés *m* (b) *Br Fam (wife)* **the old D.** la parienta
3 *adj* holandés(esa) ►► ***the D. Antilles*** las Antillas Holandesas; ***D. auction*** = subasta en la que se va bajando el precio hasta encontrar comprador; ***D. barn*** *Br* = granero metálico con el techo abovedado; *US* = granero de estilo colonial con tejado puntiagudo; ***D. cap*** *(contraceptive)* diafragma *m;* ***D. courage*** = valentía que da el alcohol; ***D. elm disease*** enfermedad *f* de los olmos; ***D. oven*** *(cooking pot)* = cazuela pesada con tapa; ***D. treat*** = salida en la que cada cual paga lo suyo; ***D. uncle:*** **to talk to sb like a D. uncle** echar una reprimenda *or Esp* rapapolvo a alguien
4 *adv* IDIOM *Fam* **to go D.** pagar cada uno lo suyo, *Esp* pagar a escote

Dutchman ['dʌtʃmən] *n* holandés *m;* IDIOM *Fam* **if that's a real diamond (then) I'm a D.** si eso es un diamante de verdad, que venga Dios y lo vea

Dutchwoman ['dʌtʃwʊmən] *n* holandesa *f*

dutiable ['dju:tɪəbəl] *adj* sujeto(a) a derechos, imponible

dutiful ['dju:tɪfʊl] *adj* obediente

dutifully ['dju:tɪfʊlɪ] *adv* obedientemente, sin rechistar

duty ['dju:tɪ] *n* (**a**) *(obligation)* deber *m*; **he did his d.** cumplió con su deber; **he failed in his d.** faltó a *or* no cumplió con su deber; **I shall make it my d. to...** yo me ocuparé de...; **it is my painful d. to inform you that...** siento mucho tener que comunicarle que... ; **it is your d. to...** tu deber es...; **he did it out of a sense of d.** lo hizo porque sentía que era su deber; **I'll have to go, d. calls** tengo que ir, el deber me llama ▸▸ ***d. call*** visita *f* de compromiso
(**b**) *(task)* **duties** tareas *fpl*; **she took up** *or* **assumed her duties** se incorporó a su puesto; **she carried out** *or* **performed her duties well** desempeñó bien su trabajo; **she handed over her duties (to her successor)** delegó sus responsabilidades (en su sucesor); **in the course of one's duties** en el desempeño de sus funciones
(**c**) *(of soldier, doctor, policeman)* **to be on d.** estar de servicio; **to be off d.** estar fuera de servicio; **to go on/off d.** empezar/terminar el turno de servicio; *Mil* **tour of d.** destino; IDIOM **to do d. as sth** hacer de algo, servir de algo ▸▸ ***d. chemist's*** farmacia *f* de turno *or* de guardia; ***d. doctor*** médico(a) *m,f* de guardia; ***d. manager*** encargado(a) *m,f* de turno; ***d. officer*** oficial *mf* de guardia; ***d. roster*** rota *f* de guardias
(**d**) *Fin (tax)* derecho *m*, impuesto *m*; **to pay d. on sth** pagar derechos *or* impuestos por algo

duty-bound ['dju:tɪbaʊnd] *adj* **to feel d. to do sth** sentirse obligado(a) a hacer algo

duty-free ['dju:tɪ'fri:] **1** *n Fam (goods)* artículos *mpl* libres de impuestos; **I'm just going to get some d.** voy a comprar algo al duty-free
2 *adj* exento(a) *or* libre de impuestos ▸▸ ***d. allowance*** cantidad *f* libre de impuestos; ***d. shop*** tienda *f* libre de impuestos

duvet ['du:veɪ] *n Br* edredón *m* ▸▸ ***d. cover*** funda *f* de edredón

DVD [di:vi:'di:] *n Comptr* (*abbr* **Digital Versatile Disk**, **Digital Video Disk**) DVD *m* ▸▸ ***D. player*** reproductor *m or* lector *m* de DVD

DVLA [di:vi:el'eɪ] *n* (*abbr* **Driver and Vehicle Licensing Agency**) ≃ Dirección *f* General de Tráfico

DVM [di:vi:'em] *n* (*abbr* **Doctor of Veterinary Medicine**) veterinario(a) *m,f*

dwarf [dwɔ:f] **1** *n* (*pl* **dwarfs** *or* **dwarves** [dwɔ:vz]) (**a**) *Mythol* enano(a) *m,f* (**b**) *(person)* enano(a) *m,f* (**c**) *(plant, tree)* variedad *f* enana
2 *adj (plant, tree)* enano(a) ▸▸ ***d. star*** estrella *f* enana
3 *vt (of building, achievements)* empequeñecer; **the church is dwarfed by the new skyscraper** el nuevo rascacielos hace pequeña a la iglesia

dweeb [dwi:b] *n US Fam* petardo(a) *m,f*

dwell [dwel] (*pt & pp* **dwelt** [dwelt]) *vi Literary (live)* morar; **to d. in one's mind** *(image, thought)* permanecer

▸ **dwell on, dwell upon** *vt insep* **to d. on sth at some length** *(in lecture, book)* explayarse *or* extenderse bastante; **why d. on the negative side of things?** ¿para qué fijarse en el lado negativo de las cosas?; **let's not** *or* **don't let's d. on it** no le demos más vueltas al asunto

-dweller ['dwelə(r)] *suffix* **cave-d.** cavernícola; **city-d.** habitante de la ciudad

dwelling ['dwelɪŋ] *n* (**a**) *Literary (abode)* morada *f*; **the gods had their d. place on Mount Olympus** los dioses moraban en el monte Olimpo (**b**) *Formal (house)* vivienda *f* ▸▸ ***d. house*** residencia *f*

dwelt *pt & pp of* **dwell**

DWEM [dwem] *n* (*abbr* **dead white European male**) = varón europeo blanco muerto

DWI ['di:dʌbəlju:'aɪ] *n US* (*abbr* **driving while intoxicated**) **he was charged with D.** le acusaron de conducir *or Am* manejar bajo los efectos del alcohol

dwindle ['dwɪndəl] *vi (hopes, savings, population)* disminuir, reducirse; **to d. (away) to nothing** quedar reducido(a) a nada

dwindling ['dwɪndlɪŋ] *adj (funds, membership)* menguante; *(enthusiasm, hopes, audience)* decreciente

DWP [di:dʌbəlju:'pi:] *n* (*abbr* **Department for Work and Pensions**) = ministerio británico de seguridad social y empleo

dye [daɪ] **1** *n* (**a**) *(for clothes, hair)* tinte *m*; **the d. has run** ha desteñido (**b**) *Literary* **a villain of the deepest d.** un malvado de la peor calaña
2 *vt (fabric, hair)* teñir; **to d. sth black/red** teñir algo de negro/rojo; **to d. one's hair** teñirse el pelo
3 *vi (fabric)* teñirse; **nylon doesn't d. well** el nylon no se tiñe bien, el nylon no coge bien el tinte

dyed-in-the-wool ['daɪdɪnðə'wʊl] *adj* acérrimo(a)

dyer ['daɪə(r)] *n* tintorero(a) *m,f*

dyestuff ['daɪstʌf] *n* tinte *m*, tintura *f*

dyeworks ['daɪwɜ:ks] *n* taller *m* de teñido, tintorería *f*

dying ['daɪɪŋ] **1** *adj (person, animal)* moribundo(a), agonizante; *(art, industry, tradition)* en vías de desaparición; **to** *or* **till my d. day** hasta el día de mi muerte; IDIOM **men like him are a d. breed** quedan pocos hombres como él ▸▸ ***d. wish*** última voluntad *f*; ***d. words*** últimas palabras *fpl*
2 *npl* **the d.** los moribundos

dyke, dike [daɪk] *n* (**a**) *(barrier)* dique *m* (**b**) *(ditch)* zanja *f* (**c**) *very Fam Pej (lesbian)* tortillera *f*

dynamic [daɪ'næmɪk] **1** *adj* (**a**) *(energetic)* dinámico(a) (**b**) *Comptr* ***d. data exchange*** intercambio *m* dinámico de datos; ***d. HTML*** HTML *m* dinámico; ***d. RAM*** RAM *f* dinámica
2 *n* dinámica *f*

dynamics [daɪ'næmɪks] **1** *npl (of change, growth)* dinámica *f*
2 *n Phys* dinámica *f*

dynamism ['daɪnəmɪzəm] *n* dinamismo *m*

dynamite ['daɪnəmaɪt] **1** *n* (**a**) *(explosive)* dinamita *f* (**b**) IDIOMS **this information is political d.** esta información es políticamente explosiva; *Fam* **it's d.!** *(marvellous)* ¡es genial!
2 *vt* dinamitar

dynamo ['daɪnəməʊ] (*pl* **dynamos**) *n* (**a**) *Elec* dinamo *f* (**b**) *Fig (person)* máquina *f*

dynamometer [daɪnə'mɒmɪtə(r)] *n Tech* dinamómetro *m*

dynastic [dɪ'næstɪk] *adj* dinástico(a)

dynasty ['dɪnəstɪ] *n* dinastía *f*

dyne [daɪn] *n Phys* dina *f*

dysentery ['dɪsəntrɪ] *n* disentería *f*

dysfunction [dɪs'fʌŋkʃən] *n (of organ)* disfunción *f*

dysfunctional [dɪs'fʌŋkʃənəl] *adj* disfuncional ▸▸ ***d. family*** familia *f* desestructurada

dyslexia [dɪs'leksɪə] *n* dislexia *f*; **to suffer from d.** ser disléxico(a), padecer dislexia

dyslexic [dɪs'leksɪk] *adj* disléxico(a)

dysmenorrhoea, *US* **dysmenorrhea** [dɪsmenə'rɪə] *n Med* dismenorrea *f*

dyspepsia [dɪs'pepsɪə] *n Med* dispepsia *f*

dyspeptic [dɪs'peptɪk] *adj* (**a**) *Med* dispéptico(a), que hace malas digestiones (**b**) *Formal (bad-tempered)* malhumorado(a); **to be in a d. mood** estar de mal humor

dysphasia [dɪs'feɪzɪə] *n Med* disfasia *f*, afasia *f* moderada

dyspnoea, *US* **dyspnea** [dɪsp'nɪə] *n Med* disnea *f*

dystrophy ['dɪstrəfɪ] *n Med* distrofia *f*

E, e

E, e [iː] *n (letter)* E, e *f*

E [iː] *n* (**a**) *Mus* mi *m* (**b**) (*abbr* **east**) E (**c**) *Sch* baja calificación *f*; **to get an E** *(in exam, essay)* obtener una baja calificación (**d**) *Fam* (*abbr* **ecstasy**) *(drug)* éxtasis *m inv* (**e**) IDIOM *Br Fam* **to give sb the big E** deshacerse de alguien, dar calabazas a alguien

ea. (*abbr* **each**) **£3.00 ea.** tres libras cada uno(a)

EACH [iːtʃ] **1** *adj* cada; **e. day** cada día; **e. one (of them)** cada uno (de ellos); **e. (and every) one of us** todos (y cada uno de) nosotros; **an e. way bet** *(in horse racing)* = apuesta que se gana si el caballo queda entre los tres primeros

2 *pron* (**a**) *(both, all)* cada uno(a); **we e. earn $300, we earn $300 e.** ganamos cada uno 300 dólares, ganamos 300 dólares cada uno; **oranges at 25 pence e.** naranjas a 25 peniques la pieza *or* cada una; **you can have one e.** pueden tomar uno cada (uno); **e. of us** cada uno de nosotros; **her novels, e. of which is a masterpiece,...** sus novelas, cada una de las cuales es una obra maestra,...; **a little of e.** un poco de cada (uno); **take one of e.** tomen uno de cada (uno); **it may seem odd, but e. to his own** aunque parezca extraño, sobre gustos no hay nada escrito

(**b**) *(reciprocal)* **to hate e. other** odiarse; **to kiss e. other** besarse; **they were made for e. other** fueron hechos el uno para el otro; **to support e. other** apoyarse mutuamente; **we used to copy e. other's homework** solíamos copiarnos los deberes; **stop screaming at e. other!** *Esp* ¡dejad de gritar!, *Am* ¡déjense de gritar!; **we write to e. other** nos escribimos; **they are always arguing with e. other** siempre están discutiendo

eager [ˈiːgə(r)] *adj (look, interest)* ávido(a), ansioso(a); *(supporter, helper)* entusiasta; *(desire, hope)* intenso(a); **to be e. for sth** estar ansioso(a) por *or* ávido(a) de algo; **to be e. for affection/for success** tener una gran necesidad de afecto/de triunfar; **the audience were e. for more** el público seguía pidiendo más; **he's e. for me to see his work** está ansioso porque yo vea su trabajo; **to be e. to do sth** estar ansioso(a) por hacer algo; **to be e. to please** estar deseoso(a) por agradar; **they were e. to learn** estaban ávidos *or* ansiosos por aprender; IDIOM *Fam* **to be an e. beaver** ser muy aplicado(a)

eagerly [ˈiːgəlɪ] *adv (to ask, say, look at)* ávidamente, ansiosamente; *(to wait)* con ansiedad *or* impaciencia; *(to listen)* con avidez; **e. awaited** ansiado(a), largamente esperado(a)

eagerness [ˈiːgənɪs] *n (impatience)* avidez *f*, ansia *f*; *(enthusiasm)* entusiasmo *m*; **his e. to please** su afán de agradar; **in her e. to leave, she forgot the key** en su afán por marcharse, se olvidó de la llave

eagle [ˈiːgəl] **1** *n* (**a**) *(bird)* águila *f*; IDIOM **under the e. eye of...** bajo la atenta mirada de... ▸▸ ***e. owl*** búho *m* real (**b**) *(in golf)* dos *m* bajo par, eagle *m*; **an e. 3** un eagle en un par 5

2 *vt (in golf)* **to e. a hole** hacer dos bajo par *or* eagle en un hoyo

eagle-eyed [ˈiːgəlˈaɪd] *adj* **to be e.** tener vista de lince

eaglet [ˈiːglɪt] *n* aguilucho *m*

E and OE *Fin* (*abbr* **errors and omissions excepted**) s.e.u.o.

ear [ˈɪə(r)] *n* (**a**) *(of person, animal) (external part)* oreja *f*; *(internal part)* oído *m*; **he has an e. infection** tiene una infección en el oído ▸▸ *Med* ***e., nose and throat specialist*** otorrinolaringólogo(a) *m,f*; *Med* ***e., nose and throat department*** departamento *m* de otorrinolaringología; ***e. piercing*** perforación *f* de las orejas; ***e. trumpet*** trompetilla *f*

(**b**) *(hearing, perception)* oído *m*; **I could scarcely believe my ears** no daba crédito a lo que estaba oyendo *or* lo que oían mis oídos; **to keep an e.** *or* **one's ears open** estar alerta *or* atento(a); **keep an e. open for the baby** está atento(a) al bebé; **to reach sb's ears** *(news, rumour)* llegar a (los) oídos de alguien; **to have a good e.** tener buen oído; **to have an e. for music** tener buen oído para la música; **to have an e. for languages** tener aptitudes para los idiomas; **to play by e.** *(instrument, tune)* tocar de oído; *Fig* **let's play it by e.** ya veremos sobre la marcha

(**c**) *(of wheat)* espiga *f*

(**d**) IDIOMS **he closed his ears to her request for help** hizo oídos sordos a su petición de ayuda; **to keep one's ears pinned back** ser todo oídos; **to keep one's e. to the ground** mantenerse al corriente; **I was listening to them with half an e.** estaba medio escuchándolos(as); **he has the boss's e.** goza de la confianza del jefe; **the house was falling down around their ears** la casa se les caía encima; *Fam* **to be up to one's ears in work/debt** estar hasta las *Esp* cejas *or Am* narices de trabajo/deudas; *Fam* **to have sth coming out of one's ears** estar hasta arriba *or Am* las narices de algo; **to go in one e. and out the other** *(words, information)* entrar por un oído y salir por el otro; *Fam* **to be (thrown) out on one's e.** ser puesto(a) de patitas en la calle; **to grin from e. to e.** sonreír de oreja a oreja; **his ears are flapping** *(he's listening closely)* está con las antenas puestas *or RP* orejas paradas; **his ears must be burning** no se habla más que de él; *Fam* **I'm all ears** soy todo oídos

earache [ˈɪəreɪk] *n* dolor *m* de oídos

ear-bashing [ˈɪəbæʃɪŋ] *n Fam* reprimenda *f*, *Esp* bronca *f*, *Méx* jalada *f*, *RP* rezongo *m*; **to give sb an e.** echar una reprimenda *or Esp* bronca a alguien, dar a alguien *Méx* una jalada *or RP* un buen rezongo

eardrops [ˈɪədrɒps] *npl* gotas *fpl* para los oídos

eardrum [ˈɪədrʌm] *n* tímpano *m*

-eared [ɪəd] *suffix* **long/short-e.** con orejas largas/cortas

earflap [ˈɪəflæp] *n (on cap)* orejera *f*

earful [ˈɪəfʊl] *n Fam* (**a**) **to give sb an e.** *(scold, criticize)* echar un sermón *or Esp* una bronca a alguien, *RP* dar a alguien un buen rezongo; **to get an e.** llevarse un sermón *or Esp* una bronca *or RP* un rezongo (**b**) **get an e. of this!** *(news, gossip)* ¡pon la antena!

ear-hole [ˈɪəhəʊl] *n* agujero *m* de la oreja

earl [ɜːl] *n* conde *m* ▸▸ ***E. Grey (tea)*** = tipo de té chino, muy popular en Gran Bretaña, con sabor suave

earldom [ˈɜːldəm] *n* título *m* de conde, condado *m*

earlier [ˈɜːlɪə(r)] **1** *adj* anterior; **I caught an e. train** tomé *or Esp* cogí un tren anterior; **her e. novels** sus novelas anteriores; **it's e. than I thought** es más temprano de lo que creía; **could I have an e. appointment?** ¿podría darme una cita a primera hora?

2 *adv* **e. (on)** antes; **a few days e.** unos días antes; **e. that day** ese mismo día con anterioridad; **no e. than tomorrow** no antes de mañana; **as we saw e.** como vimos anteriormente *or* antes

earliest [ˈɜːlɪəst] **1** *n* **at the e.** como muy pronto; **the e. I can be there is four o'clock** no podré estar ahí antes de las cuatro; **what's the e. you can make it?** ¿a qué hora puede estar?

2 *adj (opportunity, memory)* primero(a); **from the e. times** desde los primeros tiempos; **from the e. days of the century** desde principios de siglo; **at the e. possible moment** lo antes posible; **what is your e. possible delivery date?** ¿cuál es su fecha de entrega más inmediata?; *Com* **at your e. convenience** en cuanto le sea posible

earliness [ˈɜːlɪnɪs] *n* **the e. of the hour** lo temprano de la hora

earlobe [ˈɪələʊb] *n* lóbulo *m* de la oreja

EARLY [ˈɜːlɪ] **1** *adj* (*comparative* **earlier** [ˈɜːlɪə(r)], *superlative* **earliest** [ˈɜːlɪəst]) (**a**) *(in the day)* temprano(a); **at this e. hour...** a una hora tan temprana...; **the e. hours** las primeras horas de la mañana, la madrugada; **in the e. afternoon** a primera hora de la tarde; **in the e. morning** *Esp* por la mañana temprano, *Am* en *or Arg* a la mañana temprano, *Urug* de mañana temprano; **to be an e. riser** *or* **bird** ser madrugador(ora); **to have an e. night** acostarse temprano; **to make an e. start** *(on journey)* salir temprano; *Br* **it's e. closing on Wednesdays** los miércoles las tiendas abren sólo por la mañana

(**b**) *(at beginning of period of time)* temprano(a); **my e. childhood/teens** mi temprana infancia/juventud; **an e. example of...** un ejemplo temprano de...; **an e. goal** un gol temprano *or* tempranero; **this is an e. Rembrandt** éste es un Rembrandt de su primera época; **at/from an e. age** en/desde una edad temprana; **in e. summer** a principios del verano; **in the e. 1980s** a principios de los ochenta; **in my e. days as a** teacher... en mis primeros tiempos como profesor...; **in the e. days** al principio ►► ***E. American*** estilo *m* colonial americano; ***e. music*** música *f* antigua

(**c**) *(first)* primero(a); **e. aircraft were much slower** los primeros aviones eran mucho más lentos; **the e. days/stages of...** los primeros días/las primeras etapas de...; **he is in the e. stages of cancer** se encuentra en la fase inicial de un cáncer; **e. signs suggest that...** las primeras señales sugieren que... ►► ***e. man*** el hombre primitivo

(**d**) *(ahead of time) (arrival)* antes de tiempo; *(flowers, vegetables)* temprano(a); **to be e.** llegar temprano *or Esp* pronto; **I am half an hour e.** llego media hora antes *or* con media hora de adelanto; **she was e. for the interview** llegó pronto *or* temprano a la entrevista; **we were e. going to bed last night** ayer nos fuimos pronto a la cama; **it's too e. to say** es demasiado pronto para saber; **it's e. days** todavía es pronto; **to have an e. breakfast/lunch** desayunar/comer temprano; **an e. death** una muerte prematura; **the illness sent him to an e. grave** la enfermedad le ocasionó una muerte prematura; PROV **e. to bed, e. to rise (makes a man healthy, wealthy and wise)** a quien madruga, Dios le ayuda ►► ***an e. bird*** un(a) madrugador(ora); PROV **the e. bird catches the worm** a quien madruga Dios le ayuda; *US* ***e. bird special*** = menú a precio rebajado para los clientes que llegan a un restaurante antes de la hora de la cena; *Br* ***e. closing:*** **it's e. closing today** hoy cierran temprano; ***e. retirement*** jubilación *f* anticipada, prejubilación *f*; *Mil* ***e. warning system*** sistema *m* de alerta inmediata

(**e**) *(future)* pronto(a); **we need an e. decision** necesitamos una decisión rápida; **an e. reply** una pronta respuesta; **at an e. date** en fecha próxima

2 *adv* (**a**) *(in the day)* temprano, *Esp* pronto; **e. in the morning/evening** en las primeras horas de la mañana/tarde; **I'd phoned her e. that day** ya la había llamado ese mismo día; **to get up e.** levantarse temprano *or Esp* pronto

(**b**) *(at beginning of period of time)* **e. next week** a principios de la semana que viene; **e. in the year** a primeros *or* principios de año; **e. in one's life/career** al principio de la vida/carrera profesional; **they scored as e. as the fifth minute** marcaron tras sólo cinco minutos, sólo tardaron *orAm* demoraron cinco minutos en marcar; **e. on** temprano; **it became clear e. on that we would lose** ya al poco (tiempo) de comenzar quedó claro que perderíamos

(**c**) *(ahead of time)* temprano, *Esp* pronto; **he was born a month e.** nació con un mes de adelanto; **we finished e.** acabamos temprano *or Esp* pronto; **they left the party e.** se fueron temprano *orEsp* pronto de la fiesta; **to die e.** morir prematuramente; **Easter falls e. this year** este año Semana Santa cae antes *or Am* temprano; **we made our reservations e.** reservamos con antelación; **to retire e.** jubilarse anticipadamente; **as e. as possible** lo antes posible, cuanto antes; **we arrived too e.** llegamos demasiado temprano *or Esp* pronto

---

earmark ['ɪəmɑːk] **1** *n* característica *f*; **it has all the earmarks of embezzlement** tiene todas las características de un desfalco

2 *vt* (**a**) *(assign)* destinar (**for** a); **this land has been earmarked for development** estos terrenos han sido destinados para desarrollo urbano; **this money has been earmarked for research** esta partida ha sido asignada a investigación (**b**) *(sheep)* marcar en la oreja

earmuffs ['ɪəmʌfs] *npl* orejeras *fpl*

earn [ɜːn] **1** *vt* (**a**) *(money)* ganar; *(interest)* dar, devengar; **how much does he e.?** ¿cuánto gana?; **their money is earning a high rate of interest** obtienen un interés muy alto por su dinero; **to e. one's living** ganarse la vida

(**b**) *(rest, respect)* ganarse; **it earned him ten years in prison** le valió diez años en prisión, le costó diez años de cárcel; **you've earned it!** ¡te lo has ganado!, ¡te lo mereces!

2 *vi (person)* ganar dinero; **none of his children have started earning yet** ninguno de sus hijos ha comenzado a trabajar aún

►**earn out** *vi Com (cover costs, profit)* ser rentable, dar beneficios

earned income ['ɜːnd'ɪnkʌm] *n* rentas *fpl* del trabajo

earner ['ɜːnə(r)] *n* (**a**) *(person)* **(wage) e.** asalariado(a) *m,f*; **she's the only e. in the family** es la única de la familia que aporta ingresos (**b**) *Br Fam (source of income)* **the shop is a nice little e.** la tienda es una buena fuente de ingresos

earnest ['ɜːnɪst] **1** *adj* (**a**) *(serious)* serio(a); **she's terribly e.** es muy formal, todo se lo toma muy en serio (**b**) *(sincere)* **it is my e. hope/wish that...** espero/deseo de todo corazón que...

2 *n* **in e.** *(seriously)* en serio; **he spoke in deadly e.** habló muy en serio; **it's raining in e. now** se ha puesto a llover a cántaros

earnestly ['ɜːnɪstlɪ] *adv* (**a**) *(seriously)* seriamente, con gravedad (**b**) *(sincerely)* sinceramente; **we e. hope that...** esperamos sinceramente que...

earnestness ['ɜːnɪstnɪs] *n* (**a**) *(seriousness)* seriedad *f*, gravedad *f* (**b**) *(sincerity)* honestidad *f*, sinceridad *f*

earning ['ɜːnɪŋ] *n* **e. capacity** *or* **power** *(of business)* capacidad de generar ingresos, poder lucrativo; **his e. capacity** *or* **power has increased enormously** su capacidad de ganar dinero ha aumentado vertiginosamente

earnings ['ɜːnɪŋz] *npl (of person)* ingresos *mpl*; *(of company)* beneficios *mpl*, ganancias *fpl* ►► *St Exch* ***e. per share*** dividendos *mpl* por acción

earnings-related ['ɜːnɪŋzrɪ'leɪtɪd] *adj* proporcional a los ingresos ►► ***e. pension*** pensión *f* contributiva *or* retributiva

earphones ['ɪəfəʊnz] *npl* auriculares *mpl*

earpiece ['ɪəpiːs] *n (of telephone)* auricular *m*

ear-piercing ['ɪəpɪəsɪŋ] *adj (scream)* estridente

earplug ['ɪəplʌg] *n* tapón *m* para los oídos

earring ['ɪərɪŋ] *n Esp* pendiente *m*, *Am* arete *m*

earshot ['ɪəʃɒt] *n* **within e.** al alcance del oído; **out of e.** fuera del alcance del oído; **I was within e. of them** podía oírlos

ear-splitting ['ɪəsplɪtɪŋ] *adj* ensordecedor(ora)

earth [ɜːθ] **1** *n* (**a**) *(planet)* **the e.** *or* **E.** la Tierra; *Hum* **E. to John, E. calling John** John ¿estás ahí?, centro de control *orAm* monitoreo llamando a John; **on e.** en la Tierra; **life on e.** la vida en la Tierra; **on e. as it is in heaven** así en la Tierra como en el cielo ►► ***e. mother*** *(in mythology)* madre tierra *f*, diosa *f* de la fecundidad; *Fig (woman)* madraza *f*; ***e. sciences*** ciencias *fpl* de la Tierra; ***e. tremor*** temblor *m* de tierra, movimiento *m* sísmico

(**b**) *(soil)* tierra *f*; **e. floor** *(of hut)* piso *or* suelo de tierra

(**c**) *BrElec* toma *f* de tierra ►► ***e. wire*** conductor *m* de tierra, cable *m* de toma de tierra

(**d**) *(burrow)* madriguera *f*; **to go to e.** *(animal)* esconderse en la madriguera; *(person)* esconderse; *Fig* **to run sb to e.** dar con alguien

(**e**) *Fam (as intensifier)* **where/why/what/who on e....?** ¿dónde/por qué/qué/quién diantres...?; **how on e. should I know?** ¿cómo (diantres *or* demonios) quieres que yo lo sepa?; **there's no reason on e. why I should go** no tengo por qué ir

(**f**) IDIOMS *Hum* **the e. moved** *(while making love)* la tierra tembló; *Hum* **did the e. move for you?** *(while making love)* ¿fue alucinante?; *Fig* **to come back to e. (with a bump)** bajarse de la nube, bajar a la tierra; **to bring sb back down to e.** devolver a alguien a la realidad, *RP* traer de vuelta a alguien; *Fam* **to look/feel like nothing on e.** tener un aspecto/sentirse horrible *or Esp* fatal; **to cost/pay the e.** costar/pagar un ojo de la cara *orEsp* un riñón; **to promise sb the e.** prometer a alguien el oro y el moro

2 *vt Br Elec* conectar a tierra

►**earth up** *vt sep (plant)* aporcar, cubrir con tierra

earthbound ['ɜːθbaʊnd] *adj* (**a**) *(heading towards earth)* en dirección a Tierra (**b**) *Fig (uninspired)* mediocre, gris

earthen ['ɜːθən] *adj* (**a**) *(floor)* de tierra (**b**) *(pot)* de barro

earthenware ['ɜːθənweə(r)] **1** *n* loza *f*

2 *adj* de loza

earthiness ['ɜːθɪnɪs] *n (of humour, person)* descaro *m*

earthling ['ɜːθlɪŋ] *n* terrícola *mf*

earthly ['ɜːθlɪ] **1** *n Br Fam* (**a**) *(chance)* **she hasn't got an e.** no tiene la menor posibilidad (**b**) *(idea)* **I haven't got an e.** (no tengo) ni idea

2 *adj* (**a**) *(life, existence)* terrenal (**b**) *Fam (emphatic)* **there's no e. reason** no hay razón alguna; **it's no e. use** no vale absolutamente para nada

earthman ['ɜːθmæn] *n* terrícola *m*

earthmover ['ɜːθmuːvə(r)] *n* excavadora *f*, pala *f* mecánica

earthmoving ['ɜːθmuːvɪŋ] *adj* **e. equipment** maquinaria de excavaciones

earthquake ['ɜːθkweɪk] *n also Fig* terremoto *m*

earth-shaking ['ɜːθʃeɪkɪŋ], **earth-shattering** ['ɜːθʃætərɪŋ] *adj Fam (news, discovery)* extraordinario(a)

earthward ['ɜːθwəd], **earthwards** ['ɜːθwədz] *adv* rumbo a la Tierra

earthwoman ['ɜːθwʊmən] *n* terrícola *f*

earthwork ['ɜːθwɜːk] *n* (**a**) *(excavation)* movimiento *m* de tierras (**b**) *(fortification)* terraplén *m*

earthworm ['ɜːθwɜːm] *n* lombriz *f (de tierra)*

earthy ['ɜːθɪ] *adj* (**a**) *(of or like earth)* terroso(a); **e. taste/smell** sabor/olor a tierra

(**b**) *(person, humour) (coarse)* descarado(a); *(uninhibited)* directo(a), campechano(a)

earwax ['ɪəwæks] *n* cera *f* de los oídos, cerumen *m*

earwig ['ɪəwɪg] **1** *n* tijereta *f*

2 *vi (pt & pp* **earwigged)** *Fam (eavesdrop)* pegar la oreja, escuchar de *Esp* estranjis *or RP* de contrabando

earwigging ['ɪəwɪgɪŋ] *n Fam (scolding)* broncazo *m*, *Esp* rapapolvo *m*

ease [i:z] **1** *n* **(a)** *(facility)* facilidad *f*; **with e.** con facilidad; **e. of access/use** fácil acceso/manejo; **for e. of reference** para facilitar la consulta

(b) *(peace)* **at e.** a gusto; **to be** *or* **feel at e.** estar *or* sentirse a gusto; **we feel more at e. with each other now** ahora nos sentimos más a gusto juntos; **to put sb at (his** *or* **her) e.** hacer que alguien se sienta a gusto; **to put** *or* **set sb's mind at e.** tranquilizar a alguien; *Formal* **to take one's e.** descansar, reposar

(c) *(affluence, leisure)* **a life of e.** una vida desahogada

(d) *Mil* **(stand) at e.!** ¡descansen!

2 *vt* **(a)** *(alleviate) (pain, anxiety)* calmar; **to e. sb's mind** tranquilizar *or* sosegar a alguien

(b) *(relax, diminish) (pressure, tension)* disminuir; *(traffic flow)* descongestionar, hacer más fluido(a); *(sb's workload)* aliviar; *(restrictions)* relajar

(c) *(move carefully, slowly)* **she eased the heavy box onto the shelf** despacio y con cuidado, trasladó la pesada caja al estante; **she eased the rucksack from her back** se quitó la mochila con cuidado; **to e. oneself into a chair** acomodarse en una silla parsimoniosamente; **he eased himself through the gap in the wall** se deslizó por el hueco en el muro

3 *vi (pain, pressure)* disminuir, remitir; **the wind/the rain has eased** el viento/la lluvia ha amainado un poco

▸ **ease in** *vt sep* introducir con cuidado

▸ **ease off 1** *vt sep (lid)* quitar con cuidado; *(bandage)* aflojar, quitar con cuidado

2 *vi (pain)* disminuir, remitir; *(rain)* amainar; *(work)* aflojar; *(pressure)* disminuir, bajar; **the traffic tends to e. off towards late evening** al anochecer el tráfico *or Am* tránsito se hace más fluido

▸ **ease out** *vt sep* **they eased him out of the front seat** lo bajaron del asiento con cuidado; **to e. sb out** *(from position, job)* forzar la caída de alguien paulatinamente

▸ **ease up** *vi* **(a)** *(diminish) (pain)* disminuir, remitir; *(rain)* amainar **(b)** *(runner, horse)* aflojar *or* disminuir la marcha **(c)** *(take things easy)* tomarse las cosas con más calma; **to e. up on sb** no ser demasiado duro(a) con alguien; **to e. up on sth** no pasarse con algo

easel ['i:zəl] *n* caballete *m*

easily ['i:zɪlɪ] *adv* **(a)** *(without difficulty)* fácilmente; **the table would e. sit six people** a la mesa se pueden sentar seis personas con comodidad; **she is e. pleased** es fácil de complacer; **he is e. amused** se entretiene con cualquier cosa; **that's e. said** eso se dice pronto, del dicho al hecho...; **that's e. done** *(anyone can make that mistake)* le puede pasar a cualquiera; *(it's simple)* tiene fácil solución

(b) *(undoubtedly)* fácilmente; **e. the biggest** sin duda alguna el mayor; **it's e. the best of the lot** es con mucho *or* con diferencia el mejor de todos

(c) *(very possibly)* **he could e. change his mind** es muy probable que cambie de idea; **the information could (just as) e. be wrong** la información puede muy bien ser errónea

(d) *(comfortably)* cómodamente, sin dificultad

(e) *(at least)* **he's e. forty** andará por los cuarenta como poco, tendrá por lo menos cuarenta (años); **it's e. two hours from here** queda a por lo menos dos horas de aquí

(f) *(to speak)* con soltura; *(to smile, answer)* espontáneamente, con desenvoltura

easiness ['i:zɪnɪs] *n* **(a)** *(of task, question, exam)* facilidad *f* **(b)** *(of manner)* desenvoltura *f*

easing ['i:zɪŋ] *n* **(a)** *(of pain)* alivio *m* **(b)** *(of pressure)* disminución *f*; *(of restrictions)* flexibilización *f*, relajación *f*; **e. of tension** *(political)* distensión

east [i:st] **1** *n* este *m*; **to the e. (of)** al este (de); **the E. of Spain** el este de España; **the E.** *(Asia)* el Oriente; *(of Europe)* el Este; **the wind is in** *or* **(coming) from the e.** el viento sopla del este

2 *adj* **(a)** *(direction, side)* oriental, este; **the e. coast** la costa este *or* occidental; **e. London** el este de Londres ▸▸ ***e. wind*** viento *m* del este *or* de levante

(b) *(in names)* ***E. Africa*** África Oriental; ***E. Anglia*** East Anglia, = región geográfica del este de Inglaterra que incluye los condados de Norfolk y Suffolk y zonas de Cambridgeshire y Essex; ***the E. End (of London)*** = el barrio este de Londres; *Formerly* ***E. Germany*** Alemania Oriental *or* del Este; *Old-fashioned* ***the E. Indies*** *(Far East)* las Indias Orientales; *(Malay archipelago)* = el archipiélago indonesio; ***the E. Midlands*** el este de la región de Midlands *(en el centro de Inglaterra)*; ***the E. Side*** = el barrio este de Manhattan; ***E. Timor*** Timor Oriental

3 *adv (to travel, move)* hacia el este; **it's (3 miles) e. of here** está (a 3 millas) al este de aquí; **they live out e.** viven por el este; **e. by north/by south** este cuarta al nordeste/al sureste; **to face e.** *(person)* mirar hacia el este; *(room, house)* estar orientado(a) *or* mirar al este; **to go e.** ir hacia el este

eastbound ['i:stbaʊnd] *adj (train, traffic)* en dirección este; **the e. carriageway** el carril que va hacia el este

Eastender ['i:st'endə(r)] *n Br* = persona del East End londinense

Easter ['i:stə(r)] *n (period)* Semana *f* Santa; *(festival)* Pascua *f* (de Resurrección); **at E.** en Semana Santa ▸▸ ***E. Day*** Domingo *m* de Pascua *or* de Resurrección; ***E. egg*** *(chocolate egg)* huevo *m* de Pascua; *Comptr* huevo *m* de Pascua; ***E. Island*** la Isla de Pascua; ***E. Monday*** Lunes *m inv* de Pascua; ***E. Sunday*** Domingo *m* de Pascua *or* de Resurrección; ***E. week*** *(Holy Week)* Semana *f* Santa; *(following Easter)* Semana *f* de Pascua

easterly ['i:stəlɪ] **1** *n (wind)* levante *m*

2 *adj (direction)* (hacia el) este; **the most e. point** el punto más al este; **e. wind** viento de levante

eastern ['i:stən] *adj* **(a)** *(region)* del este, oriental; **the e. side of the country** la región del este *or* oriental del país ▸▸ *Formerly* ***the E. bloc*** el bloque del Este; ***E. Europe*** Europa Oriental *or* del Este; ***e. hemisphere*** hemisferio *m* oriental; ***e. kingbird*** tirano *m* real; ***E. Orthodox Church*** Iglesia *f* ortodoxa; ***e. screech owl*** autillo *m* americano; *US* ***E. Standard Time*** = hora oficial en la costa este de los EE.UU.

(b) *(religion)* oriental

Easterner ['i:stənə(r)] *n* **(a)** *(in US)* persona del este de Estados Unidos **(b)** *(oriental)* oriental *mf*

easternized ['i:stənaɪzd] *adj US* = que adoptó las costumbres del este de los EE.UU. aunque proviene de otra zona del país

easternmost ['i:stənməʊst] *adj* más oriental, más al este; **the e. island of the archipelago** la isla más al este del archipiélago

east-north-east ['i:stnɔ:θ'i:st] **1** *adj* del estenordeste *or* estenoreste

2 *adv* hacia el *or* en dirección estenordeste *or* estenoreste

east-south-east ['i:stsaʊθ'i:st] **1** *adj (direction)* estesudeste, estesureste; *(wind)* del estesudeste *or* estesureste

2 *adv* hacia el *or* en dirección estesudeste *or* estesureste

eastward ['i:stwəd] **1** *adj* hacia el este

2 *adv* hacia el este

eastwardly ['i:stwədlɪ] *adj (direction)* (hacia el) este

eastwards ['i:stwədz] *adv* hacia el este; **to face e.** *(person)* mirar hacia el este; *(room, house)* estar orientado(a) *or* mirar al este; **to go e.** ir hacia el este

East-West ['i:st'west] *adj (relations, trade)* Este-Oeste

EASY ['i:zɪ] **1** *adj* **(a)** *(not difficult)* fácil; **that's the e. answer** ésa es la salida fácil; **to take the e. option** *or* **the e. way out** optar por *or* elegir la solución fácil; **they ran out e. winners** ganaron con gran facilidad; **e. on the eye/ear** agradable a la vista/al oído; **e. to get on with** tratable, de trato fácil; **e. to install** de fácil instalación; **e. to please** fácil de contentar; **e. to talk to** tratable, de trato fácil; *Com* **by e. payments, on e. terms** con facilidades de pago; **it's within e. walking distance** se puede ir caminando *or Esp* andando perfectamente; **it's all too e. to believe such a thing of her** no es difícil creer algo así de ella; **that's e. for you to say** eso se dice muy fácil; **it's the easiest thing in the world** es lo más fácil del mundo; **that's easier said than done** es muy fácil decirlo, del dicho al hecho (hay mucho trecho); **that's far from e.** *or* **no e. matter** de fácil eso no tiene nada, eso no es nada fácil; **to make things e. for sb** ponerle *or RP* hacerle las cosas fáciles a alguien; **you're not making this e. for me** no me lo estás poniendo *or RP* haciendo nada fácil; IDIOM *Fam* **it's as e. as ABC** *or* **as anything** *or* **as pie** *or* **as falling off a log** *or* **as shelling peas** es pan comido, *RP* es un boleto *or* una papa; IDIOM *Fam* **to be e. game** *or* **meat** *or* **prey** ser presa fácil ▸▸ *Fam* ***e. money*** dinero *m* fácil

(b) *(comfortable) (pace, life)* cómodo(a), apacible; *(manners, style)* desenvuelto(a); **with an e. mind** *or* **conscience** con la conciencia tranquila; **I don't feel too e. about the idea** la idea me inquieta *or* preocupa; *Fam* **I'm e.!** *(I don't mind)* ¡por mí es igual!, ¡a mí me da lo mismo!; **my stomach feels a little easier** *(less painful)* mi estómago está algo mejor; **to have an e. time (of it)** tenerlo fácil; **I haven't been having an e. time of it recently** no lo he tenido nada fácil últimamente; IDIOM *Fam* **to be on e. street** no tener problemas económicos ▸▸ ***e. chair*** butaca *f*, sillón *m*; ***e. listening*** *(music)* música *f* ligera

(c) *Fam (woman)* fácil; *Old-fashioned* **a woman of e. virtue** una mujer de vida *Esp* alegre *or RP* ligera, *Méx* una mujer de costumbres fáciles

2 *adv Fam* **I could beat you e.** te gano fácil; **true love doesn't come**

e. el amor verdadero no se encuentra fácilmente; *Fam* **to get off e.** salir bien parado(a); **to go e. on sb** no ser demasiado duro(a) con alguien; **to go e. on sth** no pasarse con algo; **now we can rest** *or* **breathe e.** ahora podemos descansar *or* respirar tranquilos; *Fig* **I can sleep e.** puedo dormir tranquilo; *Mil* **stand e.!** ¡descansen!; **to take things** *or* **it e.** tomarse las cosas con calma, tomárselo con calma; **the doctor told me to take things e.** el doctor me dijo que no hiciera grandes esfuerzos; **take it e.!** *(relax)* ¡tranquilo!; *(goodbye)* ¡hasta pronto!; IDIOM **e. come, e. go** tal como viene, se va; *Fam* **e. does it!** ¡con cuidado!; *US* **e. over** *(egg)* frito por los dos lados

easy-care ['i:zɪkeə(r)] *adj (fabric, clothing)* fácil de lavar y planchar, que no necesita especiales cuidados

easy-cook ['i:zɪkʊk] *adj* de cocción fácil *or* rápida ►► ***e. rice*** arroz *m* vaporizado

easy-going ['i:zɪ'gəʊɪŋ] *adj (tolerant)* tolerante; *(calm)* tranquilo(a); **the police take an e. attitude to such cases** ante casos de este tipo, la policía es bastante permisiva *or* tolerante

easy-peasy ['i:zɪ'pi:zɪ] *adj Fam (in children's language)* facilísimo(a), chupado(a)

easy-to-use ['i:zɪtə'ju:z] *adj* fácil de usar

eat [i:t] (*pt* **ate** [et, eɪt], *pp* **eaten** ['i:tən]) **1** *vt* (**a**) *(food)* comer; **to e. (one's) breakfast/lunch/dinner** desayunar/almorzar/cenar; **I don't e. meat** no como carne; **they ate their way through a whole chicken** se zamparon un pollo entero

(**b**) *(of machine) (cash card, ticket)* tragarse; **the machine just ate my cash card** la máquina se me acaba de tragar la tarjeta

(**c**) IDIOMS **he/she/it looks good enough to e.** está para comérselo(a); **to e. sb out of house and home** dejar la despensa vacía a alguien; *Fam* **I could e. a horse!** ¡tengo un hambre tremenda *or Esp* canina *or RP* de la Madona!; *Fam* **he won't e. you!** ¡no te va a comer!; **he eats people like you for breakfast** se merienda a la gente viva *or* cruda; *Fam* **what's eating you?** *(worrying you)* ¿qué te preocupa?, *RP* ¿qué te pica?; **to e. one's words** tragarse (uno) sus propias palabras; *Fam* **if it works, I'll e. my hat** si esto funciona, *Esp* me meto a *or Méx* me voy de *or RP* me hago monja; *US very Fam* **e. it** *or* **me!** ¡cómemela!; *US Vulg* **e. shit and die!** ¡vete a la puta mierda!

2 *vi* comer; **to e. well** comer bien; **we usually e. at seven** normalmente comemos a las siete; **to e. for two** *(pregnant woman)* comer por dos; **e., drink and be merry!** ¡a vivir, que son dos días!; IDIOM **to have sb eating out of one's hand** tener a alguien en *Esp* el bote *orAm* el bolsillo

► **eat away (at)** *vt sep* (**a**) *(wear away) (of waves)* erosionar; *(of mice)* roer; *(of acid, rust)* corroer (**b**) *(use up) (support, resources)* agotar, consumir

► **eat in** *vi (at home)* comer en casa

► **eat into** *vt insep* (**a**) *(erode)* corroer (**b**) *(use up) (time)* gastar; *(savings)* mermar

► **eat out** **1** *vt sep Vulg (perform cunnilingus on) Esp* comer el coño a, *Méx* dar el beso francés a, *RP* chupar la concha a

2 *vi* salir a comer fuera

► **eat up** **1** *vt sep* (**a**) *(food)* terminar (de comer) (**b**) *(consume) (petrol, money)* consumir; **to e. up the miles** *(car)* devorar los kilómetros, comerse la carretera; **to be eaten up with** *(jealousy, hate, ambition)* estar consumido(a) por

2 *vi* **e. up!** ¡termina (de comer)!

eatable ['i:təbəl] **1** *adj* comestible

2 eatables *npl* provisiones *fpl*; **has everyone brought some eatables?** ¿ha traído todo el mundo algo de comer?

eaten *pp of* **eat**

eater ['i:tə(r)] *n* **to be a slow/fast e.** comer despacio/deprisa; **to be a big e.** comer mucho; **to be a fussy e.** ser un(a) quisquilloso(a) *or* tiquismiquis para la comida; **he's a messy e.** lo deja todo hecho una porquería cuando come

eatery ['i:tərɪ] *n Fam* restaurante *m*

eating ['i:tɪŋ] *n* **to be** *or* **make good e.** estar riquísimo(a) ►► ***e. apple*** manzana *f* de mesa *or* para comer; ***e. disorder*** trastorno *m* alimenticio; ***e. house*** restaurante *m*

eats [i:ts] *npl Fam* comida *f*, *Esp* manduca *f*, *RP* morfi *m*

eau de Cologne ['əʊdəkə'ləʊn] *n* (agua *f* de) colonia *f*

eau de toilette ['əʊdətwɑ:'let] *n* (agua *f* de) colonia *f*

eau de vie ['əʊdə'vi:] *n* aguardiente *m*

eaves [i:vz] *npl (of house)* alero *m* ►► *US* ***e. trough*** canalón *m*

eavesdrop ['i:vzdrɒp] (*pt & pp* **eavesdropped**) *vi* **to e. (on)** escuchar disimuladamente

eavesdropper ['i:vzdrɒpə(r)] *n* = persona que escucha con disimulo conversaciones ajenas

ebb [eb] **1** *n (of tide)* reflujo *m*; *Fig* **the e. and flow** *(of events)* los vaivenes; **to be on the e.** *(tide)* bajar; *Fig (fortunes)* estar pasando por una mala racha; IDIOM **to be at a low e.** *(person, spirits)* estar en horas bajas; **his fortunes were at their lowest e.** estaban pasando una mala racha ►► ***e. tide*** marea *f* baja, bajamar *f*

2 *vi* (**a**) *(tide)* bajar; **to e. and flow** fluir y refluir; *Fig* sufrir altibajos (**b**) *(strength, enthusiasm)* menguar, disminuir

► **ebb away** *vi* (**a**) *(water)* bajar (**b**) *(strength, enthusiasm)* menguar, disminuir; *(rage)* disiparse; *(support)* debilitarse; *(life)* escaparse, consumirse

Ebola virus ['ebələ'vaɪrəs] *n* virus *m* del Ébola

ebonics [ɪ'bɒnɪks] *n Ling* inglés *m* afroamericano

ebony ['ebənɪ] *n* (**a**) *(tree, wood)* ébano *m* (**b**) *(colour)* color *m* ébano; **e. skin** piel negra como el ébano

e-book ['i:bʊk] *n Comptr* libro *m* electrónico

EBRD [i:bi:ɑ:'di:] *n* (*abbr* **European Bank for Reconstruction and Development**) BERD *m*

ebullience [ɪ'bʌlɪəns] *n* fogosidad *f*

ebullient [ɪ'bʌlɪənt] *adj* fogoso(a); **they were in (an) e. mood** *or* **in e. spirits** estaban exultantes

e-business ['i:'bɪznɪs] *n* comercio *m* electrónico

EC [i:'si:] *n* (*abbr* **European Community**) CE *f*

e-cash ['i:kæʃ] *n Comptr* dinero *m* electrónico

ECB [i:si:'bi:] *n* (*abbr* **European Central Bank**) BCE *m*

eccentric [ek'sentrɪk] **1** *n* excéntrico(a) *m,f*

2 *adj* (**a**) *(person, clothes, behaviour)* excéntrico(a) (**b**) *(circle, orbit, wheel)* excéntrico(a)

eccentrically [ek'sentrɪklɪ] *adv* (**a**) *(to dress, talk, behave)* de forma excéntrica, excéntricamente (**b**) *(to rotate)* de forma excéntrica

eccentricity [eksen'trɪsɪtɪ] *n* (**a**) *(of person, clothes, behaviour)* excentricidad *f* (**b**) *(of circle, orbit, wheel)* excentricidad *f*

ecclesiastic [ɪkli:zɪ'æstɪk] **1** *n* clérigo *m*

2 *adj* eclesiástico(a)

ecclesiastical [ɪkli:zɪ'æstɪkəl] *adj* eclesiástico(a) ►► ***e. architecture*** arquitectura *f* religiosa

ECG [i:si:'dʒi:] *n Med* (*abbr* **electrocardiogram**) ECG *m*

echelon ['eʃəlɒn] *n* **the higher echelons** las altas esferas; **the lower echelons** los grados inferiores

echidna [ɪ'kɪdnə] *n* equidna *f*

echinoderm [ɪ'kaɪnədɜ:m] *n Zool* equinodermo *m*

echo ['ekəʊ] **1** *n* (*pl* **echoes**) (**a**) *(sound)* eco *m*; **they cheered him to the e.** se llevó una sonora ovación; *Fig* **her words found an e. in many hearts** sus palabras conmovieron a muchos ►► ***e. chamber*** cámara *f* de resonancia; ***e. sounder*** sonda *f* acústica; *Med* ***e. virus*** ecovirus *m inv*, echovirus *m inv* (**b**) *Comptr* eco *m*

2 *vt* (*pt & pp* **echoed**) *(of mountain, valley)* devolver el eco de; *(of person) (opinion, words)* repetir, hacerse eco de

3 *vi (noise, voice, music)* retumbar; *(place)* hacer eco; **the room echoed with the shouts of children** la habitación resonó con los gritos de los niños

echoic [e'kəʊɪk] *adj (onomatopoeic)* onomatopéyico(a)

echolocation ['ekəʊləʊkeɪʃən] *n* ecolocación *f*

echo-sounder ['ekəʊsaʊndə(r)] *n* ecosonda *f*, sonda *f* acústica

echt [ekt] *adj* auténtico(a), genuino(a)

éclair [eɪ'kleə(r)] *n (pastry)* petisú *m*

eclampsia [ɪ'klæmpsɪə] *n Med* eclampsia *f*

eclectic [ɪ'klektɪk] *adj* ecléctico(a)

eclecticism [ɪ'klektɪsɪzəm] *n* eclecticismo *m*

eclipse [ɪ'klɪps] **1** *n* (**a**) *(of sun)* eclipse *m*; **e. of the moon/sun** eclipse de luna/sol; **total/partial e.** eclipse total/parcial (**b**) *(loss of fame, prominence)* eclipse *m*

2 *vt* (**a**) *(sun, moon)* eclipsar (**b**) *(surpass, obscure)* eclipsar

eclogue ['eklɒg] *n Lit* égloga *f*

eco- ['i:kəʊ] *prefix* eco-; **e.-hazard** peligro ecológico

ecocide ['i:kəʊsaɪd] *n* atentado *m* contra el medio ambiente

Ecofin ['i:kəʊfɪn] *n EU* (*abbr* **European Council of Economics and Finance Ministers**) Ecofin *m*

ecofreak ['i:kəʊfri:k] *n Fam* verde *mf* radical

eco-friendly ['i:kəʊfrendlɪ] *adj* ecológico(a)

eco-industry ['i:kəʊ'ɪndəstrɪ] *n* ecoindustria *f*

eco-label ['i:kəʊleɪbəl] *n* ecoetiqueta *f*

E. coli ['i:'kəʊlaɪ] *n Biol* (*abbr* **Escherichia coli**) Escherichia coli *f*

ecological [i:kə'lɒdʒɪkəl] *adj* ecológico(a) ▸▸ ***e. disaster*** desastre *m* ecológico; ***e. pyramid*** pirámide *f* ecológica *or* trófica

ecologically [i:kə'lɒdʒɪklɪ] *adv* desde el punto de vista ecológico; **e. friendly** ecológico(a), que no daña el medio ambiente; **e. sound** razonable desde el punto de vista ecológico

ecologist [ɪ'kɒlədʒɪst] *n (scientist)* ecólogo(a) *m,f*

ecology [ɪ'kɒlədʒɪ] *n* ecología *f*

e-commerce ['i:'kɒmɜ:s] *n* comercio *m* electrónico

econometrics [ɪkɒnə'metrɪks] *n Econ* econometría *f*

economic [i:kə'nɒmɪk] *adj* (**a**) *(factor, development, crisis)* económico(a) ▸▸ ***e. agreement*** acuerdo *m* económico; ***e. growth*** crecimiento *m* económico; ***e. indicator*** indicador *m* económico; ***e. miracle*** milagro *m* económico; *Pol* ***e. refugee*** refugiado(a) *m,f* por razones económicas; ***e. sanctions*** sanciones *fpl* económicas
(**b**) *(profitable)* rentable; **it doesn't make e. sense** no tiene sentido desde el punto de vista económico; **it's more e. to buy in bulk** sale más barato *or* económico comprar grandes cantidades
(**c**) *Fam (inexpensive)* económico(a)

economical [i:kə'nɒmɪkəl] *adj* (**a**) *(inexpensive)* económico(a); **to be e. (to run)** *(car, heating)* ser económico(a), consumir poco; **he was being e. with the truth** no decía toda la verdad (**b**) *(style)* sobrio(a)

economically [i:kə'nɒmɪklɪ] *adv* (**a**) *(in economic terms)* económicamente; **e. viable** *(project, product)* económicamente viable (**b**) *(cost-effectively)* económicamente

economics [i:kə'nɒmɪks] *n* economía *f*, ciencias *fpl* económicas; **the e. of a plan** el aspecto económico de un plan

economism [ɪ'kɒnəmɪzəm] *n* economicismo *m*

economist [ɪ'kɒnəmɪst] *n* economista *mf*

economize [ɪ'kɒnəmaɪz] *vi* economizar, ahorrar (**on** en)

economy [ɪ'kɒnəmɪ] **1** *n* (**a**) *(system)* economía *f*; **the British/US e.** la economía británica/estadounidense; **a mixed/planned/market e.** una economía mixta/planificada/de mercado
(**b**) *(saving)* economía *f*; **to practise e.** ser ahorrador(ora); **to make economies** ahorrar; **e. of effort** moderación *or* economía en el esfuerzo; **e. of style** sobriedad en el estilo; **economies of scale** economías de escala ▸▸ *Av* ***e. class*** clase *f* económica *or* turista; *Fam* ***e. class syndrome*** síndrome *m* de la clase turista; ***e. drive*** *(cost-cutting campaign)* campaña *f* de ahorro; ***e. measure*** medida *f* de ahorro; ***e. size*** *(of packet)* tamaño *m* económico
2 *adv (to fly, travel)* en clase económica *or* turista

ecopolitics ['i:kəʊ'pɒlɪtɪks] *n* ecología *f* política, ecopolítica *f*

ecosphere ['i:kəʊsfɪə(r)] *n Geog* ecosfera *f*, biosfera *f*

ecosystem ['i:kəʊsɪstəm] *n* ecosistema *m*

ecotage ['i:kəʊtɑ:ʒ] *n* sabotaje *m* ecológico

ecotax ['i:kəʊtæks] *n* ecotasa *f*, impuesto *m* ecológico

ecoterrorism ['i:kəʊterərɪzəm] *n* terrorismo *m* ecológico

ecoterrorist ['i:kəʊterərɪst] *n* terrorista *mf* ecológico(a)

ecotourism ['i:kəʊtɔ:rɪzəm] *n* ecoturismo *m*, turismo *m* verde *or* ecológico

ecotourist ['i:kəʊtɔ:rɪst] *n* ecoturista *mf*

ecowarrior ['i:kəʊwɒrɪə(r)] *n* militante *mf* ecologista

ecru ['eɪkru:] **1** *n* color *m* crudo
2 *adj* de color crudo

ecstasy ['ekstəsɪ] *n* (**a**) *(emotional state)* éxtasis *m inv*; **he went into ecstasies over the food** se deshacía en elogios a la comida; **to send sb into e.** *or* **ecstasies** sumir a alguien en un estado de éxtasis (**b**) *(drug)* éxtasis *m inv* (**c**) *Rel* éxtasis *m inv*

ecstatic [ek'stætɪk] *adj* exultante, alborozado(a); **to be e. (about** *or* **over sth)** estar exultante de alegría (por algo); **I'm not e. about it** no doy saltos de alegría

ecstatically [ek'stætɪklɪ] *adv* con inmensa alegría, con gran alborozo; **e. happy** loco(a) de alegría *or* de contento

ECT [i:si:'ti:] *n Med* (*abbr* **electroconvulsive therapy**) electrochoque *m*

ectoderm ['ektəʊdɜ:m] *n Biol* ectodermo *m*

ectoparasite [ektəʊ'pærəsaɪt] *n Biol* ectoparásito *m*

ectoparasitic [ektəʊpærə'sɪtɪk] *adj Biol* ectoparásito(a)

ectopic [ek'tɒpɪk] *adj Med* ectópico(a) ▸▸ ***e. pregnancy*** embarazo *m* ectópico *or* extrauterino

ectoplasm ['ektəplæzəm] *n* (**a**) *Biol* ectoplasma *m* (**b**) *(at a seance)* ectoplasma *m*

Ecuador ['ekwədɔ:(r)] *n* Ecuador

Ecuadoran [ekwə'dɔ:rən], **Ecuadorian** [ekwə'dɔ:rɪən] **1** *n* ecuatoriano(a) *m,f*
2 *adj* ecuatoriano(a)

ecumenic(al) [i:kjʊ'menɪk(əl)] *adj Rel* ecuménico(a) ▸▸ ***e. council*** concilio *m* ecuménico

ecumenism [i:'kju:mənɪzəm] *n Rel* ecumenismo *m*

eczema ['eksɪmə] *n* eccema *m*; **to have e.** tener un eccema

ed [ed] (**a**) (*abbr* **edition**) ed. (**b**) (*abbr* **editor**) ed. (**c**) (*abbr* **edited**) editado(a)

Edam ['i:dæm] *n* queso *m* de bola

eddy ['edɪ] **1** *n* remolino *m* ▸▸ *Elec* ***e. current*** corriente *f* de Foucault
2 *vi* arremolinarse

edelweiss ['eɪdəlvaɪs] *n* edelweiss *m inv*, flor *f* de nieve

edema *US* = **oedema**

Eden ['i:dən] *n* (jardín *m* del) Edén *m*

edentate [i:'denteɪt] *Biol* **1** *n* desdentado *m*
2 *adj* desdentado(a)

edge [edʒ] **1** *n* (**a**) *(of table, road, forest)* borde *m*; *(of page)* margen *m*; *(of coin, book)* canto *m*; **at** *or* **by the water's e.** al borde *or* a la orilla del agua; **to be on the e. of** *(war, disaster, madness)* estar al borde de; *Fig* **to be on the e. of one's seat** estar (con el alma) en vilo; *Fig* **to be close to the e.** estar al borde de la desesperación; *Fig* **to push sb over the e.** llevar a alguien al límite
(**b**) *(of blade, tool)* filo *m*; IDIOM **to take the e. off sb's hunger** calmar el hambre a alguien; IDIOM **it took the e. off their victory** deslustró *or* enturbió su victoria; IDIOM **to give sth/sb that extra e.** dar a algo/alguien una ventaja adicional; **to be on e.** *(nervous)* estar tenso(a) *or* nervioso(a); **to set sb on e.** *(make nervous)* poner los nervios de punta a alguien; *US Fam* **to have an e. on** estar alegre, *Esp* tener el puntillo
(**c**) *(advantage)* ventaja *f*; **to have the e. (over** *or* **on sb)** llevar ventaja (a alguien)
2 *vt* (**a**) *(in sewing)* ribetear; **edged with lace** ribeteado(a) con encaje (**b**) *(move gradually)* **to e. one's way** abrirse camino; **to e. one's way along a ledge** ir desplazándose lentamente por una cornisa; **to e. one's chair nearer** ir acercando la silla (**c**) *US (include)* incluir
3 *vi (move slowly)* **to e. forward(s)/backward(s)** ir avanzando/retrocediendo despacio *or* poco a poco; **to e. towards** acercarse lentamente a; **to e. away (from sth/sb)** alejarse (de algo/alguien); **to e. past sb** pasar deslizándose junto a alguien; **to e. through the crowd** avanzar lentamente entre la multitud

▸**edge out 1** *vt sep (beat narrowly)* batir por muy poco a
2 *vi* escabullirse; **to e. out of a room** abandonar disimuladamente una habitación

edger ['edʒə(r)] *n (for lawn)* desbrozadora *f*, cortadora *f* de bordes

edgeways ['edʒweɪz], **edgewise** ['edʒwaɪz] *adv* de canto, de lado; **seen e. (on)...** visto(a) de lado...

edgily ['edʒɪlɪ] *adv (nervously)* tensamente, con los nervios a flor de piel

edginess ['edʒɪnɪs] *n (nervousness)* estado *m* de tensión, nerviosismo *m*

edging ['edʒɪŋ] *n (of cloth)* ribete *m*; *(of furniture)* moldura *f*

edgy ['edʒɪ] *adj (nervous)* tenso(a), con los nervios a flor de piel; **to be e.** estar tenso(a) *or* con los nervios a flor de piel

edible ['edɪbəl] **1** *adj* comestible
2 edibles *npl* provisiones *fpl*; **has everyone brought some edibles?** ¿ha traído todo el mundo algo de comer?

edict ['i:dɪkt] *n Formal* edicto *m*; *Hist* **the E. of Nantes** el edicto de Nantes

edification [edɪfɪ'keɪʃən] *n Formal* edificación *f*, instrucción *f*; *Ironic* **for your e.** para que te vayas instruyendo, para tu solaz espiritual

edifice ['edɪfɪs] *n Formal* edificio *m*

edify ['edɪfaɪ] *vt Formal* edificar

edifying ['edɪfaɪɪŋ] *adj* edificante; **a far from e. spectacle** un espectáculo nada edificante

Edinburgh ['edɪnbərə] *n* Edimburgo

edit ['edɪt] **1** *n* (**a**) *(of text)* revisión *f* (**b**) *Comptr (menu heading)* edición *f*
2 *vt* (**a**) *(correct, rewrite)* corregir (**b**) *(prepare for publication)* editar; **edited by...** edición (a cargo) de... (**c**) *Cin (cut)* montar (**d**) *(manage) (newspaper, journal)* dirigir (**e**) *Comptr* editar ▸▸ ***e. mode*** modo *m* de edición

▸**edit out** *vt sep* eliminar, excluir

editing ['edɪtɪŋ] *n* (**a**) *Cin* montaje *m* ►► ***e. desk*** mesa *f* de montaje; ***e. table*** mesa *f* de montaje (**b**) *Comptr* edición *f*

edition [ɪ'dɪʃən] *n* edición *f*; **revised/limited e.** *(of book)* edición revisada/limitada; **morning/evening e.** *(of newspaper)* edición matutina/vespertina; **in Tuesday's e. of the programme** en la edición del martes del programa

editor ['edɪtə(r)] *n* (**a**) *(of published writings)* editor(ora) *m,f* (**b**) *(proofreader, writer)* redactor(ora) *m,f* (**c**) *Cin* montador(ora) *m,f* (**d**) *(of newspaper, journal) (manager)* director(ora) *m,f*; *(journalist)* redactor(ora) *m,f*; **the political/sports e.** el jefe de la sección de política/deportes (**e**) *TV (of series of programmes)* realizador(ora) *m,f* (**f**) *Comptr (software)* editor *m*

editorial [edɪ'tɔːrɪəl] **1** *n* editorial *m*

2 *adj (decision, comment)* editorial; *(job, skills)* editorial; **changes in e. policy** cambios en la política editorial ►► ***e. staff*** (equipo *m* de) redacción *f*

editorialist [edɪ'tɔːrɪəlɪst] *n US* editorialista *mf*

editorialize [edɪ'tɔːrɪəlaɪz] *vi Journ* (**a**) *(in editorial)* **as the Times editorialized,...** como editorializó el Times,... (**b**) *Pej (be opinionated)* verter las propias opiniones, ser subjetivo(a)

editorially [edɪ'tɔːrɪəlɪ] *adv* desde el punto de vista editorial

editor-in-chief ['edɪtərɪn'tʃiːf] *n (of newspaper)* jefe(a) *m,f* de redacción, redactor(ora) *m,f* jefe

editorship ['edɪtəʃɪp] *n* (**a**) *(of newspaper)* dirección *f* (**b**) *(of series of books)* dirección *f* editorial (**c**) *TV (of programmes)* realización *f*

EDP [iːdiː'piː] *n Comptr* (*abbr* **electronic data processing**) tratamiento *m or* procesamiento *m* electrónico de datos

educable ['edjʊkəbəl] *adj Formal* educable

educate ['edjʊkeɪt] *vt* (**a**) *(school) (child, pupil)* educar; **he was educated in France/at Oxford** se educó en Francia/Oxford

(**b**) *(inform)* **the campaign aims to e. young people about the risks of drugs** el objetivo de la campaña es concienciar a los jóvenes de los riesgos de las drogas

(**c**) *(train, develop) (person, taste)* educar; **she was educated always to think of others before herself** le enseñaron a pensar en los demás antes que en ella

educated ['edjʊkeɪtɪd] *adj (person)* culto(a); *(palate)* educado(a); **an e. guess** una suposición bien fundada; **in e. speech** en la lengua culta

education [edjʊ'keɪʃən] *n* (**a**) *(process of learning)* educación *f*, aprendizaje *m*; *(process of teaching)* educación *f*, enseñanza *f*; **primary/secondary e.** enseñanza primaria/secundaria; **tertiary e.** enseñanza terciaria *or* superior; **a classical/scientific e.** una formación *or* instrucción clásica/científica; **he had** *or* **received a good e.** recibió una buena educación; **he never completed his e.** nunca concluyó sus estudios; **Faculty of E.** facultad de pedagogía; *Fam* **it was an e. working over there** trabajar allí fue muy instructivo

(**b**) *(knowledge)* educación *f*, cultura *f*; **a man without e.** un hombre sin instrucción

educational [edjʊ'keɪʃənəl] *adj* (**a**) *(system, standards, TV programme)* educativo(a); *(books, publisher)* educativo(a); *(method)* pedagógico(a); *(establishment)* docente ►► ***e. psychologist*** psicopedagogo(a) *m,f*; ***e. qualifications*** títulos *mpl* académicos; ***e. toy*** juguete *m* educativo (**b**) *(experience, visit)* instructivo(a)

educationalist [edjuː'keɪʃənəlɪst], **educationist** [edjuː'keɪʃənɪst] *n* pedagogo(a) *m,f*

educationally [edjuː'keɪʃənəlɪ] *adv* pedagógicamente hablando, desde el punto de vista pedagógico; **to be e. deprived** *or* **disadvantaged** estar en una situación desventajosa desde el punto de vista educativo; *Br Old-fashioned* **e. sub-normal** con graves problemas de aprendizaje

educationist = **educationalist**

educative ['edjʊkətɪv] *adj* educativo(a)

educator ['edjʊkeɪtə(r)] *n* educador(ora) *m,f*, docente *mf*

educe [ɪ'djuːs] *vt Formal* extraer

edutainment [edjʊ'teɪnmənt] *n* juegos *mpl* didácticos *or* educativos, material *m* lúdico-didáctico

Edward ['edwəd] *pr n* **E. I/II** Eduardo I/II

Edwardian [ed'wɔːdɪən] **1** *n* = persona de la época de Eduardo VII

2 *adj (architecture, furniture)* = de la época de Eduardo VII (1901-10)

EEC [iːiː'siː] *n Formerly* (*abbr* **European Economic Community**) CEE *f*

EEG [iːiː'dʒiː] *n Med* (**a**) (*abbr* **electroencephalogram**) EEG *m* (**b**) (*abbr* **electroencephalograph**) electroencefalógrafo *m*

eek [iːk] *exclam Fam* ¡ah!

eel [iːl] *n* anguila *f*

eelworm ['iːlwɜːm] *n* nematodo *m*, lombriz *f* radicícola

e'en [iːn] *adv Literary* = **even**

EEOC [iːiːəʊ'siː] *n* (*abbr* **Equal Employment Opportunity Commission**) = organismo público estadounidense que vela por la existencia de igualdad de oportunidades para los diferentes sexos, razas, etc.

e'er [eə(r)] *adv Literary* = **ever**

eerie ['ɪərɪ] *adj (sound, atmosphere)* espeluznante, sobrecogedor(ora); **an e. silence** *(after explosion, in empty house)* un silencio sobrecogedor

eerily ['ɪərɪlɪ] *adv* de forma espeluznante; **it was e. silent** había un silencio sobrecogedor

eeriness ['ɪərɪnɪs] *n* lo espeluznante

eff [ef] *vi Br Fam Euph* **he was effing and blinding** estaba diciendo palabrotas *or* soltando maldiciones

► **eff off** *vi Br Fam Euph* **e. off!** ¡vete por ahí!

efface [ɪ'feɪs] *vt* borrar; **to e. oneself** mantenerse en un segundo plano

EFFECT [ɪ'fekt] **1** *n* (**a**) *(result)* efecto *m*; **we did all we could, but to little** *or* **no e.** hicimos todo lo posible, pero no sirvió para nada; **with e. from...** con efecto a partir de..., que entra en vigor a partir de...; **with immediate e.** con efecto inmediato; **to come into e.** entrar en vigor *or* vigencia; **to have an e. on** tener efecto en *or* sobre; **the measures had a positive e. on inflation** las medidas incidieron positivamente en la inflación, las medidas tuvieron un impacto positivo en la inflación; **the medicine didn't have any e.** el medicamento no surtió ningún efecto; **to put sth into e.** llevar algo a la práctica; **to remain in e.** permanecer en vigor *or* vigencia; **to suffer (from) the effects of sth** sufrir los efectos de algo; **to take e.** *(drug, medicine)* hacer *or* surtir efecto; *(law)* entrar en vigor

(**b**) *(impression)* efecto *m*, impresión *f*; **they had altered the design to great e.** su cambio de diseño fue impactante; **the city is seen to best e. at night** la ciudad puede observarse en todo su esplendor de noche; **for e.** para impresionar; **to pause for e.** hacer una pausa para mantener la emoción

(**c**) *(meaning, significance)* **...or words to that e.** ...o algo por el estilo; **he said something to the e. that he wouldn't be staying long** dijo algo en el sentido de que no se quedaría mucho rato; *Formal* **you will receive a letter to this e.** recibirá una carta confirmando este hecho

(**d**) *Formal (possession)* **personal effects** efectos personales

(**e**) *(simulation)* efecto *m*; **clever use of lighting created the e. of a thunderstorm** un uso inteligente de la iluminación consiguió el efecto de una tormenta; **effects** *(in film)* efectos especiales; *(in music)* efectos

2 *vt Formal (cause) (reconciliation, cure)* lograr; *(payment, purchase)* efectuar; **to e. a change** efectuar un cambio; **to e. an entry** entrar, penetrar

3 in effect *adv (basically)* de hecho, en la práctica; **in e., what this means is that...** lo que esto viene a decir es que...

---

effective [ɪ'fektɪv] **1** *adj* (**a**) *(efficient, successful)* eficaz; **an e. way of doing sth** una manera eficaz de hacer algo

(**b**) *(actual, real)* efectivo(a); **to assume e. command** asumir el mando efectivo ►► ***e. life*** *(of product, structure)* vida *f* útil; ***e. range*** *(of firearm, missile)* alcance *m* real

(**c**) *Law (in force)* **to be** *or* **become e. (from)** entrar en vigor (desde); **to cease to be e.** *(policy, law)* dejar de tener vigencia

(**d**) *(creating effect) (colour, illustration, speaker)* impactante

2 effectives *npl Mil* efectivos *mpl*

effectively [ɪ'fektɪvlɪ] *adv* (**a**) *(efficiently)* eficazmente (**b**) *(really)* en realidad, de hecho; **they are e. the same** de hecho vienen a ser lo mismo; **the game was e. over** el partido quedó virtualmente sentenciado (**c**) *(creating effect)* con gran efecto

effectiveness [ɪ'fektɪvnɪs] *n* (**a**) *(efficiency)* eficacia *f* (**b**) *(effect) (of colour, illustration, speech)* efecto *m*; **how to improve the e. of your backhand** cómo mejorar la eficacia de tu revés

effectual [ɪ'fektjʊəl] *adj* (**a**) *(effective)* efectivo(a) (**b**) *(contract, ruling)* válido(a)

effectuate [ɪ'fektjʊeɪt] *vt Formal* efectuar, operar

effeminacy [ɪ'femɪnəsɪ] *n (of man)* afeminamiento *m*; **the e. of his voice/manner** lo afeminado de su voz/sus modales

effeminate [ɪ'femɪnət] *adj* afeminado(a)

effeminately [ɪ'femɪnətlɪ] *adv* de manera afeminada

effervesce [efə'ves] *vi* (**a**) *(liquid)* burbujear, estar en efervescencia (**b**) *(person)* estar en plena efervescencia

effervescence [efə'vesəns] *n (of liquid, person)* efervescencia *f*

effervescent [efə'vesənt] *adj (liquid, person)* efervescente
effete [ɪ'fi:t] *adj* **(a)** *(person, gesture)* afectado(a), refinado(a) en exceso **(b)** *(civilization, society)* decadente
efficacious [efɪ'keɪʃəs] *adj Formal* eficaz
efficacy ['efɪkəsɪ] *n Formal* eficacia *f*
efficiency [ɪ'fɪʃənsɪ] *n* **(a)** *(of person)* eficiencia *f* **(b)** *(of machine, method)* eficacia *f* ▸▸ *US* ***e. apartment*** cuarto *m* de alquiler
efficient [ɪ'fɪʃənt] *adj* **(a)** *(person)* eficiente; **to be e. at sth** ser eficiente en algo **(b)** *(machine, method)* eficaz; **to make more e. use of sth** hacer un uso más eficaz de algo
efficiently [ɪ'fɪʃəntlɪ] *adv* con eficiencia, eficientemente; **to organize one's time e.** organizarse el tiempo de forma eficiente
effigy ['efɪdʒɪ] *n (statue)* efigie *f*; *(for ridicule)* monigote *m*; **to burn sb in e.** quemar un monigote de alguien
effing ['efɪŋ] *Br Fam Euph* **1** *n* **e. and blinding** palabrotas
2 *adj* maldito(a), *Esp* puñetero(a); **the e. telly's not working** la maldita tele no funciona
3 *adv* **don't be so e. lazy!** ¡no seas tan vago, contra *or* caray!
efflorescence [eflə'resəns] *n* **(a)** *Bot (of plant)* floración *f* **(b)** *Chem* eflorescencia *f* **(c)** *Med* eflorescencia *f*
efflorescent [eflə'resənt] *adj Chem* eflorescente
effluent ['efluənt] *n* **(a)** *(waste, sewage)* aguas *fpl* residuales **(b)** *Geog* efluente *m*
effort ['efət] *n* **(a)** *(exertion)* esfuerzo *m*; **their efforts were rewarded** sus esfuerzos se vieron recompensados; **we appreciate your efforts on our behalf** agradecemos los esfuerzos que han hecho por nosotros; **put some e. into it!** ¡podrías hacer un esfuerzo!; **I put a lot of e. into that project** puse mucho esfuerzo *or* empeño en ese proyecto; **without much e.** sin mucho esfuerzo; **it was an e. for me to stay awake** me costó mucho mantenerme despierta; **to make an e. (to do sth)** hacer un esfuerzo (por hacer algo); **at least she made the e.** al menos lo intentó; **to make no e. to do sth** no molestarse en hacer algo, no hacer nada *or* ningún esfuerzo por hacer algo; **to make every e. to do sth** esforzarse al máximo por hacer algo; **to be worth the e.** valer la pena
(b) *(attempt)* intento *m*; **in an e. to do sth** en un intento por hacer algo
(c) *(achievement, production)* **it's not a bad e.** no está nada mal; *Fam* **what do you think of his latest e.?** ¿qué te parece su último trabajo?
(d) *Phys (of traction)* esfuerzo *m*
(e) *Br Fam (gadget)* chisme *m*; **she was wearing this awful polka-dot e.** llevaba esa cosa horrible de lunares; **he writes those historical romance efforts** escribe noveluchas románticas históricas
effortless ['efətlɪs] *adj* fácil, cómodo(a); **she makes it seem so e.** hace que parezca tan sencillo; **he won with almost e. ease** ganó con absoluta comodidad
effortlessly ['efətlɪslɪ] *adv* sin esfuerzo, fácilmente
effrontery [ɪ'frʌntərɪ] *n Formal* desfachatez *f*, descaro *m*; **he had the e. to...** tuvo la desfachatez *or* el descaro de...
effusion [ɪ'fju:ʒən] *n* **(a)** *Formal (spontaneous expression)* efusión *f* **(b)** *Med (of liquid, blood)* efusión *f*
effusive [ɪ'fju:sɪv] *adj* efusivo(a); **to be e. in one's praise/congratulations** ser efusivo(a) en los elogios/las felicitaciones; **to be e. in one's apologies** deshacerse en disculpas
effusively [ɪ'fju:sɪvlɪ] *adv* efusivamente; **to apologize e.** deshacerse en disculpas
EFL [i:ef'el] *n* (*abbr* **English as a Foreign Language**) inglés *m* como lengua extranjera
EFT [i:ef'ti:] *n* (*abbr* **electronic funds transfer**) transferencia *f* electrónica de fondos
EFTA ['eftə] *n* (*abbr* **European Free Trade Association**) EFTA *f*, AELC *f*
EFTPOS ['eftpɒs] *n* (*abbr* **electronic funds transfer at point of sale**) transferencia *f* (electrónica de fondos) en el punto de venta
e.g. [i:'dʒi:] (*abbr* **exempli gratia**) p. ej.
EGA [i:dʒi:'eɪ] *n Comptr* (*abbr* **enhanced graphics adaptor**) EGA *m*
egad [ɪ'gæd] *exclam Archaic* ¡pardiez!
egalitarian [ɪgælɪ'teərɪən] **1** *n* partidario(a) *m,f* del igualitarismo
2 *adj* igualitario(a)
egalitarianism [ɪgælɪ'teərɪənɪzəm] *n* igualitarismo *m*
egg [eg] *n* **(a)** *(of animal, food)* huevo *m*, *CAm, Méx* blanquillo *m* ▸▸ *US* ***e. crate*** huevera *f*, cartón *m* de huevos; ***e. custard*** ≃ natillas *fpl*; *US* ***e. roll*** rollo *m or* rollito *m* de primavera, *RP* arrollado *m or* arrolladito *m* primavera; ***e. white*** clara *f* (de huevo); ***e. yolk*** yema *f* (de huevo)
(b) *(reproductive cell)* óvulo *m*
(c) IDIOMS **to be a good/bad e.** *(person)* ser buena/mala gente; **to have e. on one's face** haber quedado en ridículo; *Fam* **you've got e. on your chin** *(your fly is undone)* tienes la bragueta bajada, *RP* tenés la ventana abierta; *Fam* **as sure as eggs is eggs** como que dos y dos son cuatro; PROV **don't put all your eggs in one basket** no te lo juegues todo a una sola carta, *Am* no pongas todos los huevos en la misma canasta
▸ **egg on** *vt sep* **to e. sb on (to do sth)** incitar a alguien (a hacer algo)
egg-and-spoon race ['egən'spu:nreɪs] *n* carrera *f* del huevo y la cuchara
eggbeater ['egbi:tə(r)] *n* **(a)** *(kitchen utensil)* varillas *fpl* (para batir), batidor *m* **(b)** *US Fam (helicopter)* helicóptero *m*
eggbox ['egbɒks] *n Br* huevera *f*, cartón *m* de huevos
egg-cosy ['egkəʊzɪ] *n Br* cubrehuevera *f*
eggcup ['egkʌp] *n* huevera *f (para huevos cocidos)*
egg-flip = **eggnog**
egghead ['eghed] *n Fam Hum or Pej* lumbrera *f*, cerebrito *m*
eggnog [eg'nɒg], **egg-flip** [eg'flɪp] *n* ponche *m* de huevo
eggplant ['egplænt] *n US* berenjena *f*
eggshell ['egʃel] **1** *n* cáscara *f* (de huevo); IDIOM **to walk on eggshells** andar con pies de plomo ▸▸ ***e. china*** *or* ***porcelain*** = porcelana muy fina y frágil
2 *adj (paint, finish)* semimate
egg-slice ['egslaɪs] *n* rodaja *f* de huevo
egg-timer ['egtaɪmə(r)] *n* reloj *m* de arena *(para medir el tiempo de cocción de los huevos)*
eggwhisk ['egwɪsk] *n Br* varillas *fpl* (para batir), batidor *m*
eggy ['egɪ] *adj Fam (smell, taste)* a huevo
egis *US* = **aegis**
eglantine ['egləntaɪn] *n Bot* eglantina *f*
EGM [i:dʒi:'em] *n Com* (*abbr* **extraordinary general meeting**) *n* junta *f* general extraordinaria
ego ['i:gəʊ] (*pl* **egos**) *n* **(a)** *(self-esteem)* amor *m* propio, autoestima *f*; *Psy* ego *m*, yo *m*; **he has an enormous e.** tiene un ego descomunal, es un presuntuoso; **to boost sb's e.** dar mucha moral a alguien ▸▸ *Fam* ***e. trip:*** **his public statements are just a big e. trip** sólo hace declaraciones públicas para alimentar su ego; **he's on another e. trip** ya se le han vuelto a subir los humos
(b) *Psy* ego *m*
egocentric [i:gəʊ'sentrɪk] *adj* egocéntrico(a)
egocentricity ['i:gəʊsen'trɪsɪtɪ], **egocentrism** ['i:gəʊ'sentrɪzəm] *n* egocentrismo *m*
egoism ['i:gəʊɪzəm] *n* egoísmo *m*
egoist ['i:gəʊɪst] *n* egoísta *mf*
egoistic(al) [i:gəʊ'ɪstɪk(əl)] *adj* egoísta
egomania [i:gəʊ'meɪnɪə] *n* egolatría *f*, egocentrismo *m*
egomaniac [i:gəʊ'meɪnɪæk] *n* ególatra *mf*, egocéntrico(a) *m,f*
egotism ['i:gətɪzəm] *n* egocentrismo *m*
egotist ['i:gətɪst] *n* egocéntrico(a) *m,f*
egotistic(al) [i:gə'tɪstɪk(əl)] *adj* egocéntrico(a)
egotistically ['i:gə'tɪstɪklɪ] *adv* egocéntricamente
ego-trip ['i:gəʊ'trɪp] *vi Fam* **he's ego-tripping again** ya se le han vuelto a subir los humos
egregious [ɪ'gri:dʒɪəs] *adj Formal* atroz; **an e. error** un craso error, un error mayúsculo

> **False friend**: The Spanish adjective **egregio** is not a translation for the English word **egregious**. In Spanish **egregio** means "illustrious".

egress ['i:gres] *n Formal* salida *f*
egret ['i:gret] *n* garceta *f*
Egypt ['i:dʒɪpt] *n* Egipto
Egyptian [ɪ'dʒɪpʃən] **1** *n* egipcio(a) *m,f*
2 *adj* egipcio(a) ▸▸ ***E. goose*** ganso *m* del Nilo; ***E. vulture*** alimoche *m*
Egyptologist ['i:dʒɪp'tɒlədʒɪst] *n* egiptólogo(a) *m,f*
Egyptology [i:dʒɪp'tɒlədʒɪ] *n* egiptología *f*
eh [eɪ] *exclam* **(a)** *(what did you say?)* ¿eh? **(b)** *(seeking agreement, confirmation)* ¿eh? **(c)** *(in astonishment)* ¡qué!, ¡cómo!
eider ['aɪdə(r)] *n* **e. (duck)** éider *m*, eider *m*
eiderdown ['aɪdədaʊn] *n (duvet)* edredón *m*
eidetic [aɪ'detɪk] *adj Psy (memory, image)* eidético(a)

eight [eɪt] **1** *n* (a) *(number)* ocho *m*; **e. and e. are sixteen** ocho y ocho, dieciséis; **there were e. of us** éramos ocho; **all e. of them left** se marcharon los ocho; **the e. of hearts** *(in cards)* el ocho de corazones ►► *US* ***e. ball*** bola *f* negra; IDIOM *Fam* **to be behind the e. ball** estar con el agua al cuello

(b) *(time)* las ocho; **come at e.** ven a las ocho; **it's almost e.** van a dar *or* son casi las ocho; **is e. too late?** ¿(qué tal) a las ocho? ¿o es muy tarde?

2 *adj* (a) *(number)* ocho; **they live at number e.** viven en el (número) ocho; **chapter/page e.** capítulo/página ocho; **e. hundred** ochocientos(as); *US* **e. hundred number** = número de teléfono al que se llama gratis, *Esp* ≃ número novecientos; **e. hundred men** ochocientos hombres; **e. thousand** ocho mil; **it costs e. pounds** cuesta ocho libras; **an e.-hour day** una jornada de ocho horas

(b) *(time)* ocho; **e. o'clock** las ocho (en punto); **it's e. minutes to five** son las cinco menos ocho minutos

(c) *(age)* **to be e. (years old)** tener ocho años (de edad); **she'll soon be e. (years old)** dentro de nada cumplirá (los) ocho años

eighteen [eɪ'tiːn] **1** *n* dieciocho *m*

2 *adj* dieciocho; *see also* **eight**

eighteenth [eɪ'tiːnθ] **1** *n* (a) *(fraction)* dieciochoavo *m*, decimoctava parte *f* (b) *(in series)* decimoctavo(a) *m,f* (c) *(of month)* dieciocho *m*

2 *adj* decimoctavo(a); *see also* **eleventh**

eightfold ['eɪtfəʊld] **1** *adj* óctuplo(a); **an e. increase** una subida de ocho veces

2 *adv* ocho veces

eighth [eɪtθ] **1** *n* (a) *(fraction)* octavo *m*, octava parte *f* (b) *(in series)* octavo(a) *m,f*; **Edward the E.** *(written)* Eduardo VIII; *(spoken)* Eduardo octavo (c) *(of month)* ocho *m*; **(on) the e. of May** el ocho de mayo; **we're leaving on the e.** nos vamos el (día) ocho

2 *adj* octavo(a); **the e. century** *(written)* el siglo VIII; *(spoken)* el siglo octavo *or* ocho; *US* **e. grade** = octavo (y último) curso de educación primaria en Estados Unidos; *US* **e. grader** alumno(a) de octavo de primaria ►► *US Mus* ***e. note*** corchea *f*

3 *adv* **she finished e.** acabó octava

eighties ['eɪtiːz] **1** *npl* **in the e.** *(decade)* en los (años) ochenta; **to be in one's e.** tener ochenta y tantos años; **the temperature was in the e.** *(Fahrenheit)* hacía alrededor de 30 grados

2 *adj Fam* de los ochenta; **it's terribly e.** recuerda un montón a los años ochenta; **e. look/song** pinta/canción de los (años) ochenta; **e. hairstyle** peinado estilo años ochenta

eightieth ['eɪtɪəθ] **1** *n* octogésimo(a) *m,f*

2 *adj* octogésimo(a)

eightsome reel ['eɪtsəm'riːl] *n* = danza escocesa para ocho personas

eighty ['eɪtɪ] **1** *n* ochenta *m*; **e.-one** ochenta y uno(a); **he was doing e. (miles an hour)** *(in car)* iba a unos ciento treinta (kilómetros por hora)

2 *adj* ochenta; **about e. books/passengers** unos ochenta libros/pasajeros; **e. percent of the staff** el ochenta por ciento del personal; **she's about e. (years old)** tiene unos ochenta años; **he will be e. tomorrow** mañana cumple ochenta años

eighty-six ['eɪtɪ'sɪks] *vt US Fam* (a) *(eject)* echar; **the bouncer had to e. that drunk** el gorila tuvo que poner al borracho de patitas en la calle (b) *(kill)* cepillarse a; **another drug dealer got eighty-sixed downtown** se cepillaron a otro camello en el centro

einsteinium [aɪn'staɪnɪəm] *n Chem* einstenio *m*

Eire ['eərə] *n Formerly* Eire *m (hoy la República de Irlanda)*

eisteddfod [aɪ'stedfəd] *n* = festival de música, teatro y poesía celebrado en Gales

EITHER ['aɪðə(r), 'iːðə(r)] **1** *adj* (a) *(one or other)* cualquiera de los/las dos; **e. candidate may win** puede ganar cualquiera de los (dos) candidatos; **I doubt whether e. solution can really work** dudo que ninguna de las dos soluciones funcione; **I don't like e. colour** no me gusta ninguno de los dos colores

(b) *(each of the two)* **in e. case** en los dos casos, en ambos casos; **she wore a bracelet on e. arm** llevaba una pulsera en cada brazo *or* ambos brazos; **on e. side** a cada lado; **e. way, you still have to pay the full fare** en cualquier caso vas a tener que pagar el importe completo; **I don't mind e. way** me da igual; **they said a week, but it could be a day e. way** dijeron una semana, pero podría ser un día arriba, un día abajo

2 *pron* cualquiera; **e. (of them) will do** me sirve cualquiera (de ellos); **has e. of you heard from him?** ¿alguno de los dos tiene noticias suyas?; **if e. got lost...** si se perdiese cualquiera de los dos...; **I don't believe e. of them** no les creo a ninguno de los dos; **I don't want e. of them** no quiero ninguno

3 *conj* **e.... or...** o... o..., (o) bien... o bien...; **e. you or your brother** o tú o tu hermano; **we can e. do it now or later** o lo hacemos ahora o más tarde; **I don't eat e. meat or fish** no como (ni) carne ni pescado; **you e. love it or hate it** lo amas o lo odias; **e. shut up or leave!** ¡o te callas o te vas!; **it's e. that or I lose my job** o eso o pierdo mi trabajo

4 *adv* tampoco; **if you don't go, I won't go e.** si tú no vas, yo tampoco; **I've never met her – I haven't e.** no la conozco – yo tampoco; **he can't sing, and he can't act e.** no sabe cantar ni tampoco actuar; **I don't want to and I don't see why I should e.** ni quiero ni veo por qué debería

either-or ['aɪðər'ɔː(r)] *adj* **to be in an e. situation** tener que elegir (entre lo uno o lo otro)

ejaculate [ɪ'dʒækjʊleɪt] **1** *vt* (a) *(semen)* eyacular (b) *Formal (exclaim)* exclamar

2 *vi (emit semen)* eyacular

ejaculation [ɪdʒækjʊ'leɪʃən] *n* (a) *(of semen)* eyaculación *f* (b) *Old-fashioned (exclamation)* exclamación *f*

eject [ɪ'dʒekt] **1** *vt* (a) *(troublemaker)* expulsar (b) *(CD, video)* expulsar; *(pilot)* eyectar; *(lava)* escupir, arrojar

2 *vi (from plane)* eyectarse

ejection [ɪ'dʒekʃən] *n* (a) *(of troublemaker)* expulsión *f* (b) *(of CD, video)* expulsión *f*; *(of pilot)* eyección *f*; *(of lava)* erupción *f* ►► *US* ***e. seat*** asiento *m* eyectable *or* eyector

ejector seat [ɪ'dʒektəsiːt] *n* asiento *m* eyectable *or* eyector

eke [iːk]

► **eke out** *vt sep* (a) *(make last) (rations)* estirar (b) *(scrape)* **to e. out a living** ganarse la vida a duras penas; **they eked out a miserable existence on the barren land** la árida tierra apenas les permitía subsistir

EKG ['iːkeɪdʒiː] *n US* (*abbr* **electrocardiogram**) ECG *m*

el [el] *n US Fam* (*abbr* **elevated railroad**) ferrocarril *m or* tren *m* elevado

elaborate **1** *adj* [ɪ'læbərət] *(plan, excuse, meal)* elaborado(a); *(preparations)* minucioso(a); *(drawing, description, design)* detallado(a); *(system)* sofisticado(a); *(style, costume)* muy elaborado(a); **in e. detail** minuciosamente; **he described the scene in e. detail** describió la escena con todo lujo de detalles

2 *vt* [ɪ'læbəreɪt] elaborar

3 *vi* dar detalles (**on** *or* **upon** sobre)

elaborately [ɪ'læbərətlɪ] *adv* laboriosamente; **an e. worked-out scheme** un plan cuidadosamente elaborado; **an e. decorated room** una habitación profusamente decorada

elaboration [ɪlæbə'reɪʃən] *n* (a) *(development)* elaboración *f* (b) *(adding of detail)* **to provide further e.** dar más detalles

élan [eɪ'lɑːn] *n Literary* brío *m*

eland ['iːlənd] *n* eland *m* común *or* de El Cabo

elapse [ɪ'læps] *vi* transcurrir

elasmobranch [ɪ'læzməbræŋk] *Zool* **1** *n* elasmobranquio *m*

2 *adj* elasmobranquio(a)

elastic [ɪ'læstɪk] **1** *n* (a) *(material)* elástico *m* (b) *US (rubber band)* goma *f* elástica, gomita *f*

2 *adj* (a) *(material)* flexible, elástico(a) ►► ***e. band*** goma *f* (elástica), gomita *f* (b) *(adaptable, changeable) (concept, category)* flexible; *(conscience)* indulgente; *(price, demand)* elástico(a) (c) *(springy) (step)* ágil, ligero(a)

elasticated [ɪ'læstɪkeɪtɪd] *adj* con elástico, *RP* elastizado(a)

elasticity [iːlæs'tɪsɪtɪ] *n* (a) *(of material)* elasticidad *f* (b) *(of concept, category)* flexibilidad *f*; *(of conscience)* indulgencia *f*; *(of price, demand)* elasticidad *f*

elastin [ɪ'læstɪn] *n Biochem* elastina *f*

Elastoplast® [ɪ'læstəplɑːst] *n Br Esp* tirita® *f*, *Am* curita *f*

elated [ɪ'leɪtɪd] *adj* jubiloso(a), eufórico(a); **to be** *or* **feel e. (about sth)** estar jubiloso(a) *or* eufórico(a) (por algo)

elation [ɪ'leɪʃən] *n* júbilo *m*, euforia *f*

Elbe [elb] *n* **the (River) E.** el Elba

elbow ['elbəʊ] **1** *n* (a) *(of arm, jacket)* codo *m*; **out at the elbows** *(of pullover, jacket)* con agujeros en los codos; **to be at sb's e.** *(as support)* estar al lado de alguien; *(as irritant)* estar pegado(a) a alguien ►► ***e. patch*** codera *f*

(b) *(in road)* recodo *m*; *(in pipe)* codo *m*

(c) IDIOMS **to give sb the e.** *(of employer)* despedir a alguien; *(of lover)* cortar con alguien; **he got the e.** *(employee)* lo despidieron; *(lover)* cortó con él; **to be up to one's** *or* **the elbows in sth** estar hasta arriba de algo

2 *vt* **to e. sb in the ribs** dar un codazo a alguien en las costillas; **to e. sb aside** apartar a alguien de un codazo; **to e. one's way through (a crowd)** abrirse paso a codazos (entre una multitud)

elbow-grease ['elbəʊgri:s] *n Fam* **the house is in a state, but it just needs a bit of e.** la casa está hecha un desastre, pero con un repaso a fondo quedará bien; **put some e. into it!** ¡dale fuerte! *(al sacar brillo)*

elbow-room ['elbəʊrʊm] *n* (**a**) *(space)* espacio *m or* sitio *m* (libre) (**b**) *Fam Fig (freedom)* **to have enough e.** tener un margen de libertad *or* de maniobra

elder[1] ['eldə(r)] **1** *adj* mayor; **my e. brother** mi hermano mayor; **Pitt/Pliny the E.** Pitt/Plinio el Viejo ►► ***e. statesman*** antiguo mandatario *m (que conserva su prestigio)*

2 *n* (**a**) *(older person)* mayor *mf*; **young people should respect their elders** los jóvenes deberían respetar a sus mayores; ***e. abuse*** maltrato *m* a las personas mayores (**b**) *(of tribe)* anciano(a) *m,f* (**c**) *Rel* = persona que ostenta una cargo de responsabilidad en una parroquia

elder[2] *n (tree)* saúco *m*

elderberry ['eldəberı] *n (fruit)* baya *f* de saúco

elderly ['eldəlı] **1** *adj* anciano(a); **she's getting rather e.** se está haciendo mayor; *Hum* **my rather e. VCR** mi prehistórico vídeo *or Am* video

2 *npl* **the e.** los ancianos

eldest ['eldıst] **1** *adj* mayor; **my e. daughter** la mayor de mis hijas, mi hija mayor

2 *n* **the e.** el/la mayor

elect [ı'lekt] **1** *n Rel* **the e.** los elegidos

2 *adj* electo(a); **the president e.** el presidente electo

3 *vt* (**a**) *(councillor, MP)* elegir; **to e. sb president, to e. sb to the presidency** elegir a alguien presidente; **to e. sb to office** elegir a alguien para un cargo; **to get** *or* **be elected** ser elegido(a) (**b**) *Formal (choose)* **to e. to do sth** elegir hacer algo

electable [ı'lektəbəl] *adj* elegible, con gancho electoral

elected [ı'lektıd] *adj* elegido(a)

election [ı'lekʃən] *n (event)* elecciones *fpl*; *(action)* elección *f*; **to hold an e.** celebrar unas elecciones; **to stand for e.** presentarse a las elecciones ►► *Br* ***e. agent*** representante *mf* electoral; ***e. campaign*** campaña *f* electoral; ***e. literature*** propaganda *f* electoral

electioneering [ılekʃə'nıərıŋ] **1** *n* electoralismo *m*

2 *adj (speech, campaign)* electoralista

elective [ı'lektıv] **1** *adj* (**a**) *(assembly)* electivo(a); *(official, post)* electivo(a) (**b**) *Univ (course)* optativo(a), opcional

2 *n (subject)* (asignatura *f*) optativa *f*

elector [ı'lektə(r)] *n* (**a**) *(voter)* elector(ora) *m,f*, votante *mf* (**b**) *US (member of electoral college)* miembro *mf* de un colegio electoral

electoral [ı'lektərəl] *adj Pol* electoral ►► ***e. college*** cuerpo *m* de compromisarios, colegio *m* electoral; ***e. mandate*** mandato *m* electoral; ***e. pact*** pacto *m* electoral; ***e. reform*** reforma *f* electoral; *Br, Austr* ***e. register*** censo *m* electoral; *Br, Austr* ***e. roll*** censo *m* electoral

electorate [ı'lektərət] *n* electorado *m*

Electra [ı'lektrə] *n Mythol* Electra

electric [ı'lektrık] **1** *adj* eléctrico(a); *Fig* **the atmosphere of the meeting was e.** en la reunión el ambiente estaba electrizado; **the effect of her words was e.** sus palabras tuvieron un efecto electrizante ►► *Elec* ***e. arc*** arco *m* eléctrico *or* voltaico; *esp US* ***e. bill*** factura *f* de la luz; ***e. blanket*** manta *f* eléctrica; ***e. blue*** azul *m* eléctrico; ***e. chair*** silla *f* eléctrica; ***e. charge*** carga *f* eléctrica; ***e. cooker*** cocina *f or Col, Méx* estufa *f* eléctrica; ***e. current*** corriente *f* eléctrica, fluido *m* eléctrico; ***e. eel*** anguila *f* eléctrica; ***e. eye*** célula *f* fotoeléctrica; ***e. fence*** valla *f* electrificada, cerca *f* eléctrica; ***e. field*** campo *m* eléctrico; ***e. guitar*** guitarra *f* eléctrica; ***e. motor*** electromotor *m*, motor *m* eléctrico; ***e. organ*** órgano *m* electrónico; ***e. ray*** *(fish)* torpedo *m*, tembladera *f*; ***e. razor*** máquina *f* de afeitar, maquinilla *f* eléctrica *or* de afeitar; ***e. shock*** descarga *f* eléctrica; ***e. shock therapy*** terapia *f* de electrochoque *or* electroshock; ***e. storm*** tormenta *f* eléctrica; ***e. window:* it has e. windows** tiene elevalunas eléctrico *or Am* vidrio eléctrico

2 **electrics** *npl Br Fam (of car, house)* instalación *f* eléctrica

electrical [ı'lektrıkəl] *adj* eléctrico(a) ►► ***e. appliance*** electrodoméstico *m*, aparato *m* eléctrico; ***e. engineer*** *(with university qualification)* ingeniero(a) *m,f* eléctrico(a); *(without university qualification)* técnico *mf* electricista; ***e. engineering*** electrotecnia *f*, ingeniería *f* electrónica; ***e. fault*** *Esp* fallo *m* eléctrico, *Am* falla *f* eléctrica; ***e. shock*** descarga *f* eléctrica; ***e. storm*** tormenta *f* eléctrica

electrically [ı'lektrıklı] *adv* **e. powered** *or* **operated** eléctrico(a); **e. charged** con carga eléctrica; *Fig* **an e. charged atmosphere** un ambiente cargado

electrician [ılek'trıʃən] *n* electricista *mf*

electricity [ılek'trısıtı] *n* (**a**) *(power)* electricidad *f*; **the e. (supply)** el suministro eléctrico; **to turn** *or* **to switch the e. off/on** conectar/desconectar la corriente; **to be without e.** estar sin suministro eléctrico ►► *esp Br* ***e. bill*** factura *f* de la luz; ***e. generator*** generador *m* eléctrico, grupo *m* electrógeno; ***e. pylon*** torre *f* de alta tensión

(**b**) *(tension, energy)* tensión *f*; **there was e. in the air** el ambiente estaba cargado

electrification [ılektrıfı'keıʃən] *n* electrificación *f*

electrify [ı'lektrıfaı] *vt* (**a**) *(supply)* electrificar (**b**) *(railway system)* electrificar (**c**) *Fig (excite)* electrizar

electrifying [ı'lektrıfaııŋ] *adj Fig* electrizante

electrocardiogram [ılektrə'kɑ:dıəgræm] *n Med* electrocardiograma *m*

electrocardiograph [ılektrə'kɑ:dıəgræf] *n Med* electrocardiógrafo *m*

electrochemical [ılektrə'kemıkəl] *adj* electroquímico(a)

electroconvulsive therapy [ı'lektrəʊkənvʌlsıv'θerəpı] *n* terapia *f* de electrochoque *or* electroshock

electrocute [ı'lektrəkju:t] *vt* electrocutar; **to e. oneself** electrocutarse

electrocution [ılektrə'kju:ʃən] *n* electrocución *f*

electrode [ı'lektrəʊd] *n* electrodo *m*

electrodynamics [ılektrəʊdaı'næmıks] *n* electrodinámica *f*

electroencephalogram [ılektrəʊen'sefələgræm] *n* (electro)encefalograma *m*

electroencephalograph [ılektrəʊen'sefələgræf] *n* electroencefalógrafo *m*

electrolyse, *US* **electrolyze** [ı'lektrəlaız] *vt* (**a**) *Chem* electrolizar (**b**) *(to remove hair)* hacerse la depilación eléctrica en

electrolysis [ılek'trɒlısıs] *n* (**a**) *Chem* electrólisis *f inv* (**b**) *(to remove hair)* depilación *f* eléctrica

electrolyte [ı'lektrəlaıt] *n Chem* electrólito *m*, electrolito *m*

electrolyze *US* = **electrolyse**

electromagnet [ılektrəʊ'mægnıt] *n* electroimán *m*

electromagnetic [ılektrəʊmæg'netık] *adj Phys* electromagnético(a) ►► ***e. theory*** teoría *f* electromagnética de la luz; ***e. wave*** onda *f* electromagnética

electromagnetism [ılektrəʊ'mægnətızəm] *n Phys* electromagnetismo *m*

electrometer [ılek'trɒmıtə(r)] *n* electrómetro *m*

electromotive [ılektrəʊ'məʊtıv] *adj Phys* ***e. force*** fuerza *f* electromotriz

electron [ı'lektrɒn] *n* electrón *m* ►► ***e. beam*** haz *m* de electrones; *Phys* ***e. gun*** cañón *m* electrónico *or* de electrones; ***e. microscope*** microscopio *m* electrónico

electronic [ılek'trɒnık] *adj* electrónico(a) ►► ***e. banking*** banca *f* electrónica, (servicio *m* de) telebanco *m*; ***e. book*** libro *m* electrónico; *Comptr* ***e. cash*** dinero *m* electrónico; *Comptr* ***e. commerce*** comercio *m* electrónico; ***e. crime*** delito *m* electrónico; *Comptr* ***e. data interchange*** intercambio *m* electrónico de datos; *Comptr* ***e. data processing*** tratamiento *m or* procesamiento *m* electrónico de datos; ***e. engineer*** ingeniero(a) *m,f* electrónico(a); ***e. engineering*** ingeniería *f* electrónica; ***e. flash*** flash *m* electrónico; ***e. funds transfer*** transferencia *f* electrónica de fondos; ***e. funds transfer at point of sale*** transferencia *f* (electrónica de fondos) en el punto de venta; *Comptr* ***e. journal*** periódico *m* electrónico; *Comptr* ***e. mail*** correo *m* electrónico; *Comptr* ***e. mailbox*** buzón *m* electrónico; ***e. media*** medios *mpl* de comunicación electrónicos; *Comptr* ***e. money*** dinero *m* electrónico; ***e. music*** música *f* electrónica; *Comptr* ***e. office*** oficina *f* informatizada *or* electrónica; *Comptr* ***e. organizer*** agenda *f* electrónica; ***e. payment system*** sistema *m* de pago electrónico; ***e. point of sale*** punto *m* de venta electrónico; ***e. publishing*** edición *f* electrónica; ***e. purse*** monedero *m* electrónico; *Comptr* ***e. shopping*** compras *fpl* en línea; ***e. signature*** firma *f* electrónica; ***e. surveillance*** vigilancia *f* a través de dispositivos electrónicos; ***e. tagging*** *(of criminal)* = sistema electrónico que mediante una etiqueta permite la localización de presos en libertad condicional; ***e. ticketing*** expedición *f* de *Esp* billetes *or Am* boletos *or Am* pasajes electrónicos

electronically [ılek'trɒnıklı] *adv* electrónicamente

electronics [ılek'trɒnıks] **1** *n* electrónica *f*; **e. company** casa de electrónica; **the e. industry** el sector de la electrónica

2 *npl (of machine)* sistema *m* electrónico

electronvolt [ı'lektrɒnvəʊlt] *n Phys* electronvoltio *m*

electroplate [ı'lektrəpleıt] *vt* bañar por galvanoplastia, galvanizar por electrodeposición

electroshock [ɪlektrəʊ'ʃɒk] *n Med* **e. therapy** *or* **treatment** terapia *or* tratamiento de electrochoque

electrostatics [ɪlektrə'stætɪks] *n* electrostática *f*

electrotherapy [ɪlektrə'θerəpɪ] *n* electroterapia *f*

electrotype [ɪ'lektrətaɪp] *n Typ (printing plate)* electrotipo *m*, galvanotipo *m*

elegance ['elɪgəns] *n* elegancia *f*

elegant ['elɪgənt] *adj (appearance, movement)* elegante; *(reasoning, solution)* lúcido(a); IDIOM **to have had an e. sufficiency** saciar el apetito

elegantly ['elɪgəntlɪ] *adv (to dress, move)* elegantemente; **e. arranged/proportioned** armoniosamente dispuesto(a)/proporcionado(a)

elegiac [elə'dʒaɪək] *adj* elegiaco(a), elegíaco(a)

elegy ['elɪdʒɪ] *n* elegía *f*

element ['elɪmənt] *n* **(a)** *(constituent part)* elemento *m*, componente *m*; **a key e. in selling is...** un componente fundamental de las ventas es...; **this movie has all the elements of a hit movie** esta película contiene todos los ingredientes del éxito
(b) *(factor, aspect)* componente *m*, elemento *m*; **there is an e. of risk involved** existe cierto riesgo; **the e. of surprise** el factor sorpresa; **the human/time e.** el factor humano/tiempo; **an e. of danger** un factor de peligro
(c) *(in society)* elemento *m*; **undesirable elements in society** los indeseables de la sociedad
(d) *(rudiments)* **the elements of computing** los principios básicos de la informática
(e) *Chem* elemento *m*
(f) *(of kettle, electric fire)* resistencia *f*
(g) the elements *(weather)* los elementos; **to brave the elements** desafiar a los elementos
(h) *(ideal environment)* **she was in her e.** estaba en su elemento
(i) *Rel* **the elements** *(bread and wine)* las especies eucarísticas

elemental [elɪ'mentəl] *adj* **(a)** *(basic)* elemental, primario(a); **logistics is e. to any successful military campaign** la logística es un factor fundamental en cualquier campaña militar **(b)** *(relating to the elements)* elemental, natural; **the e. force of the storm** la fuerza natural que desencadena la tormenta **(c)** *Chem* elemental

elementary [elɪ'mentərɪ] *adj* elemental, básico(a); **an e. mistake** un error básico; IDIOM **e. my dear Watson** elemental, querido Watson ►► ***e. algebra*** álgebra *f* elemental; *Phys* ***e. particle*** partícula *f* elemental; *US* ***e. school*** escuela *f* primaria

elephant ['eləfənt] *n* elefante *m*; *Hum* **like the e., he never forgets** no olvida fácilmente las cosas ►► ***e. seal*** elefante *m* marino

elephantiasis [eləfən'taɪəsɪs] *n Med* elefantiasis *f inv*

elephantine [elə'fæntaɪn] *adj* **(a)** *(in size) (body, size)* mastodóntico(a) **(b)** *(clumsy) (steps, movement)* pesado(a), de elefante

elevate ['elɪveɪt] *vt* **(a)** *(raise) (object)* elevar; *Mil (cannon)* apuntar más alto con **(b)** *(promote)* **to e. sb to the peerage** otorgar a alguien un título nobiliario **(c)** *(exalt, uplift) (person, mind)* elevar, exaltar; **the legends have been elevated into a religion** las leyendas han sido elevadas a la categoría de cultos

elevated ['elɪveɪtɪd] *adj* **(a)** *(raised) (road, platform)* elevado(a) ►► *US* ***e. railroad*** ferrocarril *m or* tren *m* elevado **(b)** *(exalted) (position, rank)* elevado(a); *(thoughts, style)* elevado(a); **to have an e. opinion of oneself** tener un concepto demasiado elevado de uno mismo

elevation [elɪ'veɪʃən] *n* **(a)** *(height)* altitud *f*; **e. above sea level** altitud (por encima del nivel del mar); **2000 metres in e.** 2.000 metros de altitud
(b) *(promotion)* ascenso *m*, elevación *f*
(c) *(of style, language)* exaltación *f*, enaltecimiento *m*
(d) *(high place)* elevación *f* (del terreno), promontorio *m*
(e) *Archit* alzado *m*; **front/side/rear e.** vista frontal/lateral/posterior; **viewed in e.** en vista alzada
(f) *Mil* ángulo *m* de tiro
(g) *Rel (of host)* elevación *f*

elevator ['elɪveɪtə(r)] *n* **(a)** *US (lift)* ascensor *m*; IDIOM *Fam Hum* **the e. doesn't go up to the top floor** no es precisamente una lumbrera ►► ***e. attendant*** ascensorista *mf*; ***e. operator*** ascensorista *mf*; ***e. shaft*** hueco *m* del ascensor; ***e. shoes*** zapatos *mpl* de plataforma **(b)** *US* **(grain) e.** silo *m* **(c)** *(for goods)* montacargas *m inv* **(d)** *(on aircraft wing)* timón *m* de profundidad

eleven [ɪ'levən] **1** *n* once *m*; **the Spanish e.** *(football team)* el once español
2 *adj* once; *see also* **eight**

eleven-plus [ɪ'levən'plʌs] *n* = prueba selectiva con la que se accede a una "grammar school" en el Reino Unido

elevenses [ɪ'levənzɪz] *npl Br Fam* tentempié *m* (de la mañana), *Am* onces *fpl*

eleventh [ɪ'levənθ] **1** *n* **(a)** *(fraction)* onceavo *m*, onceava parte *f* **(b)** *(in series)* undécimo(a) *m,f*; **Louis the E.** *(written)* Luis XI; *(spoken)* Luis once **(c)** *(in month)* once *m*; **(on) the e. of May** el once de mayo; **we're leaving on the e.** nos vamos el (día) once
2 *adj* undécimo(a); IDIOM **at the e. hour** *Esp* en el *or Am* a último momento, *Am* en el último minuto; **the e. century** *(written)* el siglo XI; *(spoken)* el siglo once

elf [elf] *(pl* **elves** [elvz]*) n* elfo *m* ►► ***e. owl*** mochuelo *m* duende

elfin ['elfɪn] *adj* delicado(a), angelical

elicit [ɪ'lɪsɪt] *vt (information)* sacar, obtener **(from** de**)**; *(reaction, response)* provocar **(from** en**)**; **to e. a smile from sb** arrancar a alguien una sonrisa

elide [ɪ'laɪd] *vt Ling* elidir

eligibility [elɪdʒə'bɪlɪtɪ] *n* **(a)** *(entitlement)* elegibilidad *f*; **they questioned his e.** cuestionaron si era apto para presentar su candidatura; **to determine sb's e. for promotion** decidir si alguien reúne los requisitos necesarios para un ascenso **(b)** *(as potential partner)* **there was no doubt as to his e.** no cabían dudas de que era un buen candidato

eligible ['elɪdʒəbəl] *adj* **(a)** *(deserving, entitled)* **to be e. for sth** reunir los requisitos para algo; **you are still not e. to join the pension scheme** usted aún no reúne los requisitos necesarios para acogerse al plan de pensiones **(b)** *(as potential partner)* **there were lots of e. men at the party** en la fiesta había muchos hombres apetecibles; **an e. bachelor** un buen partido

Elijah [ɪ'laɪdʒə] *pr n* Elías

eliminate [ɪ'lɪmɪneɪt] *vt* **(a)** *(remove) (possibility, alternative)* eliminar; *(item from diet)* suprimir; **to e. hunger and poverty from the world** terminar con el hambre y la pobreza en el mundo **(b)** *(from competition)* eliminar; **they were eliminated in the first round** cayeron eliminados en la primera ronda **(c)** *Math* eliminar **(d)** *Physiol* eliminar **(e)** *Euph (kill)* eliminar

elimination [ɪlɪmɪ'neɪʃən] *n* **(a)** *(removal) (of possibility, alternative)* eliminación *f*; **by a process of e.** por (un proceso de) eliminación **(b)** *(from competition)* eliminación *f* **(c)** *Math* eliminación *f* **(d)** *Physiol* eliminación *f* **(e)** *Euph (murder)* eliminación *f*

eliminator [ɪ'lɪmɪneɪtə(r)] *n (contest)* eliminatoria *f*

eliminatory [ɪ'lɪmɪnətərɪ] *adj (round, stage)* eliminatorio(a)

elision [ɪ'lɪʒən] *n Ling* elisión *f*

elite [eɪ'li:t] **1** *n* élite *f*
2 *adj* de élite

elitism [eɪ'li:tɪzəm] *n* elitismo *m*

elitist [eɪ'li:tɪst] **1** *n* elitista *mf*
2 *adj* elitista

elixir [ɪ'lɪksə(r)] *n Literary* elixir *m*; **the e. of life** el elixir de la vida

Elizabeth [ɪ'lɪzəbəθ] *pr n* **E. I/II** Isabel I/II; **Queen E. II (of England)** la reina Isabel (de Inglaterra)

Elizabethan [ɪlɪzə'bi:θən] **1** *n* isabelino(a) *m,f*
2 *adj* isabelino(a)

elk [elk] *n* **(a)** *(European)* alce *m* **(b)** *(North American)* ciervo *m* canadiense

ellipse [ɪ'lɪps] *n Math* elipse *f*

ellipsis [ɪ'lɪpsɪs] *(pl* **ellipses** [ɪ'lɪpsi:z]*) n Gram* elipsis *f inv*

ellipsoid [ɪ'lɪpsɔɪd] *n Math* elipsoide *m*

ellipsoidal [ɪlɪp'sɔɪdəl] *adj Math* elipsoidal

elliptic(al) [ɪ'lɪptɪk(əl)] *adj* **(a)** *Math* elíptico(a) **(b)** *Formal (remark)* solapado(a), indirecto(a)

elm [elm] *n (wood, tree)* olmo *m*

elocution [elə'kju:ʃən] *n* dicción *f*; **e. lessons/teacher** clase/profesor(ora) de dicción

elongate ['i:lɒŋgeɪt] *vt* alargar; **an elongated neck** un cuello alargado

elongation [i:lɒŋ'geɪʃən] *n* **(a)** *(act)* alargamiento *m* **(b)** *(of line)* prolongación *f*, alargamiento *m*

elope [ɪ'ləʊp] *vi* fugarse *(para casarse)*

elopement [ɪ'ləʊpmənt] *n* fuga *f (para casarse)*

eloquence ['eləkwəns] *n* elocuencia *f*

eloquent ['eləkwənt] *adj* **(a)** *(person, speech)* elocuente **(b)** *(expressive)* **an e. gesture** un gesto elocuente; **the state of the economy is an e. indictment of this policy** la actual situación económica constituye una elocuente crítica a esta política

eloquently ['eləkwəntlɪ] *adv* con elocuencia, elocuentemente

El Salvador [el'sælvədɔ:(r)] *n* El Salvador

ELSE [els] *adv* **all e. is mere speculation** todo lo demás es mera especulación; **above all e.** por encima de todo; **if all e. fails** si el resto falla, en último extremo; **anyone e.** *(any other person)* alguien más; *(in negative sentences)* nadie más; **anyone e. would have given up** cualquier otro(a) hubiera abandonado; **would anyone e. like some coffee?** ¿alguien más quiere café?; **anything e.** cualquier otra cosa; *(in negative sentences)* nada más; **I rarely eat anything e.** rara vez como otra cosa; **(can I get you) anything e.?** ¿(desea) alguna cosa más *or* algo más?; **anywhere e.** (en/a) cualquier otro sitio; **we'd never live anywhere e.** nunca viviríamos en ninguna otra parte; **is there anywhere e. I should look?** ¿debería mirar en alguna otra parte?; **everyone e.** todos los demás; **everything e.** todo lo demás; **everywhere e.** (en/a) todos los demás sitios; **how e.?** ¿cómo si no?; **how e. do you think I did it?** ¿cómo piensas si no que lo hice?, *RP* ¿cómo te pensás que lo hice?; **little e.** poca cosa más, poco más; **there's little e. we can do, there isn't much e. we can do** poco más podemos hacer, no podemos hacer mucho más; **no one e.** nadie más; **nothing e.** *(nothing different)* ninguna otra cosa; *(nothing additional)* nada más; **we'll have to have sausages, there's nothing e.** tendremos que comer salchichas, es lo único que tenemos; **if nothing e. it taught me to be more cautious** al menos me enseñó a ser más precavido; **nowhere e.** (en/a) ningún otro sitio; **there's nowhere e. for us to hide** no tenemos ningún otro sitio donde escondernos; **or e.** de lo contrario, si no; **do what I tell you or e.!** ¡como no hagas lo que te digo, te vas a enterar *or* ya verás!; **someone e.** *(different person)* otra persona; *(additional person)* alguien más; **she ran off with someone e.** se marchó con otro; **it must be someone e.'s** debe ser de otro; **something e.** *(different thing)* otra cosa; *(additional thing)* algo más; *Fam* **that meal was something e.!** ¡la comida estaba *Esp* estupenda *or Andes, CAm, Carib, Méx* chévere *or Col* tenaz *or Méx* padre *or RP* bárbara!; *Fam* **you're something e., you know!** ¡eres la repera *or Méx* lo máximo!, *RP* ¡sos de no creer!; **somewhere e.** (en/a) otro sitio; **there must be somewhere e. we can hide** tiene que haber algún otro sitio donde nos podamos esconder; **what e.?** ¿qué más?; **what e. can you do?** *(expressing resignation)* ¿qué más se puede hacer?; **I didn't know what e. to do** no sabía qué otra cosa podía hacer; **what did you get for your birthday? – socks, what e.?** ¿qué te regalaron para tu cumpleaños? – calcetines, para variar; **whatever e. you do, don't do that** hagas lo que hagas, no se te ocurra hacer eso; **when e.?** ¿en qué otro momento?; **when is he coming round? – Tuesday, when e.?** ¿cuándo va a venir? – el martes, ¿cuándo si no?; **where e.?** ¿en/a qué otro sitio?; **where is she? – in the bar, where e.?** ¿dónde está? – en el bar, ¿dónde si no?; **who e. was there?** ¿quién más estaba allí?; **who broke it? – Peter, who e.?** ¿quién lo rompió? – Peter, ¿quién si no? *or* ¿quién va a ser?; **whoever e. you tell, don't tell her** se lo digas a quien se lo digas, no se te ocurra decírselo a ella; **why e.?** ¿por qué si no?; **why e. would I do that?** ¿por qué iba a hacerlo si no?

elsewhere ['elsweə(r)] *adv (in another place)* en otro sitio; *(to another place)* a otro sitio; **e. in Europe** en otras partes de Europa; **her ambitions lie e.** tiene otras aspiraciones; *Fig* **to look e.** buscar en otro sitio

ELT [i:el'ti:] *n* (*abbr* **English Language Teaching**) enseñanza *f* del inglés

elucidate [ɪ'lu:sɪdeɪt] **1** *vt* aclarar, poner en claro
2 *vi* aclararlo, explicarse

elucidation [ɪlu:sɪ'deɪʃən] *n Formal* dilucidación *f*, aclaración *f*

elude [ɪ'lu:d] *vt (enemy, pursuers)* eludir; *(obligation, responsibility)* eludir; **success has eluded us so far** el éxito nos ha rehuido hasta ahora; **her novels e. categorization** sus novelas escapan a cualquier clasificación; **his name eludes me** no consigo recordar su nombre; **to e. sb's grasp** escapar(se) de las manos de alguien

elusive [ɪ'lu:sɪv] *adj (enemy, concept)* escurridizo(a); *(difficult to find)* esquivo(a); *(vague)* vago(a), impreciso(a); **success proved e.** el éxito se mostraba esquivo

elusiveness [ɪ'lu:sɪvnɪs] *n (of person, concept, happiness)* carácter *m* escurridizo *or* esquivo

elver ['elvə(r)] *n* angula *f*

elves *pl of* **elf**

Elysian [ɪ'lɪzɪən] *adj Mythol* **the E. fields** los Campos Elíseos

Elysium [ɪ'lɪzɪəm] *n Mythol* Elíseo

'em [əm] *pron Fam* = **them**

emaciated [ɪ'meɪsɪeɪtɪd] *adj (person)* esquelético(a), demacrado(a); *(animal, body, limbs)* esquelético(a); *(face)* demacrado(a)

emaciation [ɪmeɪsɪ'eɪʃən] *n* delgadez *f* extrema, escualidez *f*

e-mail ['i:meɪl] *Comptr* **1** *n* (**a**) *(system)* correo *m* electrónico, e-mail *m*; **to contact sb by e.** contactar con alguien por correo electrónico; **to send sth by e.** enviar algo por correo electrónico ►► ***e. account*** cuenta *f* de correo (electrónico); ***e. address*** dirección *f* de correo electrónico; ***e. bomb*** bomba *f* de correo; ***e. client*** cliente *m* de correo electrónico; ***e. program*** programa *m* de correo electrónico; ***e. software*** software *m* de correo electrónico
(**b**) *(message)* (mensaje *m* por) correo *m* electrónico, e-mail *m*
2 *vt (person)* enviar un correo electrónico a; *(file)* enviar por correo electrónico; **e. us at...** contacte con nosotros por correo electrónico en la siguiente dirección...

emanate ['emənert] **1** *vt* emanar
2 *vi (quality, smell, radiation)* emanar (**from** de); *(suggestions, noises)* provenir, proceder (**from** de); **orders emanating from headquarters** órdenes provenientes del cuartel general

emanation [emə'neɪʃən] *n* emanación *f*, efluvio *m*; **emanations of a disturbed mind** creaciones de una mente trastornada

emancipate [ɪ'mænsɪpeɪt] *vt* emancipar (**from** de)

emancipated [ɪ'mænsɪpeɪtɪd] *adj* emancipado(a)

emancipation [ɪmænsɪ'peɪʃən] *n* emancipación *f*; *US Hist* **the E. Proclamation** la Proclamación de la Emancipación

emasculate [ɪ'mæskjʊleɪt] *vt Formal* (**a**) *(castrate)* emascular, castrar (**b**) *(rights)* mutilar; *(legislation)* desvirtuar; *(group, organization)* debilitar, minar

emasculated [ɪ'mæskjʊleɪtɪd] *adj Formal* (**a**) *(castrated)* emasculado(a), castrado(a) (**b**) *(legislation)* desvirtuado(a); *(group, organization)* debilitado(a), minado(a)

embalm [ɪm'bɑ:m] *vt* embalsamar

embalmer [ɪm'bɑ:mə(r)] *n* embalsamador(ora) *m,f*

embalming [ɪm'bɑ:mɪŋ] *n* embalsamamiento *m* ►► ***e. fluid*** líquido *m* embalsamador

embankment [ɪm'bæŋkmənt] *n* (**a**) *(beside railway)* terraplén *m* (**b**) *(alongside river)* dique *m*

embargo [ɪm'bɑ:gəʊ] **1** *n* (*pl* **embargoes**) (**a**) *(on trade)* embargo *m*; **trade/arms e.** embargo comercial/de armas; **to be under (an) e.** estar sometido(a) a embargo; **to put** *or* **place** *or* **lay an e. on** imponer un embargo a; **to lift** *or* **raise an e.** levantar un embargo; **to break an e.** romper un embargo (**b**) *(on spending, activity)* prohibición *f*; **to put an e. on sth** prohibir algo
2 *vt* (*pt & pp* **embargoed**, *continuous* **embargoing**) someter a embargo

embark [ɪm'bɑ:k] **1** *vt (passengers, cargo)* embarcar
2 *vi (go on ship)* embarcar; *Fig* **to e. (up)on** *(adventure)* embarcarse en

embarkation [embɑ:'keɪʃən] *n* embarque *m*

> **False friend**: The Spanish noun **embarcación** is not a translation for the English word **embarkation**. In Spanish **embarcación** means "boat".

embarrass [ɪm'bærəs] *vt* avergonzar, abochornar, *Andes, CAm, Carib, Méx* apenar; **I won't e. you by repeating what you said** no te voy a avergonzar *or* abochornar repitiendo lo que dijiste; **to e. the government** poner en apuros al Gobierno

embarrassed [ɪm'bærəst] *adj* (**a**) *(ashamed)* avergonzado(a), *Andes, CAm, Carib, Méx* apenado(a); *(uncomfortable)* azorado(a), violento(a); **an e. laugh/grin** una risa/sonrisa de apuro; **there was an e. silence** se produjo un embarazoso *or* incómodo silencio; **to be e.** *(ashamed)* estar avergonzado(a) *or Andes, CAm, Carib, Méx* apenado(a); *(uncomfortable)* estar azorado(a) *or* violento(a); **to feel e. (about sth)** *(ashamed)* sentirse avergonzado(a) *or Andes, CAm, Carib, Méx* apenado(a) (por algo); *(uncomfortable)* estar azorado(a) *or* violento(a) (por algo); **I felt e. about asking him** *(ashamed)* me daba vergüenza *or Andes, CAm, Carib, Méx* pena preguntárselo; *(uncomfortable)* preguntárselo me hacía sentir violento; **to look e.** *(ashamed)* parecer avergonzado(a) *or Andes, CAm, Carib, Méx* apenado(a); *(uncomfortable)* parecer azorado(a) *or* violento(a)
(**b**) *(financially)* **to be (financially) e.** estar apurado(a) de dinero

> **False friend**: The Spanish adjective **embarazada** is not a translation for the English word **embarrassed**. In Spanish **embarazada** means "pregnant".

embarrassing [ɪm'bærəsɪŋ] *adj (causing shame)* vergonzoso(a), bochornoso(a); *(causing discomfort)* violento(a), embarazoso(a); **this report will be very e. for the government** este informe pondrá al gobierno en una situación muy embarazosa *or* violenta; **she was so**

bad it was e. era tan mala que daba vergüenza (ajena); **e. revelations** revelaciones escandalosas; **how e.!** ¡qué vergüenza *or Andes, CAm, Carib, Méx* pena!

embarrassingly [ɪm'bærəsɪŋlɪ] *adv (causing shame)* bochornosamente; *(causing discomfort)* violentamente; **it was e. obvious** era de una evidencia bochornosa; **it was e. easy** era tan fácil que daba vergüenza

embarrassment [ɪm'bærəsmənt] *n* (**a**) *(feeling) (shame)* vergüenza *f*, *Andes, CAm, Carib, Méx* pena *f*; *(discomfort)* apuro *m*, embarazo *m*; **(much) to my e.** para mi (gran) bochorno; **to cause sb e.** hacer pasar vergüenza *or Andes, CAm, Carib, Méx* pena a alguien

(**b**) *(person, thing)* **to be an e. to sb** ser motivo de vergüenza *or Andes, CAm, Carib, Méx* pena para alguien

(**c**) *(financial)* **to be in a state of financial e.** estar pasando apuros económicos

(**d**) *(excess)* **to have an e. of riches** estar bien surtido(a)

embassy ['embəsɪ] *n* embajada *f*; **the Spanish E.** la embajada española *or* de España

embattled [ɪm'bætəld] *adj* (**a**) *(town)* asediado(a); *(leader, government)* asediado(a), acosado(a); **to be e.** *(town, leader, government)* estar asediado(a) (**b**) *(ready for battle) (army)* preparado(a) para el combate

embed [ɪm'bed] (*pt & pp* **embedded**) *vt* (**a**) *(in wood, rock, cement)* incrustar; *(jewel)* engastar, incrustar; **to be embedded in sth** estar incrustado(a) en algo; **the bullet embedded itself in the wall** la bala se incrustó en la pared; **to be embedded in sb's memory** estar grabado(a) en la memoria de alguien

(**b**) *Comptr* incrustar

(**c**) *Ling* insertar; **an embedded clause** una oración insertada (en otra)

embellish [ɪm'belɪʃ] *vt* (**a**) *(room, design, building)* adornar (**with** con) (**b**) *(account)* adornar (**with** con) (**c**) *Mus* adornar

embellishment [ɪm'belɪʃmənt] *n* (**a**) *(of room, design, building)* adorno *m* (**b**) *(of account)* adornar (**with** con) (**c**) *Mus* floritura *f*

ember ['embə(r)] *n* brasa *f*, ascua *f*; **embers** *(of fire)* brasas, rescoldos

embezzle [ɪm'bezəl] **1** *vt (public money)* malversar; *(private money)* desfalcar

2 *vi* **to e. from a company** desfalcar a una compañía

embezzlement [ɪm'bezəlmənt] *n (of public money)* malversación *f*; *(of private money)* desfalco *m*

embezzler [ɪm'bezlə(r)] *n (of public money)* malversador(ora) *m,f*; *(of private money)* desfalcador(ora) *m,f*

embitter [ɪm'bɪtə(r)] *vt (person)* amargar; *(relations)* agriar; *(conflict)* enconar

embittered [ɪm'bɪtəd] *adj (person)* amargado(a)

embitterment [ɪm'bɪtəmənt] *n (of person)* amargura *f*

emblazon [ɪm'bleɪzən] *vt* (**a**) *(on shield)* blasonar (**with** con) (**b**) *(display) (name, headline)* estampar con grandes letras; **her name was emblazoned across the front page** su nombre aparecía en grandes titulares en primera plana

emblem ['embləm] *n* emblema *m*

emblematic [emblə'mætɪk] *adj* simbólico(a), emblemático(a); **to be e. of sth** ser el emblema de algo, simbolizar algo

embodiment [ɪm'bɒdɪmənt] *n* encarnación *f*; **she seemed the e. of reasonableness** parecía la sensatez personificada

embody [ɪm'bɒdɪ] *vt* encarnar, representar; **she embodies everything I detest** es la encarnación de todo lo que detesto; **the principles embodied in the American Constitution** los principios encarnados en la constitución americana

embolden [ɪm'bəʊldən] *vt* envalentonar; **to feel emboldened to do sth** tener el valor de hacer algo

embolism ['embəlɪzəm] *n Med* embolia *f*

embolus ['embələs] (*pl* **emboli** ['embəlaɪ]) *n Med* émbolo *m*

emboss [ɪm'bɒs] *vt (metal, leather)* repujar; *(letter, design)* grabar en relieve

embossed [ɪm'bɒst] *adj (design, notepaper)* grabado(a) en relieve; *(wallpaper)* estampado(a) en relieve; **an e. letterhead** un membrete en relieve

embouchure [ɒmbʊ'ʃʊə(r)] *n Mus* boquilla *f*

embrace [ɪm'breɪs] **1** *n* abrazo *m*; **to hold** *or* **clasp sb in an e.** estrechar a alguien entre los brazos

2 *vt* (**a**) *(person)* abrazar (**b**) *(belief, cause)* abrazar; *(opportunity)* aprovechar (**c**) *(include)* abarcar; **the view from the terrace embraces the whole valley** la vista desde la terraza abarca todo el valle; **the movement embraces people of all faiths and of none** el movimiento engloba tanto a los creyentes de cualquier fe como a los no creyentes

3 *vi* abrazarse

embrasure [ɪm'breɪʒə(r)] *n* (**a**) *Archit* alféizar *m* (**b**) *Mil* tronera *f*

embrocation [embrə'keɪʃən] *n* linimento *m*

embroider [ɪm'brɔɪdə(r)] **1** *vt* (**a**) *(garment, cloth)* bordar (**b**) *(account, report)* adornar

2 *vi* bordar

embroidered [ɪm'brɔɪdəd] *adj (garment, cloth)* bordado(a)

embroidery [ɪm'brɔɪdərɪ] *n* (**a**) *(on garment, cloth)* bordado *m* ►► ***e. frame*** bastidor *m*, tambor *m* de bordar; ***e. thread*** hilo *m* de bordar

(**b**) *(of account, report)* florituras *fpl*

embroil [ɪm'brɔɪl] *vt* **to be embroiled in sth** estar implicado(a) en algo; **to get embroiled in a debate with sb** enfrascarse *or* participar en una discusión con alguien

embroilment [ɪm'brɔɪlmənt] *n (in scandal, situation)* implicación *f*, participación *f*

embryo ['embrɪəʊ] (*pl* **embryos**) *n* embrión *m*; **I have the e. of an idea** tengo el embrión de una idea; **in e.** *(creature, plan, idea)* en estado embrionario ►► ***e. research*** investigación *f* embrionaria

embryologist [embrɪ'ɒlədʒɪst] *n* embriólogo(a) *m,f*

embryology [embrɪ'ɒlədʒɪ] *n* embriología *f*

embryonic [embrɪ'ɒnɪk] *adj* (**a**) *Biol* embrionario(a) (**b**) *(plan, idea)* en estado embrionario

emcee [em'si:] *Fam* **1** *n* presentador(ora) *m,f*, maestro(a) *m,f* de ceremonias

2 *vt* presentar

emend [ɪ'mend] *vt Formal* enmendar, corregir

emendation [i:men'deɪʃən] *n Formal* enmienda *f*, corrección *f*

emerald ['emərəld] *n* (**a**) *(gemstone)* esmeralda *f* (**b**) *(colour)* **e. (green)** verde *m* esmeralda; **the E. Isle** la Isla Esmeralda, = apelativo con que se conoce a Irlanda

emerge [ɪ'mɜ:dʒ] *vi* (**a**) *(come out) (from water)* emerger, salir a la superficie (**from** de); *(from behind or inside something)* salir (**from** de); **she emerged from hiding** salió de su escondite

(**b**) *(come through)* **to e. victorious** *or* **the winner** salir victorioso(a) *or* ganador(ora); **to e. unscathed** resultar *or* salir ileso(a)

(**c**) *(become apparent) (difficulty, truth)* aflorar, surgir; **it later emerged that...** más tarde resultó que...

(**d**) *(come into being) (new state, leader, theory)* surgir, aparecer; **new playwrights have emerged on the scene** nuevos dramaturgos han surgido *or* aparecido en escena

emergence [ɪ'mɜ:dʒəns] *n* (**a**) *(from hiding)* aparición *f* (**b**) *(of facts, truth)* revelación *f* (**c**) *(of new state, leader, theory)* surgimiento *m*, aparición *f*; **his e. on the international stage** su aparición *or* irrupción en el ámbito internacional

emergency [ɪ'mɜ:dʒənsɪ] *n* (**a**) *(crisis)* emergencia *f*; **in an e., in case of e.** en caso de emergencia; **to be prepared for any e.** estar preparado(a) para cualquier emergencia; **for e. use only** *(sign)* usar sólo en caso de emergencia ►► *US* ***e. brake*** freno *m* de mano; ***e. exit*** salida *f* de emergencia; ***e. landing*** aterrizaje *m* forzoso; ***e. services*** *(police, ambulance, fire brigade)* servicios *mpl* de urgencia; ***e. stop*** parada *f* en seco *or* de emergencia

(**b**) *Med* urgencia *f* ►► *US* ***e. room*** sala *f* de urgencias

(**c**) *Pol* **a national e.** una crisis nacional; **to declare a state of e.** declarar el estado de excepción ►► ***e. powers*** poderes *mpl* extraordinarios

emergent [ɪ'mɜ:dʒənt] *adj* pujante; **e. nations** países emergentes

emerging [ɪ'mɜ:dʒɪŋ] *adj* emergente, incipiente; *Fin* **e. markets** mercados emergentes

emeritus [ɪ'merɪtəs] *adj* emérito(a) ►► ***professor e., e. professor*** profesor(ora) *m,f* emérito(a)

emery ['emərɪ] *n* esmeril *m* ►► ***e. board*** lima *f* de uñas; ***e. paper*** (papel *m* de) lija *f*

emetic [ɪ'metɪk] **1** *n* emético *m*, vomitivo *m*

2 *adj* emético(a), vomitivo(a)

EMF [i:em'ef] *n* (**a**) (*abbr* **electromotive force**) fuerza *f* electromotriz (**b**) (*abbr* **European Monetary Fund**) FME *m*

emigrant ['emɪgrənt] *n* emigrante *mf*

emigrate ['emɪgreɪt] *vi* emigrar

emigration [emɪ'greɪʃən] *n* emigración *f*

émigré ['emɪgreɪ] *n* emigrado(a) *m,f*; *Pol* exiliado(a) *m,f*

eminence ['emɪnəns] *n* (**a**) *(importance)* eminencia *f*; **she has achieved** *or* **attained e. in her profession** ha alcanzado el prestigio en su profesión (**b**) *(high ground)* promontorio *m* (**c**) *(title of cardinal)* **Your E.** Su *or* Vuestra Eminencia (**d**) *Anat (of bone)* eminencia *f*

éminence grise ['eɪmɪnɒns'gri:z] *n* eminencia *f* gris

eminent ['emɪnənt] *adj* (**a**) *(distinguished)* eminente (**b**) *(conspicuous)* evidente, indiscutible; **it makes e. good sense** indiscutiblemente, tiene sentido (**c**) *US Law* **e. domain** dominio eminente, derecho a expropiar

eminently ['emɪnəntlɪ] *adv* sumamente; **e. suitable** sumamente apropiado(a)

emir [e'mɪə(r)] *n* emir *m*

emirate ['emɪreɪt] *n* emirato *m*

emissary ['emɪsərɪ] *n* emisario(a) *m,f*

emission [i:'mɪʃən] *n* emisión *f*, emanación *f*; **toxic emissions** emanaciones tóxicas

emit [i:'mɪt] (*pt & pp* **emitted**) *vt (heat, light, sound)* emitir; *(smell, gas)* desprender, emanar; *(radiation)* emitir; *(sparks)* soltar

Emmental ['eməntɑ:l] *n* (queso *m*) emental *m or* emmenthal *m*

Emmy ['emɪ] *n* **E. (Award)** (premio *m*) Emmy *m*

emollient [ɪ'mɒlɪənt] **1** *n Med* emoliente *m*
2 *adj* (**a**) *Med* emoliente (**b**) *(calming)* conciliador(ora), apaciguador(ora)

emolument [ɪ'mɒljʊmənt] *n Formal* emolumento *m*

e-money ['i:mʌnɪ] *n Comptr* dinero *m* electrónico

emote [ɪ'məʊt] *vi* exteriorizar las emociones

emoticon [ɪ'mɒtɪkɒn] *n Comptr* emoticón *m*, emoticono *m*

emotion [ɪ'məʊʃən] *n* (**a**) *(strong feeling)* emoción *f*; **to show no e.** no mostrar ninguna emoción; **to shake with e.** *(person, voice)* temblar de la emoción (**b**) *(particular feeling)* sentimiento *m*; **to appeal to the emotions** apelar a los sentimientos; **to be in control of one's emotions** controlar los sentimientos

emotional [ɪ'məʊʃənəl] *adj* (**a**) *(stress, problem)* emocional; *(life)* sentimental, afectivo(a); **to be an e. wreck** estar destrozado(a) emocionalmente; **an e. cripple** un(a) inmaduro(a) emocional ►► ***e. blackmail*** chantaje *m* sentimental *or* emocional; ***e. intelligence*** inteligencia *f* emocional
(**b**) *(charged with emotion) (plea, music, farewell)* emotivo(a), conmovedor(ora); **an e. speech** un discurso emotivo
(**c**) *(governed by emotions) (person)* emotivo(a); *(reaction, state)* emocional; **he felt very e.** se emocionó mucho; **to get** *or* **become e.** emocionarse; **now, now, don't get so e.** *(keep calm)* vamos, no te alteres

emotionalism [ɪ'məʊʃənəlɪzəm] *n Pej* sentimentalismo *m*

emotionally [ɪ'məʊʃənəlɪ] *adv* (**a**) *(immature, scarred)* emocionalmente; **to feel e. exhausted** *or* **drained** sentirse emocionalmente exhausto(a); **to be e. involved with sb** tener una relación sentimental con alguien; **I'm too e. involved with the whole situation** estoy demasiado implicado emocionalmente en la situación; **e. deprived** privado(a) de cariño; **to be e. disturbed** tener traumas *or* problemas emocionales
(**b**) *(to react)* emotivamente; *(to speak)* emotivamente, con emoción; **an e. charged atmosphere** un ambiente cargado de emotividad

emotionless [ɪ'məʊʃənlɪs] *adj (voice)* desapasionado(a), inexpresivo(a); *(expression)* impertérrito(a)

emotive [ɪ'məʊtɪv] *adj (words, plea)* emotivo(a); **an e. issue** un asunto que despierta encendidas pasiones

empanel [ɪm'pænəl] (*pt & pp Br* **empanelled,** *US* **empaneled**) *vt Law (jury)* constituir

empathetic [empə'θetɪk] *adj* empático(a)

empathize ['empəθaɪz] *vi* **to e. with sb** sentirse identificado(a) con alguien, empatizar con alguien

empathy ['empəθɪ] *n* empatía *f*; **there is real e. between them** hay una verdadera empatía *or* compenetración entre ellos; **to feel e. for sb** identificarse con alguien

emperor ['empərə(r)] *n* emperador *m*; IDIOM **it was a case of the e.'s new clothes** *(deception)* era un caso de autoengaño colectivo, era negarse a ver la realidad ►► ***e. moth*** pavón *m*; ***e. penguin*** pingüino *m* emperador

emphasis ['emfəsɪs] (*pl* **emphases** ['emfəsi:z]) *n* (**a**) *(importance)* énfasis *m inv*; **there is too much e. on materialism in our society** nuestra sociedad pone demasiado énfasis en *or* da demasiada importancia a las cosas materiales; **to lay** *or* **place** *or* **put e. on sth** hacer hincapié en algo, poner énfasis en algo; **a change of e.** un cambio en el orden de importancia
(**b**) *(stress) (in words)* acento *m*; **to say sth with e.** decir algo enfatizando *or* con énfasis; **he waved his arms around for e.** agitó los brazos para enfatizar *or* para recalcar

emphasize ['emfəsaɪz] *vt* (**a**) *(point, fact)* hacer hincapié en, recalcar; **she emphasized the need for caution** hizo hincapié en *or* recalcó la necesidad de ser cautos; **I can't e. this too strongly** no todo énfasis que se le dé es poco (**b**) *(physical feature)* hacer resaltar, marcar (**c**) *(word, syllable)* acentuar

emphatic [ɪm'fætɪk] *adj (gesture, tone)* enfático(a); *(denial, response, refusal)* rotundo(a), categórico(a); *(victory, scoreline)* convincente; **he was quite e. that...** hizo especial hincapié en que...; **he was quite e. on that point** recalcó mucho este punto

emphatically [ɪm'fætɪklɪ] *adv (to say)* enfáticamente; *(to refuse, deny)* rotundamente, categóricamente; **I most e. do not agree (with you)** esto en absoluto desacuerdo contigo; **most e.!** ¡absolutamente!

emphysema [emfɪ'si:mə] *n* enfisema *m*

empire ['empaɪə(r)] **1** *n also Fig* imperio *m*; **the Roman/British E.** el Imperio Romano/Británico; **a shipbuilding/newspaper e.** un imperio naviero/periodístico
2 *adj (costume, furniture)* (de) estilo imperio

empire-building ['empaɪə'bɪldɪŋ] *n (within an organization)* acumulación *f* de poder, medro *m* personal

empirical [em'pɪrɪkəl] *adj* empírico(a) ►► *Chem* ***e. formula*** fórmula *f* empírica

empirically [em'pɪrɪklɪ] *adv* empíricamente

empiricism [em'pɪrɪsɪzəm] *n Phil* empirismo *m*

empiricist [ɪm'pɪrɪsɪst] *n Phil* empirista *mf*

emplacement [ɪm'pleɪsmənt] *n Mil* **(gun) e.** puesto *m* de artillería, emplazamiento *m* de tiro

emplane [ɪm'pleɪn] **1** *vt* embarcar *(en avión)*
2 *vi* embarcar(se) *(en un avión)*, subir a bordo *(de un avión)*

employ [ɪm'plɔɪ] **1** *n Formal* **to be in sb's e.** trabajar al servicio *or* a las órdenes de alguien
2 *vt* (**a**) *(workers)* emplear; **he has been employed with the firm for twenty years** ha trabajado veinte años para la empresa; **to e. sb as a receptionist** emplear a alguien como recepcionista, tener a alguien trabajando como recepcionista; **we employed two new people last week** la semana pasada contratamos *or* empleamos a dos personas nuevas
(**b**) *(occupy)* **to e. oneself (by** *or* **in doing sth)** ocuparse (en hacer algo); **to be employed in doing sth** estar ocupado(a) con algo; **have you no better way of employing your time?** ¿no tienes una forma mejor de ocupar el tiempo?; **you would be better employed elsewhere** serías de más provecho en otra parte
(**c**) *(tool, method, force)* emplear, utilizar

employable [ɪm'plɔɪəbəl] *adj* **a good education makes you more e.** una buena formación te da más posibilidades de encontrar trabajo *or* empleo; **at her age she's no longer e.** a su edad ya nadie le quiere dar trabajo *or* empleo

employed [ɪm'plɔɪd] **1** *n* **the e.** los trabajadores, los asalariados
2 *adj (person)* empleado(a), con empleo; **the resources e. in the operation** los recursos empleados en la operación; **the methods e. were questionable** los métodos empleados eran cuestionables ►► ***e. population*** población *f* con empleo *or* asalariada

employee [ɪm'plɔɪi:] *n* empleado(a) *m,f*; **she is an e. of Ratcorp, she is a Ratcorp e.** trabaja para Ratcorp, es una empleada de Ratcorp; **management and employees** *(in negotiations)* dirección y los trabajadores *or* empleados ►► ***e. association*** asociación *f* de trabajadores; *Com* ***e. buyout*** = adquisición de una empresa por los trabajadores

employer [ɪm'plɔɪə(r)] *n (person)* empresario(a) *m,f*, patrono(a) *m,f*; *(company)* empresa *f*; **who is your e.?** ¿para quién trabajas?; **they are good employers** tratan bien a sus trabajadores; **this company is the town's largest e.** esta empresa es la que emplea a un mayor número de trabajadores en la ciudad ►► ***e.'s contribution*** *(to employee benefits)* cotizaciones *fpl* por parte de la empresa; ***e.'s liability*** responsabilidad *f* patronal *or* de la empresa; ***e.'s organization*** organización *f* empresarial *or* patronal

employment [ɪm'plɔɪmənt] *n* (**a**) *(work)* empleo *m*; **to be in e.** tener un (puesto de) trabajo, estar empleado(a); **to be without e.** no tener empleo, estar desempleado(a) *or Am* desocupado(a); **to look for** *or* **to seek e.** buscar trabajo *or* empleo; **to provide e. for sb** dar trabajo *or* empleo a alguien ►► *Com* ***e. agency*** agencia *f* de colocación; *Com* ***e. bureau*** agencia *f* de colocación; *Br Formerly* ***e. exchange*** oficina *f* de empleo; ***(the) e. figures*** las cifras de desempleo *or Esp* del paro *or Am* de desocupación
(**b**) *(use) (of tool, force)* empleo *m*, uso *m*

emporium [em'pɔːrɪəm] (*pl* **emporiums** *or* **emporia** [em'pɔːrɪə]) *n Formal* gran almacén *m*, *Am* emporio *m*

empower [ɪm'paʊə(r)] *vt* (**a**) *(authorize)* **to e. sb to do sth** autorizar a alguien para hacer algo (**b**) *(give power to)* **to e. sb** dar a alguien una sensación de poder *or* fuerza

empowering [ɪm'paʊərɪŋ] *adj* emancipador(ora); **an e. experience** una experiencia que hace sentir fuerte; **she found it e. to be able to stand up to him** le daba una sensación de poder verse capaz de enfrentarse a él

empowerment [ɪm'paʊəmənt] *n* capacitación *f*; **the e. of women** la potenciación del papel de la mujer

empress ['emprɪs] *n* emperatriz *f*

emptiness ['emptɪnɪs] *n* vacío *m*; **a feeling of e.** una sensación de vacío; **the e. of my life/days** la vacuidad de mi vida/mis días

empty ['emptɪ] **1** *adj* (**a**) *(container, room, house)* vacío(a); **the house was e. of people** en la casa no había nadie; **on an e. stomach** con el estómago vacío; PROV **e. vessels make most noise** mucho ruido y pocas nueces

(**b**) *(promise, threat)* vano(a); *(gesture)* vacío(a), vano(a)

(**c**) *(meaningless) (existence)* vacío(a); **her life seemed e. (of meaning)** su vida parecía carecer de significado *or* sentido

(**d**) *(of fuel)* **the fuel gauge was at** *or* **showing e.** el indicador de la gasolina marcaba vacío; **to be running on e.** *(car)* ir sin gasolina *or* con el depósito vacío; *Fig* **I feel like I'm running on e. at the moment** en estos momentos, me siento como si ya no me quedaran fuerzas

(**e**) *Math* ***the e. set*** el conjunto vacío

2 *vt (glass, bottle, bin)* vaciar; **to e. sth into sth** vaciar (el contenido de) algo en algo; **he emptied everything out of his pockets** se vació los bolsillos *or CAm, Méx, Perú* las bolsas por completo; **he emptied (the contents of) the bucket over her head** le vació el balde en la cabeza

3 *vi (building, street, bath)* vaciarse; **the room emptied** la habitación se quedó vacía; **the sewer emptied into the river** la cloaca vertía sus aguas *or* desaguaba en el río

4 empties *npl (bottles)* cascos *mpl*

▸**empty out 1** *vt sep (container, pockets)* vaciar

2 *vi (container)* vaciarse; *(liquid)* salir (**into** a), verterse (**into** en)

empty-handed ['emptɪ'hændɪd] *adv* con las manos vacías

empty-headed ['emptɪ'hedɪd] *adj* necio(a), bobo(a); **to be e.** tener la cabeza hueca

empyrean [empaɪ'riːən] *n Literary* **the e.** el empíreo

EMT [iːem'tiː] *n US* (*abbr* **emergency medical technician**) auxiliar *mf* sanitario(a) *(que presta primeros auxilios)*

EMU [iːem'juː] *n Fin* (*abbr* **Economic and Monetary Union**) UEM *f*

emu ['iːmjuː] *n (bird)* emú *m*

emulate ['emjʊleɪt] *vt* (**a**) *(imitate)* emular (**b**) *Comptr* emular

emulation [emjʊ'leɪʃən] *n* (**a**) *(imitation)* emulación *f*; **to do sth in e. of sb** hacer algo emulando a alguien (**b**) *Comptr* emulación *f*

emulator ['emjʊleɪtə(r)] *n Comptr* emulador *m*

emulsifier [ɪ'mʌlsɪfaɪə(r)], **emulsifying agent** [ɪ'mʌlsɪfaɪɪŋ'eɪdʒənt] *n* emulgente *m*, emulsionante *m*

emulsify [ɪ'mʌlsɪfaɪ] *vt Tech* emulsionar

emulsifying agent = **emulsifier**

emulsion [ɪ'mʌlʃən] **1** *n* (**a**) *Chem (liquid)* emulsión *f* (**b**) *Phot* emulsión *f* (**c**) **e. (paint)** pintura *f* al agua

2 *vt (paint)* pintar

enable [ɪ'neɪbəl] *vt* (**a**) *(allow)* **to e. sb to do sth** permitir a alguien hacer algo; **this device will e. closer study of chemical reactions** este dispositivo permitirá un estudio más directo de las reacciones químicas (**b**) *Comptr (function)* ejecutar; *(device, option)* activar

enabled [ɪ'neɪbəld] *adj Comptr (device, option)* activado(a)

enabler [ɪ'neɪblə(r)] *n* posibilitador(ora) *m,f*, facilitador(ora) *m,f*

enabling [ɪn'eɪblɪŋ] *n Law* capacitación *f*, autorización *f* ▸▸ ***e. act*** ley *f* de otorgamiento de poderes

enact [ɪ'nækt] *vt* (**a**) *(law)* promulgar (**b**) *(drama)* representar; *Fig* **the political drama currently being enacted in Washington** el drama político que están representando en Washington en estos momentos

enactment [ɪn'æktmənt] *n* (**a**) *(of law)* promulgación *f* (**b**) *(of drama)* representación *f*

enamel [ɪ'næməl] **1** *n* (**a**) *(on metal, glass)* esmalte *m*; **an e. plate** un plato esmaltado *or* de loza; **an e. bath** una bañera esmaltada (**b**) *(on teeth)* esmalte *m* (**c**) **e. (paint)** esmalte *m*

2 *vt* (*pt & pp* **enamelled**, *US* **enameled**) esmaltar

enamelled, *US* **enameled** [ɪ'næməld] *adj* esmaltado(a); **e. saucepan** una cacerola esmaltada

enamelling, *US* **enameling** [ɪ'næməlɪŋ] *n* esmalte *m*, esmaltado *m*

enamoured [ɪ'næməd] *adj* **to be e. of** estar enamorado(a) de; **I'm not greatly e. of the idea** no me entusiasma la idea

en bloc [ɒn'blɒk] *adv* en bloque

enc (**a**) (*abbr* **enclosure**) material *m* adjunto (**b**) (*abbr* **enclosed**) adjunto(a)

encamp [ɪn'kæmp] **1** *vt* **to be encamped** estar acampado(a)

2 *vi* acampar

encampment [ɪn'kæmpmənt] *n Mil* campamento *m*

encapsulate [ɪn'kæpsjʊleɪt] *vt* (**a**) *(summarize)* sintetizar, condensar (**b**) *Pharm* encapsular

encase [ɪn'keɪs] *vt (with lining, cover)* revestir; **to be encased in concrete** estar revestido(a) de hormigón *or Am* concreto

encash [ɪn'kæʃ] *vt Br* hacer efectivo(a), cobrar

encashment [ɪn'kæʃmənt] *n Br* cobro *m*

encaustic [en'kɔːstɪk] **1** *adj (brick, tile)* encáustico(a); *(painting)* encáustico(a)

2 *n* pintura *f* encáustica

encephalitis [ɪnsefə'laɪtɪs] *n Med* encefalitis *f inv*

encephalogram [ɪn'sefələgræm] *n Med* encefalograma *m*

encephalograph [ɪn'sefələgrɑːf] *n Med* electroencefalógrafo *m*

encephalography [ɪnsefə'lɒgrəfɪ] *n Med* encefalografía *f*

encephalomyelitis [ɪnsefələʊmaɪə'laɪtɪs] *n Med* encefalomielitis *f*

enchant [ɪn'tʃɑːnt] *vt* (**a**) *(charm)* cautivar, encantar; **her performance enchanted us all** su actuación nos cautivó a todos *or* nos dejó a todos encantados (**b**) *(put under a spell)* hechizar

"EMPTY" VERBS

Hay verbos como **have**, **take**, **make** y **give** que a menudo se usan en combinación con sustantivos o sintagmas nominales para dar lugar a una amplia gama de frases verbales. En ellas es el sustantivo el que lleva el peso de la acción; los verbos tienen poco significado en sí mismos, por lo que se les conoce como "delexical verbs" (verbos con un mínimo significado léxico). Estas expresiones a menudo equivalen a un verbo de significado pleno, que suele ser la forma verbal del sustantivo que lleva el peso de la acción:

to make a mess of something (= to mess sth up) *hacer algo desastrosamente*
to have a laugh (= to laugh) *reírse*
to take a deep breath (= to breathe deeply) *respirar profundamente*
to give a loud sigh (= to sigh loudly) *dar un suspiro sonoro*
to do the right thing *hacer lo correcto, hacer lo que se debe hacer*

Por otra parte, también hay muchas expresiones coloquiales o argóticas que usan esta estructura:

to have a go at doing sth *probar a hacer algo*
to take a powder *poner los pies en polvorosa*
I don't give a hoot *me importa un bledo*
to do a job on someone *dar una paliza a alguien*

En los diccionarios estas expresiones suelen encontrarse en la entrada correspondiente al sustantivo.

enchanted [ɪn'tʃɑːntɪd] *adj* (**a**) *(delighted)* encantado(a) (**with** con) (**b**) *(under a spell, magic)* encantado(a); **an e. wood** un bosque encantado

enchanter [ɪn'tʃɑːntə(r)] *n* mago(a) *m,f*, hechicero(a) *m,f*

enchanting [ɪn'tʃɑːntɪŋ] *adj (smile, scenery, voice, idea)* cautivador(ora); *(person, cottage)* encantador(ora)

enchantingly [ɪn'tʃɑːntɪŋlɪ] *adv* con encanto; **he sings e.** canta de forma encantadora

enchantment [ɪn'tʃɑːntmənt] *n* fascinación *f*, encanto *m*

enchantress [ɪn'tʃɑːntrɪs] *n* (**a**) *(witch)* maga *f*, hechicera *f* (**b**) *(attractive woman)* seductora *f*

enchilada [entʃɪ'lɑːdə] *n* enchilada *f*; *US Fam* **big e.** *(person)* pez gordo; **the whole e.** *(everything)* todo, toda la pesca *or RP* la bola

encircle [ɪn'sɜːkəl] *vt* rodear

encirclement [ɪn'sɜːkəlmənt] *n* cerco *m*

encl (**a**) (*abbr* **enclosure**) material *m* adjunto (**b**) (*abbr* **enclosed**) adjunto(a)

enclave ['enkleɪv] *n* enclave *m*

enclose [ɪn'kləʊz] *vt* (**a**) *(surround)* rodear; **a garden enclosed in** *or* **by high walls** un jardín rodeado de *or* cercado por un muro alto (**b**) *(include in letter)* adjuntar; **I e. a cheque for £20** adjunto un cheque por 20 libras

enclosed [ɪn'kləʊzd] *adj* (**a**) *(confined)* **an e. space** un espacio cerrado (**b**) *(in letter)* adjunto(a); **please find e....** le adjunto..., le envío adjunto(a)... (**c**) *Rel* **an e. order** una orden de clausura

enclosure [ɪn'kləʊʒə(r)] *n* (**a**) *(area)* recinto *m*, cercado *m* (**b**) *(in letter)* material *m* adjunto (**c**) *(of land)* terreno *m* cercado

encode [ɪn'kəʊd] *vt* (**a**) *(message, text)* cifrar, codificar (**b**) *Comptr* codificar

encoder [ɪn'kəʊdə(r)] *n* (**a**) *(of message, text)* codificador *m* (**b**) *Comptr* codificador *m*

encoding [ɪn'kəʊdɪŋ] *n Comptr* codificación *f*

encomium [en'kəʊmɪəm] (*pl* **encomiums** *or* **encomia** [en'kəʊmɪə]) *n Formal* encomio *m*, elogio *m*

encompass [ɪn'kʌmpəs] *vt* (**a**) *(include)* abarcar, incluir (**b**) *Formal (surround)* circundar

encore ['ɒŋkɔː(r)] **1** *n (in theatre)* bis *m*; **to call for an e.** pedir un bis; **to give an e.** *(performer)* hacer un bis

2 *exclam* ¡otra, otra!

encounter [ɪn'kaʊntə(r)] **1** *n* (**a**) *(meeting)* encuentro *m* ▸▸ *Psy* ***e. group*** grupo *m* de encuentro (**b**) *(confrontation)* enfrentamiento *m*

2 *vt (person, difficulty)* encontrar(se) con, topar(se) con; **to e. resistance/opposition** topar con *or* encontrar resistencia/oposición

encourage [ɪn'kʌrɪdʒ] *vt* (**a**) *(person)* animar; **to e. sb to do sth** animar a alguien a hacer algo; **this encouraged her in her belief that he was guilty** aquello dio pábulo a sus sospechas de que era culpable; **don't e. him!** ¡no le des más pie!, ¡no lo animes!

(**b**) *(support, promote) (growth, commerce)* promover, impulsar; *(the arts)* fomentar, promover; *(belief)* alimentar; **it's something we want to e.** es algo que pretendemos fomentar

encouragement [ɪn'kʌrɪdʒmənt] *n* apoyo *m*, aliento *m*; **to give** *or* **offer sb e.** animar *or* alentar a alguien; **to get** *or* **to receive e. (from sb)** recibir *or* tener respaldo *or* apoyo (de alguien); **shouts/words of e.** gritos/palabras de aliento

encouraging [ɪn'kʌrɪdʒɪŋ] *adj* alentador(ora)

encouragingly [ɪn'kʌrɪdʒɪŋlɪ] *adv (to smile, speak)* de forma alentadora; **e., a working party has been set up** es alentador que se haya formado un equipo de trabajo

encroach [ɪn'krəʊtʃ]

▸ **encroach on, encroach upon** *vt insep (rights)* usurpar; *(time, land)* invadir; *Fig* **to e. on sb's territory** invadir el terreno de alguien

encroachment [ɪn'krəʊtʃmənt] *n (on rights)* usurpación *f* (**on** de); *(on time, land)* invasión *f* (**on** de)

encrustation [ɪnkrʌst'eɪʃən] *n* costra *f*

encrusted [ɪn'krʌstɪd] *adj* **e. with diamonds** con diamantes incrustados; **e. with mud** con barro incrustado

encrypt [ɪn'krɪpt] *vt Comptr* encriptar

encryption [ɪn'krɪpʃən] *n Comptr* encriptación *f*

encumber [ɪn'kʌmbə(r)] *vt* (**a**) *(hamper, impede)* **to be encumbered by** *or* **with** estar *or* verse entorpecido(a) por (**b**) *Law* **an encumbered estate** *(with debts, mortgage)* una finca con cargas

encumbrance [ɪn'kʌmbrəns] *n* (**a**) *(to movement, action)* estorbo *m*; **to be an e. to sb** ser *or* representar una carga para alguien (**b**) *Law* gravamen *m*, carga *f*

encyclical [ɪn'sɪklɪkəl] *n Rel* encíclica *f*

encyclop(a)edia [ɪnsaɪklə'piːdɪə] *n* enciclopedia *f*

encyclop(a)edic [ɪnsaɪklə'piːdɪk] *adj* enciclopédico(a); **he has an e. knowledge of baseball** sus conocimientos de baloncesto son enciclopédicos ▸▸ ***e. dictionary*** diccionario *m* enciclopédico

END [end] **1** *n* (**a**) *(extremity)* extremo *m*; *(of nose, finger, stick)* punta *f*; *(of sports stadium)* fondo *m*; **a cigarette e.** una colilla; **the financial e. of the business** el lado *or* aspecto financiero del negocio; **at either e. of the political spectrum** a ambos extremos del espectro político; **aimed at the lower e. of the market** dirigido(a) al segmento bajo del mercado; **at the other e. of the line** *(on phone)* al otro lado del teléfono *or* de la línea; **we'll pick you up at the other e.** *(of journey)* te recogeremos a la llegada; **go to the e. of the** *Br* **queue** *or US* **line** ve al final de la cola; **a cylinder viewed e. on looks like a circle** un cilindro visto desde un extremo parece un círculo; **place the two tables e. to e.** junta las mesas a lo largo; **they were parked e. to e.** estaban estacionados *or Esp* aparcados en cordón; **from one e. to the other, from e. to e.** de un extremo al otro; *Sport* **to change ends** cambiar de lado; **to stand sth on (its) e.** colocar algo de pie *or Am* parado(a); **the deep/shallow e.** *(of swimming pool)* el lado más/menos hondo *or* donde cubre/no cubre ▸▸ *Comptr* ***e. key*** (tecla *f*) fin *m*; ***e. line*** línea *f* de fondo; ***e. zone*** *(in American football)* zona *f* de anotación

(**b**) *(limit in time, quantity)* final *m*, fin *m*; *(of film, book)* final *m*, desenlace *m*; **THE END** *(in film)* FIN; **I'll take questions at the e.** responderé preguntas al final; **at the e. of the week** al final de la semana; **at the e. of May/the month** a finales *or* fin de mayo/de mes; **there will be no e. to the bombings until...** los bombardeos no cesarán hasta...; **I am at the e. of my patience** se me está agotando la paciencia; **I'm not going, e. of story** *or* **and that's the e. of it** no voy, y se acabó, no voy, y no hay nada más que hablar; **his career is at an e.** su carrera ha llegado a su fin *or Am* al fin; **in the e.** al final; **to be at the e. of one's resources/one's strength** haber agotado los recursos/las fuerzas; **they have improved no e.** han mejorado un montón; *Fam* **no e. of...** la mar de...; **for hours/days on e.** durante horas y horas/días y días; **that's the e. of that!** ¡se acabó!, ¡sanseacabó!; **it's not the e. of the world** no es el fin del mundo; **to bring sth to an e.** *(interview, show)* terminar *or* acabar algo; *(speculation, uncertainty)* terminar *or* acabar con algo; **to come to an e.** concluir, llegar a su fin; *Fam* **to come to a bad** *or* **sticky e.** acabar mal; **look, take my bike and let that be the e. of it** *or* **an e. to it!** ¡toma mi bici, y no se hable más!; **to put an e. to sth** poner fin a algo; **to the e. of time** *(forever)* por siempre; IDIOM **at the e. of the day** en definitiva, al final ▸▸ ***e. product*** producto *m* final; ***e. result*** resultado *m* final; *Com & Comptr* ***e. user*** usuario(a) *m,f* final; ***e. user certificate*** certificado *m* del destinatario final

(**c**) *(death)* final *m*, fin *m*; **when the e. finally came** cuando llegó la hora final; **and that was the e. of him** y así murió; *Fam* **this job will be the e. of me!** ¡este trabajo va a acabar conmigo *or* me va a matar!; **to meet one's e.** encontrar la muerte; **to meet a bloody e.** tener un final violento

(**d**) *(aim, purpose)* fin *m*, propósito *m*; **an e. in itself** un fin en sí mismo; **to this e.** con este fin; **to what e.?** ¿con qué fin *or* propósito?; **she attained** *or* **achieved her end(s)** logró lo que se proponía; PROV **the e. justifies the means** el fin justifica los medios

(**e**) *Sport (in American football)* extremo *m*, end *m*; **defensive e.** extremo defensivo, defensive end; **tight e.** extremo cerrado, tight end

(**f**) *Sport (in bowls, curling)* tanda *f* de lanzamiento *(en una dirección)*

(**g**) IDIOMS *Fam* **it's/she's the absolute e.!** ¡es el colmo!; **to be at the e. of one's tether** *or esp US* **rope** estar hasta la coronilla; *Fam* **to beat sb all ends up** darle a alguien una paliza *or Esp* un baño; **to come to** *or* **reach the e. of the road** *or* **line** llegar al final; *Fam* **to get (hold of) the wrong e. of the stick** agarrar el rábano por las hojas, *RP* agarrar para el lado de los tomates; *Br very Fam* **to get one's e. away** mojar *Esp* el churro *or RP* bizcocho, *Méx* echarse un caldito; **I would go to the ends of the earth to be with you** iría hasta el fin del mundo para estar contigo; **we shall never hear the e. of it** nos lo van a recordar mientras vivamos; *Fam* **to keep** *or* **hold one's e. up** defenderse bien; **we've kept our e. of the bargain** por nuestra parte hemos cumplido; **to make ends meet** llegar a fin de mes; **he can't see beyond the e. of his nose** no ve más allá de sus narices; *Fam* **she can't tell one e. of a cello from the other** no tiene ni idea de violoncelos

2 *adj (house, seat, table)* del final; **it's the e. one** es el que está al final, es el del final

3 *vt* terminar, acabar; **this ends weeks of uncertainty** esto pone fin a semanas de incertidumbre; **she ended her career on a high** finalizó su carrera a lo grande; **to e. it all, to e. one's own life** *(commit suicide)* quitarse la vida; **he ended his life** *or* **days in poverty** terminó *or* acabó sus días en la pobreza; **it will be the celebration to e. all**

celebrations será una celebración de antología

4 *vi* terminar, acabar; **the similarity ends there** el parecido acaba ahí; **I must e. by thanking...** para terminar, debo dar gracias a...; **it ends in a point** acaba en punta; **the match ended in a draw** el partido terminó en empate; **it ended in disaster** terminó en desastre; *Br* **it'll all e. in tears!** ¡acabará mal!; **the book ends with everyone getting married** el libro concluye con todos casándose; *Fig* **where will it all e.?** ¿hasta dónde vamos a llegar?

5 **in the end** *adv* al final; **in the e. we decided not to go** al final decidimos no ir; **what does it matter in the e.?** ¿qué importa a fin de cuentas?

▸ **end up** *vi* acabar, terminar; **they ended up in Manchester** acabaron *or* terminaron en Manchester; **to e. up in hospital/in prison** acabar *or* terminar en el hospital/en la cárcel; **to e. up as the boss** acabar *or* terminar siendo jefe

---

endanger [ɪn'deɪndʒə(r)] *vt* poner en peligro; **such work would e. her health** un trabajo así resultaría peligroso para su salud

endangered [ɪn'deɪndʒəd] *adj* **an e. species** una especie amenazada *or* en peligro de extinción

endear [ɪn'dɪə(r)] *vt* **to e. oneself to sb** hacerse querer por alguien; **her outspokenness did not e. her to her boss** su franqueza no le ganó el favor del jefe

endearing [ɪn'dɪərɪŋ] *adj (person)* encantador(ora); *(feature, smile)* atrayente; **it's his least e. characteristic** es su característica menos atrayente

endearingly [ɪn'dɪərɪŋlɪ] *adv* de forma encantadora; **the house was e. named "Bide a Wee"** la casa tenía el encantador nombre de "Bide a Wee"

endearment [ɪn'dɪəmənt] *n* **words** *or* **terms of e.** palabras tiernas *or* cariñosas

endeavour, *US* **endeavor** [ɪn'devə(r)] *Formal* **1** *n* esfuerzo *m*; **in an e. to stop the strike** en un esfuerzo por terminar la huelga; **despite her best endeavours** a pesar de haberse esforzado al máximo; **to make every e. to do sth** procurar por todos los medios hacer algo; **a new field of human e.** un nuevo campo en los afanes de la humanidad

2 *vt* **to e. to do sth** esforzarse por hacer algo, procurar hacer algo; **we e. to please** nos esforzamos por complacer, procuramos complacer

endemic [ɪn'demɪk] *adj* endémico(a); **the problem/disease is e. to the region** el problema es endémico a la región/la enfermedad es endémica a la región

endgame ['endgeɪm] *n* **(a)** *(in chess)* final *m* (de partida) **(b)** *(in conflict)* etapa *f* final *or* desenlace *m* (de los acontecimientos)

ending ['endɪŋ] *n* **(a)** *(of nuclear tests, restrictions)* fin *m*; **he called for the e. of the ban on...** pidió que se levantase la prohibición de... **(b)** *(of story)* final *m*, desenlace *m*; **it has a happy/sad e.** tiene un final feliz/triste **(c)** *(of word)* desinencia *f*, terminación *f*; **accusative/genitive e.** desinencia *or* terminación de acusativo/genitivo

endive ['endaɪv] *n* **(a)** *(like lettuce)* **(curly) e.** escarola *f* **(b)** *esp US (chicory)* endibia *f*, achicoria *f*

endless ['endlɪs] *adj* **(a)** *(series, task)* interminable; *(variations)* innumerables, infinitos(as); *(complaining)* constante; *(patience, tolerance)* inagotable; **the long afternoons seemed e.** las largas tardes parecían eternas; **the possibilities are e.** las posibilidades son interminables *or* infinitas **(b)** *Tech (belt, screw)* sin fin

endlessly ['endlɪslɪ] *adv (to talk, discuss)* constantemente, sin parar; **the road stretched out e. before them** la carretera se extendía interminable ante ellos

endmost ['endməʊst] *adj* último(a)

endnote ['endnəʊt] *n* nota *f (al final de libro, artículo)*

endocarditis [endəʊkɑː'daɪtɪs] *n Med* endocarditis *f*

endocardium [endəʊ'kɑːdɪəm] *n Anat* endocardio *m*

endocarp [endəʊ'kɑːp] *n Biol* endocarpio *m*

endocrine ['endəkraɪn] *adj Med* endocrino(a) ▸▸ ***e. gland*** glándula *f* endocrina

endocrinologist [endəʊkrɪ'nɒlədʒɪst] *n* endocrinólogo(a) *m,f*, endocrino(a) *m,f*

endocrinology [endəkrɪ'nɒlədʒɪ] *n* endocrinología *f*

endodontics [endə'dɒntɪks] *n* endodoncia *f*

end-of-term ['endəv'tɜːm] *adj Sch & Univ (party, concert, trip) (of three-month term)* de final de trimestre; *(of four-month term)* de final de cuatrimestre ▸▸ ***e. exam*** examen *m* parcial

endogamous [en'dɒgəməs] *adj* endogámico(a)

endogamy [en'dɒgəmɪ] *n* endogamia *f*

endogenous [ɪn'dɒdʒənəs] *adj* endógeno(a)

endometriosis ['endəʊmiːtrɪ'əʊsɪs] *n Med* endometriosis *f inv*

endometritis ['endəʊmɪ'traɪtəs] *n Med* endometritis *f inv*

endometrium [endəʊ'miːtrɪəm] *n Anat* endometrio *m*

endomorph ['endəʊmɔːf] *n* endomorfo(a) *m,f*

endorheic [endə'reɪɪk] *adj Geol* endorreico(a)

endorphin [ɪn'dɔːfɪn] *n* endorfina *f*

endorse, indorse [ɪn'dɔːs] *vt* **(a)** *(document, cheque)* endosar **(b)** *(opinion, action)* apoyar, respaldar **(c)** *(commercial product)* promocionar **(d)** *Br (driving licence)* anotar una infracción en

endorsee, indorsee [endɔː'siː] *n Fin* endosatario(a) *m,f*

endorsement, indorsement [ɪn'dɔːsmənt] *n* **(a)** *(on document, cheque)* endoso *m* **(b)** *(of action, opinion)* apoyo *m*, respaldo *m* (**of** a) **(c)** *(of commercial product)* promoción *f* **(d)** *Br (on driving licence)* infracción *f* anotada

endoscope ['endəskəʊp] *n Med* endoscopio *m*

endoscopy [en'dɒskəpɪ] *n Med* endoscopia *f*

endoskeleton ['endəʊskelətən] *n Zool* endoesqueleto *m*

endosperm ['endəʊspɜːm] *n Bot* endoespermo *m*

endothelium [endəʊ'θiːlɪəm] *n Anat* endotelio *m*

endothermic [endəʊ'θɜːmɪk] *adj Chem* endotérmico(a) ▸▸ ***e. reaction*** proceso *m* endotérmico

endow [ɪn'daʊ] *vt* **(a)** *Fin* = donar (a una institución) capital o propiedades que proporcionen una renta regular **(b)** *(gift)* dotar (**with** de); **she was endowed with a lively sense of humour** estaba dotada de un gran sentido del humor

endowment [ɪn'daʊmənt] *n* **(a)** *Fin* donación *f* ▸▸ ***e. assurance*** seguro *m* de vida mixto *or* de ahorro; ***e. insurance*** seguro *m* de vida mixto *or* de ahorro; ***e. mortgage*** hipoteca-inversión *f*, = crédito hipotecario por intereses ligado a un seguro de vida **(b)** *Formal (talent)* dote *f*

endpaper ['endpeɪpə(r)] *n (in book)* guarda *f*

endurable [ɪn'djʊərəbəl] *adj* soportable

endurance [ɪn'djʊərəns] *n* resistencia *f*; **to have great powers of e.** tener gran resistencia; **beyond e.** insoportable ▸▸ ***e. test*** prueba *f* de resistencia

endure [ɪn'djʊə(r)] **1** *vt* soportar, aguantar; **it was more than she could e.** fue más de lo que era capaz de soportar; **she can't e. being kept waiting** no soporta *or* no aguanta tener que esperar

2 *vi (last) (relationship)* prolongarse; *(memory, fame, tradition)* perdurar; **he won't be able to e. for long in this temperature** no podrá sobrevivir por mucho tiempo con esta temperatura

enduring [ɪn'djʊərɪŋ] *adj (relationship)* duradero(a); *(memory, fame, tradition)* duradero(a), perdurable

endways ['endweɪz], **endwise** ['endwaɪz] *adv* **(a)** *(end forward)* de canto, de lado; **e. on** de canto, de lado; **the house stands e. on to the road** uno de los extremos de la casa mira hacia la carretera **(b)** *(end to end)* a lo largo, extremo con extremo

ENE (*abbr* **east-north-east**) ENE

enema ['enəmə] *n* enema *m*

enemy ['enəmɪ] **1** *n* **(a)** *(opponent, adversary)* enemigo(a) *m,f*; **I wouldn't wish it/him on my worst e.** no se lo desearía ni a mi peor enemigo; **she's her own worst e.** su peor enemigo es ella misma; **to make an e. of sb** ganarse la enemistad de alguien; **the e. within** el enemigo en casa *or* de dentro

(b) *(in war)* **the e.** el enemigo; **e.-occupied territory** territorio ocupado por el enemigo

2 *adj (country, ship, territory)* enemigo(a); *(losses)* en el campo enemigo; **e. alien** extranjero(a) enemigo(a); **e. fire** fuego enemigo

energetic [enə'dʒetɪk] *adj* **(a)** *(exercise, activity) (vigorous)* enérgico(a); *(demanding energy)* que requiere mucha energía; **I don't want to do anything too e.** no quiero hacer nada que requiera mucha energía; **after a very e. day** después de un día muy activo

(b) *(person)* lleno(a) de energía, enérgico(a); **to feel e.** sentirse con muchas energías; **I'm at my most e. in the morning** por las mañanas es cuando tengo más energías; **they're doing it, but they aren't being very e. about it** lo están haciendo pero no le están echando muchas ganas *or* mucho brío

(c) *(vehement) (denials, protest)* enérgico(a)

energetically [enə'dʒetɪklɪ] *adv* **(a)** *(to move, work)* con brío, con energías **(b)** *(to protest)* enérgicamente

energize ['enədʒaɪz] *vt* **(a)** *(invigorate)* dar energías a **(b)** *(machine, circuit)* energizar, activar

energy ['enədʒɪ] *n* **(a)** *(power)* energía *f*; **to save** *or* **conserve e.** ahorrar energía; **to consume** *or* **use e.** consumir *or* usar energía ►► ***e. audit*** auditoría *f* energética; ***e. conservation*** reducción *f* del consumo energético; ***e. crisis*** crisis *f* energética; ***e. source*** fuente *f* de energía
(b) *Phys* energía *f* ►► ***e. level*** nivel *m* de energía
(c) *(vitality)* energía *f*; **to lack e.** no tener energía *or* fuerzas
(d) *(effort)* energía *f*; **he is devoting** *or* **applying (all) his e.** *or* **energies to finding a job** dedica toda su energía a encontrar empleo

energy-saving ['enədʒɪseɪvɪŋ] *adj* que ahorra energía

enervated ['enəveɪtɪd] *adj Formal* enervado(a), debilitado(a)

enervating ['enəveɪtɪŋ] *adj Formal* enervante, debilitante

enervation [enə'veɪʃən] *n Formal* enervación *f*, enervamiento *m*

enfant terrible ['ɒnfɒnte'ri:blə] (*pl* **enfants terribles**) *n* enfant terrible *mf*, niño(a) *m,f* terrible

enfeeble [ɪn'fi:bəl] *vt* debilitar, enervar

enfeeblement [ɪn'fi:bəlmənt] *n* debilitamiento *m*, debilitación *f*

enfilade [enfɪ'leɪd] *Mil* **1** *n* enfilada *f*
2 *vt* enfilar

enfold [ɪn'fəʊld] *vt* rodear; **he enfolded her in his arms** la rodeó con sus brazos

enforce [ɪn'fɔ:s] *vt (law, policy, decision)* hacer cumplir, aplicar; *(discipline)* mantener; *(rights)* hacer valer; **such a law would be impossible to e.** sería imposible hacer que una ley así se cumpliese; **to e. compliance with the law/regulations** hacer que se cumpla la ley/la normativa

enforced [ɪn'fɔ:st] *adj* forzoso(a), obligado(a)

enforcement [ɪn'fɔ:smənt] *n* aplicación *f* ►► ***e. procedure*** vía *f* ejecutiva

enforcer [ɪn'fɔ:sə(r)] *n* **(a)** *US (hitman)* = persona encargada de mantener la disciplina en el seno de una banda criminal **(b)** *Sport* jugador(ora) *m,f* duro(a) **(c)** *Br Pol* = ministo encargado de que se lleve a cabo la política del gobierno

enfranchise [ɪn'fræntʃaɪz] *vt* otorgar el derecho al voto a

enfranchisement [ɪn'fræntʃaɪzmənt] *n* concesión *f* del derecho al voto (**of** a)

engage [ɪn'geɪdʒ] **1** *vt* **(a)** *(employ)* contratar; *Formal* **to e. the services of sb** contratar *or* emplear los servicios de alguien
(b) *(attract, draw)* **to e. sb's attention/interest** suscitar la atención/el interés de alguien; **there was nothing about the film that engaged me** la película no me interesó lo más mínimo; **this campaign is carefully designed to e. our sympathy** esta campaña está cuidadosamente diseñada para ganarse nuestras simpatías; **to be engaged in doing sth** estar ocupado haciendo algo; **to e. sb in conversation** entablar conversación con alguien
(c) *Mil* **to e. the enemy** entrar en liza con el enemigo
(d) *(cog, gear)* engranar; **to e. the clutch** embragar
2 *vi* **(a) to e. in sth** *(activity, sport)* dedicarse a algo; **to e. in conversation** entablar conversación; **they engaged in name-calling** se dedicaron a intercambiar insultos
(b) *(cog)* engranar; *(gear)* entrar
(c) *Mil* entablar batalla *or* combate
(d) *Formal (promise)* **to e. to do sth** comprometerse a hacer algo

engaged [ɪn'geɪdʒd] *adj* **(a)** *(to be married)* prometido(a); **to be e. (to sb)** estar prometido(a) (a *or* con alguien); **to get e. (to sb)** prometerse (con *or* a alguien); **they got e. last summer** se prometieron el verano pasado
(b) *Br* **to be e.** *(phone)* estar ocupado(a) *or Esp* comunicando; **I got the e. tone** *or* **signal** estaba ocupado *or Esp* comunicando
(c) *Br (public toilet)* ocupado(a)
(d) *(involved)* **to be e. in doing sth** estar ocupado(a) haciendo algo; **to be e. in discussions with sb** estar en discusiones con alguien; *Formal* **I am otherwise e. this evening** tengo otros compromisos esta noche

engagement [ɪn'geɪdʒmənt] *n* **(a)** *(to be married)* compromiso *m*; *(period)* noviazgo *m*; **he announced their e.** anunció *or* hizo público su compromiso; **to break off an e.** romper un compromiso ►► ***e. ring*** anillo *m* de pedida *or* de compromiso
(b) *(appointment)* compromiso *m*; **he had a prior** *or* **previous e.** tenía un compromiso previo; **e. diary/calendar** agenda/calendario de compromisos
(c) *(military action)* batalla *f*, combate *m*

engaging [ɪn'geɪdʒɪŋ] *adj* atractivo(a), encantador(ora)

engagingly [ɪn'geɪdʒɪŋlɪ] *adv* encantadoramente; **to smile e.** sonreír con encanto

engender [ɪn'dʒendə(r)] *vt Formal* generar, engendrar

engine ['endʒɪn] *n* **(a)** *(of car, plane, ship)* motor *m* ►► ***e. room*** sala *f* de máquinas; ***e. trouble*** avería *f (del motor)* **(b)** *Rail* locomotora *f* ►► *Br* ***e. driver*** maquinista *mf*; *US* ***e. house*** cochera *f* de tren; *Br* ***e. shed*** cochera *f* de tren **(c)** *(motivating force)* motor *m* **(d)** *(of computer game)* sistema *m*

engineer [endʒɪ'nɪə(r)] **1** *n* **(a)** *(for roads, machines, bridges)* ingeniero(a) *m,f*; **civil/marine/mechanical e.** ingeniero(a) civil/naval/mecánico(a)
(b) *(mechanic, repairer)* técnico(a) *m,f*
(c) *Naut* maquinista *mf*
(d) *Mil* ingeniero(a) *m,f*; **the Engineers** el cuerpo de ingenieros
(e) *US Rail* maquinista *mf*
(f) *(instigator)* artífice *mf*; **she was the e. of her own downfall** fraguó su propia ruina
2 *vt* **(a)** *(road, bridge, car)* **the bridge has been superbly engineered** el puente es una magnífica obra de ingeniería **(b)** *(bring about) (coup, confrontation)* tramar; *(downfall, defeat, escape)* maquinar; *(situation)* manipular; **he engineered things so he would get all the credit** maquinó las cosas para acaparar todo el mérito

engineering [endʒɪ'nɪərɪŋ] *n* **(a)** *(subject, activity)* ingeniería *f*; *Br* **e. work** *(on railway line)* reparaciones; **an e. company** una empresa de ingeniería **(b)** *(design, construction)* **an incredible feat of e.** una increíble hazaña de ingeniería

England ['ɪŋglənd] *n* Inglaterra; **an E. player** un(a) jugador(ora) inglés(esa)

English ['ɪŋglɪʃ] **1** *n (language)* inglés *m*; **Australian/Indian E.** inglés australiano/de la India; **E. class/teacher** clase/profesor(ora) de inglés; **in plain** *or* **simple E.** con claridad, en cristiano; **she could barely speak the King's/Queen's E.** ni siquiera sabe hablar (inglés) como Dios manda; *Hum* **E. as she is spoke** el inglés macarrónico ►► ***E. as a Foreign Language*** inglés *m* como lengua extranjera; ***E. Language Teaching*** enseñanza *f* del inglés
2 *npl (people)* **the E.** los ingleses
3 *adj* inglés(esa); **the E. Channel** el Canal de la Mancha ►► ***E. breakfast*** desayuno *m* inglés; *US Mus* ***E. horn*** corno *m* inglés; *US* ***E. muffin*** tortita *f*

Englishman ['ɪŋglɪʃmən] *n* inglés *m*; PROV **an E.'s home is his castle** el hogar de un inglés es su castillo, = refrán que alude a la importancia que los ingleses otorgan a la intimidad de sus hogares

English-speaking ['ɪŋglɪʃ'spi:kɪŋ] *adj* anglófono(a), de habla inglesa; **the E. world** los países *or* el mundo de habla inglesa

Englishwoman ['ɪŋglɪʃwʊmən] *n* inglesa *f*

engorged [ɪn'gɔ:dʒd] *adj* hinchado(a); **e. with blood** hinchado y lleno de sangre

engraft [ɪn'grɑ:ft] *vt* **(a)** *Bot* injertar **(b)** *(ideas, principles)* inculcar

engrain, engrained = **ingrain, ingrained**

engrave [ɪn'greɪv] *vt* grabar; **to have one's name engraved on sth** hacer (uno) grabar algo con su nombre; **engraved on her memory** grabado en su memoria

engraver [ɪn'greɪvə(r)] *n* grabador(ora) *m,f*

engraving [ɪn'greɪvɪŋ] *n* grabado *m*

engross [ɪn'grəʊs] *vt* **(a)** *(absorb)* absorber; **I wondered what was engrossing them** sentía curiosidad por saber qué los tenía tan absortos **(b)** *Law (manuscript, document)* redactar en forma legal

engrossed [ɪn'grəʊst] *adj* absorto(a); **to be e. (in)** estar absorto(a) (en)

engrossing [ɪn'grəʊsɪŋ] *adj* absorbente

engulf [ɪn'gʌlf] *vt (of waves, flames)* devorar; **the house was suddenly engulfed in darkness** la casa quedó súbitamente sumida en la oscuridad; **she was engulfed by despair** se sumió en la desesperación

enhance [ɪn'hɑ:ns] *vt* **(a)** *(increase, improve) (value, chances)* incrementar, aumentar; *(performance, quality)* mejorar; *(beauty, colour, taste)* realzar; *(reputation)* acrecentar, elevar **(b)** *Comptr (image)* mejorar, aumentar la calidad de **(c)** *Fin (pension)* aumentar

enhanced [ɪn'hɑ:nst] *adj Comptr* ***e. keyboard*** teclado *m* expandido

enhancement [ɪn'hɑ:nsmənt] *n* **(a)** *(of value)* aumento *m*; *(of performance, quality)* mejora *f*; *(of beauty, colour, taste)* realce *m* **(b)** *Comptr (of image)* mejora *f*, aumento *m* de calidad **(c)** *Fin (of pension)* aumento *m*

enigma [ɪ'nɪgmə] *n* enigma *m*; **he remains an e. to us** sigue siendo un enigma para nosotros

enigmatic [enɪg'mætɪk] *adj* enigmático(a)

enigmatically [enɪg'mætɪklɪ] *adv* enigmáticamente

enjambment [ɪn'dʒæmmənt] *n Lit* encabalgamiento *m*

enjoin [ɪn'dʒɔɪn] *vt Formal* (**a**) *(urge)* ordenar; **to e. sb to do sth** instar a alguien a hacer algo; **to e. sth on sb** exigir *or* imponer algo a alguien (**b**) *US (forbid)* prohibir; **to e. sb from doing sth** prohibirle a alguien (que haga) algo

enjoy [ɪn'dʒɔɪ] **1** *vt* (**a**) *(take pleasure from)* disfrutar de; **I enjoyed that!** *(book, film, meal)* ¡me ha gustado mucho!, ¡he disfrutado mucho (con eso)!; **I thoroughly enjoyed the party** lo pasé fenomenal en la fiesta; **e. your meal!** ¡que aproveche!, ¡buen provecho!; **did you e. your meal?** ¿te gustó la comida?; *(said by waiter)* ¿ha sido todo de su agrado?; **he enjoys swimming/going to the cinema** le gusta nadar/ir al cine; **I don't e. being made fun of** no me hace ninguna gracia que se rían de mí; **to e. oneself** divertirse, pasarlo bien; **to e. life** disfrutar de la vida

(**b**) *(benefit from)* gozar de, disfrutar de; **to e. good health/a high standard of living** disfrutar de buena salud/de un buen nivel de vida

2 *vi US* **e.!** *(enjoy yourself)* ¡pásalo bien!; *(in restaurant)* ¡que aproveche!, ¡buen provecho!

enjoyable [ɪn'dʒɔɪəbəl] *adj* agradable; **we had a most e. evening** pasamos una tarde de lo más agradable

enjoyably [ɪn'dʒɔɪəblɪ] *adv* agradablemente; **we spent the weekend most e.** pasamos un fin de semana muy agradable

enjoyment [ɪn'dʒɔɪmənt] *n* (**a**) *(pleasure)* disfrute *m*; **to get e. out of** *or* **from sth/doing sth** disfrutar de algo/haciendo algo; **to spoil sb's e. of sth: I won't spoil your e. by telling you the end of the movie** no te voy a robar el placer de disfrutar de la película contándote el final (**b**) *(of privilege, right)* disfrute *m*

enlarge [ɪn'lɑːdʒ] **1** *vt* (**a**) *(house, territory)* ampliar, agrandar; *(hole)* agrandar; *(business, group of friends, field of knowledge)* ampliar; *(pores)* dilatar (**b**) *(photograph)* ampliar

2 *vi (get larger)* agrandarse, aumentar; *(pores)* dilatarse

▸**enlarge (up)on** *vt insep Formal (elaborate on)* **to e. (up)on sth** explicar algo más detalladamente

enlarged [ɪn'lɑːdʒd] *adj* (**a**) *(increased)* aumentado(a); **an e. edition** *(of reference book)* una edición ampliada (**b**) *(photograph)* ampliado(a) (**c**) *Med (organ)* aumentado(a) de volumen

enlargement [ɪn'lɑːdʒmənt] *n* (**a**) *(of territory, business)* ampliación *f* (**b**) *Med (of organ)* agrandamiento *m*, aumento *m* de volumen (**c**) *(of photograph)* ampliación *f*

enlarger [ɪn'lɑːdʒə(r)] *n Phot* ampliadora *f*

enlighten [ɪn'laɪtən] *vt* aclarar; **can somebody e. me as to what is going on?** ¿podría alguien aclararme qué está ocurriendo?

enlightened [ɪn'laɪtənd] *adj* progresista, liberal ▸▸ *Hist* ***e. despotism*** despotismo *m* ilustrado

enlightening [ɪn'laɪtənɪŋ] *adj* esclarecedor(ora), informativo(a)

enlightenment [ɪn'laɪtənmənt] *n* (**a**) *(clarification)* aclaración *f* (**b**) *Hist* **the (Age of) E.** la Ilustración, el Siglo de las Luces

enlist [ɪn'lɪst] **1** *vt* (**a**) *(support, help)* conseguir; **in a blatant attempt to e. our sympathy** en un intento descarado de ganarse nuestras simpatías (**b**) *Mil (soldier)* alistar; *US* **enlisted man/woman** soldado *mf* raso

2 *vi Mil* alistarse

enlistment [ɪn'lɪstmənt] *n* (**a**) *(of support, help)* obtención *f*, consecución *f* (**b**) *Mil* alistamiento *m*

enliven [ɪn'laɪvən] *vt* animar

en masse ['ɒn'mæs] *adv* en masa

enmesh [ɪn'meʃ] *vt* **to become** *or* **get enmeshed in sth** enredarse en algo

enmity ['enmɪtɪ] *n Formal* enemistad *f* (**towards** hacia)

ennoble [ɪ'nəʊbəl] *vt* (**a**) *(confer title on)* conceder un título nobiliario a (**b**) *Fig (elevate, dignify)* ennoblecer

ennoblement [ɪ'nəʊbəlmənt] *n* (**a**) *(of commoner)* concesión *f* de un título nobiliario (**b**) *(conferral of dignity)* ennoblecimiento *m*, dignificación *f*

ennobling [ɪ'nəʊblɪŋ] *adj (effect, experience)* ennoblecedor(ora), dignificador(ora)

ennui [ɒn'wiː] *n Literary* hastío *m*

enormity [ɪ'nɔːmɪtɪ] *n* (**a**) *(of action, crime)* magnitud *f* (**b**) *Formal (atrocity)* atrocidad *f* (**c**) *(great size)* enormidad *f*; **the e. of the task** la enormidad de la tarea

enormous [ɪ'nɔːməs] *adj* (**a**) *(very large)* enorme, inmenso(a); **e. amounts of food** enormes *or* ingentes cantidades de comida; **he made one last e. effort** hizo un último y descomunal esfuerzo; **an e. difference** una enorme diferencia (**b**) *(as intensifier)* enorme; **I found e. enjoyment in watching those old films again** disfruté enormemente viendo de nuevo esas viejas películas

enormously [ɪ'nɔːməslɪ] *adv* enormemente; **it was e. successful** fue un enorme éxito

ENOUGH [ɪ'nʌf] **1** *adj* suficiente, bastante; **are there e. chairs?** ¿hay suficientes sillas?; **there'll be opportunity e. later** habrá suficientes oportunidades más adelante; **I've got problems e. of my own** ya tengo yo suficientes problemas; **do you have e. money to pay for it?** ¿te alcanza *or* llega el dinero para pagarlo?; **more than e.** *or* **quite e. money/wine** dinero/vino de sobra *or* más que suficiente; **there's not nearly e. food** no hay suficiente comida ni de lejos; **that's e. complaining for one day!** ¡ya basta de quejarte!

2 *pron* **will this be e.?** ¿bastará *or* será bastante con esto?; **I haven't got e.** no tengo suficiente(s); **have you got e. to pay the bill?** ¿te alcanza *or* llega para pagar la cuenta?; **I know e. about the subject to say that...** conozco el tema lo suficiente como para decir que...; *Ironic* **have you had e. of that cake yet?** ¿todavía no te has llenado *or* hartado de pastel *or Col, CSur* torta?; **you've had e. of a chance to apologize** has tenido (más que) suficientes ocasiones para pedir perdón; **more than e., quite e.** más que suficiente; **that's not nearly e.** con eso no basta ni mucho menos; **that's e.** *(sufficient)* es suficiente; **that's e.!** *(stop doing that)* ¡basta ya!, *Esp* ¡vale ya!; **e. is e.** ya basta; **e. of this nonsense!** ¡basta de tonterías!; *Fam* **e. said!** ¡no me digas más!, ¡ni una palabra más!; **it's e. to make you doubt your sanity!** ¡es como para volverte loco!; *Fam* **I can't get e. of that wine!** ¡no me canso de beber *or* tomar ese vino!; **to have e. to live on** tener (lo suficiente) para vivir; **to have had e. of sth/sb** estar harto(a) de algo/alguien; *US Fam* **e. already!** ¡basta!, *Esp* ¡ya vale!

3 *adv* (**a**) *(sufficiently)* suficientemente, bastante; **good e.** suficientemente bueno(a), suficiente; **it's just not good e.!** *(behaviour)* ¡esto es inaceptable!; **she is not strong/tall e. (to...)** no es lo bastante fuerte/alta (como para...); **is it warm e. in here for you?** ¿no tendrás frío aquí?; **last year was bad e., but this year is even worse** el año pasado ya fue malo, pero éste es aún peor; **I was stupid e. to listen to him** fui tan estúpido como para escucharlo; **he's friendly e., I suppose, but...** no es que no sea amable, pero...; **would you be kind e. to give me a hand?** ¿serías tan amable de ayudarme?; **you understand well e. what I'm saying** entiendes perfectamente lo que estoy diciendo

(**b**) *(reasonably)* bastante; **it's normal e. that he should want to be informed** es bastante normal que quiera estar informado; **she's a nice e. girl** es una chica agradable *or Esp* maja; **oddly** *or* **strangely e.,...** curiosamente,...

en passant [ɒn'pæsɒŋ] *adv* de pasada

enplane [en'pleɪn] *US* **1** *vt* embarcar *(en avión)*

2 *vi* embarcar(se) *(en un avión)*, subir a bordo *(de un avión)*

enquire, enquiry *etc* = **inquire, inquiry** *etc*

enrage [ɪn'reɪdʒ] *vt* enfurecer, encolerizar

enraged [ɪn'reɪdʒd] *adj* enfurecido(a), colérico(a); **he was e. to discover that...** montó en cólera *or* se enfureció cuando se enteró de que...

enrapture [ɪn'ræptʃə(r)] *vt* embelesar

enraptured [ɪn'ræptʃəd] *adj* embelesado(a); **to be e.** estar embelesado(a)

enrich [ɪn'rɪtʃ] *vt* enriquecer; **to e. oneself** enriquecerse; **enriched with vitamins** enriquecido(a) con vitaminas ▸▸ *Phys* ***enriched uranium*** uranio *m* enriquecido

enriching [ɪn'rɪtʃɪŋ] *adj* enriquecedor(ora)

enrichment [ɪn'rɪtʃmənt] *n* enriquecimiento *m*

enrol, *US* enroll [ɪn'rəʊl] (*pt & pp* **enrolled**) **1** *vt (member)* inscribir; *(student)* matricular, inscribir

2 *vi* inscribirse; **to e. on** *or* **for a course** matricularse *or* inscribirse en un curso; **to e. as a student** matricularse como estudiante

> **False friend**: The Spanish verb **enrollar** is not a translation for the English word **enrol**. In Spanish **enrollar** means "to roll up" or "to bamboozle".

enrolment, *US* enrollment [ɪn'rəʊlmənt] *n* (**a**) *(registration) (of members)* inscripción *f*; *(of students)* matrícula *f*, inscripción *f* (**b**) *(number of members)* número *m* de socios; *(number of students)* número *m* de matriculados

en route [ɒn'ruːt] *adv* de camino, por el camino; **e. for** de camino a

ensconce [ɪn'skɒns] *vt* **to e. oneself** apoltronarse, aposentarse; **to be ensconced in** estar apoltronado(a) *or* aposentado(a) en

ensemble [ɒn'sɒmbəl] *n* (**a**) *Mus* conjunto *m*; **a wind e.** un conjunto de viento (**b**) **an e. cast** *(in movie, play)* un reparto de primerísima categoría (**c**) *(of clothes)* conjunto *m* (**d**) *(whole)* conjunto *m*

enshrine [ɪn'ʃraɪn] *vt* **to be enshrined in sth** estar consagrado(a) en algo

enshroud [ɪn'ʃraʊd] *vt Literary* envolver

ensign ['ensaɪn] *n* (**a**) *(flag)* bandera *f*, enseña *f* (**b**) *US (naval officer)* alférez *m* de fragata (**c**) *Br Hist (army officer)* abanderado *m*

enslave [ɪn'sleɪv] *vt* esclavizar

ensnare [ɪn'sneə(r)] *vt (animal, criminal)* atrapar, capturar; **to e. sb into doing sth** engatusar a alguien para que haga algo

ensue [ɪn'sju:] *vi* sucederse, seguir; **a long silence ensued** siguió un largo silencio; **the problems that have ensued from this decision** los problemas que surgieron a consecuencia de esta decisión

ensuing [ɪn'sju:ɪŋ] *adj* subsiguiente

en suite ['ɒn'swi:t] *adj* **with an e. bathroom, with bathroom e.** con cuarto de baño privado

ensure [ɪn'ʃʊə(r)] *vt* asegurar, garantizar; **her support will e. your success/promotion** su apoyo te asegurará *or* garantizará el éxito

ENT [i:en'ti:] *n Med* (*abbr* **Ear, Nose and Throat**) otorrinolaringología *f* ►► ***E. specialist*** otorrinolaringólogo(a) *m,f*

entablature [ɪn'tæblətjʊə(r)] *n Archit* entablamento *m*

entail [en'teɪl] *vt* (**a**) *(involve)* implicar, conllevar; **what does the job e.?** ¿en qué consiste el trabajo? (**b**) *Law* **to e. an estate** vincular mediante testamento una propiedad

entangle [ɪn'tæŋgəl] *vt* (**a**) *(ensnare)* **to get** *or* **become entangled** *(wires)* enmarañarse, enredarse; *(animal in net)* enredarse (**b**) *(involve)* **she got entangled in the dispute** se vio envuelta *or* involucrada en la disputa; **to be romantically entangled with sb** tener relaciones amorosas con alguien

entanglement [ɪn'tæŋgəlmənt] *n* (**a**) *(of wires, cables)* enredo *m*, entramado *m*; **barbed wire entanglements** *(defences)* alambradas de púas *or* espino (**b**) *(love affair, difficult situation)* lío *m*; **his various romantic entanglements** sus diversos líos amorosos; **his entanglements with the police** sus líos con la policía

entente [ɒn'tɒnt] *n Pol* **e. (cordiale)** entente *f* (cordial)

enter ['entə(r)] **1** *vt* (**a**) *(room, house, country)* entrar en; **as we e. a new decade** ahora que entramos en *or* iniciamos una nueva década; **the war entered a new phase** la guerra entró en una nueva fase; **a note of sadness entered her voice** su voz adquirió una nota de tristeza; **it never entered my head** *or* **mind that...** jamás se me pasó por la cabeza que...

(**b**) *(race)* inscribirse en; *(exam)* presentarse a; **to e. sb for an exam/a race** inscribir a alguien en un examen/una carrera

(**c**) *(army, university)* ingresar en; *(profession)* empezar a ejercer; *(politics)* entrar en; **young graduates entering the profession** los jóvenes licenciados que comienzan a ejercer; **to e. the church** *(as priest)* ser ordenado sacerdote; *(as nun)* meterse monja

(**d**) *(formally present)* **to e. a complaint/protest** presentar una queja/un escrito de protesta

(**e**) *Law* **to e. a plea of guilty/not guilty** declararse culpable/inocente; **to e. an appeal** interponer un recurso de apelación

(**f**) *(record) (on list, in book)* anotar

(**g**) *Comptr (data)* introducir ►► ***e. key*** tecla *f* enter

2 *vi* (**a**) *(go in)* entrar; *Theat* **e. Juliet** *(stage direction)* entra Julieta (**b**) *(sign up)* **to e. for a race/an exam** inscribirse en una carrera/presentarse a un examen

▸**enter into** *vt insep* (**a**) *(service, dispute, relationship)* empezar, iniciar; **to e. into conversation with sb** entablar conversación con alguien; **to e. into discussions with sb** entablar *or* establecer un diálogo con alguien

(**b**) *(become involved in)* **to e. into partnership (with sb)** asociarse (con alguien); **to e. into an agreement with sb** llegar a un acuerdo con alguien; **to e. into the spirit of things** meterse en el ambiente

(**c**) *(have a part in)* **money doesn't e. into it** el dinero no tiene nada que ver; **an element of risk enters into every business venture** hay un elemento de riesgo en toda operación comercial

▸**enter (up)on** *vt insep* embarcarse en

enteric [en'terɪk] *adj Med* entérico(a) ►► ***e. fever*** fiebre *f* tifoidea

enteritis [entə'raɪtɪs] *n Med* enteritis *f inv*

enterprise ['entəpraɪz] *n* (**a**) *(undertaking)* empresa *f*, iniciativa *f* (**b**) *(company)* empresa *f* (**c**) *(initiative)* iniciativa *f*; **to show e.** tener *or* mostrar iniciativa ►► ***e. culture*** cultura *f* empresarial; ***e. zone*** ≃ zona *f* de urgente reindustrialización

enterprising ['entəpraɪzɪŋ] *adj (person)* emprendedor(ora); **an e. choice as a subject for a dissertation** una elección de tema para una tesina que demuestra iniciativa

entertain [entə'teɪn] **1** *vt* (**a**) *(amuse)* entretener, divertir; **to keep sb entertained** entretener a alguien, tener a alguien entretenido

(**b**) *(show hospitality towards)* **to e. guests** tener invitados, recibir visitas; **he entertained them to dinner** *(at restaurant)* los invitó a cenar; *(home)* los tuvo de invitados para la cena

(**c**) *Formal (consider) (opinion, idea)* considerar; *(fear, suspicion, hope)* albergar; **he entertains grave doubts about the scheme** alberga serias dudas respecto al plan; **I refused to e. such a suggestion** me negué a considerar tal propuesta

2 *vi* recibir (invitados)

entertainer [entə'teɪnə(r)] *n* artista *mf* (del espectáculo)

entertaining [entə'teɪnɪŋ] **1** *n* **to do a lot of e.** tener a menudo invitados, recibir muchas visitas

2 *adj* entretenido(a), divertido(a)

entertainingly [entə'teɪnɪŋlɪ] *adv* **he rather e. fell flat on his face** la forma en que calló de bruces fue de lo más divertida *or* graciosa

entertainment [entə'teɪnmənt] *n* (**a**) *(amusement)* entretenimiento *m*, diversión *f*; **for your e., we have organized...** para su diversión, hemos organizado...; **her favourite e. is reading** su distracción preferida es la lectura; **much to the e. of the crowd** para regocijo de la multitud; **we had to make our own e.** tuvimos que entretenernos solos; **I'm not doing this for my own e., you know!** ¡esto no lo hago por gusto, eh! ►► *Com* ***e. allowance*** gastos *mpl* de representación

(**b**) *Theat* espectáculo *m*; **the e. business** la industria del espectáculo ►► *Com* ***e. allowance*** gastos *mpl* de representación; ***entertainments director*** *(at hotel, holiday camp)* organizador(ora) *m,f* de actividades; ***entertainments officer*** *(on ship)* animador(ora) *m,f*

enthral, *US* **enthrall** [ɪn'θrɔ:l] (*pt & pp* **enthralled**) *vt* cautivar, hechizar

enthralling [ɪn'θrɔ:lɪŋ] *adj* cautivador(ora)

enthrone [ɪn'θrəʊn] *vt* entronizar, colocar en el trono

enthronement [ɪn'θrəʊnmənt] *n* entronización *f*

enthuse [ɪn'θju:z] **1** *vt* entusiasmar

2 *vi* entusiasmarse (**about** *or* **over** por)

enthusiasm [ɪn'θju:zɪæzəm] *n* entusiasmo *m*

enthusiast [ɪn'θju:zɪæst] *n* entusiasta *mf*; **she's a jazz e.** es una enamorada del jazz

enthusiastic [ɪnθju:zɪ'æstɪk] *adj (person)* entusiasmado(a); *(praise, applause, support, welcome)* entusiasta; **to be e. (about)** estar entusiasmado(a) (con); *Ironic* **don't sound so e.!** ¡no lo digas con tanto entusiasmo!

enthusiastically [ɪnθju:zɪ'æstɪklɪ] *adv* con entusiasmo

entice [ɪn'taɪs] *vt* **to e. sb to do sth** incitar a alguien a hacer algo; **their suggestion didn't e. me** su sugerencia no me tentó; **they enticed him into a card game** lo engatusaron para que jugase a las cartas; **she enticed him away from his wife** consiguió que se alejara de su mujer seduciéndolo

enticement [ɪn'taɪsmənt] *n (attraction)* incentivo *m*, aliciente *m*

enticing [ɪn'taɪsɪŋ] *adj* tentador(ora), atractivo(a)

entire [ɪn'taɪə(r)] *adj* (**a**) *(whole)* entero(a); **the e. building/country** el edificio/país entero; **the e. day/week** el día entero/la semana entera; **she read the e. book in an afternoon** se leyó el libro entero en una tarde

(**b**) *(complete, total)* **to be in e. agreement (with sb)** estar completamente de acuerdo (con alguien); **to enjoy sb's e. confidence** tener la completa confianza de alguien

(**c**) *(intact)* intacto(a)

entirely [ɪn'taɪəlɪ] *adv* completamente, totalmente; **I agree (with you) e., I e. agree (with you)** estoy completamente *or* totalmente de acuerdo (contigo); **it's e. my fault** es totalmente culpa mía; **that's another matter e.** eso es una cuestión completamente *or* totalmente diferente; **it's not e. clear what happened** no está completamente *or* totalmente claro lo que sucedió

entirety [ɪn'taɪərətɪ] *n* (**a**) *(completeness)* integridad *f*, totalidad *f*; **in its e.** en su totalidad, íntegramente (**b**) *(total)* totalidad *f*; **the e. of his estate** la totalidad de su patrimonio

entitle [ɪn'taɪtəl] *vt* (**a**) *(allow)* **to e. sb to sth** dar derecho a alguien a algo; **to e. sb to do sth** dar derecho a alguien a hacer algo; **to be entitled to (do) sth** tener derecho a (hacer) algo; **you're entitled to your own opinion but...** tienes todo el derecho a opinar lo que quieras pero..., tu opinión es muy respetable, pero...

(**b**) *(book, song)* titular; **his new album is entitled "Knock me Senseless"** su nuevo álbum se titula *or* llama "Knock me Senseless"

entitlement [ɪn'taɪtəlmənt] *n* derecho *m*

entity ['entɪtɪ] *n* ente *m*, entidad *f*; **it is now a separate e.** es ahora un ente independiente

entomb [ɪn'tu:m] *vt* sepultar

entomologist [entə'mɒlədʒɪst] *n* entomólogo(a) *m,f*

entomology [entə'mɒlədʒɪ] *n* entomología *f*

entourage ['ɒntʊrɑ:ʒ] *n* séquito *m*, comitiva *f*

entr'acte ['ɒntrækt] *n* intermedio *m*, entreacto *m*

entrails ['entreɪlz] *npl* entrañas *fpl*

entrain [ɪn'treɪn] **1** *vt Formal (troops)* embarcar *(en tren)*
2 *vi* subir al tren

entrance[1] ['entrəns] *n* **(a)** *(way in)* entrada *f*; **the front/rear/side e.** la entrada delantera/trasera/lateral ▸▸ ***e. hall*** vestíbulo *m*
(b) *(act of entering)* entrada *f*; *Theat & Fig* **he made his e.** hizo su aparición *or* entrada (en escena)
(c) *(access)* **to gain e. to** lograr acceder a
(d) *(admission)* entrada *f*, ingreso *m*; **to refuse** *or* **deny sb e. (to sth)** no permitirle la entrada a alguien (a algo) ▸▸ ***e. examination*** examen *m* de ingreso, prueba *f* de acceso; ***e. fee*** *(to museum)* (precio *m* de) entrada *f*; *(to join organization)* cuota *f* de ingreso; *(to sit exam)* (cuota *f* de) inscripción *f*; ***e. requirements*** *(to university, profession)* requisitos *mpl* de ingreso

entrance[2] [ɪn'trɑ:ns] *vt (charm)* cautivar, encantar

entrancing [ɪn'trɑ:nsɪŋ] *adj* cautivador(ora), encantador(ora)

entrant ['entrənt] *n* **(a)** *(in exam)* candidato(a) *m,f*, examinando(a) *m,f*; *(in race)* participante *mf* **(b)** *(to society, profession)* nuevo(a) miembro *mf*, neófito(a) *m,f*

entrap [ɪn'træp] *(pt & pp* **entrapped***)* *vt* **(a)** *(animal, bird)* atrapar **(b)** *(trick)* engañar, embaucar **(c)** *Law* **to e. sb** inducir a alguien a cometer un delito

entrapment [ɪn'træpmənt] *n Law* incitación *f or* inducción *f* al delito

entreat [ɪn'tri:t] *vt Formal* suplicar, rogar; **to e. sb to do sth** suplicar a alguien que haga algo

entreaty [ɪn'tri:tɪ] *n Formal* súplica *f*, ruego *m*; **a look of e.** una mirada de súplica

entrechat ['ɒntrəʃɑ:] *n (in ballet)* entrechat *m*, cruce *m* de pies

entrecôte ['ɒntrəkɒt] *n* entrecot *m*

entrée ['ɒntreɪ] *n* **(a)** *(introduction)* entrada *f*, acceso *m* **(b)** *Br (first course)* entrada *f*, primer plato *m* **(c)** *US (main course)* plato *m* principal

entrench [ɪn'trentʃ] *vt (establish)* consolidar

entrenched [ɪn'trentʃd] *adj* **(a)** *(troops)* **to be e.** estar atrincherado(a) **(b)** *(deep-rooted)* arraigado(a); *(opposition)* firme; **to be e.** *(custom, attitude)* estar arraigado(a); **he became more e. in his views** se reafirmó más en sus ideas

entrepreneur [ɒntrəprə'nɜ:(r)] *n* empresario(a) *m,f*

entrepreneurial [ɒntrəprə'nɜ:rɪəl] *adj (spirit, attitude)* empresarial; *(flair, skill, talent)* para los negocios

entropy ['entrəpɪ] *n Phys* entropía *f*

entrust [ɪn'trʌst] *vt* **to e. sb with sth, to e. sth to sb** confiar algo a alguien; **she entrusted her children to them** les confió a sus hijos

entry ['entrɪ] *n* **(a)** *(way in)* entrada *f*; **to deny** *or* **refuse sb e. (to)** negarle a alguien la entrada (a); **no e.** *(sign) (on door)* prohibida la entrada; *(in street)* prohibido pasar *or* el paso ▸▸ ***e. visa*** visado *m* de entrada
(b) *(act of entering)* entrada *f*; **she made her e. by a side door** hizo su entrada por la puerta lateral
(c) *(access)* **to gain e. to** lograr introducirse en
(d) *(admission) (into group, organization)* ingreso *m*; **to deny** *or* **refuse sb e. (to)** *(organization)* negarle a alguien el ingreso (en) ▸▸ ***e. requirements*** *(to university, profession)* requisitos *mpl* de ingreso
(e) *(in competition)* **we had over 1,000 entries for the competition** se recibieron más de 1.000 inscripciones para el concurso; **last year's marathon had a record number of entries** el maratón del año pasado registró un número récord de participantes ▸▸ *US* ***e. blank*** (impreso *m* de) inscripción *f*; ***e. fee*** cuota *f* de inscripción; ***e. form*** (impreso *m* de) inscripción *f*
(f) *(number of entrants)* número *m* de inscripciones
(g) *(item) (in dictionary, encyclopedia)* entrada *f*; *(in diary)* anotación *f*; *(in accounts)* asiento *m*

entryism ['entrɪɪzəm] *n Br Pol* entrismo *m*

entry-level ['entrɪlevəl] *adj* **(a)** *(computer)* de gama baja **(b)** *(job, salary)* inicial

entryphone ['entrɪfəʊn] *n Br* portero *m* automático *or* electrónico

entryway ['entrɪweɪ] *n US* entrada *f*

entwine [ɪn'twaɪn] **1** *vt* entrelazar; **to e. sth round sth** enrollar algo alrededor de algo; **to become entwined** *(one thing)* enrollarse; *(two or more things)* entrelazarse; **to become entwined with sth** enrollarse con algo
2 *vi* entrelazarse

E-number ['i:nʌmbə(r)] *n* número *m* E, aditivo *m*

enumerable [ɪ'nju:mərəbəl] *adj* enumerable; **his faults were easily e.** sus defectos se podían enumerar fácilmente

enumerate [ɪ'nju:məreɪt] *vt* enumerar

enumeration [ɪnju:mə'reɪʃən] *n* enumeración *f*

enunciate [ɪ'nʌnsɪeɪt] **1** *vt* **(a)** *(sound, word)* articular **(b)** *(opinion, view)* enunciar
2 *vi* vocalizar

enunciation [ɪnʌnsɪ'eɪʃən] *n (diction)* dicción *f*

envelop [ɪn'veləp] *vt* envolver **(in** en**)**; **enveloped in mystery** envuelto en misterio; **enveloped in mist** envuelto en (la) niebla

envelope ['envələʊp, 'ɒnvələʊp] *n* **(a)** *(for letter)* sobre *m* **(b)** *(covering)* envoltura *f*, recubrimiento *m* **(c)** IDIOMS **back of an e. calculations** cálculos hechos deprisa y corriendo; **to push the e.** romper moldes

envenom [ɪn'venəm] *vt* **(a)** *(with poison)* envenenar **(b)** *(with malice)* envenenar

enviable ['envɪəbəl] *adj* envidiable

envious ['envɪəs] *adj* envidioso(a); **to be** *or* **feel e. (of)** tener envidia (de); **I am very e. of you!** ¡me das mucha envidia!; **her success only made people e. (of her)** su éxito sólo consiguió que la gente le tuviese envidia

enviously ['envɪəslɪ] *adv* con envidia

environment [ɪn'vaɪrənmənt] *n* **(a)** *(natural surroundings)* **the e.** el medio ambiente; *Pol* **Department** *or* **Ministry of the E.** ministerio del medio ambiente **(b)** *(of animal, plant)* **(natural) e.** entorno *m or* medio *m* natural **(c)** *(context)* entorno *m*; **in a work e.** en un entorno laboral **(d)** *(atmosphere)* ambiente *m*; **a good working e.** un buen ambiente de trabajo **(e)** *Comptr* entorno *m*

environmental [ɪnvaɪrən'mentəl] *adj* **(a)** *(ecological) (planning, issue)* ambiental, medioambiental; *(pollution)* ambiental ▸▸ ***e. audit*** auditoría *f* medioambiental; ***e. conservation*** conservación *f* del medio ambiente; ***e. consultancy*** consultoría *f* de medio ambiente *or* medioambiental; ***e. damage*** daños *mpl* medioambientales *or* ecológicos; ***e. disaster*** catástrofe *f* ecológica; ***e. education*** educación *f* (medio)ambiental; ***e. group*** grupo *m* ecologista; *Br* ***E. Health Officer*** inspector(ora) *m,f* de sanidad; ***e. impact*** impacto *m* (medio)ambiental; ***e. impact assessment*** evaluación *f* de impacto ambiental; *US* ***E. Protection Agency*** = agencia gubernamental estadounidense encargada de la protección medioambiental; ***e. studies*** estudios *mpl* medioambientales *or* del medio ambiente
(b) *(of surroundings)* ambiental

environmentalism [ɪnvaɪrən'mentəlɪzəm] *n* ecologismo *m*

environmentalist [ɪnvaɪrən'mentəlɪst] *n* ecologista *mf*

environmentally [ɪnvaɪrən'mentəlɪ] *adv* ecológicamente, desde el punto de vista ecológico ▸▸ ***e. friendly*** ecológico(a), que no daña el medio ambiente; ***e. friendly manufacturing*** fabricación *f* limpia

environs [ɪn'vaɪrənz] *npl* inmediaciones *fpl*, alrededores *mpl*

envisage [ɪn'vɪzɪdʒ], **envision** [en'vɪʒən] *vt* **(a)** *(foresee)* prever; **I don't e. any major changes** no preveo ningún cambio importante **(b)** *(imagine)* imaginar; **it's not quite what I'd envisaged** yo me había hecho a la idea de otra cosa

envoy ['envɔɪ] *n (diplomat)* enviado(a) *m,f*

envy ['envɪ] **1** *n* **(a)** *(jealousy)* envidia *f*; **out of e.** por envidia **(b)** *(object of jealousy)* envidia *f*; **to be the e. of sb** ser la envidia de alguien
2 *vt (person)* envidiar; **I do e. her** la envidio; **I e. her having the chance to travel at that age** me da envidia las posibilidades de viajar que tiene a su edad; **they envied him his success** tenían envidia de *or* envidiaban su éxito; **I can't say I e. you** ¡no me das ninguna envidia!

enzyme ['enzaɪm] *n Biol* enzima *m or f*

EOC [i:əʊ'si:] *n (abbr* **Equal Opportunities Commission***)* = organismo público británico que vela por la existencia de igualdad de oportunidades para los diferentes sexos, razas, etc.

Eocene ['i:əʊsi:n] *Geol* **1** *n* **the E.** el eoceno
2 *adj (epoch)* eoceno(a)

E & OE *Fin (abbr* **errors and omissions excepted***)* s.e.u.o.

eon *US* = **aeon**

EP [i:'pi:] *n (abbr* **extended play***)* EP *m*

EPA [i:pi:'eɪ] *n (abbr* **Environmental Protection Agency***)* = agencia gubernamental estadounidense encargada de la protección medioambiental

epaulette, *US* **epaulet** ['epəlet] *n Mil* charretera *f*

epée ['epeɪ] *n (fencing sword)* espada *f (de esgrima)*

ephedrine [*Br* 'efɪdri:n, *US* ɪ'fedrən] *n Pharm* efedrina *f*

ephemera [ɪ'femərə] *npl* objetos *mpl* efímeros coleccionables

ephemeral [ɪ'femərəl] *adj* **(a)** *(short-lived)* efímero(a) **(b)** *Zool* de vida efímera

Ephesus ['efəsəs] *n* Éfeso

epic ['epɪk] **1** *n (poem, novel)* epopeya *f*; *(film)* película *f* épica
2 *adj* **(a)** *(poem, film, novel)* épico(a) **(b)** *(struggle, game)* épico(a); **on an e. scale** a gran escala

epicene ['epɪsi:n] *adj Literary (beauty)* andrógino(a)

epicentre, *US* **epicenter** ['epɪsentə(r)] *n* epicentro *m*

epicure ['epɪkjʊə(r)] *n Formal* gourmet *mf*

epicurean ['epɪkjʊə'ri:ən] **1** *n* **(a)** *Phil* **E.** epicúreo(a) *m,f* **(b)** *(gourmet)* sibarita *mf*, gourmet *mf*
2 *adj* **(a)** *Phil* **E.** epicúreo(a) **(b)** *(tastes)* sibarita, de gourmet

epidemic [epɪ'demɪk] *Med & Fig* **1** *n* epidemia *f*
2 *adj* epidémico(a); **the problem has reached e. proportions** el problema ha alcanzado una enorme magnitud

epidemiological [epɪdi:mɪə'lɒdʒɪkəl] *adj Med* epidemiológico(a)

epidemiologist [epɪdi:mɪ'ɒlədʒɪst] *n Med* epidemiólogo(a) *m,f*

epidemiology [epɪdi:mɪ'ɒlədʒɪ] *n Med* epidemiología *f*

epidermic [epɪ'dɜ:mɪk] *adj Anat* epidérmico(a)

epidermis [epɪ'dɜ:mɪs] *n Anat* epidermis *f inv*

epidural [epɪ'dju:rəl] *Med* **1** *n* (anestesia *f*) epidural *f*
2 *adj* epidural

epigastrium [epɪ'gæstrɪəm] *n Anat* epigastrio *m*

epiglottis [epɪ'glɒtɪs] (*pl* **epiglottises**) *n Anat* epiglotis *f inv*

epigram ['epɪgræm] *n* epigrama *m*

epigrammatic [epɪgrə'mætɪk] *adj* epigramático(a)

epigraph ['epɪgrɑ:f] *n* epígrafe *m*

epilepsy ['epɪlepsɪ] *n* epilepsia *f*

epileptic [epɪ'leptɪk] **1** *n* epiléptico(a) *m,f*
2 *adj* epiléptico(a) ▸▸ ***e. fit*** ataque *m* epiléptico

epilogue, *US* **epilog** ['epɪlɒg] *n* epílogo *m*

epinephrine [epɪ'nefrɪn] *n US* epinefrina *f*

epiphany [ɪ'pɪfənɪ] *n* **(a)** *Rel* **the E.** la Epifanía **(b)** *Literary (revelation)* epifanía *f*

epiphyte ['epɪfaɪt] *adj Bot* epifito(a)

episcopacy [ɪ'pɪskəpəsɪ] *n* **(a)** *(church government)* gobierno *m* episcopal **(b)** *(group of bishops)* episcopado *m*

episcopal [ɪ'pɪskəpəl] *adj* episcopal; **the E. Church** la Iglesia Episcopal

episcopalian [ɪpɪskə'peɪlɪən] *Rel* **1** *n* episcopalista *mf*
2 *adj* episcopalista

episcopate [ɪ'pɪskəpət] *n* episcopado *m*

episiotomy [epɪsɪ'ɒtəmɪ] *n Med* episiotomía *f*

episode ['epɪsəʊd] *n* **(a)** *(part of story, programme)* capítulo *m*, episodio *m* **(b)** *(incident)* episodio *m*; **I wanted to forget the whole e.** quería olvidar toda la historia **(c)** *Med* ataque *m*

episodic [epɪ'sɒdɪk] *adj* episódico(a)

epistemology [ɪpɪstə'mɒlədʒɪ] *n* epistemología *f*

epistle [ɪ'pɪsəl] *n* **(a)** *Rel* epístola *f*; **the E. of Paul to the Romans/Corinthians** la epístola de San Pablo a los Romanos/Corintios **(b)** *Hum (letter)* epístola *f*

epistolary [ɪ'pɪstələrɪ] *adj Lit (novel)* epistolar

epitaph ['epɪtɑ:f] *n* epitafio *m*

epithelial [epɪ'θi:lɪəl] *adj Anat* epitelial ▸▸ ***e. tissue*** tejido *m* epitelial

epithelium [epɪ'θi:lɪəm] *n Anat* epitelio *m*

epithet ['epɪθet] *n* epíteto *m*

epitome [ɪ'pɪtəmɪ] *n* paradigma *m*; **she's the e. of generosity** es la generosidad personificada

epitomize [ɪ'pɪtəmaɪz] *vt* ser el paradigma de; **this action epitomizes the government's attitude to education** este acto refleja a la perfección *or* es el vivo ejemplo de la actitud del gobierno respecto a la educación

epoch ['i:pɒk] *n* era *f*, época *f*

epoch-making ['i:pɒkmeɪkɪŋ], **epochal** ['epəkəl] *adj* **an e. change/event** un cambio/acontecimiento que hace/hizo/*etc* época

eponym ['epənɪm] *n* epónimo *m*

eponymous [ɪ'pɒnɪməs] *adj* epónimo(a)

EPOS ['i:pɒs] *n* (*abbr* **electronic point of sale**) punto *m* de venta electrónico

epoxy resin [ɪ'pɒksɪ'rezɪn] *n Chem* resina *f* epoxídica

EPS [i:pi:'es] *n* **(a)** *Fin* (*abbr* **earnings per share**) dividendos *mpl* por acción **(b)** *Comptr* (*abbr* **encapsulated PostScript**) EPS *m*

epsilon ['epsɪlɒn] *n* épsilon *f*

Epsom salts ['epsəm'sɔ:lts] *npl* epsomita *f*

e-publishing ['i:'pʌblɪʃɪŋ] *n Comptr* edición *f* electrónica

equable ['ekwəbəl] *adj* **(a)** *(person, temper)* ecuánime **(b)** *(climate)* estable

equably ['ekwəblɪ] *adv* con ecuanimidad, ecuánimemente

equal ['i:kwəl] **1** *n* igual *mf*; **she is his intellectual e.** tiene la misma talla intelectual que él; **to treat sb as an e.** tratar a alguien de igual a igual; **to have no e.** *(person)* no tener rival; *(achievement, work of art)* no tener parangón
2 *adj* **(a)** *(identical)* igual; **e. in size/number** de la misma talla/del mismo número; **to be e. to sth** ser igual a algo; **all other things being e.** si no hay imprevistos; **in e. measure** en igual medida; **to an e. extent** en igual medida, de la misma forma; **she speaks Spanish and German with e. ease** habla español e inglés con la misma facilidad; **to be on an e. footing with sb** estar en igualdad de condiciones con alguien; **on e. terms** en igualdad de condiciones ▸▸ ***e. opportunities*** igualdad *f* de oportunidades; **an e. opportunity employer** = una entidad que practica la igualdad de oportunidades en la selección de personal; ***e. pay*** igualdad *f* salarial *or* de retribuciones; **e. pay for e. work** el mismo salario para el mismo trabajo; ***e. rights*** igualdad *f* de derechos; *US* ***E. Rights Amendment*** = proyecto de enmienda de la Constitución estadounidense para equiparar los derechos entre mujeres y hombres que finalmente fue rechazado; *Math* **e.** *or* ***equals sign*** (signo *m* de) igual *m*
(b) *(good enough)* **to be/feel e. to (doing) sth** estar/sentirse capaz para (hacer) algo; **he proved e. to the task/challenge** se mostró a la altura de la tarea/del desafío
3 *vt* (*pt & pp* **equalled,** *US* **equaled**) **(a)** *Math* ser igual a; **four fives equal(s) twenty** cuatro por cinco (es) igual a veinte, cuatro por cinco, veinte; **let x e. 2y** si x es igual a 2y
(b) *(match) (record, offer)* igualar; **there is no one to e. him for eloquence** nadie lo iguala en elocuencia; **there is nothing to e. it in nature** no tiene parangón en la naturaleza

equality [ɪ'kwɒlɪtɪ] *n* igualdad *f*; **e. of opportunity** igualdad de oportunidades

equalize ['i:kwəlaɪz] **1** *vt* igualar
2 *vi Sport* empatar, igualar el marcador

equalizer ['i:kwəlaɪzə(r)] *n* **(a)** *Elec* ecualizador *m* **(b)** *Sport* tanto *m* del empate **(c)** *US Fam (handgun)* pipa *f*, *Am* fierro *m*

equally ['i:kwəlɪ] *adv* **(a)** *(to an equal degree)* igualmente; **she worked e. hard** se esforzó por igual; **e. talented students** estudiantes de igual talento; **they were e. responsible** fueron igualmente responsables; **it applies e. to both young and old** se aplica tanto a los jóvenes como a los viejos
(b) *(in equal amounts)* **to share** *or* **divide sth e.** dividir algo en partes iguales; **to contribute e. to the expenses** contribuir en partes iguales a los gastos; **e. spaced** a la misma distancia
(c) *(alternatively)* al mismo tiempo, del mismo modo; **e., he might be lying** por otro lado, podría estar mintiendo; **we could e. well stay at home** también podemos quedarnos en casa

equanimity [ekwə'nɪmɪtɪ] *n Formal* ecuanimidad *f*; **to recover one's e.** recobrar la compostura; **with e.** ecuánimemente

equate [ɪ'kweɪt] **1** *vt* equiparar (**with** con)
2 *vi* corresponderse (**with** con)

equation [ɪ'kweɪʒən] *n* **(a)** *Math* ecuación *f*; IDIOM **to bring sth into the e.: that's without bringing money into the e.** y eso sin tener en cuenta el dinero **(b)** *Chem* ecuación *f*

equator [ɪ'kweɪtə(r)] *n* ecuador *m*; **at** *or* **on the E.** en el Ecuador; **to cross the E.** cruzar el Ecuador *or* la línea del Ecuador

equatorial [ekwə'tɔ:rɪəl] *adj* ecuatorial; **E. Guinea** Guinea Ecuatorial

equerry ['ekwərɪ] *n* = ayuda de cámara de la casa real británica

equestrian [ɪ'kwestrɪən] **1** *n* caballista *mf*
2 *adj (statue, ability)* ecuestre

equestrianism [ɪ'kwestrɪənɪzəm] *n* equitación *f*

equidistance [ekwɪ'dɪstəns] *n* equidistancia *f*

equidistant [ekwɪ'dɪstənt] *adj* equidistante (**from** de); **to be e. (from)** equidistar (de)

equilateral [ekwɪ'lætərəl] *adj (triangle)* equilátero(a)

equilibrium [ekwɪ'lɪbrɪəm] *n* equilibrio *m*; **to maintain/lose one's e.** mantener/perder el equilibrio; **in e.** en equilibrio

equine ['ekwaɪn] *adj* **(a)** *(activities)* ecuestre; *(disease)* equino(a) **(b)** *(features)* caballuno(a), equino(a); **to have an e. face** tener cara de caballo

equinoctial [ekwɪ'nɒkʃəl] *adj* equinoccial

equinox ['ekwɪnɒks] *n* equinoccio *m*; **autumnal e.** equinoccio de otoño; **spring** *or* **vernal e.** equinoccio de primavera

equip [ɪ'kwɪp] *(pt & pp* **equipped)** *vt* **(a)** *(provide with equipment)* equipar; **to e. sb with sth** equipar a alguien con *or* de algo, proveer a alguien de algo; **she equipped herself with a tent and a sleeping bag** se equipó con *or* de una tienda y un saco de dormir; **we're not equipped to perform heart surgery** no contamos con el equipo necesario para realizar una operación de corazón

(b) *(prepare)* preparar; **to be equipped for...** estar preparado(a) para...

equipment [ɪ'kwɪpmənt] *n* **(a)** *(items)* equipo *m*; **camping e.** material de acampada; **sports e.** artículos deportivos ►► ***e. allowance*** gastos *mpl* de equipamiento **(b)** *Fig* **intellectual e.** dotación intelectual **(c)** *Formal (act)* equipamiento *m*

equitable ['ekwɪtəbəl] *adj* justo(a), equitativo(a)

equitably ['ekwɪtəblɪ] *adv* equitativamente

Equity ['ekwɪtɪ] *n (actors' union)* = sindicato británico al que todos los actores profesionales han de estar afiliados

equity ['ekwɪtɪ] *n* **(a)** *(fairness)* justicia *f*, equidad *f* **(b)** *Fin (of shareholders)* fondos *mpl* propios, neto *m* patrimonial; *(of company)* capital *m* escriturado *or* social; **equities** acciones (ordinarias) ►► ***e. capital*** capital *m* propio; ***e. markets*** mercados *mpl* de renta variable

equivalence [ɪ'kwɪvələns] *n* equivalencia *f* (**between** entre)

equivalent [ɪ'kwɪvələnt] **1** *n* equivalente *m*; **the Spanish e. for "Prime Minister"** el equivalente español del "primer ministro"; **it costs the e. of £5 per week** cuesta el equivalente de cinco libras por semana

2 *adj* equivalente (**to** a); **to be e. (to)** equivalar (a); **that would be e. to saying that...** eso equivale a decir que...

equivocal [ɪ'kwɪvəkəl] *adj* **(a)** *(ambiguous) (words, attitude)* equívoco(a) **(b)** *(dubious) (behaviour)* equívoco(a)

equivocally [ɪ'kwɪvəklɪ] *adv* **(a)** *(ambiguously)* de manera equívoca **(b)** *(dubiously)* de manera equívoca

equivocate [ɪ'kwɪvəkeɪt] *vi Formal* hablar con ambigüedad

equivocation [ɪkwɪvə'keɪʃən] *n Formal* evasivas *fpl*, ambigüedades *fpl*

> **False friend**: The Spanish noun **equivocación** is not a translation for the English word **equivocation**. In Spanish **equivocación** means "mistake".

ER [iː'ɑː(r)] *n* **(a)** *Br* (*abbr* **Elizabeth Regina**) = emblema de la reina Isabel **(b)** *US Med* (*abbr* **Emergency Room**) (sala *f* de) urgencias *fpl*

ERA ['ɪərə] *n* (*abbr* **Equal Rights Amendment**) = proyecto de enmienda de la Constitución estadounidense para equiparar los derechos entre mujeres y hombres que finalmente fue rechazado

era ['ɪərə] *n* **(a)** *(period, epoch)* era *f*, época *f*; **the end of an e.** el final de una era *or* época; **her election marked a new e. in politics** su elección marcó una nueva era en política; **the e. of horse travel** la era *or* época de los viajes a caballo **(b)** *Geol* era *f*

eradicable [ɪ'rædɪkəbəl] *adj* erradicable; **these errors are (not) easily e.** estos errores no se pueden erradicar fácilmente

eradicate [ɪ'rædɪkeɪt] *vt* erradicar

eradication [ɪrædɪ'keɪʃən] *n* erradicación *f*

erasable [*Br* ɪ'reɪzəbəl, *US* ɪ'reɪsəbəl] *adj Comptr* regrabable ►► ***e. CD-ROM*** CD-ROM *m* regrabable

erase [*Br* ɪ'reɪz, *US* ɪ'reɪs] *vt* **(a)** *(writing)* borrar; *Fig* **to e. sth from one's mind** borrar algo de la mente *or* del pensamiento **(b)** *(from tape, disk, file)* borrar; **e. button/head** botón/cabeza de borrado

eraser [*Br* ɪ'reɪzə(r), *US* ɪ'reɪsər] *n* goma *f* (de borrar)

Erasmus [ɪ'ræzməs] *pr n* Erasmo

erasure [ɪ'reɪʒə(r), *US* ɪ'reɪʃər] *n* **(a)** *(act)* borrado *m* **(b)** *(mark) (in paper)* tachadura *f*; **there were numerous erasures on the tape** había muchas secciones borradas de la cinta

erbium ['ɜːbɪəm] *n Chem* erbio *m*

ERDF [iːɑːdiː'ef] *n Fin* (*abbr* **European Regional Development Fund**) FEDER *m*

ere [eə(r)] *Literary* **1** *prep* antes de; **e. long** en breve

2 *conj* antes (de) que

erect [ɪ'rekt] **1** *adj* **(a)** *(upright)* erguido(a), erecto(a); **she holds herself very e.** va muy erguida; **with head e.** con la cabeza erguida; **the dog sat with ears e.** el perro estaba sentado con las orejas tiesas **(b)** *(penis)* erecto(a); *(nipples)* de punta, duro(a)

2 *vt* **(a)** *(build) (building, temple)* erigir, construir; *(statue, wall)* erigir, levantar; *(roadblock, scaffolding, mast)* levantar; *(tent)* montar, levantar **(b)** *(system, theory)* construir

erectile [ɪ'rektaɪl] *adj Physiol* eréctil ►► ***e. disfunction*** disfunción *f* eréctil

erection [ɪ'rekʃən] *n* **(a)** *(of building)* construcción *f*; *(of tent, scaffolding)* montaje *m*; **the sculptor was present at the e. of the statue** el escultor estaba presente cuando levantaron *or* erigieron la estatua **(b)** *(building)* construcción *f* **(c)** *(erect penis)* erección *f*; **to have** *or* **get an e.** tener una erección

erector [ɪ'rektə(r)] *n* **(a)** *Anat (muscle)* **e. (muscle)** (músculo *m*) erector *m* **(b)** *US* **E. set** = juego de construcciones de metal

erg [ɜːg] *n Phys* ergio *m*

ergative ['ɜːgətɪv] *adj Gram* ergativo(a)

ergo ['ɜːgəʊ] *adv Formal & Hum* ergo, luego

ergonomic [ɛːgə'nɒmɪk] *adj* ergonómico(a)

ergonomically [ɜːgə'nɒmɪklɪ] *adv* ergonómicamente; **e. designed** con diseño ergonómico

ergonomics [ɜːgə'nɒmɪks] *n* ergonomía *f*

ergot ['ɜːgɒt] *n* cornezuelo *m*, ergotina *f*

ergotism ['ɜːgətɪzəm] *n Med* ergotismo *m*

Erin ['erɪn] *n Literary* Erín

Eritrea [erɪ'treɪə] *n* Eritrea

Eritrean [erɪ'treɪən] **1** *n* eritreo(a) *m,f*

2 *adj* eritreo(a)

ERM [iːɑː'rem] *n Fin* (*abbr* **Exchange Rate Mechanism**) mecanismo *m* de tipos de cambio

ermine ['ɜːmɪn] *n* armiño *m*

Ernie ['ɜːnɪ] *n Br* = computadora que otorga al azar los premios a los cupones de un sorteo británico (los "premium bonds")

erode [ɪ'rəʊd] **1** *vt* **(a)** *(rock, soil, metal)* erosionar **(b)** *(confidence)* minar; *(power)* desgastar **(c)** *(savings, income)* mermar

2 *vi* **(a)** *(rock, soil, metal)* erosionarse **(b)** *(confidence, power)* minarse **(c)** *(savings, income)* mermar

erogenous [ɪ'rɒdʒɪnəs] *adj* erógeno(a) ►► ***e. zone*** zona *f* erógena

Eros ['ɪərɒs] *n Mythol* Eros

erosion [ɪ'rəʊʒən] *n* **(a)** *(of rock, soil, metal)* erosión *f*; **soil e.** erosión del terreno; **wind/wave e.** erosión eólica/marítima **(b)** *(of confidence, power)* desgaste *m* **(c)** *(of savings, income)* merma *f*

erotic [ɪ'rɒtɪk] *adj* erótico(a)

erotica [ɪ'rɒtɪkə] *npl* obras *fpl* eróticas

erotically [ɪ'rɒtɪklɪ] *adv* eróticamente; **to be e. charged** tener mucha carga erótica

eroticism [ɪ'rɒtɪsɪzəm] *n* erotismo *m*

eroticize [ɪ'rɒtɪsaɪz] *vt* erotizar

erotomania [ɪ'rɒtəʊmeɪnɪə] *n* erotomanía *f*

err [ɜː(r)] *vi* **(a)** *(make mistake)* cometer un error, errar; **to e. in one's judgement/calculations** cometer un error de juicio/de cálculo; **to e. on the side of caution** pecar de prudente; PROV **to e. is human (to forgive divine)** errar es humano (perdonar, divino) **(b)** *(stray)* descarriarse; *Rel or Hum* **to e. from the straight and narrow** apartarse del camino del bien

errand ['erənd] *n* recado *m*, *Am* mandado *m*; **to send sb on an e.** mandar a alguien a hacer un recado *or Am* mandado; **to run** *or* **do errands for sb** hacerle los recados *or Am* mandados a alguien; **an e. of mercy** una misión caritativa *or* de caridad ►► ***e. boy*** chico *m* de los recados, *RP* cadete *m*

errant ['erənt] *adj Literary* **(a)** *(behaviour)* desordenado(a), díscolo(a); *(son, daughter)* descarriado(a); *(husband)* díscolo(a), infiel **(b)** *(roaming)* errante

errata *pl of* **erratum**

erratic [ɪ'rætɪk] **1** *adj* **(a)** *(irregular, unpredictable) (service, performance)* desigual, irregular; *(course, movement)* errático(a); *(mood)* errático, variable; **her playing is e.** *(of musician)* su interpretación es muy irregular *or* desigual **(b)** *Med (heartbeat)* irregular **(c)** *Geol* **e. block** *or* **boulder** bloque errático

2 *n Geol* bloque *m* errático

erratically [ɪ'rætɪklɪ] *adv (to act, behave)* de manera errática, de forma imprevisible; *(to move)* erráticamente; **to play e.** *(sportsman, musician)* de manera irregular

erratum [e'rɑːtəm] (*pl* **errata** [e'rɑːtə]) *n Typ (mistake)* errata *f*; **errata** *(list)* fe de erratas ►► ***errata slip*** fe *f* de erratas *(en una hoja suelta)*

erring ['ɜːrɪŋ] *adj (husband, wife)* infiel; **his e. ways** sus devaneos

erroneous [ɪ'rəʊnɪəs] *adj* erróneo(a)

erroneously [ɪ'rəʊnɪəslɪ] *adv* erróneamente

error ['erə(r)] *n* **(a)** *(mistake)* error *m*; **to make** *or* **commit an e.** cometer un error, equivocarse; **an e. of judgement** un error de juicio
(b) *(mistakenness)* **in e.** por error, por equivocación; **to be in e.** *(be wrong)* estar en un error; *(have made a mistake)* haber cometido un error; **to see the e. of one's ways** darse cuenta de los propios errores
(c) *Comptr* ***e. code*** código *m* de error; ***e. message*** mensaje *m* de error

ersatz ['ɜːzæts] *adj* sucedáneo(a) ►► ***e. coffee*** sucedáneo *m* del café

Erse [ɜːs] *n* gaélico *m* irlandés

erstwhile ['ɜːstwaɪl] *adj Literary* antiguo(a), de otros tiempos

erudite ['erjʊdaɪt] *adj Formal* erudito(a)

eruditely ['erjʊdaɪtlɪ] *adv Formal* eruditamente

erudition [erjʊ'dɪʃən] *n Formal* erudición *f*

erupt [ɪ'rʌpt] *vi* **(a)** *(volcano)* entrar en erupción
(b) *(break out) (violence, war)* estallar; **the city erupted into violence** la ciudad estalló en violencia
(c) *(make an outburst)* **the stadium erupted when they scored** el estadio se vino abajo cuando marcaron; **he erupted when I told him the news** montó en cólera cuando le dije la noticia; **to e. with laughter** estallar en carcajadas
(d) *(pimples)* hacer erupción, salir; **her face erupted in spots** su cara se cubrió de una erupción de granos
(e) *(tooth)* romper, salir

eruption [ɪ'rʌpʃən] *n* **(a)** *(of volcano)* erupción *f* **(b)** *(of violence, war)* estallido *m*, explosión *f* **(c)** *(outburst)* estallido *m*, explosión *f* **(d)** *(of pimples)* erupción *f*

erysipelas [erɪ'sɪpɪləs] *n Med* erisipela *f*

erythema [erɪ'θiːmə] *n Med* eritema *m*

erythrocyte [ɪ'rɪθrəsaɪt] *n Physiol* eritrocito *m*, hematíe *m*

esc *Comptr* (*abbr* **escape**) Esc ►► ***e. key*** tecla *f* Esc

escalate ['eskəleɪt] **1** *vt (conflict, tension)* intensificar, provocar una escalada de; *(demands)* aumentar, incrementar
2 *vi* **(a)** *(prices)* aumentar; **escalating costs/prices** costos *or Esp* costes/precios cada vez más altos *or* en constante aumento **(b)** *(conflict)* intensificarse; **the conflict may e.** puede intensificarse el conflicto, puede producirse una escalada del conflicto; **to e. into...** convertirse en...

escalation [eskə'leɪʃən] *n* **(a)** *(of prices)* escalada *f*; *(of demands)* aumento *m* ►► *Com* ***e. clause*** *(for wages)* cláusula *f* de escala móvil; *(for prices)* cláusula *f* de revisión de precios **(b)** *(of conflict)* escalada *f*

escalator ['eskəleɪtə(r)] *n* **(a)** *(moving stairs)* escalera *f* mecánica **(b)** *Com* ***e. clause*** *(for wages)* cláusula *f* de escala móvil; *(for prices)* cláusula *f* de revisión de precios

> **False friend:** The Spanish noun **escalador** is not a translation for the English word **escalator**. In Spanish **escalador** means "climber".

escalope ['eskəlɒp] *n Culin* escalope *m*

escapade ['eskəpeɪd] *n* aventura *f*, correría *f*

> **False friend:** The Spanish noun **escapada** is not a translation for the English word **escapade**. In Spanish **escapada** means "escape" or "quick trip".

escape [ɪs'keɪp] **1** *n* **(a)** *(from captivity) (of person)* huida *f*, evasión *f*; *(of prisoner)* fuga *f*, evasión *f*; *(of animal)* huida *f*; **to make one's e.** escapar(se), huir ►► *Com* ***e. clause*** cláusula *f* de escape *or* de salvaguardia; ***e. hatch*** escotilla *f* de escape; ***e. road*** vía *f* de escape, zona *f* de frenado de emergencia; ***e. route*** *(from fire)* vía *f* de salida (de emergencia); *(of criminal)* vía *f* de escape; ***e. velocity*** velocidad *f* de escape
(b) *(from danger, death)* **he had a narrow** *or* **lucky e.** se salvó por poco; **a means of e. from poverty** un medio para salir de la pobreza
(c) *(diversion)* evasión *f*; **an e. from reality** una evasión de la realidad; **the cinema provided an e. from their daily routine** el cine les servía para evadirse de la monotonía cotidiana
(d) *(of gas, liquid)* escape *m* ►► *also Fig* ***e. valve*** válvula *f* de escape
(e) *Comptr* escape *m* ►► ***e. key*** tecla *f* de escape
2 *vt* **(a)** *(avoid) (danger, punishment, death)* escapar(se) de, librarse de; **to e. doing sth** librarse de hacer algo; **there's no escaping the fact that...** no se puede negar (el hecho de) que...
(b) *(elude)* **nothing escapes them** no se les escapa ni una; **to e. sb's notice** pasar inadvertido(a) a alguien; **this problem escaped detection** este problema pasó inadvertido, este problema no fue detectado; **her name escapes me** ahora no me sale su nombre
3 *vi* **(a)** *(flee)* escapar(se) **(from** de); **he escaped to Italy** (se) escapó a Italia; **to e. from reality** evadirse de la realidad
(b) *(from accident)* **she escaped uninjured** escapó *or* salió ilesa; **they escaped with a few bruises** salieron con unos cuantos cardenales
(c) *(gas, fluid)* escaparse **(from** de)
(d) *Comptr* salir

escaped [ɪ'skeɪpt] *adj (prisoner)* fugado(a); *(animal)* escapado(a)

escapee [eskeɪ'piː] *n* fugitivo(a) *m,f*

escapement [ɪ'skeɪpmənt] *n (of clock, piano)* escape *m*

escapism [ɪs'keɪpɪzəm] *n* escapismo *m*, evasión *f* de la realidad

escapist [ɪs'keɪpɪst] **1** *n* fantasioso(a) *m,f*
2 *adj* de evasión

escapologist [eskə'pɒlədʒɪst] *n* escapista *mf*

escapology [eskə'pɒlədʒɪ] *n* escapismo *m*

escarpment [ɪs'kɑːpmənt] *n* escarpa *f*, escarpadura *f*

eschatological [eskætə'lɒdʒɪkəl] *adj Rel* escatológico(a)

eschatology [eskə'tɒlədʒɪ] *n Rel* escatología *f*

eschew [ɪs'tʃuː] *vt Formal* evitar, rehuir

escort **1** *n* ['eskɔːt] **(a)** *(guard)* escolta *f*; **under e.** escoltado(a); **under armed e.** escoltado(a) por hombres armados ►► *Mil* ***e. duty*** servicio *m* de escolta **(b)** *(for convoy)* escolta *f* **(c)** *(male companion at social event)* acompañante *m* **(d)** *(hired companion) (female)* señorita *f* de compañía; *(male)* acompañante *m* ►► ***e. agency*** agencia *f* de acompañantes
2 *vt* [ɪs'kɔːt] **(a)** *(prisoner, VIP)* escoltar **(b)** *(convoy)* escoltar **(c)** *(conduct)* **to e. sb off the premises** conducir a alguien fuera del local; **kindly e. these gentlemen to the door** sírvase acompañar *or* conducir a estos señores a la puerta **(d)** *(at social event)* acompañar

escritoire [eskrɪ'twɑː(r)] *n* buró *m*, escritorio *m*

escrow ['eskrəʊ] *n Law* plica *f*; **in e.** en fideicomiso ►► ***e. account*** cuenta *f* de depósito en garantía

escudo [ɪ'skuːdəʊ] (*pl* **escudos**) *n Formerly* escudo *m*

escutcheon [ɪs'kʌtʃən] *n (shield)* escudo *m* de armas, blasón *m*

ESE (*abbr* **east-south-east**) ESE

Eskimo ['eskɪməʊ] (*pl* **Eskimos**) **1** *n* esquimal *mf*
2 *adj* esquimal ►► ***E. roll*** *(in canoeing)* = maniobra para darle la vuelta a una piragua que ha volcado sin salirse de ella; ***E. whimbrel*** *(bird)* zarapito *m* esquimal

ESL [iːes'el] *n* (*abbr* **English as a Second Language**) = inglés como segunda lengua

ESOP [iːesəʊ'piː] *n* (*abbr* **employee** *Br* **share** *or US* **stock ownership plan**) plan *m* de oferta de acciones a los empleados

esophagus *US* = **oesophagus**

esoteric [esəʊ'terɪk] *adj* esotérico(a)

ESP [iːes'piː] *n* **(a)** (*abbr* **extrasensory perception**) percepción *f* extrasensorial **(b)** (*abbr* **English for special purposes**) inglés *m* para fines específicos

esp (*abbr* **especially**) especialmente

espadrille ['espədrɪl] *n* alpargata *f*, zapatilla *f* de esparto

esparto [ɪ'spɑːtəʊ] *n* **e. (grass)** esparto *m*

especial [ɪs'peʃəl] *adj Formal* especial, singular

especially [ɪs'peʃəlɪ] *adv* **(a)** *(particularly, more than normal)* especialmente, particularmente; **we were e. lucky with the weather** tuvimos especial suerte con el tiempo; **be e. careful with this one** ten especial cuidado con éste; **I wasn't e. interested in the movie** no tenía especial *or* particular interés por la película; **it's very hot, e. in August** hace mucho calor, sobre todo *or* especialmente en agosto
(b) *(for a particular purpose)* especialmente; **he went e. to meet her** fue especialmente *or* expresamente para conocerla

Esperanto [espə'ræntəʊ] *n* esperanto *m*

espionage ['espɪənɑːʒ] *n* espionaje *m*

esplanade [esplə'neɪd] *n* paseo *m* marítimo

espousal [ɪ'spaʊzəl] *n Formal (of belief, cause)* adhesión *f* (**of** a)

espouse [ɪs'paʊz] *vt* patrocinar

espresso [es'presəʊ], **expresso** [e(k)s'presəʊ] (*pl* **espressos, expressos**) *n* café *m* exprés, *Esp* café *m* solo, *Am* café *m* negro ►► ***e. machine*** cafetera *f* exprés

esprit de corps [e'spriːdə'kɔː(r)] *n* espíritu *m* de grupo *or* cuerpo

espy [ɪ'spaɪ] *vt Literary* divisar

Esq (*abbr* **Esquire**) **Derek Wilson, E.** (Sr.) D. Derek Wilson

Esquire [ɪ'skwaɪə(r)] *n* **Derek Wilson, E.** (Sr.) D. Derek Wilson

essay ['eseɪ] **1** *n* **(a)** *(at school)* redacción *f*; *(at university)* trabajo *m* **(b)** *(literary)* ensayo *m* **(c)** *Formal (attempt)* tentativa *f*
2 *vt Formal (attempt)* intentar; **to e. a smile** tratar de *or* intentar esbozar una sonrisa

essayist ['eseɪɪst] *n* ensayista *mf*

essence ['esəns] *n* **(a)** *(most important part or quality)* esencia *f*; **the e. of her speech was that...** la esencia de su discurso era que...; **in e.** esencialmente, en esencia; **the very e. of...** la más pura esencia de...; **time is of the e.** no hay tiempo que perder **(b)** *Culin* esencia *f*; **coffee/vanilla e.** esencia de café/vainilla **(c)** *Phil* esencia *f*

essential [ɪ'senʃəl] **1** *n* **(a)** *(vital item, ingredient)* **when camping a good sleeping bag is an e.** cuando vas de camping, un buen saco de dormir es imprescindible; **just pack a few essentials** prepara sólo lo imprescindible
(b) essentials *(basic foodstuffs)* productos primarios *or* de primera necesidad; *(basic issues)* cuestiones básicas; *(basic principles)* nociones básicas, principios básicos; **in (all) essentials** en lo esencial
2 *adj* **(a)** *(basic)* esencial, básico(a) ►► ***e. oil*** aceite *m* esencial
(b) *(indispensable)* esencial, fundamental; **the e. thing** lo esencial; **good rapport is e. to success in teaching** una buena relación de comunicación es esencial *or* imprescindible para enseñar con éxito; **a balanced diet is e. for good health** una dieta equilibrada es esencial para mantener una buena salud; **it is e. that...** es esencial *or* fundamental que...

essentially [ɪ'senʃəlɪ] *adv* esencialmente, fundamentalmente; **e., it's a question of having enough money** fundamentalmente, se trata de disponer del dinero suficiente; **e., nothing has changed** en esencia, no ha cambiado nada

EST [i:es'ti:] *n US* (*abbr* **Eastern Standard Time**) = hora oficial de la costa este de los Estados Unidos

est **(a)** (*abbr* **established**) fundado(a); **Jones & Son, Butchers (e. 1879)** Carnicería Jones e hijos, fundada en 1879 **(b)** (*abbr* **estimated**) aprox.

establish [ɪs'tæblɪʃ] *vt* **(a)** *(set up, create) (business)* constituir; *(precedent)* sentar, crear; *(order, peace)* establecer, imponer; **to e. a reputation** crearse *or* labrarse una reputación; **to e. oneself in business** establecerse en el mundo de los negocios; **to e. contact with sb** entrar en *or* establecer contacto con alguien; **she has established a 6 percent lead in the polls** ha establecido una ventaja del 6 por ciento sobre sus oponentes en las encuestas
(b) *(confirm) (authority, power)* consolidar; **the movie established her as an important director** la película la consagró como una gran directora; **they established their right to vote** establecieron su derecho al voto
(c) *(prove, determine) (fact, cause)* determinar, establecer; **to e. sb's innocence/guilt** demostrar la inocencia/culpabilidad de alguien; **the police have been unable to e. a link between the two murders** la policía no ha conseguido establecer una conexión entre los dos asesinatos

established [ɪs'tæblɪʃt] *adj* **(a)** *(existing) (custom, practice)* establecido(a); **the e. order** el orden establecido **(b)** *(confirmed, successful) (reputation)* consolidado(a); *(author, star)* consagrado(a) **(c)** *(proven) (fact)* probado(a) **(d) the e. Church** la iglesia oficial

establishing shot [ɪs'tæblɪʃɪŋ'ʃɒt] *n TV & Cin* plano *m* general *or* de situación

establishment [ɪs'tæblɪʃmənt] *n* **(a)** *(founding, creation) (of company)* fundación *f*; *(of reputation)* establecimiento *m*
(b) *(of fact)* determinación *f*
(c) the E. *(established order)* el sistema, el orden establecido; *(ruling class)* la clase dirigente; **the financial/political E.** la clase dirigente económica/política
(d) *(institution)* centro *m*; *(hotel, restaurant)* establecimiento *m*
(e) *Formal (staff)* **to be on the e.** estar en plantilla
(f) *Mil* **peacetime e.** personal en tiempos de paz

estate [ɪs'teɪt] *n* **(a)** *(land)* finca *f*; **her country e.** su finca en el campo ►► *Br* ***e. agency, e. agent's*** inmobiliaria *f*, agencia *f* inmobiliaria; *Br* ***e. agent*** agente *mf* de la propiedad (inmobiliario(a))
(b) *Br (development)* **(housing) e.** urbanización *f*; **(industrial) e.** parque *m or* polígono *m* industrial
(c) *Law (of deceased person)* herencia *f* ►► *Br* ***e. duty*** impuesto *m* sobre sucesiones; *US* ***e. tax*** impuesto *m* sobre sucesiones
(d) *Br* **e. (car)** ranchera *f*, *Esp* coche *m* familiar
(e) *Formal (state, position)* **men of low/high e.** hombres de estrato social bajo/alto; **the e. of matrimony** el estado del matrimonio
(f) *Pol* estamento *m*; **the three estates** los tres estamentos

estate-bottled [ɪs'teɪt'bɒtəld] *adj (wine)* embotellado(a) en origen

estd., est'd. (*abbr* **established**) fundado(a)

esteem [ɪs'ti:m] **1** *n* estima *f*; **to hold sth/sb in high/low e.** tener algo/a alguien en gran/poca estima; **to go down/up in sb's e.** perder/ganar puntos con alguien
2 *vt* **(a)** *(respect)* apreciar **(b)** *Formal (consider)* **to e. it an honour that...** considerar un honor que...

esteemed [ɪs'ti:md] *adj Formal* estimado(a)

ester ['estə(r)] *n Chem* éster *m*

esthete, esthetic *etc US* = **aesthete, aesthetic** *etc*

estimable ['estɪməbəl] *adj Formal* estimable

estimate **1** *n* ['estɪmət] **(a)** *(calculation)* estimación *f*, cálculo *m* aproximado; **give me an e. of how much it will cost/how long it will take** dime aproximadamente cuánto va a costar/cuánto va a tardar; **at a rough e.** aproximadamente **(b)** *Com (quote)* presupuesto *m*
2 *vt* ['estɪmeɪt] **(a)** *(calculate)* estimar **(at** en); **the cost was estimated at £2,000** calcularon *or* estimaron que el costo *or Esp* coste sería de dos mil libras esterlinas; **I e. (that) it will take at least five years** calculo que llevará al menos cinco años **(b)** *(judge)* estimar

estimated ['estɪmeɪtɪd] *adj (cost, value)* estimado(a), aproximado(a); **an e. 50,000 people attended the demonstration** se calcula *or* se estima que 50.000 personas asistieron a la manifestación; **e. time of arrival** hora aproximada *or* prevista de llegada

estimation [estɪ'meɪʃən] *n* **(a)** *(calculation)* cálculo *m*, estimación *f* **(b)** *(judgement)* juicio *m*, opinión *f*; **in my e.** a mi juicio **(c)** *(esteem)* **she has gone up/down in my e.** ahora la tengo en más/menos estima

Estonia [es'təʊnɪə] *n* Estonia

Estonian [es'təʊnɪən] **1** *n* **(a)** *(person)* estonio(a) *m,f* **(b)** *(language)* estonio *m*
2 *adj* estonio(a)

estrange [ɪ'streɪndʒ] *vt* distanciar, alejar

estranged [ɪs'treɪndʒd] *adj* **his e. wife** su mujer, con la que ya no vive; **an e. couple** una pareja separada; **to be e. (from)** estar separado(a) (de)

estrangement [ɪs'treɪndʒmənt] *n* separación *f*

estrogen *US* = **oestrogen**

estrus *US* = **oestrus**

estuary ['estjʊərɪ] *n* estuario *m* ►► ***E. English*** = inglés con un acento sin connotaciones de clase, hablado por la gente joven en el sureste de Inglaterra

ET [i:'ti:] *n* (*abbr* **extraterrestrial**) extraterrestre

ETA [i:ti:'eɪ] *n* (*abbr* **estimated time of arrival**) hora *f* aproximada *or* prevista de llegada

e-tailer ['i:teɪlə(r)] *n* tienda *f* digital

e-tailing ['i:teɪlɪŋ] *n* venta *f* digital

et al [et'æl] (*abbr* **et alii**) et al.

etc (*abbr* **et cetera**) etc.

et cetera [ɪt'setərə] *adv* etcétera

etch [etʃ] *vt* grabar (al aguafuerte); *Fig* **the scene was etched on his memory** tenía la escena grabada en la memoria

etching ['etʃɪŋ] *n* **(a)** *(print)* (grabado *m* al) aguafuerte *m*; *Hum* **come up and see my etchings** ven a ver mi colección de sellos **(b)** *(technique)* grabado *m* (al aguafuerte)

ETD [i:ti:'di:] *n* (*abbr* **estimated time of departure**) hora *f* aproximada *or* prevista de salida

eternal [ɪ'tɜ:nəl] *adj* **(a)** *(everlasting)* eterno(a); **to my e. shame** para mi infinita vergüenza *or Andes, CAm, Carib, Méx* pena ►► ***the E. City*** la Ciudad Eterna; ***e. rest*** sueño *m* eterno **(b)** *(perpetual) (problem)* eterno(a); *(discussions, complaints)* constante ►► ***the e. triangle*** el triángulo amoroso

eternally [ɪ'tɜ:nəlɪ] *adv* **(a)** *(forever)* eternamente; **I shall be e. grateful to you** te estaré eternamente agradecido(a) **(b)** *(perpetually)* constantemente; **they were e. complaining about the weather** se pasaban todo el día quejándose del tiempo

eternity [ɪ'tɜ:nɪtɪ] *n* eternidad *f*; *Fam* **I waited an e.** esperé una eternidad ►► ***e. ring*** alianza *f*

ethane ['i:θeɪn] *n Chem* etano *m*

ethanol ['eθənɒl] *n Chem* etanol *m*

ethene ['eθi:n] *n Chem* etileno *m*, eteno *m*

ether ['i:θə(r)] *n* **(a)** *(chemical)* éter *m* **(b)** *Literary (sky)* **the e.** el éter **(c) over** *or* **through the e.** *(by radio)* por el éter

ethereal [ɪ'θɪərɪəl] *adj* etéreo(a)

Ethernet® ['i:θənet] *n Comptr* Ethernet® *f*

ethic ['eθɪk] *n* ética *f*, moral *f*

ethical ['eθɪkəl] *adj* ético(a) ►► *Com* ***e. audit*** auditoría *f* ética; *Fin* ***e. fund*** fondo *m* ético; *Fin* ***e. investment*** inversiones *fpl* éticas

ethically ['eθɪklɪ] *adv* éticamente

ethics ['eθɪks] **1** *n Phil* ética *f*
2 *npl (principles, morality)* ética *f*

Ethiopia [i:θɪ'əʊpɪə] *n* Etiopía

Ethiopian [i:θɪ'əʊpɪən] **1** *n* etíope *mf*
2 *adj* etíope

ethmoid bone ['eθmɔɪdbəʊn] *n Anat* etmoides *m inv*

ethnic ['eθnɪk] **1** *adj* **(a)** *(of race)* étnico(a); **the threat of e. unrest** la amenaza de disturbios étnicos ►► ***e. cleansing*** limpieza *f* étnica; ***e. minority*** minoría *f* étnica; ***e. origin*** origen *m* étnico **(b)** *(exotic) (music, clothes)* étnico(a); *(food, furniture)* exótico(a)
2 *n US* miembro *m* de la minoría étnica

ethnically ['eθnɪklɪ] *adv* étnicamente; **an e. mixed** *or* **diverse region** una región de diversidad étnica

ethnicity ['eθnɪsɪtɪ] *n* etnicidad *f*

ethnocentric [eθnəʊ'sentrɪk] *adj* etnocéntrico(a)

ethnocentrism ['eθnəʊ'sentrɪzəm] *n* etnocentrismo *m*

ethnographer [eθ'nɒgrəfə(r)] *n* etnógrafo(a) *m,f*

ethnographic [eθnə'græfɪk] *adj* etnográfico(a)

ethnography [eθ'nɒgrəfɪ] *n* etnografía *f*

ethnologist [eθ'nɒlədʒɪst] *n* etnólogo(a) *m,f*

ethnology [eθ'nɒlədʒɪ] *n* etnología *f*

ethology [ɪ'θɒlədʒɪ] *n* etología *f*

ethos ['i:θɒs] *n* espíritu *m*, valores *mpl* (morales)

ethyl ['eθɪl] *n Chem* etilo *m* ►► ***e. alcohol*** alcohol *m* etílico

ethylene ['eθɪli:n] *n Chem* etileno *m* ►► ***e. glycol*** etilenglicol *m*

e-ticket ['i:'tɪkɪt] *n Esp* billete *m or Am* boleto *m or Am* pasaje *m* electrónico

etiolated ['i:tɪəleɪtɪd] *adj* **(a)** *Bot* con etiolación **(b)** *Formal* demacrado(a)

etiology *US* = **aetiology**

etiquette ['etɪket] *n* etiqueta *f*, protocolo *m*; **professional e.** ética profesional

Etna ['etnə] *n* **(Mount) E.** el Etna

Eton ['i:tən] *n* **E. (College)** = centro privado de enseñanza secundaria de larga tradición en Inglaterra ►► ***E. crop*** corte *m* de pelo a lo garçon

Etonian [ɪ'təʊnɪən] **1** *n* alumno *m* de la escuela privada de Eton
2 *adj* de la escuela privada de Eton

Etruscan [ɪ'trʌskən] **1** *n* **(a)** *(person)* etrusco(a) *m,f* **(b)** *(language)* etrusco *m*
2 *adj* etrusco(a)

etymological [etɪmə'lɒdʒɪkəl] *adj* etimológico(a)

etymologist [etɪ'mɒlədʒɪst] *n* etimólogo(a) *m,f*

etymology [etɪ'mɒlədʒɪ] *n* etimología *f*

EU [i:'ju:] *n* (*abbr* **European Union**) UE *f*

eucalyptus [ju:kə'lɪptəs] *n* eucalipto *m* ►► ***e. oil*** aceite *m* de eucalipto

Eucharist ['ju:kərɪst] *n* **the E.** la Eucaristía

euchre ['ju:kə(r)] *US* **1** *n* = juego de veinticuatro o treinta y dos cartas parecido al whist
2 *vt Fam (cheat)* timar

Euclid ['ju:klɪd] *pr n* Euclides

Euclidean [ju:'klɪdɪən] *adj Geom* euclidiano(a)

eugenic [ju:'dʒenɪk] *adj* eugenésico(a)

eugenics [ju:'dʒenɪks] *n* eugenesia *f*

eukaryotic [ju:kærɪ'ɒtɪk] *adj Biol* eucariótico(a)

eulogist ['ju:lədʒɪst] *n* panegirista *mf*

eulogistic [ju:lə'dʒɪstɪk] *adj* panegírico(a), laudatorio(a)

eulogize ['ju:lədʒaɪz] *vt Formal* loar, alabar

eulogy ['ju:lədʒɪ] *n* panegírico *m*

eunuch ['ju:nək] *n* eunuco *m*

euphemism ['ju:fəmɪzəm] *n* eufemismo *m*

euphemistic [ju:fə'mɪstɪk] *adj* eufemístico(a)

euphemistically [ju:fə'mɪstɪklɪ] *adv* de manera eufemística, eufemísticamente; **e. known as...** conocido(a) con el eufemismo...

euphonious [ju:'fəʊnɪəs] *adj Formal* eufónico(a), armonioso(a)

euphonium [ju:'fəʊnɪəm] *n* bombardino *m*

euphony ['ju:fənɪ] *n* eufonía *f*

euphoria [ju:'fɔ:rɪə] *n* euforia *f*

euphoric [ju:'fɔ:rɪk] *adj* eufórico(a); **to be e.** estar eufórico(a)

Euphrates [ju:'freɪti:z] *pr n* **the E.** el Éufrates

Eurasia [jʊə'reɪʒə] *n* Eurasia *f*

Eurasian [jʊə'reɪʒən] **1** *n* eur(o)asiático(a) *m,f*
2 *adj* eur(o)asiático(a)

EURATOM [jʊə'rætəm] *n* (*abbr* **European Atomic Energy Community**) EURATOM *f*

eureka [jʊə'ri:kə] *exclam* ¡eureka!

eurhythmics, *US* **eurythmics** [ju:'rɪðmɪks] *n* euritmia *f*

Euribor ['jʊərɪbɔ:(r)] *n Fin* (*abbr* **Euro Inter-Bank Offered Rate**) Euribor *m*

Euripides [jʊ'rɪpɪdi:z] *pr n* Eurípides

euro ['jʊəreʊ] (*pl* **euros**) *n (European currency)* euro *m*; **the e. area** *or* **zone** la zona (del) euro

Euro- ['jʊərəʊ] *prefix* euro-

Eurobond ['jʊərəʊbɒnd] *n* eurobono *m*

Eurocentric [jʊərəʊ'sentrɪk] *adj* eurocéntrico(a)

Eurocheque ['jʊərəʊtʃek] *n Br Fin* eurocheque *m*

Eurocommunism ['jʊərəʊ'kɒmjʊnɪzəm] *n* eurocomunismo *m*

Eurocommunist ['jʊərəʊ'kɒmjʊnɪst] **1** *n* eurocomunista *mf*
2 *adj* eurocomunista

Eurocrat ['jʊərəkræt] *n* eurócrata *mf*

eurocurrency ['jʊərəʊkʌrənsɪ] *n* eurodivisa *f*

Eurodollar ['jʊərəʊdɒlə(r)] *n Fin* eurodólar *m*

Euro-election ['jʊərəʊɪ'lekʃən] *n* **the Euro-elections** las euroelecciones

Euroland ['jʊərəʊlænd] *n Fam* zona *f* (del) euro, Eurolandia

Euromarket ['jʊərəʊmɑ:kɪt] *n Fin* euromercado *m*

Euro-MP ['jʊərəʊem'pi:] *n* eurodiputado(a) *m,f*

Europa [jʊ'rəʊpə] *n Mythol* Europa

Europe ['jʊərəp] *n* **(a)** *(continent)* Europa **(b)** *Br (the EU)* la Unión Europea; **Britain went into E. in 1973** Gran Bretaña entró en la Comunidad Europea en 1973

European [jʊərə'pi:ən] **1** *n* europeo(a) *m,f*
2 *adj* europeo(a) ►► ***E. arrest warrant*** orden *f* de detención europea; *Fin* ***E. Bank for Reconstruction and Development*** Banco *m* Europeo de Reconstrucción y Desarrollo; ***E. capital of culture*** capital *f* europea de la cultura; ***E. Central Bank*** Banco *m* Central Europeo; *EU* ***E. Commission*** Comisión *f* Europea; *EU* ***E. Commissioner*** comisario(a) *m,f* europeo(a); *EU* ***E. Community*** Comunidad *f* Europea; ***E. Court of Human Rights*** Tribunal *m* Europeo de Derechos Humanos; ***E. Court of Justice*** Tribunal *m* de Justicia Europeo; ***the E. Cup*** *(in soccer)* la Copa de Europa; ***the E. Cup Winners Cup*** *(in soccer)* la Recopa de Europa; ***E. Free Trade Association*** Asociación *f* Europea de Libre Comercio; *EU* ***E. Parliament*** Parlamento *m* Europeo; *US* ***E. plan:*** **on the E. plan** por habitación sólo; *EU* ***E. Regional Development Fund*** Fondo *m* Europeo de Desarrollo Regional; *EU* ***E. Social Fund*** Fondo *m* Social Europeo; ***E. Space Agency*** Agencia *f* Espacial Europea; *EU* ***E. Union*** Unión *f* Europea

Europeanism [jʊərə'pi:ənɪzəm] *n* europeísmo *m*

Europeanization [jʊərəpi:ənaɪ'zeɪʃən] *n* europeización *f*

Europeanize [jʊərə'pi:ənaɪz] *vt* europeizar

Europhile ['jʊərəʊfaɪl] **1** *n* europeísta *mf*
2 *adj* europeísta

Europhobe ['jʊərəfəʊb] **1** *n* antieuropeísta *mf*
2 *adj* antieuropeísta

europium [jʊ'rəʊpɪəm] *n Chem* europio *m*

Europol ['jʊərəʊpɒl] *n* (*abbr* **European Police**) Europol *f*

Euro-rebel ['jʊərəʊ'rebəl] *n Br* disidente *mf* en materia de europeísmo

Eurosceptic ['jʊərəʊ'skeptɪk] *Br* **1** *n* euroescéptico(a) *m,f*
2 *adj* euroescéptico(a)

Euroscepticism ['jʊərəʊ'skeptɪsɪzəm] *n Br* euroescepticismo *m*

Eurospeak ['jʊərəʊspi:k] *n Fam* jerga *f* burocrática europea, jerga *f* comunitaria

Eurostar® ['jʊərəʊstɑ:(r)] *n* Euroestar® *m*

Eurotunnel® ['jʊərəʊtʌnəl] *n* eurotúnel® *m*

Eurovision ['jʊərəʊvɪʒən] *n* Eurovisión *f* ►► ***the E. song contest*** el Festival de Eurovisión

eurythmics *US* = **eurhythmics**

Eustachian tube [ju:'steɪʃən'tju:b] *n Anat* trompa *f* de Eustaquio

euthanasia [ju:θə'neɪzɪə] *n* eutanasia *f*

eutrophication [ju:trɒfɪ'keɪʃən] *n Biol* eutrofización *f*

evacuate [ɪ'vækjʊeɪt] *vt* (**a**) *(people)* evacuar; **children were evacuated to the countryside** los niños fueron evacuados al campo (**b**) *(building, area)* evacuar, desalojar (**c**) *Formal* **to e. the bowels** evacuar

evacuation [ɪvækjʊ'eɪʃən] *n* (**a**) *(of people)* evacuación *f* (**b**) *(of building, area)* evacuación *f*, desalojo *m* (**c**) *Formal (of bowels)* evacuación *f*

evacuee [ɪvækjʊ'i:] *n* evacuado(a) *m,f*

evade [ɪ'veɪd] *vt* (**a**) *(escape from) (pursuer)* burlar (**b**) *(avoid) (blow)* esquivar; *(question)* eludir; **he has so far evaded arrest/detection** hasta el momento, ha eludido ser detenido/descubierto; **she evaded her responsibilities** rehuyó sus responsabilidades; **success still evades him** el éxito aún le da la espalda; **to e. the issue** evitar el tema (**c**) *(tax)* **to e. tax** evadir impuestos

evader [ɪ'veɪdə(r)] *n* **tax e.** evasor(ora) fiscal

evaluate [ɪ'væljʊeɪt] *vt* (**a**) *(damages, worth)* evaluar (**b**) *(situation, evidence, reasons)* evaluar, analizar

evaluation [ɪvæljʊ'eɪʃən] *n* (**a**) *(of damages, worth)* evaluación *f* (**b**) *(of situation, evidence, reasons)* evaluación *f*, análisis *m inv*

evaluative [ɪ'væljʊətɪv] *adj* evaluador(ora), valorativo(a)

evanescence [evə'nesəns] *n Literary* evanescencia *f*

evanescent [evə'nesənt] *adj Literary* evanescente, efímero(a)

evangelical [i:væn'dʒelɪkəl] **1** *n Rel* evangélico(a) *m,f*
2 *adj* (**a**) *Rel* evangélico(a) (**b**) *(eager to persuade)* **an e. communist** un(a) comunista que siempre está predicando

evangelism [ɪ'vændʒəlɪzəm] *n* evangelismo *m*

evangelist [ɪ'vændʒəlɪst] *n* (**a**) *(gospel writer)* evangelista *mf* (**b**) *(preacher)* predicador(ora) *m,f* (**c**) *(fervent advocate)* **he was an e. for the new business methods** predicó las bondades de los nuevos métodos empresariales

evangelize [ɪ'vændʒəlaɪz] **1** *vt Rel* evangelizar, predicar el evangelio
2 *vi* (**a**) *Rel* evangelizar, predicar el evangelio (**b**) *(advocate fervently)* predicar; **he has been evangelizing about jazz for years** lleva años predicando las bondades del jazz

evaporate [ɪ'væpəreɪt] **1** *vt* evaporar; **evaporated milk** leche evaporada
2 *vi* (**a**) *(liquid)* evaporarse (**b**) *(enthusiasm, doubts, fears, opposition)* evaporarse, desvanecerse

evaporation [ɪvæpə'reɪʃən] *n* (**a**) *(of liquid)* evaporación *f* (**b**) *(of enthusiasm, doubts, fears, opposition)* desvanecimiento *m*

evasion [ɪ'veɪʒən] *n* (**a**) *(escape) (from pursuer)* evasión *f* (**b**) *(avoidance) (of question)* evasión *f*; *(of responsibility)* evasión *f*, negligencia *f* (**c**) *(evasive statement)* evasiva *f*; **I was met with the usual evasions** me dieron las evasivas de costumbre (**d**) *(of tax)* **(tax) e.** evasión *f* fiscal *or* de impuestos

evasive [ɪ'veɪsɪv] *adj* (**a**) *(person, reply)* evasivo(a); **to be e. (about sth)** andarse *or* venir con evasivas (con respecto a algo) (**b**) *Mil* **to take e. action** maniobrar para evitar el enfrentamiento; *Fig* quitarse *or Andes, RP* sacarse de en medio

evasively [ɪ'veɪsɪvlɪ] *adv* con evasivas

evasiveness [ɪ'veɪsɪvnɪs] *n* actitud *f* evasiva

Eve [i:v] *pr n* Eva

eve [i:v] *n* (**a**) *(day before)* víspera *f*; **on the e. of...** (en) la víspera de..., en vísperas de... (**b**) *Archaic or Literary (evening)* crepúsculo *m*

EVEN[1] ['i:vən] **1** *adj* (**a**) *(flat) (surface)* llano(a), liso(a); **the surface isn't very e.** la superficie no está nivelada; IDIOM **to put sth back on an e. keel** restablecer el equilibrio de algo
(**b**) *(regular) (breathing, pace)* regular, constante; *(temperature)* constante; *(coating)* uniforme; *(voice, tone)* mesurado(a); **to have an e. temper** tener un carácter pacífico
(**c**) *(equal) (contest)* igualado(a); **the scores are e.** los marcadores están igualados; **an e. distribution of wealth** una distribución equitativa de la riqueza; **to have an e. chance (of doing sth)** tener un cincuenta por ciento de posibilidades (de hacer algo); *Fig* **we're e. now** (ahora) estamos en paz *or RP* a mano; *Fig* **to get e. with sb** *(take revenge on)* vengarse *or* desquitarse de alguien; **it's e. money whether... or...** tan posible es que... como que...
(**d**) *(exactly divisible by 2)* **e. number** número par
2 *adv (for emphasis)* incluso, aún; **e. bigger/more interesting** aún *or* incluso mayor/más interesante; **e. my dad agreed** hasta mi padre estuvo de acuerdo; **it could be described as foolish, e. absurd** se podría describir como tonto, hasta absurdo; **he seemed shy, surly e.** parecía tímido, incluso arisco *or RP* chúcaro; **it would be unwise to e. consider the offer** no sería aconsejable ni plantearse siquiera la oferta; *Fam* **don't e. think about it!** ¡ni lo pienses!, ¡ni se te ocurra!; **I never e. saw it** ni siquiera llegué a verlo; **not e.** ni siquiera; **without e. speaking** sin (tan) siquiera hablar
3 *vt* (**a**) *(surface)* allanar, nivelar
(**b**) *(make equal)* igualar, equilibrar; **in order to e. the odds their team had an extra player** con el objeto de igualar el encuentro, su equipo tenía un jugador más; **to e. the score** igualar el marcador
4 even as *conj* **e. as I speak** justo a la vez que estoy hablando, incluso mientras estoy hablando; **e. as she said it, she realized she was wrong** conforme *or* mientras lo decía, se daba cuenta de que estaba equivocada
5 even if *conj* aunque; **e. if what you say is true** aunque sea verdad lo que dices, aun siendo verdad lo que dices; **e. if you run you'll be late** aunque corras llegarás tarde
6 even now *adv* incluso ahora
7 even so *adv* aun así
8 even then *adv (still)* ya entonces; *(nevertheless)* aun así
9 even though *conj* aunque, a pesar de que

▶**even out 1** *vt sep (surface, bumps, load)* nivelar; *(differences, effects)* equilibrar; **they aim to e. out social inequalities** aspiran a eliminar las desigualdades sociales; **with this account, you can e. out payments over the year** con esta cuenta, los pagos se reparten equitativamente a lo largo del año
2 *vi (differences, workload)* equilibrarse

▶**even up** *vt sep* equilibrar; **to e. things up** equilibrar las cosas; **the amateur team starts a goal ahead to e. up the odds** el equipo de aficionados empieza con un gol de más para compensar la desventaja

---

even[2] *n Archaic or Literary (evening)* tarde

even-handed ['i:vən'hændɪd] *adj* imparcial

even-handedly ['i:vən'hændɪdlɪ] *adv* imparcialmente

evening ['i:vnɪŋ] **1** *n* (**a**) *(part of day) (earlier)* tarde *f*; *(later)* noche *f*; **this e.** esta tarde/noche; **tomorrow e.** mañana por la tarde/noche; **yesterday e.** ayer (por la) tarde/noche; **the next** *or* **following e., the e. after** la tarde/noche (del día) siguiente; **the previous e., the e. before** la tarde/noche (del día) anterior; **all e.** toda la tarde; **every e.** todas las tardes/noches; **every Friday e.** todos los viernes por la tarde/noche; **in the e.** por la tarde/noche; **at seven o'clock in the e.** a las siete de la tarde; **on Wednesday e.** el miércoles por la tarde/noche; **on the e. of the twelfth** la tarde/noche del doce; **I'm on evenings this week** hago turno de tarde esta semana; **good e.!** ¡buenas tardes/noches!; *Fam* **e.!** ¡buenas (tardes/noches)!; IDIOM **to make an e. of it** aprovechar la noche; **thank you for a lovely e.** gracias por una velada tan agradable; *Fig* **in the e. of her life** en el crepúsculo de su vida ▶▶ ***e. class*** clase *f* nocturna; ***e. dress*** *(for men)* traje *m* de etiqueta; *(for women)* vestido *m or* traje *m* de noche; ***e. paper*** periódico *m* vespertino *or* de la tarde; ***e. performance*** *(of play)* función *f* de noche; ***e. primrose*** onagra *f*, hierba *f* del asno; ***e. primrose oil*** aceite *m* de onagra; ***e. showing*** *(of movie)* sesión *f* de noche; ***e. star*** lucero *m* de la tarde *or* vespertino
(**b**) *(entertainment)* velada *f*; **a musical/cultural e.** una velada musical/cultural
2 evenings *adv esp US (earlier)* por las tardes; *(later)* por las noches; **evenings he's mostly at home** por las tardes/noches normalmente está en casa

evenly ['i:vənlɪ] *adv* (**a**) *(regularly) (to spread, coat)* uniformemente; **to breathe e.** respirar con normalidad (**b**) *(calmly)* **to say sth e.** decir algo con tranquilidad (**c**) *(equally) (to divide, share)* equitativamente; **e. matched** en igualdad de condiciones; **e. spaced rows** filas con intervalos regulares

evenness ['i:vənnɪs] *n* (**a**) *(of surface)* uniformidad *f*, lisura *f* (**b**) *(regularity) (of breathing, pace)* regularidad *f*; *(of voice)* mesura *f* (**c**) *(of contest)* equilibrio *m*

evens ['i:vənz] *n (in betting)* **the odds are e.** las apuestas están 2 a 1

evensong ['i:vənsɒŋ] *n Rel* vísperas *fpl*

event [ɪ'vent] *n* (**a**) *(occurrence)* acontecimiento *m*; **in the normal course of events** en circunstancias normales; **a strange/unexpected turn of events** un giro extraño/ inesperado en el transcurso de los acontecimientos; **after the e.** a posteriori; **at all events** en todo *or* cualquier caso; **in any e.** en cualquier caso; **in either e.** en cualquiera de los casos; **in the e. it was a big success** resultó ser todo un éxito; **in the e. of fire** en caso de incendio; **in the e. of her resigning...** en caso de que dimita...; **in the unlikely e. that he comes** en el improbable supuesto de que venga
(**b**) *(organized activity)* actividad *f*; *(entertainment)* espectáculo *m*; *(banquet)* gala *f* ▶▶ ***e. management*** organización *f* de eventos; ***e. organizer*** organizador(ora) *m,f* de eventos
(**c**) *(in athletics)* prueba *f*

even-tempered ['iːvən'tempəd] *adj* ecuánime, sereno(a)

eventful [ɪ'ventfʊl] *adj (day, life)* agitado(a), azaroso(a)

eventfulness [ɪ'ventfulnɪs] *n* lo accidentado

eventide ['iːvəntaɪd] *n Old-fashioned or Literary* anochecer *m* ▸▸ *Euph* ***e. home*** residencia *f* de la tercera edad *or* de ancianos

eventual [ɪ'ventʃʊəl] *adj* final; **bad management led to the e. collapse of the company** una mala gestión finalmente llevó a la empresa a la quiebra

> **False friend**: The Spanish adjective **eventual** is not a translation for the English word **eventual**. In Spanish **eventual** means "temporary" or "possible".

eventuality [ɪventʃʊ'ælɪtɪ] *n* eventualidad *f*, posibilidad *f*; **in that e.** en ese caso; **to be ready for all eventualities** estar preparado(a) *or Am* alistado(a) para cualquier eventualidad

eventually [ɪ'ventʃəlɪ] *adv* finalmente, al final; **he'll get tired of it e.** al final se acabará cansando

> **False friend**: The Spanish adverb **eventualmente** is not a translation for the English word **eventually**. In Spanish **eventualmente** means "by chance" or "possibly".

eventuate [ɪ'ventʃʊeɪt] *vi Formal* resultar; **whatever expense may e. from these changes** cualquier gasto que pueda surgir de estos cambios; **his illness eventuated in death** la enfermedad consumó en su muerte

EVER ['evə(r)] *adv* (**a**) *(always, at any time)* **all she e. does is criticize** no hace más que criticar; **it's the only brand of coffee I e. buy** es la única marca de café que compro; **don't e. do it again!** ¡ni se te ocurra volver a hacerlo!; **before I had e. met her** antes de que la conociera, antes de conocerla; **if you e. come to Washington** si vienes a Washington alguna vez; **e. the gentleman, he opened the door for her** caballeroso como siempre, le abrió la puerta; *Literary* **it will e. be so** siempre será así; **she was as friendly as e.** estuvo *or* fue tan amable como siempre; **as e., we were the last to find out** como siempre, fuimos los últimos en saberlo; **e. since (then)** desde entonces; **e. since 1960** desde 1960; **e. since her mother died** desde que murió su madre; **for e. (and e.)** por siempre; **if e. there was a time to celebrate, this is it** ésta es una ocasión como ninguna para celebrar; **she's a liar if e. there was one** miente como ella sola, es la más mentirosa del mundo; **they all lived happily e. after** *(in story)* vivieron felices y comieron perdices; *Br* **Yours e.,** *Old-fashioned* **e. yours** *(in letter)* afectuosamente, un saludo afectuoso

(**b**) *(with comparatives, superlatives)* **the worst/best e.** el peor/mejor de todos los tiempos; **the biggest earthquake e. recorded** el mayor terremoto registrado jamás; **it's my first e. parachute jump** es mi primer salto en paracaídas; **it's my last e. performance** es mi última representación; **the biggest house I've e. seen** la casa más grande que haya visto jamás; **better/worse than e.** mejor/peor que nunca; **more than e.** más que nunca; **they are becoming e. better** son cada vez mejores

(**c**) *(with negative sense)* **hardly e.** casi nunca; **nobody had e. heard of him** nadie sabía nada de él; **not e.** nunca; **nothing e. happens** nunca pasa nada; **nothing e. upsets her** nada consigue *esp Esp* enfadarla *or esp Am* enojarla; **I don't know if I'll e. see him again** no sé si lo volveré a ver (alguna vez); **I seldom** *or* **rarely if e. see her** apenas la veo; *US* **e. and again** de cuando *or* vez en cuando

(**d**) *(in questions)* alguna vez; **do you e. go to Spain?** ¿vas a España?, ¿visitas España?; **have you e. been to Spain?** ¿has estado (alguna vez) en España?; **I can't remember e. meeting him** no recuerdo haberlo visto; **will I e. be happy?** ¿seré feliz algún día?; **can't you e. get anything right?** ¿es que no puedes hacer nada bien?; **don't you e. regret it?** ¿nunca sientes remordimientos?

(**e**) *(in exclamations, questions)* **have you e. seen the like of it!** ¡has visto algo igual!; **how e. could she say that?** ¿pero cómo ha podido decir algo así?; **what e. is the matter?** ¿se puede saber qué te ocurre?; **when e. did you manage to do it?** ¿pero cuándo te las arreglaste para hacerlo?; **where e. can it be?** ¿pero dónde puede estar?; **who e. was that?** ¿se puede saber quién era ése?; **why e. would he do such a thing?** ¿pero por qué haría una cosa así?; *US* **are you pleased? – am I e.!** ¿estás contento? – ¡ya lo creo!

(**f**) *Fam (for emphasis)* **e. so expensive** tan carísimo(a); **thanks e. so much** muchísimas *or* tantísimas gracias; **it's e. so slightly stained** tiene una mancha pero apenas se nota; **I got e. so confused** me confundí por completo; **e. such a lot of money** tantísimo dinero; **she's e. such a nice person** es una persona tan encantadora; **we had e. such a good time** nos lo pasamos de maravilla

Everest ['evərɪst] *n* **(Mount) E.** el (monte) Everest

Everglades ['evəgleɪdz] *npl* **the E.** los Everglades, = región pantanosa al sur de Florida

evergreen ['evəgriːn] **1** *n* árbol *m* de hoja perenne

2 *adj* (**a**) *(tree)* (de hoja) perenne (**b**) *(ever popular) (song, story, film)* de toda la vida, clásico (**c**) *Fin* ***e. fund*** fondo *m* de crédito permanente

everlasting [evə'lɑːstɪŋ] *adj* (**a**) *(eternal) (life)* eterno(a), perpetuo(a); **to my e. shame/regret,...** para mi infinita vergüenza *or Am* pena/infinito remordimiento,...; **Henry, to his e. credit, said nothing** Henry no dijo nada, lo cual le será eternamente reconocido (**b**) *(incessant)* continuo(a), incesante; **a life of e. misery** una vida de continuas desgracias (**c**) ***e. flower*** siempreviva *f*

evermore [evə'mɔː(r)] *adv Formal* por siempre (jamás); **for e.** para siempre

EVERY ['evrɪ] *adj* (**a**) *(each, all)* cada; **I know e. song he's ever written** conozco todas las canciones que ha escrito; **he ate e. (last) bit of it** se comió hasta el último bocado; **I enjoyed e. minute of the movie** disfruté la película enormemente; **it was worth e. penny** ha valido su precio; **she has read e. (single) one** ha leído todos y cada uno, ha leído todos sin excepción; **e. (single) one of us** todos y cada uno de nosotros; **e. time** siempre, cada vez; **e. time (that) I see her** cada vez que la veo; *US* **e. which way** en todas direcciones; **he criticizes me at e. opportunity** me critica siempre que puede; **from e. side** de todas partes; **it is in e. sense** *or* **way an improvement** supone una mejora desde todos los puntos de vista; **of e. description** *or* **kind** *or* **sort** de todo tipo; **e. man for himself!** ¡sálvese quien pueda!; **they have been watching her e. move** han estado vigilando todos sus movimientos; **they cater for your e. need** se ocupan de todas tus necesidades; **they hung on his e. word** estaban pendientes de cada una de sus palabras

(**b**) *(indicating regular occurrence)* **e. day** todos los días; **e. week** todas las semanas; **e. 20 kilometres** cada 20 kilómetros; **e. day this week** cada día de esta semana; **a baby is born e. three minutes** cada tres minutos nace un bebé; **e. second week** cada dos semanas; **e. second man was killed** uno de cada dos hombres murió; **one in e. ten** uno de cada diez; **e. few days** cada pocos días; **e. other** *or* **second day** cada dos días, *Am* día por medio; **e. other line/page** *(one in two)* cada dos líneas/páginas, *Am* línea/página por medio; **e. other house had a satellite dish** *(almost all)* casi todas las casas tenían antena parabólica; **e. so often, e. once in a while, e. now and again** *or* **then** de vez en cuando

(**c**) *(for emphasis)* **I shall give you e. assistance** haré todo lo que pueda para ayudarte; **there is e. chance the plan will succeed** lo más probable es que el plan sea un éxito; **I have e. confidence in you** confío plenamente en ti; **we are making e. effort to improve** estamos haciendo todo lo posible por mejorar; **I have e. intention of telling her** estoy completamente decidido a contárselo; **you have had e. opportunity to change** has tenido todas las oportunidades del mundo para cambiar; **you have e. right to be angry** tienes todo el derecho a estar *esp Esp* enfadado *or esp Am* enojado; **he is showing e. sign of improving** muestra todos los signos de estar recuperándose; **we wish you e. success** te deseamos mucho éxito; **e. bit as good/intelligent as...** exactamente igual de bueno/inteligente que...

EVERYBODY ['evrɪbɒdɪ], **everyone** ['evrɪwʌn] *pron* todo el mundo, todos(as); **e. I know was there** toda la gente que conozco estaba allí; **e. has their own opinion on the matter** todos tenemos nuestra propia opinión sobre el tema; **is e. here?** ¿estamos todos?; **is that e.?** *(are we all here?)* ¿estamos todos?; **not e. would agree with you** no todo el mundo estaría de acuerdo contigo; **we will send a letter to e. affected** enviaremos una carta a todos los afectados; **would e. in favour raise their hand?** los que estén a favor, que levanten la mano; **O.K. e., let's start** atención todo el mundo, vamos a empezar, *Esp* venga todos, comencemos; **e. but Jim agreed** todos estuvimos/estuvieron de acuerdo menos Jim; **e. who wants to go should put their name on the list** el que quiera ir que escriba su nombre en la lista; *Hum* **e. who is anybody** toda la gente importante

everyday ['evrɪdeɪ] *adj (event, expression)* cotidiano(a); **for e. use** para uso cotidiano; **in e. use** de uso cotidiano *or* corriente

everyone = **everybody**

everyplace ['evrɪpleɪs] *adv US* = **everywhere**

EVERYTHING ['evrɪθɪŋ] *pron* todo; **I lost e.** (lo) perdí todo; **the movie has e.** la película tiene de todo; **we have e. from sofas to fitted kitchens** tenemos de todo, desde sofás hasta cocinas integrales; **she has e. going for her** lo tiene todo a su favor; **e. (that) I did seemed to**

go wrong parecía que todo lo que hacía salía mal; **I will do e. possible** *or* **e. (that) I can** haré todo lo posible *or* todo lo que pueda; **e. went quiet** se hizo el silencio; **is e. all right?** ¿pasa algo?, ¿algún problema?; **money isn't e.** el dinero no lo es todo; **you are** *or* **mean e. to me** tú lo eres todo para mí; **does it have anything to do with me? – it has e. to do with you!** ¿tiene algo que ver conmigo? – ¡por supuesto que tiene que ver contigo!; *Fam* **the room had a minibar and e.** la habitación tenía minibar y todo; *Fam* **what with the kids and e. we haven't got time** con los niños y toda la pesca *or Méx* todas las historias *or RP* toda la pelota no tenemos tiempo; **e. must go!** *(sign in sale)* ¡hasta liquidar existencias *or RP* el stock!

EVERYWHERE ['evrıweə(r)] **1** *adv* por *or* en todas partes *or* todos lados; **we looked e.** miramos por todas partes *or* todos lados; **they go e. together** van juntos a todas partes *or* todos lados; **he follows me e.** me sigue a todas partes *or* todos lados; **e. in France** en toda Francia; **e. you go/look** dondequiera que vayas/mires; **I fly e. with British Airways** siempre vuelo con British Airways; **democrats e. were shocked by this decision** la decisión conmocionó a los demócratas de todo el mundo; **death was e.** la presencia de la muerte se dejaba *or* hacía sentir en todas partes; **I can't be e. at once!** ¡no se puede estar en todas partes a la vez *or* en todos lados al mismo tiempo!

2 *pron* **e. looks so clean** todo parece tan limpio; **e.'s fully booked** no hay lugar en ningún sitio, *Esp, Méx* no hay plazas en ningún sitio, *Andes* en ninguna parte hay campo

---

evict [ı'vıkt] *vt* desahuciar, desalojar

eviction [ı'vıkʃən] *n* desahucio *m*, desalojo *m* ►► ***e. order*** orden *f* de desahucio *or* desalojo

evidence ['evıdəns] **1** *n* **(a)** *(proof, indication)* pruebas *fpl*; **on the e. of their past performances...** a juzgar por su actuación en el pasado...; **to be in e.** ser claramente visible; **the police weren't much in e.** no se veía mucha policía; **a politician very much in e. these days** un político que en la actualidad se deja ver mucho; **to show e. of** mostrar; **there was no e. of his stay in the house** no había pruebas de su paso por la casa

(b) *Law* pruebas *fpl*; **the e. is against him** las pruebas están en su contra; **a piece of e.** una prueba; **on the e. of...** de acuerdo con el *or* sobre la base del testimonio de...; **to give e. (for/against sb)** declarar (a favor/contra alguien), testificar (a favor/contra alguien); *Br* **to turn King's** *or* **Queen's e.,** *US* **to turn State's e.** = inculpar a un cómplice ante un tribunal a cambio de recibir un trato indulgente; *Br* **anything you say may be taken down and used in e. against you** *(police caution)* todo lo que diga puede ser utilizado en su contra

2 *vt Formal* evidenciar, demostrar; **as evidenced by...** como lo demuestra...

evident ['evıdənt] *adj* evidente; **with e. pleasure** con evidente placer; **it was e. that...** era evidente que..., estaba claro que...

evidently ['evıdəntlı] *adv* **(a)** *(apparently)* evidentemente, por lo visto; **did he refuse? – e. not** ¿se negó? – por lo visto no; **their solution to the problem has e. been unsuccessful** evidentemente, la solución que han dado al problema no ha tenido éxito **(b)** *(clearly)* claramente; **he was e. in pain** se veía *or* se notaba claramente que le dolía

evil ['i:vəl] **1** *n* mal *m*; **a greater/lesser e.** un mal mayor/menor; **the evils of drink** los males de la bebida; **to speak e. of sb** hablar mal de alguien

2 *adj* **(a)** *(wicked) (person)* malo(a), malvado(a); *(action, practice)* vil, perverso(a); *(influence, effect)* nocivo(a), perjudicial; *(spirit, spell)* maligno(a); IDIOM **to have an e. tongue** tener una lengua viperina; IDIOM **to put off the e. day** *or* **hour** posponer el día *or* el momento fatídico ►► ***the e. eye*** el mal de ojo; **to give sb the e. eye** echar mal de ojo a alguien **(b)** *(smell, taste)* horrible

evildoer ['i:vəldu:ə(r)] *n Literary* malhechor(ora) *m,f*

evildoing ['i:vəldu:ıŋ] *n* maldad *f*

evil-looking ['i:vəllʊkıŋ] *adj* de aspecto siniestro

evilly ['i:vəlı] *adv* maliciosamente

evil-minded ['i:vəl'maındıd] *adj* perverso(a)

evil-smelling ['i:vəl'smelıŋ] *adj* maloliente, apestoso(a)

evil-tempered ['i:vəl'tempəd] *adj* de mal carácter

evince [ı'vıns] *vt Formal* evidenciar

eviscerate [ı'vısəreıt] *vt (disembowel)* destripar

evocation [evə'keıʃən] *n* evocación *f*

evocative [ı'vɒkətıv] *adj* evocador(ora) **(of** de**)**; **to be e. of sth** evocar algo

evoke [ı'vəʊk] *vt* **(a)** *(summon up) (memory, emotion)* evocar **(b)** *(elicit) (admiration)* suscitar; *(response, smile)* provocar

evolution [i:və'lu:ʃən] *n (gradual development)* evolución *f*; **the theory of e.** la teoría de la evolución (de las especies)

evolutionary [i:və'lu:ʃənərı] *adj* evolutivo(a)

evolutionist [i:və'lu:ʃənıst] *n* evolucionista *mf*

evolve [ı'vɒlv] **1** *vt* desarrollar

2 *vi (species)* evolucionar; *(situation)* desarrollarse; *(theory, discipline)* desarrollarse, evolucionar; **to e. from** *(species)* provenir de

ewe [ju:] *n* oveja *f* (hembra)

ewer ['ju:ə(r)] *n* aguamanil *m*, jarro *m*

ex[1] [eks] *n Fam (former spouse, girlfriend, boyfriend)* ex *mf*

ex[2] *prep* **(a)** *Com* **ex warehouse/works** en almacén/fábrica **(b)** *Fin* sin (incluir); **ex VAT** sin IVA

ex- [eks] *prefix (former)* ex-; **ex-minister/teacher** ex ministro(a)/profesor(ora); **ex-wife/husband** ex mujer/marido, exmujer/exmarido

exacerbate [eg'zæsəbeıt] *vt Formal* exacerbar

exact [ıg'zækt] **1** *adj* **(a)** *(accurate, correct)* exacto(a); **it's an e. copy** es una copia exacta

(b) *(precise) (number, amount)* exacto(a), preciso(a); **at the e. moment when...** en el preciso momento *or* instante en que...; **those were her e. words** ésas fueron exactamente sus palabras; **the e. opposite** exactamente lo contrario; **to be e.** para ser exactos; **an e. science** una ciencia exacta

2 *adv Fam* **the e. same dress** el mismísimo vestido

3 *vt (promise, apology)* arrancar **(from** a**)**; *(obedience, respect)* imponer **(from** a**)**; *(tax)* imponer el pago de **(from** a**)**

exacting [ıg'zæktıŋ] *adj (person)* exigente; *(task)* arduo(a); *(standards)* riguroso(a)

exaction [ıg'zækʃən] *n* exacción *f*

exactitude [ıg'zæktıtju:d] *n Formal* exactitud *f*

exactly [ıg'zæktlı] *adv* exactamente; **I followed her instructions e.** seguí sus instrucciones al pie de la letra; **it's e. 5 o'clock** son exactamente las cinco en punto; **the machine can reproduce this sound e.** el aparato puede reproducir este sonido con exactitud; **e.!** ¡exacto!; **not e.** *(not very)* no precisamente; *(as a reply)* no exactamente; **e. the same** exactamente lo mismo; **e. the opposite** justo lo contrario; **it's e. what I was worried about** es justo lo que me preocupaba; *Ironic* **her remarks were not e. helpful** sus comentarios no fueron lo que se dice de gran ayuda

exactness [ıg'zæktnıs] *n* exactitud *f*, precisión *f*

exaggerate [ıg'zædʒəreıt] **1** *vt* **(a)** *(overstate)* exagerar; **to e. one's own importance** darse una importancia exagerada **(b)** *(emphasize)* acentuar

2 *vi* exagerar

exaggerated [ıg'zædʒəreıtıd] *adj* exagerado(a); **to have an e. opinion of oneself** *or* **of one's own worth** tener una opinión desmesurada de la propia valía

exaggeration [ıgzædʒə'reıʃən] *n* exageración *f*; **he is given to e.** le gusta exagerar; **it would be no e. to say that...** no sería exagerado *or* una exageración decir que...

exalt [ıg'zɔ:lt] *vt Formal* **(a)** *(praise)* exaltar **(b)** *(in rank)* ascender

exaltation [egzɔl'teıʃən] *n* **(a)** *(praise)* exaltación *f*, ensalzamiento *m* **(b)** *(elation)* júbilo *m*, exultación *f*

exalted [ıg'zɔ:ltıd] *adj (high)* elevado(a)

exam [ıg'zæm] *n* examen *m*; **to take** *or* **sit an e.** examinarse, hacer un examen; **to fail an e.** *Esp* suspender *or Am* reprobar un examen; **to pass an e.** aprobar un examen; **under e. conditions** con condiciones de examen, como si fuera un examen ►► ***e. board*** tribunal *m* (de examen), junta *f* examinadora; ***e. paper*** hoja *f* de examen, examen *m*; ***e. result*** nota *f*, resultado *m*

examination [ıgzæmı'neıʃən] *n* **(a)** *(inspection, scrutiny)* examen *m*, inspección *f*; *(at customs) (of baggage)* registro *m*; **to carry out** *or* **make an e. of sth** *(gen)* examinar *or* inspeccionar algo; *(baggage)* registrar algo; **the device was removed for e.** retiraron el dispositivo para examinarlo; **on e.** tras *or* al ser examinado, después de un examen; **on closer** *or* **further e.** tras un examen más detenido, al ser examinado más de cerca; **the matter is under e.** el asunto se está estudiando

(b) *(at school, at university)* examen *m*; **to take** *or* **sit an e.** hacer un examen, examinarse; **to fail an e.** *Esp* suspender *or Am* reprobar un examen; **to pass an e.** aprobar un examen; **under e. conditions** con condiciones de examen, como si fuera un examen ►► ***e. board*** tribunal *m* (de examen), junta *f* examinadora; ***e. paper*** hoja *f* de examen, examen *m*; ***e. result*** nota *f*, resultado *m*

(c) *(of patient)* reconocimiento *m*, examen *m*

(d) *Law (of witness, suspect)* interrogatorio *m*

examine [ɪg'zæmɪn] *vt* (**a**) *(inspect) (object, evidence)* examinar; *(place)* inspeccionar; *(records)* estudiar, revisar; *(at customs) (baggage)* registrar; **to e. one's conscience** hacer examen de conciencia (**b**) *(at school, at university)* examinar (**c**) *(patient)* reconocer, examinar; IDIOM *Hum* **he needs his head examined** le falta un tornillo (**d**) *Law (witness, suspect)* interrogar

examinee [ɪgzæmɪ'ni:] *n* examinando(a) *m,f*

examiner [ɪg'zæmɪnə(r)] *n* examinador(ora) *m,f*

examining magistrate [ɪg'zæmɪnɪŋ'mædʒɪstreɪt] *n Br* juez *m* de instrucción, juez *m* de primera instancia

example [ɪg'zɑ:mpəl] *n* (**a**) *(illustration, specimen)* ejemplo *m*; **for e.** por ejemplo; **it's a classic e. of 1960's architecture** es un ejemplo clásico de la arquitectura de los años sesenta
(**b**) *(person or action to be imitated)* ejemplo *m*; **you're an e. to us all** eres un ejemplo para todos nosotros; **to hold sb up as an e.** poner a alguien como ejemplo; **to set an e.** dar ejemplo; **you're setting your little brother a bad e.** le estás dando un mal ejemplo a tu hermano pequeño; **to follow sb's e.** seguir el ejemplo de alguien; **to lead by e.** predicar con el ejemplo
(**c**) *(warning)* **let this be an e. to you!** ¡que te sirva de escarmiento!, ¡así aprenderás!; **to make an e. of sb** imponer un castigo ejemplar a alguien

exasperate [ɪg'zɑ:spəreɪt] *vt* exasperar; **to get** *or* **become exasperated (with sth/sb)** exasperarse (con algo/alguien)

exasperating [ɪg'zɑ:spəreɪtɪŋ] *adj* exasperante; **it's been an e. day** ha sido un día de volverse loco

exasperatingly [ɪg'zɑ:spəreɪtɪŋlɪ] *adv* exasperantemente; **he's e. slow** es de una lentitud exasperante *or* que saca de quicio

exasperation [ɪgzɑ:spə'reɪʃən] *n* exasperación *f*; **out of** *or* **in e.** con exasperación

ex cathedra ['ekskə'θi:drə] **1** *adj* magistral
2 *adv* ex cathedra, ex cátedra

excavate ['ekskəveɪt] **1** *vt* excavar
2 *vi* excavar

excavation [ekskə'veɪʃən] *n* (**a**) *(activity)* excavación *f*; **after months of e.** después de excavar durante meses (**b**) *(site)* lugar *m* de la excavación

excavator ['ekskəveɪtə(r)] *n* (**a**) *(machine)* excavadora *f* (**b**) *(person)* excavador(ora) *m,f*

exceed [ɪk'si:d] *vt* (**a**) *(be more than) (amount, number)* superar, exceder; **demand exceeded supply** la demanda superaba *or* excedía la oferta (**b**) *(go beyond) (expectations, hopes, fears)* superar, exceder; *(limit)* rebasar, sobrepasar; *(budget)* sobrepasar; **she exceeded her authority** se excedió en su autoridad; **do not e. the stated dose** *(on medicine label)* no exceda la dosis indicada

exceedingly [ɪk'si:dɪŋlɪ] *adv* sumamente, extremadamente

excel [ɪk'sel] (*pt & pp* **excelled**) **1** *vt esp Ironic* **to e. oneself** superarse; **you've really excelled yourself this time!** ¡esta vez te has superado a ti misma!, ¡esta vez te has lucido!
2 *vi* sobresalir (**at** *or* **in** en), distinguirse (**at** *or* **in** en)

excellence ['eksələns] *n* excelencia *f*; **to strive for e.** esforzarse por alcanzar la excelencia *or* máxima calidad

Excellency ['eksələnsɪ] *n* **Your/His E.** Su Excelencia

excellent ['eksələnt] *adj* excelente; **e.!** ¡estupendo!, *Andes, CAm, Carib, Méx* ¡chévere!, *Méx* ¡padre!, *RP* ¡bárbaro!

excellently ['eksələntlɪ] *adv* estupendamente, excelentemente

excelsior [ɪk'selsɪɔ:(r)] *n US* virutas *fpl* de embalaje

EXCEPT [ɪk'sept] **1** *prep* excepto, salvo; **everywhere e. there** en todas partes *or* todos lados menos allí; **nobody e. him** nadie salvo él; **I know nothing e. what you've told me** no sé nada aparte de lo que me has contado; **you can't get them e. by mail order** sólo los puedes conseguir por correo; **we would have lost, e. for you** de no ser *or* a no ser por ti, habríamos perdido; **the dress is ready e. for the buttons** menos *or* salvo los botones, el vestido está listo; **he's my best friend, e. for you, of course** es mi mejor amigo, aparte de ti, claro está
2 *conj* (**a**) *(apart from)* **they did everything e. win** hicieron todo menos ganar; **there is little we can do e. pray** aparte de rezar, poco podemos hacer; **e. when** salvo cuando
(**b**) *(only)* **e. (that)** sólo que; **mine's identical e. (that) it's red** el mío es igual, pero rojo; **I'd love to go, e. I haven't got time** me encantaría ir, sólo que *or* pero no tengo tiempo
3 *vt* exceptuar, excluir (**from** de); **Friday excepted, we had a nice week** con la excepción del viernes, la semana fue buena; **present company excepted** exceptuando a los aquí presentes

excepting [ɪk'septɪŋ] *prep* exceptuando, salvo; **not e....** incluyendo a...; **I got all the answers right, e. the first one** acerté todas las respuestas menos la primera

exception [ɪk'sepʃən] *n* (**a**) *(atypical case)* excepción *f*; **the e. that proves the rule** la excepción que confirma la regla (**b**) *(exemption, allowance)* excepción *f*; **to make an e. of sth/for sb** hacer una excepción con algo/con alguien; **with the e. of...** a excepción de...; **without e.** sin excepción (**c**) **to take e. to sth** *(be offended)* ofenderse por algo; *(object)* censurar algo

exceptionable [ɪk'sepʃənəbəl] *adj Formal* inaceptable, censurable

exceptional [ɪk'sepʃənəl] *adj* (**a**) *(outstanding)* excepcional (**b**) *(very special)* excepcional; **in e. circumstances** en circunstancias excepcionales

exceptionally [ɪk'sepʃənəlɪ] *adv* (**a**) *(outstandingly)* extraordinariamente (**b**) *(in very special cases)* excepcionalmente; **e., more time may be allowed** en casos excepcionales se dará más tiempo

excerpt ['eksɜ:pt] **1** *n* fragmento *m* (**from** de)
2 *vt* **the quotations were excerpted from...** las citas fueron extraídas *or* seleccionadas de...

excess [ɪk'ses] **1** *n* (**a**) *(over-indulgence)* exceso *m*; **to do sth to e.** hacer algo en exceso; **to lead a life of e.** llevar una vida de excesos (**b**) *(surplus)* exceso *m*; **in e. of** más de, por encima de; **sums in e. of £1,000** sumas superiores a *or* de más de 1.000 libras; **to pay the e.** *(on ticket)* pagar la diferencia *or* el suplemento (**c**) **excesses** *(outrages, atrocities)* excesos (**d**) *Br (in insurance policy)* franquicia *f*
2 *adj* ***e. baggage*** exceso *m* de equipaje; ***e. demand*** exceso *m* de demanda; ***e. fare*** suplemento *m*; ***e. weight*** *(obesity)* exceso *m* de peso

excessive [ɪk'sesɪv] *adj (charges, fees)* excesivo(a); **e. drinking** beber demasiado *or* en exceso

excessively [ɪk'sesɪvlɪ] *adv* excesivamente; **it was difficult, but not e. so** era difícil pero no demasiado *or* excesivamente

exchange [ɪks'tʃeɪndʒ] **1** *n* (**a**) *(of prisoners, ideas)* intercambio *m*; **in e. (for)** a cambio (de); **in e. for helping them, she was given food and lodging** a cambio de ayudarles, le dieron alojamiento y comida ►► *Com* ***e. of contracts*** firma *f* de contrato
(**b**) *(argument)* **there was a heated e.** hubo un acalorado intercambio verbal
(**c**) *(cultural, educational)* intercambio *m* ►► ***e. student*** alumno(a) *m,f* de intercambio; ***e. visit*** visita *f* de intercambio
(**d**) *Fin (of currency)* cambio *m* ►► ***e. controls*** controles *mpl* de cambio (monetario); ***e. rate*** tipo *m or Am* tasa *f* de cambio; **at the current e. rate** con el tipo *or Am* la tasa de cambio actual; ***e. rate mechanism*** mecanismo *m* de los tipos de cambio
(**e**) *Fin (place)* **(Stock) E.** mercado *m* de valores, bolsa *f*
(**f**) **(telephone) e.** *(equipment)* central *f* telefónica, centralita *f*
2 *vt* (**a**) *(insults, gifts, information)* intercambiar; *(faulty goods)* descambiar; *(prisoners)* canjear; **to e. sth for sth** cambiar algo por algo; **we exchanged places (with each other)** intercambiamos el sitio (el uno con el otro); **would you like to e. places?** ¿quieres que te cambie el sitio?, ¿quieres que me cambie de sitio contigo?; **we exchanged addresses** nos intercambiamos nuestras señas *or* direcciones; *Euph* **to e. words** tener unas palabras; **to e. glances** mirarse, intercambiar miradas; **to e. views** intercambiar impresiones
(**b**) *Fin (currency)* cambiar

exchangeable [ɪks'tʃeɪndʒəbəl] *adj (voucher, currency)* canjeable (**for** por)

exchequer [ɪks'tʃekə(r)] *n Br* **the E.** el erario público, ≃ Hacienda

excisable [ɪk'saɪzəbəl] *adj (taxable)* imponible

excise[1] ['eksaɪz] *n* **e. (duties)** *(tax)* impuesto *m* sobre el consumo

excise[2] [ɪk'saɪz] *vt Formal* (**a**) *(growth)* extirpar (**b**) *(from text)* suprimir, excluir

exciseman ['eksaɪzmæn] *n Br Hist* recaudador *m* de impuestos

excision [ek'sɪʒən] *n Formal* (**a**) *(of growth)* extirpación *f* (**b**) *(of a piece of text)* supresión *f*, eliminación *f*

excitability [ɪksaɪtə'bɪlɪtɪ] *n* excitabilidad *f*

excitable [ɪk'saɪtəbəl] *adj* excitable

excite [ɪk'saɪt] *vt* (**a**) *(person)* entusiasmar, emocionar; **the doctor said you weren't to e. yourself** el médico dijo que no debes alterarte *or* agitarte (**b**) *(arouse sexually)* excitar (**c**) *(feeling, passion)* excitar, estimular; *(envy, interest)* suscitar (**d**) *Phys* excitar

excited [ɪk'saɪtɪd] *adj* (**a**) *(enthusiastic, eager)* entusiasmado(a), emocionado(a) (**about** *or* **at** con); *(child, dog)* alborotado(a); **to get e. (about)** entusiasmarse *or* ilusionarse (con); **don't get too e.!** ¡no te hagas muchas ilusiones!; *Ironic* **well, don't sound so e.!** ¡no lo digas con tanto entusiasmo!

(**b**) *(agitated)* **don't get e.!** ¡no te alteres *or* agites!
(**c**) *(sexually)* excitado(a)
(**d**) *Phys* excitado(a)

excitedly [ɪk'saɪtɪdlɪ] *adv* (**a**) *(enthusiasticly, eagerly)* con entusiasmo, con emoción (**b**) *(agitatedly)* con alteración

excitement [ɪk'saɪtmənt] *n* (**a**) *(enthusiasm, eagerness)* emoción *f*, entusiamo *m*; **to cause great e.** provocar un gran revuelo
(**b**) *(agitation)* **to avoid e.** evitar las emociones fuertes; **what's all the e. about?** ¿a (cuento de) qué viene tanto revuelo?; **I've had enough e. for one day** he tenido suficientes emociones por un día
(**c**) *(sexual)* excitación *f*
(**d**) *(interesting events)* **we don't get much e. round here** por aquí nunca pasa nada muy emocionante; **I don't want to miss the e.** no quería perderme lo más emocionante

exciting [ɪk'saɪtɪŋ] *adj* (**a**) *(eventful, interesting)* emocionante, apasionante (**b**) *(sexually)* excitante

excl. (*abbr* **excluding**) sin (incluir)

exclaim [ɪks'kleɪm] **1** *vt* exclamar; **"but why?" he exclaimed** "pero, ¿por qué?", exclamó
2 *vi* exclamar (**at** ante)

exclamation [eksklə'meɪʃən] *n* exclamación *f* ►► ***e. mark*** signo *m* de admiración *or* exclamación; *US* ***e. point*** signo *m* de admiración *or* exclamación

exclamatory [eks'klæmətərɪ] *adj* exclamativo(a)

exclude [ɪks'klu:d] *vt* (**a**) *(bar)* excluir (**from** de); **women were excluded from power/from holding public office** a las mujeres se las excluía de las posiciones de poder/de los cargos públicos; **to feel excluded (from)** sentirse excluido(a) (de)
(**b**) *(not take into consideration)* excluir (**from** de); **the figures e. deaths from other causes** las cifras no incluyen *or* no comprenden las muertes por otras causas; **excluding...** excluyendo...
(**c**) *Br (from school)* expulsar temporalmente

exclusion [ɪks'klu:ʒən] *n* (**a**) *(barring)* exclusión *f* ►► ***e. clause*** *(in insurance policy)* cláusula *f* de exclusión; ***e. order*** orden *f* (judicial) de extrañamiento; ***e. zone*** zona *f* de exclusión (**b**) *(ignoring)* exclusión *f*; **to the e. of...** haciendo caso omiso de... (**c**) *Br (from school)* expulsión *f* temporal

exclusive [ɪks'klu:sɪv] **1** *n (in newspaper, on TV)* exclusiva *f*
2 *adj* (**a**) *(socially select)* exclusivo(a), selecto(a)
(**b**) *(rights, contract)* exclusivo(a); **e. interview** entrevista en exclusiva
(**c**) *(not including)* **e. of** *(tax, postage)* sin incluir, excluyendo; **from 14 to 19 October, e.** del 14 al 19 de octubre, ambos exclusive
(**d**) *(incompatible)* **to be mutually e.** excluirse mutuamente
(**e**) *(sole)* exclusivo(a); **for the e. use of...** para uso exclusivo de...

exclusively [ɪks'klu:sɪvlɪ] *adv (only)* exclusivamente; *(in newspaper, on TV)* en exclusiva

exclusivity [eksklu:'sɪvɪtɪ] *n* uso *m* exclusivo, exclusividad *f*

excommunicate [ekskə'mju:nɪkeɪt] *vt* excomulgar

excommunication [ekskəmju:nɪ'keɪʃən] *n* excomunión *f*

ex-convict ['eks'kɒnvɪkt], *Fam* **ex-con** ['eks'kɒn] *n* ex presidiario(a) *m,f*

excoriate [ɪks'kɔ:rɪeɪt] *vt Formal (criticize)* vituperar

excrement ['ekskrɪmənt] *n* excremento *m*

excrescence [ɪks'kresəns] *n Formal* (**a**) *(growth)* excrecencia *f* (**b**) *(eyesore)* adefesio *m*

excreta [ɪks'kri:tə] *npl Formal* excrementos *mpl*, deposiciones *fpl*

excrete [ɪks'kri:t] *Formal* **1** *vt* excretar
2 *vi* excretar

excretion [ɪks'kri:ʃən] *n Formal* (**a**) *(action)* excreción *f* (**b**) *(substance)* excreción *f*

excretory [ɪks'kri:tərɪ] *adj Formal* excretor(ora)

excruciating [ɪks'kru:ʃɪeɪtɪŋ] *adj* (**a**) *(pain, sight)* terrible, espantoso(a) (**b**) *(extremely bad)* terrible, espantoso(a); **it was e.** *(embarrassing)* era para morirse de vergüenza; *(boring)* era para morirse de aburrimiento

excruciatingly [ɪks'kru:ʃɪeɪtɪŋlɪ] *adv* (**a**) *(painfully)* terriblemente, espantosamente; **e. painful** terriblemente doloroso(a) (**b**) *(very)* **it was e. embarrassing** era de morirse de vergüenza; **it was e. boring** era para morirse de aburrimiento; **e. funny** tremendamente gracioso(a)

exculpate ['ekskʌlpeɪt] *vt Formal* exculpar; **to e. oneself** exculparse

excursion [ɪks'kɜ:ʃən] *n* (**a**) *(short trip)* excursión *f*; **to make** *or* **go on an e.** hacer una excursión, ir de excursión; **she went on a shopping e.** salió de compras ►► ***e. ticket*** *Esp* billete *m or Am* boleto *m or Am* pasaje *m* de tarifa reducida (**b**) *(into a different field)* incursión *f*

excusable [ɪk'skju:zəbəl] *adj* disculpable, perdonable

excuse 1 *n* [ɪks'kju:s] (**a**) *(explanation, justification)* excusa *f*; **to make an e., to make excuses** disculparse, excusarse; **to make one's excuses (and leave)** excusarse (y marcharse); **make my excuses to them** preséntales mis excusas; **you'd better have a good e.!** ¡más vale que tengas una buena excusa!; **there's no e. for it!** ¡no hay derecho a eso!; **ignorance is no e.** el no saber no es excusa; **that's no e. for being rude** eso no es razón para ser grosero; **by way of (an) e.** como excusa; **excuses, excuses!** ¡excusas y nada más que excusas!
(**b**) *(example)* **a poor e. for a TV show** una vergüenza de programa; **he's a poor e. for a father** llamarlo padre es mucho
(**c**) *(pretext)* excusa *f*, pretexto *m*; **an e. to do** *or* **for doing sth** una excusa *or* un pretexto para hacer algo; **any e. for a drink!** ¡cualquier excusa es buena con tal de beber algo!
2 *vt* [ɪks'kju:z] (**a**) *(justify)* justificar; **to e. oneself** justificarse
(**b**) *(forgive)* disculpar, excusar; **now, if you will e. me,...** ahora, si me disculpas...; **one could be excused for thinking that he was much younger** no sería de extrañar que alguien pensase que era mucho más joven; **e. me!** *(to attract attention)* ¡perdón!, ¡oiga (por favor)!; *(when trying to get past)* ¿me permite?; *(making objection)* ¡un momento!, ¡perdona!; **e. me?** *(what did you say?)* ¿cómo?; **well, e. me for mentioning it!** ¡tampoco es como para que te pongas así porque lo haya mencionado!
(**c**) *(exempt)* dispensar (**from** de), eximir (**from** de); **to e. sb from doing sth** dispensar a alguien de hacer algo; **he is excused gym** está dispensado de hacer gimnasia
(**d**) **to e. oneself** *(give excuse)* disculparse, excusarse; *(before leaving)* disculparse, excusarse

ex-directory [eksdɪ'rektərɪ] **1** *adj Br* **e. number** = número que no figura en la guía telefónica
2 *adv* **to go e.** = hacer que el número de uno no figure en la guía telefónica

exe ['eksi:] *n Comptr* ***e. file*** archivo *m* exe *or* ejecutable

exec [ɪg'zek] *n Fam* ejecutivo(a) *m,f*

execrable ['eksɪkrəbəl] *adj Formal* execrable

execrably ['eksɪkrəblɪ] *adv Formal* execrablemente

execrate ['eksəkreɪt] *vt Formal* (**a**) *(loathe)* detestar, abominar (**b**) *(denounce)* execrar

execration [eksɪ'kreɪʃən] *n Formal* (**a**) *(loathing)* aversión *f* (**b**) *(denunciation)* execración *f*

executable file [ɪg'zekjʊtəbəl'faɪl] *n Comptr* (fichero *m*) ejecutable *m*

execute ['eksɪkju:t] *vt* (**a**) *(prisoner)* ejecutar (**b**) *(carry out) (command)* ejecutar; *(plan, operation)* llevar a cabo; *(one's duties)* cumplir (con); **a superbly executed carving** una talla magníficamente labrada (**c**) *Law (will, deed)* otorgar (**d**) *Comptr* ejecutar

execution [eksɪ'kju:ʃən] *n* (**a**) *(of prisoner)* ejecución *f* (**b**) *(of order)* ejecución *f*; *(of duty)* cumplimiento *m* (**c**) *Law (of will, deed)* otorgamiento *m*

executioner [eksɪ'kju:ʃənə(r)] *n* verdugo *m*

executive [ɪg'zekjʊtɪv] **1** *n* (**a**) *(businessman)* ejecutivo(a) *m,f* (**b**) *(committee)* ejecutivo *m* (**c**) *(arm of government)* (poder *m*) ejecutivo *m* ►► *US* ***e. privilege*** = exención de la obligación de revelar el contenido de documentos internos por parte del ejecutivo del gobierno estadounidense; ***e. session*** sesión *f* a puerta cerrada
2 *adj (function, role)* ejecutivo(a); *(car park, canteen)* para ejecutivos; **he's not good at making e. decisions** no sirve para tomar decisiones con carácter ejecutivo ►► *Br* ***e. director*** director(ora) *m,f* ejecutivo(a); ***e. lounge*** *(in airport)* sala *f* para ejecutivos; *(in hotel)* salón *m* de ejecutivos; ***e. secretary*** secretario(a) *m,f* ejecutivo(a), secretario(a) *m,f* de sección; ***e. suite*** *(in hotel)* suite *f* para ejecutivos; *(in company)* despacho *m* de ejecutivo; ***e. toy*** = juego o artilugio para entretenerse en los ratos libres en la oficina

executor [ɪg'zekjʊtə(r)] *n Law* albacea *mf*; **to make sb one's e.** nombrar a alguien su albacea

executrix [ɪg'zekjʊtrɪks] (*pl* **executrices** [ɪg'zekjʊtrɪsi:z]) *n Law* albacea *f*

exegesis [eksə'dʒi:sɪs] (*pl* **exegeses** [eksə'dʒi:si:z]) *n Formal* exégesis *f inv*

exemplar [ɪg'zemplɑ:(r)] *n* (**a**) *(fine example)* modelo *m* (**b**) *(typical example)* ejemplo *m*

exemplary [ɪg'zemplərɪ] *adj* (**a**) *(very good) (behaviour, pupil)* ejemplar (**b**) *(serving as a warning) (punishment)* ejemplar ►► *Law* ***e. damages*** = indemnización adicional en calidad de castigo ejemplar

exemplification [ɪgzemplɪfɪ'keɪʃən] *n* ejemplificación *f*

exemplify [ɪg'zemplɪfaɪ] *vt* (**a**) *(give example of)* ilustrar (**b**) *(be example of)* ilustrar, ejemplificar

exempt [ɪg'zempt] **1** *adj* exento(a) **(from** de); **to be e. from sth** estar exento(a) de algo; **e. from taxes** exento(a) de impuestos
2 *vt* **(a)** *(from duty, obligation)* eximir **(from** de) **(b)** *(goods)* **to be exempted from tax** estar exento(a) de impuestos

exemption [ɪg'zem(p)ʃən] *n* **(a)** *(from duty, obligation)* exención *f* **(from** de) **(b)** *Br (from tax)* exención *f* **(c)** *US (tax allowance)* desgravación *f* fiscal

exercise ['eksəsaɪz] **1** *n* **(a)** *(physical)* ejercicio *m*; **I don't get much e.** no hago mucho ejercicio; **to take e.** hacer ejercicio; **I'll walk, I need the e.** iré andando, necesito hacer ejercicio ►► ***e. bike*** bicicleta *f* estática; ***e. yard*** *(in prison)* patio *m* (de ejercicios)
(b) *(school task)* ejercicio *m* ►► ***e. book*** *(book)* libro *m* de ejercicios; *(notebook)* cuaderno *m* de ejercicios
(c) *(use)* ejercicio *m*; **in the e. of one's duties** en el ejercicio de su cargo
(d) *(activity, undertaking)* ejercicio *m*, operación *f*; **a useful/futile e.** una útil/vana empresa; **this is more than just a PR e.** esto es más que un simple ejercicio de relaciones públicas
(e) *(military)* maniobra *f*; **on exercise(s)** de maniobras
2 *vt* **(a)** *(body, mind)* ejercitar; *(horse)* ejercitar; *(dog)* sacar a pasear a
(b) *(right, one's influence)* ejercer; **to e. discretion** ser discreto(a); **to e. restraint** controlarse; **to e. patience** tener paciencia; **to e. caution** ser prudente
(c) *St Exch (option)* ejercer
(d) *Formal (preoccupy)* atribular
3 *vi (physically)* hacer ejercicio

exert [ɪg'zɜːt] *vt (pressure, force, influence)* ejercer; **to e. oneself** esforzarse; *Ironic* **don't e. yourself!** ¡no te vayas a herniar!

exertion [ɪg'zɜːʃən] *n* **(a)** *(of pressure, influence)* ejercicio *m*; *(of force)* empleo *m* **(b)** *(effort)* esfuerzo *m*; **after the day's exertions** después de los esfuerzos hechos durante la jornada

exfoliate [eks'fəʊlɪeɪt] **1** *vt* exfoliar
2 *vi* exfoliarse

exfoliating cream [eks'fəʊlɪeɪtɪŋkriːm] *n* crema *f* exfoliante

ex gratia ['eks'greɪʃɪə] *adj (payment)* voluntario(a)

exhalation [ekshə'leɪʃən] *n* **(a)** *(breathing out)* espiración *f* **(b)** *(air breathed out)* exhalación *f*

exhale [eks'heɪl] **1** *vt (air)* espirar, exhalar; *(smoke)* exhalar
2 *vi (breathe out air)* espirar, exhalar; *(breathe out smoke)* exhalar

exhaust [ɪg'zɔːst] **1** *n* **(a)** *(on car)* escape *m*; **e. (pipe)** tubo *m* de escape, *RP* caño *m* de escape **(b)** *(emission)* **e. (fumes)** gases *mpl* de la combustión
2 *vt* **(a)** *(person)* agotar; **to e. oneself (doing sth)** agotarse haciendo algo **(b)** *(resources, patience)* agotar; **I think we've exhausted the subject, don't you?** creo que hemos agotado el tema ¿no?

exhausted [ɪg'zɔːstɪd] *adj* agotado(a), exhausto(a); **to be e.** estar agotado(a) *or* exhausto(a); **you look e.!** ¡pareces agotada *or* exhausta!

exhausting [ɪg'zɔːstɪŋ] *adj* agotador(ora)

exhaustion [ɪg'zɔːstʃən] *n* **(a)** *(tiredness)* agotamiento *m*; **to be suffering from e.** sufrir de agotamiento **(b)** *(of resources, patience)* agotamiento *m*

exhaustive [ɪg'zɔːstɪv] *adj* exhaustivo(a); **the list is not e.** la lista no es exhaustiva

exhaustively [ɪg'zɔːstɪvlɪ] *adv* exhaustivamente, de forma exhaustiva

exhibit [ɪg'zɪbɪt] **1** *n* **(a)** *(in art exhibition)* obra *f* expuesta; **one of the prize exhibits** una de las mejores piezas **(b)** *(in court case)* prueba *f* material; **e. A** la prueba A **(c)** *US (exhibition)* exposición *f*
2 *vt* **(a)** *(object)* exhibir **(b)** *(painting in exhibition)* exponer **(c)** *(demonstrate) (courage, self-control)* demostrar, dar muestras de; **to e. signs of stress/wear** dar muestras de estrés/desgaste
3 *vi (artist)* exponer

exhibition [eksɪ'bɪʃən] *n* **(a)** *(of art, informative)* exposición *f*; **trade e.** exposición comercial ►► ***e. centre*** centro *m* de exposiciones; *Sport* ***e. game*** partido *m* de exhibición **(b)** *Fam* **to make an e. of oneself** dar el espectáculo, *Esp* montar el número; **that was a disgraceful e.!** ¡fue un espectáculo penoso *or* bochornoso! **(c)** *Br Univ (award)* beca *f*

exhibitionism [eksɪ'bɪʃənɪzəm] *n* **(a)** *(attracting attention)* exhibicionismo *m* **(b)** *Psy* exhibicionismo *m*

exhibitionist [eksɪ'bɪʃənɪst] *n* **(a)** *(person who likes attracting attention)* exhibicionista *mf* **(b)** *Psy* exhibicionista *mf*

exhibitionistic [eksɪbɪʃə'nɪstɪk] *adj (behaviour, person)* exhibicionista

exhibitor [ɪg'zɪbɪtə(r)] *n* **(a)** *(at gallery, trade fair)* expositor(ora) *m,f* **(b)** *(cinema owner, company)* exhibidor(ora) *m,f*

exhilarate [ɪg'zɪləreɪt] *vt* entusiasmar, enardecer

exhilarated [ɪg'zɪləreɪtɪd] *adj* eufórico(a), enardecido(a); **to feel e.** sentirse eufórico(a)

exhilarating [ɪg'zɪləreɪtɪŋ] *adj* vivificante, excitante

exhilaration [ɪgzɪlə'reɪʃən] *n* euforia *f*

exhort [ɪg'zɔːt] *vt Formal* exhortar; **to e. sb to do sth** exhortar a alguien a hacer algo

exhortation [ɪgzɔː'teɪʃən] *n Formal* exhortación *f*

exhumation [ekshjuː'meɪʃən] *n Formal* exhumación *f*

exhume [eks'hjuːm] *vt* exhumar

exigency ['eksɪdʒənsɪ] *n Formal* **(a)** **exigencies** *(demands, needs)* exigencias, imperativos **(b)** *(emergency)* urgencia *f*

exigent ['eksɪdʒənt] *adj Formal* **(a)** *(manner)* exigente, imperioso(a) **(b)** *(problem)* acuciante, apremiante

exiguous [ɪg'zɪgjʊəs] *adj Formal* exiguo(a)

exile ['eksaɪl] **1** *n* **(a)** *(banishment)* exilio *m*; **to go into e.** exiliarse; **in e.** en el exilio **(b)** *(exiled person)* exiliado(a) *m,f*
2 *vt* exiliar **(from** de)

exist [ɪg'zɪst] *vi* **(a)** *(be in existence)* existir; **the species now only exists in zoos** la especie sólo se conserva en zoológicos; **there exists an ancient tradition which...** existe una vieja tradición que... **(b)** *(survive)* sobrevivir **(on** a base de); **he earns enough to e. on** gana lo suficiente para subsistir

existence [ɪg'zɪstəns] *n* **(a)** *(state of being)* existencia *f*; **to be in e.** existir; **it's the only one of its species still in e.** es el único de su especie que queda en existencia; **it's the only shop/institution of its kind still in e.** es la única tienda/institución de este tipo que aún existe; **to come into e.** nacer, ver la luz; **to go out of e.** desaparecer
(b) *(life)* existencia *f*, vida *f*; **to lead a pleasant/wretched e.** llevar una existencia *or* vida agradable/desgraciada

existent [ɪg'zɪstənt] *adj Formal* existente, actual; **under e. legislation** con la legislación actual *or* vigente

existential [egzɪs'tenʃəl] *adj* existencial

existentialism [egzɪs'tenʃəlɪzəm] *n* existencialismo *m*

existentialist [egzɪs'tenʃəlɪst] **1** *n* existencialista *mf*
2 *adj* existencialista

existing [ɪg'zɪstɪŋ] *adj* existente, actual; **under e. legislation** con la legislación actual *or* vigente

exit ['egzɪt] **1** *n* **(a)** *(way out) (from room, building, motorway)* salida *f*; **let's turn off at the next e.** vamos a tomar la próxima salida ►► *US* ***e. ramp*** carril *m* de salida *or* deceleración **(b)** *(action) (from room)* salida *f*; **to make an e.** salir ►► *Pol* ***e. poll*** sondeo *m* a la salida de los colegios electorales; ***e. visa*** visado *m* or *Am* visa *f* de salida; ***e. wound*** herida *f* de salida
2 *vt* **(a)** *(room, building)* salir de **(b)** *Comptr* salir de
3 *vi* **(a)** *(leave)* salir; **he exited through the rear door** salió por la puerta de atrás **(b)** *Theat* salir; **e. Ophelia** *(as stage direction)* sale Ofelia **(c)** *Comptr* salir

> **False friend**: The Spanish noun **éxito** is not a translation for the English word **exit**. In Spanish **éxito** means "success".

exodus ['eksədəs] *n* **(a)** *(mass departure)* éxodo *m* **(b)** **E.** *(book in Bible)* el Éxodo

ex officio ['eksə'fɪʃɪəʊ] **1** *adj (member)* en virtud del cargo
2 *adv* **to act e.** actuar en virtud del cargo

exogamous [ek'sɒgəməs] *adj Biol* exogámico(a)

exogamy [ek'sɒgəmɪ] *n Biol* exogamia *f*

exogenous [ek'sɒdʒənəs] *adj* exógeno(a)

exonerate [ɪg'zɒnəreɪt] *vt* exonerar, exculpar **(from** *or* **of** de)

exoneration [ɪgzɒnə'reɪʃən] *n* exoneración **(from** de)

exorbitant [ɪg'zɔːbɪtənt] *adj* exorbitante, exagerado(a)

exorbitantly [ɪg'zɔːbɪtəntlɪ] *adv* exorbitantemente; **it's e. expensive** es exorbitantemente caro; **it's e. priced** tiene un precio exorbitante

exorcism ['eksɔːsɪzəm] *n* exorcismo *m*; **to carry out** *or* **perform an e.** llevar a cabo un exorcismo

exorcist ['eksɔːsɪst] *n* exorcista *mf*

exorcize ['eksɔːsaɪz] *vt (evil spirits, place)* exorcizar; *Fig (past, fears)* conjurar

exoskeleton ['eksəʊskelətən] *n Zool* exoesqueleto *m*

exosphere ['eksəʊsfɪə(r)] *n Astron* exosfera *f*

exothermic [eksəʊ'θɜːmɪk] *adj Chem (reaction)* exotérmico(a)

exotic [ɪg'zɒtɪk] **1** *adj* exótico(a); **e.-sounding/-looking** de sonido/aspecto exótico
2 *n (plant)* planta *f* exótica

exotica [ɪg'zɒtɪkə] *npl* objetos *mpl* exóticos, rarezas *fpl*

exotically [ɪg'zɒtɪklɪ] *adv (dressed, decorated)* de forma exótica

exoticism [ɪg'zɒtɪsɪzəm] *n* exotismo *m*

expand [ɪks'pænd] **1** *vt* **(a)** *(enlarge) (gas)* expandir; *(metal)* expandir, dilatar; *(chest, muscles)* desarrollar
(b) *(increase) (production, output)* ampliar; *(company, empire)* expandir
(c) *(extend) (ambitions, influence)* extender, ampliar; **to e. one's horizons** ampliar horizontes; **it's an idea that could easily be expanded into a novel** es una idea que puede fácilmente ampliarse a una novela
(d) *(add detail to)* ampliar
(e) *Math (equation)* desarrollar
(f) *Comptr (memory)* ampliar, expandir
2 *vi* **(a)** *(enlarge) (gas)* expandirse; *(metal)* expandirse, dilatarse; *(chest, muscles)* desarrollarse
(b) *(increase) (production, output)* ampliarse; *(company, empire)* expandirse; *(market)* expandirse, extenderse; **we want to e. into publishing** queremos extendernos al sector editorial
(c) *(talk, write at greater length)* **could you e.?** ¿puedes hablar más *or* extenderte un poco?

▶ **expand on, expand upon** *vt insep (talk, write at greater length about)* desarrollar; **could you e. on this?** ¿puedes hablar más *or* extenderte sobre este punto?

expandable [ɪks'pændəbəl] *adj Comptr* expandible; **98MB e. to 392MB** 98MB expandibles a 392MB

expanded [ɪks'pændɪd] *adj* **(a)** *(plastic)* ***e. polystyrene*** poliestireno *m* expandido **(b)** *Comptr* ***e. keyboard*** teclado *m* expandido; ***e. memory*** memoria *f* expandida

expanding [ɪks'pændɪŋ] *adj* **(a)** *(market, economy, company)* en expansión; **the e. universe** el universo en expansión **(b)** *(extendable)* expandible; **e. watch strap** correa de reloj expandible; **e. suitcase/briefcase** maleta/maletín de fuelle

expanse [ɪks'pæns] *n (of land, water)* extensión *f*

expansion [ɪks'pænʃən] *n* **(a)** *(of solid, gas)* dilatación *f* ▸▸ ***e. bolt*** perno *m* regulable; ***e. joint*** junta *f* de dilatación **(b)** *(of production, output)* ampliación *f*; *(of company, empire, market)* expansión *f* **(c)** *Comptr* ***e. card*** tarjeta *f* de ampliación (de memoria); ***e. slot*** ranura *f* de expansión

expansionism [ɪk'spænʃənɪzəm] *n* expansionismo *m*

expansionist [ɪks'pænʃənɪst] *adj* expansionista

expansive [ɪks'pænsɪv] *adj (person, gesture)* expansivo(a), comunicativo(a); **an e. gesture** un gesto amplio; **to be in an e. mood** estar comunicativo(a)

expansively [ɪks'pænsɪvlɪ] *adv (to talk)* extensamente; *(to gesture)* ampliamente

expat ['eks'pæt] *n esp Br Fam* emigrado(a) *m,f*

expatiate [eks'peɪʃɪeɪt] *vi Formal* explayarse, hablar largo y tendido (**on** acerca de)

expatriate [eks'pætrɪət] **1** *n (voluntary)* emigrado(a) *m,f*; *(in exile)* expatriado(a) *m,f*
2 *adj* expatriado(a)
3 *vt* [eks'pætrɪeɪt] expatriar

EXPECT [ɪks'pekt] **1** *vt* **(a)** *(anticipate)* esperar; **the movie was better than I expected** la película era mejor de lo que esperaba; **I wasn't expecting that** no me esperaba eso, no contaba con eso; **I knew what to e.** ya sabía lo que me esperaba; **the police are expecting trouble** la policía prevé problemas, la policía cree que se producirán problemas; **we were expecting more people to turn up** contábamos con que viniera más gente; **e. it to be difficult** puedes contar con que será difícil; **I expected as much** ya me lo esperaba; **to e. the worst** esperarse lo peor; **to e. to do sth** esperar hacer algo; **so I'll e. to see you here on Monday** nos vemos entonces el lunes; **I'm expecting to be made redundant** estoy pendiente de que me despidan; **you can e. to pay up to $50** te puede costar hasta 50 dólares; **to e. sb to do sth** esperar que alguien haga algo; **I was expecting you to say no** me temía que dirías que no; **don't e. me to help you out** no esperes que yo te ayude; **we e. sales to drop** prevemos un descenso en las ventas; **they won, as expected** ganaron, como se esperaba; **as one might e.** como era de esperar; **it's only to be expected** era de esperar; **what do** *or* **can you e. (from him)?** ¿qué esperas *or* esperabas (de él)?; **I expected better of you** realmente esperaba más de ti
(b) *(require)* **to e. sb to do sth** esperar de alguien que haga algo; **I e. you to be punctual** confío en que serás puntual; **I don't e. you to be perfect** no pretendo que seas perfecto; **you are expected to answer all the questions** conteste a todas las preguntas; **applicants are expected to provide three references** los aspirantes deberán adjuntar tres referencias; **you can't be expected to do everything yourself** no te pueden pedir que hagas todo tú solo *or* por ti mismo; **people e. too much from marriage** la gente espera demasiado del matrimonio; **I e. absolute loyalty from you** te exijo lealtad absoluta; **I know what is expected of me** sé qué es lo que se espera de mí
(c) *(suppose)* **to e. (that)...** suponer que...; **I e. you'll be wanting something to drink** *(said grudgingly)* supongo que querrás algo de beber; **I e. so/not** supongo que sí/que no; **it is expected that they will marry in the autumn** se espera que se casen en otoño
(d) *(baby)* **she's expecting a baby** está esperando un hijo
(e) *(await)* esperar; **I'll e. you at six** te espero a las seis; **we're expecting him back any minute** lo esperamos en cualquier momento
2 *vi Fam (be pregnant)* **she's expecting** está en estado *or* esperando

---

expectancy [ɪks'pektənsɪ] *n* expectación *f*; **an air of e.** un ambiente de gran expectación; **a look of e.** una mirada expectante

expectant [ɪks'pektənt] *adj* **(a)** *(full of anticipation) (air, crowd)* expectante **(b)** *(pregnant)* **e. mother** futura madre

expectantly [ɪks'pektəntlɪ] *adv* con expectación, con aire expectante

expectation [ekspek'teɪʃən] *n* **(a)** *(anticipation)* expectativa *f*; **there is every e. that he will recover** hay muchas esperanzas de que se recupere; **in (the) e. of sth** en previsión de algo
(b) *(hope, aspiration)* expectativa *f*; **to have high expectations of** tener muchas esperanzas puestas en; **it came up to/fell short of** *or* **didn't live up to his expectations** estuvo/no estuvo a la altura de las expectativas; **contrary to all expectations** contra lo que se esperaba
(c) *Formal* **expectations** *(of inheritance)* expectativas de heredar

expected [ɪks'pektɪd] *adj* esperado(a), previsto(a); **please state e. salary** *(on application form)* por favor, indique el salario que espera percibir

expectorant [ɪks'pektərənt] *n Med* expectorante *m*

expectorate [ɪk'spektəreɪt] *Med or Formal* **1** *vi* expectorar
2 *vt* expectorar

expediency [ɪks'piːdɪənsɪ], **expedience** [ɪks'piːdɪəns] *n* **(a)** *(advisability)* conveniencia *f* **(b)** *(self-interest)* conveniencia *f*

expedient [ɪks'piːdɪənt] *Formal* **1** *n* recurso *m*
2 *adj* **(a)** *(advisable)* conveniente; **it would be e. to...** resultaría conveniente... **(b)** *(self-interested)* conveniente

expedite ['ekspɪdaɪt] *vt Formal* acelerar, apresurar; **to e. matters** para acelerar las cosas

> **False friend:** The Spanish verb **expedir** is not a translation for the English word **expedite**. In Spanish **expedir** means "to send" or "to issue".

expedition [ekspə'dɪʃən] *n* **(a)** *(journey)* expedición *f*; **to go on an e.** salir de expedición; *Fam* **getting there was quite an e.!** ¡llegar allí resultó ser toda una expedición! **(b)** *Archaic or Literary (speed)* celeridad *f*

expeditionary force [ekspə'dɪʃənərɪ'fɔːs] *n Mil* cuerpo *m or* fuerzas *fpl* expedicionarias

expeditious [ekspə'dɪʃəs] *adj Formal* diligente

expeditiously [ekspɪ'dɪʃəslɪ] *adv Formal* con diligencia

expel [ɪks'pel] (*pt & pp* **expelled**) *vt* **(a)** *(from school, party, country)* expulsar **(b)** *(gas, liquid, breath)* expulsar

expend [ɪks'pend] *vt* **(a)** *(time)* emplear (**on** en); *(effort)* dedicar (**on** a); *(energy)* consumir (**on** en); *(money, resources)* emplear, invertir (**on** en) **(b)** *(use up) (ammunition)* agotar; *(supply)* consumir, agotar

expendable [ɪks'pendəbəl] *adj* prescindible; **none of my staff was e.** todos mis empleados eran imprescindibles

expenditure [ɪks'pendɪtʃə(r)] *n* **(a)** *(act of spending) (of money, energy)* gasto *m*; **this will involve us in fairly heavy e.** esto nos obligará a realizar un desembolso considerable **(b)** *(money spent)* gasto *m* (**on** en); **arms/defence e.** gastos en armamento/defensa; **public e.** gasto público

expense [ɪks'pens] *n* **(a)** *(cost)* gasto *m*; **at no extra e.** sin costo *or Esp* coste adicional; **at my own e.** a mi costa; **it's not worth the e.** no vale lo que cuesta; **to go to great e.** gastar mucho dinero; **no e. was spared to...** no se reparó en gastos para...; **at the e. of one's health/sanity** a costa de perder la salud/cordura; **to go to the e. of doing sth** gastarse el dinero en hacer algo; **I don't want to put you to any e.** no quiero suponerte ningún gasto; **to make a joke at sb's e.** hacer un chiste a costa de alguien; **to succeed at other people's e.** tener éxito a costa de los demás (**b**) *Com* **expenses** gastos; **to meet** *or* **cover sb's expenses** correr con *or* costear los gastos de alguien; **to put sth on expenses** apuntar algo en la cuenta de gastos (de la empresa); **it's on expenses** corre a cargo de la empresa; **all expenses paid** con todos los gastos pagados ▸▸ ***e. account*** cuenta *f* de gastos

expensive [ɪks'pensɪv] *adj* caro(a); **it's an e. place to live** es un sitio donde resulta caro vivir; **to have e. tastes** tener gustos caros; **an e. mistake** un error muy caro

expensively [ɪks'pensɪvlɪ] *adv* caro; **e. dressed/furnished** con ropa cara/muebles caros; **to live e.** vivir a lo grande, llevar un tren de vida caro

expensiveness [ɪk'spensɪvnɪs] *n* lo caro

experience [ɪks'pɪərɪəns] **1** *n* (**a**) *(in life, in a job)* experiencia *f*; **he still lacks e.** todavía le falta experiencia; **to know sth from e.** saber algo por experiencia; **to speak from e.** hablar basándose en la experiencia; **to learn from e.** aprender de la experiencia; **e. shows** *or* **proves that...** la experiencia indica *or* demuestra que...; **in my e.** según mi experiencia; **to chalk it up to** *or* **put it down to e.** asumirlo como una experiencia positiva; **no e. necessary** *(in job advert)* no es necesaria *or* no se necesita experiencia

(**b**) *(event)* experiencia *f*; **she had a nasty e.** le pasó una cosa terrible; **my first e. of Spanish cooking** mi primera experiencia *or* encuentro con la cocina española; **it was the e. of a lifetime!** ¡fue una experiencia inolvidable!

2 *vt* (**a**) *(undergo) (hardship, recession, improvement)* experimentar; **it's not something I've experienced myself** no es algo por lo que yo haya pasado; **he experienced some difficulty in opening the door** tuvo alguna dificultad para abrir la puerta

(**b**) *(feel) (thrill, emotion, despair)* experimentar; **she experienced a certain feeling of fear** tuvo un poco de miedo; **he is experiencing a great deal of anxiety at the moment** está pasando por un momento de mucha ansiedad

experienced [ɪks'pɪərɪənst] *adj (person, observer)* experimentado(a) (**in** en); **we're looking for someone a bit more e.** buscamos a alguien con un poco más de experiencia; **to be e. at** *or* **in (doing) sth** tener experiencia en (hacer) algo; **to the e. eye** para el ojo avezado

experiential [ɪkspɪərɪ'enʃəl] *adj Formal* empírico(a), experiencial

experiment [ɪks'perɪmənt] **1** *n* experimento *m*; **to do** *or* **carry out** *or* **conduct an e.** hacer *or* realizar un experimento; **as an e., by way of e.** como experimento; **it's a bit of an e.** *(as modest apology)* es una prueba *or* un experimento

2 *vi* experimentar (**with/on** con); **to e. on animals** experimentar con animales, hacer experimentos con animales

experimental [ɪksperɪ'mentəl] *adj* experimental; **it's still at the e. stage** aún se encuentra en (una) fase experimental

experimentally [ɪksperɪ'mentəlɪ] *adv* de forma experimental, empíricamente

experimentation [ɪksperɪmən'teɪʃən] *n* experimentación *f*

experimenter [ɪk'sperɪmentə(r)] *n* experimentador(ora) *m,f*

expert ['ekspɜːt] **1** *n* experto(a) *m,f* (**at/on** *or* **in** en); **I'm no e., but...** no soy un experto *or* entendido pero...; **do it yourself, you're the e.!** hazlo tú, que eres el experto

2 *adj* experto(a) (**in** *or* **at** en); **an e. opinion** la opinión de un experto; **to seek e. advice** recurrir a la opinión de un experto; **to run** *or* **cast an e. eye over sth** analizar algo con ojos de experto ▸▸ *Comptr* ***e. system*** sistema *m* experto; *Law* ***e. witness*** perito(a) *m,f*

expertise [ekspɜː'tiːz] *n* destreza *f*, pericia *f*

expertize ['ekspɜːtaɪz] *US* **1** *vt* expertizar

2 *vi* dar una opinión experta *or* de especialista

expertly ['ekspɜːtlɪ] *adv* diestramente, hábilmente

expiate ['ekspɪeɪt] *vt Formal* expiar

expiation [ekspɪ'eɪʃən] *n Formal* expiación *f*; **in e. of sth** para expiar *or* enmendar algo

expiatory ['ekspɪətərɪ] *adj Formal* expiatorio(a)

expiration [ekspɪ'reɪʃən] *n Formal* (**a**) *(of contract)* vencimiento *m* (**b**) *(exhalation)* espiración *f* (**c**) *US* ***e. date*** *(of product)* fecha *f* de caducidad

expire [ɪks'paɪə(r)] *vi* (**a**) *(law)* caducar; *(deadline)* expirar, vencer; *(passport, visa, lease)* vencer; **expires end 08/04** *(on credit card)* válido hasta 08/04 (**b**) *(exhale)* espirar (**c**) *Literary (die)* expirar

expiry [ɪks'paɪərɪ] *n* vencimiento *m* ▸▸ ***e. date*** fecha *f* de caducidad

explain [ɪks'pleɪn] **1** *vt* (**a**) *(clarify) (rule, theory)* explicar; **he explained to us how the machine worked** nos explicó el funcionamiento de la máquina; **she explained that she was a tourist in the city** aclaró que estaba de turista en la ciudad

(**b**) *(account for)* explicar, aclarar; **that explains it!** ¡eso lo explica todo!, ¡acabáramos!; **that's easily explained, that is easy to e.** es fácil de explicar; **to e. oneself** explicarse

2 *vi* explicarse

▸ **explain away** *vt sep* justificar, explicar; **e. that away if you can!** a ver si puedes justificarlo

explainable [ɪk'spleɪnəbəl] *adj* explicable

explaining [ɪks'pleɪnɪŋ] *n* **he's got a lot of e. to do** tiene muchas cosas que explicar *or* muchas explicaciones que dar

explanation [eksplə'neɪʃən] *n* explicación *f*; **to give** *or* **offer an e. for sth** explicar algo; **to find an e. for sth** encontrarle una explicación a algo; **what's the e. for this?** ¿cómo se explica esto?, ¿qué explicación tiene esto?; **what can you say in e. of your conduct?** ¿cómo puedes explicar tu conducta?; **the instructions need a bit of e.** hay que explicar un poco las instrucciones; **the minister is demanding a full e.** el ministro exige una detallada explicación

explanatory [ɪks'plænətərɪ] *adj* explicativo(a) ▸▸ ***e. note*** nota *f* aclaratoria

expletive [ɪks'pliːtɪv] *n (swearword)* palabrota *f*, *Esp* taco *m*

explicable [ɪks'plɪkəbəl] *adj* explicable

explicate ['eksplɪkeɪt] *vt Formal* explicar, ofrecer una interpretación de

explication [eksplɪ'keɪʃən] *n Formal* explicación *f*

explicit [ɪks'plɪsɪt] *adj (denial, meaning, support)* explícito(a); **he was e. on this point** fue explícito al respecto; **there's too much e. sex on TV** en la tele se ve demasiado sexo explícito; **to give sb e. instructions to do sth** dar instrucciones explícitas a alguien de que haga algo

explicitly [ɪks'plɪsɪtlɪ] *adv* explícitamente

explicitness [eks'plɪsɪtnɪs] *n* lo explícito

explode [ɪks'pləʊd] **1** *vt* (**a**) *(bomb)* hacer explotar, explosionar (**b**) *(idea, theory)* reventar, desbaratar

2 *vi* (**a**) *(bomb)* explotar, estallar

(**b**) *(person) (with anger)* estallar; **to e. with laughter** echarse *or* romper a reír, soltar una carcajada

(**c**) *(change dramatically)* **the game exploded into life** el partido cobró vida repentinamente; **punk exploded onto the scene in the 1970s** el movimiento punk irrumpió en escena en los años setenta; **the population exploded over the next decade** el crecimiento de la población se disparó durante la década siguiente

exploded [ɪks'pləʊdɪd] *adj* (**a**) *(bomb)* detonado(a) (**b**) *(diagram)* en secciones, esquemático(a)

exploit **1** *n* ['eksplɔɪt] hazaña *f*, proeza *f*

2 *vt* [eks'plɔɪt] (**a**) *(take unfair advantage of)* explotar (**b**) *(use) (resources, sb's talents)* aprovechar

exploitation [eksplɔɪ'teɪʃən] *n* explotación *f*

exploitative [eks'plɔɪtətɪv] *adj* explotador(ora)

exploiter [ek'splɔɪtə(r)] *n (of workers)* explotador(ora) *m,f*

exploration [eksplə'reɪʃən] *n* (**a**) *(of place, problem)* exploración *f* (**b**) *Med* exploración *f*

exploratory [ɪks'plɒrətərɪ] *adj* exploratorio(a); **e. discussions** *or* **talks** negociaciones preliminares ▸▸ ***e. drilling*** perforación *f* exploratoria; *Med* ***e. surgery*** cirugía *f* exploratoria

explore [ɪks'plɔː(r)] **1** *vt* (**a**) *(country, town)* explorar; **she explored her new filling with the tip of her tongue** se tocaba el nuevo empaste *or RP* la nueva emplomadura con la punta de la lengua (**b**) *(issue, possibility, problem)* analizar, estudiar; *Fig* **to e. every avenue** agotar todas la posibilidades (**c**) *Med* explorar

2 *vi* explorar; **let's go exploring** *(in countryside, town)* vayamos a explorar

explorer [ɪks'plɔːrə(r)] *n* explorador(ora) *m,f*

explosion [ɪks'pləʊʒən] *n* (**a**) *(of bomb, gas)* explosión *f*, estallido *m* (**b**) *(of laughter, anger)* estallido *m*; **there was an e. of laughter from the dining room** en el comedor comenzaron a soltar carcajadas

(**c**) *(rapid increase)* **an e. in house prices** una vertiginosa escalada de los precios de la vivienda; **an e. in the number of fast-food outlets** un espectacular incremento de los establecimientos de comida rápida

explosive [ɪks'pləʊsɪv] **1** *n* explosivo *m*; **an explosives expert** un experto en explosivos

2 *adj* (**a**) *(gas)* explosivo(a) ▸▸ ***e. device*** artefacto *m* explosivo (**b**) *(likely to become violent) (temper, situation)* explosivo(a); **an e. combination** *(of personalities, factors)* una mezcla explosiva

expo ['ekspəʊ] (*pl* **expos**) *n Fam* expo *f*

exponent [ɪks'pəʊnənt] *n* (**a**) *(of theory, art)* exponente *m*; **a leading e. of...** *(supporter)* un destacado defensor de... (**b**) *Math* exponente *m*

exponential [ekspə'nenʃəl] *adj* exponencial; **e. growth/increase** crecimiento/aumento exponencial

exponentially [ekspə'nenʃəlɪ] *adv* exponencialmente

export 1 *n* ['ekspɔːt] (**a**) *(product)* artículo *m* de exportación; **exports** *(of country)* exportaciones
(**b**) *(exportation)* exportación *f*; **for e. only** sólo para exportación ▸▸ ***e. credit*** crédito *m* a la exportación; ***e. credit guarantee*** garantía *f* de créditos para la exportación; ***e. duty*** derechos *mpl* de exportación; ***e. licence*** permiso *m or* licencia *f* de exportación; ***e. trade*** comercio *m* de exportación
2 *vt* [ɪks'pɔːt] (**a**) *(goods)* exportar (**b**) *Comptr* exportar (**to** a)
3 *vi* exportar

exportation [ekspɔː'teɪʃən] *n* exportación *f*

exporter [eks'pɔːtə(r)] *n* exportador(ora) *m,f*; **the country is a big e. of oil** el país es un gran exportador de petróleo

expose [ɪks'pəʊz] *vt* (**a**) *(uncover) (wire, nerve)* exponer; *(to air, cold, danger)* exponer (**to** a); **to e. sb to sth** exponer a alguien a algo; **he was exposed to German from the age of five** estuvo en contacto con el alemán desde que tenía cinco años; **to be exposed to criticism/ridicule** estar expuesto(a) a las críticas/al ridículo
(**b**) *(crime, scandal)* sacar a la luz, revelar; **to e. sb as a traitor** revelar que alguien es un traidor
(**c**) *(sexually)* **a man exposed himself to my sister** a mi hermana le salió al paso un exhibicionista
(**d**) *Phot* exponer

exposé [eks'pəʊzeɪ] *n (article)* artículo *m* de denuncia; *(TV programme)* programa *m* de denuncia

exposed [ɪks'pəʊzd] *adj (position, hillside)* expuesto(a), desprotegido(a); *(wire)* al descubierto, sin protección; *(parts, gears)* al descubierto; *(beam)* a la vista

exposition [ekspə'zɪʃən] *n* (**a**) *(explanation)* exposición *f* (**b**) *(exhibition)* exposición *f* (**c**) *Mus* exposición *f*

expostulate [ɪks'pɒstjʊleɪt] *vi Formal* discutir

expostulation [ɪkspɒstjʊ'leɪʃən] *n Formal* protesta *f*, reclamación *f*

exposure [ɪks'pəʊʒə(r)] *n* (**a**) *(to air, cold, danger)* exposición *f*; **to die of e.** morir de hipotermia *(a la intemperie)*
(**b**) *(publicity)* publicidad *f*; **to get** *or* **receive a lot of e.** recibir mucha publicidad
(**c**) *(of crime, criminal)* denuncia *f*
(**d**) *Phot (time)* (tiempo *m* de) exposición *f*; *(photograph)* foto *f* ▸▸ ***e. meter*** fotómetro *m*
(**e**) *Fin* riesgo *m*, exposición *f or* concentración *f* crediticia
(**f**) *(position of house)* orientación *f*; **the building has a southern e.** el edificio está orientado al sur

expound [ɪks'paʊnd] *Formal* 1 *vt* explicar, dar cuenta de
2 *vi* **to e. on** hablar extensamente sobre, explayarse sobre

express [ɪks'pres] 1 *n* (**a**) *(train)* (tren *m*) rápido *m* (**b**) *(bus)* directo *m*
2 *adj* (**a**) *(explicit) (purpose, instruction)* expreso(a); **with the e. intention of...** con la expresa intención de... (**b**) *(rapid)* ***e. checkout*** caja *f* rápida; ***e. delivery*** entrega *f* urgente; ***e. letter*** carta *f* urgente; *US* ***E. Mail*** = servicio de correo de entrega en 24 horas; ***e. train*** tren *m* rápido *or* expreso
3 *adv* **to send a letter e.** enviar una carta urgente
4 *vt* (**a**) *(voice, convey) (idea, opinion, emotion)* expresar; **to e. oneself** expresarse; **to e. an interest in (doing) sth** expresar *or* manifestar interés por (hacer) algo; **they expressed optimism that a solution would be found** manifestaron su optimismo en que se hallaría una solución; **well/badly expressed** bien/mal expresado
(**b**) *Math* expresar
(**c**) *Formal (squeeze out) (juice)* exprimir; *(milk)* extraerse

expression [ɪks'preʃən] *n* (**a**) *(of feelings, thoughts, friendship)* expresión *f*; **to give e. to sth** dar expresión a algo, expresar algo; **her feelings found e. in music** expresaba sus sentimientos a través de la música; **we'd like you to have it as an e. of our gratitude** nos gustaría que lo aceptes como muestra de nuestra gratitud; **freedom of e.** libertad de expresión
(**b**) *(facial)* expresión *f*
(**c**) *(feeling) (in art, music)* sentimiento *m*; **to play/to paint with e.** tocar/pintar con sentimiento
(**d**) *(verbal)* expresión *f*; **a set** *or* **fixed e.** una frase hecha
(**e**) *Math* expresión *f*

expressionism [ɪks'preʃənɪzəm] *n* expresionismo *m*

expressionist [ɪks'preʃənɪst] 1 *n* expresionista *mf*
2 *adj* expresionista

expressionistic [ɪkspreʃə'nɪstɪk] *adj* expresionista

expressionless [ɪks'preʃənlɪs] *adj (face, voice)* inexpresivo(a)

expressive [ɪks'presɪv] *adj* expresivo(a); **to be e. of sth** ser la manifestación *or* expresión de algo

expressively [ɪks'presɪvlɪ] *adv* de un modo expresivo

expressiveness [ɪk'spresɪvnɪs] *n* expresividad *f*

expressly [ɪks'preslɪ] *adv* (**a**) *(specially)* expresamente (**b**) *(explicitly)* explícitamente, expresamente; **I e. forbid you to leave** te prohíbo expresamente que te vayas

expresso = **espresso**

expressway [ɪks'presweɪ] *n US* autopista *f*

expropriate [eks'prəʊprɪeɪt] *vt* expropiar

expropriation [eksprəʊprɪ'eɪʃən] *n* expropiación *f*

expulsion [ɪks'pʌlʃən] *n* (**a**) *(from school, party, country)* expulsión *f* (**b**) *(of gas, liquid, breath)* expulsión *f*

expunge [ɪks'pʌndʒ] *vt Formal* borrar, eliminar

expurgate ['ekspɜːgeɪt] *vt* expurgar

exquisite ['ekskwɪzɪt] *adj* (**a**) *(food, beauty, manners)* exquisito(a); *(jewellery, craftsmanship)* exquisito(a); **to have e. taste** tener un gusto exquisito (**b**) *(intense) (pleasure, pain, thrill)* intenso(a)

exquisitely [eks'kwɪzɪtlɪ] *adv* (**a**) *(beautiful, decorated)* exquisitamente; **an e. beautiful girl** una joven de una belleza exquisita (**b**) *(intensely)* intensamente

ex-serviceman [eks'sɜːvɪsmən] *n Br* excombatiente *m*

ex-servicewoman [eks'sɜːvɪswʊmən] *n Br* excombatiente *f*

ext (*abbr* **extension**) ext.

extant [eks'tænt] *adj Formal* **one of the few e. paintings of that period** una de las pocas pinturas que se conservan de aquel periodo

extemporaneous [ɪkstempə'reɪnɪəs], **extemporary** [ɪks'tempərərɪ] *adj* improvisado(a)

> **False friend**: The Spanish adjective **extemporáneo** is not a translation for the English word **extemporaneous**. In Spanish **extemporáneo** means "unseasonable" or "inopportune".

extempore [ɪks'tempərɪ] 1 *adj (speech, speaker)* improvisado(a)
2 *adv* **to speak e.** hablar improvisando

extemporize [ɪks'tempəraɪz] *vi Formal* improvisar

extend [ɪks'tend] 1 *vt* (**a**) *(stretch out) (arm, leg)* extender; *(wings)* extender, abrir; *(aerial)* desplegar
(**b**) *(make longer) (holiday, deadline, contract)* prolongar, prorrogar; *(road, runway)* prolongar, alargar
(**c**) *(make larger, widen) (frontier, knowledge, search)* ampliar; *(vocabulary)* ampliar; **to e. a house** ampliar una casa; **the company wants to e. its activities into the export market** la compañía quiere ampliar sus actividades entrando en el mercado de las exportaciones
(**d**) *(give, offer) (one's hand)* tender; *(support, thanks)* dar; **to e. an invitation to sb** invitar a alguien, enviar una invitación a alguien; **to e. a welcome to sb** dar a alguien la bienvenida; *Fin* **to e. credit to sb** conceder un crédito a alguien
(**e**) *(stretch) (horse, person)* exigir
2 *vi* (**a**) *(in space)* extenderse; **the queue extended all the way down the street** la cola llegaba hasta la calle; **the ladder extends to 15 ft** la escalera se extiende cuatro metros y medio
(**b**) *(in time)* prolongarse
(**c**) *(apply to)* **the legislation does not e. to single mothers** esta legislación no alcanza *or* incluye a las madres solteras

extendable [ɪks'tendəbəl] *adj* (**a**) *(ladder, legs)* extensible (**b**) *(lease, contract)* prorrogable

extended [ɪks'tendɪd] *adj* (**a**) *(in time) (contract)* prorrogado(a); *(leave, visit)* prolongado(a); **e. coverage** *(on radio, TV)* amplia cobertura ▸▸ *US* ***e. care*** = servicios de atención hospitalaria en consultorios externos; *US* ***e. forecast*** = pronóstico meteorológico que comprende más de dos días; ***e. warranty*** garantía *f* ampliada
(**b**) *(larger, wider) (frontiers, search)* ampliado(a), extendido(a); **the bank granted him e. credit** el banco le amplió el crédito ▸▸ ***e. family*** clan *m* familiar, *Spec* familia *f* extendida
(**c**) *Comptr* ***e. keyboard*** teclado *m* extendido; ***e. memory*** memoria *f* extendida

extended-play [ɪks'tendɪd'pleɪ] *adj* EP *inv*

extension [ɪks'tenʃən] *n* (**a**) *(of deadline)* prórroga *f*, prolongación *f*; *(for essay)* aplazamiento *m* (de la fecha de entrega)
(**b**) *(on building)* ampliación *f*; **to build an e. onto** construir una ampliación a
(**c**) *(for telephone)* extensión *f*, *RP* interno *m*; **can I have e. 946?** ¿me puede comunicar *or Esp* poner con la extensión 946?, *RP* ¿me puede dar con el interno 946? ▸▸ ***e. number*** número *m* de extensión *or RP* interno

(d) *(of frontiers)* ampliación *f*, extensión *f*; *(of legislation)* ampliación *f*; **by e.** por extensión
(e) *(action) (of arm)* extensión *f*
(f) e. (cable *or* **cord** *or Br* **lead)** alargador *m*, alargadera *f*
(g) *Comptr* extensión *f*
(h) *Univ* ***e. course*** curso *m* de extensión universitaria

extensive [ɪks'tensɪv] *adj* **(a)** *(area, knowledge, experience)* amplio(a), extenso(a); *(damage, repairs)* cuantioso(a); *(changes)* profundo(a); *(research, enquiries)* exhaustivo(a); **to make e. use of sth** utilizar algo mucho; **the issue has been given e. coverage in the media** el asunto ha recibido una amplia cobertura en los medios de comunicación **(b)** ***e. farming*** agricultura *f* extensiva

extensively [ɪks'tensɪvlɪ] *adv (to travel)* mucho, a muchas partes; *(to read)* mucho, extensamente; **to use sth e.** utilizar algo mucho; **to be e. damaged** sufrir cuantiosos daños; **e. changed/revised** profundamente transformado(a)/revisado(a)

extensor [ɪk'stensə(r)] *n Anat* **e. (muscle)** (músculo *m*) extensor *m*

extent [ɪks'tent] *n* **(a)** *(of lands)* extensión *f*; *(of problem, damage, knowledge)* alcance *m*; *(of debts, involvement, influence)* magnitud *f*; **along the entire e. of the street** en toda la extensión de la calle
(b) *(degree)* grado *m*, nivel *m*; **to what e.?** ¿hasta qué punto *or* extremo?, ¿en qué medida?; **to an e., to a certain e., to some e.** hasta cierto punto, en cierta medida; **to a great e., to a large e.** en gran medida; **to a lesser e.** en menor medida; **to the e. that..., to such an e. that...** hasta tal punto que...

extenuate [ɪk'stenjʊeɪt] *vt* atenuar; **extenuating circumstances** (circunstancias) atenuantes

extenuation [ɪkstenjʊ'eɪʃən] *n* atenuación *f*; **in e. (of)** como atenuante (de)

exterior [ɪks'tɪərɪə(r)] **1** *n* **(a)** *(outside)* exterior *m*; **beneath her calm e. she was extremely nervous** bajo su apariencia tranquila estaba sumamente inquieta **(b)** *Cin* exterior *m*
2 *adj* **(a)** *(external) (wall, surface)* externo(a), exterior **(b)** *Cin* **an e. shot** una toma en exteriores **(c)** *Math (angle)* externo(a)

exteriorize [ɪk'stɪərɪəraɪz] *vt (emotions)* exteriorizar, manifestar

exterminate [ɪks'tɜːmɪneɪt] *vt* exterminar

extermination [ɪkstɜːmɪ'neɪʃən] *n* exterminio *m*

exterminator [ɪks'tɜːmɪneɪtə(r)] *n (of insects)* técnico(a) *m,f* en desinfección; *(of rodents)* técnico(a) *m,f* en desratización

external [ɪks'tɜːnəl] **1** *adj* **(a)** *(exterior) (wall, surface, appearance)* externo(a), exterior; **for e. use** *or* **application only** *(on medicine)* (de) uso tópico, (de) aplicación externa
(b) *(from outside) (interference, pressure)* externo(a) ▸▸ *Fin* ***e. audit*** auditoría *f* externa; *Univ* ***e. degree*** licenciatura *f* a distancia; *Univ* ***e. examiner*** examinador(ora) *m,f* externo(a)
(c) *(foreign) (relations, trade)* exterior; ***e. affairs*** política *f* exterior
(d) *Comptr* ***e. command*** comando *m* externo; ***e. device*** periférico *m* externo; ***e. hard disk*** disco *m* duro externo
2 externals *npl* apariencias *fpl*

externalize [ɪks'tɜːnəlaɪz] *vt (feelings, emotions)* exteriorizar

externally [ɪks'tɜːnəlɪ] *adv* **(a)** *(outside, outwardly)* por fuera, exteriormente **(b)** *(to apply medicine)* por vía tópica, externamente **(c)** *(by outsiders)* por terceros

extinct [ɪks'tɪŋkt] *adj (species)* extinto(a), extinguido(a); *(volcano)* extinto(a), apagado(a); **to become e.** extinguirse

extinction [ɪks'tɪŋkʃən] *n* extinción *f*; **to hunt an animal to e.** cazar un animal hasta que se extinga

extinguish [ɪks'tɪŋgwɪʃ] *vt* **(a)** *(fire)* extinguir, apagar; *(light, cigarette)* apagar **(b)** *(hope, memory)* apagar, destruir

extinguisher [ɪks'tɪŋgwɪʃə(r)] *n Esp* extintor *m*, *Am* extinguidor *m*

extirpate ['ekstɜːpeɪt] *vt Formal* extirpar, erradicar

extirpation [ekstə'peɪʃən] *n Formal* extirpación *f*

extol, *US* **extoll** [ɪks'təʊl] (*pt & pp* **extolled**) *vt* ensalzar

extort [ɪks'tɔːt] *vt (money)* obtener mediante extorsión; *(promise, confession)* arrancar; **to e. money from sb** extorsionar a alguien

extortion [ɪks'tɔːʃən] *n* extorsión *f*; *Fam* **that's sheer e.!** *(very expensive)* ¡es un robo!

extortionate [ɪks'tɔːʃənɪt] *adj (demand, price)* abusivo(a)

extortionately [ɪks'tɔːʃənɪtlɪ] *adv* **to be e. expensive** tener un precio abusivo *or* exorbitante

extra ['ekstrə] **1** *n* **(a)** *(additional item)* extra *m*; **a model with many optional extras** un modelo con muchos extras; **I can't afford many little extras** *(luxuries)* no me puedo permitir muchos caprichos *or* lujos **(b)** *(on bill)* suplemento *m*, recargo *m* **(c)** *(in movie)* extra *mf* **(d)** *(edition of newspaper)* número *m* especial *or* extra
2 *adj* **(a)** *(additional)* adicional; **an e. helping of cake** una porción más de pastel, otra porción más de pastel; **there are e. towels if you need them** si necesitas toallas, hay más; **he made an e. effort to be polite** tuvo que hacer un verdadero esfuerzo por ser amable; **service/VAT is e.** el servicio/IVA no está incluido; **it was an e. $2** costó *or* valía dos dólares más; **(at) no e. charge** sin recargo ▸▸ ***e. point*** *(in American football)* punto *m* extra; ***e. time*** *(in soccer match)* prórroga *f*; **the game has gone into e. time** están jugando la prórroga
(b) *(spare)* de repuesto, de sobra
3 *adv* **(a)** *(extremely)* **be e. careful with the salt** ten muchísimo cuidado con la sal; **to work e. hard** trabajar muchísimo; **e. fast** superrápido; **e. fine** *(flour, sugar)* extrafino(a); **e. large** extragrande; **e. strong** *(paper, tissue)* superresistente; *(mint)* extra fuerte ▸▸ ***e. virgin olive oil*** aceite *m* de oliva virgen extra
(b) *(in addition)* de más; **to pay e. for a double room** pagar un suplemento por habitación doble

extract 1 *n* ['ekstrækt] **(a)** *(concentrate)* extracto *m*; **beef/malt/vegetable e.** extracto de carne/malta/vegetal **(b)** *(from book, movie)* fragmento *m*
2 *vt* [ɪks'trækt] **(a)** *(take out) (juice, oil, bullet)* extraer, sacar; *(tooth)* extraer; *(cork)* sacar; **I extracted the letter from my pocket** saqué la carta del bolsillo **(b)** *(obtain) (information)* obtener, sacar; *(money)* sacar, extraer; **to e. a confession from sb** arrancar una confesión a alguien **(c)** *Math* **to e. the square root of a number** extraer la raíz cuadrada de un número **(d)** *Comptr (zipped file)* extraer

extraction [ɪks'trækʃən] *n* **(a)** *(removal) (of juice, oil, bullet, tooth)* extracción *f* **(b)** *(social, geographical)* origen *m*, extracción *f*; **of noble/humble e.** de extracción *or* origen noble/humilde; **she is of Danish e.** es de origen danés

extractor [ɪks'træktə(r)] *n* **(a)** *(machine, tool)* extractor *m* **(b)** *(for juice)* exprimidor *m* **(c) e. (fan)** extractor *m* ▸▸ ***e. hood*** campana *f* extractora (de humos) **(d)** *(in gun)* expulsor *m*, extractor *m* de cartuchos

extracurricular ['ekstrəkə'rɪkjʊlə(r)] *adj Sch* extraescolar ▸▸ ***e. activities*** actividades *fpl* extraescolares

extraditable ['ekstrədaɪtəbəl] *adj (person)* extraditable; **e. offence** delito de extradición, delito sujeto a extradición

extradite ['ekstrədaɪt] *vt Law* extraditar

extradition [ekstrə'dɪʃən] *n Law* extradición *f* ▸▸ ***e. request*** demanda *f* de extradición; ***e. treaty*** tratado *m* de extradición

extrajudicial ['ekstrədʒuː'dɪʃəl] *adj* extrajudicial

extramarital ['ekstrə'mærɪtəl] *adj* extramarital

extramural ['ekstrə'mjʊərəl] *adj* **(a)** *Br Univ* **e. course** = curso universitario para alumnos externos; **Department of E. Studies** Departamento de Estudios Externos **(b)** *US* **e. medical care** = asistencia que se brinda fuera de la institución hospitalaria

extraneous [ɪks'treɪnɪəs] *adj Formal* **(a)** *(irrelevant)* no pertinente; **to be e. to sth** no ser pertinente en *or* para algo **(b)** *(from outside)* externo(a), ajeno(a)

extranet ['ekstrənet] *n Comptr* extranet *m*

extraordinarily [ɪks'trɔːdənərɪlɪ] *adv* **(a)** *(as intensifier)* extraordinariamente; **e. beautiful** bellísimo(a); **it took an e. long time to get there** llevó muchísimo tiempo llegar allí **(b)** *(unusually)* extraordinariamente; **e. for him, he arrived on time** por extraordinario que parezca, llegó a tiempo

extraordinary [ɪks'trɔːdənrɪ] *adj* **(a)** *(outstanding)* extraordinario(a)
(b) *(strange, unusual) (person)* extraño(a), extraordinario(a); *(behaviour, appearance, outfit)* insólito(a); **I find it e. that you did not inform the police** me parece raro que no hayas informado a la policía; **the e. thing is that...** lo extraordinario es que...; **quite e.!** ¡increíble!, ¡fabuloso!
(c) *(additional) (meeting, session)* extraordinario(a) ▸▸ ***e. general meeting*** junta *f* general extraordinaria; ***e. powers*** poderes *mpl* extraordinarios, competencias *fpl* extraordinarias

extrapolate [ɪk'stræpəleɪt] **1** *vt* **(a)** *(infer from facts)* extrapolar **(b)** *Math* extrapolar **(from** a partir de)
2 *vi* **to e. from sth** extrapolar (a partir) de algo

extrapolation [ɪkstræpə'leɪʃən] *n* extrapolación *f*

extrasensory ['ekstrə'sensərɪ] *adj* extrasensorial ▸▸ ***e. perception*** percepción *f* extrasensorial

extraterrestrial ['ekstrətɪ'restrɪəl] **1** *n* extraterrestre *mf*
2 *adj* extraterrestre

extraterritorial ['ekstrəterɪ'tɔːrɪəl] *adj (possessions, rights)* extraterritorial

extrauterine ['ekstrə'juːtəraɪn] *adj Med* extrauterino(a)

extravagance [ɪks'trævəgəns] *n* (**a**) *(excessive spending)* derroche *m*, despilfarro *m*; **his bankruptcy was due to the e. of his tastes** se arruinó por lo mucho que despilfarró (**b**) *(expensive purchase)* dispendio *m*; **to allow oneself little extravagances/the occasional e.** permitirse pequeños lujos/un lujo esporádico *or* ocasional (**c**) *(exaggeratedness) (of behaviour, dress, gesture)* exageración *f*

extravagant [ɪks'trævəgənt] *adj* (**a**) *(wasteful, profligate) (person)* derrochador(ora), manirroto(a); *(tastes)* caro(a); *(lifestyle)* de lujo; **an e. purchase** un despilfarro; **to be e. with other people's money** tirar *or* malgastar el dinero de los demás

(**b**) *(exaggerated) (behaviour, dress, gesture)* extravagante; *(comparison)* exagerado(a); *(praise)* excesivo(a); **to make e. claims for sth** atribuir a algo exageradas cualidades

extravagantly [ɪks'trævəgəntlɪ] *adv* (**a**) *(lavishly)* dispendiosamente; **to live e.** vivir a todo lujo (**b**) *(exaggeratedly) (to behave, dress)* extravagantemente; *(to praise)* exageradamente

extravaganza [ɪkstrævə'gænzə] *n* espectáculo *m* fastuoso

extravehicular ['ekstrəvɪ'hɪkjʊlə(r)] *adj (in space flight)* fuera de la nave ►► ***e. activity*** paseo *m* espacial

extraversion, extravert *etc* = **extroversion, extrovert** *etc*

Extremadura [ekstrəmə'djuːrə] *n* Extremadura

extreme [ɪks'triːm] **1** *n* extremo *m*; **to go from one e. to the other** pasar de un extremo al otro; **to go to extremes** recurrir a comportamientos extremos; **to take** *or* **carry sth to extremes** llevar algo al extremo; **to go to the opposite e.** irse al extremo opuesto; **extremes of temperature** temperaturas extremas; **in the e.** en grado sumo; **polite/careful/reckless in the e.** extremadamente amable/cuidadoso/imprudente

2 *adj* (**a**) *(intense, great) (heat, pain)* extremo(a); **they live in e. poverty** viven en la más absoluta pobreza; **to be in e. pain** sufrir un dolor terrible; **e. old age** vejez muy avanzada; *Cin & TV* **e. close-up** primerísimo plano

(**b**) *(immoderate) (views, measures, reaction)* extremo(a); **to be e. in one's beliefs** ser de creencias extremistas *or* radicales; **an e. case** un caso extremo ►► ***e. sports*** deportes *mpl* extremos

(**c**) *(furthest away)* **on the e. left/right of the screen** en el extremo izquierdo/derecho de la pantalla; **e. opposites** polos opuestos; **they are e. opposites of the political spectrum** se encuentran en extremos opuestos dentro del espectro político; *Pol* **the e. left** la extrema izquierda

(**d**) *Rel* ***e. unction*** extremaunción *f*

extremely [ɪks'triːmlɪ] *adv* extremadamente, sumamente

extremism [ɪks'triːmɪzəm] *n* extremismo *m*

extremist [ɪks'triːmɪst] **1** *n* extremista *mf*

2 *adj* extremista

extremity [ɪks'tremɪtɪ] *n* (**a**) *(end)* extremo *m* (**b**) **the extremities** *(of the body)* las extremidades (**c**) *(extreme nature) (of belief, view)* extremismo *m* (**d**) *(of situation)* gravedad *f* extrema; **to help sb in their e.** ayudar a alguien que está pasando por una situación extrema (**e**) *(extreme measure)* medida *f* extrema

extricate ['ekstrɪkeɪt] *vt* sacar, extraer; **to e. oneself from** *(danger, difficulties)* escapar *or* librarse de; *(meeting, conversation)* escabullirse de

extrinsic [eks'trɪnsɪk] *adj Formal* extrínseco(a)

extroversion, extraversion [ekstrə'vɜːʃən] *n Psy* extroversión *f*, extraversión *f*

extrovert, extravert ['ekstrəvɜːt] **1** *n* extrovertido(a) *m,f*, extravertido(a) *m,f*

2 *adj* extrovertido(a), extravertido(a)

extroverted ['ekstrəvɜːtɪd] *adj* extrovertido(a), extravertido(a)

extrude [ɪks'truːd] *vt Tech* extrudir

exuberance [ɪg'zjuːbərəns] *n* (**a**) *(of person)* euforia *f*, exultación *f*; *(of writing)* exuberancia *f*; **to be full of e.** estar exultante (**b**) *(of vegetation)* exuberancia *f*

exuberant [ɪg'zjuːbərənt] *adj* (**a**) *(person)* eufórico(a), exultante; *(style)* exuberante (**b**) *(vegetation)* exuberante

exuberantly [ɪg'zjuːbərəntlɪ] *adv* con euforia, eufóricamente

exude [ɪg'zjuːd] **1** *vt* (**a**) *(sweat, odour)* exudar, rezumar (**b**) *(health, confidence)* rebosar, rezumar

2 *vi (sap, blood)* brotar

exult [ɪg'zʌlt] *vi Formal* (**a**) *(rejoice)* alborozarse, exultar (**in** ante) (**b**) *(be triumphant)* regocijarse (**over** con)

exultant [ɪg'zʌltənt] *adj Formal* exultante

exultantly [ɪg'zʌltəntlɪ] *adv Formal* con gran júbilo, exultantemente

exultation [egzʌl'teɪʃən] *n Formal* júbilo *m*, euforia *f*

exurb [eks'ɜːb] *n US* = zona residencial ubicada en las afueras de una ciudad

exurbia [eks'ɜːbɪə] *n US* = zona en la que se encuentran diferentes barrios residenciales en las afueras de una ciudad

EYE [aɪ] **1** *n* (**a**) *(of person)* ojo *m*; **he has blue eyes** tiene los ojos azules; **I have weak eyes** tengo la vista débil; **to open/close one's eyes** abrir/cerrar los ojos; **to look sb (straight) in the e.** mirar a alguien a los ojos; **the e. of the camera** la mirada de la cámara ►► ***e. contact*** contacto *m* visual; **to establish e. contact with sb** mirar a alguien a los ojos, cruzar la mirada con alguien; *US* ***e. doctor*** óptico(a) *m,f*; ***e. gel*** gel *m* para los ojos; ***at e. level*** a la altura de los ojos; ***e. make-up*** maquillaje *m* de ojos; ***e. pencil*** lápiz *m* de ojos; ***e. socket*** cuenca *f* del ojo; ***e. test*** revisión *f* ocular *or* de la vista; ***e. tooth*** colmillo *m*

(**b**) *(gaze)* **her eyes fell on the letter** al bajar la vista vió la carta; **the film looks at the world through the eyes of a child** la película mira el mundo a través de los ojos de un niño; **to look at sth with a critical e.** mirar algo con ojo crítico

(**c**) *(of needle)* ojo *m*

(**d**) *(on potato)* ojo *m*

(**e**) **the e. of the storm** el ojo del huracán

(**f**) IDIOMS **all eyes will be on the prime minister this week** todas las miradas recaerán esta semana sobre el primer ministro; **they were all eyes** miraban con enorme atención; **as far as the e. can see** hasta donde alcanza la vista; **she's our eyes and ears at central office** nos mantiene informados de lo que ocurre en la oficina central; **he stole it before my (very) eyes** lo robó delante de mis ojos; **I couldn't believe my eyes** no podía creer lo que veía *or* estaba viendo; **to catch sb's e.** *(attract attention)* llamar la atención de alguien; **I was trying to catch your e., but you didn't notice** intentaba hacer que me miraras, pero no me viste; *Fam* **to clap eyes on** echarle el ojo *or* la vista a; **to cry one's eyes out** llorar a lágrima viva; **to disappear from the public e.** desaparecer de la escena pública; **your eyes were too big for your stomach!** ¡comiste más con los ojos *or* con la vista que con la boca!; **his eyes were popping out of his head** los ojos se le salían de las órbitas; *Fam* **her eyes were out on stalks** tenía los ojos como platos; **to feast one's eyes on sth** recrearse la vista con algo *or* mirando algo; **this is for your eyes only** esto sólo te lo enseño a ti; **to get one's e. in** *(when playing sport)* afinar la puntería; **to give sb the e.** echarle unas miraditas a; **a scene of devastation greeted** *or* **met my eyes** ante mis ojos se presentaba una escena de destrucción; **to have an e. for detail/colour/a bargain** tener buen ojo para los detalles/el color/las gangas; **to have an e. to** *or* **for the main chance** actuar de manera oportunista, estar a la que salta; **the government clearly has half an e. on the forthcoming election** el gobierno no pierde de vista las próximas elecciones; **to have a good e.** *(at billiards, tennis, shooting)* tener buen ojo; **to have one's e. on sth/sb** *(be observing)* estar vigilando algo/a alguien; **to have one's e. on sth** *(be intending to buy)* tenerle el ojo echado a algo; **to have one's e. on sb** *(be attracted to)* haberle echado el ojo a alguien; **he only has eyes for her** sólo tiene ojos para ella; **he has eyes in** *or* **at the back of his head** se entera de todo, *RP* tiene ojos en la nuca; **she has eyes like a hawk** no se le pasa ni un detalle, *RP* tiene un ojo de lince; **to be in the public e.** estar en (el) candelero; **she can do no wrong in his eyes** para él, ella es perfecta; **in the eye(s) of the law** a (los) ojos de la ley; **to keep an e. on sth/sb** vigilar algo/a alguien; **I'll keep an e. out for it/him** estaré al tanto de ello/él; **keep your e. on the ball** no pierdas de vista la pelota; **keep your eyes open for any cheap printers** estate alerta por si ves alguna impresora barata; **to keep one's eyes and ears open** mantener los ojos y los oídos bien abiertos; **to keep one's eyes peeled** *or* **skinned** no perder ojo; **to make eyes at sb** echar miradas lánguidas *or* miraditas a alguien; **I couldn't meet her eyes** no me atrevía a mirarla a los ojos; **there's more to this/him than meets the e.** es más complicado de lo que parece; *Br Fam* **that's one in the e. for him!** ¡le va a sentar *or* caer como una patada!; **to open sb's eyes to sth** abrirle a alguien los ojos en relación con algo, hacer ver algo a alguien; **to please** *or* **delight the e.** deleitar la vista; **to run** *or* **cast one's e. over sth** echar una ojeada a algo; **I don't see e. to e. with my boss** *(we don't get on)* no me llevo bien con mi jefe; **we don't see e. to e. about abortion** no compartimos las mismas ideas sobre el aborto; **I saw it with my own eyes** lo vi con mis propios ojos; **to shut** *or* **close one's eyes to sth** negarse a ver algo, no querer ver algo; **to set** *or* **lay eyes on sth** ver algo; **he couldn't take his eyes off it/her** no podía quitarle *or Andes, RP* sacarle los ojos de encima; **to my beginner's e., it seems fine** desde mi mirada de principiante, parece bien; **a story told through the eyes of a child** una historia contada desde la perspectiva de un niño; **to be up to one's eyes in work/debt** estar hasta el cuello de trabajo/

deudas; **with an e. to...** con vistas a...; **I could do it with my eyes closed** *or* **shut** lo podría hacer con los ojos cerrados; **she wanders around with her eyes closed** *or* **shut most of the time** la mayoría del tiempo no se entera de nada; **to do sth with one's eyes open** hacer algo a sabiendas; **I'd give my e. teeth to go with them** daría *Esp* un ojo de la cara *or Am* todo por ir con ellos; PROV **what the e. doesn't see, the heart doesn't grieve over** ojos que no ven, corazón que no siente; PROV **an e. for an e., a tooth for a tooth** ojo por ojo, diente por diente; **their justice is based on an e. for an e., a tooth for a tooth** su justicia se basa en la ley del talión

2 *vt* observar, mirar; **they eyed each other suspiciously** se miraron con sospecha

▸ **eye up** *vt sep Fam (ogle)* desnudar con la mirada

---

eyeball ['aɪbɔːl] **1** *n* globo *m* ocular; *Fam* **e. to e.** muy cerca, frente a frente; *Fam* **I'm up to my eyeballs in work** estoy *Esp* hasta arriba *or Am* hasta las narices de trabajo; *Fam* **doped** *or* **drugged (up) to the eyeballs** drogadísimo(a), *Esp* muy puesto(a), *RP* falopeado(a) al mango

2 *vt Fam* repasar de arriba a abajo a

eyebath ['aɪbɑːθ] *n Br* lavaojos *m inv*

eyebolt ['aɪbɒlt] *n* perno *m* de argolla

eyebrow ['aɪbraʊ] *n* ceja *f*; **to raise one's eyebrows** *(in surprise)* arquear las cejas; **this remark raised a few eyebrows** *or* **caused a few raised eyebrows** este comentario provocó estupor entre algunos ▸▸ ***e. pencil*** lápiz *m* de ojos, delineador *m*; ***e. tweezers*** pinzas *fpl* de depilar

eyecatching ['aɪkætʃɪŋ] *adj* llamativo(a)

eye-cup ['aɪkʌp] *n US* lavaojos *m inv*

eye-drops ['aɪdrɒps] *npl (medicine)* colirio *m*

eyeful ['aɪfʊl] *n* (**a**) *(of dirt, dust)* **I got an e. of sand** tengo el ojo lleno de arena (**b**) *Fam* **to get an e. of sth** *(look at)* mirar algo bien; **she's quite an e.!** ¡está para comérsela *or* como un tren!

eyeglass ['aɪglɑːs] *n* monóculo *m*

eyeglasses ['aɪglɑːsɪz] *npl US (spectacles)* gafas *fpl*

eyehole ['aɪhəʊl] *n* (**a**) *(in mask)* (agujero *m* del) ojo *m* (**b**) *(peephole)* mirilla *f* (**c**) *(eye socket)* cuenca *f* del ojo

eyelash ['aɪlæʃ] *n* pestaña *f*

eyelet ['aɪlɪt] *n* (**a**) *(hole)* ojete *m* (**b**) *(metal ring)* aro *m* (del ojete)

eyelid ['aɪlɪd] *n* párpado *m*

eyeliner ['aɪlaɪnə(r)] *n* lápiz *m* de ojos

eye-opener ['aɪəʊpənə(r)] *n Fam* (**a**) *(surprise)* revelación *f*; **it was a real e. for him** para él fue una verdadera revelación; **the experience proved a bit of an e. for us all!** la experiencia nos abrió los ojos a todos (**b**) *US (drink)* = trago que se toma de buena mañana

eyepatch ['aɪpætʃ] *n* parche *m*

eyepiece ['aɪpiːs] *n* ocular *m*

eye-popper ['aɪpɒpə(r)] *n US Fam* **her dress was a real e.** el vestido que tenía puesto era alucinante

eye-popping ['aɪpɒpɪŋ] *adj US Fam* alucinante

eyeshade ['aɪʃeɪd] *n* visera *f*

eyeshadow ['aɪʃædəʊ] *n* sombra *f* de ojos

eyesight ['aɪsaɪt] *n* vista *f*; **to have good/bad e.** tener buena/mala vista, tener bien/mal la vista; **his e. is failing** ya no ve tan bien, le comienza a fallar la vista; **to lose one's e.** perder la vista, quedarse ciego(a)

eyesore ['aɪsɔː(r)] *n (building)* engendro *m*, adefesio *m*

eyestrain ['aɪstreɪn] *n* vista *f* cansada; **it causes e.** cansa la vista

Eyetie ['aɪtaɪ] *n Br Fam Pej* = término despectivo para referirse a personas de origen italiano, *RP* tano(a) *m,f*

eyewash ['aɪwɒʃ] *n* (**a**) *(for eye)* colirio *m*, baño *m* ocular (**b**) *(nonsense)* paparruchas *fpl*

eyewear ['aɪweə(r)] *n* gafas *fpl*, *Am* anteojos *mpl*, *Am* lentes *mpl*

eyewitness ['aɪwɪtnɪs] *n* testigo *mf* presencial *or* ocular

eyrie ['ɪərɪ], *US* **aerie** ['eərɪ] *n* nido *m* de águila

Ezekiel [ɪ'ziːkɪel] *pr n* Ezequiel

e-zine ['iːziːn] *n Comptr* revista *f* electrónica

F, f

F, f [ef] *n (letter)* F, f *f*

F [ef] *n* **(a)** *Br Euph* **the F word** = eufemismo para referirse a la palabra "fuck" **(b)** *Mus* fa *m* **(c)** *Sch* muy deficiente *m*; **to get an F** *(in exam, essay)* sacar un muy deficiente **(d)** (*abbr* **Fahrenheit**) F

f **(a)** *Mus* (*abbr* **forte**) forte **(b)** (*abbr* **female**) *(person)* m.; *(animal)* h. **(c)** (*abbr* **feminine**) f., fem.

FA [ef'eɪ] *n Br* **(a)** (*abbr* **Football Association**) = federación inglesa de fútbol; **the FA Cup** = la copa de la federación inglesa de fútbol, *Esp* ≃ la Copa del Rey **(b)** *Fam Euph* (*abbr* **Fanny Adams** *or* **fuck all**) **sweet FA** nada de nada

fa [fɑː] *n Mus* fa *m*

FAA [efeɪ'eɪ] *n US* (*abbr* **Federal Aviation Administration**) Dirección *f* Federal de Aviación

fab [fæb] *adj Fam Esp* chupi, genial

Fabian ['feɪbɪən] **1** *n* fabiano(a) *m,f*

2 *adj* fabiano(a); **the F. Society** la Sociedad Fabiana

fable ['feɪbəl] *n* fábula *f*

fabled ['feɪbəld] *adj* legendario(a), fabuloso(a)

fabric ['fæbrɪk] *n* **(a)** *(cloth)* tejido *m* ►► ***f. conditioner*** suavizante *m* (para la ropa); ***f. softener*** suavizante *m* (para la ropa) **(b)** *(framework, structure)* estructura *f*; **the f. of society** el tejido social

> **False friend**: The Spanish noun **fábrica** is not a translation for the English word **fabric**. In Spanish **fábrica** means "factory".

fabricate ['fæbrɪkeɪt] *vt* **(a)** *(story)* inventar; *(evidence)* falsificar **(b)** *(manufacture)* fabricar

fabrication [fæbrɪ'keɪʃən] *n* **(a)** *(of story)* invención *f*; *(of evidence)* falsificación *f*; **it's pure f.** es pura invención **(b)** *(manufacture)* fabricación *f*

fabulist ['fæbjʊlɪst] *n Literary* **(a)** *(storyteller)* escritor(ora) *m,f* de fábulas, fabulista *mf* **(b)** *(liar)* fabulador(ora) *m,f*

fabulous ['fæbjʊləs] *adj* **(a)** *(astounding)* fabuloso(a), magnífico(a); **f. wealth** riqueza fabulosa **(b)** *Fam (marvellous)* fabuloso(a); **we had a f. time** lo pasamos estupendamente **(c)** *(mythical)* fabuloso(a)

fabulously ['fæbjʊləslɪ] *adv (as intensifier)* tremendamente

facade, façade [fə'sɑːd] *n* **(a)** *(of building)* fachada *f* **(b)** *(false appearance)* fachada *f*; **his confidence is just a f.** su seguridad es sólo una fachada

---

FACE [feɪs] **1** *n* **(a)** *(of person)* cara *f*, rostro *m*; **she has a beautiful f.** tiene una cara bonita; **he had a frown on his f.** tenía el ceño fruncido; **I never forget a f.** nunca olvido una cara; **to look sb in the f.** mirar a alguien a la cara; *Fig* **I shall never be able to look her in the f. again** nunca podré volver a mirarla a la cara; **I told him to his f.** se lo dije a *or* en la cara; **to be f. to f. with sb** estar cara a cara con alguien; **to meet sb f. to f.** encontrarse frente a frente con alguien; **to bring sb f. to f. with sth/sb** hacer que alguien se enfrente a algo/alguien ►► ***f. card*** *(playing card)* figura *f*; ***f. cloth*** toallita *f*; ***f. cream*** crema *f* facial; *Br* ***f. flannel*** toallita *f*; ***f. mask*** *(cosmetic)* mascarilla *f* (facial); *(in ice hockey)* protector *m* facial; ***f. pack*** mascarilla *f* (facial); ***f. powder*** polvos *mpl (para la cara)*; *US* ***f. time*** *(meeting)* tiempo *m* de contacto personal; **we need more f. time on TV** necesitamos más presencia en televisión

(b) *(expression)* cara *f*; **she had a sad f.** tenía la cara triste, *RP* tenía cara de triste; **his f. was a picture** su cara era un poema; **you should have seen her f. when I told her** deberías haber visto la cara que puso cuando se lo dije; **his f. dropped** *or* **fell** puso cara larga; **to keep a straight f.** quedarse serio(a); **to make** *or* **pull a f.** *(of distaste)* poner cara de asco; **to make** *or* **pull faces** hacer muecas, poner caras

(c) *(appearance)* **the changing f. of Britain** el rostro cambiante de Gran Bretaña; **the acceptable f. of capitalism** la cara más aceptable del capitalismo; **to lose f.** sufrir una humillación; **to save f.** salvar las apariencias; **the new legislation is just a f. saver** la nueva legislación sólo sirve para salvar las apariencias ►► ***f. value*** *(of stamp, note)* valor *m* nominal; *Fig* **to take sth at f. value** aceptar algo sin darle más vueltas

(d) *(person)* cara *f*; **a famous/new f.** una cara famosa/nueva; **the same old faces** las mismas caras de siempre

(e) *(surface) (of coin, mountain, cube)* cara *f*; *(of the earth)* superficie *f*, faz *f*; *(of clock)* esfera *f*; *(of coalmine)* frente *m*, tajo *m*; *(of building)* fachada *f*; *(of golf club, table tennis bat)* cara *f (con la que se golpea)*; **f. up/down** boca arriba/abajo; **to disappear off the f. of the earth** desaparecer de la faz de la tierra

(f) *Typ* tipo *m*, letra *f*; **bold f.** letra *or* tipo negrita

(g) IDIOMS *Fam* **to have a f. like the back (end) of a bus** ser un coco *or RP* cuco, *Esp* ser feo(a) con avaricia, *RP* ser más feo que el miércoles, *Andes, RP* ser un bagre; **her f. doesn't fit** *(in job, company)* no encaja bien; **the situation blew up in his f.** el problema le reventó *or* estalló en las manos; *US very Fam* **get out of my f.!** ¡piérdete!, *RP* ¡borrate!; *Fam* **in your f.** impactante, atrevido(a); *US Fam* **he's always in my f.** está siempre encima *or Am* arriba de mí; *Fam* **to be off one's f.** *(drunk) Esp, Méx* estar pedo, *RP* estar en pedo; *(on drugs)* estar colocado(a) *or Méx* grifo(a); *Fam* **to put one's f. on** *(make-up)* pintarse; **to set one's f. against sth** oponerse cerrilmente a algo; **to show one's f.** dejarse ver, hacer acto de presencia; **don't ever show your f. here again!** ¡ni se te ocurra volver a aparecer por aquí!; *very Fam* **shut your f.!** ¡cierra el pico!, ¡cállate la boca!

2 *vt* **(a)** *(look towards)* mirar a; **to f. the front** mirar al frente; **we were facing each other** estábamos el uno frente al otro; **the house faces the river** la casa da al río; **she turned to f. him** se puso cara a él

(b) *(actively confront) (difficulty, danger)* enfrentarse a; **they f. Colombia in the next round** se enfrentarán a Colombia en la próxima ronda; **I don't think I can f. her** no creo que pueda mirarla a la cara; **I don't think I can f. listening to him for another hour** no creo que pueda aguantar escucharlo otra hora más; **to f. the press** hacer frente a la prensa; **to f. facts** *or* **the truth** admitir la realidad *or* la verdad; **let's f. it** hay que admitirlo; IDIOM **to f. the music** apechugar con las consecuencias

(c) *(be confronted by)* **he faces a sentence of up to twenty years** puede recibir una condena de hasta veinte años; **the problem facing us** el problema que se nos plantea *or* que tenemos delante; **to be faced with a decision** tener que plantearse una decisión; **to be faced with the prospect of having to do sth** enfrentarse a la perspectiva de tener que hacer algo

(d) *Constr* **the building is faced with brick/stone** la fachada es de ladrillo visto/piedra

3 *vi* **(a)** *(be oriented)* **she was facing towards the camera** estaba de cara a la cámara; **he was facing away from me** me daba la espalda; **to f. north/south** *(building, window)* estar orientado(a) hacia el norte/sur; **the house faces away from the river** la casa da al lado opuesto al río

(b) *Mil* **about f.!** ¡media vuelta!

4 in the face of *prep (danger, threat)* ante

5 on the face of it *adv* a primera vista

▸ **face down** *vt sep* **he faced down his critics** se enfrentó a sus críticos y los hizo callar

▸ **face off** *vi US Sport (teams)* enfrentarse

▸ **face up to** *vt insep (person, fears)* hacer frente a

---

face-ache ['feɪseɪk] *n Fam Esp* cardo *m*, *Méx* gocho(a) *m,f*, *RP* asco *m*

-faced [feɪst] *suffix* **round/long-f.** de cara redonda/alargada

face-hardened ['feɪshɑːdənd] *adj (iron, steel)* templado(a)

faceless ['feɪslɪs] *adj* anónimo(a)

face-lift ['feɪslɪft] *n* **(a)** *(plastic surgery)* lifting *m*, estiramiento *m* de piel; **to have a f.** hacerse un lifting **(b)** *(of building)* lavado *m* de cara

face-off ['feɪsɒf] *n* **(a)** *(confrontation)* enfrentamiento *m* (a cara de perro) **(b)** *(in ice hockey)* saque *m* neutral

face-painting ['feɪspeɪntɪŋ] *n* pintado *m or* pintura *f* del rostro

face-saving ['feɪsseɪvɪŋ] *adj (agreement, manoeuvre)* para salvar las apariencias

facet ['fæsɪt] *n* **(a)** *(of gem)* faceta *f* **(b)** *(of situation)* faceta *f*

facetious [fə'siːʃəs] *adj* guasón(ona), jocoso(a); **I was being f.** estaba bromeando

facetiously [fə'siːʃəslɪ] *adv* en tono de burla *or* guasa

facetiousness [fə'siːʃəsnɪs] *n* guasonería *f*, jocosidad *f*

face-to-face ['feɪstə'feɪs] *adj (meeting, confrontation)* cara a cara

facia = **fascia**

facial ['feɪʃəl] **1** *n* **to have a f.** hacerse una limpieza de cutis
2 *adj* facial ►► ***f. hair*** vello *m* facial; ***f. sauna*** sauna *f* facial

facile ['fæsaɪl] *adj (argument, remark)* obvio(a), fácil

facilitate [fə'sɪlɪteɪt] *vt Formal* facilitar

facilitator [fə'sɪlɪteɪtə(r)] *n (person)* promotor(ora) *m,f*

facility [fə'sɪlɪtɪ] *n* **(a)** *(ease)* facilidad *f*; **to do sth with great f.** hacer algo con gran facilidad
(b) *(skill)* habilidad *f*, facilidad *f*; **to have a f. for** *or* **with languages** tener facilidad para los idiomas
(c) *(building, unit)* centro *m*, instalaciones *fpl*; **a training/research f.** un centro de entrenamiento/ investigación
(d) facilities *(resources, equipment)* instalaciones y servicios; **the university has excellent research facilities** la universidad cuenta con excelentes instalaciones y servicios de investigación; **the university has excellent computer facilities** la universidad está dotada de un excelente sistema informático; **storage facilities** lugar *or* sitio para almacenamiento; **cooking facilities** equipamiento para cocinar; **we don't have the facilities to hold a conference here** no contamos con los medios adecuados para organizar un congreso
(e) *Fin* **we offer easy credit facilities** ofrecemos un ágil servicio de préstamos; *Br* **an overdraft f.** un servicio para girar en descubierto
(f) *(device, feature)* dispositivo *m*; **it has a spell-check f.** cuenta con una herramienta de revisión ortográfica

facing ['feɪsɪŋ] **1** *adj Typ* ***f. pages*** páginas *fpl* enfrentadas
2 *n* **(a)** *(of garment)* entretela *f* **(b)** *(on wall)* revestimiento *m*

facsimile [fæk'sɪmɪlɪ] *n (copy)* facsímil *m*; **in f.** en facsímil ►► ***f. edition*** edición *f* facsímil

---

FACT [fækt] **1** *n* **(a)** *(thing that is true)* hecho *m*; **despite the f. that...** a pesar del hecho de que...; **in view of** *or* **given the f. that...** en vista de que..., dado que...; **it's a f. that...** se sabe que...; **it's a f. of life** es una realidad insoslayable *or* un hecho cierto; **the facts of life** *(sexual)* lo referente al sexo y a la reproducción; *(hard reality)* la realidad de las cosas; **I want a pay rise – is that a f.?** quiero una subida de sueldo – ¿no me digas?; **the f. (of the matter) is that...** el hecho es que...; **the f. that you didn't know it's a crime is irrelevant** el que no supieras que era delito no viene al caso; **the f. remains that it was a failure** no obstante, fue un fracaso; **the facts speak for themselves** los hechos hablan por sí mismos; **to know for a f. (that)...** saber a ciencia cierta (que)...; **to stick** *or* **keep to the facts** centrarse en los hechos; *Law* **after the f.** después de los hechos
(b) *(piece of information, detail)* dato *m*; **the book is full of interesting facts** el libro está lleno de datos interesantes; **to get one's facts right/wrong** informarse bien/mal; **facts and figures** datos ►► ***f. file*** ficha *f* técnica *(con datos de interés)*; ***f. sheet*** hoja *f* informativa
(c) *(reality)* realidad *f*; **to distinguish f. from fiction** distinguir la realidad de la ficción
2 in fact *adv* **(a)** *(giving additional or more precise information)* de hecho; **in f., it wouldn't have mattered if we had known in advance** de hecho no habría importado que lo hubiéramos sabido de antemano; **he asked us, in f. ordered us, to be quiet** nos preguntó, bueno nos mandó, que nos calláramos
(b) *(correcting)* en realidad; **he claims to be a writer, but in (actual) f. he's a journalist** asegura que es escritor, pero en realidad es periodista
(c) *(emphasizing, reinforcing)* **did she in f. say when she was going to arrive?** ¿pero dijo cuándo iba a llegar?; **he said it'd take two days and he was in f. correct** dijo que llevaría dos días y, en efecto, así fue

---

fact-finding ['fæktfaɪndɪŋ] *adj* de investigación; **a f. mission** una misión investigadora

faction[1] ['fækʃən] *n (group)* facción *f*

faction[2] *n* **(a)** *(novel)* = novela que narra hechos reales **(b)** *(TV programme)* docudrama *m*

factional ['fækʃənəl] *adj (in-fighting, disputes)* entre facciones

factionalism ['fækʃənəlɪzəm] *n* faccionalismo *m*

factious ['fækʃəs] *adj* faccioso(a)

factitious [fæk'tɪʃəs] *adj Formal* forzado(a), artificial

factoid ['fæktɔɪd] *n* = noticia poco fiable que parece veraz porque aparece repetidamente en los medios de comunicación

factor ['fæktə(r)] *n* **(a)** *(element)* factor *m*; **age is an important f.** la edad es un factor importante; **the human/time f.** el factor humano/ tiempo
(b) *Math* factor *m*; **by a f. of ten** *(increase)* en un factor diez ►► ***f. analysis*** análisis *m* factorial
(c) *Econ* ***factors of production*** factores *mpl* de producción
(d) *(in suntan cream)* **f. 6/15** factor 6/15
(e) *Scot (estate manager)* administrador(ora) *m,f*

► **factor in** *vt sep (include in calculation)* incluir, contar

factorial [fæk'tɔːrɪəl] *n Math* factorial *f*

factorize ['fæktəraɪz] *vt Math* factorizar, descomponer en factores

factory ['fæktərɪ] *n* fábrica *f*, *Am* planta *f* ►► ***f. farm*** granja *f* industrial; ***f. farming*** las granjas de cría intensiva; ***f. price*** precio *m* de fábrica; ***f. ship*** buque *m* factoría; ***f. shop*** tienda *f or* almacén *m* de fábrica; ***f. worker*** obrero(a) *m,f* industrial

factotum [fæk'təʊtəm] *n Formal* factótum *mf*

factual ['fæktʃʊəl] *adj* basado(a) en hechos reales; **a f. error** un error de hecho

factually ['fæktʃʊəlɪ] *adv* ateniéndose a los hechos; **f. accurate/ inaccurate** con datos precisos/ imprecisos

faculty ['fækəltɪ] *n* **(a)** *(of mind, body)* facultad *f*; **she is still in possession of all her faculties** tiene pleno uso de sus facultades; **the f. of reason** la razón; **the f. of speech** la facultad del habla **(b)** *(section of university)* facultad *f*; **the F. of Arts/Law/Medicine** la facultad de letras/derecho/medicina **(c)** *US (staff)* cuerpo *m* docente

fad [fæd] *n Fam* moda *f*; **his latest f. is ballroom dancing** ahora le ha dado por los bailes de salón

faddy ['fædɪ], **faddish** ['fædɪʃ] *adj Fam (fussy)* quisquilloso(a), tiquismiquis *inv*

fade [feɪd] **1** *vt* **(a)** *(cloth, colour)* desteñir **(b)** *Sport (ball)* abrir
2 *vi* **(a)** *(material)* desteñirse, perder color; *(colour)* apagarse; *(light)* oscurecerse
(b) *(flower, beauty)* marchitarse
(c) *(disappear slowly) (music, sound)* desvanecerse, desaparecer gradualmente; *(memory)* desvanecerse; *(anger, interest)* disiparse; *(hope, smile)* desvanecerse; **to f. from memory** desaparecer de la memoria
(d) *(weaken)* **to be fading fast** *(person)* apagarse por momentos
(e) *US Fam (leave)* escabullirse, *Am* hacerse humo
3 *n Cin, TV & Rad* fundido *m*

► **fade away** *vi* **(a)** *(disappear slowly) (music, sound)* desvanecerse; *(memory)* desvanecerse; *(anger, interest)* disiparse; *(hope, smile)* desvanecerse **(b)** *(weaken) (person)* debilitarse

► **fade in** *Cin, TV & Rad* **1** *vt sep (picture, sound)* fundir
2 *vi (picture, sound)* fundirse

► **fade out** *Cin, TV & Rad* **1** *vt sep (picture)* fundir en negro; *(sound)* hacer desaparecer gradualmente
2 *vi (picture)* fundirse en negro; *(sound)* desvanecerse, desaparecer gradualmente

faded ['feɪdɪd] *adj (flower)* marchito(a); *(photograph, garment)* descolorido(a)

fade-in ['feɪdɪn] *n Cin, TV & Rad* fundido *m*

fade-out ['feɪdaʊt] *n Cin, TV & Rad (of picture)* fundido *m* en negro; *(of sound)* desaparición *f* gradual

fading ['feɪdɪŋ] *adj (light)* mortecino(a)

faecal, *US* **fecal** ['fiːkəl] *adj* fecal ►► ***f. matter*** heces *fpl* fecales

faeces, *US* **feces** ['fiːsiːz] *npl* heces *fpl*

Faeroe ['feərəʊ] *n* **the F. Islands, the Faeroes** las islas Feroe

faff [fæf]

► **faff about, faff around** *vi Br Fam* enredar; **stop faffing around and make up your mind** deja de enredar *or* dar vueltas y decídete

fag [fæg] **1** *n* **(a)** *Br Fam (unpleasant job)* lata *f*, rollo *m*
(b) *US very Fam (homosexual)* maricón *m*, *Méx* tortillón *m*, *RP* trolo *m* ►► ***f. hag*** = mujer que se relaciona con hombres homosexuales
(c) *Fam (cigarette)* pitillo *m* ►► *Fam* ***f. end*** *(cigarette butt)* colilla *f*, *Am* pucho *m*; **the f. end of a conversation** los últimos coletazos *or* el final de una conversación; **stop picking up f. ends!** ¡no seas chismoso *or Esp* cotilla!
(d) *Br (at public school)* = alumno que sirve a otro de un grado superior

2 *vt* (*pt & pp* **fagged**) *Fam (exhaust)* dejar hecho polvo, matar

3 *vi Br (at public school)* **to f. for sb** servir a un alumno de un grado superior

▶ **fag out** *vt sep Fam (of work)* dejar hecho polvo, matar

fagged [fægd] *adj Fam* (**a**) *(exhausted)* **f. (out)** hecho(a) migas *or* polvo, molido(a) (**b**) *Br (bothered)* **I can't be f.** no tengo ganas, paso

faggot ['fægət] *n* (**a**) *(firewood)* haz *m* de leña (**b**) *Br (meatball)* albóndiga *f* (**c**) *US very Fam (homosexual)* maricón *m*, *Méx* tortillón *m*, *RP* trolo *m*

faggy ['fægɪ] *adj US very Fam* maricón *m*, *Méx* tortillón *m*, *RP* trolo *m*

fah [fɑː] *n Br Mus* fa *m*

Fahrenheit ['færənhaɪt] *adj* Fahrenheit; **70 degrees F.** 70 grados Fahrenheit, ≃ 21 grados centígrados ▶▶ ***F. scale*** escala *f* Fahrenheit

FAIL [feɪl] **1** *n (in exam) Esp* suspenso *m*, *Am* reprobado *m*; IDIOM **without f.** sin falta

2 *vt* (**a**) *(exam, candidate) Esp* suspender, *Am* reprobar; **to f. a drugs test** dar positivo en un control antidoping

(**b**) *(let down)* **I won't f. you** no te fallaré; **his nerve failed him** le fallaron los nervios; **words f. me** me faltan las palabras

3 *vi* (**a**) *(not succeed) (person, plan, business, marriage)* fracasar; *(in exam) Esp* suspender, *Am* reprobar; *(crops)* perderse; *(rains)* no llegar; **I tried to convince her, but I failed** intenté convencerla, pero no lo logré; **it never fails** *(strategy, excuse)* nunca falla; **if all else fails** en último extremo; **she failed in her attempt to become champion** fracasó en su intento de convertirse en campeona; **he failed in his duty** no cumplió con su obligación

(**b**) *(stop working) (brakes, kidneys, heart)* fallar

(**c**) *(grow weak) (health)* fallar; **his memory/eyesight is starting to f.** está empezando a fallarle la memoria/vista; **the light was failing** se hacía de noche, estaba oscureciendo

(**d**) **to f. to do sth** *(not do)* no hacer algo; **they failed to agree a price** no consiguieron ponerse de acuerdo en el precio; **she failed to qualify for the final** no consiguió clasificarse para la final; **I f. to see what the problem is** no acabo *or* termino de ver cuál es el problema; **you can't f. to be impressed by her skill** no se puede negar que tiene mucho talento; **I f. to be impressed** no me impresiona, no me dice nada; **it never fails to surprise me how/that...** nunca deja de sorprenderme cómo/que...

failed [feɪld] *adj (attempt, plan)* fallido(a); *(writer, actor)* fracasado(a)

failing ['feɪlɪŋ] **1** *n (fault)* defecto *m*, *Esp* fallo *m*, *Am* falla *f*; **with all her failings** con todos sus *Esp* fallos *or Am* fallas

2 *adj* (**a**) *(sight, strength)* debilitado(a) (**b**) *(business, marriage)* en serios problemas, que hace aguas; **to be in f. health** tener una salud debilitada (**c**) *US* **f. students** alumnos que no aprueban

3 *prep* a falta de; **f. that** en su defecto; **f. which** en caso contrario, si no; **f. any evidence to the contrary...** ante la falta de pruebas en sentido contrario...; **f. all else** en último extremo

fail-safe ['feɪlseɪf] *adj* (**a**) *(device)* de seguridad *or* de bloqueo (en caso de avería) (**b**) *(plan, method, excuse)* infalible

failure ['feɪljə(r)] *n* (**a**) *(lack of success)* fracaso *m*; *(in exam, course) Esp* suspenso *m*, *Am* reprobado *m*; *(of company)* quiebra *f*; *(of crop)* pérdida *f*; **to end in f.** terminar en fracaso; **doomed to f.** condenado(a) al fracaso

(**b**) *(fiasco)* fracaso *m*, fiasco *m*; **the party/plan was a total f.** la fiesta/el plan fue un absoluto fracaso

(**c**) *(person) (unsuccessful)* fracasado(a) *m,f*, fracaso *m*; *(useless)* inútil *mf*; **he's a f. as a father** es un fracaso de padre

(**d**) *(breakdown) (of machine)* avería *f*, *Esp* fallo *m*, *Am* falla *f*; **respiratory/kidney f.** insuficiencia respiratoria/renal

(**e**) *(neglect, omission)* **f. to keep a promise** incumplimiento de una promesa; **f. to pay a bill** impago de una factura; **his f. to arrive on time** el hecho de que llegara tarde; **his f. to appear meant I had to take charge** como él no apareció tuve que hacerme cargo; **the press criticized the government's f. to act** la prensa criticó la falta de respuesta *or* de acción del gobierno

fain [feɪn] *adv Old-fashioned or Literary* de (buen) grado

faint [feɪnt] **1** *n (loss of consciousness)* desmayo *m*; **she fell to the floor in a (dead) f.** se desplomó inconsciente

2 *adj* (**a**) *(slight) (light, sound, smell)* leve, tenue; *(breeze, voice)* débil; *(idea, hope, memory)* vago(a), ligero(a); *(chance, possibility)* remoto(a); *(mark, trace)* ligero(a); *(suggestion)* leve; *(smile)* ligero(a); **I haven't got the faintest idea** no tengo ni la más mínima *or* remota idea

(**b**) *(weak, dizzy)* **to feel f.** *(person)* estar *or* sentirse mareado(a); **f. with exhaustion/hunger** desmayado(a) de hambre

3 *vi (lose consciousness)* desmayarse; **to be fainting from** *or* **with hunger** estar desmayado(a) de hambre; **I almost fainted when they told me I'd got the job!** ¡cuando me dijeron que había conseguido el empleo, casi me desmayo!

faint-hearted ['feɪnt'hɑːtɪd] **1** *adj* pusilánime

2 *npl* **not for the f.** no apto para personas de corazón delicado

fainting fit ['feɪntɪŋ'fɪt] *n* desmayo *m*; **he had a f.** se desmayó

faintly ['feɪntlɪ] *adv* (**a**) *(indistinctly) (to hear, see)* apenas; *(to shine)* débilmente; *(to remember)* vagamente (**b**) *(slightly) (uneasy, ridiculous)* ligeramente; **the taste is f. reminiscent of cinnamon** tiene un ligero gusto a canela; **she smiled f.** esbozó una sonrisa

faintness ['feɪntnɪs] *n* (**a**) *(of sound, light)* levedad *f*; *(of breeze, voice)* suavidad *f*, lo imperceptible; *(of memory)* fragilidad *f*; *(of mark, trace)* levedad *f* (**b**) *(dizziness)* mareos *mpl*, desfallecimientos *mpl*

fair[1] [feə(r)] *n* (**a**) *Br (funfair)* feria *f* (ambulante) (**b**) *(trade fair)* feria *f* (comercial) (**c**) *(market)* feria *f*, mercado *m* (**d**) *(for charity)* kermesse *f*

FAIR[2] **1** *adj* (**a**) *(just)* justo(a); **it's not f.** no es justo; **it's not f. on your mother, leaving her to do everything** no es justo que tu madre tenga que hacer todo; **f.'s f., that's only f.,** hay que ser justos; **it is f. to say that...** es justo decir que...; **to be f.,...** para ser justos,...; **be f., he's not that bad!** ¡no seas injusto, no es tan malo!; **I try to be f. to** *or* **with everybody** intento ser justo con todos; *Fam* **you did it last week, so it's f. do's that he has his turn too** tú lo hiciste la semana pasada, ¿por qué no va a tener él también su oportunidad?; **what you say is f. enough, but...** no te falta razón en lo que dices, pero..., es cierto lo que dices, pero...; **f. enough!** de acuerdo *or Esp* vale, está bien; **to give sb a f. chance** dar a alguien una oportunidad decente; **that's f. comment** no te/le/*etc.* falta razón; **to get a f. hearing** *Law* tener un juicio justo; *Fig* tener la oportunidad de explicarse; **she didn't do her f. share (of the work)** no hizo su parte (del trabajo); **they all got their f. share** todos recibieron lo que les correspondía; **we've had our f. share of problems** hemos tenido bastantes problemas; **he's had more than his f. share of misfortune** ya ha sufrido más que suficiente; **to have a f. trial** tener un juicio justo; **I've given you f. warning** ya te he avisado suficientes veces; IDIOM **by f. means or foul** como sea; IDIOM **to be f. game** ser un blanco legítimo; PROV **all's f. in love and war** en la guerra y en el amor, no hay reglas; IDIOM *Br, Austr Fam* **it's a f. cop** está bien, me descubriste, *Esp* vale, me has pillado, *Méx* órale, me cachaste, *RP* está bien, me agarraste; IDIOM *Fam* **you've had a f. crack of the whip** has tenido suficientes oportunidades; *Austr, Irish Fam* **f. play to you!** ¡bien hecho! ▶▶ *Sport* ***f. play*** juego *m* limpio; ***f. trade*** comercio *m* justo

(**b**) *(quite good)* bastante bueno(a); *(average)* regular; **a f. idea** una idea bastante buena; **they have a f. chance of winning** tienen bastantes posibilidades de ganar; **f. to middling** regular

(**c**) *(quite large)* **a f. amount of luck** bastante suerte; **a f. number of people** bastante gente; **it's a f. size** es bastante grande; **we still have a f. way to go** todavía nos queda bastante camino

(**d**) *Literary (attractive)* hermoso(a); *Old-fashioned* **the fair(er) sex** el bello sexo; *Hum* **written by my own f. hand** escrito de mi puño y letra

(**e**) *(neat)* ***f. copy*** copia *f* en limpio; **to make a f. copy of sth** pasar algo *Esp* a *or Am* en limpio

(**f**) *(weather)* bueno(a); **f. weather** buen tiempo

(**g**) *(light-coloured) (hair)* rubio(a), *Méx* güero(a), *Bol* choco(a), *Col* mono(a), *Ven* catire(a); *(skin)* claro(a); **she's f.** *(fair-haired)* es rubia *or Méx* güera *or Bol* choca *or Col* mona *or Ven* catira

(**h**) *(favourable) (wind)* a favor

2 *adv* (**a**) *(to act)* justamente; **to play/fight f.** jugar/pelear limpio; **to beat sb f. and square** derrotar a alguien con todas las de la ley; **you can't say fairer than that** no se puede pedir más (**b**) *Br Fam (completely)* **you f. scared me to death!** ¡me diste un susto de muerte!

3 *vt US* (**a**) *(make smooth)* perfilar (**b**) *(join)* **to f. sth into sth** acoplar algo a algo

fairground ['feəgraʊnd] *n* (**a**) *(of funfair)* feria *f* (**b**) *(of trade fair)* recinto *m* ferial

fair-haired ['feə'heəd] *adj* rubio(a); IDIOM *US Fam* **the boss's f. boy** el favorito del jefe

fairing ['feərɪŋ] *n (of plane, car, motorbike)* carenado *m*

fairish ['feərɪʃ] *adj* (**a**) *(quite large)* **a f. number of...** un buen número de... (**b**) *(blondish)* tirando a rubio(a), más bien rubio(a)

fairly ['feəlɪ] *adv* (**a**) *(justly)* justamente; **to treat sb f.** tratar justamente a alguien

(**b**) *(honestly)* limpiamente; **to play/fight f.** jugar/pelear limpio; **to come by sth f.** conseguir algo limpiamente; **to win f. and squarely** ganar limpiamente; **to lay the blame f. and squarely on sth/sb** echarle la culpa directamente a algo/alguien

(c) *(quite) (rich, skilful)* bastante; **the paint comes off f. easily** la pintura sale *or* se quita con bastante facilidad; **it is f. certain that...** es bastante probable *or* más que probable que...
(d) *(for emphasis)* **he f. took me by surprise** la verdad es que me pilló *or Esp* cogió *or Am* agarró por sorpresa; **we were f. racing along** íbamos bastante rápido

fair-minded ['feə'maɪndɪd] *adj* imparcial, justo(a)

fairness ['feənɪs] *n* (a) *(of person)* imparcialidad *f*; *(of decision)* justicia *f*; **in all f.** para ser justos; **in f.** *or* **out of f. to sb** para hacer justicia a alguien (b) *(of hair)* color *m* rubio; *(of skin)* claridad *f*

fair-sized ['feə'saɪzd] *adj* (de tamaño) considerable

fair-skinned ['feə'skɪnd] *adj* de piel blanca

fair-spoken ['feə'spəʊkən] *adj* bien hablado(a)

fairway ['feəweɪ] *n* (a) *(in golf)* calle *f (de campo de golf)* (b) *(in river)* canal *m* navegable

fair-weather friend ['feəweðə'frend] *n* amigo(a) *m,f* sólo para lo bueno

fairy ['feərɪ] *n* (a) *(in folklore)* hada *f* ►► ***f. godmother*** hada *f* madrina; ***f. lights*** lucecitas *fpl* de colores; ***f. ring*** corro *m* de brujas *(de setas)*; ***f. story*** *or* ***tale*** *(magic story)* cuento *m* de hadas; *Fam (lie)* cuento *m* chino, patraña *f* (b) *Fam Pej (homosexual)* mariquita *m*

fairyland ['feərɪlænd] *n* país *m* de las hadas

fairy-tale ['feərɪteɪl] *adj* **a f. ending** un final feliz; **a f. romance** un romance de cuento de hadas

fait accompli ['feɪtə'kɒmpli:] (*pl* **faits accomplis** ['feɪtə'kɒmpli:]) *n* hecho *m* consumado; **to be presented with a f.** recibir un hecho consumado

faith [feɪθ] *n* (a) *(trust)* fe *f*; **to have f. in sth/sb** tener fe en algo/alguien; **to put one's f. in sth/sb** depositar la confianza en algo/alguien; **to lose one's f. in sth/sb** perder la fe *or* confianza en algo/alguien
(b) *(honesty)* **in good/bad f.** de buena/mala fe
(c) *(loyalty)* **to break f. with** romper la lealtad hacia; **to keep f. with sb** mantenerse fiel a alguien
(d) *(religious belief)* fe *f*; **f. in God** fe en Dios; **to lose one's f.** perder la fe; **Faith, Hope and Charity** Fe, Esperanza y Caridad; **an act of f.** un acto de fe ►► ***f. healer*** = persona que pretende curar a la gente gracias a la fe y la oración
(e) *(particular religion)* creencia *f*, fe *f*; **to be of the Catholic/Jewish f.** profesar la fe católica/judía

faithful ['feɪθfʊl] **1** *adj* (a) *(friend, supporter)* fiel, leal; **f. to sth/sb** fiel *or* leal a algo/alguien (b) *(accurate) (account, translation, copy)* fiel
2 *npl* (a) *Rel* **the f.** los fieles (b) *Pol* **the party f.** los incondicionales

faithfully ['feɪθfʊlɪ] *adv* (a) *(loyally)* fielmente; **she promised f. to come** dio su palabra de que vendría; **Yours f.** *(in formal letter)* (le saluda) atentamente (b) *(accurately)* fielmente

faithfulness ['feɪθfʊlnɪs] *n* (a) *(loyalty)* fidelidad *f* (b) *(of report, translation, copy)* fidelidad *f*

faithless ['feɪθlɪs] *adj* (a) *(disloyal) (husband, partner)* infiel; *(friend)* desleal (b) *Rel* infiel

faithlessness ['feɪθlɪsnɪs] *n* (a) *(dishonesty) (of husband, partner)* deslealtad *f*; *(of friend)* deslealtad *f* (b) *Rel* falta *f* de fe

fake [feɪk] **1** *n* (a) *(object)* falsificación *f* (b) *(person)* impostor(ora) *m,f*
2 *adj (passport, banknote)* falso(a); *(beard)* postizo(a); **a f. tan** un bronceado artificial *or Esp* de pote
3 *vt* (a) *(forge) (signature, document, painting)* falsificar (b) *(alter) (document)* falsificar, adulterar; *(photograph)* trucar (c) *(simulate) (illness, death, orgasm)* simular, fingir
4 *vi* fingir

fakir ['feɪkɪə(r)] *n* faquir *m*, fakir *m*

falafel = **felafel**

falcon ['fɔ:lkən] *n* halcón *m*

falconer ['fɔ:lkənə(r)] *n* cetrero(a) *m,f*, halconero(a) *m,f*

falconry ['fɔ:lkənrɪ] *n* cetrería *f*

Falkland ['fɔ:lklənd] *n* **the F. Islands, the Falklands** las (Islas) Malvinas ►► ***F. Islander*** malvinense *mf*

Falklander ['fɔ:lkləndə(r)] *n* malvinense *mf*

FALL [fɔ:l] **1** *n* (a) *(of person, besieged city)* caída *f*; *(of rock)* desprendimiento *m*; **he died after a f.** murió tras una caída; **to have a f.** sufrir una caída; **there has been a heavy f. of snow** ha caído una gran nevada; *Fig* **a f. from grace** una caída en desgracia; *Fig* **his f. from power** su caída del poder
(b) *(drop, slope)* pendiente *f*
(c) *(decrease)* caída *f*, descenso *m* (**in** de); **a f. in interest rates** una caída *or* un descenso de los tipos de interés
(d) *(ruin) (of person)* caída *f*; IDIOM **he's heading for a f.** un día de éstos se va a pegar un batacazo *or RP* porrazo; *US Fam* **to take the f. for sth** asumir la responsabilidad de algo; *US Fam* **he took the f. for his boss** pagó por lo que hizo su jefe ►► *US Fam* ***f. guy*** *(scapegoat)* chivo *m* expiatorio
(e) *(in wrestling, judo)* caída *f*
(f) *US (autumn)* otoño *m*; **in (the) f.** en (el) otoño; **the f. colours** los colores del otoño
(g) *Rel* **the F.** la Caída
(h) **falls** *(waterfall) (small)* cascada; *(larger)* catarata
2 *vi* (*pt* **fell** [fel], *pp* **fallen** ['fɔ:lən]) (a) *(trip, tumble) (person)* caerse; **she fell nastily** tuvo una caída muy mala, *RP* se llevó una caída muy fea; **the horse fell at the first (fence)** el caballo cayó en el primer obstáculo; **to f. backwards** caerse hacia atrás *or* de espaldas; **to f. down a hole** caer por un agujero; **to f. from a great height** caer desde muy alto; **be careful not to f. in!** ¡no te vayas a caer (dentro *or* adentro)!; **he fell into the water** se cayó al agua; **she fell off the ladder** se cayó de la escalera; **he fell on his ankle** se torció el tobillo al caer; **be careful you don't f. out!** ¡no te vayas a caer!; **she fell out of the window** se cayó *Esp* de *or Am* por la ventana; **she fell to her death from the tower** se cayó desde la torre y se mató; **to f. flat** *(be disappointing)* no funcionar; *also Fig* **to f. into a trap** caer en una trampa; **to f. short of doing sth** no llegar a hacer algo; IDIOM **she always seems to f. on her feet** siempre se las arregla, *RP* suele caer parada
(b) *(drop) (rain, snow, stone)* caer; *(curtain)* caer, cerrarse; **to f. at sb's feet** caer a los pies de alguien; **she fell into his arms** cayó en sus brazos; **a tin of paint fell on my head** me cayó una lata de pintura en la cabeza; **his gaze fell on her** su mirada cayó sobre ella; **she fell onto the bed** se dejó caer en la cama; **it fell out of my pocket** se me cayó del bolsillo *or CAm, Méx, Perú* de la bolsa; **a photo fell out of the book** se cayó una foto del libro; **to f. to one's knees** caer de rodillas; **the satellite fell to earth** el satélite cayó a la Tierra; **my spirits fell** me desmoralicé; **to f. from grace** caer en desgracia; *Literary* **not a word fell from his lips** sus labios no dejaron escapar ni un suspiro; **to f. into line** entrar en vereda; **suddenly everything fell into place** de pronto todo encajaba
(c) *(decrease) (price, temperature, demand, level)* caer, bajar, descender; **the dollar has fallen against the yen** el dólar ha caído *or* bajado con respecto al yen; **the temperature fell by 10°/below zero** la temperatura descendió 10°/abajo cero
(d) *(become)* **to f. asleep** dormirse; **to f. due** ser pagadero(a); **to f. foul of sb** enemistarse con alguien, ponerse a malas con alguien; **to f. foul of the law** incumplir la ley; **to f. ill** caer enfermo(a), enfermar, *RP, Ven* enfermarse; **to f. in love** enamorarse; **to f. on hard times** caer en la pobreza *or* miseria; **the book fell open at page 25** el libro cayó abierto por *or* en la página 25; **to f. out of favour with sb** dejar de contar con *or* perder el apoyo de alguien; **to f. silent** quedarse callado(a); **to f. to pieces** *(object)* romperse en pedazos; *Fig (person)* desmoronarse; **those trousers are falling to pieces!** ¡esos pantalones se caen a pedazos *or* están hechos jirones!; **to f. victim to sth** ser víctima de algo; **the match fell victim to the weather** el partido se suspendió debido al mal tiempo
(e) *(hang down)* caer; **the curtains f. right to the floor** las cortinas caen hasta el suelo
(f) *(happen, be)* **Christmas Day falls on a Thursday** el día de Navidad cae en jueves; **Easter falls late this year** este año Semana Santa cae más tarde; **the stress falls on the second syllable** el acento cae *or* recae en la segunda sílaba
(g) *(be classified)* **to f. into two categories** dividirse en dos categorías; **such matters f. under my responsibilities** esos asuntos son responsabilidad mía; **that does not f. within the scope of our agreement** eso no entra dentro de nuestro acuerdo
(h) *(empire, government)* caer, sucumbir; **to f. from power** perder el poder; **the city fell to the Gauls** la ciudad cayó en manos *or* en poder de los Galos
(i) *(be killed) (soldier)* caer, morir
(j) *(begin)* **silence/night fell** se hizo el silencio/de noche
(k) *(light, shadow)* **a shadow fell across the floor** una sombra se proyectó sobre el suelo; **a ray of sunshine fell on the table** un rayo de sol cayó sobre la mesa

► **fall about** *vi Fam* **to f. about (laughing)** partirse (de risa)

► **fall apart** *vi* (a) *(break)* romperse (b) *(marriage, deal)* fracasar; *(country, company, family, person)* venirse abajo, desmoronarse; **these trousers are falling apart!** ¡estos pantalones se caen a pedazos!; **my world fell apart** el mundo se me vino encima

► **fall away** *vi* (a) *(paint, plaster, wallpaper)* desprenderse (b) *(ground)* caer, descender (c) *(attendance)* decaer

►**fall back** *vi* (a) *(move away)* echarse atrás, retroceder; *Mil* replegarse (b) *(drop behind)* **he has fallen back into fifth place** ha retrocedido al quinto puesto (c) *(decrease)* caer, bajar, descender

►**fall back on** *vt insep (money, resources, argument)* recurrir a

►**fall behind** 1 *vt insep* **we have fallen behind our competitors** nos hemos rezagado con respecto a nuestros competidores
2 *vi (drop back)* quedarse rezagado(a); **to f. behind with one's payments** atrasarse en los pagos; **he fell behind with his work** se retrasó en su trabajo, se le acumuló el trabajo

►**fall down** *vi* (a) *(person, building)* caerse; **your trousers are falling down** se te están cayendo los pantalones; **this house is falling down!** *(is in bad condition)* ¡esta casa se cae en pedazos! (b) *(argument, plan)* fallar; **where the whole thing falls down is...** donde falla la cosa es...

►**fall for** *vt insep Fam* (a) *(fall in love with)* enamorarse de (b) *(be deceived by) (story)* tragarse; **I'm not falling for that one!** ¡no me voy a tragar eso!; **to f. for it** picar

►**fall in** *vi* (a) *(roof)* hundirse (b) *(troops)* formar; **the rest of the group fell in behind him** el resto del grupo se colocó en fila detrás suyo

►**fall into** *vt insep* (a) *(come to be in)* **to f. into the wrong hands** caer en malas manos; **to f. into disrepair** deteriorarse; **to f. into disrepute** caer en descrédito; **to f. into disuse** caer en desuso; **to f. into a stupor** quedar aletargado(a)
(b) *(habit, routine)* caer en; **to f. into conversation with sb** trabar *or* entablar conversación con alguien; **I fell into step with the rest of the troop** me puse al ritmo del resto de la tropa

►**fall in with** *vt insep* (a) *(become friendly with)* juntarse con, andar con (b) *(plan, idea)* aceptar; **I'll f. in with whatever you decide to do** aceptaré lo que decidas hacer

►**fall off** *vi* (a) *(come off)* desprenderse, caerse (b) *(profits, attendance)* decrecer

►**fall on** *vt insep* (a) *(attack) (person, food)* abalanzarse *or* caer sobre (b) *(be responsibility of)* **the responsibility falls on you** la responsabilidad recae sobre ti (c) *(encounter)* **they fell on hard times** sufrieron un revés de la fortuna

►**fall out** *vi* (a) *(teeth, hair)* **all his hair/one of his teeth has fallen out** se le ha caído todo el pelo/un diente
(b) *(quarrel)* reñir, pelearse (**with** con)
(c) *Mil* romper filas
(d) *(happen)* suceder; **as things fell out...** al final resultó que...
(e) *US Fam (fall asleep)* quedarse traspuesto(a), *RP* desmayarse

►**fall over** 1 *vt insep (stumble on)* tropezar con; IDIOM **to f. over oneself to do sth** *(be very keen)* desvivirse por hacer algo
2 *vi* caerse

►**fall through** *vi (plan, deal)* venirse abajo

►**fall to** 1 *vt insep* (a) *(begin)* **to f. to doing sth** empezar *or* comenzar a hacer algo (b) *Formal (be responsibility of)* **it falls to me to break the bad news** me corresponde a mí dar las malas noticias; **the task that falls to us is not an easy one** no es fácil la tarea que recae sobre nosotros
2 *vi (start eating)* empezar *or* comenzar a comer

►**fall under** *vt insep* **to f. under sb's influence/spell** caer bajo la influencia/el hechizo de alguien

►**fall upon** *vt insep* = **fall on**

---

fallacious [fə'leɪʃəs] *adj Formal* falaz

fallacy ['fæləsɪ] *n* falacia *f*

fall-back ['fɔːlbæk] *n* recurso *m* alternativo ►► ***f. position*** postura *f* alternativa

fallen ['fɔːlən] 1 *npl* **the f.** los caídos
2 *adj* caído(a); **a f. angel** un ángel caído; **f. arches** pies planos; *Old-fashioned* **a f. woman** una mujer perdida
3 *pp of* **fall**

fallibility [fælɪ'bɪlɪtɪ] *n* capacidad *f* de errar, falibilidad *f*

fallible ['fælɪbəl] *adj* falible; **everyone is f.** cualquiera se puede equivocar

falling ['fɔːlɪŋ] *adj (standards, prices, demand)* a la baja, en descenso; **due to f. demand/prices** debido a la caída de la demanda/los precios

falling-off ['fɔːlɪŋ'ɒf], **falloff** ['fɔːlɒf] *n (in demand, popularity)* descenso *m*, bajón *m*; *(in production)* caída *f*, disminución *f*; *(in quality)* paso *m* atrás

Fallopian tube [fə'ləʊpɪən'tjuːb] *n Anat* trompa *f* de Falopio

fallout ['fɔːlaʊt] *n* (a) *Phys* lluvia *f* radiactiva ►► ***f. shelter*** refugio *m* antinuclear (b) *(from scandal)* secuelas *fpl*

fallow ['fæləʊ] 1 *adj (uncultivated)* en barbecho; *Fig* **a f. period** un periodo improductivo ►► ***f. deer*** gamo *m*
2 *adv* **to lie f.** estar en barbecho

false [fɔːls] 1 *adj* (a) *(incorrect, mistaken)* falso(a); **to create** *or* **give a f. impression** dar una falsa impresión; **to put a f. interpretation on sth** interpretar algo equivocadamente; **the ceasefire turned out to be a f. dawn** el alto el fuego se convirtió en una esperanza frustrada; **make one f. move and I'll shoot** no hagas un solo movimiento en falso o disparo; **to bear f. witness** presentar falso testimonio ►► ***f. alarm*** falsa alarma *f*; ***a f. economy*** un falso ahorro; ***f. friend*** *(in foreign language)* falso amigo *m*; ***f. memory syndrome*** síndrome *m* de la falsa memoria; ***f. modesty*** falsa modestia *f*; *Mus & Fig* ***f. note*** nota *f* falsa; ***f. pregnancy*** embarazo *m* psicológico; ***f. rib*** falsa costilla *f*; ***f. start*** *(in race)* salida *f* nula
(b) *(dishonest, insincere)* falso(a); **to put on a f. front** ponerse una máscara, pretender ser diferente; **you got me here under f. pretences** me trajiste aquí con engaños ►► *Law* ***f. imprisonment*** encarcelamiento *m* ilegal; ***f. position:*** **to put sb in a f. position** poner a alguien en una situación comprometida *or* difícil
(c) *(unfaithful)* infiel
(d) *(simulated) (beard, nose, eyelashes, fingernails)* postizo(a); *(document, passport, identity)* falso(a) ►► ***f. bottom*** *(of container)* doble fondo *m*; ***f. ceiling*** falso techo *m*; ***f. teeth*** dentadura *f* postiza, *Col, RDom* caja *f* de dientes; ***f. wall*** pared *f* falsa
2 *adv* **to play sb f.** embaucar a alguien

falsehood ['fɔːlshʊd] *n Formal* (a) *(lie)* falsedad *f* (b) *(dishonesty)* falsedad *f*

falsely ['fɔːlslɪ] *adv* (a) *(mistakenly)* equivocadamente; **he was f. accused of theft** lo acusaron por error de haber robado (b) *(insincerely)* falsamente

falsetto [fɔːl'setəʊ] (*pl* **falsettos**) *Mus* 1 *n* falsete *m*
2 *adj (voice)* en falsete

falsies ['fɔːlsɪz] *npl Fam* rellenos *mpl (para sostén)*

falsifiable [fɔːlsɪ'faɪəbəl] *adj (theory)* refutable

falsification [fɔːlsɪfɪ'keɪʃən] *n* (a) *(forgery)* falsificación *f* (b) *(disproof)* refutación *f*

falsify ['fɔːlsɪfaɪ] *vt* (a) *(forge) (records, document, evidence)* falsificar (b) *(disprove) (theory)* refutar

falsity ['fɔːlsɪtɪ] *n* falsedad *f*

falter ['fɔːltə(r)] 1 *vt* balbucear; **"maybe... yes... perhaps...," he faltered** "quizá... sí... tal vez...", balbuceó
2 *vi* (a) *(speaker)* vacilar, titubear; *(voice)* entrecortarse (b) *(waver) (courage)* flaquear; *(memory)* fallar; **his steps faltered as he neared the room** al acercarse a la habitación su andar perdió seguridad (c) *(function unreliably) (engine)* fallar; *(economy)* tambalear

faltering ['fɔːltərɪŋ] *adj* (a) *(hesitating) (voice)* titubeante; *(attempt)* tímido (b) *(wavering) (courage)* debilitado(a); *(memory)* que falla; *(steps)* tambaleante (c) *(engine)* que falla; *(economy)* tambaleante

fame [feɪm] *n* fama *f*; **to seek f. and fortune** buscar fama y fortuna; **to rise to f.** llegar a la fama; **Mick Jagger of Rolling Stones f.** Mick Jagger, famoso por los Rolling Stones

famed [feɪmd] *adj* famoso(a), afamado(a); **he is f. for his generosity** es famoso por su generosidad

familial [fə'mɪlɪəl] *adj Formal* familiar

familiar [fə'mɪlɪə(r)] 1 *adj* (a) *(well-known)* familiar; **a f. face** un rostro familiar; **his name is f.** su nombre resulta familiar; **she's a f. sight about town** se la suele ver en la ciudad; **an all too f. story of drug addiction and homelessness** la conocida historia de adicción a las drogas y falta de hogar
(b) *(acquainted)* **to be f. with** estar familiarizado(a) con; **to become f. with sth** familiarizarse con algo
(c) *(informal)* familiar, *Am* confianzudo(a); **f. language/tone** lenguaje/tono familiar; **to be on f. terms with sb** tener trato informal con alguien; **to get too f. with sb** tomarse demasiada confianza con alguien
2 *n* (a) *(friend)* allegado *m* (b) *(in witchcraft)* familiar *m*

familiarity [fəmɪlɪ'ærɪtɪ] *n* (a) *(of face, place)* familiaridad *f*; PROV **f. breeds contempt** la confianza da asco (b) *(acquaintance) (with book, rules, language)* familiaridad *f* (**with** con); **her f. with his work** el conocimiento que posee sobre su trabajo (c) *(informality)* familiaridad *f*, confianza *f*; **she resented his excessive f. with her** le molestaba la excesiva confianza con la que la trataba

familiarization [fəmɪlɪəraɪ'zeɪʃən] *n* familiarización *f*; **a f. process** un proceso de familiarización; **after a period of f. with the method...** luego de un periodo de familiarización con el método...

familiarize [fə'mɪlɪəraɪz] *vt* (**a**) *(acquaint)* **to f. oneself with sth** familiarizarse con algo; **to f. sb with sth** familiarizar a alguien con algo (**b**) *(make widely known)* popularizar

familiarly [fə'mɪlɪəlɪ] *adv (informally)* con confianza *or* familiaridad; **f. known as...** popularmente *or* comúnmente conocido(a) como...

family ['fæmɪlɪ] *n also Biol* familia *f*; **have you any f.?** *(relatives)* ¿tienes parientes?; *(children)* ¿tienes hijos?; **of good f.** de buena familia; **to start a f.** empezar a tener hijos; **to keep sth in the f.** *(of property)* mantener algo en la familia; *(scandal)* mantener algo en familia; **they treat her as one of the f.** la tratan como si fuera de la familia; **it runs in the f.** es cosa de familia; *Fam* **she's in the f. way** está en estado; **a f. affair** *(celebration, problem)* un asunto familiar *or* de familia ►► *Br Formerly* ***f. allowance*** ayuda *f* familiar; ***f. business*** negocio *m* familiar; *US Law* ***f. court*** tribunal *m* de familia; *Br* ***f. credit*** ayuda *f or* subsidio *m* familiar; ***f. doctor*** médico *m* de cabecera *or* familia; ***f. heirloom*** joya *f* de familia; *very Fam* ***f. jewels*** *(man's genitals)* la flauta; ***f. life*** vida *f* de familia; ***f. man*** hombre *m* de familia; ***f. name*** apellido *m*; ***f. planning*** planificación *f* familiar; ***f. planning clinic*** centro *m* de planificación familiar; *US* ***f. practice*** medicina *f* general; *US* ***f. practitioner*** médico *m* de cabecera *or* familia; ***f. resemblance*** parecido *m* de familia; ***f. room*** *(in hotel)* habitación *f* familiar; *US (in house)* sala *f* de estar; *Br (in pub)* = sala en la que se permite el acceso con niños; ***f. seat*** casa *f* solariega; ***f. therapy*** terapia *f* familiar; ***f. tree*** árbol *m* genealógico; ***f. vault*** panteón *m* familiar; ***f. viewing:*** **suitable/unsuitable for f. viewing** apto(a)/no apto(a) para todos los públicos

family-run ['fæmɪlɪ'rʌn] *adj* familiar; **a f. business** un negocio familiar; **a f. hotel/restaurant** un hotel/restaurante familiar *or* regentado por una familia

family-sized ['fæmɪlɪ'saɪzd] *adj* de tamaño familiar

famine ['fæmɪn] *n* hambruna *f* ►► ***f. relief*** ayuda *f* humanitaria contra el hambre

famished ['fæmɪʃd] *adj Fam* muerto(a) de hambre; **to be f.** estar muerto(a) de hambre

famous ['feɪməs] *adj* famoso(a), célebre; **the town is f. for its gardens** la ciudad es famosa por sus jardines; **a f. victory** una victoria célebre; **so much for her f. cooking!** ¡y para esto tanto hablar de su famosa cocina!; **f. last words!** ¡que te crees tú eso!

famously ['feɪməslɪ] *adv* (**a**) *(celebratedly)* celebradamente; **as Oscar Wilde f. said...** como reza *or* dice la célebre cita de Oscar Wilde... (**b**) *Fam (very well)* **to get on f. (with sb)** llevarse genial (con alguien)

fan[1] [fæn] **1** *n (cooling device) (hand-held)* abanico *m*; *(mechanical)* ventilador *m*; **shaped like a f.** con forma de abanico; IDIOM *US Fam* **to hit the f.** destaparse, estallar ►► ***f. belt*** *(of car)* correa *f* del ventilador; ***f. heater*** convector *m*; ***f. oven*** horno *m* de convección; ***f. palm*** palma *f* enana; *Archit* ***f. vaulting*** bóveda *f* de abanico

2 *vt (pt & pp* **fanned**) (**a**) *(with fan)* abanicar; **to f. oneself** abanicarse (**b**) *(blow on)* **the coast is fanned by cool sea breezes** la fresca brisa del mar acaricia la costa (**c**) *(fire, passions)* atizar, avivar; **to f. the flames** echar (más) leña al fuego

► **fan out 1** *vt* (**a**) *(of peacock) (tail)* desplegar en abanico (**b**) *(cards)* abrir en abanico

2 *vi (police, soldiers)* desplegarse

fan[2] *n (enthusiast) (of music, art, sport)* aficionado(a) *m,f*; *(of team)* hincha *mf*; *(of artist, singer)* admirador(ora) *m,f*, fan *mf*; **I'm not a f. of electric cookers** no soy partidario de las cocinas *or Col, Méx, Ven* estufas eléctricas ►► ***f. club*** club *m* de fans; ***f. letter*** carta *f* de admirador(ora) *or* fan; ***f. mail*** cartas *fpl* de fans *or* de admiradores

fan-assisted ['fænə'sɪstɪd] *adj (oven)* con ventilación

fanatic [fə'nætɪk] **1** *n* fanático(a) *m,f*

2 *adj* fanático(a)

fanatical [fə'nætɪkəl] *adj* fanático(a) (**about** de); **he's f. about punctuality** es un fanático de la puntualidad

fanatically [fə'nætɪklɪ] *adv* con fanatismo, de un modo fanático

fanaticism [fə'nætɪsɪzəm] *n* fanatismo *m*

fanciable ['fænsɪəbəl] *adj Br Fam* atractivo(a), resultón(ona)

fancied ['fænsɪd] *adj* (**a**) *(imagined)* imaginario(a); **he was nicknamed "Clint" because of a f. resemblance to the movie actor** lo llamaban "Clint" por un imaginario *or* supuesto parecido al actor de cine (**b**) *(favoured)* favorito(a)

fancier ['fænsɪə(r)] *n* **a pigeon/bird f.** un(a) criador(ora) de palomas/pájaros

fanciful ['fænsɪfʊl] *adj* (**a**) *(imaginative)* creativo(a), imaginativo(a) (**b**) *(unrealistic)* inverosímil, descabellado(a)

fancifully ['fænsɪfʊlɪ] *adv (to suggest)* con gran derroche *or* grandes dosis de imaginación; **somewhat f. described as...** descripta, con bastante imaginación, como...

fancily ['fænsɪlɪ] *adv* extravagantemente, estrafalariamente; **they were very f. dressed** estaban vestidos de una manera estrafalaria

fancy ['fænsɪ] **1** *n* (**a**) *(imagination)* fantasía *f*; **a flight of f.** un delirio (**b**) *(whim)* capricho *m*; **he went wherever his f. took him** iba donde se le antojaba *or Esp* donde le apetecía *or Carib, Col, Méx* donde le provocaba; **it's just a passing f.** es sólo un interés *or* capricho pasajero (**c**) *(liking)* **to take a f. to sth/sb** encapricharse de algo/alguien; **the idea took** *or* **caught his f.** le atrajo *or* gustó la idea (**d**) *(notion)* fantasía *f*, impresión *f*; **I have a f. that...** me da en la nariz que...

2 *adj* (**a**) *(elaborate) (jewels, hat)* de fantasía; *(gadget)* sofisticado(a); **don't try any f. stuff, or else** no intentes nada raro ►► ***f. dress*** disfraz *m*; ***f. dress party*** fiesta *f* de disfraces; ***f. footwork*** *(of dancer)* paso *m* complicado *or* difícil; *Fig* **it took some f. footwork to see three women at the same time** tuvo que hacer malabarismos para salir con tres mujeres a la vez; *Br* ***f. goods*** obsequios *mpl*, artículos *mpl* de regalo; *Fam* ***f. man*** *(lover)* querido *m*, amiguito *m*; *Fam* ***f. woman*** *Br (lover)* querida *f*, amiguita *f*; *US (prostitute)* fulana *f*

(**b**) *(upmarket) (neighbourhood, shop, car)* exclusivo(a); *(party)* encopetado(a); *(hotel)* lujoso(a); *(food, decoration)* con muchas florituras; *Fam* **to charge f. prices** cobrar precios exorbitantes

(**c**) *(affected, pretentious) (talk, words)* afectado(a), pedante

3 *vt* (**a**) *Fam (want)* **do you f. a drink?** *Esp* ¿te apetece algo de beber?, *Carib, Col, Méx* ¿te provoca algo de beber?, *RP* ¿querés algo de tomar?; **I didn't f. the idea** no me atraía la idea; **I don't f. travelling in this weather** no me apetece viajar con este tiempo

(**b**) *Br Fam (be attracted by)* **he fancies her** le gusta ella; *Fam* **to f. the pants off sb** encontrar a alguien buenísimo(a)

(**c**) *(imagine)* imaginar; **to f. (that)...** imaginar que...; *Fam* **f. that!** ¡fíjate!, ¡lo que hay que ver!; **f. anyone wanting to do that!** ¡quién podría querer hacerlo!; **f. meeting you here!** ¡qué sorpresa encontrarte aquí!

(**d**) *Formal (believe)* creer; **she fancies herself as an intellectual** se considera una intelectual; **I f. I have seen her before** me parece que la he visto antes

(**e**) *(have good opinion of)* **he is strongly fancied to win** se cree que tiene muchas posibilidades de ganar; *Fam* **to f. oneself** tenérselo muy creído; *Fam* **she fancies herself as a writer/musician** se las da de buena escritora/música; **I don't f. their chances of winning** no creo que tengan muchas posibilidades de ganar; *Fam* **he fancies his chances of getting the job** tiene muchas esperanzas de conseguir el trabajo

fancy-Dan ['fænsɪ'dæn] *adj US Fam* fanfarrón(ona), *Esp* chulo(a)

fancy-free ['fænsɪ'friː] *adj* sin compromisos *or* responsabilidades

fancywork ['fænsɪwɜːk] *n* labor *m*

fandom ['fændəm] *n US* hinchada *f*

fanfare ['fænfeə(r)] *n* (**a**) *(on trumpets)* fanfarria *f* (**b**) *(ostentation)* fanfarría *f*; **with much f.** con *or* a bombo y platillo

fang [fæŋ] *n (of wolf, vampire)* colmillo *m*; *(of snake)* diente *m*

fanlight ['fænlaɪt] *n* montante *m* en abanico

fanny ['fænɪ] *n* (**a**) *US Fam (buttocks)* culo *m* ►► ***f. pack*** riñonera *f*, *Méx* cangurera *f* (**b**) *Br Vulg (vagina) Esp* coño *m*, *Am* concha *f*, *Méx* paloma *f*

► **fanny about, fanny around** *vi Br very Fam* dar vueltas

fantabulous [fæn'tæbjʊləs] *adj Fam Hum (marvellous)* alucinante, *Esp* flipante

fantail ['fænteɪl] *n* **f. (pigeon)** paloma *f* colipava

fan-tailed warbler ['fænteɪld'wɔːblə(r)] *n* buitrón *m*

fantasia [fæn'teɪzɪə] *n Mus* fantasía *f*

fantasist ['fæntəzɪst] *n* (**a**) *(writer)* escritor(ora) *m,f* de novela fantástica (**b**) *(over-imaginative person)* fantaseador(ora) *m,f*

fantasize ['fæntəsaɪz] *vi* fantasear (**about** sobre)

fantastic [fæn'tæstɪk] *adj* (**a**) *Fam (excellent)* fantástico(a), formidable; **we had a f. time** lo pasamos formidablemente *or* estupendamente (**b**) *(enormous) (size, amount, rate)* inmenso(a); *(price)* desorbitado(a); *(success, achievement)* descomunal, increíble (**c**) *(unbelievable)* absurdo(a); **it sounds f., but it's true** parece absurdo pero es verdad

fantastical [fæn'tæstɪkəl] *adj* fantástico(a), increíble

fantastically [fæn'tæstɪklɪ] *adv* (**a**) *Fam (enormously)* fabulosamente, increíblemente; **it's f. expensive** es increíblemente caro (**b**) *(unbelievably)* **somewhat f., the story ends happily** aunque parezca increíble, la historia tiene un final feliz *or* termina bien

fantasy ['fæntəsɪ] *n* (a) *(dream)* fantasía *f*, sueño *m*; **his f. was...** su fantasía era...
(b) *(imagination)* fantasía *f*; **to live in a f. world** vivir en un mundo imaginario *or* de fantasía ►► ***f. football*** = juego en que los participantes escogen su equipo de fútbol ideal de entre los futbolistas de un torneo y luego van sumando puntos según la actuación de éstos en la competición real, *Esp* ≃ liga *f* fantástica®; ***f. role-playing game*** juego *m* de rol
(c) *Lit* **f. (literature)** literatura *f* fantástica

fanzine ['fænzi:n] *n* fanzine *m*

FAO [efeɪ'əʊ] *n* (a) (*abbr* **Food and Agriculture Organization**) FAO *f* (b) (*abbr* **for the attention of**) a la atención de

FAQ [efeɪ'kju:] *n Comptr* (*abbr* **frequently asked questions**) preguntas *fpl* más frecuentes ►► ***F. file*** documento *m* con las preguntas más frecuentes

---

FAR [fɑ:(r)] 1 *adj* (a) *(distant)* lejano(a); **in the f. distance** allá a lo lejos; **life here is a f. cry from life in Paris** la vida aquí no se parece en nada a *or* ni se compara con la vida en París ►► ***the F. East*** el Lejano Oriente
(b) *(more distant)* **the f. end** el (otro) extremo; **the f. side of the pitch** el otro lado del campo
(c) *(extreme)* extremo(a); **on the f. left of the screen** en el extremo izquierdo de la pantalla; *Pol* **the f. left/right** la extrema izquierda/derecha; **in the f. north of the country** en el extremo norte del país
2 *adv* (*comparative* **farther** ['fɑ:ðə(r)] *or* **further** ['fɜ:ðə(r)], *superlative* **farthest** ['fɑ:ðɪst] *or* **furthest** ['fɜ:ðɪst]) (a) *(with distance)* lejos; **is it f. to Seattle?** ¿está *or* queda muy lejos Seattle?; **how f. is it to Glasgow?** ¿a cuánto estamos de Glasgow?; **how f. is it from Montreal to Toronto?** ¿a qué distancia *or* a cuánto está Montreal de Toronto?; **how f. did she jump?** ¿cuánto saltó?; **how f. did you get with your homework?** ¿hasta dónde llegaste en *or* con los deberes?; **how f. can he be trusted?** ¿hasta qué punto podemos confiar en él?; **we hadn't got f. along the road when...** no llevábamos mucho rato en la carretera cuando...; **f. away** lejos; **how f. away is it?** ¿a qué distancia está?; **f. below/above** muy abajo/arriba; *also Fig* **f. from...** lejos de...; **I was f. from satisfied** no estaba satisfecho ni mucho menos; **I didn't mean to offend you, f. from it** no quise ofenderte, todo lo contrario; **f. be it from me to criticize, but...** Dios me libre de criticar a nadie, pero...; **f. and wide** *or* **near** por todas partes; **they got as f. as the border** no pasaron de la frontera; **as f. as possible** *(as much as possible)* en la medida de lo posible, en lo posible; *Fig* **as** *or* **so f. as I can see** tal y como yo lo veo; **as** *or* **so f. as I know** que yo sepa; **as** *or* **so f. as I can remember** por lo que yo recuerdo; **as** *or* **so f. as I'm concerned** en *or* por lo que a mí respecta; **as** *or* **so f. as your salary is concerned** en *or* por lo que se refiere a tu salario; **it's all right as f. as it goes** dentro de lo que cabe, no está mal; **they came from/searched f. and wide** vinieron de/buscaron por todas partes; **he can only be trusted so f.** sólo se puede confiar en él hasta cierto punto; **you weren't f. off** *or* **out** *or* **wrong** no ibas muy desencaminado; *Fig* **to go f.** *(in career)* llegar lejos; *(of money)* dar para mucho; *Fig* **to go as** *or* **so f. as to do sth** llegar al extremo de hacer algo; **I would go so f. as to call him stupid** *Esp* yo hasta estúpido lo llamaría, *Am* yo incluso diría que es estúpido; **this has gone f. enough!** ¡esto ya pasa de castaño oscuro!; *Fig* **to go too f.** ir demasiado lejos; **if you follow my advice, you won't go f. wrong** si sigues mis consejos, no tendrás problemas; *Fig* **to take** *or* **carry sth too f.** ir demasiado lejos con algo; IDIOM *Fam* **to be f. gone** *(drunk) Esp, Méx* estar pedo, *RP* estar en pedo; *(mad)* estar enojadísimo(a) *or Esp* ido(a) *or CSur* rayado(a) *or Méx* zafado(a)
(b) *(with time)* **to work f. into the night** trabajar hasta bien entrada la noche; **we mustn't plan so f. ahead** no debemos hacer planes a tan largo plazo; **my birthday isn't f. away** no queda *or* falta mucho para mi cumpleaños; **f. back in the past** en el pasado lejano; **for as f. back as I can remember** hasta donde alcanzo a recordar; **so f.** hasta el momento; **so f. this year** en lo que llevamos de año; IDIOM **so f. so good** todo bien de momento
(c) *(much)* **f. better/worse** mucho mejor/peor; **f. above/below the average** muy por encima/por debajo del promedio; **I'd f. rather stay at home** yo desde luego *or* sin duda preferiría quedarme en casa; **her arguments f. outweigh his** sus argumentos tienen mucho más peso que los de él; **she's f. too intelligent to do that** es demasiado inteligente (como) para hacer eso; **f. too many** demasiados(as); **f. too much** demasiado; **f. and away the best** el mejor con diferencia *or RP* por lejos; **by f.** con diferencia, con mucho, *RP* por lejos

---

farad ['færəd] *n Elec* faradio *m*

faraday ['færədeɪ] *n Phys* faraday *m*

faraway ['fɑ:rəweɪ] *adj* (a) *(place)* lejano(a) (b) *(look)* ausente

farce [fɑ:s] *n* (a) *Lit* farsa *f* (b) *(ridiculous situation)* farsa *f*; **the event degenerated into a f.** el acontecimiento degeneró en *or* se transformó en una farsa

farcical ['fɑ:sɪkəl] *adj* grotesco(a)

fare [feə*r*] 1 *n* (a) *(for journey)* tarifa *f* ►► *Br* ***f. dodger***, *US* ***f. beater*** = persona que se cuela en un medio de transporte público; *Br* ***f. stage*** *(section)* zona *f* tarifaria (de un autobús) (b) *(taxi passenger)* pasajero(a) *m,f* (c) *Formal (food)* comida *f*; **hospital/prison f.** comida de hospital/de prisión
2 *vi* **to f. well/badly** *(person, team)* hacerlo bien/mal; *(industry, sector)* comportarse bien/mal; **how did she f.?** ¿cómo le salió?; **the company has fared better in recent months** en los últimos meses la compañía ha obtenido mejores resultados; **he fared better in last year's tournament** le fue mejor en el torneo del año pasado

farewell [feə'wel] *n* despedida *f*, adiós *m*; **to bid sb f.** despedirse de alguien; **to say** *or* **make one's farewells** despedirse; **f., my old friend** hasta siempre, compañero ►► ***f. dinner*** cena *f* de despedida

far-fetched ['fɑ:'fetʃt] *adj (idea, plan)* inverosímil, rebuscado(a)

far-flung ['fɑ:flʌŋ] *adj* (a) *(distant)* remoto(a) (b) *(widespread)* amplio(a), vasto(a)

farm [fɑ:m] 1 *n (small)* granja *f*; *(large)* hacienda *f*, explotación *f* agrícola, *RP* estancia *f*; **a fish f.** una piscifactoría; **a mink f.** una granja *or* un criadero de visones ►► ***f. animals*** animales *mpl* de granja; ***f. hand*** bracero *m*, peón *m or* trabajador *m* del campo; ***f. labourer*** bracero *m*, peón *m or* trabajador *m* del campo; ***f. produce*** productos *mpl* de la tierra; ***f. work*** faenas *fpl* agrícolas *or* del campo; ***f. worker*** bracero *m*, peón *m or* trabajador *m* del campo
2 *vt (land)* cultivar; *(livestock)* criar
3 *vi (grow crops)* cultivar la tierra

►**farm out** *vt sep* (a) *(work)* subcontratar (b) *(child)* **she farms her children out to an aunt** deja el cuidado de sus niños a una tía

farmer ['fɑ:mə(r)] *n (of small farm)* granjero(a) *m,f*; *(of large farm)* agricultor(ora) *m,f*; **a sheep/cattle f.** un(a) ganadero(a) ►► ***farmers' market*** = mercado en el que se venden sobre todo productos de agricultores de la zona

farmhouse ['fɑ:mhaʊs] 1 *n* granja *f*, casa *f* de labranza
2 *adj* de granja; **f. cooking** cocina artesanal

farming ['fɑ:mɪŋ] *n* agricultura *f*; **fish farming** piscicultura; **mink farming** cría de visones; **fruit/vegetable f.** cultivo frutícola/de hortalizas; **f. cooperative/machinery** cooperativa/maquinaria agrícola

farmland ['fɑ:mlænd] *n* terreno *m* agrícola

farmstead ['fɑ:msted] *n US* granja *f*, alquería *f*

farmyard ['fɑ:mjɑ:d] *n* corral *m*; **f. animal** animal de corral; **f. smells** olor a cuadra *or* establo

Faroe ['feərəʊ] *n* **the F. Islands, the Faroes** las Islas Feroe

far-off ['fɑ:'rɒf] *adj (place, time)* lejano(a)

far-out ['fɑ:'raʊt] *Fam* 1 *adj* (a) *(strange)* raro(a); *(avant-garde)* moderno(a) (b) *(excellent)* genial, formidable, *CAm, Carib, Col, Méx* chévere, *Méx* padre, *RP* bárbaro(a)
2 *exclam* ¡súper!, *Esp* ¡chachi!

farrago [fə'rɑ:gəʊ] (*pl* **farragos** *or* **farragoes**) *n* fárrago *m*, mezcolanza *f*; **a f. of lies** una sarta de mentiras

far-reaching ['fɑ:'ri:tʃɪŋ] *adj (decision, change)* de gran alcance; **to have f. consequences** tener consecuencias importantes

farrier ['færɪə(r)] *n (blacksmith)* herrador(ora) *m,f*, herrero(a) *m,f*

farrow ['færəʊ] 1 *n* camada *f* de cerdos *or* puercos *or Am* chanchos
2 *vi* parir

far-seeing ['fɑ:'si:ɪŋ] *adj (person, decision)* previsor(ora), con visión de futuro

Farsi ['fɑ:si:] *n (language)* persa *m* (moderno)

far-sighted ['fɑ:'saɪtɪd] *adj* (a) *(shrewd) (person, decision)* previsor(ora), con visión de futuro (b) *US (long-sighted)* hipermétrope

far-sightedness ['fɑ:'saɪtɪdnɪs] *n* (a) *(of person, decision)* visión *f* de futuro (b) *US (long-sightedness)* hipermetropía *f*

fart [fɑ:t] *Fam* 1 *n* (a) *(gas)* pedo *m* (b) *(person)* **a boring old f.** un(a) petardo(a), *Esp* un(a) plasta
2 *vi* tirarse un pedo

►**fart about, fart around** *vi Fam (waste time)* perder el tiempo a lo tonto

farther = **further**

farthest = **furthest**

farthing ['fɑ:ðɪŋ] *n Br Formerly* cuarto *m* de penique; *Fam* **he doesn't have a (brass) f.** no tiene (ni) un céntimo

f.a.s., FAS *Com* (*abbr* **free alongside ship**) F.A.S., franco al costado del buque

fascia, facia ['feɪʃə] (*pl* **fasciae** ['feɪʃɪiː] *or* **fascias**) *n* (**a**) *(on shop front)* rótulo *m* (**b**) *Br (in car)* tablero *m* de instrumentos, *Esp* salpicadero *m* (**c**) *Archit* faja *f*

fascinate ['fæsɪneɪt] *vt* fascinar; **she was fascinated by** *or* **with his story** estaba fascinada con su relato, su relato la fascinó

fascinating ['fæsɪneɪtɪŋ] *adj* fascinante

fascinatingly ['fæsɪneɪtɪŋlɪ] *adv* fascinantemente, de manera fascinante

fascination [fæsɪ'neɪʃən] *n* fascinación *f*; **it holds a f. for him** ejerce gran fascinación en él; **she watched/listened in f.** observó/escuchó con fascinación

fascism ['fæʃɪzəm] *n* fascismo *m*

fascist ['fæʃɪst] **1** *n* fascista *mf*
2 *adj* fascista

fascistic [fə'ʃɪstɪk] *adj* fascista

fashion ['fæʃən] **1** *n* (**a**) *(in clothes)* moda *f*; **the latest Paris fashions** los últimos modelos de París; **to follow f.** seguir la moda; **to set the f.** marcar la moda; **in f.** de moda; **out of f.** pasado(a) de moda; **to come into f.** ponerse de moda; **to go out of f.** pasar de moda; **it's becoming the f. to take holidays at home** se está poniendo de moda tomarse las vacaciones en casa; *Fam* **he was eating chocolate like** *or* **as if it was going out of f.** comía chocolate a más no poder ▸▸ ***f. boutique*** boutique *f* de señora; ***f. designer*** modisto(a) *m,f*; ***f. house*** casa *f* de moda(s); ***f. model*** modelo *mf*; ***f. parade*** desfile *m* de moda, desfile *m or* pase *m* de modelos; ***f. show*** desfile *m* de moda, desfile *m or* pase *m* de modelos; ***f. statement:*** **he wears that as a f. statement** lleva eso para dejar claro su estilo propio; *Pej* ***f. victim*** adicto(a) *m,f* a la moda
(**b**) *(manner)* manera *f*, forma *f*; **in an orderly f.** ordenadamente, de forma ordenada; **we rubbed noses, Eskimo f.** nos frotamos las narices al estilo esquimal; **after** *or* **in the f. of** al estilo de; **after** *or* **in the f. of Mozart** al estilo de Mozart, a lo Mozart; **after a f.** más o menos; **he can speak German after a f.** se defiende en alemán
2 *vt (form)* elaborar (**from** con); **he fashioned a small figure from a block of wood** modeló un figurín a partir de un bloque de madera; **to f. a log into a canoe** convertir un tronco en una canoa

fashionable ['fæʃnəbəl] *adj* de moda; **to be f.** estar de moda

fashionably ['fæʃnəblɪ] *adv (to dress)* a la moda

fashion-conscious ['fæʃənkɒnʃəs] *adj* pendiente de la moda

FAST¹ [fɑːst] **1** *adj* (**a**) *(rapid)* rápido(a); **I'm a f. reader/swimmer** leo/nado muy rápido; *Fam Fig* **he's a f. worker!** ¡no pierde un instante!; **the action was f. and furious** la acción transcurría a un ritmo vertiginoso; IDIOM *Fam* **he pulled a f. one on me** me jugó una mala pasada, *Esp* me la pegó, *RP* me jorobó ▸▸ ***f. break*** *(in basketball)* contraataque *m*; ***f. food*** comida *f* rápida; ***the f. lane*** *(of motorway)* el carril rápido; IDIOM **to live life in the f. lane** llevar un tren de vida frenético; ***f. train*** (tren *m*) rápido *m*
(**b**) *(clock, watch)* adelantado(a); **my watch is ten minutes f.** mi reloj lleva diez minutos de adelanto, mi reloj va *or* está diez minutos adelantado
(**c**) *(secure) (grip)* firme; *(rope, knot)* bien apretado(a); *(door)* bien cerrado(a); **to make sth f.** sujetar *or* atar algo
(**d**) *Phot (film)* sensible
(**e**) *(track, green, surface)* rápido(a)
(**f**) *(colour)* sólido(a), inalterable
(**g**) *(wild)* disipado(a), disoluto(a); *Fam* **a f. woman** *(promiscuous)* una mujer fácil *or Esp* casquivana
2 *adv* (**a**) *(rapidly)* rápido; **we need a doctor, f.!** ¡rápido, necesitamos un doctor!; **this species is disappearing f.** esta especie está desapareciendo rápidamente; **do it, and do it f.!** ¡hazlo, y hazlo deprisa!, *RP* ¡hacelo, y que sea rápido!; **how f. can it go?** ¿qué velocidad alcanza?; **how f. were you driving?** ¿a qué velocidad *Esp* conducías *or Am* ibas manejando?; **how f. can you finish it?** ¿para cuándo puedes tenerlo finalizado *or Am* pronto?; **not so f.!** ¡no tan deprisa *or* rápido!; **we are f. running out of options** cada vez nos quedan menos opciones; **she ran as f. as her legs could carry her** corrió como una condenada; **to play f. and loose with the truth** jugar con la verdad
(**b**) *(securely)* firmemente; **to hold f.** sujetarse bien; **he held f. to his beliefs** se mantuvo fiel a sus creencias
(**c**) *(soundly)* **f. asleep** profundamente dormido(a)

---

fast² **1** *n* ayuno *m*; **to break one's f.** romper el ayuno ▸▸ *Rel* ***f. day*** día *m* de ayuno
2 *vi* ayunar

fast-acting ['fɑːst'æktɪŋ] *adj (drug, poison)* de efecto inmediato

fastball ['fɑːstbɔːl] *n (in baseball)* bola *f* rápida

fast-breeder reactor ['fɑːstbriːdərɪ'æktə(r)] *n* reactor *m* (nuclear) reproductor rápido

fasten ['fɑːsən] **1** *vt* (**a**) *(attach)* unir; **to f. sth (onto sth) with glue/nails/string** pegar/clavar/atar algo (a algo); **he fastened the two ends together** ató *or* unió un extremo al otro; **to f. one's belt/buttons** abrocharse el cinturón/los botones; **they fastened the blame on him** le echaron la culpa a él; **f. your seatbelts** abróchense los cinturones
(**b**) *(close) (door, window)* cerrar, echar el cerrojo a
(**c**) *(eyes, attention)* fijar (**on** en)
2 *vi (garment)* abrocharse; *(bag, door, window)* cerrarse; **the trousers f. at the side** el pantalón se abrocha por el costado

▸ **fasten down** *vt sep* cerrar

▸ **fasten on** *vt insep* (**a**) *(belt, holster)* abrochar(se) (**b**) *(seize upon) (idea)* aferrarse a; **the press fastened on this admission as proof of his guilt** la prensa se aferró a aquella confesión como prueba de su culpabilidad (**c**) *(fix)* fijarse en; **her eyes fastened on the letter** se fijó en la carta, clavó la mirada en la carta

▸ **fasten onto** *vt insep* (**a**) *(seize upon) (idea)* aferrarse a (**b**) *(grip)* agarrarse a, pegarse a; **he fastened onto our group** se pegó a nuestro grupo

▸ **fasten upon** *vt insep* (**a**) *(seize upon) (idea)* aferrarse a (**b**) *(fix)* fijarse en; **her eyes fastened upon the letter** se fijó en la carta, clavó la mirada en la carta

fastener ['fɑːsnə(r)], **fastening** ['fɑːsnɪŋ] *n (of garment)* cierre *m*

fast-food ['fɑːst'fuːd] *adj (restaurant, chain)* de comida rápida

fast-forward ['fɑːst'fɔːwəd] **1** *n* avance *m* rápido ▸▸ ***f. button*** botón *m* de avance rápido
2 *vt (cassette)* pasar hacia delante

fastidious [fæ'stɪdɪəs] *adj* (**a**) *(meticulous)* meticuloso(a), puntilloso(a); **she is f. about accuracy** es muy meticulosa *or* puntillosa con la precisión (**b**) *(fussy)* quisquilloso(a)

fastidiousness [fæ'stɪdɪəsnɪs] *n* (**a**) *(meticulousness)* meticulosidad *f* (**b**) *(fussiness)* quisquillosidad *f*; **she found his f. tiresome** era tan quisquilloso que le resultaba pesado *or Am* fastidioso

> **False friend**: The Spanish adjective **fastidioso** is not a translation for the English word **fastidious**. In Spanish **fastidioso** means "annoying" or "boring".

fast-moving ['fɑːst'muːvɪŋ] *adj (vehicle)* veloz, rápido(a); *(film)* rápido(a) ▸▸ ***f. consumer goods*** productos *mpl* de venta rápida

fastness ['fɑːstnɪs] *n* (**a**) *(of colour, dye)* inalterabilidad *f* (**b**) *Literary (stronghold)* fortaleza *f*

fast-talk ['fɑːsttɔːk] *vt Fam* **he fast-talked his way into a good job** consiguió un buen empleo a base de mucha labia *or* palabrería

fast-talker [fɑːst'tɔːkə(r)] *n Fam* embaucador(ora) *m,f*, tipo(a) *m,f* con mucha labia

fast-track ['fɑːsttræk] **1** *n* vía *f* rápida
2 *adj (promotion, career)* fulgurante; *(executive)* de fulgurante carrera
3 *vt* hacer por la vía rápida

fat [fæt] **1** *n* (**a**) *(on person)* grasa *f* ▸▸ *US Fam* ***f. farm*** clínica *f* de adelgazamiento
(**b**) *(on meat, in food)* grasa *f*; **high/low in f.** alto/bajo contenido de grasa; **to fry in deep/shallow f.** freír en abundante aceite/con poco aceite ▸▸ ***f. content*** materia *f* grasa; ***f. intake*** consumo *m* de grasa
(**c**) IDIOMS *Fam* **the f.'s in the fire!** ¡la que se va a armar!; **to live off the f. of the land** vivir a cuerpo de rey
2 *adj* (**a**) *(obese)* gordo(a); **to get f.** engordar; *Fig* **to grow f. at the expense of others** *(become rich)* hacerse rico(a) a costa de los demás; IDIOM *Fam* **get this into your f. head** métetelo en esa cabezota *or* cabeza dura que tienes ▸▸ *Fig* ***f. cat*** pez *m* gordo; *Pej* ***f. cat executive*** = alto ejecutivo con un salario desproporcionado
(**b**) *(meat)* graso(a)
(**c**) *(thick)* grueso(a), voluminoso(a)
(**d**) *Fam (cheque, salary, contract)* jugoso(a); **to make a f. profit** tener unas jugosas ganancias; **the f. years** los años de vacas gordas; IDIOM *US* **to be in f. city** vivir en jauja
(**e**) *Fam Ironic (for emphasis)* **a f. lot of good that'll do you!** ¡pues sí que te va a servir de mucho!; **you're a f. lot of help!** ¡pues sí que eres tú de mucha ayuda!, ¡con tu ayuda estamos arreglados *or Esp* apañados!; **f. chance!** ¡ni soñarlo!, *Méx* ¡ya mero!

fatal ['feɪtəl] *adj* (**a**) *(deadly) (disease, injury, accident)* mortal; **this condition can prove f.** esta afección puede ser mortal
(**b**) *(ruinous) (action, consequences)* nefasto(a), fatal; *(mistake)* fatídico(a); **such a decision would be f. to our plans** semejante decisión sería nefasta para nuestros planes

(c) *Literary (ordained by fate)* fatal; **the f. hour/meeting** la hora/el encuentro fatal

(d) *Comptr* ***f. error*** error *m* fatal

fatalism ['feɪtəlɪzəm] *n* fatalismo *m*

fatalist ['feɪtəlɪst] *n* fatalista *mf*

fatalistic [feɪtə'lɪstɪk] *adj* fatalista

fatality [fə'tælɪtɪ] *n* (a) *(in accident)* víctima *f* mortal; **road fatalities** víctimas mortales de accidentes de tráfico (b) *(inevitability)* fatalidad *f*

> **False friend:** The most common sense of the English noun **fatality** is not translated by the Spanish word **fatalidad**. In Spanish **fatalidad** means "fate" or "misfortune".

fatally ['feɪtəlɪ] *adv (wounded)* mortalmente; **f. flawed** con graves defectos

fate [feɪt] *n* (a) *(destiny)* destino *m*, sino *m*; *Formal* **f. decreed otherwise** el destino no lo quiso así; **as f. would have it...** el destino quiso que...

(b) *(destined end, lot)* **to meet one's f.** encontrar la muerte; **to leave sb to his f.** abandonar a alguien a su suerte; **to suffer/share a similar f.** sufrir/compartir la misma suerte; **a f. worse than death** un sino peor que la muerte

(c) *Mythol* **the Fates** las Parcas

fated ['feɪtɪd] *adj* (a) *(destined)* predestinado(a); **they were f. to meet** estaban destinados a conocerse; **he was f. never to return** su destino era no regresar jamás (b) *(doomed)* condenado(a)

fateful ['feɪtfʊl] *adj* (a) *(decisive) (day, decision)* decisivo(a) (b) *(prophetic) (words)* profético(a)

fat-free ['fæt'fri:] *adj* sin grasas; **95 percent f.** sin grasas en un 95 por ciento de su contenido

fathead ['fæthed] *n Fam* imbécil *mf*, majadero(a) *m,f*

father ['fɑ:ðə(r)] 1 *n* (a) *(parent)* padre *m*; **f. of six** padre de seis hijos; **from f. to son** de padre a hijo; **he was like a f. to me** fue como un padre para mí; **on my f.'s side** por parte de mi padre; PROV **like f., like son** de tal palo, tal astilla; **Our F.** Padre Nuestro ►► ***F. Christmas*** Papá *m* Noel, *Chile* el viejo de Pascua; ***F.'s Day*** día *m* del padre; ***f. figure*** figura *f* paterna; **he was a f. figure to her** para ella él era como un padre; ***(Old) F. Time*** el Tiempo

(b) *(ancestor)* antepasado *m*, predecesor *m*; **like our fathers before us** como nuestros predecesores *or* antecesores

(c) *(originator)* creador *m*, padre *m*; **the f. of the atom bomb** el padre de la bomba atómica

(d) *(priest)* padre *m*; **F. Murphy** el padre Murphy ►► *Rel* ***the Fathers of the Church*** los Padres de la Iglesia; *Rel* ***f. confessor*** padre *m* espiritual

(e) *Br (of trade union)* ***F. of Chapel*** delegado *m or Esp* enlace *m* sindical *(del sector editorial y de artes gráficas)*

2 *vt* (a) *(child)* engendrar; *Fig (idea, invention)* concebir, crear (b) *(attribute)* **to f. sth on sb** achacar algo a alguien, cargar a alguien con algo; **they fathered the idea on her** le achacaron *or* atribuyeron la idea a ella

fatherhood ['fɑ:ðəhʊd] *n* paternidad *f*

father-in-law ['fɑ:ðərɪnlɔ:] (*pl* **fathers-in-law**) *n* suegro *m*, padre *m* político

fatherland ['fɑ:ðəlænd] *n* tierra *f* natal, patria *f*

fatherless ['fɑ:ðəlɪs] *adj* huérfano(a) de padre

fatherly ['fɑ:ðəlɪ] *adj* paternal; **f. advice** un consejo paternal *or* de padre

father-to-be ['fɑ:ðətə'bi:] (*pl* **fathers-to-be**) *n* futuro padre *m*

fathom ['fæðəm] 1 *n (measurement)* braza *f*

2 *vt (mystery)* desentrañar; *(person)* entender

►**fathom out** *vt sep (mystery)* desentrañar; *(person)* entender

fatigue [fə'ti:g] 1 *n* (a) *(tiredness)* fatiga *f*, cansancio *m*; **to be suffering from f.** estar agotado(a) *or* exhausto(a) (b) *(in metal)* fatiga *f* (c) *Mil* **f. (duty)** faena *f*; **fatigues** *(military clothing)* traje *m* de faena

2 *vt* (a) *(person)* fatigar, cansar (b) *(metal)* producir la fatiga de

fatigue-dress [fə'ti:g'dres] *n Mil* traje *m* de faena

fatiguing [fə'ti:gɪŋ] *adj* cansador(ora)

fatness ['fætnɪs] *n* (a) *(obesity)* gordura *f* (b) *(of meat)* grasa *f* (c) *(thickness)* grosor *m*, voluminosidad *f*

fatso ['fætsəʊ] (*pl* **fatsos**) *n Fam* gordinflón(ona) *m,f*

fatted ['fætɪd] *adj* IDIOM **to kill the f. calf** tirar la casa por la ventana

fatten ['fætən] 1 *vt* engordar, cebar

2 *vi* engordar

►**fatten up** *vt sep* engordar, cebar

fattening ['fætənɪŋ] *adj* que engorda; **it's very f.** engorda mucho

fattish ['fætɪʃ] *adj* más bien grueso(a)

fatty ['fætɪ] 1 *n Fam* gordito(a) *m,f*

2 *adj* (a) *(meat)* graso(a); **f. foods** alimentos grasos (b) *Physiol* ***f. acid*** ácido *m* graso; ***f. tissue*** tejido *m* adiposo

fatuity [fə'tju:ətɪ] *n Formal* necedad *f*

fatuous ['fætjʊəs] *adj* fatuo(a), necio(a)

fatuously ['fætjʊəslɪ] *adv (to smile)* con necedad, neciamente; **to say sth f.** decir algo de forma necia

fatuousness ['fætjʊəsnɪs] *n* necedad *f*

fatwa ['fætwɑ:] *n* fatwa *f*

faucet ['fɔ:sɪt] *n US Esp* grifo *m*, *Chile, Col, Méx* llave *f*, *RP* canilla *f*

fault [fɔ:lt] 1 *n* (a) *(flaw) (of person, product)* defecto *m*; *(of engine)* avería *f*, *Esp* fallo *m*, *Am* falla *f*; **for all her faults, in spite of her faults** a pesar de todos sus defectos; **to find f. with** encontrar defectos a; **she finds f. with everything** nada le parece bien, le encuentra defectos a todo; **she's generous to a f.** se pasa de generosa

(b) *(mistake)* error *m*; **a f. in the addition** un error en la suma

(c) *(guilt)* culpa *f*; **whose f. is it?** ¿de quién es la culpa?; **it was my f.** fue culpa mía; **it's not my f.** no es culpa mía, no tengo la culpa; **to be at f.** tener la culpa; **his memory was at f.** le fallaba la memoria; **I was late, but through no f. of my own** llegué tarde, pero no fue por culpa mía

(d) *(in tennis, badminton, squash)* falta *f*; *(in show jumping)* falta *f*

(e) *(geological)* falla *f* ►► ***f. line*** línea *f* de falla; ***f. plane*** plano *m* de falla

2 *vt* criticar, poner reparos a; **her attitude can't be faulted** no se puede criticar su actitud

fault-finding ['fɔ:ltfaɪndɪŋ] 1 *n* **her f. is losing her friends** como no para de poner defectos está perdiendo amistades

2 *adj* criticón(ona)

faultless ['fɔ:ltlɪs] *adj* impecable, intachable

faultlessly ['fɔ:ltlɪslɪ] *adv* impecablemente, de manera impecable

faulty ['fɔ:ltɪ] *adj* (a) *(machine)* defectuoso(a); **the wiring is f.** hay *Esp* un fallo *or Am* una falla en la instalación eléctrica, la instalación eléctrica es defectuosa (b) *(logic, reasoning)* incorrecto(a), equivocado(a)

faun [fɔ:n] *n (mythological creature)* fauno *m*

fauna ['fɔ:nə] *n (animal life)* fauna *f*

Faust [faʊst] *pr n* Fausto

Faustian ['faʊstɪən] *adj* de Fausto

Fauvism ['fəʊvɪzəm] *n Art* fauvismo *m*

faux ami ['fəʊzæ'mi:] (*pl* **faux amis** ['fəʊzæ'mi:z]) *n* falso amigo *m*

faux pas ['fəʊ'pɑ:] (*pl* **faux pas** ['fəʊ'pɑ:z]) *n* metedura *f or Am* metida *f* de pata

fava bean ['fɑ:vəbi:n] *n US* haba *f*

fave [feɪv] *adj Fam* favorito(a)

favour, *US* **favor** ['feɪvə(r)] 1 *n* (a) *(approval)* favor *m*; **to be in/out of f. (with)** *(of people)* ser visto(a) con buenos/malos ojos (por); *(of product, method)* gozar/no gozar de mucha aceptación (entre); **to look on sth/sb with f.** ser partidario(a) de algo/alguien; **to find f. with sb** encontrar aceptación por parte de alguien; **to fall out of f. (with sb)** caer en desgracia (con alguien); **to be in f. of (doing) sth** estar a favor de (hacer) algo; **to vote in f. (of)** votar a favor (de); **all those in f. say "aye"** los que estén a favor, digan "sí"

(b) *(act of goodwill)* favor *m*; **to ask sb a f., to ask a f. of sb** pedir un favor a alguien; **to do sb a f.** hacer un favor a alguien; *Br Fam* **do me a f. and shut up!** ¡haz el favor de callarte!; *Fam* **are you going to buy it? – do me a f.!** ¿vas a comprarlo? – ¡por favor!, ¡anda ya!

(c) *(advantage)* favor *m*; **the odds are in his f.** tiene todo a su favor; **the wind is in our f.** tenemos viento a favor; **in f. of...** *(in preference to)* en favor de...; **that's a point in her f.** eso es un punto a su favor; *Fin* **balance in your f.** saldo a su favor

(d) *Hist (badge)* emblema *m*

(e) *Literary* **a woman's favours** los favores de una mujer

2 *vt* (a) *(approve of, prefer)* estar a favor de, ser partidario(a) de

(b) *(be favourable to)* favorecer

(c) *(bestow favour on)* **she favoured him with a smile** lo honró con una sonrisa; **he favoured us with his company** nos honró con su presencia *or* compañía; **he has been favoured with good looks** ha sido agraciado con un buen aspecto físico

(d) *Old-fashioned (resemble)* parecerse a; **he favours his mother/father** ha salido *or* se parece a su madre/padre

favourable, *US* **favorable** ['feɪvrəbəl] *adj* (a) *(positive, assenting) (answer, impression)* favorable; **he seemed f. to the idea** parecía apoyar la idea

(b) *(advantageous) (terms, conditions)* favorable, ventajoso(a); *(weather, wind)* favorable; **in a f. light** desde una óptica favorable; **the election will be held at the time most f. to the government** la elección tendrá lugar en el momento que más convenga al gobierno

favourably, *US* **favorably** ['feɪvrəblɪ] *adv* favorablemente; **she spoke f. of you** habló muy bien de ti; **the movie was f. reviewed** la película recibió críticas favorables; **to be f. disposed toward(s)** tener buena disposición hacia; **I was f. impressed** me impresionó gratamente; **it compares f. with his early work** es mejor que su trabajo anterior

favoured, *US* **favored** ['feɪvəd] *adj* privilegiado(a), favorecido(a); **the f. few** los pocos privilegiados

favourite, *US* **favorite** ['feɪvərɪt] **1** *n* **(a)** *(preferred person, thing)* favorito(a) *m,f*, preferido(a) *m,f*; **let's listen to some old favourites** escuchemos algunos viejos éxitos; **he's a great f. with the old ladies** les cae muy bien a las señoras mayores; **spaghetti? my f.!** ¿espaguetis? ¡mi plato favorito *or* preferido!

(b) *(of teacher, monarch)* predilecto(a) *m,f*, elegido(a) *m,f*

(c) *(in race, competition)* favorito(a) *m,f*

(d) *Comptr* favorito *m*

2 *adj* favorito(a); **he's not one of my f. people** no es de los que mejor me cae; *US Pol* **f. son** = político que goza del favor de los delegados de su estado para convertirse en candidato de su partido a la presidencia de la nación

favouritism, *US* **favoritism** ['feɪvərɪtɪzəm] *n* favoritismo *m*

fawn[1] [fɔːn] **1** *n* **(a)** *(deer)* cervatillo *m* **(b)** *(colour)* beige *m*, *Esp* beis *m*

2 *adj (colour)* beige, *Esp* beis

fawn[2] *vi* adular **(on** a)

fawning ['fɔːnɪŋ] *adj* adulador(ora), adulón(ona)

fax [fæks] **1** *n* **(a)** *(machine)* fax *m*, telefax *m*; **to send sth by f.** enviar algo por fax ▸▸ *Comptr* ***f. modem*** módem *m* fax; ***f. number*** número *m* de fax **(b)** *(message)* fax *m*; **to send sb a f.** enviar un fax a alguien

2 *vt* mandar por fax; **to f. sb** mandar un fax a alguien; **I'll f. the figures to you** le enviaré *or* mandaré un fax con las cifras

faze [feɪz] *vt Fam* desconcertar; **he wasn't remotely fazed by the news he had won** la noticia de que había ganado no lo pilló por sorpresa en lo más mínimo

FBI [efbiː'aɪ] *n US (abbr* **Federal Bureau of Investigation)** FBI *m*

FC [ef'siː] *n (abbr* **football club)** CF *m*, FC *m*

FCC [efsiː'siː] *n (abbr* **Federal Communications Commission)** Comisión *f* Federal de Comunicaciones

FCO [efsiː'əʊ] *n Br (abbr* **Foreign and Commonwealth Office)** Ministerio *m* de Asuntos Exteriores *or Am* Relaciones Exteriores

FD [ef'diː] *n US (abbr* **Fire Department)** Cuerpo *m* de Bomberos

FDA [efdiː'eɪ] *n (abbr* **Food and Drug Administration)** = organismo encargado del control de la calidad de los alimentos y de otorgar las licencias de venta para los medicamentos

fealty ['fiːəltɪ] *n Hist* (juramento *m* de) vasallaje *m*

fear [fɪə(r)] **1** *n* **(a)** *(dread)* miedo *m*; **her f. of spiders/failure/heights** su miedo a las arañas/al fracaso/a las alturas; **have no f.!** ¡no temas!, ¡no tengas miedo!; **there is a f. amongst some groups that...** existe el temor entre algunos grupos de que...; **my fears proved unfounded** mis temores resultaron ser infundados; **fears are growing for his safety** existe una creciente preocupación *or* un miedo creciente por su seguridad; **for f. of** por miedo a; **for f. that** por miedo a que; **to be** *or* **go in f. of** tener miedo de; **she was in f. of** *or* **for her life** temía por su vida; **we live in f. of being attacked by terrorists** vivimos con el miedo en el cuerpo a un atentado terrorista; **without f. or favour** con imparcialidad

(b) *(awe)* **the f. of God** el temor a Dios; IDIOM *Fam* **to put the f. of God into sb** meter a alguien el miedo en el cuerpo

(c) *(risk)* peligro *m*; **there's no f. of her leaving** no corremos el riesgo de que se marche, es muy poco probable que se marche; *Fam* **no f.!** ¡ni pensarlo!, *Méx* ¡ya mero!

2 *vt* **(a)** *(be afraid of)* temer; **to f. that...** temer(se) que...; **they were feared dead** se temía que hubieran fallecido; **I f. so** eso me temo; **I f. not** me temo que no; **to f. the worst** temerse lo peor; **just as I had feared** tal y como yo (me) temía; **I fear it may be too late** temo que pueda ser demasiado tarde

(b) *(revere) (God)* temer

3 *vi* temer **(for** por); *Old-fashioned* **f. not!, never f.!** pierde cuidado, no hay por qué preocuparse

feared ['fɪəd] *adj* temido(a)

fearful ['fɪəfʊl] *adj* **(a)** *(pain, consequence)* terrible, espantoso(a); **she has a f. temper** tiene un carácter terrible **(b)** *Fam (noise, expense)* tremendo(a) **(c)** *(person)* temeroso(a); **to be f. of...** tener miedo de...

fearfully ['fɪəfʊlɪ] *adv* **(a)** *(in fear)* temerosamente, atemorizadamente **(b)** *Fam (extremely)* tremendamente

fearless ['fɪəlɪs] *adj* valiente, arrojado(a); **they set off, f. of the consequences** partieron, sin temor a las consecuencias

fearlessly ['fɪəlɪslɪ] *adv* sin miedo, con arrojo

fearlessness ['fɪəlɪsnɪs] *n* valentía *f*, arrojo *m*

fearsome ['fɪəsəm] *adj* terrible, espantoso(a); **the f. difficulty of the task** la tremenda dificultad de la tarea

feasibility [fiːzə'bɪlɪtɪ] *n (of plan, scheme)* viabilidad *f*, factibilidad *f* ▸▸ ***f. study*** estudio *m* de viabilidad

feasible ['fiːzəbəl] *adj* viable, factible; **a f. explanation** una explicación aceptable *or* creíble

feasibly ['fiːzəblɪ] *adv* **he could quite f. finish last** no es imposible que llegue el último

feast [fiːst] **1** *n* **(a)** *(large meal)* banquete *m*, festín *m*; **it was a real f.** fue una verdadera comilona **(b)** *(pleasant abundance)* **a f. of music/poetry** un festín de música/de poesía; **a f. for the eyes** un deleite para los ojos; IDIOM **it's either f. or famine** no hay término medio **(c)** *Rel* fiesta *f* ▸▸ ***f. day*** fiesta *f* de guardar

2 *vt* **to f. oneself on sth** darse un festín con algo; IDIOM **to f. one's eyes on sth** recrear la vista en algo

3 *vi* darse un banquete **(on** *or* **upon** de)

feasting ['fiːstɪŋ] *n* celebraciones *fpl*, festejos *mpl*

feat [fiːt] *n* hazaña *f*, hito *m*; **a major f. of engineering** un importante hito *or* logro de la ingeniería; **it was a remarkable f. of arms** fue un extraordinario hito *or* logro militar

feather ['feðə(r)] **1** *n* **(a)** *(of bird)* pluma *f* ▸▸ ***f. bed*** colchón *m* de plumas; ***f. boa*** boa *f*; ***f. duster*** plumero *m*; ***f. stitch*** punto *m* de escapulario **(b)** IDIOMS **you could have knocked me down with a f.** me quedé de piedra; **that's a f. in her cap** es un triunfo personal para ella; **to make the feathers fly** armar un buen revuelo

2 *vt* **(a)** *(put feathers on) (arrow)* emplumar; IDIOM **to f. one's nest** hacer el agosto **(b)** *Av (propeller)* poner en bandera **(c)** *(in rowing) (oar)* poner en posición horizontal

featherbed ['feðəbed] *(pt & pp* **featherbedded)** *vt (pamper, spoil)* facilitar las cosas a

featherbedding ['feðəbedɪŋ] *n Pej (of industry, business)* = práctica que consiste en contratar mano de obra que no es necesaria o limitar el rendimiento de los obreros a fin de crear puestos de trabajo o proteger los ya existentes

featherbrain ['feðəbreɪn] *n Fam* cabeza *mf* hueca

feather-brained ['feðəbreɪnd] *adj Fam* atolondrado(a), cabeza hueca

feathered ['feðəd] *adj* con plumas ▸▸ *Hum* ***f. friend*** pájaro *m*

featherweight ['feðəweɪt] *n (in boxing)* peso *m* pluma

feathery ['feðərɪ] *adj (sponge, pastry)* ligero(a), liviano(a)

feature ['fiːtʃə(r)] **1** *n* **(a)** *(of face)* rasgo *m*, facción *f*; **features** *(face)* facciones

(b) *(part, element)* elemento *m*; **it's a regular f. in the programme** es un elemento fijo del programa; **safety features** *(of car)* equipamiento de seguridad

(c) *(characteristic, quality)* característica *f*; **it's a f. of these films that...** una de las características de estas películas es que...; **the novel has just one redeeming f.** hay sólo un aspecto rescatable de la novela; **to make a f. of sth** destacar algo

(d) *Cin* **f. (film)** largometraje *m*

(e) *(in newspaper, on television, radio)* reportaje *m* ▸▸ ***features editor*** redactor(ora) *m,f* jefe *(de reportajes)*; ***f. writer*** articulista *mf*

2 *vt* **(a)** *(have as special feature) (of car, appliance, house)* contar *or* estar equipado(a) con

(b) *Cin (of movie)* **a movie featuring...** una película en la que figura...

(c) *Journ (display prominently)* **the story/the picture is featured on the front page** la historia/la fotografía aparece en la primera página

3 *vi* **(a)** *(appear, figure)* figurar, aparecer; **the millionaire featured prominently in the scandal** el multimillonario desempeñó un papel importante en el escándalo; **do I f. in your plans?** ¿cuentas conmigo?

(b) *Cin* aparecer

feature-length ['fiːtʃəleŋθ] *adj* de larga duración, de largo metraje

featureless ['fiːtʃəlɪs] *adj* uniforme, monótono(a)

Feb *(abbr* **February)** feb.

febrile ['fiːbraɪl] *adj Formal (atmosphere, state)* febril

February ['febrʊərɪ] *n* febrero *m*; *see also* **May**

fecal *US* = **faecal**

feces *US* = **faeces**

feckless ['feklɪs] *adj* abúlico(a), apático(a)

fecklessness ['feklɪsnɪs] *n* abulia *f*, apatía *f*

fecund ['fekʌnd] *adj Literary* fecundo(a)

fecundity [fə'kʌndɪtɪ] *n Literary* fecundidad *f*

Fed [fed] *n US Fam* **(a)** *(FBI agent)* agente *mf* del FBI; **the Feds** los del FBI, los federales **(b)** *Fin* **the F.** la junta de gobierno de la Reserva Federal

fed *pt & pp of* **feed**

federal ['fedərəl] *adj* **(a)** *(republic, system)* federal; IDIOM *US Fam Fig* **to make a f. case out of sth** *Esp* montar *or Am* armar un dramón por algo ▸▸ ***F. Bureau of Investigation*** FBI *m*; ***F. Republic of Germany*** República *f* Federal de Alemania; ***F. Reserve Bank*** banco *m* de la Reserva Federal; ***F. Reserve Board*** junta *f* de gobierno de la Reserva Federal **(b)** *(funding, taxes)* federal

federalese ['fedərəli:z] *n US Fam* jerga *f* burocrática federal

federalism ['fedərəlɪzəm] *n* federalismo *m*

federalist ['fedərəlɪst] **1** *n* federalista *mf*

2 *adj* federalista

federally ['fedərəlɪ] *adv* **to be f. funded** estar sufragado(a) con fondos federales

federate ['fedəreɪt] **1** *vt* federar

2 *vi* federarse

3 *adj* ['fedərət] federado(a)

federation [fedə'reɪʃən] *n* **(a)** *(organisation)* federación *f* ▸▸ ***the F. Cup*** *(in tennis)* la Copa Federación **(b)** *(unification)* federación *f*

fedora [fɪ'dɔ:rə] *n* = sombrero flexible de fieltro

fed up ['fed'ʌp] *adj Fam* **to be f. (with)** estar harto(a) (de); **I'm f. with the way you treat me!** ¡estoy harto de cómo me tratas!; **you sound f.** parece que estás harta

fee [fi:] *n* **(a)** *(of lawyer, doctor)* minuta *f*, honorarios *mpl*; *(for speaker, performer)* honorarios *mpl* **(b)** *(for entrance)* (precio *m* de) entrada *f*, *Méx* (precio *m* del) boleto *m*; *(for examination)* derechos *mpl*; *(for membership)* cuota *f*; **(school) fees** matrícula *f*; **for a small f.** por una módica suma **(c)** *Law* **f. simple** pleno dominio

feeb [fi:b] *n US Fam* bobo(a) *m,f*, cretino(a) *m,f*

feeble ['fi:bəl] *adj* **(a)** *(weak) (person, light)* débil; *Fam* **don't be so f.!** ¡no seas tan patético! **(b)** *(unconvincing) (argument, attempt, excuse)* flojo(a), pobre; *(smile)* tenue; *(joke)* malo(a)

feeble-minded ['fi:bəl'maɪndɪd] *adj* **(a)** *(irresolute)* con poco carácter **(b)** *(stupid)* lelo(a) **(c)** *Old-fashioned (mentally defective)* débil mental

feebleness ['fi:bəlnɪs] *n* **(a)** *(of person)* debilidad *f* **(b)** *(of argument, attempt, excuse)* pobreza *f*

feebly ['fi:blɪ] *adv* **(a)** *(to say, shine, wave)* débilmente **(b)** *(to argue, attempt, smile)* desganadamente

feed [fi:d] **1** *n* **(a)** *(animal food)* pienso *m* ▸▸ ***f. additive*** aditivo *m* (alimentario)

(b) *(for baby) (from breast, bottle)* toma *f*; **it's time for her next f.** ya es la hora de la siguiente toma

(c) *(meal for animal)* **the dog gets two feeds a day** al perro se le dan dos comidas diarias

(d) *Fam (meal)* comilona *f*

(e) *Tech (supply) (of fuel, material)* provisión *f*; *(device)* alimentador *m* ▸▸ ***f. pipe*** *(for fuel)* manguera *f or* tubo *m* de alimentación; *Elec* ***f. source*** fuente *f* de alimentación

(f) *Br Theat Fam (comedian's partner)* partenaire *mf*

2 *vt* (*pt & pp* **fed** [fed]) **(a)** *(give food to)* alimentar, dar de comer a; **to f. sb sth** dar de comer algo a alguien; **to f. oneself** alimentarse; **she is so ill she isn't even able to f. herself** está tan enferma que ni siquiera puede comer por sus propios medios; **he can f. himself already** ya come solo; **we were well fed** nos dieron muy bien de comer; *Fam* **to f. one's face** comer hasta reventar; **please do not f. the animals** *(sign)* se ruega no dar de comer a los animales

(b) *(give as food)* **to f. sth to sb** darle a alguien algo de comer; **they were fed to the lions** los echaron a los leones

(c) *(provide food for)* alimentar; **the country is no longer able to f. its citizens** el país ya no puede procurar alimentos para sus ciudadanos; **he earns just enough money to f. himself** gana lo justo para comer; **to f. one's family** dar de comer a la familia; **there are ten mouths to f.** son diez bocas que alimentar; *Hum* **there's enough here to f. an army!** ¡aquí hay suficiente para alimentar a un ejército *or* a un batallón!

(d) *(baby) (from breast)* amamantar, dar de mamar a; *(from bottle)* dar el biberón a

(e) *(plant, lawn)* echar fertilizante a, fertilizar

(f) *(fire, furnace)* alimentar; *(imagination, hope, rumour)* alimentar

(g) *(supply) (fuel, material)* alimentar, proveer; **to f. coins into a machine** introducir monedas en una máquina; **to f. information to sb, to f. sb with information** proporcionar información a alguien; **to f. data into a computer** introducir datos en *Esp* un ordenador *or Am* una computadora

(h) *Theat (give cue to)* dar pie a

(i) *Sport* pasar; **to f. the forwards** dar pases a los delanteros

3 *vi* **(a)** *(eat)* alimentarse **(on** de**)**; **to put the cattle out to f.** sacar el ganado para que paste; *Fig* **these demagogues f. on people's ignorance** estos demagogos se aprovechan de la ignorancia de la gente **(b)** *(suckle)* **to f. on demand** *(of nursing mother)* dar el pecho *or* de mamar cuando el bebé lo pide

▸ **feed back** *vt sep (information, results)* retroalimentar

▸ **feed into** *vt insep* abastecer; **what you study in this module feeds into the general course as well** lo que se estudia en esta asignatura *or* módulo guarda relación con el curso

▸ **feed off** *vt insep* **(a)** *(eat)* alimentarse de **(b)** *(prey on)* cebarse en *or* con

▸ **feed up** *vt sep* **to f. sb up** alimentar bien *or* hacer engordar a alguien

feedback ['fi:dbæk] *n* **(a)** *Elec* realimentación *f*; *(on guitar, microphone)* acoplamiento *m*, feedback *m*

(b) *(response)* reacción *f*; **positive/negative f.** reacción positiva/negativa; **we welcome f. from customers** apreciamos la opinión de nuestros clientes; **this will provide us with much-needed f. on public opinion** esto nos proporcionará la información que tanto necesitamos sobre la opinión pública

feedbag ['fi:dbæg] *n US (for horse)* morral *m*; *Fam* **to put on the (old) f.** comer, *Esp* papear, *RP* morfar

feeder ['fi:də(r)] *n* **(a)** *(eater)* **this baby is such a messy f.** este niño es muy sucio a la hora de comer; **to be a heavy f.** *(person, animal)* comer mucho **(b)** *(small road, railway line)* ramal *m* **(c)** *(device) (for cattle, poultry)* comedero *m* **(d)** *(for machine, printer, photocopier)* alimentador *m* **(e)** *(power line)* cable *m* de alimentación

feeding ['fi:dɪŋ] *n* alimentación *f* ▸▸ ***f. bottle*** biberón *m*; ***f. frenzy:*** **to be in a f. frenzy** *(sharks)* alterarse a la hora de atacar a su presa; *(reporters, critics)* acosar frenético(a) a su presa; *Zool* ***f. grounds*** áreas *fpl or* zonas *fpl* de alimentación; ***f. station*** *(in cycling)* avituallamiento *m (lugar)*; ***f. time*** *(for child, animal)* hora *f* de comer; *Fam* **it's like f. time at the zoo** es un descontrol total a la hora de comer

feedstock ['fi:dstɒk] *n Ind* materia *f* prima

feedstuff ['fi:dstʌf] *n* pienso *m*, comida *f* para animales

FEEL [fi:l] **1** *n* **(a)** *(act of touching)* **to have a f. of sth** tocar algo; **can I have a f.?** ¿puedo tocar?

(b) *(sense of touch)* tacto *m*

(c) *(sensation)* sensación *f*; **I don't like the f. of nylon** no me gusta la sensación que produce el nylon; **it has a silky f.** es sedoso al tacto; **the f. of silk against her skin** el roce de la seda contra su piel

(d) *(knack)* **she has a real f. for languages** tiene un don especial para los idiomas; **he soon got the f. for it** *Esp* enseguida cogió el truco *or* tranquillo, *Am* enseguida agarró la onda *or RP* le encontró la vuelta; **I haven't got a f. for the part yet** todavía no me he hecho con el personaje

(e) *(atmosphere)* **the movie has an authentic f. to it** la película da sensación de autenticidad

(f) *Sport (skill)* finura *f*

2 *vt* (*pt & pp* **felt** [felt]) **(a)** *(touch with hand)* tocar; *(examine)* palpar; **f. how hot this plate is!** ¡toca y verás lo caliente que está el plato!; **to f. one's way** *(in darkness)* andar *or* ir a tientas; *Fig (in new situation)* familiarizarse

(b) *(notice)* notar; **did it hurt? – no, I didn't f. a thing** ¿te dolió? – no, no noté nada; **I felt the floor tremble** *or* **trembling** noté que el suelo temblaba; **I felt her arm against mine** noté el contacto de su brazo contra el mío; **I could f. myself getting nervous** sentía que me estaba poniendo nervioso

(c) *(experience) (pain, despair)* sentir; **I no longer f. anything for her** ya no siento nada por ella; **I felt her death more than the others** su muerte me afectó a mí más que a los otros; **I'm beginning to f. my age** estoy empezando a sentirme viejo(a); **to f. the cold** ser *Esp* friolero(a) *or Am* friolento(a); **to f. the effects of sth** sentir los efectos de algo; *Fig* **to f. the heat** sentir la presión; **to f. the need to do sth** sentir la necesidad de hacer algo; **to f. the pace** *(athlete) & Fig* no conseguir seguir, no aguantar el ritmo; **I (can) f. it in my bones** *(have intuition)* lo presiento, me da en la nariz, *Chile, Perú* me tinca, *Méx, Ven* me late

(d) *(believe)* creer, pensar; **I f. (that)...** me parece que...; **I f. it necessary** creo que hace falta; **she felt herself (to be) better than the rest** se creía mejor que el resto

3 *vi* **(a)** *(physically) (person)* sentirse; **to f. ill/tired** sentirse enfermo(a)/cansado(a); **my legs are feeling tired** tengo las piernas cansadas; **to f. hot/cold** tener calor/frío; **to f. hungry/thirsty** tener hambre/sed; **my throat feels sore** me duele la garganta; **my foot feels better** tengo mejor el pie; **how do you f.?, how are you feeling?** ¿cómo te encuentras?, ¿cómo estás?; **not to f. oneself** no sentirse muy bien; **to f. up to doing sth** *(well enough)* sentirse con fuerzas para hacer algo; *(competent enough)* sentirse capaz de hacer algo

(**b**) *(mentally, emotionally)* sentirse; **to f. satisfied/left out** sentirse satisfecho(a)/excluido(a); **I f. as if...** me da la sensación de que...; **to f. bad about sth** sentirse mal por algo; **to f. strongly about sth** tener convicciones muy arraigadas sobre algo; **to f. sure (that)...** estar seguro(a) (de que)...; **how would you f. about going to the cinema?** ¿qué te parecería ir al cine?; **how would you f. if...?** ¿cómo te sentirías si...?; **I know exactly how you f.** te entiendo perfectamente; **to f. (like) a new man/woman** sentirse otro/otra; **it feels strange/good** es extraño/agradable; **how does it f. to be a grandfather?** ¿qué se siente siendo abuelo?; **I felt (like) an idiot** me sentí como un/una idiota; **to f. like doing sth** tener ganas de hacer algo; **I f. like a cup of coffee** *Esp* me apetece *or Carib, Col, Méx* me provoca un café, *Méx* se me antoja *or CSur* me tomaría un café; **I don't f. like it** no tengo ganas, *Esp* no me apetece; **come round whenever you f. like it** ven a vernos cuando quieras; **it felt like** *or* **as if it would never end** parecía que no iba a acabar *or* terminar nunca; **it feels like (it's going to) rain** parece que va a llover; **f. free to take as many as you like** llévate todos los que quieras; **can I have another? – f. free!** ¿puedo *Esp* tomar *or Am* agarrar otro? – ¡claro! *or* ¡por favor!

(**c**) *(feel sympathy for)* **to f. for sb** sentirlo por alguien; **I really felt for his wife** me daba mucha pena su mujer

(**d**) *(things)* **to f. hard/soft** ser duro(a)/blando(a) al tacto; **it feels soft now** ahora está blando(a); **to f. hot/cold** estar caliente/frío(a); **it feels warmer today** *(weather)* parece que hace más calor hoy; **it feels like leather** parece cuero al tacto, tiene la textura del cuero; **it feels like summer** parece como si estuviéramos en verano

(**e**) *(touch with hands)* **to f. in one's pockets** mirarse *or RP* fijarse en los bolsillos *or CAm, Méx, Perú* las bolsas; **he felt on the ground for the key** buscó la llave a tientas por el suelo

▸ **feel about** *vi (in drawer, pocket)* rebuscar; **to f. about in one's pocket for the key** rebuscar la llave en el bolsillo

▸ **feel out** *vt sep US Fam (ask opinion of)* **to f. sb out about sth** sondear *or* tantear a alguien acerca de algo

▸ **feel up** *vt sep Fam* meter mano a, sobar

---

feeler ['fi:lə(r)] *n* (**a**) *(of insect)* antena *f*; *(of snail)* cuerno *m* (**b**) **to put out feelers** *(before deal, negotiation)* tantear el terreno

feelgood ['fi:lgʊd] *adj Fam* **a f. movie/ending** una de esas películas/uno de esos finales que levantan la moral; **the f. factor** la sensación de bienestar

feeling ['fi:lɪŋ] *n* (**a**) *(sensation) (of cold, pain)* sensación *f*; **she gets a tingling f. in her fingers** le da un hormigueo en los dedos; **there's a f. of spring in the air** en el aire se siente la primavera; **a f. of unease came over her** la invadió cierta inquietud

(**b**) *(ability to feel)* **(sense of) f.** sensibilidad *f*; **to have no f. in one's right arm** tener el brazo derecho insensible

(**c**) *(emotion)* sentimiento *m*; **a f. of joy/anger** un sentimiento de alegría/ira; **to speak with f.** hablar apasionadamente; **I know the f.!** ¡sé cómo te sientes!; **his feelings towards me** sus sentimientos hacia mí; **to hurt sb's feelings** herir los sentimientos de alguien; **to show one's feelings** demostrar los sentimientos (propios); **to have no feelings** no tener sentimientos; **feelings were running high (about)** estaban los ánimos revueltos (en cuanto a); *Fam* **no hard feelings!** ¡estamos en paz!

(**d**) *(sensitivity)* sensibilidad *f*; **to have a f. for sth** tener sensibilidad para algo; **to play/sing with f.** tocar/cantar con pasión

(**e**) *(opinion)* opinión *f*; **there is a general f. that..., the general f. is that...** la impresión general es que...; **my f. is that...** pienso *or* creo que...; **I don't have any strong feelings about it (either way)** no tengo una opinión muy clara al respecto

(**f**) *(intuition)* impresión *f*; **I have a f. that somebody's watching us** tengo la sensación de que alguien nos observa; **I had a f. I might find you here** me daba la sensación *or* tenía la impresión de que te encontraría aquí; **it's just a f.** es sólo una corazonada; **to have a good/bad f. about sth/sb** tener un buen/mal presentimiento acerca de algo/alguien

feelingly ['fi:lɪŋlɪ] *adv* sentidamente

fee-paying ['fi:peɪɪŋ] *adj* ***f. school*** colegio *m* de pago

feet *pl of* **foot**

feign [feɪn] *vt (anger, surprise)* fingir, simular; **to f. illness/interest** fingir una enfermedad/interés

feigned [feɪnd] *adj (fake)* fingido(a), simulado(a)

feint[1] [feɪnt] **1** *n* amago *m*, finta *f*

2 *vi* **to f. to the left/right** hacer una finta *or* amagar a la izquierda/derecha

feint[2] *n Typ* raya *f* fina; **narrow f.** con rayas finas

feint-ruled ['feɪnt'ru:ld] *adj (paper)* rayado(a)

feisty ['faɪstɪ] *adj Fam (spirited)* combativo(a), animoso(a)

felafel, falafel [fə'læfəl] *n* falafel *m*, = especie de albóndiga a base de pasta de garbanzos, cebolla, pimiento y especias

feldspar ['feldspɑ:(r)] *n Geol* feldespato *m*

felicitous [fɪ'lɪsɪtəs] *adj Formal (choice, expression)* feliz, acertado(a)

felicitously [fɪ'lɪsɪtəslɪ] *adv Formal* acertadamente

felicity [fɪ'lɪsɪtɪ] *n Formal* (**a**) *(happiness)* dicha *f*, felicidad *f* (**b**) *(of choice, expression)* acierto *m*

feline ['fi:laɪn] **1** *n* felino *m*, félido *m*

2 *adj* felino(a)

fell[1] [fel] *vt* (**a**) *(tree)* talar (**b**) *(opponent)* derribar

fell[2] *adj* (**a**) *Archaic or Literary (evil)* maligno(a) (**b**) IDIOM **at one f. swoop** de un golpe

fell[3] *n Br (hill)* monte *m* ▸▸ ***f. running*** = deporte en el que se corre a través de páramos o colinas; ***f. walking*** senderismo *m*, excursionismo *m*

fell[4] *pt of* **fall**

fella(h), feller ['felə] *n Fam* (**a**) *(man)* tipo *m*, *Esp* tío *m*, *RP* flaco *m* (**b**) *(boyfriend)* novio *m*, *Esp* chorbo *m*

fellatio [fe'leɪʃɪəʊ] *n* felación *f*

feller = **fella(h)**

fellow ['feləʊ] **1** *n* (**a**) *(comrade)* compañero(a) *m,f*, camarada *mf*; **school f.** compañero(a) de escuela (**b**) *Fam (man)* tipo *m*, *Esp* tío *m*, *RP* flaco *m*; **my dear f.** (mi) querido amigo (**c**) *(at university)* profesor(ora) *m,f* titular (**d**) *(of academy, society)* miembro *mf* (**e**) *(of sock, glove)* compañero(a) *m,f*, pareja *f*

2 *adj* **f. citizen** conciudadano(a); **f. countryman/countrywoman** compatriota; **one's f. man** el prójimo; **f. passenger/student** compañero(a) de viaje/de estudios; **f. worker** compañero(a) de trabajo ▸▸ ***f. feeling*** (sentimiento *m* de) solidaridad *f*; ***f. traveller*** *(in politics)* simpatizante *mf*

fellowship ['feləʊʃɪp] *n* (**a**) *(friendship)* compañerismo *m*, camaradería *f* (**b**) *(association)* sociedad *f*, asociación *f* (**c**) *(at university) (of college)* título *m* de fellow; *(research grant)* beca *f* de investigación

felon ['felən] *n US Law* criminal *mf*

felonious [fe'ləʊnɪəs] *adj Formal* criminal

felony ['felənɪ] *n US Law* crimen *m*, delito *m* grave

felt[1] [felt] *n* (**a**) *(fabric)* fieltro *m* (**b**) **(roofing) f.** fieltro *m* impermeable *(para tejados)* (**c**) **f. pen** rotulador, *Méx* plumón, *RP* marcador

felt[2] *pt & pp of* **feel**

felt-tip ['felt'tɪp] *n* **f. (pen)** rotulador *m*, *Méx* plumón *m*, *RP* marcador *m*

fem [fem] *Fam* **1** *n (feminine lesbian)* lesbiana *f* femenina

2 *n* femenino(a)

female ['fi:meɪl] **1** *n* (**a**) *(person)* mujer *f* (**b**) *(animal, plant)* hembra *f*

2 *adj* (**a**) *(person)* femenino(a) ▸▸ ***f. circumcision*** circuncisión *f* femenina, ablación *f* del clítoris; ***f. condom*** preservativo *m or* condón *m* femenino; ***f. impersonator*** = comediante que se disfraza de mujer (**b**) *(animal, plant)* hembra (**c**) *Tech (plug, socket)* hembra ▸▸ ***f. connector*** conector *m* hembra; ***f. screw*** rosca *f* (hembra), hembra *f* del tornillo

feminine ['femɪnɪn] **1** *n Gram* femenino *m*

2 *adj* (**a**) *(characteristic of a woman)* femenino(a); **this house needs the f. touch** esta casa necesita el toque femenino (**b**) *Gram* femenino(a) ▸▸ ***f. gender*** género *m* femenino

femininity [femɪ'nɪnɪtɪ] *n* femin(e)idad *f*

feminism ['femɪnɪzəm] *n* feminismo *m*

feminist ['femɪnɪst] **1** *n* feminista *mf*

2 *adj* feminista

femme fatale ['fæmfə'tɑ:l] (*pl* **femmes fatales** ['fæmfə'tɑ:l]) *n* mujer *f* fatal

femoral ['femərəl] *adj Anat* femoral

femur ['fi:mə(r)] *n Anat* fémur *m*

fen [fen] *n (marshy land)* pantano *m*, ciénaga *f*; **the Fens** = tierras bajas del este de Inglaterra, especialmente Norfolk y Cambridgeshire

fence [fens] **1** *n* (**a**) *(barrier)* valla *f*, cerca *f*; *(metal)* alambrada *f*, *Am* alambrado *m* ▸▸ ***f. post*** poste *m*, estaca *f* (**b**) *(in show-jumping)* valla *f* (**c**) *Fam (receiver of stolen property)* perista *mf* (**d**) IDIOMS **to sit on**

the f. no pronunciarse, nadar entre dos aguas; **to get off the f.** pronunciarse; **to mend one's fences with sb** limar asperezas con alguien
2 *vt* (a) *(land)* vallar, cercar (b) *Fam (stolen goods)* recibir *(el perista)*
3 *vi* (a) *(as sport)* hacer esgrima (b) *(joust verbally)* polemizar, contender (c) *Fam (receive stolen goods)* ejercer de perista

▸ **fence in** *vt sep* (a) *(land)* vallar, cercar (b) *Fig (restrict)* restringir, limitar; **to feel fenced in** sentirse atrapado(a)

▸ **fence off** *vt sep* cerrar *or* separar con una valla

fencer ['fensə(r)] *n* (a) *(sportsperson)* tirador(ora) *m,f* (b) *(workman)* alambrador(ora) *m,f*

fencing ['fensɪŋ] *n* (a) *(sport)* esgrima *f* (b) *Fig (verbal)* contienda *f* (c) *(fences) (wood)* vallado *m*; *(metal)* alambrado *m*

fencing-master ['fensɪŋ'mæstə(r)] *n* maestro *m* de esgrima

fend [fend] *vi* **to f. for oneself** valerse por sí mismo(a)

▸ **fend off** *vt sep (attack)* rechazar; *(blow)* atajar, parar; *(question)* eludir

fender ['fendə(r)] *n* (a) *(for fireplace)* pantalla *f* (de chimenea), parachispas *m inv* (b) *US (of car) Esp, RP* guardabarros *m inv*, *Andes, CAm, Carib* guardafango *m*, *Méx* salpicadera *f* (c) *US (on train, tram)* quitapiedras *m inv*

fender-bender ['fendəbendə(r)] *n US Fam* toque *m*, topetazo *m*

feng shui ['fəŋʃʊiː] *n* feng shui *m*

Fenian ['fiːnɪən] *Irish Fam* 1 *n (catholic)* = término ofensivo para designar a los católicos
2 *adj* = término ofensivo referido a los católicos; **F. bastard!** ¡católico de mierda!

fenland ['fenlənd] *n* pantano *m*, ciénaga *f*

fennel ['fenəl] *n* hinojo *m*

fenugreek ['fenjʊgriːk] *n* alholva *f*, fenogreco *m*

feral ['ferəl] *adj* montaraz, salvaje

ferment 1 *n* ['fɜːment] (a) *(commotion)* agitación *f*; **in a (state of) f.** agitado(a) (b) *(substance)* fermento *m*
2 *vt* [fə'ment] (a) *(cause to ferment)* fermentar (b) *(stir up)* provocar, agitar
3 *vi (alcoholic drink)* fermentar

fermentation [fɜːmen'teɪʃən] *n* fermentación *f*

fermented [fə'mentɪd] *adj* fermentado(a)

fermium ['fɜːmɪəm] *adj Chem* fermio *m*

fern [fɜːn] *n* helecho *m*

ferocious [fə'rəʊʃəs] *adj* (a) *(fierce) (animal)* feroz; *(criticism, fighting)* feroz, encarnizado(a) (b) *(intense) (competition, opposition)* encarnizado(a); *(appetite)* voraz; *(heat, climate)* abrasador

ferociously [fə'rəʊʃəslɪ] *adv* (a) *(fiercely) (to attack, criticize)* encarnizadamente; *(to look at)* con furia, enfurecidamente (b) *(intensely) (competitive)* encarnizadamente; **it was f. hot** hacía un calor atroz

ferocity [fə'rɒsɪtɪ], **ferociousness** [fə'rəʊʃəsnɪs] *n* (a) *(of animal)* ferocidad *f*; *(criticism, fighting)* ferocidad *f*, encarnizamiento *m* (b) *(intensity) (of competition, opposition)* encarnizamiento *m*; *(of heat, climate)* furia *f*

ferret ['ferɪt] 1 *n* hurón *m*
2 *vi* (a) *(hunt with ferrets)* huronear (b) *Fam* **to f. (about** *or* **around) for sth** husmear *or* hurgar en busca de algo; **to f. about in sb's past** hurgar en el pasado de alguien

▸ **ferret out** *vt sep (object, information)* encontrar, dar con

ferric ['ferɪk] *adj* férrico(a) ▸▸ ***f. oxide*** óxido *m* férrico

Ferris wheel ['ferɪs'wiːl] *n Esp* noria *f*, *Andes* rueda *f* de Chicago, *Arg* vuelta *f* al mundo, *Chile, Urug* rueda *f* gigante, *Méx* rueda *f* de la fortuna

ferroconcrete ['ferəʊ'kɒŋkriːt] *n* hormigón *m* armado

ferrous ['ferəs] *adj* ferroso(a)

ferruginous duck [fə'ruːdʒɪnəs'dʌk] *n* porrón *m* pardo

ferrule ['feruːl] *n (on umbrella, walking stick)* virola *f*, contera *f*

ferry ['ferɪ] 1 *n* transbordador *m*, ferry *m* ▸▸ ***f. terminal*** terminal *f* de ferries
2 *vt* (a) *(by boat)* **to f. sth/sb across a river** pasar *or* llevar algo/a alguien al otro lado de un río
(b) *(by vehicle)* **the injured were ferried to hospital in taxis** los heridos fueron trasladados *or* transportados al hospital en taxis; **speakers were ferried to and fro between venues by volunteers** un equipo de voluntarios se encargaba de llevar a los conferenciantes *or Am* conferencistas a las distintas sedes

ferryboat ['ferɪbəʊt] *n* transbordador *m*, ferry *m*

ferryman ['ferɪmən] *n* barquero *m*

fertile ['fɜːtaɪl] *adj* (a) *(land, animal, person)* fértil (b) *(imagination, mind)* fértil; **to fall on f. ground** *(suggestion)* caer en terreno fértil

fertility [fɜː'tɪlɪtɪ] *n* (a) *(of land, animal, person)* fertilidad *f* ▸▸ ***f. drug*** fármaco *m or* medicamento *m* fertilizante; ***f. rate*** tasa *f* de fecundidad; ***f. symbol*** símbolo *m* de fertilidad; *Med* ***f. treatment*** tratamiento *m* de fertilidad (b) *(of imagination, mind)* fecundidad *f*, fertilidad *f*

fertilization [fɜːtɪlaɪ'zeɪʃən] *n* (a) *(of animal, plant, egg)* fecundación *f* (b) *(of land)* abono *m*

fertilize ['fɜːtɪlaɪz] *vt* (a) *(animal, plant, egg)* fecundar (b) *(land)* fertilizar

fertilizer ['fɜːtɪlaɪzə(r)] *n* fertilizante *m*

ferule ['feruːl] *n (cane, rod)* férula *f*

fervent ['fɜːvənt], **fervid** ['fɜːvɪd] *adj (hope, prayer, belief)* ferviente; *(believer, supporter)* fervoroso(a); **he is a f. believer in reincarnation** cree fervientemente en la reencarnación

fervently ['fɜːvəntlɪ] *adv (to hope, pray, believe)* fervientemente; *(to speak, beg, desire)* con fervor

fervid = **fervent**

fervour, *US* **fervor** ['fɜːvə(r)] *n* fervor *m*

fess [fes]

▸ **fess up** *vi US Fam (confess)* cantar

-fest [fest] *suffix Fam* (a) *(festival)* **filmfest** festival de cine; **songfest** festival de la canción (b) *(occasion of excess)* **drinkfest** orgía de alcohol

fester ['festə(r)] *vi* (a) *(wound)* infectarse; *also Fig* **a festering sore** una herida abierta (b) *(rubbish)* pudrirse; *Fig* **piles of dishes were festering in the kitchen** había montones de platos pudriéndose en la cocina (c) *(resentment, rivalry)* enconarse

festival ['festɪvəl] *n* (a) *(of arts, music, drama)* festival *m* (b) *(public holiday)* festividad *f* (c) *Rel* festividad *f*

festive ['festɪv] *adj (atmosphere, occasion)* festivo(a); **in f. mood** con ganas de fiesta; **there was a really f. atmosphere** había un clima muy festivo *or* alegre; **the f. season** *(Christmas)* la época navideña

festively ['festɪvlɪ] *adv* con aire festivo *or* de fiesta

festivity [fes'tɪvɪtɪ] *n* regocijo *m*; **an air of f.** un clima *or* aire de fiesta; **the festivities** la celebración, las fiestas

festoon [fes'tuːn] 1 *n* (a) *(of flowers, ribbons)* guirnalda *f* (b) *Archit* festón *m*
2 *vt* festonear, engalanar (**with** con)

feta ['fetə] *n* **f. (cheese)** queso *m* feta

fetal *US* = **foetal**

fetch [fetʃ] 1 *vt* (a) *(bring) (object, liquid)* traer, *Esp* ir a por; *(person)* ir a recoger *or* buscar a; **to f. sb from the airport** ir a recoger *or* buscar a alguien al aeropuerto; **to f. the police** llamar a la policía; **go and f. the doctor!** ¡ve a buscar a un médico!; **the noise fetched him from the cellar** el ruido hizo que regresara del sótano; **f.!** *(to dog)* ¡busca!
(b) *(be sold for)* alcanzar; **it should f. at least $50,000** debería venderse al menos por 50.000 dólares
(c) *(blow)* **to f. sb a blow** propinarle un golpe a alguien
(d) *(generate) (response, laugh)* arrancar
(e) *Literary (utter) (sigh, moan)* exhalar
2 *vi* IDIOM **to f. and carry for sb** ser el/la criado(a) de alguien

▸ **fetch up** 1 *vt sep Fam* (a) *(vomit)* **the child fetched up his dinner all over himself** el niño se devolvió toda la cena encima (b) *(bring up)* **he fetched a bottle of wine up from the cellar** subió una botella de vino de la bodega
2 *vi (end up)* ir a parar, acabar

fetching ['fetʃɪŋ] *adj* atractivo(a); **that hat's very f. on you** ese sombrero te sienta de maravilla, estás muy *Esp* guapo *or Am* lindo con ese sombrero

fête, fete [feɪt] 1 *n* = fiesta benéfica al aire libre con mercadillo, concursos, actuaciones, etc.
2 *vt* festejar, agasajar; **his book was fêted in the press/by the critics** su libro fue muy elogiado por la prensa/por los críticos

fetid ['fetɪd] *adj* fétido(a)

fetish ['fetɪʃ] *n* (a) *(idol)* fetiche *m* (b) *(obsession)* obsesión *f*; **to have a f. for sth** tener obsesión por algo, estar obsesionado(a) por algo; **to make a f. of sth** hacer de algo una obsesión

fetishism ['fetɪʃɪzəm] *n* fetichismo *m*

fetishist ['fetɪʃɪst] *n* fetichista *mf*

fetlock ['fetlɒk] *n* espolón *m*

fetter ['fetə(r)] 1 *vt* (a) *(slave, prisoner)* poner grilletes a, engrilletar (b) *(restrict)* encadenar, atar; **we are fettered by the conditions laid down in the will** estamos atados de pies y manos por las condiciones establecidas en el testamento
2 **fetters** *npl* (a) *(on slave, prisoner)* grilletes *mpl*; **in fetters** con los grilletes puestos, engrilletado(a) (b) *(on rights, freedom)* cadenas *fpl*, ataduras *fpl*

fettle ['fetəl] *n* **in good** *or* **fine f.** en plena forma

fettuccine, fettucini [fetʊ'tʃi:ni:] *n* fettuccini *mpl*

fetus *US* = **foetus**

feud [fju:d] 1 *n* disputa *f* duradera
2 *vi* pelearse (**with** con)

feudal ['fju:dəl] *adj* feudal ►► ***f. system*** feudalismo *m*

feudalism ['fju:dəlɪzəm] *n* feudalismo *m*

feuding ['fju:dɪŋ] *n* altercados *mpl*, reyertas *fpl*

fever ['fi:və(r)] *n* (a) *(illness, high temperature)* fiebre *f*; **to have** *or* **be running a f.** tener fiebre (b) *(state of excitement)* **gold/election f.** fiebre del oro/electoral; **to be in a f. (over sth)** estar revolucionado(a) *or* muy agitado(a) (por algo); **excitement had risen to f. pitch** los ánimos estaban muy exaltados

fevered ['fi:vəd] *adj* (a) *(brow)* afiebrado(a) (b) *(imagination)* febril

feverish ['fi:vərɪʃ] *adj* (a) *(patient)* con fiebre, febril; **to be/feel f.** estar/sentirse afiebrado(a) (b) *(excitement, atmosphere)* febril

feverishly ['fi:vərɪʃlɪ] *adv* febrilmente

FEW [fju:] 1 *npl* **the f. who came** los pocos que vinieron; **the many suffer abject poverty while the f. enjoy great wealth** la mayoría sufre una pobreza extrema mientras que unos pocos viven en la abundancia
2 *adj* (a) *(not many)* pocos(as); **f. people knew who she was** pocos sabían quién era; **he's one of the f. people you can trust** es uno de los pocos en los que se puede confiar; **in the last/next f. days** en los últimos/próximos días; **his visits are f. and far between** sólo viene muy de vez en cuando; **as f. as a dozen finished the race** tan sólo una docena terminó la carrera; **every f. minutes/days** cada pocos minutos/días; **so f. people came that...** vino tan poca gente que...; **only a very f. people knew** sólo lo sabía muy poca gente; **he gave too f. examples** dio muy pocos ejemplos; **we had one chair too f.** nos faltaba una silla
(b) *(some)* **a f. days/lemons** algunos días/limones; **there are only a f. tickets left** sólo quedan unas pocas entradas *or Col, Méx* boletos; **a f. hundred metres** algunos centenares de metros; **I've met him a f. times** me lo he encontrado unas cuantas veces; **have a f. more olives** come más aceitunas; **more than a f. people were shocked** mucha gente se escandalizó; **we've had quite a f.** *or* **a good f. problems** hemos tenido bastantes problemas; **to have a f. words with sb (about sth)** hablar con alguien (sobre algo)
3 *pron* (a) *(not many)* pocos(as) *m,fpl*; **f. (of them) could speak French** pocos (de ellos) hablaban francés; **he's one of the f. you can trust** es uno de los pocos en los que se puede confiar; **the last/next f.** los últimos/los siguientes; **f., if any** pocos(as) o ninguno(a), apenas alguno(a); **so f. remain that...** quedan tan pocos que...; **we have too f.** no tenemos suficientes; **there are very/too f. of us** somos muy/demasiado pocos
(b) *(some)* **a f.** algunos(as); **carrots? – just a f., please** ¿zanahorias? – unas pocas, por favor; **a f. of the survivors** algunos supervivientes *or* sobrevivientes; **a f. of us** algunos de nosotros; **all but a f. (of them) left early** casi todos se fueron temprano; **more than a f. (of us) were shocked** muchos nos escandalizamos; **there are only a f. left** sólo quedan unos pocos; **quite a f., a good f.** bastantes; *Fig* **to have had a f. (too many)** haber tomado unas cuantas copas de más

---

fewer ['fju:ə(r)] *(comparative of* **few**) 1 *adj* menos; **we have ten books f.** tenemos diez libros menos; **f. and f. people** cada vez menos gente; **no f. than thirty** no menos de treinta
2 *pron* menos *mfpl*; **there are f. (of them) than I thought** hay menos de lo que creía; **few like him, f. still respect him** pocos lo aprecian y menos aún lo respetan; **the f. the better** cuantos menos, mejor

fewest ['fju:ɪst] *(superlative of* **few**) 1 *adj* **that hospital reported the f. cases** ese hospital es el que menos casos registró; **take the road which has the f. curves** ve por la carretera que tenga menos curvas; **the f. mistakes possible** la menor cantidad de errores posible
2 *pron* **we received the f.** nosotros somos los que menos recibimos

fey [feɪ] *adj* (a) *(whimsical)* fantasioso(a) (b) *(clairvoyant)* clarividente

fez [fez] *(pl* **fezzes**) *n* fez *m*

ff *(abbr* **and the following**) y sig.

fiancé [fɪ'ɒnseɪ] *n* prometido *m*, novio *m*

fiancée [fɪ'ɒnseɪ] *n* prometida *f*, novia *f*

Fianna Fáil ['fi:ənə'fɔɪl] *n* = partido político irlandés a favor de la unificación de Irlanda

fiasco [fɪ'æskəʊ] *(pl Br* **fiascos**, *US* **fiascoes**) *n* fiasco *m*

fiat ['fi:æt] *n* (a) *Formal* decreto *m* (b) *US Fin* ***f. money*** moneda *f* fiduciaria

fib [fɪb] *Fam* 1 *n* cuento *m*; **to tell a f.** contar un cuento
2 *vi (pt & pp* **fibbed**) contar un cuento; **I'm sure he was fibbing about how much he earns** estoy seguro de que lo que dijo que ganaba era (un) cuento; **I fibbed to them about having to do some work** les metí el cuento de que tenía que trabajar

FIBA ['fi:bə] *n (abbr* **Fédération Internationale de Basket-ball Amateur**) FIBA *f*

fibber ['fɪbə(r)] *n Fam* cuentista *mf, Am* cuentero(a) *m,f*

fibre, *US* **fiber** ['faɪbə(r)] *n* (a) *(of cloth, wood)* fibra *f*; **artificial/natural fibres** fibras artificiales/naturales; **every f. of his being** lo más profundo de su ser ►► ***f. optics*** fibra *f* óptica (b) *(in diet)* fibra *f*; **high/low f. diet** dieta rica/baja en fibra (c) *(strength of character)* **(moral) f.** carácter *m*

fibreboard, *US* **fiberboard** ['faɪbəbɔ:d] *n* chapa *f or* tablero *m* de fibra

fibreglass, *US* **fiberglass** ['faɪbəglɑ:s] *n* fibra *f* de vidrio; **a f. boat** un bote de fibra de vidrio

fibre-optic, *US* **fiber-optic** [faɪbə'rɒptɪk] *adj* de fibra óptica

fibrescope, *US* **fiberscope** ['faɪbəskəʊp] *n Med* fibroscopio *m*

fibre-tip, *US* **fiber-tip** ['faɪbətɪp] *n* **f. (pen)** rotulador *m*

fibrillation [fɪbrɪ'leɪʃən] *n Med* fibrilación *f*

fibroid ['faɪbrɔɪd] 1 *n Med* fibroma *m*
2 *adj* fibrilar ►► ***f. tumour*** tumor *m* fibrilar

fibrosis [faɪ'brəʊsɪs] *n Med* fibrosis *f inv*

fibrositis [faɪbrə'saɪtɪs] *n Med* fibrositis *f inv*

fibrous ['faɪbrəs] *adj* fibroso(a)

fibula ['fɪbjʊlə] *(pl* **fibulae** ['fɪbjʊli:] *or* **fibulas**) *n Anat* peroné *m*

fiche [fi:ʃ] *n (microfiche)* microficha *f*

fickle ['fɪkəl] *adj (person)* inconstante, inconsecuente; *(weather)* cambiante, inestable; *(fate)* caprichoso(a)

fickleness ['fɪkəlnɪs] *n (of person)* insconstancia *f*; *(of weather)* inestabilidad *f*; *(of fate)* lo caprichoso

fiction ['fɪkʃən] *n* (a) *(something invented)* ficción *f*; **it's pure f.** es pura ficción; **to maintain** *or* **keep up a f.** continuar con *or* mantener un engaño *or* una farsa (b) *(short stories, novels)* ficción *f*; **a work of f.** una obra de ficción

fictional ['fɪkʃənəl] *adj (character)* de ficción; *(scene, account)* novelado(a)

fictionalize ['fɪkʃənəlaɪz] *vt* novelar, traspasar a la ficción

fictitious [fɪk'tɪʃəs] *adj* ficticio(a); **he gave her a f. address** le dio una dirección inventada *or* falsa

ficus ['faɪkəs] *n Bot* ficus *m*

fiddle ['fɪdəl] 1 *n* (a) *(violin)* violín *m (en música folk)* (b) *esp Br Fam (swindle)* timo *m*; **a tax f.** una evasión fiscal; **an insurance f.** un chanchullo para cobrar dinero del seguro; **to be on the f.** dedicarse a hacer chanchullos (c) *(tricky task)* lío *m*, enredo *m*
2 *vt Fam (cheat)* amañar; **to f. the accounts** amañar la contabilidad, *Méx* hacer una transa con la contabilidad; **to f. one's income tax** amañar la declaración de la renta; **he fiddled it so that he got the results he wanted** lo amañó para conseguir el resultado que quería
3 *vi* (a) *(play violin)* tocar el violín *(en música folk)*; IDIOM **to f. while Rome burns** tontear en un momento de crisis (b) *(fidget)* juguetear (**with** con), enredar (**with** con); **to f. with sth** juguetear *or* enredar con algo; **he fiddled with the knobs on the television** toqueteaba los controles del televisor

►**fiddle about, fiddle around** *vi (fidget)* juguetear, enredar; **to f. about** *or* **around with sth** juguetear *or* enredar con algo; **he fiddled about with the knobs on the television** toqueteaba los controles del televisor

fiddle-de-dee ['fɪdəldi:'di:] *exclam Fam Old-fashioned* ¡tonterías!

fiddle-faddle ['fɪdəlfædəl] *Fam Old-fashioned* 1 *n* tonterías *fpl*
2 *exclam* ¡tonterías!

fiddler ['fɪdlə(r)] *n* (a) *(musician)* violinista *mf (en música folk)* ►► ***f. crab*** cangrejo *m* de mar (b) *Fam (swindler)* tramposo(a) *m,f*

fiddlesticks ['fɪdəlstɪks] *exclam Fam Old-fashioned* ¡paparruchas!

fiddling ['fɪdlɪŋ] *Fam* 1 *n Br (swindling)* chanchullos *mpl*, tejemanejes *mpl*
2 *adj (trifling)* trivial

fiddly ['fɪdlɪ] *adj Br* complicado(a); **some of the parts are quite small and f.** algunas de las piezas son muy pequeñas y difíciles de manejar; **now for the really f. bit** y ahora viene la parte delicada; **to be a f. job** ser un trabajo complicado *or* de chinos

fidelity [fɪ'delɪtɪ] *n* (**a**) *(of people)* fidelidad *f* (**b**) *(of translation)* fidelidad *f* (**c**) *Elec* fidelidad *f*

fidget ['fɪdʒɪt] **1** *n (person)* enredador(ora) *m,f*, trasto *m*; **to have** *or* **get the fidgets** estar *or* ponerse inquieto

2 *vi* enredar, trastear; **stop fidgeting!** ¡quédate quieto!; **to f. with sth** juguetear *or* enredar con algo

fidgety ['fɪdʒɪtɪ] *adj* inquieto(a); **to get f.** ponerse inquieto

fiduciary [fɪ'du:ʃərɪ] *adj Fin* fiduciario(a)

fiefdom ['fi:fdəm] *n* (**a**) *Hist* feudo *m* (**b**) *(private domain)* feudo *m*

field [fi:ld] **1** *n* (**a**) *(of grass, crops)* campo *m*; **to work in the fields** trabajar en el campo; **a f. of wheat** un trigal ►► ***f. ice*** banquisa *f*; ***f. of view*** campo *m* visual; ***f. of vision*** campo *m* visual

(**b**) *(of oil, coal)* yacimiento *m*

(**c**) *(of study, activity)* campo *m*; **in the political f.** en el terreno político; **she's an expert in her f.** es una experta en su campo; **that's not my f.** eso no entra en mi campo

(**d**) *(not in office, laboratory)* **to work in the f.** hacer trabajo de campo, trabajar in situ ►► ***f. day*** día *m* de actividades al aire libre; *Mil* día *m* de maniobras; IDIOM **to have a f. day: the press had a f. day** la prensa se puso las botas; ***f. study*** *(scientific)* estudio *m* de campo; ***f. trial(s)*** prueba *f* sobre el terreno; *Sch & Univ* ***f. trip*** viaje *m or* salida *f* para (realizar) trabajo de campo

(**e**) *(for sport)* campo *m*; **the f.** *(in race, contest)* los participantes; *(in baseball, cricket)* el campo, *Am* la cancha; *also Fig* **to lead the f.** ir en cabeza; **to take the f.** *(team)* salir a la cancha, *Esp* saltar al terreno de juego; *(army)* entrar en combate; IDIOM *Fam* **to play the f.** ir de flor en flor ►► ***f. events*** *(in athletics)* pruebas *fpl* de salto y lanzamiento; ***f. goal*** *(in American football)* gol *m* de campo; *(in basketball)* tiro *m* de campo; *(in ice hockey)* gol *m* de campo; *US* ***f. hockey*** hockey *m* sobre hierba *or Am* césped; ***f. sports*** = la caza y la pesca

(**f**) *Mil* **f. (of battle)** campo *m* (de batalla); **in the f.** en el campo de batalla ►► ***f. ambulance*** ambulancia *f* de campaña; ***f. artillery*** artillería *f* de campaña; ***f. of fire*** campo *m* de fuego; ***f. glasses*** prismáticos *mpl*, gemelos *mpl*; ***f. gun*** cañón *m* de campaña; ***f. hospital*** hospital *m* de campaña; ***f. kitchen*** cocina *f* de campaña; ***f. marshal*** mariscal *m* de campo; ***f. officer*** oficial *m* superior

(**g**) *Phys (electric, magnetic)* campo *m* ►► ***f. winding*** devanado *m* inductor *or* de campo

(**h**) *Comptr* campo *m*

(**i**) *Phot* ***f. aperture*** apertura *f* de campo

(**j**) *(on coat of arms, flag)* campo *m*

2 *vt* (**a**) *(team)* alinear; *(candidates)* presentar; *(troops, unit)* poner en acción (**b**) *(deal with)* **to f. a question** contestar con destreza a una pregunta (**c**) *(in cricket, baseball) (ball)* interceptar y devolver, *Am* fildear

3 *vi (in cricket, baseball)* interceptar y devolver la pelota, *Am* fildear

fieldcraft ['fi:ldkrɑ:ft] *n* = destreza para manejarse en el campo

fielder ['fi:ldə(r)] *n (in cricket, baseball)* exterior *mf*, *Am* fildeador(ora) *m,f*; **center/left/right f.** exterior *or Am* fildeador(ora) central/izquierdo(a)/derecho(a)

fieldfare ['fi:ldfeə(r)] *n* zorzal *m* real

fieldmouse ['fi:ldmaʊs] (*pl* **fieldmice** ['fi:ldmaɪs]) *n* ratón *m* de campo

field-test ['fi:ldtest] *vt (machine)* probar *or CSur* testear sobre el terreno

fieldwork ['fi:ldwɜ:k] *n (scientific)* trabajo *m* de campo

fieldworker ['fi:ldwɜ:kə(r)] *n* investigador(ora) *m,f* de campo

fiend [fi:nd] *n* (**a**) *(demon)* demonio *m* (**b**) *Fam (evil person)* diablo *m*, demonio *m*; **sex f.** maníaco sexual (**c**) *Fam (fanatic)* entusiasta *mf*, fanático(a) *m,f*; **my boss is a f. for punctuality** mi jefe está obsesionado con la puntualidad; **dope** *or* **drug f.** adicto(a)

fiendish ['fi:ndɪʃ] *adj* (**a**) *(evil)* endiablado(a), endemoniado(a); **to take a f. delight** *or* **pleasure in doing sth** regodearse *or* entusiasmarse haciendo algo (**b**) *Fam (difficult)* endiablado(a), endemoniado(a) (**c**) *Fam (cunning) (plan, scheme)* diabólico(a), maquiavélico(a)

fiendishly ['fi:ndɪʃlɪ] *adv* (**a**) *(evilly)* diabólicamente (**b**) *(difficult, clever)* endiabladamente, endemoniadamente

fierce [fɪəs] *adj* (**a**) *(aggressive) (animal, look)* fiero(a); *(hatred, temper)* feroz; *(fighting, battle)* encarnizado(a) (**b**) *(intense) (heat, sun)* abrasador(ora); *(contest, argument, competition, criticism)* feroz, encarnizado(a); *(wind, storm)* devastador(ora); *(loyalty, desire)* fervoroso(a)

fiercely ['fɪəslɪ] *adv* (**a**) *(aggressively) (to glare)* fieramente; *(to fight)* ferozmente (**b**) *(to condemn, defend, argue)* vehementemente, apasionadamente; *(to resist)* con furia; *(to compete, criticize)* encarnizadamente; *(competitive, loyal)* extremadamente; **to be f. opposed to sth** oponerse a algo con vehemencia

fierceness ['fɪəsnɪs] *n* (**a**) *(of animal, look)* fiereza *f*; *(of hatred, temper)* furia *f*; *(of fighting, battle)* encarnizamiento *m* (**b**) *(intensity) (of heat, sun)* intensidad *f*; *(of contest, argument, competition, criticism)* ferocidad *f*; *(of wind, storm)* violencia *f*; *(of loyalty, desire)* fervor *m*

fiery ['faɪərɪ] *adj* (**a**) *(heat)* achicharrante, abrasador(ora) (**b**) *(red, sky)* encendido(a) (**c**) *(taste)* muy picante (**d**) *(person, character)* fogoso(a), ardiente; *(temper)* exaltado(a); *(speech)* encendido(a) (**e**) *US* ***the f. cross*** la cruz ardiente, = símbolo del Ku Klux Klan

fiesta [fɪ'estə] *n* fiesta *f*

FIFA ['fi:fə] *n* (*abbr* **Fédération Internationale de Football Association**) FIFA *f*

fife [faɪf] *n* pífano *m*, flautín *m*

fifteen [fɪf'ti:n] **1** *n* (**a**) *(number)* quince *m* (**b**) *Sport (rugby team)* equipo *m*

2 *adj* quince; *see also* **eight**

fifteenth [fɪf'ti:nθ] **1** *n* (**a**) *(fraction)* quinceavo *m*, quinceava parte *f* (**b**) *(in series)* decimoquinto(a) *m,f* (**c**) *(of month)* quince *m*

2 *adj* decimoquinto(a); *see also* **eleventh**

fifth [fɪfθ] **1** *n* (**a**) *(fraction)* quinto *m*, quinta parte *f* (**b**) *(in series)* quinto(a) *m,f* (**c**) *(of month)* cinco *m* (**d**) *(fifth gear)* quinta *f*; **in f.** en quinta

2 *adj* quinto(a); IDIOM *US Fam* **to feel like a f. wheel** hacer de carabina *or* de sujetavelas, *Méx* hacer mal tercio, *RP* estar de paleta ►► ***the F. Amendment*** la Quinta Enmienda; *Hum* **I plead the F. (Amendment)** tengo derecho a guardar silencio; *Pol* ***f. column*** quinta columna *f*; *Pol* ***f. columnist*** quintacolumnista *mf*; *Aut* ***f. gear*** quinta *f* (marcha *f*); *see also* **eighth**

fifthly ['fɪfθlɪ] *adv* en quinto lugar

fifties ['fɪfti:z] *npl* (años *mpl*) cincuenta *mpl*; *see also* **eighties**

fiftieth ['fɪftɪəθ] **1** *n* quincuagésimo(a) *m,f*

2 *adj* quincuagésimo(a)

fifty ['fɪftɪ] **1** *n* cincuenta *m*

2 *adj* cincuenta; *see also* **eighty**

fifty-fifty ['fɪftɪ'fɪftɪ] **1** *adj* **a f. chance of success** un cincuenta por ciento de posibilidades de éxito

2 *adv* a medias; **to go f. (on sth/with sb)** ir a medias (en algo/con alguien)

fig[1] [fɪg] *n (fruit)* higo *m*; IDIOM *Fam* **he doesn't give** *or* **care a f.** le importa un rábano ►► ***f. leaf*** *(in art)* hoja *f* de parra; *Fig* **it's just a f. leaf** no es más que una tapadera; ***f. tree*** higuera *f*

fig[2] (*abbr* **figure**) fig.

FIGHT [faɪt] **1** *n* (**a**) *(physical, verbal)* pelea *f*; *(contest, battle)* lucha *f*; *(boxing match)* combate *m*; **to get into a f. (with sb)** pelearse (con alguien); **to give in without a f.** ceder sin oponer resistencia; **to have a f. (with sb)** pelearse (con alguien); **the f. game** el boxeo, *Am* el box; **to put up a good f.** oponer resistencia; **to make a f. of it** plantar cara; **to start a f. (with sb)** pelearse (con alguien); IDIOM **it promises to be a f. to the finish** promete ser una lucha encarnizada; IDIOM **to have a f. on one's hands: you'll have a f. on your hands to convince her** te costará Dios y ayuda *or* un triunfo convencerla

(**b**) *(struggle)* lucha *f* (**for** por); **the f. against cancer** la lucha contra el cáncer

(**c**) *(spirit)* **to show some f.** demostrar espíritu de lucha; **all the f. went out of her** se quedó sin fuerzas para seguir luchando; **there was no f. left in him** no le quedaban fuerzas *or* arrestos

2 *vt* (*pt & pp* **fought** [fɔ:t]) *(person, enemy, rivals)* luchar contra; *(boxer)* pelear contra; *(disease, poverty, fire)* luchar contra, combatir; *(temptation, desire, decision)* luchar contra; *(war, battle)* librar; **he's always fighting other children** siempre se está peleando con otros niños; **to f. sb for sth** disputar algo a alguien; *Law* **she fought her case** defendió su caso *(en un juicio)*; **the Socialists fought a successful campaign** los Socialistas llevaron a cabo una campaña exitosa; **to f. a duel** enfrentarse en duelo; **to f. an election** presentarse a unas elecciones; *Pol* **to f. a seat** = presentarse como candidato por una circunscripción electoral; **to f. one's way through a crowd** abrirse paso entre una multitud; **to f. one's way to the top of one's profession** luchar por llegar a la cima de su profesión; IDIOM **to f. sb's battles for them** dar la cara por alguien; IDIOM **to f. one's corner: she fought her corner fiercely** defendió su parcela apasionadamente; IDIOM **to f. fire with fire: we'll have to f. fire with fire** combatiremos con sus mismas armas; IDIOM **to f. a losing battle** librar una batalla perdida

3 *vi* (**a**) *(physically)* luchar (**about/with** por/contra), pelearse (**about/with** por/con); *(verbally)* pelearse, discutir (**about/with** por/con); *(boxer)* pelear; **did you f. in the Second World War?** ¿combatiste en la Segunda Guerra Mundial?; **to f. over sth** pelearse por algo; **to f. fair** pelear limpio; **to f. shy of sth** evitar algo; **to f. to the death** luchar a muerte; **to go down fighting** luchar hasta el final; IDIOM **to f. like cats and dogs** pelearse como locos *or RP* como perro y gato

(**b**) *(struggle)* luchar (**for** por); **to f. for breath** luchar por respirar; **he is fighting for his life** se está debatiendo entre la vida y la muerte; **she is fighting for her political life** está luchando por salvar su carrera política

▸ **fight back 1** *vt sep (laughter, fear)* reprimir, contener; **to f. back one's tears** reprimir *or* contener las lágrimas

2 *vi* (**a**) *(respond to attack) (physically)* devolver los golpes; *(verbally)* responder; *(soldiers, company)* contraatacar (**b**) *(recover) (from near defeat)* remontar; **he fought back and made a full recovery** luchó contra la enfermedad y se recuperó por completo

▸ **fight down** *vt sep* **to f. down one's tears** tratar de contener las lágrimas

▸ **fight off** *vt sep (enemy, attack)* rechazar, ahuyentar; *(illness)* librarse de; *(sensation, sleep, impulse)* vencer

▸ **fight on** *vi* continuar luchando

▸ **fight out** *vt sep* **they'll have to f. it out (between them) for who gets the last slice** tendrán que ponerse de acuerdo para ver quién se lleva el último trozo

---

fightback ['faɪtbæk] *n* contraataque *m*, respuesta *f*

fighter ['faɪtə(r)] *n* (**a**) *(person) (in fight)* combatiente *mf*, contendiente *mf*; *(for cause)* luchador(ora) *m,f*; *(boxer)* boxeador(ora) *m,f*, púgil *mf* (**b**) *(plane)* **f. (plane)** caza *m* ▸▸ ***f. pilot*** piloto *m* de caza; ***f. squadron*** escuadrón *m* de cazas

fighter-bomber ['faɪtə'bɒmə(r)] *n* cazabombardero *m*

fighting ['faɪtɪŋ] **1** *n* (**a**) *(brawling)* peleas *fpl*; **f. broke out between police and fans** hubo enfrentamientos entre la policía y los fans (**b**) *Mil* combates *mpl*, enfrentamientos *mpl* (armados); **heavy f.** fuertes combates *or* enfrentamientos

2 *adj* IDIOM **to be in with** *or* **have a f. chance** tener posibilidad de ganar; **to be f. fit** estar en plena forma; **that's f. talk!**, *Fam Hum* **them's f. words!** *(approving)* ¡así se habla!; *(disapproving)* ¡conque ésas tenemos! ▸▸ ***f. cock*** gallo *m* de pelea; ***f. fish*** (pez *m*) combatiente *m*; ***f. forces*** fuerzas *fpl* de combate; ***f. spirit*** espíritu *m* de lucha

figment ['fɪgmənt] *n* **it's a f. of your imagination** es producto de tu imaginación

figurative ['fɪgərətɪv] *adj* (**a**) *(language, sense)* figurado(a) (**b**) *(art, painting)* figurativo(a)

figuratively ['fɪgərətɪvlɪ] *adv* en sentido figurado; **f. speaking,...** en sentido figurado,...

FIGURE ['fɪgə(r), *US* 'fɪgjə(r)] **1** *n* (**a**) *(number)* cifra *f*; **there must be a mistake in the figures** debe de haber un error en los números; **she's good at figures** tiene facilidad para los números, se le dan bien los números; **I couldn't put a f. on it** no sabría decir cuánto exactamente; **he received a f. of around $10,000** recibió una cantidad en torno a los 10.000 dólares; **unemployment is down to single figures** el desempleo ha caído por debajo del 10 por ciento; **to reach double/three figures** *(total)* alcanzar valores de dos/tres cifras; **his salary is in six figures** gana más de 100.000 libras/dólares/*etc.*

(**b**) *(body shape)* figura *f*, línea *f*; **to have a good f.** tener buen tipo; **she has kept/lost her f.** ha mantenido/ha perdido la línea; **a fine f. of a man** un hombre muy bien plantado; **to cut a sorry f.** tener un aspecto lamentable

(**c**) *(person)* figura *f*; **a leading f. in local politics** una figura destacada de la política local; **a distinguished f.** una personalidad distinguida; **he's a f. of fun** todo el mundo se ríe de él

(**d**) *(illustration)* figura *f*, ilustración *f*; **see f. 21 b** ver figura 21 b

(**e**) *(expression)* ***f. of speech*** figura *f* retórica; **I didn't mean it like that, it was just a f. of speech** no quería decir eso, era sólo una manera *or* forma de hablar

(**f**) *Geom* figura *f* ▸▸ *Br* ***f. of eight***, *US* ***f. eight*** ocho *m*; ***f. skater*** patinador(ora) *m,f* artístico(a); ***f. skating*** patinaje *m* artístico

(**g**) *(statue, in painting)* figura *f*

2 *vt US* (**a**) *(think)* figurarse; **I figured (that) you'd want me to tell her** me figuraba *or* imaginaba que querrías que se lo dijera yo; **why did you help me? – I figured I owed you one** ¿por qué me ayudaste? – te debía una (**b**) *(calculate)* calcular

3 *vi* (**a**) *(appear) (in list, book)* figurar; **that doesn't f. in my plans** eso no figura en mis planes; **where do I f. in all this?** ¿dónde entro yo en todo esto? (**b**) *Fam (make sense)* **that figures!** ¡(es) normal *or* lógico!; **it doesn't f.** no lo entiendo; *US* **go f.!** ¡a ver ahora!

▸ **figure in** *vt sep US* incluir

▸ **figure on** *vt insep Fam* **to f. on doing sth** contar con hacer algo

▸ **figure out** *vt sep Fam* (**a**) *(amount)* calcular

(**b**) *(problem)* resolver; *(solution)* encontrar; **to f. out (that)...** llegar a la conclusión de que...; **I couldn't f. out how to do it** no conseguí entender cómo había que hacerlo; **I can't f. out why he'd do such a thing** no acabo de entender por qué ha hecho algo así; **she can't f. you out at all!** ¡no te entiende en absoluto!

▸ **figure up** *vt sep US* sumar

---

figurehead ['fɪgəhed] *n* (**a**) *(on ship)* mascarón *m* de proa (**b**) *(of country, party)* testaferro *m*

figure-hugging ['fɪgəhʌgɪŋ] *adj* muy ceñido(a)

figurine [fɪgə'ri:n] *n* figurilla *f*, estatuilla *f*

> **False friend**: The Spanish noun **figurín** is not a translation for the English word **figurine**. In Spanish **figurín** means "fashion sketch".

Fiji ['fi:dʒi:] *n* (las islas) Fiyi

Fijian [fi:'dʒi:ən] **1** *n* fiyiano(a) *m,f*

2 *adj* de Fiyi

filament ['fɪləmənt] *n* (**a**) *Elec* filamento *m* (**b**) *Bot* filamento *m*

filbert ['fɪlbət] *n* avellana *f*; **f. (tree)** avellano *m*

filch [fɪltʃ] *vt Fam* afanar, *Esp* mangar

file[1] [faɪl] **1** *n (tool)* lima *f*

2 *vt (metal)* limar; **to f. one's nails** limarse las uñas; **to f. sth down/off** limar

file[2] **1** *n* (**a**) *(folder)* carpeta *f*; *(box)* archivo *m* ▸▸ ***f. card*** ficha *f*; *US* ***f. clerk*** archivero(a) *m,f*, archivista *mf*; ***f. copy*** copia *f* de archivo

(**b**) *(documents)* expediente *m*, ficha *f*; **to keep** *or* **have a f. on** tener una ficha *or* un expediente de; **to have sth on f.** tener algo archivado; **we have placed your CV on f.** *or* **in our files** hemos guardado su CV en nuestros registros, tendremos su CV presente; **the police have closed their f. on the case** la policía ha cerrado *or* archivado el caso

(**c**) *Comptr* archivo *m*, fichero *m* ▸▸ ***f. compression*** compresión *f* de archivos; ***f. conversion*** conversión *f* de archivos *or* ficheros; ***f. format*** formato *m* de archivo *or* fichero; ***f. manager*** administrador *m* de archivos; ***f. merging*** fusión *f* de archivos; ***f. name*** nombre *m* de archivo *or* fichero; ***f. name extension*** extensión *f* (del nombre) del archivo; ***f. protection*** protección *f* de ficheros *or* archivos; ***f. server*** servidor *m* de ficheros *or* archivos; ***f. transfer*** transferencia *f* de archivos *or* ficheros; ***f. transfer protocol*** protocolo *m* de transferencia de archivos

2 *vt* (**a**) *(sort and store) (documents, letters)* archivar; **to be filed under a letter/subject** estar archivado en una letra determinada/por tema

(**b**) *(present)* **to f. a claim** presentar una demanda; **to f. charges against sb** presentar cargos contra alguien; *US* **to f. one's tax return** presentar la declaración impositiva *or* (del impuesto sobre) la renta

3 *vi* **to f. for divorce** presentar una demanda de divorcio

file[3] **1** *n (line)* fila *f*; **in single** *or* **Indian f.** en fila india

2 *vi* **to f. past (sth/sb)** desfilar (ante algo/alguien); **to f. in/out** entrar/salir en fila

filet mignon ['fi:leɪmi:njɒn] *n US* solomillo *m*

filial ['fɪlɪəl] *adj* filial

filibuster ['fɪlɪbʌstə(r)] *Pol* **1** *n* discurso *m* dilatorio *(para evitar una votación)*

2 *vi* pronunciar discursos dilatorios

filigree ['fɪlɪgri:] *n* filigrana *f*

filing ['faɪlɪŋ] *n* archivación *f*, archivado *m* ▸▸ *Br* ***f. clerk*** archivero(a) *m,f*, archivista *mf*; ***f. cabinet*** archivador *m*; ***f. tray*** bandeja *f* de la correspondencia para archivar

filings ['faɪlɪŋz] *npl (of metal)* limaduras *fpl*

Filipino [fɪlɪ'pi:nəʊ] **1** *n* (*pl* **Filipinos**) (**a**) *(person)* filipino(a) *m,f* (**b**) *(language)* tagalo *m*

2 *adj* filipino(a)

FILL [fɪl] **1** *n* **we ate/drank our f.** comimos/bebimos hasta llenarnos; *Fig* **to have had one's f. of sth** estar harto(a) de algo

2 *vt* (**a**) *(container)* llenar (**with** de); *(sails)* hinchar; **to f. sb's glass** llenar el vaso a alguien; **he filled his pipe** cargó su pipa; **filled with chocolate** relleno(a) de chocolate; **to be filled with admiration/hope** estar lleno(a) de admiración/esperanza; **the smell of roses filled the air** el olor a rosas inundaba el ambiente; **the article filled three pages**

el artículo ocupaba tres páginas; **the thought fills me with dread** la idea me horroriza; IDIOM **to f. sb's shoes** reemplazar a alguien

(**b**) *(gap, hole)* rellenar; **I had a tooth filled** me hicieron un empaste *or RP* una emplomadura; **the product filled a gap in the market** el producto vino a llenar un hueco en el mercado

(**c**) *(occupy) (time)* ocupar

(**d**) **to f. a vacancy** *(employer)* cubrir una vacante; **we need someone with more experience to f. this post** necesitamos alguien con más experiencia para ocupar este puesto

(**e**) *(cover) (need, demand)* responder a; *(role)* desempeñar

(**f**) *(supply)* **to f. an order** *(for stationery, equipment)* despachar un pedido; **the waiter who filled my order** el camarero que me sirvió

3 *vi (become full)* llenarse (**with** de *or* con); *(sails)* hincharse; **her eyes filled (up) with tears** se le llenaron los ojos de lágrimas

▸**fill in** **1** *vt sep* (**a**) *(hole, space, form)* rellenar; **f. your address in here** escriba su dirección aquí; **to f. in time** matar el tiempo

(**b**) *Fam (inform)* **to f. sb in (on sth)** poner a alguien al tanto (de algo)

(**c**) *(use) (time)* ocupar, pasar; **he's just filling in time** sólo está haciendo tiempo

2 *vi* **to f. in for sb** sustituir a alguien

▸**fill out** **1** *vt sep (form, application)* rellenar

2 *vi (person)* engordar

▸**fill up** **1** *vt sep* (**a**) *(glass)* llenar (hasta el borde); *Fam* **f. her up!** *(car)* ¡lleno, por favor!; **this rice pudding should f. you up** este arroz con leche te debería llenar (**b**) *(occupy) (day, time)* ocupar, pasar

2 *vi (tank, container, stadium, theatre)* llenarse (**with** de); **we'd better f. up at the next** *Br* **petrol** *or US* **gas station** habrá que repostar en la próxima gasolinera *or Am* estación de servicio

---

filler ['fɪlə(r)] *n* (**a**) *(for cracks, holes)* masilla *f*; *(for cavity)* empaste *m* (**b**) *(in newspaper)* artículo *m* de relleno; *(on TV or radio)* programa *m* de relleno (**c**) *(in quilt, beanbag)* relleno *m* (**d**) *Aut* ***f. cap*** tapa *f* del depósito de gasolina *or RP* del tanque de nafta

fillet ['fɪlɪt] **1** *n* (**a**) *(of fish)* filete *m* (**b**) *(of meat)* filete *m*; **pork f.** lomo (de cerdo) ▸▸ ***f. steak*** filete *m*

2 *vt (fish, meat)* cortar en filetes

fill-in ['fɪlɪn] *n* (**a**) *Fam (person)* suplente *mf* (**b**) *US Fam (information)* informe *m*

filling ['fɪlɪŋ] **1** *n* (**a**) *(in tooth)* empaste *m* (**b**) *(in sandwich, pie)* relleno *m* (**c**) ***f. station*** gasolinera *f*, estación *f* de servicio

2 *adj* **a f. meal** una comida que llena mucho

fillip ['fɪlɪp] *n* impulso *m*, empujón *m*; **to give sth/sb a f.** impulsar algo/a alguien

filly ['fɪlɪ] *n* (**a**) *(horse)* potra *f* (**b**) *Fam Old-fashioned (girl)* moza *f*

film [fɪlm] **1** *n* (**a**) *(thin layer)* película *f*; **a f. of ice** una fina capa de hielo

(**b**) *esp Br (at cinema)* película *f*; **to make a f. (about sth)** hacer una película (acerca de algo); **the f. of the book** la versión cinematográfica *or* la película del libro; **French/German f.** el cine francés/alemán; **to be in films** aparecer *or* salir en películas ▸▸ ***f. actor*** actor *m* de cine; ***f. actress*** actriz *f* de cine; ***f. buff*** cinéfilo(a) *m,f*; ***f. crew*** equipo *m* de rodaje; ***f. critic*** crítico(a) *m,f* cinematográfico(a) *or* de cine; ***f. director*** director(ora) *m,f* de cine, cineasta *mf*; ***f. festival*** festival *m* de cine; ***the f. industry*** la industria cinematográfica; ***f. library*** filmoteca *f*; ***f. noir*** cine *m* negro; ***f. projector*** proyector *m* cinematográfico; ***f. script*** guión *m* de cine; ***f. set*** plató *m* cinematográfico *or* de cine; ***f. star*** estrella *f* de cine; ***f. studio*** estudio *m* cinematográfico

(**c**) *(photographic)* **a (roll of) f.** *(for camera)* un rollo, un carrete ▸▸ ***f. speed*** sensibilidad *f* (de película); ***f. strip*** tira *f* de diapositivas

(**d**) *Typ* fotolitos *mpl*; **a piece of f.** un fotolito

2 *vt (person, event, scene)* filmar, rodar; *(novel)* llevar *or* adaptar al cine

3 *vi* rodar, filmar; **to f. well** *(be photogenic)* ser fotogénico(a)

▸**film over** *vi* empañarse, nublarse; **her eyes filmed over with tears** sus ojos se empañaron *or* llenaron de lágrimas

filmable ['fɪlməbəl] *adj* **no one thought the book was f.** nadie pensaba que el libro podía ser llevado al cine

filmgoer ['fɪlmgəʊə(r)] *n* **these scenes shocked many filmgoers** estas escenas sacudieron a muchos espectadores; **as regular filmgoers will know...** como los asiduos *or* aficionados al cine ya sabrán...; **she's not a regular f.** no va al cine con regularidad

filmic ['fɪlmɪk] *adj* cinematográfico(a), fílmico(a)

filming ['fɪlmɪŋ] *n* rodaje *m*, filmación *f*

filmmaker ['fɪlmmeɪkə(r)] *n* cineasta *mf*

filmography [fɪl'mɒgrəfɪ] *n* filmografía *f*

filmsetting ['fɪlmsetɪŋ] *n Br* fotocomposición *f*

filmy ['fɪlmɪ] *adj (material)* de gasa

Filofax® ['faɪləfæks] *n* agenda *f* de anillas

filo pastry ['fiːləʊ'peɪstrɪ] *n* hojaldre *m* griego

filter ['fɪltə(r)] **1** *n* (**a**) *(for liquids)* filtro *m* ▸▸ ***f. coffee*** café *m* de filtro; ***f. paper*** papel *m* de filtro (**b**) **f. (tip)** *(on cigarette)* filtro *m* ▸▸ ***f. (tip) cigarette*** cigarrillo *m* con filtro (**c**) *Br Aut* ***f. lane*** carril *m* de giro a la derecha/izquierda; ***f. signal*** *(on traffic light)* señal *f* de giro a la derecha/izquierda (**d**) *Phot* filtro *m* (**e**) *Elec & Rad* filtro *m* (**f**) *Comptr* filtro *m*

2 *vt* filtrar

3 *vi* (**a**) *(pass) (liquid, light)* filtrarse (**through** a través de); **to f. in/out** *(people)* llegar/irse poco a poco; **the news soon filtered through** la noticia se filtró rápidamente (**b**) *Br Aut (traffic)* **to f. to the right/left** girar a la derecha/izquierda *(según la indicación del semáforo)*

▸**filter out** *vt sep (impurities, noise)* filtrar (hasta eliminar)

filtering software ['fɪltərɪŋ'sɒftweə(r)] *n Comptr* software *m* de filtrado

filter-tipped ['fɪltətɪpt] *adj (cigarette)* con filtro

filth [fɪlθ] *n* (**a**) *(dirt)* porquería *f* (**b**) *(obscenity)* obscenidades *fpl*; *(obscene books, films)* cochinadas *fpl*, *Esp* guarrerías *fpl*; **to talk f.** decir cochinadas (**c**) *Br very Fam* **the f.** la poli, *Esp* la madera

filthy ['fɪlθɪ] **1** *adj* (**a**) *(very dirty)* asqueroso(a) (**b**) *(very bad)* **to be in a f. mood** *or* **temper** tener un humor de perros; **he gave me a f. look** me atravesó con la mirada; *Br* **f. weather** tiempo de perros (**c**) *(obscene) (language, jokes)* obsceno(a); *(film, book)* indecente, *Esp* guarro(a); **to have a f. mind** tener una mente sucia; **that f. book** esa cochinada *or Esp* guarrería de libro

2 *adv Fam* **f. dirty** mugriento(a); **f. rich** asquerosamente rico(a)

filtrate ['fɪltreɪt] *n Chem* líquido *m* filtrado

filtration [fɪl'treɪʃən] *n Chem* filtración *f*

fin [fɪn] *n* (**a**) *(of fish)* aleta *f* ▸▸ ***f. whale*** rorcual *m* (**b**) *(of aircraft, rocket, bomb)* aleta *f* (**c**) *(for swimmer)* **fins** aletas (**d**) *Tech* aleta *f* (**e**) *US Fam (five-dollar bill)* = billete de cinco dólares estadounidenses

finagle [fɪ'neɪgəl] *vt US Fam* agenciarse

final ['faɪnəl] **1** *n* (**a**) *(of competition)* final *f*; **to be through to the finals** haber llegado a la fase final (**b**) *(of newspaper)* última edición *f* (**c**) *Univ* **finals** *Br* exámenes de fin de carrera; *US* exámenes finales

2 *adj* (**a**) *(last)* último(a); **the f. stages** las etapas finales, las últimas etapas; **the f. whistle** el pitido final ▸▸ *Fin* ***f. demand*** último aviso *m* de pago; *St Exch* ***f. dividend*** dividendo *m* complementario; *Hist* ***the F. Solution*** la Solución Final; ***f. warning*** última advertencia *f*

(**b**) *(definitive)* definitivo(a); **that's my f. offer** es mi última oferta; **is that your f. answer?** ¿es tu respuesta definitiva?; **the umpire's decision is f.** la decisión del árbitro es definitiva; **and that's f.!** ¡y no hay más que hablar! ▸▸ *Cin* ***f. cut*** montaje *m* definitivo

3 *vi* **to f. (in an event)** llegar a la final (en una prueba)

finale [fɪ'nɑːlɪ] *n (of concert, play)* final *m*; **grand f.** gran final; **there was a grand f. to the match** el partido tuvo un final apoteósico

finalist ['faɪnəlɪst] *n* finalista *mf*

finality [faɪ'nælɪtɪ] *n (of words, statement)* rotundidad *f*, irrevocabilidad *f*; *(of death)* carácter *m* irreversible; **there was a note of f. in his voice** lo dijo de forma un tanto rotunda *or* terminante

> **False friend**: The Spanish noun **finalidad** is not a translation for the English word **finality**. In Spanish **finalidad** means "aim, purpose".

finalization [faɪnəlaɪ'zeɪʃən] *n* ultimación *f*, conclusión *f*

finalize ['faɪnəlaɪz] *vt (details, plan, agreement)* ultimar; *(date)* concretar; **that hasn't been finalized yet** eso aún no se ha ultimado

finally ['faɪnəlɪ] *adv* (**a**) *(lastly)* por último, finalmente; **and f.,...** y por último,... (**b**) *(at last)* por fin, finalmente; **she had f. met him** por fin lo había conocido (**c**) *(irrevocably)* definitivamente; **it hasn't been decided f. yet** todavía no se ha tomado la decisión definitiva

final-year ['faɪnəl'jɪə(r)] *adj (student, exam)* de último curso

finance [faɪ'næns, fɪ'næns] **1** *n* (**a**) *(subject, business, funding)* finanzas *fpl*; **it's a problem of f.** es un problema financiero; **we don't have the necessary f.** no contamos con los recursos financieros necesarios; **F. Minister, Minister of F.** Ministro de Economía ▸▸ ***f. company*** compañía *f* financiera; ***f. department*** departamento *m* financiero; *Br* ***f. house*** compañía *f* financiera

(**b**) **finances** *(funds)* finanzas; **his finances are low** se encuentra en una mala situación financiera

2 *vt* financiar

financial [faɪˈnænʃəl, fɪˈnænʃəl] *adj* financiero(a) ▸▸ ***f. adviser*** asesor(ora) *m,f* financiero(a); ***f. assets*** activos *mpl* financieros; ***f. control*** control *m* financiero; ***f. controller*** interventor(ora) *m,f* (financiero(a)); ***f. director*** director(ora) *m,f* financiero(a); ***f. management*** gestión *f* financiera; ***f. market*** mercado *m* financiero; ***f. planning*** planificación *f* financiera; ***f. reserves*** provisión *f* de fondos; ***f. statement*** balance *m* (general); *Br* ***f. year*** *(for budget)* ejercicio *m* (económico); *(for tax)* año *m* fiscal

financially [faɪˈnænʃəlɪ, fɪˈnænʃəlɪ] *adv* económicamente; **f. sound** económicamente sólido; **is the company f. sound?** ¿la empresa tiene solidez económica?

financier [faɪˈnænsɪə(r), fɪˈnænsɪə(r)] *n* financiero(a) *m,f*

finch [fɪntʃ] *n* pinzón *m*

FIND [faɪnd] 1 *n* hallazgo *m*; **it was quite a f.** fue todo un hallazgo

2 *vt* (*pt & pp* **found** [faʊnd]) (**a**) *(discover by chance)* encontrar, hallar; **to f. sb at home** *or* **in** encontrar a alguien en casa; **I found her waiting in the hall** me la encontré esperando en la entrada; **he was found dead** lo encontraron muerto; **leave everything as you found it** deja todo tal y como lo encontraste; **they found an unexpected supporter in Richard Sanders** recibieron el inesperado apoyo de Richard Sanders; **you don't f. many people taking the bus for that journey** no mucha gente hace ese viaje en autobús; *Literary* **nightfall found us 20 miles from our destination** la noche cayó sobre nosotros a 20 millas de nuestro destino; **I f. comfort in the knowledge that...** me consuela saber que...; **they f. themselves in serious difficulty** están metidos en serias dificultades; **I often f. myself wondering...** a menudo me sorprendo preguntándome...; **I found myself feeling jealous** me di cuenta de que tenía celos

(**b**) *(discover by searching)* encontrar, hallar; **the painting has been found** han encontrado el cuadro; **we need to f. another $500** necesitamos conseguir 500 dólares más; **you won't f. a better bike for the price** por este precio no vas a encontrar una bicicleta mejor; **there wasn't a single free seat to be found** no quedaba ni un asiento (libre); **she was nowhere to be found** no la encontraron por ninguna parte *or* ningún lado; **to f. a job for sb, to f. sb a job** encontrarle un trabajo a alguien; **he found something for me to do** me encontró algo que hacer; **to f. the courage/time to do sth** encontrar el valor/el tiempo para hacer algo; **to f. fault with sth** encontrar defectos a algo; **he couldn't f. it in his heart to tell her** no halló *or* encontró fuerzas para decírselo; **the arrow/comment found its mark** la flecha/el comentario dio en el blanco; **to f. oneself** *(spiritually)* encontrarse a uno mismo; *Fig* **to f. one's feet** situarse; *Fig* **to f. one's tongue** recuperar el habla; **to f. one's way** orientarse, encontrar el camino; **this leaflet somehow found its way into my pocket** no sé cómo ha venido a parar a mi bolsillo este folleto; **the product never found its way into the shops** el producto no llegó a ser comercializado; **to f. a way to do sth** encontrar la manera de hacer algo

(**c**) *(discover by analysis)* encontrar, hallar; **to f. an answer/a solution** hallar una respuesta/una solución; **our research found that...** nuestra investigación descubrió que...; **the drug has been found to benefit cancer patients** se ha demostrado que la droga beneficia a los pacientes con cáncer

(**d**) *(experience)* **they will f. it easy/difficult** les resultará *or* lo encontrarán fácil/difícil; **she found it impossible to understand him** le resultó imposible entenderle; **he found it necessary to remind her of her duty** consideró necesario recordarle cuáles eran sus obligaciones; **how did you f. the meal/the exam?** ¿qué te pareció la comida/el examen?; **did you f. everything to your satisfaction?** ¿le ha parecido todo bien?; **I found her charming** me pareció muy simpática; **I f. that I can't bend down as easily as I used to** estoy descubriendo que ya no me puedo agachar como antes; **you'll f. (that) it gets easier the more you do it** ya verás cómo *or RP* vas a ver que te resultará más fácil con la práctica

(**e**) *(realize)* **you will f. (that) I am right** te darás *or* vas a dar cuenta de que tengo razón; **I was surprised to f. that...** me sorprendió enterarme de que...

(**f**) *Law* **to f. sb guilty/innocent** declarar a alguien culpable/inocente; **how do you f. the accused?** ¿cuál es su veredicto?

(**g**) **to be found** *(exist)* encontrarse; **this species is only found in Australia** esta especie sólo se encuentra en Australia

3 *vi Law* **to f. in favour of/against sb** fallar a favor de/en contra de alguien

▸ **find out** 1 *vt sep* (**a**) *(discover)* descubrir; *(check, confirm)* enterarse de; **we found out that she was French** descubrimos que era francesa; **go and f. out what's happening** ve y entérate de lo que está pasando; **to f. out more, write to...** para obtener más información, diríjase a...; **I found out from his wife that he had been ill for some time** me enteré por su esposa que llevaba un tiempo enfermo

(**b**) *(see through)* **to f. sb out** descubrir a alguien; **we've been found out** nos han descubierto

2 *vi* (**a**) *(discover)* enterarse (**about** de); **his wife found out about his affair** su mujer se enteró de su aventura (**b**) *(get information)* informarse (**about** de)

finder [ˈfaɪndə(r)] *n* (**a**) *(of lost object)* **the f. of the money should contact the police** quien encuentre el dinero ha de llamar a la policía; IDIOM *Fam* **finders keepers (losers weepers)** quien lo encuentre, para él (**b**) *(of telescope)* anteojo *m* buscador

finding [ˈfaɪndɪŋ] *n* (**a**) *(discovery)* descubrimiento *m* (**b**) **findings** conclusiones

fine[1] [faɪn] *Law* 1 *n* multa *f*

2 *vt* multar, poner una multa a; **to f. sb £100** poner a alguien una multa de 100 libras

FINE[2] 1 *adj* (**a**) *(excellent)* excelente; *(food)* fino(a), exquisito(a); *(furniture, china, clothes)* fino(a); **the weather was f.** hacía buen tiempo; **it will be f. tomorrow** mañana hará buen tiempo; **she's a f. woman** es una mujer extraordinaria; **one of these f. days** un día de éstos; **to appeal to sb's finer feelings** apelar a los más nobles sentimientos de alguien; **that was our finest hour** fue nuestro mejor momento ▸▸ ***f. art*** *(paintings, artefacts)* arte *m*; **she's got it down to a f. art** lo hace con los ojos cerrados, lo tiene muy controlado; ***the f. arts*** las bellas artes; ***f. wines*** vinos *mpl* selectos

(**b**) *(satisfactory)* bien; **she's f.** está bien; **everything is f.** todo está bien; **would you like wine? – water would be f.** ¿quieres vino? – con agua me basta; **more tea? – I'm f., thanks** ¿más té? – no, gracias; **that's f. by me** ¡me parece bien!, ¡por mí, *Esp* vale *or RP* dale *or Méx* órale!; **I feel f.** me encuentro bien, estoy bien

(**c**) *(thin)* fino(a); **f. grains of sand** granos finos de arena ▸▸ ***f. print*** letra *f* pequeña

(**d**) *(pointed, sharp)* fino(a); **a f. nib** una plumilla fina

(**e**) *(delicate, subtle)* fino(a); *(adjustment)* preciso(a); *(distinction)* sutil; *(features)* delicado(a); **there's a f. line between eccentricity and madness** la frontera entre la excentricidad y la locura es muy tenue; **I didn't understand some of the finer points** no entendí los aspectos más sutiles; **not to put too f. a point on it** hablando en plata

(**f**) *Ironic (great)* **you're a f. one to talk!** ¡mira quién fue a hablar!, ¡mira quién habla!; **this is another f. mess you've got us into!** ¡en menudo lío nos has vuelto a meter!, *RP* ¡otra vez nos metiste en flor de lío!; **that's a f. thing to do to your mother!** ¡eso no se le hace a tu madre!; **a f. help you are!** ¡menuda ayuda estás hecho!, *RP* ¡flor de ayuda, sos vos!; **he was in a f. (old) temper!** ¡estaba de un humor de perros!

2 *adv* bien; **that'll do (me) just f.** con eso me bastará *or RP* alcanza; **you're doing f.!** ¡lo estás haciendo muy bien!; **she's getting on** *or* **doing f.** le va bien; **they get on f.** se llevan bien; **that suits me f.** eso me viene bien; **it seems to be working f. to me** me parece que no le pasa nada

3 *exclam* **shall we meet at five? – f.** ¿nos vemos a las cinco? – muy bien *or Esp* vale *or Arg* dale *or Méx* órale; *Ironic* **oh f., you just sit there while I do all the work!** ¡fantástico, tú ahí sentado mientras yo hago todo el trabajo!

fine-grained [ˈfaɪngreɪnd] *adj* (**a**) *(rock)* de grano fino; *(wood, leather)* fino(a); **f. salt** sal fina (**b**) *(distinction)* detallado(a), minucioso(a)

finely [ˈfaɪnlɪ] *adv* (**a**) *(skilfully)* acertadamente, hábilmente (**b**) *(grated, ground, sliced)* muy fino; **f. chopped** picado(a) muy fino (**c**) *(delicately)* **f. balanced** *(contest)* muy equilibrado(a); **f. tuned** *(engine)* a punto

fineness [ˈfaɪnnɪs] *n* (**a**) *(excellence) (of clothes, manners)* refinamiento *m* (**b**) *(of sand, sugar)* finura *f* (**c**) *(thinness) (of thread, hair, nib)* finura *f* (**d**) *(delicacy, subtlety) (of features)* sutileza *f*, delicadeza *f*; *(of detail, distinction)* sutileza *f*

finery [ˈfaɪnərɪ] *n* galas *fpl*; **dressed in all one's f.** vestido(a) con las mejores galas

finesse [fɪˈnes] 1 *n* (**a**) *(elegance, tact)* finura *f*; **he handled the matter with great f.** llevó el asunto con mucha mano izquierda *or* delicadeza (**b**) *(in card games)* impasse *m*

2 *vt* (**a**) *(deal with skilfully)* sortear con destreza; **he finessed his way through the interview** sorteó la entrevista con mucha habilidad (**b**) *(in card game)* jugar de impasse

fine-tooth(ed) comb [ˈfaɪntuːθ(t)ˈkəʊm] *n* peine *m* de púas finas; IDIOM **to go through sth with a f.** mirar algo con lupa, examinar algo al detalle

fine-tune [ˈfaɪnˈtjuːn] *vt* (**a**) *(machine, engine)* afinar, poner a punto (**b**) *(economy, policy)* afinar

fine-tuning ['faɪn'tju:nɪŋ] *n* (**a**) *(of machine, engine)* ajuste *m* (**b**) *(of economy, policy)* ajuste *m*

finger ['fɪŋgə(r)] **1** *n* (**a**) *(of hand, glove)* dedo *m*; **to eat with one's fingers** comer con las manos; **to hold sth between f. and thumb** sujetar algo entre el índice y el pulgar; *Fig* **to keep one's fingers crossed** cruzar los dedos ►► ***f. bowl*** bol *m or* cuenco *m* para las manos; ***f. buffet*** bufé *m* a base de canapés y aperitivos; ***f. food*** *(snacks)* cosas *fpl* de picar; ***f. hole*** *(in musical instrument)* orificio *m*; ***f. painting*** pintura *f* con los dedos; ***f. puppet*** títere *m (para manejar con la mano)*

(**b**) *(measure)* **a f. of brandy** un dedo de coñac

(**c**) *(of land)* lengua *f*; **to cut a cake into fingers** cortar un pastel en porciones

(**d**) *Comptr* finger *m*

(**e**) IDIOMS **I'm all fingers and thumbs today** estoy de lo más torpe hoy, hoy estoy hecho un manazas; **he's got them (wrapped** *or* **twisted) round his little f.** los tiene a sus pies; **you could count them on the fingers of one hand** se pueden contar con los dedos de una mano; **to get one's fingers burnt** salir escaldado(a) *or* escarmentado(a); *Br very Fam* **get** *or* **pull your f. out!** ¡mueve el culo!, *RP* ¡mové las bolas!; *US Fam* **to give sb the f.** = hacerle un gesto grosero a alguien con el dedo corazón hacia arriba, ≃ hacerle un corte de mangas a alguien; *Br Fam* **to stick two fingers up at sb** = hacerle a alguien un gesto insultante con los dedos índice y corazón hacia arriba y el dorso de la mano hacia fuera, ≃ hacer un corte de mangas a alguien; **to have one's f. on the pulse** estar al tanto *or* a la última; **to have a f. in every pie** estar metido(a) en todo; **don't you dare lay a f. on him** no te atrevas a tocarle un pelo; **she wouldn't lift a f. to help you** no levantaría *or* movería un dedo para ayudarte; **to point the f. (of suspicion) at sb** señalar a alguien con el dedo, acusar a alguien; **who are you to point the f.?** ¿quién eres tú para acusar?; *Fam* **to put the f. on sb** *(denounce)* delatar a alguien; **to put one's f. on it** dar en el clavo; **I can't quite put my f. on it** no consigo dar con ello; **to work one's fingers to the bone** trabajar duro, matarse *Esp* a trabajar *or Am* trabajando

2 *vt* (**a**) *(feel)* tocar (**b**) *Fam (inform on)* soplar acerca de, *RP* pasar el dato de (**c**) *Vulg (woman)* masturbar con el dedo

fingerboard ['fɪŋgəbɔ:d] *n (on musical instrument)* diapasón *m*

fingering ['fɪŋgərɪŋ] *n Mus* digitación *f*

fingerless ['fɪŋgəlɪs] *adj* ***f. gloves*** mitones *mpl*

fingermark ['fɪŋgəmɑ:k] *n* marca *f or* huella *f* de los dedos

fingernail ['fɪŋgəneɪl] *n* uña *f*; IDIOM **to hang on by one's fingernails** colgar de un hilo

fingerprint ['fɪŋgəprɪnt] **1** *n* huella *f* digital *or* dactilar; **to take sb's fingerprints** tomar las huellas digitales a alguien; *Fig* **his fingerprints are all over it** lleva su firma

2 *vt (person)* tomar las huellas digitales *or* dactilares a

fingerstall ['fɪŋgəstɔ:l] *n* dedil *m*

fingertip ['fɪŋgətɪp] *n* punta *f* del dedo; **to have sth at one's fingertips** *(facts, information)* tener algo al alcance de la mano; *(subject)* conocer algo al dedillo

finicky ['fɪnɪkɪ] *adj Fam* (**a**) *(fussy)* quisquilloso(a); **to be a f. eater** ser quisquilloso con la comida (**b**) *(tricky)* **to be a f. job** ser un trabajo complicado *or* de chinos

FINISH ['fɪnɪʃ] **1** *n* (**a**) *(end) (of match, meeting)* final *m*; *(of race)* meta *f*; **to be in at the f.** presenciar el final; **it was a close f.** fue un final reñido ►► ***f. line*** línea *f* de meta

(**b**) *(surface) (of furniture, metalwork)* acabado *m*

(**c**) *(quality of workmanship, presentation)* **his prose/acting lacks f.** tiene una prosa/forma de actuar poco refinada

(**d**) *Sport* **that was a very good f. from Jones** Jones ha marcado un gol muy bueno

2 *vt* (**a**) *(end)* terminar, acabar; **the injury finished his career** la lesión terminó *or* acabó con su carrera; **to f. doing sth** terminar *or* acabar de hacer algo; **have you finished eating?** ¿has terminado *or* acabado de comer?

(**b**) *(use up)* terminar, acabar; **the milk is finished** se ha terminado *or* acabado la leche

(**c**) *(ruin, kill)* terminar con, acabar con

(**d**) *Fam (tire out)* terminar con, acabar con

(**e**) *(furniture, metalwork)* acabar; **nicely finished** con un excelente acabado, *RP* con una excelente terminación

3 *vi* (**a**) *(end)* terminar, acabar; **you didn't let me f.** no me dejaste terminar *or* acabar (lo que estaba diciendo); **school finishes on Friday/at three o'clock** el colegio termina *or* acaba el viernes/a las tres; **I would like to f. by thanking...** me gustaría concluir agradeciendo...; **to f. on an optimistic note** finalizar con una nota de optimismo; **would you like a brandy to f. with?** ¿*Esp* te apetece *or Carib, Col, Méx* te provoca *or Méx* se te antoja *or CSur* querés un brandy para terminar?

(**b**) *(in race, contest)* **to f. fourth** quedar en cuarto lugar, terminar cuarto(a); **three horses failed to f.** tres caballos no terminaron la carrera; **Mexico finished the stronger of the two teams** México terminó jugando mejor que el otro equipo

► **finish off** **1** *vt sep* (**a**) *(complete) (task, book)* terminar, acabar

(**b**) *(use up)* terminar, acabar; **we'd better f. off this ice cream** será mejor que terminemos *or* acabemos este helado

(**c**) *Fam (ruin, kill)* terminar con, acabar con

(**d**) *Fam (tire out)* terminar con, acabar con

2 *vi* terminar, acabar; **to f. off by doing sth** acabar *or* terminar haciendo algo

► **finish up** **1** *vt sep (use up)* terminar, acabar; **f. up that spinach** termínate *or* acábate las espinacas

2 *vi* (**a**) *(end up)* terminar, acabar; **to f. up doing sth** terminar *or* acabar haciendo algo; **most of the waste finishes up as recycled paper** la mayoría de los desechos son convertidos en papel reciclado

(**b**) *(finish task)* terminar, acabar

► **finish with** *vt insep* (**a**) *(stop using, talking to)* terminar con, acabar con; **have you finished with the newspaper?** ¿has terminado *or* acabado con el periódico?; **I haven't finished with you yet** todavía no he terminado *or* acabado contigo; **I'm finished with politics/journalism** he dejado la política/el periodismo

(**b**) *(end relationship with)* terminar con, acabar con

---

finished ['fɪnɪʃt] *adj* (**a**) *(completed)* terminado(a), acabado(a); **the job isn't f. yet** el trabajo no está terminado *or* acabado aún; **the joiner was f. by 4 o'clock** a las cuatro el carpintero había terminado *or* acabado; **the f. product** el producto acabado *or* terminado

(**b**) *Fam (ruined)* **he's f.!** ¡está acabado!

(**c**) *(of high quality) (performance)* logrado(a), redondo(a); *(appearance)* elaborado(a)

finishing ['fɪnɪʃɪŋ] *adj* **to put the f. touches to sth** dar los últimos (re)toques a algo ►► ***f. line*** línea *f* de meta; ***f. post*** poste *m* de llegada; ***f. school*** = escuela privada de etiqueta para señoritas

finite ['faɪnaɪt] *adj* (**a**) *(resources, number, time)* limitado(a); *Math* finito(a) (**b**) *Gram (verb)* conjugado(a)

fink [fɪŋk] *US Fam* **1** *n* (**a**) *(informer)* soplón(ona) *m,f*, *Esp* chivato(a) *m,f* (**b**) *(unpleasant person)* pelagatos *mf inv* (**c**) *(strikebreaker)* esquirol(ola) *m,f*

2 *vi* dar el chivatazo (**on** sobre)

Finland ['fɪnlənd] *n* Finlandia

Finn [fɪn] *n (person)* finlandés(esa) *m,f*

Finnish ['fɪnɪʃ] **1** *n (language)* finés *m*, finlandés *m*

2 *adj* finlandés(esa)

fiord = **fjord**

fir [fɜ:(r)] *n (wood)* (madera *f* de) abeto *m*; **f. (tree)** abeto *m* ►► ***f. cone*** piña *f*

fire ['faɪə(r)] **1** *n* (**a**) *(element)* fuego *m*; **to be afraid of f.** tenerle miedo al fuego; IDIOM **to play with f.** jugar con fuego; **f. and brimstone** fuego eterno

(**b**) *(in hearth, campsite)* fuego *m*; **to lay a f.** preparar un fuego; **to light** *or* **make a f.** encender *or* hacer un fuego; **wood/coal f.** fuego de leña/carbón ►► ***f. irons*** (juego *m* de) utensilios *mpl* para la lumbre

(**c**) *Br (heater)* estufa *f*; **electric/gas f.** estufa eléctrica/de gas

(**d**) *(large, destructive)* incendio *m*; **on f.** en llamas, ardiendo; **his forehead is on f.** *(because of fever)* tiene la frente hirviendo; **he is on f.** está ardiendo; **to cause** *or* **start a f.** provocar un incendio; **to catch f.** prenderse fuego; **to set f. to sth, to set sth on f.** prender fuego a algo; **f.!** ¡fuego!; *Fam Hum* **where's the f.?** *(what's the rush?)* ¿quién se ha muerto?; IDIOM **he'll never set the world** *or Br* **the Thames on f.** nunca será un éxito rutilante ►► ***f. alarm*** alarma *f* contra incendios; *esp Br* ***f. brigade*** (cuerpo *m* de) bomberos *mpl*; *US* ***f. chief*** jefe(a) *m,f* de bomberos; *US* ***f. department*** (cuerpo *m* de) bomberos *mpl*; ***f. door*** puerta *f* contra incendios; ***f. drill*** simulacro *m* de incendio; ***f. engine*** coche *m* de bomberos; ***f. escape*** escalera *f* de incendios; ***f. exit*** salida *f* de incendios; ***f. extinguisher*** *Esp* extintor *m*, *Am* extinguidor *m*; ***f. hazard*** = objeto o acción que supone peligro de incendio; **all those empty boxes are a f. hazard** todas esas cajas vacías pueden causar un incendio; ***f. hose*** manguera *f* de incendios; ***f. hydrant*** boca *f* de incendios; ***f. insurance*** seguro *m* contra incendios; ***f. prevention*** prevención *f* de incendios; ***f. regulations*** *(laws)* normativa *f* contra incendios; *(in building)* procedimiento *m* en caso de incendio; ***f. sale*** venta *f* de objetos dañados en un incendio; ***f. station*** parque *m* de bomberos; *US* ***f. truck*** coche *m* de bomberos

(e) *(of rifle, artillery)* fuego *m*; **to open f. (on sb)** abrir fuego (contra alguien); **to hold one's f.** dejar de disparar; **hold your f.** *(don't shoot)* no disparen; *(stop shooting)* alto el fuego; **to come under f.** caer bajo el fuego enemigo; *Fig* **to be** *or* **come under f.** *(be criticized)* recibir muchas críticas; **to return (sb's) f.** responder al fuego (de alguien)
(f) *(enthusiasm)* pasión *f*
2 *vt* (a) *(rifle, bullet, missile)* disparar (**at** contra); **to f. a shot** disparar; *Fig* **to f. a question at sb** lanzar una pregunta a alguien
(b) *Fam (dismiss)* despedir; **you're fired!** ¡quedas despedido!
(c) *(set alight, heat)* encender, *Am* prender; **oil-/gas-fired central heating** calefacción central de petróleo/gas
(d) *(inspire)* **to f. sb with enthusiasm** hacer arder de entusiasmo a alguien; **the movie fired his imagination** la película despertó su imaginación
(e) *(pottery)* cocer
3 *vi* (a) *(with gun)* disparar (**at** *or* **on** contra); **f.!** ¡fuego!; **f. at will!** ¡fuego a discreción!; *Fam Fig* **f. away!** *(to questioner)* ¡adelante! (b) *(engine)* encenderse, *Am* prenderse; *Fig* **to be firing on all cylinders** funcionar a pleno rendimiento

▸**fire off** *vt sep* (a) *(round of ammunition)* disparar (b) *Fig* **to f. off questions at sb** acribillar a alguien a preguntas, asediar a alguien con preguntas; **to f. off a memo (to)** escribir rápidamente y enviar un memorándum (a)

▸**fire up** *vt sep Fam (switch on)* encender, *Am* prender

firearm ['faɪərɑːm] *n* arma *f* de fuego; **firearms expert** experto(a) en armas de fuego; **firearms training** entrenamiento con armas de fuego

fireball ['faɪəbɔːl] *n* (a) *(ball lightning)* bola *f* de fuego (b) *(in nuclear explosion)* bola *f* de fuego (c) *Astron* bólido *m* (d) IDIOM **she's a real f.** es muy temperamental

fire-bomb ['faɪəbɒm] 1 *n* bomba *f* incendiaria
2 *vt* arrojar bombas incendiarias a

firebrand ['faɪəbrænd] *n* (a) *(burning torch)* antorcha *f* (b) *(agitator)* agitador(ora) *m,f*

firebreak ['faɪəbreɪk] *n* cortafuego *m*

firebrick ['faɪəbrɪk] *n* ladrillo *m* refractario

firebug ['faɪəbʌg] *n Fam* pirómano(a) *m,f*, incendiario(a) *m,f*

firecracker ['faɪəkrækə(r)] *n* petardo *m*

firedamp ['faɪədæmp] *n* grisú *m*

fire-eater ['faɪəriːtə(r)] *n* (a) *(performer)* tragafuegos *mf inv* (b) *(aggressive person)* belicoso(a) *m,f*, agresivo(a) *m,f*

firefight ['faɪəfaɪt] *n* tiroteo *m*

firefighter ['faɪəfaɪtə(r)] *n* bombero(a) *m,f*

firefighting ['faɪəfaɪtɪŋ] 1 *n* labores *fpl* *or* tareas *fpl* de extinción (de incendios)
2 *adj* ***f. equipment*** equipo *m* contra incendios

firefly ['faɪəflaɪ] *n* luciérnaga *f*

fireguard ['faɪəgɑːd] *n* pantalla *f* (de chimenea), parachispas *m inv*

firelight ['faɪəlaɪt] *n* luz *f* del fuego

firelighter ['faɪəlaɪtə(r)] *n* pastilla *f* para (encender *or Am* prender) el fuego

fireman ['faɪəmən] *n* (a) *(firefighter)* bombero *m* ▸▸ ***f.'s lift*** = manera de llevar a alguien a cuestas sobre un hombro y el otro brazo libre (b) *(of steam engine)* fogonero *m*

fireplace ['faɪəpleɪs] *n* chimenea *f*

fireplug ['faɪəplʌg] *n US* boca *f* de incendios

firepower ['faɪəpaʊə(r)] *n* potencia *f* de fuego

fireproof ['faɪəpruːf] *adj (door, safe, clothing)* ignífugo(a), incombustible; *(dish)* refractario(a)

fire-raiser ['faɪəreɪzə(r)] *n Br* pirómano(a) *m,f*, incendiario(a) *m,f*

fire-resistant ['faɪərɪzɪstənt] *adj* ignífugo(a), incombustible

fire-retardant ['faɪərɪtɑːdənt] *adj* de combustión lenta

firescreen ['faɪəskriːn] *n* pantalla *f* (de chimenea)

fireship ['faɪəʃɪp] *n* (a) *(for firefighting)* = barco para la extinción de incendios (b) *Hist* brulote *m*

fireside ['faɪəsaɪd] *n* **by the f.** junto a la chimenea; **f. chat** *(by politician)* conversación *or* charla informal

fire-storm ['faɪəstɔːm] *n* tormenta *f* de fuego

firetrap ['faɪətræp] *n* = local altamente peligroso en caso de incendio

firewall ['faɪəwɔːl] *n Comptr* cortafuegos *m inv*

fire-water ['faɪəwɔːtə(r)] *n Fam* aguardiente *m*

firewood ['faɪəwʊd] *n* leña *f*

firework ['faɪəwɜːk] *n* fuego *m* de artificio; **fireworks** fuegos artificiales; *Fig* **there'll be fireworks** se va a armar una buena ▸▸ ***firework(s) display*** (castillo *m* de) fuegos *mpl* artificiales, espectáculo *m* pirotécnico

firkin ['fɜːkɪn] *n* barrilete *m*

firing ['faɪərɪŋ] *n* (a) *(of weapons)* disparos *mpl*; IDIOM **to be in the f. line** estar en la línea de fuego *or* en el punto de mira ▸▸ ***f. pin*** percutor *m*; ***f. range*** *(place)* polígono *m* de tiro; **within f. range** dentro del campo de tiro; ***f. squad*** pelotón *m* de ejecución *or* de fusilamiento; **to be executed by f. squad** ser fusilado(a), ser ejecutado(a) por un pelotón de fusilamiento
(b) *(in oven)* cocción *f*

firm[1] [fɜːm] *n (company)* empresa *f*; *(of lawyers)* bufete *m*, estudio *m*

firm[2] 1 *adj* (a) *(solid, hard) (flesh, mattress)* firme; *(fruit)* duro(a); *(ground)* duro(a), firme; *Fig* **I'm on firmer ground when it comes to the computing aspects** me siento más seguro en lo relativo a la informática
(b) *(strong) (handshake, grip)* firme; **to have a f. hold** *or* **grasp** *or* **grip of sth** agarrar algo con firmeza
(c) *(steady, stable)* firme, sólido(a); *Fin* **the franc remained f.** el franco se mantuvo (firme)
(d) *(definite) (date)* firme; *(denial, refusal)* categórico(a), firme; **the f. favourite** el gran favorito; **it is my f. belief that...** creo firmemente que...; **a f. offer** una oferta en firme
(e) *(strict)* firme, estricto(a); **to be f. with sb** ser estricto(a) con alguien; **she was polite but f.** se mostró educada, pero firme
2 *adv* **to stand f.** mantenerse firme; **she held f. to her principles** se mantuvo firme en sus principios
3 *vi (prices, market)* recuperarse

▸**firm up** 1 *vt sep (plan)* concretar algo
2 *vi* (a) *(muscles)* reafirmarse (b) *Com (prices)* afianzarse, consolidarse

firmament ['fɜːməmənt] *n Literary* bóveda *f* celeste

firmly ['fɜːmlɪ] *adv* (a) *(securely) (to hold, grasp)* con firmeza, firmemente; *(shut, secured)* firmemente; **make sure you close the window f.** asegúrate de cerrar bien la ventana (b) *(definitely) (to say, deny, refuse)* categóricamente, firmemente; **I f. believe that...** creo firmemente que... (c) *(to deal with)* con firmeza

firmness ['fɜːmnɪs] *n* (a) *(hardness) (of flesh, mattress)* firmeza *f*; *(of fruit)* dureza *f*; *(of ground)* dureza *f*, firmeza *f* (b) *(strength) (of handshake, grip)* firmeza *f* (c) *(stability)* firmeza *f*, solidez *f* (d) *(definiteness) (of offer, date)* firmeza *f*; *(of denial, refusal)* firmeza *f* (e) *(strictness)* firmeza *f*

firmware ['fɜːmweə(r)] *n Comptr* firmware *m*, microprograma *m*

FIRST [fɜːst] 1 *n* (a) *(in series)* primero(a) *m,f*; **the second one was better than the f.** el segundo fue mejor que el primero; **I'm the f. on the list** soy el primero de la lista; **we were the f. to arrive** fuimos los primeros en llegar; **I'm the f. to admit that...** soy el primero en reconocer que...; **it's the f. I've heard of it** es la primera noticia que tengo (de ello), ahora me entero
(b) *(of month)* primero *m*, *Esp* uno *m*; **the f. of June** el primero de junio; **we're leaving on the f.** nos vamos el primero *or Esp* el (día) uno
(c) *(beginning)* **at f.** al principio; **it will be cloudy at f.** por la mañana estará nublado; **from f. to last** de principio a fin; **from the (very) f.** (ya) desde el principio
(d) *Br Univ* **to get a f.** *(in degree)* = licenciarse con la nota más alta en la escala de calificaciones
(e) *(first gear)* primera *f*; **in f.** en primera
(f) *(unique event)* **it was a f.** fue un acontecimiento sin precedentes
2 *adj* primero(a); *(before masculine singular noun)* primer; **the f. month** el primer mes; **he was one of the f. people to arrive** fue uno de los primeros en llegar; **the f. few days** los primeros días; **the f. century** *(written)* el siglo I; *(spoken)* el siglo uno *or* primero; **our f. priority is to...** nuestra prioridad máxima es...; **at f. hand** de primera mano; **at f. sight** a primera vista; **for the f. time** por primera vez; **in the f. place** en primer lugar; **why didn't you say so in the f. place?** ¡haberlo dicho antes!; **neither of them dared make the f. move** nadie se atrevió a dar el primer paso; **to have f. refusal on sth** tener la opción de compra sobre algo; **f. things f.!** lo primero es lo primero; **I said the f. thing that came into my head** dije lo primero que me vino a la mente; **I don't know the f. thing** *or* **haven't got the f. idea about motorbikes** no tengo ni idea de motos; **f. thing (in the morning)** a primera hora de la mañana; **it'll be ready f. thing Monday** estará listo a primera hora del lunes ▸▸ ***f. aid*** *(skill)* socorrismo *m*, primeros auxilios *mpl*; *(treatment)* primeros auxilios *mpl*; **to give sb f. aid** prestar a alguien los primeros auxilios; ***f. base*** *(in baseball) (place)* primera base *f*; *(player)* primer base *m*, *Am* inicialista *mf*; IDIOM *US Fam* **to get to f.**

base *(complete first stage)* cubrir la primera etapa; ***f. class*** *(on train)* primera *f* (clase *f*); *(for mail)* = en el Reino Unido, tarifa postal más cara y rápida que la de segunda clase; ***f. cousin*** primo(a) *m,f* hermano(a) *or* carnal; ***f. cousin once removed*** tío(a) *m,f* segundo(a); ***F. Division*** *(of league)* primera división *f*; *(in British soccer)* = la segunda división del fútbol inglés y escocés; ***f. edition*** primera edición *f*, edición *f* príncipe; *Br* ***f. eleven*** *(in soccer, cricket)* primer equipo *m*; *US* ***the f. family*** = la familia del presidente o gobernador; ***f. floor*** *Br (above ground floor)* primer piso *m*; *US (ground floor)* planta *f* baja; *Br* ***f. form*** *(at school)* primer curso *m*; *also Fig* ***the f. fruits*** los primeros frutos; *Aut* ***f. gear*** primera *f* (marcha *f*); *US* ***f. grade*** *(at school)* primer curso *m* de enseñanza primaria; *Sport* ***f. half*** primera parte *f*, primer tiempo *m*; *US* ***the F. Lady*** la primera dama; **the f. lady of rock/crime fiction** la reina del rock/de las novelas policiacas; ***f. language*** lengua *f* materna; *Sport* ***f. leg*** partido *m* de ida; *US Mil* ***f. lieutenant*** teniente *mf*; ***at f. light*** al alba; ***f. love*** primer amor *m*; *Naut* ***f. mate*** segundo *m* de a bordo; *Pol* ***F. Minister*** *(of Scottish Parliament, Northern Ireland Assembly)* presidente(a) *m,f*; ***f. name*** nombre *m* (de pila); ***f. night*** *(of play)* (noche *f* del) estreno *m*; **f. night nerves** nervios del estreno; *Law* ***f. offence*** primer delito *m*; *Law* ***f. offender*** delincuente *mf* sin antecedentes; *Naut* ***f. officer*** segundo *m* de a bordo; *Gram* ***f. person*** primera persona *f*; **in the f. person** en primera persona; ***f. prize*** *(in competition)* primer premio *m*; ***f. quarter*** *(of moon)* cuarto *m* creciente; *(of year)* primer trimestre *m*; *Pol* ***F. Secretary*** *(of Welsh Assembly)* presidente(a) *m,f*; *Mil* ***f. strike*** ataque *m* preventivo; *Sport* ***f. team*** primer equipo *m*; ***f. violin*** primer violín *m*; ***the F. World*** el primer mundo; ***the F. World War*** la Primera Guerra Mundial; ***f. year*** *(at school, university)* primer curso *m*; *(pupil, student)* estudiante *mf* de primer curso

3 *adv* (**a**) *(firstly)* primero; **f., I don't want to, and second, I can't** en primer lugar, no quiero, y en segundo (lugar), no puedo; **f. and foremost** ante todo; **she was f. and last a singer** por encima de todo era una cantante; **f. of all** antes de nada, en primer lugar; *Fam* **f. off** primero de todo

(**b**) *(for the first time)* por primera vez; **I f. met her in London** la conocí en Londres; **I f. started working here three years ago** comencé a trabajar aquí hace tres años

(**c**) *(before)* primero(a), antes; **to come f.** *(in race, contest)* quedar primero(a); *(in importance)* ser lo primero; **you go f.!** ¡tú primero!; **he puts his work f.** para él, su trabajo es lo primero; **on a f. come, f. served basis** por orden de llegada; **ladies f.!** las señoras primero

(**d**) *(rather)* **I'd resign f.** antes dimito

---

first-aid [fɜːst'eɪd] *adj* ***f. box*** botiquín *m* de primeros auxilios; ***f. certificate*** título *m* de primeros auxilios; ***f. kit*** botiquín *m* de primeros auxilios; ***f. post*** casa *f or* puesto *m* de socorro; ***f. station*** casa *f or* puesto *m* de socorro

first-born ['fɜːstbɔːn] *Literary* 1 *n* primogénito(a) *m,f*
2 *adj* primogénito(a)

first-class ['fɜːst'klɑːs] 1 *adj* (**a**) *(compartment, ticket)* de primera (clase); *(travel)* en primera (clase); *(hotel, restaurant)* de primera categoría

(**b**) *Br* ***f. mail*** = en el Reino Unido, servicio postal más caro y rápido que el de segunda clase; ***f. stamp*** = en el Reino Unido, sello correspondiente a la tarifa postal de primera clase

(**c**) *Br Univ* **f. honours degree** = licenciatura obtenida con la nota más alta en la escala de calificaciones

(**d**) *Fam (excellent)* de primera; **f.!** ¡genial!

2 *adv* **to travel f.** viajar en primera (clase); **to send a letter f.** enviar una carta utilizando la tarifa postal de primera clase

first-day cover ['fɜːstdeɪ'kʌvə(r)] *n* = sobre con un sello matasellado el día de su puesta en circulación

first-degree ['fɜːstdɪ'griː] *adj* (**a**) *Med (burns)* de primer grado (**b**) *US Law (murder)* en primer grado

first-foot ['fɜːst'fʊt] 1 *n* = primera visita en la madrugada de Año Nuevo
2 *vt* = ser el primero en visitar a alguien en la madrugada de Año Nuevo

first-former ['fɜːst'fɔːmə(r)] *n Br Sch* alumno(a) *m,f* de (primer curso de enseñanza) secundaria

first-generation ['fɜːstdʒenə'reɪʃən] *adj* de primera generación

first-grader ['fɜːst'greɪdə(r)] *n US Sch* alumno(a) *m,f* de (primer curso de enseñanza) primaria

first-hand ['fɜːst'hænd] 1 *adj* de primera mano; **I know from f. experience what it is like to be poor** sé de primera mano lo que es la pobreza, sé por experiencia propia lo que es la pobreza
2 *adv* de primera mano; **he heard it f.** se lo dijeron a él mismo

firstly ['fɜːstlɪ] *adv* en primer lugar

first-name ['fɜːst'neɪm] *adj* **to be on f. terms (with sb)** ≃ tutearse (con alguien)

first-past-the-post ['fɜːstpɑːstðə'pəʊst] *adj Pol* ***f. system*** sistema *m* de elección por mayoría simple

first-person ['fɜːst'pɜːsən] *adj* (**a**) *Gram (pronoun)* de primera persona (**b**) *Lit* **a f. narrative** una narración en primera persona

first-rate [fɜːst'reɪt] *adj* excelente, de primera clase

first-run ['fɜːstrʌn] *adj* ***f. cinema*** cine *m* de estreno

first-strike ['fɜːst'straɪk] *adj (missile)* de ataque preventivo; **a f. capability** una capacidad de ataque preventivo

first-time ['fɜːstaɪm] *n* **f. buyer** comprador(ora) de primera vivienda; **f. visitors to the country** personas que visitan el país por primera vez; **f. visitors are always puzzled by...** quienes llegan por primera se sorprenden por...

firth [fɜːθ] *n Scot* ría *f*, estuario *m*

fiscal ['fɪskəl] 1 *adj* fiscal; *US* **the budget for f. 2004** el presupuesto para el año fiscal de 2004 ►► *Econ* ***f. drag*** presión *f* fiscal en frío; ***f. policy*** política *f* fiscal; *US* ***f. year*** año *m* fiscal
2 *n Scot Law* **(procurator) f.** fiscal *mf* (del Estado)

fish [fɪʃ] 1 *n* (*pl* **fish** *or* **fishes**) (**a**) *(animal)* pez *m*; **to catch a f.** pescar ►► ***f. eagle*** águila *f* pescadora; ***f. farm*** piscifactoría *f*; ***f. farming*** piscicultura *f*; ***f. hawk*** águila *f* pescadora; ***f. hook*** anzuelo *m*; ***f. pond*** estanque *m*; ***f. tank*** acuario *m*

(**b**) *(food)* pescado *m* ►► *Br* ***f. and chips*** = pescado frito con patatas fritas; *Br* ***f.-and-chip shop*** = tienda de "fish and chips"; *Br* ***f. fingers*** palitos *mpl or* barritas *fpl* de pescado; ***f. glue*** cola *f* de pescado; *Culin* ***f. kettle*** cacerola *f* para pescado; ***f. knife*** cuchillo *m or* paleta *f* de pescado; ***f. market*** lonja *f* de pescado; ***f. meal*** harina *f* de pescado; ***f. paste*** = paté barato de pescado; ***f. shop*** pescadería *f*; ***f. slice*** pala *f or* espátula *f* (de cocina); *US* ***f. sticks*** palitos *mpl or* barritas *fpl* de pescado

(**c**) IDIOMS **there are plenty more f. in the sea** con él/ella no se acaba el mundo; **at school/work, he was a big f. in a small pond** en la escuela/el trabajo era un pez gordo, pero fuera era un don nadie; **to have bigger** *or* **other f. to fry** tener algo más importante que hacer; *Fam* **to drink like a f.** beber como un cosaco, *Am* tomar como un barril sin fondo; **she felt like a f. out of water** no se sentía en su elemento, *Am* se sentía como sapo de otro pozo; **neither f. nor fowl** ni chicha ni limoná

2 *vt* (**a**) *(river)* pescar en (**b**) *(remove)* **to f. sth from somewhere** retirar algo de un lugar

3 *vi* (**a**) *(for fish)* pescar (**b**) *Fam* **to f. for compliments** tratar de atraer elogios; **to f. for information** ir a la caza de información; **she fished around in her pocket for some change** rebuscó en el bolsillo *or CAm, Méx, Perú* la bolsa a ver si tenía monedas; IDIOM *US* **it's time to f. or cut bait** es hora de decidirse

► **fish out** *vt sep* sacar; **she fished her keys out of her bag** sacó las llaves de la cartera

► **fish up** *vt sep Fam* **where did you f. that up from?** *(object)* ¿dónde lo conseguiste?; *(idea)* ¿de dónde sacaste esa idea?; **to f. up sth from one's memory** rescatar algo de la memoria

fishbone ['fɪʃbəʊn] *n* espina *f*

fishbowl ['fɪʃbəʊl] *n* pecera *f*

fishcake ['fɪʃkeɪk] *n* pastelillo *m* de pescado

fisherman ['fɪʃəmən] *n* pescador *m*

fisherwoman ['fɪʃəwʊmən] *n* pescadora *f*

fishery ['fɪʃərɪ] *n* (**a**) *(area)* caladero *m* ►► ***f. protection vessel*** guardapesca *m* (**b**) **fisheries** *(fishing industry)* sector pesquero, industria pesquera (**c**) *(fish farm)* piscifactoría *f*

fish-eye lens ['fɪʃaɪ'lenz] *n Phot* (objetivo *m* de) ojo *m* de pez

fish-face ['fɪʃfeɪs] *n Fam* merluzo(a) *m,f*

fishing ['fɪʃɪŋ] *n* pesca *f*; **to go f.** ir de pesca *or* a pescar; **trout/salmon f.** pesca de la trucha/del salmón; **there is some good f. along this river** en este río hay buena pesca; **no f.** *(sign)* prohibido pescar ►► ***f. boat*** barco *m* de pesca; ***f. fleet*** flota *f* pesquera; ***f. grounds*** caladeros *mpl*; ***f. line*** sedal *m*; ***f. net*** red *f* de pesca; *US* ***f. pole*** caña *f* de pescar; ***f. port*** puerto *m* pesquero; ***f. rod*** caña *f* de pescar; ***f. tackle*** aparejos *mpl* de pesca; ***f. village*** aldea *f or* pueblo *m* de pescadores

fish-ladder ['fɪʃlædə(r)] *n* salmonera *f*

fishmonger ['fɪʃmʌŋgə(r)] *n (person)* pescadero(a) *m,f*; **the f.'s** la pescadería

fishnet ['fɪʃnet] 1 *n US (for catching fish)* red *f* de pesca
2 *adj* **f. stockings** *or* **tights** medias de red *or* de malla

fishplate ['fɪʃpleɪt] *n Rail* eclisa *f*

fishtail ['fɪʃteɪl] 1 *n* cola *f* de pescado
2 *vi (aircraft, car)* colear

fishwife ['fɪʃwaɪf] *n Pej* verdulera *f*

fishy ['fɪʃɪ] *adj* (a) *(smell, taste)* a pescado (b) *Fam (suspicious)* sospechoso(a); **there's something f. going on here** aquí hay gato encerrado

fissile ['fɪsaɪl] *adj* (a) *Geol* fisil, hojoso(a) (b) *Phys* fisible, fisionable

fission ['fɪʃən] *n* fisión *f*

fissure ['fɪʃə(r)] 1 *n* (a) *(in mountain, rock)* grieta *f* (b) *Med* fisura *f*
2 *vt* agrietar
3 *vi* agrietarse

fist [fɪst] *n* puño *m*; **to shake one's f. at sb** amenazar a alguien con el puño; **to clench one's f., to make a f.** apretar *or* cerrar el puño; IDIOM **to make a (good) f. of it** hacerlo bastante bien

fistfight ['fɪstfaɪt] *n* pelea *f* a puñetazos

fistful ['fɪstfʊl] *n* puñado *m*

fisticuffs ['fɪstɪkʌfs] *npl* pelea *f* a puñetazos

fistula ['fɪstjʊlə] (*pl* **fistulas** *or* **fistulae** ['fɪstjʊli:]) *n Med* fístula *f*

fit[1] [fɪt] *n* (a) *(of apoplexy, hysterics)* ataque *m*, crisis *f inv*; **(epileptic) f.** ataque *m* de epilepsia, crisis *f inv* epiléptica; *Med* **to have a f.** sufrir un ataque; *Fam Fig* **to have** *or* **throw a f.** *(get angry)* ponerse hecho(a) una furia; **she'll have a f. when she finds out** cuando se entere le da un ataque
(b) *(outburst) (of anger, pique, generosity)* ataque *m*, acceso *m*; **in a f. of temper** en un arrebato de ira; **a f. of crying** un ataque de llanto; **a f. of coughing, a coughing f.** un acceso de tos; **to get a f. of the giggles** tener un ataque de risa (tonta); IDIOM **to do sth by fits and starts** hacer algo a trompicones
(c) *Br Fam* **to be in fits** *(of laughter)* partirse de risa; **to have sb in fits (of laughter)** hacer que alguien se muera de risa

FIT[2] 1 *adj* (a) *(appropriate)* adecuado(a), apto(a); **f. to drink** potable; **f. to eat** comestible; **he's not f. to serve as a director** no está en condiciones de ejercer de director; **a meal f. for a king** una comida digna de un rey; **that's all he's f. for** no vale para más; **those trousers are only f. for the bin** esos pantalones no valen más que para tirarlos *or Am* botarlos; **you are in no f. state to be going to work** no estás en condiciones de ir al trabajo; **this is no f. way to behave** ésta no es manera de comportarse; **do as you see** *or* **think f.** haz lo que creas conveniente; **she saw f. to tell him without asking me first** le dio por contárselo sin ni siquiera preguntarme a mí primero; **they didn't see f. to inform us** no juzgaron necesario informarnos; IDIOM **he's not f. to tie her shoelaces** *or* **bootlaces** no le llega a la suela de los zapatos; IDIOM *US Fam* **to be f. to be tied: she was f. to be tied** se subía por las paredes, *Méx* estaba como agua para chocolate
(b) *(ready)* **they were f. to burst with excitement** desbordaban de entusiasmo; **she worked until she was f. to drop** trabajó hasta caer rendida
(c) *(healthy)* en forma; **she's very f. for her age** se mantiene muy en forma para su edad; **to get/keep f.** ponerse/mantenerse en forma; **he is not yet f. to go back to work** todavía no está en condiciones de volver a trabajar; IDIOM *Fam* **to be as f. as a fiddle** estar en plena forma
(d) *Br Fam (attractive)* **to be f.** estar como un tren, *Méx* estar buenón(ona)
2 *vt* (*pt & pp* **fitted**) (a) *(match)* ajustarse a, adecuarse a; **she fits the description** se ajusta a la descripción; **to make the punishment f. the crime** imponer un castigo proporcional al delito
(b) *(be the right size for)* **it fits me** me sirve, me queda bien; **this key fits the lock** esta llave entra (bien) *or* encaja en la cerradura; **this hat doesn't f. me** este sombrero me queda pequeño/grande; **the trousers had been made to f. a smaller man** los pantalones habían sido confeccionados para un hombre más pequeño; **the dress fits you like a glove** el vestido te queda como un guante
(c) *(in dressmaking)* **she's being fitted for her wedding dress** le están tomando las medidas para el traje de novia
(d) *(install)* colocar, poner; **to f. a carpet** colocar una *Esp* moqueta *or Am* alfombra; **it's fitted with an alarm** viene equipado con alarma
(e) *(insert)* **to f. sth into sth** introducir *or* encajar algo en algo; **to f. sth onto sth** colocar algo sobre algo; **we can f. another two people inside** podemos meter a dos personas más; **the lid fits over the box** la tapa se coloca *or* va en la caja; **to f. two things together** encajar dos cosas
(f) *(equip)* equipar; **to f. sth with sth** equipar algo con algo; **fitted with electronic security devices** equipado con dispositivos electrónicos de seguridad
(g) *(make suitable)* **it is her tact that fits her for the job** su tacto la hace idónea para el trabajo
3 *vi* (a) *(lid, key, plug)* encajar; **to f. (together)** encajar; **to f. into sth** caber en algo; **I can't f. into these shoes any more** estos zapatos ya no me caben; *Fig* **she doesn't f. into any of the usual categories** es inclasificable; *Fig* **there's something about her that doesn't f.** tiene algo raro
(b) *(clothes)* quedar bien (de talla); **it fits perfectly** me queda perfectamente; **this shirt doesn't f. any more** esta camisa ya no me sirve
4 *n* (a) *(of clothes)* **your coat is a good/bad f.** te queda bien/mal el abrigo; **it was a bit of a tight f.** *(in room, car)* íbamos muy justos *or* apretados; *(when parking car)* no había mucho sitio
(b) *(match)* **there must be a f. between what we offer and what they need** tiene que haber una correspondencia entre lo que ofrecemos y lo que necesitan

▶ **fit in** 1 *vt sep* (a) *(find room for) (clothes in suitcase)* **can you f. one more in?** *(in car)* ¿cabe uno más?; **how are you going to f. everyone in?** *(in room, car etc)* ¿qué vas a hacer para que quepa todo el mundo?
(b) *(in timetable)* **to f. sb in** hacer un hueco a alguien; **I don't think I'll be able to f. any shopping in** no creo que pueda sacar tiempo para ir de compras
2 *vi* (a) *(go into place)* encajar; **will we all f. in?** ¿cabremos todos?; **to f. in with** *(statement, colour scheme, plans)* encajar con; **that idea doesn't f. in with our overall strategy** esa idea no encaja en *or* con nuestra estrategia global
(b) *(person)* **he just didn't f. in** simplemente no encajaba bien (en aquel ambiente); **you're going to have to learn to f. in at school** vas a tener que aprender a integrarte en el colegio; **she doesn't f. in easily with other people** le cuesta adaptarse a la gente; **you'll just have to f. in with what I want to do** tendrás que adaptarte a lo que yo quiero hacer

▶ **fit out** *vt sep (ship)* armar (**with** de); *(room)* amueblar (**with** con); *(person)* equipar (**with** de *or* con)

▶ **fit up** *vt sep* (a) *(provide)* **to f. sb up with sth** proporcionar algo a alguien
(b) *Fam (frame)* **to f. sb up** hacer una declaración falsa *or* un montaje contra alguien

fitful ['fɪtfʊl] *adj (sleep)* intermitente; **to make f. progress** ir progresando por rachas

fitfully ['fɪtfʊlɪ] *adv (to sleep, work)* intermitentemente, a ratos

fitment ['fɪtmənt] *n Br* accesorio *m (de instalación)*

fitness ['fɪtnɪs] *n* (a) *(health)* buena forma *f* ▶▶ ***f. training*** entrenamiento *m* físico (b) *(suitability)* aptitud *f*

fitted ['fɪtɪd] *adj* (a) *(garment)* entallado(a) ▶▶ ***f. skirt*** falda *f or Am* pollera *f* a medida (b) *Br (close-fitting)* ***f. carpet*** *Esp* moqueta *f*, *Am* alfombra *f*, *RP* moquette *m*; ***f. sheet*** sábana *f* ajustable (c) *Br (built-in) (cupboard, shelves)* empotrado(a) ▶▶ ***f. kitchen*** cocina *f* amueblada a medida; ***f. wardrobe*** armario *m* empotrado (d) *(suited)* **to be f. for (doing) sth** estar capacitado para (hacer) algo

fitter ['fɪtə(r)] *n* (a) *(of machine, electrical parts)* técnico(a) *m,f* (b) *(of clothes)* probador(ora) *m,f*

fitting ['fɪtɪŋ] 1 *n* (a) *(of clothes)* prueba *f*; **I'm going for a f. tomorrow** mañana voy a probármelo ▶▶ ***f. room*** probador *m* (b) *Br (of shoe)* **have you got it in a wider/narrower f.?** ¿lo tiene con una horma más ancha/angosta? (c) **fittings** *(of office)* equipamiento; *(of bathroom)* accesorios
2 *adj (conclusion, remark)* apropiado(a); **it was only f. he should score the winning goal** no podía ser otro quien marcase el gol de la victoria

fittingly ['fɪtɪŋlɪ] *adv* muy apropiadamente; **f., he died in battle** como no podía ser de otro modo, murió en el campo de batalla

five [faɪv] 1 *n* (a) *(number)* cinco *m*; *Fam* **to take f.** descansar cinco minutos; *US Fam* **gimme f.!** ¡chócala!, ¡choca esos cinco! (b) *US Fam (five-dollar note)* billete *m* de cinco (dólares)
2 *adj* cinco; *see also* **eight**

five-and-dime ['faɪvən'daɪm], **five-and-ten** ['faɪvən'ten] *n US* = tienda en la que sólo se venden productos muy baratos

five-a-side ['faɪvəsaɪd] *Br* 1 *adj* ***f. football*** fútbol *m* sala
2 *n* fútbol *m* sala

five-day week ['faɪvdeɪ'wi:k] *n Br* semana *f* laboral de cinco días, semana *f* inglesa

five-door ['faɪv'dɔ:(r)] *adj (car)* de cinco puertas

fivefold ['faɪvfəʊld] 1 *adj* quintuplicado(a); **a f. increase (in)** cinco veces más (de) 2 *adv* cinco veces, por cinco; **to increase f.** quintuplicarse

five-o'clock shadow [faɪvəklɒk'ʃædəʊ] *n Fam* sombra *f* de barba

fiver ['faɪvə(r)] *n Fam* (a) *Br (sum)* cinco libras *fpl*; *(note)* billete *m* de cinco libras (b) *US (sum)* cinco dólares *mpl*; *(note)* billete *m* de cinco dólares

fives [faɪvz] *n Sport* = deporte británico similar al squash en el que los jugadores golpean la pelota con las manos

five-spice powder ['faɪv'spaɪs'paʊdə(r)] *n Culin* polvo *m or* mezcla *f* cinco especias

five-spot ['faɪvspɒt] *n US Fam* billete *m* de cinco (dólares)

Five-Year Plan ['faɪvjɪə'plæn] *n Hist* plan *m* quinquenal

fix [fɪks] **1** *n* (**a**) *Fam (difficulty)* **to be in a f.** estar en un lío; **to get into/out of a f.** meterse en/salir de un lío

(**b**) *Fam (of drug)* pico *m*, *Esp* chute *m*; **to give oneself a f.** picarse, *Esp* chutarse; *Fig* **my daily f. of television news** mi dosis diaria de noticias

(**c**) *Av & Naut* **to get a f. on** *(plane, ship)* establecer la posición de; *Fig (get clear idea of)* hacerse una idea de

(**d**) *Fam (set-up)* **the match/quiz was a f.** el partido/concurso estaba amañado

2 *vt* (**a**) *(attach securely)* fijar; **to f. a post in the ground** fijar un poste en el suelo; *Mil* **f. bayonets!** ¡calen las bayonetas!; **to f. sth in one's memory** fijar algo en la memoria; **to f. one's attention on sth** fijar la atención en algo; **to f. one's eyes on sb** fijar la mirada en alguien; **to f. the blame on sb** echarle la culpa a alguien; **to f. one's hopes on sth/sb** depositar las esperanzas en algo/alguien

(**b**) *(stare at)* **she fixed him with her piercing eyes** le clavó una mirada penetrante

(**c**) *(decide) (limit, price, date, place)* fijar; **nothing is fixed yet** no hay nada fijo todavía; **have you (got) anything fixed for Friday?** ¿haces algo el viernes?

(**d**) *(arrange) (meeting)* organizar; **I'll f. it so you don't have to stay overnight** lo arreglaré para que no tengas que quedarte por la noche; **I've fixed it for them to come tomorrow** lo he arreglado para que vengan mañana

(**e**) *(prepare)* **to f. sb breakfast/a drink** preparar el desayuno/una bebida a alguien

(**f**) *(repair)* arreglar; **I've been meaning to get that fixed for ages** hace tiempo que quiero arreglarlo

(**g**) *Fam (adjust, neaten) (make-up, tie)* arreglar; **just wait while I f. my hair** espera mientras me peino *or* me arreglo el pelo; *US Fam* **to f. one's face** pintarse la cara

(**h**) *Fam (settle a score with)* ajustar cuentas con; **I'll f. him!** ¡se va a enterar!; **that'll f. him!** ¡así sabrá lo que es bueno!

(**i**) *Fam (election, contest)* amañar, *Am* arreglar; **they'd fixed all the witnesses** *(bribed)* sobornaron a todos los testigos; *(threatened)* amenazaron a todos los testigos

(**j**) *US Fam* **to be fixing to do sth** tener la intención de hacer algo; **he's fixing to go on holiday** está planeando irse de vacaciones

(**k**) *Chem (nitrogen)* fijar

(**l**) *Phot (photo)* fijar

(**m**) *Art (drawing)* fijar

(**n**) *US Fam Euph (neuter)* capar

▸ **fix on** *vt insep (decide on)* decidirse por

▸ **fix up** **1** *vt sep* (**a**) *(arrange) (meeting)* preparar; **it's all fixed up** está todo preparado; **he'll try to f. something up for us** intentará arreglarnos algo; **have you got anything fixed up for this evening?** ¿haces algo esta noche?

(**b**) *(provide)* **I've fixed him up with a date** le he buscado a alguien para que salgan juntos; **I've managed to f. him up with some work** logré conseguirle algo de trabajo; **you can stay here until you get fixed up (with a place to stay)** puedes quedarte aquí hasta que consigas un lugar donde instalarte *or* quedarte

(**c**) *(prepare) (room, flat)* arreglar, acondicionar

(**d**) *(repair)* **the doctor will have you fixed up in no time** el doctor te pondrá bien rápidamente

2 *vi Fam (arrange)* quedar, *RP* arreglar

fixate [fɪk'seɪt] **1** *vt (stare at)* fijar la atención *or* la vista en

2 *vi* **to f. on sth/sb** obsesionarse con algo/alguien

fixated [fɪk'seɪtɪd] *adj* obsesionado(a) (**on** con); **to be f. on sth** estar obsesionado con algo; **he became f. on the idea of winning** se obsesionó con la idea de ganar

fixation [fɪk'seɪʃən] *n* fijación *f*; **to have a f. about sth** tener una fijación con algo

fixative ['fɪksətɪv] *n* (**a**) *(on drawing, painting)* fijador *m* (**b**) *(for dentures)* fijador *m*

fixed [fɪkst] *adj* (**a**) *(unchanging)* fijo(a); **a f. smile** una sonrisa inmutable; **to have f. ideas** tener ideas fijas; *Law* **of no f. abode** sin domicilio fijo ▸▸ *Fin* ***f. assets*** activo *m* fijo *or* inmovilizado; *Fin* ***f. costs*** costos *mpl or Esp* costes *mpl* fijos; ***f. expenses*** gastos *mpl* fijos; ***f. income*** renta *f* fija; *Fin* ***f. interest rate*** renta *f* fija; *Law* ***f. penalty*** multa *f* fija *or* estipulada; ***f. satellite*** satélite *m* fijo *or* geoestacionario

(**b**) *(definite)* **to have no f. plans** no tener planes definidos

(**c**) *Fam* **how are you f. for money/time?** ¿qué tal vas *or* andas de dinero/tiempo?; **how are you f. for accommodation/transport?** ¿cómo te las arreglas con el alojamiento/transporte?

(**d**) *Fam (election, contest) Esp* amañado(a), *Am* arreglado(a)

fixed-income ['fɪkst'ɪnkʌm] *adj US Fin* a interés fijo

fixed-interest ['fɪkst'ɪntrest] *adj Br Fin* a interés fijo

fixedly ['fɪksɪdlɪ] *adv* fijamente

fixed-rate ['fɪkstreɪt] *adj Fin* a interés fijo ▸▸ ***f. mortgage*** hipoteca *f or* crédito *m* hipotecario a interés fijo

fixed-term ['fɪkstɜːm] *adj (deposit, loan)* a plazo fijo ▸▸ ***f. contract*** contrato *m* temporal *or Am* temporario; *Br* ***f. deposit*** depósito *m* a plazo fijo

fixed-wing aircraft ['fɪkst'wɪŋ'eəkrɑːft] *n* aeronave *f* de alas fijas

fixed-yield ['fɪkst'jiːld] *adj Fin* de rentabilidad fija ▸▸ ***f. securities*** valores *mpl* de renta fija

fixer ['fɪksə(r)] *n* (**a**) *Fam (person)* intermediario(a) *m,f*, chanchullero(a) *m,f* (**b**) *Phot* fijador *m*

fixer-upper ['fɪksər'ʌpə(r)] *n US Fam (house)* casa *f* para *or* a reformar

fixing ['fɪksɪŋ] *n* (**a**) *Phot* ***f. bath*** *(container)* cubeta *f* de fijador; *(solution)* (baño *m*) fijador *m* (**b**) *US* **roast turkey with all the fixings** pavo asado con guarniciones

fixity ['fɪksɪtɪ] *n (of gaze)* fijeza *f*; **f. of purpose** determinación

fixture ['fɪkstʃə(r)] *n* (**a**) *(permanent feature)* **bathroom fixtures and fittings** saneamientos *or* sanitarios y accesorios; *Fam* **she was something of a f. at his parties** asistía invariablemente a todas sus fiestas (**b**) *Br Sport* encuentro *m*, partido *m* ▸▸ ***f. list*** calendario *mpl* de partidos, *RP* fixture *m*

fix-up ['fɪksʌp] *n US Fam (repair)* arreglo *m*

fizz [fɪz] **1** *n* (**a**) *(sound)* burbujeo *m* (**b**) *(effervescence)* efervescencia *f* (**c**) *Fam (soft drink)* refresco *m* (**d**) *Fam (champagne)* champán *m* (**e**) *Fam (excitement)* chispa *f*; **their marriage has lost its f.** su matrimonio ha perdido la chispa

2 *vi* burbujear; IDIOM *Fam* **to be fizzing** *(extremely angry)* estar cabreadísimo(a) *or RP* re-caliente, *Méx* estar como agua para chocolate

fizziness ['fɪzɪnɪs] *n (of drink)* efervescencia *f*

fizzle ['fɪzəl] **1** *n (sound)* sonido *m* crepitante

2 *vi (drink, firework)* crepitar

▸ **fizzle out** *vi Fam (plan)* quedarse en nada, quedar en agua de borrajas; *(enthusiasm, interest)* disiparse

fizzy ['fɪzɪ] *adj (wine)* espumoso(a); *(soft drink)* con gas, con burbujas

fjord, fiord ['fiːɔːd] *n* fiordo *m*

FL, Fla (*abbr* **Florida**) Florida

flab [flæb] *n Fam* grasa *f*; **to fight the f.** cuidar la silueta

flabbergast ['flæbəgɑːst] *vt Fam* **I was flabbergasted by this news** aluciné *or Esp* flipé con la noticia

flabbergasting ['flæbəgɑːstɪŋ] *adj Fam* alucinante, *Esp* flipante

flabbiness ['flæbɪnɪs] *n* (**a**) *(of person)* flac(c)idez *f* (**b**) *(of prose)* flojedad *f*

flabby ['flæbɪ] *adj* (**a**) *(person, part of body)* fofo(a) (**b**) *(argument, reasoning)* flojo(a); *(prose)* pobre

flaccid ['flæsɪd] *adj* flác(c)ido(a); **her writing style is rather f.** escribe con un estilo bastante pobre

flack [flæk] *n US* agente *mf* de prensa

flag [flæg] **1** *n* (**a**) *(of country)* bandera *f*; *(on boat)* pabellón *m*, bandera *f*; *(in golf)* bandera *f*, banderín *m*; *(for celebration)* banderín *m*, banderita *f*; *(for charity)* banderita *f* ▸▸ ***f. of convenience*** pabellón *m or* bandera *f* de conveniencia; ***F. Day*** *(in United States)* = día de la bandera en Estados Unidos, 14 de junio; *Br* ***f. day*** *(for charity)* día *m* de la banderita, día *m* de cuestación; *US* ***f. station*** *Esp* apeadero *m*, *Am* estación *f* de bandera

(**b**) *(in taxi)* banderita *f*; **the f. was down/up** el taxi estaba ocupado/libre, *Am* la bandera estaba baja/levantada

(**c**) *(flagstone)* losa *f*

(**d**) *Comptr* comentario *m*, flag *m*

(**e**) IDIOMS **to keep the f. flying** mantener alto el pabellón; **to show the f.** defender el pabellón; *Fig* hacer acto de presencia; **to go down with all flags flying** morir peleando, *Esp* caer con las botas puestas; **to put out the flags for sb** recibir a alguien con honores

2 *vt* (*pt & pp* **flagged**) **to f. (down) a taxi** llamar *or* parar a un taxi; **to f. (up) a mistake** señalar un error

3 *vi (person)* desfallecer; *(strength, enthusiasm)* flaquear; *(conversation, interest)* decaer

▸ **flag down** *vt sep (motorist, race driver)* detener

flagella *pl of* **flagellum**

flagellant ['flædʒələnt] *n Rel* flagelante *mf*

flagellate ['flædʒəleɪt] *vt* flagelar

flagellation [flædʒə'leɪʃən] *n* flagelación *f*

flagellum [flə'dʒeləm] (*pl* **flagella** [flə'dʒelə]) *n Biol* flagelo *m*

flageolet ['flædʒəʊleɪ] *n* (**a**) *(bean)* alubia *f* verdina (**b**) *Mus* flauta *f* dulce

flagged [flægd] *adj (floor)* enlosado(a)

flagging ['flægɪŋ] **1** *n (on floor)* enlosado *m*
2 *adj (strength, enthusiasm)* debilitado(a); *(conversation, interest)* decreciente

flagon ['flægən] *n* (**a**) *(bottle)* botellón *m* (**b**) *(jug)* jarra *f*

flagpole ['flægpəʊl] *n* asta *f*, mástil *m (de bandera)*; IDIOM *Fam* **let's run it up the f. (and see who salutes)** vamos a planteárselo a ver cómo reaccionan

flagrant ['fleɪgrənt] *adj (injustice, abuse)* flagrante; **a f. disregard for the safety of others** una flagrante falta de consideración por la seguridad de los demás

flagrantly ['fleɪgrəntlɪ] *adv* flagrantemente; **f. unfair** incuestionablemente injusto(a)

flagship ['flægʃɪp] *n* (**a**) *(of fleet)* buque *m* insignia (**b**) *(of range of products, policies)* buque *m* insignia, estandarte *m*

flagstaff ['flægstɑːf] *n* asta *f*, mástil *m (de bandera)*

flagstick ['flægstɪk] *n (in golf)* bandera *f or* banderín *m* del hoyo

flagstone ['flægstəʊn] *n* losa *f*

flail [fleɪl] **1** *n Agr* mayal *m*
2 *vt* (**a**) *(thresh)* trillar (**b**) *(arms, legs)* agitar; **she flailed her fists at him** trató inútilmente de golpearle
3 *vi* moverse descontroladamente; **I managed to avoid his flailing fists** conseguí evitar sus puñetazos descontrolados

▸ **flail about, flail around** *vi (arms, legs)* moverse descontroladamente; **she was flailing about in the water** se sacudía desesperadamente en el agua

flair [fleə(r)] *n* (**a**) *(stylishness)* estilo *m*; **to do sth with f.** hacer algo con estilo *or* elegancia (**b**) *(gift)* don *m*, dotes *fpl*; **to have a f. for sth** tener dotes para algo; **he has no f. for business** no tiene aptitudes para los negocios

flak [flæk] *n* (**a**) *(gunfire)* fuego *m* antiaéreo (**b**) *Fam Fig (criticism)* críticas *fpl*; **she got a lot of f. for her decision** su decisión recibió duras críticas; **to come in for a lot of f.** recibir duras críticas ▸▸ ***f. jacket*** chaleco *m* antifragmentación

flake [fleɪk] **1** *n* (**a**) *(of snow, cereal)* copo *m*; *(of skin, soap)* escama *f*; *(of paint, plaster)* desconchón *m* (**b**) *US Fam (person)* bicho *m* raro
2 *vt Culin (fish)* desmenuzar, cortar en trozos pequeños; **flaked almonds** almendras fileteadas
3 *vi* (**a**) *(skin)* descamarse; *(paint, plaster)* desconcharse (**b**) *US Fam* **to f. (on sb)** pasar (de alguien)

▸ **flake off** *vi (skin)* pelarse; *(plaster, paint)* desconcharse

▸ **flake out** *vi Fam* quedarse roque

flakiness ['fleɪkɪnɪs] *n* (**a**) *(of surface, skin)* escamosidad *f* (**b**) *US Fam (of person)* rareza *f*

flaky ['fleɪkɪ] *adj* (**a**) *(surface)* quebradizo(a); *(skin)* con escamas ▸▸ ***f. pastry*** hojaldre *m* (**b**) *US Fam (eccentric)* raro(a)

flambé ['flɒmbeɪ] (*pt & pp* **flambéed**) *vt Culin* flambear, flamear

flamboyance [flæm'bɔɪəns] *n (of person, manner)* extravagancia *f*; *(of clothes)* vistosidad *f*

flamboyant [flæm'bɔɪənt] *adj (person, manner)* extravagante; *(clothes)* vistoso(a)

flame [fleɪm] **1** *n* (**a**) *(of fire)* llama *f*; **to be in flames** *(building, car)* estar en llamas; **to go up in flames** ser pasto de las llamas; *Fig (of hopes, chances)* esfumarse, evaporarse; **to burst into flames** incendiarse; **to be shot down in flames** *(plane, pilot)* caer envuelto(a) en llamas; *Fig (politician, critic)* llevarse un tremendo varapalo ▸▸ ***f. retardant*** material *m* ignífugo
(**b**) *Literary (of passion, desire)* llama *f*; IDIOM *Fam* **he's an old f. of mine** es un antiguo amor
(**c**) *Comptr* llamarada *f*, = mensaje ofensivo ▸▸ ***f. war*** guerra *f* de llamaradas *or* dialéctica
2 *vi* (**a**) *(fire)* llamear (**b**) *(face, cheeks)* encenderse (**c**) *Comptr* lanzar llamaradas
3 *vt Comptr* lanzar llamaradas a

▸ **flame up** *vi* (**a**) *(fire)* hacer llama, llamear (**b**) *(person, anger)* encenderse

flame-coloured ['fleɪmkʌləd] *adj* de color rojo fuego

flamenco [flə'meŋkəʊ] *n* flamenco *m* ▸▸ ***f. dancing*** baile *m* flamenco; ***f. music*** el flamenco, la música flamenca

flameout ['fleɪmaut] *n (of jet engine)* extinción *f* de la llama

flame-proof ['fleɪmpruːf] *adj* resistente al fuego

flamer ['fleɪmə(r)] *n Comptr* = autor de un mensaje ofensivo

flame-resistant ['fleɪmrɪ'zɪstənt] *adj* ignífugo(a)

flame-retardant ['fleɪmrɪ'tɑːdənt] *adj* de combustión lenta

flamethrower ['fleɪmθrəʊə(r)] *n* lanzallamas *m inv*

flaming ['fleɪmɪŋ] **1** *adj* (**a**) *(burning)* en llamas (**b**) *Br Fam (extremely angry)* **a f. row** una pelea violenta; **in a f. temper** enfurecido(a) (**c**) *Br Fam (for emphasis)* maldito(a), *Méx* pinche, *RP* bendito(a); **he's got a f. cheek** ¡qué jeta que tiene el tipo!; **you f. idiot!** ¡serás imbécil!; **he's a f. pest** es un pesado de narices; **f. hell!** ¡maldición!
2 *adv Br Fam* **don't be so f. stupid** ¡mira que eres bobo!; **it was f. expensive** fue caro *Esp* del copón, *Méx* fue mucho muy caro, *RP* fue recaro; **you're f. well staying here!** ¡tú te quedas aquí!

flamingo [flə'mɪŋgəʊ] (*pl* **flamingos**) *n* flamenco *m* ▸▸ ***greater f.*** flamenco *m* común

flammable ['flæməbəl] *adj* inflamable

flan [flæn] *n* tarta *f*

> **False friend**: The Spanish noun **flan** is not a translation for the English word **flan**. In Spanish **flan** means "crème caramel".

Flanders ['flɑːndəz] *n* Flandes

flange [flændʒ] *n Tech (on wheel)* pestaña *f*; *(on pipe, tube)* reborde *m*; *(on rail)* patín *m*

flank [flæŋk] **1** *n* (**a**) *(of person, animal)* costado *m* (**b**) *(of beef, mutton)* falda *f* (**c**) *(of mountain)* ladera *f* (**d**) *(of army)* flanco *m* (**e**) *US* **f. speed** *(full speed)* velocidad máxima
2 *vt* (**a**) *(be on either side of)* flanquear; **flanked by his wife and son** flanqueado por su esposa y su hijo (**b**) *Mil* flanquear

flanker ['flæŋkə(r)] *n* (**a**) *(in rugby)* tercera línea *mf*, flánker *mf* (**b**) *(in American football)* ala *mf* libre

flannel ['flænəl] **1** *n* (**a**) *(fabric)* franela *f*; **f. shirt/nightgown** camisa/camisón de franela (**b**) *Br (face-cloth)* toallita *f* (**c**) *Br Fam (wordy talk)* palabrería *f*
2 *vi Br Fam (use empty words)* charlatanear

flannelette [flænə'let] *n* franela *f* de algodón

flannels ['flænəlz] *npl (trousers)* pantalones *mpl* de franela; **a pair of f.** unos pantalones de franela

flap [flæp] **1** *n* (**a**) *(movement) (of wings)* aleteo *m*; *(of sails)* golpeteo *m*; **the bird gave a f. of its wings** el pájaro sacudió sus alas
(**b**) *(of envelope, book cover)* solapa *f*; *(of tent)* puerta *f*; *(of counter, table)* hoja *f*
(**c**) *(of aircraft)* alerón *m*
(**d**) *Fam (panic)* **to be in/get into a f.** estar/ponerse hecho(a) un manojo de nervios *or* histérico(a); **there's a f. on at the office** hay un lío tremendo en la oficina
(**e**) *Ling* golpe *m* ligero y breve
2 *vt* (*pt & pp* **flapped**) *(wings)* batir; **she flapped her arms excitedly** agitó los brazos con excitación
3 *vi* (**a**) *(wings)* aletear; *(flag)* ondear; *(sails, washing, curtains)* agitarse; **the seagull flapped away** la gaviota echó a volar batiendo las alas (**b**) *Fam (panic)* ponerse hecho(a) un manojo de nervios *or* histérico(a); **stop flapping!** ¡tranquilízate de una vez!

flapjack ['flæpdʒæk] *n* (**a**) *Br (biscuit)* galleta *f* de avena (**b**) *US (pancake)* crepe *f*, hojuela *f*

flapper ['flæpə(r)] *n* chica *f* moderna *(de los años veinte)*

flare [fleə(r)] **1** *n* (**a**) *(signal)* bengala *f* ▸▸ *Av* ***f. path*** pista *f* iluminada; ***f. pistol*** pistola *f* de *or* lanza bengalas (**b**) *(bright flame)* llamarada *f* (**c**) *(in clothes)* campana *f*; **trousers with a wide f.** pantalones acampanados *or* de campana
2 *vt* **to f. one's nostrils** hinchar las aletas de la nariz
3 *vi* (**a**) *(fire, match)* llamear (**b**) *(temper, trouble)* estallar (**c**) *(clothes)* acampanarse

▸ **flare up** *vi* (**a**) *(fire)* llamear (**b**) *(medical condition)* exacerbarse (**c**) *(temper, trouble)* estallar; **she flares up at the least thing** se pone hecha una fiera a la mínima

flared [fleəd] *adj (trousers, skirt)* acampanado(a)

flares [fleəz] *npl (trousers)* pantalones *mpl* de campana; **a pair of f.** unos pantalones de campana

flare-up ['fleərʌp] *n* (**a**) *(of anger)* estallido *m* de ira (**b**) *(of old injury)* rebrote *m*

flash [flæʃ] **1** *n* (**a**) *(of light)* destello *m*; **a f. of lightning** un relámpago; **a f. of wit** una ocurrencia; **a f. of inspiration** una inspiración súbita; **in a f.** *(very quickly)* en un abrir y cerrar de ojos; **it came to me in a f.** de repente caí en la cuenta; IDIOM **a f. in the pan** un éxito aislado; IDIOM **quick as a f., like a f.** *(to answer)* rápido como un rayo ►► ***f. burn*** quemadura *f* por fogonazo; ***f. card*** = tarjeta grande con un dibujo o palabra empleada como material didáctico; ***f. flood*** riada *f*; *Fam* ***f. Harry*** fanfarrón *m*, *Esp* chulo *m*; ***f. point*** *Chem* punto *m* de inflamación; *(of situation)* momento *m* de máxima tensión; *(region)* zona *f* conflictiva

(**b**) *(in photography)* flash *m* ►► ***f. photography*** fotografía *f* con flash

(**c**) *(of news)* avance *m* informativo, comunicado *m* urgente

(**d**) *Mil (on uniform)* distintivo *m*

(**e**) *US Fam (flashlight)* linterna *f*

2 *adj Br Fam (showy)* llamativo(a), ostentoso(a)

3 *vt* (**a**) *(torch)* alumbrar, iluminar; **to f. a light in sb's face/eyes** enfocar una luz a la cara/los ojos de alguien; **to f. one's headlights at sb** darle las luces a alguien, hacerle señales con los faros a alguien

(**b**) *(briefly display) (card, badge)* mostrar, exhibir; *(smile, look)* lanzar (**at** a); **to f. a message (up) on the screen** mostrar *or* poner un mensaje en pantalla; IDIOM **to f. one's money around** hacer un alarde de dinero

(**c**) *Fam (expose oneself to)* exhibirse ante

4 *vi* (**a**) *(light, sign, diamond)* destellar; *(lightning)* relampaguear; **his eyes flashed with anger** sus ojos lanzaban destellos de ira

(**b**) *(move quickly)* **to f. in/out/past** entrar/salir/pasar a toda velocidad *or* como un rayo; **to f. past** *or* **by** *(time, days)* pasar rápidamente; **it flashed across my mind that...** se me ocurrió de pronto que...; **my life flashed before me** en un instante vi mi vida entera

(**c**) *Fam (expose oneself)* hacer exhibicionismo

► **flash back** *vi (in novel, film)* retroceder

► **flash forward** *vi (in novel, film)* avanzar

flashback ['flæʃbæk] *n* (**a**) *(in novel, film)* escena *f* retrospectiva, flashback *m*; **the story is told in f.** la historia está narrada retrospectivamente (**b**) *Fam (hallucination)* flash *m* de después

flashbulb ['flæʃbʌlb] *n Phot* lámpara *f or Esp* bombilla *f* de flash

flashcube ['flæʃkju:b] *n Phot* cuboflash *m*

flasher ['flæʃə(r)] *n* (**a**) *Aut (indicator)* intermitente *m* (**b**) *Fam* exhibicionista *m*

flash-fried ['flæʃ'fraɪd] *adj* frito(a) a vuelta y vuelta

flash-frozen ['flæʃ'frəʊzən] *adj* congelado(a) rápidamente

flashgun ['flæʃgʌn] *n Phot* disparador *m* del flash

flashily ['flæʃɪlɪ] *adv Pej* ostentosamente; **f. dressed** con ropa muy llamativa

flashing ['flæʃɪŋ] **1** *n* (**a**) *Fam (indecent exposure)* exhibicionismo *m* (**b**) *(on roof)* cubrejuntas *m inv*, tapajuntas *m inv*

2 *adj (light)* intermitente

flashlight ['flæʃlaɪt] *n US* linterna *f*

flashover ['flæʃəʊvə(r)] *n Elec* salto *m* (de corriente)

flashy ['flæʃɪ] *adj Pej* llamativo(a), ostentoso(a)

flask [flɑ:sk] *n* (**a**) *(in chemistry)* matraz *m* (**b**) **(hip) f.** petaca *f* (**c**) **(Thermos®) f.** termo *m*

flat [flæt] **1** *n* (**a**) *Br (apartment)* apartamento *m*, *Esp* piso *m*, *Arg* departamento *m*; **(block of) flats** (edificio *or* bloque de) apartamentos *or Esp* pisos *or Arg* departamentos

(**b**) *Fam (flat tyre)* rueda *f* desinflada; **we got a f.** *(puncture)* pinchamos

(**c**) *(flat surface) (of hand)* palma *f*; *(of blade)* cara *f*; **on the f.** en *or* sobre el llano; *(in horse racing)* en carreras sin obstáculos

(**d**) *(flat land)* **salt flats** salinas; **mud flats** marismas

(**e**) *Mus* bemol *m*

(**f**) *Theat* bastidor *m*

2 *adj* (**a**) *(surface)* llano(a), liso(a), plano(a); *(landscape, region)* llano(a); *(roof)* liso(a), plano(a); *(stomach)* plano(a); *(nose)* chato(a); **to be f. on one's back** *(with illness)* estar en *or* guardar cama; **lay the book f. on the desk** abre bien el libro sobre el escritorio; IDIOM **to be as f. as a pancake** *(surface)* ser más liso(a) que una tabla; *Fam (flat-chested)* ser plana *or Am* chata como una tabla; IDIOM **to go into a f. spin** *(airplane)* entrar en barrena (horizontal); *Fam Fig* no saber por dónde tirar *or RP* agarrar, *Méx* no saber ni qué ondas ►► *Br* ***f. cap*** = gorra de tela; ***f. feet:*** **to have f. feet** tener los pies planos; *Comptr* ***f. monitor*** monitor *m* de pantalla plana; ***f. race*** carrera *f* (de caballos) sin obstáculos; ***f. racing*** carreras *fpl* de caballos sin obstáculos; *Comptr* ***f. screen*** pantalla *f* plana; ***f. tyre*** rueda *f* desinflada

(**b**) *(monotonous, uneventful) (existence, atmosphere)* gris, monótono(a); *(voice)* monótono(a); *(stock market, business)* poco activo(a)

(**c**) *(soft drink, beer, champagne)* sin gas; **this beer is f.** esta cerveza ha perdido el gas

(**d**) *(categorical) (refusal, denial)* rotundo(a); **you're not going, and that's f.!** no vas, ¡y se acabó!

(**e**) *(fixed) (fare, charge)* fijo(a) ►► ***f. fee*** tarifa *f* fija; ***f. rate*** *Fin* tarifa *f* única; *Comptr* tarifa *f* plana

(**f**) *(tyre, balloon)* desinflado(a)

(**g**) *(battery)* descargado(a)

(**h**) *Mus (a semitone lower)* bemol; *(out of tune)* desafinado(a); **B f.** si bemol; **to be f.** *(singer)* desafinar; *(instrumentalist)* desafinar; *(instrument)* estar desafinado(a)

(**i**) *Comptr* ***f. file*** archivo *m* sin formato

3 *adv* (**a**) *(horizontal)* **he lay f. on the floor** estaba tumbado en el suelo; **to fall f. on one's face/back** caer(se) de bruces/caer de espaldas; **to stand f. against the wall** *(person)* pegarse a la pared; *(item of furniture)* quedar plano(a) contra la pared; **it folds up f.** se pliega, es plegable; *Fig* **the joke fell f.** el chiste no hizo mucha gracia

(**b**) *(completely)* **to turn sb down f.** rechazar a alguien de plano; **to work f. out** trabajar a tope; **to be going f. out** *(car, person, animal)* ir a tope; **she's going f. out to win the chairmanship** intentará conseguir la presidencia a toda costa; *Fam* **to be f. broke** estar sin un *Esp* duro *or Méx* quinto, *RP* estar en lampa y la vía

(**c**) *(exactly)* **in twenty seconds f.** en veinte segundos justos

(**d**) *Mus (to play, sing)* desafinadamente

flatbed ['flætbed] *n* (**a**) *(vehicle)* ***f. truck*** camión *m* (con semirremolque) de plataforma (**b**) *Comptr* ***f. scanner*** escáner *m* plano *or* de sobremesa

flatcar ['flætkɑ:(r)] *n US Rail* vagón *m* plataforma

flat-chested ['flæt'tʃestɪd] *adj* plana (de pecho)

flatfish ['flætfɪʃ] *n* pez *m* (de cuerpo) plano

flatfoot ['flætfʊt] *n US Fam (police officer)* poli *mf*, *Andes* paco(a) *m,f*, *RP* milico(a) *m,f*

flat-footed ['flæt'fʊtɪd] *adj* (**a**) *Med* **to be f.** tener (los) pies planos (**b**) *Fam (clumsy, tactless)* torpe (**c**) *Fam* **to catch sb f.** *(off guard)* pillar *or Am* agarrar desprevenido(a) a alguien

flat-hunting ['flæt'hʌntɪŋ] *n Br* búsqueda *f* de apartamento *or Esp* piso *or Arg* departamento; **f. takes up all my free time** buscar apartamento *or Esp* piso *or Arg* departamento me ocupa todo el tiempo libre

flat-leaf parsley ['flæt'li:f'pɑ:slɪ] *n* perejil *m* común

flatlet ['flætlɪt] *n Br* apartamento *m or Esp* piso *m or RP* departamento *m* pequeño

flatline ['flætlaɪn] *vi* **to be flatlining** *(patient)* tener las constantes vitales a cero; *(economy, career)* estar en punto muerto; *(machine)* estar paralizado(a)

flatly ['flætlɪ] *adv* (**a**) *(categorically) (to refuse, deny)* rotundamente, de plano (**b**) *(without emotion, monotonously) (to say, speak)* monótonamente, con monotonía

flatmate ['flætmeɪt] *n Br* compañero(a) *m,f* de apartamento *or Esp* piso *or Arg* departamento

flatness ['flætnɪs] *n* (**a**) *(of surface)* lisura *f*; *(of countryside)* llanura *f* (**b**) *(monotony, dullness) (of existence, atmosphere)* monotonía *f*; *(of voice)* monotonía *f* (**c**) *(of refusal, denial)* rotundidad *f*

flat-rate ['flæt'reɪt] *adj Comptr* ***f. connection*** *(to Internet)* conexión *f* con tarifa plana

flat-screen ['flæt'skri:n] *adj* de pantalla plana

flatten ['flætən] *vt* (**a**) *(make flat) (by squashing)* aplastar; *(ground)* allanar; **the earthquake flattened the village** el terremoto arrasó la aldea; **to f. oneself against a wall** pegarse bien contra la pared (**b**) *(knock down) (building, area)* arrasar; *Fam (in fight)* tumbar (**c**) *Mus (note)* bajar un semitono

► **flatten out 1** *vt sep (ground, surface)* allanar, aplanar; *(dents, tablecloth)* alisar; **to f. out a map on a table** extender un mapa en una mesa

2 *vi* (**a**) *(hills)* allanarse, hacerse más llano(a); *(prices)* estabilizarse, nivelarse (**b**) *(aircraft)* estabilizarse

flatter ['flætə(r)] *vt* (**a**) *(of person)* halagar, adular; **I felt flattered** me sentí halagado; **I f. myself that I am a good judge of character** me considero muy bueno a la hora de juzgar personalidades; **she flatters herself that she's a good cook** se piensa que es una buena cocinera; *Fam* **don't f. yourself!** ¡no te engañes! (**b**) *(of clothes, photo)* favorecer

flatterer ['flætərə(r)] *n* adulador(ora) *m,f*

flattering ['flætərɪŋ] *adj* (**a**) *(words)* halagador(ora); **it is f. to be asked** es halagador que te lo pidan; **I didn't get a very f. impression of the city/your boss** no me llevé una muy buena impresión de la ciudad/tu jefe (**b**) *(clothes, colour)* favorecedor(ora)

flattery ['flætərɪ] *n* halagos *mpl*; **f. will get you nowhere** con halagos no llegarás a ninguna parte *or* no tienes nada que hacer

flattop ['flætɒp] *n* **(a)** *(haircut)* corte *m* de pelo al cepillo **(b)** *US Fam* portaaviones *m inv*

flatulence ['flætjʊləns] *n Med* flatulencia *f*

flatulent ['flætjʊlənt] *adj* **(a)** *Med* flatulento(a); **to make sb f.** producirle gases a alguien **(b)** *(speech, style)* rimbombante, campanudo(a)

flatware ['flætweə(r)] *n US* **(a)** *(cutlery)* cubertería *f* **(b)** *(plates)* platos *mpl* y recipientes *mpl* planos

flatworm ['flætwɜːm] *n* (gusano *m*) platelminto *m*

flaunt [flɔːnt] *vt* hacer ostentación de, alardear de; *Fam* **if you've got it, f. it!** el que presume de algo es porque puede

flautist ['flɔːtɪst] *n Mus* flautista *mf*

flavour, *US* **flavor** ['fleɪvə(r)] **1** *n (of food)* sabor *m*; **chocolate/coffee f. ice-cream** helado con sabor a chocolate/café; **her stories have a Mediterranean f.** sus relatos tienen un sabor mediterráneo; IDIOM **to be f. of the month** *(be fashionable)* estar a la orden del día; **I'm not exactly f. of the month at head office** en la central no están lo que se dice encantados conmigo ►► ***f. enhancer*** aditivo *m* para potenciar el sabor

2 *vt (food) (with spices, herbs)* condimentar; *(with fruit, alcohol)* dar sabor con; **vanilla flavoured** con sabor a vainilla

flavourful, *US* **flavorful** ['fleɪvəfʊl] *adj* sabroso(a)

flavouring, *US* **flavoring** ['fleɪvərɪŋ] *n* aromatizante *m*; **strawberry/rum f.** esencia de fresa/ron

flavourless, *US* **flavorless** ['fleɪvəlɪs] *adj* insípido(a)

flavoursome, *US* **flavorsome** ['fleɪvəsəm] *adj* sabroso(a)

flaw [flɔː] **1** *n (in diamond, plan)* defecto *m*, *Esp* fallo *m*, *Am* falla *f*; *(in personality)* defecto *m*

2 *vt (sb's character)* manchar; *(beauty, object)* estropear, afear

flawed [flɔːd] *adj (object, argument)* defectuoso(a); *(work of art)* imperfecto(a); *(character)* con defectos

flawless ['flɔːlɪs] *adj (reasoning, logic)* impecable; *(plan, figure, complexion)* perfecto(a); **to speak in f. English** hablar un inglés perfecto

flawlessly ['flɔːlɪslɪ] *adv* impecablemente, a la perfección

flax [flæks] *n* lino *m*

flaxen ['flæksən] *adj* **f. hair** pelo muy rubio

flay [fleɪ] *vt* **(a)** *(skin)* desollar **(b)** *(flog)* despellejar, desollar; **I'll f. him alive!** ¡lo voy a despellejar vivo! **(c)** *(criticize) (person)* despellejar, desollar; *(performance, movie)* hacer trizas

flea [fliː] *n (insect)* pulga *f*; IDIOM *Fam* **to send sb away with a f. in his ear** echar a alguien una buena reprimenda *or Esp* bronca, *RP* dar a alguien un buen rezongo ►► ***f. circus*** circo *m* de pulgas amaestradas; ***f. collar*** (collar *m*) antiparasitario *m*; ***f. market*** mercadillo *m* callejero, rastro *m*

fleabag ['fliːbæg] *n Fam* **(a)** *Br (person)* piojoso(a) *m,f*; *(animal)* pulgoso(a) *m,f* **(b)** *US (hotel)* hotel *m* de mala muerte

fleabite ['fliːbaɪt] *n* picadura *f* de pulga

flea-bitten ['fliːbɪtən] *adj Fam (shabby)* mugriento(a)

flea-pit ['fliːpɪt] *n Br Fam (cinema)* cine *m* de mala muerte, cine *m* de barrio

fleck [flek] **1** *n* **(a)** *(of colour)* mota *f* **(b)** *(of dust, paint)* mota *f*; *(of mud)* mota *f*, salpicadura *f*

2 *vt* **(a)** *(with colour, sunlight)* motear (**with** de) **(b)** *(with mud)* salpicar; **flecked with paint** con gotas de pintura

flecked [flekt] *adj (bird, cloth)* moteado(a) (**with** de); **hair f. with grey** pelo jaspeado de canas

fled *pt & pp of* **flee**

fledged [fledʒd] *adj (bird)* con plumas, plumado

fledgling ['fledʒlɪŋ] **1** *n* **(a)** *(young bird)* polluelo *m* **(b)** *(person)* novato(a) *m,f*

2 *adj (poet)* novel; *(lawyer)* con poca experiencia; *(company, state)* naciente

flee [fliː] (*pt & pp* **fled** [fled]) **1** *vi* huir (**from** de); **they fled to safety** corrieron a ponerse a salvo

2 *vt (person, danger, temptation)* huir de; **he fled the country** huyó del país

fleece [fliːs] **1** *n* **(a)** *(of sheep)* vellón *m* **(b)** *(material) (sheepskin)* corderito *m*, borreguillo *m*; *(synthetic)* forro *m* polar **(c) f. (jacket)** forro *m* polar

2 *adj (gloves, scarf, hat)* polar

3 *vt* **(a)** *Fam (cheat)* desplumar; *(overcharge)* clavar, *Méx* desplumar, *RP* afanar **(b)** *(shear) (sheep)* esquilar

fleece-lined ['fliːs'laɪnd] *adj (with sheepskin)* forrado(a) de corderito *or* borreguillo; *(with synthetic material)* con *or* de forro polar

fleecy ['fliːsɪ] *adj* algodonoso(a)

fleet [fliːt] **1** *n* **(a)** *(of ships)* flota *f*; **fishing/merchant f.** flota pesquera/mercante ►► *US* ***f. admiral*** almirante *mf* de la flota **(b)** *(of taxis, buses)* flota *f*

2 *adj Literary (rapid)* raudo(a), ligero(a); **f. of foot** alígero(a)

fleet-footed ['fliːt'fʊtɪd] *adj Literary* alígero(a)

fleeting ['fliːtɪŋ] *adj* fugaz; **for a f. moment** por un breve instante, por un momento fugaz; **we caught a f. glimpse of her** sólo logramos atisbarla fugazmente

fleetingly ['fliːtɪŋlɪ] *adv* fugazmente, por un momento

fleetness ['fliːtnɪs] *n Literary* ligereza *f*; **f. of foot** ligereza de paso

Fleming ['flemɪŋ] *n* flamenco(a) *m,f*

Flemish ['flemɪʃ] **1** *n (language)* flamenco *m*

2 *npl* **the F.** *(people)* los flamencos

3 *adj* flamenco(a)

flesh [fleʃ] *n* **(a)** *(of person, animal)* carne *f*; **there's not much f. on her** no tiene mucha chicha; **in the f.** en persona; **to add f. to** *or* **put f. on one's argument** darle mayor peso a los argumentos de uno; **to make sb's f. creep** *or* **crawl** darle escalofríos a alguien; **his own f. and blood** los de su misma sangre; IDIOM **I'm only f. and blood, you know** soy sólo de carne y hueso, no soy una máquina; IDIOM **it's more than f. and blood can bear** *or* **stand** va más allá de lo humanamente soportable ►► ***f. wound*** herida *f* superficial

(b) *(of fruit)* pulpa *f*

(c) *Rel* carne *f*; **the pleasures/sins of the f.** los placeres/pecados de la carne; **(the spirit is willing but) the f. is weak** el espíritu está pronto, pero la carne es débil

►**flesh out** *vt sep (plan, remarks)* definir, precisar

flesh-coloured, *US* **flesh-colored** ['fleʃkʌləd] *adj* color carne *inv*

flesh-eating ['fleʃiːtɪŋ] *adj (dinosaur, insect)* carnívoro(a)

fleshpots ['fleʃpɒts] *npl Hum* antros *mpl* de lujuria y perdición

fleshy ['fleʃɪ] *adj* **(a)** *(person)* rollizo(a); *(limb)* carnoso(a) **(b)** *(fruit)* carnoso(a); *(leaf)* carnoso(a)

fleur-de-lis, fleur-de-lys [flɜːdə'liː] (*pl* **fleurs-de-lis** *or* **fleurs-de-lys** [flɜːdə'liː]) *n* flor *f* de lis

flew *pt of* **fly**[4]

flex [fleks] **1** *n Br (cable)* cable *m*, cordón *m*

2 *vt (one's arms, knees)* flexionar; **to f. one's muscles** flexionar los músculos; *Fig* **they are flexing their muscles** están haciendo una demostración de fuerza

flexibility [fleksɪ'bɪlɪtɪ] *n* **(a)** *(of object, material)* flexibilidad *f* **(b)** *(of person, plan, attitude)* flexibilidad *f*

flexible ['fleksɪbəl] *adj* **(a)** *(object, material)* flexible **(b)** *(person, plan, attitude)* flexible; **f. working hours** horario de trabajo flexible; **f. working practices** flexibilidad laboral ►► ***f. mortgage*** hipoteca *f* flexible; *Mil* ***f. response*** réplica *f* flexible

flexibly ['fleksɪblɪ] *adv* con flexibilidad

flexitime ['fleksɪtaɪm] *n* horario *m* flexible

flibbertigibbet ['flɪbətɪdʒɪbɪt] *n Fam* cabeza *mf* loca

flick [flɪk] **1** *n* **(a)** *(movement) (of finger)* toba *f*; **give the table a quick f. with a duster** da una pasada rápida a la mesa con el trapo del polvo; **a f. of the wrist** *(in tennis)* un golpe de muñeca; **at the f. of a switch** con sólo apretar un botón ►► *Br* ***f. knife*** navaja *f* automática

(b) *Br Fam Old-fashioned (movie)* peli *f*; **the flicks** *(cinema)* el cine

2 *vt* **(a)** *(hit lightly) (with finger)* dar una toba a; *(with hands, tail)* sacudir; **he flicked the horse with his whip** dio un golpe de fusta al caballo; **to f. a switch** pulsar un interruptor; **he flicked the cigarette ash onto the floor** tiró *or Am* botó la ceniza del cigarrillo al suelo; **she flicked the hair out of her eyes** se quitó *or* apartó el pelo de los ojos

(b) *(move quickly)* **the snake's tongue flicked in and out** la serpiente sacaba y metía la lengua rápidamente

►**flick off** *vt sep* **(a)** *(light, computer)* apagar **(b)** *(with finger) (ash, dust)* sacudir; **Dobbin flicked the flies off with his tail** Dobbin se sacudía las moscas con el rabo

►**flick on** *vt sep* **(a)** *(light, computer)* encender, *Am* prender **(b)** *(ball)* pasar al primer toque

►**flick through** *vt insep (book, magazine)* hojear, echar un vistazo a; **to f. through the channels** *(on TV)* cambiar de un canal a otro, hacer zapping

flicker ['flɪkə(r)] **1** *n (of flame, light, eyelids)* parpadeo *m*; **the f. of the TV screen** el parpadeo de la pantalla; **a f. of hope** un rayo de esperanza; **a f. of interest** un atisbo de interés; **she searched his face for a f.**

of recognition examinó su rostro buscando algún indicio *or* alguna muestra de que la reconocía; **a f. of a smile** un atisbo de sonrisa

2 *vi (flame, light, eyelids)* parpadear; *(instrument needle)* oscilar; **a smile flickered on** *or* **across his lips** sus labios dibujaron una ligera sonrisa

flickering ['flɪkərɪŋ] *adj (light)* parpadeante; *(image)* parpadeante; **the f. fire** el resplandor oscilante de la lumbre; **a f. hope** un incierto rayo de esperanza

flick-on ['flɪkɒn] *n (in soccer)* pase *m* al primer toque

flier, flyer ['flaɪə(r)] *n* (**a**) *(pilot)* piloto *mf*

(**b**) *(passenger)* **she's a nervous f.** se pone muy nerviosa cuando viaja en avión

(**c**) *(leaflet)* hoja *f* de propaganda

(**d**) *Fam (in race)* **to get a f.** salir disparado(a)

(**e**) *Fam (fall)* **to take a f.** resbalar y caer; **he slipped on a wet patch and took a f. into the freezer cabinet** resbaló en el suelo mojado y aterrizó en el congelador

(**f**) *US Fam (speculative venture)* operación *f* arriesgada; **it's a bit of a f., don't you think?** es un poco arriesgado, ¿no crees?

flight [flaɪt] *n* (**a**) *(act of flying)* vuelo *m*; **it's two hours' f. from Chicago** está a dos horas de vuelo desde Chicago; **to be in f.** estar volando; *Fig* **a f. of fancy** un vuelo de la imaginación ►► ***f. crew*** tripulación *f* de vuelo; ***f. deck*** *(of plane)* cabina *f* del piloto; *(of aircraft carrier)* cubierta *f* de vuelo; ***f. engineer*** mecánico(a) *m,f* de vuelo, ingeniero(a) *m,f* de a bordo; *Br* ***f. lieutenant*** teniente *mf* de aviación; ***f. log*** diario *m* de vuelo; ***f. mechanic*** mecánico(a) *m,f* de vuelo; ***f. path*** ruta *f* de vuelo; ***f. plan*** plan *m* de vuelo; ***f. recorder*** caja *f* negra; ***f. sergeant*** sargento *mf* de aviación; ***f. simulator*** simulador *m* de vuelo; ***f. time*** duración *f* de(l) vuelo

(**b**) *(journey by plane)* vuelo *m*; **my f. is at 2.15** mi vuelo sale a las 2.15; **f. BA 314 from/to Madrid** vuelo BA 314 procedente de/con destino Madrid; **how was your f.?** ¿cómo ha ido el vuelo? ►► ***f. attendant*** auxiliar *mf* de vuelo; ***f. bag*** bolso *m or* bolsa *f* de viaje; ***f. number*** número *m* de vuelo

(**c**) *(group) (of birds)* bandada *f*; *(of aircraft)* escuadrilla *f*; *Fig* **in the top f.** con los mejores, entre la élite

(**d**) *(of stairs)* **f. (of stairs)** tramo *m* (de escalera); **two flights up from me** dos pisos más arriba

(**e**) *(escape)* huida *f*, fuga *f*; **to put sb to f.** poner a alguien en fuga; **to take f.** darse a la fuga ►► *Fin* ***f. of capital*** fuga *f* de capital

(**f**) *(on arrow, dart)* pluma *f*, aleta *f*

flight-feather ['flaɪt'feðə(r)] *n (of bird)* pluma *f* de vuelo

flightless ['flaɪtlɪs] *adj* no volador(ora)

flighty ['flaɪtɪ] *adj* inconstante, voluble

flimflam ['flɪmflæm] *n Fam* rollos *mpl*, historias *fpl*

flimsily ['flɪmzɪlɪ] *adv* con poca solidez

flimsiness ['flɪmzɪnɪs] *n* (**a**) *(of structure)* lo endeble, la poca solidez (**b**) *(of material, dress)* ligereza *f* (**c**) *(of evidence, argument)* inconsistencia *f*; *(of excuse)* pobreza *f*

flimsy ['flɪmzɪ] **1** *adj* (**a**) *(structure)* endeble (**b**) *(material, dress)* ligero(a) (**c**) *(evidence, argument)* inconsistente, poco sólido(a); *(excuse)* probre

2 *n (paper)* finura *f*

flinch [flɪntʃ] *vi* (**a**) *(with pain)* estremecerse; *(with shock)* dar un respingo; **without flinching** sin inmutarse (**b**) *(shy away)* **to f. from (doing) sth** echarse atrás a la hora de (hacer) algo

fling [flɪŋ] **1** *n* (**a**) *Fam (attempt, try)* **to give sth a f., to have a f. at sth** intentar *or* probar algo; **he had given French a f. a few years before** había probado aprender francés unos años atrás

(**b**) *Fam (affair)* aventura *f*; **to have a f. (with sb)** tener una aventura (con alguien)

(**c**) *Fam (period of pleasure)* juerga *f*; **to have a f.** echar una cana al aire; **to have a final f.** echar una última cana al aire

2 *vt* (*pt & pp* **flung** [flʌŋ]) (**a**) *(throw)* arrojar, tirar; **don't just f. it, aim when you throw** cuando lo lances apunta, no lo tires de cualquier manera; **f. it in the dustbin** tíralo a la basura; **she flung the windows wide open** abrió las ventanas de par en par; **to f. one's arms around sb** rodear a alguien con los brazos; **he flung himself into an armchair** se dejó caer de golpe en un sillón; **I flung a few things into a suitcase** metí unas cosas rápidamente en una maleta; **he flung himself off the top of the cliff** se arrojó *or* tiró por el precipicio; **she was flinging insults at us** nos lanzaba insultos; IDIOM **to f. sth in sb's face** *(past mistake, promise)* echar algo en cara a alguien

(**b**) *(commit)* **to f. oneself into a campaign** meterse de lleno en una campaña; **she flung herself at him** se echó en sus brazos

► **fling about** *vt sep* **he flung his arms about wildly** *(fighting)* lanzaba golpes al aire en todas direcciones; *(gesticulating)* hacía aspavientos con vehemencia; *Fig* **to f. one's money about** derrochar *or* despilfarrar el dinero

► **fling down** *vt sep (object)* tirar, *Andes, CAm, Carib, Méx* botar, *Andes, CAm, Méx* aventar; **to f. down a challenge to sb** retar a alguien

► **fling off** *vt sep* (**a**) *(coat, dress)* quitarse rápidamente (**b**) *(attacker)* librarse de (**c**) *(casual remarks)* dejar caer; **to f. sth off** *(poem, article)* escribir algo en un periquete

► **fling out** *vt sep* (**a**) *(throw out) (object)* tirar, *Am* botar; *(person)* echar (**b**) *(extend)* **to f. out one's arm** extender el brazo rápidamente; **to f. out one's fist** lanzar un puñetazo

► **fling up** *vt sep* **he flung up his hands in horror** se echó las manos a la cabeza

flint [flɪnt] *n* (**a**) *(stone)* sílex *m inv*, pedernal *m* (**b**) *(of lighter)* piedra *f*

flintlock ['flɪntlɒk] *n* fusil *m (de chispa)*

flinty ['flɪntɪ] *adj* (**a**) *(soil)* silíceo(a) (**b**) *(person, stare)* duro(a), despiadado(a); *(heart)* duro(a), de piedra; *(manner)* arisco(a)

flip [flɪp] **1** *n* (**a**) *(flick)* **to give sth a f.** dar la vuelta a algo *(de un golpecito)*; *Fam* **the f. side** *(of record)* la cara B; *Fig (of situation)* la otra cara de la moneda ►► ***f. chart*** flip chart *m*, pizarra *f* de conferencia *(con bloc)*; ***f. top*** tapa *f* abatible (**b**) *(somersault)* salto *m* mortal, voltereta *f*

2 *vt* (*pt & pp* **flipped**) **to f. the switch** dar al interruptor; **to f. a coin** lanzar una moneda al aire; **we flipped a coin to decide who went** echamos a suertes quién iría; IDIOM *Fam* **to f. one's lid** *or US* **wig** *(get angry)* ponerse hecho(a) una fiera, *Esp* cabrearse; *(go mad)* volverse loco *or Esp* majara; *(get excited) Esp* desmadrarse, *Col, Méx, Ven* alebrestarse, *RP* pirarse; IDIOM *US* **to f. sb the bird** *(gesture at)* = hacerle un gesto grosero a alguien con el dedo corazón hacia arriba, ≃ hacerle un corte de mangas a alguien

3 *vi Fam (get angry)* ponerse hecho(a) una fiera *or Méx* como agua para chocolate; *(go mad)* volverse loco *or Esp* majara; *(get excited) Esp* desmadrarse, *Col, Méx, Ven* alebrestarse, *RP* pirarse

4 *adj Fam (flippant)* pasota

5 *exclam Fam* ¡cachis!

► **flip out** *vi Fam (get angry)* ponerse hecho(a) una fiera *or Méx* como agua para chocolate; *(go mad)* volverse loco *or Esp* majara; *(get excited) Esp* desmadrarse, *Col, Méx, Ven* alebrestarse, *RP* pirarse

► **flip over** **1** *vt sep (pancake)* dar la vuelta a; *(boat)* volcar; *(pages)* pasar

2 *vi (turn over) (boat)* volcar(se); *(car)* dar una vuelta de campana

► **flip through** *vt insep (book, magazine)* hojear, echar un vistazo a

flip-flop ['flɪpflɒp] **1** *n* (**a**) *Br (sandal)* chancleta *f*, chancla *f* (**b**) *Elec & Comptr* biestable *m*, flip-flop *m* (**c**) *(somersault)* voltereta *f* hacia atrás (**d**) *US Fam (in attitude, policy)* cambio *m* radical, giro *m* de 180°; **to do a f. (over sth)** cambiar radicalmente de idea (respecto a algo), dar un giro de 180° (respecto a algo)

2 *vi US Fam* cambiar radicalmente de idea

flippancy ['flɪpənsɪ] *n (of person, remark)* frivolidad *f*

flippant ['flɪpənt] *adj (person, remark)* frívolo(a); **he was just being f.** estaba en plan frívolo

flippantly ['flɪpəntlɪ] *adv* frívolamente, con ligereza

flipper ['flɪpə(r)] *n* (**a**) *(of seal, penguin, whale)* aleta *f* (**b**) *(for swimming)* aleta *f*

flipping ['flɪpɪŋ] *Br Fam* **1** *adj (for emphasis)* condenado(a), *Esp* puñetero(a), *Méx* pinche, *Col, RP* de miércoles; **get that f. dog out of here!** ¡saca de aquí al condenado perro este!; **f. heck!** ¡puñeta!, *Méx* ¡híjole!, *Col, RP, Ven* ¡miércoles!

2 *adv (for emphasis)* condenadamente, puñeteramente; **it was f. sore!** ¡dolía que no veas!; **don't f. well talk to me like that!** ¡a mí no se te ocurra hablarme así!

flip-top ['flɪptɒp] *adj (packet)* duro(a)

flirt [flɜːt] **1** *n (man)* ligón *m*, mariposón *m*; *(woman)* ligona *f*, coqueta *f*

2 *vi* (**a**) *(sexually)* flirtear, coquetear (**with** con) (**b**) *(entertain)* **to f. with danger/an idea** coquetear con el peligro/una idea

flirtation [flɜː'teɪʃən] *n* (**a**) *(coquetry)* coqueteo *m*, flirteo *m*; *(liaison)* flirt *m*, *Esp* ligue *m*, *RP* historia *f* (**b**) *(engagement)* **he had a brief f. with Communism/politics** tuvo un fugaz devaneo con el comunismo/la política

flirtatious [flɜː'teɪʃəs] *adj* coqueto(a)

flirtatiously [flɜː'teɪʃəslɪ] *adv* de un modo coqueto

flirty ['flɜːtɪ] *adj* coqueto(a)

flit [flɪt] **1** *n Fam* (**a**) *Br* **to do a (moonlight) f.** *(move house)* mudarse de casa a escondidas (**b**) *Scot (move house)* mudarse

2 *vi* (*pt & pp* **flitted**) **to f. about** *(bird)* revolotear; **people flitted in**

and out of his office había gente entrando y saliendo de su oficina; **an idea flitted into my mind** una idea me revoloteaba por la cabeza; *Fig* **to f. from one thing to another** saltar de una cosa a otra; **to f. from woman to woman/job to job** ir de mujer en mujer/de trabajo en trabajo

flitch [flɪtʃ] *n (of pork)* pieza *f*

float [fləʊt] **1** *n* **(a)** *(on fishing line, net)* flotador *m*, corcho *m*; *(on raft, seaplane)* flotador *m*; *(as swimming aid)* flotador *m*
(b) *(in toilet cistern)* boya *f*; *(in carburettor)* flotador *m*
(c) *(in procession)* carroza *f*
(d) *Br* **(milk) f.** = furgoneta eléctrica para el reparto de leche
(e) *Com (supply of change)* reserva *f* de cambio
(f) *US (raft)* plataforma *f* flotante
(g) *US (drink)* = refresco con un helado flotando
2 *vt* **(a)** *(ship, raft, platform)* flotar; **the timber is floated downstream to the mill** la madera llega al molino flotando río abajo
(b) *(idea, proposal)* lanzar
(c) *Fin (bonds, share issue)* flotar, lanzar al mercado; **they decided to f. the company** *(on Stock Exchange)* decidieron que la empresa comenzara a cotizar en bolsa
(d) *Fin (currency)* hacer flotar
3 *vi* **(a)** *(on water)* flotar; **the logs floated down the river** los troncos bajaron flotando por el río; **the bottle floated out to sea** la botella flotó hacia el mar; **the diver floated slowly up to the surface** el submarinista se dejó llevar lentamente hasta la superficie
(b) *(in the air) (feather)* volar; *(mist, cloud)* estar suspendido(a); *(ghost, apparition)* flotar; **music floated in through the open window** la música entraba por la ventana abierta; **she floated out of the room** se deslizó fuera de la habitación; **he seems to f. through life** *(has no worries)* parece que vive en una nube
(c) *Fin (currency)* flotar

▶**float about, float around** *Fam* **1** *vt insep (of object)* estar *or* andar por; *(of person)* dar vueltas por
2 *vi* andar por ahí; **have you seen my keys floating about** *or* **around?** ¿has visto por ahí mis llaves?; **there's a rumour floating about** *or* **around that...** se dice *or* rumorea por ahí que...

floatation = **flotation**

floater ['fləʊtə(r)] *n US* **(a)** *(multiple voter)* = elector que vota más de una vez en una misma elección **(b)** *(person who often changes jobs)* = persona que cambia de empleo con frecuencia

floating ['fləʊtɪŋ] *adj* **(a)** *(on water)* flotante ▸▸ ***f. dock*** dique *m* flotante
(b) *(mobile) (population)* fluctuante, flotante ▸▸ ***f. kidney*** riñón *m* flotante; ***f. rib*** costilla *f* flotante; *Br Pol* ***f. voter*** votante *mf* indeciso(a)
(c) *Fin (exchange rate)* flotante ▸▸ ***f. capital*** capital *m* circulante; *Br Com* ***f. charge*** garantía *f* flotante
(d) *Comptr* ***f. palette*** paleta *f* flotante; ***f. point*** coma *f* flotante; ***f. point processor*** procesador *m* de coma flotante; ***f. point unit*** unidad *f* de coma flotante; ***f. window*** paleta *f* flotante

floating-point ['fləʊtɪŋ'pɔɪnt] *adj Comptr* de coma flotante ▸▸ ***f. processor*** procesador *m* de coma flotante

floating-rate ['fləʊtɪŋ'reɪt] *adj Fin* con interés flotante

flock [flɒk] **1** *n* **(a)** *(of sheep)* rebaño *m*; *(of birds)* bandada *f* **(b)** *(of people)* tropel *m*; **they came in flocks** vinieron en tropel *or* en masa; **a f. of tourists** un tropel de turistas **(c)** *Rel (congregation)* rebaño *m*, grey *f* **(d)** *(fibre)* **f. wallpaper** papel pintado con relieve
2 *vi (gather, move)* acudir en tropel; **people flocked to see it** la gente acudió en masa para verlo, se formaron verdaderas multitudes para verlo; **audiences are flocking in** el público está acudiendo en masa *or* en tropel; **the fans flocked around him** un tropel de fans lo rodeó, una multitud de fans se apelotonó a su alrededor

floe [fləʊ] *n* témpano *m* (de hielo)

flog [flɒg] *(pt & pp* **flogged**) *vt* **(a)** *(beat)* azotar; IDIOM *Fam* **you're flogging a dead horse** te estás esforzando inútilmente; IDIOM *Fam* **to f. a subject to death** agotar completamente un tema **(b)** *Br Fam (sell)* enchufar, vender

flogging ['flɒgɪŋ] *n (beating)* azote *m*, flagelación *f*; **he was given a f.** lo azotaron

flood [flʌd] **1** *n* **(a)** *(of water)* inundación *f*; **the F.** *(in the Bible)* el diluvio (universal); **he caused a f. in the bathroom** inundó el baño; **the f. waters receded** el agua empezó a bajar; **to be in f.** *(river)* sufrir una crecida; **to be in full f.** *(river)* estar desbordado ▸▸ ***f. barrier*** barrera *f* contra las inundaciones; ***f. damage*** daños *mpl* causados por las inundaciones; ***f. plain*** llanura *f* aluvial; ***f. warning*** peligro *m* de inundación
(b) *(of applications, letters, offers)* lluvia *f*; *(of light)* **a f. of light poured into the room** el cuarto se inundó de luz; **floods of tears** un mar de lágrimas; **to be in floods of tears** llorar a mares, estar hecho(a) un mar de lágrimas
(c) *(tide)* pleamar *f*
(d) *(floodlight)* foco *m*, reflector *m*
2 *vt* **(a)** *(land, bathroom, market)* inundar; **the river flooded its banks** el río se desbordó
(b) *Aut (carburettor, engine)* ahogar
(c) *(swamp)* **to be flooded with complaints/calls** recibir un aluvión de quejas/llamadas telefónicas; **to be flooded with applications/offers** recibir una lluvia de solicitudes/ofertas; **to be flooded in light** *(room, valley)* estar inundado(a) de luz
(d) *Com* **to f. the market (with sth)** inundar el mercado (con algo)
3 *vi* **(a)** *(river)* desbordarse
(b) *Aut (carburettor, engine)* ahogarse
(c) *(move in large quantities)* **the populace flooded into the streets** el pueblo salió a la calle en tropel, el pueblo llenó las calles; **the sun's rays came flooding through the window** el sol entraba a raudales por la ventana; **new energy was flooding through his veins** una nueva energía le fluía por las venas

▶**flood back** *vi (memories)* **suddenly it all came flooding back** de repente volvía a revivirlo todo

▶**flood out 1** *vt sep (people) (from homes)* salir en tropel de, salir en masa de
2 *vi (people, words)* salir en tropel, salir en masa; **the spectators flooded out of the stadium** los espectadores salían en masa del estadio; **money flooded out of the country** el dinero salió a raudales del país

floodgate ['flʌdgeɪt] *n* compuerta *f*; IDIOM **to open the floodgates to sth** abrir las puertas de par en par a algo; **the new law will open the floodgates to all kinds of fraudulent practices** la nueva ley allanará el terreno a toda clase de práctica fraudulenta

flooding ['flʌdɪŋ] *n* inundaciones *fpl*

floodlight ['flʌdlaɪt] **1** *n* foco *m*, reflector *m*
2 *vt (pt & pp* **floodlit** ['flʌdlɪt] *or* **floodlighted**) iluminar con focos *or* reflectores

floodlighting ['flʌdlaɪtɪŋ] *n* iluminación *f* con focos *or* reflectores

floodlit ['flʌdlɪt] *adj* iluminado(a) con focos *or* reflectores; **a f. match** un partido con luz artificial

floodtide ['flʌdtaɪd] *n* pleamar *f*, marea *f* alta

floodwall ['flʌdwɔːl] *n* dique *m*

floor [flɔː(r)] **1** *n* **(a)** *(of room)* suelo *m* ▸▸ ***f. covering*** revestimiento *m* para suelos; *US* ***f. lamp*** lámpara *f* de pie; ***f. plan*** (plano *m* de) planta *f*; ***f. polish*** cera *f* para suelos; ***f. polisher*** *(machine)* enceradora *f*; ***f. show*** espectáculo *m* de variedades; ***f. space*** superficie *f* comercial, superficie *f* de venta; **let's push back the furniture so we have more f. space** vamos a retirar los muebles para tener más espacio; ***f. tile*** losa *f*, baldosa *f*; ***f. wax*** cera *f* para suelos
(b) *(bottom part) (of lift, cage)* suelo *m*; *(of forest)* suelo *m*; *(of ocean)* fondo *m*
(c) *(storey) (of building)* piso *m*, planta *f*; **on the first f.** *Br* en el primer piso, en la primera planta; *US* en la planta baja ▸▸ ***f. manager*** *(in store)* gerente *mf* de planta; *(of TV show)* regidor(ora) *m,f*
(d) *(for dancing)* pista *f*; **shall we take the f.?** ¿salimos a la pista?
(e) *(in parliament, assembly)* **the f. of the House** ≃ el hemiciclo; **to give sb the f.** *(in debate)* pasar *or* dar la palabra a alguien; **to take the f.** levantarse para tomar la palabra; **questions from the f.** preguntas del público; *Br Parl* **to cross the f. of the House** cambiar de partido ▸▸ *US* ***f. leader*** portavoz *mf (de un partido, en el Congreso o el Senado)*
(f) *(of Stock Exchange)* parquet *m* ▸▸ *US* ***f. broker*** corredor(ora) *m,f* de parquet *(para un tercero)*; *US* ***f. trader*** corredor(ora) *m,f* de parquet independiente
2 *vt* **(a)** *(building, house) (with carpet) Esp* enmoquetar, *Am* alfombrar, *RP* moquetear; *(with tiles)* embaldosar; **to f. a room with parquet/linoleum** poner parquet/linóleo en la habitación
(b) *(knock down)* derribar; **that virus really floored me** ese virus me dejó realmente por los suelos *or* hecho polvo
(c) *Fam (puzzle, baffle)* **the question floored him** la pregunta lo dejó patidifuso *or* perplejo

floorboard ['flɔːbɔːd] *n* tabla *f* del suelo *(de tarima)*; **to take the floorboards up** levantar las tablas del suelo

floorcloth ['flɔːklɒθ] *n (for cleaning)* trapo *m* del suelo

flooring ['flɔːrɪŋ] *n* suelo *m*, solado *m*

floor-through ['flɔːθruː] *adj US* **this is a f. apartment** este apartamento *or Esp* piso *or Arg* departamento ocupa toda la planta

floorwalker ['flɔːwɔːkə(r)] *n US* jefe(a) *m,f* de sección *or* planta

floozie, floozy ['flu:zɪ] *n Fam* pelandusca *f*

flop [flɒp] **1** *n* (**a**) *(failure)* fracaso *m* (**b**) *US Fam (place to sleep)* pensión *f* de mala muerte

2 *vi* (*pt & pp* **flopped**) (**a**) *(fall slackly)* dejarse caer; **she flopped into the chair** se dejó caer sobre el sillón; **her hair flopped across her face** el pelo le azotaba el rostro; **the fish flopped about on the deck** el pez rebotaba sobre la cubierta (**b**) *(fail)* fracasar

3 *adv Fam* **it went f. into the water** y plaf, se cayó al agua; **the plan went f.** el plan se fastidió

flophouse ['flɒphaʊs] *n US Fam* pensión *f* de mala muerte

floppy ['flɒpɪ] **1** *adj* (**a**) *(ears)* caído(a); *(garments)* flojo(a); *(collar, hat)* blando(a), flexible (**b**) *Comptr* ***f. disk*** disquete *m*; ***f. (disk) drive*** unidad *f* de disquetes, disquetera *f*

2 *n Comptr* disquete *m*

flora ['flɔ:rə] *n (plant life)* flora *f*; **f. and fauna** flora y fauna

floral ['flɔ:rəl] *adj* floral; **f. wreath/fabric** corona/tela de flores ►► ***f. tribute*** corona *f* de flores

Florence ['flɒrəns] *n* Florencia

Florentine ['flɒrəntaɪn] **1** *adj* florentino(a)

2 *n* (**a**) *(person)* florentino(a) *m,f* (**b**) *(biscuit)* = galleta hecha con frutos secos y cubierta de chocolate

florescence [flə'resəns] *n Bot* florescencia *f*

floret ['flɒrɪt] *n* (**a**) *Bot* flósculo *m* (**b**) **broccoli/cauliflower florets** cogollos de brécol/coliflor

florid ['flɒrɪd] *adj* (**a**) *(style)* florido(a) (**b**) *(complexion)* colorado(a)

Florida ['flɒrɪdə] *n* Florida ►► ***the F. Keys*** los cayos de Florida; ***the F. Strait*** el estrecho de Florida

Floridian [flə'rɪdɪən] **1** *n* floridano(a) *m,f*

2 *adj* floridano(a)

florin ['flɒrɪn] *n* (**a**) *Formerly (British)* florín *m* (**b**) *(Dutch)* florín *m*

florist ['flɒrɪst] *n* florista *mf*; **f.'s (shop)** floristería *f*

floss [flɒs] **1** *n* (**a**) *(of cocoon)* cadarzo *m* (**b**) **(dental) f.** hilo *m* dental

2 *vt* **to f. one's teeth** limpiarse los dientes con hilo dental

3 *vi* limpiarse (los dientes) con hilo dental

flossy ['flɒsɪ] *adj* (**a**) *(resembling floss)* algodonoso(a) (**b**) *US Fam (showy)* llamativo(a)

flotation [fləʊ'teɪʃən] *n* (**a**) *(in water)* flotación *f* ►► ***f. tank*** cámara *f* de balneoterapia; ***f. therapy*** balneoterapia *f*, talasoterapia *f* (**b**) *Com (of company)* salida *f* a bolsa; *(of share issue)* emisión *f*

flotilla [flə'tɪlə] *n* flotilla *f*

flotsam ['flɒtsəm] *n* **f. (and jetsam)** desechos *mpl* arrojados por el mar; *Fig* **the f. of the war/of society** los desechos de la guerra/de la sociedad

flounce [flaʊns] **1** *n* (**a**) *(in sewing)* volante *m*, *Chile* vuelo *m*, *RP, Ven* volado *m* (**b**) *(of indignation, impatience)* **with a f. of her skirt, she marched out of the room** salió de la habitación indignada/impaciente con un revuelo de faldas

2 *vi* **to f. in/out/off** entrar/salir/irse haciendo aspavientos

flounced [flaʊnst] *adj (skirt)* avolantado(a)

flounder ['flaʊndə(r)] **1** *n (fish)* platija *f*

2 *vi* (**a**) *(in water, mud)* debatirse; **the dolphin was floundering about in a few inches of water** el delfín nadaba con dificultad en unos centímetros de agua (**b**) *(in speech, lecture)* **somehow he floundered through his speech** a trancas y barrancas logró dar su discurso; **the economy is still floundering** la economía no consigue levantar cabeza

flour ['flaʊə(r)] **1** *n* harina *f* ►► ***f. improver*** = aditivo conservante para la harina del pan

2 *vt* enharinar

flourish ['flʌrɪʃ] **1** *n* (**a**) *(gesture)* ademán *m* floriturescο; **with an elaborate f. of his hat** con una reverencia exagerada con el sombrero (**b**) *(musical, in writing)* floritura *f*; *(in signature)* rúbrica *f*; **a f. of trumpets** un toque de trompetas

2 *vt (brandish)* blandir

3 *vi (thrive) (plant, person)* crecer con vigor; *(business, arts)* florecer; *(economy)* prosperar

flourishing ['flʌrɪʃɪŋ] *adj (plant)* vigoroso(a), lozano(a); *(business, economy)* próspero(a), floreciente

floury ['flaʊrɪ] *adj* (**a**) *(hands, surface)* lleno(a) de harina, enharinado(a); *(roll)* con harina encima (**b**) *(in texture) (potatoes)* harinoso(a)

flout [flaʊt] *vt (rule, sb's authority)* desobedecer; *(tradition, convention)* romper con

flow [fləʊ] **1** *n* (**a**) *(of liquid, electricity)* flujo *m*; *(of river)* corriente *f*, flujo *m*; *(of air)* corriente *f*

(**b**) *(amount, movement) (of goods, supplies)* circulación *f*; **the f. of traffic** la circulación; *Fin* **the free f. of capital** la libre circulación de capital; **a steady f. of tourists** un movimiento constante de turistas; *Fig* **the speaker was interrupted in full f.** el orador fue interrumpido en pleno discurso; *Fig* **to go against the f.** ir a contracorriente; *Fig* **to go with the f.** seguir la corriente ►► ***f. chart*** organigrama *m*; ***f. diagram*** organigrama *m*

(**c**) *(course, progression) (of prose, novel, piece of music)* fluidez *f*; **to follow the f. of an argument** seguir el hilo de un razonamiento; **the f. of the narrative** la fluidez del hilo narrativo

(**d**) *(of the tide)* flujo *m*

2 *vi* (**a**) *(liquid, electricity, air)* correr, fluir; **a river flows through the city** un río atraviesa la ciudad; **blood was flowing from the wound** la sangre salía de la herida; **to f. into the sea** *(river)* desembocar en el mar; *Fig* **the wine flowed freely** había vino para dar y vender

(**b**) *(traffic, crowd)* circular; *Fin (capital, money)* circular; *(ideas, conversation)* fluir; **to keep the conversation flowing** mantener viva la conversación

(**c**) *(hair, dress)* caer

(**d**) *(prose)* ser fluido(a); **this essay doesn't f. very well** el estilo de este ensayo no es muy fluido

(**e**) *(tide)* subir, crecer

(**f**) **to f. from** *(be the result of)* derivarse de

► **flow in** *vi* (**a**) *(water, liquid)* entrar (**b**) **offers are flowing in** están lloviendo las ofertas

► **flow out** *vi* (**a**) *(water, liquid)* salir (**b**) *(people, crowds)* salir en masa

flower ['flaʊə(r)] **1** *n* (**a**) *(plant, blossom)* flor *f*; **to be in f.** estar en flor; **to come into f.** florecer; **no flowers by request** *(at funeral)* se ruega no envíen flores ►► ***f. arranging*** arte *m or* decoración *f* floral; ***f. garden*** jardín *m* floral; ***f. girl*** = dama de honor de corta edad que lleva un ramo de flores en una boda; ***f. people*** hippies *mpl* pacifistas; ***f. power*** movimiento *m* pacifista hippie; ***f. show*** exposición *f* de flores

(**b**) *(best part)* **the f. of the nation's youth** el retoño de la juventud de la nación; **in the first f. of youth** en la flor de la juventud

2 *vi* (**a**) *(plant, tree)* florecer (**b**) *(artistic movement, talent)* florecer

flowerbed ['flaʊəbed] *n* parterre *m*

flowered ['flaʊəd] *adj (dress, pattern)* de flores, floreado(a)

flowering ['flaʊərɪŋ] *adj (plant, tree) (which flowers)* que da flores; *(in flower)* en flor ►► ***f. cherry*** cerezo *m* japonés

flowerpot ['flaʊəpɒt] *n* tiesto *m*, maceta *f*

flowery ['flaʊərɪ] *adj* (**a**) *(fabric, dress)* floreado(a) (**b**) *(perfume, wine)* de flores; *(smell)* de flores (**c**) *(prose, compliments)* florido(a)

flowing ['fləʊɪŋ] *adj* (**a**) *(beard, hair)* suelto(a) (**b**) *(prose, movement)* fluido(a)

flow-meter ['fləʊmi:tə(r)] *n* aforador *m*, caudalímetro *m*

flown *pp of* **fly**[4]

fl. oz. (*abbr* = **fluid ounce(s)**) onza *f* líquida *(Br = 28,4 ml; US = 29,6 ml)*

flu [flu:] *n* gripe *f*, *Am* gripa *f*; **a dose of the f.** una gripe *or Am* gripa

flub [flʌb] (*pt & pp* **flubbed**) *US Fam* **1** *n* metedura *f* de pata, pifia *f*

2 *vt* pifiarla con

3 *vi* meter la pata, pifiarla

fluctuate ['flʌktjʊeɪt] *vi* fluctuar

fluctuation [flʌktjʊ'eɪʃən] *n* fluctuación *f*

flue [flu:] *n* (**a**) *(of heater)* salida *f* de humos; *(of chimney)* tiro *m* (**b**) *Mus (of organ)* **f. (pipe)** tubo *m*

fluency ['flu:ənsɪ] *n* (**a**) *(in speaking, writing)* fluidez *f*; **f. in French required** *(in job advert)* se requiere dominio del francés (**b**) *(movement)* fluidez *f*

fluent ['flu:ənt] *adj* (**a**) *(in a foreign language)* **he is f. in French, he speaks f. French** habla francés con fluidez *or* soltura; **he replied in f. Urdu** contestó con fluidez *or* soltura en urdu; **he's a f. speaker of Italian** habla italiano con mucha fluidez *or* soltura (**b**) *(delivery, style)* fluido(a) (**c**) *(movement)* fluido(a)

fluently ['flu:əntlɪ] *adv* (**a**) *(to speak, write)* con soltura (**b**) *(to move)* con fluidez

fluey ['flu:ɪ] *adj Br Fam* griposo(a)

fluff [flʌf] **1** *n* (**a**) *(material)* pelusa *f*; *(down) (on kitten, baby's head)* pelusa *f*; *(on baby bird)* plumón *m* (**b**) *Fam* **a bit of f.**, *US* **a f.** una *Esp* chorba *or Méx* vieja *or RP* mina (**c**) *Br Fam (mistake)* metedura *f* de pata, pifia *f*

2 *vt Fam (botch)* hacer muy mal; *(lines)* decir mal; **to f. one's entrance** entrar torpemente; *Sport* **to f. a shot** pifiar el tiro

► **fluff out, fluff up** *vt sep (pillow)* mullir; *(feathers)* ahuecar

fluffy ['flʌfɪ] *adj (towel, spongecake, pastry)* esponjoso(a); *Br (toy)* de peluche

fluid ['flu:ɪd] 1 *n* fluido *m*; **to be on fluids** *(patient)* estar tomando sólo líquidos

2 *adj* (a) *(substance)* fluido(a) ►► ***f. dynamics*** dinámica *f* de fluidos; ***f. ounce*** onza *f* líquida *(Br = 28,4 ml; US = 29,6 ml)* (b) *(flowing) (movement)* fluido(a); *(match)* dinámico(a) (c) *(liable to change) (plans, ideas)* inconcreto(a); **a f. situation** una situación inestable

fluidity [flu:'ɪdɪtɪ] *n* (a) *(of substance)* fluidez *f* (b) *(of movement)* fluidez *f*; *(of match)* dinamismo *m* (c) *(of plans, ideas)* inconcreción *f*; *(of situation)* instabilidad *f*

fluke[1] [flu:k] *n Fam (stroke of luck)* chiripa *f*; **by a f.** de chiripa

fluke[2] *n (flatworm)* trematodo *m*

fluk(e)y ['flu:kɪ] *adj Fam (lucky)* suertudo(a)

flume [flu:m] *n (at swimming pool)* tobogán *m*

flummery ['flʌmərɪ] *n* (a) *(dessert)* = postre frío hecho con harina de avena (b) *Fam (pompous nonsense)* palabrería *f*

flummox ['flʌməks] *vt Fam* desconcertar

flung *pt & pp of* **fling**

flunk [flʌŋk] *US Fam* 1 *vt Esp* catear, *Am* reprobar, *Méx* tronar, *RP* desaprobar

2 *vi Esp* catear, *Am* reprobar, *Méx* tronar, *RP* desaprobar

► **flunk out** *vi US Fam* ser expulsado(a) *(por malas notas)*

flunkey ['flʌŋkɪ] *n Fam Pej* lacayo *m*

fluorescence [flʊə'resəns] *n* fluorescencia *f*

fluorescent [flʊə'resənt] *adj* fluorescente ►► ***f. light*** (luz *f*) fluorescente *m*

fluoridate ['flʊərɪdeɪt], **fluoridize** ['flʊərɪdaɪz] *vt* fluorar

fluoridation [flʊərɪ'deɪʃən] *n* fluoración *f*

fluoride ['flʊəraɪd] *n* fluoruro *m* ►► ***f. toothpaste*** dentífrico *m* con fluoruro

fluoridize = **fluoridate**

fluorine ['flʊəri:n] *n Chem* flúor *m*

fluorite ['flʊəraɪt] *n Geol* fluorina *f*, fluorita *f*

fluorocarbon ['flʊərəʊ'kɑ:bən] *n Chem* fluorocarburo *m*

flurried ['flʌrɪd] *adj* aturullado(a); **to get f.** aturullarse

flurry ['flʌrɪ] *n* (a) *(of snow, wind)* torbellino *m* (b) **a f. of activity** un torbellino *or* frenesí de actividad; **to be in a f. of excitement** estar todo(a) aturullado(a)

flush [flʌʃ] 1 *n* (a) *(redness of face)* rubor *m*, sonrojo *m*; **to bring a f. to sb's cheeks** *(compliment, crude joke)* hacer ruborizar *or* sonrojar a alguien; *(wine)* hacer que alguien se ponga colorado(a)

(b) *(beginning)* **in the first f. of youth** en la primera juventud; **in the first f. of enthusiasm** en el primer momento de entusiasmo

(c) *(in cards)* color *m*

(d) *(toilet mechanism)* cisterna *f*, cadena *f*; **to pull the f., to give the toilet a f.** tirar de la cadena

2 *adj* (a) *(even)* **the door is f. with the wall** la puerta no sobresale de la pared (b) *Fam (person)* **to be f.** estar *or* andar bien de dinero (c) *Comptr & Typ* **f. left/right** alineado(a) a la izquierda/derecha

3 *vt* (a) *(cheeks, face)* **the exercise had flushed their cheeks** tenían las mejillas sonrojadas *or* coloradas por el ejercicio (b) *(toilet)* **to f. the toilet** tirar de la cadena; **to f. sth down the toilet** tirar algo por el váter (c) *(birds, game)* levantar

4 *vi* (a) *(blush)* ruborizarse, sonrojarse; **to f. with embarrassment** sonrojarse *or* ruborizarse de vergüenza (b) *(toilet)* **the lavatory isn't flushing properly** la cisterna (del váter) no funciona bien

► **flush away** 1 *vt sep* tirar *or Am* botar al váter, tirar por el váter

2 *vi* irse al tirar de la cadena

► **flush out** *vt sep* (a) *(clean out) (container)* limpiar; *(pipe)* purgar; *(dirt, waste)* limpiar (b) *(force to emerge) (animal, person in hiding)* hacer salir, sacar; *(truth)* revelar

flushed [flʌʃt] *adj (face)* ruborizado(a); **f. with** *(joy, pride)* rebosante de; *(success)* enardecido(a) por

fluster ['flʌstə(r)] 1 *n* **to be in a f.** estar nervioso(a); **to get in a f.** ponerse nervioso(a), aturullarse

2 *vt* poner nervioso(a), aturullar; **to get flustered** ponerse nervioso(a), aturullarse

3 *vi* **he doesn't f. easily** no se pone nervioso *or* no se aturulla fácilmente

flute [flu:t] *n* (a) *(musical instrument)* flauta *f* (traversera) (b) *(glass)* copa *f* de flauta *or* de champán (c) *Archit (groove on column)* estría *f*

fluted ['flu:tɪd] *adj* (a) *Archit* acanalado(a), estriado(a) (b) ***f. glass*** vidrio *m* ondulado

fluting ['flu:tɪŋ] *n Archit* acanaladura *f*

flutist ['flu:tɪst] *n US Mus* flautista *mf*

flutter ['flʌtə(r)] 1 *n* (a) *(of wings)* aleteo *m*; *(of eyelids)* parpadeo *m*; **with a f. of her eyelashes** pestañeando con coquetería ►► ***f. kick*** *(in swimming)* patada *f* de crol

(b) *Fam (nervous state)* **to be all in** *or* **of a f.** estar todo(a) agitado(a); **in a f. of excitement** en un revuelo de emoción

(c) *Br Fam (bet)* apuesta *f*; **to have a f.** hacer una pequeña apuesta; **to have a f. on the horses/Stock Exchange** probar suerte en los caballos/la bolsa

(d) *Elec (in hi-fi system)* oscilación *f*

(e) *Med (of heart)* palpitaciones *fpl*

2 *vt* **to f. its wings** *(bird)* batir las alas; **she fluttered her eyelashes at him** lo miró pestañeando con coquetería

3 *vi* (a) *(birds, insects)* revolotear; **to f. away** marcharse revoloteando

(b) *(flag)* agitarse; *(wings)* agitarse

(c) *(fall) (leaves, paper)* **the letter fluttered to the ground** la carta revoloteó hasta acabar en el suelo

(d) *(person)* revolotear; **to f. in/out** entrar/salir revoloteando

(e) *(heart)* palpitar rápidamente; IDIOM **to make sb's heart f.** hacer palpitar el corazón de alguien, *RP* dar taquicardia a alguien

flutterboard ['flʌtəbɔ:d] *n US, Austr* corcho *m*

fluvial ['flu:vɪəl] *adj* fluvial

flux [flʌks] *n* (a) *(constant change)* **in a state of f.** *(universe)* en constante fluctuación; *(situation, government)* en constante cambio (b) *Phys* flujo *m* ►► ***f. density*** densidad *f* de flujo (c) *Med* flujo *m* (d) *Tech (in soldering)* fundente *m*

fly[1] [flaɪ] *n* (a) *(of trousers)* **f., flies** bragueta *f*; **his f. is** *or* **flies are open** *or* **undone** lleva la bragueta bajada *or* abierta (b) *(entrance to tent)* puerta *f*; *(covering for tent)* doble techo *m* (c) ***f. half*** *(in rugby)* medio *m* (de) apertura, apertura *mf* (d) *Theat* **the flies** bambalinas

fly[2] *Br Fam* 1 *n* **to do sth on the f.** *(craftily, secretively)* hacer algo de tapadillo *or Esp* de extranjis

2 *adj (cunning)* astuto(a), listo(a)

fly[3] *n* (a) *(insect)* mosca *f* ►► ***f. agaric*** amanita *f* muscaria, falsa oronja *f*

(b) *(for fishing)* mosca *f*

(c) IDIOMS **he wouldn't hurt a f.** es incapaz de matar una mosca; **they were dropping like flies** caían como moscas *or* chinches; **a f. in the ointment** un pero, *Esp* una pequeña pega; *Fam* **there are no flies on him** se las sabe todas; **I wish I could be a f. on the wall** me encantaría espiar por un agujerito

fly[4] *(pt* **flew** [flu:], *pp* **flown** [fləʊn]) 1 *vt* (a) *(plane, helicopter)* pilotar; **to f. Concorde** *(pilot)* pilotar el Concorde; *(passenger)* volar en Concorde; **to f. Air India** volar con Air India

(b) *(transport) (troops)* aerotransportar; *(passengers)* transportar *(por aire)*; *(goods)* mandar por avión

(c) *(route, distance)* cubrir; **to f. the Atlantic** *(pilot, passenger, plane)* cruzar el Atlántico

(d) *(combat mission)* **you had to f. twenty missions before being eligible for leave** tenías que participar en veinte misiones aéreas para tener derecho a un permiso

(e) *(kite)* volar; **the ship/town hall was flying the Polish flag** la bandera polaca ondeaba en el barco/ayuntamiento; IDIOM **to f. the flag** *(be patriotic)* defender los (propios) colores

(f) *(flee)* huir de, escapar de; **to f. the nest** *(bird, child)* volar del *or* abandonar el nido; IDIOM *Fam* **to f. the coop** *(escape)* ahuecar el ala

2 *vi* (a) *(bird, plane)* volar; *(arrow, bullet, missile)* volar; *(passenger)* ir en avión, volar; **to f. over London** sobrevolar Londres; **to f. across the Atlantic** cruzar el Atlántico en avión; **have you ever flown** *Br* **in** *or US* **with Concorde?** ¿has ido *or* volado alguna vez en Concorde?; **he flies for an American airline** trabaja de piloto para una compañía aérea americana; **which airline did you f. with?** ¿con qué compañía volaste?; **this plane flies well** este avión es fácil de pilotar; **the trapeze artist flew through the air** la trapecista voló por los aires; *Fig* **to be flying high** *(doing well)* estar en un muy buen momento; IDIOM **to f. by the seat of one's pants** hacer las cosas a base de intuición

(b) *(flag, hair)* ondear; *(kite)* volar

(c) *(in wind) (coat, hair)* ondear

(d) *(move quickly) (person)* ir volando; *(time)* pasar volando; **I must f.** tengo que salir volando; **she flew down the stairs** bajó las escaleras volando *or* como una exhalación; **she flew out of the room** salió volando *or* como una exhalación de la habitación; **he came flying round the corner** dobló la esquina a toda velocidad; **sparks/dust flew into the air** saltaron chispas por los aires/se levantó una polvareda; *Literary* **he flew to her rescue** corrió a rescatarla; **the door flew open** la puerta se abrió de golpe; **his hat went flying across the room** su sombrero voló por los aires y cruzó la habitación; *Fam* **to send** *or* **knock sth/sb flying** mandar algo/a alguien por los aires; **to f. into a rage** *or* **temper** enfurecerse, ponerse hecho(a) una furia; **to f. in the face of sth** ir totalmente en contra de algo; **to f. in the face of reason** ir en contra de la razón; IDIOM *Fam* **to f. off the handle** perder los estribos

(**e**) *(attack)* **to f. at sb** lanzarse sobre alguien; **to let f. at** *(physically, verbally)* emprenderla *or* arremeter contra

3 *n* (**a**) *(in aircraft)* **to go for a f.** ir a dar una vuelta en avión (**b**) *US* ***f. ball*** *(in baseball)* fly *m*, = bola golpeada hacia lo alto y a lo lejos (**c**) *US Fam* **on the f.** *(ball)* por el aire; **to live on the f.** ir siempre escopeteado(a)

▸ **fly about** *vi* (**a**) *(bird, insect)* revolotear (**b**) *(rumours, accusations)* correr

▸ **fly away** *vi* (**a**) *(bird)* salir volando; *(plane, pilot)* despegar (**b**) *(papers)* volarse

▸ **fly by** *vi (time, days)* pasar volando

▸ **fly in** 1 *vt sep (transport by aircraft)* traer *(por aire)*
2 *vi (arrive by aircraft)* llegar *(por aire)*

▸ **fly into** *vt insep* aterrizar; **which airport are you flying into?** ¿a qué aeropuerto vuelas?

▸ **fly off** 1 *vt sep* (**a**) *(from oil rig, island)* sacar *(por aire)*; *(evacuate)* evacuar (**b**) *(transport by plane)* transportar *(por aire)*
2 *vi* (**a**) *(bird, insect)* alejarse volando; *(plane, person)* volar (**b**) *(leave quickly)* irse corriendo, salir volando (**c**) *(hat)* volar por los aires, salir volando; *(lid, button)* salir disparado(a)

▸ **fly out** 1 *vt sep (transport by aircraft)* transportar *(por aire)*
2 *vi* (**a**) *(leave by aircraft)* salir *(por aire)*; **which airport did you f. out of?** ¿desde qué aeropuerto saliste *or* volaste? (**b**) *(come out quickly) (from hand, box, pocket)* salir disparado(a)

▸ **fly past** *vi* (**a**) *(plane, bird)* pasar volando (**b**) *(time, days)* pasar volando

flyaway ['flaɪəweɪ] *adj (hair)* suelto(a)

flyblown ['flaɪbləʊn] *adj* (**a**) *(food)* infestado(a) de moscarda (**b**) *(shabby)* mugriento(a)

fly-boy ['flaɪbɔɪ] *n US Fam* piloto *m* de las fuerzas aéreas

fly-by ['flaɪbaɪ] (*pl* **fly-bys**) *n* (**a**) *(of spacecraft)* acercamiento *m*, sobrevuelo *m* orbital de un astro (**b**) *US* desfile *m* aéreo

fly-by-night ['flaɪbaɪnaɪt] *Fam Pej* 1 *n* pirata *mf*, = empresa o empresario que no es de fiar
2 *adj (company)* nada fiable *or Am* confiable

fly-by-wire ['flaɪbaɪ'waɪə(r)] *adj Av* fly-by-wire, controlado(a) por señales electrónicas

flycatcher ['flaɪkætʃə(r)] *n (bird)* papamoscas *m inv*

fly-drive ['flaɪ'draɪv] *n* **f. (holiday)** vacaciones *fpl* con vuelo y alquiler de coche *or Am* carro *or RP* auto incluido

flyer = **flier**

fly-fish ['flaɪfɪʃ] *vi* pescar con mosca

fly-fishing ['flaɪfɪʃɪŋ] *n* pesca *f* con mosca; **to go f.** ir a pescar con mosca

flying ['flaɪɪŋ] 1 *n* **she loves f.** le encanta volar; **to be afraid of f.** tener miedo a ir en avión ▸▸ ***f. boat*** hidroavión *m*; ***f. circus*** *(group)* escuadrón *m* de acrobacias aéreas; *(exhibition)* espectáculo *m* de acrobacias aéreas; ***f. club*** aeroclub *m*; ***f. hours*** horas *fpl* de vuelo; ***f. lessons*** lecciones *fpl* de vuelo; *Old-fashioned* ***f. machine*** máquina *f* voladora, aeroplano *m*; ***f. officer*** ≃ teniente *mf* de aviación; ***f. suit*** traje *m* de vuelo; ***f. time*** horas *fpl* de vuelo

2 *adj* (**a**) *(in flight, capable of flight)* volador(ora); IDIOM **to pass an exam with f. colours** aprobar un examen con muy buena nota ▸▸ *Hist* ***f. bomb*** bomba *f* volante *(en la Segunda Guerra Mundial)*; ***f. buttress*** arbotante *m*; ***f. doctor*** = médico que hace uso del avión o del helicóptero para visitar a pacientes en zonas remotas o de difícil acceso; *Mythol* ***the F. Dutchman*** el holandés errante; ***f. fish*** pez *m* volador; ***f. fox*** panique *m*; ***f. saucer*** platillo *m* volante; ***f. squirrel*** ardilla *f* voladora

(**b**) *(rapid, energetic)* **f. leap** *or* **jump** salto con carrerilla; **to get off to a f. start** *(runner)* salir bien; *Fig (person, project, campaign)* comenzar con muy buen pie ▸▸ ***f. tackle*** placaje *m* en plancha

(**c**) *(mobile) Mil* ***f. column*** columna *f* volante; ***f. picket*** piquete *m* volante; ***f. squad*** brigada *f* volante

(**d**) *(visit)* ***f. visit*** visita *f* relámpago

flyleaf ['flaɪli:f] (*pl* **flyleaves** ['flaɪli:vz]) *n (of book)* guarda *f*

Flymo® ['flaɪməʊ] *n* = cortacésped que funciona mediante una corriente de aire

fly-on-the-wall ['flaɪɒnðə'wɔ:l] *adj* **a f. documentary** = un documental en el que la cámara actúa con la mayor discreción posible para mostrar un retrato realista

flyover ['flaɪəʊvə(r)] *n* (**a**) *Br* paso *m* elevado (**b**) *US* desfile *m* aéreo

flypaper ['flaɪpeɪpə(r)] *n* papel *m* atrapamoscas

fly-past ['flaɪpɑ:st] *n Br Av* desfile *m* aéreo

flyposting ['flaɪpəʊstɪŋ] *n Br* = fijar carteles en lugares donde no está permitido

flysheet ['flaɪʃi:t] *n (of tent)* doble techo *m*

flyspeck ['flaɪspek] *n* (**a**) *(of fly)* cagada *f* de mosca (**b**) *(tiny spot)* mota *f*

flyspray ['flaɪspreɪ] *n* (espray *m*) matamoscas *m inv*

flyswat ['flaɪswɒt], **flyswatter** ['flaɪswɒtə(r)] *n* matamoscas *m inv*

fly-tipping ['flaɪtɪpɪŋ] *n Br* vertido *m* ilegal (de residuos)

flytrap ['flaɪtræp] *n Bot* atrapamoscas *m inv*

flyweight ['flaɪweɪt] *n (in boxing)* peso *m* mosca

flywheel ['flaɪwi:l] *n Tech* volante *m (de motor)*

flywhisk ['flaɪwɪsk] *n* matamoscas *m inv (con forma de cepillo)*

FM [ef'em] *n Rad* (*abbr* **frequency modulation**) FM *f*

FMCG [efemsi:'dʒi:] *n Com* (*abbr* **fast-moving consumer goods**) productos *mpl* de venta rápida

f-number ['efnʌmbə(r)] *n Phot* número *m* f

FO [ef'əʊ] *n Br Pol* (*abbr* **Foreign Office**) Ministerio *m* de Asuntos Exteriores *or Am* Relaciones Exteriores

foal [fəʊl] 1 *n* potro *m*, potrillo *m*; **to be in f.** estar preñada
2 *vi* parir

foam [fəʊm] 1 *n* (**a**) *(on beer, sea)* espuma *f*; *(at mouth)* espuma *f*; **a f. bath** un baño de espuma *or* con burbujas (**b**) *(used in fire-fighting)* espuma *f* (**c**) *(for padding, packing)* espuma *f* ▸▸ ***f. rubber*** gomaespuma *f*
2 *vi (sea, beer)* hacer espuma; **to f. at the mouth** echar espuma por la boca

▸ **foam up** *vi* hacer espuma

foamy ['fəʊmɪ] *adj* espumoso(a)

fob [fɒb] *n (chain)* cadena *f* (de reloj), leontina *f*; *(on keyring)* colgante *m* (de llavero) ▸▸ ***f. watch*** reloj *m* de bolsillo

▸ **fob off** (*pt & pp* **fobbed**) *vt sep Fam* **to f. sb off with sth** quitarse a alguien de encima con algo; **to f. sth off on sb** colocarle *or* encasquetarle algo a alguien

f.o.b. *Com* (*abbr* **free on board**) f.a.b., f.o.b.

focal ['fəʊkəl] *adj* (**a**) *Phys & Phot* focal ▸▸ ***f. distance*** distancia *f* focal; ***f. length*** distancia *f* focal; ***f. plane*** plano *m* focal; ***f. point*** *(of lens)* foco *m* (**b**) *(most important)* central; ***f. point*** *(centre of attraction)* núcleo *m*, foco *m* de atención

foci *pl of* **focus**

fo'c'sle = **forecastle**

focus ['fəʊkəs] 1 *n* (*pl* **focuses** *or* **foci** ['fəʊkaɪ]) (**a**) *(of lens)* foco *m*; **in f.** *(binoculars, camera, projector)* enfocado(a); *(picture, image)* (bien) enfocado(a); **out of f.** *(binoculars, camera, projector)* desenfocado(a); *(picture, image)* desenfocado(a), mal enfocado(a); **to bring an image into f.** enfocar una imagen; *Fig* **let's try and get the problem into f.** vamos a intentar definir claramente el problema

(**b**) *(of interest)* foco *m*; *(of discussion)* tema *m*; **the issue became a f. of people's discontent** el tema se convirtió en un exponente del descontento de la gente; **the f. of the conference is on human rights** el tema central de la conferencia son los derechos humanos; **she was the f. of attention** fue el centro de la atención; **the government is trying to shift the f. of the debate** el gobierno está intentando desviar el énfasis del debate ▸▸ *Com & Pol* ***f. group*** grupo *m* muestra

(**c**) *Med (of infection)* foco *m*

2 *vt* (*pt & pp* **focussed** *or* **focused**) (**a**) *Phys (rays of light)* enfocar
(**b**) *(camera, microscope)* enfocar
(**c**) *(eyes)* **he couldn't f. his eyes** no podía enfocar la mirada; **all eyes were focused on him** todas las miradas estaban centradas en él
(**d**) *(one's interest, energy)* concentrar (**on** en); *(attention)* centrar (**on** en)

3 *vi* (**a**) *(camera, microscope)* enfocar (**b**) *(with eyes)* enfocar la vista (**on** en) (**c**) *(concentrate)* **to f. on sth** *(debate, speaker)* centrarse en algo

focussed ['fəʊkəst] *adj* **she's very f.** tiene muy claro lo que quiere

fodder ['fɒdə(r)] *n (for animal)* forraje *m*; *Fig* **this is f. for the tabloids** esto da mucho que hablar a la prensa sensacionalista

FOE [efəʊ'i:] *n* (*abbr* **Friends of the Earth**) Amigos *mpl* de la Tierra

foe [fəʊ] *n* enemigo(a) *m,f*

foetal, *US* **fetal** ['fi:təl] *adj* fetal ▸▸ ***f. distress*** sufrimiento *m* fetal; ***f. position*** posición *f* fetal

foetus, *US* **fetus** ['fi:təs] *n* feto *m*

fog [fɒg] 1 *n* (**a**) *(mist)* niebla *f* ▸▸ ***f. bank*** banco *m* de niebla; *Aut* ***f. lamp*** faro *m* antiniebla; *Aut* ***f. light*** faro *m or* luz *f* antiniebla (**b**) *(mental)* **to be in a f.** *(confused)* estar confuso(a), encontrarse confundido(a) (**c**) *Phot (on film, negative)* velo *m*

2 *vt* (**a**) *(glass, mirror)* empañar (**b**) *(confuse)* confundir (**c**) *Phot (film, negative)* velar

3 *vi* (**a**) **to f. (over** *or* **up)** *(glass, mirror)* empañarse (**b**) *Phot (film, negative)* velarse

fogbound ['fɒgbaʊnd] *adj (port, airport)* paralizado(a) por la niebla

fogey, fogy ['fəʊgɪ] *(pl* **fogeys, fogies***)* *n Fam* **old f.** carroza, *Am* carcamán; *Hum* **young f.** nene(a) carca

fogeyish ['fəʊgɪɪʃ] *adj Fam* carca, carroza

foggy ['fɒgɪ] *adj* (**a**) *(misty)* neblinoso(a); **a f. day** un día de niebla; **it's f.** hay (mucha) niebla ▸▸ *Fam* ***F. Bottom*** = apelativo usado para referirse al Ministerio de Asuntos Exteriores estadounidense (**b**) IDIOM *Fam* **I haven't (got) the foggiest (idea)!** ¡no tengo ni la menor *or* ni la más remota idea!

foghorn ['fɒghɔ:n] *n (on ship)* sirena *f* de niebla; IDIOM **a voice like a f.** un vozarrón

fogy = **fogey**

foible ['fɔɪbəl] *n* manía *f*

foie gras ['fwa:'gra:] *n* **(pâté de) f.** foie-gras *m*

foil [fɔɪl] 1 *n* (**a**) *(tinfoil)* papel *m* de aluminio, *Esp* papel *m* Albal® (**b**) *(counterweight, contrast)* contrapunto *m*; **to act as a f. (to** *or* **for)** servir de contrapunto (a *or* para) (**c**) *(sword)* florete *m* (**d**) *(hydrofoil)* hidroaleta *f*

2 *vt (thwart)* frustrar, malograr; *Hum* **(curses!,) foiled again!** (¡maldición!) ¡he fallado nuevamente!

foist [fɔɪst] *vt* (**a**) *(unload)* **to f. sth on sb** endosar algo a alguien (**b**) *(impose on)* imponer (**on** a); **he foisted himself on us for the weekend** se nos colocó en casa durante todo el fin de semana

fold[1] [fəʊld] *n* **(sheep) f.** redil *m*; IDIOM **to return to the f.** volver al redil

fold[2] 1 *n* (**a**) *(crease)* pliegue *m*; **folds of fat** pliegues de grasa (**b**) *Geol* pliegue *m*

2 *vt (cloth, paper)* doblar; *(chair, table)* plegar; **to f. sth in two** *or* **in half** doblar algo por la mitad; **she sat with her legs folded under her** se sentó sobre los talones; **she sat with her hands folded in her lap** se sentó con las manos recostadas sobre el regazo; **the bird folded its wings** el pájaro dobló *or* cerró las alas; **to f. one's arms** cruzarse de brazos; **he folded her in his arms** la estrechó entre sus brazos

3 *vi* (**a**) *(chair, table)* plegarse (**b**) *Fam (business)* quebrar

▸ **fold away** 1 *vt sep* plegar

2 *vi (chair, table)* plegarse

▸ **fold back** 1 *vt sep (sheets)* doblar; *(sleeves)* remangar; *(shutters, partition)* plegar

2 *vi (shutters, partition)* plegarse

▸ **fold down** *vt sep (sheet)* doblar (hacia fuera); **he folded down a corner of the page** dobló una esquina de la página

▸ **fold in** *vt sep Culin* incorporar

▸ **fold up** 1 *vt sep* doblar

2 *vi (map, chair)* plegarse

-fold [fəʊld] *suffix* **it's a six/twelve-f. increase** se ha multiplicado por seis/doce

foldaway ['fəʊldəweɪ] *adj* plegable

folder ['fəʊldə(r)] *n* (**a**) *(file, document wallet)* carpeta *f*; *(ring binder)* carpeta *f* de anillas (**b**) *Comptr* carpeta *f*

folding ['fəʊldɪŋ] *adj* (**a**) *(chair, table)* plegable ▸▸ ***f. doors*** puertas *fpl* plegables (**b**) *Fam* ***f. money*** billetes *mpl*

foldout ['fəʊldaʊt] *n (in a book)* (página *f*) desplegable *m*

foliage ['fəʊlɪɪdʒ] *n* follaje *m*

folic acid ['fɒlɪk'æsɪd] *n Biochem* ácido *m* fólico

folio ['fəʊlɪəʊ] *(pl* **folios***)* *n* (**a**) *(of paper)* folio *m*; *Typ (page number)* folio *m* (**b**) *(book)* libro *m* en folio, infolio *m* (**c**) *(paper size)* folio *m*

folk [fəʊk] 1 *npl Fam* (**a**) *(people)* gente *f*; **the f. I work with** la gente con la que trabajo; **most folk(s) just want a quiet life** la mayor parte de la gente quiere una vida tranquila; **old/young folk(s)** los viejos/la gente joven; **city/country folk(s)** la gente de ciudad/campo; **hi folks!** ¡qué hay! (**b**) **my/your folks** *(family)* mi/tu familia, mi/tu gente; *US (parents)* mis/tus padres

2 *n (music)* música *f* folk *or* popular

3 *adj (traditional)* ***f. art*** artesanía *f* popular *or* tradicional; ***f. dance*** baile *m* popular *or* regional; ***f. etymology*** etimología *f* popular; ***f. hero*** héroe *m* popular; ***f. medicine*** medicina *f* tradicional; ***f. memory*** acervo *m* popular, memoria *f* de la gente; ***f. music*** música *f* folk *or* popular; ***f. rock*** folk rock *m*; ***f. singer*** cantante *mf* de folk; ***f. song*** canción *f* folk *or* tradicional; ***f. tale*** cuento *m* popular

folklore ['fəʊklɔ:(r)] *n* folclor *m*, folclore *m*

folklorist ['fəʊklɔ:rɪst] *n* folklorista *mf*

folksy ['fəʊksɪ] *adj Fam* (**a**) *US (friendly)* simpático(a) (**b**) *(simple, down-to-earth)* simplón(ona)

follicle ['fɒlɪkəl] *n* folículo *m*

FOLLOW ['fɒləʊ] 1 *vt* (**a**) *(go after) (person, path, route)* seguir; **I think we're being followed** creo que nos están siguiendo; **the road follows the coast** la carretera va a lo largo de la costa; **f. that!** ¡toma ya!, *RP* ¡ahí tenés!; **to f. suit** *(in cards)* seguir el palo; *Fig* seguir el ejemplo; IDIOM **to f. the crowd** dejarse llevar por la masa; IDIOM **to f. one's nose** *(go straight ahead)* seguir todo recto *or* derecho; *(act instinctively)* guiarse por el instinto

(**b**) *(come after)* seguir a; **in the years that followed his death** en los años posteriores a su muerte; **the news will f. this programme** a este programa le seguirán las noticias; **roast chicken followed by ice cream** pollo asado y de postre, helado

(**c**) *(be guided by) (example, fashion, instructions)* seguir; *(career)* hacer, seguir; **she followed a strict fitness regime** siguió un estricto programa de preparación física; **f. your instincts** sigue tus instintos

(**d**) *(understand)* seguir; **I don't quite f. you** no te sigo bien

(**e**) *(pay attention to)* seguir; **are you following events in Afghanistan?** ¿te mantienes al tanto de los acontecimientos en Afganistán?; **to f. a tune** seguir una melodía; **to f. sb's progress** seguir el progreso de alguien

(**f**) *(support) (team, leader)* ser de; **I f. the Bears** soy de los Bears

(**g**) *(believe in) (religion, method)* seguir

2 *vi* (**a**) *(come after)* seguir; **there follows a special newsflash** a continuación un avance informativo especial; **what followed would change the course of history** lo que siguió cambió el transcurso de la historia; **in the years that followed** en los años posteriores; **proceed as follows** proceda de la siguiente forma; **their names are as follows** sus nombres son los siguientes

(**b**) *(result)* **it follows that...** se sigue *or* deduce que...; **just because I was late once it doesn't f. that I will be again** porque llegara tarde una vez no quiere decir que lo vaya a volver hacer; **it follows from X that Y...** de X se deduce que Y...

(**c**) *(understand)* entender; **I don't f.** no (lo) entiendo

▸ **follow around** *vt sep* seguir por todas partes

▸ **follow on** *vi* continuar, seguir; **to f. on from my earlier remarks...** a lo anteriormente dicho quisiera añadir *or Am* agregar...

▸ **follow through** 1 *vt sep (argument, development)* desarrollar; **to f. a project through (to the end)** llevar a cabo un proyecto (hasta el final)

2 *vi* (**a**) *(complete task)* llegar hasta el final

(**b**) *Sport* acompañar el golpe

▸ **follow up** *vt sep* (**a**) *(advantage, success)* acrecentar; **they followed up their debut single with a platinum album** a su single de debut le siguió un disco de platino

(**b**) *(continue) (contact, job opportunity)* hacer un seguimiento de; **they didn't f. up their complaint** presentaron una queja pero no persistieron en ella; **f. up your initial phone call with a letter** confirma tu llamada inicial por escrito; **to f. up a clue** seguir una pista

---

follower ['fɒləʊə(r)] *n* (**a**) *(devotee, disciple)* seguidor(ora) *m,f*; **as followers of this programme will be aware...** como los seguidores de este programa sabrán...; **a f. of fashion** un seguidor de la moda (**b**) *(attendant)* vasallo(a) *m,f*

following ['fɒləʊɪŋ] 1 *n (of team)* seguidores *mpl*; *(of politician, political party)* partidarios *mpl*; *(of TV programme)* audiencia *f*; *(of novelist, pop group)* admiradores *mpl*

2 *pron* **the f. is the full list** a continuación figura la lista completa

3 *adj* siguiente; **on the f. day** al día siguiente; **a f. wind** un viento favorable *or* a favor

follow-my-leader ['fɒləʊmaɪ'li:də(r)], *US* **follow-the-leader** ['fɒləʊðə'li:də(r)] *n* = juego en el que los participantes han de imitar lo que hace el primero de la fila

follow-on ['fɒləʊ'ɒn] *n (continuation)* continuación *f*

follow-the-leader *US* = **follow-my-leader**

follow-through ['fɒləʊθru:] *n* (**a**) *(consolidation)* seguimiento *m*, continuidad *f* (**b**) *Sport (of stroke)* acompañamiento *m* (del golpe)

follow-up ['fɒləʊʌp] *n* (**a**) *(to event, research)* continuación *f* ►► ***f. interview*** *(for job, research)* segunda entrevista *f*; ***f. programme*** *(on TV)* continuación *f*; ***f. research*** investigación *f* complementaria (**b**) *Com (to bill, letter)* seguimiento *m*; **a f. phone call/letter** una llamada/carta de seguimiento (**c**) *Med (checkup)* revisión *f*

folly ['fɒlɪ] *n* (**a**) *(foolishness)* locura *f*; **an act of f.** una locura; **it would be (sheer) f. to continue** sería una (verdadera) locura seguir (**b**) *Archit* pequeño edificio *m* ornamental (**c**) *Theat* **follies** revista

foment [fə'ment] *vt (unrest, ill feeling)* fomentar

fond [fɒnd] *adj* (**a**) **to be f. of sb** *(like)* tener cariño *or* aprecio a alguien; **to be f. of (doing) sth** gustar a alguien (hacer) algo; **I'm very f. of sweet things** me gustan mucho los dulces; **to become f. of sb** encariñarse con alguien; **she was f. of the occasional whisky** le gustaba tomarse un whisky de vez en cuando; **he is rather too f. of the sound of his own voice** le encanta escucharse a sí mismo

(**b**) *(loving) (friend, wife, parent, embrace)* cariñoso(a); **f. memories** recuerdos entrañables; **with fondest love** *(in letter)* con mucho cariño

(**c**) *(hope, belief)* vano(a)

fondant ['fɒndənt] *n* fondant *m*

fondle ['fɒndəl] *vt* acariciar

fondly ['fɒndlɪ] *adv* (**a**) *(lovingly)* cariñosamente (**b**) *(naively)* ingenuamente; **to f. imagine that...** creer ingenuamente que...

fondness ['fɒndnɪs] *n* (**a**) *(affection)* cariño *m*, afecto *m* (**for** por) (**b**) *(liking)* afición *f* (**for** a), gusto *m* (**for** por); **to have a f. for drink** tener afición a la bebida

fondue ['fɒndu:] *n* fondue *f* ►► ***f. set*** fondue *f (utensilios)*

font [fɒnt] *n* (**a**) *Rel* pila *f* bautismal (**b**) *Typ & Comptr* tipo *m* (de letra), fuente *f*

fontanelle, *US* **fontanel** [fɒntə'nel] *n Anat* fontanela *f*

food [fu:d] *n* comida *f*; **we gave them f.** les dimos comida *or* algo de comer; **take some f. for the journey** lleva algo de comida para el viaje; **exotic/imported food(s)** alimentos exóticos/de importación; **f. and drink** comida y bebida; **to be off one's f.** estar desganado(a); **to give sb f. for thought** dar a alguien en qué pensar ►► ***f. additive*** aditivo *m* (alimentario); *Biol* ***f. chain*** cadena *f* trófica; ***f. colouring*** colorante *m* alimenticio; ***f. combining*** combinación *f* de alimentos; ***f. court*** = plaza o zona de un centro comercial dedicada al consumo de comida rápida; ***f. critic*** crítico(a) *m,f* gastronómico(a); ***f. hall*** departamento *m* de alimentación; ***f. industry*** industria *f* alimentaria; ***f. mixer*** batidora *f*; ***f. parcel*** paquete *m* de alimentos; ***f. poisoning*** intoxicación *f* alimentaria; ***f. processor*** robot *m* de cocina; *US* ***f. stamp*** = cupón que se da a gentes con bajos ingresos para la adquisición de alimentos; ***f. technology*** tecnología *f* de la alimentación; ***f. value*** valor *m* alimenticio *or* nutricional

foodie ['fu:dɪ] *n Fam* sibarita *mf* de la cocina

foodstuffs ['fu:dstʌfs] *npl* alimentos *mpl*, (productos *mpl*) comestibles *mpl*

fool[1] [fu:l] **1** *n* (**a**) *(stupid person)* idiota *mf*; **she was a f. to go/agree** cometió una estupidez al ir/acceder; **some f. of a politician** algún político idiota; **any f. could do it** cualquier necio podría hacerlo; **to play** *or* **act the f.** hacer el tonto; **to make a f. of sb** poner a alguien en ridículo; **to make a f. of oneself** hacer el ridículo; **(the) more f. you!** ¡peor para ti!; **I felt such a f.** me sentí como un tonto; **she's no** *or* **nobody's f.** no tiene un pelo de tonta; **to send sb on a f.'s errand** hacer perder el tiempo a alguien; IDIOM **they're living in a f.'s paradise** viven en las nubes; PROV **there's no f. like an old f.** no hay peor tonto que un viejo tonto; PROV **a f. and his money are soon parted** poco le dura el dinero a quien mal lo administra; PROV **fools rush in where angels fear to tread** la ignorancia es osada ►► ***f.'s gold*** pirita *f*

(**b**) *(jester)* bufón *m*

2 *adj US Fam* estúpido(a), insensato(a); **that's just the kind of f. thing he'd do** ésa es justo la típica estupidez propia de él; **that f. brother of mine** el estúpido *or* insensato de mi hermano

3 *vt (deceive)* engañar; **they had me completely fooled** me engañaron por completo; **to f. sb into doing sth** engañar a alguien para que haga algo; **he fooled me into believing it** me lo hizo creer; **(I) fooled you!** ¡te engañé!, ¡has caído!; **you can't f. me** a mí no me engañas; **he's an expert? you could have fooled me!** ¿que es un experto? ¡quién lo hubiera dicho!

4 *vi* (**a**) *(act foolishly)* hacer el tonto *or* el indio; **stop fooling!** ¡deja de hacer el tonto! (**b**) *(joke)* bromear; **I was only fooling** estaba de broma (**c**) *(trifle)* **you'd better not f. with him/me** más vale que no le/me toques mucho las narices

► **fool about, fool around** *vi* (**a**) *(act foolishly)* hacer el tonto *or* el indio

(**b**) *(fiddle)* juguetear, enredar; **to f. about** *or* **around with sth** enredar con algo

(**c**) *(waste time)* perder el tiempo

(**d**) *Fam (have affair)* tener una aventura (**with** con); **her husband was always fooling around** su marido siempre tenía algún lío de faldas

(**e**) *Fam (couple)* besuquearse, *Esp* morrearse

► **fool away** *vt sep US (money)* despilfarrar, malgastar; *(time)* malgastar

fool[2] *n Culin* = crema de frutas con nata

foolery ['fu:lərɪ] *n Fam* idioteces *fpl*, *Am* pendejadas *fpl*

foolhardiness ['fu:lhɑ:dɪnɪs] *n* temeridad *f*

foolhardy ['fu:lhɑ:dɪ] *adj* temerario(a)

foolish ['fu:lɪʃ] *adj* (**a**) *(stupid, ridiculous)* tonto(a); **to make sb look f.** dejar a alguien en ridículo; **I felt rather f.** me sentí como un idiota (**b**) *(imprudent) (decision, choice)* insensato(a), imprudente; **to do sth f.** hacer una imprudencia; **I was f. enough to believe her** fui lo suficientemente insensato *or* imprudente como para creerla

foolishly ['fu:lɪʃlɪ] *adv (to act)* irreflexivamente; **f., I agreed to do it, I f. agreed to do it** con gran imprudencia por mi parte acepté hacerlo

foolishness ['fu:lɪʃnɪs] *n (of action, decision)* estupidez *f*, imprudencia *f*; **I don't want any more f.!** ¡no quiero más tonterías!

foolproof ['fu:lpru:f] *adj (method, plan)* infalible

foolscap ['fu:lskæp] *n Br* pliego *m* común *(de 43 x 34 cm)*

foosball ['fu:zbɔ:l] *n US* fútbol *m* de mesa, *Esp* futbolín *m*, *Arg* metegol *m*, *Chile* taca-taca *m*, *Méx, Urug* futbolito *m*

FOOT [fʊt] (*pl* **feet** [fi:t]) **1** *n* (**a**) *(of person)* pie *m*; *(of animal, chair)* pata *f*; **a f. injury** una lesión en el pie; **the dog lay at her feet** el perro estaba tumbado a sus pies; **on f.** a pie, caminando, *Esp* andando; **she is on her feet all day** se pasa el día entero de pie *or Am* parada; **to be on one's feet again** *(after illness)* estar recuperado(a); **we'll soon have you back on your feet** *(better)* dentro de poco estarás recuperado; **to get to one's feet** levantarse, ponerse de pie, *Am* pararse; **to jump to one's feet** levantarse *or* ponerse de pie *or Am* pararse de un salto; **to put one's feet up** *(rest)* descansar; **I was so tired I could barely put one f. in front of the other** estaba tan cansado que apenas podía caminar; **to set f. in/on** poner los pies en ►► ***f. bath*** baño *m* de pies; ***f. brake*** freno *m* de pie; ***f. fault*** *(in tennis)* falta *f* de pie; ***f. passenger*** pasajero(a) *m,f* peatón; *Mil* ***f. patrol*** patrulla *f* de infantería; ***f. pedal*** pedal *m*; ***f. soldier*** soldado *mf* de infantería; ***f. spa*** masaje *m* para pies

(**b**) *(lower part) (of mountain, stairs, page)* pie *m*; **at the f. of** al pie de

(**c**) *(measurement)* pie *m (= 30,48 cm)*; **three f.** *or* **feet six (inches)** tres pies y seis pulgadas *(= 1,06 m)*; **at 2,000 feet** a dos mil pies *(= 609,6 m)*

(**d**) *(in poetry)* pie *m*

(**e**) IDIOMS **the job's not much, but it's a f. in the door** el trabajo no es gran cosa, pero supone un primer paso; **to find one's feet** *(in new surroundings, activity)* familiarizarse; **to get off on the right/wrong f.** empezar con buen/mal pie, *RP* empezar con el pie derecho/izquierdo; **to have feet of clay** tener (los) pies de barro; **to have a f. in both camps** tener intereses en los dos bandos; **to have one's** *or* **both feet (firmly) on the ground** tener los pies en la tierra; **to have one f. in the grave** tener un pie en la tumba; **I was out on my feet** *(exhausted)* estaba que no me tenía en pie; **she hasn't put a f. wrong** no ha cometido un solo error; *Fam* **my f.!** ¡ni loco!, *Esp* ¡y un jamón!, *Méx* ¡ni yendo a bailar a Chalma!, *RP* ¡tu abuela!; **to put one's f. down** *(be firm) Esp* ponerse serio(a), *Am* no ceder; *(refuse)* negarse *Esp* en redondo *or Am* rotundamente; *(drive faster)* apretar el acelerador, pisar fuerte; *Fam* **to put one's f. in it, to put one's f. in one's mouth** meter la pata; **we've been rushed off our feet** no hemos parado ni un instante; **we had to think on our feet** tuvimos que tomar una decisión en el momento; **the children have been under my feet all day** los niños han estado incordiándome todo el día

2 *vt* **to f. the bill** pagar la cuenta

footage ['fʊtɪdʒ] *n Cin* secuencias *fpl*; *TV* imágenes *fpl*

foot-and-mouth disease [fʊtən'maʊθdɪzi:z] *n* glosopeda *f*, fiebre *f* aftosa

football ['fʊtbɔ:l] *n* (**a**) *Br (soccer)* fútbol *m*; *(ball)* balón *m* (de fútbol) ►► ***f. club*** club *m* (de fútbol); ***f. colours*** colores *mpl* del equipo; ***f. fan*** hincha *mf*, forofo(a) *m,f*; ***f. ground*** estadio *m* de fútbol; ***f. hooligan*** hooligan *mf*, hincha *mf* violento(a); ***f. hooliganism*** hooliganismo *m*, violencia *f* futbolística; ***f. league*** liga *f* de fútbol; ***f. match*** partido *m* de fútbol; ***f. pitch*** campo *m* de fútbol; ***f. player*** futbolista *mf*; **f. *pools*** quiniela *f*; **f. *stadium*** estadio *m* de fútbol; **f. *strip*** uniforme *m* del equipo; **f. *supporter*** hincha *mf*, forofo(a) *m,f*; **f. *team*** equipo *m* (de fútbol)

(**b**) *US (American football)* fútbol *m* americano; *(ball)* balón *m* (de fútbol americano) ►► **f. *fan*** hincha *mf*, forofo(a) *m,f*; **f. *field*** campo *m* de fútbol; **f. *game*** partido *m* de fútbol americano; **f. *league*** liga *f* de fútbol americano; **f. *pitch*** campo *m* de fútbol americano; **f. *player*** futbolista *mf*, jugador(ora) *m,f* de fútbol americano; **f. *stadium*** estadio *m* de fútbol americano; **f. *supporter*** hincha *mf*, forofo(a) *m,f*; **f. *team*** equipo *m* (de fútbol americano)

(**c**) IDIOM **the abortion issue has become a political f.** el aborto se ha convertido en un tema con el que los políticos intentan marcar puntos

footballer ['fʊtbɔːlə(r)] *n* futbolista *mf*

footboard ['fʊtbɔːd] *n (on bed)* pies *mpl*

footbridge ['fʊtbrɪdʒ] *n* puente *m* peatonal

-footed ['fʊtɪd] *suffix* **swift-f.** de paso ligero

-footer ['fʊtə(r)] *suffix* **the boat is a 15-f.** la barca mide seis pies de eslora

footer ['fʊtə(r)] *n Typ* pie *m* de página

footfall ['fʊtfɔːl] *n* (**a**) *(sound)* pisada *f* (**b**) *Com (customers)* número *m* de clientes

footgear ['fʊtgɪə(r)] *n* calzado *m*

foothills ['fʊthɪlz] *npl* estribaciones *fpl*

foothold ['fʊthəʊld] *n* punto *m* de apoyo; **to gain a f.** *(climber)* afianzar el pie; *Fig* introducirse; *Com* **to get** *or* **secure a f. in a market** introducirse *or* entrar en un mercado

footie, footy ['fʊtɪ] *n Br Fam* fútbol *m*, *RP* fóbal *m*

footing ['fʊtɪŋ] *n* (**a**) *(balance)* **to lose one's f.** *(on hill, ladder)* perder el equilibrio (**b**) *(basis)* **on an equal f.** de igual a igual; **on a sound financial f.** con una base económica sólida; **on a war f.** en pie de guerra; **to be on a friendly f. with sb** tener buenas relaciones con alguien

footle ['fuːtəl]

▸**footle about, footle around** *vi Fam (potter)* perder el tiempo

footless ['fʊtlɪs] *adj* (**a**) *(tights)* sin pie (**b**) *US (inept)* torpe

footlights ['fʊtlaɪts] *npl Theat* candilejas *fpl*

footling ['fuːtlɪŋ] *adj Fam (objection)* nimio(a); *(sum)* irrisorio(a)

footloose ['fʊtluːs] *adj* libre de ataduras; **to be f. and fancy-free** ser libre como el viento

footman ['fʊtmən] *n* lacayo *m*

footmark ['fʊtmɑːk] *n* huella *f*, pisada *f*

footnote ['fʊtnəʊt] *n* nota *f* a pie de página; **as a f. I should just mention...** a modo de haciendo un inciso, debería mencionar...; *Fig* **he was a mere f. to history** no fue más que una gota en el océano de la historia

footpath ['fʊtpɑːθ] *n* sendero *m*, senda *f*

footplate ['fʊtpleɪt] *n Br* plataforma *f* del maquinista

footprint ['fʊtprɪnt] *n* (**a**) *(of foot)* huella *f*, pisada *f* (**b**) *(of satellite)* (zona *f* de) cobertura *f* (**c**) *Comptr* = espacio físico que ocupa un sistema informático

footpump ['fʊtpʌmp] *n* bomba *f* de pie

footrest ['fʊtrest] *n (under desk, on motorcycle)* reposapiés *m inv*

Footsie ['fʊtsɪ] *n St Exch* (*abbr* **Financial Times-Stock Exchange 100 Index**) Footsie *m*

footsie ['fʊtsɪ] *n Fam* **to play f. with sb** *(under the table)* = acariciar a alguien con el pie por debajo de la mesa; *(collaborate with)* entenderse con alguien

footsore ['fʊtsɔː(r)] *adj* con los pies doloridos

footstep ['fʊtstep] *n* paso *m*; IDIOM **to follow in sb's footsteps** seguir los pasos de alguien

footstool ['fʊtstuːl] *n* escabel *m*, reposapiés *m inv*

footswitch ['fʊtswɪtʃ] *n (for guitar)* interruptor *m* de pie

foot-up [fʊt'ʌp] *n (in soccer)* juego *m* peligroso *(por levantar la pierna)*

footwear ['fʊtweə(r)] *n* calzado *m*

footwork ['fʊtwɜːk] *n* (**a**) *(in dancing, sports)* juego *m* de pies; *Fig* **fancy f.** *(in difficult situation)* malabarismos (**b**) *(walking)* **the job entails a lot of f.** el trabajo supone andar mucho

footy *Fam* = **footie**

fop [fɒp] *n Pej* petimetre *m*

foppish ['fɒpɪʃ] *adj* peripuesto(a)

FOR [fɔː(r), *unstressed* fə(r)] 1 *prep* (**a**) *(reason)* por; **what did you say that f.?** ¿por qué has dicho eso?; **they chose him f. his looks** lo eligieron por su buena apariencia; **they fined him f. speeding** lo multaron por exceso de velocidad; **she couldn't sleep f. the pain** no pudo dormir a causa del dolor; **to jump f. joy** dar saltos de alegría; **there must be a reason f. him to be so quiet** debe estar callado por alguna razón; **if it weren't f. you** si no hubiera sido por ti; **if it hadn't been f. the weather** si no hubiera sido por el tiempo; **he did five years f. robbery** cumplió cinco años por robo; **he was operated on f. cancer** le operaron de un cáncer

(**b**) *(purpose)* para; **what's it f.?** ¿para qué es?; **underwear f. men** ropa interior de hombre; **a table f. two** una mesa para dos; **there's no time f. that** no hay tiempo para eso; **bring that chair over f. me to sit on** acércame esa silla para que me pueda sentar; **can you give me something f. the pain?** ¿me puede dar algo para el dolor?; **to ask sb round f. dinner** invitar a alguien a cenar; **f. hire** se alquila, *Méx* se renta; **f. sale** se vende, en venta

(**c**) *(in order to get)* **I always go to my uncle f. advice** siempre voy a pedirle consejo a mi tío; **will you go f. the paper?** ¿podrías traer el periódico?, *Esp* ¿podrías ir a por el periódico?; **he reached f. his wallet** sacó su cartera; **we had to run f. the bus** tuvimos que correr para alcanzar el autobús; **I've sent off f. details** he pedido que me envíen más detalles; **we did it f. a laugh** lo hicimos por divertirnos *or* por diversión

(**d**) *(destination)* para; **to leave f. France** salir hacia *or* para Francia; **the plane f. Dallas** el avión de *or* para Dallas; **it's f. you** es para ti; **there's a prize f. the winner** hay un premio para el ganador; **her love f. him** el amor que siente por él; *Br Fam* **I'm f. bed** me voy a la cama

(**e**) *(on the occasion of)* para; **what do you want f. your birthday?** ¿qué quieres para tu cumpleaños?; **what's f. dinner?** ¿qué hay para *or* de cenar?

(**f**) *(in exchange for)* **I bought it f. £10** lo compré por 10 libras; **it is insured f. $5,000** está asegurado en 5.000 dólares; **you get a lot f. your money at that restaurant** la comida de ese restaurante sale muy bien de precio; **I wouldn't do that f. all the world** *or* **f. anything** no lo haría ni por todo el oro del mundo

(**g**) *(with regard to, considering)* para; **he is big f. his age** es grande para su edad; **f. a woman of your age...** para una mujer de tu edad...; **he's quite nice f. an Australian** para ser australiano no es mala persona; **that's f. you to decide** eso lo tienes que decidir tú; **f. me, she's the best** para mí, es la mejor; **how are we f. time?** ¿cómo vamos de tiempo?; **they sell ten red bikes f. every black one** se venden diez bicicletas de color rojo por cada una de color negro; **as f. him/that,...** en cuanto a él/eso,...

(**h**) *(representing, on behalf of)* **A f. Andrew** A de Andrés; **what's the Russian f. "book"?** ¿cómo se dice "libro" en ruso?; **he plays f. Boca Juniors** juega en (el) Boca Juniors; **I work f. an insurance company** trabajo para una aseguradora; **I can't speak f. her** no puedo hablar por ella; **to be happy f. sb** estar contento(a) por alguien

(**i**) *(duration)* durante; **cook f. an hour** cocinar durante una hora; **I was there f. a month** pasé un mes allí; **I've been here f. a month** llevo *or Am* tengo un mes aquí; **I will be here f. a month** voy a pasar un mes aquí; **I haven't been there f. a month** hace un mes que no voy (por allí); **we have enough food f. two days** tenemos comida suficiente para dos días

(**j**) *(point in time)* **f. the first/last time** por primera/última vez; **it's time f. lunch** es la hora de comer *or* almorzar; **can I book a table f. eight o'clock?** querría reservar una mesa para las ocho; **I need it f. Friday** lo necesito (para) el viernes; **can you do it f. next Monday?** ¿lo puedes hacer para el lunes que viene?; **be there at five f. five thirty** estáte ahí entre las cinco y las cinco y media

(**k**) *(distance)* **we ran f. miles** corrimos varias millas

(**l**) *(in favour of)* **to be f. sth** estar a favor de algo; **who's f. a game of chess/a glass of wine?** ¿quién quiere jugar una partida de ajedrez/un vaso de vino?, ¿a quién *Esp* le apetece *or Carib, Col, Méx* le provoca *or Méx* se le antoja una partida de ajedrez/un vaso de vino?; **to vote f. sth** votar a favor de *or* por algo; **I'm all f. it!** ¡estoy absolutamente a favor!

(**m**) *(introducing an infinitive clause)* **it is too early f. me to decide** es demasiado pronto para decidirme; **it's time f. us to act** ya es hora de que actuemos; **it will be difficult/easy f. her to come** lo va a tener difícil/fácil para venir, le va a ser difícil/fácil venir; **it took an hour f. us to get there** tardamos *or Am* demoramos una hora en llegar; **it's rare f. her to be late** no es normal que llegue tarde

(**n**) *(despite)* a pesar de; **f. all his wealth, he was still unhappy** a pesar de todo su dinero, no era feliz; **f. all that, we're still good friends** a pesar de eso, seguimos siendo buenos amigos

(**o**) *(to the liking of)* para; **she's too quiet f. me** es demasiado tranquila para mi gusto; **it's too small f. you** es demasiado pequeño para ti

(**p**) *(in phrases)* **now f. the moment you've all been waiting for** y ahora el momento que todos esperaban; *Fam* **he's f. it!** ¡se la va a cargar!, *RP* ¡se va a ligar una!; **f. all the good it will do!** ¡para lo que va a servir!; **f. all I care** para lo que me importa; **I f. one am going to stay** yo por lo menos me voy a quedar; **f. one thing..., f. another...** por un lado..., por el otro...; **that's men f. you!** ¡los hombres, ya se sabe!; *Ironic* **there's gratitude f. you!** ¡los he visto más agradecidos!
2 *conj Literary (because)* dado que

forage ['fɒrɪdʒ] **1** *n* (**a**) *(search)* búsqueda *f*; **to have a f. for sth** buscar algo (**b**) *(animal food)* forraje *m* (**c**) *Mil* ***f. cap*** gorra *f* militar
2 *vt* (**a**) *(obtain)* reunir (**b**) *(feed)* dar forraje a
3 *vi* **to f. (about** *or* **around) for** buscar

foray ['fɒreɪ] *n* (**a**) *(raid)* incursión *f* (**into** en) (**b**) *(excursion)* incursión *f* (**into** en); **she was on one of her forays round the bookshops** estaba en una de sus expediciones por las librerías; **he made a brief f. into politics** hizo una breve incursión en el mundo de la política

forbade *pt of* **forbid**

forbear [fɔː'beə(r)] (*pt* **forbore** [fɔː'bɔː(r)], *pp* **forborne** [fɔː'bɔːn]) **1** *vi Formal* **to f. from doing sth** abstenerse de hacer algo, contenerse para no hacer algo; **I forbore to point out it had been my idea all along** omití *or* me abstuve de señalar que la idea había sido mía
2 = **forebear**

forbearance [fɔː'beərəns] *n* paciencia *f*, tolerancia *f*

forbearing [fɔː'beərɪŋ] *adj* paciente, tolerante

forbid [fə'bɪd] (*pt* **forbade** [fə'bæd, fə'beɪd], *pp* **forbidden** [fə'bɪdən]) *vt* (**a**) *(not allow)* prohibir; **to f. sb to do sth** prohibir a alguien que haga algo; **he was forbidden from seeing her again** le prohibieron volver a verla; **to f. oneself sth** prohibirse algo (**b**) *(prevent)* **God** *or* **Heaven f.!** ¡Dios no lo quiera!

forbidden [fə'bɪdən] *adj* prohibido(a); **smoking/talking (is) f.** (está) prohibido fumar/hablar ►► ***f. fruit*** fruta *f* prohibida; ***f. territory*** *(literally)* zona *f* prohibida, territorio *m* vedado; *Fig (subject, topic)* tema *m* tabú *or* prohibido

forbidding [fə'bɪdɪŋ] *adj (appearance, look)* severo(a); *(sky)* amenazador(ora); *(landscape)* agreste; *(task)* dificultoso(a); **it was a f. prospect** era una perspectiva aterradora

forbiddingly [fə'bɪdɪŋlɪ] *adv* **the castle towered f. over the town** el castillo se elevaba amenazadoramente *or* imponentemente sobre la ciudad; **f. difficult/complex** de una dificultad/complejidad insalvable

forborе *pt of* **forbear**

forborne *pp of* **forbear**

FORCE [fɔːs] **1** *n* (**a**) *(strength, violence)* fuerza *f*; **to use f.** emplear la fuerza; **by (sheer** *or* **brute) f.** por la fuerza; **they won by f. of numbers** ganaron por superioridad numérica
(**b**) *(power, influence)* fuerza *f*; **the f. of gravity** la fuerza de la gravedad; **the forces of Nature** las fuerzas de la naturaleza; **a f. 9 gale** un viento de fuerza 9; **various forces conspired to bring about his downfall** diversas causas contribuyeron a su caída; **a f. for good** una fuerza del bien; **the forces of evil** las fuerzas del mal; **f. of circumstance(s)** causas de fuerza mayor; **she is a f. to be reckoned with** es alguien a tener en cuenta; **I did it from f. of habit** lo hice por la fuerza de la costumbre ►► ***f. field*** campo *m* de fuerza
(**c**) *(group)* fuerza *f*; **the (armed) forces** las fuerzas armadas; **the police f.** la policía, el cuerpo de policía; **to join forces (to do sth)** unir fuerzas (para hacer algo); **they turned out in (full) f.** se presentaron en gran número
(**d**) **to be in f.** *(law)* estar en vigor; **to come into f.** entrar en vigor
2 *vt* (**a**) *(compel)* forzar, obligar; **to f. a smile** forzar una sonrisa; **to f. sb to do sth** *or* **into doing sth** forzar *or* obligar a alguien a hacer algo; **she was forced into accepting the offer** se vio obligada a aceptar la oferta; **to f. sth on sb** imponer algo a alguien; **to f. oneself to do sth** forzarse a hacer algo; *Fam* **I can't manage any more chocolate – go on, f. yourself!** no me cabe más chocolate – ¡vamos, haz un esfuerzo *or RP* dale, castigate un poco!
(**b**) *(use force on) (door, lock)* forzar; **to f. a vehicle off the road** obligar a un vehículo a salirse de la carretera; **to f. a door open** abrir una puerta a la fuerza; **to f. one's way through a crowd** abrirse paso a través de una multitud; **they forced his head under the water** le hundieron la cabeza en el agua a la fuerza; **to f. an entry** entrar por la fuerza; **to f. sb's hand** forzar a alguien a tomar una decisión; **to f. the issue** acelerar las cosas; **to f. oneself on sb** *(sexually)* intentar forzar a alguien
(**c**) *(quicken)* **to f. the pace** forzar el ritmo
(**d**) *(flowers, plants)* forzar
(**e**) *Comptr* **to f. quit** forzar la salida

► **force back** *vt sep* **they forced the enemy back** obligaron a retroceder al enemigo; **to f. back the tears** contener *or* reprimir las lágrimas

► **force down** *vt sep* (**a**) *(medicine, food)* tragar a la fuerza
(**b**) *(aircraft)* **the plane was forced down** el avión se vio obligado a aterrizar
(**c**) *(prices, interest rates)* hacer bajar

► **force open** *vt sep* abrir forzudo

► **force out** *vt sep* **he forced out an apology** pidió perdón de una manera forzada; **I always have to f. the truth out of you** siempre tengo que extraerte la verdad con pinzas

► **force up** *vt sep (prices, interest rates)* hacer subir

forced [fɔːst] *adj* (**a**) *(manner, laugh)* forzado(a) (**b**) *(compulsory)* ***f. labour*** trabajos *mpl* forzados; *Av* ***f. landing*** aterrizaje *m* forzoso; *Mil* ***f. march*** marcha *f* forzada

force-feed ['fɔːs'fiːd] (*pt & pp* **force-fed** ['fɔːs'fed]) *vt* dar de comer a la fuerza

forceful ['fɔːsfʊl] *adj* (**a**) *(person)* con mucha personalidad; *(language)* enérgico(a), lleno(a) de fuerza (**b**) *(argument)* poderoso(a), contundente

forcefully ['fɔːsfʊlɪ] *adv (to act, speak)* enérgicamente; *(to argue, reason)* de forma contundente

force majeure ['fɔːsmæ'ʒɜː(r)] *n Law* fuerza *f* mayor

forcemeat ['fɔːsmiːt] *n Br Culin* (picadillo *m* de) relleno *m*

forceps ['fɔːseps] *npl Med* **(a pair of) f.** (unos) fórceps *m inv* ►► ***f. delivery*** parto *m* con fórceps

forcible ['fɔːsɪbəl] *adj* (**a**) *(reminder)* contundente (**b**) *Law* ***f. entry*** *Esp* allanamiento *m* de morada, *Am* invasión *f* de domicilio

forcibly ['fɔːsɪblɪ] *adv* (**a**) *(by force)* por la fuerza; **they were f. removed from the premises** los sacaron por la fuerza del local (**b**) *(powerfully)* **I was f. reminded of his father by these words** estas palabras me recordaron vivamente a su padre

forcing ['fɔːsɪŋ] *n* (**a**) *Culin* ***f. bag*** manga *f* (pastelera) (**b**) *(in gardening)* ***f. house*** *(for plants)* maduradero *m*; *Fam Fig* **it's just an academic f. house** lo único que les importa en ese colegio son los resultados académicos

ford [fɔːd] **1** *n* vado *m*
2 *vt* vadear

fordable ['fɔːdəbəl] *adj* vadeable

fore [fɔː(r)] **1** *n* **he was always to the f. at such times** en momentos como ése, él siempre aparecía *or* se dejaba ver; **to come to the f.** cobrar importancia, pasar a primer plano; **the revolt brought these issues to the f.** la revuelta ha hecho pasar estos temas a un primer plano; **this question has been very much to the f. in the talks** esta pregunta ha estado muy presente en las conversaciones
2 *adj* (**a**) *(front)* delantero(a), anterior (**b**) *Naut* de proa; **f. hatch/cabins** escotilla/camarotes de proa
3 *adv Naut* **they searched the ship f. and aft** registraron el barco de proa a popa

forearm ['fɔːrɑːm] *n* antebrazo *m*

forearmed [fɔːr'ɑːmd] *adj* **he came f.** vino preparado

forebear, forbear ['fɔːbeə(r)] *n* antepasado(a) *m,f*, ancestro *m*

forebode [fɔː'bəʊd] *vt Formal* augurar, presagiar

foreboding [fɔː'bəʊdɪŋ] *n* presentimiento *m* ominoso; **the news filled us with f.** la noticia nos llenó de desasosiego

forebrain ['fɔːbreɪn] *n Anat* prosencéfalo *m*

forecast ['fɔːkɑːst] **1** *n* pronóstico *m*; *Com* previsión *f*; **the (weather) f.** *(prediction)* el pronóstico meteorológico; *(programme)* el parte meteorológico, el tiempo
2 *vt* (*pt & pp* **forecast(ed)**) pronosticar; **showers are f. for tomorrow** el pronóstico para mañana es de lluvias

forecaster ['fɔːkɑːstə(r)] *n* **weather f.** meteorólogo(a); **political/economic f.** analista político(a)/económico(a)

forecastle, fo'c'sle ['fəʊksəl] *n Naut* castillo *m* de proa

foreclose [fɔː'kləʊz] *Fin* **1** *vt* **to f. a mortgage** ejecutar una hipoteca
2 *vi* **to f. (on a mortgage/a loan)** ejecutar (una hipoteca/un crédito)

foreclosure [fɔː'kləʊʒə(r)] *n Fin* ejecución *f*

forecourt ['fɔːkɔːt] *n (of petrol station)* explanada *f* delantera

foredeck ['fɔːdek] *n* cubierta *f* de proa

forefathers ['fɔːfɑːðəz] *npl* ancestros *mpl*

forefinger ['fɔːfɪŋgə(r)] *n* (dedo *m*) índice *m*

forefoot ['fɔːfʊt] *n* pata *f* delantera

forefront ['fɔ:frʌnt] *n* **to be at** *or* **in the f. (of)** estar a la vanguardia (de); **it was at the f. of my mind** lo tenía siempre en mente

foregather = **forgather**

for(e)go [fɔ:'gəʊ] (*pt* **for(e)went** [fɔ:'went], *pp* **for(e)gone** [fɔ:'gɒn]) *vt Formal* renunciar a

foregoing [fɔ:'gəʊɪŋ] *Formal* 1 *n* **the f.** lo anterior, lo anteriormente dicho
2 *adj* precedente, anterior

foregone ['fɔ:gɒn] *adj* **the result was a f. conclusion** el resultado ya se conocía de antemano

foreground ['fɔ:graʊnd] 1 *n* primer plano *m*; **in the f.** *(in picture)* en primer plano; **to keep the issue in the f.** mantener el asunto en el primer plano de actualidad *or* en el candelero
2 *vt* poner de relieve

forehand ['fɔ:hænd] 1 *n (tennis stroke)* drive *m*
2 *adj (tennis stroke)* de drive ►► ***f. smash*** mate *m* (de drive); ***f. volley*** volea *f* de drive

forehead ['fɒrɪd, 'fɔ:hed] *n* frente *f*

foreign ['fɒrɪn] *adj* (**a**) *(from another country)* extranjero(a); *(trade, policy)* exterior; **she sounded f.** tenía acento extranjero ►► ***f. affairs*** política *f* exterior, asuntos *mpl* exteriores; ***f. aid*** *(to another country)* ayuda *f* (al) exterior; *(from another country)* ayuda *f* extranjera *or* (del) exterior; *Br* ***F. and Commonwealth Office*** Ministerio *m* de Asuntos Exteriores *or Am* Relaciones Exteriores; *Journ* ***f. correspondent*** corresponsal *mf* (en el extranjero); ***f. currency reserves*** reservas *fpl* de divisas; ***f. debt*** deuda *f* exterior *or* externa; ***f. exchange*** *(currency)* divisas *fpl*; *(system)* mercado *m* de divisas; ***f. investment*** inversión *f* extranjera; ***F. Legion*** legión *f* extranjera; ***F. Minister*** ministro(a) *m,f* de Asuntos Exteriores *or Am* Relaciones Exteriores; *Br* ***F. Office*** Ministerio *m* de Asuntos Exteriores *or Am* Relaciones Exteriores; ***f. policy*** política *f* exterior; *Br* ***F. Secretary*** ministro(a) *m,f* de Asuntos Exteriores *or Am* Relaciones Exteriores; *US* ***f. service*** = funcionariado en las embajadas y consulados estadounidenses; ***f. trade*** comercio *m* exterior
(**b**) *(not characteristic)* ajeno(a); **this is f. to our traditions** esto es ajeno a nuestras tradiciones
(**c**) *Med* ***f. body*** cuerpo *m* extraño

foreigner ['fɒrɪnə(r)] *n* extranjero(a) *m,f*

forejudge [fɔ:'dʒʌdʒ] *vt* prejuzgar

foreknowledge ['fɔ:nɒlɪdʒ] *n Formal* conocimiento *m* previo

foreland ['fɔ:lænd] *n* promontorio *m*, lengua *f* de tierra

foreleg ['fɔ:leg] *n* pata *f* delantera

forelock ['fɔ:lɒk] *n* mechón *m* de pelo (sobre los ojos); IDIOM **to touch** *or* **tug one's f.** hacer una reverencia

foreman ['fɔ:mən] *n* (**a**) *Ind* capataz *m*, encargado *m* (**b**) *(of jury)* presidente *m or* portavoz *m* (del jurado)

foremast ['fɔ:mɑ:st] *n Naut* trinquete *m*

foremost ['fɔ:məʊst] *adj* principal; **one of our f. citizens** uno de nuestros más ilustres *or* insignes ciudadanos; **the matter was f. in my mind** el asunto ocupaba la mayor parte de mis pensamientos

forename ['fɔ:neɪm] *n* nombre *m* (de pila)

forensic [fə'rensɪk] *adj Law* forense ►► ***f. evidence*** pruebas *fpl* forenses; ***f. medicine*** medicina *f* legal *or* forense; ***f. scientist*** forense *mf*; ***f. skill*** pericia *f* legal

forepaw ['fɔ:pɔ:] *n (of dog)* uña *f*; *(of cat)* zarpa *f*

foreplay ['fɔ:pleɪ] *n* juego *m* amoroso *(antes del coito)*

forequarter ['fɔ:kwɔ:tə(r)] *n (of meat)* espaldilla *f*, cuarto *m* delantero; **forequarters** *(of animal)* cuartos delanteros

forerunner ['fɔ:rʌnə(r)] *n* predecesor(ora) *m,f*

foresee [fɔ:'si:] (*pt* **foresaw** [fɔ:'sɔ:], *pp* **foreseen** [fɔ:'si:n]) *vt* prever; **this could not have been foreseen** esto era imposible de prever

foreseeable [fɔ:'si:əbəl] *adj* previsible; **in the f. future** en un futuro próximo *or* no muy lejano; **for the f. future** en tiempos venideros, en el futuro inmediato

foreseen *pp of* **foresee**

foreshadow [fɔ:'ʃædəʊ] *vt* presagiar, anunciar

foreshore ['fɔ:ʃɔ:(r)] *n* franja *f* costera intermareal

foreshorten [fɔ:'ʃɔ:tən] *vt* escorzar

foreshortened [fɔ:'ʃɔ:tənd] *adj* en escorzo, escorzado(a)

foresight ['fɔ:saɪt] *n* previsión *f*; **she had the f. to see what would probably happen** supo prever lo que podría ocurrir; **lack of f.** falta de previsión

foreskin ['fɔ:skɪn] *n* prepucio *m*

forest ['fɒrɪst] *n* bosque *m*; *Fig* **a f. of hands** una multitud de manos ►► ***f. fire*** incendio *m* forestal; *US* ***f. ranger*** guarda *mf* forestal, guardabosques *mf inv*

forestall [fɔ:'stɔ:l] *vt* (**a**) *(preempt)* anticiparse a, adelantarse a (**b**) *(prevent)* impedir

forestay ['fɔ:steɪ] *n Naut* estay *m* de proa

forester ['fɒrɪstə(r)] *n (keeper)* guardabosque *mf*, guarda *mf* forestal; *(technical specialist)* ingeniero(a) *m,f* de montes

forestry ['fɒrɪstrɪ] *n* silvicultura *f* ►► ***the F. Commission*** = organismo oficial británico dedicado al cuidado y explotación forestales; ***f. worker*** trabajador(ora) *m,f* forestal

foretaste ['fɔ:teɪst] *n* anticipo *m*; **to give** *or* **offer (sb) a f. of sth** ofrecer (a alguien) un anticipo de algo

foretell [fɔ:'tel] (*pt & pp* **foretold** [fɔ:'təʊld]) *vt* predecir; **nobody could have foretold what happened next** nadie podría haber anticipado lo que ocurrió a continuación

forethought ['fɔ:θɔ:t] *n* previsión *f*; **lack of f.** falta de previsión; **if you had given it some f....** si antes lo hubieses pensado un poco...

foretold *pt & pp of* **foretell**

forever [fə'revə(r)] 1 *n Fam* **to take f. (to do sth)** tardar un siglo (en hacer algo), *Am* demorar una eternidad (en hacer algo)
2 *adv* (**a**) *(until the end of time)* para siempre; **it won't last f.** no durará eternamente *or* para siempre; **Scotland f.!** ¡viva Escocia!
(**b**) *(for good)* para siempre; **dinosaurs have vanished f.** los dinosaurios se han extinguido para siempre
(**c**) *Fam (a long time)* eternamente; **we can't wait f.** no podemos esperar eternamente
(**d**) *(repeatedly)* constantemente; **he was f. changing his mind** siempre estaba cambiando de opinión

forevermore [fɔ:revə'mɔ:(r)] *adv Literary* por el resto de los días, para siempre jamás

forewarn [fɔ:'wɔ:n] *vt* advertir; PROV **forewarned is forearmed** hombre prevenido vale por dos

forewent *pt of* **forego**

forewoman ['fɔ:wʊmən] *n* (**a**) *Ind* capataza *f*, encargada *f* (**b**) *(of jury)* presidenta *f or* portavoz *f* (del jurado)

foreword ['fɔ:wɜ:d] *n* prólogo *m*

forfeit ['fɔ:fɪt] 1 *n* (**a**) *(in game)* prenda *f*; **to play forfeits** jugar a las prendas; **to pay a f.** pagar una prenda (**b**) *(penalty)* multa *f*; **one's privacy is the f. one pays for success** la pérdida de la intimidad es el precio que hay que pagar por el éxito (**c**) *Law (confiscation)* sanción *f*
2 *vt Formal (right, property, sb's respect)* renunciar a, sacrificar; **to f. one's life** sacrificar la vida; *Fin* **to f. a deposit** renunciar al depósito
3 *adj Formal (subject to confiscation)* decomisable; *(confiscated)* decomisado(a); **her life could be f.** le podría costar la vida

forfeiture ['fɔ:fɪtʃə(r)] *n* pérdida *f*

forfend [fɔ:'fend] *vt Archaic or Literary* **heaven f.!** ¡Dios no lo quiera!

forgather, foregather [fɔ:'gæðə(r)] *vi Formal* congregarse

forgave *pt of* **forgive**

forge [fɔ:dʒ] 1 *n (factory)* fundición *f*; *(of blacksmith)* forja *f*, fragua *f*
2 *vt* (**a**) *(metal, alliance)* forjar; **a friendship forged in adversity** una amistad forjada en la adversidad (**b**) *(counterfeit)* falsificar
3 *vi (go forward)* seguir adelante, avanzar; **we forged on, hoping to reach the village by nightfall** seguimos adelante *or* avanzamos, con la esperanza de llegar al pueblo antes de que cayera la noche; **to f. into the lead** ponerse a la cabeza

► **forge ahead** *vi* (**a**) *(make progress)* progresar a pasos agigantados; **to f. ahead with one's plans** seguir adelante con los planes (**b**) *(in competition)* tomar la delantera

forged [fɔ:dʒd] *adj (banknote, letter)* falso(a), falsificado(a); *(signature)* falsificado(a)

forger ['fɔ:dʒə(r)] *n* falsificador(ora) *m,f*

forgery ['fɔ:dʒərɪ] *n* (**a**) *(crime)* falsificación *f* (**b**) *(forged object, signature)* falsificación *f*; **it's a f.** es una falsificación

FORGET [fə'get] (*pt* **forgot** [fə'gɒt], *pp* **forgotten** [fə'gɒtən]) 1 *vt* (**a**) *(not recall)* olvidar; **I'll never f. you** nunca te olvidaré; **I've forgotten her name, I f. her name** se me ha olvidado su nombre; **I want to f. everything for a few days** quiero olvidarme de todo durante unos días; *Fam* **you can f. the holiday** ya puedes decir adiós a las vacaciones, *RP* andá despidiéndote de las vacaciones; **to f. to do sth** olvidarse de hacer algo; **I'll never f. meeting him for the first time** nunca olvidaré la primera vez que lo vi; **to f. how to do sth** olvidar cómo se hace algo, olvidarse de cómo se hace algo; **to be forgotten (by)** caer en el olvido (de); **that has all been forgotten now** eso ya ha quedado

olvidado *or* pasó al olvido; **the whole affair is best forgotten** es mejor que olvidemos el asunto; **to f. (that)...** olvidar que...; **f. I mentioned it** como si no hubiera dicho nada, *RP* hacé de cuenta que no dije nada; **it's my idea and don't you f. it!** es idea mía, que no se te olvide; **I'd like to thank all my friends, not forgetting my family** quisiera dar las gracias a todos mis amigos, sin olvidarme de mi familia; *Fam* **f. it!** *(in reply to apology)* olvídalo, *RP* no fue nada; *(in reply to thanks)* no hay de qué; *(stop talking about it)* dejémoslo, *RP* dejémoslo así; *(no way)* ¡ni hablar!; **I'm in charge and don't you f. it!** yo soy el que manda, ¡ni se te ocurra olvidarlo!; **to f. oneself** perder el control
(**b**) *(leave behind)* olvidar(se); **I forgot my coat at their place** (me) olvidé el abrigo en su casa
2 *vi* olvidarse (**about** de); **before I f.** antes de que (se) me olvide; **don't f.** no te olvides; **let's f. about it** olvidémoslo, *RP* dejémoslo así; *Fam* **you can f. about the holiday** ya puedes decir adiós a las vacaciones, *RP* andá despidiéndote de las vacaciones

> Hay una serie de verbos en inglés que pueden ir seguidos tanto como de infinitivo como de gerundio sin que apenas cambie su significado; por ejemplo **begin, bother, continue, hate, like** o **try.** Sin embargo, **forget** es uno de los pocos verbos en los que existe una clara diferencia entre ambas opciones:
> **I forgot to close the door** *se me olvidó cerrar la puerta*
> **he won't forget meeting you!** *¡no se olvidará de haberte conocido!*

forgetful [fə'getfʊl] *adj* olvidadizo(a); **how f. of me!** ¡qué olvido por mi parte!; **to be f. of sth** *(one's duties)* desatender algo
forgetfulness [fə'getfʊlnɪs] *n* mala memoria *f*
forget-me-not [fə'getmi:nɒt] *n* nomeolvides *m inv*
forgettable [fə'getəbəl] *adj* poco memorable; **a very f. performance** una actuación para olvidar *or* el olvido
forgivable [fə'gɪvəbəl] *adj* perdonable
forgivably [fə'gɪvəblɪ] *adv* comprensiblemente
forgive [fə'gɪv] (*pt* **forgave** [fə'geɪv], *pp* **forgiven** [fə'gɪvən]) **1** *vt* (**a**) *(pardon)* perdonar; **to f. sb (for sth)** perdonar (algo) a alguien; **can you ever f. me?** ¿me podrás perdonar alguna vez?; **I'll never f. myself if he dies** si llegara a morir nunca me lo perdonaría; **one could be forgiven for finding this strange** no es de extrañar que a uno esto le parezca raro; **f. my ignorance, but who was this Galsworthy?** disculpa mi ignorancia, pero ¿quién era Galsworthy?
(**b**) *(debt, payment)* **to f. (sb) a debt** perdonar una deuda (a alguien)
2 *vi* **to f. and forget** perdonar y olvidar
forgiveness [fə'gɪvnɪs] *n* (**a**) *(pardon)* perdón *m*; **to ask (sb) for f.** pedir perdón (a alguien) (**b**) *(indulgence)* indulgencia *f*; **he was full of f.** era muy indulgente
forgiving [fə'gɪvɪŋ] *adj* indulgente
forgo = **forego**
forgone *pp of* **forgo**
forgot *pt of* **forget**
forgotten [fə'gɒtən] **1** *adj (obscure)* olvidado(a)
2 *pp of* **forget**
forint ['fɒrɪnt] *n* forint *m inv*, forinto *m*
fork [fɔ:k] **1** *n* (**a**) *(for food)* tenedor *m*, *Am* trinche *m* (**b**) *(for lifting hay)* horca *f* (**c**) *(in road)* bifurcación *f*; **take the left f.** tomar el desvío a *or* de la izquierda (**d**) *(of bicycle, motorbike)* horquilla *f* (**e**) **a f. of lightning** un relámpago *(bifurcado)*
2 *vt* (**a**) **he forked the food into his mouth** se llevó la comida a la boca con el tenedor (**b**) **they were forking hay onto the truck** cargaban heno con la horca en el camión
3 *vi* (**a**) *(road, river)* bifurcarse (**b**) *(driver)* desviarse; **f. right for the airport** desvíate *or* toma la desviación a la derecha para ir al aeropuerto
▸ **fork out** *Fam* **1** *vt sep (money)* aflojar, *Esp* apoquinar, *RP* garpar
2 *vi* aflojar (**for** por), *Esp* apoquinar (**for** por), *RP* garpar (**for** por)
forked [fɔ:kt] *adj (tongue)* bífido(a); *(tail)* ahorquillado(a); *(stick)* bifurcado(a); IDIOM *Hum* **to speak with f. tongue** hablar con dobleces ▸▸ ***f. lightning*** relámpagos *mpl (bifurcados)*
fork-lift ['fɔ:klɪft] *n* **f. (truck)** carretilla *f* elevadora
forlorn [fə'lɔ:n] *adj* (**a**) *(wretched)* desdichado(a); **a f. cry** un grito de desesperado (**b**) *(lonely) (place)* abandonado(a); *(look, appearance)* desamparado(a) (**c**) *(desperate) (belief, attempt)* desesperado(a); **in the f. hope that...** con la vana esperanza de que...
forlornly [fə'lɔ:nlɪ] *adv* desesperanzadamente, apesadumbradamente

FORM [fɔ:m] **1** *n* (**a**) *(shape)* forma *f*; **in the f. of...** en forma de...; **the news came in the f. of a fax** las noticias llegaron por fax; **to take f.** tomar forma; **to take the f. of...** consistir en...; **f. and content** forma y fondo *or* contenido
(**b**) *(type)* forma *f*; **it's a f. of madness** es una forma de locura; **some f. of apology would be nice** no estaría mal que te disculparas de una manera u otra; **a f. of address** una fórmula de tratamiento; **f. of transport** forma *or* modalidad de transporte
(**c**) *(formality)* **as a matter of f., for f.'s sake** por guardar las formas
(**d**) *(for applications, orders)* formulario *m*, impreso *m*, *Méx* forma *f*; **to fill in** *or* **out a f.** rellenar un formulario *or* un impreso *or Méx* una forma ▸▸ *Comptr* ***f. feed*** avance *m* de página; ***f. letter*** carta *f* general
(**e**) *(condition)* forma *f* (física); **to be in (good) f.** estar en (buena) forma
(**f**) *(recent performances) (of athlete, player, team)* forma *f*; *(in horse-racing)* reciente historial *m*; **on current f., this team is unlikely to win** tal y como está jugando últimamente es poco probable que este equipo gane; **on current f., the government is unlikely to last long** de seguir así, este gobierno no durará mucho; **this tennis player is in** *or* **on (good) f.** este tenista está en plena forma *or* jugando (muy) bien; *Fig* **you're on (good) f. today!** ¡hoy estás en vena *or* forma!; **this sprinter is out of** *or* **off f.** este esprínter no está en plena forma *or* corriendo (muy) bien; *Fig* **I'm a bit off f. at the moment** no estoy muy en forma últimamente; *Fig* **true to f., he failed to turn up** como de costumbre, no se presentó; **to upset the f. book** ganar contra pronóstico
(**g**) *Br Sch (class)* clase *f*; *(year)* curso *m* ▸▸ ***f. room*** = aula asignada a cada curso para pasar lista, guardar material escolar, etc.; ***f. teacher*** tutor(ora) *m,f*
(**h**) *(body, figure)* silueta *f*; **a slender f. appeared at the door** una delgada silueta apareció en la puerta
(**i**) *Old-fashioned (etiquette)* **it's good/bad f.** es de buena/mala educación
(**j**) *(mould)* molde *m*
(**k**) *Gram* forma *f*
(**l**) *Br Fam (criminal record)* ficha *f*
(**m**) *Br (bench)* banco *m (sin respaldo)*
2 *vt* (**a**) *(shape)* formar; **to f. a line** ponerse en fila; **she formed her hands into a cup** puso las manos en forma de cuenco
(**b**) *(organization, party, committee)* formar, fundar
(**c**) *(develop) (relationship, friendship)* establecer; *(plan)* concebir; *(habit)* adquirir; **to f. an idea/opinion** formarse una idea/opinión; **I formed the impression that she wasn't interested** me dio la impresión de que no estaba interesada
(**d**) *(constitute) (obstacle, basis)* constituir; **the river forms a natural barrier** el río constituye *or* forma una barrera natural; **to f. part of sth** formar parte de algo
(**e**) *Gram (past tense, imperative etc)* formar; **the plural is formed by adding an "s"** el plural se forma añadiendo *or Am* agregando una "s"
3 *vi* formarse; **they formed into a circle** se pusieron en círculo

formal ['fɔ:məl] *adj* (**a**) *(ceremonious)* formal; **a f. dinner** una cena de gala; **a f. occasion** un acto de gala ▸▸ ***f. dress*** *(for men)* traje *m* de etiqueta; *(for women)* vestido *m* largo *or* de noche
(**b**) *(correct) (person, language)* ceremonioso(a), solemne; *(behaviour)* ceremonioso(a), solemne; **he's very f.** es muy ceremonioso *or* solemne; **don't be so f.** olvídate las formalidades; **"usted" is the f. pronoun** "usted" es el pronombre de tratamiento de cortesía
(**c**) *(official)* formal; **he has no f. qualifications** no tiene titulación oficial; **a f. application** una solicitud oficial; **we gave him a f. warning** lo amonestamos por escrito ▸▸ ***f. education*** formación *f* académica
(**d**) *(ordered)* ***f. garden*** jardín *m* francés *or* racionalista
(**e**) *Ling* formal
(**f**) *Phil* ***f. language*** lenguaje *m* formal
formaldehyde [fɔ:'mældəhaɪd] *n Chem* formaldehído *m*
formalin ['fɔ:məlɪn] *n Chem* formol *m*, formalina *f*
formalism ['fɔ:məlɪzəm] *n* formalismo *m*
formalist ['fɔ:məlɪst] **1** *n* formalista *mf*
2 *adj* formalista
formality [fɔ:'mælɪtɪ] *n* (**a**) *(ceremoniousness)* formalidad *f* (**b**) *(procedure)* formalidad *f*; **it's a mere f.** no es más que un trámite *or* una formalidad; **let's skip the formalities** vamos a dejarnos de formalidades
formalization [fɔ:məlaɪ'zeɪʃən] *n* formalización *f*
formalize ['fɔ:məlaɪz] *vt* formalizar
formally ['fɔ:məlɪ] *adv* (**a**) *(with ceremony)* formalmente
(**b**) *(correctly) (to speak)* con solemnidad; *(to behave)* ceremoniosamente; **he expresses himself very f.** se expresa de una manera muy solemne

(**c**) *(officially)* oficialmente, formalmente; **to be f. educated** haber seguido una enseñanza reglada, tener formación académica; **f. announced/agreed** anunciado/acordado de manera oficial

formant ['fɔːmənt] *n Phys & Ling* formante *m*

format ['fɔːmæt] **1** *n* (**a**) *(size)* formato *m*; *Typ* **A f.** = formato de un libro de 110 por 178 milímetros; **B f.** = formato de un libro de 130 por 198 milímetros (**b**) *(design, layout)* formato *m*, presentación *f*; **the news on TV now has a new f.** los *Esp* telediarios *or Am* noticieros tienen ahora un nuevo formato *or* una nueva presentación (**c**) *Comptr* formato *m*

2 *vt* (*pt & pp* **formatted**) *Comptr (disk, page, text)* formatear

formation [fɔː'meɪʃən] *n* (**a**) *(establishment) (of committee, government)* formación *f*; *(of club, company)* fundación *f* (**b**) *(development)* desarrollo *m* (**c**) *(arrangement)* formación *f*; *Sport* esquema *m* (de juego); **in battle f.** en formación de combate ►► ***f. dancing*** baile *m* sincronizado; ***f. flying*** vuelo *m* en formación (**d**) *Mil (unit)* formación *f* (**e**) *Geol* formación *f*

formative ['fɔːmətɪv] *adj* formativo(a); **the f. years** los años de formación

formatted ['fɔːmætɪd] *adj (disk, text, page)* formateado(a)

formatting ['fɔːmætɪŋ] *n Comptr* (**a**) *(action) (of disk, text)* formateado *m* (**b**) *(format) (of text)* formato *m*

former ['fɔːmə(r)] **1** *adj* (**a**) *(earlier, previous) (pupil, colleague)* antiguo(a); **in a f. life** en una vida anterior; **in f. times** antiguamente; **he is a mere shadow of his f. self** no es más que una sombra de lo que fue; **the f. Soviet Union** la antigua Unión Soviética (**b**) *(first)* primero(a); **I prefer the f. suggestion** prefiero la primera sugerencia

2 *pron* **the f.** *(singular)* el/la primero(a); *(plural)* los/las primeros(as)

formerly ['fɔːməlɪ] *adv* anteriormente; **Burkina Faso, f. Upper Volta** Burkina Faso, antes *or* anteriormente llamado Alto Volta

form-filling ['fɔːm'fɪlɪŋ] *n* papeleo *m*; **there was a lot of f.** hubo mucho papeleo, hubo que rellenar muchos formularios

Formica® [fɔː'maɪkə] *n* formica® *f*

formic acid ['fɔːmɪk'æsɪd] *n Chem* ácido *m* fórmico

formidable [fɔː'mɪdəbəl] *adj* (**a**) *(daunting) (opponent)* temible, terrible; *(task, difficulty, obstacle)* tremendo(a) (**b**) *(impressive) (performance, talent)* formidable, extraordinario(a); *(achievement, skills)* extraordinario(a); **a f. intellect** un intelecto extraordinario

formidably ['fɔːmɪdəblɪ] *adv* (**a**) *(dauntingly) (difficult)* tremendamente (**b**) *(impressively) (talented, thorough)* extraordinariamente

formless ['fɔːmlɪs] *adj* informe, sin forma

formlessness ['fɔːmlɪsnɪs] *n* falta *f* de forma

formula ['fɔːmjʊlə] (*pl* **formulas** *or* **formulae** ['fɔːmjʊliː]) *n* (**a**) *(recipe, procedure)* fórmula *f*; **the f. for success** la clave del éxito; **a peace/pay f.** una fórmula para la paz/de pago

(**b**) *(form of words)* fórmula *f*; **a polite f.** una fórmula de cortesía; **a f. acceptable to both sides** una fórmula aceptable para ambas partes

(**c**) *Math & Phys* fórmula *f*

(**d**) *Chem* fórmula *f*

(**e**) *Sport* ***F. One*** Fórmula *f* 1

(**f**) *US (baby milk)* leche *f* maternizada

formulaic [fɔːmjʊ'leɪɪk] *adj* formulario(a)

formulate ['fɔːmjʊleɪt] *vt* formular; **it's difficult to f. in words** es difícil expresarlo en palabras

formulation [fɔːmjʊ'leɪʃən] *n* (**a**) *(of plan)* formulación *f*; *(of idea)* formulación *f*, expresión *f* (**b**) *(of medicine, cosmetics)* fórmula *f*

fornicate ['fɔːnɪkeɪt] *vi Formal* fornicar

fornication [fɔːnɪ'keɪʃən] *n Formal* fornicación *f*

fornicator ['fɔːnɪkeɪtə(r)] *n Formal* fornicador(ora) *m,f*

forsake [fə'seɪk] (*pt* **forsook** [fə'sʊk], *pp* **forsaken** [fə'seɪkən]) *vt Literary* (**a**) *(abandon)* abandonar (**b**) *(give up)* renunciar a

forsaken [fə'seɪkən] *adj* abandonado(a)

forsook *pt of* **forsake**

forsooth [fə'suːθ] *exclam Archaic* ¡en efecto!

forswear [fɔː'sweə(r)] (*pt* **forswore** [fɔː'swɔː(r)], *pp* **forsworn** [fɔː'swɔːn]) *vt Formal* (**a**) *(renounce)* renunciar firmemente a (**b**) *(deny)* negar rotundamente (**c**) **to f. oneself** *(commit perjury)* perjurar

forsythia [fɔː'saɪθɪə] *n* forsitia *f*

fort [fɔːt] *n Mil* fortaleza *f*, fuerte *m*; *Fig* **to hold** *or US* **hold down the f.** quedarse al cargo

forte ['fɔːtɪ] **1** *n (strong point)* fuerte *m*

2 *adj Mus* forte

3 *adv Mus* forte

forth [fɔːθ] *adv* (**a**) *Literary (out, forward)* **to go** *or* **set f.** partir; **to send f.** enviar; **to walk back and f.** ir de aquí para allá (**b**) *Literary (forwards in time)* **from that day f.** a partir de ese día (**c**) **and (so on and) so f.** y así sucesivamente

Forth Bridge ['fɔːθ'brɪdʒ] *n* **the F.** el puente Forth; IDIOM *Br Hum* **it's like painting the F.** es el cuento de nunca acabar

forthcoming [fɔːθ'kʌmɪŋ] *adj* (**a**) *(imminent) (election)* próximo(a); *(book)* de próxima aparición; *(movie)* de próximo estreno (**b**) *(available)* **no money/help was f.** no había dinero/ayuda disponible; **no answer was f.** no se ofreció ninguna respuesta (**c**) *(informative)* comunicativo(a); **he wasn't very f. (on the subject)** no estuvo muy comunicativo (respecto a ese asunto)

forthright ['fɔːθraɪt] *adj* directo(a), franco(a)

forthwith [fɔːθ'wɪθ] *adv Formal* en el acto

forties ['fɔːtɪz] *npl* **the f.** los (años) cuarenta; *see also* **eighties**

fortieth ['fɔːtɪəθ] **1** *n* cuadragésimo(a) *m,f*

2 *adj* cuadragésimo(a)

fortification [fɔːtɪfɪ'keɪʃən] *n* (**a**) *(action)* fortificación *f* (**b**) *(structure)* fortificación *f*

fortified ['fɔːtɪfaɪd] *adj* (**a**) *(town)* fortificado(a) (**b**) ***f. wine*** = vino fuerte tipo Oporto o Jerez

fortify ['fɔːtɪfaɪ] *vt* (**a**) *Mil (place)* fortificar (**b**) *(strengthen)* **to f. oneself** fortalecerse, tomar *or* cobrar fuerzas (**c**) *(wine)* fortificar; **fortified with vitamins** *(food, drink)* enriquecido con vitaminas

fortissimo [fɔː'tɪsɪməʊ] *Mus* **1** *adj* fortissimo

2 *adv* fortissimo

fortitude ['fɔːtɪtjuːd] *n* fortaleza *f*, entereza *f*

fortnight ['fɔːtnaɪt] *n Br* quincena *f*; **a f. today** en quince días; **a f.'s holiday** quince días de vacaciones

fortnightly ['fɔːtnaɪtlɪ] *Br* **1** *adj* quincenal

2 *adv* quincenalmente, cada quince días

3 *n (magazine)* publicación *f* quincenal

FORTRAN ['fɔːtræn] *n Comptr* FORTRAN *m*

fortress ['fɔːtrɪs] *n* fortaleza *f*

fortuitous [fɔː'tjuːɪtəs] *adj* casual, fortuito(a)

fortuitously [fɔː'tjuːɪtəslɪ] *adv* por casualidad, de manera fortuita

fortuitousness [fɔː'tjuːɪtəsnɪs] *n* lo fortuito

fortunate ['fɔːtʃənət] *adj* afortunado(a); **to be f. enough to do sth** tener la suerte de hacer algo; **he is f. in his friends** tiene suerte con sus amigos; **how f.!** ¡qué suerte!; **we should help those less f. than ourselves** debemos ayudar a los que son menos afortunados que nosotros

fortunately ['fɔːtʃənətlɪ] *adv* afortunadamente

fortune ['fɔːtʃən] *n* (**a**) *(riches)* fortuna *f*; **to make a f.** ganar una fortuna; **to make one's f.** hacer una fortuna; **to come into a f.** heredar una fortuna; **there are fortunes to be made in computing** con la informática se puede uno hacer de oro; *Fam* **it cost me a (small) f.** me ha costado un dineral *or* una fortuna

(**b**) *(luck)* suerte *f*, fortuna *f*; **good/bad f.** buena/mala suerte; **by good f.** por suerte *or* fortuna; **to try one's f.** probar fortuna ►► ***f. cookie*** galleta *f* de la suerte

(**c**) *(chance, fate)* **f. smiles on him** la fortuna le sonríe; **the changing fortunes of...** los avatares *or* las vicisitudes de...; **the fortunes of war** los avatares *or* las vicisitudes de la guerra

(**d**) *(future)* **to tell sb's f.** decir a alguien la buenaventura

fortune-hunter ['fɔːtʃənhʌntə(r)] *n Fam Pej* cazadotes *m inv*

fortune-teller ['fɔːtʃəntelə(r)] *n* adivino(a) *m,f*

forty ['fɔːtɪ] **1** *n* cuarenta *m*

2 *adj* cuarenta; *Fam* **to have f. winks** echarse una siestecita; *US* **the lower f.-eight** = los Estados Unidos sin incluir a Alaska y Hawai; *see also* **eighty**

forty-five ['fɔːtɪ'faɪv] *n* (**a**) *(record)* disco *m* de cuarenta y cinco (revoluciones) (**b**) *US (pistol)* pistola *f* del calibre 45

forum ['fɔːrəm] *n* (**a**) *(place, publication for debate)* foro *m*; **a f. for debate** un foro de debate (**b**) *Hist* **the F.** el Foro (**c**) *Comptr* fórum *m*

forward ['fɔːwəd] **1** *n Sport* delantero(a) *m,f*; *(in basketball)* alero(a) *m,f*

2 *adj* (**a**) *(position)* delantero(a); *(movement)* hacia delante ►► *Mil* ***f. area*** área *f* de vanguardia; *Com* ***f. integration*** integración *f* vertical; *Sport* ***f. line*** línea *f* delantera; *Fin* ***f. market*** mercado *m* de futuros; ***f. pass*** *(in rugby)* pase *m* adelantado, avant *m*; ***f. planning*** planificación *f* (de futuro); ***f. roll*** *(in gymnastics)* voltereta *f* hacia adelante;

Comptr **f.** ***search*** búsqueda *f* hacia adelante; ***f. slash*** barra *f* inclinada *(hacia adelante)*
(**b**) *(impudent, bold)* atrevido(a)
3 *adv* (**a**) *(of time)* **from this/that day f.** desde este/ese día en adelante; **to put the clocks f.** adelantar los relojes
(**b**) *(of direction)* hacia delante; **keep going straight f.** sigue todo recto hacia adelante; **to run/jump f.** correr/saltar hacia adelante; **he reached f. to tap her on the shoulder** alargó la mano y le dio unos toquecitos en el hombro; *Mil* **f., march!** ¡de frente, marchen!
(**c**) *(of position)* delante; **we're too far f.** estamos demasiado delante; **the project is no further f.** el proyecto no ha progresado nada
4 *vt* (**a**) *(letter)* reexpedir, remitir; *(e-mail)* remitir; **to f. sth to sb** enviar algo a alguien; **I've arranged to have my mail forwarded** he pedido que me remitan el correo; **please f.** *(on envelope)* = expresión que se escribe en una carta para indicar que ésta debe ser enviada a una nueva dirección
(**b**) *Com (goods)* enviar, expedir
(**c**) *(one's career, interests, a cause)* promover

forwarding ['fɔːwədɪŋ] *adj* ***f. address*** = dirección a la que se reexpide una carta; *Com* ***f. agent*** transitario(a) *m,f*

forward-looking ['fɔːwədlʊkɪŋ] *adj* con visión de futuro, progresista

forwards ['fɔːwədz] *adv* = **forward**

forwent *pt of* **forgo**

Fosbury flop ['fɒzbərɪ'flɒp] *n Sport* salto *m* al estilo Fosbury

fossil ['fɒsəl] *n* (**a**) *(of plant, animal)* fósil *m* ►► ***f. fuel*** combustible *m* fósil (**b**) *Fam (person)* **an old f.** un carcamal *or Am* carcamán

fossilize ['fɒsəlaɪz] *vi* (**a**) *(remains)* fosilizar (**b**) *(attitudes, opinions)* anquilosarse (**c**) *(second language)* fosilizarse, quedarse estancado(a)

fossilized ['fɒsəlaɪzd] *adj* (**a**) *(remains)* fosilizado(a) (**b**) *(attitudes, opinions)* anquilosado(a) (**c**) *Ling (form)* fosilizado(a)

foster ['fɒstə(r)] **1** *adj* ***f. child*** niño(a) *m,f* en régimen de acogida; ***f. home*** hogar *m* de acogida; ***f. mother*** madre *f* adoptiva; ***f. parents*** familia *f* de acogida
2 *vt* (**a**) *(child) (of family, person)* adoptar (temporalmente), acoger; *(of authorities, court)* colocar con una familia de acogida (**b**) *(idea, hope, friendship)* fomentar, alimentar

fostering ['fɒstərɪŋ] *n* acogida *f* familiar *(de un niño)*

fought *pt & pp of* **fight**

foul [faʊl] **1** *n Sport* falta *f*
2 *adj* (**a**) *(disgusting) (smell, taste)* asqueroso(a); *(air)* viciado(a); *(breath)* fétido(a)
(**b**) *Fam (horrible, unpleasant) (weather)* espantoso(a); **to be in a f. mood** *or* **temper** estar de un humor de perros; **he has a f. temper** tiene un genio de mil demonios; **to be f. to sb** tratar muy mal *or Esp* fatal a alguien; **he was being perfectly f.** estuvo de lo más desagradable ►► ***f. language*** lenguaje *m* soez
(**c**) *Literary (vile)* vil
(**d**) *(illegal)* ***f. ball*** *(in baseball)* pelota *f* nula; ***f. line*** *(in baseball, bowling)* línea *f* de límites; *Sport* ***f. play*** juego *m* sucio; *Law* **f. play is not suspected** no hay sospecha de que exista un acto delictivo
3 *adv* **to smell/taste f.** oler/saber asqueroso(a) *or Esp* fatal; **to fall f. of the law** incumplir la ley
4 *vt* (**a**) *(make dirty)* ensuciar; *(pollute)* contaminar; *Br* **it is an offence to allow a dog to f. the pavement** es una infracción dejar que el perro haga sus necesidades en la calle; IDIOM **to f. one's own nest** tirar piedras sobre el propio tejado
(**b**) *(entangle)* **weeds had fouled the propeller** unas algas atascaron la hélice
(**c**) *Sport* **to f. sb** hacerle (una) falta a alguien
5 *vi* (**a**) *(rope, anchor)* enredarse (**b**) *Sport (in soccer, hockey)* hacer falta; *(in basketball)* hacer (falta) personal

►**foul up** *Fam* **1** *vt sep (ruin)* estropear
2 *vi (fail)* meter la pata, *Méx* regarla

foully ['faʊlɪ] *adv* (**a**) *(to speak)* groseramente (**b**) *(to behave)* vilmente; **to treat sb f.** tratar a alguien vilmente (**c**) *Literary* **he was f. murdered** fue vilmente asesinado

foul-mouthed ['faʊl'maʊðd] *adj* grosero(a), soez

foulness ['faʊlnɪs] *n* (**a**) *(of breath, smell)* hedor *m*, pestilencia *f*; *(of taste)* lo repugnante; *(of air)* lo viciado (**b**) *(of weather)* inclemencia *f*; *(of language)* lo grosero (**c**) *(unpleasant behaviour)* grosería *f*, malos modos *mpl*

foul-smelling ['faʊl'smelɪŋ] *adj* pestilente

foul-tempered ['faʊl'tempəd] *adj* malhumorado(a), arisco(a); **to be f.** tener muy mal genio

foul-up ['faʊlʌp] *n Fam* metedura *f or Am* metida *f* de pata

found[1] [faʊnd] *vt* (**a**) *(city, organization)* fundar; *(business)* crear, abrir; **our society is founded on the idea of equality** nuestra sociedad está fundada *or* basada en la idea de la igualdad (**b**) *(suspicions, hope)* fundar, basar (**on** en); **the story is founded on fact** la historia se basa en hechos reales (**c**) *(cast)* fundir

found[2] **1** *pt & pp of* **find**
2 *adj Br* **£30 a week all f.** 30 libras a la semana con todo incluido

foundation [faʊn'deɪʃən] *n* (**a**) *(act of founding)* fundación *f*
(**b**) *(institution)* fundación *f*; **a charitable f.** una fundación benéfica
(**c**) *(basis) (of theory, belief)* fundamento *m*; **the rumour is without f.** el rumor no tiene fundamento
(**d**) *Constr* **the foundations** los cimientos; **to lay the foundations of sth** sentar las bases de algo, poner los cimientos de algo; *Fig* **the foundations of modern society** los pilares de la sociedad moderna ►► *Univ* ***f. course*** curso *m* introductorio *or* de iniciación; ***f. garment*** prenda *f* de corsetería; ***f. stone*** primera piedra *f*
(**e**) *(make-up)* **f. (cream)** (crema *f* de) base *f*

founder[1] ['faʊndə(r)] *n* (**a**) *(of hospital, school)* fundador(ora) *m,f* ►► *Br* ***f. member*** miembro *mf* fundador(ora); ***f. partner*** socio(a) *m,f* fundador(ora) (**b**) *(of statue, bell)* fundidor(ora) *m,f*

founder[2] *vi* (**a**) *(ship)* **the boat foundered on the rocks** el barco chocó contra las rocas y se fue a pique (**b**) *(vehicle)* **the carriage foundered in the mud** el coche se atascaba en el barro (**c**) *(project, talks)* irse a pique (**on** debido a) (**d**) *(horse) (go lame)* dar un traspié

founding father ['faʊndɪŋ'fɑːðə(r)] *n* padre *m*, fundador *m*; *US Hist* **the Founding Fathers** = los redactores de la constitución y fundadores de los Estados Unidos

foundling ['faʊndlɪŋ] *n Old-fashioned* expósito(a) *m,f* ►► ***f. home*** casa *f* cuna

foundry ['faʊndrɪ] *n* fundición *f*

fount [faʊnt] *n* (**a**) *Literary (spring)* fuente *f* (**b**) *(source)* fuente *f*; **a f. of knowledge** una fuente de conocimientos; **the f. of all wisdom** la fuente de toda sabiduría (**c**) *Br Typ* fundición *f*

fountain ['faʊntɪn] *n* (**a**) *(ornamental)* fuente *f*; *Mythol* **the F. of Youth** la fuente de la juventud (**b**) ***f. pen*** pluma *f* (estilográfica), *CSur* lapicera *f* fuente

four [fɔː(r)] **1** *n* (**a**) *(number)* cuatro *m*; **on all fours** a gatas, a cuatro patas (**b**) *(in cricket)* = cuatro carreras que se otorgan al bateador cuando la pelota lanzada por él da en el duelo y luego sale fuera del perímetro del campo marcado por la cuerda
2 *adj* cuatro; **the f. winds** los cuatro vientos; **to the f. corners of the earth** a todos los rincones del orbe ►► *Rel* ***the f. horsemen of the Apocalypse*** los cuatro jinetes del Apocalipsis; *see also* **eight**

fourball ['fɔːbɔːl] *n (in golf)* fourball *m*, cuatro bolas *m*

four-by-four ['fɔːbaɪ'fɔː(r)] *n (vehicle)* todoterreno *m*

four-colour ['fɔː'kʌlə(r)] *adj Comptr & Typ* ***f. process*** cuatricromía *f*; ***f. separation*** separación *f* de colores

four-cycle ['fɔː'saɪkəl] *adj US (engine, cylinder)* de cuatro tiempos

four-dimensional ['fɔːdaɪ'menʃənəl] *adj* cuatridimensional

four-door ['fɔː'dɔː(r)] *adj* de cuatro puertas ►► ***f. hatchback*** cinco puertas *m*; ***f. saloon*** berlina *f*

four-engined ['fɔːr'endʒɪnd] *adj (plane)* cuatrimotor

four-eyes ['fɔːraɪz] *n Fam* cuatro ojos *mf inv*, *Esp* gafotas *mf inv*, *Méx* cuatro lámparas *mf inv*, *RP* anteojudo(a) *m,f*

Four-F ['fɔːr'ef] *n US Mil* inútil *m (para el servicio militar)*

four-figure ['fɔː'fɪgə(r)] *adj* de cuatro cifras; **a f. sum** una suma de dinero de cuatro cifras

four-flusher ['fɔː'flʌʃə(r)] *n US Fam* fantasma *mf*, fanfarrón(ona) *m,f*

fourfold ['fɔːfəʊld] **1** *adj* cuatriplicado(a); **a f. increase (in)** cuatro veces más (de)
2 *adv* por cuatro, cuatro veces; **to increase f.** cuadruplicarse

four-footed ['fɔː'fʊtɪd] *adj* cuadrúpedo(a) ►► *Hum* ***f. friend*** amigo *m* cuadrúpedo

four-in-hand ['fɔːrɪn'hænd] *n (carriage)* coche *m* tirado por cuatro caballos

four-leaf clover ['fɔːliːf'kləʊvə(r)] *n* trébol *m* de cuatro hojas

four-legged ['fɔː'legɪd] *adj* cuadrúpedo(a) ►► *Hum* ***f. friend*** amigo *m* cuadrúpedo

four-letter word ['fɔːletə'wɜːd] *n* palabrota *f*, *Esp* taco *m*

four-ply ['fɔːplaɪ] *adj* (**a**) *(wool)* de cuatro hebras (**b**) *(wood)* de cuatro capas

four-poster ['fɔː'pəʊstə(r)] *n* **f. (bed)** cama *f* de dosel

fourscore ['fɔːskɔː(r)] *Old-fashioned* **1** *n* ochenta *m*
2 *adj* ochenta

foursome ['fɔːsəm] *n* (**a**) *(people)* cuarteto *m* (**b**) *(for tennis match, card game)* dos parejas *fpl*; *(in golf)* foursome *m*

four-square ['fɔːskweə(r)] **1** *adj (steady)* firme; *(solid)* sólido(a)
2 *adv* **they stood f. behind her** la apoyaron firmemente *or* decididamente

four-star ['fɔːstɑː(r)] *Br* **1** *n* súper *f*
2 *adj (petrol)* súper

four-stroke ['fɔːstrəʊk] *adj* de cuatro tiempos

fourteen [fɔː'tiːn] **1** *n* catorce *m*
2 *adj* catorce; *see also* **eight**

fourteenth [fɔː'tiːnθ] **1** *n* (**a**) *(fraction)* catorceavo *m*, catorceava parte *f* (**b**) *(in series)* decimocuarto(a) *m,f* (**c**) *(of month)* catorce *m*
2 *adj* decimocuarto(a); *see also* **eleventh**

fourth [fɔːθ] **1** *n* (**a**) *(in series)* cuarto(a) *m,f* (**b**) *(of month)* cuatro *m* ►► ***the F. of July*** el cuatro de julio (**c**) *(fourth gear)* cuarta *f*; **in f.** en cuarta (**d**) *Mus* cuarta *f*
2 *adj* cuarto(a) ►► ***f. dimension*** cuarta dimensión *f*; ***the f. estate*** *(the press)* el cuarto poder; *Aut* ***f. gear*** cuarta *f* (marcha *f*); ***f. official*** *(in soccer)* cuarto árbitro *m*; ***the F. World*** el Cuarto Mundo
3 *adv* en cuarto lugar; *see also* **eighth**

fourthly ['fɔːθlɪ] *adv* en cuarto lugar

four-wheel drive ['fɔːwiːl'draɪv] *n* tracción *f* a las cuatro ruedas; **a f. (vehicle)** un todoterreno, un cuatro por cuatro

fowl [faʊl] *(pl* **fowl**) *n* (**a**) *(farmyard bird)* ave *f* de corral ►► ***f. pest*** influenza *f or* peste *f* aviaria (**b**) *Archaic or Literary (bird)* ave *f*

fowling ['faʊlɪŋ] *n* **to go f.** ir a cazar aves ►► ***f. piece*** escopeta *f (para cazar aves)*

fox [fɒks] **1** *n* (**a**) *(animal)* zorro *m*; *Fig* **a sly old f.** *(cunning person)* un viejo zorro; IDIOM **it's like setting the f. to mind the geese** es como dejar al lobo cuidando a los corderos ►► ***f. cub*** cría *f* de zorro; ***f. hunt*** cacería *f* del zorro; ***f. hunting*** la caza del zorro; ***f. terrier*** foxterrier *m* (**b**) *US Fam (woman)* nena *f*, *Esp* tía *f* buena
2 *vt* (**a**) *Fam (perplex)* confundir; **the problem had us foxed** el problema nos tenía confundidos (**b**) *Fam (deceive)* burlar, engañar (**c**) *(paper)* manchar
3 *vi (paper)* mancharse

fox-bat ['fɒksbæt] *n* zorro *m* volador

foxglove ['fɒksglʌv] *n* digital *f*, dedalera *f*

foxhole ['fɒkshəʊl] *n* (**a**) *(of fox)* madriguera *f (de zorro)* (**b**) *Mil* hoyo *m* trinchera

foxhound ['fɒkshaʊnd] *n* perro *m* raposero

foxhunting ['fɒkshʌntɪŋ] *n* caza *f* del zorro; **to go f.** ir a la caza del zorro

foxtrot ['fɒkstrɒt] **1** *n* foxtrot *m*
2 *vi (pt & pp* **foxtrotted**) bailar el foxtrot

foxy ['fɒksɪ] *adj Fam* (**a**) *(cunning)* astuto(a), zorro (**b**) *US (sexy)* sexy

foyer ['fɔɪeɪ] *n* (**a**) *(of cinema, theatre)* vestíbulo *m*, *RP* foyer *m*; *(of hotel)* vestíbulo *m* (**b**) *US (of house)* recibidor *m*

FP [ef'piː] *n* (**a**) *Br* (*abbr* **former pupil**) ex alumno(a) *m,f* (**b**) *US* (*abbr* **fireplug**) boca *f* de incendios

FPU [efpiː'juː] *n Comptr* (*abbr* **floating-point unit**) FPU *f*, unidad *f* de coma flotante

Fr (*abbr* **Father**) P.

fracas ['frækɑː] *(pl* **fracas** ['frækɑːz]) *n* gresca *f*, refriega *f*

> **False friend:** The Spanish noun **fracaso** is not a translation for the English word **fracas**. In Spanish **fracaso** means "failure".

fractal ['fræktəl] *n Math* fractal *m* ►► ***f. geometry*** geometría *f* fractal *or* de fractales

fraction ['frækʃən] *n* (**a**) *Math* fracción *f*, (número *m*) quebrado *m* (**b**) *(small part)* fracción *f*; **a f. too small/large** un poquitín pequeño/grande; **at a f. of the cost** por una mínima parte del costo *or Esp* coste; **he escaped death by a f. of a second** se libró de la muerte por una milésima *or* una fracción de segundo (**c**) *Fin (of share)* fracción *f* (**d**) *Chem (of distillation)* fracción *f*

fractional ['frækʃənəl] *adj* (**a**) *(very small) (amount)* ínfimo(a); *(difference, alteration)* mínimo(a); *(decline, hesitation)* mínimo(a), ligero(a) (**b**) *Chem* ***f. distillation*** destilación *f* fraccionada

fractionally ['frækʃənəlɪ] *adv* mínimamente

fractious ['frækʃəs] *adj* (**a**) *(unruly)* díscolo(a), revoltoso(a) (**b**) *(irritable)* irritable; **to be f.** *or* **in a f. mood** estar irritable

fractiously ['frækʃəslɪ] *adv (irritably)* con irritación

fracture ['fræktʃə(r)] **1** *n* (**a**) *Med* fractura *f* (**b**) *(split, crevice)* fisura *f*, grieta *f*
2 *vt (bone, limb)* fracturar; **fractured skull/ribs** cráneo fracturado/costillas fracturadas; *Fig* **their withdrawal fractured the alliance** su retirada quebró la alianza
3 *vi* fracturarse

fragile ['frædʒaɪl] *adj* (**a**) *(object, material)* frágil (**b**) *(alliance, peace)* frágil; *(health)* delicado(a), frágil (**c**) *(person)* vulnerable; *Fam* **I'm feeling a bit f.** me siento un poco débil

fragility [frə'dʒɪlɪtɪ] *n* fragilidad *f*

fragment **1** *n* ['frægmənt] *(of object, story)* fragmento *m*; **the report contains not a f. of truth** el informe no contiene ni un ápice de verdad
2 *vt* [fræg'ment] *(object)* romper en pedazos, hacer añicos; *(organization)* fragmentar
3 *vi (object)* romperse en pedazos, hacerse añicos; *(organization)* fragmentarse

fragmentary [fræg'mentərɪ] *adj* fragmentario(a)

fragmentation [frægmen'teɪʃən] *n* (**a**) *(breaking up)* fragmentación *f* ►► ***f. bomb*** bomba *f* de fragmentación (**b**) *Comptr* fragmentación *f*

fragmented [fræg'mentɪd] *adj* fragmentado(a)

fragrance ['freɪgrəns] *n* fragancia *f*

fragrant ['freɪgrənt] *adj* fragante

fraidy cat ['freɪdɪkæt] *n US Fam* gallina *mf*, *Esp* miedica *mf*

frail [freɪl] *adj* (**a**) *(person, health)* delicado(a), frágil; *(object, structure)* frágil (**b**) *(beauty, happiness)* frágil

frailty ['freɪltɪ] *n (of person, health, alliance)* fragilidad *f*; **human f.** la flaqueza humana

frame [freɪm] **1** *n* (**a**) *(border) (of picture, door)* marco *m*; *(of window)* marco *m*; *(for embroidery)* bastidor *m*, tambor *m*
(**b**) *(structure) (of building, bridge)* estructura *f*; *(of bicycle)* cuadro *m*; *(of spectacles)* montura *f*; *(of racket)* marco *m*; *(for walking)* andador *m* ►► ***f. backpack*** mochila *f* con armazón; ***f. house*** casa *f* de madera
(**c**) *(of person, animal)* cuerpo *m*
(**d**) *Fig* **f. of mind** humor, estado de ánimo; **I was in the wrong f. of mind to take the test** no me sentía con ánimos para hacer el examen; **to get oneself into the right f. of mind** prepararse mentalmente para algo; **f. of reference** sistema de referencia
(**e**) *(of film)* fotograma *m*; *(of comic strip)* viñeta *f*
(**f**) *(in snooker, pool, billiards)* set *m*; *(in bowling)* juego *m*
(**g**) *(in gardening)* marco *m*
(**h**) *Comptr (on Web page)* cuadro *m*, marco *m*
2 *vt* (**a**) *(picture)* enmarcar; **he stood framed in the doorway** estaba de pie *orAm* parado(a) en el vano de la puerta; **her face was framed by a white silk scarf** su cara estaba enmarcada por un pañuelo de seda blanca
(**b**) *Phot, Cin & TV (subject)* encuadrar
(**c**) *(answer, legislation)* formular
(**d**) *Fam (falsely incriminate)* tender una trampa a; **I've been framed!** ¡me han cargado con el muerto!

frame-up ['freɪmʌp] *n Fam* trampa *f*, montaje *m*

framework ['freɪmwɜːk] *n* (**a**) *(of structure)* estructura *f* (**b**) *(for talks)* marco *m*; **the bill seeks to provide a legal f. for divorce** el proyecto de ley intenta proporcionar un marco legal para el divorcio; **within the f. of the UN/EU** dentro del marco de la ONU/UE; **a f. agreement** un acuerdo marco

franc [fræŋk] *n (currency)* franco *m*; *Formerly* **Belgian/French f.** franco belga/francés; **Swiss f.** franco suizo

France [frɑːns] *n* Francia

franchise ['fræntʃaɪz] **1** *n* (**a**) *Pol* sufragio *m* (**b**) *Com (for shop, fast-food chain)* franquicia *f*; *(for radio, TV station)* licencia *f* ►► ***f. agreement*** contrato *m* de franquicia (**c**) *Com (shop, outlet)* franquicia *f*
2 *vt Com* franquiciar

franchisee [fræntʃaɪ'ziː] *n Com (from company)* franquiciado(a) *m,f*, concesionario(a) *m,f*

franchising ['fræntʃaɪzɪŋ] *n Com* franquicia *f*, franchising *m*

Francis ['frɑːnsɪs] *pr n* **F. I/II** Francisco I/II

Franciscan [fræn'sɪskən] **1** *n* franciscano(a) *m,f*
2 *adj* franciscano(a)

francium ['frænsɪəm] *n Chem* francio *m*

Franco- ['fræŋkəʊ] *prefix* franco-; **F.-German cooperation** cooperación franco-alemana

Francoism ['fræŋkəʊɪzəm] *n* franquismo *m*

Francoist ['fræŋkəʊɪst] 1 *n* franquista *mf*
2 *adj* franquista

francophile ['fræŋkəfaɪl] 1 *n* francófilo(a) *m,f*
2 *adj* francófilo(a)

francophilia [fræŋkə'fɪlɪə] *n* francofilia *f*

francophobe ['fræŋkəfəʊb] 1 *n* francófobo(a) *m,f*
2 *adj* francófobo(a)

francophobia [fræŋkə'fəʊbɪə] *n* francofobia *f*

francophone ['fræŋkəʊfəʊn] 1 *n* francófono(a) *m,f*
2 *adj* francófono(a)

frangipane ['frændʒɪpeɪn] *n Culin* franchipán *m*

frangipani [frændʒɪ'pɑ:nɪ] *n (plant)* franchipaniero *m*; *(perfume)* esencia *f* de franchipaniero

franglais ['frɒŋgleɪ] *n Hum* francés *m* lleno de anglicismos

Frank [fræŋk] *n Hist* franco(a) *m,f*

frank [fræŋk] 1 *adj* (a) *(candid) (person, discussion)* franco(a); **to be f.,...** francamente,... (b) *(undisguised) (distaste, admiration)* manifiesto(a)
2 *vt Br (letter)* franquear
3 *n* (a) *Br (on letter)* franqueo *m* (b) *US Fam (sausage)* salchicha *f* de Fráncfort

Frankenstein ['fræŋkɪnsteɪn] *n* **F., F.'s monster** *(the character)* (el monstruo del doctor) Frankenstein; *Fig* **the committee has turned into a F.'s monster** el comité se ha convertido en un monstruo descontrolado que se ha vuelto contra su creador ►► *Br Fam* ***F. food*** *(genetically modified)* alimentos *mpl* transgénicos

Frankfurt ['fræŋkfɜ:t] *n* Fráncfort

frankfurter ['fræŋkfɜ:tə(r)] *n (sausage)* salchicha *f* de Fráncfort

frankincense ['fræŋkɪnsens] *n* incienso *m*

franking machine ['fræŋkɪŋmə'ʃi:n] *n* máquina *f* de franquear cartas

Frankish ['fræŋkɪʃ] 1 *adj Hist* franco(a)
2 *n (language)* franco *m*

frankly ['fræŋklɪ] *adv* francamente; **a f. disastrous performance** una actuación francamente *or* realmente desastrosa; **f., I couldn't care less** la verdad, me da igual

frankness ['fræŋknɪs] *n* franqueza *f*

frantic ['fræntɪk] *adj* (a) *(rush, pace)* frenético(a); **things are pretty f. at the office** estamos que no paramos en la oficina (b) *(agitated)* **f. with worry** fuera de sí de preocupación; **to drive sb f.** poner a alguien frenético(a) *or* al borde de la desesperación

frantically ['fræntɪklɪ] *adv* frenéticamente; **we're f. busy at the moment** estamos ocupadísimos este momento

frappé [*Br* 'fræpeɪ, *US* fræ'peɪ] *n* (a) *(alchoholic)* = cóctel alcohólico servido con hielo picado (b) *(milkshake)* batido *m*

frat [fræt] *n US Fam* ***f. boy*** = miembro de una "fraternity" universitaria; ***f. house*** = residencia perteneciente a una "fraternity" universitaria

fraternal [frə'tɜ:nəl] *adj* fraterno(a), fraternal ►► ***f. twins*** gemelos *mpl* bivitelinos, mellizos *mpl*

fraternity [frə'tɜ:nɪtɪ] *n* (a) *(brotherliness)* fraternidad *f* (b) *(religious group)* hermandad *f*, cofradía *f*; **the medical/banking f.** el gremio médico/de la banca (c) *US Univ* = asociación de estudiantes que suele funcionar como club social ►► ***f. house*** = residencia perteneciente a dicha asociación

fraternization [frætənaɪ'zeɪʃən] *n* confraternización (**with** con)

fraternize ['frætənaɪz] *vi* confraternizar (**with** con)

fratricidal [frætrɪ'saɪdəl] *adj* fratricida

fratricide ['frætrɪsaɪd] *n* (a) *(act)* fratricidio *m* (b) *(person)* fratricida *mf*

fraud [frɔ:d] *n* (a) *(person)* farsante *mf* (b) *(deception)* fraude *m*; **credit card f.** fraude con tarjetas de crédito; **computer f.** delito informático; **to obtain sth by f.** conseguir algo por medios fraudulentos ►► ***f. squad*** brigada *f* de delitos económicos, brigada anticorrupción (c) *(product, work)* engaño *m*

fraudster ['frɔ:dstə(r)] *n Br Fam* estafador(ora) *m,f*

fraudulence ['frɔ:djʊləns], **fraudulency** ['frɔ:djʊlənsɪ] *n* fraudulencia *f*

fraudulent ['frɔ:djʊlənt] *adj* fraudulento(a)

fraudulently ['frɔ:djʊləntlɪ] *adv* de forma fraudulenta, fraudulentamente

fraught [frɔ:t] *adj* (a) *(tense) (situation)* tenso(a), tirante; *(person)* tenso(a); **I've had a particularly f. week** he tenido una semana de mucha tensión (b) *(filled)* **f. with danger/emotion** cargado(a) de peligro/emoción; **f. with difficulty** plagado(a) de dificultades

fray[1] [freɪ] *n (brawl)* contienda *f*, combate *m*; **to enter** *or* **join the f.** entrar en liza; **to return to the f.** *(after rest, illness)* volver a estar en la brecha

fray[2] 1 *vt* (a) *(material, garment)* deshilachar; **her jacket was frayed at the cuffs** tenía los puños de la chaqueta deshilachados (b) *(nerves)* crispar; **his questions were fraying my nerves** sus preguntas estaban empezando a crisparme los nervios
2 *vi* (a) *(material)* deshilacharse; IDIOM **to f. around** *or* **at the edges** *(agreement, system)* hacer aguas; **the team were starting to f. around the edges** se estaban empezando a ver señales de tensión en el equipo (b) *(nerves, tempers)* crisparse

frazzle ['fræzəl] *Fam* 1 *n* **to be burnt to a f.** estar (totalmente) carbonizado(a); **worn to a f.** *(person)* hecho(a) polvo, *RP* destruido(a); **my nerves were worn to a f.** tenía los nervios destrozados
2 *vt* (a) *(exhaust)* reventar, hacer polvo (b) *(burn)* carbonizar; **I got frazzled on the beach** me freí en la playa

frazzled ['fræzəld] *adj Fam (worn out)* **to be f.** estar hecho(a) polvo *or RP* destruido(a)

FRCP [efɑ:si:'pi:] *n* (*abbr* **Fellow of the Royal College of Physicians**) = miembro del colegio británico de médicos

FRCS [efɑ:si:'es] *n* (*abbr* **Fellow of the Royal College of Surgeons**) = miembro del colegio británico de cirujanos

freak [fri:k] 1 *n* (a) *(bizarre example) (person)* engendro *m*, monstruo *m*; *(event)* fenómeno *m*, caso *m* insólito; **just because I choose not to eat meat, that doesn't make me a f.** sólo porque no coma carne no significa que sea un bicho raro; **by some f. (of chance)** por una casualidad rara; **by a f. of fortune** por un capricho del destino ►► ***f. show*** = espectáculo que consiste en exhibir a personas con extrañas anomalías físicas
(b) *Fam (enthusiast)* fanático(a) *m,f*; **jazz/film f.** fanático(a) del jazz/cine
2 *adj* insólito(a); **a f. occurrence** un caso excepcional *or* insólito; **a f. storm** una tormenta inesperada
3 *vt Fam (shock)* alucinar; *(scare)* asustar
4 *vi* = **freak out**

► **freak out** *Fam* 1 *vt sep (shock)* alucinar; *(scare)* meter canguelo *or Méx* mello *or RP* cuiqui a
2 *vi* (a) *(become angry)* ponerse hecho(a) una furia; **I freaked out** *(panicked)* me entró el pánico *or* la neura (b) *Fam (dance with abandon)* bailar como descosido(a)

freaking ['fri:kɪŋ] *US Fam* 1 *adj (for emphasis)* **where are those f. kids?** ¿dónde están esos demonios de chicos?
2 *adv (for emphasis)* **it's f. cold out there** hace un frío de mil pares de narices; **I don't f. know!** ¡no lo sé, narices!

freakish ['fri:kɪʃ] *adj (bizarre)* extrafalario(a), raro(a)

freaky ['fri:kɪ] *adj Fam* muy raro(a)

freckle ['frekəl] *n* peca *f*

freckled ['frekəld], **freckly** ['freklɪ] *adj* pecoso(a)

Frederick ['fredrɪk] *pr n* **F. I/II** Federico I/II

FREE [fri:] 1 *adj* (a) *(at liberty)* libre (**from** *or* **of** de); **f. and easy** relajado(a); **to be f. to do sth** ser libre de hacer algo; **you are f. to do as you please** eres libre de hacer lo que quieras; **feel f. to borrow the books** toma los libros cuando quieras; **feel f. to help yourself to tea** sírvete té si quieres; **she didn't feel f. to...** no se atrevía a...; **to set sb f.** liberar a alguien; **to have f. use of sth** poder utilizar algo sin restricciones; **to be a f. agent** *(in general)* poder obrar a su antojo; *(of sports player)* tener la carta de libertad; IDIOM **as f. as a bird** libre como el viento; IDIOM **to give sb/to have a f. hand** dar a alguien/tener carta blanca ►► ***f. association*** asociación *f* libre; ***F. Church*** iglesia *f* no conformista; ***f. climbing*** escalada *f* libre; *Ind* ***f. collective bargaining*** negociación *f* colectiva libre; ***f. diving*** (buceo *m* en) apnea *f*; ***f. drop:*** **to take a f. drop** *(in golf)* dropar una bola sin penalización; ***f. enterprise*** libre empresa *f*; ***f. fall*** *(of parachutist)* caída *f* libre; *(of economy)* caída *f* en *Esp* picado *or Am* picada; ***f. hit*** *(in hockey)* falta *f*, tiro *m* libre; ***f. house*** = "pub" británico que no depende de ninguna cervecera y puede vender cualquier marca de cerveza; ***f. jazz*** free jazz *m*, jazz *m* libre; ***f. kick*** *(in soccer)* falta *f*, golpe *m* franco, tiro *m* libre; ***f. love*** amor *m* libre; *Econ* ***f. market*** libre mercado *m*; ***f. market economics*** liberalismo *m* económico; ***f. market economy*** economía *f* de libre mercado; *Econ* ***f. marketeer*** librecambista *mf*, partidario(a) *m,f* de la economía de libre mercado; *Econ* ***f. movement*** *(of capital, workers)* libertad *f* de circulación, libre circulación *f*; *Br Law* ***f. pardon:*** **to give sb a f. pardon** conceder el indulto a alguien; *Com* ***f. port*** puerto *m* franco *or* libre; ***a f. press*** una prensa libre; ***f. skating*** programa *m* libre; ***f. speech*** libertad *f* de expresión; ***f. spirit:*** **she's a f. spirit** no se conforma con una vida convencional; ***f.***

throw *(in basketball)* tiro *m* libre; ***f. throw line*** *(in basketball)* línea *f* de tiros libres; ***f. trade*** libre cambio *m*, libre comercio *m*; ***f. trade area*** área *f* de libre cambio *or* comercio; ***f. verse*** verso *m* libre; ***f. vote*** voto *m* libre; ***f. will*** *(generally)* propia voluntad *f*; *(in philosophy, theology)* libre albedrío *m*; **to do sth of one's own f. will** hacer algo por iniciativa propia; ***the f. world*** el mundo libre
(**b**) *(unoccupied)* libre; **I am f. tomorrow** mañana estoy libre; **is this seat f.?** ¿está libre este asiento?; **she closed the door with her f. hand** cerró la puerta con la mano libre ►► *Br Sch* ***f. period*** = hora sin clase; ***f. time*** tiempo *m* libre
(**c**) *(without charge)* gratuito(a), gratis; **to be f.** ser gratuito(a) *or* gratis; *Com* **f. on board** franco a bordo; IDIOM **there's no such thing as a f. lunch** nadie regala nada ►► ***f. gift*** obsequio *m* (promocional); ***f. postage*** franquicia *f* postal; ***f. sample*** muestra *f* gratuita *or RP* gratis
(**d**) *(loose, not touching)* **you take the f. end** agarra el extremo que queda libre; **they pulled him f. of the rubble** lo sacaron de los escombros; **to get f.** liberarse; **the bolt had worked itself f.** el cerrojo se había soltado
(**e**) *(not having)* **the country will never be completely f. from** *or* **of unemployment** el país nunca se librará por completo del desempleo; **none of us is f. from** *or* **of guilt** ninguno de nosotros está libre de culpa; **this product is f. from** *or* **of artificial colouring** este producto no contiene colorantes artificiales; **it's nice to be f. of the children for once** no está mal estar sin los niños por una vez
(**f**) *(translation)* libre
(**g**) *(generous)* **to make f. with sth** no regatear algo; *Ironic* **he is very f. with his advice** es demasiado pródigo a la hora de dar consejos
(**h**) *Chem* libre ►► ***f. radical*** radical *m* libre
2 *adv* (**a**) *(without charge)* gratis, gratuitamente; **to do sth f. of charge** hacer algo gratis *or* gratuitamente; **for f.** gratis; *Fam Fig* **I won't be inviting you back again, I'll tell you that much for f.** no te voy a volver a invitar, eso lo tengo muy claro
(**b**) **to go** *or* **walk f.** *(prisoner)* salir libre
3 *vt* (*pt & pp* **freed** [fri:d]) *(prisoner, funds, mechanism)* liberar (**from** de); *(time, place)* desocupar; *(something stuck)* soltar; **this tool belt frees your hands for other jobs** este cinturón para herramientas te deja las manos libres para otras tareas; **they freed her from the wreckage** la sacaron de los restos del accidente; **losing my job frees me to do other things** el haber perdido el trabajo me deja tiempo para hacer otras cosas; **to f. oneself from** *or* **of sth** librarse de algo
► **free up** *vt sep (time, person)* dejar libre; *(funds)* liberar; **this system frees up space on your hard disk** este sistema libera espacio en el disco duro

---

-free [fri:] *suffix* **additive-f.** sin aditivos; **a problem-f. transition** una transición sin problemas; **we will replace it cost-f.** lo substituiremos gratuitamente
freebase ['fri:beɪs] *vi Fam* hacerse un chino de coca
freebie, freebee ['fri:bi:] *n Fam (gift)* regalito *m*; **the company sent him on a f. to Prague** la empresa le pagó un viaje a Praga
freeboard ['fri:bɔ:d] *n Naut* obra *f* muerta
freebooter ['fri:bu:tə(r)] *n Hist* filibustero *m*
freeborn ['fri:bɔ:n] *adj* nacido(a) libre
freedman ['fri:dmən] *n Hist* liberto *m*
freedom ['fri:dəm] *n* (**a**) *(lack of restriction)* libertad *f*; **to have the f. to do sth** tener libertad para hacer algo
(**b**) *(liberty, as right)* libertad *f*; **f. of conscience/thought** libertad de conciencia/pensamiento; **f. of association/speech/worship** libertad de asociación/expresión/culto; **f. of the press** libertad de prensa ►► ***f. fighter*** revolucionario(a) *m,f*
(**c**) *(exemption, absence)* **f. from fear/interference** total ausencia de miedos/intromisiones; **he was granted f. from prosecution** le eximieron de ser juzgado
(**d**) *(unrestricted access)* **she had the f. of the whole house** tenía toda la casa a su disposición, podía utilizar toda la casa con entera libertad; **to give** *or* **grant sb the f. of the city** entregar la(s) llave(s) de la ciudad a alguien; **the f. of the seas** la libertad de los mares; **f. of information** libertad de información ►► *Law* ***F. of Information Act*** ley *f* del derecho a la información
freedwoman ['fri:dwʊmən] *n Hist* liberta *f*
Freefone® ['fri:fəʊn] *adj Br* **a F. number** un (número de) teléfono gratuito, *Esp* ≃ un teléfono 900
free-for-all ['fri:fərɔ:l] *n Fam (fight, discussion)* bronca *f*, gresca *f*, *Méx* agarrón *m*; **it turned into a f.** degeneró en una bronca *or* gresca *or Méx* un agarrón
free-form ['fri:'fɔ:m] *adj* de estilo libre; **f. jazz** free jazz
freehand ['fri:hænd] **1** *adj* a mano alzada
2 *adv* a mano alzada
free-handed ['fri:'hændɪd] *adj* generoso(a), desprendido(a)
freehold ['fri:həʊld] *Law* **1** *n* propiedad *f* absoluta
2 *adv* en propiedad (absoluta)
freeholder ['fri:həʊldə(r)] *n* propietario(a) *m,f* absoluto(a)
freelance ['fri:lɑ:ns] **1** *n* colaborador(ora) *m,f* externo(a), free-lance *mf*
2 *adj* free-lance
3 *adv* **to work f.** trabajar como autónomo(a) *or* free-lance
4 *vi* trabajar como autónomo(a) *or* free-lance
freelancer ['fri:lɑ:nsə(r)] *n* colaborador(ora) *m,f* externo(a), free-lance *mf*
free-living ['fri:'lɪvɪŋ] *adj* (**a**) *(person)* desmadrado(a) (**b**) *Biol* autónomo(a)
freeload ['fri:ləʊd] *vi Fam* gorrear, *Esp, Méx* gorronear, *RP* garronear
freeloader ['fri:ləʊdə(r)] *n Fam* gorrero(a) *m,f*, *Esp, Méx* gorrón(ona) *m,f*, *RP* garronero(a) *m,f*
freely ['fri:lɪ] *adv* (**a**) *(without constraint) (to give, speak, move, travel)* con libertad, libremente; **to be f. available** encontrarse fácilmente
(**b**) *(voluntarily)* **I would f. do it again** lo haría otra vez de buena gana; **I f. admit I was wrong** no me cuesta reconocer que estaba equivocado
(**c**) *(translate)* libremente
(**d**) *(generously) (to spend)* libremente
(**e**) *(copiously) (to perspire, weep)* copiosamente; **the wine was flowing f.** el vino fluía copiosamente *or* en abundancia
freeman ['fri:mən] *n* (**a**) *(not a slave)* hombre *m* libre (**b**) *(as honour)* ciudadano *m* honorífico *or* de honor
Freemason ['fri:meɪsən] *n* masón *m*, francmasón *m*
Freemasonry ['fri:meɪsənrɪ] *n* masonería *f*, francmasonería *f*
freenet ['fri:net] *n Comptr* red *f* ciudadana
Freepost® ['fri:pəʊst] *n Br* ≃ franqueo *m* pagado
free-range ['fri:'reɪndʒ] *adj (egg, chicken)* de corral, de granja
freesheet ['fri:ʃi:t] *n Br* periódico *m* gratuito
freesia ['fri:zɪə] *n* fresia *f*
free-standing ['fri:'stændɪŋ] *adj* independiente
freestone ['fri:stəʊn] *n* piedra *f* franca
freestyle ['fri:staɪl] *n (in swimming)* estilo *m* libre ►► ***f. wrestling*** lucha *f* libre
freethinker [fri:'θɪŋkə(r)] *n* librepensador(ora) *m,f*
freethinking ['fri:θɪŋkɪŋ] **1** *n* librepensamiento *m*
2 *adj* librepensador(ora)
free-trade ['fri:'treɪd] *adj* de libre comercio ►► ***f. zone*** zona *f* franca
freeware ['fri:weə(r)] *n Comptr* freeware *m*, programa *m* de dominio público *(y gratuito)*
freeway ['fri:weɪ] *n US* autopista *f*
freewheel [fri:'wi:l] **1** *n (on bicycle)* piñón *m* libre
2 *vi* (**a**) *(on bicycle)* ir sin pedalear (**b**) *(in car)* ir en punto muerto (**c**) *(act in carefree fashion)* **to f. through life** vivir sin plantearse nada
freewheeling [fri:'wi:lɪŋ] *adj Fam* **he took a f. approach to bringing up his children** se planteaba la educación de sus hijos sin convencionalismos ni restricciones
freewoman ['fri:wʊmən] *n* (**a**) *(not a slave)* mujer *f* libre (**b**) *(as honour)* ciudadana *f* honorífica *or* de honor
freeze [fri:z] **1** *n* (**a**) *(in weather)* helada *f*
(**b**) *(control) (of sb's assets)* congelación *f*; **price/wage f.** congelación de los precios/los salarios
(**c**) *(halt)* **they called for a f. in the production of nuclear weapons** solicitaron una suspensión total en la fabricación de armas nucleares
2 *vt* (*pt* **froze** [frəʊz], *pp* **frozen** ['frəʊzən]) (**a**) *(water, food)* congelar; *(river, earth, pipes)* helar; *Fig* **she froze them with a look** los fulminó con la mirada; **to be frozen to death** morir congelado
(**b**) *(wages, prices, assets)* congelar
(**c**) *Cin (image)* congelar
(**d**) *(anaesthetize)* dormir
3 *vi* (**a**) *(weather)* **it may f. tonight** puede que hiele esta noche
(**b**) *(liquid)* congelarse; *(river, earth, pipes)* helarse; **food had frozen solid** la comida estaba completamente congelada; **does it f. well?** *(food)* ¿se puede congelar?; **to f. to death** morirse de frío; *Fam* **I'm freezing!** ¡me estoy congelando!; *Fig* **her blood froze** se le heló la sangre en las venas
(**c**) *(person) (stand still)* quedarse paralizado(a); **f.!** ¡quieto(a)!; **she froze (in her tracks)** se quedó completamente inmóvil; **the smile**

froze on his lips se le heló la sonrisa en los labios
(**d**) *Cin (image)* congelarse
(**e**) *Comptr (screen, computer)* bloquearse

▸ **freeze out** *vt sep Fam* **to f. sb out of the conversation** excluir a alguien de la conversación

▸ **freeze over** *vi (pond, river)* helarse

▸ **freeze up** *vi* (**a**) *(pond, mechanism)* helarse (**b**) *Fam (person)* quedarse paralizado(a)

freeze-dried ['fri:z'draɪd] *adj* liofilizado(a)

freeze-dry ['fri:z'draɪ] *vt* liofilizar

freeze-frame ['fri:z'freɪm] *n Cin* imagen *f* congelada ▸▸ ***f. function*** congelación *f* de imagen

freezer ['fri:zə(r)] *n* (**a**) *(deep-freeze)* congelador *m*; **in the f. section of your supermarket** en la sección de congelados de su supermercado ▸▸ ***f. bag*** bolsa *f* para congelados (**b**) **f. (compartment)** *(of fridge)* congelador *m*

freeze-up ['fri:zʌp] *n Fam* ola *f* de frío

freezing ['fri:zɪŋ] **1** *adj (rain, wind)* helado(a); *(weather, temperature)* muy frío(a); **f. temperatures** temperaturas bajo cero; **it's f.** *(very cold)* hace un frío espantoso; **your hands are f.** tienes las manos heladas
2 *n* (**a**) *(temperature)* **it's two degrees above/below f.** hay dos grados/dos grados bajo cero ▸▸ ***f. point*** punto *m* de congelación (**b**) *(of food)* congelación *f*; **(not) suitable for f.** (no) se puede congelar ▸▸ ***f. instructions*** instrucciones *fpl* de congelación
3 *adv* **it's f. cold outside** hace un frío espantoso

freight [freɪt] *Com* **1** *n* (**a**) *(transport)* transporte *m or* flete *m* de mercancías; **to send goods by f.** enviar algo por flete ▸▸ ***f. charges*** gastos *mpl* de transporte
(**b**) *(goods)* flete *m*, carga *f* ▸▸ *US* ***f. car*** vagón *m* de mercancías; *US* ***f. elevator*** montacargas *m inv*; ***f. terminal*** terminal *f* de carga, terminal *f* de mercancías; *(in airports)* terminal *f* de carga; ***f. train*** tren *m* de mercancías, tren *m* de carga
(**c**) *(price)* flete *m*, porte *m*
2 *vt (transport)* fletar, transportar; **we'll f. it to you tomorrow** se lo fletaremos mañana

freighter ['freɪtə(r)] *n (ship)* carguero *m*

French [frentʃ] **1** *npl (people)* **the F.** los franceses
2 *n (language)* francés *m*; **F. class/teacher** clase/profesor(ora) de francés; *Hum* **pardon** *or* **excuse my F.!** *(after swearing)* ¡con perdón!
3 *adj* francés(esa) ▸▸ ***F. bean*** *Esp* judía *f* verde, *Bol, RP* chaucha *f*, *Chile* poroto *m* verde, *Carib, Col* habichuela *f*, *Méx* ejote *m*; ***F. bread*** pan *m* francés *or* de barra; ***F. Canadian*** francocanadiense *mf*; ***F. chalk*** jaboncillo *m*, jabón *m* de sastre; *Tech* ***F. curve*** plantilla *f* de curvas; ***F. doors*** (puerta *f*) cristalera *f*; ***F. dressing*** vinagreta *f*; ***F. fries*** *Esp* patatas *fpl or Am* papas *fpl* fritas; ***F. Guiana*** Guayana Francesa; *Mus* ***F. horn*** trompa *f*; ***F. kiss*** beso *m* con lengua *or Esp* de tornillo; *Br* ***F. knickers*** culot *m*; ***F. leave:*** **to take F. leave** escaquearse; *Br Old-fashioned* ***F. letter*** condón *m*; *Br* ***F. loaf*** barra *f* de pan; ***F. polish*** barniz *m* de muñequilla *or* muñeca; *Br* ***F. stick*** barra *f* de pan; ***F. toast*** torrija *f*; ***F. window*** (puerta *f*) cristalera *f*
4 *vt US* (**a**) *(cook) (beans)* cortar en juliana; *(meat)* cortar en filetes (**b**) *Vulg* hacer un francés a

Frenchified ['frentʃɪfaɪd] *adj (manners, ideas)* afrancesado(a)

Frenchify ['frentʃɪfaɪ] *vt Fam* afrancesar

French-kiss [frentʃ'kɪs] **1** *vt* dar un beso con lengua *or Esp* de tornillo a
2 *vi* dar un beso con lengua *or Esp* de tornillo

Frenchman ['frentʃmən] *n* francés *m*

French-polish ['frentʃ'pɒlɪʃ] *vt* dar barniz de muñequilla *or* muñeca a

French-speaking ['frentʃspi:kɪŋ] *adj* francófono(a)

Frenchwoman ['frentʃwʊmən] *n* francesa *f*

Frenchy ['frentʃɪ] *n Fam* franchute(a) *m,f*

frenetic [frə'netɪk] *adj* frenético(a)

frenetically [frə'netɪklɪ] *adv* frenéticamente

frenzied ['frenzɪd] *adj* frenético(a); **f. with rage** fuera de sí (de ira); **f. with worry** angustiado(a)

frenzy ['frenzɪ] *n* (**a**) *(fury, passion)* frenesí *m*; **to work oneself into a f.** ponerse frenético(a) (**b**) *(fit, outburst)* **in a f. of anger** en un arrebato de furia; **the department was in a f. of activity** había una actividad frenética en el departamento

frequency ['fri:kwənsɪ] *n* (**a**) *(of occurrence, event)* frecuencia *f*; **the increasing f. of his absences** sus ausencias cada vez más frecuentes (**b**) *Phys* frecuencia *f* ▸▸ *Rad* ***f. band*** banda *f* de frecuencia(s); *Rad* ***f. modulation*** frecuencia *f* modulada (**c**) *Math* ***f. distribution*** distribución *f* de frecuencias

frequent 1 *adj* ['fri:kwənt] frecuente; **it is a f. occurrence** ocurre con frecuencia; **it is a f. sight in the summer months** se puede ver con frecuencia durante los meses de verano; **he became a f. visitor to our house** se convirtió en asiduo visitante de nuestra casa ▸▸ ***f. flyer club*** = programa de fidelización de pasajeros habituales de una compañía aérea
2 *vt* [frɪ'kwent] *Formal* frecuentar

frequently ['fri:kwəntlɪ] *adv* con frecuencia, frecuentemente; **how f.?** ¿con qué frecuencia?

fresco ['freskəʊ] (*pl* **frescos** *or* **frescoes**) *n Art* fresco *m*

fresh [freʃ] **1** *adj* (**a**) *(food)* fresco(a); *(bread)* reciente; *(air)* puro(a); *(taste, smell)* refrescante; **to get some f. air** tomar un poco el aire ▸▸ ***f. water*** *(not salty)* agua *f* dulce
(**b**) *(rested, untired)* descansado(a); **I felt fresher after a shower** la ducha me despejó; **a f. complexion** un cutis fresco; IDIOM **as f. as a daisy** (fresco(a)) como una rosa
(**c**) *(new) (page, attempt, drink)* nuevo(a); *(tracks, footprint)* reciente; *(troops)* de refresco; **the paint was still f.** la pintura aún no estaba seca; **he put on a f. shirt** se puso una camisa limpia; **to make a f. start** empezar de nuevo; **it is still f. in my mind** todavía lo tengo fresco en la memoria; IDIOM **to look for f. fields and pastures new** ampliar horizontes
(**d**) *(original) (approach, writing)* fresco(a), original
(**e**) *(cold) (breeze, weather)* fresco(a); **it's a bit f. today** hoy hace fresco *or* fresquito
(**f**) *US Fam (cheeky)* descarado(a), impertinente; **don't get f. with me, young man!** ¡no me sea descarado *or* no se me ponga impertinente, jovencito!
(**g**) *US Fam (sexually bold)* fresco(a), aprovechado(a); **to get f. with sb** propasarse con alguien
2 *adv* **f. from...** recién salido(a) de...; **f. from** *or* **out of university** recién salido de la universidad; **the vegetables are f. from the garden** las verduras están recién cogidas del huerto; **f. cut flowers** flores frescas; **we're f. out of lemons** se nos acaban de terminar los limones

freshen ['freʃən] **1** *vt US (drink)* rellenar
2 *vi (wind)* soplar más fuerte; *(weather)* refrescar

▸ **freshen up** *vi (wash)* refrescarse

fresher ['freʃə(r)] *n Br Univ* novato(a) *m,f*

fresh-faced ['freʃ'feɪst] *adj* lozano(a)

freshly ['freʃlɪ] *adv* recién; **f. baked/made/painted** recién horneado/hecho/pintado

freshman ['freʃmən] *n Univ* novato(a) *m,f*, estudiante *mf* de primer año

freshness ['freʃnɪs] *n* (**a**) *(of food)* frescura *f*; *(of air)* pureza *f*; *(of taste, smell)* frescor *m* (**b**) *(of complexion)* frescura *f*, lozanía *f* (**c**) *(of approach, writing)* frescura *f*, originalidad *f* (**d**) *(of breeze, weather)* frescura *f*, frescor *m*

freshwater ['freʃwɔ:tə(r)] *adj* de agua dulce ▸▸ ***f. fish*** pez *m* de río *or* de agua dulce

fret[1] [fret] **1** *n Fam* **to be/get in a f.** estar/ponerse de los nervios
2 *vt* (*pt & pp* **fretted**) **don't f. yourself!** ¡no te pongas nervioso!, ¡tranquilízate!
3 *vi (worry)* ponerse nervioso(a); **don't f.!** ¡no te pongas nervioso!, ¡tranquilízate!; **to f. for sth/sb: the dog was fretting for its owner** el perro estaba nervioso por la ausencia de su dueño

fret[2] *n Mus* traste *m*

fretful ['fretfʊl] *adj* (**a**) *(anxious)* inquieto(a) (**b**) *(peevish)* quejoso(a); **the baby is getting f.** el niño se está poniendo nervioso

fretfully ['fretfəlɪ] *adv* (**a**) *(anxiously)* con nerviosismo (**b**) *(peevishly)* **"no one ever believes me," she said f.** "nadie me cree nunca", dijo quejándose *or* en tono de queja

fretsaw ['fretsɔ:] *n (manual)* segueta *f*; *(electrical)* sierra *f* de calar

fretwork ['fretwɜ:k] *n* calado *m* (de marquetería)

Freudian ['frɔɪdɪən] **1** *n* freudiano(a) *m,f*
2 *adj* freudiano(a) ▸▸ ***F. slip*** lapsus *m inv* (linguae)

FRG [efɑ:'dʒi:] *n* (*abbr* **Federal Republic of Germany**) RFA *f*

Fri (*abbr* **Friday**) viern.

friable ['fraɪəbəl] *adj* desmenuzable, *Spec* friable

friar ['fraɪə(r)] *n* fraile *m*; **F. Edmund** Fray Edmund

friary ['fraɪərɪ] *n* monasterio *m*

fricassee [frɪkə'si:] **1** *n* fricasé *m*
2 *vt* hacer un fricasé de

fricative ['frɪkətɪv] *Ling* **1** *n* fricativa *f*
2 *adj* fricativo(a)

friction ['frɪkʃən] n (a) (rubbing) fricción f ▸▸ Comptr f. feed avance m de papel por fricción; US f. tape cinta f aislante (b) (disagreement) fricción f; the decision is bound to cause f. ésta es una decisión que va a provocar roces or levantar ampollas (c) Phys rozamiento m

Friday ['fraɪdɪ] n viernes m inv; F. the 13th ≃ martes y trece; see also Saturday

fridge [frɪdʒ] n nevera f, Esp frigorífico m, Méx refrigerador m, RP heladera f ▸▸ f. magnet imán m para el frigorífico

fridge-freezer ['frɪdʒ'fri:zə(r)] n combi m, Esp frigorífico-congelador m

fried [fraɪd] adj (a) (meat, fish, vegetables) frito(a) ▸▸ a f. egg un huevo frito; f. food frituras fpl, fritos mpl; f. rice arroz m frito (b) US Fam (drunk) trompa; (on drugs) colocado(a)

friend [frend] n (a) (intimate, close acquaintance) amigo(a) m,f; he's a f. of the family es un amigo de la familia; to be friends with sb, to be sb's f. ser amigo de alguien; he's been a real f. to us se ha portado como un verdadero amigo con nosotros; to make friends with sb hacerse amigo de alguien; she makes friends easily hace amigos fácilmente; he's been good f. to me se ha portado como un buen amigo conmigo; that's what friends are for para eso están los amigos; we're just good friends sólo somos buenos amigos; they wanted to part friends querían dejarlo como amigos; he's no f. of mine no es amigo mío; any f. of yours is a f. of mine tus amigos son mis amigos; to have friends in high places tener amigos influyentes; with friends like that, who needs enemies? ten amigos para esto, con amigos así ¿a quién le hacen falta enemigos?; PROV a f. in need is a f. indeed en la adversidad se conoce a los amigos
(b) (supporter) to be a f. of the arts ser un mecenas de las artes; the Friends of the National Gallery la Asociación de Amigos de la Galería Nacional; she's no f. of trade unionism no simpatiza con el sindicalismo ▸▸ Friends of the Earth Amigos mpl de la Tierra
(c) (addressing someone) my dear f. querido(a) amigo(a); listen, (my) f. mira amigo; friends, we are gathered here tonight... amigos, estamos aquí reunidos esta noche...; f. or foe? (said by sentry) ¿quién vive?
(d) Rel the (Society of) Friends la Sociedad de los Amigos, los cuáqueros

friendless ['frendlɪs] adj to be f. no tener amigos; a f. childhood una infancia sin amigos

friendliness ['frendlɪnɪs] n amabilidad f, simpatía f

friendly ['frendlɪ] 1 n Sport (partido m) amistoso m
2 adj (a) (person) simpático(a), agradable; (animal) simpático(a); (smile) agradable, amable; (face) conocido(a); (greeting) cálido(a), amistoso(a); (place) agradable, acogedor(ora); to be f. to or towards sb estar simpático or agradable con alguien; to be f. with sb llevarse bien con alguien; they became f. se hicieron amigos(as); that wasn't very f. of him! ¡qué poco amable!; to be on f. terms with sb llevarse bien con alguien; let me give you some f. advice te voy a dar un consejo como amigo ▸▸ Br Fin f. society mutua f, mutualidad f
(b) (not hostile) (argument, rivalry) amistoso(a); Sport (match, game) amistoso(a); a f. nation una nación amiga; Fin a f. takeover bid una oferta pública de adquisición amistosa, una OPA amistosa
(c) Mil (troops, forces, planes) amigo(a) ▸▸ f. fire fuego m del propio bando, fuego m amigo

friendship ['frendʃɪp] n amistad f; its aim is to promote f. between nations su objetivo es fomentar la amistad entre las naciones; he did it out of f. for her lo hizo por amistad (hacia ella), lo hizo por la amistad que tenía con ella; to form a f. with sb forjar una amistad con alguien; to lose sb's f. perder la amistad de alguien

frier = fryer

fries [fraɪz] npl US (French) f. Esp patatas fpl or Am papas fpl fritas

Friesian, Frisian ['fri:ʒən] 1 n (a) (person) frisón(ona) m,f (b) (language) frisón m (c) (cow) vaca f frisona or holandesa
2 adj frisón(ona)

frieze [fri:z] n (a) Art & Archit friso m (b) (decorative strip on wall) greca f

frig [frɪg] 1 exclam very Fam f. (it)! ¡mierda!
2 vt Vulg (a) (have sex with) Esp follarse a, Am cogerse a, RP fifar (b) (masturbate) hacer una or Am la paja a
3 vi Vulg (masturbate) hacerse una or Am la paja

▸ **frig about, frig around** vi very Fam (a) (act foolishly) Esp hacer el gilipollas, Am pendejear, RP boludear (b) (waste time) Esp hacer el gilipollas, Am pendejear, RP boludear

frigate ['frɪgət] n fragata f ▸▸ f. bird rabihorcado m, fragata f

frigging ['frɪgɪŋ] very Fam 1 adj (for emphasis) Esp puñetero(a), Méx pinche, RP reverendo(a); what a f. waste of time! ¡esto es Esp una puñetera or Méx pinche or RP reverenda pérdida de tiempo!; shut your f. mouth! ¡cierra el pico, carajo or Esp joder!
2 adv (for emphasis) don't f. lie to me! ¡a mí no me vengas jodiendo or Méx chingando con mentiras!; I'm f. freezing! ¡tengo un frío del carajo!

fright [fraɪt] n (a) (scare) susto m; his face was pale with f. estaba pálido del susto; to take f. asustarse; to get a f. darse un susto, asustarse; to get the f. of one's life llevarse (uno) el susto de su vida; to give sb a f. dar un susto a alguien (b) Fam to look a f. estar horroroso(a)

frighten ['fraɪtən] 1 vt asustar; to f. sb into doing sth asustar a alguien para que haga algo; to f. sb out of doing sth asustar a alguien para que no haga algo; Fam to f. the life or the wits out of sb, to f. sb to death dar a alguien un susto Esp de muerte or Méx de la madre or RP de miércoles
2 vi I don't f. easily no me asusto fácilmente

▸ **frighten away, frighten off** vt sep ahuyentar, espantar; the burglars were frightened away by the police siren la sirena de la policía asustó a los ladrones

frightened ['fraɪtənd] adj asustado(a) (of de); to be f. of heights/spiders tener miedo a las alturas/las arañas; there's nothing to be f. of no hay de qué tener miedo; to be f. to do sth tener miedo de hacer algo; I was f. to say anything me daba miedo decir nada

frighteners ['fraɪtnəz] npl Br Fam to put the f. on sb meterle el miedo en el cuerpo a alguien

frightening ['fraɪtnɪŋ] adj escalofriante, aterrador(ora); it's f. to think what might have happened da miedo pensar en lo que puede haber pasado

frighteningly ['fraɪtnɪŋlɪ] adv tremendamente, terriblemente

frightful ['fraɪtfʊl] adj (a) (terrible) terrible, espantoso(a); the soldier had f. wounds el soldado tenía unas heridas terribles or espantosas (b) Fam (as intensifier) terrible, espantoso(a); she's a f. bore es una pesada terrible; what f. nonsense! ¡qué bobada más enorme!

frightfully ['fraɪtfʊlɪ] adv Fam (as intensifier) terriblemente, tremendamente; I'm f. tired tengo un cansancio terrible or tremendo; it's f. boring es aburrido de solemnidad; I'm f. sorry lo siento muchísimo

frigid ['frɪdʒɪd] adj (a) (smile, atmosphere) glacial (b) (sexually) frígida (c) Geog f. zones zonas fpl glaciales

frigidity [frɪ'dʒɪdɪtɪ] n (a) (of smile, atmosphere) frialdad f (b) (sexual) frigidez f

frill [frɪl] n (a) (of cloth) volante m; (of paper) fleco m (b) IDIOM without frills (of ceremony) sencillo(a), sin florituras; a cheap package holiday with no frills unas vacaciones organizadas baratas y sin lujos

frilly ['frɪlɪ] adj (shirt, skirt) de volantes, RP, Ven de volados ▸▸ f. underwear ropa f interior de fantasía

fringe [frɪndʒ] 1 n (a) (on clothes, lampshade) flecos mpl; (on rug, carpet) flecos; a f. of trees una hilera de árboles
(b) Br (of hair) flequillo m
(c) (edge) borde m; the fringes of the party la periferia del partido; to be on the fringes of society ser un/una marginado(a), vivir en la marginalidad ▸▸ f. benefits ventajas fpl adicionales or extras; Pol f. group grupo m marginal; f. theatre teatro m alternativo, teatro m off
(d) (of golf green) borde m (del green)
2 vt (rug, carpet) poner flecos a; the path was fringed with rosebushes el sendero estaba bordeado de rosales

frippery ['frɪpərɪ] n trivialidad f, fruslería f

Frisbee® ['frɪzbi:] n frisbee® m, disco m or plato m volador

Frisco ['frɪskəʊ] n US Fam San Francisco

Frisian = Friesian

frisk [frɪsk] 1 n (a) (gambol) to go for a f. in the park ir a retozar or juguetear al parque (b) (search) cacheo m; to give sb a f. hacer un cacheo a alguien
2 vt (search) cachear, registrar
3 vi to f. about (gambol) retozar, juguetear

frisky ['frɪskɪ] adj (person) lleno(a) de vitalidad; (animal) retozón(ona), saltarín(ina); to be f. (person) (energetic) estar lleno(a) de vitalidad; (sexually) estar retozón(ona) or juguetón(ona)

frisson ['fri:sɒn] n (of excitement, fear) estremecimiento m

fritter ['frɪtə(r)] n buñuelo m

▸ **fritter away** vt sep (money) despilfarrar; (time) desperdiciar

fritz [frɪts] n US Fam to be on the f. (TV, machine) estar estropeado(a) or Esp escacharrado(a)

▸ **fritz out** *vi US Fam* estropearse, *Esp* escacharrarse

frivolity [frɪ'vɒlɪtɪ] *n* frivolidad *f*

frivolous ['frɪvələs] *adj* frívolo(a); **a f. waste of time** una pérdida de tiempo inútil

frivolously ['frɪvələslɪ] *adv* frívolamente, con poca seriedad

frizz [frɪz] **1** *n* rizos *mpl* muy pequeños
2 *vt* rizar (con rizos muy pequeños)
3 *vi* rizar (con rizos muy pequeños)

frizzle ['frɪzəl] **1** *vt (overcook)* achicharrar
2 *vi (cook noisily)* chisporrotear

frizzy ['frɪzɪ] *adj* ensortijado(a)

fro [frəʊ] *adv* **to and f.** de aquí para allá; **to go to and f.** ir y venir (de un lado para otro)

frock [frɒk] *n (dress)* vestido *m* ▸▸ ***f. coat*** levita *f*

frog [frɒg] **1** *n* **(a)** *(animal)* rana *f*; IDIOM *Fam* **to have a f. in one's throat** tener carraspera ▸▸ ***f.'s legs*** ancas *fpl* de rana **(b)** *Br Fam* **F.** *(French person)* franchute(a) *m,f*, *Esp* gabacho(a) *m,f*
2 *adj Br Fam (French)* franchute(a), *Esp* gabacho(a)

frogman ['frɒgmən] *n* hombre *m* rana

frogmarch ['frɒgmɑːtʃ] *vt* llevar por la fuerza; **they frogmarched her out of the room** la sacaron por la fuerza de la habitación

frogspawn ['frɒgspɔːn] *n Br* huevos *mpl* de rana

frolic ['frɒlɪk] **1** *n* **to go for a f. in the park** ir a juguetear *or* retozar al parque
2 *vi (pt & pp* **frolicked***)* juguetear, retozar

frolicsome ['frɒlɪksəm] *adj* juguetón(ona), retozón(ona)

FROM [frɒm, *unstressed* frəm] *prep* **(a)** *(expressing place)* de; *(expressing specific location or origin)* desde; **f. above/the outside** desde arriba/fuera *or Am* afuera; **there's a great view f. the top** desde la cima la vista es magnífica; **it fell f. a great height** cayó desde gran altura; **he watched them f. behind a tree** los observó desde detrás *or Am* atrás de un árbol; **hanging f. the ceiling** colgado(a) del techo; **to travel f. Edinburgh to Madrid** viajar de Edimburgo a Madrid; **the train f. Guadalajara** el tren (procedente) de Guadalajara; **the road f. Bakersfield** la carretera de Bakersfield; **10 km f. Barcelona** a 10 km de Barcelona; **to return f. abroad** volver del extranjero

(b) *(expressing time)* desde; **f. now on** de ahora en adelante, a partir de ahora; **f. then (on)** desde entonces; **f. that day on** a partir de aquel día, desde aquel día; **f. tomorrow** a partir de mañana; **f. six to seven (o'clock)** de (las) seis a (las) siete; **f. morning to** *or* **till night** de la mañana a la noche; **f. the beginning** desde el principio; **five years f. now** de aquí a cinco años; **to be blind f. birth** ser ciego(a) de nacimiento; **they date f. the twelfth century** datan del siglo doce; **we are still many years f. finding a cure** todavía han de pasar muchos años hasta que encontremos una cura

(c) *(expressing range)* **f.... to...** de... a...; **for children f. seven to nine (years)** para niños de siete a nueve años; **we receive anything f. twenty to fifty calls an hour** recibimos entre veinte y cincuenta llamadas por hora; **it will benefit everyone, f. the poor to the rich** beneficiará a todos, desde los pobres hasta los ricos; **wine f. $7 a bottle** vinos desde 7 dólares la botella; **prices start f. $20** precios desde 20 dólares

(d) *(expressing change)* **unemployment has gone down f. 10 to 9 percent** el desempleo ha caído del 10 al 9 por ciento; **he has changed f. being opposed to the idea to supporting it** ha pasado de oponerse a la idea a estar a favor de ella; **to go f. bad to worse** ir de mal en peor; **to go f. door to door** ir puerta a puerta, ir de puerta en puerta

(e) *(expressing source)* de; **who's this letter f.?** ¿de quién es esta carta?; **I bought it f. a friend** se lo compré a un amigo; **I bought it f. an antique shop** lo compré en una tienda de antigüedades; **I caught chickenpox f. my cousin** mi primo me contagió la varicela; **where are you f.?, where do you come f.?** ¿de dónde eres?; **she's f. Portugal** es de Portugal; **to drink f. a cup/bottle** beber de una taza *or* en taza/de una botella; **a quotation f. the Bible** una cita de la Biblia; **the wind is blowing f. the north** el viento sopla del norte; **made f. rubber** hecho(a) de goma; **you can tell her f. me that...** le puedes decir de mi parte que...

(f) *(on cards, faxes, in e-mails)* **f. Dave** de Dave

(g) *(expressing removal)* **to take sth f. sb** quitar *or Andes, RP* sacar algo a alguien; **take** *or* **subtract seven f. ten** réstale siete a diez; **she took a coin f. her pocket** sacó una moneda del bolsillo; **he was banned f. the club** fue expulsado del club; **she ran f. the room** salió corriendo de la habitación

(h) *(expressing cause)* **he died f. cancer/his burns** murió de cáncer/a causa de las quemaduras; **she suffers f. a rare disease** padece una enfermedad rara

(i) *(on the basis of)* **to act f. conviction** actuar por convicción; **you could tell he was angry f. his expression** se sabía que estaba *esp Esp* enfadado *or esp Am* enojado por su expresión; **f. what I heard/saw...** (a juzgar) por lo que yo he oído/visto...; **f. what she has said we can conclude that...** por lo que ha dicho podemos concluir que...; **f. my point of view** desde mi punto de vista

(j) *(expressing protection)* **to protect sb f. sth** proteger a alguien de algo; **we sheltered f. the rain** nos resguardamos de la lluvia

(k) *(expressing prevention)* **to keep sb f. doing sth** impedir que alguien haga algo; **we kept the information f. them** les ocultamos la información; **she has been banned f. driving** le han retirado el carnet de *Esp* conducir *or Am* manejar

(l) *(expressing comparison)* **to be different f. sth/sb** ser diferente de algo/alguien; **it's hard to tell one f. the other** es difícil diferenciarlos

fromage frais ['frɒmɑːʒ'freɪ] *n* crema *f* de queso fresco

frond [frɒnd] *n (of fern)* fronda *f*; *(of palm)* (hoja *f* de) palma *f*

FRONT [frʌnt] **1** *n* **(a)** *(forward part)* parte *f* delantera; *(of building)* fachada *f*; *(cover of book)* portada *f*, *RP* tapa *f*; *(of shirt, dress)* parte *f* de delante; *(of queue)* principio *m*; **on the f. of the book** en la portada *or RP* tapa del libro; **at the f. of the book** al principio del libro; **at the f. of the lecture hall** en la parte de delante *or Am* adelante del aula; **let's sit at the f.** sentémonos delante *or Am* adelante; **I sat in the f.** *(of car)* me senté delante *or Am* adelante; **lie on your f.** túmbate *or RP* tirate boca abajo; **she pushed her way to the f.** se abrió camino hasta la parte de delante *or Am* adelante; *Theat* **f. of house** = conjunto de actividades que se desarrollan dentro del teatro y que implican contacto con el público

(b) *(outward appearance)* fachada *f*; **his kindness is only a f.** su amabilidad es pura fachada; **the company is a f. for their arms dealing** la empresa es una tapadera *or RP* pantalla para el tráfico de armas ▸▸ *Fam* ***f. man*** *(of TV, radio programme)* presentador *m*; *(of pop group)* líder *m*; *(of organization)* cabeza *f* visible

(c) *Mil & Pol* frente *m*; *Fig* **to make progress on all fronts** hacer progresos en todos los frentes; **on the domestic** *or* **home f.** *(at national level)* en el frente nacional; **how are things on the work f.?** ¿cómo van las cosas en el trabajo?

(d) *Met* frente *m*; **warm/cold f.** frente cálido/frío

(e) *Br* **the f.** *(at seaside)* el paseo marítimo, *Arg* la costanera, *Cuba* el malecón, *Urug* la rambla

(f) *Br Fam (cheekiness)* cara *f*; **to have the f. to do sth** tener la cara de hacer algo

2 *adj* delantero(a) ▸▸ *Br Parl* ***f. benches*** = las filas de escaños ocupados por los ministros y sus homólogos en la oposición; ***f. burner:*** IDIOM *US* **to put sth on the f. burner** poner algo al principio de la lista; *Rail* ***f. carriage*** vagón *m* delantero; ***f. cover*** *(of magazine, book)* portada *f*, *RP* tapa *f*; ***f. desk*** *(reception)* recepción *f*; ***f. door*** puerta *f* principal; *Br* ***f. garden*** jardín *m* delantero *or Am* de adelante; ***f. line*** *Mil* frente *m* (de batalla); *(in soccer)* línea *f* delantera; *Fig* **we are in the f. line of the fight against crime** estamos en la primera línea de la lucha contra la delincuencia; ***the f. nine*** *(in golf)* los primeros nueve hoyos; ***f. page*** *(of newspaper)* portada *f*, primera plana *f*; ***f. room*** salón *m*, sala *f* de estar, *RP* living *m*; ***f. row:*** **in the f. row** en la primera fila; *Theat* **to have a f. row seat** tener asiento de primera fila; *Fig* ser espectador privilegiado; ***f. seat*** *(in car)* asiento *m* delantero *or Am* de adelante; ***f. teeth*** palas *fpl*, paletas *fpl*; ***f. view*** vista *f* frontal; ***f. wheel*** rueda *f* delantera; *US* ***f. yard*** jardín *m* delantero *or Am* de adelante

3 *vt* **(a)** *(government)* encabezar; *(TV programme)* presentar; *(organization)* dirigir; *(pop group)* liderar

(b) *Constr* **the building is fronted with...** la fachada del edificio está recubierta de...

(c) *(stand in front of)* **tall bushes f. the building** hay altos arbustos delante del edificio

(d) *US Fam (pay in advance)* adelantar; **the cashier can f. you the money** el cajero le puede adelantar el dinero

(e) *US Fam (give, lend money to)* prestar, *Esp* dejar; **can you f. me five bucks?** ¿puedes prestarme *or Esp* dejarme cinco dólares?

4 *vi (building)* **the house fronts onto the river** la casa da al río

5 in front *adv (in race, contest)* en cabeza, por delante; **to be in f.** ir ganando; **the person in f.** la persona de delante *or Am* adelante; **I sat in f.** *(of car)* me senté delante *or Am* adelante; **you go on in f.** ve tú delante *or Am* adelante

6 in front of *prep (in queue, opposite)* delante de, *Am* adelante de; *(in presence of)* delante de, en presencia de; **we have a lot of work in f. of us** tenemos un montón de trabajo delante de nosotros *or Am* por delante

7 out front *adv Fam (of building)* fuera, afuera

8 **up front** *adj Fam* **to be up f. about sth** ser claro(a) en cuanto a algo
9 **up front** *adv Fam (to pay)* por adelantado

frontage ['frʌntɪdʒ] *n* fachada *f*; **the house has a garden with river f.** la fachada de la casa da al río ▸▸ *US* ***f. road*** vía *f* de servicio

frontal ['frʌntəl] *adj* (a) *Anat* frontal ▸▸ ***f. lobes*** lóbulos *mpl* frontales; ***f. lobotomy*** lobotomía *f* frontal (b) *Mil (attack)* frontal (c) *Met* ***f. system*** sistema *m* frontal

front-bench ['frʌnt'bentʃ] *adj Br Parl* ***f. spokesperson*** *(government)* portavoz *mf* del gobierno; *(opposition)* portavoz *mf* de la oposición

frontbencher [frʌnt'bentʃə(r)] *n Br Parl* = diputado con cargo ministerial en el gobierno u homólogo en la oposición

front-end ['frʌnt'ənd] *adj* (a) *Comput* frontal (b) *Fin* inicial

frontier ['frʌntɪə(r)] *n* (a) *(border)* frontera *f* ▸▸ ***f. guard*** guardia *mf* fronterizo(a); ***f. town*** ciudad *f* fronteriza (b) *(limit)* límite *m*; **the frontiers of human knowledge** los límites del conocimiento humano (c) *US Hist* **the F.** la frontera; **the f. spirit** el espíritu de los hombres de la frontera

frontiersman [frʌn'tɪəzmən] *n* colonizador *m*

frontispiece ['frʌntɪspi:s] *n* frontispicio *m*

front-line ['frʌnt'laɪn] *adj* (a) *Mil (troops, defences)* de primera línea (b) *Pol* **the f. states** los estados fronterizos *(de un país en guerra)*

front-loader ['frʌnt'ləʊdə(r)] *n* lavadora *f* de carga frontal

front-loading ['frʌnt'ləʊdɪŋ] *adj* de carga frontal

front-of-house ['frʌntəv'haʊs] *adj Theat (staff)* en contacto directo con el público ▸▸ ***f. manager*** director(ora) *m,f* administrativo(a)

front-page ['frʌntpeɪdʒ] *adj* de portada, de primera plana *or* página ▸▸ ***f. news*** noticias *fpl* de primera plana *or* página; **it was f. news** salió en primera plana *or* página

front-runner ['frʌnt'rʌnə(r)] *n* (a) *Sport (horse)* caballo *m* en cabeza; *(athlete)* corredor(ora) *m,f* en cabeza; **to be the f.** ir en cabeza (b) *(in election)* favorito(a) *m,f*

frontwards ['frʌntwədz] *adv* hacia delante, hacia el frente

front-wheel drive ['frʌntwi:l'draɪv] *n* tracción *f* delantera

frosh [frɒʃ] *n US Fam* novato(a) *m,f*, estudiante *mf* de primer año

frost [frɒst] 1 *n* (a) *(freezing weather)* helada *f*; **there was a f.** cayó una helada; **eight degrees of f.** ocho grados bajo cero (b) *(frozen dew)* escarcha *f*
2 *vt* (a) *(freeze)* helar; *(cover with frost)* cubrir de escarcha (b) **the rim of the glass was frosted with sugar** el reborde de la copa estaba escarchado con azúcar (c) *US (cake)* glasear

▸ **frost over, frost up** *vi (window)* cubrirse de escarcha

frostbite ['frɒstbaɪt] *n* congelación *f*; **he got f. in his toes** se le congelaron los dedos de los pies; **the climber died of f.** el escalador murió congelado

frostbitten ['frɒstbɪtən] *adj (fingers, toes)* con síntomas de congelación; **his fingers were f.** sus dedos mostraban síntomas de congelación

frosted ['frɒstɪd] *adj* (a) *(covered with frost) (field, grass)* escarchado(a); *(car)* cubierto(a) de hielo (b) *(glass)* esmerilado(a) (c) *(lipstick, nail varnish)* nacarado(a) (d) *US (cake)* glaseado(a)

frostily ['frɒstɪlɪ] *adv* con gelidez *or* frialdad

frosting ['frɒstɪŋ] *n US (on cake)* glaseado *m*

frosty ['frɒstɪ] *adj* (a) *(night, air)* gélido(a), helado(a) (b) *(welcome, smile)* glacial, gélido(a)

froth [frɒθ] 1 *n* (a) *(foam)* espuma *f* (b) *(insubstantial talk, entertainment)* insustancialidades *fpl*, banalidades *fpl*
2 *vi* hacer espuma; **he was frothing at the mouth** *(with rage)* echaba espuma por la boca
3 *vt* **to f. the milk (with steam)** dar vapor a la leche para que espume

frothy ['frɒθɪ] *adj* (a) *(liquid)* espumoso(a) (b) *Pej (novel, style)* insustancial, banal (c) *(dress, lace)* ligero(a), vaporoso(a)

frown [fraʊn] 1 *n* **he gave a disapproving f.** frunció el ceño en señal de desaprobación
2 *vi* fruncir el ceño; **she frowned at my remark** frunció el ceño al escuchar mi comentario; **to f. at sb** mirar a alguien con el ceño fruncido

▸ **frown on, frown upon** *vt insep (disapprove of)* **her parents f. upon their friendship** los padres de ella no miran su amistad con buenos ojos; **such behaviour is rather frowned upon** este tipo de comportamiento no está muy bien visto

frowsy ['fraʊzɪ] *adj* (a) *(person, clothing)* desaliñado(a) (b) *(atmosphere)* con olor a cerrado

froze *pt of* **freeze**

frozen ['frəʊzən] 1 *adj* (a) *(food)* congelado(a); **to be f. (stiff)** estar (totalmente) congelado(a); *Fig* **f. with terror** congelado *or* paralizado por el terror ▸▸ ***f. carrots*** zanahorias *fpl* congeladas; ***f. yoghurt*** yogur *m* helado, helado *m* de yogur
(b) *Fam (very cold)* congelado(a), helado(a); **my feet are f.!** ¡tengo los pies congelados!
(c) *Med* ***f. shoulder*** hombro *m* congelado
(d) *Comptr (screen, computer)* bloqueado(a)
2 *pp of* **freeze**

FRS [efɑ:'res] *n* (a) (*abbr* **Fellow of the Royal Society**) miembro *mf* de la Real Academia de las Ciencias Británica (b) *US* (*abbr* **Federal Reserve System**) Sistema *m* de la Reserva Federal, = banco central de EE.UU.

fructose ['frʌktəʊs] *n* fructosa *f*

frugal ['fru:gəl] *adj* (a) *(person, life)* frugal; **she's very f. with her money** es muy ahorradora (b) *(meal)* frugal

frugality [fru:'gælɪtɪ] *n* frugalidad *f*

frugally ['fru:gəlɪ] *adv* frugalmente

fruit [fru:t] *n* (a) *(for eating)* fruta *f*; *(on plant)* fruto *m*; **a piece of f.** una (pieza de) fruta; **the fruits of the earth** los frutos de la tierra; **to bear f.** *(tree)* dar fruto; *Fig* **the f. of her womb** el fruto de su vientre ▸▸ ***f. bat*** murciélago *m* frugívoro, zorro *m* volador; ***f. bowl*** frutero *m*; ***f. cocktail*** cóctel *m* de frutas, macedonia *f* (de frutas); ***f. cup*** *(dessert)* cóctel *m* de fruta, macedonia *f*; *(drink)* ≃ sangría *f*, *RP* ≃ clericó *m*; ***f. drop*** caramelo *m* de fruta; ***f. fly*** mosca *f* de la fruta; *Br* ***f. gum*** goma *f* de mascar *or* chicle *m* de fruta; ***f. juice*** *Esp* zumo *m or Am* jugo *m* de frutas; ***f. knife*** cuchillo *m* de fruta; *Br* ***f. machine*** (máquina *f*) tragaperras *f inv*; ***f. salad*** macedonia *f* (de frutas), ensalada *f* de frutas; ***f. sugar*** fructosa *f*; ***f. tree*** (árbol *m*) frutal *m*
(b) *(result)* **their plans have never borne f.** sus planes nunca han dado fruto; **his book is the f. of much research** su libro es el fruto de muchas investigaciones
(c) *Br Fam Old-fashioned (term of address)* **old f.** compadre
(d) *US Fam (homosexual)* mariquita *m*, sarasa *m*

fruitcake ['fru:tkeɪk] *n* (a) *(cake)* bizcocho *m* de frutas (b) *Fam (mad person)* chiflado(a) *m,f*, chalado(a) *m,f*

fruiterer ['fru:tərə(r)] *n Br* frutero(a) *m,f*; **the f.'s** la frutería

fruitful ['fru:tfʊl] *adj* fructífero(a)

fruitfully ['fru:tfʊlɪ] *adv* provechosamente, de modo fructífero

fruition [fru:'ɪʃən] *n* **to come to f.** *(effort)* fructificar; *(plan)* realizarse; **to bring sth to f.** llevar algo a buen término

fruitless ['fru:tlɪs] *adj* infructuoso(a); **at least the trip won't have been entirely f.** al menos el viaje no habrá sido en vano

fruitlessly ['fru:tlɪslɪ] *adv* infructuosamente

fruity ['fru:tɪ] *adj* (a) *(taste, perfume, wine)* afrutado(a) (b) *Fam (voice)* profundo(a) y sonoro(a) (c) *Br Fam (joke, story)* picante, subido(a) de tono

frump [frʌmp] *n Fam* **she's a f.** es muy rancia en la manera de vestir

frumpish ['frʌmpɪʃ], **frumpy** ['frʌmpɪ] *adj Fam* **to be f.** ser anticuado(a) *or* rancio(a) en la manera de vestir; **she wears rather f. clothes** usa ropa bastante anticuada

frustrate [frʌs'treɪt] *vt (person, plan)* frustrar; **he was frustrated in his attempt to escape** su intento de fuga fue frustrado

frustrated [frʌs'treɪtɪd] *adj* frustrado(a); **to be f.** estar frustrado(a)

frustrating [frʌs'treɪtɪŋ] *adj* frustrante

frustratingly [frʌs'treɪtɪŋlɪ] *adv* desesperantemente; **f., he refused to help** para mayor frustración mía, se negó a ayudarme

frustration [frʌs'treɪʃən] *n (emotion)* frustración *f*; **in f.** de (la) rabia, de desesperación; **to the point of f.** hasta desesperarse

fry [fraɪ] 1 *vt* (a) *(cook)* freír (b) *US Fam (electrocute)* electrocutar, achicharrar en la silla eléctrica
2 *vi* (a) *(cook)* freírse (b) *US Fam (convict)* morir electrocutado(a) *or* achicharrado(a) en la silla eléctrica
3 *n* (a) *US (meal)* parrillada *f* al aire libre (b) *(offal)* asaduras *fpl*, *RP* achuras *fpl*
4 *npl Zool (young fish)* pececillos *mpl*; *(frogs)* renacuajos *mpl*

▸ **fry up** *vt sep* freír

fryer, frier ['fraɪə(r)] *n* **(deep fat) f.** freidora *f*

frying ['fraɪɪŋ] *n* fritura *f* ▸▸ ***f. pan*** sartén *f*; IDIOM **to jump out of the f. pan into the fire** ir de Guatemala a Guatepeor

fry-pan ['fraɪpæn] *n US* sartén *f*

fry-up ['fraɪʌp] *n Br* fritura *f*

f-stop ['efstɒp] *n Phot* posición *f* del número f

FT [ef'ti:] *n* (*abbr* **Financial Times**) Financial Times *m*; **FT Index** índice (FT) de la bolsa de Londres

ft (*abbr* **foot** *or* **feet**) pie *m* (= *30,48 cm*); **20 ft** 20 pies

FTC [efti:'si:] *n US* (*abbr* **Federal Trade Commission**) Comisión *f* Federal de Comercio

FTP [efti:'pi:] *n Comptr* (*abbr* **File Transfer Protocol**) FTP *m* ▸▸ ***F. server*** servidor *m* FTP

FT-SE ['fʊtsɪ] *n* **F. (Index)** índice *m* (FTSE *or* FOOTSIE) de la bolsa de Londres

fuchsia ['fju:ʃə] *n (plant, colour)* fucsia *f*

fuck [fʌk] *Vulg* **1** *n* (**a**) *(intercourse)* polvo *m*, *Méx* acostón *m*, *Cuba* palo *m*; **to have a f.** echar un polvo, *Esp* follar, *Am* coger, *Méx* chingar, *RP, Ven* clavar

(**b**) *(person)* **to be a good f.** *Esp* follar bien, *Méx* ser un buen acostón, *RP* coger como los dioses; **you stupid f.!** ¡tonto *or Esp* gilipollas *or RP* forro de mierda!

(**c**) *(expressing surprise, contempt, irritation)* **f.!** ¡carajo!, *Esp* ¡joder!; **what the f....?** ¿qué *Esp* cojones *or Col, Méx* chingados *or RP* mierda...?; **who/why the f....?** ¿quién/por qué *Esp* cojones *or Col, Méx* chingados *or RP* mierda...?; **get to f.!** *Esp* ¡vete a tomar por (el) culo!, *Méx* ¡vete a la chingada!, *RP* ¡andate a la puta que te parió!; **can I borrow your bike? – can you f.** *or* **like f. you can!** ¿me prestas tu moto? – ¡y un huevo!; **shut the f. up!** ¡cállate de una puta vez!; **for f.'s sake!** ¡me cago en la puta!; **f. knows why he came!** ¡para qué *Esp* cojones *or Col, Méx* chingados *or RP* mierda habrá venido!

(**d**) *(for emphasis)* **I don't give a f.** me importa un huevo; **who gives a f.!** ¡a quién carajo le importa!, *Esp* ¡a quién cojones le importa!; **I can't really afford it, but what the f.!** no me lo puedo permitir pero ¡qué *Esp* cojones *or RP* mierda! *or Méx* ¡me vale madre!; **he's as stupid/rich as f.** es más bobo/rico que el carajo *or Esp* la hostia *or RP* la mierda; **he ran like f.** corría que se las pelaba *or Esp* que de la hostia; **it costs a f. of a lot of money** cuesta un huevo, *Esp* es caro de cojones

2 *vt* (**a**) *(have sex with) Esp* follar, *Am* coger, *Méx* chingar

(**b**) *(expressing surprise, contempt, irritation)* **f. it!** ¡carajo!, *Esp* ¡joder!; **f. me!** ¡no me jodas!, *Esp* ¡coño!; **f. you!** *Esp* ¡que te den por culo!, *Méx* ¡chinga tu madre!, *RP* ¡andate a la puta que te parió!; **I'm fucked if I know!** ¡no tengo ni puta idea!

3 *vi Esp* follar, *Am* coger, *Méx* chingar; **don't f. with me!** ¡no me jodas!

4 fuck all *n (nothing)* **he's done f. all this week** se ha tocado los huevos *or RP* rascado las bolas toda la semana, *Méx* estuvo de huevón toda la semana; **to know f. all about sth** no tener ni puta idea de algo

▸ **fuck about, fuck around** *Vulg* **1** *vt sep* **to f. sb about** *or* **around** *(treat badly)* joder *or Méx* chingar a alguien; *(waste time of)* andar jodiendo *or RP* hinchando a alguien

2 *vi (act foolishly)* hacer el *Esp* gilipollas *or Am* pendejo (**with** con); *(waste time)* tocarse los cojones, *RP* rascarse las bolas; **to f. about** *or* **around with sth** joder con algo

▸ **fuck off** *Vulg* **1** *vt sep* **to f. sb off** joder a alguien, *Arg* hincharle las pelotas a alguien; **to be fucked off (with sth/sb)** estar hasta los huevos (de algo/alguien)

2 *vi (go away)* largarse, *RP* tomarse el raje; **f. off!** *Esp* ¡vete a tomar por (el) culo!, *Méx* ¡vete a la chingada!, *RP* ¡andate a la puta que te parió!

▸ **fuck over** *vt sep Vulg* **to f. sb over** *Esp* tangar *or Méx* chingar *or RP* joder a alguien

▸ **fuck up** *Vulg* **1** *vt sep* **to f. sth up** *(bungle)* joder bien algo; **he's really fucked up emotionally** emocionalmente está hecho una mierda

2 *vi (bungle)* cagarla (bien cagada), *Méx* regarla

fuckable ['fʌkəbəl] *adj Vulg Esp* follable, *Am* cogible

fucked [fʌkt] *adj Vulg* **to be f.** *(exhausted) Esp* estar hecho(a) una braga *or Méx* chingado(a) *or RP* hecho(a) una mierda; *(broken)* estar jodido(a); **my leg's f.** se me ha jodido una pierna; **if they don't win this game, they're f.** si no ganan este partido se van a tomar por culo *or* al carajo

fucker ['fʌkə(r)] *n Vulg* (**a**) *(person)* cabrón(ona) *m,f*, hijo(a) *m,f* de puta *or Méx* de la chingada; **stupid/lazy f.** tonto/vago de mierda *or Esp* de los cojones (**b**) *(thing)* **I can't get the f. to start** este hijo (de) puta *or Méx* de la chingada no arranca

fuckface ['fʌkfeɪs], **fuckhead** ['fʌkhed] *adj Vulg* tonto(a) *m,f* del culo *or RP* de mierda, *Am* pendejo *m*

fucking ['fʌkɪŋ] *Vulg* **1** *adj* **he's a f. idiot!** ¡es un *Esp* gilipollas *or Am* pendejo *or RP* boludo!; **where's the f. key?** ¿dónde está la puta llave?; **he's a f. bastard!** ¡es un hijo de puta!; **you f. idiot!** ¡imbécil de mierda!; *US* **f. A!** ¡de puta madre!, *Méx* ¡de poca madre!, *RP* ¡de (la) mierda!; **f. hell!** ¡joder!; **where the f. hell have you been?** ¿dónde *Esp* cojones *or Méx* chingados *or RP* mierda te habías metido?

2 *adv* **it's f. brilliant!** ¡está de puta madre *or Méx* de la chingada!; **it's f. cold!** ¡hace un frío *Esp* de cojones *or Méx* de la chingada *or RP* de mierda!; **I'm f. (well) sick of it!** ¡estoy hasta las pelotas *or Esp* los cojones de ello!; **f. stop it!** ¡basta, carajo *or Esp* coño!; **I don't f. know!** ¡no sé, carajo *or Esp* joder!

fuck-me ['fʌkmɪ] *adj Vulg* de puta

fuck-off ['fʌkɒf] *n US Vulg (person)* vago(a) *m,f* de mierda

fuck-up ['fʌkʌp] *n Vulg* (**a**) *(disaster)* cagada *f*; **to make a f. of sth** cagarla *or Méx* chingarla con algo (**b**) *US (bungler)* **he's a real f.** la caga siempre

fuckwit ['fʌkwɪt] *n Vulg* tonto(a) *m,f* del culo *or RP* de mierda, *Am* pendejo *m*

fuddle ['fʌdəl] **1** *n* aturdimiento *m*; **in a f.** aturdido(a)

2 *vt* aturdir; **to get fuddled** aturdirse

fuddy-duddy ['fʌdɪdʌdɪ] **1** *n Fam* **an old f.** un carcamal *or Am* carcamán

2 *adj* de *Esp* carcamal *or Am* carcamán

fudge [fʌdʒ] **1** *n* (**a**) *(sweet)* = dulce blando de azúcar, leche y mantequilla (**b**) *Fam Pej (compromise)* apaño *m or Am* arreglo *m* (para salir del paso)

2 *vt Fam Pej* (**a**) *(avoid)* **to f. an issue** eludir un asunto, *Esp* echar balones fuera (**b**) *(distort, obscure)* **to f. the figures** amañar las cifras

3 *vi Fam* **stop fudging!** ¡déjate de evasivas!; **the President fudged on the budget issue** el Presidente eludió el tema del presupuesto

4 *exclam Fam Euph* ¡caray!

fuel ['fjʊəl] **1** *n* combustible *m*; **fossil/nuclear f.** combustible fósil/nuclear; IDIOM **to add f. to the flames** *(of situation, crisis)* echar leña al fuego ▸▸ ***f. bill*** factura *f* de combustible; *Aut* ***f. consumption*** consumo *m* de combustible; *Aut* ***f. gauge*** indicador *m* del nivel de gasolina *or RP* nafta; *Aut* ***f. injection*** inyección *f* (de combustible); ***f. oil*** fuel *m* oil; ***f. pipe*** manguera *f* de combustible; ***f. pump*** bomba *f* de (la) gasolina *or RP* nafta; ***f. rod*** *(for nuclear reactor)* barra *f* de combustible; ***f. tank*** depósito *m* de combustible

2 *vt* (*pt & pp* **fuelled**, *US* **fueled**) (**a**) *(furnace)* alimentar; **it is fuelled by...** *(vehicle, plane)* utiliza... (**b**) *Fig (hatred, speculation)* avivar, dar pábulo a; *(argument)* avivar

▸ **fuel up** *vi Br* echar gasolina, *Am* cargar gasolina, *RP* cargar nafta

fuel-air ['fjʊəl'eə(r)] *adj* aire-carburante *inv* ▸▸ ***f. explosive bomb*** bomba *f* explosiva de aire-combustible

fuel-injection ['fjʊəlɪn'dʒekʃən] *adj* ***f. engine*** motor *m* de inyección

fug [fʌg] *n Fam* ambiente *m* cargado, aire *m* viciado

fugitive ['fju:dʒɪtɪv] **1** *n* fugitivo(a) *m,f*; **she's a f. from justice** huye de la justicia, es una fugitiva de la justicia

2 *adj* (**a**) *(debtor, slave)* fugitivo(a) (**b**) *Literary (temporary)* fugaz, pasajero(a)

fugue [fju:g] *n* (**a**) *Mus* fuga *f* (**b**) *Psy* fuga *f*

Führer ['fjʊərə(r)] *n* (**a**) *Hist* Führer *m* (**b**) *Fam (dictator, boss)* nazi *mf*, dictador(ora) *m,f*

Fuji ['fu:dʒi:], **Fujiyama** [fu:dʒi:'ɑ:mə] *n* **(Mount) F.** el Fujiyama

fulcrum ['fʊlkrəm] *n* fulcro *m*, punto *m* de apoyo

fulfil, *US* **fulfill** [fʊl'fɪl] (*pt & pp* **fulfilled**) *vt* (**a**) *(carry out) (plan, task)* realizar, cumplir; *(function, role)* desempeñar; *(promise)* cumplir

(**b**) *(satisfy) (condition, regulation)* cumplir; *(need, requirement)* satisfacer; *(obligation)* cumplir con; **to feel fulfilled** *(person)* sentirse realizado(a); **she fulfilled herself both as an artist and as a mother** se realizó como artista y como madre

(**c**) *(achieve) (ambition, dream)* realizar, cumplir; **to f. one's potential** desarrollar todo su potencial

(**d**) *Com (order, contract)* ejecutar

fulfilling [fʊl'fɪlɪŋ] *adj (life, career, experience)* pleno(a), satisfactorio(a); **I want a more f. job** quiero un trabajo que me satisfaga más

fulfilment, *US* **fulfillment** [fʊl'fɪlmənt] *n* (**a**) *(of plan, task)* realización *f*, cumplimiento *m*; *(of function, role)* desempeño *m*; *(of promise)* cumplimiento *m*

(**b**) *(of condition, regulation, obligation)* cumplimiento *m*; *(of need, requirement)* satisfacción *f*; **to find** *or* **achieve f.** realizarse, hallar satisfacción; **to seek f.** buscar la realización personal; **she gets a sense** *or* **feeling of f. from her work** su trabajo le hace sentir realizada

(**c**) *(of ambition, dream)* realización *f*, cumplimiento *m*

(**d**) *Com (of order, contract)* ejecución *f*

FULL [fʊl] **1** *adj* (**a**) *(container, room)* lleno(a); *(day, schedule)* completo(a); **to be f. (up)** *(person, bus, container)* estar lleno(a); *(hotel)* estar lleno(a) *or* completo(a); **to be half f.** estar a medio llenar *or* medio lleno(a); **don't speak with your mouth f.** no hables con la boca llena; *Fig* **my heart is f.** mi corazón rebosa de emociones; **to be f. of** estar lleno(a) de; **f. of holes** lleno(a) de agujeros; **to be f. of energy**

rebosar energía; **to be f. of praise for sb** no tener más que elogios para alguien; **to be f. of oneself** *or* **of one's own importance** tenérselo muy creído, estar muy pagado(a) de sí (mismo(a)); *Fam* **he was f. of the joys of spring** estaba que se salía de alegría; *Vulg* **you're f. of shit** no dices más que *Esp* gilipolleces *or Am* pendejadas *or RP* boludeces; *Fam* **he's f. of it** no dice más que bobadas; **f. to the brim** (lleno(a)) hasta el borde; *Br* **to be f. to bursting** *(person, bus)* estar hasta arriba; **on a f. stomach** con el estómago lleno

(**b**) *(complete) (amount, support)* total; *(explanation, recovery, range)* completo(a); **this is our last f. day** es nuestro último día completo *or* entero; **I waited two f. days for news** estuve esperando noticias (durante) dos días enteros; **the f. extent of the damage** el alcance real del daño; **he drew himself up to his f. height** se levantó cuan largo era; **the f. horror** todo el horror; **the f. implications** todas las implicaciones; **to take f. responsibility for sth** asumir plena responsabilidad por algo; **she gave me the f. story** me lo contó todo; **to lead a f. life** llevar una vida plena; **I waited two f. hours** *or* **a f. two hours** esperé dos horas enteras; **to ask for fuller information about sth** pedir más información acerca de algo; **to be in f. agreement** estar completamente de acuerdo; *also Fig* **to be in f. bloom** estar en pleno florecimiento; **in f. flow** *(speaker)* en pleno discurso; **to be in f. swing** *(party)* estar en pleno apogeo; **in f. view** completamente a la vista; **to come f. circle** volver al punto de partida ►► *BrAut* ***f. beam*** luces *fpl* de carretera, (luces *fpl*) largas *fpl*; ***f. board*** pensión *f* completa; *Phot* ***in f. colour*** a todo color; ***f. dress*** traje *m* de gala; *Rail* ***f. fare*** precio *m or* tarifa *f* normal; ***f. house*** *(in theatre)* lleno *m*; *(in cards)* full *m*; *(in bingo)* cartón *m* completo; *Comptr* ***f. Internet access*** acceso *m* completo a Internet; ***f. member*** miembro *mf* de pleno derecho; ***f. moon*** luna *f* llena; ***f. name*** nombre *m* y apellidos, nombre *m* completo; ***f. nelson*** *(in wrestling)* doble nelson *f*; *Comptr* ***f. page display*** monitor *m* de página completa; ***f. pay*** sueldo *m* completo; ***f. point*** *(punctuation)* punto *m*; ***f. price*** *(of theatre ticket)* precio *m* completo; ***f. stop*** *(punctuation)* punto *m*; **you can't go, f. stop** no puedes ir, y punto; **the talks have come to a f. stop** se han roto las negociaciones; ***f. time*** *(in sports)* final *m* del tiempo reglamentario

(**c**) *(maximum)* **at f. blast** *(heater, air conditioning)* a plena potencia, *RP* a todo vapor; *(radio, TV)* a todo volumen; **at f. pelt** *or* **tilt** a toda marcha *or Esp* pastilla; **(at) f. speed** a toda velocidad; **at f. steam** a toda marcha; **f. steam ahead!** ¡a toda máquina!, *RP* ¡a todo vapor!; **at f. stretch** a pleno rendimiento; **to make f. use of sth** aprovechar algo al máximo ►► ***f. employment*** pleno empleo *m*; ***f. marks*** *(in exam)* nota *f or* puntuación *f* máxima; **f. marks for observation!** ¡qué observador eres!

(**d**) *(skirt, sleeve)* de vuelo

(**e**) *(plump) (face)* redondo(a); **a woman with a f. figure** una mujer rellenita; **f. lips** labios carnosos

(**f**) *(flavour, smell)* rico(a)

2 *n* **to pay in f.** pagar el total; **name in f.** nombre y apellidos; **to live life to the f.** disfrutar la vida al máximo

3 *adv* (**a**) *(entirely, completely)* **I turned the heat f. on** puse la calefacción al máximo; **I know it f. well** lo sé perfectamente

(**b**) *(directly, exactly)* **it hit him f. in the face** le dio en plena cara; **to look sb f. in the face** mirar a alguien directamente a la cara

---

fullback ['fʊlbæk] *n* (**a**) *(in soccer)* (defensa *mf*) lateral *mf* (**b**) *(in American football)* fullback *mf* (**c**) *(in rugby)* zaguero *m*, defensa *mf* de cierre (**d**) *(in hockey)* defensa *mf*, fullback *mf*

full-blooded ['fʊl'blʌdɪd] *adj* (**a**) *(thoroughbred)* de pura raza (**b**) *(enthusiastic) (attempt)* vigoroso(a), decidido(a); *(argument)* ardoroso(a); **a f. Socialist** un socialista de pura cepa

full-blown ['fʊl'bləʊn] *adj* (**a**) *(flower)* florecido(a) (**b**) *(war, scandal)* declarado(a); *(argument)* verdadero(a); **to have f. AIDS** haber desarrollado la enfermedad del sida (por completo)

full-bodied ['fʊl'bɒdɪd] *adj (wine)* con cuerpo

full-court press ['fʊlkɔːt'pres] *n* (**a**) *(in basketball)* presión *f* en toda la cancha (**b**) *US (all-out effort)* ofensiva *f* a gran escala

full-cream ['fʊl'kriːm] *adj* ***f. milk*** leche *f* entera

full-dress ['fʊl'dres] *adj* ***f. uniform*** uniforme *m* de gala; *Theat* ***f. rehearsal*** ensayo *m* general

fuller's earth ['fʊləz'ɜːθ] *n* tierra *f* de batán

full-face(d) ['fʊl'feɪs(t)] 1 *adj* de frente

2 *adv* de frente

full-fashioned *US* = **fully-fashioned**

full-fat ['fʊl'fæt] *adj (cheese, yoghurt)* con toda su grasa ►► ***f. milk*** leche *f* entera

full-fledged *US* = **fully-fledged**

full-frontal ['fʊl'frʌntəl] 1 *n* desnudo *m* integral

2 *adj* (**a**) *(photograph)* con desnudo integral; **f. nudity** desnudo integral (**b**) *(unrestrained)* directo(a), frontal

full-grown ['fʊl'grəʊn] *adj* plenamente desarrollado(a); **to be f.** estar plenamente desarrollado(a)

full-length ['fʊl'leŋθ] 1 *adj (portrait, mirror)* de cuerpo entero; *(dress, skirt)* largo(a); **f. film** largometraje

2 *adv* **he was lying f. on the floor** estaba tendido en el suelo cuan largo era

fullness ['fʊlnɪs] *n* (**a**) *(of container)* **because of the f. of the bucket** por lo lleno que estaba el balde; **I had an unpleasant feeling of f.** tenía una desagradable sensación de estar muy lleno

(**b**) *(completeness)* **I was amazed at the f. of his recovery** me sorprendió su completa recuperación; **in the f. of time** en su momento

(**c**) *(of skirt, sleeve)* amplitud *f*; *(of person's figure)* **he likes the f. of my figure** le gusto rellenita

(**d**) *(of flavour)* intensidad *f*

full-on ['fʊl'ɒn] *adj Fam (argument)* en serio; **to have f. sex** llegar hasta el final; **things were heading for a f. war** la situación iba camino de una guerra total

full-page ['fʊl'peɪdʒ] *adj (advert, illustration)* a toda página ►► *Comptr* ***f. display*** pantalla *f* de página completa

full-scale ['fʊl'skeɪl] *adj* (**a**) *(model)* (de) tamaño natural (**b**) *(search, reorganization)* exhaustivo(a), a gran escala; **f. war** guerra a gran escala

full-screen ['fʊl'skriːn] *adj Comptr* a pantalla completa

full-size(d) ['fʊl'saɪz(d)] *adj* (**a**) *(life size) (drawing, model)* de tamaño real *or* natural (**b**) *(fully grown) (animal, plant)* adulto(a) (**c**) *(bed)* de adulto

full-strength ['fʊl'streŋθ] *adj (solution)* puro(a), sin diluir; *(team)* completo(a)

full-throated ['fʊl'θrəʊtɪd] *adj (singing)* a pleno pulmón

full-time ['fʊl'taɪm] 1 *adj* (**a**) *(job, employment, contract)* a tiempo completo; *(teacher, housewife)* con dedicación exclusiva, de plena dedicación; *Fig* **looking after the children is a f. job** *or* **occupation** cuidar de los niños es un trabajo de plena dedicación (**b**) *Sport* **the f. score** el resultado final

2 *adv (to work)* a tiempo completo

full-timer ['fʊl'taɪmə(r)] *n* trabajador(ora) *m,f or* empleado(a) *m,f* a tiempo completo

fully ['fʊlɪ] *adv* (**a**) *(completely) (to agree)* totalmente; *(to understand)* perfectamente; *(aware, satisfied)* plenamente; **I f. expected to be arrested** no esperaba otra cosa que ser arrestado; **I f. intended to return the money** no tenía otra intención que devolver el dinero; **f. clothed** vestido(a) de arriba abajo; **f. grown** hecho(a) y derecho(a); **f. licensed** *(hotel, restaurant)* autorizado(a) a vender bebidas alcohólicas; **he is not yet f. qualified as a doctor** todavía no tiene el título de médico

(**b**) *(thoroughly) (to answer, examine, explain)* detalladamente; **this topic is dealt with more f. below** este tema se trata con más detalle abajo

(**c**) *(at least)* **it takes f. two hours** lleva dos horas largas; **f. half of the planes were faulty** al menos la mitad de los aviones eran defectuosos

fully-fashioned ['fʊlɪ'fæʃənd], *US* **full-fashioned** ['fʊl'fæʃənd] *adj (knitwear, hosiery)* ajustado(a)

fully-fledged ['fʊlɪ'fledʒd], *US* **full-fledged** ['fʊl'fledʒd] *adj* (**a**) *(bird)* que ya puede volar, volandero(a) (**b**) *Fig (doctor)* titulado(a); *(member)* de pleno derecho; **a f. atheist** un ateo puro y duro

fulmar ['fʊlmɑː(r)] *n* fulmar *m*

fulminate ['fʊlmɪneɪt] *vi* tronar, arremeter (**against** contra)

fulmination [fʌlmɪ'neɪʃən] *n* ataque *m*, crítica *f*, diatriba *f*

fulness = **fullness**

fulsome ['fʊlsəm] *adj* excesivo(a), exagerado(a); **to be f. in one's praise of sth/sb** alabar algo/a alguien en exceso

fumarole ['fjuːmərəʊl] *n* fumarola *f*

fumble ['fʌmbəl] 1 *vt* **he fumbled his lines** se confundió al decir sus líneas; **the goalkeeper fumbled the ball** al portero *or Am* arquero se le escapó la pelota de las manos; **she fumbled her way down the dark corridor** fue por el oscuro pasillo a tientas

2 *vi* **she fumbled in her pocket for a tissue** revolvió en el bolsillo buscando un pañuelo; **to f. for words** no encontrar las palabras adecuadas, titubear; **he fumbled with the controls** trató torpemente de accionar los mandos; **he fumbled (about** *or* **around) in the dark for**

the light switch tanteó en la oscuridad buscando el interruptor de la luz
3 *n (in American football)* = pérdida del balón al caérsele a un jugador de las manos

fumbling ['fʌmblɪŋ] *adj* torpe

fume [fju:m] 1 *n* **fumes** *(of factory, traffic)* gases; *(of tobacco)* humo ►► ***f. cupboard*** campana *f* de laboratorio
2 *vi* **(a)** *(give off fumes)* despedir gases **(b)** *(be angry)* **to be fuming** echar humo (por las orejas)
3 *vt* **"this is your fault," she fumed** "es culpa tuya", le espetó

> **False friend**: The Spanish verb **fumar** is not a translation for the English word **fume**. In Spanish **fumar** means "to smoke".

fumigate ['fju:mɪgeɪt] *vt* fumigar

fumigation [fju:mɪ'geɪʃən] *n* fumigación *f*

fun [fʌn] 1 *n* diversión *f*; **to be f.** *(person, activity)* ser divertido(a); **it's not much f.** no es muy divertido; **it won't be half as much f. without you** sin ti no será tan divertido; **to have f.** divertirse; **have f.!** ¡diviértete!; **they get a lot of f. out of the bicycle** se divierten muchísimo con la bicicleta; **it was good** *or* **great f.** fue muy divertido(a); **to make f. of, to poke f. at** burlarse de; **to say sth in f.** decir algo en broma; **to do sth for f., to do sth for the f. of it** hacer algo por diversión; **to join in the f.** unirse a la diversión; **to take the f. out of sth** quitar la gracia a algo; **what f.!** ¡qué divertido!; IDIOM **there'll be f. and games** *(trouble)* se va a armar una buena
2 *adj Fam* divertido(a) ►► ***f. fur*** piel *f* sintética; ***f. run*** carrera *f* popular

function ['fʌŋkʃən] 1 *n* **(a)** *(of machine, person, institution)* función *f*; **to carry out one's f.** llevar a cabo sus funciones; **my f. in life is to...** mi papel consiste en... **(b)** *(celebration)* celebración *f*; *(official occasion)* acto *m* ►► ***f. room*** salón *m* de fiestas **(c)** *Math* función *f*; **X is a f. of Y** X es función de Y **(d)** *Ling* función *f* ►► ***f. word*** palabra *f* funcional **(e)** *Comptr* función *f* ►► ***f. key*** tecla *f* de función
2 *vi* funcionar; **to f. as** *(room)* servir de, hacer de; **it can f. as an adverb** puede funcionar como adverbio

functional ['fʌŋkʃənəl] *adj* **(a)** *(practical) (design, furniture, building)* funcional **(b)** *(operational)* operativo(a); **to be f.** estar en funcionamiento, funcionar; *Fam* **I'm barely f. before ten o'clock** antes de las diez no sirvo para nada ►► ***f. illiterate*** analfabeto(a) *m,f* funcional **(c)** *Med (disease)* funcional

functionalism ['fʌŋkʃənəlɪzəm] *n* funcionalismo *m*

functionality [fʌŋkʃə'nælɪtɪ] *n* funcionalidad *f*

functionally ['fʌŋkʃənəlɪ] *adv* funcionalmente; **to be f. equivalent to sth** tener la misma función que algo; **to be f. illiterate** ser analfabeto(a) funcional

functionary ['fʌŋkʃənərɪ] *n* funcionario(a) *m,f*

functioning ['fʌŋkʃənɪŋ] 1 *n* funcionamiento *m*
2 *adj* en funcionamiento

fund [fʌnd] 1 *n* **(a)** *(charitable, for investment)* fondo *m*; **they've set up a f. for the earthquake victims** han creado un fondo para las víctimas del terremoto ►► *Fin* ***f. management*** administración *f* de fondos; *Fin* ***f. manager*** gestor(ora) *m,f* de fondos
(b) *(available money)* **funds** fondos; **to be in/out of funds** tener/no tener fondos; **I'm a bit short of funds** estoy un poco escaso de fondos
(c) *(of information, jokes)* fuente *f*; **she has a large f. of amusing anecdotes** tiene un amplio repertorio de divertidas anécdotas
2 *vt* **(a)** *(project, company)* financiar **(b)** *Fin (debt)* financiar

> **False friend**: The Spanish verb **fundar** is not a translation for the English word **fund**. In Spanish **fundar** means "to found".

fundamental [fʌndə'mentəl] 1 *adj* **(a)** *(basic)* fundamental; **a knowledge of economics is f. to a proper understanding of the problem** para comprender de verdad el problema es fundamental poseer conocimientos de economía; **of f. importance** de vital importancia ►► *Phys* ***f. frequency*** frecuencia *f* fundamental; *Phys* ***f. particle*** partícula *f* elemental
(b) *(inherent)* **the f. inequalities in society** las desigualdades básicas *or* estructurales de la sociedad; **her f. honesty** su honradez inherente
2 *n* **(a)** **fundamentals** principios básicos **(b)** *Mus* nota *f* fundamental

fundamentalism [fʌndə'mentəlɪzəm] *n* integrismo *m*, fundamentalismo *m*

fundamentalist [fʌndə'mentəlɪst] 1 *n* integrista *mf*, fundamentalista *mf*
2 *adj* integrista, fundamentalista

fundamentally [fʌndə'mentəlɪ] *adv* fundamentalmente; **they are f. different** tienen diferencias fundamentales; **it's f. important** es (de una importancia) fundamental; **we disagree f.** tenemos desacuerdos fundamentales; **she seems hard but f. she's good-hearted** parece dura pero es, en esencia, una persona de buen corazón; **f., there's nothing wrong with the idea** la idea en sí no es mala

fundholder ['fʌndhəʊldə(r)] *n Br* = centro de salud o médico con autonomía en la gestión financiera

funding ['fʌndɪŋ] *n* **(a)** *(for project) (act of resourcing)* financiación *f*, financiamiento *m*; *(resources)* fondos *mpl*; **BP will put up half of the f.** BP financiará la mitad **(b)** *Fin (of debt)* financiación *f*, financiamiento *m*

fund-raiser ['fʌndreɪzə(r)] *n* **(a)** *(person)* recaudador(ora) *m,f* de fondos **(b)** *(event)* acto *m* para recaudar *or* captar fondos

fundraising ['fʌndreɪzɪŋ] *n* recaudación *f* de fondos, captación *f* de fondos

funeral ['fju:nərəl] *n* entierro *m*; IDIOM *Fam* **that's your f.!** ¡eso es cosa tuya *or* tu problema! ►► ***f. chapel*** capilla *f* ardiente; ***f. cortège*** cortejo *m* fúnebre; ***f. director*** encargado(a) *m,f* de la funeraria; *Am* ***f. home*** funeraria *f*; *Mus* ***f. march*** marcha *f* fúnebre; ***f. oration*** oración *f* fúnebre; *Br* ***f. parlour*** funeraria *f*; ***f. procession*** cortejo *m* fúnebre; ***f. service*** honras *fpl* fúnebres; ***f. wreath*** corona *f* fúnebre

funerary ['fju:nərərɪ] *adj* funerario(a)

funereal [fjʊ'nɪərɪəl] *adj* fúnebre

funfair ['fʌn'feə(r)] *n* feria *f* (ambulante)

funfest ['fʌnfest] *n US* fiesta *f (con actividades programadas)*

fun-filled ['fʌn'fɪld] *adj* divertido(a)

fungal ['fʌŋgəl] *adj* fúngico(a), de los hongos; **a f. infection** una micosis

fungi *pl of* **fungus**

fungicidal [fʌŋgɪ'saɪdəl] *adj* fungicida

fungicide ['fʌŋgɪsaɪd] *n* fungicida *m*

fungus ['fʌŋgəs] *(pl* **fungi** ['fʌŋgaɪ]*) n* **(a)** *(mushroom, toadstool)* hongo *m* **(b)** *(on walls, fruit)* moho *m* **(c)** *(on skin)* hongos *mpl*

funicular [fjʊ'nɪkjʊlə(r)] *n* **f. (railway)** funicular *m*

funk [fʌŋk] 1 *n* **(a)** *Fam Old-fashioned (fright)* **to be in a (blue) f.** estar muerto(a) de miedo; **he got into a f.** le entró mieditis *or Méx* el mello *or RP* el cuiqui **(b)** *(music)* funk *m*, funky *m*
2 *vt (out of fear)* **I funked telling him** no me atreví a contárselo

funkhole ['fʌŋkhəʊl] *n Fam* **(a)** *Mil* escondrijo *m*, agujero *m* **(b)** *(civilian job)* = trabajo que permite eludir el servicio militar

funky ['fʌŋkɪ] *adj* **(a)** *Fam (fashionable, excellent)* genial, *Esp* muy guapo(a), *Andes, CAm, Carib, Méx* muy chévere, *Méx* muy padre **(b)** *Mus* funky **(c)** *US Fam (smelly)* apestoso(a), maloliente

fun-loving ['fʌnlʌvɪŋ] *adj* amante de las diversiones

funnel ['fʌnəl] 1 *n* **(a)** *(of locomotive, steamship)* chimenea *f* **(b)** *(for filling bottle)* embudo *m* **(c)** *(for ventilation)* conducto *m*, tubo *m*
2 *vt (pt & pp* **funnelled**, *US* **funneled)** **(a)** *(liquid)* echar con un embudo **(b)** *(direct) (crowd, funds)* canalizar
3 *vi* **the crowd funnelled out of the gates** la multitud salía encauzada por las puertas

funnel-web ['fʌnəlweb] *n* **f. (spider)** = araña muy venenosa de Australia que teje una telaraña acanalada

funnily ['fʌnɪlɪ] *adv* **(a)** *(strangely)* de forma rara; **f. enough...** curiosamente..., por raro que parezca... **(b)** *(amusingly)* de una manera divertida

funny ['fʌnɪ] 1 *adj* **(a)** *(amusing)* gracioso(a); **to be f.** tener gracia, ser gracioso(a); **to seem f.** parecer gracioso(a); **it didn't seem f. to me** a mí no me hizo gracia; **she didn't see the f. side of it** no le veía la gracia; **are you trying to be f.?** ¿te estás haciendo el gracioso?; *Ironic* **very f.!** ¡muy gracioso! ►► ***f. bone*** hueso *m* de la risa; ***f. man*** *(comedian)* humorista *m*, cómico *m*; *Ironic* gracioso *m*; *US* ***f. papers*** *(in newspaper)* historietas *fpl*
(b) *(strange)* raro(a), curioso(a); **to look/sound f.** parecer/sonar raro; **this butter tastes/smells f.** esta mantequilla sabe/huele raro; *Fam* **to go all f.** *(person)* ponerse raro; *(machine)* ir mal; **(that's) f., I thought I'd locked the door** qué curioso, creía que había cerrado la puerta con llave; **(it's) f. you should say that** es curioso que digas eso; *Fam* **she's f. that way** es bastante particular en ese sentido
(c) *(dubious, suspicious)* raro(a), extraño(a); **there's something f. going on here** aquí pasa *or* sucede algo raro; *Fam* **I don't want any f. business!** ¡nada de trucos!; *Fam* **there was some f. business about the will** había gato encerrado en lo del testamento ►► ***f. money*** *(fake)* dinero *m* falso; *(dishonest)* dinero *m* negro
(d) *(ill)* **I feel a bit f.** no me siento muy allá; **my stomach's a bit f.** tengo el estómago un poco revuelto

(**e**) *Fam (slightly crazy)* raro(a); **he went a bit f. in his old age** *(eccentric)* se volvió un poco raro con los años ►► *Fam* ***f. farm*** manicomio *m*, renopático *m*
2 *adv Fam (to walk, talk)* raro
3 *n US* (**a**) *Fam (joke)* chiste *m*; **to make a f.** hacer un chiste (**b**) **the funnies** *(in newspaper)* las historietas, *RP* los chistes

funny-ha-ha ['fʌnɪhɑː'hɑː] *adj Fam* divertido(a), gracioso(a)

funny-peculiar ['fʌnɪpɪ'kjuːlɪə(r)] *adj Fam* curioso(a), raro(a)

fun-packed ['fʌn'pækt] *adj* de mucha diversión

fur [fɜː(r)] 1 *n* (**a**) *(on animal)* pelo *m*; *(animal skin)* piel *f*; IDIOM *Fam* **the f. was flying** se armó la marimorena; **her remark made the f. fly** *or* **set the f. flying** su comentario armó un revuelo ►► ***f. coat*** abrigo *m* de piel; ***f. farm*** criadero *m* de animales para piel; ***f. seal*** lobo *m* marino; ***f. trade*** comercio *m* de pieles (**b**) *(on tongue)* sarro *m* (**c**) *Br (in kettle, pipe)* sarro *m*
2 *vt* (*pt & pp* **furred**) *Br* **to f. (up)** *(kettle, pipe)* cubrir de sarro *(por dentro)*

► **fur up** *vi (kettle, pipe)* cubrirse de sarro *(por dentro)*

furbish ['fɜːbɪʃ] *vt* (**a**) *(polish)* limpiar (**b**) *(renovate)* remozar, renovar

furious ['fjʊərɪəs] *adj* (**a**) *(angry)* furioso(a); **to be f. (with sb)** estar furioso(a) (con alguien); **to be f. with oneself** tirarse de los pelos; **to be in a f. temper** estar de un humor de perros (**b**) *(intense) (struggle)* feroz; *(sea, storm)* violento(a); **at a f. pace** a un ritmo frenético *or* vertiginoso; **at a f. speed** a una velocidad de vértigo

furiously ['fjʊərɪəslɪ] *adv* (**a**) *(to answer, look)* con furia, furiosamente (**b**) *(to fight, work)* frenéticamente; **the fire was blazing f.** el fuego ardía con furia

furl [fɜːl] *vt (flag, sail)* enrollar, recoger; *(umbrella)* plegar

furlong ['fɜːlɒŋ] *n* = 201 metros *(unidad utilizada en las carreras de caballos)*

furlough ['fɜːləʊ] *US* 1 *n Mil* permiso *m*; **to be on f.** estar de permiso *or CSur, Méx* franco
2 *vt* (**a**) *Mil (grant leave of absence)* dar permiso *or CSur, Méx* franco a (**b**) *(lay off)* despedir temporalmente

furnace ['fɜːnɪs] *n* horno *m*; **it's like a f. in here!** ¡esto es un horno!

furnish ['fɜːnɪʃ] *vt* (**a**) *(house, flat)* amueblar (**b**) *Formal (provide) (supplies, food)* proporcionar, suministrar; *(information, reason, opportunity)* proporcionar; **to f. sb with sth** proporcionar algo a alguien; **they furnished the ship with provisions** aprovisionaron el barco; **they had furnished themselves with the necessary information** habían hecho acopio de la información necesaria

furnished ['fɜːnɪʃd] *adj (flat, room)* amueblado(a); **to be f.** estar amueblado(a) ►► ***f. accommodation*** viviendas *fpl* amuebladas

furnishings ['fɜːnɪʃɪŋz] *npl* mobiliario *m*

furniture ['fɜːnɪtʃə(r)] *n* (**a**) *(for house)* muebles *mpl*, mobiliario *m*; **a piece of f.** un mueble; **office/garden f.** mobiliario de oficina/jardín; IDIOM **she treats me as if I were part of the f.** me trata como si fuera un mueble ►► *US* ***f. mover*** empleado(a) *m,f* de una empresa de mudanzas; ***f. polish*** abrillantador *m* de muebles, *CSur* lustramuebles *m inv*; *Br* ***f. remover*** empleado(a) *m,f* de una empresa de mudanzas; ***f. shop*** tienda *f* de muebles; ***f. showroom*** salón *m* de exposición y venta de muebles; ***f. van*** camión *m* de mudanzas
(**b**) *(accessories)* **street f.** mobiliario urbano; **door f.** herrajes

furore [fʊ'rɔːrɪ], *US* **furor** ['fjʊrɔː(r)] *n (uproar)* revuelo *m*, escándalo *m*; **there's been a great f. over the sex scenes** hubo un gran revuelo *or* escándalo con las escenas de sexo; **to cause a f.** levantar un gran revuelo

furred [fɜːd] *adj* (**a**) *(animal)* peludo(a) (**b**) *(kettle, pipe, tongue)* lleno(a) de sarro

furrier ['fʌrɪə(r)] *n* peletero(a) *m,f*

furrow ['fʌrəʊ] 1 *n* (**a**) *(in field)* surco *m* (**b**) *(on face)* surco *m*
2 *vt* (**a**) *(field, soil)* surcar (**b**) *Literary* **the lines which furrowed his brow** las arrugas que le surcaban la frente; **his brow was furrowed with worry** fruncía el ceño con preocupación
3 *vi* **her brow furrowed** frunció el ceño

furry ['fɜːrɪ] *adj* (**a**) *(animal)* peludo(a); *(toy)* de peluche (**b**) *(kettle, pipe)* con sarro; **to have a f. tongue** tener la lengua llena de sarro

further ['fɜːðə(r)], **farther** ['fɑːðə(r)] (*comparative of* **far**) 1 *adv* (**a**) *(in distance)* más lejos; **f. along the beach** más adelante en la playa; **have you much f. to go?** ¿te queda mucho camino?; **f. (to the) north/south** más al *or* hacia el norte/sur; **she's never been f. north than Leicester** nunca ha estado más allá de Leicester; **how much f. is it to the station?** ¿cuánto queda para la estación?; **f. away** más lejos; **he got f. and f. away from the shore** se alejaba cada vez más de la orilla; **f. back** *(in space)* más atrás; *(in time)* antes; **f. on** *(in space, time)* más adelante; **she's f. on than the rest of the students** está más adelantada que el resto de los alumnos; **we got no f. than the river** no pasamos del río; **that doesn't get us much f.** eso no nos ayuda mucho; **I've got no f. with finding a job** no he avanzado mucho en la búsqueda de trabajo; **I can go no f.** *(walking)* no puedo seguir; *(speaking)* no puedo decir más; **this mustn't go any f.** *(don't tell anyone else)* esto no debe salir de aquí; **to go no f. into the matter** no profundizar más en el asunto; **I would go (even) f. and say he's a genius** yo iría aun más lejos y diría que es un genio; **by being careful he made his money go f.** siendo cuidadoso pudo sacar más partido a su dinero; **they fell f. and f. into debt** cada vez tenían más deudas; **if you want financial advice, look no f. (than me)!** si necesitas un asesor financiero ¡ése soy yo *or* aquí me tienes!; **nothing could be f. from the truth** nada más lejos de la realidad; **nothing could be f. from my mind** ni se me había pasado por la cabeza
(**b**) *(more)* más; **I didn't question him any f.** no le pregunté más; **I want nothing f. to do with him/it** no quiero tener nada más que ver con él/eso; **until you hear f.** hasta que tengas más noticias; **don't try my patience any f.** no agotes mi paciencia; **the police want to question him f.** la policía quiere interrogarlo nuevamente; **the committee wanted to take the matter f.** *(issue, suggestion)* el comité quería profundizar más en el asunto; *(complaint)* el comité quería seguir adelante con el asunto
(**c**) *(to a greater degree)* **the issue is f. confused by...** el asunto se complica más si cabe por...; **her arrival only complicated things f.** su llegada sólo complicó aun más las cosas
(**d**) *(additionally)* además; *Formal* **I would f. suggest that...** es más, yo sugeriría que...; *Formal* **f. to your recent letter...** en respuesta a su última carta...; **f. to our discussion/conversation** con relación a nuestra discusión/conversación
2 *adj* (**a**) *(more distant)* más alejado(a)
(**b**) *(additional)* **do you have any f. questions?** ¿tiene alguna otra pregunta?; **for f. information** para mayor información; **I need a f. £90** necesito 90 libras más; **I have nothing f. to say** no tengo nada más que añadir *or Am* agregar; **I have no f. use for it** ya no me sirve; **upon f. consideration** tras considerarlo de nuevo; **until f. notice** hasta nuevo aviso; **without f. ado** sin más preámbulos; **without f. delay** sin más demoras; **without f. warning** sin más aviso ►► *Br* ***f. education*** = enseñanza no universitaria para adultos, ≃ formación *f* continua; *Br* ***f. education college*** = centro de enseñanza donde se pueden cursar estudios de formación profesional y bachillerato
3 *vt (cause, one's interests, career)* favorecer

furtherance ['fɜːðərəns] *n Formal* promoción *f*, fomento *m*; **in f. of** para favorecer

furthermore [fɜːðə'mɔː(r)] *adv Formal* es más

furthermost ['fɜːðəməʊst] *adj Literary* último(a), más alejado(a)

furthest ['fɜːðɪst], **farthest** ['fɑːðɪst] (*superlative of* **far**) 1 *adj* **the f.** el/la más alejado(a), el/la más distante; **her house is the f. away** su casa es la que queda más lejos; **when it's f. from the sun** cuando se encuentra a mayor distancia del sol; **this is the f. north I've ever been** nunca he ido más al norte que esto
2 *adv* más lejos; **it's 10 miles at the f.** a lo sumo queda a 10 millas

furtive ['fɜːtɪv] *adj* furtivo(a)

furtively ['fɜːtɪvlɪ] *adv (to glance)* furtivamente, con disimulo; *(to creep)* sigilosamente

fury ['fjʊərɪ] *n* (**a**) *(anger)* furia *f*, ira *f*; **to be in a f.** estar furioso(a); **he was beside himself with f.** estaba fuera de sí (**b**) *(violence) (of storm, wind)* furia *f*; *(of struggle, battle)* ferocidad *f*; *Fam* **to work/run like f.** trabajar/correr como loco(a) (**c**) *(frenzy)* frenesí *m*; **to be in a f. of activity** tener una actividad frenética (**d**) *Mythol* **the Furies** las Furias

furze [fɜːz] *n* aliaga *f*, aulaga *f*

fuse [fjuːz] 1 *n* (**a**) *Elec* fusible *m*; IDIOM *Fam* **she blew a f.** *(became angry)* se puso como una fiera ►► ***f. box*** cuadro *m* eléctrico, caja *f* de fusibles; ***f. wire*** fusible *m* (**b**) *(for dynamite)* mecha *f*; *(in bomb)* espoleta *f*; IDIOM *Fam* **to have a short f.** *(be short-tempered)* saltar a la mínima, *RP* ser muy calderita
2 *vt* (**a**) *(join, melt)* fundir (**b**) *(unite)* fundir; **an attempt to f. traditional and modern methods** un intento por fundir métodos modernos con tradicionales (**c**) *Br Elec* **a surge of power fused the lights** se fundieron los plomos y se fue la luz por una subida de corriente
3 *vi* (**a**) *(metals)* fundirse (**b**) *(organizations, parties)* fundirse (**c**) *Br Elec* **the lights have fused** se han fundido los plomos y se ha ido la luz

fused [fjuːzd] *adj Elec (plug, appliance)* provisto(a) de fusible

fuselage ['fjuːzəlɑːʒ] *n* fuselaje *m*

fusilier [fjuːzɪ'lɪə(r)] *n* fusilero *m*

fusillade ['fjuːzɪleɪd] *n (of bullets)* descarga *f* cerrada; *Fig (of criticism, questions)* lluvia *f*

fusion ['fjuːʒən] *n* **(a)** *(of metal)* fundición *f*, fusión *f*
(b) *Phys* fusión *f* ▸▸ ***f. bomb*** bomba *f* de fusión; ***f. reactor*** reactor *m* de fusión
(c) *(of ideas, parties)* fusión *f*
(d) *(in music, culture)* fusión *f*, mestizaje *m* ▸▸ ***f. cookery*** cocina *f* de fusión

fuss [fʌs] **1** *n* **(a)** *(excitement, commotion)* alboroto *m*, escándalo *m*; **a lot of f. about** *or* **over nothing** mucho ruido y pocas nueces; **I don't see what all the f. is about** no veo a qué viene tanto alboroto; **with as little f. as possible** lo más discretamente posible; **to make** *or Fam* **kick up a f. (about** *or* **over sth)** armar un alboroto *or* un escándalo (por algo); **I don't want any f. made when I retire** para mi jubilación no

FUTURE

El inglés no tiene una conjugación verbal simple para expresar el futuro.

a) Para ello suelen usarse **will** + INFINITIVO o **be going to** + INFINITIVO, con una variación de significado que a menudo es mínima. Hay, sin embargo, una serie de diferencias entre ambas:

WILL se usa cuando uno se compromete a hacer algo, por lo que es frecuente a la hora de manifestar una promesa, un ofrecimiento, una amenaza, etc.

I'll be home by six at the latest *estaré en casa a las seis como muy tarde*
I'll never let you down *nunca te voy a fallar*
we'll help clean up - it won't take long *te ayudamos a recoger – no va a llevar mucho tiempo*
I'll smash your face in! *¡te voy a partir la cara!*

Will se usa además para predecir acontecimientos futuros:

we'll have a tough time persuading Nancy to help *nos va a costar convencer a Nancy para que nos ayude*
there will be scattered showers in northern parts *habrá chubascos aislados en el norte*

GOING TO se usa para hablar de intenciones claras, de decisiones que ya se han tomado:

we're going to move to the country *vamos a irnos a vivir al campo*
John is going to start, so you can be next if you like *va a empezar John, así que si quieres tú puedes ser el segundo*

Going to se usa también para hacer una predicción basada en lo que ocurre en el presente:

it looks like it's going to rain *parece que va a llover*

b) Algunas FORMAS DE PRESENTE que se pueden usar para expresar el futuro:

PRESENTE SIMPLE
Se usa hablando de horarios o de acontecimientos muy predecibles, como en español:

we get to Rome on Friday *llegamos a Roma el viernes*
the Festival starts next week *el Festival empieza la semana que viene*
what time does the sun rise tomorrow? *¿a qué hora sale el sol mañana?*

A menudo se usa también para referirse al futuro en oraciones condicionales que comienzan con **if** o con conjunciones temporales como **before, after, until,** etc.:

if you pay him some money he'll take you there himself *si le pagas algo él mismo te llevará allí*
by the time we get there, there'll be no food left *para cuando lleguemos allí ya no quedará comida*

PRESENTE CONTINUO
Se usa a menudo cuando el hecho futuro ha sido decidido entre el hablante y otras personas:

I'm seeing Pamela for lunch tomorrow *voy a ver a Pamela para comer mañana*
we're having a party on Saturday *damos una fiesta el sábado*

be to + *INFINITIVO*
Esta forma se usa para indicar o referirse a un mandato:

we are to assemble here at four o'clock *tenemos que reunirnos aquí a las cuatro*
forms are to be returned no later than next Friday *los impresos han de ser devueltos el próximo viernes como muy tarde*

c) Otras FORMAS DE FUTURO son:

FUTURO CONTINUO
Con él se transmite al futuro el énfasis que confiere el presente continuo al hecho de que la acción se está realizando:

I'll be lying on the beach this time next week *la semana que viene a estas horas estaré tumbado en la playa*

Asimismo puede indicar que se da por hecho que la acción va a ocurrir, y por ello a menudo se usa antes de pedir un favor:

will you be taking your car to the party? *¿vas a ir en coche a la fiesta?*

FUTURO PERFECTO
Se usa para referirse a una acción ya realizada cuando se llegue el tiempo futuro mencionado en la oración:

I'll have been here for ten years come next March *en marzo hará diez años que estoy aquí*
will you have finished by Friday? *¿habrás terminado para el viernes?*

quiero que hagan fiesta ni despedida

(**b**) **to make a f. of** *or* **over sb** *(show affection to)* mimar a alguien; **he always makes a f. of his grandchildren** se deshace en atenciones cada vez que está con sus nietos; **he likes to be made a f. over** le gusta que lo mimen y le presten atención

2 *vt* (**a**) *Fam* **I'm not fussed** *(I don't mind)* me da lo mismo (**b**) *(make nervous, annoy)* fastidiar; **don't f. me!** ¡no me fastidies!

3 *vi* (**a**) *(be agitated)* **to f. (about** *or* **around)** estar inquieto(a); **don't f., we'll be on time** no te preocupes, llegaremos a tiempo; **stop fussing!** ¡estate quieto! (**b**) *(fiddle)* **to f. with sth** juguetear con algo, toquetear algo; **she kept fussing with her hair** no dejaba de juguetear con *or* toquetearse el pelo

▸ **fuss over** *vt insep* mimar, cuidar; **stop fussing over me!** ¡déjame!; **he fussed over his grandchildren** se deshacía en atenciones con sus nietos

fussbudget ['fʌsbʌdʒət] *n US Fam* quisquilloso(a) *m,f*

fussily ['fʌsɪlɪ] *adv* (**a**) *(to react, comment)* quisquillosamente (**b**) *(dressed, decorated)* recargadamente

fussiness ['fʌsɪnɪs] *n* (**a**) *(fastidiousness)* meticulosidad *f*, exigencia *f* (**b**) *(of dress, decoration)* lo recargado

fusspot ['fʌspɒt] *n Fam* quisquilloso(a) *m,f*, tiquismiquis *mf inv*

fussy ['fʌsɪ] *adj* (**a**) *(person)* quisquilloso(a), exigente; **I'm not f.** *(I don't mind)* me da lo mismo (**b**) *(dress, decor)* recargado(a)

fustian ['fʌstɪən] *n* (**a**) *(cloth)* fustán *m* (**b**) *(pompous language)* grandilocuencia *f*, prosopopeya *f*

fusty ['fʌstɪ] *adj* (**a**) *(furniture, carpets)* con olor a humedad; *(place)* con olor a cerrado (**b**) *(person, attitude)* rancio(a), anticuado(a)

futile ['fju:taɪl] *adj (attempt, protest)* inútil, vano(a); *(remark, suggestion)* fútil; **it's f. trying to reason with him** es inútil intentar razonar con él

futility [fju:'tɪlɪtɪ] *n (of attempt, protest)* inutilidad; *(of remark, suggestion)* futilidad *f*

futon ['fu:tɒn] *n* futón *m*

future ['fju:tʃə(r)] **1** *n* (**a**) *(time)* futuro *m*; **in the f.** en el futuro; **in f.** de ahora en adelante, en el futuro; **in the near/distant f.** en un futuro próximo/lejano; **who knows what the f. holds** *or* **has in store?** ¿quién sabe qué traerá el futuro?; **to look into the f.** mirar al futuro

(**b**) *(prospects)* futuro *m*, porvenir *m*; **the f. of the company/country** el futuro de la empresa/del país; **he has a great f. ahead of him as an actor** tiene un gran futuro como actor; **she has a job with a (good) f.** tiene un trabajo con (mucho) futuro; **the f. looks bright** el futuro se presenta inmejorable; **there's no f. in it** no tiene futuro

(**c**) *Gram* **f. (tense)** futuro *m*; **f. perfect (tense)** futuro perfecto

(**d**) *Fin* **futures** futuros; **sugar/coffee futures** futuros de azúcar/café ▸▸ ***futures market*** mercado *m* de futuros

2 *adj* futuro(a); **my f. wife** mi futura esposa; **at some f. date** en una fecha futura; **for f. reference** por si pudiera ser de interés en el futuro

future-proof ['fju:tʃəpru:f] *adj (computer)* actualizable

futurism ['fju:tʃərɪzəm] *n Art & Lit* futurismo *m*

futurist ['fju:tʃərɪst] *Art & Lit* **1** *n* futurista *mf*

2 *adj* futurista

futuristic [fju:tʃə'rɪstɪk] *adj* futurista

futurologist [fju:tʃə'rɒlədʒɪst] *n* futurólogo(a) *m,f*

futurology [fju:tʃə'rɒlədʒɪ] *n* futurología *f*

fuze [fju:z] *n US (for dynamite)* mecha *f*; *(in bomb)* espoleta *f*

fuzz [fʌz] *n* (**a**) *(down) (on peach, skin)* pelusa *f* (**b**) *(frizzy hair)* pelo *m* crespo (**c**) *Fam* **the f.** *(the police)* la poli, *Esp* la pasma, *Méx* los pitufos, *RP* la cana (**d**) *US (lint)* pelusa *f*

fuzziness ['fʌzɪnɪs] *n (lack of definition) (of outline, image, sound)* falta *f* de nitidez; *(mental)* embotamiento *m*

fuzzy ['fʌzɪ] **1** *adj* (**a**) *(hair)* crespo(a) (**b**) *(ill-defined) (outline, image, sound)* borroso(a); *(idea)* vago(a) ▸▸ *Comptr* ***f. logic*** lógica *f* difusa *or* borrosa

2 *vt US* **to f. (up) the issue** embrollar el tema

fwd (*abbr* **forward**) reexpedir (al destinatario)

FWIW (*abbr* **for what it's worth**) si sirve de algo

FX (*abbr* **special effects**) efectos *mpl* especiales

fyi (*abbr* **for your information**) para tu información

FYROM ['efwaɪɑ:rəʊ'em] *n* (*abbr* **Former Yugoslavian Republic of Macedonia**) ARYM *f*

G, g

G, g [dʒiː] *n (letter)* G, g *f*

G [dʒiː] **1** *n* **(a)** *Mus* sol *m* **(b)** *Phys* **(gravity)** G
2 *adj US Cin* ≃ (apta) para todos los públicos

g (*abbr* **gramme**) g

G7 ['dʒiː'sevən] *n* (*abbr* **Group of Seven**) G7 *m*; **the G7 countries** el grupo de los siete

G8 ['dʒiː'eɪt] *n* (*abbr* **Group of Eight**) G8 *m*

GA (*abbr* **Georgia**) Georgia

gab [gæb] *Fam* **1** *n (chatter)* charla *f*; **we had a good g. on the phone** estuvimos de charla *or Esp* palique *or Méx* plática por teléfono; IDIOM **to have the gift of the g.** tener un pico de oro
2 *vi* (*pt & pp* **gabbed**) **(a)** *(talk, gossip)* darle al pico **(b)** *(to police, press)* dar el soplo, *Méx* soplar, *RP* pasar el dato

gabardine, gaberdine [gæbə'diːn] *n* **(a)** *(material)* gabardina *f* **(b)** *(coat)* gabardina *f*

gabble ['gæbəl] **1** *n* algarabía *f*; **a g. of voices** una algarabía de voces; **to talk at a g.** parlotear
2 *vt* farfullar; **she gabbled (out) her an apology** farfulló una disculpa
3 *vi* **(a)** *(geese)* graznar **(b)** *(person)* farfullar; **they g. (away) for hours** parlotean durante horas

gabby ['gæbɪ] *adj Fam* charlatán(ana)

gaberdine = **gabardine**

gabfest ['gæbfest] *n US Fam* charla *f*, tertulia *f*

gable ['geɪbəl] *n (of house)* hastial *m*, gablete *m* ►► ***g. end*** hastial *m*; ***g. roof*** tejado *m* a dos aguas

gabled ['geɪbəld] *adj (house)* con el tejado a dos aguas; *(roof)* a dos aguas

Gabon [gæ'bɒn] *n* Gabón

Gabonese [gæbə'niːz] **1** *n* gabonés(esa) *m,f*
2 *adj* gabonés(esa)

Gad [gæd] *exclam Archaic or Hum* **(by) G.!** ¡Señor mío!

gad [gæd] (*pt & pp* **gadded**) *vi Fam* **to g. (about** *or* **around)** pendonear, zascandilear

gadabout ['gædəbaʊt] *n Fam (person)* pendón *m*, zascandil *mf*

Gadarene ['gædəriːn] *adj (in Bible)* **the miracle of the G. swine** el milagro del endemoniado gadareno; *Fig* **the G. rush to buy into the new technology** la avalancha ciega para adquirir las últimas tecnologías

gadfly ['gædflaɪ] *n* **(a)** *(insect)* tábano *m* **(b)** *(person)* provocador(ora) *m,f*

gadget ['gædʒɪt] *n* artilugio *m*, gadget *m*

gadgetry ['gædʒɪtrɪ] *n* artilugios *mpl*

gadwall ['gædwɔːl] *n* ánade *m* friso

Gael [geɪl] *n* = persona de origen celta oriunda de Irlanda o Escocia

Gaelic ['geɪlɪk, 'gælɪk] **1** *n (language)* gaélico *m*
2 *adj* gaélico(a) ►► *Br* ***G. coffee*** café *m* irlandés; *Sport* ***G. football*** fútbol *m* gaélico, = deporte irlandés a medio camino entre el fútbol y el rugby

Gaeltacht ['geɪltæxt] *n* **the G.** = región de Irlanda donde se habla el gaélico

gaff [gæf] *n* **(a)** *(in fishing)* garfio *m* **(b)** *Naut (spar)* pico *m* **(c)** *Br Fam (home)* casa *f*, *Esp* queli *f* **(d)** *US Fam* **to stand the g.** aguantar

gaffe [gæf] *n (blunder)* desliz *m*, metedura *f or Am* metida *f* de pata; **to commit** *or* **make a g.** cometer un desliz

> **False friend**: The Spanish noun **gafe** is not a translation for the English word **gaffe**. In Spanish **gafe** means "jinxed person".

gaffer ['gæfə(r)] *n Br Fam* **(a)** *(boss)* mandamás *mf* **(b)** *(soccer manager)* míster *m* **(c)** *(old man)* **an old g.** un vejete

gaffsail ['gæfseɪl] *n* vela *f* cangreja

gag [gæg] **1** *n* **(a)** *(on mouth)* mordaza *f* **(b)** *(on press)* mordaza *f*; **they want to put a g. on the press** quieren amordazar *or* silenciar a la prensa ►► *US* ***g. law*** = ley que limita la libertad de expresión; *US Pol* ***g. resolution*** *or* ***rule*** = norma que fija un tiempo límite a quienes toman la palabra en un debate parlamentario **(c)** *Fam (joke)* chiste *m*
2 *vt* (*pt & pp* **gagged**) *(silence) (person, the press)* amordazar, silenciar; IDIOM *US Fam Hum* **g. me with a spoon!** ¡qué asco!, *Esp* ¡es como para echar hasta la primera papilla!
3 *vi* **(a)** *(retch)* tener arcadas; **to make sb g.** provocar arcadas a alguien; **I just g. at the idea of eating raw fish** me dan arcadas sólo de pensar en comer pescado crudo; **he gagged on a fishbone** se atragantó con una espina **(b)** *Vulg* **to be gagging for it** perder el culo por un polvo, *Esp* tener unas ganas locas de follar, *Am* estar recaliente

gaga ['gɑːgɑː] *adj Fam* **(a)** *Br (senile)* chocho(a), gagá; **to go g.** empezar a chochear, ponerse gagá **(b)** *(crazy)* chiflado(a) **(c)** *(besotted)* **to be g. about** *or* **over sb** estar chiflado(a) por alguien

gage *US* = **gauge**

gagging ['gægɪŋ] *n (of person, press)* silenciamiento *m*, amordazamiento *m*; **g. order** *or* **writ** = prohibición del juez de publicar algo

gaggle ['gægəl] *n (of geese)* bandada *f*; *Fig* **a g. of journalists** una manada de periodistas

gagman ['gægmən] *n US (writer)* guionista *mf or Am* libretista *mf* cómico(a)

gaiety ['geɪətɪ] *n* alegría *f*

gaily ['geɪlɪ] *adv* **(a)** *(happily)* alegremente, con alegría; **they went g. on, as if nothing had happened** ellos siguieron tan felices *or* panchos, como si nada hubiera pasado **(b)** *(brightly)* alegremente; **g. coloured clothes** ropa de colores alegres *or* vivos

gain [geɪn] **1** *n* **(a)** *(profit)* beneficio *m*, ganancia *f*; **gains and losses** ganancias y pérdidas; **my loss is your g.** uno pierde lo que el otro gana; **there have been major gains on the Stock Exchange** la bolsa ha generado fuertes ganancias; **for personal g.** en beneficio propio
(b) *(increase)* aumento *m* (**in** de); **a g. in speed/weight** un aumento de velocidad/peso
(c) *(improvement, advance)* **the real gains of the revolution** los verdaderos beneficios *or* las verdaderas mejoras que ha aportado la revolución
(d) *(in election)* **a g. for the Republicans/Liberals** una victoria *or* un escaño para los republicanos/liberales; **to make gains** ganar terreno
(e) *Elec* ganancia *f*
2 *vt* **(a)** *(win) (advantage, reputation)* cobrar, ganar; *(experience, popularity, prestige)* adquirir, ganar; *(victory)* obtener; *(sympathy)* granjearse, ganarse; **to g. access** *or* **entry to** lograr acceder a; **to g. control of sth** hacerse con el control de algo; **to g. ground** ganar terreno; **to g. ground on sb** ganarle *or* comerle terreno a alguien; **to g. a share of the market** conseguir *or* ganar una cuota del mercado; **we have everything/nothing to g. from this proposal** con esta propuesta podemos ganar mucho/no ganamos nada; **what would we (have to) g. by joining?** ¿qué ganamos uniéndonos?; **we're not losing a daughter, but gaining a son** no perdemos una hija sino que ganamos un hijo; **he gained the impression that...** le dio la impresión de que...
(b) *(increase)* ganar; **the party has gained support** el partido ha ganado apoyo; **the share index gained two points** el índice de cotizaciones ha subido dos puntos; **to g. weight** aumentar de *or* ganar peso; **to g. speed** cobrar velocidad; **to g. time** ganar tiempo
(c) *(in election)* **to g. seats (for/from)** conseguir escaños (para/a costa de)
(d) *(of clock, watch)* adelantar; **my watch gains ten minutes a day** mi reloj adelanta diez minutos al día
(e) *Literary (reach)* alcanzar; **they finally gained the other shore** finalmente alcanzaron la otra orilla
3 *vi* **(a)** *(benefit)* **to g. by sth** beneficiarse de algo, ganar con algo;

who stands to g. by this deal? ¿quién se beneficia *or* quién gana con este acuerdo?
(**b**) *(increase)* **to g. in confidence** adquirir *or* ganar confianza; **to g. in popularity** hacerse cada vez más popular
(**c**) *(clock)* adelantar(se)

▸ **gain on** *vt insep* **to g. on one's competitors** ganar terreno a los competidores; **they're gaining on us!** ¡los tenemos cada vez más cerca!

gainful ['geɪnfʊl] *adj (employment)* remunerado(a)

gainfully ['geɪnfʊlɪ] *adv* **to be g. employed** tener un empleo remunerado

gainsay [geɪn'seɪ] (*pt & pp* **gainsaid** [geɪn'sed]) *vt Formal* negar; **there is no gainsaying her achievement** es innegable lo que ha conseguido

gait [geɪt] *n* paso *m*, manera *f* de caminar *or Esp* andar; **to walk with an unsteady g.** caminar de una manera insegura

gaiter ['geɪtə(r)] *n* polaina *f*

gal [gæl] *n Old-fashioned Fam* moza *f*

gal. (*abbr* **gallon**) galón *m (GB = 4,546 litros; EE.UU. = 3,785 litros)*

gala ['gɑːlə] *n* (**a**) *(festivity)* gala *f* ▸▸ ***g. evening*** noche *f* de gala; ***g. performance*** (actuación *f* de) gala *f* (**b**) *Br* **swimming g.** concurso de natación

galactic [gə'læktɪk] *adj* galáctico(a)

Galapagos [gə'læpəgəs] *npl* **the G. (Islands)** las (Islas) Galápagos

galaxy ['gæləksɪ] *n* (**a**) *Astron* galaxia *f* (**b**) *(gathering, array)* pléyade *f*; **a g. of stars** un gran elenco de estrellas

gale [geɪl] *n* (**a**) *(wind)* vendaval *m*; **a force 9 g.** un viento de fuerza 9; **it's blowing a g.** hay un viento terrible ▸▸ ***g. warning*** aviso *m* de temporal (**b**) *(outburst)* **a g. of laughter** un torrente de carcajadas

gale-force ['geɪlfɔːs] *adj* **g. winds** vientos huracanados

galena [gə'liːnə] *n* galena *f*

Galicia [gə'lɪsɪə] *n* (**a**) *(in Spain)* Galicia (**b**) *(in Eastern Europe)* Galitzia

Galician [gə'lɪsɪən] **1** *n* (**a**) *(from Spain)* gallego(a) *m,f* (**b**) *(language)* gallego *m* (**c**) *(from Eastern Europe)* galitzio(a) *m,f*
2 *adj* (**a**) *(from Spain)* gallego(a) (**b**) *(from Eastern Europe)* galitzio(a)

Galilean[1] [gælɪ'liːən] **1** *n* galileo(a) *m,f*; **the G.** el Galileo
2 *adj* galileo(a)

Galilean[2] [gælɪ'leɪən] *adj* galileano(a)

Galilee ['gælɪliː] *n* Galilea ▸▸ ***the Sea of G.*** el lago Tiberíades

gall [gɔːl] **1** *n* (**a**) *Med* bilis *f inv* ▸▸ ***g. bladder*** vesícula *f* biliar (**b**) *(bitterness)* rencor *m*, hiel *f* (**c**) *(impudence)* insolencia *f*; **she had the g. to...** tuvo la insolencia de... (**d**) *(on tree)* agalla *f*
2 *vt (annoy)* irritar, dar rabia a; **much though it galls me to admit it...** aunque me duela *or* reviente reconocerlo...

gallant ['gælənt] **1** *adj* (**a**) *(brave)* valiente, gallardo(a) (**b**) *(dashing)* apuesto(a), gallardo(a) (**c**) *(attentive, courteous)* galante
2 *n Literary (young man)* galán *m*

gallantly ['gæləntlɪ] *adv* (**a**) *(bravely)* valientemente, con gallardía (**b**) *(attentively, courteously)* galantemente

gallantry ['gæləntrɪ] *n* (**a**) *(bravery)* valentía *f*, gallardía *f*; **a medal for g.** una medalla al valor (**b**) *(attentiveness, courtesy)* galantería *f*

galleon ['gælɪən] *n* galeón *m*

galleria [gælə'rɪə] *n (in shopping centre)* galería *f* central

gallery ['gælərɪ] *n* (**a**) **(art) g.** *(for sale)* galería *f* de arte; *(for exhibition)* museo *m* (de arte) (**b**) *(balcony)* galería *f* (**c**) *(walkway)* galería *f* (**d**) *(in theatre)* galería *f*; IDIOM **to play to the g.** *(of politician)* actuar para la galería (**e**) *(in mine, burrow)* galería *f* (**f**) *Sport (spectators)* público *m*

galley ['gælɪ] *n* (**a**) *(ship)* galera *f*; **to be sent to the galleys** ser enviado a galeras ▸▸ ***g. slave*** galeote *m*; *Fam Hum* esclavo(a) *m,f* (**b**) *(kitchen on ship, plane)* cocina *f* (**c**) *Typ* **g. (proof)** galerada *f*

Gallic ['gælɪk] *adj* (**a**) *(French)* galo(a) (**b**) *Hist (of Gaul)* galo(a), gálico(a)

gallicism ['gælɪsɪzəm] *n Ling* galicismo *m*

galling ['gɔːlɪŋ] *adj* mortificante; **a g. admission** un reconocimiento mortificante

gallium ['gælɪəm] *n Chem* galio *m*

gallivant ['gælɪvænt]

▸ **gallivant about, gallivant around** *vi* pendonear

gallon ['gælən] *n* galón *m (GB = 4,546 litros; EE.UU. = 3,785 litros)*

gallop ['gæləp] **1** *n* galope *m*; **to go for a g.** ir a galopar; **the pony broke into a g.** el pony hechó a galopar; *also Fig* **at a g.** al galope
2 *vt (horse)* hacer galopar a
3 *vi* (**a**) *(horse, rider)* galopar; **to g. off** *or* **away** salir galopando *or* al galope (**b**) *Fig* **he came galloping down the stairs** bajó las escaleras al galope; **the country has galloped ahead of its rivals** el país ha dejado descolgados a sus competidores; **she galloped through her work** despachó rápidamente su trabajo

galloping ['gæləpɪŋ] *adj* galopante

gallows ['gæləʊz] *npl* horca *f*, patíbulo *m*; **to be sent to the g.** ser enviado a la horca *or* al patíbulo ▸▸ ***g. humour*** humor *m* negro *or* macabro

gallstone ['gɔːlstəʊn] *n* cálculo *m* biliar; **to have gallstones** tener cálculos *or* piedras en la vesícula

Gallup Poll ['gæləp'pəʊl] *n* sondeo *m* de opinión *(llevado a cabo por la empresa Gallup)*

galoot [gə'luːt] *n Scot, US Fam* zoquete *m*, *Am* sonso(a) *m,f*

galore [gə'lɔː(r)] *adv Fam* a montones; **we've got food g.** tenemos comida a montones

galoshes, goloshes [gə'lɒʃɪz] *npl* chanclos *mpl*

galumph [gə'lʌmf] *vi Fam (walk clumsily)* caminar con torpeza; **he came galumphing down the stairs** bajó las escaleras con torpeza

galvanize ['gælvənaɪz] *vt* (**a**) *Tech* galvanizar (**b**) *(stimulate)* galvanizar; **to g. sb into action** mover a alguien a la acción

galvanized ['gælvənaɪzd] *adj* galvanizado(a) ▸▸ ***g. steel*** acero *m* galvanizado

galvanizing ['gælvənaɪzɪŋ] *adj* **to have a g. effect on sth/sb** hacer reaccionar a algo/alguien

galvanometer [gælvə'nɒmɪtə(r)] *n Phys* galvanómetro *m*

Gambia ['gæmbɪə] *n* **(the) G.** Gambia

Gambian ['gæmbɪən] **1** *n* gambiano(a) *m,f*, gambio(a) *m,f*
2 *adj* gambiano(a), gambio(a)

gambit ['gæmbɪt] *n* (**a**) *(in chess)* gambito *m* (**b**) *(in negotiation, diplomacy)* jugada *f*, maniobra *f*; **opening g.** primer envite

gamble ['gæmbəl] **1** *n* (**a**) *(wager)* apuesta *f* (**b**) *(risk)* riesgo *m*; **to take a g.** arriesgarse; **it's a g. we have to take** es un riesgo que debemos asumir *or* afrontar; **it's a bit of a g. whether it'll work or not** es una lotería (saber) si funcionará o no; **I know it's a g. but...** sé que es un riesgo pero...; **his g. paid off** su jugada funcionó
2 *vt* jugarse; **to g. one's future/reputation on sth** jugarse el porvenir/la reputación en algo
3 *vi* jugar, apostar dinero; **to g. on sth** *(bet money on)* apostar a algo; **to g. on the Stock Exchange** jugar a la Bolsa; **they're gambling on there not being an inspector on the train** confían en que no haya un inspector en el tren; *Fig* **Napoleon gambled and lost** Napoleón se arriesgó y perdió

▸ **gamble away** *vt sep* **to g. sth away** perder algo en el juego

gambler ['gæmblə(r)] *n* jugador(ora) *m,f*

gambling ['gæmblɪŋ] *n* juego *m* ▸▸ ***g. debts*** deudas *fpl* de juego; ***g. den*** timba *f*, garito *m*

gambol ['gæmbəl] (*pt & pp* **gambolled**, *US* **gamboled**) *vi* retozar

game [geɪm] **1** *n* (**a**) *(activity, sport)* juego *m*; *(of cards, chess)* partida *f*; *(of football, tennis, golf)* partido *m*; **games of chance/skill** juegos de azar/destreza; **the children were playing a g. of hide-and-seek** los niños jugaban al escondite; **politics is just a g. to them** la política no es más que un juego para ellos; **I'm off my g. today** hoy no tengo un buen día; **it put me right off my g.** me desconcentró completamente ▸▸ ***g. of chance*** juego *m* de azar; ***g. plan*** plan *m or* estrategia *f* de juego; ***g. point*** *(in tennis)* punto *m or* pelota *f* de juego; ***g. show*** programa *m* concurso; ***g. theory*** teoría *f* de juegos
(**b**) *(division of match) (in tennis, bridge)* juego *m*; **g., set, and match** juego, set y partido; **(one) g. all** iguales *or* empatados a uno
(**c**) **games** *(sporting event)* juegos; *Br (school subject)* deportes; **the Commonwealth Games** los Juegos de la Commonwealth; **the Olympic Games** los Juegos Olímpicos
(**d**) *Fam (undertaking, operation)* **at this stage in the g.** a estas alturas del juego; **to be ahead of the g.** ir por delante
(**e**) *Fam (activity)* **I'm new to this g.** soy nuevo en esto; **I've been in this g. a long time** llevo mucho tiempo metido en esto
(**f**) *(in hunting)* caza *f*; **g. bird** ave de caza; **g. fish** = pez que se pesca por deporte; *Fig* **to be easy g.** ser presa fácil ▸▸ ***g. laws*** reglamentos *mpl* de caza; ***g. licence*** permiso *m* de caza; ***g. park*** reserva *f* animal; ***g. pie*** pastel *m* de carne de caza; ***g. preserve*** coto *m or* reserva *f* de caza; ***g. reserve*** coto *m or* reserva *f* de caza; ***g. warden*** guarda *mf* de caza
(**g**) IDIOMS **to play the g.** jugar limpio; **to play games with sb** jugar con alguien; **to play (along with) sb's g.** seguir el juego a alguien; **let's stop playing games and come to the point** dejémonos de *Esp* juegos *or Am* vueltas y vayamos al grano; **two can play at that g.**

donde las dan las toman; **to beat sb at his own g.** vencer a alguien con sus propias armas; **to give the g. away** desvelar el secreto; **what's his g.?** ¿qué pretende?; **I know what your g. is** sé a qué estás jugando; **the g.'s up for him** para él se acabó lo que se daba; *Br* **the g. is not worth the candle** no vale la pena; *Br Fam* **to be on the g.** *(prostitute)* hacer la calle
2 *adj* **(a)** *(brave)* valiente **(b)** *(willing)* **to be g. (to do sth)** apuntarse (a hacer algo); **he's g. for anything** se apunta a todo; **I'm g. if you are!** si tú te animas, yo también **(c)** *Br Old-fashioned (lame)* **he's got a g. leg** es cojo
3 *vi* **(a)** *Formal (gamble)* jugar **(b)** *(play computer games)* jugar con juegos de *Esp* ordenador *or Am* computadora

gamebag ['geɪmbæg] *n* morral *m*

gamecock ['geɪmkɒk] *n* gallo *m* de pelea, *Andes, RP* gallo *m* de riña

gamekeeper ['geɪmki:pə(r)] *n* guarda *mf* de caza

gamelan ['gæməlæn] *n* gamelán *m*

gamely ['geɪmlɪ] *adv* valientemente

gameplay ['geɪmpleɪ] *n* gameplay *m*

gamer ['geɪmə(r)] *n* **(a)** *(of computer games)* aficionado(a) *m,f* a los juegos de *Esp* ordenador *or Am* computadora **(b)** *US (athlete, sportsperson)* jugador(ora) *m,f* competitivo(a)

gamesmanship ['geɪmzmənʃɪp] *n* estrategia *f* inteligente *(sin infringir las reglas del juego)*

gamester ['geɪmstə(r)] *n (gambler)* jugador(ora) *m,f*

gamete ['gæmi:t] *n Biol* gameto *m*

gamey = **gamy**

gamine ['gæmi:n] *adj* con aspecto de muchacho; **a g. haircut** un corte a lo garçon

gaming ['geɪmɪŋ] *n* **(a)** *(gambling)* juego *m*, juegos *mpl* de azar; **he lost everything on the g. tables** perdió todo en la mesa de juego ►► ***g. laws*** = legislación que rige los juegos de azar **(b)** *(on computers)* juegos *mpl* de *Esp* ordenador *or Am* computadora

gamma ['gæmə] *n* **(a)** *(Greek letter)* gamma *f* **(b)** *Phys* ***g. radiation*** radiación *f* gamma; ***g. rays*** rayos *mpl* gamma **(c)** *Biol* ***g. globulin*** gammaglobulina *f*

gammon ['gæmən] *n* jamón *m* ►► ***g. steak*** = loncha de jamón a la plancha

gammy ['gæmɪ] *adj Fam* **a g. leg** una pata coja *or Andes, RP* renga *or Esp* chula

gamut ['gæmət] *n* gama *f*; **to run the g. of** pasar por toda la gama de

gamy, gamey ['geɪmɪ] *adj* **(a)** *(of flavour)* de *or* a caza **(b)** *(salacious, scandalous)* escabroso(a)

gander ['gændə(r)] *n* **(a)** *(male goose)* ganso *m* **(b)** *Fam* **to have** *or* **take a g. (at)** *(look)* echar un ojo *or* un vistazo (a)

G and T ['dʒi:ən'ti:] *n Br* gin-tonic *m*

gang [gæŋ] *n* **(a)** *(of criminals)* banda *f*; *(of violent youths)* pandilla *f*, panda *f* ►► ***g. rape*** violación *f* colectiva
(b) *(of children, friends)* pandilla *f*; *Fam* **the whole g.** *(of friends, colleagues)* toda la pandilla ►► ***g. show*** scout *m* show, = espectáculo de variedades organizado por los scouts
(c) *(of workers, convicts)* cuadrilla *f*

►**gang together** *vi* juntarse, formar una banda *or* panda

►**gang up** *vi* **to g. up on/with sb** confabularse contra/con alguien

gang-bang ['gæŋ'bæŋ] *very Fam* 1 *n* **(a)** *(group rape)* violación *f* colectiva **(b)** *(orgy)* orgía *f (de varios hombres con una mujer)*
2 *vt* violar en grupo a

gangbuster ['gæŋbʌstə(r)] *n US Fam* = policía de la brigada especial contra bandas criminales; IDIOM **like gangbusters** a lo bestia

ganger ['gæŋə(r)] *n Br (foreman)* capataz *m*

Ganges ['gændʒi:z] *n* **the G.** el Ganges

gangland ['gæŋlænd] *n (underworld)* hampa *f*; **a g. killing** un ajuste de cuentas entre bandas; **g. warfare** guerra entre bandas

ganglia *pl of* **ganglion**

gangling ['gæŋglɪŋ] *adj* larguirucho(a)

ganglion ['gæŋglɪən] (*pl* **ganglia** ['gæŋglɪə]) *n Anat* ganglio *m*

gangplank ['gæŋplæŋk] *n Naut* pasarela *f*, plancha *f*

gang-rape ['gæŋ'reɪp] *vt* violar en grupo a

gangrene ['gæŋgri:n] *n* gangrena *f*; **to have g.** tener gangrena

gangrenous ['gæŋgrɪnəs] *adj* gangrenoso(a); **to go** *or* **turn g.** gangrenarse

gangsta ['gæŋstə] *n* **(a)** *(music)* **g. (rap)** gangsta *m* **(b)** *(rapper)* gangsta *mf*

gangster ['gæŋstə(r)] *n* gángster *m* ►► ***g. movie*** película *f* de gángsters

gangway ['gæŋweɪ] *n* **(a)** *Theat (passage)* pasillo *m*; **g.!** ¡paso! **(b)** *Naut (gangplank)* pasarela *f*, plancha *f*

ganja ['gændʒə] *n Fam* maría *f*, hierba *f*

gannet ['gænət] *n* **(a)** *(bird)* alcatraz *m* **(b)** *Fam (greedy person)* glotón(ona) *m,f*

gantry ['gæntrɪ] *n* **(a)** *(for crane)* pórtico *m* **(b)** *(for rocket)* torre *f* de lanzamiento **(c)** *(for theatre lighting)* pasarela *f* de focos *or* luces, rejilla *f* de iluminación **(d)** *(for barrel)* combo *m* **(e)** *(in pub)* botellero *m*

GAO [dʒi:eɪ'əʊ] *n US* (*abbr* **General Accounting Office**) Oficina *f* General de Contabilidad

gaol [dʒeɪl] *Br* 1 *n* cárcel *f*, prisión *f*; **to be in g.** estar en la cárcel; **to go to g.** ir a la cárcel
2 *vt* encarcelar

gaolbird ['dʒeɪlbɜ:d] *n Br Fam* preso(a) *m,f* reincidente

gaolbreak ['dʒeɪlbreɪk] *n Br* fuga *f*, evasión *f*

gaoler ['dʒeɪlə(r)] *n Br (in prison)* carcelero(a) *m,f*; *(of hostages)* captor(ora) *m,f*

gap [gæp] *n* **(a)** *(physical opening) (in wall, defences)* hueco *m*; *(in mountains)* desfiladero *m*, paso *m*; *(in spark plug)* separación *f*; **the sun shone through a g. in the clouds** los rayos del sol se filtraban a través de un hueco en las nubes
(b) *(space between objects)* espacio *m*; **a g. of 2 cm, a 2 cm g.** un espacio de 2 cm; **there was a g. of a few metres between each house** entre cada casa había un espacio de unos metros; **he has a g. between his front teeth** tiene los dientes de adelante separados; **a g. in the curtains** un resquicio *or* una abertura en las cortinas ►► ***g. site*** solar *m (entre dos edificios)*
(c) *(interruption) (in time)* intervalo *m*; **after a g. of some years/months** tras un lapso *or* intervalo de varios años/meses ►► ***g. year*** = año que muchos jóvenes utilizan, una vez concluida la educación secundaria y antes de ingresar a la universidad, para viajar por el mundo o trabajar
(d) *(inequality, disparity) (in age, ability)* diferencia *f*, distancia *f*; **the g. between rich and poor is huge** la distancia entre ricos y pobres es enorme; **a technology g.** una gran distancia tecnológica
(e) *(lack) (in knowledge, story)* laguna *f*; *(in text)* espacio *m* en blanco; **to fill in the gaps** *(in knowledge, story)* cubrir las lagunas, tapar los huecos; **his death leaves a g. in all of our lives** su muerte deja un vacío en la vida de todos nosotros; *Com* **a g. in the market** un hueco en el mercado

gape [geɪp] *vi* **(a)** *(stare)* **to g. (at sth/sb)** mirar (algo/a alguien) boquiabierto(a); **to g. (at sth/sb) in astonishment** mirar (algo/a alguien) estupefacto(a); **what are you gaping at?** ¿qué miras con esa cara de asombro? **(b)** *(open one's mouth wide)* quedarse boquiabierto(a) **(c)** *(open)* **to g. (open)** abrirse; **the cave/crater gaped in front of them** la caverna/el cráter se abría frente a ellos

gaping ['geɪpɪŋ] *adj* **(a)** *(onlookers)* boquiabierto(a) **(b)** *(hole, chasm)* enorme; *(wound)* abierto(a)

gappy ['gæpɪ] *adj* **(a)** *(account, knowledge)* disperso(a), con muchas lagunas **(b)** **to have g. teeth** tener los dientes separados; **a g. smile** una sonrisa desdentada

gap-toothed ['gæptu:θt] *adj (with noticeable spaces)* con los dientes separados; *(with missing teeth)* mellado(a), desdentado(a)

garage ['gærɑ:ʒ, 'gærɪdʒ, *US* gə'rɑ:ʒ] 1 *n* **(a)** *(for storing cars)* garaje *m*, *Am* cochera *f*; **there is g. space for two cars** en el garaje hay espacio para dos coches, *Am* en la cochera hay espacio para dos carros ►► *US* ***g. sale*** = mercadillo en casa de un particular
(b) *Br (where fuel is sold)* gasolinera *f*, estación *f* de servicio
(c) *(for repairing cars)* taller *m* (de reparaciones), garaje *m* ►► ***g. mechanic*** mecánico(a) *m,f*
(d) *Mus* **g. (music)** (música *f*) garaje *m* ►► ***g. band*** grupo *m* de rock de aficionados
2 *vt (vehicle)* meter en un garaje *or Am* una cochera

garam masala ['gærəmmə'sɑ:lə] *n Culin* = mezcla de especias de la cocina india

garb [gɑ:b] *n Literary* atuendo *m*, atavío *m*

garbage ['gɑ:bɪdʒ] *n* **(a)** *US (household waste)* basura *f* ►► ***g. can*** cubo *m or Am* bote *m* de la basura; ***g. dump*** basurero *m*, *CSur* basural *m*; ***g. heap*** montón *m* de basura; ***g. truck*** camión *m* de la basura
(b) *Fam (nonsense) Esp* chorradas *fpl*, *Am* pendejadas *fpl*; **he's talking g.** está diciendo *Esp* chorradas *or Am* pendejadas; **that's g.!** ¡(eso no son más que) *Esp* chorradas *or Am* pendejadas!
(c) *Fam (worthless, useless things)* porquería *f*; **their new album is (a load of) g.** su nuevo disco es una porquería

(**d**) *Comptr* **g. in, g. out** si se cargan datos erróneos, se obtienen resultados erróneos
(**e**) ***g. time*** *(in basketball)* minutos *mpl* de la basura

garbageman ['gɑːbɪdʒmæn] *n US* basurero *m*

garbanzo [gɑː'bɑːnzəʊ] (*pl* **garbanzos**) *n US* **g. (bean)** garbanzo *m*

garble ['gɑːbəl] *vt* (**a**) *(involuntarily) (story, message)* embrollar (**b**) *(deliberately) (facts)* tergiversar

garbled ['gɑːbəld] *adj (story, explanation, quotation)* embrollado(a), confuso(a); **the message had become g. in transmission** con la transmisión el mensaje resultaba indescifrable

garda ['gɑːdə] (*pl* **gardai** ['gɑːdiː]) *n* policía *mf (de la república de Irlanda); Irish* **the Gardai,** *Br* **the G.** la policía *(de la república de Irlanda)*

garden ['gɑːdən] **1** *n* (**a**) *(with flowers)* jardín *m*; *(for vegetables)* huerta *f*, huerto *m*; **back/front g.** jardín trasero/delantero; IDIOM **everything in the g. is rosy** todo es de color de rosa, todo marcha de maravilla; IDIOM *Fam* **to lead sb up the g. path** *(mislead)* engañar a alguien ▸▸ *US* ***g. apartment*** apartamento *m or Esp* piso *m or Arg* departamento *m* (en planta baja) con jardín; ***g. centre*** centro *m* de jardinería; ***g. city*** ciudad *f* jardín; ***G. of Eden*** jardín *m* del Edén; *Br* ***g. flat*** apartamento *m or Esp* piso *m or Arg* departamento *m* (en planta baja) con jardín; ***g. furniture*** mobiliario *m* de jardín; ***g. gnome*** enanito *m* de jardín; ***g. party*** recepción *f* al aire libre; ***g. shed*** cobertizo *m*; *Br* ***g. suburb*** = urbanización con grandes zonas ajardinadas; ***g. tools*** útiles *mpl* de jardinería; ***g. warbler*** curruca *f* mosquitera
(**b**) *(park)* **public garden(s)** jardines públicos ▸▸ ***g. of remembrance*** = jardín en memoria de los difuntos
(**c**) *(fertile region)* **the G. of England** = apelativo referido a la región inglesa de Kent, célebre por su producción agrícola
(**d**) *(in street names)* **Gardens** = nombre dado a ciertas calles en Gran Bretaña
2 *vi* cuidar el jardín, trabajar en el jardín

gardener ['gɑːdnə(r)] *n* jardinero(a) *m,f*

gardenia [gɑː'diːnɪə] *n* gardenia *f*

gardening ['gɑːdnɪŋ] *n* jardinería *f*; **g. book/gloves** libro/guantes de jardinería; **to do the g.** cuidar el jardín

garden-variety ['gɑːdənvə'raɪətɪ] *adj US* común y corriente

garganey ['gɑːgənɪ] *n* cerceta *f* carretona

gargantuan [gɑː'gæntjʊən] *adj (in general)* colosal; *(meal)* pantagruélico(a)

gargle ['gɑːgəl] **1** *n* (**a**) *(action)* gargarismo *m*; **to have a g.** hacer gárgaras (**b**) *(liquid)* gargarismo *m*
2 *vi* hacer gárgaras

gargoyle ['gɑːgɔɪl] *n* gárgola *f*

garish ['geərɪʃ] *adj (clothes, colour)* chillón(ona), estridente; *(light)* deslumbrante

garishly ['geərɪʃlɪ] *adv* con colores chillones

garland ['gɑːlənd] **1** *n* guirnalda *f*
2 *vt* adornar con guirnaldas

garlic ['gɑːlɪk] *n* ajo *m*; **a head/clove of g.** una cabeza/un diente de ajo ▸▸ ***g. bread*** pan *m* de ajo; ***g. butter*** mantequilla *f or RP* manteca *f* aromatizada con ajo; ***g. press*** triturador *m* de ajos, prensaajos *m inv*; ***g. salt*** sal *f* de ajo; ***g. sausage*** embutido *m* al ajo; ***g. soup*** sopa *f* de ajo

garlicky ['gɑːlɪkɪ] *adj (food)* con mucho ajo; *(smell, taste, breath)* a ajo

garment ['gɑːmənt] *n* prenda *f* (de vestir); *US* **the g. industry** la industria de la confección; *US* **g. workers** obreros *or* trabajadores de la confección ▸▸ ***g. bag*** portatrajes *m inv*

garner ['gɑːnə(r)] *vt* hacer acopio de

garnet ['gɑːnɪt] *n* (**a**) *(stone)* granate *m* (**b**) *(colour)* granate *m*

garnish ['gɑːnɪʃ] **1** *n Culin* guarnición *f*
2 *vt* guarnecer, adornar (**with** con)

garnishee [gɑːnɪ'ʃiː] *n Law* ***g. order*** orden *f* de embargo

Garonne [gə'rɒn] *n* **the G.** el Garona

garret ['gærət] *n* buhardilla *f*

garrison ['gærɪsən] **1** *n* guarnición *f* ▸▸ ***g. duty*** servicio *m* en una guarnición; ***g. town*** ciudad *f* con guarnición
2 *vt (troops)* acuartelar; **the fort was garrisoned with regular troops** el fuerte tenía una guarnición de tropas regulares

garrotte, *US* **garrote** [gə'rɒt] **1** *n* garrote *m* vil
2 *vt* dar garrote vil a

garrulity = **garrulousness**

garrulous ['gærələs] *adj* gárrulo(a), parlanchín(ina)

garrulousness ['gærələsnɪs], **garrulity** [gə'ruːlɪtɪ] *n* garrulería *f*, charlatanería *f*

garter ['gɑːtə(r)] *n* (**a**) *(circular) (for stockings)* liga *f*; *(for socks)* elástico *m*; *(for sleeves)* liga *f* ▸▸ ***g. snake*** culebra *f* de jaretas; ***g. stitch*** punto *m* del derecho (**b**) *US (strap)* liguero *m* ▸▸ *US* ***g. belt*** liguero *m* (**c**) *Br* **Knight of the (Order of the) G.** Caballero de la Orden de la Jarretera

gas [gæs] **1** *n* (**a**) *(for cooking, heating)* gas *m*; **to have g.** *(as anaesthetic)* recibir anestesia gaseosa ▸▸ ***g. bill*** factura *f* del gas; ***g. burner*** mechero *m* de gas; ***g. chamber*** cámara *f* de gas; ***g. chromatography*** cromatografía *f* de gases; ***g. cooker*** cocina *f or Col, Méx, Ven* estufa *f* de gas; ***g. cylinder*** bombona *f* de gas; ***g. fire*** estufa *f* de gas; ***g. fitter*** técnico(a) *m,f* instalador(ora) de gas; ***g. heater*** *(for heating)* estufa *f* de gas; *(for hot water)* calentador *m* de gas; ***g. holder*** gasómetro *m*, tanque *m* de gas; ***g. lamp*** lámpara *f* de gas; ***g. main*** tubería *f* del gas, gasoducto *m*; ***g. man*** técnico *m* de la compañía del gas; ***g. mask*** máscara *f* antigás; ***g. meter*** contador *m* del gas; ***g. oven*** horno *m* de gas; ***g. ring*** quemador *m*
(**b**) *US (gasoline)* gasolina *f*, *RP* nafta *f*; *Fam* **to step on the g.** *(accelerate)* pisar el acelerador; **to be out of g.** quedarse sin gasolina *or RP* nafta; *Fam Fig (exhausted)* estar rendido(a), haberse quedado sin fuelle ▸▸ ***g. pedal*** acelerador *m*; ***g. station*** gasolinera *f*, estación *f* de servicio; ***g. tank*** depósito *m* de la gasolina *or RP* nafta
(**c**) *Fam (amusing thing, situation)* **what a g.!** ¡qué divertido!; **the movie was a real g.!** ¡la película era divertidísima *or Esp* muy cachonda!
(**d**) *Br Fam (chatter)* cháchara *f*, *Esp* palique *m*; **they had a good g. on the phone** estuvieron de palique *or* cháchara por teléfono
(**e**) *US (in stomach, intestines)* gases *mpl*
(**f**) *Med* ***g. gangrene*** gangrena *f* gaseosa
2 *vt* (*pt & pp* **gassed**) gasear; **to g. oneself** suicidarse con gas
3 *vi Fam (chat)* estar de cháchara *or Esp* palique

▸ **gas up** *US* **1** *vt sep* llenar de gasolina *or RP* nafta
2 *vi* echar gasolina, *Am* cargar gasolina, *RP* cargar nafta

gasbag ['gæsbæg] *n Fam* charlatán(ana) *m,f*, cotorra *f*

Gascon ['gæskən] **1** *n* (**a**) *(person)* gascón(ona) *m,f* (**b**) *(language)* gascón *m*
2 *adj* gascón(ona)

Gascony ['gæskənɪ] *n* Gascuña *f*

gas-cooled reactor ['gæskuːldrɪ'æktə(r)] *n* reactor *m* nuclear refrigerado por gas

gaseous ['geɪsɪəs] *adj* gaseoso(a)

gasfield ['gæsfiːld] *n* yacimiento *m* de gas natural

gas-fired ['gæs'faɪəd] *adj Br* de gas

gas-guzzler ['gæs'gʌzlə(r)] *n Fam* = vehículo que consume mucho combustible

gash [gæʃ] **1** *n* (**a**) *(wound)* herida *f* (profunda), corte *m* (profundo) (**b**) *(in wood, metal)* brecha *f* (**c**) *Vulg (woman's genitals)* raja *f*
2 *vt* (**a**) *(knee, hand, face)* hacerse una herida *or* un corte en (**b**) *(material)* cortar, hacer un corte en

gasket ['gæskɪt] *n Aut* junta *f* de culata; IDIOM *Fam* **he blew a g.** se salió de sus casillas

gaslight ['gæslaɪt] *n* (**a**) *(lamp)* lámpara *f* de gas (**b**) *(light)* luz *f* de gas

gaslit ['gæslɪt] *adj* iluminado(a) con lámparas de gas

gasohol ['gæsəhɒl] *n* carburol *m*, gasohol® *m*

gasoline ['gæsəliːn] *n US* gasolina *f*, *RP* nafta *f*

gasometer [gæ'sɒmɪtə(r)] *n* gasómetro *m*

gasp [gɑːsp] **1** *n (breath)* jadeo *m*; *(of surprise)* grito *m* ahogado; **to be at one's last g.** estar en las últimas
2 *vt* (**a**) *(short of breath)* **she gasped (out) an explanation** dio una explicación entrecortada (**b**) *(in shock, surprise)* **"what?" he gasped** "¿qué?", dijo con un grito ahogado
3 *vi* (**a**) *(be short of breath)* jadear; **she gasped for breath** *or* **air** respiraba jadeando (**b**) *(in shock, surprise)* lanzar un grito ahogado (**with** *or* **in** de); **to make sb g.** dejar boquiabierto(a) a alguien (**c**) *Br Fam* **to be gasping for a cigarette/a drink** morirse por un cigarrillo/algo de beber *or Am* tomar

gasper ['gɑːspə(r)] *n Br Fam* pito *m*, *Andes, RP* pucho *m*

gas-permeable ['gæs'pɜːmɪəbəl] *adj* **g. (contact) lenses** lentes (de contacto) de gas permeable

gassed [gæst] *adj Fam (drunk)* borracho(a) como una cuba

gasser ['gæsə(r)] *n US Fam (amusing thing, situation)* **what a g.!** ¡qué divertido!; **the movie was a real g.!** ¡la película era divertidísima *or Esp* muy cachonda!

gassiness ['gæsɪnəs] *n (of beer, drink)* **it's the g. I don't like** lo que no me gusta es que tiene mucho gas

gassy ['gæsɪ] *adj* (a) *(beer)* con mucho gas (b) *Fam (person)* charlatán(ana)

gastric ['gæstrɪk] *adj* gástrico(a) ▸▸ ***g. flu*** gripe *f* gastrointestinal; ***g. juices*** jugos *mpl* gástricos; ***g. ulcer*** úlcera *f* de estómago

gastritis [gæs'traɪtɪs] *n* gastritis *f inv*

gastroenteritis [gæstrəʊəntə'raɪtɪs] *n* gastroenteritis *f inv*

gastroenterologist ['gæstrəʊentə'rɒlədʒɪst] *n Med* gastroenterólogo(a) *m,f*

gastroenterology ['gæstrəʊentə'rɒlədʒɪ] *n Med* gastroenterología *f*

gastronome ['gæstrənəʊm] *n* gastrónomo(a) *m,f*

gastronomic [gæstrə'nɒmɪk] *adj* gastronómico(a)

gastronomy [gæs'trɒnəmɪ] *n* gastronomía *f*

gastropod ['gæstrəpɒd] *n Biol* gasterópodo *m*

gasworks ['gæswɜːks] *n* fábrica *f or Am* planta *f* de gas

gate [geɪt] 1 *n* (a) *(into garden, field, city)* puerta *f*; *(with metal bars)* verja *f* (b) *(at station, stadium)* barrera *f* (c) *(at airport)* puerta *f* (de embarque); **g. (number) 15** puerta número 15 (d) *(on canal)* **lock gates** compuertas (e) *Sport (spectators)* entrada *f*; *(takings)* recaudación *f* (f) *Elec* puerta *f* (g) *(in skiing, canoeing)* puerta *f* (h) *(in horse racing)* **(starting) g.** cajón *m* de salida
 2 *vt Br Sch* **they were gated for a week** les castigaron a quedarse después de clase una semana

gâteau ['gætəʊ] (*pl* **gâteaux** ['gætəʊz]) *n* pastel *m*, *Esp* tarta *f*, *Col, CSur* torta *f*

gatecrash ['geɪtkræʃ] *Fam* 1 *vt (party, concert)* colarse en
 2 *vi* colarse

gatecrasher ['geɪtkræʃə(r)] *n Fam* intruso(a) *m,f*

gated ['geɪtɪd] *adj* (a) *Br (pupil)* sin permiso para salir (b) ***g. community*** = urbanización protegida con vigilantes

gatefold ['geɪtfəʊld] *n (in book, magazine)* (página *f*) desplegable *m*

gatehouse ['geɪthaʊs] *n (of park, castle)* casa *f* del guarda; *(of house, estate)* casa *f* del portero

gatekeeper ['geɪtkiːpə(r)] *n* (a) *(of park, castle)* guarda *mf*; *(of house, estate)* portero(a) *m,f* (b) *(who controls access)* guardián(ana) *m,f*

gateleg table ['geɪtleg'teɪbəl] *n* mesa *f* (plegable) de hojas

gatepost ['geɪtpəʊst] *n* poste *m* (de la verja); IDIOM *Fam* **between you, me and the g.** entre tú y yo, que quede entre nosotros

gateway ['geɪtweɪ] *n* (a) *(entrance)* entrada *f*; *Fig* **the g. to the East** la vía de entrada a Oriente; *Fig* **the g. to success** la clave del éxito ▸▸ *US* ***g. drug*** droga *f* de iniciación (b) *Comptr* pasarela *f*

gather ['gæðə(r)] 1 *vt* (a) *(collect)* reunir; *(fruit, flowers)* recoger; **to g. the harvest** recoger la cosecha, cosechar; **we are gathered here today...** estamos hoy aquí reunidos...; **he gathered her in his arms** la tomó entre sus brazos; **he gathered the children to him** reunió a los niños en torno a él; **to g. all one's strength to do sth** hacer acopio de fuerzas para hacer algo; IDIOM *Literary* **to be gathered to one's fathers** estar reunido(a) con sus antepasados
 (b) *(put in order)* **to g. one's wits** recobrarse; **he gathered his thoughts** puso en orden sus ideas
 (c) *(accumulate) (dirt, dust)* acumular, llenarse de; *Fig* **to be gathering dust** *(plan, project)* estar arrinconado(a); **to g. strength** cobrar fuerza; **to g. speed** *or* **momentum** adquirir velocidad
 (d) *(in sewing)* fruncir; **the dress is gathered at the waist** el vestido está fruncido en la cintura
 (e) *(conclude, understand)* **to g. that...** deducir que..., entender que...; **as far as I can g.** por lo que se ve; **as you may already have gathered...** como te habrás imaginado...; **I had (already) gathered as much** *(it was not news to me)* ya me lo había imaginado; **so I g.** eso parece
 2 *vi (people)* reunirse, congregarse; *(things)* acumularse; **tears were gathering in her eyes** se le llenaron los ojos de lágrimas; **a storm is gathering** se está formando una tormenta; **to g. round the fire/the radio** reunirse en torno al fuego/a la radio
 3 **gathers** *npl (in sewing)* frunces *mpl*

▸ **gather in** *vt sep* (a) *(harvest)* recoger; *(books, exam papers)* recoger (b) *(in sewing)* **gathered in at the waist** fruncido(a) en la cintura

▸ **gather round** *vi* formar corro, agruparse; **g. round, children!** ¡a ver, niños, acérquense!

▸ **gather together** 1 *vt sep (belongings, evidence)* reunir
 2 *vi (people)* reunirse

▸ **gather up** *vt sep* (a) *(objects, belongings)* recoger; **he gathered her up in his arms** la tomó en sus brazos (b) *(skirts, hair)* recoger; **her hair was gathered up into a bun** tenía el pelo recogido en un moño

gathered ['gæðəd] *adj* fruncido(a) ▸▸ ***g. skirt*** falda *f or RP* pollera *f* fruncida

gathering ['gæðərɪŋ] 1 *n (group)* grupo *m*; *(meeting)* reunión *f*
 2 *adj (darkness, speed)* creciente; *also Fig* **the g. storm** la tormenta que se viene preparando

gator ['geɪtə(r)] *n US Fam* caimán *m*

GATS [gæts] *n* (*abbr* **General Agreement on Trade in Services**) AGCS *m*

GATT [gæt] *n* (*abbr* **General Agreement on Tariffs and Trade**) GATT *m*

gauche [gəʊʃ] *adj* torpe, desmañado(a)

gaucheness ['gəʊʃnɪs] *n* torpeza *f*

gaucho ['gaʊtʃəʊ] (*pl* **gauchos**) *n* gaucho *m*

gaudily ['gɔːdɪlɪ] *adv* con colores chillones

gaudiness ['gɔːdɪnɪs] *n* estilo *m* chillón *or* llamativo

gaudy ['gɔːdɪ] *adj* chillón(ona), llamativo(a)

gauge, *US* **gage** [geɪdʒ] 1 *n* (a) *(size) (of screw, wire, shotgun)* calibre *m*
 (b) *(of railway track)* ancho *m* de vía; **narrow g. railway** vía estrecha
 (c) *(instrument)* calibrador *m*; **water/oil g.** indicador del nivel de agua/aceite; *Aut* **petrol** *or* **fuel g.** indicador del nivel de gasolina *or RP* nafta
 (d) *(indicator)* indicador *m*; **the poll is a useful g. of public opinion** los sondeos son un útil indicador de la opinión pública
 2 *vt* (a) *(assess, estimate) (amount, difficulty)* calcular, precisar; **to g. the temperature of the political situation** medir la temperatura de la situación política; **it was difficult to g. how interested they were** era difícil evaluar *or* juzgar lo interesados que estaban (b) *(predict)* preveer; **he tried to g. what her reaction would be** intentó preveer su reacción

Gaul [gɔːl] *n Hist* (a) *(region)* Galia *f* (b) *(inhabitant)* galo(a) *m,f*

Gaulish ['gɔːlɪʃ] *Hist* 1 *n (language)* galo *m*
 2 *adj* galo(a)

Gaullism ['gɔːlɪzəm] *n Pol* gaullismo *m*

Gaullist ['gɔːlɪst] *n Pol* gaullista *mf*

gaunt [gɔːnt] *adj* (a) *(emaciated) (person, features)* demacrado(a) (b) *(desolate) (landscape)* desolado(a)

gauntlet ['gɔːntlɪt] *n* (a) *(glove)* guante *m* (largo); *Hist* guantelete *m*, manopla *f*; IDIOM **to throw** *or* **fling down the g.** arrojar el guante, *Am* desafiar a alguien; IDIOM **to take up the g.** recoger el guante, aceptar el reto *or* desafío
 (b) *Hist & Mil* **to run the g.** recorrer el pasillo *(recibiendo golpes de los que lo forman)*; *Fig* **to run the g. of sth** exponerse a algo; **to run the g. of an angry mob** soportar el acoso de una multitud enojada

gauze [gɔːz] *n* gasa *f*

gave *pt of* **give**

gavel ['gævəl] *n* martillo *m*, maceta *f (de subastador, juez)*

gavel-to-gavel ['gævəltə'gævəl] *adj US* integral, completo(a)

gavotte [gə'vɒt] *n* gavota *f*

Gawd [gɔːd] *exclam Br Fam* ¡Dios!

gawk = **gawp**

gawky ['gɔːkɪ] *adj Fam* desgarbado(a)

gawp [gɔːp], **gawk** [gɔːk] *vi Fam* quedarse papando moscas; **to g. at sth/sb** mirar boquiabierto(a) algo/a alguien; **what are you gawping at?** ¿qué miras?

gay [geɪ] 1 *adj* (a) *(homosexual)* gay *inv* ▸▸ *Fam Old-fashioned* ***g. plague*** peste *f* gay; ***g. rights*** derechos *mpl* de los homosexuales
 (b) *Old-fashioned (happy)* alegre; **he's a g. (old) dog** está hecho un golfo; **to have a g. old time** pasarlo estupendamente; **with g. abandon** con alegre despreocupación
 (c) *Old-fashioned (bright) (colours, lights)* alegre; **the streets were g. with coloured flags/flowers** las banderas de colores/las flores alegraban las calles
 2 *n (man)* homosexual *m*, gay *m*; *(woman)* lesbiana *f*

gay-basher ['geɪbæʃə(r)] *n* = persona que ataca a los homosexuales

gay-bashing ['geɪbæʃɪŋ] *n* ataques *mpl* contra homosexuales

gayness ['geɪnɪs] *n (homosexuality)* homosexualidad *f*

Gaza ['gɑːzə] *n* Gaza ▸▸ ***the G. Strip*** la Franja de Gaza

gaze [geɪz] 1 *n* mirada *f* (fija); **to meet** *or* **return sb's g.** devolver la mirada a alguien; **exposed to the public g.** expuesto(a) a las miradas del público
 2 *vi* **to g. at** mirar fijamente; **to g. into space** *or* **the middle distance** mirar al vacío

gazebo [gə'ziːbəʊ] (*pl* **gazebos** *or* **gazeboes**) *n* belvedere *m*, mirador *m*

gazelle [gə'zel] *n* gacela *f*

gazette [gəˈzet] **1** *n (official journal)* boletín *m* oficial
2 *vt Br* publicar en el boletín oficial

gazetteer [gæzɪˈtɪə(r)] *n (book)* diccionario *m* geográfico

gazillion [gəˈzɪljən] *n US Fam* tropecientos(as) *m,fpl*

gazump [gəˈzʌmp] *vt Br Fam* **we've been gazumped** le han vendido la casa que teníamos ya apalabrada a otros que pagan más

GB[1] [dʒiːˈbiː] *n* (*abbr* **Great Britain**) GB

GB[2] *Comptr* (*abbr* **gigabyte**) GB

GBH [dʒiːbiːˈeɪtʃ] *n Br Law* (*abbr* **grievous bodily harm**) lesiones *fpl* graves

GC [dʒiːˈsiː] *n Br* (*abbr* **George Cross**) = condecoración civil concedida por actos de heroísmo

GCE [dʒiːsiːˈiː] *n Br Sch Formerly* (*abbr* **General Certificate of Education**) = certificado de enseñanza secundaria

GCHQ [dʒiːsiːeɪtʃˈkjuː] *n Br* (*abbr* **Government Communications Headquarters**) = servicio británico de espionaje electrónico

G-clef [ˈdʒiːklef] *n Mus* clave *f* de sol

GCSE [dʒiːsiːesˈiː] *n Br Sch* (*abbr* **General Certificate of Secondary Education**) = certificado de enseñanza secundaria

g'day [gəˈdeɪ] *exclam Austr Fam* ¡buenas!, ¡buenos días!

Gdns (*abbr* **Gardens**) = abreviatura utilizada en los nombres de algunas calles

GDP [dʒiːdiːˈpiː] *n Econ* (*abbr* **gross domestic product**) PIB *m*

GDR [dʒiːdiːˈɑː(r)] *n Formerly* (*abbr* **German Democratic Republic**) RDA *f*

gear [gɪə(r)] **1** *n* **(a)** *(in car, on bicycle) (speed)* marcha *f*, velocidad *f*; *(mechanism)* engranaje *m*; **first/second g.** primera/segunda marcha *or* velocidad; **in/out of g.** *(car)* con una marcha puesta/en punto muerto; **put the car in g.** mete una marcha; **to get in g.** meter una marcha; *also Fig* **to** *Br* **change** *or US* **shift g.** cambiar de marcha; *US Fam Fig* **to get it in g., to get into g.** moverse; *Fig* **to put sb's plans out of g.** desbaratar los planes de alguien; *Fig* **I'm back in g. again now** estoy de nuevo en marcha; *Fig* **to step** *or* **move up a g.** superarse, ir a más ►► *Aut Br* ***g. lever*** palanca *f* de cambios; ***g. ratio*** relación *f* de marchas *or* velocidades; *Aut* ***g. stick*** palanca *f* de cambios
(b) *(cogwheel)* engranaje *m*
(c) *Fam (equipment)* equipo *m*; *(in kitchen)* aparatos *mpl*; **climbing g.** equipo de alpinismo *or* montañismo; **fishing g.** aparejos de pesca
(d) *Fam (belongings)* cosas *fpl*
(e) *Fam (clothes)* ropa *f*; **jogging/swimming g.** ropa de jogging/de baño; **I like the g.** me gusta el equipo
(f) *Br Fam (drugs)* material *m*, mandanga *f*
2 *vt (adapt, equip)* preparar; *(design)* diseñar; **the army was not geared for modern warfare** el ejército no estaba preparado para la guerra moderna; **the government's policies were not geared to cope with an economic recession** la política del gobierno no estaba pensada *or* diseñada para hacer frente a una recesión económica

► **gear down** **1** *vt sep* **(a)** *(reduce)* reducir, disminuir **(b)** *(simplify)* simplificar
2 *vi (factory, work force)* reducir *or* disminuir la marcha

► **gear to** *vt sep* **(a)** *(adapt)* **to g. sth to sth** adaptar algo a algo **(b)** *Fin (link)* **salaries are geared to the cost of living** los salarios están asociados al costo de vida

► **gear towards** *vt sep* **to be geared towards sth/sb** estar dirigido(a) *or* orientado(a) a algo/alguien

► **gear up** **1** *vt sep* **(a)** *(prepare)* **to g. sb up** preparar a alguien; **to g. oneself up** prepararse **(b)** *(increase)* aumentar; **we must g. up production to meet the demand** debemos aumentar la producción para satisfacer la demanda
2 *vi (prepare)* prepararse; **the sprinters were gearing up for the race** los velocistas se estaban preparando para la carrera

gearbox [ˈgɪəbɒks] *n* caja *f* de cambios

gearing [ˈgɪərɪŋ] *n Br Fin* apalancamiento *m*, nivel *m* de endeudamiento relativo al capital

gearshift [ˈgɪəʃɪft] *n US* palanca *f* de cambios

gearwheel [ˈgɪəwiːl] *n* piñón *m*, rueda *f* dentada

gecko [ˈgekəʊ] (*pl* **geckos** *or* **geckoes**) *n* geco *m*

GED [dʒiːiːˈdiː] *n US* (*abbr* **General Equivalency Diploma**) = diploma de estudios secundarios para aquellos que no siguieron la ruta tradicional del bachillerato

gee [dʒiː] *exclam* **(a)** *(to horse)* **g. up!** ¡arre! **(b)** *US* **g. (whizz)!** ¡anda!; **aw g., you shouldn't have!** ¡anda! *or* ¡bueno! ¿para qué te has molestado?; **g. thanks!** gracias, ¿eh?

► **gee up** *vt sep Fam* **to g. sb up** hacer espabilar a alguien, meter caña a alguien

gee-gee [ˈdʒiːdʒiː] *n Fam (in children's language)* caballito *m*

geek [giːk] *n US Fam* lelo(a) *m,f*, tontaina *mf*; **a computer g.** un monstruo de la informática

geeky [ˈgiːkɪ] *adj US Fam* ridículo(a)

geese *pl of* **goose**

geezer [ˈgiːzə(r)] *n Br Fam (man)* tipo *m*, *Esp* tío *m*; **an old g.** un vejestorio

Geiger counter [ˈgaɪgəˈkaʊntə(r)] *n* contador *m* Geiger

geisha [ˈgeɪʃə] (*pl* **geisha** *or* **geishas**) *n* **g. (girl)** geisha *f*, geisa *f*

gel[1] [dʒel] **1** *n* **(a)** *(substance)* gel *m* **(b)** *(for hair)* gel *m* moldeador, gomina *f* **(c)** *Theat* filtro *m*
2 *vi* (*pt & pp* **gelled**) **(a)** *(liquid)* aglutinarse **(b)** *(ideas, plans, team)* cuajar

gel[2] [gel] *n Br Hum* niña *f*

gelatin(e) [ˈdʒelətiːn] *n* gelatina *f*

gelatinous [dʒɪˈlætɪnəs] *adj* gelatinoso(a)

geld [geld] *vt* capar, castrar

gelding [ˈgeldɪŋ] *n* caballo *m* castrado

gelignite [ˈdʒelɪgnaɪt] *n* gelignita *f* (explosiva)

gelt [gelt] *n US Fam Esp* pasta *f*, *Am* plata, *Méx* lana, *Esp RP* guita *f*

gem [dʒem] *n* **(a)** *(precious stone)* gema *f* **(b)** *(person)* **he's an absolute g.** es una verdadera joya, es un verdadero tesoro **(c)** *(prize specimen)* joya *f*; **the g. of the collection** la joya de la colección

Gemini [ˈdʒemɪnaɪ] *n (sign of zodiac)* Géminis *m inv*; **to be (a) G.** ser Géminis

gemstone [ˈdʒemstəʊn] *n* piedra *f* preciosa, gema *f*

gen [dʒen] *n Br Fam (information)* información *f*, datos *mpl*

► **gen up** (*pt & pp* **genned**) *Br Fam* **1** *vt sep* poner al tanto *or* al día a (**on** de)
2 *vi* **to g. up on sth** ponerse al día de algo, informarse bien sobre algo

Gen. (*abbr* **General**) Gral.

gen. **(a)** (*abbr* **general**) gral. **(b)** (*abbr* **generally**) gralte.

gendarme [ˈʒɒndɑːm] *n* gendarme *mf*

gender [ˈdʒendə(r)] *n* **(a)** *Gram* género *m* **(b)** *(sex)* sexo *m* ►► ***g. gap*** diferencia *f* entre los sexos; *Univ* ***g. studies*** estudios *mpl* de género

gender-bender [ˈdʒendəˈbendə(r)] *n Fam* travestí *mf*, transformista *mf*

gender-specific [ˈdʒendəspəˈsɪfɪk] *adj* exclusivo(a) de un sexo

gene [dʒiːn] *n Biol* gen *m*; **to have sth in one's genes** *(talent, trait)* llevar algo en los genes *or* en la sangre ►► ***g. bank*** genoteca *f*, banco *m* de ADN; ***g. pool*** acervo *m* genético *or* génico; ***g. therapy*** terapia *f* génica

genealogical [dʒiːnɪəˈlɒdʒɪkəl] *adj* genealógico(a)

genealogist [dʒiːnɪˈælədʒɪst] *n* genealogista *mf*

genealogy [dʒiːnɪˈælədʒɪ] *n* genealogía *f*

genera *pl of* **genus**

general [ˈdʒenərəl] **1** *n* **(a)** *Mil* general *m* ►► *US* ***g. of the army*** capitán(ana) *m,f* general; ***g. officer*** oficial *mf* general **(b)** *(not particular)* **to go from the g. to the particular** ir de lo general a lo particular; **in g.** en general
2 *adj* **(a)** *(universal, collective)* general; **there was a g. movement to leave the room** todo el mundo se preparó como para abandonar la sala; **as a g. rule** por norma *or* regla general ►► ***G. Agreement on Tariffs and Trade*** Acuerdo *m* General sobre Aranceles y Comercio; ***g. anaesthetic*** anestesia *f* general; ***g. election(s)*** elecciones *fpl* generales; *Law* ***g. legatee*** legatario(a) *m,f* universal; *Com* ***g. and limited partnership*** sociedad *f* comanditaria *or* en comandita; ***g. meeting*** asamblea *f* general; ***g. partnership*** sociedad *f* colectiva; ***g. strike*** huelga *f* general; *Phys* ***g. theory of relativity*** teoría *f* de la relatividad general
(b) *(common, widespread)* general; **in g. use** de uso general; **in the g. interest** en interés de todos; **there is g. agreement on the matter** existe consenso sobre esta cuestión
(c) *(overall) (outline, plan, impression)* general; **the g. effect is quite pleasing** el efecto general es bastante agradable; **in g. charge** a cargo de todo; **I get the g. idea** me hago una idea general; **the g. tone of her remarks was that...** lo que vino a decir más o menos fue que... ►► *US* ***G. Accounting Office*** Oficina *f* General de Contabilidad; ***G. Assembly*** *(of United Nations)* Asamblea *f* General; *(of presbyterian church)* Asamblea *f* General; ***g. manager*** director(ora) *m,f* general; *Br* ***G. Medical Council*** ≃ colegio *m* de médicos; *Br* ***g. post office***

(oficina *f*) central *f* de correos; ***G. Secretary*** secretario(a) *m,f* general; *Mil* ***g. staff*** estado *m* mayor; ***G. Synod*** *(of Church of England)* Sínodo *m* General

(**d**) *(non-specialist, non-specific)* general; **the g. reader** el lector no especializado; **in g. terms** en términos generales ▸▸ ***g. hospital*** hospital *m* general; ***g. knowledge*** cultura *f* general; *Med* ***g. practice*** medicina *f* general; *Med* ***g. practitioner*** médico(a) *m,f* de cabecera *or* de familia; ***the g. public*** el gran público, el público en general; *US* ***g. store*** tienda *f* *(que vende de todo)*; *Univ* ***g. studies*** = cursos de enseñanza no reglada

(**e**) *(approximate)* **their house is over in that g. direction** su casa queda por aquella dirección; **there are lots of shops in the g. area** hay muchas tiendas por la zona

(**f**) *US* ***g. delivery*** lista *f* de correos

generalissimo [dʒenərə'lɪsɪməʊ] (*pl* **generalissimos**) *n* generalísimo *m*

generalist ['dʒenərəlɪst] *n* generalista *mf*

generality [dʒenə'rælɪtɪ] *n* (**a**) *(abstractness)* generalidad *f* (**b**) *(general statement)* generalidad *f*, generalización *f* (**c**) *Formal (majority)* **the g. of men** la generalidad *or* la mayoría de los hombres

generalization [dʒenərəlaɪ'zeɪʃən] *n* generalización *f*

generalize ['dʒenərəlaɪz] **1** *vt* **to become generalized** *(practice, belief)* generalizarse; *(infection, cancer)* generalizarse

2 *vi* generalizar

generally ['dʒenrəlɪ] *adv* (**a**) *(taken overall)* en general; **g. speaking** en términos generales

(**b**) *(as a general rule)* generalmente, por lo general; **he g. comes in the afternoon** generalmente *or* por lo general viene por la tarde

(**c**) *(by most people)* en general; **it was g. regarded as a success** se lo consideró en general como un éxito; **it is not g. known that...** la gente en general no sabe que...; **his decision was g. approved of** su decisión tuvo la aprobación general; **this information is not g. available** esta información no se encuentra a disposición del público

general-purpose ['dʒenrəl'pɜːpəs] *adj* multiuso *inv*

generalship ['dʒenərəlʃɪp] *n* (**a**) *(command)* generalato *m* (**b**) *(leadership qualities)* don *m* de mando; *(tactics)* táctica *f*

generate ['dʒenəreɪt] *vt* (**a**) *(electricity, noise, income)* generar (**b**) *(reaction, interest)* provocar; *(excitement)* despertar (**c**) *Ling* generar

generating station ['dʒenəreɪtɪŋ'steɪʃən] *n* central *f* eléctrica, *Andes, RP* usina *f* eléctrica

generation [dʒenə'reɪʃən] *n* (**a**) *(of people)* generación *f*; **the present g.** la generación actual; **our parents' g.** la generación de nuestros padres; **a new g. of writers/footballers** una nueva generación de escritores/futbolistas; **the younger/older g.** la generación joven/vieja; **from g. to g.** de generación en generación ▸▸ ***g. gap*** conflicto *m* generacional; ***G. X*** Generación *f* X

(**b**) *(by birth)* **she is second/third g. Irish** es irlandesa de segunda/tercera generación

(**c**) *(period of time)* generación *f*; **the house has been in the family for three generations** la casa ha pertenecido a la familia durante tres generaciones

(**d**) *(model)* generación *f*; **a third/fourth g. computer** un *Esp* ordenador *or Am* computador de tercera/cuarta generación

(**e**) *(production) (of electricity, ideas)* producción *f*

generative ['dʒenərətɪv] *adj* generativo(a) ▸▸ *Ling* ***g. grammar*** gramática *f* generativa

generator ['dʒenəreɪtə(r)] *n* (**a**) *Elec* generador *m* (**b**) *(of income)* generador *m*

generic [dʒɪ'nerɪk] *adj* genérico(a); **it has become the g. term for vacuum cleaners** se ha convertido en el término genérico para las aspiradoras ▸▸ ***g. drug*** (medicamento *m*) genérico *m*; ***g. name*** nombre *m* genérico

generically [dʒɪ'nerɪklɪ] *adv* genéricamente

generosity [dʒenə'rɒsɪtɪ] *n* generosidad *f*; **g. of spirit** grandeza de espíritu

generous ['dʒenərəs] *adj* (**a**) *(person) (with money, in spirit)* generoso(a) (**to** *or* **towards** con); **she's always g. with her time** siempre tiene tiempo para los demás; **he was very g. in his praise** no se quedó corto en elogios

(**b**) *(in value) (gift, sum, salary)* generoso(a); **a g. offer** una oferta generosa

(**c**) *(in size)* amplio(a); *Euph* **to have g. curves** tener formas generosas

(**d**) *(in quantity)* generoso(a), abundante; **a g. portion** una ración generosa *or* abundante; **to be g. with the parmesan/pepper** no escatimar el parmesano/la pimienta; **don't be over g. with the salt** no te pases con la sal; **food and drink were in g. supply** había comida y bebida en abundancia

generously ['dʒenərəslɪ] *adv* (**a**) *(unsparingly)* generosamente; **to give g.** ser generoso(a); **his family were g. provided for** su familia quedó en una situación económica muy holgada

(**b**) *(kindly) (to agree, offer)* generosamente, con generosidad; **she g. acknowledged our contribution** reconoció con generosidad nuestra aportación

(**c**) *(in size)* **the jacket is g. cut** la chaqueta tiene un corte amplio; *Euph* **to be g. built** *or* **proportioned** ser de formas generosas

(**d**) *(copiously)* **a plate of fish g. sprinkled with salt** un plato de pescado con abundante sal; **the soup was rather g. salted** *(oversalted)* la sopa estaba bastante salada

genesis ['dʒenɪsɪs] (*pl* **geneses** ['dʒenɪsiːz]) *n* (**a**) *Formal (origin)* génesis *f inv*, origen *m* (**b**) **(the Book of) G.** (el Libro del) Génesis *m*

genetic [dʒɪ'netɪk] *adj* genético(a); **g. parents** padres biológicos ▸▸ ***g. code*** código *m* genético; ***g. counselling*** asesoramiento *m* genético; ***g. engineering*** ingeniería *f* genética; ***g. fingerprinting*** pruebas *fpl* de(l) ADN, pruebas *fpl* de identificación genética; ***g. screening*** = pruebas para la detección precoz de enfermedades hereditarias en pacientes de alto riesgo

genetically [dʒɪ'netɪklɪ] *adv* genéticamente

genetically-modified [dʒɪ'netɪklɪ'mɒdɪfaɪd] *adj (plant, food)* transgénico(a), modificado(a) genéticamente

geneticist [dʒɪ'netɪsɪst] *n* genetista *mf*

genetics [dʒɪ'netɪks] *n* genética *f*

Geneva [dʒɪ'niːvə] *n* Ginebra; **Lake G.** el Lago Leman ▸▸ ***the G. Convention*** la Convención de Ginebra

Genevan [dʒɪ'niːvən] **1** *n* ginebrino(a) *m,f*, ginebrés(esa) *m,f*

2 *adj* ginebrino(a), ginebrés(esa)

Genghis Khan ['geŋgɪs'kɑːn] *pr n* Gengis Kan; IDIOM **a little to the right of G.** más de derechas que Mussolini

genial ['dʒiːnɪəl] *adj* (**a**) *(friendly)* cordial, amable (**b**) *Literary (clement) (weather, climate)* benigno(a)

> **False friend**: The Spanish adjective **genial** is not a translation for the English word **genial**. In Spanish **genial** means "great" or "of genius".

geniality [dʒiːnɪ'ælɪtɪ] *n* cordialidad *f*, amabilidad *f*

> **False friend**: The Spanish noun **genialidad** is not a translation for the English word **geniality**. In Spanish **genialidad** means "genius" or "stroke of genius".

genially ['dʒiːnɪəlɪ] *adv* cordialmente, amablemente

> **False friend**: The Spanish adverb **genialmente** is not a translation for the English word **genially**. In Spanish **genialmente** means "brilliantly".

genie ['dʒiːnɪ] (*pl* **genies** *or* **genii** ['dʒiːnɪaɪ]) *n* duende *m*, genio *m*; IDIOM **to let the g. out of the bottle** abrir la caja de Pandora

genital ['dʒenɪtəl] **1** *adj* genital ▸▸ ***g. herpes*** herpes *m* genital

2 genitals *npl* (órganos *mpl*) genitales *mpl*

genitalia [dʒenɪ'teɪlɪə] *npl Formal* (órganos *mpl*) genitales *mpl*

genitive ['dʒenɪtɪv] *Gram* **1** *n* genitivo *m*

2 *adj* genitivo(a) ▸▸ ***g. case*** (caso *m*) genitivo *m*

genito-urinary ['dʒenɪtəʊ'jʊərɪnərɪ] *adj Med* genitourinario(a), urogenital

genius ['dʒiːnɪəs] *n* (**a**) *(gifted person)* genio *m*

(**b**) *(special gift)* don *m*; **to have a g. for...** tener un don (natural) para...; **man/work of g.** hombre/obra genial; **her g. lies in her power to evoke atmosphere** su don es la capacidad para crear determinados ambientes; *Ironic* **he has a g. for putting his foot in it** tiene una habilidad especial para meter la pata; *Fam* **that goal was pure** *or* **sheer g.** ese gol fue una genialidad

(**c**) *Literary (distinctive character) (of system, epoch, place)* genio *m*

(**d**) *(spirit, demon)* genio *m*; **evil g.** genio maligno

Genoa ['dʒenəʊə] *n* Génova

genocidal [dʒenə'saɪdəl] *adj* genocida

genocide ['dʒenəsaɪd] *n* genocidio *m*

Genoese [dʒenəʊ'iːz] (*pl* **Genoese**) **1** *n* genovés(esa) *m,f*

2 *adj* genovés(esa)

genome ['dʒiːnəʊm] *n Biol* genoma *m*

genotype ['dʒiːnəʊtaɪp] *n Biol* genotipo *m*

genre [ˈʒɒnrə] *n (of film, novel)* género *m*; **g. cinema/painting** cine/pintura de género

gent [dʒent] *n Br Fam* **(a)** *(gentleman)* caballero *m*, señor *m*; **he's a (real) g.** es (todo) un caballero; **gents' footwear** calzado de caballero **(b) the gents** *(toilets)* el baño *or Esp* servicio *or CSur* la toilette de caballeros

genteel [dʒenˈtiːl] *adj* **(a)** *(delicate)* fino(a); *Pej* afectado(a) **(b)** *(respectable)* respetable

> **False friend**: The Spanish adjective **gentil** is not a translation for the English word **genteel**. In Spanish **gentil** means "kind, nice".

gentian [ˈdʒenʃən] *n* genciana *f* ▸▸ *Br* ***g. violet*** violeta *f* de genciana

Gentile [ˈdʒentaɪl] **1** *n* gentil *mf*
2 *adj* gentil

gentility [dʒenˈtɪlɪtɪ] *n* **(a)** *(good manners)* refinamiento *m*, finura *f* **(b)** *Pej (affected politeness)* afectación *f*, cursilería *f*

gentle [ˈdʒentəl] *adj* **(a)** *(kind, mild) (person, manner, voice)* tierno(a); **the g.** *or* **gentler sex** el bello sexo; IDIOM **as g. as a lamb** como un corderillo
(b) *(not harsh, rough) (treatment, handling)* cuidadoso(a); *(shampoo, detergent)* suave; **be g. with that vase** trata el jarrón con cuidado
(c) *(light) (push, breeze, slope)* suave; *(heat, friction)* suave, ligero(a); *(rain)* ligero(a); *(exercise)* leve, moderado(a)
(d) *(moderate, discreet) (hint)* discreto(a); *(reminder, rebuke)* sutil; *Hum* **the g. art of persuasion** el sutil arte de la persuasión
(e) *(gradual) (rise, fall)* suave; **a g. transition** una suave transición; **to come to a g. halt** detenerse suavemente
(f) *Literary (noble)* noble, de alcurnia; **of g. birth** de noble linaje; **g. reader** amable lector

gentlefolk [ˈdʒentəlfəʊk] *npl Old-fashioned* gente *f* de buena familia *or* de prosapia

gentleman [ˈdʒentəlmən] *n* **(a)** *(man)* caballero *m*; **show the g. in** haga pasar al caballero; **come in, gentlemen!** ¡adelante, caballeros!; **Gentlemen** *(sign)* Caballeros
(b) *(well-bred man)* caballero *m*; **he's a real g.** es todo un caballero; **the word of a g.** la palabra de un caballero; **a g.'s agreement** un pacto de *or* entre caballeros
(c) *(man of substance)* hombre *m* de fortuna ▸▸ ***g. farmer*** terrateniente *m*, latifundista *m*; *Old-fashioned* ***a g.'s g.*** un criado *or* sirviente

gentleman-at-arms [ˈdʒentəlmənətˈɑːmz] *n Br* miembro *m* de la comitiva real

gentlemanly [ˈdʒentəlmənlɪ] *adj* caballeroso(a), cortés

gentleness [ˈdʒentəlnɪs] *n* **(a)** *(of person, nature, voice)* ternura *f*, afectuosidad *f* **(b)** *(of treatment, handling)* cuidado *m*, delicadeza *f*; *(of shampoo, detergent)* suavidad *f* **(c)** *(of push, breeze, slope)* suavidad *f* **(d)** *(of hint)* discreción *f*; *(of reminder, rebuke)* sutileza *f* **(e)** *(of rise, fall)* suavidad *f*

gentlewoman [ˈdʒentəlwʊmən] *n Hist* dama *f*, señora *f*

gently [ˈdʒentlɪ] *adv* **(a)** *(kindly, mildly) (to speak, smile)* con ternura, afectuosamente
(b) *(not harshly, roughly) (to treat, handle)* con cuidado; **g. does it!** ¡con cuidado!, ¡despacio!
(c) *(lightly)* ligeramente, suavemente
(d) *(discreetly) (to hint, remind, rebuke)* discretamente, con tacto; **break it to him g.** díselo con delicadeza
(e) *(gradually)* suavemente; **g. rolling hills** colinas suaves
(f) *(slowly)* suavemente; **a g. flowing river** un río que fluye suavemente

gentrification [dʒentrɪfɪˈkeɪʃən] *n (of area)* aburguesamiento *m (de barrio obrero)*

gentrified [ˈdʒentrɪfaɪd] *adj* **(a)** *(area, street)* aburguesado(a) **(b)** *(accent, manners)* aburguesado(a)

gentrify [ˈdʒentrɪfaɪ] *vt (area, street)* aburguesar

gentry [ˈdʒentrɪ] *npl* alta burguesía *f (terrateniente)*

genuflect [ˈdʒenjʊflekt] *vi* hacer una genuflexión

genuflection [dʒenjʊˈflekʃən] *n* genuflexión *f*

genuine [ˈdʒenjʊɪn] *adj* **(a)** *(authentic) (manuscript, painting)* auténtico(a), genuino(a); **this isn't a fake Rolls, it's the g. article** no es falso, es un Rolls auténtico *or* de verdad; **he's the g. article, a real aristocrat** es un aristócrata auténtico *or* de verdad; **g. leather** cuero auténtico; **g. silver** plata auténtica
(b) *(sincere)* sincero(a); **it is my g. belief that he is innocent** estoy convencido de que es inocente; **a g. mistake** un error no intencionado
(c) *(serious) (application)* serio(a); **g. enquiries only** *(in advert)* abstenerse curiosos

genuinely [ˈdʒenjʊɪnlɪ] *adv (sincerely)* realmente; **he seemed g. surprised** parecía sorprendido de verdad

genuineness [ˈdʒenjʊɪnnɪs] *n* **(a)** *(authenticity)* autenticidad *f* **(b)** *(sincerity)* sinceridad *f*

genus [ˈdʒiːnəs] *(pl* **genera** [ˈdʒenərə]*) n Biol* género *m*

geo- [ˈdʒiːəʊ] *prefix* geo-

geocentric [dʒiːəʊˈsentrɪk] *adj* geocéntrico(a)

geochemistry [dʒiːəʊˈkemɪstrɪ] *n* geoquímica *f*

geode [ˈdʒiːəʊd] *n Geol* geoda *f*

geodemographics [dʒiːəʊdeməˈgræfɪks] *n Com* geodemografía *f*

geodesic dome [dʒɪəʊˈdiːsɪkˈdəʊm] *n* cúpula *f* geodésica

geodesy [dʒiːˈɒdɪsɪ] *n* geodesia *f*

geodynamics [dʒiːəʊdaɪˈnæmɪks] *n Geol* geodinámica *f*

geographer [dʒɪˈɒgrəfə(r)] *n* geógrafo(a) *m,f*

geographic(al) [dʒɪəˈgræfɪk(əl)] *adj* geográfico(a)

geographically [dʒɪəˈgræfɪklɪ] *adv* geográficamente

geography [dʒɪˈɒgrəfɪ] *n* **(a)** *(science)* geografía *f* **(b)** *(layout)* **I don't know the g. of the building** no me oriento muy bien en el edificio

geological [dʒɪəˈlɒdʒɪkəl] *adj* geológico(a) ▸▸ ***g. survey*** estudio *m* geológico

geologist [dʒɪˈɒlədʒɪst] *n* geólogo(a) *m,f*

geology [dʒɪˈɒlədʒɪ] *n* geología *f*

geomagnetic [ˈdʒiːəʊmægˈnetɪk] *adj* geomagnético(a)

geomagnetism [ˈdʒiːəʊˈmægnɪtɪzəm] *n* geomagnetismo *m*, magnetismo *m* terrestre

geometric(al) [dʒɪəˈmetrɪk(əl)] *adj* geométrico(a) ▸▸ ***g. progression*** progresión *f* geométrica

geometry [dʒɪˈɒmɪtrɪ] *n* geometría *f*

geomorphology [dʒiːəʊmɔːˈfɒlədʒɪ] *n* geomorfología *f*

geophysical [ˈdʒiːəʊˈfɪzɪkəl] *adj* geofísico(a)

geophysicist [dʒiːəʊˈfɪzɪsɪst] *n* geofísico(a) *m,f*

geophysics [ˈdʒiːəʊˈfɪzɪks] *n* geofísica *f*

geopolitical [ˈdʒiːəʊpəˈlɪtɪkəl] *adj* geopolítico(a)

Geordie [ˈdʒɔːdɪ] *Br Fam* **1** *n* **(a)** *(person)* persona de la región de Tyneside *(Inglaterra)* **(b)** *(dialect)* geordie *m*, = dialecto hablado en la región inglesa de Tyneside *(Inglaterra)*
2 *adj* de la región de Tyneside *(Inglaterra)*

George [dʒɔːdʒ] *n* **(a)** *Fam Old-fashioned* **by G.!** ¡cáspita!, ¡caramba! **(b)** *(in proper names)* **Saint G.** San Jorge; **G. I/II** Jorge I/II ▸▸ ***G. Cross*** = medalla al mérito civil del Reino Unido; ***G. Medal*** = medalla al mérito civil y militar del Reino Unido

georgette [dʒɔːˈdʒet] *n* crepé *m* georgette

Georgia [ˈdʒɔːdʒə] *n* **(a)** *(country)* Georgia **(b)** *(US state)* Georgia

Georgian [ˈdʒɔːdʒən] **1** *n* **(a)** *(person) (from country)* georgiano(a) *m,f*; *(from US state)* georgiano(a) *m,f* **(b)** *(language)* georgiano *m*
2 *adj* **(a)** *(of country)* georgiano(a) **(b)** *(of US state)* georgiano(a) **(c)** *(architecture, furniture)* de estilo georgiano **(d)** *(in British poetry)* pre-modernista

geosphere [ˈdʒɪəsfɪə(r)] *n* geosfera *f*

geostationary [ˈdʒiːəʊˈsteɪʃənərɪ] *adj* geoestacionario(a); **in g. orbit** en órbita geoestacionaria

geothermal [ˈdʒiːəʊˈθɜːməl], **geothermic** [dʒiːəʊˈθɜːmɪk] *adj* geotérmico(a) ▸▸ ***g. energy*** energía *f* geotérmica

geranium [dʒəˈreɪnɪəm] *n* geranio *m*

gerbil [ˈdʒɜːbɪl] *n* jerbo *m*, gerbo *m*

geriatric [dʒerɪˈætrɪk] **1** *n* **(a)** *Med* anciano(a) *m,f* **(b)** *Fam Pej* vejestorio *m*
2 *adj* geriátrico(a); **g. hospital** hospital geriátrico; **g. ward** servicio de geriatría

geriatrician [dʒerɪəˈtrɪʃən] *n Med* geriatra *mf*

geriatrics [dʒerɪˈætrɪks] *n Med* geriatría *f*

germ [dʒɜːm] *n* **(a)** *Med (micro-organism)* germen *m*, microbio *m* ▸▸ ***g. warfare*** guerra *f* bacteriológica **(b)** *Bot* germen *m* **(c)** *(origin, beginning)* **the g. of an idea** el germen de una idea

German [ˈdʒɜːmən] **1** *n* **(a)** *(person)* alemán(ana) *m,f* **(b)** *(language)* alemán *m*; **G. class/teacher** clase/profesor(ora) de alemán
2 *adj* alemán(ana) ▸▸ *Formerly* ***G. Democratic Republic*** República *f* Democrática Alemana; ***G. measles*** rubeola *f*; ***G. shepherd*** pastor *m* alemán

germane [dʒɜːˈmeɪn] *adj Formal* pertinente; **that's not entirely g. to the matter** eso no concierne mucho al asunto

Germanic [dʒɜːˈmænɪk] 1 *n Ling* germánico *m*
2 *adj* germánico(a)

Germanist [ˈdʒɜːmənɪst] *n* germanista *mf*

germanium [dʒɜːˈmeɪnɪəm] *n Chem* germanio *m*

germanize [ˈdʒɜːmənaɪz] *vt* germanizar

germanophile [dʒɜːˈmænəfaɪl] *n* germanófilo(a) *m,f*

germanophilia [dʒɜːˈmænəfɪlɪə] *n* germanofilia *f*

germanophobe [dʒɜːˈmænəfəʊb] *n* germanófobo(a) *m,f*

germanophobia [dʒɜːmænəˈfəʊbɪə] *n* germanofobia *f*

Germany [ˈdʒɜːmənɪ] *n* Alemania

germ-free [ˈdʒɜːmˈfriː] *adj* aséptico(a)

germicidal [dʒɜːmɪˈsaɪdəl] *adj* germicida

germicide [ˈdʒɜːmɪsaɪd] *n* germicida *m*

germinate [ˈdʒɜːmɪneɪt] 1 *vt* hacer germinar
2 *vi* germinar

germination [dʒɜːmɪˈneɪʃən] *n* germinación *f*

gerontocracy [dʒerɒnˈtɒkrəsɪ] *n* gerontocracia *f*

gerontology [dʒerɒnˈtɒlədʒɪ] *n Med* gerontología *f*

gerrymander [ˈdʒerɪmændə(r)] *vt Pol* **(a)** *(constituency)* = alterar los límites de un distrito electoral para que un partido obtenga mejores resultados **(b)** *(results)* manipular

gerrymandering [ˈdʒerɪmændərɪŋ] *n Pol* = alteración de los límites de un distrito electoral para que un partido obtenga mejores resultados

gerund [ˈdʒerənd] *n Gram* gerundio *m*

gesso [ˈdʒesəʊ] (*pl* **gessoes**) *n* gesso *m*

gestalt [gəˈʃtælt] *n Psy* gestalt *f* ►► ***G. psychology*** (escuela *f* de la) Gestalt *f*, psicología *f* gestáltica

Gestapo [geˈstɑːpəʊ] *n* Gestapo *f*; *Fig* **G. tactics** tácticas al estilo de la Gestapo

gestate [dʒesˈteɪt] *vi* **(a)** *Biol (mother)* gestar, estar en estado de gestación; *(young)* gestarse, permanecer en el útero **(b)** *(idea, plan)* gestarse

gestation [dʒesˈteɪʃən] *n* **(a)** *Biol* gestación *f* ►► ***g. period*** periodo *m* de gestación **(b)** *(of idea, plan)* gestación *f*

gesticulate [dʒesˈtɪkjʊleɪt] *vi* gesticular

gesticulation [dʒestɪkjʊˈleɪʃən] *n* gesticulación *f*

gestural [ˈdʒestʃərəl] *adj* gestual

gesture [ˈdʒestʃə(r)] 1 *n* **(a)** *(expressive movement)* gesto *m*; **they communicated by gestures** se comunicaban por gestos; **to make a g. of acknowledgement** saludar con un ademán, hacer un gesto de reconocimiento; **to make a g. of dismissal** despedir a alguien con un ademán *or* gesto; **to make a g. of assent** hacer un ademán *or* gesto de aprobación
(b) *(sign, token)* gesto *m*; **as a g. of friendship** en señal de amistad; **it was a nice g.** fue todo un detalle; **a hollow** *or* **empty g.** un gesto vacío ►► ***g. politics*** política *f* efectista
2 *vi (single action)* hacer un gesto; *(repeatedly)* gesticular, hacer gestos; **he gestured to me to stand up** me hizo un gesto para que me levantara; **to g. towards sth** *(point)* señalar *or* indicar hacia algo

gesundheit [gəˈzʊnthaɪt] *exclam US* ¡salud!, ¡Jesús!

GET [get] (*pt & pp* **got** [gɒt], *US pp* **gotten** [ˈgɒtən])

> En las expresiones que aparecen bajo **(r)** y **(s)**, **get** suele ser opcional. Cuando se omite **get**, **have** no se contrae. Para los casos en que se puede omitir, véase **have**.

1 *vt* **(a)** *(obtain)* conseguir (**from** *or* **off** de); *(buy)* comprar (**from** *or* **off** a); *(mark)* sacar; **to g. sth for sb, to g. sb sth** *(present)* comprar algo a alguien; **could you g. me some sweets from the supermarket?** ¿me traes unos caramelos del supermercado?; **shall we g. a bite to eat?** ¿comemos algo?; **let me g. this round** *(pay for)* deja que pague yo esta ronda *or RP* vuelta; **we usually g. "The Sun"** normalmente compramos "The Sun"; **could you g. me extension 340?** *(on phone)* ¿me podría comunicar *or Esp* poner con la extensión 340?, *RP* ¿me podría pasar con el interno 340?; **to g. a job** encontrar trabajo; **I got the idea from a book** saqué la idea de un libro; **to g. the right/wrong answer** dar la respuesta correcta/equivocada; **the food there is as good as you can g.** la comida de ahí es insuperable; **to g. oneself a job/girlfriend** conseguir un trabajo/una novia; **I got myself a new suit** me compré un traje nuevo
(b) *(receive) (present, reply)* recibir; **I always g. chocolates for Christmas** siempre me dan *or* regalan bombones para Navidad; **how did you g. that scar?** ¿cómo te hiciste esa cicatriz?; **to g. £18,000 a year** ganar 18.000 libras anuales; **we can't g. Channel 9 here** aquí no recibimos *or* no captamos *or* no llega el Canal 9; **we got a lot of rain this summer** este verano llovió mucho; **I got $50 for my old fridge** me dieron 50 dólares por la nevera *or RP* heladera vieja; **he got ten years for rape** lo condenaron a diez años por violación; **she gets her figure from her mother** tiene el tipo de su madre; **I g. the feeling** *or* **impression that...** me da *or* tengo la impresión de que..., *Chile, Perú* me tinca que..., *Méx, Ven* me late que...; **to g. pleasure from doing sth** disfrutar haciendo algo; **to g. promotion** ser ascendido(a); **she got a surprise/shock** se llevó una sorpresa/un susto
(c) *(catch) (person, disease) Esp* coger, *Am* agarrar; *(train, bus)* tomar, *Esp* coger, *Am* agarrar; **he got her by the throat** la agarró del cuello; **I got this cold off** *or* **from my sister** mi hermana me pegó *Esp, Méx* resfriado *or Andes, RP* resfrío; *Fam* **g. him!** *(look at him)* ¡mira éste!; *Fam* **g. you!** *(look at you)* ¡míralo!; *Fam* **what's the capital of Somalia? – you've got me there!** ¿cuál es la capital de Somalia? – ¡ahí me has pillado! *or RP* ¡ahí me agarraste!; *Fam* **the bit where she dies always gets me** el momento en el que muere siempre me emociona
(d) *(fetch)* **to g. sth for sb, to g. sb sth** traerle algo a alguien; **g. me the hammer** tráeme el martillo; **go and g. a doctor** ve a buscar a un médico; **I'm going to g. my mother from the hospital** voy a recoger *or* buscar a mi madre al hospital
(e) *(prepare, make) (meal, cocktail)* preparar; **can I g. you a glass of wine?** ¿te pongo *or* sirvo un vaso de vino?; **g. yourself a drink** ponte *or* sírvete algo de beber *or Am* tomar
(f) *(reach)* **put it where the children can't g. it** ponlo donde los niños no lleguen *or* alcancen
(g) *(answer) (phone, door)* contestar a; **would you g. that for me?** ¿te importaría contestar?
(h) *Fam* **to g. it** *(be reprimanded)* cobrar; **I'll g. you for that!** ¡me las pagarás!
(i) *Fam (annoy)* molestar, fastidiar; **what really gets me is his attitude** lo que de verdad me molesta *or* fastidia es su actitud
(j) *Fam (understand)* entender; *(hear)* (alcanzar a) oír; **now I g. you!** ¡ahora te entiendo!; **I didn't quite g. what you said** no oí bien lo que dijiste; **oh, I g. it, you're trying to be funny** ah, ahora lo entiendo, estás haciéndote el gracioso; **you just don't g. it, do you? I'm leaving** ¿es que no te quieres enterar? me marcho, *RP* no te das cuenta ¿no?, que me voy; **to g. a joke** pescar *or Esp* coger *or Am* cachar un chiste; **I don't g. your meaning** no entiendo *or Esp* cojo lo que quieres decir; **I g. the message!** ¡entendido!; **don't g. me wrong!** ¡no me malinterpretes!; **g. (a load of) that haircut!** ¡fíjate qué corte de pelo!
(k) *(send)* **to g. sth to sb** mandar *or* enviar algo a alguien; **I got a message to them** les mandé *or* envié un mensaje
(l) *(cause to be in a certain state)* **to g. sth dry/wet** secar/mojar algo; **I can't g. it clean** no consigo limpiarlo; **to g. sth dirty** ensuciar algo; **to g. sth fixed** arreglar algo; **I like to g. things done** me gusta acabar las cosas rápidamente; **I got my wallet stolen** me robaron la cartera; **she got her work finished** terminó su trabajo; **to g. sb pregnant** dejar embarazada a alguien; **you've got him worried** lo has dejado preocupado; **the movie got everyone talking** la película dio que hablar a todo el mundo; **to g. sb into trouble** meter a alguien en líos; **to g. the children to bed** acostar a los niños; **arguing will g. you nowhere** discutir no lleva a ninguna parte
(m) *(move)* **g. the washing inside, quick!** mete la ropa, ¡rápido!; **we got him past the guards** conseguimos pasarlo sin que lo vieran los guardias; **you'll never g. that piano through the door** nunca conseguirás pasar el piano por la puerta
(n) *(cause to do)* **she got me to help her** me pidió que la ayudara *(y la ayudé)*; **why don't you g. your mother to do it?** ¿por qué no le pides a tu madre que lo haga ella?; **I finally got my mother to do it** por fin conseguí que lo hiciera mi madre; **you can g. them to wrap it for you** puedes pedir que te lo envuelvan; **we g. our paper delivered** nos traen el periódico; **can I g. you to write your address here?** ¿te importaría escribir tu dirección aquí?; **I can't g. the motorbike to start** no consigo que arranque la moto
(o) *(do gradually)* **to g. to know sb** llegar a conocer a alguien; **you'll g. to like him** con el tiempo te va a caer bien; **you're getting to be quite good at chess** juegas cada vez mejor al ajedrez; **she soon got to thinking that...** pronto empezó a pensar que...
(p) *(have opportunity)* **I'll do it when I g. the time/chance** lo haré cuando tenga tiempo/la ocasión; **to g. to do sth** llegar a hacer algo; **you g. to travel a lot in this job** en este trabajo se viaja mucho; **I finally got to see her** por fin pude *or* conseguí verla
(q) *(find)* **you don't g. many eagles round here** no se ven muchas águilas por aquí; **we don't g. many visitors here** no viene mucha gente por aquí
(r) *(possess) (with* **have***)* **they've got a big house** tienen una casa grande; **she hasn't got a boyfriend** no tiene novio; **he's got black**

hair tiene el pelo negro; **she's got measles/AIDS** tiene (el) sarampión/SIDA; **we've got a choice** tenemos una alternativa; **I've got something to do** tengo algo que hacer; **what's that got to do with it?** ¿y eso qué tiene que ver?

(s) *(must) (with* **have***)* **I've got to go** me tengo que ir; **have you got to work?** ¿tienes que trabajar?; **it's got to be done** hay que hacerlo

2 *vi* (a) *(arrive, progress)* llegar (**to** a); **to g. home** llegar a casa; **how do you g. there?** ¿cómo se llega?; **how did this motorbike g. here?** ¿cómo ha llegado hasta aquí esta moto?, ¿qué hace esta moto acá?; **he got as far as Chapter Five** llegó hasta el quinto capítulo; **when it got to Friday, I started to worry** cuando llegó el viernes, comencé a preocuparme; **I was about to g. to that** estaba a punto de mencionar eso; **we're not getting anywhere** (así) no vamos a ninguna parte; **how's the project coming on? – we're getting there** ¿cómo va el proyecto? – vamos avanzando

(b) *(move)* **g. behind that bush!** ¡escóndete detrás de ese arbusto!; **to g. in the way** ponerse en medio; **to g. in the way of sb, to g. in sb's way** ponerse delante de alguien; **he got onto the table** se subió a la mesa; **she got over the wall** sorteó *or* pasó el muro; **I got to my feet** me puse de pie, me levanté, *Am* me paré

(c) *(become)* **to g. angry** *esp Esp* enfadarse, *esp Am* enojarse; **to g. better** mejorar; **it's getting dark/chilly** está oscureciendo/empezando a hacer frío; **it's getting late** se está haciendo tarde; **to g. drunk** emborracharse; **to g. old** envejecer; **this is getting ridiculous** esto es cada vez más ridículo

(d) *(in passive-type constructions)* **to g. broken** romperse; **to g. captured** ser capturado(a); **I didn't g. invited** no me invitaron; **to g. lost** *(person)* perderse; *(object)* perderse, extraviarse; **to g. stolen** ser robado(a)

(e) *(in reflexive-type constructions)* **to g. dressed** vestirse; **to g. married** casarse; **to g. ready for sth** prepararse *or Am* alistarse *or RP* aprontarse para algo

(f) *(start)* **to g. going** *(leave)* irse, marcharse; *(start working)* empezar a funcionar; **let's g. moving** *or* **going!** ¡en marcha!; **to g. talking with sb** empezar a hablar con alguien

3 *exclam (go away)* ¡fuera!

4 *n* (a) *Br very Fam (person) Esp* capullo(a) *m,f*, *Am* pendejo(a) *m,f*
(b) *Fam (in tennis)* salvada *f*

▸**get about** *vi* (a) *(move around)* moverse; **I don't g. about much these days** no me muevo mucho últimamente; **you g. about a lot!** *(travel)* ¡viajas mucho! (b) *(news, rumour)* difundirse, trascender

▸**get above** *vt insep* **to g. above oneself** darse muchos humos

▸**get across** 1 *vt insep (cross)* cruzar

2 *vt sep* (a) *(take across)* **how are we going to g. the van across the river?** ¿cómo vamos a cruzar la furgoneta a la otra orilla? (b) *(convey)* **to g. an idea/a message across** hacer entender una idea/un mensaje; **to g. sth across to sb** hacer que alguien entienda algo

3 *vi (cross)* cruzar

▸**get ahead** *vi (in life)* abrirse paso *or* camino

▸**get along** *vi* (a) *(leave)* marcharse, irse; **we must be getting along** tenemos que marcharnos *or* irnos

(b) *(progress)* **how are you getting along in your new job?** ¿cómo te va en el nuevo trabajo?; **we can g. along without them** podemos seguir sin ellos

(c) *(have good relationship)* llevarse bien; **she's easy to g. along with** se lleva bien con el mundo

▸**get around** 1 *vt insep* (a) *(avoid) (problem)* evitar; **we got around the rule** conseguimos evitar tener que cumplir la norma (b) *(persuade)* **he knows how to g. around his mother** sabe cómo ganarse a su madre

2 *vi* = **get about**

▸**get around to** *vt insep* **to g. around to doing sth** sacar tiempo para hacer algo; **I haven't got around to telling her yet** no he sacado tiempo para decírselo

▸**get at** *vt insep* (a) *(gain access to)* acceder a, llegar a; *(reach)* alcanzar; **to g. at the truth** dar con la verdad

(b) *(imply)* **what are you getting at?** ¿qué (es lo que) quieres decir?

(c) *Fam (criticize unfairly) (person)* meterse con, chinchar

(d) *Fam (influence) (witness, jury)* atemorizar

▸**get away** 1 *vt sep (move)* **to g. sth/sb away from sth/sb** apartar algo/a alguien de algo/de alguien

2 *vi (escape)* irse, escaparse; *(have a holiday)* tomarse unas vacaciones; *(leave work)* salir de trabajar; **g. away from me!** ¡aléjate de mí!; *Br Fam* **g. away (with you)!** *(expressing disbelief) Esp* ¡anda *or* venga ya!, *Méx* ¡no me cuentes!, *RP* ¡dale!; **we need to g. away from that way of thinking** tenemos que abandonar esa manera de ver las cosas; **you can't g. away** *or* **there's no getting away from the fact that...** es imposible ignorar el hecho de que...; **to g. away from it all** escaparse de todo

▸**get away with** *vt insep (crime)* salir impune de; **I don't know how you g. away with speaking to your mother like that** no entiendo cómo tu madre te permite que le hables así; **he got away with a small fine** sólo le han puesto una pequeña multa; IDIOM **that child gets away with murder!** ¡ese niño se sale siempre con la suya!

▸**get back** 1 *vt sep* (a) *(recover)* recuperar; **he got his job back** recuperó el trabajo; **we got our money back** nos devolvieron el dinero

(b) *(return)* **how are we going to g. these packages back home?** ¿cómo vamos a llevar estos paquetes a casa?; **I'll g. it back to you by Monday at the latest** te lo devolveré el lunes como muy tarde

(c) *Fam (take revenge on)* **I'll g. you back for this!** ¡me las pagarás!

2 *vi* (a) *(move)* echarse atrás, apartarse; **g. back!** ¡atrás!

(b) *(return)* volver, regresar; **to g. back to normal** volver a la normalidad; **let's g. back to the point** centrémonos de nuevo en el tema; **to g. back to sleep** volverse a dormir

(c) *(contact later)* **can I g. back to you?** *(on phone)* ¿te puedo llamar dentro de un rato?; **can I g. back to you on that? I'm busy just now** ahora estoy ocupado, ¿te puedo contestar más tarde?

▸**get back at** *vt insep* **to g. back at sb (for sth)** vengarse de alguien (por algo)

▸**get back together** *vi (couple)* volver a juntarse

▸**get behind** 1 *vt insep (support)* apoyar

2 *vi (become delayed)* atrasarse, quedarse atrás

▸**get by** *vi (manage)* arreglárselas; **we g. by on just $150 a week** nos las arreglamos con sólo 150 dólares a la semana; **we can g. by without him** podemos arreglarnos sin él; **I g. by in Spanish** me defiendo en español

▸**get down** 1 *vt sep* (a) *(move)* bajar; **could you g. that book down for me?** ¿me podrías bajar ese libro?

(b) *(reduce) (costs, temperature)* reducir; **to g. one's weight down** perder peso

(c) *(write)* anotar

(d) *(depress)* **to g. sb down** desanimar *or* deprimir a alguien

(e) *(swallow)* tragar; *Fam* **g. this whisky down you!** ¡métete este whisky en el cuerpo!

GET

Get es uno de los verbos más frecuentes en inglés. Por sí solo puede traducirse por muchos verbos distintos en español, como puede verse en la entrada. También se usa en combinación con preposiciones y adverbios para formar verbos frasales y junto a sustantivos y adjetivos para crear expresiones verbales que indican distintas acciones o estados:

> **I got up** *(me levanté)* **at seven, got myself showered** *(me duché)* **and dressed** *(me vestí)* **and then got breakfast** *(desayuné)* **in a local cafe. I got to work** *(llegué al trabajo)* **early and got through** *(terminé)* **a pile of stuff before lunchtime. I got a bite to eat** *(comí un bocado)* **in a new bar near the office. In the afternoon I got myself into trouble** *(tuve problemas)* **with the boss because she needed work I hadn't had time to get finished** *(terminar)* **yet, so I got home** *(llegué a casa)* **in a bad mood.**

Este uso excesivo de **get** a menudo se considera incorrecto y no sería apropiado en inglés escrito en un registro formal, si bien es frecuente en el inglés hablado informalmente.

Por otra parte, **get** + ADJETIVO suele equivaler a un verbo reflexivo en español:

get angry	*enfadarse*	**get tired**	*cansarse*
get worried	*preocuparse*	**get bored**	*aburrirse*

2 *vi* (**a**) *(descend)* bajarse (**from** de); **g. down, he's going to shoot!** ¡agáchate, va a disparar!; **to g. down on one's hands and knees** ponerse a cuatro patas
(**b**) *Fam (dance with abandon)* soltarse
(**c**) *US Fam (get to work, begin)* ponerse a trabajar
(**d**) *US Fam (have sex)* enrollarse

▸ **get down to** *vt insep* ponerse a; **to g. down to doing sth** ponerse a hacer algo; **to g. down to the facts** ir (directamente) a los hechos; **to g. down to work** poner manos a la obra; **I just can't seem to g. down to work today** no consigo centrarme en el trabajo hoy; **when you g. down to it...** en el fondo...

▸ **get in** 1 *vt sep* (**a**) *(bring inside) (washing)* meter; *(harvest)* recoger
(**b**) *(fit in)* meter; **I couldn't g. a word in** *(in conversation)* no pude meter baza
(**c**) *(stock up with) (food, coal)* hacer acopio de
(**d**) *(call) (plumber, expert)* llamar
(**e**) *(submit)* entregar, presentar; **we have to g. the application in by next week** tenemos que entregar *or* presentar la solicitud antes del final de la semana que viene
(**f**) *Br Fam (pay for)* invitar a; **he got the next round in** invitó a la siguiente ronda
2 *vi* (**a**) *(arrive) (train, person)* llegar (**b**) *(enter)* entrar; **water is getting in through the roof** está entrando agua por el techo (**c**) *(be elected)* salir elegido(a), ganar las elecciones

▸ **get in on** *vt insep Fam (take part in)* apuntarse a

▸ **get into** 1 *vt insep* (**a**) *(enter) (house, car)* entrar en; **to g. into the habit of doing sth** *Am* agarrar *or Esp* coger la costumbre de hacer algo; **to g. into a temper** agarrar una pataleta, *Esp* coger una rabieta; **to g. into trouble** meterse en un lío; *Fam* **I don't know what's got into her** no sé qué mosca le ha picado
(**b**) *(put on) (clothes, boots)* ponerse; **she got into her dress** se puso el vestido; **I can't g. into this jacket** no me entra la chaqueta
(**c**) *(arrive at) (station, work)* llegar a
(**d**) *(be accepted)* **to g. into Parliament** salir elegido(a) parlamentario(a); **to g. into college** ser admitido(a) en la universidad
(**e**) *Fam* **I really got into it** *(book, activity)* me enganchó muchísimo
2 *vt sep* (**a**) *(fit)* meter (**b**) *(involve in)* meter; **you're the one who got us into this** tú eres el que nos ha metido en esto (**c**) *(make interested in)* meter; **he got me into jazz** él me metió en el jazz

▸ **get in with** *vt insep (ingratiate oneself with)* congraciarse con

▸ **get off** 1 *vt insep* (**a**) *(descend from)* bajar(se) de; **g. off that table!** ¡baja *or* bájate de esa mesa! (**b**) *(bus, train)* bajarse de
2 *vt sep* (**a**) *(remove) (lid, wrapper)* quitar, *Andes, RP* sacar; **g. your feet off the table!** ¡quita *or Andes, RP* saca los pies de la mesa!; **g. your hands off me!** ¡quítame las manos de encima!
(**b**) *(save from punishment)* **to g. sb off** librar *or* salvar a alguien
(**c**) *(avoid)* **to g. off having to do sth** librarse de tener que hacer algo
(**d**) *(cause to be)* **to g. the children off to school** mandar a los niños al colegio; **to g. a baby off (to sleep)** dormir a un niño
(**e**) *(send)* enviar
(**f**) *(leave) (work)* salir de; **g. off my land!** ¡fuera de mis tierras!
3 *vi* (**a**) *(descend from vehicle)* bajarse, apearse; *Fig* **I told him where to g. off** *(rebuked him)* lo mandé a paseo
(**b**) *(go unpunished)* librarse; **he got off with a small fine** sólo le han puesto una pequeña multa; *Fig* **to g. off lightly** salir bien librado(a)
(**c**) **to g. off (to sleep)** dormirse, quedarse dormido(a); **to g. off to a good/bad start** empezar con buen/mal pie
(**d**) *(start journey)* salir; **we'd best be getting off** deberíamos marcharnos *or* irnos
(**e**) *(leave work)* salir (del trabajo)
(**f**) *(leave alone)* **g. off!** ¡déjame en paz!
(**g**) *US very Fam (have orgasm) Esp* correrse, *Col, Méx* venirse, *RP* irse

▸ **get off on** *vt insep Fam (sexually)* **he gets off on blue movies** le ponen a cien las películas porno; *Fig* **he really gets off on ordering people about** eso de mandar le encanta

▸ **get off with** *vt insep Br Fam* **to g. off with sb** enrollarse con alguien

▸ **get on** 1 *vt insep* (**a**) *(move onto)* **g. on the table** súbete a la mesa (**b**) *(board) (train, bus, plane)* montar en, subir a
2 *vt sep* (**a**) *(put on)* **to g. one's clothes/trousers on** ponerse la ropa/los pantalones; **I can't g. my trousers on** no me entran *or* caben los pantalones (**b**) *US Fam* **to g. it on (with sb)** *(have sex) Esp* enrollarse (con alguien), *Am* coger (con alguien)
3 *vi* (**a**) *(board)* montarse, subirse
(**b**) *(succeed, progress)* **how are you getting on?** ¿cómo te va?; **I'm getting on well/badly** me va bien/mal; **do you know how you got on in the exam?** ¿sabes qué te han puesto en el examen?; **we're getting on fine without you** nos va muy bien sin ti; **you'll never g. on in life** *or* **in the world with that attitude!** ¡con esa actitud nunca llegarás a ninguna parte!
(**c**) *(have good relationship)* llevarse bien; **to g. on well/badly with sb** llevarse bien/mal con alguien; **how do you g. on with her?** ¿qué tal te llevas con ella?
(**d**) *(with time)* **it's getting on, we should go** se hace tarde, tenemos que irnos; **to be getting on (in years)** ser bastante mayor
(**e**) *(leave)* **I must be getting on** me tengo que ir

▸ **get on at** *vt insep Fam* **to g. on at sb (about sth)** meterse con alguien (por algo)

▸ **get on for** *vt insep* **he must be getting on for fifty** debe de tener cerca de los cincuenta; **it was getting on for midnight** era cerca de medianoche; **there were getting on for 10,000 people there** debía haber allí cerca de 10.000 personas

▸ **get onto** *vt insep* (**a**) *(move)* **g. onto the table** súbete a la mesa
(**b**) *(board) (train, bus, plane)* montar en, subir a
(**c**) *(contact)* ponerse en contacto con
(**d**) *(move onto subject of)* pasar a (hablar de); **they eventually got onto (the subject of) money** finalmente pasaron a hablar de (asuntos de) dinero
(**e**) *(be elected to) (committee, board)* ser elegido(a) como miembro de
(**f**) *(start to deal with)* comenzar a tratar

▸ **get on with** *vt insep (continue with)* seguir, continuar; **g. on with it!** *(hurry up)* ¡date prisa!, *Am* ¡apúrate!; **here's $20 to be getting on with** aquí tienes 20 dólares para ir empezando; *Fam* **why can't you just let me g. on with my work?** ¿por qué no me dejas trabajar en paz?

▸ **get out** 1 *vt sep* (**a**) *(remove) (tools, books, money)* sacar; *(nail, splinter)* sacar, extraer; *(stain)* quitar, *Andes, RP* sacar; **he got his wallet out** sacó su cartera (**b**) *(publish)* publicar, sacar (**c**) *(manage to say)* **I couldn't g. the words out** no me salían las palabras
2 *vi* (**a**) *(leave)* salir; *(escape)* salir, escapar; **g. out!** ¡vete de aquí!; **g. out of here!** *(leave)* ¡vete de aquí!; *US Fam (I don't believe it)* ¡anda ya! (**b**) *(from car)* salir, bajarse (**c**) *(socialize)* salir; **we don't g. out much** no salimos mucho (**d**) *(news)* filtrarse; **the secret got out** se descubrió el secreto

▸ **get out of** 1 *vt insep* (**a**) *(car, bus, train)* salir de, bajar de; **to g. out of the way** apartarse, quitarse de en medio; **he got out of bed** se levantó de la cama; **how are we going to g. out of this mess?** ¿cómo vamos a salir de este lío? (**b**) *(avoid)* **to g. out of sth/doing sth** librarse de algo/de hacer algo
2 *vt sep* (**a**) *(benefit from)* **what do I g. out of it?** ¿y yo qué saco (de ello)?; **to g. a lot of enjoyment out of sth** disfrutar mucho con algo (**b**) *(help to avoid)* **to g. sb out of doing sth** ayudar a alguien a librarse de tener que hacer algo; **to g. sb out of trouble** sacar a alguien de un apuro (**c**) *(extract)* **to g. the truth/a confession out of sb** extraer la verdad/una confesión de alguien

▸ **get over** 1 *vt insep* (**a**) *(cross) (road, river)* cruzar; *(wall, fence)* franquear
(**b**) *(recover from) (illness, trauma)* recuperarse de; **you'll g. over it** se te pasará; **I can't g. over how stupidly he behaved** no me puedo creer lo estúpido que fue; **I'll never g. over her** nunca la voy a olvidar
(**c**) *(overcome) (problem)* superar
2 *vt sep (communicate)* hacer llegar, transmitir
3 *vi* (**a**) *(cross) (over road, river)* cruzar; *(over wall, fence)* pasar al otro lado (**b**) *(come)* **g. over here as soon as possible** ven aquí tan pronto como puedas

▸ **get over with** *vt sep* **to g. sth over with** terminar con algo

▸ **get round** 1 *vt insep* = **get around**
2 *vi* = **get about**

▸ **get round to** = **get around to**

▸ **get through** 1 *vt insep* (**a**) *(pass through) (hole, roof)* entrar por
(**b**) *(survive) (test, interview)* pasar, superar; *(exam)* aprobar; *(period of time)* superar, aguantar; **the bill finally got through Parliament** el proyecto de ley fue finalmente aprobado por el parlamento
(**c**) *(finish) (work)* terminar, acabar; **I got through an enormous amount of work** terminé *or* acabé una cantidad de trabajo enorme
(**d**) *(consume) (food, drink)* consumir; *(money)* gastar; **I g. through two packs of cigarettes a day** me fumo dos paquetes de cigarrillos al día
2 *vt sep* (**a**) *(communicate)* **to g. sth through to sb** hacer ver algo a alguien (**b**) *(help to overcome)* **to g. sb through sth** ayudar a alguien a superar algo; **to g. a bill through Parliament** conseguir que un proyecto de ley se apruebe en el parlamento
3 *vi* (**a**) *(pass through)* pasar

(**b**) *(arrive) (news, messenger, supplies)* llegar
(**c**) **to g. through to sb** *(on telephone)* (lograr) comunicarse con alguien; *Fig (communicate with)* conectar con alguien; **the idea had finally got through to him** la idea le entró por fin en la cabeza
(**d**) *(qualify)* clasificarse
(**e**) *US (finish)* terminar, acabar; **call me when you g. through** llámame cuando termines *or* acabes

▸ **get to** 1 *vt insep Fam* (**a**) *(annoy)* fastidiar, molestar; **don't let it g. to you** no dejes que eso te afecte (**b**) *US* **they got to the witnesses** *(bribed)* compraron a los testigos; *(killed)* acabaron con los testigos
2 *vi* **where has Alistair/my wallet got to?** ¿adónde ha ido a parar Alistair/mi cartera?

▸ **get together** 1 *vt sep (organize) (petition)* organizar; *(band, team)* montar, juntar; **to g. some money together** juntar algo de dinero; **we got our belongings together** juntamos *or* recogimos nuestros efectos personales; **let me g. my thoughts together** déjame poner en claro mis ideas; **I've finally got it** *or* **myself together** finalmente he puesto mi vida en orden; *Fam* **they finally got it together last week** *(became lovers)* finalmente comenzaron a salir la semana pasada
2 *vi (meet)* quedar, verse

▸ **get up** 1 *vt insep (hill, cliff, tree)* subir a; **I couldn't g. up the stairs** no podía subir las escaleras; IDIOM **to g. up sb's nose** *(annoy)* fastidiar a alguien, *Esp* tocar a alguien las narices
2 *vt sep* (**a**) *(wake up)* **to g. sb up** levantar *or* despertar a alguien
(**b**) *(cause to rise to feet)* levantar
(**c**) *(dress up)* **he got himself up in his best clothes** se puso sus mejores ropas; **to g. oneself up as sth/sb** disfrazarse de algo/alguien
(**d**) *(arouse) (appetite, enthusiasm)* despertar; **don't g. your hopes up** no te hagas ilusiones; **to g. up the courage to do sth** armarse de valor para hacer algo; **to g. up speed** coger velocidad
(**e**) *(organize)* organizar, juntar
(**f**) *very Fam* **he couldn't g. it up** *(achieve erection)* no se le *Esp* empinaba *or Am* paraba
3 *vi* (**a**) *(in morning)* levantarse
(**b**) *(stand up)* levantarse, ponerse de pie, *Am* pararse; **he got up from the table** se levantó *or Am* paró de la mesa
(**c**) *(wind, storm)* levantarse

▸ **get up to** *vt insep* (**a**) *(reach)* **I've got up to Chapter Two** he llegado hasta el segundo capítulo (**b**) *Fam (do)* **what have you been getting up to recently?** ¿qué has estado haciendo últimamente?; **to g. up to mischief** hacer de las suyas; **he's been getting up to his old tricks** ha vuelto a las andadas

---

get-at-able [get'ætəbəl] *adj Fam (high shelf, person)* accesible

getaway ['getəweɪ] *n* (**a**) *(escape)* fuga *f*, huida *f*; **to make one's g.** huir, escaparse ▸▸ ***g. car*** vehículo *m* utilizado en la fuga (**b**) *Aut (start)* arranque *m*; *(in racing)* salida *f* (**c**) *US (short holiday)* escapada *f*

get-go ['getgəʊ] *n US Fam* **from the g.** *(from the beginning)* desde el principio

get-out ['getaʊt] *n* (**a**) (means of escape) salida *f*, escapatoria *f* ▸▸ ***g. clause*** cláusula *f* de salvaguardia (**b**) *Fam* **as drunk/mad as (all) g.** como una cuba/cabra

get-rich-quick [getrɪtʃ'kwɪk] *adj Fam* **a g. scheme** un proyecto para enriquecerse rápidamente

get-there ['getðeə(r)] *n US Fam* empuje *m*, *RP* polenta *f*

get-together ['gettəgeðə(r)] *n Fam* reunión *f*; **we're having a g. with some friends** nos vamos a juntar con unos cuantos amigos

get-up ['getʌp] *n Fam (clothes)* indumentaria *f*; *(fancy dress)* disfraz *m*

get-up-and-go ['getʌpən'gəʊ] *n Fam (energy)* dinamismo *m*, iniciativa *f*; *Hum* **my g. has got up and went** *or* **gone** se me acabaron las pilas

get-well card [get'welkɑːd] *n* = tarjeta con que se desea a un enfermo su mejoría

gewgaw ['gjuːgɔː] *n Old-fashioned* baratija *f*

geyser ['giːzə(r)] *n* (**a**) *Geog* géiser *m* (**b**) *Br Old-fashioned (water heater)* calentador *m* (de agua)

G-force ['dʒiːfɔːs] *n* fuerza *f* de gravedad

Ghana ['gɑːnə] *n* Ghana

Ghanaian [gɑː'neɪən] 1 *n* ghanés(esa) *m,f*
2 *adj* ghanés(esa)

ghastliness ['gɑːstlɪnɪs] *n* (**a**) *(of crime)* lo horrendo, lo espantoso (**b**) *(of place, sight, situation)* lo horrible, lo horroroso(a)

ghastly ['gɑːstlɪ] *adj* (**a**) *(horrific)* horroroso(a), horrible (**b**) *Fam (very bad)* horroroso(a), horrible; **he looked g.** tenía un aspecto horroroso *or* horrible; **how g.!** ¡qué horror!; **she wore the most g. outfit** llevaba un vestido horroroso; **it was all a g. mistake** todo fue un tremendo error (**c**) *Fam (ill)* **I feel g.** me siento horrible *or Esp* fatal

ghee [giː] *n* mantequilla *f* clarificada *(empleada en la cocina india)*

Ghent [gent] *n* Gante

gherkin ['gɜːkɪn] *n* pepinillo *m*

ghetto ['getəʊ] *(pl* **ghettos**) *n* gueto *m*

ghetto-blaster ['getəʊ'blɑːstə(r)] *n Fam (cassette player)* radiocasete *m* portátil *(de gran tamaño)*

ghettoize ['getəʊaɪz] *vt* marginar (como en un gueto)

ghillie = **gillie**

ghost [gəʊst] 1 *n* (**a**) *(spirit)* fantasma *m*; **to believe in ghosts** creer en fantasmas; **you look as if you've just seen a g.!** ¡ni que hubieras visto un fantasma!; IDIOM *US Fam* **to get g.** desaparecer; IDIOM **to give up the g.** pasar a mejor vida; IDIOM **to lay the g. of sth to rest** enterrar el fantasma de algo ▸▸ ***g. story*** relato *m* de fantasmas; ***g. town*** pueblo *m* fantasma; ***g. train*** tren *m* fantasma
(**b**) *(trace, hint)* **the g. of a smile** la sombra de una sonrisa; **she doesn't have the g. of a chance** no tiene ni la más remota posibilidad
(**c**) ***g. writer*** negro(a) *m,f*, escritor(ora) *m,f* anónimo(a)
2 *vt* **to g. a book for sb** escribir anónimamente un libro para alguien

ghostly ['gəʊstlɪ] *adj* fantasmal, fantasmagórico(a)

ghostwrite ['gəʊstraɪt] *vt* **to g. a book for sb** escribir anónimamente un libro para alguien

ghoul [guːl] *n* (**a**) *(evil spirit)* espíritu *m* maligno (**b**) *(morbid person)* morboso(a) *m,f*; **don't be such a g.!** ¡no seas morboso!

ghoulish ['guːlɪʃ] *adj* morboso(a)

ghoulishly ['guːlɪʃlɪ] *adv* morbosamente

GHQ [dʒiːeɪtʃ'kjuː] *n Mil* (*abbr* **General Headquarters**) cuartel *m* general

GHz *Elec* (*abbr* **gigahertz**) GHz

GI [dʒiː'aɪ] *n US Fam* soldado *m* raso; **GI Joe** soldado estadounidense ▸▸ ***GI bill*** = ley por la que se facilitó la formación de los veteranos de guerra; ***GI bride*** = esposa extranjera de un soldado americano

giant ['dʒaɪənt] 1 *n* (**a**) *(in size)* gigante(a) *m,f*; **a g. of a man** un hombre enorme, un gigante ▸▸ ***g. killer*** *(in sport)* matagigantes *mf inv* (**b**) *(in importance, achievement)* **a literary g.** un gigante de la literatura; **an industrial g.** *(company)* un gigante industrial
2 *adj* colosal, gigantesco(a); **with g. strides** con enormes zancadas; **the campaign has made g. strides (forward)** la campaña ha avanzado enormemente ▸▸ ***g. panda*** (oso *m*) panda *m*, panda *m* gigante; ***g. redwood*** secuoya *f* gigante; ***g. slalom*** *(in skiing)* eslalon *m or* slalom *m* gigante; ***g. tortoise*** tortuga *f* gigante

giantess ['dʒaɪəntes] *n* giganta *f*

giant-size(d) ['dʒaɪəntsaɪz(d)] *adj (pack)* de tamaño gigante

Gib [dʒɪb] *n Fam* el Peñón

gibber ['dʒɪbə(r)] *vi* (**a**) *(monkey)* parlotear (**b**) *(talk incoherently)* farfullar

gibbering ['dʒɪbərɪŋ] *adj* incoherente, desvariado(a); **I was a g. wreck!** ¡no podía articular una sola frase!; *Fam* **a g. idiot** un perfecto idiota

gibberish ['dʒɪbərɪʃ] *n (unintelligible speech, writing)* galimatías *m inv*; *(nonsense)* tonterías *fpl*, memeces *fpl*; **it's complete g. to me** me resulta totalmente ininteligible; **to talk g.** decir tonterías *or* memeces

gibbet ['dʒɪbɪt] *n* horca *f*

gibbon ['gɪbən] *n* gibón *m*

gibe [dʒaɪb] 1 *n* burla *f*
2 *vi* **to g. at sb** hacer burla de alguien

giblets ['dʒɪbləts] *npl* menudillos *mpl*

Gibraltar [dʒɪ'brɔːltə(r)] *n* Gibraltar

Gibraltarian [dʒɪbrɔːl'teərɪən] *n* gibraltareño(a) *m,f*

giddily ['gɪdɪlɪ] *adv* (**a**) *(dizzily)* vertiginosamente (**b**) *(frivolously)* frívolamente, con frivolidad

giddiness ['gɪdɪnɪs] *n* (**a**) *(dizziness)* mareo *m*; *(from height)* vértigo *m* (**b**) *(frivolity)* frivolidad *f*

giddy ['gɪdɪ] *adj* (**a**) *(dizzy)* **to be g.** estar mareado(a); *(from height)* tener vértigo; **I feel g. just watching them** me da vértigo sólo mirarlos; **a g. round of parties** una racha frenética de fiestas
(**b**) *(lofty)* **g. heights** altas cotas *or* cumbres; *Ironic* **to reach the g. heights of deputy assistant inspector** alcanzar el alto honor de ser ayudante del subinspector
(**c**) *(frivolous) (person, behaviour)* atolondrado(a); *Br Fam Old-fashioned* **my g. aunt!** ¡vaya por Dios!

▸ **giddy up** 1 *vt sep* presionar, apurar
2 *exclam (to horse)* ¡arre!

GIF [dʒɪf] *n Comptr* (*abbr* **Graphics Interchange Format**) GIF *m*

gift [gɪft] 1 *n* (**a**) *(present)* regalo *m*, obsequio *m*; **a g. from the gods** *or* **from God** un regalo de Dios, una bendición divina; PROV **never look a g. horse in the mouth** a caballo regalado no le mires el diente ▸▸ *US* ***g. certificate*** vale *m* de regalo; ***g. shop*** tienda *f* de artículos de regalo; *Br* ***g. token*** vale *m* de regalo; *Rel* ***the g. of tongues*** el don de lenguas; *Br* ***g. voucher*** vale *m* de regalo; ***g. wrap*** papel *m* de regalo; ***g. wrapping*** papel *m* de regalo
(**b**) *(talent)* don *m*; **to have a g. for mathematics** tener un don especial para las matemáticas; **he has a great g. for telling jokes** tiene mucho talento para contar chistes; **she has a g. for putting her foot in it** tiene un don especial para meter la pata, lo de meter la pata se le da como a nadie; IDIOM **to have the g. of the gab** tener un pico de oro
(**c**) *Fam (bargain)* **at £5, it's a g.** a 5 libras está regalado
(**d**) *Fam (easy thing)* **that exam question was a g.** la pregunta del examen estaba tirada
(**e**) *(power of donation)* **to be in sb's g.** estar en manos de alguien
2 *vt* (**a**) *US Formal (present)* donar; **gifted by Mr Evans** *(on plaque)* donado por el Sr. Evans, donación del Sr. Evans (**b**) *(give away)* entregar, regalar

gifted ['gɪftɪd] *adj (talented)* dotado(a); *(unusually talented)* superdotado(a)

giftwrap ['gɪftræp] *vt* envolver con papel de regalo; **would you like it giftwrapped?** ¿se lo envuelvo para regalo?

gig [gɪg] *n* (**a**) *(carriage)* calesa *f* (**b**) *Fam (concert)* actuación *f*, concierto *m*

gigabyte ['dʒɪgəbaɪt, 'gɪgəbaɪt] *n Comptr* gigabyte *m*

gigahertz ['dʒɪgəhɜːts, 'gɪgəhɜːts] *n Elec* gigahercio *m*

gigantic [dʒaɪ'gæntɪk] *adj* gigantesco(a)

gigantism [dʒaɪ'gæntɪzəm] *n Med* gigantismo *m*

giggle ['gɪgəl] 1 *n* (**a**) *(laugh)* risita *f*, risa *f* floja; **to get the giggles, to have a fit of the giggles** tener un ataque de risa tonta (**b**) *esp Br Fam (source of amusement)* **the evening was a g. from start to finish** la tarde fue superdivertida; **to do sth for a g.** hacer algo de broma
2 *vi* soltar risitas

giggly ['gɪglɪ] *adj* **she goes all g.** le entra la risa tonta; **two g. girls at the back of the class** dos niñas soltando risitas al fondo de la clase

GIGO ['gaɪgəʊ] *Comptr* (*abbr* **garbage in garbage out**) = información errónea genera resultados erróneos

gigolo ['dʒɪgələʊ] (*pl* **gigolos**) *n* gigoló *m*

gigot ['dʒɪgət] *n* pierna *f* de cordero

Gila monster ['hiːləmɒnstə(r)] *n* monstruo *m* de Gila

gild [gɪld] (*pt & pp* **gilded** *or* **gilt** [gɪlt]) *vt* dorar; IDIOM **to g. the lily** rizar el rizo

gilded ['gɪldɪd] *adj* dorado(a); IDIOM **to be like a bird in a g. cage** estar en una jaula de oro ▸▸ ***g. youth*** dorada juventud *f*

gilding ['gɪldɪŋ] *n* dorado *m*

gill[1] [gɪl] *n* (**a**) **gills** *(of fish)* branquias; IDIOM **to be/go green about the gills** *(look unwell)* estar/ponerse blanco(a) como la cera (**b**) *(of mushroom)* lámina *f*

gill[2] [dʒɪl] *n (liquid measure)* cuarto *m* de pinta *(= 0,142 litros)*

gillie, ghillie ['gɪlɪ] *n Scot (for hunting, fishing)* ayudante *m*

gillyflower ['dʒɪlɪflaʊə(r)] *n* clavellina *f*, clavel *m* silvestre

gilt [gɪlt] 1 *n* (**a**) *(gilding)* (baño *m*) dorado *m*; IDIOM **to take the g. off the gingerbread** quitarle la gracia a algo (**b**) *Br Fin* **gilts** valores del Estado
2 *adj* dorado(a)
3 *pt & pp of* **gild**

gilt-edged ['gɪlt'edʒd] *adj* (**a**) *Fin* ***g. securities*** *or* ***stock*** *Br* títulos *mpl* de deuda pública, valores *mpl* del Estado; *US* títulos *mpl* or valores *mpl* de máxima garantía (**b**) *(book, page)* de bordes dorados (**c**) *(opportunity)* único(a), de oro

gimbals ['dʒɪmbəlz] *npl Tech* soporte *m* cardánico, suspensión *f* universal

gimcrack ['dʒɪmkræk] *adj* de pacotilla

gimlet ['gɪmlɪt] *n* (**a**) *(tool)* barrena *f*; **his g. eyes** su mirada penetrante (**b**) *(cocktail)* = cóctel hecho con vodka o ginebra y lima

gimme ['gɪmiː] *Fam* 1 = **give me**
2 *n* (**a**) *US* IDIOM **she has the gimmes** la vuelven loca los regalos ▸▸ *US* ***g. cap*** *or* ***hat*** gorra *f* de béisbol con logo publicitario (**b**) *(easy question)* pregunta *f* facilona

gimmick ['gɪmɪk] *n* reclamo *m*, truco *m*; **an advertising g.** un reclamo publicitario; **it's just a sales g.** es sólo un reclamo para vender más; **the voters aren't fooled by election gimmicks** los votantes no se dejan engañar por reclamos electoralistas

gimmickry ['gɪmɪkrɪ] *n* reclamos *mpl*, trucos *mpl*

gimmicky ['gɪmɪkɪ] *adj* artificioso(a)

gimp [gɪmp] *n US very Fam (person with limp)* cojo(a) *m,f*, *Esp* cojitranco(a) *m,f*

gin [dʒɪn] *n* (**a**) *(drink)* ginebra *f*; **g. and tonic** gin-tonic; **g. and it** martini, = cóctel a base de ginebra y vermú italiano ▸▸ *Br Fam* ***g. palace*** pub *m* tradicional; ***g. sling*** gin sling *m*, = cóctel a base de ginebra con mucho hielo, limón y licor de cerezas (**b**) *(trap)* ***g. trap*** lazo *m (trampa de caza)* (**c**) *(machine)* limpiadora *f* de algodón (**d**) *(card game)* **g. (rummy)** gin rummy *m*

ginger ['dʒɪndʒə(r)] 1 *n* (**a**) *(spice)* jengibre *m*; **root** *or* **fresh g.** jengibre fresco; **ground** *or* **powdered g.** jengibre en polvo ▸▸ ***g. ale*** ginger ale *m*; ***g. beer*** refresco *m* de jengibre; *Br* ***g. nut*** galleta *f* de jengibre; ***g. snap*** galleta *f* de jengibre; ***g. wine*** vino *m* de jengibre (**b**) *(colour)* rojo *m* anaranjado (**c**) *(redhead)* **oi g.!** ¡pelirrojo! (**d**) *Br* ***g. group*** grupo *m* de presión
2 *adj* **she has g. hair** es pelirroja; **a g. cat** un gato rojizo

▸ **ginger up** *vt sep Fam* animar

gingerbread ['dʒɪndʒəbred] *n* (**a**) *(cake)* pan *m* de jengibre (**b**) *(biscuit)* galleta *f* de jengibre ▸▸ ***g. man*** galleta *f* de jengibre *(con forma de figura humana)*

gingerly ['dʒɪndʒəlɪ] 1 *adv* con mucho tiento *or* cuidado
2 *adj* delicado(a), suave; **to do sth in a g. fashion** hacer algo con mucho tiento *or* cuidado

gingery ['dʒɪndʒərɪ] *adj* (**a**) *(colour)* bermejo(a); *(hair)* pelirrojo(a) (**b**) *(taste)* a jengibre

gingham ['gɪŋəm] *n* guinga *f*, = tela de algodón a cuadros

gingivitis [dʒɪndʒɪ'vaɪtɪs] *n Med* gingivitis *f inv*

gingko ['gɪŋkəʊ] *n Bot* ginkgo *m*

gink [gɪŋk] *n US Fam* bicho *m* raro

ginormous [dʒaɪ'nɔːməs] *adj Fam* requetegrande

ginseng ['dʒɪnseŋ] *n* ginseng *m*

gippo ['dʒɪpəʊ] (*pl* **gippoes**) *n Br Fam Pej* gitano(a) *m,f*

gippy tummy ['dʒɪpɪ'tʌmɪ] *n Br Fam Esp* descomposición *f*, *Am* descompostura *f*; **to have a g.** estar descompuesto(a)

gipsy = **gypsy**

giraffe [dʒɪ'rɑːf] *n* jirafa *f*

gird [gɜːd] (*pt & pp* **girded** *or* **girt** [gɜːt]) *vt Literary* IDIOM **to g. (up) one's loins** armarse para la batalla; **a sea-girt country** un país rodeado de mar

girder ['gɜːdə(r)] *n* viga *f*

girdle ['gɜːdəl] 1 *n* (**a**) *(corset)* faja *f* (**b**) *Literary (belt)* cinturón *m* (**c**) *Anat* **pelvic/pectoral g.** anillo pélvico/pectoral
2 *vt Literary* ceñir

girl [gɜːl] *n*

girl [gɜːl] *n* (**a**) *(child, baby)* niña *f*; **I'd known him since we were girls** lo conocía desde que éramos niñas
(**b**) *(young woman)* chica *f* ▸▸ ***g. band*** grupo *m* musical de mujeres; ***g. Friday*** chica *f* para todo; *Br* ***G. Guide*** scout *f*, escultista *f*; *US* ***G. Scout*** scout *f*, escultista *f*
(**c**) *(daughter)* niña *f*, hija *f*; *(older)* hija *f*; **they have three girls** tienen tres niñas *or* hijas; **the Smiths' g.** la niña *or* hija de los Smith; **their little g.** su niña
(**d**) *(female adult)* chica *f*; **he's gone out with the girls from the office** ha salido con las chicas de la oficina
(**e**) *Fam (term of address)* **my dear g.** mi querida niña; **that's my g.!** *(well done)* ¡muy bien!; *Br* **how are you, old g.?** ¿cómo estás, cielo?
(**f**) *Fam Old-fashioned (girlfriend)* chica *f*
(**g**) *(addressing dog, horse)* **down, g.!** ¡échate, linda!

girlfriend ['gɜːlfrend] *n* (**a**) *(in relationship)* novia *f* (**b**) *(friend)* amiga *f* (**c**) *US Fam (term of address)* **g., you're way out of line** tú exageras, chica

girlhood ['gɜːlhʊd] *n* niñez *f*

girlie, girly ['gɜːlɪ] *Fam* 1 *n* chica *f*, nena *f*, *Arg* piba *f*, *Méx* chava *f*
2 *adj* (**a**) *Pej (girlish)* de chica *or Arg* piba *or Méx* chava; **g. things** cosas de chicas; **it looks a bit g. on you** tienes pinta de chica con eso; *Br* **to have a g. chat** charlar de cosas de chicas (**b**) ***g. mag*** revista *f* de chicas desnudas; ***g. magazine*** revista *f* de chicas desnudas

girlish ['gɜːlɪʃ] *adj* (**a**) *(of girl, young woman)* de niña (**b**) *(man)* afeminado(a)

giro ['dʒaɪrəʊ] *(pl* **giros***) n Br* (**a**) *Fin* **to pay by bank g.** pagar con giro bancario ▸▸ ***g. account*** cuenta *f* de giros postales (**b**) *Fam (unemployment cheque)* cheque *m* del desempleo *or Esp* paro

girt *pt & pp of* **gird**

girth [gɜːθ] *n* (**a**) *(of tree)* contorno *m* (**b**) *(stoutness)* barriga *f* (**c**) *(of saddle)* cincha *f*

gism = **jism**

gismo, gizmo ['gɪzməʊ] *(pl* **gismos, gizmos***) n Fam* chisme *m*, aparato *m*

gist [dʒɪst] *n* esencia *f*; **the g. of what she was saying was...** la esencia de lo que decía era...; **give me the g. of the discussion** cuéntame qué fue, en esencia, lo que se discutió; **to get the g. (of sth)** entender la esencia *or* el sentido general (de algo)

git[1] [gɪt] *n Br very Fam Esp* capullo(a) *m,f*, *Am* pendejo(a) *m,f*

git[2] *exclam US Fam* ¡fuera!

GIVE [gɪv] **1** *vt (pt* **gave** [geɪv], *pp* **given** ['gɪvən]) (**a**) *(in general)* dar; *(blood, sperm)* dar, donar; *(as present)* regalar; **to g. sth to sb, to g. sb sth** dar algo a alguien; *(as present)* regalar algo a alguien; **g. it to me** dámelo; **g. the money to John** dale el dinero a John; **we were each given different orders** cada uno de nosotros recibió diferentes órdenes; **to g. sb sth to eat** dar algo de comer a alguien; **to g. sb a present** dar a alguien un regalo, regalar algo a alguien; **to g. a child a name** ponerle nombre a un niño; **g. her my love** dale recuerdos *or Am* cariños de mi parte; **I'll g. you $20 for it** te doy 20 dólares por él; **can you g. me something for the pain?** ¿me podría dar algo para el dolor?; **I wouldn't g. much for their chances** no creo que tengan muchas posibilidades; **g. me a good book any day** *or* **every time** prefiero un buen libro mil veces; *Br Vulg* **to g. sb one** *(have sex with)* echar un polvo con alguien; **she gives as good as she gets** sabe defenderse

(**b**) *(organize) (party, dinner, dance)* dar, hacer

(**c**) *(cause)* dar; **to g. sb trouble** molestar a alguien; **to g. sb a fright** dar un susto a alguien; **to g. sb a headache** dar dolor de cabeza a alguien; **to g. sb an illness** contagiarle *or* pegarle una enfermedad a alguien; **he gives me the impression that he couldn't care less** me da la impresión de que no le importa nada

(**d**) *(allow)* dar; *(rights, power)* dar, conceder; **to g. sb a choice** dar a alguien una elección; **given the chance (again)** si se presentara (de nuevo) la ocasión *or* oportunidad; **given the choice, I'd emigrate to Canada** si pudiera elegir, emigraría a Canadá; **she has been given six months to live** le han dado seis meses de vida

(**e**) *(devote)* **I'll g. my full attention to the matter** pondré toda mi atención en el asunto; **to g. a lot of thought to sth** considerar algo a fondo; **he gave his all, he gave it everything he'd got** dio todo de sí

(**f**) *(lend)* **it gives her an air of distinction** le da un aire de distinción; **his name gives authority to the study** su nombre (le) confiere autoridad al estudio

(**g**) *(tell)* **he gave his age as twenty** declaró que tenía veinte años; **the clock gave the time as midnight** el reloj marcaba la medianoche; *Formal* **she gave me to understand that...** me dio a entender que...; *Formal* **I was given to understand that...** se me dio a entender que...; **g. it to me straight!** *(tell me the truth)* ¡sé franco conmigo!; *Fam* **don't g. me that (nonsense)!** ¡no me vengas con ésas!

(**h**) *(sentence to)* imponer, sentenciar a; **he was given ten years** le cayeron diez años; **she was given a fine** le pusieron una multa

(**i**) *(concede)* **he's intelligent, I'll g. you that, but I still don't like him** es inteligente, de acuerdo, pero me sigue sin gustar

(**j**) *Sport (adjudge)* **the referee gave a penalty** el árbitro señaló penalti *or RP* penal, *CSur* el juez cobró penal; **the umpire gave the ball out** el juez de silla decidió que la bola había salido

(**k**) *(estimate the duration of)* dar; **I g. him one week at most** le echo *or* doy como mucho una semana

(**l**) *Formal (present)* **ladies and gentlemen, I g. you the mayor of Boston!** ¡damas y caballeros, con ustedes el alcalde de Boston!

(**m**) *Old-fashioned* **to g. oneself to sb** *(have sex with)* entregarse a alguien

(**n**) *(with noun, to form verbal expressions)* **to g. evidence** testificar, prestar declaración, *RP* atestiguar; **to g. sb a kick** dar una patada a alguien; **to g. a laugh** soltar una carcajada; **she gave me a strange look** me lanzó una extraña mirada; **to g. a sigh** dar *or* lanzar un suspiro; **to g. sb a smile** sonreírle a alguien; **to g. a speech** dar *or* pronunciar un discurso; **she gave the soup a stir** removió *or* revolvió la sopa; **he gave his face a wash** se lavó la cara

2 *vi* (**a**) *(donate)* hacer donativos *or Am* donaciones; **please g. generously** por favor, sea generoso en sus donativos *or Am* donaciones; **he gave of his free time to the cause** dedicó parte de su tiempo libre a la causa; **he gave of his best** dio lo mejor de sí mismo; **to g. of oneself** entregarse a los demás

(**b**) *(bend, stretch)* dar de sí, ceder; *(break)* ceder, romperse; **she refused to g. on the question of money** se negó a ceder en la cuestión del dinero; **we can't continue like this, something will have to g.** no podemos seguir así, algo va a tener que cambiar

(**c**) *US Fam* **what gives?** ¿qué pasa?

3 *n* elasticidad *f*; **this fabric hasn't got much g.** este tejido no da mucho de sí *or* no cede demasiado

4 give or take *prep* **g. or take a few minutes/pesos** minuto/peso arriba o abajo, minuto/peso más o menos

▸ **give away** *vt sep* (**a**) *(give for nothing)* regalar; **it was in such bad condition, I couldn't even g. it away** estaba en tal malas condiciones que no lo podía dar ni regalado

(**b**) *(prize)* repartir

(**c**) *(by mistake, carelessness) (chance, opportunity)* regalar; **they gave away an easy goal** regalaron un gol fácil

(**d**) *(at wedding)* **to g. the bride away** llevar a la novia al altar; **she was given away by her father** su padre la llevó hasta el altar

(**e**) *(reveal)* revelar; **to g. away details/a secret** revelar detalles/un secreto; **he didn't g. much away in the interview** no reveló mucho en la entrevista

(**f**) *(betray)* delatar; **his accomplices gave him away (to the police)** sus cómplices lo delataron (a la policía); **his accent gave him away** su acento lo delató; **to g. oneself away** delatarse, descubrirse

▸ **give back** *vt sep* devolver; **to g. sth back to sb, to g. sb sth back** devolver algo a alguien

▸ **give in 1** *vt sep (hand over)* entregar

2 *vi (surrender)* rendirse (**to** a); *(admit defeat)* rendirse, darse por vencido(a); **we will not g. in to their demands** no cederemos ante sus demandas; **I gave in to the pressure** cedí ante la presión; **I nearly gave in to the urge to hit him** casi no me aguanto y le pego

▸ **give off** *vt sep (smell, heat)* despedir

▸ **give onto** *vt insep (of window, door)* dar a

▸ **give out 1** *vt sep* (**a**) *(money, food)* repartir; *(information)* divulgar (**b**) *(announce)* anunciar; **it was given out that he was leaving** anunciaron que se marchaba (**c**) *(noise, heat)* emitir; *(cry)* dar, lanzar

2 *vi (supplies, patience)* agotarse; *(luck)* acabarse; *(machine)* estropearse; *(heart)* pararse

▸ **give over 1** *vt sep* (**a**) *(hand over) (money, objects)* entregar (**b**) *(devote)* dedicar; **most of the land is given over to agriculture** la mayor parte de la tierra está dedicada a usos agrarios; **to g. oneself over to sth** entregarse a algo

2 *vi Br Fam* (**a**) *(stop)* **g. over, will you?** déjalo ya, ¿quieres?; **g. over criticizing!** ¡ya basta de criticar! (**b**) *(expressing disbelief)* **we're getting married – g. over!** nos vamos a casar – ¡anda ya!

▸ **give up 1** *vt sep* (**a**) *(possessions, activity, hope)* abandonar, renunciar a; *(boyfriend, girlfriend)* abandonar; **to g. up one's job** dejar el trabajo; **I'm giving up chocolate for Lent** voy a renunciar al chocolate durante la cuaresma; **she gave her seat up to an old man** cedió su asiento a un hombre mayor; **to g. up smoking** dejar de fumar; **I've given up hoping** he perdido la esperanza; **to g. sb up for adoption** dar a alguien en adopción; **to g. sb up for dead** dar a alguien por muerto(a)

(**b**) *(denounce)* delatar; **he gave his accomplices up (to the police)** delató a sus cómplices (a la policía); **to g. oneself up** *(to police)* entregarse

(**c**) *(devote) (time)* dedicar

(**d**) *Fam* **g. it up for sb: give it up for our next guest** un gran aplauso para nuestro próximo invitado

2 *vi (stop trying)* rendirse, darse por vencido(a); **I g. up, I don't know the answer** me rindo, no sé la respuesta; **I g. up, there's clearly no point trying to convince you** me rindo *or* me doy por vencido, está claro que no vale la pena intentar convencerte; **to g. up on sth/sb** *(lose faith, hope in)* dejar algo/a alguien por imposible; **the doctors have given up on her** los médicos la han desahuciado; **we had given up on ever finding them** habíamos perdido todas las esperanzas de encontrarlos; **we've been waiting since five, we'd almost given up on you** llevamos esperando desde las cinco, casi pensábamos que no venías

▸ **give up to** *vt sep* **they gave themselves up to a life of pleasure** se entregaron a una vida de placer; **he gave his life up to caring for the elderly** dedicó su vida a cuidar a los ancianos

▸ **give way** *vi* (**a**) *(collapse)* ceder, hundirse (**b**) *(yield) (in argument)* ceder (**to** ante); *(in car)* ceder el paso (**to** a); **g. way** *(sign)* ceda el paso (**c**) *(be superseded)* verse desbancado(a) (**to** por); **her tears gave way to laughter** las lágrimas dieron paso a la risa

give-and-take ['gɪvən'teɪk] *n* (**a**) *(compromise)* concesiones *fpl* mutuas, toma y daca *m* (**b**) *(in conversation)* intercambio *m*

giveaway ['gɪvəweɪ] *n Fam* (**a**) *(revelation)* señal *f* reveladora; **her guilty expression was a dead g.** la delató su cara de culpa (**b**) *(free gift)* obsequio *m*; **a g. budget** un presupuesto que beneficia al contribuyente ▸▸ ***g. price*** precio *m* de saldo

giveback ['gɪvbæk] *n Fam* vuelta *f*

given ['gɪvən] **1** *adj* (**a**) *(specific) (time, place)* dado(a), determinado(a); **at any g. time** en todo momento, en cualquier momento; **at a g. point** en un momento dado ▸▸ ***g. name*** nombre *m* (de pila)
(**b**) **to be g. to** *(in the habit of)* ser dado(a) a; *(prone to)* ser propenso(a) a; **to be g. to doing sth** ser dado(a) a hacer algo; **he's g. to attacks of depression** es propenso a las depresiones
(**c**) *Formal (on official statement)* **g. in Melbourne on the sixth day of March** emitido(a) en Melbourne el seis de marzo
2 *conj* (**a**) *(considering)* dado(a); **g. the nature of the case** dada la naturaleza del caso; **g. that we need a new carpet anyway...** dado que necesitamos una alfombra de todos modos... (**b**) *Math* **g. the rectangle ABCD...** dado el rectángulo ABCD...
3 *n (sure fact)* hecho *m*
4 *pp of* **give**

giver ['gɪvə(r)] *n (of money, present)* **the g. of the largest donation** quien haga la mayor donación

giving ['gɪvɪŋ] *adj* desprendido(a), generoso(a)

gizmo = **gismo**

gizzard ['gɪzəd] *n* molleja *f*; IDIOM **it sticks in my g.** se me atraganta

glacé ['glæseɪ] *adj Culin* confitado(a), escarchado(a), *Col, Méx* cristalizado(a), *RP* abrillantado(a) ▸▸ ***g. cherries*** cerezas *fpl* confitadas; ***g. icing*** baño *m* de azúcar *Esp, Méx* glas *or Chile* flor *or Col* pulverizado *or RP* impalpable

glacial ['gleɪsɪəl, *US* 'gleɪʃəl] *adj* (**a**) *Geol (erosion, valley)* glacial ▸▸ ***g. period*** glaciación *f*, periodo *m* glacial (**b**) *Fam (temperatures, wind)* glacial (**c**) *(manner, atmosphere)* glacial

glaciation [gleɪsɪ'eɪʃən] *n* glaciación *f*

glacier ['glæsɪə(r), *US* 'gleɪʃər] *n* glaciar *m*

glad [glæd] *adj* (**a**) *(happy)* **to be g. (about sth)** alegrarse (de algo); **I'm feeling a lot better today – I am g.!** hoy me siento mucho mejor – ¡me alegro!; **I'm (so) g. you came** me alegro (mucho) de que hayas venido; **I'm g. about that** me alegro; **to be g. to do sth** estar encantado(a) de hacer algo; **I'd be only too g. to help** me encantaría poder ayudar; **could you do me a favour? – I'd be g. to** ¿podrías hacerme un favor? – con mucho gusto *or* encantado; IDIOM **to give sb the g. eye** mirar a alguien de forma insinuante *or* provocadora; IDIOM **to give sb the g. hand** dar apretones de manos efusivos a alguien ▸▸ *Fam* ***g. rags*** ropa *f* elegante; **to put on one's g. rags** acicalarse
(**b**) *(grateful)* **to be g. of sth** agradecer algo
(**c**) *Literary (news, occasion)* feliz ▸▸ ***g. tidings*** buenas nuevas *fpl*

gladden ['glædən] *vt* alegrar, llenar de contento; **it gladdens my heart to see them** verlos me alegra el corazón

glade [gleɪd] *n Literary* calvero *m*, claro *m*

glad-hand ['glædhænd] *vt US Fam* dar apretones de manos efusivos a

gladiator ['glædɪeɪtə(r)] *n Hist* gladiador *m*

gladiatorial [glædɪə'tɔːrɪəl] *adj* (**a**) *Hist (combat, contest)* de gladiadores (**b**) *(combative)* combativo(a); **g. politics** política de confrontación

gladiolus [glædɪ'əʊləs] (*pl* **gladioli** [glædɪ'əʊlaɪ]) *n* gladiolo *m*

gladly ['glædlɪ] *adv* con mucho gusto

gladness ['glædnɪs] *n* alegría *f*, regocijo *m*

glam [glæm] *n Fam* glamour *m* ▸▸ *Mus* ***g. rock*** (música *f*) glam *m*, glam rock *m*

▸ **glam up** *vt sep Fam* arreglar, acicalar; **to g. oneself up** acicalarse

glamor *US* = **glamour**

glamorization [glæməraɪ'zeɪʃən] *n* idealización *f*

glamorize ['glæməraɪz] *vt* dar una visión idealizada de

glamorous ['glæmərəs] *adj* glamouroso(a), sofisticado(a); **working in the film industry is not always g.** trabajar en el cine no es siempre tan glamouroso como parece; **a g. grandmother** *or Fam* **granny** una abuela que aún se conserva

glamorously ['glæmərəslɪ] *adv* con una elegancia deslumbrante

glamorpuss *US* = **glamourpuss**

glamour, *US* **glamor** ['glæmə(r)] *n* glamour *m*, sofisticación *f*; **there isn't much g. in this job** este trabajo no tiene nada de glamour ▸▸ *Fam* ***g. boy*** *Esp* guaperas *m inv*, *Am* guapetón *m*; ***g. girl*** bombón *m*, *Am* muñequita *f*

glamourpuss, *US* **glamorpuss** ['glæməpʊs] *n Fam* bombón *m*, cara *f* bonita

glance [glɑːns] **1** *n* vistazo *m*, ojeada *f*; **to have** *or* **take a g. at** echar un vistazo a; **he cast an affectionate/anxious g. in her direction** le lanzó una mirada de afecto/preocupación; **to give sb a sidelong g.** mirar a alguien rápidamente de reojo; **at a g.** de un vistazo; **at first g.** a primera vista
2 *vi* (**a**) *(look)* **to g. at** echar un vistazo a; **he glanced away** miró a otro sitio; **he glanced back** miró hacia atrás; **he glanced up** miró hacia arriba; **he glanced down** miró hacia abajo, bajó los ojos; **she glanced round the room** echó un vistazo por la habitación; **I glanced towards the door** miré hacia la puerta
(**b**) *(read quickly)* **to g. through** *(book, magazine)* dar un vistazo a, ojear; **she glanced through** *or* **over the letter** le dio un vistazo a *or* ojeó la carta
(**c**) *(gleam)* destellar, fulgurar

▸ **glance off 1** *vt insep (of blow, missile)* rebotar en
2 *vi (blow, missile)* desviarse

glancing ['glɑːnsɪŋ] *adj (blow)* de lado, de refilón

gland [glænd] *n Anat* glándula *f*

glandes *pl of* **glans**

glandular ['glændjʊlə(r)] *adj* glandular ▸▸ ***g. fever*** mononucleosis *f inv* infecciosa

glans [glænz] (*pl* **glandes** ['glændiːz]) *n Anat* **g. (penis)** glande *m*

glare [gleə(r)] **1** *n* (**a**) *(angry stare)* mirada *f* feroz (**b**) *(bright light)* resplandor *m*; **he stood in the g. of the headlights** se quedó parado ante la luz deslumbrante de los faros; *Fig* **in the full g. of publicity** en el punto de mira de toda la gente ▸▸ *Comptr* ***g. filter*** filtro *m* de pantalla; *Comptr* ***g. screen*** filtro *m* de pantalla
2 *vt* **to g. hatred/defiance at sb** lanzar a alguien una mirada iracunda/desafiante
3 *vi* (**a**) *(stare angrily)* **to g. at sth/sb** mirar algo/a alguien con furia; **he glared angrily at me** me lanzó una mirada de furia (**b**) *(sun, light)* resplanceder, fulgurar; **the sun glared down on them** un sol de plomo les deslumbraba

glaring ['gleərɪŋ] *adj* (**a**) *(light)* deslumbrante (**b**) *(omission, mistake, injustice)* flagrante

glaringly ['gleərɪŋlɪ] *adv* **g. obvious** clarísimo(a), de una claridad meridiana

glasnost ['glæznɒst] *n Pol* glásnost *f*, apertura *f* política

glass [glɑːs] *n* (**a**) *(material)* vidrio *m*, *Esp* cristal *m*; **to grow sth under g.** cultivar algo en invernadero; **a g. bottle** una botella de vidrio *or Esp* cristal ▸▸ ***g. case*** vitrina *f*; *Fig* ***g. ceiling*** *(in career)* barreras *fpl* laborales *or* profesionales; ***g. eye*** ojo *m* de vidrio *or Esp* cristal; ***g. factory*** fábrica *f* de vidrio; *US* ***g. fiber*** fibra *f* de vidrio; *Br* ***g. fibre*** fibra *f* de vidrio; *Fam* ***g. jaw:*** **to have a g. jaw** tener mandíbula de cristal; ***g. wool*** lana *f* de vidrio
(**b**) *(vessel)* vaso *m*; *(with stem)* copa *f*; **a g. of wine** un vaso de vino; **a champagne/wine g.** una copa de champán/vino; **to sell wine by the g.** vender copas de vino; **to raise one's g. to sb** *(in toast)* alzar la copa *or* brindar por alguien
(**c**) *(glassware)* cristalería *f*
(**d**) *(mirror)* **(looking) g.** espejo *m*
(**e**) *Old-fashioned (telescope)* anteojo *m*
(**f**) *Old-fashioned (barometer)* **the g. is falling** la presión está bajando
(**g**) ***g. snake*** lagarto *m* de cristal

▸ **glass in** *vt sep (bookcase, porch)* acristalar

glass-blower ['glɑːsbləʊə(r)] *n* soplador(ora) *m,f* de vidrio

glass-blowing ['glɑːsbləʊɪŋ] *n* soplado *m* de vidrio

glasscutter ['glɑːskʌtə(r)] *n (implement)* cortavidrios *m*

glasses ['glɑːsɪz] *npl (spectacles)* gafas *fpl*, *Am* anteojos *mpl*, *Am* lentes *mpl*; **he wears g.** lleva gafas ▸▸ ***g. case*** funda *f* de (las) gafas

glassful ['glɑːsfʊl] *n* vaso *m*

glasshouse ['glɑːshaʊs] *n Br* (**a**) *(for plants)* invernadero *m* (**b**) *Mil Fam (military prison)* calabozo *m*, *Esp* trullo *m*

glassily ['glɑːsɪlɪ] *adv (to stare)* con ojos vidriosos

glasspaper ['glɑːspeɪpə(r)] *n Br* papel *m* de lija

glassware ['glɑːsweə(r)] *n* cristalería *f*

glassworks ['glɑːswɜːks] *n* fábrica *f* de vidrio

glasswort ['glɑːswɜːt] *n* barrilla *f*

glassy ['glɑːsɪ] *adj* (**a**) *(water, lake)* cristalino(a); *(surface)* vítreo(a), bruñido(a) (**b**) *(expression)* vidrioso(a); **a g. look** una mirada vidriosa

glassy-eyed ['glɑːsɪ'aɪd] *adj* de mirada vidriosa; **he looked at me g.** me miraba con los ojos vidriosos

Glaswegian [glæz'wi:dʒən] **1** *n* (**a**) *(person)* persona de Glasgow *(Escocia)* (**b**) *(dialect)* = dialecto de Glasgow *(Escocia)*
2 *adj* de Glasgow *(Escocia)*

glaucoma [glɔ:'kəʊmə] *n Med* glaucoma *m*

glaucous ['glɔ:kəs] *adj Bot* de piel verdosa

glaze [gleɪz] **1** *n* (**a**) *(on pottery)* vidriado *m* (**b**) *(on paper, photograph)* brillo *m* (**c**) *Art* glaseado *m* (**d**) *(on pastry)* glaseado *m* (**e**) *US (ice)* verglás *m* ▸▸ *Br* ***g. ice*** verglás *m*
2 *vt* (**a**) *(window)* acristalar (**b**) *(pottery)* vidriar (**c**) *(pastry)* glasear

▸ **glaze over** *vi (eyes)* velarse

glazed [gleɪzd] *adj* (**a**) *(roof, door)* acristalado(a) (**b**) *(pottery)* vidriado(a) (**c**) *(look)* vidrioso(a)

glazier ['gleɪzɪə(r)] *n* cristalero *m*, vidriero *m*

glazing ['gleɪzɪŋ] *n* (**a**) *(installation)* acristalamiento *m* (**b**) *(glass)* vidrios *mpl*, cristales *mpl*

gleam [gli:m] **1** *n (of light)* destello *m*; *Fig* **a g. of hope** un destello de esperanza; **she had a strange g. in her eye** tenía un brillo extraño en los ojos; IDIOM *Hum* **when you were just a g. in your father's eye** cuando aún andabas por el éter
2 *vi (metal, polished surface)* relucir; *Fig* **her eyes gleamed with anticipation/mischief** le brillaban los ojos de expectación/picardía

gleaming ['gli:mɪŋ] *adj* reluciente

glean [gli:n] *vt* (**a**) *(information)* averiguar; **to g. information from sth** extraer información de algo; **I couldn't g. much from the brochure** no pude sacar gran cosa del folleto (**b**) *Agr* espigar

gleaner ['gli:nə(r)] *n (at harvest)* espigador(ora) *m,f*

gleanings ['gli:nɪŋz] *npl* (**a**) *(information)* fragmentos *mpl* sueltos (**b**) *Agr* espigas *fpl* sueltas

glee [gli:] *n* (**a**) *(delight)* regocijo *m*, contento *m*; *(malicious pleasure)* regodeo *m* (**b**) *Mus* composición *f* coral a capella *(para tres o más voces)* ▸▸ ***g. club*** coral *f*

gleeful ['gli:fʊl] *adj (happy)* regocijado(a); **to be g.** *(to be maliciously happy)* regodearse

gleefully ['gli:fʊlɪ] *adv (joyfully)* con regocijo; *(maliciously)* con malicia, regodeándose

glen [glen] *n Scot* cañada *f*

glengarry [glen'gærɪ] *n* = gorra militar escocesa

glib [glɪb] *adj (salesman, politician)* con mucha labia, *CAm, Ecuad, Méx* labioso(a); *(talk)* simplista; *(excuse, answer)* fácil; **he's rather too g.** tiene mucha labia

glibly ['glɪblɪ] *adv (fluently)* con labia; *(simplistically)* simplistamente

glibness ['glɪbnɪs] *n* labia *f*

glide [glaɪd] **1** *vi* (**a**) *(slide)* deslizarse; **to g. in/out** *(servant, waiter)* entrar/salir silenciosamente; *(imposing person)* entrar/salir con paso majestuoso; **the swans glided across the lake** los cisnes se deslizaban por el lago; **the motorcade glided past** la caravana pasó silenciosamente (**b**) *(aircraft, bird)* planear; *(pilot)* volar sin motor ▸▸ ***g. path*** trayectoria *f* de descenso
2 *n* (**a**) *(movement, dance)* deslizamiento *m* (**b**) *(of glider, aircraft)* planeo *m* (**c**) *Mus (for trombone)* bomba *f* (**d**) *Ling* semivocal *f*

glider ['glaɪdə(r)] *n* (**a**) *Av* planeador *m* (**b**) *US (swing)* mecedora *f*

gliding ['glaɪdɪŋ] *n Av* vuelo *m* sin motor; **to go g.** hacer vuelo sin motor

glimmer ['glɪmə(r)] **1** *n* brillo *m* tenue; *Fig* **a g. of hope** un resquicio de esperanza; **not the slightest g. of intelligence/sympathy** ni el más mínimo atisbo de inteligencia/compasión
2 *vi (light)* lucir tenuemente; *(water, metal)* relucir

glimmering ['glɪmərɪŋ] *adj (light)* tenue

glimpse [glɪmps] **1** *n* vistazo *m* fugaz, atisbo *m*; **to catch a g. of** entrever, ver fugazmente; **a g. of the future** un atisbo del futuro
2 *vt* entrever, ver fugazmente

glint [glɪnt] **1** *n* destello *m*, reflejo *m*; **with a g. in her eye** con un brillo en los ojos
2 *vi (metal, eyes)* destellar, lanzar destellos

glissade [glɪ'seɪd] *n* (**a**) *(in ballet)* deslizamiento *m* (**b**) *(in mountaineering)* deslizamiento *m*

glissando [glɪ'sændəʊ] *(pl* **glissandos** *or* **glissandi** [glɪ'sændi:]) *n Mus* glissando *m*

glisten ['glɪsən] *vi* brillar, relucir

glitch [glɪtʃ] *n Fam Esp* pequeño fallo *m*, *Am* pequeña falla *f*

glitter ['glɪtə(r)] **1** *n* (**a**) *(sparkle)* brillo *m*, resplandor *m* (**b**) *(glamour) (of occasion)* esplendor *m*, brillantez *f* (**c**) *(decoration)* purpurina *f*
2 *vi* lanzar destellos, relucir; **her eyes glittered with excitement** le brillaban los ojos de emoción; PROV **all that glitters is not gold** no es oro todo lo que reluce

glitterati [glɪtə'rɑ:tɪ] *npl Fam* famosos *mpl*, *Esp* gente *f* guapa, *Méx* popis *mpl*, *RP* crema *f*

glittering ['glɪtərɪŋ] *adj* (**a**) *(jewels)* brillante, resplandeciente (**b**) *(occasion, career)* rutilante

glittery ['glɪtərɪ] *adj* llamativo(a), de relumbrón

glitz [glɪts] *n Fam* boato *m*, pompa *f*

glitzy ['glɪtsɪ] *adj Fam (party)* espectacular, despampanante

gloaming ['gləʊmɪŋ] *n Literary* crepúsculo *m*; **in the g.** en el crepúsculo

gloat [gləʊt] **1** *vi* regodearse (**about** *or* **over** de); **don't g.!** ¡no te regodees!
2 *n* **to have a g.** regodearse

gloating ['gləʊtɪŋ] *adj (smile, look)* de regodeo

glob [glɒb] *n Fam* pegote *m*

global ['gləʊbəl] *adj* (**a**) *(worldwide)* mundial, global ▸▸ ***g. economy*** economía *f* global; ***the g. village*** la aldea global; ***g. warming*** calentamiento *m* global (**b**) *(comprehensive) (solution, view)* global (**c**) *Comptr (search, change)* global

globalism ['gləʊbəlɪzəm] *n* globalismo *m*

globalization [gləʊbəlaɪ'zeɪʃən] *n* mundialización *f*, globalización *f*

globally ['gləʊbəlɪ] *adv* (**a**) *(world-wide)* globalmente (**b**) *(comprehensively)* globalmente

globe [gləʊb] *n* (**a**) *(sphere)* esfera *f*, bola *f*; *(with map)* globo *m* terráqueo, bola *f* del mundo (**b**) **the g.** *(the Earth)* el globo, el planeta; **to travel the g.** viajar por todo el mundo (**c**) *Austr (lightbulb) Esp* bombilla *f*, *Andes, Méx* foco *m*, *CAm, Carib* bombillo *m*, *RP* lamparita *f* (**d**) ***g. artichoke*** alcachofa *f*, *RP* alcaucil *m* (**e**) *Fam* **globes** *(breasts)* melones, *Méx* chichís, *RP* lolas

globefish ['gləʊbfɪʃ] *n* pez *m* globo

globeflower ['gləʊbflaʊə(r)] *n* ranúnculo *m*

globetrotter ['gləʊbtrɒtə(r)] *n Fam* trotamundos *mf inv*

globetrotting ['gləʊbtrɒtɪŋ] *n* viajes *mpl* por todo el mundo

globo-cop ['gləʊbəʊkɒp] *n Fam* policía *m or f* global

globular ['glɒbjʊlə(r)] *adj* globular ▸▸ *Astron* ***g. cluster*** grupo *m* globular

globule ['glɒbju:l] *n* gota *f*

glockenspiel ['glɒkənʃpi:l] *n* carillón *m*

glom [glɒm] *(pt & pp* **glommed**) *vt US Fam (seize)* agarrar

▸ **glom onto** *vt insep US Fam (seize)* agarrar

gloom [glu:m] *n* (**a**) *(darkness)* oscuridad *f*, tinieblas *fpl* (**b**) *(melancholy)* abatimiento *m*, tristeza *f*; *(pessimism)* pesimismo *m*; **to cast** *or* **throw a g. over sth** enturbiar algo; **g. and doom** oscuros presagios; **the papers were full of g. and doom about the economy** todos los periódicos auguraban un oscuro porvenir para la economía

gloomily ['glu:mɪlɪ] *adv (unhappily)* sombríamente, tenebrosamente

gloominess ['glu:mɪnɪs] *n* (**a**) *(darkness)* oscuridad *f* (**b**) *(melancholy)* abatimiento *m*, tristeza *f*

gloomy ['glu:mɪ] *adj* (**a**) *(dark)* oscuro(a); **g. weather** tiempo gris; **to become g.** ponerse oscuro, oscurecer (**b**) *(melancholy)* abatido(a), decaído(a); **g. thoughts** pensamientos sombríos (**c**) *(pessimistic)* pesimista; **the future looks g.** el futuro se presenta sombrío *or RP* pinta oscuro; **to paint a g. picture of sth** pintar algo muy negro

glop [glɒp] *n US Fam* plomo *m*, *Esp* plasta *mf*

glorification [glɔ:rɪfɪ'keɪʃən] *n* glorificación *f*

glorified ['glɔ:rɪfaɪd] *adj Fam* **it's just a g. typewriter** no es más que una máquina de escribir con un nombre más pomposo

glorify ['glɔ:rɪfaɪ] *vt* (**a**) *(extol)* glorificar, ensalzar; **his films g. violence** sus películas ensalzan la violencia (**b**) *Rel* glorificar; **to g. God** glorificar a Dios

glorious ['glɔ:rɪəs] *adj* (**a**) *(reign, victory)* glorioso(a); **our army's g. deeds** las gloriosas hazañas de nuestro ejército
(**b**) *(view, weather)* espléndido(a), magnífico(a)

gloriously ['glɔ:rɪəslɪ] *adv* (**a**) *(heroically) (to die)* gloriosamente (**b**) *(wonderfully)* **three g. sunny days** tres días con un sol espléndido; **g. fine weather** un tiempo espléndido; **it was g. successful** tuvo un éxito maravilloso

glory ['glɔːrɪ] *n* **(a)** *(honour, praise)* gloria *f*; **to be covered in g.** estar cubierto(a) de gloria; **to get all the g.** recibir todos los elogios; **to live on past glories** vivir de glorias pasadas; **to have one's hour of g.** tener su hora de gloria
(b) *(splendour, beauty)* esplendor *m*; **the glories of the Irish countryside** el esplendor de la campiña irlandesa; **Hollywood in all its g.** Hollywood en todo su esplendor; **the g. of it is that...** lo genial es que... ▸▸ ***g. days*** días *mpl* gloriosos; *Fam* ***g. hole*** *(for junk)* trastero *m*
(c) *Rel* **g. be to God** gloria a Dios; **to the greater g. of God** para mayor gloria de Dios; *Fam* **g. be!** ¡bendito sea!
(d) *(heaven)* gloria *f*; *Euph* **he has gone to g.** ha pasado a mejor vida

▸ **glory in** *vt insep* deleitarse; **to g. in doing sth** deleitarse haciendo algo

Glos (*abbr* **Gloucestershire**) (condado *m* de) Gloucestershire

gloss[1] [glɒs] **1** *n (in text)* glosa *f*
2 *vt (text)* glosar, explicar

gloss[2] **1** *n* **(a)** *(shininess) (of paint)* lustre *m*, brillo *m* ▸▸ ***g. finish*** *(of paint)* acabado *m* brillante; *(of photograph)* brillo *m* **(b)** **g. (paint)** pintura *f* al esmalte **(c)** *(appearance)* barniz *m*; **a g. of politeness/respectability** un barniz de cortesía/decencia; IDIOM **to take the g. off sth** deslucir algo
2 *vt (paint)* pintar al esmalte

▸ **gloss over** *vt insep (difficulty, mistake)* mencionar muy de pasada

glossary ['glɒsərɪ] *n* glosario *m*

glossolalia [glɒsəʊ'leɪlɪə] *n* glosolalia *f*

glossy ['glɒsɪ] **1** *adj* **(a)** *(shiny) (fur, hair, surface)* brillante, lustroso(a); *(leather, satin, leaves)* con brillo ▸▸ ***g. ibis*** morito *m* **(b)** *(photo)* con brillo; **a g. brochure** un folleto en papel cuché ▸▸ ***g. magazine*** revista *f* de papel satinado *or* cuché; ***g. paper*** papel *m* satinado *or* cuché **(c)** *(superficially attractive)* **underneath the g. surface** bajo el brillo de la superficie
2 *n Fam* **the glossies** *(magazines)* las revistas de papel satinado *or* cuché

glottal stop ['glɒtəl'stɒp] *n Ling* oclusión *f* glotal

glottis ['glɒtɪs] *n Anat* glotis *f inv*

glottochronology [glɒtəʊkrə'nɒlədʒɪ] *n Ling* glotocronología *f*

glove [glʌv] *n* guante *m*; **a pair of gloves** unos guantes, un par de guantes; IDIOM **to fit like a g.** quedar como un guante; IDIOM **the gloves are off** se terminaron los miramientos ▸▸ *Aut* ***g. box*** guantera *f*; ***g. compartment*** guantera *f*; ***g. counter*** *or* ***department*** *(in large store)* sección *f* de guantes; *Br* ***g. puppet*** títere *m*, marioneta *f* (de guiñol)

gloved [glʌvd] *adj* enguantado(a), con guante(s)

glover ['glʌvə(r)] *n* guantero(a) *m,f*

glow [gləʊ] **1** *n* **(a)** *(of light, fire)* resplandor *m*; *(of embers, heated metal)* rojo *m* encendido; *(of sky, sunset)* resplandor *m* crepuscular; *(of colours)* luminosidad *f* **(b)** *(on cheeks)* rubor *m*; **to have a healthy g.** *(person)* tener buen color; **he had a g. of pride/satisfaction** se le iluminaba la cara de orgullo/satisfacción; **it gives you a warm g.** *(news, scene)* te da una sensación de bienestar
2 *vi* **(a)** *(light, fire, sky, colour)* resplandecer; *(embers, heated metal)* estar al rojo; **to g. in the dark** brillar en la oscuridad **(b)** *(person)* resplandecer; **he was glowing with pride/pleasure** resplandecía de orgullo/placer; **to be glowing with health** rebosar salud

glower ['glaʊə(r)] **1** *n* mirada *f* de cólera
2 *vi* **to g. at sb** mirar con furia a alguien; **she sat glowering in a corner** estaba sentada en un rincón, con una mirada de cólera

glowing ['gləʊɪŋ] *adj* **(a)** *(cigarette, coal)* encendido(a) **(b)** *(flattering) (report)* elogioso(a); **he spoke of you in g. terms** habló de ti en términos elogiosos; IDIOM **to paint sth in g. colours** pintar algo de color de rosa

glowingly ['gləʊɪŋlɪ] *adv* **to speak g. of sth/sb** hablar elogiosamente de algo/alguien

glow-worm ['gləʊwɜːm] *n* luciérnaga *f*

glucose ['gluːkəʊs] *n* glucosa *f*

glue [gluː] **1** *n (in general)* pegamento *m*; *(thicker, for wood, metal)* cola *f*; IDIOM **he stuck to them like g.** se les pegó como una lapa ▸▸ *Med* ***g. ear*** otitis *f* serosa
2 *vt* **(a)** *(in general)* pegar; *(wood, metal)* encolar, pegar; **to g. sth down/on** pegar algo; **to g. sth (back) together** volver a pegar algo **(b)** *Fig (fix)* **he was glued to the spot** se había quedado pegado; **to be glued to the television** estar pegado(a) a la televisión; **he kept his eyes glued on** *or* **to the ball** mantuvo los ojos fijos en el balón

gluepot ['gluːpɒt] *n* bote *m* de cola

glue-sniffer ['gluːsnɪfə(r)] *n* persona *f* que inhala pegamento

glue-sniffing ['gluːsnɪfɪŋ] *n* inhalación *f* de pegamento

gluey ['gluːɪ] *adj* pegajoso(a)

glug [glʌg] **1** *n* **g. g.** gluglú *m*
2 *vt* tragar

glum [glʌm] *adj* abatido(a), triste; **to be** *or* **feel g.** estar abatido(a) *or* triste

glumly ['glʌmlɪ] *adv* con abatimiento, con aire sombrío

gluon ['gluːɒn] *n Phys* gluón *m*

glut [glʌt] **1** *n Com* saturación *f*; **there's a g. of fruit on the market** el mercado está saturado de fruta
2 *vt* (*pt & pp* **glutted**) **(a)** *Com* saturar **(b)** **to g. oneself (with** *or* **on)** saturarse (de); **to be glutted with television** estar saturado(a) de televisión

glutamate ['gluːtəmeɪt] *n Chem* glutamato *m*

glutamic acid [gluː'tæmɪk'æsɪd] *n Biochem* ácido *m* glutámico

gluten ['gluːtən] *n Biochem* gluten *m*

gluten-free ['gluːtən'friː] *adj* sin gluten

gluteus ['gluːtɪəs] *n Anat* glúteo *m* ▸▸ ***g. maximus*** glúteo *m* mayor

glutinous ['gluːtɪnəs] *adj (substance)* viscoso(a), glutinoso(a); *(rice)* apelmazado(a)

glutton ['glʌtən] *n (greedy person)* glotón(ona) *m,f*; *Fig* **she's a g. for work** nunca se harta de trabajar; IDIOM **you're a g. for punishment** eres masoquista

gluttonous ['glʌtənəs] *adj* glotón(ona)

gluttonously ['glʌtənəslɪ] *adv* con gula

gluttony ['glʌtənɪ] *n* gula *f*, glotonería *f*

glyceride ['glɪsəraɪd] *n Chem* glicérido *m*

glycerin ['glɪsərɪn], **glycerine** ['glɪsəriːn], **glycerol** ['glɪsərɒl] *n Chem* glicerina *f*

glycogen ['glaɪkədʒən] *n Biochem* glucógeno *m*

glycol ['glaɪkɒl] *n Chem* glicol *m*

GM [dʒiː'em] **1** *n Com* (*abbr* **general manager**) director(ora) *m,f* general
2 *adj* (*abbr* **genetically modified**) transgénico(a), modificado(a) genéticamente ▸▸ ***GM food*** (alimentos *mpl*) transgénicos *mpl*

gm (*abbr* **gram, gramme**) gr., g.

G-man ['dʒiːmæn] *n Fam US* agente *m* del FBI

GMAT ['dʒiːmæt] *n US* (*abbr* **Graduate Management Admissions Test**) = examen de ingreso a una escuela de administración

GMB [dʒiːem'biː] *n* (*abbr* **General and Municipal and Boilerworkers (Union)**) = importante sindicato británico que incluye trabajadores de varios sectores

GMC [dʒiːem'siː] *n Br* (*abbr* **General Medical Council**) ≃ colegio *m* de médicos

GMO [dʒiːem'əʊ] *n* (*abbr* **genetically-modified organism**) OMG *m*, organismo *m* modificado genéticamente

GMT [dʒiːem'tiː] *n* (*abbr* **Greenwich Mean Time**) hora *f* del meridiano de Greenwich

gnarled [nɑːld] *adj (tree)* retorcido(a) y nudoso(a); *(hands, fingers)* nudoso(a)

gnarly ['nɑːlɪ] *adj US Fam* **(a)** *(excellent)* alucinante **(b)** *(terrible)* muy mal, *Esp* fatal

gnash [næʃ] *vt* **he was gnashing his teeth (with rage)** le rechinaban los dientes (de rabia)

gnashers ['næʃəz] *npl Fam Hum* dientes *mpl*, *Esp* piños *mpl*

gnat [næt] *n* mosquito *m (muy pequeño)* ▸▸ *very Fam* ***g.'s piss*** *(drink)* bebida *f* intragable, *Esp* meado *m*

gnaw [nɔː] **1** *vt* **(a)** *(of animal)* roer **(b)** *Fig* **he was constantly gnawed by remorse** le remordía la conciencia
2 *vi* **(a)** *(animal)* **to g. through sth** roer algo **(b)** *Fig (doubt)* **to g. (away) at sb** corroer a alguien; **hunger gnawed at him** el hambre lo consumía

gnawing ['nɔːɪŋ] *adj* **(a)** *(pain, hunger)* persistente **(b)** *Fig* **he suffered from a g. sense of guilt** le corroía el sentimiento de culpa

gneiss [naɪs] *n Geol* gneis *m*

gnocchi ['njɒkɪ] *npl Culin* ñoquis *mpl*

gnome [nəʊm] *n* gnomo *m*; **(garden) g.** enanito *m* de jardín; *Fam* **the gnomes of Zurich** los banqueros suizos

gnomic ['nəʊmɪk] *adj* enigmático(a)

gnomish ['nəʊmɪʃ] *adj (appearance)* de gnomo

gnostic ['nɒstɪk] **1** *n* gnóstico(a) *m,f*
2 *adj* gnóstico(a)

gnosticism ['nɒstɪsɪzəm] *n* gnosticismo *m*

GNP [dʒi:en'pi:] *n Econ* (*abbr* **Gross National Product**) PNB *m*

gnu [nu:] *n* ñu *m*

GNVQ [dʒi:envi:'kju:] *n Br Educ* (*abbr* **General National Vocational Qualification**) = curso de formación profesional de dos años para mayores de dieciséis años

GO[1] [gəʊ] **1** *n* (*pl* **goes**) **(a)** *(energy)* **to be full of go** estar lleno(a) de vitalidad

(b) *(turn)* turno *m*; **(it's) your go!** ¡te toca a ti!; **can I have a go on the swing?** ¿me dejas subirme al columpio?, *RP* ¿me prestás la hamaca?; **this ride is £1 a go** esta atracción es a una libra el viaje, *RP* en este juego sale una libra la vuelta

(c) *(try)* intento *m*; **I did it (at the) first go** lo hice al primer intento *or* a la primera; **at one go** de una vez; **to give sth a go** intentar *or* probar algo; **I've decided to give it a go as a musician** he decidido probar suerte como músico; **to have a go at doing sth** probar a *or* intentar hacer algo; **let's have a go!** ¡probemos!, ¡intentémoslo!; **let me have a go** déjame probar

(d) *Fam (success)* **to make a go of sth** sacar algo adelante; **they're going to make a go of their marriage** van a intentar sacar adelante su matrimonio

(e) IDIOMS **from the word "go"** desde el principio, desde el primer momento; **it's all go** hay mucha actividad; *Fam* **I asked her if she'd help, but it was no go** le pregunté si ayudaría, pero me dijo que nones; *Fam* **she had a go at me** *(told me off)* me echó una reprimenda *or Esp* la bronca, *RP* me relajó todo; *Fam* **he was dying to have a go at me** *(attack)* se moría de ganas de meterse conmigo; **to make a go of sth** sacar algo adelante; **I've been on the go all day** *(active)* no he parado en todo el día; **she had three boyfriends on the go at the same time** tenía tres novios al mismo tiempo

2 *vi* (*3rd person singular* **goes** [gəʊz], *pt* **went** [went], *pp* **gone** [gɒn]) **(a)** *(in general)* ir; **to go closer** acercarse; **to go home** irse a casa; **go right/left** tuerce *or* gira *or* dobla a la derecha/izquierda; **to go by bus/train** ir en autobús/en tren; **to go to Spain/the doctor** ir a España/al médico; **to go to prison** ir a la cárcel; **I had to go into hospital** tuve que ser ingresado (en el hospital), *RP* me tuvieron que internar; **to go to church/school** ir a la iglesia/al colegio; **to go to bed** ir a la cama; **to go hunting/skiing** ir de caza/a esquiar; **the glass went flying** el vaso salió volando; *Fam* **don't go wasting your money** no vayas por ahí derrochando el dinero; **I'd better go and tell them,** *US* **I'd better go tell them** será mejor que vaya y se lo diga, es mejor que vaya a decírselo; **go and play outside** sal a jugar fuera *or Am* afuera; *Fam* **now look what you've gone and done!** ¡mira la que has armado!; *Fam* **you've really gone and done it this time!** ¡esta vez la has hecho buena!; **to go for a swim/walk** ir a darse un baño/a dar un paseo; **to go on television** salir en televisión; *Mil* **who goes there?** ¿quién va?; **there goes Bob!** ¡ahí va Bob!; *Fam* **there** *or* **bang goes my chance of getting the job!** ¡adiós mis posibilidades de conseguir el trabajo!; *Fam* **there you go** *(when giving sth)* aquí tienes; *(I told you so)* ¿qué te dije?; *(there's nothing to be done about it)* ¿qué le vamos a hacer?; **where do we go from here?** *(what do we do next?)* y ahora, ¿qué hacemos?; **it's not bad, as fast-food restaurants go** como restaurante de comida rápida, no está mal; *US* **two white coffees to go** *(to take away)* dos cafés con leche para llevar

(b) *(leave) (person)* irse, marcharse; *(train, bus)* salir; **we'd better be going** deberíamos irnos *or* salir ya; **that dog will have to go!** ¡tenemos que librarnos de ese perro!; *Euph* **I'm afraid we're having to let you go** *(make redundant)* me temo que vamos a tener que prescindir de tus servicios; *Euph* **when I am gone** cuando yo falte

(c) *(move quickly)* **watch him go!** ¡mira cómo corre!; **this bike can really go** esta moto corre lo suyo

(d) *(start)* empezar; **we're ready to go** estamos listos para empezar; **you go now** *(have turn)* ahora tú; **go!** *(at start of race, contest)* ¡ya!; **let's get going** vámonos; **to go to sleep** dormirse; *Fam* **here goes!, here we go!** ¡vamos allá!, *RP* ¡dale!; **she went to pick the phone up...** *(was about to)* fue a contestar el teléfono...

(e) *(be sent)* **this letter must go by tonight/by courier** esta carta hay que enviarla esta noche/por mensajero

(f) *(extend)* **the garden goes down to the river** el jardín llega *or* se extiende hasta el río; **the path goes down to the beach** el camino lleva hasta la playa; **this road goes to Miami** esta carretera va *or* lleva a Miami; **the river goes from north to south** el río fluye de norte a sur

(g) *(function)* funcionar; *(bell)* sonar; **I can't get my car going** no consigo arrancar el coche; **to keep the conversation going** mantener viva la conversación; **to start** *or* **set** *or* **get things going** animar la cosa

(h) *(progress)* ir; **to go well/badly** ir bien/mal; **how did the exam go?** ¿qué tal fue el examen?; **to go wrong** ir mal, *Am* descomponerse, *Andes* malograrse; *Fam* **how's it going?, how are things going?** ¿qué tal?; **if all goes well** si todo va bien; **the way things are going...** tal y como van las cosas...; **how does the song/story go?** ¿cómo es la canción/historia?; **the legend goes that...** según la leyenda...

(i) *(time)* **the time went quickly** el tiempo pasó muy rápido; **it's just gone eight** acaban de dar las ocho; **there are only five minutes to go** sólo quedan cinco minutos; **I only have two days to go** sólo me quedan dos días

(j) *(disappear)* desaparecer; **the pain has gone** el dolor ha desaparecido; **where has my wallet gone?** ¿adónde ha ido a parar mi cartera *or RP* billetera?; **five hundred jobs are to go** se van a perder quinientos puestos de trabajo; **most of my money goes on food** la mayor parte del dinero se me va en comida

(k) *(deteriorate, be damaged)* **his nerve went** perdió la calma; **her sight/hearing is going** está perdiendo vista/oído; **my voice is going** me estoy quedando afónico; **the fuse has gone** se ha fundido *or RP* quemado el fusible; **the batteries are going** se están acabando las pilas; **my jumper is going at the elbows** se me está desgastando el suéter por *or* en los codos; **the jacket went at the seams** se descosió la chaqueta

(l) *(forming future)* **to be going to do sth** ir a hacer algo; **I was going to walk there** iba a ir caminando *or Esp* andando; **it's going to rain** va a llover; **I'm going to be a doctor** voy a ser médico; **are you going to be at home tonight?** ¿vas a estar en casa esta noche?

(m) *(match)* ir bien, pegar (**with** con); **these colours go/don't go** estos colores pegan/no pegan; **red wine goes well with cheese** el vino tinto va bien con el queso

(n) *(be available)* **there's a job going at the factory** hay una (plaza) vacante en la fábrica; **is there any wine going?** ¿hay vino?

(o) *(be sold)* venderse; **has the sofa you advertised gone yet?** ¿ha vendido el sofá que anunciaba?; **laptops are going cheap at the moment** los portátiles están muy baratos ahora; **it went for $12** se vendió por 12 dólares; **20,000, going (once), going (twice), gone!** *(at auction)* ¡20.000 a la de una, 20.000 a la de dos, 20.000 a la de tres!, ¡adjudicado!

(p) *(be given)* **the job went to a woman** le dieron el trabajo a una mujer; **first prize went to a sculpture** el primer premio fue para una escultura; **the proceeds will go to charity** las ganancias se destinarán a obras de beneficencia; **a lot of praise went to him for his performance** recibió muchos elogios por su actuación

(q) *(belong)* ir; **the plates go in the cupboard** los platos van en el armario; **this strap goes around your arm** esta correa se pone alrededor del brazo

(r) *(fit)* caber; **the piano won't go through the door** el piano no cabe por la puerta

(s) *Math* **four into three won't go** tres no es divisible entre cuatro, tres entre cuatro no cabe; **two goes into six three times** seis entre dos, tres

(t) *(become)* **to go bad** echarse a perder; **to go bankrupt** quebrar, ir a la quiebra; **to go blind** quedarse ciego(a); **to go cold** enfriarse; **to go crazy** volverse loco(a); **he's going grey** le están saliendo canas; **to go red** enrojecer, ponerse rojo(a); **to go wild with excitement** enloquecer, *RP* enloquecerse

(u) *(be)* **her protests went unheard** nadie escuchó sus protestas; **to go topless** ir *or Am* andar en topless; **I don't want the children to go hungry** no quiero que los niños pasen hambre; **I go in fear of my life** temo por mi vida

(v) *(be the rule)* **what she says goes** ella es la que manda; **anything goes** todo vale; **that rule goes for everyone** esa norma vale para todos

(w) *(gesture)* **he went like this with his tongue** hizo esto con su lengua

(x) *(undergo)* **to go to a lot of trouble** tomarse muchas molestias; **to go to a lot of expense** gastar mucho dinero

(y) *Fam (urinate)* **I really need to go** ya no me aguanto

(z) *Fam (believe)* **I had you going for a while there!** ¡casi caes!

3 *vt* **(a)** *(travel)* hacer; **we went 20 miles in a day** hicimos 20 millas en un día; **to g. one's own way** ir a lo suyo

(b) *Fam (say)* decir; **"get lost!" he went** "¡piérdete! *or RP* ¡borrate!", dijo; **so she goes "you're lying!" and I go "no, I'm not!"** y entonces ella va y me dice "¡estás mintiendo!" y yo "que no"

(c) *(make sound)* **dogs go "woof"** los perros hacen "guau"; **it went bang** estalló

(d) IDIOMS **to go it alone** ir por libre, montárselo por su cuenta, *RP* estar por cuenta propia; **to go one better than sb** superar a alguien; **last year they finished third, this year they went one better** el año pasado acabaron terceros, este año han mejorado un puesto; *Fam* **I could really go a beer!** ¡me tomaría una cerveza ahora mismo!

Para una comparación de **be going to** con otras formas de expresar el futuro en inglés, ver el panel FUTURE.

▸ **go about** 1 *vt insep* (a) *(travel) (country)* viajar por (b) *(tackle) (task)* abordar; **I went about my business calmly** me ocupé tranquilamente de mis asuntos; **to go about doing sth** *(start)* ponerse a hacer algo; **how do I go about getting a licence?** ¿qué hay que hacer para conseguir un permiso?
2 *vi* (a) *(circulate) (person)* ir por ahí; *(rumour)* circular, correr; **he goes about wearing nothing but a hat** va por ahí sin llevar otra cosa que un sombrero; **there's a virus going about** hay un virus suelto por ahí; **she goes about with some strange people** sale por ahí con unos tipos raros; **you can't just go about lying to everyone** no puedes ir por ahí mintiendo a todo el mundo
(b) *Naut* virar

▸ **go across** 1 *vt insep* cruzar, atravesar
2 *vi* **to go across to the States** ir a los Estados Unidos

▸ **go after** *vt insep (pursue)* ir tras; *Fig (job, prize, person)* estar detrás de, *Esp* ir a por

▸ **go against** *vt insep* (a) *(conflict with) (principles, instincts)* ir (en) contra de (b) *(disregard)* **he went against my advice** no siguió mis consejos; **he went against my wishes** actuó en contra de mis deseos (c) *(be unfavourable to)* **the decision went against him** la decisión le fue desfavorable

▸ **go ahead** *vi* (a) *(proceed)* seguir adelante; **we've decided to go ahead and buy the tickets anyway** a pesar de todo hemos decidido comprar las entradas *or Am* los boletos; **to go ahead with sth** seguir (adelante) con algo; **may I say something? – go ahead** ¿puedo hablar? – adelante; **can I smoke? – go ahead** ¿puedo fumar? – adelante
(b) *(go in front)* ir delante
(c) *(take the lead)* **Paraguay went ahead after five minutes** Paraguay se puso por delante a los cinco minutos

▸ **go along** *vi* (a) *(proceed)* avanzar; **she went along with them to the fair** fue con ellos a la feria; **to do sth as one goes along** hacer algo sobre la marcha (b) *(attend)* acudir (**to** a)

▸ **go along with** *vt insep* estar de acuerdo con, aceptar; **she wouldn't go along with it** no quiso tomar parte en ello

▸ **go around** = **go round**

▸ **go at** *vt insep (person, food)* atacar; *(task)* emprender; *(problem)* enfrentarse con decisión a; *Fam* **to go at it** *(fight)* darse de bofetadas *or Esp* de hostias *or Méx* de machazos *or RP* a los golpes

▸ **go away** *vi (leave)* irse; *(disappear)* desaparecer; **go away!** ¡vete!; **this should make the pain go away** esto hará que desaparezca el dolor; **to go away on business** irse en viaje de negocios; **to go away for the weekend** irse a pasar el fin de semana fuera

▸ **go back** *vi* (a) *(return)* volver; **she's gone back to her husband** ha vuelto con su marido; **to go back to sleep** volver a dormirse; **going back to what you said earlier...** volviendo a lo que dijiste antes...; **to go back to one's old ways** volver a las andadas; **to go back to doing sth** volver a hacer algo; **once you've signed, there's no going back** una vez que has firmado, ya no te puedes echar atrás
(b) *(retreat)* ir para atrás; **go back!** ¡vete para atrás!
(c) *(be put back)* **the clocks go back tonight** hay que retrasar los relojes esta madrugada
(d) *(date back)* **to go back to** remontarse a, datar de; **this building goes back to the Revolution** este edificio se remonta a *or* data de la Revolución; *Fam* **we go back a long way** nos conocemos desde hace mucho

▸ **go back on** *vt insep (promise, one's word)* faltar a

▸ **go before** 1 *vt insep* **to go before the court** *(defendant)* comparecer ante el juez, ir a juicio; *(case)* verse
2 *vi (precede)* **we can't ignore what has gone before** no podemos ignorar lo que ha pasado antes

▸ **go below** *vi Naut* bajar

▸ **go by** 1 *vt insep* (a) *(be guided by)* guiarse por; **if their last performance is anything to go by, they'll lose** si nos guiamos por su última actuación, perderán; **to go by appearances** fiarse de las apariencias; **to go by the rules** seguir las reglas; **going by her accent, I'd say she's from New York** por su acento yo diría que es de Nueva York
(b) *(be known by)* **to go by the name of...** ser conocido(a) con el nombre de...
2 *vi* (a) *(pass)* pasar; **to watch people going by** mirar a la gente que pasa; **we can't let this chance go by** no podemos dejar pasar esta oportunidad (b) *(elapse) (time)* pasar, transcurrir; **hardly a day goes by that I don't think of him** no pasa un día en el que no piense en él; *Literary* **in days gone by** antaño

▸ **go down** 1 *vt insep (descend) (hill, ladder)* bajar por; **I was going down the road, when...** iba por la carretera, cuando...
2 *vi* (a) *(descend)* bajar; *(sun)* ponerse; *(theatre curtain)* caer; *(ship)* hundirse; *(plane)* caer; **to go down on one's knees** arrodillarse, ponerse de rodillas; **we're going down to Florida/the park** vamos a ir a Florida/al parque
(b) *(fall down) (in soccer, boxing)* caer
(c) *(be defeated)* perder (**to** contra), caer (**to** ante); *(be relegated)* descender; **they went down to the second division** descendieron a segunda división; **I'm not going to go down without a fight** no voy a rendirme sin luchar
(d) *(decrease) (flood, temperature, prices)* bajar, caer, descender; *(swelling)* bajar; *(tyre, balloon)* desinflarse; **to go down in price** bajar de precio; **he's gone down in my estimation** ahora lo tengo en menos estima
(e) *(stop working) (computer network)* caerse
(f) *(become dimmer) (lights)* atenuarse
(g) *(be received)* **to go down well/badly (with sb)** ser bien/mal acogido(a) (por alguien); IDIOM *Br Fam* **to go down like a ton of bricks** *or* **a lead balloon** sentar como una patada en el estómago, *Méx* caer como una bomba
(h) *(be remembered, recorded)* **this must go down as one of the worst days of my life!** ¡éste pasará a la historia como uno de los peores días de mi vida!; **he went down in history as a tyrant** pasó a la historia como un tirano
(i) *(food, drink)* **the pill won't go down** no consigo tragar la píldora; *Fam* **that beer went down a treat!** ¡la cerveza me sentó de maravilla!; **to go down the wrong way** *(food)* irse por otro lado *(la comida al tragar)*
(j) *Fam (be sent to prison)* **he went down for ten years** le cayeron diez años en la cárcel *or Esp* en chirona *or Méx* en el bote *or Andes, RP* en la cana
(k) *Fam (happen)* **what's going down?** ¿qué te cuentas?, *CAm, Col, Méx* ¡qué hubo!; **when's the robbery going down?** ¿cuándo va a ser el robo?
(l) *Br (leave university) (after graduating)* licenciarse; *(at end of term)* = dejar la universidad al acabar el trimestre

▸ **go down on** *vt insep Vulg (man)* mamársela *or* chupársela a; *(woman)* darle una chupadita a, *Esp* comer el conejo a

▸ **go down with** *vt insep Fam (illness)* agarrar, *Esp* coger

▸ **go for** *vt insep* (a) *(attack)* lanzarse contra, atacar
(b) *(try to get) (job, title)* intentar conseguir, *Esp* ir a por; **he went for the ball** se lanzó a por *or Esp* fue a por la pelota; *Fam* **if you really want the job, go for it!** si realmente te interesa el trabajo, ¡lánzate *or Esp* a por él!
(c) *(like)* **I don't really go for that idea** no estoy por esa idea; **she goes for strong types** le van los tipos fuertes
(d) *(choose)* escoger, elegir
(e) *(favour)* **he has got a lot going for him** tiene mucho a su favor; **the play didn't have a lot going for it** la obra no valía demasiado la pena
(f) *(apply to)* valer para; **the same goes for you** lo mismo te digo a ti *or* vale para ti
(g) *(continue for)* **we went for three days without any food** pasamos tres días sin comer

▸ **go forward** *vi* (a) *(progress)* pasar; **the two top teams go forward to the next round** los primeros dos equipos pasan a la siguiente ronda (b) *(be put forward)* **the clocks go forward tomorrow** hay que adelantar los relojes esta madrugada

▸ **go in** *vi* (a) *(enter)* entrar; *Fig* **do you want to go in with us on this project?** ¿quieres unirte a nosotros en este proyecto? (b) *(fit)* caber; **this rod goes in here** esta barra entra *or* se mete aquí (c) *(disappear)* **the sun has gone in** se ha nublado

▸ **go in for** *vt insep* (a) *(competition)* tomar parte en; *(exam)* presentarse a (b) *(hobby, sport)* practicar; *(profession)* dedicarse a; **have you ever thought about going in for teaching?** ¿has pensado alguna vez dedicarte a la enseñanza? (c) *(like)* **she doesn't go in for cooking/sports** no le atrae la cocina/el deporte

▸ **go into** *vt insep* (a) *(enter) (place, program)* entrar en; *(hospital)* ingresar en; *(career)* entrar en, meterse en; *(trade, market)* introducirse en; **to go into business with sb** montar un negocio con alguien
(b) *(hit)* chocar con; **I went into the car in front of me** choqué con el coche *or Am* carro *or RP* auto de delante
(c) *(begin) (speech, description)* comenzar, empezar; **to go into production** comenzar *or* empezar a ser fabricado; **to go into a spin** *(car)* comenzar a dar vueltas; *(plane)* entrar en barrena; **to go into a sulk** enfurruñarse; **to go into a trance** entrar en trance
(d) *(be devoted to)* dedicarse a; **a lot of time and effort has gone into**

this manual se ha dedicado mucho tiempo y esfuerzo a este manual
(**e**) *(examine) (question, matter)* tratar; **to go into detail** entrar en detalle

▸ **go off** 1 *vt insep (lose liking for)* **I've gone off wine** ya no me gusta el vino; **I've gone off the idea** me ha dejado de gustar la idea
2 *vi* (**a**) *(leave)* marcharse, irse; *Theat* salir; *(from sports field)* retirarse; **to go off with sb** *(elope)* escaparse con alguien; **to go off with sth** *(steal)* irse con algo, llevarse algo
(**b**) *(milk, meat, fish)* echarse a perder
(**c**) *Br (get worse)* empeorar
(**d**) *(gun)* dispararse; *(bomb)* explotar; *(alarm)* saltar, sonar
(**e**) *(event)* transcurrir; **to go off well** *or* **smoothly** salir bien
(**f**) *(electricity, heating)* apagarse; **the lights went off** *(because of fault)* se fue la luz
(**g**) *(go to sleep)* dormirse, quedarse dormido(a)

▸ **go on** 1 *vt insep* (**a**) *(enter) (boat, train)* subir a
(**b**) *(start)* **to go on a course** hacer un curso; **to go on a diet** ponerse a dieta; **to go on the pill** empezar a tomar la píldora
(**c**) *(be guided by)* guiarse por; **the police have nothing to go on** la policía carece de pistas
(**d**) *(approach)* **she's two, going on three** tiene dos años, casi tres; **it's going on eight years that I've worked here** llevo casi ocho años trabajando aquí
2 *vi* (**a**) *(continue)* seguir, continuar (**with** con); **you go on (ahead)** tú sigue adelante; **the weather will improve as the day goes on** el tiempo mejorará conforme avanza el día; **the contest went on for two days** la competición *or Am* competencia duró dos días; **as time went on...** a medida que pasaba el tiempo...; **the movie went on and on** parecía que la película no se iba a acabar nunca; **the way he's going on, he'll kill himself soon** tal y como va, acabará matándose pronto; *Br Fam* **here's £10 to be going on with** aquí tienes diez libras para ir empezando; *Br Fam* **go on with you!** *(expressing disbelief)* ¡anda ya!, *Méx* ¡no me cuentes!, *RP* ¡dale!
(**b**) *(proceed)* **to go on to (do) sth** pasar a (hacer) algo; **we had a meal and went on to a bar afterwards** cenamos y después fuimos a un bar
(**c**) *(talk excessively)* hablar sin parar, enrollarse; **to go on (and on) about sth** no parar de hablar de algo, enrollarse con algo
(**d**) *(happen)* pasar, ocurrir; **what's going on here?** ¿qué pasa aquí?; **do you think there's anything going on between them?** ¿crees que hay algo entre ellos?
(**e**) *(progress)* **how's the project going on?** ¿cómo va el proyecto?
(**f**) *(appear) (on stage)* salir
(**g**) *(electricity, lights, heating)* encenderse, *Am* prenderse
(**h**) *(as encouragement)* **go on, try it!** ¡vamos *or Esp* venga *or Méx* ándale *or RP* dale, pruébalo!; **no, you can't have a go – oh, go on!** no, no puedes – ¡*Esp* hala *or Méx* ándale *or RP* dale, por favor!; **I bet I can do it – go on, then** ¿a que puedo hacerlo? – adelante pues; **more cake? – go on then, just a small slice** ¿más tarta? – bueno, pero sólo un trocito

> Hay una serie de verbos en inglés que pueden ir seguidos tanto como de infinitivo como de gerundio sin que apenas cambie su significado; por ejemplo **begin**, **bother**, **continue**, **hate**, **like** o **try**. Sin embargo, **go on** es uno de los pocos verbos en los que existe una clara diferencia entre ambas opciones:
> **she went on to mention his many publications** *a continuación mencionó sus numerosas publicaciones*
> **they went on making a noise even after we complained** *siguieron haciendo ruido incluso después de que nos quejáramos*

▸ **go on at** *vt insep Fam* **to go on at sb** dar la paliza a alguien; **he's always going on at his wife about money** siempre está dando la paliza a su mujer con el dinero; **I went on at my mother to go and see the doctor** estuve dando la paliza a mi madre para que fuera a ver al médico

▸ **go out** *vi* (**a**) *(leave)* salir; **to go out of the room** salir de la habitación; **to go out for a breath of fresh air** salir a tomar el aire; **he's going out to China** se va a China; **to go out (on strike)** ponerse *or* declararse en huelga; *Fig* **all the fight went out of her** se quedó sin fuerzas para seguir luchando
(**b**) *(for entertainment)* salir; **are you going out tonight?** ¿vas a salir esta noche?; **to go out for a meal** salir a comer fuera
(**c**) *(date)* **to go out with sb** salir con alguien; **they are going out together** salen juntos
(**d**) *(tide)* bajar
(**e**) *(fire, light)* apagarse
(**f**) *(become unfashionable)* pasar de moda
(**g**) *Sport (be eliminated)* quedar eliminado(a); **Italy went out to England** Italia fue eliminada por Inglaterra
(**h**) *TV & Rad (be transmitted)* emitirse
(**i**) *(be sent)* **the forms went out yesterday** los impresos salieron ayer
(**j**) *(intend)* **I didn't go out to hurt him** no pretendía hacerle daño
(**k**) *(feel sympathy)* **my heart goes out to them** comparto su sufrimiento; *(on death)* los acompaño en el sentimiento; **our sympathy goes out to the relatives of the victim** expresamos nuestras condolencias a los familiares de la víctima
(**l**) *(in card games)* cerrar

▸ **go over** 1 *vt insep* (**a**) *(road, bridge)* cruzar
(**b**) *(examine) (accounts, report)* estudiar, examinar; **the police went over the apartment** la policía registró el apartamento; **to go over sth in one's mind** repasar algo mentalmente
(**c**) *(practise, revise)* repasar; **let's go over it one more time** repasémoslo una vez más
(**d**) *(explain)* explicar; **could you go over the first bit again?** ¿podrías explicar la primera parte otra vez?
(**e**) *(clean)* **she went over the mantelpiece with a cloth** pasó un trapo *or RP* repasador por la repisa
2 *vi* (**a**) *(cross)* **to go over to sb** aproximarse a alguien, acercarse hasta alguien; **I'm going over to Europe** voy a ir a Europa
(**b**) *(switch)* **to go over to a different system** cambiar de sistema; **to go over to the enemy** pasarse a las filas del enemigo; **we now go over to our correspondent in Chicago** y pasamos ahora a nuestro corresponsal en Chicago; **I've gone over to smoking cigars** he pasado a fumar puros
(**c**) *(be received)* **to go over well/badly** tener buena/mala acogida; IDIOM *US Fam* **to go over like a lead balloon** sentar como una patada en el estómago, *Méx* caer como una bomba
(**d**) *TV & Rad* **let's go over now to our Birmingham studios** vamos ahora a nuestros estudios de Birmingham

▸ **go past** 1 *vt insep* **we went past a castle on the way** pasamos un castillo de camino; **he went right past me without saying hello** pasó a mi lado sin saludarme
2 *vi* pasar

▸ **go round** 1 *vt insep* (**a**) *(of person)* **to go round town/the shops** recorrer la ciudad/las tiendas; **to go round the world** dar la vuelta al mundo (**b**) *(of rumour)* circular por, correr por
2 *vi* (**a**) *(move in circle)* dar vueltas
(**b**) *(visit)* **I said I'd go round (and see her)** dije que me pasaría (a visitarla); **she's gone round to a friend's** ha ido a casa de un amigo
(**c**) *(circulate) (rumour)* circular, correr; **there's a virus going round** hay un virus suelto por ahí; **she goes round with some strange people** sale por ahí con unos tipos raros; **you can't just go round lying to everyone** no puedes ir por ahí mintiendo a todo el mundo
(**d**) *(suffice) (food, drink)* llegar, alcanzar; **are there enough plates to go round?** ¿tenemos suficientes platos?; **there should be enough money to go round** debería llegarnos el dinero

▸ **go through** 1 *vt insep* (**a**) *(penetrate)* atravesar
(**b**) *(experience, suffer)* pasar (por), atravesar; **I can't face going through all that again** no puedo pasar por eso otra vez; **in spite of all she had gone through...** a pesar de todo lo que le había pasado...
(**c**) *(complete) (formalities)* cumplir con
(**d**) *(be dealt with via)* **your application must go through the proper channels** su solicitud debe seguir los trámites *or* cauces apropiados
(**e**) *(examine) (document, accounts)* estudiar, examinar; *(suitcase, house)* registrar; **he went through his pockets looking for the letter** rebuscó en los bolsillos buscando la carta
(**f**) *(practise)* repasar; **let's go through it one more time** repasémoslo una vez más
(**g**) *(explain)* explicar; **could you go through the first bit again?** ¿podrías explicar la primera parte otra vez?
(**h**) *(use up) (money, food)* acabar con, gastar; **we've gone through six bottles of milk** hemos gastado seis botellas de leche
2 *vi* (**a**) *(enter)* pasar, entrar; **you can go through to the interview room** puede pasar a la oficina de entrevistas (**b**) *(be approved) (proposal, bill)* aprobarse; *(deal, divorce)* consumarse (**c**) *(qualify)* clasificarse

▸ **go through with** *vt insep (carry out)* llevar a término

▸ **go together** *vi* (**a**) *(harmonize)* pegar, ir bien; **red wine and fish don't go together** el vino tinto y el pescado no combinan bien; **youth and innocence don't always go together** la juventud y la inocencia no siempre van unidas (**b**) *Fam (have relationship)* salir juntos

▸ **go towards** *vt insep (contribute to)* **this money can go towards your new bicycle** aquí tienes una contribución para tu nueva bicicleta

▸ **go under** 1 *vt insep* **this product goes under the name of...** este producto se comercializa con el nombre de...
2 *vi* (**a**) *(drowning person)* hundirse; *(ship)* naufragar (**b**) *(go bankrupt)* quebrar, ir a la quiebra

▸ **go up** 1 *vt insep (ascend) (hill, ladder)* subir; **I'm just going up the road to the shop** voy un momento a la tienda
2 *vi* (**a**) *(climb, rise)* subir; *Theat (curtain)* levantarse; *(building)* subir; **a notice went up saying...** pusieron un aviso que decía...; **the wall went up overnight** construyeron el muro de un día a otro; **to go up to bed** subir a acostarse; **we're going up to Canada** vamos a subir a Canadá; *Fig* **he's gone up in my opinion** ahora lo tengo en más estima; IDIOM **to go up in the world** prosperar
(**b**) *(prices, temperature, standard)* subir; **to go up in price** subir de precio
(**c**) *(be promoted)* subir; **to go up to the first division** subir a primera (división)
(**d**) *(explode)* estallar; **to go up (in flames)** ser pasto de las llamas
(**e**) *(be heard)* **a shout went up from the crowd** se elevó un grito desde la multitud

▸ **go up to** *vt insep* (**a**) *(approach)* acercarse a, aproximarse a (**b**) *(reach)* **the book only goes up to the end of the war** el libro sólo llega hasta el final de la guerra (**c**) *Br (university)* ir a

▸ **go with** *vt insep* (**a**) *(accompany)* ir con; **private health insurance goes with the job** el puesto lleva aparejado un seguro privado de salud; **the consequences that go with heavy drinking** las consecuencias de beber *or Am* tomar en exceso; IDIOM *Fam* **to go with the flow** dejarse llevar por la corriente
(**b**) *(harmonize with)* pegar con; **red wine doesn't go with fish** el vino tinto no combina con el pescado
(**c**) *(agree with, accept) (decision)* aceptar; **we've decided to go with the original plan** hemos decidido seguir el plan original
(**d**) *Fam (have sexual relationship with)* acostarse con

▸ **go without** 1 *vt insep (not have)* prescindir de, quedarse sin; **it goes without saying that...** no hace falta decir que...
2 *vi* pasar privaciones; **they haven't got any, so we'll just have to go without** no les quedan, así que habrá que apañárselas (sin ellos)

---

go[2] *n (game)* go *m*

goad [gəʊd] 1 *n* (**a**) *(prod)* aguijada *f*, *Am* picana *f* (**b**) *(remark, criticism)* acicate *m*
2 *vt* (**a**) *(animal)* aguijonear (**b**) *(sb's curiosity, interest)* suscitar; **to g. sb into doing sth** pinchar a alguien para que haga algo; **he goaded me into losing my temper** tanto me provocó *or* pinchó que perdí los estribos; **it goaded them into action** les incitó a la acción; **he was goaded by these remarks** estos comentarios le sirvieron de acicate

▸ **goad on** *vt sep* **to g. sb on** *(motivate)* espolear *or* acicatear a alguien

go-ahead ['gəʊəhed] 1 *n* visto *m* bueno; **to give sth/sb the g.** dar luz verde a algo/alguien
2 *adj (enterprising)* dinámico(a), emprendedor(ora)

goal [gəʊl] *n* (**a**) *(aim)* objetivo *m*, meta *f*; **what's your g. in life?** ¿cuál es tu objetivo *or* meta en la vida?; **to achieve** *or* **attain a g.** alcanzar un objetivo *or* una meta; **to define one's goals** concretar *or* definir los objetivos; **to set oneself a g.** marcarse un objetivo *or* una meta
(**b**) *Sport (point)* gol *m*; *(goalmouth)* portería *f*, *Am* arco *m*; **to score a g.** marcar *or* meter un gol; **to be in** *or* **play in** *or* **keep g. (for)** jugar de guardameta *or* portero *or Am* arquero ▸▸ ***g. area*** área *f* (de meta); ***g. average*** promedio *m* de goles; ***g. difference*** gol *m* average; ***g. kick*** saque *m* de puerta; ***g. kicker*** *(in American football)* goal kicker *m*; ***g. line*** *(at end of field)* línea *f* de fondo; *(between goalposts)* línea *f* de gol *or* meta; *(in rugby)* línea *f* de marca, *RP* ingoal *m*; ***g. scorer*** goleador(ora) *m,f*

goalkeeper ['gəʊlki:pə(r)], *Fam* **goalie** ['gəʊlɪ] *n* portero(a) *m,f*, guardameta *mf*, *Am* arquero(a) *m,f*, *Am* guardavallas *mf inv*, *RP* golero(a) *m,f*

goalkeeping ['gəʊlki:pɪŋ] *n* defensa *f* de la portería *or Am* del arco; **that was an excellent piece of g.** ha sido una sensacional parada ▸▸ ***g. gloves*** guantes *mpl* de portero *or Am* arquero

goalless ['gəʊllɪs] *adj Sport* ***g. draw*** empate *m* a cero

goalminder ['gəʊlmaɪndə(r)] *n Br (in hockey, ice hockey)* portero(a) *m,f*, *Am* arquero(a) *m,f*

goalmouth ['gəʊlmaʊθ] *n (in soccer)* portería *f*, *Am* arco *m* ▸▸ ***g. scramble*** melé *f* en el área pequeña

goalpost ['gəʊlpəʊst] *n* poste *m*; **the goalposts** la portería, la meta, *Am* el arco; IDIOM **to move** *or* **shift the goalposts** cambiar las reglas del juego

goaltender ['gəʊltendə(r)] *n* portero(a) *m,f*, *Am* arquero(a) *m,f*

Goan ['gəʊən], **Goanese** [gəʊə'ni:z] 1 *n* goanés(esa) *m,f*
2 *adj* goanés(esa)

go-as-you-please ['gəʊəzju:'pli:z] *adj (informal)* informal

goat [gəʊt] *n* (**a**) *(animal)* cabra *f* ▸▸ ***g.'s milk*** leche *f* de cabra (**b**) *Fam* **(old) g.** *(lecherous man)* viejo *m* verde; **you silly g.!** ¡melón! (**c**) IDIOMS *Br* **to act** *or* **play the g.** hacer el indio, hacer el ganso; *Fam* **it really gets my g.!** ¡me pone negro(a) *or* a cien *or RP* de la nuca!

goatee ['gəʊti:] *n* perilla *f*

goatherd ['gəʊthɜ:d] *n* cabrero(a) *m,f*

goatskin ['gəʊtskɪn] *n* (**a**) *(hide)* piel *f* de cabra (**b**) *(container)* odre *m*

goatsucker ['gəʊtsʌkə(r)] *n* chotacabras *m inv* (gris)

gob [gɒb] 1 *n* (**a**) *esp Br very Fam (mouth)* pico *m*; **shut your g.!** ¡cierra el pico!; **he's got a bit of a g. on him** es un bocazas (**b**) *Br Fam (spittle)* escupitajo *m*, gargajo *m* (**c**) *US Fam* **gobs of** montones de; **gobs of money** dinero a patadas, montones de dinero
2 *vi (pt & pp* **gobbed**) *Br Fam (spit)* escupir, echar lapos

gobbet ['gɒbɪt] *n* (**a**) *(of food, substance)* trozo *m*, cacho *m*; **a g. of information** un dato, una información (**b**) *Fam (extract from text)* trozo *m*, cacho *m*

gobble ['gɒbəl] 1 *vt* (**a**) *(eat)* engullir (**b**) *Vulg (fellate)* chupar
2 *vi (turkey)* gluglutear

▸ **gobble up** *vt sep* engullir; **to g. up one's food** engullir la comida; **to g. up money/resources** *(of project)* consumir mucho dinero/muchos recursos

gobbledygook, gobbledegook ['gɒbəldɪgu:k] *n Fam (jargon)* jerga *f* incomprensible; *(nonsense)* galimatías *m inv*

gobbler ['gɒblə(r)] *n US (turkey)* pavo *m*, *Méx* guajolote *m*

gobby ['gɒbɪ] *adj Br Fam* **to be g.** ser un bocazas

go-between ['gəʊbɪtwi:n] *n* mediador(ora) *m,f*; **to act** *or* **serve as a g.** actuar como mediador, mediar

Gobi ['gəʊbɪ] *n* **the G. (Desert)** el desierto de Gobi

goblet ['gɒblɪt] *n* copa *f*

goblin ['gɒblɪn] *n* duende *m*

gobshite ['gɒbʃaɪt] *n Br Vulg Esp* gilipollas *mf inv*, *Am* pendejo(a) *m,f*

gobsmacked ['gɒbsmækt] *adj Br Fam* **I was g.** me quedé atónito *or Esp* flipado

gobstopper ['gɒbstɒpə(r)] *n Br* = caramelo grande y redondo

goby ['gəʊbɪ] *n Zool* gobio *m* (de mar)

go-by ['gəʊbaɪ] *n Fam* **to give sb the g.** no hacer caso de alguien, pasar de alguien

GOC [dʒi:əʊ'si:] *n Mil* (*abbr* **General Officer Commanding**) oficial *mf* general al mando

go-cart ['gəʊkɑ:t] *n* (**a**) *(motorized)* kart *m* ▸▸ ***g. racing*** carreras *fpl* de karts (**b**) *(home-made)* carro *m* de juguete (**c**) *US (pushchair)* cochecito *m* (de bebé) (**d**) *US (babywalker)* andador *m*

God [gɒd] *n* (**a**) *(supreme being)* Dios *m*; **G. the Father, the Son and the Holy Ghost** el Padre, el Hijo y el Espíritu Santo; **G. bless you!** ¡que Dios te bendiga!; **G. help us** que Dios nos agarre *or Esp* coja confesados; **please G.** te lo ruego, Señor; **G. willing** si Dios quiere ▸▸ ***G. mode*** *(in computer game)* modo *m* Dios; *Fam* ***G. slot*** la hora del Señor, el programa de la misa; *Fam* ***the G. squad*** los beatos *(que intentan convertir a los demás)*
(**b**) *(deity)* dios *m*; **the g. of War/Fire** el dios de la Guerra/del Fuego; **profit is their only g.** las ganancias son lo único que les interesa; *Hum* **ye gods!** ¡cielo santo!
(**c**) *Fam (in interjections and expressions)* **oh G.!, my G.!** ¡Dios mío!; **G. Almighty!** ¡Santo Dios!; **G. forbid!** ¡Dios no lo quiera!; **for G.'s sake!, for the love of G.!** ¡por (el amor de) Dios!; **for G.'s sake, don't tell him!** por Dios ¡no se lo digas!; **thank G.** menos mal, gracias a Dios; **thank G. for that** menos mal; **I wish to G....** ojalá...; **G. help you!** *(in warning, in sympathy)* ¡pobre de tí!; **G. (only) knows** sabe Dios; **in G.'s name, in the name of G.** por el amor de Dios; **what in G.'s name are you doing?** pero por el amor de Dios, ¿qué haces?; **G.'s truth!** lo juro por Dios, es la pura verdad
(**d**) *Fam Theat* **the gods** *(gallery)* el gallinero
(**e**) IDIOMS **to play G.** jugar a ser Dios; *Fam* **he thinks he's G.'s gift** se cree que es lo mejor que hay; *Fam* **he thinks he's G.'s gift to women** se cree que las mujeres se vuelven locas por él

god-awful ['gɒdɔ:fəl] *adj Fam* horroroso(a)

god-botherer ['gɒdbɒðərə(r)] *n Fam* beato(a) *m,f (que intenta convertir a los demás)*

godchild ['gɒdtʃaɪld] *n* ahijado(a) *m,f*

goddam(n) ['gɒdæm] *Fam* 1 *adj* maldito(a), *Esp* dichoso(a), *Méx* pinche; **he's a g. fool!** ¡es un maldito imbécil!
2 *adv* **that was g. stupid!** ¡eso fue una auténtica estupidez!
3 *exclam* **g. (it)!** ¡maldita sea!, *Méx* ¡híjole!, *RP* ¡miércoles!

goddaughter ['gɒddɔːtə(r)] *n* ahijada *f*

goddess ['gɒdɪs] *n* diosa *f*; *Fig* **a g. of the (silver) screen, a screen g.** una diosa del cine

godfather ['gɒdfɑːðə(r)] *n* (**a**) *(godparent)* padrino *m* (**b**) *(criminal)* padrino *m*

god-fearing ['gɒdfɪərɪŋ] *adj* temeroso(a) de Dios

godforsaken ['gɒdfəseɪkən] *adj* dejado(a) de la mano de Dios; **what a g. place!** ¡qué lugar de mala muerte!

god-given ['gɒdgɪvən] *adj* divino(a); **she sees it as her g. right** lo ve como un derecho otorgado por la gracia divina

Godhead ['gɒdhed] *n Formal* **the G.** Dios *m*, el Señor

godless ['gɒdlɪs] *adj* impío(a)

godlessness ['gɒdlɪsnɪs] *n* impiedad *f*

godlike ['gɒdlaɪk] *adj* divino(a)

godliness ['gɒdlɪnɪs] *n* piedad *f*, devoción *f*

godly ['gɒdlɪ] *adj* pío(a), piadoso(a); **to lead a g. life** llevar una vida piadosa

godmother ['gɒdmʌðə(r)] *n* madrina *f*

godparent ['gɒdpeərənt] *n* padrino *m*, madrina *f*; **my godparents** mis padrinos

godsend ['gɒdsend] *n* regalo *m* del cielo; **this money is a g. to him** este dinero le viene como llovido del cielo

godson ['gɒdsʌn] *n* ahijado *m*

Godspeed ['gɒdspiːd] *exclam Archaic* ¡vaya con Dios!; **we wished them G. on their journey** les deseamos feliz viaje

godwit ['gɒdwɪt] *n* aguja *f*; **bar-tailed g.** aguja colipinta; **black-tailed g.** aguja colinegra

goer ['gəʊə(r)] *n Br Fam* (**a**) *(fast person, vehicle, animal)* bala *f*; **this horse is a real g.** este caballo es una bala (**b**) *(woman)* **she's quite a g.** es una calentona, *Esp* le va la marcha

-goer ['gəʊə(r)] *suffix* **concert/opera-g.** aficionado(a) a los conciertos/a la ópera

go-faster stripes ['gəʊfɑːstə'straɪps] *npl Fam (on car)* embellecedores *mpl* laterales

gofer ['gəʊfə(r)] *n Fam* recadero(a) *m,f*, chico(a) *m,f* de los recados *or RP* mandados

go-getter ['gəʊ'getə(r)] *n Fam* **he's a real g.** es ambicioso y decidido

go-getting ['gəʊ'getɪŋ] *adj Fam (person, approach)* audaz, osado(a)

goggle ['gɒgəl] *vi* mirar con ojos desorbitados; **to g. at sth/sb** mirar algo/a alguien con los ojos como platos

goggle-box ['gɒgəlbɒks] *n Br Fam* caja *f* tonta, tele *f*

goggle-eyed ['gɒgəlaɪd] *adv Fam* con ojos como platos *or RP* como dos huevos fritos

goggles ['gɒgəlz] *npl (for swimmer, skier, motorcyclist)* gafas *fpl*, *CSur* antiparras *fpl*; *(for diver)* gafas *fpl* de buceo, *RP* lentes *mpl* de natación; **safety g.** gafas protectoras, *CSur* antiparras protectoras

go-go ['gəʊ'gəʊ] *n* ***g. dancer*** gogó *f*; ***g. dancing*** baile *m* de gogós

going ['gəʊɪŋ] 1 *n* (**a**) *(leaving)* partida *f*
(**b**) *(progress)* **we made good g. on the return journey** fuimos a buena marcha en el viaje de vuelta; **that's very good g.!** ¡es un buen ritmo!; **it's slow g.** se avanza lentamente
(**c**) *(condition of path)* camino *m*; *(in horseracing)* terreno *m*; **the g. is good** el terreno está en buen estado; *Fig* **to get out while the g. is good** retirarse mientras las cosas van bien; **heavy g.** *(film, book)* pesado(a); **it's hard g. on these mountain roads** es difícil avanzar por estas rutas de montaña; *Fig* **it's heavy g. getting him to talk** cuesta mucho hacerlo hablar; PROV **when the g. gets tough, the tough get g.** al mal tiempo buena cara
2 *adj* (**a**) *(functioning)* **a g. concern** *(successful business)* un negocio en marcha y rentable (**b**) *(current)* **the g. price** *or* **rate** *(for purchase)* la tasa *or* el precio vigente; **the g. rate** *(for job)* la tarifa vigente; **the best novelist g.** el mejor novelista de la actualidad

going-away ['gəʊɪŋə'weɪ] *adj* **g. dress/outfit** vestido/conjunto de luna de miel; **a g. party/present** una fiesta/un regalo de despedida

going-over ['gəʊɪŋ'əʊvə(r)] *n Fam* (**a**) *(check-up)* revisión *f*; **the auditors gave the accounts a thorough g.** los auditores miraron las cuentas de arriba abajo *or* con lupa
(**b**) *(clean-up)* limpieza *f*; **the house needs a good g.** la casa necesita una buena pasada *or* limpieza
(**c**) **to give sb a g.** *(beating)* dar una paliza a alguien; *(criticism)* echar una reprimenda *or Esp* bronca a alguien, *RP* dar a alguien un buen rezongo; **the burglars had given the house a real g.** los ladrones habían dejado la casa manga por hombro

goings-on ['gəʊɪŋz'ɒn] *npl Fam* (**a**) *Pej (behaviour)* tejemanejes *mpl*; **there are some funny g. in that house** en aquella casa pasan cosas raras (**b**) *(events)* acontecimientos *mpl*

goitre, *US* **goiter** ['gɔɪtə(r)] *n* bocio *m*

go-kart ['gəʊkɑːt] *n* (**a**) *(motorized)* kart *m* ▸▸ ***g. racing*** carreras *fpl* de karts (**b**) *(home-made)* carro *m* de juguete

Golan Heights ['gəʊlæn'haɪts] *npl* **the G.** los Altos del Golán

gold [gəʊld] 1 *n* (**a**) *(metal)* oro *m* ▸▸ ***g. bullion*** lingotes *mpl* de oro; ***g. dust*** oro *m* en polvo; IDIOM **tickets are like g. dust** es casi imposible conseguir una entrada *or Méx* un boleto; ***g. fever*** fiebre *f* del oro; ***g. filling*** *(in tooth)* empaste *m* de oro; ***g. foil*** pan *m* de oro, oro *m* batido; ***g. leaf*** pan *m* de oro, oro *m* batido; *Sport* ***g. medal*** medalla *f* de oro; ***g. mine*** mina *f* de oro; *Fig* mina *f* (de oro); ***g. plate*** *(decoration)* baño *m* de oro; *(dishes)* vajilla *f* de oro; *Fin* ***g. reserves*** reservas *fpl* de oro; ***g. rush*** fiebre *f* del oro; ***g. standard*** patrón *m* oro
(**b**) *(gold medal)* medalla *f* de oro; **to go for g.** *Esp* ir a por *orAm* ir en procura de la medalla de oro
(**c**) *(colour)* dorado *m*
2 *adj* (**a**) *(of gold)* de oro (**b**) *(colour)* dorado(a) ▸▸ ***g. braid*** galón *m* de oro; ***g. card*** tarjeta *f* oro; ***g. disc*** disco *m* de oro; ***g. lamé*** lamé *m* dorado; ***g. star*** *(given to schoolchildren)* = estrella dorada de papel, símbolo de buenas notas o de buena conducta
3 *adv* **to go g.** *(record)* convertirse en disco de oro

goldbrick ['gəʊldbrɪk] *US Fam* 1 *n* (**a**) *(shirker)* **to be a g.** esquivarse, *Esp* escaquearse, *RP* zafarse (**b**) IDIOM **to sell sb a g.** vender a alguien gato por liebre
2 *vt (swindle)* vender gato por liebre a
3 *vi (not work)* esquivarse, *Esp* escaquearse, *RP* zafarse

gold-coloured ['gəʊldkʌləd] *adj* dorado(a), de color oro

goldcrest ['gəʊldkrest] *n* reyezuelo *m* sencillo

gold-digger ['gəʊld'dɪgə(r)] *n Fam Pej (mercenary woman)* cazafortunas *f inv*

golden ['gəʊldən] *adj* (**a**) *(made of gold)* de oro ▸▸ ***the g. calf*** el becerro de oro; ***the g. goose*** la gallina de los huevos de oro
(**b**) *(gold-coloured)* dorado(a); **g. brown** tostado(a) ▸▸ ***g. eagle*** águila *f* real; ***g. oriole*** oropéndola *f*; ***g. pheasant*** faisán *m* dorado; ***g. pipit*** bisbita *m* dorado; ***g. plover*** chorlito *m* dorado común; ***g. retriever*** retriever *m* dorado, = raza de perro cobrador; *Br* ***g. syrup*** melaza *f* de caña
(**c**) *(excellent)* **a g. opportunity** una oportunidad de oro; **the g. boy/girl of...** el chico/la chica de oro de...; **his last book won him g. opinions from the critics** su último libro recibió excelentes críticas ▸▸ ***the G. Age*** *Mythol* la edad de oro; *(of Spanish literature)* el Siglo de Oro; ***g. goal*** *(in soccer)* gol *m* de oro; ***the g. mean*** el punto medio; ***g. oldie*** clásico *m*, viejo éxito *m*; ***g. rule*** regla *f* de oro; ***g. section*** sección *f* áurea; *Fin* ***g. share*** acción *f* de oro, participación *f* de control; ***the g. triangle*** el triángulo dorado *or* de oro
(**d**) *(marking 50 years)* ***g. jubilee*** quincuagésimo aniversario *m*, cincuentenario *m*; ***g. wedding*** bodas *fpl* de oro
(**e**) *Com* ***g. handcuffs*** contrato *m* blindado; ***g. handshake*** *(retirement bonus)* gratificación *f* voluntaria por jubilación; ***g. hello*** = cuantiosa gratificación ofrecida como incentivo para ingresar en una empresa; ***g. parachute*** contrato *m* blindado
(**f**) *(in proper names)* ***G. Delicious*** (manzana *f*) golden *f*; ***the G. Fleece*** el Vellocino de Oro; ***the G. Gate (Bridge)*** el (puente) Golden Gate

goldeneye ['gəʊldənaɪ] *n* porrón *m* osculado

goldenrod ['gəʊldənrɒd] *n Bot* vara *f* de oro *(planta)*

goldfield ['gəʊldfiːld] *n* yacimiento *m* de oro

goldfinch ['gəʊldfɪntʃ] *n* jilguero *m*

goldfish ['gəʊldfɪʃ] *n* pez *m* de colores ▸▸ ***g. bowl*** pecera *f*; IDIOM **it's like living in a g. bowl** es como estar expuesto(a) en una vitrina

goldilocks ['gəʊldɪlɒks] *n Fam* ricitos *mpl* de oro, rubiales *mf inv*

gold-plated ['gəʊld'pleɪtɪd] *adj* bañado(a) en oro

gold-rimmed ['gəʊld'rɪmd] *adj (spectacles)* con montura de oro

goldsmith ['gəʊldsmɪθ] *n* orfebre *mf*

golf [gɒlf] 1 *n* golf *m* ▸▸ ***g. bag*** bolsa *f* de golf; ***g. ball*** pelota *f* de golf; *(on typewriter, printer)* esfera *f or* bola *f* de impresión; *Br* ***g. buggy*** carrito *m* de golf (eléctrico); ***g. cart*** carrito *m* de golf (eléctrico); ***g. club*** *(stick)* palo *m* de golf; *(association)* club *m* de golf; ***g. course*** campo *m* de golf; ***g. glove*** guante *m* de golf; ***g. links*** campo *m* de golf; ***g. shoes*** zapatos *mpl* de golf; *Br* ***g. trolley*** carrito *m* de golf; ***g.***

umbrella sombrilla *f* de golf; *Hum* **g.** ***widow*** = esposa de un golfista que pasa todo su tiempo libre jugando al golf
2 *vi* jugar al golf

golfer ['gɒlfə(r)] *n* jugador(ora) *m,f* de golf, golfista *mf*; **to be a good g.** jugar bien al golf

golfing ['gɒlfɪŋ] *n* el golf; **g. holiday** = vacaciones dedicadas a jugar al golf

Goliath [gə'laɪəθ] *n* **(a)** *(in the Bible)* Goliat **(b)** *(powerful person, company)* gigante *m*

golliwog, gollywog ['gɒlɪwɒg], *Fam* **golly** ['gɒlɪ] *n (doll)* muñeca *f* negra de trapo *(hoy día considerada racista)*

golly ['gɒlɪ] *exclam Fam Old-fashioned* ¡caramba!; **he said he'd buy it, and by g., so he did!** dijo que lo compraría y ¡vaya si lo hizo!

gollywog = **golliwog**

goloshes = **galoshes**

GOM [dʒiːəʊ'em] *n* (*abbr* **Grand Old Man**) gran mito *m* viviente, leyenda *f* viva

gonad ['gəʊnæd] *n* **(a)** *Biol* gónada *f* **(b)** *very Fam Hum* **gonads** pelotas, huevos

gondola ['gɒndələ] *n* **(a)** *(boat)* góndola *f* **(b)** *(of cable car)* cabina *f* **(c)** *(on airship, balloon)* góndola *f* **(d)** *Mktg* góndola *f* ▸▸ ***g. end*** cabecera *f* de góndola **(e)** *US Rail* **g. (car)** batea *f*

gondolier [gɒndə'lɪə(r)] *n* gondolero *m*

gone [gɒn] **1 (a)** *(past)* **those days are g. now** eso ya se acabó; **g. is the time when you could...** se acabó aquello de poder...
(b) *Literary or Hum (away)* **be g. with you!** ¡desaparece de mi vista!
(c) *Fam (on drugs, drink)* puesto(a); **to be far** *or* **well g.** *Esp* estar muy puesto(a), llevar un buen colocón
(d) *Fam (pregnant)* **to be six months g.** estar de seis meses; **how far g. is she?** ¿de cuánto está?
(e) *Fam (infatuated)* **to be g. on sth/sb** estar colado(a) por algo/alguien
2 *prep (past)* **it's g. ten o'clock** son las diez pasadas
3 *pp of* **go**

goner ['gɒnə(r)] *n Fam* **I thought she was a g.** *(thought she would die)* creí que la palmaba; **I'm a g. if she finds out** *(will be in trouble)* si se entera, me mata

gong [gɒŋ] *n* **(a)** *(for striking)* gong *m* **(b)** *Br Fam (medal)* medalla *f*

gonna ['gənə] *Fam* = **going to**

go-no-go [gəʊ'nəʊgəʊ] *adj US Fam* definitivo(a)

gonorrhoea, *US* **gonorrhea** [gɒnə'rɪə] *n* gonorrea *f*

gonzo ['gɒnzəʊ] *adj US Fam* extravagante ▸▸ ***g. journalism*** = estilo de periodismo extravagante y muy subjetivo

goo [guː] *n Fam* **(a)** *(sticky substance)* porquería *f* pringosa **(b)** *(sentimentality)* cursilería *f*, *Esp* cursiladas *fpl*

goober ['guːbə(r)] *n US* **(a)** *(peanut)* **g. (pea)** cacahuete *m*, *Andes, Carib, RP* maní *m*, *CAm, Méx* cacahuate *m* **(b)** *Fam (idiot)* melón *m*, zoquete *m*

GOOD [gʊd] **1** *n* **(a)** *(in general)* bien *m*; **g. and evil** el bien y el mal; **he's up to no g.** está tramando algo malo; **to do g.** hacer el bien; **to see the g. in sth/sb** ver el lado bueno de algo/alguien
(b) *(benefit)* bien *m*; **what's the g. of that?, what g. is that?** ¿para qué sirve eso?; **I did it for your own g.** lo hice por tu bien; **for the g. of his health** por motivos de salud; *Hum* **I'm not doing this (just) for the g. of my health!** ¡no lo hago por amor al arte!; **for the common g.** por el bien de todos; **it was all to the g.** todo fue para bien; **I'm £50 to the g.** tengo 50 libras más; **it will do you g.** te sentará bien, te vendrá bien, *RP* te va a hacer bien; **the measures will do a lot of g.** las medidas harán mucho bien; **is his new book any g.?** ¿es bueno su nuevo libro?; **it won't do any g.** *(make any difference)* no cambiará nada; **it's no g. complaining** quejarse no sirve de nada; **he's no g.** *(incompetent)* no sirve para nada; *(morally bad)* no es bueno; **the food there's no g.** *or* **not much g.** la comida de allí no es muy buena; **no g. will come of it** no puede acabar *or RP* terminar bien; PROV **you have to take the g. with the bad** hay que estar a las duras y a las maduras, *RP* hay que estar en las buenas y en las malas
2 *npl* **the g.** los buenos
3 *adj* (*comparative* **better** ['betə(r)], *superlative* **best** [best]) **(a)** *(of positive quality)* bueno(a), buen *(before singular masculine noun)*; **to be g.** *(person, movie, book)* ser bueno(a); *(food, drink)* estar bueno(a); **g. to eat** comestible; **he's a g. friend** es un buen amigo; **he used his g. arm** utilizó el brazo bueno; **did you have a g. trip?** ¿tuviste un buen viaje?; *Sch* **"g."** "bien"; **g. luck!** ¡buena suerte!; **we had g. luck** tuvimos buena suerte; **g. luck to her!** ¡me alegro por ella!; *Br Old-fashioned* **g. show!** ¡bien hecho!; **you're late again, it's just not g. enough!** has vuelto a llegar tarde, ¡esto es inaceptable!; **it's g. to see you** me alegro de verte; **I don't feel too g.** no me encuentro *or* siento muy bien; **that feels g.!** ¡así!, ¡así!; **I feel g. about my decision** me siento bien tras haber tomado la decisión; **that cake looks g.** ese pastel tiene buen aspecto; **it looks g. on you** te queda bien; **she looks g. in that hat** le queda muy bien ese sombrero; **to sound/taste g.** sonar/saber bien; **I told him to get lost – g. for you!** lo mandé a paseo – ¡bien hecho!; **if it's g. enough for you, it's g. enough for me** si a ti te sirve *or Esp* vale, a mí también; **to have g. cause** *or* **reason to do sth** tener buenos motivos para hacer algo; **in g. faith** de buena fe; **it was g. fun** fue muy divertido(a); **to have a g. nature** ser bueno(a) por naturaleza; *Br Fam* **Anne's a g. laugh** Anne es muy divertida; *Br Fam* **the party was a g. laugh** lo pasamos genial en la fiesta; **to earn g. money** ganar un buen sueldo; **the g. old days** los viejos tiempos; *Fam* **have a g. one!** ¡que lo pases bien!; *Fam* **that's a g. one!** *(I don't believe you)* ¡no me digas!, *Esp* ¡venga ya!; **she had the g. sense to keep quiet** fue lo suficientemente sensata como para callarse; **to have a g. time** pasarlo bien; **to show sb a g. time** *(entertain)* sacar a alguien a divertirse por ahí; *Fam* **I'll show you a g. time** *(said by prostitute)* te lo voy a hacer pasar de maravilla; **all in g. time** todo llegará; **to arrive in g. time** llegar a tiempo; **I'll do it in my own g. time** lo haré cuando lo considere oportuno; **she was as g. as her word** cumplió lo prometido; **too g. to be true** demasiado bueno para ser verdad; **he's been really nice to me recently, it's too g. to last** se ha portado muy bien conmigo últimamente, esto no puede durar mucho; **I suppose he thinks he's too g. for us** debe pensar que es más que nosotros; **she's too g. for him** es demasiado buena para él; PROV **all g. things come to an end** todo lo bueno se acaba ▸▸ ***the G. Book*** la Biblia; IDIOM **to be in sb's g. books** estar a buenas con alguien, *RP* estar en buenos términos con alguien; ***a g. cause*** una buena causa; ***G. Friday*** Viernes *m inv* Santo; *Fam* ***the g. guys*** los buenos; ***the g. life*** la buena vida; ***g. looks*** atractivo *m*; ***g. news*** buenas noticias *fpl*; *US Fam* **g. *old*** *or* ***ole*** *or* ***ol' boy*** = blanco sureño tradicionalista; *Rel & Fig* ***G. Samaritan*** buen samaritano *m*; *Rel* ***the G. Shepherd*** el Buen Pastor
(b) *(advantageous, beneficial)* bueno(a); **a g. opportunity** una buena ocasión; **to be g. for business** ser bueno(a) para los negocios; **I got a g. deal on this holiday** las vacaciones me salieron muy baratas; **he doesn't know what's g. for him** no sabe lo que le conviene; **to be in a g. position to do sth** estar en una buena posición para hacer algo; **to use sth to g. purpose** hacer buen uso de algo; **things are looking g.** la cosa tiene buena pinta; **to be on to a g. thing** tener entre manos algo bueno; **she never has a g. word for anyone** nunca habla bien de nadie; **to put in a g. word for sb** decir unas palabras en favor de alguien; PROV **you can have too much of a g. thing** lo bueno, si breve, dos veces bueno
(c) *(appropriate, suitable)* **it's a g. day for mowing the lawn** es un buen día para cortar el césped; **is now a g. moment?** ¿es éste un buen momento?; **now's as g. a time as any** ahora, ¿por qué no?; **tomorrow is g. for me** mañana me *Esp* va *or Am* viene bien; **it's a g. job** *or* **thing we were here** menos mal que estábamos aquí; **g. riddance!** ¡ya era hora de que desapareciera!
(d) *(healthy)* bueno(a); **this medicine is very g. for coughs** este medicamento es muy bueno para la tos; **exercise is g. for you** el ejercicio es bueno para la salud, el ejercicio hace bien
(e) *(useful)* **that's a g. thing to know** es bueno saber eso; **this sofa is g. for a few years yet** este sofá durará unos cuantos años más; **he's g. for nothing** no sirve para nada, es un inútil; **he's g. for $25,000** *(has in credit)* tiene un activo de 25.000 dólares; *(will contribute)* aportará 25.000 dólares; *Fam* **she's always g. for a laugh** *(entertaining)* con ella siempre nos lo pasamos bien; **that should be g. for a laugh** ya verás como nos reímos
(f) *(skilful)* bueno(a); **he is a g. swimmer** es un buen nadador, nada muy bien; **she is g. at chemistry** tiene facilidad para la química, se le da bien la química, *Am* es buena en química; **he is g. at languages** tiene facilidad para los idiomas, se le dan bien los idiomas, *Am* es bueno para los idiomas; **to be g. with one's hands** ser habilidoso(a) con las manos *or Esp* muy manitas; **she is g. with children** se lleva bien con los niños, se le dan bien los niños; **he's g. with people** tiene don de gentes; **to be g. in bed** ser bueno(a) en la cama
(g) *(well-behaved)* bueno(a); **be g.!** *(to child)* ¡sé bueno!, ¡pórtate bien!; **g. boy/girl!** ¡qué bueno/buena eres!; **g. dog!** ¡buen chico!; **g. behaviour** *or* **conduct** buena conducta, buen comportamiento; **to lead a g. life** llevar una vida ejemplar; IDIOM **to be as g. as gold** ser más bueno(a) que el pan
(h) *(kind)* amable; **she's a g. person** es una buena persona; **to be g. to sb** ser amable *or* bueno con alguien; *Formal* **would you be so g. as to** *or* **g. enough to...?** ¿serías tan amable de...?; **he was very g. about it** fue muy comprensivo al respecto; **that's very g. of you** es muy amable de tu parte; **g. old Bob's got dinner for us!** ¡el bueno de

Bob nos ha preparado la cena!; **g. deed** buena obra; **to do sb a g. turn** hacer un favor a alguien

(i) *(valid)* **the ticket is g. for two weeks** el *Esp* billete *or Am* boleto *or Am* pasaje es válido durante dos semanas; **(that's a) g. point** es verdad; **(that's a) g. question** buena pregunta; **a g. reason** una buena razón; **I have g. reason to believe that...** tengo buenas razones para creer que...; **there is no g. reason why...** no hay razón alguna por la que...

(j) *Sport (goal, try, touchdown)* válido(a); **the ball was g.** *(in tennis)* la bola ha entrado

(k) *(thorough)* bueno(a); **to have a g. cry (about)** llorar a gusto (por), *Esp* echarse una buena llantina (por); **to have a g. look (at sth/sb)** mirar bien (algo/a alguien); **have a g. think about it** piénsalo bien

(l) **to make g.** *(person)* prosperar; **he was ordered to make g. the company's losses** fue condenado a indemnizar a la empresa por las pérdidas; **they made g. their promise/threat** cumplieron su promesa/amenaza; **he made g. his escape** consiguió escapar

(m) *(at least)* **a g. ten hours/miles** por lo menos diez horas/millas

(n) *(large)* **the room is a g. size** la habitación es bastante grande; **you've got a g. chance** tienes bastantes posibilidades; **there's a g. chance the game will be postponed** es muy probable que se aplace *or Am* postergue el partido; **a g. deal better** mucho mejor; **a g. deal of** mucho(s), mucha(s); **a g. few** bastantes; **a g. many** muchos(as); **we've come a g. way** hemos progresado mucho; **it took a g. while** llevó un buen rato

(o) *(in greetings)* **g. afternoon!** ¡buenas tardes!; **g. day!** *Austr, US (hello)* ¡hola!; *Br Old-fashioned (hello)* ¡buenas!; *(goodbye)* ¡adiós!; **g. evening!** ¡buenas tardes/noches!; **g. morning!** ¡buenos días!; **g. night!** ¡buenas noches!, ¡hasta mañana!; **to say g. night (to sb)** dar las buenas noches (a alguien); **a g. night kiss** un beso de buenas noches

(p) *Fam (in exclamations)* **g. God!, g. grief!, g. heavens!, g. Lord!, g. gracious!** ¡santo cielo!, ¡dios mío!, *Esp* ¡madre mía!

(q) *(in horse-racing) (ground)* en buen estado

4 *adv* (a) *(for emphasis)* bien, muy; **a g. hard bed** una cama bien dura; **a g. long time** un rato bien largo, mucho tiempo; *Fam* **her soup is always g. and hot** su sopa siempre está bien calentita; *Fam* **I'll do it when I'm g. and ready** lo haré cuando crea conveniente; *Fam* **they beat us g. and proper** nos dieron una buena paliza

(b) *(as comment, answer)* bien, estupendo, *Andes, CAm, Carib, Méx* chévere, *Méx* padre, *RP* bárbaro; **I feel better today – g.** hoy me encuentro mejor – estupendo *or Andes, CAm, Carib, Méx* chévere *or Méx* padre *or RP* bárbaro; **g., it's a relief to know you're all right** me alegro mucho de saber que estás bien; **I've finished that piece of work – g.!** he acabado ese trabajo – ¡muy bien!; **g., so we'll meet at eight, then** de acuerdo, nos veremos a las ocho; *Br* **very g., sir!** *(yes)* sí, señor

(c) *US Fam (well)* bien; **I played real g.** jugué muy bien; **listen and listen g.!** ¡escucha bien!

5 for good *adv (permanently)* para siempre; *US* **for g. and all** por siempre jamás

6 as good as *adv (almost)* **it's as g. as new** está como nuevo; **if she hears about it, I'm as g. as dead** si se entera, me puedo dar por muerto; **he as g. as called me a liar** prácticamente me llamó mentiroso

---

goodbye ['gʊd'baɪ] *n* despedida *f*, adiós *m*; **g.!** ¡adiós!; **to say g.** despedirse; **to say g. to sb** decir adiós a alguien, despedir a alguien; **to give sb a g. kiss/hug** dar a alguien un beso/un abrazo de despedida; **they said their goodbyes** dijeron adiós, se despidieron; **he can say g. to his chances of winning** puede despedirse del triunfo

good-for-nothing ['gʊdfə'nʌθɪŋ] **1** *n* inútil *mf*, bala *m* perdida
2 *adj* inútil

good-hearted [gud'hɑ:tɪd] *adj (person)* de buen corazón; *(action)* bien intencionado(a)

good-humoured, *US* **good-humored** ['gʊd'hju:məd] *adj (discussion)* afable; *(joke, remark)* sin mala intención; **a g. fellow** un tipo de buen carácter; **he's always g.** siempre está de buen humor

good-humouredly, *US* **good-humoredly** ['gʊd'hju:mədlɪ] *adv* con buen humor

goodie = **goody**

goodish ['gʊdɪʃ] *adj Fam* (a) *(quite good)* bastante bueno(a) (b) *(number, size)* bastante grande; **add a g. pinch of salt** agrega una buena pizca de sal

good-looker ['gʊd'lʊkə(r)] *n Fam* **to be a g.** estar bueno(a)

good-looking ['gʊd'lʊkɪŋ] *adj Esp* guapo(a), *Am* lindo(a); **hey, g.!** *(to woman)* ¡oye, preciosa *or Esp* guapa!; *(to man) Esp* ¡oye, guapo!, *Am* ¡ey, buen mozo!

goodly ['gʊdlɪ] *adj Literary (amount, size)* considerable, importante; **a g. sum of money** una importante suma de dinero

good-natured ['gʊd'neɪtʃəd] *adj (person)* bondadoso(a); *(discussion, disagreement)* amigable

goodness ['gʊdnɪs] *n* (a) *(of person)* bondad *f*; **out of the g. of my heart** por lo bueno que soy

(b) *(of food)* valor *m* nutritivo; **if you boil it, you lose all the g.** si lo hierves, pierde todas sus propiedades *or* todo su valor nutritivo

(c) *(in exclamations)* **g. (me)!** ¡santo cielo!; **(my) g.!** ¡madre mía!; **thank g.!** ¡gracias a Dios!; **for g. sake, be quiet!** ¡por el amor de Dios, cállate!; **g. knows** sabe Dios; **I wish to g. he would shut up!** ¡quiera Dios que se calle la boca!

good-oh ['gʊdəʊ] *exclam Fam* ¡bien!, ¡qué bueno!

goods [gʊdz] *npl* (a) *(possessions)* bienes *mpl*; **he gave up all his worldly g.** abandonó todas sus posesiones ▸▸ *Br* ***g. and chattels*** enseres *mpl*

(b) *(articles, merchandise)* artículos *mpl*, productos *mpl*; **leather g.** artículos *or* productos de cuero

(c) *Br (freight)* ***g. depot*** almacén *m* de mercancías; ***g. train*** tren *m* de mercancías; ***g. van*** vagón *m* de mercancías; ***g. wagon*** vagón *m* de mercancías; ***g. yard*** almacén *m* de mercancías

(d) IDIOMS **to come up with the g.** cumplir; **to deliver the g.** estar a la altura de las circunstancias; *US Fam* **to have the g. on sb** tener pruebas contra alguien

good-sized ['gʊd'saɪzd] *adj* grande, de buen tamaño

good-tempered ['gʊd'tempəd] *adj (person)* afable

good-time girl ['gʊdtaɪm'gɜ:l] *n Fam* chica *f* de vida alegre

goodwill ['gʊd'wɪl] *n* (a) *(benevolence, willingness)* buena voluntad *f*; **a gesture of g., a g. gesture** un gesto de buena voluntad; **to retain sb's g.** conservar el favor de alguien ▸▸ ***g. ambassador*** embajador *m* en misión de buena voluntad; ***g. visit*** visita *f* de buena voluntad

(b) *Com* fondo *m* de comercio

(c) *US* ***G. shop*** = tienda perteneciente a una entidad benéfica en la que normalmente se venden artículos de segunda mano

goody, goodie ['gʊdɪ] *Fam* **1** *n* (a) *(person)* buenazo(a) *m,f*; **the goodies and the baddies** los buenos y los malos (b) **goodies** *(food)* golosinas; *(presents, prizes)* regalos (c) *US Fam* **goodies** *(genitals) Esp* paquete, *Méx* cosa *f*, *RP* bulto *m* (d) *US Fam* **goodies** *(breasts)* melones, *Esp* peras, *Méx* chichís, *RP* lolas
2 *exclam* ¡viva!, *Esp* ¡qué chupi!

goody-goody ['gʊdɪgʊdɪ] *Fam Pej* **1** *n* niño(a) *m,f* modelo
2 *adj* modélico(a)

gooey ['gu:ɪ] *adj Fam* (a) *(sticky)* pegajoso(a) (b) *(sentimental)* empalagoso(a), sentimentaloide; **she goes all g. over babies** los bebés la ponen tonta

goof [gu:f] *US Fam* **1** *n* (a) *(blunder)* metedura *f or Am* metida *f* de pata; *(in movie)* gazapo *m* (b) *(idiot)* bobo(a) *m,f*
2 *vi* (a) *(make mistake)* meter la pata (b) *(joke)* hacer el bobo; **to g. (with) sb** *(tease)* tomar el pelo a alguien (c) *(stare)* **to g. at** mirar como un(a) bobo(a) a

▸ **goof about, goof around** *vi US Fam (mess around)* hacer el bobo

▸ **goof off** *US Fam* **1** *vt insep* **to g. off work** no ir a trabajar *or Esp* currar
2 *vi (waste time)* holgazanear, gandulear

▸ **goof up** *US Fam* **1** *vt sep* **to g. sth up** meter la pata con algo
2 *vi* meter la pata

goofball ['gu:fbɔ:l] *n US Fam* (a) *(person)* bobalicón(ona) *m,f*, *Esp* zampabollos *mf inv* (b) *(barbiturate)* barbitúrico *m*, somnífero *m*

goofy ['gu:fɪ] *adj Fam* (a) *(stupid)* bobalicón(ona), *Esp* zampabollos *inv* (b) *Br (buck-toothed)* dentón(ona), dentudo(a)

googly ['gu:glɪ] *n (in cricket)* = pelota lanzada con efecto que sorprende al bateador; IDIOM *Br* **to bowl sb a g.** salirle a alguien con una pregunta inesperada

goo-goo ['gu:'gu:] **1** *adj US (loving)* **to make g. eyes at sb** hacer ojitos a alguien
2 *adv Fam* **to go g.** *(baby)* hacer ojitos

gook [gu:k] *n US* (a) *very Fam (oriental)* = término ofensivo para referirse a una persona de China, Vietnam, Corea, etc. (b) *Fam (muck)* porquería *f* pringosa

goolies ['gu:lɪz] *npl Br very Fam (testicles)* pelotas *fpl*, huevos *mpl*

goombah ['gu:mbə] *n US Fam* (a) *(gang member)* miembro *m* de una banda (b) *(associate)* amigo(a) *m,f*, *Esp* colega *mf*, *Méx* cuate *mf*

goon [gu:n] *n Fam* (a) *(stupid person)* bobo(a) *m,f*, lerdo(a) *m,f* (b) *US (thug)* matón *m* ▸▸ ***g. squad*** banda *f* de matones

goosander [guː'sændə(r)] *n* serreta *f* grande

goose [guːs] 1 *n* (*pl* **geese** [giːs]) (**a**) *(bird)* ganso *m*, oca *f* ►► ***g. egg*** huevo *m* de ganso; *US (bump on head)* chichón *m*; *US (zero)* cero *m*; ***pink-footed g.*** ánsar *m* piquicorto; ***red-breasted g.*** barnacla *f* cuellirroja; ***white-fronted g.*** ánsar *m* careto

(**b**) *Old-fashioned Fam (fool)* ganso(a) *m,f*; **don't be such a g.!** ¡no seas ganso!

(**c**) IDIOMS **his g. is cooked** se va a caer con todo el equipo; **to kill the g. that lays the golden eggs** matar la gallina de los huevos de oro ►► *US* ***g. bumps*** carne *f* de gallina; ***g. pimples*** carne *f* de gallina; **I came out in** *or* **got g. pimples** se me puso la carne de gallina

2 *vt Fam* **to g. sb** dar un pellizco en el trasero a alguien

gooseberry ['gʊzbərɪ] *n* grosella *f* silvestre; IDIOM *Br Fam* **to play g.** *Esp* hacer de carabina *or* de sujetavelas, *Méx* hacer mal tercio, *RP* estar de paleta ►► ***g. bush*** grosellero *m* silvestre; IDIOM *Hum* **we found you under a g. bush** te trajo la cigüeña

gooseflesh ['guːsfleʃ] *n* carne *f* de gallina

gooseneck ['guːsnek] *n US* cuello *m* de cisne ►► ***g. lamp*** lámpara *f* de cuello flexible, flexo *m*

goose-step ['guːsstep] 1 *n* paso *m* de la oca

2 *vi* (*pt & pp* **goose-stepped**) marchar al paso de la oca

GOP [dʒiːəʊ'piː] *n Fam* (*abbr* **Grand Old Party**) Partido *m* Republicano *(de Estados Unidos)*

gopher ['gəʊfə(r)] *n* (**a**) *(pocket gopher)* tuza *f* (**b**) *(ground squirrel)* ardilla *f* de tierra (**c**) *(tortoise)* tortuga *f* de tierra (**d**) *Fam (messenger)* recadero(a) *m,f*, chico(a) *m,f* de los recados *or RP* mandados (**e**) *Comptr* gopher *m*

gorblim(e)y [gɔː'blaɪmɪ] 1 *exclam Br Fam* ¡demonios!, ¡caramba!

2 *adj* **a g. accent** un acento "cockney" cerrado

Gordian knot ['gɔːdɪən'nɒt] *n* IDIOM **to cut the G.** cortar el nudo gordiano, resolver el asunto de un plumazo

Gordon Bennett ['gɔːdən'benɪt] *exclam Br Fam* ¡caray!, *Esp* ¡jolín!

gore [gɔː(r)] 1 *n (blood)* sangre *f* (derramada); **there's plenty of g. in this movie** en esta película hay sangre por doquier

2 *vt (of bull)* cornear; **the matador was gored by the bull** el matador recibió una cornada

gorge [gɔːdʒ] 1 *n* (**a**) *(valley)* garganta *f*, desfiladero *m* (**b**) *(throat)* IDIOM **it makes my g. rise** me revuelve el estómago

2 *vt* **to g. oneself (on sth)** atiborrarse (de algo); **don't g. yourself with** *or* **on sweets** no te atiborres de caramelos

3 *vi* atiborrarse (**on** de)

gorgeous ['gɔːdʒəs] *adj* (**a**) *(wonderful) (meal, weather)* estupendo(a), magnífico(a); *(baby, dress)* precioso(a) (**b**) *(attractive) (woman, man) Esp* guapísimo(a), *Am* lindísimo(a) (**c**) *(sumptuous) (fabric, clothing)* magnífico(a)

gorgeously ['gɔːdʒəslɪ] *adv* magníficamente; **g. decorated** con una decoración magnífica

gorgon ['gɔːgən] *n* (**a**) *(in mythology)* gorgona *f* (**b**) *Fam (fierce woman)* bruja *f*, arpía *f*

Gorgonzola [gɔːgən'zəʊlə] *n* (queso *m*) gorgonzola *m*

gorilla [gə'rɪlə] *n* (**a**) *(animal)* gorila *m* (**b**) *Fam (thug)* gorila *m*

gormless ['gɔːmlɪs] *adj Br Fam (person, expression)* idiota, *Esp* memo(a); **a g. idiot** un completo idiota

gorp [gɔːp] *n US* mezcla *f* de frutos secos

gorse [gɔːs] *n* tojo *m*, aulaga *f*; **a g. bush** un arbusto *or* una mata de tojo

gory ['gɔːrɪ] *adj* (**a**) *(film, crime)* sangriento(a); *Fig & Hum* **in g. detail** con pelos y señales (**b**) *(covered in blood)* ensangrentado(a)

gosh [gɒʃ] *exclam Fam* ¡vaya!, *Esp* ¡jolines!, *Méx* ¡híjole!

goshawk ['gɒshɔːk] *n* azor *m*

gosling ['gɒzlɪŋ] *n* ansarón *m*

go-slow ['gəʊ'sləʊ] *n Br* huelga *f* de celo

gospel ['gɒspəl] *n* (**a**) *(in Bible)* evangelio *m*; **St Mark's Gospel, the G. according to St Mark** el evangelio según San Marcos; *Fig* **the g. of monetarism** el evangelio del monetarismo; IDIOM **to take sth as g.: he takes what she says as g.** para él lo que ella dice va a misa; IDIOM **it's the g. truth** es la pura verdad

(**b**) *(music)* **g. (music)** (música *f*) gospel *m* ►► ***g. singer*** cantante *mf* (de) gospel

gossamer ['gɒsəmə(r)] *n* (**a**) *(spider's thread)* (hilos *mpl* de) telaraña *f* (**b**) *(fabric)* gasa *f*

gossip ['gɒsɪp] 1 *n* (**a**) *(person)* chismoso(a) *m,f*, *Esp* cotilla *mf*

(**b**) *(talk)* chismorreo *m*, *Esp* cotilleo *m*; **to have a g. (about)** chismorrear *or Esp* cotillear (sobre)

(**c**) *(rumour)* chismorreo *m*, *Esp* cotilleo *m*; **have you heard the latest (bit of) g.?** ¿has oído el último chismorreo *or Esp* cotilleo?; **that's just (idle) g.** son sólo habladurías *or Esp* cotilleos ►► ***g. column*** ecos *mpl* de sociedad; ***g. columnist*** cronista *mf* de sociedad

2 *vi* chismorrear, *Esp* cotillear

gossiping ['gɒsɪpɪŋ] 1 *n* chismorreo *m*, *Esp* cotilleo *m*

2 *adj* chismoso(a), *Esp* cotilla

gossipmonger ['gɒsɪpmʌngə(r)] *n* chismoso(a) *m,f*, *Esp* cotilla *mf*

gossipy ['gɒsɪpɪ] *adj* **he's very g.** es muy chismoso *or Esp* cotilla; **a g. letter** una carta llena de chismorreos *or Esp* cotilleos

got *pt & pp of* **get**

gotcha ['gɒtʃə] *exclam Br Fam* (= **I got you**) *(I understand) Esp* ¡ya!, *Am* ¡entiendo!; *(on catching someone)* ¡te agarré *or Esp* pillé!; *(in triumph)* ¡toma ya!, ¡chúpate esa!

Goth [gɒθ] *n* (**a**) *Hist* godo(a) *m,f* (**b**) *(music fan)* siniestro(a) *m,f*

Gotham ['gɒθəm] *n US Fam* Nueva York

Gothic ['gɒθɪk] 1 *n* (**a**) *(artistic style)* gótico *m* (**b**) *(language)* gótico *m* (**c**) *Typ* letra *f* gótica

2 *adj* gótico(a) ►► ***G. arch*** arco *m* apuntado; ***G. novel*** novela *f* gótica

gotta ['gɒtə] *Fam* = **got to**

gotten *US pp of* **get**

gouache [gʊ'ɑːʃ] *n* (**a**) *(paint)* guache *m*, aguada *f* (**b**) *(painting)* guache *m*, aguada *f*

Gouda ['gaʊdə] *n* queso *m* Gouda

gouge[1] [gaʊdʒ] 1 *n (tool)* gubia *f*

2 *vt (hole)* hacer, abrir

► **gouge out** *vt sep (hole)* cavar; *(eye)* arrancar

gouge[2] *vt US Fam* clavar, *RP* afanar

goujons ['guːʒɒnz] *npl Culin* escalopines *mpl*

goulash ['guːlæʃ] *n* gulach *m*

gourd ['gʊəd] *n* (**a**) *(vegetable)* calabaza *f*, *Bol, CSur* zapallo *m*, *Col, Ven* ahuyama *f* (**b**) *(container)* calabaza *f*; IDIOM *US Fam* **to be out of one's g.** estar mal de la azotea

gourmand ['gʊəmənd] *n* gourmand *mf*

gourmet ['gʊəmeɪ] *n* gastrónomo(a) *m,f*, gourmet *mf* ►► ***g. cooking*** alta *or* buena cocina *f*

gout [gaʊt] *n (illness)* gota *f*

gouty ['gaʊtɪ] *adj (leg, person)* gotoso(a)

Gov (**a**) (*abbr* **government**) gobierno *m* (**b**) (*abbr* **governor**) gobernador(ora) *m,f*

govern ['gʌvən] 1 *vt* (**a**) *(state, country)* gobernar (**b**) *(determine) (behaviour, actions)* regir, regular; *(of scientific law)* regir; **her behaviour was governed by a desire for revenge** le movía el deseo de venganza (**c**) *(control) (emotions)* dominar (**d**) *Gram* regir

2 *vi* gobernar

governable ['gʌvənəbəl] *adj* gobernable

governance ['gʌvənəns] *n Formal* gobernanza *f*

governess ['gʌvənɪs] *n* institutriz *f*

governing ['gʌvənɪŋ] *adj* (**a**) *(ruling) (party, coalition)* gobernante ►► ***g. body*** órgano *m* rector (**b**) *(determining) (concept, principle)* rector(ora)

government ['gʌvənmənt] *n* (**a**) *(governing body)* gobierno *m*; **to form a g.** formar gobierno; **the g. has fallen** ha caído el gobierno ►► ***g. bonds*** bonos *mpl* del Estado, papel *m* del Estado; ***g. health warning*** advertencia *f* del gobierno sobre los riesgos para la salud; ***G. House*** *(in Australia)* = residencia del Gobernador General; *Hist (in colony)* = residencia del gobernador; ***g. issue*** propiedad *f* del Estado; ***g. policy*** política *f* gubernamental; ***g. securities*** efectos *mpl* públicos; ***g. spending*** gasto *m* público

(**b**) *(system)* gobierno *m*, régimen *m*; **democratic/civilian g.** gobierno *or* régimen democrático/civil; **the demonstrators are calling for a return to democratic g.** los manifestantes reclaman el regreso a la democracia

(**c**) *(process of governing)* gobierno *m*; **good g.** buen gobierno; **strong g.** gobierno fuerte

governmental [gʌvən'mentəl] *adj* gubernamental

governor ['gʌvənə(r)] *n* (**a**) *(head) (of colony, central bank)* gobernador(ora) *m,f*; *Br (of prison)* director(ora) *m,f* (**b**) *US* **(state) g.** gobernador(ora) *m,f* (**c**) *Br (of school)* miembro *mf* del consejo escolar (**d**) *Br Fam* **the g.** *(boss)* el/la mandamás (**e**) *Br Fam (form of address)* **where to, g.?** ¿adónde vamos, jefe? (**f**) *(of engine)* regulador *m*

governor-general ['gʌvənə'dʒenərəl] *n* gobernador(ora) *m,f* general

governorship ['gʌvənəʃɪp] *n* gobernación *f*

Govt (*abbr* **government**) gobierno *m*

gown [gaʊn] *n* (a) *(of woman)* vestido *m* (largo) (b) *(of magistrate, academic, teacher)* toga *f* (c) *(of surgeon)* bata *f*

goy [gɔɪ] (*pl* **goys** *or* **goyim** ['gɔɪɪm]) *n Fam* = para los judíos, un no creyente, un gentil

GP [dʒiː'piː] *n* (*abbr* **general practitioner**) médico(a) *m,f* de familia *or* de cabecera

GPO [dʒiːpiː'əʊ] *n* (a) *Br Formerly* (*abbr* **General Post Office**) ≃ (Administración *f* Central de) Correos *mpl* (b) *US* (*abbr* **Government Printing Office**) = imprenta (oficial) del Estado

GPS [dʒiːpiː'es] *n* (*abbr* **global positioning system**) GPS

gr (*abbr* **gramme(s)**) g

grab [græb] 1 *n* (a) *(movement)* **to make a g. at** *or* **for sth** tratar de agarrar algo; IDIOM *Fam* **to be up for grabs** ser para quien lo quiera; **is that last chocolate up for grabs?** ¿me puedo comer esa última chocolatina? ►► ***g. bag*** *(at party, fair)* bolsa *f* sorpresa; *(assortment)* colección *f* (b) *esp Br (for excavating)* pala *f*
2 *vt* (*pt & pp* **grabbed**) (a) *(snatch)* **to g. (hold of) sth/sb** agarrar algo/a alguien; **to g. sth off sb** arrebatar algo a alguien; **he grabbed the book out of my hand** me quitó el libro de las manos
(b) *(seize) (opportunity)* aprovechar; *(land)* apropiarse de; *(attention)* llamar; *(power)* tomar, hacerse con; **they grabbed power from their opponents** le quitaron el poder a sus oponentes
(c) *Fam (take hurriedly)* **g. a chair** agarra *or* pilla una silla; **to g. a bite to eat** comer algo en cualquier parte
(d) *Fam (attract, interest)* **how does that g. you?** ¿qué te parece?; **the idea doesn't g. me** no me entusiasma la idea
3 *vi* **to g. at sth/sb** tratar de agarrar algo/a alguien; **don't g.!** ¡sin agarrar!

grace [greɪs] 1 *n* (a) *(of movement, dancer, language)* gracia *f*, elegancia *f*
(b) *(of manners)* **he lacks the social graces, he has no social graces** carece de modales; **to do sth with (a) good/bad g.** hacer algo de buena/mala gana; **to have the (good) g. to do sth** tener la delicadeza de hacer algo
(c) *(favour)* **to be in/get into sb's good graces** gozar del/ganarse el favor de alguien
(d) *(for payment of a bill)* **to give a debtor seven days' g.** conceder a un moroso una prórroga de siete días
(e) *Rel* **in a state of g.** en estado de gracia; **to fall from g.** caer en desgracia; **the g. of God** la gracia de Dios; **there, but for the g. of God, go I** nos podría haber pasado a cualquiera; *Old-fashioned* **in the year of g. 1066** en el año de gracia de 1066
(f) *(prayer before meal)* **to say g.** bendecir la mesa
(g) *(form of address)* **Your G.** *(bishop)* (Su) Ilustrísima; *(duke, duchess)* (Su) Excelencia
(h) *Mus* ***g. note*** (nota *f* de) adorno *m*, floritura *f*
(i) *Mythol* **the three Graces** las Tres Gracias
2 *vt* (a) *(honour)* honrar; *Ironic* **she rarely graces us with her presence** raras veces nos honra con su presencia *or* se digna a acompañarnos (b) *(ornament)* adornar

grace-and-favour ['greɪsən'feɪvə(r)] *adj Br* **g. residence** = vivienda cedida por la corona

graceful ['greɪsfʊl] *adj* (a) *(person, movement)* elegante, airoso(a); *(speech, style)* elegante (b) *(apology)* cortés

gracefully ['greɪsfʊlɪ] *adv* (a) *(to dance, move)* con elegancia (b) *(to apologize)* cortésmente; **to accept/decline g.** aceptar/declinar cortésmente

gracefulness ['greɪsfʊlnɪs] *n* (a) *(of movement)* elegancia *f*, gracia *f* (b) *(of apology, acceptance)* cortesía *f*

graceless ['greɪslɪs] *adj* (a) *(inelegant) (person, movement)* falto(a) de elegancia *or* gracia (b) *(apology, behaviour)* descortés

gracious ['greɪʃəs] *adj* (a) *(generous, kind)* magnánimo(a); **to be g. to** *or* **towards sb** portarse con magnanimidad con alguien; **God has been g. to us** Dios ha sido misericordioso con nosotros (b) *(elegant)* elegante, refinado(a); **g. living** la vida refinada (c) *Old-fashioned (exclamation)* **g. (me)!, good(ness) g.!** ¡santo cielo!, ¡Dios bendito!; **good g. no!** ¡por Dios, no!

graciously ['greɪʃəslɪ] *adv* con magnanimidad; **to g. accept** dignarse a aceptar

graciousness ['greɪʃəsnɪs] *n* (a) *(kindness, politeness)* magnanimidad *f* (b) *(elegance)* elegancia *f*

grad [græd] *n Fam* estudiante *mf* de posgrado ►► *US* ***g. school*** escuela *f* de posgrado

gradation [grə'deɪʃən] *n* gradación *f*; **subtle gradations of meaning** matices sutiles del significado

grade [greɪd] 1 *n* (a) *(rank)* grado *m*, rango *m*; **the top grades of the civil service** los escalafones superiores de la administración pública
(b) *(quality)* clase *f*, calidad *f*; **a high g. of coal** un carbón de alta calidad; IDIOM **to make the g.** dar la talla; *US* **to be up to g.** ser de suficiente calidad
(c) *US Sch (mark)* nota *f* ►► ***g. point average*** nota *f* media
(d) *US (year at school)* curso *m* ►► ***g. school*** escuela *f* primaria
(e) *US Rail* ***g. crossing*** paso *m* a nivel
2 *vt* (a) *(classify)* clasificar (b) *US Educ* **to g. essays** calificar los trabajos (c) *US (level)* nivelar

graded ['greɪdɪd] *adj* graduado(a), escalonado(a); **g. exercises** ejercicios escalonados según su dificultad

grader ['greɪdə(r)] *n* (a) *US (pupil)* **a first/second g.** un alumno de primero/segundo (b) *(machine)* niveladora *f*

gradient ['greɪdɪənt] *n* (a) *(of slope)* pendiente *f*; **a g. of one in four, a one in four g.** una pendiente del 25 por ciento (b) *(of temperature)* gradiente *m*, curva *f* de temperaturas (c) *Comptr* ***g. fill*** degradado *m* lineal

gradual ['grædjʊəl] *adj* gradual

gradualism ['grædjʊəlɪzəm] *n* transformación *f* gradual

gradually ['grædjʊəlɪ] *adv* gradualmente

graduate ['grædjʊət] 1 *n* (a) *Univ* licenciado(a) *m,f*; **biology/history g.** licenciado(a) en biología/historia; **she's an Oxford g.** *or* **a g. of Oxford** es licenciada por la Universidad de Oxford ►► *US* ***G. Record Exam*** = examen previo a un curso de posgrado (b) *US (from high school)* ≃ bachiller *mf*
2 *adj US (postgraduate)* ***g. studies*** estudios *mpl* de posgrado
3 *vt* ['grædjʊeɪt] (a) *US (student)* conferir *or* dar el título a; **I graduated college last May** terminé la carrera en mayo pasado (b) *(thermometer, measuring vessel)* graduar
4 *vi* (a) *Univ* obtener la licenciatura, licenciarse; **he graduated in linguistics** obtuvo la licenciatura en lingüística
(b) *US (from high school)* ≃ sacar el bachillerato
(c) *(progress)* **to g. to** pasar a; **she learnt on a cheap violin before graduating to a better instrument** aprendió con un violín corriente antes de pasar a tocar con uno mejor; **he soon graduated from marijuana to cocaine** pronto pasó *or* dio el paso de la marihuana a la cocaína

graduated ['grædjʊeɪtɪd] *adj (thermometer)* graduado(a) ►► *Comptr* ***g. fill*** degradado *m* lineal; ***g. income tax*** impuesto *m* sobre la renta progresivo

graduation [grædjʊ'eɪʃən] *n* (a) *(from school, university)* graduación *f* ►► ***g. ceremony*** ceremonia *f* de graduación (b) *(progression)* paso *m*

Graeco-Roman, *US* **Greco-Roman** [griːkəʊ'rəʊmən] *adj* grecorromano(a) ►► ***G. wrestling*** lucha *f* grecorromana

graffiti [græ'fiːtiː] *n* graffiti *mpl*; **a piece of g.** un graffiti; **there's some g. on the wall** hay graffiti en la pared ►► ***g. artist*** artista *mf* de graffiti

graft[1] [grɑːft] 1 *n (of skin, plant)* injerto *m*; **bone/skin g.** injerto óseo/de piel
2 *vt* (a) *(skin, plant)* injertar (**onto** en) (b) *Fig (idea, method)* insertar (**onto** en)

graft[2] *Fam* 1 *n* (a) *Br (work)* **the job involves a lot of hard g.** en ese trabajo hay que trabajar mucho *or Esp* currar a tope *or Méx* chambear duro *or RP* laburar como loco (b) *US (bribery, corruption)* corruptelas *fpl*
2 *vi Br (work hard)* trabajar mucho, *Esp* currar a tope, *Méx* chambear duro, *RP* laburar como loco

grafter ['grɑːftə(r)] *n Fam* (a) *Br (hard worker)* trabajador(ora) *m,f*, *Esp* currante *mf*, *Col* camellador(ora) *m,f*, *RP* laburador(ora) *m,f* (b) *US (corrupt person, official)* corrupto(a) *m,f*, *Andes, RP* coimero(a) *m,f*

graham ['greɪəm] *adj US* ***g. cracker*** galleta *f* integral; ***g. flour*** harina *f* integral

Grail [greɪl] *n* (a) *Mythol* **the (Holy) G.** el (Santo) Grial (b) *Fig (tantalising goal)* ideal *m*; **the G. of full employment/world peace** el ideal del pleno empleo/de la paz mundial

grain [greɪn] *n* (a) *(particle) (of wheat, salt, sand)* grano *m*; **a g. of truth** una pizca de verdad
(b) *(cereal)* cereal *m*, grano *m*; **g. market** mercado de cereal ►► ***g. alcohol*** alcohol *m* de grano; *US* ***g. elevator*** silo *m*
(c) *(of photo)* grano *m*
(d) *(of leather, stone)* grano *m*; *(of wood) (fibre)* grano *m*; *(pattern)* veta *f*; **to cut wood against the g.** cortar la madera a contrahilo;

IDIOM **it goes against the g. for me to do it** me cuesta mucho hacer eso
(**e**) *(unit of weight)* grano *m* (= 0,065 gramos)

grainy ['greɪnɪ] *adj (photo, TV or cinema image)* granuloso(a), con mucho grano

gram[1] [græm] *n* gramo *m* ►► *Chem* ***g. atom*** átomo-gramo *m*

gram[2] *n* ***g. flour*** harina *f* de garbanzo

graminivorous [græmɪ'nɪvərəs] *adj* granívoro(a)

grammar ['græmə(r)] *n* (**a**) *(rules, discipline, knowledge)* gramática *f*; **English/Spanish g.** gramática inglesa/española; **it's bad g. to say that** eso está mal dicho; **her g. is terrible** comete muchos errores gramaticales ►► *Comptr* ***g. checker*** corrector *m* de gramática
(**b**) *(text)* **g. (book)** gramática *f*
(**c**) *Br* ***g. school*** centro *m* de enseñanza secundaria *(al que sólo se accede tras superar un examen de ingreso)*

grammarian [grə'meərɪən] *n* gramático(a) *m,f*

grammatical [grə'mætɪkəl] *adj (mistake, rule)* gramatical; **a g. sentence** una oración gramaticalmente correcta

grammaticality [grəmætɪ'kælɪtɪ] *n* gramaticalidad *f*

grammatically [grə'mætɪklɪ] *adv* gramaticalmente; **to speak/write g.** hablar/escribir con una gramática correcta

gramme [græm] *n Br* gramo *m*

Grammy ['græmɪ] *n US* **G. (award)** (premio *m*) Grammy *m*

gramophone ['græməfəʊn] *n Old-fashioned* gramófono *m* ►► ***g. record*** disco *m* de gramófono

gramps [græmps] *n US Fam* abuelo *m*, yayo *m*

grampus ['græmpəs] *n* (**a**) *(dolphin)* delfín *m* gris (**b**) *(whale)* orca *f*

gran [græn] *n Fam (grandmother)* abuela *f*, *Esp* yaya *f*

granary ['grænərɪ] *n* (**a**) *(store)* granero *m* (**b**) *Br* ***g. bread*** pan *m* de semillas; *Br* ***g. loaf*** pan *m* de semillas

grand [grænd] **1** *adj* (**a**) *(imposing, impressive)* grandioso(a); *(plan, scheme)* ambicioso(a); **on a g. scale** a gran escala; **to entertain on a g. scale** agasajar a lo grande; **in (a) g. style** a lo grande; **this dress is a bit too g. for me** este vestido me resulta demasiado ostentoso ►► ***the G. Canyon*** el Gran Cañón (del Colorado); ***g. finale*** final *m* apoteósico, apoteosis *f inv* final; *US Law* ***g. jury*** jurado *m* de acusación; *Br* ***the G. National*** el Grand National, = carrera hípica de obstáculos que se celebra anualmente en Aintree, Gran Bretaña; ***g. opera*** gran ópera *f*; ***g. piano*** piano *m* de cola; ***g. prix*** *(motor race)* gran premio *m*; ***g. slam*** *(in tennis, bridge, rugby)* gran slam *m*; **a g. slam tournament** *(in tennis)* un torneo de(l) gran slam; *Hist* ***the G. Tour*** = gira por Europa que se consideraba parte de la educación de los jóvenes de la alta sociedad británica
(**b**) *(of highest rank)* ***g. duchess*** gran duquesa *f*; ***g. duchy*** gran ducado *m*; ***g. duke*** gran duque *m*; ***G. Master*** *(in Freemasonry)* Gran Maestro *m*
(**c**) *(overall)* global; **it was all part of his g. design** todo era parte de su plan maestro ►► ***g. total*** total *m*; **a g. total of £35,000** un total de 35.000 libras; *Phys* ***g. unified theory*** teoría *f* de la gran unificación
(**d**) *(revered)* **the g. old man of car racing** el gran mito viviente *or* la leyenda viva del automovilismo ►► ***the G. Old Party*** = el Partido Republicano *(de Estados Unidos)*
(**e**) *Fam (excellent)* genial, *Andes, CAm, Carib, Méx* chévere, *Méx* padre, *RP* bárbaro; **we had a g. time** lo pasamos genial; *Ironic* **we had a g. old time trying to find the house!** ¡lo pasamos genial buscando la casa!; **I'm not feeling too g.** no me siento muy bien
2 *n Fam* (**a**) *(thousand pounds)* mil libras *fpl*; *(thousand dollars)* mil dólares *mpl*; **ten g.** diez mil (**b**) *(piano)* piano *m* de cola

grandad ['grændæd] *n Fam* abuelito *m*, yayo *m* ►► ***g. collar*** cuello *m* alto (de camisa); ***g. shirt*** camisa *f* de cuello alto

grandaddy ['grændædɪ] *n Fam* (**a**) *(grandfather)* abuelo *m*, yayo *m* (**b**) *(first, best example)* **the g. of them all** el padre de todos ellos

grand-aunt ['grænd'ɑːnt] *n* tía *f* abuela

grandchild ['græntʃaɪld] *n* nieto(a) *m,f*

granddaughter ['grændɔːtə(r)] *n* nieta *f*

grandee [græn'diː] *n* (**a**) *(nobleman)* grande *m* (**b**) *Fam (important person)* pez *m* gordo

grandeur ['grændjə(r)] *n (of place, building)* grandiosidad *f*; *(personal status)* grandeza *f*

grandfather ['grænfɑːðə(r)] *n* abuelo *m* ►► ***g. clock*** reloj *m* de pie *or* de pared

grandfatherly ['grændfɑːðəlɪ] *adj* de abuelo; **in a g. way** como un abuelo

grandiloquence [græn'dɪləkwəns] *n Formal* grandilocuencia *f*

grandiloquent [græn'dɪləkwənt] *adj Formal* grandilocuente

grandiloquently [græn'dɪləkwəntlɪ] *adv Formal* con grandilocuencia

grandiose ['grændɪəʊs] *adj* grandioso(a); **on a g. scale** en plan grandioso

grandly ['grændlɪ] *adv* grandiosamente; **a book g. entitled "A History of the Universe"** un libro con el grandioso título de "Una historia del universo"

grandma ['grænmɑː] *n Fam* abuela *f*, *Esp* yaya *f*

grandmamma ['grænməmɑː] *n Old-fashioned* abuela *f*, *Esp* yaya *f*

grandmaster ['grænd'mɑːste(r)] *n (in chess)* gran maestro(a) *m,f*

grandmother ['grænmʌðə(r)] *n* abuela *f*

grandmotherly ['grænmʌðəlɪ] *adj* de abuela; **in a g. way** como una abuela

grand-nephew ['græn'nefjuː] *n* sobrino *m* nieto

grandness ['grændnɪs] *n (of behaviour, gesture)* grandilocuencia *f*; *(of lifestyle)* opulencia *f*; *(of appearance)* ostentosidad *f*

grand-niece ['græn'niːs] *n* sobrina *f* nieta

grandpa ['grænpɑː] *n Fam* abuelito *m*, yayo *m*

grandpapa ['grænpəpɑː] *n Old-fashioned* abuelo *m*, yayo *m*

grandparent ['grænpeərənt] *n* abuelo(a) *m,f*; **grandparents** abuelos

grandson ['grænsʌn] *n* nieto *m*

grandstand ['grænstænd] **1** *n (in stadium)* tribuna *f*; **to have a g. view of sth** presenciar algo desde una posición privilegiada
2 *vi US Fam* figurar, pavonearse, *Esp* darse pisto

grand-uncle ['grænd'ʌŋkəl] *n* tío *m* abuelo

grange [greɪndʒ] *n* (**a**) *Br (house)* casa *f* solariega (**b**) *US (farm)* granja *f*

granite ['grænɪt] *n* granito *m*

grannie, granny ['grænɪ] *n Fam* abuelita *f*, *Esp* yaya *f* ►► *US* ***g. dumping*** = abandono de un familiar anciano en la recepción de un hospital; ***g. flat*** = apartamento anexo a una casa o en su interior dedicado al alojamiento de un familiar anciano; ***g. glasses*** gafas *fpl* de aro; ***g. knot*** nudo *m* mal hecho; ***Granny Smith*** manzana *f* Granny Smith

granola [grə'nəʊlə] *n US* muesli *m* de avena

grant [grɑːnt] **1** *n* (**a**) *(financial aid)* subvención *f*; *(for student)* beca *f* (**b**) *(transfer) (of property, land)* cesión *f*, concesión *f*
2 *vt* (**a**) *(allow) (permission, request)* conceder; *(favour, privilege)* otorgar, conceder; **to g. sb an interview** conceder una entrevista a alguien; *Literary* **God g. you good fortune** que Dios le proteja; IDIOM **to take sth for granted** dar algo por supuesto *or* por sentado; **she felt that she was being taken for granted** sentía que no la apreciaban debidamente
(**b**) *(award) (credit, loan, money, subsidy)* conceder
(**c**) *(admit)* reconocer, admitir; **I g. that he's talented, but...** reconozco *or* admito que tiene talento, pero...; **I g. (you) he was mistaken, but he meant well** de acuerdo que estaba equivocado, pero lo hizo con buena intención; **granted, he's not very intelligent, but...** de acuerdo, no es muy inteligente pero...

grantee [grɑːn'tiː] *n Law* cesionario(a) *m,f*

grant-in-aid ['grɑːntɪn'eɪd] *n* subvención *f*, subsidio *m*

grant-maintained ['grɑːntmeɪn'teɪnd] *adj Br* **g. school** = escuela subvencionada directamente por el Estado, no por las autoridades locales

grantor [grɑːn'tɔː(r)] *n Law* cesionista *mf*

granular ['grænjʊlə(r)] *adj (surface, texture)* granuloso(a)

granulated ['grænjʊleɪtɪd] *adj* granulado(a), en gránulos; **g. sugar** azúcar granulado(a)

granule ['grænjʊl] *n* gránulo *m*; **coffee/tea granules** gránulos de café/té

grape [greɪp] *n* uva *f* ►► ***g. harvest*** vendimia *f*; ***g. juice*** mosto *m*, *Esp* zumo *m or Am* jugo *m* de uva; ***g. picker*** vendimiador(ora) *m,f*; ***g. sugar*** azúcar *f* de uva, dextrosa *f*

grapefruit ['greɪpfruːt] *n* pomelo *m*, *Am* toronja *f* ►► ***g. juice*** *Esp* zumo *m or Am* jugo *m* de pomelo

grapeshot ['greɪpʃɒt] *n* metralla *f*

grapevine ['greɪpvaɪn] *n* (**a**) *(plant) (on ground)* vid *f*; *(climbing)* parra *f* (**b**) IDIOM *Fam* **I heard on the g. that...** me ha dicho un pajarito que...

graph [grɑːf] **1** *n* gráfico *m*, gráfica *f* ►► ***g. paper*** papel *m* milimetrado
2 *vt* hacer un gráfico *or* una gráfica de

grapheme ['græfiːm] *n Ling* grafema *m*

graphic ['græfɪk] *adj* **(a)** *Math (in graph form)* gráfico(a) **(b)** *(stark, explicit) (description, language)* gráfico(a); **in g. detail** sin escatimar detalle, con todo lujo de detalles **(c)** *Art* gráfico(a) ►► ***g. artist*** artista *mf* gráfico(a); ***g. arts*** artes *fpl* gráficas; ***g. design*** diseño *m* gráfico; ***g. designer*** diseñador(ora) *m,f* gráfico(a), grafista *mf*; ***g. novel*** novela *f* ilustrada **(d)** *Elec* ***g. equalizer*** ecualizador *m* gráfico **(e)** *Comptr* ***g. accelerator*** acelerador *m* gráfico; ***g. display*** representación *f* gráfica; ***g. mode*** modo *m* gráfico

graphical ['græfɪkəl] *adj Comptr* ***g. (user) interface*** interfaz *f* gráfica

graphically ['græfɪklɪ] *adv (to describe, portray)* gráficamente

graphics ['græfɪks] **1** *n Art* diseño *m* gráfico, grafismo *m*
2 *npl* **(a)** *(illustrations)* diseño *m* gráfico **(b)** *Comptr* gráficos *mpl* ►► ***g. accelerator*** acelerador *m* gráfico; ***g. card*** tarjeta *f* gráfica; ***g. mode*** modo *m* gráfico; ***g. tablet*** tableta *f* gráfica

graphite ['græfaɪt] *n* grafito *m*

graphologist [græ'fɒlədʒɪst] *n* grafólogo(a) *m,f*

graphology [græ'fɒlədʒɪ] *n* grafología *f*

grapnel ['græpnəl] *n* rezón *m*

grapple ['græpəl] **1** *vt US (person)* **to g. sb to the floor** forcejear con alguien para tirarlo al suelo
2 *vi (fight)* forcejear (**with** con); **to g. with a problem** debatirse *or* batallar con un problema; **to g. with inflation** luchar contra la inflación

grappling hook ['græplɪŋ'hʊk], **grappling iron** ['græplɪŋ'aɪən] *n* rezón *m*

GRAS [dʒiːɑːreɪ'es] *adj US* (*abbr* **generally recognized as safe**) = declarado no perjudicial por las autoridades sanitarias estadounidenses

grasp [grɑːsp] **1** *n* **(a)** *(hold)* asimiento *m*; **to have a strong g.** tener mucha fuerza en las manos; **to wrest sth from sb's g.** arrancar algo de las manos de alguien
(b) *Fig (reach)* **within one's g.** al alcance de uno; **beyond one's g.** fuera del alcance de uno; **success is now within her grasp** el éxito está ahora a su alcance; **the opportunity had slipped from her g.** la oportunidad se le había ido de las manos
(c) *(understanding)* comprensión *f*; **his g. of the problem was poor** no comprendía bien el problema; **to have a good g. of modern history** conocer bien la historia moderna
2 *vt* **(a)** *(hold firmly)* agarrar, asir; **to g. (hold of) sb's hand** agarrar *or* asir con fuerza la mano de alguien; **he grasped the book to his chest** apretó el libro contra el pecho; *Fig* **to g. the opportunity** aprovechar la oportunidad; IDIOM **to g. the nettle** agarrar al toro por los cuernos
(b) *(understand)* comprender; **to g. the importance of sth** comprender bien la importancia de algo

► **grasp at** *vt insep (attempt to seize)* intentar agarrar; *(accept eagerly)* aprovechar; **to g. at an opportunity** no dejar escapar una oportunidad, aprovechar una oportunidad

grasping ['grɑːspɪŋ] *adj* avaricioso(a)

grass [grɑːs] **1** *n* **(a)** *(plant)* hierba *f*; IDIOM **she doesn't let the g. grow under her feet** *(is very decisive)* no pierde el tiempo; PROV **the g. is always greener (on the other side of the fence)** siempre anhelamos lo que no tenemos ►► *Fig* ***the g. roots*** *(of organization)* las bases; ***g. skirt*** borde *m* de césped; ***g. snake*** culebra *f* de agua; ***g. widow*** = mujer cuyo marido está siempre fuera; ***g. widower*** = hombre cuya mujer está siempre fuera
(b) *(lawn)* césped *m*, hierba *f*; **to cut** *or* **mow the g.** cortar el césped *or* la hierba; **keep off the g.** *(sign)* prohibido pisar el césped ►► ***g. box*** *(of lawnmower)* recogecésped *m*; ***g. court*** *(in tennis)* pista *f* de hierba
(c) *(pasture)* pasto *m*; **to put a horse out to g.** sacar un caballo a pastar; *Fig* **to put sb out to g.** jubilar a alguien
(d) *Fam (marijuana)* maría *f*, hierba *f*
(e) *Br Fam (informer)* soplón(ona) *m,f*, *Esp* chivato(a) *m,f*
2 *vt* **to g. (over)** *(field)* plantar hierba en
3 *vi Br Fam (inform)* cantar; **to g. on sb** delatar a alguien, dar el soplo sobre alguien

► **grass up** *vt sep Br Fam* **to g. sb up** delatar a alguien, dar el soplo sobre alguien

grass-cutter ['grɑːskʌtə(r)] *n* cortacésped *m or f*

grasshopper ['grɑːshɒpə(r)] *n* **(a)** *(insect)* saltamontes *m inv* ►► ***g. warbler*** buscarla *f* pintoja **(b)** IDIOM **he's got a g. mind** mariposea de un tema a otro constantemente

grassland ['grɑːslænd] *n* pradera *f*, pastizal *m*

grass-roots ['grɑːs'ruːts] *adj* **at g. level** al nivel de las bases; **g. opinion** la opinión de las bases; **g. support/opposition** apoyo/oposición de las bases

grassy ['grɑːsɪ] *adj* poblado(a) de hierba

grate[1] [greɪt] *n (of hearth)* parrilla *f*, rejilla *f*

grate[2] **1** *vt (cheese, nutmeg)* rallar; **grated cheese** queso rallado; **grated lemon rind** ralladura de limón
2 *vi* **(a)** *(machinery)* chirriar, rechinar; **the bones grated against each other** los huesos rechinaban entre sí **(b)** *Fig* **his cheerfulness starts to g. after a while** al cabo de un rato, su jovialidad comienza a crispar; **to g. on the ear** *(voice, sound)* hacer daño al oído; **it really grates on my nerves** me ataca los nervios

G-rated ['dʒiːreɪtɪd] *adj US (movie)* apto(a) para todos los públicos

grateful ['greɪtfʊl] *adj* agradecido(a); **to be g. (to sb/for sth)** estar agradecido(a) (a alguien/por algo); **I am extremely g. to you** te estoy sumamente agradecido; **I'm g. for all you've done** te agradezco todo lo que has hecho; **be g. for what you've got** agradece lo que tienes; **I would be g. if you could let me know as soon as possible** le agradecería que me lo comunicara lo antes posible

gratefully ['greɪtfʊlɪ] *adv* agradecidamente, con gratitud; **to smile g.** sonreír con gratitud; **all donations g. accepted** se agradece cualquier donación

grater ['greɪtə(r)] *n (for cheese, nutmeg)* rallador *m*

graticule ['grætɪkjuːl] *n* **(a)** *(in microscope, telescope)* retícula *f* **(b)** *(on map)* coordenadas *fpl* geográficas, cuadrícula *f*

gratification [grætɪfɪ'keɪʃən] *n* satisfacción *f*; **I noticed to my g. that...** para mi satisfacción, noté que...

> **False friend:** The Spanish noun **gratificación** is not a translation for the English word **gratification**. In Spanish **gratificación** means "reward" or "bonus".

gratified ['grætɪfaɪd] *adj* **to be g. (by)** estar satisfecho(a) (con); **I was g. by the news** las noticias me produjeron gran satisfacción

gratify ['grætɪfaɪ] *vt* **(a)** *(person)* satisfacer; **it gratified him to learn/know that...** le produjo gran satisfacción *or* le fue muy grato enterarse de/saber que... **(b)** *(whim, wish)* satisfacer

gratifying ['grætɪfaɪɪŋ] *adj* satisfactorio(a), gratificante; **it's g. to know that...** es grato saber que...

grating[1] ['greɪtɪŋ] *adj* **(a)** *(noise)* chirriante; *(voice)* chillón(ona) **(b)** *(irritating)* crispante

grating[2] *n (grille)* reja *f*

gratis ['grætɪs] *adv* gratis

gratitude ['grætɪtjuːd] *n* gratitud *f*; **to show one's g. (to** *or* **towards sb)** demostrar su gratitud (a alguien); **to express one's g. (for sth)** expresar su gratitud (por algo); **this is how they show their g. for all our help!** ¡así es como nos demuestran su gratitud por la ayuda que les dimos!

gratuitous [grə'tjuːɪtəs] *adj (unjustified)* gratuito(a); **g. violence** violencia gratuita

gratuitously [grə'tjuːɪtəslɪ] *adv (without good reason)* gratuitamente

gratuitousness [grə'tjuːɪtəsnɪs] *n* gratuidad *f*

gratuity [grə'tjuːɪtɪ] *n Formal (tip)* propina *f*, gratificación *f*

gravadlax = **gravlax**

grave[1] [greɪv] **1** *n* **(a)** *(for burial)* tumba *f*; **to be in one's g.** estar en la tumba ►► ***g. clothes*** mortaja *f*; ***g. robber*** ladrón(ona) *m,f* de tumbas
(b) IDIOM **he took his secret with him to the g.** se llevó el secreto a la tumba; **from beyond the g.** del más allá, de ultratumba; **he drank himself into an early g.** la bebida se lo llevó a la tumba prematuramente; **to make sb turn in his g.** hacer que alguien se revuelva en su sepultura; **to have one foot in the g.** estar con un pie en la tumba
2 *adj* **(a)** *(matter, mistake, accusation)* grave **(b)** *(manner, voice)* grave

grave[2] [grɑːv] *Ling* **1** *n* acento *m* grave
2 *adj* grave

gravedigger ['greɪvdɪgə(r)] *n* sepulturero(a) *m,f*

gravel ['grævəl] **1** *n* **(a)** *(small stones)* grava *f*, gravilla *f* ►► ***g. path*** camino *m* de grava; ***g. pit*** yacimiento *m* de grava, gravera *f* **(b)** *Med* arenilla *f*
2 *vt* (*pt & pp* **gravelled**, *US* **graveled**) cubrir de grava

gravelled, *US* **graveled** ['grævəld] *adj* de grava

gravelly ['grævəlɪ] *adj* **(a)** *(sand, soil)* pedregoso(a) **(b) a g. voice** una voz áspera

gravely ['greɪvlɪ] *adv* **(a)** *(seriously)* gravemente; **g. wounded** gravemente herido(a); **g. ill** muy grave; **to be g. mistaken** estar sumamente equivocado(a) **(b)** *(solemnly)* con gravedad

graven ['greɪvən] *adj (in the Bible)* **g. image** ídolo

graveside ['greɪvsaɪd] *n* **at sb's g.** al pie de la *or* junto a la tumba de alguien

gravestone ['greɪvstəʊn] *n* lápida *f*

graveyard ['greɪvjɑːd] *n* **(a)** *(burial place)* cementerio *m* **(b)** *Fig* **this town is a g.** este pueblo es como un cementerio; **the battle was the g. of Napoleon's hopes** la batalla sepultó las esperanzas de Napoleón ►► ***g. shift*** *(in factory)* turno *m* de noche; ***g. slot*** *(on radio, TV)* horario *m* de menor audiencia

gravid ['grævɪd] *adj Med* grávida

graving dock ['greɪvɪŋ'dɒk] *n* dique *m* seco

gravitate ['grævɪteɪt] *vi* **to g. towards** verse atraído(a) por; **many young people g. towards the big cities** muchos jóvenes se ven atraídos por las grandes ciudades; **most of the guests had gravitated towards the bar** casi todos los invitados se habían ido desplazando hacia el bar

gravitation [grævɪ'teɪʃən] *n* **(a)** *Phys* gravitación *f* **(b)** *(gradual movement)* desplazamiento *m*; **his slow g. towards the right of the party** su desplazamiento gradual hacia la derecha del partido

gravitational [grævɪ'teɪʃənəl] *adj (force, field)* gravitatorio(a) ►► ***g. pull*** atracción *f* gravitatoria

gravity ['grævɪtɪ] *n* **(a)** *(force)* gravedad *f* ►► *Tech* ***g. feed*** alimentación *f* por gravedad **(b)** *(of matter, mistake, accusation)* gravedad *f* **(c)** *(of person, manner)* gravedad *f*

gravlax ['grævlæks], **gravadlax** ['grævədlæks] *n* gravlax *m*, salmón *m* marinado

gravy ['greɪvɪ] *n* **(a)** *(for meat)* salsa *f (hecha con el jugo de la carne)* ►► ***g. boat*** salsera *f* **(b)** *Fam* ***g. train:*** **to be on the g. train** estar apuntado(a) al *Esp* chollo *or Am* chance de la temporada **(c)** *US Fam (easy money, bonus)* **it's g.** es dinero regalado

gray, gray-haired *etc US* = **grey, grey-haired** *etc*

grayling ['greɪlɪŋ] *n (fish)* tímalo *m*, timo *m*

graze[1] [greɪz] **1** *vt* **(a)** *(of farmer) (cattle, herd)* apacentar **(b)** *(of cattle) (grass)* pastar; *(field)* pastar en

2 *vi* **(a)** *(cattle)* pastar, pacer **(b)** *(person)* picar

graze[2] **1** *n* rasguño *m*

2 *vt (scrape)* rasguñar; *(touch lightly)* rozar; **to g. one's knee** hacerse un rasguño en la rodilla; **she grazed her elbow on the wall** se raspó el codo contra la pared; **the bullet grazed his cheek** la bala le rozó la mejilla

grazing ['greɪzɪŋ] *n (pasture)* pastos *mpl*, pastizales *mpl*

grease [griːs] **1** *n* **(a)** *(in cooking)* grasa *f*, *RP* grasitud *f* **(b)** *(for machine)* grasa *f* ►► ***g. gun*** *(pump)* pistola *f* de engrase; *US Fam (submachine gun)* subfusil *m*; *Fam* ***g. monkey*** mecánico(a) *m,f*

2 *vt* **(a)** *(cake tin)* engrasar **(b)** *(machine)* engrasar, lubricar **(c)** **to g. back one's hair** engominarse el pelo **(d)** IDIOMS *Fam* **to g. sb's palm** *(bribe)* untar a alguien, *Andes, RP* coimear a alguien, *CAm, Méx* dar una mordida a alguien; **to g. the wheels** engrasar el mecanismo; *Fam* **to move like greased lightning** moverse con la velocidad del rayo

greasepaint ['griːspeɪnt] *n Theat* maquillaje *m* de teatro; IDIOM **the smell of g.** el ambiente teatral

greaseproof ['griːspruːf] *adj Br* ***g. paper*** papel *m* de cera *or* parafinado

greaser ['griːsə(r)] *n Fam* **(a)** *(biker)* motero(a) *m,f* **(b)** *US Pej (Latin American)* latino(a) *m,f*, sudaca *mf*

grease-stained ['griːssteɪnd] *adj* con manchas de grasa

greasiness ['griːsɪnɪs] *n* **(a)** *(of food, hair, skin)* grasa *f*, *RP* grasitud *f* **(b)** *(of hands, clothes)* grasa *f*, *RP* grasitud *f* **(c)** *(of manner)* adulación *f*, lisonja *f*

greasy ['griːsɪ] *adj* **(a)** *(containing, covered in grease) (food)* grasiento(a); *(hair, skin)* graso(a) ►► *Fam* ***g. spoon*** *(cheap restaurant)* restaurante *m* barato **(b)** *(grease-stained)* manchado(a) de grasa **(c)** *Fam (manner)* adulador(ora), *Méx, RP* arrastrado(a)

GREAT [greɪt] **1** *adj* **(a)** *(large, considerable)* grande, gran *(before singular noun)*; **this is a g. improvement over her previous novel** ha mejorado mucho respecto a su anterior novela; **to reach a g. age** llegar a una edad avanzada; **to take g. care** poner *or* tener mucho cuidado; **in g. detail** en *or* con gran detalle; **with the greatest of ease/pleasure** con suma facilidad/sumo placer; **it gives me g. pleasure to announce that...** es un auténtico placer para mí anunciar que...; **I have g. respect for them** siento enorme respeto por ellos; **he slept for the greater part of the afternoon** durmió la mayor parte de la tarde; **a g. deal better** muchísimo mejor; **a g. deal of...** muchísimo(a)...; **a g. many** muchos(as) ►► ***g. ape*** gran simio *m* antropoide; ***g. cormorant*** cormorán *m* grande; ***g. crested grebe*** somormujo *m* lavanco; ***g. grey shrike*** alcaudón *m* real; ***g. reed warbler*** carricero *m* tordal; ***g. skua*** págalo *m* grande; ***g. tit*** carbonero *m* común

(b) *(important)* grande, gran *(before singular noun)*; **a g. artist** un(a) gran artista; **the g. Jesse Owens** el gran Jesse Owens; **to be the greatest** ser el mejor; **g. deeds** grandes hazañas; **he seems destined for g. things** parece destinado a hacer grandes cosas; *Hum* **g. minds think alike** los genios siempre tenemos las mismas ideas

(c) *(accomplished)* grande, gran *(before singular noun)*; **a g. player/painting** un gran jugador/cuadro; **he's g. at cooking** cocina de maravilla; **to have a g. eye for detail** tener un ojo excelente para los detalles

(d) *Fam (very good)* genial, *Andes, CAm, Carib, Méx* chévere, *Méx* padre, *RP* bárbaro; **this knife is g. for chopping carrots** este cuchillo es genial para picar zanahorias; **it's g. that you'll be living so near us!** *Esp* ¡qué genial que vayáis a vivir tan cerca de nosotros!, ¡qué *Andes, CAm, Carib, Méx* chévere *or Méx* padre *or RP* bárbaro que vengan a vivir tan cerca de nosotros!; **it's g. to see you again!** ¡qué alegría verte de nuevo!; **to have a g. time** pasarlo muy bien; **he's a g. guy** es un tipo excelente; **the g. thing about this printer is...** y lo mejor de esta impresora es que...; **(that's) g.!** ¡genial!, *Andes, CAm, Carib, Méx* ¡chévere!, *Méx* ¡padre!, *RP* ¡bárbaro!; *Ironic* **oh, (that's) g., now what are we going to do?** oh, fantástico, ¿y ahora qué hacemos?

(e) *(enthusiastic, committed)* **I'm a g. fan of hers** soy un gran admirador suyo; **they are g. friends** son muy buenos amigos; **she's a g. hillwalker** es muy aficionada al montañismo; **he's a g. one for having everything planned in advance** nadie como él para tener todo planeado de antemano

(f) *(in proper names)* **Alexander the G.** Alejandro Magno ►► ***the G. Barrier Reef*** la Gran Barrera de Coral; *Astron* ***the G. Bear*** la Osa Mayor; ***G. Britain*** Gran Bretaña; ***G. Dane*** gran danés *m*; *Hist* ***the G. Depression*** la Gran Depresión; ***the G. Divide*** la División Continental; ***the G. Lakes*** los Grandes Lagos; ***Greater London*** el Gran Londres, el área metropolitana de Londres; ***the G. Plains*** las Grandes Llanuras (de Norteamérica); ***the G. Salt Lake*** el Gran Lago Salado; ***the G. Wall of China*** la Gran Muralla china; *Hist* ***the G. War*** la Gran Guerra, la Primera Guerra Mundial

2 *n (person)* grande *mf*

3 *npl* **the g. and the good** las personalidades más importantes de la vida pública

4 *adv Fam* **(a)** *(well)* estupendamente; **I feel g.!** ¡me siento estupendamente!; **he's doing g.** *(in health)* se está recuperando muy bien

(b) *(for emphasis)* **a g. big dog** un perrazo enorme; **you g. fat slob!** ¡so vago *or Esp* gandulazo!, ¡pedazo de *Andes, Méx* flojo *or RP* haragán!; **you g. big idiot!** ¡pero qué tontorrón *or Am* papanatas eres!; **a huge g. mountain** una montaña gigantesca

great-aunt ['greɪt'ɑːnt] *n* tía *f* abuela

greatcoat ['greɪtkəʊt] *n* abrigo *m*, gabán *m*

great-grandchild ['greɪt'græntʃaɪld] *n* bisnieto(a) *m,f*

great-granddaughter ['greɪt'grændɔːtə(r)] *n* bisnieta *f*

great-grandfather ['greɪt'grænfɑːðə(r)] *n* bisabuelo *m*

great-grandmother ['greɪt'grænmʌðə(r)] *n* bisabuela *f*

great-grandparents ['greɪt'grænpeərənts] *npl* bisabuelos *mpl*

great-grandson ['greɪt'grænsʌn] *n* bisnieto *m*

great-great-grandchild ['greɪt'greɪt'græntʃaɪld] *n* tataranieto(a) *m,f*

great-great-granddaughter ['greɪt'greɪt'grændɔːtə(r)] *n* tataranieta *f*

great-great-grandfather ['greɪt'greɪt'grænfɑːðə(r)] *n* tatarabuelo *m*

great-great-grandmother ['greɪt'greɪt'grænmʌðə(r)] *n* tatarabuela *f*

great-great-grandparents ['greɪt'greɪt'grænpeərənts] *npl* tatarabuelos *mpl*

great-great-grandson ['greɪt'greɪt'grænsʌn] *n* tataranieto *m*

greatly ['greɪtlɪ] *adv* **g. changed** muy cambiado(a); **he was g. influenced by his father** estaba muy influido por su padre; **it's g. improved** ha mejorado mucho; **you'll be g. missed** tu ausencia se va a sentir mucho; **g. though I admired/respected him...** aunque lo admiraba/respetaba enormemente...

great-nephew ['greɪt'nefjuː] *n* sobrino *m* nieto

greatness ['greɪtnɪs] *n (of person)* talla *f*, grandeza *f*; *(of action)* grandeza *f*; **to achieve g.** *(writer, politician)* convertirse en uno de los grandes

great-niece ['greɪt'niːs] *n* sobrina *f* nieta

great-uncle ['greɪt'ʌŋkəl] *n* tío *m* abuelo

grebe [griːb] *n* somormujo *m*; **black-necked g.** zampullín cuellinegro

Grecian ['griːʃən] *adj* helénico(a), griego(a) ►► ***G. nose*** nariz *f* griega

Greece [griːs] *n* Grecia

greed [griːd], **greediness** ['griːdɪnɪs] *n* (**a**) *(for food)* glotonería *f*; *(for material things)* codicia *f* (**for** de) (**b**) *(for fame, power, knowledge, success)* avidez *f* (**for** de)
greedily ['griːdɪlɪ] *adv* (**a**) *(to eat)* con glotonería (**b**) *(to look, behave)* codiciosamente
greediness = **greed**
greedy ['griːdɪ] *adj* (**a**) *(for food)* glotón(ona); *(for material things)* codicioso(a) (**b**) **to be g. for sth** *(fame, power, knowledge, success)* estar ávido(a) de algo
greedy-guts ['griːdɪgʌts] *n Fam* tragón(ona) *m,f*
Greek [griːk] 1 *n* (**a**) *(person)* griego(a) *m,f*; PROV **beware of Greeks bearing gifts** no te fíes de las apariencias (**b**) *(language)* griego *m*; **ancient/modern G.** griego clásico/moderno; IDIOM *Fam* **it's all G. to me** me suena a chino
2 *adj* griego(a) ►► ***G. god*** dios *m* griego; ***G. goddess*** diosa *f* griega; ***G. Orthodox Church*** iglesia *f* ortodoxa griega; *Comptr* ***G. text*** texto *m* simulado
green [griːn] 1 *n* (**a**) *(colour)* verde *m* (**b**) **greens** *(vegetables)* verdura (**c**) **(village) g.** = en los pueblos, parque o zona verde céntricos de uso público (**d**) *(in golf)* green *m*; **to hit/miss the g.** alcanzar/no alcanzar el green ►► (**e**) *Pol* **the Greens** los verdes, los ecologistas (**f**) *US (money) Esp* pasta *f*, *Am* plata *f*
2 *adj* (**a**) *(colour)* verde; **to go** *or* **turn g.** *(traffic lights)* cambiar a *or* ponerse (en) verde; *(tree)* echar las hojas; *Fam (person)* ponerse blanco(a) *or* pálido(a); **the g. shoots (of recovery)** un atisbo de recuperación ►► ***g. bean*** *Esp* judía *f* verde, *Bol, RP* chaucha *f*, *Carib, Col* habichuela *f*, *Chile* poroto *m* verde, *Méx* ejote *m*; ***g. belt*** *(around city)* cinturón *m* verde; *US* ***G. Beret*** boina verde *mf*; ***g. card*** *US (work permit)* permiso *m* de trabajo, carta *f* verde; *(car insurance)* carta *f* verde; ***the g. channel*** *(at customs)* el canal verde, la puerta verde; ***G. Cross Code*** = código británico de seguridad vial infantil; *Sport* ***the g. jersey*** el maillot verde; *Br* ***the g. man*** *(at pedestrian crossing)* la señal de paso para peatones; **wait for the g. man** espera que se ponga (en) verde; *Hum* **little g. men** hombrecitos verdes; *US* ***g. onion*** cebolleta *f*, *RP* cebolla *f* de verdeo; *Br Parl* ***g. paper*** libro *m* verde; ***g. pepper*** pimiento *m* verde; *Br* ***the g. pound*** = el valor de la libra en el mercado agrícola europeo; ***the g. revolution*** la revolución verde; ***g. salad*** ensalada *f* verde; ***g. sandpiper*** andarríos *m inv* grande; ***g. tea*** té *m* verde; ***g. woodpecker*** pito *m* real
(**b**) *(undried) (timber)* verde
(**c**) *(unripe)* verde; **these tomatoes are still g.** estos tomates aún están verdes
(**d**) *Fam (young, inexperienced)* inexperto(a), novato(a); *(naive)* ingenuo(a)
(**e**) *(environmentalist)* ecologista, verde ►► ***g. audit*** auditoría *f* ambiental; ***the G. Party*** el partido ecologista *or* de los verdes; ***g. tourism*** turismo *m* verde
(**f**) IDIOMS **to be g. with envy** estar muerto(a) de envidia; **to have** *Br* **g. fingers** *or US* **a g. thumb** tener buena mano para *or Esp* con las plantas; **to give sb the g. light (to do sth)** dar a alguien luz verde (para hacer algo); **to keep sb's memory g.** mantener viva la memoria de alguien
greenback ['griːnbæk] *n US Fam* billete *m (dólar estadounidense)*, *RP* verde *m*
greenery ['griːnərɪ] *n (plants, trees)* vegetación *f*; *(as decoration for cut flowers)* verde *m*
green-eyed ['griːnaɪd] *adj* de ojos verdes; *Literary* **the g. monster** *(jealousy)* los celos
greenfield site ['griːnfiːld'saɪt] *n (for factory, houses)* terreno *m* edificable *(fuera del casco urbano)*
greenfinch ['griːnfɪntʃ] *n* verderón *m* común
green-fingered ['griːn'fɪŋgəd] *adj Br* con buena mano para las plantas
greenfly ['griːnflaɪ] *n* pulgón *m*
greengage ['griːngeɪdʒ] *n (fruit)* ciruela *f* claudia
greengrocer ['griːngrəʊsə(r)] *n Br* verdulero(a) *m,f*; **g.'s (shop)** verdulería *f*
greenhorn ['griːnhɔːn] *n Fam* novato(a) *m,f*
greenhouse ['griːnhaʊs] *n* invernadero *m* ►► ***the g. effect*** el efecto invernadero; ***g. gas*** gas *m* productor del efecto invernadero
greening ['griːnɪŋ] *n* ecologización *f*, concienciación *f* ecológica
greenish ['griːnɪʃ] *adj* verdoso(a)
greenkeeper ['griːnkiːpə(r)] *n* técnico(a) *m,f* de mantenimiento *or* cuidador(ora) *m,f* de campo de golf
Greenland ['griːnlənd] *n* Groenlandia ►► ***G. halibut*** fletán *m* negro
Greenlander ['griːnləndə(r)] *n* groenlandés(esa) *m,f*
Greenlandic [griːn'lændɪk] 1 *n (language)* groenlandés *m*
2 *adj* groenlandés(esa)
greenlight ['griːnlaɪt] *vt US (approve)* dar luz verde a
greenmail ['griːnmeɪl] *n US Com* órdago *m*, = compra de acciones para su posterior reventa a la misma entidad emisora
greenness ['griːnnɪs] *n* (**a**) *(colour)* verdor *m*, verde *m*; *(of field, landscape)* verdor *m*, verde *m* (**b**) *(of fruit)* falta *f* de madurez (**c**) *(of person) (inexperience)* inexperiencia *f*; *(naivety)* ingenuidad *f* (**d**) *(environmental awareness)* concienciación *f* ambiental
greenroom ['griːnruːm] *n Theat* sala *f* de descanso *(para actores)*
greenshank ['griːnʃæŋk] *n* archibebe *m* claro
greenstick fracture ['griːnstɪk'fræktʃə(r)] *n Med* fractura *f* de tallo verde
greenstuff ['griːnstʌf] *n* (**a**) *(vegetables)* verdura *f* (**b**) *US Fam (money) Esp* pasta *f*, *Am* plata *f*, *Méx* lana *f*, *RP* guita *f*
green-wellie [griːn'welɪ] *adj Br Fam Hum* ***the g. brigade*** los terratenientes (británicos), los señoritos del campo (británicos)
Greenwich ['grenɪtʃ] *n* ***G. Mean Time*** hora *f* del meridiano cero *or* de Greenwich; ***the G. meridian*** el meridiano de Greenwich
greenwood ['griːnwʊd] *n Archaic or Literary* floresta *f*
greeny ['griːnɪ] *adj* verdoso(a)
greet [griːt] *vt* (**a**) *(say hello to)* saludar
(**b**) *(welcome) (person, idea)* recibir, acoger; **to g. sth/sb with open arms** recibir *or* acoger algo/a alguien con los brazos abiertos
(**c**) *(receive, respond to)* recibir, acoger; **her speech was greeted with wild applause** su discurso fue recibido *or* acogido con una enardecida ovación
(**d**) *(be immediately apparent to)* **a strange sound greeted our ears** nos llegó a los oídos un extraño sonido; **an awful sight greeted their eyes** un horrendo espectáculo se ofrecía ante sus ojos
greeter ['griːtə(r)] *n (in restaurant)* relaciones *mf inv* públicas
greeting ['griːtɪŋ] *n* saludo *m*; **to send greetings to sb** enviar saludos *or CAm, Col, Ecuad* saludes a alguien; **New Year/birthday greetings** felicitaciones de Año Nuevo/cumpleaños ►► *US* ***g.*** *or Br* ***greetings card*** tarjeta *f* de felicitación
gregarious [grɪ'geərɪəs] *adj (animal)* gregario(a); *(person)* sociable
gregariousness [grɪ'geərɪəsnɪs] *n (of animal)* gregarismo *m*; *(of person)* sociabilidad *f*
Gregorian [grɪ'gɔːrɪən] *adj* ***G. calendar*** calendario *m* gregoriano; ***G. chant*** canto *m* gregoriano
Gregory ['gregərɪ] *pr n* **Saint G.** San Gregorio; **G. I/II** Gregorio I/II
gremlin ['gremlɪn] *n Fam* duende *m*
Grenada [grə'neɪdə] *n* Granada *(país)*
grenade [grə'neɪd] *n* granada *f*; **g. attack** ataque con granadas ►► ***g. launcher*** lanzagranadas *m inv*
Grenadian [grə'neɪdɪən] 1 *n* granadino(a) *m,f*
2 *adj* granadino(a)
grenadier [grenə'dɪə(r)] *n* granadero *m*
grenadine ['grenədiːn] *n (drink)* granadina *f*
grew *pt of* **grow**
grey, *US* **gray** [greɪ] 1 *n* (**a**) *(colour)* gris *m* (**b**) *(horse)* rucio(a) *m,f*
2 *adj* (**a**) *(in colour)* gris ►► ***Grey Friar*** fraile *m* franciscano; ***g. heron*** garza *f* real; *St Exch* ***g. knight*** = agente de bolsa que opera en el mercado gris; *Comptr* ***g. levels*** niveles *mpl* de gris; *St Exch* ***g. market*** mercado *m* gris, preapertura *f*; ***g. matter*** *(brain)* materia *f* gris; *Fam* **to exercise the g. matter** hacer trabajar la materia gris; ***g. mullet*** mújol *m*; ***g. partridge*** perdiz *f* pardilla; ***g. plover*** chorlito *m* gris; ***the g. pound*** el poder adquisitivo de los mayores; ***g. seal*** foca *f* gris; ***g. squirrel*** ardilla *f* gris; ***g. wagtail*** lavandera *f* cascadeña; ***g. wolf*** lobo *m* gris
(**b**) *(hair)* cano(a), gris; **he's going** *or* **turning g.** le están saliendo canas; **g. hairs** canas
(**c**) *(overcast)* gris
(**d**) *(boring)* gris
(**e**) *(unclear)* **a g. area** una zona gris, una zona poco definida
3 *vi (hair)* encanecer
greybeard, *US* **graybeard** ['greɪbɪəd] *n Literary* anciano *m*
grey-haired, *US* **gray-haired** ['greɪ'heəd] *adj* canoso(a)
Greyhound® ['greɪhaʊnd] *n US* **G. (bus)** = autobús de largo recorrido
greyhound ['greɪhaʊnd] *n (dog)* galgo *m* ►► ***g. race*** carrera *f* de galgos; ***g. racing*** carreras *fpl* de galgos; ***g. stadium*** canódromo *m*
greying, *US* **graying** ['greɪɪŋ] *adj (hair)* encanecido(a); *(population)* envejecido(a)

greyish, *US* **grayish** ['greɪɪʃ] *adj* grisáceo(a)

greylag ['greɪlæg] *n* **g. (goose)** ánsar *m* (común)

greyness, *US* **grayness** ['greɪnɪs] *n* (**a**) *(of paint, skin, sky)* color *m* gris; **the g. of the weather** el tiempo gris (**b**) *(dullness)* **the g. of London when I was a child** lo gris que era la vida en Londres cuando yo era niño

greyscale, *US* **grayscale** ['greɪskeɪl] *n Comptr & Typ* escala *f* de grises

grid [grɪd] *n* (**a**) *(bars)* reja *f* (**b**) *(on map, chart)* cuadrícula *f* ►► ***g. layout*** *(of town)* trazado *m* cuadricular, planta *f* cuadriculada; ***g. reference*** coordenadas *fpl* (**c**) *(for electricity)* red *f* eléctrica (**d**) *(electrode)* electrodo *m* (**e**) *(on motor racing track)* parrilla *f* de salida; **he was second on the g.** ocupaba el segundo lugar en la parrilla de salida

griddle ['grɪdəl] *n* plancha *f* ►► *US* ***g. cake*** crepe *m*, *Am* panqueque *m*

gridiron ['grɪdaɪən] *n* (**a**) *(for cooking)* parrilla *f* (**b**) *US (field)* campo *m* de fútbol americano

gridline ['grɪdlaɪn] *n Comptr* cuadrícula *f*

gridlock ['grɪdlɒk] *n* (**a**) *(traffic jam)* paralización *f* del tráfico (**b**) *(in negotiations)* estancamiento *m*

gridlocked ['grɪdlɒkt] *adj* (**a**) *(roads)* **the town centre is g.** el tráfico está paralizado; **I was g. for an hour** estuve una hora metido en un atasco (**b**) *(negotiations)* estancado(a)

grief [gri:f] *n* (**a**) *(sorrow)* dolor *m*, aflicción *f*; IDIOM **to come to g.** venirse abajo (**b**) *Fam (hassle)* **to give sb g. (about sth)** dar la vara *or* la lata a alguien (con algo), *RP* hinchar a alguien (con algo); **I'm getting a lot of g. from my parents** mis padres no paran de darme la vara *or* la lata (**c**) *(as exclamation) Fam* **good g.!** ¡santo Dios!

grief-stricken ['gri:fstrɪkən] *adj* afligido(a); **to be g.** estar afligido(a)

grievance ['gri:vəns] *n* (**a**) *(resentment)* (sentimiento *m* de) agravio *m*; **to harbour** *or* **nurse a g.** sentirse agraviado(a) (**b**) *(complaint)* motivo *m* de queja; **they voiced** *or* **aired their grievances** expresaron sus quejas ►► *Ind* ***g. procedure*** procedimiento *m* de quejas

grieve [gri:v] **1** *vt* apenar, afligir; **it grieves me to have to tell you that...** me apena tener que decirte que...; **I was grieved to discover that...** me apenó mucho descubrir que...

2 *vi* (**a**) *(feel grief)* **her husband died five years ago and she is still grieving** su marido murió hace cinco años y sigue sufriendo por su muerte *or Psy* aún está en proceso de duelo; **to g. for** *or* **over sb** sufrir por la muerte de alguien, llorar la muerte de alguien; **he is grieving for his lost dominions** llora la pérdida de sus dominios

(**b**) *(express grief)* **to g. for the dead** llorar a los muertos

grieving ['gri:vɪŋ] **1** *n* duelo *m*; **the g. process** el proceso de duelo

2 *adj* desconsolado(a)

grievous ['gri:vəs] *adj* (**a**) *Formal (serious) (loss, injury, error)* grave; **you have done me g. wrong** me has hecho mucho mal (**b**) *Br Law* ***g. bodily harm*** lesiones *fpl* graves

grievously ['gri:vəslɪ] *adv Formal (seriously)* seriamente; **to be g. wounded** estar gravemente herido(a); **you are g. mistaken** estás en un grave error

griffin ['grɪfən] *n (mythological creature)* grifo *m*

griffon ['grɪfən] *n* (**a**) *(dog)* grifón *m* (**b**) ***g. vulture*** buitre *m* leonado

grift [grɪft] *vi US Fam* vivir del timo

grifter ['grɪftə(r)] *n US Fam* timador(ora) *m,f*

grill [grɪl] **1** *n* (**a**) *Br (on cooker)* grill *m* (**b**) *(for open fire)* parrilla *f* (**c**) *(food)* parrillada *f*; **a mixed g.** una parrillada de carne (**d**) *(room in restaurant, hotel)* asador *m*, parrilla *f*; *(restaurant)* asador *m*, parrilla *f*

2 *vt* (**a**) *(cook)* asar (a la parrilla); **grilled meat** carne a la parrilla (**b**) *Fam (interrogate)* acribillar a preguntas

grille [grɪl] *n* (**a**) *(bars, grating)* reja *f*; *(made of wire)* alambrada *f*, *Am* alambrado *m* (**b**) *Aut* **(radiator) g.** rejilla *f* del radiador

grilling ['grɪlɪŋ] *n Fam (interrogation)* **to give sb a g.** acribillar a alguien a preguntas

grillroom ['grɪlru:m] *n* asador *m*, parrilla *f (restaurante)*

grilse [grɪls] *n* = salmón joven que remonta por primera vez para el desove

grim [grɪm] *adj* (**a**) *(depressing, gloomy) (account, news, prospects)* desalentador(ora), sombrío(a); *(mood)* sombrío(a); *(landscape)* desolado(a); **the situation looks g.** el panorama es desalentador

(**b**) *(unpleasant, gruesome) (reality)* duro(a); **it was a g. reminder of his years in prison** era un sombrío recuerdo de los años que pasó en la cárcel

(**c**) *(stern) (expression, smile)* adusto(a); **to look g.** *(person)* tener la cara larga ►► ***the g. reaper*** la muerte, = la figura con guadaña que simboliza la muerte, *Andes, Cuba, RP* la Pelada

(**d**) *(relentless)* **he showed g. determination** demostró una determinación implacable; **I hung on** *or* **held on like g. death** me agarré como si me fuera la vida en ello

(**e**) *Fam (bad)* **his new film is pretty g.** su nueva película es bastante mala; **I've had a g. day** tuve un día pésimo

(**f**) *Fam (unwell, depressed) Esp* fatal, *Am* pésimo(a); **how do you feel? – pretty g.!** ¿cómo te sientes? – *Esp* ¡fatal! *or Am* ¡pésimo!

grimace [grɪ'meɪs] **1** *n* mueca *f*

2 *vi (once)* hacer una mueca; *(more than once)* hacer muecas

grime [graɪm] *n* mugre *f*, porquería *f*

griminess ['graɪmɪnɪs] *n* apariencia *f* sombría

grimly ['grɪmlɪ] *adv* (**a**) *(gravely) (to speak, smile)* sombríamente (**b**) *(relentlessly) (to fight, hold on)* con determinación

grimness ['grɪmnɪs] *n* (**a**) *(gloominess) (of news, report)* lo desalentador, lo sombrío; *(mood)* lo sombrío; *(of landscape)* desolación *f*; **the g. of his situation** lo deprimente de su situación (**b**) *(sternness)* adustez *f*

grimy ['graɪmɪ] *adj* mugriento(a)

grin [grɪn] **1** *n (smile)* (amplia) sonrisa *f*; **take** *or* **wipe that stupid g. off your face!** ¡deja ya de sonreír como un imbécil!

2 *vi (smile)* sonreír ampliamente; **what are you grinning at?** ¿de qué te sonríes?; **to g. from ear to ear** sonreír de oreja a oreja; IDIOM **to g. and bear it** poner al mal tiempo buena cara

grind [graɪnd] **1** *n* (**a**) *(texture)* **a fine/coarse g.** un molido fino/grueso (**b**) *Fam (work)* **the daily g.** la rutina diaria; **what a g.!** ¡qué rollo de trabajo! (**c**) *US Fam (hard worker)* esclavo(a) *m,f*; *(student) Esp* empollón(ona) *m,f*, *Méx* matado(a) *m,f*, *RP* traga *mf*

2 *vt* (*pt & pp* **ground** [graʊnd]) (**a**) *(grain, coffee, pepper)* moler; *US (meat)* picar

(**b**) *(crush)* aplastar; **he ground his feet into the sand** hundió sus pies en la arena; **he ground the cigarette under his heel** aplastó el cigarrillo con el talón; *Fig* **to g. the faces of the poor** oprimir a los pobres

(**c**) *(rub together)* **to g. one's teeth** *(in frustration)* apretar los dientes; *(in one's sleep)* hacer rechinar los dientes; **to g. the gears** *(driver)* hacer rascar las marchas

(**d**) *(polish) (glass)* esmerilar

(**e**) *(sharpen) (knife, axe)* afilar

(**f**) *(turn handle)* moler; **to g. a pepper mill** moler pimienta en el molinillo; **to g. a barrel-organ** dar cuerda a un organillo

(**g**) *US Fam (irritate)* cabrear

3 *vi* (**a**) *(move noisily) (wheels, gears)* chirriar; **to g. to a halt** *or* **standstill** *(vehicle, machine)* detenerse con estrépito; *(project)* acabar estancado(a) (**b**) *(study hard) Esp* empollar, *Méx* matarse (estudiando), *RP* tragar

► **grind away** *vi Fam (work hard)* trabajar sin parar (**at** en); *(study hard)* darle como un loco (**at** a)

► **grind down** *vt sep* (**a**) *(reduce)* pulverizar, moler (**b**) *Fig (opposition, resistance)* desgastar, minar; *Fam* **don't let them g. you down!** ¡no te dejes avasallar por ellos!

► **grind on** *vi (proceed relentlessly)* proseguir machaconamente; **he was still grinding on about taxes when I left** cuando me fui todavía seguía dándole al tema de los impuestos

► **grind out** *vt sep (music)* interpretar trabajosamente; *(novel, essay)* escribir trabajosamente

grinder ['graɪndə(r)] *n* (**a**) *(for coffee, pepper)* molinillo *m* (**b**) *(industrial) (crusher)* trituradora *f* (**c**) *(for polishing)* pulidora *f* (**d**) *(tooth)* muela *f* (**e**) *US Fam (sandwich) Esp* bocadillo *m*, *Am* sándwich *m (hecho con una barra estrecha y larga)*

grinding ['graɪndɪŋ] *adj* (**a**) *(sound)* **a g. noise** un chirrido; **to come to a g. halt** *(of car, machine)* pararse en seco; *(of project)* acabar estancado(a); **to bring sth to a g. halt** *(production)* detener algo completamente; *(country, rail network)* paralizar algo (**b**) *(oppressive) (boredom, worry)* insufrible, insoportable; **g. poverty** pobreza absoluta

grindstone ['graɪndstəʊn] *n* (**a**) *(for sharpening)* muela *f*, piedra *f* de afilar; IDIOM **to keep** *or* **have one's nose to the g.** trabajar como un negro (**b**) *(for milling)* rueda *f* de molino

gringo ['grɪŋgəʊ] (*pl* **gringos**) *n US Fam* gringo(a) *m,f*

grinning ['grɪnɪŋ] *adj (face, person)* risueño(a); **I was surrounded by g. idiots** me rodeaban imbéciles de sonrisa tonta

grip [grɪp] **1** *n* (**a**) *(hold, grasp)* sujeción *f*; *(in tennis, golf)* sujeción *f*, forma *f* de agarrar; *(of tyres on road)* adherencia *f*, agarre *m*; **your g. is wrong** *(in tennis)* agarras mal la raqueta; *(in golf)* agarras mal el palo; **to get a g. on** *or* **of sth** *(rope, handle)* agarrar algo; **to tighten/loosen**

one's g. on sth agarrar algo con más fuerza/menos fuerza; **to lose one's g.** soltarse; **to lose one's g. on sth** soltar algo; *Fig* **to be in the g. of a disease/a crisis/despair** ser presa de una enfermedad/una crisis/la desesperación; *Fig* **the country was in the g. of the worst winter for years** el país estaba asolado por el peor invierno desde hacía años

(**b**) *(handclasp)* **to have a strong g.** agarrar con fuerza; **she held his hand in a vice-like g.** le agarraba la mano una fuerza bruta

(**c**) *(control)* **he's losing his g.** está perdiendo el control; **to lose one's g. on reality** perder el contacto con la realidad; **to get** *or* **come to grips with** *(new situation)* asimilar, asumir; *(subject, method, problem)* conseguir entender; *Fam* **to get a g. on oneself** dominarse, contenerse; *Fam* **get a g.!** *(control yourself)* ¡no desvaríes!; *(don't be ridiculous)* pero, ¡por favor!; **to have a firm g. on a situation** dominar una situación

(**d**) *(handle) (of oar, handlebars, racket)* empuñadura *f*

(**e**) *(pin)* **(hair) g.** horquilla *f*

(**f**) *US (bag)* bolsa *f* de viaje

(**g**) *Theat* ayudante *mf* de puesta en escena

(**h**) *Cin & TV* maquinista *mf*

2 *vt* (*pt & pp* **gripped**) (**a**) *(seize)* agarrar

(**b**) *(hold)* sujetar; **tyres that g. the road** neumáticos *or Col, Méx* llantas *or RP* gomas que se adhieren (bien) a la carretera; *Fig* **to be gripped by panic/fear** ser presa del pánico/miedo

(**c**) *(hold interest of)* **the play gripped the audience** la obra tuvo en vilo al público; **go on, I'm gripped!** ¡sigue, que me tienes en vilo!; **the trial gripped the nation** todo el país estaba pendiente del juicio

3 *vi (tyre)* adherirse

gripe [graɪp] **1** *n* (**a**) *Fam (complaint)* queja *f*; **what's your g.?** ¿qué tripa se te ha roto? (**b**) *Br* ***g. water*** (medicamento *m*) carminativo *m*, agua *f* de anís

2 *vi Fam (complain)* quejarse (**about** de)

gripping ['grɪpɪŋ] *adj (book, story)* apasionante

grisly ['grɪzlɪ] *adj* espeluznante, horripilante

grist [grɪst] *n* IDIOM **it's all g. to his mill** todo lo aprovecha

gristle ['grɪsəl] *n* ternilla *f*

gristly ['grɪslɪ] *adj (meat)* lleno(a) de ternilla

grit [grɪt] **1** *n* (**a**) *(gravel)* gravilla *f* (**b**) *(dust)* **I have a piece of g. in my eye** tengo una mota en el ojo (**c**) *Fam (courage, determination)* coraje *m*; **to have a lot of g.** tener mucho coraje

2 *vt* (*pt & pp* **gritted**) (**a**) *Br (put grit on)* **to g. a road** echar gravilla en una carretera (**b**) *(clench)* **to g. one's teeth** apretar los dientes

grits [grɪts] *npl US* gachas *fpl* de sémola de maíz *or Andes, RP* choclo

gritter ['grɪtə(r)] *n Br (lorry)* = camión que va esparciendo gravilla por la carretera cuando está resbaladiza por el hielo o la nieve

gritty ['grɪtɪ] *adj* (**a**) *(sandy)* arenoso(a); **it tastes g.** sabe a arenilla (**b**) *Fam (determined)* resuelto(a); **g. determination** una determinación implacable (**c**) *(grim)* **g. realism** realismo descarnado

grizzle ['grɪzəl] *vi (complain)* lloriquear

grizzled ['grɪzəld] *adj (hair, person) (grey)* canoso(a); *(greyish)* entrecano(a)

grizzly ['grɪzlɪ] **1** *n* **g. (bear)** oso *m* pardo *(norteamericano)*

2 *adj (hair, person)* canoso(a)

groan [grəʊn] **1** *n* (**a**) *(of pain)* gemido *m*; **to let out a g.** dejar escapar un gemido (**b**) *(of dismay)* gemido *m* (**c**) *(creak)* crujido *m*

2 *vt* **"oh no!" he groaned** "¡oh no!", gimió

3 *vi* (**a**) *(in pain)* gemir (**b**) *(in dismay)* gemir; **to g. inwardly** ahogar un gemido (**c**) *(creak)* crujir (**d**) *(be weighed down by)* **the shelves groaned under the weight of books** la estantería cedía con el peso de los libros (**e**) *(complain)* quejarse

groaning ['grəʊnɪŋ] *n* gemidos *mpl*

groat [grəʊt] *n* moneda *f* de cuatro peniques

groats [grəʊts] *npl* = cereal descascarado y molido grueso

grocer ['grəʊsə(r)] *n* tendero(a) *m,f*; *Br* **g.'s (shop)** *Esp* tienda *f* de comestibles, *CSur* almacén *m*, *Col, Méx* tienda *f* de abarrotes

groceries ['grəʊsərɪz] *npl (shopping)* comestibles *mpl*

grocery ['grəʊsərɪ] *n esp US* **g. (store)** *Esp* tienda *f* de comestibles, *CSur* almacén *m*, *Col, Méx* tienda *f* de abarrotes

grody ['grəʊdɪ] *adj US Fam* asqueroso(a); **g. to the max** *Esp* más asqueroso(a) que la leche, *Méx* putrefacto(a), *RP* más asqueroso(a) que la miércoles

grog [grɒg] *n Fam* (**a**) *(drink)* grog *m*, ponche *m* (**b**) *Austr (any alcoholic drink)* bebida *f*, *Am* trago *m*

groggily ['grɒgɪlɪ] *adv Fam* con aire aturdido

groggy ['grɒgɪ] *adj Fam* atontado(a), grogui; **to be g.** estar atontado(a) *or* grogui

grogshop ['grɒgʃɒp] *n Austr Fam* = tienda de bebidas alcohólicas

groin[1] [grɔɪn] *n* (**a**) *Anat* ingle *f* ►► ***g. strain*** lesión *f* en la ingle (**b**) *Br Euph (testicles)* entrepierna *f* (**c**) *Archit* arista *f*

groin[2] *US* = **groyne**

grommet ['grɒmɪt] *n* (**a**) *(eyelet)* arandela *f* (**b**) *Med (in ear)* diábolo *m* (**c**) *Fam (in surfing, skateboarding)* principiante *mf*

groom [gru:m] **1** *n* (**a**) *(of horse)* mozo *m* de cuadra (**b**) *(at wedding)* novio *m* (**c**) *(in royal household)* ayudante *m* de cámara

2 *vt* (**a**) *(keep clean) (horse)* almohazar, cepillar; **cats g. themselves** los gatos se asean a sí mismos (**b**) *(keep smart, neat) (person)* **to g. oneself** asearse (**c**) *(prepare) (candidate)* preparar

grooming ['gru:mɪŋ] *n (smart, neat appearance)* buena presencia *f*

groove [gru:v] **1** *n* (**a**) *(slot)* ranura *f* (**b**) *(of record)* surco *m* (**c**) *Mus (in dance music)* ritmo *m* (**d**) *Fam (rut)* **to get into a g.** estancarse; **to be stuck in a g.** estar estancado(a) (**e**) IDIOM *Fam* **to be in the g.** estar metido(a) en ello

2 *vi US Fam* **I g. on it** *Esp* me mola, *Méx* me late, *RP* me copa pila

groovy ['gru:vɪ] *Fam* **1** *adj Esp* chachi, *Méx* padre, *RP* bárbaro(a)

2 *exclam Esp* ¡chachi!, ¡qué *Méx* padre *or RP* bárbaro!

grope [grəʊp] **1** *n Fam (sexual)* **to give sb a g.** meter mano a alguien; **they were having a g.** se estaban metiendo mano

2 *vt* (**a**) *(move in the dark)* **to g. one's way in the dark** ir a tientas en la oscuridad; **to g. one's way forward** avanzar a tientas (**b**) *Fam (sexually)* meter mano a

3 *vi* **to g. (about** *or* **around) for sth** buscar algo a tientas; **to g. for words** buscar torpemente las palabras adecuadas

grosbeak ['grəʊsbi:k] *n* **pine g.** camachuelo *m* picogrueso

gross [grəʊs] **1** *n* (**a**) *(whole amount)* **the g.** los ingresos brutos (**b**) *(twelve dozen)* gruesa *f*, doce docenas *fpl*; **two g.** dos gruesas

2 *adj* (**a**) *(blatant) (error, ignorance)* craso(a); *(stupidity, incompetence, injustice)* flagrante ►► ***g. misconduct*** *(at work)* falta *f* grave; *Law* ***g. negligence*** negligencia *f* grave

(**b**) *(profit, income, interest)* bruto(a) ►► *Econ* ***g. domestic product*** producto *m Esp* interior *or Am* interno bruto; ***g. margin*** beneficio *m or* margen *m* bruto; *Econ* ***g. national product*** producto *m* nacional bruto; ***g. weight*** peso *m* bruto; ***g. yield*** rendimiento *m* bruto

(**c**) *(vulgar) (joke, person)* basto(a), grosero(a)

(**d**) *Fam (disgusting)* asqueroso(a)

(**e**) *(fat)* gordo(a)

3 *vt (earn) (of firm)* tener una ganancia bruta de; **she grosses £40,000 a year** gana 40.000 libras brutas al año

▸**gross out** *vt sep US Fam* **to g. sb out** revolver las tripas a alguien

▸**gross up** *vt sep Fin* **to g. sth up** expresar algo en bruto

grossly ['grəʊslɪ] *adv* (**a**) *(coarsely)* groseramente, crudamente (**b**) *(as intensifier) (exaggerated, negligent)* tremendamente, enormemente; **g. unfair** sumamente injusto(a)

grossness ['grəʊsnɪs] *n* (**a**) *(of abuse, error)* gravedad *f* (**b**) *(vulgarity)* vulgaridad *f* (**c**) *(obesity)* obesidad *f*

gross-out ['grəʊsaʊt] *n US Fam* asco *m*; **a g. scene** una escena que revuelve las tripas

grot [grɒt] *n Br Fam* porquería *f*, cochambre *f*

grotesque [grəʊ'tesk] **1** *n* (**a**) *Art* **the g.** lo grotesco (**b**) *(caricature)* personaje *m* grotesco

2 *adj* (**a**) *(hideous, bizarre)* grotesco(a) (**b**) *(outrageous) (injustice, waste)* de escándalo; *(distortion)* burdo(a)

grotesquely [grəʊ'tesklɪ] *adv* grotescamente; **he was g. fat** era de una gordura grotesca; **it's g. unfair** es una injusticia de escándalo

grotto ['grɒtəʊ] (*pl* **grottoes** *or* **grottos**) *n* gruta *f*

grotty ['grɒtɪ] *adj esp Br Fam (house, job)* malo(a), *Esp* cutre, *Méx* gacho(a), *RP* roñoso(a); **to feel g.** sentirse *Esp* fatal *or Am* pésimo(a)

grouch [graʊtʃ] *Fam* **1** *n* (**a**) *(person)* gruñón(ona) *m,f* (**b**) *(complaint)* queja *f*

2 *vi* refunfuñar

grouchiness ['graʊtʃɪnɪs] *n Fam* mal genio *m*, malas pulgas *fpl*

grouchy ['graʊtʃɪ] *adj Fam* **(to be) g.** *(inherent quality)* (ser) refunfuñón(ona); *(temporary mood)* (estar) enfurruñado(a) *or Am* enojado(a)

GROUND [graʊnd] **1** *n* (**a**) *(earth, soil)* tierra *f*; *(surface of earth)* suelo *m*; **to fall to the g.** caer al suelo; **to sit on the g.** sentarse en el suelo; *Fig* **on the g.** *(in the field)* sobre el terreno; **opinion on the g. seems to be in favour** la opinión pública parece estar a favor; **above g.** sobre la tierra; **to come above g.** salir a la superficie; **below g.** bajo tierra; **burnt to the g.** completamente destruido(a) por el fuego; IDIOM

to be on dangerous/safe g. estar en terreno peligroso/seguro; IDIOM **to get off the g.** *(project)* ponerse en marcha; IDIOM **to go to g.** ocultarse, desaparecer de la circulación; IDIOM **to run sb to g.** dar por fin con alguien; IDIOM **it suits you down to the g.** te sienta de maravilla; IDIOM **to work** *or* **drive oneself into the g.** matarse *Esp* a trabajar *or* *Am* trabajando ►► ***g. bait*** carnada *f*; ***g. ball*** *(in baseball)* = bola bateada a ras de suelo; *Av* ***g. control*** control *m* de tierra; ***g. cover*** maleza *f*; *Av* ***g. crew*** personal *m* de tierra; ***g. floor*** planta *f* baja; *Fig* **to get in on the g. floor** estar metido(a) desde el principio; *Mil* ***g. forces*** ejército *m* de tierra; ***g. frost*** escarcha *f*; ***at g. level*** a nivel del suelo; ***g. plan*** *Archit* planta *f*; *Fig* plan *m* básico; ***g. rules:* to establish the g. rules** establecer las normas básicas; *Av* ***g. speed*** velocidad *f* en tierra; ***g. squirrel*** ardilla *f* terrestre; *Av* ***g. staff*** personal *m* de tierra; ***g. stroke*** *(in tennis)* golpe *m* (tras el bote); ***g. war*** guerra *f* terrestre; ***g. zero*** zona *f* cero

(b) *(area of land)* terreno *m*; **high g.** terreno elevado; **he's on home g.** *or* **on his own g.** está en su terreno; *also Fig* **to gain g. on sb** *(catch up on)* ganarle terreno a alguien; *also Fig* **to lose** *or* **give g. to sb** perder *or* ceder terreno ante alguien; IDIOM **to cover a lot of g.** *(book, lecture)* abarcar mucho; IDIOM **the idea is gaining g.** la idea está ganando terreno; IDIOM **to go over the same g.** volver a abordar la misma temática; *Pol* **the middle g.** el centro; IDIOM **to prepare the g. for sth** preparar el terreno para algo; IDIOM **to stand** *or* **hold one's g.** mantenerse firme ►► ***g. rent*** = alquiler que se paga al dueño del solar donde está edificada una vivienda

(c) *(stadium)* campo *m*, estadio *m* ►► ***g. staff*** personal *m* de mantenimiento (del campo de juego)

(d) *(area used for specific purpose)* **fishing grounds** caladero; **training g.** campo de entrenamiento

(e) *(area of knowledge)* **to find common g. for negotiations** hallar un terreno común para las negociaciones; **to be on familiar/firm g.** pisar terreno conocido/firme; **to be on shaky g.** pisar un terreno resbaladizo; **he's very sure of his g.** está muy seguro de lo que hace/dice; **to break new** *or* **fresh g.** abrir nuevas vías *or* nuevos caminos; **to change** *or* **shift one's g.** cambiar la línea de argumentación

(f) **grounds** *(of school, hospital)* terrenos; *(of country house)* jardines

(g) *(reason)* **grounds** motivo, razón; **to have (good) g.** *or* **grounds for doing sth** tener (buenos) motivos para hacer algo; **g.** *or* **grounds for complaint** motivo de queja; **on grounds of ill health** por motivos de salud; *Law* **grounds for divorce** motivo de divorcio

(h) **grounds** *(of coffee)* posos

(i) *US Elec* toma *f* de tierra

(j) *(background)* fondo *m*; **on a green g.** *(painting)* sobre fondo verde

2 *adj (coffee, pepper)* molido(a) ►► ***g. glass*** *(powder)* vidrio *m* pulverizado; *(opaque)* vidrio *m* esmerilado; *US* ***g. meat*** *Esp, RP* carne *f* picada, *Am* carne *f* molida

3 *vt* **(a)** *(base)* fundamentar, basar; **their argument is not grounded in fact** su argumento no se basa en hechos reales

(b) *(educate)* **to g. sb in a subject** enseñar a alguien los principios de una materia; **to be well grounded in sth** tener buenos conocimientos de algo

(c) *US Elec (current)* conectar a tierra

(d) *(prevent from moving)* **the plane was grounded by bad weather** el avión no salió a causa del mal tiempo; **the ship was grounded on a sandbank** el barco encalló en un banco de arena; *US Fig* **her parents grounded her** sus padres la castigaron con no salir, como castigo, sus padres no la dejaron salir; *US Fig* **you're grounded for a week!** ¡te quedas sin salir una semana!

(e) *Sport (ball)* poner en tierra

4 *vi (ship)* encallar

5 *pt & pp of* **grind**

groundbreaking ['graʊndbreɪkɪŋ] *adj* innovador(ora)

groundcloth ['graʊndklɒθ] *n US (of tent)* suelo *m*

grounded ['graʊndɪd] *n Fam* **he's very g.** tiene muy claro lo que es importante en la vida

groundhog ['graʊndhɒg] *n* marmota *f* ►► ***G. Day*** = 2 de febrero, fecha en la que la marmota sale de su hibernación, según una tradición estadounidense

grounding ['graʊndɪŋ] *n* base *f*; **a thorough g. in economics** una base sólida de economía

groundless ['graʊndlɪs] *adj (suspicion, fear)* infundado(a); **her fears proved g.** sus temores resultaron ser infundados

groundling ['graʊndlɪŋ] *n* **(a)** *(fish)* pez *m* de fondo **(b)** *(plant)* planta *f* de fondo **(c)** *Hist (in Elizabethan theatre)* = espectador de patio

groundnut ['graʊndnʌt] *n* cacahuete *m*, *Am* maní *m*, *CAm, Méx* cacahuate *m* ►► ***g. oil*** aceite *m* de cacahuete *or Am* maní *or CAm, Méx* cacahuate

groundsel ['graʊnsəl] *n* hierba *f* cana, zuzón *m*

groundsheet ['graʊndʃiːt] *n (of tent)* suelo *m*

groundsman ['graʊndzmən] *n Br* encargado(a) *m,f* del mantenimiento del campo de juego

groundspeed ['graʊndspiːd] *n Av* velocidad *f* en tierra

groundswell ['graʊndswel] *n* **(a)** *(at sea)* oleada *f*, mar *m* de fondo **(b)** *Fig* **there has been a g. of support for the proposal** ha habido un apoyo masivo de la propuesta

groundwater ['graʊndwɔːtə(r)] *n Geol* aguas *fpl* subterráneas

groundwork ['graʊndwɜːk] *n* **to do** *or* **lay the g.** preparar el terreno

group [gruːp] **1** *n* **(a)** *(of people)* grupo *m* ►► ***g. decision*** decisión *f* colectiva; ***g. dynamics*** dinámica *f* de grupo; ***g. photograph*** fotografía *f* de grupo; ***g. sex*** cama *f* redonda; ***g. therapy*** terapia *f* de grupo; ***g. work*** *(in school, at seminar)* trabajo *m* en grupo

(b) *(of objects)* grupo *m* ►► ***g. dialling*** *(on fax machine)* marcado *m* múltiple, *Andes, RP* discado *m* múltiple; *Econ* ***G. of Eight*** Grupo *m* de los Ocho; *Econ* ***G. of Seven*** Grupo *m* de los Siete; *Math* ***g. theory*** teoría *f* de grupos

(c) *(in business)* grupo *m*; **they're in the Thistle g.** están en el grupo Thistle ►► ***g. turnover*** facturación *f* del grupo

(d) *(band)* grupo *m*; **a pop/rock g.** un grupo música pop/rock

(e) *(in air force)* grupo *m* ►► *Br* ***g. captain*** coronel *mf* de aviación

(f) *US Mil* = unidad compuesta por dos o más batallones

2 *vt* **(a)** *(bring together)* agrupar **(b)** *(put in groups)* agrupar; **the teacher grouped all the eight-year-olds together** el maestro colocó juntos *or* agrupó a todos los niños de ocho años

3 *vi* agruparse; **they grouped round their leader** se agruparon en torno al líder

grouper ['gruːpə(r)] *n (fish)* mero *m*

groupie ['gruːpɪ] *n Fam* groupie *mf*, grupi *mf*

grouping ['gruːpɪŋ] *n* **(a)** *(combination)* agrupación *f* **(b)** *(group)* agrupación *f*

groupthink ['gruːpθɪŋk] *n* pensamiento *m* grupal

grouse[1] [graʊs] *(pl* **grouse***)* *n (bird)* lagópodo *m* escocés ►► ***g. moor*** coto *m* de caza de lagópodos

grouse[2] *Fam* **1** *n (complaint)* queja *f*; **to have a g. about sth** tener una queja sobre algo

2 *vi* quejarse **(about** de)

grouser ['graʊsə(r)] *n Fam (complainer)* quejica *mf*

grout [graʊt] **1** *n (for tiles)* lechada *f*

2 *vt (tiles)* enlechar

grouting ['graʊtɪŋ] *n* cemento *m* blanco

grove [grəʊv] *n (of trees)* arboleda *f*; **a beech g.** un bosquecillo de hayas; **an olive g.** un olivar; IDIOM **the groves of academe** el mundo académico

grovel ['grɒvəl] *(pt & pp* **grovelled**, *US* **groveled***)* *vi* **(a)** *(act humbly)* arrastrarse; **to g. to sb** arrastrarse ante alguien **(b)** *(crawl on floor)* arrastrarse

groveller, *US* **groveler** ['grɒvələ(r)] *n* persona *f* servil

grovelling, *US* **groveling** ['grɒvəlɪŋ] **1** *n* servilismo *m*

2 *adj (tone, remark)* servil; **a g. apology** una disculpa servil

grow [grəʊ] *(pt* **grew** [gruː], *pp* **grown** [grəʊn]) **1** *vt* **(a)** *(vegetables)* cultivar; **I g. roses in my garden** tengo rosas en mi jardín ►► ***g. bag*** = bolsa de compost en la que crecen plantas

(b) **to g. a beard** dejarse (crecer la) barba; **I've decided to g. my hair long** he decidido dejarme el pelo largo; **I'm growing my nails** me estoy dejando crecer las uñas

(c) *(increase in size by)* **it has grown 5 centimetres** ha crecido 5 centímetros

(d) *Com (profits, business)* incrementar

2 *vi* **(a)** *(increase in size)* crecer; **you've grown since I last saw you!** ¡cuánto has crecido desde la última vez que te vi!; **our profits have grown by 5 percent** nuestros beneficios han crecido *or* aumentado un 5 por ciento; **fears are growing for their safety** se teme cada vez más por su seguridad; **his influence grew** su influencia se acrecentó; **a growing number of people think that...** cada vez más gente piensa que...; **to g. as a person** madurar como persona; **to g. in wisdom/beauty** ganar en sabiduría/belleza

(b) *(become)* hacerse; **to g. accustomed to sth** ir acostumbrándose a algo; **to g. angry** *esp Esp* enfadarse, *esp Am* enojarse; **to g. big** *or* **bigger** crecer; **to g. dark** oscurecer; **to g. old** envejecer; **she grew more and more suspicious of him** cada vez sospechaba más de él; **to g. worse** empeorar

(c) *(come eventually)* **he grew to respect her** la llegó a respetar; **they grew to like the house** les llegó a gustar la casa

▸ **grow apart** *vi (people)* distanciarse (**from** de); **they have grown apart from each other** se han distanciado

▸ **grow back** *vi (hair, nail, plant)* volver a crecer

▸ **grow from** *vt insep (result from)* resultar de

▸ **grow into** *vt insep* (**a**) *(clothes)* **this T-shirt's too big for him, but he'll g. into it** ahora le queda grande la camiseta, pero cuando crezca podrá llevarlo; **to g. into a role/job** hacerse con un papel/trabajo (**b**) *(become)* convertirse en; **he had grown into a handsome young man** se había convertido en un joven muy *Esp* guapo *or Am* lindo

▸ **grow on** *vt insep Fam* **it'll g. on you** *(music, book)* te va a gustar *or* enganchar con el tiempo

▸ **grow out** *vi (dye, perm)* irse, desaparecer

▸ **grow out of** *vt insep* (**a**) *(become too large for)* **he's grown out of his shoes** se le han quedado pequeños los zapatos (**b**) *(become too old for)* **she grew out of her dolls** dejó de jugar con muñecas al hacerse mayor; **he's obsessed with Madonna – don't worry, he'll g. out of it** está obsesionado con Madonna – no te preocupes, ya se le pasará (**c**) *(result from)* resultar de

▸ **grow together** *vi* ir intimando

▸ **grow up** *vi* (**a**) *(become adult)* crecer; **I want to be a doctor when I g. up** de mayor quiero ser médico; **we didn't have television when I was growing up** cuando era pequeño no teníamos televisión; **I grew up in the countryside** me crié en el campo; *Fam* **g. up!** ¡no seas niño *or* crío!
(**b**) *(develop) (town, village)* surgir; **the industry has grown up out of nothing** la industria ha surgido de la nada

grower ['grəʊə(r)] *n* (**a**) *(person)* cultivador(ora) *m,f*; **a vegetable g.** un(a) horticultor(ora); **a rose g.** un cultivador de rosas (**b**) *(plant, tree)* **a fast/slow g.** una planta de crecimiento rápido/lento

growing ['grəʊɪŋ] **1** *adj* (**a**) *(child)* en edad de crecer (**b**) *(increasing, developing) (town, population)* en aumento, en crecimiento; *(debt, discontent, friendship)* creciente; **g. numbers of people** un número de personas que va en aumento; **there was a g. fear that...** aumentaba el temor de que...
2 *n* ***g. pains*** *(of person)* dolores *mpl* del crecimiento; *(of firm, country)* dificultades *fpl* del desarrollo; ***the g. season*** la época de crecimiento

growl [graʊl] **1** *n (of dog, person)* gruñido *m*; *(from stomach)* gruñido *m*
2 *vt (answer, instructions)* mascullar, farfullar
3 *vi (dog, person)* gruñir (**at** a); **his stomach was growling again** le sonaban otra vez las tripas

growling ['graʊlɪŋ] *n (of dog, person)* gruñidos *mpl*; *(from stomach)* ruidos *mpl*

grown [grəʊn] **1** *adj* adulto(a); **a g. woman** una mujer adulta; **fully g.** completamente desarrollado(a); **their children are all g. up now** todos sus hijos son ya mayores
2 *pp of* **grow**

grown-up **1** *n* ['grəʊnʌp] adulto(a) *m,f*; **the grown-ups** los adultos, los mayores
2 *adj* [grəʊn'ʌp] *(person, attitude)* maduro(a); **he's very g. for his age** es muy maduro para su edad; **he was very g. about it** reaccionó con mucha madurez

growth [grəʊθ] *n* (**a**) *(development) (of child, animal, plant)* crecimiento *m*; *(of friendship)* desarrollo *m*, crecimiento *m*; *(of organization)* expansión *f*, crecimiento *m*; **intellectual/spiritual g.** desarrollo intelectual/espiritual ▸▸ *Physiol* ***g. hormone*** hormona *f* del crecimiento; ***g. ring*** *(in tree)* anillo *m* de crecimiento
(**b**) *(increase) (in numbers, amount)* aumento *m*; *(of influence, knowledge)* aumento *m*; *(of market, industry)* aumento *m*, crecimiento *m* ▸▸ ***a g. area*** un área de crecimiento; ***g. industry*** industria *f* en expansión; *Econ* ***g. market*** mercado *m* en expansión; ***g. rate*** tasa *f* de crecimiento; *Fin* ***g. stock*** valores *mpl or* títulos *mpl* de crecimiento
(**c**) *(of hair, weeds)* mata *f*; **a week's g. of beard** una barba de una semana
(**d**) *(lump)* bulto *m*; **benign/malignant g.** tumor benigno/maligno

groyne, *US* **groin** [grɔɪn] *n* escollera *f*

grub [grʌb] *n* (**a**) *(larva)* larva *f*, gusano *m* (**b**) *Fam (food)* comida *f*, *Esp* manduca *f*, *RP* morfi *m*; **g.'s up!** ¡a comer! (**c**) *Tech* ***g. screw*** tornillo *m* de cabeza hendida

▸ **grub about, grub around** *vi* (*pt & pp* **grubbed**) rebuscar (**for sth** algo)

▸ **grub up** *vt sep* arrancar

grubbiness ['grʌbɪnɪs] *n* falta *f* de aseo, suciedad *f*

grubby ['grʌbɪ] *adj* (**a**) *(dirty)* sucio(a), mugriento(a); **I don't want him getting his g. hands on these documents** no quiero que meta mano a estos documentos (**b**) *(immoral, dishonest)* sucio(a), inmoral

grubstake ['grʌbsteɪk] *n US* = préstamo concedido a un buscador de oro o a un empresario a cambio de una participación en los beneficios

Grub Street ['grʌbstri:t] *n Br Fam* = el mundillo de los que escriben por dinero; **a G. hack** un escritor de pacotilla

grudge [grʌdʒ] **1** *n* rencor *m*; **to bear sb a g., to have** *or* **hold a g. against sb** guardar rencor a alguien; **he's not one to bear grudges** no es rencoroso ▸▸ ***a g. fight*** un ajuste de cuentas; ***a g. match*** un ajuste de cuentas
2 *vt* (**a**) *(give unwillingly)* **to g. sb sth** dar algo a regañadientes a alguien; **he paid, but he grudged them every penny** les pagó, pero escatimándoles cada penique (**b**) *(resent)* **she grudges him his success** le tiene rencor por su éxito; **I don't g. spending the money but...** no me duele gastar el dinero pero...

grudging ['grʌdʒɪŋ] *adj* **he felt g. respect for her** sentía respeto por ella a pesar de sí mismo; **to be g. in one's praise** ser reacio(a) a alabar; **they helped, but they were very g. about it** ayudaron, pero muy a regañadientes *or* de muy mala gana

grudgingly ['grʌdʒɪŋlɪ] *adv* de mala gana, a regañadientes

gruel ['gru:əl] *n* gachas *fpl* (de avena)

gruelling, *US* **grueling** ['gru:əlɪŋ] *adj* agotador(ora)

gruesome ['gru:səm] *adj* horripilante, espantoso(a); **in g. detail** sin ahorrar detalles truculentos

gruff [grʌf] *adj (tone, manner)* seco(a), hosco(a); *(voice)* áspero(a)

gruffly ['grʌflɪ] *adv* secamente, bruscamente

grumble ['grʌmbəl] **1** *n* queja *f*; **she obeyed without so much as a g.** obedeció sin rechistar
2 *vt* **"I do all the work here," he grumbled** "soy yo el que hace todo el trabajo", se quejó
3 *vi* (**a**) *(person)* quejarse (**about** de); *Fam* **how are things? – mustn't g.!** ¿cómo te va? – ¡no me puedo quejar! (**b**) *(stomach)* gruñir

grumbler ['grʌmblə(r)] *n* quejica *mf*, gruñón(ona) *m,f*

grumbling ['grʌmblɪŋ] **1** *n* quejas *fpl*
2 *adj* (**a**) *(person)* quejumbroso(a) (**b**) *Med* ***g. appendix*** dolores *mpl* intermitentes de apéndice

grump [grʌmp] *n Fam (person)* gruñón(ona) *m,f*; IDIOM **to have the grumps** estar de mal humor, *RP* estar cruzado(a)

grumpily ['grʌmpɪlɪ] *adv* de mal humor

grumpiness ['grʌmpɪnɪs] *n* mal genio *m*, malas pulgas *fpl*

grumpy ['grʌmpɪ] *adj* gruñón(ona); **don't be so g.!** ¡no seas tan gruñón!

grunge [grʌndʒ] *n (music)* (música *f*) grunge *m*

grungy ['grʌndʒɪ] *adj US Fam* asqueroso(a), *Esp* cutre, *Méx* gacho(a), *RP* roñoso(a)

grunt [grʌnt] **1** *n* (**a**) *(of pig, person)* gruñido *m*; **to give a g.** dar un gruñido (**b**) *US Fam (foot soldier)* soldado *mf* de infantería
2 *vt* **"what?" he grunted** "¿qué?", gruñó
3 *vi (pig, person)* gruñir

grunting ['grʌntɪŋ] *n* gruñidos *mpl*

Gruyère [gru:'jeə(r)] *n* (queso *m* de) gruyère *m*

gryphon ['grɪfən] *n* grifo *m*

GSM [dʒi:es'em] *n Tel* (*abbr* **global system for mobile communication**) GSM *m*

g-spot ['dʒi:spɒt] *n* punto *m* G

GST [dʒi:es'ti:] *n* (*abbr* **goods and services tax**) = impuesto del estado en Canadá y Australia

G-string ['dʒi:strɪŋ] *n* (**a**) *(garment)* tanga *m* (**b**) *Mus* cuerda *f* de sol

g-suit ['dʒi:su:t] *n Av & Astron* traje *m* espacial presurizado

gt (*abbr* **great**) gran

GTG (*abbr* **got to go**) te dejo

GTi [dʒi:ti:'aɪ] *n (car)* GTi *m*

Guadeloupe [gwɑ:də'lu:p] *n* Guadalupe

guano ['gwɑ:nəʊ] *n* guano *m*

guarantee [gærən'ti:] **1** *n* (**a**) *(assurance)* garantía *f*; **we have no g. that she was telling the truth** nada nos garantiza que dice la verdad; **she gave me her g. that it wouldn't happen again** me aseguró que no volvería a pasar
(**b**) *(for goods, services) (warranty, document)* garantía *f*; **this printer has a five-year g.** esta impresora tiene cinco años de garantía; **under g.** en garantía ▸▸ ***g. certificate*** certificado *m* de garantía
(**c**) *Law (for debt) (agreement)* aval *m*; *(person)* avalista *mf*, garante

mf; **to act as g. (for sb)** ser el *or* salir de garante (de alguien)
2 *vt* (a) *(assure)* garantizar; **I can't g. that everything will go to plan** no puedo garantizar que todo salga según lo previsto; **our success is guaranteed** nuestro éxito está asegurado *or* garantizado
(b) *(goods)* garantizar; **the watch is guaranteed for two years** el reloj tiene una garantía de dos años
(c) *(loan, cheque)* avalar; *Fin* **to g. sb against loss** ofrecer a alguien una garantía contra posibles pérdidas

guaranteed [gærən'ti:d] *adj* garantizado(a)

guarantor [gærən'tɔ:(r)] *n* avalista *mf*, garante *mf*

guard [gɑ:d] 1 *n* (a) *(sentry)* guardia *mf*; *US (in prison)* funcionario(a) *m,f* de prisiones, guardián(ana) *m,f*
(b) *Mil (body of sentries)* guardia *f*; **call out the g.!** ¡llamen a la guardia!; **the changing of the g.** el cambio de guardia ▸▸ ***g. of honour*** guardia *f* de honor
(c) *(watch, supervision)* **under g.** bajo custodia; **to put a g. on sth/sb** hacer vigilar a algo/alguien; **to stand g.** montar guardia; **to keep g. over** custodiar, vigilar; **to be on g. duty** estar de guardia ▸▸ ***g. dog*** perro *m* guardián
(d) *(readiness)* **to be on one's g.** estar en guardia; **on g.!** *(in fencing)* ¡en guardia!; **you should be on g. against pickpockets** debes estar en guardia con los carteristas; **to put sb on his g.** poner en guardia a alguien; **to put sb off his g.** desarmar a alguien; **to catch sb off his g.** agarrar *or Esp* coger a alguien desprevenido
(e) *(in boxing)* guardia *f*; **to keep one's g. up** *(in boxing)* mantener la guardia alta; *Fig (be alert)* mantenerse en guardia; *also Fig* **to drop** *or* **lower one's g.** bajar la guardia
(f) *(protective shield, screen) (on machine)* protección *f*; *(for fire)* guardallamas *m inv*; **as a g. against...** como protección contra...
(g) *Br (on train)* jefe *m* de tren ▸▸ ***g.'s van*** furgón *m* de equipajes
(h) *(in basketball)* base *mf*
(i) *(in American football)* defensa *mf*
(j) *Br Mil* **the Guards** la Guardia real; **a Guards regiment** un regimiento de la Guardia real
2 *vt* (a) *(protect, watch over)* vigilar; **the house was heavily guarded** la casa estaba muy vigilada; **a closely guarded secret** un secreto muy bien guardado; **g. this letter with your life** cuida de esta carta con tu vida (b) *(control)* **g. your tongue!** ¡cuidado con lo que dices!

▸**guard against** *vt insep (frost, flooding)* protegerse contra; **to g. against a repetition of the scandal** tomar precauciones para evitar que se repita el escándalo; **to g. against doing sth** evitar hacer algo; **to g. against sth happening** evitar que suceda algo

guarded ['gɑ:dɪd] *adj (cautious)* cauteloso(a), cauto(a)

guardedly ['gɑ:dɪdlɪ] *adv* con cautela, cautamente

guardhouse ['gɑ:dhaʊs] *n* (a) *(for guards)* cuartel *m* (b) *(prison)* edificio *m* con calabozos

guardian ['gɑ:dɪən] *n* (a) *(of standards)* guardián(ana) *m,f* ▸▸ ***g. angel*** ángel *m* custodio *or* de la guarda (b) *Law (of minor)* tutor(ora) *m,f*

guardianship ['gɑ:dɪənʃɪp] *n Law* tutela *f*

guardrail ['gɑ:dreɪl] *n* (a) *(on ship, staircase, train)* pasamanos *m inv*, *Esp* barandilla *f* (b) *US (on road)* barrera *f* de protección, *RP* guardarail *m*

guardroom ['gɑ:dru:m] *n Mil* cuartel *m* del cuerpo de guardia; *(for prisoners)* celda *f*

guardsman ['gɑ:dzmən] *n* (a) *Br Mil* miembro *m* de la Guardia real (b) *US* soldado *m* de la Guardia Nacional

Guatemala [gwætɪ'mɑ:lə] *n* Guatemala

Guatemalan [gwætɪ'mɑ:lən] 1 *n* guatemalteco(a) *m,f*
2 *adj* guatemalteco(a)

guava ['gwɑ:və] *n (fruit)* guayaba *f* ▸▸ ***g. jelly*** jalea *f* de guayaba; ***g. tree*** guayabo *m*

gubbins ['gʌbɪnz] *n Br Fam* (a) *(person)* bobo(a) *m,f*, *Esp* memo(a) *m,f* (b) *(worthless object)* chisme *m*

gubernatorial [gu:bənə'tɔ:rɪəl] *adj Formal* del/de la gobernador(ora); **a g. candidate/election** un candidato/unas elecciones a gobernador

guck [gʌk] *n US Fam* porquería *f* pringosa

gudgeon ['gʌdʒən] *n (fish)* gobio *m* (de agua dulce)

Guernsey ['gɜ:nzɪ] *n* (a) *(island)* (la isla de) Guernesey (b) *(breed of cattle)* vaca *f* de Guernesey (c) *(sweater)* suéter *m or Esp* jersey *m or Col* saco *m or RP* pulóver *m* tipo chaleco

guerrilla [gə'rɪlə] *n* guerrillero(a) *m,f* ▸▸ ***g. tactics*** tácticas *fpl* de guerrilla; ***g. war*** guerra *f* de guerrillas; ***g. warfare*** guerra *f* de guerrillas

guess [ges] 1 *n* conjetura *f*, suposición *f*; **to have** *or* **make** *or* **take a g.** intentar adivinar; **have a g.** a ver si lo adivinas; **he made a good g.** lo adivinó; **he made a wild g.** dijo lo primero que se le ocurrió; **it was a lucky g.** lo adivinó por casualidad; **I'll give you three guesses** te doy tres oportunidades (para intentar adivinarlo); **at a g.** a ojo (de buen cubero); **my g. is that he won't come** me parece que no va a venir; **it's anybody's g.** ¿quién sabe?; **your g. is as good as mine** vete a saber
2 *vt* (a) *(estimate)* adivinar; **you've guessed it!** ¡lo adivinaste!; **I guessed as much** me lo imaginaba; **I guessed him to be twenty-five** calculé que tendría veinticinco años; *Fam* **g. what!** ¿a que no sabes qué?; *Fam* **g. who!** ¿a que no sabes quién?; **g. who I saw!** ¿a que no sabes a quién he visto?
(b) *(suppose)* suponer; **I g. you're right** supongo que tienes razón; **I g. so/not** supongo que sí/no
3 *vi* adivinar; **(try to) g.!** ¡adivina!, ¡a ver si lo adivinas!; *Ironic* **I would never have guessed** nunca me lo hubiera imaginado; **to g. right** acertar, adivinarlo; **to g. wrong** no acertar, no adivinarlo; **you'll never g. (who/what/why...)** no te imaginas (quién/qué/porqué...); **to keep sb guessing** tener a alguien en vilo; **to g. at sth** hacer suposiciones *or* conjeturas acerca de algo; **we can only g. as to the real reason** los verdaderos motivos no podemos más que suponerlos

guessable ['gesəbəl] *adj* **it's g.** se puede acertar *or* adivinar

guessing game ['gesɪŋ'geɪm] *n* (juego *m* de las) adivinanzas *fpl*

guesstimate *Fam* 1 *n* ['gestɪmət] *(mental)* cálculo *m* aproximado; *(by eye)* cálculo *m* a ojo
2 *vt* ['gestɪmeɪt] *(mentally)* hacer un cálculo aproximado de; *(by eye)* calcular a ojo

guesswork ['geswɜ:k] *n* conjeturas *fpl*; **it's pure** *or* **sheer g.** son sólo conjeturas

guest [gest] 1 *n* (a) *(person invited) (to home, party, by club member)* invitado(a) *m,f*; **be my g.!** ¡por favor!, ¡no faltaba más!; **g. of honour** invitado(a) de honor ▸▸ *Br* ***g. beer*** = cerveza de barril que se vende por una temporada en un pub, junto a las cervezas habituales; ***g. list*** lista *f* de invitados; ***g. night*** *(in club)* = noche en la que los socios pueden llevar invitados; ***g. room*** habitación *f* de los invitados, cuarto *m* de los huéspedes; ***g. speaker*** orador(ora) *m,f* invitado(a); ***g. worker*** = extranjero con permiso de trabajo
(b) *(at hotel)* huésped *mf*
(c) *(on TV programme)* invitado(a) *m,f*; **a g. appearance by...** una aparición como artista invitado(a) de... ▸▸ ***g. artist*** artista *mf* invitado(a); ***g. star*** estrella *f* invitada
(d) *Comptr* invitado(a) *m,f*
2 *vi* (a) *TV & Rad* **to g. on sb's show** aparecer como invitado en el programa de alguien (b) *Mus* **another guitarist guested on one of the numbers** otro guitarrista tocó como invitado en uno de los temas

guestbook ['gestbʊk] *n* (a) *(in hotel, B & B)* libro *m* de huéspedes (b) *Comptr (on Web page)* libro *m* de visitas

guesthouse ['gesthaʊs] *n Br (hotel)* casa *f* de huéspedes

guff [gʌf] *n Fam* paparruchas *fpl*, *Esp* chorradas *fpl*, *Am* pendejadas *fpl*; **the movie was a load of g.** la película era una *Esp* chorrada *or Am* pendejada

guffaw [gʌ'fɔ:] 1 *n* carcajada *f*
2 *vt* **"of course!" he guffawed** "¡por supuesto!", dijo con una carcajada
3 *vi* carcajearse

GUI ['gu:ɪ] *n Comptr* (*abbr* **Graphical User Interface**) interfaz *f* gráfica

Guiana [gaɪ'ɑ:nə] *n* **G., the Guianas** (la) Guayana, las Guayanas

Guianan [gaɪ'ɑ:nən], **Guianese** [gaɪə'ni:z] 1 *n* guayanés(esa) *m,f*
2 *adj* guayanés(esa)

guidance ['gaɪdəns] *n* (a) *(advice, supervision)* orientación *f*; **to ask for/seek g.** pedir/buscar orientación; **under the g. of...** bajo la dirección de...
(b) *(information)* información *f*; **diagrams are given for your g.** aparecen diagramas a título informativo
(c) *(for missile)* dirección *f*, teledirección *f* ▸▸ ***g. system*** sistema *m* de guiado
(d) *Sch US* ***g. counsellor*** asesor(ora) *m,f* de orientación profesional; *Br* ***g. teacher*** tutor(ora) *m,f* (de curso)

guide [gaɪd] 1 *n* (a) *(person)* guía *mf*; IDIOM **let your conscience be your g.** haz lo que te dicte la conciencia ▸▸ ***g. dog*** (perro *m*) lazarillo *m*
(b) *(book)* guía *f* **(to** de); **a g. to France** una guía de Francia
(c) *(indication)* guía *f*; **as a (rough) g.** como guía (aproximada); **to take sth as a g.** guiarse por algo; **are these tests a good g. to future performance?** ¿dan estas pruebas una idea real de cómo va a ser su rendimiento en el futuro?
(d) *Br* **(Girl) G.** scout *f*, exploradora *f*
(e) *(machine part)* guía *f*, riel *m*

2 *vt* (**a**) *(show, lead) (person)* guiar; **the children guided us through the old city** los chicos nos guiaron por la ciudad antigua; **I'll drive and you g. me** yo *Esp* conduzco *or Am* manejo y tú me guías; **to g. sb in/out** acompañar a alguien a la entrada/salida
(**b**) *(control, steer) (investigation, conversation)* conducir, dirigir; *(vehicle) Esp* conducir, *Am* manejar; **he guided the country through some difficult times** condujo al país en momentos difíciles
(**c**) *(advise)* **I will be guided by your advice** me guiaré por tus consejos; **he simply won't be guided** es que no atiende a razones
(**d**) *(machine part)* dirigir

guidebook ['gaɪdbʊk] *n* guía *f*

guided ['gaɪdɪd] *adj* ***g. missile*** misil *m* teledirigido; ***g. tour*** visita *f* guiada

guideline ['gaɪdlaɪn] *n (indication)* directriz *f*, línea *f* general; **guidelines** directrices; **as a general g.** como orientación general

guiding ['gaɪdɪŋ] *adj (controlling, directing)* **the g. principle of his life** el principio que rige su vida ▸▸ ***g. hand*** mano *f* que guía; *Fig* ***g. light*** guía *mf*; **he's been the g. light of my career** ha sido el norte por el que me ha guiado en mi trayectoria profesional; ***g. star*** guía *mf*

guild [gɪld] *n* (**a**) *Hist (professional)* gremio *m* (**b**) *(association)* agrupación *f*, asociación *f*; **women's g.** agrupación de mujeres; **church g.** agrupación eclesiástica

guilder ['gɪldə(r)] *n Formerly* florín *m*

guildhall ['gɪldhɔːl] *n* sede *f or* casa *f* gremial

guile [gaɪl] *n* astucia *f*; **he was totally without g.** carecía de malicia

guileless ['gaɪllɪs] *adj* ingenuo(a), cándido(a)

guilelessly ['gaɪllɪslɪ] *adv* ingenuamente, cándidamente

guillemot ['gɪlɪmɒt] *n* arao *m* (común)

guillotine ['gɪlətiːn] **1** *n* (**a**) *(for executions)* guillotina *f*; **he was sent to the g.** lo llevaron a la guillotina (**b**) *(for cutting paper)* guillotina *f* (**c**) *Br Parl* **to put a g. on a bill** = limitar el plazo de discusión de un proyecto de ley
2 *vt (person, paper)* guillotinar

guilt [gɪlt] **1** *n* (**a**) *(blame)* culpa *f*; **an admission of g.** una declaración de culpabilidad; **the g. does not lie with him alone** él no es el único culpable (**b**) *(emotion)* culpabilidad *f*, culpa *f*; **to feel g.** tener un sentimiento de culpabilidad *or* culpa; *Fam* **to be on a g. trip** culpabilizarse ▸▸ ***g. complex*** complejo *m* de culpa *or* culpabilidad
2 *vt Fam* **to g. sb into (doing) sth: he guilted me into doing it** me hizo sentir tan culpable que acabé haciéndolo

guiltily ['gɪltɪlɪ] *adv* con aire culpable

guiltless ['gɪltlɪs] *adj* inocente

guilty ['gɪltɪ] *adj* (**a**) *(of crime)* culpable; **to find sb g./not g.** declarar a alguien culpable/inocente; **g. of murder/theft** culpable de asesinato/robo; **the g. party** la parte culpable; **a g. verdict** una sentencia condenatoria; **he's g. of a terrible lack of sensitivity** ha dado pruebas de una terrible falta de sensibilidad
(**b**) *(emotionally)* **to feel g.** sentirse culpable; **to have a g. conscience** tener remordimientos; **he gave me a g. look** me lanzó una mirada culpable
(**c**) *(shameful)* **a g. secret** un secreto vergonzante

Guinea ['gɪnɪ] *n* Guinea

guinea ['gɪnɪ] *n* (**a**) *Br (coin)* guinea *f (moneda equivalente a 21 chelines)* (**b**) ***g. fowl*** pintada *f*, gallina *f* de Guinea (**c**) ***g. pig*** cobaya *m or f*, conejillo *m* de Indias; *Fig* **to be a g. pig** hacer de conejillo de Indias (**d**) *US Fam (Italian)* = término ofensivo para referirse a un italiano

Guinea-Bissau ['gɪnɪbɪ'saʊ] *n* Guinea-Bissau

Guinean [gɪ'neɪən] **1** *n* guineano(a) *m,f*
2 *adj* guineano(a)

guise [gaɪz] *n* (**a**) *(appearance)* apariencia *f*, aspecto *m*; **in** *or* **under the g. of...** bajo la apariencia de...; **in a different g.** con un aspecto distinto; **the same old policies in a new g.** la misma política de siempre pero con otro nombre (**b**) *Archaic (costume)* vestimenta *f*

guitar [gɪ'tɑː(r)] *n* guitarra *f*

guitarist [gɪ'tɑːrɪst] *n* guitarrista *mf*

Gujarati [gʊdʒə'rɑːtɪ] *n (language)* gujaratí *m*

gulag ['guːlæg] *n* gulag *m*

gulch [gʌltʃ] *n US (valley)* garganta *f*, hoz *f*

gulf [gʌlf] *n* (**a**) *(bay)* golfo *m*; **the (Persian) G.** el Golfo (Pérsico) ▸▸ ***the G. of California*** el golfo de California, *Méx* el mar de Cortés; ***the G. of Mexico*** el Golfo de México; ***the G. States*** los países del Golfo; ***the G. Stream*** la Corriente del Golfo; ***the G. of Tonkin*** el golfo de Tonkín; ***the G. of Venezuela*** el golfo de Venezuela; ***the G. War*** la guerra del Golfo; ***G. War syndrome*** síndrome *m* de la guerra del Golfo
(**b**) *(between people, ideas)* abismo *m*

gull[1] [gʌl] *n* gaviota *f* (cana); **black-headed g.** gaviota reidora; **lesser black-backed g.** gaviota sombría

gull[2] *Archaic or Literary* **1** *n (dupe)* papanatas *mf*
2 *vt* embaucar

gullet ['gʌlɪt] *n* esófago *m*; IDIOM *Fam* **it really sticks in my g.** lo tengo atravesado (en la garganta)

gulley = **gully**

gullibility [gʌlɪ'bɪlɪtɪ] *n* credulidad *f*, ingenuidad *f*

gullible ['gʌlɪbəl] *adj* crédulo(a), ingenuo(a)

gully, gulley ['gʌlɪ] *n* barranco *m*

gulp [gʌlp] **1** *n* (**a**) *(act of gulping)* trago *m*; **in** *or* **at one g.** de un trago; **"what money?" he said, with a g.** "¿qué dinero?" dijo, tragando saliva (**b**) *(mouthful)* trago *m*
2 *vt (swallow)* tragar, engullir
3 *vi (with surprise)* tragar saliva

▸**gulp back** *vt sep* **she gulped back her tears** se tragó las lágrimas

▸**gulp down** *vt sep (swallow)* tragar, engullir

gum [gʌm] **1** *n* (**a**) *(in mouth)* encía *f* ▸▸ ***g. disease*** gingivitis *f inv* (**b**) *(adhesive)* pegamento *m*, goma *f* (**c**) **(chewing) g.** chicle *m* (**d**) *Br (sweet)* chicle *m*, goma *f* de mascar (**e**) *(resin)* ***g. arabic*** goma *f* arábiga; ***g. tree*** eucalipto *m*; IDIOM *Br Fam* **to be up a g. tree** estar metido(a) en un buen lío
2 *vt (pt & pp* **gummed**) *(stick)* pegar
3 *exclam Br Fam Old-fashioned* **by g.!** ¡caray!

▸**gum up** *vt sep (mechanism)* pegar; **the kitten's eyes were all gummed up** el gatito tenía los ojos pegados

gumball ['gʌmbɔːl] *n US* chicle *m (en forma de bola)*

gumbo ['gʌmbəʊ] (*pl* **gumbos**) *n US* (**a**) *(soup)* = sopa de verduras con carne o pescado y espesada con quingombó (**b**) *(okra)* quingombó *m*

gumboil ['gʌmbɔɪl] *n* flemón *m*

gumboot ['gʌmbuːt] *n* bota *f* de agua *or* goma *or Méx, Ven* caucho

gumdrop ['gʌmdrɒp] *n* pastilla *f* de goma, *Esp* ≃ gominola *f*

gummed [gʌmd] *adj (label)* engomado(a)

gummy ['gʌmɪ] *adj* (**a**) *(toothless)* desdentado(a), mellado(a) (**b**) *(sticky)* pegajoso(a)

gumption ['gʌmʃən] *n Fam* (**a**) *(common sense)* sensatez *f*, sentido *m* común (**b**) *(courage)* agallas *fpl*

gumshield ['gʌmʃiːld] *n Sport* protector *m* bucal

gumshoe ['gʌmʃuː] *n US Fam (detective)* sabueso *m*, detective *m*

gun [gʌn] **1** *n* (**a**) *(pistol)* pistola *f*; *(rifle)* rifle *m*; *(shotgun)* escopeta *f*; *(any portable firearm)* arma *f* (de fuego); **the burglar had a g.** el ladrón iba armado; **to draw** *or* **pull a g. on sb** apuntar a alguien con un arma ▸▸ ***g. barrel*** cañón *m*; ***g. battle*** tiroteo *m*, *Am* balacera *f*; ***g. cotton*** algodón *m* pólvora; ***g. dog*** perro *m* de caza; ***g. laws*** legislación *f* sobre armas de fuego; ***g. licence*** licencia *f* de armas; *US* ***the g. lobby*** = los que están en contra del control sobre las armas de fuego
(**b**) *(artillery piece)* cañón *m*; **a 21-g. salute** una salva de 21 cañonazos ▸▸ ***g. carriage*** cureña *f*; ***g. crew*** personal *m* de artillería
(**c**) *(hunter)* = miembro de una partida de caza
(**d**) *Fam (gunman)* pistolero *m*, matón *m*; **hired g.** pistolero a sueldo
(**e**) *(dispenser)* pistola *f*; **grease g.** pistola de engrase; **paint g.** pistola *(para pintar)*
(**f**) IDIOMS *Fam* **big g.** *(important person)* pez gordo; *Fam* **to bring out the** *or* **one's big guns** recurrir a la artillería pesada; **to be going great guns** *(enterprise)* ir a pedir de boca; **she was going great guns** le estaba yendo a pedir de boca; *US* **to be under the g.** sentirse presionado(a); **to stick to one's guns** no dar el brazo a torcer; **to jump the g.** *(in race)* salir antes de tiempo; *Fig* precipitarse
2 *vt (pt & pp* **gunned**) **to g. the engine** dar acelerones

▸**gun down** *vt sep (kill)* matar a tiros

▸**gun for** *vt insep* **he's gunning for us** la tiene tomada con nosotros; **he's gunning for the heavyweight title** aspira al título de los pesos pesados; **she's gunning for my job** tiene las miras puestas en mi trabajo

gunboat ['gʌnbəʊt] *n* cañonera *f* ▸▸ ***g. diplomacy*** la diplomacia de los cañones

gundeck ['gʌndek] *n* cubierta *f* de batería

gunfight ['gʌnfaɪt] *n* tiroteo *m*

gunfighter ['gʌnfaɪtə(r)] *n* pistolero(a) *m,f*

gunfire ['gʌnfaɪə(r)] *n* (**a**) *(from pistols, rifles)* disparos *mpl*, tiros *mpl* (**b**) *(from artillery)* cañonazos *mpl*

gunge [gʌndʒ] *n Br Fam* porquería *f*, pringue *f*

gung-ho ['gʌŋ'həʊ] *adj (enthusiastic)* exaltado(a); *(eager for war)* belicoso(a); **to be g. about sth** lanzar las campanas al vuelo con relación a algo

gungy ['gʌndʒɪ] *adj Fam* pringoso(a), asqueroso(a)

gunk [gʌŋk] *n Fam* porquería *f*, pringue *f*

gunman ['gʌnmən] *n (armed criminal)* hombre *m* armado; *(assassin, terrorist)* pistolero *m*

gunmetal ['gʌnmetəl] **1** *n* **(a)** *(alloy)* bronce *m* para cañones **(b)** *(colour)* gris *m* plomo
2 *adj* gris oscuro(a)

gunnel ['gʌnəl] *n* **(a)** *(eel)* blenio *m* **(b)** = **gunwale**

gunner ['gʌnə(r)] *n* artillero *m*

gunnery ['gʌnərɪ] *n* artillería *f* ►► ***g. officer*** oficial *mf* de artillería

gunny ['gʌnɪ] *n* arpillera *f*, tela *f* de saco; **g. (sack)** saco *m* de arpillera

gunplay ['gʌnpleɪ] *n* tiroteo *m*

gunpoint ['gʌnpɔɪnt] *n* **at g.** a punta de pistola

gunpowder ['gʌnpaʊdə(r)] *n* pólvora *f* ►► ***the G. Plot*** = conspiración encabezada por Guy Fawkes en 1605 para volar el parlamento inglés

gunroom ['gʌnru:m] *n* **(a)** *(in house)* sala *f* de armas **(b)** *(on ship)* sala *f* de suboficiales

gunrunner ['gʌnrʌnə(r)] *n* contrabandista *mf* de armas

gunrunning ['gʌnrʌnɪŋ] *n* contrabando *m* de armas

gunship ['gʌnʃɪp] *n* avión *m* equipado con armamento; **a helicopter g.** un helicóptero artillado

gunshot ['gʌnʃɒt] *n* **(a)** *(shot)* disparo *m*, tiro *m* ►► ***g. wound*** herida *f* de bala **(b)** *(range)* **to be out of g.** estar fuera de tiro; **to be within g.** estar a tiro

gun-shy ['gʌnʃaɪ] *adj* **to be g.** asustarse con el ruido de las armas

gunslinger ['gʌnslɪŋə(r)] *n Fam* pistolero(a) *m,f*

gunsmith ['gʌnsmɪθ] *n* armero *m*

gunstock ['gʌnstɒk] *n* culata *f*

gunwale, gunnel ['gʌnəl] *n Naut* borda *f*, regala *f*

guppy ['gʌpɪ] *n* guppy *m*, lebistes *m inv*

gurgle ['gɜ:gəl] **1** *n* **(a)** *(of liquid)* borboteo *m*, gorgoteo *m* **(b)** *(of baby)* gorjeo *m*; **a g. of delight** un gorjeo de placer
2 *vi* **(a)** *(liquid)* borbotear, gorgotear **(b)** *(baby)* gorjear; **to g. with delight** gorjear de placer

Gurkha ['gɜ:kə] *n* gurja *mf*, gurka *mf*

gurnard ['gɜ:nəd], **gurnet** ['gɜ:nɪt] *n* bejel *m*

gurney ['gɜ:nɪ] *n US* camilla *f*

guru ['gʊru:] *n also Fig* gurú *m*

gush [gʌʃ] **1** *n* *(of spring, fountain)* chorro *m*; **a g. of words** un torrente de palabras **(b)** *(of emotion)* efusión *f*; **a sudden g. of enthusiasm** un repentino ataque de entusiasmo
2 *vt* **(a)** *(emit)* **to g. water/oil** chorrear agua/aceite **(b)** *Pej (say effusively)* **"how wonderful to see you!" she gushed** "¡qué estupendo verte!", dijo con excesivo entusiasmo
3 *vi* **(a)** *(spurt, pour)* manar; **blood was gushing from his arm** le manaba sangre del brazo **(b)** *Pej (talk effusively)* **to g. about sth** hablar con excesivo entusiasmo de algo; **everyone was gushing over the baby** todos se deshacían en halagos con el bebé

gusher ['gʌʃə(r)] *n (oil well)* pozo *m* (petrolífero) surgente

gushing ['gʌʃɪŋ], **gushy** ['gʌʃɪ] *adj Pej (person, praise)* excesivamente efusivo(a)

gusset ['gʌsɪt] *n (in clothing)* escudete *m*

gust [gʌst] **1** *n (of wind, rain, air)* ráfaga *f*
2 *vi (wind)* soplar racheado *or* en ráfagas; **winds gusting up to 50 mph were recorded** se registraron ráfagas de hasta 50 millas por hora

gusto ['gʌstəʊ] *n* entusiasmo *m*; **with g.** con entusiasmo

gusty ['gʌstɪ] *adj (wind)* racheado(a); **it's a bit g.** hay mucho viento, hay fuertes rachas de viento; **a g. day** un día de mucho viento; **g. weather** tiempo con viento racheado

gut [gʌt] **1** *n* **(a)** *(intestine)* intestino *m*
(b) *Fam (stomach)* panza *f*, barriga *f*, tripa *f*; **a g. feeling** *(intuition)* una intuición, una corazonada; **I have a g. feeling that...** tengo la intuición *or* corazonada de que...; *Fam* **to bust a g.** *(make big effort)* herniarse; *(laugh uncontrollably)* morirse *or* troncharse de risa ►► *US Fam* ***g. course*** asignatura *f* fácil, *Esp* maría *f*; ***g. reaction*** *(intuitive)* reacción *f* instintiva
(c) *Fam* **guts** *(of person, machine)* tripas; IDIOM **to work** *or* **sweat one's guts out** dejarse la piel; IDIOM **she hates my guts** no me puede ver ni en pintura; IDIOM **I'll have his guts for garters** lo haré picadillo
(d) *Fam* **guts** *(courage)* agallas, arrestos; **I didn't have the guts to tell them** no tuve agallas para decírselo
(e) *(catgut) (for racquets, violins)* cuerda *f* de tripa; *(in surgery)* catgut *m*, hilo *m* de sutura
2 *vt* (*pt & pp* **gutted**) **(a)** *(fish, poultry)* limpiar **(b)** *(building)* **the house had been gutted by the fire** el fuego destruyó por completo el interior de la casa; **she gutted the house and completely redecorated it** despojó la casa de todos sus enseres y la decoró de nuevo por completo **(c)** *(book)* sacar los puntos principales de

gutless ['gʌtlɪs] *adj Fam* cobarde

gutrot ['gʌtrɒt] *n Br Fam* **(a)** *(drink)* matarratas *m inv* **(b)** *(stomach upset)* dolor *m* de tripa

gutsy ['gʌtsɪ] *adj Fam* **(a)** *(brave)* con agallas, corajudo(a) **(b)** *(spirited) (performance, singer)* con garra **(c)** *(greedy)* glotón(ona)

gutta-percha ['gʌtə'pɜ:tʃə] *n* gutapercha *f*

gutted ['gʌtɪd] *adj Br Fam (disappointed)* **to be g.** llevarse un chasco enorme, quedarse hecho(a) polvo

gutter ['gʌtə(r)] **1** *n* **(a)** *(in street)* cuneta *f*
(b) *(on roof)* canalón *m*
(c) *Typ* margen *m* interior
(d) *(in ten-pin bowling)* canalón *m*, *Bol, CSur* canaleta *f*
(e) IDIOMS **to end up in the g.** terminar en el arroyo; **to drag oneself out of the g.** salir del arroyo; **the language of the g.** el lenguaje barriobajero ►► *Fam Pej* ***g. journalism*** periodismo *m* amarillo *or* sensacionalista; *Fam Pej* ***g. press*** prensa *f* amarilla *or* sensacionalista
2 *vi (flame)* parpadear

guttering ['gʌtərɪŋ] *n* canalones *mpl*

guttersnipe ['gʌtəsnaɪp] *n Fam Old-fashioned* pillo(a) *m,f*, golfillo(a) *m,f*

guttural ['gʌtərəl] *adj* gutural

gut-wrenching ['gʌtrentʃɪŋ] *adj Fam* desgarrador(ora)

guv [gʌv], **guv'nor, guvnor** ['gʌvnə(r)] *n Br Fam (boss)* patrón *m*, jefe *m*; *(form of address)* jefe *m*, amigo *m*

guy[1] [gaɪ] **1** *n* **(a)** *Fam (man)* tipo *m*, *Esp* tío *m*; **a great g.** un gran tipo; **a tough g.** un tipo duro **(b)** *esp US Fam* **hi guys!** ¡hola, amigos(as) *or Esp* tíos(as)!; **what are you guys doing tonight?** ¿qué *Esp* vais *or Am* van a hacer esta noche? **(c)** *Fam (boyfriend)* novio *m* **(d)** *Br (effigy)* = muñeco que representa a Guy Fawkes y que se quema en las hogueras la noche del 5 de noviembre
2 *vt (make fun of)* burlarse de

guy[2] *n* **g. (rope)** *(for tent)* viento *m*

Guyana [gaɪ'ænə] *n* Guyana

Guyanese [gaɪə'ni:z] **1** *n* guyanés(esa) *m,f*
2 *adj* guyanés(esa)

Guy Fawkes Night ['gaɪ'fɔ:ks'naɪt] *n Br* = fiesta del 5 de noviembre, en la que se conmemora el fracaso del atentado de Guy Fawkes contra el parlamento en 1605

guzzle ['gʌzəl] **1** *vt Fam (food)* engullir, tragar; *(drink)* tragar; **this car really guzzles gas** este auto sí que traga gasolina *or RP* nafta
2 *vi (eat)* engullir, tragar; *(drink)* tragar

gym [dʒɪm] *n* **(a)** *(gymnasium)* gimnasio *m* **(b)** *(activity, school subject)* gimnasia *f* ►► ***g. shoes*** zapatillas *fpl* de gimnasia *or* de deporte; *Br* ***g. slip*** bata *f*; *Br Fam* ***g.-slip mum*** mamá *f* colegiala

gymkhana [dʒɪm'kɑ:nə] *n* gincana *f* hípica

gymnasium [dʒɪm'neɪzɪəm] (*pl* **gymnasiums** *or* **gymnasia** [dʒɪm'neɪzɪə]) *n* gimnasio *m*

gymnast ['dʒɪmnæst] *n* gimnasta *mf*

gymnastic [dʒɪm'næstɪk] *adj* gimnástico(a)

gymnastics [dʒɪm'næstɪks] **1** *n* gimnasia *f*
2 *npl Fig* **mental g.** gimnasia mental

gynaecological, *US* **gynecological** [gaɪnɪkə'lɒdʒɪkəl] *adj* ginecológico(a)

gynaecologist, *US* **gynecologist** [gaɪnɪ'kɒlədʒɪst] *n* ginecólogo(a) *m,f*

gynaecology, *US* **gynecology** [gaɪnɪ'kɒlədʒɪ] *n* ginecología *f*

gyp [dʒɪp] **1** *n Br Fam* **my tooth/leg is giving me g.** la muela/pierna me está matando; **he's been giving me g. about my decision** no para de darme la barrila por mi decisión
2 *vt (cheat)* estafar, timar

gyppo ['dʒɪpəʊ] (*pl* **gyppos**) *n Br Fam* = término ofensivo para referirse a una persona de Egipto

gypsum ['dʒɪpsəm] *n* yeso *m*

gypsy, gipsy ['dʒɪpsɪ] *n* gitano(a) *m,f*; **she's a g. at heart** tiene alma de gitana ►► ***g. caravan*** carromato *m* de gitanos; ***g. moth*** lagarta *f*

gyrate [dʒaɪ'reɪt] *vi* rotar, girar

gyration [dʒaɪ'reɪʃən] *n* rotación *f*, giro *m*

gyratory [dʒaɪ'reɪtərɪ] *adj* giratorio(a)

gyrfalcon ['dʒɜːfɔːlkən] *n* halcón *m* gerifalte

gyrocompass ['dʒaɪrəʊkʌmpəs] *n* brújula *f* giroscópica

gyroplane ['dʒaɪrəpleɪn] *n* autogiro *m*

gyroscope ['dʒaɪrəskəʊp] *n* giróscopo *m*, giroscopio *m*

gyrostabilizer ['dʒaɪrəʊ'steɪbɪlaɪzə(r)] *n* giroestabilizador *m*

gyrus ['dʒaɪrəs] (*pl* **gyri** ['dʒaɪraɪ]) *n* *Anat* circunvolución *f* cerebral

H, h

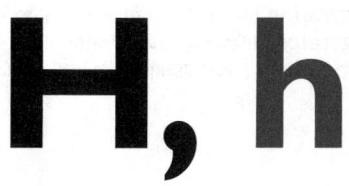

H, h [eɪtʃ] *n (letter)* H, h *f*

H [eɪtʃ] *n* (**a**) ***H. bomb*** bomba *f* H (**b**) *Fam* (*abbr* **heroin**) heroína *f*, *Esp* caballo *m*

ha, hah [hɑː] *exclam* (**a**) *(in triumph, sudden comprehension)* ¡ajá!; **ha, that's where it was!** ¡ajá! ¡conque allí estaba! (**b**) *(in contempt)* ¡ja!; **ha! is that all you were worried about?** ¡ja! ¿es eso lo que te preocupaba?

habeas corpus ['heɪbɪəs'kɔːpəs] *n Law* habeas corpus *m*

haberdasher ['hæbədæʃə(r)] *n* (**a**) *Br (draper)* propietario(a) *m,f* de una mercería, mercero(a) *m,f* (**b**) *US (men's outfitter)* propietario(a) *m,f* de una tienda de confección de caballero

haberdashery ['hæbədæʃərɪ] *n* (**a**) *Br (sewing items, shop)* mercería *f* (**b**) *US (men's clothes)* ropa *f* de caballero; *(shop)* tienda *f* de confección de caballero

habit ['hæbɪt] *n* (**a**) *(custom, practice)* costumbre *f*, hábito *m*; **good/bad habits** buenas costumbres/malos hábitos; **get rid of those bad habits** abandona esos malos hábitos; **to be in the h. of doing sth** tener la costumbre de hacer algo; **to get into the h. of doing sth** adquirir la costumbre *or* el hábito de hacer algo; **to get out of the h. of doing sth** quitarse la costumbre de hacer algo; **you must get out of the h. of always blaming other people** tienes que dejar de echar siempre la culpa a los demás; **to get sb into/out of the h. of doing sth** acostumbrar a alguien a hacer algo/quitar a alguien la costumbre de hacer algo; **to make a h. of doing sth** *Esp* coger la costumbre de hacer algo, *Am* hacerse a la costumbre de hacer algo; **don't make a h. of it** que no se convierta en una costumbre; **from force of h., out of h.** por la fuerza de la costumbre
(**b**) *Fam (addiction)* vicio *m*; **he steals to pay for his h.** roba para pagarse el vicio; **to have a drug h.** ser drogadicto(a), tener adicción a las drogas
(**c**) *(costume) (for monk, nun)* hábito *m*; **(riding) h.** ropa *f* de montar *or* de equitación

habitable ['hæbɪtəbəl] *adj* habitable

habitat ['hæbɪtæt] *n* hábitat *m*

habitation [hæbɪ'teɪʃən] *n* (**a**) *(occupation)* habitación *f*; **there were few signs of h.** había pocos rastros de habitantes; **fit/unfit for h.** apto/no apto para su uso como vivienda (**b**) *Formal (dwelling place)* vivienda *f*

habit-forming ['hæbɪtfɔːmɪŋ] *adj (drug)* adictivo(a); *Hum* **surfing the Web can be h.** navegar por Internet puede ser adictivo *or* puede crear adicción

habitual [hə'bɪtjʊəl] *adj* (**a**) *(customary) (generosity, rudeness)* habitual, acostumbrado(a) (**b**) *(persistent) (liar, drunk)* empedernido(a); **h. offenders** reincidentes, delincuentes habituales

habitually [hə'bɪtjʊəlɪ] *adv* habitualmente; **he would h. insult his customers** solía insultar a sus clientes

habituate [hə'bɪtjʊeɪt] *vt* habituar (**to** a); **to become habituated to sth** habituarse a algo

habituation [həbɪtjʊ'eɪʃən] *n* acostumbramiento *m*, habituación *f*

habitué [hə'bɪtʃʊeɪ] *n* asiduo(a) *m,f*

Habsburg = **Hapsburg**

hacienda [hæsɪ'endə] *n* hacienda *f*

hack[1] [hæk] *n* (**a**) *Fam Pej (journalist)* gacetillero(a) *m,f*; **h. (writer)** escritor(ora) *m,f* mercenario(a)
(**b**) *Fam Pej (political activist)* político(a) *m,f* de carrera
(**c**) *(horse) (for riding)* caballo *m* de silla *or* paseo; *(for hire)* caballo *m* de alquiler; *(old horse, nag)* jamelgo *m*, *RP* matungo *m*
(**d**) *(horseride)* **to go for a h.** ir a dar un paseo a caballo
(**e**) *(cough)* tos *f* seca *or* perruna
(**f**) *US Fam (taxi)* taxi *m*, *Esp* pelas *m inv*, *RP* tacho *m*
(**g**) *US Fam (taxi driver)* taxista *mf*, *RP* tachero(a) *m,f*
(**h**) *US Fam (prison officer)* carcelero(a) *m,f*, *Esp* boqueras *mf inv*

hack[2] **1** *n* (**a**) *(cut)* tajo *m*; **to take a h. at sth/sb** dar un tajo a algo/alguien (**b**) *(kick)* patada *f*; **to take a h. at sb** darle una patada a alguien
2 *vt* (**a**) *(cut)* cortar; **to h. sth to pieces** hacer algo trizas; **to h. sb to pieces** descuartizar a alguien; *Fig (criticize)* destrozar a alguien; **to h. sb to death with a machete/an axe** matar a alguien a machetazos/hachazos; **to h. one's way through the jungle** abrirse paso a machetazos por la jungla
(**b**) *(in soccer)* dar un hachazo a
(**c**) *Fam (cope with)* **he can't h. it** no puede con ello
(**d**) *Comptr* **they hacked their way into the system** accedieron al sistema burlando los códigos de seguridad
3 *vi* (**a**) *(cut)* **to h. (away) at sth** dar tajos (sin parar) a algo (**b**) *(cough)* toser con fuerza (**c**) *(on horseback)* pasear a caballo; **to go hacking** salir a pasear a caballo (**d**) *Comptr* **to h. into a computer system** introducirse ilegalmente en un sistema informático

►**hack down** *vt sep* (**a**) *(tree)* talar, cortar; *(person)* destrozar (**b**) *(soccer player)* derribar, entrar en falta a

►**hack off** *vt sep* (**a**) *(chop off) (branch, limb)* cortar (**b**) *Fam* **to h. sb off** enfurecer *or* mosquear a alguien; **to be hacked off (with sth/sb)** estar furioso(a) *or* mosqueado(a) (con algo/alguien)

hacker ['hækə(r)] *n Comptr Fam* (**a**) *(illegal user)* pirata *mf* informático(a) (**b**) *(expert)* usuario(a) *m,f* experto(a), hacker *mf*

hackette [hæ'ket] *n Br Fam Pej* gacetillera *f*

hackie ['hækɪ] *n US Fam* taxista *mf*, *RP* tachero(a) *m,f*

hacking ['hækɪŋ] **1** *n* (**a**) *Comptr Fam (illegal use)* pirateo *m* informático, piratería *f* informática (**b**) ***h. jacket*** chaqueta *f* de montar
2 *adj* **a h. cough** una tos seca *or* perruna

hackle ['hækəl] *n (of bird)* pluma *f* de cuello, collar *m*

hackles ['hækəlz] *npl (of dog)* pelo *m* del cuello; **the dog's h. were up** al perro se le erizaron los pelos del cuello; IDIOM **my h. rose** me indigné; IDIOM **to make sb's h. rise** enfurecer a alguien

hackney cab ['hæknɪ'kæb], **hackney carriage** ['hæknɪ'kærɪdʒ] *n* (**a**) *Formal (taxi)* taxi *m* (**b**) *(horse-drawn)* coche *m* de alquiler

hackneyed ['hæknɪd] *adj* manido(a), trillado(a)

hacksaw ['hæksɔː] *n* sierra *f* para metales

hackwork ['hækwɜːk] *n Fam* trabajo *m* de pacotilla; **she dismissed her article as mere h.** descartó su artículo por considerarlo una chapucería

had *pt & pp of* **have**

haddock ['hædək] *n* abadejo *m*

hadn't ['hædənt] = **had not**

Hades ['heɪdiːz] *n* el Hades

hadj = **hajj**

Hadrian ['heɪdrɪən] *pr n* Adriano ►► ***H.'s Wall*** la Muralla de Adriano

hadron ['hædrɒn] *n Phys* hadrón *m*

haematite, *US* **hematite** ['hiːmətaɪt] *n Geol* hematites *m inv*

haematologist, *US* **hematologist** [hiːmə'tɒlədʒɪst] *n* hematólogo(a) *m,f*

haematology, *US* **hematology** [hiːmə'tɒlədʒɪ] *n* hematología *f*

haematoma, *US* **hematoma** [hiːmə'təʊmə] (*pl* **haematomas** *or* **haematomata** [hiːmə'təʊmətə]) *n* hematoma *m*

haemoglobin, *US* **hemoglobin** [hiːməʊ'gləʊbɪn] *n* hemoglobina *f*

haemophilia, *US* **hemophilia** [hiːməʊ'fɪlɪə] *n* hemofilia *f*

haemophiliac, *US* **hemophiliac** [hiːməʊ'fɪlɪæk] *n* hemofílico(a) *m,f*

haemophilic, *US* **hemophilic** [hiːmə'fɪlɪk] *adj* hemofílico(a)

haemorrhage, *US* **hemorrhage** ['hemərɪdʒ] **1** *n* (**a**) *(bleeding)* hemorragia *f* (**b**) *Fig (of people, resources)* fuerte pérdida *f*
2 *vi* (**a**) *Med* sangrar, sufrir una hemorragia (**b**) *Fig (support, funds)* decrecer por momentos; **party membership was haemorrhaging badly** el partido padecía la deserción masiva de sus afiliados
haemorrhoids, *US* **hemorrhoids** ['hemərɔɪdz] *npl Med* hemorroides *fpl*; **to have h.** tener hemorroides
hafnium ['hæfnɪəm] *n Chem* hafnio *m*
haft [hɑːft] *n (of axe)* astil *m*; *(of knife)* mango *m*; *(of sword)* empuñadura *f*
hag [hæg] *n* (**a**) *Pej (old woman)* bruja *f*, arpía *f* (**b**) *(witch)* bruja *f*, arpía *f*
hagfish ['hægfɪʃ] *n* lamprea *f* glutinosa
haggard ['hægəd] *adj* demacrado(a)
haggis ['hægɪs] *n* = plato típico escocés a base de asaduras de cordero mezcladas con harina de avena y embutidas en una tripa
haggle ['hægəl] *vi* (**a**) *(over price)* regatear; **to h. about** *or* **over the price of sth** regatear el precio de algo (**b**) *(argue)* negociar; **they haggled about who should be on the committee** negociaron la composición de la junta
haggling ['hæglɪŋ] *n* (**a**) *(over price)* regateo *m* (**b**) *(arguing)* tira y afloja *m*
hagiographic(al) [hægɪə'græfɪk(əl)] *adj* hagiográfico(a)
hagiography [hægɪ'ɒgrəfɪ] *n* hagiografía *f*
hag-ridden ['hægrɪdən] *adj Literary (tormented)* atormentado(a)
Hague [heɪg] *n* **the H.** La Haya
hah = **ha**
ha-ha[1] ['hɑː'hɑː], **haw-haw** ['hɔː'hɔː] *exclam (laughter, mockery)* ¡ja, ja!; *Ironic* **h., very funny!** ¡ja, ja, muy gracioso!
ha-ha[2] *n (fence in ditch)* valla *f* (en zanja)
hahnium ['hɑːnɪəm] *n Chem* hahnio *m*
haiku ['haɪkuː] *n* hai kai *m*, haiku *m*
hail[1] [heɪl] **1** *n* (**a**) *(hailstones)* granizo *m* (**b**) *(of blows, bullets, insults)* lluvia *f*; **he died in a h. of bullets** murió bajo una lluvia de balas, *Am* murió en una balacera
2 *vi* **it's hailing** está granizando
▸ **hail down** *vi (blows, stones)* llover; **blows/rocks hailed down on us** nos cayó encima una lluvia de golpes/piedras; **criticism hailed down on him** le llovieron las críticas
hail[2] **1** *exclam* **h. Caesar!** ¡ave, César!; **h. Mary** avemaría
2 *vt* (**a**) *(attract attention of) (person)* llamar; *(ship)* saludar; *(taxi)* parar, hacer señas a; **to be within hailing distance of sth/sb** estar a suficiente distancia de algo/alguien como para llamarle *or* hacerle señas (**b**) *(acclaim)* aclamar (**as** como); **she has been hailed as the greatest novelist of the century** fue aclamada como la mejor novelista del siglo
3 *n Literary (call)* llamada *f*, saludo *m*; **within h.** al alcance de la voz
▸ **hail from** *vt insep* proceder de; **where does he h. from?** ¿de dónde es?, ¿cuál es su procedencia?
hail-fellow-well-met [heɪlfeləʊwel'met] *adj* demasiado campechano(a); **he greeted his boss with a h. slap on the shoulder** saludó a su jefe con una informal y campechana palmada en el hombro
hailstone ['heɪlstəʊn] *n* (piedra *f* de) granizo *m*
hailstorm ['heɪlstɔːm] *n* granizada *f*
hair [heə(r)] *n* (**a**) *(on head)* pelo *m*, cabello *m*; *(on body)* vello *m*; *(of animal)* pelo *m*; **my h. is a mess** mi pelo es un desastre; **to have long/short h.** tener el pelo largo/corto; **to do one's h.** peinarse; **to get one's h. done** peinarse (en la peluquería); **who does your h.?** ¿quién es tu peluquero?, ¿quién te peina?; **I like the way you've done your h.** me gusta como te peinaste; **to brush/comb/wash one's h.** cepillarse/peinarse/lavarse el pelo; **to have** *or* **get one's h. cut** cortarse el pelo; **she put her h. up** se sujetó el pelo; **she let her h. down** se soltó el pelo ▸▸ ***h. clippers*** maquinilla *f*; ***h. colorant*** tinte *m or RP* tinta *f* para el pelo; *Br* ***h. curlers*** rulos *mpl*, ruleros *mpl*; ***h. gel*** gel *m* moldeador, gomina *f*; ***h. implants*** implantes *mpl* capilares; ***h. lacquer*** fijador *m* para el pelo; ***h. lotion*** loción *f* capilar; ***h. remover*** crema *f* depilatoria; ***h. restoration clinic*** clínica *f* capilar; ***h. restorer*** producto *m* contra la calvicie, crecepelo *m*; ***h. shirt*** cilicio *m*; ***h. transplant*** trasplante *m* capilar
(**b**) *(single hair)* pelo *m*; **she never has a h. out of place** va siempre muy arreglada ▸▸ ***h. follicle*** folículo *f* piloso
(**c**) ***h. trigger*** *(on gun)* gatillo *m* muy sensible; *Fig* **to be on a h. trigger** *(temper)* estar a punto de estallar; *(situation)* pender de un hilo
(**d**) IDIOMS **she never has a h. out of place** *(is immaculate)* siempre está perfecta; **if you harm one single h. of** *or* **on his head...** si le tocas un pelo...; **to make sb's h. stand on end** ponerle a alguien los pelos de punta; *Fam* **keep your h. on!** ¡no te sulfures!; *Fam* **to get in sb's h.** fastidiar a alguien, dar la lata a alguien; *Fam* **keep him out of my h.** quítamelo de encima; **I'll keep out of your h.** te dejo tranquilo, no te molestaré; **to let one's h. down** *(lose inhibitions)* soltarse el pelo *or* la melena; **to win/lose by a h.** ganar/perder por un pelo; **to a h.** *(perfectly)* a la perfección; **without turning a h.** sin pestañear; **she didn't turn a h. when I told her about the accident/that I had won** no se le movió un pelo cuando le conté acerca del accidente/que había ganado; *Fam Hum* **that'll put hairs on your chest!** esto levanta a un muerto; *Fam* **to have sb by the short hairs** tener a alguien en un puño; **to make one's h. curl** poner a uno los pelos de punta; *Fam* **do you fancy a h. of the dog (that bit you)?** *(for hangover)* ¿quieres algo de alcohol para quitarte la resaca *or Méx* cruda?
hairball ['heəbɔːl] *n* bola *f* de pelo
hairband ['heəbænd] *n* cinta *f* (para el pelo)
hairbreadth = **hair's-breadth**
hairbrush ['heəbrʌʃ] *n* cepillo *m*
haircare ['heəkeə(r)] **1** *n* cuidado *m* del cabello *or* pelo
2 *adj* para el cuidado del cabello *or* pelo; **h. products** productos capilares
hairclip ['heəklɪp] *n* clip *m* para el pelo, horquilla *f*
haircut ['heəkʌt] *n* corte *m* de pelo; **to have a h.** cortarse el pelo; **to give sb a h.** cortar el pelo a alguien
hairdo ['heəduː] (*pl* **hairdos**) *n Fam* peinado *m*
hairdresser ['heədresə(r)] *n* peluquero(a) *m,f*; **h.'s** peluquería *f*
hairdressing ['heədresɪŋ] *n* peluquería *f* ▸▸ ***h. salon*** salón *m* de peluquería
hairdryer ['heədraɪə(r)] *n* secador *m* (de pelo)
-haired [heəd] *suffix* **long/short/curly-h.** de pelo largo/corto/rizado; **white/grey-h.** canoso(a), entrecano(a)
hairgrip ['heəgrɪp] *n Br* horquilla *f*, *Chile* pinche *m*, *Col, Méx, Perú, Ven* gancho *m*, *Cuba* presilla *f*, *Méx* pasador *m*
hairless ['heəlɪs] *adj (head, body)* sin pelo; *(face)* lampiño(a); *(infant, puppy)* pelón(ona)
hairline ['heəlaɪn] *n* (**a**) *(of person)* nacimiento *m* del pelo; **to have a receding h.** tener entradas; IDIOM *US* **to a h.** *(perfectly)* a la perfección (**b**) ***h. crack*** *(in pipe, wall)* fisura *f* muy pequeña; ***h. fracture*** *(of bone)* fisura *f* (de hueso)
hairnet ['heənet] *n* redecilla *f* para el pelo
hairpiece ['heəpiːs] *n (for man)* peluquín *m*; *(for woman)* postizo *m*, *RP* aplique *m*
hairpin ['heəpɪn] *n* horquilla *f*, *Chile* pinche *m*, *Col, Méx, Perú, Ven* gancho *m*, *Cuba* presilla *f*, *Méx* pasador *m* ▸▸ ***h. bend,*** *US* ***h. turn*** *(on road)* curva *f* muy cerrada
hair-raising ['heəreɪzɪŋ] *adj* espeluznante
hair's-breadth ['heəzbredθ], **hairbreadth** ['heəbredθ] *n* **by a h.** por un pelo; **to be within a h. of** estar al borde de
hairslide ['heəslaɪd] *n Br* pasador *m* (para el pelo)
hair-splitting ['heəsplɪtɪŋ] **1** *n* sutilezas *fpl*
2 *adj* **that's a h. argument** es un argumento muy rebuscado; **that's a h. distinction** es una distinción muy sutil
hairspray ['heəspreɪ] *n* laca *f* (de pelo)
hairspring ['heəsprɪŋ] *n* espiral *f (de reloj)*
hairstyle ['heəstaɪl] *n* peinado *m*
hairstylist ['heəstaɪlɪst] *n* estilista *mf*
hairy ['heərɪ] *adj* (**a**) *(hair-covered)* velludo(a), peludo(a) (**b**) *Fam (scary)* **there were a few h. moments when the car broke down** hubo algunos momentos que nos pusieron los pelos de punta como cuando se rompió el auto (**c**) *Fam (uncomfortable, tricky)* peliagudo(a)
Haiti ['heɪtɪ] *n* Haití
Haitian ['heɪʃən] **1** *n* haitiano(a) *m,f*
2 *adj* haitiano(a)
hajj, hadj [hɑːdʒ] *n* peregrinación *f* a la Meca
haka ['hɑːkə] *n* haka *m*, danza *f* guerrera maorí
hake [heɪk] *n* merluza *f*
halal [hə'lɑːl] **1** *n* carne *f* halal, = carne sacrificada según la ley musulmana
2 *adj* **h. butcher** = carnicero que vende carne hahal ; **h. meat** carne halal, = carne sacrificada según la ley musulmana
halation [hə'leɪʃən] *n Phot* halo *m*, *Spec* halación *f*
halberd ['hælbəd] *n Hist* alabarda *f*

halberdier [hælbəˈdiːə(r)] *n Hist* alabardero *m*

halcyon days [ˈhælsɪənˈdeɪz] *npl Literary* días *mpl* felices

hale [heɪl] 1 *adj* sano(a); **to be h. and hearty** estar como una rosa
2 *vt US (haul)* arrastrar; **to h. sb in/out** meter/sacar a alguien a rastras, arrastrar a alguien para adentro/afuera

---

HALF [hɑːf] 1 *n* (*pl* **halves** [hɑːvz]) **(a)** *(in general)* mitad *f*; *(six months)* semestre *m*; **the lower h. of the page** la mitad inferior de la página; **h. of it** la mitad; **h. of them** la mitad (de ellos); **h. of the time you can't understand her** la mitad del tiempo no se le entiende; *Fam* **I haven't told you the h. of it** y todavía no te he contado lo mejor; **to increase sth by h.** aumentar algo en un 50 por ciento; **to reduce sth by h.** reducir algo a la mitad; **she is too clever/arrogant by h.** se pasa de lista *or RP* viva/arrogante; **she doesn't do things by halves** no le gusta hacer las cosas a medias; **to fold/cut sth in h.** doblar/cortar algo por la mitad; *Hum* **my better** *or* **other h.** mi media naranja; **the king wanted to see how the other h. lives** el rey quería enterarse de cómo viven los pobres; **to go halves with sb (on sth)** ir a medias con alguien (en algo)
(b) *(fraction)* medio *m*; **three and a h.** tres y medio; **an hour and a h.** una hora y media; **three and a h. thousand** tres mil quinientos(as); *Fam Fig* **that was a goal and a h.!** ¡menudo gol!; *Fam Fig* **a party/hangover and a h.** un (buen) fiestón/resacón, *Esp* una fiesta/resaca de aúpa, *CSur* flor de fiesta/resaca
(c) *(period of sports match)* parte *f*; **first/second h.** primera/segunda parte, primer/segundo tiempo; **France was in the lead in the first h.** Francia fue por delante durante la primera parte
(d) *(area of sports pitch)* medio campo *m*; **almost the entire game took place in the opposition's h.** casi todo el juego se desarrolló en el medio campo del contrario
(e) *Br (ticket) (for child) Esp* billete *m orAm* boleto *m orAm* pasaje *m* infantil
(f) *Br (half pint)* media pinta *f*
(g) *(in golf)* hoyo *m* empatado
2 *adj* medio(a); **at h. speed** a medio gas; **h. an hour** media hora; **h. past twelve,** *US* **h. after twelve,** *Fam* **h. twelve** las doce y media; **it's h. past** son y media; **h. a dozen** media docena; **h. the students failed** suspendió *or Am* reprobó *or RP* perdió la mitad de los alumnos; **getting started is h. the battle** lo más difícil es empezar; **given h. a chance** a la mínima oportunidad; **that's h. the problem** eso es parte del problema; **but that's only h. the story** pero aún hay más; **she's h. the writer she used to be** es una sombra de la escritora que era antes; **to have h. a mind to do sth** estar tentado(a) de hacer algo; **the plan went off at h. cock** el plan salió mal por falta de preparación ▸▸ ***h. board*** media pensión *f*; *Fam* ***h. buck*** medio dólar *m*; ***h. dollar*** medio dólar *m*; ***h. hour*** media hora *f*; **every h. hour** cada media hora; ***h. mast:*** **at h. mast** *(flag)* a media asta; *Br Hum (trousers, socks)* medio caídos, medio bajados; ***h. nelson*** *(in wrestling)* media nelson *f*; *US Mus* ***h. note*** blanca *f*; ***h. pay:*** **to be on h. pay** tener el sueldo reducido a la mitad, cobrar medio sueldo; ***h. price:*** **at h. price** a mitad de precio; ***h. shell:*** **on the h. shell** abierto(a) y en su concha; *US* ***h. staff:*** **at h. staff** *(flag)* a media asta; *US Mus* ***h. step*** semitono *m*; ***h. volley*** media volea *f*
3 *adv* **(a)** *(with verb)* a medias; *(before adjective)* medio; **to h. do sth** hacer algo a medias; **you're h. my age** tienes la mitad de años que yo, te doblo la edad; **the bottle was h. full/empty** la botella estaba medio llena/vacía; **the painting is only h. finished** el cuadro está por la mitad; **I'm h. Canadian** soy medio canadiense; **she was h. naked** estaba medio desnuda; **you're h. right** tienes razón a medias; **you look h. starved** pareces un muerto de hambre; **he was only h. joking** hablaba medio en broma, estaba medio bromeando; **I was h. expecting him to say no** medio me esperaba que me dijera que no; **she was h. laughing, h. crying** reía y lloraba al mismo tiempo; **the novel is h. as long as her last one** la novela es la mitad de larga que la anterior; **this movie isn't h. as good as his last one** esta película no es ni la mitad de buena que la anterior; **I earn h. as much as him** gano la mitad que él; **you need h. as much again** necesitas la mitad más
(b) *Br Fam (for emphasis)* **not h.!** ¡y que lo digas!; **it isn't h. cold!** ¡menudo frío (que) hace!, ¡no hace frío ni nada!, *RP* ¡hace un frío de novela!; **he didn't h. get angry** ¡no se *esp Esp* enfadó *or esp Am* enojó ni nada!, ¡menudo *esp Esp* enfado *or esp Am* enojo se agarró!; **you don't h. talk rubbish** ¡anda, que no dices tonterías!

---

half- [hɑːf] *prefix* **h.-asleep/dead** medio dormido(a)/muerto(a)

half-(a-)crown [ˈhɑːf(ə)kraʊn] *n Br Formerly* media corona *f*

half-and-half [ˈhɑːfənˈhɑːf] *n* **(a)** *esp Br (beer)* = combinado de dos tipos de cerveza a partes iguales **(b)** *US (for coffee)* leche *f* con *Esp* nata *orAm* crema

half-arsed [ˈhɑːfˈɑːst], *US* **half-assed** [ˈhɑːfˈæst] *adj very Fam (attempt, plan)* penoso(a), chapucero(a)

halfback [ˈhɑːfbæk] *n* **(a)** *(in rugby)* **the halfbacks** el medio de melé y el medio de apertura **(b)** *(in American football)* corredor *m*

half-baked [hɑːfˈbeɪkt] *adj Fam (theory, plan)* mal concebido(a)

half-binding [ˈhɑːfˈbaɪndɪŋ] *n Typ* (encuadernación *f* de) media pasta *f*, encuadernación *f* a la holandesa

halfbreed [ˈhɑːfbriːd] *n Pej* mestizo(a) *m,f*

half-brother [ˈhɑːfbrʌðə(r)] *n (on father's side)* hermano *m* por parte de padre, hermanastro *m*; *(on mother's side)* hermano *m* por parte de madre, hermanastro *m*

half-caste [ˈhɑːfkɑːst] *Pej* 1 *n* mestizo(a) *m,f*
2 *adj* mestizo(a)

half-close [ˈhɑːfˈkləʊz] *vt* entornar

half-closed [ˈhɑːfˈkləʊzd] *adj* entornado(a)

half-cock [ˈhɑːfˈkɒk] *n* posición *f* de disparo con el seguro echado; IDIOM *Br* **to go off at h.** *(plan)* irse a pique *or* al garete; **we don't want to go off at h. on this one** hay que procurar no precipitarse esta vez

half-cocked [ˈhɑːfˈkɒkt] *adj (gun, pistol)* con el seguro echado; **to go off h.** *(plan)* irse a pique *or* al garete; **we don't want to go off h. on this one** hay que procurar no precipitarse esta vez

half-crown = **half-a-crown**

half-cut [hɑːfˈkʌt] *adj Br Fam (drunk) Esp, Méx* pedo *inv*, *Col* caído(a), *RP* en pedo

half-day [ˈhɑːfˈdeɪ] 1 *n* media jornada *f*
2 *adj* **a h. holiday** medio día festivo

half-dozen [hɑːfˈdʌzən] *n* media docena *f*; **a h. eggs** media docena de huevos

half-full [ˈhɑːfˈfʊl] *adj* medio lleno(a)

half-hardy [ˈhɑːfˈhɑːdɪ] *adj (plant)* resistente *(salvo a fuertes heladas)*

half-hearted [ˈhɑːfˈhɑːtɪd] *adj (effort, performance)* desganado(a); *(belief, support)* tibio(a); **he was very h. about it** no le entusiasmaba la idea, no se le veía muy entusiasmado *or* con muchas ganas; **they were very h. about accepting** les costaba mucho aceptarlo; **a h. apology** una disculpa de compromiso

half-heartedly [ˈhɑːfˈhɑːtɪdlɪ] *adv* sin (muchas) ganas

half-hitch [ˈhɑːfˈhɪtʃ] *n* nudo *m* sencillo *(de una vuelta)*

half-holiday [ˈhɑːfˈhɒlɪdeɪ] *n Br* medio día *m* festivo

half-hourly [hɑːfˈaʊəlɪ] 1 *adj* cada media hora; **at h. intervals** cada media hora
2 *adv* cada media hora

half-inch [hɑːfˈɪntʃ] *vt Br Fam* birlar, afanar

half-jokingly [hɑːfˈdʒəʊkɪŋlɪ] *adv (to say, suggest)* medio en broma

half-length [ˈhɑːflenθ] *adj (portrait)* de medio cuerpo

half-life [ˈhɑːflaɪf] *n Phys* media vida *f*

half-light [ˈhɑːflaɪt] *n* penumbra *f*, media luz *f*

half-marathon [hɑːfˈmærəθən] *n* media maratón *f*

half-measures [ˈhɑːfˈmeʒəz] *npl* **we won't be satisfied with h.** no nos conformaremos con soluciones que se queden a medio camino

half-moon [hɑːfˈmuːn] *n* **(a)** *(in sky)* media luna *f* **(b)** *(on fingernail)* blanco *m* de la uña, *Spec* lúnula *f* **(c)** ***h. glasses*** gafas *fpl* de media luna

half-open [hɑːfˈəʊpən] *adj (eyes, window)* entreabierto(a), entornado(a)

halfpenny, ha'penny [ˈheɪpnɪ] *n Br Formerly* medio penique *m*; **he didn't have two ha'pennies to rub together** no tenía ni un real *or* un chavo

halfpennyworth [ˈheɪpnɪwɜːθ], **hap'orth** [ˈheɪpəθ] *n Br* **(a)** *Formerly (amount)* medio penique *m* **(b)** *Fam (trifling amount)* miaja *f*, chispa *f*; **it doesn't make a h. of difference** se mire por donde se mire, da igual

half-pint [ˈhɑːfpaɪnt] 1 *n Fam (small person)* retaco *m*, tapón *m*
2 *adj* **a h. glass** un vaso de media pinta

half-price [ˈhɑːfˈpraɪs] 1 *adj (goods, ticket)* a mitad de precio
2 *adv* a mitad de precio; **children get in h.** los niños sólo pagan la mitad

half-seas-over [ˈhɑːfsiːzˈəʊvə(r)] *adj Br Fam (drunk)* borracho(a) como una cuba

half-sister [ˈhɑːfˈsɪstə(r)] *n (on father's side)* hermana *f* por parte de padre, hermanastra *f*; *(on mother's side)* hermana *f* por parte de madre, hermanastra *f*

half-size ['hɑːf'saɪz] *n* (**a**) *(for clothing)* talla *f* intermedia (**b**) *(for shoes)* número *m* intermedio

half-term ['hɑːf'tɜːm] *n Br* **h. (holiday)** vacaciones *fpl* de mitad de trimestre

half-timbered [hɑːf'tɪmbəd] *adj* con entramado de madera

half-time ['hɑːf'taɪm] *n* (**a**) *(of game)* descanso *m*; **the h. score** el resultado al descanso (**b**) *(in work)* media jornada *f*; **to be on h.** trabajar media jornada, tener un trabajo de media jornada

half-title [hɑːf'taɪtəl] *n Typ* portadilla *f*

halftone ['hɑːftəʊn] *n* (**a**) *Phot* grabado *m* reticulado (**b**) *Comptr* medio tono *m*

half-track ['hɑːftræk] *n (vehicle)* (vehículo *m*) semioruga *m or f*, autooruga *m*

half-truth ['hɑːf'truːθ] *n* verdad *f* a medias

halfway ['hɑːf'weɪ] 1 *adj (point, stage)* intermedio(a); **work has reached the h. stage** el trabajo ha llegado a su fase intermedia; **at the h. point of his career** en el punto medio *or* intermedio de su carrera; **they're at the h. mark** *(in race)* están en el punto intermedio *or* a mitad de la carrera ►► ***h. house*** *(for former prisoners, addicts)* centro *m* de reinserción; *Fig (compromise)* término *m* medio; ***h. line*** *(on soccer pitch)* línea *f* divisoria *or* de medio campo

2 *adv* (**a**) *(on route)* a mitad de camino; **it's h. between New York and Washington** está a mitad de camino entre Nueva York y Washington; **we're h. there (already)** ya llevamos la mitad del camino, ya estamos a mitad de camino; **we had got h. to Manchester** nos quedaba la mitad del camino para llegar a Manchester; **they have now travelled h. to the Moon** llevan hecha la mitad del trayecto a la Luna; **h. through the programme/film/year** a mitad de programa/película/año; **I'm h. through chapter six** voy por la mitad del capítulo seis; **the path stops h. up/down** el sendero se termina en mitad de la cuesta; **we had climbed h. up the mountain** habíamos escalado media montaña *or* hasta la mitad de la montaña; **this will go h. towards covering the costs** con esto cubriremos (una) parte de los gastos; **to meet sb h.** *(on journey)* encontrarse con alguien a mitad de camino; *(compromise)* llegar a una solución de compromiso con alguien

(**b**) *Fam (adequately)* mínimamente, medio; **some h. decent food/accommodation** una comida/un alojamiento mínimamente *or* medio decente

halfwit ['hɑːfwɪt] *n Fam* bobo(a) *m,f*, *Esp* memo(a) *m,f*

halfwitted [hɑːf'wɪtɪd] *adj Fam (person)* bobo(a), *Esp* memo(a); **a h. idea** una bobada, *Esp* una memez

half-yearly ['hɑːf'jɪəlɪ] 1 *adj* semestral, bianual

2 *adv* semestralmente, cada seis meses

halibut ['hælɪbət] *(pl* **halibut**) *n* fletán *m*

halide ['heɪlaɪd] *n Chem* haluro *m*, halogenuro *m*

halite ['heɪlaɪt] *n* sal *f* gema, *Spec* halita *f*

halitosis [hælɪ'təʊsɪs] *n Med* halitosis *f inv*

hall [hɔːl] *n* (**a**) *(entrance room) (gen)* vestíbulo *m*; *(of house, flat)* recibidor *m*, vestíbulo *m*; *(of hotel)* vestíbulo *m*, hall *m* ►► ***h. porter*** conserje *mf*; ***h. stand***, *US* ***h. tree*** perchero *m*

(**b**) *(corridor)* pasillo *m*

(**c**) *(for concerts, meetings) (large room)* salón *m* de actos; *(building)* auditorio *m*

(**d**) *Br Univ* ***h. of residence*** residencia *f* de estudiantes, *Esp* colegio *m* mayor; **to live in h.** vivir en una residencia de estudiantes *or Esp* un colegio mayor

(**e**) *Br Sch & Univ* **(dining) h.** comedor *m*; **(banqueting** *or* **great) h.** *(of castle, stately home)* salón *m* principal, gran sala *f*

(**f**) *US Sport* ***H. of fame*** panteón *m* de celebridades del deporte; ***H. of famer*** = deportista que ha entrado en el panteón de celebridades

(**g**) *(mansion, large country house)* mansión *f*, casa *f* solariega

hallelujah, halleluia [hælɪ'luːjə] *exclam* ¡aleluya!

Halley's comet ['hælɪz'kɒmɪt] *n* el cometa Halley

hallmark ['hɔːlmɑːk] *n* 1 (**a**) *(on silver)* contraste *m* (**b**) *(of idea, plan)* sello *m* característico; **to have all the hallmarks of sth/sb** llevar el sello característico de algo/alguien

2 *vt (precious metals)* contrastar, grabar el contraste a

hallo = **hello**

halloo [hə'luː] 1 *exclam* ¡hala, tuso!, ¡tus!

2 *n (pl* **halloos**) grito *m (para azuzar a los perros)*

3 *vi (pt & pp* **hallooed**) gritar *(para azuzar a los perros)*

hallowed ['hæləʊd] *adj* sagrado(a); **h. be thy name** santificado sea tu nombre; *also Fig* **h. ground** terreno sagrado

Hallowe'en [hæləʊ'iːn] *n* = víspera de Todos los Santos en la que los niños se disfrazan de brujas y fantasmas

hallucinate [hə'luːsɪneɪt] *vi* alucinar; **I must be hallucinating!** ¡debo de estar alucinando!, ¡debo de estar viendo visiones!

hallucination [həluːsɪ'neɪʃən] *n* alucinación *f*; **to have hallucinations** sufrir *or* tener alucinaciones

hallucinatory [hə'luːsɪnətərɪ] *adj* alucinatorio(a)

hallucinogen [hə'luːsɪnədʒən] *n* alucinógeno *m*

hallucinogenic [həluːsɪnə'dʒenɪk] *adj* alucinógeno(a)

hallway ['hɔːlweɪ] *n* (**a**) *(entrance room)* vestíbulo *m* (**b**) *(corridor)* pasillo *m*

halo ['heɪləʊ] *(pl* **halos** *or* **haloes**) *n* (**a**) *(of saint, angel)* halo *m*, aureola *f* (**b**) *(round sun, moon)* halo *m*

halogen ['hælədʒən] *n* halógeno *m* ►► ***h. lamp*** lámpara *f* halógena

halt [hɒlt] 1 *n* (**a**) *(stop)* alto *m*, parada *f*; **to come to a h.** detenerse, parar(se); **until the aircraft comes to a complete h.** hasta que el aparato se detenga por completo; **the project has come to a h.** el proyecto se ha parado; **to bring sth to a h.** detener *or* interrumpir algo; **to call a h. to sth** interrumpir algo; **let's call a h. for today** vamos a dejarlo por hoy (**b**) *Br (small railway station)* apeadero *m*

2 *npl Literary* **the h. and the lame** los tullidos y los lisiados

3 *vt (gen)* detener; *(production)* detener, interrumpir

4 *vi* detenerse; *Mil* **h.! (who goes there?)** ¡alto! (¿quién va?)

halter ['hɔːltə(r)] *n* (**a**) *(for horse)* ronzal *m* (**b**) *(on women's clothing)* tira *f*, tirante *m (que se ata al cuello)* (**c**) *(noose)* soga *f*, dogal *m*

halterneck ['hɔːltənek] 1 *n* top *m* con tiras *or* tirantes que se atan al cuello

2 *adj (dress, top)* con tiras *or* tirantes que se atan al cuello

halting ['hɔːltɪŋ] *adj (voice, progress)* vacilante, titubeante; **he spoke in h. French** hablaba francés con dificultad

haltingly ['hɔːltɪŋlɪ] *adv (to walk)* con paso vacilante; *(to speak)* con la voz entrecortada

halva ['hælvə] *n* halva *f*, = dulce hecho con frutos secos, miel, azafrán y semillas de sésamo

halve [hɑːv] *vt* (**a**) *(divide in two)* dividir (en dos); *(number)* dividir por *or* entre dos; *(cake, fruit)* partir por la mitad (**b**) *(reduce by half)* reducir a la mitad (**c**) *(in golf)* **to h. a hole** empatar (en) un hoyo

halves *pl of* **half**

halyard ['hæljəd] *n Naut* driza *f*

ham [hæm] 1 *n* (**a**) *(meat)* jamón *m* (cocido *or Esp* de York); **cured h.** jamón (serrano) (**b**) *Fam (actor)* actor *m* exagerado, actriz *f* exagerada ►► ***h. acting*** sobreactuación *f*, histrionismo *m* (**c**) **(radio) h.** radioaficionado(a) *m,f* (**d**) *Fam (of leg)* jamón *m*

2 *vt (pt & pp* **hammed**) *Fam (of actor)* **to h. it up** sobreactuar

3 *vi* sobreactuar

Hamburg ['hæmbɜːg] *n* Hamburgo

hamburger ['hæmbɜːgə(r)] *n* (**a**) *(in bun)* hamburguesa *f* (**b**) *US (minced beef)* carne *f* picada

ham-fisted ['hæm'fɪstɪd], **ham-handed** ['hæm'hændɪd] *adj Fam (person)* torpe, manazas *inv*; *(workmanship, attempt)* torpe

hamlet ['hæmlɪt] *n* aldea *f*

hammer ['hæmə(r)] 1 *n* (**a**) *(tool)* martillo *m*; **the h. and sickle** la hoz y el martillo ►► *Archit* ***h. beam*** imposta *f*; *Br* ***h. drill*** taladro *m or* taladradora *f* de percusión

(**b**) *(of auctioneer)* mazo *m*; **to come** *or* **go under the h.** salir a subasta

(**c**) *(of piano)* macillo *m*

(**d**) *(of firearm)* percutor *m*

(**e**) *(in ear)* martillo *m*

(**f**) *Sport (ball on wire)* martillo *m*; *(event)* lanzamiento *m* de martillo

(**g**) IDIOMS **to go at it h. and tongs** *(argue)* tener una acalorada discusión; *(try hard)* poner mucho empeño *or* esfuerzo; *US* **to let the h. down** pisar a fondo (el acelerador), pisar el acelerador

2 *vt* (**a**) *(hit with hammer)* martillear; *(hit with fist)* dar puñetazos a; **to h. a nail into sth** clavar un clavo en algo; **to h. sth flat/straight** aplanar/enderezar algo a martillazos; **to h. home** *(nail, argument)* remachar; **she hammered home her advantage** se aseguró su ventaja; IDIOM **to h. sth into sb** meter algo a alguien en la cabeza, inculcar algo a alguien; **I had it hammered into me that I mustn't do that type of thing** a mí me inculcaron que esas cosas no se hacen; **they're always hammering it into us that...** andan siempre recordándonos que...

(**b**) *Fam (defeat)* dar una paliza a, *Esp* machacar

(**c**) *Br Fam (criticize)* poner por los suelos a

3 *vi* (**a**) *(pound) (person)* martillear, dar martillazos; *(rain, hail)* martillear, golpetear; *(heart)* latir con fuerza; **to h. on the table/door**

(with fist) aporrear la mesa/puerta **(b)** *Fam (go fast, drive fast)* ir a toda mecha *or* a todo tren *or* a todo trapo; **he came hammering round the final bend** enfiló a todo tren la última curva

▸ **hammer away at** *vt insep Fig* **to h. away at a problem** ponerse en serio con un problema

▸ **hammer out** *vt sep* **(a)** *(dent)* quitar a martillazos **(b)** *(tune, rhythm)* tocar aporreando el piano **(c)** *(agreement)* alcanzar, llegar a

hammered ['hæməd] *adj Fam (drunk) Esp* ciego(a), *Méx* cuete, *RP* en pedo

hammerhead ['hæməhed] *n* **h. (shark)** pez *m* martillo

hammering ['hæmərɪŋ] *n* **(a)** *(noise)* martilleo *m* **(b)** *Fam (defeat)* paliza *f*; **to give sb a h.** dar una paliza a alguien, *Esp* machacar a alguien; **we got a real h.** nos dieron un palizón **(c)** *Fam (criticism)* **to give sth/sb a h.** poner por los suelos algo/a alguien; **the new policy got a h. in the press** la prensa puso por los suelos las nuevas medidas

hammer-toe ['hæmətəʊ] *n* dedo *m* en martillo

hammock ['hæmək] *n* hamaca *f*

hammy ['hæmɪ] *adj (actor, performance)* sobreactuado(a), histriónico(a)

hamper[1] ['hæmpə(r)] *n* **(a)** *(for food)* cesta *f*, cesto *m*; **(Christmas) h.** cesta *f* de Navidad **(b)** *(for laundry)* cesta *f or* cesto *m* de la ropa

hamper[2] *vt (hinder)* dificultar, entorpecer

hamster ['hæmstə(r)] *n* hámster *m*

hamstring ['hæmstrɪŋ] **1** *n* tendón *m* de la corva; **to pull a h.** sufrir un tirón en el tendón de la corva ▸▸ ***h. injury*** rotura *f* de ligamentos (de la rodilla)

2 *vt* (*pt & pp* **hamstrung** ['hæmstrʌŋ]) **(a)** *(cripple) (animal)* desjarretar; *(person)* lisiar de una pierna **(b)** *(incapacitate)* incapacitar, paralizar; **we are hamstrung by these regulations** nos vemos incapacitados por culpa de la normativa; **the project is hamstrung (by lack of money)** el proyecto está paralizado (por falta de dinero)

HAND [hænd] **1** *n* **(a)** *(part of body)* mano *f*; **to be good with one's hands** tener habilidad manual; **to hold hands** agarrarse de la mano; **to hold sth in one's h.** sostener algo en la mano; **to take sb by the h.** coger a alguien de la mano; **by h.** *(make, wash, write)* a mano; *(on envelope)* en propia mano; **to deliver sth by h.** entregar algo en mano *or* personalmente; **h. in h.** (cogidos) de la mano; **autograph book in h., he approached the star** con el libro de autógrafos en mano *or* en ristre, se acercó a la estrella; **on one's hands and knees** a cuatro patas; **hands off!** ¡las manos fuera!; **get your hands off me!** ¡quítame las manos de encima!; **hands up!** *(in robbery)* ¡manos arriba!; **hands up anyone who knows the answer** que levante la mano quien sepa la respuesta ▸▸ ***h. baggage*** equipaje *m* de mano; *Br* ***h. basin*** lavabo *m*, *Am* lavamanos *m*; ***h. cream*** crema *f* de manos; ***h. drill*** taladro *m* manual; ***h. grenade*** granada *f* de mano; ***h. grip*** *(on racket)* empuñadura *f*; *(on bicycle)* mango *m* (del manillar); ***h. lotion*** loción *f* para las manos; ***h. luggage*** equipaje *m* de mano; ***h. mirror*** espejo *m* de mano; ***h. puppet*** títere *m or* marioneta *f* (de guiñol); ***h. saw*** serrucho *m*; ***h. towel*** toalla *f* (de manos)

(b) *(of clock, watch)* manecilla *f*

(c) *(worker)* brazo *m*; **all hands on deck!** ¡todos a cubierta!; **to be an old h. at sth** ser veterano(a) en algo

(d) *(handwriting)* letra *f*; **in his own h.** de su puño y letra

(e) *(in cards)* mano *f*; **to play a h. of poker** jugar *or* echar una mano de poker; *Fig* **to show one's h.** poner las cartas boca arriba *or* sobre la mesa, *RP* mostrar el juego; *Fig* **to strengthen/weaken sb's h.** reforzar/debilitar la posición de alguien

(f) *(influence)* mano *f*; **you can see the h. of the CIA in this decision** se nota la mano de la CIA en esta decisión; **I had a h. in designing the course** tuve que ver *or* puse de mi parte en el diseño del curso; **the government is suspected of having had a h. in the decision** se sospecha que el gobierno ha tenido *or* metido mano en esta decisión

(g) *(help)* **to give** *or* **lend sb a h.** echar *or* dar una mano a alguien; **do you need a h. with that box?** ¿necesitas que te eche *or* dé una mano con esa caja?

(h) *(unit of measurement)* = unidad para medir la altura de los caballos, de aproximadamente 10 cm

(i) *(of bananas)* cacho *m*

(j) IDIOMS **at h., close at h.** a mano; **luckily, help was at h.** por suerte, teníamos quien nos ayudara; **the day is almost at h. when...** no está lejano el día en que...; **to suffer/die at sb's hands** sufrir/morir a manos de alguien; **to ask for sb's h. (in marriage)** pedir la mano de alguien; **to change hands** *(money, car)* cambiar de mano; **it came into my hands via an acquaintance** llegó a mis manos por medio de un conocido; **we'll use whatever comes to h.** utilizaremos lo que haya por ahí; **to fall into the wrong hands** caer en malas manos *or* manos equivocadas; **just wait till I get** *or* **lay my hands on him!** ¡espera a que le ponga la mano encima!; **the situation has got out of h.** la situación se nos ha escapado de las manos; **the children got out of h.** los niños se desmandaron; **to give sb a big h.** *(applaud)* dar un gran aplauso a alguien; **she gave me her h. on the deal** sellamos el trato con un apretón de manos; **to be h. in glove with sb** colaborar estrechamente con alguien; **to go from h. to h.** ir *or* pasar de mano en mano; **success and fame go h. in h.** el éxito y la fama van juntos; **to have one's hands full** estar ocupadísimo(a); **I have my hands tied, my hands are tied** tengo las manos atadas; **I don't need you to hold my h. any more** no te necesito, ya puedo hacerlo solo; **we still have a few days in h.** todavía tenemos unos días; **they have a game in h.** han jugado un partido menos; **concentrate on the job in h.** concéntrate en lo que estás haciendo; **to have a situation in h.** tener una situación bajo control; **to take sb in h.** hacerse cargo de alguien; **to be in good** *or* **safe hands** estar en buenas manos; **the city is in enemy hands** la ciudad está en manos enemigas; **we are putting the matter in the hands of our lawyer** vamos a poner el asunto en manos de nuestro abogado; **her fate is in her own hands** su destino está en sus manos; **to keep one's h. in** no perder la práctica; *Fam* **they can't keep their hands off each other** están todo el día uno encima del otro; **to keep a firm h. on sth** controlar algo con mano dura; **the left h. doesn't know what the right h. is doing** no se aclaran *or* entienden; **to live from h. to mouth** vivir de forma precaria; **to lose money h. over fist** perder dinero a raudales; **to make money h. over fist** ganar dinero a espuertas *or* a lo loco; **a doctor is always on h.** siempre hay un médico disponible; **on the one h.** por una parte; **on the other h.** por otra parte; **to have time on one's hands** tener tiempo libre; **we've got a real problem on our hands here** nos enfrentamos a un problema serio; **it's out of my hands** no está en mi mano; **to dismiss a suggestion out of h.** rechazar una sugerencia sin más ni más; **to put one's h. in one's pocket** *(pay)* echar mano al bolsillo; **I can put my h. on my heart and say...** puedo decir con la mano en el corazón que...; **I've never raised a h. to her** nunca le he levantado la mano; **we need a safe pair of hands for this job** necesitamos a alguien fiable *or Am* confiable para hacer este trabajo; **to have sth to h.** tener algo a mano; **to try one's h. at sth** intentar algo alguna vez; **he turned his h. to painting** se puso a pintar, empezó a dedicarse a la pintura; **to win hands down** ganar con comodidad; PROV **many hands make light work** compartir el trabajo aligera la carga

2 *vt* dar, pasar; **to h. sth to sb, to h. sb sth** dar *or* pasar algo a alguien; *Fig* **to h. sth to sb (on a plate)** ponerle algo a alguien en bandeja; *Fig* **you've got to h. it to him** tienes que reconocérselo

▸ **hand around** *vt sep* = **hand round**

▸ **hand back** *vt sep (return)* devolver

▸ **hand down** *vt sep* **(a)** *(pass)* pasar **(b)** *(bequeath)* dejar en herencia; **the story had been handed down from one generation to the next** la historia había pasado de generación en generación; **these trousers were handed down from my sister** heredé estos pantalones de mi hermana **(c)** *(sentence, verdict)* dictar

▸ **hand in** *vt sep (give)* entregar; *(resignation)* presentar

▸ **hand on** *vt sep* pasar

▸ **hand out** *vt sep (money, food)* repartir; *(advice)* dar; *(justice)* administrar

▸ **hand over** **1** *vt sep* **(a)** *(give)* dar, entregar; *(hostages, ransom)* entregar **(b)** *(control, responsibility)* ceder **(c)** *(on phone)* **I'll h. you over to my boss** te paso con mi jefe

2 *vi* **to h. over to sb** dar paso a alguien

▸ **hand round** *vt sep (circulate)* pasar

hand- [hænd] *prefix* a mano; **h.-stitched** cosido(a) a mano; **h.-knitted** tejido(a) a mano

handbag ['hændbæg] **1** *n* **(a)** *Br (woman's) Esp* bolso *m*, *Col, CSur* cartera *f*, *Méx* bolsa *f* **(b)** *(small travelling bag)* bolso *m* de mano

2 *vt Br Fam (attack verbally)* **she handbagged him** lo puso de vuelta y media

handball *n* ['hændbɔːl] **(a)** *(team game)* balonmano *m*, *Am* handball *m* **(b)** *(individual sport)* pelota *f* (vasca), frontón *m* **(c)** *(in soccer)* (falta *f* de) mano *f*

handbell ['hændbel] *n* campanilla *f*

handbill ['hændbɪl] *n* panfleto *m* (de propaganda)

handbook ['hændbʊk] *n* manual *m*

handbrake ['hændbreɪk] *n Br (of car)* freno *m* de mano ▸▸ ***h. turn*** trompo *m* *(al poner el freno de mano)*

h and c, h & c (*abbr* **hot and cold**) **all rooms with h.** todas las habitaciones disponen de agua caliente

handcar ['hændkɑː(r)] *n US* vagón *m* plataforma de tracción manual *(con balancín)*

handcart ['hændkɑːt] *n* carretilla *f*

handclap ['hændklæp] *n Br* **a slow h.** = palmas lentas del público en señal de desaprobación

handclasp ['hændklɑːsp] *n US* apretón *m* de manos

handcraft ['hændkrɑːft] *vt* realizar a mano; **all items are lovingly handcrafted** todos los artículos están elaborados artesanalmente con el mayor esmero

handcrafted ['hændkrɑːftɪd] *adj* artesanal, de artesanía

handcuff ['hændkʌf] *vt* esposar; **he was handcuffed to the radiator** estaba esposado al radiador

handcuffs ['hændkʌfs] *npl* esposas *fpl*; **to be in h.** estar *or* ir esposado(a)

hand-drier ['hænd'draɪə(r)] *n* secador *m* de manos, secamanos *m inv*

-hander ['hændə(r)] *suffix* **two/three-h.** *(play)* obra (de teatro) para dos/tres personajes

hand-feed ['hændfiːd] *vt* **(a)** *(animal)* dar de comer manualmente a **(b)** *(machine, printer)* alimentar manualmente **(c)** *(paper, blanks)* cargar manualmente

handful ['hændfʊl] *n* **(a)** *(of sand, rice)* puñado *m* **(b)** *(of people)* puñado *m* (de gente) **(c)** IDIOM **to be a real h.: that child is a real h.** ese niño es un terremoto *or* una buena pieza; **my grandfather is a real h.** con mi abuelo hay que andarse con cien ojos

handgun ['hændgʌn] *n* pistola *f*

hand-held ['hænd'held] *adj (camera)* de mano, portátil ►► ***h. computer*** *Esp* ordenador *m or Am* computadora *f* de bolsillo; ***h. scanner*** escáner *m* de mano

handhold ['hændhəʊld] *n* punto *m* de agarre *or* sujeción, asidero *m*

handicap ['hændɪkæp] **1** *n* **(a)** *(disadvantage)* desventaja *f*; *(impediment)* obstáculo *m*, hándicap *m* **(b)** *(disability)* discapacidad *f*, minusvalía *f*; **physical/mental h.** discapacidad *or* minusvalía física/mental **(c)** *(in golf)* hándicap *m* **(d)** *(in horse racing) (race)* hándicap *m*; *(extra weight)* hándicap *m*, (compensación *f* de) peso *m*, *Arg, Perú* plomo *m*

2 *vt (pt & pp* **handicapped) (a)** *(disadvantage)* suponer una desventaja para; *(impede)* suponer un obstáculo para; **to be handicapped by...** verse perjudicado(a) por... **(b)** *(player)* asignar un hándicap a

handicapped ['hændɪkæpt] **1** *adj* discapacitado(a), minusválido(a); **mentally/physically h.** discapacitado(a) psíquico(a)/físico(a)

2 *npl* **the h.** los discapacitados *or* minusválidos

handicapper ['hændɪkæpə(r)] *n* **(a)** *(in horse racing)* handicapper *mf*, = encargado de asignar el hándicap o compensación de peso a un caballo **(b)** *(in golf)* jugador(ora) *m,f* con hándicap; **I'm a 10 h.** tengo un hándicap 10

handicraft ['hændɪkrɑːft] *n* **(a)** *(skill)* artesanía *f* **(b)** *(object)* objeto *m* de artesanía; **local handicrafts** (objetos de) artesanía local

handily ['hændɪlɪ] *adv* **(a)** *(conveniently)* cómodamente, convenientemente **(b)** *(within reach)* a mano; **the switch is h. placed next to the steering wheel** el interruptor se halla muy a mano junto al volante **(c)** *US (easily)* con facilidad

handiness ['hændɪnɪs] *n* **(a)** *(convenience)* comodidad *f*, conveniencia *f* **(b)** *(skill)* habilidad *f*, destreza *f*; **his h. about the home** lo habilidoso *or Esp* manitas que es para las cosas de la casa

handiwork ['hændɪwɜːk] *n* **(a)** *(craftwork)* trabajos *mpl* manuales, manualidades *fpl* **(b)** *(product of work)* obra *f*, trabajo *m*; **she stood back to admire her h.** retrocedió para admirar su obra *or* trabajo **(c)** *Ironic* **this mess looks like Clara's h.!** este desorden parece obra de Clara

hand-job ['hænddʒɒb] *n Vulg* **to give sb a h.** hacer una paja *or Am* la paja a alguien

handkerchief ['hæŋkətʃɪf] *n* pañuelo *m*; **(paper) h.** pañuelo *m* de papel

hand-knit ['hænd'nɪt] **1** *n* prenda *f* (de punto) tejida a mano

2 *vt* tejer a mano

handle ['hændəl] **1** *n* **(a)** *(of screwdriver, saucepan)* mango *m*; *(of broom)* palo *m*; *(of gun, knife)* empuñadura *f*, mango *m*; *(of racket, bat)* empuñadura *f*; *(of suitcase, cup)* asa *f*

(b) *(of door, drawer) (lever-like)* picaporte *m*, manija *f*, manilla *f*; *(round)* pomo *m*

(c) *Fam (name)* nombre *m*; *(of citizens' band user)* código *m*

(d) *Comptr* manejador *m*

(e) IDIOMS **to fly off the h.** *(lose one's temper)* perder los estribos; *Fam* **I can't get a h. on it** *(understand)* no sé por dónde agarrarlo; *(manage, control)* se me va *or* escapa de las manos; **I'll get back to you once I've got a h. on the situation** te vuelvo a llamar cuando sepa qué hacer con este asunto; **the first thing to do is to get a h. on the export market** lo primero es aprender a manejarse en el mercado de las exportaciones

2 *vt* **(a)** *(touch, hold)* manipular, tocar; **wash your hands before you h. food** lávese las manos antes de manipular *or* tocar alimentos; **pesticides should be handled with caution** los pesticidas deben manipularse con precaución; **h. with care** *(sign)* frágil; **to h. the ball** *(in soccer)* hacer (falta con la) mano

(b) *(cope with, control) (situation, crisis)* manejar; *(people)* tratar; **you handled that very well** lo has hecho muy bien, saliste adelante muy bien; **the situation was badly handled** no se manejó bien la situación; **I don't know how to h. her when she's in this state** cuando se pone así, no sé cómo tratarla; **he's good at handling people** sabe cómo tratar *or* manejar a la gente; **he knows how to h. himself in a crisis** sabe manejarse bien en medio de una crisis; **four babies are a lot for one person to h.** cuatro bebés son muchos bebés para una sola persona; **now he knows the truth he can't h. it** ahora que sabe lo que pasó no puede soportarlo; **how is she handling it?** ¿qué tal lo lleva?; **I'll h. this** déjame a mí, yo me encargo de esto; **it's nothing I can't h.** me las puedo apañar solo

(c) *(operate) (ship, car)* manejar; *(gun)* manejar; **have you any experience of handling horses?** ¿tiene experiencia en el manejo de caballos?

(d) *(deal with, process) (business, contract, client)* encargarse de; **we h. all the large orders** nosotros llevamos todos los pedidos grandes; **she handles my tax for me** ella me lleva los asuntos fiscales; **the airport handles two hundred planes a day** el aeropuerto tiene un tráfico diario de doscientos aviones; **to h. stolen goods** traficar *or* comerciar con mercancía robada

3 *vi (car, boat)* responder

handlebar moustache ['hændəlbɑːmə'stɑːʃ] *n* bigote *m* retorcido

handlebars ['hændəlbɑːz] *npl (of bicycle, motorbike)* manillar *m*, *Am* manubrio *m*; **she went right over the h.** salió despedida de la bicicleta hacia delante

handler ['hændlə(r)] *n* **(a)** *(of animals)* adiestrador(ora) *m,f* **(b)** *(of spy, agent)* contacto *m* **(c)** *(of boxer) (trainer)* preparador(ora) *m,f*; *(second)* cuidador(ora) *m,f*

handling ['hændlɪŋ] *n* **(a)** *(touching, holding)* manipulación *f*; **it's not designed to be subjected to so much h.** no está diseñado para ser objeto de tanta manipulación; **the animals react badly to too much h.** los animales reaccionan mal si se les toca mucho

(b) *(of situation, problem)* manejo *m*; **her h. of the enquiry has been seriously questioned** la manera en la que ha llevado a cabo la investigación ha sido puesta en tela de juicio; **her h. of the interview was very professional** manejó *or* llevó la entrevista con mucha profesionalidad

(c) *(of car, aircraft, boat)* manejo *m*

(d) *(of order, contract)* gestión *f*, tramitación *f*; *(of goods, baggage)* porte *m*; *(of stolen goods)* tráfico *m*, comercio *m* ►► *Fin* ***h. charges*** gastos *mpl* de gestión *or* tramitación

handloom ['hændluːm] *n* telar *m* de mano

handmade ['hænd'meɪd] *adj* hecho(a) a mano; **to be h.** estar hecho(a) a mano

handmaid(en) ['hændmeɪd(ən)] *n* **(a)** *Old-fashioned (female servant)* doncella *f* **(b)** *Fig* **logic is the h. of mathematics** la lógica es un valioso instrumento *or* una valiosa herramienta para las matemáticas

hand-me-down ['hændmɪdaʊn] *n Fam* **this suit is a h. from my father** este traje lo heredé de mi padre; **he wore his brother's hand-me-downs** llevaba ropa heredada de su hermano

hand-operated ['hænd'ɒpəreɪtɪd] *adj* manual

handout ['hændaʊt] *n* **(a)** *(donation)* donativo *m*, limosna *f*; **we don't want to live off handouts** no queremos vivir de (las) limosnas **(b)** *(printed sheet or sheets) (at lecture)* hoja(s) *f(pl)* informativa(s) *(para distribuir entre los asistentes)*; **press h.** nota de prensa **(c)** *(publicity leaflet) (small brochure)* folleto *m*; *(piece of paper)* octavilla *f*

handover ['hændəʊvə(r)] *n* entrega *f*

handpick ['hænd'pɪk] *vt* **(a)** *(fruit, vegetables)* escoger **(b)** *(people, team)* seleccionar cuidadosamente

hand-picked ['hænd'pɪkt] *adj* **(a)** *(fruit, vegetables)* escogido(a) **(b)** *(person, team)* cuidadosamente seleccionado(a)

handrail ['hændreɪl] *n (on stairway)* pasamanos *m inv*, baranda *f*, *Esp* barandilla *f*; *(on footbridge, ship)* baranda *f*, *Esp* barandilla *f*

hands-down ['hænz'daʊn] *adj US (winner, favourite)* indiscutible

handset ['hændset] *n (of telephone)* auricular *m*

handsewn ['hænd'səʊn] *adj* cosido(a) a mano

hands-free ['hænz'friː] *adj (phone, dialling)* de manos libres; **phone with h. facility** teléfono con (opción de) manos libres

handshake ['hændʃeɪk] *n* (**a**) *(greeting)* apretón *m* de manos (**b**) *Comptr* diálogo *m* de establecimiento de comunicación

handshaking ['hændʃeɪkɪŋ] *n Comptr* establecimiento *m* de comunicación *or* diálogo

hands-off ['hæn'zɒf] *adj* (**a**) *(approach, style)* no intervencionista (**b**) *(machine, device)* de funcionamiento automático

handsome ['hænsəm] *adj* (**a**) *(man)* atractivo, *Esp* guapo, *Am* lindo; *(woman)* distinguida; *(animal)* hermoso(a), bello(a); *(building)* elegante, bello(a); PROV **h. is as h. does** = a la gente hay que juzgarla por sus obras, no por su aspecto, ≃ el hábito no hace al monje

(**b**) *(generous) (reward, compliment)* generoso(a), bonito(a); *(praise, apology)* generoso(a); **a h. gesture** un bonito *or* noble gesto

(**c**) *(substantial) (price, profit)* considerable

handsomely ['hænsəmlɪ] *adv* (**a**) *(dressed, furnished)* elegantemente (**b**) *(to reward, compliment)* generosamente; *(to praise, apologize, pay)* generosamente (**c**) *(substantially) (to profit)* considerablemente; **to win h.** vencer ampliamente or holgadamente

hands-on ['hæn'zɒn] *adj* (**a**) *(practical, involved) (approach)* práctico(a); **he has a h. management style** le gusta implicarse en todos los aspectos del negocio ►► ***h. training*** formación *f* práctica (**b**) *(exhibition)* = que ofrece la posibilidad de tocar lo expuesto

handspan ['hændspæn] *n* anchura *f* de la mano

handspring ['hændsprɪŋ] *n* voltereta *f*

handstand ['hændstænd] *n* **to do a h.** hacer el pino

hand-to-hand ['hæntə'hænd] **1** *adj* **h. combat** combate cuerpo a cuerpo

2 *adv* **to fight h.** luchar cuerpo a cuerpo

hand-to-mouth ['hæntə'maʊθ] **1** *adj* **a h. existence** una existencia precaria

2 *adv* **to live h.** vivir de forma precaria

hand-tool ['hæntuːl] *vt* trabajar a mano

hand-tooled ['hæntuːld] *adj* trabajado(a) a mano

handwash ['hændwɒʃ] **1** *vt* lavar a mano

2 *n* **I'm doing a h.** voy a lavar unas cosas a mano

handwork ['hændwɜːk] *n* trabajo *m* manual

handwriting ['hændraɪtɪŋ] *n* letra *f*, caligrafía *f*; **her h. is terrible** tiene una letra horrible; **a h. expert** un calígrafo, un perito caligráfico

handwritten ['hændrɪtən] *adj* manuscrito(a), escrito(a) a mano

handy ['hændɪ] *adj* (**a**) *(useful)* práctico(a), útil; **that's h.!** ¡mira qué bien!; **to come in h.** venir bien; **don't throw it away, it might come in h. one day** no lo tires, algún día podría venirnos bien

(**b**) *(conveniently situated)* bien situado(a); **the house is very h. for the shops** la casa queda muy cerca de las tiendas; **living in the centre is h. for work** viviendo en el centro el trabajo queda cerca

(**c**) *(within reach)* a mano; **have you got a pencil h.?** ¿tienes un lápiz a mano?

(**d**) *(skilful)* habilidoso(a), *Esp* mañoso(a); **to be h. at doing sth** tener maña *or* habilidad para hacer algo; **he's very h. in the kitchen** se le da muy bien la cocina *or* cocinar; **he's h. about the house** es muy habilidoso *or Esp* mañoso para las cosas de la casa; **he's h. with his fists** tiene la mano muy larga, enseguida se lía a puñetazos; **she's very h. with a paintbrush** es muy hábil con la brocha

handyman ['hændɪmæn] *n (person good at odd jobs)* persona *f* habilidosa, *Esp* manitas *mf inv*; **get the h. to have a look at it** llama a un técnico para que le eche un vistazo

HANG [hæŋ] **1** *n* (**a**) *(of garment, fabric)* caída *f*

(**b**) IDIOMS *Fam* **to get the h. of sth** pillar el truco *or Esp* el tranquillo a algo, *Méx* pescar algo, *RP* agarrar la mano a algo; *Br Fam* **he doesn't give a h.** *(couldn't care less)* le importa un bledo

2 *vt* (*pt & pp* **hung** [hʌŋ]) (**a**) *(suspend) (wallpaper, door)* poner, colocar; *(meat, painting)* colgar

(**b**) *(lower)* **to h. one's head** bajar la cabeza; **he hung his head in shame** bajó la cabeza avergonzado

(**c**) *(decorate)* decorar; **the walls were hung with rugs** había tapices colgados de las paredes, las paredes estaban decoradas con tapices

(**d**) IDIOM **to h. fire** *(delay)* esperar, no hacer nada por el momento

(**e**) *Fam (damn)* **h. it (all)!** ¡al diablo *or* a la porra con todo!; **h. the cost!** ¡al diablo *or* a la porra el precio!

(**f**) *US Fam (take turning)* **h. a left/right!** ¡tuerce *or* dobla a la izquierda/derecha!

(**g**) (*pt & pp* **hanged**) *(execute)* ahorcar, colgar (**for** por); **to h. oneself** ahorcarse, colgarse; **he was hanged, drawn and quartered** lo colgaron, lo destriparon y lo descuartizaron; *Fam* **I'll be hanged if I'm going to let her do that!** ¡no la pienso dejar hacer eso ni de broma!

3 *vi* (**a**) *(be suspended)* colgar; **the painting hangs in the Metropolitan museum/on the wall** el cuadro está en el Metropolitan/en la pared; **a string of pearls hung around her neck** llevaba un collar de perlas al cuello; **her hair hung loose around her shoulders** los cabellos sueltos caían sobre sus hombros; **their future is hanging by a thread** su futuro pende *or* está pendiente de un hilo; **their future is hanging in the balance** su futuro es incierto *or* está en el aire

(**b**) *(hover)* **the bird hung in the air for a moment, then dived** el ave permaneció inmóvil en el aire unos instantes y se lanzó *Esp* en picado *or Am* en picada; **the smoke hung in the air for some time** el humo permaneció en el aire durante un rato

(**c**) *(be executed)* ser ahorcado(a) *or* colgado(a) (**for** por); *Fam* **he can go h. for all I care!** ¡por mí, como si se muere *or* que se muera!

(**d**) *(material, clothes)* caer, colgar; **the suit hangs well on you** el traje te cae *or* sienta *or* queda bien

(**e**) *US Fam (hang out)* **what are you doing? – nothing, just hanging** ¿qué haces? – ya ves *or* nada; **to h. loose** estar tranqui, no perder los nervios; **h. loose!** ¡tranqui!; **to h. tough** aguantar (bien) el tipo

(**f**) *Fam* **how's it hanging?** *(how are you?)* ¿qué tal?, *Esp* ¿qué pasa?, *Carib, Col, Méx* ¿quihu?, *RP* ¿qué talco?

► **hang about, hang around** *Fam* **1** *vt insep* **we used to h. about** *or* **around the mall after school** solíamos rondar por el centro comercial después de clase

2 *vi* (**a**) *(wait)* esperar; **he kept me hanging about** *or* **around for hours** me tuvo esperando horas; *Br* **h. about, there's something odd going on here** un momento, aquí pasa algo raro

(**b**) *(be slow)* **stop hanging about** *or* **around and get a move on!** ¡deja de perder el tiempo y ponte en marcha!; **she didn't h. about!** ¡no perdió ni un segundo!

(**c**) *(spend time)* **to h. about or around with one's friends** andar por ahí con los amigos; **I don't h. about** *or* **around with them any more** ya no voy *or* salgo con ellos

► **hang back** *vi* (**a**) *(stay behind)* quedarse atrás (**b**) *(hesitate)* dudar, titubear

► **hang down** *vi* colgar (**from** de)

► **hang in** *vi Fam (persevere)* aguantar; **h. in there!** ¡aguanta!

► **hang on** **1** *vi* (**a**) *(hold)* agarrarse; **h. on tight!** ¡agárrate bien!

(**b**) *Fam (wait)* esperar; **h. on (a minute)!** ¡espérate (un minuto)!

(**c**) *(survive)* resistir, aguantar; **Germany hung on for a draw** Alemania aguantó y consiguió un empate; *Fam* **h. on in there!** *(don't give up)* ¡aguanta!

2 *vt insep (depend on)* depender de; **everything hangs on his answer** todo depende de su respuesta; **she hung on his every word** estaba totalmente pendiente de sus palabras

3 *vt sep* (**a**) *(put blame on)* **he hung it on me** me colgó el muerto a mí

(**b**) *US Fam* **to h. one on** *(get drunk)* agarrarla, agarrarse una buena cogorza

(**c**) *US Fam* **to h. one on sb** *(hit)* cascar *or Esp* atizar a alguien

► **hang on to** *vt insep* (**a**) *(hold)* agarrarse a (**b**) *(keep)* conservar; **I'd h. on to those documents if I were you** yo, en tu lugar, me quedaría con esos documentos

► **hang open** *vi* **her mouth hung open in dismay** se le quedó la boca abierta de consternación

► **hang out** **1** *vt sep (washing)* tender; *(flags)* colgar

2 *vi* (**a**) *(protrude)* **his tongue/shirt was hanging out** tenía la lengua/camisa fuera; **she always has a cigarette hanging out of her mouth** siempre tiene un cigarrillo en la boca; *Fam* **just let it all h. out** ¡tranqui!

(**b**) *Fam (spend time)* **to h. out with one's friends** andar por ahí con los amigos; **he usually hangs out in the Bronx Café** normalmente va por el Café Bronx; **what are you doing? – nothing, just hanging out** ¿qué haces? – ya ves *or* nada

(**c**) *(survive, resist)* **they won't be able to h. out for more than another two days** no podrán sobrevivir más de otros dos días; **they're hanging out for 10 percent** no pactarán hasta conseguir el 10 por ciento

► **hang over** *vt insep* **the threat of relegation has been hanging over them all season** la amenaza del descenso se ha cernido sobre ellos durante toda la temporada; **a question mark hangs over his reliability** su fiabilidad se encuentra en entredicho

► **hang together** *vi* (**a**) *(argument, statements)* encajar, concordar (**b**) *(help each other)* cooperar

► **hang up** **1** *vt sep* (**a**) *(suspend) (hat, picture)* colgar; IDIOM **to h. up one's hat** retirarse, colgar los hábitos; IDIOM **to h. up one's boots** *(soccer, rugby player)* colgar las botas (**b**) *Fam* **to be hung up on** *(obsessed)* estar obsesionado(a) *or* paranoico(a) con; **he's really hung up on her** está obsesionado con ella (**c**) *US Fam* **to h. it up** *(stop)* dejarlo, abandonar

2 *vi (on telephone)* colgar; **to h. up on sb** colgarle (el teléfono) a alguien

---

hangar ['hæŋə(r)] *n Av* hangar *m*

hangdog ['hæŋdɒg] *adj* **a h. look** *or* **expression** una expresión avergonzada *or Andes, CAm, Carib, Méx* apenada

hanger ['hæŋə(r)] *n (for clothes)* percha *f*

hanger-on [hæŋə'rɒn] (*pl* **hangers-on**) *n Fam Pej* parásito(a) *m,f*; **the mayor and his hangers-on** el alcalde y su cohorte

hang-glide ['hæŋglaɪd] *vi* volar en ala delta, hacer ala delta

hang-glider ['hæŋglaɪdər] *n* ala *f* delta

hang-gliding ['hæŋglaɪdɪŋ] *n* vuelo *m* libre; **to go h.** hacer ala delta

hanging ['hæŋɪŋ] 1 *n* (**a**) *(execution)* ahorcamiento *m*, ejecución *f* en la horca; **a h. offence** un delito castigado con la horca; *Fam* **a h. judge** un juez muy duro (**b**) **hangings** *(curtains, drapes)* colgaduras *fpl*; *(tapestries)* tapices *mpl* (**c**) *Art* ***h. committee*** comité *m* seleccionador

2 *adj* ***h. garden*** jardín *m* colgante; *Typ* ***h. indent*** sangría *f* francesa; *Geog* ***h. valley*** valle *m* suspendido *or* colgado

hangman ['hæŋmən] *n* (**a**) *(person)* verdugo *m* (**b**) *(game)* (juego *m* del) ahorcado *m*

hangnail ['hæŋneɪl] *n* padrastro *m*

hang-out ['hæŋaʊt] *n Fam* guarida *f*, sitio *m* predilecto; **it's a real student h.** es un garito donde se suelen juntar los estudiantes

hangover ['hæŋəʊvə(r)] *n* (**a**) *(from drinking)* resaca *f*; **to have a h.** tener resaca (**b**) *(practice, belief)* vestigio *m*; **a h. from the past** un vestigio del pasado

hang-up ['hæŋʌp] *n Fam (complex)* complejo *m*, paranoia *f*; **to have a h. about sth** estar acomplejado(a) por algo

hank [hæŋk] *n (of wool)* madeja *f*; *(of rope)* rollo *m*

hanker ['hæŋkə(r)] *vi* **to h. after** *or* **for sth** anhelar algo

hankering ['hæŋkərɪŋ] *n* **to have a h. after** *or* **for sth** sentir anhelo de algo

hankie, hanky ['hæŋkɪ] *n Fam* pañuelo *m*

hanky-panky ['hæŋkɪ'pæŋkɪ] *n Fam* (**a**) *(sexual activity) Esp* ñacañaca *m*, *Méx* cuchi-cuchi *m* (**b**) *(underhand behaviour)* chanchullos *mpl*, tejemanejes *mpl*

Hannibal ['hænɪbəl] *pr n* Aníbal

Hanoi [hæ'nɔɪ] *n* Hanoi

Hanoverian [hænə'vɪərɪən] 1 *n* hannoveriano(a) *m,f*, miembro *m* de la casa de Hannover *(dinastía real británica, 1714-1901)*

2 *adj* hannoveriano(a), de la casa de Hannover

Hansard ['hænsɑːd] *n Br Pol* = actas oficiales y diario de sesiones del parlamento británico

hansom ['hænsəm] *n* **h. (cab)** cabriolé *m*, cab *m* inglés

Hants [hænts] (*abbr* **Hampshire**) Hampshire

Hanukkah ['hɑːnəkə] *n Rel* Janucá *f*, = fiesta judía de ocho días celebrada en diciembre para conmemorar la dedicación del templo

ha'penny = **halfpenny**

haphazard [hæp'hæzəd] *adj (choice, decision)* arbitrario(a), incoherente; *(attempt)* desorganizado(a); **the whole thing was a bit h.** todo estaba bastante mal organizado; **in a h. fashion** de cualquier manera, al azar

haphazardly [hæp'hæzədlɪ] *adv* descuidadamente; **everything was lying h. on the floor** todo estaba tirado de cualquier manera por el suelo

hapless ['hæplɪs] *adj* infortunado(a)

haploid ['hæplɔɪd] *adj Biol* haploide

hap'orth = **halfpennyworth**

happen ['hæpən] 1 *vi* (**a**) *(take place)* pasar, ocurrir, suceder; **what's happened?** ¿qué ha pasado *or* ocurrido *or* sucedido?; **where did the accident h.?** ¿dónde ocurrió *or* sucedió el accidente?; **it happened ten years ago** pasó hace diez años; **it all happened so quickly** todo ocurrió tan deprisa; **he acted as if nothing had happened** él actuó como si no hubiera pasado *or* ocurrido nada; **what has happened to him?** ¿qué le ha pasado?; **whatever happened to him?** ¿qué fue de él?; **what's happening to us?** ¿qué nos está pasando?; **what has happened to my keys?** *(where are they?)* ¿dónde estarán mis llaves?; **it couldn't h./have happened to a nicer person** no podía pasarle/haberle pasado a nadie mejor; **a funny thing happened to me last night** anoche me pasó algo muy raro; **what happened next?** ¿qué pasó después?, ¿cómo sigue la historia?; **whatever happens, stay calm** pase lo que pase, no te pongas nervioso; **don't let it h. again** que no vuelva a ocurrir, que no se vuelva a repetir; **these things h.** son cosas que pasan; *Euph* **if anything happens** *or* **should h. to me** si me pasara algo, si algo me ocurriera; **as (so) often happens** como suele ocurrir, como es habitual; **don't worry, it'll never h.** no te preocupes, que no va a pasar; **it's all been happening this morning** esta mañana ha pasado de todo; *Fam* **it's all happening!** ¡qué movida!; *US Fam* **what's happening?** *(greeting) Esp* ¿qué pasa?, *Carib, Col, Méx* ¿quihu?, *RP* ¿qué talco?

(**b**) *(occur by chance)* **to h. to meet sb** encontrarse con alguien por casualidad; **I happened to mention it to the boss** dio la casualidad de que se lo comenté al jefe; **I h. to know that...** resulta que sé que...; **I h. to know her** da la casualidad de que la conozco; **he happens to be my father** resulta que es mi padre; **do you h. to know when she's coming?** ¿no sabrás por casualidad cuándo viene?; **you wouldn't h. to have a pencil I could borrow, would you?** ¿no tendrías por ahí un lápiz para dejarme?; **you wouldn't happen to know where I could find him, would you?** ¿no sabría usted por casualidad dónde puedo encontrarlo?; **if you h. to see him, could you give him this?** si por casualidad *or* si acaso lo ves, ¿podrías darle esto?; **it just so happens that I DO know the answer** pues mira por dónde sí que sé la respuesta; **as it happens...** precisamente..., casualmente...; **as it happened, we were going there anyway** casualmente, nosotros íbamos para allí de todas maneras

2 *adv Br Fam (maybe)* a lo mejor, quizá

▸ **happen along, happen by** *vi* aparecer

▸ **happen on, happen upon** *vt insep (person)* encontrarse con; *(object, place)* dar con, encontrar

happening ['hæpənɪŋ] 1 *n* (**a**) *(occurrence)* suceso *m* (**b**) *Theat* happening *m*, performance *f*

2 *adj Fam* **this club is a really h. place** esta discoteca está de moda *or* a la última

happenstance ['hæpənstæns] *n US* casualidad *f*; **by h.** por casualidad

happily ['hæpɪlɪ] *adv* (**a**) *(with pleasure, contentedly)* alegremente; **we were sitting there quite h. watching television** estábamos allí sentados viendo tranquilamente la televisión; **she's h. married** ella es feliz en su matrimonio; **Jane and Paul are h. married** Jane y Paul son un matrimonio feliz; **they lived h. ever after** fueron felices y comieron perdices

(**b**) *(gladly, willingly)* de buena gana, con mucho gusto; **I could quite h. live here** de buena gana viviría aquí, no me importaría (nada) vivir aquí; **she said she would h. give her consent** dijo que con mucho gusto daría su consentimiento; **I'd quite h. do it** no me importaría para nada hacerlo, lo haría con mucho gusto; **I could quite h. strangle him** de buena gana *or* con gusto lo estrangularía; **he'll quite h. say one thing and do the opposite** te dice una cosa, luego hace lo contrario y se queda tan tranquilo

(**c**) *(fortunately)* afortunadamente, por suerte; **h., no-one was hurt** afortunadamente *or* por suerte, nadie resultó herido

(**d**) *(appropriately)* acertadamente; **a h. chosen turn of phrase** una expresión muy afortunada *or* acertada

happiness ['hæpɪnɪs] *n* felicidad *f*; **we wish you every h.** *or* **all the h. in the world** (te deseamos) que seas muy feliz

happy ['hæpɪ] *adj* (**a**) *(in a state of contentment)* feliz; *(pleased)* contento(a); *(cheerful)* alegre, feliz; **I'm so h. they've come** estoy muy contento de que hayan venido; **I want you to be h.** quiero que seas feliz; **their h. smiling faces** sus rostros alegres *or* felices y sonrientes; **h. birthday/Christmas/New Year!** ¡feliz cumpleaños/Navidad/Año Nuevo!; **those were h. days** (aquellos) eran tiempos felices; **to be h. with** *or* **about sth** estar contento(a) con algo; **I'm not at all h. about your decision** no estoy nada contento con tu decisión; **to be h. for sb** alegrarse por alguien; **I'm very h. for you** me alegro mucho por ti; **to make sb h.** hacer feliz a alguien; **to keep sb h.** tener contento(a) a alguien; **that should keep the kids h.** con esto tendremos contentos a los niños; *Ironic* **there, are you h. now?** ¿qué? estarás contento, ¿no?; IDIOM **as h. as a lark** *or* **a sandboy** *or Br, Austr* **Larry** *or US* **a clam** más contento(a) que un niño con zapatos nuevos *or* que unas castañuelas; IDIOM *Fam Hum* **he's not a h. camper** *or Br* **chappy** *Esp* tiene un mosqueo de narices, *Méx* está como agua para chocolate, *RP* está más furioso que la miércoles ▸▸ ***the h. couple*** la feliz pareja; ***a h. ending*** *(of book, film, true story)* un final feliz; *Fam* ***the h. event*** el feliz acontecimiento, el nacimiento del niño; ***h. families*** *(card game)* juego *m* de las familias; *Fig* **to play h. families** hacer que se tiene la familia ideal; ***h. hour*** = periodo del día en que las bebidas son más baratas en el bar; ***h. hunting ground*** *Rel* = paraíso de los indios de Norteamérica; *Fig* paraíso *m*

(**b**) *(willing)* encantado(a); **to be h. to do sth** hacer algo con mucho gusto *or* encantado(a); **I'd be only too h. to help** me encantaría poder ayudar, yo ayudaría con mucho gusto *or* encantado; **h. to oblige** no hay de qué

(c) *(fortunate) (coincidence)* feliz; **the h. few** los pocos afortunados; **in happier times** en otros tiempos mejores; **in happier circumstances** en mejores circunstancias

(d) *(appropriate) (choice, phrase)* afortunado(a), acertado(a); **it wasn't a h. choice of words** no eligió las palabras más acertadas; **(to strike) a h. medium** (llegar a) un satisfactorio término medio

(e) *Fam (drunk)* alegre, achispado(a)

happy-clappy ['hæpɪ'klæpɪ] *Br Fam* **1** *n* = evangélico de los que cantan y dan palmas con gran fervor

2 *adj* = de los evangélicos que cantan y dan palmas con gran fervor

happy-go-lucky ['hæpɪgəʊ'lʌkɪ] *adj* despreocupado(a)

Hapsburg, Habsburg ['hæpsbɜːg] *n* **the Hapsburgs** *(in general)* los Habsburgo; *(Spanish royal house)* los Austrias, la casa de Austria

hara-kiri [hærə'kɪrɪ] *n also Fig* haraquiri *m*; **to commit h.** hacerse el haraquiri

harangue [hə'ræŋ] **1** *n* arenga *f*

2 *vt* arengar, soltar una arenga a (**about** sobre); **to h. sb into doing sth** arengar *or* soltar una arenga a alguien para convencerle de algo

harass [hə'ræs, 'hærəs] *vt* **(a)** *(pester)* acosar, hostigar; **he was harassing me for money** me perseguía para pedirme dinero; **to h. sb into doing sth** acosar a alguien para que haga algo; **to sexually h. sb** acosar sexualmente a alguien **(b)** *(attack)* asediar

harassed [hə'ræst, 'hærəst] *adj* acelerado(a)

harassment [hə'ræsmənt, 'hærəsmənt] *n* acoso *m*; **police h.** acoso por parte de la policía; **sexual h.** acoso sexual

harbinger ['hɑːbɪndʒə(r)] *n Literary* heraldo *m*, precursor *m*; **the announcement was viewed as a h. of doom** recibieron el anuncio como un mal presagio

harbour, *US* **harbor** ['hɑːbə(r)] **1** *n* puerto *m* ►► ***h. dues*** derechos *mpl* portuarios *or* de puerto; ***h. master*** capitán(ana) *m,f* de puerto

2 *vt* **(a)** *(fugitive)* acoger, proteger **(b)** *(contain) (dirt, germs)* albergar, contener **(c)** *(hope, suspicion)* albergar; **to h. a grudge against sb** guardar rencor a alguien

HARD [hɑːd] **1** *adj* **(a)** *(substance)* duro(a); **to become h.** endurecerse; **as h. as iron** *or* **stone** *or* **a rock** (duro) como una piedra ►► ***h. cash*** dinero *m* contante y sonante; **in h. cash** en metálico; ***h. core*** *(of supporters, movement)* núcleo *m* duro; ***h. court*** *(for tennis)* pista *f* de cemento; ***h. currency*** divisa *f* fuerte; *US* ***h. goods*** bienes *mpl* de consumo duraderos; ***h. hat*** casco *m*; *US Fam (worker)* albañil *mf*, obrero(a) *m,f* de la construcción; *US Fam (reactionary)* retrógrado(a) *m,f*; ***h. lenses*** *Esp* lentillas *fpl* duras, *Am* lentes *mpl* de contacto duros; *Anat* ***h. palate*** paladar *m* (duro); *Br Aut* ***h. shoulder*** *Esp* arcén *m*, *Méx* acotamiento *m*, *RP* banquina *f*, *Ven* hombrillo *m*

(b) *(fact, evidence)* concreto(a), real; **h. science** ciencia (pura)

(c) *(difficult)* difícil; **it's h. to read** es difícil de leer; **it's h. to say...** no es fácil decir...; **to be h. to come by** ser difícil de conseguir; **to be h. to please** ser muy exigente; **I find it h. to believe that...** me cuesta creer que...; **it's h. to beat** *(value for money)* es difícil de superar; **it's h. to beat a good cigar** hay pocas cosas como un buen puro, no hay nada como un buen puro; **the book/job is h. going** es un libro/trabajo difícil *or* duro; **why do you always have to do things the h. way?** ¿por qué tienes que hacerlo todo tan difícil?; **to learn the h. way** aprender por las malas; **h. of hearing** duro(a) de oído

(d) *(harsh, tough) (person, conditions, life)* duro(a); **a h. frost** una helada muy fuerte; **a h. winter** un invierno muy duro; *Fam* **a h. case** *(man)* un tipo duro; *(woman)* una tipa dura; *Fam* **a h. man** un hombre duro; *Fam* **a h. nut** *(person)* un desgraciado, *Esp* un macarra; **to be h. on sb** ser (muy) duro(a) con alguien; **this type of work is h. on the eyes** este tipo de trabajo cansa la vista *or* los ojos; **it was h. on them losing both parents** fue muy duro para ellos perder a sus padres; **to give sb a h. time** hacérselo pasar mal a alguien; **he's been having a h. time of it recently** está pasando por una mala racha; **I had a h. time convincing them** me costó mucho convencerlos; **to fall on h. times** pasar apuros; *Fam* **no h. feelings?** ¿hacemos las paces?; **to take a h. line on sth** ponerse duro(a) con (respecto a) algo; *Fam* **h. luck!, h. cheese!,** *Br* **h. lines!** ¡mala pata *or* suerte!; IDIOM **to be as h. as nails** *(unfeeling)* ser insensible, *Esp* ser un hueso, *RP* ser de terror; *(tough)* ser duro(a) de pelar

(e) *(forceful)* **to give sth a h. kick/push** darle una buena patada/un buen empujón a algo ►► *Com* ***h. sell*** venta *f* agresiva; *Fig* **to give sth the h. sell** montar una campaña para vender algo

(f) *(intense) (work, climb, run)* duro(a); **I've had a h. day** he tenido un día muy duro; **to be a h. worker** ser muy trabajador(ora); **we need to take a long h. look at our strategy** tenemos que examinar con ojo muy crítico nuestra estrategia; **she's h. work** *(difficult to get on with)* cuesta tratar con ella; *(difficult to make conversation with)* cuesta hablar con ella; **you're making h. work of that job** te estás complicando demasiado la vida para hacer ese trabajo ►► ***h. drinker*** alcohólico(a) *m,f*; *Law* ***h. labour*** trabajos *mpl* forzados

(g) *(extreme) Pol* **h. left/right** izquierda/derecha radical

(h) *(strong, powerful)* ***h. drink*** bebida *f* fuerte; ***h. drugs*** drogas *fpl* duras; *US* ***h. liquor*** bebida *f* fuerte; *Fam* ***h. porn*** porno *m* duro; *Mus* ***h. rock*** rock *m* duro; *Fam* ***the h. stuff*** *(spirits)* el alcohol, las bebidas fuertes

(i) *Comptr* ***h. copy*** copia *f* impresa; ***h. disk*** disco *m* duro; ***h. drive*** unidad *f* de disco duro; ***h. return*** retorno *m* manual; ***h. space*** espacio *m* indivisible

(j) *(water)* duro(a)

(k) *Gram* fuerte

2 *adv* **(a)** *(work)* duro, duramente; *(think, consider)* detenidamente; *(push, hit)* fuerte; *(laugh, cry)* ruidosamente, *Am* fuerte; **I work h. and play h.** yo trabajo duro y vivo la vida al máximo; **to be h. at work** estar muy metido(a) en el trabajo; **we have been h. hit by the cutbacks** nos han afectado mucho los recortes; **I'd be h. pushed** *or* **put** *or* **pressed to finish any earlier** me va a ser muy difícil terminar antes; **to feel h. done by** sentirse injustamente tratado(a); **to listen h.** escuchar bien; **to look h. at sb** mirar fijamente a alguien; **it's raining h.** está lloviendo mucho; **to take sth h.** tomarse algo (a) mal; **to try h.** esforzarse

(b) *(sharply)* **turn h. left/right** gira *or* dobla *or* tuerce totalmente a la izquierda/derecha; *Naut* **h. a port!** ¡todo a babor!

(c) *(solid)* **the ground was frozen h.** se había congelado la tierra; **the ice-cream's frozen h.** el helado está hecho un bloque de hielo *or* una piedra

(d) *(close)* **h. by** muy cerca; **h. by sth** muy cerca de algo; **to follow h. upon** *or* **behind sb** seguir a alguien muy de cerca

3 hard up *adj Fam* **to be h. up** estar en apuros *or Am* problemas; **I'm a bit h. up for cash** ando mal de dinero

---

hard-and-fast ['hɑːdən'fɑːst] *adj* **there are no h. rules** no hay reglas fijas

hard-ass ['hɑːdæs] *n US very Fam (person)* hueso *m* duro de roer

hard-assed ['hɑːdæst] *adj US very Fam* cabrón(ona), *Esp* borde, *RP* de terror

hardback ['hɑːdbæk], **hardcover** ['hɑːdkʌvə(r)] **1** *n (book)* edición *f* de pasta dura; **available in h.** disponible en (edición de) pasta dura

2 *adj* de pasta dura

hardball ['hɑːdbɔːl] *n US (baseball)* béisbol *m*; IDIOM **to play h. (with sb)** ponerse duro(a) (con alguien), adoptar una línea dura (con alguien)

hard-bitten ['hɑːd'bɪtən] *adj* curtido(a)

hardboard ['hɑːdbɔːd] *n* cartón *m* madera

hard-boiled [hɑːd'bɔɪld] *adj* **(a)** *(egg)* duro(a), cocido(a) **(b)** *(person) (tough)* duro(a), curtido(a)

hardcore ['hɑːdkɔː(r)] **1** *n* **(a)** *Constr* balasto *m*, capa *f or* lecho *m* de grava **(b)** *Mus* hard core *m*

2 *adj* **(a)** *(support)* incondicional, acérrimo(a) **(b)** ***h. porn(ography)*** porno *m* duro

hardcover = **hardback**

hard-drinking ['hɑːd'drɪŋkɪŋ] *adj* muy bebedor(ora)

hard-earned [hɑːd'ɜːnd] *adj (money, reputation)* ganado(a) con mucho esfuerzo; *(victory, holiday, reward)* merecido(a)

harden ['hɑːdən] **1** *vt* **(a)** *(substance)* endurecer; *(steel, glass)* templar; *(skin)* curtir **(b)** *(person) (physically, emotionally)* endurecer; **to h. oneself to sth** insensibilizarse a algo; **to h. one's heart** endurecerse; **the bombing only hardened their resolve** el bombardeo reforzó aún más si cabe su determinación

2 *vi* **(a)** *(snow, concrete, mortar, clay)* endurecerse; *(skin)* curtirse; *(steel)* templarse **(b)** *(person, attitude)* endurecerse **(c)** *Med (arteries)* endurecerse **(d)** *Fin (prices, market)* consolidarse, estabilizarse

► **harden off** *vt sep (plant)* aclimatar

hardened ['hɑːdənd] *adj* **(a)** *(emotionally)* **to become h. to sth** hacerse *or* acostumbrarse a algo **(b)** *(steel)* endurecido(a), templado(a) **(c)** *(unrepentant) (drinker)* empedernido(a); *(sinner)* impenitente; **a h. criminal** un delincuente habitual

hardener ['hɑːdnə(r)] *n (for glue, fingernails)* endurecedor *m*

hardening ['hɑːdənɪŋ] *n* **(a)** *(of substance)* endurecimiento *m*; *(of steel, glass)* temple *m* **(b)** *(of person, attitude)* endurecimiento *m* **(c)** ***h. of the arteries*** arteriosclerosis *f inv* **(d)** *Fin (of prices)* consolidación *f*, estabilización *f*

hard-faced ['hɑːd'feɪst] *adj Fam* duro(a), *Esp* borde, *RP* de terror

hard-fought ['hɑːd'fɔːt] *adj (election, contest)* (muy) reñido(a), (muy) disputado(a)

hard-hat ['hɑːd'hæt] *adj US Fam (attitude)* retrógrado(a)

hard-headed ['hɑːd'hedɪd] *adj* (**a**) *(tough, shrewd) (person, decision)* pragmático(a); *(realism)* a ultranza (**b**) *US (stubborn) (person, attitude)* tozudo(a), testarudo(a)

hard-hearted ['hɑːd'hɑːtɪd] *adj* duro(a), insensible

hard-hit [hɑːd'hɪt] *adj* castigado(a), seriamente afectado(a)

hard-hitting [hɑːd'hɪtɪŋ] *adj (criticism, report)* contundente

hardiness ['hɑːdɪnɪs] *n* fortaleza *f*, reciedumbre *f*

hard-line ['hɑːdlaɪn] *adj (policy, doctrine)* inflexible, intransigente; *(politician)* intransigente, de línea dura

hardliner [hɑːd'laɪnə(r)] *n (politician, activist)* intransigente *mf*, partidario(a) *m,f* de la línea dura

hardly ['hɑːdlɪ] *adv* (**a**) *(scarcely)* apenas; **he can h. read** apenas sabe leer; **there are h. any left** no queda apenas ninguno(a); **I could h. hear myself think** no había quien oyera nada; **you can h. move in here for furniture** aquí hay tantos muebles que uno apenas puede moverse *or* que uno no puede ni moverse; **h. anyone/anything** casi nadie/nada; **h. ever** casi nunca; **I h. ever see you these days** últimamente no te veo casi nunca, últimamente apenas te veo; **I can h. believe it** me cuesta creerlo; **I can h. wait till the holidays!** tengo unas ganas enormes de que lleguen las vacaciones; *Ironic* **a new Woody Allen movie? I can h. wait!** ¿otra de Woody Allen? ¡qué ganas de verla!; **I need h. say that...** ni que decir tiene que...; **h. had we begun when...** no habíamos hecho más que empezar cuando...; **h. a week goes by without a letter from her** no hay semana que no mande una carta

(**b**) *(not at all)* **she's h. likely to agree** raro sería que dijera que sí; **I could h. have refused** no podía negarme; **it's h. surprising** no tiene nada de extraño, no es en absoluto de extrañar; **it's h. MY fault!** ¡desde luego yo no tengo la culpa!; **this is h. the time to ask him** éste no es momento para preguntárselo; **did she invite you to her party? – h.!** ¿te invitó a su fiesta? – ¡qué va!

hardness ['hɑːdnɪs] *n* (**a**) *(of substance)* dureza *f* (**b**) *(of problem)* dificultad *f* (**c**) *(of person) (severity)* dureza *f*; **h. of heart** dureza, insensibilidad (**d**) **h. of hearing** sordera *(en mayor o menor grado)*, discapacidad auditiva

hard-nosed ['hɑːdnəʊzd] *adj Fam* duro(a), contundente

hard-on ['hɑːdɒn] *n Vulg* (**a**) *(erection)* **to have a h.** *Esp* estar empalmado, *Am* tenerla parada; **he got a h.** se le puso dura, *Esp* se empalmó, *Am* se le paró (**b**) *US* **to have a h. for sth/sb** *(be enthusiastic about)* estar (uno) que no mea por algo/alguien, estar loquito(a) con algo/alguien; *(dislike)* tenerla tomada con algo/alguien

hard-pressed [hɑːd'prest], **hard-pushed** [hɑːd'pʊʃt] *adj* **to be h. to do sth** tenerlo difícil para hacer algo; **to be h. for time/money** estar (muy) apurado(a) de tiempo/dinero

hard-shell(ed) ['hɑːdʃel(d)] *adj* (**a**) *(crab)* crustáceo(a) (**b**) *US (fundamentalist)* integrista

hardship ['hɑːdʃɪp] *n (suffering)* sufrimiento *m*, penalidades *fpl*; *(deprivation)* privación *f*; **to suffer** *or* **undergo great h.** pasar muchas penalidades *or* privaciones; **the hardships of life at sea** la dureza *or* las penalidades de la vida en alta mar; **to live in h.** vivir en la miseria; **that would be no great h.** eso no supondría un tremendo sacrificio ▸▸ ***h. fund*** = fondo de solidaridad para ayudar en casos de necesidad

hardtack ['hɑːdtæk] *n Hist* galleta *f*

hardtop ['hɑːdtɒp] *n (car)* automóvil *m* no descapotable

hardware ['hɑːdweə(r)] *n* (**a**) *(tools)* ferretería *f*; **(military) h.** *(weapons)* armamento *m* ▸▸ *US* ***h. store*** ferretería *f* (**b**) *Fam (guns)* armas *fpl* (**c**) *Comptr* hardware *m*, soporte *m* físico ▸▸ ***h. problem*** problema *m* de hardware

hard-wearing [hɑːd'weərɪŋ] *adj* resistente

hard-wired ['hɑːd'waɪəd] *adj Comptr* integrado(a)

hard-won ['hɑːd'wʌn] *adj* ganado(a) a pulso

hardwood ['hɑːdwʊd] *n* (**a**) *(timber)* madera *f* noble (**b**) *(tree)* árbol *m* caducifolio de madera dura

hard-working ['hɑːd'wɜːkɪŋ] *adj* trabajador(ora)

hardy ['hɑːdɪ] *adj* (**a**) *(strong) (person)* recio(a); *(plant)* resistente (al frío) ▸▸ ***h. annual*** planta *f* anual (de jardín); ***h. perennial*** planta *f* resistente a las heladas; *Fig (conversation topic)* eterna cuestión *f*, tema *m* clásico (**b**) *(intrepid) (explorer, pioneer)* esforzado(a), valeroso(a)

hardy har har ['hɑːdɪ'hɑː'hɑː] *exclam Fam* ¡me parto de risa!, ¡no sé si reír o echar a llorar!

hare [heə(r)] **1** *n* (**a**) *(animal)* liebre *f* ▸▸ ***h. coursing*** caza *f* de liebres con perros (**b**) IDIOMS *Br* **to raise** *or* **start a h.** levantar la liebre, sacar un tema; **to run with the hares and hunt with the hounds** nadar entre dos aguas

2 *vi Br* **to h. across/down/out** cruzar/bajar/salir disparado(a); **to h. off** salir disparado(a)

harebell ['heəbel] *n* campanilla *f*

harebrained ['heəbreɪnd] *adj* disparatado(a)

harelip ['heəlɪp] *n* labio *m* leporino

harem [hɑː'riːm] *n* harén *m*

haricot ['hærɪkəʊ] *n* **h. (bean)** alubia *f*, *Esp* judía *f* blanca, *Andes, CAm, Carib, Méx* frijol *m* blanco, *Andes, RP* poroto *m* blanco

hark [hɑːk] *exclam* (**a**) *Literary* ¡escucha!, ¡atención! (**b**) *Br Fam* **h. at him!** ¿has oído lo que dice?

▸ **hark back** *vi* **to h. back to sth** recordar algo; **he's always harking back to his youth** siempre está recordando su juventud; **the style harks back to the 1940s** el estilo recuerda a *or* tiene el sabor de los años cuarenta

harken = **hearken**

harlequin ['hɑːləkwɪn] *n* (**a**) *Theat* arlequín *m* (**b**) ***h. duck*** pato *m* harlequín

harlot ['hɑːlət] *n Literary* ramera *f*, meretriz *f*

harm [hɑːm] **1** *n* daño *m*; **to do sb h.** hacer daño a alguien; **adverse publicity will do their cause a great deal of h.** la publicidad adversa perjudicará enormemente su causa; **to do oneself h.** hacerse daño; **it will do more h. than good** hará más mal que bien; **you will come to no h.** no sufrirás ningún daño; **no h. will come of it** no pasará nada; **I see no h. in it** no veo que tenga nada de malo; **where's the h. in that?** ¿qué tiene eso de malo?; **(there's) no h. done** no ha pasado nada, no ha sido nada; **there's no h. in trying** no se pierde nada por intentarlo, por intentarlo que no quede; **they didn't mean any h.** no lo hicieron *or* dijeron con mala intención, no tenían mala intención; **out of h.'s way** en lugar seguro

2 *vt* (**a**) *(person, animal)* hacer daño a; *(crops)* dañar; *(environment)* perjudicar, dañar (**b**) *(reputation, image, quality)* dañar; *(chances, interests, business)* perjudicar

harmful ['hɑːmfʊl] *adj* (**a**) *(effect)* perjudicial, dañino(a); *(influence)* pernicioso(a), perjudicial (**b**) *(substance)* nocivo(a), perjudicial (**to** para)

harmless ['hɑːmlɪs] *adj* (**a**) *(animal, person)* inofensivo(a); *(substance)* inocuo(a), inofensivo(a); **he's h.** no hace daño a nadie, es inofensivo (**b**) *(fun, amusement, comment)* inocente, sin malicia

harmlessly ['hɑːmlɪslɪ] *adv* (**a**) *(not harming)* sin causar daños (**b**) *(innocently)* sin malicia

harmlessness ['hɑːmlɪsnɪs] *n* (**a**) *(of animal, person)* carácter *m* inofensivo; *(of substance)* inocuidad *f* (**b**) *(innocence)* inocencia *f*, ausencia *f* de malicia

harmonic [hɑː'mɒnɪk] **1** *n* (**a**) *Phys* armónico *m* (**b**) *Mus* armónico *m*

2 *adj* (**a**) *Phys & Math* armónico(a) ▸▸ ***h. motion*** movimiento *m* armónico, oscilación *f* armónica; ***h. progression*** progresión *f* armónica (**b**) *Mus* armónico(a)

harmonica [hɑː'mɒnɪkə] *n* armónica *f*

harmonics [hɑː'mɒnɪks] *n* armonía *f*

harmonious [hɑː'məʊnɪəs] *adj* armonioso(a)

harmoniously [hɑː'məʊnɪəslɪ] *adv (to live)* en armonía; *(to blend)* armoniosamente

harmonium [hɑː'məʊnɪəm] *n* armonio *m*

harmonization [hɑːmənaɪ'zeɪʃən] *n* (**a**) *Mus* armonización *f* (**b**) *(of norms, practices, standards)* armonización *f*

harmonize ['hɑːmənaɪz] **1** *vt* (**a**) *Mus* armonizar, dar armonía a (**b**) *(blend together)* armonizar

2 *vi* (**a**) *Mus* cantar en armonía (**b**) *(blend together)* armonizar, estar en armonía

harmony ['hɑːmənɪ] *n* (**a**) *Mus* armonía *f*; **to sing in h.** cantar en armonía; **a three-part h.** una armonía para tres voces (**b**) *(agreement) (of colours)* armonía *f*; *(of temperaments, people, ideas)* armonía *f*; **in h. with** en armonía con; **to live in h. (with)** vivir en armonía *or* en paz (con)

harness ['hɑːnɪs] **1** *n* (**a**) *(of horse)* arreos *mpl* (**b**) *(for safety, of parachute)* arnés *m* (**c**) IDIOMS **to work in h. with sb** trabajar hombro con hombro con alguien; **to be back in h.** volver al tajo; **to die in h.** morir antes de jubilarse

2 *vt* (**a**) *(horse)* arrear, aparejar; **the pony was harnessed to the cart** el poni iba enganchado al carro (**b**) *(resources, energy)* emplear, hacer uso de

harp [hɑːp] *n* arpa *f*

▸**harp on** 1 *vt insep* dar vueltas a, insistir sobre

2 *vi Fam* **to h. on (at sb) about sth** dar la lata (a alguien) con algo, *RP* hinchar (a alguien) con algo; **don't keep harping on!** ¡deja ya de darle vueltas!, ¡deja ya de dar la lata con el tema!

harpist ['hɑːpɪst] *n* arpista *mf*

harpoon [hɑː'puːn] 1 *n* arpón *m*

2 *vt* arponear

harpsichord ['hɑːpsɪkɔːd] *n* clave *m*, clavicémbalo *m*

harpy ['hɑːpɪ] *n* **(a)** *Mythol* arpía *f* **(b)** *(woman)* arpía *f* **(c)** ***h. eagle*** harpía *f*

harridan ['hærɪdən] *n Literary* vieja *f* gruñona, arpía *f*

harrier ['hærɪə(r)] *n* **(a)** *Sport (runner)* corredor(ora) *m,f* de cross **(b)** *(hunting dog)* lebrel *m* **(c)** *(bird)* aguilucho *m*

Harris ['hærɪs] *n* **(a)** *Pol* ***H. poll*** sondeo *m* de opinión *(llevado a cabo por la empresa Harris)* **(b)** ***H. Tweed*** ® tweed *m* de la isla de Harris

harrow ['hærəʊ] 1 *n (farm equipment)* grada *f*

2 *vt* **(a)** *Agr* gradar, pasar la grada por **(b)** *(distress) (person)* angustiar

harrowing ['hærəʊɪŋ] *adj (experience, sight)* angustioso(a); **the report makes h. reading** la lectura del informe resulta espeluznante

harry ['hærɪ] *vt* **(a)** *(enemy)* hostigar **(b)** *(pester, harass)* hostigar, agobiar

harsh [hɑːʃ] *adj* **(a)** *(voice, sound)* áspero(a); *(climate, environment)* duro(a), riguroso(a); *(light)* cegador(ora); *(colour)* chillón(ona); *(landscape)* inhóspito(a) **(b)** *(punishment, treatment, sentence, person)* duro(a), severo(a); **to be h. with** *or* **on sb** ser duro(a) *or* severo(a) con alguien; **to use h. words** expresarse en *or* con términos muy duros

harshly ['hɑːʃlɪ] *adv (to punish, treat, judge)* con dureza *or* severidad; **don't speak so h. of him** no hables de él con tanta severidad, no seas tan duro *or* severo al hablar de él

harshness ['hɑːʃnɪs] *n* **(a)** *(of voice, sound)* aspereza *f*; *(of climate, environment)* dureza *f*, rigurosidad *f*; *(of light)* aspereza *f*, crudeza *f*; *(of colour)* tono *m* chillón; *(of landscape)* carácter *m* inhóspito **(b)** *(of punishment, treatment, sentence, person)* dureza *f*, severidad *f*

hart [hɑːt] *n* venado *m*, ciervo *m*

harum-scarum ['heərəm'skeərəm] *Fam* 1 *adj* alocado(a)

2 *adv* alocadamente

harvest ['hɑːvɪst] 1 *n* **(a)** *(gathering) (of cereal, crops)* cosecha *f*, siega *f*; *(of fruit, vegetables)* cosecha *f*, recolección *f*; *(of grapes)* vendimia *f*; **at h. (time)** en la cosecha, en época de cosecha ▸▸ *Br* ***h. festival*** = fiesta con que se celebra la recogida de la cosecha; ***h. moon*** luna *f* llena del (equinoccio de) otoño; ***h. mouse*** ratón *m* de las mieses

(b) *(yield) (of cereal, fruit, vegetables, grapes)* cosecha *f*; **a good/poor h.** una buena/mala cosecha

(c) *Fig (from experience, research)* resultados *mpl*, fruto *m*; **it yielded a rich h. of information** produjo un amplio caudal de información

2 *vt* **(a)** *(cereal, crops)* cosechar, segar; *(fruit, vegetables)* cosechar, recolectar; *(grapes)* vendimiar **(b)** *Med* **to h. organs** = extraer órganos de un animal o una persona para su transplante o investigación

3 *vi* cosechar, hacer la cosecha

harvester ['hɑːvɪstə(r)] *n* **(a)** *(machine)* cosechadora *f* **(b)** *(person) (of cereals)* segador(ora) *m,f*; *(of fruit)* recolector(ora) *m,f*

harvestman ['hɑːvɪstmən] *n (insect)* segador *m*, falangio *m*

has *3rd person singular of* **have**

has-been ['hæzbiːn] *n Fam Pej* vieja gloria *f*

hash [hæʃ] 1 *n* **(a)** *(stew)* guiso *m* de carne con *Esp* patatas *or Am* papas, *Andes, Méx* ahogado *m* de carne con papas; IDIOM **to fix** *or* **settle sb's h.** poner a alguien en su sitio ▸▸ *US* ***h. browns*** = fritura de *Esp* patata *or Am* papa y cebolla; *US Fam* ***h. house*** ≃ casa *f* de comidas; *US Fam* ***h. slinger*** cocinero(a) *m,f* de poca monta *or* de tres al cuarto

(b) *Fam (mess)* **to make a h. of sth** pifiarla con algo, *Esp* hacer algo fatal *or* de pena; **he certainly made a h. of putting that shelf up!** ¡la pifió pero bien *or* menuda chapuza hizo al poner esa estantería!; **I made a real h. of the interview** la entrevista me salió fatal *or* de pena, la pifié en la entrevista

(c) *(symbol)* ***h. mark*** *Comptr & Typ* = el símbolo '#'; *(on telephone)* almohadilla *f*, numeral *m*; *(in music)* sostenido *m*

(d) *US* ***h. mark*** *(on uniform)* = galón del uniforme militar, que indica 3 ó 4 años de servicio

(e) *Fam (hashish)* chocolate *m*, *Esp* costo *m* ▸▸ *US* ***h. head*** porrero(a) *m,f*

2 *vt Culin* trocear

▸**hash out, hash over** *vt sep US Fam (discuss)* hablar largo y tendido de

▸**hash up** *vt sep Br Fam (mess up)* echar a perder; **I'm afraid I completely hashed up the interview** me temo que eché a perder la entrevista *or* que la pifié en la entrevista *or Esp* que la entrevista me salió fatal

hashish ['hæʃiːʃ] *n* hachís *m*

Hasidic [hæ'sɪdɪk] *adj Rel* hasídico(a)

haslet ['hæzlɪt] *n* = fiambre de asaduras de cerdo, ≃ chicharrones *mpl*

hasn't ['hæznt] = **has not**

hasp [hɑːsp] *n (for door)* pestillo *m*; *(for box, book)* aldabilla *f*, cierre *m*

hassle ['hæsəl] *Fam* 1 *n* **(a)** *(trouble, inconvenience)* lío *m*, *Esp* follón *m*; **it's too much h.** es demasiado lío; **it's a real h. buying a house** comprarse una casa es un lío tremendo; **to give sb h.** dar la lata a alguien; **no h.** no es ninguna molestia, no hay problema **(b)** *(quarrel)* trifulca *f*, pelotera *f*

2 *vt (annoy, nag)* dar la lata a; **don't h. me about it** no me des la lata con eso; **he keeps hassling me for money** anda siempre detrás de mí para que le deje dinero; **Yvonne's always hassling him to stop smoking** Yvonne no para de darle la lata para que deje de fumar; **to h. sb into doing sth** dar la lata a alguien para que haga algo

hassle-free ['hæsəl'friː] *adj Fam* sin líos, *Esp* sin follones, *Am* sin relajo, *Méx* sin argüende

hassock ['hæsək] *n* **(a)** *(cushion in church)* cojín *m*, almohadón *m (para arrodillarse)* **(b)** *(tuft of grass)* mata *f* de hierba

hast [hæst] *Literary & Rel 2nd pers singular of* **have**

haste [heɪst] *n* prisa *f*, *Am* apuro *m*; **in h.** a toda prisa, *Am* con apuro; **in my h., I forgot my hat** con las prisas olvidé el sombrero; **in my h. to get away I forgot my passport** tenía tanta prisa por irme que olvidé el pasaporte; **to make h.** apresurarse, *Am* apurarse; PROV **more h. less speed** vísteme despacio que tengo prisa

hasten ['heɪsən] 1 *vt* **(a)** *(speed up) (process, decline)* acelerar; *(event, death)* precipitar, adelantar **(b)** *(urge on) (person)* meter prisa a, apresurar, *Am* apurar; **we were hastened along a corridor** nos condujeron a toda prisa por un pasillo **(c)** *(say quickly)* **she hastened to assure us that all would be well** se apresuró a garantizarnos que todo iría bien; **it wasn't me, I h. to add** que conste que no fui yo

2 *vi* apresurarse, *Am* apurarse; **to h. away** alejarse a toda prisa; **to h. back** volver a toda prisa

hastily ['heɪstɪlɪ] *adv* **(a)** *(quickly)* deprisa, apresuradamente **(b)** *(rashly)* precipitadamente, apresuradamente; **to judge sth h.** juzgar algo a la ligera

hastiness ['heɪstɪnɪs] *n* **(a)** *(speed)* celeridad *f*; **in his h. to leave he knocked over a table** tenía tanta prisa por marcharse que tiró una mesa **(b)** *(rashness)* precipitación *f*

hasty ['heɪstɪ] *adj* **(a)** *(quick, hurried)* apresurado(a), rápido(a); **I sent him a h. note** le mandé una nota rápida *or* escrita a toda prisa; **to make a h. exit** marcharse apresuradamente *or* a toda prisa

(b) *(rash)* precipitado(a); **a h. decision** una decisión precipitada; **don't be too h.** no te precipites; **to jump to a h. conclusion** sacar conclusiones apresuradas

(c) *(angry, irritated)* **h. words** palabras fuera de tono

(d) *Culin* ***h. pudding*** *Br* = budín hecho a base de leche endulzada y espesada con sémola o tapioca; *US* = papilla a base harina de maíz y melaza

hat [hæt] *n* **(a)** *(headgear)* sombrero *m*; *also Fig* **to take one's h. off to sb** descubrirse ante alguien, quitarse el sombrero ante alguien ▸▸ *US* ***h. tree*** perchero *m*; ***h. trick*** *(of goals)* tres goles *mpl (en el mismo partido)*; *(of victories)* tres victorias *fpl* consecutivas

(b) *Fam (role)* **I'm wearing three different hats at the moment** ahora estoy haciendo tres cosas distintas; **I'm saying that with my lawyer's h. on** digo esto como abogado que soy *or* desde mi posición de abogado

(c) IDIOMS **to pass the h. round** *(collect money)* pasar la gorra; **to throw one's h. in the ring** *(enter contest)* echarse al ruedo; **to go h. in hand to sb** ir a mendigarle a alguien; *Fam* **to keep sth under one's h.** no decir ni media de algo a nadie; *Fam* **to talk through one's h.** no decir más que bobadas *or* tonterías

hatband ['hætbænd] *n* cinta *f* del sombrero

hatbox ['hætbɒks] *n* sombrerera *f*

hatch[1] [hætʃ] *n* **(a)** *(in wall, floor)* trampilla *f* **(b)** *(in aircraft)* portezuela *f*; *(in spaceship)* escotilla *f*, compuerta *f* **(c)** *Naut* escotilla *f* **(d)** **(serving) h.** ventanilla *f* **(e)** *Fam* **down the h.!** ¡salud!

hatch[2] 1 *vt* **(a)** *(eggs)* incubar; *(chickens)* empollar **(b)** *(scheme, plan)* tramar, urdir; **to h. (up) a plot** tramar *or* urdir un plan

2 *vi* **the egg** *or* **chicken hatched (out)** el pollo salió del cascarón

hatch[3] *vt (drawing)* sombrear

hatchback ['hætʃbæk] *n* **(a)** *(car) (3-door)* tres puertas *m inv*; *(5-door)* cinco puertas *m inv* **(b)** *(door)* puerta *f* trasera, portón *m* (trasero)

hatcheck ['hættʃek] *adj US* **h. clerk/girl** empleado(a)/chica del guardarropa

hatchery ['hætʃərɪ] *n* criadero *m*

hatchet ['hætʃɪt] *n* hacha *f (pequeña)*; IDIOM *Fam* **to do a h. job on sth/sb** *(critic, reviewer)* ensañarse con algo/alguien ►► *Fam* ***h. man*** *(person who does sb's dirty work)* = encargado del trabajo sucio; *(killer)* asesino *m* a sueldo, sicario *m*

hatchet-faced ['hætʃɪtfeɪst] *adj* de rostro enjuto y anguloso

hatching ['hætʃɪŋ] *n (in drawing)* sombreado *m*

hatchway ['hætʃweɪ] *n* **(a)** *(in wall, floor)* trampilla *f* **(b)** *(in aircraft)* portezuela *f*; *(in spaceship)* escotilla *f*, compuerta *f* **(c)** *Naut* escotilla *f*

hate [heɪt] **1** *n* **(a)** *(hatred)* odio *m* ►► *US* ***h. crime*** = delito de carácter xenófobo, racista, antihomosexual, etc.; ***h. mail*** = cartas que contienen amenazas o fuertes críticas; *US Fam* ***h. sheet*** = publicación de carácter xenófobo, racista, antihomosexual, etc. **(b)** *(thing detested)* fobia *f*; **one of my pet hates is...** una de las cosas que más odio es...

2 *vt* **(a)** *(detest)* odiar, detestar; **I h. her for what she has done** la odio *or* detesto por lo que ha hecho; **I h. getting up early** odio *or* detesto tener que madrugar, me sienta muy mal tener que madrugar; **he hates to be contradicted** no soporta que lo contradigan; **she hates having her hair washed** no le gusta nada *or* no soporta que le laven la cabeza; **I h. it when you do that** detesto *or* me enferma que hagas eso; **I h. it when he's in a bad mood** cuando está de mal humor, no lo soporto; **to h. oneself** odiarse a sí mismo(a); **I h. myself for letting them down** me sabe muy mal *or* siento en el alma haberles fallado

(b) *(not want)* **I h. to admit it but I think he's right** me cuesta admitirlo, pero creo que tiene razón; **I'd h. to see anything go wrong** no me haría ninguna gracia que fallara algo; **I h. to think what might have happened otherwise** no quiero ni pensar qué hubiera ocurrido de no ser así; **I h. to bother you, but could I use your phone?** perdone la molestia *or* perdone que lo moleste, pero ¿podría usar su teléfono?; *Fam* **I h. to tell you, but I think you've missed your train** lo siento mucho, pero me parece que has perdido el tren

hated ['heɪtɪd] *adj* odiado(a)

hateful ['heɪtfʊl] *adj* odioso(a), detestable; **the very idea is h. to him** la sola idea le resulta odiosa *or* repugnante

hater ['heɪtə(r)] *n* enemigo(a) *m,f*

hath [hæθ] *Literary or Rel 3rd pers singular of* **have**

hatmaker ['hætmeɪkə(r)] *n* sombrerero(a) *m,f*

hatpin ['hætpɪn] *n* alfiler *m* (de sombrero)

hatred ['heɪtrɪd] *n* odio *m*; **he had an intense h. of the police** odiaba a la policía, le tenía odio a la policía; **to feel h. for sb** sentir odio por *or* hacia alguien

hatstand ['hætstænd] *n* perchero *m*

hatter ['hætə(r)] *n* sombrerero(a) *m,f*

haughtily ['hɔːtɪlɪ] *adv* con altanería

haughtiness ['hɔːtɪnɪs] *n* altanería *f*

haughty ['hɔːtɪ] *adj* altanero(a)

haul [hɔːl] **1** *n* **(a)** *(money, of stolen goods)* botín *m*; *(of drugs)* alijo *m*; *(fish caught)* captura *f*

(b) *(pull)* tirón *m*, *Andes, CAm, Carib, Méx* jalón *m*; **to give a h. on a rope** dar un tirón *or Andes, CAm, Carib, Méx* jalón a una cuerda, tirar *or Andes, CAm, Carib, Méx* jalar de una cuerda

(c) **to be a long h.: it was a long h. from Austin to Detroit** de Austin a Detroit había un largo trecho *or* camino *or* trayecto; **training to be a doctor is a long h.** lleva mucho tiempo formarse para ser médico

2 *vt* **(a)** *(pull)* arrastrar; **they hauled the boat out of the water** sacaron la barca del agua arrastrándola; **to h. up/down a flag/sail** izar/arriar una bandera/vela

(b) *Fam (bring by force)* **he was hauled in for questioning** se lo llevaron para interrogarlo; **they were hauled in front of** *or* **before a judge** les hicieron comparecer ante un juez

(c) *(move with effort)* **he hauled himself into a sitting position** se incorporó (hasta quedar sentado); **he hauled himself out of bed** con gran esfuerzo salió de la cama

(d) IDIOMS *US Vulg* **to h. ass** *Esp* ir a toda hostia, *Méx* ir hecho(a) la raya, *RP* ir a los santos pedos; *Fam* **to h. sb over the coals** *(reprimand)* echar una reprimenda *or Esp* una bronca a alguien, dar *Méx* una jalada *or RP* un rezongo a alguien

(e) *(transport)* transportar

3 *vi (pull)* **to h. on sth** tirar de algo, *Andes, CAm, Carib, Méx* jalar de algo

► **haul off 1** *vt sep (take away)* llevar(se); **he was hauled off to prison** lo metieron en la cárcel

2 *vi US Fam* prepararse, *Esp* atarse *or* apretarse los machos; **she hauled off and slugged him** agarró y le dio un tortazo

► **haul up** *vt sep* llamar al orden a; **she was hauled up before the headmaster** la llevaron al despacho del director; **he was hauled up before the court** tuvo que ir a juicio

haulage ['hɔːlɪdʒ] *n* **(a)** *(transportation)* transporte *m* (de mercancías) ►► ***h. firm*** empresa *f* de transportes, transportista *m* **(b)** *(costs)* portes *mpl*

haulier ['hɔːlɪə(r)], *US* **hauler** ['hɔːlə(r)] *n* **(a)** *(company)* empresa *f* de transportes, transportista *m* **(b)** *(person)* transportista *mf*

haunch [hɔːntʃ] *n* **(a)** *(of person)* cadera *f*; **to sit** *or* **squat on one's haunches** ponerse en cuclillas **(b)** *(of meat)* pierna *f*

haunt [hɔːnt] **1** *n (favourite place)* lugar *m* predilecto; **it's one of his favourite haunts** es uno de sus lugares predilectos; **we couldn't find her in any of her usual haunts** no la encontramos en los sitios por donde solía parar *or* que solía frecuentar

2 *vt* **(a)** *(of ghost) (house)* aparecerse en; *(person)* aparecerse a **(b)** *(of thought, memory)* asaltar; **he was haunted by the fear that...** le asaltaba el temor de que...; **these problems have returned to h. us** estos problemas vuelven a ser un quebradero de cabeza para nosotros; **she is haunted by her unhappy childhood** vive obsesionada por su infeliz infancia; **his past continues to h. him** el fantasma de su pasado le acompaña *or* persigue a todas partes

(c) *(frequent)* frecuentar

haunted ['hɔːntɪd] *adj* **(a)** *(by ghost)* **they say the castle is h.** dicen que hay fantasmas *or* un fantasma en el castillo **(b)** *(worried)* **he has a h. look** tiene una mirada atormentada

haunting ['hɔːntɪŋ] *adj* fascinante, hechizante

hauntingly ['hɔːntɪŋlɪ] *adv* **h. beautiful** de una belleza fascinante *or* hechizante

haute couture [əʊtkʊ'tʃʊə(r)] *n* alta costura *f*

haute cuisine [əʊtkwɪ'ziːn] *n* alta cocina *f*

hauteur [əʊ'tɜː(r)] *n Formal* altivez *f*, soberbia *f*

Havana [hə'vænə] *n* La Habana ►► ***H. cigar*** (puro *m*) habano *m*

HAVE [hæv] **1** *n* **the haves and the have-nots** los ricos y los pobres

2 *vt* (*3rd person singular* **has** [hæz], *pt & pp* **had** [hæd])

> En el inglés hablado, y en el escrito en estilo coloquial, el verbo auxiliar **have** se contrae de forma que **I have** se transforma en **I've**, **he/she/it has** se transforman en **he's/she's/it's** y **you/we/they have** se transforman en **you've/we've/they've**. Las formas de pasado **I/you/he** *etc* **had** se transforman en **I'd/you'd/he'd** *etc*. Las formas negativas **has not**, **have not** y **had not** se transforman en **hasn't**, **haven't** y **hadn't**

(a) *(possess, own)* tener; **they've got** *or* **they h. a big house** tienen una casa grande; **she hasn't got** *or* **doesn't h. a cat** no tiene gato; **she's got** *or* **she has blue eyes** tiene los ojos azules; **I've got** *or* **I h. something to do** tengo algo que hacer; **we've got** *or* **we h. a choice** tenemos una alternativa; **I don't h. time** no tengo tiempo; **I've got no sympathy for them** no me dan ninguna pena; **he had them in his power** los tenía en su poder; **now I h. the house all to myself** ahora tengo toda la casa para mí solo; **she had her eyes closed** tenía los ojos cerrados; **I haven't got** *or* **don't h. the document with me** no tengo el documento aquí; **what's that got to do with it?** ¿qué tiene que ver eso?; *Fam* **well done, I didn't know you had it in you!** ¡muy bien, no pensé que fueras a ser capaz de hacerlo!

(b) *(suffer from) (disease)* tener; **she's got** *or* **she has measles/AIDS** tiene (el) sarampión/el sida; **I've got** *or* **I h. a bad knee** tengo una rodilla mal

(c) *(take, receive, accept)* **can I h. a beer and a brandy, please?** ¿me daría *or Esp* pone una cerveza y un coñac, (por favor)?; **can I h. some more bread?** ¿puedo comer *or Esp* tomar más pan?; **I'll h. the soup** yo tomaré una sopa; **which one will you h.?** ¿cuál prefieres?; **here, h. my pen** toma mi bolígrafo; **I haven't had any more news** no he tenido más noticias; **we're having friends to stay** tenemos amigos durmiendo *or* quedándose en casa

(d) *(eat)* comer, *Esp* tomar; *(drink)* tomar; **to h. something to eat/drink** comer/beber algo; **what are we having for lunch?** ¿qué vamos a comer *or* almorzar?; **h. some more cheese** come *or Esp* toma más queso; **h. some more wine** toma más vino; **to h. breakfast** desayunar; **to h. dinner** cenar; **to h. lunch** comer, almorzar

(e) *(with noun, to denote activity)* **to h. a bath** darse un baño; **to h. a meeting** tener una reunión; **to h. a nap** echarse una siesta; **to h. sex** tener relaciones sexuales; **to h. a shave** afeitarse; **to h. a swim** darse un baño; **to h. a walk** dar un paseo; **to h. a wash** lavarse

(f) *(give birth to)* tener; **she has had a baby girl** ha tenido una niña

(g) *(experience)* pasar; **to h. an accident** tener *or* sufrir un accidente;

I'm having the operation next week me operan la semana que viene; **I had a pleasant evening** pasé una agradable velada; **to h. a good/bad time** pasarlo bien/mal; **to h. a surprise** llevarse una sorpresa; **we didn't h. any trouble** no tuvimos ningún problema

(h) *(causative)* **I had him do it again** le hice repetirlo; **h. her call me as soon as she knows** que me llame en cuanto lo sepa; **he had them killed** los mandó *or* hizo matar; **I'll h. it ready by Friday** lo tendré listo para el viernes; **he had us in fits of laughter** nos reímos muchísimo con él; **some people would h. you believe she's a saint** algunos te harían creer que es una santa; **I'll h. you know that...!** ¡has de saber que...!, *RP* ¡te diré que...!

(i) *(in passive-type constructions)* **to h. one's hair cut** cortarse el pelo; **I'm having my television repaired** me están arreglando el televisor; **I had my watch stolen** me robaron el reloj; **the house had all its windows blown out** estallaron todas las ventanas de la casa

(j) *(allow)* **I will not h. such conduct!** ¡no toleraré ese comportamiento!; **I won't h. you causing trouble!** ¡no permitiré que crees problemas!; **as luck would h. it...** mira qué casualidad..., mira por dónde...; *Fam* **I asked her for some money, but she wasn't having any of it** le pedí dinero, pero pasó de mí *or RP* no me dio bola

(k) *(be compelled)* **to h. to do sth** tener que hacer algo; **I h.** *or* **I've got to go** me tengo que ir; **do you h. to work?, h. you got to work?** ¿tienes que trabajar?; **it's got** *or* **it has to be done** hay que hacerlo; **I h. to admit that...** he de *or* tengo que admitir que...; **I'm not going unless I h. to** no voy a ir a no ser que me obliguen; **do you h. to keep singing that song?** ¿tienes que cantar esa canción todo el rato?; **that has to be the best wine I've ever had** debe de ser el mejor vino que he tomado nunca

(l) *(grip)* **he had me by the throat** me tenía sujeto *or* agarrado del cuello; *Fam* **you've got** *or* **you h. me there!** *(I don't know)* ¡ahí me has *Esp* pillado *or Am* agarrado *or Méx* cachado!

(m) *(obtain)* **there were no tickets to be had** no quedaban entradas *or Col, Méx* boletos; **can I h. your address?** ¿me puedes dar tu dirección?; **could I h. extension 238?** *(on phone)* ¿me pasa *or Esp* pone con la extensión 238?, *RP* ¿me pasa con el interno 238?; **I h. it on good authority that...** sé por fuentes fidedignas que...

(n) *(assert, state)* **some people would h. it that there's nothing wrong with drugs** para algunas personas las drogas no son malas; **tradition has it that...** según *or* de acuerdo con la tradición...

(o) *Fam (cheat)* **you've been had!** ¡te han timado!, *Méx* ¡te chingaron!, *RP* ¡te embromaron!

(p) *Fam* **I've had it if she finds out!** ¡si se entera, me la cargo *or RP* la quedo!; **this coat has had it** este abrigo está para el arrastre, *RP* este saco ya cumplió; *US* **to h. had it** *(be exhausted)* estar hecho(a) polvo; **I've had it (up to here) with your sarcastic comments!** ¡ya estoy harto *or* hasta aquí de tus comentarios sarcásticos!; *Fam* **she really let him h. it when she found out what he'd done** *(told him off)* le echó una buena reprimenda *or Esp* bronca *or RP* le dio un buen rezongo cuando se enteró de lo que había hecho; *(hit him)* le dio una buena paliza cuando se enteró de lo que había hecho

(q) *very Fam (have sex with) Esp* tirarse a, *Am* cogerse a, *Méx* chingarse a

(r) *Fam (beat up)* **I could h. him** *Esp* a ese le puedo, *Am* a ese le gano

3 *v aux* haber; **I/we/they h. seen it** lo he/hemos/han visto; **you h. seen it** *(singular)* lo has visto; *(plural) Esp* lo habéis visto, *Am* lo vieron; **he/she/it has seen it** lo ha visto; **I h. worked here for three years** llevo *or Am* tengo tres años trabajando aquí; **I would h. left immediately** yo me habría ido *or* marchado inmediatamente; **they had already gone** ya se habían ido *or* marchado; **had I known earlier...** si lo hubiera sabido antes..., de haberlo sabido antes...; **having reached the border, our next problem was how to get across** una vez llegados a la frontera, nuestro siguiente problema fue cómo cruzarla; **you HAVE been working hard!** ¡sí que has trabajado!, *RP* ¡trabajaste como loco!; **he has been in prison before – no he hasn't!** ha estado ya antes en la cárcel – ¡no!; **h. you been to Paris? – yes I h.** ¿has estado en París? – sí; **I've bought a new car – h. you?** me he comprado un coche *or Am* carro *or RP* auto – ¿ah sí?; **you haven't forgotten, have you?** no te habrás olvidado, ¿no? *or* ¿verdad?; **they've split up, haven't they?** han roto, ¿no?, cortaron, ¿no?; **you've gone and told him, haven't you?** ya se lo has tenido que decir, ¿no?; **I've resigned from my job – you haven't (have you)?** he dejado el trabajo – ¿de verdad? *or* ¿en serio?

▸ **have around** *vt sep* **he's a useful person to h. around** conviene tenerlo cerca

▸ **have away** *vt sep Br very Fam (have sex)* **to h. it away (with sb)** echar un polvo *or Cuba* palo (con alguien), *Am* cogerse (a alguien)

▸ **have back** *vt sep* **you shall h. it back tomorrow** te lo devolveré mañana; **will you h. him back?** ¿vas a volver con él?

▸ **have in** *vt sep* (a) *(have supply of)* tener; **do we h. any coffee in?** ¿tenemos café?

(b) *(invite)* **I'm having some friends in for a drink this evening** esta noche vienen unos amigos a casa a tomar una copa; **the boss had him in for a chat** el jefe lo llamó a su despacho para hablar con él

(c) *(workman)* **we had the plumber in to fix the pipes** vino el fontanero *or RP* plomero para arreglar las tuberías

(d) *Fam* **to h. it in for sb** tenerla tomada con alguien

▸ **have off** *vt sep* (a) *(time)* **I had a week off work with a cold** estuve una semana sin ir a trabajar porque tenía un resfriado; **we've got next Monday off** el lunes que viene libramos, tenemos el lunes que viene libre

(b) *Br very Fam (have sex)* **to h. it off (with sb)** echar un polvo *or Cuba* palo (con alguien), *Am* cogerse (a alguien)

▸ **have on** *vt sep* (a) *(wear)* llevar puesto; **they had nothing on** estaban desnudos

(b) *(be carrying)* **I haven't got any money on me** no llevo dinero encima; **do you h. a pen on you?** ¿tienes un bolígrafo?

(c) *(have switched on)* tener encendido(a) *or Am* prendido(a)

(d) *Fam (fool)* **to h. sb on** tomarle el pelo *or Esp, Carib, Méx* vacilar a alguien; **you're having me on!** ¡me estás tomando el pelo *or Esp, Carib, Méx* vacilando!

(e) *(have arranged)* **he has a lot on this week** esta semana tiene mucho que hacer; **I haven't got anything on on Tuesday** el martes lo tengo libre

▸ **have out** *vt sep* (a) *(have extracted)* **I had my tonsils out** me operaron de amígdalas, me sacaron las amígdalas; **I had a tooth out** me sacaron una muela

(b) **to h. it out (with sb)** *(resolve)* poner las cosas en claro (con alguien)

▸ **have over** *vt sep* = **have round**

▸ **have round** *vt sep (friends, guests)* invitar; **I'm having some friends round this evening** he invitado a unos amigos esta noche

▸ **have up** *vt sep Br Fam* **to be had up (for sth)** tener que ir a juicio (por algo)

---

have-a-go hero ['hævəgəʊ'hɪərəʊ] *n Br Fam* héroe *m* espontáneo

haven ['heɪvən] *n* (a) *(refuge)* refugio *m*; *Literary* **the garden was a h. of peace and tranquillity** el jardín era un remanso de paz y tranquilidad (b) *Literary (harbour)* puerto *m*

have-nots ['hæv'nɒts] *npl* **the h.** los pobres

haven't ['hævnt] = **have not**

haver ['heɪvə(r)] *vi Br* (a) *(dither)* titubear, vacilar; **stop havering and make up your mind** no le des más vueltas y decídete (b) *Scot (talk nonsense)* decir disparates

haversack ['hævəsæk] *n* mochila *f*

havoc ['hævək] *n* estragos *mpl*; **to cause** *or* **wreak h.** hacer estragos; **to play h. with** hacer estragos en; **this will play h. with our plans** esto desbaratará *or* trastocará todos nuestros planes; **it played h. with the timetable** causó estragos en los horarios; **the meal played h. with my digestion** la comida me sentó muy mal (al estómago)

haw[1] [hɔː] *n* (a) *(berry)* baya *f* del espino (b) *(shrub)* espino *m* (albar)

haw[2] *vi see* **hum**

Hawaii [hə'waiː] *n* Hawai

Hawaiian [hə'waɪən] 1 *n* hawaiano(a) *m,f*

2 *adj* hawaiano(a) *m,f* ▸▸ ***H. guitar*** guitarra *f* hawaiana; ***H. shirt*** camisa *f* hawaiana

hawfinch ['hɔːfɪntʃ] *n* picogordo *m*

haw-haw = **ha-ha**

hawk[1] [hɔːk] 1 *n* (a) *(bird)* halcón *m*; IDIOM **to watch sth/sb like a h.** mirar algo/a alguien con ojos de lince; IDIOM **he has eyes like a h.** tiene (una) vista de lince *or* águila ▸▸ ***h. owl*** lechuza *f* gavilana (b) ***h. moth*** esfinge *f (mariposa)* (c) *Pol* halcón *m*, partidario(a) *m,f* de la línea dura *(en política exterior)*

2 *vi (hunt)* cazar con aves rapaces, hacer cetrería

hawk[2] *vt* **to h. one's wares** hacer venta ambulante

hawk[3] *vi (clear throat)* carraspear; *(spit)* escupir

▸ **hawk up** *vt sep* esputar carraspeando

hawker ['hɔːkə(r)] *n* vendedor(ora) *m,f* ambulante

hawkeye ['hɔːkaɪ] *n Fam* (persona *f* con vista de) lince *m*

hawk-eyed ['hɔːkaɪd] *adj* con vista *or* ojos de lince

hawking ['hɔːkɪŋ] *n* (a) *(hunting)* cetrería *f* (b) *(of goods)* venta *f* ambulante

hawkish ['hɔːkɪʃ] *adj Pol* partidario(a) de la línea dura *(en política exterior)*

hawknosed ['hɔːknəʊzd] *adj (person)* de nariz aguileña

hawksbill ['hɔːksbɪl] *n* **h. (turtle)** (tortuga *f*) carey *m*

hawser ['hɔːzə(r)] *n* cable *m*, estacha *f*

hawthorn ['hɔːθɔːn] *n* espino *m* (albar)

hay [heɪ] *n* heno *m*; **to make h.** dejar secar la paja; *Fig (use to advantage)* aprovechar(se), sacar partido; *Fam* **to hit the h.** *(go to bed)* irse al sobre; PROV **make h. while the sun shines** aprovecha mientras puedas ►► ***h. fever*** fiebre *f* del heno, alergia *f* al polen

haycock ['heɪkɒk] *n* almiar *m*

hayfork ['heɪfɔːk] *n* horca *f*

hayloft ['heɪlɒft] *n* henal *m*, henil *m*

haymaker ['heɪmeɪkə(r)] *n* **(a)** *(person)* segador(ora) *m,f*; *(machine)* segadora *f* **(b)** *Fam (punch)* directo *m*

hayrick ['heɪrɪk] *n* almiar *m*

hayseed ['heɪsiːd] *n* **(a)** *Agr* granzas *fpl* **(b)** *US Fam Esp* paleto(a) *m,f*, *Méx* paisa *mf*, *RP* pajuerano(a) *m,f*

haystack ['heɪstæk] *n* almiar *m*

haywire ['heɪwaɪə(r)] *adv Fam* **to go h.** *(plan)* desbaratarse; *(mechanism)* volverse loco(a)

hazard ['hæzəd] **1** *n* **(a)** *(danger)* peligro *m*, riesgo *m*; **the hazards of smoking** el peligro *or* riesgo que conlleva fumar; **a health h.** un peligro para la salud; **a fire h.** una causa potencial de incendio ►► *Aut* ***h. (warning) lights*** luces *fpl* de emergencia; *US* ***h. pay*** prima *f or* plus *m* de peligrosidad **(b)** *(in golf)* trampa *f*

2 *vt* **(a)** *(one's life, fortune)* arriesgar, poner en peligro **(b)** *(opinion, guess)* aventurar; **would you care to h. a guess as to the weight?** ¿podría aventurar *or* tratar de adivinar cuál es su peso?

hazardous ['hæzədəs] *adj* peligroso(a) ►► ***h. waste*** residuos *mpl* peligrosos

haze[1] [heɪz] *n* **(a)** *(of mist)* neblina *f*; *(shimmer)* calima *f*, calina *f* **(b)** *(of doubt, confusion)* nube *f*; **my mind was in a h.** tenía la mente nublada

haze[2] *vt US Fam (students, new recruits)* hacer novatadas a

hazel ['heɪzəl] **1** *n* **(a)** *(colour)* color *m* avellana **(b) h. (tree)** avellano *m* **(c)** *(nut)* avellana *f*

2 *adj* color avellana

hazelnut ['heɪzəlnʌt] *n* avellana *f*; **h. (tree)** avellano *m*

hazily ['heɪzɪlɪ] *adv (remember)* vagamente

haziness ['heɪzɪnɪs] *n* **(a)** *(of weather) (mistiness)* ambiente *m* neblinoso; *(shimmer)* calima *f*, calina *f* **(b)** *(of memory)* vaguedad *f*

hazing ['heɪzɪŋ] *n US Fam (of students, new recruits)* novatadas *fpl*

hazy ['heɪzɪ] *adj* **(a)** *(weather) (misty)* neblinoso(a); *(shimmery)* calinoso(a), con calima **(b)** *(image, memory)* vago(a), confuso(a); **to be h. about sth** no tener algo nada claro; **things get a bit h. after that** no recuerdo con claridad nada de lo que pasó después

h & c = **h and c**

HD *Comptr* **(a)** *(abbr* **hard drive)** disco *m* duro **(b)** *(abbr* **high density)** alta densidad *f*

HDTV [eɪtʃdiːtiː'viː] *n (abbr* **high-definition television)** televisión *f* de alta definición

HE *(abbr* **His/Her Excellency)** S. E., Su Excelencia

HE [hiː] **1** *pron* él *(usually omitted in Spanish, except for contrast)*; **he's Scottish** es escocés; **he likes red wine** le gusta el vino tinto; **who's he?** *(pointing at sb)* ¿quién es ése?; **HE hasn't got it!** ¡él no lo tiene!; *Formal* **he who believes this...** quien se crea *or* aquel que se crea esto...

2 *n* **it's a he** *(of animal)* es macho

HEAD [hed] **1** *n* **(a)** *(of person)* cabeza *f*; **my h. hurts** me duele la cabeza; **a fine h. of hair** una buena cabellera; **to be a h. taller than sb** sacar *or RP* llevar una cabeza a alguien; **from h. to foot** *or* **toe** de la cabeza a los pies; **to stand on one's h.** hacer el pino (con la cabeza sobre el suelo), *RP* hacer un paro de cabeza; *Fig* **to stand** *or* **turn the situation on its h.** trastornar completamente la situación; **to win by a h.** *(horse)* ganar por una cabeza ►► *Med* ***h. cold*** catarro *m*; ***h. count*** recuento *m* (de personas), *RP* conteo *m*; *Med* ***h. injuries*** lesiones *fpl* craneales; ***h. louse*** piojo *m*; ***h. restraint*** reposacabezas *m inv*; *Cin & TV* ***h. shot*** primer plano *m*; ***h. start*** *(advantage)* ventaja *f*; **to give sb a h. start** dar ventaja a alguien; **to have a h. start on** *or* **over sb** tener ventaja sobre alguien; ***h. torch*** lámpara *f* frontal

(b) *(intellect, mind)* cabeza *f*; **you need a clear h. for this sort of work** hay que tener la mente despejada para hacer este tipo de trabajo; **to clear one's h.** despejarse la cabeza; **say the first thing that comes into your h.** decir lo primero que te viene a la cabeza *or* mente; **to do sums in one's h.** sumar mentalmente; **it never entered my h. that...** nunca se me pasó por la cabeza que...; **I can't get that song/Susan out of my h.** no puedo quitarme *or Am* sacarme esa canción/a Susan de la cabeza; **to have a good h. on one's shoulders** tener la cabeza sobre los hombros *or RP* bien puesta; **to have a (good) h. for business/figures** tener (buena) cabeza para los negocios/los números; **to have a (good) h. for heights** no tener vértigo; **to put ideas into sb's h.** meter ideas a alguien en la cabeza; **he has taken** *or* **got it into his h. that...** se le ha metido en la cabeza que...; **use your h.!** ¡usa la cabeza!

(c) *(of pin, hammer, golf club, list, pimple)* cabeza *f*; *(of arrow)* punta *f*; *(of plant, flower)* flor *f*; *(of page, stairs)* parte *f* superior; *(of bed, table, river)* cabecera *f*; *(on beer)* espuma *f*; **to be at the h. of a list/queue** encabezar una lista/cola

(d) *(person in charge) (of family, the Church)* cabeza *mf*; *(of business, department)* jefe(a) *m,f*; *Br Sch* **h. (teacher)** director(ora) *m,f* ►► *Br Sch* ***h. boy*** delegado *m* de toda la escuela; ***h. chef*** primer chef *m*; ***h. gardener*** jardinero *m* jefe; *Br Sch* ***h. girl*** delegada *f* de toda la escuela; ***h. of government*** jefe(a) *m,f* de gobierno; ***h. office*** sede *f*, central *f*; ***h. of state*** jefe *m* de Estado; ***h. waiter*** maître *m*

(e) heads or tails? *(when tossing coin)* ¿cara o cruz?; *Chile, Col* ¿cara o sello?, *Méx* ¿águila o sol?, *RP* ¿cara o ceca?; *Hum* **heads I**

HE O SHE?

Cuando no se conoce el sexo del sujeto

Tradicionalmente, cuando se hacía referencia a una persona sin determinación de sexo, (por ejemplo a la hora de expresar ciertas normas o hacer generalizaciones), lo normal era usar el género masculino:

if a member fails to renew his subscription, he will be sent only one reminder
si un miembro no renueva su suscripción, sólo se le enviará un aviso

Hoy día este uso se considera sexista, aunque no hay consenso aún sobre cuál sería una alternativa aceptable. Una posibilidad es el uso de **he or she** (o **he/she**), si bien esta solución no siempre es la más elegante:

if a member fails to renew his or her subscription, he or she will be sent only one reminder

Otra solución frecuente es usar el pronombre plural **they** en su lugar, para evitar el masculino o femenino:

if a member fails to renew their subscription, they will be sent only one reminder

Para algunos, esta posibilidad es gramaticalmente incorrecta, por lo que es mejor evitarla en contextos formales, si bien tiene más aceptación cuando se usa con pronombres indefinidos como **someone**, **anyone** o **no one**:

anyone who fails to renew their subscription will be sent only one reminder

La forma más sencilla de evitar este problema a menudo consiste en usar el plural:

if members fail to renew their subscriptions, they will be sent only one reminder

win, tails you lose cara, gano yo, cruz, pierdes tú
(f) *(on tape recorder, VCR)* cabeza *f* (magnética), cabezal *m* ▸▸ ***h. cleaner*** limpiacabezales *m inv*
(g) *(unit)* **to pay £10 per** *or* **a h.** pagar 10 libras por cabeza; **six h. of cattle** seis cabezas de ganado, seis reses
(h) **a h. of cabbage** un repollo; **a h. of lettuce** una lechuga
(i) *Geog (of land)* promontorio *m*
(j) *(pressure of water)* presión *f (del agua)*
(k) *Naut (toilet on ship)* baño *m*, váter *m*
(l) *US Fam (toilet)* baño *m*, váter *m*
(m) *(in rugby)* **to win a scrum against the h.** robar la posesión del balón en una melé
(n) *Vulg* **to give sb h.** *(oral sex)* chupársela *or Esp* hacerle una mamada a alguien
(o) IDIOMS **she's h. and shoulders above the other candidates** está muy por encima de los demás candidatos; **to be h. over heels in love (with sb)** estar locamente enamorado(a) (de alguien); **to bite** *or* **snap sb's h. off** saltarle a alguien, *Esp* ponerse borde con alguien; *Fam* **don't bother your h. about it** no te comas la cabeza con eso; **to bring sth to a h.** *(conflict, situation)* llevar algo a un punto crítico; **to build up a h. of steam** *(person, campaign)* tomar ímpetu; **to bury** *or* **have one's h. in the sand** adoptar la estrategia del avestruz; **to come to a h.** *(conflict, situation)* alcanzar un punto crítico; *Br Fam* **to do sb's h. in** fastidiar *or* mosquear a alguien; *Fam* **he's funny** *or* **not right in the h.** no está bien de la cabeza; **we need to get our heads down** *(start working hard)* tenemos que ponernos a trabajar en serio; **when will you get it into your h. that I refuse to lend you any more money?** ¿cuándo te va a entrar en la cabeza que no te voy a prestar más dinero?; *Fam* **I can't get my h. round the idea of him leaving** no puedo hacerme a la idea de que se haya ido; **to give sb his h.** *(allow to take decisions)* dar libertad a alguien; **to go over sb's h.** *(appeal to higher authority)* pasar por encima de alguien; **it went** *or* **was over my h.** *(I didn't understand it) Esp* no me enteré de nada, *Am* no me di cuenta de nada; **the wine/praise went to his h.** se le subió a la cabeza el vino/tanto halago; **to have one's h. in the clouds** tener la cabeza en las nubes; **they'll have your h. (on a plate) for this** vas a pagar con el pellejo por esto; **she has her h. screwed on** tiene la cabeza sobre los hombros *or RP* bien puesta, es una mujer sensata; **she has a good h. on her shoulders** tiene la cabeza sobre los hombros *or RP* bien puesta; **he has an old h. on young shoulders** es muy maduro para su edad; **you can hold your h. (up) high** puedes andar con la cabeza bien alta; **he's in over his h.** no puede con la situación; *Fam* **to keep one's h.** mantener la cabeza fría; **to keep one's h. above water** mantenerse a flote; **to keep one's h. down** mantenerse en segundo plano; *Fam* **to laugh one's h. off** morirse *or* desternillarse de risa; *Fam* **to lose one's h.** perder la cabeza; **I can't make h. or tail of this** no le encuentro ni pies ni cabeza a esto; *Fam* **she needs her h. examined** está como una cabra, está para que la encierren; *Fam* **to be off one's h.** estar mal de la cabeza; **off the top of one's h.** sin pararse a pensar; **on your own h. be it** allá tú con lo que haces; *Fam* **he was out of his h.** *(drunk, stoned)* tenía un colocón tremendo, *Col, Méx* estaba zafadísimo, *RP* estaba voladísimo; **to put** *or* **get one's h. down** *(sleep)* echarse a dormir; *Fam* **to get one's h. together** ponerse las pilas, organizarse; **we put our heads together** entre todos nos pusimos a pensar; **when the report is published, heads will roll** cuando se publique el informe *or CAm, Méx* reporte van a rodar muchas cabezas; *Fam* **to shout one's h. off** desgañitarse, vociferar; PROV **two heads are better than one** dos cabezas piensan mejor que una, dos mentes discurren más que una sola
2 *vt* (a) *(lead) (organization, campaign)* estar a la cabeza de; *(list, procession)* encabezar; **the organization is headed by a famous businessman** la organización está dirigida por un famoso hombre de negocios
(b) *(direct)* conducir; **one of the locals headed me in the right direction** un lugareño me indicó el camino; **which way are you headed?** ¿hacia dónde vas?
(c) *(put a title on) (page, chapter)* encabezar, titular; **the first chapter is headed "Introduction"** el primer capítulo se titula "Introducción"
(d) *(in soccer)* **to h. the ball** cabecear el balón *or* la pelota, darle al balón *or* a la pelota de cabeza; **to h. a goal** meter un gol de cabeza
3 *vi (move)* dirigirse; **where are you heading?** ¿hacia dónde vas?; **we should be heading home** deberíamos irnos ya a casa; **they were heading out of town** salían de la ciudad; **they headed north/south** se dirigieron hacia el norte/sur

▸**head back** *vi* volver, regresar

▸**head for** *vt insep* dirigirse a; **when I saw him, I headed for the exit** cuando lo vi, me fui hacia la salida; **to be heading** *or* **headed for disaster** ir camino de la ruina; **you're heading** *or* **headed for trouble** vas a tener problemas

▸**head off** 1 *vt sep* (a) *(intercept)* interceptar (b) *(prevent)* evitar
2 *vi (depart)* marcharse

▸**head up** *vt sep (lead) (organization, campaign)* estar a la cabeza de

-head [hed] *suffix Fam* **she's a bit of a jazz-h.** es una enamorada del jazz, la vuelve loca el jazz; **he's a real tea-h.** bebe té a todas horas, es un bebedor de té empedernido

headache [ˈhedeɪk] *n* (a) *(pain)* dolor *m* de cabeza; **I have a terrible h.** me duele muchísimo la cabeza (b) *Fam (problem)* quebradero *m* de cabeza; **it can be a h. finding somewhere to park** lo de estacionar se puede convertir en una pesadilla

headachy [ˈhedeɪkɪ] *adj Fam* **I'm feeling a bit h.** me duele un poquillo la cabeza

headband [ˈhedbænd] *n* cinta *f* para la cabeza

headbanger [ˈhedbæŋə(r)] *n Fam* (a) *(heavy metal fan)* (fan *mf* del) heavy *mf* (b) *Br (crazy person)* descerebrado(a) *m,f*, bruto(a) *m,f*

headboard [ˈhedbɔːd] *n (of bed)* cabecero *m*

head-butt [ˈhedbʌt] 1 *n* cabezazo *m*
2 *vt* dar un cabezazo a

headcase [ˈhedkeɪs] *n Fam (lunatic)* chiflado(a) *m,f*

headcheese [ˈhedtʃiːz] *n US* queso *m* de cerdo, *Esp* cabeza *f* de jabalí

headdress [ˈheddres] *n* tocado *m*

headed [ˈhedɪd] *adj* **h. (note)paper** papel *m* con membrete

-headed [ˈhedɪd] *suffix* **a silver-h. cane** un bastón de punta *or* contera plateada; **a three-h. dragon** un dragón tricéfalo *or* de tres cabezas

header [ˈhedə(r)] *n* (a) *Typ* encabezamiento *m* (b) *(in soccer)* cabezazo *m* (c) *Fam (fall)* caída *f* de cabeza; *(dive)* salto *m* de cabeza; **he took a h. into the ditch** se tiró de cabeza a la zanja (d) *Br Aut* **h. (tank)** depósito *m* de igualación *or* de compensación (e) *(brick)* (ladrillo *m* colocado a) tizón *m*

headfirst [ˈhedˈfɜːst] *adv* (a) *(dive, fall, jump)* de cabeza; **he dived h. into the pool** se tiró de cabeza a la piscina (b) *(rashly)* sin pensarlo, precipitadamente; **to jump h. into sth** meterse sin pensarlo *or* de forma precipitada en algo

headgear [ˈhedgɪə(r)] *n* tocado *m*

headguard [ˈhedgɑːd] *n* protector *m* para la cabeza

headhunt [ˈhedˈhʌnt] *vt Com* captar, cazar

headhunter [ˈhedhʌntə(r)] *n* (a) *(member of tribe)* cazador(ora) *m,f* de cabezas (b) *Com* cazatalentos *mf inv*

headhunting [ˈhedhʌntɪŋ] *n* (a) *(by tribes)* casa *f* de cabezas (b) *Com* caza *f* de talentos ▸▸ ***h. agency*** empresa *f* de caza talentos

headiness [ˈhedɪnɪs] *n* (a) *(of wine)* efecto *m* embriagador; *(of perfume)* aroma *m* embriagador (b) *(excitement)* emoción *f*, excitación *f*; **the h. of the early sixties** la excitante efervescencia de los primeros años sesenta

heading [ˈhedɪŋ] *n* (a) *(of chapter, article)* encabezamiento *m* (b) *(topic)* tema *m*; **it comes** *or* **falls under the h. of...** entra dentro de la categoría de... (c) *(letterhead)* membrete *m* (d) *(compass direction)* rumbo *m*

headlamp [ˈhedlæmp] *n (on car, train)* faro *m*

headland [ˈhedlənd] *n* promontorio *m*

headless [ˈhedlɪs] *adj* (a) *(creature, figure)* sin cabeza; *(corpse)* decapitado(a); IDIOM *Fam* **to run about like a h. chicken** ir *or* andar de aquí para allá sin parar (b) *(company, organization)* sin dirección, acéfalo(a)

headlight [ˈhedlaɪt] *n (on car, train)* faro *m*

headline [ˈhedlaɪn] 1 *n* (a) *(of newspaper, TV news)* titular *m*, *Méx, RP* encabezado *m*; **pollution has been in the headlines a lot recently** la contaminación ha ocupado muchos titulares últimamente; **to hit the headlines** saltar a los titulares; **to be** *or* **make h. news** ser noticia de portada; **the hijacking made the headlines** el secuestro fue noticia (de portada)
(b) *Rad & TV* **headlines** *(news summary)* resumen *m or* sumario *m* de las principales noticias, titulares *mpl*, *Méx, RP* encabezados *mpl*; **here are today's news headlines** les ofrecemos el resumen *or* sumario de las principales noticias
(c) *Com* ***h. rate*** *(of inflation)* tasa *f* de inflación *(en la que se incluyen los tipos de interés hipotecarios)*
2 *vt* (a) *(article, story)* titular; **the article was headlined "The New Poor"** el artículo se titulaba "Los nuevos pobres" (b) *(have top billing in)* encabezar el cartel de; **he is to h. the channel's flagship news programme** él se hallará al frente del principal programa informativo de la cadena

headliner [ˈhedlaɪnə(r)] *n US* actuación *f* estelar, cabeza *mf* de cartel

headlock [ˈhedlɒk] *n* presa *f or* llave *f* de cabeza

headlong ['hedlɒŋ] 1 *adv* (a) *(dive, fall)* de bruces; **she tripped and fell h. on the floor** tropezó y cayó de bruces al suelo (b) *(rashly)* precipitadamente; **they rushed h. into marriage** se casaron precipitadamente

2 *adj* **there was a h. rush for the bar** se produjo una estampida hacia el bar; **the crowd made a h. dash for the exit** la multitud se precipitó hacia la salida

headman ['hedmən] *n (of a tribe)* jefe *m*

headmaster [hed'mɑːstə(r)] *n Sch* director *m*

headmistress [hed'mɪstrɪs] *n Sch* directora *f*

head-on ['he'dɒn] 1 *adj* (a) *(crash, collision)* frontal, de frente (b) *(confrontation)* directo(a), frontal

2 *adv* (a) *(collide, hit)* de frente, frontalmente (b) *(confront)* directamente, frontalmente; **to meet sb h.** encontrarse de frente con alguien; **to meet a problem h.** afrontar directamente un problema

headphones ['hedfəʊnz] *npl* auriculares *mpl*

headpin ['hedpɪn] *n* primer bolo *m*, (bolo *m* de) cabecera *f*

headquarter ['hedkwɔːtə(r)] *US* 1 *vt* **to be headquartered in Houston** tener su sede *or* central en Houston

2 *vi (company)* **to h. in Houston** tener su sede *or* central en Houston

headquarters [hed'kwɔːtəz] *npl* (a) *(of organization)* sede *f*, central *f* (b) *Mil* cuartel *m* general

headrest ['hedrest] *n* reposacabezas *m inv*

headroom ['hedruːm] *n* (a) *(under bridge)* gálibo *m*; **max h. 10 metres** *(sign)* altura máxima permitida: 10 metros, prohibido el paso a vehículos de altura superior a 10 metros (b) *(inside car)* altura *f* de la cabeza al techo (c) *(inside room)* **there's not much h. in the attic** el ático tiene el techo muy bajo

headscarf ['hedskɑːf] *n* pañuelo *m (para la cabeza)*

headset ['hedset] *n (earphones)* auriculares *mpl*, cascos *mpl*

headship ['hedʃɪp] *n Br (of school)* dirección *f*

headshrinker ['hedʃrɪŋkə(r)] *n* (a) *Fam (psychiatrist)* psiquiatra *mf* (b) *(member of tribe)* reductor(ora) *m,f* de cabezas

headsman ['hedzmən] *n Hist (executioner)* verdugo *m*

headsquare ['hedskweə(r)] *n* pañuelo *m (para la cabeza)*

headstall ['hedstɔːl] *n (for horse)* cabezada *f*

headstand ['hedstænd] *n* **to do a h.** hacer el pino

headstone ['hedstəʊn] *n* (a) *(on grave)* lápida *f* (b) *(in arch)* clave *f*

headstrong ['hedstrɒŋ] *adj (person)* testarudo(a), tozudo(a); *(action, insistence)* tenaz

head-to-head ['hedtə'hed] 1 *n (confrontation)* enfrentamiento *m* cara a cara

2 *adv* **to meet** *or* **clash h.** tener un enfrentamiento cara a cara

head-up display ['hedʌpdɪs'pleɪ] *n (in aircraft, car)* pantalla *f* virtual a la altura de la vista

heads-up ['hedzʌp] *n US Fam* **to give sb the h.** informar a alguien

headwaters ['hedwɔːtəz] *npl* cabecera *f* (del río)

headway ['hedweɪ] *n* **to make h.** avanzar

headwind ['hedwɪnd] *n* viento *m* contrario *or* de cara

headword ['hedwɜːd] *n (in dictionary)* lema *m*

heady ['hedɪ] *adj* (a) *(drink, perfume)* embriagador(ora) (b) *(exciting) (atmosphere, experience, days)* emocionante, excitante; *(feeling)* excitante, embriagador(ora)

heal [hiːl] 1 *vt* (a) *(wound)* curar; *Fig* **wounds which only time would h.** heridas que sólo el tiempo podría cerrar (b) *(differences)* subsanar; **I'd do anything to h. the breach between them** haría lo que fuera por cerrar esa brecha que los separa

2 *vi (wound)* **to h. (up** *or* **over)** curarse, sanar

healer ['hiːlə(r)] *n* curandero(a) *m,f*; PROV **time is a great h.** el tiempo todo lo cura

healing ['hiːlɪŋ] 1 *n* curación *f*

2 *adj* (a) *(treatment, ointment)* curativo(a); **h. hands** manos que curan (b) *(soothing) (words, influence)* benéfico(a), beneficioso(a)

health [helθ] *n* (a) *(general condition)* salud *f*; **his h. has never been good** nunca ha estado bien de salud, su salud siempre ha sido frágil; **to be in good/poor h.** estar bien/mal de salud; **the economy is in good h.** la economía goza de buena salud; **the Department of H.** el Ministerio de Sanidad ▸▸ ***h. care*** atención *f* sanitaria; *Br* ***h. centre*** centro *m* de salud, ambulatorio *m*; ***h. club*** gimnasio *m*; *Fin* ***h. cover*** cobertura *f* sanitaria; ***h. education*** educación *f* sanitaria *or* para la salud; ***h. farm*** clínica *f* de adelgazamiento; ***h. food*** comida *f* integral; ***h. food shop*** tienda *f* de alimentos integrales, ≃ herbolario *m*; ***h. hazard*** peligro *m* para la salud; *Fin* ***h. insurance*** seguro *m* de enfermedad; ***h. resort*** centro *m* de reposo; ***h. risk*** peligro *m* para la salud; *Br Ind* ***h. and safety*** seguridad *f* e higiene en el trabajo, prevención *f* de riesgos laborales; *Br* ***the H. Service*** el sistema de sanidad pública británico; ***h. visitor*** enfermero(a) *m,f* visitante

(b) *(good condition)* (buena) salud *f*; **has he regained his h.?** ¿vuelve a estar bien de salud?; **to nurse sb back to h.** cuidar a alguien hasta devolverle la salud *or* hasta su restablecimiento; **she's the picture of h.** es la viva imagen de la salud *or* de una persona sana

(c) *(in toast)* **to drink (to) sb's h.** brindar a la salud de alguien, brindar por alguien; **(your) good h.!** ¡a tu/su/*etc.* salud!, ¡salud!

healthily ['helθɪlɪ] *adv (to eat, live)* de un modo sano, saludablemente

healthy ['helθɪ] *adj* (a) *(in good health) (person)* sano(a), saludable; *(animal, plant)* sano(a); **he's always been very h.** siempre ha estado muy sano *or* ha tenido buena salud

(b) *(showing good health) (colour, skin)* saludable, sano(a); **to have a h. appetite** comer bien; **it is a h. sign that...** es un buen síntoma que...

(c) *(beneficial) (climate, diet, lifestyle)* sano(a), saludable; *(exercise)* sano(a), saludable

(d) *(thriving) (economy, business)* boyante, próspero(a)

(e) *(substantial) (profits, sum)* sustancioso(a), pingüe

(f) *(sensible) (attitude, respect)* saludable; **he has a h. disrespect for authority** demuestra una saludable falta de respeto ante la autoridad; **she had developed a h. respect for guard dogs** le tenía un respeto más que razonable a los perros guardianes

heap [hiːp] 1 *n* (a) *(pile)* montón *m*; **her things were piled in a h.** sus cosas estaban amontonadas *or* apiladas; **he collapsed in a h. on the floor** se desplomó sobre el suelo; *Fig* **people at the top/bottom of the h.** los de arriba/abajo; **he started at the bottom of the h. and worked his way up** empezó desde abajo *or* desde lo más bajo y fue ascendiendo; *Fam* **to be struck** *or* **knocked all of a h.** quedarse de una pieza

(b) *Fam* **heaps,** *US* **a (whole) h.** *(large amount)* un montón, montones *mpl*; **we've got heaps** *or US* **a h. of time** tenemos un montón de tiempo; **she had heaps** *or US* **a h. of children** tenía montones *or* un montón *or* una pila de hijos; **it's heaps** *or US* **a h. better** es muchísimo *or* infinitamente mejor; **it's heaps** *or US* **a h. faster to go by train** se va muchísimo más rápido en tren

(c) *Fam (car)* cacharro *m*, *Esp* carraca *f*

(d) *Comptr* zona *f*

2 *vt* (a) *(pile)* amontonar; **she heaped roast beef onto his plate** le echó un montón de rosbif en el plato; **the table was heaped with food** había montones *or* un montón de comida en la mesa (b) *(lavish)* **to h. riches/praise/insults on sb** colmar a alguien de riquezas/alabanzas/insultos

▸**heap up** *vt sep* (a) *(pile) (books, furniture)* amontonar, apilar (b) *(collect) (money, riches)* amasar, acumular; *Fig* **she's heaping up trouble for herself** no hace más que buscarse problemas

heaped [hiːpt], *US* **heaping** ['hiːpɪŋ] *adj (spoonful)* colmado(a)

HEAR [hɪə(r)] *(pt & pp* **heard** [hɜːd]) 1 *vt* (a) *(perceive)* oír; **can you h. me?** ¿me oyes?; **to h. sb speak** *or* **speaking** oír hablar a alguien; **I could hardly h. myself speak** apenas se oía; **I could hardly h. myself think** no había quien oyera nada; **she was struggling to make herself heard over the noise** se esforzaba por hacerse oír en medio del ruido; **he was heard to say that he didn't care** parece que dijo que le daba igual; **I've heard it said that...** he oído que...; **to h. her talk you'd think she was some sort of expert** oyéndola hablar cualquiera diría que es una experta; **let's h. it for...** aplaudamos a...; *Fam* **I h. you, I h. what you're saying** bueno *or Esp* vale, tienes razón; **have you heard the one about ...?** *(introducing a joke)* ¿sabes el de...?; *Fam* **I've heard that one before!** ¡no me vengas con ésas!, *Esp* ¡a otro perro con ese hueso!; *Fam Hum* **he said he'd do the dusting – I must be hearing things!** dijo que él limpiaría el polvo – ¡ha ocurrido un milagro!

(b) *(listen to)* escuchar; **h.!, h.!** *(at meeting)* ¡sí señor!, ¡eso es!; **OK, let's h. it then** *(tell me the news)* vamos, suéltalo; **the priest hears confession on Saturdays** el sacerdote confiesa los sábados; *Law* **to h. a case** ver un caso

(c) *(find out)* oír; **I heard (that) she was in Spain** he oído (decir) que estaba en España; **I h. (that) you're getting married** me han dicho que te vas a casar; **I'm glad to h. (that) you're better** me alegra saber que estás mejor; **have you heard the news?** ¿has oído la noticia?; **from what I've heard it was a bit of a disaster** por lo que he oído, fue más bien un desastre; **she had a baby – so I heard** ha tenido un niño – sí, ya lo sabía

2 *vi* oír; **I can't h. properly** no oigo bien; **that's quite enough, do you h.?** basta ya, ¿me oyes?

▸**hear about** *vt insep* **to h. about sth** saber de algo; **have you heard about the job yet?** ¿sabes algo del trabajo ya?; **did you h. about the**

train crash yesterday? ¿te has enterado del accidente de tren que hubo ayer?; **I've heard a lot about you** he oído hablar mucho de ti

▸ **hear from** *vt insep* **to h. from sb** tener noticias de alguien, saber de alguien; **I look forward to hearing from you** *(in letter)* quedo a la espera de recibir noticias suyas; **you'll be hearing from my lawyer!** ¡mi abogado se pondrá en contacto con usted!

▸ **hear of** *vt insep* **I've never heard of her** nunca he oído hablar de ella; **they were never heard of again** nunca se supo nada más de ellos; **that's the first I've heard of it!** es la primera noticia que tengo; **I've never heard of such a thing!** ¡nunca he oído hablar de nada semejante!; **I won't h. of it!** ¡no quiero ni oír hablar de ello!

▸ **hear out** *vt sep* **h. me out** escúchame antes

hearer ['hɪərə(r)] *n* oyente *mf*

hearing ['hɪərɪŋ] *n* **(a)** *(sense)* oído *m*; **cats have better h. than humans** los gatos tienen el (sentido del) oído más desarrollado que los humanos; **my h. is getting worse** cada vez oigo menos *or* peor; **his h. gradually deteriorated** se fue quedando sordo, cada vez oía peor; **he has very little h. left** ya apenas oye nada; **the h. impaired** las personas con discapacidad auditiva ▸▸ ***h. aid*** audífono *m*; ***h. loss*** pérdida *f* de audición; ***h. threshold*** umbral *m* de audición
(b) *(earshot)* **to be within/out of h.** estar/no estar lo suficientemente cerca como para oír; **he's never said it in my h.** nunca lo ha dicho en mi presencia, yo nunca le he oído decirlo
(c) *(chance to explain)* **to give sb a fair h.** dejar a alguien que se explique; **to condemn sb without a h.** condenar a alguien sin haberlo escuchado antes
(d) *Law (enquiry)* vista *f*

hearken, harken ['hɑːkən] *vi Archaic or Literary* **to h. to** *or* **unto sth/sb** escuchar algo/a alguien

hearsay ['hɪəseɪ] *n* rumores *mpl*; **I only know (it) by** *or* **from h.** sólo lo sé de oídas ▸▸ *Law* ***h. evidence*** pruebas *fpl* basadas en rumores

hearse [hɜːs] *n* coche *m* fúnebre

HEART [hɑːt] **1** *n* **(a)** *(organ)* corazón *m*; **to have h. trouble, to have a weak** *or* **bad h., to have a h. condition** tener problemas cardíacos *or* de corazón; *Fam* **just look at her tap dancing, eat your h. out, Fred Astaire!** mira como baila el claqué, ¡chúpate esa *or* toma del frasco, Fred Astaire!; *Fig* **my h. skipped** *or* **missed a beat** me dio un vuelco el corazón; *Fig* **my h. stood still** tenía el corazón en un puño *or Am* en la boca ▸▸ ***h. attack*** ataque *m* al corazón, infarto *m*; *Fig* **you nearly gave me a h. attack!** ¡casi me matas del susto!; ***h. disease*** cardiopatía *f*; ***h. failure*** *(condition)* insuficiencia *f* cardíaca; *(cessation of heartbeat)* paro *m* cardíaco; *Fig* **I nearly had h. failure when they told me I'd won** casi me da un ataque (al corazón) cuando me dijeron que había ganado; ***h. murmur*** soplo *m* cardíaco, soplo *m* en el corazón; ***h. surgery*** cirugía *f* cardíaca; ***h. transplant*** trasplante *m* de corazón
(b) *(seat of the emotions)* corazón *m*; **a h. of gold** un corazón de oro; **a h. of stone** un corazón duro *or* de piedra; **affairs** *or* **matters of the h.** asuntos *or* cosas del corazón; **he's a man after my own h.** es uno de los míos; *Ironic* **my h. bleeds for you** ¡qué pena me das!; **to break sb's h.** *(of lover)* romperle el corazón a alguien; **it breaks my h. to see them suffer** me rompe el corazón verlos sufrir; **the subject is very close** *or* **dear to my h.** este tema es muy importante para mí; **I can't find it in my h. to feel sorry for them** aunque lo intento, la verdad es que no los compadezco; **I speak from the h.** estoy hablando con el corazón en la mano; **from the bottom of one's h.** *(thank, congratulate)* de todo corazón; **my h. goes out to them** comparto su sufrimiento; *(on death)* los acompaño en el sentimiento; **have a h.!** ¡no seas cruel!; **to have a big h.** tener un gran corazón; **she has a kind** *or* **good h.** tiene muy buen corazón; **to have one's h. in one's mouth** tener el corazón en un puño *or Am* en la boca; **her h. is in the right place** tiene un gran corazón; **in my h. (of hearts)** en el fondo (de mi corazón); **my h. leapt at the news** el corazón me dio un vuelco al oír la noticia; *Literary* **to lose one's h. to sb** caer perdidamente enamorado(a) de alguien; **he loved her h. and soul** *or* **with all his h.** la amaba con toda su alma; **to pour one's h. out to sb** abrirle el corazón a alguien; **my h. sank at the news** la noticia me dejó hundido; **he had set his h. on it** lo deseaba con toda el alma; **to take sth to h.** tomarse algo a pecho; **to one's h.'s content** hasta saciarse; **to wear one's h. on one's sleeve** no ocultar los sentimientos; *Literary* **to win sb's h.** ganarse el corazón *or* amor de alguien; **with a heavy h.** con aflicción
(c) *(enthusiasm, courage)* **to be in good h.** tener la moral alta; **it gives me h. to know that** me anima saberlo; **to take/lose h.** animarse/desanimarse; **they can take h. from these results** estos resultados son alentadores para ellos; **he tried to convince them but his h. wasn't in it** trató de convencerlos, pero sin mucho empeño; **I didn't have the h. to tell him** no tuve coraje para decírselo; **she put her h. and soul into it** puso todo su empeño en ello
(d) *(centre)* **the h. of the city** el corazón de la ciudad; **the h. of the matter** el meollo del asunto; **in the h. of the forest** en el corazón del bosque; **in the h. of winter** en pleno invierno
(e) *(of lettuce, cabbage)* corazón *m*; *(of artichoke)* corazón *m*, fondo *m*
(f) *(in cards)* corazón *m*; **hearts** *(suit)* corazones *mpl*; **ace/nine of hearts** as/nueve de corazones
2 at heart *adv* en el fondo; **to have sb's welfare/interests at h.** preocuparse de veras por el bienestar/los intereses de alguien
3 by heart *adv* de memoria

heartache ['hɑːteɪk] *n* dolor *m*, tristeza *f*; **he caused her a lot of h.** la hizo sufrir mucho, le hizo mucho daño

heartbeat ['hɑːtbiːt] *n* latido *m* (del corazón); **she could hear his h.** oía los latidos de su corazón; **the doctor checked his h.** el médico le comprobó el ritmo cardíaco; **to be a h. away from sth** estar a un paso de algo; *US* **in a h.** *(at once)* al momento, enseguida; *(willingly)* sin pensarlo dos veces

heartbreak ['hɑːtbreɪk] *n (sorrow)* congoja *f*, pena *f*; *(in love)* desengaño *m* amoroso; **I've had my share of heartbreak(s)** yo he sufrido lo mío

heartbreaker ['hɑːtbreɪkə(r)] *n* rompecorazones *mf inv*

heartbreaking ['hɑːtbreɪkɪŋ] *adj* desolador(ora), desgarrador(ora)

heartbroken ['hɑːtbrəʊkən] *adj* abatido(a), descorazonado(a); **he was left h. by the news** la noticia lo dejó abatido *or* destrozado

heartburn ['hɑːtbɜːn] *n (indigestion)* acidez *f* (de estómago), ardor *m* de estómago

hearten ['hɑːtən] *vt* alentar, animar; **we were heartened by the news** la noticia nos alentó *or* animó mucho

heartening ['hɑːtənɪŋ] *adj* alentador(ora)

heartfelt ['hɑːtfelt] *adj (apology, thanks)* sincero(a); **with our h. wishes for a speedy recovery** *(on card)* con nuestros más sentidos *or* sinceros deseos de una pronta recuperación

hearth [hɑːθ] *n* **(a)** *(fireplace)* chimenea *f* ▸▸ ***h. rug*** alfombrilla *f* de chimenea **(b)** *(home)* hogar *m*; **h. and home** el hogar

heartily ['hɑːtɪlɪ] *adv* **(a)** *(enthusiastically, warmly) (to say, thank, congratulate, welcome)* de todo corazón; *(to laugh)* campechanamente; *(to eat)* con ganas; **I can h. recommend it** lo recomiendo encarecidamente
(b) *(wholeheartedly)* totalmente, completamente; **I h. agree** yo estoy totalmente *or* completamente de acuerdo, yo pienso exactamente lo mismo; **to be h. sick of sth** estar totalmente *or* completamente harto de algo

heartiness ['hɑːtɪnɪs] *n (of thanks, congratulations, welcome)* efusividad *f*, cordialidad *f*; *(of laughter)* campechanía *f*, jovialidad *f*; *(of appetite)* voracidad *f*

heartland ['hɑːtlænd] *n* núcleo *m*; **the h. of North America** el corazón de Norteamérica; **Mexico's industrial h. was devastated by the depression** la recesión asoló el núcleo *or* el corazón industrial de México

heartless ['hɑːtlɪs] *adj* inhumano(a), despiadado(a)

heartlessly ['hɑːtlɪslɪ] *adv* despiadadamente

heartlessness ['hɑːtlɪsnɪs] *n* crueldad *f*

heart-lung ['hɑːt'lʌŋ] *adj Med* ***h. machine*** (máquina *f* de) corazón-pulmón *m* artificial; ***h. transplant*** trasplante *m* cardiopulmonar

heart-rending ['hɑːtrendɪŋ] *adj* desgarrador(ora)

heart-searching ['hɑːtsɜːtʃɪŋ] *n* **after much h.** tras un profundo examen de conciencia

heartsease ['hɑːtsiːz] *n* trinitaria *f*

heart-shaped ['hɑːtʃeɪpt] *adj* con forma de corazón, en forma de corazón, *Spec* acorazonado(a)

heartsick ['hɑːtsɪk] *adj* desconsolado(a)

heart-stopping ['hɑːtstɒpɪŋ] *adj* emocionantísimo(a)

heartstrings ['hɑːtstrɪŋz] *npl* **to tug** *or* **pull at sb's h.** tocar la fibra sensible de alguien

heart-throb ['hɑːtθrɒb] *n Fam* ídolo *m*; **he's the office h.** en la oficina arrasa, *Esp* es el guaperas de la oficina

heart-to-heart ['hɑːtə'hɑːt] **1** *n* **to have a h. with sb** tener una charla íntima con alguien
2 *adj* íntimo(a)

heart-warming ['hɑːtwɔːmɪŋ] *adj* conmovedor(ora)

heartwood ['hɑːtwʊd] *n Spec* duramen *m*

hearty ['hɑːtɪ] 1 *adj* (a) *(jovial, warm) (person, laugh)* campechano(a), jovial; *(welcome)* cordial, efusivo(a); **my heartiest congratulations** felicidades de todo corazón (b) *(wholehearted) (approval)* caluroso(a); *(dislike)* profundo(a) (c) *(substantial) (meal)* copioso(a); *(appetite)* voraz
2 *n Archaic or Hum* **me hearties!** ¡camaradas!, ¡mis valientes!

heat [hiːt] 1 *n* (a) *(high temperature)* calor *m*; **the radiator gives off a lot of h.** el radiador calienta mucho *or* da mucho calor; **you shouldn't go out in this h.** no deberías salir con este calor *or* con el calor que hace; **in the h. of the day** con todo el calor del día; PROV **if you can't stand** *or* **take the h., get out of the kitchen** si no puedes con ello, ya sabes dónde está la puerta ►► *Phys* ***h. exchanger*** cambiador *m* de calor; ***h. exhaustion*** colapso *m* por exceso de calor; ***h. haze*** calima *f*; ***h. loss*** pérdida *f* de calor; ***h. pump*** bomba *f* de calor; ***h. rash*** sarpullido *m (por el calor)*; ***h. shield*** pantalla *f* térmica, escudo *m* térmico; *Comptr* ***h. sink*** disipador *m or* sumidero *m* térmico; ***h. treatment*** *Med* termoterapia *f*; *Tech* tratamiento *m* térmico
(b) *(on cooker)* **to cook at a high/moderate/low h.** cocinar a fuego vivo/moderado/lento; **to turn up/down the h.** subir/bajar el fuego
(c) *(heating)* calefacción *f*; **to turn the h. off/on/up** apagar/encender/subir la calefacción
(d) *(passion)* calor *m*; **she replied with (some) h.** contestó (un tanto) acalorada; **in the h. of the moment/of the argument** con el acaloramiento del momento/de la pelea; **in the h. of battle** con el calor *or* ardor de la batalla
(e) *Fam (pressure)* **to turn up the h. on sb** presionar a alguien; **the h. is on** ha llegado la hora de la verdad; **lie low until the h. is off** procura pasar desapercibido hasta que la cosa se calme; **this decision took the h. off us** esta decisión supuso un respiro para nosotros
(f) *(of female animal)* **in** *or Br* **on h.** en celo
(g) *(in sport)* serie *f*, eliminatoria *f*
(h) *very Fam US (police)* **the h.** la poli, *Esp* la pasma, *Méx* los pitufos, *RP* la cana
2 *vt (food)* calentar; *(air, room)* calentar, caldear
3 *vi* calentarse

► **heat through** 1 *vt sep (food)* calentar bien
2 *vi (food)* calentarse bien

► **heat up** 1 *vt sep (air, room)* calentar, caldear; *(food)* calentar, recalentar
2 *vi* (a) *(food, air, room)* calentarse, caldearse; *(food)* calentarse (b) *(argument, contest)* subir de tono, acalorarse

heated ['hiːtɪd] *adj* (a) *(room, building)* caldeado(a); *(swimming pool)* climatizado(a); *(towel rail)* caliente; **h. rear window** luneta térmica
(b) *(argument, words)* acalorado(a); **h. words were exchanged** se dijeron cosas muy fuertes *or* muy subidas de tono; **to become h.** *(person)* acalorarse; *(argument, discussion)* subir de tono, acalorarse; **he became quite h. about it** se acaloró mucho con *or* por esto; **things got a bit h.** los ánimos se caldearon bastante

heatedly ['hiːtɪdlɪ] *adv (to debate, argue)* acaloradamente; *(to deny, refuse)* con indignación

heater ['hiːtə(r)] *n* (a) *(radiator)* radiador *m*; *(electric, gas)* estufa *f* (b) *US Fam (pistol)* pipa *m*

heath [hiːθ] *n* (a) *(moor)* brezal *m*, páramo *m* (b) *(plant)* brezo *m*

heathen ['hiːðən] 1 *n* pagano(a) *m,f*
2 *npl* **the h.** los paganos
3 *adj* pagano(a)

heather ['heðə(r)] *n* brezo *m*

Heath Robinson [hiːθ'rɒbɪnsən] *adj Br* complicadísimo(a)

heating ['hiːtɪŋ] *n* calefacción *f*; **to put the h. on** poner *or* encender la calefacción ►► ***h. engineer*** (técnico(a) *m,f*) calefactor(ora) *m,f*

heatproof ['hiːtpruːf] *adj* termorresistente, refractario(a)

heat-resistant ['hiːtrɪzɪstənt] *adj* resistente al calor, refractario(a)

heat-seeking ['hiːtsiːkɪŋ] *adj (missile)* de guiado térmico, termodirigido(a)

heatstroke ['hiːtstrəʊk] *n Med* insolación *f*

heatwave ['hiːtweɪv] *n* ola *f* de calor

heave [hiːv] 1 *vt* (a) *(pull)* tirar de; *(push)* empujar; *(lift)* subir; **she heaved herself out of her chair** se levantó de la silla con dificultad (b) *(throw)* arrojar, lanzar; **he heaved a rock at the bear** le arrojó *or* lanzó una piedra al oso (c) *(sigh)* dar, exhalar; **to h. a sigh of relief** dar *or* exhalar un (profundo) suspiro de alivio, suspirar aliviado(a)
2 *vi* (a) *(pull)* **they heaved on the rope** tiraron *or Andes, CAm, Carib, Méx* jalaron de la cuerda; **h.!** ¡tira!, *Andes, CAm, Carib, Méx* ¡jala!
(b) *(deck, ground)* subir y bajar; *(bosom)* palpitar; **his shoulders heaved with suppressed laughter** de tanto contener la risa, le temblaban *or* se le agitaban los hombros
(c) *Fam (retch)* tener arcadas; *(vomit)* devolver, vomitar; **the sight made my stomach** *or* **me h.** al verlo tuve *or* me dieron arcadas
(d) *Naut* (*pt* **hove** [həʊv]) **to h. into view** *(ship)* aparecer; *Fig Hum (person)* aparecer por el horizonte
(e) *Br Fam* **to be heaving** *(extremely busy)* estar hasta los topes, *Esp* estar hasta la bandera, *RP* estar repleto(a)
3 *n* (a) *(pull)* tirón *m*; *(push)* empujón *m*; **one more h. and we're there** un último esfuerzo y ya está (b) *Fam (dismissal)* **to give sb the h.** *(employee)* poner a alguien en la calle; *(boyfriend, girlfriend)* dar calabazas a alguien; **to get the h.** *(employee)* irse a la calle; *(boyfriend, girlfriend)* quedarse compuesto(a) y sin novio(a)

► **heave to** (*pp* **hove** [həʊv]) *vi Naut (ship)* ponerse al pairo

heave-ho [hiːv'həʊ] 1 *exclam Naut* ¡tira!
2 *n Fam Hum* **to give sb the (old) h.** *(employee)* poner a alguien de patitas en la calle; *(boyfriend, girlfriend)* dar calabazas a alguien; **to get the (old) h.** *(employee)* irse a la calle; *(boyfriend, girlfriend)* quedarse compuesto(a) y sin novio(a)

heaven ['hevən] *n* (a) *(place)* cielo *m*; *(state)* gloria *f*, paraíso *m*; **in h.** en el cielo; *Fig (overjoyed)* en la gloria; **to go to h.** ir al cielo; **this is h.!** ¡esto es gloria *or* el paraíso!; IDIOM **it was like h. on earth** era idílico, era un paraíso; IDIOM **to move h. and earth to do sth** mover *or* remover Roma con Santiago para hacer algo
(b) **the heavens** *(sky)* el cielo; **the heavens opened** cayó un aguacero; IDIOM *Fam* **it stinks to high h.** ¡huele que apesta!
(c) *(in exclamations)* **(good) heavens!, heavens above!** ¡madre mía!, ¡Dios mío!; **thank h. (for that)!** ¡gracias a Dios!; **h. forbid!** ¡Dios no lo quiera!; **h. help you** *(warning)* que Dios te ayude; *(in sympathy)* que Dios lo bendiga; **h. help us** que Dios nos ayude, *Esp* que Dios nos coja confesados; **h. knows!** ¡sabe Dios!; **h. knows we've tried to help!** ¡sabe Dios que hemos hecho cuanto estaba en nuestra mano por ayudar!; **she bought books, magazines and h. knows what (else)** compró libros, revistas y sabe Dios *or* qué sé yo cuántas cosas más; **in h.'s name** por el amor de Dios; **why in h.'s name are you dressed up like that?** por el amor de Dios ¿por qué vas vestido así?; **who in h.'s name told you that?** ¿a ti quién demonios te ha dicho eso?; **for h.'s sake!** ¡por el amor de Dios!

heavenly ['hevənlɪ] *adj* (a) *(of heaven)* celestial; **Our H. Father** Dios Padre (b) *Fam (weather, food)* divino(a); **to have a h. evening** pasar una noche divina *or* de ensueño; **what h. peaches!** ¡qué maravilla de melocotones *or Am* duraznos! (c) *Astron* ***h. body*** cuerpo *m* celeste

heaven-sent ['hevənsent] *adj* como caído(a) del cielo; **a h. opportunity** una ocasión de oro

heavenward ['hevənwəd] 1 *adv (ascend, point, look)* al cielo
2 *adj* dirigido(a) al cielo; **with a h. glance** mirando al cielo

heavenwards ['hevənwədz] *adv (ascend, point, look)* al cielo

heavily ['hevɪlɪ] *adv* (a) *(to fall, walk, sleep)* pesadamente; *(to breathe)* profundamente; **h. built** corpulento(a); **h. laden** muy cargado(a), cargado(a) hasta arriba; IDIOM **to come down h. on sth/sb** *(to penalize, criticize)* pegarle duro a algo/alguien
(b) *(densely)* **h. populated** densamente poblado; **h. wooded** muy boscoso
(c) *(a lot)* **it was raining h.** llovía a cántaros, llovía con fuerza; **it was snowing h.** nevaba intensamente *or* con fuerza; **to drink/smoke h.** beber *or Am* tomar/fumar mucho; **to gamble h.** darle mucho al juego, jugar mucho; **to rely** *or* **depend h. on sth** depender mucho de algo; **to criticize sth/sb h.** criticar duramente algo/a alguien; **to be h. defeated** perder estrepitosamente; **they lost h.** *(team)* perdieron estrepitosamente; *(gamblers, investors)* tuvieron enormes pérdidas; **to be h. taxed** estar sometido(a) a fuertes impuestos; **they were h. involved in training guerillas** estaban metidos de lleno en el adiestramiento de guerrilleros; *Fam* **to be h. into sth** estar metido(a) a tope en algo

heaviness ['hevɪnɪs] *n* (a) *(of load)* peso *m* (b) *(of features)* tosquedad *f*; *(of build)* robustez *f* (c) *(of food)* pesadez *f* (d) *(of rain)* fuerza *f*; *(of responsibilities)* envergadura *f*; *(of defeat, fine, sentence)* dureza *f*

HEAVY ['hevɪ] 1 *adj* (a) *(in weight)* pesado(a); **how h. is it?** ¿cúanto pesa?; **he's twice as h. as I am** pesa el doble que yo; **the branches were h. with apples** las ramas se doblaban bajo el peso de las manzanas; **her eyes were h. with sleep** se le caían los ojos de sueño; *Literary* **she was h. with child** estaba grávida *or* embarazada ►► *Mil* ***h. artillery*** artillería *f* pesada; *US* ***h. cream*** *Esp* nata *f* para montar, *Am* crema *f* líquida enriquecida, *RP* crema *f* doble; *Br* ***h. goods vehicle*** vehículo *m* pesado *or* de gran tonelaje; ***h. industry*** industria *f* pesada; ***h. machinery*** maquinaria *f* pesada; ***h. metal*** *Chem* metal *m* pesado; *(music)* rock *m* duro, heavy metal *m*; *Chem* ***h. water*** agua *f* pesada
(b) *(large, thick) (coat, shoes)* grueso(a); *(features)* tosco(a); *(build)* robusto(a), fornido(a)
(c) *(food)* pesado(a)

(**d**) *(clumsy)* **to be h. on one's feet** ser torpe, ser de movimientos torpes; **a h. hint** una indirecta obvia *or* clara

(**e**) *(intense) (fighting)* enconado(a); *(rain, showers, blow, thud, spending)* fuerte; *(snowfall)* intenso(a), fuerte; *(defeat, fine, sentence)* duro(a); *(period)* abundante; *(drinker, smoker)* empedernido(a); *(sarcasm)* duro(a); **we place h. emphasis on this** hacemos mucho hincapié en esto; **the traffic was very h.** había mucho tráfico *or Am* tránsito; **a h. cold** *(illness)* un fuerte resfriado *or RP* resfrío; **to make h. demands on sb** exigir mucho a alguien; **the project is placing h. demands on our company's resources** el proyecto supone una gran carga financiera para nuestra empresa; **he's a h. drinker** bebe mucho, es un alcohólico; **h. losses** grandes pérdidas; **they hadn't gone further than h. petting** se pegaron un buen lote pero no llegaron a más, *RP* se amasijaron un poco, pero no fueron más lejos; **h. responsibility** gran responsabilidad; **to be a h. sleeper** dormir profundamente; **for h. use** para uso continuado; **we came under h. fire** *Mil* no dejaron de dispararnos; *Fig* recibimos una lluvia de críticas

(**f**) *(oppressive) (smell)* fuerte; *(sky)* cargado(a), plomizo(a); *(clouds)* plomizo(a); *(air, atmosphere)* cargado(a), pesado(a); **you're making h. weather of that job** te estás complicando demasiado la vida para hacer ese trabajo

(**g**) *(hard) (work, day, schedule)* duro(a); *(breathing)* jadeante; **h. breathing** *(on phone)* jadeos; **h. seas** mar gruesa

(**h**) *(soil)* **it was h. underfoot** el suelo estaba embarrado *or* enfangado; **the going is h.** *(in horseracing)* el suelo está embarrado *or* enfangado; *Fig* **the book was h. going** el libro era muy denso

(**i**) *(boring) (book, lecture)* pesado(a), aburrido(a)

(**j**) *Fam (serious, threatening) (situation)* complicado(a), *Esp* chungo(a), *Méx* gocho(a), *RP* fulero(a); **things started to get a bit h.** las cosas empezaron a ponerse complicadas *or Esp* chungas *or Méx* gochas *or RP* fuleras; **to get h. with sb** emplear la mano dura con alguien; **I don't want things to get too h. in our relationship** no quiero una relación demasiado seria

2 *adv* **the lie weighed h. on her conscience** la mentira le pesaba en la conciencia, la mentira le remordía la conciencia; **now he's retired, time hangs h. on his hands** ahora que está jubilado, las horas se le hacen eternas

3 *n* (**a**) *Fam (person)* gorila *m*, matón *m*

(**b**) *Scot (beer)* = cerveza tostada de gusto amargo con poco gas

---

heavy-duty ['hevɪ'dju:tɪ] *adj* (**a**) *(clothing, furniture, boots)* resistente; *(cleaning product)* fuerte, potente; *(equipment)* de gran potencia (**b**) *Fam (serious, major)* **we've got to do some h. socialising** nos va a tocar alternar de lo lindo *or* a base de bien

heavy-handed ['hevɪ'hændɪd] *adj* (**a**) *(clumsy)* torpe; *(tactless, unsubtle) (compliment)* poco sutil; **a h. attempt at humour** un burdo *or* torpe intento de parecer gracioso(a) (**b**) *(harsh) (person)* severo(a), con mano dura; *(policy)* de mano dura; *(action)* duro(a)

heavy-handedness ['hevɪ'hændɪdnɪs] *n* (**a**) *(clumsiness)* torpeza *f*; *(of compliment)* falta *f* de sutileza; *(of humour)* ordinariez *f*, vulgaridad *f* (**b**) *(harshness) (of person)* severidad *f*, mano *f* dura; *(of policy, action)* dureza *f*

heavy-hearted ['hevɪ'hɑ:tɪd] *adj* afligido(a), desconsolado(a)

heavy-set ['hevɪ'set] *adj (solidly built)* fornido(a), corpulento(a)

heavyweight ['hevɪweɪt] **1** *n* (**a**) *(in boxing)* peso *m* pesado (**b**) *Fam (important person)* peso *m* pesado; **a literary h.** un peso pesado de las letras *or* la literatura

2 *adj* (**a**) *(cloth, coat, sweater)* grueso(a) (**b**) *Fam (important)* de peso; **a h. newspaper** un periódico serio *or* de peso (**c**) *(championship, fight)* de los pesos pesados; *(boxer)* de la categoría de los pesos pesados; **the h. title** el título de los pesos pesados

hebe [hi:b] *n US Fam Pej* = término ofensivo para referirse a un judío, *RP* ruso(a) *m,f*

Hebraic [hɪ'breɪɪk] *adj* hebraico(a), hebreo(a)

Hebrew ['hi:bru:] **1** *n* (**a**) *(person)* hebreo(a) *m,f*; **the Hebrews** los hebreos; **the Epistle of Paul to the Hebrews** la epístola de Pablo a los hebreos (**b**) *(language)* hebreo *m*

2 *adj* hebreo(a); **H. script** escritura *f* hebrea

Hebridean [hebrɪ'di:ən] *adj* de las Hébridas

Hebrides ['hebrɪdi:z] *npl* **the (Outer/Inner) H.** las Hébridas (Exteriores/Interiores)

heck [hek] *Fam* **1** *n* **what/who/why the h....?** ¿qué/quién/por qué demonios *or* diablos...?; **what the h. are you doing here?** ¿qué demonios *or* diablos *or Esp* narices haces aquí?; **what the h.!** *(when taking risk)* ¡qué demonios!; **to do sth just for the h. of it** hacer algo porque sí; **we saw a h. of a good movie** vimos una película súper buena *or Esp* tela de buena; **you've got a h. of a cheek coming here** menuda cara le echas viniendo aquí; **a h. of a lot** un montón; **not a h. of a lot** no mucho

2 *exclam* **h., if you don't like it don't buy it!** ¡vaya, hombre!, si no te gusta no lo compres

heckle ['hekəl] **1** *vt* interrumpir (con comentarios impertinentes)

2 *vi* interrumpir (con comentarios impertinentes)

heckler ['heklə(r)] *n* espectador(ora) *m,f* molesto(a)

heckling ['hekəlɪŋ] *n* interrupciones *fpl* impertinentes

hectare ['hektɑ:(r)] *n* hectárea *f*

hectic ['hektɪk] *adj* (**a**) *(eventful, rushed) (lifestyle)* ajetreado(a); *(pace)* vertiginoso(a), frenético(a); *(day, week)* ajetreado(a), agitado(a); **I've had a h. day** no he parado en todo el día, he tenido un día de lo más ajetreado *or* agitado; **things are getting pretty h.** esto ya es no parar (**b**) *Med (fever, flush)* hético(a)

hectogram ['hektəgræm] *n* hectogramo *m*

hectolitre, *US* **hectoliter** ['hektəli:tə(r)] *n* hectolitro *m*

hectometre, *US* **hectometer** ['hektəmi:tə(r)] *n* hectómetro *m*

hector ['hektə(r)] *vt* intimidar; **she tried to h. me into agreeing** trató de intimidarme para que accediera

hectoring ['hektərɪŋ] *adj* intimidante, intimidatorio(a)

he'd [hi:d] = **he had, he would**

hedge [hedʒ] **1** *n* (**a**) *(in field, garden)* seto *m* ►► ***h. sparrow*** acentor *m*; ***h. trimmer*** cortasetos *m or f inv* (**b**) *(protection)* **a h. against inflation** una protección contra la inflación (**c**) *(statement)* excusa *f*, evasiva *f*

2 *vt* (**a**) *(field)* cercar con un seto; **the field was hedged with beech** el campo estaba rodeado de hayas (**b**) **to h. one's bets** *(in betting)* jugar seguro diversificando apuestas; *Fig* cubrirse las espaldas

3 *vi* (**a**) *(in discussion)* responder con evasivas (**b**) *Fin* compensar riesgos *(con operaciones en el mercado de futuros)*

►**hedge about, hedge around** *vt sep* constreñir; **the offer was hedged about with conditions** la oferta estaba plagada de condiciones

►**hedge in** *vt sep* (**a**) *(surround with hedge)* cercar con un seto (**b**) *(person)* **hedged in by restrictions** constreñido(a) or limitado(a) por las restricciones; **I'm feeling hedged in** me siento atado

►**hedge off** *vt sep (area)* limitar con un seto; *(part of area)* separar con un seto

hedgehog ['hedʒhɒg] *n* erizo *m*; **to curl up like a h.** hacerse un ovillo *or* una bola como los erizos

hedge-hop ['hedʒhɒp] *vi* volar a ras de tierra

hedgerow ['hedʒrəʊ] *n* seto *m*

hedonism ['hedənɪzəm] *n* hedonismo *m*

hedonist ['hedənɪst] *n* hedonista *mf*

hedonistic [hedə'nɪstɪk] *adj* hedonista

heebie-jeebies [hi:bɪ'dʒi:bɪz] *npl Fam* **it gives me the h.** me da canguelo *or Méx* mello *or RP* cuiqui

heed [hi:d] **1** *vt* (**a**) *(warning, advice)* prestar atención a, hacer caso de (**b**) *(person)* hacer caso a

2 *n* **to pay** *or* **give h. to, to take h. of** hacer caso de *or* a; **to pay no h. to, to take no h. of** hacer caso omiso de; **he pays little h. to criticism** no hace mucho *or* gran caso de *or* a las críticas; **take h.!** ¡ten cuidado!

heedful ['hi:dfʊl] *adj* consciente; **she's h. of the importance of secrecy** es consciente de la importancia que tiene mantener el secreto

heedless ['hi:dlɪs] *adj* **to be h. of** hacer caso omiso de; **h. of my warning, he drove on** haciendo caso omiso de mi advertencia, siguió conduciendo

heedlessly ['hi:dlɪslɪ] *adv* (**a**) *(without thinking or noticing)* despreocupadamente, sin preocuparse (**b**) *(inconsiderately)* con gran irresponsabilidad

hee-haw ['hi:hɔ:] **1** *n* (**a**) *(noise of donkey)* rebuzno *m* (**b**) *(guffaw)* risotadas *fpl*, carcajada *f*

2 *vi* (**a**) *(donkey)* rebuznar (**b**) *(person)* soltar risotadas, carcajearse

heel [hi:l] **1** *n* (**a**) *(of foot)* talón *m*; **to turn on one's h.** dar media vuelta; **he had the police at his heels** la policía le venía pisando los talones; **to be close** *or* **hard** *or* **hot on sb's heels** ir pisándole los talones a alguien; **famine followed hard on the heels of drought** la sequía le siguió la hambruna sin solución de continuidad; IDIOM **to take to one's heels** poner pies en polvorosa; IDIOM **to come to h.** *(dog)* someterse, obedecer; *Fam (person, party)* doblegarse, doblar la rodilla; IDIOM *Fam* **to cool** *or* **kick one's heels** *(wait)* quedarse esperando un largo rato; IDIOM **to bring sb to h.** meter a alguien en cintura ►► *Br* ***h. bar*** tienda *f* de reparaciones de calzado en el acto

(**b**) *(of sock)* talón *m*; *(of shoe)* tacón *m*, *Am* taco *m*; **high heels**

(shoes) zapatos de tacón *or Am* taco alto; *Fig* **under the h. of fascism** bajo el yugo del fascismo
(**c**) *(of hand)* **the h. of the hand** la parte inferior de la palma de la mano
(**d**) *Fam (contemptible person)* canalla *mf*, desgraciado(a) *m,f*
(**e**) *(of golf club)* talón *m*
(**f**) *(of bread)* cuscurro *m*, punta *f*
2 *vt* (**a**) *(shoe)* poner un tacón *or Am* taco nuevo a (**b**) *(in rugby)* talonar
3 *vi* **h.!** *(to dog)* ¡ven aquí!

▸ **heel over** *vi (ship)* escorar(se)

heft [heft] *Fam* 1 *n* (**a**) *(weight)* peso *m* (**b**) *US (importance, influence)* peso *m*, entidad *f*
2 *vt* (**a**) *(hoist)* subir, levantar (**b**) *(test weight of)* calcular el peso de

hefty ['heftɪ] *adj Fam* (**a**) *(strong) (person)* robusto(a), fornido(a) (**b**) *(heavy) (person)* grueso(a), gordinflón(ona); *(suitcase, box)* pesado(a) (**c**) *(bill, fine, salary)* morrocotudo(a) (**d**) *(blow, slap)* fuerte

hegemony [hɪ'gemənɪ] *n* hegemonía *f*

heifer ['hefə(r)] *n* (**a**) *(young cow)* novilla *f*, vaquilla *f* (**b**) *Fam Pej (fat woman)* vaca *f*, foca *f*

heigh-ho ['heɪhəʊ] *exclam* ¡vaya!, ¡qué se le va a hacer!

height [haɪt] *n* (**a**) *(of person)* estatura *f*, altura *f*; **h.: 1 m 80** *(on form)* estatura: 1,80 m; **of medium** *or* **average h.** de mediana estatura, de estatura media; **what h. are you?** ¿cuánto mides?
(**b**) *(of building, mountain, tree)* altura *f*; **(at/from) a h. of 20,000 metres** (a/desde) una altura de 20.000 metros; **to gain/lose h.** *(of plane)* ganar/perder altura
(**c**) *(high position)* altura *f*; **to fall from a great h.** caer desde gran altura; **the heights above the city** los altos *or* las cumbres que dominan la ciudad; **to be afraid of heights** tener vértigo
(**d**) *(peak)* **the tourist season is at its h.** la temporada turística está en pleno auge; **at the h. of summer** en pleno verano; **at its h. the organization had nearly a million members** en sus mejores momentos *or* en su momento cumbre la organización tenía casi un millón de miembros; **at the h. of the battle** en el momento álgido *or* punto culminante de la batalla; **at the h. of the storm** en plena tormenta; **she's at the h. of her powers** está en plenas facultades; **she's at the h. of her career** está en la cumbre de su carrera; **to reach new heights** *(of talent, career)* alcanzar nuevas cotas; **the h. of fashion** el último grito, la última moda; **to dress in the h. of fashion** vestir a la última (moda); **it's the h. of fashion** es el último grito; **the h. of ignorance/stupidity** el colmo *or* el súmmum de la ignorancia/estupidez; **it's the h. of madness/bad manners!** ¡es el colmo de la locura/mala educación!

heighten ['haɪtən] 1 *vt (fear, pleasure)* intensificar, aumentar; *(effect, contrast, impression)* realzar, acentuar; *(speculation)* alimentar, aumentar; **to h. sb's awareness (of sth)** elevar el grado de concienciación de alguien (sobre algo), concienciar bien a alguien (de algo)
2 *vi (fear, pleasure, tension)* aumentar

heightened ['haɪtənd] *adj (fear, pleasure, tension)* mayor; **a h. sense of injustice** una mayor conciencia de la injusticia

heightening ['haɪtənɪŋ] *adj (fear, expectation, tension)* creciente, cada vez mayor

Heimlich manoeuvre ['haɪmlɪkmə'nu:və(r)] *n* maniobra *f* de Heimlich, abrazo *m* de oso *(para desobstruir tráquea)*

heinie ['hi:nɪ] *n US Fam* (**a**) *(buttocks)* culo *m*, trasero *m* (**b**) *Pej (German)* cabeza *mf* cuadrada, teutón(ona) *m,f*

heinous ['heɪnəs] *adj Formal (crime)* execrable, infame

heir [eə(r)] *n* heredero *m*; **to be h. to sth** ser heredero de algo; **the h. to the throne** el heredero al trono ▸▸ *Law* ***h. apparent*** heredero *m* forzoso; *Fig* heredero *m* natural; *Law* ***h. presumptive*** heredero *m* presunto

heiress ['eərɪs] *n* heredera *f*

heirless ['eəlɪs] *adj* sin herederos

heirloom ['eəlu:m] *n* reliquia *f* familiar

heist [haɪst] *US Fam* 1 *n* golpe *m*, atraco *m*; **to pull a h.** dar un golpe
2 *vt* (**a**) *(money)* afanar, robar (**b**) *(bank)* dar un golpe en, atracar

held *pt & pp of* **hold**

helical ['helɪkəl] *adj* helicoidal

helices *pl of* **helix**

helicopter ['helɪkɒptə(r)] 1 *n* helicóptero *m* ▸▸ ***h. gunship*** helicóptero *m* de guerra
2 *vt* trasladar en helicóptero; **they managed to h. in provisions** lograron llevar provisiones en *or* por helicóptero

helideck ['helɪdek] *n* helipuerto *m* en cubierta

heliocentric [hi:lɪəʊ'sentrɪk] *adj Astron* heliocéntrico(a)

heliograph ['hi:lɪəgrɑ:f] *n* heliógrafo *m*

heliotrope ['hi:lɪətrəʊp] *n* (**a**) *(plant)* heliotropo *m* (**b**) *(colour)* azul *m* heliotropo *or* lila

helipad ['helɪpæd] *n* helipuerto *m*

heliport ['helɪpɔ:t] *n* helipuerto *m*

helium ['hi:lɪəm] *n Chem* helio *m*

helix ['hi:lɪks] *(pl* **helices** ['hi:lɪsi:z] *or* **helixes)** *n* (**a**) hélice *f* (**b**) *Anat* hélix

hell [hel] *n* (**a**) *Rel* infierno *m*; **to go to h.** *(be damned)* ir al infierno
(**b**) ***Hell's Angels*** *(bikers)* los ángeles del infierno
(**c**) *Fam (expressing annoyance)* **h.!** ¡mierda!; **go to h.!** ¡vete a la mierda!; **what the h. do you think you're doing?** ¿me quieres decir qué demonios estás haciendo?; **who the h. are you?** ¿y tú quién diablos *or Esp* leches eres?; **why the h.** *or* **in h.'s name...?** ¿por qué demonios *or* diablos...?; **how the h. should I know?** ¿y yo cómo demonios voy a saberlo?; **are you going? – like** *or* **the h. I am!, am I h.!** ¿vas a ir? – *Esp* ¡y un cuerno voy a ir! *or Méx* ¡ni yendo a bailar a Chalma voy a ir! *or RP* ¡ni en joda voy a ir!; **I'm leaving – like h. you are!** me marcho – ¡ni hablar! *or Esp* ¡de eso nada, monada!; **to h. with it!** ¡que se vaya al infierno!, *Esp* ¡que le den por saco!; **to h. with what they think!** ¡me importa un carajo lo que piensen!; **h.'s bells** *or Br* **teeth!** ¡madre de Dios *or* del amor hermoso!
(**d**) *Fam (as intensifier)* **a h. of a lot of...** una porrada de..., *Méx* un chorro de..., *RP* un toco de...; **it could have been a h. of a lot worse** podría haber sido muchísimo peor; **to have a h. of a time** *(good)* pasárselo como Dios *or RP* como los dioses; *(bad)* pasarlas negras *or Esp* moradas; **we had a h. of a time convincing her** nos costó muchísimo trabajo *or Esp* Dios y ayuda convencerla; **he put up a h. of a fight** opuso muchísima resistencia; **he's one** *or* **a h. of a guy** *Esp* es una pasada de tío, *Am* es un tipo de primera; **she is in a h. of a mess** está metida en un lío de mil demonios *or Esp* de aquí te espero; **a h. of a price** un precio altísimo; **to hurt like h.** doler un montón; **to run like h.** correr como alma que lleva el diablo; **get the h. out of here!** ¡largo de aquí!; **get the h. out of there!** ¡lárgate de allí!; **I wish to h. I knew** ¡ojalá yo lo supiera!; **I just hope to h. he leaves** a ver si se marcha de una maldita vez, que se marche ya por Dios; **did you agree? – h., no!** ¿dijiste que sí? – ¡claro que no! *or Esp* ¡qué va, hombre!
(**e**) *Fam* IDIOMS **it was h. (on earth)** fue un infierno *or* una pesadilla; *US* **it was h. on wheels** fue una pasada; *US* **he's h. on wheels** es un camorrista; **it's colder/hotter than h.** hace un frío/calor de mil demonios; **to be h. on sth** ser criminal *or Esp* fatal para algo; **to go to h. and back** pasarlas negras *or Esp* moradas; **I'll see him in h. before I speak to him again** antes muerta que volver a dirigirle la palabra; **you can wait till h. freezes over** puedes esperar hasta que las ranas críen pelo; **it'll be a cold day in h. before I apologize** no pienso disculparme por nada en el mundo; **the boyfriend/neighbours from h.** una pesadilla de novio/vecinos; **to feel like h.** sentirse muy mal *or Esp* fatal; **to give sb h.** *Esp* hacérselas pasar canutas *or Am* negras a alguien; **give them h.!** *Esp* ¡dales caña!, *Am* ¡reviéntalos!; **these shoes are giving me h.** estos zapatos me están matando; **to knock h. out of sb** pegarle una paliza de muerte a alguien; **to make sb's life h.** amargarle a alguien la vida; **to play (merry) h. with sb** traer a alguien por la calle de la amargura; **to play (merry) h. with sth** hacer estragos en algo; **to go h. for leather** ir a toda mecha; **come h. or high water** pase lo que pase; **all h. broke loose** se armó la gorda *or* la marimorena; **there'll be h. to pay if...** alguien lo va a pasar muy mal si...; **to do sth for the h. of it** hacer algo porque sí; **what the h., you only live once!** ¡qué demonios! ¡sólo se vive una vez! ▸▸ *US* ***h. week*** semana *f* de novatadas *(entre estudiantes)*

he'll [hi:l] = **he will, he shall**

hellacious [he'leɪʃəs] *adj US Fam* (**a**) *(bad, unpleasant)* demencial, *Esp* fatal (**b**) *(excellent)* genial, *Esp* guay (del Paraguay), *Andes, CAm, Carib, Méx* chévere, *Méx* padre, *RP* bárbaro(a)

hellbent ['helbent] *adj Fam* **to be h. on doing sth** tener entre ceja y ceja hacer algo, estar empeñado(a) en hacer algo; **he's h. on going** se le ha metido entre ceja y ceja que tiene que ir

hellcat ['helkæt] *n* bruja *f*, arpía *f*

hellebore ['helɪbɔ:(r)] *n (black)* eléboro *m* (negro); *(white)* eléboro *m* blanco, vedegambre *m*

Hellenic [hɪ'li:nɪk] *adj* helénico(a)

Hellenism ['helənɪzəm] *n* helenismo *m*

Hellenize ['helɪnaɪz] *vt* helenizar

hellfire ['helfaɪə(r)] *n* el fuego del infierno; **a h. preacher/sermon** un predicador/sermón incendiario

hellhole ['helhəʊl] *n Fam (place)* infierno *m*, agujero *m* infecto

hellhound ['helhaʊnd] *n Literary (cruel person)* canalla *mf*, desalmado(a) *m,f*

hellion ['helɪən] *n US Fam* demonio *m*

hellish ['helɪʃ] *adj Fam* infernal, horroroso(a); **I feel h.** me siento horrible *or Esp* fatal *or Esp* de pena

hellishly ['helɪʃlɪ] *adv Fam* endiabladamente, horrorosamente; **it was h. hot** hacía un calor de mil demonios

hellishness ['helɪʃnɪs] *n* atrocidad *f*; **the h. of war** las atrocidades de la guerra

hello [he'ləʊ] **1** *exclam* **(a)** *(as greeting)* ¡hola!; **to say h. to sb** saludar a alguien; **say h. to him for me** salúdalo de mi parte, dale recuerdos de mi parte; **say h. to the lady** dile hola a la señora
(b) *(to attract attention)* ¡eh!, ¡oye!, *Am* ¡ey!; **h. there, wake up!** ¡eh, despierta!
(c) *(on phone) (when answering)* ¿sí?, *Esp* ¿diga?, *Esp* ¿dígame?, *Am* ¿aló?, *Carib, RP* ¿oigo?, *Méx* ¿bueno?, *RP* ¿hola?; *(when calling)* ¡hola!
(d) *(indicating surprise)* **h., what's this?** caramba, ¿qué es esto?
2 *n (greeting)* hola *m*

hell-raiser ['helreɪzə(r)] *n Fam* camorrista *mf*

hell-raising ['helreɪzɪŋ] *n Fam* camorras *fpl*, broncas *fpl*

helluva ['heləvə] *Fam* = **hell of a**

helm [helm] *n* **(a)** *(of ship)* timón *m*; **to be at the h.** *(of ship)* estar al (mando del) timón; *(of party, country)* estar al frente; **to take the h.** *(of ship)* hacerse cargo del timón; *(of party, country)* ponerse al frente, tomar las riendas **(b)** *Archaic (helmet)* yelmo *m*

helmet ['helmɪt] *n* **(a)** *(for policeman, bike rider, soldier)* casco *m* **(b)** *(for knight)* yelmo *m*

helmsman ['helmzmən] *n (on ship)* timonel *m*

HELP [help] **1** *n* **(a)** *(aid)* ayuda *f*; **do you need any h. with that box?** ¿necesitas ayuda para llevar esa caja?; **his directions weren't much h.** sus indicaciones no fueron de mucha ayuda; **to be of h. to sb** ser de ayuda para alguien; **shall I carry this box? – thanks, that would be a h.** ¿llevo esta caja? – sí, sería de gran ayuda; **thank you, you've been a great h.** gracias, has sido de gran ayuda; *Ironic* **you've been a great h.!** ¡gracias por tu ayuda!; **with the h. of sb, with sb's h.** con la ayuda de alguien; **to be beyond h.** no tener remedio; **go and get h.** ve a buscar ayuda ▸▸ ***h. desk*** *(for queries)* servicio *m* de asistencia
(b) *Comptr* ayuda *f* ▸▸ ***h. button*** botón *m* de ayuda; ***h. menu*** menú *m* de ayuda; ***h. screen*** pantalla *f or* ventana *f* de ayuda
(c) *(cleaning woman)* asistenta *f*
(d) *Br Fam (alternative)* **there's no h. for it but to...** no hay más remedio que...
2 *vt* **(a)** *(aid)* ayudar; **to h. sb (to) do sth** ayudar a alguien a hacer algo; **can I h. you?** *(in shop)* ¿en qué puedo servirle?; **this tablet will h. the pain** esta pastilla aliviará el dolor; **the measures should h. growth** estas medidas deberían fomentar el crecimiento; **his comments did little to h. the situation** sus comentarios no fueron una gran ayuda para resolver la situación; **to h. sb across the road** ayudar a alguien a cruzar; **to h. sb on/off with their coat** ayudar a alguien a ponerse/quitarse *or Am* sacarse el abrigo; **h. me up!** ¡ayúdame a subir!; **a man is helping police with their enquiries** la policía esta llevando a cabo el interrogatorio de un sospechoso; **to h. one another** ayudarse mutuamente, ayudarse el uno al otro; **we must h. the poor to h. themselves** debemos ayudar a los pobres a ser autosuficientes; **God** *or* **heaven h. us if they ever find out!** ¡que Dios nos proteja si se enteran!
(b) *(prevent)* **I can't h. it** no lo puedo evitar; **I can't h. it if he won't listen** si él no escucha yo no puedo hacer nada; **it can't be helped** no tiene remedio; **I can't h. being short** no puedo remediar ser bajito; **I can't h. laughing** no puedo evitar reírme; **don't move more than you can h.** muévete lo menos posible; **she couldn't h. overhearing** *or* **but overhear** no pudo evitar oír (la conversación); **I can't h. thinking it's a bit unfair** no puedo evitar pensar que es un poco injusto; **I didn't mean to laugh, but I couldn't h. myself** no quería reírme, pero no lo pude evitar; **not if I can h. it!** ¡no, si lo puedo evitar!
(c) *(take)* **to h. oneself to sth** agarrar *or Esp* coger algo
(d) *(serve)* **can I h. you to some more carrots?** ¿te sirvo más zanahorias?; **h. yourself!** ¡sírvete!
3 *vi* ayudar; **can I h.?** ¿puedo ayudar?; **would it h. if I closed the door?** ¿sirve de algo que cierre la puerta?; **every little helps** toda contribución (ya sea grande o pequeña) es importante; **these measures will h. to reduce unemployment** estas medidas contribuirán a reducir el desempleo *or Am* la desocupación
4 *exclam* **h.!** ¡socorro!

▸ **help out 1** *vt sep* ayudar; **they h. each other out** se ayudan mutuamente
2 *vi* ayudar

helper ['helpə(r)] *n* **(a)** *(assistant)* ayudante *mf* **(b)** *US (apprentice)* aprendiz(iza) *m,f* **(c)** *Comptr* ***h. application*** aplicación *f* auxiliar

helpful ['helpfʊl] *adj* **(a)** *(person) (willing to help)* servicial; **you've been very h.** nos has sido de gran ayuda; **I was only trying to be h.!** ¡sólo trataba de ayudar! **(b)** *(advice, book)* útil; **this book isn't very h.** este libro no es muy útil *or* no es de gran ayuda; **it's often h. to talk to your doctor about it** suele servir de ayuda hablar de ello con el médico

helpfully ['helpfʊlɪ] *adv* **"have you tried asking Sue?" he suggested h.** "¿has probado a preguntar a Sue?" sugirió, tratando de ser útil; **a translation is h. provided** como ayuda se incluye una traducción

helping ['helpɪŋ] **1** *n (portion)* ración *f*; **I had a second h. of spaghetti** repetí (de) espagueti
2 *adj* **to give** *or* **lend a h. hand** echar una mano

helpless ['helplɪs] *adj* **(a)** *(powerless)* impotente; **he gave me a h. look** me lanzó una mirada de impotencia; **we were h. to prevent it** no pudimos evitarlo; **to be h. with laughter** no poder dejar de reír **(b)** *(incapacitated)* incapacitado(a); **he lay h. on the ground** yacía en el suelo incapaz de moverse **(c)** *(defenceless)* indefenso(a)

helplessly ['helplɪslɪ] *adv (powerlessly)* impotentemente, sin poder hacer nada; **he looked on h.** él observaba impotente; **"what can I do?" he said h.** "¿qué puedo hacer?" dijo él, presa de la impotencia; **they giggled h.** no podían parar de reír

helplessness ['helplɪsnɪs] *n* **(a)** *(powerlessness)* impotencia *f* **(b)** *(incapacity)* incapacidad *f* **(c)** *(defencelessness)* indefensión *f*

helpline ['helplaɪn] *n (for people in distress)* teléfono *m* de asistencia *or* ayuda; *(for customers)* servicio *m* de atención *or* asistencia telefónica

helpmate ['helpmeɪt] *n (companion)* compañero(a) *m,f*; *(helper)* ayudante *mf*; *(spouse)* esposo(a) *m,f*

helpmeet ['helpmiːt] *Archaic (companion)* compañero(a) *m,f*; *(helper)* ayudante *mf*; *(spouse)* esposo(a) *m,f*

Helsinki [hel'sɪŋkɪ] *n* Helsinki

helter-skelter ['heltə'skeltə(r)] **1** *n Br (at fairground)* tobogán *m*
2 *adj (rush, account)* atropellado(a)
3 *adv (in disorder)* atropelladamente, a lo loco

hem[1] [hem] **1** *n* dobladillo *m*; **to take up/let down a h.** meter *or* subir/sacar *or* bajar el dobladillo; **she let the h. down on her skirt** le sacó *or* bajo el dobladillo a la falda; **your h.'s coming down** llevas el dobladillo suelto
2 *vt* (*pt & pp* **hemmed**) hacer el dobladillo a

▸ **hem in** *vt sep (surround)* cercar, rodear; **he felt hemmed in** *(in relationship)* se sentía atado; *Fig* **hemmed in by rules** constreñido(a) por las normas

hem[2] [həm] **1** *exclam* ¡ejem!
2 *vi* IDIOM **to h. and haw** titubear, vacilar; **he hemmed and hawed before getting to the point** carraspeó y titubeó un rato antes de abordar el asunto

he-man ['hiːmæn] *n Fam* machote *m*, *Esp* hombretón *m*

hematite, hematologist etc *US* = **haematite, haematologist** *etc*

hemidemisemiquaver ['hemɪ'demɪ'semɪ'kweɪvə(r)] *n Mus* semifusa *f*

hemiplegia [hemɪ'pliːdʒɪə] *n Med* hemiplejia *f*, hemiplejía *f*

hemisphere ['hemɪsfɪə(r)] *n* **(a)** *Geog & Anat* hemisferio *m* **(b)** *Geom* semiesfera *f*

hemispheric(al) [hemɪs'ferɪk(əl)] *adj Geom* semiesférico(a)

hemline ['hemlaɪn] *n* bajo *m*; **hemlines are going up this year** este año se van a llevar las faldas y los vestidos más cortos

hemlock ['hemlɒk] *n* cicuta *f*

hemoglobin, hemophilia etc *US* = **haemoglobin, haemophilia** *etc*

hemp [hemp] *n* **(a)** *(fibre, plant)* cáñamo *m* **(b)** *(drug)* cannabis *m inv*

hemstitch ['hemstɪtʃ] *n* vainica *f*

hen [hen] *n* gallina *f* ▸▸ ***h. coop*** gallinero *m*; ***h. harrier*** aguilucho *m* pálido; *Fam* ***h. party*** *or Br* ***night*** *(before wedding)* despedida *f* de soltera; *(women only)* juerga *f* solo para chicas; ***h. run*** gallinero *m*

henbane ['henbeɪn] *n* beleño *m* negro

hence [hens] *adv* **(a)** *(thus)* de ahí; **he was born on Christmas Day, h. the name Noel** nació el día de Navidad, de ahí el nombre Noel; **they are cheaper and h. more popular** son más baratos y por tanto más populares **(b)** *(from now)* **five years h.** de aquí a cinco años **(c)** *Archaic or Hum (from here)* **(get thee) h.!** ¡atrás!, ¡fuera!

henceforth [hens'fɔːθ], **henceforward** [hens'fɔːwəd] *adv Formal* en lo sucesivo, de ahora/ahí en adelante

henchman ['henʃmən] *n Pej* sicario *m*, secuaz *m*

hencoop ['henku:p] *n* gallinero *m*

henhouse ['henhaʊs] *n* gallinero *m*

henna ['henə] 1 *n* henna *f*
2 *vt (hair)* darse henna en

henpecked ['henpekt] *adj* **a h. husband** un calzonazos

Henry ['henrɪ] *pr n* **H. I/II** Enrique I/II

hepatitis [hepə'taɪtɪs] *n Med* hepatitis *f inv*; **h. A/B** hepatitis A/B

hepatologist [hepə'tɒlədʒɪst] *n Med* hepatólogo(a) *m,f*

hepatology [hepə'tɒlədʒɪ] *n Med* hepatología *f*

heptagon ['heptəgɒn] *n* heptágono *m*

heptagonal [hep'tægənəl] *adj* heptagonal

heptathlete [hep'tæθli:t] *n* heptatleta *mf*

heptathlon [hep'tæθlɒn] *n* heptatlón *m*

HER [hɜ:(r), *unstressed* hə(r)] 1 *possessive adj* **(a)** *(singular)* su; *(plural)* sus; **h. dog** su perro; **h. parents** sus padres; **I took h. motorbike** tomé su moto; *(contrasting with his or theirs)* tome el moto de ella; **what's h. name?** ¿cómo se llama?; **it wasn't HER idea!** ¡no fue idea suya!; **they were upset at h. mentioning it** les sentó *or* cayó mal que lo mencionara; **that wasn't h. understanding** no lo entendió así; **h. sails billowed in the wind** *(of ship)* sus velas ondeaban al viento
(b) *(for parts of body, clothes)* **h. eyes are blue** tiene los ojos azules; **she hit h. head** se dio un golpe en la cabeza; **she washed h. face** se lavó la cara; **she put h. hands in h. pockets** se metió las manos en los bolsillos
2 *pron* **(a)** *(direct object)* la; **I hate h.** la odio; **I like h.** me gusta; **kill h.!** ¡mátala!; **I can forgive her son but not HER** puedo perdonar a su hijo, pero no a ella; **fill h. up!** *(of car)* lleno, por favor
(b) *(indirect object)* le; **I gave h. the book** le di el libro; **I gave it to h.** se lo di; **give it to h.** dáselo (a ella)
(c) *(after preposition)* ella; **I talked to h.** hablé con ella; **her mother lives near h.** su madre vive cerca de su casa; **it was meant for you, not for HER** iba dirigido a ti, no a ella
(d) *(as complement of verb* **to be***)* ella; **it's h.!** ¡es ella!; **it was h. who did it** lo hizo ella; **the coat isn't really h.** el abrigo no va mucho con ella
(e) *Br Fam Hum* **h. indoors** *Esp* la parienta, *Méx* la prenda *or* cobija, *RP* la patrona

---

herald ['herəld] 1 *n* **(a)** *Hist (messenger)* heraldo *m* **(b)** *Literary (forerunner)* heraldo *m*; **a h. of spring** un anuncio *or* presagio de la primavera **(c)** *(record keeper)* heraldo *m*
2 *vt* **(a)** *(announce)* presagiar, anunciar; **the dark sky heralded a storm** el oscuro cielo presagiaba *or* anunciaba tormenta; **his rise to power heralded a new era** su acceso al poder presagiaba la llegada de una nueva era **(b)** *(hail)* anunciar

heraldic [hə'rældɪk] *adj* heráldico(a)

heraldry ['herəldrɪ] *n* heráldica *f*

herb [hɜ:b, *US* ɜ:rb] *n* hierba *f* ►► ***h. garden*** jardín *m* de hierbas; ***h. tea*** infusión *f*

herbaceous [hɜ:'beɪʃəs, *US* ɜ:'beɪʃəs] *adj* herbáceo(a) ►► ***h. border*** arriate *m* de plantas y flores

herbal ['hɜ:bəl, *US* 'ɜ:rbəl] *adj* de hierbas ►► ***h. cigarettes*** cigarrillos *mpl* de hierbas; ***h. medicine*** medicina *f* a base de hierbas; ***h. remedies*** = remedios a base de hierbas medicinales; ***h. tea*** infusión *f*

herbalist ['hɜ:bəlɪst, *US* 'ɜ:rbəlɪst] *n* herbolario(a) *m,f*; **h.'s (shop)** herbolario *m*, herboristería *f*

herbarium [hɜ:'beərɪəm, *US* ɜ:'beərɪəm] *n* herbario *m*

herbicide ['hɜ:bɪsaɪd, *US* 'ɜ:rbɪsaɪd] *n* herbicida *m*

herbivore ['hɜ:bɪvɔ:(r), *US* 'ɜ:rbɪvɔ:(r)] *n* herbívoro *m*

herbivorous [hɜ:'bɪvərəs, *US* ɜ:r'bɪvərəs] *adj* herbívoro(a)

herculean [hɜ:kjʊ'lɪən] *adj (strength)* hercúleo(a), titánico(a); *(struggle, effort)* titánico(a); *(task)* ingente, titánico(a)

Hercules ['hɜ:kjʊli:z] *n Mythol* Hércules

herd [hɜ:d] 1 *n* **(a)** *(of cattle, sheep)* rebaño *m*; *(of horses, elephants)* manada *f* **(b)** *(of people)* rebaño *m*, manada *f*; **to follow the h.** dejarse llevar por la masa ►► ***the h. instinct*** el instinto gregario
2 *vt* **(a)** *(bring together)* juntar, reunir; *(look after)* criar **(b)** *(drive) (cattle, people)* conducir; **the cattle were herded into the barn** metieron al ganado en el pajar, condujeron el ganado hasta el pajar; **the prisoners were herded onto trucks** los prisioneros fueron hacinados en camiones
3 *vi* **to h. (together)** juntarse, apiñarse

herder ['hɜ:də(r)] *n esp US (of cattle)* vaquero(a) *m,f*; *(of sheep)* pastor(ora) *m,f*; *(of goats)* cabrero(a) *m,f*

herdsman ['hɜ:dzmən] *n (of cattle)* vaquero *m*; *(of sheep)* pastor *m*; *(of goats)* cabrero *m*

HERE [hɪə(r)] 1 *n* **the h. and now** el aquí y ahora
2 *adv* **(a)** *(referring to position)* aquí; **come h.!** ¡ven aquí!; **h. she comes** aquí viene; **she's not h.** no está aquí; **they're still not h.** todavía no están aquí, todavía no llegaron; **h. it/he is** aquí está; **h. you are, we couldn't find you!** ¡estás aquí, no te encontrábamos por ninguna parte!; **h. we are in San Francisco** estamos en San Francisco; **h.'s Nick** aquí está *or* llega Nick; **my friend h.** mi amigo(a), este(a) amigo(a) mío(a); **h.'s what you have to do** esto es lo que tienes que hacer; **in/out h.** aquí dentro/fuera; **over h.** aquí; **round h.** por aquí; **up/down h.** aquí arriba/abajo; **what have we h.?** ¿qué es esto?, ¿qué tenemos aquí?; *Fam* **give it h.!** trae, dámelo; **h.!** *(at roll call)* ¡presente!; **h.!, come and look at this** ¡ven!, echa un vistazo a esto; **h., let me try** a ver, déjame que pruebe, *RP* ¡che!, ¿qué hacés?; **h. boy!** *(to dog)* ¡ven aquí!; *Br* **h., you, what are you doing?** ¡oye, tú!, ¿qué haces?; **h. and now** aquí y ahora; **h. and there** aquí y allá; *Fig* **that's neither h. nor there** eso es irrelevante; **h., there and everywhere** por *or* en todas partes; **h. goes!** ¡vamos allá!; **h. we go again!** ¡ya estamos otra vez con lo mismo!; **it looks like mobile phones are h. to stay** parece que los teléfonos móviles no son una moda pasajera; **now where's her address? ah, h. we are!** a ver, ¿dónde está su dirección? ¡ah, aquí está!
(b) *(referring to time)* ahora, aquí; **what you need to remember h. is...** ahora *or* aquí lo que tienes que recordar es...; **the moment we've all been waiting for is finally h.** por fin ha llegado el momento que todos estábamos esperando; **where do we go from h.?** ¿y ahora qué hacemos?
(c) *(when giving)* **h.'s that tape I promised you** aquí tienes la cinta que te prometí; **h. you are!** *(when giving something)* aquí tienes, toma; **h. (you are), have some of this whisky** toma un poco de este whisky
(d) *(in toasts)* **h.'s to the future!** ¡por el futuro!; **h.'s to you!** ¡por ti!, ¡(a tu) salud!

---

hereabout(s) ['hɪərəbaʊt(s)] *adv* por aquí

hereafter [hɪər'ɑ:ftə(r)] 1 *adv Formal* de aquí *or* de hoy en adelante; *(in document)* en adelante, en lo sucesivo
2 *n Literary* **the h.** el más allá

hereby [hɪə'baɪ] *adv Formal (in writing)* por la presente; *(in speech)* por el presente acto; **I h. declare my intention to...** y quiero anunciar mi intención de...; **I h. pronounce you man and wife** desde ahora os declaro marido y mujer

hereditary [hɪ'redɪtərɪ] *adj* hereditario(a) ►► *Br Parl* ***h. peer*** noble *m* hereditario; *Br Parl* ***h. peerage*** título *m* de nobleza hereditario

heredity [hɪ'redɪtɪ] *n* herencia *f*

herein [hɪə'rɪn] *adv* **(a)** *Law (in this document)* aquí, en este documento; **the letter h. enclosed** la carta que aquí se adjunta **(b)** *Formal (in this respect)* **h. lies the difference between them** aquí radica la diferencia entre ellos

hereinafter ['hɪərɪn'ɑ:ftə(r)] *adv Formal or Law* (de aquí) en adelante, en lo sucesivo

hereof [hɪə'rɒv] *adv Formal or Law* al respecto

hereon [hɪə'rɒn] *adv Formal or Law* al respecto

heresiarch [he'ri:zɪɑ:k] *n* heresiarca *mf*

heresy ['herəsɪ] *n* herejía *f*

heretic ['herətɪk] *n* hereje *mf*

heretical [hɪ'retɪkəl] *adj* herético(a)

hereto [hɪə'tu:] *adv Law (to this document)* con este documento

heretofore [hɪətʊ'fɔ:(r)] *adv Formal or Law* hasta ahora

hereunder [hɪə'rʌndə(r)] *adv Formal or Law* **(a)** *(below)* a continuación **(b)** *(by this document)* por el presente documento

hereupon [hɪərə'pɒn] *adv Formal or Law* **(a)** *(immediately after this)* a partir de aquí **(b)** *(upon this subject)* al respecto

herewith [hɪə'wɪð] *adv Formal or Law* con este documento; **enclosed h. is the information you requested** le enviamos adjunta la información que solicitó

heritable ['herɪtəbəl] *adj* **(a)** *(property)* heredable **(b)** *(characteristic)* hereditario(a)

heritage ['herɪtɪdʒ] *n* (a) *(of nation, people)* patrimonio *m*; **their rich cultural h.** su rico patrimonio cultural ▸▸ ***h. centre*** = edificio con museo en un lugar de interés histórico o cultural; ***h. site*** lugar *m* declarado de interés histórico-artístico (b) *(of person)* herencia *f*, patrimonio *m*

herky-jerky ['hɜːkɪ'dʒɜːkɪ] *adj Fam (movement)* brusco(a);

hermaphrodite [hɜː'mæfrədaɪt] 1 *n* hermafrodita *mf*
2 *adj* hermafrodita

hermeneutic(al) [hɜːmə'njuːtɪk(əl)] *adj* hermenéutico(a)

hermeneutics [hɜːmə'njuːtɪks] *n* hermenéutica *f*

hermetic [hɜː'metɪk] *adj* hermético(a)

hermetically [hɜː'metɪklɪ] *adv* herméticamente; **h. sealed** herméticamente cerrado(a)

hermit ['hɜːmɪt] *n* ermitaño(a) *m,f* ▸▸ ***h. crab*** cangrejo *m* ermitaño

False friend: The Spanish noun **ermita** is not a translation for the English word **hermit**. In Spanish **ermita** means "country chapel" or "hermitage".

hermitage ['hɜːmɪtɪdʒ] *n* ermita *f*

hernia ['hɜːnɪə] *n Med* hernia *f*

herniated ['hɜːnɪeɪtɪd] *adj Med* ***h. disc*** hernia *f* discal

hero ['hɪərəʊ] (*pl* **heroes**) *n* (a) *(brave man)* héroe *m*; *(in fiction)* protagonista *m*; **they gave him a h.'s welcome** lo recibieron como a un héroe (b) *(idol)* ídolo *m*; *Fam* **my h.!** ¡mi ídolo *or* héroe! ▸▸ ***h. worship*** idolatría *f* (c) *US Fam (sandwich) Esp* flauta *f*, = sándwich hecho con una barra de pan larga y estrecha, rellena de varios ingredientes

Herod ['herəd] *pr n* Herodes

heroic [hɪ'rəʊɪk] *adj* (a) *(person, effort, sacrifice)* heroico(a) (b) *Lit* ***h. couplets*** pareados *mpl* en verso heroico

heroically [hɪ'rəʊɪklɪ] *adv* heroicamente

heroics [hɪ'rəʊɪks] *npl* (a) *(behaviour)* heroicidades *fpl*; **we don't want any h.** nada de heroicidades, que nadie intente hacerse el héroe (b) *(language)* palabras *fpl* hueras

heroin ['herəʊɪn] *n (drug)* heroína *f* ▸▸ ***h. addict*** heroinómano(a) *m,f*

heroine ['herəʊɪn] *n (female hero)* heroína *f*

heroism ['herəʊɪzəm] *n* heroísmo *m*

heron ['herən] *n* garza *f*

hero-worship ['hɪərəʊwɜːʃɪp] (*pt & pp* **hero-worshipped**) *vt* idolatrar

herpes ['hɜːpiːz] *n* herpes *m inv* ▸▸ *Med* ***h. simplex*** herpes *m* simple; *Med* ***h. zoster*** herpes *m* zóster

herring ['herɪŋ] (*pl* **herring** *or* **herrings**) *n* arenque *m* ▸▸ ***h. gull*** gaviota *f* argéntea

herringbone ['herɪŋbəʊn] *n* (a) *(on cloth)* espiguilla *f*, espiga *f* ▸▸ ***h. stitch*** punto *m* de espiga (b) *(in skiing)* tijera *f*

hers [hɜːz] *possessive pron* (a) *(singular)* el suyo *m*, la suya *f*; *(plural)* los suyos *mpl*, las suyas *fpl*; *(to distinguish)* el/la/los/las de ella; **my house is big but h. is bigger** mi casa es grande, pero la suya es mayor; **he didn't have a book so she gave him h.** no tenía libro así que ella le dio el suyo; **it must be one of h.** debe de ser uno de los suyos/una de las suyas; **it wasn't his fault, it was HERS** no fue culpa de él, sino de ella; **h. is the work I admire most** su obra es la que más admiro
(b) *(used attributively) (singular)* suyo(a); *(plural)* suyos(as); **this book is h.** este libro es suyo; **a friend of h.** un amigo suyo; **I can't stand that boyfriend/dog of h.** no soporto a ese novio/perro que tiene
(c) *Fam (her house, flat)* su casa

herself [hɜː'self] *pron* (a) *(reflexive)* se; **she hurt h.** se hizo daño; **she introduced h.** se presentó; **she bought h. a coat** se compró un abrigo; **she could see h. reflected in the water** vio su imagen reflejada *or* se vio reflejada en el agua
(b) *(unaided, alone)* ella sola; **she can do it h.** (ella) puede hacerlo sola; **she made the pattern h.** ella sola hizo el diseño
(c) *(emphatic)* ella misma; **she told me h.** me lo dijo ella misma; **she h. did not believe it** ella misma no se lo creía; **she h. saw them leave** ella (misma) los vio salir con sus propios ojos
(d) *(her usual self)* **she's not h. today** hoy está un poco rara; **she's feeling h. again** vuelve a sentirse la de siempre
(e) *(after preposition)* ella; **she talks about h. a lot** habla mucho de sí misma; **she did it all by h.** lo hizo ella misma *or* ella sola; **she lives by h.** vive sola; **she was all by h.** estaba (completamente) sola; **she bought it for h.** se lo compró para ella; **she talks to h.** habla sola; **"how unfair!" she thought to h.** "¡qué injusto!" pensó para sus adentros
(f) *(replacing 'her')* **it is meant for people like h.** está pensado para gente como ella

Herts [hɑːts] (*abbr* **Hertfordshire**) Hertfordshire

hertz [hɜːts] (*pl* **hertz**) *n Phys* hercio *m*

he's [hiːz] = **he is, he has**

hesitancy ['hezɪtənsɪ] *n* duda *f*, vacilación *f*

hesitant ['hezɪtənt] *adj (speaker, smile, gesture)* vacilante, dubitativo(a); *(speech, voice)* vacilante, titubeante; **to be/seem h.** estar/parecer indeciso(a); **to be h. about doing sth** tener dudas a la hora de hacer algo; **I'm h. about sending her to a new school** no me decido a cambiarla de colegio; **I would be h. to...** no me atrevería a...

hesitantly ['hezɪtəntlɪ] *adv (to act, try)* con indecisión, sin demasiada convicción; *(to answer, speak)* con vacilación, de modo vacilante

hesitate ['hezɪteɪt] *vi* dudar, vacilar; **she wrote to them after hesitating for some time** tras dudarlo un tiempo, se decidió a escribirles; **he will h. at nothing** no duda *or* vacila ante nada; **he wouldn't h. to have you shot** no dudaría un momento en ordenar que te fusilaran; **I h. to say this, but...** no sé si debería decir esto, pero...; **don't h. to ask for advice** no dude en pedir ayuda; **don't h. to call me** llámame, no dudes en llamarme; PROV **he who hesitates is lost** camarón que se duerme, se lo lleva la corriente

hesitatingly ['hezɪteɪtɪŋlɪ] *adv* con vacilación, de modo vacilante

hesitation [hezɪ'teɪʃən] *n* vacilación *f*, titubeo *m*; **after much h.** tras dudarlo mucho; **she answered with some h.** dudó *or* vaciló *or* titubeó un poco al contestar; **I would have no h. in recommending her** no dudaría en recomendarla, la recomendaría sin dudarlo un momento; **without (a moment's) h.** sin vacilar

hessian ['hesɪən] 1 *n* arpillera *f*
2 *adj* de arpillera

hetero ['hetərəʊ] *Fam* 1 *n* (*pl* **heteros**) hetero *mf*, heterosexual *mf*
2 *adj* hetero, heterosexual

heterodox ['hetərədɒks] *adj* heterodoxo(a)

heterodoxy ['hetərədɒksɪ] *n* heterodoxia *f*

heterogeneity [hetərəʊdʒɪ'niːɪtɪ] *n* heterogeneidad *f*

heterogeneous [hetərə'dʒiːnɪəs] *adj* heterogéneo(a)

heteronym ['hetərənɪm] *n Gram* heterónimo *m*

heterosexual [hetərəʊ'seksjʊəl] 1 *n* heterosexual *mf*
2 *adj* heterosexual

heterosexuality [hetərəseksjʊ'ælɪtɪ] *n* heterosexualidad *f*

het up ['het'ʌp] *adj Fam (angry)* furioso(a), *Esp* mosqueado(a); *(tense)* nervioso(a); **to get (all) h. (about sth)** *(angry)* enfurecerse *or Esp* mosquearse (por algo); *(tense)* ponerse nervioso (por algo)

heuristic [hjʊə'rɪstɪk] 1 *n (program, method)* método *m* heurístico
2 *adj* heurístico(a)

heuristics [hjuː'rɪstɪks] *npl* heurística *f*

hevea ['hiːvɪə] *n* hevea *m*

HEW [eɪtʃiː'dʌbəljuː] *n US Formerly* (*abbr* **(Department of) Health, Education and Welfare**) = ministerio estadounidense de educación, sanidad y seguridad social

hew [hjuː] (*pp* **hewn** [hjuːn] *or* **hewed**) 1 *vt (cut down)* cortar; *(shape)* tallar; *(coal)* picar; **they hewed a path through the jungle** abrieron un sendero por la selva; **it was hewn from a single block of stone** fue tallado de una sola pieza de piedra; **the cavern had been hewn out of the rock** la caverna había sido excavada en la roca
2 *vi US (conform)* ajustarse; **they hewed to the company line** se ajustaron a *or* siguieron la política de la empresa

hex[1] [heks] *US* 1 *n* (a) *(spell)* hechizo *m*, maldición *f*; **to put a h. on sb** hechizar a alguien, echar una maldición a alguien (b) *(witch)* bruja *f*
2 *vt* hechizar, echar una maldición a

hex[2] *n Comptr Fam* (sistema *m*) hexadecimal *m*

hexadecimal [heksə'desɪməl] *adj Comptr* hexadecimal ▸▸ ***h. system*** sistema *m* hexadecimal

hexagon ['heksəgən] *n* hexágono *m*

hexagonal [hek'sægənəl] *adj* hexagonal

hexahedron [heksə'hiːdrən] *n* hexaedro *m*

hexameter [hek'sæmɪtə(r)] *n* hexámetro *m*

hexasyllabic [heksəsɪ'læbɪk] *adj* hexasílabo(a)

hey [heɪ] *exclam (to draw attention)* ¡eh!, ¡oye!, ¡oiga!; *(to show surprise, protest)* ¡eh!, ¡oye!; *Br* **h. presto!** ¡ale-hop!

heyday ['heɪdeɪ] *n* apogeo *m*, auge *m*; **in his/its h.** en pleno apogeo, en su mejor época; **the h. of British theatre** el apogeo *or* auge del teatro británico

HF (*abbr* **high frequency**) frecuencia *f* alta, HF

HGV [eɪtʃdʒiː'viː] *n Br* (*abbr* **heavy goods vehicle**) vehículo *m* pesado *or* de gran tonelaje; **an H. licence** un permiso para conducir vehículos pesados *or* de gran tonelaje, *Esp* ≃ un permiso de conducir del tipo C

HHS [eɪtʃeɪtʃ'es] *n US* (*abbr* **(Department of) Health and Human Services**) = ministerio estadounidense de sanidad y seguridad social

HI (*abbr* **Hawaii**) Hawai

hi [haɪ] *exclam Fam* ¡hola!

hiatus [haɪ'eɪtəs] *n* **(a)** *(interruption)* interrupción *f*, paréntesis *m inv* **(b)** *(blank space)* laguna *f* **(c)** *Med* ***h. hernia*** hernia *f* de hiato

hibernate ['haɪbəneɪt] *vi* hibernar

hibernation [haɪbə'neɪʃən] *n* hibernación *f*; **to go into h.** hibernar, entrar en estado de hibernación

Hibernian [haɪ'bɜːnɪən] **1** *n* hibernés(esa) *m,f*, irlandés(esa) *m,f*
 2 *adj* hibernés(esa), irlandés(esa)

hibiscus [hɪ'bɪskəs] *n* hibisco *m*

hiccup, hiccough ['hɪkʌp] **1** *n* **(a)** *(sound)* hipo *m*; **to have (the) hiccups** tener hipo; **it gave me the hiccups** me dio hipo **(b)** *Fam (minor problem)* traspié m, desliz *m*; **there's been some sort of h. with the delivery** parece que ha habido algún problemilla con la entrega
 2 *vi* (*pt & pp* **hiccupped**) *(repeatedly)* tener hipo; *(once)* hipar

hick [hɪk] *US Fam* **1** *n* pueblerino(a) *m,f*, *Esp* paleto(a) *m,f*, *Méx* paisa *mf*, *RP* pajuerano(a) *m,f*
 2 *adj* de pueblo, *Esp* paleto(a), *Méx* paisa, *RP* de afuera; **a h. town** una aldeúcha

hickey ['hɪkɪ] *n US Fam* **(a)** *(lovebite)* marca *f* (de un beso), *Esp* chupetón *m*, *Am* chupón *m* **(b)** *(gadget)* cacharro *m*, chisme *m*, *CAm, Carib, Col* vaina *f*, *RP* coso *m*

hickory ['hɪkərɪ] *n (tree, wood)* nogal *m* americano

hickory-smoked ['hɪkərɪ'sməʊkt] *adj (ham, cheese)* ahumado(a) con leña de nogal americano

hid *pt of* **hide**

hidden ['hɪdən] **1** *adj* oculto(a); **to be h.** estar oculto(a); **she has h. talents** tiene algunos talentos ocultos ►► ***h. agenda*** objetivo *m* secreto; ***h. extras*** gastos *mpl* extras; *Comptr* ***h. file*** archivo *m or* fichero *m* oculto; ***h. hand*** mano *f* oculta *or* negra; *Comptr* ***h. text*** texto *m* oculto; ***h. unemployment*** desempleo *m* encubierto
 2 *pp of* **hide**

hide[1] [haɪd] **1** *vt* (*pt* **hid** [hɪd], *pp* **hidden** ['hɪdən]) **(a)** *(conceal)* esconder **(from** de); **they hid him from the police** lo escondieron de la policía *or* para que no lo encontrara la policía; **the town was hidden from view** no se podía ver el pueblo; **to h. oneself** esconderse; **where have you been hiding yourself recently?** ¿dónde te metes últimamente?; **to h. one's face in one's hands** taparse la cara con las manos; IDIOM **to h. one's light under a bushel** no hacer alardes de las propias cualidades **(b)** *(not reveal) (emotions, truth)* ocultar; **to h. the truth from sb** ocultarle la verdad a alguien; **to have nothing to h.** no tener nada que ocultar
 2 *vi* esconderse **(from** de); **to h. behind an excuse/statistics** parapetarse tras *or* ampararse en alguna excusa/las estadísticas
 3 *n Br (for birdwatching)* puesto *m* de observación

►**hide away 1** *vt* esconder; **to h. oneself away** esconderse
 2 *vi* esconderse

►**hide out** *vi* esconderse

hide[2] *n* **(a)** *(skin)* piel *f* **(b)** IDIOMS **to save one's h.** salvar el pellejo; *Fam* **to tan sb's h.** dar una buena paliza *or* tunda a alguien; **I'll have your h. for that** como te agarre, te despellejo; **I haven't seen h. nor hair of her** no le he visto el pelo

hide-and-seek ['haɪdən'siːk], *US* **hide-and-go-seek** ['haɪdəngəʊ'siːk] *n* escondite *m*, *Am* escondidas *fpl*; **to play h.** jugar al escondite

hideaway ['haɪdəweɪ] *n* escondite *m*, escondrijo *m*

hidebound ['haɪdbaʊnd] *adj (person, attitude)* retrógrado(a), encorsetado(a)

hideous ['hɪdɪəs] *adj* **(a)** *(physically ugly)* horrendo(a), horroroso(a) **(b)** *(horrific) (conditions, situation)* terrible, espantoso(a); *(cruelty, crime)* atroz, espantoso(a)

hideously ['hɪdɪəslɪ] *adv* **(a)** *(deformed, wounded)* horrorosamente, espantosamente **(b)** *(cruel)* horrorosamente, espantosamente **(c)** *(as intensifier)* **h. expensive** terriblemente *or* tremendamente caro, carísimo; **h. embarrassing** terriblemente *or* tremendamente embarazoso

hideout ['haɪdaʊt] *n* guarida *f*, escondite *m*

hidey-hole ['haɪdɪhəʊl] *n Fam* escondite *m*, escondrijo *m*

hiding[1] ['haɪdɪŋ] *n* **to be in h.** *(criminal, celebrity)* estar escondido(a); *(for political reasons)* estar en la clandestinidad; **to go into h.** *(criminal, celebrity)* esconderse; *(for political reasons)* pasar a la clandestinidad; **to come out of h.** *(criminal, celebrity)* salir del escondite; *(for political reasons)* salir de la clandestinidad ►► ***h. place*** escondite *m*

hiding[2] *n Fam (beating, defeat)* paliza *f*; **to give sb a h.** dar una paliza a alguien; IDIOM *Br* **to be on a h. to nothing** no tener nada que hacer, estar perdiendo el tiempo

hie [haɪ] *Archaic or Hum* **1** *vt* **h. thee hence!** ¡id presto!
 2 *vi* apresurarse, ir presto

hierarchic(al) [haɪə'rɑːkɪk(əl)] *adj* jerárquico(a) ►► *Comptr* ***h. file system*** sistema *m* de archivos jerárquicos; *Comptr* ***h. menu*** menú *m* jerárquico

hierarchically [haɪə'rɑːkɪklɪ] *adv* jerárquicamente

hierarchy ['haɪərɑːkɪ] *n* jerarquía *f*

hieroglyph ['haɪərəglɪf] *n* jeroglífico *m*

hieroglyphics [haɪərə'glɪfɪks] *npl* jeroglíficos *mpl*; *Fam Fig (handwriting)* garabatos *mpl*

hi-fi ['haɪ'faɪ] **1** *n* **(a)** *(stereo system)* equipo *m* de alta fidelidad **(b)** *(reproduction)* alta fidelidad *f*
 2 *adj* de alta fidelidad; **h. set** *or* **system** equipo de alta fidelidad

higgledy-piggledy ['hɪgəldɪ'pɪgəldɪ] *Fam* **1** *adj* embarullado(a)
 2 *adv* de cualquier manera, a la buena de Dios

HIGH [haɪ] **1** *n* **(a)** *(peak)* punto *m* álgido; *Fam (from drugs)* colocón *m*; **to reach a new h.** *(in career, performance)* alcanzar nuevas cotas de éxito; *(unemployment, inflation)* alcanzar un nuevo máximo *or* récord; **prices are at an all-time h.** los precios han alcanzado un máximo histórico; **to be on a h.** *(from drugs)* estar colocado(a); *(from success)* estar ebrio(a) de triunfo; **highs and lows** altibajos; **there have been more highs than lows** ha habido más momentos buenos que malos
 (b) *(setting)* **I put the oven/iron on h.** puse la temperatura del horno/de la plancha en el máximo
 (c) *Met (area of high pressure)* anticiclón *m*; *(highest temperature)* máxima *f*
 (d) *Rel* **on h.** en el cielo; **the Most H.** el Altísimo; *Fig* **an order from on h.** una orden de arriba
 2 *adj* **(a)** *(mountain, building)* alto(a); **how h. is it?** ¿qué altura tiene?; **it's 2 metres h.** tiene 2 metros de altura; **at h. altitude** a mucha altitud; **the sun was h. in the sky** el sol estaba alto; *Fig* **this reform is h. on the agenda** *or* **list** esta reforma es prioritaria; *Fig* **to get on one's h. horse about sth** echar un sermón sobre algo; **on the h. seas** en alta mar ►► ***h. board*** *(in diving)* palanca *f*; ***h. diving*** salto *m* de trampolín; ***h. ground*** terreno *m* elevado; **to gain the moral h. ground** erigirse como autoridad moral; ***h. heels*** tacones *mpl or Am* tacos *mpl* altos; ***h. jump*** salto *m* de altura, *Am* salto *m* alto; IDIOM *Br Fam* **you'll be for the h. jump** *(will be punished)* vas a cobrar, *Esp* te vas a enterar de lo que vale un peine; ***h. jumper*** saltador(ora) *m,f* de altura; ***h. tide*** marea *f* alta; ***h. wire*** cuerda *f* floja
 (b) *(price, speed, number, score, standards)* alto(a), elevado(a); *(frequency, temperature, voltage)* alto(a); *(risk, danger)* grande; *(reputation)* bueno(a), excelente; **the h. quality of our products** la gran calidad de nuestros productos; **to be h. in calories/fibre** tener alto contenido calórico/en fibra; **our chances of success remain h.** aún tenemos muchas posibilidades de éxito; **we had h. hopes of winning** teníamos muchas esperanzas de ganar; **to have a h. opinion of sb** tener una buena opinión de alguien; *Pej* **to have a h. opinion of oneself** tener una alta opinión de sí mismo(a); **to hold sb in h. esteem** *or* **regard** tener a alguien en gran estima; **the total could be as h. as 150** el total podría alcanzar los 150; **at h. speed** a gran velocidad; **the figure is in the h. sixties** la cifra se acerca a setenta ►► *US Aut* ***h. beam*** luces *fpl* largas *or Am* altas, luces *fpl* de carretera; ***h. explosive*** explosivo *m* de gran potencia; ***h. fidelity*** alta fidelidad *f*; *Aut* ***h. gear*** directa *f*, marcha *f* alta; *Fig* **they moved into h. gear** comenzaron a dar todo de sí; *Fam* ***h. jinks*** juerga *f*, jarana *f*; *Ironic* **there'll be h. jinks if my parents find out** como se enteren mis padres, se arma la gorda *or* les da un patatús; ***h. point*** punto *m or* momento *m* culminante; *US Fam* ***h. roller*** *(gambler)* jugador(ora) *m,f*; ***the h. season*** la temporada alta; ***h. spot*** punto *m or* momento *m* culminante; ***h. technology*** alta tecnología *f*; *Law* ***h. treason*** alta traición *f*; ***h. winds*** viento *m* fuerte
 (c) *(rank, position)* elevado(a), alto(a); *(honour, award, priority)* alto(a); **to have a h. profile** ser muy prominente *or* destacado(a); **to act all h. and mighty** comportarse de forma arrogante; **he took a very h. moral tone** adoptó un tono moral elevado; **to lead** *or* **live the h. life** darse *or* pegarse la gran vida; **the pressures of h. office** las presiones de ocupar un alto cargo ►► *Rel* ***h. altar*** altar *m* mayor; ***h. camp:*** **in a**

style of h. camp con mucha pluma; *Rel* ***H. Church*** = sección de la iglesia anglicana más próxima al catolicismo; *Mil* ***h. command*** alto mando *m*; ***H. Commission*** = embajada de un país de la Commonwealth en otro; ***H. Commissioner*** = embajador de un país de la Commonwealth en otro; ***H. Court*** Tribunal *m* Supremo; ***h. fashion*** alta costura *f*; ***h. finance*** altas finanzas *fpl*; ***H. German*** alto alemán *m*; ***H. Mass*** misa *f* solemne; ***the H. Middle Ages*** la Alta Edad Media; ***h. priest*** sumo sacerdote *m*; *Fig* **the h. priests of fashion** los reyes de la alta costura; ***h. priestess*** suma sacerdotisa *f*; *Fig* **the h. priestess of rock** la reina del rock; *Old-fashioned* ***h. road*** carretera *f* principal; *Fig* **the h. road to success** la vía directa hacia el éxito; ***h. school*** *(in US)* instituto *m* de enseñanza secundaria *(de 14 a 18 años)*; *(in UK)* instituto *m* de enseñanza secundaria *(de 11 a 18 años)*; ***h. society*** alta sociedad *f*; *Br* ***h. street*** calle *f* principal; *Br* **the h. street has been badly hit by the recession** el pequeño comercio se ha visto gravemente afectado por la recesión; *Br* ***h. table*** = mesa reservada para los profesores en los comedores de las universidades británicas, especialmente en Oxford y Cambridge

(**d**) *(forehead)* amplio(a), ancho(a); **to have h. cheekbones** tener los pómulos salientes

(**e**) *(river)* crecido(a), alto(a)

(**f**) *(in tone, pitch)* agudo(a); *Fig* **h. note** *(of career, performance)* punto culminante

(**g**) *(excited, cheerful)* **in h. spirits** muy animado(a); **spirits are h. amongst the staff** el personal está muy animado; **we had a h. old time** nos lo pasamos estupendamente

(**h**) *(intensely emotional)* **moments of h. drama** momentos de gran dramatismo; **a tale of h. adventure** una historia de emocionantes aventuras

(**i**) *Br (complexion)* **to have a h. colour** tener los colores subidos

(**j**) *(of time)* **it's h. time you got yourself a job** ya es hora de que te busques un trabajo ▸▸ ***h. noon*** *(midday)* mediodía *m*; ***h. summer*** pleno verano *m*; *Br* ***h. tea*** merienda *f* cena

(**k**) *(in cards)* **aces are h.** el as es el más alto

(**l**) *Comptr* ***h. memory*** memoria *f* alta; ***h. resolution*** alta resolución *f*

(**m**) *(meat)* pasado(a)

(**n**) *Geog (latitude)* alto(a)

(**o**) *Ling (vowel)* alto(a)

(**p**) *(traditional)* **a h. Tory** un conservador de los de la vieja escuela; **h. Anglicans** = miembros de la iglesia anglicana más próximos al catolicismo en sus creencias y ceremonias

(**q**) *Fam* **to be h.** *(on drugs)* estar colocado(a) *or RP* entregado(a); *Fig (on success, excitement)* estar eufórico(a) (**on** de); *US* **to be h. on sth** *(keen, enthusiastic)* estar muy metido(a) en; **to be as h. as a kite** *(from drugs)* estar totalmente colocado(a), tener un colocón tremendo; *Br (very excited)* estar loco(a) de contento, *Esp* estar como una moto, *Am* estar saltando en una pata; **to get h. (on sth)** *(on drugs)* colocarse (de algo), agarrar un colocón (de algo); *Fig (on success)* ponerse como una moto (con algo)

3 *adv* (**a**) *(with position) (to jump)* alto; **the plate was piled h. with cakes** el plato estaba lleno a rebosar de pasteles; **the building rose h. above them** el edificio se elevaba hasta el cielo ante ellos; **prices have risen higher than ever before** los precios han subido más que nunca; *Fig* **to aim h.** apuntar alto, ponerse metas altas; **to be h. up** *(above ground)* estar muy alto(a); *(in organization)* ocupar un puesto importante; **to hunt h. and low for sth** buscar algo por todas partes

(**b**) *(at or to a greater degree than normal)* **they set the price/standards too h.** han puesto el precio/nivel demasiado alto; **I turned the heating up h.** puse la temperatura de la calefacción alta; **he rose higher in my esteem** mi admiración por él aumentó mucho; **feelings were running h.** los ánimos estaban exaltados *or* caldeados

(**c**) *Mus* **to sing h.** cantar en tono agudo

(**d**) IDIOMS *Fam* **to be left h. and dry** quedarse en la estacada; *US Fam* **to live h. on** *or* **off the hog** vivir a todo lujo *or* tren, *Esp* pegarse la vida padre

---

-high [haɪ] *suffix* **shoulder-h.** por los hombros, hasta los hombros, a la altura de los hombros; **waist-h.** por la cintura, hasta la cintura, a la altura de la cintura

high-angle [ˈhaɪˈæŋgəl] *adj Cin* **h. shot** toma desde un ángulo alto

highball [ˈhaɪbɔːl] *US* **1** *n (drink)* highball *m* ▸▸ ***h. glass*** vaso *m* alto *or Esp* de tubo

2 *vi* avanzar a toda marcha

highbinder [ˈhaɪbaɪndə(r)] *n US (politician)* político(a) *m,f* corrupto(a)

high-born [ˈhaɪbɔːn] *adj* de alta alcurnia

highboy [ˈhaɪbɔɪ] *n US* cómoda *f* alta

highbrow [ˈhaɪbraʊ] **1** *n* intelectual *mf*

2 *adj (tastes, movie, novel)* intelectual, culto(a)

high-chair [ˈhaɪtʃeə(r)] *n* trona *f*

high-class [haɪˈklɑːs] *adj (of high quality)* de (alta) categoría; *(person)* de clase alta; **a h. prostitute** una prostituta de lujo

high-coloured [haɪˈkʌləd] *adj* colorado(a), rubicundo(a)

high-definition [haɪdefɪˈnɪʃən] *adj* de alta definición ▸▸ ***h. graphics*** gráficos *mpl* de alta definición; ***h. screen*** pantalla *f* de alta definición; ***h. television*** televisión *f* de alta definición

high-density [haɪˈdensɪtɪ] *adj* (**a**) *(housing)* con muchos vecinos (**b**) *Comptr* de alta densidad

high-end [ˈhaɪend] *adj Comptr* de gama alta

high-energy [haɪˈenədʒɪ] *adj (food, diet)* con alto contenido energético

Higher [ˈhaɪe(r)] *n* (**a**) *Scot Sch* = examen final de estudios preuniversitarios (**b**) *Br Educ* ***H. National Certificate*** = título de escuela técnica de grado medio (un año); ***H. National Diploma*** = título de escuela técnica de grado superior (dos años)

higher [ˈhaɪə(r)] *adj* (**a**) *(at greater height)* más alto(a) (**b**) *(advanced)* superior; **at a h. level** a un nivel superior *or* más alto; **h. animals** animales superiores; **institute of h. learning** instituto de estudios superiores ▸▸ ***h. degree*** título *m* de pos(t)grado; ***h. education*** educación *f* superior, estudios *mpl* superiores

higher-up [haɪəˈrʌp] *n Fam* **the higher-ups** los de arriba, los mandamases

highest [ˈhaɪəst] **1** *n* máximo *m*

2 *adj* **I have it on the h. authority that...** sé de muy buena fuente que...; **this is the h. temperature ever recorded** esta es la máxima temperatura jamás registrada; **she speaks of you in the h. terms** te pone por todo lo alto ▸▸ *Math* ***h. common denominator*** máximo común denominador *m*; *Math* ***h. common factor*** máximo común divisor *m*

highfalutin [haɪfəˈluːtɪn] *adj Fam* pretencioso(a), petulante

high-fibre, *US* **high-fiber** [ˈhaɪfaɪbə(r)] *adj (food, diet)* rico(a) en fibra

high-five [ˈhaɪˈfaɪv] *n US Fam* palmada *f* en el aire *(saludo entre dos)*

high-flier, high-flyer [ˈhaɪˈflaɪə(r)] *n (ambitious, successful person)* persona *f* brillante y ambiciosa; **he's one of the company's high-fliers** es uno de los que más futuro tiene *or* que más promete en la empresa

high-flown [haɪˈfləʊn] *adj* (**a**) *(language)* altisonante, pomposo(a) (**b**) *(ideas)* vano(a)

high-flyer = **high-flier**

high-flying [ˈhaɪˈflaɪɪŋ] *adj* (**a**) *(aircraft, bird)* apto(a) para el vuelo de altura (**b**) *(person)* brillante y ambicioso(a), con un futuro prometedor

high-frequency [haɪˈfriːkwənsɪ] *adj* de alta frecuencia

high-grade [ˈhaɪgreɪd] *adj (beef, fruit)* de primera calidad; *(minerals, coal)* de alto grado (de pureza)

high-handed [ˈhaɪˈhændɪd] *adj* despótico(a)

high-handedly [ˈhaɪˈhændɪdlɪ] *adv* despóticamente, de modo despótico

high-handedness [ˈhaɪˈhændɪdnɪs] *n* despotismo *m*

high-hat, hi-hat [ˈhaɪhæt] **1** *n* (**a**) *Mus* charles *m inv*, chaston *m* (**b**) *Fam (snob)* engreído(a) *m,f*; **to give sb the h.** mirar a alguien por encima del hombro, darse aires con alguien

2 *adj Fam* engreído(a)

high-heeled [ˈhaɪˈhiːld] *adj* de tacón, *Am* de taco alto

high-income [ˈhaɪˈɪnkəm] *adj* de altos ingresos

highjack, highjacker *etc* = **hijack, hijacker** *etc*

highland [ˈhaɪlənd] *adj* (**a**) *(in general)* de montaña (**b**) **H.** *(of Scotland)* de las Tierras Altas ▸▸ ***H. cattle*** = raza de ganado vacuno escocés de pelo largo rojizo y largos cuernos; ***H. dress*** = traje regional típico de las Tierras Altas de Escocia; ***H. fling*** = danza individual de ritmo vivo originaria de las Tierras Altas escocesas; ***H. games*** juegos *mpl* escoceses, = fiesta al aire libre con concursos de música tradicional, deportes rurales, etc., que se celebra en distintas localidades escocesas

highlander [ˈhaɪləndə(r)] *n* (**a**) *(mountain dweller)* montañés(esa) *m,f* (**b**) *(Scottish)* **H.** habitante *mf* de las Tierras Altas de Escocia

Highlands [ˈhaɪləndz] *npl* **the H.** *(of Scotland)* las Tierras Altas de Escocia; **the Kenyan/Guatemalan H.** las zonas montañosas *or* tierras altas de Kenia/Guatemala

high-level ['haɪlevəl] *adj* (**a**) *(talks, delegation, contacts)* de alto nivel (**b**) *Comptr* ***h. format*** formateado *m* de alto nivel; ***h. language*** lenguaje *m* de alto nivel

highlight ['haɪlaɪt] **1** *n* (**a**) *(of performance, career)* momento *m* cumbre; **the h. of the party** el punto *or* momento culminante de la fiesta; **the news highlights** las noticias más destacadas; **highlights** *(of game)* (repetición *f* de las) jugadas *fpl* más interesantes, mejores momentos *mpl*

(**b**) *(in hair)* **highlights** *(individual hairs)* reflejos *mpl*; *(thicker streaks)* mechas *fpl*; **she has had highlights (put in her hair)** se ha dado reflejos/mechas (en el pelo)

2 *vt* (**a**) *(problem, difference)* poner de relieve, destacar (**b**) *(with pen)* resaltar *(con rotulador fluorescente)* (**c**) *(hair)* dar reflejos/mechas en (**d**) *Comptr (text)* resaltar

highlighter ['haɪlaɪtə(r)] *n (pen)* rotulador *m* fluorescente, *Col, RP* resaltador *m*, *Méx* marcador *m*

highly ['haɪlɪ] *adv* (**a**) *(very)* muy; **h. dangerous** muy peligroso(a), tremendamente peligroso(a); **h. intelligent** muy inteligente, enormemente inteligente; **h. paid** (muy) bien pagado(a); **it is h. recommended** es altamente recomendable; **h. seasoned** muy condimentado(a) (**b**) *(well)* **to think h. of sb** tener buena opinión de alguien; **to speak h. of sth/sb** hablar bien de algo/alguien

highly-strung ['haɪlɪ'strʌŋ] *adj* **to be h.** ser muy nervioso(a)

high-minded ['haɪ'maɪndɪd] *adj* noble, elevado(a)

high-mindedness ['haɪ'maɪndɪdnɪs] *n* nobleza *f*, espíritu *m* elevado

high-necked ['haɪ'nekt] *adj* de cuello alto

Highness ['haɪnɪs] *n* **His/Her Royal H.** Su Alteza Real

high-octane [haɪ'ɒkteɪn] *adj* de alto octanaje

high-performance ['haɪpə'fɔːməns] *adj* de alto rendimiento

high-pitched ['haɪpɪtʃt] *adj* (**a**) *(sound, voice)* agudo(a) (**b**) *(roof)* empinado(a)

high-powered ['haɪ'paʊəd] *adj* (**a**) *(engine, car, telescope, rifle)* potente, de gran potencia (**b**) *(person, job)* de gran importancia, de altos vuelos

high-pressure ['haɪ'preʃə(r)] **1** *adj* (**a**) *(substance, container)* a gran presión (**b**) *Met* **h. area** área de altas presiones (**c**) *(methods, sales campaign)* agresivo(a); *(job, profession)* de mucha responsabilidad

2 *vt US Fam* apretar las tuercas *or* las clavijas a, presionar

high-profile ['haɪ'prəʊfaɪl] *adj* (**a**) *(person)* prominente, destacado(a) (**b**) *(campaign)* de gran alcance

high-ranking ['haɪ'ræŋkɪŋ] *adj* de alto rango; **a h. officer/official** un alto mando/funcionario

high-resolution ['haɪrezə'luːʃən] *adj (screen, graphics)* de alta resolución

high-rise ['haɪ'raɪz] **1** *n (block of flats)* bloque *m*, torre *f*

2 *adj* ***h. building*** bloque *m*, torre *f*

high-risk ['haɪrɪsk] *adj* (**a**) *(dangerous) (strategy, investment)* de alto riesgo; *(sport)* de riesgo (**b**) *(at risk)* de riesgo

high-roast [haɪ'rəʊst] *adj (coffee)* torrefacto(a)

high-season ['haɪsiːzən] *adj (prices)* de temporada alta

high-sounding ['haɪsaʊndɪŋ] *adj* altisonante

high-speed ['haɪ'spiːd] *adj* de alta velocidad

high-spirited [haɪ'spɪrɪtɪd] *adj (person)* muy animado(a), exultante; *(horse)* brioso(a)

high-street ['haɪstriːt] *adj Br* **h. banks** bancos comerciales; **h. shops** las tiendas principales del centro de la ciudad

high-strung ['haɪ'strʌŋ] *adj US* **to be h.** ser muy nervioso(a)

hightail ['haɪteɪl] *vt US Fam* **to h. it** largarse corriendo, *Esp, RP* pirarse, pirárselas; **he hightailed it home/out of there** se largó a su casa/de allí corriendo

high-tech, hi-tech ['haɪ'tek] *adj* (**a**) *(industry, equipment)* de alta tecnología (**b**) *(furniture)* de estilo high tech *or* industrial; *(style)* high tech, industrial

high-tension ['haɪ'tenʃən] *adj* de alta tensión

high-toned ['haɪ'təʊnd] *adj* (**a**) *(elevated) (discussion)* de tono elevado, de mucho nivel (**b**) *(superior) (person)* con aires de superioridad; *(attitude)* de superioridad

high-up ['haɪʌp] *adj Fam* importante

high-voltage ['haɪ'vɒltɪdʒ] *adj* de alta tensión, de alto voltaje

high-water [haɪ'wɔːtə(r)] *n* marea *f* alta ▸▸ ***h. mark*** *(of tide)* nivel *m* de pleamar; *(of river)* nivel *m* de crecida; *Fig (of career)* cumbre *f*, cima *f*

highway ['haɪweɪ] *n* (**a**) *US (main road)* carretera *f*; *(freeway)* autopista *f*; IDIOM **it's h. robbery!** ¡es un atraco a mano armada! ▸▸ ***h. patrol*** *(organization)* policía *f* de carreteras, *RP* policía *f* caminera; *(unit)* patrulla *f* de carreteras; ***h. patrolman*** policía *m* de carreteras, *RP* policía *m* caminero

(**b**) *Br Formal (road)* carretera *f*; *Fig* **to travel the highways and byways** recorrer hasta el último camino; *Fig* **he knows all the highways and byways of the subject/law** conoce todos los intríngulis *or* vericuetos de la materia/ley ▸▸ ***H. Code*** código *m* de (la) circulación

highwayman ['haɪweɪmən] *n* bandolero *m*, salteador *m* de caminos

hi-hat = **high-hat**

hijack ['haɪdʒæk] **1** *n* secuestro *m*

2 *vt* (**a**) *(plane, car, train)* secuestrar; *(goods)* robar *or* interceptar en un asalto (**b**) *(campaign, public meeting)* apropiarse de

hijacker ['haɪdʒækə(r)] *n (of plane)* secuestrador(ora) *m,f*, pirata *mf* aéreo(a) *or* del aire; *(of car, train)* secuestrador(ora) *m,f*

hijacking ['haɪdʒækɪŋ] *n (of plane, car, train)* secuestro *m*; *(of goods)* robo *m* mediante asalto

hike [haɪk] **1** *n* (**a**) *(walk)* excursión *f*, caminata *f*; **to go on** *or* **for a h.** darse una caminata; *Fam* **it's a bit of a h. into town** de aquí al centro hay un buen paseo *or* una buena caminata; *US Fam* **(go) take a h.!** ¡vete a paseo *or* al diablo! (**b**) *(increase)* subida *f*; **price/tax h.** subida de precios/impuestos

2 *vt (price, tax, interest rate)* subir

3 *vi (walk)* caminar

▸ **hike up** *vt sep* (**a**) *(hitch up) (one's skirt, trousers)* subirse, remangarse (**b**) *(price, tax, interest rate)* subir

hiker ['haɪkə(r)] *n* excursionista *mf*, senderista *mf*

hiking ['haɪkɪŋ] *n* senderismo *m*, excursionismo *m*; **to go h.** hacer senderismo *or* excursionismo ▸▸ ***h. boots*** botas *fpl* de senderismo *or* excursionismo

hilarious [hɪ'leərɪəs] *adj* divertidísimo(a), graciosísimo(a); **we had a h. time last night** ¡lo que nos pudimos reír anoche!

hilariously [hɪ'leərɪəslɪ] *adv* **h. funny** divertidísimo(a), graciosísimo(a); **a h. inappropriate comment/dress** un comentario/vestido tan fuera de tono que resulta risible

hilarity [hɪ'lærɪtɪ] *n* hilaridad *f*

hill [hɪl] *n* (**a**) *(small mountain)* colina *f*, monte *m* ▸▸ ***h. country*** montes *mpl*, sierra *f*; ***h. farm*** granja *f* de montaña; ***h. farmer*** granjero(a) *m,f* montañés(esa)

(**b**) *(slope)* cuesta *f*; **to go down/up the h.** ir cuesta abajo/arriba ▸▸ ***h. start*** *(for car)* arranque *m* en cuesta

(**c**) *US Pol* **on the H.** en el Capitolio, en el Congreso

(**d**) IDIOMS **to be over the h.** *(past one's best)* no estar ya para muchos trotes; *US* **to go over the h.** *(go AWOL)* ausentarse sin permiso; *(disappear)* esfumarse; **up h. and down dale, over h. and dale** *(everywhere)* por todas partes; *US Fam* **it isn't worth a h. of beans** no vale para nada

hillbilly ['hɪlbɪlɪ] *n US Pej* palurdo(a) *m,f* de la montaña ▸▸ ***h. music*** música *f* country

hillfort ['hɪlfɔːt] *n (Roman)* atalaya *f*; *(pre-Roman)* castro *m*

hilliness ['hɪlɪnɪs] *n* carácter *m* accidentado *or* montañoso

hillock ['hɪlək] *n* cerro *m*, collado *m*

hillside ['hɪlsaɪd] *n* ladera *f*

hilltop ['hɪltɒp] **1** *n* cima *f*, cumbre *f*

2 *adj (village)* en la cima de un monte

hillwalker ['hɪlwɔːkə(r)] *n Br* senderista *mf*

hillwalking ['hɪlwɔːkɪŋ] *n Br* senderismo *m*

hilly ['hɪlɪ] *adj (with hills)* con muchas colinas; *(with mountains)* accidentado(a), montañoso(a)

hilt [hɪlt] *n (of sword, dagger)* puño *m*, empuñadura *f*; IDIOM **to the h.: to back sb to the h.** *(support)* apoyar sin reservas a alguien; **to be mortgaged (up) to the h.** *(person)* estar hipotecado(a) hasta el cuello; *(property)* estar todo hipotecado

---

HIM [hɪm] *pron* (**a**) *(direct object)* lo; **I hate h.** lo odio; **I like h.** me gusta; **kill h.!** ¡mátalo!; **I can forgive his son but not HIM** puedo perdonar a su hijo, pero no a él

(**b**) *(indirect object)* le; **I gave h. the book** le di el libro; **I gave it to h.** se lo di; **give it to h.** dáselo (a él)

(**c**) *(after preposition)* él; **I talked to h.** hablé con él; **his mother lives near h.** su madre vive cerca de su casa; **it was meant for you, not for HIM** iba dirigido a ti, no a él

(**d**) *(as complement of verb* **to be***)* él; **it's h.!** ¡es él!; **it was h. who did it** lo hizo él; *Fam* **the coat isn't really h.** el abrigo no va mucho con él

Himalayan [hɪmə'leɪən] *adj* himalayo(a)

Himalayas [hɪmə'leɪəz] *npl* **the H.** el Himalaya

himbo ['hɪmbəʊ] *n Fam Esp* guaperas *m or Am* lindo *m* con poco seso

himself [hɪm'self] *pron* (**a**) *(reflexive)* se; **he hurt h.** se hizo daño; **he introduced h.** se presentó; **he bought h. a coat** se compró un abrigo; **he could see h. reflected in the water** vio su imagen reflejada *or* se vio reflejado en el agua
(**b**) *(unaided, alone)* él solo; **he can do it h.** (él) puede hacerlo solo; **he made the pattern h.** él solo hizo el diseño
(**c**) *(emphatic)* él mismo; **he told me h.** me lo dijo él mismo; **he h. did not believe it** él mismo no se lo creía; **he h. saw them leave** él (mismo) los vio salir con sus propios ojos
(**d**) *(his usual self)* **he's not h. today** hoy está un poco raro; **he's feeling h. again** vuelve a sentirse el de siempre
(**e**) *(after preposition)* él; **he talks about h. a lot** habla mucho de sí mismo; **he did it all by h.** lo hizo él mismo *or* él solo; **he lives by h.** vive solo; **he was all by h.** estaba (completamente) solo; **he bought it for h.** se lo compró para él; **he talks to h.** habla solo; **"how unfair!" he thought to h.** "¡qué injusto!" pensó para sus adentros
(**f**) *(replacing 'him')* **it is meant for people like h.** está pensado para gente como él

hind[1] [haɪnd] *adj* trasero(a), de atrás; **h. legs** patas traseras; IDIOM *Fam* **she could talk the h. legs off a donkey** habla como una cotorra, habla por los codos

hind[2] *n (female deer)* cierva *f*

hinder ['hɪndə(r)] *vt (person)* estorbar; *(movements, operation, negotiations)* entorpecer; **progress was hindered by the weather** el avance se vio entorpecido por el mal tiempo; **to h. sb in his/her work** suponer un obstáculo para el trabajo de alguien; **his shyness hindered him from making friends** su timidez le impedía hacer amigos

Hindi ['hɪndɪ] **1** *n* hindi *m*
2 *adj* hindi, del hindi

hindmost ['haɪndməʊst] *adj* posterior, postrero(a)

hindquarters ['haɪndkwɔːtəz] *npl* cuartos *mpl* traseros

hindrance ['hɪndrəns] *n* (**a**) *(person)* estorbo *m*; *(thing)* impedimento *m*, traba *f*; **you'll be more of a h. than a help** vas a estorbar, más que ayudar (**b**) *(action)* **without any h. from the authorities** sin que las autoridades pusieran ningún impedimento

hindsight ['haɪndsaɪt] *n* retrospección *f*; **with the benefit** *or* **wisdom of h.** con la perspectiva que da el tiempo

Hindu ['hɪnduː] **1** *n* hindú *mf*
2 *adj* hindú *mf*

Hinduism ['hɪnduːɪzəm] *n* hinduismo *m*

Hindustan [hɪndʊ'stɑːn] *n* el Indostán

Hindustani ['hɪndʊ'stɑːnɪ] **1** *n (language)* indostaní *m*
2 *adj* indostánico(a), indostaní

hinge [hɪndʒ] **1** *n* (**a**) *(of door, lid, box)* bisagra *f*; **to take a door off its hinges** sacar una puerta del quicio ►► ***h. joint*** (articulación *f* de) charnela *f* (**b**) **(stamp) h.** charnela *f*
2 *vt (door, box)* poner bisagras a

► **hinge on, hinge upon** *vt insep (depend on)* depender de

hinged [hɪndʒd] *adj* con bisagras, de bisagra

hinky ['hɪŋkɪ] *adj US Fam* raro(a)

hint [hɪnt] **1** *n* (**a**) *(allusion)* indirecta *f*, insinuación *f*; **to give** *or* **drop sb a h.** lanzar a alguien una indirecta; **to be able to take a h.** saber pillar *or Esp* coger *or Am* agarrar una indirecta; **OK, I can take a h.** eso va por mí ¿no?, vale, ya entiendo; *Hum* **I just love plain chocolate, h., h.** me encanta el chocolate: a buen entendedor... (pocas palabras bastan)
(**b**) *(clue)* pista *f*; **give me a h.** dame una pista
(**c**) *(sign, trace)* atisbo *m*, rastro *m*; **a h. of irony/anger** un atisbo de ironía/enojo; **not a h. of surprise** ni un asomo de sorpresa; **a h. of garlic** un ligero gusto a ajo; **a h. of green/red** un toque de verde/rojo; **there's a h. of spring in the air** ya se notan atisbos de la primavera
(**d**) *(piece of advice)* consejo *m*; **I gave her a few helpful hints** le di algunos consejos útiles
2 *vt* **to h. that...** insinuar que...
3 *vi (give clues)* dar pistas

► **hint at** *vt insep* insinuar, hacer alusión a; **what are you hinting at?** ¿qué insinúas *or* estás insinuando?

hinterland ['hɪntəlænd] *n* región *f* interior

hip[1] [hɪp] *n* (**a**) *(part of body)* cadera *f*; **with one's hands on one's hips** con los brazos en jarras; **to be broad/narrow in the hips** ser ancho(a)/estrecho(a) de caderas; IDIOM **to shoot from the h.** *(speak bluntly)* llamar a las cosas por su nombre, no andar mordiéndose la lengua; *(speak rashly)* hablar a la ligera ►► *Br* ***h. bath*** baño *m* de asiento; ***h. bone*** hueso *m* de la cadera; ***h. flask*** petaca *f*; ***h. joint*** articulación *f* de la cadera; ***h. operation*** (operación *f* de) trasplante *m* de cadera; ***h. pocket*** bolsillo *m* trasero; *Med* ***h. replacement*** (operación *f* de) trasplante *m* de cadera
(**b**) *Constr (part of roof)* lima *f* tesa

hip[2] *n (berry)* escaramujo *m*

hip[3] *Fam* **1** *adj (trendy)* moderno(a), a la última, *Am* de onda; **she's h. to all the latest trends** está al tanto de todas las nuevas tendencias
2 *vt US* **to h. sb to sth** poner a alguien al tanto de algo

hip-hop ['hɪphɒp] *n Mus* hip-hop *m*

hip-huggers ['hɪphʌgəz] *npl US* pantalones *mpl* de cintura baja, pantalones *mpl* por la cadera

hipped [hɪpt] *adj US Fam* **to be h. on sth/sb** estar como loco(a) con algo/alguien

-hipped [hɪpt] *suffix* **broad/narrow-h.** ancho(a)/estrecho(a) de caderas

hippie = **hippy**[1]

hippo ['hɪpəʊ] (*pl* **hippos**) *n Fam* hipopótamo *m*

hippocampus [hɪpəʊ'kæmpəs] (*pl* **hippocampi** [hɪpəʊ'kæmpaɪ]) *n Anat* hipocampo *m*

Hippocrates [hɪ'pɒkrətiːz] *pr n* Hipócrates

Hippocratic oath [hɪpə'krætɪk'əʊθ] *n* juramento *m* hipocrático

hippodrome ['hɪpədrəʊm] *n* (**a**) *(theatre)* teatro *m* de variedades (**b**) *Hist (racecourse)* circo *m*, hipódromo *m*

hippopotamus [hɪpə'pɒtəməs] (*pl* **hippopotami** [hɪpə'pɒtəmaɪ]) *n* hipopótamo *m*

hippy[1], **hippie** ['hɪpɪ] **1** *n* hippy *mf*
2 *adj* hippy

hippy[2] *adj* ancho(a) de caderas

hipsters ['hɪpstəz] *npl* pantalones *mpl* de cintura baja, pantalones *mpl* por la cadera

hire ['haɪə(r)] **1** *n* (**a**) *Br (of car, room, suit)* alquiler *m*, *Méx* renta *f*; **for h.** *(taxi)* libre; **bicycles for h.** *(sign)* se alquilan *or Méx* se rentan bicicletas; **it's out on h.** está alquilado(a) ►► ***h. car*** coche *m or Am* carro *m or CSur* auto *m* de alquiler, *Méx* carro *m* rentado (**b**) *(cost) (of car, boat)* alquiler *m*; *(of worker)* salario *m*
2 *vt* (**a**) *Br (car, room, suit)* alquilar, *Méx* rentar (**b**) *(lawyer, worker)* contratar
3 *vi (recruit staff)* contratar personal; **with authority to h. and fire** con libertad para contratar y despedir a la gente

► **hire on** *vi US (take a job)* conseguir trabajo, colocarse

► **hire out** **1** *vt sep Br (boat, bicycle)* alquilar, *Méx* rentar; *(one's services)* ofrecer
2 *vi US* **to h. out as** *(offer one's services)* ofrecerse como, trabajar de

hired ['haɪəd] *adj (car)* alquilado(a), *Méx* rentado(a) ►► ***h. gun*** *(killer)* pistolero *m* a sueldo; *Pej (expert)* mercenario(a) *m,f*; ***h. gunman*** pistolero *m* a sueldo; ***h. hand*** *(on farm)* jornalero(a) *m,f*; ***h. killer*** asesino(a) *m,f* a sueldo

hireling ['haɪəlɪŋ] *n Pej* mercenario(a) *m,f*

hire-purchase ['haɪə'pɜːtʃɪs] *n Br Com* compra *f* a plazos; **to buy sth on h.** comprar algo a plazos ►► ***h. agreement*** contrato *m* de compra a plazos

hi-res ['haɪ'rez] *adj Fam* (*abbr* **high-resolution**) de alta resolución

hirsute ['hɜːsjuːt] *adj Literary* hirsuto(a)

HIS [hɪz] **1** *possessive adj* (**a**) *(singular)* su; *(plural)* sus; **h. dog** su perro; **h. parents** sus padres; **I took h. motorbike** tomé su moto; *(contrasting with hers or theirs)* tomé el moto de él; **what's h. name?** ¿cómo se llama?; **it wasn't HIS idea!** ¡no fue idea suya!; **they were upset at h. mentioning it** les sentó mal que lo mencionara; **that wasn't h. understanding** no lo entendió así
(**b**) *(for parts of body, clothes)* **h. eyes are blue** tiene los ojos azules; **he hit h. head** se dio un golpe en la cabeza; **he washed h. face** se lavó la cara; **he put h. hands in h. pockets** se metió las manos en los bolsillos
2 *possessive pron* (**a**) *(singular)* el suyo *m*, la suya *f*; *(plural)* los suyos *mpl*, las suyas *fpl*; *(to distinguish)* el/la/los/las de él; **my house is big but h. is bigger** mi casa es grande, pero la suya es mayor; **she didn't have a book so I gave her h.** ella no tenía libro, así que le di el de él; **it must be one of h.** debe de ser uno de los suyos; **it wasn't her fault, it was HIS** no fue culpa de ella, sino de él; **h. is the work I admire most** su obra es la que más admiro; **a set of h. and hers towels** un juego de toallas para él y para ella

(**b**) *(used attributively) (singular)* suyo(a); *(plural)* suyos(as); **this book is h.** este libro es suyo; **a friend of h.** un amigo suyo; **I can't stand that girlfriend/dog of h.** no soporto a su novia/perro, no soporto a esa novia/ese perro que tiene
(**c**) *Fam (his house, flat)* su casa; **we all went back to h.** volvimos todos a su casa

Hispanic [hɪs'pænɪk] **1** *n US* hispano(a) *m,f*
2 *adj* hispánico(a), hispano(a)

Hispanic-American [hɪs'pænɪkə'merɪkən] **1** *n* hispano(a) *m,f*
2 *adj* hispano(a)

Hispanicist = **Hispanist**

hispanicize [hɪs'pænɪsaɪz] *vt* hispanizar

Hispanist ['hɪspənɪst], **Hispanicist** [hɪs'pænɪsɪst] *n* hispanista *mf*

Hispanophile [hɪs'pænəfaɪl] *n* hispanófilo(a) *m,f*

hiss [hɪs] **1** *n* (**a**) *(sound) (of gas, snake)* silbido *m*; *(of goose)* graznido *m* (**b**) *(of person) (to attract sb's attention)* siseo *m*, *Andes, RP* chistido *m*; *(to express disapproval)* silbido *m*
2 *vt* (**a**) *(say quietly)* susurrar, musitar; **"come here!" he hissed** "¡ven aquí!" susurró (**b**) *(express disapproval of) (bad performer, speaker)* silbar, abuchear; **the audience hissed its disapproval** el público silbó en señal de desaprobación
3 *vi* (**a**) *(gas, snake)* silbar; *(goose)* graznar (**b**) *(expressing disapproval)* silbar

hissy ['hɪsɪ] *US Fam* **1** *n* rabieta *f*
2 *adj* **to have a h. fit** agarrar *or Esp* coger una rabieta

hist [hɪst] *exclam* ¡chsss!, ¡chist!, ¡chis!

histamine ['hɪstəmi:n] *n Biochem* histamina *f*

histogram ['hɪstəgræm] *n* histograma *m*

histological [hɪstə'lɒdʒɪkəl] *adj* histológico(a)

histologist [hɪs'tɒlədʒɪst] *n* histólogo(a) *m,f*

histology [hɪ'stɒlədʒɪ] *n* histología *f*

histopathological ['hɪstəʊpæθə'lɒdʒɪkəl] *adj* histopatológico(a)

histopathology ['hɪstəʊpə'θɒlədʒɪ] *n* histopatología *f*

historian [hɪs'tɔ:rɪən] *n* historiador(ora) *m,f*

historic [hɪs'tɒrɪk] *adj* (**a**) *(memorable, significant)* memorable, histórico(a); **a** *or* **an h. event** un acontecimiento *or* hecho histórico (**b**) *(of time past)* histórico(a); **h. buildings/monuments** edificios/monumentos históricos

historical [hɪs'tɒrɪkəl] *adj* (**a**) *(relating to history, the past)* histórico(a); **it's a** *or* **an h. fact** es un hecho histórico; **to be of (merely) h. interest** ser de interés (meramente *or* puramente) histórico ►► ***h. linguistics*** lingüística *f* histórica; ***h. method*** método *m* histórico; ***h. novel*** novela *f* histórica (**b**) *Phil* ***h. materialism*** materialismo *m* histórico (**c**) *Gram* ***h. present*** presente *m* histórico

historically [hɪs'tɒrɪklɪ] *adv* históricamente; **h., such attempts have usually failed** a lo largo de la historia *or* tradicionalmente, ha sido habitual el fracaso de intentos de este tipo

historicism [hɪ'stɒrɪsɪzəm] *n* historicismo *m*

historicity [hɪstə'rɪsɪtɪ] *n* veracidad *f* (histórica), carácter *m* verídico

historiography [hɪstɒrɪ'ɒgrəfɪ] *n* historiografía *f*

history ['hɪstərɪ] *n* (**a**) *(the past, subject)* historia *f*; **the h. of Spain, Spanish h.** la historia de España, la historia española; **ancient/modern h.** historia antigua/moderna; **h. book/teacher** libro/profesor(ora) de historia; **throughout h.** a través de *or* a lo largo de (toda) la historia; **the worst crash in aviation h.** *or* **the h. of aviation** el peor accidente de la historia de la aviación; **to go down in h. as...** pasar a (los anales de) la historia como...; **to make h.** hacer historia; **the rest is h....** el resto *or* lo demás ya es historia, el resto es ya algo sabido
(**b**) *(account)* historia *f*; **Shakespeare's histories** *or* **h. plays** las obras históricas de Shakespeare
(**c**) *(record)* **employment h.** trayectoria *or* historial profesional; **medical h.** historia clínica, historial médico *or* clínico; **to have a h. of...** *Med* tener antecedentes en el historial clínico de...; *(by reputation)* tener un largo historial de...; **the entire family has a h. of political activity** toda la familia cuenta con una larga trayectoria política; *Fam* **there's a lot of h. between them** han ocurrido muchas cosas entre ellos, *Am* ha pasado mucha agua bajo ese puente
(**d**) *Fam Fig (finished, irrelevant)* **that's h.** eso pasó a la historia; **they used to date but they're h. now** solían salir *or Esp* quedar juntos, pero eso ya pasó a la historia; **you're h.!** ¡de ésta no te salva nadie!, ¡estás perdido, amigo!

histrionic [hɪstrɪ'ɒnɪk] *adj Pej* histriónico(a), teatral

histrionically [hɪstrɪ'ɒnɪklɪ] *adv (to say, behave)* histriónicamente

histrionics [hɪstrɪ'ɒnɪks] *npl Pej* histrionismo *m*, teatralidad *f*

HIT [hɪt] **1** *n* (**a**) *(blow)* golpe *m*; *(in American football, rugby)* placaje *m*; *(in fencing)* tocado *m*; *(in shooting)* impacto *m*; **to score a direct h.** dar de lleno en el blanco; **the air base took a direct h.** la bomba alcanzó directamente a la base aérea
(**b**) *(critical remark)* pulla *f*; **that was a h. at me** la pulla iba dirigida a mí
(**c**) *(in baseball)* hit *m*, batazo *m* de base
(**d**) *(success)* éxito *m*; *(record)* (disco *m* de) éxito *m*; **she had two top-ten hits** dos de sus discos estuvieron entre los diez más vendidos; **The Rolling Stones' Greatest Hits** los grandes éxitos de los Rolling Stones; **the canapés were a real h.** los canapés fueron todo un éxito; **you were a real h. with my friends** le caíste fenomenal a mis amigos ►► *Old-fashioned* ***h. parade*** lista *f* de éxitos
(**e**) *Comptr (visit to website)* acceso *m*, visita *f*; *(in search)* aparición *f*; **this website counted 20,000 hits last week** 20.000 personas han visitado esta página web durante la semana pasada
(**f**) *Fam (murder)* asesinato *m* ►► ***h. list*** lista *f* negra; ***h. man*** asesino *m* a sueldo; ***h. squad*** banda *f* de asesinos
(**g**) *Fam (of drug) (puff)* tiro *m*, *Méx* fumada *f*, *RP* pitada *f*; *(injection)* pico *m*, *RP* pichicata *f*
2 *adj (successful)* de mucho éxito; **h. record** (disco de) éxito
3 *vt* (*pt & pp* **hit**) (**a**) *(of person)* golpear; **he hits his wife** pega a su mujer; **to h. one's hand/knee (on** *or* **against sth)** darse un golpe en la mano/rodilla (con algo); **he h. me in the face/on the head** me pegó en la cara/cabeza; **to h. a ball** golpear una pelota *or* bola; *Fig* **he didn't know what had h. him** no sabía lo que le pasaba; *Fig* **to h. sb when they are down** ensañarse con alguien; *Fig* **to h. sb where it hurts** dar a alguien donde más le duele
(**b**) *(of vehicle) (tree, bus)* chocar contra; *(person)* atropellar; **the boat h. a reef** el barco chocó contra un arrecife
(**c**) *(attack) (enemy)* atacar
(**d**) *(reach) (target)* alcanzar; **his shot h. the post** su disparo dio en el poste; **the bullet h. him in the leg** la bala le dio en *or* le alcanzó la pierna; **the air base was h. by the bomb** la bomba alcanzó la base aérea; **to h. a note** llegar a *or* dar una nota; **to h. the jackpot** ganar el premio gordo; **his insult h. the mark** su insulto dio en el blanco; *Fam* **that whisky really h. the spot!** este whisky es justo lo que necesitaba
(**e**) *(arrive at) (barrier, difficulty)* toparse *or* encontrarse con; **we h. the outskirts of Paris just after dawn** llegamos a las afueras de París justo después del amanecer; **the typhoon h. the capital at midday** el tifón alcanzó la ciudad a mediodía; **the circus hits town tomorrow** el circo llega mañana a la ciudad; **it hits the shops next week** estará a la venta la próxima semana; **to h. 90 (miles an hour)** alcanzar las 90 millas por hora; **to have h. an all-time low** *(investment)* haber alcanzado un mínimo histórico; *Fig (relationship)* estar por los suelos; **to h. the headlines** salir en los titulares
(**f**) *(affect)* afectar; **the company has been badly h. by the recession** la empresa se ha visto muy afectada por la recesión; **to be hard h. by...** verse muy afectado(a) por...; **the worst h. areas** las áreas más afectadas
(**g**) *(operate) (button, switch)* darle a; *Comptr (key)* pulsar; **to h. the brakes** pisar el freno
(**h**) *(score)* **to h. a home run** *(in baseball)* hacer un home-run, *Am* jonronear
(**i**) *(occur to)* **it suddenly h. me that...** de repente me di cuenta de que...; **the solution suddenly h. me** de repente se me ocurrió la solución, de repente di con la solución
(**j**) *Fam* **to h. sb for sth** *(ask favour from)* sacar algo a alguien
(**k**) *Fam (murder)* cargarse a, *Méx* echarse a, *RP* amasijar a
(**l**) IDIOMS *Fam* **to h. the big time** alcanzar la fama; *US* **to h. the bricks** *(go on strike)* ir a la huelga; **to h. the ceiling** *or* **the roof** *(lose one's temper)* ponerse hecho(a) una furia; *Fig* **to h. the ground running** empezar con brío; *US Fam* **to h. the books** hacer codos; *Fam* **to h. the bottle** empinar el codo; *US Fam* **to h. the gas** pisar el acelerador, darle al acelerador; *Fam* **to h. the hay** irse al sobre; **to h. the nail on the head** dar en el clavo; *Fam* **to h. the road** *(leave)* ponerse en marcha, largarse; *Fam* **to h. the sack** irse al sobre
4 *vi* (**a**) *(strike)* golpear
(**b**) *(collide)* estrellarse, chocar
(**c**) *(reach target) (bullet, bomb)* dar en el blanco
(**d**) *(arrive)* llegar; **the hurricane h. at midday** el huracán llegó a mediodía; **the full implications only h. home later** no nos dimos cuenta de todas las consecuencias hasta más tarde

► **hit back 1** *vt sep* **to h. sb back** devolver el golpe a alguien; **to h. the ball back** devolver la pelota
2 *vi (return blow)* devolver el golpe; *Fig (with answer, accusation,*

criticism) responder (**at** a); **to h. back at the enemy** responder al enemigo

▸ **hit off** *vt sep* (**a**) *Fam* **to h. it off** *(get on well)* caerse bien; **I didn't h. it off with them** no nos caímos bien (**b**) *(depict) (in impersonation)* imitar; *(in painting, drawing)* retratar; *(in prose description)* describir

▸ **hit on** *vt insep* (**a**) *(idea, solution)* dar con (**b**) *US Fam (flirt with)* intentar seducir a, *Esp* tirar los tejos a, *Méx* echarle los perros a, *RP* cargar a

▸ **hit out** *vi (physically)* lanzar golpes (**at** contra); *(verbally)* lanzar ataques (**at** *or* **against** contra)

▸ **hit up** *vt sep* (**a**) *US Fam* **she h. me up for $10** me sacó 10 dólares (**b**) *Fam* **to h. it up** *(inject drugs)* inyectarse, *Esp* chutarse, *RP* picarse

▸ **hit upon** *vt insep (idea, solution)* dar con

---

hit-and-miss = **hit-or-miss**

hit-and-run ['hɪtən'rʌn] *adj* **he was knocked down in a h. accident** lo atropelló un coche que se dio a la fuga; *Mil* **a h. attack** un ataque relámpago ▸▸ ***h. driver*** = conductor que huye tras atropellar a alguien

hitch [hɪtʃ] **1** *n* (**a**) *(difficulty)* contratiempo *m*; **there's been a h.** ha surgido un contratiempo *or* una contrariedad *or* un problema; **without a h.** sin ningún contratiempo
(**b**) *(knot)* nudo *m*
(**c**) *(pull, lift)* **to give sth a h. (up)** subir algo de un tirón
(**d**) *(ride)* viaje *m* en coche, *CAm, Méx* aventón *m*, *Col* chance *m*, *Cuba* botella *f*, *Perú* jalada *f*, *Ven* cola *f*
(**e**) ***h. kick*** *(in long jump)* movimiento *m* de pedaleo
(**f**) *US (limp)* cojera *f*, renquera *f*
(**g**) *US (towbar)* barra *f* de remolque *or* tracción
(**h**) *US Fam (length of time)* período *m*; **he did a three-year h. in prison/the army** pasó un período de tres años en la cárcel/el ejército (de tierra)
2 *vt* (**a**) *(attach)* enganchar (**to** a); *Fig* **the opportunists who have hitched themselves to her campaign** los oportunistas que se han subido al carro de su campaña
(**b**) *Fam* **to get hitched** *(marry)* casarse
(**c**) *Fam* **to h. a lift to...** ir en autostop *or* a dedo a..., *CAm, Méx* irse de aventón a..., *Ven* conseguir cola hasta...; **she has hitched her way round Europe** ha recorrido Europa a dedo *or CAm, Méx* de aventón
3 *vi Fam* hacer autoestop *or* dedo, pedir *CAm, Méx* aventón *or Col* chance *or Cuba* botella *or Perú* una jalada *or Ven* cola

▸ **hitch up** *vt sep* (**a**) *(trousers, skirt)* subirse, remangarse (**b**) *(horse, oxen)* enganchar; *(caravan, trailer)* enganchar

hitcher ['hɪtʃə(r)] *n* autoestopista *mf*, *Ven* colero(a) *m,f*

hitchhike ['hɪtʃhaɪk] **1** *vt* **to h. one's way round Europe** recorrer(se) Europa a dedo *or CAm, Méx* de aventón, viajar por Europa en *or* haciendo autostop *or CAm, Méx* de aventón
2 *vi* hacer autoestop *or* dedo, pedir *CAm, Méx* aventón *or Col* chance *or Cuba* botella *or Perú* una jalada *or Ven* cola; **to h. to London** ir a Londres a dedo, *CAm, Méx* ir hasta Londres de aventón

hitchhiker ['hɪtʃhaɪkə(r)] *n* autoestopista *mf*, *Ven* colero(a) *m,f*

hi-tech = **high-tech**

hither ['hɪðə(r)] *adv Literary* acá; **h. and thither** de acá para allá

hitherto ['hɪðə'tu:] *adv Formal* hasta la fecha

Hitlerism ['hɪtlərɪzəm] *n* hitlerismo *m*

Hitlerite ['hɪtləraɪt] **1** *n* hitleriano(a) *m,f*
2 *adj* hitleriano(a)

Hitler Youth ['hɪtlə'ju:θ] *n* Juventudes *fpl* Hitlerianas

hit-or-miss ['hɪtɔ:'mɪs], **hit-and-miss** [hɪtən'mɪs] *adj (method, approach)* al azar, al tuntún, *RP* a la que te criaste; **it's all a bit h.** todo sale un poco a la buena de Dios; **the service here is a bit h.** el servicio aquí nunca se sabe cómo va a ser

HIV [eɪtʃaɪ'vi:] *n* (*abbr* **human immuno-deficiency virus**) VIH *m*, virus *m inv* de la inmunodeficiencia humana; **to be H. positive/negative** ser/no ser seropositivo(a)

hive [haɪv] *n (for bees)* colmena *f*; *(group of bees)* enjambre *m*; *Fig* **a h. of activity** un hervidero de actividad

▸ **hive off** *vt sep (sell)* desprenderse de; **they intended to h. off the profitable parts of the company then shut the remainder down** tenían la intención de vender por separado el sector más rentable de la empresa y liquidar el resto

hives [haɪvz] *npl Med* urticaria *f*

hiya ['haɪjə] *exclam Fam* ¡hola!, ¿qué hay?

HM [eɪtʃ'em] (*abbr* **Her/His Majesty**) S. M.

HMG [eɪtʃem'dʒi:] *n Br* (*abbr* **Her/His Majesty's Government**) el Gobierno de Su Majestad

HMI [eɪtʃem'aɪ] *n Educ Formerly* (**a**) (*abbr* **Her/His Majesty's Inspectorate**) = organismo británico de inspección de enseñanza (**b**) (*abbr* **Her/His Majesty's Inspector**) inspector(ora) *m,f* de enseñanza

HMMV ['hʌmvi:] *n US* (*abbr* **high-mobility multipurpose vehicle**) vehículo *m* polivalente de alta movilidad, *Esp* ≃ VAMTAC

HMO [eɪtʃem'əʊ] *n US* (*abbr* **Health Maintenance Organization**) = Organización para el Mantenimiento de la Salud

HMS [eɪtʃem'es] *n Naut* (*abbr* **Her/His Majesty's Ship**) = título que precede a los nombres de buques de la marina británica

HMSO [eɪtʃemes'əʊ] *n Br Formerly* (*abbr* **Her/His Majesty's Stationery Office**) = imprenta (oficial) del Estado

HNC [eɪtʃen'si:] *n Br Educ* (*abbr* **Higher National Certificate**) = título de escuela técnica de grado medio (un año)

HND [eɪtʃen'di:] *n Br Educ* (*abbr* **Higher National Diploma**) = título de escuela técnica de grado superior (dos años)

HO [eɪtʃ'əʊ] *n US* (*abbr* **habitual offender**) delicuente *mf* habitual, reincidente *mf*

ho [həʊ] *exclam* (**a**) *(attracting attention)* ¡eh!, ¡oye!, *RP* ¡ey! (**b**) *(imitating laughter)* **ho ho!** ¡jo, jo!

hoagie ['həʊgɪ] *n US Fam (sandwich) Esp* bocadillo *m or Am* sándwich *m or Méx* torta *f or RP* refuerzo *m* en una barra entera de pan

hoar [hɔ:(r)] *Literary* **1** *n (hoarfrost)* escarcha *f*
2 *adj (white)* canoso(a)

hoard [hɔ:d] *n* **1** *(of food)* provisión *f*; *(of money)* reserva *f* (secreta); **he has a whole h. of stories** tiene todo un repertorio *or* toda una colección de historias; **a squirrel's h. of nuts** la provisión de frutos secos de una ardilla
2 *vt (food)* hacer acopio de; *(money)* atesorar
3 *vi* acopiar *or* acaparar provisiones

hoarder ['hɔ:də(r)] *n* acaparador(ora) *m,f*

hoarding ['hɔ:dɪŋ] *n* (**a**) *(of food, money)* acaparamiento *m*, acopio *m* (**b**) *Br (display board)* valla *f* publicitaria (**c**) *(temporary fence)* valla *f* (provisional)

hoarfrost ['hɔ:frɒst] *n* escarcha *f*

hoarse [hɔ:s] *adj* ronco(a); **to be** *or* **sound h.** estar ronco(a); **to shout oneself h.** desgañitarse, gritar hasta ponerse ronco(a)

hoarsely ['hɔ:slɪ] *adv* con la voz ronca

hoarseness ['hɔ:snɪs] *n* ronquera *f*, ronquedad *f*

hoary ['hɔ:rɪ] *adj* (**a**) *(white)* canoso(a) (**b**) *(old)* viejo(a); **a h. old joke** un chiste muy antiguo *or* antediluviano

hoatzin [həʊ'ætsɪn] *n* hoatzin *m*, chenchena *f*

hoax [həʊks] **1** *n* engaño *m*; **the story turned out to be a h.** la historia resultó ser falsa *or Esp* un bulo; **to play a h. on sb** engañar a alguien; **bomb h.** falso aviso de bomba ▸▸ ***h. caller*** = persona que da falsas alarmas por teléfono
2 *vt* engañar

hoaxer ['həʊksə(r)] *n* bromista *mf*

hob [hɒb] *n* (**a**) *(on cooker)* fuego *m*, *Andes, Esp, Méx* hornilla *f*, *RP* hornalla *f* (**b**) *(on hearth)* plancha *f*

hobble ['hɒbəl] **1** *vi* cojear, *Andes, RP* renguear; **she hobbled across the street** atravesó la calle cojeando
2 *vt (horse)* apear, maniatar
3 *n* (**a**) *(limp)* cojera *f*, *Andes, RP* renguera *f*; **to walk with a h.** cojear, *Andes, RP* renguear (**b**) *(for horse)* maniota *f*, manea *f* (**c**) ***h. skirt*** falda *f* larga de tubo

hobbledehoy ['hɒbəldɪhɔɪ] *n* zangolotino *m*

hobby ['hɒbɪ] *n* (**a**) *(pastime)* afición *f*, hobby *m* (**b**) *(bird)* alcotán *m*

hobbyhorse ['hɒbɪhɔ:s] *n* (**a**) *(toy)* caballito *m* de juguete (**b**) *(favourite subject)* tema *m* favorito; **he's off on his h. again** ya está con la misma cantinela *or* canción de siempre

hobbyist ['hɒbɪɪst] *n* aficionado(a) *m,f*

hobgoblin [hɒb'gɒblɪn] *n* diablillo *m*, duende *m*

hobnail ['hɒbneɪl] *n* tachuela *f*

hobnail(ed) boot ['hɒbneɪl(d)'bu:t] *n* bota *f* de suela claveteada

hobnob ['hɒbnɒb] (*pt & pp* **hobnobbed**) *vi Fam* **to h. with sb** codearse con alguien

hobo ['həʊbəʊ] (*pl* **hoboes** *or* **hobos**) *n US* (**a**) *(tramp)* vagabundo(a) *m,f*, indigente *mf* (**b**) *(itinerant worker)* peón *m*, jornalero(a) *m,f*

Hobson's choice ['hɒbsənz'tʃɔɪs] *n* **it's H.** no hay otra elección, *Esp* esto son lentejas, si quieres las tomas y si no, las dejas

hock[1] [hɒk] *n (wine)* = vino blanco alemán del valle del Rin

hock[2] *n* (a) *(joint)* corvejón *m*, jarrete *m* (b) *(piece of meat)* codillo *m*

hock[3] *Fam* 1 *n* **in h.** *(in pawn)* empeñado(a); *(in debt)* endeudado(a), entrampado(a); **to get sth out of h.** desempeñar algo; **to be in h. to the bank** tener una deuda con el banco
2 *vt (pawn)* empeñar

hockey ['hɒkɪ] *n* (a) *(on grass)* hockey *m* (sobre hierba *or Am* césped) ▸▸ ***h. pitch*** campo *m* de hockey; ***h. stick*** stick *m*, palo *m* de hockey (b) *US (on ice)* hockey *m* (sobre hielo) ▸▸ ***h. rink*** pista *f* de hockey sobre hielo; ***h. stick*** stick *m*, palo *m* de hockey

hockshop ['hɒkʃɒp] *n US Fam* casa *f* de empeños *or* préstamos, monte *m* de piedad

hocus-pocus ['həʊkəs'pəʊkəs] *n* (a) *(trickery)* camelo *m*, embaucamiento *m*; **all that religion stuff is just h.** todo eso de la religión no es más que un engañabobos; **they think a bit of h. with interest rates will turn round the economy** creen que algunos pases mágicos con las tasas de interés modificarán drásticamente la economía (b) *(magician's chant)* abracadabra *m*

hod [hɒd] *n* = artesa abierta por los lados utilizada para acarrear ladrillos ▸▸ ***h. carrier*** peón *m* de albañil *or* de albañilería

hodad ['həʊdæd] *n US Fam* (a) *(at beach)* = persona que frecuenta las playas de surf fingiendo ser un surfista (b) *(loser)* fracasado(a) *m,f*

hodgepodge = **hotchpotch**

Hodgkin's disease ['hɒdʒkɪnzdɪziːz], **Hodgkin's lymphoma** ['hɒdʒkɪnzlɪm'fəʊmə] *n* linfoma *m* de Hodgkin

hoe [həʊ] 1 *n* azada *f*, azadón *m*
2 *vt* remover con la azada

hoedown ['həʊdaʊn] *n US* contradanza *f*

hog [hɒg] 1 *n* (a) *Br (castrated pig)* cerdo *m* castrado
(b) *US (pig)* cerdo *m*, puerco *m*, *Am* chancho *m* ▸▸ ***h. cholera*** peste *f* porcina
(c) *(glutton)* glotón(ona) *m,f*
(d) *US Fam (motorbike)* motaza *f*, moto *f* grande
(e) IDIOMS **to go the whole h.** *(be extravagant)* tirar *or Andes, CAm, Carib, Méx* botar la casa por la ventana; **why don't we go the whole h. and order champagne?** ya puestos (a despilfarrar)... ¿por qué no pedimos champán?; *US Fam* **to be in h. heaven** estar más contento(a) que un chico con zapatos nuevos *or* que unas castañuelas
2 *vt* (*pt & pp* **hogged**) *Fam* acaparar; **she hogs all the best bits for herself** ella siempre se queda con la mejor parte; **to h. the limelight** acaparar *or* monopolizar la atención; **to h. the middle of the road** estar en medio del paso, ocupar el paso

hogback ['hɒgbæk], **hog's-back** ['hɒgzbæk] *n (hill)* risco *m*, montaña *f* escarpada

Hogmanay [hɒgmə'neɪ] *n Scot* Nochevieja *f*

hog's-back = **hogback**

hogshead ['hɒgzhed] *n* tonel *m*

hogtie ['hɒgtaɪ] *vt US (person)* atar de pies y manos a; *(animal)* atar las cuatro patas a; *Fig* **this new legislation has hogtied us** esta nueva legislación nos ha dejado atados de pies y manos *or* nos impide (por completo) actuar

hogwash ['hɒgwɒʃ] *n* (a) *Fam (nonsense)* sandeces *fpl*, tonterías *fpl*; **that's a load of h.!** ¡eso es una sandez!, ¡eso no son más que tonterías! (b) *(pigswill)* bazofia *f*, desperdicios *mpl*

hog-wild ['hɒg'waɪld] *adj US Fam* descontrolado(a), desenfrenado(a); **to go h.** descontrolarse, desenfrenarse, *Esp* desmadrarse; **she won the lottery and went h.** le tocó la lotería y se desmelenó

hoik, hoick [hɔɪk] *vt Br Fam* levantar de golpe

hoi polloi [hɔɪpə'lɔɪ] *n* **the h.** el populacho, la plebe

hoist [hɔɪst] 1 *n* (a) *(device) (pulley system)* aparejo *m* para izar; *(elevator)* elevador *m*, montacargas *m* (b) **to give sb a h. up** *(lift)* aupar *or Am* alzar a alguien
2 *vt (equipment, person)* subir, elevar; *(flag, sail)* izar; **she hoisted herself on to the wall** se subió *or Esp* aupó a la tapia; IDIOM **she was h. with her own petard** le salió el tiro por la culata

hoity-toity ['hɔɪtɪ'tɔɪtɪ] *adj Fam* creído(a), presumido(a); **to go all h.** ufanarse, hincharse como un pavo, *Esp* ponerse ancho(a)

hokey ['həʊkɪ] *adj US Fam* (a) *(nonsensical)* majadero(a), necio(a) (b) *(sentimental)* sensiblero(a)

hokey cokey ['həʊkɪ'kəʊkɪ] *n Br* = canción y danza que se baila en corro a su ritmo; **to do the h.** bailar el hokey cokey

hokum ['həʊkəm] *n esp US Fam* (a) *(nonsense) Esp* majaderías *fpl*, *Am* pendejadas *fpl* (b) *(sentimental or unreal play, movie)* cursilería *f*, *Esp* ñoñez *f*

HOLD [həʊld] 1 *n* (a) *(grip)* **to catch** *or* **take h. of** agarrarse a; **get h. of the other end of the table** sujeta *or Esp* coge *or RP* agarrá el otro extremo de la mesa; **to have h. of sth** tener algo *Esp* cogido *or Am* agarrado; **to keep h. of sth** no soltar algo; **you'd better keep h. of the money** mejor que guardes tú el dinero; **to let go one's h. on sth** soltar algo; **he lost h. of the rope** se le escapó la cuerda; **to loosen one's h. on sth** aflojar la presión sobre algo; **to tighten one's h. on sth** apretar más algo; *Fig* **to get h. of sb** *(make contact with)* localizar a alguien; *Fig* **to get h. of sth** *(obtain)* hacerse con algo; **where did you get h. of that idea?** ¿de dónde has sacado esa idea?; **just wait till the newspapers get h. of the story!** ¡ya verás cuando se enteren los periódicos!; **to lose one's h. on reality** perder el contacto con la realidad
(b) *(place to grip) (when climbing)* agarre *m*, apoyo *m*
(c) *(in wrestling)* llave *f*; *Fig* **there were no holds barred in the election campaign** la campaña electoral fue una batalla campal
(d) *(control)* control *m* (on sobre); **to have a h. on** *or* **over sb** tener poder sobre alguien; **to keep a h. on sth** contener algo; **get a h. on yourself!, keep a h. of yourself!** ¡mantén la compostura!; *US* **they put a h. on all the rooms in the hotel** reservaron todas las habitaciones del hotel; **the fire was beginning to take h.** el incendio estaba empezando a extenderse; **all sorts of wild ideas had begun to take h. of the populace** toda clase de ideas descabelladas se habían apoderado de la población
(e) *(of ship, plane)* bodega *f*
2 *vt* (*pt & pp* **held** [held]) (a) *(grip)* coger, sujetar, *Am* agarrar; *(embrace)* abrazar; **h. this!** ¡sujeta esto!; **he held the child in his arms** sostuvo al niño en brazos; **she held her lover in her arms** sostuvo a su amante en brazos; **she held a knife (in her hand)** tenía un cuchillo en la mano; **will you h. my coat a second?** ¿me aguantas *or* sostienes el abrigo un momento?; **they held hands** estaban agarrados de la mano; **to h. one's head in dismay** hundir la cara entre las manos consternado(a); **to h. one's nose** taparse la nariz; **to h. sth in position** *or* **place** sujetar algo sin que se mueva; **he held the door open for her** le sujetó la puerta para que pasara; **to h. sth/sb tight** sujetar *or Esp* coger *or Am* agarrar algo/a alguien fuerte
(b) *(carry, support)* **the chair couldn't h. his weight** la silla no resistió su peso; **to h. one's head high** llevar la cabeza bien alta; **to h. oneself well** mantenerse erguido(a)
(c) *(contain)* contener; **this bottle holds two litres** en esta botella caben dos litros; **the stadium holds over 50,000** el estadio tiene capacidad *or* cabida para más de 50.000 espectadores; **will this box h. all our things?** ¿nos cabrá todo en esta caja?; **nobody knows what the future holds** nadie sabe lo que deparará el futuro; **this letter holds the key to the murder** esta carta contiene la clave del asesinato; **it holds no interest for me** no tiene ningún interés para mí; **this photo holds fond memories for me** esta foto me trae gratos recuerdos; **he can't h. his drink** *or US* **liquor** el alcohol se le sube a la cabeza muy rápido; IDIOM **to h. water** *(theory, story)* no hacer agua; **it doesn't h. water** hace agua
(d) *(possess) (shares, passport, account, degree, ticket)* tener; *(title, rank)* poseer; *(job, position)* ocupar; *(record)* ostentar; **she had held office before** ya antes había ocupado un cargo; *Fig* **to h. all the cards** tener las mejores cartas; **she holds the world record for the javelin** posee el récord mundial de (lanzamiento de) jabalina
(e) *(keep)* mantener; **we h. details of all our customers** tenemos detalles de todos nuestros clientes; **she held her seat at the last election** mantuvo su escaño en las últimas elecciones; **to h. sb's interest/attention** mantener el interés/la atención de alguien; **to h. an audience** mantener la atención del público; **to h. the floor** *(in debate)* tener la palabra; **to h. one's own** defenderse (bien); **to h. one's own against sb** no desmerecer frente a alguien; **to h. one's ground** mantenerse en sus trece
(f) *(keep against will)* retener, tener; **to h. sb prisoner/hostage** tener a alguien prisionero/como rehén; **the police are holding him for questioning** la policía lo tiene retenido para interrogarlo; *Mil* **to h. a town** tener tomada una ciudad
(g) *(maintain without change)* **to h. one's position/course** mantener la posición/el rumbo; *Mus* **to h. a note** sostener una nota
(h) *(reserve, set aside) (room, table)* reservar
(i) *(retain)* **she held her arms by** *or* **at her sides** tenía los brazos pegados al cuerpo; **her hair was held in place with hairpins** tenía el pelo sujeto con horquillas
(j) *(restrain)* sujetar; **to h. one's breath** contener la respiración; *Fig* **don't h. your breath!** puedes esperar sentado; **there's no holding him** no hay quien lo pare; *Fig* **h. your tongue!** ¡cierra la boca!; *US* **one burger, h. the mustard!** *(in restaurant order)* una hamburguesa sin mostaza
(k) *(keep in check)* **we held them to a draw** les sacamos un empate; **we have held costs to a minimum** hemos contenido los costos *or Esp* costes en el mínimo

(**l**) *(delay) (start)* retrasar; **they held the plane for him** retrasaron el avión por él; **h. everything until further notice** paraliza todo hasta nueva orden; *Fam* **h. it!, h. your horses!** ¡para el carro!; *Tel* **h. all my calls for the next hour** no me pases llamadas durante la próxima hora; **to h. one's fire** *(not shoot)* no disparar; *(not criticize)* no empezar a criticar; *Journ* **h. the front page!** ¡para la portada!

(**m**) *(conduct) (negotiations, meeting)* celebrar; *(inquiry)* realizar; *(conversation)* mantener; *(interview)* hacer; *(party)* dar; *(protest, demonstration)* hacer, celebrar; **to h. an election/elections** celebrar una elección/elecciones; **the classes are held in the evening** las clases se imparten por la tarde; **to h. talks** mantener conversaciones

(**n**) *(assert, believe)* sostener; **the Constitution holds that we all have equal rights** la Constitución dice *or* sostiene que todos tenemos los mismos derechos; **she holds strong views on the subject** sostiene opiniones firmes sobre el asunto; **I h. the opinion that...** soy de la opinión de que...

(**o**) *(consider)* **to h. sb responsible** hacer responsable a alguien; **to be held in respect** ser respetado(a); **to h. sb in contempt** sentir desdén por alguien; **to h. that...** *(person)* sostener que...; **the appeal court held the evidence to be insufficient** el tribunal de apelación consideró que las pruebas no eran determinantes

(**p**) *Comptr* almacenar; **the information is held in a temporary buffer** la información se almacena en un búffer temporal

(**q**) *Aut* **to h. the road well** tener buen agarre, agarrarse a la carretera

(**r**) *Tel* **h. the line** espere un momento, no cuelgue

3 *vi* (**a**) *(person)* **h. fast** *or* **tight!** ¡agárrate bien *or* fuerte!; **h. still!** ¡quieto!; **to h. fast to a belief** aferrarse a una idea

(**b**) *(remain secure) (rope, shelf, branch)* resistir, aguantar; **their resolve held fast** *or* **firm despite fierce opposition** se mantuvieron firmes en su empeño a pesar de la encarnizada oposición; **the pound held firm against the dollar** la libra se mantuvo sólida frente al dólar

(**c**) *(remain valid) (agreement)* mantenerse; **my offer/invitation still holds** mi oferta/invitación sigue en pie; **the same holds (true) for everyone** lo mismo es válido para todos

(**d**) *(last) (good weather)* mantenerse; **if your luck holds** si sigues teniendo suerte

(**e**) *Tel* esperar; **the line's busy just now – I'll h.** la línea está ocupada en estos momentos – me espero

(**f**) *Av* esperar para aterrizar

4 **on hold** *adv* **to put sth on h.** suspender algo temporalmente; *Tel* **to put sb on h.** poner a alguien a la espera

▸**hold against** *vt sep* **to h. sth against sb** tener algo contra alguien; **he never held it against me** nunca me lo reprochó

▸**hold back** 1 *vt sep* (**a**) *(restrain) (person, animal)* frenar, contener; *(army, crowd, flood)* contener; *(progress, project)* impedir el avance de; **she held back her tears/laughter** contuvo las lágrimas/la risa; **his difficulties with maths are holding him back** sus dificultades con las matemáticas lo están dejando atrás

(**b**) *(not tell)* **he's holding something back** se está guardando algo

(**c**) *(keep in reserve)* reservar, guardar

(**d**) *US Sch* **they held him back a year** le hicieron repetir curso

2 *vi* (**a**) *(stay back)* quedarse atrás (**b**) *(refrain)* contenerse; **to h. back from doing sth** abstenerse de hacer algo; **don't h. back, express yourself!** ¡no te cortes, expresa lo que sientes!

▸**hold down** *vt sep* (**a**) *(restrain) (person)* sujetar; *(carpet)* sujetar, fijar; *(taxes, prices)* mantener en un nivel bajo

(**b**) **to h. down a job** *(keep)* conservar un trabajo

(**c**) *Comptr (key, mouse button)* mantener apretado(a)

▸**hold forth** *vi* explayarse (**on** acerca de)

▸**hold in** *vt sep* **to h. one's stomach in** meter el estómago; **he held his emotions in** no exteriorizaba sus emociones

▸**hold off** 1 *vt sep* (**a**) *(keep at bay)* rechazar; **the troops held off the enemy/the attack** las tropas repelieron al enemigo/el ataque; **I can't h. the reporters off any longer** no puedo darles más largas a los periodistas

(**b**) *(delay, put off)* posponer; **she held off making a decision until she had more information** pospuso su decisión hasta disponer de más datos

2 *vi (delay)* **the rain is holding off** no se decide a llover; **he ordered the mob to h. off** ordenó a la multitud que se contuviera

▸**hold on** 1 *vt sep (attach)* **it was held on with glue** estaba pegado con pegamento

2 *vi* (**a**) *(continue, persevere)* resistir, aguantar

(**b**) *(wait)* esperar; **h. on (a minute)!** ¡espera (un momento)!; **h. on (a minute), there's something funny going on here** espera (un momento), aquí pasa algo raro

(**c**) *(brace oneself)* **h. on (tight)!** ¡agárrate (bien *or* fuerte)!

▸**hold on to** *vt insep* (**a**) *(grip tightly) (to stop oneself from falling)* agarrarse a; *(to stop something from falling)* agarrar; *Fig (idea, hope, power)* aferrarse a; IDIOM **h. on to your hat!** ¡agárrate (a la silla)!

(**b**) *(keep) (property)* guardar; *(memories)* conservar

▸**hold out** 1 *vt sep (one's hand, object)* tender; **h. your arms out in front of you** extiende los brazos hacia delante

2 *vt insep (hope, opportunity)* ofrecer; **I don't h. out much hope of...** tengo pocas esperanzas de que...

3 *vi* (**a**) *(resist)* resistirse; **they held out against the changes** se resistieron a los cambios; **to h. out for a better offer** aguantar a la espera de una oferta mejor

(**b**) *(last) (supplies)* durar; **will the engine h. out till we get home?** ¿aguantará el motor hasta llegar a casa?

▸**hold out on** *vt insep Fam* resistirse a; **you're holding out on me!** *(not telling truth)* ¡me estás escondiendo algo!

▸**hold over** *vt sep* (**a**) *(postpone)* diferir, posponer

(**b**) *US (keep on)* **the play was held over for another three weeks** mantuvieron la obra en cartel tres semanas más

(**c**) *(use to blackmail)* **to h. sth over sb** sobornar a alguien con algo

▸**hold to** 1 *vt insep (belief, opinion)* aferrarse a; **you must h. to your principles** tienes que ser fiel a tus principios

2 *vt sep* **to h. sb to his promise** hacer que alguien cumpla su promesa; **I'll h. you to that!** ¡lo prometido es deuda!, ¡te lo recordaré!

▸**hold together** 1 *vt sep (party, marriage, alliance)* mantener unido(a); *(with glue, string, rope)* sujetar

2 *vi (party, marriage, alliance)* mantenerse unido(a)

▸**hold up** 1 *vt sep* (**a**) *(support)* soportar, aguantar; **my trousers were held up with safety pins** me aguantaba los pantalones con alfileres

(**b**) *(raise)* levantar, alzar; **h. your head up above the water** mantén la cabeza fuera del agua; *Fig* **she would never be able to h. her head up again** no podría mirar más a la gente a la cara; **to h. sth up to the light** poner algo a contraluz

(**c**) *(present)* **to h. sb up as an example** poner a alguien como ejemplo; **to h. sb up to ridicule** dejar a alguien en ridículo

(**d**) *(delay)* retrasar; **I was held up in the traffic** me retrasé por culpa del tráfico; **the project was held up for lack of funds** el proyecto se retrasó por falta de fondos

(**e**) *(rob)* atracar

2 *vi (theory, alibi)* tenerse en pie; *(good weather)* aguantar; **she's holding up well under the pressure** está aguantando bien las presiones

▸**hold with** *vt insep* **I don't h. with swearing** soy enemigo de que la gente use palabrotas; **I don't h. with his opinions** no estoy de acuerdo con sus opiniones

---

holdall ['həʊldɔːl] *n esp Br* bolsa *f (de viaje o de deporte)*

holder ['həʊldə(r)] *n* (**a**) *(of record, trophy)* poseedor(ora) *m,f*; **the current h. of the record** el actual poseedor del récord, *Am* el recordista (**b**) *(of ticket)* poseedor(ora) *m,f*; *(of passport, licence, permit)* titular *mf*; *(of stock, shares)* accionista *mf*, titular *mf*; *(of belief, opinion)* defensor(ora) *m,f* (**c**) *(device)* soporte *m*

holding ['həʊldɪŋ] *n* (**a**) *(property)* propiedad *f*; *(of shares)* participación *f* ▸▸ *Com* ***h. company*** holding *m* (**b**) *Mil* ***h. operation*** maniobra *f* de contención (**c**) *Av* ***h. pattern*** vuelo *m* de espera para el aterrizaje

holdover ['həʊldəʊvə(r)] *n US* (**a**) *Cin & Theat* obra *f or* película *f* que permanece en cartel (**b**) *(relic)* reliquia *f*, vestigio *m*

hold-up ['həʊldʌp] *n* (**a**) *(delay) (in plan)* retraso *m*, *Am* demora *f*; *(of traffic)* retención *f*, embotellamiento *m* (**b**) *(armed robbery)* atraco *m*

hole [həʊl] 1 *n* (**a**) *(in roof, clothing)* agujero *m*; *(in ground)* hoyo *m*, agujero *m*; **his sock/shoe has a h. in it** tiene un agujero en el calcetín/zapato; **to make a h. in sth** hacer un agujero en algo, agujerear algo; **to wear a h. in sth** hacerle *or* hacérsele un agujero a algo (como consecuencia del uso), agujerear *or* agujerearse algo; **the holiday made a h. in their savings** las vacaciones dejaron maltrecha su economía; *Fig* **to pick holes in sth** *(in argument, theory)* encontrar defectos en *or* a algo; **his argument's full of holes** su argumento *or* razonamiento está lleno de lagunas, *Andes, RP* su argumento hace agua por todos lados; IDIOM *Fam* **I need this like a h. in the head** ¡es lo que me faltaba!; IDIOM *Fam* **you're talking through a h. in your head** hablas a tontas y a locas, estás diciendo bobadas, no sabes lo que dices ▸▸ *Med* ***h. in the heart*** comunicación *f* interventricular congénita; ***h. punch*** perforadora *f*; *Fam* ***h. in the wall*** *(place)* lugar *m* insignificante, rincón *m* de mala muerte; *Br (cash machine)* cajero *m* automático

(**b**) *(animal's burrow)* madriguera *f*

(**c**) *(in golf)* hoyo *m*; **a h. in one** un hoyo en uno; *Hum* **the nineteenth h.** = el bar del club de golf

(**d**) *Fam (awkward situation)* **to be in a h.** *(in difficulty)* estar en un apuro *or* brete; **to get sb out of a h.** sacar a alguien de un aprieto
(**e**) *Fam (room, house)* cuchitril *m*; *(town)* lugar *m* de mala muerte; **what a h.!** *(town)* ¡qué mísero rincón!, ¡qué miserable pueblucho!, *Am* ¡qué agujero!; **this is an awful h.!** *(house, bar, disco)* ¡esto es un bohío *or* bujío *or* tugurio de mala muerte!
(**f**) *Vulg (vagina)* coño *m*, *Andes, RP* concha *f*; *Br* **to get one's h.** echar un polvo, *Esp* follar, *Am* coger, *Méx* chingar
2 *vt* (**a**) *(make a hole in)* agujerear; **the ship was holed below the waterline** el buque tenía una vía de agua por debajo de la línea de flotación (**b**) *(in golf)* **to h. a shot/putt** embocar un golpe/putt; **he holed the fourteenth in four** hizo el hoyo 14 en cuatro golpes
3 *vi (in golf)* embocar, hacer un hoyo; **to h. in four** embocar *or* hacer un hoyo en cuatro golpes
▸ **hole out** *vi (in golf)* embocar (la bola)
▸ **hole up** *Fam* **1** *vt sep* **they're holed up in a hotel** están refugiados *or* escondidos en un hotel
2 *vi (hide)* esconderse

hole-and-corner ['həʊlən'kɔːnə(r)] *adj* clandestino(a)

hole-in-the-wall ['həʊlɪnðəwɔːl] *adj* insignificante, de mala muerte

holey ['həʊlɪ] *adj Fam (socks)* con tomates, *Andes, RP* con papas; *(jumper)* lleno(a) de agujeros

holiday ['hɒlɪdeɪ] **1** *n* (**a**) *esp Br (vacation)* vacaciones *fpl*; **summer/Christmas h.** *or* **holidays** vacaciones de verano/Navidad; **to be/go on h.** estar/irse de vacaciones; **to take a h./two months' h.** tomarse *or Esp* cogerse (unas) vacaciones/dos meses de vacaciones; **the Krügers could do with** *or* **need a h.** a los Krüger les irían bien unas vacaciones; **I wish I could take a h. from the kids for a few days** ojalá pudiera alejarme de los niños por unos días; **there was a h. mood in the office** se respiraba un ambiente festivo en la oficina; **the h. rush has started** ha comenzado la desbandada del período vacacional; **h. with pay, paid holidays** vacaciones retribuidas; **we had the h. of a lifetime** fueron unas vacaciones inolvidables ▸▸ ***h. brochure*** folleto *m* turístico; ***h. camp*** centro *m* turístico, colonia *f* turística *or Am* de vacaciones; ***h. entitlement*** derecho *m* a vacaciones; ***h. home*** segunda residencia *f*, casa *f* para las vacaciones; ***h. resort*** centro *m* turístico, lugar *m* de veraneo, *RP* balneario *m*; ***h. season*** temporada *f* de vacaciones
(**b**) *(day off) Esp* (día *m* de) fiesta *f*, *Am* feriado *m*; *(public holiday)* día *m* festivo, *Am* día *m* feriado; **tomorrow is a h.** mañana es fiesta *or Am* feriado ▸▸ *Rel* ***h. of obligation*** fiesta *f* de guardar *or* de prefecto
(**c**) *US* **the holidays** *(Christmas)* las fiestas *or* vacaciones (de Navidad); **happy holidays!** ¡felices fiestas!
2 *vi* pasar las vacaciones; *(in summer)* veranear

holidaymaker ['hɒlɪdeɪ'meɪkə(r)] *n esp Br* turista *mf*; *(in summer)* veraneante *mf*

holier-than-thou ['həʊlɪəðən'ðaʊ] *adj (religiously)* santurrón(ona); *(morally in general)* con aires de superioridad moral; **he always sounds so h.** habla siempre como si él estuviera más allá del bien y del mal

holiness ['həʊlɪnɪs] *n* santidad *f*; **Your H.** Su Santidad

holistic [həʊ'lɪstɪk] *adj* holístico(a) ▸▸ ***h. medicine*** medicina *f* holística

Holland ['hɒlənd] *n* Holanda

hollandaise sauce ['hɒləndeɪz'sɔːs] *n* salsa *f* holandesa

holler ['hɒlə(r)] *Fam* **1** *vi* gritar, dar voces; **if you need anything, just h.** si necesitas algo, dame una voz *or* pégame un grito
2 *vt* gritar, chillar
3 *n* grito *m*, chillido *m*

hollow ['hɒləʊ] **1** *n* (**a**) *(in wall, tree)* hueco *m* (**b**) *(in ground)* depresión *f* (**c**) *(in hand, back)* hueco *m*
2 *adj* (**a**) *(container, log)* hueco(a); *(cheek, eyes)* hundido(a); *Fig* **to have a h. feeling in one's stomach** *(be hungry)* tener un vacío *or RP* un agujero en el estómago; *Fig* **to feel h.** *(emotionally)* sentirse vacío(a); IDIOM *Fam* **you must have h. legs** *or* **a h. leg!** *(can eat a lot)* debes de tener una solitaria; *(can drink a lot)* eres una esponja
(**b**) *(sound)* hueco(a), resonante; **in a h. voice** con voz hueca; **a h. laugh** una risa sardónica
(**c**) *(promise, guarantee)* vacío(a); **h. victory** victoria deslucida; **h. promises** promesas vanas
3 *adv* (**a**) *(empty)* **to sound h.** *(tree, wall)* sonar a hueco(a); *(laughter, excuse, promise)* sonar a falso(a) (**b**) *Fam* **to beat sb h.** *or US* **all h.** dar una (buena) paliza a alguien
4 *vt* **to h. sth (out)** ahuecar *or* vaciar algo

hollow-cheeked ['hɒləʊ'tʃiːkt] *adj* de mejillas hundidas

hollow-eyed ['hɒləʊwaɪd] *adj* de ojos hundidos

hollowly ['hɒləʊlɪ] *adv (to laugh)* sardónicamente

hollowness ['hɒləʊnɪs] *n* (**a**) *(of tree, container)* oquedad *f*; **the h. of his eyes/cheeks** lo hundido de sus ojos/mejillas (**b**) *(of laughter, excuse, promise)* falsedad *f*; **the h. of their victory** lo insustancial de su victoria

holly ['hɒlɪ] *n (leaves)* hojas *fpl* de acebo ▸▸ ***h. berry*** fruto *m* del acebo; ***h. tree*** acebo *m*

hollyhock ['hɒlɪhɒk] *n* malvarrosa *f*

holly-oak ['hɒlɪəʊk] *n* encina *f*

holmium ['hɒlmɪəm] *n Chem* holmio *m*

holm-oak ['həʊməʊk] *n* encina *f*

holocaust ['hɒləkɔːst] *n* holocausto *m*; **nuclear h.** holocausto nuclear; *Hist* **the H.** el holocausto judío

Holocene ['hɒləsiːn] *Geol* **1** *n* **the H.** el holoceno
2 *adj (era)* holoceno(a)

hologram ['hɒləgræm] *n* holograma *m*

holograph ['hɒləgrɑːf] **1** *n* (h)ológrafo *m*
2 *adj* (h)ológrafo(a)

holographic [hɒlə'græfɪk] *adj* holográfico(a)

holography [hɒ'lɒgrəfɪ] *n* holografía *f*

hols [hɒlz] *npl Br Fam* vacaciones *fpl*

Holstein ['hɒlstaɪn] *n US (cow)* vaca *f* (de la raza) Holstein

holster ['həʊlstə(r)] *n* pistolera *f*

holt [hɒlt] *n* guarida *f*, madriguera *f*

holy ['həʊlɪ] *adj* (**a**) *(sacred)* santo(a) ▸▸ ***the H. Bible*** la Sagrada Biblia; ***the H. City*** la Ciudad Santa; ***H. Communion*** la comunión; **to take H. Communion** comulgar, recibir la Eucaristía *or* a Dios, *Am* tomar la comunión; ***h. day*** fiesta *f* de guardar; ***the H. Family*** la Sagrada Familia; ***the H. Father*** el Santo Padre; ***the H. Ghost*** el Espíritu Santo; ***the H. Grail*** el Santo Grial; ***h. of holies*** *(place)* santuario *m*, sanctasanctórum *m*; *(thing)* cosa *f* sacrosanta; *Fam Pej* ***H. Joe*** *(religious person)* santurrón(ona) *m,f*, meapilas *mf inv*, *RP* chupacirios *mf*; *(chaplain, parson)* cura *m*; ***the H. Land*** Tierra Santa; ***H. Mother Church*** la Santa Madre Iglesia; ***h. matrimony*** santo *or Am* sagrado matrimonio *m*; **to be joined in h. matrimony** unirse en santo *or Am* sagrado matrimonio; ***the H. Office*** el santo Oficio; ***the h. oils*** los santos óleos; ***h. orders*** sagradas órdenes *fpl*; **to take h. orders** ordenarse sacerdote; *US Pej* ***H. Roller*** = miembro de algunas sectas religiosas en las que el fervor espiritual se expresa mediante gritos y movimientos violentos del cuerpo; *Hist* ***H. Roman Empire*** Sacro Imperio *m* Romano Germánico; ***the H. See*** la Santa Sede; ***the H. Spirit*** el Espíritu Santo; ***h. war*** guerra *f* santa; ***h. water*** agua *f* bendita; ***H. Week*** Semana *f* Santa; ***H. Writ*** las Sagradas Escrituras; **it's not H. Writ!** ¡eso no es el Evangelio!; ***H. Year*** año *m* de jubileo *or Am* jubilar, año *m* santo
(**b**) *(devout)* santo(a)
(**c**) *Fam (as intensifier)* **that child is a h. terror** *(mischievous)* ese niño es un verdadero diablillo; **to have a h. fear** *or* **dread of sth** tenerle verdadero miedo *or Am* pavor a algo; **h. cow** *or* **smoke** *or* **mackerel!** ¡madre de Dios *or* del amor hermoso!; *Vulg* **h. shit!** *Esp* ¡hostias!, *Méx* ¡chingado!, *RP* ¡carajo!

homage ['hɒmɪdʒ] *n* homenaje *m*; **to pay** *or* **do h. to sth/sb** rendir homenaje a algo/alguien

hombre ['ɒmbreɪ] *n US Fam* tipo *m*, individuo *m*, fulano *m*

homburg ['hɒmbɜːg] *n* sombrero *m* de fieltro

HOME [həʊm] **1** *n* (**a**) *(house)* casa *f*; **my h. phone number** mi número de teléfono particular; **at h.** en casa; *Formal* **Mrs Carr is not at h. on Mondays** los lunes Mrs Carr no recibe visitas; **to be away from h.** *(not in house)* estar fuera (de casa); **to feel at h.** sentirse como en casa; **I am** *or* **feel very much at h. with modern technology** me siento cómodo utilizando las nuevas tecnologías; **he doesn't yet feel at h. with the machine** todavía no domina el manejo del aparato; *Fam* **we'll have to find a h. for this new vase** tendremos que encontrar un sitio para este jarrón nuevo; **to give a h. to an orphan** acoger a un huérfano; **to have a h. of one's own** tener casa propia; **to leave h.** *(in the morning)* salir de casa; *(one's parents' home)* independizarse, irse de casa; **to make sb feel at h.** hacer que alguien se sienta cómodo(a); **make yourself at h.** estás en tu casa, ponte cómodo; **to make one's h. in...** asentarse en...; **to work from h.** trabajar en casa; *Br Fam* **what's a "cotyledon" when it's at h.?** ¿qué diablos es un cotiledón?, ¿qué es un cotiledón en cristiano?; *Br* **it's a h. from h.**, *US* **it's a h. away from h.** es como estar en casa; *Fig* **to be h. and dry** estar sano(a) y salvo(a); *US* **to be h. free** haber pasado lo peor; IDIOM **to tell sb a few h. truths** decirle a alguien cuatro verdades ▸▸ ***h. address*** domicilio *m*; ***h. banking*** telebanco *m*; ***h. birth*** parto *m* en casa; ***h. computer*** *Esp* ordenador *m* doméstico, *Am* computadora *f* doméstica; ***h. cooking***

comida *f* casera; ***h. delivery*** entrega *f or* reparto *m* a domicilio; ***h. delivery service*** servicio *m* a domicilio; ***h. economics*** *(school subject)* economía *f* doméstica; *Br* ***h. help*** ayuda *f* doméstica; ***h. improvements*** reformas *fpl* del hogar; *Fin* ***h. loan*** crédito *m* hipotecario, hipoteca *f*; ***h. movie*** vídeo *m or Am* video *m* casero *or* doméstico, película *f* casera; ***h. owner*** propietario(a) *m,f* (de una vivienda); ***h. remedy*** remedio *m* casero; *US Sch* ***h. room*** = aula donde cada alumno debe presentarse todas las mañanas; ***h. run*** *(last leg of trip)* trayecto *m* final; ***h. schooling*** enseñanza *f* doméstica *or* en el hogar; ***h. shopping*** telecompra *f*; ***h. shopping channel*** teletienda *f*; ***h. town*** ciudad *f*/pueblo *m* natal; ***h. video*** vídeo *m or Am* video *m* doméstico; ***h. visits*** *(by nurse, doctor)* asistencia *f* a domicilio, atención *f* domiciliaria; ***h. worker*** teletrabajador(ora) *m,f*

(**b**) *(family abode)* hogar *m*; **to come from a good h.** ser de buena familia; PROV **h. is where the heart is** = el hogar se encuentra donde uno tiene a los seres queridos; PROV **there's no place like h.** no hay nada como el hogar ►► ***h. comforts*** comodidades *fpl* hogareñas; ***h. life*** vida *f* doméstica

(**c**) *(country, region)* tierra *f*; **people at h. are very different** en mi país la gente es muy diferente; **at h. and abroad** nacional e internacionalmente; **Mexico has been her h. for twenty years** vivió veinte años en México; **an example nearer h.** un ejemplo más cercano; **Milan, the h. of fashion** Milán, la meca *or* la cuna de la moda; **the region is h. to thousands of refugees** en la región habitan miles de refugiados ►► ***h. front*** frente *m* civil; *Br Hist* ***the H. Guard*** = fuerza de reservistas que se quedó para defender Gran Bretaña durante la segunda Guerra Mundial; *Br Pol* ***H. Office*** Ministerio *m* del Interior; *Pol* ***h. rule*** autonomía *f*, autogobierno *m*; *Br Pol* ***the H. Secretary*** el ministro del Interior; ***h. waters*** aguas *fpl* nacionales

(**d**) *(of animal, plant)* hábitat *m*; **it's another species which has made its h. in this country** es otra de las especies que se han instalado en este país

(**e**) *(institution)* **(children's) h.** residencia *f* infantil; **(mental) h.** hospital *m* psiquiátrico; **(old people's) h.** residencia *f* de ancianos; **dog's/cat's h.** residencia canina/para gatos; **they put the child in a h.** metieron al niño en un centro de acogida

(**f**) *Br* ***the H. Counties*** = los condados de alrededor de Londres

(**g**) *Comptr* ***h. key*** tecla *f* de inicio; ***h. page*** *(initial page)* portada *f*, página *f* inicial *or* de inicio; *(personal page)* página *f* personal

(**h**) *Sport* **to be** *or* **play at h.** jugar en casa; **to be** *or* **play away from h.** jugar fuera de casa; **they're at h. to Sweden next week** la semana que viene juegan en casa contra Suecia ►► *also Fig* ***the h. straight*** *or esp US* ***stretch*** la recta final

(**i**) *(in baseball)* home *m* ►► ***h. base*** home *m*, base *f* meta; ***h. plate*** home *m*, base *f* meta; ***h. run*** carrera *f* completa, home-run *m*, *Am* jonrón *m*

2 *adj* (**a**) *Sport (team, game, ground, supporters)* local, de casa; **to have h. advantage** (tener la ventaja de) jugar en casa; *Fig* **to be on h. ground** *(familiar place)* conocer el terreno; *(familiar subject)* conocer el tema; **a h. win** una victoria local; **the h. strip** el equipaje *or* indumentaria habitual

(**b**) *(national) (market)* nacional, doméstico(a) ►► *TV & Journ* ***h. news*** noticias *fpl* nacionales

3 *adv* (**a**) *(in general)* a casa; **to be h.** estar en casa; **to go/come h.** ir/venir a casa; **to send sb h.** mandar a alguien a casa; **to see sb h.** acompañar a alguien a casa; **my friends back h.** los amigos que dejé en mi ciudad/pueblo/país; **to be h. alone** estar solo(a) en casa; **how much do you take h.?** ¿cuánto ganas?; **Fido, h.!** ¡Fido, a casa!

(**b**) *(all the way)* **he drove the knife h.** hundió el cuchillo hasta el fondo; **she really drove the message h.** dejó bien claro su mensaje; **to bring sth h. to sb** dejar bien claro algo a alguien; **the danger really came h. to me when...** verdaderamente me di cuenta del peligro cuando...

► **home in on** *vt insep (on target)* dirigirse a; *(on mistake, evidence)* señalar, concentrarse en

---

home-baked ['həʊm'beɪkt] *adj (bread, cakes)* casero(a), hecho(a) en casa

homebody ['həʊmbɒdɪ] *n Fam* persona *f* hogareña *or* amante del hogar

homebound ['həʊmbaʊnd] *adj* (**a**) *(going home)* de vuelta *or* en viaje de vuelta (a casa), camino del hogar (**b**) *(confined to home)* (metido(a)) entre cuatro paredes, metido(a) *or* encerrado(a) en casa; *(of sick people)* recluido(a) en casa

homeboy ['həʊmbɔɪ] *n US Fam* (**a**) *(man from one's home town, district)* paisano *m* (**b**) *(friend)* amiguete *m*, *Esp* colega *m*, *Méx, CAm* cuate *m* (**c**) *(fellow gang member)* compinche *m*, *Méx, CAm* cuate *m*

home-brew ['həʊm'bruː] *n* cerveza *f* casera

homebuyer ['həʊmbaɪə(r)] *n* comprador(ora) *m,f* de vivienda

homecoming ['həʊmkʌmɪŋ] *n* (**a**) *(to family, country)* regreso *m or* vuelta *f* a casa (**b**) *US Sch & Univ* fiesta *f* anual de antiguos alumnos

homegirl ['həʊmgɜːl] *n US Fam* (**a**) *(woman from one's home town, district)* paisana *f* (**b**) *(friend)* amigueta *f*, *Esp* colega *f*, *CAm, Méx* cuata *f* (**c**) *(fellow gang member)* compinche *f*, *CAm, Méx* cuata *f*

home-grown ['həʊm'grəʊn] *adj (from own garden)* de cosecha propia; *(not imported) (food)* del país; *Fig (singer, sportsperson)* de la tierra, nacional

homeland ['həʊmlænd] *n* (**a**) *(native country)* tierra *f or* país *m* natal (**b**) *Formerly (in South Africa)* homeland *m*, = territorio donde se confinaba a la población negra

homeless ['həʊmlɪs] **1** *adj* sin techo, sin hogar

2 *npl* **the h.** las personas sin techo, los sin techo

homelessness ['həʊmlɪsnɪs] *n* carencia *f* de hogar; **h. is becoming a huge problem** el problema de la gente sin techo *or* sin hogar está alcanzando proporciones enormes

homely ['həʊmlɪ] *adj* (**a**) *(welcoming) (person)* afable; *(atmosphere)* acogedor(ora), cálido(a) (**b**) *(unpretentious)* llano(a), sencillo(a); **the food is good if a little h.** sirven buenos platos aunque es comida sencilla *or* casera (**c**) *US (ugly)* feúcho(a)

home-made ['həʊm'meɪd] *adj* casero(a); **a h. bomb** una bomba (de fabricación) casera; **it's hard to believe your dress is h.** es increíble que ese vestido lo hayas hecho tú sola en casa

homemaker [həʊm'meɪkə(r)] *n* ama *f* de casa

homeopath ['həʊmɪəʊpæθ] *n* homeópata *mf*

homeopathic [həʊmɪəʊ'pæθɪk] *adj* homeopático(a)

homeopathy [həʊmɪ'ɒpəθɪ] *n* homeopatía *f*

Homer ['həʊmə(r)] *pr n* Homero; PROV **even H. nods, H. sometimes nods** el mejor escribano echa un borrón, nadie es perfecto

homer ['həʊmə(r)] *US Fam* **1** *n (in baseball)* carrera *f* completa, home-run *m*, *Am* jonrón *m*

2 *vi* hacer una carrera completa *or* un home run *or Am* un jonrón

Homeric [həʊ'merɪk] *adj* homérico(a)

homesick ['həʊmsɪk] *adj* nostálgico(a); **to be** *or* **feel h.** tener nostalgia *or Esp* morriña *or Ven* guayabo, *RP* extrañar; **he's h. for his family** echa de menos a *or esp Am* extraña a su familia

homesickness ['həʊmsɪknɪs] *n* nostalgia *f*, *Esp* morriña *f*, *Ven* guayabo *m*

homespun ['həʊmspʌn] **1** *adj* (**a**) *(cloth)* hilado(a) *or* tejido(a) en casa, hilado(a) *or* tejido(a) de manera artesanal *or* a mano (**b**) *(wisdom, advice)* de andar por casa, *Am* de entrecasa

2 *n (cloth)* tela *f* tejida en casa, tejido *m* de fabricación casera *or* artesanal

homestead ['həʊmsted] *n* finca *f*, hacienda *f* ►► *US Hist* ***the H. Act*** la ley de garantía de la propiedad, = ley sobre la cesión de tierras a los colonos por parte del Estado a cambio del cultivo de las mismas

homesteader ['həʊmstedə(r)] *n US* colono *m*

homeward ['həʊmwəd] **1** *adj* de vuelta a casa

2 *adv* a casa; **to be h. bound** estar de regreso a casa

homewards ['həʊmwədz] *adv* a casa

homework ['həʊmwɜːk] *n* (**a**) *Sch* deberes *mpl*; *also Fig* **to do one's h.** hacer los deberes; **the minister hadn't done his h.** el ministro no se había preparado para la ocasión (**b**) *(paid work)* teletrabajo *m*, trabajo *m* que se hace desde su propio domicilio

homeworker ['həʊmwɜːkə(r)] *n* teletrabajador(ora) *m,f*, persona *f* que trabaja desde su propio domicilio

homey ['həʊmɪ] *US* **1** *n Fam* = **homeboy, homegirl**

2 *adj* acogedor(ora), afable

homicidal [hɒmɪ'saɪdəl] *adj* homicida; **a h. maniac** un(a) maníaco(a) homicida

homicide ['hɒmɪsaɪd] *n* (**a**) *(act)* homicidio m; **accidental h.** homicidio involuntario *or* accidental; **justifiable h.** homicidio inculpable (**b**) *(person)* homicida *mf* (**c**) *US Fam (police department)* departamento *m* de homicidios, *Esp* policía *f* criminal

homily ['hɒmɪlɪ] *n* (**a**) *Rel* homilía *f* (**b**) *Fig (speech)* sermón *m*

homing ['həʊmɪŋ] *adj* ***h. instinct*** instinto *m* de volver al hogar, querencia *f*; ***h. missile*** misil *m* autodirigido; ***h. pigeon*** paloma *f* mensajera

hominid ['hɒmɪnɪd] *n* homínido *m*

hominoid ['hɒmɪnɔɪd] **1** *n* primate *m*

2 *adj* antropomorfo(a), *Spec* hominoideo(a)

hominy ['hɒmɪnɪ] *n US* sémola *f* de maíz ►► ***h. grits*** copos *mpl or Esp* gachas *fpl* de sémola de maíz

homo ['həʊməʊ] *n Fam Pej (homosexual)* marica *m*

homogeneity [həʊməʊdʒə'neɪtɪ] *n* homogeneidad *f*

homogeneous [hɒmə'dʒi:nɪəs, hə'mɒdʒɪnəs] *adj* homogéneo(a)

homogenize [hɒ'mɒdʒənaɪz] *vt* homogeneizar; **homogenized milk** leche homogeneizada

homograph ['hɒməgrɑ:f] *n* homógrafo *m*

homologous [hə'mɒləgəs] *adj Biol & Chem* homólogo(a)

homonym ['hɒmənɪm] *n* homónimo *m*

homophobe ['həʊməfəʊb] *n* homófobo(a) *m,f*

homophobia [hɒmə'fəʊbɪə] *n* homofobia *f*

homophobic [həʊmə'fəʊbɪk] *adj* homófobo(a)

homophone ['hɒməfəʊn] *n Ling* homófono *m*

Homo sapiens ['həʊməʊ'sæpɪenz] *n* homo sapiens *m inv*

homosexual [hɒmə'seksjʊəl] **1** *n* homosexual *mf*
2 *adj* homosexual

homosexuality [hɒməseksjʊ'ælɪtɪ] *n* homosexualidad *f*

homunculus [hə'mʌŋkjʊləs] (*pl* **homunculi** [hə'mʌŋkjʊlaɪ]) *n* homúnculo *m*

Hon *Br Parl* (*abbr* **Honourable**) **the H. member (for...)** el/la señor(ora) diputado(a) (por...)

hon [hʌn] *n US Fam* (*abbr* **honey**) *(term of address)* cielo *m*, cariño *m*

honcho ['hɒntʃəʊ] *n esp US Fam* **the head h.** el/la mandamás

Honduran [hɒn'djʊərən] **1** *n* hondureño(a) *m,f*
2 *adj* hondureño(a)

Honduras [hɒn'djʊərəs] *n* Honduras

hone [həʊn] **1** *n (stone)* piedra *f* de afilar *or* amolar
2 *vt* (**a**) *(knife, blade)* afilar (**b**) *(skill)* pulir; **finely honed arguments** argumentos muy afinados; **practice will h. your reflexes** la práctica agudizará tus reflejos
3 *vi US Fam (yearn)* **to h. after sth** ansiar algo, anhelar algo

▸**hone in on** *vt insep US (on target)* dirigirse a; *(on mistake, evidence)* señalar, concentrarse en

honest ['ɒnɪst] **1** *adj* (**a**) *(trustworthy)* honrado(a); **he has an h. face** tiene aspecto de honrado; IDIOM **he's as h. as the day is long** es todo honradez, es la honradez en persona ▸▸ ***h. broker*** mediador(ora) *m,f* imparcial
(**b**) *(truthful)* sincero(a); **the h. truth** la pura verdad; **give me your h. opinion** dame tu sincera opinión; **I don't think he was being h. with me** creo que no me estaba diciendo la verdad; **to be h., I don't know** la verdad es que no lo sé; **let's be h., it's not working, is it?** seamos sinceros, la cosa no marcha, ¿verdad?
(**c**) *(legitimate)* **to earn an h. living** ganarse la vida honradamente; **to make an h. profit** obtener beneficios legítimos; **an h. day's work** una digna jornada laboral; IDIOM **to earn** *or* **turn an h. penny** ganarse la vida honradamente; IDIOM *Hum* **to make an h. woman of sb** *(marry)* llevar a alguien al altar
2 *adv Fam* **I didn't mean it, h.!** no fue mi intención, de verdad *or* en serio; **h. to goodness** *or* **God!** ¡palabra (de honor)! ¡te lo juro (por Dios *or* por mi honor)!

honestly ['ɒnɪstlɪ] *adv* (**a**) *(legitimately)* honradamente; **to obtain sth h.** conseguir algo honradamente
(**b**) *(sincerely)* sinceramente; **h.!** ¡palabra (de honor)!; **I can h. say that...** puedo decir sin faltar a la verdad que...; **h., I'm fine/it doesn't matter** en serio que estoy bien/no importa; **quite h., I don't see the problem** francamente, no veo qué problema hay, la verdad, no veo dónde está el problema; **I can't h. remember** la verdad es que no me acuerdo
(**c**) *(expressing indignation)* **well h.!** ¡desde luego!, ¡hay que ver!; **h.! some people!** ¡desde luego, hay cada uno por ahí!

honest-to-goodness ['ɒnɪstə'gʊdnɪs] *adj* genuino(a), auténtico(a)

honesty ['ɒnɪstɪ] *n* (**a**) *(trustworthiness)* honradez *f*, honestidad *f*; **a man of irreproachable h.** un hombre de una honradez *or* rectitud intachable (**b**) *(truthfulness)* sinceridad *f*; **in all h.** para ser francos; PROV **h. is the best policy** lo mejor es decir la verdad

honey ['hʌnɪ] *n* (**a**) *(food)* miel *f* ▸▸ ***h. bear*** *(Asian)* oso *m* malayo; *(South American)* oso *m* melero, tamandua *m*, kinkajú *m*; ***h. bee*** abeja *f*; ***h. buzzard*** halcón *m* abejero (**b**) *esp US Fam (term of endearment)* cariño *m*, cielo *m* (**c**) *Fam* **he's a h.** *(good-looking)* es un bombón, está como un tren; *(nice)* es un cielo, *Esp* es majísimo; **a h. of a motorbike/dress** una maravilla de moto/vestido

honeybun ['hʌnɪbʌn], **honeybunch** ['hʌnɪbʌntʃ] *n esp US Fam* cariño *m*, cielo *m*

honeycomb ['hʌnɪkəʊm] **1** *n* panal *m*
2 *vt* **the mountain is honeycombed with tunnels** el interior de la montaña es un entramado de túneles

honeydew ['hʌnɪdju:] *n* (**a**) ***h. melon*** melón *m* francés, = variedad muy dulce de melón (**b**) *(from aphids)* miel *f*

honeyed ['hʌnɪd] *adj (voice, words)* meloso(a)

honeymoon ['hʌnɪmu:n] **1** *n* (**a**) *(period, trip)* luna *f* de miel, viaje *m* de novios; **they're on (their) h.** están de luna de miel, están en viaje de luna de miel *or* en viaje de novios (**b**) *Fig (for new leader, boss)* **a h. period** una luna de miel, un periodo idílico; **the h. is over** se acabó el periodo de gracia
2 *vi* pasar la luna de miel, estar de viaje de novios

honeymooner ['hʌnɪmu:nə(r)] *n* recién casado(a) *m,f* (en viaje de novios); **honeymooners** parejas de recién casados (en viaje de novios)

honeysuckle ['hʌnɪsʌkəl] *n* madreselva *f*

honeytrap ['hʌnɪtræp] *n* trampa *f* de amor

Hong Kong ['hɒŋ'kɒŋ] *n* Hong Kong

honk[1] [hɒŋk] **1** *n* (**a**) *(of goose)* graznido *m* (**b**) *(of car horn)* bocinazo *m*
2 *vi* (**a**) *(goose)* graznar (**b**) *(car driver)* tocar la bocina *or* el claxon, dar bocinazos

honk[2] *vi Br Fam* (**a**) *(smell bad)* apestar, *Esp* cantar (**b**) *(vomit)* devolver, echar la papilla

honky, honkie ['hɒŋkɪ] *n US very Fam* = término ofensivo para referirse a un blanco

honky-tonk ['hɒŋkɪtɒŋk] *Fam* **1** *n* (**a**) *(music)* = variedad del ragtime tocada en piano vertical (**b**) *US (nightclub)* cafetucho *m*, cabaretucho *m*, *RP* cafetín *m*
2 *adj* = típico de o relacionado con la música "honky-tonk"

Honolulu [hɒnə'lu:lu:] *n* Honolulú

honor, honorable *etc US* = **honour, honourable** *etc*

honorarium [ɒnə'reərɪəm] (*pl* **honorariums** *or* **honoraria** [ɒnə'reərɪə]) *n* honorarios *mpl*

honorary ['ɒnərərɪ] *adj (title, member)* honorífico(a), honorario(a); **h. president** *or* **chairman** presidente de honor ▸▸ *Univ* ***h. degree*** título *m* honoris causa; ***h. secretary*** secretario(a) *m,f* honorario(a)

honorific [ɒnə'rɪfɪk] **1** *n* título *m* honorífico
2 *adj* honorífico(a)

honour, *US* **honor** ['ɒnə(r)] **1** *n* (**a**) *(self-respect, good name)* honor *m*, honra *f*; **the affair cost him his h.** el asunto le costó la honra; **peace with h.!** ¡paz y honor!; **on my (word of) h.!** ¡palabra de honor!; **to be on one's h. to do sth** estar moralmente obligado(a) a hacer algo; PROV **(there is) h. among thieves** hasta los ladrones tienen sus reglas ▸▸ *US* ***h. system*** sistema *m* de honor
(**b**) *(pleasure)* **this is a great h.** es un gran honor; **to have the h. of doing sth** tener el honor de hacer algo; *Hum* **to what do I owe this h.?** ¿a qué debo semejante honor *or* privilegio?; **may I have the h. of your company/the next dance?** ¿me concede el honor de acompañarla/de bailar conmigo?; *Hum* **to do the honours** *(serve food or drink)* hacer los honores; *(make introductions)* hacer las presentaciones
(**c**) *(credit)* honra *f*, orgullo *m*; **your children do you great h.** puedes estar muy orgulloso(a) de tus hijos; **she's an h. to her profession** es un orgullo para su profesión
(**d**) *(respect, mark of respect)* honor *m*; **in h. of** en honor de; **he was buried with full military honours** fue enterrado con todos los honores militares; **to do sb the h. of doing sth** hacerle *or* concederle a alguien el honor de hacer algo; **all h. to him!** ¡bendita sea su alma!; **he may be our enemy, but all h. to him for his generalship** puede que sea nuestro enemigo, pero sus dotes de mando son dignas de admiración ▸▸ *US* ***h. guard*** guardia *f* de honor
(**e**) **Your H.** *(judge)* Señoría
(**f**) *(award)* honor *m*, distinción *f*; **honours degree** licenciatura *f* ▸▸ *Br* ***honours list*** = relación de los ciudadanos condecorados por el monarca británico por los servicios aportados a la sociedad; *US* ***h. roll*** lista *f* de honor académica
(**g**) *(in golf)* **to have the h.** abrir el par, dar el primer golpe de salida
2 *vt* (**a**) *(person)* honrar; **I felt honoured that they had invited me** me honró mucho su invitación; *Formal* **I'm most honoured to be here tonight** me siento muy honrado(a) de estar aquí esta noche, es un honor para mí estar aquí esta noche; *Ironic* **the manager honoured us with his presence today** el director nos ha honrado hoy con su presencia
(**b**) *(fulfil) (commitment, obligation)* cumplir; *(contract, agreement)* cumplir
(**c**) *(debt, cheque)* pagar

honourable, *US* **honorable** ['ɒnərəbəl] *adj* (**a**) *(worthy of honour)* honorable; **he's an h. man** es un hombre honorable; **to do the h. thing** *(marry)* hacer lo que Dios manda y casarse; *(resign)* tomar la salida más honrosa y dimitir *or Am* renunciar; **he got an h. discharge** *(from army)* lo licenciaron *or* fue dado de baja con honores; *Hum* **are his intentions h.?** ¿viene con buenas intenciones?; **h. mention** mención honorífica
(**b**) *Br (aristocratic title)* = título honorífico aplicado a los hijos de condes, vizcondes y barones
(**c**) *Br Parl* **the H. member for Caithness** el señor diputado por Caithness

honourably, *US* **honorably** ['ɒnərəblɪ] *adv* honorablemente

honour-bound ['ɒnə'baʊnd] *adj* obligado(a) moralmente; **to be/feel h. to do sth** estar/sentirse obligado(a) moralmente a hacer algo, tener/sentir la obligación moral de hacer algo

Hons (*abbr* **honours degree**) licenciatura *f*

Hon Sec (*abbr* **honorary secretary**) secretario(a) *m,f* honorario(a)

hooch, hootch [huːtʃ] *n US Fam (liquor)* alcohol *m (destilado clandestinamente)*

hood [hʊd] **1** *n* (**a**) *(of coat, cloak)* capucha *f*; *(on academic gown)* capirote *m*; *(enclosing head) (with eyeholes)* pasamontaña *m*, pasamontañas *m inv*; *(without eyeholes)* capucha *f*; *(for falcons)* capirote *m*, capillo *m*
(**b**) *Br (of car, pram)* capota *f*
(**c**) *US (car bonnet)* capó *m*, *CAm, Méx* cofre *m*
(**d**) *(over cooker, fireplace)* campana *f* (extractora); *(on machine)* cubierta *f*; *(of hairdryer)* casco *m*
(**e**) *US Fam (gangster)* matón(ona) *m,f*
(**f**) *US Fam (neighbourhood)* **the h.** el barrio
2 *vt (prisoner)* encapuchar; *(falcon)* encapirotar, encapillar

hooded ['hʊdɪd] *adj (item of clothing)* con capucha; *(person)* encapuchado(a) ►► ***h. crow*** corneja *f* cenicienta

hoodlum ['huːdləm] *n Fam* matón(ona) *m,f*

hoodoo ['huːduː] *n US Fam* cenizo *m*, *Esp* gafe *m*

hoodwink ['hʊdwɪŋk] *vt Fam* engañar, timar; **I was hoodwinked into signing** me embaucaron para que firmara; **he hoodwinked me into coming** me engatusó para que viniera

hooey ['huːɪ] *n Fam* tonterías *fpl*, *Esp* majaderías *fpl*

hoof [huːf] **1** *n* (*pl* **hooves** [huːvz]) *(of horse)* casco *m*; *(of cattle, deer, sheep)* pezuña *f*, pata *f*; **on the h.** *(alive)* en pie; *Fig (on ad hoc basis)* sobre la marcha; **I had lunch on the h.** comí deprisa y corriendo
2 *vt Fam* **to h. it** ir a pata, ir en el coche de San Fernando

hoofbeat ['huːfbiːt] *n* **the (horse's) hoofbeats came closer** el repicar de los cascos se oía cada vez más cerca

hoofer ['huːfə(r)] *n Fam* bailarín(ina) *m, f*

hoofprint ['huːfprɪnt] *n* huella *f* de herradura

hoo-ha ['huːhɑː] *n Fam (fuss)* alboroto *m*, jaleo *m*; **there was a lot of h. about it at the time** se armó un gran revuelo entonces

hook [hʊk] **1** *n* (**a**) *(in general)* gancho *m*; *(for coats)* colgador *m*; *(for hanging pictures)* escarpia *f*, alcayata *f*; IDIOM *Fam* **to get one's hooks into sb** poner a alguien las garras encima; IDIOM *Fam* **to get sb off the h.** sacar a alguien del apuro; IDIOM *Fam* **that lets you off the h.** eso te libra, *Esp* eso te salva de la quema; IDIOM *Fam* **by h. or by crook** sea como sea
(**b**) *(for fishing)* anzuelo *m*; IDIOM *Fam* **he swallowed it h., line and sinker** *(believed it)* se tragó el anzuelo
(**c**) *(on dress)* corchete *m* ►► ***h. and eye*** corchete *m*
(**d**) *(of telephone)* **to leave the phone off the h.** dejar el teléfono descolgado; **to put the phone back on the h.** colgar el teléfono
(**e**) *(in boxing)* gancho *m*, crochet *m*; **left/right h.** gancho de izquierda/derecha
(**f**) *(in basketball)* gancho *m*
(**g**) *(in golf)* hook *m*
(**h**) *(of song)* gancho *m*
(**i**) *(for advertising campaign)* gancho *m* (publicitario)
2 *vt* (**a**) *(catch)* enganchar; **to h. a fish** enganchar un pez; **to h. one's legs around sth** enroscar las piernas en algo; **h. the rope around the tree** ata la cuerda alrededor del árbol (**b**) *Fam Hum* **she'll never manage to h. a man** nunca conseguirá enganchar *or* cazar *or* pescar a un hombre (**c**) *(in golf)* **to h. the ball** golpear la bola de hook (**d**) *(in rugby)* talonar
3 *vi* (**a**) *(fasten)* abrocharse (con corchetes *or RP* ganchitos), cerrarse con corchetes *or RP* ganchitos; **the dress hooks at the back/side** el vestido se abrocha (con corchetes *or RP* ganchitos) por la espalda/en el costado (**b**) *US (work as prostitute)* hacer la calle *or* la carrera (**c**) *US Fam* **to h. it** esfumarse, largarse, *Esp* pirárselas

►**hook on 1** *vt sep* enganchar, abrochar, encorchetar
2 *vi* engancharse, abrocharse

►**hook up 1** *vt sep* (**a**) *(trailer)* enganchar; *(horse, oxen)* enganchar, uncir; **they hooked up an extra coach to the train** engancharon un vagón adicional al tren (**b**) *(dress)* abrochar; **could you h. me up, please?** ¿me puedes abrochar, por favor? (**c**) *Fam (install) TV & Comptr* conectar
2 *vi* (**a**) *(dress)* abrocharse (**b**) *US Fam* **to h. up with sb** *(meet)* unirse a alguien, reunirse *or* juntarse con alguien, *RP* engancharse; *(be in relationship)* iniciar una relación con alguien, *RP* engancharse con alguien (**c**) *Rad, TV & Comptr* conectar (**with** con *or* a); **they h. up on the network to play Quake** se conectan con *or* a la red para jugar a Quake

hookah ['hʊkə] *n* narguile *m*

hooked [hʊkt] *adj* (**a**) *(hook-shaped)* en forma de gancho, curvado(a); **a h. nose** una nariz aguileña (**b**) *Fam* **to be/get h. on sth** estar enganchado(a)/engancharse a algo; **he got h. on hard drugs** se quedó enganchado a las drogas duras; **to get h. on chess** engancharse al ajedrez; **one bite and I was h.** me envicié con un solo bocado

hooker ['hʊkə(r)] *n* (**a**) *Br (in rugby)* talon(e)ador *m* (**b**) *US Fam (prostitute)* fulana *f*, puta *f*

hookey, hooky ['hʊkɪ] *n US Fam* **to play h.** *Esp* hacer novillos, *Col* capar clase, *Méx* irse de pinta, *RP* hacerse la rabona

hook-nosed ['hʊknəʊzd] *adj* de nariz aguileña

Hook of Holland ['hʊkəv'hɒlənd] *n* Hoek van Holland

hook-up ['hʊkʌp] *n* (**a**) *Rad & TV* conexión *f*; **a satellite h.** una conexión vía satélite; **a live h. with Hollywood** una conexión en directo con Hollywood (**b**) *US Fam (alliance)* alianza *f*

hookworm ['hʊkwɜːm] *n* anquilostoma *m* ►► ***h. disease*** anquilostomiasis *f inv*

hooky = **hookey**

hooligan ['huːlɪgən] *n* vándalo(a) *m,f*, *Esp* gamberro(a) *m,f*

hooliganism ['huːlɪgənɪzəm] *n* vandalismo *m*, *Esp* gamberrismo *m*

hoop [huːp] *n* (**a**) *(ring)* aro *m*; *(on sports strip)* raya *f* (horizontal) ►► ***h. earrings*** aretes *mpl*, aros *mpl* (**b**) *Fam* **hoops** *(basketball)* básquet *m*; **to shoot hoops** echar unos tiros (**c**) IDIOMS **to put sb through the hoops** *(test thoroughly)* poner a alguien a prueba; **I had to jump through hoops to get the job** *Esp* me las vi y me las deseé *or Am* me las vi negras para conseguir el trabajo

hoop-la ['huːplɑː] *n* (**a**) *Br (game)* = juego de feria en el que se intentan colar aros en los premios (**b**) *US (noise, bustle)* alboroto *m*; **there was a lot of h. about the new design** hubo mucho revuelo en torno al nuevo diseño (**c**) *US (nonsense)* bobadas *fpl*

hoopoe ['huːpuː] *n* abubilla *f*

hoorah [hʊ'rɑː] *exclam* ¡hurra!

hooray [hʊ'reɪ] **1** *exclam* ¡hurra!; **h. for Simon!** ¡un hurra por Simón!
2 *n* (**a**) *(shout)* hurra *m* (**b**) *Br* ***H. Henry*** niño *m* bien *or Esp* pijo

hoosegow ['huːsgaʊ] *n US Fam Esp* chirona *f*, *Andes, RP* cana *f*, *Méx* bote *m*; **in the h.** en *Esp* chirona *or Andes, RP* la cana *or Méx* el bote

Hoosier ['huːzɪə(r)] *n* persona de Indiana

hoot [huːt] **1** *n* (**a**) *(of owl)* ululato *m*
(**b**) *(of car horn)* bocinazo *m*, pitido *m*; *(of factory whistle)* sirena *f*; *(of train)* pitido *m*, silbido *m*
(**c**) *(shout)* grito *m*, chillido *m*, alarido *m*; *(jeer)* abucheo *m*, silba *f*, pitada *f*; **there were hoots from the audience when he finished the speech** el público lo silbó *or* lo abucheó al terminar el discurso; **hoots of laughter** risotadas; IDIOM *Fam* **I don't give** *or* **care a h.** *or* **two hoots** me importa un pepino *or* bledo
(**d**) *Fam (amusing person, situation)* **he's a h.!** ¡es divertidísimo!, *Esp* ¡es un cachondo!; **it was a h.!** ¡fue divertidísimo!, *Esp* ¡fue un cachondeo!
2 *vt* (**a**) *(car horn)* tocar, hacer sonar (**b**) *(jeer) (actor, speaker)* abuchear, silbar, pitar; *(play)* silbar, pitar; **they hooted him down** los abucheos le impidieron continuar
3 *vi* (**a**) *(owl)* ulular (**b**) *(car, driver)* dar bocinazos; *(train)* pitar, silbar (**c**) *(shout)* chillar, gritar; *(jeer)* silbar; **to h. with laughter** reírse a carcajadas

hootch = **hooch**

hootenanny ['huːtənænɪ] *n US* (**a**) *(gadget)* chisme *m*, *CAm, Carib, Col* vaina *f*, *RP* coso *m* (**b**) *(informal concert)* fiesta *f* folk

hooter ['huːtə(r)] *n Br* (**a**) *(of ship, factory)* sirena *f*; *(of car)* bocina *f*, claxon *m* (**b**) *Fam (nose)* napias *fpl*

hoover® ['hu:və(r)] *Br* **1** *n* (**a**) *(machine)* aspiradora *f*, aspirador *m* (**b**) *(clean)* **I'll give the room a h.** pasaré la aspiradora por la habitación

2 *vt (room, carpet)* aspirar, pasar la aspiradora por

▸ **hoover up** *vt sep Br (dirt, dust)* aspirar; *Fam* **he hoovered up the bar snacks** se ventiló los aperitivos en un santiamén

hooves *pl of* **hoof**

hop [hɒp] **1** *n* (**a**) *(jump)* salto *m*, brinco *m*; IDIOM *Fam* **to catch sb on the h.** agarrar *or Esp* coger desprevenido(a) a alguien; IDIOM *Fam* **to keep sb on the h.** mantener a alguien ocupado(a) (**b**) *Fam (on plane)* vuelo *m* corto (**c**) *Fam (dance)* baile *m*, bailongo *m*

2 *vt (pt & pp* **hopped**) *Fam* (**a**) **to h. it** *(clear off)* largarse, tomar las de Villadiego, *RP* tomárselas; **h. it!** ¡lárgate! (**b**) *US (bus, subway) (legally)* subir a, *Esp* coger, *Am* tomar; *(illegally)* subirse sin pagar a, colarse en

3 *vi* (**a**) *(jump)* saltar, brincar; *(on one leg)* saltar con *or Am* en un pie, saltar a la pata coja

(**b**) *Fam (move quickly, lightly)* **to h. out of bed** salir de la cama de un salto; **to h. into bed with sb** acostarse con alguien, meterse con alguien en la cama; **to h. on/off the bus** subirse al/bajarse del autobús (de un salto); **h. in!** *(into car)* ¡sube!

(**c**) *Fam (travel by plane)* **we hopped across to Paris for the weekend** hicimos una escapada (en avión) a París durante el fin de semana

▸ **hop off** *vi Fam* largarse

HOPE [həʊp] **1** *n* (**a**) *(desire, expectation)* esperanza *f*; **he's one of his country's young hopes** es una de las jóvenes promesas de su país; **in the h. of (doing) sth** con la esperanza de (hacer) algo; **in the h. that...** con la esperanza de que...; **there's h. for him yet** aún tiene posibilidades de salvarse; **the situation is beyond h.** la situación es desesperada; **hopes are fading of a settlement to the dispute** cada vez hay menos esperanzas de que se resuelva la situación; **to get one's hopes up** hacerse ilusiones; **to give up** *or* **lose h.** perder la esperanza *or* las esperanzas; *Hum* **we live in h.!, h. springs eternal!** la esperanza es lo último que se pierde; **to raise (sb's) hopes** dar esperanzas (a alguien)

(**b**) *(chance)* esperanza *f*; **there is little h. (of)** hay pocas esperanzas (de); **there is no h. (of)** no hay esperanza(s) (de); *Fam* **do you think they'll agree? – not a h.!** ¿tú crees que aceptarán? – ¡ni de casualidad!; **she hasn't got a h. of winning** no tiene posibilidad alguna de ganar; *Fam* **they haven't got a h. in hell of winning** no van a ganar ni de casualidad; **her best h. is if her opponent doesn't turn up** su mayor esperanza es que su adversario no se presente; **my only** *or* **last h. is to ask for a second opinion** mi única *or* última esperanza es pedir una segunda opinión; *Ironic* **what a h.!, some h.!** ¡no caerá esa breva!

(**c**) *Rel* esperanza *f*

(**d**) *US* ***h. chest*** ajuar *m*

2 *vt* **to h. to do sth** esperar hacer algo; **I h. to see you again** espero volverte a ver; **you're feeling better, I h.** te encuentras mejor, ¿no?, espero que ya te encuentres mejor; **I h. (that) your brother is better** espero que tu hermano esté mejor; **I h. (to God that) you are right** ojalá tengas razón; **I h. you don't mind me calling** espero que no te moleste que te llame; **let's h. we're not too late** esperemos que no sea demasiado tarde; **I'm hoping they won't notice** espero que no se den cuenta; **we h. and pray that...** ojalá que...

3 *vi* esperar; **don't h. for too much** no esperes demasiado; **a victory was always going to be too much to h. for** esperar la victoria hubiera sido demasiado optimista; **I'm hoping for promotion** espero conseguir un ascenso; **we're hoping for a nice day** esperamos que haga buen día; **to h. for the best** confiar en la suerte; **we must h. against h. that...** no debemos perder la esperanza de que...; *Fam* **wouldn't it be nice if she got the job? – here's hoping** estaría bien que consiguiera el trabajo – sí, ojalá; **I h. so** eso espero; **I h. not** espero que no; *Br* **he got sacked as a result – I should h. so too!** como resultado, lo echaron – ¡y con razón!

---

hopeful ['həʊpfʊl] **1** *n Fam* **a young h.** una joven promesa

2 *adj* (**a**) *(full of hope)* esperanzado(a), optimista; **we are h. that...** esperamos que...; **he says he'll come, but I'm not that h.** dice que vendrá, pero no creo que lo haga; **he didn't seem very h. that he would win** no parecía tener grandes *or* muchas esperanzas en su victoria

(**b**) *(inspiring hope) (situation, sign)* prometedor(ora), alentador(ora); **the signs are h. that he will recover** hay indicios que alimentan la esperanza de una recuperación

hopefully ['həʊpfʊlɪ] *adv* (**a**) *(in a hopeful manner)* esperanzadamente, confiadamente; **it is better to travel h. than to arrive** caminar con esperanza *or* optimismo es mejor que llegar

(**b**) *Fam (it is to be hoped)* **h. not** esperemos que no, *Am* ojalá que no; **will you get it finished today? – h.!** ¿lo tendrás listo hoy? – ¡eso espero!, *Am* ¡ojalá (que sí)!; **h. we will have found him by then** con un poco de suerte, para entonces ya le habremos encontrado

hopeless ['həʊplɪs] *adj* (**a**) *(without hope) (person)* desesperanzado(a), sin esperanza; *(situation)* desesperado(a); **it's h.!** ¡es inútil!; **it's h. trying to explain to him** es inútil intentar explicárselo; **a h. cause** una causa perdida; **a h. case** *(incompetent person)* un caso perdido; *(in court)* una causa perdida; *(patient)* un caso (de enfermedad) incurable; **to be in a h. condition** encontrarse *or* estar en una situación desesperada

(**b**) *(inveterate) (drunk, liar)* empedernido(a), contumaz

(**c**) *Fam (incompetent)* malísimo(a), negado(a); **to be h. at maths/cooking** ser nulo(a) *or* un(a) negado(a) para las matemáticas/la cocina; **he's h.!** ¡es un inútil!; **I'm h. at this** yo, para esto, soy un desastre

hopelessly ['həʊplɪslɪ] *adv* (**a**) *(inconsolably)* desesperanzadamente, sin esperanza (**b**) *(completely)* totalmente, completamente; **he was h. in love with her** estaba desesperadamente enamorado de ella; **by this time we were h. late/lost** para entonces nuestro retraso era irremediable/estábamos completamente perdidos

hopelessness ['həʊplɪsnɪs] *n* (**a**) *(despair)* desesperanza *f* (**b**) *(irremediable nature)* **the h. of the situation** lo desesperado de la situación, el carácter irremediable de la situación

hophead ['hɒphed] *n US Fam* yonqui *mf*, *Esp* drogata *mf*

hopper ['hɒpə(r)] *n (for storage, loading)* tolva *f*

hopping ['hɒpɪŋ] *adv Fam* **to be h. mad** estar hecho(a) una furia, *Méx* estar como agua para chocolate

hops [hɒps] *npl* lúpulo *m*

hopscotch ['hɒpskɒtʃ] *n* tejo *m*, rayuela *f*; **to play (at) h.** jugar al tejo

horde [hɔ:d] *n* (**a**) *(crowd)* multitud *f*, *Am* horda *f*; **hordes of tourists** legiones *or Am* hordas de turistas (**b**) *(nomadic)* horda *f*

horizon [hə'raɪzən] *n* (**a**) *(between sky and earth or sea)* horizonte *m*; **there is a general election on the h.** hay elecciones generales a la vista (**b**) **horizons** *(perspectives)* horizontes *mpl*; **to broaden one's horizons** ampliar (uno sus) horizontes

horizontal [hɒrɪ'zɒntəl] **1** *n* horizontal *f*

2 *adj* (**a**) *(position)* horizontal; *Fam* **I was h. for a few days with the flu** pasé varios días en la cama con gripe ▸▸ *Sport* ***h. bar*** barra *f* fija; *Comptr* ***h. justification*** justificación *f* horizontal; *Comptr* ***h. orientation*** orientación *f* horizontal (**b**) *Com (communication, integration)* horizontal, al mismo nivel; **he asked for a h. move** solicitó un cambio de puesto de trabajo dentro de su misma categoría

horizontally [hɒrɪ'zɒntəlɪ] *adv* horizontalmente

hormonal [hɔ:'məʊnəl] *adj* hormonal

hormone ['hɔ:məʊn] *n* hormona *f* ▸▸ *Med* ***h. replacement therapy*** terapia *f* hormonal sustitutiva

horn [hɔ:n] *n* (**a**) *(of mammal, snail)* cuerno *m*; **the h. of plenty** el cuerno de la abundancia; IDIOM **to be on the horns of a dilemma** estar entre la espada y la pared; IDIOM **to draw** *or* **pull in one's horns** *(back off)* echarse para atrás, bajar el tono, *Am* bajarse del caballo; *(spend less)* apretarse el cinturón

(**b**) *(material)* cuerno *m*, *Am* asta *m*

(**c**) *(musical instrument)* trompa *f* ▸▸ ***h. player*** trompa *mf*; ***h. section*** sección *f* de trompetas

(**d**) *(on car)* bocina *f*, claxon *m*; **to sound one's h.** *(in car)* tocar la bocina *or* el claxon

(**e**) *Geog* ***the H. of Africa*** el Cuerno de África

(**f**) *Br very Fam (erection)* **to have the h.** tenerla dura *or* empinada *or Am* parada; **to give sb the h.** *(arouse) Esp, Méx* poner a alguien cachondo(a) *or RP* caliente, *Am* calentar a alguien

(**g**) *US Fam (telephone)* teléfono *m*; **to get on the h. to sb** dar un telefonazo a alguien

▸ **horn in** *vi Fam (on conversation)* entrometerse, meterse (donde no lo llaman); *(on a deal)* meter (mi, tu *etc.*) cuchara, meter la mano *or* las manos, sacar tajada

hornbeam ['hɔ:nbi:m] *n* carpe *m*

hornbill ['hɔ:nbɪl] *n* cálao *m*

horned [hɔ:nd] *adj* con cuernos ▸▸ ***h. toad*** lagarto *m* cornudo, frinosoma *m*

hornet ['hɔ:nɪt] *n* avispón *m*; *Fig* **to stir up a h.'s nest** remover un avispero

hornpipe ['hɔ:npaɪp] *n (dance, music)* aire *m* marinero

horn-rimmed ['hɔ:nrɪmd] *adj* **h. spectacles** *or* **glasses** gafas de (montura de) concha *or RP* carey

hornswoggle ['hɔ:nswɒgəl] *vt Fam* embaucar, camelar

horny ['hɔːnɪ] *adj* (**a**) *(hands)* calloso(a), encallecido(a) (**b**) *very Fam (sexually aroused) Esp, Méx* cachondo(a), *Esp* calentorro(a), *CAm, Col, Méx, Ven* arrecho(a), *RP* caliente (**c**) *Br very Fam (sexually attractive) Esp* buenorro(a), *Carib, Col, Méx* buenón(ona), *RP* fuerte

horoscope ['hɒrəskəʊp] *n* horóscopo *m*

horrendous [hɒ'rendəs] *adj* (**a**) *(horrifying)* horrendo(a), espantoso(a) (**b**) *Fam (very bad)* espantoso(a), horrible, tremendo(a)

horrendously [hɒ'rendəslɪ] *adv Fam (expensive, complicated)* terriblemente

horrible ['hɒrɪbəl] *adj* (**a**) *(horrific)* horroroso(a), espantoso(a), terrorífico(a); **a h. tragedy/scream** una espantosa tragedia/un grito terrorífico

(**b**) *(unpleasant)* horrible; **to say h. things about sb** hablar muy mal de alguien; **I have a h. feeling she's right** me da la desagradable sensación de que tiene razón; **the room was in a h. mess** la habitación era un tremendo caos; **how h.!** ¡qué horror!

(**c**) *(unkind)* antipático(a); **to be h. to sb** ser muy antipático(a) con alguien

horribly ['hɒrɪblɪ] *adv* (**a**) *(nastily)* horriblemente, de una manera horrible *or* espantosa; **she was h. murdered** fue asesinada de una forma horrible (**b**) *(as intensifier)* espantosamente, horriblemente; **it all went h. wrong** todo salió rematadamente mal

horrid ['hɒrɪd] *adj* (**a**) *(unpleasant)* horrendo(a), repelente (**b**) *(unkind)* antipático(a); **to be h. to sb** ser muy antipático(a) con alguien; **to say h. things about sb** decir cosas muy desagradables de alguien

horrific [hɒ'rɪfɪk] *adj* horrible, espantoso(a)

horrifically [hɒ'rɪfɪklɪ] *adv* (**a**) *(gruesomely)* de un modo horrible, espantosamente (**b**) *(as intensifier)* **h. expensive** tremendamente *or* terriblemente caro(a), carísimo(a)

horrified ['hɒrɪfaɪd] *adj* horrorizado(a); **a h. expression** una expresión de horror

horrify ['hɒrɪfaɪ] *vt* horrorizar

horrifying ['hɒrɪfaɪɪŋ] *adj* horroroso(a), *Am* aterrorizante

horror ['hɒrə(r)] *n* (**a**) *(feeling)* horror *m*; **to my h. I saw that...** me horroricé al ver que...; **to have a h. of sth** tener pánico *or* horror a algo; **to have the horrors** sentir pavor *or* espanto; *Fam* **to give sb the horrors** dar pavor *or* espantar a alguien, poner la carne de gallina *or* los pelos de punta a alguien ►► ***h. film*** película *f* de terror *or* miedo; ***h. movie*** película *f* de terror *or* miedo; ***h. story*** cuento *m* de terror; *Fam Fig* **they had some real h. stories about their holiday** habían vivido auténticas pesadillas durante las vacaciones

(**b**) *(person, thing)* horror *m*, espanto *m*; **I began to see the h. of it all** comencé a ver lo espantoso *or* terrible de todo el asunto; **the horrors of war** los horrores de la guerra; *Fam* **that child's a little h.** ese niño es un monstruito; *Fam Hum* **h. of horrors,...** ¡(qué) horror!; *Br Fam* **oh, horrors!** ¡válgame Dios, qué horror!

horror-stricken ['hɒrəstrɪkən], **horror-struck** ['hɒrəstrʌk] *adj* horrorizado(a)

hors d'oeuvre [ɔː'dɜːv] (*pl* **hors d'oeuvres** [ɔː'dɜːvr]) *n* entremeses *mpl*

horse [hɔːs] *n* (**a**) *(animal)* caballo *m*; *Fam* **the horses** *(horse racing)* los caballos, las carreras de caballos; **I like h. riding** me gusta montar *or RP* andar a caballo ►► ***h. apple*** *(dung)* boñigo *m*; ***h. blanket*** manta *f* para caballería; ***h. brass*** jaez *m* de latón; ***h. chestnut*** *(tree)* castaño *m* de Indias; *(fruit)* castaña *f* de Indias; *US Fam Hum* ***h. opera*** película *f* del Oeste; ***h. race*** carrera *f* hípica *or* de caballos; ***h. racing*** carreras *fpl* de caballos; ***h. riding*** equitación *f*, *Esp* monta *f* de caballos; ***h. show*** concurso *m* hípico, *Esp* exhibición *f* de monta de caballos; ***h. trials*** concurso *m* hípico

(**b**) *(gym apparatus)* caballo *m*

(**c**) *Mil & Hist (cavalry)* caballería *f*, soldado *m* de caballería; **a regiment of h.** un regimiento de caballería ►► ***h. artillery*** artillería *f* montada *or* a caballo

(**d**) IDIOMS **to eat like a h.** comer muchísimo *or Esp* como una lima; **(I'm so hungry) I could eat a h.** tengo un hambre que no veo, tengo un hambre canina; **that's a h. of a different colour** eso es harina de otro costal; **to change horses in midstream** cambiar de idea (*or* de táctica/bando etc) a mitad de camino; **to get (up) on one's high h.** darse ínfulas; **to hear sth (straight) from the h.'s mouth** oír algo de boca del propio interesado ►► ***h. laugh*** risotada *f*; *Fam* ***h. sense*** sentido *m* común

►**horse about, horse around** *vi* hacer el indio

horseback ['hɔːsbæk] *n* **on h.** a caballo ►► *US* ***h. riding*** equitación *f*; *US* **to go h. riding** montar *or RP* andar a caballo

horsebox ['hɔːsbɒks] *n Br* remolque *m* para caballos

horsecar ['hɔːskɑː(r)] *n US (trailer)* remolque *m* para caballos

horse-drawn ['hɔːsdrɔːn] *adj* de tiro, de caballos

horseflesh ['hɔːsfleʃ] *n* (**a**) *(horse meat)* carne *f* de caballo (**b**) *(horses collectively)* caballos *mpl*; **he's a good judge of h.** es un entendido en caballos

horsefly ['hɔːsflaɪ] *n* tábano *m*

horsehair ['hɔːsheə(r)] *n* crin *f*, crines *fpl* ►► ***h. mattress*** colchón *m* de crin

horseman ['hɔːsmən] *n* jinete *m*

horsemanship ['hɔːsmənʃɪp] *n* equitación *f*, manejo *m* del caballo

horsemeat ['hɔːsmiːt] *n* carne *f* de caballo

horseplay ['hɔːspleɪ] *n* retozo *m*, jugueteo *m*

horsepower ['hɔːspaʊə(r)] *n Tech* caballos *mpl* (de vapor); **a 10-h. motor** un motor de diez caballos

horseradish ['hɔːsrædɪʃ] *n* rábano *m* silvestre ►► ***h. sauce*** salsa *f* de rábano picante

horseshit ['hɔːsʃɪt] *n US Vulg (nonsense) Esp* gilipolleces *fpl*, *Am* pendejadas *fpl*

horseshoe ['hɔːsʃuː] *n* herradura *f* ►► ***h. arch*** arco *m* de herradura; ***h. crab*** cacerola *f or* cangrejo *m* de las Molucas, límulo *m*

horsetail ['hɔːsteɪl] *n* (**a**) *(tail of horse)* cola *f* de caballo (**b**) *(plant)* cola *f* de caballo, equiseto *m*

horse-trading ['hɔːstreɪdɪŋ] *n Fam* negociaciones *fpl* entre bastidores, tira y afloja *m*, *Esp* chalaneo *m*

horsewhip ['hɔːswɪp] **1** *n* fusta *f*

2 *vt* (*pt & pp* **horsewhipped**) azotar

horsewoman ['hɔːswʊmən] *n* amazona *f*

horsey, horsy ['hɔːsɪ] *adj* (**a**) *(horse-like)* caballuno(a) (**b**) *(keen on horses)* aficionado(a) a los caballos (**c**) *Br Fam (upper class) Esp* pijo(a), *Am* de la hípica; **he mixes with a very h. crowd** *Esp* alterna con gente pija aficionada a los caballos, *Am* alterna con gente de la hípica

horticultural [hɔːtɪ'kʌltʃərəl] *adj* hortícola ►► ***h. show*** exposición *f* hortícola

horticulturalist [hɔːtɪ'kʌltʃərəlɪst] *n* horticultor(ora) *m,f*

horticulture ['hɔːtɪkʌltʃə(r)] *n* horticultura *f*

hosanna [həʊ'zænə] **1** *n* hosanna *m*

2 *exclam* ¡hosanna!

hose [həʊz] **1** *n* (**a**) *(pipe)* manguera *f* (**b**) *Old-fashioned (stockings)* calcetas *fpl*, medias *fpl* (**c**) *Hist* **doublet and h.** calzas y jubón

2 *vt* regar con manguera

►**hose down** *vt sep* limpiar con manguera

hosepipe ['həʊzpaɪp] *n* manguera *f* ►► ***h. ban*** restricciones *fpl* de agua *(para usos no básicos)*

hosiery ['həʊzɪərɪ] *n* calcetines *mpl* y medias; **the (men's/women's) h. department** la sección de medias *or* calcetines (de señoras/caballeros) *(en una gran tienda)*

hospice ['hɒspɪs] *n (for the terminally ill)* hospital *m* para enfermos terminales

hospitable [hɒs'pɪtəbəl] *adj* hospitalario(a) (**to** con)

hospitably [hɒs'pɪtəblɪ] *adv* hospitalariamente

hospital ['hɒspɪtəl] *n* hospital *m*; **to go into h.** *or US* **the h.** ingresar en el hospital, ser hospitalizado(a); **h. ship/train** barco *or* buque/tren hospital ►► ***h. bed*** cama *f* de hospital; ***h. care*** atención *f* hospitalaria; ***h. treatment*** tratamiento *m* hospitalario

hospitality [hɒspɪ'tælɪtɪ] *n* hospitalidad *f* ►► ***h. room*** sala *f* de recepción; ***h. suite*** sala *f* de recepción

hospitalization [hɒspɪtəlaɪ'zeɪʃən] *n* hospitalización *f*

hospitalize ['hɒspɪtəlaɪz] *vt* (**a**) *(admit to hospital)* hospitalizar (**b**) *(injure severely)* **a couple of thugs hospitalized him** acabó *Esp* ingresado *or Am* internado por la paliza que le dieron un par de matones

host[1] [həʊst] **1** *n* (**a**) *(at home, party)* anfitrión *m*; **h. country** país anfitrión *or* organizador; **the h. city for the Olympic Games** la sede de los Juegos Olímpicos (**b**) *(on TV)* presentador(ora) *m,f* (**c**) *Biol (of parasite)* huésped *m* ►► ***h. cell*** célula *f* huésped (**d**) *Comptr* **h. (computer)** host *m*, sistema *m* central ►► ***h. system*** sistema *m* host

2 *vt* (**a**) *(party)* dar; **the city will h. the next Olympics** la ciudad albergará las próximas olimpiadas (**b**) *(TV show)* presentar (**c**) *Comptr (website)* hospedar

host[2] *n* (**a**) *(great number)* **a whole h. of** un sinfín de, (una) infinidad de (**b**) *Rel* **the Lord of Hosts** el Señor *or* Dios de los ejércitos

host[3] *n Rel (consecrated bread)* hostia *f*

hostage ['hɒstɪdʒ] *n* rehén *m*; **to take/hold sb h.** tomar/tener a alguien como rehén; IDIOM **that's offering a h. to fortune** eso supone hipotecar el futuro

hostel ['hɒstəl] *n* (a) **(youth) h.** albergue *m* juvenil (b) *esp Br (for students, nurses)* residencia *f*; *(for the homeless)* albergue *m*, hogar *m*

hostelling, *US* **hosteling** ['hɒstəlɪŋ] *n* **to go (youth) h.** ir de albergues

hosteller, *US* **hosteler** ['hɒstələ(r)] *n* **(youth) h.** alberguista *mf*

hostelry ['hɒstəlrɪ] *n Old-fashioned or Hum (pub)* bar *m*

hostess ['həʊstɪs] *n* (a) *(in private house)* anfitriona *f*
(b) *(on TV)* presentadora *f*
(c) *(at exhibition, conference)* azafata *f*, *Méx* edecán *f*, *RP* recepcionista *f* (de exposiciones y congresos *or* de ferias y congresos)
(d) *(in nightclub)* chica *f* de alterne, *RP* copera *f*; **a h. agency** una agencia de acompañantes *or* de señoritas de compañía
(e) **(air) h.** azafata *f* ►► ***h. trolley*** carro *m* caliente, = carrito con compartimentos para mantener la comida caliente

hostile ['hɒstaɪl, *US* 'hɒstəl] *adj* (a) *(aggressive)* hostil (**to** *or* **towards** a *or* con); **why are you always so h. to me?** ¿por qué eres tan arisco conmigo? (b) *(opposed)* hostil (**to** *or* **towards** a *or con)*; **to be h. to** ser hostil a, mostrarse hostil ante; **people who are h. to change** gente contraria *or* opuesta al cambio (c) *Mil* **h. forces** fuerzas hostiles (d) *Com* **h. takeover bid** OPA *f* hostil

hostility [hɒs'tɪlɪtɪ] *n* (a) *(aggression, opposition)* hostilidad *f* (**to** hacia) (b) *Formal* **hostilities** *(war)* hostilidades *fpl*

hosting ['həʊstɪŋ] *n Comptr* hospedaje *m*

HOT [hɒt] *adj* (a) *(in temperature) (food, plate, stove, water)* caliente; *(day, summer, climate)* caluroso(a); **we sat in the h. sun** nos sentamos al calor del sol; **I'd like a h. bath** me apetece un baño caliente; **to be h.** *(of person)* tener calor; *(of thing)* estar caliente; **this jacket's too h.** esta chaqueta abriga demasiado; **it's h.** *(of weather)* hace calor; **this is h. work** aquí se suda la gota gorda ►► ***h. chocolate*** batido *m* de cacao (caliente); ***h. cross bun*** = bollo con pasas y una cruz dibujada encima que se suele comer el día de Viernes Santo; ***h. dog*** perrito *m* caliente, *Col, Méx* perro *m* caliente, *RP* pancho *m*; *US Med* ***h. flashes*** sofocos *mpl*; *Med* ***h. flushes*** sofocos *mpl*; ***h. spring*** manantial *m* de aguas termales; *US* ***h. tub*** jacuzzi® *m*
(b) *(spicy)* picante ►► ***h. pepper*** guindilla *f*, *Méx* chile *m*, *Andes, RP* ají *m*
(c) *(close)* **you're getting h.** *(in guessing game)* caliente, caliente; **to be h. on sb's/sth's trail** estar pisando los talones a alguien/algo
(d) *Fam (good)* cosa fina; **that's one h. bike** esa moto es cosa fina; **to be h. on sth** *(be knowledgeable about)* estar muy puesto(a) en algo, *RP* estar muy por dentro de algo; *(attach importance to)* ser muy quisquilloso(a) con algo; **it wasn't such a h. idea** no fue una idea tan buena; **how are you? – not so h.** ¿qué tal? – regular; *very Fam* **h. shit** de puta madre, *Andes, CAm, Carib, Méx* chévere, *Méx* padrísimo(a), *RP* de la puta; *very Fam* **she's pretty h. shit when it comes to statistics** es un genio de las estadísticas, es una *Méx* chingona *or RP* bestia para las estadísticas, *Esp* se le dan genial *or* de puta madre las estadísticas; *Fam* **to be h. stuff** *(excellent) Esp* ser cosa fina, ser *CAm, Carib, Col, Méx* chévere *or Méx* padrísimo(a) *or RP* bárbaro(a); *(person)* estar buenísimo(a), estar como un tren ►► *Fam* ***h. date*** cita *f* íntima; ***a h. favourite*** *(in race)* un(a) gran favorito(a); ***h. gossip*** chismorreo *m or Esp* cotilleo *m or RP* chusmerío *m* jugoso; ***h. news*** noticias *fpl* frescas
(e) *Fam (in demand, popular)* popular; **this hairstyle is really h. just now** este peinado está *or* se ha puesto muy de moda; **he's really h. property** se lo rifa todo el mundo
(f) *Fam (sexually attractive)* sexy; *(sexually aroused) Esp, Méx* cachondo(a), *CAm, Col, Méx, Ven* arrecho(a), *RP* alzado(a); **to be h. to trot** estar *Esp, Méx* cachondo(a) *or CAm, Col, Méx, Ven* arrecho(a) *or RP* alzado(a)
(g) *Fam (dangerous)* **things were getting too h. for us** las cosas se estaban poniendo feas; **too h. to handle** *(issue)* demasiado comprometido(a) *or* comprometedor(ora) ►► *Fam* ***h. potato*** *(controversial issue)* asunto *m* espinoso, *Esp* patata *f* caliente; *US Fam* ***the h. seat*** *(electric chair)* la silla eléctrica; *Fig* **to be in the h. seat** ser el responsable; ***h. spot*** *(trouble spot)* zona *f* conflictiva
(h) *Fam (stolen)* afanado(a), *Esp* chorizado(a), *RP* choreado(a)
(i) *Fam* ***h. air*** *(meaningless talk)* palabras *fpl* vanas, música *f* celestial, *Esp* rollo *m* patatero; *Fam* **it's all h. air** no son más que fanfarronadas
(j) *Fam* ***h. jazz*** hot jazz *m*
(k) ***h. pants*** minishorts *mpl*
(l) ***h. rod*** *(car)* coche *m* trucado
(m) ***h. spot sprint*** *(in cycling)* sprint *m* especial, meta *f* volante
(n) *Com* ***h. desking*** sistema *m* de mesa compartida, = sistema de trabajo en el que los trabajadores carecen de un escritorio propio y ocupan el que se encuentre libre
(o) *Comptr* ***h. key*** tecla *f* personalizada; ***h. swap*** *(of devices)* reemplazo *m* en caliente
(p) *Tel* ***h. line*** línea *f* directa, teléfono *m* rojo; ***h. line support*** asistencia *f* por línea directa
(q) IDIOMS **h. from** *or* **off the press** *(of news)* caliente; *(of book)* recién salido(a) (de la imprenta); **they're selling like h. cakes** se venden como pan caliente *or Esp* churros *or Esp* rosquillas; **to have a h. temper** tener mal genio; **to get h. under the collar** *(become indignant)* acalorarse; **h. and bothered** agobiado(a); *Fam* **to be in h. water** *(in difficult situation)* estar en un lío *or* en apuros; *Fam* **to get into h. water** meterse en un lío *or* en apuros

► **hot up** *(pt & pp* **hotted**) *vi Fam (situation, contest) Esp* calentarse, *Am* ponerse bravo(a)

hot-air balloon ['hɒteəbə'lu:n] *n* globo *m* de aerostático, aerostato *m*

hotbed ['hɒtbed] *n* **a h. of rebellion/intrigue** un foco de rebelión/intrigas

hot-blooded ['hɒt'blʌdɪd] *adj* (a) *(passionate)* ardiente (b) *(excitable)* irascible

hotcake ['hɒtkeɪk] *n US* crepe *f*, panqueque *m*, *Esp* tortita *f*

hotchpotch ['hɒtʃpɒtʃ], **hodgepodge** ['hɒdʒpɒdʒ] *n Fam* revoltijo *m*, *Esp* batiburrillo *m*

hot-dog ['hɒtdɒg] *vi (pt & pp* **hotdogged**) (a) *US Fam (show off)* alardear, fanfarronear (b) *(in skiing)* hacer acrobacias

hotel [həʊ'tel] *n* hotel *m*; **the h. industry** el sector hotelero, la industria hotelera ►► ***h. manager*** director(ora) *m,f* de hotel; ***h. reception*** recepción *f* (de hotel); ***h. room*** habitación *f* (de hotel)

hotelier [həʊ'teljeɪ] *n* hotelero(a) *m,f*

hotfoot ['hɒt'fʊt] *Fam* **1** *adv* a la carrera, zumbando, *Esp* escopetado(a)
2 *vt* **to h. it** ir a la carrera, ir zumbando, *Esp* ir escopetado(a)

hothead ['hɒthed] *n* impulsivo(a) *m,f*, impetuoso(a) *m,f*

hot-headed ['hɒt'hedɪd] *adj* impulsivo(a), impetuoso(a)

hothouse ['hɒthaʊs] *n* (a) *(glasshouse)* invernadero *m* (b) *(place with intense atmosphere)* hervidero *m*

hotly ['hɒtlɪ] *adv (to reply, protest)* acaloradamente; *(to deny)* enérgicamente; **h. contested** ferozmente disputado(a)

hotplate ['hɒtpleɪt] *n* (a) *(on cooker)* placa *f* (b) *(for keeping food warm)* = placa para mantener la comida caliente

hotpot ['hɒtpɒt] *n (stew)* estofado *m*, *Am* ahogado *m*

hots [hɒts] *npl very Fam* **she had the h. for Fred** Fred la ponía a cien *or* muy caliente, *RP* estaba recaliente con Fred

hotshot ['hɒtʃɒt] *n Fam* **1** *n (expert)* as *m*, *Esp* hacha *m*
2 *adj* **a h. lawyer** un abogado estrella

hotsy-totsy ['hɒtsɪ'tɒtsɪ] *adj US Fam* estupendo(a), de primera, *Esp* dabuten

hot-tempered ['hɒt'tempəd] *adj esp Esp* enfadadizo(a) *or esp Am* enojadizo(a), con mal genio

Hottentot ['hɒtəntɒt] **1** *n* (a) *(person)* hotentote *mf* (b) *(language)* lengua *f* hotentote
2 *adj* hotentote

hottie, hotty ['hɒtɪ] *n US Fam* **to be a h.** estar muy bueno(a)

hot-water [hɒt'wɔ:tə(r)] *adj* de agua caliente ►► ***h. bottle*** bolsa *f* de agua caliente

hot-wire ['hɒtwaɪə(r)] *vt Fam* hacer un puente a

hound [haʊnd] **1** *n* (a) *(hunting dog)* perro *m* de caza (b) *Fam (dog)* chucho *m*, *RP* pichicho *m*
2 *vt (persecute)* acosar; **she was hounded by the press** la prensa la acosaba; **he was hounded out of town** lo echaron de la ciudad

hound's-tooth ['haʊndztu:θ] *n (fabric)* pata *f* de gallo

hour ['aʊə(r)] *n* (a) *(period of time)* hora *f*; **an h. and a half** una hora y media; **half an h., a half h.** media hora; **it's an h. long** dura una hora; **at 60 km an** *or* **per h.** a 60 kilómetros por hora; **he gets £10 an h.** le pagan *or* gana diez libras por hora; **it's a two-h. walk from here** está a dos horas a pie; **we're three hours ahead of Fresno** estamos a tres horas de Fresno; **to pay sb by the h.** pagar a alguien por horas; **to take hours over sth** tardar *or Am* demorar horas en algo; **we've been waiting for hours** llevamos horas esperando; **to work long hours** trabajar muchas horas; **what are your hours?, what hours do you work?** ¿cuál es tu horario de trabajo?, ¿qué horario de trabajo tienes?; **the situation is deteriorating by the h.** la situación se deteriora

(a) cada hora que pasa ►► ***h. hand*** *(of watch, clock)* manecilla *f* de las horas

(**b**) *(time of day)* **at this h.!** ¡a estas horas!; **after hours** fuera de horas, a deshora; **every h. (on the h.)** cada hora (en punto); **till all hours** hasta las tantas; **people come and go at all hours** hay gente yendo y viniendo a toda(s) hora(s); **to keep late hours** acostarse muy tarde, *Andes* trasnocharse

(**c**) *(decisive moment)* **where were you in my h. of need?** ¿dónde estabas cuando te necesitaba *or* te precisé?; **his h. has come** ha llegado su hora; **the man of the h.** el hombre *or* la figura del momento

hourglass ['aʊəglɑːs] *n* reloj *m* de arena; **an h. figure** una cintura de avispa

hourly ['aʊəlɪ] **1** *adj* (**a**) *(each hour)* **at h. intervals** con intervalos de una hora; **hourly departures** salidas cada hora (**b**) *(per hour) (earnings, rate)* por hora

2 *adv* (**a**) *(every hour)* cada hora (**b**) *(at any time)* en cualquier momento; **we expect them hourly** los esperamos en cualquier instante *or* de un momento a otro

house 1 *n* [haʊs] (**a**) *(dwelling)* casa *f*; **to move h.** mudarse de casa; **to set up h. (together)** irse a vivir juntos; **to keep h. (for sb)** encargarse de (las cosas de) la casa (de alguien), llevarle (a alguien) (las cosas de) la casa; **h. for sale** *(sign)* se vende; *also Fig* **a h. of cards** un castillo de naipes; **h. of ill fame** *or* **repute** casa de lenocinio, prostíbulo; **the h. of God** la casa del Señor; IDIOM **to set** *or* **put one's h. in order** poner sus cosas *or* asuntos en orden, *Am* poner la casa en orden; IDIOM **to get on like a h. on fire** llevarse estupendamente; IDIOM *Br Fam* **all round the houses: the bus goes all round the houses** el autobús va dando un rodeo, ese *Arg* micro *or Urug* ómnibus es un carro lechero; *Fam* **to go all round the houses** *(not get to the point)* dar un rodeo, divagar, irse por las ramas *or Esp* por los cerros de Úbeda ►► *US Fam Hum* ***h. ape*** mono(a) *m,f or* mico(a) *m,f* de la casa; *Law* ***h. arrest*** arresto *m* domiciliario; ***h. call*** visita *f* a domicilio; ***h. guest*** huésped *mf*, invitado(a) *m,f*; ***h. husband*** amo *m* de casa; ***h. martin*** avión *m* (común); ***h. painter*** pintor(ora) *m,f* de brocha gorda; ***h. party*** fiesta *f (en una casa de campo)*; ***h. surgeon*** *(in hospital)* cirujano(a) *m,f* residente; ***h. sparrow*** gorrión *m*; *US* ***h. trailer*** caravana *f*, roulotte *f*, *RP* casa *f* rodante; ***h. wren*** chochín *m* casero

(**b**) *Com (company)* casa *f*, empresa *f*; **banking h.** banco; **publishing h.** (casa) editorial ►► *US* ***h. detective*** = guardia sin uniforme contratado por un hotel; ***h. journal*** boletín *m* interno (de una empresa); ***h. style*** política *f* (de estilo) de la casa

(**c**) *Pol* **the H. of Commons/Lords** la Cámara de los Comunes/Lores; **the Houses of Parliament** el Parlamento británico; **the H. of Representatives** la Cámara de Representantes

(**d**) *(household)* casa *f*, familia *f*; **the whole h. was down with flu** toda la familia tenía gripe; **don't wake up the whole h.!** ¡no despiertes a toda la casa!

(**e**) *(royal family)* casa *f*; **the H. of Stuart** la casa de los Estuardo, los Estuardo

(**f**) *(restaurant)* **on the h.** por cuenta de la casa ►► ***h. wine*** vino *m* de la casa

(**g**) *Theat* **an empty/a good h.** un público escaso/numeroso; **to bring the h. down** hacer que el teatro se venga abajo, meterse al público en el bolsillo; **h. full** *(sign)* no hay localidades *or* entradas, *Am* entradas agotadas; **the first/second h.** la primera/segunda función ►► ***h. lights*** luces *fpl* de sala

(**h**) *(music)* **h. (music)** (música *f*) house *m*

(**i**) *Br Sch* = división que se hace de los alumnos de cada curso para la realización de actividades no académicas

(**j**) *(in debate)* **this h. believes that...** somos de la opinión que...

2 *exclam (in bingo)* ¡bingo!

3 *vt* [haʊz] (**a**) *(person)* alojar; **many families are still badly housed** muchas familias permanecen alojadas en hogares inadecuados

(**b**) *(store) (collection, library)* alojar; **the library cannot h. any more books** la biblioteca ya no puede albergar más libros; **the archives are housed in the basement** el archivo se encuentra *or* está ubicado en el sótano

(**c**) *(mechanism)* alojar; **this section houses the main engines** en esta sección se encuentran las principales máquinas

houseboat ['haʊsbəʊt] *n* barco-vivienda *m*

housebound ['haʊsbaʊnd] *adj* **to be h.** estar confinado(a) en casa

houseboy ['haʊsbɔɪ] *n* mozo *m*, sirviente *m*, criado *m*

housebreaker ['haʊsbreɪkə(r)] *n* ladrón(ona) *m,f*

housebreaking ['haʊsbreɪkɪŋ] *n* robos *mpl* de casas, *RP* escruche *m*

housebroken ['haʊsbrəʊkən] *adj US (pet)* = que ya ha aprendido a no hacer sus necesidades en casa

houseclean ['hauskli:n] *vi US* hacer la limpieza de la casa, limpiar la casa

housecoat ['haʊskəʊt] *n* bata *f* de (estar en) casa

housefather ['haʊsfɑːðə(r)] *n* = hombre responsable del bienestar de los internos en un orfanato o en un reformatorio

housefly ['haʊsflaɪ] *n* mosca *f* (doméstica)

household ['haʊshəʊld] *n* hogar *m*, *Esp* unidad *f* familiar; **the head of the h.** *Esp* el/la cabeza de familia, *Am* el jefe/la jefa del hogar; **households with more than two children** *Esp* familias con más de dos hijos, *Am* hogares con más de dos niños; **to be a h. name** *(of famous person)* ser un nombre conocidísimo; *(of brand name)* ser una marca famosa *or* muy conocida ►► ***h. appliance*** electrodoméstico *m*; ***h. chores*** tareas *fpl* domésticas *or* del hogar

householder ['haʊshəʊldə(r)] *n* ocupante *mf* de vivienda

house-hunting ['haʊshʌntɪŋ] *n* búsqueda *f* de vivienda

housekeeper ['haʊskiːpə(r)] *n* (**a**) *(employee)* ama *f* de llaves *or Esp* de gobierno, *Am* encargado(a) *m,f*, *Am* casero(a) *m,f* (**b**) *(housewife)* **she's a good/bad h.** es una buena/mala ama de casa

housekeeping ['haʊskiːpɪŋ] *n* (**a**) *(work)* tareas *fpl* domésticas, economía *f* doméstica (**b**) **h. (money)** dinero *m* para los gastos domésticos (**c**) *Comptr* mantenimiento *m*

housemaid ['haʊsmeɪd] *n* doncella *f*, sirvienta *f*, criada *f* ►► ***h.'s knee*** *(inflammation)* bursitis *f inv* de rodilla

houseman ['haʊsmən] *n Br Med* médico(a) *m,f* interno(a) residente

housemaster ['haʊsmɑːstə(r)] *n Br Sch* = profesor a cargo de una "house" (división para actividades no académicas)

housemistress ['haʊsmɪstrɪs] *n Br Sch* = profesora a cargo de una "house" (división para actividades no académicas)

housemother ['haʊsmʌðə(r)] *n* = mujer responsable del bienestar de los internos en un orfanato o en un reformatorio

house-owner ['haʊsəʊnə(r)] *n* propietario(a) *m,f* (de una vivienda)

houseparent ['haʊspeərənt] *n* = persona responsable del bienestar de los internos en un orfanato o en un reformatorio

houseplant ['haʊsplɑːnt] *n* planta *f* de interior

house-proud ['haʊspraʊd] *adj* **she's very h.** es una mujer muy de su casa

houseroom ['haʊsruːm] *n* **I wouldn't give it h.** *(piece of furniture)* yo no lo pondría en mi casa; *(theory, suggestion)* yo no lo aceptaría

house-shopping ['haʊsʃɒpɪŋ] *n US* búsqueda *f* de vivienda

house-sit ['haʊssɪt] *vi* quedarse cuidando la casa (**for** de)

house-to-house ['haʊstə'haʊs] *adj (search, enquiries)* de casa en casa, casa por casa

housetop ['haʊstɒp] *n* IDIOM **to shout** *or* **proclaim sth from the housetops** proclamar algo a los cuatro vientos

house-train ['haʊstreɪn] *vt Br* (**a**) *(pet)* amaestrar, educar, enseñar; **has the dog been house-trained?** ¿el perro está educado? (**b**) *Hum (husband, children)* acostumbrar *or* enseñar (a hacer las cosas de la casa), domesticar

house-trained ['haʊstreɪnd] *adj Br* (**a**) *(dog)* = que ya ha aprendido a no hacer sus necesidades en casa (**b**) *Hum (husband, children)* bien enseñado(a), domesticado(a)

house-warming ['haʊswɔːmɪŋ] *n* **h. (party)** fiesta *f* de inauguración *(de apartamento, piso, casa)*

housewife ['haʊswaɪf] *n* ama *f* de casa

housework ['haʊswɜːk] *n* tareas *fpl* domésticas; **to do the h.** realizar *or* hacer las faenas del hogar *or* domésticas; **we share the h.** compartimos las labores domésticas

housing ['haʊzɪŋ] *n* (**a**) *(accommodation)* vivienda *f*; **the government has no long-term h. strategy** el gobierno no cuenta con una estrategia de creación de viviendas a largo plazo; **thousands still live in substandard h.** miles de personas residen aún en viviendas que no cumplen los niveles exigidos de habitabilidad; **there's a lot of new h. being built in the area** se están construyendo muchas viviendas nuevas en la zona ►► *Br* ***h. association*** cooperativa *f* de viviendas; *Br* ***h. benefit*** = subsidio para el pago del alquiler *or Méx* de la renta; ***h. cooperative*** cooperativa *f* de viviendas; *Br* ***h. estate*** *(public housing)* = urbanización con viviendas de protección oficial; *(private housing)* urbanización *f*, *Am* condominio *m*; ***h. market*** mercado *m* inmobiliario; *US* ***h. project*** = urbanización con viviendas de protección oficial; ***h. scheme*** plan *m* de vivienda; *US* ***h. starts*** índices *mpl* de construcción de nuevas viviendas

(**b**) *(of machinery)* cubierta *f* protectora

HOV [eɪtʃəʊ'viː] *n* (*abbr* **High Occupancy Vehicle**) *US* **H. lane** carril VAO, carril para vehículos de alta ocupación

hove *Naut pp of* **heave**

hovel ['hɒvəl] *n Pej Esp* chabola *f*, *Méx* jacal *m*, *CSur*, *Ven* rancho *m*

hover ['hɒvə(r)] *vi* (**a**) *(bird)* cernerse, cernirse; *(insects)* revolotear; *(helicopter)* permanecer inmóvil en el aire

(**b**) *(linger) (person)* rondar; *(smile)* asomarse, dibujarse; **it's no use hovering over the phone like that** de nada sirve que estés tan pendiente del teléfono; **a smile hovered round his lips** sus labios esbozaron una sonrisa; **a waitress was hovering near our table** una camarera andaba dando vueltas cerca de nuestra mesa; **she hovered between life and death** se debatía entre la vida y la muerte

(**c**) *(hesitate)* dudar, titubear; **I'm hovering between the two possible options** estoy indeciso *or* dudando entre las dos posibilidades; **he seemed to be hovering on the brink of saying something** parecía estar a punto de decir algo

hovercraft ['hɒvəkrɑːft] *n* aerodeslizador *m*, hovercraft *m*

hoverport ['hɒvəpɔːt] *n* puerto *m* de aerodeslizadores

HOW [haʊ] **1** *adv* (**a**) *(in what way, by what means)* cómo; **h. did they find out?** ¿cómo se enteraron?; **h. do you pronounce this word?** ¿cómo se pronuncia esta palabra?; **h. can you be so insensitive?** ¿cómo puedes ser tan insensible?; **tell me h. he did it** dime cómo lo hizo; *Fam* **I can behave h. I like** me porto como me da la gana; **it's incredible h. they stay so calm** es increíble lo tranquilos que están; **do you remember h. we used to hide behind the shed?** ¿te acuerdas de cuando nos escondíamos detrás del cobertizo?; *Fam* **h. come, h. so?** ¿cómo es eso?; *Fam* **h. come they told you and not me?** ¿por qué te lo dijeron a ti y a mí no?; *Fam* **h. do you mean?** *(I don't understand)* ¿cómo?; *Fam* **and h.!** ¡y cómo!

(**b**) *(to what extent)* **h. big is it?** ¿cómo es de grande?; **h. far is it to Houston?** ¿a cuánto está Houston de aquí?; **h. fast is the train?** ¿qué velocidad alcanza el tren?; **h. heavy is it?** ¿cuánto pesa?; **h. high is the mountain?** ¿qué altura tiene la montaña?; **h. interested are you in politics?** ¿hasta qué punto te interesa la política?; **h. long have you been here?** ¿cuánto tiempo llevas *or Méx, Ven* tienes aquí?; **h. many** cuántos(as); **h. many times?** ¿cuántas veces?; **h. much** cuánto; **h. much time is left?** ¿cuánto tiempo queda?; **h. much (is it)?** ¿cuánto es?, ¿cuánto cuesta?; **h. much longer will you be?** ¿cuánto te queda para terminar?; **h. often?** ¿con qué frecuencia?; **h. often do you go swimming?** ¿cada cuánto vas a la piscina?; **h. old are you?** ¿cuántos años tienes?; **h. soon will it be ready?** ¿(para) cuándo estará listo?; **h. tall are you?** ¿cuánto mides?; **I was surprised by h. easy it was** me sorprendió lo fácil que era; **you know h. useful he is to me** sabes lo útil que me resulta; **h. stupid can you get?** ¡qué tonto(a)!

(**c**) *(greetings, enquiries after health, quality, success)* **h. are you?** ¿cómo estás?, ¿qué tal estás?; **h. was the movie?** ¿qué tal fue la película?; **h. was it for you?** ¿y tú qué tal?; **h. did you like the meal?** ¿te gustó la comida?; **h. did the interview go?** ¿qué tal fue la entrevista?; *Fam* **h. are things?, how's everything?, how's it going?** ¿qué tal?; **h.'s business?** ¿qué tal el negocio?; *Formal* **h. do you do?** encantado(a) de conocerlo; *Fam* **h. goes it?** ¿qué tal?, ¿cómo te va?

(**d**) *(in exclamations)* qué; **h. brave she is!** ¡qué valiente es!; **h. disgusting!** ¡qué asco!; **h. silly of me!** ¡qué tonto!; **h. she has changed!** ¡cómo ha cambiado!; **h. nice to see you again!** ¡cuánto me alegro de verte otra vez!; **h. I miss them!** ¡cuánto los echo de menos!, *Am* ¡cuánto los extraño!; **well h. about that!** ¡caramba!, ¡fíjate!; **well h. do you like that, she left without even saying thank you!** ¿qué te parece?, se fue sin ni siquiera dar las gracias!

(**e**) *(in suggestions)* **h. about a game of cards?, h. would you like a game of cards?** ¿quieres jugar a las cartas?, ¿te *Esp* apetece *or Carib, Col, Méx* provoca jugar a las cartas?; **h. about going out for a meal?, h. would you like to go out for a meal?** ¿quieres salir a comer?, ¿te *Esp* apetece *or Carib, Col, Méx* provoca salir a comer?; **h. about it?** ¿qué te parece?; **h. about next week?** ¿qué te parece la semana que viene?; **h. about painting it blue?** ¿y si lo pintamos de azul?; **h. about you/Mike?** ¿y tú/Mike?

2 *n* **the h. and the why of sth** el cómo y el por qué de algo

3 *exclam Hum* ¡jau!

howdah ['haʊdə] *n* = silla para montar en elefante

howdy ['haʊdɪ] *exclam US Fam* ¡hola!, ¿qué hay?, *CAm, Col, Méx* ¡quihubo!

however [haʊ'evə(r)] **1** *adv* (**a**) *(to whatever degree)* **h. clever she is** por muy lista que sea; **h. hard she tried, she couldn't do it** por mucho que lo intentaba no podía hacerlo; **h. long it takes, finish it** tardes lo que tardes, termínalo; **all contributions will be welcome, h. small** se agradecerá cualquier contribución, por pequeña que sea

(**b**) *(in whatever way)* **h. you look at it,...** se mire como se mire,...; **h. did she find out?** pero, ¿cómo se pudo enterar?

2 *conj* sin embargo, no obstante

howitzer ['haʊɪtsə(r)] *n* obús *m*

howl [haʊl] **1** *n (of animal, person)* aullido *m*; **to let out a h. of pain** lanzar un fuerte grito *or* un alarido de dolor; **howls of derision** gritos de burla, abucheos

2 *vt* gritar; **they howled their defiance at the guards** desafiaron a los guardias a gritos

3 *vi* (**a**) *(animal, person)* aullar; **to h. with laughter** desternillarse de risa; **to h. with rage** montar en cólera, gritar de furia (**b**) *Fam (cry)* berrear

▸**howl down** *vt sep (silence by shouting)* acallar con gritos

howler ['haʊlə(r)] *n* (**a**) *Fam (mistake)* error *m* grave *or Esp* de bulto (**b**) ***h. monkey*** mono *m* aullador

howling ['haʊlɪŋ] **1** *n* aullidos *mpl*

2 *adj* (**a**) *(wolf)* aullador(ora); *(gale, wind)* violento(a), salvaje (**b**) *Fam* **it wasn't exactly a h. success** no fue un éxito clamoroso, que digamos

howsoever [haʊsəʊ'evə(r)] *adv Formal* comoquiera que

how's-your-father ['haʊzjə'fɑːðə(r)] *n Br Fam Hum (sexual intercourse)* **he fancied a bit of h.** tenía ganas de hacer ñacañaca *or Méx* el cuchi-cuchi

how-to ['haʊ'tuː] *adj US* sobre cómo (hacer algo), para aprender a (hacer algo); **a h. book** un libro de aprendizaje, un manual (de instrucción *or* de instrucciones); **he loves those h. cookery programmes** le encantan los programas de cocina

hoy [hɔɪ] *exclam* ¡eh!

hoyden ['hɔɪdən] *n* niña *f* revoltosa

HP, hp [eɪtʃ'piː] *n* (**a**) *Tech* (*abbr* **horsepower**) C.V. (**b**) *Br Com* (*abbr* **hire-purchase**) compra *f* a plazos

HQ [eɪtʃ'kjuː] *n* (*abbr* **headquarters**) sede *f*, central *f*

hr (*abbr* **hour**) h.

HRH [eɪtʃɑː'reɪtʃ] *n Br* (*abbr* **Her/His Royal Highness**) S.A.R.

HRT [eɪtʃɑː'tiː] *n Med* (*abbr* **hormone replacement therapy**) terapia *f* hormonal sustitutiva

HS (*abbr* **High School**) instituto *m* de enseñanza secundaria

HSE [eɪtʃes'iː] *n* (*abbr* **Health and Safety Executive**) inspección *f* de trabajo

HT (*abbr* **high tension**) AT

HTH *Comptr* (*abbr* **hope this helps**) espero que (esto) te sirva

HTML [eɪtʃtiːem'el] *n Comptr* (*abbr* **Hyper Text Markup Language**) HTML *m* ▸▸ ***H. editor*** editor *m* de HTML

HTTP [eɪtʃtiːtiː'piː] *n Comptr* (*abbr* **Hyper Text Transfer Protocol**) HTTP *m*

hub [hʌb] *n* (**a**) *(of wheel)* cubo *m* (**b**) *(of community)* centro *m* (**c**) **h. (airport)** aeropuerto *m* principal *(con múltiples conexiones)* (**d**) *Comptr* hub *m*

hub-and-spoke ['hʌbənd'spəʊk] *adj* (**a**) *Av (network, system)* hub and spoke, = en el que el tráfico se concentra en un aeropuerto principal y desde allí continúa a su destino final (**b**) *US (holiday tour)* con excursiones de un día desde el lugar de *Esp* estancia *or Am* estadía

hubba-hubba ['hʌbə'hʌbə] *exclam US Fam* ¡guau!, *Am* ¡uau!

hubbub ['hʌbʌb] *n* griterío *m*, algarabía *f*

hubby ['hʌbɪ] *n Fam (husband)* maridito *m*

hubcap ['hʌbkæp] *n (of wheel)* tapacubos *m inv*, *RP* taza *f*

hubris ['hjuːbrɪs] *n Literary* orgullo *m* desmedido, ensoberbecimiento *m*

huckleberry ['hʌkəlbərɪ] *n* = especie de arándano norteamericano

huckster ['hʌkstə(r)] *n* (**a**) *Old-fashioned (pedlar)* buhonero(a) *m,f* (**b**) *Fam US (swindler)* charlatán(ana) *m,f* (**c**) *US Fam Pej (advertising copywriter)* agente *mf* de publicidad *or* publicitario(a), publicitario(a) *m,f*, publicista *mf*

huddle ['hʌdəl] **1** *n* (**a**) *(of people, houses)* piña *f*, *RP* montonera *f*; **to go into a h.** hacer un grupo aparte, reunirse en petit comité (**b**) *(in American football)* reunión *f* en corro *or RP* ronda

2 *vi* (**a**) *(crowd together)* amontonarse, apiñarse; **to h. round sth** apiñarse en torno a algo (**b**) *(crouch)* acurrucarse; **she was huddling under a blanket** estaba bajo una manta, hecha un ovillo

▸**huddle together, huddle up** *vi* apiñarse

Hudson Bay ['hʌdsən'beɪ] *n* bahía *f* de Hudson

hue[1] [hjuː] *n (colour)* tonalidad *f*; *Fig* **political opinions of every h.** opiniones políticas de todo signo

hue[2] *n* **h. and cry** revuelo tremendo; **to raise a h. and cry about sth** poner el grito en el cielo por algo

-hued [hjuːd] *suffix* **dark/light-h.** de tonalidad oscura/clara, de un tono oscuro/claro

huff [hʌf] **1** *n Fam* **to be in a h.** estar mosqueado(a) *o* enfurruñado(a); **to go (off) in a h., to take the h.** mosquearse, enfurruñarse
2 *vi* **to h. and puff** *(blow)* resoplar; *Fig (show annoyance)* refunfuñar

huffily ['hʌfɪlɪ] *adv Fam (sulkily)* enfurruñadamente, con tono ofendido *or Esp* de mosqueo

huffy ['hʌfɪ] *adj Fam* **to be h.** *(in bad mood)* estar mosqueado(a) *or* enfurruñado(a); *(by nature)* ser un(a) refunfuñón(ona), ser muy picajoso(a)

hug [hʌg] **1** *n* abrazo *m*; **to give sb a h.** dar un abrazo a alguien
2 *vt (pt & pp* **hugged)** **(a)** *(embrace)* abrazar; **she hugged the child to her** abrazó al niño; **she hugged herself with delight** no cabía en sí de alegría, se volvió loca de alegría; **her dress hugged her figure** el vestido se ceñía a su cuerpo **(b)** *Fig (ground, shore)* no alejarse de

huge [hju:dʒ] *adj* enorme; **he's making a h. mistake** comete un craso error *or* un error gravísimo; **the cost will be h.** costará una fortuna; *Fam* **they're h. in the States** son superpopulares *or* tienen mucho éxito en Estados Unidos

hugely ['hju:dʒlɪ] *adv* enormemente; **I enjoyed myself h.** me divertí a lo grande, (me) lo pasé en grande

hugger-mugger ['hʌgəmʌgə(r)] *adv (in disorder)* al tuntún, manga por hombro; *(in secrecy)* en secreto, bajo cuerda; **piled together h.** apilados(as) de cualquier manera

Huguenot ['hju:gənəʊ] **1** *n* hugonote *mf*
2 *adj* hugonote

huh [hʌh] *exclam* **(a)** *(expressing disbelief, inquiry)* ¿eh?, ¿qué? **(b)** *(expressing disgust, scorn)* ¡ja!

hula ['hu:lə] *n* ***h. hoop*** hula-hoop *m*; ***h. skirt*** falda *f or RP* pollera *f* de paja *(para bailar el hula-hula)*

hulk [hʌlk] *n* **(a)** *(of ship)* casco *m*, carcasa *f* **(b)** *(large thing)* armatoste *m*; *(large person)* mole *f*, mastodonte *m* **(c)** *Hist (used as prison)* buque *m* prisión

hulking ['hʌlkɪŋ] *adj* descomunal, mastodóntico(a); **you h. great oaf!** ¡pedazo de zoquete!

hull [hʌl] **1** *n* **(a)** *(of ship, tank, aircraft)* casco *m* **(b)** *(of peas, beans)* vaina *f* **(c)** *(of strawberry, raspberry)* rabillo *m*
2 *vt* **(a)** *(peas, beans)* desgranar **(b)** *(strawberries, raspberries)* quitar el rabillo a

hullabaloo [hʌləbə'lu:] *n Fam* alboroto *m*, jaleo *m*; **the press made a real h. about it** la prensa *Esp* montó *or Am* armó un verdadero escándalo en torno al asunto

hullo = **hello**

hum [hʌm] **1** *n* **(a)** *(noise)* zumbido *m*, murmullo *m*; **the distant h. of traffic** el lejano rumor del tráfico **(b)** *Br Fam (bad smell)* pestilencia *f*, tufo *m*, *Esp* olor *m* a chotuno
2 *vt (pt & pp* **hummed)** *(tune)* tararear, canturrear
3 *vi* **(a)** *(make noise) (person)* tararear; *(insect, engine)* zumbar; *(spinning top)* zumbar; **to h. and haw** *(mumble)* mascullar; *(hesitate)* titubear, vacilar; *Fig* **everything was humming along nicely** todo iba viento en popa, todo marchaba bien; **to h. with activity** bullir de actividad **(b)** *Br Fam (smell)* apestar

human ['hju:mən] **1** *n* ser *m* humano
2 *adj* humano(a); **to have the h. touch** tener calor humano, tener un toque de humanidad; **he's only h.** es sólo un ser humano; **I can't do all that work alone, I'm only h.!** no puedo hacer sola todo ese trabajo, ¡no soy sobrehumana! ►► ***h. being*** ser *m* humano; ***h. error*** error *m* humano; ***the H. Genome Project*** el Proyecto Genoma Humano; ***h. geography*** geografía *f* humana; *Med* ***h. immunodeficiency virus*** virus *m inv* de la inmunodeficiencia humana; ***h. interest*** interés *m* humano; **a h. interest story** una historia de interés humano; ***h. nature*** la naturaleza humana; ***the h. race*** la raza humana; ***h. resources*** recursos *mpl* humanos; ***h. rights*** derechos *mpl* humanos; ***h. shield*** escudo *m* humano

humane [hjʊ'meɪn] *adj* **(a)** *(compassionate)* humano(a); **a h. method of killing animals** un método humanitario de matar animales ►► ***h. society*** *(for animals)* sociedad *f* protectora de animales, asociación *f* para la protección de los animales; *(for good works)* asociación *f* humanitaria **(b)** *Literary (education)* humanístico(a)

humanely [hjʊ'meɪnlɪ] *adv* humanamente

humanism ['hju:mənɪzəm] *n* humanismo *m*

humanist ['hju:mənɪst] **1** *n* humanista *mf*
2 *adj* humanista

humanistic [hjʊmə'nɪstɪk] *adj* humanístico(a)

humanitarian [hjʊmænɪ'teərɪən] **1** *n* persona *f* humanitaria
2 *adj* humanitario(a)

humanity [hjʊ'mænɪtɪ] *n* **(a)** *(the human race)* la humanidad **(b)** *(compassion)* humanidad *f*; **to lack h.** no tener humanidad **(c)** *Univ* **the humanities** humanidades *fpl*, letras *fpl*

humanize ['hju:mənaɪz] *vt* humanizar

humankind [hjʊmən'kaɪnd] *n* la humanidad, la raza humana

humanly ['hju:mənlɪ] *adv* humanamente; **to do everything h. possible** hacer todo lo humanamente posible

humanoid ['hju:mənɔɪd] **1** *n* humanoide *mf*
2 *adj* humanoide

humble ['hʌmbəl] **1** *adj* **(a)** *(meek)* humilde; **in my h. opinion** en mi humilde opinión; *Formal* **please accept my h. apologies** le ruego que acepte mis humildes disculpas IDIOM **to eat h. pie** *(admit one was wrong)* tragarse (uno) sus palabras
(b) *(modest, unpretentious)* humilde; **to come from h. origins** *or* **a h. background** proceder de familia humilde; *Hum* **welcome to my h. abode** bienvenido(a) a mi humilde morada
2 *vt (defeat)* humillar, poner en su sitio a; **to h. oneself before sth/sb** humillarse *or* arrodillarse ante algo/alguien; **to be humbled (by sth)** sacar una lección de humildad (de algo)

humbling ['hʌmbəlɪŋ] *adj* **a h. experience** una lección de humildad

humbly ['hʌmblɪ] *adv* **(a)** *(speak, ask)* humildemente, con modestia; **most h.** con la mayor humildad **(b)** *(live)* humildemente, modestamente; **h. born** de origen humilde

humbug ['hʌmbʌg] *n* **(a)** *(nonsense)* embustes *mpl*, patrañas *fpl* **(b)** *(hypocrite)* embaucador(ora) *m,f* **(c)** *Br (sweet)* caramelo *m* de menta

humdinger ['hʌmdɪŋə(r)] *n Fam* **a h. of a movie** una película bestial *or* genial *or Méx* padrísima; **they had a real h. of a row!** tuvieron una pelotera colosal *or* bárbara

humdrum ['hʌmdrʌm] *adj* anodino(a), monótono(a); **the h. tasks of everyday life** la rutina (de la vida) diaria

humerus ['hju:mərəs] *n Anat* húmero *m*

humid ['hju:mɪd] *adj* húmedo(a)

humidifier [hjʊ'mɪdɪfaɪə(r)] *n* humidificador *m*

humidify [hjʊ'mɪdɪfaɪ] *vt* humidificar

humidity [hjʊ'mɪdɪtɪ] *n* humedad *f*

humidor ['hju:mɪdɔ:(r)] *n* humidificador *m*

humiliate [hjʊ'mɪlɪeɪt] *vt* humillar; **he refused to h. himself by apologizing to them** se negó a rebajarse a pedirles perdón; **to feel humiliated** sentirse humillado(a)

humiliating [hjʊ'mɪlɪeɪtɪŋ] *adj* humillante

humiliatingly [hjʊ'mɪlɪeɪtɪŋlɪ] *adv* de manera humillante, humillantemente

humiliation [hjʊmɪlɪ'eɪʃən] *n* humillación *f*

humility [hjʊ'mɪlɪtɪ] *n* humildad *f*

hummingbird ['hʌmɪŋbɜ:d] *n* colibrí *m*

humming-top ['hʌmɪŋtɒp] *n* peonza *f*, trompo *m*

hummock ['hʌmək] *n (knoll)* montículo *m*, *Esp* mogote *m*

hummus ['hʊməs] *n* hum(m)us *m inv*, puré *m* de garbanzos

humongous, humungous [hju:'mʌŋgəs] *adj Fam* grandísimo(a), *Esp* gansísimo(a)

humor, humorless *US* = **humour, humourless**

humorist ['hju:mərɪst] *n* humorista *mf*

humorous ['hju:mərəs] *adj (person, remark)* gracioso(a), cómico(a); *(play, magazine)* humorístico(a); **there's nothing h. about cancer/losing your job** el cáncer/quedarse sin trabajo es algo que no tiene ninguna gracia; **she had a h. twinkle in her eye** tenía un brillo divertido en la mirada

humorously ['hju:mərəslɪ] *adv* con humor, con gracia

humour, *US* **humor** ['hju:mə(r)] **1** *n* **(a)** *(wit, fun) (in general)* humor *m*; *(of a situation, a story)* gracia *f*; **the h. of the situation** lo cómico *or* gracioso de la situación; **sense of h.** sentido del humor; **to see the h. in sth** verle la gracia a algo
(b) *Formal (mood)* humor *m*, talante *m*; **to be in good/bad h.** estar de buen/mal humor; **he's in no h. to talk to anybody** no está de humor para hablar con nadie; **to be out of h.** no estar de (buen) humor, estar de mal humor
(c) *Archaic (bodily fluid)* **the four humours** los cuatro humores
2 *vt (indulge)* **to h. sb** seguir la corriente a alguien; **don't try to h. me** no me digas que sí como a los tontos *or* locos

humourless, *US* **humorless** ['hju:məlɪs] *adj (person)* sin sentido del humor; *(book, situation)* sin gracia; **a h. smile** una sonrisa forzada *or* fingida

hump [hʌmp] 1 *n* (**a**) *(lump, bump) (on back)* joroba *f*; *(of camel)* joroba *f*; *(on road)* bache *m (convexo)*; IDIOM **we're over the h. now** ya hemos pasado lo peor (**b**) *Br Fam* **to have** *or* **get** *or* **take the h.** *(be annoyed)* enfurecerse, mosquearse; **to give sb the h.** poner de mal humor a alguien, mosquear a alguien
2 *vt* (**a**) *esp Br Fam (carry)* acarrear (**b**) *Vulg (have sex with)* tirarse a
3 *vi Vulg (have sex) Esp* joder, *Am* coger, *Méx* chingar

humpback ['hʌmpbæk] *n* (**a**) *Br* ***h. bridge*** puente *m* peraltado (**b**) ***h. whale*** rorcual *m* jiboso, yubarta *f*

humpbacked ['hʌmpbækt] *adj* (**a**) *(person)* jorobado(a) (**b**) ***h. bridge*** puente *m* peraltado

humongous = **humungous**

humus ['hju:məs] *n (in soil)* humus *m inv*

humvee ['hʌmvi:] *n US Fam* vehículo *m* polivalente de alta movilidad, *Esp* ≃ Vehículo de Alta Movilidad Táctico

Hun [hʌn] (*pl* **Huns** *or* **Hun**) *n* (**a**) *Hist* huno(a) *m,f* (**b**) *Fam Pej* **the H.** los cabezas cuadradas, = término ofensivo para referirse a los alemanes

hunch [hʌntʃ] 1 *n (intuition)* presentimiento *m*, corazonada *f*; **to act on a h.** actuar por instinto; **to have a h. that...** tener el presentimiento *or* la corazonada de que...; **to play** *or* **follow one's h.** dejarse llevar por la intuición, seguir (uno) su propia intuición; **my h. paid off... he was there** mi corazonada *or* intuición resultó ser cierta... él estaba allí; **it's only a h., but...** es sólo una corazonada, pero...; **my h. is that...** a mí me da en la nariz que..., *Méx, Ven* a mí me late que...
2 *vt* **to h. one's back** encorvar la espalda, encorvarse; **to h. one's shoulders** encorvar los hombros, encorvarse
3 *vi* **to h. over sth** inclinarse sobre algo encorvándose

hunchback ['hʌntʃbæk] *n* (**a**) *(person)* jorobado(a) *m,f* (**b**) *(hump)* joroba *f*

hunchbacked ['hʌntʃbækt] *adj* jorobado(a)

hunched [hʌntʃt] *adj* encorvado(a); **he sat h. in a corner** se sentó encorvado en un rincón

hundred ['hʌndrəd] 1 *n* (**a**) *(in general and before "thousand", "million", etc)* cien *m*; *(before other numbers)* ciento *m*; **one** *or* **a h.** cien; **one** *or* **a h. and one** ciento uno; **two h.** doscientos; **two hundred and one** doscientos uno; **about a h.,** *Fam* **a h. odd** unos(as) cien; **one** *or* **a h. thousand/million** cien mil/millones; **a h. and twenty-five books** ciento veinticinco libros; **two h. books** doscientos libros; **they were dying in their hundreds** *or* **by the h.** morían a centenares, *Am* morían de a cientos; **to live to be a h.** vivir hasta los cien años
(**b**) *(in dates)* **in nineteen h.** en mil novecientos; **in nineteen h. and ten** en mil novecientos diez
(**c**) *Fam Fig (lots)* **a h. and one details** mil y un detalles; **I've told you hundreds of times** te lo he dicho cientos de veces
(**d**) *Culin* ***hundreds and thousands*** gragea *f or* anises *mpl* de colores
2 *adj* cien; **a h. kilometres an hour** cien kilómetros por hora; **one** *or* **a h. per cent** cien por cien, ciento por ciento, *Am* cien por ciento; **to be a h. per cent certain** estar seguro(a) al cien por cien *or Am* cien por ciento; **I'm not feeling a h. per cent** no me encuentro del todo bien; **to give a** *or* **one h. per cent** rendir el *or* al ciento por ciento, rendir el *or* al cien por cien, *Am* rendir al cien por ciento ▸▸ ***the h. metres*** *(in athletics)* los cien metros (lisos); *Hist* ***the H. Years' War*** la Guerra de los Cien Años

hundredfold ['hʌndrədfəʊld] 1 *adj* centuplicado(a)
2 *adv* **to increase a h.** multiplicar por cien

hundredth ['hʌndrədθ] 1 *n* (**a**) *(fraction)* centésimo *m*, centésima parte *f* (**b**) *(in series)* centésimo(a) *m,f*
2 *adj* centésimo(a); *Fam* **for the h. time, no!** por enésima vez, ¡no!

hundredweight ['hʌndrədweɪt] *n* (**a**) *(metric)* 50 kg (**b**) *(imperial) Br* = 50,8 kg; *US* = 45,36 kg

hundred-year-old ['hʌndrəd'jɪər' əʊld] *adj* centenario(a)

hung [hʌŋ] 1 *adj* (**a**) *(without a clear majority)* **h. jury** jurado dividido; **h. parliament** parlamento sin mayoría (**b**) *very Fam* **to be h. like a horse** *Esp* tener un buen paquete, estar bien *Méx* dado *or RP* armado
2 *pt & pp of* **hang**

Hungarian [hʌŋ'geərɪən] 1 *n* (**a**) *(person)* húngaro(a) *m,f* (**b**) *(language)* húngaro *m*
2 *adj* húngaro(a)

Hungary ['hʌŋgərɪ] *n* Hungría

hunger ['hʌŋgə(r)] *n* hambre *f*; **to have h. pains** *or* **pangs** sentir los dolores del hambre; *Fig* **to have a h. for truth/knowledge** tener ansias de verdad/de conocimientos; **he was driven by a h. for truth/knowledge** lo impulsaba la sed de verdad/de conocimientos ▸▸ ***h. march*** = marcha de protesta de desempleados o necesitados; ***h. strike*** huelga *f* de hambre; **to go on (a) h. strike** ponerse en huelga de hambre; ***h. striker*** persona *f* en huelga de hambre

▸ **hunger after, hunger for** *vt insep* ansiar; **he hungered for revenge** tenía sed de venganza

hungrily ['hʌŋgrɪlɪ] *adv* (**a**) *(eat)* vorazmente (**b**) *(stare)* con avidez; **they stared h. at the women** devoraban a las mujeres con la mirada

hungry ['hʌŋgrɪ] *adj* (**a**) *(for food)* hambriento(a); **a h. look** una mirada de hambre; **to be h.** tener hambre; **to be as h. as a wolf** tener un hambre canina; **he still felt h.** seguía con *or* teniendo hambre; **to go h.** pasar hambre; **that night he went h.** esa noche se quedó sin comer; **this is h. work!** ¡este trabajo te abre el apetito *or* las ganas de comer!
(**b**) *Fig* **to be h. for knowledge** tener ansias de conocimiento; **she was h. for news of her family** estaba ansiosa por tener noticias de su familia; *Fam* **you have to be h. to make it to the top** hay que tener ganas de comerse el mundo para llegar a la cumbre

hung-up ['hʌŋ'ʌp] *adj Fam* (**a**) *(anxious, disturbed)* acomplejado(a) (**about** con) (**b**) *(obsessed)* obsesionado(a) (**on** con)

hunk [hʌŋk] *n* (**a**) *(large piece of bread, meat, cheese)* pedazo *m*, trozo *m* (**b**) *Fam (attractive man)* tipo *m or Esp* tío *m* bueno; **he's a real h.** está buenísimo, *Esp* es un auténtico cachas

hunker ['hʌŋkə(r)]

▸ **hunker down** *vi (crouch)* agacharse; *Fig* **I have to h. down and work this semester** debo ponerme a trabajar en serio este semestre

hunkers ['hʌŋkəz] *npl Fam* jamones *mpl*, *Esp* cachas *fpl*; **he was sitting on his h.** estaba en cuclillas

hunky ['hʌŋkɪ] *adj Fam (man)* fortachón, *Esp* cachas *inv*

hunky-dory [hʌŋkɪ'dɔ:rɪ] *adj Fam* **everything's h.** todo es de color de rosa, todo va de perlas

hunt [hʌnt] 1 *n* (**a**) *(for animals)* caza *f*; **a tiger/bear h.** una caza del tigre/oso
(**b**) *(search) (for person, work)* búsqueda *f*, caza *f*; **to be on the h. for sth** ir *or* andar a la caza de algo, ir en busca de algo; **the h. is on (for)** ha comenzado la búsqueda (de); **I've had a h. for your scarf** he buscado tu bufanda por todas partes
(**c**) *Br (fox-hunting group)* partida *f* de caza ▸▸ ***h. ball*** baile *m* de cazadores; ***h. saboteur*** saboteador(ora) *m,f* de cacerías
2 *vt* (**a**) *(for food, sport) (fox, deer)* cazar; **they were hunted to extinction** su caza indiscriminada provocó la extinción de la especie
(**b**) *(pursue)* **to h. a criminal** ir tras la pista de un delincuente
(**c**) *(drive out)* expulsar, echar; **people were hunted from their homes** la gente se vio forzada a abandonar sus hogares
(**d**) *(area)* recorrer
3 *vi* (**a**) *(search)* **to h. for** ir en busca de; **I've hunted for it high and low** lo he buscado por todas partes; **I hunted all over town for a linen jacket** me he recorrido toda la ciudad en busca de una chaqueta de lino (**b**) *(kill animals)* cazar; **they h. by night/in packs** salen a cazar de noche/en grupos; **to go hunting** ir de caza *or* de cacería, ir a cazar

▸ **hunt about for, hunt around for** *vt insep* buscar

▸ **hunt down** *vt sep (animal)* cazar; *(person)* atrapar, capturar; *(information, book)* conseguir; **I finally managed to h. down the book in Zurich** por fin me hice con el libro en Zurich

▸ **hunt out, hunt up** *vt sep* (**a**) *(find) (person)* dar con, lograr encontrar (**b**) *(look for) (thing)* buscar

hunted ['hʌntɪd] *adj (look, appearance)* angustiado(a)

hunter ['hʌntə(r)] *n* (**a**) *(person)* cazador(ora) *m,f* (**b**) *(horse)* caballo *m* especialmente adiestrado para la caza (**c**) *(watch)* saboneta *f*, reloj *m* de bolsillo (con tapa)

hunter-gatherer [hʌntə'gæðərə(r)] *n* cazador-recolector *m*

hunter-killer [hʌntə'kɪlə(r)] *n (submarine)* submarino *m* de ataque

hunting ['hʌntɪŋ] *n* caza *f* ▸▸ ***h. dog*** perro *m* de caza; ***h. ground*** terreno *m* de caza; *Fig* **the bazaar is a (happy) h. ground for tourists** el bazar es un buen sitio donde los turistas pueden encontrar todo tipo de curiosidades; ***h. knife*** navaja *f* de caza; ***h. licence*** licencia *f* de caza; ***h. lodge*** pabellón *m* de caza; ***h. season*** temporada *f* de caza

hunting-horn ['hʌntɪŋhɔ:n] *n* cuerno *m* de caza

Huntington's chorea ['hʌntɪŋtənzkə'rɪə] *n Med* corea *f* de Huntington

huntress ['hʌntrɪs] *n* cazadora *f*

huntsman ['hʌntsmən] *n* cazador *m*

hurdle ['hɜ:dəl] 1 *n* (**a**) *(in race)* valla *f*, *Am* obstáculo *m*; **hurdles** *(event)* (prueba *f* de) vallas *fpl or Am* obstáculos *mpl*; **the 400-metre hurdles** los 400 metros valla *or Am* obstáculo (**b**) *(obstacle)* obstáculo *m*; **to overcome a h.** vencer un obstáculo; **she took that h. in her**

stride salvó ese obstáculo sin dificultad (**c**) *(for fences)* zarzo *m*
2 *vt (obstacle)* saltar
3 *vi* saltar obstáculos

hurdler ['hɜːdlə(r)] *n Sport* vallista *mf*

hurdling ['hɜːdlɪŋ] *n Sport* carreras *fpl* de vallas

hurdy-gurdy ['hɜːdɪ'gɜːdɪ] *n* (**a**) *(barrel organ)* organillo *m* (**b**) *(medieval instrument)* zanfoña *f*

hurl [hɜːl] 1 *vt* (**a**) *(throw)* lanzar, arrojar; **he hurled a vase at him** le tiró *or Andes, CAm, Méx* aventó un jarrón; **they were hurled to the ground by the explosion** salieron despedidos contra el suelo por la explosión; **the boat was hurled onto the rocks** el barco fue lanzado contra las rocas; **to h. oneself at sb** abalanzarse sobre alguien; **to h. oneself into the fray/one's work** lanzarse a combatir/trabajar, meterse de lleno en el combate/trabajo; **she hurled herself off the bridge** se tiró desde el puente
(**b**) *(insults)* proferir
2 *vi Fam (vomit)* devolver, echar la papilla, *RP* arrojar

hurling ['hɜːlɪŋ], **hurley** ['hɜːlɪ] *n (Irish game)* = deporte irlandés a medio camino entre el hockey y el rugby

hurly-burly ['hɜːlɪ'bɜːlɪ] *n Fam* tumulto *m*, barullo *m*

hurrah [hʊ'rɑː], **hurray** [hʊ'reɪ] *exclam* ¡hurra!

hurricane ['hʌrɪkən, *US* 'hʌrɪkeɪn] *n* huracán *m*; **h. force winds** vientos de fuerza huracanada ►► ***h. lamp*** farol *m*

hurried ['hʌrɪd] *adj (meeting, reply)* precipitado(a), apresurado(a); *(departure, footsteps)* apresurado(a), precipitado(a); *(work)* hecho(a) a la carrera *or RP* a las corridas; **to be h.** tener prisa, *Am* estar apurado(a); **to have a h. meal** comer deprisa y corriendo *or* a la carrera, *RP* comer a las corridas; **I wrote a h. note to reassure her** le escribí una breve nota para tranquilizarla

hurriedly ['hʌrɪdlɪ] *adv* apresuradamente; **she passed h. over the unpleasant details** mencionó de pasada *or* superficialmente los detalles desagradables; **he h. excused himself and left** se disculpó precipitadamente y se marchó

hurry ['hʌrɪ] 1 *n* prisa *f*, *Am* apuro *m*; **to be in a h. (to do sth)** tener prisa *or Am* apuro (por hacer algo); **to be in a tearing** *or* **an awful h.** tener muchísima prisa, *Am* estar apuradísimo(a); **he was in no h. to finish** no tenía ninguna prisa *or Am* ningún apuro por terminar; **to do sth in a h.** hacer algo deprisa *or Am* rápido; **it was obviously written in a h.** sin duda fue escrito a la carrera *or RP* a las corridas; **to leave in a h.** marcharse apresuradamente; **in his** *or* **the h. to leave he forgot his umbrella** con las prisas *or Am* con *or* en el apuro, se dejó olvidado el paraguas; **there's no h.** no hay prisa *or Am* apuro, no corre prisa; **what's the** *or* **your h.?** ¿a qué tanta prisa *or Am* tanto apuro?; IDIOM **I won't do that again in a h.** no lo volveré a hacer sin pensarlo antes; IDIOM *Br* **a young man in a h.** un joven con grandes ambiciones *or* que quiere llegar lejos
2 *vt* (**a**) *(person)* meter prisa a, apremiar, *Am* apurar; **she won't be hurried, you can't h. her** a ella no hay quien le meta prisa *or Am* la apure, no hay forma de meterle prisa *or Am* apurarla; **they hurried him through customs** lo hicieron pasar rápidamente por la aduana; **he was hurried into making a choice** lo hicieron elegir precipitadamente
(**b**) *(work, decision)* apresurar, realizar con prisas; **this decision/work can't be hurried** esta decisión no puede tomarse/este trabajo no puede hacerse a la ligera *or* precipitadamente
(**c**) *(send hastily)* enviar rápidamente; *(transport hastily)* llevar rápidamente; **aid was hurried to the stricken town** se envió urgentemente ayuda a la ciudad afectada; **she was hurried to hospital** la llevaron apresuradamente al hospital
3 *vi* (**a**) *(make haste)* **to h. (to do sth)** apresurarse *or Am* apurarse (a hacer algo); **he's hurrying to finish some work** está dándose prisa *or Am* se está apurando para terminar un trabajo; **I must** *or* **I'd better h.** será mejor que me dé prisa *or Am* me apure; **you don't have to h. over that report** ese informe no corre prisa *or Am* no tiene apuro; **h.! it's already started** ¡date prisa *or Am* apúrate, que ya ha empezado!
(**b**) *(move quickly)* **to h. into a room** entrar apresuradamente en una habitación; **to h. out of a room** salir apresuradamente de una habitación; **he hurried down the stairs** corrió escaleras abajo, bajó las escaleras a toda prisa; **he hurried (over) to the bank** se fue corriendo al banco

► **hurry along** 1 *vt sep* (**a**) *(person)* meter prisa a, *Am* apurar (**b**) *(work)* acelerar
2 *vi* irse rápido; **to h. along towards** precipitarse hacia; **we'd better be hurrying along** será mejor que nos vayamos rápido

► **hurry away** *vi* marcharse a toda prisa *or Am* con apuro

► **hurry back** *vi* volver corriendo

► **hurry on** 1 *vt sep* (**a**) *(person)* meter prisa a, *Am* apurar (**b**) *(work)* acelerar
2 *vi (proceed quickly) (person)* seguir sin pararse; **he hurried on to the next shelter** se apresuró a cobijarse en el siguiente refugio; **can we h. on to the next item on the agenda?** ¿podemos pasar rápidamente al próximo punto del orden del día?; **to h. on with sth** continuar algo deprisa *or Am* rápido

► **hurry up** 1 *vt sep* (**a**) *(person)* meter prisa a, *Am* apurar (**b**) *(work)* acelerar
2 *vi* apresurarse, darse prisa, *Am* apurarse; **h. up!** ¡date prisa!, *Am* apúrate!

hurry-up ['hʌrɪʌp] *adj US Fam (meal)* a la carrera, *RP* a las corridas; *(manner, procedure)* precipitado(a); **everyone was in a h. mode** todo el mundo iba acelerado

---

HURT [hɜːt] 1 *n* (**a**) *(physical pain)* dolor *m*
(**b**) *(emotional)* dolor *m*; **he wanted to make up for the h. he had caused her** quería resarcirla por el dolor que le había causado
2 *adj* (**a**) *(physically)* **are you h.?** *(after falling)* ¿te has hecho daño?; *(wounded)* ¿estás herido?
(**b**) *(emotionally) (person)* dolido(a); *(look)* dolorido(a); *(feelings)* herido(a)
(**c**) *US (damaged)* **h. books** libros defectuosos
3 *vt* (*pt & pp* **hurt**) (**a**) *(physically)* hacer daño a; *Fig (chances, prospects)* perjudicar; **my leg is hurting me** me duele la pierna; **to h. one's foot** hacerse daño en un pie; **nobody was h. in the accident** nadie resultó herido en el accidente; **the measures really h. small businesses** las medidas perjudicaron mucho a las pequeñas empresas; **to get h.** hacerse daño; *Fam* **do as I say and no one gets h.!** ¡hagan lo que les digo y nadie saldrá herido!; **to h. oneself** hacerse daño; *Fig* **it wouldn't h. him to do the dishes once in a while** no le se van a caer los anillos por lavar los platos de vez en cuando; **a bit of exercise never h. anyone** un poco de ejercicio nunca le hizo mal a nadie
(**b**) *(emotionally)* herir; **I'm very h. by what you said** me duele mucho lo que me dijiste; **I don't want to get h. again** no quiero que me vuelvan a hacer daño; **to h. sb's feelings** herir los sentimientos de alguien; **you're only hurting yourself** te estás haciendo daño a ti mismo
4 *vi* (**a**) *(cause pain)* doler; **it hurts** me duele; **where does it h.?** ¿dónde te duele?; **my foot hurts** me duele el pie; *Fig* **it hurts to admit it, but...** me da rabia admitirlo, pero...; *Fam* **one more chocolate won't h.** por un bombón más no va a pasar nada; *Fam* **it wouldn't h. to say sorry** no pasaría nada por que pidieras perdón, no estaría mal que pidieras perdón; *Fam* **it won't h. to check first** no estará de más que lo comprobemos antes
(**b**) *(feel pain)* **the athlete is really hurting now** el atleta está pasándolo mal ahora
(**c**) *(emotionally)* resultar doloroso(a), doler; **it hurts that you didn't come** me dolió que no vinieras; *esp US* **he's still hurting from not getting the job** todavía le pesa no haber conseguido el empleo

---

hurtful ['hɜːtfʊl] *adj (remark)* hiriente; **that was a h. thing to say** ese fue un comentario de los que hacen daño *or* de lo más hiriente

hurtle ['hɜːtəl] *vi* **to h. along** pasar zumbando; **the cars hurtled round the track** los coches recorrían el circuito a toda velocidad; **to h. down the street** bajar por la calle a todo correr; **he went hurtling down the stairs** bajó las escaleras volando; **a rock hurtled through the air** una piedra *or* un peñasco surcó velozmente el aire; **to h. towards** precipitarse hacia; **the motorbike came hurtling towards him** la moto se abalanzó *or* se precipitó sobre él, la moto se le echó encima

husband ['hʌzbənd] 1 *n* marido *m*; **h. and wife** marido y mujer
2 *vt Formal (one's resources)* economizar; *(one's strength)* guardar, reservar

husbandry ['hʌzbəndrɪ] *n* (**a**) *Agr* agricultura *f*; **animal h.** ganadería (**b**) *Formal (management)* gestión *f*, administración *f*; **good h.** buena administración

hush [hʌʃ] 1 *n (quiet)* silencio *m*; **a h. fell over the room** se hizo el silencio en la sala; **h.!** ¡silencio! ►► *Fam* ***h. money*** soborno *m*, *RP* coima *f*
2 *vt* acallar; *Fam* **(well) h. my mouth!** ¡no he dicho nada!, ¡me callo, entonces!

► **hush up** *vt sep* (**a**) *(scandal)* echar tierra a (**b**) *(noisy person)* callar, hacer callar

hushed [hʌʃt] *adj* susurrado(a); **to speak in h. tones** hablar susurrando *or* en voz muy baja *or Am* despacio

hush-hush ['hʌʃhʌʃ] *adj Fam* secreto(a); **it's all very h.** es todo muy secreto *or* supersecreto

hush-puppy [ˈhʌʃpʌpɪ] *n US* = masa de harina de maíz frita con forma de bolita

husk [hʌsk] **1** *n (of seed)* cáscara *f*, cascarilla *f*; *(of corn)* farfolla *f*, *Andes, RP* chala *f*
2 *vt (grain)* pelar

huskily [ˈhʌskɪlɪ] *adv (hoarsely)* con voz ronca, con tono ronco; *(attractively)* con voz grave

huskiness [ˈhʌskɪnɪs] *n (of voice, sound) (hoarseness)* aspereza *f*; *(attractive)* tonalidad *f* grave

husky[1] [ˈhʌskɪ] *adj* (**a**) *(voice)* áspero(a); *(attractive)* grave ▸ (**b**) *Fam (robust)* fornido(a), robusto(a)

husky[2] *n (dog)* husky *m*

hussar [hʊˈzɑː(r)] *n Mil* húsar *m*

hussy [ˈhʌsɪ] *n Old-fashioned or Hum* pelandusca *f*; **you shameless** *or* **brazen h.!** ¡desvergonzada!, *Esp* ¡pendón, que eres un pendón!

hustings [ˈhʌstɪŋz] *npl* mítines *mpl* electorales; **on the h.** en campaña electoral

hustle [ˈhʌsəl] **1** *n* (**a**) *(commotion)* agitación *f*, bullicio *m*; **h. and bustle** ajetreo, bullicio (**b**) *US Fam (swindle)* lío *m*, chanchullo *m*, tejemaneje *m*
2 *vt* (**a**) *(shove, push)* empujar; **I was hustled into a small room** me metieron a empujones en un cuartito; **the doctor was hustled through the crowd** llevaron al médico a empujones a través del gentío; **he was hustled away** *or* **off by two men** se lo llevaron apresuradamente entre dos
(**b**) *(persuade quickly)* **to h. sb into (doing) sth** meter prisa *or* presionar a alguien para que haga algo, *Am* apurar a alguien para que haga algo
(**c**) *Fam (obtain dishonestly)* quedarse con
(**d**) *US Fam (swindle)* estafar; **to h. sb out of sth** birlarle algo a alguien; **he hustled the old lady for her savings** con artimañas, le sacó a la anciana sus ahorros; **to h. some pool** jugar al billar por dinero
(**e**) *US Fam (sell)* vender; **he made a living hustling used bottles for dimes** vivía de vender botellas usadas por unos centavos
3 *vi Fam* (**a**) *(shove, jostle)* empujar (**b**) *(hurry)* darse prisa, *Esp* aligerar(se), *Am* apurar(se) (**c**) *US (work as prostitute)* hacer la calle *or Méx* la esquina (**d**) *(promote oneself aggressively)* venderse, hacerse *or* dejarse notar, *RP* batirse el parche

hustler [ˈhʌslə(r)] *n US Fam* (**a**) *(energetic person)* persona *f* dinámica, trabajador(ora) *m,f* incansable, *RP* laburador(ora) *m,f* (**b**) *(swindler)* estafador(ora) *m,f*, timador(ora) *m,f* (**c**) *(prostitute)* puto(a) *m,f*

hut [hʌt] *n* (**a**) *(shed)* cobertizo *m* (**b**) *(dwelling)* cabaña *f*, choza *f*

hutch [hʌtʃ] *n (for rabbit)* jaula *f* para conejos

HV (*abbr* **high voltage**) AV

hyacinth [ˈhaɪəsɪnθ] *n* jacinto *m*

hybrid [ˈhaɪbrɪd] **1** *n* híbrido *m*
2 *adj* híbrido(a)

hybridize [ˈhaɪbrɪdaɪz] **1** *vt* hibridar, hibridizar
2 *vi* hibridarse, hibridizarse

hydra [ˈhaɪdrə] *n* (**a**) *Zool* hidra *f* (**b**) *(in Greek mythology)* **the H.** la Hidra

hydrangea [haɪˈdreɪndʒə] *n* hortensia *f*

hydrant [ˈhaɪdrənt] *n* boca *f* de incendios

hydrate **1** *n* [ˈhaɪdreɪt] *Chem* hidrato *m*; **chloral h.** hidrato de cloral
2 *vt* [haɪˈdreɪt] hidratar

hydration [haɪˈdreɪʃən] *n Chem* hidratación *f*

hydraulic [haɪˈdrɔːlɪk] *adj* hidráulico(a) ▸▸ ***h. brake*** freno *m* hidráulico; ***h. press*** prensa *f* hidráulica; ***h. suspension*** suspensión *f* hidráulica

hydraulics [haɪˈdrɔːlɪks] *npl* hidráulica *f*

hydride [ˈhaɪdraɪd] *n Chem* hidruro *m*

hydro [ˈhaɪdrəʊ] *n* (**a**) *Br (spa) Esp* balneario *m*, *Am* termas *fpl* (**b**) *(power)* energía *f* hidroeléctrica

hydrocarbon [haɪdrəʊˈkɑːbən] *n* hidrocarburo *m*

hydrocephalic [ˈhaɪdrəʊseˈfælɪk] *adj Med* hidrocefálico(a), hidrocéfalo(a)

hydrocephalus [ˈhaɪdrəʊˈsefələs] *n Med* hidrocefalia *f*

hydrochloric acid [ˈhaɪdrəˈklɒrɪkˈæsɪd] *n* ácido *m* clorhídrico

hydrocortisone [haɪdrəʊˈkɔːtɪzəʊn] *n* hidrocortisona *f*

hydrodynamic [haɪdrəʊdaɪˈnæmɪk] *adj* hidrodinámico(a)

hydrodynamics [haɪdrəʊdaɪˈnæmɪks] *n* hidrodinámica *f*

hydroelectric [haɪdrəʊɪˈlektrɪk] *adj* hidroeléctrico(a) ▸▸ ***h. power*** energía *f* hidroeléctrica; ***h. power station*** central *f* hidroeléctrica

hydroelectricity [haɪdrəʊelɪkˈtrɪsɪtɪ] *n* hidroelectricidad *f*

hydrofoil [ˈhaɪdrəfɔɪl] *n* (**a**) *(device)* hidroaleta *f* (**b**) *(boat)* hidroala *m*, *RP* alíscafo *m*

hydrogen [ˈhaɪdrədʒən] *n Chem* hidrógeno *m* ▸▸ ***h. bomb*** bomba *f* de hidrógeno; ***h. bond*** enlace *m or* puente *m* de hidrógeno; ***h. chloride*** cloruro *m* de hidrógeno; ***h. ion*** ion *m* hidrógeno, protón *m*; ***h. peroxide*** agua *f* oxigenada, *Spec* peróxido *m* de hidrógeno; ***h. sulphide*** ácido *m* sulfhídrico, sulfuro *m* de hidrógeno

hydrogenate [haɪˈdrɒdʒɪneɪt] *vt Chem* hidrogenar

hydrogenated [haɪˈdrɒdʒɪneɪtɪd] *adj Chem* hidrogenado(a) ▸▸ ***h. vegetable oil*** aceite *m* vegetal hidrogenado

hydrogenation [haɪˈdrɒdʒɪneɪʃən] *n Chem* hidrogenación *f*

hydrogenous [haɪˈdrɒdʒɪnəs] *adj* de hidrógeno

hydrographic(al) [haɪdrəˈgræfɪk(əl)] *adj* hidrográfico(a)

hydrography [haɪˈdrɒgrəfɪ] *n* hidrografía *f*

hydrologic(al) [ˈhaɪdrəˈlɒdʒɪk(əl)] *adj* hidrológico(a)

hydrology [haɪˈdrɒlədʒɪ] *n* hidrología *f*

hydrolyse [ˈhaɪdrəlaɪz] *vt Chem* hidrolizar; **hydrolysed vegetable protein** proteína *f* vegetal hidrolizada

hydrolysis [haɪˈdrɒlɪsɪs] *n Chem* hidrólisis *f inv*

hydrolyte [ˈhaɪdrəlaɪt] *n Chem* hidrólito *m*

hydrometer [haɪˈdrɒmɪtə(r)] *n Phys* hidrómetro *m*

hydrometry [haɪˈdrɒmɪtrɪ] *n* hidrometría *f*

hydronaut [ˈhaɪdrənɔːt] *n US* hidronauta *m*

hydrophobia [haɪdrəˈfəʊbɪə] *n Med (rabies)* hidrofobia *f*

hydrophobic [haɪdrəˈfəʊbɪk] *adj* (**a**) *Chem* hidrófobo(a) (**b**) *Med (with rabies)* hidrófobo(a)

hydroplane [ˈhaɪdrəpleɪn] **1** *n* (**a**) *(boat)* hidroala *m*, *RP* alíscafo *m* (**b**) *US (seaplane)* hidroavión *m* (**c**) *(on submarine)* timón *m* de inmersión
2 *vi US (car)* hacer aquaplaning, patinar

hydroponics [haɪdrəˈpɒnɪks] *n Bot* cultivo *m* hidropónico, hidroponía *f*

hydrosphere [ˈhaɪdrəʊsfɪə(r)] *n* hydrosfera *f*

hydrostatic [ˈhaɪdrəʊˈstætɪk] *adj* hidrostático(a)

hydrostatics [ˈhaɪdrəʊˈstætɪks] *n* hidrostática *f*

hydrotherapy [haɪdrəʊˈθerəpɪ] *n* hidroterapia *f*

hydrothermal [haɪdrəʊˈθɜːməl] *adj* hidrotermal

hydrous [ˈhaɪdrəs] *adj Chem* hidratado(a)

hydroxide [haɪˈdrɒksaɪd] *n Chem* hidróxido *m*; **sodium h.** hidróxido sódico

hydroxyl [haɪˈdrɒksɪl] *n Chem* hidroxilo *m*

hyena [haɪˈiːnə] *n* hiena *f*

hygiene [ˈhaɪdʒiːn] *n* higiene *f*

hygienic [haɪˈdʒiːnɪk] *adj* higiénico(a)

hygienically [haɪˈdʒiːnɪklɪ] *adv* con higiene, de un modo higiénico

hygienist [ˈhaɪdʒiːnɪst] *n* higienista *mf*

hygrometer [haɪˈgrɒmətə(r)] *n* higrómetro *m*

hygrometry [haɪˈgrɒmətrɪ] *n* higrometría *f*

hygroscopic [haɪgrəˈskɒpɪk] *adj* higroscópico(a)

hymen [ˈhaɪmen] *n Anat* himen *m*

hymn [hɪm] **1** *n* himno *m*; **a h. to nature** un himno *or* canto a la naturaleza ▸▸ ***h. book*** libro *m* de himnos, himnario *m*
2 *vt Literary* loar, alabar

hymnal [ˈhɪmnəl] *n Rel* himnario *m*, libro *m* de himnos

hype [haɪp] *Fam* **1** *n (publicity)* bombo *m*, revuelo *m* publicitario; **I was put off by all the h.** se me quitaron *or Am* fueron las ganas con tanta propaganda publicitaria
2 *vt (publicize)* dar mucho bombo a; **her latest novel has been heavily hyped** han publicitado exageradamente su última novela

▸ **hype up** *vt sep* (**a**) *(publicize)* dar mucho bombo a; **it's been so hyped up in the media** lo han publicitado muchísimo en los medios de comunicación (**b**) **to be hyped up** *(excited)* estar hecho(a) un manojo de nervios

hyper [ˈhaɪpə(r)] *adj Fam (overexcited)* acelerado(a)

hyperactive [haɪpəˈræktɪv] *adj* (**a**) *(thyroid)* hiperactivo(a) (**b**) *(child, person)* hiperactivo(a)

hyperactivity [haɪpəˈræktɪvɪtɪ] *n* hiperactividad *f*

hyperbola [haɪˈpɜːbələ] *n Math* hipérbola *f*

hyperbole [haɪˈpɜːbəlɪ] *n* hipérbole *f*

hyperbolic [haɪpəˈbɒlɪk] *adj* (**a**) *Math* hiperbólico(a) (**b**) *Lit* hiperbólico(a)

hyperbolically [haɪpəˈbɒlɪk(ə)lɪ] *adv* hiperbólicamente

hypercorrection [haɪpəkəˈrekʃən] *n* hipercorrección *f*

hypercritical [haɪpəˈkrɪtɪkəl] *adj* criticón(ona), hipercrítico(a)

hyperglycaemia, *US* **hyperglycemia** [haɪpəglaɪˈsiːmɪə] *n Med* hiperglucemia *f*, *Am* hiperglicemia *f*

hyperglycaemic, *US* **hyperglycemic** [haɪpəglaɪˈsiːmɪk] *adj Med* hiperglucémico(a), *Am* hiperglicémico(a)

hyperinflation [haɪpərɪnˈfleɪʃən] *n Econ* hiperinflación *f*

hyperlink [ˈhaɪpəlɪŋk] *n Comptr* hiperenlace *m*

hypermarket [ˈhaɪpəmɑːkɪt] *n* hipermercado *m*

hypermedia [ˈhaɪpəmiːdɪə] *n Comptr* hipermedia *f*

hyperon [ˈhaɪpərɒn] *n Phys* hiperón *m*

hyperplasia [haɪpəˈpleɪʒə] *n Med* hiperplasia *f*

hyperrealism [haɪpəˈrɪəlɪzəm] *n Art* hiperrealismo *m*

hyperrealist [haɪpəˈrɪəlɪst] *Art* **1** *n* hiperrealista *mf*
 2 *adj* hiperrealista

hypersensitive [haɪpəˈsensɪtɪv] *adj* hipersensible, muy susceptible

hypersensitivity [ˈhaɪpəsensɪˈtɪvɪtɪ] *n* hipersensibilidad *f*

hypersonic [haɪpəˈsɒnɪk] *adj* hipersónico(a)

hyperspace [ˈhaɪpəspeɪs] *n* (**a**) *Math* hiperespacio *m* (**b**) *(in science fiction)* hiperespacio *m*

hypertension [haɪpəˈtenʃən] *n Med* hipertensión *f*

hypertensive [haɪpəˈtensɪv] *Med* **1** *adj* hipertenso(a)
 2 *n* hipertenso(a) *m,f*

hypertext [ˈhaɪpətekst] *n Comptr* hipertexto *m* ▸▸ ***h. link*** enlace *m* hipertextual

hyperthermia [haɪpəˈθɜːmɪə] *n Med* hipertermia *f*

hyperthyroidism [haɪpəˈθaɪrɔɪdɪzəm] *n Med* hipertiroidismo *m*

hypertrophy [haɪˈpɜːtrəfɪ] *n Med* hipertrofia *f*

hyperventilate [haɪpəˈventɪleɪt] *vi* hiperventilar

hyperventilation [ˈhaɪpəventɪˈleɪʃən] *n* hiperventilación *f*

hypervitaminosis [ˈhaɪpəvɪtəmɪˈnəʊsɪs] *n Med* hipervitaminosis *f*

hyphen [ˈhaɪfən] *n* guión *m*

hyphenate [ˈhaɪfəneɪt] *vt (word)* escribir con guión

hyphenated [ˈhaɪfəneɪtɪd] *adj* (**a**) *(word)* con guión (**b**) *US* **h. American** medio americano(a)

hyphenation [haɪfəˈneɪʃən] *n* partición *f* de palabras *or* silábica

hypnosis [hɪpˈnəʊsɪs] *n* hipnosis *f inv*; **under h.** hipnotizado(a), en estado de hipnosis; **to put sb under h.** hipnotizar a alguien

hypnotherapy [hɪpnəˈθerəpɪ] *n* terapia *f* hipnótica, hipnoterapia *f*

hypnotic [hɪpˈnɒtɪk] **1** *adj* hipnótico(a); **in a h. trance** en trance hipnótico; *Fig* **to have a h. effect on sb** tener un efecto hipnotizante sobre alguien
 2 *n (drug)* hipnótico *m*

hypnotism [ˈhɪpnətɪzəm] *n* hipnotismo *m*

hypnotist [ˈhɪpnətɪst] *n* hipnotizador(ora) *m,f*

hypnotize [ˈhɪpnətaɪz] *vt* hipnotizar

hypo [ˈhaɪpəʊ] *n Fam* jeringuilla *f*

hypoallergenic [haɪpəʊæləˈdʒenɪk] *adj* hipoalergénico(a), hipoalérgico(a)

hypocentre, *US* **hypocenter** [ˈhaɪpəʊsentə(r)] *n* hipocentro *m*

hypochondria [haɪpəˈkɒndrɪə] *n Med* hipocondría *f*

hypochondriac [haɪpəˈkɒndrɪæk] **1** *n* hipocondríaco(a) *m,f*
 2 *adj* hipocondríaco(a)

hypocrisy [hɪˈpɒkrɪsɪ] *n* hipocresía *f*

hypocrite [ˈhɪpəkrɪt] *n* hipócrita *mf*

hypocritical [hɪpəˈkrɪtɪkəl] *adj* hipócrita

hypocritically [hɪpəˈkrɪtɪklɪ] *adv* hipócritamente, con hipocresía

hypodermic [haɪpəˈdɜːmɪk] **1** *n* **h. (syringe)** (jeringuilla *f*) hipodérmica *f*
 2 *adj* hipodérmico(a)

hypoglycaemia, *US* **hypoglycemia** [ˈhaɪpəʊglaɪˈsiːmɪə] *n Med* hipoglucemia *f*, *Am* hipoglicemia *f*

hypoglycaemic, *US* **hypoglycemic** [ˈhaɪpəʊglaɪˈsiːmɪk] *adj Med* hipoglucémico(a), *Am* hipoglicémico(a)

hyponym [ˈhaɪpənɪm] *n Ling* hipónimo *m*

hypostasis [haɪpəʊˈsteɪsɪs] *n* hipóstasis *f*

hypotaxis [haɪpəˈtæksɪs] *n Gram* hipotaxis *f*

hypotension [haɪpəʊˈtenʃən] *n Med* hipotensión *f*

hypotensive [haɪpəʊˈtensɪv] *Med* **1** *adj* hipotenso(a)
 2 *n* hipotenso(a) *m,f*

hypotenuse [haɪˈpɒtənjuːz] *n Geom* hipotenusa *f*

hypothalamus [haɪpəʊˈθæləməs] *n Anat* hipotálamo *m*

hypothermia [haɪpəʊˈθɜːmɪə] *n Med* hipotermia *f*

hypothesis [haɪˈpɒθəsɪs] (*pl* **hypotheses** [haɪˈpɒθəsiːz]) *n* hipótesis *f inv*; **to put forward** *or* **advance a h.** formular *or* plantear una hipótesis

hypothesize [haɪˈpɒθəsaɪz] **1** *vt* plantear como hipótesis, conjeturar
 2 *vi* plantear hipótesis, conjeturar

hypothetic(al) [haɪpəˈθetɪk(əl)] *adj* hipotético(a)

hypothetically [haɪpəˈθetɪklɪ] *adv* en teoría, hipotéticamente

hypothyroidism [haɪpəʊˈθaɪrɔɪdɪzəm] *n Med* hipotiroidismo *m*

hypotonia [haɪpəʊˈtəʊnɪə] *n Med* hipotonía *f*

hysterectomy [hɪstəˈrektəmɪ] *n Med* histerectomía *f*; **she has had a h.** le han hecho una histerectomía

hysteresis [hɪstəˈriːsɪs] *n Phys* histéresis *f inv*

hysteria [hɪsˈtɪərɪə] *n* (**a**) *Psy* histeria *f* (**b**) *(panic)* histeria *f*, histerismo *m*; **an atmosphere of barely controlled h. reigned in the office** en la oficina reinaba un clima de histeria apenas controlado; **a country in the grip of war h.** un país dominado por la psicosis de la guerra (**c**) *(laughter)* grandes carcajadas *fpl*, hilaridad *f*

hysteric [hɪsˈterɪk] *n* histérico(a) *m,f*

hysterical [hɪsˈterɪkəl] *adj* (**a**) *Psy* histérico(a) (**b**) *(uncontrolled)* histérico(a); **he's the h. type** es el típico histérico; **he was h. with grief** estaba histérico de dolor; **h. laughter** carcajadas histéricas (**c**) *Fam (very funny)* graciosísimo(a), divertidísimo(a), *Esp* la monda

hysterically [hɪsˈterɪklɪ] *adv* (**a**) *(uncontrolledly)* histéricamente; **he was waving his arms h.** agitaba los brazos como un histérico (**b**) *(hilariously)* **h. funny** para morirse de risa

hysterics [hɪsˈterɪks] *npl* (**a**) *(panic)* ataque *m* de histeria; **to go into** *or* **have (a fit of) h.** tener un ataque de histeria (**b**) *(laughter)* **we were in h.** nos desternillábamos de risa; **he had me in h.** me tenía muerto(a) *or* partido(a) *or Esp* tronchado(a) *or Esp* mondado(a) de risa

Hz *Elec* (*abbr* **Hertz**) Hz

I, i

I, i [aɪ] *n (letter)* I, i *f*

I [aɪ] *pron* yo *(usually omitted in Spanish, except for contrast)*; **I'm Canadian** soy canadiense; **I like red wine** me gusta el vino tinto; **I haven't got it!** ¡yo no lo tengo!; **my friend and I** mi amigo y yo; **I, for one, am in favour** yo, desde luego, estoy a favor; *Formal* **it is I** soy yo; *Formal* **it was I who did it** yo fui el que lo hizo

IA (*abbr* **Iowa**) Iowa

IAAF [aɪdʌbəleɪ'ef] *n* (*abbr* **International Amateur Athletics Federation**) IAAF *f*

IAEA [aɪeiː'eɪ] *n* (*abbr* **International Atomic Energy Agency**) AIEA *f*

iamb ['aɪæmb] *n* yambo *m*

iambic [aɪ'æmbɪk] *adj* yámbico(a) ▸▸ ***i. pentameter*** pentámetro *m* yámbico

IAP [aɪeɪ'piː] *n Comptr* (*abbr* **Internet Access Provider**) PSI *m*, proveedor *m* de servicios Internet

IATA [aɪ'ɑːtə] *n* (*abbr* **International Air Transport Association**) IATA *f*

IBA [aɪbiː'eɪ] *n* (*abbr* **Independent Broadcasting Authority**) = organismo regulador de las cadenas privadas de radio y televisión británicas

I-beam ['aɪbiːm] *n* (**a**) *Constr* viga *f* de doble T (**b**) *Comptr* ***I. pointer*** puntero *m* en forma de I

Iberia [aɪ'bɪərɪə] *n* Iberia *f*

Iberian [aɪ'biːrɪən] **1** *n* ibero(a) *m,f*, íbero(a) *m,f*
2 *adj* ibérico(a); **the I. peninsula** la península Ibérica

ibex ['aɪbeks] (*pl* **ibex** *or* **ibexes**) *n* íbice *m*, cabra *f* montés

IBF [aɪbiː'ef] *n* (*abbr* **International Boxing Federation**) IBF *f*, Federación *f* Internacional de Boxeo

ibid ['ɪbɪd] *adv* (*abbr* **ibidem**) ibíd., ib.

ibidem ['ɪbɪdem] *adv* ibídem

ibis ['aɪbɪs] (*pl* **ibis** *or* **ibises**) *n* ibis *m inv*

IBM [aɪbiː'em] *n Mil* (*abbr* **intercontinental ballistic missile**) misil *m* balístico intercontinental

IBRD [aɪbiːɑː'diː] *n* (*abbr* **International Bank for Reconstruction and Development**) BIRD *m*, Banco *m* Mundial

ibuprofen [aɪbjuː'prəʊfən] *n Pharm* ibuprofén *m*

i/c (*abbr* **in charge, in command**) al mando

Icarus ['ɪkərəs] *n Mythol* Ícaro

ICBM [aɪsiːbiː'em] *n* (*abbr* **intercontinental ballistic missile**) misil *m* balístico intercontinental

ice [aɪs] **1** *n* (**a**) *(frozen water)* hielo *m*; **to turn to i.** helarse, congelarse; **her feet were like i.** tenía los pies helados *or* como témpanos ▸▸ ***i. age*** glaciación *f*; ***i. axe*** piolet *m*; ***i. climbing*** cascadismo *m*; ***i. dance*** *or* ***dancing*** patinaje *m* artístico por parejas en la modalidad de danza; ***i. field*** campo *m* de hielo; ***i. floe*** témpano *m* (de hielo); ***i. hockey*** hockey *m* sobre hielo; ***i. pack*** *(pack ice)* banco *m* de hielo; *(ice bag)* bolsa *f* de hielo; ***i. rink*** pista *f* de hielo; ***i. scraper*** rascador *m* de hielo; ***i. sheet*** capa *f* de hielo; ***i. skate*** patín *m (de hielo)*; ***i. storm*** tormenta *f* de hielo; ***i. yacht*** rompehielos *m inv*
(**b**) *(ice cubes)* hielo *m*; **with i.?** *(in drink)* ¿con hielo? ▸▸ ***i. bucket*** cubitera *f*, *Am* cubetera *f*; ***i. cube*** cubito *m* de hielo; ***i. pick*** pico *m* para el hielo; ***i. tray*** bandeja *f* de los cubitos de hielo, *Am* cubetera *f*; ***i. water*** *(for drinking)* agua *f* con hielo
(**c**) *(edible)* **(chocolate/strawberry) i. cream** helado (de chocolate/de fresa); *Br* **an i.** un helado ▸▸ *Br* ***i. lolly*** polo *m*, *Bol, Col, Perú* paleta *f*, *RP* palito *m*
(**d**) *Fam (diamonds)* brillantes *mpl*
(**e**) IDIOMS **to put a project on i.** suspender *or Esp* aparcar un proyecto; **to break the i.** *(socially)* romper el hielo; **to be skating** *or* **treading on thin i.** estar jugándosela; **that cuts no i. with me** eso me deja frío *or RP* no me mueve un pelo
2 *vt* (**a**) *(chill) (drink)* poner *or* echar hielo en *or* a (**b**) *(cake)* glasear, *RP* cubrir con fondant (**c**) *Fam (kill)* dejar tieso, eliminar, liquidar

▸**ice over** **1** *vt sep* **to be iced over** *(pond, river)* estar helado(a) *or* congelado(a); *(window)* estar cubierto(a) de hielo *or* helado(a)
2 *vi (pond, river)* cubrirse de hielo, helarse; *(window)* cubrirse de hielo, helarse

▸**ice up** **1** *vt sep* **to be iced up** *(lock, windscreen)* estar cubierto(a) de hielo *or* helado(a); *(road)* estar cubierto(a) de hielo *or* helado(a)
2 *vi (lock, windscreen)* cubrirse de hielo, helarse; *(road)* cubrirse de hielo, helarse

iceberg ['aɪsbɜːg] *n* iceberg *m*; IDIOM **that's just the tip of the i.** eso es sólo la punta del iceberg ▸▸ ***i. lettuce*** lechuga *f* iceberg *or* repolluda

icebound ['aɪsbaʊnd] *adj (ship, port)* bloqueado(a) por el hielo

icebox ['aɪsbɒks] *n* (**a**) *Br (in fridge)* congelador *m* (**b**) *US (fridge)* nevera *f*, *RP* heladera *f*, *Méx* refrigerador *m*

icebreaker ['aɪs'breɪkə(r)] *n* (**a**) *(ship)* rompehielos *m inv* (**b**) *(at social occasion)* **this game's a good i.** este juego viene muy bien para romper el hielo

icecap ['aɪskæp] *n (on mountain)* nieves *fpl* perpetuas; *(at poles)* casquete *m* polar *or* glaciar

ice-cold ['aɪs'kəʊld] *adj* helado(a)

ice-cream ['aɪskriːm] *adj* ***i. cone*** helado *m* de cucurucho; *Br* ***i. cornet*** helado *m* de cucurucho; *US* ***i. parlor*** heladería *f*; *US* ***i. soda*** helado *m* con soda, *Esp* = helado de mantecado mezclado con agua con gas y algún sabor; *Br* ***i. van*** furgoneta *f* de helados

iced [aɪst] *adj* (**a**) *(containing ice)* ***i. tea*** té *m* frío *or* helado; ***i. water*** agua *f* con hielo (**b**) *(cake)* glaseado(a)

Iceland ['aɪslənd] *n* Islandia ▸▸ ***I. spar*** espato *m* de Islandia

Icelander ['aɪsləndə(r)] *n* islandés(esa) *m,f*

Icelandic [aɪs'lændɪk] **1** *n (language)* islandés *m*
2 *adj* islandés(esa)

iceman ['aɪsmæn] *n US* vendedor *m or* repartidor *m* de hielo

ice-skate ['aɪs'skeɪt] **1** *n* patín *m (de hielo)*
2 *vi* patinar sobre hielo

ice-skater ['aɪsskeɪtə(r)] *n* patinador(ora) *m,f* (sobre hielo)

ice-skating ['aɪs'skeɪtɪŋ] *n* patinaje *m* sobre hielo

I Ching [aɪ'tʃɪŋ] *n* I Ching *m*

ichthyologist [ɪkθɪ'ɒlədʒɪst] *n* ictiólogo(a) *m,f*

ichthyology [ɪkθɪ'ɒlədʒɪ] *n* ictiología *f*

ichthyosaur ['ɪkθɪəsɔː(r)], **ichthyosaurus** [ɪkθɪə'sɔːrəs] *n* ictiosauro *m*

icicle ['aɪsɪkəl] *n* carámbano *m*

icily ['aɪsɪlɪ] *adv (to look, say)* con gran frialdad; **to answer i.** contestar muy fríamente

iciness ['aɪsɪnɪs] *n* (**a**) *(of wind, water)* **I was surprised by the i. of the wind** me sorprendió lo gélido del viento (**b**) *(of voice, stare)* frialdad *f*

icing ['aɪsɪŋ] *n* (**a**) *(on cake)* glaseado *m*; IDIOM **the i. on the cake** la guinda ▸▸ *Br* ***i. sugar*** azúcar *m Esp, Méx* glas *or Esp* de lustre *or Chile* flor *or Col* pulverizado *or RP* impalpable (**b**) *(formation of ice)* formación *f* de hielo (**c**) *(in ice hockey)* icing *m*

icky ['ɪkɪ] *adj Fam* (**a**) *(repulsive)* asqueroso(a) (**b**) *(sentimental)* sentimentaloide, *Esp* ñoño(a)

icon ['aɪkɒn] *n* (**a**) *Art & Rel* icono *m* (**b**) *(symbol)* símbolo *m*, icono *m*; **a 60's i.** un símbolo *or* icono de los sesenta; **a gay i.** un icono gay (**c**) *Comptr* icono *m*

iconic [aɪ'kɒnɪk] *adj* icónico(a)

iconoclasm [aɪ'kɒnəklæzəm] *n* iconoclasia *f*, iconoclastia *f*

iconoclast [aɪ'kɒnəklæst] *n* iconoclasta *mf*

iconoclastic [aɪkɒnəʊ'klæstɪk] *adj* iconoclasta

iconographic(al) [aɪkɒnə'græfɪk(əl)] *adj* iconográfico(a)

iconography [aɪkə'nɒgrəfɪ] *n* iconografía *f*

iconology [aɪkə'nɒlədʒɪ] *n* iconología *f*

icosahedron [aɪkɒzəˈhiːdrən] *n Geom* icosaedro *m*

ICRC [aɪsiːɑːˈsiː] *n* (*abbr* **International Committee of the Red Cross**) CICR *m*

ICU [aɪsiːˈjuː] *n* (*abbr* **intensive-care unit**) UCI *f*, UVI *f*

ICVC [aɪsiːviːˈsiː] *n Fin* (*abbr* **investment company with variable capital**) SICAV *f*

icy [ˈaɪsɪ] *adj* (**a**) *(road)* con hielo; *(weather, water, wind)* helado(a), glacial; *(hands)* helado(a), congelado(a); **there are i. patches on some roads** hay placas de hielo en algunas carreteras (**b**) *(reception, stare, reply)* muy frío(a), gélido(a)

ID[1] [ˈaɪˈdiː] 1 *n* documentación *f* ▸▸ ***ID card*** carné *m* de identidad, *Esp* ≃ DNI *m*

2 *vt Fam* **to ID sb** identificar a alguien; **to be** *or* **to get ID'd** ser identificado(a)

ID[2] (*abbr* **Idaho**) Idaho

I'd [aɪd] = **I had, I would**

id [ɪd] *n Psy* id *m*

IDA [aɪdiːˈeɪ] *n* (*abbr* **International Development Association**) *Esp* AID *f*, *Am* AIF *f*

IDE [aɪdiːˈiː] *n Comptr* (*abbr* **integrated drive electronics**) IDE *m*

idea [aɪˈdɪə] *n* (**a**) *(individual notion, suggestion)* idea *f*; **I've had an i.** se me ha ocurrido una idea; **the i. of leaving you never entered my head** jamás se me pasó por la cabeza la idea de dejarte; **that's** *or* **there's an i.!** ¡ésa es una buena idea!; **what a good i.!** ¡qué buena idea!; **it seemed like a good i. at the time** entonces no parecía una mala idea; **it's a good i. to check first** no sería mala idea *or* no estaría mal comprobarlo antes; **it's a bad i. to do this alone** no es buena idea hacer esto solo; **it was a nice i. to phone** fue buena idea llamar; **he's an ideas man** es un hombre de ideas; **what gave you that i.?, what put that i. into your head?** ¿qué te hizo pensar eso?; **it wasn't MY i.!** ¡no fue idea mía!; **the very i.!** ¡es el colmo!, ¡vaya ideas!; *Fam* **what's the big i.?** ¿a qué viene esto?

(**b**) *(concept)* idea *f*, concepto *m*; **our ideas about the universe** nuestra idea *or* nuestro concepto del universo; **to get the i.** captar la idea, *Esp* enterarse; **to get ideas** hacerse ilusiones; **to give sb ideas, to put ideas into sb's head** meter ideas en la cabeza a alguien; **is this is your i. of a joke?** ¡pues vaya lo que entiendes tú por broma!; **you've got a funny i. of loyalty** tienes un curioso concepto de la lealtad; **sorry, but this is not my i. of fun** lo siento, pero no es esto lo que yo entiendo por diversión; **(I've) no i.** (no tengo) ni idea; **she had no i. what the time was** no tenía ni idea de la hora que era; **I had no i. that...** no tenía ni idea de que...; **I have a rough i. of what happened** tengo una vaga idea de lo que ocurrió; **I haven't the faintest** *or* **foggiest** *or* **slightest** *or* **remotest i.** no tengo (ni) la menor *or* (ni) la más remota idea

(**c**) *(plan)* **I thought the i. was for them to come here** creí que la idea era que ellos vinieran aquí; **the general i. is to...** la idea general es...

(**d**) *(objective, intention)* idea *f*, finalidad *f*; **the i. of the game** la finalidad del juego; **that's the whole i.!** ¡de eso se trata, precisamente!

(**e**) *(suspicion)* **to have an i. that...** tener la sensación de que...; **she had an i. that something was going to happen** tenía la sensación de que algo iba a suceder; **I've an idea that he'll succeed** me da la impresión de que lo va a conseguir

(**f**) *(estimate)* idea *f*; **can you give me an i. of how much it will cost?** ¿puede darme una idea de cuánto va a costar?

ideal [aɪˈdɪəl] 1 *n* (**a**) *(perfect example)* ideal *m*; **the Greek i. of beauty** el ideal de belleza griego (**b**) *(principle)* ideal *m*

2 *adj* ideal; **it's not i., but it'll have to do** no es lo ideal, pero ya nos arreglaremos; **in an i. world** en un mundo ideal ▸▸ *Phys* ***i. gas*** gas *m* ideal *or* perfecto

idealism [aɪˈdɪəlɪzəm] *n* idealismo *m*

idealist [aɪˈdɪəlɪst] *n* idealista *mf*

idealistic [aɪdɪəˈlɪstɪk] *adj* idealista

idealization [aɪdɪəlaɪˈzeɪʃən] *n* idealización *f*

idealize [aɪˈdɪəlaɪz] *vt* idealizar

ideally [aɪˈdɪəlɪ] *adv* (**a**) *(perfectly)* **they're i. matched** están hechos el uno para el otro; **i. situated** en una posición ideal (**b**) *(in a perfect world)* **i., we should all be there** lo ideal sería que estuviéramos todos

idée fixe [iːdeɪˈfiːks] (*pl* **idées fixes**) *n* idea *f* fija

idem [ˈaɪdem] *adv* en el lugar ya mencionado

ident [ˈaɪdent] *n TV* logo *m*

identical [aɪˈdentɪkəl] *adj* (**a**) *(exactly similar)* idéntico(a) (**to** *or* **with** a); **they were wearing i. dresses** llevaban el mismo modelo (de vestido) (**b**) *(one and the same)* mismísimo(a), exactamente el (la) mismo(a); **it was the i. one I'd seen before** era exactamente el mismo que yo había visto antes (**c**) ***i. twins*** gemelos(as) *m,fpl*

identically [aɪˈdentɪklɪ] *adv* exactamente igual, de manera idéntica

identifiable [aɪdentɪˈfaɪəbəl] *adj* identificable; **it was not easily i.** no se podía identificar fácilmente

identification [aɪdentɪfɪˈkeɪʃən] *n* (**a**) *(of body, criminal)* identificación *f* ▸▸ *Br* ***i. parade*** rueda *f* de reconocimento *or* identificación (**b**) *(documents)* documentación *f*; **the police asked me for i.** la policía me pidió los documentos (**c**) *(association)* identificación *f*

identifier [aɪˈdentɪfaɪə(r)] *n Comptr* identificador *m*

identify [aɪˈdentɪfaɪ] 1 *vt* (**a**) *(recognize, name)* identificar; **to i. oneself** identificarse; **the winner has asked not to be identified** el ganador ha pedido que no se revele su identidad

(**b**) *(distinguish) (of physical feature, badge)* identificar; **she wore a red rose to i. herself** llevaba una rosa roja para que se la pudiera identificar; **his accent immediately identified him as an outsider** su acento en seguida lo identificó como alguien de fuera

(**c**) *(acknowledge) (difficulty, issue)* identificar; **the report identifies two major problems** el informe identifica dos problemas fundamentales

(**d**) *(associate)* **to i. sth with sth** identificar algo con algo; **to i. oneself with a cause** sentirse identificado(a) *or* identificarse con una causa; **he has long been identified with right-wing groups** hace tiempo que se lo identifica *or* asocia con grupos de la derecha

2 *vi* **to i. with sth/sb** identificarse con algo/alguien; **I can i. with the way she feels** me imagino cómo se siente

identifying mark [aɪˈdentɪfaɪɪŋˈmɑːk] *n* seña *f* de identidad

Identikit® [aɪˈdentɪkɪt] *n* **I. (picture)** retrato *m* robot

identity [aɪˈdentɪtɪ] *n* (**a**) *(name, set of characteristics)* identidad *f*; **to reveal/conceal sb's i.** revelar/ocultar la identidad de alguien; **a case of mistaken i.** un caso de identificación errónea ▸▸ ***i. badge*** tarjeta *f* identificativa; ***i. bracelet*** pulsera *f* de identificación; ***i. card*** carné *m* de identidad, *Esp* ≃ DNI *m*; *Br Mil* ***i. disc*** placa *f* de identificación; *Br* ***i. parade*** rueda *f* de reconocimento *or* identificación; *Mil* ***i. tag*** placa *f* de identificación

(**b**) *(sense of self)* identidad *f* ▸▸ ***i. crisis*** crisis *f inv* de identidad

ideogram [ˈɪdɪəgræm], **ideograph** [ˈɪdɪəgrɑːf] *n* ideograma *m*

ideographical [ɪdɪəˈgræfɪkəl] *adj* ideográfico(a)

ideography [ɪdɪˈɒgrəfɪ] *n* ideografía *f*

ideological [aɪdɪəˈlɒdʒɪkəl] *adj* ideológico(a)

ideologically [aɪdɪəˈlɒdʒɪklɪ] *adv* ideológicamente

ideologist [aɪdɪˈɒlədʒɪst] *n* ideólogo(a) *m,f*

ideologue [ˈaɪdɪəlɒg] *adj Pej* ideólogo(a) *m,f*

ideology [aɪdɪˈɒlədʒɪ] *n* ideología *f*

ides [aɪdz] *n Hist* idus *mpl*; **the I. of March** los idus de marzo

idiocy [ˈɪdɪəsɪ] *n* idiotez *f*, estupidez *f*

idiolect [ˈɪdɪəlekt] *n Ling* idiolecto *m*

idiom [ˈɪdɪəm] *n* (**a**) *(expression)* modismo *m*, giro *m* (**b**) *(dialect)* lenguaje *m* (**c**) *(style) (of music, writing)* lenguaje *m*, estilo *m*, corte *m*, aire *m*

idiomatic [ɪdɪəˈmætɪk] *adj* **his English isn't very i.** su inglés no suena muy natural ▸▸ ***i. expression*** modismo *m*, giro *m*

idiomatically [ɪdɪəˈmætɪklɪ] *adv* con modismos *or* giros idiomáticos

idiosyncrasy [ɪdɪəʊˈsɪŋkrəsɪ] *n* peculiaridad *f*, particularidad *f*

idiosyncratic [ɪdɪəʊsɪŋˈkrætɪk] *adj* peculiar, particular

idiot [ˈɪdɪət] *n* (**a**) *(fool)* idiota *mf*, estúpido(a) *m,f*; **you i.!** ¡idiota!, ¡imbécil!; **don't be an i.!** ¡no seas bobo(a) *or Esp* memo(a)!; **that i. Harry** el idiota de Harry ▸▸ *Fam* ***i. board*** teleapuntador *m*; *US* ***i. light*** chivato *m* (**b**) *(retarded person)* idiota *mf* ▸▸ *Psy* ***i. savant*** idiot *m* savant, idiota *m* sabio

idiotic [ɪdɪˈɒtɪk] *adj* idiota, estúpido(a)

idiotically [ɪdɪˈɒtɪklɪ] *adv* estúpidamente; **he behaved i.** se comportó como un idiota; **he smiled i.** sonrió de un modo estúpido

idiot-proof [ˈɪdɪətpruːf] *Fam* 1 *adj (system, machine)* a prueba de idiotas

2 *vt* garantizar a prueba de idiotas

idle [ˈaɪdəl] 1 *adj* (**a**) *(unoccupied, unused) (person)* ocioso(a), desocupado(a); *(factory, machine)* inactivo(a); **an i. moment** un momento libre; **to lie i.** *(factory)* permanecer parado(a); *(money)* permanecer improductivo(a); **1,500 men have been made i.** 1.500 hombres se han quedado sin trabajo

(**b**) *(lazy)* vago(a); **he's an i. good-for-nothing** es un holgazán *or Esp* penco que no sirve para nada; **the i. rich** los rentistas *or* ricos ociosos

(**c**) *(futile) (threat, boast)* vano(a); *(gossip, rumour)* frívolo(a); **it would be i. to speculate** sería ocioso hacer conjeturas

(**d**) *(casual)* **an i. glance** una mirada ocasional *or* casual; **i. curiosity** mera curiosidad

2 *vt US (make unemployed)* dejar sin empleo *or Esp* en el paro *or Am* desocupado(a)
3 *vi (engine)* estar en punto muerto
▸**idle away** *vt sep* pasar ociosamente

idleness ['aɪdəlnɪs] *n* (**a**) *(inaction)* ociosidad *f*, inactividad *f* (**b**) *(laziness)* vagancia *f* (**c**) *(futility)* banalidad *f*; **the i. of the threats** la banalidad de las amenazas

idler ['aɪdlə(r)] *n (lazy person)* vago(a) *m,f*

idly ['aɪdlɪ] *adv* (**a**) *(inactively)* ociosamente; **to stand i. by** estar sin hacer nada (**b**) *(lazily)* indolentemente (**c**) *(casually)* despreocupadamente

idol ['aɪdəl] *n* ídolo *m*; **a 1970s pop i.** un ídolo del pop de los setenta

idolater [aɪ'dɒlətə(r)] *n* idólatra *mf*

idolatress [aɪ'dɒlətrɪs] *n* idólatra *f*

idolatrous [aɪ'dɒlətrəs] *adj* idólatra

idolatry [aɪ'dɒlətrɪ] *n* idolatría *f*

idolize ['aɪdəlaɪz] *vt* idolatrar

idyll ['ɪdɪl] *n* idilio *m*

idyllic [ɪ'dɪlɪk] *adj* idílico(a)

idyllically [ɪ'dɪlɪklɪ] *adv* idílicamente

i.e. ['aɪ'iː] (*abbr* **id est**) i.e., es decir

IF [ɪf] **1** *n* **ifs and buts** *Esp* pegas *fpl*, *Am* peros *mpl*; **no ifs(, ands) or buts** no hay pero que valga; **if we win, and it's a big if,...** en el caso hipotético de que ganáramos,...
2 *conj* (**a**) *(conditional)* si; **if the weather's good** si hace buen tiempo; **if you hadn't arrived right then...** si no hubieras llegado en ese momento...; **if I were rich** si fuese rico; **if I were you** yo en tu lugar, yo de ti; **would you mind if I smoked?** ¿te importa que fume?; **sorry if I've upset you** perdona si te he disgustado
(**b**) *(whenever)* si, cuando; **if you click here, a help menu appears** si *or* cuando haces clic aquí, aparece un menú de ayuda
(**c**) *(whether)* si; **I asked if it was true** pregunté si era verdad
(**d**) *(conceding)* si bien; **the movie was good, if rather long** la película fue buena, si bien un poco larga
(**e**) *(qualifying)* **we get little, if any snow** nieva muy poco, a veces nada; **which, if any, do you prefer?** ¿cuál prefieres, si es que te gusta alguno?; **if anything it's better** en todo caso, es mejor, si acaso, es mejor; **he sees them rarely, if at all** *or* **if ever** apenas los ve; **I'll be finished by Monday, if not earlier** habré terminado el lunes, si no antes
(**f**) *(in polite requests)* **if I could just interrupt for a second...** ¿me permites una pequeña interrupción?; **would you like me to wrap it for you? – if you would, please** ¿quiere que se lo envuelva? – si me hace el favor
(**g**) *(in phrases)* **if and when...** en caso de que...; **I'll talk to her if and when the occasion arises** hablaré con ella sólo si se presenta la ocasión; **if ever someone deserved the award it's her** si hay alguien que de verdad se merezca *or Am* amerite ese premio, es ella; **that's a pathetic excuse if ever there was one!** ¡es la peor excusa que he oído en mi vida!; **if it isn't my old friend James!** ¡caramba, pero si es mi amigo James!; **if necessary** si es preciso *or* necesario; **if not** si no; **it's colourful, if nothing else** por lo menos no se puede decir que no sea colorido; **if so** en ese caso; **if you ask me** si quieres saber mi opinión
3 **if only** *conj* (**a**) *(providing a reason)* **I'll let you go, if only to keep you quiet** te dejaré ir, aunque sólo sea para que te calles
(**b**) *(expressing a wish)* ¡ojalá!; **if only I had more money!** ¡ojalá tuviera más dinero!; **if only they knew!, if they only knew!** ¡si ellos supieran!; **if only we'd known** si lo hubiéramos sabido

---

IFA [aɪef'eɪ] *n Br* (*abbr* **independent financial adviser**) asesor(ora) *m,f* financiero(a) independiente

iffy ['ɪfɪ] *adj Fam* (**a**) *(doubtful, unreliable)* dudoso(a); *Br* **my stomach's been a bit i. lately** estoy un poco pachucho del estómago últimamente; **the brakes are a bit i.** los frenos no van *or* andan demasiado bien (**b**) *(suspicious)* sospechoso(a); **it all sounded rather i.** todo aquello daba muy mala espina

igloo ['ɪgluː] (*pl* **igloos**) *n* iglú *m*

igneous ['ɪgnɪəs] *adj Geol (rock)* ígneo(a)

ignite [ɪg'naɪt] **1** *vt (fire, conflict)* prender, encender
2 *vi (fire, conflict)* prender, encenderse

ignition [ɪg'nɪʃən] *n* (**a**) *Aut* encendido *m*, contacto *m*; **to turn on the i.** arrancar, dar al contacto; **the key was still in the i.** la llave aún estaba en el contacto ▸▸ ***i. coil*** bobina *f* de encendido; ***i. key*** llave *f* de contacto (**b**) *Chem* ***i. temperature*** temperatura *f* de combustión *or* ignición

ignoble [ɪg'nəʊbəl] *adj* innoble, indigno(a)

ignominious [ɪgnə'mɪnɪəs] *adj* ignominioso(a)

ignominiously [ɪgnə'mɪnɪəslɪ] *adv* de forma ignominiosa, ignominiosamente

ignominy ['ɪgnəmɪnɪ] *n* ignominia *f*

ignoramus [ɪgnə'reɪməs] *n* ignorante *mf*

ignorance ['ɪgnərəns] *n* ignorancia *f*; **out of** *or* **through i.** por ignorancia; **to keep sb in i. (of)** mantener a alguien en la ignorancia (acerca de); **forgive my i., but...** disculpa mi ignorancia, pero...; **i. of the law is no excuse** el desconocimiento de la ley no exime de su cumplimiento; PROV **i. is bliss** es mejor no saber

ignorant ['ɪgnərənt] *adj* (**a**) *(uneducated)* inculto(a); **I'm really i. about classical music/politics** soy un perfecto ignorante en materia de música clásica/política (**b**) *(lacking knowledge)* ignorante; **to be i. of sth** ignorar algo; **I was i. as to his whereabouts** desconocía su paradero; **he was i. of the facts** ignoraba los hechos (**c**) *Fam (bad-mannered)* grosero(a), maleducado(a)

ignore [ɪg'nɔː(r)] *vt* (**a**) *(pay no attention to) (person)* no hacer caso a; *(remark)* no prestar atención a; *(letter, signal)* hacer caso omiso de; **she completely ignored me all evening** me hizo el vacío toda la tarde, *Esp* pasó de mí por completo toda la tarde; **I'll i. that!** *(what you said)* ¡yo no he oído nada!; **just i. him!** ¡no le hagas caso!
(**b**) *(take no account of) (warning, advice, order)* no hacer caso de, no tomar en cuenta; **he ignored the doctor's advice and continued smoking** hizo oídos sordos del consejo del médico y siguió fumando
(**c**) *(overlook)* **we can't i. it this time!** ¡esta vez debemos tenerlo en cuenta!; **the report ignores certain crucial facts** el informe pasa por alto determinados hechos decisivos

iguana [ɪg'wɑːnə] *n* iguana *f*

iguanodon [ɪ'gwɑːnədɒn] *n* iguanodonte *m*

IIRC *Comptr* (*abbr* **if I remember correctly**) si mal no recuerdo

ikon = **icon**

IL (*abbr* **Illinois**) Illinois

ileum ['ɪlɪəm] (*pl* **ilea** ['ɪlɪə]) *n Anat* íleon *m*

ilex ['aɪleks] *n Bot* (**a**) *(shrub)* ilicínea *f* (**b**) *(holm oak)* encina *f*

ilium ['ɪlɪəm] (*pl* **ilia** ['ɪlɪə]) *n Anat* ilion *m*, íleon *m*

ilk [ɪlk] *n* **of that i.** por el estilo

I'll [aɪl] = **I will, I shall**

ill [ɪl] **1** *n* (**a**) *Literary (evil)* mal *m*; **for good or i.** *(whatever happens)* para bien o para mal (**b**) *(difficulty, trouble)* mal *m*; **the nation's ills** los males que aquejan a la nación
2 *adj* (**a**) *(unwell)* enfermo(a); **to be i.** estar enfermo(a) *or* malo(a); **to fall** *or* **be taken i.** caer enfermo(a) *or* malo(a); **that smell is making me i.** ese olor me está *Esp* poniendo enfermo(a) *or Am* enfermando; **I feel i. just thinking about it** *Esp* me pongo malo(a) *or Am* me enfermo sólo de pensarlo
(**b**) *(bad, poor)* **i. effects** efectos indeseables; **i. feeling** rencor; **i. fortune** *or* **luck** mala suerte *or* fortuna; **to be in i. health** tener mala salud; **to be** *or* **feel i. at ease** no sentirse a gusto, sentirse incómodo(a); **i. will** rencor; PROV **it's an i. wind (that blows nobody any good)** no hay mal que por bien no venga
3 *adv* (**a**) *(badly)* mal; **to speak/think i. of sb** hablar/pensar mal de alguien; **it i. becomes** *or* **befits you to criticize** ¡mira quién habla!; **to augur** *or* **bode i. (for)** no augurar nada bueno (para) (**b**) *(hardly)* **I can i. afford it** apenas me lo puedo permitir; **we can i. afford to wait** prácticamente no podemos esperar

ill. (*abbr* **illustration**) ilustración *f*

ill-advised ['ɪləd'vaɪzd] *adj* imprudente, desacertado(a); **you'd be i. to complain** harías mal en quejarte

ill-advisedly ['ɪləd'vaɪzɪdlɪ] *adv* de manera imprudente

ill-assorted ['ɪlə'sɔːtɪd] *adj (group, collection)* dispar, variopinto(a); *(couple)* incompatible

ill-bred ['ɪl'bred] *adj* maleducado(a)

ill-concealed ['ɪlkən'siːld] *adj (disappointment, disgust)* mal disimulado(a)

ill-considered ['ɪlkən'sɪdəd] *adj (remark, decision)* irreflexivo(a), precipitado(a)

ill-defined ['ɪldɪ'faɪnd] *adj* difuso(a)

ill-disposed ['ɪldɪs'pəʊzd] *adj (unfriendly, unhelpful)* **to be i. towards sb** tener mala disposición hacia alguien; **to be i. towards an idea/a proposal** ser contrario(a) *or* refractario(a) a una idea/propuesta

illegal [ɪ'liːgəl] *adj* (**a**) *(unlawful)* ilegal, ilícito(a); **i. immigrant** *or US* **alien** inmigrante ilegal (**b**) *Comptr (character, instruction)* ilegal

illegality [ɪlɪ'gælɪtɪ] *n* ilegalidad *f*

illegally [ɪ'li:gəlɪ] *adv* ilegalmente, de forma ilegal; **to be i. parked** estar estacionado(a) *or Esp* aparcado(a) en lugar prohibido

illegibility [ɪledʒɪ'bɪlɪtɪ] *n* ilegibilidad *f*

illegible [ɪ'ledʒɪbəl] *adj* ilegible

illegibly [ɪ'ledʒəblɪ] *adv* de manera ilegible

illegitimacy [ɪlɪ'dʒɪtɪməsɪ] *n* **(a)** *(of child)* ilegitimidad *f* **(b)** *(of activity, claim)* ilicitud *f*, ilegalidad *f* **(c)** *(of argument)* falta *f* de validez

illegitimate [ɪlɪ'dʒɪtɪmət] *adj* **(a)** *(child)* ilegítimo(a) **(b)** *(activity, claim)* ilícito(a), ilegal **(c)** *(argument)* inválido(a)

ill-equipped ['ɪlɪ'kwɪpd] *adj* **(a)** *(lacking equipment)* mal equipado(a) **(b)** *(lacking skill, experience)* **to be i. to do sth** no estar preparado(a) para hacer algo; **he is i. to handle the situation** no está capacitado para hacer frente a la situación

ill-fated ['ɪl'feɪtɪd] *adj (day, occasion)* aciago(a); *(enterprise)* infausto(a), desdichado(a)

ill-favoured, *US* **ill-favored** [ɪl'feɪvəd] *adj (unattractive)* poco agraciado(a)

ill-fitting ['ɪl'fɪtɪŋ] *adj* **an i. dress** un vestido que no queda bien; **an i. lid** una tapa que no ajusta bien

ill-founded ['ɪl'faʊndɪd] *adj* infundado(a)

ill-gotten gains ['ɪlgɒtən'geɪnz] *npl* ganancias *fpl* obtenidas por medios ilícitos

ill-humoured, *US* **ill-humored** ['ɪl'hju:məd] *adj* malhumorado(a); **to be i.** estar de mal humor; **an i. comment** un comentario destemplado

illiberal [ɪ'lɪbərəl] *adj Formal* **(a)** *(narrow-minded)* intolerante **(b)** *(ungenerous)* cicatero(a), mezquino(a)

illicit [ɪ'lɪsɪt] *adj* ilícito(a); **an i. still** una destilería ilegal

illicitly [ɪ'lɪsɪtlɪ] *adv* de manera ilícita, ilícitamente

ill-informed ['ɪlɪn'fɔ:md] *adj* **(a)** *(having the wrong information) (person)* mal informado(a) **(b)** *(having insufficient information)* poco informado(a); **an i. decision** una decisión basada en datos incompletos; **we continue to be i. about their intentions** seguimos sin saber bien cuáles son sus intenciones

ill-intentioned ['ɪlɪn'tenʃənd] *adj* malintencionado(a)

illiteracy [ɪ'lɪtərəsɪ] *n* analfabetismo *m*

illiterate [ɪ'lɪtərət] **1** *adj* **(a)** *(unable to read or write)* analfabeto(a) **(b)** *(ignorant)* **to be scientifically i.** no tener conocimientos científicos **(c)** *(usage, style)* analfabeto(a), ignorante
2 *n* analfabeto(a) *m,f*

ill-judged ['ɪldʒʌdʒd] *adj* imprudente; **an i. move** un error de cálculo

ill-kempt ['ɪl'kempt] *adj* **(a)** *(hair)* desordenado(a), despeinado(a); *(personal appearance)* descuidado(a), *RP* desprolijo(a) **(b)** *(garden)* abandonado(a), descuidado(a)

ill-mannered ['ɪl'mænəd] *adj* maleducado(a); **an i. reply** una respuesta grosera *or* descortés

ill-natured ['ɪl'neɪtʃəd] *adj* malévolo(a)

illness ['ɪlnɪs] *n* enfermedad *f*

illocutionary [ɪlə'kju:ʃənərɪ] *adj Ling* ilocutivo(a), ilocucionario(a); **i. force** fuerza ilocutiva *or* ilocucionaria

illogical [ɪ'lɒdʒɪkəl] *adj* ilógico(a)

illogicality [ɪlɒdʒɪ'kælɪtɪ] *n* falta *f* de lógica, incongruencia *f*

illogically [ɪ'lɒdʒɪklɪ] *adv* de forma ilógica, de manera incongruente

ill-prepared ['ɪlprɪ'peəd] *adj* poco preparado(a)

ill-qualified ['ɪl'kwɒlɪfaɪd] *adj (lacking knowledge)* poco capacitado(a) *or* cualificado(a); *(lacking experience)* poco capacitado(a)

ill-spoken ['ɪl'spəʊkən] *adj* malhablado(a)

ill-starred ['ɪl'stɑ:d] *adj Literary (person)* desventurado(a), malaventurado(a); *(plan, attempt)* malhadado(a), desafortunado(a)

ill-suited ['ɪl'su:tɪd] *adj (not appropriate)* inadecuado(a) (**to** para); **arts graduates are i. to this job** los licenciados en letras no se adecuan bien a este trabajo

ill-tempered ['ɪl'tempəd] *adj (person)* malhumorado(a); *(meeting, exchange)* agrio(a); *(match, occasion)* brusco(a), áspero(a)

ill-timed ['ɪl'taɪmd] *adj* inoportuno(a)

ill-treat ['ɪl'tri:t] *vt* maltratar

ill-treatment [ɪl'tri:tmənt] *n* malos tratos *mpl*; **to be subjected to i.** ser objeto de *or* recibir malos tratos

illuminate [ɪ'lu:mɪneɪt] *vt* **(a)** *(light up)* iluminar **(b)** *(clarify)* ilustrar **(c)** *(manuscript)* iluminar

illuminated [ɪ'lu:mɪneɪtɪd] *adj (manuscript)* iluminado(a) ►► ***i. sign*** anuncio *m or* letrero *m* luminoso

illuminating [ɪ'lu:mɪneɪtɪŋ] *adj* ilustrativo(a), iluminador(ora)

illumination [ɪlʊmɪ'neɪʃən] *n* **(a)** *(lighting)* iluminación *f*; **a candle was the only means of i.** la única fuente de luz era una vela **(b)** *(clarification)* explicación *f*, aclaración *f*; **his answer provided little i.** su respuesta no resultó muy ilustrativa **(c) illuminations** *(decorative lights)* iluminación *f*

illumine [ɪ'lju:mɪn] *vt Literary* iluminar

ill-use 1 *n* ['ɪl'ju:s] maltrato *m*
2 *vt* ['ɪl'ju:z] maltratar; **to feel ill-used** sentirse maltratado(a)

illusion [ɪ'lu:ʒən] *n* **(a)** *(false impression)* ilusión *f*; **mirrors give an i. of space** los espejos crean *or* dan sensación de espacio **(b)** *(false belief)* ilusión *f*; **to be under the i. that...** hacerse la ilusión de que...; **I was under no illusions about the risk** no me engañaba respecto al peligro; **she has no illusions about her chances of success** no se hace ilusiones acerca de las posibilidades de éxito

illusionist [ɪ'lu:ʒənɪst] *n* ilusionista *mf*

illusory [ɪ'lu:sərɪ] *adj Formal* ilusorio(a)

illustrate ['ɪləstreɪt] *vt* **(a)** *(with pictures)* ilustrar; **the lecture will be illustrated by slides** la conferencia irá acompañada de una proyección de diapositivas **(b)** *(demonstrate)* evidenciar, manifestar; **this clearly illustrates the danger** esto evidencia claramente el peligro existente

illustrated ['ɪləstreɪtɪd] *adj* ilustrado(a) ►► ***i. feature*** *(in magazine)* reportaje *m* gráfico

illustration [ɪləs'treɪʃən] *n* **(a)** *(picture)* ilustración *f* **(b)** *(example)* ejemplo *m*; **by way of i.** a modo de ejemplo **(c)** *Comptr* ***i. software*** software *m* de diseño gráfico

illustrative ['ɪlʌstrətɪv] *adj* ilustrativo(a); **to be i. of sth** ilustrar algo; **this crisis is i. of the problems in the economy** esta crisis ilustra bien a las claras *or* pone de manifiesto los problemas de la economía; **i. examples** ejemplos ilustrativos

illustrator ['ɪləstreɪtə(r)] *n* ilustrador(ora) *m,f*

illustrious [ɪ'lʌstrɪəs] *adj* ilustre, insigne

ILO [aɪe'ləʊ] *n* (*abbr* **International Labour Organization**) OIT *f*

I'm [aɪm] = **I am**

image ['ɪmɪdʒ] *n* **(a)** *(mental picture)* imagen *f*; **you have the wrong i. of life in New York** tienes una falsa imagen de lo que es vivir en Nueva York
(b) *(public appearance)* imagen *f*; **to improve one's i.** mejorar la imagen; **the party wants to change its i.** el partido quiere cambiar de imagen; **they have an i. problem** tienen un problema de imagen ►► ***i. consultant*** asesor(a) *m,f* de imagen; ***i. maker*** creador(ora) *m,f* de imagen
(c) *(likeness)* imagen *f*; **man was made in God's i.** Dios hizo al hombre a su imagen (y semejanza); **he's the i. of his father** es la viva imagen *or* el vivo retrato de su padre
(d) *(in art, literature)* imagen *f*
(e) *Comptr & Phot* imagen *f* ►► ***i. bank*** banco *m* de imágenes; ***i. enhancement*** realce *m or* mejora *f* de imagen; ***i. format*** formato *m* de imagen; ***i. intensifier*** *(in radiology)* intensificador *m* de imagen; ***i. processing*** tratamiento *m* de imagen

image-conscious ['ɪmɪdʒ'kɒnʃəs] *adj* preocupado(a) por la propia imagen; **film stars are very i.** a las estrellas de cine les preocupa mucho su imagen

imagery ['ɪmɪdʒərɪ] *n* **(a)** *(pictures)* imágenes *fpl* **(b)** *(in literature)* imaginería *f*

imagesetter ['ɪmɪdʒsetə(r)] *n* filmadora *f*

imaginable [ɪ'mædʒɪnəbəl] *adj* imaginable; **the best/worst thing i.** lo mejor/peor que se pueda imaginar

imaginary [ɪ'mædʒɪnərɪ] *adj* **(a)** *(danger, being)* imaginario(a), ficticio(a); **i. being** ente de razón **(b)** *Math* ***i. number*** número *m* imaginario

imagination [ɪmædʒɪ'neɪʃən] *n* imaginación *f*; **to have no i.** no tener imaginación; **to capture sb's i.** atraer *or* despertar el interés de alguien; **she tends to let her i. run away with her** tiende a dar rienda suelta a la imaginación; **it's all in your i.** son imaginaciones *or Am* fantasías tuyas; **is it just my i., or...** son imaginaciones *or Am* fantasías mías o...; **use your i.!** ¡usa la imaginación!

imaginative [ɪ'mædʒɪnətɪv] *adj* imaginativo(a)

imaginatively [ɪ'mædʒɪnətɪvlɪ] *adv* imaginativamente, con imaginación; **an i. designed collection** una colección de imaginativos *or* originales diseños

imagine [ɪ'mædʒɪn] **1** *vt* **(a)** *(mentally picture)* imaginar, imaginarse; **i. (that) you're on a beach** imagínate que estás en una playa; **to i. sb doing sth** imaginarse a alguien haciendo algo; **i. winning all that money!** ¡imagínate ganar todo ese dinero!; **i. meeting you here!** ¡qué sorpresa verte aquí!; **I had imagined it to be very different** me lo había imaginado de otra forma; **I can't i. what he wants** no tengo ni idea de qué es lo que quiere; **you can't i. how awful it was!** ¡no te imaginas lo espantoso que fue!; **i. my disgust/surprise** imagínate *or* figúrate mi indignación/sorpresa

(**b**) *(mistakenly see, hear, remember)* imaginar, imaginarse; **you must have imagined it** te lo habrás imaginado; **you're imagining things** son imaginaciones *or Am* fantasías tuyas

(**c**) *(suppose, think)* imaginar, imaginarse; **I i. that you must be very tired** (me) imagino que debes de estar muy cansado; **as you can i., I was most annoyed** como te puedes figurar *or* imaginar, estaba muy enojado; **I i. so** me lo imaginaba *or* figuraba; **don't i. I'll help you again** no creas que voy a volver a ayudarte

2 *vi* **just i.** imagínate; **what could he want with a barrel organ? – I can't i.** ¿para qué querrá un organillo? – no me lo puedo imaginar; **it was hilarious – I can i.!** fue divertidísimo – ¡(ya) me (lo) imagino!

imagines *pl of* **imago**

imaginings [ɪ'mædʒɪnɪŋs] *npl* imaginaciones *fpl*, figuraciones *fpl*, *Am* fantasías *fpl*; **never in my worst i. did I think it would come to this** jamás en la vida imaginé que podría acabar así

imagism ['ɪmədʒɪzəm] *n Lit* imaginismo *m*, imagismo *m*

imagist ['ɪmədʒɪst] *Lit* 1 *n* imaginista *mf*, imagista *mf*

2 *adj* imaginista, imagista; **i. poetry** poesía imaginista *or* imagista

imago [ɪ'meɪgəʊ] (*pl* **imagos** *or* **imagines** [ɪ'meɪdʒɪni:z]) *n* (**a**) *Zool* imago *m* (**b**) *Psy* imago *f*

imam [ɪ'mɑ:m] *n Rel* imán *m*, imam *m*

IMAX® ['aɪmæks] *n Cin* Imax® *m*

imbalance [ɪm'bæləns] *n* desequilibrio *m*

imbecile ['ɪmbɪsi:l] *n* (**a**) *(idiot)* imbécil *mf*, idiota *mf* (**b**) *Old-fashioned Psy* imbécil *mf*

imbecility [ɪmbɪ'sɪlɪtɪ] *n Formal (stupidity)* imbecilidad *f*, idiotez *f*

imbibe [ɪm'baɪb] 1 *vt* (**a**) *Formal or Hum (drink)* ingerir (**b**) *(knowledge, ideas)* absorber, embeber

2 *vi Hum* libar

imbroglio [ɪm'brɒlɪəʊ] *n* embrollo *m*

imbue [ɪm'bju:] *vt Formal* **to i. sb with sth** inculcar algo a alguien; **to be imbued with sth** estar imbuido(a) de algo; **his words were imbued with resentment** sus palabras rezumaban resentimiento

IMF [aɪe'mef] *n* (*abbr* **International Monetary Fund**) FMI *m*

IMHO *Comptr* (*abbr* **in my humble opinion**) IMHO, = en mi humilde opinión

imitable ['ɪmɪtəbəl] *adj* imitable

imitate ['ɪmɪteɪt] *vt* (**a**) *(copy) (person)* imitar; **to i. sb's style** imitar el estilo de alguien (**b**) *(mimic) (person, bird)* imitar; **to i. its surroundings** *(of insect)* confundirse con su entorno

imitation [ɪmɪ'teɪʃən] 1 *n* (**a**) *(action)* imitación *f*; **to learn by i.** aprender por imitación; **in i. of** a imitación de, imitando a; PROV **i. is the sincerest form of flattery** no hay halago mejor que el ser objeto de imitación (**b**) *(copy)* imitación *f*; **beware of imitations** *(sign)* rechace imitaciones, *Am* cuidado con las imitaciones

2 *adj* ***i. fur*** piel *f* sintética; ***i. jewellery*** bisutería *f*, *RP* bijouterie *f*; ***i. leather*** *Esp, Méx* piel *f* sintética, *Andes, CAm, Carib, RP* cuero *m* sintético

imitative ['ɪmɪtətɪv] *adj* imitativo(a); **its colouring is i. of a poisonous butterfly** su color imita el de una mariposa venenosa

imitator ['ɪmɪteɪtə(r)] *n* imitador(ora) *m,f*

immaculate [ɪ'mækjʊlət] *adj* (**a**) *(very clean, tidy)* inmaculado(a) (**b**) *(performance, rendition, taste)* impecable (**c**) *Rel* ***the I. Conception*** la Inmaculada Concepción

immaculately [ɪ'mækjʊlətlɪ] *adv* (**a**) *(clean, tidy)* inmaculadamente; **i. turned out/dressed** impecablemente arreglado(a)/vestido(a) (**b**) *(performed, played)* impecablemente

immanence ['ɪmənəns], **immanency** ['ɪmənənsɪ] *n* inmanencia *f*

immanent ['ɪmənənt] *adj* inmanente

immaterial [ɪmə'tɪərɪəl] *adj* (**a**) *(unimportant)* irrelevante; **that's quite i.** eso no tiene ninguna importancia; **whether I was there or not is i.** si estuve o no allí es totalmente irrelevante (**b**) *(incorporeal)* inmaterial

immature [ɪmə'tjʊə(r)] *adj* (**a**) *(childish)* inmaduro(a); **stop being so i.!** ¡deja de actuar como un(a) niño(a), ¡no seas inmaduro(a)! (**b**) *(animal, fruit)* inmaduro(a)

immaturely [ɪmə'tjʊəlɪ] *adv* con poca madurez, de forma inmadura

immaturity [ɪmə'tjʊərɪtɪ] *n* (**a**) *(childishness)* inmadurez *f* (**b**) *(of animal, fruit)* inmadurez *f*

immeasurable [ɪ'meʒərəbəl] *adj* (**a**) *(size, distance)* inconmensurable (**b**) *Fig* incalculable, inmenso(a); **to have an i. influence on sth** tener una enorme influencia en algo

immeasurably [ɪ'meʒərəblɪ] *adv* (**a**) *(long, high)* inmensamente, infinitamente (**b**) *(better, improved)* infinitamente, sumamente

immediacy [ɪ'mi:dɪəsɪ] *n* inmediatez *f*, proximidad *f*; **the i. of the danger** la inminencia *or* proximidad del peligro

immediate [ɪ'mi:dɪət] *adj* (**a**) *(instant)* inmediato(a); **the problem needs i. attention** el problema requiere atención inmediata; **to come into** *or* **have i. effect** entrar en vigor de manera inmediata

(**b**) *(close in time)* inmediato(a); **in the i. future** en un futuro inmediato; **enough to satisfy i. needs** suficiente para cubrir las necesidades más inmediatas *or* perentorias; **my i. objective** mi objetivo inmediato; **I have no i. plans to retire** la jubilación no figura entre mis planes inmediatos

(**c**) *(nearest)* inmediato(a), cercano(a); **the i. family** la familia más cercana; **my i. superior** mi superior más inmediato *or* directo; **in the i. vicinity** en las inmediaciones

(**d**) *(direct) (cause, influence)* directo(a)

immediately [ɪ'mi:dɪətlɪ] 1 *adv* (**a**) *(at once)* inmediatamente; **it was not i. apparent** no era algo que saltara a la vista (**b**) *(directly)* directamente; **it does not affect me i.** no me afecta directamente (**c**) *(just)* justamente, justo; **i. above the window** justo encima de la ventana

2 *conj* **i. I saw her I knew...** en cuanto la vi supe...; **phone me i. she arrives** llámame en cuanto llegue

immemorial [ɪmɪ'mɔ:rɪəl] *adj Literary* inmemorial, ancestral; **from time i.** desde tiempo(s) inmemorial(es)

immense [ɪ'mens] *adj* inmenso(a)

immensely [ɪ'menslɪ] *adv (interesting, enjoyable, difficult)* enormemente; *(problematic, rich, powerful)* inmensamente; **to enjoy sth i.** disfrutar enormemente de algo; **I'm i. grateful to you** te estoy inmensamente agradecido(a)

immensity [ɪ'mensɪtɪ] *n* inmensidad *f*

immerse [ɪ'mɜ:s] *vt* (**a**) *(in liquid)* sumergir (**in** en) (**b**) *(in activity)* sumergir (**in** en); **to i. oneself in sth** sumergirse en algo; **I immersed myself in my work** me enfrasqué en mi trabajo; **she went to London to i. herself in the English language** fue a Londres para sumergirse una temporada en la lengua inglesa

immersion [ɪ'mɜ:ʃən] *n* (**a**) *(in liquid)* inmersión *f* ►► ***i. heater*** calentador *m* de agua eléctrico (**b**) *(in activity)* enfrascamiento *m* ►► ***i. course*** curso *m* de inmersión (lingüística)

immigrant ['ɪmɪgrənt] 1 *n* inmigrante *mf*

2 *adj* inmigrante

immigrate ['ɪmɪgreɪt] *vi* inmigrar

immigration [ɪmɪ'greɪʃən] *n* (**a**) *(act of immigrating)* inmigración *f*; **the government wants to reduce i.** el Gobierno quiere reducir la inmigración (**b**) *(control section)* **i. (control)** control *m* de inmigración; **to go through i.** pasar por el control de pasaportes ►► ***i. officer*** agente *mf* de inmigración

imminence ['ɪmɪnəns] *n* inminencia *f*

imminent ['ɪmɪnənt] *adj* inminente

immobile [ɪ'məʊbaɪl] *adj* inmóvil

immobility [ɪmə'bɪlɪtɪ] *n* inmovilidad *f*

immobilization [ɪməʊbɪlaɪ'zeɪʃən] *n* inmovilización *f*

immobilize [ɪ'məʊbɪlaɪz] *vt* inmovilizar

immobilizer [ɪ'məʊbɪlaɪzə(r)] *n (for vehicle)* inmovilizador *m* (antirrobo)

immoderate [ɪ'mɒdərət] *adj* desmedido(a), inmoderado(a); **to an i. degree** en sumo grado, en demasía; **i. behaviour** comportamiento desmedido; **i. drinking** ingestión excesiva de alcohol; **to be i. in one's habits/views** tener unos hábitos/unas opiniones desmesurados(as)

immoderately [ɪ'mɒdərətlɪ] *adv* de forma desmedida

immodest [ɪ'mɒdɪst] *adj* (**a**) *(vain)* inmodesto(a), vanidoso(a) (**b**) *(indecent)* deshonesto(a), impúdico(a)

immodestly [ɪ'mɒdɪstlɪ] *adv* (**a**) *(vainly)* sin ninguna modestia (**b**) *(indecently)* impúdicamente

immodesty [ɪ'mɒdɪstɪ] *n* (**a**) *(vanity)* inmodestia *f*, vanidad *f* (**b**) *(indecency)* impudicia *f*

immolate ['ɪməleɪt] *vt Literary* inmolar

immolation [ɪmə'leɪʃən] *n Literary* inmolación *f*

immoral [ɪ'mɒrəl] *adj* inmoral ►► *Law* ***i. earnings*** ganancias *fpl* procedentes del proxenetismo

immorality [ɪmə'rælɪtɪ] *n* inmoralidad *f*

immorally [ɪ'mɒrəlɪ] *adv* de forma inmoral

immortal [ɪ'mɔːtəl] **1** *n* inmortal *mf*
2 *adj* inmortal; **in the i. words of Churchill...** citando las inmortales palabras de Churchill...

immortality [ɪmɔː'tælɪtɪ] *n* inmortalidad *f*

immortalize [ɪ'mɔːtəlaɪz] *vt* inmortalizar

immovable [ɪ'muːvəbəl] *adj* (**a**) *(object)* inamovible, fijo(a) (**b**) *(opposition)* inflexible; **on this point she is quite i.** a este respecto es muy inflexible (**c**) *Law* **i. property** propiedad inmobiliaria

immune [ɪ'mjuːn] *adj* (**a**) *(invulnerable)* inmune; **to be i. to a disease** ser inmune a una enfermedad ►► *Med **i. response*** respuesta *f* inmunitaria *or* inmunológica; *Med **i. system*** sistema *m* inmunológico (**b**) *(unaffected)* **i. to criticism** inmune a la crítica; **to be i. to temptation/flattery** ser inmune a la tentación/los halagos (**c**) *(exempt)* **i. from taxation** exento(a) de impuestos, con inmunidad tributaria *or* fiscal; *Law* **i. from prosecution** con inmunidad procesal, que goza de inmunidad procesal

immunity [ɪ'mjuːnɪtɪ] *n* (**a**) *Med* inmunidad *f* (**to** contra) (**b**) *Law* **i. (from prosecution)** inmunidad *f* (procesal) (**c**) *(exemption)* **i. from taxation** inmunidad tributaria *or* fiscal; **diplomatic/parliamentary i.** inmunidad diplomática/parlamentaria

immunization [ɪmjʊnaɪ'zeɪʃən] *n Med* inmunización *f* (**against** contra)

immunize ['ɪmjʊnaɪz] *vt Med* inmunizar (**against** contra)

immunoassay [ɪmjʊnəʊ'æseɪ] *n Biol* inmunoensayo *m*, ensayo *m* inmunológico

immunodeficiency [ɪmjʊnəʊdə'fɪʃənsɪ] *n* inmunodeficiencia *f*

immunodeficient [ɪmjʊnəʊdɪ'fɪʃənt] *adj* inmunodeficiente

immunodepressant [ɪmjʊnəʊdɪ'presənt] *n* inmunodepresor *m*

immunoglobulin [ɪmjʊnəʊ'glɒbjʊlɪn] *n* inmunoglobulina *f*

immunological [ɪmjʊnə'lɒdʒɪkəl] *adj* inmunológico(a)

immunologist [ɪmjʊ'nɒlədʒɪst] *n* inmunólogo(a) *m,f*

immunology [ɪmjʊ'nɒlədʒɪ] *n* inmunología *f*

immunosuppressant [ɪmjʊnəʊsə'presənt] *n Med* inmunosupresor *m*

immunosuppression [ɪmjʊnəʊsə'preʃən] *n Med* inmunosupresión *f*

immunosuppressive [ɪmjʊnəʊsə'presɪv] *adj Med* inmunosupresor(ora)

immunotherapy ['ɪmjʊnəʊ'θerəpɪ] *n* inmunoterapia *f*

immure [ɪ'mjʊə(r)] *vt Formal* confinar (entre cuatro paredes); **he had immured himself in the library** se había enclaustrado en la biblioteca

immutability [ɪmjuːtə'bɪlɪtɪ] *n Formal* inmutabilidad *f*

immutable [ɪ'mjuːtəbəl] *adj Formal* inmutable

immutably [ɪ'mjuːtəblɪ] *adv Formal* de forma inmutable

imp [ɪmp] *n* (**a**) *(devil)* diablillo *m* (**b**) *(child)* diablillo *m*; **she's a little imp!** ¡es un (pequeño) diablillo!

impact **1** *n* ['ɪmpækt] (**a**) *(collision)* impacto *m*; **on i.** en el momento del impacto ►► ***i. adhesive*** cola *f* de impacto; ***i. printer*** impresora *f* de impacto (**b**) *(impression)* impresión *f*; *(result)* impacto *m*; **you made** *or* **had quite an i. on him** lo dejaste impresionado; **the scandal had little i. on the election results** el escándalo tuvo escasa repercusión en el resultado de las elecciones
2 *vt* [ɪm'pækt] (**a**) *(collide with)* impactar en, chocar con (**b**) *(influence)* repercutir en
3 *vi (affect)* **to i. on** repercutir en

impacted [ɪm'pæktɪd] *adj* (**a**) *(tooth)* **to have i. wisdom teeth** tener las muelas del juicio impactadas *or* incluidas ►► *Med **i. fracture*** fractura *f* impactada (**b**) *US (affected)* afectado(a); **the area i. by the floods** la zona afectada por las inundaciones

impair [ɪm'peə(r)] *vt* (**a**) *(sight, hearing)* dañar; **performance is impaired in wet conditions** la humedad afecta negativamente el rendimiento (**b**) *(relations, chances)* perjudicar

impaired [ɪm'peəd] *adj* **i. hearing** problemas de audición, *Esp* oído dañado; **i. vision** problemas de visión, vista dañada

impairment [ɪm'peəmənt] *n (in sight, hearing)* deterioro *m*, pérdida *f*; **to have a hearing i.** tener una deficiencia auditiva; **i. in hearing is one side effect of the drug** la pérdida de la audición es uno de los efectos colaterales de la droga; **the progressive i. of his mental faculties by these conditions** el deterioro progresivo de sus facultades mentales originado por estas circunstancias

impala [ɪm'pɑːlə] (*pl* **impalas** *or* **impala**) *n* impala *m*

impale [ɪm'peɪl] *vt* empalar (**on** en); **he impaled himself on the railings when he fell** la reja le atravesó el cuerpo al caer

impalpable [ɪm'pælpəbəl] *adj* (**a**) *(by touch)* intangible, inmaterial (**b**) *(difficult to grasp, understand)* inaprehensible

impanel [ɪm'pænəl] (*pt & pp* **impaneled**) *vt US Law (jury)* constituir

impart [ɪm'pɑːt] *vt Formal* (**a**) *(heat, light)* desprender (**b**) *(quality, flavour)* conferir (**c**) *(knowledge)* impartir; *(news)* revelar

impartial [ɪm'pɑːʃəl] *adj* imparcial

impartiality [ɪmpɑːʃɪ'ælɪtɪ] *n* imparcialidad *f*

impartially [ɪm'pɑːʃəlɪ] *adv* imparcialmente, de manera imparcial

impassable [ɪm'pɑːsəbəl] *adj (river, barrier)* infranqueable; *(road)* intransitable

impasse ['æmpæs] *n* punto *m* muerto, callejón *m* sin salida; **there's no way out of this i.** no hay ninguna posibilidad de salir de esta crisis; **the talks have reached an i.** las conversaciones *or* negociaciones han llegado a un punto muerto

impassioned [ɪm'pæʃənd] *adj* apasionado(a)

impassive [ɪm'pæsɪv] *adj* impasible, impertérrito(a)

impassively [ɪm'pæsɪvlɪ] *adv* impasiblemente

impassivity [ɪmpæ'sɪvɪtɪ] *n* impasibilidad *f*

impasto [ɪm'pæstəʊ] *n Art* empaste *m*

impatience [ɪm'peɪʃəns] *n* (**a**) *(lack of patience)* impaciencia *f*; **with i.** con impaciencia (**b**) *(eagerness)* impaciencia *f* (**c**) *(irritation)* impaciencia *f*, fastidio *m*; **I fully understand your i. at the delay** comprendo perfectamente tu fastidio por el retraso (**d**) *(intolerance)* **he was known for his i. of sloppy work** tenía fama de impacientarse con el trabajo mal hecho

impatient [ɪm'peɪʃənt] *adj* (**a**) *(lacking patience)* impaciente; **she's terribly i. with her children** no tiene ninguna paciencia con sus hijos
(**b**) *(anxious, eager)* impaciente, ansioso(a); **to be i. (to do sth)** estar impaciente (por hacer algo); **to be i. for change** esperar con impaciencia el cambio
(**c**) *(irritated)* impaciente, fastidiado(a); **to get i. (with sb)** impacientarse (con alguien)
(**d**) *(intolerant)* **he's i. with people who always ask the same questions** se impacienta con la gente que hace siempre las mismas preguntas

impatiently [ɪm'peɪʃəntlɪ] *adv* impacientemente, con impaciencia

impeach [ɪm'piːtʃ] *vt* (**a**) *Br Law* = acusar de traición u otro delito grave contra el Estado (a un alto cargo público) (**b**) *US Law* iniciar un proceso de destitución *or* un impeachment contra (**c**) *Formal (cast doubt on)* poner en entredicho *or* en tela de juicio

impeachment [ɪm'piːtʃmənt] *n* (**a**) *Br Law* formulación *f* de cargos contra un alto funcionario (**b**) *US Law* proceso *m* de incapacitación, impeachment *m*

impeccable [ɪm'pekəbəl] *adj* impecable

impeccably [ɪm'pekəblɪ] *adv* impecablemente; **he was i. well behaved** tenía un comportamiento exquisito

impecunious [ɪmpɪ'kjuːnɪəs] *adj Literary* menesteroso(a)

impedance [ɪm'piːdəns] *n Phys* impedancia *f*

impede [ɪm'piːd] *vt* entorpecer, dificultar

impediment [ɪm'pedɪmənt] *n* (**a**) *(barrier, obstacle)* impedimento *m* (**to** para); **an i. to marriage** un impedimento para el matrimonio (**b**) **(speech) i.** defecto *m* del habla, trastorno *m* del lenguaje

impedimenta [ɪmpedɪ'mentə] *npl Formal or Hum (baggage, equipment)* impedimenta *f*

impel [ɪm'pel] (*pt & pp* **impelled**) *vt* (**a**) *(urge, incite)* impeler; **to feel impelled to do sth** sentirse *or* verse impelido(a) a hacer algo (**b**) *(propel)* impeler

impending [ɪm'pendɪŋ] *adj* inminente; **an atmosphere of i. doom** una atmósfera de fatalidad inminente

impenetrability [ɪmpenɪtrə'bɪlɪtɪ] *n* (**a**) *(of forest, fog, defences, mystery)* impenetrabilidad *f* (**b**) *(of jargon, system, motives)* impenetrabilidad *f*, incomprensibilidad *f*

impenetrable [ɪm'penɪtrəbəl] *adj* (**a**) *(forest, fog, defences, mystery)* impenetrable (**b**) *(jargon, system, motives)* impenetrable, indescifrable

impenitence [ɪm'penɪtəns] *n* impenitencia *f*

impenitent [ɪm'penɪtənt] *adj* impenitente; **to be i. about sth** no arrepentirse de algo

imperative [ɪm'perətɪv] **1** *n* (**a**) *Gram* imperativo *m* (**b**) *(absolute need)* imperativo *m*
2 *adj* (**a**) *(need)* imperioso(a), acuciante; **it is i. that he should come** es imprescindible que venga (**b**) *(categorical) (orders, voice, tone)* imperioso(a), categórico(a) (**c**) *Gram* imperativo(a)

imperceptible [ɪmpə'septɪbəl] *adj* imperceptible

imperceptibly [ɪmpə'septɪblɪ] *adv* imperceptiblemente, de forma imperceptible

imperceptive [ɪmpə'septɪv] *adj* obtuso(a), insensible

imperfect [ɪm'pɜːfɪkt] **1** *n Gram* imperfecto *m*
2 *adj* (**a**) *(not perfect)* imperfecto(a); **she has an i. grasp of the facts** tiene una visión inexacta de los hechos; **her i. command of English** su deficiente dominio del inglés; **it's slightly i.** *(of item for sale)* tiene imperfecciones (**b**) *Gram* imperfecto(a)

imperfection [ɪmpə'fekʃən] *n* (**a**) *(imperfect state)* imperfección *f*; **he had a vast tolerance for human i.** era muy tolerante con los defectos del ser humano (**b**) *(fault)* imperfección *f*

imperfectly [ɪm'pɜːfɪktlɪ] *adv* de un modo imperfecto

imperial [ɪm'pɪərɪəl] *adj* (**a**) *(of empire)* imperial; **His/Her I. Majesty** Su Majestad Imperial (**b**) *(majestic)* majestuoso(a), solemne (**c**) *(weights and measures)* británico(a), imperial *(que utiliza pesos y medidas anglosajones: la pulgada, la libra, el galón, etc)* ▸▸ ***i. gallon*** galón *m* británico *(= 4,546 litros)*

imperialism [ɪm'pɪərɪəlɪzəm] *n* imperialismo *m*

imperialist [ɪm'pɪərɪəlɪst] **1** *n* imperialista *mf*
2 *adj* imperialista *mf*

imperialistic [ɪmpɪərɪə'lɪstɪk] *adj* imperialista

imperially [ɪm'pɪərɪəlɪ] *adv* de forma suprema *or* absoluta

imperil [ɪm'perɪl] (*pt & pp* **imperilled**, *US* **imperiled**) *vt* poner en peligro

imperious [ɪm'pɪərɪəs] *adj* imperioso(a), autoritario(a)

imperiously [ɪm'pɪərɪəslɪ] *adv* imperiosamente

imperishable [ɪm'perɪʃəbəl] *adj* (**a**) *(goods)* no perecedero(a) (**b**) *(quality, truth)* imperecedero(a)

impermanence [ɪm'pɜːmənəns] *n* provisionalidad *f*, temporalidad *f*

impermanent [ɪm'pɜːmənənt] *adj* provisional, pasajero(a)

impermeability [ɪmpɜːmɪə'bɪlɪtɪ] *n* impermeabilidad *f*

impermeable [ɪm'pɜːmɪəbəl] *adj* impermeable

impermissible [ɪmpə'mɪsəbəl] *adj* inadmisible

impersonal [ɪm'pɜːsənəl] *adj* (**a**) *(objective)* imparcial, desapasionado(a) (**b**) *(cold, anonymous)* impersonal (**c**) *Gram* impersonal

impersonally [ɪm'pɜːsənəlɪ] *adv* de forma impersonal

impersonate [ɪm'pɜːsəneɪt] *vt* (**a**) *(pretend to be)* hacerse pasar por (**b**) *(do impression of)* imitar, hacer una imitación de

impersonation [ɪmpɜːsə'neɪʃən] *n* (**a**) *(illegal)* suplantación *f* de personalidad; **he was sent to prison for i. of a diplomat** fue encarcelado por hacerse pasar por un diplomático (**b**) *(impression)* imitación *f*

impersonator [ɪm'pɜːsəneɪtə(r)] *n* (**a**) *(impostor)* impostor(ora) *m,f* (**b**) *(impressionist)* imitador(ora) *m,f*

impertinence [ɪm'pɜːtɪnəns] *n* impertinencia *f*

impertinent [ɪm'pɜːtɪnənt] *adj* (**a**) *(rude)* impertinente; **to be i. to sb** ser impertinente con alguien (**b**) *Formal (irrelevant)* improcedente

impertinently [ɪm'pɜːtɪnəntlɪ] *adv* de un modo impertinente, impertinentemente

imperturbable [ɪmpə'tɜːbəbəl] *adj* imperturbable

imperturbably [ɪmpə'tɜːbəblɪ] *adv* de un modo imperturbable

impervious [ɪm'pɜːvɪəs] *adj* (**a**) *(to water)* impermeable (**b**) *(to threats, persuasion)* insensible; **she is i. to reason** es imposible que razone; **i. to criticism** inmune a las críticas; **he was i. to her charm** era insensible a sus encantos; **he remained i. to our suggestions** no se dejó convencer por nuestras sugerencias

imperviousness [ɪm'pɜːvɪəsnɪs] *n (to threats, persuasion, reason)* insensibilidad *f*, impasibilidad *f*

impetigo [ɪmpɪ'taɪgəʊ] *n Med* impétigo *m*

impetuosity [ɪmpetjʊ'ɒsɪtɪ] *n* impetuosidad *f*

impetuous [ɪm'petjʊəs] *adj* impetuoso(a)

impetuously [ɪm'petjʊəslɪ] *adv* impetuosamente, de manera impetuosa

impetuousness [ɪm'petjʊəsnɪs] *n* impetuosidad *f*

impetus ['ɪmpɪtəs] *n* (**a**) *(momentum)* ímpetu *m* (**b**) *(incentive, drive)* ímpetu *m*, impulso *m*; **to gain/lose i.** ganar/perder impulso; **to be carried by** *or* **under one's own i.** dejarse llevar por el propio impulso; **the news gave an added i. to the campaign** la noticia le proporcionó mayor ímpetu a la campaña

impiety [ɪm'paɪətɪ] *n* (**a**) *(lack of piety)* impiedad *f* (**b**) *(act)* acto *m* impío; *(remark)* frase *f* irreverente, blasfemia *f*

impinge [ɪm'pɪndʒ]

▸ **impinge on** *vt insep* (**a**) *(affect)* incidir en, influir en; **it impinges in a big way on all our lives** incide de manera notable en nuestra vida; **to i. on sb's conscious mind** influir en la consciencia de alguien; **in so far as it impinges on our department** en la medida en que afecta a nuestro departamento (**b**) *(infringe on)* vulnerar

impious ['ɪmpɪəs] *adj* impío(a)

impiously ['ɪmpɪəslɪ] *adv* de un modo impío

impish ['ɪmpɪʃ] *adj* travieso(a)

impishly ['ɪmpɪʃlɪ] *adv* malévolamente, con picardía

impishness ['ɪmpɪʃnɪs] *n* picardía *f*

implacable [ɪm'plækəbəl] *adj* implacable

implacably [ɪm'plækəblɪ] *adv* implacablemente

implant 1 *n* ['ɪmplɑːnt] *Med* implante *m*; **breast/hair i.** implante mamario/capilar
2 *vt* [ɪm'plɑːnt] (**a**) *Med* implantar (**b**) *(opinion, belief)* inculcar

implantation [ɪmplɑːn'teɪʃən] *n* (**a**) *Med* implantación *f* (**b**) *(of opinion, belief)* inculcación *f*

implausibility [ɪmplɔːzɪ'bɪlɪtɪ] *n* inverosimilitud *f*

implausible [ɪm'plɔːzɪbəl] *adj* inverosímil, poco convincente

implausibly [ɪm'plɔːzɪblɪ] *adv* de forma inverosímil

implement 1 *n* ['ɪmplɪmənt] utensilio *m*; **gardening implements** herramientas *or* útiles de jardinería; **kitchen implements** utensilios de cocina
2 *vt* ['ɪmplɪment] *(plan, agreement, proposal)* poner en práctica, llevar a cabo

implementation [ɪmplɪmen'teɪʃən] *n (of plan, agreement, proposal)* puesta *f* en práctica

implicate ['ɪmplɪkeɪt] *vt* (**a**) *(show involvement of)* implicar, involucrar; **they are all implicated in the crime** todos están implicados *or* involucrados en el delito (**b**) *Formal (imply)* implicar, significar, suponer

implication [ɪmplɪ'keɪʃən] *n* (**a**) *(effect)* consecuencia *f*, *Esp* implicación *f*, *Am* implicancia *f*; **I don't think you understand the implications of what you are saying** no creo que seas consciente del alcance de tus palabras; **the full implications are not yet clear** aún no se puede determinar claramente cuál va a ser la repercusión final
(**b**) *(inference)* insinuación *f*; **the i. was that we would be punished** se daba a entender que seríamos castigados; **by i.** indirectamente, implícitamente

implicit [ɪm'plɪsɪt] *adj* (**a**) *(implied)* implícito(a); **his feelings were i. in his words** sus palabras revelaban sus sentimientos; **it was i. in his remarks** estaba implícito en sus comentarios (**b**) *(total) (confidence, obedience)* absoluto(a), sin reservas; **i. faith** fe inquebrantable

implicitly [ɪm'plɪsɪtlɪ] *adv* (**a**) *(by implication)* de manera implícita, implícitamente (**b**) *(believe, trust)* ciegamente, de manera inquebrantable

implied [ɪm'plaɪd] *adj* implícito(a)

implode [ɪm'pləʊd] *vi* (**a**) *(collapse inward)* sufrir una implosión, implosionar (**b**) *(organization, economy)* destruirse, desmoronarse

implore [ɪm'plɔː(r)] *vt* implorar; **to i. sb to do sth** implorar a alguien que haga algo; **I i. you!** ¡te lo imploro!

imploring [ɪm'plɔːrɪŋ] *adj* implorante

imploringly [ɪm'plɔːrɪŋlɪ] *adv* con aire implorante, con aire de súplica; **to look at sb i.** mirar implorante a alguien

implosion [ɪm'pləʊʒən] *n Phys* implosión *f*

imply [ɪm'plaɪ] *vt* (**a**) *(insinuate)* insinuar; **what are you implying?** ¿qué insinúas?; **your silence implies that you are guilty** el que calla otorga (**b**) *(involve)* implicar; **it implies a lot of hard work** implica *or* supone muchísimo trabajo

impolite [ɪmpə'laɪt] *adj* maleducado(a); **to be i. to sb** ser descortés con alguien

impolitely [ɪmpə'laɪtlɪ] *adv* maleducadamente, con mala educación

impoliteness [ɪmpə'laɪtnɪs] *n* mala educación *f*

impolitic [ɪm'pɒlɪtɪk] *adj Formal* inoportuno(a), imprudente; **it would have been i. to invite both of them** hubiera sido una ligereza *or* una imprudencia invitarlos a ambos

imponderable [ɪm'pɒndərəbəl] **1** *n* (factor *m*) imponderable *m*
2 *adj* imponderable

import 1 *n* ['ɪmpɔːt] (**a**) *(item)* artículo *m* de importación; *Fig (activity)* importación *f* ▸▸ ***i. controls*** control *m* de importaciones; ***i. duty*** derechos *mpl* de importación *or* de aduana; ***i. licence*** licencia *f* de importación; ***i. surcharge*** recargo *m* a la importación
(**b**) *Formal (importance, significance)* significación *f*, importancia *f*; **a matter of some/great i.** un asunto de cierta/gran importancia *or* consideración; **the full i. of these changes** el alcance *or* la trascendencia total de estos cambios
(**c**) *Formal (meaning)* significado *m*
2 *vt* [ɪm'pɔːt] (**a**) *(goods)* importar (**from** de) (**b**) *Comptr* importar (**from** de)

importance [ɪm'pɔːtəns] *n* importancia *f*; **it is of no great i.** no tiene mucha importancia; **to be of i. (to sth/sb)** ser de importancia *or* importante (para algo/alguien); **to attach** *or* **give i. to sth** dar importancia a algo; **a position of i.** un puesto importante *or* de relevancia; **to be full of one's own i.** darse aires, estar pagado(a) de sí mismo(a)

important [ɪm'pɔːtənt] *adj* importante; **my job is i. to me** mi empleo es importante para mí; **it's not i.** no tiene importancia; **it is i. to send regular reports** es importante que se envíen informes con regularidad; **an i. book/writer** *(influential, significant)* un libro/escritor importante; **stop trying to look i.** deja de dártelas de importante, *Esp* deja de darte pisto

importantly [ɪm'pɔːtəntlɪ] *adv (speak)* dándose importancia; **but, more i....** pero, lo que es más importante...

importation [ɪmpɔː'teɪʃən] *n (of goods)* importación *f*

importer [ɪm'pɔːtə(r)] *n* (**a**) *(person, company)* importador(ora) *m,f* (**b**) *(country)* país *m* importador, importador *m*; **we are a net i. of technology** somos un país netamente importador de tecnología

import-export ['ɪmpɔːt'ekspɔːt] *n* **i. (trade)** importación-exportación *f*, comercio *m* exterior

importunate [ɪm'pɔːtjʊnət] *adj (beggar, demands, questions)* importuno(a), pertinaz

importune [ɪm'pɔːtjuːn] **1** *vt* (**a**) *Formal (pester)* importunar; **to i. sb with questions** importunar a alguien con preguntas (**b**) *Br (of prostitute)* abordar

2 *vi Br (prostitute)* ejercer la prostitución

importunity [ɪmpɔː'tjuːnətɪ] *n Formal (harassment)* importunidad *f*

impose [ɪm'pəʊz] **1** *vt (silence, one's will, restrictions)* imponer (**on** a); **to i. a tax on sth** gravar algo con un impuesto; **to i. a fine on sb** poner *or* imponer a alguien una multa; **he tried to i. his opinions on us** intentó imponernos sus puntos de vista; **to i. oneself on sb** imponérsele a alguien, imponerle (uno) su voluntad a alguien

2 *vi* molestar, resultar molesto(a); **I don't want to i., but...** no quisiera molestar, pero...

▸**impose on, impose upon** *vt insep (take advantage of, inconvenience)* abusar de; **to i. on sb's generosity/hospitality** abusar de la generosidad/hospitalidad de alguien

imposing [ɪm'pəʊzɪŋ] *adj* imponente

imposition [ɪmpə'zɪʃən] *n* (**a**) *(of tax, fine)* imposición *f* (**b**) *(unfair demand)* abuso *m*; **it was a bit of an i.** fue un poco abusivo *or* de abuso (**c**) *Typ* imposición *f*

impossibility [ɪmpɒsɪ'bɪlɪtɪ] *n* imposibilidad *f*; **it's a physical i.** es físicamente imposible

impossible [ɪm'pɒsɪbəl] **1** *n* **the i.** lo imposible; **to ask the i.** pedir lo imposible; **to attempt the i.** intentar lo imposible

2 *adj* (**a**) *(not possible)* imposible; **it's i. for me to leave before 6 p.m.** me es imposible salir antes de las 6 de la tarde; **to make it i. for sb to do sth** imposibilitar a alguien hacer algo; **you make it i. for me to be civil to you** no hay forma de poder ser amable contigo; **it's i. to say when we'll finish** es imposible saber cuándo terminaremos; **it's not i. that...** no es imposible que...; **but that's i.!** *(it can't be true)* ¡(eso es) imposible!

(**b**) *(unbearable)* imposible, insufrible; **you're i.!** ¡eres imposible!; **an i. position/situation** una posición/situación insostenible

impossibly [ɪm'pɒsɪblɪ] *adv* increíblemente; **i. difficult** sumamente *or* extremadamente difícil; **the film is i. long** la película es exageradamente larga; **he's i. stupid** es increíblemente estúpido; **to behave i.** portarse de forma insoportable, portarse tremendamente mal

impostor, imposter [ɪm'pɒstə(r)] *n* impostor(ora) *m,f*

imposture [ɪm'pɒstʃə(r)] *n Formal* impostura *f*

impotence ['ɪmpətəns] *n* (**a**) *(sexual)* impotencia *f* (**b**) *(powerlessness)* impotencia *f*

impotent ['ɪmpətənt] *adj* (**a**) *(sexually)* impotente (**b**) *(powerless)* impotente

impound [ɪm'paʊnd] *vt* (**a**) *Law* embargar (**b**) *(car)* llevar al depósito municipal (por infracción) (**c**) *(dog)* llevar a la perrera (municipal)

impoverish [ɪm'pɒvərɪʃ] *vt* (**a**) *(person, country)* empobrecer; **we are all impoverished by his death** su muerte significa una pérdida para todos; **the arts have been impoverished** las artes se han venido a menos (**b**) *(soil)* empobrecer

impoverished [ɪm'pɒvərɪʃd] *adj* (**a**) *(person, country)* empobrecido(a); **to be i.** estar empobrecido(a) (**b**) *(soil)* empobrecido(a)

impoverishment [ɪm'pɒvərɪʃmənt] *n* (**a**) *(of person, country)* empobrecimiento *m* (**b**) *(of soil)* empobrecimiento *m*

impracticability [ɪmprækt ɪkə'bɪlɪtɪ] *n* inviabilidad *f*, imposibilidad *f* de realizarse

impracticable [ɪm'præktɪkəbəl] *adj* irrealizable, impracticable

impractical [ɪm'præktɪkəl] *adj* (**a**) *(person)* poco práctico(a); **he's completely i.** no es nada práctico (**b**) *(plan, suggestion)* poco práctico(a)

impracticality [ɪmpræktɪ'kælɪtɪ] *n* (**a**) *(of person)* falta *f* de pragmatismo (**b**) *(of plan, suggestion)* falta *f* de sentido práctico

imprecation [ɪmprɪ'keɪʃən] *n Formal* imprecación *f*

imprecise [ɪmprɪ'saɪs] *adj* impreciso(a)

imprecisely [ɪmprɪ'saɪslɪ] *adv* de forma imprecisa

imprecision [ɪmprɪ'sɪʒən] *n* imprecisión *f*

impregnable [ɪm'pregnəbəl] *adj* (**a**) *(fortress, defences)* inexpugnable (**b**) *(argument)* incontestable; **to have an i. lead** llevar una ventaja inalcanzable, ser el/la líder indiscutible; **his position is i.** su posición es invencible

impregnate ['ɪmpregneɪt] *vt* (**a**) *Formal (fertilize)* fecundar (**b**) *(soak)* impregnar (**with** de)

impregnation [ɪmpreg'neɪʃən] *n* (**a**) *Formal (fertilization)* fecundación *f* (**b**) *(soaking)* impregnación *f*

impresario [ɪmpre'sɑːrɪəʊ] (*pl* **impresarios**) *n* empresario(a) *m,f*, organizador(ora) *m,f* de espectáculos

impress [ɪm'pres] **1** *vt* (**a**) *(make an impression on)* impresionar; **she was impressed with** *or* **by it** aquello la impresionó; **to i. sb favourably/unfavourably** causar buena/mala impresión a alguien; **the witness impressed the jury** el testigo dejó impresionado al jurado; **I'm not impressed** no me parece gran cosa

(**b**) *(emphasize to sb)* **to i. sth on sb** recalcarle a alguien la importancia de algo

(**c**) *(imprint)* **to i. sth on(to) sth** imprimir algo en algo; **to i. sth on sb's mind** imprimir algo en la mente de alguien; **her words are impressed on my memory** sus palabras están grabadas en mi memoria

2 *vi (make a favourable impression)* causar buena impresión; *(stronger)* impresionar; **he was eager to i.** tenía muchas ganas de dejar una buena impresión; **he was dressed to i.** se había vestido con la idea de impresionar

impression [ɪm'preʃən] *n* (**a**) *(effect)* impresión *f*; **to make a good/bad i. (on sb)** dar *or* causar buena/mala impresión (a alguien); **he made a strong i. on them** les causó una notable impresión; **he always tries to make an i.** siempre trata de impresionar *or* de causar sensación; **my words made no i. on him whatsoever** mis palabras no le causaron la más mínima impresión; **our artillery made little i. on their defences** nuestra artillería causó pocos estragos en su defensa

(**b**) *(idea, thought)* impresión *f*; **what were your impressions of Tokyo?** ¿qué impresión te causó Tokio?; **to be under the i. that...** tener la impresión de que...; **I was under the i. that you were unable to come** tenía la impresión de que no podías venir; **to give the i. that...** dar la impresión de que...; **I don't know where she got that i. (from)** no sé qué le ha hecho pensar eso, no sé de dónde ha sacado esa idea; **to create** *or* **give the i. that...** dar la impresión de que...; **to create a false i.** dar una impresión falsa; **it's my i.** *or* **I have the i. that she's rather annoyed with us** tengo *or* me da la impresión de que está algo enojada con nosotros

(**c**) *(imprint) (in wax, snow)* marca *f*, impresión *f*; **to take an i. of sth** sacar el molde de algo

(**d**) *(of book)* impresión *f*, tirada *f*

(**e**) *(imitation)* imitación *f*; **to do impressions** hacer imitaciones

impressionable [ɪm'preʃənəbəl] *adj* (**a**) *(easily influenced)* influenciable; **an i. age** una edad en la que todo te influye (**b**) *(easily shocked)* impresionable

impressionism [ɪm'preʃənɪzəm] *n Art* impresionismo *m*

impressionist [ɪm'preʃənɪst] **1** *n* (**a**) *Art* impresionista *mf* (**b**) *(impersonator)* imitador(ora) *m,f*

2 *adj Art* impresionista

impressionistic [ɪmpreʃə'nɪstɪk] *adj* impresionista

impressive [ɪm'presɪv] *adj* impresionante; **his appearance was very i.** su aspecto era bastante imponente; **the report was most i.** el informe era excepcional

impressively [ɪm'presɪvlɪ] *adv* de un modo impresionante; **I thought you dealt with that guy very i.** a mí me pareció que lidiaste con aquel tipo de forma admirable; **an i. big room** una habitación inmensa

imprest ['ɪmprest] *n Fin* crédito *m* oficial ▸▸ *Com* ***i. system*** sistema *m* de fondo fijo (de caja)

imprimatur [ɪmprɪ'meɪtə(r)] *n* (**a**) *Rel* imprimátur *m* (**b**) *Formal (permission)* visto *m* bueno

imprint 1 *n* [ˈɪmprɪnt] (**a**) *(of seal)* marca *f*; *(of hand, feet)* huella *f* (**b**) *(of experience)* huella *f*, impronta *f*; **the i. of suffering on her face** la huella del sufrimiento en su cara; **the war had left its i. on all of us** la guerra había dejado su impronta en todos nosotros (**c**) *(of publisher) (name and address)* pie *m* de imprenta; *(series name)* sello *m* (editorial)
2 *vt* [ɪmˈprɪnt] (**a**) *(on paper)* imprimir (**on** en); *(in sand, mud)* marcar (**on** en) (**b**) *(fix)* **her words were imprinted on my memory** sus palabras se me quedaron grabadas en la memoria

imprinter [ɪmˈprɪntə(r)] *n (for credit cards)* máquina *f* de validación

imprison [ɪmˈprɪzən] *vt* (**a**) *(put in prison)* encarcelar (**b**) *(confine, restrain)* confinar, aprisionar; **he felt imprisoned** se sentía aprisionado

imprisonment [ɪmˈprɪzənmənt] *n* encarcelamiento *m*; **to be sentenced to six months' i.** ser condenado(a) a seis meses de prisión

improbability [ɪmprɒbəˈbɪlɪtɪ] *n* (**a**) *(unlikelihood)* improbabilidad *f* (**b**) *(strangeness)* inverosimilitud *f*

improbable [ɪmˈprɒbəbəl] *adj* (**a**) *(unlikely)* improbable; **I think it highly i. that they ever met** me parece muy improbable que hayan podido conocerse (**b**) *(strange, unusual)* inverosímil

improbably [ɪmˈprɒbəblɪ] *adv* increíblemente; **i. enough, they turned out to be twin brothers** por inverosímil que parezca, resultó que eran hermanos gemelos

impromptu [ɪmˈprɒmptju:] 1 *adj (speech, party)* improvisado(a)
2 *adv (unexpectedly)* de improviso; *(ad lib)* improvisadamente
3 *n* improvisación *f*

improper [ɪmˈprɒpə(r)] *adj* (**a**) *(incorrect) (use, purpose)* indebido(a) (**b**) *(inappropriate) (dress)* inadecuado(a) (**c**) *(indecent) (words, action)* inadecuado(a); *(suggestion, behaviour)* indecoroso(a) ▸▸ ***i. suggestion*** proposición *f* deshonesta (**d**) *(dishonest)* impropio(a), irregular ▸▸ *Law* ***i. practices*** actuaciones *fpl* irregulares (**e**) *Math* ***i. fraction*** fracción *f* impropia

improperly [ɪmˈprɒpəlɪ] *adv* (**a**) *(incorrectly)* incorrectamente (**b**) *(inappropriately)* inadecuadamente; **he was i. dressed** iba inadecuadamente vestido (**c**) *(indecently)* indecorosamente; **he behaved most i.** su comportamiento fue de lo más indecoroso (**d**) *(dishonestly)* deshonestamente

impropriety [ɪmprəˈpraɪətɪ] *n* (**a**) *(unlawfulness)* irregularidad *f* (**b**) *(inappropriateness)* impropiedad *f*, incorrección *f* (**c**) *(indecency)* falta *f* de decoro

improve [ɪmˈpru:v] 1 *vt* (**a**) *(make better) (work, facilities, result)* mejorar; **to i. one's chances** ampliar *or* multiplicar (uno) sus posibilidades; **if you cut your hair it would i. your looks** un corte de pelo realzaría tu imagen; **a little basil will greatly i. the flavour** un poco de albahaca le dará mucho mejor gusto; **she's gone to Madrid to i. her Spanish** se ha ido a Madrid a perfeccionar su español
(**b**) *(cultivate)* **to i. oneself** cultivarse; **she was eager to i. her mind** estaba ansiosa por ampliar sus conocimientos; **reading improves the mind** la lectura cultiva la mente *or* inteligencia
(**c**) **to i. a property** hacer mejoras en un inmueble
2 *vi* mejorar; **to i. with time/age/use** mejorar con el tiempo/la edad/el uso; **he improves on acquaintance** gana mucho cuando se lo conoce, gana con el trato; **things are improving at work** las cosas van mejor en el trabajo

▸ **improve on, improve upon** *vt insep* (**a**) *(result, work)* mejorar; **it's difficult to see how her performance can be improved on** sería difícil mejorar sus resultados (**b**) *(offer)* mejorar, superar

improved [ɪmˈpru:vd] *adj (system, design)* mejorado(a); **he is much i.** ha mejorado mucho

improvement [ɪmˈpru:vmənt] *n* (**a**) *(in situation, quality, behaviour)* mejora *f*; *(in health)* mejoría *f*; **there has been a slight/some/a considerable i. in his work** su trabajo presenta ligeras/algunas/considerables mejoras; **to be an i. on** ser mejor que; **her new boyfriend's a bit of an i.** ha salido ganando con su nuevo novio; **there's room for i.** se puede mejorar
(**b**) *(in building, road)* mejora *f*; **(home) improvements** mejoras (domésticas); **to make improvements (to)** *(home)* hacer mejoras (en)

improvidence [ɪmˈprɒvɪdəns] *n Formal* imprevisión *f*

improvident [ɪmˈprɒvɪdənt] *adj Formal* poco previsor(ora), imprudente

improving [ɪmˈpru:vɪŋ] *adj (book)* instructivo(a), educativo(a); *(influence, environment)* formativo(a)

improvisation [ɪmprəvaɪˈzeɪʃən] *n* improvisación *f*

improvise [ˈɪmprəvaɪz] 1 *vt* improvisar
2 *vi* improvisar; **you will have to i.** *(make do)* tendrás que improvisar

imprudence [ɪmˈpru:dəns] *n Formal* imprudencia *f*

imprudent [ɪmˈpru:dənt] *adj Formal* imprudente; **an i. investment** una inversión desaconsejable; **she's rather i. in her choice of friends** es algo desatinada eligiendo a sus amigos

imprudently [ɪmˈpru:dəntlɪ] *adv Formal* imprudentemente

impudence [ˈɪmpjʊdəns] *n* desvergüenza *f*, insolencia *f*

impudent [ˈɪmpjʊdənt] *adj* desvergonzado(a), insolente

> **False friend:** The Spanish adjective **impúdico** is not a translation for the English word **impudent**. In Spanish **impúdico** means "immodest, indecent".

impudently [ˈɪmpjʊdəntlɪ] *adv* con insolencia, con descaro

impugn [ɪmˈpju:n] *vt Formal* poner en tela de juicio, cuestionar

impulse [ˈɪmpʌls] *n* (**a**) *(desire, instinct)* impulso *m*; **to do sth on i.** hacer algo guiado(a) por un impulso; **to act on i.** actuar por impulso *or* instinto; **I'm sorry, I did it on i.** lo siento, lo hice sin pensar; **on a sudden i., he kissed her** en un arranque inesperado la besó; **I felt an irresistible i. to hit him** me entraron unas ganas irresistibles de pegarle; **a sudden i. made me start running** un repentino impulso me hizo echar a correr; **it was an i. buy** me dio por comprarlo, lo compré por impulso ▸▸ ***i. buying*** compra *f* impulsiva
(**b**) *Formal (impetus)* impulso *m*; **government grants have given an i. to trade** las subvenciones del Gobierno han dado un impulso al comercio
(**c**) *Elec & Physiol* impulso *m*

impulsive [ɪmˈpʌlsɪv] *adj* impulsivo(a); **try to be less i.** intenta ser menos impulsivo(a)

impulsively [ɪmˈpʌlsɪvlɪ] *adv (to buy, act)* por un impulso; **he i. grabbed her and kissed her** la agarró y la besó de forma impulsiva

impulsiveness [ɪmˈpʌlsɪvnɪs] *n* impulsividad *f*

impunity [ɪmˈpju:nɪtɪ] *n* impunidad *f*; **with i.** impunemente

impure [ɪmˈpjʊə(r)] *adj* (**a**) *(unclean) (air, milk)* impuro(a) (**b**) *(adulterated) (drug)* adulterado(a) (**c**) *Literary (sinful) (thought, deed)* impuro(a); *(motive)* deshonesto(a)

impurity [ɪmˈpju:rɪtɪ] *n* (**a**) *(in air, milk)* impureza *f* (**b**) *(in drug)* adulteración *f* (**c**) *Literary (of thought, deed)* impureza *f*; *(of motive)* carácter *m* deshonesto

imputation [ɪmpjʊˈteɪʃən] *n Formal* (**a**) *(accusation)* imputación *f* (**b**) *(attribution)* imputación *f*; **no i. of guilt is intended** no se pretende hacer una imputación de culpa

impute [ɪmˈpju:t] *vt Formal* **to i. sth to sb** imputar algo a alguien

IN *(abbr* **Indiana***)* Indiana

in[1] *(abbr* **inch** *or* **inches***)* pulgada *f (= 2,54 cm)*

IN[2] [ɪn] 1 *prep* (**a**) *(with place)* en; **in Spain** en España; **to arrive in Spain** llegar a España; **somewhere in Argentina** en algún lugar de Argentina; **it was cold in the bar** dentro del bar *or* en el bar hacía frío; **those records in the corner are mine** los discos del rincón son míos; **I'd like the hat in the window** quiero el sombrero de la ventana; **get in the bath!** ¡a la bañera!; **to be deaf in one ear** estar sordo(a) de un oído; **she was shot in the chest** le dispararon en el pecho; **in bed** en la cama; **in hospital** en el hospital; **in prison** en la cárcel; **in the rain** bajo la lluvia; **in the sun** al sol; **in here** aquí dentro; **in there** allí dentro
(**b**) *(forming part of)* **are you in this** *Br* **queue** *or US* **line?** ¿estás en esta cola?; **do you take milk in your tea?** ¿tomas el té con leche?; **I'm in a jazz band** toco en un grupo de jazz; **she's the best player in the team** es la mejor jugadora del equipo; **what do you look for in a manager?** ¿qué esperas de un buen jefe?; **in Graham, we have an excellent leader** con Graham tenemos un excelente líder
(**c**) *(with expressions of time)* en; **in 1927/April/spring** en 1927/abril/primavera; **in the eighties** en los ochenta; **he did it in three hours/record time** lo hizo en tres horas/en un tiempo récord; **he'll be here in three hours** llegará dentro de tres horas; **in the morning/afternoon** por la mañana/tarde; **at three o'clock in the afternoon** a las tres de la tarde; **it rained in the night** llovió por la noche; **for the first time in years** por primera vez en años *or* desde hace años; **I haven't seen her in years** hace años que no la veo
(**d**) *(expressing manner)* **in Spanish** en español; **to write in pen/pencil/ink** escribir con bolígrafo/a lápiz/a tinta; **in a loud/quiet voice** en voz alta/baja; **to stand in a circle** formar un corro; **arranged in groups of six** distribuidos(as) en grupos de seis; **a programme in three parts** un programa en *or* de *or* con tres partes; **this model comes in pink or blue** este modelo viene en rosa y en azul; **piano concerto in C major** concierto de piano en do mayor; **covered in snow** cubierto(a) de nieve; **she was dressed in white** iba vestida de blanco; **in full colour** a todo color; **in horror/surprise** con horror/sorpresa; **she left in a hurry** se fue rápidamente; **to live in luxury** vivir a todo lujo; **to speak to sb in private/secret** hablar con alguien en privado/secreto; **in this way** de este modo, de esta manera

(**e**) *(expressing quantities, denominations, ratios)* **in twos** de dos en dos; **one in ten** uno de cada diez; **she has a one in ten chance of getting the disease** tiene un diez por ciento de posibilidades de contraer *or Esp* coger *or Am* agarrarse la enfermedad; **2 metres in length/height** 2 metros de longitud/altura; **in small/large quantities** en pequeñas/grandes cantidades; **in dollars** en dólares; **he's in his forties** anda por los cuarenta; **the temperature was in the nineties** ≃ hacía (una temperatura de) treinta y tantos grados; **they are dying in (their) thousands** están muriendo a millares

(**f**) *(expressing state)* en; **in good condition** en buenas condiciones; **I'm not going for a walk in this rain** no pienso salir a dar un paseo con esta lluvia; **in danger** en peligro

(**g**) *(with gerund)* **he had no difficulty in doing it** no tuvo dificultad en hacerlo; **in taking this decision, we considered several factors** al tomar esta decisión, tuvimos en cuenta varios factores; **in saying this, I don't mean to imply that...** no quiero dar a entender con esto que...

(**h**) *(regarding)* **a rise/fall in inflation** una subida/bajada de la inflación; **a diet lacking in vitamins** una dieta pobre en vitaminas; **better in every sense** mejor en todos los sentidos; **in such cases** en esos casos

(**i**) *(wearing)* **the man in the suit** el hombre del traje; **you look lovely in pink** estás preciosa vestida de rosa; **the soldiers were in uniform** los soldados iban de uniforme

(**j**) *(as)* **in answer to** en respuesta a; **in return** a cambio

(**k**) *(with field of activity)* **to be in insurance/marketing** dedicarse a los seguros/al marketing; **a degree in biology** una licenciatura en biología

(**l**) *(in phrases) Fam* **I didn't think she had it in her (to...)** no la creía capaz (de...); **there's not much in it** *(not much difference)* no hay mucha diferencia; **there's nothing in it for me** *(no advantage)* no tiene ninguna ventaja para mí

2 *adv* (**a**) *(inside)* dentro; **shall I bring the clothes in?** ¿meto la ropa?; **come in!** ¡adelante!; **come in, the water's lovely!** ¡métete, el agua está estupenda!; **to go in** entrar

(**b**) *(at home, office)* **is your mother in?** ¿está tu madre (en casa)?; **will you be in (at the office) next week?** ¿estarás en la oficina la semana que viene?; **to have an evening in** pasar una tarde en casa; **to stay in** quedarse en casa, no salir

(**c**) *(arrived, returned)* **is the train in yet?** ¿ha llegado ya el tren?; **when's the flight due in?** ¿a qué hora está previsto que llegue el vuelo?; **applications should be in by next week** las solicitudes deberán llegar antes de la semana que viene; **we should get some more in next week** la semana que viene recibiremos más

(**d**) *(tide)* **to be in** estar alto(a)

(**e**) *(inwards)* hacia dentro; **the photo was curling in at the edges** la foto tenía los bordes curvados hacia dentro

(**f**) *(fashionable)* **to be in** estar de moda; **mini-skirts are in** se llevan *or RP* se usan las minifaldas

(**g**) *Sport (within field of play)* **the ball was in!** ¡la bola entró!; **the umpire called the shot in** el juez de silla dijo que la bola había entrado

(**h**) *Sport (in baseball, cricket)* **he's been in for an hour** lleva bateando una hora; **the umpire gave him in** el árbitro decidió que no quedaba eliminado

(**i**) *(participating)* **are you in or not?** ¿te apuntas o no?

(**j**) IDIOMS **she is in for a surprise** le espera una sorpresa; **we're in for some heavy showers** nos esperan unos buenos chaparrones; *Fam* **he's in for it** se va a enterar de lo que es bueno *or Esp* de lo que vale un peine; *Fam* **he's got it in for me** la *Esp* tiene tomada *or Méx* trae conmigo, *RP* se la agarró conmigo; **to be in on a plan** estar al corriente de un plan; *Fam* **to be in with sb** tener amistad *or Esp* mano con alguien; *Br Fam* **she's well in there!** *Esp* ¡menudo chollo ha encontrado!, *Méx* ¡qué churro ha encontrado!, *RP* ¡qué curro se consiguió!

3 *adj* (**a**) *(fashionable)* **it's the in place to go** es el lugar de moda; **the in crowd** la gente selecta; **roller-blading was the in thing last year** el patinaje en línea fue la moda del año pasado ►► *Comptr* **in box** *(for e-mail)* buzón *m* de entrada

(**b**) *(understood by the few)* **an in joke** un chiste privado

4 *n* **the ins and outs** los pormenores

5 in all, in total *adv* en total

6 in that *conj* en el sentido de que; **it's rather complicated in that...** es bastante complicado en el sentido de que...

inability [ɪnə'bɪlɪtɪ] *n* incapacidad *f* (**to do sth** para hacer algo); **our i. to help them** nuestra incapacidad para ayudarlos

in absentia [ɪnæb'sentɪə] *adv Formal* en su ausencia

inaccessibility [ɪnæksesɪ'bɪlɪtɪ] *n* inaccesibilidad *f*

inaccessible [ɪnæk'sesɪbəl] *adj* (**a**) *(impossible to reach)* inaccesible; **the village is i. by car** no se puede llegar al pueblo en coche *or Am* carro *or RP* auto (**b**) *(unavailable) (person)* inaccesible; **he's been i. all morning** ha estado ilocalizable toda la mañana (**c**) *(obscure) (film, book, subject)* incomprensible

inaccuracy [ɪn'ækjʊrəsɪ] *n* (**a**) *(imprecision) (of information)* inexactitud *f*; *(of calculation, report, measurement)* inexactitud *f*; *(of translation, portrayal)* falta *f* de fidelidad, inexactitud *f* (**b**) *(mistake)* imprecisión *f*, error *m*; **the report was full of inaccuracies** el informe estaba lleno de imprecisiones (**c**) *(of firearm, shot)* imprecisión *f*

inaccurate [ɪn'ækjʊrət] *adj* (**a**) *(information)* inexacto(a); *(calculation, report, measurement)* inexacto(a); *(translation, portrayal)* poco fiel, inexacto(a) (**b**) *(firearm, shot)* impreciso(a), poco certero(a)

inaccurately [ɪn'ækjʊrətlɪ] *adv* (**a**) *(to calculate, measure, report)* sin exactitud, sin precisión; *(to translate, portray)* de forma inexacta (**b**) *(shoot)* sin precisión, de forma poco certera

inaction [ɪn'ækʃən] *n* pasividad *f*, inactividad *f*

inactive [ɪn'æktɪv] *adj* (**a**) *(person, animal)* inactivo(a), en reposo (**b**) *(lazy)* inactivo(a), pasivo(a) (**c**) *(inoperative) (machine)* inactivo(a), parado(a) (**d**) *(dormant) (volcano)* inactivo(a); *(virus)* inactivo(a) (**e**) *Chem* inactivo(a)

inactivity [ɪnæk'tɪvɪtɪ] *n* inactividad *f*

inadequacy [ɪn'ædɪkwəsɪ] *n* (**a**) *(of explanation, measures)* insuficiencia *f* (**b**) *(of person)* incapacidad *f*; **feelings of i.** sensación de incompetencia *or* de no dar la talla

inadequate [ɪn'ædɪkwət] *adj* (**a**) *(explanation, measures)* insuficiente; **we were given i. resources for the task** los recursos que nos facilitaron para realizar la labor eran insuficientes (**b**) *(person)* inepto(a), incompetente; **I feel i.** *Esp* siento que no doy la talla; **to feel i. to the task** no sentirse capacitado(a) para la tarea; **he's socially i.** es un inadaptado social

inadequately [ɪn'ædɪkwətlɪ] *adv* insuficientemente; **i. trained/equipped** mal *or* insuficientemente preparado(a)/equipado(a); **the vehicle performed i. on rough terrain** el vehículo funcionaba deficientemente en terrenos escabrosos

inadmissible [ɪnəd'mɪsɪbəl] *adj Law (evidence)* inadmisible

inadvertent [ɪnəd'vɜːtənt] *adj* fortuito(a), inintencionado(a); **an i. error** un error involuntario

inadvertently [ɪnəd'vɜːtəntlɪ] *adv* sin darse cuenta, inadvertidamente

inadvisability [ɪnədvaɪzə'bɪlɪtɪ] *n* **she pointed out the i. of such a move** señaló lo poco aconsejable que era tal paso

inadvisable [ɪnəd'vaɪzəbəl] *adj* poco aconsejable, desaconsejable

inalienable [ɪn'eɪlɪənəbəl] *adj Formal* inalienable; **an i. right** un derecho inalienable

inane [ɪ'neɪn] *adj (person, behaviour)* estúpido(a), necio(a); *(remark, laugh)* estúpido(a)

inanely [ɪ'neɪnlɪ] *adv* **to grin i.** esbozar una sonrisa estúpida

inanimate [ɪn'ænɪmət] *adj* inanimado(a); **an i. object** un objeto inanimado

inanition [ɪnə'nɪʃən] *n Formal (lethargy)* letargo *m*

inanity [ɪ'nænɪtɪ] *n* (**a**) *(stupidity)* estupidez *f*, necedad *f* (**b**) *(stupid remark)* sandez *f*, estupidez *f*

inapplicable [ɪn'æplɪkəbəl] *adj* inaplicable (**to** a); **delete where i.** táchese lo que no proceda

inapposite [ɪn'æpəzɪt] *adj Formal* inapropiado(a), inoportuno(a)

inappropriate [ɪnə'prəʊprɪət] *adj (behaviour, remark)* inadecuado(a), improcedente; *(dress)* inadecuado(a), impropio(a); *(present, choice)* inapropiado(a); *(time, moment)* inoportuno(a); **it would be i. for me to comment** no estaría bien que yo me pronunciara

inappropriately [ɪnə'prəʊprɪətlɪ] *adv* de modo inadecuado; **to be i. dressed** no ir vestido de un modo adecuado; **i. timed** inoportuno(a)

inappropriateness [ɪnə'prəʊprɪətnɪs] *n (of remark, behaviour)* lo inadecuado, lo improcedente; *(of dress)* lo inadecuado, lo impropio; *(of present, choice)* lo inapropiado

inapt [ɪn'æpt] *adj* inapropiado(a)

inaptly [ɪn'æptlɪ] *adv* inapropiadamente

inarticulate [ɪnɑː'tɪkjʊlɪt] *adj* (**a**) *(sound)* inarticulado(a) (**b**) **to be i.** *(of person)* expresarse mal; **she was i. with rage** estaba tan *esp Esp* enfadada *or esp Am* enojada que no podía ni hablar (**c**) *Biol* inarticulado(a)

inarticulately [ɪnɑː'tɪkjʊlɪtlɪ] *adv* (**a**) *(to mumble)* de forma ininteligible (**b**) *(to express oneself)* mal, con dificultad

inartistic [ɪnɑː'tɪstɪk] *adj* (**a**) *(lacking artistic taste)* sin sensibilidad artística (**b**) *(lacking artistic talent)* sin talento artístico

inasmuch as [ɪnəz'mʌtʃəz], **insomuch as** [ɪnsəʊ'mʌtʃəz] *conj Formal* (**a**) *(given that)* dado que, puesto que (**b**) *(insofar as)* en la medida en que, en tanto en cuanto

inattention [ɪnəˈtenʃən] *n* falta *f* de atención; **a moment's i. can lead to an accident** un momento de descuido *or* distracción puede dar lugar a un accidente; **your essay shows i. to detail** tu redacción muestra una falta de atención a los detalles

inattentive [ɪnəˈtentɪv] *adj* (**a**) *(paying no attention)* distraído(a), desatento(a); **most of the students seemed i. until I mentioned her sex life** la mayoría de los alumnos parecían estar desatentos hasta el momento en que mencioné su vida sexual; **to be i. to** no poner suficiente atención a *or* en
(**b**) *(neglectful)* negligente, descuidado(a); **to be i. to** *or* **towards sb** descuidar a alguien, no prestar la debida atención a alguien

inattentively [ɪnəˈtentɪvlɪ] *adv* distraídamente, sin prestar atención

inattentiveness [ɪnəˈtentɪvnɪs] *n* falta *f* de atención

inaudibility [ɪnɔːdɪˈbɪlɪtɪ] *n* falta *f* de audibilidad

inaudible [ɪnˈɔːdɪbəl] *adj* inaudible

inaudibly [ɪnˈɔːdɪblɪ] *adv* de forma inaudible

inaugural [ɪˈnɔːgjʊrəl] **1** *n US (speech)* discurso *m* inaugural; *(ceremony)* acto *m* inaugural; **the President's i.** *(speech)* el discurso de investidura del presidente; *(ceremony)* el acto de investidura del presidente, la toma de posesión del presidente
2 *adj* inaugural; *(ceremony)* de investidura

inaugurate [ɪˈnɔːgjʊreɪt] *vt* (**a**) *(event, scheme)* inaugurar; **this inaugurates a new era in global politics** esto da comienzo a una nueva era en materia de política global (**b**) *Pol* **the President will be inaugurated in January** el presidente tomará posesión de su cargo en enero

inauguration [ɪnɔːgjʊˈreɪʃən] *n* (**a**) *(of event, scheme)* inauguración *f*; **the i. of a new era in global politics** el comienzo de una nueva era en materia de política global (**b**) *(of president)* toma *f* de posesión ►► ***I. Day*** = día de la toma de posesión del presidente de los Estados Unidos

inauspicious [ɪnɔːsˈpɪʃəs] *adj (circumstances)* desafortunado(a); *(start, moment)* aciago(a)

inauspiciously [ɪnɔːsˈpɪʃəslɪ] *adv* de forma poco propicia; **to start i.** tener un comienzo aciago

inauthentic [ɪnɔːˈθentɪk] *adj* no auténtico(a), falso(a)

in-between [ɪnbɪˈtwiːn] *adj* intermedio(a)

inborn [ˈɪnˈbɔːn] *adj* innato(a)

inbound [ˈɪnbaʊnd] *adj (flight, passenger)* de llegada

inbred [ˈɪnˈbred] *adj* (**a**) *(animals, people)* endogámico(a) (**b**) *(innate)* innato(a)

inbreeding [ˈɪnbriːdɪŋ] *n* endogamia *f*

in-built [ˈɪnˈbɪlt] *adj (tendency, weakness)* inherente; *(feature)* incorporado(a); **his height gives him an i. advantage** su altura le proporciona una ventaja de entrada

Inc [ɪŋk] *adj US Com* (*abbr* **Incorporated**) ≃ S.A.

inc (**a**) (*abbr* **including**) incl. (**b**) (*abbr* **inclusive**) incl.

Inca [ˈɪŋkə] **1** *n* inca *mf*
2 *adj* incaico(a), inca

incalculable [ɪnˈkælkjʊləbəl] *adj* incalculable

incalculably [ɪnˈkælkjʊləblɪ] *adv* inmensamente

in camera [ɪnˈkæmərə] *adv Law* a puerta cerrada

incandescence [ɪnkænˈdesəns] *n* incandescencia *f*

incandescent [ɪnkænˈdesənt] *adj* incandescente; *Fig* **to be i. with rage** estar rojo(a) de ira ►► ***i. lamp*** lámpara *f* de incandescencia

incantation [ɪnkænˈteɪʃən] *n* conjuro *m*

incantatory [ɪnˈkæntətərɪ] *adj* mágico(a), fascinante

incapability [ɪnkeɪpəˈbɪlɪtɪ] *n* incapacidad *f*

incapable [ɪnˈkeɪpəbəl] *adj* (**a**) *(not able)* incapaz (**of doing sth** de hacer algo); **she would be i. of such an act** sería incapaz de hacer algo así; **she is i. of kindness/deceit** es incapaz de ser amable/engañar a nadie; **the stroke left him i. of speech** el derrame le dañó totalmente el habla
(**b**) *(helpless)* inepto(a), inútil
(**c**) *Formal (not allowing)* que no admite, que no se presta a; **feelings i. of expression** sentimientos imposibles de expresar; **the problem is i. of a simple solution** el problema no admite una solución sencilla
(**d**) *Law* **to be declared i.** ser declarado(a) incapaz, obtener la declaración de incapacidad

incapacitate [ɪnkəˈpæsɪteɪt] *vt* (**a**) *(deprive of strength, power)* incapacitar; **to be incapacitated** quedar incapacitado(a) *or* impedido(a) (**b**) *Law* incapacitar

incapacity [ɪnkəˈpæsɪtɪ] *n* (**a**) *(inability)* incapacidad *f* (**b**) *Law* incapacidad *f*

in-car [ˈɪnkɑː(r)] *adj* de automóvil; **an i. stereo** un autorradio

incarcerate [ɪnˈkɑːsəreɪt] *vt Formal* encarcelar, recluir

incarceration [ɪnkɑːsəˈreɪʃən] *n Formal* encarcelamiento *m*, reclusión *f*

incarnate [ɪnˈkɑːneɪt] **1** *adj* personificado(a); **beauty i.** la belleza personificada; **the devil i.** el diablo en persona
2 *vt* encarnar

incarnation [ɪnkɑːˈneɪʃən] *n* (**a**) *(personification)* encarnación *f*; **he's the very i. of humility** es la humildad personificada; **in a previous i.** en una encarnación anterior, en otra vida (**b**) *Rel* **the I.** la Encarnación

incautious [ɪnˈkɔːʃəs] *adj* incauto(a), imprudente

incautiously [ɪnˈkɔːʃəslɪ] *adv* incautamente, imprudentemente

incendiary [ɪnˈsendɪərɪ] **1** *n* (**a**) *(bomb)* bomba *f* incendiaria (**b**) *(arsonist)* incendiario(a) *m,f*, pirómano(a) *m,f*
2 *adj (bomb, device, remarks)* incendiario(a)

incense[1] [ˈɪnsens] *n* incienso *m* ►► ***i. burner*** incensario *m*

incense[2] [ɪnˈsens] *vt (anger)* encolerizar, enfurecer; **he was incensed by** *or* **at her indifference** lo exacerbaba su indiferencia; **I was absolutely incensed** estaba indignadísimo(a)

incensed [ɪnˈsenst] *adj* enfurecido(a); **to get** *or* **become i.** enfurecerse

incent [ɪnˈsent] *vt US* incentivar

incentive [ɪnˈsentɪv] *n* (**a**) *(stimulus, motivation)* incentivo *m*; **they have lost their i.** han perdido el estímulo; **he has no i. to work harder** no tiene ningún incentivo para empeñarse más en su trabajo; **to offer sb an i.** ofrecer un incentivo a alguien; **the price offers a real i.** el precio supone un verdadero aliciente (**b**) *(payment)* incentivo *m*; **tax incentives** incentivos fiscales ►► *US* ***i. plan*** plan *m* de incentivos; *Br* ***i. scheme*** plan *m* de incentivos

incentivize [ɪnˈsentɪvaɪz] *vt US* incentivar

inception [ɪnˈsepʃən] *n Formal* comienzo *m*, inicio *m*

incessant [ɪnˈsesənt] *adj* incesante, continuo(a)

incessantly [ɪnˈsesəntlɪ] *adv* incesantemente, sin parar

incest [ˈɪnsest] *n* incesto *m*

incestuous [ɪnˈsestjʊəs] *adj* (**a**) *(sexually)* incestuoso(a) (**b**) *Fig (environment, group)* endogámico(a)

inch [ɪntʃ] **1** *n* (**a**) *(measurement)* pulgada *f* (= 2,54 cm); **it's about 6 inches wide** mide unas 6 pulgadas de ancho; **it's a few inches shorter** es unas pulgadas más corto; **i. by i.** palmo a palmo; **the car missed me by inches** no me atropelló el coche por cuestión de centímetros
(**b**) IDIOMS **I know every i. of the town** me conozco la ciudad como la palma de la mano; **we'll have to fight every i. of the way** tendremos que luchar palmo a palmo; **he's every i. the gentleman** es todo un caballero; **to be within an i. of doing sth** estar en un tris de hacer algo; **to beat sb to within an i. of their life** estar en un tris de matar a alguien; **she won't give an i.** no cederá ni un ápice; **the government won't budge** *or* **give an i.** el Gobierno no cederá (en) lo más mínimo; **give her an i. and she'll take a mile** dale la mano y se tomará el brazo
2 *vt* **to i. one's way across/forward/up** ir cruzando/avanzando/subiendo poco a poco
3 *vi* **to i. in/out** entrar/salir muy despacio *or* poco a poco; **he inched towards the door** se acercó poco a poco a la puerta

►**inch along** *vi* avanzar poco a poco; **he inched along the ledge** avanzó lentamente por la cornisa

►**inch forward** *vi* avanzar poco a poco; **he inched forward on his hands and knees until he could see out of the window** gateó muy despacio hasta alcanzar a ver por la ventana

inchoate [ɪnˈkəʊeɪt] *adj Formal* incipiente

inchoative [ɪnˈkəʊətɪv] *adj Gram* incoativo(a)

inchworm [ˈɪntʃwɜːm] *n* oruga *f* geómetra

incidence [ˈɪnsɪdəns] *n* (**a**) *(frequency)* índice *m* (**of** de); *(of disease)* incidencia *f* (**of** de); **there is a higher/lower i. of crime** hay un mayor/menor índice de delincuencia (**b**) *Phys* incidencia *f*; **angle of i.** ángulo de incidencia

incident [ˈɪnsɪdənt] *n* incidente *m*; **the demonstration passed off without i.** la manifestación se desarrolló sin incidentes ►► ***i. room*** *(in police investigation)* centro *m* de investigaciones policiales

incidental [ɪnsɪˈdentəl] *adj* incidental, accesorio(a); **the project will have other i. benefits** el proyecto traerá aparejados otros beneficios adicionales; **the risks i. to such an enterprise** los riesgos propios de semejante iniciativa; **the fatigue i. to such work** el cansancio inherente a ese tipo de trabajo ►► ***i. expenses*** gastos *mpl* imprevistos; *Cin Theat* ***i. music*** música *f* de acompañamiento

incidentally [ɪnsɪˈdentəlɪ] *adv* (**a**) *(by the way)* por cierto; **i., have you seen Mark?** por cierto, ¿has visto a Mark? (**b**) *(to mention, deal with)* de pasada

incinerate [ɪnˈsɪnəreɪt] *vt* incinerar

incineration [ɪnsɪnəˈreɪʃən] *n* incineración *f*

incinerator [ɪnˈsɪnəreɪtə(r)] *n* incineradora *f*

incipient [ɪnˈsɪpɪənt] *adj Formal* incipiente

incise [ɪnˈsaɪz] *vt (engrave, carve)* burilar, grabar

incision [ɪnˈsɪʒən] *n* incisión *f*; **to make an i. in sth** hacer una incisión en algo

incisive [ɪnˈsaɪsɪv] *adj (comment, analysis)* agudo(a), incisivo(a); *(mind)* sagaz, incisivo(a)

incisively [ɪnˈsaɪsɪvlɪ] *adv (to comment)* con agudeza; *(to think)* con sagacidad

incisiveness [ɪnˈsaɪsɪvnɪs] *n (of comment)* mordacidad *f*; *(of thought)* agudeza *f*

incisor [ɪnˈsaɪzə(r)] *n* incisivo *m*

incite [ɪnˈsaɪt] *vt* incitar, instigar; **to i. sb to do sth** incitar a alguien a que haga algo; **to i. sb to violence** incitar a alguien a la violencia; **they were accused of inciting racial hatred** se los acusó de instigar el odio racial

incitement [ɪnˈsaɪtmənt] *n* incitación *f*; **i. to riot/violence** incitación al amotinamiento/a la violencia

incivility [ɪnsɪˈvɪlɪtɪ] *n Formal* descortesía *f*

incl (a) (*abbr* **including**) incl. (b) (*abbr* **inclusive**) incl.

inclemency [ɪnˈklemənsɪ] *n Formal (of weather)* inclemencia *f*

inclement [ɪnˈklemənt] *adj Formal (weather)* inclemente

inclination [ɪnklɪˈneɪʃən] *n* (a) *(tendency)* inclinación *f*, tendencia *f*, propensión *f*; **a decided i. towards laziness** una clara tendencia a la vagancia; **by i.** por naturaleza; **he was by i. a loner** era un solitario por naturaleza
(b) *(liking, wish)* inclinación *f*; **to have lost all i. for sth** haber perdido el gusto *or* la afición por algo; **to have no i. to do sth** no sentir ninguna inclinación por *or* a hacer algo; **my own i. would be to say yes** instintivamente diría que sí; **you should follow your own i. in the matter** deberías dejarte llevar por tu instinto en este asunto; **I do it from necessity, not from i.** lo hago por necesidad, no por inclinación natural
(c) *(slant, lean)* inclinación *f*, pendiente *f*
(d) *(action)* inclinación *f*; **a slight i. of the head** una ligera inclinación de la cabeza

incline 1 *n* [ˈɪnklaɪn] *(slope)* cuesta *f*, pendiente *f*
2 *vt* [ɪnˈklaɪn] (a) *(motivate, cause)* inclinar; **her remarks don't i. me to be sympathetic** sus comentarios no me mueven a ser comprensivo (b) *(lean)* inclinar; **she inclined her head towards him** inclinó la cabeza hacia él
3 *vi* (a) *(tend)* **to i. to** *or* **towards** inclinarse a; **to i. to the belief that...** inclinarse a pensar que... (b) *(lean)* inclinarse

inclined [ɪnˈklaɪnd] *adj* (a) *(having a tendency)* **he's i. to exaggeration** tiene tendencia a exagerar; **he's i. to put on weight** es propenso a engordar; **these drawers are i. to stick** estos cajones se atascan fácilmente; **I'm not musically i.** *(don't like music)* no siento inclinación *or* no tengo afición por la música; *(have no talent)* no tengo talento *or* aptitudes para la música
(b) *(disposed)* **to be i. to do sth** tener tendencia *or* tender a hacer algo; **I'm i. to agree with you** soy de tu misma opinión; **to be well i. towards sth/sb** inclinarse a favor de algo/alguien; **if you are so i.** *(if you want to)* si así lo deseas, si eso es lo que quieres
(c) *(sloping)* inclinado(a) ▸▸ ***i. plane*** plano *m* inclinado

inclose = **enclose**

inclosure = **enclosure**

include [ɪnˈkluːd] *vt* incluir; *(in letter)* adjuntar; **my duties i. sorting the mail** una de mis obligaciones es clasificar la correspondencia; **my name was not included on the list** mi nombre no figuraba en la lista; **does that i. me?** ¿yo también?, ¿eso me incluye a mí también?; **if you i. Christmas Day** contando con el día de Navidad; **to i. sb among one's friends** incluir a alguien en el círculo de amistades personales; **the price does not i. accommodation** el alojamiento no está incluido en el precio; **included in the price are two excursions** el precio incluye dos excursiones; **everyone, myself included, was surprised** todos nos sorprendimos, incluido yo; **all his property was sold, his house included** vendieron todo lo que poseía, incluida la casa

▸ **include in** *vt sep Br Fam* **i. me in!** ¡cuenta conmigo!, *RP* ¡contáme!

▸ **include out** *vt sep Br Fam Hum* **you can i. me out!** ¡no cuentes conmigo!, ¡de mí olvídate!

including [ɪnˈkluːdɪŋ] *prep* **$4.99 i. postage and packing** 4,99 dólares incluyendo gastos de envío; **five books, i. one I hadn't read** cinco libros, incluyendo uno que no había leído; **up to and i. page 40/next Friday** hasta la página 40/el viernes próximo inclusive; **not i.** sin contar, sin incluir

inclusion [ɪnˈkluːʒən] *n* inclusión *f*

inclusive [ɪnˈkluːsɪv] *adj* (a) **i. of** *(including)* incluido(a), incluyendo; **i. of VAT** IVA incluido; **an i. price/sum** un precio/una cifra con todo incluido (b) *(with dates)* **from the 4th to the 12th February i.** del 4 al 12 de febrero, ambos inclusive; **from July to September i.** desde principios de julio hasta finales de septiembre (c) *(comprehensive)* completo(a), integral

incognito [ɪnkɒgˈniːtəʊ] *adv* de incógnito; **to remain i.** mantener el anonimato

incoherence [ɪnkəʊˈhɪərəns] *n* incoherencia *f*

incoherent [ɪnkəʊˈhɪərənt] *adj* incoherente; **he was i. with rage** estaba tan furioso que le fallaban las palabras

incoherently [ɪnkəʊˈhɪərəntlɪ] *adv* incoherentemente; **to mutter i.** murmurar de un modo incoherente

incombustible [ɪnkəmˈbʌstɪbəl] *adj* incombustible

income [ˈɪnkəm] *n (of person) (from work)* ingresos *mpl*; *(from shares, investment)* rendimientos *mpl*, réditos *mpl*; *(from property)* renta *f*; *(in accounts)* ingresos *mpl*; **a high/low i.** un elevado/bajo nivel de ingresos; **to live within/beyond one's i.** vivir (uno) dentro de/por encima de sus posibilidades ▸▸ ***i. bracket*** tramo *m* de renta; ***incomes policy*** política *f* de rentas; *Br* ***i. support*** = ayuda gubernamental a personas con muy bajos ingresos o desempleadas pero sin derecho al subsidio de desempleo; ***i. tax*** impuesto *m* sobre la renta; ***i. tax return*** declaración *f* de la renta *or* del impuesto sobre la renta

incomer [ˈɪnkʌmə(r)] *n Br* forastero(a) *m,f* recién llegado(a)

incoming [ˈɪnkʌmɪŋ] *adj* (a) *(from outside)* **i. calls** llamadas *or Am* llamados de fuera; **i. flights** vuelos de llegada; **i. mail** correo recibido (b) *(tide)* ascendente (c) *Mil (fire)* (procedente del) enemigo; **the i. missile** el misil que se aproximaba (d) *(government, president)* entrante

incommensurable [ɪnkəˈmenʃərəbəl] *adj Formal* incompatible (**with** con)

incommensurate [ɪnkəˈmenʃərət] *adj Formal* desproporcionado(a) (**with** con relación a, en relación con)

incommodious [ɪnkəˈməʊdɪəs] *adj Formal (uncomfortable)* incómodo(a)

incommunicable [ɪnkəˈmjuːnɪkəbəl] *adj* incomunicable, inexpresable

incommunicado [ɪnkəmjuːnɪˈkɑːdəʊ] *adv* **to hold** *or* **keep sb i.** dejar incomunicado(a) a alguien; *Fig* **I'll be i. while I'm on holiday** estaré ilocalizable durante mis vacaciones

in-company [ˈɪnkʌmpənɪ] *adj esp Br* ***i. training*** fomación *f* en el lugar de trabajo

incomparable [ɪnˈkɒmpərəbəl] *adj* (a) *(without equal)* incomparable; **her i. beauty** su belleza sin igual; **with i. ease/skill** con incomparable soltura/maestría (b) *(cannot be compared)* **the two cases are quite i.** no hay comparación entre ambos casos

incomparably [ɪnˈkɒmpərəblɪ] *adv* incomparablemente, infinitamente

incompatibility [ɪnkəmpætɪˈbɪlɪtɪ] *n* (a) *(of people, statements)* incompatibilidad *f* (**with** con) (b) *(as grounds for divorce)* incompatibilidad *f* de caracteres (c) *Comptr* incompatibilidad *f* (**with** con)

incompatible [ɪnkəmˈpætɪbəl] *adj* (a) *(people, statements)* incompatible (**with** con) (b) *Comptr* incompatible (**with** con)

incompetence [ɪnˈkɒmpɪtəns] *n* (a) *(lack of skill, ability)* incompetencia *f* (b) *Law* incapacidad *f*

incompetent [ɪnˈkɒmpɪtənt] 1 *adj* (a) *(lacking skill, ability)* incompetente (b) *Law (judge, court)* incompetente
2 *n* incompetente *mf*

incompetently [ɪnˈkɒmpɪtəntlɪ] *adv* incompetentemente, de modo incompetente

incomplete [ɪnkəmˈpliːt] *adj* (a) *(unfinished)* inconcluso(a), inacabado(a); **the building remained i.** el edificio quedó sin terminar (b) *(lacking something)* incompleto(a); **his i. understanding of what was involved** su comprensión parcial del alcance de los hechos

incompletely [ɪnkəmˈpliːtlɪ] *adv* de forma incompleta

incompleteness [ɪnkəmˈpliːtnɪs] *n* (a) *(unfinished nature)* **there's a feeling of i. about his paintings** sus pinturas producen la sensación de estar incompletas *or* inacabadas (b) *(in logic)* incompletud *f*

incomprehensibility [ɪnkɒmprɪhensɪˈbɪlɪtɪ] *n* incomprensibilidad *f*

incomprehensible [ɪnkɒmprɪ'hensɪbəl] *adj* incomprensible

incomprehensibly [ɪnkɒmprɪ'hensɪblɪ] *adv* incomprensiblemente

incomprehension [ɪnkɒmprɪ'henʃən] *n* incomprensión *f*; **to the utter i. of those present...** ante la total perplejidad *or* el total asombro de los presentes...

inconceivable [ɪnkən'si:vəbəl] *adj* inconcebible

inconceivably [ɪnkən'si:vəblɪ] *adv* inconcebiblemente

inconclusive [ɪnkən'klu:sɪv] *adj (evidence, investigation)* no concluyente; **the results are i.** los resultados no son concluyentes; **the meeting was i.** la reunión no sirvió para aclarar las cosas

inconclusively [ɪnkən'klu:sɪvlɪ] *adv* sin una conclusión clara; **the meeting ended i.** la reunión terminó sin que se llegase a una conclusión clara

inconclusiveness [ɪnkən'klu:sɪvnɪs] *n* carácter *m* no concluyente *or* no decisivo

incongruity [ɪnkɒŋ'gru:ɪtɪ] *n* incongruencia *f*; **there were many startling incongruities to be found in his account** su informe estaba lleno de incongruencias sorprendentes

incongruous [ɪn'kɒŋgrʊəs] *adj* incongruente; **he was an i. figure among the factory workers** era un personaje singular entre los obreros de la fábrica

incongruously [ɪn'kɒŋgrʊəslɪ] *adv* de forma incongruente

inconsequential [ɪnkɒnsɪ'kwenʃəl] *adj* **(a)** *(unimportant, trivial) (matter, remarks)* trivial, intrascendente; **an i. little man** un hombrecillo insignificante **(b)** *Formal (not following)* inconsecuente, ilógico(a)

inconsequentiality ['ɪnkɒnsɪkwenʃɪ'ælɪtɪ] *n* **(a)** *(of matter, remarks)* trivialidad *f*, intrascendencia *f* **(b)** *Formal (illogicality)* falta *f* de lógica

inconsiderable [ɪnkən'sɪdərəbəl] *adj* **it is not an i. sum of money** es una suma de dinero nada despreciable; **he had difficulty moving his not i. bulk** tenía dificultad en desplazar de acá para allá su considerable corpulencia

inconsiderate [ɪnkən'sɪdərɪt] *adj (person, action, remark)* desconsiderado(a); **that was very i. of you** fue una falta de consideración por tu parte; **to be i. towards sb** no tener consideración con alguien; **don't be so i.** no seas desconsiderado(a), ten un poco de consideración

inconsiderately [ɪnkən'sɪdərɪtlɪ] *adv* desconsideradamente

inconsistency [ɪnkən'sɪstənsɪ] *n* **(a)** *(lack of logic, illogical statement)* incoherencia *f*, incongruencia *f*; **there are several inconsistencies in your argument** hay varias contradicciones en tu razonamiento **(b)** *(uneven quality)* irregularidad *f*

inconsistent [ɪnkən'sɪstənt] *adj* **(a)** *(contradictory) (statement)* incongruente, incoherente; **you're being i.** *(in saying that)* te estás contradiciendo; *(in doing that)* estás siendo inconsecuente *or* incoherente; **his words are i. with his conduct** sus palabras no están en consonancia con sus actos **(b)** *(uneven)* irregular

inconsistently [ɪnkən'sɪstəntlɪ] *adv* **(a)** *(to behave)* de manera inconsecuente *or* ilógica; *(to argue)* sin coherencia, de forma incongruente **(b)** *(unevenly)* irregularmente, de forma irregular

inconsolable [ɪnkən'səʊləbəl] *adj* inconsolable, desconsolado(a)

inconsolably [ɪnkən'səʊləblɪ] *adv* desconsoladamente

inconspicuous [ɪnkən'spɪkjʊəs] *adj* discreto(a); **to be i.** pasar desapercibido(a) *or* inadvertido(a); **she tried to make herself as i. as possible** trató de pasar lo más inadvertida posible

inconspicuously [ɪnkən'spɪkjʊəslɪ] *adv* con discreción

inconstancy [ɪn'kɒnstənsɪ] *n Formal* **(a)** *(fickleness)* inconstancia *f*, volubilidad *f* **(b)** *(instability, impermanence)* variabilidad *f*, inestabilidad *f*

inconstant [ɪn'kɒnstənt] *adj Formal* **(a)** *(fickle)* inconstante, voluble **(b)** *(unstable, impermanent)* variable, inestable; **the i. nature of this world** la naturaleza inestable *or* cambiante de este mundo

incontestable [ɪnkən'testəbəl] *adj* incontestable, indiscutible

incontestably [ɪnkən'testəblɪ] *adv* indiscutiblemente, de manera incontestable

incontinence [ɪn'kɒntɪnəns] *n* **(a)** *Med* incontinencia *f* ►► ***i. pants*** pañales *mpl* (para adultos) **(b)** *Formal (in one's passions)* incontinencia *f*

incontinent [ɪn'kɒntɪnənt] *adj* **(a)** *Med* incontinente **(b)** *Formal (in one's passions)* incontinente

incontrovertible [ɪnkɒntrə'vɜ:tɪbəl] *adj* incontrovertible, indiscutible; **i. evidence** pruebas irrefutables

incontrovertibly ['ɪnkɒntrə'vɜ:təblɪ] *adv* indiscutiblemente, de manera incontrovertible

inconvenience [ɪnkən'vi:njəns] **1** *n* **(a)** *(awkwardness) (of time, place)* inconveniencia *f*, inoportunidad *f*; **the i. of a small house** los inconvenientes *or* las desventajas de una casa pequeña

(b) *(trouble, difficulty)* molestia *f*; **we apologize for any i.** disculpen las molestias; **to be an i. to sb** suponer una molestia para alguien; **I don't want to put you to any i.** no quiero ocasionarles *or* causarles ninguna molestia

(c) *(problem, drawback)* inconveniente *m*

2 *vt* causar molestias a; **please don't i. yourselves on my account!** ¡por mí no se molesten, se lo ruego!

inconvenient [ɪnkən'vi:njənt] *adj* **(a)** *(awkward) (time, request)* inoportuno(a); *(place)* mal situado(a); **if it's not i.** si no es molestia, si no hay inconveniente; **I'm afraid four thirty would be i.** (me temo que) las cuatro y media no me viene bien *or* no es buena hora; **he has chosen to ignore any i. facts** ha decidido pasar por alto los datos que no le convienen

(b) *(impractical)* **it's very i. living so far from town** resulta muy incómodo vivir tan lejos de la ciudad; **this house is very i. for the shops** esta casa es muy poco práctica a la hora de ir de compras

inconveniently [ɪnkən'vi:njəntlɪ] *adv* inoportunamente; **the announcement was i. timed** el anuncio se produjo en un momento inadecuado *or* inoportuno; **the shop is i. situated** la tienda no está en buen sitio *or* no queda muy a mano

inconvertible [ɪnkən'vɜ:təbəl] *adj (currency)* inconvertible

incorporate [ɪn'kɔ:pəreɪt] *vt* **(a)** *(integrate)* incorporar (**into** a) **(b)** *(include)* incluir, comprender; **to i. amendments into a text** introducir modificaciones en un texto; **the report incorporates the latest research** el informe *or CAm, Méx* reporte incorpora las investigaciones más recientes **(c)** *Com* **to i. a company** constituir (en sociedad) una empresa

incorporated [ɪn'kɔ:pəreɪtɪd] *adj US (company)* legalmente constituido(a) en sociedad anónima; **Bradley, Wells & Jones I.** Bradley, Wells & Jones S.A.

incorporation [ɪnkɔ:pə'reɪʃən] *n* **(a)** *(integration)* incorporación *f* **(b)** *(inclusion)* incorporación *f* **(c)** *Com* constitución *f* en sociedad anónima

incorporeal [ɪnkɔ:'pɔ:rɪəl] *adj Literary* incorpóreo(a)

incorrect [ɪnkə'rekt] *adj* **(a)** *(wrong) (amount, figure)* incorrecto(a); *(information, use, spelling)* incorrecto(a); **it would be i. to say that...** sería incorrecto decir que...; **to prove i.** resultar ser incorrecto(a) **(b)** *(person, behaviour)* incorrecto(a), inapropiado(a)

incorrectly [ɪnkə'rektlɪ] *adv* **(a)** *(wrongly)* incorrectamente; **the letter was i. addressed** la dirección a la que iba dirigida la carta era incorrecta; **he was i. diagnosed with cancer** se equivocaron al diagnosticarle que tenía cáncer **(b)** *(improperly)* incorrectamente, inapropiadamente; **he behaved most i.** se comportó muy inadecuadamente, su comportamiento fue de lo más inadecuado

incorrigible [ɪn'kɒrɪdʒɪbəl] *adj* incorregible; **he is quite i.** es incorregible, no tiene remedio

incorruptibility [ɪnkərʌptɪ'bɪlɪtɪ] *n* **(a)** *(of person)* incorruptibilidad *f* **(b)** *(of material)* incorruptibilidad *f*

incorruptible [ɪnkə'rʌptɪbəl] *adj* **(a)** *(person)* incorruptible **(b)** *(material)* incorruptible

increase 1 *n* ['ɪnkri:s] aumento *m* (**in** de); *(in price, temperature)* aumento *m*, subida *f* (**in** de); **an i. in productivity/the cost of living** un incremento *or* aumento de (la) productividad/del costo *or Esp* coste de (la) vida; **to be on the i.** ir en aumento

2 *vt* [ɪn'kri:s] aumentar; *(price, temperature)* aumentar, subir; **to i. productivity** aumentar *or* incrementar la productividad; **recent events have increased speculation** los últimos acontecimientos han acrecentado la especulación; **to i. one's efforts** esforzarse más; **to i. one's speed** acelerar, aumentar la velocidad

3 *vi* aumentar; *(price, temperature)* aumentar, subir; **to i. in size/length** aumentar de tamaño/longitud; **to i. in intensity/frequency** aumentar de *or* en intensidad/frecuencia; **to i. in price** subir de precio; **to i. in value** aumentar de valor

increasing [ɪn'kri:sɪŋ] *adj* creciente; **an i. number of complaints/cases** un creciente número de quejas/casos, un número de quejas/casos cada vez más elevado; **to make i. use of sth** hacer un uso cada vez mayor de algo

increasingly [ɪn'kri:sɪŋlɪ] *adv* cada vez más; **it's i. difficult...** cada vez es más difícil...; **i., people are saying that...** cada vez más la gente dice que...

incredible [ɪn'kredɪbəl] *adj* (**a**) *(unbelievable)* increíble; **I find it i. that she didn't know** me resulta increíble que no lo supiera; *Fam* **the really i. thing is....** lo increíble (del caso) es que... (**b**) *Fam (excellent)* increíble, extraordinario(a)

incredibly [ɪn'kredɪblɪ] *adv* (**a**) *(unbelievably)* increíblemente; **i., no one was killed** aunque parezca increíble, no murió nadie (**b**) *Fam (very)* increíblemente; **i. good** increíblemente bueno(a)

incredulity [ɪnkrɪ'dju:lɪtɪ] *n* incredulidad *f*

incredulous [ɪn'kredjʊləs] *adj* incrédulo(a); **an i. look** una mirada incrédula *or* de incredulidad

incredulously [ɪn'kredjʊləslɪ] *adv* con incredulidad

increment ['ɪnkrɪmənt] *n* (**a**) *(increase)* incremento *m*; **a salary with yearly increments of £500** un sueldo con incremento anual de 500 libras (**b**) *Math* incremento *m*

incremental [ɪnkrə'mentəl] *adj* progresivo(a) ►► *Comptr* ***i. plotter*** plotter *m* incremental

incriminate [ɪn'krɪmɪneɪt] *vt* incriminar; **to i. sb in sth** incriminar a alguien en algo; **to incriminate oneself** incriminarse

incriminating [ɪn'krɪmɪneɪtɪŋ], **incriminatory** [ɪnkrɪmɪ'neɪtərɪ] *adj* incriminador(ora)

incubate ['ɪnkjʊbeɪt] *vt* **1** *vt* (**a**) *(eggs)* incubar (**b**) *(plot, idea)* incubar, madurar

2 *vi* (**a**) *(egg)* incubarse (**b**) *Med (virus)* incubarse (**c**) *(plan, idea)* incubarse, madurar

incubation [ɪnkjʊ'beɪʃən] *n* (**a**) *(of egg)* incubación *f* (**b**) *Med (of disease)* incubación *f* ►► ***i. period*** período *m* de incubación

incubator ['ɪnkjʊbeɪtə(r)] *n (for eggs, babies)* incubadora *f*

inculcate ['ɪnkʌlkeɪt] *vt Formal* **to i. sth in sb, to i. sb with sth** inculcar algo en alguien

inculcation [ɪnkʌl'keɪʃən] *n* inculcación *f*

incumbency [ɪn'kʌmbənsɪ] *n (office)* mandato *m*; **during the i. of my predecessor** durante el mandato de mi predecesor(ora)

incumbent [ɪn'kʌmbənt] **1** *n* titular *mf*

2 *adj Formal* (**a**) *(obligatory)* **to be i. on sb to do sth** incumbir *or* atañer a alguien hacer algo (**b**) *(in office)* en ejercicio; **the i. mayor** el alcalde en ejercicio, el titular de la alcaldía

incur [ɪn'kɜ:(r)] *(pt & pp* **incurred**) *vt (blame, expense, penalty)* incurrir en; *(sb's anger)* provocar, incurrir en; *(debt)* contraer; *(losses)* experimentar, sufrir

incurable [ɪn'kjʊərəbəl] *adj* (**a**) *(disease)* incurable (**b**) *(optimist, romantic)* incorregible

incurably [ɪn'kjʊərəblɪ] *adv* (**a**) *(ill)* **to be i. ill** padecer una enfermedad incurable (**b**) *(incorrigibly)* **he's i. romantic/optimistic** es un romántico/optimista incorregible; **to be i. lazy** ser un(a) vago(a) sin remedio

incurious [ɪn'kjʊərɪəs] *adj* poco curioso(a)

incursion [ɪn'kɜ:ʃən] *n Formal* incursión *f* (**into** en)

Ind (**a**) *Pol* (*abbr* **Independent**) independiente (**b**) (*abbr* **Indiana**) Indiana

indebted [ɪn'detɪd] *adj* (**a**) *(financially)* endeudado(a); **to be i. to sb** estar endeudado(a) con alguien (**b**) **to be i. to sb** *(for help, advice)* estar en deuda con alguien; **I am i. to you for your loyal support** te estoy muy agradecido(a) por tu fiel apoyo; **his style is heavily i. to Joyce** mucho es lo que su estilo le debe a Joyce

indebtedness [ɪn'detɪdnɪs] *n* (**a**) *(financial)* endeudamiento *m* (**b**) *(for help, advice)* deuda *f* (**to** con), agradecimiento *m* (**to** a); **his i. to the Surrealists** su deuda (para) con los surrealistas

indecency [ɪn'di:sənsɪ] *n* indecencia *f*

indecent [ɪn'di:sənt] *adj* (**a**) *(improper)* indecente ►► *Law* ***i. assault*** abusos *mpl* deshonestos; *Law* ***i. exposure*** exhibicionismo *m* (**b**) *(unreasonable, excessive)* indecoroso(a); **to do sth with i. haste** apresurarse descaradamente a hacer algo

indecently [ɪn'di:səntlɪ] *adv* indecentemente; **to be i. assaulted** ser víctima de abusos deshonestos; **to expose oneself i.** realizar exhibicionismo

indecipherable [ɪndɪ'saɪfərəbəl] *adj* indescifrable

indecision [ɪndɪ'sɪʒən] *n* indecisión *f*

indecisive [ɪndɪ'saɪsɪv] *adj* (**a**) *(person)* indeciso(a) (**b**) *(battle, election)* no concluyente

indecisively [ɪndɪ'saɪsɪvlɪ] *adv* (**a**) *(showing indecision)* con indecisión (**b**) *(inconclusively)* sin una conclusión clara; **the argument/battle ended i.** la discusión/batalla no fue conclusiva

indecisiveness [ɪndɪ'saɪsɪvnɪs] *n* indecisión *f*, falta *f* de decisión

indecorous [ɪn'dekərəs] *adj Formal* indigno(a), indecoroso(a)

indecorously [ɪn'dekərəslɪ] *adv Formal* indecorosamente

indecorum [ɪndɪ'kɔ:rəm] *n Formal* falta *f* de decoro

INDEED [ɪn'di:d] *adv* (**a**) *(confirming)* efectivamente, ciertamente; **this is i. the case** de hecho, es así; **she confessed that she had i. stolen the money** confesó que, efectivamente, había robado el dinero; **(yes) i.!** ¡ciertamente!; **did you see the movie? – i. I did!** ¿viste la película? – ¡ya lo creo (que la vi)!; **you've been to Venice, haven't you? – i. I have!** has estado en Venecia, ¿verdad? – ¡ya lo creo!

(**b**) *(qualifying)* **few, if i. any, remain** quedan pocos, si es que queda alguno; **it is difficult, i. virtually impossible, to get in** es difícil, si no imposible, entrar

(**c**) *(for emphasis)* **this is a sad day i.** hoy es un día tristísimo; **that is praise i.** es un gran elogio; **very happy i.** contentísimo(a); **it was a very pleasant journey i.** fue un viaje muy agradable; **I am very glad i.** me alegro muchísimo; **thank you very much i.** muchísimas gracias; **did you join in? – i. not!** ¿te apuntaste? – ¡por supuesto que no!

(**d**) *(what is more)* es más; **it is a serious problem, i. it could mean the end of the project** es un problema grave, de hecho podría suponer el fin del proyecto; **I think so, i. I am sure of it** creo que sí, es más, estoy seguro

(**e**) *(expressing ironic surprise)* **have you i.?** ¿ah, sí?, ¿no me digas?; **why would he do that? – why i.?** ¿por qué haría una cosa así? – ¡desde luego! *or* exactamente, ¿por qué?

(**f**) *(expressing scorn)* **"marketing manager" i.! he's just a glorified salesman** mucho "director *or Am* gerente de márketing" pero no deja de ser un mero vendedor

---

indefatigable [ɪndɪ'fætɪgəbəl] *adj Formal* infatigable, incansable

indefatigably [ɪndɪ'fætɪgəblɪ] *adv Formal* infatigablemente, incansablemente

indefensible [ɪndɪ'fensɪbəl] *adj (remark, conduct, opinion)* indefendible, injustificable

indefensibly [ɪndɪ'fensɪblɪ] *adv* de manera injustificable, inexcusablemente

indefinable [ɪndɪ'faɪnəbəl] *adj* indefinible

indefinite [ɪn'defɪnɪt] *adj* (**a**) *(period of time, number)* indefinido(a); **for an i. period** por un período indefinido; **an i. strike** una huelga indefinida (**b**) *(ideas, promises)* indefinido(a), vago(a) (**c**) *Gram* indeterminado(a), indefinido(a) ►► ***i. article*** artículo *m* indeterminado *or* indefinido

indefinitely [ɪn'defɪnɪtlɪ] *adv* indefinidamente; **we can't go on like this i.** no podemos continuar así indefinidamente

indelible [ɪn'delɪbəl] *adj (ink)* indeleble; *(marker)* de tinta indeleble; *Fig (impression)* indeleble, imborrable

indelibly [ɪn'delɪblɪ] *adv (to print, mark)* de forma indeleble; *Fig* **the incident was i. imprinted on my memory** el incidente quedó grabado indeleblemente en mi memoria

indelicacy [ɪn'delɪkəsɪ] *n* falta *f* de delicadeza

indelicate [ɪn'delɪkət] *adj* grosero(a)

indemnify [ɪn'demnɪfaɪ] *vt* (**a**) *(compensate)* **to i. sb for sth** indemnizar a alguien por algo (**b**) *(insure)* **to i. sb against sth** asegurar a alguien contra algo

indemnity [ɪn'demnɪtɪ] *n* (**a**) *(guarantee)* indemnidad *f* (**b**) *(money)* indemnización *f* (**c**) *(exemption) (from prosecution)* inmunidad *f*

indent 1 *n* ['ɪndent] (**a**) *(in paragraph)* sangría *f*, sangrado *m* (**b**) *(in surface)* hendidura *f*

2 *vt* [ɪn'dent] (**a**) *(paragraph)* sangrar (**b**) *(in surface)* grabar

indentation [ɪnden'teɪʃən] *n* (**a**) *(on edge)* muesca *f* (**b**) *(dent)* abolladura *f* (**c**) *(in paragraph)* sangría *f*, sangrado *m*

indented [ɪn'dentɪd] *adj* (**a**) *(edge)* dentado(a) (**b**) *(coastline)* recortado(a); **a heavily i. coastline** un litoral muy recortado (**c**) *(line, paragraph)* sangrado(a)

indenture [ɪn'dentʃə(r)] **1** *n* **indenture(s)** contrato *m* de aprendizaje

2 *vt Old-fashioned* contratar como aprendiz; **he was indentured to a carpenter** lo contrataron como aprendiz de carpintero

independence [ɪndɪ'pendəns] *n* independencia *f*; **the country has recently gained its i.** el país conquistó la independencia recientemente ►► ***I. Day*** el Día de la Independencia

independent [ɪndɪ'pendənt] **1** *adj* (**a**) *(free, autonomous) (person, country, inquiry)* independiente; **to be i. of** ser independiente de; **to become i.** *(person)* independizarse; *(country)* conseguir la independencia, independizarse; **he is incapable of i. thought/action** es incapaz de pensar/actuar por sí mismo

(**b**) *(separate, unrelated)* independiente, diferente; **the rumour has**

been confirmed by two i. sources el rumor ha sido confirmado por dos fuentes diferentes

(**c**) *(financially)* **she is i. of her parents** es (económicamente) independiente de sus padres; **a woman of i. means** una mujer que vive de sus rentas

(**d**) *Br (not state-run)* ***i. school*** colegio *m* privado; ***i. television*** televisión *f* privada

(**e**) *Gram* ***i. clause*** oración *f* independiente

2 *n Pol* independiente *mf*

independently [ɪndɪˈpendəntlɪ] *adv* (**a**) *(on one's own) (work, live)* independientemente; **he left the company to set up i.** abandonó la empresa para establecerse como por su cuenta; **to be i. wealthy** vivir de las rentas; **she's very i. minded** es muy independiente en su forma de pensar

(**b**) *(separately)* por separado; **she was warned by three people i.** la avisaron tres personas por separado, tres personas distintas la avisaron; **i. of other considerations...** al margen de otras consideraciones...

in-depth [ˈɪnˈdepθ] *adj* a fondo, exhaustivo(a)

indescribable [ɪndɪsˈkraɪbəbəl] *adj (pain, beauty)* indescriptible; **i. boredom** un aburrimiento indecible *or* inenarrable

indescribably [ɪndɪsˈkraɪbəblɪ] *adv* indescriptiblemente; **i. tedious/boring** indeciblemente tedioso(a)/aburrido(a); **he was i. handsome** con palabras no se puede describir lo atractivo que era

indestructible [ɪndɪsˈtrʌktəbəl] *adj* indestructible

indestructibility [ɪndɪstrʌktɪˈbɪlɪtɪ] *n* indestructibilidad *f*

indeterminable [ɪndɪˈtɜːmɪnəbəl] *adj (unmeasurable)* indeterminable

indeterminacy [ɪndɪˈtɜːmɪnəsɪ] *n* indeterminación *f*

indeterminate [ɪndɪˈtɜːmɪnət] *adj* (**a**) *(unspecified)* indeterminado(a); **for an i. period** por un período indeterminado (**b**) *Math* indeterminado(a)

index [ˈɪndeks] **1** *n* (*pl* **indexes** *or* **indices** [ˈɪndɪsiːz]) (**a**) *(of book, database)* índice *m* (**b**) *(in library)* índice *m* ►► ***i. card*** ficha *f* (**c**) ***i. finger*** (dedo *m*) índice *m* (**d**) *(scale) (financial)* índice *m* ►► *Fin* ***i. fund*** fondo *m* indexado *or* índice; ***i. number*** índice *m* (**e**) *(indication)* índice *m*; **it is a good i. of the current political mood** es un buen índice del actual talante político

2 *vt* (**a**) *(book)* indizar; *(database)* indizar, indexar; *(word, name)* incluir en un índice; **you'll find it indexed under "science"** figura en el índice bajo el epígrafe "ciencia" (**b**) *Fin (wages)* indexar; **pensions are indexed to inflation** las pensiones están indexadas a la tasa de inflación

indexation [ɪndekˈseɪʃən] *n Fin* indexación *f*

index-linked [ˈɪndeksˈlɪŋkt] *adj Fin (wages, pension)* indexado(a)

India [ˈɪndɪə] *n* (**a**) *(country)* (la) India (**b**) ***I. rubber*** *(material)* caucho *m*; *(eraser)* goma *f* (de borrar) (**c**) *US* ***I. ink*** tinta *f* china

Indiaman [ˈɪndɪəmən] *n Br Hist* = barco destinado al comercio con la India/las Indias Orientales

Indian [ˈɪndɪən] **1** *n* (**a**) *(native of India)* indio(a) *m,f*, hindú *mf* (**b**) *(Native American)* indio(a) *m,f*, indígena *mf* (**c**) *Br Fam (meal)* comida *f* india *or* hindú

2 *adj* (**a**) *(from India)* indio(a), hindú ►► ***I. club*** maza *f*; ***I. elephant*** elefante *m* asiático; *Br* ***I. ink*** tinta *f* china; *Hist* ***the I. Mutiny*** la sublevación de los cipayos; ***the I. Ocean*** el Océano Índico; ***I. rope-trick*** = truco atribuido a los indios de trepar por una soga suspendida en el aire

(**b**) *(Native American)* indio(a), *Am* indígena ►► *US* ***I. agent*** = representante del gobierno federal en las reservas de los indios americanos; ***I. corn*** maíz *m*, *Andes, RP* choclo *m*; ***I. file*** fila *f* india; *US* ***I. giver:*** **don't be an I. giver, Tommy!** ¡santa Rita, santa Rita, lo que se da no se quita, Tommy!; ***I. hemp*** cáñamo *m* indio; ***I. summer*** *(in northern hemisphere)* veranillo *m* de San Martín; *(in southern hemisphere)* veranillo *m* de San Juan

indicate [ˈɪndɪkeɪt] **1** *vt* (**a**) *(point to, signpost)* señalar, indicar; **to i. the way** indicar el camino; **the exits are clearly indicated** las salidas están claramente señalizadas

(**b**) *(of dial, instrument)* indicar, señalar

(**c**) *(show, suggest)* indicar, apuntar a; **all the pointers i. a rise in unemployment later in the year** todos los indicadores apuntan a un aumento de la tasa de desempleo antes de que acabe el año

(**d**) *(state, make clear)* manifestar, indicar; **he indicated his willingness to help** manifestó su disposición a ayudar; **she indicated that the interview was over** indicó que la entrevista había terminado; **as I have already indicated** como ya he señalado

(**e**) *(require)* convenir, ser lo indicado; **surgery is indicated** conviene operar, lo (más) indicado es operar

2 *vi Br (car-driver)* poner el intermitente

indication [ɪndɪˈkeɪʃən] *n* (**a**) *(sign)* indicio *m*; **she gave no i. of her feelings** no dio ningún indicio de cuáles eran sus sentimientos; **he gave early indications of his talent** pronto dio muestras de su talento; **he gave us a clear i. of his intentions** nos dejó ver claramente sus intenciones, nos dio claros indicios de cuáles eran sus intenciones; **there is every i. that he was speaking the truth** todo parece indicar que dijo la verdad; **all the indications are that..., there is every i. that...** todo indica que..., todo apunta a que...

(**b**) *Med* indicación *f*

indicative [ɪnˈdɪkətɪv] **1** *n Gram* indicativo *m*

2 *adj* (**a**) *(symptomatic)* indicativo(a) (**of** de); **this behaviour is i. of a strong personality** ese comportamiento denota una personalidad fuerte (**b**) *Gram* ***i. mood*** modo *m* indicativo

indicator [ˈɪndɪkeɪtə(r)] *n* (**a**) *(instrument)* indicador *m* (**b**) *(sign)* indicador *m*; **it's a good i. of future performance** es un buen indicador del desempeño futuro; **economic indicators** indicadores económicos (**c**) ***i. board*** *(at station, in airport)* panel *m* de información (**d**) *Br Aut* intermitente *m*, *Bol* guiñador *m*, *Chile* señalizador *m*, *Col, Ecuad, Méx* direccional *m*, *Urug* señalero *m*

indices *pl of* **index**

indict [ɪnˈdaɪt] *vt Law* acusar (formalmente) (**for** de)

indictable [ɪnˈdaɪtəbəl] *adj Law* ***i. offence*** delito *m* procesable *or* grave

indictment [ɪnˈdaɪtmənt] *n* (**a**) *Law (document)* acta *f or* escrito *m* de acusación formal; *(act)* acusación *f* formal(**b**) *(condemnation)* **it is an i. of our society** pone en tela de juicio a nuestra sociedad

indie [ˈɪndɪ] *Fam* **1** *n* productor(a) *m,f* independiente

2 *adj (music, movie)* independiente

indifference [ɪnˈdɪfərəns] *n* (**a**) *(lack of interest)* indiferencia *f* (**to** *or* **towards** a); **with total i.** con total indiferencia (**b**) *(unimportance)* **it's a matter of complete i. to me** es un asunto que me trae sin cuidado (**c**) *(mediocrity)* mediocridad *f*

indifferent [ɪnˈdɪfərənt] *adj* (**a**) *(not interested)* indiferente (**to** a); **he was i. to her pleas** fue indiferente a sus súplicas; **i. to the danger** indiferente al peligro (**b**) *(unimportant)* **it's entirely i. to me whether they go or stay** me es totalmente indiferente si se van o se quedan (**c**) *(mediocre)* mediocre, regular; **good, bad or i.** bueno(a), malo(a) o regular

indifferently [ɪnˈdɪfərəntlɪ] *adv* (**a**) *(uninterestedly)* con indiferencia (**b**) *(mediocrely)* de forma mediocre

indigence [ˈɪndɪdʒəns] *n Formal* indigencia *f*

indigenous [ɪnˈdɪdʒɪnəs] *adj* indígena (**to** de), autóctono(a); **rabbits are not i. to Australia** los conejos no son autóctonos de Australia

indigent [ˈɪndɪdʒənt] *adj Formal* indigente

indigestible [ɪndɪˈdʒestɪbəl] *adj* (**a**) *(food)* indigesto(a), indigerible (**b**) *(writing)* intragable, indigesto(a)

indigestion [ɪndɪˈdʒestʃən] *n* indigestión *f*; **to have i.** tener una indigestión; **spicy food gives me i.** la comida muy condimentada me produce indigestión

indignant [ɪnˈdɪgnənt] *adj* indignado(a); **he was i. at her attitude** lo indignaba su actitud; **to get i. about sth** indignarse por algo

indignantly [ɪnˈdɪgnəntlɪ] *adv* indignadamente, con indignación

indignation [ɪndɪgˈneɪʃən] *n* indignación *f*

indignity [ɪnˈdɪgnɪtɪ] *n* indignidad *f*, humillación *f*; **the i. of it!** ¡lo humillante que resultaba!, ¡la humillación que supone!

indigo [ˈɪndɪgəʊ] **1** *n* añil *m*

2 *adj* añil

indirect [ɪndɪˈrekt] *adj* (**a**) *(not direct)* indirecto(a); **by an i. route** por *or* siguiendo un camino indirecto ►► *Com* ***i. costs*** costos *or Esp* costes *mpl* indirectos; ***i. free kick*** tiro *m* libre indirecto; ***i. lighting*** iluminación *f* indirecta; *Fin* ***i. taxation*** impuestos *mpl* indirectos (**b**) *Gram* ***i. object*** complemento *m or* objeto *m* indirecto; ***i. question*** oración *f* interrogativa indirecta; ***i. speech*** estilo *m* indirecto

indirectly [ɪndɪˈrektlɪ] *adv* indirectamente; **I heard about it i.** me he enterado indirectamente; **she felt i. responsible** se sentía indirectamente responsable

indirectness [ɪndɪˈrektnɪs] *n* tortuosidad *f*, sinuosidad *f*

indiscernible [ɪndɪˈsɜːnɪbəl] *adj* indiscernible

indiscipline [ɪnˈdɪsɪplɪn] *n* indisciplina *f*

indiscreet [ɪndɪsˈkriːt] *adj* indiscreto(a)

indiscreetly [ɪndɪsˈkriːtlɪ] *adv* con indiscreción

indiscretion [ɪndɪs'kreʃən] *n* (**a**) *(lack of discretion)* indiscreción *f* (**b**) *(unwise act)* imprudencia *f*, falta *f*; *(unwise remark)* indiscreción *f*

indiscriminate [ɪndɪs'krɪmɪnɪt] *adj* indiscriminado(a); **it was i. slaughter** fue una masacre indiscriminada; **to distribute i. punishment/praise** repartir castigos/elogios de manera indiscriminada; **to be i. in one's praise** hacer elogios indiscriminadamente; **children are i. in their television viewing** los niños no son selectivos a a la hora de mirar la televisión

indiscriminately [ɪndɪs'krɪmɪnɪtlɪ] *adv* indiscriminadamente; **he reads i.** no tiene criterio en cuestión de lectura; **they fired i. into the crowd** dispararon de forma indiscriminada contra la multitud; **the plague struck rich and poor i.** la epidemia atacó por igual a ricos y pobres

indispensable [ɪndɪs'pensəbəl] *adj* indispensable, imprescindible; **to make oneself i.** hacerse indispensable *or* imprescindible

indisposed [ɪndɪs'pəʊzd] *adj Formal* (**a**) *(ill)* indispuesto(a); **to be i.** hallarse indispuesto(a) (**b**) *(unwilling)* **to be i. to do sth** no estar dispuesto(a) a hacer algo

indisposition [ɪndɪspə'zɪʃən] *n Formal (illness)* indisposición *f*

indisputable [ɪndɪs'pju:təbəl] *adj* indiscutible; **it is i. that...** es indiscutible que..., no cabe duda de que...; **she has built up an i. lead over the others** ha ido ganando una indiscutible supremacía sobre los demás

indisputably [ɪndɪs'pju:təblɪ] *adv* indiscutiblemente; **he is i. the best in his field** indiscutiblemente *or* sin lugar a dudas, es el mejor en su especialidad

indissoluble [ɪndɪ'sɒljʊbəl] *adj Formal* indisoluble

indissolubly [ɪndɪ'sɒljʊblɪ] *adv Formal* indisolublemente

indistinct [ɪndɪs'tɪŋkt] *adj* indistinto(a), impreciso(a); **it was just an i. blur on the horizon** tan sólo era un perfil borroso en el horizonte

indistinctly [ɪndɪs'tɪŋktlɪ] *adv (to speak)* ininteligiblemente; *(to see, remember)* de forma imprecisa *or* confusa

indistinguishable [ɪndɪs'tɪŋgwɪʃəbəl] *adj* indistinguible (**from** de); **the twins are i.** los gemelos son indistinguibles entre sí

indium ['ɪndɪəm] *n Chem* indio *m*

individual [ɪndɪ'vɪdjʊəl] **1** *n* (**a**) *(not member of a group)* individuo *m*; **no one i. is responsible for the accident** nadie en particular es responsable del accidente; **as a private i.** a título personal (**b**) *Fam (person)* individuo *m*, sujeto *m*; **a bizarre i.** un individuo *or* tipo extrañísimo

2 *adj* (**a**) *(of or for one person, thing)* individual; **i. portions** porciones individuales; **his pupils get i. attention** sus alumnos reciben atención personalizada ►► *Sport* ***i. medley*** *(in swimming)* prueba *f* de estilos individual; ***i. pursuit*** *(in cycling)* persecución *f* individual; ***i. time trial*** *(in cycling)* contrarreloj *f* individual

(**b**) *(characteristic)* personal; **she has a very i. way of working** tiene un forma de trabajar muy personal

(**c**) *(single)* individual; **the i. hospitals are responsible for running their own affairs** cada hospital lleva sus propios asuntos; **no i. person is responsible, but...** individualmente ninguna persona es responsable, pero...; **each i. incident** cada uno de los hechos

individualism [ɪndɪ'vɪdjʊəlɪzəm] *n* individualismo *m*

individualist [ɪndɪ'vɪdjʊəlɪst] *n* individualista *mf*

individualistic [ɪndɪvɪdʒʊə'lɪstɪk] *adj* individualista

individuality [ɪndɪvɪdjʊ'ælɪtɪ] *n* individualidad *f*

individualize [ɪndɪ'vɪdjʊəlaɪz] *vt* individualizar

individually [ɪndɪ'vɪdjʊəlɪ] *adv (separately)* individualmente; **he spoke to us all i.** nos habló a todos uno por uno *or* por separado; **i. wrapped** envuelto(a) por separado *or* individualmente

indivisibility [ɪndɪvɪzɪ'bɪlɪtɪ] *n* indivisibilidad *f*

indivisible [ɪndɪ'vɪzɪbəl] *adj* indivisible

Indo- ['ɪndəʊ] *prefix* indo-; **an I.-Pakistani agreement** un acuerdo indopaquistaní

Indochina ['ɪndəʊ'tʃaɪnə] *n Formerly* Indochina

Indochinese ['ɪndəʊtʃaɪ'ni:z] *Formerly* **1** *n* indochino(a) *m,f*

2 *adj* indochino(a)

indoctrinate [ɪn'dɒktrɪneɪt] *vt* adoctrinar; **he indoctrinated his pupils with his prejudices** inculcó sus prejuicios a los alumnos

indoctrination [ɪndɒktrɪ'neɪʃən] *n* adoctrinamiento *m*

Indo-European ['ɪndəʊjʊərə'pɪən] **1** *n* indoeuropeo(a) *m,f*

2 *adj* indoeuropeo(a)

indolence ['ɪndələns] *n Formal* indolencia *f*

indolent ['ɪndələnt] *adj Formal* indolente

indomitable [ɪn'dɒmɪtəbəl] *adj Formal* indómito(a)

Indonesia [ɪndə'ni:zɪə] *n* Indonesia

Indonesian [ɪndə'ni:ʒən] **1** *n* (**a**) *(person)* indonesio(a) *m,f* (**b**) *(language)* indonesio *m*

2 *adj* indonesio(a)

indoor ['ɪndɔ:(r)] *adj (plant, photography)* de interior; *(toilet)* interior; *(clothing)* de estar en *or* por casa, *Esp* de andar por casa, *RP* de entre casa; *(tennis court, swimming pool)* cubierto(a) ►► ***i. athletics*** atletismo *m* en pista cubierta; ***i. five-a-side*** fútbol *m* sala; ***i. games*** *(sports)* juegos *mpl* en pista cubierta *or* instalaciones cerradas; *(board games, charades)* juegos *mpl* de mesa *or* interior; ***i. track*** pista *f* cubierta; ***i. trial*** trial *m* indoor

indoors [ɪn'dɔ:z] *adv* dentro (de casa); **to go i.** entrar en casa; **it's much cooler i.** hace mucho más fresco dentro (de la casa)

Indo-Pakistan ['ɪndəʊpɑ:kɪ'stɑ:n] *adj (war, relations)* indopaquistaní

indorse, indorsee *etc* = **endorse, endorsee** *etc*

indraught, *US* **indraft** ['ɪndrɑ:ft] *n (of liquid, air)* absorción *f*, succión *f*

indrawn [ɪn'drɔ:n] *adj* **i. breath** inspiración *f*, aspiración *f*

indubitable [ɪn'dju:bɪtəbəl] *adj Formal* indudable

indubitably [ɪn'dju:bɪtəblɪ] *adv Formal* indudablemente, sin (lugar a) duda

induce [ɪn'dju:s] *vt* (**a**) *(persuade)* inducir; **to i. sb to do sth** inducir a alguien a hacer algo; **nothing would i. me to change my mind** nada me llevaría *or* induciría a cambiar de opinión (**b**) *(cause)* provocar, producir (**c**) *Med* **to i. labour** provocar *or* inducir el parto; **she had to be induced** tuvieron que provocarle el parto (**d**) *Elec* inducir

inducement [ɪn'dju:smənt] *n (incentive)* aliciente *m*, incentivo *m*; **he was offered considerable financial inducements to leave his company** le ofrecieron jugosos incentivos para que abandonara la empresa

induct [ɪn'dʌkt] *vt* (**a**) *(to job, rank)* investir (**b**) *US Mil* reclutar

inductance [ɪn'dʌktəns] *n Phys* inductancia *f*

inductee ['ɪndʌk'ti:] *n US Mil* recluta *mf*

induction [ɪn'dʌkʃən] *n* (**a**) *(into new job, group)* iniciación *f* ►► *esp Br* ***i. course*** cursillo *m* introductorio

(**b**) *Phys & Elec* inducción *f* ►► ***i. coil*** bobina *f* de inducción; ***i. heating*** calefacción *f* por inducción; ***i. loop system*** = sistema de transmisión inductivo para audífonos; ***i. motor*** motor *m* de inducción

(**c**) *(logical reasoning)* inducción *f*

(**d**) *Med (of labour)* inducción *f*

(**e**) *US Mil* incorporación *f* a filas

inductive [ɪn'dʌktɪv] *adj (reasoning)* inductivo(a)

inductively [ɪn'dʌktɪvlɪ] *adv* inductivamente, de manera inductiva

indulge [ɪn'dʌldʒ] **1** *vt* consentir; **they indulged his every whim** le consentían todos los caprichos; **to i. oneself** darse un capricho *or* un gusto

2 *vi* **to i. in alcohol** darse a la bebida; **to i. in idle speculation** entregarse a especulaciones vanas; **no thank you, I don't i.** *(drink, smoke)* no gracias, no tengo la costumbre

indulgence [ɪn'dʌldʒəns] *n* (**a**) *(tolerance, generosity)* indulgencia *f*; **he watched their antics with i.** observaba complacido sus travesuras

(**b**) *(gratification)* **the i. of his every desire** la satisfacción de todos sus deseos; **he criticized their excessive i. in alcohol** criticó su abuso del alcohol

(**c**) *(pleasure, treat)* **I allow myself the occasional i.** de vez en cuando me permito algún capricho; **smoking is my only i.** el tabaco es mi único vicio

(**d**) *Rel* indulgencia *f*

indulgent [ɪn'dʌldʒənt] *adj* indulgente (**to** con); **you shouldn't be so i. with your children** no deberías ser tan indulgente con tus hijos

indulgently [ɪn'dʌldʒəntlɪ] *adv* con indulgencia

Indus ['ɪndəs] *n* **the I.** el (río) Indo

industrial [ɪn'dʌstrɪəl] *adj* industrial; **for i. use only** sólo para uso industrial; **in i. quantities** en cantidades industriales ►► ***i. accident*** accidente *m* laboral; ***i. action*** movilizaciones *fpl* (obreras); **to take i. action** movilizarse; ***i. archaeology*** arqueología *f* industrial; ***i. belt*** cinturón *m* industrial; ***i. democracy*** democracia *f* económica *or* empresarial; ***i. design*** diseño *m* industrial; ***i. designer*** diseñador(ora) *m,f* industrial; ***i. diamond*** diamante *m* industrial; ***i. disability*** incapacidad *f* laboral; *Br* ***i. disablement*** incapacidad *f* laboral; ***i. disease*** enfermedad *f* laboral; *Br* ***i. dispute*** conflicto *m* laboral; ***i. engineer*** ingeniero(a) *m,f* industrial; ***i. espionage*** espionaje *m* industrial; *Br* ***i. estate*** polígono *m* industrial; ***i. goods*** bienes *mpl* de producción; ***i.***

injury lesión *f* laboral; *US* ***i. park*** polígono *m* industrial; ***i. relations*** relaciones *fpl* laborales; *Hist* ***the I. Revolution*** la Revolución Industrial; *Br Law* ***i. tribunal*** tribunal *m* laboral, *Esp* magistratura *f* de trabajo; ***i. unrest*** conflictividad *f* laboral; ***i. waste*** residuos *mpl* industriales

industrialism [ɪn'dʌstrɪəlɪzəm] *n Econ* industrialismo *m*

industrialist [ɪn'dʌstrɪəlɪst] *n* industrial *mf*

industrialization [ɪndʌstrɪəlaɪ'zeɪʃən] *n* industrialización *f*

industrialize [ɪn'dʌstrɪəlaɪz] **1** *vt* industrializar
2 *vi* industrializarse

industrialized [ɪn'dʌstrɪəlaɪzd] *adj* industrializado(a)

industrial-strength [ɪn'dʌstrɪəlstreŋθ] *adj (glue, material)* de uso industrial; *Hum (coffee)* muy fuerte

industrious [ɪn'dʌstrɪəs] *adj (pupil, worker)* aplicado(a), afanoso(a); *(research)* laborioso(a)

industriously [ɪn'dʌstrɪəslɪ] *adv* afanosamente, con afán *or* ahínco

industriousness [ɪn'dʌstrɪəsnɪs] *n* afán *m*, aplicación *f*

industry ['ɪndʌstrɪ] *n* **(a)** *(in general)* industria *f*; **heavy/light i.** industria pesada/ligera; **both sides of i.** la patronal y los sindicatos; **European i. is facing recession** la industria europea se enfrenta a una recesión
(b) *(particular sector)* sector *m*, industria *f*; **the aircraft/mining/shipping i.** el sector aeronáutico/minero/naviero, la industria aeronáutica/minera/naviera; **the tourist i.** el sector turístico; **the entertainment i.** la industria *or* el sector del espectáculo
(c) *Formal (hard work)* aplicación *f*

inebriate *Formal* **1** *n* [ɪ'ni:brɪət] bebedor(ora) *m,f*
2 *adj* ebrio(a), embriagado(a)
3 *vt* [ɪ'ni:brɪeɪt] embriagar

inebriated [ɪn'i:brɪeɪtɪd] *adj Formal* ebrio(a); **to be i.** estar ebrio(a)

inebriation [ɪni:brɪ'eɪʃən] *n Formal* ebriedad *f*, embriaguez *f*

inedible [ɪn'edɪbəl] *adj* **(a)** *(not edible)* incomestible **(b)** *(unpalatable)* incomible

ineducable [ɪn'edjʊkəbəl] *adj* imposible de educar, incapacitado(a) para el aprendizaje

ineffable [ɪn'efəbəl] *adj Formal* inefable, indescriptible

ineffably [ɪn'efəblɪ] *adv Formal* inefablemente, indescriptiblemente

ineffective [ɪnɪ'fektɪv] *adj (measure, drug)* ineficaz; *(attempt)* inútil; *(teacher, chairman)* incompetente; **to render sth i.** inutilizar algo

ineffectiveness ['ɪnɪ'fektɪvnɪs] *n (of measure, drug)* ineficacia *f*; *(of attempt)* infructuosidad *f*, improductividad *f*; *(of teacher, chairman)* ineptitud *f*, incompetencia *f*

ineffectual [ɪnɪ'fektjʊəl] *adj* **(a)** *(person)* inepto(a) **(b)** *(measure)* ineficaz

ineffectually [ɪnɪ'fektjʊəlɪ] *adv* de forma ineficaz

inefficacious [ɪnefɪ'keɪʃəs] *adj Formal* ineficaz

inefficiency [ɪnɪ'fɪʃənsɪ] *n* ineficiencia *f*; **he was sacked for i.** lo echaron del trabajo por ineficiente *or* incompetente

inefficient [ɪnɪ'fɪʃənt] *adj* ineficiente; **an i. use of resources** un empleo *or* uso ineficiente de los recursos

inefficiently [ɪnɪ'fɪʃəntlɪ] *adv* de forma ineficiente

inelastic [ɪnɪ'læstɪk] *adj* **(a)** *(material)* rígido(a) **(b)** *(principles)* rígido(a) **(c)** *Phys (collision)* inelástico(a)

inelegant [ɪn'elɪgənt] *adj* vulgar, poco elegante

inelegantly [ɪn'elɪgəntlɪ] *adv* sin elegancia, con poca elegancia

ineligibility [ɪnelɪdʒə'bɪlɪtɪ] *n* ausencia *f* del derecho (**for** a)

ineligible [ɪn'elɪdʒɪbəl] *adj* **(a)** *(unqualified)* **to be i. for sth** no tener derecho a algo; **he is i. for the post** no reúne las condiciones *or* requisitos necesarias para ocupar el puesto; **to be i. for military service** no ser apto para (hacer) el servicio militar; **they are i. for unemployment benefit** no tienen derecho al subsidio por desempleo; **they are i. to vote** no pueden votar, no tienen derecho al voto
(b) *(for election)* inelegible

ineluctable [ɪnɪ'lʌktəbəl] *adj Literary* ineluctable, insoslayable

ineluctably [ɪnɪ'lʌktɪblɪ] *adv Literary* ineluctablemente, inevitablemente

inept [ɪn'ept] *adj* **(a)** *(clumsy)* inhábil, torpe (**at** para) **(b)** *(inappropriate)* inapropiado(a)

ineptitude [ɪn'eptɪtju:d], **ineptness** [ɪ'neptnɪs] *n* ineptitud *f*

ineptly [ɪn'eptlɪ] *adv* con bastante ineptitud

inequality [ɪnɪ'kwɒlɪtɪ] *n* desigualdad *f*

inequitable [ɪn'ekwɪtəbəl] *adj Formal* injusto(a), no equitativo(a)

inequity [ɪn'ekwətɪ] *n Formal* injusticia *f*

ineradicable [ɪnɪ'rædɪkəbəl] *adj* indeleble, imposible de borrar; **being jilted at the altar left an i. scar in his mind** el que lo dejaran plantado en el altar lo marcó para siempre

inert [ɪ'nɜ:t] *adj (motionless)* inmóvil ▸▸ *Chem* ***i. gas*** gas *m* noble *or* inerte

inertia [ɪ'nɜ:ʃɪə] *n* inercia *f* ▸▸ *Br* ***i. selling*** venta *f* por inercia

inertia-reel [ɪn'ɜ:ʃəri:l] *adj Aut* ***i. seat belt*** cinturón *m* de seguridad autotensable *or* con pretensor

inescapable [ɪnɪ'skeɪpəbəl] *adj (conclusion)* inevitable, ineludible; *(consequence, result)* inevitable, ineluctable; **it is an i. fact that...** no se puede ignorar que...

inescapably [ɪnɪ'skeɪpəblɪ] *adv* inevitablemente, ineluctablemente

inessential [ɪnɪ'senʃəl] **1** *n* cosa *f* superflua *or* innecesaria; **to do without inessentials** prescindir de todo lo que sea superfluo *or* innecesario
2 *adj* superfluo(a), innecesario(a)

inestimable [ɪn'estɪməbəl] *adj Formal* inestimable, inapreciable; **of i. value** de incalculable *or* inestimable valor

inevitability [ɪnevɪtə'bɪlɪtɪ] *n* inevitabilidad *f*

inevitable [ɪn'evɪtəbəl] **1** *n* **we resigned ourselves to the i.** nos resignamos a *or* ante lo inevitable
2 *adj* inevitable; **war seems i.** la guerra parece inevitable; **it's i. that someone will feel left out** es inevitable que alguien se sienta excluido

inevitably [ɪn'evɪtəblɪ] *adv* inevitablemente; **i., some will feel disappointed** inevitablemente, habrá quien se sienta decepcionado

inexact [ɪnɪg'zækt] *adj* inexacto(a); **it's an i. science** es una ciencia inexacta

inexactly [ɪnɪg'zæktlɪ] *adv* inexactamente, con inexactitud

inexcusable [ɪnɪks'kju:zəbəl] *adj* inexcusable, injustificable

inexcusably [ɪnɪks'kju:zəblɪ] *adv* injustificablemente; **an i. violent attack** un ataque de una virulencia inexcusable *or* fuera de lugar; **quite i., I had left the papers at home** había olvidado los papeles en casa, lo cual era del todo imperdonable

inexhaustible [ɪneg'zɔ:stɪbəl] *adj* **(a)** *(source, energy, patience)* inagotable; **she had an i. supply of jokes** tenía un repertorio de chistes inagotable **(b)** *(person)* infatigable, incansable

inexorability [ɪneksərə'bɪlɪtɪ] *n* inexorabilidad *f*

inexorable [ɪn'eksərəbəl] *adj* inexorable

inexorably [ɪn'eksərəblɪ] *adv* inexorablemente

inexpedient [ɪnɪk'spi:dɪənt] *adj Formal* desacertado(a)

inexpensive [ɪnɪks'pensɪv] *adj* económico(a), barato(a)

inexpensively [ɪnɪks'pensɪvlɪ] *adv (to live)* con pocos gastos; *(to buy, sell)* a bajo precio; *(to eat)* barato

inexperience [ɪnɪks'pɪərɪəns] *n* inexperiencia *f*

inexperienced [ɪnɪks'pɪərɪənst] *adj* inexperto(a); **to the i. eye/ear** para el ojo/oído inexperto; **he's i. in handling staff** no tiene experiencia en cuestiones de personal

inexpert [ɪn'ekspɜ:t] *adj* inexperto(a); **an i. attempt** un torpe intento

inexpertly [ɪn'ekspɜ:tlɪ] *adv* con torpeza

inexplicable [ɪnɪks'plɪkəbəl] *adj* inexplicable

inexplicably [ɪnɪks'plɪkəblɪ] *adv* inexplicablemente

inexpressible [ɪnɪks'presɪbəl] *adj* indescriptible, indecible

inexpressive [ɪnɪks'presɪv] *adj* inexpresivo(a)

inextinguishable [ɪnɪks'tɪŋgwɪʃəbəl] *adj* inextinguible; *Fig* **an i. thirst for liberty** una sed insaciable de libertad

in extremis [ɪneks'tri:mɪs] *adv Formal* **(a)** *(in extreme situation)* en un caso extremo **(b)** *(about to die)* in extremis

inextricable [ɪnɪk'strɪkəbəl] *adj* inextricable

inextricably [ɪneks'trɪkəblɪ] *adv* inseparablemente

infallibility [ɪnfælɪ'bɪlɪtɪ] *n* infalibilidad *f*

infallible [ɪn'fælɪbəl] *adj* infalible

infallibly [ɪn'fælɪblɪ] *adv* **(a)** *(without mistakes)* de forma infalible, sin un sólo error **(b)** *(inevitably, as usual)* indefectiblemente

infamous ['ɪnfəməs] *adj* **(a)** *(notorious)* infame, despreciable; **to be i. for sth** ser tristemente famoso(a) por algo **(b)** *(shocking) (conduct)* infame, innoble

infamy ['ɪnfəmɪ] *n Formal* infamia *f*

infancy ['ɪnfənsɪ] *n* **(a)** *(childhood)* infancia *f*; *Fig* **when medicine was still in its i.** cuando la medicina daba sus primeros pasos **(b)** *Law* minoría *f* de edad

infant ['ɪnfənt] **1** *n* **(a)** *(baby)* bebé *m*, *Andes* guagua *f*, *RP* bebe(a) *m,f*; *(small child)* niño(a) *m,f* pequeño(a), *Andes* pelado(a) *m,f*, *RP* nene(a) *m,f* ▸▸ *Med* ***i. mortality*** mortalidad *f* infantil

(**b**) *Br Educ* niño(a) *m,f* (de unos 5 a 7 años), párvulo(a) *m,f* ►► ***i. class*** clase *f* de párvulos; ***i. school*** colegio *m* de párvulos, escuela *f* infantil
(**c**) *Law* menor *mf* de edad
2 *adj (organization)* naciente, nuevo(a); **the i. Church** la Iglesia naciente

infanticide [ɪn'fæntɪsaɪd] *n* (**a**) *(act)* infanticidio *m* (**b**) *(person)* infanticida *mf*

infantile ['ɪnfəntaɪl] *adj* (**a**) *Pej (childish)* pueril, infantil (**b**) *Med* infantil

infantilism [ɪn'fæntɪlɪzəm] *n Psy* infantilismo *m*

infantry ['ɪnfəntrɪ] *n* infantería *f*

infantryman ['ɪnfəntrɪmən] *n* soldado *m* de infantería, infante *m*

infatuated [ɪn'fætjʊeɪtɪd] *adj* **to be/become i. with** estar/quedarse prendado(a) de, estar encaprichado(a) con

infatuation [ɪnfætjʊ'eɪʃən] *n* encaprichamiento *m* (amoroso)

infect [ɪn'fekt] *vt* (**a**) *(with disease)* infectar; **to become** *or* **get infected** *(of wound)* infectarse; **to i. sb with sth** contagiar algo a alguien; **he infected all his friends with the flu** le pegó *or* contagió la gripe a todos sus amigos (**b**) *(food, water, area)* contaminar, infectar (**c**) *Fig (with prejudice)* emponzoñar; **her enthusiasm infected us all** nos contagió a todos su entusiasmo (**d**) *Comptr (with virus)* infectar

infection [ɪn'fekʃən] *n* (**a**) *(of person)* contagio *m*; *(of wound)* infección *f*; **to guard against i. by bacteria** proteger contra una infección bacteriana; **a throat i.** una infección de garganta (**b**) *(of food, water, area)* contaminación *f*, infección *f*

infectious [ɪn'fekʃəs] *adj* (**a**) *(disease)* infeccioso(a) (**b**) *(person)* **is he still i.?** ¿puede contagiar todavía su enfermedad?, ¿todavía contagia? (**c**) *(laughter, enthusiasm)* contagioso(a)

infectiousness [ɪn'fekʃəslɪ] *adv* (**a**) *(of disease)* naturaleza *f* infecciosa (**b**) *(of laughter, enthusiasm)* contagiosidad *f*

infelicitous [ɪnfɪ'lɪsɪtəs] *adj Formal (comment)* desafortunado(a)

infer [ɪn'fɜː(r)] (*pt & pp* **inferred**) *vt* (**a**) *(deduce)* inferir, deducir (**from** de); **what are we to i. from their silence?** ¿cómo debemos interpretar su silencio? (**b**) *(considered incorrect) (imply)* insinuar; **what are you inferring?** ¿qué insinúas?

inferable = **inferrable**

inference ['ɪnfərəns] *n* inferencia *f*, deducción *f*; **what i. can we draw from this?** ¿qué conclusión podemos sacar de esto?; **by i.** por deducción

inferential [ɪnfə'renʃəl] *adj* deductivo(a)

inferior [ɪn'fɪərɪə(r)] **1** *n* inferior *mf*; **to be sb's i.** ser inferior a alguien
2 *adj* (**a**) *(more junior)* inferior; **an i. officer** un (oficial) inferior (**b**) *(in quality, worth, status)* inferior (**to** a); **to make sb feel i.** hacer sentir inferior a alguien

inferiority [ɪnfɪərɪ'ɒrɪtɪ] *n* inferioridad *f* (**to** respecto de, con respecto a) ►► ***i. complex*** complejo *m* de inferioridad

infernal [ɪn'fɜːnəl] *adj* (**a**) *(diabolical)* infernal, diabólico(a); **the i. flames** las llamas del infierno (**b**) *Fam (awful)* infernal, de mil *or* de todos los demonios; **stop that i. racket** *or* **din!** ¡para con ese ruido del demonio!; **that i. little man!** ¡esa peste de hombre!

infernally [ɪn'fɜːnəlɪ] *adv Fam* **I have i. noisy neighbours** tengo unos vecinos que arman un ruido infernal *or* de mil demonios; **she takes an i. long time getting ready to go out** el tiempo que tarda *or Am* demora en arreglarse para salir es como para desesperar al más pintado

inferno [ɪn'fɜːnəʊ] (*pl* **infernos**) *n* (**a**) *(fire)* incendio *m* devastador *or* pavoroso; **the building was soon an i.** rápidamente se desató un pavoroso *or* devastador incendio en el edificio (**b**) *(hell)* infierno *m*

inferable, inferrable [ɪn'fɜːrəbəl] *adj* deducible (**from** de)

infertile [ɪn'fɜːtaɪl] *adj (land)* estéril, yermo(a); *(person)* estéril

infertility [ɪnfɜː'tɪlɪtɪ] *n* esterilidad *f*, infertilidad *f*; **i. clinic/treatment** clínica/tratamiento de fertilidad

infest [ɪn'fest] *vt* infestar; **to be infested with** *or* **by sth** estar infestado(a) de algo

infestation [ɪnfes'teɪʃən] *n (of insects, weeds)* plaga *f*; *(of lice)* infección *f*

infibulation [ɪnfɪbjʊ'leɪʃən] *n* infibulación *f*

infidel ['ɪnfɪdel] **1** *n Rel* infiel *mf*
2 *adj* infiel, irreligioso(a)

infidelity [ɪnfɪ'delɪtɪ] *n* (**a**) *(betrayal)* deslealtad *f*, traición *f*; *(sexual)* infidelidad *f* (**b**) *(lack of faith)* infidelidad *f*, falta *f* de fe

infield ['ɪnfiːld] *n (in baseball)* diamante *m* (interior)

infielder ['ɪnfiːldə(r)] *n (in baseball)* jugador(ora) *m,f* (del diamante) interior

infighting ['ɪnfaɪtɪŋ] *n* (**a**) *(within group)* lucha *f* interna (**b**) *(in boxing)* lucha *f* cuerpo a cuerpo

infill ['ɪnfɪl] *n* relleno *m*, material *m* de relleno

infiltrate ['ɪnfɪltreɪt] **1** *vt* infiltrar; **the organization had been infiltrated by spies** se habían infiltrado espías en la organización; **they infiltrated an informer into the central committee** infiltraron a un informante en el comité central
2 *vi (liquid, gas)* infiltrarse

infiltration [ɪnfɪl'treɪʃən] *n* (**a**) *(of group)* infiltración *f* (**b**) *(by liquid)* infiltración *f* (**into/through** en/por)

infiltrator ['ɪnfɪltreɪtə(r)] *n* infiltrado(a) *m,f*

infinite ['ɪnfɪnɪt] **1** *n* **the i.** el infinito
2 *adj* (**a**) *(not finite)* infinito(a) (**b**) *(very great)* infinito(a); **he showed i. patience** demostró una paciencia infinita; **to take i. pains over something** esmerarse muchísimo en algo (**c**) *Rel or Hum* **in his i. wisdom** en su infinita sabiduría

infinitely ['ɪnfɪnɪtlɪ] *adv* infinitamente; **that would be i. preferable** eso sería infinitamente mejor *or* preferible

infinitesimal [ɪnfɪnɪ'tesɪməl] *adj* (**a**) *Math* infinitesimal ►► ***i. calculus*** cálculo *m* infinitesimal (**b**) *(tiny)* infinitesimal, minúsculo(a)

infinitesimally [ɪnfɪnɪ'tesɪməlɪ] *adv* mínimamente, microscópicamente

infinitive [ɪn'fɪnɪtɪv] *Gram* **1** *n* infinitivo *m*; **in the i.** en infinitivo
2 *adj* de infinitivo

infinitude [ɪn'fɪnɪtjuːd] *n Literary* infinitud *f*, inmensidad *f*

infinity [ɪn'fɪnɪtɪ] *n* (**a**) *(of space)* infinito *m*; **it stretches to i.** se prolonga *or* extiende hasta el infinito (**b**) *Fig (vast number)* infinidad *f*, multitud *f*; **there is an i. of names to choose from** hay un sinfín de nombres entre los que elegir (**c**) *Math* infinito *m*

infirm [ɪn'fɜːm] **1** *npl* **the i.** los enfermos
2 *adj* (**a**) *(weak, sickly)* enfermizo(a), achacoso(a) (**b**) *Literary (in moral resolution)* **to be i. of purpose** ser irresoluto(a), carecer de determinación

infirmary [ɪn'fɜːmərɪ] *n* (**a**) *(hospital)* hospital *m*, clínica *f* (**b**) *(in school, prison)* enfermería *f*

infirmity [ɪn'fɜːmɪtɪ] *n (weakness)* debilidad *f*; **the infirmities of old age** los achaques de la edad

infix ['ɪnfɪks] *n Ling* infijo *m*

in flagrante (delicto) [ɪnflə'græntɪ(dɪ'lɪktəʊ)] *adv* in fraganti

inflame [ɪn'fleɪm] *vt* (**a**) *(desire, curiosity)* despertar; *(crowd)* enardecer (**b**) *(of wound, part of body)* **to become inflamed** inflamarse

inflammable [ɪn'flæməbəl] *adj* (**a**) *(substance)* inflamable (**b**) *(situation)* explosivo(a)

inflammation [ɪnflə'meɪʃən] *n* inflamación *f*

inflammatory [ɪn'flæmətrɪ] *adj* (**a**) *(speech)* incendiario(a); **his words had an i. effect on the crowd** sus palabras inflamaron a la multitud (**b**) *Med* inflamatorio(a)

inflatable [ɪn'fleɪtəbəl] **1** *n (rubber dinghy)* barca *f* hinchable
2 *adj* hinchable

inflate [ɪn'fleɪt] **1** *vt* (**a**) *(tyre, balloon)* inflar, hinchar; *(sail)* hinchar; *(lungs, chest)* llenar (de aire), hinchar (**b**) *(exaggerate)* inflar, exagerar (**c**) *(prices, economy)* inflar
2 *vi (tyre, balloon)* hincharse, inflarse; *(sail)* hincharse; *(lungs, chest)* llenarse (de aire), hincharse

inflated [ɪn'fleɪtɪd] *adj* (**a**) *(balloon, tyre)* inflado(a), hinchado(a) (**b**) *(exaggerated)* **she has an i. opinion of herself** se cree mejor de lo que es (**c**) *(prices, salary)* desorbitado(a) (**d**) *(pompous)* pomposo(a), grandilocuente

inflation [ɪn'fleɪʃən] *n Econ* inflación *f*; **i. is down/up on last year** la inflación ha disminuido/aumentado respecto del año pasado; **i. now stands at 5 percent** la inflación se sitúa actualmente en el 5 por ciento

inflationary [ɪn'fleɪʃənrɪ] *adj Econ* inflacionista; **i. spiral** espiral inflacionaria *or Esp* inflacionista

inflation-proof [ɪn'fleɪʃən'pruːf] *adj Econ* protegido(a) contra la inflación; **i. pension** pensión revisable de acuerdo con la inflación

inflect [ɪn'flekt] **1** *vt* (**a**) *Gram (verb)* conjugar; *(noun, pronoun, adjective)* declinar (**b**) *(voice)* modular
2 *vi Gram (verb)* conjugarse; *(noun, pronoun, adjective)* declinarse; **adjectives do not i. in English** en inglés no se declinan los adjetivos, el adjetivo inglés no es declinable

inflected [ɪn'flektɪd] *adj Gram (language)* flexivo(a); *(word, form)* flexivo(a)

inflection [ɪn'flekʃən] *n* (**a**) *(of word) (change)* flexión *f*; *(suffix)* desinencia *f*, terminación *f* (**b**) *(in voice)* inflexión *f*

inflectional [ɪn'flekʃənəl] *adj Ling* flexivo(a)

inflexibility [ɪnfleksɪ'bɪlɪtɪ] *n* rigidez *f*, inflexibilidad *f*

inflexible [ɪn'fleksɪbəl] *adj* (**a**) *(material)* rígido(a), inflexible (**b**) *(person, principles)* rígido(a), inflexible

inflexibly [ɪn'fleksɪblɪ] *adv* inflexiblemente, de manera inflexible

inflict [ɪn'flɪkt] *vt (suffering, punishment, defeat)* infligir (**on** a); **he was inflicting himself on us** teníamos que estar aguantando su presencia; **I won't i. myself** *or* **my company on you any longer** no te voy a seguir molestando con mi presencia

infliction [ɪn'flɪkʃən] *n (action)* imposición *f*; **to take pleasure in the i. of pain** disfrutar causando *or* infligiendo dolor

in-flight ['ɪn' flaɪt] *adj* ***i. entertainment*** distracciones *fpl* ofrecidas durante el vuelo; ***i. meal*** comida *f* (servida) a bordo; ***i. refuelling*** reabastecimiento *or Esp* repostaje *m* en vuelo

inflow ['ɪnfləʊ] *n* (**a**) *(of water, gas)* entrada *f* (**b**) *(of people, goods)* afluencia *f*, entrada *f*; **the i. of capital** la entrada *or* afluencia de capital

influence ['ɪnflʊəns] **1** *n* (**a**) *(power)* influencia *f*; **to have i. over/with sb** tener influencia sobre/con alguien; **to bring one's i. to bear on sth/sb** valerse (uno) de su poder para influir en algo/alguien; **a man of i.** un hombre influyente; **under the i. (of drink)** bajo los efectos del alcohol

(**b**) *(person, thing exercising power)* **to be a good/bad i. on sb** tener buena/mala influencia en alguien; **she is a disruptive i.** su influencia es negativa; **you can see the i. of Caravaggio in his paintings** se puede apreciar la influencia de Caravaggio en su pintura

2 *vt* influir en, influenciar; **her style was strongly influenced by cubism** su estilo estuvo muy influenciado por el cubismo; **don't let yourself be influenced by them** no dejes que te influyan *or* que influyan en ti; **he is easily influenced** se deja influir fácilmente

influential [ɪnflʊ'enʃəl] *adj* influyente; **to be very i.** ser muy influyente, tener mucha influencia; **he was i. in persuading them to accept the treaty** fue fundamental a la hora de convencerlos de que aceptaran el tratado

influenza [ɪnflʊ'enzə] *n* gripe *f*, *Col, Méx* gripa *f*; **to have i.** tener gripe

influx ['ɪnflʌks] *n (of people, goods, cash)* afluencia *f* (masiva); **an i. of capital** una entrada *or* afluencia de capital

info ['ɪnfəʊ] *n Fam* información *f*

infoaddict ['ɪnfəʊædɪkt] *n Comptr* infoadicto(a) *m,f*

infobahn ['ɪnfəʊbɑːn] *n Comptr* infopista *f*, autopista *f* de la información

infold = **enfold**

infomercial ['ɪnfəʊmɜːʃəl] *n TV* publirreportaje *m*

inform [ɪn'fɔːm] **1** *vt* (**a**) *(give information to)* informar *or CAm, Méx* reportar (**of/about** de/sobre); **keep me informed of what is happening** manténme informado de lo que pase; **why was I not informed (of this)?** ¿por qué no se me informó (de esto *or* al respecto)?; **I regret to have to i. you that...** siento tener que comunicarle *or* informarle que...; **we are writing to i. you of the dispatch of...** nos dirigimos a usted(es) para informarle(s) del envío de...

(**b**) *Formal (pervade)* impregnar, informar

2 *vi* **to i. on** *or* **against sb** delatar a alguien

informal [ɪn'fɔːməl] *adj* (**a**) *(dress, manner)* informal; **British offices tend to be more i. than German ones** las oficinas británicas tienden a ser más informales que las alemanas (**b**) *(word, language)* coloquial, informal (**c**) *(meeting, talks)* informal; **I had an i. chat with the boss** tuve una charla informal con el jefe

informality [ɪnfɔː'mælɪtɪ] *n* (**a**) *(of dress, manner)* informalidad *f* (**b**) *(of word, language)* coloquialismo *m*, informalidad *f* (**c**) *(of meeting, talks)* informalidad *f*

informally [ɪn'fɔːməlɪ] *adv* (**a**) *(to dress, behave)* informalmente, de manera informal (**b**) *(to speak, address sb)* coloquialmente, informalmente (**c**) *(to hold talks, inform)* informalmente

informant [ɪn'fɔːmənt] *n* (**a**) *(for police)* confidente *mf* (**b**) *(for research study)* informante *mf*

informatics [ɪnfə'mætɪks] *n Comptr* informática *f*

information [ɪnfə'meɪʃən] *n* (**a**) *(news, facts)* información *f*; **a piece** *or* **bit of i.** una información, un dato; **according to my i.,...** según la información de que dispongo..., según los datos con los que cuento...; **an i. gathering exercise** una operación de recopilación de datos; **for your i.** para tu información; **for your i., I'm not stupid** para que te enteres, no soy estúpido; **for your i., I've done the dishes for the past week!** para que lo sepas, he sido yo quien ha estado haciendo el fregado toda la semana ►► ***i. blackout:*** **the government is operating an i. blackout** el Gobierno está llevando a cabo un bloqueo informativo; ***i. bureau*** oficina *f* de información; ***i. desk*** mostrador *m* de información; ***i. office*** oficina *f* de información; ***i. officer*** documentalista *mf*; ***i. overload*** sobrecarga *f* de información

(**b**) *Comptr* ***i. highway*** autopista *f* de la información; ***i. processing*** proceso *m* de datos; ***i. retrieval*** recuperación *f* de la información; ***i. science*** informática *f*; ***i. society*** sociedad *f* de la información; ***i. superhighway*** autopista *f* de la información; ***i. technology*** tecnologías *f* de la información, informática *f*; ***i. theory*** teoría *f* de la información

(**c**) *US Tel* información *f*, *Am* informaciones *fpl*; **to call i.** llamar a información *or* al servicio de información

informative [ɪn'fɔːmətɪv] *adj* informativo(a); **he wasn't very i. about his future plans** no dio muchos datos sobre sus planes futuros

informed [ɪn'fɔːmd] *adj* (**a**) *(having information)* informado(a); **according to i. sources** según fuentes bien informadas; **she's very well i.** está muy bien informada ►► *Med* ***i. consent*** consentimiento *m* informado

(**b**) *(based on information)* **an i. choice** una elección informada; **it will allow us to make an i. choice** nos permitirá tomar una decisión informada; **an i. guess/decision** una conjetura/decisión bien fundada

informer [ɪn'fɔːmə(r)] *n* confidente *mf*; **a police i.** un informante *or* confidente de la policía

infotainment [ɪnfəʊ'teɪnmənt] *n TV* programas *mpl* informativos de entretenimiento

infraction [ɪn'frækʃən] *n Formal* infracción *f*

infra dig ['ɪnfrə'dɪg] *adj Fam Old-fashioned* ordinario(a), *Esp* cutre, *Méx* gacho(a), *RP* roñoso(a)

infrared ['ɪnfrə'red] *adj Phys* infrarrojo(a); **i. radiation** *or* **rays** rayos infrarrojos ►► ***i. photography*** fotografía *f* infrarroja

infrasonic [ɪnfrə'sɒnɪk] *adj Phys* infrasónico(a)

infrasound ['ɪnfrəsaʊnd] *n Phys* infrasonido *m*

infrastructure ['ɪnfrəstrʌktʃə(r)] *n* infraestructura *f*

infrequency [ɪn'friːkwənsɪ] *n* infrecuencia *f*, escasa frecuencia *f*

infrequent [ɪn'friːkwənt] *adj* poco frecuente, infrecuente; **an i. visitor to our shores** un visitante poco habitual de nuestras costas; **a not i. occurence** un acontecimiento nada infrecuente

infrequently [ɪn'friːkwəntlɪ] *adv* con poca frecuencia, raras veces

infringe [ɪn'frɪndʒ] *vt* (**a**) *(rule)* infringir (**b**) *(right)* violar, vulnerar; **to i. copyright** violar los derechos *or* el derecho de autor

► **infringe on, infringe upon** *vt insep* infringir

infringement [ɪn'frɪndʒmənt] *n* (**a**) *(of rule, law)* infracción *f* (**b**) *(of right)* violación *f*, vulneración *f*; **i. of copyright** violación de los derechos *or* del derecho de autor

infuriate [ɪn'fjʊːrɪeɪt] *vt* exasperar, enfurecer

infuriating [ɪn'fjʊːrɪeɪtɪŋ] *adj* exasperante; **it's i. the way she's always right** es exasperante *or* lo saca a uno de sus casillas que siempre tenga razón

infuriatingly [ɪn'fjʊːrɪeɪtɪŋlɪ] *adv* **she's an i. nice person** de tan buena persona que es resulta exasperante; **she remained i. polite/reasonable throughout** se mantuvo irritantemente correcta/razonable todo el tiempo; **the movie was i. boring** la película era desesperantemente aburrida

infuse [ɪn'fjuːz] **1** *vt* (**a**) *(instil)* infundir (**into** en); **to i. sb with sth** infundir algo a *or* en alguien; **her speech infused them with courage** su discurso les infundió valor (**b**) *(tea)* infundir

2 *vi* reposar *(una infusión)*

infusion [ɪn'fjuːʒən] *n* (**a**) *(drink)* infusión *f* (**b**) *(of money, high spirits)* inyección *f* (**c**) *Med* infusión *f*

ingenious [ɪn'dʒiːnɪəs] *adj* ingenioso(a); **she was i. at making economies** se le ocurrían muy buenas ideas para ahorrarse dinero

ingeniously [ɪn'dʒiːnɪəslɪ] *adv* ingeniosamente

ingénue ['ænʒeɪnuː] *n* joven *f* ingenua

ingenuity [ɪndʒɪ'njuːɪtɪ] *n* ingenio *m*

ingenuous [ɪn'dʒenjʊəs] *adj* (**a**) *(naive)* ingenuo(a) (**b**) *(frank)* franco(a), natural

ingenuously [ɪn'dʒenjʊəslɪ] *adv* (**a**) *(naively)* ingenuamente (**b**) *(frankly)* francamente, con naturalidad

ingenuousness [ɪn'dʒenjʊəsnɪs] *n* (**a**) *(naivety)* ingenuidad *f* (**b**) *(frankness)* franqueza *f*, naturalidad *f*

ingest [ɪn'dʒest] *vt Formal (food, liquid)* ingerir

ingestion [ɪn'dʒestʃən] *n Formal* ingestión *f*, ingesta *f*

inglenook [ˈɪŋgəlnʊk] *n* rincón *m* de la chimenea

inglorious [ɪnˈglɔːrɪəs] *adj Formal* deshonroso(a), vergonzoso(a)

ingloriously [ɪnˈglɔːrɪəslɪ] *adv Formal* ignominiosamente, deshonrosamente

in-goal area [ˈɪngəʊlˈeərɪə] *n (in rugby)* zona *f* de marca

ingot [ˈɪŋgət] *n* lingote *m*

ingrain, engrain [ɪnˈgreɪn] *vt* inculcar

ingrained, engrained [ɪnˈgreɪnd] *adj* (**a**) *(dirt)* incrustado(a) (**b**) *(prejudice, habit)* arraigado(a)

ingrate [ˈɪŋgreɪt] *n Formal* ingrato(a) *m,f*

ingratiate [ɪnˈgreɪʃɪeɪt] *vt* **to i. oneself (with sb)** congraciarse (con alguien)

ingratiating [ɪnˈgreɪʃɪeɪtɪŋ] *adj* obsequioso(a); **an i. smile** una sonrisa zalamera; **an i. manner** un talante obsequioso *or* lisonjero

ingratiatingly [ɪnˈgreɪʃɪeɪtɪŋlɪ] *adv* de manera obsequiosa

ingratitude [ɪnˈgrætɪtjuːd] *n* ingratitud *f*

ingredient [ɪnˈgriːdɪənt] *n* (**a**) *(of food)* ingrediente *m*; **ingredients: sugar, water...** ingredientes: azúcar, agua... (**b**) *(component)* ingrediente *m*, elemento *m*; **rapport is an essential i. in a good comedian** la capacidad de comunicación es un elemento fundamental en un buen comediante; **the missing i.** lo que falta/faltaba

ingress [ˈɪŋgres] *n Formal* acceso *m*

in-group [ˈɪngruːp] *n* camarilla *f*, pandilla *f*

ingrowing toenail [ˈɪngrəʊɪŋˈtəʊneɪl], **ingrown toenail** [ˈɪngrəʊnˈtəʊneɪl] *n Med* uña *f* encarnada

inguinal [ˈɪŋgwɪnəl] *adj Anat* inguinal

inhabit [ɪnˈhæbɪt] *vt* habitar

inhabitable [ɪnˈhæbɪtəbəl] *adj* habitable

> **False friend**: The Spanish adjective **inhabitable** is not a translation for the English word **inhabitable**. In Spanish **inhabitable** means "uninhabitable".

inhabitant [ɪnˈhæbɪtənt] *n* habitante *mf*

inhabited [ɪnˈhæbɪtɪd] *adj* habitado(a); **the island is no longer i.** la isla ya no está habitada

> **False friend**: The Spanish adjective **inhabitado** is not a translation for the English word **inhabited**. In Spanish **inhabitado** means "uninhabited".

inhalant [ɪnˈheɪlənt] *n* (sustancia *f*) inhalante *m*

inhalation [ɪnhəˈleɪʃən] *n* inhalación *f*

inhale [ɪnˈheɪl] **1** *vt (gas, fumes)* inhalar; *(cigarette smoke)* aspirar
2 *vi* inspirar; *(when smoking)* tragarse el humo

inhaler [ɪnˈheɪlə(r)] *n (for asthmatics)* inhalador *m*

inharmonious [ɪnhɑːˈməʊnɪəs] *adj Formal (colours)* poco armónico(a), sin armonía; *(sounds, music)* inarmónico(a)

inhere [ɪnˈhɪə(r)] *vi Formal* ser inherente a, ser propio(a) de; **the powers which i. in the state** los poderes propios del Estado

inherent [ɪnˈherənt] *adj* inherente (**in** a); **an i. fault in the design** *Esp* un fallo *orAm* una falla inherente al diseño

inherently [ɪnˈherəntlɪ] *adv* intrínsecamente; **the theory is i. flawed** la teoría es intrínsecamente errónea

inherit [ɪnˈherɪt] **1** *vt* heredar (**from** de); **the problems inherited from the previous government** los problemas heredados del Gobierno anterior; *Fam* **I inherited this jacket from my older brother** heredé esta chaqueta de mi hermano mayor
2 *vi* heredar

inheritable [ɪnˈherɪtəbəl] *adj (title, property)* heredable, transmisible por herencia; *(trait)* heredable

inheritance [ɪnˈherɪtəns] *n* (**a**) *(legacy)* herencia *f*; **to come into an i.** heredar, recibir una herencia ►► ***i. tax*** impuesto *m* sobre sucesiones (**b**) *(process)* herencia *f*, sucesión *f*; **it came into the family by i.** la familia lo obtuvo por herencia; **to claim sth by right of i.** reclamar algo haciendo uso del derecho de sucesión (**c**) *(heritage)* **cultural/artistic i.** patrimonio *or* legado cultural/artístico

inherited [ɪnˈherɪtɪd] *adj* heredado(a)

inheritor [ɪnˈherɪtə(r)] *n* heredero(a) *m,f*

inhibit [ɪnˈhɪbɪt] *vt* (**a**) *(feeling, person)* cohibir, inhibir; **to i. sb from doing sth** impedir a alguien hacer algo; **a law which inhibits free speech** una ley que limita la libertad de expresión (**b**) *(progress, growth)* impedir, coartar; *(breathing)* inhibir (**c**) *Chem* inhibir

inhibited [ɪnˈhɪbɪtɪd] *adj* cohibido(a)

inhibiter = **inhibitor**

inhibition [ɪnɪˈbɪʃən] *n* (**a**) *(feeling)* inhibición *f*; **to lose one's inhibitions** dejar de sentirse cohibido(a); **to have no inhibitions about doing sth** no sentir ninguna vergüenza *or CAm, Col, Ven* pena a la hora de hacer algo (**b**) *Chem* inhibición *f*

inhibitor, inhibiter [ɪnˈhɪbɪtə(r)] *n Chem* inhibidor *m*

inhibitory [ɪnˈhɪbɪtərɪ] *adj* inhibidor(ora)

inhospitable [ɪnhɒˈspɪtəbəl] *adj* (**a**) *(person)* inhospitalario(a), poco hospitalario(a) (**b**) *(town, climate)* inhóspito(a)

inhospitably [ɪnhɒˈspɪtəblɪ] *adv* de forma poco hospitalaria

in-house [ˈɪnˈhaʊs] **1** *adj* ***i. journal*** boletín *m* interno (de una empresa); ***i. staff*** personal *m* en plantilla; ***i. training*** formación *f* en el lugar de trabajo
2 *adv* **the work was done i.** el trabajo se hizo en la misma empresa

inhuman [ɪnˈhjuːmən] *adj* inhumano(a); **i. cruelty** crueldad inhumana; *Fam* **a six o'clock start? that's i.!** ¿empezar a las seis? ¡eso es inhumano!

inhumane [ɪnhjuːˈmeɪn] *adj* inhumano(a)

inhumanely [ɪnhjuːˈmeɪnlɪ] *adv* de forma inhumana; **the hostages were treated i.** los rehenes recibieron un trato inhumano

inhumanity [ɪnhjuːˈmænɪtɪ] *n* (**a**) *(quality)* falta *f* de humanidad; IDIOM **man's i. to man** la crueldad del hombre hacia el propio hombre (**b**) *(act)* atrocidad *f*, brutalidad *f*

inimical [ɪˈnɪmɪkəl] *adj Formal* (**a**) *(unfavourable)* adverso(a) (**to** a) (**b**) *(unfriendly)* hostil, poco amigable

inimitable [ɪˈnɪmɪtəbəl] *adj* inimitable

iniquitous [ɪˈnɪkwɪtəs] *adj Formal* inicuo(a)

iniquitously [ɪˈnɪkwɪtəslɪ] *adv Formal* injustamente, sin justificación

iniquity [ɪˈnɪkwɪtɪ] *n Formal* iniquidad *f*

initial [ɪˈnɪʃəl] **1** *n* inicial *f*; **initials** iniciales *fpl*
2 *adj* (**a**) *(payment, impression)* inicial; **my i. reaction** mi primera reacción; **the i. stages** la fase *or* etapa inicial; **we expect a few problems in the i. stages** contamos con que habrá algunos problemas en la etapa inicial *or* al principio; **the project is still in its i. stages** el proyecto está aún en fase inicial; **the i. letter** la letra inicial (**b**) *Ling* **in i. position** en posición inicial
3 *vt* (*pt & pp* **initialled**, *US* **initialed**) *(document)* poner las iniciales en

initialization [ɪnɪʃəlaɪˈzeɪʃən] *n Comptr* inicialización *f*

initialize [ɪˈnɪʃəlaɪz] *vt Comptr* inicializar

initially [ɪˈnɪʃəlɪ] *adv* inicialmente; **an i. favourable response** una respuesta de entrada favorable; **i. she was against the idea** en un principio no aprobaba la idea *or* estaba en contra de la idea

initiate **1** *vt* [ɪˈnɪʃɪeɪt] (**a**) *Formal (begin) (talks, debate)* iniciar; *(policy, measures)* emprender, poner en marcha; **I find it hard to i. a conversation with him** me resulta difícil entablar (una) conversación con él (**b**) *Law* **to i. proceedings (against sb)** emprender una acción legal (contra alguien) (**c**) *(into secret society, gang)* iniciar (**into** en)
2 *n* [ɪˈnɪʃɪət] iniciado(a) *m,f*

initiation [ɪnɪʃɪˈeɪʃən] *n* (**a**) *Formal (beginning) (of talks, debate)* iniciación *f*; *(of policy, measure)* puesta *f* en marcha; **he fought for the i. of new policies** luchó por la puesta en marcha de nuevas políticas (**b**) *(into secret society, gang)* iniciación *f* (**into** en) ►► ***i. ceremony*** ceremonia *f* iniciática *or* de iniciación; ***i. rites*** rito *m* iniciático

initiative [ɪˈnɪʃətɪv] *n* (**a**) *(drive)* iniciativa *f*; **she's certainly got i.** no cabe duda de que tiene iniciativa; **to act on one's own i.** actuar por propia iniciativa, obrar motu proprio; **she lacks i.** le falta iniciativa; **you'll have to use your i.** tendrás que actuar por ti mismo(a)
(**b**) *(first step)* iniciativa *f*; **to take the i.** tomar la iniciativa
(**c**) *(lead)* iniciativa *f*; **to have the i.** tener la iniciativa; **they lost the i. to foreign competition** la competencia extranjera les sobrepasó
(**d**) *(scheme)* iniciativa *f*

initiator [ɪˈnɪʃɪeɪtə(r)] *n* (**a**) *(of scheme, process)* iniciador(ora) *m,f* (**b**) *Chem* iniciador *m*

inject [ɪnˈdʒekt] *vt* (**a**) *(substance)* inyectar (**into** en); **to i. sb with a drug** inyectar un medicamento a alguien; **have you been injected against tetanus?** ¿te has puesto la inyección *or* vacuna del tétanos?
(**b**) *(money)* inyectar (**into** en); **they've injected billions of dollars into the economy** le han inyectado a la economía miles de millones de dólares
(**c**) *(quality)* infundir; **to i. sb with enthusiasm** infundir entusiasmo a alguien; **to i. new life into sth** infundir nueva vida a algo; **he tried to i. some humour into the situation** trató de inyectarle un poco de humor a la situación

injectable [ɪnˈdʒektəbəl] *adj* inyectable

injection [ɪn'dʒekʃən] *n* (**a**) *(of substance)* inyección *f*; **to give sb an i.** poner una inyección a alguien ►► ***i. moulding*** moldeo *m* por inyección; ***i. pump*** bomba *f* de inyección (**b**) *(of money)* inyección *f* (**c**) *(of quality)* inyección *f*

injudicious [ɪndʒʊ'dɪʃəs] *adj Formal* imprudente, poco juicioso(a)

injudiciously [ɪndʒʊ'dɪʃəslɪ] *adv Formal* imprudentemente

injunction [ɪn'dʒʌnkʃən] *n* (**a**) *Law* requerimiento *m* judicial (**b**) *Formal (order, warning)* orden *f*; **she smokes despite her father's injunctions against it** fuma en contra de las órdenes de su padre

injure ['ɪndʒə(r)] *vt* (**a**) *(physically)* herir, lesionar; **to i. oneself** lesionarse; **to i. one's leg** lesionarse una pierna (**b**) *(feelings)* herir; **only his pride was injured** sólo vio herido su orgullo, sólo le hirieron el orgullo (**c**) *(reputation, interests)* dañar, perjudicar

injured ['ɪndʒəd] **1** *npl* **the i.** los heridos
2 *adj* (**a**) *(physically)* herido(a), lesionado(a) (**b**) *(offended) (tone, voice)* resentido(a); **to feel i.** sentirse ofendido(a), sentirse dolido(a) (**c**) *Law* **the i. party** la parte perjudicada

injurious [ɪn'dʒʊrɪəs] *adj Formal* perjudicial (**to** para); **actions i. to the public good** actuaciones perniciosas para el bien público

injury ['ɪndʒərɪ] *n* (**a**) *(open wound)* herida *f*; *(broken bone, damaged muscle)* lesión *f*; **to do oneself an i.** *esp Esp* hacerse daño, *esp Am* lastimarse (**b**) *(harm) (physical)* lesiones *fpl*; **he escaped without i.** escapó ileso; **i. to sb's feelings** ofensa a *or* contra los sentimientos de alguien ►► *Br Sport* ***i. time*** tiempo *m* de descuento (**c**) *(injustice, wrong)* daño *m*, ofensa *f*

injustice [ɪn'dʒʌstɪs] *n* injusticia *f*; **you do her an i.** estás siendo injusto con ella

ink [ɪŋk] **1** *n* (**a**) *(for writing, printing)* tinta *f*; **in i.** con tinta; **an i. drawing** un dibujo (hecho) a plumilla ►► ***i. blotter*** tampón *m*; ***i. bottle*** bote *m or* frasco *m* de tinta; ***i. cartridge*** *(for pen, printer)* cartucho *m* de tinta; ***i. eraser*** goma *f* de tinta (**b**) *(of squid, octopus etc)* tinta *f* ►► ***i. sac*** bolsa *f* de tinta
2 *vt* (**a**) *(surface)* entintar (**b**) *US (sign)* firmar, aprobar

► **ink in** *vt sep* marcar *or* repasar con tinta

inkblot ['ɪŋkblɒt] *n (on clothes, table)* mancha *f* de tinta; *(on paper)* borrón *m* de tinta ►► ***i. test*** prueba *f or* test *m* de Rorschach

inkjet printer ['ɪŋkdʒet'prɪntə(r)] *n Comptr* impresora *f* de chorro de tinta

inkling ['ɪŋklɪŋ] *n* **to have an i. of sth** tener una vaga *or* ligera idea de algo; **I had some i. of the** *or* **as to the real reason** tenía una ligera sospecha de cuáles eran los verdaderos motivos; **she had no i. of what they were up to** no tenía ni idea de lo que estaban tramando

inkpad ['ɪŋkpæd] *n* tampón *m*

inkpot ['ɪŋkpɒt] *n* tintero *m*

inkstand ['ɪŋkstænd] *n* escribanía *f*

inkwell ['ɪŋkwel] *n* tintero *m*

inky ['ɪŋkɪ] *adj* (**a**) *(stained with ink)* manchado(a) de tinta (**b**) *(in colour)* **i. (black)** negro(a) (como el carbón)

inlaid [ɪn'leɪd] **1** *adj (with wood)* taraceado(a); *(with jewels)* incrustado(a) **2** *pp of* **inlay**

inland **1** *adj* ['ɪnlænd] (**a**) *(not coastal) (town, sea)* interior, del interior (**b**) *Br (not foreign)* interior, nacional; **i. mail** correo interior ►► *Br* ***the I. Revenue*** *Esp* ≃ la Agencia Tributaria, *Am* ≃ la Dirección General Impositiva
2 *adv* [ɪn'lænd] *(to travel)* al interior; *(to live)* en el interior; **the town is several miles i.** la ciudad está varias millas hacia el interior *or* tierra adentro, la ciudad está a varias millas de la costa

in-laws ['ɪnlɔːz] *npl* familia *f* política

inlay **1** *n* ['ɪnleɪ] (**a**) *(in wood)* taracea *f*, incrustación *f*; *(in metal)* incrustación *f* (**b**) *(in dentistry)* empaste *m*, *Am* emplomadura *f*, *Chile* tapadura *f*, *Col* calza *f*
2 *vt* [ɪn'leɪ] *(pt & pp* **inlaid***) (in wood)* taracear, hacer una taracea en (**with** con); *(in metal)* hacer incrustaciones en (**with** de)

inlet ['ɪnlet] *n* (**a**) *(of sea)* ensenada *f* (**b**) *(of pipe, machine)* entrada *f*; **air/fuel i.** entrada *or* toma de aire/combustible

inline ['ɪnlaɪn] *adj* (**a**) *Comptr* ***i. image*** imagen *f* integrada (**b**) *Aut* ***i. engine*** motor *m* de cilindros en línea (**c**) ***i. skates*** patines *mpl* en línea

in loco parentis [ɪn'ləʊkəʊpə'rentɪs] *adv Formal* en nombre de los padres

inmate ['ɪnmeɪt] *n* (**a**) *(in prison)* recluso(a) *m,f* (**b**) *(in mental hospital)* paciente *mf*

in medias res [ɪn'miːdɪæs'reɪz] *adv Formal* in media res

in memoriam ['ɪnme'mɔːrɪæm] *adv* in memóriam

inmost = **innermost**

inn [ɪn] *n* (**a**) *(pub)* bar *m*, tasca *f*; *(small hotel)* posada *f*, mesón *m* (**b**) *Law* ***I. of Court*** = cada una de las asociaciones privadas de abogados británicos

innards ['ɪnədz] *npl also Fig* tripas *fpl*

innate [ɪ'neɪt] *adj* innato(a)

innately [ɪ'neɪtlɪ] *adv* por naturaleza; **an i. kind person** una persona amable por naturaleza

inner ['ɪnə(r)] *adj* (**a**) *(chamber, lining)* interior ►► ***i. city*** = área céntrica y degradada de una ciudad; *Anat* ***i. ear*** oído *m* interno; ***I. London*** el casco céntrico de Londres; *Astron* ***i. planets*** planetas *mpl* interiores; ***i. tube*** cámara *f* (de aire)
(**b**) *(thought, feeling)* íntimo(a) ►► ***i. circle*** *(of friends)* círculo *m* restringido *or* privado; **her i. circle of advisers** el círculo de sus asesores más allegados *or* de mayor confianza; **the i. circles of power** los círculos próximos al poder; ***the i. man*** *(soul)* el espíritu del hombre; ***i. peace*** paz *f* interior; ***the i. woman*** *(soul)* el espíritu de la mujer

inner-city ['ɪnə'sɪtɪ] *adj* **i. crime** delincuencia en los barrios céntricos deprimidos; **i. housing** viviendas de los barrios céntricos deprimidos

innermost ['ɪnəməʊst], **inmost** ['ɪnməʊst] *adj* (**a**) *(most intimate, secret)* **i. thoughts** pensamientos más íntimos; **in her i. being** en lo más profundo *or* recóndito de su ser (**b**) *(central)* **i. part** parte más interior; **in the i. depths of the cave** en lo más recóndito de la cueva

inning ['ɪnɪŋ] *n (in baseball)* turno *m* para batear, *Am* inning *m*

innings ['ɪnɪŋz] *n (in cricket)* turno *m* para batear; *Br Fig* **she had a good i.** *(a long life)* tuvo una vida larga y plena

innkeeper ['ɪnkiːpə(r)] *n* mesonero(a) *m,f*, posadero(a) *m,f*

innocence ['ɪnəsəns] *n* (**a**) *(lack of guilt)* inocencia *f*; **to protest one's i.** declararse inocente; **to prove one's i.** demostrar (uno) su inocencia (**b**) *(naivety, lack of guile)* inocencia *f*, ingenuidad *f*; **in all i.** con toda *or* la mayor inocencia

innocent ['ɪnəsənt] **1** *adj* (**a**) *(not guilty)* inocente (**of** de); **the bomb killed several i. bystanders** la bomba mató a varias personas inocentes que se encontraban en la zona; *Fam* **to act all i.** hacerse el/la inocente (**b**) *(naive, guileless)* inocente; **an i. remark** un comentario inocente *or* sin malicia (**c**) *Formal (devoid)* **i. of** desprovisto(a) de, libre de
2 *n* inocente *mf*; **what an i. you are!** ¡qué inocente eres!; **don't play the i.!** ¡no te hagas el inocente!

innocently ['ɪnəsəntlɪ] *adv* inocentemente, con inocencia

innocuous [ɪ'nɒkjʊəs] *adj* inocuo(a)

innocuously [ɪ'nɒkjʊəslɪ] *adv* de forma inocua

innovate ['ɪnəveɪt] *vi* innovar

innovation [ɪnə'veɪʃən] *n* innovación *f*

innovative ['ɪnəveɪtɪv], **innovatory** ['ɪnəveɪtərɪ] *adj* innovador(ora)

innovator ['ɪnəveɪtə(r)] *n* innovador(ora) *m,f*

innovatory = **innovative**

innuendo [ɪnjʊ'endəʊ] *(pl* **innuendos***) n* (**a**) *Pej (in remarks)* indirecta *f*, insinuación *f*; **to discredit sb by i.** desacreditar a alguien mediante insinuaciones (**b**) *(in jokes)* doble sentido *m*, juegos *mpl* de palabras *(sobre sexo)*

Innuit = **Inuit**

innumerable [ɪ'njuːmərəbəl] *adj* innumerable; **on i. occasions** en innumerables ocasiones

innumeracy [ɪ'njuːmərəsɪ] *n* falta *f* de conocimientos de aritmética

innumerate [ɪ'njuːmərət] *adj* falto(a) de conocimientos de aritmética

inoculate [ɪ'nɒkjʊleɪt] *vt* inocular; **to i. sb with sth** inocular algo a alguien; **to i. sb against sth** vacunar a alguien de algo

inoculation [ɪnɒkjʊ'leɪʃən] *n* inoculation *f*

inoffensive [ɪnə'fensɪv] *adj* inofensivo(a)

inoffensively [ɪnə'fensɪvlɪ] *adv* inofensivamente; **she was sitting there quite i., when...** estaba allí sentada sin hacerle daño a nadie, cuando...

inoperable [ɪn'ɒpərəbəl] *adj* (**a**) *Med* **to be i.** no ser operable (**b**) *(unworkable)* impracticable, inviable

inoperative [ɪn'ɒpərətɪv] *adj* (**a**) *(rule)* inoperante (**b**) **to be i.** *(of machine)* no funcionar

inopportune [ɪn'ɒpətjuːn] *adj* inoportuno(a)

inordinate [ɪn'ɔːdɪnət] *adj Formal* desmesurado(a); **it cost an i. amount of money** costó una cantidad desorbitada de dinero; **they spent an i. amount of time on it** emplearon *or* le dedicaron una cantidad excesiva de tiempo

inordinately [ɪn'ɔːdɪnətlɪ] *adv Formal* desmesuradamente

inorganic [ɪnɔː' gænɪk] *adj* inorgánico(a) ▸▸ *Chem* ***i. chemistry*** química *f* inorgánica; ***i. fertilizer*** abono *m* químico

in-patient ['ɪnpeɪʃənt] *n* paciente *mf* interno(a)

input ['ɪnpʊt] **1** *n* (**a**) *(contribution) (to project)* aportación *f*, aporte *m*; **we'd like some i. from the marketing department on this issue** queremos consultar al departamento de marketing en este tema (**b**) *(to manufacturing process)* materias *fpl* primas (**c**) *Elec* entrada *f* (**d**) *Comptr* input *m*, entrada *f* (de información) ▸▸ ***i. device*** dispositivo *m* de entrada

2 *vt Comptr* **to i. data** introducir datos

input/output ['ɪnpʊt'aʊtpʊt] *adj Comptr* ***i. device*** dispositivo *m* de entrada y salida; ***i. system*** sistema *m* de entrada y salida

inquest ['ɪnkwest] *n* investigación *f* (**into** sobre); *Law* **to hold an i.** *(of coroner)* determinar las causas de la muerte; *(in politics, business)* investigar

inquire, enquire [ɪn'kwaɪə(r)] **1** *vt (ask)* preguntar; **he inquired why I was there** me preguntó por qué estaba allí; **why, might I i., are you here?** ¿y tú qué haces aquí, si es que puede saberse?

2 *vi* preguntar; **to i. as to** *or* **about...** informarse sobre...; **I'm inquiring about the post advertised in "The Guardian"** quisiera información sobre la oferta de empleo publicada en "The Guardian"; **i. within** *(sign)* razón aquí

▸**inquire after, enquire after** *vt insep* preguntar por; **she inquired after your health** ha preguntado *or* se ha interesado por tu salud

▸**inquire into, enquire into** *vt insep* investigar, indagar; **it doesn't do to i. into these things too deeply** no hay que ahondar demasiado en estos asuntos; **they should i. into how the money was spent** deberían averiguar en qué se empleó el dinero

inquirer, enquirer [ɪn'kwaɪərə(r)] *n* investigador(ora) *m,f*

inquiring, enquiring [ɪn'kwaɪrɪŋ] *adj (mind)* inquisitivo(a); *(look)* de interrogación

inquiringly, enquiringly [ɪn'kwaɪrɪŋlɪ] *adv* de un modo inquisitivo; **she looked at him i.** lo miró con ojos inquisidores

inquiry, enquiry [ɪn'kwaɪrɪ, *US* 'ɪnkwərɪ] *n* (**a**) *(official investigation)* investigación *f* (oficial); **to hold** *or* **conduct an i. (into sth)** realizar una investigación (sobre algo); **the police are making inquiries** la policía está haciendo indagaciones *or* averiguaciones; **a man is helping police with their inquiries** la policía está interrogando a una persona sospechosa *or* a un presunto implicado

(**b**) *(request for information)* consulta *f*; **to make inquiries (about sth/sb)** consultar *or* informarse (sobre algo/alguien); **to make inquiries into sth** hacer averiguaciones *or* indagaciones sobre algo; **a look of i.** una mirada inquisitiva *or* inquisitoria; **a tone of i.** un tono inquisitivo *or* inquisitorio; **on further i.** indagando un poco más ▸▸ ***i. desk, inquiries*** (mostrador *m* de) información *f*

inquisition [ɪnkwɪ'zɪʃən] *n* (**a**) *(interrogation)* interrogatorio *m*; **the interview turned into an i.** la entrevista se convirtió en un interrogatorio (**b**) *Hist* **the I.** la Inquisición

inquisitive [ɪn'kwɪzɪtɪv] *adj* curioso(a)

inquisitively [ɪn'kwɪzɪtɪvlɪ] *adv* con curiosidad

inquisitiveness [ɪn'kwɪzɪtɪvnɪs] *n* curiosidad *f*

inquisitor [ɪn'kwɪzɪtə(r)] *n* (**a**) *Hist* inquisidor *m* (**b**) *(questioner)* interrogador(ora) *m,f*

inquisitorial [ɪnkwɪzɪ'tɔːrɪəl] *adj* inquisitorial

inquorate [ɪn'kwɔːrət] *adj Br Formal (meeting)* sin quórum

inroads ['ɪnrəʊdz] *npl* **to make i. into enemy territory** adentrarse en territorio enemigo; **I had to make i. into my savings** tuve que recurrir a mis propios ahorros; **to make i. into the market** penetrar en el mercado; **the Nationalists had made i. into the Socialist vote** los nacionalistas se habían hecho con parte del voto socialista

inrush ['ɪnrʌʃ] *n* (**a**) *(of people)* aluvión *m* (**b**) *(of air)* ráfaga *f*

INS [aɪen'es] *n* (*abbr* **Immigration and Naturalization Service**) = departamento estadounidense de inmigración y naturalización

ins. (**a**) (*abbr* **inches**) pulgadas *fpl* (**b**) (*abbr* **insurance**) seguro *m*

insalubrious [ɪnsə'luːbrɪəs] *adj Formal (climate, atmosphere)* insalubre; *(district, surroundings)* sórdido(a)

insane [ɪn'seɪn] **1** *adj* (**a**) *(person)* demente, loco(a); **to be i.** *(of person)* estar loco(a); **to go i.** trastornarse, volverse loco(a); **to drive sb i.** volver loco(a) a alguien; **to be i. with grief/jealousy** enloquecer de dolor/celos ▸▸ *US* ***i. asylum*** manicomio *m* (**b**) *(desire, scheme)* demencial, descabellado(a)

2 *npl* **the i.** los enfermos mentales, los locos

insanely [ɪn'seɪnlɪ] *adv* disparatadamente; **i. jealous** loco(a) de celos

insanitary [ɪn'sænɪtrɪ] *adj* antihigiénico(a)

insanity [ɪn'sænɪtɪ] *n* (**a**) *(of person)* demencia *f*, locura *f* (**b**) *(of desire, scheme)* demencialidad *f*, locura *f*; **it would be sheer i. to do that** sería una auténtica locura hacer eso

insatiability [ɪnseɪʃɪə'bɪlɪtɪ] *n* insaciabilidad *f*

insatiable [ɪn'seɪʃəbəl] *adj* insaciable

insatiably [ɪn'seɪʃəblɪ] *adv* insaciablemente; **i. curious** de una curiosidad insaciable

inscribe [ɪn'skraɪb] *vt* (**a**) *(write, engrave)* inscribir; **he had the ring inscribed with her name** *or* **her name inscribed on the ring** tenía grabado *or* inscrito su nombre en el anillo; *Fig* **it's inscribed on my memory** está grabado en mi memoria (**b**) *(dedicate)* dedicar; **an inscribed copy of the book** un ejemplar dedicado del libro (**c**) *Geom* inscribir

inscription [ɪn'skrɪpʃən] *n* (**a**) *(on stone, coin)* inscripción *f* (**b**) *(in book)* dedicatoria *f*

inscrutability [ɪnskruːtə'bɪlɪtɪ] *n* impenetrabilidad *f*, inescrutabilidad *f*

inscrutable [ɪn'skruːtəbəl] *adj* inescrutable

insect ['ɪnsekt] *n* insecto *m* ▸▸ ***i. bite*** picadura *f* de insecto; ***i. repellent*** repelente *m* contra insectos

insecticide [ɪn'sektɪsaɪd] *n* insecticida *m*

insectivore [ɪn'sektɪvɔː(r)] *n* insectívoro *m*

insectivorous [ɪnsek'tɪvərəs] *adj* insectívoro(a)

insecure [ɪnsɪ'kjʊə(r)] *adj* (**a**) *(person)* inseguro(a); **he's terribly i.** tiene mucha inseguridad (**b**) *(nail, scaffolding)* poco seguro(a) (**c**) *(position, situation)* poco seguro(a); **an i. position within the company** una posición inestable dentro de la empresa

insecurely [ɪnsɪ'kjʊəlɪ] *adv* (**a**) *(not confidently)* de forma insegura, con inseguridad (**b**) *(not safely)* de forma poco segura; **i. fastened** mal sujeto(a); **i. tied** mal atado(a)

insecurity [ɪnsɪ'kjʊərɪtɪ] *n* inseguridad *f*; **job i.** precariedad laboral

inseminate [ɪn'semɪneɪt] *vt* inseminar

insemination [ɪnsemɪ'neɪʃən] *n* inseminación *f*

insensate [ɪn'senseɪt] *adj Formal (crazed)* insensato(a), vesánico(a), *(fury)* desbocado(a); **he was driven i. with rage** se puso fuera de sí de rabia

insensible [ɪn'sensɪbəl] *adj Formal* (**a**) *(unconscious)* inconsciente; **to be i.** estar inconsciente; **she was knocked i. by her fall** perdió el conocimiento a consecuencia de la caída

(**b**) *(cold, indifferent)* **i. to the suffering of others** insensible al sufrimiento ajeno

(**c**) *(unaware)* **to be i. of** *or* **to sth** no ser consciente de algo; **I am not i. of the great honour you do me with this award, but...** reconozco el gran honor que representa recibir este galardón, pero...; **I am not i. of the risks involved** soy consciente de los riesgos que entraña

(**d**) *(imperceptible)* imperceptible

insensitive [ɪn'sensɪtɪv] *adj* (**a**) *(emotionally)* insensible; **what an i. person!** ¡qué poca sensibilidad!, ¡qué falta de sensibilidad!; **that was an i. thing to say** qué poco tacto has tenido al decir eso; **the government's reaction was highly i.** la reacción del Gobierno reflejó una enorme falta de sensibilidad (**b**) *(physically)* insensible; **my fingers/gums had been rendered i.** no sentía nada en los dedos/las encías

insensitively [ɪn'sensɪtɪvlɪ] *adv (tactlessly)* con muy poca sensibilidad

insensitivity [ɪnsensɪ'tɪvɪtɪ] *n* (**a**) *(lack of tact)* insensibilidad *f* (**b**) *(lack of sensation)* insensibilidad *f*, falta *f* de sensibilidad

inseparable [ɪn'sepərəbəl] *adj* inseparable (**from** de); **they were i.** eran inseparables

inseparably [ɪn'sepərəblɪ] *adv* inseparablemente

insert 1 *n* ['ɪnsɜːt] (**a**) *(in magazine)* encarte *m* (**b**) *Comptr* ***i. key*** tecla *f* de inserción; ***i. mode*** modo *m* de inserción

2 *vt* [ɪn'sɜːt] *(key, finger, coin)* introducir (**into** en); *(clause, advertisement)* insertar (**in** en); *(contact lenses)* colocar, poner; **to i. a name on a list** incluir un nombre en una lista

insertion [ɪn'sɜːʃən] *n* (**a**) *(act)* inserción *f* (**b**) *Comptr* ***i. point*** punto *m* de inserción

in-service ['ɪnsɜːvɪs] *adj* ***i. training*** formación *f* en el lugar de trabajo

INSET ['ɪnset] *n Br Sch* (*abbr* **in-service training**) formación *f* en el lugar de trabajo

inset ['ɪnset] 1 *n* (a) *(in map, picture)* recuadro *m* (b) *(in clothing)* añadido *m*, entredós *m*
2 *vt (pt & pp* **inset**) (a) *(in map, picture)* insertar (en recuadro) (b) *(cloth)* añadir; *(jewel, wood, metal)* incrustar; **i. with** incrustado(a) de

inshore [ɪn'ʃɔ:(r)] 1 *adj (navigation)* costero(a); *(fishing)* de bajura; **i. waters** aguas costeras
2 *adv (to sail, blow)* hacia la costa; **the boat kept close i.** el barco se mantenía cerca de la costa

INSIDE 1 *n* ['ɪn'saɪd] (a) *(interior) (of house, vehicle, container)* interior *m*; **on/from the i.** en/desde el interior; **a chocolate which is hard on the outside, but soft on the i.** un bombón que es duro por fuera y blando por dentro; *Fig* **we need someone on the i.** necesitamos un infiltrado
(b) *(part facing towards one)* **the i. of one's wrist/leg** la parte interior de la muñeca/pierna
(c) *(of pavement, road)* **to overtake on the i.** *(in Britain)* adelantar por la izquierda; *(in Europe, USA)* adelantar por la derecha; **the athlete went past her on the i.** la atleta la adelantó por dentro *or* por el interior
(d) *Fam* **insides** *(internal organs)* tripas *fpl*
2 *adj* ['ɪnsaɪd] interior; **the i. pages** *(of newspaper)* las páginas interiores; **to have i. information/help** tener información/ayuda confidencial; *Fam* **it must have been an i. job** *(robbery, fraud)* debe de haber sido un trabajo realizado desde dentro *or Am* adentro, *RP* debe haber sido un trabajo entregado; **to know the i. story** conocer la historia de cerca *or* de primera mano ►► ***i. lane*** *Aut (in Britain)* carril *m* de la izquierda; *(in Europe, USA)* carril *m* de la derecha; *Sport Esp* calle *f* de dentro, *Am* carril *m* de adentro; ***i. left*** *(in soccer)* interior *m* izquierdo; *Br* ***i. leg*** *(measurement)* (medida *f* interior de la) pernera *f*; ***i. pocket*** bolsillo *m* interior; ***i. right*** *(in soccer)* interior *m* derecho; ***i. track*** *Sport Esp* calle *f* de dentro, *Am* carril *m* de adentro; IDIOM *esp US* **to have the i. track** estar en una posición ventajosa
3 *adv* (a) *(to be, stay)* dentro, *Am* adentro; *(to look, run)* adentro; **come i.!** *(to guest)* ¡pasa!; *(to children playing outside)* ¡vamos para dentro!; **shall we go i.?** *(into house)* ¿entramos?, ¿pasamos dentro *or Am* adentro?; **they painted the house i. and out** pintaron la casa por dentro y por fuera
(b) *(within oneself)* **i. she was angry** por dentro estaba *esp Esp* enfadada *or esp Am* enojada
(c) *Fam (in prison) Esp* en chirona, *Méx* en bote, *RP* en cana
4 *prep* [ɪn'saɪd] (a) *(with position)* dentro de; **he ran i. the house** corrió al interior de la casa, *RP* corrió para adentro; *Fam* **get this whisky i. you and you'll feel better** métete este whisky en el cuerpo y te sentirás mejor
(b) *(with time)* **i. a week/an hour** en menos de una semana/hora; **his time was just i. the world record** su marca batió el récord mundial por muy poco
(c) *(with emotions)* **i. herself she was angry** por dentro estaba *esp Esp* enfadada *or esp Am* enojada; **something i. me made me feel she was lying** algo me dijo que estaba mintiendo
5 **inside of** *prep (be, stay)* dentro de; *(look, run)* adentro de; **i. of a week/an hour** en menos de una semana/hora
6 **inside out** *adv* **his shirt is i. out** lleva la camisa del revés, *Am* dio vuelta la camiseta; *Fig* **to know sth i. out** saberse algo al dedillo; **she turned her T-shirt i. out** dio la vuelta a la camiseta *(de dentro a fuera)*; *Fig* **they turned the room i. out** pusieron la habitación patas arriba; *Fig* **this news has turned our plans i. out** esta noticia ha trastornado por completo nuestros planes

insider [ɪn'saɪdə(r)] *n* = persona que cuenta con información confidencial ►► *Fin* ***i. dealing*** uso *m* de información privilegiada; ***i. trading*** uso *m* de información privilegiada

insidious [ɪn'sɪdɪəs] *adj Formal* insidioso(a), larvado(a)

insidiously [ɪn'sɪdɪəslɪ] *adv Formal* de manera larvada

insight ['ɪnsaɪt] *n* (a) *(perspicacity)* perspicacia *f*, penetración *f*; **she has great i.** es muy perspicaz (b) *(understanding)* idea *f* (**into** de); *(revealing comment)* revelación *f*, aclaración *f* (**into** sobre); **to get** *or* **gain an i. into sth** hacerse una idea de algo; **the article gives us an i. into the causes of the conflict** el artículo nos permite entender las causas del conflicto

insightful ['ɪnsaɪtfʊl] *adj* penetrante, revelador(ora)

insignia [ɪn'sɪgnɪə] *n* insignia *f*

insignificance [ɪnsɪg'nɪfɪkəns] *n* insignificancia *f*; **my problems pale** *or* **fade into i. beside yours** mis problemas son insignificantes comparados con los tuyos

insignificant [ɪnsɪg'nɪfɪkənt] *adj* insignificante; **a not i. sum of money** una considerable suma de dinero, una suma nada despreciable de dinero

insincere [ɪnsɪn'sɪə(r)] *adj* falso(a); **did you think I was being i.?** ¿creíste que mentía?

insincerely [ɪnsɪn'sɪəlɪ] *adv* de un modo poco sincero

insincerity [ɪnsɪn'serɪtɪ] *n* falsedad *f*, insinceridad *f*

insinuate [ɪn'sɪnjʊeɪt] *vt* (a) *(hint)* insinuar; **he insinuated that you were lying** insinuó que mentías (b) *Formal (introduce)* **to i. oneself into sb's favour** ganarse arteramente el favor de alguien; **she managed to i. his name into the conversation at several points** logró introducir su nombre en varios momentos de la conversación

insinuating [ɪn'sɪnjʊeɪtɪŋ] *adj* insinuante

insinuation [ɪnsɪnjʊ'eɪʃən] *n* (a) *(hint)* insinuación *f*, indirecta *f* (b) *(practice)* insinuación *f*

insipid [ɪn'sɪpɪd] *adj (food)* insípido(a), soso(a); *(character)* soso(a)

insipidity [ɪnsɪ'pɪdɪtɪ], **insipidness** [ɪn'sɪpɪdnɪs] *n (of taste)* insipidez *f*; *(of person)* sosería *f*

insist [ɪn'sɪst] 1 *vt* (a) *(demand)* **I i. that you tell no-one** no le permito que se lo diga a nadie; **you should i. that you be paid** debes exigir que te paguen (b) *(maintain)* **to i. that...** insistir en que...; **she insists that she locked the door** insiste en que cerró la puerta con llave
2 *vi* (a) *(demand)* **she insists on absolute punctuality/real champagne** exige absoluta puntualidad/champán de verdad; **very well, if you i.** bueno, si insistes; **you must stay for dinner, I i. (on it)!** te tienes que quedar a cenar, ¡faltaría más!
(b) *(persist)* **to i. on doing sth** empeñarse en hacer algo; **he insists on doing everything himself** se empeña en hacerlo todo él; **if you i. on doing that, I'm leaving** como sigas haciendo eso, yo me marcho; **he insisted on his innocence** insistió en que era inocente
(c) *(emphasize)* **to i. on sth** hacer hincapié en algo; **I must i. on this point** debo hacer hincapié en este punto

> En inglés culto o elevado, y especialmente en inglés americano, **insist** puede ir seguido de **that** más un verbo en subjuntivo (ver el panel SUBJUNCTIVE):
> **we insist that he cease his campaign of slander against us**
> *exigimos que cese su campaña de difamación contra nosotros*
> Lo mismo también podría decirse del siguiente modo:
> **we insist that he ceases his campaign of slander against us**

insistence [ɪn'sɪstəns] *n* (a) *(demand)* exigencia *f*; **their i. on secrecy has hindered negotiations** sus exigencias de la confidencialidad han entorpecido las negociaciones; **I came here at her i.** vine porque ella insistió
(b) *(persistence, assertion)* **because of his i. on paying for us** por su empeño en invitarnos; **in spite of her i. that she locked the door** a pesar de que insistió en que había cerrado la puerta con llave
(c) *(emphasis)* hincapié *m*; **his i. on the role of the economy** el hincapié que hace en el papel de la economía

insistent [ɪn'sɪstənt] *adj* (a) *(demand)* insistente; **to be i. about sth** insistir sobre *or* en algo; (b) *(rhythm, noise)* insistente

insistently [ɪn'sɪstəntlɪ] *adv* insistentemente, con insistencia

in situ [ɪn'sɪtju:] *adv Formal* en su lugar original, in situ

insofar as ['ɪnsəʊ'fɑ:rəz] *adv* en la medida en que; **I'll help her i. I can** la ayudaré en la medida de mis posibilidades; **i. it's possible** en la medida de lo posible

insole ['ɪnsəʊl] *n (of shoe)* plantilla *f*

insolence ['ɪnsələns] *n* insolencia *f*

insolent ['ɪnsələnt] *adj* insolente; **he's i. to his teachers** es insolente con sus profesores *or* maestros

insolently ['ɪnsələntlɪ] *adv* insolentemente, de un modo insolente

insolubility [ɪnsɒljʊ'bɪlɪtɪ] *n* (a) *(of substance)* insolubilidad *f* (b) *(of problem)* insolubilidad *f*

insoluble [ɪn'sɒljʊbəl] *adj* (a) *(substance)* insoluble, indisoluble (b) *(problem)* irresoluble

insolvency [ɪn'sɒlvənsɪ] *n Fin* insolvencia *f*

insolvent [ɪn'sɒlvənt] *adj Fin* insolvente; **to be declared i.** *(person, firm)* ser declarado(a) insolvente

insomnia [ɪn'sɒmnɪə] *n* insomnio *m*

insomniac [ɪn'sɒmnɪæk] *n* insomne *mf*

insomuch as = **inasmuch as**

insouciance [ɪn'su:sɪəns] *n Formal* despreocupación *f*

insouciant [ɪn'su:sɪənt] *adj Formal* despreocupado(a)

inspect [ɪn'spekt] *vt* (a) *(examine)* examinar, inspeccionar; **she inspected his body for bruises** le examinó *or* revisó el cuerpo en busca de moretones *or* magulladuras (b) *(check officially) (school, factory)* inspeccionar; *(accounts)* revisar; *(machinery, vehicle)* revisar; *(passport, luggage)* examinar, inspeccionar (c) *(troops)* pasar revista a

inspection [ɪn'spekʃən] *n* (a) *(examination)* examen *m*, inspección *f*; **on closer i.** tras un examen más detallado ►► ***i. copy*** *(of book)* ejemplar *m* de muestra (b) *(official check) (of school, factory)* inspección *f*; *(of accounts)* revisión *f*; *(of machinery, vehicle)* revisación *f*, *Am* revisión *f*; *(of passport, luggage)* examen *m*, inspección *f* (c) *(of troops)* revista *f*

inspector [ɪn'spektə(r)] *n* (a) *(of schools, factories)* inspector(ora) *m,f*; *Br* **i. of taxes, tax i.** inspector(ora) de Hacienda (b) *Br (on train, bus)* revisor(ora) *m,f* (c) *Br* **(police) i.** inspector(ora) de policía

inspectorate [ɪn'spektərət] *n* (departamento *m* de) inspección *f*

inspiration [ɪnspɪ'reɪʃən] *n* (a) *(source of ideas)* inspiración *f*; **to draw i. from sth** inspirarse en algo; **to be an i. to sb** ser una fuente de inspiración para alguien; **your enthusiasm and dedication have been an i. to us all** tu entusiasmo y dedicación han sido una fuente de inspiración para todos nosotros

(b) *(bright idea)* idea *f* brillante *or* genial; **hey, I've had an i.!** ¡he tenido una idea brillante!

(c) *Formal (inhalation)* inspiración *f*

inspirational [ɪnspɪ'reɪʃənəl] *adj* inspirador(ora)

inspire [ɪn'spaɪə(r)] **1** *vt* (a) *(person, work of art)* inspirar; **the poem was inspired by a visit to Italy** el poema estaba inspirado en una visita a Italia; **to be divinely inspired** ser fruto de una inspiración divina; **to i. sb to do sth: what inspired me to do it was...** lo que me dio la idea de hacerlo fue...; **what inspired you to choose that name?** ¿qué te llevó a elegir ese nombre?

(b) *(arouse) (feeling)* inspirar, suscitar; **a name which inspires respect/fear** un nombre que inspira respeto/miedo; **to i. confidence in sb, to i. sb with confidence** inspirar confianza a alguien; **to i. courage in sb** infundir coraje a alguien

(c) *Formal (inhale)* inspirar

2 *vi Formal (inhale)* inspirar

inspired [ɪn'spaɪəd] *adj* inspirado(a); **I'm not feeling very i. today** hoy no estoy muy inspirado; **it was an i. choice/decision** fue una elección/decisión inspirada; **their performance was nothing short of i.** su actuación fue más que *or* muy inspirada; **to make an i. guess** acertar por casualidad

inspiring [ɪn'spaɪərɪŋ] *adj* estimulante; **the menu wasn't very i.** el menú no era muy interesante

inst. (*abbr* **instant**) *Com Old-fashioned* **your letter of the 9th i.** su carta del 9 del corriente *or* del mes en curso

instability [ɪnstə'bɪlɪtɪ] *n* inestabilidad *f*; **emotional/political i.** inestabilidad emocional/política

install, *US* **instal** [ɪn'stɔːl] *vt* (a) *(machinery, equipment, software)* instalar; **we're having central heating installed** nos están instalando la calefacción central ►► *Comptr* ***i. program*** programa *m* de instalación

(b) *(settle) (person)* instalar; **to i. oneself in an armchair** instalarse en una butaca

(c) *(manager, president)* investir; **to i. sb in a post** colocar a alguien en un puesto; **the Tories were installed with a huge majority** los conservadores asumieron el poder con una amplia mayoría

installation [ɪnstə'leɪʃən] *n* (a) *(of machinery, equipment, software)* instalación *f* ►► *Comptr* ***i. disk*** disco *m* de instalación; ***i. manual*** manual *m* de instalación; ***i. program*** programa *m* de instalación (b) *(in post)* investidura *f* (c) *Art* instalación *f* (d) *(military base)* instalación *f* militar

installer [ɪn'stɔːlə(r)] *n Comptr* instalador *m*

instalment, *US* **installment** [ɪn'stɔːlmənt] *n* (a) *(part payment)* plazo *m*; **monthly instalments** cuotas mensuales; **to pay in** *or* **by instalments** pagar a plazos ►► *US Com* ***i. plan*** compra *f* a plazos *or Am* en cuotas; **to buy sth on an i. plan** comprar algo a plazos *or RP* en cuotas

(b) *(of radio, TV programme)* episodio *m*; **the last i. of our special report on Brazil** *(on TV)* la última entrega de nuestro informe *or Andes, CAm, Méx, Ven* reporte especial sobre Brasil; **to publish sth in instalments** publicar algo por entregas

instance ['ɪnstəns] **1** *n* (a) *(case)* caso *m*; *(example)* ejemplo *m*; **for i.** por ejemplo; **in this i.** en este caso; **in the first i.** en primer lugar (b) *Formal (request)* **at the i. of** a instancias de

2 *vt Formal* (a) *(cite)* citar, dar como ejemplo (b) *(exemplify)* demostrar, ejemplificar

instant ['ɪnstənt] **1** *n (moment)* instante *m*; **at that i.** en ese momento; **the next i. he had disappeared** un instante después había desaparecido; **do it this i.!** ¡hazlo ahora mismo!; **let me know the i. he gets here** avísame en cuanto llegue; **the i. I saw him** en cuanto lo vi; **not an i. too soon** justo a tiempo; **in an i.** en un instante; **he left on the i.** se fue de inmediato; **I don't believe it for one i.** no lo creo ni por casualidad

2 *adj* (a) *(immediate)* instantáneo(a), inmediato(a); **I took an i. dislike to him** me cayó mal instantáneamente; **there's are no i. solutions** no hay soluciones inmediatas ►► ***i. access*** *(to money)* acceso *m* inmediato; ***i. access account*** cuenta *f* a la vista; *Comptr* ***i. message*** mensaje *m* instantáneo; *Comptr* ***i. messaging*** mensajería *f* instantánea; *US TV* ***i. replay*** repetición *f*

(b) *(coffee, soup, mashed potato)* instantáneo(a)

(c) *Com Old-fashioned* **your letter of the 9th i.** su carta del 9 del corriente *or* del mes en curso

instantaneous [ɪnstən'teɪnɪəs] *adj* instantáneo(a)

instantaneously [ɪnstən'teɪnɪəslɪ] *adv* instantáneamente, al instante

instantly ['ɪnstəntlɪ] *adv* al instante; **he was killed i.** murió en el acto; **i. forgettable** muy fácil de olvidar; **i. recognizable** reconocible al instante

instate [ɪn'steɪt] *vt* instalar

in-state ['ɪn'steɪt] *adj US* del (propio) estado

INSTEAD [ɪn'sted] *adv* **she couldn't come so he came i.** como ella no podía venir, vino él en su lugar; **we haven't got any green ones, would you like a blue one i.?** no tenemos verdes, ¿quiere uno azul?; **I was going to buy the green one but I bought the blue one i.** iba a comprar el verde, pero al final compré el azul; **I decided against going to Spain and to buy a motorbike i.** decidí que, en lugar de gastarme el dinero en ir a España, me compraría una moto; **I should have kept quiet, but i. I spoke up** en vez de callarme, que es lo que tendría que haber hecho, dije lo que pensaba; **i. of** en vez de, en lugar de; **he came i. of me** vino en mi lugar; **i. of doing sth** en lugar *or* vez de hacer algo

instep ['ɪnstep] *n* (a) *(of foot)* empeine *m* (b) *(of shoe)* empeine *m*

instigate ['ɪnstɪgeɪt] *vt* (a) *(strike, unrest, violence)* instigar (b) *(inquiry, search, changes)* iniciar

instigation ['ɪnstɪgeɪʃən] *n* (a) *(of strike, unrest, violence)* instigación *f*; **at sb's i.** a instancias de alguien (b) *(of inquiry, search, changes)* instigación *f*

instigator ['ɪnstɪgeɪtə(r)] *n* (a) *(of strike, unrest, violence)* instigador(ora) *m,f* (b) *(of inquiry, search, changes)* iniciador(ora) *m,f*

instil, *US* **instill** [ɪn'stɪl] (*pt & pp* **instilled**) *vt* inculcar (**in** *or* **into** en); **to i. certain principles/ideals into sb** inculcar a alguien ciertos principios/ideales; **to i. fear into sb** amedrentar a alguien

instinct ['ɪnstɪŋkt] *n* instinto *m*; **to have an i. for sth** tener buen olfato para algo; **to follow one's instincts** dejarse guiar por la intuición; **(all) my instincts told me to say no** el *or* mi instinto me decía que dijera que no; **my first i. was to run away** mi primer impulso fue irme *or* salir corriendo; **he is by i. a rebel** es rebelde por instinto; **to work by i.** trabajar por instinto

instinctive [ɪn'stɪŋktɪv] *adj* instintivo(a); **to take an i. dislike to sb** sentir una antipatía instintiva por alguien

instinctively [ɪn'stɪŋktɪvlɪ] *adv* instintivamente, por instinto

instinctual [ɪn'stɪŋktjʊəl] *adj* instintivo(a)

institute ['ɪnstɪtjuːt] **1** *n* instituto *m*

2 *vt* (a) *(set up) (system, procedure)* instaurar (b) *(start) (search)* emprender; *Law (enquiry)* emprender; *Law* **to i. proceedings (against sb)** emprender una acción legal (contra alguien)

institution [ɪnstɪ'tjuːʃən] *n* (a) *(organization)* institución *f*; **the institutions of the state** las instituciones del estado

(b) *(mental hospital)* (hospital *m*) psiquiátrico *m*; *(old people's home)* residencia *f* de ancianos, asilo *m*; *(children's home)* centro *m* de menores; **he had lived most of his life in institutions** había vivido la mayor parte de su vida en instituciones de distinto tipo

(c) *(custom, political or social structure)* institución *f*; **the i. of marriage** la institución del matrimonio; *Fig* **to become a national i.** *(event, TV programme, person)* convertirse en una institución (nacional); **our Friday lunches have become an office i.** en la oficina, nuestros almuerzos de los viernes se han convertido en una institución

(d) *Formal (of system, procedure)* institución *f*, instauración *f*

(e) *Formal (of search)* inicio *m*; *Law (of enquiry)* instrucción *f*; *Law* **the i. of proceedings (against sb)** la instrucción de un proceso (contra alguien)

institutional [ɪnstɪ'tjuːʃənəl] *adj* (**a**) *(of hospital, prison, school)* institucional; **after years of i. life** después de años de vida institucional; **i. care** cuidado *or* atención institucional (**b**) *Com* institucional; **i. investors** instituciones inversionistas *or* inversoras

institutionalize [ɪnstɪ'tjuːʃənəlaɪz] *vt* (**a**) *(put in a mental hospital)* internar en un psiquiátrico; *(put in an old people's home)* internar en un asilo (**b**) *(turn into an institution)* institucionalizar

institutionalized [ɪnstɪ'tjuːʃənəlaɪzd] *adj* (**a**) *(person)* **to become i.** desarrollar una fuerte dependencia institucional *(de la vida carcelaria, hospitalaria, etc)* (**b**) *(practice)* **this practice had become i.** esta práctica se había institucionalizado ►► ***i. racism*** racismo *m* institucionalizado

in-store ['ɪnstɔː(r)] *adj* de la tienda, dentro de la tienda; **i. advertising/promotion** publicidad/promoción en la tienda *or RP* el local

instruct [ɪn'strʌkt] *vt* (**a**) *(teach)* instruir (**in** en)
(**b**) *(command)* dar instrucciones a; **to i. sb to do sth** ordenar a alguien que haga algo; **I have been instructed to say nothing** se me ha ordenado no decir nada, tengo instrucciones de no decir nada
(**c**) *(inform)* informar; **I have been instructed that the meeting has been cancelled** me han informado que se ha cancelado la reunión
(**d**) *(lawyer) (engage)* contratar los servicios de; *(inform)* dar instrucciones a; *(jury)* instruir

► **instruct in** *vt sep* **to i. sb in sth** dar clases a alguien de algo; **she instructed everyone in how to use the machine** enseñó a todos a usar la máquina

instruction [ɪn'strʌkʃən] *n* (**a**) *(training)* instrucción *f*, adiestramiento *m*; **we received i. in using the machines** nos enseñaron cómo utilizar las máquinas
(**b**) *(order)* instrucción *f*; **to give sb instructions to do sth** dar a alguien instrucciones de hacer algo; **they were given instructions not to let him out of their sight** recibieron instrucciones de no perderlo de vista; **she gave instructions for the papers to be destroyed** dio instrucciones de que se destruyeran los documentos; **to act in accordance with/contrary to instructions** actuar/no actuar según las instrucciones; **our instructions are to arrest him** recibimos instrucciones de arrestarlo
(**c**) *Comptr* instrucción *f*
(**d**) **instructions** *(directions)* instrucciones *fpl*; **instructions for use** instrucciones de uso, modo de empleo ►► ***i. manual*** manual *m* de instrucciones

instructional [ɪn'strʌkʃənəl] *adj* de instrucción, de adiestramiento

instructive [ɪn'strʌktɪv] *adj* instructivo(a)

instructor [ɪn'strʌktə(r)] *n* (**a**) *(teacher)* instructor(ora) *m,f*; **driving i.** profesor(ora) de autoescuela; **ski i.** monitor(ora) de esquí (**b**) *US (university lecturer)* profesor(ora) *m,f* de universidad

instructress [ɪn'strʌktrɪs] *n (teacher)* instructora *f*, profesora *f*

instrument ['ɪnstrʊmənt] *n* (**a**) **(musical) i.** instrumento *m*
(**b**) *(implement)* instrumento *m*; **scientific instruments** instrumentos científicos; **surgical instruments** el instrumental quirúrgico
(**c**) *Av* **instruments** instrumentos *mpl*; **to fly by** *or* **on instruments** volar por instrumentos ►► ***i. board*** tablero *m* de mandos, panel *m* de instrumentos; ***i. panel*** tablero *m* de mandos, panel *m* de instrumentos
(**d**) *(means)* instrumento *m* ; **to serve as the i. of sb's vengeance** ser el instrumento de la venganza de alguien
(**e**) *Fin* documento *m*, instrumento *m*; **an i. of payment** un instrumento de pago

instrumental [ɪnstrʊ'mentəl] **1** *n Mus* (pieza *f*) instrumental *m*
2 *adj* (**a**) *(involved)* fundamental; **she was i. in negotiating the agreement** desempeñó un papel fundamental en la negociación del acuerdo (**b**) *Mus* instrumental

instrumentalist [ɪnstrʊ'mentəlɪst] *n Mus* instrumentista *mf*

instrumentation [ɪnstrʊmen'teɪʃən] *n* (**a**) *Mus* instrumentación *f* (**b**) *Tech* instrumentos *mpl*

insubordinate [ɪnsə'bɔːdɪnət] *adj* insubordinado(a)

insubordination [ɪnsəbɔːdɪ'neɪʃən] *n* insubordinación *f*

insubstantial [ɪnsəb'stænʃəl] *adj* (**a**) *(flimsy) (structure, garment)* endeble, frágil; *(argument, reasoning)* frágil (**b**) *(not satisfying) (meal)* poco sustancioso(a); *(book)* intrascendente, insustancial (**c**) *(imaginary)* imaginario(a)

insufferable [ɪn'sʌfrəbəl] *adj* insufrible, insoportable; **she was being quite i.** estaba bastante insoportable

insufferably [ɪn'sʌfrəblɪ] *adv* insoportablemente; **he's i. arrogant** es insoportablemente arrogante

insufficiency [ɪnsə'fɪʃənsɪ] *n* (**a**) *(inadequacy)* insuficiencia *f*; **the i. of our equipment** lo inadecuado de nuestro equipamiento (**b**) *Med* **cardiac/renal i.** insuficiencia cardíaca/renal

insufficient [ɪnsə'fɪʃənt] *adj* insuficiente; **i. evidence** pruebas insuficientes; **i. funds** fondos insuficientes

insufficiently [ɪnsə'fɪʃəntlɪ] *adv* insuficientemente; **he was i. cautious** no fue lo suficientemente cauto

insular ['ɪnsjʊlə(r)] *adj* (**a**) *(people, views)* provinciano(a); **he leads a very i. existence** lleva una vida muy aislada del mundo exterior (**b**) *(of an island)* insular

insularity [ɪnsjʊ'lærɪtɪ] *n* provincianismo *m*; **the i. of the press** lo provinciana que es la prensa

insulate ['ɪnsjʊleɪt] *vt* (**a**) *(against cold, heat, radiation)* aislar; **insulated sleeping bag** saco *or* bolsa de dormir térmica (**b**) *(electrically)* aislar; **insulated screwdriver** destornillador con aislante (**c**) *(protect)* proteger; **insulated from the outside world** aislado del mundo exterior

insulating tape ['ɪnsjʊleɪtɪŋ'teɪp] *n Br* cinta *f* aislante

insulation [ɪnsjʊ'leɪʃən] *n* (**a**) *(against heat loss)* aislamiento *m* térmico (**b**) *(electrical)* aislamiento *m* (**c**) *(material)* aislante *m* (**d**) *(protection)* protección *f*

insulator ['ɪnsjʊleɪtə(r)] *n* (**a**) *(material)* aislante *m* (**b**) *(device)* aislador *m*

insulin ['ɪnsjʊlɪn] *n* insulina *f*

insult **1** *n* ['ɪnsʌlt] *(words, action)* insulto *m*; **it's an i. to our intelligence** es un insulto a nuestra inteligencia; **their adverts are an i. to women** sus anuncios son un insulto a la mujer; **to add i. to injury...** para colmo...
2 *vt* [ɪn'sʌlt] insultar; **don't be insulted if I don't tell you everything** no te ofendas si no te lo cuento todo

insulting [ɪn'sʌltɪŋ] *adj* insultante; **it is i. to suggest that...** es insultante sugerir que

insultingly [ɪn'sʌltɪŋlɪ] *adv (to speak, act)* de un modo insultante; **they made me an i. low offer** me hicieron una oferta tan baja que resultaba insultante

insuperable [ɪn'suːpərəbəl] *adj* insuperable, infranqueable

insuperably [ɪn'suːpərəblɪ] *adv* insuperablemente; **i. difficult** extremadamente difícil

insupportable [ɪnsə'pɔːtəbəl] *adj Formal* (**a**) *(intolerable)* insoportable (**b**) *(indefensible)* indefendible, insustentable

insurable [ɪn'ʃʊərəbl] *adj* asegurable

insurance [ɪn'ʃʊərəns] *n* (**a**) *(against fire, theft, accident)* seguro *m*; **to take out i. (against sth)** hacerse un seguro (contra algo), asegurarse (contra algo); **to have i. (against sth)** estar asegurado(a) (contra algo); **he's in i.** trabaja en *or Am* con seguros; **he bought himself a stereo out of the i.** con lo del seguro se compró un equipo de música ►► ***i. broker*** agente *mf* (libre) *or Am* corredor(ora) *m,f* de seguros; ***i. claim*** reclamación *f or Col, CSur* reclamo *m* al seguro; ***i. company*** aseguradora *f*, compañía *f* de seguros; ***i. cover*** cobertura *f*; ***i. policy*** *Fin also Fig* póliza *f* de seguros; ***i. premium*** prima *f* (del seguro); ***i. salesman*** agente *m* de seguros; ***i. saleswoman*** agente *f* de seguros
(**b**) *(safeguard)* protección *f*; **an alarm is a good i. against theft** una alarma es una buena protección contra los robos; **I took Sam with me, just as (an) i.** me llevé a Sam, por si acaso

insure [ɪn'ʃʊə(r)] *vt* (**a**) *(car, building, person)* asegurar (**against** contra); **to i. one's life** hacerse un seguro de vida (**b**) *(protect)* proteger; **what strategy can i. (us) against failure?** ¿qué estrategia podría garantizar(nos) el éxito?

insured [ɪn'ʃʊəd] **1** *n Fin* **the i.** el asegurado
2 *adj* asegurado(a); **to be i.** estar asegurado(a) ►► *Fin* ***i. value*** valor *m* asegurado

insurer [ɪn'ʃʊərə(r)] *n* asegurador(ora) *m,f*

insurgency [ɪn'sɜːdʒənsɪ] *n* insurgencia *f*

insurgent [ɪn'sɜːdʒənt] **1** *n* insurgente *mf*, insurrecto(a) *m,f*
2 *adj* insurgente, insurrecto(a)

insurmountable [ɪnsə'maʊntəbəl] *adj Formal* insuperable, insalvable

insurrection [ɪnsə'rekʃən] *n* insurrección *f*

insurrectionary [ɪnsə'rekʃənərɪ] *adj* insurrecto(a), sedicioso(a)

insurrectionist [ɪnsə'rekʃənɪst] *n* insurrecto(a) *m,f*, sedicioso(a) *m,f*

intact [ɪn'tækt] *adj* intacto(a); **to be i.** estar intacto(a); **to remain i.** permanecer intacto(a)

intaglio [ɪn'tɑːlɪəʊ] *n* (**a**) *(in jewellery)* entalle *m* (**b**) *(in printing)* intaglio *m*

intake ['ɪnteɪk] *n* (**a**) *(of alcohol, calories)* consumo *m*, ingesta *f*; **a sharp i. of breath** una brusca inspiración (**b**) *(of pupils, recruits)* **this year's i. of pupils** la matrícula de este año; **our i. of refugees** la cantidad de refugiados admitidos en nuestro país (**c**) *(pipe, vent)* toma *f*; **i. valve** válvula de admisión

intangibility [ɪntændʒɪ'bɪlɪtɪ] *n* intangibilidad *f*

intangible [ɪn'tændʒɪbəl] **1** *n* valor *m* intangible
2 *adj* intangible ►► *Fin* ***i. assets*** bienes *mpl* inmateriales

integer ['ɪntɪdʒə(r)] *n Math* (número *m*) entero *m*

integral ['ɪntɪgrəl] **1** *n Math* integral *f*
2 *adj* (**a**) *(essential)* esencial; **to be** *or* **form an i. part of sth** formar parte integrante de algo (**b**) *(built-in)* incorporado(a) (**c**) *Math* **an i. number** un número entero ►► ***i. calculus*** cálculo *m* integral

integrate ['ɪntɪgreɪt] **1** *vt* (**a**) *(combine in a larger unit)* integrar (**into** en); **the two systems have been integrated** los dos sistemas han sido integrados; **to i. sb into a group** integrar a alguien en un *or* al grupo; **his brief was to i. the new building into the historic old quarter** su tarea era integrar el nuevo edificio al viejo barrio histórico (**b**) *(end segregation of)* integrar, eliminar la segregación de (**c**) *Math* integrar
2 *vi* (**a**) *(fit in)* integrarse (**into** en) (**b**) *(desegregate)* integrarse, eliminar la segregación

integrated ['ɪntɪgreɪtɪd] *adj* (**a**) *(combined in a larger unit)* integrado(a) (**b**) *(desegregated)* integrado(a), no segregacionista (**c**) *Elec* ***i. circuit*** circuito *m* integrado (**d**) *Comptr* ***i. package*** paquete *m* integrado; ***i. services digital network*** red *f* digital de servicios integrados; ***i. software*** software *m* integrado

integration [ɪntɪ'greɪʃən] *n* (**a**) *(process of integrating)* integración *f* (**b**) *(desegregation)* integración *f*, no segregación *f* (**c**) *Math* integración *f*

integrity [ɪn'tegrɪtɪ] *n* (**a**) *(uprightness)* integridad *f*; **she's a woman of great i.** es una mujer muy íntegra (**b**) *(wholeness)* integridad *f*; **cultural i.** integridad cultural

integument [ɪn'tegjʊmənt] *n Biol & Zool* tegumento *m*

intellect ['ɪntɪlekt] *n* (**a**) *(intelligence)* intelecto *m*; **a man of i.** un hombre muy inteligente (**b**) *(person)* cerebro *m*, inteligencia *f*

intellectual [ɪntɪ'lektjʊəl] **1** *n* intelectual *mf*
2 *adj* intelectual; **interests of an i. nature** intereses de carácter intelectual ►► *Law* ***i. property*** propiedad *f* intelectual

intellectualize [ɪntɪ'lektjʊəlaɪz] **1** *vt* intelectualizar, dar un tono intelectual a
2 *vi* filosofar

intellectually [ɪntɪ'lektjʊəlɪ] *adv* intelectualmente, desde el punto de vista intelectual

intelligence [ɪn'telɪdʒəns] *n* (**a**) *(faculty)* inteligencia *f*; **to have the i. to do sth** tener la inteligencia de hacer algo; **her decision shows real i.** la suya es una decisión sumamente inteligente; **use your i.!** ¡piensa! ►► *Psy* ***i. quotient*** cociente *m* intelectual; ***i. test*** test *m* de inteligencia
(**b**) *(information)* información *f*; **we received the i. that...** hemos recibido la información de que...
(**c**) *Mil & Pol* inteligencia *f*, información *f*; **he used to work in i.** trabajaba en inteligencia *or* información ►► ***i. agency*** servicio *m* de inteligencia *or* información; ***i. officer*** agente *mf* de inteligencia *or* información; ***i. service*** servicio *m* de inteligencia *or* información

intelligent [ɪn'telɪdʒənt] *adj* inteligente; **is there i. life on other planets?** ¿hay vida inteligente en otros planetas? ►► *Comptr* ***i. terminal*** terminal *m* inteligente

intelligently [ɪn'telɪdʒəntlɪ] *adv* con inteligencia, inteligentemente

intelligentsia [ɪntelɪ'dʒensɪə] *n* **the i.** la intelectualidad

intelligibility [ɪntelɪdʒə'bɪlɪtɪ] *n* inteligibilidad *f*

intelligible [ɪn'telɪdʒɪbəl] *adj* inteligible

intelligibly [ɪn'telɪdʒɪblɪ] *adv* de manera inteligible

intemperance [ɪn'tempərəns] *n Formal* (**a**) *(lack of restraint)* intemperancia *f* (**b**) *(overindulgence in alcohol)* exceso *m* en la bebida, intemperancia *f*

intemperate [ɪn'tempərət] *adj* (**a**) *(unrestrained) (person, behaviour)* inmoderado(a), intemperante; **her statements became increasingly i.** sus comentarios se fueron volviendo cada vez más intemperantes (**b**) *(drunken)* descontrolado(a) (**c**) *(climate)* riguroso(a)

intend [ɪn'tend] *vt* (**a**) *(plan, have in mind)* **to i. to do sth, to i. doing** *or US* **on doing sth** tener la intención de hacer algo; **to i. sth for sb** *(plan to give to)* tener pensado dar algo a alguien; **I didn't i. her to see it yet** no quería que ella lo viera todavía; **those comments were intended for you** esos comentarios iban por ti *or* destinados a ti; **I told her to do it, and I i. to be obeyed** le dije que lo hiciera, y vaya si lo hará
(**b**) *(mean)* **was that intended?** ¿ha sido a propósito?; **it was intended as a joke/compliment** pretendía ser una broma/un cumplido; **his statement was intended to mislead** el objetivo de su comentario era confundir; **no pun intended!** no es un juego de palabras, ¿eh?
(**c**) *(destine)* **a movie intended for children** una película para niños *or* dirigida a los niños; **the device is intended to reduce pollution** la función del dispositivo es reducir la contaminación; **the reform is intended to limit the dumping of toxic waste** la reforma busca limitar el vertido de desechos tóxicos

> En inglés culto o elevado, y especialmente en inglés americano, **intend** puede ir seguido de **that** más un verbo en subjuntivo (ver el panel SUBJUNCTIVE):
> **I had intended that there be more time for discussion**
> *había pensado que hubiera más tiempo para discusión*
> Lo mismo también podría decirse del siguiente modo:
> **I had intended that there should be more time for discussion**

intended [ɪn'tendɪd] **1** *n Old-fashioned or Hum (future spouse)* prometido(a) *m,f*
2 *adj* (**a**) *(planned) (outcome, reaction)* esperado(a), deseado(a); **I had to cancel our i. trip** tuve que cancelar el viaje que habíamos planeado; **as i.** como estaba calculado (**b**) *(insult, mistake)* intencionado(a)

intense [ɪn'tens] *adj* (**a**) *(great, heavy)* intenso(a); **to my i. satisfaction/annoyance** para mi gran satisfacción/tremendo fastidio (**b**) *(person)* muy serio(a); **he gets terribly i.** se toma las cosas muy a pecho

intensely [ɪn'tenslɪ] *adv* (**a**) *(highly, extremely)* enormemente; **i. painful** sumamente doloroso; **i. annoyed** extremadamente *Esp* enfadado *or Am* enojado; **to dislike sb i.** sentir un profundo rechazo por alguien (**b**) *(strongly, deeply)* intensamente; **i. moving/emotional** profundamente conmovedor/emotivo

intensification [ɪntensɪfɪ'keɪʃən] *n* intensificación *f*

intensifier [ɪn'tensɪfaɪə(r)] *n Gram* intensivo *m*, intensificador *m*

intensify [ɪn'tensɪfaɪ] **1** *vt* intensificar; **to i. one's efforts (to do sth)** redoblar los esfuerzos (por hacer algo); **the police have intensified their search for the child** la policía ha intensificado la búsqueda del niño
2 *vi* intensificarse

intensity [ɪn'tensɪtɪ] *n* (**a**) *(of emotion, colour)* intensidad *f*; **the i. of the debate** la intensidad del debate (**b**) *Phys* intensidad *f*

intensive [ɪn'tensɪv] *adj* intensivo(a); **despite an i. search, nothing was found** a pesar de la intensa búsqueda, no se encontró nada ►► *Med* ***i. care*** cuidados *mpl* intensivos, *Méx, RP* terapia *f* intensiva; *Med* ***i. care unit*** unidad *f* de cuidados intensivos *or* de vigilancia intensiva *or Méx, RP* de terapia intensiva; *Educ* ***i. course*** curso *m* intensivo; *Agr* ***i. farming*** agricultura *f* intensiva

intensively [ɪn'tensɪvlɪ] *adv (to farm)* intensivamente; *(to study)* profundamente, exhaustivamente

intent [ɪn'tent] **1** *n* intención *f*; **to do sth with i.** hacer algo con premeditación; **with good/evil i.** con buena/mala intención; **to all intents and purposes** a todos los efectos
2 *adj* (**a**) *(concentrated) (look, expression)* intenso(a), concentrado(a); **he was silent, i. on the meal** estaba en silencio, concentrado en la comida (**b**) *(determined)* **to be i. on doing sth** estar empeñado(a) en hacer algo; **they were i. on murder** estaban decididos a llevar a cabo el asesinato; **a woman i. on success** una mujer decidida a triunfar

intention [ɪn'tenʃən] *n* intención *f*; **good/bad intentions** buenas/malas intenciones; **he went to Australia with the i. of making his fortune** fue a Australia con la intención de hacer fortuna; **it was with this i. that I wrote to him** le escribí con esa intención, fue esa mi intención al escribirle; **to have no i. of doing sth** no tener ninguna intención de hacer algo; **to have every i. of doing sth** tener toda la intención de hacer algo; *Old-fashioned or Hum* **my intentions are entirely honourable** tengo la mejor de las intenciones

intentional [ɪn'tenʃənəl] *adj* intencionado(a); **it wasn't i.** no fue adrede *or* a propósito

intentionally [ɪn'tenʃənəlɪ] *adv* adrede, a propósito; **he didn't do it i.** no lo hizo adrede; **I i. didn't invite her** no la invité a propósito

intently [ɪn'tentlɪ] *adv (to listen)* atentamente; *(to look at)* intensamente

inter [ɪn'tɜː(r)] *(pt & pp* **interred***) vt Formal* inhumar, sepultar

interact [ɪntə'rækt] *vi* (**a**) *(people)* interrelacionarse (**with** con); **a person who doesn't i. well with others** una persona que no se relaciona bien con los demás (**b**) *(factors, events)* combinarse (**with** con); **the cold air interacts with the warm** se produce una reacción entre el aire frío y caliente (**c**) *Comptr* interactuar (**with** con)

interaction [ɪntə'rækʃən] *n* interacción *f*

interactive [ɪntə'ræktɪv] *adj* interactivo(a) ►► *Comptr **i. CD*** CD *m* interactivo; *Comptr **i. video*** vídeo *m or Am* video *m* interactivo

interactively [ɪntər'æktɪvlɪ] *adv Comptr* interactivamente

inter alia [ɪntə'reɪlɪə] *adv Formal* entre otras cosas

interbank [ɪntə'bæŋk] *adj* interbancario(a) ►► ***i. deposit rate*** interés *m* interbancario; ***i. market*** mercado *m* interbancario

interbreed [ɪntə'bri:d] **1** *vt* cruzar

2 *vi* (**a**) *(crossbreed)* cruzarse (**b**) *(within family, community)* reproducirse entre sí

intercede [ɪntə'si:d] *vi* interceder (**with/for** ante/por); **to i. on sb's behalf** interceder por alguien

intercept [ɪntə'sept] **1** *vt* (**a**) *(letter, blow, missile)* interceptar (**b**) *(in football)* interceptar (**c**) *Math* cortar, intersectar

2 *n* (**a**) **radio intercepts** mensajes *mpl* de radio interceptados (**b**) *Math* intersección *f*

interception [ɪntə'sepʃən] *n* (**a**) *(of letter, blow, missile)* interceptación *f*, intercepción *f* (**b**) *(in football)* intercepción *f*

interceptor [ɪntə'septə(r)] *n (aircraft)* interceptor *m*

intercession [ɪntə'seʃən] *n Formal* intercesión *f*

interchange **1** *n* ['ɪntətʃeɪndʒ] (**a**) *(exchange)* intercambio *m* (**b**) *(of roads)* enlace *m*, nudo *m* de carreteras

2 *vt* [ɪntə'tʃeɪndʒ] intercambiar

interchangeable [ɪntə'tʃeɪndʒəbəl] *adj* intercambiable (**with** con)

interchangeably [ɪntə'tʃeɪndʒəblɪ] *adv* de forma intercambiable, indistintamente

intercity ['ɪntə'sɪtɪ] **1** *n (train) Esp* intercity *m*, *Am* interurbano *m*

2 *adj* intercity ►► ***i. bus*** *Esp* autobús *m* de línea, *Am* bus *m* interurbano

intercollegiate [ɪntəkə'li:dʒɪət] *adj US (between universities)* interuniversitario(a)

intercom ['ɪntəkɒm] *n* interfono *m*

intercommunicate [ɪntəkə'mju:nɪkeɪt] *vi* (**a**) *(people)* comunicarse (**b**) *(rooms)* comunicarse

intercommunication [ɪntəkəmju:nɪ'keɪʃən] *n* intercomunicación *f*

intercommunion [ɪntəkə'mju:njən] *n Rel* intercomunión *f*

intercompany [ɪntə'kʌmpənɪ] *adj* entre empresas

interconnect [ɪntəkə'nekt] **1** *vt* interconectar (**with** con); **interconnected corridors** pasillos comunicados; **the buildings are interconnected by underground walkways** los edificios están comunicados por pasajes subterráneos

2 *vi (ideas, lives)* interrelacionarse (**with** con); *(rooms, buildings)* comunicarse (**with** con); *(computers, circuits)* interconectarse (**with** con)

interconnecting [ɪntəkə'nektɪŋ] *adj (rooms)* comunicado(a)

interconnection [ɪntəkə'nekʃən] *n* interconexión *f*; **there are lots of interconnections between the two fields of study** hay muchos puntos de contacto entre los dos campos de estudio

intercontinental [ɪntəkɒntɪ'nentəl] *adj* intercontinental ►► *Mil **i. ballistic missile*** misil *m* balístico intercontinental

intercostal [ɪntə'kɒstəl] *adj Anat* intercostal ►► ***i. muscle*** músculo *m* intercostal

intercourse ['ɪntəkɔ:s] *n* (**a**) *(sexual)* coito *m*, cópula *f*; **to have i. (with sb)** realizar el coito *or* el acto sexual (con alguien) (**b**) *Formal (dealings)* trato *m*; **social i.** relaciones sociales

intercut [ɪntə'kʌt] *vt Cin* intercalar

interdenominational ['ɪntədɪnɒmɪ'neɪʃənəl] *adj* interconfesional, entre religiones

interdepartmental ['ɪntə'di:pɑ:t'mentəl] *adj* interdepartamental

interdependence ['ɪntədɪ'pendəns] *n* interdependencia *f*

interdependent ['ɪntədɪ'pendənt] *adj* interdependiente

interdict **1** *n* ['ɪntədɪkt] (**a**) *Law* interdicción *f*, prohibición *f* por orden judicial (**b**) *Rel* entredicho *m*

2 *vt* [ɪntə'dɪkt] (**a**) *Law* someter a interdicción a (**b**) *Rel* poner en entredicho a (**c**) *Mil* destruir

interdiction [ɪntə'dɪkʃən] *n Mil* destrucción *f*

interdisciplinary ['ɪntədɪsə'plɪnərɪ] *adj* interdisciplinar

interest ['ɪntrest] **1** *n* (**a**) *(curiosity)* interés *m*; **of i.** de interés; **with i.** *(watch, say)* con interés, interesado(a); **to have no i. in (doing) sth** no tener ningún interés en (hacer) algo *or* por (hacer) algo; **to lose i. (in sth)** perder el interés (por algo); **to hold sb's i.** mantener a alguien interesado(a); **to show/express an i. (in sth)** mostrar/expresar interés (en *or* por algo); **to take an i. (in sth)** interesarse (por algo); **the book created** *or* **aroused a great deal of i.** el libro suscitó un gran interés

(**b**) *(appeal)* **to be of i./of no i. to sb** interesar/no interesar a alguien; **politics has** *or* **holds no i. for me** la política no me interesa

(**c**) *(hobby)* interés *m*, afición *f*; **we share the same interests** compartimos los mismos intereses *or* las mismas aficiones; **to have outside interests** tener otros intereses, tener otras aficiones

(**d**) *(stake)* interés *m*; **to declare an i.** *or* **one's interests** declararse parte interesada; **to have an i. in sth** *(in general)* tener interés en *or* por algo; *Fin* tener intereses *or* participación en algo ►► ***i. group*** grupo *m* con intereses comunes

(**e**) *(benefit)* **to act in sb's interests** obrar en interés de alguien; **to act against one's own interests** obrar en contra de los propios intereses; **the public i.** el interés general *or* público; **it's in my i. to do it** hacerlo va en mi propio interés, me interesa hacerlo; **it's in all our interests to cut costs** reducir costos va en interés de todos, reducir costos nos interesa a todos; **I have your (best) interests at heart** estoy considerando lo que es mejor para ti; **in the interests of accuracy/hygiene** en pro de la precisión/higiene

(**f**) *(group)* **foreign interests** grupos *mpl* de poder extranjeros; **big business interests** intereses *mpl* corporativos

(**g**) *Fin (on investment)* interés *m*; **to pay i. on a loan** pagar interés sobre un préstamo; **the investment will bear 6 percent i.** la inversión dará un interés del 6 por ciento; **to pay sb back with i.** devolver el dinero a alguien con intereses; *Fig (exact revenge)* vengarse con creces de alguien ►► ***i. charges*** intereses *mpl* (devengados); ***i. due*** intereses *mpl* vencidos; ***i. rate*** tipo *m or* tasa *f* de interés

2 *vt* interesar; **it may i. you to know that...** tal vez te interese saber que...; **to i. sb in sth** interesar a alguien en algo

interest-bearing ['ɪntrest'beərɪŋ] *adj (account)* que da *or* devenga interés

interested ['ɪntrestɪd] *adj* (**a**) *(look, audience)* interesado(a); **to be i. in sth** estar interesado(a) en algo, interesarse por algo; **would you be i. in meeting him?** ¿te interesaría conocerlo?; **they seem i. in the offer** parecen interesados en el ofrecimiento; **I've got a free ticket for the opera here... anyone i.?** tengo una entrada gratis para la ópera...¿le interesa a alguien?; **I'd be i. to know what you think** me gustaría saber qué opinas

(**b**) *(concerned)* interesado(a); **the i. party** la parte interesada

interest-free ['ɪntrest'fri:] *adj (loan)* sin intereses

interesting ['ɪntrestɪŋ] *adj* interesante

interestingly ['ɪntrestɪŋlɪ] *adv (to speak)* de manera *or* forma interesante; **i., she said she couldn't remember anything** es interesante recalcar que ella dijo que no se acordaba de nada; **i. enough** curiosamente

interface ['ɪntəfeɪs] **1** *n* (**a**) *(interaction)* interacción *f* (**with/between** con/entre); **the patient-doctor i.** la interacción médico-paciente (**b**) *Comptr* interface *m o f*, interfaz *m o f*

2 *vi* (**a**) *(interact)* relacionarse (**with** con) (**b**) *Comptr* **to i. with** comunicarse con

interfere [ɪntə'fɪə(r)] *vi* (**a**) *(meddle)* interferir, entrometerse (**in** en); **he's always interfering** siempre se está entrometiendo

(**b**) *(tamper)* **to i. with sth** andar con *or* tocar algo; **the safety lock had been interfered with** alguien había andado con *or* tocado la cerradura de seguridad; **don't i. with my papers** no enredes en *or* no toques mis papeles

(**c**) *(clash, conflict)* **to i. with sth** interferir en *or* afectar a algo; **he lets his pride/personal feelings i. with his judgment** suele dejar que su orgullo/sus sentimientos personales influyan en sus opiniones; **not if it interferes with my work** no si afecta mi trabajo

(**d**) *Rad & TV* **to i. with sth** interferir con algo

(**e**) *Phys (waves)* causar *or* provocar interferencia

(**f**) *Euph* **to i. with a child** *(sexually)* abusar de un niño

interference [ɪntə'fɪərəns] *n* (**a**) *(meddling)* intromisión *f*; **she won't tolerate i. in** *or* **with her plans** no va a tolerar ninguna injerencia *or* interferencias en sus planes (**b**) *Rad & TV* interferencia *f* (**c**) *Phys (waves)* interferencia *f*

interfering [ɪntə'fɪərɪŋ] *adj* entrometido(a)

interferon [ɪntə'fɪərɒn] *n Biochem* interferón *m*

intergalactic [ɪntəgə'læktɪk] *adj* intergaláctico(a)

interglacial [ɪntəˈgleɪʃəl] *adj Geol* interglacial ▸▸ ***i. stage*** período *m* interglacial

intergovernmental [ˈɪntəgʌvənˈmentəl] *adj* intergubernamental

interim [ˈɪntərɪm] **1** *n* **in the i.** entre tanto, en el ínterin

2 *adj (agreement, report, appointment)* provisional, *Am* provisorio; **as an i. measure** como medida provisional *or Am* provisoria ▸▸ *Fin* ***i. dividend*** dividendo *m* a cuenta; ***i. government*** gobierno *m* de transición; ***i. payment*** pago *m* a cuenta

interior [ɪnˈtɪərɪə(r)] **1** *n* **(a)** *(of building, country)* interior *m*; **the French Minister of the I.** el Ministro de Interior de Francia; **Secretary/Department of the I.** Ministro(a)/Ministerio del Interior **(b)** *Art* interior *m* **(c)** *Cin &TV* interior *m*; **the interiors were all shot in London** todos los interiores se rodaron en Londres

2 *adj* **(a)** *(inside) (wall, room)* interior ▸▸ ***i. decoration*** interiorismo *m*; ***i. decorator*** interiorista *mf*, *Am* decorador(ora) *m,f* de interiores; ***i. design*** interiorismo *m*, decoración *f* de interiores; ***i. designer*** interiorista *mf*; *Aut* ***i. trim*** revestimientos *mpl* interiores **(b)** *Cin &TV* interior *m* **(c)** *Lit* ***i. monologue*** monólogo *m* interior **(d)** *Geom* ***i. angle*** ángulo *m* interno

interiority [ɪntɪərɪˈɒrɪtɪ] *n* interioridad *f*

interior-sprung [ɪnˈtɪərɪəˈsprʌŋ] *adj Br (mattress)* de muelles *or* resortes

interject [ɪntəˈdʒekt] *vt (question, comment)* interponer; **"not like that," he interjected** "así no", interrumpió

interjection [ɪntəˈdʒekʃən] *n* **(a)** *Gram* interjección *f* **(b)** *(interruption)* interrupción *f*

interlace [ɪntəˈleɪs] **1** *vt* **(a)** *(entwine)* entrelazar **(b)** *(mix, intersperse)* intercalar

2 *vi* entrelazarse

interlaced [ɪntəˈleɪst] *adj Comptr (monitor)* entrelazado(a)

interlard [ɪntəˈlɑːd] *vt Pej* entreverar *or* salpicar (**with** de)

interleaf [ˈɪntəliːf] *n* hoja *f* interfoliada

interleave [ɪntəˈliːv] *vt* **(a)** *(book)* intercalar, interfoliar **(b)** *Comptr* intercalar

interlibrary [ˈɪntəˈlaɪbrərɪ] *adj* **i. loan** préstamo interbibliotecario

interline [ɪntəˈlaɪn] *vt* **(a)** *(text)* interlinear, intercalar comentarios *or* notas en un texto **(b)** *(garment)* entretela *f*

interlinear [ˈɪntəˈlɪnɪə(r)] *adj (word, gloss)* interlineal, entre líneas

interlining [ɪntəˈlaɪnɪŋ] *n (fabric)* entretela *f*

interlink [ˈɪntəlɪŋk] *vt* enlazar; **the problems are interlinked** los problemas están interrelacionados

interlock [ɪntəˈlɒk] **1** *vt (entwine)* trabar, entrelazar

2 *vi* **(a)** *(parts)* trabarse, entrelazarse; *(cogs)* engranarse **(b)** *(groups, issues)* imbricarse

3 *n* [ˈɪntəlɒk] *Tex* interlock *m*

4 *adj (garment)* de interlock

interlocking [ɪntəˈlɒkɪŋ] *adj* interconectado(a)

interlocutor [ɪntəˈlɒkjʊtə(r)] *n Formal* interlocutor(ora) *m,f*

interloper [ˈɪntələʊpə(r)] *n* intruso(a) *m,f*

interlude [ˈɪntəluːd] *n* **(a)** *(period)* intervalo *m* **(b)** *(intermission) (at cinema)* intermedio *m*, descanso *m*; *(in theatre)* entreacto *m*, intermedio *m* **(c)** *Lit (short play)* sainete *m* corto, entremés *m* **(d)** *Mus* interludio *m*

intermarriage [ɪntəˈmærɪdʒ] *n* **(a)** *(within family, clan)* matrimonio *m* endogámico **(b)** *(between different groups)* matrimonio *m* mixto *(entre personas de distintas razas, religiones o comunidades)*

intermarry [ɪntəˈmærɪ] *vi* **(a)** *(within family, clan)* casarse con personas de la misma familia o grupo; **the tribe no longer intermarries** los miembros de la tribu ya no se casan entre sí **(b)** *(between different groups)* casarse *(personas de diferente raza, religión o comunidad)*; **Catholics and Protestants rarely intermarried** católicos y protestantes raras veces se casaban entre sí

intermediary [ɪntəˈmiːdɪərɪ] **1** *n (mediator)* intermediario(a) *m,f*, mediador(ora) *m,f*

2 *adj* **(a)** *(mediating)* intermediario(a) **(b)** *(intermediate)* intermedio(a)

intermediate [ɪntəˈmiːdɪət] *adj* intermedio(a); **an i. course** un curso de nivel medio ▸▸ ***i. technology*** tecnología *f* de nivel medio

interment [ɪnˈtɜːmənt] *n Formal* sepelio *m*

intermezzo [ɪntəˈmetsəʊ] (*pl* **intermezzos** *or* **intermezzi** [ɪntəˈmetsiː]) *n Mus* intermezzo *m*

interminable [ɪnˈtɜːmɪnəbəl] *adj* interminable

interminably [ɪnˈtɜːmɪnəblɪ] *adv* interminablemente; **his talk was i. long** su conferencia se hizo interminable; **the discussions dragged on i.** las conversaciones se extendieron interminablemente

intermingle [ɪntəˈmɪŋgəl] **1** *vt* mezclar (**with** con)

2 *vi* mezclarse (**with** con)

intermission [ɪntəˈmɪʃən] *n (at cinema)* intermedio *m*, descanso *m*; *(in theatre)* entreacto *m*, intermedio *m*

intermittent [ɪntəˈmɪtənt] *adj* intermitente; **sunny weather with i. showers** tiempo soleado con chaparrones aislados

intermittently [ɪntəˈmɪtəntlɪ] *adv* de forma intermitente, a intervalos; **she interrupted i.** cada cierto rato decía algo

intermodal [ɪntəˈməʊdəl] *adj (transport)* intermodal; **i. transport system** sistema de transporte intermodal

intermolecular [ɪntəməˈlekjʊlə(r)] *adj* intermolecular

intern **1** *n* [ˈɪntɜːn] *US* **(a)** *(doctor)* médico(a) *m,f* interno(a) residente **(b)** *(teacher)* practicante *mf*

2 *vt* [ɪnˈtɜːn] recluir

3 *vi US* **(a)** *(in hospital)* internarse **(b)** *(in school)* hacer prácticas

internal [ɪnˈtɜːnəl] *adj* **(a)** *(inside object)* interno(a) ▸▸ *Comptr* ***i. clock*** reloj *m* interno; *Tech* ***i. combustion engine*** motor *m* de combustión interna; *Comptr* ***i. command*** comando *m* interno; *Comptr* ***i. drive*** unidad *f* de disco interna

(b) *(inside body) (bleeding, injuries)* interno(a) ▸▸ ***i. examination*** examen *m* interno; *US* ***i. medicine*** medicina *f* interna

(c) *(inside text)* **i. evidence suggests it was written between 1609 and 1612** la información que se desprende del texto sugiere que fue escrito entre 1609 y 1612 ▸▸ *Lit* ***i. rhyme*** rima *f* interna

(d) *(inside country)* interno; **to interfere in another country's i. affairs** interferir en los asuntos internos de otro país ▸▸ *Econ* ***i. debt*** deuda *f* interior *or* interna; ***i. flight*** vuelo *m* doméstico

(e) *(inside organization, institution)* interno(a) ▸▸ *US* ***(Department of) I. Affairs*** (Secretaría *f or* Ministerio *m* de) Asuntos Internos *mpl*; *Fin* ***i. audit*** auditoría *f* interna; *Univ* ***i. examiner*** examinador(ora) *m,f* interno(a); ***i. mail*** correo *m* interno; *US* ***the I. Revenue Service*** *Esp* ≃ la Agencia Tributaria, *Am* ≃ la Dirección General Impositiva

internalization [ɪntɜːnəlaɪˈzeɪʃən] *n (of values, behaviour)* incorporación *f*, *Am* internalización *f*

internalize [ɪnˈtɜːnəlaɪz] *vt* interiorizar, *Am* internalizar

internally [ɪnˈtɜːnəlɪ] *adv* **(a)** *(within body)* internamente; **he was bleeding i.** tenía una hemorragia interna; **not to be taken i.** *(on medicine container)* para uso externo **(b)** *(within organization, institution)* internamente

international [ɪntəˈnæʃənəl] **1** *adj* internacional ▸▸ *Hist* ***the I. Brigade*** las Brigadas Internacionales; ***i. call*** llamada *f or Am* llamado *m* internacional; ***I. Court of Justice*** Tribunal *m* Internacional de Justicia; ***I. Date Line*** línea *f* de cambio de fecha; *US* ***i. dial code*** indicativo *m* internacional; *Br* ***i. dialling code*** indicativo *m* internacional; **an *i. incident*** un incidente internacional; ***I. Labour Organization*** Organización *f* Internacional del Trabajo; ***i. law*** derecho *m* internacional; *Fin* ***I. Monetary Fund*** Fondo *m* Monetario Internacional; ***I. Phonetic Alphabet*** Alfabeto *m* Fonético Internacional; ***i. relations*** relaciones *fpl* internacionales; ***I. Standards Organization*** Organización *f* Internacional de Normalización; ***i. waters*** aguas *fpl* internacionales

2 *n* **(a)** *Sport (player)* (jugador(ora) *m,f*) internacional *mf*; *(game)* partido *m* internacional **(b)** *Pol* **the Second/Third I.** la segunda/tercera Internacional; **the Socialist I.** la Internacional Socialista

Internationale [ɪntənæʃəˈnɑːl] *n* **the I.** la Internacional

internationalism [ɪntəˈnæʃənəlɪzəm] *n* internacionalismo *m*

internationalist [ɪntəˈnæʃənəlɪst] **1** *n* internacionalista *mf*

2 *adj* internacionalista

internationalization [ɪntənæʃənəlaɪˈzeɪʃən] *n* internacionalización *f*

internationalize [ɪntəˈnæʃənəlaɪz] *vt* internacionalizar; **to become internationalized** internacionalizarse

internationally [ɪntəˈnæʃənəlɪ] *adv* internacionalmente; **i. acclaimed** de fama internacional; **she is well known i., but comparatively ignored at home** es conocida a nivel internacional pero, comparativamente, en su país se la ignora

internaut [ˈɪntənɔːt] *n Comptr* internauta *mf*

internecine [ɪntəˈniːsaɪn] *adj Formal* intestino(a), interno(a); **i. struggles** luchas intestinas; **i. rivalry/feuding** rivalidad/contienda interna

internee [ɪntɜːˈniː] *n* recluso(a) *m,f*

Internet [ˈɪntənet] *n Comptr* **the I.** Internet *f*; **to surf the I.** navegar por Internet ▸▸ ***I. access*** acceso *m* a Internet; ***I. access provider*** proveedor *m* de acceso a Internet; ***I. account*** cuenta *f* de Internet; ***I.***

address dirección *f* de Internet; ***I. banking*** banca *f* por Internet, banca *f* electrónica; ***I. café*** cibercafé *m*; ***I. connection*** conexión *f* a Internet; ***I. number*** número *m* de Internet; ***I. phone*** teléfono *m* por Internet; ***I. protocol*** protocolo *m* de Internet; ***I. Relay Chat*** charla *f* interactiva por Internet; ***I. service provider*** proveedor *m* de (acceso a) Internet; ***I. surfer*** internauta *mf*; ***I. surfing*** navegación *f* por Internet; ***I. user*** internauta *mf*

internist [ɪn'tɜːnɪst] *n US Med* internista *mf*, especialista *mf* en medicina interna

internment [ɪn'tɜːnmənt] *n* reclusión *f*; **i. without trial** reclusión sin juicio ▸▸ ***i. camp*** campo *m* de reclusión

internship ['ɪntɜːnʃɪp] *n US* (**a**) *(in hospital) Esp* ≃ MIR *m*, *Am* internado *m* (**b**) *(in school)* prácticas *fpl*

interparty [ɪntə'pɑːtɪ] *adj (talks, negotiations)* interpartidario(a)

interpellate [ɪn'tɜːpeleɪt] *vt Pol* interpelar

interpenetrate [ɪntə'penətreɪt] *vt* imbuir

interpersonal [ɪntə'pɜːsənəl] *adj* interpersonal ▸▸ ***i. skills*** habilidades *fpl* interpersonales

interplanetary [ɪntə'plænɪtrɪ] *adj Astron* interplanetario(a) ▸▸ ***i. travel*** viaje *m* interplanetario

interplay ['ɪntəpleɪ] *n* interacción *f* (**of** de)

Interpol ['ɪntəpɒl] *n* Interpol *f*

interpolate [ɪn'tɜːpəleɪt] *vt* (**a**) *Formal (in text, conversation)* interpolar (**into** en) (**b**) *Math* interpolar

interpolation [ɪntɜːpə'leɪʃən] *n* (**a**) *Formal (in text, conversation)* interpolación *f* (**b**) *Math* interpolación *f*

interpose [ɪntə'pəʊz] **1** *vt* (**a**) *(between objects)* interponer (**between** entre) (**b**) *(interject)* interponer; **"that simply isn't true!" he interposed** "¡eso no es verdad!", exclamó

2 *vi* interponerse

interpret [ɪn'tɜːprɪt] **1** *vt* interpretar

2 *vi* interpretar; **can you i. for me?** ¿puedes hacerme de intérprete?

interpretation [ɪntɜːprɪ'teɪʃən] *n* (**a**) *(understanding, analysis)* interpretación *f*; **she puts quite a different i. on the facts** ella hace una interpretación muy diferente de los hechos; **she wasn't sure what i. to put on the remarks** no estaba segura de cómo interpretar los comentarios; **it's open to several** *or* **various** *or* **different interpretations** se puede interpretar de diversas formas ▸▸ ***i. centre*** *(at historic site, country park)* centro *m* de interpretación

(**b**) *(translation)* interpretación *f*

(**c**) *(artistic expression)* interpretación *f*

interpretative [ɪn'tɜːprɪtətɪv], **interpretive** [ɪn'tɜːprɪtɪv] *adj* interpretativo(a) ▸▸ ***i. centre*** centro *m* de interpretación

interpreter [ɪn'tɜːprɪtə(r)] *n* (**a**) *(person)* intérprete *mf* ▸▸ ***i.'s booth*** cabina *f* de interpretación *or* traducción (**b**) *Comptr* intérprete *mf*

interpreting [ɪn'tɜːprɪtɪŋ] *n (occupation)* interpretación *f*

interpretive = **interpretative**

interracial [ɪntə'reɪʃəl] *adj* interracial

Inter-Rail ['ɪntəreɪl] *Br* **1** *n* Inter-Rail *m*, Inter-Raíl *m*

2 *vi* hacer Inter-Rail

interregnum [ɪntə'regnəm] *(pl* **interregnums** *or* **interregna** [ɪntə'regnə]) *n* (**a**) *(between monarchs, governments)* interregno *m* (**b**) *Br Hist* **the I.** el Interregno

interrelate [ɪntərɪ'leɪt] *vi* interrelacionarse

interrelated [ɪntərɪ'leɪtɪd] *adj* interrelacionado(a)

interrelation [ɪntərɪ'leɪʃən], **interrelationship** [ɪntərɪ'leɪʃənʃɪp] *n* interrelación *f*; **the i. between poverty levels and inflation** la interrelación entre niveles de pobreza e inflación

interrogate [ɪn'terəgeɪt] *vt* (**a**) *(suspect)* interrogar (**b**) *Comptr (database)* interrogar

interrogation [ɪnterə'geɪʃən] *n* (**a**) *(of suspect)* interrogatorio *m*; **to undergo (an) i.** pasar por un interrogatorio (**b**) *Comptr (of database)* interrogatorio *m* (**c**) *Gram* ***i. mark*** signo *m* de interrogación; *US Gram* ***i. point*** signo *m* de interrogación

interrogative [ɪnte'rɒgətɪv] **1** *n Gram (voice)* forma *f* interrogativa; *(word)* interrogativo *m*

2 *adj* (**a**) *(look, tone)* interrogativo(a) (**b**) *Gram* interrogativo(a)

interrogatively [ɪntə'rɒgətɪvlɪ] *adv (questioningly)* con aire interrogativo, interrogativamente

interrogator [ɪn'terəgeɪtə(r)] *n* interrogador(ora) *m,f*

interrogatory [ɪntə'rɒgətərɪ] *adj* interrogativo(a)

interrupt [ɪntə'rʌpt] **1** *vt* (**a**) *(person, lecture, conversation)* interrumpir; **don't i. me when I'm speaking to you!** ¡no me interrumpas cuando te hablo!

(**b**) *(process, activity)* interrumpir; **we i. this programme for a news flash** interrumpimos este programa para brindar *or* poner en el aire un flash informativo

(**c**) *(uniformity)* interrumpir; **only an occasional tree interrupted the monotony of the landscape** sólo algún árbol ocasional interrumpía la monotonía del paisaje

2 *vi* interrumpir; **sorry to i. but...** perdón por interrumpir pero...

interrupter, interruptor [ɪntə'rʌptə(r)] *n Elec* interruptor *m*

interruption [ɪntə'rʌpʃən] *n* interrupción *f*; **without i.** sin interrupción

interruptor = **interrupter**

interscholastic [ɪntəskɒ'læstɪk] *adj US* interescolar; **the i. championship/tournament** el campeonato/torneo interescolar

intersect [ɪntə'sekt] **1** *vt (of line, street)* cruzar, atravesar

2 *vi* cruzarse

intersection [ɪntə'sekʃən] *n* (**a**) *(of lines)* cruce *m*, intersección *f* (**b**) *US (of roads)* cruce *m*, intersección *f*

interservice ['ɪntə'sɜːvɪs] *adj* entre armas; **i. rivalry is strongest between the army and the navy** la rivalidad entre armas es mayor en el caso del ejército y la marina

intersperse [ɪntə'spɜːs] *vt* **our conversation was interspersed with long silences** largos silencios se fueron intercalando en nuestra conversación; **plain-clothes officers were interspersed throughout the crowd** oficiales de civil estaban desperdigados entre la multitud; **sunny weather interspersed with the odd shower** tiempo soleado con ocasionales chaparrones

interstate ['ɪntəsteɪt] *US* **1** *n* autopista *f* interestatal

2 *adj* entre estados

interstellar [ɪntə'stelə(r)] *adj* interestelar

interstice [ɪn'tɜːstɪs] *n Formal* intersticio *m*

interterritorial ['ɪntəterɪ'tɔːrɪəl] *adj* interterritorial

intertextual [ɪntə'tekstjʊəl] *adj Lit* intertextual

intertextuality [ɪntətekstjʊ'ælɪtɪ] *n Lit* intertextualidad *f*

intertidal [ɪntə'taɪdəl] *adj* intermareal

intertwine [ɪntə'twaɪn] **1** *vt* entrelazar, entretejer (**with** con); **his fate seemed to be intertwined with hers** sus destinos parecían estar entrelazados

2 *vi* entrelazarse

interurban ['ɪntə'ɜːbən] *adj* interurbano(a)

interval ['ɪntəvəl] *n* (**a**) *(of time)* intervalo *m*, lapso *m*; **I saw him again after an i. of six months** volví a verlo después de un intervalo de seis meses; **at regular intervals** a intervalos regulares; **at weekly/monthly intervals** a intervalos semanales/mensuales; **rainy weather with sunny intervals** tiempo lluvioso con intervalos soleados

(**b**) *(of space)* intervalo *m*; **at two-metre intervals** cada dos metros; **trees planted at regular intervals** árboles plantados a intervalos regulares

(**c**) *Br (at cinema)* intermedio *m*, descanso *m*; *(in theatre)* entreacto *m*, intermedio *m*

(**d**) *Mus* intervalo *m*

(**e**) *Math* ***i. scale*** escala *f* de intervalos

inter-varsity ['ɪntə'vɑːsɪtɪ] *adj* interuniversitario(a); **i. match/championship** un encuentro/campeonato interuniversitario

intervene [ɪntə'viːn] *vi* (**a**) *(person, government)* intervenir (**in** en); **the government intervened to save the dollar from falling** el gobierno intervino para evitar que cayera el dólar; **if I might just i. here...** si me permiten una intervención...

(**b**) *(event)* sobrevenir; **he was about to go to college when war intervened** estaba por empezar la universidad cuando sobrevino la guerra

(**c**) *(time)* transcurrir, pasar; **three months intervened between the agreement and actually signing the contract** transcurrieron tres meses entre el acuerdo y la firma del contracto

intervening [ɪntə'viːnɪŋ] *adj (years, months)* mediante, transcurrido(a); *(miles)* intermedio(a); **in the i. period** en el ínterin

intervention [ɪntə'venʃən] *n (by person, government)* intervención *f*; **local people have called for government i. to avoid closure** los habitantes del lugar han solicitado la intervención del gobierno para evitar el cierre; **armed i.** intervención armada ▸▸ *EU* ***i. price*** precio *m* mínimo garantizado

interventionism [ɪntə'venʃənɪzəm] *n* intervencionismo *m*

interventionist [ɪntə'venʃənɪst] **1** *n* intervencionista *mf*

2 *adj* intervencionista

interview ['ɪntəvju:] **1** *n* (**a**) *(for job, university place)* entrevista *f*; **to invite** *or* **call sb for i.** invitar a alguien a *or* llamar a alguien para una entrevista (**b**) *(for newspaper, on TV)* entrevista *f*; **she gave him an exclusive i.** le concedió una entrevista exclusiva (**c**) *(with police)* interrogatorio *m*, toma *f* de declaración (**d**) *(in survey, for research)* entrevista *f*

2 *vt* (**a**) *(for job, university place)* entrevistar; **we have interviewed ten people for the post** hemos entrevistado a diez personas para el puesto (**b**) *(for newspaper, on TV)* entrevistar (**c**) *(of police)* interrogar, tomar declaración a (**d**) *(in survey, for research)* encuestar

3 *vi* entrevistar; **they're interviewing for the new post** están entrevistando para el nuevo puesto; **I'm interviewing all day** voy a estar todo el día haciendo entrevistas; **he interviews well/badly** *(candidate)* sale bien parado/mal parado de sus entrevistas; *(celebrity)* da buenas/malas entrevistas

interviewee [ɪntəvju:'i:] *n* (**a**) *(for job, university place)* entrevistado(a) *m,f* (**b**) *(celebrity)* entrevistado(a) *m,f* (**c**) *(by police)* interrogado(a) *m,f*

interviewer ['ɪntəvju:ə(r)] *n* (**a**) *(for job, university place)* entrevistador(ora) *m,f* (**b**) *(of celebrity)* entrevistador(ora) *m,f* (**c**) *(police officer)* interrogador(ora) *m,f*

intervocalic [ɪntəvə'kælɪk] *adj Ling* intervocálico(a)

interwar ['ɪntə'wɔ:(r)] *adj* **the i. period** *or* **years** el período *or* los años de entre guerras

interweave [ɪntə'wi:v] (*pt* **interwove** [ɪntə'wəʊv], *pp* **interwoven** [ɪntə'wəʊvən]) **1** *vt* entretejer; *Fig* **our lives have become closely interwoven** nuestras vidas están ahora íntimamente entrelazadas

2 *vi* entretejerse

intestate [ɪn'testeɪt] *adv Law* **to die i.** morir intestado(a)

intestinal [ɪntes'taɪnəl] *adj* intestinal ►► ***i. flora*** flora *f* (gastro)intestinal; *Hum* ***i. fortitude*** agallas *fpl*

intestine [ɪn'testaɪn] *n Anat* intestino *m*; **large/small i.** intestino grueso/delgado

intimacy ['ɪntɪməsɪ] *n* (**a**) *(of relationship, atmosphere)* intimidad *f* (**b**) *(intimate remark)* comentario *m* íntimo (**c**) *Euph (sexual)* relaciones *fpl* (sexuales); **i. took place on more than one occasion** hubo relaciones íntimas en más de una oportunidad

intimate ['ɪntɪmət] **1** *n (close friend, associate)* íntimo(a) *m,f*, allegado(a) *m,f*

2 *adj* (**a**) *(friend, relationship)* íntimo(a); **to be i. with sb, to be on i. terms with sb** *(friendly)* ser amigo(a) íntimo(a) de alguien

(**b**) *(restaurant)* íntimo(a); **an i. dinner party** una cena íntima

(**c**) *(personal, private)* íntimo(a); **he revealed the i. details of their friendship** desveló los detalles más íntimos de su amistad; *Hum* **spare me the i. details!** ¡ahórrate los detalles más íntimos!

(**d**) *Euph* **to be i. with sb** *(sexually)* tener relaciones (sexuales) con alguien

(**e**) *(close, detailed)* profundo(a); **to have an i. knowledge of sth** conocer algo a fondo; **an i. link** un profundo nexo

3 *vt* ['ɪntɪmeɪt] *Formal* (**a**) *(hint, imply)* dar a entender, sugerir; **her speech intimated strong disapproval** con lo que dijo dio a entender que estaba en total desacuerdo (**b**) *(make known)* comunicar, hacer saber

intimately [ɪn'tɪmətlɪ] *adv* (**a**) *(in a friendly way)* íntimamente

(**b**) *Euph* **to know sb i.** *(sexually)* haber tenido relaciones (sexuales) con alguien

(**c**) *(closely)* a fondo; **the two questions are i. related** las dos preguntas están íntimamente relacionadas; **to be i. acquainted with sth** conocer algo a fondo; **to be i. acquainted with sb** conocer bien a alguien, conocer a alguien en la intimidad; **to be i. involved in sth** estar metido(a) de lleno en algo

intimation [ɪntɪ'meɪʃən] *n (clue, sign)* indicio *m*; **we had no i. that disaster was imminent** nada nos hacía suponer que el desastre era inminente

intimidate [ɪn'tɪmɪdeɪt] *vt* intimidar; **to i. sb into doing sth** intimidar a alguien para que haga algo; **don't let him i. you** no dejes que te intimide, no te dejes intimidar por él

intimidating [ɪn'tɪmɪdeɪtɪŋ] *adj (experience)* imponente, aterrador(ora); *(person)* avasallador(ora)

intimidation [ɪntɪmɪ'deɪʃən] *n* intimidación *f*

intimidatory [ɪntɪmɪ'deɪtərɪ] *adj* intimidatorio(a)

INTO ['ɪntʊ] *prep* (**a**) *(with motion, direction)* en; **to go i. a house** entrar en una casa *or Am* a una casa; **she went out i. the garden** salió al jardín; **to get i. a car** subirse a *or* montarse en un automóvil; **to get i. bed** meterse en la cama; **to get i. one's trousers** ponerse los pantalones; **she fell i. the water** cayó al agua; **the car crashed i. a tree** el automóvil chocó contra un árbol; **speak i. the microphone** habla frente al micrófono

(**b**) *(with change)* en; **to change i. sth** convertirse en algo; **to grow i. a man** hacerse (un) hombre; **to translate sth i. English** traducir algo al inglés; **to break sth i. pieces** romper algo en pedazos; **mix the ingredients i. a paste** se mezclan los ingredients hasta formar una pasta

(**c**) *(regarding)* de; **an inquiry i. the accident** una investigación del accidente

(**d**) *(with time)* **three days i. the term** a los tres días del comienzo del trimestre; **rain continued to fall well i. the summer** siguió lloviendo hasta bien entrado el verano; **I was reading late i. the night** estuve leyendo hasta bien entrada la noche; **he must be well i. his forties** debe de tener ya sus cuarenta años largos, debe de estar ya bien metido en la cuarentena

(**e**) *(with career)* **to go i. politics** meterse en política

(**f**) *(indicating result)* **to fool sb i. believing that...** hacer creer a alguien que...; **to talk sb i. doing sth** convencer a alguien de que haga algo

(**g**) *(indicating division)* **cut it i. three** córtarlo en tres partes; **divide the cake i. three** divide el pastel en tres partes; **three i. six goes twice** seis entre tres cabe a dos; **three i. five doesn't** *or* **won't go** cinco entre tres, no cabe

(**h**) *Fam (keen on)* **she's really i. folk music** le gusta *or Esp* va mucho la música folk; **I'm not i. Mexican food** no me gusta *or Esp* va mucho la comida mexicana; **they're really i. the idea of getting married** se les ve muy entusiasmados con la idea de casarse; **he's really i. my sister** le gusta un montón *or Esp* mogollón *or Méx* un chingo *or RP* pila mi hermana, *RP* le copa mi hermana; **he's i. drugs** toma drogas, anda en drogas

(**i**) *US Fam (indebted)* **to be i. sb for sth** estar endeudado(a) con alguien

---

intolerable [ɪn'tɒlərəbəl] *adj (heat, conditions)* insoportable; *(price, behaviour)* intolerable; **I find it i. that...** me parece intolerable que ...

intolerably [ɪn'tɒlərəblɪ] *adv (to behave)* de un modo intolerable, muy mal; **unemployment figures are still i. high** las cifras de desempleo *or Am* desocupación continúan en unos niveles intolerables; **he had been i. rude** había sido insoportablemente grosero

intolerance [ɪn'tɒlərəns] *n* (**a**) *(to people, beliefs)* intolerancia *f* (**b**) *(to drug)* intolerancia *f*

intolerant [ɪn'tɒlərənt] *adj* (**a**) *(to people, beliefs)* intolerante (**of** con) (**b**) *(to drug)* intolerante

intolerantly [ɪn'tɒlərəntlɪ] *adv* con intolerancia

intonation [ɪntə'neɪʃən] *n* entonación *f*

intone [ɪn'təʊn] *vt* (**a**) *(say)* decir solemnemente (**b**) *(chant)* entonar

in toto [ɪn'təʊtəʊ] *adv* por completo, íntegramente

intoxicant [ɪn'tɒksɪkənt] *n Formal (alcohol)* bebida *f* alcohólica; *(drug)* estupefaciente *m*

intoxicate [ɪn'tɒksɪkeɪt] *vt* (**a**) *(make drunk)* embriagar, emborrachar (**b**) *(excite)* embriagar, embargar

intoxicated [ɪn'tɒksɪkeɪtɪd] *adj* (**a**) *(drunk)* **to be i.** estar embriagado(a) *or* ebrio(a) (**b**) *(excited)* ebrio(a); **i. with power** ebrio de poder; **i. by success** embriagado por el éxito

intoxicating [ɪn'tɒksɪkeɪtɪŋ] *adj also Fig* embriagador(ora), embriagante; **i. liquor** bebida alcohólica

intoxication [ɪntɒksɪ'keɪʃən] *n* (**a**) *(drunkenness)* embriaguez *f*, ebriedad *f* (**b**) *(excitement)* embriaguez *f* (**c**) *Med (poisoning)* intoxicación *f*

intractability [ɪntræktə'bɪlɪtɪ] *n Formal* (**a**) *(of person)* intransigencia *f*, obstinación *f* (**b**) *(of problem)* la inextricabilidad

intractable [ɪn'træktəbəl] *adj Formal* (**a**) *(person)* intratable (**b**) *(problem)* arduo(a)

intramural [ɪntrə'mjʊərəl] *adj (at school, college)* del propio centro, interno(a)

intramuscular [ɪntrə'mʌskjʊlə(r)] *adj Med* intramuscular

intranet ['ɪntrənet] *n Comptr* intranet *f*

intransigence [ɪn'trænzɪdʒəns] *n Formal* intransigencia *f*

intransigent [ɪn'trænzɪdʒənt] *Formal* **1** *n* intransigente *mf*

2 *adj* intransigente

intransitive [ɪn'trænzɪtɪv] *Gram* **1** *n* verbo *m* intransitivo

2 *adj* intransitivo(a)

intransitively [ɪn'trænzɪtɪvlɪ] *adv Gram* intransitivamente

intrapreneur [ɪntrəprə'nɜ:(r)] *n* = empresario que realiza sus negocios dentro de una gran organización

intrastate ['ɪntrə'steɪt] *adj US* intraestatal

intrauterine [ˈɪntrəˈjuːtəraɪn] *adj Med* intrauterino(a) ▸▸ ***i. device*** dispositivo *m* intrauterino, DIU *m*

intravenous [ˈɪntrəˈviːnəs] *adj Med* ***i. drip*** gota a gota *m*; ***i. injection*** inyección *f* intravenosa

intravenously [ˈɪntrəˈviːnəslɪ] *adv Med* por vía intravenosa

in-tray [ˈɪntreɪ] *n* bandeja *f* de trabajos pendientes

intrepid [ɪnˈtrepɪd] *adj* intrépido(a)

intrepidity [ɪntreˈpɪdɪtɪ] *n* intrepidez *f*

intrepidly [ɪnˈtrepɪdlɪ] *adv* intrépidamente

intricacy [ˈɪntrɪkəsɪ] *n* (**a**) *(complicated detail)* complejidad *f*, complicación *f*; **the intricacies of...** los entresijos de...; **he knows all the legal intricacies** él conoce todas las complejidades legales (**b**) *(complexity)* complejidad *f*

intricate [ˈɪntrɪkət] *adj* intrincado(a), complicado(a)

intricately [ˈɪntrɪkətlɪ] *adv* intrincadamente, con gran complejidad

intrigue 1 *n* [ˈɪntriːg] (**a**) *(plotting)* intriga *f* (**b**) *(plot, treason)* conspiración *f*, intriga *f* (**c**) *(love affair)* aventura *f*

2 *vt* [ɪnˈtriːg] *(interest)* intrigar; **I was intrigued to hear of your plan** tenía curiosidad por conocer tu plan, me intrigaba mucho tu plan; **I'd be intrigued to know where they met** tengo cierta intriga por saber dónde se conocieron

3 *vi (conspire)* intrigar, conspirar (**against** contra)

intriguing [ɪnˈtriːgɪŋ] *adj* intrigante; **it's an i. idea!** ¡es una idea fascinante!

intriguingly [ɪnˈtriːgɪŋlɪ] *adv* curiosamente; **did he turn up on time? – i. enough, he did** ¿llegó a tiempo? – curiosamente, sí

intrinsic [ɪnˈtrɪnsɪk] *adj* intrínseco(a); **the object has little i. value** el objeto en sí (mismo) tiene poco valor; **such ideas are i. to my argument** dichas ideas son parte esencial de mi razonamiento

intrinsically [ɪnˈtrɪnsɪklɪ] *adv* intrínsecamente; **the story is not i. interesting** la historia en sí *or* de por sí tiene poco interés

intro [ˈɪntrəʊ] *n Fam* (**a**) *(to song)* entrada *f* (**b**) *(to person)* presentación *f*

introduce [ɪntrəˈdjuːs] *vt* (**a**) *(person)* presentar; **may I i. you?** ¿me permites que te presente?; **let me i. myself, I'm John** permíteme que me presente, soy John; **has everyone been introduced?** ¿se han hecho todas las presentaciones?; **to i. oneself** presentarse; **allow me to i. you to Mr Black** permítame presentarle al Sr. Black; **we haven't been introduced, have we?** creo que no nos han presentado, ¿verdad?; **to be introduced to society** *(débutante)* ser presentada en sociedad

(**b**) *(present) (radio or TV programme)* presentar; **to i. a speaker** presentar a un(a) orador(ora)

(**c**) *(initiate)* **to i. sb to sth** introducir *or* iniciar a alguien en algo

(**d**) *(bring in) (reform, practice)* introducir; **this custom was introduced by missionaries** esta costumbre la trajeron los misioneros; **when were rabbits introduced into Australia?** ¿cuándo se introdujeron los conejos en Australia?; **he introduced a note of humour into proceedings** introdujo una nota de color *or* humor en la reunión; **her arrival introduced a note of sadness into the festivities** su llegada trajo una nota de tristeza a la celebración

(**e**) *(laws, legislation)* presentar, introducir; **the government hopes to i. the new bill next week** el gobierno planea presentar el nuevo proyecto de ley la semana próxima

(**f**) *Cin (in credits)* **introducing Simon McLean** con la actuación por primera vez en pantalla de Simon McLean

(**g**) *(insert)* introducir; **to i. one thing into another** meter una cosa dentro de otra, introducir una cosa en otra

introduction [ɪntrəˈdʌkʃən] *n* (**a**) *(of person)* presentación *f*; **to make** *or* **do the introductions** hacer las presentaciones; **the next speaker needs no i.** nuestro siguiente invitado a la tribuna de oradores no necesita presentación

(**b**) *(to experience)* **that was my i. to life in Mexico** aquella fue mi primera experiencia de lo que era la vida en México; **this was my i. to Shakespeare** ese fue mi primer contacto con Shakespeare; **this record is a good i. to her work** este disco es una buena introducción a su trabajo

(**c**) *(to book, piece of music)* introducción *f*; **a short i. to linguistics** *(book title)* una breve introducción a la lingüística

(**d**) *(bringing in) (of reform, practice)* introducción *f*; **the i. of computer technology into schools** la introducción de la informática en las escuelas

(**e**) *(of law, legislation)* presentación *f*, introducción *f*

(**f**) *(insertion)* introducción *f*; **the i. of a new species** la introducción de una nueva especie

introductory [ɪntrəˈdʌktərɪ] *adj* introductorio(a); **an i. course** un curso introductorio *or* de introducción; **i. remarks** comentarios preliminares ▸▸ *Com* ***i. offer*** oferta *f* de lanzamiento; *Com* ***i. price*** precio *m* de lanzamiento

introit [ˈɪntrɔɪt] *n Mus & Rel* introito *m*

introspection [ɪntrəˈspekʃən] *n* introspección *f*

introspective [ɪntrəˈspektɪv] *adj* introspectivo(a)

introversion [ɪntrəˈvɜːʃən] *n Psy* introversión *f*

introvert [ˈɪntrəvɜːt] *n* introvertido(a) *m,f*

introverted [ɪntrəˈvɜːtɪd] *adj* introvertido(a)

intrude [ɪnˈtruːd] 1 *vi* (**a**) *(impose oneself)* **to i. on sb** molestar *or* importunar a alguien; **I hope I'm not intruding** espero no molestar

(**b**) *(interfere)* **her work intrudes on her family life** el trabajo invade su vida familiar; **to i. on sb's privacy** perturbar *or* invadir la intimidad de alguien; **I felt I was intruding on their grief** tenía la sensación de que estaba invadiendo su intimidad en momentos de dolor

(**c**) *Geol* penetrar

2 *vt Formal* introducir; **a doubt intruded itself into my mind** una duda se filtró en mi mente

intruder [ɪnˈtruːdə(r)] *n* intruso(a) *m,f*

intrusion [ɪnˈtruːʒən] *n* (**a**) *(imposition)* intromisión *f*; **pardon the i.** disculpen la molestia (**b**) *(interference)* **it's an i. into our privacy** es una intromisión en nuestra privacidad (**c**) *Geol* intrusión *f*

intrusive [ɪnˈtruːsɪv] *adj* (**a**) *(person, question)* molesto(a), importuno(a); **he was an i. presence in the house** su presencia en la casa importunaba; **far away from the i. sounds of the city** lejos de los molestos ruidos de la ciudad; **the police presence was rather i.** la presencia policial fue bastante invasiva (**b**) *Geol* ***i. rock*** roca *f* intrusiva (**c**) *Ling* ***i. consonant*** consonante *f* de apoyo *or* intrusiva

intrusiveness [ɪnˈtruːsɪvnɪs] *n* impertinencia *f*, indiscreción *f*

intubate [ˈɪntʃʊbeɪt] *vt Med* intubar, entubar

intuit [ɪnˈtjuːɪt] *vt Formal* intuir

intuition [ɪntjuːˈɪʃən] *n* intuición *f*; **(my) i. tells me he won't be coming** mi intuición me dice que no vendrá; **I had an i. something was wrong** tenía la intuición de que algo andaba mal

intuitive [ɪnˈtjuːɪtɪv] *adj* intuitivo(a); **an i. understanding** una comprensión intuitiva; **he's very i.** es muy intuitivo

intuitively [ɪnˈtjuːɪtɪvlɪ] *adv* de manera intuitiva, por intuición; **I knew i. that she was lying** intuitivamente supe que estaba mintiendo

Inuit, Innuit [ˈɪnʊɪt] 1 *n* inuit *mf*

2 *adj* inuit

inundate [ˈɪnʌndeɪt] *vt* (**a**) *Formal (flood)* inundar (**b**) *(overwhelm)* inundar (**with** de); **we've been inundated with phone calls/letters** nos han inundado de llamadas/cartas; **I'm inundated with work just now** en este momento estoy inundado de trabajo

inundation [ɪnʌnˈdeɪʃən] *n Formal (flood)* inundación *f*

inure [ɪnˈjʊə(r)]

▸ **inure to** *vt Formal* inmunizar ante, habituar a; **to become inured to sth** habituarse a algo; **he became inured to the pain** se inmunizó contra el dolor

in utero [ɪnˈjuːtərəʊ] 1 *adj* intrauterino(a)

2 *adv* intrauterinamente

invade [ɪnˈveɪd] 1 *vt* (**a**) *(with army)* invadir (**b**) *(overwhelm)* **the village was invaded by reporters** el pueblo fue invadido por periodistas; **her mind was invaded by sudden doubts** súbitas dudas la asaltaron; **to i. sb's privacy** perturbar *or* invadir la intimidad de alguien

2 *vi* invadir

invader [ɪnˈveɪdə(r)] *n* invasor(ora) *m,f*

invading [ɪnˈveɪdɪŋ] *adj* invasor(ora)

invalid[1] [ɪnˈvælɪd] *adj* (**a**) *(document, argument)* nulo(a); **to declare sth i.** declarar nulo(a) algo (**b**) *Comptr (file name)* inválido(a)

invalid[2] [ˈɪnvəlɪd] 1 *n (disabled person)* inválido(a) *m,f*; **I'm not an i.!** ¡no soy ningún inválido! ▸▸ ***i. car*** automóvil *m* para discapacitados

2 *adj* **his i. mother** su madre inválida

3 *vt* **to i. sb home** mandar a alguien a casa con un parte de baja

▸ **invalid out** *vt sep* **to i. sb out** dar de baja a alguien por invalidez

invalidate [ɪnˈvælɪdeɪt] *vt* (**a**) *(theory, argument)* invalidar (**b**) *(document, contract)* anular, invalidar

invalidation [ɪnvælɪˈdeɪʃən] *n* (**a**) *(of theory, argument)* invalidación *f* (**b**) *(of document, agreement)* invalidación *f*

invalidity [ɪnvəˈlɪdɪtɪ] *n* (**a**) *(of theory, argument)* invalidez *f*, falta *f* de validez (**b**) *(of document, agreement)* invalidez *f* (**c**) *(of person)* invalidez *f* ▸▸ *Br* ***i. benefit*** pensión *f* por invalidez transitoria

invaluable [ɪnˈvæljʊəbəl] *adj* inestimable, inapreciable; **to be i. for sth/to sb** ser de gran valor para algo/alguien; **your help has been i. (to me)** tu ayuda ha sido invalorable (para mí); **she's an i. asset (to the company)** es sumamente importante (para la compañía)

invariable [ɪnˈveərɪəbəl] *adj* invariable

invariably [ɪnˈveərɪəblɪ] *adv* invariablemente; **she was i. dressed in black** estaba, como siempre, vestida de negro

invariance [ɪnˈveərɪəns] *n Math* invariancia *f*

invariant [ɪnˈveərɪənt] *adj Math* invariante

invasion [ɪnˈveɪʒən] *n* (**a**) *(with army)* invasión *f*; **the Roman i. of England** la invasión romana de Inglaterra ▸▸ ***i. force*** fuerzas *fpl* de invasión (**b**) *Fig* invasión *f*; **a pitch i.** una invasión del campo de juego; **we expect the usual i. of tourists this summer** este verano esperamos la usual invasión de turistas; **it's an i. of my privacy** es una intromisión en mi vida privada

invasive [ɪnˈveɪsɪv] *adj Med (cancer)* con metástasis, invasivo(a) ▸▸ ***i. surgery*** cirugía *f* invasiva

invective [ɪnˈvektɪv] *n* invectivas *fpl*; **a stream of i.** una catarata de improperios

inveigh [ɪnˈveɪ] *vi Formal* **to i. against** lanzar invectivas contra

inveigle [ɪnˈveɪgəl] *vt* **to i. sb into doing sth** engatusar a alguien para que haga algo

invent [ɪnˈvent] *vt* (**a**) *(new machine, process)* inventar (**b**) *(lie, excuse)* inventar; **she had invented the whole thing** se lo había inventado todo

invention [ɪnˈvenʃən] *n* (**a**) *(action)* invención *f*; *(thing invented)* invento *m*, invención *f*; **a device/method of his own i.** un dispositivo/método de su propia invención; **television is a wonderful i.** la televisión es un invento maravilloso (**b**) *(lie)* invención *f*; **it was pure i.** fue pura invención (**c**) *(creativity)* inventiva *f*; **she has great powers of i.** tiene mucha inventiva

inventive [ɪnˈventɪv] *adj* (**a**) *(creative) (person, mind)* inventivo(a), imaginativo(a) (**b**) *(ingenious) (plan, solution)* ingenioso(a)

inventiveness [ɪnˈventɪvnəs] *n* inventiva *f*

inventor [ɪnˈventə(r)] *n* inventor(ora) *m,f*

inventory [ˈɪnvəntərɪ, ˈɪnvəntrɪ] **1** *n* (**a**) *(list)* inventario *m*; **to draw up** *or* **make an i. (of sth)** hacer un inventario (de algo) (**b**) *Com (stock)* existencias *fpl* ▸▸ ***i. replenishment cost*** costo *m* de reaprovisionamiento

2 *vt* inventariar, hacer un inventario de

inverse **1** *n* [ˈɪnvɜːs] **the i.** lo contrario

2 *adj* [ɪnˈvɜːs] inverso(a); **in i. proportion to** inversamente proporcional a, en proporción inversa a ▸▸ *Comptr* ***i. video*** vídeo *m* or *Am* video *m* inverso

inversely [ɪnˈvɜːslɪ] *adv* a la inversa, inversamente; **i. proportional** inversamente proporcional

inversion [ɪnˈvɜːʃən] *n* (**a**) *(reversal)* inversión *f* (**b**) *Mus* inversión *f* (**c**) *Old-fashioned Psy* **(sexual) i.** inversión *f* (sexual)

invert **1** *vt* [ɪnˈvɜːt] invertir

2 *n* [ˈɪnvɜːt] *Old-fashioned Psy* invertido(a) *m,f*

3 *adj Biochem* ***i. sugar*** azúcar *m* invertido

invertebrate [ɪnˈvɜːtɪbrɪt] **1** *n* invertebrado *m*

2 *adj* invertebrado(a)

inverted [ɪnˈvɜːtɪd] *adj* invertido(a) ▸▸ ***i. commas*** comillas *fpl*; **in i. commas** entre comillas; **her "best friend", in i. commas, ran off with her husband** su "mejor amiga", entre comillas, se escapó con su marido; ***i. snob*** = persona que busca identificarse con una clase social inferior a la suya

invest [ɪnˈvest] **1** *vt* (**a**) *(money)* invertir (**in** en)

(**b**) *(time, effort)* invertir (**in** en); **I've invested a lot in this relationship** yo he puesto mucho de mi parte en esta relación; **we've invested a lot of time and energy in this project** hemos invertido mucho dinero y energía en este proyecto

(**c**) *Formal (confer on)* **to i. sb with sth** investir a alguien con algo; **by the authority invested in me...** por la autoridad que me ha sido conferida...; **his novels i. criminality with too much glamour** en sus novelas, el crimen aparece como algo demasiado glamoroso

(**d**) *(install)* investir

(**e**) *Archaic (besiege)* sitiar

2 *vi* invertir (**in** en); *Fam* **you ought to i. in a new coat** te tendrías que comprar un abrigo

investigate [ɪnˈvestɪgeɪt] **1** *vt (allegation, crime, accident)* investigar; *(complaint, problem, situation)* examinar, estudiar; **we must i. what happened to those supplies** hay que averiguar qué ha pasado con esos suministros

2 *vi (police)* realizar una investigación; **what's that noise? – I'll just go and i.** ¿qué ha sido ese ruido? – iré a echar un vistazo

investigation [ɪnvestɪˈgeɪʃən] *n* investigación *f*; **to make investigations** hacer investigaciones; **to be under i.** estar siendo investigado(a), ser objeto de una investigación; **your case is currently under i.** tu caso está siendo estudiado en este momento; **on further i., the ruins turned out to be much more recent** nuevas investigaciones revelaron que las ruinas eran mucho más recientes

investigative [ɪnˈvestɪgətɪv] *adj* de investigación, investigador(ora) ▸▸ ***i. journalism*** periodismo *m* de investigación

investigator [ɪnˈvestɪgeɪtə(r)] *n* investigador(ora) *m,f*

investigatory [ɪnvestɪˈgeɪtərɪ] *adj* de investigación

investiture [ɪnˈvestɪtʃə(r)] *n* investidura *f*

investment [ɪnˈvestmənt] *n* (**a**) *(of money)* inversión *f*; **property is no longer such a safe i.** los inmuebles *or* las propiedades ya no son una inversión tan segura ▸▸ ***i. account*** cuenta *f* de inversiones; ***i. analyst*** analista *mf* financiero(a) *or* de inversiones; ***i. bank*** banco *m* de inversiones; ***i. company*** sociedad *f* de inversión; ***i. fund*** fondo *m* de inversión; ***i. income*** rendimientos *mpl (de una inversión)*; ***i. portfolio*** cartera *f* de valores, valores *mpl* en cartera; ***i. trust*** sociedad *f* de inversión

(**b**) *(of time, effort)* inversión *f*

investor [ɪnˈvestə(r)] *n* inversor(ora) *m,f*

inveterate [ɪnˈvetərɪt] *adj (gambler, smoker, reader)* empedernido(a); *(liar)* redomado(a)

invidious [ɪnˈvɪdɪəs] *adj (choice, comparison)* odioso(a); **to be in an i. position** estar en una posición ingrata

> **False friend:** The Spanish adjective **envidioso** is not a translation for the English word **invidious**. In Spanish **envidioso** means "envious".

invigilate [ɪnˈvɪdʒɪleɪt] *Br* **1** *vt (exam)* vigilar

2 *vi* vigilar

invigilation [ɪnvɪdʒɪˈleɪʃən] *n Br (in exam)* vigilancia *f* de un examen

invigilator [ɪnˈvɪdʒɪleɪtə(r)] *n Br (in exam)* vigilante *mf*

invigorate [ɪnˈvɪgəreɪt] *vt* tonificar, vigorizar; **she felt invigorated by the cold wind** se sintió vigorizada por el viento frío

invigorating [ɪnˈvɪgəreɪtɪŋ] *adj (bath, air)* tonificante; *(walk)* vigorizante; **it's i. just talking to her** el mero hecho de hablar con ella es estimulante

invincibility [ɪnvɪnsɪˈbɪlɪtɪ] *n* invencibilidad *f*

invincible [ɪnˈvɪnsɪbəl] *adj (army, enemy)* invencible; *(belief, faith)* inquebrantable; **an i. argument** un argumento irrefutable

inviolable [ɪnˈvaɪələbəl] *adj Formal* inviolable

inviolate [ɪnˈvaɪələt] *adj Formal* inviolado(a); **to remain i.** permanecer inmaculado(a)

invisibility [ɪnvɪzɪˈbɪlɪtɪ] *n* invisibilidad *f*

invisible [ɪnˈvɪzɪbəl] *adj* (**a**) *(not seen)* invisible; **i. to the naked eye** invisible a simple vista ▸▸ *Comptr* ***i. file*** archivo *m* invisible; ***i. ink*** tinta *f* simpática *or* invisible; ***i. mending*** zurcido *m* invisible (**b**) *Fin* ***i. assets*** activos *mpl* invisibles *or* intangibles; ***i. earnings*** (ganancias *fpl*) invisibles *mpl*; ***i. exports*** exportaciones *fpl* invisibles

invisibly [ɪnˈvɪzɪblɪ] *adv* sin ser visto(a)

invitation [ɪnvɪˈteɪʃən] *n* (**a**) *(request to attend)* invitación *f*; **we have an open** *or* **a standing i.** *(to house)* estamos invitados a ir siempre que queramos; **she's here at my i.** está aquí porque yo la invité; **by i. (only)** sólo con invitación

(**b**) *(card, letter)* invitación *f*; **have you sent out the wedding invitations?** ¿has enviado las invitaciones de la boda?

(**c**) *(encouragement, enticement)* invitación *f*, incitación *f*; **it's an open i. to burglars** es pedir a gritos que entren a robar en tu casa

invite **1** *vt* [ɪnˈvaɪt] (**a**) *(guest)* invitar; **the Thomsons have invited us over** los Thomson nos han invitado a su casa; **to i. sb in/up** invitar a alguien a entrar/subir; **to i. sb to dinner** invitar a alguien a cenar; **an invited audience** un público invitado

(**b**) *(request)* **to i. sb to do sth** invitar a alguien a que haga algo; **several leading writers were invited to contribute to the magazine** varios escritores de prestigio fueron invitados a escribir en la revista; **I've been invited for interview** me han citado para una entrevista; **applications are invited for the post of...** se admiten candidaturas para el puesto de...; **we i. suggestions from readers** las sugerencias de nuestros lectores serán tomadas en cuenta

(c) *(trouble, criticism)* buscarse, provocar; **they're inviting disaster by building it so quickly** construirlo tan rápido es una invitación al desastre; **his garbled answers simply invited disbelief** sus confusas respuestas sólo provocaron incredulidad

2 *n* ['ɪnvaɪt] *Fam* invitación *f*

▸ **invite out** *vt sep* invitar a salir (a alguien)

inviting [ɪn'vaɪtɪŋ] *adj (offer, prospect)* atractivo(a); *(eyes, smile)* provocativo(a), seductor(ora); *(meal)* apetecible, apetitoso(a); **the water looks i.** el agua está tentadora; **the prospect was far from i.** el panorama no era nada alentador

invitingly [ɪn'vaɪtɪŋlɪ] *adv* de forma incitante; **he gestured i.** hacía gestos incitantes; **the door stood i. ajar** la puerta estaba tentadoramente entreabierta

in vitro fertilization [ɪn'viːtrəʊfɜːtɪlaɪ'zeɪʃən] *n* fertilización *f or* fecundación *f* in vitro

invocation [ɪnvə'keɪʃən] *n Formal* invocación *f*

invoice ['ɪnvɔɪs] *Com* 1 *n* factura *f*; **to make out an i.** extender *or* hacer una factura; **as per i.** según factura; **within 30 days of i.** dentro de los 30 días de la fecha de factura

2 *vt (goods)* facturar; *(person, company)* facturar; **to i. sb for sth** facturar algo a alguien, hacer una factura a alguien por algo

invoicing ['ɪnvɔɪsɪŋ] *n (of goods)* facturación *f*; **i. address/instructions** domicilio/instrucciones de facturación ▸▸ *Comptr* ***i. software*** programas *mpl or* software *m* para facturación

invoke [ɪn'vəʊk] *vt Formal* (a) *(cite)* acogerse a, invocar; **she invoked the principle of free speech** se acogió al principio de libre expresión (b) *(call upon)* invocar; **they invoked the help of the gods** invocaron la ayuda de los dioses (c) *(summon up)* invocar, conjurar; **to i. evil spirits** conjurar espíritus malignos

involuntarily [ɪn'vɒləntərəlɪ, 'ɪnvɒlən'teərəlɪ] *adv* involuntariamente; **she smiled i.** sonrió sin querer

involuntary [ɪn'vɒləntərɪ] *adj* involuntario(a) ▸▸ *Anat* ***i. muscle*** músculo *m* liso

involuted ['ɪnvəluːtɪd] *adj* (a) *Formal (intricate)* intrincado(a), complicado(a) (b) *Bot* involuto(a)

involve [ɪn'vɒlv] *vt* (a) *(implicate, concern)* **to i. sb in sth** implicar *or* involucrar a alguien en algo; **we try to i. the parents in the running of the school** intentamos que los padres participen en el manejo de la escuela; **to i. oneself in sth** meterse en algo, tomar parte activa en algo; **I'm not going to i. myself in their private affairs** no me pienso inmiscuir en sus asuntos privados; **this doesn't i. you** esto no tiene nada que ver contigo; **the matter involves your family** el asunto afecta a tu familia; **over 200 people were involved in planning the event** más de 200 personas participaron en la planificación del evento; **there are too many accidents involving children** hay demasiados accidentes que involucran a niños

(b) *(entail) (work, expense)* implicar, suponer; **there's a lot of work involved in launching a new product** el lanzamiento de un nuevo producto implica *or* supone mucho trabajo; **it won't i. you in much expense** no va a implicar mucho gasto para ti; **my job involves a lot of travel** mi trabajo requiere que viaje mucho; **what does the job i.?** ¿en qué consiste el trabajo?

(c) *(absorb, engage)* **the novel doesn't really i. the reader** el lector no se llega a sentir implicado en la novela

involved [ɪn'vɒlvd] *adj* (a) *(implicated)* **to be i. in sth** *(crime, affair)* estar implicado(a) *or* involucrado(a) en algo; **to be i. in an accident** verse envuelto(a) en un accidente; **to be i. in teaching/banking** dedicarse a la enseñanza/banca; **to get** *or* **become i. in sth** involucrarse en algo; **I don't want to get i.** no quiero tener nada que ver

(b) *(emotionally)* **to be i. with sb** tener una relación (sentimental) con alguien; **he doesn't want to get i. with anyone just now** en este momento no quiere ninguna relación seria *or* nada serio por ahora

(c) *(entailed)* **he had no idea of the problems i.** no tenía idea de los problemas que implicaba; **the amount of work i. is enormous** el trabajo que implica es descomunal

(d) *(engrossed)* **to get i. in a book/movie** enfrascarse en un libro/una película; **she's too i. in her work to notice** está tan metida en su trabajo que no se dio cuenta

(e) *(complicated)* complicado(a), embrollado(a); **the highly i. plots of his novels** los argumentos sumamente intrincados de sus novelas

involvement [ɪn'vɒlvmənt] *n* (a) *(participation)* participación *f* (**in** en); *(role)* relación *f* (**in** con); **they were against American i. in the war** se oponían a la participación de los Estados Unidos en la guerra (b) *(commitment)* implicación *f*, compromiso *m* (c) *(relationship)* relación *f* sentimental; **her i. with him was short-lived** su relación con él duró poco

invulnerability [ɪnvʌlnərə'bɪlɪtɪ] *n* invulnerabilidad *f*

invulnerable [ɪn'vʌlnərəbəl] *adj* invulnerable

inward ['ɪnwəd] 1 *adj* (a) *(motion)* hacia dentro (b) *(thoughts)* interno(a), interior (c) *Econ* ***i. investment*** inversión *f* del exterior

2 *adv* = **inwards**

inward-bound ['ɪnwəd'baʊnd] *adj* **i. flight** vuelo de llegada

inward-looking ['ɪnwəd'lʊkɪŋ] *adj (person)* introvertido(a); *(community)* cerrado(a)

inwardly ['ɪnwədlɪ] *adv* por dentro; **she said nothing but went home i. rejoicing** no dijo nada pero se fue a casa con una gran satisfacción interna; **he smiled i.** sonrió para sus adentros; **i. he knew that she was right** en su fuero interno sabía que ella tenía razón

inward(s) ['ɪnwəd(z)] *adv* (a) *(to turn, face)* hacia dentro; **the doors open i.** las puertas se abren hacia adentro (b) *(into one's own heart, soul)* interiormente, en el interior; **my thoughts turned i.** me puse más introspectivo; **he said we should look i. to find our true selves** dijo que para encontrar nuestra verdadera esencia debíamos buscar en nuestro interior

in-your-face ['ɪnjɔː'feɪs], **in-yer-face** ['ɪnjə'feɪs] *adj Fam (style)* descarado(a); *(movie, advert)* impactante, fuerte; **his act is pure i. aggression** su número es pura agresión gratuita

I/O *Comptr* (*abbr* **input/output**) E/S, entrada/salida

IOC [aɪəʊ'siː] *n* (*abbr* **International Olympic Committee**) COI *m*, Comité *m* Olímpico Internacional

iodide ['aɪədaɪd] *n Chem* yoduro *m*

iodine ['aɪədiːn] *n Chem* yodo *m*

iodize ['aɪədaɪz] *vt Chem* yodar

IOM (*abbr* **Isle of Man**) isla *f* de Man

ion ['aɪən] *n* ion *m* ▸▸ ***i. engine*** motor *m* iónico; *Chem* ***i. exchange*** cambio *m or* intercambio *m* iónico

Ionian [aɪ'əʊnɪən] *n* **the I. (Sea)** el mar Jónico; **the I. Islands** las Islas Jónicas

Ionic [aɪ'ɒnɪk] *adj Archit* jónico(a)

ionic [aɪ'ɒnɪk] *adj Phys & Chem* iónico(a) ▸▸ *Chem* ***i. bond*** enlace *m* iónico

ionization [aɪənaɪ'zeɪʃən] *n Phys & Chem* ionización *f*

ionize ['aɪənaɪz] *vt Phys & Chem* ionizar

ionizer ['aɪənaɪzə(r)] *n* ionizador *m*

ionosphere [aɪ'ɒnəsfɪə(r)] *n Met* ionosfera *f*

iota [aɪ'əʊtə] *n* ápice *m*; **not an i. of truth** ni un ápice de verdad

IOU [aɪəʊ'juː] *n (= I owe you)* pagaré *m*

IOW (*abbr* **Isle of Wight**) isla *f* de Wight

Iowan ['aɪəwən] 1 *n* = persona de Iowa

2 *adj* de Iowa

IP [aɪ'piː] *n Comptr* (*abbr* **Internet Protocol**) ***I. address*** dirección *f* IP; ***I. number*** número *m* IP

IPA [aɪpiː'eɪ] *n Ling* (*abbr* **International Phonetic Alphabet**) AFI *m*, Alfabeto *m* Fonético Internacional

ipso facto ['ɪpsəʊ'fæktəʊ] *adv* por esto, por este mismo hecho

IQ [aɪ'kjuː] *n Psy* (*abbr* **intelligence quotient**) coeficiente *m* intelectual ▸▸ ***I. test*** prueba *f or* test *m* de inteligencia

IRA [aɪɑː'reɪ] *n* (a) (*abbr* **Irish Republican Army**) IRA *m* (b) *US* (*abbr* **individual retirement account**) cuenta *f* de retiro *or* jubilación individual

Iran [ɪ'rɑːn] *n* Irán

Iranian [ɪ'reɪnɪən] 1 *n* (a) *(person)* iraní *mf* (b) *(language)* iraní *m*

2 *adj* iraní

Iraq [ɪ'rɑːk] *n* Iraq, Irak

Iraqi [ɪ'rɑːkɪ] 1 *n* iraquí *mf*, irakí *mf*

2 *adj* iraquí, irakí

irascibility [ɪræsɪ'bɪlɪtɪ] *n Formal* irascibilidad *f*

irascible [ɪ'ræsɪbəl] *adj Formal* irascible

irascibly [ɪ'ræsɪblɪ] *adv Formal* de manera irascible

irate [aɪ'reɪt] *adj* airado(a), furioso(a); **she got most i. about it** se puso furiosa por eso; **an i. letter** una carta furibunda

irately [aɪ'reɪtlɪ] *adv* airadamente

IRBM [aɪɑːbiː'em] *n* (*abbr* **intermediate range ballistic missile**) misil *m* balístico de alcance intermedio

IRC [aɪɑː'siː] *n Comptr* (*abbr* **Internet Relay Chat**) IRC *m* ▸▸ ***I. channel*** canal *m* IRC

ire ['aɪə(r)] *n Literary* ira *f*

Ireland ['aɪələnd] *n* Irlanda; **the Republic of I.** la República de Irlanda

iridescence [ɪrɪ'desəns] *n* iridiscencia *f*

iridescent [ɪrɪ'desənt] *adj* iridiscente, irisado(a)

iridium [ɪ'rɪdɪəm] *n Chem* iridio *m*

iridology [ɪrɪ'dɒlədʒɪ] *n* iridología *f*

iris ['aɪrɪs] *n* (**a**) *(of eye)* iris *m inv* (**b**) *(flower)* lirio *m*

Irish ['aɪrɪʃ] **1** *npl (people)* **the I.** los irlandeses
2 *n (language)* irlandés *m*
3 *adj* (**a**) *(gen)* irlandés(esa) ►► ***I. coffee*** café *m* irlandés; ***I. gaelic*** (gaélico *m)* irlandés *m*; ***the I. Republic*** la República Irlandesa; ***the I. Sea*** el Mar de Irlanda; ***I. setter*** setter *m* irlandés; ***I. stew*** guiso *m* de carne con *Esp* patatas *or Am* papas; ***I. wolfhound*** lebrel *m* irlandés
(**b**) *Fam (nonsensical)* **that's a bit I.!** ¡qué tontería! ►► *Br* ***I. joke*** ≃ chiste *m* de Lepe

Irishman ['aɪrɪʃmən] *n* irlandés *m*

Irishwoman ['aɪrɪʃwʊmən] *n* irlandesa *f*

irk [ɜːk] *vt* fastidiar, irritar; **I was irked by his attitude** me fastidiaba *or* irritaba su actitud

irksome ['ɜːksəm] *adj* molesto(a), irritante

iron ['aɪən] **1** *n* (**a**) *(metal)* hierro *m*; **made of i.** de hierro; **the i. and steel industry** la industria siderúrgica; *Fig* **a will of i.** una voluntad de hierro ►► ***the I. Age*** la Edad del Hierro; ***the I. Curtain*** el telón de acero, *Am* la cortina de hierro; ***i. filings*** limaduras *fpl* de hierro; ***i. foundry*** fundición *f* de hierro; *US Hist* ***the i. horse*** el caballo de hierro; *Br* ***the I. Lady*** la Dama de Hierro; *Med* ***i. lung*** pulmón *m* de acero; *Hist* ***i. maiden*** dama *f* de hierro, caja *f* de pinchos; ***i. ore*** mineral *m or* mena *f* de hierro; ***i. oxide*** óxido *m* de hierro; ***i. pyrites*** pirita *f*
(**b**) *(nutrient)* hierro *m* ►► ***i. deficiency*** deficiencia *f* de hierro; *Br* ***i. rations*** raciones *fpl* de campaña; ***i. tablet*** comprimido *m* de hierro
(**c**) *(for clothes) (tool)* plancha *f*; *(action) Esp* plancha *f*, *Am* planchada *f*; **your shirt needs an i.** a tu camisa le hace falta una plancha *or Am* planchada; IDIOM **to have several irons in the fire** estar *or* andar metido(a) en muchos asuntos
(**d**) *(in golf)* hierro *m*; **a six i.** un hierro del seis
(**e**) **irons** *(chains)* grilletes *mpl*; **clap them in irons!** ¡pónganles grilletes!
2 *adj* (**a**) *(made of iron)* de hierro (**b**) *(strong, unyielding)* de hierro; **he has an i. constitution** está hecho un roble; **i. discipline** disciplina férrea; **with an i. hand** *or* **fist** con mano dura *or* de hierro; **an i. hand** *or* **fist in a velvet glove** mano dura en guante de seda; **an i. resolve** una férrea determinación; **an i. will** una voluntad de hierro, una férrea voluntad
3 *vt (clothes)* planchar
4 *vi (clothes)* planchar

► **iron out** *vt sep* (**a**) *(crease)* planchar (**b**) *(problem, difficulty)* allanar, solventar; **have they ironed out their differences?** ¿han limado asperezas?

ironbound ['aɪənbaʊnd] *adj* (**a**) *(cask)* revestido(a) en hierro (**b**) *(rule, tradition)* inflexible, rígido(a)

ironclad ['aɪənklæd] **1** *n Hist (ship)* acorazado *m*
2 *adj* (**a**) *(ship)* acorazado(a) (**b**) *(rule)* rígido(a), inflexible

iron-grey, *US* **iron-gray** ['aɪən'greɪ] *adj* gris plomo *inv*; **i. hair** pelo entrecano

ironic(al) [aɪ'rɒnɪk(əl)] *adj* irónico(a); **isn't it i. that...?** ¿no es irónico que...?

ironically [aɪ'rɒnɪklɪ] *adv* (**a**) *(humorously)* irónicamente; **I meant it i.** lo decía en el sentido irónico (**b**) *(paradoxically)* irónicamente, paradójicamente; **i. enough, he was the only one to remember** paradójicamente, él fue el único que lo recordó

ironing ['aɪənɪŋ] *n* (**a**) *(action)* planchado *m*, *Am* planchada *f*; **I've got a lot of i. to do** tengo mucho que planchar; **to do the i.** planchar ►► ***i. board*** tabla *f* de planchar (**b**) *(clothes) (to be ironed)* ropa *f* para planchar; *(recently ironed)* ropa *f* planchada

ironist ['aɪrənɪst] *n* ironista *mf*

ironmaster ['aɪənmɑːstə(r)] *n Br* = dueño de una fundición

ironmonger ['aɪənmʌŋgə(r)] *n Br* ferretero(a) *m,f*; **i.'s (shop)** ferretería *f*

ironmongery ['aɪənmʌŋgərɪ] *n Br* artículos *mpl* de ferretería

iron-on ['aɪən'ɒn] *adj (patch, transfer)* para fijar con plancha

ironstone ['aɪənstəʊn] *n* mineral *m* de hierro

ironware ['aɪənweə(r)] *n* utensilios *mpl* de hierro

iron-willed ['aɪən'wɪld] *adj* muy tenaz, de voluntad férrea

ironwork ['aɪənwɜːk] *n (articles)* herrajes *mpl*

ironworks ['aɪənwɜːks] *n (where iron is smelted)* fundición *f*; *(where iron is made into goods)* herrería *f*, forja *f*

irony ['aɪrənɪ] *n* ironía *f*; **the i. is that...** lo paradójico del asunto es que...; **one of life's little ironies** una de las pequeñas ironías de la vida; **and, i. of ironies, his prediction turned out to be true** y el colmo de la ironía es que su pronóstico resultó acertado

irradiate [ɪ'reɪdɪeɪt] *vt* (**a**) *(tumour)* someter a radiación, irradiar (**b**) *(food)* irradiar

irradiation [ɪreɪdɪ'eɪʃən] *n* (**a**) *(of tumour)* irradiación *f*, radiación *f* (**b**) *(of food)* irradiación *f*

irrational [ɪ'ræʃənəl] *adj* (**a**) *(person, behaviour, fear)* irracional (**b**) *Math* ***i. number*** número *m* irracional

irrationality [ɪræʃə'nælɪtɪ] *n* irracionalidad *f*

irrationally [ɪ'ræʃənəlɪ] *adv* irracionalmente

irreconcilable [ɪrekən'saɪləbəl] *adj* (**a**) *(aims, views, beliefs)* irreconciliable; **his religious beliefs are i. with his work** sus creencias religiosas son incompatibles con su trabajo (**b**) *(conflict, disagreement)* irreconciliable; **to be i. enemies** ser enemigos(as) irreconciliables

irreconcilably [ɪrekən'saɪləblɪ] *adv* irreconciliablemente

irrecoverable [ɪrɪ'kʌvərəbəl] *adj* irrecuperable

irrecoverably [ɪrɪ'kʌvərəblɪ] *adv* irrecuperablemente, de forma irrecuperable

irredeemable [ɪrɪ'diːməbəl] *adj* (**a**) *(loss, damage, wrong)* irremediable; *(person)* irredimible (**b**) *Fin (share)* no amortizable

irredeemably [ɪrɪ'diːməblɪ] *adv* irremediablemente; **he is i. lazy** es un vago incorregible

irredentism [ɪrɪ'dentɪzəm] *n Pol* irredentismo *m*

irredentist [ɪrɪ'dentɪst] *Pol* **1** *n* irredentista *mf*
2 *adj* irredentista

irreducible [ɪrɪ'djuːsɪbəl] *adj* irreductible

irrefutable [ɪrɪ'fjuːtəbəl] *adj* irrefutable

irrefutably [ɪrɪ'fjuːtəblɪ] *adv* irrefutablemente

irregular [ɪ'regjʊlə(r)] **1** *n (soldier)* irregular *m*, no regular *m*; **i. forces** fuerzas irregulares *or* no regulares
2 *adj* (**a**) *(shape, surface)* irregular (**b**) *(in frequency)* irregular; **she works i. hours** tiene un horario irregular; **i. breathing** respiración irregular (**c**) *(against rule)* irregular; **this is highly i.** esto va totalmente en contra de las normas (**d**) *Gram* ***i. verb*** verbo *m* irregular

irregularity [ɪregjʊ'lærɪtɪ] *n* (**a**) *(in shape, surface)* irregularidad *f* (**b**) *(in frequency)* irregularidad *f* (**c**) *(nonconformity with rule)* irregularidad *f*; **there were some irregularities in the paperwork** había algunas irregularidades en los papeles (**d**) *Gram* irregularidad *f*

irregularly [ɪ'regjʊləlɪ] *adv* (**a**) *(in shape)* irregularmente, de forma irregular (**b**) *(in frequency)* sin regularidad, irregularmente

irrelevance [ɪ'reləvəns], **irrelevancy** [ɪ'reləvənsɪ] *n* falta *f* de pertinencia; **whether he did it or not is really an i.** que lo hiciera o no realmente no viene al caso; **the monarchy has become an i.** la monarquía ya no tiene sentido

irrelevant [ɪ'reləvənt] *adj* carente de pertinencia (**to** a); **an i. objection/remark** una objeción/un comentario que no viene al caso; **age is i.** la edad no importa; **that's i.** eso no viene al caso

irreligion [ɪrɪ'lɪdʒən] *n* irreligiosidad *f*

irreligious [ɪrɪ'lɪdʒəs] *adj* irreligioso(a), impío(a)

irremediable [ɪrɪ'miːdɪəbəl] *adj Formal* irreparable, irremediable

irremediably [ɪrɪ'miːdɪəblɪ] *adv Formal* irreparablemente, irremediablemente

irreparable [ɪ'repərəbəl] *adj* irreparable

irreparably [ɪ'repərəblɪ] *adv* de forma irreparable, irreparablemente

irreplaceable [ɪrɪ'pleɪsəbəl] *adj* irreemplazable

irrepressible [ɪrɪ'presɪbəl] *adj (need, desire, urge)* irreprimible; *(optimism)* incontenible; *(good humour)* incontenible, irrefrenable; **she is quite i.** no hay quien la pare

irrepressibly [ɪrɪ'presɪblɪ] *adv* **i. optimistic/enthusiastic** irreprimiblemente optimista/entusiasta; **i. good-humoured** de irrefrenable buen humor

irreproachable [ɪrɪ'prəʊtʃəbəl] *adj* irreprochable, intachable

irreproachably [ɪrɪ'prəʊtʃəblɪ] *adv* de manera irreprochable, irreprochablemente

irresistible [ɪrɪ'zɪstɪbəl] *adj* irresistible

irresistibly [ɪrɪ'zɪstɪblɪ] *adv* irresistiblemente; **i. beautiful** de una belleza irresistible; **I was being i. drawn to the conclusion that...** cada vez estaba más seguro de que...

irresolute [ɪ'rezəluːt] *adj Formal* irresoluto(a)

irresolutely [ɪ'rezəluːtlɪ] *adv Formal* de manera indecisa, con indecisión

irresoluteness [ɪ'rezəlu:tnɪs], **irresolution** [ɪrezə'lu:ʃən] *n Formal* irresolución *f*

irrespective [ɪrɪ'spektɪv] **1** *adj* **i. of** independientemente de
2 *adv Fam* igualmente; **we'll help you i.** te ayudaremos igualmente

irresponsibility [ɪrɪspɒnsɪ'bɪlɪtɪ] *n* irresponsabilidad *f*, falta *f* de responsabilidad

irresponsible [ɪrɪ'spɒnsɪbəl] *adj* irresponsable

irresponsibly [ɪrɪ'spɒnsɪblɪ] *adv* irresponsablemente, de forma irresponsable

irretrievable [ɪrɪ'tri:vəbəl] *adj Formal (loss, money)* irrecuperable; *(mistake, situation, damage)* irreparable, irremediable

irretrievably [ɪrɪ'tri:vəblɪ] *adv Formal* irremediablemente, de forma irremediable; **to break down i.** *(marriage)* fracasar irremediablemente

irreverence [ɪ'revərəns] *n* irreverencia *f*, falta *f* de respeto

irreverent [ɪ'revərənt] *adj* irreverente; **an i. sense of humour** un sentido del humor irreverente

irreverently [ɪ'revərəntlɪ] *adv* con falta de respeto, irrespetuosamente

irreversible [ɪrɪ'vɜ:sɪbəl] *adj (decision, process)* irreversible

irreversibly [ɪrɪ'vɜ:sɪblɪ] *adv* de manera irreversible, irreversiblemente

irrevocable [ɪ'revəkəbəl] *adj Formal* irrevocable

irrevocably [ɪ'revəkəblɪ] *adv Formal* de forma irrevocable, irrevocablemente

irrigable ['ɪrɪgəbəl] *adj* irrigable; **that is an i. plot** aquélla es una parcela *or* un terreno de regadío

irrigate ['ɪrɪgeɪt] *vt* **(a)** *(land)* regar **(b)** *Med (wound, cavity)* irrigar

irrigation [ɪrɪ'geɪʃən] *n* **(a)** *(of land)* riego *m*, irrigación *f* ►► ***i. canal*** acequia *f*; ***i. channel*** acequia *f*; ***i. ditch*** acequia *f* **(b)** *Med (of wound, cavity)* irrigación *f*

irritability [ɪrɪtə'bɪlɪtɪ] *n* irritabilidad *f*

irritable ['ɪrɪtəbəl] *adj* **(a)** *(person, mood)* irritable; *(tone, response)* irritado(a); **to be i.** *(by nature)* ser irritable; *(by circumstances)* estar irritado(a); **to get i.** irritarse **(b)** *Med* ***i. bowel syndrome*** colon *m* irritable

irritably ['ɪrɪtəblɪ] *adv* con irritación, irritadamente

irritant ['ɪrɪtənt] *n* **(a)** *(to eyes, skin)* agente *m* irritante **(b)** *(to person, government)* molestia *f*

irritate ['ɪrɪteɪt] *vt* **(a)** *(annoy)* irritar, fastidiar **(b)** *Med* irritar

irritated ['ɪrɪteɪtɪd] *adj* **(a)** *(annoyed)* irritado(a); **don't get i.!** *Esp* ¡no te enfades!, *Am* ¡no te enojes! **(b)** *Med (eyes, skin)* irritado(a)

irritating ['ɪrɪteɪtɪŋ] *adj* **(a)** *(annoying)* irritante, exasperante; **how i.!** ¡qué exasperante! **(b)** *Med* irritante

irritatingly ['ɪrɪteɪtɪŋlɪ] *adv* de un modo irritante; **i. slow** de una lentitud exasperante

irritation [ɪrɪ'teɪʃən] *n* **(a)** *(annoyance)* irritación *f*; **I discovered, to my intense i., that...** me irritó profundamente descubrir que...; **she tried to hide her i.** procuró ocultar lo irritada que estaba; **it's just one of life's little irritations** es tan sólo una de las pequeñas vicisitudes de la vida **(b)** *Med* irritación *f*

irrupt [ɪ'rʌpt] *vi Formal* irrumpir

irruption [ɪ'rʌpʃən] *n Formal* irrupción *f* (**into** en)

IRS [aɪɑ:'res] *n US* (*abbr* **Internal Revenue Service**) **the I.** *Esp* ≃ la Agencia Tributaria, *Am* ≃ la Dirección General Impositiva

is [ɪz] *3rd person singular of* **be**

ISA ['aɪsə] *n Br* (*abbr* **individual savings account**) ≃ cuenta *f* de ahorro personal

Isaac ['aɪzək] *pr n* Isaac

Isaiah [aɪ'zaɪə] *pr n* Isaías

ISBN [aɪesbi:'en] *n* (*abbr* **International Standard Book Number**) ISBN *m*

ischaemia [ɪs'ki:mɪə] *n Med* isquemia *f*

ischium ['ɪskɪəm] *n Anat* isquion *m*

ISDN [aɪesdi:'en] *Comptr* (*abbr* **Integrated Services Delivery Network**)
1 *n* RDSI *f* ►► ***I. line*** línea *f* RDSI; ***I. modem*** módem *m* RDSI
2 *vt* enviar por RDSI

-ish [ɪʃ] *suffix* **(a)** *(with adjective)* **blueish** azulado(a); **shortish** más bien corto(a), tirando a corto(a) **(b)** *(with time, numbers etc)* **around eightish** cerca de las ocho; **he's fortyish** anda en los cuarenta

isinglass ['aɪzɪŋglɑ:s] *n* cola *f* de pescado, mica *f*

Islam ['ɪzlɑ:m] *n* (el) islam *m*

Islamic [ɪz'læmɪk] *adj* islámico(a)

Islamicist [ɪz'læmɪsɪst] **1** *n (scholar)* islamista *mf*
2 *adj* islamista

Islamist [ɪz'læmɪst] **1** *n* **(a)** *(scholar)* islamista *mf* **(b)** *(fundamentalist)* islamista *mf*
2 *adj* **(a)** *(studies)* islámico(a), islamista **(b)** *(fundamentalist)* islamista

island ['aɪlənd] *n* **(a)** *(in sea, river)* isla *f*; **i. customs** costumbres isleñas *or* de la isla; **an i. nation** una isla-nación; *Fig* **an i. of calm** un remanso **(b)** *(in road)* isleta *f* **(c)** *(for displaying goods)* isla *f*

islander ['aɪləndə(r)] *n* isleño(a) *m,f*

island-hop ['aɪləndhɒp] *vi* ir de isla en isla

isle [aɪl] *n* isla *f* ►► ***the I. of Dogs*** la Isla de los Perros; ***the I. of Man*** la isla de Man; ***the I. of Wight*** la isla de Wight

islet ['aɪlət] *n* islote *m*

ism ['ɪzəm] *n Fam Pej* ismo *m*

isn't ['ɪzənt] = **is not**

ISO [aɪes'əʊ] *n* (*abbr* **International Standards Organization**) ISO *f*, Organización *f* Internacional de Normalización

isobar ['aɪsəʊbɑ:(r)] *n* isobara *f*

isobaric [aɪsəʊ'bærɪk] *adj* isobárico(a)

isogloss ['aɪsəʊglɒs] *n* isoglosa *f*

isolate ['aɪseleɪt] *vt* **(a)** *(separate)* aislar (**from** de); **she isolated herself from other people** se aisló de los demás **(b)** *(identify)* aislar **(c)** *(quarantine)* aislar

isolated ['aɪseleɪtɪd] *adj* **(a)** *(alone, remote)* aislado(a); **to be i. (from)** estar aislado(a) (de) **(b)** *(single)* aislado(a)

isolation [aɪse'leɪʃən] *n* **(a)** *(separation)* aislamiento *m*; **to deal with sth in i.** tratar algo aisladamente **(b)** *(identification)* identificación *f* **(c)** *Med* ***i. ward*** pabellón *m* de enfermedades infecciosas

isolationism [aɪsə'leɪʃənɪzəm] *n Pol* aislacionismo *m*

isolationist [aɪsə'leɪʃənɪst] *Pol* **1** *n* aislacionista *mf*
2 *adj* aislacionista

isomer ['aɪsəmə(r)] *n Chem* isómero *m*

isometric [aɪsə'metrɪk] *adj* **(a)** *(paper)* isométrico(a) **(b)** *(exercise)* isométrico(a)

isometrics [aɪsə'metrɪks] *n* isometría *f*

isomorph ['aɪsəmɔ:f] *n Chem* isomorfo *m*

isomorphic [aɪsəʊ'mɔ:fɪk] *adj Chem* isomorfo(a)

isosceles [aɪ'sɒsɪli:z] *adj* isósceles *inv* ►► ***i. triangle*** triángulo *m* isósceles

isotherm ['aɪsəθɜ:m] *n* isoterma *f*

isothermal [aɪsəʊ'θɜ:məl] *adj* isotérmico(a), isotermo(a)

isotonic [aɪsə'tɒnɪk] *adj (drink)* isotónico(a)

isotope ['aɪsətəʊp] *n Phys* isótopo *m*

isotopic [aɪsəʊ'tɒpɪk] *adj Phys* isótopo(a)

ISP [aɪes'pi:] *n Comptr* (*abbr* **Internet Service Provider**) PSI *m*, proveedor *m* de servicios Internet, proveedor *m* de (acceso a) Internet

I-spy ['aɪ'spaɪ] *n Br* veo-veo *m*; *Hum* **I. with my little eye...** veo-veo...

Israel ['ɪzreɪəl] *n* Israel

Israeli [ɪz'reɪlɪ] **1** *n* israelí *mf*
2 *adj* israelí *mf*

Israelite ['ɪzrəlaɪt] *n Hist* israelita *mf*

issue ['ɪʃu:] **1** *n* **(a)** *(matter, topic)* tema *m*, cuestión *f*; **where do you stand on the abortion i.?** ¿cuál es tu posición acerca del aborto?; **the i. was raised at the meeting** sacaron *or* plantearon el tema en la reunión; **the issues of the day** los temas de actualidad; **it has become an international i.** se ha convertido en un tema de repercusión internacional; **that's not the i.** no se trata de eso; **to avoid** *or* **duck** *or* **evade the i.** evitar el tema; **to cloud** *or* **confuse the i.** complicar el asunto
(b) *(cause of disagreement)* tema *m or* punto *m* de desacuerdo; **to make an i. of sth** hacer de algo un problema; **to take i. with sb** discrepar de alguien; **I take i. with him on only one point** hay sólo un tema en el que no estoy de acuerdo con él; **at i.** en cuestión; **the point at i. is not the coming election** no es de la próxima elección que se habla; **her competence is not at i.** su capacidad no está en cuestión; **to be at i. with sb (over sth)** estar en conflicto con alguien (acerca de algo); IDIOM *US* **to have issues (with sb/sth)** tener problemas (con alguien/algo)
(c) *(result)* **to await the i.** esperar el resultado
(d) *(giving out) (of clothes, rations)* entrega *f*, reparto *m*; *(permit, visa)* entrega *f*, expedición *f*
(e) *(of banknotes, stamps)* emisión *f*; *Fin (of shares, bonds)* emisión *f*;

Navy i. boots botas de la Armada; **jackets were standard i. to prisoners** a todos los presos se les entregaban chaquetas

(**f**) *(of magazine, newspaper)* número *m*; **the latest i. of the magazine** el último número de la revista

(**g**) *(discharge) (of blood, pus)* flujo *m*

(**h**) *Formal (offspring)* descendencia *f*; *Law* **to die without i.** morir sin dejar descendencia

2 *vt* (**a**) *(give out) (banknote, stamp)* emitir, poner en circulación; *(permit, visa)* expedir, entregar; **to i. sb with sth** *(ticket, pass)* proporcionar algo a alguien; *(permit, visa)* expedir *or* entregar algo a alguien; **we were all issued with rations** nos dieron raciones a todos; **the Bank of Scotland issues its own notes** el Banco de Escocia emite sus propios billetes

(**b**) *(order, instructions)* dar; **to i. a statement** emitir un comunicado; **the government has issued a denial** el gobierno ha emitido un desmentido

(**c**) *Law (warrant, writ)* expedir, dictar; **to i. a summons** enviar una citación judicial

3 *vi Formal* (**a**) *(come or go out) (blood)* manar (**from** de); *(noise)* surgir (**from** de); *(smoke)* brotar (**from** de); **delicious smells issued from the kitchen** deliciosos aromas emanaban de la cocina (**b**) *(result, originate)* **to i. from** originarse en, surgir de

▸ **issue forth** *vi Literary* surgir

issuing [ˈɪʃuːɪŋ] *adj* emisor(ora) ▸▸ *Fin* ***i. house*** entidad *f* emisora de acciones en bolsa

Istanbul [ɪstænˈbʊl] *n* Estambul

isthmus [ˈɪsməs] *n* istmo *m*

IT [aɪˈtiː] *n Comptr* (*abbr* **information technology**) tecnologías *fpl* de la información, informática *f*

IT [ɪt] *pron* (**a**) *(subject) (usually omitted in Spanish)* **it is red** es rojo(a); **it escaped** se escapó

(**b**) *(direct object)* lo *m*, la *f*; **I don't want it** no lo/la quiero; **I like it** me gusta; **give it to him** dáselo

(**c**) *(indirect object)* le; **give it something to eat** dale algo de comer

(**d**) *(prepositional object) (masculine)* él; *(feminine)* ella; *(referring to uncountable nouns)* ello; **from it** de él/ella/ello; **with it** con él/ella/ello; **I don't want to talk about it** no quiero hablar de ello; **they gave me half of it** me dieron la mitad; **is there any meat in it?** ¿tiene carne?; **a table with a bowl of fruit on it** una mesa con un frutero encima; **put some newspaper under it** pon papel de periódico debajo

(**e**) *(impersonal uses)* **it's Friday** es viernes; **it's raining** está lloviendo, llueve; **it's ten o'clock** son las diez (en punto); **it's cold today** hoy hace frío; **it's twenty miles to New York** de aquí a Nueva York hay veinte millas; **it says on the packet that...** en el paquete dice que...; **it should be remembered that...** hay que recordar que...; **it seems unlikely** no parece probable; **it is rumoured that...** se rumorea que..., corre el rumor de que...; **it's not that I don't like her** no es que no me caiga bien; **it's his constant complaining I can't stand** lo que no aguanto son sus continuas quejas; **I'll stay in London for a while, because I like it here** me voy a quedar en Londres una temporada, porque me gusta esta ciudad; **I find it easier to use a credit card** me parece más sencillo usar una tarjeta de crédito; **I love it when we go on a picnic** me encanta ir de picnic; **I couldn't bear it if she left** si me dejara no lo podría soportar

(**f**) *(as complement of verb* **to be***)* **who is it?** ¿quién es?; **it's me** soy yo; **who's that? – it's Jack** ¿quién es? – Jack; **it was she who told me** fue ella la que me lo dijo; **that's it for today** eso es todo por hoy

(**g**) *(referring to baby)* **is it a boy or a girl?** ¿es (un) niño o (una) niña?, *RP* ¿es (una) nena o (un) varón?

(**h**) *(certain quality)* **you've either got it or you haven't** se tiene o no se tiene

(**i**) *Fam (in children's games)* **you're it!** ¡tú la llevas!

(**j**) *Fam (sexual intercourse)* **did they do it?** ¿lo hicieron?

(**k**) **that's it!** *(expressing annoyance)* ¡se acabó!; *(after finishing sth)* ¡esto es todo!; *(expressing approval)* ¡así!, ¡muy bien!

(**l**) *Fam (most important person)* **she thinks she's IT** es muy creída ▸▸ *Br* ***it girl*** = joven cuya ocupación es ser famosa

---

Italian [ɪˈtælɪən] 1 *n* (**a**) *(person)* italiano(a) *m,f* (**b**) *(language)* italiano *m*; **I. class/teacher** clase/profesor(ora) de italiano

2 *adj* italiano(a)

Italianate [ɪˈtælɪəneɪt] *adj* de estilo italiano, italianizante

Italianize [ɪˈtælɪənaɪz] *vt* italianizar

italic [ɪˈtælɪk] 1 *n Typ* **italic(s)** cursiva *f*; **in italics** en cursiva; **the italics are mine** *(footnote to quotation)* la cursiva es mía

2 *adj* cursiva

italicize [ɪˈtælɪsaɪz] *vt* poner en cursiva; **the italicized words** las palabras en cursiva *or* bastardilla

Italy [ˈɪtəlɪ] *n* Italia

ITC [aɪtiːˈsiː] *n* (*abbr* **Independent Television Commission**) = organismo regulador de las televisiones privadas británicas

itch [ɪtʃ] 1 *n* (**a**) *(on skin)* picor *m* (**b**) *Fam (desire)* **to have an i. to do sth** tener muchas ganas de hacer algo; IDIOM **if you've got an i., scratch it** si deseas hacer algo, hazlo

2 *vi* (**a**) *(be itchy)* picar; **my leg is itching** me pica la pierna; **I'm itching all over** me pica todo el cuerpo; **this sweater itches terribly** este pulóver pica muchísimo (**b**) *(be eager)* **to be itching to do sth** tener muchas ganas de hacer algo; **to be itching for trouble/a fight** estar deseando meterse en líos/buscar pelea

itchiness [ˈɪtʃɪnɪs] *n* (**a**) *(of skin)* picor *m* (**b**) *(of material)* **I don't wear wool because of its i.** no suelo usar lana porque pica

itching [ˈɪtʃɪŋ] *n* picor *m* ▸▸ ***i. powder*** polvos *mpl* (de) picapica

itchy [ˈɪtʃɪ] *adj* **to be i.** picar; **I've got an i. hand, my hand's i.** me pica la mano; **this material is very i.** esta tela pica mucho; IDIOM **to have i. feet: he has always had i. feet** nunca le ha gustado estar mucho tiempo en un sitio; **I'm beginning to get i. feet** ya me están entrando ganas de irme a otro sitio

it'd [ˈɪtəd] (**a**) = **it had** (**b**) = **it would**

item [ˈaɪtəm] 1 *n* (**a**) *(object) (in collection, on display)* artículo *m*; **the items in the shop window** los artículos de la vidriera; **an i. of clothing** una prenda de vestir; **personal items** objetos personales

(**b**) *(on list, agenda)* punto *m*; **there are two important items on the agenda** hay dos puntos importantes en la agenda; **I've several items of business to attend to** me tengo que ocupar de varias cosas de trabajo

(**c**) *Journ, TV & Rad* noticia *f*; **there was an i. on the news about it yesterday** ayer salió una noticia acerca de eso; **and here are today's main news items** y a continuación las principales noticias *or* los principales titulares del día

(**d**) *Comptr (on menu)* ítem *m*

(**e**) *Fam* **they're an i.** salen juntos; **they're no longer an i.** ya no salen (juntos)

2 *adv Old-fashioned (when listing)* ítem

itemize [ˈaɪtəmaɪz] *vt* (**a**) *(contents)* hacer una lista de (**b**) *(bill, list)* detallar

iterate [ˈɪtəreɪt] *vt Comptr & Math* iterar, repetir

iterative [ˈɪtərətɪv] *adj Comptr & Math* iterativo(a)

itinerant [ɪˈtɪnərənt] *adj* itinerante

itinerary [aɪˈtɪnərərɪ] *n* itinerario *m*

it'll [ˈɪtəl] = **it will**

ITN [aɪtiːˈen] *n Br* (*abbr* **Independent Television News**) = servicio de noticias del canal privado de televisión ITV

ITO [aɪtiːˈəʊ] *n* (*abbr* **International Trade Organization**) OIC *f*

its [ɪts] 1 *possessive adj (singular)* su; *(plural)* sus; **the lion returned to i. den** el león volvió a su guarida; **the bear hurt i. paw** el oso se hizo daño en la zarpa; **the plane lost one of i. engines** el avión perdió uno de los motores

2 *possessive pron* el suyo, la suya; **the dog can't eat chocolate so I'll have i.** el perro no puede comer chocolate así que me comeré el suyo *or* que le toca a él

it's [ɪts] (**a**) = **it is** (**b**) = **it has**

itself [ɪtˈself] *pron* (**a**) *(reflexive)* se; **the dog hurt i.** el perro se hizo daño; **the company has got i. into debt** la empresa se ha endeudado; **the dog saw i. reflected in the water** el perro se vio reflejado en el agua

(**b**) *(emphatic)* **this method is simplicity i.** este método es la sencillez misma; **she was politeness i.** era la educación personificada; **the town i. isn't very interesting** la ciudad en sí (misma) no es muy interesante

(**c**) *(after preposition)* **by/in i.** por/en sí mismo(a); **the house stands by i. at the end of the street** es la única casa al final de la calle; **the delay in i. isn't a problem, but...** el retraso *or Am* la demora en sí no supone un problema, pero...

itsy-bitsy [ˈɪtsɪˈbɪtsɪ], *US* **itty-bitty** [ˈɪtɪˈbɪtɪ] *adj Fam* chiquitito(a), pequeñito(a)

ITV [aɪtiːˈviː] *n* (*abbr* **Independent Television**) = canal privado de televisión británico

IUD [aɪjuːˈdiː] *n Med* (*abbr* **intra-uterine device**) DIU *m*

IV [aɪ'viː] *Med* (*abbr* **intravenous**) **1** *adj* intravenoso(a) ►► ***IV drip*** gota a gota *m*
2 *n Fam (IV drip)* gota a gota *m*

Ivan ['aɪvən] *pr n* **I. the Terrible** Iván el Terrible

I've [aɪv] = **I have**

IVF [aɪviː'ef] *n Med* (*abbr* **in vitro fertilization**) fertilización *f* in vitro

ivied ['aɪvɪd] *adj* cubierto(a) de hiedra

ivory ['aɪvərɪ] **1** *n* (**a**) *(substance)* marfil *m* ►► ***the I. Coast*** la Costa de Marfil; ***i. nut*** marfil *m* vegetal; *Fig* ***i. tower*** torre *f* de marfil (**b**) *(colour)* color *m* marfil
2 *adj* (**a**) *(made of ivory)* de marfil (**b**) *(ivory-coloured)* color marfil, marfil

ivy ['aɪvɪ] *n (plant)* hiedra *f*; *US* **the halls of i.** el mundo académico ►► *US* ***I. League*** = grupo de ocho universidades de gran prestigio del nordeste de Estados Unidos

J, j

J, j [dʒeɪ] *n (letter)* J, j *f*

J *Elec* (*abbr* **Joule(s)**) J

jab [dʒæb] **1** *n* (**a**) *(with elbow)* codazo *m*; *(with finger)* movimiento *m* seco (**b**) *(in boxing)* golpe *m* corto, directo *m* (**c**) *Br Fam (injection)* inyección *f*, pinchazo *m*; **I've got to get a tetanus j.** me tengo que vacunar contra el tétano

2 *vt* (*pt & pp* **jabbed**) (**a**) *(poke, prick)* **he jabbed her in the leg with a pencil** le clavó un lápiz en la pierna; **he nearly jabbed my eye out!** ¡casi me saca un ojo! (**b**) *(thrust)* **to j. a finger at sb** señalar a alguien con el dedo

3 *vi* (**a**) *(poke, prick)* **he jabbed at me with a stick** me pinchó con un palo; **to j. at sb with a knife** herir a alguien con un cuchillo; **to j. at sb with an umbrella** clavarle el paraguas a alguien (**b**) *(in boxing)* tirar *or* echar un jab (**at** a); **he feinted with his right then jabbed with his left** amagaba con la derecha y luego tiraba un jab de izquierda

jabber ['dʒæbə(r)] *Fam* **1** *vi* parlotear; **they were all jabbering away in different languages** estaban todos parloteando en distintos idiomas

2 *vt* **to j. (out)** mascullar

3 *n (noise)* ruido *m*, barullo *m*

jacana [dʒə'kɑːnə] *n* jacana *f*

jacaranda [dʒækə'rændə] *n Bot* jacarandá *m*

Jack [dʒæk] *n* IDIOM *Br Fam* **before you could say J. Robinson** en menos que canta un gallo, antes de que puedas decir esta boca es mía; IDIOM *Br Fam* **he's a real J. the Lad** es un mujeriego ►► ***J. Frost*** la escarcha, la helada; ***J. the Ripper*** Jack el Destripador; ***J. Russell (terrier)*** Jack Russell (terrier) *m*; *Br Old-fashioned* ***J. Tar*** lobo *m* de mar

jack [dʒæk] *n* (**a**) *(person)* **every man j. of them** todo quisque

(**b**) *(for car)* gato *m*

(**c**) *(in cards)* jota *f*; *(in Spanish cards)* sota *f*

(**d**) *Elec (plug)* clavija *f*, ficha *f*; *(socket)* clavijero *m* ►► ***j. plug*** enchufe *m* macho, enchufe *m* de clavija

(**e**) *(in bowls)* boliche *m*

(**f**) **jacks** *(game)* tabas *fpl*

(**g**) ***j. rabbit*** *(North American hare)* liebre *f* americana

(**h**) *Vulg* **j. shit** un carajo; **he knows j. shit about it** no tiene ni puta idea del tema

►**jack around** *US Fam* **1** *vt sep* **to j. sb around** *(treat badly)* maltratar, *Urug* botijear; *(waste time of)* hacer perder el tiempo a alguien, enrollar a alguien; **stop jacking me around — just tell me what I want to know** no me hagas perder más el tiempo – sólo dime lo que quiero saber

2 *vi (waste time)* perder el tiempo, *RP* boludear

►**jack in** *vt sep Br Fam (job)* dejar, largar

►**jack off** *Vulg* **1** *vt sep* **to j. sb off** hacer una *or Am* la paja a alguien

2 *vi* hacerse una *or Am* la paja

►**jack up** **1** *vt sep* (**a**) *(car)* levantar (con el gato) (**b**) *Fam (price, salaries)* subir

2 *vi Br Fam (inject oneself)* inyectarse

jackal ['dʒækəl] *n* (**a**) *(animal)* chacal *m* (**b**) *(henchman)* secuaz *m*

jackass ['dʒækæs] *n* (**a**) *(male donkey)* burro *m*, asno *m* (**b**) *Fam (person)* burro(a) *m,f*, animal *mf*

jackboot ['dʒækbuːt] *n* bota *f* militar; *Fig* **under the j. of a military dictatorship** bajo el yugo de una dictadura militar; **j. tactics** tácticas dictatoriales

jackbooted ['dʒækbuːtɪd] *adj* con botas hasta la rodilla

jackdaw ['dʒækdɔː] *n* grajilla *f*

jacket ['dʒækɪt] *n* (**a**) *(coat) (formal)* chaqueta *f*, americana *f*, *Am* saco *m*; *(casual)* cazadora *f*, *CSur* campera *f*, *Méx* chamarra *f*

(**b**) *Culin* **j. potatoes, potatoes (cooked) in their jackets** = *Esp* patatas *or Am* papas asadas con piel que se suelen comer con un relleno

(**c**) *(of book)* sobrecubierta *f*

(**d**) *US (of record)* funda *f*

(**e**) *(of boiler)* funda *f*

(**f**) *(of bullet)* camisa *f*

jackfruit ['dʒækfruːt] *n* nanjea *f*, jaca *f*

jackhammer ['dʒækhæmə(r)] *n* martillo *m* neumático

jack-in-office [dʒækɪn'ɒfɪs] *n Br Pej* funcionario(a) *m,f* de tres al cuarto

jack-in-the-box ['dʒækɪnðəbɒks] *n* caja *f* sorpresa; IDIOM *Fam* **to jump up and down like a j.** ir para arriba y para abajo como un muñeco de resortes

jackknife **1** ['dʒæknaɪf] *n* (**a**) *(knife)* navaja *f* (**b**) **j. (dive)** salto *m* de carpa

2 *vi (articulated lorry)* hacer la tijera, derrapar por el remolque

jack-of-all-trades ['dʒækəv'ɔːltreɪdz] *n* **he's a j.** hace *or* sabe hacer un poco de todo; IDIOM **to be a j., and master of none** saber un poco de todo (y mucho de nada)

jack-o'-lantern ['dʒækə'læntən] *n US (Hallowe'en lantern)* = farolillo hecho con una calabaza hueca y una vela dentro

jackpot ['dʒækpɒt] *n (in lottery, card games)* (premio *m*) gordo *m*; **he hit** *or* **won the j.** le tocó el gordo; **she hit the j. with her latest book/film** con su último libro/última película se sacó la lotería

jacksie, jacksy ['dʒæksɪ] *n Br Fam* (**a**) *(buttocks) Esp* culo *m*, *Am* cola *f* (**b**) *(anus)* ojete *m*, ojo *m* del culo

jackstraws ['dʒækstrɔːz] *n* palitos *mpl* chinos, mikado *m*

Jacob ['dʒeɪkəb] *n (in Bible)* Jacob ►► ***J.'s ladder*** *(plant)* valeriana *f* griega

Jacobean [dʒækə'bɪən] *adj* jacobino(a), = relativo al periodo del reinado de Jacobo I de Inglaterra (1603-1625)

Jacobin ['dʒækəbɪn] *Hist* **1** *n* jacobino(a) *m,f*

2 *adj* jacobino(a)

Jacobite ['dʒækəbaɪt] **1** *n* jacobita *mf*

2 *adj* jacobita

Jacuzzi® [dʒə'kuːzɪ] *n* jacuzzi® *m*

jade[1] [dʒeɪd] **1** *n (stone)* jade *m*; *(colour)* verde *m* jade

2 *adj (colour)* verde jade

jade[2] *n Archaic* (**a**) *(horse)* jamelgo *m* (**b**) *(woman)* mujerzuela *f*

jaded ['dʒeɪdɪd] *adj* hastiado(a); **this is something to tempt even the most j. of palates** esto tentará incluso a aquellos que ya lo han probado todo

Jag [dʒæg] *n Fam (car)* Jaguar *m*

jag [dʒæg] *Fam* **1** *n* (**a**) *(bout)* **to go on a (drinking) j.** ir de borrachera; **he had a crying j.** le dio la llorera (**b**) *Scot (injection)* pinchazo *m*

2 *vt* (*pt & pp* **jagged**) *(prick)* pinchar

jagged ['dʒægɪd] *adj (coastline)* accidentado(a); *(rock)* irregular; *(crest)* escarpado(a); *(blade)* dentado(a)

jaguar [*Br* 'dʒægjʊə(r), *US* 'dʒægwɑː(r)] *n* jaguar *m*

jai alai [dʒaɪə'laɪ] *n US* pelota *f* vasca, cesta *f* punta

jail [dʒeɪl] **1** *n* cárcel *f*; **to be in j.** estar en la cárcel; **to go to j.** ir a la cárcel

2 *vt* encarcelar; **he was jailed for ten years** le condenaron a diez años de cárcel

jailbait ['dʒeɪlbeɪt] *n very Fam* **she's j.** es menor y puede meterte en líos

jailbird ['dʒeɪlbɜːd] *n Fam* preso(a) *m,f* reincidente

jailbreak ['dʒeɪlbreɪk] *n* fuga *f*, evasión *f*

jailer, jailor ['dʒeɪlə(r)] *n (in prison)* carcelero(a) *m,f*; *(of hostages)* captor(ora) *m,f*

jailhouse ['dʒeɪlhaʊs] *n US* cárcel *f*

jailor = **jailer**

Jakarta, Djakarta [dʒəˈkɑːtə] *n* Yakarta

jalop(p)y [dʒəˈlɒpɪ] *n Fam* cacharro *m*, cafetera *f*

jam[1] **1** [dʒæm] *n* (**a**) *(crowd) (of people)* muchedumbre *f*, multitud *f*; **traffic j.** atasco, embotellamiento (**b**) *Fam (difficult situation)* **to be in/get into a j.** estar/meterse en un aprieto (**c**) *(improvised performance)* **j. (session)** jam-session *f*, = sesión improvisada de jazz o rock

2 *vt* (*pt & pp* **jammed**) (**a**) *(pack tightly) (objects)* embutir (**into** en); *(container)* atestar (**with** de); **we were jammed in like sardines** estábamos (apretados) como sardinas en lata; **I was jammed (up) against the wall** (yo) estaba aplastado contra la pared

(**b**) *(ram)* encajar, clavar; **she jammed her hat on** se encasquetó el sombrero; **to j. one's foot on the brake(s)** pisar fuerte el freno

(**c**) *(block) (radio broadcast, station)* provocar interferencias en; *(switchboard)* bloquear; **traffic jammed the streets** el tráfico colapsaba las calles

(**d**) *(make stick) (gun, mechanism)* atascar, trabar; **something has jammed the mechanism** algo ha trabado el mecanismo; **the drawer is jammed** el cajón se ha atascado; **he jammed the window open** enganchó *or* trabó la ventana para que quedara abierta

3 *vi* (**a**) *(crowd)* apiñarse; **people jammed into the hall** la gente se apiñaba en la sala (**b**) *(stick) (drawer, window, machine)* atascarse, *Am* trancarse; *(gun)* encasquillarse; *(brakes, paper in printer)* atascarse, *Am* trancarse (**c**) *Mus* improvisar *(con un grupo)*

►**jam in** **1** *vt sep* (**a**) *(wedge in)* meter; **the crowd were jamming him in** la multitud lo empujaba hacia adentro; **her car was jammed in by a large truck** un camión enorme se le incrustó en el auto (**b**) *(pack or press tightly in)* meter; **I only had one bag and managed to j. in all my clothes** sólo tenía un bolso y me las arreglé para meter toda la ropa

2 *vi (crowd in)* apretujarse; **we all managed to j. in somehow** de alguna manera todos logramos apretujarnos adentro

►**jam on** *vt sep* **to j. on the brakes** frenar en seco

jam[2] *n* (**a**) *(fruit preserve)* mermelada *f*; **strawberry j.** mermelada de fresas *or Bol, CSur, Ecuad* frutillas; **raspberry j.** mermelada de frambuesa ►► ***j. jar*** tarro *m* de mermelada; ***j. tart*** pastel *m or Col, CSur* torta *f* de mermelada (**b**) IDIOMS *Br* **it's a case of j. tomorrow** no son más que vanas promesas; *Br* **to want j. on it** quererlo todo

Jamaica [dʒəˈmeɪkə] *n* Jamaica

Jamaican [dʒəˈmeɪkən] **1** *n* jamaicano(a) *m,f*

2 *adj* jamaicano(a)

jamb [dʒæm] *n* jamba *f*

jamboree [dʒæmbəˈriː] *n* (**a**) *(scouts' meeting)* encuentro *m* de boy-scouts (**b**) *Fam (celebration)* jolgorio *m*, fiesta *f*

James [dʒeɪmz] *pr n* **J. I/II** Jacobo I/II (de Inglaterra)

jamming [ˈdʒæmɪŋ] *n Rad* interferencias *fpl*

jammy [ˈdʒæmɪ] *adj* (**a**) *(covered with jam)* cubierto(a) de mermelada (**b**) *Br Fam (lucky)* suertudo(a); **you j. thing!** ¡qué potra *or Méx* chance *or RP* tarro tienes!

jam-packed [ˈdʒæmˈpækd] *adj* **to be j. (with)** estar atestado(a) *or* abarrotado(a) (de); **this magazine is j. with interesting articles** esta revista está repleta de artículos interesantes

Jan (*abbr* **January**) ene.

Jane Doe [ˈdʒeɪnˈdəʊ] *n US* (**a**) *(average person)* la estadounidense media (**b**) *(unidentified woman)* = nombre con el que se hace referencia a una desconocida

jangle [ˈdʒæŋgəl] **1** *n (of keys, chain)* tintineo *m*

2 *vt (keys, chain)* hacer tintinear

3 *vi (keys, chain)* tintinear; *Fig* **her voice made his nerves j.** su voz le ponía los nervios de punta

jangly [ˈdʒæŋglɪ] *adj (keys, chain)* tintineante

janitor [ˈdʒænɪtə(r)] *n* (**a**) *US, Scot (caretaker)* conserje *m*, bedel *m* (**b**) *(doorkeeper)* portero(a) *m,f*

Jansenism [ˈdʒænsənɪzəm] *n Rel* jansenismo *m*

Jansenist [ˈdʒænsənɪst] *Rel* **1** *adj* jansenista

2 *n* jansenista *mf*

January [ˈdʒænjʊərɪ] *n* enero *m*; *see also* **May**

Janus [ˈdʒeɪnəs] *n* Jano *m*

JAP [dʒæp] *n US Fam* (*abbr* **Jewish American Princess**) niña *f* bien *or Esp* pija judía

Jap [dʒæp] *Fam* **1** *n* = término ofensivo para referirse a los japoneses, *RP* ponja *mf*

2 *adj* japonés(esa), *RP* ponja

Japan [dʒəˈpæn] *n* Japón

Japanese [dʒæpəˈniːz] **1** *n* (**a**) *(person)* japonés(esa) *m,f* (**b**) *(language)* japonés *m*; **J. class/teacher** clase/profesor(ora) de japonés

2 *npl* **the J.** los japoneses

3 *adj* japonés(esa)

japanned [dʒəˈpænd] *adj* lacado(a)

jape [dʒeɪp] *n* broma *f*

japonica [dʒəˈpɒnɪkə] *n Bot* membrillo *m* japonés

jar[1] [dʒɑː(r)] **1** *n (jolt, shock)* sacudida *f*; **the news gave him a nasty j.** la noticia supuso una desagradable sorpresa para él

2 *vt* (*pt & pp* **jarred**) *(knock)* sacudir, golpear; *Fig (surprise)* alterar, sacudir

3 *vi* (**a**) *(make unpleasant sound)* rechinar; **to j. on the ears** rechinar en los oídos; **to j. on the nerves** crispar los nervios (**b**) *(clash)* **to j. (with each other)** *(colours)* desentonar; *(ideas)* chocar (entre sí)

jar[2] *n* (**a**) *(container)* tarro *m* (**b**) *Br Fam (beer)* **to have a j.** tomarse una birra

jardinière [ʒɑːdɪˈnjeə(r)] *n* (**a**) *(ornamental plant pot)* jardinera *f* (**b**) *Culin (mixed vegetables)* jardinera *f*

jargon [ˈdʒɑːgən] *n Pej* jerga *f*; **to talk (in) j.** hablar en jerga

jarring [ˈdʒɑːrɪŋ] *adj (noise, voice)* estridente; *(blow)* contundente

jasmine [ˈdʒæzmɪn] *n (plant)* jazmín *m*

jasper [ˈdʒæspə(r)] *n (stone)* jaspe *m*

jaundice [ˈdʒɔːndɪs] *n Med* ictericia *f*

jaundiced [ˈdʒɔːndɪst] *adj (attitude, opinion)* negativo(a), resentido(a); **to look on things with a j. eye** ver las cosas desde una posición muy negativa

jaunt [dʒɔːnt] *n* excursión *f*, paseo *m*; **to go on** *or* **for a j.** ir de excursión *or* paseo

jauntily [ˈdʒɔːntɪlɪ] *adv* desenfadadamente

jauntiness [ˈdʒɔːntɪnɪs] *n* desenfado *m*

jaunty [ˈdʒɔːntɪ] *adj* desenfadado(a); **he wore his cap at a j. angle** llevaba la gorra torcida, con desenfado

Java[1] [ˈdʒɑːvə] *n (island)* Java

Java[2]® *nm Comptr* Java®; **J. script** lenguaje Java

java [ˈdʒɑːvə] *n US Fam (coffee)* café *m*

Javanese [dʒɑːvəˈniːz] **1** *n* (**a**) *(person)* javanés(esa) *m,f* (**b**) *(language)* javanés *m*

2 *npl* **the J.** los javaneses

3 *adj* javanés(esa)

javelin [ˈdʒævlɪn] *n* (**a**) *(weapon, in sport)* jabalina *f* (**b**) *(sporting event)* lanzamiento *m* de jabalina

jaw [dʒɔː] **1** *n* (**a**) *(of person, animal)* mandíbula *f*; **jaws** fauces *fpl*; **his j. dropped** se quedó boquiabierto; IDIOM **the jaws of death** las garras de la muerte; IDIOM **to snatch victory from the jaws of defeat** dar vuelta un resultado (**b**) **jaws** *(of tool)* mordaza *f* (**c**) *Fam (chat)* **to have a good old j.** tener una buena charla (**d**) *(of snooker, pool pocket)* borde *m* del agujero

2 *vi Fam (chat)* charlar, *CAm, Méx* platicar

jawbone [ˈdʒɔːbəʊn] **1** *n* maxilar *m* inferior

2 *vt US Fam* presionar

jawbreaker [ˈdʒɔːbreɪkə(r)] *n Fam* (**a**) *(unpronounceable word)* trabalenguas *m inv* (**b**) *(sweet)* caramelo *m* duro

jawline [ˈdʒɔːlaɪn] *n* mentón *m*

jay [dʒeɪ] *n* arrendajo *m*

jaywalk [ˈdʒeɪwɔːk] *vi* cruzar la calle sin prudencia

jaywalker [ˈdʒeɪwɔːkə(r)] *n* peatón(ona) *m,f* imprudente

jaywalking [ˈdʒeɪwɔːkɪŋ] *n* imprudencia *f* peatonal

jazz [dʒæz] *n* (**a**) *(music)* jazz *m*; **j. band** banda de jazz; **j. trumpeter** trompetista de jazz (**b**) *Fam (rigmarole)* lío *m*, *Esp* follón *m*, *RP* historia *f*; **and all that j.** y otras cosas por el estilo, *Esp* y todo el rollo, *RP* y toda esa historia

►**jazz up** *vt sep Fam* (**a**) *(music, song)* sincopar, jazzear; **to j. up a song** jazzear una canción *or* un tema; **it's jazzed up Beethoven** es una versión popular de Beethoven (**b**) *(enliven)* animar

jazzy [ˈdʒæzɪ] *adj* (**a**) *(tune)* jazzístico(a) (**b**) *(clothes, pattern)* llamativo(a)

JCB® [dʒeɪsiːˈbiː] *n Br* pala *f* excavadora

JCR [dʒeɪsiːˈɑː(r)] *n Br Univ* (*abbr* **junior common room**) sala *f* de estudiantes

jealous [ˈdʒeləs] *adj* (**a**) *(envious)* envidioso(a); **to be j. of sb** tener envidia de alguien; **he just wants to make you j.** sólo quiere darte envidia

(**b**) *(possessive) (lover, husband)* celoso(a); **to make sb j.** hacer

poner celoso(a) a alguien; **he gets terribly j.** le entran unos celos terribles; **a j. God** un Dios celoso
(**c**) *(protective)* **she is j. of her reputation** es celosa de su reputación, vela por su reputación

jealously ['dʒeləslɪ] *adv* (**a**) *(enviously)* con envidia (**b**) *(possessively)* celosamente (**c**) *(protectively)* **a j. guarded secret** un secreto celosamente guardado

jealousy ['dʒeləsɪ] *n* (**a**) *(envy)* envidia *f* (**b**) *(possessiveness)* celos *mpl*; **a fit of j.** un ataque de celos

jeans [dʒiːnz] *npl* (pantalones *mpl*) vaqueros *mpl*, *Col* bluejeans *mpl*, *Méx* pantalones *mpl* de mezclilla, *Ven* bluyín *m*; **a pair of j.** unos (pantalones) vaqueros

Jeep® [dʒiːp] *n* todoterreno *m*, jeep *m*

jeepers ['dʒiːpəz] *exclam US Fam* **j. (creepers)** ¡caramba!, *Esp* ¡jolín!

jeer [dʒɪə(r)] **1** *n (boo)* abucheo *m*; *(derision)* burla *f*
2 *vt (boo)* abuchear; *(mock)* burlarse de
3 *vi (boo)* abuchear (**at** a); *(mock)* burlarse (**at** de)

jeering ['dʒɪərɪŋ] **1** *n (booing)* abucheo *m*; *(mocking)* burlas *fpl*
2 *adj* burlón(ona)

Jeez, Jeeze [dʒiːz] *exclam Fam* ¡caray!

Jehovah [dʒɪ'həʊvə] *n* Jehová ►► ***J.'s Witness*** testigo *mf* de Jehová

jejune [dʒə'dʒuːn] *adj Formal* (**a**) *(dull, banal)* tedioso(a), vacuo(a) (**b**) *(naive)* pueril

jejunum [dʒə'dʒuːnəm] *n Anat* yeyuno *m*

Jekyll and Hyde ['dʒekələn'haɪd] *adj* esquizoide; **to have a J. personality** tener doble personalidad

jell [dʒel] *vi* (**a**) *(liquid)* aglutinarse (**b**) *Fig (ideas, plans, team)* cuajar

jellied ['dʒelɪd] *adj Culin* en gelatina; **j. eels** anguilas en gelatina

Jell-O®, **jello** ['dʒeləʊ] *n US* gelatina *f*, jalea *f*

jelly ['dʒelɪ] *n* (**a**) *Br (dessert)* gelatina *f*, jalea *f*; **to turn to j.** volverse de mantequilla; **my legs just turned to j.** se me aflojaron las piernas (**b**) *esp US (jam)* mermelada *f*, confitura *f* ►► *US* ***j. roll*** brazo *m* de gitano (**c**) *Br* ***j. baby*** *(sweet)* = pastilla de goma en forma de niño; ***j. bean*** pastilla *f* de goma, *Esp* gominola *f* (**d**) *Fam (gelignite)* gelignita *f* (explosiva) (**e**) *Br (drug)* = pastilla de temazepam

jellyfish ['dʒelɪfɪʃ] (*pl* **jellyfish** *or* **jellyfishes**) *n* medusa *f*, *Col, Méx* aguamala *f*, *RP* aguaviva *f*

jemmy [dʒemɪ], *US* **jimmy** ['dʒɪmɪ] **1** *n* palanqueta *f*
2 *vt* **to j. the door (open)** forzar la puerta con una palanqueta (para abrirla)

je ne sais quoi [ʒənəseɪ'kwɑː] *n* **to have a certain j.** tener un no sé qué

jeopardize ['dʒepədaɪz] *vt* poner en peligro

jeopardy ['dʒepədɪ] *n* **in j.** en peligro; **to put sth/sb in j.** poner en peligro algo/a alguien

jerboa [dʒɜː'bəʊə] *n* jerbo *m*, gerbo *m*

jeremiad [dʒerə'maɪəd] *n Literary* jeremiada *f*

Jeremiah [dʒerə'maɪə] *pr n also Fig* Jeremías

Jericho ['dʒerɪkəʊ] *n* Jericó

jerk[1] [dʒɜːk] **1** *n* (**a**) *(sudden movement)* sacudida *f*; **with a j. of his head he indicated that I should leave** con un brusco movimiento de la cabeza indicó que me tenía que ir; **the train came to a halt with a j.** el tren se detuvo con una sacudida; **to wake up with a j.** despertarse con un sobresalto (**b**) *(pull)* tirón *m*; **to give sth a j.** sacudir algo (**c**) *(in weightlifting)* envión *m*, segundo tiempo *m*
2 *vt* (**a**) *(move suddenly)* sacudir (**b**) *(pull) (once)* dar un tirón a; *(in order to move)* mover a tirones; **he jerked the door open** abrió la puerta de un tirón; IDIOM *US Fam* **to j. sb's chain** *(tease)* tomar el pelo a alguien; *(bring under control)* cortar las alas a alguien
3 *vi* **to j. awake** despertarse con un sobresalto; **to j. forward** *(car)* dar una sacudida hacia delante; *(head)* caer hacia delante; **to j. to a halt** detenerse con una sacudida; **the train jerked violently from side to side** el tren se sacudía violentamente de un lado a otro

► **jerk around** *vt sep US Fam* **to j. sb around** tomar a alguien *Esp* por el pito del sereno *or Méx* de botana *or RP* para la joda

► **jerk off** *Vulg* **1** *vt sep (masturbate)* **to j. sb off** hacer una *or Am* la paja a alguien
2 *vi* hacerse una *or Am* la paja

jerk[2] *n Fam (person)* imbécil *mf*, majadero(a) *m,f*

jerkily ['dʒɜːkɪlɪ] *adv (to move)* a sacudidas; *(to speak)* entrecortadamente

jerkin ['dʒɜːkɪn] *n (sleeveless jacket)* chaqueta *f* sin mangas; *Hist* jubón *m*

jerk-off ['dʒɜːkɒf] *n US Vulg* cabrón(ona) *m,f*

jerkwater ['dʒɜːkwɔːtə(r)] *adj US Fam* de mala muerte; **a j. town** un pueblo de mala muerte

jerky[1] ['dʒɜːkɪ] *adj* (**a**) *(movement)* brusco(a); *(speech)* entrecortado(a); **a j. ride** un viaje a los saltos; IDIOM **things got off to a j. start** las cosas empezaron a andar a los tumbos (**b**) *US Fam (contemptible)* estúpido(a), imbécil; **what a j. thing to do/say** qué estupidez hacer/decir eso

jerky[2] *n US* tasajo *m*, cecina *f*

jerrican, jerry can ['dʒerɪkæn] *n* bidón *m*

Jerry ['dʒerɪ] *n Br Fam* cabeza cuadrada *mf*, = término a veces ofensivo para referirse a los alemanes

jerry-built ['dʒerɪbɪlt] *adj* chapucero(a)

jerry can = **jerrican**

Jersey ['dʒɜːzɪ] *n* (**a**) *(island)* Jersey (**b**) **J. (cow)** vaca *f* de Jersey (**c**) *US Fam (New Jersey)* Nueva Jersey

jersey ['dʒɜːzɪ] *n* (**a**) *(garment)* suéter *m*, *Esp* jersey *m*, *Col* saco *m*, *RP* pulóver *m* (**b**) *(in sport)* camiseta *f* (**c**) *(in cycling)* maillot *m*; **the green/yellow j.** el maillot verde/amarillo; **the polka-dot j.** el maillot de lunares (**d**) *(fabric)* tejido *m* de punto, *Am* jersey *m*

Jerusalem [dʒə'ruːsələm] *n* Jerusalén ►► ***J. artichoke*** aguaturma *f*, cotufa *f*

jest [dʒest] **1** *n* broma *f*; **in j.** en broma, de broma; **half in j.** medio en broma medio en serio
2 *vi* bromear

jester ['dʒestə(r)] *n* bufón *m*

jesting ['dʒestɪŋ] *adj (remark, tone)* de broma

Jesuit ['dʒezjʊɪt] **1** *n* jesuita *m*
2 *adj (church, priest)* jesuita; *(education)* jesuítica

Jesuitical [dʒezjʊ'ɪtɪkəl] *adj Pej (argument, reasoning)* retorcido(a), jesuítico(a)

Jesus ['dʒiːzəs] *n* (**a**) *Rel* Jesús *m* ►► ***J. Christ*** Jesucristo *m*; *Fam Pej* ***J. freak*** hippy *mf* cristiano(a); *Br Fam* ***J. sandals*** sandalias *fpl* (**b**) *Fam (in exclamations)* **J. (Christ)!** ¡Santo Dios!; **J. wept!** *Esp* ¡(la) leche!, *Col, RP* ¡miércoles!, *Méx* ¡híjole!; *US* **J. H. Christ!** ¡Dios Santo!

jet[1] [dʒet] **1** *n* (**a**) *(plane)* reactor *m*, avión *m* a reacción ►► ***j. engine*** motor *m* de reacción, reactor *m*; ***j. fighter*** caza *m*; ***j. lag*** desfase *m* horario, jet-lag *m*; ***j. propulsion*** propulsión *f* a reacción *or* a chorro; ***the j. set*** *Esp* la jet(-set), *Am* el jet-set; ***j. ski*** moto *f* náutica *or* acuática; ***j. stream*** corriente *f* en chorro (**b**) *(of liquid, steam, gas)* chorro *m* (**c**) *(nozzle)* boquilla *f*
2 *vt Fam* (*pt & pp* **jetted**) *(transport by jet)* llevar en avión; **supplies are being jetted into** *or* **to the disaster area** las provisiones se están mandando por avión a la zona del desastre
3 *vi* (**a**) *Fam (travel by plane)* **to j. in/off** llegar/salir en avión (**b**) *(liquid)* salir a chorros *or* en un chorro; **the fuel jetted across the room before catching fire** un chorro de combustible atravesó la sala antes de encenderse

jet[2] **1** *n (stone)* azabache *m*
2 *adj* **j. (black)** (negro) azabache

jet-black ['dʒet'blæk] *adj* negro azabache

jetfoil ['dʒetfɔɪl] *n* alíscafo *m* de pasajeros con motor a reacción

jet-lagged ['dʒetlægd] *adj* afectado(a) por el desfase horario, con jet-lag; **I'm still a bit j.** todavía tengo un poco de jet-lag

jetliner ['dʒetlaɪnə(r)] *n* jet *m* comercial

jet-powered [dʒet'paʊəd], **jet-propelled** [dʒetprə'peld] *adj* a reacción

jetsam ['dʒetsəm] *n* restos *mpl* del naufragio *(sobre la arena)*

jet-setter ['dʒetsetə(r)] *n* integrante *mf* de la jet(-set)

jettison ['dʒetɪsən] *vt* (**a**) *(bombs, cargo, fuel) (from ship)* tirar *or* echar *or Andes, CAm, Carib, Méx* botar por la borda; *(from plane)* lanzar (**b**) *(unwanted possession)* tirar *or* echar *or Am* botar por la borda; *(theory, belief, principle)* deshacerse de, liberarse de

jetty ['dʒetɪ] *n* (**a**) *(landing stage)* malecón *m*; *(breakwater)* espigón *m* (**b**) *(for boarding aircraft)* pasarela *f or* manga *f* telescópica

Jew [dʒuː] *n* (**a**) *(Hebrew)* judío(a) *m,f* ►► ***J.'s harp*** birimbao *m*, guimbarda *f* (**b**) *Old-fashioned Pej (miser)* judío(a) *m,f*

Jew-baiter ['dʒuːbeɪtə(r)] *n* = persona que persigue a los judíos

Jew-baiting ['dʒuːbeɪtɪŋ] *n* persecución *f* de judíos

jewel ['dʒuːəl] *n* (**a**) *(gem, piece of jewellery)* joya *f*, alhaja *f*; *(in watch)* rubí *m*; **j. box** *or* **case** alhajero; *Fig* **the j. in the crown** la joya de la corona (**b**) *(person, thing)* joya *f*

jeweller, *US* **jeweler** ['dʒuːələ(r)] *n* joyero(a) *m,f*; **j.'s (shop)** joyería *f*

jewellery, *US* **jewelry** ['dʒuːəlrɪ] *n* joyas *fpl*, alhajas *fpl*; **a piece of j.** una joya *or* alhaja ▸▸ ***j. box*** joyero *m*

Jewess [dʒuː'es] *n Old-fashioned* judía *f*

Jewish ['dʒuːɪʃ] *adj* judío(a)

Jewry ['dʒuːərɪ] *n* **(a)** *(community)* los judíos; **British J.** la comunidad judía británica **(b)** *Hist (part of town)* judería *f*

Jezebel ['dʒezəbel] *n* **(a)** *(in the Bible)* Jezabel **(b)** *(scheming woman)* mala pécora *f*

jib[1] [dʒɪb] *n* **(a)** *(sail)* foque *m*; IDIOM **I don't like the cut of his j.** me da muy mala espina, no me gusta nada la pinta que tiene **(b)** *(of crane)* aguilón *m*

jib[2] *(pt & pp* **jibbed**) *vi* **to j. at doing sth** resistirse a hacer algo

jibe [dʒaɪb] **1** *n* burla *f*
2 *vi* **(a)** *(mock)* **to j. at sb** burlarse de alguien **(b)** *US Fam (agree)* encajar, cuadrar, *RP* cerrar

jiff [dʒɪf], **jiffy** ['dʒɪfɪ] *n Fam* **in a j.** en un segundo; **to do sth in a j.** hacer algo en un periquete

Jiffy bag® ['dʒɪfɪbæg] *n* sobre *m* acolchado

jig [dʒɪg] **1** *n (dance, music)* giga *f*, jiga *f*; *US* **the j. is up** se acabó la fiesta, *RP* se pudrió todo
2 *vi (pt & pp* **jigged**) **(a)** *(dance)* bailar una giga *or* jiga **(b) to j. (around** *or* **about)** *(move)* brincar; **stop jigging around** *or* **about** deja de brincar

jigger[1] ['dʒɪgə(r)] *n* **(a)** *(measure of alcohol)* dedal *m*, medida *f* de licor *(= 42 ml)* **(b)** *US Fam (thingummy)* chisme *m* **(c)** *(insect)* nigua *f*

jigger[2] *vt Fam (damage)* descuajeringar

jiggered ['dʒɪgəd] *adj Fam* **(a)** *(TV, microwave)* descuajeringado(a); *(back, knee) Esp* descoyuntado(a), *Am* reventado(a) **(b)** *(as expletive)* **well, I'll be j.!** ¡atiza!; **I'm j. if I'll do it!** ¡ni muerto lo hago! **(c)** *Br (exhausted)* rendido(a), molido(a)

jiggery-pokery ['dʒɪgərɪ'pəʊkərɪ] *n Br Fam* tejemanejes *mpl*

jiggle ['dʒɪgəl] **1** *vt* mover, menear
2 *vi* moverse, menearse

▸**jiggle about, jiggle around 1** *vt sep* = **jiggle**
2 *vi* = **jiggle**

jiggy ['dʒɪgɪ] *adj US Fam* **to get j. (with it)** *(dance)* ponerse a brincar; **to get j. with sb** *(have sex with) Esp* enrollarse con alguien, *Am* coger con alguien; **to get j. with sth** *(get involved with)* verse metido(a) en algo

jigsaw ['dʒɪgsɔː] *n* **(a)** *(saw)* sierra *f* de calar *or* de vaivén, caladora *f* **(b)** *(game)* **j. (puzzle)** rompecabezas *m inv*, puzzle *m*; IDIOM **the pieces of the j. were beginning to fall into place** las piezas del rompecabezas comenzaban a caer en su lugar

jihad [dʒɪ'hæd] *n* guerra *f* santa, yihad *f* (islámica)

jilt [dʒɪlt] *vt* dejar plantado(a)

Jim Crow ['dʒɪm'krəʊ] *n US Fam* **(a)** *(black person)* = término generalmente ofensivo para referirse a un negro **(b)** *(racist policies)* segregacionismo *m*, racismo *m* ▸▸ ***J. laws*** leyes *fpl* segregacionistas *or* racistas

jim-dandy ['dʒɪm'dændɪ] *adj US Fam* fabuloso(a), sensacional

jimjams ['dʒɪmdʒæmz] *npl Fam* **(a)** *(nervous excitement)* nerviosismo *m*, nervios *mpl*; **I've really got the j.** estoy hecho un manojo de nervios **(b)** *Br (pyjamas)* pijama *m*, *Am* piyama *m or f*

jimmy *US* = **jemmy**

jingle ['dʒɪŋgəl] **1** *n* **(a)** *(of bells, keys)* tintineo *m* **(b)** *Rad & TV* melodía *f* (de un anuncio), sintonía *f*
2 *vt (bells, keys)* hacer tintinear
3 *vi* tintinear

jingo ['dʒɪŋgəʊ] *n Fam Old-fashioned* patriotero(a) *m,f*; **by j.** ¡demontre!, ¡diablos!

jingoism ['dʒɪŋgəʊɪzəm] *n Pej* patrioterismo *m*

jingoistic ['dʒɪŋgəʊ'ɪstɪk] *adj Pej* patriotero(a)

jink [dʒɪŋk] **1** *n (movement)* amago *m*
2 *vi* amagar; **he jinked to the left** amagó hacia la izquierda; **he jinked through the defence** esquivó a la defensa dando bandazos

jinx [dʒɪŋks] *Fam* **1** *n (spell, curse)* **to put a j. on sth/sb** embrujar algo/a alguien, *Esp* gafar algo/a alguien, *Méx* echarle la sal a algo/a alguien, *RP* enyetar algo/a alguien; **there's a j. on this team** este equipo está embrujado *or Esp* gafado *or Méx* salado, *RP* este equipo tiene yeta
2 *vt* **to be jinxed** estar embrujado(a) *or Esp* gafado(a) *or Méx* salado(a), *RP* tener yeta

jism, gism ['dʒɪzəm] *n* **(a)** *Vulg (semen)* leche *f*, *Esp* lefa *f* **(b)** *US (energy)* brío *m*, empuje *m*

JIT [dʒɪt] *adj Ind* (*abbr* **just in time**) ***J. production*** producción *f* "justo a tiempo" *(con minimización de stocks)*

jitterbug ['dʒɪtəbʌg] **1** *n* jitterbug *m*, = baile de movimientos enérgicos de los años cuarenta
2 *vi* bailar el jitterbug

jitters ['dʒɪtəz] *npl Fam* **the j.** *(anxiety)* canguelo, *Méx* mello, *RP* cuiqui; **I got the j.** me entró canguelo *or Méx* mello *or RP* cuiqui; **to give sb the j.** poner nervioso a alguien

jittery ['dʒɪtərɪ] *adj Fam (anxious)* histérico(a); **to be/get j.** estar/ponerse histérico

jiu-jitsu = **ju-jitsu**

jive [dʒaɪv] **1** *n* **(a)** *(music, dance)* swing *m* **(b)** *(slang)* **j. (talk)** = jerga de los negros norteamericanos, en especial usada por músicos de jazz **(c)** *US Fam (lies, nonsense)* bobadas *fpl*, *Esp* chorradas *fpl*, *RP* boludeces *fpl*; **don't give me all that j.** no me vengas con bobadas *or Esp* chorradas *or RP* boludeces
2 *vt US Fam (tease)* tomar el pelo a
3 *vi (dance)* bailar el swing

Jnr (*abbr* **Junior**) **Nigel Molesworth, J.** Nigel Molesworth, hijo

Job [dʒəʊb] *n* Job; **J.'s comforter** = persona que intenta dar ánimos pero sólo consigue empeorar las cosas; IDIOM **to have the patience of J.** tener la paciencia de un santo

JOB [dʒɒb] **1** *n* **(a)** *(post)* (puesto *m* de) trabajo *m*, empleo *m*; **to change jobs** cambiar de trabajo; **to give up** *or* **leave one's j.** dejar el trabajo; **she's got a j. as a cleaner** trabaja de limpiadora; **I've lost my j.** he perdido mi trabajo; *Euph* **I'm between jobs at the moment** ahora mismo no estoy haciendo nada; **we learned on the j.** aprendimos con la práctica, aprendimos sobre el terreno; **he was accused of drinking on the j.** le acusaron de beber en horas de trabajo; **I've been on the j. for ten years** llevo *or Am* tengo diez años en el trabajo; **to be out of a j.** estar sin trabajo *or* empleo; *Br Fam* **it's more than my job's worth to let you in** me juego el puesto si te dejo entrar; IDIOM *Br Fam* **jobs for the boys: it's a clear case of jobs for the boys** es un caso claro de amiguismo *or Esp* enchufismo *or Col, Méx, RP* palanca ▸▸ *US* ***j. action*** huelga *f* de celo; ***j. applicant*** demandante *mf* de empleo; ***j. application*** demanda *f* de empleo; *Br* ***j. club*** = centro de apoyo y formación para los desempleados; ***j. creation*** creación *f* de empleo; ***j. cuts*** recortes *mpl* de personal, despidos *mpl*; ***j. description*** responsabilidades *fpl* del puesto; ***j. hunting:* to go j. hunting** buscar trabajo; ***j. interview*** entrevista *f* de trabajo; ***j. losses*** despidos *mpl*; ***j. market*** mercado *m* de trabajo; ***j. offer*** oferta *f* de empleo; ***j. opportunities*** ofertas *fpl* de empleo; ***j. satisfaction*** satisfacción *f* laboral; ***j. security*** estabilidad *f* laboral; ***j. seeker*** persona *f* en busca de empleo; *Br* ***j. seeker's allowance*** subsidio *m* de desempleo *or Am* desocupación; ***j. share*** empleo *m* compartido; ***j. sharing*** el empleo compartido; ***j. title*** cargo *m*, nombre *m* del puesto
(b) *(piece of work, task, responsibility)* tarea *f*; **I have a few jobs around the house to do** tengo algunas cosas que hacer en la casa; **I have (been given) the j. of writing the report** me han encargado redactar el informe; **it's not my j. to tell you what to do** no creo que me corresponda a mí decirte lo que tienes que hacer; **a (good) j. well done** un trabajo bien hecho; **to do a good j.** hacerlo bien; **you've made a really good j. of this report** has hecho un informe excelente; **he made a good j. of cleaning the kitchen** dejó la cocina impecable; *US* **good j.!** *(well done)* ¡muy bien!, ¡estupendo!, *CAm, Carib, Col, Méx* ¡chévere!, *Méx* ¡padre!, *RP* ¡bárbaro!; *Fam Fig* **to do the j.** *(serve purpose)* servir, funcionar; *Fig* **to fall down on the j.** no cumplir; **he's (just) the man for the j.** es el hombre indicado ▸▸ *Com* ***j. lot*** lote *m*
(c) *(difficulty, trouble)* **it was quite a j.** *or* **I had a j. getting her to come** me costó mucho convencerla para que viniera; *Fam* **they've got a real j. on their hands with that baby** ese niño les da muchísimo trabajo; **it's a j. and a half** es una paliza
(d) *Comptr* tarea *f*
(e) *Fam (referring to activity)* **to give sth a paint j.** pintar algo, darle una manita de pintura a algo; **it looks like it's going to be a crowbar j.** parece que vamos a tener que usar una palanqueta; *Fig* **to do a demolition j. on sth/sb** poner a algo/alguien de vuelta y media, *Méx* barrer *or RP* dar vuelta a algo/alguien
(f) *Fam (thing, object)* cacharro *m*, chisme *m*, *CAm, Col, Ven* vaina *f*; **what do you call those little plastic jobs?** ¿cómo se llaman esos cacharros de plástico?; **her new car is one of those sporty jobs** su nuevo coche *or Am* carro *or RP* auto es uno de esos modelos deportivos
(g) *Fam (crime)* **to do** *or* **pull a j.** dar un golpe
(h) *Br Fam Hum (excrement)* mierda *f*, caca *f*; **to do a j.** cagar, *Méx* chingar
(i) *Br very Fam* **to be on the j.** *(having sex)* estar dale que te pego
(j) IDIOMS *Br Fam* **it's a good j. (that)...!** ¡menos mal que...!; *Br Fam*

she never saw him when he was ill, and a good j. too. nunca lo vio mientras estuvo enfermo, y menos mal; *Br Fam* **that's just the j.!** eso me viene que ni pintado; *Fam* **to do a j. on sth** *(ruin, damage)* cargarse algo; *Fam* **to do a j. on sb** *(beat up)* dar una paliza a alguien; **that journalist did a real j. on him** ese periodista lo puso por los suelos; *Br* **to give sth up as a bad j.** dejar algo por imposible; **to make the best of a bad j.** poner al mal tiempo buena cara
2 *vi* (*pt & pp* **jobbed**) hacer trabajos eventuales

---

jobber ['dʒɒbə(r)] *n St Exch* corredor(ora) *m,f or* agente *mf* de bolsa

jobbery ['dʒɒbərı] *n Fam (corruption)* corrupción *f*, trapicheos *mpl*

jobbing ['dʒɒbıŋ] *adj Br (carpenter, electrician)* eventual

Jobcentre ['dʒɒbsentə(r)] *n Br* oficina *f* de empleo

jobholder ['dʒɒbhəʊldə(r)] *n US* empleado(a) *m,f*

job-hop ['dʒɒbhɒp] *vi US* ir de un trabajo en otro

jobless ['dʒɒblıs] **1** *npl* **the j.** los desempleados, *Esp* los parados, *Am* los desocupados
2 *adj* desempleado(a), *Esp* parado(a), *Am* desocupado(a)

Jobseekers allowance ['dʒɒbsi:kəzə'laʊəns] *n Br* subsidio *m* de desempleo *or Am* de desocupación

job-share ['dʒɒbʃeə(r)] **1** *vi* compartir un empleo
2 *n* **they do the work as a j.** comparten el empleo

jobsworth ['dʒɒbzwɜ:θ] *n Fam* = persona que trabaja de cara al público y que rehúye a modificar las normas para facilitar las cosas

Joburg, Jo'burg ['dʒəʊbɜ:g] *n Fam* Johannesburgo, Johanesburgo

Jock [dʒɒk] *n Br Fam (Scottish person)* = término a veces ofensivo para referirse a los escoceses

jock [dʒɒk] *n US Fam* (**a**) *(athlete)* deportista *m* (**b**) *(disc jockey)* DJ *mf*

jockey ['dʒɒkı] **1** *n* jockey *m*, jinete *m*
2 *vt* (**a**) *(horse)* montar (**b**) *(trick)* **they jockeyed him into lending them money** lo embaucaron para que les prestara dinero; **to j. sb out of a job** quitar el puesto a alguien a base de engaños y manejos
3 *vi* **to j. for position** luchar por tomar posiciones

Jockey® shorts ['dʒɒkıʃɔ:ts] *npl US* calzoncillos *mpl*, *Chile* fundillos *mpl*, *Col* pantaloncillos *mpl*, *Méx* calzones *mpl*, *Méx* chones *mpl*

jockstrap ['dʒɒkstræp] *n* suspensorio *m*

jocose [dʒə'kəʊs] *adj Literary* jocoso(a)

jocular ['dʒɒkjʊlə(r)] *adj* jocoso(a)

jocularity [dʒɒkjʊ'lærıtı] *n* jocosidad *f*

jocularly ['dʒɒkjʊləlı] *adv* jocosamente, en tono jocoso; **he was j. known as "the Walrus"** se lo conocía, en tono jocoso, como "la morsa"

jocund ['dʒɒkənd] *adj Literary* jocundo(a)

jodhpurs ['dʒɒdpəz] *npl* pantalones *mpl* de montar

Joe [dʒəʊ] *n Fam* hombre *m* cualquiera; *US* **he's an ordinary J.** es un tipo del montón ►► *Br* ***J. Bloggs*** *or* ***Public***, *US* ***J. Blow*** *or* ***Schmo*** el ciudadano de a pie *or RP* común y silvestre; *US* ***J. Six-pack*** el típico obrero *or Esp* currito *or RP* laburante

joey ['dʒəʊı] *n Austr Fam (kangaroo)* cría *f* de canguro

jog [dʒɒg] **1** *n* (**a**) *(push)* empujoncito *m*; **to give sb's memory a j.** refrescar la memoria de alguien (**b**) *(run)* trote *m*; **to break into a j.** echar a correr lentamente; **to go for a j.** ir a hacer footing *or* jogging, ir a correr
2 *vt* (*pt & pp* **jogged**) *(push)* **don't j. my arm!** ¡no me des en el brazo!; **ok, try jogging the machine** a ver, dale un empujoncito a la máquina; **to j. sb's memory** refrescar la memoria a alguien; **to j. sb into action** poner a alguien en acción *or* movimiento
3 *vi* (**a**) *(run)* hacer footing *or* jogging, correr (**b**) *(bump)* dar golpes; **his rifle jogged against his back** el rifle golpeaba contra su espalda

►**jog along** *vi* (**a**) *(run)* correr lentamente (**b**) *(in job)* **it's jogging along quite happily** avanza poco a poco, pero va bien; **I'm tired of just jogging along** estoy harto de no hacer más progresos

jogger ['dʒɒgə(r)] *n* corredor(ora) *m,f* de footing *or* jogging ►► *Fam* ***j.'s nipple*** = irritación de los pezones de una persona que practica footing o realiza carreras de fondo debido al roce con la ropa

jogging ['dʒɒgıŋ] *n* footing *m*, jogging *m*; **to go j.** ir a hacer footing *or* jogging ►► *Br* ***j. bottoms*** pantalones *mpl* de *Esp* chándal *or RP* jogging *or Ven* mono, *Méx* pants; *US* ***j. pants*** pantalones *mpl* de *Esp* chándal *or RP* jogging *or Ven* mono, *Méx* pants

joggle ['dʒɒgəl] **1** *vt* menear
2 *vi* sacudirse, traquetear; **the truck joggled along the track** el camión iba traqueteando por el camino

jog-trot ['dʒɒgtrɒt] *n* paseo *m* a caballo (a medio trote)

Johannesburg [dʒəʊ'hænızbɜ:g] *n* Johannesburgo, Johanesburgo

John [dʒɒn] *pr n* **King J.** *(of England)* Juan sin Tierra; **(Saint) J. the Baptist** san Juan Bautista; **(Pope) J. Paul I/II** Juan Pablo I/II

john [dʒɒn] *n US Fam* (**a**) **the j.** *(lavatory)* el váter (**b**) *(prostitute's client)* cliente *m*

John Bull ['dʒɒn'bʊl] *n* (**a**) *(Englishman)* el inglés de a pie *or RP* común y silvestre (**b**) *(England)* = la personificación de Inglaterra

John Doe ['dʒɒn'dəʊ] *n US* (**a**) *(average person)* el estadounidense medio (**b**) *(unidentified man)* = nombre con el que se hace referencia a un desconocido

John Dory [dʒɒn'dɔ:rı] *n (fish)* gallo *m*, pez *m* de San Pedro

John Hancock [dʒɒn'hænkɒk] *n US Fam (signature)* firma *f*

johnny ['dʒɒnı] *n Br Fam* (**a**) *(condom)* goma *f*, condón *m* (**b**) *Old-fashioned (chap)* tipo *m*, *Esp* gachó *m*

johnny-come-lately [dʒɒnıkʌm'leıtlı] (*pl* **johnny-come-latelys**) *n Fam* novato(a) *m,f*, recién llegado(a) *m,f*

John Q. Public ['dʒɒnkju:'pʌblık] *n US* el ciudadano de a pie *or RP* común y silvestre

johnson ['dʒɒnsən] *n US Fam* pito *m*, cola *f*

John Thomas ['dʒɒn'tɒməs] *n Fam (penis)* pito *m*

joie de vivre ['ʒwɑ:də'vi:vrə] *n* alegría *f* de vivir

join [dʒɔın] **1** *n* juntura *f*, unión *f*; *(in sewing)* costura *f*
2 *vt* (**a**) *(unite, connect)* unir; **to j. two things/places together** unir dos cosas/lugares; **to be joined in marriage** *or* **matrimony** estar unidos en matrimonio; **to j. battle** entablar batalla; **to j. the dots** unir los puntos con una línea; **to j. hands** *(in prayer)* unir las manos; *(link hands)* tomarse de las manos; **we joined forces with them** unimos nuestras fuerzas con ellos *or* a las de ellos; **she joined forces with her brother** se alió a su hermano
(**b**) *(become a member of) (club)* ingresar en; *(political party, union)* afiliarse a; *(army)* alistarse en; *(discussion, game)* unirse a; **to j. the queue** ponerse a la cola; **to j. the ranks of sth** incorporarse a las filas de algo; **to j. the ranks of the unemployed** pasar a engrosar las listas del desempleo *or Esp* paro; IDIOM **so you've been burgled too? j. the club!** ¿así que te han robado? ¡bienvenido al club!
(**c**) *(join company with, meet)* encontrarse con, juntarse con; **I'll j. you later** los encuentro más tarde; **may I j. you?** *(to sb at table)* ¿puedo sentarme contigo?; **they joined/will be joining us for lunch** almorzaron/almorzarán con nosotros; **to j. sb for a drink** tomarse una copa con alguien; **my wife joins me in offering our sincere condolences** en nombre mío y en el de mi esposa, reciban nuestras sinceras condolencias; *Naut* **to j. one's ship** embarcarse; *Mil* **to j. one's regiment** unirse a su regimiento
(**d**) *(of river, road)* desembocar en; **does this path j. the main road?** ¿este sendero desemboca en la carretera principal?; **where the path joins the road** donde el camino empalma con la carretera
3 *vi* (**a**) *(pipes, roads, rivers)* juntarse, unirse (**b**) *(enrol) (in club)* ingresar; *(in political party, union)* afiliarse (**c**) *(unite)* unirse; **they joined together to fight drug trafficking** se unieron para combatir el tráfico de drogas; **they joined with us in condemning the attack** suscribieron nuestra condena del ataque

►**join in** **1** *vt insep (game, discussion)* participar en
2 *vi* participar; **she started singing and the others joined in** comenzó a cantar y los demás se le unieron

►**join on** **1** *vt sep* enganchar
2 *vi* engancharse; **where does this part j. on?** ¿dónde se engancha esta pieza?

►**join up** **1** *vt sep (pipes, electric cables, vehicles)* empalmar, unir; *(letters)* unir, juntar
2 *vi* (**a**) *Mil* alistarse (**b**) **to j. up with sb** unirse a alguien

joined-up ['dʒɔınd'ʌp] *adj* (**a**) *Sch* **can you do j. writing yet?** ¿ya sabes unir las letras al escribir? (**b**) *Br Pol* ***j. government:*** **we must strive for j. government** debemos esforzarnos para que todas las áreas del gobierno trabajen de una forma integrada

joiner ['dʒɔınə(r)] *n* (**a**) *(carpenter)* carpintero(a) *m,f* (de obra) (**b**) *Fam* **I'm not a great j.** no me gusta *or Esp* va mucho unirme a grupos

joinery ['dʒɔınərı] *n* carpintería *f* (de obra); **piece of j.** un trabajo de carpintería

joining ['dʒɔınıŋ] *n* ***j. fee*** tarifa *f* de alta

joint [dʒɔınt] **1** *n* (**a**) *Anat* articulación *f*; **out of j.** dislocado(a); **to put one's shoulder out of j.** dislocarse el hombro; *Fig* **these changes have put** *or* **thrown everything out of j.** estos cambios han desacomodado todo; IDIOM *Br* **to put sb's nose out of j.** *(upset)* desairar a alguien
(**b**) *(in woodwork)* junta *f*, juntura *f*
(**c**) *(of meat) (raw)* pieza *f*; *(roasted)* asado *m*
(**d**) *Fam (nightclub, restaurant)* garito *m*, local *m*

(**e**) *US Fam (house)* casa *f*, *Arg* cueva *f*; **nice j. you have here!** tu casa no está mal, ¿eh?

(**f**) *Fam (cannabis cigarette)* porro *m*, canuto *m*

(**g**) *US Fam (prison) Esp* chirona *f*, *Andes, RP* cana *f*, *Méx* bote *m*; **in the j.** *Esp* en chirona, *Andes, RP* en cana, *Méx* en el bote

(**h**) *US very Fam (penis) Esp* polla *f*, *Esp* picha *f*, *Am* verga *f*, *Chile* pico *m*, *Chile* penca *f*, *Méx* pito *m*, *RP* pija *f*, *Ven* pinga *f*

2 *adj* (**a**) *(united, combined)* conjunto(a); **to take j. action** iniciar una acción conjunta; **thanks to their j. efforts...** gracias a su esfuerzo conjunto... (**b**) *(shared, collective)* conjunto(a) ►► ***j. author*** coautor(ora) *m,f*; *Fin* ***j. account*** cuenta *f* indistinta *or* conjunta; *US Mil* ***the J. Chiefs of Staff*** los Jefes del Estado Mayor Conjunto; ***j. committee*** comisión *f* mixta; ***a j. communiqué*** un comunicado conjunto; *Law* ***j. custody*** custodia *f* compartida; ***j. heir*** coheredero(a) *m,f*; *Br Univ* ***j. honours*** = licenciatura en dos áreas distintas; ***j. leader*** colíder *mf*; ***j. owner*** copropietario(a) *m,f*; ***j. ownership*** copropiedad *f*; *US Pol* ***j. resolution*** resolución *f* conjunta; *Law* ***j. and several liability*** responsabilidad *f* solidaria; ***j. venture*** empresa *f* conjunta

3 *vt* (**a**) *(chicken)* trinchar (**b**) *(connect with a joint)* articular

jointly ['dʒɔɪntlɪ] *adv* conjuntamente; **to be j. responsible for sth** ser corresponsable de algo

joint-stock company ['dʒɔɪnt'stɒk'kʌmpənɪ] *n* sociedad *f* anónima

jointure ['dʒɔɪntʃə(r)] *n Law (widow's property)* bienes *mpl* gananciales (de la esposa)

joist [dʒɔɪst] *n (beam)* viga *f*, vigueta *f*

jojoba [həʊ'həʊbə] *n* jojoba *f*, yoyoba *f*

joke [dʒəʊk] 1 *n* (**a**) *(witty remark)* broma *f*; *(funny story)* chiste; **to tell** *or* **crack a j.** contar un chiste; **to make a j. about sth** hacer una broma *or* bromear sobre algo; **to make a j. of sth** quitar importancia a algo bromeando; **to see the j.** verle la gracia (a la cosa); **to say/do sth for** *or* **as a j.** decir/hacer algo en *or* de broma; **she can't take a j.** no sabe aguantar una broma; **that's** *or* **it's no j.!** *(serious, not easy)* ¡no es cosa de broma!; **it's getting beyond a j.** esto ya pasa de castaño oscuro

(**b**) *(prank, trick)* broma; **to play a j. on sb** gastar una broma a alguien; **the j. is on you this time** esta vez te ha salido el tiro por la culata

(**c**) *Fam (object of derision)* **to be a j.** *(of person)* ser un(a) inútil, no valer *Esp* un duro *or Am* ni cinco; *(of thing)* ser de chiste, *RP* ser joda; **the security precautions were a j.** las medidas de seguridad eran un chiste *or RP* una joda; **his staff regard him as a j.** los empleados lo consideran un gilipollas, *RP* para los empleados es un boludo; **what a j.!** *(how ridiculous)* ¡qué ridículo!

2 *vi* bromear; **to j. about sth** bromear acerca de algo; **it's not something to j. about** con eso no se bromea; **to j. with sb** bromear con alguien; **I'm not joking** (hablo) en serio; **I was only joking** estaba de broma; **you're joking!, you must be joking!** *(expressing surprise)* ¡no hablarás en serio!; *(expressing refusal)* ¡ni hablar!

joker ['dʒəʊkə(r)] *n* (**a**) *(clown)* bromista *mf*, gracioso(a) *m,f*; *(incompetent person)* inútil *mf*; **some j. has stolen my umbrella** algún gracioso me ha robado el paraguas (**b**) *(in cards)* comodín *m*; IDIOM **the j. in the** *Br* **pack** *or US* **deck** la gran incógnita (**c**) *US (clause)* cláusula *f* escondida

jokey, joky ['dʒəʊkɪ] *adj* jocoso(a)

jokily ['dʒəʊkɪlɪ] *adv* en tono de broma

jokiness ['dʒəʊkɪnɪs] *n* jocosidad *f*, humor *m*

joking ['dʒəʊkɪŋ] 1 *adj* jocoso(a); **I'm not in a j. mood** no estoy para bromas

2 *n* **the j. must stop** basta de bromas; **j. apart** *or* **aside...** bromas aparte..., fuera de broma...

jokingly ['dʒəʊkɪŋlɪ] *adv* en broma

joky = **jokey**

joliotium [dʒɒlɪ'əʊtɪəm] *n Chem* jolita *f*

jollies ['dʒɒlɪz] *npl US Fam* **to get one's j. (doing sth)** divertirse (haciendo algo)

jollification [dʒɒlɪfɪ'keɪʃən] *n Fam* jolgorio *m*, jarana *f*; **jollifications** festejos *mpl*, fastos *mpl*

jolliness ['dʒɒlɪnɪs], **jollity** ['dʒɒlɪtɪ] *n* regocijo *m*, alegría *f*

jolly ['dʒɒlɪ] 1 *adj* (**a**) *(cheerful)* alegre; IDIOM *Br* **she's very j. hockey sticks** tiene la típica jovialidad y entusiasmo de las niñas bien ►► ***the J. Roger*** la bandera pirata (**b**) *Br (enjoyable)* agradable; **we had a very j. time** nos divertimos mucho, lo pasamos muy bien

2 *adv Br Fam (very)* bien; **j. good!** ¡estupendo!, *CAm, Carib, Col, Méx* ¡chévere!, *Méx* ¡padre!, *RP* ¡bárbaro!; **a j. good fellow** un tío muy majo, *RP* un flaco genial; **and a j. good thing too!** ¡y por suerte fue así!, *RP* ¡y menos mal!; **it serves him j. well right!** ¡se lo tiene bien merecido!; **you'll j. well do what you're told!** ¡haz lo que se te diga y se acabó *or RP* punto!; **yes, I j. well DID do it!** sí, fui yo ¿qué pasa?

3 *vt* **to j. sb into doing sth** animar a alguien a hacer algo; **to j. sb along** animar a alguien

►**jolly up** *vt sep* **to j. sb up** dar ánimos *or* animar a alguien

jolt [dʒəʊlt] 1 *n* (**a**) *(jar)* sacudida *f*; **to wake up with a j.** despertarse con un sobresalto (**b**) *(shock, surprise)* susto *m*; **it gave me a bit of a j.** me dio un buen susto

2 *vt* (**a**) *(shake)* sacudir; **the passengers were jolted about in the bus** los pasajeros iban sacudiéndose en el autobús (**b**) *(shock, surprise)* sacudir, alterar; **to j. sb into action** empujar a alguien a actuar; **to j. sb out of a depression** hacer salir a alguien de una depresión

3 *vi (shake)* dar sacudidas; **to j. along** avanzar dando sacudidas; **to j. forward** dar una sacudida hacia adelante; **his head jolted forward/back** *(on impact)* la cabeza le dio una sacudida hacia adelante/atrás; **to j. to a stop** *(vehicle)* pararse en seco

Jonah ['dʒəʊnə] *n* (**a**) *(in the Bible)* Jonás (**b**) *(person bringing bad luck)* cenizo *m*, *Esp* gafe *mf*

Joneses ['dʒəʊnzɪz] *npl* IDIOM **to keep up with the J.** no ser menos que el vecino

jonquil ['dʒɒŋkwɪl] *n* junquillo *m*

Jordan ['dʒɔːdən] *n* (**a**) *(country)* Jordania (**b**) **the (River) J.** el Jordán

Jordanian [dʒɔː'deɪnɪən] 1 *n* jordano(a) *m,f*

2 *adj* jordano(a)

Joseph ['dʒəʊzɪf] *pr n* **Saint J.** san José; **J. of Arimathea** José de Arimatea

josh [dʒɒʃ] *Fam* 1 *vt (tease)* tomar el pelo a

2 *vi* **I was only joshing** sólo te estaba tomando el pelo

Joshua ['dʒɒʃʊə] *pr n* Josué

joss-stick ['dʒɒsstɪk] *n* pebete *m*, varilla *f* aromática

jostle ['dʒɒsəl] 1 *vt* empujar; **she was jostled by the demonstrators** los manifestantes la empujaron; **to j. sb out of the way** quitar *or Am* sacar a alguien de en medio a empujones; **to j. one's way through** abrirse paso a empellones; **to j. one's way out** salir a empellones

2 *vi (push)* empujarse; **to j. for position** *(in contest, job)* luchar por tomar posiciones

jot [dʒɒt] *n Fam* **not a j.** ni pizca; **he doesn't care a j.** le importa un comino; **there isn't a j. of truth in what you say** no hay ni un ápice de verdad en lo que dices; *Literary* **not one j. or tittle** ni un ápice

►**jot down** *vt sep* apuntar, anotar

jotter ['dʒɒtə(r)] *n Br* libreta *f*

jottings ['dʒɒtɪŋz] *npl* anotaciones *fpl*

joule [dʒuːl] *n Phys* julio *m*

journal ['dʒɜːnəl] *n* (**a**) *(publication)* revista *f (especializada)*, boletín *m* (**b**) *(diary)* diario *m*; **to keep a j.** llevar *or* escribir un diario (**c**) *Naut (logbook)* diario *m or* cuaderno *m* de navegación (**d**) *Fin (for transactions)* libro *m* diario

> **False friend**: The Spanish noun **jornal** is not a translation for the English word **journal**. In Spanish **jornal** means "day's wage".

journalese [dʒɜːnə'liːz] *n Fam Pej* jerga *f* periodística

journalism ['dʒɜːnəlɪzəm] *n* periodismo *m*

journalist ['dʒɜːnəlɪst] *n* periodista *mf*

journalistic [dʒɜːnə'lɪstɪk] *adj* periodístico(a)

journey ['dʒɜːnɪ] 1 *n* viaje *m*; **a train/plane/boat j.** un viaje en tren/avión/barco; **it is a two-day j. on foot** es un viaje de dos días a pie, son dos días de marcha; **my j. to work takes me thirty-five minutes** ir al trabajo me lleva treinta y cinco minutos; **have a good j.!** ¡buen viaje!; **it was quite a j. to get here** fue todo un viaje llegar hasta aquí; **to make a j.** hacer un viaje; **to set off** *or* **out on a j.** salir de viaje; **to go (away) on a j.** ir(se) de viaje; **to get to** *or* **reach the end of one's j.** llegar al final del viaje

2 *vi* viajar

journeyman ['dʒɜːnɪmən] *n (qualified craftsman)* oficial *m*

journo ['dʒɜːnəʊ] (*pl* **journos** *or* **journoes**) *n Br Fam* periodista *mf*

joust [dʒaʊst] 1 *n Hist* justa *f*

2 *vi* (**a**) *Hist* justar (**b**) *(compete)* pugnar, estar en liza (**with** con)

jousting ['dʒaʊstɪŋ] *n* (**a**) *Hist* justas *fpl*; **a j. match** un torneo de justas (**b**) *(competition)* competencia *f*

Jove [dʒəʊv] *n* Júpiter; *Br Fam Old-fashioned* **by J.!** ¡cáspita!

jovial ['dʒəʊvɪəl] *adj* jovial

joviality [dʒəʊvɪ'ælɪtɪ] *n* jovialidad *f*

jovially ['dʒəʊvɪəlɪ] *adv* jovialmente

jowl [dʒaʊl] *n* (**a**) *(jaw)* mandíbula *f* (**b**) *(cheek)* carrillo *m*, mejilla *f*; **he had heavy jowls** tenía mucha papada

jowly ['dʒaʊlɪ] *adj* con los carrillos fofos, *Am* mofletudo(a), *RP* cachetón(ona)

joy [dʒɔɪ] *n* (**a**) *(happiness)* alegría *f*, gozo *m*; **to wish sb j.** desear a alguien lo mejor; **to shout with** *or* **for j.** dar un grito de alegría; **she moved out, to the great j. of her neighbours** se mudó, para alegría de sus vecinos; *Ironic* **oh j.!** ¡qué alegría!
(**b**) *(pleasure)* placer *m*, maravilla *f*; **the joys of gardening/having a car** los placeres de la jardinería/tener un auto; **it was a j. to see him laughing again** fue un placer verlo reír de nuevo; **she's a j. to be with, it's a j. to be with her** su compañía es muy placentera; **he's a j. to work for** es una maravilla de jefe; **her style is a j. to watch** es una delicia observar su estilo
(**c**) *Br Fam (success)* **(did you have** *or* **get) any j.?** ¿hubo suerte?; **I didn't get** *or* **have any j.** no conseguí nada; **I had no j. finding a hotel** no conseguí encontrar un hotel; **you won't get any j. from him** no vas a conseguir nada de él

Joycean ['dʒɔɪsɪən] *adj* joyceano(a)

joyful ['dʒɔɪfʊl] *adj* alegre

joyfully ['dʒɔɪfəlɪ] *adv* alegremente

joyless ['dʒɔɪlɪs] *adj* triste

joyous ['dʒɔɪəs] *adj* jubiloso(a); **on this j. day** en este día de júbilo

joyously ['dʒɔɪəslɪ] *adv* con júbilo

joypad ['dʒɔɪpæd] *n Comptr* joypad *m*, control *m* (para juegos)

joypop ['dʒɔɪpɒp] *vi Fam* consumir drogas esporádicamente

joyride ['dʒɔɪraɪd] **1** *n (in stolen car)* **to go for a j.** ir a dar una vuelta en un coche *or Am* carro *or RP* auto robado
2 *vi* **to go joyriding** robar un coche *or Am* carro *or RP* auto para hacer locuras y divertirse; **they were arrested for joyriding** los arrestaron por robar coches *or Am* carros *or RP* autos para divertirse

joyrider ['dʒɔɪraɪdə(r)] *n* = persona que roba coches para darse una vuelta por diversión

joyriding ['dʒɔɪraɪdɪŋ] *n* = robo de coches para darse una vuelta por diversión

joystick ['dʒɔɪstɪk] *n* (**a**) *Av* palanca *f* de mando (**b**) *Comptr* joystick *m*

JP [dʒeɪ'pi:] *n Br Law* (*abbr* **justice of the peace**) juez *mf* de paz

JPEG ['dʒeɪpeg] *n Comptr* (*abbr* **Joint Photographic Experts Group**) JPEG *m*

Jr (*abbr* **Junior**) **Nigel Molesworth, Jr** Nigel Molesworth, hijo

jubilant ['dʒu:bɪlənt] *adj (shouts, expression)* de júbilo; *(person, celebration)* jubiloso(a); *(crowd)* exultante; **to be j. (at** *or* **about** *or* **over sth)** estar encantado(a) (con algo)

jubilation [dʒu:bɪ'leɪʃən] *n* júbilo *m*

jubilee ['dʒu:bɪli:] *n* aniversario *m*; **silver/golden j.** vigésimo quinto/quincuagésimo aniversario

Judaea [dʒu:'dɪə] *n* Judea

Judaeo-, Judeo- [dʒu:'di:əʊ] *prefix* judeo-

Judaeo-Christian, Judeo-Christian [dʒu:'di:əʊ'krɪstʃən] *adj* judeocristiano(a)

Judaic [dʒu:'deɪɪk] *adj* judaico(a)

Judaism ['dʒu:deɪɪzəm] *n* judaísmo *m*

Judas ['dʒu:dəs] *n* (**a**) *(in Bible)* **J. (Iscariot)** Judas (Iscariote) (**b**) *(traitor)* judas *mf* ►► ***J. kiss*** beso *m* de Judas

judder ['dʒʌdə(r)] *Br* **1** *n* sacudida *f*, temblor *m*; **a j. went through the whole building** todo el edificio se sacudió
2 *vi* dar sacudidas; **to j. to a halt** pararse en seco

Judeo- = **Judaeo-**

Judeo-Christian = **Judaeo-Christian**

judge [dʒʌdʒ] **1** *n* (**a**) *Law* juez *mf*, juez(a) *m,f*; IDIOM **to appoint oneself j., jury and executioner** nombrarse juez y verdugo ►► *Mil* ***j. advocate*** juez *mf* togado(a) militar
(**b**) *(in competition)* jurado *m*, juez *m*; **the judges were divided** la opinión de los jueces estaba dividida, el jurado estaba dividido; **the judges' decision is final** la decisión del jurado es inapelable
(**c**) *(assessor)* **to be a good/poor j. of sth** tener buen/mal ojo para (juzgar) algo; **to be a good j. of character** tener buen ojo para la gente; **I'm not sure he's the best j. of such things** no estoy seguro de que él sea la persona indicada para evaluar estas cosas; **I will be the j. of that** lo juzgaré por mí mismo; **I'll let you be the j. of that** evalúalo tú mismo
2 *vt* (**a**) *(in court)* juzgar; **to j. a case** juzgar un caso
(**b**) *(be adjudicator at)* **the contest was judged by a panel of critics** el jurado del concurso estaba formado por varios críticos; **they asked me to j. the competition** me pidieron que fuera jurado del concurso
(**c**) *(deem)* considerar; **to j. sth/sb a success/failure** considerar algo/a alguien un éxito/fracaso; **her latest novel has been judged a failure by the critics** los críticos consideran que su última novela es un fracaso; **to j. it necessary to do sth** juzgar *or* considerar necesario hacer algo; **I'd j. him to be about thirty** yo diría que anda por los treinta *or* que tiene unos treinta
(**d**) *(pass judgement on)* juzgar; **don't j. him too harshly** no lo juzgues muy duramente
(**e**) *(assess)* **can you j. the distance?** ¿puedes calcular la distancia?; **I find it hard to j. which is heavier** no sabría decir cuál pesa más; **to j. sb by** *or* **on sth** juzgar a alquien por algo
3 *vi* **it's wrong to j. by appearances** no hay que juzgar por las apariencias; **as far as I can j.** en mi opinión; **j. for yourself** júzgalo tú mismo, juzga por ti mismo; **judging by** *or* **from...** a juzgar por...

judgement, judgment ['dʒʌdʒmənt] *n* (**a**) *(decision)* juicio *m*; *(of judge, in court)* fallo *m*; *Law* **to sit in j.** deliberar; *Law* **to pass j.** pronunciar *or* emitir el veredicto; *Fig* **to sit in** *or* **pass j. on sb** emitir juicios sobre alguien, juzgar a alguien ►► *Rel* ***Judg(e)ment Day*** el día del Juicio Final
(**b**) *(opinion)* juicio *m*, parecer *m*; **she gave her j. on the performance** dio su parecer acerca de la actuación; **to form a j.** formarse un juicio; **in my j.** a mi juicio
(**c**) *(discernment)* juicio *m*; **he is a man of j.** es una persona con criterio *or* criteriosa; **political/financial j.** opinión política/financiera; **good j.** buen juicio; **to lack (good** *or* **sound) j.** carecer de criterio, no tener criterio; **to show poor j.** demostrar tener poco juicio; **to trust sb's j.** fiarse (del juicio) de alguien; **against my better j.** a pesar de no estar plenamente convencido

judgemental, judgmental [dʒʌdʒ'mentəl] *adj (attitude, remarks)* sentencioso(a); **to be j.** erigirse en juez; **I don't want to seem j. but...** no quiero parecer sentencioso pero...

judicial [dʒu:'dɪʃəl] *adj* judicial ►► *Law* ***j. review*** = revisión de un fallo judicial o de una ley ante su posible inconstitucionalidad; *Br Law* ***j. separation*** separación *f* judicial

judicially [dʒu:'dɪʃəlɪ] *adv* judicialmente

judiciary [dʒu:'dɪʃɪərɪ] *n* (**a**) *(judges)* judicatura *f*, magistratura *f* (**b**) *(branch of authority)* poder *m* judicial

judicious [dʒu:'dɪʃəs] *adj* sensato(a), acertado(a); **he was most j. in his remarks** sus observaciones fueron sumamente acertadas

judiciously [dʒu:'dɪʃəslɪ] *adv* juiciosamente

judiciousness [dʒu:'dɪʃəsnɪs] *n* buen juicio *m*

judo ['dʒu:dəʊ] *n* judo *m* ►► ***j. expert*** judoka *mf*, yudoka *mf*; ***j. player*** judoka *mf*, yudoka *mf*

judogi [dʒu:'dəʊgɪ] *n* judogui *m*

judoka [dʒu:'dəʊkə] *n* judoka *mf*, yudoka *mf*

jug [dʒʌg] **1** *n* (**a**) *(for wine, water, milk)* jarra *f* ►► ***j. kettle*** tetera *f*, *Arg* pava *f*, *Urug* caldera *f* eléctrica (**b**) *Fam (prison)* **in the j.** en la cárcel *or Esp* chirona *or Andes, RP* la cana *or Méx* el bote (**c**) *very Fam* **jugs** *(breasts)* tetas *fpl*, *Esp* melones *mpl*, *Méx* chichís *fpl*, *RP* lolas *fpl*
2 *vt Culin* hervir

jug-eared ['dʒʌgɪəd] *adj Fam* con orejas tipo Dumbo

jugful ['dʒʌgfʊl] *n* jarra *f* (llena)

jugged hare ['dʒʌgd'heə(r)] *n Culin* estofado *m or* caldereta *f* de liebre

juggernaut ['dʒʌgənɔ:t] *n* (**a**) *Br (large lorry)* camión *m* grande, tráiler *m* (**b**) *(force)* gigante(a) *m,f*, coloso(a) *m,f*; **the j. of history/war** el coloso de la historia/guerra

juggins ['dʒʌgɪnz] *n Br Fam Old-fashioned (simpleton)* simplón(ona) *m,f*

juggle ['dʒʌgəl] **1** *vt (balls, figures)* hacer malabarismos *or* juegos malabares con; **I think it'll be OK if I j. the dates around** si juego un poco con las fechas creo que es posible; **she juggles her home life and her career** hace malabarismos para poder compatibilizar su vida doméstica con su carrera
2 *vi* hacer malabarismos, hacer juegos malabares; **to j. with sth** *(balls)* hacer malabarismos *or* juegos malabares con algo; *(figures, dates)* hacer malabarismos con algo, jugar con algo

juggler ['dʒʌglə(r)] *n* malabarista *mf*

juggling ['dʒʌglɪŋ] *n* juegos *mpl* malabares, malabarismo *m*

jugular ['dʒʌgjʊlə(r)] **1** *n* yugular *f*; *Fig* **to go for the j.** *(in argument)* entrar a degüello
2 *adj* yugular

juice [dʒuːs] **1** *n* (**a**) *(of fruit) Esp* zumo *m*, *Am* jugo *m*; *(of meat)* jugo *m* ►► ***j. extractor*** exprimidor *m* eléctrico
(**b**) *Physiol* **gastric/digestive juices** jugos gástricos/digestivos
(**c**) *Fam (petrol)* gasolina *f*, *Esp* gasofa *f*, *RP* nafta *f*; *(electricity)* electricidad *f*, corriente *f*
(**d**) *US Fam (alcoholic drink)* bebida *f*, *Méx, RP* chupe *m*; **he's on the j. again** le está dando a la bebida *or Méx, RP* al chupe otra vez
(**e**) *US Fam (influence)* **to have a lot of j. with sb** tener mucha mano con alguien
2 *vt (fruit)* exprimir

► **juice up** *vt sep US Fam (enliven)* animar, alegrar

juiced [dʒuːst] *adj US Fam* **j. (up)** *(drunk)* pedo, *Esp* mamado(a)

juicehead [ˈdʒuːshed] *n US Fam (alcoholic)* borracho(a) *m,f*, *Esp* bolinga *mf*, *RP* curda *mf*

juicer [ˈdʒuːsə(r)] *n* (**a**) *(utensil)* exprimidor *m* (**b**) *US Fam (alcoholic)* borracho(a) *m,f*, *Esp* bolinga *mf*, *RP* curda *mf*

juiciness [ˈdʒuːsɪnɪs] *n* (**a**) *(of fruit)* jugosidad *f*; **the j. of the orange** lo jugosa que es la naranja (**b**) *(of gossip)* **the j. of the gossip** lo picante *or* jugoso del chisme

juicy [ˈdʒuːsɪ] *adj* (**a**) *(fruit, steak)* jugoso(a) (**b**) *Fam (profitable, attractive)* jugoso(a); **a j. contract** un contrato jugoso; **a j. proposal** una propuesta jugosa (**c**) *Fam (gossip)* jugoso(a), sabroso(a); **let's hear all the j. details** escuchemos los detalles jugosos

ju-jitsu, jiu-jitsu [dʒuːˈdʒɪtsuː] *n* jiu-jitsu *m*

juju [ˈdʒuːdʒuː] *n (charm)* amuleto *m*, hechizo *m*

jukebox [ˈdʒuːkbɒks] *n* máquina *f* de discos

Jul (*abbr* **July**) jul.

julep [ˈdʒuːlɪp] *n* (**a**) *US (alcoholic drink)* julep *m*, julepe *m*; **(mint) j.** mint julep *m*, julepe *m* de menta (**b**) *(medicated drink)* julepe *m*

julienne [dʒuːlɪˈen] *Culin* **1** *n* sopa *f* juliana
2 *adj* en juliana, cortado(a) en juliana

Julius [ˈdʒuːlɪəs] *pr n* **J. Caesar** Julio César

July [dʒuːˈlaɪ] *n* julio *m*; *see also* **May**

jumble [ˈdʒʌmbəl] **1** *n* (**a**) *(disordered mass) (of things, ideas, words)* revoltijo *m*, batiburrillo *m*; **in a j.** *(papers)* revueltos; *(ideas)* confusas (**b**) *Br (articles for sale)* objetos *mpl* usados ►► ***j. sale*** rastrillo *m* benéfico
2 *vt (things, ideas, words)* revolver; **the pages got all jumbled** las páginas se mezclaron todas; **her clothes were all jumbled (up** *or* **together) in a suitcase** sus ropas estaban todas revueltas en una maleta; **his essay was just a collection of jumbled ideas** su ensayo no era más que una cantidad de ideas desordenadas

► **jumble up** *vt sep* **to j. things up** revolver las cosas, revolverlo todo

jumbo [ˈdʒʌmbəʊ] **1** *adj* gigante ►► ***j. jet*** jumbo *m*
2 *n (plane)* jumbo *m*

jumbo-size(d) [ˈdʒʌmbəʊˈsaɪz(d)] *adj* (de tamaño) gigante

JUMP [dʒʌmp] **1** *n* (**a**) *(leap)* salto *m*; **parachute j.** salto en paracaídas; *Fam Fig* **go take a j.!** ¡vete a freír espárragos!, *RP* ¡andá a freír churros!; *Fig* **to be one j. ahead** ir (un paso) por delante; *Fam* **to get a j. on one's competitors** adelantar a la competencia ►► ***j. ball*** *(in basketball)* salto *m* entre dos, lucha *f*; *Cin* ***j. cut*** corte *m* con discontinuidad; *Av* ***j. jet*** reactor *m* de despegue vertical; *Br Aut* ***j. leads*** pinzas *fpl or* cables *mpl* (de arranque) de batería; *US* ***j. rope*** *Esp* comba *f*, *Am* cuerda *f* de saltar; ***j. seat*** asiento *m* plegable *or RP* rebatible; ***j. shot*** *(in basketball)* tiro *m* en suspensión
(**b**) *(in surprise)* sobresalto *m*; **I woke up with a j.** desperté sobresaltado
(**c**) *(rise)* salto *m* (**in** en)
(**d**) *(fence on racecourse)* obstáculo *m* ►► *Br* ***j. jockey*** jockey *m* de carreras de obstáculos
2 *vt* (**a**) *(hedge, ditch)* saltar; **she jumped seven metres** saltó (una distancia de) siete metros; **to j. the gun** *(in race)* hacer una salida en falso; *Fig* precipitarse; *US* **to j. rope** saltar a la cuerda *or Esp* comba; *US Fam* **to j. sb's bones** tirarse a alguien, *Esp* pasarse a alguien por la piedra, *RP* darle a alguien
(**b**) *(horse)* hacer saltar; **she jumped her horse over the stream** saltó el riachuelo con el caballo
(**c**) *(miss out) (word, paragraph, page)* saltarse; **to j. the lights** *(in car)* saltarse un semáforo, *RP* comerse la luz roja; **to j.** *Br* **the queue** *or US* **the line** colarse
(**d**) *(leave)* **to j. bail** huir durante la libertad bajo fianza; **to j. town** abandonar la ciudad; **to j. ship** desertar, abandonar el barco
(**e**) *(attack)* asaltar
(**f**) *(in board games)* adelantar
(**g**) *US (train, bus) (get on quickly)* montarse en, *RP* saltar al; *(get on without paying)* colarse en
3 *vi* (**a**) *(leap) (person, animal)* saltar; **they jumped across the stream** cruzaron el arroyo de un salto; **to j. (down) from a wall/tree** saltar de *or* desde un muro/árbol; **to j. from a train** tirarse de un tren; **he jumped into the pool** se tiró a la piscina; **she jumped out of the window** se tiró por la ventana; **he jumped up onto the table** se subió a la mesa de un salto; **to j. up and down** *(to keep warm etc)* pegar saltos; *(with excitement)* pegar brincos *or* saltos; *(be annoyed)* estar hecho(a) una furia; *Fig* **let's wait and see which way she jumps** esperemos a ver por dónde sale *or RP* para dónde salta; **to j. for joy** saltar de alegría; *Fig* **to j. out at sb** *(mistake, surprising detail)* saltarle a alguien a la vista; IDIOM *Fam* **to j. down sb's throat** ponerse hecho(a) una furia con alguien; IDIOM *Fam* **go j. in the lake!** ¡vete a freír espárragos!, *RP* ¡andá a freír churros *or* bañarte!; IDIOM **to j. in with both feet** lanzarse con los ojos cerrados, *RP* tirarse al agua (de traje)
(**b**) *(move quickly)* **she jumped from her seat** se levantó de un salto *or* brinco; **to j. out of bed** levantarse (de la cama) de un salto, saltar de la cama; **to j. to one's feet** ponerse en pie de un salto, *Am* pararse de un salto; **we jumped up and started running** nos pusimos en pie de un brinco y salimos corriendo, *Am* nos paramos de un salto y salimos corriendo; *Fam Fig* **I wouldn't j. into bed with just anyone** yo no me metería en la cama con cualquiera; **to j. to conclusions** sacar conclusiones precipitadas; **to j. to sb's defence** saltar en defensa de alguien; **j. to it!** ¡manos a la obra!
(**c**) *(go directly)* **to j. from one subject to another** saltar de un tema a otro; **the movie then jumps to the present/jumps back to his childhood** luego la película da un salto hasta el presente/da un salto atrás hasta su infancia
(**d**) *(rise rapidly) (unemployment, prices)* dispararse, aumentar rápidamente; **inflation has jumped from 5 to 10 percent** la inflación se ha disparado de un 5 a un 10 por ciento
(**e**) *(make sudden movement) (person)* dar un salto, saltar; *(TV picture, CD, record)* saltar; **you made me j.!** ¡qué susto me has dado!; **my heart jumped** me dio un vuelco el corazón; **we nearly jumped out of our skins** nos dimos un susto de muerte; *Fam* **to be jumping** *(club, party)* estar muy animado, *Esp* estar a tope de marcha, *RP* estar de lo más

► **jump about, jump around** *vi* dar saltos

► **jump aboard** **1** *vt insep (boat)* saltar a bordo de; *(train, bus)* subir de un salto a; **to j. aboard the environmental bandwagon** subirse al carro de la ecología
2 *vi (on boat)* saltar a bordo; *(on train, bus)* subir de un salto

► **jump at** *vt insep* **to j. at an offer/a chance** no dejar escapar una oferta/una oportunidad

► **jump in** **1** *vt insep* **j. in the back!** ¡móntate (en la parte de) atrás!
2 *vi* (**a**) *(get in car)* **j. in!** ¡monta!, ¡sube! (**b**) *(interrupt)* interrumpir (**c**) *(intervene)* intervenir

► **jump into** *vt insep (taxi, car)* montar en

► **jump on** *vt insep* (**a**) *(train, bus)* coger, tomar (**b**) *(attack)* asaltar (**c**) *Fam (reprimand)* **to j. on sb (for doing sth)** echarse encima de alguien (por haber hecho algo)

jumped-up [ˈdʒʌmpˈtʌp] *adj Br Fam Pej* presuntuoso(a), con muchos humos; **she's just a j. shop assistant** no es más que una empleada cualquiera con humos

jumper [ˈdʒʌmpə(r)] *n* (**a**) *Br (sweater)* suéter *m*, *Esp* jersey *m*, *Col* saco *m*, *RP* pulóver *m* (**b**) *US (sleeveless dress) Esp* pichi *m*, *CSur, Méx* jumper *m* (**c**) *Comptr* jumper *m*, puente *m* (**d**) *Fam (in basketball) (jump shot)* tiro *m* en suspensión (**e**) *US Aut* ***j. cables*** pinzas *fpl or* cables *mpl* (de arranque) de batería

jumpiness [ˈdʒʌmpɪnɪs] *n* nerviosismo *m*

jumping-bean [ˈdʒʌmpɪŋbiːn] *n Esp* judía *f* saltarina, *Am* fríjol *m* brincador

jumping-jack [ˈdʒʌmpɪŋˈdʒæk] *n* (**a**) *(toy)* títere *m* (**b**) *(firework)* buscapiés *m inv*

jumping-off place [ˈdʒʌmpɪŋˈɒfˈpleɪs], **jumping-off point** [ˈdʒʌmpɪŋˈɒfˈpɔɪnt] *n* punto *m* de partida

jump-off [ˈdʒʌmpɒf] *n (in showjumping)* recorrido *m* de desempate

jump-start [ˈdʒʌmpstɑːt] *vt (car) (with leads)* arrancar utilizando pinzas de batería; *(by pushing)* arrancar (un vehículo) empujándolo; *Fig* **to j. the economy** hacer arrancar la economía

jumpsuit [ˈdʒʌmpsuːt] *n* mono *m (de vestir)*

jumpy [ˈdʒʌmpɪ] *adj* (**a**) *Fam (edgy)* nervioso(a); **to be j.** estar nervioso(a) (**b**) *(jerky)* **the picture is a bit j.** la imagen se mueve un poco

Jun (*abbr* **June**) jun.

junction ['dʒʌŋkʃən] *n* (**a**) *(of roads, railway lines)* cruce *m*, nudo *m*; *Br* **j. 20** *(on motorway)* salida 20 (**b**) *Elec* ***j. box*** caja *f* de empalmes

juncture ['dʒʌŋktʃə(r)] *n* (**a**) *Formal (moment)* coyuntura *f*; **at this j.** en esta coyuntura (**b**) *Formal (joining point)* unión *f*, juntura *f* (**c**) *Ling* juntura *f*

June [dʒu:n] *n* junio *m*; *see also* **May**

Jungian ['jʊŋɪən] **1** *n* junguiano(a) *m,f*
2 *adj* junguiano(a)

jungle ['dʒʌŋgəl] *n* (**a**) *(forest)* selva *f*, jungla *f* ►► *very Fam* ***j. bunny*** = término ofensivo para referirse a un negro; *Med* ***j. fever*** paludismo *m*; *Br Fam* ***j. juice*** alcohol *m* duro *or* fuerte
(**b**) *(dangerous place)* jungla *f*; **the world of business is a real j.** el mundo de los negocios es una verdadera jungla; **it's a j. out there** la calle está hecha una jungla
(**c**) *(confusion)* maraña *f*, confusión *f*; **the j. of tax laws** la maraña de las leyes tributarias
(**d**) *US* ***j. gym*** = en los parques, estructura de hierro o madera para que trepen los niños

junior ['dʒu:njə(r)] **1** *adj* (**a**) *(in age)* **to be j. to sb** ser más joven que alguien; **Nigel Molesworth J.** Nigel Molesworth hijo ►► *US* ***j. high (school)*** *(between 11 and 15)* escuela *f* secundaria; *Br* ***j. school*** *(between 7 and 11)* escuela *f* primaria; *US* ***j. year*** tercer año *m* de secundaria
(**b**) *(in rank)* de rango inferior; **to be j. to sb** tener un rango inferior al de alguien ►► *US Univ* ***j. college*** = centro educativo en el que se hacen cursos de dos años, normalmente equivalentes a los dos primeros años de la universidad; *Br Univ* ***j. common room*** sala *f* de estudiantes; *Br Parl* ***j. minister*** ≃ secretario(a) *m,f* de Estado; ***j. partner*** socio(a) *m,f* menor *or* subalterno(a)
(**c**) *(small)* pequeño(a), *Am* chico(a); **j. portions available** *(in restaurant)* hay raciones para niños
2 *n* (**a**) *(in age)* **to be sb's j.** ser más joven que alguien; **he's three years my j.** es tres años menor que yo (**b**) *(in rank)* subalterno(a) *m,f* (**c**) *Br (pupil)* alumno(a) *m,f* de primaria; **she teaches juniors** da clase en primaria (**d**) *US Sch & Univ* alumno(a) *m,f* de tercero; **she's a j.** está en tercero (**e**) *US Fam* **hi, j.!** ¡hola, hijo!; **bring J. with you next time** la próxima vez trae a tu hijo

juniper ['dʒu:nɪpə(r)] *n* **j. (tree)** enebro *m* ►► ***j. berry*** enebrina *f*, baya *f* de enebro

junk¹ [dʒʌŋk] **1** *n* (**a**) *(worthless things)* trastos *mpl*; *Fam* **his new book is a pile of j.** su nuevo libro es una mierda *or RP* cagada ►► *Fin* ***j. bond*** bono *m* basura; *Comptr* ***j. e-mail*** correo *m* basura; ***j. fax*** propaganda *f* por fax; *Pej* ***j. food*** comida *f* basura; ***j. mail*** propaganda *f* (postal); ***j. room*** (cuarto *m*) trastero *m*
(**b**) *(second-hand or unwanted goods)* cosas *fpl* usadas, cachivaches *mpl* ►► ***j. shop*** cacharrería *f*, baratillo *m*
(**c**) *Fam (stuff)* cosas *fpl*; **move all that j. of yours off the bed** saca todas tus cosas de encima de la cama; **what's/whose is all that j. in the hall?** ¿qué/de quién son todas esas cosas que están en la entrada?
(**d**) *Fam (drug)* caballo *m*, heroína *f*
2 *vt Fam (discard)* deshacerse de; **the last batch of parts from them had so many faults it had to be junked** el último lote de piezas que recibimos de ellos tenía tantas fallas que tuvimos que tirarlo

junk² *n (boat)* junco *m*

junker ['dʒʌŋkə(r)] *n US Fam (car)* cacharro *m* (viejo)

junket ['dʒʌŋkɪt] **1** *n* (**a**) *(food)* cuajada *f* (**b**) *Fam (festive occasion)* fiesta *f*, juerga *f* (**c**) *Fam Pej (trip)* viaje *m* pagado
2 *vi* (**a**) *Fam (feast)* festejar (**b**) *Fam Pej (go on trip)* viajar gratis; **councillors go junketing off to Canada on a "fact-finding trip"** los concejales se hacen un viajecito gratis a Canadá en misión investigadora

junkie, junky ['dʒʌŋkɪ] *n Fam (drug addict in general)* drogadicto(a) *m,f*, *Esp* drogata *mf*; *(heroin addict)* yonqui *mf*; **a game-show j.** un adicto a los concursos; **a chocolate j.** un devorador de chocolate

junkman ['dʒʌŋkmæn] *n US* trapero

junky = **junkie**

junkyard ['dʒʌŋkjɑ:d] *n (for metal)* chatarrería *f*, depósito *m* de chatarra

Juno ['dʒu:nəʊ] *n* Juno *m*

junoesque [dʒu:nəʊ'esk] *adj (woman)* escultural

junta ['dʒʌntə, *US* 'hʊntə] *n Pej* junta *f* militar

Jupiter ['dʒu:pɪtə(r)] *n* Júpiter *m*

Jurassic [dʒʊ'ræsɪk] *Geol* **1** *n* **the J.** el jurásico
2 *adj (era)* jurásico(a)

juridical [dʒʊ'rɪdɪkəl] *adj* jurídico(a)

jurisdiction [dʒʊərɪs'dɪkʃən] *n* (**a**) *Law* jurisdicción *f*; **to have j. over** tener jurisdicción sobre; **within** *or* **under the j. of...** bajo la jurisdicción de...; **to come** *or* **fall within the jurisdiction of** estar dentro de la jurisdicción de (**b**) *(field of activity)* competencia *f*; **this matter does not come within** *or* **is not in** *or* **falls outside our j.** esta cuestión está fuera de nuestra competencia

jurisdictional ['dʒʊərɪs'dɪkʃənəl] *adj* jurisdiccional; *US* **a j. dispute** una disputa jurisdiccional

jurisprudence [dʒʊərɪs'pru:dəns] *n* jurisprudencia *f*

jurist ['dʒʊərɪst] *n* (**a**) *Formal (legal expert)* jurista *mf* (**b**) *US (judge)* magistrado(a) *m,f*

juror ['dʒʊərə(r)] *n Law* (miembro *m* del) jurado *m*

jury ['dʒʊərɪ] *n* (**a**) *Law* jurado *m*; **to be** *or* **serve on the j.** ser miembro del jurado; **members of the j.** *(term of address)* miembros del jurado; **the j. is out** el jurado está deliberando; IDIOM **the j. is still out on the reforms** aún está por ver la conveniencia de las reformas ►► ***j. box*** tribuna *f* del jurado; ***j. service*** *or* ***duty:*** **to do j. service** *or* **duty** formar parte de un jurado (popular) (**b**) *(in contest)* jurado *m*

juryman ['dʒʊərɪmən] *n* miembro *m* del jurado

jury-rig ['dʒʊərɪ'rɪg] (*pt & pp* **jury-rigged**) *vt US (improvise)* improvisar

jury-rigging ['dʒʊərɪ'rɪgɪŋ] *n* manipulación *f* del jurado

jurywoman ['dʒʊərɪwʊmən] *n* miembro *m* del jurado

just¹ [dʒʌst] *adj (fair)* justo(a); **it's only j. that...** es justo que...; **to have j. cause to do sth** estar plenamente justificado(a) para hacer algo; **he got his j. deserts** recibió su merecido; **her promotion is j. reward for her hard work** su ascenso es una justa recompensa por haber trabajado duro

JUST² **1** *adv* (**a**) *(exactly)* justamente, justo; **that's j. what I told her** eso es exactamente *or* justo lo que le dije; **you look j. like your brother** eres idéntico a tu hermano; **that's j. the point!** ¡de eso se trata, precisamente!; **that's j. it!** *(said in agreement)* ¡justamente!, ¡exactamente!; **I can j. see her as a doctor** me la imagino perfectamente como médica; **I can j. smell the sea air!** ¡casi puedo oler el aire del mar!; **he told her to get lost j. like that** le dijo que se largara así sin más; **j. as I was leaving...** justo en el momento en que me iba...; **it's j. as good/difficult as...** es igual de bueno/difícil que...; **I've got j. as much as you** tengo justo lo mismo que tú; **he's busy j. now** está ocupado en este (preciso) momento; *Br* **j. on ten o'clock** a las diez en punto justas; **this soufflé is j. right** este suflé está justo en su punto; **j. so** *(neat and tidy)* en orden, en su sitio *or* lugar; *Old-fashioned (said in agreement)* exacto, eso es; **j. then** justo entonces; **this liquidizer is j. the thing for making soups** esta batidora viene de maravilla para hacer sopas; **I can't tell you j. yet** todavía no te lo puedo decir; **that dress is j. you** ese vestido te va de maravilla
(**b**) *(only)* sólo, solamente; **it costs j. £10** sólo cuesta 10 libras; **I'll j. have a sandwich, thanks** comeré sólo un sándwich, gracias; **she's j. a baby** no es más que una niña; **I was j. wondering whether you could help** estaba pensando si podrías echar *or* dar una mano; **I knew j. by looking at her that she was upset** sólo con mirarla supe que estaba mal; **could you move j. a little to the right?** ¿te podrías mover *or* correr un poquito hacia la derecha?; **I'd love to help, it's j. that I'm too busy** me encantaría ayudar, pero (es que) estoy demasiado ocupado; **j. a minute** *or* **moment** *or* **second!** ¡un momento!; **j. for once** por una vez; **j. in case** por si acaso; **j. this once** sólo (por) esta vez
(**c**) *(simply)* **j. add water** simplemente añade *or* agrega agua; **j. ask if you need money** si necesitas dinero, no tienes más que pedirlo; **j. put it on the table** déjalo (ahí mismo) en la mesa; **we did it j. for fun** lo hicimos sólo por diversión *or* para divertirnos; **I wouldn't lend it to j. anybody** no se lo prestaría a cualquiera; **you'll j. have to put up with it** ¡pues te aguantas!; **don't j. sit there!** ¡no te quedes ahí sin hacer nada!; **it's j. not fair!** ¡es que no es justo!; **j. listen to this!** ¡escucha esto!; **it was j. wonderful/dreadful!** ¡fue sencillamente maravilloso/horroroso!; **he j. refuses to listen!** ¡es que se niega a escuchar!; **j. because you're older than me doesn't mean I have to do what you say** ¡no tengo que hacer lo que tú digas sólo porque seas mayor que yo!
(**d**) *(barely)* justo; **you could j. see the top of the mountain** se veía apenas la cumbre de la montaña; **j. before/after** justo antes/después; **j. over/under $50** poco más/menos de 50 dólares; *also Ind* **j. in time** justo a tiempo; **it's only j. big enough** tiene el tamaño justo; **we only j. got there on time** llegamos muy justos de tiempo; **it's j. enough to live on** llega *or* alcanza justo para vivir; **they j. caught/missed the train** *Esp* cogieron/perdieron el tren por los pelos, *Am* no cogieron/perdieron el tren por un pelo; **they live j. round the corner** viven a la vuelta de la esquina
(**e**) *(recently)* **they have j. arrived** acaban de llegar; **I had j. arrived**

when... acababa de llegar cuando...; **I was j. telling Jim about your accident** justamente le estaba contando a Jim lo de tu accidente; **I'm only j. beginning to come to terms with it** sólo ahora empiezo a aceptarlo; **j. last year** tan sólo *or RP* recién el año pasado; **I saw him j. now** lo acabo de ver; **j. recently** hace muy poco; **j. yesterday** ayer mismo

(**f**) *(now)* **I'm j. coming** ¡ya voy!; **I was j. leaving, actually** ya me iba; **I'll j. finish my coffee, then we can go** me termino el café y nos vamos

(**g**) *(in exclamations)* **j. (you) try/wait!** ¡inténtalo/espera y verás *or* vas a ver!; **j. shut up, will you?** ¡cállate ya!, ¿quieres?; **(that's) j. as well!** ¡menos mal!; **isn't that j. my luck!** ¡vaya mala suerte que tengo!, ¡qué mala suerte la mía!; **j. imagine, never having to work again!** ¡imagínate no tener que trabajar nunca más!

(**h**) *Fam (for emphasis)* **it's rather cold in here – isn't it j.?** hace mucho frío aquí – ¿verdad que sí?

(**i**) *(expressing preference)* **I'd j. as soon you didn't tell her** preferiría que no se lo dijeras

2 just about *adv (almost)* casi; **they're j. about the same** son casi iguales; **I can j. about manage** me las puedo arreglar más o menos; **to be j. about to do sth** estar a punto de hacer algo

---

justice ['dʒʌstɪs] *n* (**a**) *(power of law)* justicia *f*; **to bring sb to j.** llevar a alguien a juicio; **j. was done** se hizo justicia; PROV **j. must be done, and be seen to be done** no sólo hay que ser justo, hay que parecerlo ►► *US* ***the J. Department, the Department of J.*** Ministerio *m* de Justicia

(**b**) *(fairness)* justicia *f*; **they believe in the j. of their cause** creen en lo justo de su causa; **there's simply no j.** no es justo; **this photograph doesn't do him j.** esta fotografía no le hace justicia; **to do him j., he wasn't told beforehand** para ser justos, hay que tener en cuenta que no le avisaron antes; **he didn't do himself j. in the exam/interview** no dio lo mejor de sí en el examen/la entrevista; **to do j. to a meal** hacerle honor a una comida

(**c**) *Law (judge)* juez *mf*, juez(a) *m,f*; *Br* **Mr J. Ramsbottom** *(title)* el Sr. Juez Ramsbottom ►► ***J. of the Peace*** juez *mf* de paz

justifiable ['dʒʌstɪfaɪəbəl] *adj* justificable ►► *Law* ***j. homicide*** homicidio *m* justificado

justifiably ['dʒʌstɪfaɪəblɪ] *adv* justificadamente; **she was j. angry** estaba enojada con toda razón

justification [dʒʌstɪfɪ'keɪʃən] *n* (**a**) *(gen)* justificación *f*; **in j. of** para justificar; **there is no j. for such behaviour** ese comportamiento es injustificable *or* no tiene justificación; **poverty is no j. for theft** la pobreza no justifica el robo; **he was accused of carelessness, with some j.** se lo acusó de descuido, con cierta razón

(**b**) *(of text)* justificación *f*

(**c**) *Rel* **j. by faith** (dogma de la) redención por la fe

justified ['dʒʌstɪfaɪd] *adj* (**a**) *(right, fair) (action, belief)* justificado(a); **to be j. in doing sth** tener justificación para hacer algo (**b**) *(text)* justificado(a)

justify ['dʒʌstɪfaɪ] *vt* (**a**) *(show to be reasonable)* justificar; **nothing can j. such cruelty** no hay justificativos para semejante crueldad; **to j. oneself** justificarse (**b**) *(text)* justificar

just-in-time ['dʒʌstɪntaɪm] *adj Com* ***j. production*** producción *f* "justo a tiempo" *(con minimización de stocks)*

justly ['dʒʌstlɪ] *adv (fairly, rightly)* justamente, con justicia; **j. famous** justamente *or* merecidamente famoso(a)

justness ['dʒʌstnɪs] *n* **the j. of their cause/demand** lo justificado de su causa/reivindicación

jut [dʒʌt] (*pt & pp* **jutted**) *vi* sobresalir, proyectarse

►**jut out** 1 *vt sep (chin)* sacar

2 *vi (balcony, rock)* sobresalir

jute [dʒu:t] *n (plant, fibre)* yute *m*

juvenile ['dʒu:vɪnaɪl] **1** *adj* (**a**) *(for young people)* juvenil ►► *Law* ***j. court*** tribunal *m* (tutelar) de menores; ***j. delinquency*** delincuencia *f* juvenil; ***j. delinquent*** delincuente *mf* juvenil; ***j. offender*** delincuente *mf* juvenil (**b**) *Pej (childish)* infantil, pueril

2 *n* (**a**) *Law* menor *mf* (**b**) *Theat* galán *m*

juvenilia [dʒu:və'nɪlɪə] *n* obras *fpl* de juventud

juxtapose [dʒʌkstə'pəʊz] *vt* yuxtaponer

juxtaposition [dʒʌkstəpə'zɪʃən] *n* yuxtaposición *f*

K, k

K, k [keɪ] *n (letter)* K, k *f*

K [keɪ] *n* (**a**) *(thousand)* mil; **he earns 30K** gana treinta mil (**b**) *Comptr* (*abbr* **kilobyte**) K *m*

Kabul ['kɑːbʊl] *n* Kabul

kaffeeklatsch ['kæfeɪklætʃ] *n US* tertulia *f (en la que se reúnen las mujeres y toman café)*

Kaffir ['kæfə(r)] *n SAfr very Fam* negraco(a) *m,f,* = término ofensivo para referirse a los negros

Kafkaesque [kæfkə'esk] *adj* kafkiano(a)

kaftan ['kæftæn] *n* caftán *m*

kagoule [kə'guːl] *n Br* chubasquero *m*

Kaiser ['kaɪzə(r)] *n* káiser *m*

kala-azar [kɑːləə'zɑː(r)] *n Med* kala-azar *m*

Kalahari [kælə'hɑːrɪ] *n* **the K. (Desert)** el (desierto de) Kalahari

kalashnikov [kə'læʃnɪkɒv] *n* (rifle *m*) Kaláshnikov *m*

kale [keɪl] *n* col *f* rizada, *CSur* repollo *m* rizado

kaleidoscope [kə'laɪdəskəʊp] *n* caleidoscopio *m*, calidoscopio *m*

kaleidoscopic [kəlaɪdə'skɒpɪk] *adj* caleidoscópico(a), calidoscópico(a)

kamikaze [kæmɪ'kɑːzɪ] **1** *n* kamikaze *mf*
2 *adj* (**a**) *(pilot, plane)* kamikaze (**b**) *Fam (tactics)* kamikaze

Kampala [kæm'pɑːlə] *n* Kampala

Kampuchea [kæmpuː'tʃɪə] *n Formerly* Kampuchea

kangaroo [kæŋgə'ruː] (*pl* **kangaroos**) *n* canguro *m* ▸▸ *Pej* ***k. court*** tribunal *m* irregular; *Zool* ***k. rat*** rata *f* canguro

kaoline, kaolin ['keɪəlɪn] *n* caolín *m*

kaon ['keɪɒn] *n Phys* kaón *m*

kapok ['keɪpɒk] *n* capoc *m*; **k. tree** capoquero

Kaposi's sarcoma [kə'pəʊziːzsɑː'kəʊmə] *n Med* sarcoma *m* de Kaposi

kaput [kə'pʊt] *adj Fam* **to be k.** *Esp* estar cascado(a), *esp Am* estar roto(a) *or* estropeado(a), *Andes* estar malogrado(a), *RP* haber sonado; **to go k.** *(machine, car) Esp* cascarse, *esp Am* romperse, *esp Am* descomponerse, *Andes* malograrse, *RP* sonar; *(business, plan)* irse al garete

karabiner [kærə'biːnə(r)] *n (in mountaineering)* mosquetón *m*

karaoke [kærɪ'əʊkɪ] *n* karaoke *m* ▸▸ ***k. bar*** (bar *m* con) karaoke *m*; ***k. machine*** (aparato *m* de) karaoke *m*

karat ['kærət] *n US (of gold)* quilate *m*; **18-k. gold** oro *m* de 18 quilates

karate [kə'rɑːtɪ] *n* kárate *m* ▸▸ ***k. chop*** golpe *m* de kárate; ***k. expert*** karateka *mf*

karateka [kærə'teɪkə] *n* karateka *mf*

karma ['kɑːmə] *n* (**a**) *Rel* karma *m* (**b**) *Fam Fig* **good/bad k.** buenas/malas vibraciones *or Am* ondas, *Esp* buen/mal rollo

karst ['kɑːst] *n Geol* karst *m*

karstic ['kɑːstɪk] *adj Geol* kárstico(a)

kart [kɑːt] *n* kart *m*

karting ['kɑːtɪŋ] *n Sport* carreras *fpl* de karts, karting *m*; **to go k.** ir a correr en karts

karzey, karzy, kazi ['kɑːzɪ] *n Br Fam* váter *m*, *Esp* meódromo *m*

kasbah ['kæzbɑː] *n* kasbah *f*

Kashmir [kæʃ'mɪə(r)] *n* Cachemira

Kashmiri [kæʃ'mɪərɪ] **1** *n* persona de Cachemira
2 *adj* de Cachemira

kata ['kætə] *n* kata *m*

Katmandu [kætmæn'duː] *n* Katmandú

katydid ['keɪtɪdɪd] *n US* chicharra *f*

kayak ['kaɪæk] *n* canoa *f*, kayak *m*

Kazak, Kazakh [kə'zæk] *n* kazaco(a) *m,f*, kazajo(a) *m,f*

Kazakhstan, Kazakstan [kæzæk'stɑːn] *n* Kazajistán

kazi = **karz(e)y**

kazoo [kə'zuː] *n* chifla *f*, trompetilla *f*

KB *Comptr* (*abbr* **kilobyte**) KB

Kb *Comptr* (*abbr* **kilobit**) Kb

kbps [keɪbiːpiː'es] *Comptr* (*abbr* **kilobytes per second**) kbps

KC [keɪ'siː] *n Law* (*abbr* **King's Counsel**) = abogado británico de alto rango

kcal (*abbr* **kilocalorie**) kcal, kilocaloría *f*

Keatsian ['kiːtsɪən] *adj* keatsiano(a)

kebab [kə'bæb] **1** *n* (**a**) *(on skewer)* brocheta *f*, pincho *m* moruno (**b**) **(doner) k.** = pan de pitta relleno de carne de cordero asada
2 *vt Br Fam* (**a**) *(impale)* **he almost kebabbed me with a kitchen knife** por poco me ensarta el cuchillo de cocina (**b**) *(verbally)* **he was kebabbed by the interviewer's questioning** el entrevistador lo frió a preguntas

ke(c)ks [keks] *npl Br Fam* pantalones *mpl*

kedgeree [kedʒə'riː] *n* = plato especiado de arroz, pescado y huevo duro

keel [kiːl] *n Naut* quilla *f*; IDIOM **on an even k.: to keep things on an even k.** mantener las cosas en calma, hacer que las cosas sigan su curso normal; **to be back on an even k.** *(situation)* volver a la normalidad; **to put a company/the economy back on an even k.** reestabilizar una empresa/la economía

▸ **keel over** *vi* (**a**) *(boat)* volcar (**b**) *Fam (person)* derrumbarse

keelhaul ['kiːlhɔːl] *vt* (**a**) *Naut* pasar por la quilla (**b**) *Fam Fig (rebuke severely)* reprender, *Esp* echar una bronca, *RP* reventar

keen[1] [kiːn] *adj* (**a**) *(enthusiastic)* entusiasta; **she's a k. gardener** le encanta la jardinería; **she's a k. swimmer** es una nadadora entusiasta; **to be k. to do sth** tener muchas ganas de hacer algo; **to be k. for sth to happen** tener muchas ganas de que ocurra algo; **I'm k. that they should get a second chance** me interesa mucho que les den una segunda oportunidad; **she's k. on Mike** le gusta Mike; **he wasn't k. on the idea** no le entusiasmaba la idea; **they aren't so k. on going out tonight** no tienen muchas ganas de salir esta noche; **to take a k. interest in sth** mostrar gran interés por algo; IDIOM *Fam* **to be as k. as mustard** *(enthusiastic)* estar entusiasmadísimo(a)
(**b**) *(acute, perceptive) (mind)* penetrante; *(eyesight)* agudo(a); *(sense of smell)* fino(a); **to have a k. eye for detail** tener buen ojo para el detalle; **to have a k. awareness of sth** ser profundamente consciente de algo
(**c**) *(sharp)* **a k. blade** una hoja afilada; **a k. wind** un viento cortante
(**d**) *(intense) (sorrow, regret)* profundo(a); **a k. appetite** un apetito voraz; **to have a k. appetite for success/power** tener sed de éxito/poder; **k. competition** competencia feroz
(**e**) *Br (competitive)* **k. prices** precios competitivos
(**f**) *US Fam (very good)* genial, *Andes, CAm, Carib, Méx* chévere, *Méx* padre, *RP* bárbaro(a)

keen[2] *vi* penar

keen-eyed [kiːn'aɪd] *adj* observador(ora)

keening ['kiːnɪŋ] *n (wailing)* llanto *m* fúnebre, lamento *m* fúnebre

keenly ['kiːnlɪ] *adv* (**a**) *(enthusiastically)* con entusiasmo (**b**) *(intensely)* profundamente; **a k. contested election** unas elecciones muy reñidas; **he felt her death k.** su muerte lo afectó profundamente

keenness ['kiːnnɪs] *n* (**a**) *(enthusiasm)* entusiasmo *m*; **there's no doubting her k. to help** no hay dudas de que está deseosa de ayudar (**b**) *(acuteness) (of vision, insight)* agudeza *f*; **k. of mind** agudeza intelectual (**c**) *(sharpness) (of blade, knife)* filo *m* (**d**) *(intensity) (of competition, rivalry)* ferocidad *f*

keen-sighted ['kiːn'saɪtɪd] *adj* con buena vista

KEEP [ki:p] 1 *n* (a) *(maintenance)* **he gives his mother £50 a week for his k.** le da 50 libras a su madre por la comida y el alojamiento; **to earn one's k.** ganarse el sustento; **to pay for one's k.** pagarse la manutención

(b) *(of castle)* torre *f* del homenaje

2 *vt* (*pt & pp* **kept** [kept]) (a) *(retain)* quedarse con, guardar; **k. the change** quédese con el cambio; **you can k. it** te puedes quedar con él, te lo puedes quedar; *Fam* **if that's your idea of a holiday, you can k. it!** si esa es tu idea de unas vacaciones, quédatela tú; *Fam* **tell him he can k. his rotten job!** ¡que se quede con *or* que se guarde su maldito trabajo!; **to k. sb's attention** mantener la atención de alguien; **to k. its colour** *(garment)* no desteñir; **to k. one's job** conservar el trabajo; **she kept her sense of humour** no perdió el sentido del humor; **to k. its shape** *(garment)* no deformarse

(b) *(save)* guardar; **to k. sth for sb** guardar algo para alguien; **can you k. my seat?** me puedes guardar el sitio?; **we'll k. the tickets for you until Wednesday** te guardaremos las entradas hasta el miércoles

(c) *(store)* guardar; **where do you k. the playing cards?** ¿dónde guardas las cartas?; **I always k. my comb in my pocket** siempre tengo el peine en el bolsillo; **how long can you k. fish in the freezer?** ¿cuánto tiempo se puede dejar el pescado en el congelador?

(d) *(maintain)* **to k. count of sth** llevar la cuenta de algo; **to k. a diary** llevar un diario; **to k. a note of sth** anotar algo; **to k. order** mantener el orden; *Law* **to k. the peace** mantener el orden (público); **to k. a record of sth** registrar algo, llevar un registro de algo; **to k. a secret** guardar un secreto; **to k. good time** *(clock, watch)* ir a la hora, funcionar bien; *(person)* ser puntual, no llegar nunca tarde; **to k. watch (over sth/sb)** vigilar (algo/a alguien)

(e) *(maintain in a certain condition)* mantener; **I think I'll k. this picture where it is** creo que dejaré este cuadro donde está; **they kept the prisoner in a tiny cell** tenían al prisionero en una celda diminuta; **they kept her in hospital overnight** la dejaron ingresada hasta el día siguiente; **a well-/badly-kept garden** un jardín bien/mal cuidado; **to k. sb awake** mantener *or* tener despierto(a) a alguien; **to k. sth clean/secret** mantener algo limpio/en secreto; **the doors are kept locked** las puertas siempre están cerradas con llave; **the weather kept us indoors** el mal tiempo nos impidió salir; **this sandwich should k. you going until dinnertime** con este sándwich aguantarás hasta la cena; **I don't know how long I'll manage to k. the business going** no sé cuánto tiempo voy a poder seguir con el negocio; **it wasn't easy to k. the conversation going** costaba trabajo mantener la conversación; **to k. sb in order** tener a alguien controlado(a) *or* bajo control; **you k. her talking while I sneak out of the room** tú dale conversación mientras yo salgo subrepticiamente de la habitación; **to k. sb waiting** tener a alguien esperando; **we like to k. the house warm** nos gusta mantener la casa caliente

(f) *(look after) (animals, shop)* tener; *Sport* **to k. goal** defender la portería *orAm* el arco

(g) *(support) (mistress)* mantener; **I've got a family to k.** tengo una familia que mantener; **to k. oneself** mantenerse; **they k. a maid and a gardener** tienen una criada y un jardinero; **it keeps me in cigarette money** me da para el tabaco

(h) *(detain)* entretener; **I hope I haven't kept you** espero no haberte entretenido; **what kept you?** ¿por qué llegas tan tarde?

(i) *(observe) (promise)* cumplir; *(appointment)* acudir a; *(law)* respetar; *Formal (festival, holiday)* observar; **she kept her word** mantuvo su palabra; **to k. late hours** trasnochar

(j) *Com (have in stock)* tener; **I'm afraid we don't k. this item** pues no tenemos ese producto

3 *vi* (a) *(remain, stay)* mantenerse; **I'm keeping busy** hago unas cosas y otras, me mantengo ocupado; **to k. quiet** estar callado(a); **k. quiet!** ¡cállate!; **to k. still** estarse quieto(a); **k. still!** ¡estate quieto!; **we kept warm by huddling up together** nos abrazábamos para darnos calor

(b) *(continue)* **to k. straight on** seguir todo recto *or* derecho; **to k. (to the) left/right** ir *or* circular por la izquierda/derecha; **to k. doing sth** *(continue doing)* seguir haciendo algo; **to k. going** *(not give up)* seguir adelante; **he kept getting into trouble** siempre se estaba metiendo en líos; **she keeps nagging me** no hace más que fastidiarme *or* darme la lata; **the bunches of flowers just kept coming** no paraban de llegar ramos de flores; **I k. forgetting to call her** nunca me acuerdo de llamarla; **I wish you wouldn't k. saying that** me gustaría que no dijeras eso todo el tiempo

(c) *(referring to health)* **how are you keeping?** ¿qué tal estás?; **I hope you're keeping well** espero que estés bien

(d) *(food)* conservarse; *Fig* **it will k.** *(problem)* puede esperar

(e) *Sport* **he kept very well** defendió muy bien su portería *orAm* arco

4 **for keeps** *adv Fam* para siempre

▸**keep at** 1 *vt insep* **to k. at it** seguir adelante *or* con ello; **k. at him until he listens to you** insiste hasta que te haga caso

2 *vt sep* **to k. sb at it: the sergeant kept us hard at it all morning** el sargento nos hizo trabajar toda la mañana

▸**keep away** 1 *vt sep* **the fire kept the wolves away** el fuego mantenía alejados a los lobos; **to k. sb away from sth** mantener a alguien alejado(a) de algo; **k. that dog away from me!** ¡no me acerques ese perro!

2 *vi* mantenerse alejado(a) (**from** de); **I felt my visits were unwelcome and so I kept away** me daba la impresión de que no era bienvenido, asi que no volví por allí

▸**keep back** 1 *vt sep* (a) *(crowd, tears)* contener

(b) *(delay)* entretener; **he was kept back by his lack of qualifications** su falta de titulación le impidió progresar

(c) *(hold in reserve) (wages, funds)* retener

(d) *(not reveal) (names, facts)* ocultar; **to k. sth back from sb** *(information)* ocultar algo a alguien

(e) *(detain)* **to be kept back after school** quedarse castigado(a) después de clase

2 *vi (not approach)* no acercarse (**from** a); **k. back!** ¡no te acerques!

▸**keep behind** *vt sep* (a) *(detain) (as punishment)* dejar castigado(a); **he kept me behind after the meeting** me pidió que me quedara un momento después de la reunión (b) *(delay)* retrasar

▸**keep down** 1 *vt sep* (a) *(not raise)* **to k. one's voice down** hablar bajo, hablar en voz baja; **to k. one's head down** *(physically)* mantener la cabeza agachada; *Fig* esconder la cabeza; *Fam* **k. it down!** *(be quiet)* ¡baja la voz!

(b) *(not vomit)* **I can't k. my food down** vomito todo lo que como

(c) *(repress)* reprimir; IDIOM **you can't k. a good man down** una persona que vale siempre sale adelante

(d) *(control) (vermin, weeds)* contener

(e) *(prices, number, inflation)* mantener bajo(a); **I'm trying to k. my weight down** estoy tratando de no engordar

(f) *Sch* **to be kept down a year** tener que repetir un año

2 *vi (not stand up)* mantenerse cuerpo a tierra; **k. down!** ¡no te levantes!

▸**keep from** 1 *vt sep* (a) *(prevent)* **to k. sth/sb from doing sth** impedir que algo/alguien haga algo; **I could hardly k. myself from laughing** casi no podía contener la risa; **to k. sb from their work** no dejar trabajar a alguien

(b) *(protect)* **to k. sb from harm** proteger a alguien

(c) *(hide)* **to k. sth from sb** ocultar algo a alguien

2 *vt insep (avoid)* **I couldn't k. from laughing** no podía contener la risa

▸**keep in** 1 *vt sep* (a) *(not allow out) (pupil)* castigar sin salir; **the bad weather kept us in** el mal tiempo nos impidió salir; **they decided to k. her in overnight** *(in hospital)* decidieron dejarla ingresada hasta el día siguiente

(b) *(stomach)* meter

2 *vi (not go out)* quedarse en casa, no salir

▸**keep in with** *vt insep Fam* **to k. in with sb** cultivar la amistad de alguien

▸**keep off** 1 *vt sep* **k. your hands off that!** ¡no toques eso!; **k. your hands off me!** ¡no me toques!; **wear a hat to k. the sun off** ponte un sombrero para protegerte del sol; **this cream will k. the mosquitoes off** esta crema te protegerá contra los mosquitos; **it's best to k. her off the subject of politics** lo mejor es evitar que empiece a hablar de política

2 *vt insep* **k. off the grass** *(sign)* prohibido pisar el césped; **I've been told to k. off alcohol** me han dicho que no beba alcohol; **to k. off a subject** evitar un tema

3 *vi (stay away) (person)* mantenerse al margen; **the rain kept off** no llovió

▸**keep on** 1 *vt sep* (a) *(not take off)* dejarse puesto(a)

(b) *(not switch off)* dejar encendido(a) *orAm* prendido(a)

(c) *(continue to employ)* mantener en el puesto

2 *vi* (a) *(continue)* continuar, seguir; **to k. on doing sth** *(continue doing)* seguir haciendo algo; **he kept on nagging me** no paraba de darme la lata; **she kept on getting into trouble** siempre se estaba metiendo en líos

(b) *Fam (talk continually)* **to k. on about sth** dar la lata con algo

▸**keep on at** *vt insep Fam* **to k. on at sb (to do sth)** dar la lata a alguien (para que haga algo)

▸**keep out** 1 *vt sep (wind, sun, rain)* proteger de; *(intruders, foreign imports)* impedir el paso a; *(shot)* parar; **she used her hand to k. the sun out of her eyes** se protegía los ojos del sol con la mano; **I want my name kept out of this** quiero que mi nombre se mantenga fuera de todo esto; **he's in such good form, he's keeping me out of the team** está jugando tan bien que me ha quitado la titularidad

2 *vi (avoid, stay away from)* **to k. out of sth** no meterse en algo; **k. out of the water** no te metas en el agua; **to k. out of trouble** no meterse en líos; **to k. out of an argument** mantenerse al margen de una discusión; **k. out** *(sign)* prohibida la entrada, prohibido el paso

▸**keep to 1** *vt sep* **(a)** *(hold)* **to k. sb to a promise** hacer que alguien cumpla una promesa; **to k. delays to a minimum** reducir al mínimo *or* minimizar los retrasos

(b) *(not reveal)* **to k. sth to oneself** no contar algo; **I k. myself to myself** yo voy a lo mío; **you can k. your remarks to yourself!** ¡guárdate los comentarios!

2 *vt insep* **(a)** *(promise, agreement, schedule)* cumplir

(b) *(not leave)* **k. to the path** no salirse del camino; **she kept to her room** no salió de su habitación; **to k. to the point** no divagar; **to k. to a subject** ceñirse a un tema

▸**keep together 1** *vt sep (family, country)* mantener unido(a); **I k. all the papers together in this folder** guardo todos los papeles juntos en esta carpeta

2 *vi* no separarse

▸**keep under** *vt sep* **(a)** *(repress)* someter

(b) *(with drug)* **he's being kept under with ether** lo tienen inconsciente con éter

▸**keep up 1** *vt sep* **(a)** *(prevent from falling) (shelf, roof)* sostener; *(prices, interest rates, standards)* mantener; **I need a belt to k. my trousers up** necesito un cinturón para que no se me caigan los pantalones; **to k. the troops' morale up** mantener la moral de la tropa; **to k. one's spirits up** mantener los ánimos

(b) *(maintain) (custom)* mantener; **I can't k. up this pace much longer** no puedo mantener este ritmo mucho tiempo; **to k. up the payments** llevar al día los pagos; **to k. up the pressure (on sb)** no dar tregua (a alguien); **k. it up!, k. up the good work!** ¡sigue así!; **to k. up appearances** guardar las apariencias

(c) *(not allow to deteriorate) (house, garden)* cuidar; **I want to k. my French up** quiero mantener mi (nivel de) francés; **to k. one's strength up** mantenerse fuerte

(d) *(keep awake)* tener en vela; **I don't mean to k. you up past your bedtime** no quiero que te acuestes tarde por mí

2 *vi* **(a)** *(rain, snow)* continuar; **if this noise keeps up much longer, I'll scream** como continúe mucho tiempo este ruido me voy a poner a gritar

(b) *(not fall) (prices)* mantenerse; **how are their spirits keeping up?** ¿cómo anda su moral?

(c) *(remain level, go at same speed)* no quedarse atrás; **things change so quickly I can't k. up** las cosas cambian tan rápido que no consigo mantenerme al tanto

▸**keep up with** *vt insep* **(a)** *(stay abreast of)* **to k. up with sb** seguir el ritmo de alguien; **we need to do this to k. up with the competition** tenemos que hacer esto para no ser menos que la competencia; *Fig* **to k. up with the latest developments** mantenerse informado(a) *or* estar al corriente de los últimos acontecimientos; **to k. up with the news** estar al corriente de las noticias; **to k. up with the times** adaptarse a los tiempos; IDIOM **to k. up with the Joneses** no ser menos que el vecino

(b) *(keep in touch with)* seguir en contacto con; **have you kept up with your cousins in Australia?** ¿sigues en contacto con tus primos de Australia?

---

keeper ['ki:pə(r)] *n* **(a)** *(in zoo, park)* guarda *mf*; *(in museum)* conservador(ora) *m,f* **(b)** *(gamekeeper)* guardabosque *m* **(c)** *Br Fam (goalkeeper)* portero *m*, guardameta *m*, *Am* arquero *m*

keep-fit ['ki:p'fɪt] *n Br* ***k. class*** clase *f* de mantenimiento, clase *f* de gimnasia; ***k. exercises*** ejercicios *mpl* de mantenimiento; ***k. fanatic*** = persona obsesionada por mantenerse en forma

keeping ['ki:pɪŋ] *n* **(a)** *(care, charge)* **to have sth/sb in one's k.** tener algo/a alguien bajo la custodia de uno

(b) *(appropriacy)* **in k. with...** de acuerdo con...; **it's in k. with everything I have been told about her** coincide con todo lo que me han contado acerca de ella; **out of k. with...** en desacuerdo con...; **it was rather out of k. with the spirit of the occasion** desentonaba bastante con el espíritu de la ocasión

keepnet ['ki:pnet] *n Br (for fishing)* nasa *f*, buitrón *m*

keepsake ['ki:pseɪk] *n* recuerdo *m*

keepy-up ['ki:pɪ'ʌp] *n Fam (in soccer)* toques *mpl*; **to play k.** dar toques

keg [keg] *n* barrica *f*, barrilete *m* ▸▸ ***k. beer*** cerveza *f* de barril

keister ['ki:stə(r)] *n US Fam (buttocks)* trasero *m*

keks = **kecks**

kelp [kelp] *n* laminaria *f*, varec *m*

kelvin ['kelvɪn] *n* kelvin *m* ▸▸ ***K. scale*** escala *f* Kelvin

ken [ken] **1** *n* **to be beyond sb's k.** estar fuera del alcance de alguien

2 *Scot vt* saber, conocer

kendo ['kendəʊ] *n Sport* kendo *m*

kennel ['kenəl] *n* **(a)** *(doghouse)* caseta *f* (del perro) **(b)** *Br* **kennels** *(establishment)* criadero *m* de perros, guardería *f* de animales; **to put a dog into kennels** dejar a un perro en una residencia canina ▸▸ ***k. maid*** cuidadora *f* de perros; ***k. man*** cuidador *m* de perros **(c)** *US (for boarding or breeding)* residencia *f* para perros, criadero *m* de perros

kentia ['kentɪə] *n* kentia *f*

Kentish ['kentɪʃ] *adj* de Kent

Kentuckian [ken'tʌkɪən] **1** *n* persona *f* de Kentucky

2 *adj* de Kentucky

Kenya ['kenjə, 'ki:njə] *n* Kenia

Kenyan ['kenjən] **1** *n* keniano(a) *m,f*, keniata *mf*

2 *adj* keniano(a), keniata

kepi ['keɪpɪ] *n* quepis *m inv*, kepis *m*

kept [kept] **1** *pt & pp of* **keep**

2 *adj* **to be a k. man** ser un mantenido, vivir a costa de la mujer; **to be a k. woman** ser una mantenida, vivir a costa del marido

keratin ['kerətɪn] *n Biochem* queratina *f*

kerb [kɜ:b] *n Br* bordillo *m* (de la acera), *Chile* solera *f*, *Col, Perú* sardinel *m*, *CSur* cordón *m* (de la vereda), *Méx* borde *m* (de la banqueta) ▸▸ ***k. drill*** forma *f* correcta de cruzar la calle; ***k. weight*** *(of vehicle)* tara *f*

kerb-crawler ['kɜ:bkrɔ:lə(r)] *n Br* = persona que busca prostitutas conduciendo lentamente junto a la acera

kerb-crawling ['kɜbkrɔ:lɪŋ] *n Br* = conducir despacio en busca de prostitutas

kerbside ['kɜ:bsaɪd] *n Br* borde *m* de la acera *or CSur* vereda *or Méx* banqueta

kerbstone, *US* **curbstone** ['kɜ:bstəʊn] *n Br* adoquín *m* (del bordillo)

kerchief ['kɜ:tʃi:f] *n Old-fashioned* pañuelo *m*

kerfuffle [kə'fʌfəl] *n Br Fam* lío *m*, jaleo *m*

kermis ['kɜ:mɪs] *n US (charity fair)* fiesta *f* benéfica, *Am* kermés *f*, *Am* quermés *f*

kerning ['kɜ:nɪŋ] *n Comptr* interletraje *m*

kernel ['kɜ:nəl] *n* **(a)** *(of nut)* pepita *f*, fruto *m*; *(of grain)* grano *m* **(b)** *(heart, core) (of problem)* núcleo *m*; **there's a k. of truth in the accusation** hay un elemento de verdad en la acusación

kerosene ['kerəsi:n] *n* queroseno *m*, *Am* querosén *m* ▸▸ ***k. lamp*** lámpara *f* de queroseno

kestrel ['kestrəl] *n* cernícalo *m*

ketch [ketʃ] *n (small boat)* queche *m*

ketchup ['ketʃəp] *n* **(tomato) k.** ketchup *m*, catchup *m*

ketone ['ki:təʊn] *n Chem* cetona *f*

kettle [ketəl] *n* **(a)** *(for boiling water) (on stove)* tetera *f*; *(electric)* hervidor *m* (eléctrico); **I'll put the k. on** pondré el agua a hervir **(b)** *(for fish)* cacerola *f* para pescado; IDIOM **that's a different k. of fish** eso es harina de otro costal; IDIOM *Fam* **this is a fine** *or* **pretty k. of fish!** ¡menudo problema!, ¡menudo plan!, *RP* ¡lindo despelote *or* quilombo!

kettledrum ['ketəldrʌm] *n* timbal *m*

key [ki:] **1** *n* **(a)** *(of door)* llave *f*; *(of clock, mechanical toy)* cuerda *f*; **he was given the keys to the city** recibió las llaves de la ciudad; IDIOM **to get the k. of the door** llegar a la edad de la independencia ▸▸ *Br* ***k. bar*** = lugar donde se hacen copias de llaves; ***k. money*** derecho *m* de llave; ***k. ring*** llavero *m*

(b) *(of piano, typewriter)* tecla *f*; *(on wind instrument)* llave *f* ▸▸ *Comptr* ***k. combination*** combinación *f* de teclas

(c) *(to problem, situation)* clave *f*, llave *f*; **the k. to happiness/success** la clave de la felicidad/del éxito

(d) *(answers, guide) (of map)* clave *f*; *(to exercises)* respuestas *fpl*

(e) *Mus* tono *m*; **major/minor k.** tono mayor/menor; **in the k. of C** en clave de do; **to be off k.** estar desafinado(a); **to play in/off k.** tocar en tono/fuera de tono *or* desafinado ▸▸ *Mus* ***k. signature*** armadura *f*

(f) *(islet)* cayo *m*

(g) *(in basketball)* **the k.** la zona, la botella

(h) *Fam (of drugs)* kilo *m*

2 *adj (most important)* clave; **a k. factor** un factor clave; **one of the**

k. issues in the election uno de los temas claves de la elección; **he's the k. man in the team** es el hombre clave del equipo ►► *Cin* ***k. grip*** jefe(a) *m,f* de maquinistas; *Br Educ* ***k. stage*** etapa *f* educativa

3 *vt* (**a**) *(data, text)* teclear, *Am* tipear (**b**) *(adjust, adapt)* adecuar, adaptar; **his remarks were keyed to the occasion** sus comentarios se adecuaron a la ocasión (**c**) *(reference)* referir, relacionar (**d**) *(surface)* preparar

► **key in** *vt sep Comptr* teclear, *Am* tipear

keyboard ['ki:bɔ:d] **1** *n* (**a**) *(of piano, organ)* teclado *m*; **on keyboards** al teclado, a los teclados ►► ***k. player*** teclista *mf* (**b**) *(of computer)* teclado *m* ►► ***k. layout*** disposición *f* del teclado; ***k. shortcut*** atajo *m* de teclado

2 *vt (data, text)* teclear, *Am* tipear

keyboarder ['ki:bɔ:də(r)] *n* teclista *mf*, operador(a) *m,f*

keycard ['ki:kɑ:d] *n (for door)* tarjeta *f* de acceso

keyed up [ki:d'ʌp] *adj Fam (excited)* alterado(a), nervioso(a)

keyhole ['ki:həʊl] *n* (ojo *m* de la) cerradura *f*; **he looked through the k.** miró por el ojo de la cerradura ►► ***k. saw*** sierra *f* de calar; ***k. surgery*** cirugía *f* endoscópica

keying error ['ki:ɪŋerə(r)] *n* error *m* tipográfico *or Am* de tipeo

Keynesian ['keɪnzɪən] **1** *adj* keynesiano(a)

2 *n* keynesiano(a) *m,f*

keynote ['ki:nəʊt] **1** *n* (**a**) *(main point)* nota *f* dominante; **promoting industrial recovery is the k. of government policy** promover la recuperación industrial es el tema central de la política gubernamental (**b**) *Mus* tónica *f*

2 *adj (speech, speaker)* principal

3 *vt* exponer, formular

keypad ['ki:pæd] *n Comptr* teclado *m* numérico

keypunch ['ki:pʌntʃ] *n* perforadora *f*

keystone ['ki:stəʊn] *n* (**a**) *Archit* clave *f (de un arco)* (**b**) *(of argument, policy)* piedra *f* angular

keystroke ['ki:strəʊk] *n Comptr* pulsación *f*; **keystrokes per minute/hour** (ingreso de) caracteres por minuto/hora

keyword ['ki:wɜ:d] *n* (**a**) *(informative word)* palabra *f* clave (**b**) *Comptr* palabra *f* clave

KG [keɪ'dʒi:] *n Br* (*abbr* **Knight of the Order of the Garter**) Caballero de la Orden de la Jarretera

kg (*abbr* **kilogram**) kg

KGB [keɪdʒi:'bi:] *n Formerly* KGB *m*

khaki ['kɑ:kɪ] **1** *n* caqui *m*

2 *adj* caqui *inv*; **k. shorts** pantalones cortos caqui; *US* **khakis** pantalones de soldado

khan [kɑ:n] *n (title)* kan *m*

Khmer [kmɜ:(r)] **1** *n* (**a**) *(person)* jemer *mf*; **the K. Rouge** los jemeres rojos (**b**) *(language)* jemer *m*

2 *adj* jemer

kHz *Elec* (*abbr* **kilohertz**) kHz

KIA [keɪaɪ'eɪ] *adj US Mil* (*abbr* **killed in action**) muerto en acción

kibble ['kɪbəl] *vt (cereal)* moler

kibbutz [kɪ'bʊts] (*pl* **kibbutzim** [kɪbʊt'si:m]) *n* kibbutz *m*, kibutz *m*

kibitz ['kɪbɪts] *vi US Fam* meter la cuchara

kibitzer ['kɪbɪtsə(r)] *n US Fam* mirón(ona) *m,f*, metido(a) *m,f*

kibosh, kybosh ['kaɪbɒʃ] *n Fam* **to put the k. on sth** echar algo abajo *or* a pique

kick [kɪk] **1** *n* (**a**) *(with foot)* patada *f*, puntapié *m*; *(of horse)* coz *f*; **to give sth/sb a k.** dar una patada a algo/alguien; *Fam Fig* **she needs a k. in the pants** *or* **up the backside** *or Vulg* **up the arse** necesita una buena patada en el trasero *or Vulg* culo; *Fig* **that was a k. in the teeth for him** le sentó como una patada en la boca ►► *Sport* ***k. boxing*** kick boxing *m*; ***k. turn*** *(in skiing, skateboarding)* cambio *m* brusco de dirección

(**b**) *(of gun)* retroceso *m*

(**c**) **to have a k.** *(drink)* estar fuerte *(aunque entre bien)*

(**d**) *Fam (thrill)* **to get a k. from** *or* **out of sth** disfrutar con algo; **to get a k. out of doing sth** disfrutar haciendo algo; **to do sth for kicks** hacer algo por gusto, regodearse haciendo algo

(**e**) *Fam (temporary interest)* **I'm on a fitness k.** me ha dado por mantenerme en forma

(**f**) *(in swimming)* patada *f*

2 *vt* (**a**) *(once)* dar una patada a; *(several times)* dar patadas a; **to get kicked** *(once)* recibir una patada, *(several times)* recibir patadas; **she kicked the ball over the wall** pateó la pelota al otro lado de la pared; **I kicked the door open** abrí la puerta de una patada; **he was kicked to death** lo mataron a patadas; **the baby kicked his legs in the air** el niño daba patadas en el aire

(**b**) IDIOMS **I could have kicked myself** era para tirarme de los pelos, *Esp* me hubiera dado de bofetadas; **they must be kicking themselves** se deben estar dando la cabeza contra la pared; **to k. a man when he's down** atacar a alguien cuando ya está derrotado; *US Vulg* **to k. sb's ass** *(defeat)* dar un buen palizón a alguien; *US Vulg* **to k. ass** *(be bossy)* tratar a todo el mundo a patadas; *(be excellent)* ser *Esp* cojonudo(a) *or CAm, Carib, Col, Méx* chévere *or Méx* padrísimo(a) *or RP* bárbaro(a); *Fam* **to k. the bucket** estirar la pata, *CAm, Méx* doblar *or* liar el petate; *Fam* **to k. the habit** *(stop taking drugs)* dejar el vicio; **to k. sb upstairs** ascender a alguien para que no moleste

3 *vi* (**a**) *(once)* dar una patada; *(several times)* dar patadas; *(animal)* dar coces

(**b**) *(athlete)* apretar el ritmo; *(swimmer)* mover las piernas

(**c**) *(gun)* hacer el retroceso

(**d**) *(in dance)* levantar una pierna, dar una patada al aire

(**e**) IDIOMS *Fam* **to k. against sth** *(rebel against)* patalear contra algo; **he was always trying to k. against the system** siempre intentaba rebelarse contra el sistema; *Fam* **to k. against the pricks** rebelarse

► **kick about, kick around** **1** *vt insep (spend time in)* **to k. about** *or* **around the world/Africa** recorrer el mundo/África; **is my purse kicking about** *or* **around the kitchen somewhere?** ¿has visto mi monedero por la cocina?

2 *vt sep* (**a**) *(play with)* **to k. a ball about** *or* **around** pelotear, dar patadas a un balón; *Fam* **to k. an idea about** *or* **around** darle vueltas a una idea (**b**) *(mistreat)* **don't let them k. you about** *or* **around** no dejes que te traten a patadas

3 *vi Fam* estar *or* andar por ahí; **can you see my lighter kicking about** *or* **around?** ¿está *or* anda por ahí mi encendedor?, ¿has visto mi encendedor por ahí?; **I think I've got one kicking about** *or* **around somewhere** debo tener alguno por ahí; **who are you kicking about** *or* **around with these days?** ¿con quién andas últimamente?

► **kick back** *vi US Fam (relax)* relajarse

► **kick down** *vt sep (door)* echar abajo *or* derribar a patadas

► **kick in** **1** *vt sep* (**a**) *(door)* abrir de una patada; *Fam* **to k. sb's head in** romper la cabeza a alguien; *Fam* **I'll k. his teeth in!** ¡le voy a partir la cara! (**b**) *US Fam (contribute)* poner

2 *vi Fam (come into effect) (clause)* ponerse en marcha, entrar en vigor; *(drug)* hacer efecto

► **kick off** **1** *vt sep* (**a**) *(remove)* **to k. one's shoes off** quitarse *or Am* sacarse los zapatos a patadas; **he kicked me off his land** me echó a patadas de sus tierras (**b**) *(begin)* comenzar, empezar

2 *vi* (**a**) *(in soccer, rugby)* hacer el saque inicial (**b**) *(begin)* comenzar, empezar (**with** con)

► **kick out** **1** *vt sep Fam* **he was kicked out** *(of job, house)* lo echaron, le dieron la patada

2 *vi* **to k. out (at sb)** intentar dar una patada (a alguien)

► **kick over** *vt insep* IDIOM **to k. over the traces** desmandarse

► **kick up** *vt insep Fam* **to k. up a fuss** *or* **a row** *or* **a stink** armar *or Esp* montar un escándalo; **to k. up a din** *or* **a racket** armar *or Esp* montar un alboroto

kickabout ['kɪkəbaʊt] *n Fam (soccer game)* peloteo *m*

kickback ['kɪkbæk] *n Fam* (**a**) *(payment)* **he got a k. for doing it** le *Esp* untaron *or Andes, RP* coimearon *or CAm, Méx* dieron una mordida para que lo hiciera (**b**) *US (repercussion)* pataleo *m*, reacción *f*

kickdown ['kɪkdaʊn] *n (in car)* = método para cambiar automáticamente de marcha pisando el acelerador a fondo

kicker ['kɪkə(r)] *n Sport* pateador(ora) *m,f*

kicking [kɪkɪŋ] **1** *n Br* **to give sb a k.** reprender a alguien; **to get a k.** ser reprendido

2 *adj Fam Esp* ¡guay (del Paraguay)!, *Andes, Perú* superchévere, *Méx* padrísimo(a), *RP* supergenial

kick-off ['kɪkɒf] *n* (**a**) *(in soccer, rugby)* saque *m* inicial; **the k. is at 3pm** el partido empieza a las 3 de la tarde, *Am* el puntapié inicial será a las 3 de la tarde (**b**) IDIOM *Fam* **for a k.** *(to start with)* para empezar

kickstand ['kɪkstænd] *n (on bike, motorcycle)* soporte *m*

kick-start ['kɪkstɑ:t] **1** *n (on motorbike)* pedal *m or* palanca *f* de arranque

2 *vt* (**a**) *(motorbike, engine)* arrancar a patada *(con el pedal)* (**b**) *(economy)* reactivar

kid [kɪd] **1** *n* (**a**) *Fam (child)* niño(a) *m,f*, crío(a) *m,f*, *Arg* pibe(a) *m,f*, *CAm* chavalo(a) *m,f*, *Chile* cabro(a) *m,f*, *Col* chino(a) *m,f*, *Méx* chavo(a) *m,f*, *Urug* botija *mf*; **my k. brother** mi hermano pequeño; *Br* **our k.** *(brother)* el pequeño, *Am* el chico; *(sister)* la pequeña, *Am* la chica; **she's just a k.** es sólo una niña, no es más que una niña; **it's**

k.'s stuff *(easy, childish)* eso es cosa de niños

(**b**) *(young goat)* cabrito *m*; *(skin)* cabritilla *f* ▸▸ ***k. gloves*** guantes *mpl* de cabritilla; IDIOM **to handle sb with k. gloves** tratar a alguien con mucho tacto *or Am* guantes de seda; ***k. leather*** cabritilla *f*

2 *vt* (*pt & pp* **kidded**) *Fam* (**a**) *(tease)* tomar el pelo a, *RP* cargar a; **they kidded him about his accent** le tomaban el pelo por su acento, *RP* lo cargaban por el acento que tenía (**b**) *(fool)* tomar el pelo a, *Esp, Carib, Méx* vacilar, *Esp* quedarse con; **to k. oneself** engañarse; **who do you think you're kidding?** ¿a quién crees que engañas?; **I k. you not** no es broma, no te estoy tomando el pelo

3 *vi Fam* **to be kidding** estar bromeando; **don't get upset, I was just kidding** no te enfades, sólo estaba bromeando; **I'm going, no kidding** voy a ir, te lo digo en serio; **no kidding!** *(surprise)* ¡no me digas!, ¡qué fuerte!; **no kidding?** ¿en serio?; **you're not kidding!** ¡ya lo creo!, *Esp* ¡descarado!

▸ **kid on** *Fam* **1** *vt sep* tomar el pelo a, *Esp, Carib, Méx* vacilar, *Esp* quedarse con

2 *vi* tomar el pelo, *Esp, Carib, Méx* vacilar

kidder ['kɪdə(r)] *n Fam* bromista *mf*

kiddie, kiddy ['kɪdɪ] *n Fam* nene(a) *m,f*, crío(a) *m,f*

kiddiewink, kiddywink ['kɪdɪwɪŋk] *n Br Fam* pequeñín(ina) *m,f*, chiquitín(ina) *m,f*

kiddo ['kɪdəʊ] *n Fam* nene(a) *m,f*

kiddy = **kiddie**

kiddywink = **kiddiewink**

kid-glove ['kɪd'glʌv] *adj* **to give sb the k. treatment** tratar a alguien con mucho tacto *or Am* guantes de seda

kidnap ['kɪdnæp] **1** *n* secuestro *m*, rapto *m*; **k. attempt** intento de secuestro

2 *vt* (*pt & pp* **kidnapped**) secuestrar, raptar

kidnapper ['kɪdnæpə(r)] *n* secuestrador(ora) *m,f*, raptor(ora) *m,f*

kidnapping ['kɪdnæpɪŋ] *n* secuestro *m*, rapto *m*

kidney ['kɪdnɪ] *n* (**a**) *(organ, as food)* riñón *m* ▸▸ ***k. beans*** *Esp* judías *fpl*, *Esp* alubias *fpl*, *Andes, CAm, Carib, Méx* frijoles *mpl*, *Andes, RP* porotos *mpl*; *Br* ***k. dish*** = bandeja metálica en forma de riñón; ***k. failure*** insuficiencia *f* renal; ***k. donor*** donante *mf* de riñón; ***k. machine*** riñón *m* artificial, aparato *m* de diálisis; ***k. stone*** piedra *f* en el riñón, cálculo *m* renal

(**b**) *Literary (temperament, kind)* especie *f*, tipo *m*; **a man of (quite) a different k.** un hombre (claramente) cortado por otro patrón

kidney-shaped ['kɪdnɪʃeɪpt] *adj* (en forma) de riñón

kidologist [kɪ'dɒlədʒɪst] *n Fam* bromista *mf*

kidology [kɪ'dɒlədʒɪ] *n Fam* arte *m* de tomar el pelo

kid-on ['kɪdɒn] *n Fam* tomadura *f* de pelo, *Esp, Carib, Méx* vacile *m*, *RP* joda *f*

kidskin ['kɪdskɪn] *n* cabritilla *f*

kidvid ['kɪdvɪd] *n US Fam* vídeo *or Am* video *m* infantil

Kiev ['ki:ev] *n* Kiev

kif [kɪf] *n* kif *m*

kike [kaɪk] *n US Fam* = término ofensivo para referirse a los judíos, *RP* ruso(a) *m,f*

Kilimanjaro [kɪlɪmæn'dʒɑ:rəʊ] *n* el Kilimanjaro

kill [kɪl] **1** *n* (**a**) *(act of killing)* **to make a k.** matar; *also Fig* **to be in at the k.** no perderse el desenlace, estar presente en el momento culminante; *also Fig* **to move in for the k.** lanzarse al ataque (**b**) *(number killed)* piezas *fpl* cobradas (**c**) *(prey)* presa *f* (**d**) *Mil (enemy plane, ship, tank destroyed)* baja *f* enemiga, enemigo *m* derribado

2 *vt* (**a**) *(person, animal)* matar; **twelve people were killed** resultaron muertas doce personas; **to k. oneself** matarse; *Fam Fig* **to k. oneself laughing** morirse de risa; *Ironic* **don't k. yourself!** *(to sb not working very hard)* ¡cuidado, no te vayas a herniar!; **he didn't exactly k. himself to find a job** no se ha esforzado demasiado para encontrar un empleo, *RP* tampoco se mató para encontrar un trabajo; **I'll finish it even if it kills me** lo terminaré aun si me cuesta la vida; **my feet/these shoes are killing me** los pies/estos zapatos me están matando

(**b**) *(pain)* acabar con; *(sound)* amortiguar; **this injection should k. the pain (for a while)** esta inyección debería eliminar el dolor (durante un rato)

(**c**) *(put an end to)* poner fin a, acabar con; **the speech killed his chances of promotion** el discurso acabó con sus posibilidades de ascenso; **the editor decided to k. the story** el director decidió no publicar la noticia; **the government killed the bill** el gobierno impidió que prosperara el proyecto de ley

(**d**) *Fam (switch off) (engine, lights)* apagar

(**e**) IDIOMS *Fam* **this one'll k. you** *(joke)* este es buenísimo; **to k. sb with kindness** pasarse de bueno(a) con alguien; **to k. two birds with one stone** matar dos pájaros de un tiro; **to k. time** matar el tiempo

3 *vi* matar; *Fam* **I'd k. for a beer** haría cualquier cosa por una cerveza; IDIOM **it's a case of k. or cure** hay que jugárselo a todo o nada

▸ **kill off** *vt sep* acabar con; **to k. off a character** *(in novel, TV series)* matar a un personaje; **high prices could k. off the tourist trade** los altos precios podrían acabar con la industria del turismo

killer ['kɪlə(r)] *n* (**a**) *(murderer)* asesino(a) *m,f*; **tuberculosis was once a major k.** en el pasado, la tuberculosis fue una gran causa de mortandad; **a k. road** un camino de la muerte; *Fig* **he lacks the k. instinct** *(of sportsman)* le falta garra para terminar con su contrincante ▸▸ ***k. whale*** orca *f*

(**b**) *Fam (sth very difficult)* **those steps were a k.!** ¡esos escalones me han dejado muerto!; **the maths exam was a k.** el examen de matemáticas era matador

(**c**) *Fam (sth very good)* **this one's a k.** *(joke)* este es buenísimo; **it has a k. plot** tiene un argumento de lo más interesante; **what's been a k. app for 20 years?** ¿qué programa de aplicación ha mantenido su éxito durante 20 años?

killing ['kɪlɪŋ] **1** *n (of person)* asesinato *m*; *(of animals)* matanza *f*; IDIOM *Fam* **to make a k.** *(financially)* forrarse de dinero

2 *adj* (**a**) *Fam (exhausting)* matador(ora) (**b**) *Fam (very amusing)* desternillante

killingly ['kɪlɪŋlɪ] *adv* **it was k. funny** era desternillante, era para morirse de risa

killjoy ['kɪldʒɔɪ] *n* aguafiestas *mf inv*

kiln [kɪln] *n* horno *m (para cerámica, ladrillos)*

kilo ['ki:ləʊ] (*pl* **kilos**) *n* kilo *m*

kilo- ['kɪlə] *prefix* kilo-

kilobit ['kɪləbɪt] *n Comptr* kilobit *m*

kilobyte ['kɪləbaɪt] *n Comptr* kilobyte *m*

kilocalorie ['kɪləkælərɪ] *n* kilocaloría *f*

kilocycle ['kɪləsaɪkəl] *n* kilociclo *m*

kilogram, kilogramme ['kɪləgræm] *n* kilogramo *m*

kilohertz ['kɪləhɜ:ts] *n* kilohercio *m*, kilohertz *m*

kilojoule ['kɪlədʒu:l] *n* kilojulio *m*

kilolitre, *US* **kiloliter** ['kɪləli:tə(r)] *n* kilolitro *m*

kilometre, *US* **kilometer** ['kɪləmi:tə(r), kɪ'lɒmɪtə(r)] *n* kilómetro *m*

kilometric [kɪlə'metrɪk] *adj* kilométrico(a)

kilopond ['kɪləpɒnd] *n Phys* kilopondio *m*

kiloton ['kɪlətʌn] *n* kilotón *m*

kilovolt ['kɪləvəʊlt] *n* kilovoltio *m*

kilowatt ['kɪləwɒt] *n* kilovatio *m* ▸▸ ***k. hour*** kilovatio-hora *m*; **1000 k. hours** 1000 kilovatios-hora

kilt [kɪlt] *n* falda *f or RP* pollera *f* escocesa

kilted ['kɪltɪd] *adj* (**a**) *(person)* vestido(a) con falda *or RP* pollera escocesa (**b**) *(pleated)* plisado(a)

kilter ['kɪltə(r)] *n Fam* **out of k.** *(machine part)* descuajeringado(a), *Esp* escacharrado(a), *Méx* madreado(a); *(schedule)* manga por hombro; **to be out of k. with sth** estar desfasado(a) *or* andar desacompasado(a) en relación con algo

kimono [kɪ'məʊnəʊ] (*pl* **kimonos**) *n* quimono *m*, kimono *m*

kin [kɪn] *n* parientes *mpl*, familiares *mpl*; **next of k.** parientes *or* familiares más cercanos(as); **are they k. to** *or* **with you?** ¿son parientes tuyos?

KIND[1] [kaɪnd] **1** *n* (**a**) *(type, sort)* clase *f*, tipo *m*; **this k. of mistake is very common** este tipo de errores es muy común; **all kinds of...** toda clase *or* todo tipo de...; **in a k. of a way** en cierto sentido; **I never said anything of the k.!** ¡yo nunca dije nada parecido!; **nothing of the k.** nada por el estilo; **you were drunk last night – I was nothing of the k.!** ayer estabas borracho – ¡qué va!; **something of the k.** algo así; **well, it's coffee of a k., I suppose** bueno, es una especie de café; **the money was consolation of a k.** el dinero fue un pequeño consuelo; **this is my k. of party!** ¡este es el estilo de fiestas que me gusta!; **he's that k. of person** es de esa clase de personas, él es así; **we don't have that k. of money** no tenemos ese dinero; **is this the k. of thing you're looking for?** ¿estás buscando algo así?; **what k. of a meal do you call this?** ¿a esto le llamas comida?; **what k. of a parent would abandon their child?** ¿qué clase de padre abandonaría a su hijo?; *Fam* **are you some k. of nut?** ¿estás chiflado or *Esp* majara?; **I'm not the marrying k.** yo no soy de los que se casan; **she's not the k. to complain** no es de las que se quejan

(**b**) *(class of person, thing)* **he's a traitor to his k.** ha traicionado a los suyos; **we're two of a k.** estamos hechos de la misma pasta; **she's**

one of a k. es única; **it's the only one of its k.** es único en su género; **I hate him and his k.** lo odio a él y a los de su calaña

(**c**) *Fam (slightly, more or less)* **you look k. of tired** pareces como cansado; **I was k. of surprised to find you here** la verdad es que me sorprendió bastante encontrarte aquí; **she's k. of cute** es bastante mona; **I k. of expected this** me esperaba algo así, me lo temía; **I was k. of hoping you'd come with me** la verdad es que esperaba que vinieras conmigo; **do you like it? – k. of** ¿te gusta? – más o menos, *Esp* vaya; **it was a k. of saucer-shaped thing** era una especie de objeto con forma de plato

2 in kind *adj (payment)* en especie

3 in kind *adv* **to pay sb in k.** pagar en especie; *Fig* **to answer** *or* **react in k.** responder con la misma moneda

---

kind² *adj* (**a**) *(good-natured, considerate)* amable; **k. words** palabras amables; **to be k. to sb** ser amable con alguien; **it's very k. of you (to help us)** es muy amable de tu parte (ayudarnos); **she was k. enough to say nothing** tuvo la amabilidad *or* consideración de no decir nada; *Formal* **would you be k. enough to** *or* **so k. as to...?** ¿le importaría...?; **by k. permission of...** con el consentimiento de... (**b**) *(delicate, not harmful)* suave, delicado(a); **k. to the skin** *(on detergent, soap package)* no irrita la piel

kinda ['kaɪndə] *Fam* = **kind of**

kindergarten ['kɪndəgɑ:tən] *n* jardín *m* de infancia, guardería *f*

kind-hearted ['kaɪnd'hɑ:tɪd] *adj* bondadoso(a); **she's very k.** tiene muy buen corazón

kind-heartedly ['kaɪnd'hɑ:tɪdlɪ] *adv* bondadosamente

kind-heartedness ['kaɪnd'hɑ:tɪdnɪs] *n* bondad *f*, buen corazón *m*

kindle ['kɪndəl] **1** *vt* (**a**) *(flame, fire)* encender, *Am* prender (**b**) *(emotions, interest)* despertar

2 *vi* (**a**) *(wood)* encenderse, *Am* prenderse (**b**) *(emotions, interest)* despertarse

kindliness ['kaɪndlɪnɪs] *n* amabilidad *f*

kindling ['kɪndlɪŋ] *n* leña *f* (menuda)

kindly ['kaɪndlɪ] **1** *adv* (**a**) *(good-naturedly, considerately)* amablemente; **he has always treated me k.** siempre me ha tratado con amabilidad

(**b**) *(obligingly)* generosamente; **she has k. offered to help us** generosamente nos ha ofrecido su ayuda

(**c**) *(favourably)* **to look k. on sth/sb** tener un buen concepto de algo/alguien; **to speak k. of sb** hablar bien de alguien; **she didn't take k. to being criticized** no se tomaba bien las críticas

(**d**) *Formal (in polite requests)* **would** *or* **will you k. pass the salt?** ¿tendría la amabilidad de pasarme la sal?; **k. refrain from smoking** se agradece la atención de no fumar

(**e**) *Formal (in anger or annoyance)* **(would you) k. be quiet!** ¿serías tan amable de callarte?; **will you k. sit down!** ¡ten la bondad de sentarte!

2 *adj* amable

kindness ['kaɪndnɪs] *n* (**a**) *(good-nature, consideration)* amabilidad *f* (**to** *or* **towards** con *or* hacia); **an act of k.** un gesto de amabilidad; **to show k. to sb** mostrarse amable con alguien; **she did it out of the k. of her heart** lo hizo desinteresadamente; *Formal* **would you have the k. to...?** ¿tendría la bondad de...?

(**b**) *(considerate act)* favor *m*; **to do sb a k.** hacer un favor a alguien; *Formal* **please do me the k. of replying** le ruego tenga la amabilidad de responder

kindred ['kɪndrɪd] *adj* por el estilo; **k. spirits** almas gemelas

kinesitherapy ['kɪni:zɪ'θerəpɪ] *n* kinesioterapia *f*, kinesiterapia *f*

kinetic [kɪ'netɪk] *adj* cinético(a) ▸▸ ***k. art*** arte *m* cinético; *Phys* ***k. energy*** energía *f* cinética

kinetics [kɪ'netɪks] *n Phys & Chem* cinética *f*

kinfolk *US* = **kinsfolk**

king [kɪŋ] *n* (**a**) *(of country, in cards, chess)* rey *m*; *(in draughts)* dama *f*; **the three Kings** *(in the Bible)* los Reyes Magos; **(the book of) Kings** *(in Bible)* (el Libro de) los Reyes; **the k. of (the) beasts** el rey de la selva; **the k. of the castle** el dueño y señor; *Fig* **the hamburger k.** el rey de la hamburguesa; **a k.'s ransom** un dineral; **for k. and country** por la patria; IDIOM **to live like a k.** vivir como un rey ▸▸ ***K. Charles spaniel*** King Charles spaniel *m*; ***k. cobra*** cobra *f* real; ***k. crab*** cacerola *f* *or* cangrejo *m* de las Molucas, límulo *m*; ***k. penguin*** pájaro *m* bobo real, pingüino *m* real; *Br* ***k. prawn*** langostino *m*; ***k. vulture*** rey *m* de los zopilotes

(**b**) *Br Law* ***K.'s Bench*** = división del tribunal supremo británico; ***K.'s Counsel*** = abogado británico de alto rango; *Br* ***the K.'s English*** el inglés oficial *or* estándar (en Gran Bretaña); ***K.'s evidence:*** **to turn K.'s evidence** = inculpar a un cómplice ante un tribunal a cambio de recibir un trato indulgente

kingbird ['kɪŋbɜ:d] *n* tirano *m*

kingdom ['kɪŋdəm] *n* (**a**) *(realm)* reino *m*; **the k. of God/Heaven** el Reino de Dios/los Cielos; **Thy k. come** el Juicio Final (**b**) *(division)* **the animal/plant k.** el reino animal/vegetal (**c**) IDIOMS *Fam* **till k. come** hasta el día del Juicio Final; *Fam* **to send sb to k. come** mandar a alguien al otro mundo *or* a mejor vida

kingfisher ['kɪŋfɪʃə(r)] *n* martín *m* pescador

kingly ['kɪŋlɪ] *adj* regio(a); **to behave in a k. manner** comportarse con modales dignos de un rey *or* con aire regio

kingmaker ['kɪŋmeɪkə(r)] *n* hombre *m* fuerte, persona *f* influyente

kingpin ['kɪŋpɪn] *n* (**a**) *(of organization, company)* eje *m* (**b**) *(in tenpin bowling)* bolo *m* central

kingship ['kɪŋʃɪp] *n (state, dignity)* realeza *f*; *(office)* reinado *m*

king-size(d) ['kɪŋ'saɪz(d)] *adj* (de) tamaño gigante; *(bed)* extragrande; *(cigarette)* extralargo(a); *Fam* **I've got a k. hangover** tengo una resaca tremenda *or RP* tamaño baño

kink [kɪŋk] **1** *n* (**a**) *(in wire, rope)* retorcimiento *m*; *(in hair)* rizo *m*, rulo *m* (**b**) *(in character)* manía *f*

2 *vt (rope, cable)* enroscar, retorcer

3 *vi (rope, cable)* enroscarse

kinkajou ['kɪŋkədʒu:] *n* mapache *m*

kinky ['kɪŋkɪ] *adj* (**a**) *(hair)* rizado(a), *Chile, Col* crespo(a), *Méx* quebrado(a), *RP* enrulado(a) (**b**) *Fam (person, sex)* pervertido(a); *(erotic, pornographic)* erótico(a); **he likes k. sex** le gustan los números raros

kinsfolk ['kɪnzfəʊk], *US* **kinfolk** ['kɪnfəʊk] *npl* parientes *mpl*

kinship ['kɪnʃɪp] *n* (**a**) *(family relationship)* parentesco *m* (**b**) *(affinity)* afinidad *f* (**with** con)

kinsman ['kɪnzmən] *n Literary* pariente *m*

kinswoman ['kɪnzwʊmən] *n Literary* pariente *f*

kiosk ['ki:ɒsk] *n* (**a**) *(for newspapers, magazines)* quiosco *m*, kiosco *m* (**b**) *Comptr* terminal *f* interactiva

kip [kɪp] *Br Fam* **1** *n* (**a**) *(sleep)* sueño *m*; **to have a k.** echar un sueño; **to get some k.** dormir algo (**b**) *(bed)* cama *f*, sobre *m*

2 *vi* (*pt & pp* **kipped**) *(sleep)* dormir

▸ **kip down** *vi Br Fam* pasar la noche, (quedarse a) dormir

kipper ['kɪpə(r)] *n* (**a**) *(smoked fish)* arenque *m* ahumado (**b**) *Fam* ***k. tie*** = corbata ancha de los años setenta

kir [kɪə(r)] *n* = bebida a base de vino blanco y casis

Kirbigrip®, kirby grip ['kɜ:bɪgrɪp] *n* horquilla *f*

Kirghiz ['kɜ:gɪz] **1** *adj* kirguizo(a)

2 *n* kirguizo(a) *m,f*

Kirg(h)izia [kɜ:'gi:zɪə], **Kirg(h)izstan** [kɜ:gɪz'stæn] *n* Kirguizistán

Kiribati [kɪrɪ'bætɪ] *n* Kiribati

kirk [kɜ:k] *n Scot* iglesia *f*; **the K.** la Iglesia de Escocia

kirsch [kɪəʃ] *n* kirsch *m*

kiskadee ['kɪskədi:] *n* **great k.** benteveo, cristofué

KISS [kɪs] *adj US Fam* (*abbr* **keep it simple, stupid**) sencillo(a), básico(a)

kiss [kɪs] **1** *n* (**a**) *(with lips)* beso *m*; **to give sb a k.** dar un beso a alguien; **to give sb the k. of life** hacer el boca a boca a alguien; **it could be the k. of life for the building trade** podría ser la salvación para la industria de la construcción; IDIOM **the news was the k. of death for the project** la noticia dio el golpe de gracia al proyecto ▸▸ ***k. curl*** caracolillo *m (en la frente o la mejilla)*

(**b**) *(in snooker, pool)* quite *m*, roce *m*

2 *vt* (**a**) *(with lips)* besar; **to k. sb good night/goodbye** dar un beso de buenas noches/de despedida a alguien; **you can k. your chances of promotion goodbye** ya puedes despedirte de tu ascenso; **I'll k. it better** vamos a darle un beso para que se cure; *Vulg* **to k. sb's** *Br* **arse** *or US* **ass** lamer el culo a alguien; *Vulg* **k. my** *Br* **arse** *or US* **ass!** *Esp* ¡anda y que te den por culo!, *Méx* ¡vete a la chingada!, *RP* ¡andate a la puta que te parió!

(**b**) *(touch lightly)* tocar; **the white ball kissed the pink** la bola blanca tocó la rosa

3 *vi* besarse; **to k. and make up** reconciliarse; **to k. and tell** = tener un lío con un famoso y luego contárselo a la prensa

▸ **kiss off** *vt sep US Fam* **to k. sb off** *(get rid of)* mandar a alguien a paseo; *(employee)* poner a alguien de patitas en la calle

kissable ['kɪsəbəl] *adj* **he's so k.** dan unas ganas tremendas de besarlo; **k. lips** labios tentadores

kiss-and-tell [kɪsən'tel] *adj (journalism)* del corazón; **k. stories/revelations** historias/secretos de alcoba

kisser ['kɪsə(r)] *n* (**a**) *(person)* **to be a great k.** besar muy bien (**b**) *Fam (mouth)* morros *mpl*, boca *f*

kissing ['kɪsɪŋ] *n* besos *mpl*; **there was a lot of k. and cuddling going on** no paraban de besarse y acariciarse ▸▸ *US Fam* ***k. cousin*** primo(a) *m,f* lejano(a); ***k. gate*** puerta *f* en (forma de) V

kiss-off ['kɪsɒf] *n US Fam* **to give sb the k.** *(get rid of)* mandar a alguien a paseo; *(employee)* poner a alguien de patitas en la calle

kissogram ['kɪsəgræm] *n Br* = servicio en el que se contrata a una persona para que felicite a otra dándole un beso

kit [kɪt] *n* (**a**) *(equipment)* equipo *m*; **tool k.** juego de herramientas; IDIOM *Fam* **the whole k. and caboodle** absolutamente todo
(**b**) *(soldier's gear)* equipo *m*; **in full battle k.** en equipo de combate
(**c**) *(sports clothes)* equipo *m*
(**d**) *Br Fam (clothes)* **to get one's k. off** quedarse en pelotas
(**e**) *(for assembly)* kit *m*, modelo *m* para armar; **to make sth from a k.** montar algo, armar algo; **in k. form** para montar
(**f**) *Comptr* kit *m*

▸ **kit out** *vt sep Br* equipar (**with** con); **we kitted ourselves out for a long trip** nos equipamos para un viaje largo; **he was kitted out for golf** estaba equipado para jugar al golf

kitbag ['kɪtbæg] *n* petate *m*

kitchen ['kɪtʃɪn] *n* cocina *f* ▸▸ ***k. cabinet*** *(cupboard)* armario *m* de cocina; *Pol Fam* camarilla *f* de asesores; ***k. foil*** papel *m* de aluminio, *Esp* papel *m* Albal®; ***k. garden*** huerto *m*; ***k. knife*** cuchillo *m* de cocina; ***k. paper*** (rollo *m* de) papel *m* de cocina; ***k. roll*** (rollo *m* de) papel *m* de cocina; ***k. salt*** sal *f* de cocina *or Esp* gorda *or Am* gruesa; ***k. scales*** balanza *f* de cocina; ***k. sink*** fregadero *m*, *Chile, Col, Méx* lavaplatos *m inv*, *RP* pileta *f*; IDIOM *Fam* **he took everything but the k. sink** se llevó hasta el colchón; ***k. unit*** módulo *m* de cocina

kitchenette [kɪtʃɪ'net] *n* cocina *f* pequeña

kitchen-sink drama ['kɪtʃɪn'sɪŋk'drɑːmə] *n* obra *f* de realismo social

kitchenware ['kɪtʃɪnweə(r)] *n* menaje *m* de cocina

kite [kaɪt] **1** *n* (**a**) *(toy)* cometa *f*, *CAm, Méx* papalote *m*, *Chile* volantín *m*, *Par* pandorga *f*, *RP* barrilete *m* ▸▸ *Br* ***K. mark*** = marchamo oficial de calidad (**b**) *(bird)* milano *m* (**c**) *Br Fam Old-fashioned (aircraft)* aeroplano *m* (**d**) IDIOMS **to fly a k.** lanzar un globo sonda (para tantear el terreno); *Fam* **go fly a k.!** ¡vete a freír churros *or* espárragos!
2 *vt US Fam (cheque)* = extender un cheque sin fondos esperando que para cuando se cobre los haya, *RP* diferir

kith [kɪθ] *n Literary* **k. and kin** parientes y amigos

kitsch [kɪtʃ] **1** *n* kitsch *m*
2 *adj* kitsch *inv*

kitschy ['kɪtʃɪ] *adj* kitsch *inv*

kitten ['kɪtən] *n (young cat)* gatito(a) *m,f*; IDIOM **she had kittens** *(was shocked)* le dio un soponcio

kittenish ['kɪtənɪʃ] *adj* coqueto(a), juguetono(a)

kittiwake ['kɪtɪweɪk] *n* gaviota *f* tridáctila

kitty ['kɪtɪ] *n* (**a**) *Fam (cat)* gatito(a) *m,f*, minino(a) *m,f*; **here, k. k.** minino, minino, ven aquí (**b**) *(for bills)* fondo *m or* caja *f* común; *(for drinks)* fondo *m*; *(in cards)* posturas *fpl*, puesta *f*

kitty-corner ['kɪtɪkɔːnə(r)], **kitty-cornered** ['kɪtɪkɔːnəd] *US Fam* **1** *adj* diagonal
2 *adv* en diagonal, diagonalmente

kiwi ['kiːwiː] *n* (**a**) *(bird)* kiwi *m* (**b**) *Fam* **K.** *(New Zealander)* neozelandés(esa) *m,f* (**c**) *(fruit)* **k. (fruit)** kiwi *m*

KKK [keɪkeɪ'keɪ] *n* (*abbr* **Ku Klux Klan**) KKK *m*

Klan [klæn] *n* **the K.** el Ku Klux Klan

Klansman ['klænzmən] *n* miembro *m* del Ku Klux Klan

klaxon ['klæksən] *n Aut* bocina *f*, claxon *m*

Kleenex® ['kliːneks] *n* kleenex® *m inv*, pañuelo *m* de papel

kleptomania [kleptə'meɪnɪə] *n* cleptomanía *f*

kleptomaniac [kleptə'meɪnɪæk] *n* cleptómano(a) *m,f*

klieg light ['kliːglaɪt] *n* lámpara *f* de arco; *US Fig* **under the k. lights** bajo los focos

klutz [klʌts] *n US Fam (stupid person)* bobo(a) *m,f*, *Esp* chorra *mf*; *(clumsy person)* torpe, *Esp* patoso(a) *m,f*

km (*abbr* **kilometre**) km

km/h, kmph (*abbr* **kilometres per hour**) km/h *mpl*

knack [næk] *n* habilidad *f*, maña *f*; **there's a k. to it** tiene su complicación *or* truco; **to have the k. of** *or* **a k. for doing sth** tener habilidad *or* darse maña para hacer algo; **he's got a k. of turning up at mealtimes** le ha tomado *or Esp* cogido el gusto a presentarse a la hora de las comidas; **to get the k. of sth** pillar el truco *or Esp* tranquillo a algo

knacker ['nækə(r)] *Br* **1** *n* (**a**) *(for horses)* matarife *m* de caballos; **k.'s yard** matadero de caballos (**b**) *very Fam* **knackers** *(testicles)* pelotas *fpl*, huevos *mpl*
2 *vt Fam* (**a**) *(exhaust)* dejar hecho(a) polvo *or* reventado(a) (**b**) *(break, wear out)* hacer polvo

knackered ['nækəd] *adj Br Fam* **to be k.** *(tired)* estar hecho(a) polvo *or* reventado(a); *(broken, damaged)* estar hecho(a) polvo

knapsack ['næpsæk] *n* mochila *f*

knapweed ['næpwiːd] *n* centaura *f*

knave [neɪv] *n* (**a**) *(in cards) (English pack)* jota *f*; *(Spanish pack)* sota *f* (**b**) *Literary (scoundrel)* villano *m*

knavish ['neɪvɪʃ] *adj* vil, bribón(ona)

knead [niːd] *vt* (**a**) *(dough)* amasar (**b**) *(muscles)* masajear, dar un masaje a

knee [niː] **1** *n* (**a**) *(part of body)* rodilla *f*; **we were up to our knees in snow** la nieve nos llegaba a las rodillas; **to be on one's knees** estar arrodillado(a) *or* de rodillas; **the country was on its knees** el país se hallaba postrado; **to go down on one's knees** arrodillarse, ponerse de rodillas; **to fall to one's knees** caer de rodillas; *Fig* **to bring a country to its knees** *(state of collapse)* llevar a un país a una situación catastrófica; *(at one's mercy)* doblegar a un país; *Literary* **to bend** *or* **bow the k. to** *or* **before sb** hincarse de rodillas ante alguien ▸▸ ***k. joint*** articulación *f* de la rodilla
(**b**) *(of trousers)* rodilla *f*; **worn at the knees** con las rodillas gastadas
(**c**) *(lap)* regazo *m*, falda *f*; **come and sit on my k.** ven a sentarte en mi regazo *or* falda; **quiet or I'll put you over my k.** como no te calles te voy a dar un azote
2 *vt (hit with knee)* dar un rodillazo a; **he kneed me in the groin** me dio un rodillazo en la entrepierna

knee-breeches ['niːbriːtʃɪz] *npl* bermudas *fpl*

kneecap ['niːkæp] **1** *n* rótula *f*
2 *vt Br* (*pt & pp* **kneecapped**) castigar disparando en la rótula

kneecapping ['niːkæpɪŋ] *n* = castigo que consiste en disparar en la rótula a alguien

knee-deep ['niː'diːp] *adj* **the snow/mud was k.** la nieve/el barro llegaba hasta las rodillas; **she was k. in water** le llegaba el agua por la rodilla; *Fig* **she was k. in work** estaba hasta el cuello de trabajo

knee-high ['niː'haɪ] *adj* hasta (la altura de) la rodilla; **the grass was k.** la hierba llegaba a la altura de las rodillas; IDIOM *Fam* **when I was k. to a grasshopper** cuando era pequeño *or* canijo, *Am* cuando era *or Col* estaba chiquito

kneehole ['niːhəʊl] *n* = lugar para colocar las rodillas en un escritorio o mueble; **k. desk** escritorio con espacio para las rodillas

knee-jerk ['niːdʒɜːk] **1** *n (reflex)* reflejo *m* rotular
2 *adj (reaction, response)* visceral; *(opposition, condemnation)* automático(a)

kneel [niːl] (*pt & pp* **knelt** [nelt]) *vi (go down on one's knees)* arrodillarse, ponerse de rodillas; *(be on one's knees)* estar de rodillas; **after the battle they knelt in prayer** tras la batalla se arrodillaron para rezar; **the monks were kneeling in prayer** los monjes rezaban arrodillados; **to k. before sb** arrodillarse ante alguien

▸ **kneel down** *vi* arrodillarse, ponerse de rodillas

knee-length ['niːleŋθ] *adj* hasta la rodilla ▸▸ ***k. boots*** botas *fpl* de caña alta; ***k. socks*** medias *fpl* tres cuartos

kneeler ['niːlə(r)] *n (cushion)* cojín *m*, almohadón *m*

kneepad ['niːpæd] *n* rodillera *f*

knees-up ['niːzʌp] *n Br Fam* pachanga *f*, juerga *f*

knee-trembler ['niːtremblə(r)] *n Br very Fam* polvo *m* de pie; **to have a k.** echar un polvo de pie

knell [nel] *n Literary* tañido *m* fúnebre, toque *m* de difuntos; *Fig* **to toll** *or* **sound the (death) k. for sth/sb** suponer el (principio del) fin para algo/alguien

knelt *pt & pp of* **kneel**

knew *pt of* **know**

knickerbocker glory ['nɪkəbɒkə'glɔːrɪ] *n* = copa de helado con fruta y *Esp* nata *or Am* crema

knickerbockers ['nɪkəbɒkəz], *US* **knickers** ['nɪkəz] *npl* bombachos *mpl*

knickers ['nɪkəz] **1** *npl* **(a)** *Br (underwear) Esp* bragas *fpl, Chile, Col, Méx* calzones *mpl, Col* blúmers *mpl, Ecuad* follones *mpl, RP* bombacha *f*; IDIOM *Fam* **he got his k. in a twist** *(angry)* se salió de sus casillas; *(agitated)* se puso hecho un manojo de nervios; IDIOM *very Fam* **to get into sb's k.** echar un polvo a alguien, *Am* comerse a alguien **(b)** *US* = **knickerbockers**

2 *exclam Br Fam* ¡bobadas!

knick-knack ['nɪknæk] *n Fam* chuchería *f*, baratija *f*

knife [naɪf] **1** *n* (*pl* **knives** [naɪvz]) **(a)** *(cutlery)* cuchillo *m*; *(penknife)* navaja *f* ►► ***k. block*** taco *m or* tajo *m* portacuchillos; ***k. grinder*** afilador(ora) *m,f*; ***k. pleat*** *(on trousers)* pinza *f*; *(on skirt)* tabla *f*; ***k. sharpener*** afilador *m* de cuchillos

(b) *(weapon)* navaja *f*, cuchillo *m*; **to carry a k.** llevar (una) navaja ►► ***k. fight*** pelea *f* con navajas; ***k. wound*** puñalada *f*, cuchillada *f*

(c) *Elec* ***k. switch*** interruptor *m* de cuchilla

(d) IDIOMS **the knives are out for the Prime Minister** el primer ministro tiene los días contados; *Fam* **to go under the k.** *(have operation)* ser operado(a), pasar por (el) quirófano; **to go through sth like a (hot) k. through butter** *(of tool)* cortar algo como si fuera mantequilla; *(through opposition, market)* penetrar en algo con la mayor facilidad; **to have one's k. into sb** tenérsela jurada a alguien; **to stick the k. in** ensañarse; **to turn** *or* **twist the k. (in the wound)** hurgar en las heridas

2 *vt (stab)* apuñalar, acuchillar; **he was knifed in the back** recibió una puñalada por la espalda

knife-edge ['naɪfedʒ] *n Fig* **he has been on a k. all day** *(nervous)* ha estado todo el día con los nervios de punta; *Fig* **the situation/the game is balanced on a k.** la situación/el partido pende de un hilo

knife-point ['naɪfpɔɪnt] *n* **to be robbed at k.** ser robado(a) a punta de cuchillo

knifing ['naɪfɪŋ] *n* apuñalamiento *m*, acuchillamiento *m*

knight [naɪt] **1** *n* **(a)** *(person)* caballero *m*; *Fig* **a k. in shining armour** un salvador; *Fam* **a k. of the road** *(tramp)* un vagabundo ►► *Literary* ***k. errant*** caballero *m* andante **(b)** *Br (honorary title)* caballero *m*; **he was made a k.** fue nombrado caballero ►► ***K. of (the Order of) the Garter*** Caballero (de la Orden) de la Jarretera **(c)** *(in chess)* caballo *m*

2 *vt* ordenar caballero a

knighthood ['naɪthʊd] *n (title)* título *m* de caballero; **to receive** *or* **be given a k.** recibió *or* le otorgaron el título de caballero

knit [nɪt] (*pt & pp* **knitted** *or* **knit**) **1** *vt* **(a)** *(sweater)* tejer; **he knitted himself a scarf** se tejió una bufanda **(b)** *(in instructions)* **k. two purl two** tejer dos puntos del derecho y dos del revés, *Am* tejer dos puntos para abajo y dos para arriba **(c)** *(unite)* unir, aunar; IDIOM **to k. one's brows** fruncir el ceño

2 *vi* **(a)** *(with wool)* hacer punto **(b)** *(broken bones)* soldarse

3 *adj* **closely** *or* **tightly k.** muy unido(a); **a loosely k. coalition of parties** una coalición de partidos sin vinculaciones rígidas

4 *n (garment)* prenda *f Esp* de punto *orAm* tejida

▸**knit together** *vi (broken bones)* soldarse

knitted ['nɪtəd] *adj* de punto

knitter ['nɪtə(r)] *n* tejedor(ora) *m,f*, persona *f* que hace punto

knitting ['nɪtɪŋ] *n* **(a)** *(item)* (labor *f* de) punto *m*, *Am* tejido *m* **(b)** *(activity)* labor *f* de punto, *Am* tejido *m*; **have you finished your k.?** ¿has terminado de hacer punto?, *Am* ¿terminaste el tejido?; IDIOM *US* **to stick to one's (own) k.** dedicarse a lo suyo ►► ***k. machine*** *Esp* tricotosa *f*, *Am* máquina *f* de tejer; ***k. needle*** aguja *f* de punto *orAm* de tejer

knitwear ['nɪtweə(r)] *n* prendas *fpl* de punto *or Am* tejidas

knives *pl of* **knife**

knob [nɒb] **1** *n* **(a)** *(on banisters, door, drawer)* pomo *m*; *(on cane)* empuñadura *f*, puño *m*; IDIOM *Br Fam* **the same to you with knobs on!** ¡y tú más!, *Esp* ¡me rebota (y en tu culo explota)!, *Méx* ¡soy un espejo y me reflejo! **(b)** *(on radio)* botón *m*, mando *m* **(c)** *(lump)* **a k. of butter** una nuez de mantequilla *or RP* manteca **(d)** *Br very Fam (penis)* verga *f*, pijo *m*

2 *vt Br very Fam (have sex with)* chingar *orAm* coger con

knobbly ['nɒblɪ], *US* **knobby** ['nɒbɪ] *adj* nudoso(a); **k. knees** rodillas huesudas

knock [nɒk] **1** *n* **(a)** *(blow)* golpe *m*; **give it a k. with a hammer** dale un golpe con un martillo, dale un martillazo; **I got a nasty k. on the elbow** me he dado un golpe de muerte en el codo, me he golpeado el codo de mala manera; **the car's had a few knocks, but nothing serious** el coche tiene algunos golpes *or* algunas abolladuras, pero nada grave

(b) *(on door)* **there was a k. at the door** se oyó un golpe en la puerta; **she gave three knocks on the door** llamó tres veces a la puerta, dio tres golpes en la puerta; **no one answered my k.** nadie contestó cuando llamé; **can you give me a k. tomorrow morning?** ¿podrías llamar a mi puerta por la mañana?; **k.! k.!** ¡toc! ¡toc!

(c) *Fam (criticism)* palo *m*; **she's taken a few knocks from the press** la prensa le ha dado unos cuantos palos

(d) *(to sb's pride, chances)* revés *m*; **to take a k.** sufrir un serio revés

(e) *Aut (in engine)* golpeteo *m*

2 *vt* **(a)** *(hit)* golpear; **to k. a nail in** clavar un clavo; **he was knocked into the ditch** lo tiraron a la cuneta de un golpe; **to k. sb to the ground** tumbar a alguien *(a golpes)*; **the explosion knocked us to the floor** *or* **off our feet** la explosión nos tiró al suelo; **he was knocked off balance by the blow** el golpe le hizo perder el equilibrio; **the news knocked him off balance** la noticia le dejó de una pieza; **to k. sb unconscious** dejar a alguien inconsciente; **to k. one's head on** *or* **against sth** golpearse la cabeza contra algo; **to k. a hole in sth** abrir un agujero de un golpe en algo; **to k. holes in an argument** echar por tierra *or* desbaratar un argumento; **to k. some sense into sb** meter un poco de sentido común en la cabeza a alguien

(b) *Fam (criticize)* criticar; **don't k. it till you've tried it!** no lo critiques sin probarlo antes; **he's always knocking his colleagues** siempre está poniendo verde a *or* criticando a sus compañeros

(c) *(damage)* **his confidence had been knocked** su confianza había sufrido un serio revés

(d) IDIOMS *Fam* **to k. sb dead** *(impress)* dejar de piedra a alguien; *Fam* **k. 'em dead** ¡a por ellos!, *Esp* ¡valor y al toro!; *Br Fam* **to k. sth on the head** *(put a stop to)* cortar algo de raíz; *Br Fam* **k. it on the head, will you!** ¡ya basta! ¿no?; **to k. sth/sb into shape** poner algo/a alguien a punto; *Fam* **to k. sb sideways** *or US* **for a loop** dejar a alguien de piedra

3 *vi* **(a)** *(hit)* dar golpes, golpear; **to k. on the window** dar golpes *or* golpear en la ventana; **his knees were knocking** le temblaban las rodillas

(b) *(on door)* llamar, *Am* golpear; **to k. at** *or* **on the door** llamar a la puerta (con los nudillos); **please k. before entering** por favor, llamar antes de entrar; **she came in without knocking** entró sin llamar *orAm* golpear; **don't come knocking at my door if you need help in future** a partir de ahora no llames a mi puerta cuando necesites ayuda

(c) *(bump)* golpearse, chocar; **to k. against** *or* **into sth** chocar con *or* contra algo; **my elbow knocked against the door frame** me golpeé el codo contra el marco de la puerta

(d) *(engine)* golpetear

▸**knock about, knock around** **1** *vt sep* **(a)** *(jolt)* **the furniture has been badly knocked about** *or* **around** han tratado muy mal los muebles; **we really got knocked about in the back of that truck** acabamos molidos en la parte trasera del camión ese **(b)** *Fam (beat up)* maltratar, pegar **(c)** *Fam (idea, suggestion)* dar vueltas a

2 *vt insep Fam* **are my keys knocking about** *or* **around the kitchen somewhere?** ¿están *or* andan mis llaves por la cocina?; **she knocked about** *or* **around Australia for a few years** estuvo unos cuantos años por Australia; **these clothes are OK for knocking about the house in** esta ropa va bien para estar por casa, *Am* esta ropa sirve para entrecasa

3 *vi Fam* **has anyone seen my keys knocking about** *or* **around?** ¿ha visto alguien mis llaves por ahí?; **to k. about** *or* **around with sb** andar con alguien

▸**knock back** *vt sep Fam* **(a)** *(swallow)* **to k. back a drink** *Esp* atizarse una copa, *Am* hacer fondo blanco con algo de beber; **he certainly knocks it back!** *Esp* priva *orAm* chupa como una esponja

(b) *Br (idea, proposal)* rechazar; **to k. sb back** dar calabazas a alguien

(c) *Br (cost)* costar; **that must have knocked you back a bit!** ¡eso te ha tenido que costar un ojo de la cara *or* un dineral!

(d) *(shock)* **she was knocked back by the news** la noticia le impactó muchísimo

▸**knock down** *vt sep* **(a)** *(boxer, assailant)* derribar **(b)** *(pedestrian)* atropellar **(c)** *(building, wall)* derribar **(d)** *(price)* rebajar; **I knocked her down to £30** conseguí que me lo dejara en 30 libras **(e)** *(at auction)* adjudicar; **it was knocked down to her for £300** se lo adjudicaron por 300 libras

▸**knock off** **1** *vt sep* **(a)** *(cause to fall off) (object, person)* tirar; **he was knocked off his bike by a car** un coche *orAm* carro *or RP* auto lo tiró de la bicicleta; **the arm of the statue had been knocked off** le habían roto un brazo a la estatua, la estatua había perdido un brazo; IDIOM *Fam* **to k. sb's head** *or* **block off** romper la cabeza a alguien; IDIOM *Fam* **to k. sb's socks off** dejar alucinado(a) a alguien; IDIOM *Fam* **to k. spots off sb** darle cien *or* mil vueltas a alguien

(b) *Fam (deduct) (point, mark)* quitar, *Am* sacar; **I managed to get something knocked off the price** conseguí que me rebajaran algo el precio; **the salesman knocked 10 percent off (for us)** el vendedor nos hizo una rebaja del 10 por ciento

(**c**) *Fam (steal) Esp* mangar, *Am* volar; **to k. off a bank/jeweller's** dar un golpe en un banco/una joyería

(**d**) *Fam (kill)* asesinar, cepillarse a

(**e**) *Fam* **k. it off!** *(stop it)* ¡basta ya!

(**f**) *Fam (produce quickly) (letter, report, song)* despachar; **she can k. off an article in half an hour** es capaz de despachar *or Esp* ventilarse un artículo en media hora

(**g**) *Br very Fam (have sex with)* cepillarse *or Am* comerse a

2 *vi Fam (finish work)* terminar de trabajar, *Esp* plegar

▶**knock on 1** *vt sep (in rugby)* **to k. the ball on** incurrir en *or* realizar un adelantado

2 *vi* incurrir en *or* realizar un adelantado

▶**knock out** *vt sep* (**a**) *(remove)* **one of his teeth had been knocked out** le habían saltado un diente; **he knocked out his pipe** vació la pipa (con unos golpecitos); IDIOM *Fam* **to k. sb's brains/teeth out** partirle la cabeza/la boca a alguien

(**b**) *(eliminate from competition)* eliminar; **we were knocked out in the first round** nos eliminaron en la primera ronda

(**c**) *(put out of action) (power supply, enemy artillery)* inutilizar; **it can k. out a tank at 2,000 metres** puede inutilizar un tanque a 2.000 metros

(**d**) *(make unconscious)* dejar sin sentido; *(in boxing match)* dejar fuera de combate; *Fam* **the sleeping pill knocked her out for ten hours** el somnífero la dejó K.O. *or* grogui durante diez horas

(**e**) *Fam (astound)* alucinar; **I was knocked out by the special effects** los efectos especiales me dejaron alucinado

(**f**) *Fam (exhaust)* hacer polvo a, reventar; **I'm not going to knock myself out working for him** no me voy a reventar *or* matar trabajando para él

▶**knock over** *vt sep* (**a**) *(container, table)* volcar (**b**) *(pedestrian)* atropellar; *(boxer)* derribar (**c**) *US Fam (rob)* atracar

▶**knock together** *vt sep Fam* (**a**) *(hit together)* **they need their heads knocking together, those two** esos dos necesitan que les den una buen regañina (**b**) *(make hastily) (meal, report, speech)* hacer deprisa y corriendo

▶**knock up 1** *vt sep* (**a**) *(make hastily)* hacer deprisa y corriendo (**b**) *Br (waken)* despertar (**c**) *Br Fam (exhaust)* hacer polvo, reventar (**d**) *very Fam (make pregnant)* dejar preñada a

2 *vi (in tennis)* pelotear

knockabout ['nɒkəbaʊt] **1** *n* astracanada *f*

2 *adj (comedy, comedian)* bullanguero(a)

knock-back ['nɒkbæk] *n Fam (refusal)* patada *f* en el trasero, negativa *f*; **to get a k.** llevarse una patada en el trasero

knockdown ['nɒkdaʊn] **1** *n (in boxing)* knockdown *m*

2 *adj* (**a**) *Fam (argument)* contundente, *Esp* impepinable (**b**) *(reduced)* **at a k. price** a un precio de risa (**c**) *(easy to dismantle)* desmontable, desarmable; **the furniture is sold in k. form** los muebles los venden desmontados *or* desarmados

knocker ['nɒkə(r)] *n* (**a**) *(on door)* llamador *m*, aldaba *f* (**b**) *Fam (critic)* crítico(a) *m,f* (**c**) *very Fam* **knockers** *(breasts)* domingas *fpl*, *Méx* chichís *fpl*, *RP* lolas *fpl*

knock-for-knock agreement ['nɒkfənɒkə'gri:mənt] *n Br (in car insurance)* = acuerdo amistoso entre aseguradoras automovilísticas

knocking ['nɒkɪŋ] *n* (**a**) *(at door, window)* golpes *mpl* (**b**) *(of engine)* golpeteo *m* (**c**) *Br Fam (injury, defeat)* **to take a k.** *(in fight)* llevarse una paliza *or* tunda de palos; *(in match)* llevarse una paliza (**d**) *Br very Fam* ***k. shop*** prostíbulo *m*, burdel *m* (**e**) *Com* **k. copy** = publicidad que ataca o desacredita a la competencia

knock-kneed ['nɒk'ni:d] *adj* patizambo(a), zambo(a), *Am* chueco(a)

knock-knees ['nɒk'ni:z] *npl* **to have k.** ser zambo(a) *or* patizambo(a), *Am* ser chueco(a)

knock-on ['nɒk'ɒn] **1** *n (in rugby)* adelantado *m*

2 *adj* **k. effect** efecto dominó

knockout ['nɒkaʊt] **1** *n* (**a**) *(in boxing)* K.O. *m*, fuera de combate *m*; *Fig (to chances)* golpe *m* de gracia; **to win by a k.** ganar por K.O. (**b**) *Fam (sensation)* **to be a k.** causar sensación; **he's a k.** *(attractive)* está imponente

2 *adj* (**a**) **k. blow** *(in boxing)* golpe que pone fuera de combate; *Fig* **to deliver the k. blow** *(to chances)* asestar el golpe de gracia ▶▶ *Fam* ***k. drops*** gotas *fpl* de un bebedizo *(para dejar inconsciente)* (**b**) *(in sport)* **a k. competition** una competición *or Am* competencia por eliminatorias

knock-up ['nɒkʌp] *n Br (in tennis)* peloteo *m*

knoll [nɒl] *n* loma *f*, altozano *m*

knot [nɒt] **1** *n* (**a**) *(in rope, string)* nudo *m*; *(in ribbon)* lazo *m*, lazada *f*; **to tie/untie a k.** atar/desatar un nudo, hacer/deshacer un nudo; IDIOM *Fam* **to tie the k.** *(get married)* casarse

(**b**) *(tangle)* nudo *m*, enredo *m*; **the wool is full of knots** la lana tiene muchos nudos; **my hair is full of knots** tengo el cabello enredado; IDIOM *Fam* **to tie oneself in knots** hacerse un lío enorme

(**c**) *(in muscle)* nódulo *m*; *Fig* **my stomach was in knots** tenía un nudo en el estómago

(**d**) *(in wood)* nudo *m*

(**e**) *Naut (unit of speed)* nudo *m*; **we are doing 15 knots** vamos a 15 nudos

(**f**) *(group of people)* corro *m*

(**g**) *(bird)* correlimos *m inv* gordo

2 *vt (pt & pp* **knotted**) *(piece of string)* anudar, atar; **he knotted the rope around his waist** se ató la cuerda a la cintura

3 *vi (muscle)* agarrotarse; **my stomach knotted up with fear** del miedo se me hizo un nudo en el estómago

knotgrass ['nɒtgrɑ:s] *n* centinodia *f*, correhuela *f*

knothole ['nɒthəʊl] *n* hueco *m* (de un nudo) en la madera

knotted ['nɒtɪd] *adj* (**a**) *(handkerchief, rope)* con nudos; *(hair)* enredado(a), enmarañado(a) (**b**) *Br very Fam* **get k.!** ¡vete al cuerno!, *Esp* ¡que te den!

knotty ['nɒtɪ] *adj* (**a**) *Fam (problem)* espinoso(a) (**b**) *(wood)* nudoso(a)

knotweed ['nɒtwi:d] *n* disciplina *f* de monja

knout [naʊt] *n* knut *m*

KNOW [nəʊ] **1** *n Fam* **to be in the k.** estar enterado(a), estar en el ajo, *RP* estar en el mojo

2 *vt (pt* **knew** [nju:], *pp* **known** [nəʊn]) (**a**) *(be acquainted with)* conocer; **to get to k. sb** conocer a alguien; **it took a while for me to get to k. them** me llevó tiempo conocerlos bien; **she had long hair when I first knew her** cuando la conocí tenía el pelo largo; **do you k. Miami?** ¿conoces Miami?; **the end of life as we k. it** el final de la vida tal y como la conocemos; **I k. her only as a colleague** sólo la conozco del trabajo; **I k. him better than to believe he'd say such a thing** lo conozco lo suficiente como para saber que él nunca diría una cosa así; **to k. sb by name/sight** conocer a alguien de nombre/vista; **I k. her for a hard worker** sé que es una buena trabajadora; **I k. him to say hello to** lo conozco de hola y adiós nada más; **knowing HIM...** conociéndolo...; **knowing my luck...** con la suerte que tengo...; **I had a call from you k. who** me llamó quien tú ya sabes; *Fam* **(do) you k. Mike? he was in a car crash** ¿te acuerdas de Mike? tuvo un accidente

(**b**) *(have knowledge of)* saber; **to k. (that)...** saber que...; **to k. the answer** saber la respuesta; **to k. a lot/very little about sth** saber mucho/muy poco de algo; **she knows what she is talking about** sabe de lo que está hablando; **he thinks he knows it all** *or* **everything** se cree que lo sabe todo; **she knows all there is to k. about the subject** lo sabe todo del tema, sabe todo sobre ese tema; **this substance is known to cause cancer** se sabe que esta sustancia produce cáncer; **we k. her to be a Russian agent** sabemos que es una agente rusa; **I knew it, I could have told you he'd say that!** ¡lo sabía, sabía que diría eso!; **that's not true and you k. it** eso no es verdad y tú lo sabes (perfectamente); *Fam* **don't I k. it!** ¡dímelo a mí!, ¡a mí me lo vas a decir!; **I don't k. that that's a very good idea** no estoy seguro de que sea una buena idea; **before you k. where you are, the next thing you k.** en un abrir y cerrar de ojos, antes de que puedas decir esta boca es mía; **for all I k., he could be dead** por lo que sé, podría haber muerto; **to k. sth backwards** saberse algo al dedillo; **to k. sth for a fact** saber algo a ciencia cierta; **to k. one's own mind** tener las ideas claras; **she knows her place** sabe cuál es su sitio; *Fam* **to k. a thing or two** saber alguna que otra cosa, saber un rato; **I don't k. the first thing about genetics** no tengo ni la más mínima idea de genética; **he knows his way around the office** conoce bien la oficina; **you'll keep away from him if you k. what's good for you** si sabes lo que te conviene, aléjate de él; **he knows what's what** tiene la cabeza sobre los hombros *or RP* bien puesta; **heaven** *or* **God (only)** *or* **goodness knows!** ¡sabe Dios!; **I might have known I'd find you here!** ya sabía que te encontraría aquí; **there's no knowing how they'll react** no hay manera de saber cómo van a reaccionar; **what do they k., anyway?** ¡qué sabrán ellos!; *Fam Hum* **what do you k.?, waddaya k.?** ¡anda, mira!, *Esp* ¡hombre, qué sorpresa!, *RP* ¡mirá, vos!; *Fam* **you k. that shop that used to be on the corner?** ¿te acuerdas de *or* sabes aquella tienda que había en la esquina?; *Fam* **(do) you k. what? I think he may be right** ¿sabes qué te digo? que puede que tenga razón, *RP* ¿sabés qué? talvez tenga razón; *Fam* **she's a bit slow, (you) k. what I mean?** es un poco corta, tu ya me entiendes

(**c**) *(recognize, distinguish)* distinguir, reconocer; **I knew her by her walk** la distinguí *or* la reconocí por su forma de caminar *or esp Esp* andar; **I'd k. her anywhere** la reconocería a la legua; **the town has**

changed so much you wouldn't k. it la ciudad ha cambiado tanto que no la reconocerías; **he knows a good business opportunity when he sees one** sabe reconocer un buen negocio (cuando lo tiene delante); *Fam* **she wouldn't k. a good wine if it hit her in the face** *or* **if she fell over one** no tiene ni la más remota idea de vino; **to k. right from wrong** distinguir lo bueno de lo malo; **my joy knows no bounds** mi alegría no tiene límites

(**d**) *(experience)* **I've never known anything like it** nunca he visto nada igual; **I've never known him to be shy** nunca lo he visto comportarse con timidez; **such coincidences have been known** coincidencias de ésas han pasado a veces; **she has been known to lose her temper** en alguna ocasión ha perdido los estribos; *Literary* **I have never known true love** nunca he conocido el verdadero amor

(**e**) *(language, skill)* **to k. Spanish** saber español; **to k. how to do sth** saber hacer algo

(**f**) *Archaic (have sex with)* conocer

3 *vi* (**a**) *(in general)* saber; **he's not very clever – I k.** no es muy inteligente - ya lo sé; **maybe Peter will k.** quizá Peter lo sepa; **what's her name? – I don't k.** ¿cómo se llama? - no (lo) sé; **it has been a hard week – I k.** *(expressing agreement)* ha sido una semana muy dura - ¡desde luego! *or* ¡sin duda!; **I k., why don't we go to the cinema?** ya sé, ¿por qué no vamos al cine?; **I k., I k., I'm late again** ya lo sé, ya lo sé, otra vez llego tarde; *Fam* **I don't k., whatever is he going to do next?** de verdad, ¿qué se le ocurrirá ahora?; **she's not very friendly – oh, I don't k., I find her quite pleasant** no es muy simpática - no sé, a mí me parece muy agradable; **the insurance company didn't want to k.** la compañía de seguros se desentendió; **to k. about sth** saber de algo; **she had known about it all along** ella lo sabía desde el principio; **did you k. about Jerry?** ¿sabes lo de Jerry?; **I don't k. about you, but I'm going to bed** no sé tú (qué harás), pero yo me voy a la cama; **I k. all about hard work** ¡qué me vas a contar a mí de trabajo duro (que yo no sepa)!; **as** *or* **so far as I k.** que yo sepa; **how should I k.?** ¿cómo voy a saberlo yo?; **it's not easy, I should k.!** no es fácil, créeme; **if you must k., she's my sister** ya que insistes tanto, es mi hermana; **you never k.** nunca se sabe; **is that the killer? – I wouldn't k.** ¿es ése el asesino? - yo no sé nada; **to k. best** *or* **better** saber lo que hay que hacer; **he always thinks he knows best** *or* **better** siempre se cree que lo sabe todo; **you should k. better than that by now!** ¡a estas alturas ya podías saber que eso no se hace!; **she knew better than to ask again** como es lógico, no se le ocurrió volver a preguntar; **he doesn't k. whether he's coming or going** no sabe por dónde se anda, no sabe si va o viene, *RP* no tiene idea de dónde está parado; **I didn't k. whether to laugh or to cry** no sabía si reír o llorar

(**b**) *Fam* **you shouldn't smoke so much, you k.** no deberías fumar tanto ¿sabes?; **I have been there before, you k.** yo he estado allí, ¿eh?; **it wasn't quite what I was expecting, you k.** en fin, no era lo que me esperaba; **I was walking along the street, you k., minding my own business,...** iba por la calle, ¿no?, a lo mío,...; **James, you k., my cousin...** James, ya sabes, mi primo...

▸ **know of** *vt insep* saber de, conocer; **not that I k. of** que yo sepa, no; **to get to k. of sth** enterarse de algo

know-all ['nəʊɔːl] *n esp Br Fam* sabihondo(a) *m,f*, sabelotodo *mf*

know-how ['nəʊhaʊ] *n* conocimientos *mpl* prácticos, know how *m*; *Com* técnica *f*, conocimientos *mpl* técnicos

knowing ['nəʊɪŋ] 1 *n* **there's no k.** no hay manera de saberlo
2 *adj (look, smile)* cómplice, de complicidad

knowingly ['nəʊɪŋlɪ] *adv* (**a**) *(act)* a sabiendas (**b**) *(look, smile)* de forma cómplice, con complicidad

know-it-all ['nəʊɪtɔːl] *n Fam* sabihondo(a) *m,f*, sabelotodo *mf*

knowledge ['nɒlɪdʒ] *n* (**a**) *(awareness)* conocimiento *m*; **(not) to my k.** que yo sepa (no); **to the best of my k.** por lo que yo sé; **without my k.** sin que yo tuviera conocimiento, sin que yo lo supiera; **I had no k. of it** no tenía conocimiento de ello; **to have full k. of sth** saber algo perfectamente; **it is common k. that...** todo el mundo sabe que..., de todos es sabido que...; **he brought the theft to my k.** me dio cuenta del robo; *Formal* **it has come to our k. that...** ha llegado a nuestro conocimiento que...

(**b**) *(learning)* conocimientos *mpl*; **to have a k. of several languages** saber varios idiomas; **she has a basic/thorough k. of physics** tiene conocimientos elementales/profundos de física; **her k. is immense** tiene enormes conocimientos; PROV **k. is power** el poder llega por el conocimiento

(**c**) *Comptr* ***k. base*** base *f* de conocimientos; ***the k. economy*** la economía del conocimiento

knowledgeable ['nɒlɪdʒəbəl] *adj* entendido(a); **to be k. about sth** ser un(a) (gran) entendido(a) en algo

knowledgeably ['nɒlɪdʒəblɪ] *adv* con conocimiento, con erudición; **he speaks k. about music** habla de música con gran erudición

knowledge-based ['nɒlɪdʒbeɪst] *adj Comptr* ***k. system*** sistema *m* experto

known [nəʊn] 1 *adj* (**a**) *(notorious)* conocido(a); **he's a k. drugs dealer** es un traficante conocido (**b**) *(recognized)* conocido(a); **it's a k. fact** es un hecho conocido; **to make oneself k.** darse a conocer; **to let it be k.** dar a conocer, sacar a la luz; **k. reserves** *(of oil)* reservas de petróleo conocidas
2 *pp of* **know**

knuckle ['nʌkəl] *n* (**a**) *(of finger)* nudillo *m*; *Fam Hum* **to give sb a k. sandwich** darle un piñazo a alguien, *Esp* arrearle una castaña a alguien; IDIOM *Fam* **near the k.** *(of remark, joke)* rayano(a) en la vulgaridad, hiriente ►► *US Fam* ***k. buster*** máquina *f* de validación, *Esp* bacaladera *f* (**b**) *(of pork)* codillo *m*

▸ **knuckle down** *vi Fam* **to k. down (to sth)** ponerse (a algo) en serio

▸ **knuckle under** *vi Fam* pasar por el aro, rendirse

knucklebone ['nʌkəlbəʊn] *n* (**a**) *Anat* falange *f* (**b**) *Culin* hueso *m* de codillo

knuckle-duster ['nʌkəldʌstə(r)] *n* puño *m* americano

knucklehead ['nʌkəlhed] *n Fam* (pedazo *m* de) alcornoque *m*, cabeza *mf* de chorlito

knurl [nɜːl] *n* (**a**) *(in wood)* nudo *m* (**b**) *(on screw)* moleteado *m*

KO ['keɪ'əʊ] *Fam* 1 *n* (*pl* **KO's** ['keɪ'əʊz]) *(in boxing)* K.O. *m*
2 *vt* (*pp & pt* **KO'd** ['keɪ'əʊd]) *(in boxing)* dejar fuera de combate, noquear

koala [kəʊ'ɑːlə] *n* **k. (bear)** koala *m*

Kodiak ['kəʊdɪæk] *n* **K. (bear)** (oso *m*) kodiak *m*

kohl [kəʊl] *n (eyeliner)* lápiz *m* de ojos; *(powder)* kohl *m*

kohlrabi [kəʊl'rɑːbɪ] *n* colinabo *m*, col *f* rábano

kola ['kəʊlə] *n (tree)* cola *f* ►► ***k. nut*** nuez *f* de cola

Komodo dragon [kə'məʊdəʊ'drægən] *n* dragón *m* de Komodo

kook [kuːk] *n US Fam* chiflado(a) *m,f*, *Esp* majara *mf*

kookaburra ['kʊkəbʌrə] *n* cucaburra *m or f*

kookie, kooky ['kuːkɪ] *adj US Fam* chiflado(a), *Esp* majara

kopeck, kopek ['kəʊpek] *n (subdivision of rouble)* kopek *m*, copec *m*

Koran [kə'rɑːn] *n* **the K.** el Corán

Koranic [kə'rænɪk] *adj* coránico(a)

Korea [kə'rɪə] *n* Corea; **North/South K.** Corea del Norte/del Sur

Korean [kə'rɪən] 1 *n* (**a**) *(person)* coreano(a) *m,f* (**b**) *(language)* coreano *m*
2 *adj* coreano(a); **the K. War** la guerra de Corea

korma ['kɔːmə] *n Culin* = plato suave de la cocina india consistente en verduras o carne cocidas en su jugo y mezcladas con yogur

kosher ['kəʊʃə(r)] *adj* (**a**) *(in Judaism)* kosher, conforme a la ley judaica; **k. meat** carne kosher (**b**) *Fam (legitimate)* legal

Kosovan ['kɒsəvən], **Kosovar** ['kɒsəvɑː(r)] 1 *n* kosovar *mf*
2 *adj* kosovar

Kosovan-Albanian ['kɒsəvənæl'beɪnɪən] 1 *n* albanokosovar *mf*
2 *adj* albanokosovar

Kosovo ['kɒsəvəʊ] *n* Kosovo

kowtow ['kaʊ'taʊ] *vi* postrarse; *Fig* **to k. to sb** postrarse ante alguien

kph (*abbr* **kilometres per hour**) km/h

Krakow ['krækaʊ] *n* Cracovia

Kraut [kraʊt] *Fam* 1 *n* cabeza cuadrada *mf*, = término generalmente ofensivo para referirse a los alemanes
2 *adj* de cabeza cuadrada, = término generalmente ofensivo para referirse a los alemanes

Kremlin ['kremlɪn] *n* **the K.** el Kremlin

Kremlinologist [kremlɪ'nɒlədʒɪst] *n* kremlinólogo(a) *m,f*

krill [krɪl] (*pl* **krill**) *n* kril *m*

Kriss Kringle ['krɪs'krɪŋgəl] *n US* Papá *m* Noel

krona ['kreʊnə] *n Formerly* corona *f* (sueca)

krone ['kreʊnə] *n* corona *f* (danesa *or* noruega)

Krugerrand ['kruːgərænd] *n* krugerrand *m*, = moneda de oro sudafricana

krypton ['krɪptɒn] *n Chem* criptón *m*, kriptón *m*

KS (*abbr* **Kansas**) Kansas

Kt (**a**) (*abbr* **kiloton**) Kt, kilotón *m* (**b**) *Br* (*abbr* **knight**) caballero *m*

Kuala Lumpur [kwɑːlə'lʊmpʊə(r)] *n* Kuala Lumpur

kudos ['kju:dɒs] *n* gloria *f*, renombre *m*; *US* **k. to the organizers for making the event so special** vaya nuestro reconocimiento a los que han organizado un acontecimiento tan especial

kudu ['ku:du:] *n* cudú *m*

Ku Klux Klan [ku:klʌks'klæn] *n* Ku Klux Klan *m*

kumquat ['kʌmkwɒt] *n* naranjilla *f* china, kumquat *m*

kung fu [kʌŋ'fu:] *n* kung-fu *m*

Kurd [kɜ:d] **1** *n* kurdo(a) *m,f*
2 *adj* kurdo(a)

Kurdish ['kɜ:dɪʃ] **1** *n (language)* kurdo *m*
2 *adj* kurdo(a)

Kurdistan [kɜ:dɪ'stæn] *n* Kurdistán

Kuriles [kʊə'ri:lz] *npl* **the K.** las (islas) Kuriles

Kuwait [kʊ'weɪt] *n* Kuwait

Kuwaiti [kʊ'weɪtɪ] **1** *n* kuwaití *mf*
2 *adj* kuwaití

kV (*abbr* **kilovolt**) kK

kvell [kvel] *vi US Fam (feel proud, delighted)* **he must be kvelling at the news** estará encantado con la noticia

kvetch [kvetʃ] *vi US Fam (complain)* quejarse, dar la murga con quejas

kW (*abbr* **kilowatt**) kW

kwanza(a) ['kwænzə] *n US* = festival afroamericano que se celebra del 26 de diciembre al 1 de enero

kwashiorkor [kwɒʃɪ'ɔ:kɔ:(r)] *n* kwashiorkor *m*

kWh (*abbr* **kilowatt-hour**) kvh, kWh

KY (*abbr* **Kentucky**) Kentucky

KY jelly® ['keɪwaɪ'dʒelɪ] *n* KY *m*, = lubricante soluble en agua

kybosh = **kibosh**

Kyoto [ki:'əʊtəʊ] *n* Kioto

kyrie ['kɪrɪeɪ] *n Rel* kirie *m* ▸▸ ***k. eleison*** kirieleisón *m*

L, l

L, l [el] *n (letter)* L, l *f*

L [el] *n* (**a**) (*abbr* **lake**) L. (**b**) (*abbr* **large**) L, G (**c**) (*abbr* **left**) izq., izqda. (**d**) *Br Aut* **L-plate** placa *f* de la "L"

l (*abbr* **litre(s)**) l.

LA [el'eɪ] *n* (**a**) (*abbr* **Los Angeles**) Los Ángeles (**b**) (*abbr* **Louisiana**) Luisiana

la, lah [lɑː] *n Mus* la *m*

Lab (**a**) *Br Pol* (*abbr* **Labour**) laborista (**b**) (*abbr* **Labrador**) Labrador

lab [læb] *n Fam* (*abbr* **laboratory**) laboratorio *m* ►► ***l. coat*** bata *f* blanca; ***l. technician*** técnico(a) *m,f* de laboratorio

label ['leɪbəl] **1** *n* (**a**) *(on parcel, bottle, suitcase, clothes)* etiqueta *f*; *Fig* **he objects to having a l. like "nonconformist" stuck on him** no está de acuerdo con la etiqueta de inconformista que le han puesto (**b**) *(of record company)* sello *m* discográfico, casa *f* discográfica

2 *vt* (*pt & pp* **labelled,** *US* **labeled**) (**a**) *(parcel, bottle, suitcase)* etiquetar; **you must l. your clothes clearly** debes marcar tu ropa claramente; **the bottle was labelled "poison"** la botella tenía una etiqueta que decía "veneno" (**b**) *(describe)* tildar de; **to l. sb a liar** tildar a alguien de mentiroso(a)

labelling, *US* **labeling** ['leɪblɪŋ] *n* etiquetado *m*, etiquetaje *m*; **this l. of children as failures at the age of 11 or 14 is very negative** tildar de fracasados a niños de 11 o 14 años es muy negativo, *Esp* colgarles el sambenito de fracasados a niños de 11 o 14 años es muy negativo

labia ['leɪbɪə] *npl Anat* labios *mpl* (vulvares); **l. minora/majora** labios menores/mayores

labial ['leɪbɪəl] *Ling* **1** *n* labial *f*

2 *adj* labial

labialization [leɪbɪəlaɪ'zeɪʃən] *n Ling* labialización *f*

labialize ['leɪbɪəlaɪz] *vt Ling* labializar

labile ['leɪbɪl] *adj Chem* inestable

labiodental [leɪbɪəʊ'dentəl] *Ling* **1** *n* labiodental *f*

2 *adj* labiodental

labor, labored *etc US* = **labour, laboured** *etc*

laboratory [lə'bɒrətrɪ] *n* laboratorio *m*; **tested under l. conditions** sometido(a) a pruebas de laboratorio ►► ***l. assistant*** ayudante *mf* de laboratorio

Labor Day ['leɪbədeɪ] *n US* = día del trabajador en Estados Unidos, celebrado el primer lunes de septiembre

laborious [lə'bɔːrɪəs] *adj (work, explanation)* laborioso(a), arduo(a)

laboriously [lə'bɔːrɪəslɪ] *adv* laboriosamente, arduamente

labour, *US* **labor** ['leɪbə(r)] **1** *n* (**a**) *(work)* trabajo *m* ►► ***l. camp*** campo *m* de trabajo

(**b**) *(workers)* mano *f* de obra, trabajadores *mpl* ►► ***l. costs*** costos *mpl or Esp* costes *mpl* de mano de obra; ***Labour Day*** día *m* de los trabajadores; ***l. dispute*** conflicto *m* laboral; *Br Formerly* ***l. exchange*** bolsa *f* de trabajo; ***l. force*** mano *f* de obra; ***l. law*** derecho *m* laboral *or* del trabajo; ***l. lawyer*** abogado(a) *m,f* laboralista; ***l. market*** mercado *m* laboral *or* de trabajo; ***the l. movement*** el movimiento obrero; ***l. relations*** relaciones *fpl* laborales; ***l. shortage*** escasez *f* de mano de obra; *US* ***l. union*** sindicato *m*

(**c**) *Br Pol* **the Labour Party** el partido laborista; **a Labour MP** un diputado laborista; **to vote Labour** votar a los laboristas

(**d**) *(task)* esfuerzo *m*, tarea *f*; **a l. of love** un trabajo hecho por amor al arte; *Mythol* **the (twelve) labours of Hercules** los (doce) trabajos de Hércules

(**e**) *(childbirth)* parto *m*; **it was a difficult l.** fue un parto difícil; **to be in l.** estar de parto; **to go into l.** ponerse de parto ►► ***l. pains*** dolores *mpl* del parto; ***l. ward*** sala *f* de partos

2 *vt* **to l. a point** repetir lo mismo una y otra vez

3 *vi* (**a**) *(work)* trabajar (**b**) *(struggle) (person)* trabajar afanosamente (**at** *or* **over** en); **to l. in vain** trabajar en vano; **to be labouring under a misapprehension** *or* **delusion** estar en un error (**c**) *(move with difficulty) (engine)* funcionar con dificultad; **the ship was labouring through heavy seas** el barco a duras penas avanzaba por mar gruesa; **he laboured up the hill** subió la cuesta con gran esfuerzo

laboured, *US* **labored** ['leɪbəd] *adj* (**a**) *(breathing)* fatigoso(a), trabajoso(a) (**b**) *(style)* farragoso(a); *(joke)* pesado(a)

labourer, *US* **laborer** ['leɪbərə(r)] *n* obrero(a) *m,f*

labouring, *US* **laboring** ['leɪbərɪŋ] *adj* **he did a number of l. jobs** trabajó de obrero en varias ocasiones

labour-intensive, *US* **labor-intensive** ['leɪbərɪn'tensɪv] *adj* que absorbe mucha mano de obra

labour-saving, *US* **labor-saving** ['leɪbəseɪvɪŋ] *n* ***l. device*** aparato *m* que permite ahorrarse trabajo

labrador ['læbrədɔː(r)] *n (dog)* labrador *m*

laburnum [lə'bɜːnəm] *n* codeso *m*

labyrinth ['læbərɪnθ] *n* laberinto *m*

labyrinthine [læbe'rɪnθaɪn] *adj* laberíntico(a)

lace [leɪs] **1** *n* (**a**) *(cloth)* encaje *m*; **l. handkerchief** pañuelo de encaje (**b**) *(of shoe)* cordón *m*

2 *vt* (**a**) *(shoes)* atar (los cordones de); **to do up** *or* **tie one's laces** atarse los cordones (**b**) *(drink)* **to l. a drink** *(with alcohol)* echar un chorro de licor a una bebida; *(with drug)* echar un narcótico en una bebida; *(with poison)* adulterar una bebida; *Fig* **he laced his story with salacious details** aderezó el relato con detalles obscenos

► **lace up 1** *vt sep* **to l. one's shoes up** atarse los zapatos

2 *vi (shoes, corset)* atarse; **they l. up at the sides/back** se atan a los lados/atrás

lacemaker ['leɪsmeɪkə(r)] *n* encajero(a) *m,f*

lacemaking ['leɪsmeɪkɪŋ] *n* labor *m* de encaje

lacerate ['læsəreɪt] *vt* lacerar; *Fig* **the experience left her emotions lacerated** la experiencia hirió sus sentimientos profundamente

laceration [læsə'reɪʃən] *n* laceración *f*

lace-up ['leɪsʌp] **1** *n (shoe)* zapato *m* de cordones

2 *adj (shoe)* de cordones

lacework ['leɪswɜːk] *n* encaje *m*

lachrymal, lacrimal ['lækrɪməl] *adj Anat (gland)* lacrimal

lachrymose ['lækrɪməʊs] *adj Literary* (**a**) *person)* lacrimoso(a) (**b**) *(film, story)* lacrimógeno(a)

lack [læk] **1** *n* falta *f*, carencia *f* (**of** de); **for** *or* **through l. of...** por falta de...; **not for l. of...** no por falta de...; **there's no l. of volunteers** no faltan voluntarios; **there was no l. of enthusiasm** había mucho entusiasmo; **it wasn't for l. of trying** y no es que no se intentase

2 *vt* carecer de; **he lacks confidence** carece de confianza; **what the town lacks in modern amenities it makes up for in picturesque charm** lo que al pueblo le falta de servicios modernos lo compensa con su encanto pintoresco

3 *vi* **they l. for nothing** no les falta (de) nada; **time was lacking** faltaba tiempo; **she is lacking in confidence/experience** le falta confianza/experiencia; **I find his work lacking in humour** encuentro que su obra carece de humor

lackadaisical [lækə'deɪzɪkəl] *adj* dejado(a); **he did the work, but he was most l. about it** realizó el trabajo, pero fue de lo más dejado al respecto

lackey ['lækɪ] *n* (**a**) *Pej* lacayo *m* (**b**) *Old-fashioned (footman)* lacayo *m*

lacklustre, *US* **lackluster** ['læklʌstə(r)] *adj* deslucido(a)

laconic [lə'kɒnɪk] *adj* lacónico(a)

laconically [lə'kɒnɪklɪ] *adv* lacónicamente

lacquer ['lækə(r)] **1** *n* laca *f*

2 *vt* (**a**) *(furniture)* lacar, laquear (**b**) *(hair)* aplicar laca a

lacquered ['lækəd] *adj* (**a**) *(furniture)* lacado(a) (**b**) *(hair)* con laca

lacquer-ware ['lækəweə(r)] *n* lacas *fpl*

lacrimal = **lachrymal**

lacrosse [lə'krɒs] *n Sport* lacrosse *m* ►► ***l. stick*** bastón *m or* stick *m* de lacrosse

lactate 1 *n* ['lækteɪt] *Biochem* lactato *m*
2 *vi* [læk'teɪt] *Physiol* segregar leche

lactation [læk'teɪʃən] *n Physiol* lactancia *f*

lactic acid ['læktɪk'æsɪd] *n* ácido *m* láctico

lactose ['læktəʊs] *n Biochem* lactosa *f*

lacuna [lə'kju:nə] (*pl* **lacunae** [lə'kju:ni:] *or* **lacunas**) *n* laguna *f*

lacustrine [lə'kʌstraɪn] *adj* lacustre

lacy ['leɪsɪ] *adj (made of lace)* de encaje; **the ice formed a l. pattern on the window** el hielo hacía formas de encaje en la ventana

lad [læd] *n* **(a)** *(boy)* muchacho *m*, chaval *m*, *Arg* pibe *m*, *CAm, Méx* chavo *m*, *Chile* cabro *m*; **when I was a l.** cuando era un chaval
(b) *Br Fam (fellow)* tipo *m*, *Esp* tío *m*; **the lads** *(friends)* los amiguetes, *Esp* los colegas, *Méx* los cuates; **come on, lads!** ¡vamos, *Esp* tíos *or Am* compadres!; **he's one of the lads** *(one of us)* es de los nuestros
(c) *Br Fam (macho young man)* **he's a bit of** *or* **quite a l.** es un *Esp* golfete *or Col, RP* indio *or Méx* gandalla ►► ***l. mag*** = revista para hombres donde destacan las secciones de deporte, chicas, motor, etc.

ladder ['lædə(r)] 1 *n* **(a)** *(for climbing)* escalera *f*; **the social l.** la escala social; *Fig* **to get one's foot on the l.** dar el primer paso; *Fig* **to reach the top of the l.** llegar a la cumbre **(b)** *Br (in stocking)* carrera *f*
2 *vt Br (stocking)* hacer una carrera en
3 *vi Br (stocking)* hacerse una carrera

ladderproof ['lædəpru:f] *adj Br* indesmallable

laddie ['lædɪ] *n Fam* muchacho *m*, *CAm, Méx* chavalo *m*

laddish ['lædɪʃ] *adj Br Fam* = referente a un estilo de vida en el que abundan las salidas con los amigos, el alcohol y las actitudes machistas

laden ['leɪdən] *adj* cargado(a) **(with** de**)**; **I was l. (down) with shopping** iba cargada con las compras; **apple-l. trees** árboles cargados *or* repletos de manzanas; **a heavily l. ship** un barco cargadísimo

ladette [læ'det] *n Br Fam* = chica con un estilo de vida en el que abundan las salidas con los amigos y el alcohol

la-di-da, lah-di-dah [lɑ:dɪ'dɑ:] *adj Fam Pej (accent, manner) Esp* pijo(a), *Méx* fresa, *RP* fifí

lading ['leɪdɪŋ] *n (cargo)* carga *f*

ladle ['leɪdəl] 1 *n* cucharón *m*, cazo *m*
2 *vt* servir *(con cucharón)*

►**ladle out** *vt sep* **(a)** *(soup)* servir *(con cucharón)* **(b)** *Fig (sympathy, praise, advice)* prodigar

lady ['leɪdɪ] *n* **(a)** *(woman)* señora *f*; *(in literature, of high status)* dama *f*; **a young l.** *(unmarried)* una señorita; *(married)* una (señora) joven; **an old l.** una señora mayor; *Old-fashioned* **a l. doctor** una doctora; *Old-fashioned* **his young l.** su novia; **ladies and gentlemen!** ¡señoras y señores!; **he's a ladies' man** es un mujeriego ►► ***ladies' fingers*** *(okra)* quingombó *m*, okra *f*; ***l. friend*** querida *f*, amiga *f*; ***the l. of the house*** la señora de la casa; ***l. of leisure*** mujer *f* ociosa; ***l. of the night*** *(plant)* duraznillo *m* fragante, galán *m* de noche; *Euph (prostitute)* mujer *f* de la noche
(b) *(by birth or upbringing)* dama *f*; **she's a real l.** es una verdadera dama
(c) the ladies, *US* **the ladies' room** el baño *or Esp* servicio *or CSur* toilette de señoras; **Ladies** *(sign)* señoras, damas
(d) *Rel* **Our L.** Nuestra Señora
(e) *US Fam (term of address)* señora *f*
(f) *Old-fashioned (wife)* señora *f*; **this is my l. wife** esta es mi señora esposa
(g) *(title)* **L. Browne** Lady Browne; **L. Luck** la diosa Fortuna; IDIOM *Br* **to play L. Bountiful** dárselas de dadivosa; IDIOM *Br Fam* **she's acting like L. Muck** se porta como una señoritinga

ladybird ['leɪdɪbɜ:d], *US* **ladybug** ['leɪdɪbʌg] *n* mariquita *f*

ladyboy ['leɪdɪbɔɪ] *n Fam* = joven transexual asiático

ladybug = **ladybird**

lady-in-waiting ['leɪdɪn'weɪtɪŋ] *n* dama *f* de honor

lady-killer ['leɪdɪkɪlə(r)] *n Fam* castigador *m*, casanova *m*

ladylike ['leɪdɪlaɪk] *adj* femenino(a), propio(a) de una señorita/señora

ladylove ['leɪdɪlʌv] *n Literary or Hum* **his l.** su amada

ladyship ['leɪdɪʃɪp] *n* **Her/Your L.** su señoría

lag [læg] 1 *n* **(a)** *(gap)* intervalo *m*, lapso *m* **(b)** *Br Fam (prisoner)* **old l.** presidiario
2 *vt* (*pt & pp* **lagged**) *(pipes, boiler)* revestir con un aislante
3 *vi* quedarse atrás

►**lag behind** 1 *vt insep (competitor)* quedarse atrás con respecto a, quedarse a la zaga de; **wages are lagging behind inflation** los salarios se están quedando atrás con respecto a la inflación
2 *vi* quedarse atrás, rezagarse; **the youngest children were lagging behind** los niños más pequeños se estaban quedando atrás *or* rezagados; **our country is lagging behind in medical research** el país se está quedando atrás en cuanto a investigación médica

lager ['lɑ:gə(r)] *n* cerveza *f (rubia)* ►► *Br Fam* ***l. lout*** borracho *m* peligroso *or Esp* gamberro

laggard ['lægəd] *n* rezagado(a) *m,f*

lagging ['lægɪŋ] *n (on pipes, boiler)* revestimiento *m*

lagoon [lə'gu:n] *n* laguna *f*

lah = **la**

lah-di-dah = **la-di-da**

laid *pt & pp of* **lay**

laid-back [leɪd'bæk] *adj Fam* tranquilo(a), *Esp* cachazudo(a); **he was very l. about it** se lo tomó con mucha pachorra

lain [leɪn] *pp of* **lie**[2]

lair [leə(r)] *n also Fig* guarida *f*

laird [leəd] *n Scot* terrateniente *m*

laissez-faire [leseɪ'feə(r)] 1 *n Econ* liberalismo *m*, no intervencionismo *m*
2 *adj* **(a)** *(in general)* permisivo(a) **(b)** *Econ* liberalista, no intervencionista

laity ['leɪɪtɪ] *n* **the l.** el sector laico, los seglares

lake [leɪk] *n* lago *m*; *Fig* **a wine/milk l.** *(surplus)* un excedente de vino/leche; **the Lake District, the Lakes** la Región de los Lagos *(en el noroeste de Inglaterra)* ►► ***Lake Constance*** el lago Constanza; ***Lake Como*** el lago Como; ***Lake Erie*** el lago Erie; ***Lake Garda*** el lago Garda; ***Lake Geneva*** el Lago Leman; ***Lake Huron*** el lago Hurón; ***Lake Michigan*** el lago Michigan; ***Lake Ontario*** el lago Ontario; ***Lake Superior*** el lago Superior; ***Lake Titicaca*** el lago Titicaca; ***Lake Victoria*** el lago Victoria

lakeside ['leɪksaɪd] *adj* a la orilla de un lago

La-la land ['lɑ:lɑ:lænd] *n US Fam* Los Ángeles; IDIOM **to be in L.** estar colgado(a)

lam [læm] *US Fam* 1 *n (escape)* fuga *f*; **on the l.** en fuga, fugado(a); **to take it on the l.** fugarse *or* huir
2 *vt* (*pt & pp* **lammed**) *(thrash)* destrozar, *Esp* machacar

►**lam into** *vt insep Br Fam* **to l. into sb** *(physically)* zurrar a alguien, dar una paliza a alguien; *(verbally)* poner verde a alguien

lama ['lɑ:mə] *n* lama *m*

lamb [læm] 1 *n* **(a)** *(animal, meat)* cordero *m*; IDIOM **like lambs to the slaughter** como corderos al matadero ►► ***l. chop*** chuleta *f* de cordero; ***l.'s lettuce*** valeriana *f*, hierba *f* de los canónigos; *Fam* ***l.'s tails*** candelillas *fpl or* amentos *mpl* del avellano **(b)** *(person)* **she's a l.** es un trozo de pan; **be a l. and fetch my glasses** sé bueno y alcánzame las gafas; **poor l.!** ¡pobrecillo! **(c)** *Rel* **the L. (of God)** el Cordero de Dios
2 *vi* parir *(la oveja)*

lambada [læm'bɑ:də] *n* lambada *f*

lambast [læm'bæst] *vt* vapulear

lambent ['læmbənt] *adj Literary (light, flame)* refulgente

lambing ['læmɪŋ] *n* **l. (time)** (tiempo *m* del) nacimiento *m* de los corderos

lambskin ['læmskɪn] 1 *n* piel *f* de cordero, borrego *m*
2 *adj* de borrego *or* de piel de cordero

lambswool ['læmswʊl] 1 *n* lana *f* de cordero
2 *adj* de lana de cordero

lame [leɪm] 1 *adj* **(a)** *(person, animal)* cojo(a); **to be l.** *(permanently)* ser cojo(a) *or Am* rengo(a); *(temporarily)* estar cojo(a) *or Am* rengo(a); **to go l.** quedarse cojo(a) *or Am* rengo(a); **he's l. in his left leg, his left leg is l.** cojea de la pierna izquierda ►► ***a l. duck*** *(business, organization)* un fracaso; *(person)* una nulidad; *US* **a l. duck president** un presidente saliente *(cuando ya ha sido elegido su sucesor)*
(b) *(weak) (excuse, argument)* endeble, pobre; **what a l. joke!** ¡qué chiste más malo!
(c) *US Fam (conventional)* soso(a), pavo(a)
2 *vt* dejar cojo(a)
3 *n US Fam (conventional person)* soso(a) *m,f*, pavo(a) *m,f*
4 *npl* **the l.** los cojos, *Am* los rengos

lamé ['lɑ:meɪ] *n* lamé *m*; **a gold l. dress** un vestido de lamé dorado

lamebrain ['leɪmbreɪn] *n US Fam* idiota *mf*, *Esp* cenutrio(a) *m,f*

lamely ['leɪmlɪ] *adv (to apologize)* sin convicción

lameness ['leɪmnɪs] *n* (**a**) *(of person)* cojera *f*, *Esp* renqueo *m*, *Am* renguera *f* (**b**) *(of excuse, argument)* endeblez *f*, pobreza *f*

lament [lə'ment] **1** *n* (**a**) *(complaint)* lamento *m* (**b**) *Mus* canto *m* elegíaco, treno *m* (**c**) *(poem)* elegía *f*

2 *vt* lamentar; **she lamented the passing of her youth** lamentó el paso de su juventud; **it is to be lamented that this was not done sooner** es de lamentar que esto no se hiciera antes

3 *vi* lamentarse (**over** de)

lamentable ['læməntəbəl] *adj* lamentable

lamentably ['læməntəblɪ] *adv* lamentablemente

lamented [lə'mentɪd] *adj* **the late l. Mr Jones** el llorado difunto Sr. Jones

lamentation [læmən'teɪʃən] *n* lamentación *f*

laminar ['læmɪnə(r)] *adj* laminar ▸▸ *Phys* ***l. flow*** flujo *m* laminar

laminate ['læmɪneɪt] **1** *n* laminado *m*

2 *vt* (**a**) *(form from thin sheets) (glass, plastic)* laminar (**b**) *(cover with thin sheet) (paper, identity card)* plastificar; *(wood)* laminar

laminated ['læmɪneɪtɪd] *adj* (**a**) *(glass, plastic)* laminado(a) (**b**) *(paper, identity card)* plastificado(a); **the wood is l. with plastic** la madera está laminada en plástico

lammergeyer, lammergeier ['læməgaɪə(r)] *n* quebrantahuesos *m inv*

lamp [læmp] *n* (**a**) *(in house)* lámpara *f*; **electric/gas l.** lámpara eléctrica/de gas (**b**) *(in street)* farola *f*, farol *m* (**c**) *(on car, train)* faro *m*, *Am* luz *f*

lampblack ['læmpblæk] *n* negro *m* de humo

lamplight ['læmplaɪt] *n* luz *f* de una lámpara; **to work/read by l.** trabajar/leer a la luz de una lámpara

lamplighter ['læmplaɪtə(r)] *n Hist* farolero *m*

lamplit ['læmplɪt] *adj (street)* iluminado(a) con faroles

lampoon [læm'puːn] **1** *n* sátira *f*

2 *vt* satirizar

lamppost ['læmppəʊst] *n* farola *f*

lamprey ['læmprɪ] *n* lamprea *f*

lampshade ['læmpʃeɪd] *n* pantalla *f* (de lámpara)

lampstand ['læmpstænd] *n* pie *m* de lámpara

LAN [eleɪ'en] *n Comptr* (*abbr* **local area network**) red *f* de área local

Lancastrian [læŋ'kæstrɪən] **1** *n (from Lancaster)* = persona de Lancaster *(Inglaterra)*; *(from Lancashire)* = persona del condado de Lancashire *(Inglaterra)*

2 *adj (from Lancaster)* de Lancaster *(Inglaterra)*; *(from Lancashire)* del condado de Lancashire *(Inglaterra)*

lance [lɑːns] **1** *n (weapon)* lanza *f*

2 *vt Med* sajar, abrir con una lanceta

> **False friend:** The Spanish noun **lance** is not a translation for the English word **lance**. In Spanish **lance** means "event", "dispute" or "predicament".

lance corporal ['lɑːns'kɔːpərəl] *n Mil* soldado *mf* de primera

Lancelot ['lɑːnsəlɒt] *n Mythol* Lanzarote

lancer ['lɑːnsə(r)] *n (soldier)* lancero *m*

lancet ['lɑːnsɪt] *n* (**a**) *(scalpel)* lanceta *f* (**b**) *Archit* ▸▸ ***l. arch*** arco *m* ojival; ***l. window*** ventana *f* ojival

Lancs [læŋks] (*abbr* **Lancashire**) (condado *m* de) Lancashire

land [lænd] **1** *n* (**a**) *(not sea)* tierra *f*; **they sighted l.** avistaron tierra; **by l.** por vía terrestre; **on l.** en tierra; **over l. and sea** por tierra y mar ▸▸ *Mil* ***l. forces*** ejército *m* de tierra

(**b**) *(for farming)* tierras *fpl*; *(for building)* terrenos *mpl*, solares *mpl*; **a piece of l.** *(for farming)* unas tierras; *(for building)* un solar; **to live off the l.** vivir de la tierra; **to go back to the l.** volver a la vida rural; IDIOM **to see how the l. lies, to find out the lie** *or* **lay of the l.** tantear el terreno

(**c**) *(property)* tierras *fpl*, terrenos *mpl*; **their lands were confiscated** confiscaron sus tierras; **get off my l.!** ¡fuera de mi propiedad! ▸▸ ***l. agent*** *(manager)* administrador(ora) *m,f* de fincas; *(seller)* agente *mf* inmobiliario(a), corredor(ora) *m,f* de fincas; *US* ***l. bank*** banco *m o* caja *f* rural; *Econ* ***l. consolidation*** concentración *f* parcelaria; ***l. reform*** reforma *f* agraria; ***l. register*** registro *m* catastral; ***l. registrar*** registrador(ora) *m,f* de títulos de propiedad; ***l. registry (office)*** registro *m* de la propiedad; *Formerly* ***l. tax*** contribución *f* territorial *or* rústica

(**d**) *Literary (country)* tierra *f*; **her name was known throughout the l.** la conocían en toda la región; **he came from a distant l.** venía de una tierra lejana; **in a l. of** *or* **flowing with milk and honey** en jauja; *Fam Hum* **he's still in the l. of the living** todavía está en el reino de los vivos; **she lives in a l. of make-believe** vive en un mundo de colores *or Am* color de rosa; **in the L. of Nod** en los brazos de Morfeo ▸▸ ***the l. of the Rising Sun*** la tierra del Sol Naciente

2 *vt* (**a**) *(from ship, aircraft) (passengers)* desembarcar; *(cargo)* descargar; **they have landed a man on the moon** han llevado a un hombre a la Luna

(**b**) *(aircraft) (on land)* hacer aterrizar; *(on sea)* hacer amerizar

(**c**) *(fish)* capturar

(**d**) *Fam (obtain)* agenciarse, conseguir

(**e**) *Fam (cause to end up)* **the blow nearly landed me in the water** del golpe casi acabo en el agua; **that will l. you in prison** eso hará que des con tus huesos en la cárcel; **this could l. us in real trouble** esto nos puede meter en un lío; **to l. sb in it** poner a alguien en un serio aprieto, meter a alguien en un buen lío; **to l. oneself in it** meterse en un buen lío *or* una buena

(**f**) *Fam (hit)* **to l. sb a punch** arrear un puñetazo a alguien

3 *vi* (**a**) *(aircraft) (on land)* aterrizar, tomar tierra; *(on sea)* amerizar; **we landed in New York** aterrizamos en Nueva York; **to l. on the moon** alunizar, aterrizar en la luna

(**b**) *(arrive in boat)* desembarcar; **they landed at Vigo** desembarcaron en Vigo

(**c**) *(gymnast, somebody falling)* caer, caerse; *(ball, bomb)* caer; *(parachutist)* tomar tierra; **to l. on one's feet** caer de pie; *Fig* **he always lands on his feet** las cosas siempre le salen bien; **if you l. on a red square** *(in board game)* si caes en una casilla roja

(**d**) *Fam (finish up)* acabar en, terminar en; **his letter landed on my desk** su carta apareció en mi mesa; **the bicycle landed in the ditch** la bicicleta acabó en la cuneta; **he landed in jail** terminó en la cárcel

▸ **land up** *vi* ir a parar *or* dar (**in** a); **you'll l. up in jail!** ¡irás a parar a la cárcel!; **we finally landed up at a friend's house** fuimos a parar a casa de un amigo

▸ **land with** *vt sep Fam* **he was landed with the problem/the children** le endosaron el problema/los niños; **as usual, I got landed with all the work** como de costumbre me endosaron *or RP* enchufaron todo el trabajo; **they landed me with the bill** me endilgaron la factura

landau ['lændɔː] *n* landó *m*

land-based ['lændbeɪst] *adj* de tierra

landed ['lændɪd] *adj* ***l. gentry*** aristocracia *f* terrateniente; ***the l. interest*** los intereses de los hacendados; ***l. proprietor*** terrateniente *mf*

landfall ['lændfɔːl] *n Naut* **to make l.** avistar tierra; **our first l. for three months** la primera vez que avistamos tierra en tres meses

landfill ['lændfɪl] *n* (**a**) *(technique)* enterramiento *m* de residuos (**b**) *(refuse)* residuos *mpl* (**c**) **l. (site)** vertedero *m* controlado *(en el que se entierran los residuos)*

landing ['lændɪŋ] *n* (**a**) *(of ship)* desembarco *m*, desembarque *m* ▸▸ ***l. card*** tarjeta *f* de inmigración; ***l. party*** avanzadilla *f*, avanzada *f* (**b**) *(of plane)* aterrizaje *m* ▸▸ ***l. lights*** luces *fpl* de aterrizaje (**c**) *(of skier, athlete, gymnast)* caída *f*; **he made a bad l.** cayó mal (**d**) *(of staircase)* descansillo *m*, rellano *m*

landing-craft ['lændɪŋkrɑːft] *n* lancha *f* de desembarco

landing-field ['lændɪŋfiːld] *n Av* campo *m* de aterrizaje

landing-gear ['lændɪŋgɪə(r)] *n* tren *m* de aterrizaje

landing-net ['lændɪŋnet] *n* salabardo *m*

landing-stage ['lændɪŋsteɪdʒ] *n* desembarcadero *m*

landing-strip ['lændɪŋstrɪp] *n* pista *f* de aterrizaje

landlady ['lændleɪdɪ] *n* (**a**) *(owner of rented accommodation)* casera *f*, dueña *f* (**b**) *(woman who runs boarding house, pub)* patrona *f*

landless ['lændlɪs] *adj* sin tierra

landlocked ['lændlɒkt] *adj (country)* sin salida al mar, interior

landlord ['lændlɔːd] *n* (**a**) *(owner of rented accommodation)* casero *m*, dueño *m* (**b**) *(man who runs pub)* patrón *m* (**c**) *(landowner)* terrateniente *m*

landlubber ['lændlʌbə(r)] *n Old-fashioned or Hum* **to be a l.** ser de secano, ser un marinero de agua dulce

landmark ['lændmɑːk] *n* (**a**) *(distinctive feature)* punto *m* de referencia; **the cathedral is one of the city's most famous landmarks** la catedral es uno de los monumentos más famosos de la ciudad (**b**) *(in history)* hito *m*; **a l. decision** una decisión histórica; **a l. judgement** un juicio histórico *or* decisivo

landmass ['lændmæs] *n* masa *f* terrestre

landmine ['lændmaɪn] *n* mina *f* terrestre

landowner ['lændəʊnə(r)] *n* terrateniente *mf*

landowning ['lændəʊnɪŋ] *adj* **the l. classes** la clase terrateniente

Landrover® ['lændrəʊvə(r)] *n* Land Rover® *m*

landscape ['lændskeɪp] **1** *n* (**a**) *(land)* paisaje *m*; *Fig* **the political l.** el panorama político ►► ***l. gardener*** paisajista *mf (jardinero)*; ***l. gardening*** jardinería *f* ornamental *or* paisajística (**b**) *(painting)* paisaje *m* ►► ***l. painter*** paisajista *mf (pintor)* (**c**) *Comptr* **l. (orientation)** formato *m* apaisado; **to print in l.** imprimir en apaisado
2 *vt* ajardinar

landscapist ['lændskeɪpɪst] *n* paisajista *mf*

landslide ['lændslaɪd] *n* (**a**) *Geog* corrimiento *m or* desprendimiento *m* de tierras (**b**) *Pol* **to win by a l.** ganar por una mayoría aplastante ►► ***l. victory*** victoria *f* aplastante; ***l. win*** victoria *f* aplastante

landslip ['lændslɪp] *n Br* desprendimiento *m or* corrimiento *m* de tierras

landward ['lændwəd] *adj Naut* **on the l. side** en el lado de tierra *or* más cercano a tierra; **a l. breeze** una brisa en dirección a tierra

landwards ['lændwədz] *adv Naut* hacia tierra

land-yacht ['lændjɒt] *n* velero *m* con ruedas

lane [leɪn] *n* (**a**) *(in country)* vereda *f*, camino *m*; *(in town)* callejón *m* (**b**) *(on road)* carril *m*; **to be in the wrong l.** circular por el carril equivocado; **a three/four-l. road** una carretera de tres/cuatro carriles; **traffic is reduced to two lanes** se ha limitado el tráfico a dos carriles; **traffic was held up by l. closures** había detenciones (de tráfico) debido al cierre de carriles
(**c**) *(for shipping)* ruta *f* de navegación; *(for aircraft)* pasillo *m* aéreo
(**d**) *(for runner, swimmer)* calle *f*, *RP* andarivel *m*
(**e**) *(in bowling alley)* pista *f*

langoustine ['lɒŋgʊstiːn] *n* cigala *f*

language ['læŋgwɪdʒ] *n* (**a**) *(faculty)* lenguaje *m* ►► ***l. acquisition*** adquisición *f* del lenguaje
(**b**) *(specific tongue)* idioma *m*, lengua *f*; **the English/Spanish l.** la lengua inglesa/española; **to study languages** estudiar idiomas; **l. and literature** lengua y literatura; IDIOM *Fam* **we don't talk the same l.** no hablamos el mismo idioma ►► ***the l. barrier*** la barrera del idioma; ***l. laboratory*** laboratorio *m* de idiomas; ***l. learning*** aprendizaje *m* de idiomas; ***l. school*** academia *f* de idiomas; ***l. teaching*** enseñanza *f* de idiomas
(**c**) *(style of speech or writing)* lenguaje *m*; **medical/legal l.** lenguaje médico/legal
(**d**) *(coarse words)* palabrotas *fpl*, lenguaje *m* soez; **(mind your) l.!** ¡no seas malhablado!, ¡no digas palabrotas!; **you should have heard the l. they were using!** ¡tenías que haber oído el lenguaje que empleaban!
(**e**) *Comptr* lenguaje *m*

langue [lɒŋg] *n Ling* lengua *f*

languid ['læŋgwɪd] *adj* lánguido(a)

languidly ['læŋgwɪdlɪ] *adv* lánguidamente

languish ['læŋgwɪʃ] *vi* (**a**) *(endure discomfort)* languidecer; **to l. in prison** pudrirse en la cárcel (**b**) *(lose energy)* **to l. in the heat** *(plant, person)* languidecer en el calor; **the project was languishing for lack of funds** el proyecto languidecía por falta de fondos (**c**) *Literary (pine)* anhelar; **he languished for love of his lady** anhelaba el amor de su amada

languor ['læŋgə(r)] *n* languidez *f*

languorous ['læŋgərəs] *adj* lánguido(a)

lank [læŋk] *adj (hair)* lacio(a)

lanky ['læŋkɪ] *adj* larguirucho(a)

lanolin(e) ['lænəlɪn] *n* lanolina *f*

lantern ['læntən] *n* (**a**) *(lamp)* farol *m* (**b**) *Archit* linterna *f*

lantern-jawed ['læntən'dʒɔːd] *adj* demacrado(a)

lanthanide ['lænθənaɪd] *n Chem* lantánido *m* ►► ***l. series*** lantánidos *mpl*

lanthanum ['lænθənəm] *n Chem* lantano *m*

lanyard ['lænjəd] *n* (**a**) *(cord worn round neck)* cordel *m* (**b**) *Naut* acollador *m*

Lao [laʊ] *n (language)* laosiano *m*

Laos [laʊs] *n* Laos

Laotian ['laʊʃən] **1** *n* (**a**) *(person)* laosiano(a) *m,f* (**b**) *(language)* laosiano *m*
2 *adj* laosiano(a)

lap[1] [læp] *n* (**a**) *(of person)* regazo *m*; **to sit on sb's l.** sentarse en el regazo de alguien ►► ***l. belt*** cinturón *m* (de seguridad) abdominal; ***l. dancer*** bailarina *f* de striptease *(para un único cliente)*; ***l. dancing*** striptease *m (para un único cliente)* (**b**) IDIOMS **it's in the l. of the gods** está en el aire; **he expects everything to fall** *or* **drop into his l.** espera que todo le llueva *or Am* caiga del cielo; **to drop** *or* **dump sth in sb's l.** endosar algo a alguien; **to live in the l. of luxury** vivir a cuerpo de rey

lap[2] **1** *n* (**a**) *(in race)* vuelta *f* ►► ***l. of honour*** vuelta *f* de honor (**b**) *(of journey)* etapa *f*
2 *vt* (**a**) *(overtake)* doblar (**b**) *(time)* **he was lapped at over 100 mph** iba a una velocidad media de más de 160 km/h (por vuelta)
3 *vi (complete a lap)* **he was lapping at 120 mph** giraba a más de 190 km/h

lap[3] *(pt & pp* **lapped**) **1** *vt* (**a**) *(of animal)* beber a lengüetadas (**b**) *(of waves)* lamer
2 *vi* **to l. against sth** *(waves)* lamer algo

► **lap up** *vt sep* (**a**) *(drink)* beber a lengüetadas (**b**) *Fam (enjoy)* **he laps up every word she says** se bebe sus palabras; **they were all paying her compliments and she was just lapping it up** se deleitaba con los cumplidos que le hacían todos

lap[4] *n* (**a**) *Cin* ***l. dissolve*** fundido *m* encadenado (**b**) *Constr* ***l. joint*** junta *f* de solape

laparoscope ['læpərəskəʊp] *n* laparoscopio *m*

laparoscopic [læpərəʊ'skɒpɪk] *adj Med* laparoscópico(a)

laparoscopy [læpə'rɒskəpɪ] *n Med* laparoscopia *f*

laparotomy [læpə'rɒtəmɪ] *n Med* laparotomía *f*

La Paz [læ'pæz] *n* La Paz

lapdog ['læpdɒg] *n* perrito *m* faldero

lapel [lə'pel] *n* solapa *f* ►► *Br* ***l. badge*** insignia *f* de solapa; ***l. mike*** micro *m* de solapa; ***l. pin*** insignia *f* de solapa

lapidary ['læpɪdərɪ] *adj* (**a**) *(engraved in stone)* tallado(a) en piedra (**b**) *(writing style)* lapidario(a)

lapilli [læ'pɪlɪ] *npl Geol* lapilli *mpl*

lapis lazuli ['læpɪs'læzjʊliː] *n Geol* lapislázuli *m*

Lapland ['læplænd] *n* Laponia

Laplander ['læplændə(r)] *n* lapón(ona) *m,f*

Lapp [læp] **1** *n* (**a**) *(person)* lapón(ona) *m,f* (**b**) *(language)* lapón *m*
2 *adj* lapón(ona)

lapse [læps] **1** *n* (**a**) *(failure) (in behaviour)* desliz *m*; *(in standards)* bajón *m*; **a l. of memory** *Esp* un fallo *or Am* una falla de la memoria; **a l. in concentration** un momento de distracción (**b**) *(of time)* lapso *m*; **after a l. of six months** tras un lapso de seis meses (**c**) *(of permit, membership)* vencimiento *m*; *(of legal right)* extinción *f*
2 *vi* (**a**) *(err)* tener un desliz; *(morally)* reincidir; **his concentration lapsed for a split second** le falló la concentración durante una fracción de segundo; **if standards of education are allowed to l.** si permiten que decaiga la calidad de la educación
(**b**) *(drift)* **she lapsed into a coma** entró en coma; **he soon lapsed (back) into his old ways** pronto volvió a las andadas; **to l. into silence** sumirse en el silencio; **she kept lapsing into Russian** se le escapaba el ruso constantemente
(**c**) *(pass)* **weeks lapsed before I saw her again** pasaron semanas hasta que la volví a ver
(**d**) *(permit, membership)* caducar, vencer; *(legal right)* extinguirse; **he let his insurance l.** dejó que venciera su seguro

lapsed [læpst] *adj Rel* **a l. Catholic** un/una católico(a) no practicante

laptop ['læptɒp] *n Comptr* **l. (computer)** *Esp* ordenador *m or Am* computadora *f* portátil

lapwing ['læpwɪŋ] *n* avefría *f*

larceny ['lɑːsənɪ] *n Law* (delito *m* de) robo *m or* latrocinio *m*

larch [lɑːtʃ] *n* alerce *m*

lard [lɑːd] **1** *n (fat)* manteca *f or RP* grasa *f* de cerdo; *Fam* **he's a tub of l.** es una bola de sebo *or RP* grasa
2 *vt* (**a**) *(meat) (smearing)* untar, engrasar; *(with strips)* mechar (**b**) *Fam (sprinkle)* **he larded his writings with quotations** sus escritos estaban recargados de citas

lard-arse ['lɑːdɑːs], *US* **lard-ass** ['lɑːrdæs] *n Vulg* gordo(a) *m,f* seboso(a), *RP* gordo(a) *m,f* cerdo(a)

larder ['lɑːdə(r)] *n* despensa *f*

larding needle ['lɑːdɪŋ'niːdəl] *n Culin* aguja *f* de mechar

---

LARGE [lɑːdʒ] **1** *n* (**a**) *(size)* tamaño *m* grande
(**b**) *US* **in l.** en su totalidad, en conjunto
2 *adj* (**a**) *(in size)* grande; **l. size** *(of clothes)* talla grande; *(of product)* tamaño grande; **she's a l. woman** es una mujer grande; **to grow** *or* **get larger** crecer; **to make sth larger** agrandar algo; **as l. as life** en persona; **larger than life** singular, que se sale de la norma ►► ***l. intestine*** intestino *m* grueso
(**b**) *(extensive, significant)* **to a l. extent** en gran medida; **a l. part of**

my job involves... gran parte de mi trabajo implica...
(**c**) *(liberal) (views)* liberal; *(heart)* grande
3 *adv Br Fam (to a large extent)* **Arsenal got thrashed l.** le dieron una monumental paliza al Arsenal; *very Fam* **we got pissed l. last night** agarramos una borrachera como un castillo anoche
4 at large *adj (at liberty)* **to be at l.** andar suelto(a)
5 at large *adv* (**a**) *(as a whole)* **the country at l.** el país en general; **people/the public at l.** la gente/el público en general
(**b**) *(in detail)* en detalle, en profundidad
6 by and large *adv* en general

False friend: The Spanish adjective **largo** is not a translation for the English word **large**. In Spanish the main meaning of **largo** is "long".

largely ['lɑːdʒlɪ] *adv (to a great extent)* en gran medida; *(mostly)* principalmente; **it's l. due to me that he won** en gran medida se debe a mí que ganara

False friend: The Spanish adverb **largamente** is not a translation for the English word **largely**. In Spanish **largamente** means "for a long time", "easily" or "generously".

largemouth bass ['lɑːdʒmaʊʃ'bæs] *n* perca *f* americana
largeness ['lɑːdʒnɪs] *n (in size)* gran tamaño *m*; *(of sum)* lo elevado *m*
large-print ['lɑːdʒ'prɪnt] *adj* **l. book** libro impreso en cuerpo (de letra) grande
large-scale ['lɑːdʒ'skeɪl] *adj* (**a**) *(map, model)* a gran escala (**b**) *Comptr* **l. integration** integración a gran escala
largesse [lɑː'ʒes] *n* magnanimidad *f*
largish ['lɑːdʒɪʃ] *adj (in size)* más bien grande; *(sum)* bastante elevado(a)
largo ['lɑːgəʊ] *Mus* **1** *n (pl* **largos**) largo *m*
2 *adv* largo
lariat ['lærɪət] *n* (**a**) *US (lasso)* lazo *m (para ganado)* (**b**) *(for tethering animals)* ronzal *m*
lark[1] [lɑːk] *n (bird)* alondra *f*; IDIOM **to be up** *or* **rise with the l.** levantarse con el gallo ►► ***greater short-toed l.*** terrera *f*; ***lesser short-toed l.*** terrera *f* marismeña
lark[2] *n Br Fam* (**a**) *(joke)* broma *f*; **to do sth for a l.** hacer algo por diversión; **what a l.!** ¡qué divertido! (**b**) *(activity)* **I don't like this fancy dress l.** no me gusta este asunto *or Esp* rollo *or Carib, Col, Ecuad* esta vaina de la fiesta de disfraces; **are you still at the teaching l.?** ¿todavía estás metida en la enseñanza?; *Fam* **stuff this for a l.!** ¡a tomar viento!, *Andes, RP* ¡al cuerno!
► **lark about, lark around** *vi Br Fam* jugar, *Esp* trastear
larkspur ['lɑːkspɜː(r)] *n* espuela *f* de caballero
larva ['lɑːvə] *(pl* **larvae** ['lɑːviː]) *n* larva *f*
larval ['lɑːvəl] *adj* larvario(a), larval
laryngeal [lærɪn'dʒiːəl] *adj* laríngeo(a)
laryngitis [lærɪn'dʒaɪtɪs] *n* laringitis *f inv*
laryngologist [lærɪn'gɒlədʒɪst] *n Med* laringólogo(a) *m,f*
laryngology [lærɪn'gɒlədʒɪ] *n Med* laringología *f*
laryngoscopy [lærɪn'gɒskəpɪ] *n Med* laringoscopia *f*
laryngotomy [lærɪn'gɒtəmɪ] *n Med* laringotomía *f*
larynx ['lærɪŋks] *n* laringe *f*
lasagne, lasagna [lə'sænjə] *n* lasaña *f*
lascivious [lə'sɪvɪəs] *adj* lascivo(a)
lasciviously [lə'sɪvɪəslɪ] *adv* lascivamente
laser ['leɪzə(r)] *n* láser *m* ►► ***l. beam*** rayo *m* láser; ***l. disc*** láser disc *m*; *Comptr* ***l. printer*** impresora *f* láser; *Comptr* ***l. quality*** calidad *f* láser; ***l. show*** espectáculo *m* con láser; *Med* ***l. surgery*** cirugía *f* con láser
lash [læʃ] **1** *n* (**a**) *(whip)* látigo *m*; **the l.** *(punishment)* latigazos *mpl* (**b**) *(blow with whip)* latigazo *m*; *Fig* **he'd often felt the l. of her tongue** había sufrido a menudo su lengua viperina (**c**) *(eyelash)* pestaña *f*
2 *vt* (**a**) *(with whip)* azotar, vapulear; *(of rain, waves)* azotar (**b**) *(move)* **the tiger lashed its tail** el tigre meneó la cola bruscamente (**c**) *(tie)* amarrar (**to** a) (**d**) *Fam (criticize)* emprenderla con, *Esp* cebarse con, *Méx* viborear a, *RP* dejar por el piso a
3 *vi* **to l. against sth** *(of rain, waves)* azotar algo; **the rain** *or* **it was lashing down** caían chuzos *or Am* baldes; **its tail lashed from side to side** meneaba bruscamente la cola de un lado para otro
► **lash into** *vt insep Br Fam (criticize)* arremeter contra
► **lash out 1** *vt sep Br Fam (spend)* **I lashed out £10 on a bottle of wine** gasté 10 libras en una botella de vino, *Esp* me he pulido *or RP* me rifé 10 libras en una botella de vino
2 *vi* (**a**) *(physically)* **to l. out at sb** atacar *or* agredir a alguien; **she lashed out in all directions** lanzaba golpes en todas las direcciones (**b**) *(verbally)* **to l. out at sb** arremeter contra alguien (**c**) *Br Fam (spend extravagantly)* tirar *or Andes, CAm, Carib, Méx* botar la casa por la ventana (**on** por)
lashing ['læʃɪŋ] **1** *n* (**a**) *(with whip)* latigazos *mpl*; **to give sb a l.** dar latigazos a alguien (**b**) *Fig (scolding)* reprimenda *f*, regañina *f* (**c**) *(rope)* cuerda *f*; **they cut the lashings which secured the cargo to the deck** cortaron el cabo que fijaba la mercancía a cubierta (**d**) *Br Fam Old-fashioned* **lashings of** *(lots)* un montón de
2 *adj (rain)* torrencial
lass [læs] *n Scot or Literary* chica *f*, muchacha *f*
Lassa fever ['læsə'fiːvə(r)] *n* fiebre *f* de Lassa
lassie ['læsɪ] *n Scot* chica *f*, muchacha *f*
lassitude ['læsɪtjuːd] *n Formal* lasitud *f*
lasso [læ'suː] **1** *n (pl* **lassos** *or* **lassoes**) lazo *m (para ganado)*
2 *vt* capturar con lazo, *CSur* lacear

LAST[1] [lɑːst] **1** *n* (**a**) *(final one)* **the l.** el/la último(a); **the l. but one** el/la penúltimo(a); **the l. but three** el/la cuarto(a) empezando por el final; **redundancies were on a l. in first out basis** empezaron por despedir a los últimos que habían entrado en la empresa; **the l. of the Romanovs** el/la último(a) Romanov
(**b**) *(previous one)* **the night before l.** anteanoche; **the week before l.** hace dos semanas; **the time before l.** la penúltima vez
(**c**) *(end)* **we'll never hear the l. of it** nos lo recordará eternamente; **you haven't heard the l. of this!** ¡esto no va a quedar así!; **I don't think we've heard the l. of him** creo que volveremos a oír hablar de él; **that's the l. I saw of him** fue la última vez que lo vi; **the l. I heard, she was working as a waitress** lo último que sé es que estaba trabajando de camarera; **that's the l. of the wine** es lo último que quedaba del vino; **to leave sth until l.** dejar algo para el final; **at the l.** justo antes de morir; **she was there at the l.** estuvo allí hasta el final; **to** *or* **till the l.** hasta el fin; **at (long) l.** por fin
2 *adj* (**a**) *(final)* último(a); **this is your l. chance** es tu última oportunidad; **you are my l. hope** eres mi última esperanza; **he's always the l. one to arrive** siempre llega (el) último; **to reach the l. four/eight** *(in competition)* llegar a las semifinales/a los cuartos de final; **down to the l. penny/detail** hasta el último penique/detalle; **at the l. count there were ten left** la última vez que contamos quedaban diez; **he ate every l. one of them** se comió hasta el último; **to have the l. laugh** reír (el) último; **at the l. moment** *or* **minute** en el último momento *or* minuto; **to leave it to the l. moment** *or* **minute** dejarlo para el último momento *or* minuto; *Br* **l. orders, please!** ¡vayan pidiendo las últimas bebidas!; **as a l. resort** como último recurso; **l. thing (at night)** justo antes de acostarme/se/*etc*; **to have the l. word** tener la última palabra; **the l. word in comfort** el no va más en comodidad, el súmmum de la comodidad; **the l. word in fashion design** el último grito en moda *or* de la moda; IDIOM **to be on one's l. legs** estar en las últimas, *Esp* estar para el arrastre; **this television is on its l. legs** este televisor está en las últimas *or* está para el arrastre; IDIOM **that was the l. straw** fue la gota que colmó el vaso ►► *Rel* ***the L. Judgment*** el Juicio Final; ***l. lap*** *(in race)* última vuelta *f*; IDIOM **we're on the l. lap** estamos en la recta final; ***l. name*** apellido *m*; ***l. post*** *(collection)* último correo *m*; *Br Mil* ***the l. post*** *(at funeral)* toque *m* de difuntos; *(at night)* toque *m* de retreta; ***l. quarter*** *(of moon)* cuarto *m* menguante; *Rel* ***l. rites*** extremaunción *f*; *Rel* ***the L. Supper*** la Última Cena; *Formal* ***l. will and testament*** testamento *m*, última voluntad *f*
(**b**) *(most recent)* último(a); **the l. time I saw him** la última vez que lo vi; **for the l. five minutes** (durante) los últimos cinco minutos; **l. January** en enero (del año) pasado; **l. Tuesday, on Tuesday l.** el martes pasado; **l. month** el mes pasado; **l. night** anoche; **l. week** la semana pasada
(**c**) *(least likely, desired)* **he's the l. person I'd ask to help me** es la última persona a la que pediría ayuda; **that's the l. thing I'd do in your position** eso es lo último que haría si estuviera en tu lugar; **the l. thing I wanted was to upset you** lo último que quería era disgustarte
3 *adv* (**a**) *(in final place)* **I rang Jane l.** llamé a Jane en último lugar; **to come l.** llegar en último lugar; **to finish l.** terminar (el) último; *(in race)* llegar en último lugar; **l. but not least** por último, pero no por ello menos importante; **l. of all** por último
(**b**) *(most recently)* **when I l. saw him** la última vez que lo vi

last[2] *n (for shoe)* horma *f*

last[3] 1 *vt* durar; **have we got enough to l. us until tomorrow?** ¿tenemos suficiente para que nos dure hasta mañana?; **it will l. me a lifetime** me durará toda la vida; **it has lasted him well** le ha durado bastante

2 *vi* (**a**) *(continue)* durar; **it lasted for three weeks** duró tres semanas; **it's too good to l.** es demasiado bueno para que dure; **their romance didn't l. (for) long** su romance no duró demasiado

(**b**) *(survive)* sobrevivir; **how long can we l. without water?** ¿cuánto tiempo podemos sobrevivir sin agua?; **he won't l. long in that job** no durará mucho en ese trabajo; **she won't l. the night** no llegará a mañana

(**c**) *(continue to function)* durar; **built/made to l.** construido/fabricado para que dure

(**d**) *(be enough for)* **we've got enough food to l. another week** tenemos suficiente comida para que nos dure otra semana

► **last out** 1 *vt sep* **to l. the year/weekend out** llegar a fin de año/al fin de semana

2 *vi* (**a**) *(person)* aguantar, resistir (**b**) *(supplies)* durar

last-chance saloon ['lɑːstʃɑːnssə'luːn] *n Br Fam Hum* **they are drinking in the l.** les queda sólo una bala en el cargador

last-ditch ['lɑːst'dɪtʃ] *adj* desesperado(a), último(a); **a l. attempt/effort** un intento/esfuerzo desesperado

lasting ['lɑːstɪŋ] *adj* duradero(a); **to my l. regret/shame I didn't refuse** me arrepentiré/avergonzaré eternamente de no haberlo rechazado

lastly ['lɑːstlɪ] *adv* por último

last-minute [lɑːst'mɪnɪt] *adj* de última hora

lat *Geog* (*abbr* **latitude**) lat.

latch [lætʃ] 1 *n* pestillo *m*; **to be on the l.** tener el pestillo echado

2 *vt* echar el pestillo a

► **latch onto** *vt insep Fam* (**a**) *(attach oneself to)* **to l. onto sb** pegarse a alguien; *Fig* **to l. onto an idea** meterse una idea en la cabeza (**b**) *(understand)* **to l. onto sth** darse cuenta *or Esp* enterarse de algo

latchkey ['lætʃkiː] *n* llave *f (de la puerta de entrada)* ►► ***l. kid*** = niño que llega a casa antes que sus padres, que están trabajando

LATE [leɪt] 1 *adj* (**a**) *(not on time)* **to be l. (for sth)** llegar tarde (a algo); **the train is ten minutes l.** el tren tiene *or* lleva diez minutos de retraso *or Am* demora; **the train was ten minutes l.** el tren llegó diez minutos tarde, el tren llegó con diez minutos de retraso *or Am* demora; **to be l. with the rent** retrasarse en el pago del alquiler; **to make sb l. for sth** hacer que alguien llegue tarde a algo; **we apologize for the l. departure of this flight** les pedimos disculpas por el retraso *or Am* la demora en la salida de este vuelo; **some l. news has come in** acaba de llegar una noticia de última hora; **l. payment may result in a fine** el retraso *or Am* la demora en el pago se sancionará con una multa; **we had a l. start today** hoy hemos empezado tarde; **to be a l. developer** *or US* **bloomer** madurar tarde ►► ***l. tackle*** *(in soccer)* entrada *f* a jugador que no lleva la pelota

(**b**) *(after usual time)* **the daffodils were l. this year** los narcisos salieron tarde este año; **Easter is l. this year** este año la Semana Santa cae muy tarde; **to have a l. breakfast** desayunar tarde

(**c**) *(far on in time)* tarde; **it is getting l.** se está haciendo tarde; **in the l. afternoon** al final de la tarde, *CSur* de tardecita; **in l. summer** al final del verano; **in l. March** a últimos *or* fines de marzo; **to be in one's l. thirties** tener treinta y muchos años, *RP* tener treinta y pico; **in the l. eighties** a finales *or* fines de los ochenta; **they scored a l. goal** marcaron un gol hacia el final del partido; **the l. movie** la película de la noche; **it's l. shopping tonight** hoy las tiendas abren hasta tarde; **this work is typical of l. Rembrandt** esta obra es típica de la última época de Rembrandt; **why are you awake at this l. hour?** ¿qué haces despierto a estas horas?; **to keep l. hours** acostarse tarde; *Fig* **it's a bit l. in the day to...** ya es un poco tarde para... ►► ***l. booking*** reservas *fpl* de última hora

(**d**) *(dead)* difunto(a); **my l. husband** mi difunto marido

(**e**) *(former)* **the l. leader of the party** el anterior líder del partido; *Formal* **Mr B. Hall, l. of Main Rd** el Sr. B. Hall, que antes residía en Main Rd

(**f**) **to be l.** *(with one's period)* retrasarse; **I'm a week l.** se me ha retrasado una semana

2 *adv* (**a**) *(not on time)* tarde; **to arrive l.** llegar tarde; **to arrive ten minutes l.** llegar diez minutos tarde; PROV **better l. than never** más vale tarde que nunca

(**b**) *(far on in time)* tarde; **he came home very l.** llegó a casa muy tarde; **to go to bed/get up l.** acostarse/levantarse tarde; **we left it a bit l.** tendríamos que haberlo hecho antes; **she married l.** se casó ya mayor; **we are open l.** abrimos hasta tarde; **to work l.** trabajar hasta tarde; **an appointment for l. tomorrow afternoon/l. next week** una cita para mañana al final de la tarde/el final de la semana que viene; **she left l. last night** se marchó anoche tarde; **l. at night** bien entrada la noche; **this l. in the day** *(at this stage)* a estas alturas; **l. into the night** hasta (altas horas de) la madrugada; **l. in the year** a finales de año; **l. in life** a una edad avanzada

(**c**) *(recently)* **as l. as last week** incluso la semana pasada; **of l.** recientemente

latecomer ['leɪtkʌmə(r)] *n* rezagado(a) *m,f*; **latecomers will not be admitted** no se podrá entrar después de comenzada la función; **he was a l. to football** comenzó a jugar a fútbol tarde

lateen sail [lə'tiːn'seɪl] *n* vela *f* latina

lately ['leɪtlɪ] *adv* recientemente, últimamente; **until l.** hasta hace poco

latency ['leɪtənsɪ] *n* (estado *m* de) latencia *f*

lateness ['leɪtnɪs] *n* (**a**) *(of person, train)* retraso *m*, demora *f* (**b**) *(late time)* **the l. of the hour** lo avanzado de la hora

late-night ['leɪtnaɪt] *adj (in late evening)* nocturno(a); *(after midnight)* de madrugada ►► ***l. opening*** = horario de apertura prolongado tras la hora normal de cierre; ***l. shopping*** = apertura prolongada de las tiendas tras la hora normal de cierre

latent ['leɪtənt] *adj (disease, tendency)* latente ►► *Phys* ***l. heat*** calor *m* latente; *Med* ***l. period*** periodo *m* de incubación *or* latente

late-onset ['leɪt'ɒnset] *adj (disease)* de aparición tardía ►► ***l. diabetes*** diabetes *f inv* de aparición tardía

later ['leɪtə(r)] 1 *adj* posterior; **I caught a l. train** tomé *or Esp* cogí otro tren más tarde; **his l. novels** sus novelas posteriores; **in l. life** en la madurez; **l. events proved that...** sucesos posteriores desmostraron que...; **at a l. date/stage** en fecha/una etapa posterior

2 *adv* **l. (on)** más tarde; **a few days l.** unos días más tarde; **it was only l. that I realized he had been right** sólo más tarde me di cuenta de que él tenía razón; **l. that day** ese mismo día con posterioridad; **no l. than tomorrow** mañana como muy tarde; **as we shall see l.** como veremos más adelante; *Fam* **see you l.!** ¡hasta luego!

lateral ['lætərəl] 1 *adj* lateral ►► ***l. thinking*** pensamiento *m* lateral, = capacidad para darse cuenta de aspectos no inmediatamente evidentes de los problemas

2 *n Ling* lateral *f*

laterally ['lætərəlɪ] *adv* lateralmente

latest ['leɪtɪst] 1 *n* (**a**) *(most recent news)* **have you heard the l.?** ¿has oído las últimas noticias?; **what's the l. on the trial?** ¿qué es lo último que se sabe del juicio? (**b**) *(in time)* **at the l.** como muy tarde; **the l. I can stay is four o'clock** sólo puedo quedarme hasta las cuatro

2 *adj* (**a**) *(in time)* último(a); **the l. train that will get us there** el último tren que nos lleva allí (**b**) *(most recent, up to date)* último(a); **her l. work** su última obra; **the l. news** las últimas noticias; **the l. edition** la última edición; **the l. fashions** la última moda

latex ['leɪteks] 1 *n* látex *m*

2 *adj* de látex

lath [lɑːθ] *n (strip of wood)* listón *m*

lathe [leɪð] *n* torno *m* ►► ***l. operator*** tornero(a) *m,f*

lather ['læðə(r)] 1 *n* (**a**) *(from soap)* espuma *f* (**b**) *(on horse)* sudor *m*; IDIOM *Fam* **to work** *or* **get oneself into a l. (about** *or* **over sth)** acalorarse (por algo)

2 *vt (apply soap to)* enjabonar; **to l. one's face** enjabonarse la cara

3 *vi (soap)* formar *or* hacer espuma

Latin ['lætɪn] 1 *n* (**a**) *(language)* latín *m* (**b**) *(person)* latino(a) *m,f*

2 *adj* latino(a) ►► ***L. lover*** latin lover *m*, amante *m* latino; ***L. Quarter*** barrio *m* latino

Latin America ['lætɪnə'merɪkə] *n* América Latina, Latinoamérica

Latin American ['lætɪnə'merɪkən] 1 *n* latinoamericano(a) *m,f*

2 *adj* latinoamericano(a)

Latinate ['lætɪneɪt] *adj (writing style)* con sabor latino; *(vocabulary)* latino(a), derivado(a) del latín

Latinist ['lætɪnɪst] *n* latinista *mf*

Latino [lə'tiːnəʊ] *n* latino(a) *m,f*

latish ['leɪtɪʃ] 1 *adj* tardío(a); **it is l.** es bastante tarde; **at a l. hour** más bien tarde

2 *adv* bastante tarde, más bien tarde

latitude ['lætɪtjuːd] *n* (**a**) *Geog* latitud *f*; **at a l. of 50° south** a 50° de latitud sur; **few animals live in these latitudes** raros son los animales que viven en estas latitudes (**b**) *(freedom)* libertad *f*; **they don't allow** *or* **give the children much l. for creativity** no les dan mucha rienda suelta a los niños para que sean creativos

latitudinal [lætɪ'tjuːdɪnəl] *adj Geog* latitudinal, de latitud

latrine [lə'triːn] *n* letrina *f*

latter ['lætə(r)] **1** *adj* **(a)** *(of two)* último(a), segundo(a) **(b)** *(last)* último(a); **the l. half** *or* **part of June** la segunda mitad de junio; **the l. days of the empire** las postrimerías del imperio, los últimos días del imperio; **in the l. years of her life** en los últimos años de su vida

2 *pron* **the former..., the l....** *(singular)* el/la primero(a)..., el/la segundo(a)...; *(plural)* los/las primeros(as)..., los/las segundos(as)...

latter-day ['lætə'deɪ] *adj* moderno(a), de hoy; **a l. St Francis** un San Francisco moderno ►► *Rel* ***the L. Saints*** los Mormones

latterly ['lætəlɪ] *adv* **(a)** *(recently)* recientemente, últimamente **(b)** *(towards the end)* hacia el final, en las postrimerías

lattermost ['lætəməʊst] *adj* último(a), postrero(a)

lattice ['lætɪs] *n* **(a)** *(fence, frame)* celosía *f* ►► ***l. window*** vidriera *f* de celosía **(b)** *(on pastry)* cuadriculado *m* **(c)** *Chem* red *f* cristalina

latticework ['lætɪswɜːk] *n* celosía *f*, enrejado *m*

Latvia ['lætvɪə] *n* Letonia

Latvian ['lætvɪən] **1** *n* **(a)** *(person)* letón(ona) *m,f* **(b)** *(language)* letón *m*

2 *adj* letón(ona)

laud [lɔːd] *vt Formal or Literary* loar, alabar

laudable ['lɔːdəbəl] *adj* loable

laudably ['lɔːdəblɪ] *adv* de forma loable *or* plausible

laudanum ['lɔːdənəm] *n* láudano *m*

laudatory ['lɔːdətərɪ] *adj Formal* laudatorio(a), elogioso(a)

laugh [lɑːf] **1** *n* **(a)** *(sound, act)* risa *f*; **to have a l.** reírse; **we had a good l. at his expense** nos reímos mucho a su costa; IDIOM **it's a l. a minute** te mueres de risa; *Ironic* **Wittgenstein? that must be a l. a minute!** ¿Wittgenstein? cómo te lo tienes que pasar ¿eh?; IDIOM **to have the last l.** reírse el último

(b) *Fam (fun)* **to have (a bit of) a l.** divertirse; **to do sth for a l.** hacer algo para pasarlo bien; *Br* **he's a good l.** es muy divertido; **he's always good for a l.** con él siempre lo pasamos bien

(c) *Fam (joke)* **what a l.!** ¡es para partirse de risa!; *Ironic* **that's a l.!** ¡no me hagas reír!; **the l. is on them** la broma les salió rana

2 *vi* **(a)** *(in amusement)* reírse (**at** *or* **about** de); **to l. aloud** *or* **out loud** reír(se) a carcajadas; **he was laughing to himself** se reía solo; **she knows how to l. at herself** sabe reírse de sí misma; **I can l. about it now but at the time it was very painful** ahora me río, pero en el momento fue muy doloroso; **we laughed until we cried** nos reímos hasta que se nos saltaron las lágrimas; **they didn't know whether to l. or cry** no sabían si reír o llorar; **it's easy** *or* **all right for you to l.!** para ti es fácil reírse; *Fam* **don't make me l.!** ¡no me hagas reír!; *Fam* **you've got to l.** es mejor reírse porque si no..., uno no sabe si reírse o llorar

(b) *(in contempt, ridicule)* reírse, mofarse (**at** de); **they laughed in my face** se rieron en mi cara

(c) IDIOMS *Fam* **he'll be laughing on the other side of his face when...** se llevará un buen chasco cuando...; *Br Fam* **if we win this match, we'll be laughing** ganamos este partido y a vivir; **to l. up one's sleeve** reírse para sus adentros; *Fam* **to l. all the way to the bank** hacer el agosto; PROV **he who laughs last laughs** *Br* **longest** *or US* **best** el que ríe el último ríe mejor

3 *vt* **(a)** *(in amusement) Fam* **to l. one's head off, to l. oneself silly** partirse *or Esp* mondarse de risa **(b)** *(in ridicule)* **he was laughed off the stage** se rieron tanto de él que lo hicieron salir del escenario; **they laughed him to scorn** se rieron de él con desdén; IDIOM **you'll be laughed out of court** se te reirán en la cara

► **laugh off** *vt sep (failure, insult)* tomarse a risa *or* broma

laughable ['lɑːfəbəl] *adj (excuse, attempt)* ridículo(a), risible; *(sum)* irrisorio(a)

laughably ['lɑːfəblɪ] *adv* ridículamente; **it was a l. silly idea** era una idea de lo más ridículo

laughing ['lɑːfɪŋ] **1** *n* risa *f*

2 *adj (eyes)* risueño(a); **it's no l. matter** no es ninguna tontería; **I'm in no l. mood** no estoy para bromas ►► ***l. falcon*** aguilucho *m* lagartero; ***l. gas*** gas *m* hilarante; ***l. hyena*** hiena *f* manchada; ***l. jackass*** cucaburra *f*

laughingly ['lɑːfɪŋlɪ] *adv* **(a)** *(cheerfully)* **he said l.** dijo risueño **(b)** *(inappropriately)* **this noise is l. called music** este ruido algunos lo llaman música

laughing-stock ['lɑːfɪŋ'stɒk] *n* hazmerreír *m*; **they were the l. of the factory** eran el hazmerreír de la fábrica; **he made a l. of himself** hizo el ridículo

laughter ['lɑːftə(r)] *n* risas *fpl*; **a burst of l.** un estallido de risas; **to cause l.** provocar la risa; **there was much l. over the incident** el incidente provocó carcajadas

launch [lɔːntʃ] **1** *n* **(a)** *(boat)* lancha *f*

(b) *(act of launching) (of ship)* botadura *f*; *(of rocket)* lanzamiento *m* ►► ***l. pad*** plataforma *f* de lanzamiento; ***l. site*** base *f* de lanzamiento; ***l. vehicle*** lanzador *m* espacial; ***l. window*** *(for space rocket)* ventana *f* de lanzamiento

(c) *(of product)* lanzamiento *m*; **a book l.** el lanzamiento de un libro; **the l. of a new job creation scheme** la puesta en marcha de un nuevo plan para la creación de empleos ►► ***l. party*** fiesta *f* de presentación; ***l. price*** precio *m* de lanzamiento

2 *vt* **(a)** *(ship)* botar; *(rocket)* lanzar **(b)** *(product)* lanzar **(c)** *(start) (business, enquiry)* emprender; **to l. sb on a career** *(of event)* marcar el inicio de la carrera de alguien; **to l. an attack on sb** lanzar un ataque contra alguien; **the newspaper launched an attack on government policy** el periódico inició una campaña contra la política del gobierno **(d)** *Comptr* arrancar, abrir

► **launch into** *vt insep (attack, story)* emprender; *(complaint)* embarcarse en

► **launch out** *vi* embarcarse, lanzarse; **she's just launched out on her own** acaba de ponerse por su cuenta

launcher ['lɔːntʃə(r)] *n (for missiles)* lanzamisiles *m inv*; *(for rocket, spacecraft)* lanzador *m*, lanzacohetes *m inv*

launching ['lɔːntʃɪŋ] *n* **(a)** *(of ship)* botadura *f*; *(of rocket)* lanzamiento *m* ►► ***l. vehicle*** vehículo *m* lanzador **(b)** *(of product)* lanzamiento *m*

launching-pad ['lɔːntʃɪŋ'pæd] *n also Fig* plataforma *f* de lanzamiento

launder ['lɔːndə(r)] *vt* **(a)** *(clothes)* lavar (y planchar) **(b)** *(money)* blanquear

launderette = **laundrette**

laundress ['lɔːndrɪs] *n* lavandera *f*

laundrette, launderette [lɔːn'dret], *US* **Laundromat®** ['lɔːndrəmæt] *n* lavandería *f*

laundry ['lɔːndrɪ] *n* **(a)** *(dirty clothes)* ropa *f* sucia; *(clean clothes)* ropa *f* limpia, *Esp* colada *f*; **to do the l.** lavar la ropa, *Esp* hacer la colada ►► ***l. basket*** cesto *m* de la ropa sucia; ***l. room*** *(in hotel, hospital etc)* lavandería *f*; *(in house)* lavadero *m*; ***l. van*** camión *m* de la lavandería **(b)** *(place)* lavandería *f*

laureate ['lɔːrɪət] *n* laureado(a) *m,f*, galardonado(a) *m,f*; **a Nobel l.** un premio Nobel

laurel ['lɒrəl] *n* **(a)** *(tree)* laurel *m* ►► ***l. wreath*** corona *f* de laurel **(b)** IDIOMS **to rest on one's laurels** dormirse en los laureles; **you'll have to look to your laurels** no te duermas en los laureles

LAUTRO ['laʊtrəʊ] *(abbr* **Life Assurance and Unit Trust Regulatory Organization)** *n* = organismo regulador de la actividad de las compañías de seguros de vida y de los fondos de inversión

lav [læv] *n Br Fam* retrete *m*, servicio *m*, *Am* baño *m*

lava ['lɑːvə] *n* lava *f* ►► ***l. lamp*** lámpara *f* de lava

lavatorial [lævə'tɔːrɪəl] *adj (humour)* escatológico(a)

lavatory ['lævətrɪ] *n* **(a)** *(room)* cuarto *m* de baño, servicio *m*, *Am* baño *m*; **to go to the l.** ir al baño ►► ***l. humour*** chistes *mpl* escatológicos; ***l. paper*** papel *m* higiénico *or Cuba* sanitario *or Guat, Ven* toilette, *Chile* confort *m*

(b) **public l.** servicios públicos, *Esp* aseos públicos, *Am* baños públicos ►► ***l. attendant*** = persona que cuida los servicios públicos

(c) *(receptacle)* váter *m*, retrete *m* ►► ***l. bowl*** taza *f* del váter; ***l. pan*** taza *f* del váter

lavender ['lævɪndə(r)] **1** *n (shrub)* espliego *m*, lavanda *f* ►► ***l. water*** agua *f* de lavanda

2 *adj (colour)* lila *inv*, violeta *inv*

lavish ['lævɪʃ] **1** *adj* **(a)** *(person)* generoso(a) (**with** con), pródigo(a) (**with** en); **he was l. with his praise** fue pródigo en halagos; **to be l. with one's money** ser generoso(a) con el dinero de uno(a) **(b)** *(expenditure, decor)* espléndido(a)

2 *vt* prodigar; **they l. all their attention on their son** le prodigan toda la atención a su hijo; **to l. gifts/praise on sb** colmar de regalos/alabanzas a alguien

lavishly ['lævɪʃlɪ] *adv* **(a)** *(generously, extravagantly)* generosamente, pródigamente; **she spends/entertains l.** gasta dinero/recibe visitas pródigamente **(b)** *(luxuriously)* espléndidamente; **l. decorated/furnished** lujosamente *or* fastuosamente decorado/amueblado

lavishness ['lævɪʃnɪs] *n* **(a)** *(generosity, extravagance)* generosidad *f* **(b)** *(luxuriousness)* fastuosidad *f*

law [lɔː] *n* **(a)** *(rule)* ley *f*; **the laws of rugby** las reglas del rugby; **there's no l. against it** no hay ninguna ley que lo prohíba; *Hum* **there ought to be a l. against it!** ¡eso tendría que estar prohibido!; **she is a l. unto herself** hace lo que le viene en gana *or* lo que le da la gana; **there's one**

l. for the rich and another for the poor hay una ley para el rico y otra para el pobre

(**b**) *(scientific principle)* ley *f* ►► ***the l. of gravity*** la ley de la gravedad; ***the l. of supply and demand*** la ley de la oferta y la demanda; ***the l. of averages*** las leyes de la estadística

(**c**) *(set of rules)* ley *f*; **it's the l.** es la ley; **the l. of the land** las leyes del país; **to become l.** *(of parliamentary bill)* entrar en vigor; **to break/observe the l.** quebrantar/cumplir (con) la ley; **to be above the l.** estar por encima de la ley; **it's against the l. to sell alcohol** va contra la ley vender bebidas alcohólicas; **by l.** por ley; **in** *or* **under British l.** según *or* bajo la ley británica; **you can't take the l. into your own hands** no te puedes tomar la justicia por tu mano; *Fig* **her word is l.** lo que ella dice va a misa ►► *Br* ***l. centre*** servicio *m* público de asesoría jurídica; ***the L. Courts*** el palacio de Justicia; ***l. enforcement*** mantenimiento *m* de la ley y el orden; ***l. enforcement agency*** cuerpo *m* de seguridad del Estado; ***l. enforcement officer*** agente *mf* de policía; ***l. firm*** bufete *m* de abogados; ***the l. of the jungle*** la ley de la selva; *Br* ***L. Lord*** = miembro de la Cámara de los Lores que forma parte del Tribunal Supremo; ***the l. of nature*** las leyes de la naturaleza; ***l. officer*** agente *mf* de la ley; ***l. and order*** el orden público; **the problem of l. and order** la inseguridad ciudadana; *Br* ***the L. Society*** el colegio de abogados de Inglaterra y Gales

(**d**) *(system of justice, subject)* derecho *m*; **a l. student** un(a) estudiante de derecho; **to practise l.** ejercer la abogacía; *Br* **to go to l.** acudir a los tribunales ►► ***l. school*** facultad *f* de derecho

(**e**) *Fam* **the l.** *(police)* la poli; **I'll get** *or* **have the l. on you!** ¡voy a llamar a la policía!

law-abiding ['lɔːəbaɪdɪŋ] *adj* respetuoso(a) de la ley

law-and-order ['lɔːənd'ɔːdə(r)] *adj* **l. issues** asuntos de orden público; **he presents himself as the l. candidate** se define como el candidato que mantendrá la ley y el orden

lawbreaker ['lɔːbreɪkə(r)] *n* delincuente *mf*

lawcourt ['lɔːkɔːt] *n* juzgado *m*

lawful ['lɔːfʊl] *adj (legal)* legal; *(rightful)* legítimo(a); *(not forbidden)* lícito(a); **to go about one's l. business** ocuparse de sus asuntos sin meterse con nadie; **to be your l. wedded wife** ser tu legítima esposa

lawfully ['lɔːfʊlɪ] *adv (legally)* legalmente

lawgiver ['lɔːgɪvə(r)] *n* legislador(ora) *m,f*

lawks [lɔːks] *exclam Fam Old-fashioned* ¡recórcholis!

lawless ['lɔːlɪs] *adj* sin ley; **a l. mob** una muchedumbre anárquica

lawlessness ['lɔːlɪsnɪs] *n* anarquía *f*

lawmaker ['lɔːmeɪkə(r)] *n* legislador(ora) *m,f*

lawman ['lɔːmæn] *n US* agente *m* de la ley

lawn[1] [lɔːn] *n (grass)* césped *m*; **to mow** *or* **cut the l.** cortar el césped ►► ***l. tennis*** tenis *m* en pista de hierba

lawn[2] *n (fabric)* batista *f*

lawnmower ['lɔːnməʊə(r)] *n* cortadora *f* de césped, cortacésped *m or f*

Lawrence ['lɒrəns] *pr n* **Saint L.** san Lorenzo

lawrencium [lə'rensɪəm] *n Chem* laurencio *m*

lawsuit ['lɔːs(j)uːt] *n* pleito *m*; **to bring a l. against sb** entablar pleito contra alguien

lawyer ['lɔːjə(r)] *n* abogado(a) *m,f*

lax [læks] *adj (morals, discipline)* relajado(a), laxo(a); *(person)* negligente, poco riguroso(a); *(security, standards)* descuidado(a), poco riguroso(a); **he's been rather l. in his timekeeping recently** últimamente se toma sus horarios con mucha calma

laxative ['læksətɪv] **1** *n* laxante *m*

2 *adj* laxante

laxity ['læksɪtɪ], **laxness** ['læksnɪs] *n (of morals, discipline)* laxitud *f*, *Esp* relajo *m*; *(of person)* negligencia *f* (**in doing sth** al hacer algo); *(of security, standards)* falta *f* de rigor

lay[1] [leɪ] *adj Rel* laico(a), lego(a) ►► ***l. preacher*** predicador(ora) *m,f* laico(a); ***l. reader*** ***(religious)*** = persona que tiene potestad para encargarse de ciertos oficios religiosos, sin incluir la eucaristía; *(non-expert)* lector(ora) *m,f* profano(a) en la materia

LAY[2] **1** *n very Fam* **he's a good l.** *Esp* folla genial, *Am* coge como los dioses, *Méx* es un buen acostón; **she's an easy l.** es un polvo *or Carib, Méx* una vieja *or RP* una mina fácil

2 *vt* (*pt & pp* **laid** [leɪd]) (**a**) *(place)* dejar, poner; **to l. a book on the table** dejar un libro encima de la mesa; **he laid his hand on my shoulder** me puso la mano en el hombro; **she laid the baby in its cot** acostó al bebé *or Andes* a la guagua en la cuna; **to l. a newspaper flat on the table** extender un periódico en la mesa; **the blast laid the building flat** la explosión arrasó el edificio; **to l. sb flat** *(hit)* tumbar *or CSur* voltear a alguien (de un golpe); **to l. eyes on sth/sb** ver algo/a alguien; **if you l. a finger on her...** como le pongas un solo dedo encima...; **to l. one's hands on sth** *(find)* dar con algo; **she reads everything she can l. her hands on** lee todo lo que cae en sus manos; **to have nowhere to l. one's head** no tener dónde caerse muerto(a); *Formal* **to l. sb to rest** *(bury)* dar sepultura a alguien; **to l. sb's fears to rest** apaciguar los temores de alguien; **they finally laid (to rest) the ghost of their defeat ten years ago** por fin han superado el trauma de su derrota de hace diez años; **this decision lays bare her true intentions** esta decisión deja claro cuáles son sus verdaderas intenciones; **to l. the blame on sb** *or* **at sb's door** echar la culpa a alguien; **to l. a charge against sb** presentar un cargo contra alguien; **to l. claim to sth** reclamar algo; **to l. a curse on sb** echar una maldición a alguien; **to l. emphasis on sth** hacer hincapié en algo; **to l. the facts before sb** exponer los hechos a alguien; **to l. it on the line** *(express clearly)* dejar las cosas claras; **to l. one's job/reputation on the line** jugarse el puesto/la reputación; *Literary* **he laid his opponent low with a fierce blow** derribó a su adversario de un violento golpe; **the illness laid her low** la enfermedad la dejó fuera de combate; **to l. oneself open to criticism** exponerse a (las) críticas; **the bomb laid waste the area** *or* **laid the area to waste** la bomba asoló la zona

(**b**) *(foundations, carpet, mine, pipes)* colocar, poner; *(cable)* tender; *(bricks)* poner; **the reforms l. the basis** *or* **foundation for economic growth** las reformas sentaron las bases para el crecimiento económico

(**c**) *(prepare, arrange) (fire)* preparar; *(trap)* tender; **to l. plans to do sth** hacer planes para hacer algo

(**d**) *(set)* **to l. the table** poner la mesa; **I'll l. another place for the guest** pondré otro cubierto para el invitado

(**e**) *(eggs)* poner; IDIOM *US Fam* **to l. an egg** *(person, performer)* pifiarla; *(play, film)* ser un desastre

(**f**) *(bet) (money)* apostar (**on** a, por); **to l. a bet** hacer una apuesta; *Fig* **he'll never do it, I'll l. money** *or* **odds on it!** ¡apuesto a que no lo hace!

(**g**) *very Fam (have sex with)* echar un polvo con, *Am* cogerse a, *Méx* chingarse a; **he went out hoping to get laid** salió en busca de rollo, *RP, Ven* salió de levante

3 *vi (bird)* poner (huevos)

4 *pt of* **lie**[2]

► **lay about** *vt insep Literary (attack)* acometer, asaltar; **she laid about her with her umbrella** la emprendió a golpes con el paraguas

► **lay aside** *vt sep* (**a**) *(put aside)* **she laid aside her book** dejó a un lado el libro

(**b**) *(money)* reservar, apartar; *(time)* reservar

(**c**) *(prejudices, doubt)* dejar a un lado

► **lay back** *vt sep Sport* **to l. the ball back** colocar la pelota hacia atrás

► **lay before** *vt sep Formal* **to l. sth before sb** *(plan, proposal)* presentar algo a alguien

► **lay by** *vt sep (money)* reservar, apartar

► **lay down** *vt sep* (**a**) *(put down)* dejar; **to l. down one's arms** dejar *or* deponer las armas; **he laid down his life for his beliefs** dio su vida por sus creencias

(**b**) *(principle, rule)* establecer; **it is laid down in the rules that...** el reglamento estipula que...; **she's always laying down the law** siempre está dando órdenes

(**c**) *(wine)* guardar

(**d**) *Mus (song, track)* grabar

(**e**) *(field, land)* plantar

► **lay in** *vt sep (supplies, food)* abastecerse de

► **lay into** *vt insep Fam* (**a**) *(attack, criticize)* arremeter contra

(**b**) *(eat greedily)* emprenderla con

► **lay off 1** *vt sep (make redundant)* despedir *(por reducción de plantilla)*

2 *vt insep Fam (leave alone)* dejar; **to l. off drink** *or* **drinking** dejar la bebida; **l. off it, will you!** ¡déjalo ya!, ¿no?

3 *vi Fam* **l. off!** ¡déjame en paz!

► **lay on** *vt sep* (**a**) *(provide) (party, entertainment)* organizar, preparar; *(transport)* organizar; **they'd laid on a huge banquet for the cast** se habían encargado de organizar un enorme banquete para el reparto; *Br* **the caravan has electricity laid on** la caravana tiene electricidad

(**b**) *(spread) (paint, plaster)* aplicar; IDIOM *Fam* **to l. it on (a bit thick** *or* **with a trowel)** *(exaggerate)* recargar las tintas

(**c**) *Fam* **to l. one on sb** *(hit)* meter una a alguien

(**d**) *US Fam (tell)* **to l. sth on sb** delatar a alguien, *Esp* chivarse de alguien, *RP* alcahuetear a alguien

▸ **lay out** *vt sep* (**a**) *(arrange, display)* colocar, disponer; *(page, essay)* presentar; **we laid the map out on the floor** extendimos el mapa en el suelo
(**b**) *(plan) (road)* trazar; *(town)* diseñar el trazado de; **the house is badly laid out** la casa no tiene una buena distribución
(**c**) *(explain)* exponer
(**d**) *(dead body)* amortajar
(**e**) *Fam (spend)* gastarse
(**f**) *Fam (knock unconscious)* tumbar, dejar K.O.
(**g**) *Fam* **to l. oneself out (for sb)** *(make a great effort)* matarse (por alguien), dejarse la piel (por alguien)

▸ **lay over** *vi US* hacer una parada

▸ **lay up** *vt sep* (**a**) *Fam* **I've been laid up with flu all week** he estado toda la semana en cama con gripe *or Am* gripa
(**b**) *(store up) (supplies)* acumular; **you're laying up problems for yourself** estás acumulando problemas para el futuro
(**c**) *(ship, car)* estar fuera de circulación

layabout ['leɪəbaʊt] *n Br Fam* holgazán(ana) *m,f*, gandul(ula) *m,f*, *Méx* flojo(a) *m,f*, *RP* fiaca *mf*

lay-by ['leɪbaɪ] *n Br* área *f* de descanso

layer ['leɪə(r)] **1** *n* (**a**) *(of skin, paint, fabric)* capa *f*; **put on several layers of clothing to keep warm** ponte bastante ropa para ir bien abrigado; **to have one's hair cut in layers** cortarse el pelo a capas; **the poem has many layers of meaning** el poema tiene varios niveles *or* varias lecturas ▸▸ ***l. cake*** pastel *m* de varias capas
(**b**) *(of rock)* estrato *m*
(**c**) *(of plant)* acodo *m*
(**d**) *(hen)* gallina *f* ponedora
(**e**) *Comptr (of graphics)* capa *f*
2 *vt* (**a**) *(arrange in layers)* poner en capas (**b**) *(hair)* **to have one's hair layered** cortarse el pelo a capas (**c**) *(plant)* acodar

layered ['leɪəd] *adj (hair)* a capas

layering ['leɪərɪŋ] *n Comptr* disposición *f* en capas

layette [leɪ'et] *n* ajuar *m* de bebé

laying ['leɪɪŋ] *n Rel* **l. on of hands** imposición de manos

layman ['leɪmən] *n* (**a**) *Rel* laico *m*, lego *m* (**b**) *(non-specialist)* profano *m*, lego *m*; **a l.'s guide to the stock market** una guía dirigida a los noveles en el mercado de valores

lay-off ['leɪɒf] *n (dismissal)* despido *m (por reducción de plantilla)*

layout ['leɪaʊt] *n* (**a**) *(of town)* trazado *m*; *(of house)* distribución *f*; *(garden)* disposición *f*; **the l. of the controls is very straightforward** la disposición de los controles es muy sencilla (**b**) *(of text)* composición *f*; *(of magazine, letter)* diseño *m*, formato *m* (**c**) *Comptr* diseño *m*, formato *m* ▸▸ ***l. application*** programa *m* de maquetación

layover ['leɪəʊvə(r)] *n US (on land journey)* parada *f*; *(on air journey)* escala *f*

layperson ['leɪpɜːsən] *n* (**a**) *Rel* laico(a) *m,f*, lego(a) *m,f* (**b**) *(non-specialist)* profano(a) *m,f*, lego(a) *m,f*

lay-up ['leɪʌp] *n (in basketball)* bandeja *f*

laywoman ['leɪwʊmən] *n* (**a**) *Rel* laica *f*, lega *f* (**b**) *(non-specialist)* profana *f*, lega *f*

Lazarus ['læzərəs] *pr n* Lázaro

laze [leɪz] *vi* **to l. (about/around)** holgazanear, gandulear; **we spent the summer lazing on the beach** nos pasamos el verano vagando *or Esp* haciendo el vago en la playa

lazily ['leɪzɪlɪ] *adv* perezosamente

laziness ['leɪzɪnɪs] *n* pereza *f*

lazy ['leɪzɪ] *adj (person)* perezoso(a), vago(a); *(movement)* indolente; *(afternoon)* ocioso(a); **those l. summer days** aquellos ociosos días estivales ▸▸ *Med* ***l. eye*** ojo *m* vago; ***l. Susan*** *(tray on table)* bandeja *f* giratoria

lazybones ['leɪzɪbəʊnz] *n Fam* holgazán(ana) *m,f*

lb (*abbr* **pound**) libra *f (= 0,45 kg)*; **3 lb** *or* **lbs** 3 libras

LC *US* (*abbr* **Library of Congress**) Biblioteca *f* del Congreso

lc (*abbr* **lower case**) c.b., caja *f* baja

LCD [elsiː'diː] *n Elec & Comptr* (*abbr* **liquid crystal display**) LCD, pantalla *f* de cristal líquido

LCM [elsiː'em] *n Math* (*abbr* **lowest common multiple**) m.c.m.

LDC [eldiː'siː] *n Econ* (*abbr* **less-developed country**) país *m* menos desarrollado

L-dopa [el'dəʊpə] *n Pharm* L-dopa *f*

L-driver ['eldraɪvə(r)] *n (before getting licence)* conductor(ora) *m,f* en prácticas

LEA [eliː'eɪ] *n Br Pol* (*abbr* **Local Education Authority**) = organismo local encargado de la enseñanza, *Esp* ≃ consejería *f* de educación

lea [liː] *n Literary* prado *m*

leach [liːtʃ] **1** *vt Chem & Tech* lixiviar
2 *vi* filtrarse

lead[1] [led] *n* (**a**) *(metal)* plomo *m*; **l. pipe/shot** cañería/granalla de plomo ▸▸ ***l. crystal*** cristal *m* de plomo; ***l. poisoning*** saturnismo *m*
(**b**) *(for pencil)* mina *f* ▸▸ ***l. pencil*** lápiz *m* (de mina)
(**c**) **leads** *(on roof, window)* emplomado *m*
(**d**) IDIOMS **to go** *Br* **down** *or US* **over like a l. balloon** fracasar estrepitosamente; *Fam* **they filled** *or* **pumped him full of l.** le llenaron el cuerpo de plomo, lo llenaron de plomo; *US Fam* **to get the l. out (of one's pants)** moverse, *Esp* ir espabilando; *very Fam* **that'll put l. in your pencil!** ¡eso levanta a un muerto!; *Fam* **to swing the l.** escurrir el bulto

LEAD[2] [liːd] **1** *n* (**a**) *(advantage)* ventaja *f*; **to be in the l.** ir *or* estar a la cabeza *or* en cabeza; **to go into** *or* **take the l.** ponerse a la *or* en cabeza; **to have a two-point l. over sb** sacarle dos puntos a alguien; **to lose the l. (to sb)** perder la primera posición (a manos de alguien)
(**b**) *(example)* ejemplo *m*; **to follow sb's l.** seguir el ejemplo de alguien; **follow my l.** *(do as I do)* haz lo que yo; **to give sb a l.** dar un ejemplo a alguien; **to take the l.** *(initiative)* tomar la iniciativa; **to take one's l. from sb** seguir el ejemplo de alguien
(**c**) *(clue)* pista *f*; **the police have several leads** la policía tiene varias pistas
(**d**) *(in cardgame)* mano *f*; **it's your l.** tú eres mano, tú llevas la mano
(**e**) *Theat & Cin (role)* papel *m* protagonista; *(actor, actress)* protagonista *mf*; **to play the l.** ser el/la protagonista ▸▸ ***on l. guitar*** a la guitarra solista; ***l. guitarist*** guitarra *mf* solista; ***l. singer*** solista *mf*
(**f**) *(newspaper article)* **l. (story)** artículo *m* de primera plana
(**g**) *(for dog)* correa *f*; **to let the dog off the l.** soltar al perro, quitarle *or Am* sacarle la correa al perro; **dogs must be kept on the l.** los perros deberán llevar correa
(**h**) *(cable)* cable *m*
(**i**) *Ind* ***l. time*** *(for production)* tiempo *m or* período *m* de producción; *(for delivery)* tiempo *m* de entrega
2 *vt* (*pt & pp* **led** [led]) (**a**) *(show the way to)* llevar, conducir; **she led us through the forest** nos guió por el bosque; **she led us into the ambush** nos condujo a la emboscada; **he led his men into battle/to victory** dirigió a sus hombres a la batalla/hacia la victoria; *Rel* **l. us not into temptation** no nos dejes caer en la tentación; **to l. the way** mostrar el camino; *Fig* **our country leads the way in human rights** nuestro país está a la cabeza en la lucha por los derechos humanos; **to be easily led** dejarse influir con facilidad; **this leads me to the conclusion that...** esto me lleva a la conclusión de que...; **this leads me to my next point** esto me lleva a mi siguiente punto; **to l. the applause** iniciar el aplauso; **to l. the conversation around to a subject** llevar la conversación hacia un asunto; *Fig* **to l. sb astray** llevar a alguien por el mal camino; *Fam* **to l. sb a merry chase** *or* **dance** traer a alguien a mal traer; *Fam Fig* **to l. sb by the nose** tener dominado(a) a alguien, *RP* llevar a alguien de las narices
(**b**) *(cause)* **to l. sb to do sth** llevar a alguien a hacer algo; **despair led him to commit suicide** la desesperación le llevó a suicidarse; **that leads me to believe that...** eso me hace creer que...; **I was led to believe that the meal would be free** me dieron a entender que la comida sería gratis
(**c**) *(live)* **to l. a happy/sad life** tener *or* llevar una vida feliz/triste
(**d**) *(be in charge of) (team, attack, country, inquiry)* dirigir; *(discussion, debate)* moderar
(**e**) *(be ahead of)* **to l. sb by eight points** llevar a alguien ocho puntos de ventaja; **England are leading Italy by two goals to nil** Inglaterra va ganando a Italia por dos goles a cero; **to l. the field** estar *or* ir a la cabeza; *Fig* **to l. the field in sth** estar a la cabeza *or* a la vanguardia en algo; **he led the race from start to finish** fue a la cabeza durante toda la carrera; **the Broncos l. the table** los Broncos van a la cabeza de la clasificación; **we l. the world in this field** somos los líderes mundiales en este campo
(**f**) *(be at front of) (procession)* encabezar; **this leads a long list of complaints** esta es la primera de una larga lista de quejas
(**g**) *Law (witness)* hacer una pregunta capciosa a
(**h**) *(in cards)* abrir con
3 *vi* (**a**) *(road)* conducir, llevar (**to** a); **the stairs led (up/down) to his study** las escaleras llevaban a su estudio; **the door led into a cellar** la puerta daba a una bodega; **the question led into a debate on divorce** la pregunta abrió un debate sobre el divorcio; *Fig* **this is leading nowhere!** ¡así no vamos a ninguna parte!
(**b**) *(go ahead)* **you l. and I'll follow** tú vas delante y yo te sigo
(**c**) *(in competition, race)* ir en cabeza; **she leads by just ten seconds**

lleva la delantera por tan sólo diez segundos

(**d**) *(in cardgame)* salir (**with** con); **Peter to l.** sale Peter

(**e**) *(in dancing)* llevar

(**f**) *(in boxing)* **to l. with one's left/right** atacar con la izquierda/derecha

(**g**) *(newspaper)* **the Herald Tribune leads with an article on education** el artículo de primera plana del Herald Tribune trata sobre educación

(**h**) *(show leadership)* **to l. by example** *or* **from the front** predicar con el ejemplo

▸**lead away** *vt sep* **to l. sb away** llevarse a alguien; **to l. the conversation away from a subject** llevar la conversación hacia otro tema

▸**lead back 1** *vt sep (person)* llevar de vuelta a; **she led the conversation back to the question of money** volvió a llevar la conversación al tema del dinero

2 *vi* **this path leads back to the beach** este sendero lleva de vuelta a la playa

▸**lead off 1** *vt sep* (**a**) *(person)* llevar; **they were led off to jail** les llevaron a la cárcel

(**b**) *(discussion)* empezar

2 *vi* (**a**) *(road, corridor)* salir, bifurcarse (**from** de)

(**b**) *(in discussion)* comenzar, empezar

(**c**) *(at dance)* abrir el baile

(**d**) *(in baseball)* ser el primer bateador

▸**lead on 1** *vt sep* (**a**) *(deceive)* tomar el pelo a

(**b**) *(give false hopes to)* ilusionar a; **you shouldn't l. him on like that** no deberías ilusionarle así

(**c**) *(in progression)* **this leads me on to my second point** esto me lleva a mi segundo punto

2 *vi (go ahead)* **you l. on and I'll follow** tú vas delante y yo te sigo

▸**lead to** *vt insep (cause)* llevar a; **years of effort led to him finally solving the problem** tras años de trabajo finalmente solucionó el problema; **I didn't mean to kiss her, but one thing led to another** no tenía la intención de besarla, pero unas cosas llevaron a otras; **what's all this leading to?** ¿a dónde lleva todo esto?

▸**lead up to** *vt insep* (**a**) *(path, road)* llevar; **those stairs l. up to the attic** esa escalera lleva al ático

(**b**) *(in reasoning)* **what are you leading up to?** ¿a dónde quieres ir a parar (con todo esto)?; **she led up to her request by saying that...** introdujo su petición *or Am* pedido diciendo que...

(**c**) *(precede, cause)* llevar a, conducir a; **the period leading up to the war** el período previo *or* que precedió a la guerra; **in the weeks leading up to the wedding** en las semanas previas a la boda

---

leaded ['ledɪd] *adj* (**a**) ***l. window*** vidriera *f* (emplomada) (**b**) *US* ***l. gasoline*** gasolina *f or RP* nafta *f* con plomo; *Br* ***l. petrol*** gasolina *f or RP* nafta *f* con plomo

leaden ['ledən] *adj* (**a**) *(made of lead)* de plomo, plúmbeo(a) (**b**) *(sky)* plomizo(a) (**c**) *(heavy)* pesado(a), plúmbeo(a); *(heart)* de acero, de hierro, *Am* de piedra; **he walked with l. steps** andaba con pies de plomo; **his l. delivery** su discurso farragoso; **his l. acting** su actuación farragosa

leader ['li:də(r)] *n* (**a**) *(head) (of group, association, party)* líder *mf*; *(of strike, protest, riot)* cabecilla *mf*; **to be a born l.** ser un líder nato

(**b**) *(in race) (athlete, horse)* líder *mf*, cabeza *mf* (de carrera); *(in championship, league)* líder *mf*, primero(a) *m,f*; **she caught up with the leaders** alcanzó a los que iban en cabeza

(**c**) *(foremost in field) (product, company)* líder *mf*; **the institute is a world l. in cancer research** el instituto va a la cabeza mundial en la investigación contra el cáncer

(**d**) *Br Parl* ***L. of the House of Commons*** presidente *mf* de la Cámara de los Comunes; ***L. of the House of Lords*** presidente *mf* de la Cámara de los Lores; ***L. of the Opposition*** líder *mf* de la oposición

(**e**) *US Com (loss leader)* artículo *m* de reclamo, = producto que se vende por debajo del precio de coste para atraer a la clientela

(**f**) *Mus Br (first violin)* primer violín *mf*; *US (conductor)* director(ora) *m,f*

(**g**) *(for film)* guía *f*

(**h**) *Br (in newspaper)* editorial *m* ▸▸ ***l. writer*** editorialista *mf*

leaderboard ['li:dəbɔ:d] *n (in golf)* tabla *f* de clasificación; *Fig* **to be top of the l.** ir en cabeza

leadership ['li:dəʃɪp] *n* (**a**) *(people in charge)* dirección *f*

(**b**) *(position)* liderazgo *m*, liderato *m*; **during** *or* **under her l.** durante *or* bajo su liderazgo *or* liderato ▸▸ ***l. battle*** batalla *f* por el liderazgo *or* liderato; ***l. contest*** lucha *f or* pugna *f* por el liderazgo *or* liderato

(**c**) *(quality)* capacidad *f* de liderazgo, dotes *fpl* de mando; **it's the president's job to provide l.** el presidente debe desempeñar el papel de líder ▸▸ ***l. qualities*** dotes *fpl* de mando

lead-foot ['led'fʊt] *vt US Fam (in car)* pisar a fondo

lead-footed ['led'fʊtɪd] *adj US Fam* (**a**) *(clumsy)* torpe (**b**) *(driver)* fitipaldi

lead-free ['led'fri:] *adj* sin plomo

lead-in ['li:dɪn] *n TV & Rad* presentación *f*

leading[1] ['ledɪŋ] *n Typ* interlineado *m*

leading[2] ['li:dɪŋ] *adj* (**a**) *(best, most important)* principal, destacado(a); **one of Europe's l. electronics firms** una de las principales empresas europeas de electrónica; **a l. authority in the field** una destacada autoridad en la materia; **they played a l. part in the discussions** desempeñaron un papel destacado en las negociaciones ▸▸ ***l. lady*** *(in play)* primera actriz *f*; *(in movie)* protagonista *f*; ***l. light*** *(in politics, society)* figura *f* prominente; ***l. man*** *(in play)* primer actor *m*; *(in movie)* protagonista *m*; *Cin & Theat* ***l. role*** papel *m* protagonista

(**b**) *(team, runner)* líder; **the l. group** *(in race)* el grupo de cabeza; **to be in the l. position** ir a la cabeza

(**c**) *Av* ***l. edge*** *(of propeller, wing)* borde *m* de ataque; *Fig* vanguardia *f*

(**d**) *Journ* ***l. article*** *Br (editorial)* editorial *m*; *US (main story)* artículo *m* principal

(**e**) ***l. question*** *(seeking to elicit answer)* pregunta *f* capciosa

leading-edge ['li:dɪŋ'edʒ] *adj (technology, company)* de vanguardia, puntero(a)

lead-off ['li:dɒf] *n* comienzo *m*, principio *m*; **this is the l. edition in a series of programmes** éste es el primero de una serie de programas; **as a l.** para empezar, de aperitivo

lead-up ['li:dʌp] *n* periodo *m* previo (**to** a); **in the l. to** en el periodo previo a

leaf [li:f] (*pl* **leaves** [li:vz]) *n* (**a**) *(of plant, book)* hoja *f*; **to be in l.** tener hojas; **to come into l.** echar hojas, reverdecer ▸▸ ***l. insect*** insecto *m* hoja; ***l. mould*** mantillo *m* de hojas (**b**) *(of book)* hoja *f*; IDIOM **to turn over a new l.** hacer borrón y cuenta nueva; IDIOM **to take a l. out of sb's book** seguir el ejemplo de alguien (**c**) *(of table)* hoja *f* abatible (**d**) *(of metal)* hoja *f* (**e**) *Tech* ***l. spring*** ballesta *f*

▸**leaf through** *vt insep (book, magazine)* hojear

leafless ['li:flɪs] *adj* sin hojas, deshojado(a)

leaflet ['li:flɪt] **1** *n* (**a**) *(small brochure)* folleto *m*; *(piece of paper)* octavilla *f*; *(political)* octavilla *f*, panfleto *m* (**b**) *Bot* folíolo *m*

2 *vt* **to l. an area** repartir folletos en una zona

leafy ['li:fɪ] *adj (tree)* frondoso(a); **a l. avenue** una avenida arbolada; **a l. suburb** una zona residencial muy verde

league [li:g] *n* (**a**) *Sport* liga *f*; **the l. champions** los campeones de liga; **a l. match** un partido de liga ▸▸ ***l. championship*** campeonato *m* de liga; *Br* ***l. table*** *(in sports)* (tabla *f* de) clasificación *f* de la liga; *(of performance)* clasificación *f*, ránking *m*

(**b**) *(class, category)* **to be in the big l.** estar en la categoría reina, estar en primera división; **to be in a different** *or* **another l.** estar a otro nivel; **that's way out of our l.** está muy por encima de nuestras posibilidades

(**c**) *(alliance)* liga *f*; **to be in l. with sb** estar compinchado(a) con alguien; **they're all in l. against me** se han compinchado en mi contra ▸▸ *Hist* ***the L. of Nations*** la Sociedad de Naciones

(**d**) *(measurement)* legua *f*

leak [li:k] **1** *n* (**a**) *(hole) (in container, pipe)* agujero *m*; *(in roof)* gotera *f*; *(in ship)* vía *f* de agua (**b**) *(escape) (of liquid, gas)* fuga *f*, escape *m*; *(of information)* filtración *f* (**c**) *Fam* **to take** *or Br* **have a l.** echar una meadita

2 *vt* (**a**) *(liquid, gas)* tener una fuga *or* un escape de, perder; **the can leaked oil onto my trousers** la lata me goteó aceite sobre los pantalones (**b**) *(information)* filtrar; **someone leaked the news to the press** alguien filtró la noticia a la prensa

3 *vi* (**a**) *(allow liquid through) (pipe)* tener una fuga *or* un escape; *(roof)* tener goteras; *(shoe)* calar; *(ship)* hacer agua; **this bucket's leaking** este balde pierde; **his pen leaked in his pocket** el bolígrafo se le reventó en el bolsillo (**b**) *(escape, enter)* **to l. (out)** *(liquid, gas)* salirse, escaparse; *(information)* filtrarse; **the rain had leaked (in) through a crack in the wall** la lluvia se había filtrado por una grieta de la pared

leakage ['li:kɪdʒ] *n* (**a**) *(of liquid, gas)* fuga *f*, escape *m* (**b**) *(of information)* filtración *f*

leaky ['li:kɪ] *adj* **(a)** *(bucket)* con agujeros; *(pipe)* con fugas *or* escapes; *(roof)* con goteras; *(shoe)* que cala; *(ship)* que hace agua; *(tap)* que gotea **(b)** *Fam* **this department is very l.** este departamento se va demasiado de la lengua

lean[1] [li:n] **1** *adj* **(a)** *(person, animal)* delgado(a), flaco(a); *Fig* **the company is now fitter and leaner than it was before** la empresa está más saneada que antes **(b)** *(meat)* magro(a) **(c)** *(year)* de escasez; *(harvest)* escaso(a); **we had a l. time of it** fue una época de vacas flacas
2 *n (meat)* carne *f* magra

lean[2] (*pt & pp* **leaned** *or Br* **leant** [lent]) **1** *vt* **(a)** *(prop)* **to l. sth against sth** apoyar algo contra algo **(b)** *(rest) (head, elbows)* apoyar **(c)** *(incline)* **to l. one's head back/forward** inclinar la cabeza hacia atrás/delante; **she leaned** *or Br* **leant her head to one side** ladeó la cabeza, inclinó la cabeza hacia un lado
2 *vi* **(a)** *(building, tree)* inclinarse **(b)** *(bend)* **to l. back/forward** echarse hacia atrás/inclinarse hacia delante; **to l. out of the window** asomarse a la ventana **(c)** *(for support) (person, object)* **to l. on/against sth** apoyarse en/contra algo; **the ladder was leaning against the wall** la escalera estaba apoyada en *or* contra la pared

▸ **lean on** *vt insep* **(a)** *(rely on)* apoyarse en **(b)** *(pressurize)* presionar a

▸ **lean over 1** *vt insep* **he leaned over the fence** se asomó por encima de la valla
2 *vi* inclinarse; *Fig* **to l. over backwards (to do sth)** hacer lo imposible *or* todo lo posible (por hacer algo); **to l. over backwards for sb/to please sb** desvivirse por alguien

▸ **lean towards** *vt insep (tend towards)* inclinarse por, decantarse por; **I l. towards his point of view** me inclino por su punto de vista; **politically she leans towards the right** políticamente se inclina hacia la derecha

lean-burn ['li:nbɜ:n] *adj (engine)* de mezcla pobre

leaning ['li:nɪŋ] **1** *n (tendency)* inclinación *f*, tendencia *f*; **to have artistic leanings** tener tendencias *or* inclinaciones artísticas
2 *adj (tree, wall)* inclinado(a); **the L. Tower of Pisa** la torre inclinada de Pisa

leanness ['li:nnɪs] *n (of person)* delgadez *f*

leant *Br pt & pp of* **lean**

lean-to ['li:ntu:] **1** *n (shack)* cobertizo *m*
2 *adj* **l. roof** tejado a un agua

leap [li:p] **1** *n* salto *m*, brinco *m*; **it's a great l. forward in medical research** es un gran avance en la investigación médica; **his heart gave a l.** le dio un vuelco el corazón; IDIOM **to take a l. in the dark** dar un salto al vacío; IDIOM **to advance by leaps and bounds** avanzar a pasos agigantados ▸▸ ***l. year*** año *m* bisiesto **(b)** *(in prices, temperature)* subida *f* brusca
2 *vt* (*pt & pp* **leapt** [lept] *or* **leaped**) saltar
3 *vi* **(a)** *(person, animal)* saltar; **to l. over sth** saltar por encima de algo; **to l. into the air** *(leave the ground)* dar un salto en el aire; *(when startled)* dar un respingo; **to l. to one's feet** ponerse en pie de un salto *or* brinco; **to l. for joy** dar saltos de alegría; **we leapt back in fright** dimos un respingo atemorizados; IDIOM **she nearly leapt out of her skin** casi le dio un patatús
(b) *Fig (move quickly)* **he leapt to the wrong conclusion** sacó inmediatamente la conclusión equivocada; **she leapt on his mistake** se cebó de inmediato con él por su error; **the answer almost leapt off the page at me** tenía la respuesta delante de las narices; **to l. at the chance** no dejar escapar la oportunidad
(c) *(prices, temperature)* subir bruscamente

▸ **leap about, leap around 1** *vt insep* saltar *or* brincar por
2 *vi* saltar, brincar

leapfrog ['li:pfrɒg] **1** *n* **to play l.** jugar a pídola
2 *vt* (*pt & pp* **leapfrogged**) saltar por encima de
3 *vi* **to l. over** *(rivals)* saltar por encima de

leapt [lept] *pt & pp of* **leap**

learn [lɜ:n] (*pt & pp* **learned** *or Br* **learnt** [lɜ:nt]) **1** *vt* **(a)** *(language, skill)* aprender; **he's learning the violin** está aprendiendo (a tocar el) violín; **to l. (how) to do sth** aprender a hacer algo; **I've learned to be more careful since then** desde entonces he aprendido a ser más cuidadoso; **to l. sth by heart** aprender algo de memoria; *Fig* **he has learnt his lesson** ha aprendido la lección; *Fig* **when will she l. her lesson?** ¿cuándo aprenderá? **(b)** *(find out about)* saber; **we are sorry to l. that...** sentimos mucho haber sabido que... **(c)** *Fam (teach)* **that'll l. you!** ¡a ver si así aprendes!
2 *vi* **(a)** *(acquire knowledge)* aprender; **to l. about sth** aprender algo; **to l. by** *or* **from one's mistakes** aprender de los errores; **they learnt the hard way** aprendieron a base de palos; **will you never l.!** ¡nunca aprenderás! PROV **it's never too late to l.** nunca es tarde para aprender **(b)** *(find out)* **to l. of** *or* **about sth** saber de algo

▸ **learn off** *vt sep Br (dates, facts)* aprenderse (de memoria)

learned ['lɜ:nɪd] *adj* **(a)** *(erudite) (person)* erudito(a), sabio(a); *(subject, journal)* especializado(a); *(society)* académico(a) **(b)** *Br Law* **my l. friend** mi estimado colega

learner ['lɜ:nə(r)] *n (beginner)* principiante *mf*; *(student)* estudiante *mf*; **to be a quick l.** aprender deprisa; **to be a slow l.** ser lento(a) *(para aprender)* ▸▸ ***l. driver*** conductor(ora) *m,f* en prácticas; *US* ***l.'s permit*** = permiso de *Esp* conducir *or Am* manejar provisional que recibe un conductor en prácticas

learning ['lɜ:nɪŋ] *n* **(a)** *(process)* aprendizaje *m*; **to regard sth as a l. experience** considerar algo como una experiencia positiva ▸▸ ***l. curve*** curva *f* de aprendizaje; **we're on a l. curve** estamos en proceso de aprendizaje; ***l. disabilities*** discapacidad *f* psíquica; ***l. support*** clases *fpl* de apoyo **(b)** *(knowledge)* conocimientos *mpl*; **a man of great l.** un hombre de gran erudición; PROV **a little l. is a dangerous thing** qué malo es saber las cosas a medias

learnt *Br pt & pp of* **learn**

lease [li:s] **1** *n* (contrato *m* de) arrendamiento *m or* alquiler *m*; **to take (out) a l. on a house, to take a house on l.** arrendar *or* alquilar una casa; IDIOM **to give sth/sb a new l. on** *or Br* **of life** insuflar nueva vida en algo/a alguien
2 *vt* **(a)** *(of owner) (house, land, equipment)* arrendar, alquilar (**to** a) **(b)** *(of tenant) (house, land, equipment)* arrendar, alquilar; **we l. it from them** se lo arrendamos *or* alquilamos a ellos

▸ **lease back** *vt sep* hacer una operación de cesión-arrendamiento *or* retroarriendo con

▸ **lease out** *vt sep* arrendar, alquilar

leaseback ['li:sbæk] *n* **(sale and) l.** cesión-arrendamiento *m*, retroarriendo *m*

leased line ['li:st'laɪn] *n Comptr (for Internet connection)* línea *f* arrendada *or* alquilada

leasehold ['li:shəʊld] *n* arriendo *m* ▸▸ ***l. property*** propiedad *f* arrendada

leaseholder ['li:shəʊldə(r)] *n* arrendatario(a) *m,f*

leash [li:ʃ] *n (for dog)* correa *f*; **dogs must be kept on a l.** *(sign)* los perros deben ir atados; *Fig* **to keep sb on a tight l.** atar corto a alguien

leasing ['li:sɪŋ] *n Com* arrendamiento *m*, alquiler *m* ▸▸ ***l. agreement*** contrato *m* de arriendo *or* alquiler

---

LEAST [li:st] **1** *n* **the l.** lo menos; **this one costs the l.** este es el que cuesta menos; **it's the l. I can do** es lo menos que puedo hacer; **that's the l. of my worries** eso es lo que menos me preocupa; **at the (very) l. they should pay your expenses** como mínimo deberían pagar tus gastos; **not in the l.** en absoluto; **I wasn't in the l. surprised** no me sorprendió en lo más mínimo; **it doesn't matter in the l.** no tiene la menor importancia; **it was difficult, to say the l.** fue difícil, por no decir otra cosa peor; PROV **l. said, soonest mended** cuanto menos se diga, mejor
2 *adj* (*superlative of* **little**) *(smallest)* menor; **the l. thing annoys her** la menor cosa le molesta; **I have the l. time of everyone** yo soy el que menos tiempo tiene de todos; **she wasn't the l. bit interested** no le interesaba en lo más mínimo; **I don't have the l. idea** no tengo ni la más mínima idea ▸▸ *Math* ***l. common denominator*** mínimo común denominador *m*; ***l. sandpiper*** correlimos *m inv* menudillo
3 *adv* menos; **the l. interesting/difficult** el menos interesante/difícil; **he is the candidate who is l. likely to succeed** de todos los candidatos, él es el que tiene menos posibilidades de éxito; **when I was l. expecting it** cuando menos lo esperaba; **I like this one l. of all** éste es el que menos me gusta de todos; **nobody believed me, l. of all her** nadie me creyó y ella menos que nadie; **I am disappointed, not l. because I trusted you** estoy decepcionado, sobre todo porque confiaba en ti
4 at least *adv* por lo menos, al menos; **at l. as old/expensive as...** por lo menos tan viejo/caro como...; **you could at l. have phoned** por lo *or* al menos podías haberme llamado; **at l. we've got an umbrella** por lo *or* al menos tenemos un paraguas; **he's leaving, at l. that's what I've heard** se va, o por lo *or* al menos eso he oído

---

least-cost ['li:st'kɒst] *n Com* costo *m or Esp* coste *m* mínimo

leastways ['li:stweɪz], *US* **leastwise** ['li:stwaɪz] *adv Fam* al menos, por lo menos

leather ['leðə(r)] **1** *n* **(a)** *(material)* cuero *m*, *Esp, Méx* piel *f*; **leathers** *(of motorcyclist)* ropa *f* de cuero **(b)** *(for polishing)* **(wash** *or* **window) l.** gamuza *f*

2 *adj* (**a**) *(jacket, shoes, sofa, bag)* de cuero *or Esp, Méx* piel ►► ***l. binding*** encuadernación *f* en cuero *or Esp, Méx* piel; ***l. goods*** marroquinería *f*, artículos *mpl* de cuero *or Esp, Méx* piel (**b**) *(for sadomasochists) (bar, club)* sadomasoquista

3 *vt Fam (beat)* cascar, zurrar, *Méx* madrear

leather-back ['leðəbæk] *n (sea turtle)* tortuga *f* laúd

leather-bound ['leðəbaʊnd] *adj (book)* encuadernado(a) en cuero *or Esp, Méx* piel

leatherette® [leðə'ret] *n* skay *m*, cuero *m* sintético

leathering ['leðərɪŋ] *n Fam (beating)* tunda *f*, zurra *f*

leathern ['leðən] *adj Archaic* de cuero *or Esp, Méx* piel

leatherneck ['leðənek] *n US Fam* marine *mf*

leathery ['leðərɪ] *adj* (**a**) *(face, skin)* curtido(a) (**b**) *(meat)* correoso(a)

LEAVE [li:v] **1** *n* (**a**) *Formal (permission)* permiso *m*; **to ask l. to do sth** pedir permiso para hacer algo; **to grant** *or* **give sb l. to do sth** conceder *or* dar permiso a alguien para hacer algo; **by** *or* **with your l.** con su permiso; **without so much as a by your l.** sin tan siquiera pedir permiso

(**b**) *(holiday)* permiso *m*; **to go/be on l.** irse/estar de permiso *or Am* licencia; **unpaid l.** baja no retribuida *or* sin sueldo, *Am* licencia sin goce de sueldo ►► ***l. of absence*** permiso *m*, *Am* licencia *f*

(**c**) *(farewell)* **to take one's l. (of sb)** despedirse (de alguien); **to take l. of one's senses** perder el juicio

2 *vt* (*pt & pp* **left** [left]) (**a**) *(depart from) (place)* irse de, marcharse de; *(room, house)* salir de; *(person, group)* dejar; *(plane, train)* bajar de; **she left London yesterday** se fue de Londres ayer; **the train left the station** el tren salió de la estación; **to l. the table** levantarse de la mesa; **I left work at five** salí de trabajar a las cinco; **I left him lying on the sofa** lo dejé tirado en el sofá; **his eyes never left her** sus ojos no se apartaban de ella; **I'll l. you to it, then** entonces, te dejo con ello, bueno, te dejo tranquilo; **I left them to their work** los dejé que siguieran trabajando

(**b**) *(abandon)* abandonar, dejar; *(company)* dejar; **he left his wife (for another woman)** dejó a su esposa (por otra mujer); **the number of people leaving the Catholic church is increasing** cada vez más gente abandona la fe católica; **they left her to die** la dejaron morir; **to l. home** irse de casa; **to l. one's job** dejar el trabajo; **to l. school** dejar el colegio; *Fam* **to l. go** *or* **hold of sth** soltar algo; **to l. sb in the lurch** dejar a alguien en la estacada; **to l. sb to sb's tender mercies** dejar a alguien a merced de alguien; **to be left to sb's tender mercies** quedar a merced de alguien; **I was left penniless** me quedé sin un céntimo; **I was left with the bill** me quedé con la cuenta; **we were left with a feeling of disappointment** nos quedamos decepcionados

(**c**) *(put, deposit)* **to l. sth somewhere** *(deliberately)* dejar algo en algún sitio; *(by mistake)* dejarse algo en algún sitio; **to l. a message for sb** dejar un recado *or* mensaje para alguien, *Col, Méx, Ven* dejar razón para alguien; **I've left the kids with their uncle** he dejado a los niños con su tío; **take it or l. it** lo tomas o lo dejas

(**d**) *(allow to remain)* dejar; **to l. sb sth, to l. sth for sb** dejar algo a alguien; **to l. a mark/stain** dejar marca/mancha; **to l. the door open** dejar la puerta abierta; **his comments l. the door open for a future change of policy** sus comentarios dejan la puerta abierta a un futuro cambio de política; **l. my things alone!** ¡deja mis cosas tranquilas *or* en paz!; **l. me alone!, l. me be!** ¡déjame en paz!; **I think we should l. (it) well alone** creo que sería mejor no meterse *or* dejar las cosas como están; **to l. sth unfinished** dejar algo sin terminar; **to l. sth unsaid** callarse algo; **to l. a lot to be desired** dejar mucho que desear; **l. the engine running** deja el motor encendido *or Am* prendido; **he left his audience wanting more** dejó al público con ganas de más; **let's l. it at that** vamos a dejarlo aquí; **to l. oneself open to criticism** exponerse a las críticas; **to l. sb to do sth** dejar a alguien hacer algo; **it leaves much** *or* **a lot to be desired** deja mucho que desear; *Fig* **his music leaves me cold** su música no me dice nada; **to l. sb to their own devices** dejar que alguien se las arregle solo; IDIOM **to l. sb standing** *(be much better than)* dar cien *or* mil vueltas a alguien

(**e**) *(with cause)* dejar; **the bullet left a scar on his cheek** la bala le dejó una cicatriz en la mejilla; **the bomb left six people dead** la bomba dejó seis muertos; **this leaves me £5 better off** de esta forma salgo ganando 5 libras; **that leaves me $100 for spending money** eso me deja 100 dólares para gastos; *Fig* **her words left an unpleasant taste in my mouth** sus palabras me dejaron un mal sabor de boca

(**f**) *(bequeath)* **to l. sth to sb, to l. sb sth** legar *or* dejar algo a alguien; **he leaves a wife and three children** deja mujer y tres hijos

(**g**) *(delay, not do)* dejar; **let's l. that subject for later** dejemos ese asunto para más tarde; **to l. sth till last** dejar algo para el final; **we left it a bit late** deberíamos haberlo hecho antes

(**h**) *(with decisions)* **l. it to me** déjamelo a mí; **I'll l. (it to) you to decide** decide tú mismo; **to l. sth to chance** dejar algo al azar; **l. it with me** *(problem)* déjamelo a mí; **you l. me with no choice but to...** no me dejas otra alternativa que...

(**i**) *(not eat)* dejarse; **don't l. your vegetables!** ¡no (te) dejes las verduras!

(**j**) *Math* **three from seven leaves four** siete menos tres son cuatro; **what does 29 from 88 l.?** ¿cuántas son 88 menos 29?

(**k**) *(in tennis)* **to l. the ball** dejar salir la pelota

(**l**) **to be left** *(remain)* quedar; **how many are there left?** ¿cuántos quedan?; **have you got any wine left?** ¿te queda vino?

3 *vi* (**a**) *(depart)* salir; *(go away)* irse, marcharse; **when are you leaving?** ¿cuándo te vas?; **which station do you l. from?** ¿de qué estación sales?; **he's just left for lunch** se acaba de ir a comer

(**b**) *(end relationship)* **Charles, I'm leaving!** Charles, te dejo

(**c**) *(in tennis)* **well left!** ¡bien dejada!

► **leave aside** *vt sep* dejar aparte *or* de lado; **leaving aside the question of money for the moment...** dejando aparte *or* de lado la cuestión del dinero de momento...; **leaving aside your salary, is there anything else you want to talk about?** aparte del sueldo, ¿hay alguna otra cosa de la que quieras hablar?

► **leave behind** *vt sep* **to l. sth behind** *(deliberately)* dejar algo; *(by mistake)* dejarse algo; **to l. sb behind** dejar a alguien; **he left the other athletes far behind** dejó a los demás atletas muy atrás; **quick, or we'll get left behind!** ¡date prisa *or Am* apúrate o nos quedaremos atrás!; **I got left behind at school** siempre iba retrasada en el colegio; **we don't want to get left behind our competitors** tenemos que evitar que nuestros competidores nos adelanten; **I've left all those problems behind (me)** he superado esos problemas

► **leave for** *vt insep (set off for)* salir hacia *or* para

► **leave in** *vt sep (retain)* dejar

► **leave off 1** *vt insep Fam* **to l. off doing sth** dejar de hacer algo; **to l. off work** dejar el trabajo

2 *vt sep* (**a**) *(not put on)* **who left the top of the toothpaste off?** ¿quién ha dejado la pasta de dientes sin cerrar?; **you can l. your jacket off** no hace falta que te pongas la chaqueta; **to l. sth/sb off a list** omitir algo/a alguien de una lista

(**b**) *(not switch on)* **to l. the light/TV off** dejar la luz/televisión apagada

3 *vi (stop)* **where did we l. off?** ¿dónde lo dejamos?; **the rain left off after lunch** dejó de llover después de la comida; **once the boss had gone, the party continued where it had left off** cuando el jefe se hubo marchado, la fiesta continuó donde la habíamos dejado; *Br Fam* **l. off, will you!** ¡ya basta!, ¿no?

► **leave on** *vt sep* (**a**) *(not take off) (garment)* dejarse puesto(a); *(top, cover)* dejar; **don't l. the price tag on** quítale el precio

(**b**) *(not switch off)* **to l. the light/TV on** dejar la luz/televisión encendida *or Am* prendida

► **leave out** *vt sep* (**a**) *(omit)* omitir; **he left out any mention of my contribution** omitió toda mención a mi colaboración; **to l. sb out of the team** dejar a alguien fuera del equipo

(**b**) *(not involve)* **to l. sb out of sth** dejar a alguien al margen de algo; **to feel left out** sentirse excluido(a)

(**c**) *(leave ready, available)* **I'll l. your dinner out on the table for you** te dejaré la cena encima de la mesa; **l. the disks out where I can see them** deja los disquetes donde pueda verlos

(**d**) *(not put away)* **we l. the car out on the street** dejamos el coche *or Am* carro *or RP* auto en la calle; **who left the milk out?** ¿quién ha dejado la leche fuera?

(**e**) *Br Fam* **l. it out!** *(stop it)* ¡basta ya!, *Esp* ¡vale ya!; *(expressing disbelief)* ¡anda ya!

► **leave over** *vt sep* **to be left over** *(of food, money)* sobrar; **we have a couple of apples left over** nos quedan un par de manzanas; **ten divided by three is three and one left over** diez entre tres cabe a tres y sobra una

► **leave up to** *vt sep (decision)* dejar en manos de; **I'll l. it up to you to decide** decide tú mismo

---

leaven ['levən] **1** *n* (**a**) *Culin* levadura *f* (**b**) *(improving element)* **he brought a l. of humour to the dullest occasion** aportaba su chispa de humor hasta en los momentos más aburridos

2 *vt* (**a**) *Culin* hacer fermentar (**b**) *(occasion, atmosphere)* amenizar

leaves *pl of* **leaf**

leave-taking ['li:vteɪkɪŋ] *n Literary* despedida *f*

leaving ['li:vɪŋ] *adj* **a l. ceremony** una ceremonia de despedida; **a l. present** un regalo de despedida ►► *Irish Sch* ***l. certificate*** = certificado de educación secundaria

leavings ['li:vɪŋz] *npl* sobras *fpl*, desperdicios *mpl*

Lebanese [lebə'ni:z] 1 *npl (people)* **the L.** los libaneses
2 *n* libanés(esa) *m,f*
3 *adj* libanés(esa)

Lebanon ['lebənən] *n* **(the) L.** el Líbano

lech [letʃ] *Fam* 1 *n (person)* sátiro *m*, salido(a) *m,f*, *Esp, Méx* cachondo(a); *(act)* calentura *f*
2 *vi* estar salido(a) *or Esp, Méx* cachondo(a) perdido(a) *or RP* caliente; **to l. after sb** ir detrás de alguien, *Esp* trajinarse *or Am* cogerse *or Méx* chingarse a alguien

lecher ['letʃə(r)] *n* sátiro *m*, obseso *m*

lecherous ['letʃərəs] *adj* lascivo(a), lujurioso(a)

lecherously ['letʃərəslɪ] *adv* lascivamente

lechery ['letʃərɪ] *n* lascivia *f*, lujuria *f*

lecithin ['lesɪθɪn] *n Biochem* lecitina *f*

lectern ['lektən] *n* atril *m*

lector ['lektə(r)] *n* **(a)** *Univ* profesor(ora) *m,f* **(b)** *Rel* = persona que lee las Sagradas Escrituras en misa

lecture ['lektʃə(r)] 1 *n* **(a)** *(public speech)* conferencia *f* ▸▸ ***l. hall*** sala *f* de conferencias; *US* ***l. theater*** sala *f* de conferencias; ***l. theatre*** sala *f* de conferencias **(b)** *(university class)* clase *f* ▸▸ ***l. hall*** aula *f*; ***l. notes*** *(of student)* apuntes *mpl* (de clase); *(published)* notas *fpl* de clase; ***l. theatre*** aula *f* **(c)** *Fam (reprimand)* sermón *m*; **to give sb a l.** echar un sermón a alguien, sermonear a alguien
2 *vt Fam (reprimand)* echar un sermón a, sermonear
3 *vi* **(a)** *(give public lectures)* dar conferencias **(b)** *(at university)* dar *or Am* dictar clases (**on/in** sobre/de)

lecturer ['lektʃərə(r)] *n* **(a)** *(speaker)* conferenciante *mf*, *Am* conferencista *mf* **(b)** *Br Univ* profesor(ora) *m,f* de universidad; **she's a l. in Physics at the University of Dublin** es profesora de física en la Universidad de Dublín; **is she a good l.?** ¿es buena profesora?; **assistant l.** profesor(ora) auxiliar

lectureship ['lektʃəʃɪp] *n Univ* plaza *f* de profesor(ora) de universidad

LED [eli:'di:] *n Elec* (*abbr* **light-emitting diode**) LED *m*, diodo *m* emisor de luz

led *pt & pp of* **lead**

ledge [ledʒ] *n* **(a)** *(on cliff)* saliente *m* **(b)** *(shelf)* repisa *f*; *(of window)* alféizar *m (exterior)*; *(on building)* cornisa *f*

ledger ['ledʒə(r)] *n* **(a)** *(for accounts)* libro *m* mayor **(b)** *Mus* ***l. line*** línea *f* auxiliar *or* suplementaria

lee [li:] 1 *n* **(a)** *Naut* sotavento *m* **(b)** *(shelter)* abrigo *m*; **in the l. of a hill** al abrigo de una colina
2 *adj* **l. shore** costa de sotavento

leech [li:tʃ] *n* **(a)** *(animal)* sanguijuela *f*; IDIOM **to cling** *or* **stick to sb like a l.** pegarse a alguien como una lapa **(b)** *Pej (parasitical person)* sanguijuela *f*, chupóptero(a) *m,f*

▸ **leech off** *vt insep Fam* **to l. off sb** chupar la sangre a alguien

▸ **leech on to** *vt insep Fam* **to l. on to sb** pegarse a alguien como una lapa

leek [li:k] *n* puerro *m*

leer ['lɪə(r)] 1 *n* mirada *f* lasciva
2 *vi* **to l. at sb** mirar lascivamente a alguien

leering ['lɪərɪŋ] *adj* lascivo(a)

leery ['lɪərɪ] *adj Fam* listo(a), avispado(a); **to be l. of sth/sb** recelar de algo/alguien

lees [li:z] *npl (of wine)* madre *f*, heces *fpl*; IDIOM **to drink life to the l.** acar el máximo jugo a la vida

leeward ['li:wəd] 1 *n* sotavento *m*; **to l.** a sotavento
2 *adj* de sotavento ▸▸ ***the L. Islands*** las Islas de Sotavento

leeway ['li:weɪ] *n* **(a)** *(freedom)* **she was given plenty of l.** le dieron mucha libertad de acción *or* mucho margen de maniobra; **half an hour doesn't give us much l.** media hora no nos da mucho margen **(b)** *(lost time, progress)* **we have a lot of l. to make up** tenemos que recuperar el retraso que llevamos **(c)** *Av & Naut (drift)* deriva *f*

LEFT[1] [left] 1 *n* **(a)** *(position)* izquierda *f*; **she's second from the l. in the picture** es la segunda por *or Am* desde la izquierda en la fotografía; **on** *or* **to the l. (of)** a la izquierda (de); **the one on the l.** el/la de la izquierda; **on my l.** a mi izquierda; **turn to the l.** girar *or* torcer a la izquierda; *US* **to make** *or* **take a l.** girar *or* torcer a la izquierda
(b) *Pol* **the l.** la izquierda; **she is further to the l. than her husband** está más a la izquierda que su marido
(c) *(in boxing)* **a l. to the jaw** un izquierdazo *or* zurdazo en la mandíbula
2 *adj* **(a)** *(in position)* izquierdo(a); **to take a l. turn** girar *or* torcer a la izquierda; IDIOM **to have two l. feet** ser un pato mareado bailando, *Am* ser un pata dura ▸▸ ***l. back*** lateral *m* izquierdo; ***the L. Bank*** la orilla izquierda (del Sena); ***l. field*** *(in baseball)* extracampo *m or* exterior *m* izquierdo; IDIOM *US* **to be out in l. field** ser totalmente excéntrico(a); IDIOM **to come out of l. field: his question came out of l. field** hizo una pregunta totalmente inesperada; ***l. fielder*** *(in baseball)* exterior *m* izquierdo; ***l. hook*** *(in boxing)* gancho *m* izquierdo
(b) *Pol (party)* de izquierda; **the l. wing** la izquierda; **a l. of centre party** un partido de centro-izquierda
(c) *Comptr* ***l. arrow*** flecha *f* izquierda; ***l. arrow key*** tecla *f* de flecha izquierda
3 *adv* a la izquierda; **take the first/second l.** métete por la primera/segunda a la izquierda; *Fig* **l., right and centre** por todas partes

---

left[2] *pt & pp of* **leave**

left-click [left'klɪk] 1 *vt* hacer click con el botón izquierdo en
2 *vi* hacer click con el botón izquierdo

left-field ['left'fi:ld] *adj US Fam (unexpected)* inesperado(a)

left-footer [left'fʊtə(r)] *n Br Fam (Roman Catholic)* católico(a) *m,f*

left-hand ['left'hænd] *adj* de la izquierda; **on the l. side** a la izquierda; **in the top/bottom l. corner** en el ángulo superior/inferior izquierdo ▸▸ ***l. drive*** *(vehicle)* vehículo *m* con el volante a la izquierda

left-handed [left'hændɪd] 1 *adj* **(a)** *(person)* zurdo(a) **(b)** *(scissors, golf clubs)* para zurdos **(c)** *(blow, punch, shot)* con la izquierda **(d)** *(ambiguous)* **to say that I was smart for a girl was a l. compliment** decir que para ser una chica era inteligente me pareció un elogio insultante
2 *adv* con la izquierda *or* zurda

left-hander [left'hændə(r)] *n* **(a)** *(person)* zurdo(a) *m,f* **(b)** *(blow)* izquierdazo *m*, zurdazo *m*

leftie = **lefty**

leftism ['leftɪzəm] *n* izquierdismo *m*

leftist ['leftɪst] *Pol* 1 *n* izquierdista *mf*
2 *adj* izquierdista, de izquierdas

left luggage ['left'lʌgɪdʒ] *n Br* **l. (office)** consigna *f*

left-of-centre ['leftəv'sentə(r)] *adj Pol* de centroizquierda

leftover ['leftəʊvə(r)] 1 *npl* **leftovers** *(food)* sobras *fpl*
2 *adj (food, paint)* sobrante

leftward ['leftwəd] 1 *adj* a la izquierda
2 *adv* = **leftwards**

leftwards ['leftwədz] *adv* a la izquierda

left-wing ['leftwɪŋ] *adj Pol* izquierdista, de izquierdas

left-winger ['left'wɪŋə(r)] *n* **(a)** *Pol* izquierdista *mf* **(b)** *(in field sports)* izquierda *mf*

lefty, leftie ['leftɪ] *n Fam* **(a)** *Pol* izquierdoso(a) *m,f*, izquierdista *mf*, *RP* zurdo(a) *m,f* **(b)** *US (left-handed person)* zocato(a) *m,f*, zurdo(a) *m,f*

leg [leg] 1 *n* **(a)** *(of person)* pierna *f*; *(of animal)* pata *f*; **his legs went from under him** le cedieron las piernas; **she ran as fast as her legs could carry her** corrió tan deprisa como pudo
(b) *Culin (of lamb, pork)* pierna *f*; *(of chicken)* muslo *m*
(c) *(of trousers)* pernera *f*
(d) *(of table, chair, tripod)* pata *f*
(e) *(stage) (of journey, race)* etapa *f*; *(of relay race)* relevo *m*; **they won the first/second l.** ganaron la primera/segunda etapa
(f) IDIOMS **to pull sb's l.** tomar el pelo a alguien; **shake a l.!** ¡muévete!; **to show a l.** *(get up)* levantarse; **you don't have a l. to stand on** no tienes a qué agarrarte; **he was given a l. up** *(was helped)* le echaron una mano *or* un cable, *RP* le dieron una mano; *Br very Fam* **to get one's l. over** *(have sex)* echar un polvo *or Cuba* palo, *Am* coger, *Méx* chingar
2 *vt* (*pt & pp* **legged**) *Fam* **to l. it** *(hurry)* salir zumbando; *(flee)* esfumarse, abrirse

legacy ['legəsɪ] *n* **(a)** *(legal inheritance)* legado *m*; **to come into a l.** heredar **(b)** *(leftover)* legado *m*; **the crisis left a l. of bitterness** la crisis dejó un legado amargo; **this problem is a l. of the last government's neglect** este problema es herencia directa de la negligencia del anterior gobierno

legal ['li:gəl] 1 *adj* **(a)** *(lawful, legitimate)* legal; **the procedure is entirely l.** el procedimiento es totalmente legal; **to make sth l.** legalizar algo; **to be l. and binding** ser válido(a) y de obligado cumplimiento; **to be the l. owner** ser el/la propietario(a) legítimo(a), ser el/la dueño(a) en derecho; **they're below the l. age** no tienen la edad legal; **to be above the l. limit** *(for drinking)* exceder la tasa *or* el límite legal (de alcoholemia) ▸▸ *US* ***l. holiday*** día *m* festivo
(b) *(concerning the law)* legal, jurídico(a); **the l. profession** la

profesión jurídica; **to take l. action (against sb)** presentar una demanda (contra alguien); **to initiate l. proceedings against sb** iniciar un procedimiento judicial contra alguien ►► ***l. advice*** asesoría *f* jurídica *or* legal; **to take l. advice** asesorarse jurídicamente; ***l. aid*** asistencia *f* jurídica de oficio; ***l. aid lawyer*** abogado(a) *m,f* de oficio; ***l. costs*** costas *fpl* (judiciales); ***l. eagle*** *(successful lawyer)* = abogado de éxito, especialmente joven, brillante y dinámico; *US* ***l. pad*** bloc *m* de notas *(de 216mm x 356mm)*; ***l. status*** personalidad *f* jurídica; ***l. system*** sistema *m* legal; ***l. technicality*** tecnicismo *m* legal; ***l. tender*** moneda *f* de curso legal; ***l. vacuum*** vacío *m* legal

2 *n (paper size)* = tamaño de papel de 216mm x 356mm, utilizado sobre todo en Estados Unidos

legalese [li:gə'li:z] *n Fam Pej* jerga *f* legal

legalistic [li:gə'lɪstɪk] *adj* legalista

legality [lɪ'gælɪtɪ] *n* legalidad *f*

legalization [li:gəlaɪ'zeɪʃən] *n* legalización *f*

legalize ['li:gəlaɪz] *vt* legalizar

legally ['li:gəlɪ] *adv* legalmente; **to be l. entitled to (do) sth** tener el derecho legal a (hacer) algo; **to be held l. responsible for sth** tener la responsabilidad legal de algo; **to be l. binding** ser (legalmente) vinculante; **l., there is no reason why...** legalmente, no hay ninguna razón por la que...

legate ['legɪt] *n Rel* nuncio *m*

legatee [legə'ti:] *n Law* legatario(a) *m,f*

legation [lɪ'geɪʃən] *n (diplomatic mission)* legación *f*

legend ['ledʒənd] *n* **(a)** *(traditional story)* leyenda *f*; **to be a l. in one's own lifetime** ser una leyenda viva; *Fam Hum* **he's a l. in his own lunchtime** es muy conocido en su casa a la hora de comer **(b)** *(on map)* leyenda *f*, signos *mpl* convencionales **(c)** *(inscription)* leyenda *f*

legendary ['ledʒəndərɪ] *adj* legendario(a)

legerdemain [ledʒədə'meɪn] *n (trickery)* tejemanejes *mpl*

-legged ['legɪd, legd] *suffix* **short/hairy-l.** *(person)* de piernas cortas/vellosas; *(animal)* de patas cortas/peludas

leggings ['legɪŋz] *npl (of woman)* mallas *fpl*

leggy ['legɪ] *adj* **a l. blonde** una rubia todo piernas

legibility [ledʒɪ'bɪlɪtɪ] *n* legibilidad *f*

legible ['ledʒɪbəl] *adj* legible

legibly ['ledʒɪblɪ] *adv* de forma legible

legion ['li:dʒən] **1** *n Hist* legión *f*

2 *adj Formal* **such cases are l.** los casos así son innumerables *or* incontables

legionary ['li:dʒənərɪ] *n* legionario *m*

legionnaire [li:dʒə'neə(r)] *n* legionario *m* ►► *Med* ***Legionnaire's Disease*** enfermedad *f* del legionario, legionella *f*, legionela *f*

leg-iron ['legaɪən] *n (shackle)* grillete *m*

legislate ['ledʒɪsleɪt] *vi* legislar (**against/in favour of** en contra de/a favor de); **it is difficult to l. for every eventuality** es difícil que la legislación prevea todos los casos; **child labour had been legislated out of existence by 1900** en 1900 la legislación había erradicado ya el trabajo de los menores

legislation [ledʒɪs'leɪʃən] *n* legislación *f*; **the existing l. is inadequate** la actual legislación *or* la legislación en vigor resulta insuficiente; **a piece of l.** una ley; **to bring in new l. against/in favour of sth** introducir *or* aprobar nuevas leyes en contra de/a favor de algo

legislative ['ledʒɪslətɪv] *adj* legislativo(a); **a l. assembly** una asamblea legislativa

legislator ['ledʒɪsleɪtə(r)] *n* legislador(ora) *m,f*

legislature ['ledʒɪslətjə(r)] *n* asamblea *f* legislativa; **the three branches of government: the l., the executive and the judiciary** los tres poderes: legislativo, ejecutivo y judicial

legit [lɪ'dʒɪt] *adj Fam* legal

legitimacy [lɪ'dʒɪtɪməsɪ] *n* legitimidad *f*

legitimate **1** *adj* [lɪ'dʒɪtɪmət] **(a)** *(legal, lawful)* legítimo(a); **l. child** hijo(a) legítimo(a); **l. heir** legítimo(a) heredero(a) **(b)** *(valid, reasonable)* legítimo(a), justificado(a); **a l. cause for complaint** un motivo de queja justificado *or* legítimo; *Formal* **it would be l. to question her right to the property** cabe poner en tela de juicio su derecho a la propiedad **(c)** *Theat* ***l. theatre*** teatro *m* tradicional

2 *vt* [lɪ'dʒɪtɪmeɪt] legitimar

legitimately [lɪ'dʒɪtɪmətlɪ] *adv* **(a)** *(legally, lawfully)* legítimamente **(b)** *(validly, reasonably)* **one may l. doubt this story** uno puede con razón llegar a dudar de esta historia

legitimize [lɪ'dʒɪtɪmaɪz] *vt* legitimar

legless ['leglɪs] *adj* **(a)** *(without legs) (person)* sin piernas; *(animal)* sin patas **(b)** *Br Fam (drunk) Esp, Méx* pedo *inv*, *Col* caído(a), *Méx* cuete, *RP* en pedo

leg-man ['legmæn] *n US* **(a)** *Journ* reportero *m* en la calle **(b)** *(errand boy)* chico *m* de los recados

Lego® ['legəʊ] *n* Lego® *m*

leg-of-mutton ['legəv'mʌtən] *adj (sleeve)* de jamón, ceñida abajo

leg-pull ['legpʊl] *n Fam* tomadura *f* de pelo, vacile *m*

legroom ['legrʊm] *n* espacio *m* para las piernas

legume ['legju:m] *n Bot* legumbre *f*

leguminous [le'gju:mɪnəs] *adj* leguminoso(a)

legwarmers ['legwɔ:məz] *npl* calentadores *mpl*, calientapiernas *mpl*

legwork ['legwɜ:k] *n* **who's going to do the l.?** *(walking)* ¿quién se va a patear la calle?; **she got the credit after I'd done all the l.** *(hard work)* ella se llevó los elogios, después de que me lo había trabajado yo

Le Havre [lə'hɑ:vrə] *n* el Havre

lei [leɪ] (*pl* **leis**) *n* collar *m* de flores, pancarpia *f (de bienvenida)*

Leics (*abbr* **Leicestershire**) (condado *m* de) Leicester

leisure ['leʒə(r), *US* 'li:ʒər] *n* ocio *m*; **a life of l.** una vida de ocio; **he's a man of l.** lleva una vida de ocio; **to have the l. to do sth** disponer de tiempo para hacer algo; **take these leaflets and read them at your l.** llévate estos folletos y léetelos con tranquilidad ►► ***l. activities*** actividades *fpl* para el tiempo libre; ***l. centre*** polideportivo *m*; ***the l. industry*** la industria del ocio; ***the l. sector*** el sector cuaternario; ***the l. society*** la sociedad del ocio; ***l. time*** tiempo *m* de ocio; ***l. wear*** ropa *f* de sport

leisured ['leʒəd, *US* 'li:ʒəd] *adj* ocioso(a); **the l. classes** la gente que lleva una vida de ocio

leisurely ['leʒəlɪ, *US* 'li:ʒərlɪ] *adj* pausado(a), tranquilo(a); **at a l. pace** con ritmo pausado; **to do sth in a l. fashion** hacer algo con tranquilidad

leitmotif, leitmotiv ['laɪtməʊti:f] *n (in novel, music)* leitmotiv *m*

lemme ['lemɪ] *exclam Fam* = **let me**

lemming ['lemɪŋ] *n* lemming *m*; IDIOM **they followed him like lemmings** lo siguieron ciegamente

lemon ['lemən] **1** *n* **(a)** *(fruit)* limón *m*, *Méx, Ven* limón *m* francés ►► ***l. cheese*** crema *f* de limón; *Br* ***l. curd*** crema *f* de limón; ***l. drop*** caramelo *m* de limón; *US* ***l. juicer*** exprimidor *m*, exprimelimones *m inv*; ***l. meringue pie*** tarta *f* de limón y merengue, *Méx* pay de limón; ***l. peel*** piel *f or RP* cáscara *f* de limón; *Br* ***l. squash*** (refresco *m*) concentrado *m* de limón; ***l. squeezer*** exprimidor *m*, exprimelimones *m inv*; ***l. tea*** té *m* con limón; ***l. tree*** limonero *m*

(b) *(colour)* **l. (yellow)** amarillo *m* limón

(c) *(plant)* ***l. balm*** melisa *f*, toronjil *m*; ***l. grass*** lemongrass *m*; ***l. verbena*** hierbaluisa *f*

(d) ***l. sole*** mendo *m* limón

(e) *Br Fam* **I felt like a real l.** me sentí como un verdadero merluzo

(f) *Fam (worthless, useless thing or person)* desastre *m*, *Esp* patata *f* ►► *US* ***l. law*** = ley que obliga a los fabricantes de vehículos a reembolsar o reemplazar las piezas defectuosas

2 *adj* **l. (coloured)** (color) amarillo limón

lemonade [lemə'neɪd] *n* **(a)** *(still)* limonada *f* **(b)** *Br (fizzy) Esp, Arg* gaseosa *f*, *Am* gaseosa *f* de lima *or* limón

lemony ['lemənɪ] *adj (taste)* a limón; *(sauce)* con sabor a limón; *(colour)* amarillo(a) limón

lempira [lem'pɪərə] *n (currency of Honduras)* lempira *f*

lemur ['li:mə(r)] *n* lémur *m*

lend [lend] (*pt & pp* **lent** [lent]) *vt* **(a)** *(money, book, pen)* prestar; **to l. sb sth, to l. sth (out) to sb** prestar algo a alguien; **to l. sb a (helping) hand** echar una mano a alguien; **to l. an ear** *or* **one's ear to...** escuchar de buena gana a...; **to l. one's name to sth** prestar su nombre para algo

(b) *(dignity, support, credibility)* proporcionar, prestar (**to** a); **to l. weight to a theory** dar peso a *or* reforzar una teoría

(c) *(be amenable)* **her work doesn't l. itself to being filmed** su obra no se presta a ser llevada al cine

lender ['lendə(r)] *n Fin (person)* prestamista *mf*; *(institution)* entidad *f* de crédito

lending ['lendɪŋ] *n Fin* préstamos *mpl*, créditos *mpl* ►► *Fin* ***l. institution*** entidad *f* de crédito; ***l. library*** biblioteca *f* de préstamo; *Fin* ***l. rate*** tipo *m or Am* tasa *f* de interés de los préstamos *or* créditos

length [leŋθ] *n* **(a)** *(in space)* longitud *f*, largo *m*; **it's 4.5 metres in l.** tiene 4,5 metros de longitud *or* largo; **what l. is the room?** ¿cuánto mide de largo la habitación?, *Am* ¿qué largo tiene la habitación?; **we walked the l. of the garden** caminamos hasta el final del jardín;

flower beds ran the l. of the street había parterres a lo largo de la calle; **the ship can turn in its own l.** el barco puede virar sobre sí mismo; **to travel the l. and breadth of the country** viajar a lo largo y ancho del país
(b) *(in time)* duración *f*; **the l. of time required to do sth** el tiempo necesario para hacer algo; **at (great) l.** extensamente; **at l., I realized that...** con el tiempo, me di cuenta de que...; **a great l. of time** un largo periodo de tiempo; **l. of service** antigüedad en la empresa
(c) *(of text)* extensión *f*; **articles must be less than 5,000 words in l.** los artículos deben tener una extensión menor de 5.000 palabras; **his essay was a bit over/under l.** su trabajo era un tanto extenso/breve
(d) *(effort)* **to go to the l. of doing sth** llegar incluso a hacer algo; **to go to considerable** *or* **great lengths to do sth** tomarse muchas molestias para hacer algo; **I never dreamed that they would go to such lengths** nunca habría imaginado que llegarían a esos extremos; **he would go to any lengths (to do sth)** estaría dispuesto a cualquier cosa (con tal de hacer algo)
(e) *(piece) (of string)* trozo *m*; *(of pipe)* tramo *m*; *(of wallpaper)* tira *f*; *(of fabric)* largo *m*; **cut the plank into four equal lengths** corte el tablón a lo largo en cuatro trozos iguales; **what l. of material do I need to make these curtains?** ¿cuántos metros de tela necesito para hacer estas cortinas?
(f) *(of swimming pool)* largo *m*; **to swim twenty lengths** hacerse veinte largos
(g) *(in horse racing, rowing)* cuerpo *m*; **to win by a l./by half a l.** ganar por un cuerpo/medio cuerpo
(h) *Ling (of syllable, vowel)* longitud *f*

lengthen ['leŋθən] **1** *vt* (a) *(garment)* alargar (b) *(holiday, visit)* alargar (c) *Ling (vowel)* alargar
2 *vi (shadow, day)* alargarse

lengthily ['leŋθɪlɪ] *adv* extensamente, dilatadamente

lengthiness ['leŋθɪnɪs] *n* **the l. of the novel means few read it today** como la novela es tan extensa *or* larga pocos la leen hoy en día; **the l. of the wait began to annoy them** la larga espera comenzó a enojarlos

lengthways ['leŋθweɪz], **lengthwise** ['leŋθwaɪz] **1** *adj* longitudinal
2 *adv* a lo largo, longitudinalmente

lengthy ['leŋθɪ] *adj* largo(a), dilatado(a)

leniency ['li:nɪənsɪ], **lenience** ['li:nɪəns] *n (of person)* indulgencia *f*, benevolencia *f*; *(of punishment)* poca severidad *f*

lenient ['li:nɪənt] *adj (person)* indulgente, benévolo(a) (**to** *or* **with** con); *(punishment)* poco severo(a)

leniently ['li:nɪəntlɪ] *adv* con indulgencia, benévolamente

Leningrad ['lenɪngræd] *n Formerly* Leningrado

Leninism ['lenɪnɪzəm] *n* leninismo *m*

Leninist ['lenɪnɪst] **1** *n* leninista *mf*
2 *adj* leninista

lens [lenz] *n* (a) *(of glasses)* cristal *m*, lente *f*, *Am* vidrio *m*; **(contact) lenses** *Esp* lentillas *fpl*, *Am* lentes *fpl* de contacto, *Méx* pupilentes *fpl* (b) *(of camera)* objetivo *m*, lente *f*; *(of microscope, telescope)* lente *f* ►► ***l. cap*** tapa *f* del objetivo; ***l. hood*** parasol *m* (c) *(of eye)* cristalino *m*

Lent [lent] *n Rel* cuaresma *f*; **I've given up sugar for L.** durante la cuaresma he dejado de tomar azúcar

lent *pt & pp of* **lend**

lentil ['lentɪl] *n* lenteja *f*; **l. soup/stew** sopa/guiso de lentejas

lento ['lentəʊ] *Mus* (a) *n* (*pl* **lentos**) lento *m* (b) *adv* lento

Leo ['li:əʊ] *n (sign of zodiac)* Leo *m*; **to be (a) L.** ser Leo

leonine ['li:ənaɪn] *adj Literary* leonino(a)

leopard ['lepəd] *n* leopardo *m*; PROV **a l. never changes its spots** la cabra siempre tira al monte

leopardess [lepə'des] *n* leopardo *m* hembra

leopard-skin ['lepədskɪn] *adj* de piel de leopardo

leotard ['li:ətɑ:d] *n* malla *f*

LEP [eli:'pi:] *n US* (*abbr* **limited English proficiency**) = clasificación otorgada a personas con conocimientos limitados de inglés, quienes reciben clases especiales del idioma; **L. students** alumnos con conocimientos limitados de inglés

leper ['lepə(r)] *n* (a) *Med* leproso(a) *m,f* ►► ***l. colony*** leprosería *f*, lazareto *m* (b) *Fig* **a moral l.** un indeseable; **a social l.** un paria

lepidopterist [lepɪ'dɒptərɪst] *n* especialista *mf* en lepidópteros

leprechaun ['leprəkɔ:n] *n* duende *m (de las leyendas irlandesas)*

leprosy ['leprəsɪ] *n* lepra *f*

leprous ['leprəs] *adj* leproso(a)

lepton ['leptɒn] *n Phys* leptón *m*

lesbian ['lezbɪən] **1** *n* lesbiana *f*
2 *adj* lésbico(a), lesbiano(a)

lesbianism ['lezbɪənɪzəm] *n* lesbianismo *m*

lesbo ['lezbəʊ] *n very Fam Pej* tortillera *f*, *Esp* bollera *f*

lese-majesty [leɪz'mædʒəstɪ] *n (treason)* delito *m* de lesa majestad

lesion ['li:ʒən] *n Med* lesión *f*

Lesotho [lɪ'su:tu:] *n* Lesoto

LESS [les] **1** *adj* (*comparative of* **little**) menos; **I drink l. beer these days** ahora bebo menos cerveza; **the distance is l. than we thought** la distancia es menor de lo que pensábamos
2 *prep* menos; **a year l. two days** un año menos dos días; **I've got £50, l. what I spent on food** tengo 50 libras, menos lo que me he gastado en comida
3 *pron* menos; **the more I get to know him, the l. I like him** cuanto más lo conozco, menos me gusta; **can I have l. of the soup?** ¿podría tomar un poco menos de sopa?; **I see l. of her nowadays** la veo menos ahora; **it is l. of an issue these days** ahora es menos polémico; **I don't think any (the) l. of you** no pienso peor de ti; **despite what happened, I don't respect you any the l.** a pesar de lo que ocurrió, te sigo respetando tanto como antes; **in l. than an hour** en menos de una hora; **in l. than no time** instantáneamente; **I eat l. than before** como menos que antes; **I was l. hurt than disappointed** no estaba tanto dolido como decepcionado; **the l. said about it the better** cuanto menos se hable de ello, mejor; **she was driving a Rolls, no l.** conducía nada menos que un Rolls; **who should I meet there but the Queen, no l.!** ¿qué te parece? ¡conocí nada menos que a la reina!; **I expected no l. from you** no esperaba menos de ti; **there were no l. than 10,000 people there** había por lo menos 10.000 personas; **no more, no l.** ni más ni menos; IDIOM **l. is more** cuanto menos mejor; *Fam* **l. of that!** ¡basta ya!, *Méx* ¡ya párale!; *Fam* **I'll have l. of your lip!** no seas insolente
4 *adv* menos; **you should think l. and act more** deberías pensar menos y actuar más; **we go there l. often** vamos menos por allí; **l. and l.** cada vez menos; **it's l. than a week's work** es menos de una semana de trabajo; **you're being l. than generous** no estás siendo nada generoso; **it looked l. like a kitchen than a cupboard** parecía más un armario que una cocina; **they haven't got a fridge, much l. a freezer** no tienen nevera y mucho menos congelador; **nothing l. than** nada menos que; **still l., even l.** todavía menos

---

-less [ləs] *suffix* **expressionless** inexpresivo; **shameless** desvergonzado; **trouserless** sin pantalones

lessee [le'si:] *n Law* arrendatario(a) *m,f*

lessen ['lesən] **1** *vt (pain)* aliviar; *(risk, danger, intensity)* reducir, disminuir; *(impact)* amortiguar; *(damage, effect)* mitigar, paliar
2 *vi (pain)* aliviarse; *(risk, danger, intensity)* disminuir, reducirse

lesser ['lesə(r)] *adj* menor; **to a l. extent** *or* **degree** en menor medida; **a l. person** una persona de menor valía; *Hum* **l. mortals like me** simples mortales como yo; IDIOM **the l. of two evils** el mal menor ►► ***l. kestrel*** cernícalo *m* primilla; ***l. whitethroat*** curruca *f* zarcerilla

lesser-known ['lesə'nəʊn] *adj* menos conocido(a)

lesson ['lesən] *n* (a) *(session)* clase *f*; **a geography l.** una clase de geografía; **a dancing l.** una clase de baile; **to give a l.** dar una clase; **to take lessons in sth** recibir clases de algo
(b) *(in book)* lección *f*; **Spanish in 30 lessons** español en 30 lecciones
(c) *(example)* lección; **her downfall was a l. to us all** su caída nos sirvió de lección a todos; **he has learnt his l.** ha aprendido la lección; **to teach sb a l.** dar una lección a alguien; **let that be a l. to you!** ¡que te sirva de lección *or* escarmiento!
(d) *Rel* lectura *f*

lessor [le'sɔ:(r)] *n Law* arrendador(ora) *m,f*

lest [lest] *conj Literary* (a) *(in case)* para que no, por si; **they whispered l. the children should hear** susurraban para que no lo oyesen los niños; **l. we forget...** para que no olvidemos... (b) *(after verbs of fearing)* **I feared l. he should fall** temía que se cayera

let[1] [let] *n (in tennis)* servicio *m* nulo, net *m*; **to play a l.** repetir un punto *(de net)*

let[2] **1** *n* (a) *Br (property)* **a short l.** un alquiler *or Méx* una renta por un periodo corto; **she took a six-month l. on the house** alquiló *or Méx* rentó la casa por seis meses (b) *Law* **without l. or hindrance** sin obstáculo *or* impedimento alguno
2 *vt* (*pt & pp* **let**) *Br (rent out)* alquilar, *Méx* rentar; **to l.** *(sign)* se alquila, *Méx* se renta

---

LET[3] **1** *vt* (*pt & pp* **let**) (a) *(allow)* **to l. sb do sth** dejar a alguien hacer algo; **to l. sth happen** dejar que ocurra algo; **to l. one's beard grow** dejarse (crecer la) barba; **l. the engine cool down** deja que se enfríe el motor; **don't l. yourself be fooled** no te dejes engañar no dejes que te engañen; **l. me help you with that box** deja que te ayude con esa caja; **l. me begin by saying how grateful I am** para comenzar, deseo decirles lo agradecido que estoy; **l. me explain what I mean** déjame que te explique (lo que quiero decir); **l. him say what he likes, I don't care** que diga lo que quiera, me da igual; **don't l. it be said I didn't try** que no se diga que no lo intenté; **don't l. it get to you** *or* **get you down** no dejes que eso pueda contigo; **to l. go of sth, to l. sth go** soltar algo; **to l. sb go** *(release)* soltar a alguien; **l. go, it hurts!** ¡suelta, que me duele!; **whatever you do, don't l. go** *(of rope, support)* hagas lo que hagas, no sueltes; **to l. go of one's inhibitions** desinhibirse; **it hurt terribly to l. her go** me dolió muchísimo perderla; **we have decided to l. the matter go** hemos decidido pasar por alto el asunto; **I'm afraid we'll have to l. you go** *(on making somebody redundant)* me temo que vamos a tener que prescindir de usted; **to l. oneself go** *(lose restraint)* descontrolarse, soltarse *Esp* el pelo *or Méx* la greña *or Ven* el moño; *(stop caring for one's appearance)* abandonarse, *RP* venirse abajo; **I never l. a day go by without...** no dejo pasar un día sin...; **I l. him have my bike** le dejé mi bicicleta; **can you l. me have it back tomorrow?** ¿me lo puedes devolver mañana?; *Fam* **she really l. me have it when she found out** me hizo saber lo que es bueno cuando se enteró; **to l. sb know sth** avisar a alguien de algo; **she l. it be known that she was not happy** dejó claro que no era feliz; **to l. loose** *(person, animal)* soltar; **we l. the children loose on the food** dejamos que los niños se abalanzaran sobre la comida; **to l. sth pass** *or* **go** *(not criticize, comment on)* dejar pasar algo, pasar algo por alto; **l. me see** *(show me)* déjame ver; *(when answering)* veamos, a ver; **don't l. me see you here again!** ¡que no te vuelva a ver por aquí!; **I was nervous, but I tried not to l. it show** estaba nervioso, pero traté de que no se notara; **l. me think** ¿a ver...?, déjame pensar; **to l. sb be** *or* **alone** dejar a alguien en paz; **to l. things be** dejar las cosas como están; *Fig* **to l. it drop** dejarlo, olvidarse del tema; *Fam Fig* **to l. it all hang out** descontrolarse, soltarse *Esp* la melena *or Méx* la greña *or Ven* el moño; *Fig* **to l. it lie** olvidar el tema; *Fig* **to l. sth ride** no hacer nada por evitar algo; *Fig* **to l. things slide** tener las cosas abandonadas, dejar que las cosas degeneren; **he l. it slip that...** *(unintentionally)* se le escapó que...; *(intentionally)* dejó caer que...

(**b**) *(with suggestions, orders)* **let's go!** ¡vamos!; **let's hurry!** ¡deprisa!; **l. them wait!** ¡que esperen!; **let's dance!** vamos a bailar; **let's have the day off!** ¿por qué no nos tomamos el día libre?; **shall we go to the cinema? – oh yes, let's** *or* **do let's!** ¿vamos al cine? – ¡sí, sí, vamos!; **l. HER explain, it's nothing to do with me** que lo explique ella, yo no tengo nada que ver; **let's get this clear** vamos a dejar esto claro; **l. us move on to the next point** pasemos al siguiente punto; **let's see what we can do** a ver qué podemos hacer; **l. the dancing begin!** ¡que empiece el baile!; **let's not have an argument about it!** ¡no nos peleemos por eso!; **now, don't let's have any nonsense!** ¡bueno, y nada de tonterías!; **just l. him try!** ¡que lo intente (y verá)!; *Formal* **l. he who disagrees speak now** quien no esté de acuerdo, que hable ahora; *Rel* **l. there be light** hágase la luz; *Rel* **l. us pray** oremos

(**c**) *(with hypotheses)* **l. us suppose that...** supongamos que...; *Math* **l. AB be equal to CD** sea AB igual a CD; **let's say (that) they do win** pongamos que ganan; **take any number, let's say seven** tomemos un número, por ejemplo (el) siete; **how did she react? – let's just say she wasn't delighted** ¿cómo reaccionó? – digamos que no se puso a dar saltos de alegría

(**d**) *(to express wish)* **please don't l. it be true!** ¡por favor, que no sea verdad!; **let's hope she's right** esperemos que tenga razón

2 *vi* **to l. drop that...** dejar caer que...; **to l. fly** *or* **rip** *(lose temper)* ponerse hecho(a) una furia

3 let alone *conj* mucho menos, menos aún; **I can't even speak French, l. alone Chinese** no hablo francés, y menos aún chino

▸ **let by** *vt sep (allow to pass)* **to l. sb by** dejar pasar a alguien

▸ **let down** *vt sep* (**a**) *(move downwards) (rope, package, person)* bajar; *Fig* **to l. sb down gently** darle la noticia a alguien suavemente; *Fig* **to l. one's hair down** soltarse el pelo

(**b**) *(hem, skirt, trousers)* bajar

(**c**) *(tyre)* deshinchar, desinflar

(**d**) *Fam (disappoint, fail)* **to l. sb down** fallar a alguien; **the car l. us down again** el coche *or Am* carro *or RP* auto nos dejó tirados otra vez; **Woods was l. down by his inexperience** a Woods lo perdió su falta de experiencia; **I feel l. down** siento que me has/han/*etc* fallado; *Br Fig* **don't l. the side down!** ¡no nos falles!, ¡no nos dejes tirados!

▸ **let in** *vt sep* (**a**) *(allow to enter)* dejar pasar *or* entrar; **l. me in!** ¡déjame pasar *or* entrar!; **I l. myself in** *(to house)* entré con mi llave; **to l. in the light** dejar que entre la luz; **my shoes are letting in water** me están calando los zapatos; **he l. in three goals** le metieron tres goles

(**b**) *Aut* **to l. in the clutch** embragar

▸ **let in for** *vt sep Fam* **do you know what you are letting yourself in for?** ¿tienes idea de en qué te estás metiendo?

▸ **let in on** *vt sep* **to l. sb in on a secret/plan** contar a alguien un secreto/plan; **they decided to let him in on the deal** decidieron dejarle entrar en el trato

▸ **let into** *vt sep* (**a**) *(allow to enter)* dejar entrar en; **I l. myself into the house** entré en la casa con mi llave

(**b**) *Constr* **to l. a window into a wall** abrir *or* hacer una ventana en un muro

(**c**) *(tell)* **I'll l. you into a secret** te contaré un secreto

▸ **let off 1** *vt sep* (**a**) *(bomb, firework)* hacer explotar; *(gun)* disparar

(**b**) *(emit) (gas)* emitir, despedir; *Fig* **to l. off steam** desfogarse

(**c**) *(forgive)* perdonar; **they l. him off with a fine** sólo le pusieron una multa; **we were l. off lightly** salimos bien librados; *Fam* **sorry! – I'll l. you off** ¡perdón! – te perdono, no pasa nada

(**d**) *(allow to leave)* **we were l. off school early** nos dejaron salir pronto del colegio; **they l. us off the bus** nos dejaron salir del autobús

(**e**) *(allow not to do)* **I've been l. off doing the cleaning** me he librado de hacer la limpieza; **she l. me off the £5** me perdonó las 5 libras

2 *vi Br Fam (fart)* tirarse un pedo

▸ **let on 1** *vi Fam* **to l. on about sth** contar algo, decir algo; **don't l. on that I was there** no digas que estuve allí; **he was more ill than he l. on** estaba más enfermo de lo que decía

2 *vt sep (allow to embark)* dejar subir

▸ **let out 1** *vt sep* (**a**) *(release)* dejar salir; **l. me out!** ¡déjame salir!; **he l. himself out of the back door** salió sin que nadie le acompañara por la puerta trasera; **to l. out the air from sth** desinflar *or* deshinchar algo; **to l. out a yell** soltar un grito

(**b**) *(jacket, trousers)* agrandar

(**c**) *Aut* **to l. out the clutch** desembragar

(**d**) *(rent)* alquilar

2 *vi US (finish)* terminar, acabar

▸ **let through** *vt sep* (**a**) *(allow to pass) (person)* dejar pasar

(**b**) *(overlook) (mistake)* **we can't afford to l. any mistakes through** no podemos permitir que se nos pase ni un error

▸ **let up** *vi* (**a**) *(diminish) (weather)* amainar; **the rain didn't l. up all day** la lluvia no amainó en todo el día

(**b**) *(relax)* **they l. up in the second half** en la segunda parte aflojaron; **once he's started he never lets up** una vez que empieza ya no se detiene; *Fam* **l. up on him a bit** déjale ya

---

let-down ['letdaʊn] *n Fam* chasco *m*, decepción *f*; **the party was a bit of a l.** la fiesta fue una decepción

lethal ['li:θəl] *adj* mortal, letal; *Fam* **that vodka's l.!** ¡ese vodka es fortísimo! ▸▸ ***l. dose*** dosis *f inv* mortal *or* letal; ***l. weapon*** arma *f* mortífera

lethargic [lɪ'θɑ:dʒɪk] *adj (drowsy)* aletargado(a); *(inactive)* apático(a)

lethargically [lɪ'θɑ:dʒɪklɪ] *adv* apáticamente

lethargy ['leθədʒɪ] *n (drowsiness)* sopor *m*, letargo *m*; *(inactivity)* apatía *f*

Lethe ['li:θɪ] *n Mythol* Lete, Leteo

let-out ['letaʊt] *n Br Fam (from obligation)* **I've been invited but I'm looking for a l.** me han invitado pero estoy buscando una excusa para no ir ▸▸ ***l. clause*** cláusula *f* de salvaguardia

Letraset® ['letrəset] *n* Letraset® *m*, letras *fpl* transferibles

let's [lets] = **let us**

letter ['letə(r)] **1** *n* (**a**) *(of alphabet)* letra *f*; **the l. of the law** la interpretación literal de la ley; **to obey to the l.** obedecer al pie de la letra; IDIOM *Br* **to have letters after one's name** tener títulos

(**b**) *(written message)* carta *f*; **l. of acknowledgement** carta de acuse de recibo; **l. of condolence/introduction/thanks** carta de pésame/presentación/agradecimiento; **he's a bad/good l. writer** escribe pocas/muchas cartas; **by l.** por carta; **the letters page** *(of newspaper, magazine)* la sección *or* página de cartas de los lectores; **the letters of Henry James** la correspondencia de Henry James ▸▸ ***l. bomb*** carta *m* bomba *inv*; ***l. box*** buzón *m*; ***l. opener*** abrecartas *m inv*; ***l. rack*** casillero *m* de cartas; ***l. rate*** franqueo *m (para cartas)*

(**c**) *(official document)* ***letters of credence*** *(of ambassador)* cartas *fpl* credenciales; *Com* ***l. of credit*** carta *f* de crédito; *Com* ***l. of exchange*** letra *f* de cambio; *Law* ***letters patent*** (certificado *m* de) patente *f*; ***letters patent of nobility*** carta *f* de hidalguía; *Naut* ***l. of reprisal*** carta *f* de contramarca

(**d**) *Formal* **English letters** *(literature)* las letras inglesas; **a man of letters** un hombre de letras

(**e**) *(paper size)* = tamaño de papel de 216mm x 279mm, utilizado sobre todo en Estados Unidos

(**f**) *US* = emblema con la letra inicial del centro educativo, concedido a un alumno por sus victorias deportivas

2 *vt* (**a**) *(write)* **the title was lettered in gilt** el título estaba escrito en letras doradas (**b**) *(mark, identify)* **the files are lettered from A to K**

los archivos están señalados con letras de la A a la K

3 *vi US* = obtener el emblema con la letra inicial del centro educativo, por sus victorias deportivas

letter-box ['letəbɒks] *adj Cin* **l. format** formato buzón

lettered ['letəd] *adj (well-educated)* ilustrado(a), culto(a)

letterhead ['letəhed] *n* membrete *m*

lettering ['letərɪŋ] *n* (**a**) *(action, inscription) (in ink, paint)* rotulación *f*; *(carved, engraved)* inscripción *f* (**b**) *(characters)* letra *f*, caracteres *mpl*

letter-perfect [letə'pɜ:fɪkt] *adj US* impecable

letterpress ['letəpres] *n (technique)* tipografía *f*

letting ['letɪŋ] *n Br (of house, property)* alquiler *m* ►► ***l. agency*** inmobiliaria *f*

Lettish ['letɪʃ] *n (language)* letón *m*

lettuce ['letɪs] *n* (**a**) *(vegetable)* lechuga *f*; **a l. leaf** una hoja de lechuga (**b**) *US Fam (money) Esp* pasta *f*, *Am* plata *f*

let-up ['letʌp] *n Fam* tregua *f*, descanso *m*; **they worked fifteen hours without a l.** trabajaron quince horas sin descanso

leucocyte, *US* **leukocyte** ['lu:kəsaɪt] *n Anat* leucocito *m*

leucoma [lu:'kəʊmə] *n Med* leucoma *m*

leucorrhoea, *US* **leukorrhea** [lu:kə'rɪə] *n Med* leucorrea *f*

leukaemia, *US* **leukemia** [lu:'ki:mɪə] *n Med* leucemia *f*

leukocyte, leukorrhea *US* = **leucocyte, leucorrhoea**

Levant [lə'vænt] *n* **the L.** el Levante mediterráneo

Levantine [lə'væntaɪn] *adj* del Levante mediterráneo

levee ['levɪ] *n* (**a**) *US (embankment)* dique *m* (**b**) *(quay)* muelle *m*, embarcadero *m* (**c**) *Br Hist* audiencia *f* matinal

---

LEVEL ['levəl] **1** *n* (**a**) *(position, height)* nivel *m*; **the l. of the river has risen overnight** el nivel del río ha subido por la noche; **at eye l.** a la altura de los ojos; **to be on a l. with** *(at same height as)* estar al mismo nivel *or* a la misma altura que; IDIOM *Fam* **to be on the l.** *(honest)* ser honrado(a)

(**b**) *(amount)* nivel *m*; **noise levels are far too high** los niveles de ruido son demasiado altos; **inflation has reached new levels** la inflación ha alcanzado nuevas cotas

(**c**) *(standard)* nivel *m*; **his l. of English is poor** no tiene un buen nivel de inglés; **this win is on a l. with their 1966 victory** este triunfo está a la altura de su victoria de 1966; **to come down to sb's l.** ponerse al nivel de alguien; **you'll soon find your own l.** pronto encontrarás tu nivel; **to sink to sb's l.** rebajarse al nivel de alguien

(**d**) *(rank)* **at ministerial/international l.** a nivel ministerial/internacional; **a decision taken at the highest l.** una decisión tomada en los más altos niveles

(**e**) *(plane)* **on a personal l.** a nivel personal; **on a practical l.** a nivel práctico; **on a deeper l., the novel is about...** en un plano más profundo, la novela trata de...

(**f**) *(storey)* piso *m*; **l. 3** *(on sign)* tercero, 3°; **the whole building is on one l.** el edificio tiene un solo piso

(**g**) *US (spirit level)* nivel *m* de burbuja

(**h**) *Comptr* **levels of grey** niveles de gris

2 *adj* (**a**) *(flat)* nivelado(a), liso(a), horizontal; **a l. spoonful** una cucharada rasa; *Fig* **a l. playing field** igualdad de condiciones ►► *Br Rail* ***l. crossing*** paso *m* a nivel

(**b**) *(equal)* **the scores are l.** van igualados *or* empatados; **are the two shelves completely l. (with each other)?** ¿están los dos estantes exactamente a la misma altura *or* al mismo nivel?; **l. with...** *(of position)* a la altura de...; **the two teams/athletes are now l. with each other** los dos equipos/atletas van igualados en este momento; **to draw l. with** *(in race)* alcanzar, ponerse a la altura de; *(in match)* conseguir el empate contra; *(in contest)* igualar a; **the two teams finished l.** los dos equipos terminaron igualados; **she did her l. best** hizo todo lo que estaba a su alcance *or* en su mano; **the two parties are l. pegging** los dos partidos están empatados ►► ***l. par*** *(in golf)* par *m*

(**c**) *(voice, tone, gaze)* sereno(a); **to keep a l. head** mantener la cabeza fría

(**d**) *Fam (honest)* **you're not being l. with me** no estás siendo franco conmigo

3 *vt* (*pt & pp* **levelled,** *US* **leveled**) (**a**) *(make flat)* nivelar; *(raze)* arrasar

(**b**) *(make equal)* **to l. the score** igualar el marcador

(**c**) *(aim)* **to l. a blow at sb** propinar *or* asestar un golpe a alguien; **to l. a gun at sb** apuntar a alguien con un arma, dirigir un arma contra alguien; **to l. accusations at sb** lanzar acusaciones contra alguien; **to l. criticism at sb** dirigir críticas a alguien

► **level off, level out 1** *vt (make flat)* allanar

2 *vi (ground)* nivelarse, allanarse; *(prices, demand)* estabilizarse; *(graph)* nivelarse, estabilizarse; *(aircraft)* enderezarse

► **level with** *vt insep Fam* ser franco(a) con

---

leveler *US* = **leveller**

level-headed ['levəl'hedɪd] *adj* sensato(a)

leveling *US* = **levelling**

leveller, *US* **leveler** ['levələ(r)] *n (equalizer)* nivelador(ora) *m,f*; **death is a great l.** la muerte nos hace a todos iguales

levelling, *US* **leveling** ['levəlɪŋ] *n* **a l. up/down of salaries** una equiparación salarial al alza/a la baja; **a l. off of inflation** una estabilización de la inflación

lever ['li:və(r), *US* 'levə(r)] **1** *n (device, on machine)* palanca *f*; **he used his popularity as a l.** utilizó su fama como trampolín

2 *vt* **to l. a box open** abrir una caja haciendo palanca; *Fig* **to l. sb into a job** aupar a alguien a un puesto

► **lever off** *vt sep (lid)* abrir haciendo palanca; *(tyre)* sacar haciendo palanca

► **lever out** *vt sep (remove from office)* echar

leverage ['li:vərɪdʒ, *US* 'levərɪdʒ] *n* (**a**) *Tech* apalancamiento *m*; **I can't get enough l.** no puedo hacer suficiente palanca (**b**) *(influence, pressure)* influencia *f*; **to bring l. to bear on** *(pressurize)* ejercer presión sobre (**c**) *US Fin* apalancamiento *m*, relación *f* deudas-capital propio

leveraged buyout ['li:vərɪdʒd'baɪaʊt, *US* 'levərɪdʒd'baɪaʊt] *n Fin* compra *f* apalancada

lever-arch file ['li:vərɑ:tʃ'faɪl] *n* carpeta *f* archivadora *(de palanca)*

leveret ['levərət] *n* lebrato *m*

leviathan [lə'vaɪəθən] *n* (**a**) *(monster)* leviatán *m* (**b**) *(thing, institution)* coloso *m*, gigante *m*

Levis® ['li:vaɪz] *npl* Levis® *mpl*; **a pair of L.** unos Levis

levitate ['levɪteɪt] **1** *vt* hacer levitar

2 *vi* levitar

levitation [levɪ'teɪʃən] *n* levitación *f*

levity ['levɪtɪ] *n* frivolidad *f*

levodopa [li:vəʊ'dəʊpə] *n Pharm* levodopa *f*

levy ['levɪ] **1** *n* (**a**) *(action)* exacción *f*; **an annual l.** una exacción anual (**b**) *(tax)* impuesto *m*, tasa *f* (**on** sobre); **a l. of ten percent** un impuesto *or* una tasa del diez por ciento (**c**) *Mil (recruitment)* reclutamiento *m* *(forzoso)*, leva *f*; *(troops)* tropas *fpl*

2 *vt* (**a**) *(tax)* aplicar (**on** a); **to l. a tax on sth** gravar algo con un impuesto (**b**) *Mil (troops)* reclutar *(forzosamente)*

lewd [lu:d] *adj* lascivo(a), procaz

lewdly ['lu:dlɪ] *adv* lascivamente, procazmente

lewdness ['lu:dnɪs] *n* lascivia *f*, procacidad *f*

lexeme ['leksi:m] *n Ling* lexema *m*

lexical ['leksɪkəl] *adj* léxico(a)

lexicalization [leksɪkəlaɪ'zeɪʃən] *n Ling* lexicalización *f*

lexicalize ['leksɪkəlaɪz] *vt Ling* lexicalizar

lexicographer [leksɪ'kɒgrəfə(r)] *n* lexicógrafo(a) *m,f*

lexicographic(al) [leksɪkə'græfɪk(əl)] *adj* lexicográfico(a)

lexicography [leksɪ'kɒgrəfɪ] *n* lexicografía *f*

lexicological [leksɪkə'lɒdʒɪkəl] *adj* lexicológico(a)

lexicologist ['leksɪ'kɒlədʒɪst] *n* lexicólogo(a) *m,f*

lexicology ['leksɪ'kɒlədʒɪ] *n* lexicología *f*

lexicon ['leksɪkən] *n* (**a**) *(dictionary)* lexicón *m* (**b**) *(vocabulary)* léxico *m*

lexis ['leksɪs] *n Ling* léxico *m*

ley [leɪ] *n* **l. (line)** = línea que une hitos del paisaje y a la que se atribuyen antecedentes prehistóricos

lez [lez], **lezzy** ['lezɪ] *n very Fam Pej* tortillera *f*, *Esp* bollera *f*

LI (*abbr* **Long Island**) Long Island

liability [laɪə'bɪlɪtɪ] *n* (**a**) *Law (responsibility)* responsabilidad *f* (**for** de); **to accept** *or* **admit l. for sth** responsabilizarse de algo ►► ***l. insurance*** seguro *m* de responsabilidad civil

(**b**) *(eligibility)* sujeción *f*; **l. for tax** responsabilidad fiscal; **l. for military service** obligaciones militares

(**c**) *Fin* **liabilities** pasivo *m*, deudas *fpl*; **to meet one's liabilities** hacer frente a los compromisos contraídos

(**d**) *(disadvantage)* **the house he had inherited was a real l.** la casa que había heredado no le trajo más que complicaciones; **she's a real l.** no es más que un estorbo; **more of a l. than an asset** un lastre más que un beneficio

(**e**) *(tendency)* **l. to do sth** propensión a hacer algo

liable ['laɪəbəl] *adj* (**a**) *Law (responsible)* responsable (**for** de); **you'll be l. for any damages** será responsable de los daños; **to be held l. for sth** ser considerado responsable de algo
(**b**) *(eligible) (for tax, fine)* sujeto(a) (**to/for** a); **to be l. for military service** estar obligado(a) a hacer el servicio miltar
(**c**) *(likely)* **if you don't remind him, he's l. to forget** si no se lo recuerdas, se le puede olvidar; **the weather is l. to change** el tiempo puede cambiar

liaise [liː'eɪz] *vi* **to l. with sb** *(be in contact with)* estar en contacto con alguien; *(work together with)* colaborar con alguien

liaison [lɪ'eɪzɒn] *n* (**a**) *(cooperation)* coordinación *f* ►► *Mil* ***l. officer*** oficial *m* de enlace (**b**) *(love affair)* relación *f* (amorosa) (**c**) *Ling* ligazón *f*, enlace *m* (**d**) *Culin* trabazón *f*

liana [lɪ'ɑːnə] *n* liana *f*

liar ['laɪə(r)] *n* mentiroso(a) *m,f*

Lib (*abbr* **Liberal**) liberal

lib [lɪb] *n Fam* liberación *f*; **gay/women's l.** la liberación gay/de la mujer

libation [laɪ'beɪʃn] *n* (**a**) *Literary (offering)* libación *f* (**b**) *Hum* **can I offer you a small l.?** ¿puedo ofrecerle algo de beber?

libber ['lɪbə(r)] *n Fam* **gay/women's l.** partidario(a) de la liberación gay/de la mujer

Lib-Dem [lɪb'dem] *n Br Pol* (*abbr* **Liberal Democrat**) demócrata *mf* liberal

libel ['laɪbəl] *Law* **1** *n* libelo *m*; **to sue sb for l.** demandar a alguien por libelo ►► ***l. action*** juicio *m* por libelo; ***l. laws*** legislación *f* sobre el libelo
2 *vt* (*pt & pp* **libelled,** *US* **libeled**) calumniar

libellous, *US* **libelous** ['laɪbələs] *adj* calumnioso(a)

Liberal ['lɪbərəl] *Pol* **1** *n* liberal *mf*
2 *adj* liberal; *Br* **the L. Democrats** el partido demócrata liberal

liberal ['lɪbərəl] **1** *n (tolerant person)* liberal *mf*
2 *adj* (**a**) *(tolerant)* liberal ►► ***l. arts*** artes *fpl* liberales; *US* ***l. arts college*** facultad *f* de letras; ***l. education*** educación *f* liberal
(**b**) *(generous) (person)* desprendido(a), generoso(a); *(portion)* generoso(a); *(interpretation)* libre; **he was a bit too l. with the salt** se le fue un poco la mano con la sal; **this was a very l. interpretation of the rules** esa era una interpretación muy libre de las normas
(**c**) *(abundant)* abundante, generoso(a)

liberalism ['lɪbərəlɪzəm] *n* liberalismo *m*

liberality [lɪbə'rælɪtɪ] *n* (**a**) *(tolerance)* tolerancia *f* (**b**) *(generosity)* liberalidad *f*, generosidad *f*

liberalization [lɪbərəlaɪ'zeɪʃən] *n* liberalización *f*

liberalize ['lɪbərəlaɪz] *vt* liberalizar

liberally ['lɪbərəlɪ] *adv (generously)* generosamente; *(freely)* libremente; **salt the dish l.** añada sal en abundancia

liberate ['lɪbəreɪt] *vt* (**a**) *(prisoner, country)* liberar; *Fin* **to l. capital** liberar capital (**b**) *Chem (gas, heat)* liberar (**c**) *Hum (steal)* sustraer

liberated ['lɪbəreɪtɪd] *adj (persona)* liberado(a); *(ideas)* liberal; **a l. woman** una mujer liberada

liberating ['lɪbəreɪtɪŋ] *adj* liberador(ora)

liberation [lɪbə'reɪʃən] *n* (**a**) *(of prisoner, country)* liberación *f* ►► ***l. movement*** movimiento *m* de liberación; ***l. theology*** teología *f* de la liberación (**b**) *Chem (of gas, heat)* liberación *f*

liberationist [lɪbə'reɪʃənɪst] *n* partidario(a) *m,f* de la liberación

liberator ['lɪbəreɪtə(r)] *n* libertador(ora) *m,f*, liberador(ora) *m,f*

Liberia [laɪ'bɪərɪə] *n* Liberia

Liberian [laɪ'bɪərɪən] **1** *n* liberiano(a) *m,f*
2 *adj* liberiano(a)

libertarian [lɪbə'teərɪən] **1** *n* libertario(a) *m,f (esp. no anarquista)*
2 *adj* libertario(a) *(esp. no anarquista)*

libertarianism [lɪbə'teərɪənɪzəm] *n* libertarismo *m*

libertine ['lɪbətiːn] *n Literary* libertino(a) *m,f*

liberty ['lɪbətɪ] *n* libertad *f*; **at l.** *(free)* en libertad; **to be at l. to do sth** tener libertad para hacer algo; **I'm not at l. to say** no puedo decirlo, no lo puedo revelar; **to take the l. of doing sth** tomarse la libertad de hacer algo; **to take liberties with** tomarse (excesivas) libertades con; **what a l.!** ¡qué cara más dura! ►► ***l. cap*** gorro *m* frigio; ***L. Hall*** la casa de tócame Roque

libidinal [lɪ'bɪdɪnəl] *adj* libidinal

libidinous [lɪ'bɪdɪnəs] *adj (lustful)* libidinoso(a)

libido [lɪ'biːdəʊ] (*pl* **libidos**) *n* libido *f*

Lib-Lab ['lɪb'læb] *adj Br Fam* **a L. pact** un pacto entre el partido laborista y el demócrata liberal

LIBOR ['laɪbɔː(r)] *n Br Fin* (*abbr* **London Inter-Bank Offered Rate**) Líbor *f*

Libra ['liːbrə] *n (sign of zodiac)* Libra *m*; **to be (a) L.** ser Libra

Libran ['liːbrən] **1** *n* Libra *mf*
2 *adj* de Libra

librarian [laɪ'breərɪən] *n* bibliotecario(a) *m,f*

> **False friend:** The Spanish noun **librero** is not a translation for the English word **librarian.** In Spanish **librero** means "bookseller" or (in parts of Latin America) "bookcase".

librarianship [laɪ'breərɪənʃɪp] *n* (**a**) *(work)* trabajo *m* de bibliotecario(a) (**b**) *(discipline)* biblioteconomía *f*

library ['laɪbrərɪ] *n* (**a**) *(room, building)* biblioteca *f* ►► ***l. book*** libro *m* de biblioteca; ***l. card*** carné *m* de biblioteca; ***l. edition*** edición *f* para bibliotecas; *US* ***l. science*** biblioteconomía *f* (**b**) *(collection) (of books)* biblioteca *f*; **a film l.** una filmoteca; **a music l.** una discoteca ►► *TV* ***l. pictures*** imágenes *fpl* de archivo (**c**) *Comptr* librería *f*

> **False friend:** The Spanish noun **librería** is not a translation for the English word **library**, except in the computing sense. In Spanish **librería** means "bookshop" or (in Spain) "bookcase".

librettist [lɪ'bretɪst] *n Mus* libretista *mf*

libretto [lɪ'bretəʊ] (*pl* **librettos** *or* **libretti** [lɪ'bretiː]) *n Mus* libreto *m*

Libya ['lɪbɪə] *n* Libia

Libyan ['lɪbɪən] **1** *n* libio(a) *m,f*
2 *adj* libio(a)

lice *pl of* **louse**

licence, *US* **license** ['laɪsəns] *n* (**a**) *(permit)* licencia *f*, permiso *m*; *Com* **under l.** bajo licencia, con autorización; (*Br* **driving** *or US* **driver's**) **l.** carné *m or* permiso *m* de *Esp* conducir *or RP* conductor, licencia *f Carib* de conducir *or Méx* para conducir; IDIOM **it's a l. to print money** es una ocasión para hacerse de oro ►► *Br TV* ***l. fee*** = tarifa de la licencia de uso de la televisión; *Aut* ***l. number*** *(of car)* (número *m* de) matrícula *f*; *US Aut* ***l. plate*** (placa *f* de) matrícula *f*
(**b**) *(freedom)* licencia *f*
(**c**) *Formal (excessive freedom)* libertinaje *m*
(**d**) *Comptr* ***l. agreement*** acuerdo *m* de licencia

license ['laɪsəns] **1** *n US* = **licence**
2 *vt* (**a**) *Com* autorizar; **to be licensed to carry a gun** tener permiso *or* licencia de armas (**b**) *(allow)* **to l. sb to do sth** autorizar a alguien a hacer algo

licensed ['laɪsənst] *adj* (**a**) *(qualified) (practitioner)* autorizado(a) para ejercer; *(pilot)* con permiso *or* licencia (**b**) *Br (to sell or serve alcohol)* ***l. premises*** = establecimiento donde se pueden vender bebidas alcohólicas; ***l. restaurant*** = restaurante con licencia para vender bebidas alcohólicas; ***l. victualler*** = dueño de un bar con licencia para la venta y el consumo de bebidas alcohólicas

licensee [laɪsən'siː] *n* (**a**) *(licence holder)* titular *mf* de una licencia (**b**) *Br (of pub)* = persona con licencia para vender bebidas alcohólicas

licensing ['laɪsənsɪŋ] *n* (**a**) *Com* ***l. agreement*** contrato *m or* acuerdo *m* de licencia (**b**) *Br (for sale of alcohol)* ***l. hours*** = horario en el que está permitido servir bebidas alcohólicas; ***l. laws*** = legislación sobre la venta de bebidas alcohólicas

licentiate [laɪ'senʃɪət] *n (certificate)* licenciatura *f*; *(certificate holder)* licenciado(a) *m,f*

licentious [laɪ'senʃəs] *adj* licencioso(a)

licentiousness [laɪ'senʃəsnɪs] *n* licenciosidad *f*

lichen ['laɪkən] *n* liquen *m*

lichgate = **lychgate**

licit ['lɪsɪt] *adj Formal (lawful)* lícito(a)

lick [lɪk] **1** *n* (**a**) *(with tongue)* lametazo *m*, lamida *f*; **can I have a l. of your ice-cream?** ¿me dejas probar tu helado?; IDIOM *Fam* **to give sth a l. and a promise** dar a algo un lavado muy por encima, *RP* dar a algo una lamida; IDIOM *US Fam* **to get** *or* **have last licks: we got our last licks on the beach before the weather changed** aprovechamos los ultimos días en la playa antes de que cambiara el tiempo; **he starts the debate so you get last licks** él empieza el debate, así que el último eres tú
(**b**) *Fam* **a l. of paint** una pequeña mano de pintura
(**c**) *Fam (speed)* **at a great** *or* **tremendous l.** a toda máquina *or Esp* pastilla
(**d**) *Mus Fam* lick *m*, = frase corta que se suele intercalar en solos
2 *vt* (**a**) *(with tongue)* lamer; **he licked the jam off the bread** se comió la mermelada a lametazos; **the dog licked its bowl clean** el perro dejó el cuenco limpio a lametazos; **to l. one's lips** lamerse; *Fig (in*

anticipation) relamerse; *Fig* **to l. one's wounds** lamerse las heridas; *Fam* **to l. sb's boots** darle coba a alguien; *Vulg* **to l. sb's** *Br* **arse** *or US* **ass** lamer *or RP* chupar el culo a alguien; *Fam* **to l. sth/sb into shape** poner algo/a alguien a punto

(**b**) *(of flame)* lamer, rozar; **the flames licked the walls of the house** las llamas lamían *or* rozaban las paredes de la casa

(**c**) *Fam (defeat)* **to get licked** llevarse una soberana paliza; **to have sth/sb licked** dejar algo/a alguien hecho trizas; **we've finally got the problem licked** por fin nos hemos quitado el problema de encima

▸ **lick out** *vt sep Br Vulg* **to l. sb out** comer el coño a alguien, *Andes, RP* chupar la concha a alguien

lickety-split [ˈlɪkətɪˈsplɪt] *adv US Fam* en un periquete

licking [ˈlɪkɪŋ] *n Fam* **to get** *or* **take a l.** *(physically)* llevarse una buena zurra; *(in game, competition)* llevarse una soberana paliza

lickspittle [ˈlɪkspɪtəl] *n Fam* lameculos *mf inv*

licorice *US* = **liquorice**

lid [lɪd] *n* (**a**) *(of pot, jar)* tapa *f* (**b**) *(of eye)* párpado *m* (**c**) IDIOMS **to blow** *or* **take the l. off sth** destapar algo, sacar algo a la luz; *Fam* **to blow** *or* **flip one's l.** *(get angry)* ponerse hecho(a) una furia, *Méx* ponerse como agua para chocolate; **to keep the l. on sth** mantener oculto algo; **to put the l. on sth** poner fin a algo; *Br* **that puts the (tin) l. on it!** ¡eso ya es el colmo!

lidded [ˈlɪdɪd] *adj* (**a**) *(box)* con tapa (**b**) **heavy-l. eyes** ojos con párpados pesados

lido [ˈliːdəʊ] *(pl* **lidos**) *n* (**a**) *(pool)* piscina *f*, *Méx* alberca *f*, *RP* pileta *f* (**b**) *(resort)* complejo *m* deportivo acuático

lie[1] [laɪ] **1** *n* mentira *f*; **to tell a l.** decir una mentira, mentir; *Fam* **I tell a l.** no, miento; **to give the l. to sth** desmentir algo; IDIOM **there are lies, damned lies and statistics** hay tres clases de mentiras: las mentiras, las grandes mentiras y las estadísticas ▸▸ ***l. detector*** detector *m* de mentiras

2 *vi* mentir; **"it wasn't me," she lied** "no fui yo", mintió; **he lied about his age** mintió sobre su edad; **to l. through one's teeth** mentir descaradamente

LIE[2] **1** *n* (**a**) *(in golf)* posición *f* de la pelota; **he's got a good/bad l.** la pelota está en una buena/mala posición

(**b**) *Fig* **the l. of the land** el estado de las cosas

2 *vi* (*pt* **lay** [leɪ], *pp* **lain** [leɪn]) (**a**) *(person, animal) (be still)* estar acostado(a) *or Esp, Méx* tumbado(a) *or Andes* echado(a) *or RP* tirado(a); *(get down)* acostarse, *Esp, Méx* tumbarse, *Andes* echarse, *RP* tirarse; **to l. in bed** estar en la cama; **I've been lying in the sun** he estado acostado *or Esp, Méx* tumbado *or Andes* echado *or RP* tirado al sol; **she was lying on her back/front** estaba acostada *or Esp, Méx* tumbada *or Andes* echada *or RP* tirada boca arriba/abajo; **I lay awake all night** permanecí despierto toda la noche; **Jones lay dead before me** Jones yacía muerto delante de mí; **could you l. still a minute?** ¿puedes estarte quieto un minuto?; **here lies...** *(on gravestone)* aquí yace...; *Fig* **to l. low** permanecer en un segundo plano; **to l. in state** estar expuesto(a) en capilla ardiente; **to l. in wait for sb** permanecer *or* estar a la espera de alguien; *Fig* esperar a alguien

(**b**) *(object)* estar; **the ball is lying in the middle of the fairway** la pelota está en mitad de la calle; **whose coat is that lying on the bed?** ¿de quién es el abrigo que está en la cama?; **papers lay all over her desk** había papeles esparcidos por toda la mesa; **a tree lay across our path** había un árbol atravesado en el camino; **a vast plain lay before us** ante nosotros se extendía una vasta llanura; **the village lies in a valley** el pueblo se encuentra en un valle; **several warships lay off the French coast** había varios buques de guerra frente a las costas francesas; **snow lay on the ground** había nieve en el suelo; **the building has lain empty for several years** el edificio ha permanecido vacío varios años; **the coffin lay open** el ataúd estaba abierto; **to l. in ruins** *(building)* estar en ruinas; *(career, hopes)* estar arruinado(a); **the obstacles that l. in our way** los impedimentos que obstaculizan nuestro camino

(**c**) *(abstract thing)* estar, hallarse; **they know where their true interests l.** saben dónde se hallan sus verdaderos intereses; **a lot of work lies ahead of us** nos espera mucho trabajo; **a brilliant future lies before her** tiene ante sí un brillante futuro; **what lies behind this uncharacteristic generosity?** ¿qué hay detrás de esta inusual generosidad?; **my future lies elsewhere** mi futuro está en otra parte; **the guilt lies heavy on her** el sentimiento de culpabilidad la abruma; **to l. heavy on sb** ser un gran peso psicológico para alguien; **the cause of the problem lies in...** la causa del problema radica en...; **the difference lies in that...** la diferencia radica en que...; **the future lies in telematics** el futuro está en la telemática; **that lies outside my remit** eso queda fuera del ámbito de mi cometido

(**d**) *Br (in competition)* **they are currently lying second** *or* **in second position** en estos momentos se encuentran en segunda posición

(**e**) *(settle)* **the snow did not l.** la nieve no cuajó

▸ **lie about, lie around** *vi (person, thing)* estar tirado(a); **she had left her papers lying around** había dejado sus papeles tirados; **have you got any change lying around?** ¿tienes suelto por ahí?; **he spends all day lying around doing nothing** se pasa el día tirado sin hacer nada

▸ **lie back** *vi* recostarse; **just l. back and enjoy yourself** relájate y disfruta

▸ **lie down** *vi (get down)* echarse, acostarse; **she was lying down on the floor** estaba tumbada en el suelo; *Fig* **to l. down on the job** flojear (en el trabajo); *Fig* **I'm not going to take this lying down** no voy a quedarme de brazos cruzados ante esto

▸ **lie in** *vi* (**a**) *(stay in bed)* quedarse en la cama hasta tarde

(**b**) *Archaic* estar en la cama de parto

▸ **lie to** *vi Naut* fondear

▸ **lie up** *vi* (**a**) *(hide)* esconderse

(**b**) *(stay in bed)* guardar cama

▸ **lie with** *vt insep* (**a**) *(belong to)* **the responsibility lies with the author** la responsabilidad recae sobre el autor; **this decision lies with us** esta decisión nos corresponde tomarla a nosotros

(**b**) *Literary (sleep with)* yacer con

Liechtenstein [ˈlɪktənstaɪn] *n* Liechtenstein

lie-down [ˈlaɪˈdaʊn] *n Br Fam* **to have a l.** echarse un rato

Liège [liːˈeʒ] *n* Lieja

liege [liːdʒ] *n Hist* **l. (lord)** señor *m* feudal; **my l.** mi señor ▸▸ ***l. man*** vasallo *m*

lie-in [ˈlaɪˈɪn] *n Br Fam* **to have a l.** quedarse en la cama hasta tarde

lien [ˈlɪən] *n Law (on property)* derecho *m* de retención

lieu [ljuː, luː] *n Formal* **time in l.** días libres en lugar de dinero; **I'm working on Saturday, so I'm going to take Monday off in l.** trabajo el sábado, así que voy a tomarme el lunes de vacaciones; **two weeks' salary in l. of notice** dos semanas de sueldo a modo de notificación de despido

Lieut (*abbr* **Lieutenant**) Tte.

Lieut Col (*abbr* **Lieutenant Colonel**) Tte. Cor.

lieutenant [*Br* lefˈtenənt, *US* luːˈtenənt] *n* (**a**) *Mil* teniente *mf*; *Naut* teniente *mf* de navío ▸▸ *Mil* ***l. colonel*** teniente *mf* coronel; ***l. commander*** capitán *m* de corbeta; ***l. general*** *(in army)* teniente *mf* general; *(in US airforce)* general *mf* de división (**b**) *US (police officer)* oficial *mf* de policía (**c**) *(deputy, assistant)* lugarteniente *mf* ▸▸ ***l. governor*** *(in Canada)* vicegobernador(ora) *m,f*; *(in US)* vicegobernador(ora) *m, f*

LIFE [laɪf] (*pl* **lives** [laɪvz]) *n* (**a**) *(existence)* vida *f*; **l. is hard here** aquí la vida es dura; **animal l.** fauna; **bird l.** aves; **marine l.** fauna y flora marinas; **plant l.** flora; **a matter of l. and death** una cuestión de vida o muerte; **l. after death** la vida después de la muerte; **to bring sb back to l.** devolver la vida a alguien, resucitar a alguien; **to escape with one's l.** salir con vida; **she is fighting for her l.** *(of patient)* está entre la vida y la muerte; **to give** *or* **lay down one's l. for sth/sb** dar la vida por algo/alguien; **to lose one's l.** perder la vida; **no lives were lost** no hubo que lamentar víctimas *or* ninguna muerte; **to risk one's l., to risk l. and limb** arriesgar la vida; **to scare** *or* **frighten the l. out of sb** dar a alguien un susto de muerte; **to take sb's l.** quitar la vida a alguien; **to take one's own l.** quitarse la vida; **to take one's l. in one's hands** jugarse la vida; **he held on to the rope for dear l.** se aferró a la cuerda con todas sus fuerzas; **run for your lives!** ¡sálvese quien pueda!; *Fam* **I couldn't for the l. of me remember** por más que lo intentaba, no conseguía recordar; **from l.** *(to draw, paint)* del natural; *Fam* **not on your l.!** ¡ni en broma!, ¡ni soñarlo!; **l. isn't a bowl of cherries, you know** la vida no es de color de rosa *or* un lecho de rosas, ¿sabes?; **it's all part of l.'s rich tapestry** forma parte del variado retablo de la vida; PROV **l. begins at forty** la vida empieza a los cuarenta; PROV **l. is for living** la vida es para vivirla ▸▸ ***l. belt*** flotador *m*, salvavidas *m inv*; ***l. buoy*** flotador *m*; ***l. cycle*** ciclo *m* vital; ***l. force*** fuerza *f* vital; ***l. form*** forma *f* de vida; ***l. jacket*** chaleco *m* salvavidas; *US* ***l. preserver*** *(life belt)* cinturón *m* de seguridad; *(life jacket)* chaleco *m* salvavidas; ***l. raft*** lancha *f* salvavidas; ***l. sciences*** ciencias *fpl* naturales *or* biológicas; *US* ***l. vest*** chaleco *m* salvavidas

(**b**) *(period of existence)* vida *f*; **private/working l.** vida privada/laboral; **it changed my l.** me cambió la vida, cambió mi vida; **the song started l. as a ballad** la canción empezó siendo una balada; **in the next l.** *(Heaven)* en el Más Allá; **in a past l.** en una vida anterior; **he never finished his life's work** nunca terminó la obra de su vida; **she**

worked all her l. trabajó toda su vida; **I've never eaten caviar in (all) my l.** no he comido caviar (nunca) en mi vida; **this commitment is for l.** se trata de un compromiso de por vida; **a job for l.** un trabajo para toda la vida; **you gave me the fright of my l.** me diste un susto de muerte *or RP* morir; **she ran the race of her l.** hizo la mejor carrera de su vida; **he told me his l. story** me contó su vida; **to be given a l. sentence,** *Fam* **to get l.** ser condenado(a) a cadena perpetua ►► *Fin* ***l. annuity*** anualidad *f* vitalicia, renta *f* vitalicia; *Br* ***l. assurance*** seguro *m* de vida; ***l. expectancy*** *(of human, animal)* esperanza *f* de vida; *(of machine)* vida *f* útil; ***l. member*** socio(a) *m,f* vitalicio(a); *Br Pol* ***l. peer*** = miembro vitalicio de la Cámara de los Comunes; *Br Pol* ***l. peerage:* he was given a l. peerage** fue hecho miembro vitalicio de la Cámara de los Lores; *Pol* ***l. peeress*** = mujer que es miembro vitalicio de la Cámara de los Comunes; *Fin* ***l. pension*** pensión *f* vitalicia; ***l. savings*** ahorros *mpl* de toda la vida; ***l. span*** vida; ***l. subscription*** suscripción *f* vitalicia

(**c**) *(mode of existence)* vida *f*; **city l.** la vida en la ciudad; **university l.** la vida universitaria; **way of l.** modo de vida; **my job is my l.** mi trabajo es mi vida; *Fam* **get a l.!** hazme el favor, ¿es que no tienes nada mejor que hacer?; **l. goes on** la vida sigue; **to make a new l. for oneself, to start a new l.** construirse una nueva vida, comenzar una nueva vida; **you're just trying to make l. difficult for me** estás intentando hacerme la vida imposible; **having a man sent off didn't make l. any easier for them** la expulsión de un jugador no les ayudó nada; **to make sb's l. hell** convertir la vida de alguien en un infierno; **he makes her l. a misery** le amarga la vida; **to make l. worth living** hacer que la vida merezca la pena; **to have seen l.** tener mucho mundo; **the man/woman in your l.** el hombre/la mujer que hay en tu vida; **l. at the top isn't easy** cuando estás en la cumbre, la vida no es fácil; *Fam* **how's l.?** ¿qué tal?, ¿cómo va eso?, *CAm, Col, Méx* ¿quihubo?; *Fam* **how's l. treating you?** ¿cómo te va la vida?; *Fam* **such is l.!, that's l.!** ¡así es la vida!, ¡la vida es así!; *Fam* **this is the l.!** ¡esto es vida!; *Fam* **what a l.!** ¡qué vida ésta!; IDIOM *Fam* **to live** *or* **lead the l. of Riley** vivir como un pachá *or* rajá

(**d**) *(liveliness)* vida *f*; **to breathe new l. into** *(person, company)* dar nuevos bríos a; **to bring sth/sb to l.** *(make livelier)* animar algo/a alguien; **to come to l.** cobrar vida; *Fig* animarse; **that's her to the l.** es su vivo retrato; **the machine roared into l.** la máquina arrancó con un rugido; **the l. and soul of the party** el alma de la fiesta; **there's l. in the old dog yet** todavía le queda mucha cuerda

(**e**) *(of battery, machine)* vida *f*; *(of agreement)* vigencia *f*; **during the l. of this parliament** durante esta legislatura

(**f**) *(in game)* vida *f*; **if you get hit, you lose a l.** si te dan, pierdes una vida

(**g**) *(biography)* **a l. of Tolstoy** una biografía de Tolstói

(**h**) *Art* ***l. class*** clase *f* del natural; ***l. drawing*** dibujo *m* del natural

---

lifeblood ['laɪfblʌd] *n* (**a**) *(blood)* sangre *f* (**b**) *(key part)* motor *m*; **the l. of the economy** el motor de la economía; **the government are draining the l. from small businesses** el gobierno está sangrando a los pequeños negocios

lifeboat ['laɪfbəʊt] *n* (**a**) *(from coast)* lancha *f* de salvamento ►► ***l. station*** estación *f* de salvamento (**b**) *(on ship)* bote *m or* lancha *f* salvavidas

lifeboatman ['laɪfbəʊtmən] *n* = miembro de un equipo de salvamento

lifebuoy ['laɪfbɔɪ] *n* salvavidas *m inv*, flotador *m*

life-giving ['laɪfgɪvɪŋ] *adj* salvador(ora)

lifeguard ['laɪfgɑːd] *n* socorrista *mf*; **to be on l. duty** estar de socorrista

lifeless ['laɪflɪs] *adj* (**a**) *(body)* sin vida; **she fell l. to the floor** cayó inerte al suelo (**b**) *(where no life exists)* sin vida (**c**) *(dull) (eyes, hair)* apagado(a); *(town, performance)* aburrido(a), soso(a)

lifelessly ['laɪflɪslɪ] *adv* sin vida

lifelike ['laɪflaɪk] *adj* realista

lifeline ['laɪflaɪn] *n* (**a**) *(rope)* cabo *m* (salvavidas); *also Fig* **to throw sb a l.** echar un cabo a alguien (**b**) *(means of rescue, survival)* salvavidas *m inv* (**c**) *(for diver)* cuerda *f* de seguridad

lifelong ['laɪflɒŋ] *adj* de toda la vida; **a l. friend** un(a) amigo(a) de toda la vida; **it's been my l. ambition to meet her** el sueño de mi vida ha sido conocerla ►► *Educ* ***l. learning*** aprendizaje *m* a continuo

lifer ['laɪfə(r)] *n Fam (prisoner)* condenado(a) *m,f* a cadena perpetua

life-saver ['laɪfseɪvə(r)] *n* (**a**) *(lifeguard)* socorrista *mf* (**b**) *Fam* **it was a l.** *(provide relief)* me salvó la vida

life-saving ['laɪfseɪvɪŋ] *adj* **a l. drug** un medicamento que salva muchas vidas; **he had a l. operation** la operación le salvó la vida

life-size(d) ['laɪfsaɪz(d)] *adj* (de) tamaño natural

lifestyle ['laɪfstaɪl] *n* estilo *m* de vida; **it's a l. choice** es una opción de vida ►► ***l. supplement*** suplemento *m* moda y estilo

life-support ['laɪfsəpɔːt] *n Med* ***l. machine*** equipo *m* de ventilación *or* respiración asistida; ***l. system*** equipo *m* de ventilación *or* respiración asistida

life-threatening ['laɪfθretnɪŋ] *adj Med* **l. condition** *or* **disease** enfermedad mortífera *or* que puede ocasionar la muerte; **l. situation** situación de peligro mortal

lifetime ['laɪftaɪm] *n (of person)* vida *f*; *(of machine)* vida *f* (útil); **in** *or* **during my l.** durante mi vida; **it won't happen in my l.** no viviré para verlo; **it's the chance** *or* **opportunity of a l.** es la oportunidad de mi/tu/su *etc* vida; **the holiday of a l.** las vacaciones de mi/tu/su *etc* vida; **the sort of thing that happens once in a l.** esa clase de cosas que sólo pasan una vez en la vida; **it is unlikely within the l. of this parliament** no es probable que suceda durante la presente legislatura parlamentaria; **a l. supply** un suministro de por vida ►► ***l. guarantee*** garantía *f* vitalicia *or* de por vida

LIFFE [laɪf, 'lɪfɪ] *n* (*abbr* **London International Financial Futures Exchange**) LIFFE *m*, Mercado *m* Internacional de Futuros Financieros de Londres

LIFO ['laɪfəʊ] (*abbr* **last in first out**) el último en entrar es el primero en salir

---

LIFT [lɪft] **1** *n* (**a**) *Br (elevator)* ascensor *m* ►► ***l. attendant*** ascensorista *mf*; ***l. shaft*** hueco *m* del ascensor

(**b**) *(car ride)* **to give sb a l.** llevar a alguien (en el coche), *CAm, Méx* dar aventón *or Col* chance *or Cuba* botella *or Perú* una jalada *or Ven* cola a alguien; **could you give me a l. to the station?** ¿puedes llevarme *or* acercarme a la estación?, *CAm, Méx* ¿puedes darme *CAm, Méx* aventón *or Col* chance *or Cuba* botella *or Perú* una jalada *or Ven* cola hasta la estación?; **my l. couldn't make it today** hoy no me han podido traer, no me han podido dar *CAm, Méx* aventón *or Col* chance *or Cuba* botella *or Perú* una jalada *or Ven* cola

(**c**) *Fam (boost)* **that really gave me a l.!** ¡eso me levantó muchísimo el ánimo!; **the song needs a l. towards the middle** esta canción necesita un poco de animación *or Esp* marcha hacia la mitad

(**d**) *(act of raising)* **to give sth a l.** levantar algo

(**e**) *Av* sustentación *f*

2 *vt* (**a**) *(raise, move)* levantar; **to l. one's arm/eyes** levantar el *or* un brazo/los ojos; **to l. one's voice** levantar la voz; **l. the table over here** levanta la mesa y tráela aquí; **can you l. the lid off?** ¿puedes levantar la tapa?; **he lifted the vase out of the box** sacó el jarrón de la caja; **she lifted the glass to her mouth** se llevó el vaso a la boca; **to have one's breasts lifted** hacerse una operación para reafirmar el pecho; **he won't l. a finger to help** no moverá un dedo para ayudar; **to l. sb's spirits** animar a alguien; *Literary* **the church lifts its spire to the skies** la aguja de la iglesia se alza hasta el cielo

(**b**) *(transport by plane)* aerotransportar

(**c**) *(increase) (exports, level)* subir, elevar

(**d**) *(remove) (restrictions, siege)* levantar

(**e**) *Fam (take, steal)* afanar, birlar, *Am* volar

(**f**) *Fam (copy)* copiar; **he's lifted this passage from a famous author/my book** ha copiado este pasaje de un escritor famoso/mi libro

(**g**) *Fam (arrest)* detener, trincar

(**h**) *(vegetables)* recoger

3 *vi* (**a**) *(move upwards) (curtain, eyes)* subir, elevarse; **the balloon lifted into the sky** el globo se elevó en el cielo; **our spirits lifted at the news** la noticia nos subió la moral

(**b**) *(mist, fog)* disiparse; *(depression, bad mood)* desaparecer, disiparse

► **lift down** *vt sep* bajar

► **lift off** *vi (rocket)* despegar

► **lift up** *vt sep* levantar; **to l. sb up** *(after fall)* levantar a alguien; **to l. a child up** *(in one's arms)* coger a un niño en brazos; *Literary* **let us l. up our hearts to the Lord** elevemos nuestras plegarias al Señor

---

lift-off ['lɪftɒf] *n (of rocket, economy)* despegue *m*, *Am* decolaje *m*; **we have l.!** ¡se ha efectuado el despegue *or Am* decolaje!

lig [lɪg] (*pt & pp* **ligged**) *vi Br Fam* (**a**) *(lounge about)* holgazanear (**b**) *(freeload)* gorrear, *Esp, Méx* gorronear, *RP* garronear

ligament ['lɪgəmənt] *n* ligamento *m*; **to tear a l.** romperse un ligamento

ligature ['lɪgətʃə(r)] *n Med, Mus & Typ* ligadura *f*

ligger ['lɪgə(r)] *n Br Fam* (**a**) *(idler)* vago(a) *m,f* (**b**) *(freeloader)* gorrero(a) *m,f*, *Esp, Méx* gorrón(ona) *m,f*, *RP* garronero(a) *m,f*

LIGHT[1] [laɪt] **1** *n* (a) *(illumination)* luz *f*; **artificial/electric l.** luz artificial/eléctrica; **he uses l. well in his paintings** tiene un buen dominio de la luz en sus cuadros; **to be in sb's l.** taparle la luz a alguien; **come into the l.** ponte a la luz; **to hold sth up to the l.** poner algo a contraluz; **by the l. of the moon** a la luz de la luna ▸▸ *Phot* ***l. meter*** fotómetro *m*; *Comptr* ***l. pen*** lápiz *m* óptico; *Phys* ***l. wave*** onda *f* luminosa; *Astron* ***l. year*** año *m* luz; *Fig* **they are l. years ahead of us** nos llevan años luz de ventaja; *Fig* **it seems like l. years ago** parece que fue hace milenios

(b) *(daylight)* luz; **the l. was fading fast** estaba oscureciendo rápidamente

(c) *(lamp)* luz *f*; **(traffic) lights** semáforo *m*; **a red/green l.** *(traffic light)* un semáforo en rojo/verde; **to put** *or* **turn off the l.** apagar la luz; **to put** *or* **turn on the l.** encender *or Am* prender la luz; **he shone a l. into the cellar** alumbró la bodega con una linterna; *Cin* **lights, camera, action!** ¡luces, cámaras, acción!; *Theat* **the lights went down** se apagaron las luces; *Aut* **you've left your lights on** te has dejado las luces encendidas; *Fam* **it's lights out at ten o'clock** a las diez en punto se apagan las luces; IDIOM *Fam Hum* **the lights are on but there's nobody home** no hay nada algo ahí dentro ▸▸ ***l. box*** caja *f* luminosa; ***l. bulb*** *Esp* bombilla *f*, *Andes, Méx* foco *m*, *CAm, Carib* bombillo *m*, *RP* lamparita *f*; ***l. show*** *(at concert)* espectáculo *m* de luces; ***l. switch*** interruptor *m* de la luz

(d) *(fire)* **to set l. to sth** prender fuego a algo; **have you got a l.?** ¿tienes fuego?

(e) *(look, glint)* **she had a mischievous l. in her eyes** tenía un brillo travieso en los ojos

(f) *Old-fashioned* **lights** *(sheep's or pig's lungs)* bofe *m*

(g) IDIOMS **you are the l. of my life** eres la luz de mi vida; *Formal* **according to your own lights** según tu criterio; **to bring sth to l.** sacar algo a la luz; **to come to l.** salir a la luz; *Fam* **to go out like a l.** *(fall asleep)* quedarse planchado(a) *or Esp* traspuesto(a); **to see the l.** *(understand, be converted)* ver la luz; **to see the l. at the end of the tunnel** ver la luz al final del túnel; **these paintings never see the l. of day** estos cuadros nunca ven la luz del sol; **the project is unlikely to see the l. of day** probablemente su proyecto nunca llegue a ver la luz; **to see sth/sb in a new** *or* **different l.** ver algo/a alguien desde un punto de vista diferente; **to see sth in a positive** *or* **favourable l.** ver algo desde una óptica positiva *or* favorable; **to be seen in a good l.** ofrecer una buena imagen; **to show sth/sb in a bad l.** dar una mala imagen de algo/alguien; **to throw** *or* **shed** *or* **cast l. on sth** arrojar luz sobre algo; **things will look different in the cold** *or* **hard l. of day** verás las cosas distintas cuando las pienses con calma; **in (the) l. of...** *(considering)* a la luz de..., en vista de...

2 *adj* (a) *(room)* luminoso(a); **it will soon be l.** pronto será de día; **it's getting l.** está amaneciendo, se está haciendo de día; **the evenings are getting lighter** ya hay mas claridad por las tardes

(b) *(hair, complexion, colour)* claro(a); **l. blue/brown** azul/marrón claro

3 *vt* (*pt & pp* **lit** [lɪt]) (a) *(fire)* prender, encender; *(cigarette)* encender, *Am* prender

(b) *(room, street)* iluminar, alumbrar; **the guard lit our way with a torch** el guardia nos alumbró el camino con una linterna

4 *vi (catch fire)* encenderse, prenderse

▸ **light up 1** *vt sep* (a) *(brighten) (house, room)* iluminar; **a smile lit up her face** una sonrisa le iluminó el rostro; **his performance lit up the evening** su actuación animó la velada (b) *(cigarette)* encender

2 *vi* (a) *(sky, display)* iluminarse; **his eyes lit up** se le encendieron los ojos (b) *Fam (smoker)* encender un cigarrillo

LIGHT[2] **1** *npl* **lights** *(low-tar cigarettes)* cigarrillos *mpl* light

2 *adj* (a) *(not heavy)* ligero(a), *esp Am* liviano(a); **he was several kilos too l. to be a heavyweight** le faltaban varios kilos para poder ser un peso pesado; IDIOM **to be as l. as a feather** ser ligero(a) *or esp Am* liviano(a) como una pluma; **to be l. on one's feet** tener los pies ligeros *or Am* rápidos; IDIOM **to have l. fingers** ser amigo(a) de lo ajeno; **to have a l. touch** *(writer)* tener un estilo ágil ▸▸ *Av* ***l. aircraft*** avioneta *f*; *Mil* ***l. artillery*** artillería *f* ligera; ***l. cavalry*** caballería *f* ligera; ***l. industry*** industria *f* ligera; *Mil* ***l. infantry*** infantería *f* ligera; *Br* ***l. railway*** tren *m* ligero

(b) *(not intense) (job, work, exercise)* ligero(a), *esp Am* liviano(a); *(rain)* fino(a); *(wind)* ligero(a), leve; *(tap, kiss)* leve; *(sound)* suave; **there was l. traffic** había poco tráfico; **to be a l. smoker/drinker** fumar/beber moderadamente; **to be a l. sleeper** tener el sueño ligero *or esp Am* liviano

(c) *(not severe)* **a l. sentence** una sentencia benévola

(d) *(food, drink) (not strong in flavour)* suave; *(easily digested, spongy)* ligero(a), *esp Am* liviano(a); *(low in alcohol)* sin alcohol, light; *(low-calorie)* light, bajo(a) en calorías; **to have a l. meal** comer *or Esp* tomar una comida ligera *or esp Am* liviana ▸▸ ***l. ale*** = cerveza sin burbujas, clara y suave; *US* ***l. cream*** *Esp* nata *f* líquida, *Am* crema *f* de leche

(e) *(not serious)* alegre; *(music)* ligero(a); **with a l. heart** alegremente; **it is no l. matter** es un asunto serio; **on a lighter note** en un tono menos serio; **it provided a little l. relief** fue una nota de desenfado; **she made l. of her problems** no dio importancia a sus problemas; **they made l. of the fact that they had had a man sent off** no les afectó el hecho de que les expulsaran a un jugador; **they made l. work of the washing-up** lavaron los platos como si nada ▸▸ ***l. entertainment*** espectáculos *mpl* de variedades; ***l. opera*** opereta *f*; ***l. reading*** lectura *f* ligera; ***l. verse*** poesía *f* ligera

(f) *Fam (lacking)* **the novel is l. on substance** a la novela le falta sustancia

3 *adv* **to travel l.** viajar ligero(a) *or esp Am* liviano(a) de equipaje

▸ **light on, light upon** (*pt & pp* **lighted**) *vt insep Literary (of bird)* posarse en; *(solution)* dar con; **his eyes lighted on the picture** su mirada se posó en el cuadro

▸ **light out** *vi US Fam* largarse

▸ **light upon** = **light on**

light-coloured, *US* **light-colored** *adj* [ˈlaɪtkʌləd] de color claro

light-emitting diode [ˈlaɪtɪmɪtɪŋˈdaɪəʊd] *n Elec* diodo *m* emisor de luz

lighten [ˈlaɪtən] **1** *vt* (a) *(make brighter)* iluminar (b) *(colour, hair)* aclarar (c) *(make less heavy)* aligerar; *Fig* **to l. sb's load** aligerar la carga de alguien, quitarle peso de encima a alguien (d) *(make more cheerful)* aligerar

2 *vi* (a) *(sky)* aclararse (b) *(mood, atmosphere)* distenderse

▸ **lighten up** *vi Fam* animarse; **oh come on, l. up!** ¡vamos, anímate!

lighter[1] [ˈlaɪtə(r)] *n (for cigarettes)* encendedor *m*, *Esp* mechero *m*; *(for gas cooker)* encendedor *m* ▸▸ ***l. fluid*** gas *m* (licuado) para encendedores

lighter[2] *n (boat)* barcaza *f*

lighter-than-air [ˈlaɪtəðənˈeə(r)] *adj (aircraft)* ultraligero(a)

light-fingered [laɪtˈfɪŋgəd] *adj Fam* amigo(a) de lo ajeno

light-footed [laɪtˈfʊtɪd] *adj (nimble)* ágil, ligero(a)

light-headed [laɪtˈhedɪd] *adj* (a) **to feel l.** *(dizzy)* estar mareado(a); *(with excitement)* estar eufórico(a) (b) *(frivolous)* frívolo(a)

light-headedness [laɪtˈhedɪdnɪs] *n* (a) *(dizziness)* mareo *m*; *(with excitement)* euforia *f* (b) *(frivolousness)* frivolidad *f*

light-hearted [ˈlaɪtˈhɑːtɪd] *adj* alegre; **the programme takes a l. look at politics** el programa trata el tema de la política con desenfado

light-heartedly [ˈlaɪtˈhɑːtɪdlɪ] *adv* alegremente, con desenfado

light-heavyweight [ˈlaɪtˈhevɪweɪt] **1** *n* peso *m* semipesado

2 *adj (championship, fight)* de peso semipesado

lighthouse [ˈlaɪthaʊs] *n* faro *m* ▸▸ ***l. keeper*** farero(a) *m,f*

lighting [ˈlaɪtɪŋ] *n (act, system)* iluminación *f*; **artificial/gas/neon l.** iluminación artificial/de gas/de neón; **street l.** alumbrado público ▸▸ *Cin* ***l. cameraman*** director *m* de fotografía; *Theat* ***l. effects*** juego *m* de luces

lighting-up time [ˈlaɪtɪŋˈʌptaɪm] *n Br (for cars)* = hora de encender los faros

lightly [ˈlaɪtlɪ] *adv* (a) *(not heavily)* ligeramente; **it was raining l.** llovía ligeramente, lloviznaba; **l. armed troops** tropas ligeras; **l. dressed** con poca ropa

(b) *(not intensely) (to rest, touch, kiss)* levemente; *(populated)* escasamente; **l. fry the onions** fría las cebollas ligeramente; **to sleep l.** tener el sueño ligero

(c) *(not severely)* **to get off l.** salir bien parado(a); **to let sb off l.** dejar marchar a alguien por las buenas

(d) *(not seriously)* a la ligera; **to speak l. of sth/sb** hablar a la ligera de algo/alguien; **it was not a decision she took l.** no tomó la decisión a la ligera; **"I'm getting married tomorrow," he said l.** "me caso mañana", dijo sin darle importancia

light-middleweight [ˈlaɪtˈmɪdəlweɪt] **1** *n* peso *m* semiligero

2 *adj (championship, fight)* de peso semiligero

lightness [ˈlaɪtnɪs] *n* (a) *(brightness) (of room, colour, hair)* claridad *f* (b) *(in weight) (of object, fabric)* ligereza *f*, liviandad *f*; *(of rain)* suavidad *f*; **his l. of touch** su delicadeza (c) *(in intensity) (of exercise, wind, sound, tap)* suavidad *f* (d) *(in severity) (of sentence)* benevolencia *f* (**e**) *(of food, meal) (in flavour, texture)* suavidad *f*; *(in digestibility)* ligereza *f* (**f**) *(of mood)* alegría *f*; **l. of heart** euforia, ligereza de espíritu

lightning ['laɪtnɪŋ] 1 *n (bolt)* rayo *m*; *(sheet)* relámpago *m*; **a flash of l.** un relámpago; **he was hit** *or* **struck by l.** lo alcanzó un rayo; *(killed)* cayó fulminado por un rayo; IDIOM **as quick as l.** como el rayo; PROV **l. never strikes twice (in the same place)** la misma desgracia no va a ocurrir dos veces ►► *US* ***l. bug*** luciérnaga *f*; ***l. conductor*** pararrayos *m inv*; ***l. rod*** pararrayos *m inv*

2 *adj* **with l. speed** como el rayo ►► ***l. strike*** *(in industry)* huelga *f* relámpago *or* sin previo aviso; *(military attack)* ataque *m* relámpago; ***l. visit*** visita *f* relámpago

lightproof ['laɪtpru:f] *adj (container, door)* opaco(a)

light-sensitive ['laɪtsensɪtɪv] *adj* sensible a la luz

lightship ['laɪtʃɪp] *n Naut* buque *m* faro

lightweight ['laɪtweɪt] 1 *n* (**a**) *(in boxing)* peso *m* ligero (**b**) *Pej* **an intellectual l.** un personaje de poca talla intelectual

2 *adj* (**a**) *(garment)* ligero(a) (**b**) *(in boxing)* de peso ligero

lignite ['lɪgnaɪt] *n Geol* lignito *m*

lignum vitae ['lɪgnəm'vaɪti:] *n* palo *m* santo

likable = **likeable**

LIKE[1] [laɪk] 1 *n* **you're not comparing l. with l.** esas dos cosas no son comparables; **he and his l.** él y los de su clase; **it's not for the likes of me** no es para gente como yo; **music, painting and the l.** música, pintura y cosas así *or* y cosas por el estilo; **a wonderful dessert, the l. of which I haven't tasted since** un postre fabuloso, como no he vuelto a probar otro; **I've never seen the l. (of it)** nunca he visto nada parecido *or* nada igual; **we won't see her l. again** nunca habrá nadie como ella

2 *adj* (**a**) *(similar)* parecido(a), similar; **l. poles repel** los polos del mismo signo, se repelen; **they are of l. temperament** tienen un temperamento parecido; **they are as l. as two peas (in a pod)** son como dos gotas de agua; **we were treated in l. manner** nos trataron de forma parecida *or* similar

(**b**) *Old-fashioned (likely)* **to be l. to do sth** ser susceptible de hacer algo

3 *prep* (**a**) *(similar to)* como; **people l. you** la gente como tú; **to be l. sth/sb** ser como algo/alguien; **what's the weather l.?** ¿qué tiempo hace?; **what is he l.?** ¿cómo es (él)?; **you know what she's l.** ya sabes cómo es; **it was shaped l. a pear** tiene forma de pera; **to look l. sth/sb** parecerse a algo/alguien; **what does he look l.?** ¿qué aspecto tiene?; **to taste l. sth** saber a algo; **we don't have anything l. as many as that** no tenemos tantos, ni muchísimo menos; **it wasn't anything l.** *or* **it was nothing l. I expected** no fue en absoluto como me lo esperaba; **she is nothing l. as intelligent as you** no es ni mucho menos tan inteligente como tú; **there's nothing l. a nice cup of coffee** no hay nada como una buena taza de café; **there's nothing l. it!** ¡no hay nada igual!; **it costs something l. £10** cuesta unas 10 libras, cuesta algo así como 10 libras; **something l. that** algo así; **I've got one just l. it** ¡tengo uno igual!; **that's just l. him!** ¡es típico de él!; **they said tomorrow, but it'll be more l. Friday** dijeron mañana, pero será más bien el viernes; **that's more l. it** eso está mejor; **that's not l. him** no es su estilo; **it's not l. her to be so quiet** ¿por qué estará tan callada?; PROV **l. father, l. son** de tal palo tal astilla, *Am* lo que se hereda no se roba

(**b**) *(in the manner of)* como; **just l. anybody else** como todo el mundo; **l. so** así; **l. that** así; **l. this** así; **sorry to turn up all of a sudden l. this** perdón por presentarme así de pronto; *Fam* **don't be l. that** no seas así; **to run l. blazes** *or* **mad** correr como alma que lleva el diablo; *Fam* **to work l. crazy** trabajar como loco(a)

(**c**) *(such as)* como (por ejemplo); **take more exercise, l. jogging** haz más ejercicio, como (por ejemplo) correr

4 *adv* (**a**) *Fam* **there were l. three thousand people there** había como trescientas personas allí; **I was just walking down the street, l.** pues iba yo andando por la calle; **it was, l., really warm** hacía pero que mucho calor, hacía mucho pero mucho calor; **I was busy, l., that's why I didn't call you** es que estaba ocupado, por eso no te llamé; **as l. as not, l. enough** casi seguro, seguramente

(**b**) *very Fam (in reported speech)* **I was l. "no way"** y yo: "ni hablar"; **so he was l. "in your dreams, pal!"** entonces él va y dice: "eso quisieras tú, *Esp* colega *or Am* compadre", *RP* entonces él agarra y dice: "ni te sueñes, loco"

5 *conj Fam* **do it l. I said** hazlo como te dije; **it feels l. ages since I saw you** parece que hace siglos que no te veo; **he looked l. he'd seen a ghost** parecía como si *or* que hubiera visto una aparición *or* un fantasma; **it sounds l. she should see a doctor** por lo que me dices, debería ir al médico; **it's not l. he's ill or anything** no es que esté enfermo

LIKE[2] 1 *n* **likes** preferencias *fpl*; **likes and dislikes** preferencias y aversiones

2 *vt* (**a**) *(person)* **she likes John** *(as friend)* le cae bien John; *(is attracted to)* le gusta John; **I don't l. him** no me cae bien; **I don't l. his friends** no me caen bien sus amigos; **I don't think she likes me** creo que no le caigo bien; **they l. each other** se gustan; **she is well liked** es muy querida (por todo el mundo)

(**b**) *(object, situation)* **she likes it** le gusta; **she likes cats** le gustan los gatos; **Dave likes cheese** a Dave le gusta el queso; **I l. my men intelligent** a mí me gustan los hombres inteligentes; **you'd l. it there** te gustaría (el sitio); **I don't l. it** no me gusta; **they l. it** les gusta; **do you l. Italian food?** ¿te gusta la comida italiana?; **she likes reading** le gusta leer; *Fam* **I l. it!** *(expressing satisfaction)* ¡qué bien *or* bueno!; **what I l. most about the book is...** lo que más me gusta del libro es que...; **I l. to leave before five** me gusta irme antes de las cinco; **we l. our staff to wear suits** preferimos que nuestro personal use traje; **he doesn't l. people to talk about it** no le gusta que la gente hable de eso; **I l. to think my father would have agreed** me gusta pensar que mi padre habría estado de acuerdo; **I l. to think of myself as quite an expert on the subject** me gusta pensar que soy un experto en el tema; **I didn't l. to mention it** no quise mencionarlo; **I don't l. to seem fussy, but...** no quiero parecer quisquilloso, pero...; **I'd l. to see you do any better!** ¡como si tú supieras hacerlo mejor!; **how do you l. your coffee?** ¿cómo tomas el café?; **how do you l. my dress?** ¿te gusta mi vestido?; *Fam Ironic* **how do you l. that!** ¡qué te parece!; *Fam Ironic* **I l. the way he thinks because I'm a woman I should do the cleaning** me encanta, piensa que como soy mujer, tengo que hacer la limpieza; *Fam Ironic* **well, I l. that!** ¿qué te parece?, ¡tiene gracia la cosa!; **(whether you) l. it or not** te guste o no; *Fam* **(you can) l. it or lump it** lo tomas o lo dejas; *Fam* **if you don't l. it you can lump it** esto son lentejas; si quieres las tomas y si no, las dejas

(**c**) *(want)* querer; **what would you l.?** ¿qué quieres?, *Carib, Col, Méx* ¿qué te provoca?, *Méx* ¿qué se te antoja?; **I'd l. the soup** quiero la sopa, *Esp* tomaré la sopa; **I'd l. a kilo of rice** póngame *or* deme un kilo de arroz; **would you l. a cigarette?** ¿quieres un cigarrillo?; **would you l. me to help you?** ¿quieres que te ayude?; **I'd l. you to come with me** me gustaría que vinieras conmigo; **would you l. to give me a hand with this box?** me ayudas con esta caja, ¿por favor?; **I would** *or* **should very much l. to go** me encantaría ir; **I would** *or* **should l. to know whether...** me gustaría saber si...; **I would l. nothing better than...** nada me gustaría más que...; **will you pass? – I would** *or* **should l. to think so** ¿aprobarás? – creo que sí; **how would you l. a cup of tea?** ¿quieres un té?, *Esp* ¿te apetece un té?, *Carib, Col, Méx* ¿te provoca un té?, *Méx* ¿se te antoja un té?; **how would you l. to have to stand in the rain for an hour?** ¿te gustaría que te hicieran esperar una hora bajo la lluvia?; **he thinks he can do anything he likes** se cree que puede hacer lo que quiera; **whatever/when you l.** lo que/cuando quieras

3 *vi* **as much/often/many as you l.** tanto/tan a menudo/tantos(as) como quieras; **you can't always do just as you l.!** ¡no puedes hacer siempre lo que te dé la gana!; **go, if you l.** si quieres, ve; **shall we get the bus? – if you l.** ¿tomamos el autobús? – si quieres *or* como quieras; **it is, if you l., a kind of poetry for the masses** es, si quieres, una poesía para el gran público

-like [laɪk] *suffix* **ghost-l.** fantasmagórico(a); **jelly-l.** gelatinoso(a)

likeable, likable ['laɪkəbəl] *adj* simpático(a)

likelihood ['laɪklɪhʊd] *n* probabilidad *f*; **in all l.** con toda probabilidad; **there is every l. of an agreement** hay muchas probabilidades para que se llegue a un acuerdo; **there is little l. of finding it** hay pocas probabilidades de encontrarlo; **the l. is that...** lo más probable es que...

likely ['laɪklɪ] 1 *adj* (**a**) *(probable)* probable; **a l. outcome** un resultado probable; **it's not very l.** no es muy probable; **it's more than l.** es más que probable; **it's l. to rain** es probable que llueva; **she is l. to come** es probable venga; **are the neighbours l. to object?** ¿se van a quejar los vecinos?; **it's not** *or* **hardly l. to happen** no es probable que pase; **rain is l. in the east** es probable que llueva en el este; *Ironic* **a l. story!** ¡y yo me lo creo!

(**b**) *(suitable)* apropiado(a), adecuado(a); **a l. candidate** un posible candidato; **a l.(-looking) spot for a picnic** un lugar apropiado *or* adecuado para un picnic; **I've looked in all the l. places** he mirado en todos los sitios donde podía estar

2 *adv* **very l., most l.** muy probablemente; **they'll very l.** *or* **most l. forget** lo más probable es que se olviden; **as l. as not she's already home** es bastante probable que ya esté en casa; *Fam* **not l.!** ¡ni hablar!

like-minded [laɪk'maɪndɪd] *adj (having same views)* con la misma mentalidad; *(having same purpose)* de la misma opinión

liken ['laɪkən] *vt* comparar (**to** a *or* con)

likeness ['laɪknɪs] *n* (**a**) *(similarity)* parecido *m*; **a close l.** un parecido muy marcado; **family l.** parecido familiar; **God created man in his own l.** Dios creó al hombre a su imagen y semejanza (**b**) *(portrait)* retrato *m*; **it's a good l. (of him)** guarda un gran parecido (con él)

likewise ['laɪkwaɪz] *adv (similarly)* también, asimismo; **to do l.** hacer lo mismo; **nice to meet you – l.** encantado de conocerte – lo mismo digo

liking ['laɪkɪŋ] *n* (**a**) *(affection, fondness)* **to have a l. for sth** ser aficionado(a) a algo; **she has a l. for expensive jewellery** le gustan *or* es muy aficionada a joyas caras; **to take a l. to sth** tomar *or Esp* coger gusto a algo, aficionarse a algo; **to take a l. to sb** tomar *or Esp* coger simpatía a alguien

(**b**) *(taste)* gusto *m*, agrado *m*; **is it to your l.?** ¿es de su gusto *or* agrado?; **it's too sweet for my l.** es demasiado dulce para mi gusto

lilac ['laɪlək] **1** *n* (**a**) *(tree)* lilo *m*, lila *f*; *(flower)* lila *f* (**b**) *(colour)* lila *m*

2 *adj* lila

Lilliputian [lɪlɪ'pju:ʃən] **1** *n* liliputiense *mf*

2 *adj* liliputiense

Lilo® ['laɪləʊ] *(pl* **Lilos**) *n Br* colchoneta *f* (inflable)

lilt [lɪlt] *n (in speech)* modulación *f*, entonación *f*; *(in music)* cadencia *f*; **to speak with a Welsh l.** hablar con entonación galesa

lilting ['lɪltɪŋ] *adj* cadencioso(a)

lily ['lɪlɪ] *n* lirio *m* ►► ***l. pad*** hoja *f* de nenúfar; ***l. of the valley*** lirio *m* de los valles

lily-livered ['lɪlɪlɪvəd] *adj* cobarde, pusilánime

lily-white [lɪlɪ'waɪt] *adj* (**a**) *(colour)* blanco(a) como la nieve (**b**) *Fam (character)* intachable

Lima ['li:mə] *n* Lima

lima bean ['li:mə'bi:n] *n Esp* judía *f* blanca (limeña), *Andes, CAm, Carib, Méx* frijol *m* blanco, *Andes, RP* poroto *m* blanco

limb [lɪm] *n* (**a**) *(of body)* miembro *m*, extremidad *f*; **several passengers suffered broken limbs** varios pasajeros tenían un brazo o una pierna rota; **to tear sb l. from l.** descuartizar a alguien (**b**) *(of tree)* rama *f* (**c**) IDIOMS **to be out on a l.** quedarse solo(a); **to go out on a l. for sb** jugársela por alguien; **I'm going out on a l. here, but I think it was in 1928** no quisiera equivocarme, pero me parece que fue en 1928

limber ['lɪmbə(r)] *adj* flexible

► **limber up** *vi* hacer el calentamiento; *Fig* **they're limbering up for a fight with the unions** se están preparando para la refriega con los sindicatos

limbic system ['lɪmbɪk'sɪstəm] *n Anat* sistema *m* límbico

limbless ['lɪmlɪs] *adj (person)* desmembrado(a), mutilado(a); *(tree)* sin ramas

limbo[1] ['lɪmbəʊ] *n Rel* limbo *m*; IDIOM **to be in l.** *(person)* estar perdido(a); *(negotiations, project)* estar en el aire

limbo[2] *n (dance)* limbo *m* ►► ***l. dancer*** bailador(ora) *m,f* de limbo

lime[1] [laɪm] *n* (**a**) *(fruit)* lima *f*, *Méx* limón *m*; *(tree)* lima *f*, limero *m*, *Méx* limonero *m* ►► ***l. juice*** *Esp* zumo *m or Am* jugo *m* de lima; ***l. green*** verde *m* lima (**b**) *(linden tree)* tilo *m*

lime[2] **1** *n* (**a**) *Chem* cal *f* (**b**) *(birdlime)* liga *f*

2 *vt* (**a**) *(soil)* abonar con cal (**b**) *(with birdlime) (branch)* untar con liga; *(bird)* cazar *or* atrapar con liga

limeade [laɪm'eɪd] *n* = bebida hecha con zumo de lima, azúcar y agua

limekiln ['laɪmkɪln] *n* calera *f*, horno *m* de cal

limelight ['laɪmlaɪt] *n* (**a**) *Theat Old-fashioned* luz *f* de calcio (**b**) *(glare of publicity)* **to be in the l.** estar en candelero; **to seek the l.** buscar publicidad; **to steal the l.** acaparar la atención; **to stay out of the l.** alejarse de la publicidad

limerick ['lɪmərɪk] *n* = estrofa humorística de cinco versos que riman siguiendo este orden: aabba

limestone ['laɪmstəʊn] *n* (piedra *f*) caliza *f*

limey ['laɪmɪ] *US Fam* **1** *n (British person)* = término peyorativo para referirse a un británico

2 *adj* = término peyorativo para referirse a un británico

limit ['lɪmɪt] **1** *n* (**a**) *(boundary, greatest extent)* límite *m*; **the eastern limits of the empire** los límites occidentales del imperio; **there's a l. to my patience/tolerance** mi paciencia/tolerancia tiene límite; **the limits of decency** los límites de la decencia; **to know no limits** no conocer límites; **I know my limits** conozco mis límites; **the bar's off limits to servicemen** los militares tienen al acceso prohibido a este bar; **within limits** dentro de un límite; **to be stretched to the l.** *(of factory, company)* estar trabajando al límite de sus posibilidades; **our resources are stretched to the l.** nuestros recursos no dan más de sí; *Fam* **he's/that's the l.!** ¡es el colmo!

(**b**) *(restriction)* límite *m*; **to put** *or* **set** *or* **impose a l. on sth** poner *or* establecer *or* imponer un límite a algo; **age/height/weight l.** límite de edad/altura/peso; *Br* **to be over the l.** *(driver)* superar el límite en el control de alcoholemia

2 *vt* limitar; **we're trying to l. costs** tratamos de limitar *Esp* costes *or Am* costos; **to l. oneself to sth** limitarse a algo; **I will l. myself to observing that...** me limitaré a mencionar que...

limitation [lɪmɪ'teɪʃən] *n* (**a**) *(restriction, control)* limitación *f*; **arms l. talks** negociaciones para la reducción de armamento (**b**) *(shortcoming)* limitación *f*; **we all have our limitations** todos tenemos nuestras limitaciones; **I know my limitations** conozco mis limitaciones

limited ['lɪmɪtəd] *adj* (**a**) *(restricted)* limitado(a); **our resources are l.** nuestros recursos son limitados; **only a l. number of players will be successful** únicamente un número reducido de jugadores tendrá éxito; **the choice was rather l.** había pocas opciones; **the play met with only l. success** la obra no tuvo más que un éxito relativo; **to a l. extent** en cierta medida, hasta cierto punto ►► ***l. edition*** edición *f* limitada (**b**) *Com* ***l. (liability) company*** sociedad *f* (de responsabilidad) limitada; ***l. liability*** responsabilidad *f* limitada (**c**) *US (train)* semidirecto(a); *(bus)* = que se detiene en un número reducido de paradas

limiting ['lɪmɪtɪŋ] *adj* restrictivo(a)

limitless ['lɪmɪtlɪs] *adj* ilimitado(a)

limo ['lɪməʊ] *(pl* **limos**) *n Fam* limusina *f*

limousine ['lɪməzi:n] *n* limusina *f*

limp[1] [lɪmp] **1** *n* cojera *f*; **to have a l., to walk with a l.** cojear; **the accident left him with a l.** el accidente le dejó cojo, sufre una cojera por culpa del accidente

2 *vi* cojear; **he limped into the room** entró cojeando en la habitación; *Fig* **the ship limped into harbour** la embarcación entró en el puerto trabajosamente

limp[2] *adj* (**a**) *(handshake, body)* lánguido(a), flojo(a); *(lettuce)* mustio(a); **his body went completely l.** el cuerpo le cayó flácido; **to feel l.** *(person)* sentirse sin fuerzas; **to be l. with exhaustion** estar extenuado(a) (**b**) *(book, binding)* flexible

limpet ['lɪmpɪt] *n* lapa *f*; IDIOM **to stick** *or* **cling (to sth/sb) like a l.** pegarse (a algo/alguien) como una lapa ►► *Mil* ***l. mine*** mina *f* lapa, mina *f* magnética

limpid ['lɪmpɪd] *adj* límpido(a), cristalino(a)

limpkin ['lɪmpkɪn] *n* caraú *m*

limply ['lɪmplɪ] *adv (to hang, lie)* con aire mustio, sin fuerzas; *(weakly)* lánguidamente, débilmente

limpness ['lɪmpnɪs] *n (of handshake, bearing)* languidez *f*; *(of lettuce)* aspecto *m* mustio

limp-wristed [lɪmp'rɪstɪd] *adj Pej* amariposado(a), afeminado(a)

limy ['laɪmɪ] *adj (containing lime)* calizo(a)

linage = **lineage**[2]

linchpin ['lɪntʃpɪn] *n* (**a**) *Tech* pezonera *f* (**b**) *Fig (of team, policy)* eje *m* central

Lincs [lɪŋks] *(abbr* **Lincolnshire**) (condado *m* de) Lincolnshire

linctus ['lɪŋktəs] *n* jarabe *m* para la tos

linden ['lɪndən] *n* **l. (tree)** tilo *m*

LINE[1] [laɪn] **1** *n* (**a**) *(mark, boundary)* línea *f*; *(on face)* arruga *f*; **the painting consisted of no more than a few lines** el cuadro consistía en unas cuantas rayas nada más; *US* **county/state l.** la frontera del condado/estado; **the ball didn't cross the l.** la pelota no cruzó la línea; **to cross the l.** *(in athletics, horseracing)* cruzar la (línea de) meta; *(equator)* cruzar el ecuador; **to draw a l. through sth** *(delete)* tachar algo; **there's a fine l. between self-confidence and arrogance** de la confianza en uno mismo a la arrogancia hay un paso; *Fig* **to be on the l.** *(of job, reputation)* correr peligro, estar en juego; **she's putting** *or* **laying her life/reputation on the l.** está poniendo su vida/reputación en juego ►► ***l. drawing*** dibujo *m (sin sombreado)*; *Geog* ***l. of latitude*** paralelo *m*; *Geog* ***l. of longitude*** meridiano *m*

(**b**) *(row of people or things)* fila *f*; **they arranged the chairs in a l.** colocaron las sillas en fila; **they were standing in a l.** estaban en fila; **to fall into** *or* **in l.** *(of troops, children)* alinearse, ponerse en fila; *Fig* entrar en vereda; *Fig* **to keep sb in l.** tener a alguien controlado(a); *Fig* **you were out of l. saying that** te pasaste (de la raya) al decir eso; *Fig* **to get out of l.** *(be disobedient)* saltarse las normas; *Fig* **to step out of l.** pasarse de la raya ►► ***l. dancing*** baile *m* en línea, = baile al ritmo de música country en el que los participantes se colocan en hileras y dan los mismos pasos; *Com* ***l. management*** gestión *f* de línea; *Com* ***l. manager*** gerente *mf or* jefe(a) *m,f* de línea

(**c**) *US (queue)* fila *f*; **to stand in l.** hacer cola; **to cut in l.** colarse
(**d**) *Mil* línea *f*; **to go behind enemy lines** cruzar las líneas enemigas; *Fig* **a healthy diet is the first l. of defence against heart disease** una dieta sana es la primera medida contra las afecciones cardíacas
(**e**) *(of text)* línea *f*; *(of poem, song)* verso *m*; **there's this really funny l. in the movie when she says...** hay un momento muy divertido en la película, cuando ella dice...; **his character gets all the best lines** su personaje tiene los mejores diálogos; **he came out with some good lines** tuvo algunos buenos golpes; *Br Sch* **we were given a hundred lines** tuvimos que copiar cien veces una frase; *Theat* **to learn one's lines** aprenderse el papel; *Theat* **to forget one's lines** olvidarse del papel; *Fig* **to drop sb a l.** mandar unas líneas *or* escribir a alguien; *Fig* **to feed** *or* **shoot sb a l.** contarle una historieta *or* un rollo a alguien; *Fam Fig* **don't give me the l. about being skint** no me vengas con (el cuento de) que estás pelado(a) *or Esp* sin blanca *or Méx* bruja *or RP* un mango; *Fig* **to read between the lines** leer entre líneas
(**f**) *(rope, for washing)* cuerda *f*; *(for fishing)* sedal *m*, *RP* tanza *f*; **to hang the washing on the l.** tender la ropa; **the lines are down** *(power cables)* se ha ido la luz, *RP* hay apagón
(**g**) *Sport* **defensive l.** *(in soccer, American football)* línea de defensa; **forward l.** *(in soccer)* línea de ataque; **offensive l.** *(in American football)* línea de ataque ►► ***l. back*** *(in American football)* line back *m*; ***l. call*** *(in tennis)* decisión *f (respecto a si la bola ha entrado o no)*; ***l. drive*** *(in baseball)* línea *f*, linietazo *m*; ***l. judge*** *(in tennis)* juez *mf* de línea; ***l. of scrimmage*** *(in American football)* línea *f* de scrimmage
(**h**) *Tel* línea *f*; **it's a good/bad l.** te oigo bien/mal; **I'm afraid her l. is busy at the moment** *Esp* lo siento, pero está comunicando en este momento, *Am* lo siento, la línea está ocupada en este momento; **the lines open in half an hour** las líneas entrarán en funcionamiento en media hora; **there's a Mr Jackson on the l. for you** el Sr. Jackson al teléfono para usted; *Fig* **I got my lines crossed** se me cruzaron los cables ►► ***l. noise*** ruido *m* en la línea; ***l. rental*** alquiler *m or Méx* renta *f* de la línea
(**i**) *Comptr* **to be off/on l.** estar desconectado(a)/conectado(a); *Fig* **the new installation comes on l. next week** la nueva instalación empieza a funcionar la semana que viene ►► ***l. break*** salto *m* de línea; ***l. feed*** avance *m* de línea; ***lines per inch*** líneas *fpl* por pulgada; ***l. noise*** ruido *m* en la línea; ***l. printer*** impresora *f* de líneas; ***l. spacing*** interlineado *m*
(**j**) *Rail (track)* vía *f*; *(route)* línea *f*; *Fig* **all along the l.** *(from the beginning)* desde el principio; *Fig* **somewhere along the l.** en algún momento; *Fig* **we need to consider what could happen down the l.** tenemos que plantearnos lo que podría pasar en el futuro; *Fig* **he supports us right down the l.** nos apoya totalmente
(**k**) *(alignment)* ángulo *m* de tiro; **to be in l.** *(properly aligned)* estar alineados(as); **that's in l. with what I expected** esto corresponde a lo que me esperaba; **our salaries are in l. with the rest of the sector** nuestros salarios son equivalentes a los del resto del sector; **our pay rise was in l. with inflation** nuestro aumento de sueldo era acorde con la inflación; **she is in l. for promotion** ella debería ser la siguiente en obtener un ascenso; **he is in l. to become the first British author to win this prize** hay muchas posibilidades de que sea el primer autor británico en ganar este premio; *Fig* **to bring sth into l. with sth** armonizar algo con algo; **to be off l.** *(of shot)* ir desviado(a); **to be on l.** *(of shot)* ir bien dirigido(a); *Fig* **to be out of l. with sth** estar en desacuerdo con algo
(**l**) *(direction)* línea *f*; **a community divided along ethnic lines** una comunidad dividida según criterios étnicos; **we think along similar/different lines** pensamos de manera parecida/diferente; **along the lines of...** similar a...; **she said something along the lines that...** dijo algo del estilo de que...; **on the same lines as** en la misma línea que; **to be on the right/wrong lines** estar en el buen/mal camino ►► ***l. of argument*** hilo *m* argumental; ***l. of attack*** línea *f or* plan *m* de ataque; *also Fig* ***l. of fire*** *(of projectile)* trayectoria *f*; *Fig* **in the l. of fire** en el punto de mira; ***l. of inquiry*** línea *f* de investigación; ***l. of reasoning*** razonamiento *m*; ***l. of sight*** ángulo *m* de mira; ***l. of vision*** ángulo *m* de mira
(**m**) *(policy)* línea *f*, política *f*; **the party l.** la línea del partido; **maybe we should try a different l.** tal vez deberíamos probar un enfoque distinto; **to take a hard** *or* **firm l. with sb** tener mano dura con alguien; **they take the l. that it is not their responsibility** adoptan la postura de decir que no es responsabilidad suya; **the l. of least resistance** el camino más corto *or* fácil
(**n**) *Mus (part)* **I like the guitar l.** me gusta la guitarra
(**o**) *(succession)* línea *f*; **male/female l.** línea paterna/materna; **this is the latest in a long l. of gaffes** esta es la última de una larga serie de meteduras de pata; **in (a) direct l.** por línea directa; **he is first in l. to the throne** es el primero en la línea de sucesión al trono; **Thomson is next in l. for this job** Thomson es el siguiente para este trabajo
(**p**) *(job, interest)* especialidad *f*; **what l. (of work) are you in?** ¿a qué te dedicas?; **you don't get many women in this l. of business** en este negocio no hay muchas mujeres; **killed in the l. of duty** muerto en el cumplimento de su deber; *Fig* **outdoor sports are more (in) my l.** a mí me van más los deportes al aire libre
(**q**) *Com (of goods)* línea *f*; **they do a very good l. in sofas** tienen una línea de sofás muy buena; *Fig* **she has a good l. in witty ripostes** tiene un buen repertorio de salidas ingeniosas
(**r**) *(company)* **shipping l.** líneas marítimas
(**s**) *US Fin* ***l. of credit*** línea *f* de crédito, descubierto *m* permitido
(**t**) *Fam (information)* **have we got a l. on him?** ¿sabemos algo sobre él?
(**u**) *Fam (of cocaine)* raya *f*, línea *f*
(**v**) **lines** *(appearance, design)* línea *f*
2 *vt* (**a**) *(border)* bordear; **the crowd lined the street** la muchedumbre bordeaba la calle; **the river was lined with willows** había una hilera de sauces en cada orilla del río
(**b**) *(mark with lines)* **a face lined with worry** una cara llena de arrugas provocadas por la preocupación

► **line up** **1** *vt sep* (**a**) *(form into a line)* alinear, poner en fila; *Fam* **l. them up!** *(drinks)* ¡que sean varios!
(**b**) *(align)* disponer en fila; **to l. up a shot** apuntar
(**c**) *(prepare)* **have you got anyone lined up for the job?** ¿tienes algún candidato firme *or* a alguien pensado para el trabajo?; **have you got anything lined up for this evening?** ¿tienes algo pensado para esta noche?; **I've got a meeting lined up for Tuesday** el martes tengo una reunión; **we've lined up some very distinguished guests for you** les vamos a traer a unos invitados muy distinguidos
2 *vi* (**a**) *(form a line)* alinearse; **l. up, children!** ¡niños, poneos en fila!; **several senior politicians lined up behind him** *(supported him)* varios políticos importantes le dieron su apoyo
(**b**) *(start match)* jugar; **to l. up against sb** *(in race)* enfrentarse a alguien

---

line[2] *vt* (**a**) *(provide with lining) (clothes, curtains, drawer)* forrar; **the bird lines its nest with feathers** el ave recubre el nido de plumas; IDIOM **to l. one's pockets** forrarse (**b**) *(cover)* recubrir; **the nose is lined with mucus** el interior de la nariz está recubierto de mucosidad; **the walls were lined with books** había hileras de libros en las paredes

lineage[1] ['lɪnɪɪdʒ] *n (ancestry)* linaje *m*

lineage[2], **linage** ['laɪnɪdʒ] *n (for newspaper ad, article)* número *m* de líneas

lineal ['lɪnɪəl] *adj (descent)* por línea directa

lineaments ['lɪnɪəmənts] *npl Literary* particularidades *fpl*

linear ['lɪnɪə(r)] *adj* lineal ►► *Phys* ***l. accelerator*** acelerador *m* lineal; *Math* ***l. equation*** ecuación *f* lineal; *Art* ***l. perspective*** perspectiva *f* lineal; *Comptr* ***l. programming*** programación *f* lineal

linebacker ['laɪnbækə(r)] *n (in American football)* apoyador(ora) *m,f*, linebacker *mf*

lined [laɪnd] *adj* (**a**) *(paper)* rayado(a), con rayas (**b**) *(face)* arrugado(a) (**c**) *(clothes, curtains, drawer)* forrado(a) (**with** de *or* con)

lineman ['laɪnmən] *n US* (**a**) *(in American football)* lineman *m*, = jugador que se sitúa en la línea de "scrimmage" al inicio de cada "down" (**b**) *Elec & Tel* = técnico en instalación y mantenimiento de tendidos eléctricos y líneas telefónicas

linen ['lɪnɪn] *n* (**a**) *(fabric)* lino *m*; **a l. tablecloth/sheet** un mantel/una sábana de lino (**b**) *(clothes)* ropa *f* blanca, lencería *f* ►► ***l. basket*** cesto *m* de la ropa sucia; *US* ***l. closet*** armario *m* de la ropa blanca; ***l. cupboard*** armario *m* de la ropa blanca; ***l. room*** *(in hospital, hotel)* lencería *f*

line-out ['laɪnaʊt] *n (in rugby)* touche *f*, lanzamiento *m* de lateral

liner ['laɪnə(r)] *n* (**a**) *(ship)* transatlántico *m* (**b**) *(eyeliner)* lápiz *m* de ojos (**c**) *US* ***l. notes*** texto *m* de la carátula

linesman ['laɪnzmən] *n* (**a**) *(in sport)* juez *m* de línea, linier *m* (**b**) *Elec & Tel* = técnico en instalación y mantenimiento de tendidos eléctricos y líneas telefónicas

line-up ['laɪnʌp] *n* (**a**) *(of team)* alineación *f*; *(of band)* formación *f*; **we have an all-star l. for tonight's programme** tenemos unos invitados de lujo en el programa de esta noche (**b**) *(of police suspects)* rueda *f* de reconocimiento *or* identificación

ling [lɪŋ] *n* (**a**) *(fish) (saltwater)* maruca *f*; *(freshwater)* lota *f* (**b**) *(heather)* brezo *m*

linger ['lɪŋgə(r)] *vi* (**a**) *(custom, memory, smell)* perdurar, persistir; **a doubt lingered (on) in my mind** la duda perduró en mi memoria (**b**) *(person)* entretenerse; **they lingered over their coffee** se entretuvieron tomando el café; **her gaze lingered on the painting** su mirada se demoró en el cuadro; **to l. behind** rezagarse (**c**) *(stay alive)* **she might l. on for years yet** puede que subsista durante muchos años

lingerie ['lɔːnʒəri] *n* lencería *f* (fina), ropa *f* interior femenina

lingering ['lɪŋgərɪŋ] *adj* (**a**) *(persistent)* **l. fears** un resto de temor; **l. hopes** un poso de esperanza; **there are still some l. doubts** quedan aún algunas dudas que despejar, aún persiste un resto de duda (**b**) *(prolonged) (look, embrace, kiss)* prolongado(a); **a l. illness** una larga *or* prolongada enfermedad; **she died a l. death** tuvo una muerte lenta

lingo ['lɪŋgəʊ] *n Fam* (**a**) *(language)* idioma *m* (**b**) *(jargon)* jerga *f*

lingua franca ['lɪŋgwə'fræŋkə] *n* lengua *f or* lingua *f* franca

linguini [lɪŋ'gwiːnɪ] *n* linguinis *mpl,* linguini *mpl*

linguist ['lɪŋgwɪst] *n* (**a**) *(specialist in linguistics)* lingüista *mf* (**b**) *(who speaks foreign languages)* persona *f* con idiomas; *(student)* filólogo(a) *m,f*; **to be a good l.** hablar idiomas

linguistic [lɪŋ'gwɪstɪk] *adj* lingüístico(a); **he had no l. ability** no tiene aptitud para los idiomas ►► ***l. atlas*** atlas *m inv* lingüístico

linguistically [lɪŋ'gwɪstɪklɪ] *adv* desde el punto de vista lingüístico, lingüísticamente (hablando); **l. gifted** dotado(a) para los idiomas

linguistics [lɪŋ'gwɪstɪks] *n* lingüística *f*

liniment ['lɪnɪmənt] *n* linimento *m*

lining ['laɪnɪŋ] *n (of clothes, curtains)* forro *m*; *(of drawers)* papel *m* de forro; *(of brakes)* revestimiento *m*; *(of stomach)* pared *f*

link [lɪŋk] **1** *n* (**a**) *(of chain)* eslabón *m*; *Fig* **the weak l.** *(in argument, team)* el punto débil

(**b**) *(connection)* conexión *f*, nexo *m* (**between/with** entre/con); *(between countries, people)* relación *f*; **the l. between inflation and unemployment** la conexión entre la inflación y el desempleo; **she has severed all links with her family** ha roto la relación con su familia; **Britain's trade links with Spain** las relaciones comerciales del Reino Unido con España ►► *Br TV & Rad* ***l. man*** presentador *m*

(**c**) *(road, railway line)* enlace *m*

(**d**) *Comptr* enlace *m*, vínculo *m* (**to** a)

(**e**) *(cufflink)* gemelo *m*

(**f**) *Sport* **links** campo *m* de golf *(cerca del mar)*

(**g**) *(measure of length)* = medida equivalente a 7,92 pulgadas o 20 centímetros

2 *vt* (**a**) *(relate) (facts, events, situations)* relacionar; **the two crimes are linked** ambos crímenes están relacionados; **she has been linked to** *or* **with the mafia** se la ha asociado con la mafia; **wages are linked to the cost of living** los sueldos suben paralelamente al costo *or Esp* coste de la vida (**b**) *(connect physically) (places)* comunicar; *(computers, radio stations)* conectar; **to l. arms** tomarse *or Esp* cogerse del brazo; **to l. hands** enlazar las manos

► **link up 1** *vt sep Comptr* conectar (**to** a)

2 *vi* (**a**) *(roads, travellers)* encontrarse (**with** con); *(spacecraft)* ensamblarse, acoplarse; *(troops)* encontrarse, reunirse (**b**) *(form a partnership)* asociarse (**with** con) (**c**) *(be connected)* conectarse (**with** con)

linkage ['lɪŋkɪdʒ] *n* (**a**) *(connection)* conexión *f* (**b**) *Pol* vinculación *f* política

link-up ['lɪŋkʌp] *n* (**a**) *(of spacecraft)* acoplamiento *m*; *(of troops)* encuentro *m* (**b**) *(connection, partnership)* asociación *f*, acuerdo *m* comercial (**c**) *Tel* conexión *f*; **a satellite l.** una conexión vía satélite

linnet ['lɪnɪt] *n* pardillo *m*

lino ['laɪnəʊ] *n Fam* linóleo *m* ►► ***l. tile*** loseta *f* de linóleo

linocut ['laɪnəʊkʌt] *n (design)* grabado *m* sobre linóleo; *(print)* lámina *f* de linóleo

linoleum [lɪ'nəʊlɪəm] *n* linóleo *m*

Linotype® ['laɪnəʊtaɪp] *n* (**a**) *(machine, process)* linotipia *f* (**b**) *(type)* línea *f* bloque

linseed ['lɪnsiːd] *n* linaza *f* ►► ***l. oil*** aceite *m* de linaza

lint [lɪnt] *n* (**a**) *(for wounds)* hilas *fpl* (**b**) *(fluff)* pelusa *f*

lintel ['lɪntəl] *n* dintel *m*

lion ['laɪən] *n* (**a**) *(animal)* león *m*; **to feed** *or* **throw sb to the lions** echar a alguien a los leones; IDIOM **the l.'s share** la mejor parte ►► ***l. cub*** cachorro *m* de león; ***l. tamer*** domador(ora) *m,f* de leones (**b**) *(courageous person)* jabato(a) *m,f* (**c**) *(celebrity)* gran figura *f*; **a literary l.** una gran figura literaria

lioness ['laɪənes] *n* leona *f*

lion-hearted ['laɪənhɑːtɪd] *adj* valeroso(a), valiente

lionize ['laɪənaɪz] *vt (treat as celebrity)* encumbrar

lip [lɪp] *n* (**a**) *(of mouth)* labio *m* ►► ***l. balm*** protector *m* labial, *Esp* cacao *m*; ***l. gloss*** brillo *m* de labios; *esp Br* ***l. salve*** protector *m* labial, *Esp* cacao *m*

(**b**) *(of cup, glass, crater)* borde *m*; *(of jug)* pico *m*

(**c**) *Fam (impudence)* **less** *or* **enough of your l.!** ¡no seas impertinente!

(**d**) IDIOMS **my lips are sealed** no diré ni mu *or* ni pío; **her name is on everyone's lips** su nombre está en boca de todos; **to read sb's lips** leer los labios a alguien; *Fam* **read my lips** *(believe what I say)* haz caso de lo que digo; **the government is only paying l. service to fighting crime** el gobierno dice luchar contra la delincuencia, el gobierno sólo lucha contra la delincuencia de boquilla

► **lip off** *vi US Fam (be rude)* ser un(a) malhablado(a); *(boast)* fanfarronear, *Esp* tirarse el moco; *(complain)* lloriquear

lipid ['lɪpɪd] *n Biochem* lípido *m*

liposuction ['lɪpəʊsʌkʃən] *n* liposucción *f*

-lipped [lɪpt] *suffix* **thin/full-l.** de labios finos/gruesos

lippy ['lɪpɪ] *Fam* **1** *n Br (lipstick)* pintalabios *m inv*, *Esp* carmín *m*, *Méx* bilet *m*

2 *adj (cheeky)* fresco(a), *Esp* chulo(a)

lip-read ['lɪpriːd] *vi* leer los labios

lip-reader ['lɪpriːdə(r)] *n* persona *f* que lee los labios

lip-smacking ['lɪpsmækɪŋ] *adj Fam* riquísimo(a)

lipstick ['lɪpstɪk] *n* (**a**) *(substance)* carmín *m*, pintalabios *m inv*; **I never wear l.** nunca me pinto los labios ►► *Fam* ***l. lesbian*** lesbiana *f* sofisticada (**b**) *(stick)* lápiz *m or Esp* barra *f* de labios, *CSur* lápiz *m* rouge, *Méx* bilet *m*

lip-sync(h) ['lɪpsɪŋk] *vi* hacer play-back

liquefied ['lɪkwɪfaɪd] *adj* ***l. natural gas*** gas *m* natural licuado; ***l. petroleum gas*** gas *m* licuado de petróleo

liquefy ['lɪkwɪfaɪ] **1** *vt* licuar

2 *vi* licuarse

liqueur [lɪ'kjʊə(r)] *n* (**a**) *(drink)* licor *m* ►► ***l. glass*** copa *f* de licor (**b**) *(sweet)* **l. (chocolate)** bombón *m* relleno de licor

liquid ['lɪkwɪd] **1** *n* (**a**) *(fluid)* líquido *m* (**b**) *Ling (consonant)* líquida *f*

2 *adj* (**a**) *(fluid)* líquido(a) ►► ***l. crystal display*** pantalla *f* de cristal líquido; *Fam Hum* ***l. lunch:*** **we had a l. lunch** almorzamos a base de alcohol; ***l. oxygen*** oxígeno *m* líquido; ***l. paper***® película *f* correctora; ***l. paraffin*** aceite *m* de parafina (**b**) *Fin* líquido(a) ►► ***l. assets*** activo *m* líquido *or* disponible (**c**) *(clear) (eyes, sound)* cristalino(a) (**d**) *Ling (consonant)* líquido(a)

liquidate ['lɪkwɪdeɪt] *vt* (**a**) *Fin* liquidar (**b**) *Euph (kill)* liquidar

liquidation [lɪkwɪ'deɪʃən] *n* (**a**) *Fin* liquidación *f*; **to go into l.** *(of company)* ir a la quiebra (**b**) *Euph (killing)* asesinato *m*, liquidación *f*

liquidator ['lɪkwɪdeɪtə(r)] *n Fin* liquidador(ora) *m,f*

liquidity [lɪ'kwɪdɪtɪ] *n Fin* liquidez *f* ►► ***l. ratio*** coeficiente *m or* ratio *m or f* de liquidez

liquidize ['lɪkwɪdaɪz] *vt* licuar

liquidizer ['lɪkwɪdaɪzə(r)] *n Br Esp* batidora *f*, *Am* licuadora *f*

liquor ['lɪkə(r)] *n* (**a**) *US (alcohol) US* bebida *f* alcohólica, alcohol *m* ►► ***l. store*** tienda *f* de bebidas alcohólicas (**b**) *Culin* caldo *m*

► **liquor up** *vt sep US Fam* **to get liquored up** agarrarse una curda, *Méx* ponerse una peda

liquorice, *US* **licorice** ['lɪkərɪʃ] *n* regaliz *m* ►► ***l. allsorts*** surtido *m* de caramelos de regaliz; ***l. root*** regaliz *m*, *Am* palo *m* dulce

lira ['liːrə] (*pl* **lire** ['liːrə]) *n Formerly* lira *f*

Lisbon ['lɪzbən] *n* Lisboa

lisle [laɪl] *n (fine thread)* = hilo muy fino de algodón

lisp [lɪsp] **1** *n* ceceo *m*; **to have a l., to speak with a l.** cecear

2 *vt* decir ceceando

3 *vi* cecear

lissom, lissome ['lɪsəm] *adj Literary (shape, body, movement)* grácil

list¹ [lɪst] **1** *n* (**a**) *(of items)* lista *f*; **to make out** *or* **draw up a l.** hacer *or* confeccionar una lista; **it's not high on my l. of priorities** no es una de mis prioridades ►► ***l. price*** *(in catalogue)* precio *m* de catálogo

(**b**) *(of publisher)* catálogo *m*

(**c**) *Comptr* ***l. server*** servidor *m* de listas

(**d**) IDIOMS **it's at the top of my l.** es lo primero que tengo en mente hacer; **to enter the lists (for/against sb)** entrar en liza (a favor de/en contra de alguien)

2 *vt* (**a**) *(write down)* hacer una lista con *or* de; *(say out loud)* enumerar; **he listed his demands** enumeró sus exigencias; **his phone number isn't listed in the directory** su número de teléfono no aparece *or* figura en la guía *or Am* en el directorio

(**b**) *(classify, order)* ordenar, clasificar; **they are listed by family name** están ordenados *or* clasificados por apellido; **to l. names in alphabetical order** poner nombres en orden alfabético; **it was officially listed as suicide** oficialmente lo catalogaron como suicidio (**c**) *(price)* **what are the new laptops listed at?** ¿a qué precio están los nuevos portátiles?

(**d**) *Comptr* listar

3 *vi US* **this car lists (at** *or* **for) $10,000** este automóvil vale 10.000 dólares

list[2] *Naut* **1** *n* escora *f*

2 *vi (ship)* escorarse

listed ['lɪstɪd] *adj* incluido(a) en lista ►► *Archit Br* ***l. building*** edificio *m* de interés histórico-artístico; *Com* ***l. company*** empresa *f* con cotización en bolsa; *St Exch* ***l. securities*** valores *mpl* admitidos a cotización en bolsa

listen ['lɪsən] **1** *n* **to have a l. to sth, to give sth a l.** escuchar algo

2 *vi* (**a**) *(try to hear)* escuchar; **to l. to sth/sb** escuchar algo/a alguien; **she listened to the rain falling outside** escuchaba cómo caía la lluvia fuera; **to l. with half an ear** medio escuchar

(**b**) *(pay attention, follow advice)* **to l. to sb** hacer caso a alguien; **if only I'd listened to my mother!** ¡si hubiera hecho caso a mi madre!; **he wouldn't l.** no hizo (ningún) caso; **you're not listening to a word I'm saying!** ¡no me estás escuchando!; **to l. to reason** atender a razones; **l., I think this is a mistake** mira, me parece que esto es un malentendido

► **listen for** *vt insep* estar pendiente de; **to l. (out) for the postman/doctor** estar pendiente del cartero/médico; **she tapped on the wall, listening for a hollow sound** dio golpecitos en la pared, a la escucha de un sonido hueco

► **listen in** *vi* escuchar; **l. in tomorrow at the same time** escúchenos mañana a la misma hora; **to l. in on** *or* **to sth** escuchar algo; **it's rude to l. in on other people's conversations** es de mala educación escuchar las conversaciones de otras personas

► **listen out for** = **listen for**

► **listen up** *vi US Fam* **l. up!** ¡escuchad!

listener ['lɪsnə(r)] *n* (**a**) **to be a good l.** saber escuchar (**b**) *(to radio programme)* oyente *mf*

listening ['lɪsnɪŋ] *n* **l. (comprehension)** comprensión *f* auditiva ►► ***l. device*** dispositivo *m* de escucha; ***l. post*** *Mil* puesto *m* de escucha; *(in music store)* puesto *m* de escucha

listeria [lɪ'stɪərɪə] *n (bacteria)* listeria *f*; *(illness)* listeriosis *f inv*

listeriosis [lɪstɪərɪ'əʊsɪs] *n Med* listeriosis *f inv*

listing ['lɪstɪŋ] *n* (**a**) *(list)* listado *m*, lista *f*; *(entry on a list)* entrada *f*; **do you have a l. for N. Molesworth?** *(in phone book)* ¿aparece N. Molesworth en la guía *or Am* el directorio? (**b**) **listings** *(in newspaper)* cartelera *f*; **listings magazine** = guía de espectáculos y ocio

listless ['lɪstlɪs] *adj (lacking energy)* desfallecido(a), cansino(a); *(lacking enthusiasm)* desanimado(a), apático(a)

listlessly ['lɪstlɪslɪ] *adv (without energy)* cansinamente, lánguidamente; *(without enthusiasm)* apáticamente

listlessness ['lɪstlɪsnɪs] *n (lack of energy)* desfallecimiento *m*, falta *f* de fuerzas; *(lack of enthusiasm)* desánimo *m*, apatía *f*

lit[1] [lɪt] **1** *pt & pp of* **light**

2 *adj* (**a**) *(illuminated)* iluminado(a); **the room is well/badly l.** la habitación está bien/mal iluminada (**b**) *US Fam (drunk)* piripi

lit[2] *n Fam* **she teaches English l.** da clases *or* enseña literatura inglesa

litany ['lɪtənɪ] *n* (**a**) *Rel* letanía *f* (**b**) *(of complaints)* letanía *f*

lit crit [lɪt'krɪt] *n Fam* crítica *f* literaria

litchi *US* = **lychee**

lite [laɪt] *adj (low-calorie)* light *inv*, bajo(a) en calorías

liter *US* = **litre**

literacy ['lɪtərəsɪ] *n* alfabetización *f*; **adult l.** alfabetización de adultos; **the work requires a high degree of l.** el trabajo requiere un gran dominio lingüístico elevado ►► ***l. campaign*** campaña *f* de alfabetización; ***l. rate*** índice *m* de alfabetización

literal ['lɪtərəl] **1** *adj (translation, sense)* literal; **to take sth in a l. sense** tomar algo al pie de la letra; **don't be so l.!** ¡échale un poco de imaginación!

2 *n Typ* errata *f*

literalist ['lɪtərəlɪst] *n* (**a**) *(unimaginative person)* **to be a l.** tomarse las cosas al pie de la letra (**b**) *Pej (in art, film, literature)* realista *mf*

literally ['lɪtərəlɪ] *adv* (**a**) *(not figuratively)* literalmente; **to translate sth l.** traducir algo literalmente; **to take sth l.** tomar algo al pie de la letra; **he was l. bleeding to death** se estaba desangrando vivo; **it was l. this big!** ¡era sin exagerar así de grande! (**b**) *Fam (in exaggeration)* **she l. flew down the stairs** bajó las escaleras volando; **he l. blew up with rage** se puso hecho una furia

literal-minded ['lɪtərəl'maɪndɪd] *adj* poco imaginativo(a)

literary ['lɪtərərɪ] *adj (language, style)* literario(a); **a l. man** un hombre de letras ►► ***l. agent*** agente *mf* literario(a); ***l. critic*** crítico(a) *m,f* literario(a); ***l. criticism*** crítica *f* literaria

literate ['lɪtərɪt] *adj* (**a**) **to be l.** *(able to read and write)* saber leer y escribir (**b**) *(style)* culto(a) (**c**) *(educated)* culto(a), instruido(a)

> **False friend:** The Spanish word **literato** is not a translation for the English word **literate**. In Spanish **literato** means "writer, author".

literati [lɪtə'rɑːtɪ] *npl Formal* literatos *mpl*, gente *f* de las letras

literature ['lɪtərɪtʃə(r)] *n* (**a**) *(fiction, poetry)* literatura *f*; **Spanish l.** literatura española (**b**) *(of academic subject)* bibliografía *f* (**c**) *Com (leaflets)* folletos *mpl*

lithe [laɪð] *adj* ágil

lithiasis [lɪ'θaɪəsɪs] *n Med* litiasis *f*

lithium ['lɪθɪəm] *n Chem* litio *m*

lithograph ['lɪθəgræf] **1** *n* litografía *f*

2 *vt* litografiar

lithographic [lɪθə'græfɪk] *adj* litográfico(a)

lithography [lɪ'θɒgrəfɪ] *n* litografía *f*

lithosphere ['lɪθəsfɪə(r)] *n Geol* litosfera *f*

Lithuania [lɪθjʊ'eɪnɪə] *n* Lituania

Lithuanian [lɪθjʊ'eɪnɪən] **1** *n* (**a**) *(person)* lituano(a) *m,f* (**b**) *(language)* lituano *m*

2 *adj* lituano(a)

litigant ['lɪtɪgənt] *n Law* litigante *mf*, pleiteante *mf*

litigate ['lɪtɪgeɪt] *vi Law* litigar, pleitear

litigator ['lɪtɪgeɪtə(r)] *n Law* (**a**) *(lawyer)* abogado(a) *m,f* litigante (**b**) *(plaintiff, defendant)* litigante *mf*

litigation [lɪtɪ'geɪʃən] *n Law* litigio *m*, pleito *m*

litigious [lɪ'tɪdʒəs] *adj Formal* litigante, litigioso(a); **a l. person** una persona siempre metida en pleitos

litmus ['lɪtməs] *n* ***l. paper*** papel *m* de tornasol; *Fig* ***l. test*** prueba *f* definitiva

litotes ['laɪtəʊtiːz] *(pl* **litotes**) *n Lit* lítote *f*, lítotes *f inv*

litre, *US* **liter** ['liːtə(r)] *n* litro *m*

litter ['lɪtə(r)] **1** *n* (**a**) *(rubbish)* basura *f*; **no l.** *(sign)* no tirar basura; **his desk was covered in a l. of papers** tenía la mesa a rebosar de papeles revueltos ►► *Br* ***l. bin*** cubo *m* de basura; *Fam* ***l. lout*** = persona que arroja desperdicios en la vía pública; **don't be a l. lout** no tires la basura al suelo

(**b**) *(of animal)* camada *f*

(**c**) *(for cat)* arena *f* absorbente ►► ***l. tray*** cama *f or* bandeja *f* para la arena del gato

(**d**) *Agr (of straw, hay) (to bed animals)* lecho *m* de paja

(**e**) *(for carrying wounded)* camilla *f*

(**f**) *Hist (conveyance)* litera *f*

2 *vt* (**a**) *(cover with litter)* **don't l. the streets** no tires basura a la calle

(**b**) *(cover, strew)* **clothes littered the room, the room was littered with clothes** había ropa tirada por todas partes en la habitación; **don't l. the table (up) with your tools** no me llenes la mesa de herramientas; **her works are littered with allusions to the classics** sus obras están repletas de referencias a los clásicos; **his life is littered with failed love affairs** su vida está repleta de fracasos amorosos

3 *vi* (**a**) *(give birth)* parir (**b**) *US (with rubbish)* **no littering** *(sign)* no tirar basura

litterbug ['lɪtəbʌg] *n Fam* = persona que arroja desperdicios en la vía pública; **don't be a l.** no tires la basura al suelo

LITTLE ['lɪtəl] **1** *n* poco *m*; **l. of the castle remains** quedan pocos restos del castillo; **there is l. to be gained from such a policy** una política así no va a beneficiarnos mucho; **to eat l. or nothing** apenas comer; **a l.** un poco; **a l. hot/slow** un poco caliente/lento(a); **a l. more** un poco más, algo más; **a l. over half the participants** algo más de la mitad de los participantes; **she ate as l. as possible** comió lo mínimo (indispensable); **for as l. as $50** por sólo 50 dólares; **every l. helps** todo cuenta aunque sea poco, cualquier cantidad sirve; **there's precious l. to be pleased about** hay muy pocos motivos para sentirse satisfecho; **he knows very l.** no sabe casi nada; **I see very l. of her** apenas la veo; **they took what l. we had, they took the l. that we had** se llevaron lo poco que teníamos; **l. by l.** poco a poco; **to be too l. too late** llegar mal y tarde

2 *adj* (**a**) *(small)* pequeño(a), *esp Am* chico(a); **a l. girl** una niña pequeña *or esp Am* chica; **a l. house** una casita; **a l. bit** un poco; **we still have a l. way to go** todavía nos queda un poco para llegar; **wait a l. while!** ¡espera un poco!; **a l. while ago** hace poco; **could I have a l. word with you?** ¿puedo hablar contigo un momento?; **you need to**

try just that l. bit harder tienes que esforzarte un poquito más; I've brought a l. something to say thanks he traído una cosilla para darte las gracias, *RP* te traje una pavadita como agradecimiento; *Ironic* they owe me the l. sum of £50,000 me deben la módica suma de 50.000 libras; *Fig* how do you know? – a l. bird told me ¿cómo lo sabes? – me lo dijo un pajarito; PROV l. things amuse l. minds todos los tontos se ríen de las mismas tonterías ▸▸ ***L. Bear*** Osa *f* Menor; ***l. bittern*** avetorillo *m*; ***l. egret*** garceta *f*; *Br Aut* ***l. end*** pie *m* de biela; ***l. Englander*** = inglés patriota y xenófobo; ***l. finger*** (dedo *m*) meñique *m*; IDIOM to twist sb round one's l. finger hacer de alguien una marioneta; ***l. grebe*** zampullín *m* chico; *Hum* ***l. green men*** marcianitos *mpl*; ***l. gull*** gaviota *f* enana; ***l. owl*** mochuelo *m*; ***l. penguin*** pingüino *m* enano; ***the l. people*** *(fairies)* las hadas; ***l. slam*** *(in bridge)* pequeño slam *m*; ***l. swift*** vencejo *m* moro; ***l. tern*** charrancito *m*; ***l. toe*** meñique *m* del pie

(b) *(young)* pequeño(a), *esp Am* chico(a); **when I was l.** cuando era pequeño(a) *or esp Am* chico(a); **my l. brother/sister** mi hermano pequeño *or Am* chico/hermana pequeña *or Am* chica; **they have a l. boy/girl** tienen un hijo pequeño *or Am* chico/una hija pequeña *or Am* chica; **the l. ones** *(children)* los niños, *esp Am* los nenes ▸▸ ***L. League*** *(in baseball)* = liga de béisbol infantil celebrada durante el verano y patrocinada por empresas

(c) *(for emphasis) Fam* **a l. old man/lady** un viejecito/una viejecita, un viejito/una viejita; **what a strange l. man!** ¡qué hombre tan raro!; **a lovely l. house** una casita preciosa; **the poor l. thing!** ¡pobrecillo!, ¡pobrecito!; **that child is a l. terror!** ¡ese niño es un diablillo!; **it might take a l. while** puede que tarde un rato, *Am* puede llegar a demorar un rato

(d) (*comparative* **less**, *superlative* **least**) *(not much)* poco(a); **a l. money/luck** un poco de dinero/suerte; **we had too l. money** no teníamos suficiente dinero; **there is l. hope/doubt...** quedan pocas esperanzas/dudas...; **it makes l. sense** no tiene mucho sentido; **they have l. or no chance** prácticamente no tienen posibilidades, *Esp* no tienen apenas posibilidades; **l. wonder she was upset!** ¡no me extraña que estuviera disgustada!; **they took what l.** *or* **the l. money we had** se llevaron el poco dinero que teníamos

3 *adv* (*comparative* **less** *superlative* **least**) poco; **l. known** poco conocido; **the theory is l. understood** pocos entienden realmente la teoría; **a l.** un poco; **I was more than a l.** *or* **not a l. annoyed** estaba bastante *esp Esp* enfadado *or esp Am* enojado; **l. did we know that...** no nos imaginábamos que..., no teníamos ni idea de que...; **l. did I think that...** poco me podía imaginar que...; **you're l. better than they are** tú no eres mucho mejor que ellos; **l. more than an hour ago** hace poco más de una hora; **that's l. short of bribery** eso es poco menos que un soborno; **we let her in, l. though we wanted to** la dejamos entrar, aunque no por gusto; **to make l. of sth** no dar importancia a algo; **to think l. of sth/sb** no tener muy buen concepto de algo/alguien

---

littoral ['lɪtərəl] *Geog* 1 *n* litoral *m*

2 *adj* litoral *m*

liturgical [lɪ'tɜːdʒɪkəl] *adj Rel* litúrgico(a)

liturgy ['lɪtədʒɪ] *n Rel* liturgia *f*

livable = **liveable**

live[1] [laɪv] 1 *adj* (a) *(person, animal)* vivo(a); *Fam* **a real l. film star** un estrella de carne y hueso; **a l. issue** un tema candente; *US Fam* **a l. one** un(a) ingenuo(a) *or Esp* memo(a) (b) *(TV, radio broadcast)* en directo; **recorded before a l. audience** grabado(a) con público en directo; **a l. performance** una actuación en vivo ▸▸ *Comptr* ***l. cam*** webcam *f* (c) *(ammunition) (unused)* sin utilizar; *(not blank)* real (d) *Elec* ***l. wire*** cable *m* con corriente; *Fig* **she's a l. wire** rebosa energía

2 *adv (to broadcast, perform)* en directo

LIVE[2] [lɪv] 1 *vt* vivir; **to l. a happy/long life** vivir una vida feliz/larga; **to l. a life of depravity** llevar una vida depravada; **to l. a lie** vivir en la mentira; **to l. life to the full** vivir la vida al máximo; **I want to l. my own life** quiero vivir mi vida; **she lived the life of a movie star for six years** vivió como una estrella de cine durante seis años; **I lived every moment of the match** realmente viví cada minuto de ese partido; **to l. and breathe sth** vivir por y para algo

2 *vi* (a) *(be or stay alive)* vivir; **they don't think she will l.** no creen que viva; **I've been given a year to l.** me han dado un año de vida; **the greatest pianist that ever lived** el mejor pianista de todos los tiempos; **to l. for a hundred years** vivir cien años; **he lived to the age of ninety** vivió hasta los noventa años; **if I l. to be a hundred, I'll still never understand** aunque viva cien años, nunca lo entenderé; **I hope I will l. to see humankind set foot on Mars** espero llegar a ver la llegada del hombre a Marte; **you may l. to regret that decision** puede que al final te arrepientas de esa decisión; **as long as I l.** mientras viva; *Fam* **are you all right? – I'll l.** ¿estás bien? – sobreviviré; **Elvis lives!** ¡Elvis está vivo!; **l. and let l.** vive y deja vivir; **you l. and learn** ¡vivir para ver!; **you only l. once** sólo se vive una vez; *Fig* **to l. to fight another day** sobrevivir para volver a luchar; *Fig* **I lived to tell the tale** viví para contarlo

(b) *(have a specified way of life)* vivir; **we l. in fear of our lives** vivimos con el temor de morir; **to l. in the past** vivir en el pasado; **to l. in poverty/luxury** vivir en la pobreza/el lujo; **they all lived happily ever after** vivieron felices y comieron perdices; *Old-fashioned or Hum* **to l. in sin** vivir en pecado; **to l. like a king** *or* **lord** vivir a cuerpo de rey, vivir como un señor

(c) *(experience life)* **I want to l. a little** quiero disfrutar un poco de la vida; **you haven't lived until you've been to San Francisco** si no has visto San Francisco no has visto nada

(d) *(reside)* vivir; **where does she l.?** ¿dónde vive?; **I l. in** *or* **on Bank Street** vivo en Bank Street; **the giant tortoise lives mainly in the Galapagos** la tortuga gigante habita principalmente en las Islas Galápagos; **he practically lives in the library** prácticamente vive en la biblioteca; *Fam* **where does this saucepan l.?** ¿dónde va esta cacerola?

▸ **live by** *vt insep* **she lives by her writing** vive de lo que escribe; **he lived by the sword and died by the sword** la espada lo acompañó durante su vida y finalmente le dio la muerte; **to l. by one's principles** ser un hombre/una mujer de principios; **she lived by her wits** vivió de su ingenio

▸ **live down** *vt sep (mistake, one's past)* relegar al olvido, enterrar; **I'll never l. it down** nunca lograré que se olvide

▸ **live for** *vt insep* **there's nothing left to l. for** no quedan razones para vivir; **to l. for one's work** vivir para el trabajo; **I l. for the day when...** vivo esperando el día en que...; **to l. for the day** *or* **moment** vivir el presente

▸ **live in** *vi (housekeeper, pupil)* estar interno(a)

▸ **live off** *vt insep (depend on)* vivir de; **to l. off the land** vivir de la tierra; **to l. off the state** vivir del dinero del estado

▸ **live on** 1 *vt insep (depend on)* vivir de; **she lives on chocolate** no come más que chocolate; **I l. on $150 a week** vivo con 150 dólares a la semana; **it's not enough to l. on** no da para vivir; **she's living on her wits** vive de su ingenio

2 *vi (continue to live) (person)* sobrevivir, vivir; *(memory)* perdurar

▸ **live out** 1 *vt sep* (a) *(spend)* **she lived out the rest of her life in Spain** pasó el resto de su vida en España; **she lived out her life** *or* **days in poverty/sadness** acabó sus días sumida en la pobreza/tristeza

(b) *(fulfil)* **to l. out a fantasy** vivir *or* realizar una fantasía

2 *vi* estar externo(a)

▸ **live out of** *vt insep* **to l. out of tins** *or* **cans** vivir a base de latas de conserva; **I've been living out of a suitcase for the past month** llevo *or Am* tengo un mes viviendo en hoteles

▸ **live through** *vt insep (survive)* sobrevivir a; *(experience)* pasar por

▸ **live together** *vi (cohabit)* vivir juntos(as); **why can't we all l. together in peace?** ¿por qué no podemos vivir todos juntos en paz?

▸ **live up** *vt sep Fam* **to l. it up** pasarlo bien, divertirse

▸ **live up to** *vt insep (expectations)* responder a, estar a la altura de; **to fail to l. up to expectations** no estar a la altura de las expectativas; **he lives up to his principles** vive de acuerdo con sus principios

▸ **live with** *vt insep* (a) *(cohabit with)* vivir con; **they l. with each other** viven juntos

(b) *(put up with)* **she has been living with this knowledge for some time** hace algún tiempo que lo sabe; **I can l. with that** eso no es problema; **he'll have to l. with this for the rest of his life** *(to suffer from the memory of)* tendrá que vivir con ese recuerdo durante el resto de su vida; **you'll just have to l. with it!** ¡tendrás que aceptarlo!

(c) *(match, keep up with)* **he couldn't l. with the pace** no pudo aguantar el ritmo; **Ivanisevic couldn't l. with Becker** Ivanisevic era claramente inferior a Becker

(d) *(remain with)* **this memory will l. with us for a long time** guardaremos este recuerdo durante mucho tiempo

▸ **live without** *vt insep* **you'll just have to learn to l. without it!** ¡tendrás que aprender a vivir sin ello!

---

liveable, livable ['lɪvəbəl] *adj* (a) *(house, city)* habitable (b) *(bearable)* **his visits made her life l.** sus visitas le hacían la vida más llevadera; *Fam* **she is not l. with** no hay quien viva con ella

lived-in ['lɪvdɪn] *adj (home, room)* acogedor(ora); **to have a l. feel (to it)** tener un aspecto acogedor; **a l. face** un rostro curtido

live-in ['lɪvɪn] *adj (chauffeur, nanny)* interno(a); **she has a l. lover** su amante vive con ella

livelihood ['laɪvlɪhʊd] *n* sustento *m*; **tourism is our l.** vivimos del turismo, nuestro sustento es el turismo; **it's not a hobby, it's my l.** no es una distracción, así me gano la vida; **to earn** *or* **gain one's l.** ganarse la vida; **to lose one's l.** perder el sustento

liveliness ['laɪvlɪnɪs] *n* (**a**) *(of person)* vivacidad *f*, viveza *f*; *(of place, debate)* animación *f*; *(of music)* alegría *f* (**b**) *(of imagination)* vivacidad *f* (**c**) *(of colours, decor)* alegría *f*

livelong ['lɪvlɒŋ] *adj Literary (complete)* **the l. day** todo el santo día; **the l. night** toda la santa noche

lively ['laɪvlɪ] *adj* (**a**) *(energetic, full of life) (person, place, debate)* animado(a); *(music)* alegre; *(dance)* movido(a); **the town gets a bit livelier in summer** la ciudad se anima un poco en verano; *Fam* **to make things l. for sb** ponérselo difícil a alguien; *Fam* **look l.!** ¡vamos, muévete!

(**b**) *(keen) (interest, imagination)* vivo(a); **to take a l. interest in sth** estar vivamente interesado(a) por algo, interesarse vivamente por algo; **a l. mind** una mente despierta

(**c**) *(colours, decor)* alegre

liven ['laɪvən]

▸ **liven up 1** *vt sep* animar, alegrar; **some pictures would l. up the text a bit** algunas ilustraciones le darían más vida al texto

2 *vi* animarse

liver[1] ['lɪvə(r)] *n* hígado *m*; **a l. complaint** una enfermedad del hígado ▸▸ ***l. fluke*** *(flatworm)* duela *f* del hígado; *Br* ***l. salts*** sal *f* de frutas; ***l. sausage*** embutido *m* de paté de hígado; ***l. spot*** *(on skin)* mancha *f* de vejez

liver[2] *n (person)* **to be a fast** *or* **high l.** llevar una vida disoluta

liveried ['lɪvərɪd] *adj* con librea

liverish ['lɪvərɪʃ] *adj* (**a**) *Fam (unwell)* empachado(a); **to be** *or* **to feel l.** estar *or* sentirse empachado(a) (**b**) *(irritable)* enojadizo(a)

Liverpool ['lɪvəpu:l] *n* Liverpool

Liverpudlian [lɪvə'pʌdlɪən] **1** *n* persona de Liverpool *(Inglaterra)*

2 *adj* de Liverpool *(Inglaterra)*

liverwort ['lɪvəwɜ:t] *n* hepática *f*

liverwurst ['lɪvəwɜ:st] *n US* embutido *m* de paté de hígado

livery ['lɪvərɪ] *n* (**a**) *(of servant)* librea *f* (**b**) *(of company)* distintivo *m* (**c**) ***l. stable*** *(for keeping horses)* cuadra *f*, caballeriza *f*; *(for hiring horses)* picadero *m*

lives *pl of* **life**

livestock ['laɪvstɒk] *n* ganado *m*

liveware ['laɪvweə(r)] *n Fam Comptr* elemento *m* humano

livid ['lɪvɪd] *adj* (**a**) *(angry)* **to be l. (with rage)** estar colérico(a) *or* enfurecido(a) (**b**) *(bluish-grey)* lívido(a)

living ['lɪvɪŋ] **1** *n* (**a**) *(way of life)* vida *f*; **to be fond of good l.** ser aficionado a la buena vida; **plain l.** vida sencilla (**b**) *(livelihood)* sustento *m*; **to earn one's l.** ganarse la vida; **to make a l.** ganarse la vida; **what does he do for a l.?** ¿a qué se dedica?; **I have to work for a l.** tengo que trabajar para ganarme la vida (**c**) *Br Rel* beneficio *m* (eclesiástico)

2 *npl* **the l.** los vivos

3 *adj* (**a**) *(not dead)* vivo(a); **she is our finest l. artist** es nuestra mejor artista viva; **there is not a l. soul to be seen** no se ve ni un alma; **the best/worst within l. memory** lo mejor/peor que se recuerda; **to be l. proof of sth** ser la prueba palpable de algo ▸▸ ***l. fossil*** fósil *m* viviente; ***l. wage*** salario *m* decente *or* digno; ***l. will*** testamento *m* en vida

(**b**) *(for day-to-day life) (space)* vital; **the l. area is separated from the bedrooms** la zona de estar está separada de los dormitorios ▸▸ ***l. conditions*** condiciones *fpl* de vida; ***l. expenses*** gastos *mpl (cotidianos)*; ***l. quarters*** *(for servants)* habitaciones *fpl* del servicio; *(on ship)* camarotes *mpl* de la tripulación; ***l. standards*** nivel *m* de vida

(**c**) IDIOMS **a l. death: it was a l. death for him** para él fue como una muerte en vida; **he made my life a l. hell** convirtió mi vida en un infierno *or* una pesadilla; *Fam* **to scare the l. daylights out of sb** dar un susto de muerte a alguien; *Fam* **to beat** *or* **knock** *or* **thrash the l. daylights out of sb** dar una buena paliza *or* tunda a alguien

living-flame ['lɪvɪŋ'fleɪm] *adj* **l. gas fire** = estufa de gas con efecto llama, que imita a una chimenea

living-room ['lɪvɪŋru:m] *n* sala *f or* cuarto *m* de estar, salón *m*

Livy ['lɪvɪ] *pr n* Tito Livio

lizard ['lɪzəd] *n (small)* lagartija *f*; *(large)* lagarto *m*

llama ['lɑ:mə] *n (animal)* llama *f*

LLB [elel'bi:] *n* (*abbr* **Bachelor of Laws**) (**a**) *(qualification)* licenciatura *f* en derecho (**b**) *(person)* licenciado(a) *m,f* en derecho

LLD [elel'di:] *n* (*abbr* **Doctor of Laws**) (**a**) *(qualification)* doctorado *m* en derecho (**b**) *(person)* doctorado(a) *m,f* en derecho

lo [ləʊ] *exclam* (**a**) *Archaic or Literary* ¡mirad! (**b**) *Literary or Hum* **lo and behold...** hete aquí que...

loach ['ləʊtʃ] *n* lobo *m*, locha *f*

LOAD [ləʊd] **1** *n* (**a**) *(of vehicle, person)* carga *f*; **a l. of gravel** una carga de grava; **we moved all the stuff in ten loads** nos llevamos todo en diez viajes; **maximum l. 50 tonnes** *(sign)* carga máxima 50 toneladas

(**b**) *(burden)* carga *f*; **I've got a heavy/light teaching l.** tengo muchas/pocas horas de clase; **to share/spread the l.** compartir/repartir el trabajo; **that's a l. off my mind!** ¡me quito *or Am* saco un peso de encima!; *US Fam* **to have a l. on** ir borracho(a), *Esp* ir ciego(a), *Méx* ir hasta atrás, *RP* andar en pedo

(**c**) *(of washing)* **put another l. in the washing machine** pon otra lavadora; **half l.** media carga

(**d**) *Elec* carga *f*

(**e**) *Fam (lot)* **a l. (of), loads (of)** un montón (de); **it's a l. of rubbish!** *(nonsense)* ¡no son más que tonterías!; *(very bad)* ¡es nefasto(a) *or* de pena!; **we've got loads of time/money** tenemos tiempo/dinero de sobra; **there was loads to drink** había un montón de bebida; **it's loads better** es muchísimo mejor; **get a l. of this!** ¡no te lo pierdas!, *Esp* ¡al loro con esto!

2 *vt* (**a**) *(vehicle, goods)* cargar; **to l. sth into** *or* **onto sth** cargar algo en algo; **l. the bags into the taxi** mete las bolsas en el taxi; **the ship is loading grain** están cargando el barco de cereales

(**b**) *(gun)* cargar; **l. the film into the camera** introduzca el carrete *or* rollo en la cámara

(**c**) *Comptr* cargar; **to l. a program onto a computer** cargar un programa en *Esp* un ordenador *or Am* una computadora

(**d**) *(bias)* **to l. the dice** trucar los dados; **to be loaded in favour of/against sb** favorecer/perjudicar a alguien

3 *vi* (**a**) *(truck, person)* cargar

(**b**) *Comptr* cargarse

▸ **load down** *vt sep* **to be loaded down with sth** *(shopping, bags)* estar cargado(a) de algo; *(guilt, responsibility)* cargar con algo

▸ **load up 1** *vt sep* cargar (**with** con)

2 *vi* cargar (**with** con)

load-bearing ['ləʊdbeərɪŋ] *adj (wall)* maestro(a)

loaded ['ləʊdɪd] *adj* (**a**) *(vehicle)* cargado(a)

(**b**) **to be l. with** *(charged with)* estar cargado(a) de; **his words were l. with sarcasm** sus palabras estaban cargadas de sarcasmo

(**c**) *(gun, camera)* cargado(a); **to be l.** estar cargado(a)

(**d**) *(dice)* trucado(a)

(**e**) *(comment)* capcioso(a), intencionado(a); **a l. question** una pregunta capciosa

(**f**) *Fam (rich)* **to be l.** estar forrado(a)

(**g**) *US Fam (drunk) Esp, RP* mamado(a), *Méx* hasta atrás; *(on drugs)* colocado(a), *RP* falopeado(a)

loader ['ləʊdə(r)] *n* (**a**) *(person)* cargador(ora) *m,f* (**b**) *(mechanism)* cargador *m* (**c**) *Comptr* cargador *m*

loading ['ləʊdɪŋ] *n (of lorry)* carga *f* ▸▸ ***l. bay*** zona *f* de carga y descarga; *Rail* ***l. gauge*** gálibo *m* de carga

loadline ['ləʊdlaɪn] *n Naut* línea *f* de carga

loadmaster ['ləʊdmɑ:stə(r)] *n Av* supervisor(ora) *m,f* de carga

loadsa- ['ləʊdzə] *prefix Br Fam* **loadsamoney** un dineral; **loadsawork** un montonazo de trabajo, *Esp* (un) mogollón de trabajo

loadstar = **lodestar**

loadstone = **lodestone**

loaf [ləʊf] (*pl* **loaves** [ləʊvz]) *n (of bread)* pan *m*; **a l. of bread** *(in general)* un pan; *(brick-shaped)* un pan de molde, *Col* un pan tajado, *RP* un pan lactal; *(round and flat)* una hogaza de pan; IDIOM *Br* **use your l.!** ¡utiliza la mollera!; PROV **half a l. is better than no bread** a falta de pan, buenas son tortas ▸▸ *US* ***l. bread*** pan *m* de molde *or Col* pan tajado *or RP* lactal; ***l. sugar*** pan *m* de azúcar; ***l. tin*** molde *m* para pan

▸ **loaf about, loaf around** *vi* haraganear, gandulear

loafer ['ləʊfə(r)] *n* (**a**) *(person)* haragán(ana) *m,f*, gandul(ula) *m,f* (**b**) *(shoe)* mocasín *m*

loam [ləʊm] *n (soil)* marga *f*

loan [ləʊn] **1** *n* (**a**) *(money)* préstamo *m*; **he asked me for a l.** me pidió dinero prestado; **to take out a l.** *(from bank, loan company)* obtener un préstamo *or* crédito *or Méx* prestamiento ▸▸ ***l. capital*** recursos *m* ajenos (a largo plazo); *Fam* ***l. shark*** usurero(a) *m,f* (**b**) *(act of lending)* **to give sb a l. of sth** prestar algo a alguien; **may I have the l. of your typewriter?** ¿me prestas *or Esp* dejas la máquina de escribir?; *Fam* **let**

me have a l. of your scissors te cojo *or* pillo las tijeras; **to be on l.** estar en préstamo; **on l. from the Louvre** prestado(a) por el Louvre; **she's on l. from head office** la han trasladado temporalmente desde la central

2 *vt* prestar; **to l. sb sth, to l. sth to sb** prestar algo a alguien; **he asked me to l. him £20** me pidió que le prestara *or Esp* dejara 20 libras

loanword ['ləʊnwɜːd] *n Ling* préstamo *m* (lingüístico)

loath, loth [ləʊθ] *adj* **I'm very l. to admit it, but...** me cuesta mucho admitirlo pero...; **they were l. to leave** les costaba mucho irse; **nothing l.** solícitamente, con gusto

loathe [ləʊð] *vt* aborrecer; **to l. doing sth** aborrecer hacer algo

loathing ['ləʊðɪŋ] *n* aborrecimiento *m*; **it fills me with l.** me repugna

loathsome ['ləʊðsəm] *adj (person, character, behaviour)* odioso(a), detestable

loaves *pl of* **loaf**

lob [lɒb] 1 *n Sport (in tennis)* globo *m*, lob *m*; *(in soccer)* vaselina *f*

2 *vt* (*pt & pp* **lobbed**) (**a**) *(stone, grenade)* lanzar (en parábola); **she lobbed the ball over my head** lanzó la pelota por encima de mi cabeza (**b**) *Sport (in tennis)* hacer un globo *or* lob a; **he lobbed the goalkeeper** le hizo una vaselina al portero

lobby ['lɒbɪ] 1 *n* (**a**) *(of hotel)* vestíbulo *m*; *(apartment block)* portería *f*

(**b**) *Pol (pressure group)* grupo *m* de presión, lobby *m*

(**c**) *Br Pol (room for meeting public)* = sala en la Cámara de los Comunes destinada a encuentros entre los políticos y el público; **(division) l.** = pasillo de la Cámara de los Comunes al que van los parlamentarios cuando se dividen para votar ►► *Journ* ***l. correspondent*** enviado(a) *m,f* (especial) en el parlamento

2 *vt Pol* **to l. an MP** presionar a un diputado

3 *vi Pol* presionar; **to l. for/against sth** hacer presión a favor de/en contra de algo

lobbying ['lɒbɪɪŋ] *n Pol* presiones *fpl* políticas

lobbyist ['lɒbɪɪst] *n Pol* miembro *m* de un lobby *or* grupo de presión

lobe [ləʊb] *n* (**a**) *(of ear)* lóbulo *m* (**b**) *(of brain, liver, lung)* lóbulo *m* (**c**) *(of leaf)* lóbulo *m*

lobelia [ləʊ'biːlɪə] *n* lobelia *f*

lobotomize [lə'bɒtəmaɪz] *vt* practicar una lobotomía a

lobotomy [lə'bɒtəmɪ] *n* lobotomía *f*

lobster ['lɒbstə(r)] *n (with pincers)* bogavante *m*; **(spiny** *or* **rock) l.** *(without pincers)* langosta *f*; IDIOM **he was as red as a l.** *(sunburnt)* estaba rojo como un cangrejo ►► ***l. pot*** nasa *f*; *Culin* ***l. thermidor*** langosta *f* thermidor

local ['ləʊkəl] 1 *n* (**a**) *(person)* lugareño(a) *m,f*; **the locals** los lugareños, los paisanos (**b**) *Br Fam (pub)* bar *m* habitual (**c**) *US (train)* = tren que hace parada en todas las estaciones; *(bus)* = autobús que se detiene en todas las paradas (**d**) *US (union branch)* delegación *f* sindical local (**e**) *Fam (anaesthetic)* anestesia *f* local

2 *adj* (**a**) *(of, from the area)* local; **a l. man/woman** un lugareño/una lugareña; **the murderer was a l. man** el asesino era de la zona; **l. produce** los productos de la región; **the l. shops sell everything I need** las tiendas del barrio venden todo lo que necesito ►► ***l. call*** llamada *f or Am* llamado *m* local *or* urbano(a); ***l. colour*** *(in story)* color *m* local; *Br* ***l. derby*** *(match)* derby *m* local; ***l. newspaper*** periódico *m* local; ***l. radio*** emisora *f* local; *Br* ***l. rate*** tarifa *f* local; ***l. time*** hora *f* local

(**b**) *Pol (services, council)* local ►► *Br* ***l. authority*** administración *f* local; ***l. council*** junta *f* municipal; *Br* ***l. education authority*** = organismo local encargado de la enseñanza; ***l. elections*** elecciones *fpl* municipales; ***l. government*** gobierno *m* local; *Br* ***l. health authority*** = organismo local encargado de la salud

(**c**) *Med (infection, pain)* local ►► ***l. anaesthetic*** anestesia *f* local

(**d**) *Comptr* ***l. area network*** red *f* de área local; ***l. bus*** bus *m* local

locale [ləʊ'kɑːl] *n* emplazamiento *m*, lugar *m*

locality [ləʊ'kælɪtɪ] *n* vecindad *f*, zona *f*; **in the l.** en las inmediaciones

localization [ləʊkəlaɪ'zeɪʃən] *n Comptr* localización *f*

localize ['ləʊkəlaɪz] *vt (restrict)* localizar; **they aim to l. the effect of the strike** tratan de contener el impacto de la huelga

localized ['ləʊkəlaɪzd] *adj (restricted)* localizado(a); **a l. infection** una infección localizada; **to become l.** *(disease, pain)* localizarse

locally ['ləʊkəlɪ] *adv* localmente; **these issues must be decided l., not nationally** estos asuntos deben resolverse localmente *or* a nivel local, no en el ámbito nacional; **l. manufactured goods** productos fabricados en la zona; **she was well known l.** era muy conocida entre las gentes del lugar; **I live/work l.** vivo/trabajo cerca; **we shop l.** hacemos las compras en el vecindario

locate [ləʊ'keɪt] 1 *vt* (**a**) *(find)* localizar; **they have located the cause of the trouble** han localizado la causa del problema (**b**) *(situate)* emplazar, situar, ubicar; **the house is conveniently located for shops and public transport** la casa está situada cerca de las tiendas y del transporte público

2 *vi* (**a**) *(company)* establecerse, instalarse (**b**) *US (person)* establecerse, instalarse

location [ləʊ'keɪʃən] *n* (**a**) *(place)* emplazamiento *m*, ubicación *f*; **what a beautiful l. for a campus!** ¡es un lugar precioso para un campus!; **what is your present l.?** ¿dónde te encuentras ahora? (**b**) *Cin* lugar *m* de filmación; **on l.** en exteriores; **filmed entirely on l. in Guatemala** filmado íntegramente en exteriores guatemaltecos ►► ***l. shot*** toma *f* en exteriores (**c**) *Comptr (of web page)* dirección *f*

locative ['lɒkətɪv] *Gram* 1 *n* locativo *m*

2 *adj* locativo(a)

loc cit [lɒk'sɪt] (*abbr* **loco citato**) loc. cit.

loch [lɒχ, lɒk] *n Scot (lake)* lago *m*; *(open to sea)* ría *f*, fiordo *m*

loci *pl of* **locus**

lock[1] [lɒk] 1 *n* (**a**) *(on door, drawer, car)* cerradura *f*; **to be under l. and key** estar encerrado(a) bajo llave; IDIOM **l., stock and barrel** íntegramente; **the family has moved l., stock and barrel to Canada** la familia al completo se ha mudado a Canadá

(**b**) *(in wrestling)* llave *f*, inmovilización *f*; IDIOM *US* **to have a l. on sth** tener control total sobre algo; IDIOM *US* **to be a l.** ser seguro(a)

(**c**) *(on canal)* esclusa *f* ►► ***l. gate*** compuerta *f*; ***l. keeper*** esclusero(a) *m,f*

(**d**) *Br Aut* ángulo *m* de giro; **on full l.** con las ruedas giradas a tope

(**e**) **l. (forward)** *(in rugby)* segunda línea *mf*

2 *vt* (**a**) *(door, drawer, car)* cerrar (con llave); **l. all these papers in the safe** guarda estas hojas en la caja fuerte

(**b**) *(hold tightly)* **they were locked in each other's arms** estaban fundidos en un fuerte abrazo; **the unions were locked in a dispute with the management** los sindicatos estaban enzarzados en un conflicto con la dirección; **they were locked into the agreement** el acuerdo los había atado de pies y manos; **to l. arms** *(police cordon)* formar una barrera; **to l. horns** *(stags)* entrelazar la cornamenta; IDIOM **to l. horns with sb** enzarzarse en una disputa con alguien

(**c**) *Comptr* bloquear

3 *vi* (**a**) *(door, drawer)* cerrarse (**b**) *(engage)* trabarse (**c**) *(car wheels)* bloquearse

►**lock away** *vt sep (valuables)* guardar bajo llave; *(criminal)* encerrar

►**lock in** *vt sep* encerrar; **he locked himself in** se encerró

►**lock onto** *vt insep (of radar beam, missile)* captar, localizar

►**lock out** *vt sep* (**a**) *(of house)* **her father threatened to l. her out if she was late home** su padre la amenazó con dejarla en la calle si regresaba tarde a casa; **I locked myself out (of my house)** al salir me dejé las llaves dentro (de casa) (**b**) *Ind* **the workers were locked out** hubo un cierre patronal

►**lock up** 1 *vt sep* (**a**) *(criminal)* encerrar; *(valuables)* guardar bajo llave; **he should be locked up!** ¡a ése tendrían que encerrarlo! (**b**) *(house, premises)* cerrar (con llave) (**c**) *(capital)* inmovilizar; **all my money is locked up in this business** tengo todo mi dinero inmovilizado en mi negocio

2 *vi* cerrar (con llave)

lock[2] *n (of hair)* mechón *m*; **her golden locks** sus cabellos dorados

lockable ['lɒkəbəl] *adj* **it's lockable from inside** se puede cerrar por dentro

locked [lɒkt] *adj* (**a**) *(door, room)* cerrado(a) (con llave) (**b**) *US Fam* ***l. bowels*** estreñimiento *m*

locker ['lɒkə(r)] *n* (**a**) *(for luggage)* taquilla *f* (**b**) *(in school)* taquilla *f* ►► *US* ***l. room*** vestuarios *mpl*

locker-room ['lɒkə'ruːm] *adj (humour, joke)* muy de macho; **there's a l. atmosphere in the office** se respira un ambiente muy de macho en la oficina

locket ['lɒkɪt] *n* guardapelo *m*

lockjaw ['lɒkdʒɔː] *n Old-fashioned* tétanos *m inv*; **to have l.** padecer tétanos

locknut ['lɒknʌt] *n* tuerca *f* de seguridad, contratuerca *f*

lockout ['lɒkaʊt] *n* cierre *m* patronal

locksmith ['lɒksmɪθ] *n* cerrajero *m*

lockup ['lɒkʌp] *n* (**a**) *Fam (police cells)* calabozo *m* (**b**) *Br (for storage)* **l. (garage)** garaje *m*, *Am* cochera *f* (**c**) *Br* **l. (shop)** tienda *f (sin vivienda para el comerciante)*

loco [ˈləʊkəʊ] *Fam* **1** *n* locomotora *f*
2 *adj US (mad)* pirado(a), *CSur* rayado(a), *Méx* zafado(a)

locomotion [ləʊkəˈməʊʃən] *n* locomoción *f*

locomotive [ləʊkəˈməʊtɪv] **1** *n (train)* locomotora *f*
2 *adj* locomotor(ora)

locoweed [ˈləʊkəʊwi:d] *n US* (**a**) *(plant)* astrágalo *m or* tragacanto *m* americano (**b**) *Fam (marijuana)* maría *f*, grifa *f*, *Méx* mota *f*

locum [ˈləʊkəm] *n Br (doctor, vet)* suplente *mf*, sustituto(a) *m,f*

locus [ˈləʊkəs] (*pl* **loci** [ˈləʊsaɪ]) *n* (**a**) *Math* lugar *m* geométrico (**b**) *Biol* locus *m inv*

locust [ˈləʊkəst] *n* (**a**) *(insect)* langosta *f* (**b**) **l. (tree)** *(false acacia)* falsa acacia *f*, acacia *f* blanca *or* bastarda; *(carob tree)* algarrobo *m* ►► ***l. bean*** algarroba *f*

locution [ləˈkju:ʃən] *n Formal* locución *f*

lode [ləʊd] *n (of metallic ore)* veta *f*, filón *m*

loden [ˈləʊdən] *adj (jacket)* de loden; **a l. coat** un loden

lodestar, loadstar [ˈləʊdstɑ:(r)] *n* (**a**) *(Pole star)* estrella *f* polar (**b**) *(guide, example)* norte *m*

lodestone, loadstone [ˈləʊdstəʊn] *n (magnetite)* magnetita *f*, piedra *f* imán

lodge [lɒdʒ] **1** *n* (**a**) *(of porter)* garita *f*, portería *f*; *(of gatekeeper)* garita *f*, casa *f* del guarda (**b**) *(for hunters)* pabellón *m* de caza; *(skiers)* refugio *m* (**c**) *(hotel)* hotel *m* (**d**) *(of beaver)* madriguera *f* (**e**) *(of freemasons, fraternal society)* logia *f* (**f**) *US (union branch)* delegación *f* sindical local (**g**) *(of Native Americans)* choza *f*
2 *vt* (**a**) *(accommodate)* hospedar, alojar
(**b**) *(stick, embed)* **a fish bone lodged itself in his throat** le clavó una espina en la garganta; **his words were lodged in my memory** tenía sus palabras grabadas en la memoria
(**c**) *Law* **to l. an appeal** presentar una apelación, apelar; **he lodged a complaint with the authorities** presentó una queja ante las autoridades
(**d**) *(deposit for safekeeping)* **to l. sth with sb** depositar algo en manos de alguien
3 *vi* (**a**) *(live)* hospedarse, alojarse; **he is lodging at Mrs Smith's** *or* **with Mrs Smith** se hospeda *or* se aloja en casa de la señora Smith
(**b**) *(become fixed)* alojarse; **the bullet had lodged in his lung** la bala se le había alojado en el pulmón; **a fishbone lodged in her throat** tenía una espina clavada en la garganta; **the name had lodged in her memory** el nombre se le había quedado grabado en la memoria

lodger [ˈlɒdʒə(r)] *n* huésped *mf*, huéspeda *f*; **to take (in) lodgers** acoger huéspedes

lodging [ˈlɒdʒɪŋ] *n* alojamiento *m*; **board and l.** alojamiento y comida; **he took up lodgings with a local family** alquiló una habitación con una familia de la zona; **to live in lodgings** vivir en una habitación alquilada *(en casa de la persona que la alquila)* ►► ***l. house*** casa *f* de huéspedes

loess [ˈləʊɪs] *n Geol* loes *m inv*

loft [lɒft] **1** *n* (**a**) *(attic)* buhardilla *f*, ático *m*, desván *m* (**b**) *(in church)* galería *f* (**c**) *US (warehouse apartment)* = almacén reformado y convertido en apartamento (**d**) *(for hay)* pajar *m* (**e**) *(for pigeons)* palomar *m* (**f**) *(of golf club)* loft *m*, ángulo *m (de la cara del palo)*
2 *vt (ball)* lanzar por lo alto

loftily [ˈlɒftɪlɪ] *adv* (**a**) *(haughtily)* con arrogancia, con altanería (**b**) *(exaltedly)* con nobleza, insignemente

lofty [ˈlɒftɪ] *adj* (**a**) *(high) (mountain)* elevado(a); *(tree, building)* alto(a); **a l. room** un salón de techo alto (**b**) *(haughty) (person, manner)* arrogante, altanero(a); **with l. disdain** con arrogante desdén (**c**) *(exalted) (aim, desire)* noble, elevado(a); *(style, prose)* elevado(a), sublime

log[1] [lɒg] **1** *n* (**a**) *(tree-trunk)* tronco *m*; *(firewood)* leño *m*; IDIOM **to sleep like a l.** dormir como un tronco ►► ***l. cabin*** cabaña *f*; ***l. fire*** fuego *m* de leña (**b**) *(record)* registro *m*; *(of ship)* diario *m* de a bordo (**c**) *Br very Fam* **to drop a l.** *(defecate)* jiñar (**d**) *Comptr* ***l. file*** registro *m* de actividad
2 *vt* (*pt & pp* **logged**) (**a**) *(record)* registrar (**b**) *(speed, distance, time)* **he has logged 2,000 hours flying time** ha acumulado *or* tiene 2.000 horas de vuelo
3 *vi (cut down trees)* talar árboles

►**log in** *vi Comptr (user)* entrar, abrir una sesión; *(to remote user)* establecer comunicación

►**log off** *vi Comptr* salir

►**log on** = **log in**

►**log out** = **log off**

►**log up** *vt sep Br (do, achieve)* conseguir; **the team logged up yet another victory** el equipo se apuntó una nueva victoria

log[2] *n Math* (*abbr* **logarithm**) logaritmo *m* ►► ***l. tables*** tablas *fpl* de logaritmos

loganberry [ˈləʊgənberɪ] *n (plant)* frambueso *m* de Logan; *(berry)* frambuesa *f* de Logan

logarithm [ˈlɒgərɪðəm] *n Math* logaritmo *m*

logarithmic [lɒgəˈrɪðmɪk] *adj Math* logarítmico(a) ►► ***l. scale*** escala *f* logarítmica

logbook [ˈlɒgbʊk] *n* (**a**) *(for ship)* cuaderno *m* de bitácora; *(for plane)* diario *m* de vuelo (**b**) *Br (for car)* permiso *m* de circulación

logger [ˈlɒgə(r)] *n (lumberjack)* leñador(ora) *m,f*

loggerheads [ˈlɒgəhedz] *n Fam* **to be at l. with sb** estar peleado(a) *or Esp* andar a la greña con alguien

loggerhead turtle [ˈlɒgəhedˈtɜ:təl] *n* tortuga *f* boba

loggia [ˈlɒdʒɪə] *n* logia *f*

logging [ˈlɒgɪŋ] *n (cutting trees)* tala *f* (de árboles); **l. company/town** empresa/población maderera

logic [ˈlɒdʒɪk] *n* (**a**) *(reasoning)* lógica *f*; **the l. of his argument was impeccable** su argumento era de una lógica aplastante; **...if you follow my l.** ...si entiendes lo que quiero decir; **that's typical male l.!** ¡esos son los típicos argumentos machistas! (**b**) *Comptr* ***l. board*** placa *f* lógica; ***l. bomb*** bomba *f* lógica; ***l. card*** tarjeta *f* lógica; ***l. circuit*** circuito *m* lógico; ***l. operator*** operador *m* lógico

logical [ˈlɒdʒɪkəl] *adj* lógico(a); **let's try to be l. about this** tratemos de ser sensatos al respecto; **it's a l. impossibility** es lógicamente imposible ►► *Comptr* ***l. operator*** operador *m* lógico; *Phil* ***l. positivism*** positivismo *m* lógico

logicality [lɒdʒɪˈkælɪtɪ] *n* lógica *f*

logically [ˈlɒdʒɪklɪ] *adv* lógicamente; **l., there should be no problem** lo lógico es que no hubiera ningún problema

logician [lɒˈdʒɪʃən] *n* lógico(a) *m,f*

login [ˈlɒgɪn] *n Comptr* conexión *f* ►► ***l. name*** nombre *m* del usuario

logistic(al) [ləˈdʒɪstɪk(əl)] *adj* logístico(a), organizativo(a); **it's a l. nightmare** es un rompecabezas logístico *or* organizativo

logistically [ləˈdʒɪstɪklɪ] *adv* logísticamente

logistics [lɒˈdʒɪstɪks] *npl* logística *f*; **the l. of the situation** la logística de la situación

logjam [ˈlɒgdʒæm] *n* (**a**) *(in river)* = obstrucción causada por la acumulación de troncos en un río (**b**) *(deadlock)* punto *m* muerto, impasse *m*

logo [ˈləʊgəʊ] (*pl* **logos**) *n* logo *m*, logotipo *m*

logocentrism [lɒgəʊˈsentrɪzəm] *n* logocentrismo *m*

logoff [ˈlɒgɒf] *n Comptr* desconexión *f*

logorrhoea, *US* **logorrhea** [lɒgəˈrɪə] *n* (**a**) *Med* logorrea *f* (**b**) *Fam (verbal diarrhoea)* verborrea *f*

log-rolling [ˈlɒgrəʊlɪŋ] *n* (**a**) *(sport)* = deporte consistente en manejar troncos flotantes con los pies (**b**) *US Pol (exchange of favours)* comercio *m* de favores

logwood [ˈlɒgwʊd] *n* campeche *m*

loin [lɔɪn] *n* (**a**) *Euph (genital area)* **loins** pubis *m inv*, bajo vientre *m*; *Literary* **sprung from the loins of** salido(a) de las entrañas de (**b**) *(of meat)* lomo *m* ►► ***l. chop*** chuleta *f* de lomo

loincloth [ˈlɔɪnklɒθ] *n* taparrabos *m inv*

Loire [lwɑ:(r)] *n* **the L.** el Loira

loiter [ˈlɔɪtə(r)] *vi (delay)* entretenerse; *(suspiciously)* merodear; *Law* **to l. (with intent)** merodear

loll [lɒl] *vi* (**a**) *(lounge)* repanti(n)garse, repanchi(n)garse (**b**) *(tongue)* colgar; **his tongue lolled out** le colgaba la lengua

►**loll about, loll around** *vi* holgazanear, haraganear

lollapalooza [lɒləpəˈlu:zə] *n US Fam* **her latest film is a l.** su última película es el no va más *or Esp* es una pasada

lollipop [ˈlɒlɪpɒp] *n* (**a**) *(disc)* piruleta *f*; *(ball) Esp* Chupa Chups® *m inv*; *(disc, ball) Chile* chupete *m*, *Col* colombina *f*, *Méx* paleta *f*, *RP* chupetín *m*, *Ven* chupeta *f* (**b**) *Br Fam* **l. man/lady** = persona encargada de ayudar a cruzar la calle a los colegiales

lollop [ˈlɒləp] *vi Fam* **to l. along** avanzar con paso desgarbado; **the rabbit lolloped off** el conejo avanzaba torpemente

lolly [ˈlɒlɪ] *n Br Fam* (**a**) *(frozen)* **(ice) l.** polo *m* (**b**) *(lollipop) (disc)* piruleta *f*; *(ball) Esp* Chupa Chups® *m inv*; *(disc, ball) Chile* chupete *m*, *Col* colombina *f*, *Méx* paleta *f*, *RP* chupetín *m*, *Ven* chupeta *f* (**c**) *(money) Esp* pasta *f*, *Am* plata *f*, *Méx* lana *f*

Lombard [ˈlɒmbəd] **1** *n* lombardo(a) *m,f*
2 *adj* lombardo(a)

Lombardy ['lɒmbədɪ] *n* Lombardía ►► ***L. poplar*** álamo *m* negro

London ['lʌndən] **1** *n* Londres ►► *Br* ***L. weighting*** = compensación salarial que sirve para equilibrar el coste de la vida en Londres
2 *adj* londinense

Londoner ['lʌndənə(r)] *n* londinense *mf*

lone [ləʊn] *adj (solitary)* solitario(a) ►► ***l. parent*** madre *f* soltera, padre *m* soltero; ***the L. Ranger*** el Llanero Solitario; *Fig* ***a l. wolf*** una persona solitaria

loneliness ['ləʊnlɪnɪs] *n* soledad *f*

lonely ['ləʊnlɪ] *adj* (**a**) *(person)* solo(a); **to be** *or* **feel very l.** sentirse muy solo(a) ►► ***l. heart*** *(person)* corazón *m* solitario; ***l. hearts club*** club *m* de contactos; *Journ* ***l. hearts column*** sección *f* de contactos (**b**) *(place)* solitario(a); **the house seems l. without you** sin ti, la casa parece vacía; **he went back to his l. room** regresó a su solitaria habitación

loner ['ləʊnə(r)] *n* solitario(a) *m,f*

lonesome ['ləʊnsəm] **1** *n Fam* **to be on one's l.** estar solito
2 *adj US* solitario(a); **to be/feel l.** *(of person)* estar/sentirse solo(a)

LONG[1] [lɒŋ] **1** *n* **the l. and the short of it is that...** el caso es que...
2 *adj* (**a**) *(in size, distance)* largo(a); **she has l. hair** tiene el pelo largo; **how l. is the table?** ¿cuánto mide *or* tiene la mesa de largo?, *Am* ¿qué largo tiene la mesa?; **it's 4 metres l.** mide *or* tiene cuatro metros de largo; **how l. is the novel? – it's 500 pages l.** ¿cuántas páginas tiene la novela? – tiene 500 páginas; **the ball was l.** *(in tennis)* la bola *or* pelota fue demasiado larga; **the pass was l.** *(in soccer)* el pase fue demasiado largo; **we're a l. way from Dublin, it's a l. way to Dublin** estamos muy lejos de Dublín; **to go the l. way (round)** ir por el camino más largo; *also Fig* **we have a l. way to go** todavía queda mucho camino por recorrer; *Fig* **the best by a l. way** con mucho *or* de lejos el/la mejor; *Fig* **they have come a l. way** han progresado mucho; *Fig* **she'll go a l. way** llegará lejos; *Fig* **to go a l. way towards doing sth** contribuir mucho a hacer algo; *Fig* **a little of this detergent goes a l. way** este detergente *Esp* cunde *or Am* rinde muchísimo; *Fig* **we go back a l. way** nos conocemos desde hace mucho tiempo; *Fam Fig* **to be l. in the tooth** estar entrado(a) en años; *Fig* **a list as l. as your arm** una lista más larga que un día sin pan *or RP* que esperanza de pobre; **the l. arm of the law** el largo brazo de la ley; *Fig* **to have/pull a l. face** tener/poner cara triste *or* larga; **it's a l. shot, but it's our only hope** es difícil que funcione, pero es nuestra única esperanza; **they are a l. shot for the title** no tienen muchas posibilidades de conseguir el título; **not by a l. shot** *or* **chalk** ni muchísimo menos; **physics isn't my l. suit** la física no es mi fuerte ►► ***l. ball*** *(in soccer)* pase *m* largo; *Math* ***l. division*** división *f (de números de varias cifras)*; ***l. drink*** *(alcoholic)* combinado *m*, *RP* trago *m* largo; *(non-alcoholic)* refresco *m*; ***l. johns*** calzoncillos *mpl* largos; ***l. jump*** *Esp* salto *m* de longitud, *Am* salto *m* largo; ***l. jumper*** saltador(ora) *m,f* de longitud; ***l. ton*** tonelada *f* (aproximada) *(= 1.016 kilos)*; ***l. trousers*** pantalón *m* largo; ***l. wave*** onda *f* larga
(**b**) *(in time)* largo(a); **how l. is the movie?** ¿cuánto dura la película?; **it's three hours l.** dura tres horas; **a l. time ago** hace mucho tiempo; **it's a l. time since I had a holiday** hace mucho tiempo que no tengo vacaciones; **it was a l. time before we were told of their decision** pasó mucho tiempo antes de que nos informaran de su decisión; **for a l. time** durante mucho tiempo; *Fam* **l. time, no see** dichosos los ojos; **it's been a l. day** ha sido un día muy largo; **it took us a l. half hour** tardamos *or Am* demoramos media hora larga; **the days are getting longer** se están alargando los días; **three days at the longest** tres días como mucho; **he took a l. draught of the beer** bebió un gran trago de cerveza; **it's a l. haul** *(journey)* hay un tirón *or* una buena tirada; **I got my degree, but it was a l. haul** me saqué la licenciatura, pero me costó lo mío; **this team is well-equipped for the l. haul** este equipo está bien dotado a largo plazo; **to work l. hours** trabajar muchas horas; **it looks like being a l. job** parece que el trabajo va a llevar mucho tiempo; **to take a l. look at sth** mirar algo largamente; **to have a l. memory** tener buena memoria; **it's a l. story** es una historia muy larga; **to take the l. view of sth** considerar algo a largo plazo; **at l. last** por fin; **in the l. term** *or* **run** a largo plazo, a la larga ►► *Br Univ* ***l. vacation*** vacaciones *fpl* de verano; ***l. weekend*** fin de semana *m* largo, puente *m* (corto)
(**c**) *Fam* **to be l. on charm/good ideas** *(full of)* estar lleno(a) de *or Esp* andar sobrado(a) de encanto/buenas ideas, *RP* tener pila de encanto/buenas ideas; **his speeches are l. on rhetoric but short on substance** sus discursos están cargados de retórica pero carecen de contenido
(**d**) *Ling* largo(a)
(**e**) *St Exch (position)* largo(a)
(**f**) *Fam (in tennis)* **that serve was l.** el saque *or* servicio salió fuera *(pasándose de largo)*
(**g**) *(in betting)* **they're giving l. odds** pagan las apuestas muy altas; **the odds against that happening are pretty l.** hay muy pocas posibilidades de que ocurra eso
3 *adv* (**a**) *(for a long period)* durante mucho tiempo, mucho; **I didn't wait l.** no esperé mucho; **it won't take l.** no llevará mucho tiempo; **she won't be l.** no tardará *or Am* demorará mucho; **it won't be l. before things change** no pasará mucho tiempo antes de que cambien las cosas; **how l. have you known her?** ¿cuánto (tiempo) hace que la conoces?; **how l. have you lived here?** ¿desde cuándo vives aquí?, ¿cuánto (tiempo) hace que vives aquí?; **five minutes longer** cinco minutos más; **I've lived here longer than you** llevo *or Am* tengo más tiempo que tú viviendo aquí, vivo aquí desde hace más tiempo que tú; **I could no longer hear him** ya no lo oía; **I couldn't wait any longer** no podía esperar más; **to think l. and hard (about sth)** reflexionar profundamente (sobre algo); **I have l. been convinced of it** llevo mucho tiempo convencido de eso; **we have l. suspected that this was the case** hace tiempo que sospechábamos que era eso lo que sucedía; **it has l. been known that...** hace tiempo que se sabe que...; **she is not l. for this world** no le queda mucho tiempo de vida; **l. live the King/Queen!** ¡viva el Rey/la Reina!; **l. may they continue to do so!** ¡que sigan así por mucho tiempo!; **take as l. as you need** tómate todo el tiempo que necesites; **it's been like that for as l. as I can remember** que yo recuerde, siempre ha sido así; **as l. as he is alive,...** mientras viva,...; **it could take as l. as a month** podría tardar *or Am* demorar hasta un mes; **as** *or* **so l. as** *(providing)* mientras, siempre que; **as** *or* **so l. as you don't tell anyone** siempre y cuando no se lo digas a nadie, siempre que no se lo digas a nadie; **before l.** pronto; **I won't stay for l.** no me voy a quedar mucho tiempo; **it's so l. since I had a holiday** hace tanto tiempo que no tengo vacaciones; *Fam* **so l.!** ¡hasta luego!; **l. ago** hace mucho (tiempo); **as l. ago as 1956** ya en 1956; **l. before/after** mucho antes/después; **l. before/after you were born** mucho antes/después de que nacieras; **I had l. since given up hope** ya había perdido la esperanza hacía tiempo
(**b**) *(for the duration of)* **all day/winter l.** todo el día/invierno, el día/invierno entero; **her whole life l.** toda su vida

long[2] *vi* **to l. for sth/sb** desear algo/a alguien; **to l. for the day when...** desear que llegue el día en que...; **to l. for sth to happen** desear que ocurra algo; **to l.** *or* **be longing to do sth** desear *or* anhelar hacer algo

long[3] *Geog* (*abbr* **longitude**) long.

long-awaited ['lɒŋə'weɪtɪd] *adj* largamente esperado(a)

longboat ['lɒŋbəʊt] *n Hist (on sailing ship)* chalupa *f*, lancha *f* de remos; **Viking l.** barco vikingo

longbow ['lɒŋbəʊ] *n* arco *m*

long-dated ['lɒŋ'deɪtɪd] *adj Fin (securities)* a largo plazo

long-distance ['lɒŋ'dɪstəns] **1** *adj* **a l. (telephone) call** una conferencia ►► *Br* ***l. lorry driver*** camionero(a) *m,f (que hace viajes largos)*; ***l. race*** carrera *f* de fondo; ***l. runner*** corredor(ora) *m,f* de fondo
2 *adv* **to telephone l.** poner una conferencia

long-drawn-out ['lɒŋdrɔːn'aʊt] *adj (argument, dispute, story, explanation)* interminable, eterno(a)

long-eared owl ['lɒŋɪəd'aʊl] *n* búho *m* chico

longed-for ['lɒŋdfɔː(r)] *adj* ansiado(a); **a l. holiday** unas ansiadas vacaciones

long-established ['lɒŋɪs'tæblɪʃt] *adj (tradition)* antiguo(a); *(firm)* con solera

longevity [lɒn'dʒevɪtɪ] *n Formal* longevidad *f*

long-faced [lɒŋ'feɪst] *adj* con cara larga

long-forgotten ['lɒŋfə'gɒtən] *adj* olvidado(a)

long-grain rice ['lɒŋgreɪn'raɪs] *n* arroz *m* de grano largo

long-hair ['lɒŋheə(r)] *n* (**a**) *Fam Old-fashioned (intellectual)* progre *mf* (**b**) *Fam (hippie)* melenudo(a) *m,f* (**c**) *(cat)* gato *m* de pelo largo

longhaired ['lɒŋ'heəd] *adj* de pelo largo

longhand ['lɒŋhænd] *n* escritura *f* normal a mano; **in l.** escrito(a) a mano

long-haul ['lɒŋhɔːl] *adj (flight)* de larga distancia; **l. carriers** aerolíneas intercontinentales

longhorn ['lɒŋhɔːn] *n US* buey *m* colorado de Tejas

long-house ['lɒŋhaʊs] *n* = construcción comunitaria tradicional con forma alargada propia de Malaisia, Indonesia y de ciertas tribus de indios americanos

longing ['lɒŋɪŋ] **1** *n (desire)* deseo *m*, anhelo *m* (**for** de); *(for home, family, old days)* añoranza *f* (**for** de)
2 *adj* deseoso(a), anhelante

longingly ['lɒŋɪŋlɪ] *adv* con deseo, con anhelo; **to think l. of the past** recordar el pasado con anhelo

longish ['lɒŋɪʃ] *adj* más bien largo(a), bastante largo(a)

longitude ['lɒndʒɪtju:d] *n* longitud *f (coordenada)*; **at a l. of 50° east** a 50° longitud este

longitudinal [lɒndʒɪ'tju:dɪnəl] *adj* longitudinal ►► *Phys* ***l. wave*** onda *f* longitudinal

long-lasting [lɒŋ'lɑ:stɪŋ] *adj* duradero(a)

long-legged [lɒŋ'leg(ɪ)d] *adj (person)* de piernas largas; *(animal)* de patas largas

long-life ['lɒŋ'laɪf] *adj Br (battery, milk)* de larga duración

long-lived ['lɒŋ'lɪvd] *adj (person)* anciano(a); *(animal, plant)* longevo(a); *(campaign, friendship)* perdurable; *(prejudice, superstition)* viejo(a)

long-lost ['lɒŋ'lɒst] *adj* perdido(a) tiempo atrás; **his l. brother returned** regresó su hermano al que no veía desde hacía mucho tiempo; **he welcomed me like a l. friend** me recibió como a un amigo que hubiera perdido tiempo atrás

long-playing record ['lɒŋpleɪɪŋ'rekɔ:d] *n* LP *m*, elepé *m*

long-range ['lɒŋ'reɪndʒ] *adj* **(a)** *(missile, bomber)* de largo alcance **(b)** *(forecast)* a largo plazo

long-running ['lɒŋ'rʌnɪŋ] *adj* **(a)** *(play)* que lleva *or Méx, Ven* tiene mucho tiempo en cartelera; *(programme)* que lleva *or Méx, Ven* tiene mucho tiempo en antena **(b)** *(battle, dispute)* que viene de largo; *(agreement)* duradero(a)

longship ['lɒŋʃɪp] *n Hist* drakkar *m*, drakar *m*, barco *m* vikingo

longshoreman [lɒŋ'ʃɔ:mən] *n US* estibador *m*

long-sighted [lɒŋ'saɪtɪd] *adj* **(a)** *Med* hipermétrope **(b)** *(policy, decision)* previsor(ora)

long-sleeved [lɒŋ'sli:vd] *adj* de manga larga

long-standing [lɒŋ'stændɪŋ] *adj (arrangement, friendship, rivalry)* antiguo(a), viejo(a)

long-stay ['lɒŋsteɪ] *adj* **(a)** *(hospital, ward, patient)* de estancia prolongada **(b)** *(car park)* para estacionamiento prolongado

long-suffering ['lɒŋ'sʌfərɪŋ] *adj* sufrido(a)

long-tailed ['lɒŋteɪld] *adj* ***l. cormorant*** cormorán *m* africano; ***l. duck*** pato *m* havelda; ***l. skua*** págalo *m* rabero; ***l. tit*** mito *m*

long-term ['lɒŋtɜ:m] **1** *adj* a largo plazo; **a l. commitment** un compromiso a largo plazo; **l. planning** planificación a largo plazo; **the l. unemployed** los desempleados *or Esp* parados de larga duración; **the l. outlook is good** las perspectivas a largo plazo son buenas ►► *Br* ***l. car park*** parking *m or Esp* aparcamiento *m* de larga duración; *US* ***l. parking lot*** parking *m or Esp* aparcamiento *m* de larga duración; *Fin* ***l. debt*** deuda *f* a largo plazo; ***l. memory*** memoria *f* a largo plazo; ***l. unemployment*** desempleo *m* de larga duración

2 *adv* a largo plazo

long-time ['lɒŋtaɪm] *adj* antiguo(a); **her l. boyfriend** su novio de toda la vida

longueur [lɒŋ'gɜ:(r)] *n Formal (period of tedium)* rato *m* tedioso

long-waisted ['lɒŋ'weɪstɪd] *adj* de talle largo

long-wave ['lɒŋweɪv] *adj* de onda larga

longways ['lɒŋweɪz], **longwise** ['lɒŋwaɪz] *adv* a lo largo

long-winded [lɒŋ'wɪndɪd] *adj* prolijo(a)

longwise = **longways**

loo [lu:] *(pl* **loos**) *n Br Fam* baño *m*, váter *m*; **to go to the l.** ir al baño ►► ***l. paper*** papel *m* higiénico *or* de baño, *Chile* confort *m*; ***l. roll*** rollo *m* de papel higiénico *or* de baño

loofa, loofah ['lu:fə] *n* esponja *f* vegetal

LOOK [lʊk] **1** *n* **(a)** *(act of looking)* **to have** *or* **take a l. at sth** mirar algo; **let me have a l.** déjame ver; **have a l. and see if the post has arrived yet** mira a ver si ya ha llegado el correo; **the doctor wants to have a l. at you** el médico te quiere examinar; **we will be taking a l. at all aspects of our policy** examinaremos todos los aspectos de nuestra política; **I took one l. at it and decided not to buy it** un vistazo me bastó para decidir no comprarlo; **to have a l. round the town** (ir a) ver la ciudad; **can I have a l. round the garden?** ¿puedo echarle un vistazo al jardín?; **have** *or* **take a look through the telescope** mira por el telescopio; **to have a l. through some magazines** ojear unas revistas; **the castle is worth a l.** el castillo merece *or Am* amerita una visita; **the programme is a humorous l. at the Reagan years** el programa hace un recorrido en clave de humor de la época de Reagan

(b) *(search)* **to have a l. for sth** buscar algo; **I had a good l. but it I couldn't find it** he buscado por todas partes y no lo encontré

(c) *(glance)* mirada *f*; **to give a suspicious/an angry l.** mirar algo con recelo/*esp Esp* enfado *or esp Am* enojo; **to give sb a surprised l.** mirar a alguien sorprendido(a); **we got some very odd looks** nos miraron con cara rara; **if looks could kill...** si las miradas mataran...

(d) *(expression)* **she had a l. of disbelief on her face** tenía una expresión incrédula; *Fam* **take that stupid l. off your face!** ¡cambia ya esa expresión de memo!

(e) *(appearance)* aspecto *m*; **this sample has an unusual l. to it** esta muestra tiene un aspecto extraño; **I like the l. of those cakes** ¡qué buena pinta tienen esos pasteles *or CSur* esas tortas!; *Fig* **I don't like the l. of this at all** no me gusta nada el cariz *or* la pinta que tiene esto; *Fig* **I don't like the l. of him** me da mala espina; **I don't like the l. of those clouds** no me gusta la pinta de esas nubes; **by the l.** *or* **looks of it** por lo que parece

(f) *(fashion)* look *m*, imagen *f*; **they have gone for the 70s l.** se han decidido por el look de los 70; **what do you think of my new l.?** ¿qué te parece mi nuevo look?

(g) *(personal appearance)* **(good) looks** atractivo *m*, (buena) apariencia *f*; **looks don't matter** la belleza no es lo principal; **she has lost her looks** ha perdido su atractivo físico; **he's kept his looks** sigue siendo igual de atractivo

2 *vt* **(a)** *(observe)* **I can never l. him in the eye** *or* **face again** nunca podré volver a mirarlo a la cara; **to l. sb up and down** mirar a alguien de arriba abajo; **to l. one's last on sth** mirar algo por última vez; **l. what you've done!** ¡mira lo que has hecho!; **l. where you're going!** ¡mira por dónde vas!; **l. who's here!** ¡mira quién está aquí!; **l. who's talking!** ¡mira quién fue a hablar!

(b) *(appear to be)* **he doesn't l. his age** no aparenta la edad que tiene; **I'm sixty – you don't l. it** tengo sesenta años – ¡pues no lo pareces! *or* ¡pues no los representas!; **to l. one's best (for sb)** estar lo más atractivo(a) posible (para alguien); **to l. the part** tener toda la pinta, *Esp* dar el pego

3 *vi* **(a)** *(in general)* mirar; **l., here she is!** ¡mira, aquí está!; **I'm just looking, thank you** *(in shop)* sólo estoy mirando; *Educ* **l. and say** = método de aprender a leer sin descomponer las palabras en letras individuales; **to l. on the bright side** mirar el lado bueno (de las cosas); *Fig* **to l. the other way** hacer la vista gorda; PROV **l. before you leap** hay que pensar dos veces (antes de actuar)

(b) *(face)* **to l. north/south** dar al norte/sur; **the castle looks across a valley** el castillo tiene vistas sobre un valle; **the dining-room looks (out) onto the garden** el comedor da al jardín

(c) *(search)* buscar; **we've looked everywhere** hemos buscado *or* mirado por todas partes, *RP* nos fijamos en todas partes; **I haven't looked in the kitchen/under the table** no he buscado *or* mirado en la cocina/debajo de la mesa, *RP* no me fijé en la cocina/abajo de la mesa

(d) *(appear)* **you l. terrific!** ¡estás fantástico!; **you're looking well!** ¡qué buen aspecto tienes!; **those new curtains l. great** esas cortinas nuevas quedan estupendas; **how do I l. in this dress?** ¿qué tal me queda este vestido?; **that shirt looks nice on you** esa camisa te queda muy bien; **she looks pale** está pálida; **she looks about twenty** parece que tuviera veinte años; **what does she l. like?** ¿cómo es?, ¿qué aspecto tiene?; **to l. like sb** parecerse a alguien; **it looks like a rose** parece una rosa; **she looks like a nice person** parece simpática; **he was holding what looked like a knife** tenía en la mano algo que parecía un cuchillo

(e) *(seem)* parecer; **to l. old/ill** parecer viejo(a)/enfermo(a); **he made me l. stupid** me dejó *or* puso en ridículo; **you don't l. yourself** no pareces tú; **things are looking good/bad** las cosas van bien/mal; **it would l. bad if you didn't come** quedaría mal que no fueras; **how is she? – it doesn't l. good** ¿cómo está? – la cosa no tiene buen aspecto; **l. lively** *or* **sharp!** ¡espabila!, *RP* ¡despertate!; **it looks like** *or* **as if** *or* **as though...** parece que...; **you l. as if** *or* **though you've slept badly** tienes aspecto de haber dormido mal; **will they win? – it looks like it** ¿ganarán? – eso parece; **they don't l. like winning** no parece que vayan a ganar; **it looks like rain** parece que va a llover; *Fig* **to l. like thunder** *(person)* tener cara de pocos amigos

(f) *(in exclamations)* **l., why don't we just forget about it?** mira, ¿por qué no lo olvidamos?; **l. here!** ¡mire usted!; **(now) l.!** ¡mira!

► **look after** *vt insep (person, property, possessions)* cuidar; *(shop)* cuidar de, atender; *(customer, guest)* atender a; *(process, arrangements, finances)* hacerse cargo de; **they l. after our interests in Europe** velan por *or* se ocupan de nuestros intereses en Europa; **I'm perfectly capable of looking after myself** soy perfectamente capaz de cuidar de mí mismo; *Fam* **l. after yourself!** ¡cuídate!, *Am* ¡qué estés bien!; **to l. after number one** cuidarse de los propios intereses; **they l. after their own** cuidan de los suyos

► **look ahead** *vi (think of future)* pensar en el futuro; **looking ahead three or four years** a tres o cuatro años vista

► **look around, look round** **1** *vt insep* **we looked around a museum** visitamos un museo; **I looked around the cell for a way out** miré por toda la celda en busca de una salida; **l. around you, times have changed!** ¡espabila, que los tiempos han cambiado!

2 *vi* **she looked around to see if anyone was following** miró a su alrededor para ver si alguien la seguía; **I went into the centre of town to l. around** fui al centro a dar una vuelta; **when I l. around, all I see is suffering** cuando miro a mi alrededor, lo único que veo es sufrimiento; **we looked around for shelter** miramos a nuestro alrededor en busca de un refugio; **I've been looking around for something better** he estado buscando para ver si encontraba algo mejor

▸ **look at** *vt insep* (**a**) *(generally)* mirar; **he looked at himself in the mirror** se miró en el espejo; **we looked at each other** nos miramos el uno al otro; **what are you looking at?** ¿qué miras?; **I haven't looked at another woman in the last forty years** no he mirado a otra mujer en (los últimos) cuarenta años; **he's a famous athlete, though you'd never guess it to l. at him** es un atleta famoso, aunque al verlo uno nunca lo diría; *Fam* **he's not much to l. at** no es ninguna belleza; **oh dear, l. at the time!** ¡vaya, mira qué hora es!; *Fam* **well, l. at that, she didn't even say thank you!** ¿qué te parece? ¡no dio ni las gracias!

(**b**) *(examine)* examinar; **could you l. at my printer?** ¿puedes echarle un vistazo a mi impresora?

(**c**) *(consider)* ver; **we've been looking at different solutions** hemos estado estudiando diversas soluciones; **l. at the problem from my point of view** tienes que ver el problema desde mi punto de vista; **I don't l. at it that way** yo no lo veo de esa manera; **they won't even l. at the idea** ni siquiera estudiarán la idea

(**d**) *Fam (face)* **you're looking at a bill of $3,000** estamos hablando de una factura de 3.000 dólares

▸ **look away** *vi* mirar hacia otro lado

▸ **look back** *vi* (**a**) *(in space)* mirar atrás, volver la vista atrás; **she walked away without looking back** se marchó sin volver la vista atrás

(**b**) *(in time)* **looking back (on it), we could have done better** viéndolo en retrospectiva, podíamos haberlo hecho mejor; **don't l. back, think of the future** no mires atrás, piensa en el futuro; **he has never looked back since that day** desde ese día no ha hecho más que progresar; **to l. back on sth** recordar algo; **the programme looks back over eleven years of Thatcherism** el programa es una retrospectiva de once años de thatcherismo

▸ **look down** *vi (from above)* mirar hacia abajo; *(lower one's eyes)* bajar la mirada *or* la vista

▸ **look down on** *vt insep (despise)* desdeñar

▸ **look for** *vt insep* (**a**) *(seek)* buscar; **that's just what I was looking for!** ¡ése es precisamente lo que andaba buscando!; **what do you l. for in a man?** ¿qué buscas en un hombre?; **you're looking for trouble** estás buscándote un lío *or* problemas

(**b**) *(expect)* esperar; **it's not the result we were looking for** no es el resultado que esperábamos

▸ **look forward to** *vt insep* **to l. forward to sth** *(party, event)* estar deseando que llegue algo; **I was looking forward to my holidays/a good breakfast** tenía muchas ganas de empezar las vacaciones/de un buen desayuno; **I'm really looking forward to this movie** creo que esta película va a ser muy buena; **I'm looking forward to our next meeting** confío en que nuestra próxima reunión será de sumo interés; **I'm sure we're all looking forward to a productive couple of days' work** seguro que vamos a disfrutar de dos días de fructífero trabajo; **we are looking forward to a further drop in unemployment** esperamos otra bajada de las cifras del desempleo *orAm* de la desocupación; **to l. forward to doing sth** estar deseando hacer algo, tener muchas ganas de hacer algo; **I l. forward to hearing from you** *(in letter)* quedo a la espera de recibir noticias suyas

▸ **look in** *vi* **to l. in (on sb)** *(visit)* hacer una visita (a alguien); **I looked in at the office** pasé por la oficina

▸ **look into** *vt insep (investigate)* investigar, examinar

▸ **look on** 1 *vt insep (consider)* considerar; **to l. on sth/sb as...** considerar algo/a alguien...; **I look on her as a friend** la considero una amiga

2 *vt sep* **to l. kindly on sth/sb** ver algo/a alguien con buenos ojos; **they would l. favourably on such an offer** verán con buenos ojos una oferta así

3 *vi* quedarse mirando

▸ **look out** 1 *vt sep Br* **to l. sth out for sb** encontrar algo para *or* a alguien

2 *vi* (**a**) *(person)* mirar; **to l. out of the window** mirar por la ventana

(**b**) *(room, window)* **the bedroom looks out on(to)** *or* **over the garden** el dormitorio da al jardín, desde el dormitorio se ve el jardín

(**c**) *(be careful)* tener cuidado; **l. out!** ¡cuidado!

▸ **look out for** *vt insep* (**a**) *(look for)* buscar; **l. out for the special offer packs** no se pierda los packs *or* lotes en oferta especial

(**b**) *(be on guard for)* estar al tanto de; **you have to l. out for snakes** tienes que estar al tanto de las serpientes

(**c**) *(take care of)* cuidar de; **to l. out for oneself** preocuparse de uno(a) mismo(a)

▸ **look over** 1 *vt insep (house, property)* inspeccionar

2 *vt sep (document)* mirar por encima, repasar

▸ **look round** = **look around**

▸ **look through** *vt insep* (**a**) *(window, telescope)* mirar por; *Fig* **she looked straight through me** miró hacia mí, pero no me vio

(**b**) *(inspect)* examinar

(**c**) *(glance through)* echar un vistazo a

▸ **look to** *vt insep* (**a**) *(rely on)* **to l. to sb (for sth)** dirigirse a alguien (en busca de algo); **we are looking to you to help us** contamos con que nos ayudes

(**b**) *(think about)* **we must l. to the future** debemos mirar hacia el futuro; **he should l. to his reputation** debería mirar por su reputación

(**c**) *(aim to)* **to be looking to do sth** querer hacer algo, tener la intención de hacer algo

(**d**) *(ensure)* **l. to it that you...** asegúrate de que...

▸ **look towards** *vt insep* **we are looking towards finishing the project by May** esperamos terminar el proyecto en mayo

▸ **look up** 1 *vt sep* (**a**) *(in dictionary, address book)* buscar (**b**) *(visit)* **to l. sb up** visitar a alguien

2 *vi* (**a**) *(from below)* mirar hacia arriba; *(raise one's eyes)* levantar la mirada *or* la vista

(**b**) *(improve)* **things are looking up** las cosas están mejorando

▸ **look upon** 1 *vt insep* = **look on**

2 *vt sep* = **look on**

▸ **look up to** *vt insep* admirar

---

lookalike ['lʊkəlaɪk] *n (person)* doble *mf*; *(object)* réplica *f*

looked-for ['lʊkdfɔː(r)] *adj* ansiado(a), anhelado(a)

looker ['lʊkə(r)] *n Fam* **she's a real l.** es un bombón, es monísima; **he's not much of a l.** no es muy *Esp* guapo *orAm* lindo que digamos

looker-on ['lʊkər'ɒn] (*pl* **lookers-on**) *n (spectator)* curioso(a) *m,f*

look-in ['lʊkɪn] *n Fam* **he won't get a l.** no tendrá ninguna oportunidad; **she talked so much that I didn't get a l.** habló tanto que no pude decir ni pío

-looking ['lʊkɪŋ] *suffix* **kind-l.** de aspecto amable *or* agradable; **filthy-l.** mugriento(a), de aspecto mugriento

looking-glass ['lʊkɪŋglɑːs] *n Old-fashioned* espejo *m*; IDIOM **a l. world** un mundo al revés

lookout ['lʊkaʊt] *n* (**a**) *(person)* centinela *mf*, vigilante *mf* (**b**) *(place)* **l. (post)** puesto *m* de vigilancia; **l. tower** atalaya (**c**) *(action)* **to keep a l. for sth/sb** estar alerta por si se ve algo/a alguien; **to be on the l. for sth/sb** estar buscando algo/a alguien (**d**) *Br Fam (concern, problem)* **that's your l.!** ¡allá tú!; IDIOM **it's a poor l. when...** algo no va bien *or* no marcha cuando...

look-see ['lʊksiː] *n Fam* **to have** *or* **take a l.** echar un vistazo

look-up table ['lʊkʌp'teɪbəl] *n Comptr* tabla *f* de referencia

loom[1] [luːm] *n (for making cloth)* telar *m*

loom[2] *vi* (**a**) *(appear)* emerger; **above us loomed a high cliff** por encima de nuestras cabezas emergió un imponente acantilado

(**b**) *(approach threateningly)* cernerse, cernirse; **dangers l. ahead** los peligros nos acechan; **with the elections/exams looming** con las elecciones/los exámenes a la vuelta de la esquina

(**c**) *(appear important)* **to l. large** cobrar relevancia; **these factors l. large in our calculations** estos factores tienen mucho peso en nuestros cálculos

loon [luːn] *n* (**a**) *(idiot) Fam* lunático(a) *m,f*, chalado(a) *m,f*, *Méx* zafado(a) (**b**) *US (bird)* colimbo *m*

loon(e)y ['luːnɪ] *Fam* 1 *n* lunático(a) *m,f*, chalado(a) *m,f*, *Méx* zafado(a)

2 *adj (person)* chalado(a), lunático(a); *(idea)* disparatado(a); *Pej* **the l. left** la izquierda radicalizada

loony-bin ['luːnɪbɪn] *n Fam* loquero *m*, *Esp* frenopático *m*

loop [luːp] 1 *n* (**a**) *(shape)* curva *f* ▸▸ ***l. aerial*** antena *f* de cuadro

(**b**) *(of rope, ribbon)* lazo *m*

(**c**) *(of audiotape, film)* bucle *m*; **the film/the tape runs in a (continuous) l.** la misma película/la cinta se reproduce una y otra vez

(**d**) *(of river)* recodo *m* pronunciado

(**e**) *(of fingerprint)* lazo *m*

(**f**) *(contraceptive device)* DIU *m*, dispositivo *m* intrauterino

(**g**) *Comptr* bucle *m*, referencia *f* circular

(**h**) *Elec* circuito *m* cerrado

(i) *Rail* **l. (line)** = desvío de una vía principal que se vuelve a unir a ésta tras un corto trecho

(j) *US Fam* **to be out of the l.** no estar al corriente; **to cut sb out of the l.** dejar a alguien fuera de juego

2 *vt* (a) *(string)* enrollar; **to l. sth around sth** enrollar algo alrededor de algo (b) *Av* **to l. the l.** rizar el rizo

3 *vi (bird, aircraft)* trazar *or* describir un rizo; **the path looped round the side of the mountain** el sendero serpenteaba por la ladera de la montaña; **the river loops back on itself** el río gira y vuelve sobre sí mismo

loophole ['lu:phəʊl] *n* (a) *(in law)* resquicio *m* legal (b) *(in fortified wall)* aspillera *f*, tronera *f*

loopy ['lu:pɪ] *adj Fam (person)* majareta, chiflado(a); *(idea)* disparatado(a); **to be l.** *(of person)* estar chiflado(a) *or Esp* majareta *or Méx* zafado(a)

LOOSE [lu:s] 1 *n (freedom)* **to be on the l.** andar suelto(a)

2 *adj* (a) *(not firmly fixed) (tooth, connection)* suelto(a), flojo(a); *(skin)* colgante; **a dangerous animal is l. in the area** hay un animal peligroso suelto en la zona; **to break l.** soltarse; **to come l.** aflojarse; **we let the horse l. in the field** dejamos al caballo suelto en el campo; *Fam* **don't let him l. in the kitchen!** ¡no lo dejes suelto en la cocina!; **they let** *or* **set their dogs l. on us** nos soltaron *or* echaron a los perros; **they let** *or* **set the riot police l. on the crowd** soltaron a los antidisturbios entre la multitud; **they let** *or* **set us l. on the project** nos dieron rienda suelta para trabajar en el proyecto; **they let l. a volley of machine-gun fire** dispararon una ráfaga de ametralladora; **to let l. a torrent of abuse** soltar una sarta de improperios; **the screw had worked itself l.** el tornillo se había aflojado ►► *Br* ***l. cover*** *(of cushion)* funda *f* de quita y pon; ***l. end:*** **to be at a l. end** *or US* **at l. ends** no tener nada que hacer; *Fig* **to tie up the l. ends** *(in investigation)* atar cabos sueltos; ***l. head (prop)*** *(in rugby)* pilar *m* izquierdo

(b) *(not tight) (piece of clothing)* suelto(a), holgado(a); *(knot, weave)* suelto(a), flojo(a)

(c) *(not tightly packed) (sweets, olives)* suelto(a), a granel; *(soil, gravel)* suelto(a); **you look better with your hair l.** te queda mejor el pelo suelto ►► ***l. change*** cambio *m*, *Esp* suelto *m*, *Andes, CAm, Méx* sencillo *m*

(d) *(not close) (alliance, network)* informal

(e) *(not precise) (translation, interpretation)* poco exacto(a)

(f) *(uncontrolled)* **my bowels are l.** tengo *Esp* descomposición *or Am* descompostura; IDIOM **he's a l. cannon** es un descontrolado, *Am* es un(a) bala perdida ►► ***a l. cough*** una tos con flemas, *RP* un catarro; ***l. talk*** indiscreciones *fpl*

(g) *(immoral) (morals, lifestyle)* disoluto(a) ►► ***l. living*** vida *f* disoluta *or* disipada; ***a l. woman*** una mujer de vida alegre

(h) *US Fam (relaxed)* **to hang** *or* **stay l.** estar tranqui

3 *vt Literary* (a) *(arrow)* disparar; *(string of insults)* proferir

(b) *(animal)* soltar; *(prisoner)* liberar; *(knot)* deshacer; *(hair)* desenredar; **to l. one's grip on sth** soltar algo

4 *adv* **to buy sth l.** comprar algo a granel

►**loose off** 1 *vt sep (fire) (bullet, arrow, gun)* disparar; *(curses)* soltar

2 *vi (with gun)* disparar; *US (with insults, criticism)* **to l. off at sb** despotricar contra alguien

loose-fitting ['lu:s'fɪtɪŋ] *adj* suelto(a), holgado(a)

loose-leaf ['lu:sli:f] *adj* ***l. binder*** cuaderno *m or* carpeta *f* de anillas; ***l. folder*** cuaderno *m or* carpeta *f* de anillas

loose-limbed ['lu:s'lɪmd] *adj* suelto(a)

loosely ['lu:slɪ] *adv* (a) *(not firmly)* sin apretar; **the rope hung l.** *(unattached)* la cuerda colgaba suelta; *(slackly)* la cuerda colgaba laxa *or* poco tirante; **the sign is l. attached to the wall** el letrero no está pegado a la pared con firmeza; **he's l. attached to headquarters** mantiene cierta relación con la central; **l. packed** *(snow, earth)* suelto(a)

(b) *(not closely)* **the dress is l. gathered at the waist** el vestido queda bastante holgado a la altura de la cintura

(c) *(approximately, vaguely)* sin demasiado rigor, vagamente; **the movie is only l. based on my book** la película es una adaptación libre de mi libro; **l. speaking** hablando en términos generales; **l. translated** traducido(a) muy libremente

loosen ['lu:sən] 1 *vt* (a) *(screw, knot, belt)* aflojar; **the punch loosened several of his teeth** el puñetazo le aflojó unos cuantos dientes; **it loosens the bowels** aligera el vientre; **to l. the soil with a hoe** remover la tierra con una azada; **to l. one's grip** soltar, aflojar la presión; **to l. sb's tongue** soltar la lengua a alguien (b) *(restrictions)* suavizar

2 *vi* aflojarse

►**loosen up** *vi* (a) *(before exercise)* calentar (b) *(relax)* relajarse; **l. up (a bit)!** ¡relájate (un poco)!, ¡tómatelo con calma!

looseness ['lu:snɪs] *n* (a) *(of nail, screw)* falta *f* de fijeza (b) *(of rope, knot)* flojedad *f*; *(of clothing)* holgura *f* (c) *(of translation)* imprecisión *f* (d) *(of morals, lifestyle)* disipación *f*, *Esp* relajo *m*

loosening ['lu:sənɪŋ] *n (of policy, rules)* flexibilización *f*

loot [lu:t] 1 *n* (a) *(booty)* botín *m* (b) *Fam (money) Esp* pasta *f*, *Am* plata *f*, *Méx* lana *f*

2 *vt* saquear

looter ['lu:tə(r)] *n* saqueador(ora) *m,f*

looting ['lu:tɪŋ] *n* saqueo *m*, pillaje *m*

lop [lɒp] *vt* (a) *(tree)* podar (b) *(sum of money, item of expenditure)* recortar

►**lop off** *vt sep* (a) *(branch)* cortar; **he lopped the branches off the tree** podó las ramas del árbol; *Fig* **he lopped ten pages off the report** eliminó *or* cortó diez páginas del informe (b) *(price, time)* recortar; **the new motorway will l. 30 minutes off travelling time** la nueva autopista recortará los desplazamientos en 30 minutos

lope [ləʊp] 1 *n (of person)* zancadas *fpl*; *(of animal)* trote *m*

2 *vi (person)* caminar a zancadas; *(animal)* trotar

lop-eared ['lɒpɪəd] *adj (animal)* de orejas gachas *or* caídas

lopsided ['lɒp'saɪdɪd] *adj* (a) *(at the wrong angle) (picture)* torcido(a) (b) *(asymmetrical)* torcido(a); **a l. grin** una sonrisa torcida (c) *(unbalanced)* descompensado(a), desequilibrado(a); **her handwriting is all l.** tiene una letra muy desigual *or* irregular; **the article presents a rather l. picture of events** el artículo presenta los hechos de forma desequilibrada

loquacious [lɒ'kweɪʃəs] *adj Formal* locuaz

loquacity [lɒ'kwæsɪtɪ] *n Formal* locuacidad *f*

loquat ['ləʊkwɒt] *n (tree, berry)* níspero *m* del Japón

lor [lɔ:(r)] *exclam Br Fam Old-fashioned* ¡pardiez!, ¡cáspita!

lord [lɔ:d] 1 *n* (a) *(aristocrat)* señor *m*, lord *m*; *Br* **the (House of) Lords** la cámara de los lores ►► ***L. Advocate*** *(in Scotland)* ≃ fiscal *mf* general del Estado; ***L. Chamberlain*** el lord chambelán, = primer chambelán de la casa real británica; ***L. Chancellor*** = presidente de la Cámara de los Lores y responsable de justicia en Inglaterra y Gales; ***L. Chief Justice*** = juez británico de alto rango que depende del "Lord Chancellor" y preside el tribunal supremo; ***the L. Mayor*** = alcalde en algunas ciudades de Inglaterra y Gales que desempeña funciones ceremoniales; *Br Fam* ***L. Muck:*** **he's acting like L. Muck** se porta como un señoritingo; ***L. Provost*** = alcalde en algunas ciudades de Escocia que desempeña funciones ceremoniales; ***Lords Spiritual*** = dignatarios de la Iglesia anglicana que forman parte de la Cámara de los Lores; ***Lords Temporal*** = miembros laicos de la Cámara de los Lores

(b) *(term of address)* **my L.** *(to nobleman)* mi señor; *(to judge)* señoría; *(to bishop)* ilustrísima

(c) *Rel* **the L.** el Señor; **Our L. (Jesus Christ)** Nuestro Señor (Jesucristo); **in the year of our L. 1898** en el año de Nuestro Señor de 1898 ►► ***the Lord's Day*** el día del Señor; ***the Lord's Prayer*** el padrenuestro; ***the Lord's Supper*** la eucaristía *f*

(d) *Fam (in exclamations)* **good Lord!** ¡Dios mío!; **oh Lord!** ¡ay, Señor!; **L. knows if...** sabe Dios si...

(e) *Sport* **Lord's** = el campo de críquet más famoso del Reino Unido, situado en Londres

2 *vt* **to l. it over sb** tratar despóticamente a alguien

lordly ['lɔ:dlɪ] *adj* altanero(a)

Lordship ['lɔ:dʃɪp] *n* **His/Your L.** *(to nobleman)* su señoría; *(to judge)* (su) señoría; *(to bishop)* (su) ilustrísima; *Fam Hum* **what did his L. want, then?** ¿qué deseaba el señor?

lordy ['lɔ:dɪ] *exclam US Fam* ¡Jesús!

lore [lɔ:(r)] *n* (a) *(folk legend)* leyenda *f* (b) *(traditional knowledge)* saber *m* popular; **she knows all the countryside l.** domina a la perfección el saber popular del mundo rural

lorgnette [lɔ:n'jet] *n* impertinentes *mpl*

loris ['lɒrɪs] *n* loris *m inv*

lorry ['lɒrɪ] *n Br* camión *m*; *Fam Euph* **it fell off the back of a l.** *(was stolen)* es de trapicheo, *Méx* es chueco(a), *RP* es trucho(a) ►► ***l. driver*** camionero(a) *m,f*

lorry-load ['lɒrɪləʊd] *n Br* camión *m*; **he had a l. of bricks to deliver** tenía que entregar un camión (cargado) de ladrillos

Los Angeles [lɒs'ændʒəli:z] *n* Los Ángeles

LOSE [lu:z] (*pt & pp* **lost** [lɒst]) 1 *vt* (a) *(mislay)* perder, extraviar; **to l. one's way** perderse; *Fig* **he lost his way in his later years** se fue por el mal camino hacia el final de su vida; *Fig* **she lost her way in the second set** en el segundo set empezó a fallar; **to be lost at sea** desaparecer *or* morir en el mar; **she had lost herself in a book/in her work**

se quedó absorta en la lectura de un libro/en su trabajo; *Fam* **you've lost me** *(I don't understand)* no te sigo

(**b**) *(no longer have)* perder; **she lost a leg** perdió una pierna; **she lost both parents/the baby** perdió a sus padres/el niño; **several paintings were lost in the fire** se perdieron varios cuadros en el incendio; **to l. one's balance** perder el equilibrio; **I lost everything** lo perdí todo; **he had lost interest in his work** había perdido el interés por su trabajo; **three people lost their lives in the accident** tres personas perdieron la vida en el accidente; **to l. one's sight** perder la vista; **to l. sight of sth/sb** perder algo/a alguien de vista; **I wouldn't l. any sleep over it** yo no perdería el sueño por eso; **to l. one's voice** quedarse afónico(a); **you have nothing to l.** no tienes nada que perder; **it loses something in translation** al traducirlo, pierde algo; *Fam* **to l. it** descontrolarse; *Fam* **I think I'm losing it** *(going mad)* creo que estoy perdiendo la cabeza; *Fam* **to l. one's cool** mosquearse; **to l. one's head** perder los estribos; *Fam Hum* **to l. one's marbles** volverse loco(a) *or Esp* majara, *CSur* rayarse, *Méx* zafarse; **to l. one's mind** perder la cabeza; *Br Fam* **he's lost the plot** no se da cuenta de nada, no se entera de nada; *Br Fam* **to l. the place** empezar a chochear; *Fam* **to l. one's** *or* **the rag** salirse de sus casillas; *Fig* **to l. one's shirt (on sth)** perder hasta la camisa (en algo)

(**c**) *(allow to escape)* **to l. blood/heat** perder sangre/calor; **to l. height** *(aircraft)* perder altura; **we are losing a lot of business to them** nos están quitando *or Am* sacando un montón de clientes

(**d**) *(get rid of)* **to l. one's inhibitions** desinhibirse; **to l. weight** adelgazar, perder peso; **we lost him in the crowd** le dimos esquinazo entre la multitud, conseguimos despistarlo en la multitud

(**e**) *(waste)* perder; **to l. an opportunity** perder *or* dejar escapar una oportunidad; **he lost no time in correcting me** no tardó *or Am* demoró ni un minuto en corregirme; **there's no time to l.** no hay tiempo que perder; **the joke/irony was lost on him** no entendió el chiste/la ironía

(**f**) *(not win) (match, argument)* perder

(**g**) *(cause not to win)* **that mistake lost him the match** ese error hizo que perdiera el partido

(**h**) *(of clock, watch)* **my watch loses five minutes a day** mi reloj (se) atrasa cinco minutos al día

2 *vi* (**a**) *(in contest)* perder (**to** contra); **they lost two-nil to Chile** perdieron por dos a cero contra Chile

(**b**) *(have less)* **to l. in value** perder valor; **I lost on the deal** salí perdiendo (en el trato)

(**c**) *(clock, watch)* atrasar

▸**lose out** *vi* salir perdiendo (**to** en beneficio de); **to l. out on sth** salir perdiendo en algo

---

loser ['lu:zə(r)] *n* (**a**) *(in contest)* perdedor(ora) *m,f*; **to be a good/bad l.** ser buen/mal perdedor(ora); **you'll be the l.** tú saldrás perdiendo; **they're the losers by it** ellos han salido perdiendo (**b**) *Fam (in life)* fracasado(a); **he's a (born) l.** es un fracasado; **what a l.!** ¡vaya *or* menudo fracasado!

losing ['lu:zɪŋ] *adj* (**a**) *(failing, being defeated)* **the l. side** los vencidos; IDIOM **to fight a l. battle** luchar por una causa perdida (**b**) *(unprofitable)* **it's a l. proposition** la propuesta no es rentable

losingest ['lu:zɪŋəst] *adj US Fam* **the l. team/season** la peor formación/temporada

loss [lɒs] *n* (**a**) *(gen)* pérdida *f*; **l. of vision** pérdida de visión; **her leaving will be a great l. to us all** su marcha representará una gran pérdida para todos nosotros; **it's no great l.** no es una gran pérdida; **it's your l.** tú te lo pierdes; **to feel a sense of l.** sentir un gran vacío; **without l. of face** sin perder la dignidad; **to be at a l. to explain...** no saber cómo explicar...; **she's never at a l. for an answer** siempre sabe qué contestar

(**b**) *(of life)* **the l. of a close relative** la pérdida de un familiar cercano; **there was great l. of life** hubo muchas pérdidas humanas; **despite the damage there was no l. of life** a pesar de los desperfectos no hubo pérdidas humanas; **to suffer/inflict heavy losses** *(casualties)* sufrir/causar gran número de bajas (mortales); *Euph* **we were sorry to hear of your l.** *(bereavement)* lamentamos mucho enterarnos de tan dolorosa pérdida

(**c**) *(financial)* **losses** pérdidas *fpl*; **to make a l.** tener pérdidas; **we made a l. of 10 percent on the deal** perdimos un 10 por ciento en la transacción; **to sell at a l.** vender con pérdidas; **to cut one's losses** reducir pérdidas; *Fig* evitar problemas cortando por lo sano; **l. of earnings** pérdida de ingresos, descenso de los ingresos ▸▸ ***l. adjuster*** *(in insurance)* perito(a) *m,f* tasador(ora) de seguros; *Com* ***l. leader*** producto *m or* artículo *m* de reclamo

loss-maker ['lɒsmeɪkə(r)] *n (company)* empresa *f* deficitaria; *(product)* producto *m* deficitario

loss-making ['lɒsmeɪkɪŋ] *adj Br* con pérdidas

lost [lɒst] **1** *adj* (**a**) *(missing)* perdido(a); **to be l.** estar perdido(a); **to get l.** perderse, desaparecer; **to give sth/sb up for l.** dar algo/a alguien por perdido(a) ▸▸ ***l. cause*** *(aim, ideal)* causa *f* perdida; *(person)* caso *m* perdido; *US* ***l. and found*** objetos *mpl* perdidos; *US* ***l. and found office*** oficina *f* de objetos perdidos; ***l. generation*** *(soldiers)* = los caídos en la Primera Guerra Mundial; *(writers)* generación *f* perdida; ***l. property*** objetos *mpl* perdidos; ***l. property office*** oficina *f* de objetos perdidos; ***l. sheep*** oveja *f* descarriada

(**b**) *(unable to find one's way)* perdido(a); **to be l.** estar perdido(a); **to get l.** perderse; **I'm l.** me he perdido; *Fam* **get l.!** ¡lárgate!, ¡vete a paseo!; *Fam* **she told him to get l.** lo mandó a paseo *or* a freír churros

(**c**) *(presumed dead) Mil* **l. in action** desaparecido(a) en combate; **30 people were reported l. at sea** 30 personas se dieron por desaparecidas en alta mar

(**d**) *(beyond saving, retrieval)* **a l. soul** un alma descarriada; *Old-fashioned* **a l. woman** una perdida; **he was l. to us a long time ago** se volvió un extraño para nosotros hace mucho tiempo; **all is not (yet) l.** no todo está perdido

(**e**) *(wasted)* **to make up for l. time** recuperar el tiempo perdido; **the allusion was l. on me** no entendí la indirecta

(**f**) *(engrossed)* absorto(a); **she was l. in her book** estaba absorta en su libro; **he was l. in thought** estaba absorto en sus pensamientos; **he was l. to the world while he studied the report** estuvo ensimismadísimo mientras estudiaba el informe

(**g**) *(confused, disoriented)* perdido(a); **I'm l., start again!** me he perdido, comienza otra vez; **to seem** *or* **look l.** tener un aire de perdido(a), parecer perdido(a); **I'd be l. without my diary** yo sin mi agenda estaría perdido *or* no sabría qué hacer; **to be l. for words** no encontrar palabras, no saber qué decir

2 *pt & pp of* **lose**

LOT [lɒt] **1** *n* (**a**) *(large quantity)* **a l., lots** *(singular)* mucho(a); *(plural)* muchos(as); **a l. of, lots of** *(singular)* mucho(a); *(plural)* muchos(as); **he eats a l.** *or* **lots** come mucho; **I had several, but I've lost a l.** tenía varios, pero he perdido muchos de ellos; **a l.** *or* **lots has been written about her death** se ha escrito mucho sobre su muerte; **we had lots and lots to eat** comimos muchísimo; **there wasn't a l. we could do** no podíamos hacer gran cosa; **a l.** *or* **lots of people** mucha gente; **a l.** *or* **lots of questions** muchas preguntas; **a l. of my time is taken up with administration** gran parte del tiempo lo paso haciendo tareas de gestión; **I saw quite a l. of her in Paris** la vi mucho en París; **we had a l.** *or* **lots of fun** nos divertimos mucho; *Fam* **I've got the flu – there's a l. of it about** tengo (la) gripe *or Col, Méx* gripa – mucha gente la tiene; **you've got a l. of explaining to do** tienes muchas cosas que explicar; **do you like it? – not a l.** ¿te gusta? – no mucho; **I've got quite a l. of work/students** tengo bastante trabajo/bastantes alumnos; **I've had such a l. of luck/presents!** ¡he tenido tanta suerte/tantos regalos!; **what a l. of food!** ¡cuánta comida!; **what a l. of dresses you have!** ¡cuántos vestidos tienes!; **I have a l. on my mind** tengo muchas cosas en la cabeza; *Fig* **I've got a l. on my plate at the moment** tengo muchas cosas entre manos en estos momentos

(**b**) *(destiny)* fortuna *f*, suerte *f*; **he was happy with his l.** estaba contento con su suerte; **to throw in one's l. with sb** compartir la suerte de alguien, unir (uno) su suerte a la de alguien

(**c**) *(chance)* **to choose sb by l.** elegir a alguien por sorteo; **to draw** *or* **cast lots for sth** sortear algo, echar algo a suertes

(**d**) *(group of things, batch)* lote *m*; **we'll finish this l. and then stop** terminamos este lote y paramos; **here's another l. of papers for you to sign** aquí tienes otro lote de papeles para firmar; **the (whole) l.** todo; **I bought the l.** lo compré todo; *Fam* **that's your l., I'm afraid** lo siento, pero esto es todo

(**e**) *Fam (group of people)* grupo *m*; **they're a hopeless l.** son unos inútiles; **that l. next door** los de al lado; **I'm fed up with the l. of you!** ¡me tenéis todos harto!; **listen, you l.!** *Esp* ¡escuchadme bien!, *Am* ¡oigan, ustedes!; **are your l. coming too?** ¿los tuyos también vienen?; IDIOM **he's a bad l.** es un elemento de cuidado

(**f**) *(piece of land)* terreno *m*; *(film studio)* plató *m*; *US (car park)* estacionamiento *m*, *Esp* aparcamiento *m*, *Bol, Col, Cuba* parqueo *m*, *Col, Ven* parqueadero *m*

(**g**) *(at auction)* lote *m*; **in lots** por lotes; **l. number 56** lote número 56

2 *adv* **a l., lots** mucho; **are you feeling better now? – oh, lots, thank you** ¿te encuentras mejor? – muchísimo mejor, gracias; **a l.** *or* **lots bigger** mucho más grande; **we go there a l. on holiday** vamos mucho allí de vacaciones; **thanks a l.** muchas gracias

---

loth = **loath**

Lothario [lə'θɑ:rɪəʊ] *n* crápula *m*

lotion ['ləʊʃən] *n* loción *f*

lottery ['lɒtərɪ] *n* lotería *f*; *Fig* **it's a l.** es una lotería ▸▸ ***l. outlet*** administración *f* de loterías; ***l. ticket*** billete *m or Am* boleto *m* de lotería

lotto ['lɒtəʊ] *n (game)* = juego parecido al bingo

lotus ['ləʊtəs] *n* loto *m* ▸▸ ***l. position*** posición *f* del loto

lotus-eater ['ləʊtəsi:tə(r)] *n* (a) *(in Greek mythology)* lotófago(a) *m,f* (b) *(lazy person)* persona *f* indolente

loud [laʊd] **1** *adj* (a) *(noise, bang, explosion, applause)* fuerte; *(music, radio)* alto(a); *(protest)* sonoro(a); **he has a l. voice** tiene una voz muy fuerte; **he spoke in a l. voice** habló en voz alta; **to be l. in one's praise/condemnation of sth** elogiar/condenar algo rotundamente
(b) *Pej (person)* escandaloso(a); **he's a bit l., isn't he?** es un poco escandaloso, ¿no crees?
(c) *(garish) (colour, clothes, decor)* llamativo(a), chillón(ona); **he wore a suit with a l. check** llevaba un traje con unos cuadros llamativos
2 *adv* alto; **the music was turned up l.** la música estaba muy alta; **to read out l.** leer en voz alta; **to think out l.** pensar en alto; **louder!** ¡más alto!; **l. and clear** alto y claro; **I hear you l. and clear** *(on radio)* te oigo alto y claro; *Fam (I understand)* me ha quedado perfectamente claro; **to complain l. and long (about sth)** quejarse amargamente (de algo)

loudhailer [laʊd'heɪlə(r)] *n Br* megáfono *m*

loudly ['laʊdlɪ] *adv* (a) *(to speak)* alto, en voz alta; *(to complain)* en voz alta; *(to shout)* muy fuerte *or* alto (b) *(garishly)* llamativamente, chillonamente

loud-mouth ['laʊdmaʊθ] *n Fam* **to be a l.** ser un(a) bocazas

loud-mouthed ['laʊdmaʊðd] *adj Fam* bocazas *inv*

loudness ['laʊdnɪs] *n* (a) *(of noise, bang, explosion, applause)* fuerza *f*, intensidad *f*; *(of voice, music, radio)* volumen *m* (alto); *(protest)* clamor *m* (b) *(of colour, clothes, decor)* tono *m* chillón *or* llamativo

loudspeaker [laʊd'spi:kə(r)] *n* altavoz *m*, *Am* altoparlante *m*, *Méx* bocina *f*

lough [lɒχ, lɒk] *n Irish (lake)* lago *m*; *(open to sea)* ría *f*

Louis ['lu:ɪ] *pr n* **L. I/II** Luis I/II

Louisiana [lu:i:zɪ'ænə] *n* Luisiana

lounge [laʊndʒ] **1** *n (in house, hotel)* salón *m*; *(in airport)* sala *f* (de espera) ▸▸ *Fam* ***l. lizard*** = hombre que gusta de codearse con la alta sociedad, tal vez en busca de una mujer rica; *Br* ***l. suit*** traje *m* de calle (b) *Br* **l. (bar)** = en ciertos "pubs" y hoteles, sala más cómoda que la del "public bar" (c) *(rest)* **to have a l. in the sun** descansar al sol
2 *vi* (a) *(recline)* recostarse; *(sprawl)* repantigarse; **he spent the afternoon lounging on the sofa reading** se pasó la tarde leyendo repantigado en el sofá; **he lounged against the counter** estaba recostado sobre el mostrador (b) *(laze, hang around)* holgazanear, gandulear

▸ **lounge about, lounge around** *vi* holgazanear, gandulear

lounger ['laʊndʒə(r)] *n* (a) *(chair)* tumbona *f* (b) *(person)* holgazán(ana) *m,f*, gandul(ula) *m,f*

lour = **lower**[3]

louse [laʊs] (*pl* **lice** [laɪs]) *n* (a) *(insect)* piojo *m* (b) *Fam (person)* canalla *mf*

▸ **louse up** *vt sep Fam* fastidiar, jorobar

lousily ['laʊzɪlɪ] *adv Fam Esp* fatal, *Am* pésimo

lousy ['laʊzɪ] *adj* (a) *Fam (very bad, unpleasant)* pésimo(a), horroroso(a); **I'm l. at tennis, I'm a l. tennis player** soy desastroso *or* penoso jugando al tenis; **he's in a l. mood** está de un humor de perros; **to feel l.** sentirse *Esp* fatal *or Am* pésimo; **we had a l. time on holiday** lo pasamos *Esp* fatal *or Am* pésimo durante las vacaciones
(b) *Fam (annoying, trifling)* **I've got these l. letters to write!** ¡tengo que escribir estas malditas cartas!; **all for a l. $5** todo por cinco dólares de mala muerte, *Am* todo por cinco dólares de porquería
(c) *Fam (mean)* **that's a l. thing to do** *or* **say** eso es una canallada; **a l. trick** una jugarreta, una mala pasada
(d) *Fam* **to be l. with** *(overrun with)* estar hasta los topes de; **they're l. with money** están forrados
(e) *(lice-infested)* con piojos, piojoso(a)

lout [laʊt] *n* (a) *(thuggish person)* salvaje *m*, *Esp* gamberro *m*, *Arg* barra *m* brava (b) *(uncouth, clumsy person)* zopenco(a) *m,f*

loutish ['laʊtɪʃ] *adj* grosero(a), *Esp* gamberro(a), *Arg* barra brava

louvre, *US* **louver** ['lu:və(r)] *n* (a) *(on door, window)* lama *f*, listón *m* (b) *(on roof)* lumbrera *f*

louvred, *US* **louvered** ['lu:vəd] *adj* **l. door** puerta *f* (tipo) persiana *or* de listones

lovable, loveable ['lʌvəbəl] *adj* adorable, encantador(ora); **a l. rogue** un pillo encantador

lovage ['lʌvɪdʒ] *n* levístico *m*, apio *m* de monte

LOVE [lʌv] **1** *n* (a) *(between lovers or members of a family)* amor *m*; **to be in l. with sb** estar enamorado(a) de alguien; **they are in l. (with each other)** están enamorados; *Fam Pej* **he's in l. with himself** es un engreído; **to fall in l. with sb** enamorarse de alguien; **they fell in l. (with each other)** se enamoraron; **to make love with** *or* **to sb** *(have sex)* hacer el amor con *or* a alguien; *Old-fashioned* **to make l. to sb** *(court)* cortejar a alguien; **make l. not war!** haz el amor y no la guerra; **it was l. at first sight** fue un flechazo; IDIOM **for love (n)or money: I wouldn't do it for l. or money** no lo haría por nada del mundo; *Fam* **you can't get a taxi for l. nor money round here** por aquí no encuentras un taxi ni a la de tres; PROV **l. is blind** el amor es ciego ▸▸ ***l. affair*** aventura *f* (amorosa); **the nation's l. affair with soap operas** la pasión del país por las telenovelas; *Br* ***l. bite*** marca *f* (de un beso), *Esp* chupetón *m*, *Am* chupón *m*; *Euph* ***l. child*** hijo(a) *m,f* ilegítimo(a); *Fam* ***l. handles*** *Esp* michelines *mpl*, *Méx* llantas *fpl*, *RP* rollos *mpl*; ***l. letter*** carta *f* de amor; ***l. life*** vida *f* amorosa *or* sentimental; **how's your l. life?** ¿qué tal tu vida amorosa *or* sentimental?; ***l. match*** matrimonio *m* por amor; ***l. nest*** nido *m* de amor; ***l. poem*** poema *m* de amor; ***l. potion*** filtro *m or* poción *f* de amor; *Br Fam* ***l. rat*** = persona que se comporta de forma rastrera con su pareja; ***l. scene*** escena *f* de amor; ***l. seat*** *(S-shaped)* tu-y-yó *m inv*; *US (small sofa)* confidente *m*; ***l. song*** canción *f* de amor; ***l. story*** historia *f* de amor; ***l. token*** recuerdo *m* (amoroso); ***l. triangle*** triángulo *m* amoroso
(b) *(person)* amor *m*; **the l. of my life** el amor de mi vida; **(my) l.** *(term of endearment)* mi amor; *Br Fam* **have you got the time, (my) l.?** ¿tienes hora, *esp Esp* guapa *or Am* mamita?; *Fam* **you're a real l.** eres un encanto; *Fam* **be a l. and pass me the newspaper, pass me the newspaper, there's a l.** sé buen chico/buena chica y pásame el periódico
(c) *(affection)* cariño *m*; **l. of one's country** cariño por el propio país; **give my l. to your parents** saluda a tus padres de mi parte; **Bill sends his l.** Bill manda recuerdos; **with l., l. (from), lots of l., all my l.** *(at end of letter)* con cariño; *Fam* **for the l. of God** *or* **Mike** por el amor de Dios; **there's no** *or* **little l. lost between them** no se pueden ni ver
(d) *(liking, interest)* afición *f* (**of** *or* **for** a *or por*); **cricket is his one l. in life** su única pasión en la vida es el críquet; **to do sth for the l. of it** hacer algo por placer *or Esp* gusto
(e) *(in tennis)* **fifteen/thirty l.** quince/treinta nada; **he won by three sets to l.** ganó por tres sets a cero; **she won the game to l.** la ganó con un juego el blanco ▸▸ ***l. game*** juego *m* en blanco
2 *vt* (a) *(lover)* amar, querer; **I l. you** te quiero; **they l. each other** se quieren; *Fam Pej* **he really loves himself** realmente es un engreído; *Fig* **she loves me, she loves me not** me quiere, no me quiere; IDIOM **l. me, l. my dog** si me quieres a mí, tendrás que quererme con todas las consecuencias
(b) *(family member)* querer; **I never felt loved as a child** de niño nunca me sentí querido; *Fam Hum* **I'm going to have to l. you and leave you** *(I must go)* lo siento, pero tengo que irme
(c) *(like very much)* **I l. Chinese food** me encanta la comida china; **I'd l. some coffee** un café me vendría de maravilla; **don't you just l. champagne!** ¿no te encanta el champán?; **they l. to go for walks, they l. going for walks** les encanta ir de paseo; **I'd l. to come** me encantaría ir; **I'd l. you to come** me encantarías que vinieras; **I l. it!** *(expressing amusement)* ¡qué bueno!; *also Ironic* **you're going to l. this...** esto te va a encantar...; **l. them or hate them, mobile phones are here to stay** te gusten o no, los teléfonos móviles no son una moda pasajera
3 *vi* amar, querer; **it's better to have loved and lost (than never to have loved at all)** es mejor haber amado y perdido (que nunca haber amado)

---

loveable = **lovable**

lovebird ['lʌvbɜ:d] *n* (a) *(bird)* inseparable *m* (b) *Fam (lover)* **a pair of lovebirds** un par de tortolitos

loved up ['lʌvd'ʌp] *adj Br Fam* con un subidón de éxtasis

love-hate [lʌv'heɪt] *adj* **a l. relationship** una relación de amor y odio

love-in ['lʌvɪn] *n* = protesta en forma de encierro para manifestar amor, característica de los hippies en los años sesenta; *Ironic* **the occasion turned into yet another a l. between the president and his predecessor** la ocasión se convirtió en un intercambio de flores entre el presidente y su predecesor

loveless ['lʌvlɪs] *adj* sin amor, carente de amor

loveliness ['lʌvlɪnɪs] *n* (a) *(in appearance) (of person)* belleza *f*; *(of room, garden)* belleza *f*, encanto *f* (b) *(enjoyableness) (of weather, smell)* lo agradable

lovelorn ['lʌvlɔ:n] *adj Literary or Hum* apesadumbrado(a) *(por amor)*

lovely ['lʌvlɪ] *adj* **(a)** *(in appearance) (person)* bello(a), *Esp* guapo(a), *Am* lindo(a); *(curtains, room, garden)* precioso(a), *Am* lindo(a); **what a l. dress!** ¡qué preciosidad de vestido!
(b) *(enjoyable, pleasing) (weather, idea, smell)* estupendo; **it's been l. to see you!** ¡ha sido estupendo verte!; **what a l. thing to say!** ¡qué cosa más preciosa has dicho!; **to have a l. time** pasárselo estupendamente; **Clara's coming – oh l.!** viene Clara – ¡estupendo!
(c) *(in character)* encantador(ora); **what a l. woman!** ¡qué señora más encantadora!; **her parents are l. people** sus padres son encantadores; **they were l. to my sister** se portaron muy bien con mi hermana
(d) *Br Fam (as intensifier)* **it's l. and warm** hace un tiempo estupendo

lovemaking ['lʌvmeɪkɪŋ] *n* **(a)** *(sexual intercourse)* **during their l.** mientras hacían el amor; **a night of passionate l.** una noche de pasión amorosa **(b)** *Archaic (courtship)* cortejo *m*

lover ['lʌvə(r)] *n* **(a)** *(of person)* amante *mf*; *Fam* **she's gone out with l. boy** ha salido con su *Esp* noviete *or Am* noviecito **(b)** *(of nature, good food)* amante *mf*, aficionado(a) *m,f*; **I'm not a dog l. myself** los perros no me entusiasman; **she's a great l. of the cinema** es muy aficionada al cine, es una amante del cine

lovesick ['lʌvsɪk] *adj* con mal de amores, enfermo(a) de amor

lovey-dovey ['lʌvɪ'dʌvɪ] *adj Fam Pej* almibarado(a), acaramelado(a)

loving ['lʌvɪŋ] *adj* cariñoso(a), afectuoso(a); **your l. daughter, Jane** *(at end of letter)* un abrazo cariñoso de tu hija, Jane ►► ***l. kindness*** cariño *m*, afecto *m*

-loving ['lʌvɪŋ] *suffix* **wine-l.** amante del vino; **home-l.** hogareño(a)

loving-cup ['lʌvɪŋkʌp] *n* copa *f* de la amistad

lovingly ['lʌvɪŋlɪ] *adv (with affection)* con cariño, afectuosamente; *(with care, attention)* con mimo, con esmero

LOW[1] [ləʊ] **1** *n* **(a)** *Met (area of low pressure)* zona *f* de bajas presiones; *(lowest temperature)* mínima *f*
(b) *(minimum)* mínimo *m*; **to reach a new l.** *(of price, popularity)* alcanzar un nuevo mínimo; *(of country, reputation)* caer aún más bajo; **an all-time l.** un mínimo histórico; **that defeat marked an all-time l. for me** esa derrota fue mi peor momento; **there were more lows than highs** hubo más momentos malos que buenos
2 *adj* **(a)** *(not high)* bajo(a); **a l. bow** una reverencia profunda; **the sun is l. in the sky** el sol está bajo; **their fortunes are at a l. ebb** están pasando por un mal momento ►► ***the L. Countries*** los Países Bajos; ***l. tide*** marea *f* baja; ***l. water*** marea *f* baja
(b) *(not loud, not intense)* bajo(a); **there was a l. murmur from the crowd** de la multitud emergió un sordo murmullo; **I had the radio on l.** tenía la radio baja; *Aut* **to be on l. beam** llevar las luces cortas *or* de cruce puestas; **to cook sth over a l. heat** cocinar algo a fuego lento; **l. lighting** iluminación suave; **l. pitch** tono grave; **an area of l. pressure** un área de baja presión ►► *Br* ***l. season*** temporada *f* baja
(c) *(small in size, quantity) (number, cost, temperature)* bajo(a); **it's a number in the l. thirties** son treinta y pocos; **prices are getting lower** los precios están bajando; **to play a l. card** jugar una carta baja ►► *Elec* ***l. frequency*** baja frecuencia *f*; *Aut* ***a l. gear*** una marcha corta *or RP* baja; *Comptr* ***l. resolution*** baja resolución *f*
(d) *(bad) (quality, standard)* malo(a); **to have l. self-esteem** tener poca autoestima; **to have l. expectations** tener pocas expectativas; **to have a l. opinion of sb** tener mala opinión de alguien; **the l. point of her career** el peor momento de su carrera; **a l. quality carpet** una alfombra *or Am* un tapete de poca calidad
(e) *(of lesser status, priority)* bajo(a); **of l. birth** de baja extracción ►► ***l. comedy*** *(farcical)* comedia *f* grotesca; ***L. German*** bajo alemán *m*; ***L. Latin*** bajo latín *m*
(f) *(in short supply)* **fuel is getting l.** nos estamos quedando sin combustible; **the battery is l.** quedan pocas pilas; **our stock of food is rather l.** nos queda bastante poca comida; **morale is l. amongst the troops** las tropas andan con la moral baja; **this cheese is l. in fat** este queso tiene un bajo contenido de materia grasa; **the evening was l. on excitement** no fue una velada muy interesante
(g) *(deep) (sound, note, voice)* bajo(a), grave
(h) *(depressed)* **to feel l.** estar un poco deprimido(a); **in l. spirits** desanimado(a)
(i) *(ignoble) Fig* **a l. blow** un golpe bajo; **that's a l. trick!** ¡eso es una mala pasada! ►► ***l. life*** *(world)* hampa *f*
(j) *(low-cut) (dress)* escotado(a); **a l. neckline** un escote amplio
(k) *Rel* ***L. Church*** Baja Iglesia *f*, = corriente del anglicanismo más alejada del catolicismo; ***L. Mass*** misa *f* rezada
3 *adv* **(a)** *(not high)* bajo; **l. to the left of the screen** en la parte inferior izquierda de la pantalla; **to bow l.** hacer una reverencia profunda; **the dress is cut l.** el vestido tiene un escote amplio; **to fly l.** volar bajo; *Fig* **how could anyone sink** *or* **stoop so l.?** ¿cómo se puede caer tan bajo?
(b) *(not loud)* **turn the music/the lights down l.** baja la música/las luces
(c) *(badly)* **the l. paid** los que perciben salarios bajos
(d) *(short)* **we're running l. on fuel/food** nos estamos quedando sin combustible/comida; **the battery is running l.** quedan pocas pilas
(e) *(deeply)* **I can't sing that l.** no puedo cantar (en un tono) tan bajo
(f) *(cheaply)* **to buy l.** comprar barato

---

low[2] **1** *n (of cattle)* mugido *m*
2 *vi* mugir

low-alcohol [ləʊ'ælkəhɒl] *adj* bajo(a) en alcohol

low-born ['ləʊbɔːn] *adj* de condición humilde

lowboy ['ləʊbɔɪ] *n US* cómoda *f (tipo escritorio)*

lowbrow ['ləʊbraʊ] **1** *n* persona *f* sin pretensiones intelectuales
2 *adj (tastes, interests)* vulgar, de las masas; *(novel, movie)* popular chero(a)

low-budget [ləʊ'bʌdʒɪt] *adj (movie, holiday)* de bajo presupuesto

low-cal ['ləʊ'kæl] *adj (drink)* bajo(a) en calorías

low-calorie ['ləʊ'kælərɪ] *adj* bajo(a) en calorías; **a l. diet** una dieta baja en calorías

low-class ['ləʊklɑːs] *adj* de clase baja

low-cost ['ləʊ'kɒst] *adj (mortgage)* de bajo costo *or Esp* coste; *(flight)* económico(a)

low-cut ['ləʊ'kʌt] *adj (dress)* escotado(a)

low-density housing ['ləʊ'densɪtɪ'haʊzɪŋ] *n* = zona de viviendas con baja densidad de población

lowdown ['ləʊdaʊn] *n Fam* **to give sb the l. on sth** explicar de pe a pa a alguien los pormenores de algo

low-down ['ləʊdaʊn] *adj Fam* sucio(a), rastrero(a); **that was a l. trick to play!** ¡fue una jugarreta de lo más sucio!

low-end ['ləʊend] *adj Comptr* de gama baja

lower[1] ['ləʊə(r)] *vt* **(a)** *(drop, let down)* bajar; *(flag, sail)* arriar; **she lowered her eyes** bajó la mirada; **l. your aim a bit** apunta un poco más bajo; **to l. one's guard** bajar la guardia; **to l. the lifeboat** arriar el bote salvavidas; **to l. oneself into sth** entrar en algo; **to l. oneself onto sth** bajar hasta algo
(b) *(reduce) (price)* rebajar; *(pressure, standard, temperature)* reducir; **he lowered his voice** bajó la voz; **to l. the volume** bajar *or* reducir el volumen; **a surplus will l. prices** un exceso de producción hará bajar los precios
(c) *(degrade, diminish)* rebajar, denigrar; **to l. oneself to do sth** rebajarse a hacer algo; **to l. morale** desmoralizar, minar la moral; **to l. the tone of the debate/evening** hacer caer el tono del debate/de la velada

lower[2] ['ləʊə(r)] **1** *adj* inferior; **the l. deck** *(of ship)* cubierta inferior; **l. vertebrates** vertebrados inferiores; **the l. (reaches of the) Nile** el curso bajo del Nilo ►► ***l. case*** minúsculas *fpl*, *Spec* caja *f* baja; *Pol* ***l. chamber*** cámara *f* baja; ***the l. classes*** las clases bajas; *US Fam* ***the l. forty-eight*** = expresión referida a los estados continentales de los Estados Unidos, a excepción de Alaska; *Pol* ***l. house*** cámara *f* baja; ***l. middle class*** clase *f* media alta/baja; *Mil* ***l. ranks*** soldados *mpl* rasos *or* de rango inferior; *Educ* ***l. sixth*** = el primero de los dos últimos cursos del bachillerato en Inglaterra, Gales e Irlanda del Norte
2 *adv* **the l. paid** las personas con ingresos más bajos

lower[3], lour ['laʊə(r)] *vi Literary* **(a)** *(person)* mirar amenazadoramente; **he lowered at me** me lanzó una mirada amenazadora **(b)** *(sky)* estar tormentoso(a); **a lowering sky** un cielo de panza de burro

lower-case ['ləʊə'keɪs] *adj Typ* en minúsculas, *Spec* en caja baja

lower-class ['ləʊə'klɑːs] *adj* de clase baja

lowermost ['ləʊəməʊst] *adj* el/la más bajo(a); **the l. layer/level** la capa más baja/el nivel más bajo

lowest ['ləʊəst] **1** *n* **the l. of the low** lo más bajo
2 *adj* **the l. temperature ever recorded** la temperatura mínima *or* más baja que se ha registrado ►► *Math* ***l. common denominator*** mínimo común denominador *m*; *Fig* **to reduce sth to the l. common denominator** hacer caer algo en la mayor vulgaridad; *Math* ***l. common multiple*** mínimo común múltiplo *m*

low-fat ['ləʊ'fæt] *adj (food, diet)* bajo(a) en grasas

low-flying ['ləʊ'flaɪɪŋ] *adj* que vuela bajo

low-frequency ['ləʊ'friːkwənsɪ] *adj* de baja frecuencia

low-grade ['ləʊ'greɪd] *adj (in quality)* de baja calidad

lowing ['ləʊɪŋ] *n (of cattle)* mugido *m*

low-key ['ləʊ'kiː] *adj (manner, approach)* discreto(a); **the meeting was a very l. affair** la reunión fue muy discreta *or* contenida

lowland ['ləʊlənd] *adj* de las tierras bajas; **L.** *(in Scotland)* de las Tierras Bajas de Escocia ►► ***L. Scots*** = variedad escocesa del inglés hablada en las Tierras Bajas de Escocia

lowlander ['ləʊləndə(r)] *n* habitante *mf* de las tierras bajas; **L.** *(in Scotland)* habitante *mf* de las Tierras Bajas de Escocia

lowlands ['ləʊləndz] *npl* tierras *fpl* bajas; **the L.** *(in Scotland)* las Tierras Bajas de Escocia

low-level ['ləʊ'levəl] *adj* **(a)** *(discussion)* de bajo nivel **(b)** *(low-intensity)* ***l. radiation*** radiación *f* de baja intensidad **(c)** *Comptr* ***l. language*** lenguaje *m* de bajo nivel **(d)** ***l. flight*** vuelo *m* rasante

low-life ['ləʊlaɪf] **1** *n Fam (bad person)* canalla *mf*; *(delinquent)* maleante *mf*
2 *adj* canalla

low-loader ['ləʊ'ləʊdə(r)] *n Br (railcar)* vagón *m* de plataforma; *(road vehicle)* vehículo *m* de plataforma

lowly ['ləʊlɪ] *adj* humilde; **of l. birth** de origen humilde

low-lying ['ləʊ'laɪɪŋ] *adj (area, mist)* bajo(a)

low-maintenance ['ləʊ'meɪntənəns] *adj* **(a)** *(pet, garden)* que da poco trabajo; *(hairstyle)* práctico(a), que exige pocos cuidados **(b)** *Fam Hum (girlfriend)* poco exigente, que da poco trabajo

low-necked *adj* ['ləʊ'nekt] escotado(a)

lowness ['ləʊnɪs] *n* **(a)** *(in height, altitude) (of wall, building)* poca altura *f*; *(of land)* lo bajo
(b) *(of voice, sound)* gravedad *f*
(c) *(of prices)* baratura *f*; **the l. of the temperature means few plants can grow** las bajas temperaturas hacen que crezcan pocas plantas; **the l. of the wages meant a shortage of skilled workers** los bajos salarios provocaron la escasez de trabajadores cualificados
(d) *(of mood)* desánimo *m*
(e) *(ignobility)* bajeza *f*

low-octane [ləʊ'ɒkteɪn] *adj* de bajo octanaje

low-paid ['ləʊ'peɪd] **1** *npl* **the l.** los mal remunerados
2 *adj (person)* mal pagado(a); **a l. job** un empleo mal pagado *or* remunerado

low-pitched ['ləʊ'pɪtʃt] *adj* **(a)** *(voice, note)* grave **(b)** *(roof)* poco pronunciado(a)

low-pressure ['ləʊ'preʃə(r)] *adj Met* de bajas presiones

low-profile ['ləʊ'prəʊfaɪl] *adj* **(a)** *(talks, visit)* discreto(a); **the police maintained a l. presence throughout** la presencia de la policía fue discreta todo el tiempo **(b)** *Aut* **l. tyre** neumático de perfil bajo

low-rent ['ləʊ'rent] *adj* **(a)** *(housing)* de alquiler barato, *Méx* de renta barata **(b)** *Pej (low-quality)* de poca monta

low-resolution ['ləʊrezə'lu:ʃən] *adj (screen, graphics)* de baja resolución

low-rise ['ləʊraɪz] **1** *n* edificio *m* bajo
2 *adj (housing)* bajo(a), de poca altura

low-slung ['ləʊ'slʌŋ] *adj Aut (chassis)* de chasis bajo

low-spirited ['ləʊ'spɪrɪtɪd] *adj* desanimado(a)

low-tar ['ləʊ'tɑ:(r)] *adj (cigarettes)* bajo(a) en nicotina, de bajo nivel de nicotina

low-tech ['ləʊ'tek] *adj* rudimentario(a), elemental

low-tension ['ləʊ'tenʃən] *adj Elec* de baja tensión

low-water mark [ləʊ'wɔ:təmɑ:k] *n* **(a)** *(level of low tide)* línea *f* de bajamar **(b)** *Fig (lowest point)* nivel *m* mínimo

lox [lɒks] *n Culin* salmón *m* ahumado

loyal ['lɔɪəl] *adj* leal, fiel (**to** a); **to be/stay l. to one's friends/principles** ser/permanecer (uno) fiel a sus amigos/principios

loyalist ['lɔɪəlɪst] *n* **(a)** *(to government, party)* leal *mf*, adicto(a) *m,f* **(b)** *Br Pol (in Northern Ireland)* unionista *mf* **(c)** *Hist (in Spanish Civil War)* leal *mf*, republicano(a) *m,f*; *(in American War of Independence)* leal *mf (a la corona británica)*

loyally ['lɔɪəlɪ] *adv* lealmente, fielmente

loyalty ['lɔɪəltɪ] *n* lealtad *f*, fidelidad *f* (**to** a); **you'll have to decide where your loyalties lie** tienes que decidir con quién estás; **she had divided loyalties** sus lealtades estaban divididas ►► ***l. card*** tarjeta *f or* carné *m* de fidelización

lozenge ['lɒzɪndʒ] *n* **(a)** *(shape)* rombo *m* **(b)** *(cough sweet)* pastilla *f* para la tos

LP [el'pi:] *n* (*abbr* **long player**) LP *m*, elepé *m*

LPG [elpi:'dʒi:] *n* (*abbr* **liquefied petroleum gas**) GLP *m*, gas *m* licuado de petróleo

LSD [eles'di:] *n* (*abbr* **lysergic acid diethylamide**) LSD *m*

L.S.D., l.s.d. [eles'di:] *n Br Formerly* (*abbr* **librae, solidi, denarii**) = sistema monetario británico compuesto por libras, chelines y peniques empleado antes de la introducción del sistema decimal en 1971

LSE [eles'i:] *n* (*abbr* **London School of Economics**) LSE *f*, = Escuela de Economía y Ciencia Política de Londres

L-shaped ['elʃeɪpt] *adj* en (forma de) L

LSI [eles'aɪ] *n Comptr* (*abbr* **large scale integration**) *n* integración *f* a gran escala, IGE *f*

Lt *Mil* (*abbr* **Lieutenant**) Tte.

lt (*abbr* **litres**) l.

Ltd *Br Com* (*abbr* **limited**) S.L.

LTR [elti:'ɑ:(r)] *n US* (*abbr* **long-term relationship**) relación *f* duradera

luau ['lu:aʊ] *n US* = banquete de comida hawaiana

lube [lu:b] *Fam* **1** *n* lubricante *m*
2 *vt* lubricar

lubricant ['lu:brɪkənt] **1** *n* lubricante *m*
2 *adj* lubricante

lubricate ['lu:brɪkeɪt] *vt* lubricar

lubricating oil ['lu:brɪkeɪtɪŋ'ɔɪl] *n* aceite *m* lubricante

lubrication [lu:brɪ'keɪʃən] *n* **(a)** *(to reduce friction)* lubricación *f* **(b)** *Fam Hum (alcohol)* carburante *m*

lubricious [lu:'brɪʃəs] *adj Literary* lúbrico(a)

lubricity [lu:'brɪsɪtɪ] *n Literary (lewdness)* lubricidad *f*

lucerne [lu:'sɜ:n] *n Br Bot* alfalfa *f*

lucid ['lu:sɪd] *adj* **(a)** *(clear-headed)* lúcido(a); **he still has l. moments** todavía tiene momentos de lucidez **(b)** *(clear) (style, account)* lúcido(a)

lucidity [lu:'sɪdɪtɪ] *n* **(a)** *(of mind)* lucidez *f* **(b)** *(of style, account)* lucidez *f*

lucidly ['lu:sɪdlɪ] *adv* con lucidez

Lucifer ['lu:sɪfə(r)] *n* Lucifer

luck [lʌk] *n* **(a)** *(fortune)* suerte *f*; **good l.** (buena) suerte; **good l.!** ¡(buena) suerte!; *Ironic* **good l. to him!** ¡que le sea leve!, ¡que le vaya bien!; **good l. in your new job!** ¡buena suerte con tu nuevo empleo!; **bad l.** mala suerte; **it's bad l. to spill salt** trae mala suerte tirar *or* derramar la sal; **bad** *or* **hard l.!** *(sympathetic)* ¡qué lástima *or* pena!; **hard** *or* **tough l.!** *(mocking)* ¡qué lástima *or* pena!; **to bring sb good/bad l.** traer buena/mala suerte a alguien; **just my l.!** ¡qué mala suerte!; **as l. would have it...** quiso el destino que...; IDIOM **the l. of the draw** el azar **(b)** *(good fortune)* (buena) suerte *f*; **that's a bit of l.!** ¡eso sí que es suerte!; **l. was with us** *or* **on our side** teníamos la suerte de cara; **he couldn't believe his l.** no podía creerse la suerte que tenía; **some people have all the l.** hay quien nace con estrella; **to wish sb l.** desear suerte a alguien; **(did you have) any l.?** ¿hubo suerte?; **for l.** de propina; **to be in l.** estar de suerte; **to be out of l.** no tener suerte; **to be down on one's l.** no estar de suerte; **to try one's l.** probar suerte; **to push one's l.** tentar a la suerte; **don't push your l.!** *(said in annoyance)* ¡no me busques las cosquillas!; **no such l.!** ¡ojalá!; **with l.** con un poco de suerte; **with any l. he'll still be there** con un poco de suerte, todavía estará allí; **more by l. than judgement** más por suerte que por otra cosa; IDIOM **to have the l. of the devil** *or* **the Irish** tener una suerte loca

► **luck into** *vt insep Fam* **to l. into sth** conseguir algo por suerte; **he lucked into an amazing job** tuvo la potra de conseguir un trabajo formidable

► **luck out** *vi US Fam (get lucky)* tener mucha potra *or Méx* chance, *RP* tener mucho tarro

► **luck upon** *vt insep US Fam (find by chance)* tropezarse con, toparse con

luckily ['lʌkɪlɪ] *adv* por suerte, afortunadamente; **l. for us, he was at home** por suerte para nosotros estaba en casa

luckless ['lʌklɪs] *adj (person)* desafortunado(a), infortunado(a)

lucky ['lʌkɪ] *adj* **(a)** *(person)* afortunado(a); **to be l.** tener suerte; **to make a l. guess** tener la suerte de acertar, acertar por suerte; *Fam* **l. you!** ¡qué potra (la tuya)!; *Fam* **(you) l. devil** *or* **thing!, (you) l. beggar!** ¡qué suertudo!; **it's l. you came when you did** fue una suerte que llegaras en ese momento; **she's l. to be alive** tiene suerte de estar con vida; **that was l.** ¡qué suerte!; *Fam* **to have a l. break** tener un golpe de suerte; **to have a l. escape** escapar por los pelos; **to strike it l.** tener suerte; *Ironic* **you'll be l.!** ¡ni lo sueñes!, ¡no caerá esa breva!; **I should be so l.** ¡ojalá!, ¡no caerá esa breva!; **count yourself l. I didn't tell anyone** tienes suerte de que no se lo contara a nadie; **it's l. for you that...** tienes suerte de que...; **who's the l. man?** *(she's going to marry)* ¿quién es el afortunado? ►► *Br* ***l. bag*** bolsa *f* de sorpresas; *Br* ***l. dip*** caja *f* de sorpresas; *Sport* ***l. loser*** repescado(a) *m,f* (**b**) *(bringing luck) (jumper, shirt)* de la suerte; **it's my l. day** hoy es mi día (de suerte); **it's not my l. day** hoy no es mi día (de suerte); **my l. number** mi número de la suerte; **you can thank your l. stars she didn't see you!** ¡da gracias al cielo por que no te viera! ▸▸ ***l. charm*** amuleto *m*

lucrative ['lu:krətɪv] *adj* lucrativo(a)

lucratively ['lu:krətɪvlɪ] *adv* lucrativamente

lucre ['lu:kə(r)] *n Pej or Hum (money)* vil metal *m*; **to do sth for filthy l.** hacer algo por el vil metal

Luddite ['lʌdaɪt] *n* ludita *mf*

ludic ['lu:dɪk] *adj* lúdico(a)

ludicrous ['lu:dɪkrəs] *adj* ridículo(a), esperpéntico(a)

ludicrously ['lu:dɪkrəslɪ] *adv* de forma ridícula, esperpénticamente; **l. cheap/expensive** increíblemente barato/caro

ludicrousness ['lu:dɪkrəsnɪs] *n* lo ridículo, lo esperpéntico

ludo ['lu:dəʊ] *n Br* parchís *m*

luff [lʌf] *vi (in sailing)* orzar

lug[1] [lʌg] (*pt & pp* **lugged**) *vt Fam* arrear con, cargar con

▸**lug about, lug around** *vt sep Fam* arrear con, cargar con; **he always has to l. his little sister about with him** siempre tiene que cargar con su hermanita

lug[2] *n* (**a**) *(projection)* asa *f*, agarradera *f* (**b**) *Br Fam (ear)* oreja *f*, *Esp* soplillo *m*

luge [lu:ʒ] *n Sport (toboggan, event)* luge *m*

luggage ['lʌgɪdʒ] *n* equipaje *m*; **a piece of l.** un bulto (de equipaje) ▸▸ ***l. label*** etiqueta *f* identificativa del equipaje; ***l. locker*** taquilla *f* (para equipaje); ***l. rack*** *(in train, bus)* portaequipajes *m inv*; *(on car)* baca *f*; ***l. trolley*** carrito *m* de equipajes; *Br* ***l. van*** *(on train)* furgón *m* de equipajes

lugger ['lʌgə(r)] *n* lugre *m*

lughole ['lʌghəʊl] *n Br Fam* oreja, *Esp* soplillo *m*

lugsail ['lʌgseɪl] *n Naut* vela *f* al tercio

lugubrious [lə'gu:brɪəs] *adj* lúgubre

lugubriously [lə'gu:brɪəslɪ] *adv* con aire lúgubre, lúgubremente

lugworm ['lʌgwɜ:m] *n* lombriz *f* de tierra

Luke [lu:k] *pr n* **Saint L.** san Lucas

lukewarm ['lu:kwɔ:m] *adj* (**a**) *(water, soup)* tibio(a) (**b**) *(response)* tibio(a); **a l. reception** *(of person)* un recibimiento tibio; *(of book, film)* una acogida tibia; **she was rather l. about my suggestion** recibió mi sugerencia con bastante tibieza

lull [lʌl] **1** *n (in conflict, fighting)* periodo *m* de calma, respiro *m*; *(in conversation)* pausa *f*; *Fig* **the l. before the storm** la calma que precede a la tormenta

2 *vt (calm) (anxiety, fear)* calmar, sosegar; **to l. sb to sleep** dormir a alguien; **to l. sb into a false sense of security** dar a alguien una falsa sensación de seguridad

lullaby ['lʌləbaɪ] *n* nana *f*, canción *f* de cuna

lulu ['lu:lu:] *n US Fam* **it's a l.!** *(wonderful, amazing)* ¡es genial!, *Esp* ¡es cojonudo!, *RP* ¡es recopado *or* recopante!; **a l. of a mistake** un error descomunal

lumbago [lʌm'beɪgəʊ] *n* lumbago *m*

lumbar ['lʌmbə(r)] *adj Anat* lumbar ▸▸ *Med* ***l. puncture*** punción *f* lumbar

lumber ['lʌmbə(r)] **1** *n* (**a**) *(junk)* trastos *mpl* (viejos) ▸▸ ***l. room*** (cuarto *m*) trastero *m* (**b**) *US (wood)* madera *f*, maderos *mpl* ▸▸ ***l. mill*** aserradero *m*, serrería *f*

2 *vt* **to l. sb with sth** hacerle a alguien cargar con algo; **I got lumbered with a huge bill** me hicieron pagar una factura enorme

3 *vi* (**a**) *(move slowly and heavily)* **to l. about** *or* **around** caminar pesadamente; **he lumbered into the room** entró en la habitación caminando pesadamente (**b**) *US (produce timber)* talar árboles

lumbering ['lʌmbərɪŋ] *adj (walk)* pesado(a)

lumberjack ['lʌmbədʒæk] *n* leñador(ora) *m,f* ▸▸ ***l. shirt*** camisa *f* de leñador, *RP* camisa *f* leñadora

lumberjacket ['lʌmbədʒækɪt] *n* zamarra *f* de leñador

lumberyard ['lʌmbəjɑ:d] *n US* almacén *m* maderero, maderería *f*, *RP* barraca *f* maderera

luminary ['lu:mɪnərɪ] *n* figura *f*, lumbrera *f*

luminescence [lu:mɪ'nesəns] *n* luminiscencia *f*

luminescent [lu:mɪ'nesənt] *adj* luminiscente

luminosity [lu:mɪ'nɒsɪtɪ] *n* luminosidad *f*

luminous ['lu:mɪnəs] *adj* (**a**) *(glowing in the dark) (strip, road sign)* reflectante; *(paint, colour, socks)* fluorescente, fosforito(a) (**b**) *(glow)* luminoso; *(beauty)* radiante (**c**) *Phys* ***l. intensity*** intensidad *f* luminosa

lummox ['lʌməks] *n Fam* bruto(a) *m,f*, patán *m*

lump [lʌmp] **1** *n* (**a**) *(piece) (of earth, sugar)* terrón *m*; *(of stone, coal)* trozo *m*; *(in sauce)* grumo *m*; **there are lots of lumps in this mattress** hay muchos bultos en este colchón; IDIOM **it brought a l. to my throat** *(made me sad)* me hizo sentir un nudo en la garganta; IDIOM *US Fam* **you've got to take your lumps** tienes que apechugar con las consecuencias ▸▸ ***l. sugar*** azúcar *m or f* en terrones

(**b**) *(swelling) (on head)* chichón *m*; *(on breast)* bulto *m*

(**c**) *(of money)* **you don't have to pay it all in one lump** no tienes que pagarlo todo de golpe ▸▸ *Fin* ***l. sum*** pago *m* único, suma *f* global

(**d**) *Fam (person)* zoquete *m*

(**e**) *Br Fam* **the l.** *(casual building workers)* los jornaleros de la construcción; **to work on the l.** trabajar como jornalero(a) de la construcción

2 *vt* (**a**) *(group)* **all such payments were lumped under "additional expenses"** todos esos pagos estaban agrupados bajo el epígrafe de "gastos adicionales"; **you shouldn't l. them together just because they're brothers** no deberías tratarlos de la misma manera sólo porque sean hermanos (**b**) *Fam (endure)* **you'll just have to (like it or) l. it!** ¡no te queda más remedio que aguantar!

lumpectomy [lʌm'pektəmɪ] *n Med* extirpación *f* de un tumor en el pecho

lumpen ['lʌmpən] *adj* aborregado(a)

lumpenproletariat ['lʌmpənprəʊlɪ'teərɪæt] *n* lumpenproletariado *m*

lumpfish ['lʌmpfɪʃ] *n* ciclóptero *m*

lumpish ['lʌmpɪʃ] *adj (person)* desmañado(a), torpe

lumpy ['lʌmpɪ] *adj (sauce)* grumoso(a), lleno(a) de grumos; *(mattress)* lleno(a) de bultos

lunacy ['lu:nəsɪ] *n* locura *f*, demencia *f*; *Fam* **it's sheer l.** ¡es demencial!

lunar ['lu:nə(r)] *adj* lunar ▸▸ ***l. eclipse*** eclipse *m* de luna; ***l. landing*** alunizaje *m*; ***l. module*** módulo *m* lunar; ***l. month*** mes *m* lunar

lunatic ['lu:nətɪk] **1** *n* loco(a) *m,f*, lunático(a) *m,f*; *Fam* **he's a complete l.!** ¡está loco de remate! ▸▸ ***l. asylum*** manicomio *m*

2 *adj (idea, behaviour)* demencial; **the l. fringe** el sector fanático *or* intransigente

lunch [lʌntʃ] **1** *n* comida *f*, almuerzo *m*; **to have l.** comer, almorzar; **she's gone out for l.** ha salido para comer; IDIOM *Fam* **to be out to l.** *(be crazy)* estar chiflado(a) *or* chalado(a); *(absent-minded)* estar ido(a), estar en la luna (de Valencia); IDIOM *Fam* **to lose one's l.** *(vomit)* devolver, *Esp* echar la papa, *Am* arrojar ▸▸ ***l. break*** hora *f* de la comida; *US* ***l. bucket*** tartera *f*, fiambrera *f*, *Méx, RP* vianda *f*; *US* ***l. counter*** = en un bar o restaurante, mostrador donde se sirven comidas; ***l. hour*** hora *f* de comer; *US* ***l. pail*** tartera *f*, fiambrera *f*, *Méx, RP* vianda *f*

2 *vi* comer, almorzar; **we lunched on sandwiches** comimos sándwiches

lunchbox ['lʌntʃbɒks] *n* (**a**) *(container)* tartera *f*, fiambrera *f*, *Méx, RP* vianda *f* (**b**) *Br Fam Hum (man's genitals) Esp* paquete *m*, *Méx* cosa *f*, *RP* bulto *m*

luncheon ['lʌntʃən] *n Formal* almuerzo *m*, comida *f* ▸▸ ***l. meat*** fiambre *m* de lata; *Br* ***l. voucher*** vale *m* de comida

lunchroom ['lʌntʃru:m] *n US* comedor *m*

lunchtime ['lʌntʃtaɪm] *n* hora *f* de comer *or* del almuerzo; **a l. meeting** una reunión durante la hora de comer *or* del almuerzo

lung [lʌŋ] *n* pulmón *m*; **to shout at the top of one's lungs** gritar a pleno pulmón ▸▸ ***l. cancer*** cáncer *m* de pulmón

lunge [lʌndʒ] **1** *n* embestida *f*, acometida *f*; **to make a l. for sth/sb** embestir contra algo/alguien

2 *vi* **to l. at sb (with sth)** embestir contra alguien (con algo); **to l. forward** embestir

lungfish ['lʌŋfɪʃ] *n* dipnoo *m*, pez *m* pulmonado

lungful ['lʌŋfʊl] *n* **to take a l. of air** llenar los pulmones de aire, inspirar profundamente

lunkhead ['lʌŋkhed] *n US Fam* cabeza *f* hueca

lupin, *US* **lupine** ['lu:pɪn] *n* altramuz *m*

lupine ['lu:paɪn] *adj* lupino(a)

lupus ['lu:pəs] *n Med* lupus *m inv*

lurch [lɜ:tʃ] **1** *n (of ship, car)* bandazo *m*; **a l. to the right/left** *(of politician, party)* un giro brusco a la derecha/izquierda; *Fam* **to leave sb in the l.** dejar a alguien en la estacada

2 *vi (ship, car)* dar bandazos; *(person)* tambalearse; **he lurched into the room** entró tambaleándose en la habitación; **to l. to the left/right** *(politician, party)* dar un giro brusco a la izquierda/derecha; **the car lurched out of control** el coche *orAm* carro *or RP* auto dio un bandazo y perdió el control

lurcher ['lɜːtʃə(r)] *n Br (dog)* = perro de caza cruce de galgo y collie

lure ['lʊə(r)] **1** *n* (**a**) *(attraction)* atractivo *m*; **she was drawn by the l. of the big city** la sedujo el reclamo de la gran cuidad (**b**) *(for fishing)* cebo *m*, carnada *f* (**c**) *(for falcon)* señuelo *m*, reclamo *m*

2 *vt (into trap, ambush)* atraer (**into** hasta); **nothing could l. her away from the computer** nada conseguía alejarla *Esp* del ordenador *orAm* de la computadora; **he was lured away by the higher salary** se marchó atraído por un mejor sueldo

Lurex® ['ljʊəreks] **1** *n* Lurex® *m*, = tejido con hilo brillante

2 *adj* de Lurex®

lurgy ['lɜːgɪ] *n Br Fam Hum* **to have the (dreaded) l.** caer malo(a), *Esp* ponerse chungo(a)

lurid ['lʊərɪd] *adj* (**a**) *(sensational)* escabroso(a); **in l. detail** con detalles escabrosos (**b**) *(colour, clothes)* chillón(ona); *(sky, sunset)* deslumbrante

lurk [lɜːk] *vi* (**a**) *(person, animal)* estar al acecho, merodear; *(danger)* ocultarse, esconderse; **the assassin was lurking in the trees** el asesino merodeaba *or* estaba al acecho entre los árboles; **a doubt still lurked in his mind** su mente todavía albergaba una duda (**b**) *Comptr (in newsgroup)* mirar, fisgar

lurker ['lɜːkə(r)] *n Comptr* mirón(ona) *m,f*, fisgón(ona) *m,f*

lurking ['lɜːkɪŋ] *adj (suspicion, doubt)* latente; *(danger)* amenazante

luscious ['lʌʃəs] *adj* (**a**) *(woman, lips)* voluptuoso(a) (**b**) *(fruit)* jugoso(a); *(colour)* atractivo(a)

lush[1] [lʌʃ] *adj* (**a**) *(vegetation, garden)* exuberante (**b**) *(luxurious)* lujoso(a), suntuoso(a)

lush[2] *n Fam (alcoholic)* borrachín(ina) *m,f*

lushness ['lʌʃnɪs] *n* (**a**) *(of vegetation, garden)* exuberancia *f* (**b**) *(luxuriousness)* lujo *m*, suntuosidad *f*

lust [lʌst] *n* (**a**) *(sexual)* lujuria *f* (**b**) *(for power, knowledge)* sed *f*, ansia *f* (**for** de); **l. for life** ansias de vivir

► **lust after** *vt insep* **to l. after sb** beber los vientos por alguien; **to l. after sth** desvivirse por *or* ansiar algo

luster *US* = **lustre**

lustful ['lʌstfʊl] *adj* lujurioso(a)

lustfully ['lʌstfʊlɪ] *adv* con lujuria

lustily ['lʌstɪlɪ] *adv* con ganas, con fuerza

lustre, *US* luster ['lʌstə(r)] *n* (**a**) *(sheen)* lustre *m* (**b**) *(glory)* lustre *m*, gloria *f*

lustreware, *US* lusterware ['lʌstəweə(r)] *n* cerámica *f* vidriada

lustrous ['lʌstrəs] *adj* lustroso(a)

lusty ['lʌstɪ] *adj (person)* lozano(a), vigoroso(a); *(cry)* sonoro(a); *(singing)* vibrante

lute [luːt] *n* laúd *m*

lutetium [luː'tiːʃəm] *n Chem* lutecio *m*

Lutheran ['luːθərən] **1** *n* luterano(a) *m,f*

2 *adj* luterano(a)

Lutheranism ['luːθərənɪzəm] *n* luteranismo *m*

lutz [lʊts] *n (in ice skating)* lutz *m*

luvvie, luvvy [lʌvɪ] *n Br Fam* (**a**) *(term of endearment)* cielo *m*, corazón *m* (**b**) *Pej (actor)* = persona del mundo de la farándula propensa a la efusividad

Luxembourg, Luxemburg ['lʌksəmbɜːg] *n* Luxemburgo

Luxembourger, Luxemburger ['lʌksəmbɜːgə(r)] *n* luxemburgués(esa) *m,f*

luxuriance [lʌg'zjʊərɪəns] *n* exuberancia *f*

luxuriant [lʌg'zjʊərɪənt] *adj* exuberante

luxuriantly [lʌg'zjʊərɪəntlɪ] *adv* exuberantemente; **the vegetation spread l. before them** la vegetación exuberante se extendía ante ellos

luxuriate [lʌg'zjʊərɪeɪt] *vi* deleitarse (**in** con)

luxurious [lʌg'zjʊərɪəs] *adj* lujoso(a); **a l. lifestyle** una vida de lujo

luxuriously [lʌg'zjʊərɪəslɪ] *adv (decorated, furnished)* lujosamente

luxury ['lʌkʃərɪ] **1** *n* (**a**) *(great comfort)* lujo *m*; **a life of l.** una vida llena de lujos; **to live in (the lap of) l.** vivir a todo lujo *or* rodeado(a) de lujos ►► ***l. tax*** impuesto *m* de lujo (**b**) *(treat)* lujo *m*; **it's a l. we can't afford** no nos podemos permitir ese lujo

2 *adj (car, apartment)* de lujo ►► ***l. goods*** productos *mpl or* artículos *mpl* de lujo

> **False friend:** The Spanish noun **lujuria** is not a translation for the English word **luxury**. In Spanish **lujuria** means "lust".

LV [el'viː] *n Br* (*abbr* **Luncheon Voucher**) vale *m* de comida

LW *Rad* (*abbr* **Long Wave**) LW, OL

LWOP [eldʌbəljuːəʊ'piː] *n US* (**a**) (*abbr* **leave without pay**) excedencia *f* sin sueldo, *Méx, RP* licencia *f* sin goce de sueldo (**b**) (*abbr* **life without parole**) = cadena perpetua sin libertad condicional

lychee, *US* litchi ['laɪtʃiː] *n* lichi *m*

lychgate, lichgate ['lɪtʃgeɪt] *n* = zaguán de entrada al patio o camposanto de una iglesia

Lycra® ['laɪkrə] **1** *n* lycra® *f*, licra® *f*

2 *adj* de lycra®, de licra®

lye [laɪ] *n Chem* lejía *f*

lying ['laɪɪŋ] **1** *n* mentiras *fpl*

2 *adj* mentiroso(a), embustero(a); **her l. words took me in completely** me embaucó por completo con sus embustes; *Fam* **you l. swine!** ¡cochino embustero!

lying-in [laɪɪŋ'ɪn] *n Med Old-fashioned* parto *m*

lymph [lɪmf] *n Anat* linfa *f* ►► ***l. gland*** ganglio *m* linfático; ***l. node*** ganglio *m* linfático

lymphatic [lɪm'fætɪk] *adj Anat* linfático(a) ►► ***l. system*** sistema *m* linfático

lymphocyte ['lɪmfəsaɪt] *n Anat* linfocito *m*

lymphoma [lɪm'fəʊmə] *n Med* linfoma *m*

lynch [lɪntʃ] *vt* linchar ►► ***l. law*** ley *f* del linchamiento; ***l. mob*** turba *f* con sed de linchamiento; *Fig* turbamulta *f*

lynching ['lɪntʃɪŋ] *n* linchamiento *m*

lynx [lɪŋks] *n* lince *m*

lynx-eyed ['lɪŋksaɪd] *adj (sharp-sighted)* con ojos *or* vista de lince

lyre ['laɪə(r)] *n (musical instrument)* lira *f*

lyrebird ['laɪəbɜːd] *n* ave *f* lira

lyric ['lɪrɪk] **1** *n* (**a**) *(poem)* poema *m* lírico (**b**) **lyrics** *(of song)* letra *f*

2 *adj* lírico(a)

lyrical ['lɪrɪkəl] *adj* lírico(a); **he got quite l. on the subject** se tomó el asunto con mucha efusividad

lyrically ['lɪrɪklɪ] *adv* con lirismo

lyricism ['lɪrɪsɪzəm] *n* lirismo *m*

lyricist ['lɪrɪsɪst] *n* letrista *mf*

M, m

M, m [em] *n (letter)* M, m *f*

M (**a**) *Br Aut* (*abbr* **motorway**) A *f* (**b**) (*abbr* **medium**) M (**c**) (*abbr* **male**) H

m (**a**) (*abbr* **metre(s)**) m (**b**) (*abbr* **mile(s)**) milla(s) *f(pl)* (**c**) (*abbr* **million**) millón(ones) *m(pl)*

MA [em'eɪ] *n* (**a**) *Univ* (*abbr* **Master of Arts**) máster *m or Am* maestría *f* (en Humanidades); **to have an M. in linguistics** tener un máster en Lingüística; **Frederick Watson, M.** Frederick Watson, licenciado con máster (en Humanidades) (**b**) (*abbr* **Massachusetts**) Massachusetts

ma [mɑː] *n Fam* mamá *f*; **M. Watson** Mamá Watson

ma'am [mɑːm] *n Old-fashioned* señora *f*

Mac [mæk] *n* (**a**) *US Fam (term of address)* jefe *m*, *Esp* colega *m* (**b**) *Comptr* Mac *m*

mac [mæk] *n Br Fam (raincoat)* impermeable *m*, gabardina *f*

macabre [mə'kɑːbrə] *adj* macabro(a)

macadam [mə'kædəm] *n US* macadam *m*, macadán *m*

macadamia [mækə'deɪmɪə] *n* ***m. nut*** nuez *f* de macadamia; ***m. tree*** árbol *m* de la macadamia

macadamize [mə'kædəmaɪz] *vt* pavimentar con macadam *or* macadán

macaque [mə'kæk] *n* macaco *m*

macaroni [mækə'rəʊnɪ] *n* macarrones *mpl* ►► ***m. cheese*** macarrones *mpl* con queso

macaroon [mækə'ruːn] *n* mostachón *m*

macaw [mə'kɔː] *n* guacamayo *m*

Mace® [meɪs] *n* gas *m* lacrimógeno *(en spray)*

mace[1] [meɪs] *n (weapon, symbol of office)* maza *f*

mace[2] *n (spice)* macis *f inv*

Macedonia [mæsə'dəʊnɪə] *n* Macedonia

Macedonian [mæsə'dəʊnɪən] **1** *n* (**a**) *(person)* macedonio(a) *m,f* (**b**) *(language)* macedonio *m*
2 *adj* macedonio(a)

macerate ['mæsəreɪt] *vt Culin* macerar

Mach [mæk] *n Phys* **M. (number)** (número *m* de) Mach *m*; **to fly at M. 3** volar a mach 3

machete [mə'ʃetɪ] *n* machete *m*

Machiavellian [mækɪə'velɪən] *adj* maquiavélico(a)

machinations [mæʃɪ'neɪʃənz] *npl* maquinaciones *fpl*

machine [mə'ʃiːn] **1** *n* (**a**) *(device)* máquina *f*; *Fam Fig* **he's a m.!** ¡es (como) una máquina! ►► ***the m. age*** la era de las máquinas; ***m. pistol*** subfusil *m*; ***m. shop*** taller *m* de máquinas; ***m. tool*** máquina *f* herramienta; ***m. tool operator*** operario(a) *m,f* de máquina herramienta
(**b**) *(system)* **party/propaganda m.** aparato del partido/propagandístico
(**c**) *(computer) Esp* ordenador *m*, *Am* computadora *m* ►► *Comptr* ***m. code*** código *m* máquina; *Comptr* ***m. language*** lenguaje *m* máquina; ***m. translation*** traducción *f* automática
(**d**) *Fam (car, motorbike)* máquina *f*; *(plane)* aparato *m*
2 *vt* (**a**) *Ind (manufacture)* producir a máquina; **the pieces are then machined to the right size** el tamaño correcto de las piezas se consigue después a máquina (**b**) *(with sewing machine)* coser a máquina

machined [mə'ʃiːnd] *adj Ind (pieza)* acabado(a) a máquina; **a m. finish** un acabado a máquina

machine-gun [mə'ʃiːngʌn] **1** *n (hand-held)* metralleta *f*; **(heavy) m.** *(with stand)* ametralladora *f* (pesada)
2 *vt* (*pt & pp* **machine-gunned**) ametrallar

machine-gunner [mə'ʃiːngʌnə(r)] *n* = soldado que maneja una ametralladora pesada

machine-made [mə'ʃiːn'meɪd] *adj* hecho(a) a máquina

machine-readable [mə'ʃiːn'riːdəbəl] *adj Comptr* legible para *Esp* el ordenador *or Am* la computadora

machinery [mə'ʃiːnərɪ] *n* (**a**) *(machines)* maquinaria *f*; *(mechanism)* mecanismo *m* (**b**) *Fig (system)* maquinaria *f*; **the m. of state/government** la maquinaria del estado/gobierno

machine-stitch [mə'ʃiːnstɪtʃ] *vt* coser a máquina

machine-washable [mə'ʃiːn'wɒʃəbəl] *adj* lavable a máquina

machinist [mə'ʃiːnɪst] *n* (**a**) *(operator)* operario(a) *m,f*; *(of sewing machine)* cosedor(ora) *m,f* (**b**) *(repairer)* mecánico(a) *m,f*

machismo [mæ'tʃɪzməʊ] *n* machismo *m*

macho ['mætʃəʊ] **1** *n Fam (person)* macho *m*
2 *adj (remark, attitude)* muy de macho; **to be m.** *(person)* (presumir de) ser muy macho

macintosh = **mackintosh**

mack [mæk] *n US Fam (pimp)* proxeneta *m*, *Esp* chulo *m*

► **mack on** *vt insep US Fam* **to m. on sb** intentar seducir a alguien, *Esp* tirar los tejos a alguien, *Méx* echar los perros a alguien, *RP* cargar a alguien

mackerel ['mækrəl] *n* caballa *f* ►► ***m. shark*** tintorera *f*; ***m. sky*** cielo *m* aborregado

mac(k)intosh ['mækɪntɒʃ] *n* impermeable *m*, gabardina *f*

macramé [mə'krɑːmeɪ] *n* macramé *m*

macro ['mækrəʊ] (*pl* **macros**) *n Comptr* macro *f* ►► ***m. language*** lenguaje *m* macro; ***m. virus*** virus *m* de macro

macrobiotic ['mækrəʊbaɪ'ɒtɪk] *adj* macrobiótico(a); **a m. diet** una dieta macrobiótica

macrobiotics ['mækrəʊbaɪ'ɒtɪks] *n* macrobiótica *f*

macrocephalic [mækrəʊsə'fælɪk], **macrocephalous** [mækrəʊ'sefələs] *adj Med* macrocéfalo(a)

macrocephaly [mækrəʊ'sefəlɪ] *n Med* macrocefalia *f*

macrocosm ['mækrəʊkɒzəm] *n Astron* macrocosmos *m inv*

macroeconomic ['mækrəʊiːkə'nɒmɪk] *adj* macroeconómico(a)

macroeconomics ['mækrəʊiːkə'nɒmɪks] *n* macroeconomía *f*

macroinstruction ['mækreʊɪn'strʌkʃən] *n Comptr* macroinstrucción *f*

macromolecule ['mækrəʊ'mɒlɪkjuːl] *n Chem* macromolécula *f*

macron ['mækrɒn] *n Ling & Typ* macron *m*, acento *m* largo

macrophage ['mækrəʊfeɪdʒ] *n Biol* macrófago *m*

macroscopic [mækrəʊ'skɒpɪk] *adj* macroscópico(a)

macula ['mækjʊlə] (*pl* **maculae** ['mækjuliː]) *n Anat* mácula *f* ►► ***m. lutea*** mácula *f* lútea

mad [mæd] **1** *adj* (**a**) *(insane) (person)* loco(a); *(dog)* rabioso(a); **to be m.** *(person)* estar loco(a); **to go m.** volverse loco(a), enloquecer; **have you gone m.?** ¿te has vuelto loco?; **it's patriotism gone m.** es patriotismo sacado de quicio; *Fam* **don't go m. with the flowers** no te pases con las flores; **to drive sb m.** volver loco(a) a alguien; **you must have been m. to do it** ¡qué locura por tu parte haber hecho eso!; **to be m. with joy** estar loco(a) *or* rebosante de alegría; **m. with fear** aterrorizado(a); **barking m.** totalmente loco(a), *Esp* como una regadera, *RP* de remate; IDIOM **as m. as a hatter** *or* **a March hare** como un cencerro, más loco(a) que una cabra ►► *Fam* ***m. cow disease*** el mal *or* la enfermedad de las vacas locas
(**b**) *(absurd, foolish) (idea, plan)* disparatado(a)
(**c**) *(frantic)* **there was a m. rush for the door** la gente se precipitó como loca hacia la puerta; *Fam* **I'm in a m. rush** voy escopeteada; *Fam* **I'm in a m. rush to get this finished before Friday** estoy como loco intentando acabar esto para el viernes; *Fam* **to run/shout/work like m.** correr/gritar/trabajar como (un(a)) loco(a)
(**d**) *Fam (enthusiastic)* **to be m. about** *or* **on sth** estar loco(a) por algo; **to be m. about sb** estar loco(a) por alguien; **I can't say I'm m. about going** la verdad es no me muero de ganas de ir; *Br* **to be m. for it** *(raring to go)* estar super entusiasmado(a)
(**e**) *esp US Fam (angry) esp Esp* enfadado(a), *esp Am* enojado(a); **to**

be m. (with *or* **at sb)** estar muy *esp Esp* enfadado(a) *or esp Am* enojado(a) (con alguien); **to go** *or* **get m. (with** *or* **at sb)** *esp Esp* enfadarse (con alguien), *esp Am* enojarse (con alguien); **she makes me m.** me saca de quicio, me pone histérico

2 *adv Br Fam* **he's m. keen on** *or* **about golf** el golf lo vuelve loco; **he's m. keen on** *or* **about the girl next door** está coladito por la vecina

-mad [mæd] *suffix* **he is football/sex-m.** le vuelve loco el fútbol/sexo

Madagascan [mædə'gæskən] 1 *n* malgache *mf*

2 *adj* malgache

Madagascar [mædə'gæskə(r)] *n* Madagascar

madam ['mædəm] *n* (**a**) *(as form of address)* señora *f*; **Dear M.** Estimada señora; **M. Chairman** presidenta (**b**) *Br Fam Hum (child)* **she's a proper little m.** es una señoritinga; **we've had enough nonsense from you, m.!** ¡ya basta de tonterías, señorita! (**c**) *(of brothel)* madam *f*, madama *f*

madcap ['mædkæp] *adj (scheme, idea)* disparatado(a)

madden ['mædən] *vt* enloquecer

maddening ['mædənɪŋ] *adj* irritante, exasperante

maddeningly ['mædənɪŋlɪ] *adv* **the waiters were m. slow** los camareros eran de una lentitud exasperante

madder ['mædə(r)] *n* (**a**) *(plant)* rubia *f* (**b**) *(dye, colour)* rubia *f*

made *pt & pp of* **make**

-made [meɪd] *suffix* **factory-m.** manufacturado(a); **British-m.** hecho(a) en Gran Bretaña

Madeira [mə'dɪərə] *n* (**a**) *(island)* Madeira (**b**) *(wine)* madeira *m*, vino *m* de Madeira ►► *Br* ***M. cake*** bizcocho *m (compacto)*

made-to-measure ['meɪdtə'meʒə(r)], **made-to-order** ['meɪdtə'ɔːdə(r)] *adj* a medida

made-up [meɪ'dʌp] *adj* (**a**) *(story, excuse)* inventado(a) (**b**) *(lips)* pintado(a); *(face)* maquillado(a); **to be heavily m.** ir muy maquillado(a) (**c**) *Br Fam (delighted)* encantado(a), contentísimo(a) (**about** por)

madhouse ['mædhaʊs] *n Fam (lunatic asylum)* frenopático *m*, casa *f* de locos; *Fig* **this place is a m.!** ¡esto es una casa de locos!

madly ['mædlɪ] *adv* (**a**) *(insanely)* enloquecidamente; **m. jealous** muerto(a) de celos (**b**) *(frantically) (rush, struggle)* como loco(a) (**c**) *Fam (enthusiastically)* tremendamente; **m. in love** locamente enamorado(a); **I can't say I'm m. interested in it** no es que me interese tremendamente

madman ['mædmən] *n* loco *m*, demente *m*; *Fig* **he's a complete m.!** ¡está loco de remate!

madness ['mædnɪs] *n* (**a**) *(insanity)* locura *f*, demencia *f* (**b**) *Fam (folly)* locura *f*; **it's sheer m.!** ¡es una locura!

Madonna [mə'dɒnə] *n* (**a**) *Rel* **the M.** la Virgen (**b**) *Art* Madona *f*; **M. and Child** la Madona y el Niño

Madras [mə'dræs] *n* Madrás

madras [mə'dræs] *n* = curry bastante picante; **chicken/lamb m.** curry de pollo/cordero bastante picante

Madrid [mə'drɪd] *n* Madrid

madrigal ['mædrɪgəl] *n Mus* madrigal *m*

madwoman ['mædwʊmən] *n* loca *f*, demente *f*

maelstrom ['meɪlstrəm] *n* (**a**) *(whirlpool)* vorágine *f* (**b**) *(confusion)* vorágine *f*; **the m. of modern life** la vorágine de la vida moderna

maestro ['maɪstrəʊ] (*pl* **maestros**) *n* maestro *m*

mafia ['mæfɪə] *n* (**a**) *(criminal organisation)* mafia *f*; **the M.** la Mafia ►► ***M. boss*** capo *m* mafioso (**b**) *(clique)* mafia *f*

Mafioso [mæfɪ'əʊsəʊ] (*pl* **Mafiosi** [mæfɪ'əʊsiː]) *n* mafioso *m*

mag [mæg] *n Fam* revista *f*

magazine [mægə'ziːn] *n* (**a**) *(publication)* revista *f* ►► ***m. programme*** *(on radio, TV)* magazine *m*, programa *m* de variedades; ***m. rack*** revistero *m* (**b**) *(part of gun)* cargador *m* (**c**) *(ammunition store)* polvorín *m* (**d**) *(on movie camera)* cargador *m*; *(for slides)* carro *m*

magenta [mə'dʒentə] 1 *n* magenta *m*

2 *adj* magenta

maggot ['mægət] *n* gusano *m*

maggoty ['mægətɪ] *adj (food)* con gusanos

Maghreb [mæ'greb] *n* **the M.** el Magreb

Maghrebi [mæ'grebɪ] 1 *n* magrebí *mf*

2 *adj* magrebí

Magi ['meɪdʒaɪ] *npl* **the M.** los Reyes Magos

magic ['mædʒɪk] 1 *n* (**a**) *(supernatural power)* magia *f*; **black/white m.** magia negra/blanca; **as if by m.** como por arte de magia; **the medicine worked like m.** el medicamento hizo milagros

(**b**) *(conjuring)* magia *f*

(**c**) *(charm, special quality)* magia *f*, encanto *m*; **it has lost its m. (for me)** (para mí,) ha perdido el encanto; **the m. had gone out of their marriage** la magia de su matrimonio se había evaporado

2 *adj* (**a**) *(spell, trick)* mágico(a); **just say the m. words** sólo tienes que decir las palabras mágicas; *Fam* **say the m. word!** *(say "please")* ¿cómo se pide? ►► ***m. bullet*** *(drug)* remedio *m* específico; ***m. carpet*** alfombra *f* voladora *or* mágica; ***m. eye*** *(security device)* célula *f* fotoeléctrica; ***m. lantern*** linterna *f* mágica; ***m. mushroom*** psilocibe *m*, *Esp* seta *f* alucinógena, *Méx, CSur* hongo *m* alucinógeno; *Lit* ***m. realism*** realismo *m* mágico; *Br Fam* ***m. sponge*** *or* ***spray*** *(in soccer)* agua *f* milagrosa; *Math* ***m. square*** cuadrado *m* mágico; ***m. wand*** varita *f* mágica

(**b**) *Fam (excellent)* genial, *Esp* guay, *Andes, CAm, Carib, Méx* chévere, *Méx* padrísimo(a), *RP* bárbaro(a)

► **magic away** (*pt & pp* **magicked**) *vt sep* hacer desaparecer

► **magic up** (*pt & pp* **magicked**) *vt sep* sacarse de la manga; **he magicked a meal up in minutes** en pocos minutos se sacó de la manga una comida

magical ['mædʒɪkəl] *adj* mágico(a) ►► ***m. realism*** realismo *m* mágico

magically ['mædʒɪklɪ] *adv* mágicamente, por arte de magia

magician [mə'dʒɪʃən] *n* mago(a) *m,f*

magisterial [mædʒɪs'tɪərɪəl] *adj* (**a**) *(domineering)* autoritario(a) (**b**) *(authoritative)* magistral

magisterially [mædʒɪ'stɪərɪəlɪ] *adv* magistralmente

magistrate ['mædʒɪstreɪt] *n Br Law* juez *mf* de primera instancia ►► ***magistrates' court*** juzgado *m* de primera instancia

magma ['mægmə] *n* magma *m*

Magna Carta ['mægnə'kɑːtə] *n Hist* Carta *f* Magna

magna cum laude ['mægnəkʊm'laʊdeɪ] *adv US Univ* **to graduate m.** = licenciarse con una nota media

magnanimity [mægnə'nɪmɪtɪ] *n* magnanimidad *f*

magnanimous [mæg'nænɪməs] *adj* magnánimo(a)

magnanimously [mæg'nænɪməslɪ] *adv* magnánimamente

magnate ['mægneɪt] *n* magnate *mf*; **a press/oil m.** un magnate de la prensa/del petróleo

magnesia [mæg'niːzɪə] *n (magnesium oxide)* magnesia *f*

magnesium [mæg'niːzɪəm] *n Chem* magnesio *m*

magnet ['mægnɪt] *n* (**a**) imán *m* (**b**) *Fig (for tourists, investors)* foco *m* de atracción; *Fam* **his new car's a babe** *or* **chick m.** con su coche *or Am* carro *or CSur* auto nuevo las chicas van a caer como moscas

magnetic [mæg'netɪk] *adj* (**a**) *(force, pole)* magnético(a) ►► ***m. compass*** brújula *f*; ***m. card*** tarjeta *f* magnética; *Comptr* ***m. disk*** disco *m* magnético; ***m. equator*** ecuador *m* magnético; ***m. field*** campo *m* magnético; *Comptr* ***m. media*** soporte *m* magnético; ***m. mine*** mina *f* magnética; ***m. north*** norte *m* magnético; ***m. pole*** *(of magnet, Earth)* polo *m* magnético; *Med* ***m. resonance imaging*** resonancia *f* magnética; ***m. storm*** tormenta *f* magnética; ***m. strip*** banda *f* magnética; ***m. tape*** cinta *f* magnética

(**b**) *(personality, charm)* cautivador(ora)

magnetically [mæg'netɪklɪ] *adv* magnéticamente

magnetism ['mægnɪtɪzəm] *n* (**a**) *Phys* magnetismo *m* (**b**) *(attraction)* magnetismo *m*

magnetite ['mægnətaɪt] *n* magnetita *f*

magnetize ['mægnətaɪz] *vt* (**a**) *Phys* magnetizar (**b**) *(charm)* hechizar

magneto [mæg'niːtəʊ] (*pl* **magnetos**) *n* magneto *m*

magneto-optical [mæg'netəʊ'ɒptɪkəl] *adj Comptr* magneto-óptico(a)

magnetron ['mægnɪtrɒn] *n* magnetrón *m*

magnificat [mæg'nɪfɪkæt] *n Rel & Mus* Magnificat *m*

magnification [mægnɪfɪ'keɪʃən] *n* ampliación *f*; **a lens with a m. of x 7** una lente de siete aumentos

magnificence [mæg'nɪfɪsəns] *n* magnificencia *f*

magnificent [mæg'nɪfɪsənt] *adj* magnífico(a)

magnificently [mæg'nɪfɪsəntlɪ] *adv* magníficamente, estupendamente

magnifico [mæg'nɪfɪkəʊ] (*pl* **magnificos** *or* **magnificoes**) *n* prócer *m*, prohombre *m*

magnify ['mægnɪfaɪ] *vt* (**a**) *(of lens, telescope)* ampliar, aumentar (**b**) *(exaggerate)* exagerar, desorbitar; **the incident was magnified out of all proportion** el incidente se exageró desproporcionadamente (**c**) *Rel (exalt)* exaltar, glorificar

magnifying glass ['mægnɪfaɪɪŋ'glɑːs] *n* lupa *f*

magnitude ['mægnɪtju:d] *n* (**a**) *(scale)* magnitud *f*; *Math* magnitud *f*; **m. 7 on the Richter scale** magnitud *or* intensidad 7 en la escala de Richter (**b**) *(importance, size)* magnitud *f*; **a problem of the first m.** un problema de primer orden (**c**) *Astron* magnitud *f*; **a star of the first m.** una estrella de primera magnitud

magnolia [mæg'nəʊlɪə] *n* (**a**) *(flower)* magnolia *f* (**b**) *(colour)* rosa *m* pálido, blanco *m* rosáceo

Magnox® reactor ['mægnɒksrɪ'æktə(r)] *n* reactor *m* Magnox®

magnum ['mægnəm] *n* (**a**) *(bottle)* mágnum *f* (**b**) **M.**® *(gun)* Magnum® *f*

magnum opus ['mægnəm'əʊpəs] *n* obra *f* maestra

magpie ['mægpaɪ] *n* (**a**) *(bird)* urraca *f* ►► ***azure-winged m.*** rabilargo *m* (**b**) *Br Fam (hoarder)* **he's a bit of a m.** parece un trapero (**c**) *US Fam (chatterbox)* cotorra *f*, papagayo *m*

Magyar ['mægjɑ:(r)] **1** *n* (**a**) *(person)* magiar *mf* (**b**) *(language)* magiar *m*

2 *adj* magiar

maharaja(h) [mɑ:hə'rɑ:dʒə] *n* marajá *m*

maharani [mɑ:hə'rɑ:ni:] *n* maharaní *f*

maharishi [mɑ:hə'ri:ʃɪ] *n* = guía espiritual hindú

mah-jong(g) ['mɑ:'dʒɒŋ] *n* = tipo de dominó chino

mahogany [mə'hɒgənɪ] **1** *n* (**a**) *(wood)* caoba *f* (**b**) *(colour)* (color *m*) caoba *m*

2 *adj* de caoba

mahout [mə'haʊt] *n* = cuidador de elefantes en la India

MAI [emeɪ'aɪ] *n* (*abbr* **multilateral agreement on investment**) AMI *m*, acuerdo *m* multilateral de inversión

maid [meɪd] *n* (**a**) *(servant)* sirvienta *f*; *(in hotel)* camarera *f* ►► ***m. of honour*** *(to queen)* dama *f* de honor; *US (at wedding)* dama *f* de honor (**b**) *Literary (girl)* doncella *f*; *Hist* **the M. of Orleans** la Doncella de Orleans

maiden ['meɪdən] **1** *n Literary (girl)* doncella *f*

2 *adj* (**a**) *(first) (flight)* inaugural ►► *Parl* ***m. speech*** primer discurso *m* como parlamentario(a); ***m. voyage*** viaje *m* inaugural, primer trayecto *m* (**b**) *(unmarried)* ***m. aunt*** tía *f* soltera; ***m. name*** apellido *m* de soltera (**c**) *(in cricket)* **m. (over)** = entrada en la que no se consigue ninguna carrera

maidenhair ['meɪdənheə(r)] *n (fern)* culantrillo *m* ►► ***m. tree*** gingo *m*

maidenhead ['meɪdənhed] *n Old-fashioned or Literary* (**a**) *(hymen)* himen *m*, virgo *m* (**b**) *(virginity)* virginidad *f*

maidenhood ['meɪdənhʊd] *n* doncellez *f*

maidenly ['meɪdənlɪ] *adj Literary* de doncella

maidservant ['meɪdsɜ:vənt] *n* doncella *f*

mail[1] [meɪl] **1** *n* (**a**) *(postal system)* correo *m*; **to send sth by m.** enviar algo por correo; **the package got lost in the m.** el paquete se perdió en el correo; **your cheque is in the m.** le he enviado el cheque por correo ►► *US* ***m. drop*** *(letter)* buzón *m*; *(PO box)* apartado *m* de correos, *Am* casilla *f* postal, *Andes, RP* casilla *f* de correos, *Col* apartado *m* aéreo; *Com* ***m. order*** venta *f* por correo; **to buy sth by m. order** comprar algo por correo; ***m. train*** tren *m* correo; *US* ***m. truck*** furgoneta *f* del correo; *Br* ***m. van*** furgoneta *f* del correo

(**b**) *(letters or parcels received)* correo *m*, correspondencia *f*; **it came in the m.** vino en el correo

(**c**) *Comptr* ***m. address*** dirección *f* de correo electrónico; ***m. forwarding*** opción *f or* posibilidad *f* de remitir correo; ***m. gateway*** pasarela *f* de correo; ***m. manager*** gestor *m* de correos; ***m. path*** = camino que ha seguido un correo electrónico; ***m. reader*** lector *m* de correo electrónico; ***m. server*** servidor *m* de correo electrónico

2 *vt* (**a**) *esp US (by postal system) (letter, parcel)* enviar *or* mandar (por correo); **to m. sb (with) sth** enviar *or* mandar algo (por correo) a alguien (**b**) *(by e-mail) (file)* enviar *or* mandar (por correo electrónico); *(person)* enviar *or* mandar un correo electrónico a

mail[2] *n (armour)* malla *f*

mailbag ['meɪlbæg] *n* saca *f* de correos; **she gets a huge m.** *(celebrity, politician)* recibe muchísimas cartas

mailbomb ['meɪlbɒm] *n* bombardeo *m* de correo

mailbox ['meɪlbɒks] *n* (**a**) *US (for sending, receiving)* buzón *m* (**b**) *Comptr* buzón *m*

mailer ['meɪlə(r)] *n* (**a**) *esp US (sender)* remitente *mf*; *(in office)* auxiliar *mf* de clasificación y reparto de correspondencia (**b**) *(container)* tubo *m* de cartón *(para enviar documentos)* (**c**) *US (machine)* franqueadora *f* (**d**) *(leaflet)* mailing *m*

mailing ['meɪlɪŋ] *n (mailshot)* mailing *m* ►► ***m. list*** lista *f* de direcciones *(para envío de publicidad)*; *Comptr* lista *f* de correo *or* de distribución

mailman ['meɪlmæn] *n US* cartero *m*

mailmerge ['meɪlmɜ:dʒ] *n Comptr* combinación *f* de correspondencia ►► ***m. program*** programa *m* para combinar correspondencia

mail-order [meɪl'ɔ:dər] *adj Fam* ***m. bride*** = novia obtenida por catálogo; ***m. catalogue*** catálogo *m* de venta por correo; ***m. firm*** empresa *f* de ventas por correo; ***m. retailing*** venta *f* por correo; ***m. sale*** venta *f* por correo; ***m. selling*** venta *f* por correo

mailshot ['meɪlʃɒt] *n Br (leaflet)* carta *f* publicitaria; *(campaign)* mailing *m*

maim [meɪm] *vt* (**a**) *(physically)* lisiar; **six people were maimed in the attack** seis personas quedaron lisiadas tras el atentado (**b**) *(psychologically)* **the experience maimed her for life** la experiencia le dejó secuelas psíquicas de por vida

main [meɪn] **1** *n* (**a**) *(pipe)* (tubería *f*) general *f*; *(cable)* cable *m* principal; **the mains** *(water, gas)* la (tubería) general; *(electricity)* la red eléctrica; **to turn the electricity off at the m.** desconectar la luz desde el interruptor principal; **to turn the gas off at the m.** cerrar la llave de paso del gas ►► ***mains supply*** suministro *m* eléctrico; ***mains switch*** interruptor *m* general

(**b**) **in the m.** *(generally)* en general

(**c**) *Archaic* **the m.** *(ocean)* el piélago; **the Spanish M.** = las costas españolas del Caribe

2 *adj* (**a**) *(principal)* principal; **our m. branch/office** nuestra sede/oficina central; **the m. thing is to...** lo principal es...; **you're safe, that's the m. thing** estás a salvo y eso es lo principal ►► *Gram* ***m. clause*** oración *f* principal; ***m. course*** plato *m* principal; *Naut* ***m. deck*** cubierta *f* (principal); *US Fam* ***m. drag*** calle *f* principal; ***m. entrance*** entrada *f* principal; ***m. line*** *Rail* línea *f* principal; *US (road)* carretera *f* principal; *Fam (vein)* vena *f*; *US Fam* ***m. man*** *Esp* colega *m*, *Am* compay *m*; *Br Fam* **when it comes to scoring goals, he's the m. man** a la hora de marcar goles, se queda solo; *Comptr* ***m. memory*** memoria *f* principal; ***m. road*** carretera *f* general; ***m. square*** plaza *f* mayor; *Fam* ***m. squeeze*** *(boyfriend, girlfriend)* novio(a) *m,f*, *Esp* chorbo(a) *m,f*; ***m. street*** calle *f* principal; *US Fig* ***M. Street*** = el norteamericano medio

(**b**) *Literary (sheer)* **to do sth by m. force** usar la fuerza bruta para hacer algo

mainbrace ['meɪnbreɪs] *n* braza *f (de la vela mayor)*; IDIOM *Naut or Hum* **to splice the m.** beber *or Am* tomar *(para celebrar algo)*

Maine [meɪn] *n* Maine

mainframe ['meɪnfreɪm] *n Comptr* **m. (computer)** *Esp* ordenador *m or Am* computadora *f* central

mainland ['meɪnlænd] *n* tierra *f* firme; **m. Europe** la Europa continental; **on the m.** en tierra firme; **he escaped from the island to the Canadian m.** escapó de la isla hacia tierra firme canadiense

mainlander ['meɪnlændə(r)] *n* habitante *mf* de la tierra firme

mainline ['meɪnlaɪn] *Fam* **1** *vt (inject)* picarse, *Esp* chutarse

2 *vi (inject drugs)* picarse, *Esp* chutarse

mainly ['meɪnlɪ] *adv* principalmente; **the accident was caused m. by carelessness** la imprudencia fue la principal causa del accidente; **the passengers were m. Spanish** los pasajeros eran en su mayoría españoles; **we m. go out on Saturday evenings** los sábados por la noche solemos salir

mainmast ['meɪnmɑ:st] *n* palo *m* mayor

mainsail ['meɪnseɪl] *n* vela *f* mayor

mainsheet ['meɪnshi:t] *n* escota *f* mayor

mains-operated ['meɪnzɒpəreɪtɪd] *adj* que funciona con *or* a corriente

mainspring ['meɪnsprɪŋ] *n* (**a**) *(of clock, watch)* muelle *m* real, resorte *m* principal (**b**) *(of change, revolution)* móvil *m* principal

mainstay ['meɪnsteɪ] *n* (**a**) *(main support) (of economy, philosophy)* pilar *m* fundamental; **she was the m. of the family** ella era el pilar que sostenía a la familia (**b**) *Naut* estay *m* mayor

mainstream ['meɪnstri:m] **1** *n* corriente *f* principal *or* dominante; **to live outside the m. of society** vivir al margen de las convenciones sociales

2 *adj (politics, ideas, tastes)* convencional; *(movie, literature)* comercial; **m. America** el norteamericano medio; **their music is hardly what you'd call m.!** su música no es precisamente convencional

mainstreaming ['meɪnstri:mɪŋ] *n Educ* = introducción de niños con dificultades de aprendizaje en los colegios normales

mainstreeting ['meɪnstri:tɪŋ] *n Can Pol* **to go m.** echarse a la calle en busca de votos

maintain [meɪn'teɪn] *vt* (**a**) *(sustain) (correspondence, friendship, advantage, composure)* mantener; **to m. law and order** mantener la ley y el orden (**b**) *(keep in good order)* mantener; **the grounds are well maintained** los terrenos se conservan bien *or* están bien conservados

(**c**) *(support financially)* mantener

(**d**) *(argue, insist)* **to m. (that)...** mantener *or* sostener que...; **he maintained his innocence to the end** sostuvo que era inocente hasta el final

maintainable [meɪn'teɪnəbəl] *adj (attitude, opinion, position)* defendible

maintained [meɪn'teɪnd] *adj* (**a**) *Br (school)* subvencionado(a) (**b**) *(cared for)* mantenido(a)

maintenance ['meɪntənəns] *n* (**a**) *(of car, equipment, roads)* mantenimiento *m*; **m. engineer/vehicle** técnico/vehículo de mantenimiento ▸▸ ***m. contract*** contrato *m* de mantenimiento; ***m. costs*** costos *mpl or Esp* costes *mpl* de mantenimiento

(**b**) *Law (alimony)* pensión *f* alimenticia ▸▸ ***m. order:*** **she got a m. order** el juez le ha asignado una pensión alimenticia

(**c**) *Br Univ Formerly* ***m. allowance*** *or* ***grant*** beca *f* para la manutención

(**d**) *(sustaining, continuation)* mantenimiento *m*

maisonette [meɪzə'net] *n* dúplex *m inv*

maître d' ['meɪtrə'diː] *n US* maître *mf* (d'hôtel)

maître d'hôtel ['metrədəʊ'tel] *n* maître *mf* (d'hôtel)

maize [meɪz] *n* maíz *m*, *Andes, RP* choclo *m*

Maj (**a**) *Mil* (*abbr* **Major**) comandante *m* (**b**) *Mus* (*abbr* **Major**) mayor

majestic [mə'dʒestɪk] *adj* majestuoso(a)

majestically [mə'dʒestɪklɪ] *adv* majestuosamente

majesty ['mædʒəstɪ] *n* (**a**) *(splendour)* majestad *f*, majestuosidad *f*; **God in all His m.** Dios en toda su majestad (**b**) *(as title)* **His/Her/Your M.** Su Majestad ▸▸ *Br* ***His/Her Majesty's Prison Service*** = el servicio penitenciario británico; *Br* ***His/Her Majesty's Stationery Office*** = el servicio oficial de publicaciones británico

Maj Gen *Mil* (*abbr* **major general**) general *m* de división

majolica [mə'dʒɒlɪkə] *n* mayólica *f*

major ['meɪdʒə(r)] **1** *n* (**a**) *Mil* comandante *m* ▸▸ ***m. general*** general *m* de división (**b**) *US Univ (subject)* especialidad *f*; **Tina is a physics m.** Tina cursó la especialidad de física (**c**) *Mus* mayor *m* (**d**) *US (big company)* **the oil majors** las grandes petroleras; **the Majors** *(movie companies)* los grandes estudios cinematográficos (**e**) *(big golf tournament)* torneo *m* del Grand Slam

2 *adj* (**a**) *(main)* **the m. part of our time/research** la mayor parte del tiempo/de la investigación; **m. road** carretera principal; **m. town** localidad de importancia

(**b**) *(significant, important) (decision, change, factor, event)* importante, de primer orden; *(repairs)* importante, de envergadura; **a m. role** *(in play, film)* un papel destacado *or* importante; **to launch a m. offensive** lanzar una ofensiva a gran escala; **she underwent m. surgery** se sometió a una operación de importancia; **of m. importance** de enorme importancia; **any damage? – nothing m.** ¿ha sufrido daños? – nada de importancia; **in a m. way: we invested in steel in a m. way** invertimos en acero a lo grande; **he's taken up Spanish in a m. way** se ha puesto a estudiar español a conciencia ▸▸ ***m. league*** *(in baseball)* = liga profesional de béisbol estadounidense; *Fig* **a m. league company** una de las grandes empresas del sector; *Fam* **he's a m. league jerk** es un imbécil integral

(**c**) *Mus* mayor; **m. seventh/third** séptima/tercera mayor ▸▸ ***m. key*** tono *m* mayor; ***m. mode*** modo *m* mayor

(**d**) *Phil* ***m. premise*** mayor *f*

(**e**) *Br Sch Old-fashioned* **Smith m.** Smith, el hermano mayor

(**f**) *Astron* ***m. planet*** planeta *m* mayor

(**g**) *(in cards)* **m. suit** palo que pinta, triunfos

3 *vi US Univ* **to m. in** *(subject)* especializarse en

Majorca [mə'jɔːkə] *n* Mallorca

Majorcan [mə'jɔːkən] **1** *n* (**a**) *(person)* mallorquín(ina) *m,f* (**b**) *(language)* mallorquín *m*

2 *adj* mallorquín(ina)

majordomo ['meɪdʒə'dəʊməʊ] (*pl* **majordomos**) *n* mayordomo *m*

majorette [meɪdʒə'ret] *n* majorette *f*

majority [mə'dʒɒrɪtɪ] *n* (**a**) *(of a group)* mayoría *f*; **to be in a** *or* **the m.** ser mayoría; **the m. was** *or* **were in favour** la mayoría estaba a favor; **in the m. of cases** en la mayoría de los casos ▸▸ *Fin* ***m. holding*** *or* ***interest*** participación *f* mayoritaria; ***m. shareholder*** *or US* ***stockholder*** socio(a) *m,f or* accionista *mf* mayoritario(a); ***the m. world*** los paises en vías de desarrollo

(**b**) *(in vote)* mayoría *f*; **by a narrow/large m.** por una estrecha/amplia mayoría; **a two-thirds m.** una mayoría de dos tercios; **a m. government** un gobierno con mayoría ▸▸ ***m. decision*** decisión *f* por mayoría; *US Pol* ***m. leader*** = líder de la formación mayoritaria en el senado o el congreso estadounidense; ***m. rule*** representación *f* de la mayoría; *Law* ***m. verdict*** veredicto *m* mayoritario; *Pol* ***m. vote*** votación *f* por mayoría

(**c**) *Law (age)* mayoría *f* de edad; **to attain** *or* **reach one's m.** alcanzar la mayoría de edad

---

MAKE [meɪk] **1** *n* (**a**) *(brand)* marca *f*; **what m. is it?** ¿de qué marca es?

(**b**) IDIOM *Fam* **to be on the m.** *(financially)* buscar sólo el propio beneficio; *(sexually)* ir a ligar *or RP, Ven* de levante

2 *vt* (*pt & pp* **made** [meɪd]) (**a**) *(produce, prepare, perform)* hacer; *(manufacture)* hacer, fabricar; *(payment, transaction)* realizar, efectuar; *(speech)* pronunciar; *(decision)* tomar; *(mistake)* cometer; **I m. my own clothes** (me) hago mis propias ropas; **to m. the bed** hacer la cama; **we m. no charge for delivery** no cobramos por la entrega; **to m. a choice** elegir; **everybody m. a circle** todos, *Esp* formad *or Am* formen un círculo; **to m. progress** progresar; **to m. a promise** hacer una promesa; **to m. a record** grabar un disco; **m. room for your sister** hazle sitio *or* espacio *or Andes* campo a tu hermana; **to m. time to do sth** encontrar tiempo para hacer algo; **made from** *or* **out of** hecho(a) con *or* de; **it's made of silver** es de plata; **made in Spain** fabricado(a) en España; *Fig* **that coat was made for you** ese abrigo está hecho a tu medida; **they were made for each other** estaban hechos el uno para el otro; *Fam* **I'll show them what I'm made of** les voy a demostrar quién soy yo; *Fam* **I'm not made of money!** ¡que no soy millonario *or* de oro!, *RP* ¡que yo la plata no la saco de un árbol!; **I'll m. a man of you yet!** ¡te he de convertir en un hombre!; **to m. something of oneself** convertirse en una persona de provecho

(**b**) *(earn) (money)* ganar; **to m. a loss** tener *or* sufrir pérdidas; **to m. a profit** obtener *or* sacar beneficios; **I made $100 on the deal** saqué 100 dólares (de beneficio) del trato; **to m. a living** ganarse la vida; **she has made a lot of enemies** se ha creado muchos enemigos; **she has made a lot of friends** ha hecho muchos amigos; **to m. a name for oneself** crearse *or* labrarse una reputación, hacerse un nombre

(**c**) *(cause)* **to m. a difference** cambiar mucho las cosas (a mejor); **it doesn't m. any difference, it makes no difference** da lo mismo; **stop making a noise** deja de hacer ruido; **to m. a success of sth** tener éxito con algo; **to m. trouble** crear problemas; **it made his hair fall out** hizo que se le cayera el pelo; **it made me smile** me hizo sonreír; **he made her cry** la hizo llorar; **don't m. me laugh!** ¡no me hagas reír!; **what made her say that?** ¿qué la hizo decir eso?; **it makes me want to give up** me da ganas de dejarlo; **the photo makes me look older than I am** la foto me hace parecer más viejo de lo que soy; **she made herself look foolish** quedó como una tonta

(**d**) *(cause to be)* hacer; **that made me angry** eso me *esp Esp* enfadó *or esp Am* enojó; **to m. sb happy** hacer feliz a alguien; **to m. sb sad** entristecer a alguien; **to m. sb hungry** dar hambre a alguien; **it makes me nervous** me pone nervioso; **to m. sb tired** cansar a alguien; **she has been made captain** la han nombrado capitana; **to m. a fool of sb** poner a alguien en ridículo; **to m. a fool of oneself** hacer el ridículo; **quantum mechanics made easy** *(book title)* introducción básica a la mecánica cuántica; **his goal made the score two-nil** su gol puso el marcador en dos a cero; **you've made the house really nice** has dejado la casa bien bonita; **m. yourself comfortable** ponte cómodo; **to m. oneself heard** hacerse oír; **to m. oneself known to sb** ponerse en contacto con alguien; **do I m. myself understood?** ¿queda bien claro?; **to m. sb a present of sth** regalar algo a alguien; **m. mine a gin and tonic** para mí un gin-tonic

(**e**) *(cause to be successful)* **this book made her** este libro le dio la fama; **what really makes the film is the photography** lo que hace que la película sea tan buena es la fotografía; **to m. it (to the top)** *(be successful)* tener éxito, llegar a la cima; **to m. it big** triunfar; **you've got it made** lo tienes todo hecho; **this record will m. or break her career** este disco decidirá su carrera; **it made my day** me alegró el día

(**f**) *(compel)* **to m. sb do sth** hacer que alguien haga algo; **they made us wear suits, we were made to wear suits** nos hicieron llevar traje, nos obligaron a llevar traje; **she made herself keep running** se obligó a seguir corriendo

(**g**) *(estimate, calculate)* **what time do you m. it?** ¿qué hora debe ser?, *Am* ¿qué horas serán?; **what do you m. the answer?** ¿cuál crees que es la respuesta?; **I m. it $50 in total** calculo un total de 50 dólares; **£19, please – m. it £20** 19 libras, por favor – cóbrese 20

(**h**) *(amount to)* **two and two m. four** dos y dos son cuatro; **that makes $50 in total** y con eso el total son 50 dólares; **that makes five times she has called me this week!** ¡ésta es la quinta vez que me llama esta semana!; *Fam* **I'm exhausted – that makes two of us!** estoy agotado – ¡ya somos dos!

(**i**) *(attain, achieve) (goal)* alcanzar; **we made all our production targets** hemos alcanzado todos nuestros objetivos de producción; **to**

m. the charts *(record)* llegar a las listas de éxitos; **to m. the cut** *(in golf)* meterse en el corte; **to m. a deadline** cumplir un plazo; **to m. the first team** *(be selected)* conseguir entrar en el primer equipo; **to m. the front page** *(news)* aparecer en (la) portada; **we've made good time** hemos ido bien rápido; **to m. it** *(arrive in time)* llegar (a tiempo); *(finish in time)* terminar a tiempo; **the doctors don't think he'll m. it** *(live)* los doctores no creen que vaya a vivir; **I don't know how I made it through the day** no sé cómo conseguí pasar el día

(**j**) *(reach)* **do you think we'll m. the five o'clock train?** ¿llegaremos al tren de las cinco?; **we should make Houston by evening** llegaremos a Houston esta tarde

(**k**) *(manage to attend) (show, meeting)* llegar a; **I can m. two o'clock** puedo estar allí para las dos; **can you m. it next week?** ¿puedes venir la próxima semana?; **I can't m. it on Friday, I'm afraid** me temo que el viernes no podré ir

(**l**) *(become, be)* ser; **he'll m. a good doctor/singer** será un buen médico/cantante; **this old shirt would m. a good duster** esta camisa vieja irá muy bien para quitar *or Am* sacar el polvo; **it will m. interesting reading** será interesante leerlo

(**m**) *(score) (in baseball, cricket)* hacer

(**n**) *US (in directions)* **m. a right/left** torcer a la derecha/izquierda

(**o**) *(in golf)* **to m. a putt** embocar un putt

(**p**) *(in American football)* **he made 34 yards** avanzó 34 yardas

(**q**) *US Fam (have sex with)* **to m. sb, to m. it with sb** hacérselo con alguien

3 *vi* (**a**) *(act)* **to m. as if** *or* **as though to do sth** hacer como si se fuera a hacer algo; **to m. believe (that)...** imaginarse que...; **to m. to do sth** hacer como si se fuera a hacer algo

(**b**) *US Fam (pretend)* **she makes like she's an expert** se las da de experta; **m. like you don't know anything** haz ver que no sabes nada, *RP* hacé de cuenta que no sabés nada

(**c**) *(succeed)* **it's m. or break** es la hora de la verdad

(**d**) **to m. sure** *or* **certain (of sth)** asegurarse (de algo); **to m. sure** *or* **certain (that)...** asegurarse de que...

▶**make after** *vt insep* **to m. after sb** *(chase)* salir en persecución de alguien

▶**make away with** *vt insep* (**a**) = **make off with**

(**b**) *Old-fashioned (kill)* acabar con

▶**make do** *vi* arreglárselas (**with/without** con/sin); **there's no olive oil left, so you'll have to m. do without** no queda aceite de oliva, tendrás que arreglártelas sin él

▶**make for** *vt insep* (**a**) *(head towards)* dirigirse hacia; **when it started to rain everyone made for the trees** cuando se puso a llover todo el mundo se dirigió hacia los árboles

(**b**) *(contribute to)* facilitar, contribuir a; **her presence made for an interesting evening** su presencia dio interés a la velada

▶**make into** *vt sep (convert)* **to m. sth/sb into sth** convertir algo/a alguien en algo

▶**make of** *vt sep* (**a**) *(have opinion about)* **what do you m. of the new boss?** ¿qué te parece el nuevo jefe?; **I don't know what to m. of that remark** no sé cómo interpretar ese comentario; **can you m. anything of these instructions?** ¿entiendes algo de lo que dicen las instrucciones?

(**b**) *(get out of)* **I want to m. something of my life** quiero ser algo en la vida; **to m. the most of sth** aprovechar algo al máximo; **why don't we m. a day/evening of it?** ¿por qué no aprovechamos para pasar el día/la tarde?

(**c**) *(give importance to)* **I think you're making too much of this problem** creo que estás exagerando este problema

▶**make off** *vi Fam (leave)* largarse

▶**make off with** *vt insep Fam (steal)* largarse con, llevarse

▶**make out** 1 *vt insep Fam (claim)* **to m. out (that)...** decir *or* pretender que...; **it's not as bad as it's made out to be** no es tan malo como dicen

2 *vt sep* (**a**) *(write) (list)* elaborar, hacer; *(cheque)* extender (**to** a)

(**b**) *Fam (claim)* **she made herself out to be an expert** se las daba de experta; **it's not as bad as everyone makes out** no es tan malo como dicen todos

(**c**) *(understand, decipher)* entender; *(see)* distinguir; *(hear)* oír; **can you m. out what it says here?** ¿distingues lo que dice aquí?; **I just can't m. him out** no consigo entenderlo; **as far as I can m. out** por lo que entiendo

(**d**) *(explain)* **to m. out a case for/against sth** exponer los argumentos a favor/en contra de algo

3 *vi US* (**a**) *(get on)* llevarse bien; **how did you m. out at the interview?** ¿cómo te fue en la entrevista? (**b**) *Fam (sexually) (neck)* meterse mano, *Esp* darse el lote; *(have sex)* enrollarse

▶**make over** *vt sep* (**a**) *(transfer)* **she has made the estate over to her granddaughter** ha nombrado a su nieta heredera de sus propiedades

(**b**) *US (convert)* **to m. sth over into sth** convertir algo en algo

(**c**) *US (change the appearance of)* hacer una reforma total de

▶**make towards** *vt insep* dirigirse hacia

▶**make up** 1 *vt sep* (**a**) *(story, song, excuses)* inventar

(**b**) *(deficit, loss)* enjugar, recuperar; **we should be able to m. up the hour we lost later** deberíamos poder recuperar más adelante la hora perdida

(**c**) *(complete) (team, amount)* completar; **my uncle is going to m. up the difference** mi tío va a pagar la diferencia; **I felt like I was only there to m. up the numbers** sentí que estaba ahí sólo para hacer cuentas

(**d**) *(constitute)* formar, componer; **the community is made up primarily of old people** la comunidad se compone principalmente de ancianos; **road accidents m. up 70 percent of the total** los accidentes de carretera representan *or* suponen un 70 por ciento del total; **a group made up of left-wing politicians** un grupo integrado por políticos de izquierdas

(**e**) *(prepare) (list)* elaborar, hacer; *(parcel, bed)* hacer; *(prescription)* preparar; *(curtains, dress)* hacer

(**f**) *Typ* componer

(**g**) *(apply make-up to)* **to m. sb up (as sb)** maquillar a alguien (de alguien); **to m. oneself up** maquillarse

(**h**) *(resolve)* **to m. up one's mind** decidirse; **I've made up my mind never to return** he decidido no volver nunca

2 *vi (end quarrel)* reconciliarse (**with** con)

▶**make up for** *vt insep (losses)* compensar; **he bought me flowers to m. up for his behaviour** me compró flores para disculparse por su comportamiento; **to m. up for lost time** recuperar el tiempo perdido

▶**make up to** 1 *vt insep Br Fam (ingratiate oneself with)* **to m. up to sb** *Esp* hacer la pelota a *or Col* pasar el cepillo a *or Méx* lambisconear a *or RP* chuparle las medias a alguien

2 *vt sep (compensate)* **I'll m. it up to you later, I promise** te prometo que te recompensaré (por ello) más adelante

---

make-believe ['meɪkbɪli:v] 1 *n* **it's only m.** no es más que ficción; **to live in a land** *or* **world of m.** vivir en un mundo de fantasías

2 *adj* ficticio(a); **they turned the bed into a m. raft** convirtieron la cama en una balsa imaginaria

make-do ['meɪkdu:] *adj* improvisado(a); **it was a case of m. and mend** hubo que improvisar

make-or-break ['meɪkə'breɪk] *adj* decisivo(a); **it's m. time** es el momento de la verdad

makeover ['meɪkəʊvə(r)] *n* (**a**) *(of building, room)* reforma *f* total (**b**) *(of person)* cambio *m or* renovación *f* de imagen

maker ['meɪkə(r)] *n* (**a**) *(manufacturer)* fabricante *mf* (**b**) *Euph* **to (go to) meet one's M.** *(to die)* entregar el alma a Dios

-maker ['meɪkə(r)] *suffix* (**a**) *(manufacturer)* **furniture/motorcycle-m.** fabricante de muebles/motocicletas (**b**) *(machine)* **coffee/ice cream-m.** máquina de café/helados

makeshift ['meɪkʃɪft] 1 *n* parche *m*; **the repair is only a m.** la reparación sólo sirve para salir del paso

2 *adj* improvisado(a); **the accommodation was very m.** el alojamiento era de lo más improvisado

make-up ['meɪkʌp] *n* (**a**) *(cosmetics)* maquillaje *m*; **to put (one's) m. on** maquillarse; **to take one's m. off** quitarse el maquillaje, desmaquillarse; **she had a lot of m. on** llevaba mucho maquillaje ▶▶ ***m. artist*** maquillador(ora) *m,f*; ***m. bag*** bolsa *f* del maquillaje; ***m. remover*** desmaquillador *m*

(**b**) *(composition) (of team, group)* composición *f*; **she changed the m. of the cabinet** cambió la composición del gabinete

(**c**) *(of person)* temperamento *m*, carácter *m*; **spontaneous generosity is not really in** *or* **part of her m.** la generosidad desinteresada no forma parte de su carácter

(**d**) *Typ* composición *f*

(**e**) *US (test, exam)* **m. (test)** = examen que se realiza más tarde si no se pudo hacer en su día

makeweight ['meɪkweɪt] *n* relleno *m*; **as a m.** de relleno

making ['meɪkɪŋ] *n* (**a**) *(manufacture) (of goods)* fabricación *f*, manufactura *f*; *(of movie)* rodaje *f*; **the film was three years in the m.** llevó tres años realizar la película; **this is history in the m.** se está haciendo historia (aquí y ahora); **a musician in the m.** un músico en ciernes; **the problem is of her own m.** el problema se lo ha buscado ella; **it will be the m. of her** será la llave de su éxito (**b**) *(potential)* **he has the makings of an actor** tiene madera de actor; **the story has all the makings of a national scandal** la historia tiene todos los ingredientes para convertirse en un escándalo nacional

mako shark ['mɑːkəʊ'ʃɑːk] *n* marrajo *m* (dientuso)

malacca [mə'lækə] *n* (**a**) *(material)* caña *f* de Indias (**b**) *Geog* **the M. Straits** el estrecho de Malaca

malachite ['mæləkaɪt] *n* malaquita *f*

maladjusted [mælə'dʒʌstɪd] *adj* inadaptado(a)

maladjustment [mælə'dʒʌstmənt] *n* (**a**) *(psychological, social)* inadaptación *f* (**b**) *(of engine, mechanism)* desajuste *m*

maladministration [mælədmɪnɪ'streɪʃən] *n Formal* mala gestión *f*

maladroit [mælə'drɔɪt] *adj* inepto(a), desmañado(a)

maladroitly [mælə'drɔɪtlɪ] *adv* con ineptitud

malady ['mælədɪ] *n Formal* mal *m*

Malaga ['mæləgə] *n* Málaga

Malagasy ['mæləgæsɪ] **1** *n* (**a**) *(person)* malgache *mf* (**b**) *(language)* malgache *m*
2 *adj* malgache

malaise [mæ'leɪz] *n Formal* malestar *m*

malapropism ['mæləprɒpɪzəm] *n* gazapo *m*

malaria [mə'leərɪə] *n* malaria *f*, paludismo *m*; **to have m.** tener malaria *or* paludismo

malarial [mə'leərɪəl] *adj (fever, swamp)* palúdico(a); **a m. district** una zona de malaria *or* paludismo

malark(e)y [mə'lɑːkɪ] *n Fam* (**a**) *(ridiculous behaviour)* payasadas *fpl*, majaderías *fpl* (**b**) *(ridiculous explanation)* sandeces *fpl*, majaderías *fpl*

Malawi [mə'lɑːwɪ] *n* Malaui

Malawian [mə'lɑːwɪən] **1** *n* malaui *mf*
2 *adj* malaui

Malay [mə'leɪ] **1** *n* malayo(a) *m,f*
2 *adj* malayo(a); **the M. Peninsula** la península de Malaca

Malayan [mə'leɪən] **1** *n* (**a**) *(person)* malayo(a) *m,f* (**b**) *(language)* malayo *m*
2 *adj* malayo(a)

Malaysia [mə'leɪzɪə] *n* Malaisia

Malaysian [mə'leɪzɪən] **1** *n* malaisio(a) *m,f*
2 *adj* malaisio(a)

malcontent ['mælkəntent] *n Formal* insatisfecho(a) *m,f*

Maldives ['mɔːldiːvz] *npl* **the M.** las Maldivas

male [meɪl] **1** *n (person)* varón *m*, hombre *m*; *(animal)* macho *m*
2 *adj* (**a**) *(person)* masculino(a); *(animal)* macho; **a m. friend** un amigo ►► ***m. bonding:*** **he's gone down the pub for some m. bonding** se ha ido al bar para estar con sus amigotes; **m. bonding rituals** ritos típicos de hombres; ***m. chauvinism*** machismo *m*; ***m. chauvinist*** machista *m*; *Fam* ***m. chauvinist pig*** cerdo *m* machista; ***m. fern*** helecho *m* macho; *Euph* ***the m. member*** el miembro viril; *Fam Hum* ***m. menopause*** menopausia *f* masculina; ***m. model*** modelo *m*; ***m. nurse*** enfermero *m*; *Br* ***m. voice choir*** coro *m* de voces masculinas
(**b**) *(plug)* macho ►► ***m. connector*** conector *m* macho; ***m. to female adaptor*** adaptador *m* de macho a hembra

malefactor ['mælɪfæktə(r)] *n Literary* malhechor(ora) *m,f*

maleness ['meɪlnɪs] *n* masculinidad *f*

malevolence [mə'levələns] *n* malevolencia *f*

malevolent [mə'levələnt] *adj* malévolo(a)

malevolently [mə'levələntlɪ] *adv* malévolamente

malfeasance [mæl'fiːzəns] *n Law* infracción *f*

malformation [mælfɔː'meɪʃən] *n* malformación *f*

malformed [mæl'fɔːmd] *adj (organ, baby)* con malformación, deforme

malfunction [mæl'fʌŋkʃən] **1** *n Esp* fallo *m*, *Am* falla *f*; **a m. of the kidneys** una disfunción renal
2 *vi* averiarse

Mali ['mɑːlɪ] *n* Malí, Mali

Malian ['mɑːlɪən] **1** *n* malí *mf*, malense *mf*
2 *adj* malí, malense

malic acid ['mælɪk'æsɪd] *n* ácido *m* málico

malice ['mælɪs] *n* (**a**) *(ill will)* malicia *f*; **she bears you no m.** no te guarda rencor; **out of** *or* **through m.** con malicia (**b**) *Law* **with m. aforethought** con premeditación y alevosía

malicious [mə'lɪʃəs] *adj* (**a**) *(person, gossip)* malicioso(a); **she has a m. tongue** tiene una lengua viperina *or* de víbora (**b**) *Law* ***m.*** *Br* ***damage*** *or US* ***mischief*** agravio *m* malicioso

maliciously [mə'lɪʃəslɪ] *adv* maliciosamente

maliciousness [mə'lɪʃəsnɪs] *n* malicia *f*

malign [mə'laɪn] **1** *adj* perjudicial, pernicioso(a)
2 *vt* difamar; **our much maligned government** nuestro denostado gobierno

malignancy [mə'lɪgnənsɪ] *n* (**a**) *Med (of tumour)* malignidad *f* (**b**) *(of person)* maldad *f*, perversidad *f*

malignant [mə'lɪgnənt] *adj* (**a**) *Med (tumour)* maligno(a) (**b**) *(person)* maligno(a)

malinger [mə'lɪŋgə(r)] *vi* fingir una enfermedad (para no ir a trabajar)

malingerer [mə'lɪŋgərə(r)] *n* = persona que se finge enferma (para no ir a trabajar)

mall [mɔːl] *n* (**a**) *esp US (shopping centre)* centro *m* comercial (**b**) *(avenue)* paseo *m*

mallard ['mælɑːd] *n* **m. (duck)** ánade *m* real

malleability [mælɪə'bɪlɪtɪ] *n* maleabilidad *f*

malleable ['mælɪəbəl] *adj (person, metal)* maleable

mallet ['mælɪt] *n* mazo *m*

Mallorcan [mə'jɔːkən] **1** *n* (**a**) *(person)* mallorquín(ina) *m,f* (**b**) *(language)* mallorquín *m*
2 *adj* mallorquín(ina)

mallow ['mæləʊ] *n (plant)* malva *f*

malnourished [mæl'nʌrɪʃt] *adj* desnutrido(a)

malnutrition [mælnjuː'trɪʃən] *n* desnutrición *f*

malodorous [mæl'əʊdərəs] *adj Formal* (**a**) *(smelly)* hediondo(a) (**b**) *(conduct, scandal)* repugnante

malpractice [mæl'præktɪs] *n* negligencia *f* (profesional) ►► *esp US Law* ***m. suit*** demanda *f* por negligencia (profesional)

malt [mɔːlt] *n* (**a**) *(substance)* malta *f* ►► ***m. extract*** extracto *m* de malta; *US* ***m. liquor*** cerveza *f* de malta; *Br* ***m. loaf*** = bizcocho denso de malta y frutas secas; ***m. vinegar*** vinagre *m* de malta (**b**) **m. (whisky)** whisky *m* de malta (**c**) *US (malted milk)* leche *f* malteada con helado

Malta ['mɔːltə] *n* Malta

maltase ['mɔːlteɪz] *n Biochem* maltasa *f*

malted ['mɔːltɪd] **1** *n US* leche *f* malteada con helado
2 *adj* malteado(a) ►► ***m. milk*** *Br* leche *f* malteada; *US* leche *f* malteada con helado

Maltese [mɔːl'tiːz] **1** *n* (**a**) *(person)* maltés(esa) *m,f* (**b**) *(language)* maltés *m*
2 *npl (people)* **the M.** los malteses
3 *adj* maltés(esa) ►► ***M. cross*** cruz *f* de Malta

Malthusian [mæl'θuːzɪən] **1** *n* maltusiano(a) *m,f*
2 *adj* maltusiano(a)

maltose ['mɔːltəʊs] *n Chem* maltosa *f*

maltreat [mæl'triːt] *vt* maltratar

maltreatment [mæl'triːtmənt] *n* maltrato *m*, malos tratos *mpl*

malty ['mɔːltɪ] *adj* a malta; **it tastes m., it has a m. taste** sabe a malta

mam [mæm] *n Br Fam* mamá *f*

mama = **mamma**

mamba ['mæmbə] *n* mamba *f*

mambo ['mæmbəʊ] (*pl* **mambos**) *n* mambo *m*

mameluke ['mæmɪluːk] *n Hist* mameluco *m*

mamilla, *US* **mammilla** [mə'mɪlə] *n Anat* mamila *f*

mam(m)a[1] ['mæmə] *n US Fam* (**a**) *(mother)* mamá *f*, mami *f*; **he's a real m.'s boy** está enmadrado (**b**) *(woman) Esp* tía *f*, *Am* mamita *f* (**c**) **big m.** *(object)* armatoste *m*

mam(m)a[2] [mə'mɑː] *n Br Old-fashioned (mother)* mamá *f*

mammal ['mæməl] *n* mamífero *m*

mammalian [mə'meɪlɪən] *adj* **m. characteristics** características propias de los mamíferos

mammary ['mæmərɪ] *adj Anat* mamario(a) ►► ***m. glands*** mamas *fpl*, glándulas *fpl* mamarias

mammilla = **mamilla**

mammogram ['mæməgræm], **mammograph** ['mæməgrɑːf] *n Med* mamografía *f*

mammography [mæ'mɒgrəfɪ] *n Med* mamografía *f*

Mammon ['mæmən] *n Literary* el vil metal

mammoth ['mæməθ] **1** *n (animal)* mamut *m*
2 *adj (huge)* gigantesco(a), enorme; *(task)* ingente

mammy ['mæmɪ] *n Fam* **(a)** *(mother)* mamá *f*, mami *f* **(b)** *US Old-fashioned (black nanny)* = niñera negra

MAN [mæn] **1** *n* (*pl* **men** [men]) **(a)** *(adult male)* hombre *m*; **a young m.** un joven; **an old m.** un anciano; **I'm a busy/lucky m.** soy un hombre ocupado/afortunado; **he's an Oxford m.** *(from Oxford)* es de Oxford; *(who studied at Oxford University)* estudió en la Universidad de Oxford; **a family m.** un hombre de familia; **I'm not a betting m.** no soy amigo de las apuestas; **I'm a whisky m.** siempre bebo *or* tomo whisky; **he is very much the president's m.** es un incondicional del presidente; *Br Old-fashioned* **my (dear** *or* **good) m.!** mi querido amigo; **that's our m.!** *(the man we're looking for)* ¡ése es nuestro hombre!; *Fam* **if it's insurance you need, I'm your m.** si necesitas un seguro, soy la persona que buscas; **a m.'s shirt/bicycle** una camisa/bicicleta de hombre; **the men's 100 metres** los 100 metros masculinos; *Euph* **the men's room** el servicio *or RP* toilette de caballeros; **he's a m. child** es un inmaduro; **a m. of action** un hombre de acción; **to be a m. for all seasons** ser un hombre de recursos; **a m. of God** *or* **the cloth** un clérigo; **a m. of letters** un literato, un hombre de letras; **a m. of many parts** un hombre versátil *or* polifacético; **a m. of the people** un hombre popular; **a m. of science** un hombre de ciencias; **a m. of straw** *(weak person)* un pusilánime; *(front man)* un testaferro, un hombre de paja; **he's a m. of his word** es un hombre de palabra; **he's a m. of few words** es hombre de pocas palabras *or* parco en palabras; **a m. of the world** un hombre de mundo; *Fam* **the men in grey suits** los altos jerarcas, los grandes popes; **he's just the m. for the job** es el hombre indicado (para el trabajo); **the m. in the street** el hombre de la calle; **the m. of the moment** el protagonista del momento; *Fam Hum* **the men in white coats** los loqueros, *RP* los hombrecitos de blanco; **I worked there m. and boy** trabajé allí desde pequeño; **be a m. and tell her!** ¡sé hombre y díselo!; **to be m. enough to do sth** tener el valor suficiente para hacer algo; **he's a m.'s m.** le gustan las cosas de hombres; **to be one's own m.** ser dueño de sí mismo; **the army will make a m. of him** el ejército lo hará un hombre; **this will separate the men from the boys** así se verá quién vale de verdad; **to talk to sb m. to m.** hablar con alguien de hombre a hombre; **he took it like a m.** lo aceptó como un hombre; IDIOM **are you a m. or a mouse?** ¡no seas gallina!; PROV **a m.'s gotta do what a m.'s gotta do** no queda más remedio
(b) *(individual, person)* hombre *m*, persona *f*; **any m.** cualquiera; **few men** pocos, pocas personas; **I've never met the m.** no lo conozco; **they replied as one m.** respondieron como un solo hombre; **they were patriots to a m.** hasta el último de ellos era un patriota; **every m. has his price** todos tenemos un precio; **here it's every m. for himself** aquí es un sálvese quien pueda; *Fam* **every m. jack (of them)** todo el mundo, *Esp* todo quisque; **m.'s best friend** *(dog)* el mejor amigo del hombre; PROV **you can't keep a good m. down** el que vale, vale; PROV **one m.'s meat is another m.'s poison** sobre gustos no hay nada escrito
(c) *esp US Fam (in exclamations)* **m., am I tired!** ¡estoy que me caigo de cansancio!; **stop that, m.!** ¡déjalo ya, *Esp* tío *or Andes, CAm, Carib, Méx* mano!, *RP* ¡parala, che!; **my m.!** *(greeting) Esp* ¡colega!, *Méx* ¡compadre!, *Andes, CAm, Carib, Méx* ¡mano!, *RP* ¡flaco!; **oh m., that's terrible!** ¡amigo, esto es terrible!, ¡*Esp* jolín *or RP* pero che, qué terrible! **hey m., what are you doing?** oye, *Esp* tío *or Am* compadre *or Andes, CAm, Carib, Méx* mano, ¿qué haces?, *RP* ¡parala, loco!; **hey m., that's great!** amigo, ¡qué bien!, ¡*Esp* ostras *or Méx* ándale *or RP* pero che, qué bien!
(d) *(husband)* marido *m*; *Fam (boyfriend)* hombre *m*; **to live as m. and wife** vivir como marido y mujer; *Old-fashioned* **your young m.** tu galán; *Fam* **to have m. trouble** tener problemas de amores
(e) *(humanity)* el hombre; **prehistoric m.** el hombre prehistórico; **m.'s cruelty to m.** la crueldad del hombre hacia su prójimo; **one of the most toxic substances known to m.** una de las sustancias más tóxicas que se conocen; PROV **m. cannot live by bread alone** no sólo de pan vive el hombre
(f) *(employee) (in factory)* trabajador *m*; *(servant)* criado *m*; *(soldier)* hombre *m*; **an insurance m.** un vendedor de seguros; **our m. in Rome** *(spy)* nuestro agente en Roma; *(diplomat)* nuestro representante en Roma; *(reporter)* nuestro corresponsal en Roma ►► ***a M. Friday*** un chico para todo; ***m. management:*** **his m. management skills are not very good** no sabe cómo tratar al personal
(g) *Sport (player)* hombre *m*; **to lose one's m.** desmarcarse ►► ***men's doubles*** dobles *mpl* masculinos; ***m. of the match*** el jugador más destacado del partido
(h) *(in chess)* pieza *f*; *(in draughts)* ficha *f*
(i) *US Fam* **the m., the M.** *(police)* la policía, *Esp* la pasma, *Andes* los pacos, *Col* los tombos, *Méx* los pitufos, *RP* la cana; *(drug dealer)* el traficante, el camello, *RP* el dealer; *(white people)* el hombre blanco
2 *vt* (*pt & pp* **manned**) *(machine)* manejar; *(plane, boat)* tripular; *(phone, reception desk)* atender; **m. the lifeboats!** ¡todo el mundo a los botes salvavidas!; **a manned flight** un vuelo tripulado; **the office is manned by a skeleton staff** la oficina sólo hay un mínimo de personal

man-about-town ['mænəbaʊt'taʊn] *n* urbanita *m* sofisticado

manacle ['mænəkəl] *vt* esposar; **his wrists were manacled** estaba esposado

manacles ['mænəkəlz] *npl* esposas *fpl*

manage ['mænɪdʒ] **1** *vt* **(a)** *(company, hotel, project)* dirigir; *(the economy, resources)* gestionar, administrar; *(shop)* llevar, regentar; *(property, estate)* administrar; **I'm very bad at managing money** soy un desastre para administrar el dinero; **he manages Melchester United** es el director deportivo del Melchester United; **to m. sb's affairs** gestionar los asuntos de alguien
(b) *(deal with, handle) (situation)* manejar, tratar; **to know how to m. sb** saber cómo tratar a alguien
(c) *(accomplish)* **you'll m. it** te las apañarás; **she managed a smile** se las arregló para sonreír; **to m. to do sth** conseguir hacer algo; *Ironic* **somehow, he always manages to arrive at meal times** no sé cómo se las arregla para llegar siempre a la hora de la comida
(d) *(be available for)* **can you m. dinner on Thursday?** ¿te iría bien cenar el jueves?; **I can't m. Friday** el viernes no me viene bien
(e) *(cope with)* poder con; **I can't m. three suitcases** no puedo con tres maletas *or Am* valijas; **he can't m. the stairs any more** ya no puede con las escaleras; **he still can't m. parking** todavía no sabe estacionar *or Esp* aparcar; **£100 is the most I can m.** no puedo dar más de 100 libras
(f) *(eat or drink)* **I think I could m. another slice** creo que aún puedo comerme otra rebanada; **I couldn't m. another thing** ya no puedo más
2 *vi (cope)* arreglárselas, apañárselas; **he'll never m. on his own** no lo podrá hacer él solo; **to m. on sth** *(amount of money, food)* sobrevivir con algo; **to m. without sth/sb** arreglárselas *or* apañárselas sin algo/alguien

manageable ['mænɪdʒəbəl] *adj (object)* manejable; *(hair)* fácil de peinar; *(level, proportions)* razonable; *(task)* realizable, factible; **the smaller suitcase is a more m. size** la maleta pequeña es más manejable; **it will reduce the pain to a m. level** reducirá la intensidad del dolor a un nivel soportable

managed ['mænɪdʒd] *adj Fin* ***m. fund*** fondo *m* de inversión dirigido

management ['mænɪdʒmənt] *n* **(a)** *(activity) (of company, hotel, project, soccer club)* dirección *f*, gestión *f*; *(of economy, resources)* gestión *f*, administración *f*; *(of shop)* administración *f*; *(of property, estate)* administración *f*; **all their problems are due to bad m.** todos sus problemas se deben a una mala gestión ►► *Fin* ***m. accountant*** *Esp* contable *mf* de costes *or* gestión, *Am* contador(ora) *m,f* de costos *or* gestión; *Fin* ***m. accounting*** contabilidad *f* de gestión; ***m. consultant*** consultor(ora) *m,f* en administración de empresas; ***m. information system*** sistema *m* de gestión de la información; ***m. studies*** estudios *mpl* de gestión empresarial *or* administración de empresas; ***m. style*** estilo *m* de dirección
(b) *(handling) (of situation, crisis)* manejo *m*
(c) *(people in charge)* **the m.** la dirección, la gerencia; **to complain to the m.** presentar una queja a la dirección; **under new m.** *(sign)* nuevos propietarios; **the m. cannot accept responsibility for any loss or damage** la dirección no se responsabiliza de las pérdidas o desperfectos ►► ***m. buyout*** = adquisición de una empresa por sus directivos; ***m. team*** equipo *m* de dirección
(d) *(as a class)* la patronal; **m. and unions** la patronal y los sindicatos

manager ['mænɪdʒə(r)] *n* **(a)** *(of bank, company, hotel, project)* director(ora) *m,f*; *(of shop, bar, restaurant)* encargado(a) *m,f*; *(of property, estate)* administrador(ora) *m,f* **(b)** *(of boxer, singer)* representante *mf*, mánager *mf* **(c)** *(of sports team) (executive)* director(ora) *m,f* deportivo(a); *(coach)* entrenador(ora) *m,f*

manageress [mænɪdʒə'res] *n (of bank, company, hotel, project)* directora *f*; *(of shop, bar, restaurant)* encargada *f*

managerial [mænɪ'dʒɪərɪəl] *adj* de gestión, directivo(a); **at m. level** en el ámbito directivo ►► ***m. skills*** capacidad *f* de gestión; ***m. staff*** directivos *mpl*

managership ['mænɪdʒəʃɪp] *n (of sports team)* dirección *f* técnica

managing ['mænɪdʒɪŋ] *n esp Br* ***m. director*** director(ora) *m,f* gerente; ***m. editor*** director(ora) *m,f*

man-at-arms ['mænət'ɑːmz] *n* hombre *m* armado

manatee ['mænətiː] *n* manatí *m*

Manchuria [mæn'tʃʊərɪə] *n* Manchuria

Manchurian [mæn'tʃʊərɪən] **1** *n (person)* manchuriano(a) *m,f*
2 *adj* manchuriano(a)

Mancunian [mæŋ'kju:nɪən] **1** *n* persona *f* de Manchester *(Inglaterra)*
2 *adj* de Manchester *(Inglaterra)*

mandala [mæn'dɑ:lə] *n Rel & Art* mandala *m*

Mandarin ['mændərɪn] *n (language)* **M. (Chinese)** mandarín *m*

mandarin ['mændərɪn] *n* (**a**) *Hist (Chinese official)* mandarín *m* ►► ***m. collar*** cuello *m* estilo mandarín (**b**) *(high civil servant)* alto(a) burócrata *mf* (**c**) *(fruit)* **m. (orange)** mandarina *f* (**d**) *(bird)* ***m. duck*** pato *m* mandarín

mandate ['mændeɪt] **1** *n* (**a**) *Pol (authority)* autoridad *f*; **to have a m. to do sth** tener autoridad para hacer algo; **to obtain/give a m.** obtener/conferir autoridad *or* permiso
(**b**) *Fin (payment order)* orden *f* de pago, autorización *f*
(**c**) *Hist (administration of a territory)* mandato *m*; **under British m.** bajo mandato británico; **the British M. in Palestine** el mandato británico en Palestina
2 *vt* (**a**) *(authorize)* autorizar; **to m. sb to do sth** autorizar a alguien para hacer algo (**b**) *(territory)* **the territory was mandated to France after WWI** después de la Primera Guerra Mundial confirieron a Francia el mandato del territorio

mandatory ['mændətərɪ] *adj* obligatorio(a)

mandated ['mændeɪtɪd] *adj Hist* ***m. territory*** territorio *m* bajo mandato

man-day ['mæn'deɪ] *n Econ* día-hombre *m*, día *m* de mano de obra

mandible ['mændɪbəl] *n* (**a**) *(of insect)* mandíbula *f* (**b**) *(of vertebrate)* mandíbula *f*

mandolin(e) ['mændəlɪn] *n* mandolina *f*

mandrake ['mændreɪk] *n* mandrágora *f*

mandrill ['mændrɪl] *n* mandril *m*

mane [meɪn] *n (of lion)* melena *f*; *(of horse)* crines *fpl*; *Fig* **a m. of golden hair** una melena dorada

man-eater ['mæni:tə(r)] *n* (**a**) *(animal)* devorador(ora) *m,f* de hombres (**b**) *Fam (woman)* devoradora *f* de hombres

man-eating ['mæni:tɪŋ] *adj (tiger, lion)* devorador(ora) de hombres

maneuver, maneuverability etc *US* = **manoeuvre, manoeuvrability** etc

manful ['mænfʊl] *adj (courageous)* valiente

manfully ['mænfʊlɪ] *adv* con hombría, valientemente

manganese ['mæŋgəni:z] *n Chem* manganeso *m* ►► ***m. steel*** acero *m* al manganeso

mange [meɪndʒ] *n (animal disease)* sarna *f*

mangel-wurzel ['mæŋgəlwɜ:zəl], *US* **mangel** ['mæŋgəl] *n* = tipo de remolacha

manger ['meɪndʒə(r)] *n* pesebre *m*

mangetout [mɒnʒ'tu:] *n* **m. (pea)** tirabeque *m*

mangey = **mangy**

mangle ['mæŋgəl] **1** *n (for clothes)* escurridor *m* de rodillos *(para ropa)*
2 *vt* (**a**) *(body)* mutilar; *(vehicle)* destrozar (**b**) *(quotation, text)* tergiversar (**c**) *(laundry, linen)* escurrir *(con escurridor de rodillos)*

mangled ['mæŋgəld] *adj* (**a**) *(body)* mutilado(a); *(vehicle)* destrozado(a) (**b**) *(quotation, text)* tergiversado(a)

mango ['mæŋgəʊ] (*pl* **mangos** *or* **mangoes**) *n (fruit, tree)* mango *m*

mangosteen ['mæŋgəsti:n] *n (fruit, tree)* mangostán *m*

mangrove ['mæŋgrəʊv] *n* mangle *m* ►► ***m. swamp*** manglar *m*

mangy, mangey ['meɪndʒɪ] *adj* (**a**) *(animal)* sarnoso(a) (**b**) *Fam (carpet, coat)* raído(a)

manhandle ['mænhændəl] *vt* **they manhandled him into the van** lo metieron en la furgoneta a empujones; **they manhandled the piano down the stairs** acarrearon a duras penas el piano escaleras abajo

Manhattan [mæn'hætən] *n* (**a**) *(island)* Manhattan (**b**) *(cocktail)* manhattan *m*

manhole ['mænhəʊl] *n* (boca *f* de) alcantarilla *f* ►► ***m. cover*** tapa *f* de alcantarilla

manhood ['mænhʊd] *n* (**a**) *(maturity)* madurez *f*; **to reach m.** alcanzar la madurez (**b**) *(masculinity)* hombría *f*; **he proved his m.** demostró su hombría (**c**) *(men collectively)* **Scottish m.** los hombres escoceses (**d**) *Fam (genitals)* **his m.** sus partes

man-hour ['mænaʊə(r)] *n Econ* hora-hombre *f*; **300 man-hours** 300 horas-hombre

manhunt ['mænhʌnt] *n* persecución *f*

mania ['meɪnɪə] *n* (**a**) *Med* manía *f* (**b**) *(strong interest)* pasión *f* (**for** por); **to have a m. for doing sth** tener pasión por hacer algo

maniac ['meɪnɪæk] *n* (**a**) *Med* maniaco(a) *m,f*; IDIOM **to drive like a m.** *Esp* conducir *or Am* manejar como un(a) loco(a) (**b**) *(fan)* fanático(a) *m,f*; **he's a football m.** es un fanático del fútbol

maniacal [mə'naɪəkəl] *adj (crazy)* maniaco(a); **m. laughter** risa desquiciada

maniacally [mə'naɪəklɪ] *adv* desquiciadamente

manic ['mænɪk] *adj (person, behaviour)* histérico(a) ►► ***m. depression*** psicosis *f inv* maniaco-depresiva

manic-depressive ['mænɪkdɪ'presɪv] *Psy* **1** *n* maniaco(a)-depresivo(a) *m,f*
2 *adj* maniaco(a)-depresivo(a)

Manichean [mænɪ'ki:ən] *Rel* **1** *n* maniqueo(a) *m,f*
2 *adj* maniqueo(a)

Manicheism [mænɪ'ki:ɪzəm] *n Rel* maniqueísmo *m*

manicure ['mænɪkjʊə(r)] **1** *n* manicura *f*; **to give sb a m.** hacerle la manicura a alguien; **to have a m.** hacerse la manicura ►► ***m. set*** juego *m or* estuche *m* de manicura
2 *vt* **to m. one's nails** hacerse la manicura; **a manicured lawn** un césped muy bien cuidado

manicurist ['mænɪkjʊərɪst] *n* manicuro(a) *m,f*

manifest ['mænɪfest] **1** *n (of ship, aircraft)* manifiesto *m*
2 *adj* manifiesto(a), patente; **to make sth m.** poner algo de manifiesto
3 *vt* manifestar; **her insecurity manifests itself as arrogance** su inseguridad se manifiesta en forma de arrogancia
4 *vi (ghost, spirit)* aparecerse

manifestation [mænɪfes'teɪʃən] *n* (**a**) *(demonstration, display)* manifestación *f* (**b**) *(of ghost, spirit)* aparición *f*

manifestly ['mænɪfestlɪ] *adv* manifiestamente, claramente

manifesto [mænɪ'festəʊ] (*pl* **manifestos** *or* **manifestoes**) *n Pol* manifiesto *m*; **a m. commitment** *or* **pledge** una promesa electoral

manifold ['mænɪfəʊld] **1** *n Tech* colector *m*
2 *adj Formal (numerous)* múltiple

manikin = **mannikin**

Manila [mə'nɪlə] *n* Manila

mani(l)la [mə'nɪlə] *n* (**a**) *(paper)* papel *m* manila; **m. envelope** sobre de papel manila (**b**) *(hemp)* abacá *m*

manioc ['mænɪɒk] *n* mandioca *f*

manipulate [mə'nɪpjʊleɪt] *vt* (**a**) *(controls, tool)* manipular, manejar (**b**) *(people, statistics)* manipular (**c**) *Med* manipular

manipulation [mənɪpjʊ'leɪʃən] *n* (**a**) *(of controls, tool)* manipulación *f*, manejo *m* (**b**) *(of people, statistics)* manipulación *f* (**c**) *Med* manipulación *f*

manipulative [mə'nɪpjʊlətɪv] *adj Pej* manipulador(ora)

manipulator [mə'nɪpjʊleɪtə(r)] *n* manipulador(ora) *m,f*

mankind [mæn'kaɪnd] *n* la humanidad; **for the good of m.** por el bien de la humanidad

manky ['mæŋkɪ] *adj Br Fam (dirty)* mugriento(a), cochambroso(a)

manliness ['mænlɪnɪs] *n* hombría *f*, virilidad *f*

manly ['mænlɪ] *adj* viril, varonil; **he looks very m. in uniform** se ve muy varonil de uniforme

man-made ['mænmeɪd] *adj (fabric, fibre, product)* sintético(a), artificial; *(lake, beach, structure)* artificial; **m. disaster** catástrofe provocada por el hombre

manna ['mænə] *n also Fig* maná *m*; **m. from heaven** maná caído del cielo

manned [mænd] *adj* tripulado(a)

mannequin ['mænɪkɪn] *n* (**a**) *(dummy)* maniquí *m* (**b**) *(person)* modelo *mf*, maniquí *mf*

manner ['mænə(r)] *n* (**a**) *(way, method)* manera *f*, modo *m*; **in the same m.** de la misma manera, del mismo modo; **it's just a m. of speaking** es sólo un decir; **in a m. of speaking** en cierto modo; **(as if) to the m. born** como si lo llevara haciendo toda su vida
(**b**) *(style)* estilo *m*; **in the m. of Rembrandt/Haydn** al estilo de Rembrandt/Haydn
(**c**) *(type)* **all m. of** toda clase de; *Formal* **what m. of man is he?** ¿qué clase de hombre es?; **by no m. of means, not by any m. of means** en absoluto; *Formal* **by all m. of means** *(of course)* por descontado, sin lugar a dudas
(**d**) *(attitude, behaviour)* actitud *f*; **I don't like his m.** no me gusta su actitud; **she's got a very unpleasant m.** es muy arisca; **he has a good telephone m.** sabe hablar bien por teléfono
(**e**) *(etiquette)* **(good) manners** buenos modales; **bad manners** malos

modales; **it's bad manners to...** es de mala educación...; **he's got no manners** no tiene modales, es un maleducado; **where are your manners?** *(say "thank you")* ¿es que no sabes decir gracias?; *(behave properly)* ¡compórtate!; **I'm forgetting my manners, would you like some tea?** qué falta de cortesía por mi parte, ¿le apetece un poco de té?
(f) *Literary* **manners** *(social customs)* usos *mpl*

mannered ['mænəd] *adj* afectado(a), amanerado(a)

mannerism ['mænərɪzəm] *n* (a) *(characteristic, habit)* tic *m*, peculiaridad *f* (b) *Art* **M.** manierismo *m*

Mannerist ['mænərɪst] *Art* **1** *n* manierista *mf*
2 *adj* manierista

mannerly ['mænəlɪ] *adj* educado(a)

man(n)ikin ['mænɪkɪn] *n* (a) *(dwarf)* enano *m* (b) = **mannequin**

mannish ['mænɪʃ] *adj* varonil, masculino(a)

manoeuvrability, *US* **maneuverability** [mənuːvrə'bɪlɪtɪ] *n* maniobrabilidad *f*

manoeuvrable, *US* **maneuverable** [mə'nuːvrəbəl] *adj* manejable

manoeuvre, *US* **maneuver** [mə'nuːvə(r)] **1** *n* (a) *(movement)* maniobra *f*; *Fig* **there wasn't much room for m.** no había mucho margen de maniobra (b) *(tactic)* maniobra *f* (c) *Mil* **to be on manoeuvres** estar de maniobras
2 *vt* (a) *(physically)* **he manoeuvred the ladder through the window** maniobró para meter la escalera por la ventana; **they manoeuvred the animal into the pen** guiaron *or* condujeron al animal al interior del corral; **we manoeuvred the piano up the stairs** subimos el piano con cuidado por la escalera
(b) *(by influence, strategy)* **she manoeuvred her way to the top** se abrió paso hasta llegar a lo más alto; **they manoeuvred him into resigning** lo hicieron dimitir mediante artimañas
3 *vi* maniobrar; *also Fig* **to m. for position** tratar de ponerse en una buena posición

manoeuvring, *US* **maneuvering** [mə'nuːvərɪŋ] *n* (a) *(moving)* maniobra *f* (b) *Pej (plotting)* artimaña *f*, treta *f*

man-of-war = **man-o'-war**

manometer [mə'nɒmɪtə(r)] *n* manómetro *m*

manor ['mænə(r)] *n* (a) *Hist (estate)* señorío *m*; **lord/lady of the m.** el señor/la señora (b) *(house)* **m. (house)** casa *f* solariega

manorial [mə'nɔːrɪəl] *adj Hist* señorial

man-o'-war, man-of-war [mænə'wɔː(r)] (*pl* **men-o'-war, men-of-war**) *n* (a) *(warship)* buque *m* de guerra (b) *(jellyfish)* **(Portuguese) m.** = tipo de medusa venenosa

manpower ['mænpaʊə(r)] *n* mano *f* de obra; **we don't have the necessary m.** no tenemos suficiente mano de obra; **a m. shortage** falta de mano de obra

manqué [mɒŋ'keɪ] *adj Formal* fallido(a), frustrado(a); **a poet/composer m.** un poeta/compositor frustrado

mansard ['mænsɑːd] *n Archit* **m. (roof)** mansarda *f*

manse [mæns] *n Scot* casa *f* del vicario; **son/daughter of the m.** hijo/hija del vicario

manservant ['mænsɜːvənt] (*pl* **menservants** ['mensɜːvənts]) *n* criado *m*

mansion ['mænʃən] *n* mansión *f*

man-sized ['mænsaɪzd], *Br* **man-size** ['mænsaɪz] *adj* grande

manslaughter ['mænslɔːtə(r)] *n Law* homicidio *m* (involuntario)

manta ['mæntə] *n* **m. (ray)** manta *f*

mantel(piece) ['mæntəl(piːs)] *n (shelf)* repisa *f* (de la chimenea); *(surround)* chimenea *f*

mantelshelf ['mæntəlʃelf] *n* repisa *f* (de la chimenea)

mantilla [mæn'tɪlə] *n (scarf)* mantilla *f*

mantis ['mæntɪs] *n US* mantis *f inv* religiosa

mantissa [mæn'tɪsə] *n Math* mantisa *f*

mantle ['mæntəl] **1** *n* (a) *(of lava, snow)* manto *m*, capa *f*; **a m. of fog** un manto de niebla (b) *(of gas lamp)* camisa *f*, manguito *m* incandescente (c) *(cloak)* capa *f*; *Fig* **to take on the m. of office** asumir las responsabilidades del puesto (d) *Geol* manto *m*
2 *vt Literary* envolver; **the town was mantled in fog** la ciudad estaba envuelta en la niebla

> **False friend:** The Spanish noun **mantel** is not a translation for the English word **mantle**. In Spanish **mantel** means "tablecloth".

man-to-man [mæntʊ'mæn] **1** *adj (discussion)* de hombre a hombre ▸▸ ***m. defence*** *(in basketball)* defensa *f* (al) hombre; ***m. marking*** *(in soccer)* marcaje *m* individual *or* al hombre
2 *adv* de hombre a hombre; **to talk (to sb) m.** hablar con alguien de hombre a hombre

mantra ['mæntrə] *n* (a) *(in meditation)* mantra *m* (b) *(slogan)* consigna *f*

mantrap ['mæntræp] *n* trampa *f*

manual ['mænjʊəl] **1** *n* (a) *(handbook)* manual *m* (b) *(of organ)* teclado *m* (c) *Fam (car)* coche *m or Am* carro *m or CSur* auto *m* con cambio manual (d) *(mode of operation)* **to be on m.** estar en modo manual
2 *adj (work, worker)* manual; **m. dexterity** destreza *or* habilidad manual; *Aut* **m. gearbox/transmission** cambio (de marchas)/transmisión manual

manually ['mænjʊəlɪ] *adv* a mano, manualmente

manufacture [mænjʊ'fæktʃə(r)] **1** *n* (a) *(act)* fabricación *f*, manufactura *f*; **of recent/foreign m.** de fabricación reciente/extranjera (b) **manufactures** *(products)* productos *mpl* manufacturados
2 *vt* (a) *(cars, clothes)* fabricar; **manufactured goods** productos manufacturados (b) *(invent, fabricate) (excuse)* inventarse; *(evidence)* sacarse de la manga; **to m. an opportunity to do sth** crear *or* generar la oportunidad para hacer algo

manufacturer [mænjʊ'fæktʃərə(r)] *n Ind* fabricante *mf*; **send it back to the manufacturers** devuélvalo al fabricante ▸▸ ***m.'s liability*** responsabilidad *f* del fabricante

manufacturing [mænjʊ'fæktʃərɪŋ] *n Ind* fabricación *f*; **the decline of m.** el declive de la industria manufacturera ▸▸ ***m. base*** capacidad *f* de producción; ***m. capacity*** capacidad *f* de fabricación; ***m. defect*** defecto *m* de fábrica *or* fabricación; ***m. industries*** industrias *fpl* manufactureras *or* de transformación

manure [mə'njʊə(r)] **1** *n* estiércol *m*, abono *m*
2 *vt* abonar, estercolar

manuscript ['mænjʊskrɪpt] **1** *n* (a) *(of book)* manuscrito *m*; **I read the book in m.** leí el manuscrito del libro (b) **m. (paper)** *(for music)* papel *m* pautado
2 *adj* manuscrito(a)

Manx [mæŋks] **1** *npl* **the M.** los habitantes de la Isla de Man
2 *n (language)* lengua *f* de la Isla de Man
3 *adj* de la Isla de Man ▸▸ ***M. cat*** gato *m* de la Isla de Man

Manxman ['mæŋksmən] *n* hombre *m* de la Isla de Man

Manxwoman ['mæŋkswʊmən] *n* mujer *f* de la Isla de Man

MANY ['menɪ] **1** *adj* (*comparative* **more**, *superlative* **most**) muchos(as); **m. people** mucha gente; **m. times** muchas veces; **there weren't m. houses** no había muchas casas, había pocas casas; **one of the m. people to whom I am grateful** una de las muchas personas a quien estoy agradecido; **I have as m. books as you** tengo tantos libros como tú; **we have ten times/twice as m. points as them** tenemos diez veces más/el doble de puntos que ellos; **they scored three goals in as m. minutes** marcaron tres goles en tres minutos; **a good** *or* **great m. people agree** un buen número de personas está de acuerdo; **how m. times?** ¿cuántas veces?; **she asked how m. people had come** preguntó cuánta gente había venido *or* cuántos habían venido; **in m. ways** de muchas maneras; **I think he's stupid and I told him in so m. words** creo que es estúpido y así se lo dije; **not in so m. words** no exactamente; **not m. people know that** poca gente sabe eso; **not that m. people came** no vino tanta gente; **so m.** tantos(as); **so m. people** tanta gente; **too m.** demasiados(as); **too m. people** demasiada gente; **we've spent m. a happy evening with them** hemos pasado muchas tardes agradables con ellos; **m.'s the time I've done that** lo he hecho muchas veces
2 *pron* muchos(as) *m,f pl*; **m. consider him the greatest poet ever** muchos consideran que es el mejor poeta de todos los tiempos; **one of the m. I have known** uno de los muchos que he conocido; **m. of us** muchos de nosotros; **I need as m. again** necesito la misma cantidad otra vez; **ten times as m.** diez veces esa cantidad; **twice as m.** el doble; **as m. as you like** todos los que quieras; **there were as m. as 500 people there** había hasta 500 personas allí; **I've read a good** *or* **great m. of his novels** he leído un buen número de sus novelas; **how m.?** ¿cuántos(as)?; **not (very** *or* **that) m.** no muchos(as); **so m.** tantos(as); **too m.** demasiados(as); **I've got one too m.** tengo uno de más; *Fam* **to have had one too m.** llevar una copa de más, haber bebido *or Am* tomado más de la cuenta
3 *npl* **the needs of the m. outweigh the needs of the few** el interés de la mayoría está por encima del de la minoría

many-coloured ['menɪ'kʌləd] *adj* multicolor

man-year ['mæn'jɪə(r)] *n Econ* año-hombre *m*

Maoism ['maʊɪzəm] *n* maoísmo *m*

Maoist ['maʊɪst] **1** *n* maoísta *mf*
2 *adj* maoísta

Mao jacket ['maʊ'dʒækɪt] *n* chaqueta *f* Mao

Maori ['maʊrɪ] **1** *n* (**a**) *(person)* maorí *mf* (**b**) *(language)* maorí *m*
2 *adj* maorí

map [mæp] **1** *n* (**a**) *(of country, world)* mapa *m*; *(of town, network)* plano *m*; *Fig* **the city was wiped off the m.** la ciudad fue borrada del mapa; *Fig* **this will put Stonybridge on the m.** esto dará a conocer a Stonybridge ►► ***m. reference*** coordenadas *fpl* (**b**) *US Fam (face)* jeta *f*, *Esp* careto *m*
2 *vt* (*pt & pp* **mapped**) (**a**) *(region)* trazar un mapa de (**b**) *Math* representar

►**map out** *vt sep (route)* indicar en un mapa; *(plan, programme)* proyectar; **she had her career all mapped out** tenía su carrera profesional planeada paso por paso

maple ['meɪpəl] *n (tree, wood)* arce *m* ►► ***m. leaf*** hoja *f* de arce; ***m. syrup*** jarabe *m* de arce

mapmaking ['mæpmeɪkɪŋ] *n* cartografía *f*

mapping ['mæpɪŋ] *n Math* representación *f*

map-reading ['mæpri:dɪŋ] *n* interpretación *f* de mapas

maquette [mæ'ket] *n Archit* maqueta *f*

maquis [mæ'ki:] *n (guerrilla)* maquis *m*, maqui *m*; **the M.** el Maquis *(francés)*

Mar (*abbr* **March**) mar.

mar [mɑ:(r)] (*pt & pp* **marred**) *vt* deslucir, empañar; **to make or m. sb** decidir el futuro de alguien; **today will make or m. their future** hoy se decide su futuro

marabou ['mærəbu:] *n* marabú *m*

marabout ['mærəbu:] *n Rel* morabito *m*, marabuto *m*

maracas [mə'rækəz] *npl Mus* maracas *fpl*

maraschino [mærə'ʃi:nəʊ] *n* marrasquino *m* ►► ***m. cherry*** cereza *f* al marrasquino

marathon ['mærəθən] *n* maratón *m or f*; **a m. speech** un discurso maratoniano ►► ***m. runner*** corredor(ora) *m,f* de maratón

marathoner ['mærəθənə(r)] *n* maratonista *mf*

maraud [mə'rɔ:d] *vi* merodear; **to go marauding** ir a merodear

marauder [mə'rɔ:də(r)] *n* merodeador(ora) *m,f*

marauding [mə'rɔ:dɪŋ] *adj (gangs, people)* merodeador(ora); **m. animals** animales en busca de su presa

marble ['mɑ:bəl] *n* (**a**) *(stone)* mármol *m* (**b**) *(statue)* estatua *f* de mármol (**c**) *(glass ball)* canica *f*; **to play marbles** jugar a las canicas (**d**) *Culin* ***m. cake*** = pastel con aspecto semejante al del mármol (**e**) IDIOM *Fam* **to lose one's marbles** *(go mad)* volverse loco(a) *or Esp* majareta; **she still has all her marbles at ninety** a los noventa años tiene todas sus facultades intactas

marbled ['mɑ:bəld] *adj* (**a**) *(halls, interior)* de mármol (**b**) *(paper)* jaspeado(a) (**c**) *(meat)* con vetas

marbling ['mɑ:blɪŋ] *n* (**a**) *(on paper)* jaspeado *m*, veteado *m* (**b**) *(of fat in meat)* vetas *f*

March [mɑ:tʃ] *n* marzo *m*; *see also* **May**

march [mɑ:tʃ] **1** *n* (**a**) *(of soldiers)* marcha *f*; **on the m.** en marcha; *Fig* **the middle classes are on the m.** la clase media se está movilizando; **a m. of 20 km** una marcha de 20 kilómetros; **their camp was a day's m. away** su campamento se encontraba a un día de camino ►► ***m. past*** desfile *m*
(**b**) *(demonstration)* marcha *f*, manifestación *f*; **to go on a m.** ir a una marcha *or* manifestación
(**c**) *Fig (of time, events)* transcurso *m*
(**d**) *(music)* marcha *f*; **a slow/quick m.** una marcha lenta/rápida
(**e**) *Hist (frontier)* **the Welsh/Scottish Marches** la Marca galesa/escocesa
2 *vt (troops)* hacer marchar; **he was marched into the manager's office** lo llevaron (por la fuerza) al despacho del gerente; **the children were marched off to bed** llevaron a los niños (a la fuerza) a la cama
3 *vi* (**a**) *(soldiers) (in the field)* marchar; *(at ceremony, on parade)* desfilar; **to m. off to war/into battle** partir a la guerra/al combate; **to m. by** *or* **past (sth/sb)** desfilar (ante algo/alguien); **to m. on a city** marchar sobre una ciudad
(**b**) *(walk purposefully)* caminar con paso decidido; **to m. up to sb** dirigirse hacia alguien con paso decidido; **he marched upstairs** subió las escaleras con paso decidido
(**c**) *(demonstrators)* manifestarse; **to m. against sth** manifestarse en contra de algo; **they marched on parliament** los manifestantes se dirigieron hacia el parlamento
(**d**) *(time, seasons)* transcurrir; **time marches on** el tiempo pasa

marcher ['mɑ:tʃə(r)] *n (demonstrator)* manifestante *mf*

marching ['mɑ:tʃɪŋ] *adj* **the sound of m. feet** el ruido de pasos que avanzan; IDIOM *Fam* **to give sb his m. orders** mandar a paseo a alguien, *Andes, RP* mandar a alguien a bañarse; **when she found out he got his m. orders** cuando se enteró, lo mandó a paseo *or Andes, RP* a bañarse

marchioness [mɑ:ʃə'nes] *n* marquesa *f*

Mardi Gras ['mɑ:dɪgrɑ:] *n* martes *m inv* de Carnaval

mare [meə(r)] *n* (**a**) *(female horse)* yegua *f*; IDIOM **a m.'s nest** un espejismo, una quimera (**b**) *Br Fam (nightmare)* pesadilla *f*; **it was a complete m.!** ¡fue una pesadilla!; **her new boyfriend's a complete m.** su nuevo novio es insoportable

margarine [mɑ:dʒə'ri:n] *n* margarina *f*

margarita [mɑ:gə'ri:tə] *n* margarita *m*

margay ['mɑ:geɪ] *n* tigrillo *m*, margay *m*

marge [mɑ:dʒ] *n Br Fam* margarina *f*

margin ['mɑ:dʒɪn] *n* (**a**) *(on page)* margen *m*; **to set the margins** *(on typewriter, computer)* fijar los márgenes; **written in the m.** escrito al margen
(**b**) *(leeway)* margen *m* ►► ***m. of error*** margen *m* de error
(**c**) *(distance, gap)* margen *m*; **to win by a narrow/an enormous m.** ganar por un estrecho/amplio margen
(**d**) *Com (profit)* margen *m*; **to have a low/high m.** tener un margen de beneficios bajo/alto; **the margins are very tight** los márgenes están muy ajustados
(**e**) *(edge) (of field)* margen *f*; *(of lake)* orilla *f*; *(of wood)* extremo *m*; **on the margin(s) of society** en la marginación

marginal ['mɑ:dʒɪnəl] **1** *n Br Pol (constituency)* = circunscripción electoral con mayoría muy estrecha
2 *adj* (**a**) *(improvement, increase)* marginal; **of only m. relevance** de escasa importancia (**b**) *(note)* al margen, marginal (**c**) *Br Pol (seat, constituency)* muy reñido(a) (**d**) *Fin* ***m. cost*** costo *m or Esp* coste *m* marginal

marginalia [mɑ:gɪ'neɪlɪə] *npl Lit* acotaciones *fpl*

marginalization [mɑ:dʒɪnəlaɪ'zeɪʃən] *n* marginalización *f*

marginalize ['mɑ:dʒɪnəlaɪz] *vt* marginar

marginally ['mɑ:dʒɪnəlɪ] *adv* ligeramente

marguerite [mɑ:gə'ri:t] *n* margarita *f*

marigold ['mærɪgəʊld] *n* caléndula *f*

marihuana, marijuana [mærɪ'hwɑ:nə] *n* marihuana *f*

marimba [mə'rɪmbə] *n* marimba *f*

marina [mə'ri:nə] *n* puerto *m* deportivo

marinade [mærɪ'neɪd] *Culin* **1** *n* adobo *m*
2 *vt* = **marinate**
3 *vi* = **marinate**

marinate ['mærɪneɪt] *Culin* **1** *vt* adobar, marinar
2 *vi* adobar, marinar

marine [mə'ri:n] **1** *n* (**a**) *(soldier)* marine *mf*; infante *mf* de marina, *Am* fusilero *m* naval; IDIOM *Fam* **(go) tell it to the marines!** ¡eso cuéntaselo a tu abuela! ►► ***M. Corps*** cuerpo *m* de marines, infantería *f* de marina (**b**) *(ships collectively)* marina *f*
2 *adj* marino(a) ►► ***m. biologist*** biólogo(a) *m,f* marino(a); ***m. biology*** biología *f* marina; ***m. engineer*** ingeniero(a) *m,f* naval; ***m. engineering*** ingeniería *f* naval; ***m. insurance*** seguro *m* marítimo; ***m. life*** fauna *f* y flora marinas

mariner ['mærɪnə(r)] *n Literary* marinero *m*

Mariolatry [meərɪ'ɒlətrɪ] *n Pej* = veneración exagerada de la Virgen

marionette [mærɪə'net] *n* marioneta *f*

marital ['mærɪtəl] *adj* marital ►► *Euph* ***m. aid*** juguete *m* sexual; ***m. bliss*** felicidad *f* conyugal; ***m. status*** estado *m* civil

maritime ['mærɪtaɪm] *adj* marítimo(a) ►► *Can* ***the M. Provinces*** = provincias de Canadá que limitan con el Atlántico

marjoram ['mɑ:dʒərəm] *n* mejorana *f*

Mark [mɑ:k] *pr n* **Saint M.** san Marco

mark[1] [mɑ:k] *n (German currency)* marco *m* (alemán)

MARK[2] **1** *n* (**a**) *(scratch, symbol)* marca *f*; *(stain)* mancha *f*; **a scratch m.** *(on car)* una raya, *RP* un rayón; *(on skin)* un rasguño
(**b**) *(sign, proof)* signo *m*, señal *f*; **it was a m. of her confidence that...** fue un signo de su confianza el que...; **his composure under pressure is the m. of a true champion** su compostura ante la presión es característica de un auténtico campeón; **as a m. of respect** en señal de respeto; **years of imprisonment had left their m. on him** había quedado marcado por años de reclusión; **to make one's m.** *(succeed)* dejar huella
(**c**) *(target)* **unemployment has passed the three million m.** el

número de desempleados *or Am* desocupados ha rebasado la barrera de los tres millones; **to be close** *or* **near to the m.** no ir *or* andar nada descaminado(a), dar casi en el clavo; **her accusation was off** *or* **wide of the m.** su acusación estaba lejos de ser cierta; **he's not up to the m.** no está a la altura de las circunstancias; **the work just isn't up to the m.** el trabajo no está a la altura; *Old-fashioned* **I don't feel up to the m.** no me encuentro del todo bien

(**d**) *(score)* nota *f*, calificación *f*; *(point)* punto *m*; **what m. did you get?** ¿qué sacaste?; **to get good** *or* **high marks** sacar buenas notas; **full marks** nota máxima; **I give it full marks for an innovative design** le doy un diez por su diseño innovador; **I'd give them full marks for effort** hay que reconocer que se han esforzado al máximo; **no marks for guessing what she did next!** ¿a que no adivinan lo que hizo a continuación?

(**e**) *(in race)* **on your marks! get set! go!** preparados *or RP* prontos, listos, ¡ya!; **the athletes returned to their marks** los atletas volvieron a sus puestos de salida *or RP* marcas; **to be quick/slow off the m.** *(in race)* salir rápido/despacio; *Fig* reaccionar con rapidez/lentitud

(**f**) *(of machine)* **m. II/III** versión *f* II/III

(**g**) *(on cooker)* **cook at (gas) m. 4** cocínese con el mando en el 4, *RP* cocinar a temperatura 4

(**h**) *(in rugby)* **to call for the m.** hacer una parada de volea

2 *vt* (**a**) *(scratch)* marcar; *(stain)* manchar; **the experience had marked him for life** *(emotionally)* la experiencia lo marcó de por vida

(**b**) *(indicate)* marcar; **the envelope was marked "FAO Mr Black"** en el sobre ponía "a la atención de Mr Black"; **the teacher marked him present** el profesor anotó que estaba presente; **X marks the spot** una X señala el lugar; **this decision marks a change in policy** esta decisión marca un cambio de política; **to m. time** *(musician)* marcar el compás *or* el tiempo; *(soldier)* marchar sin moverse del sitio; *Fig (wait)* hacer tiempo

(**c**) *(commemorate)* marcar; **let's have some champagne to m. the occasion** vamos a tomar champán para celebrarlo

(**d**) *(characterize)* marcar, caracterizar; **his comments were marked by their sarcasm** sus comentarios se caracterizaban por el sarcasmo

(**e**) *(homework, exam)* corregir, calificar; **to m. sth right/wrong** dar/no dar algo por bueno(a), *RP* considerar algo bien/mal; **it's marked out of ten** está puntuado sobre diez

(**f**) *(pay attention to)* **m. my words** fíjate en lo que te digo

(**g**) *Sport Br (opponent)* marcar; **he marked him out of the game** su marcaje lo borró del partido

(**h**) **to m. one's ball** *(in golf)* marcar la situación de la bola

3 *vi* (**a**) *(get stained)* **this carpet marks easily** esta alfombra se mancha con facilidad

(**b**) *Old-fashioned (pay attention)* **I'm not trying to defend her, m. you** fíjate, no es que pretenda defenderla

▸ **mark down** *vt sep* (**a**) *(make note of)* anotar, apuntar; **they had him marked down as a troublemaker** lo tenían fichado como alborotador

(**b**) *(price, goods)* rebajar; **everything has been marked down to half price** todo está rebajado a la mitad de precio

(**c**) *Sch* bajar la nota a

▸ **mark off** *vt sep* (**a**) *(divide) (area, line, road)* delimitar; **one corner of the square had been marked off with barriers** una esquina de la plaza estaba vallada

(**b**) *(measure) (distance)* medir

(**c**) *(distinguish)* **what marks him off from other people is...** lo que lo diferencia de otros es...

(**d**) *(tick off)* poner una marca en

▸ **mark out** *vt sep* (**a**) *(area)* marcar (**b**) *(identify, distinguish)* distinguir; **her composure marks her out as a future champion** su compostura permite pensar en ella como futura campeona

▸ **mark up** *vt sep* (**a**) *(on notice)* anotar; **the menu is marked up on the blackboard** el menú está anotado en el tablón

(**b**) *(price)* subir; *(goods)* subir de precio

(**c**) *Sch* subir la nota a

(**d**) *Typ (proofs)* corregir; *(corrections)* anotar

---

mark-down ['mɑːkdaʊn] *n (price reduction)* rebaja *f*, reducción *f* (de precio)

marked [mɑːkt] *adj* (**a**) *(significant) (difference)* marcado(a); *(improvement)* notable (**b**) *(identified)* **to be a m. man** tener los días contados ▸▸ ***m. cards*** cartas *fpl* marcadas (**c**) *Com* ***m. price*** precio *m* marcado

markedly ['mɑːkɪdlɪ] *adv* notablemente, considerablemente

marker ['mɑːkə(r)] *n* (**a**) *(of essay, exam)* examinador(ora) *m,f*, corrector(ora) *m,f* de exámenes; **he's a hard m.** es muy severo al corregir

(**b**) **m. (pen)** rotulador *m*, *Col* marcador *m*, *Méx* plumón *m*

(**c**) *(indicator)* señal *f*; **he was putting down a m.** estaba poniendo de manifiesto cuáles eran sus intenciones ▸▸ *Av* ***m. beacon*** radiobaliza *f*; ***m. buoy*** baliza *f*

(**d**) *Sport* marcador(ora) *m,f*; **to lose one's m.** desmarcarse

(**e**) *US Fam (IOU)* pagaré *m*; *Fig* **to call in one's m.** pasar la factura

market ['mɑːkɪt] **1** *n* (**a**) *(place)* mercado *m*, *RP* feria *f*, *CAm, Méx* tianguis *m*; **to go to (the) m.** ir al mercado ▸▸ ***m. day*** día *m* de mercado; *Br* ***m. garden*** huerto *m*; *(larger)* huerta *f*; *Br* ***m. gardener*** horticultor(ora) *m,f*; ***m. square*** (plaza *f* del) mercado *m*; *Br* ***m. stall*** puesto *m* del mercado; ***m. town*** localidad *f* con mercado; *Br* ***m. trader*** puestero(a) *m,f*

(**b**) *(trading activity)* mercado *m*; **the job/property m.** el mercado laboral/inmobiliario; **the Australian/teenage m.** el mercado australiano/adolescente; **the most economical model on the m.** el modelo más económico del mercado; **to be in the m. for sth** tener intenciones de comprar algo; **to be on the m.** estar a la venta; **to come onto the m.** salir al mercado; **to put sth on the m.** sacar algo al mercado; **to take sth off the m.** retirar algo del mercado *or* de la venta; **to find a m. for sth** encontrar un mercado para algo ▸▸ *Fin* ***m. capitalization*** capitalización *f* bursátil; *Econ* ***m. economy*** economía *f* de mercado; *Econ* ***m. forces*** fuerzas *fpl* del mercado; *Com* ***m. leader*** líder *mf* del mercado; *Com* ***m. penetration*** penetración *f* de mercado; *Econ* ***m. price*** precio *m* de mercado; *Com* ***m. research*** estudio *m or* investigación *f* de mercado; *Com* ***m. share*** cuota *f* de mercado; *Com* ***m. survey*** estudio *m* de mercados; ***m. trends*** tendencias *fpl* de mercado; ***m. value*** valor *m* de mercado

(**c**) *(stock market)* mercado *m* (de valores), bolsa *f*; **the m. has risen ten points** la bolsa *or* el mercado ha subido diez puntos; **to play the m.** jugar a la bolsa ▸▸ ***m. analyst*** analista *mf* de mercados; ***m. conditions*** la situación del mercado; ***m. fluctuation*** fluctuación *f* del mercado; ***m. growth*** crecimiento *m* del mercado; ***m. maker*** creador *m* de mercado; ***m. order*** orden *f* al mercado; ***m. report*** información *f* bursátil

(**d**) *US (supermarket)* supermercado *m*

2 *vt* comercializar

3 *vi US (go shopping)* **to go marketing** ir a la compra

marketability [mɑːkɪtə'bɪlɪtɪ] *n* comerciabilidad *f*

marketable ['mɑːkɪtəbəl] *adj* comercializable

market-driven ['mɑːkɪt'drɪvən] *adj* motivado(a) por el mercado

marketer ['mɑːkɪtə(r)] *n Com* operador(ora) *m,f* de mercado

marketing ['mɑːkɪtɪŋ] *n Com (study, theory)* márketing *m*, mercadotecnia *f*; *(promotion)* comercialización *f* ▸▸ ***m. campaign*** campaña *f* de márketing *or* de publicidad; ***m. department*** departamento *m* de márketing; ***m. manager*** director(ora) *m,f* comercial, director(ora) *m,f* de márketing; ***m. mix*** marketing mix *m*, = síntesis de los elementos básicos de mercado; ***m. strategy*** estrategia *f* de márketing; ***m. techniques*** técnicas *fpl* de venta

market-led [mɑːkɪt'led] *adj Com* provocado(a) por el comportamiento del mercado

marketplace ['mɑːkətpleɪs] *n* (**a**) *(in town)* mercado *m* (**b**) *Com* mercado *m*

marking ['mɑːkɪŋ] *n* (**a**) **markings** *(on animal)* marcas *fpl*, manchas *fpl*; *(on plane)* distintivo *m* ▸▸ ***m. ink*** tinta *f* indeleble (**b**) *(of essay, exam)* corrección *f*; **I've got a lot of exam m. to do** tengo que corregir muchos exámenes ▸▸ ***m. scheme*** = pautas para la corrección de exámenes (**c**) *Sport* marcaje *m*

markka ['mɑːkə] *n Formerly (Finnish currency)* marco *m* finlandés

marksman ['mɑːksmən] *n* tirador *m*

marksmanship ['mɑːksmənʃɪp] *n* puntería *f*

markswoman ['mɑːkswʊmən] *n* tiradora *f*

mark-up ['mɑːkʌp] *n (on price)* recargo *m*

marlin ['mɑːlɪn] *n* marlín *m*, pez *m* espada

marlinspike ['mɑːlɪnspaɪk] *n Naut* pasador *m*

marmalade ['mɑːməleɪd] **1** *n* mermelada *f* (de naranja) ▸▸ ***m. orange*** naranja *f* agria

2 *adj (cat)* con estrías naranjas y marrones

Marmite® ['mɑːmaɪt] *n Br* = crema para untar hecha de levadura y extractos vegetales

marmoreal [mɑː'mɔːrɪəl] *adj Literary* marmóreo(a)

marmoset ['mɑːməzet] *n* tití *m*

marmot ['mɑːmət] *n* marmota *f*

maroon[1] [mə'ruːn] *n* (**a**) *(colour)* granate *m* (**b**) *(firework)* bengala *f* de auxilio *(en el mar)*

maroon[2] *vt (sailor)* abandonar; *Fig* **we were marooned by the floods** nos quedamos aislados *or* incomunicados por la inundación

marque [mɑːk] *n (brand)* marca *f*

marquee [mɑː'kiː] *n* (**a**) *Br (tent)* carpa *f* (**b**) *US (of building)* marquesina *f*

marquess ['mɑːkwəs] *n* marqués *m*

marquetry ['mɑːkətrɪ] *n* marquetería *f*

marquis ['mɑːkwɪs] *n* marqués *m*

marquise [mɑː'kiːz] *n* marquesa *f*

Marrakesh ['mærəkeʃ] *n* Marraquech

marriage ['mærɪdʒ] *n* (**a**) *(wedding)* boda *f*, *Andes* matrimonio *m*, *RP* casamiento *m*; *(institution, period, relationship)* matrimonio *m*; **m. of convenience** matrimonio de conveniencia; **to give sb in m.** entregar a alguien en matrimonio; **to take sb in m.** tomar a alguien en matrimonio; **uncle by m.** tío político ▸▸ *Br* ***m. bureau*** agencia *f* matrimonial; ***m. certificate*** certificado *m or* partida *f* de matrimonio; ***m. contract*** contrato *m* matrimonial; ***m. guidance counsellor*** consejero(a) *m,f* matrimonial; ***m. licence*** licencia *f* matrimonial; ***m. settlement*** acuerdo *m* matrimonial; ***m. vows*** votos *mpl* matrimoniales
(**b**) *(of ideas, organizations)* unión *f*; **a m. of minds** una perfecta sintonía

marriageable ['mærɪdʒəbəl] *adj* **a girl of m. age** una muchacha casadera

married ['mærɪd] **1** *adj* casado(a); **a m. couple** un matrimonio; **to be m.** estar *or Am* ser casado(a); **to get m.** casarse; **just m.** *(sign)* recién casados ▸▸ ***m. life*** vida *f* matrimonial; ***m. name*** apellido *m* de casada; *Mil* ***m. quarters*** = residencia para oficiales casados y sus familias
2 *npl* **young marrieds** recién casados *mpl*

marrow ['mærəʊ] *n* (**a**) *(of bone)* médula *f*; IDIOM **to be frozen to the m.** estar helado(a) hasta la médula *or* hasta los tuétanos (**b**) *Br (vegetable)* = especie de calabacín de gran tamaño

marrowbone ['mærəʊbəʊn] *n* hueso *m* de caña

marrowfat pea ['mærəʊfæt'piː] *n* = tipo de guisante grande

marry ['mærɪ] **1** *vt* (**a**) *(get married to)* casarse con; *(of priest, parent)* casar; **will you m. me?** ¿quieres casarte conmigo?; *Fig* **he's married to his job** es esclavo de su trabajo (**b**) *(combine)* casar, combinar; **a style which marries the traditional and the modern** un estilo que combina lo tradicional con lo moderno
2 *vi* casarse; **she married beneath/above herself** se casó con alguien de clase inferior/superior; **to m. for money** casarse por dinero; **to m. into money** casarse con alguien que tiene dinero; **to m. into a wealthy family** casarse con un miembro de una familia adinerada; PROV **m. in haste, repent at leisure** antes que te cases, mira lo que haces
(**b**) *(combine)* combinar; **the flavours m. well** es una buena mezcla de sabores

▸ **marry off** *vt sep* casar

▸ **marry up 1** *vt sep (bring together)* casar
2 *vi (line up)* casar

marrying ['mærɪɪŋ] *adj* **he's not the m. kind** no es de los que se casan

Mars [mɑːz] *n* (**a**) *(god)* Marte (**b**) *(planet)* Marte *m*

Marseille(s) [mɑː'seɪ] *n* Marsella

marsh [mɑːʃ] *n (of freshwater)* pantano *m*; *(of seawater)* marisma *f* ▸▸ ***m. gas*** gas *m* de los pantanos; ***m. harrier*** aguilucho *m* lagunero; *US* ***m. hawk*** aguilucho *m* pálido; ***m. mallow*** *(plant)* malvavisco *m*; ***m. marigold*** (hierba *f*) centella *f*; ***m. tit*** carbonero *m* palustre; ***m. warbler*** carricero *m* políglota

marshal ['mɑːʃəl] **1** *n* (**a**) *(army officer)* mariscal *m* (**b**) *(at race, demonstration)* miembro *m* del servicio de orden (**c**) *(in law court)* oficial *mf* de justicia, ordenanza *mf* (**d**) *US (police chief)* jefe(a) *m,f* de policía; *(fire chief)* jefe(a) *m,f* de bomberos; *(police officer)* policía *mf*; *(in Wild West)* ayudante *mf* del sheriff
2 *vt* (*pt & pp* **marshalled**, *US* **marshaled**) (**a**) *(people, troops)* dirigir; **the troops were marshalled into the square** congregaron a las tropas en la plaza; **she marshalled the children out of the room** sacó a los niños de la habitación (**b**) *(arguments, thoughts)* poner en orden; **he's trying to m. support for his project** trata de organizar el respaldo para su proyecto

marshalling-yard ['mɑːʃəlɪŋjɑːd] *n Rail* estación *f* de clasificación

marshland ['mɑːʃlænd] *n (of freshwater)* zona *f* pantanosa; *(of seawater)* marismas *fpl*

marshmallow [mɑːʃ'mæləʊ] *n (food)* = dulce de consistencia esponjosa

marshy ['mɑːʃɪ] *adj* pantanoso(a)

marsupial [mɑː'suːpɪəl] **1** *n* marsupial *m*
2 *adj* marsupial

mart [mɑːt] *n* tienda *f*, almacén *m*

martello tower [mɑː'teləʊ'taʊə(r)] *n* bastión *m (cilíndrico)*

marten ['mɑːtɪn] *n* marta *f*

martial ['mɑːʃəl] *adj* marcial; **m. music** música militar ▸▸ ***m. arts*** artes *fpl* marciales; ***m. law:*** **to declare m. law** declarar la ley marcial

Martian ['mɑːʃən] **1** *n* marciano(a) *m,f*
2 *adj* marciano(a)

martin ['mɑːtɪn] *n* avión *m*

martinet [mɑːtɪ'net] *n* tirano(a) *m,f*

martingale ['mɑːtɪngeɪl] *n (for horse)* amarra *f*

Martini® [mɑː'tiːniː] *n (vermouth)* vermú *m*, martini *m*

martini [mɑː'tiːniː] *n (cocktail)* martini *m* seco

Martinican [mɑːtɪ'niːkən] **1** *n* martiniqués(esa) *m,f*
2 *adj* martiniqués(esa)

Martinique [mɑːtɪ'niːk] *n* Martinica

Martinmas ['mɑːtɪnməs] *n* (día *m* de) San Martín

martyr ['mɑːtə(r)] **1** *n* mártir *mf*; **to die a m.** morir como un/una mártir; *Fig* **to be a m. to rheumatism** estar martirizado(a) por el reúma; *Fig* **to make a m. of oneself** hacerse el/la mártir
2 *vt* martirizar, hacer mártir

martyrdom ['mɑːtədəm] *n* martirio *m*

martyred ['mɑːtəd] *adj* de mártir, martirizado(a)

marvel ['mɑːvəl] **1** *n* (**a**) *(miracle)* maravilla *f*; **to do** *or* **work marvels** hacer maravillas; **if we survive this it'll be a m.** si salimos de ésta será un milagro (**b**) *Fam (marvellous person)* **you're a m.!** ¡eres un genio!
2 *vi* (*pt & pp* **marvelled**, *US* **marveled**) maravillarse, asombrarse (**at** de)

marvellous, *US* **marvelous** ['mɑːvələs] *adj* maravilloso(a)

marvellously, *US* **marvelously** ['mɑːvələslɪ] *adv* maravillosamente

Marxism ['mɑːksɪzəm] *n* marxismo *m*

Marxism-Leninism ['mɑːksɪzəm'lenɪnɪzəm] *n* marxismo-leninismo *m*

Marxist ['mɑːksɪst] **1** *n* marxista *mf*
2 *adj* marxista

Marxist-Leninist ['mɑːksɪst'lenɪnɪst] **1** *n* marxista-leninista *mf*
2 *adj* marxista-leninista

Mary ['meərɪ] *pr n* **(the Virgin) M.** (la virgen) María; **M. Magdalene** María Magdalena

Maryland ['meərɪlənd] *n* Maryland

marzipan ['mɑːzɪpæn] *n* mazapán *m*; **a m. mouse** un ratón de mazapán

mascara [mæs'kɑːrə] *n* rímel *m*

mascaraed, mascara'd [mæs'kɑːrəd] *adj* **heavily m. eyelashes** pestañas con mucho rímel

mascarpone [mæskə'pəʊnɪ] *n* mascarpone *m*, = queso cremoso italiano

mascot ['mæskət] *n* mascota *f*

masculine ['mæskjʊlɪn] **1** *n Gram* (género *m*) masculino *m*
2 *adj* masculino(a)

masculinity [mæskjʊ'lɪnɪtɪ] *n* masculinidad *f*

MASH [mæʃ] *n* (*abbr* **mobile army surgical hospital**) quirófano *m* militar de campaña

mash [mæʃ] **1** *n* (**a**) *Fam (mashed potato)* puré *m* de *Esp* patatas *or Am* papas (**b**) *(for pigs, poultry)* frangollo *m* (**c**) *(in brewing)* templa *f*
2 *vt (squash, crush)* machacar; *(vegetables)* majar, hacer puré de; **to m. sth up** hacer puré algo

mashed potato(es) [mæʃtpə'teɪtəʊ(z)] *npl* puré *m* de *Esp* patatas *or Am* papas

masher ['mæʃə(r)] *n (for potatoes)* pasapuré *m*

mask [mɑːsk] **1** *n* (**a**) *(for face) (for disguise)* máscara *f*, careta *f*; *(for protection, surgeon)* máscara *f*, mascarilla *f*; *Fig* **his m. had slipped** se le había caído la máscara; *Fig* **a m. of happiness/confidence** una máscara de felicidad/seguridad (**b**) *(in photography)* máscara *f*
2 *vt* (**a**) *(face)* enmascarar (**b**) *(conceal) (truth, feelings)* ocultar; *(flavour, smell)* disimular, camuflar (**c**) *(in painting, photography)* tapar, cubrir

masked [mɑːskt] *adj* enmascarado(a) ▸▸ ***m. ball*** baile *m* de máscaras

masking tape ['mɑːskɪŋteɪp] *n* cinta *f* adhesiva de pintor

masochism ['mæsəkɪzəm] *n* masoquismo *m*

masochist ['mæsəkɪst] *n* masoquista *mf*

masochistic [mæsə'kɪstɪk] *adj* masoquista

mason ['meɪsən] *n* (a) *(builder)* cantero(a) *m,f*, picapedrero(a) *m,f* (b) *(Freemason)* **M.** masón *m*

Masonic [mə'sɒnɪk] *adj* masón(ona); **M. lodge** logia masónica

masonry ['meɪsənrɪ] *n* (a) *(stonework)* albañilería *f*, obra *f*; **she was hit by a piece of falling m.** le cayó encima un cascote que se había desprendido del edificio ►► ***m. drill*** taladro *m* de albañilería (b) *(Freemasonry)* **M.** la masonería

masque [mɑːsk] *n Theat* = espectáculo teatral representado durante los siglos XVI y XVII

masquerade [mæskə'reɪd] **1** *n* (a) *(pretence)* mascarada *f* (b) *US (masked ball)* baile *m* de máscaras

2 *vi* **to m. as** hacerse pasar por

Mass (*abbr* **Massachusetts**) Massachusetts

mass[1] [mæs] **1** *n* (a) *(large number)* sinnúmero *m*; *Fam* **I've got masses (of things) to do** tengo un montón de cosas que hacer; *Fam* **there's masses of room** hay muchísimo espacio; **in the m.** en (su) conjunto

(b) *(shapeless substance)* masa *f* ►► *Gram* ***m. noun*** nombre *m* incontable (de sustancia)

(c) *Pol* **the masses** las masas

(d) *Phys* masa *f* ►► ***m. number*** número *m* másico; ***m. spectrograph*** espectrógrafo *m* de masas; ***m. spectrometer*** espectrómetro *m* de masas

2 *adj (communication)* de masas; *(education)* para todos; *(resignation, starvation, suicide)* en masa; **this product will appeal to a m. audience** este producto tendrá aceptación entre el gran público ►► ***m. extinction*** extinción *f* masiva; ***m. grave*** fosa *f* común; ***m. hysteria*** histeria *f* colectiva; ***m. market*** mercado *m* de masas; ***m. media*** medios *mpl* de comunicación (de masas); ***m. meeting*** mítin *m* multitudinario; ***m. murderer*** asesino(a) *m,f* múltiple; ***m. production*** fabricación *f* en serie, producción *f* en cadena; *Comptr* ***m. storage*** almacenamiento *m* masivo; ***m. unemployment*** desempleo *m* generalizado *or* masivo, *Am* desocupación *f* generalizada *or* masiva

3 *vt (troops)* concentrar, apelotonar

4 *vi (troops, people)* concentrarse, apelotonarse; *(clouds)* acumularse

►**mass together** **1** *vt sep* aglomerar

2 *vi* aglomerarse

mass[2] *n Rel* misa *f*; **to go to m.** ir a misa; **to say m.** decir misa; *Mus* **M. in B Minor** misa en si menor

Massachusetts [mæsə'tʃuːsɪts] *n* Massachusetts

massacre ['mæsəkə(r)] *n* **1** (a) *(slaughter)* masacre *f* ►► ***the M. of the Innocents*** la matanza de los Inocentes (b) *Fam* **it was a m.** *(in sport, election)* fue una auténtica paliza

2 *vt* (a) *(kill)* masacrar (b) *Fam* **they were massacred** *(in sport, election)* les dieron una buena paliza

massage ['mæsɑːʒ] **1** *n* masaje *m*; **a foot m.** un masaje en los pies ►► ***m. parlour*** salón *m* de masajes; *Euph* sauna *f*

2 *vt* (a) *(body, scalp)* dar un masaje a, masajear (b) *(manipulate) (data, information)* maquillar; **to m. the figures** maquillar las cifras

massed [mæst] *adj* (a) *(crowds, soldiers)* apelotonado(a); **m. bands** pandillas apelotonadas (b) *(collective)* **the m. weight of public opinion** el peso de la opinión pública en conjunto

masseter [mə'siːtə(r)] *n Anat* masetero *m*

masseur [mæ'sɜː(r)] *n* masajista *m*

masseuse [mæ'sɜːz] *n* masajista *f*

massif [mæ'siːf] *n Geol* macizo *m*

massive ['mæsɪv] *adj (structure, building, majority)* enorme, inmenso(a); *(dose, increase, explosion)* enorme; *(heart attack, stroke)* masivo(a)

massively ['mæsɪvlɪ] *adv* (a) *(bulkily)* **the mountain towered m. above the village** la enorme montaña se erguía sobre el pueblo; **m. built** enorme, inmenso(a) (b) *(extremely)* enormemente; **it was m. successful** obtuvo un éxito fabuloso; **m. over-rated** enormemente sobrevalorado

mass-market ['mæs'mɑːkət] *adj* de alto consumo

mass-produce ['mæsprə'djuːs] *vt Ind* fabricar en serie

mass-produced ['mæsprə'djuːst] *adj* producido(a) a gran escala

mast[1] [mɑːst] *n* (a) *(of ship)* mástil *m*; *Old-fashioned* **before the m.** de marinero (b) *(of radio, TV transmitter)* torre *f*

mast[2] *n (animal food)* montanera *f*

mastectomy [mæs'tektəmɪ] *n Med* mastectomía *f*

-masted ['mɑːstɪd] *suffix Naut* **three/four-m.** con tres/cuatro mástiles

master ['mɑːstə(r)] **1** *n* (a) *(of household, servants)* señor *m*; *(of slaves)* amo(a) *m*; *(of dog)* amo *m*, dueño *m*; *(of ship)* patrón *m*; **the m. of the house** el señor de la casa; **to be one's own m.** ser dueño(a) de sí mismo(a); **to be m. of the situation** ser dueño(a) de la situación ►► ***m. of ceremonies*** maestro *m* de ceremonias; *Br Law* ***M. of the Rolls*** = juez presidente de la sección civil del Tribunal de Apelación

(b) *(skilled person)* maestro(a) *m,f*; *Ironic* **he's a (past) m. at the art of avoiding work** es experto en el arte de no dar golpe ►► *Mus* ***m. class*** clase *f* magistral; ***m. of disguise*** maestro(a) *m,f* del disfraz

(c) *(instructor)* **fencing/dancing m.** maestro de esgrima/danza; **French/geography m.** profesor de francés/geografía

(d) *Univ* **M. of Arts/Science** *(degree)* máster en humanidades/ciencias; *(person)* licenciado(a) con máster en humanidades/ciencias; **m.'s (degree)** máster *m*; **she has a m.'s (degree) in economics** tiene un máster en *or* de economía

(e) *Univ (head of college)* director(ora) *m,f*

(f) *Old-fashioned (young boy)* **M. David Thomas** señorito David Thomas; **M. David** *(said by servant)* señorito David

(g) *Art* **an old m.** *(painter, painting)* un clásico de la pintura antigua

(h) **the Masters** *(golf tournament)* el Masters

(i) *US Mil* ***m. sergeant*** ≃ brigada *mf*

2 *adj* (a) *(main, principal)* principal ►► ***m. bedroom*** dormitorio *m* *or Am* cuarto *m or CAm, Col, Méx* recámara *f* principal; ***m. race*** raza *f* superior

(b) *(skilled)* **a m. thief** un ladrón astuto; **a m. spy** un espía consumado ►► ***m. builder*** maestro albañil; ***m. carpenter*** maestro carpintero

(c) *(controlling)* ***m. key*** llave *f* maestra; ***m. plan*** plan *m* maestro; ***m. switch*** interruptor *m* principal

(d) *(original)* ***m. copy*** original *m*; *Comptr* ***m. disk*** disco *m* maestro; *Comptr* ***m. file*** archivo *m* maestro

3 *vt* (a) *(control) (person, animal)* dominar; *(one's emotions)* controlar, dominar; *(situation)* dominar, controlar (b) *(learn) (language, subject, instrument)* dominar

master-at-arms ['mɑːstərət'ɑːmz] (*pl* **masters-at-arms**) *n* contramaestre *m*

masterful ['mɑːstəfʊl] *adj* (a) *(dominating)* **he was so m.** tenía tal poderío; **she was wrapped in his m. arms** sus poderosos brazos la envolvían (b) *(skilfull)* magistral, imponente

masterfully ['mɑːstəfʊlɪ] *adv* (a) *(in a dominating manner)* con poderío (b) *(skilfully)* magistralmente

masterly ['mɑːstəlɪ] *adj* magistral

mastermind ['mɑːstəmaɪnd] **1** *n* cerebro *m*

2 *vt (project, plot)* dirigir, ser el cerebro de

masterpiece ['mɑːstəpiːs] *n* obra *f* maestra

masterstroke ['mɑːstəstrəʊk] *n* golpe *m* maestro

masterwork ['mɑːstəwɜːk] *n* obra *f* maestra

mastery ['mɑːstərɪ] *n* (a) *(control) (of person, animal)* dominio *m*; **m. of a situation** dominio *or* control de una situación; **to gain m. over sth/sb** imponerse sobre algo/alguien (b) *(of language, subject, instrument)* dominio *m*

masthead ['mɑːsthed] *n* (a) *Naut* tope *m* (b) *Journ* cabecera *f*

mastic ['mæstɪk] *n* (a) *(gum)* mástique *m* (b) *Constr (putty)* masilla *f*

masticate ['mæstɪkeɪt] *Formal* **1** *vt* masticar

2 *vi* masticar

mastication [mæstɪ'keɪʃən] *n* masticación *f*

mastiff ['mæstɪf] *n* mastín *m*

mastitis [mæs'taɪtɪs] *n Med* mastitis *f inv*

mastodon ['mæstədɒn] *n* mastodonte *m*

mastoid ['mæstɔɪd] *Anat* **1** *n* mastoides *m inv*

2 *adj* ***m. process*** mastoides *m inv*

mastoiditis [mæstɔɪ'daɪtɪs] *n Anat* mastoiditis *f inv*

masturbate ['mæstəbeɪt] **1** *vt* masturbar

2 *vi* masturbarse

masturbation [mæstə'beɪʃən] *n* masturbación *f*; *Fig Pej* **mental m.** onanismo mental

mat [mæt] **1** *n* (a) *(on floor)* alfombrilla *f*; *(at door)* felpudo *m* (b) *(to protect surface)* **(table) m.** salvamanteles *m inv*; **(drink) m.** posavasos *m inv* (c) *(in gym)* colchoneta *f* (d) IDIOMS *Fam* **to be on the m.** estar contra las cuerdas; *Fam* **to have sb on the m.** tener a alguien contra las cuerdas; *US Fam* **to go to the m.** tener una agarrada con alguien

2 *vt* (*pt & pp* **matted**) *(hair, fibres)* apelmazar, enredar

3 *vi (hair, fibres)* apelmazarse, enredarse

matador ['mætədɔː(r)] *n* matador *m*, diestro *m*

match[1] [mætʃ] *n* fósforo *m*, *Esp* cerilla *f*, *Am* cerillo *m*; **a box/book of matches** una caja/un librillo de fósforos *or Esp* cerillas *or Am* cerillos; **to light** *or* **strike a m.** encender *or* prender un fósforo *or Esp* una cerilla *or Am* un cerillo; **to put a m. to sth** prender fuego a algo *(con un fósforo)*

match[2] **1** *n* **(a)** *(in sport)* partido *m*; *(in boxing)* combate *m*; **a rugby/cricket m.** un partido de rugby/críquet ►► ***m. play*** *(in golf)* match-play *m*, juego *m* por hoyos; ***m. point*** *(in tennis)* punto *m* de partido
(b) *(in design, colour) (in suitable colour, design)* combinación *f*; **it's difficult to find a m. for something in green** es difícil encontrar algo que haga juego con el verde; **this paint's not quite a perfect m. with the old stuff** esta pintura no es exactamente igual que la vieja; **they're a good m.** *(clothes)* pegan, combinan bien
(c) *(in ability)* **to be a m. for sth/sb** estar a la altura de algo/alguien; **to be no m. for sb** no ser rival para alguien; **they were more than a m. for us** eran muy superiores a nosotros; **he had met his m.** había encontrado la horma de su zapato
(d) *(marriage)* **to make a good m.** casarse bien; **he would be a good m.** sería un buen partido
2 *vt* **(a)** *(equal in quality, performance)* igualar, llegar a la altura de; **his arrogance is matched only by that of his father** a arrogante sólo lo iguala su padre; **this restaurant can't be matched for quality** este restaurante no tiene rival en cuanto a calidad; **we can't m. their prices** no podemos igualar sus precios; **to m. an offer** igualar una oferta; **to be well matched** *(teams, players)* estar muy igualados(as)
(b) *(pair up)* emparejar; **m. the names to the faces** poner nombres a las caras; **to be a well matched couple** hacer buena pareja
(c) *(as rival)* **to m. sb against sb** enfrentar a alguien con alguien; **m. your skill against the experts** mide tu habilidad con los expertos
(d) *(go with) (of colours, clothes)* hacer juego con, combinar con; *(of description, account)* coincidir con; **his jacket doesn't m. his trousers** su chaqueta no combina con los pantalones; **the music didn't m. her mood** la música no iba con su estado de ánimo
(e) *(satisfy, be appropriate to)* **we have the facilities to m. your needs** tenemos las instalaciones para satisfacer sus necesidades; **we have kitchens to m. every budget** tenemos cocinas para todos los presupuestos *or* bolsillos
3 *vi (colours, clothes)* hacer juego, combinar; *(descriptions, stories)* coincidir, casar; **none of the glasses matched** no había dos vasos iguales; **a sofa with armchairs to m.** un sofá con sillones a juego

►**match up** **1** *vt sep (colours, clothes)* hacer juego con, combinar con
2 *vi (clothes, colours)* hacer juego, combinar; *(explanations)* coincidir; **to m. up to sb's expectations** estar a la altura de las expectativas de alguien

matchboard ['mætʃbɔːd] *n* tabla *f* machiembrada

matchbook ['mætʃbʊk] *n* librito *m* de *Esp* cerillas *or Am* cerillos

matchbox ['mætʃbɒks] *n* caja *f* de *Esp* cerillas *or Am* cerillos

match-fit ['mætʃfɪt] *adj Br (player)* en condiciones de jugar

match-fixing ['mætʃ'fɪksɪŋ] *n Br* **they were accused of m.** los acusaron de amañar partidos

matching ['mætʃɪŋ] *adj* a juego; **a blue suit with a m. tie** un traje azul con corbata a juego

matchless ['mætʃlɪs] *adj* sin par, sin igual

matchmaker ['mætʃmeɪkə(r)] *n* **(a)** *(arranger of marriages)* casamentero(a) *m,f* **(b)** *(manufacturer)* fabricante *mf* de *Esp* cerillas *or Am* cerillos

matchmaking ['mætʃmeɪkɪŋ] *n* alcahueteo *m*; **m. was her favourite hobby** le encantaba hacer de casamentera *or* alcahuetear

matchstick ['mætʃstɪk] *n Esp* cerilla *f*, *Am* cerillo *m*; **to have m. legs** tener las piernas como palillos ►► ***m. man*** *or* ***figure*** monigote *m (dibujo hecho con palotes)*

matchwood ['mætʃwʊd] *n* **to reduce sth to m.** hacer astillas algo

mate[1] [meɪt] **1** *n* **(a)** *(male animal)* macho *m*; *(female animal)* hembra *f*; *(person)* pareja *f*
(b) *Br, Austr Fam (friend)* amigo(a) *mf*, *Esp* colega *mf*, *Méx* cuate *mf*
(c) *Br, Austr Fam (form of address) Esp* colega *m*, *Esp* tío *m*, *Andes, CAm, Carib, Méx* mano *m*, *RP* flaco *m*
(d) *(assistant)* ayudante *mf*; **plumber's m.** ayudante de fontanero
(e) *(on ship)* oficial *mf*; **(first) m.** primer oficial, segundo de a bordo; **second m.** segundo oficial
2 *vt (animals)* aparear
3 *vi (animals)* aparearse

mate[2] *(in chess)* **1** *n* jaque *m* mate
2 *vt* dar jaque mate a

mater ['meɪtə(r)] *n Br Old-fashioned or Hum* **(the) m.** madre

material [mə'tɪərɪəl] **1** *n* **(a)** *(for construction, manufacture)* material *m*; **building materials** material de construcción
(b) *(ideas, data) (for book)* documentación *f*, material *m*
(c) *(for act)* **she writes all her own m.** *(singer, musician)* ella sola compone toda su música; *(comedian)* prepara sus propios guiones
(d) *(cloth)* tela *f*, tejido *m*
(e) *(equipment)* **cleaning materials** productos de limpieza; **reading m.** (material de) lectura, lecturas; **writing materials** objetos de papelería *or* escritorio
(f) *(suitable person or persons)* **he isn't officer m.** no tiene madera de oficial; **he's not university m.** no está hecho para ir a la universidad
2 *adj* **(a)** *(physical)* material; **the m. world** el mundo material **(b)** *(important, significant)* sustancial, relevante; **of m. benefit** de gran provecho; **the point is m. to my argument** es un punto pertinente para mi razonamiento **(c)** *Law (evidence)* sustancial; *(witness)* esencial, importante

materialism [mə'tɪərɪəlɪzəm] *n* materialismo *m*

materialist [mə'tɪərɪəlɪst] **1** *n* **(a)** *(acquisitive person)* materialista *mf* **(b)** *Phil* materialista *mf*
2 *adj* **(a)** *(acquisitive)* materialista **(b)** *Phil* materialista

materialistic [mətɪərɪə'lɪstɪk] *adj* materialista

materialize [mə'tɪərɪəlaɪz] *vi* **(a)** *(hope, something promised)* materializarse **(b)** *(spirit)* aparecer

materially [mə'tɪərɪəlɪ] *adv* **(a)** *(in money, goods)* materialmente **(b)** *(appreciably)* sustancialmente

matériel [mətɪərɪ'el] *n Mil* pertrechos *mpl*

maternal [mə'tɜːnəl] *adj* **(a)** *(feelings, instinct, love)* maternal **(b)** *(relative, genes)* materno(a); **m. grandfather** abuelo materno

maternity [mə'tɜːnɪtɪ] *n* maternidad *f* ►► ***m. dress*** vestido *m* premamá; ***m. hospital*** (hospital *m* de) maternidad *f*; ***m. leave*** baja *f* por maternidad; ***m. ward*** pabellón *m* de maternidad

mateship ['meɪtʃɪp] *n Austr Fam* camaradería *f* entre hombres

matey ['meɪtɪ] *Br Fam* **1** *n (form of address) Esp* colega *m*, *Esp* tío *m*, *Andes, CAm, Carib, Méx* mano *m*, *RP* flaco *m*
2 *adj* **he's been very m. with the boss recently** se ha hecho muy amigo *or Esp* colega del jefe últimamente

math [mæθ] *n US* matemáticas *fpl* ►► *Comptr* ***m. coprocessor*** coprocesador *m* matemático

mathematical [mæθə'mætɪkəl] *adj* matemático(a); **I haven't got a m. mind** no se me dan bien las matemáticas

mathematically [mæθə'mætɪklɪ] *adv* matemáticamente

mathematician [mæθəmə'tɪʃən] *n* matemático(a) *m,f*

mathematics [mæθə'mætɪks] *n (subject)* matemáticas *fpl*; **the m. of the problem is** *or* **are quite complex** el problema entraña una complicada aritmética

maths [mæθs] *n Br* matemáticas *fpl* ►► *Comptr* ***m. coprocessor*** coprocesador *m* matemático

matinée ['mætɪneɪ] *n* **(a)** *(of play)* función *f* de tarde; *(of film)* sesión *f* de tarde, primera sesión *f* ►► ***m. idol*** galán *m* **(b)** *Br* ***m. coat*** *or* ***jacket*** chaqueta *f* de bebé

matiness ['meɪtɪnɪs] *n Br Fam* **I found his m. rather off-putting** me molestan las confianzas que se toma con la gente

mating ['meɪtɪŋ] *n* apareamiento *m* ►► ***m. call*** llamada *f* nupcial; ***m. season*** época *f* de celo *or* apareamiento

matins ['mætɪnz] *n* **(a)** *(Roman Catholic)* maitines *mpl* **(b)** *(Episcopalian)* oficio *m* de la mañana

matriarch ['meɪtrɪɑːk] *n* matriarca *f*

matriarchal [meɪtrɪ'ɑːkəl] *adj* matriarcal

matriarchy ['meɪtrɪɑːkɪ] *n* matriarcado *m*

matric card [mə'trɪk'kɑːd] *n Br Fam Univ* carné *m* universitario

matrices *pl of* **matrix**

matricide ['mætrɪsaɪd] *n* **(a)** *(crime)* matricidio *m* **(b)** *(person)* matricida *mf*

matriculate [mə'trɪkjʊleɪt] *vi (enrol)* matricularse

matriculation [mətrɪkjʊ'leɪʃən] *n (enrolment)* matrícula *f* ►► ***m. fee*** derechos *mpl* de matrícula

matrilineal [mætrɪ'lɪnɪəl] *adj* por línea materna

matrimonial [mætrɪ'məʊnɪəl] *adj* matrimonial

matrimony ['mætrɪmənɪ] *n* matrimonio *m*; *Rel* **to be joined in holy m.** ser unidos en santo matrimonio

matrix ['meɪtrɪks] (*pl* **matrixes** ['meɪtrɪksɪz], **matrices** ['meɪtrɪsiːz]) *n* matriz *f*

matron ['meɪtrən] *n* (**a**) *(in school, orphanage)* = mujer a cargo de la enfermería; *Old-fashioned (in hospital)* enfermera *f* jefe (**b**) *(married woman)* matrona *f* ▸▸ ***m. of honour*** dama *f* de honor (**c**) *US (in prison)* directora *f*, alcaidesa *f*

matronly ['meɪtrənlɪ] *adj* (**a**) *(sedate, dignified)* matronil (**b**) *Euph (figure)* corpulento(a), robusto(a)

matt [mæt] *adj (colour, finish)* mate

matted ['mætɪd] *adj (hair)* apelmazado(a), enredado(a); **his hair was m. with blood** tenía el cabello apelmazado por la sangre

MATTER ['mætə(r)] **1** *n* (**a**) *(substance)* materia *f*; **all m. is made of atoms** toda materia está compuesta de átomos; **printed m.** impresos; **reading m.** lectura; **the subject m.** el tema; **vegetable m.** materia vegetal; **waste m.** residuos

(**b**) *(affair, issue)* asunto *m*, cuestión *f*; **military/business matters** cuestiones militares/de negocios; **that's a m. for the police** eso es asunto de la policía; **that's a m. for the boss (to decide)** le corresponde al jefe (decidir); **the m. in** *or US* **at hand** el asunto que nos concierne; **this is a m. of some concern to us** nos preocupa bastante este asunto; **a m. of conscience** una cuestión de conciencia; **a m. of life and death** una cuestión de vida o muerte; **that's a m. of opinion/taste** es una cuestión de opinión/gustos; **it's a m. of regret for me that...** siento mucho que...; **it's a m. of time** es cuestión de tiempo; **it's only a m. of time before he makes a mistake** no tardará *or Am* demorará mucho en cometer un error; **within** *or* **in a m. of hours** en cuestión de horas; **I consider the m. (to be) closed** considero cerrado el asunto; **that's a different** *or* **quite another m.** eso es otra cuestión; *Hum* **there's still the little m. of remuneration** y todavía queda el asuntillo *or RP* temita de la remuneración; **it's no easy m.** no es asunto fácil; **it's no laughing m.** no es cosa de risa; **as a m. of course** automáticamente; **as a m. of interest** por curiosidad; **we check them as a m. of policy** nuestra política es comprobarlos; **I refuse to go there as a m. of principle** me niego por principio a ir ahí; **as matters stand** tal como están las cosas; **I ought to be going and for that m. so should you** tendría que irme ya, y en realidad tú también; **he doesn't like it and nor do I for that m.** a él no le gusta y a mí de hecho tampoco; **that didn't help matters** eso no ayudó mucho; **to make matters worse** para colmo de males

(**c**) *(problem)* **what's the m.?** ¿qué pasa?; **what's the m. with you?** ¿qué (es lo que) te pasa?; **what's the m. with Ana?** ¿qué le pasa a Ana?; **what's the m. with doing that?** ¿qué tiene de malo hacer eso?; **is anything** *or* **something the m.?** ¿ocurre *or* pasa algo?; **there's something the m.** hay algo que no va bien; **there's something the m. with the aerial** hay un problema con la antena; **nothing's the m. with me** no me pasa nada

(**d**) *(with "no")* **no m.!** ¡no importa!; **no m. how hard I push** por muy fuerte que empuje; **no m. how much it costs** cueste lo que cueste; **no m. what I do** haga lo que haga; **don't tell her, no m. what** por ninguna razón del mundo se lo digas; **no m. who/where** quien/donde sea; **no m. who I ask** pregunte a quien pregunte; **no m. where I look for it** por mucho que lo busque

2 *vi* importar (**to** a); **does it really m.?** ¿de verdad importa?; **nothing else matters** lo demás no importa; **what matters is to do your best** lo que importa es que lo hagas lo mejor que puedas; **what does it m. if...?** ¿qué importa si...?; **it doesn't m.** no importa; **it doesn't m. to me/her** no me/le importa; **it doesn't m. what you do, he always complains** hagas lo que hagas, siempre se queja

3 as a matter of fact *adv* **as a m. of fact, I've never met her** de hecho *or* en realidad, no la conozco; **I don't suppose you liked it – as a m. of fact, I did** supongo que no te gustó – pues mira por dónde *or RP* ¿sabés que sí?, sí que me gustó

Matterhorn ['mætəhɔːn] *n* **the M.** el Cervino

matter-of-fact ['mætərə'fækt] *adj (tone, voice)* pragmático(a); **he was very m. about it** se lo tomó como si tal cosa

matter-of-factly ['mætərəv'fæktlɪ] *adv* impasiblemente, fríamente

Matthew ['mæθjuː] *pr n* **Saint M.** san Mateo

matting ['mætɪŋ] *n* estera *f*

mattock ['mætək] *n Agr* azadón *m*

mattress ['mætrɪs] *n* colchón *m*

maturation [mætjʊ'reɪʃən] *n* maduración *f*

mature [mə'tjʊə(r)] **1** *adj* (**a**) *(in age) (person)* maduro(a); *(animal)* adulto(a), plenamente desarrollado(a); **a man of m. years** un hombre de edad madura; *Br Euph* **would suit a m. person** *(in job advertisement)* conveniente para una persona madura ▸▸ *Br Univ* ***m. student*** ≃ estudiante *mf* mayor de veinticinco años

(**b**) *(in attitude)* maduro(a); **to be m. for one's age** *or* **years** ser maduro(a) para su edad; **on m. reflection** tras reflexionar cuidadosamente

(**c**) *(wine)* de crianza; *(cheese)* curado(a)

(**d**) *Fin (insurance policy, bond)* vencido(a)

2 *vt* madurar; *(wine)* criar

3 *vi* (**a**) *(in age) (person)* madurar; *(animal)* llegar a la madurez, desarrollarse; **she had matured into a sophisticated young woman** al madurar se convirtió en una joven muy sofisticada

(**b**) *(in attitude)* madurar

(**c**) *Fig (plan)* madurar

(**d**) *(wine, spirits)* envejecer, criarse; *(cheese)* madurar, curarse

(**e**) *Fin (insurance policy, bond)* vencer

maturely [mə'tjʊəlɪ] *adv* como un/una adulto(a)

maturity [mə'tjʊərɪtɪ] *n* (**a**) *(in age) (of person, animal)* madurez *f*; **to reach m.** llegar a la madurez (**b**) *(in attitude)* madurez *f*; **she lacks m.** le hace falta madurar (**c**) *(of wine)* crianza *f*; *(of cheese)* maduración *f*, curación *f* (**d**) *Fin* **(date of) m.** vencimiento *m* ▸▸ ***m. value*** valor *m* al vencimiento

matzo(h) ['mætsəʊ] *n* matzá *mf*, pan *m* ácimo ▸▸ ***m. ball*** = pan ácimo que se toma en ciertas celebraciones judías

maudlin ['mɔːdlɪn] *adj* lacrimoso(a); **to be m.** estar lacrimoso(a)

maul [mɔːl] **1** *n (in rugby)* maul *m*

2 *vt* (**a**) *(attack) (of animal, person)* acometer; **he was mauled by a tiger** fue gravemente herido por un tigre (**b**) *(criticize)* vituperar; **the book was mauled by the critics** los críticos destrozaron el libro (**c**) *Fam (sexually) (grope)* sobar

3 *vi* (**a**) *(fight)* pelearse (**b**) *(in rugby)* disputar un maul

mauling ['mɔːlɪŋ] *n* (**a**) **to get a m.** *(from a lion)* quedar malherido(a) (**b**) *Fam* **they got a m.** *(by enemy troops, opposing team, critics)* les dieron una paliza

maunder ['mɔːndə(r)] *vi* (**a**) *(in speech)* **to m. (on)** divagar (**b**) *(idle about)* **to m. (about)** holgazanear

Maundy ['mɔːndɪ] *n* ***M. money*** = monedas de plata que la monarquía distribuye el Jueves Santo; ***M. Thursday*** Jueves Santo

Mauritania [mɒrɪ'teɪnɪə] *n* Mauritania

Mauritanian [mɒrɪ'teɪnɪən] **1** *n* mauritano(a) *m,f*

2 *adj* mauritano(a)

Mauritian [mə'rɪʃən] **1** *n* mauriciano(a) *m,f*

2 *adj* mauriciano(a)

Mauritius [mə'rɪʃəs] *n* Mauricio

mausoleum [mɔːsə'liːəm] (*pl* **mausoleums, mausolea** [mɔːsə'liːə]) *n* mausoleo *m*

mauve [məʊv] **1** *n* malva *m*

2 *adj* malva

maven ['meɪvən] *n US Fam* entendido(a) *m,f*

maverick ['mævərɪk] **1** *n* (**a**) *(person)* inconformista *mf*, disidente *mf* (**b**) *US (stray animal)* orejano(a) *m,f*

2 *adj* inconformista, disidente

maw [mɔː] *n Literary* (**a**) *(of animal)* fauces *fpl* (**b**) *Fig (of person)* fauces *fpl*

mawkish ['mɔːkɪʃ] *adj Pej* empalagoso(a)

mawkishly ['mɔːkɪʃlɪ] *adv* empalagosamente

mawkishness ['mɔːkɪʃnɪs] *n* empalago *m*

max [mæks] (*abbr* **maximum**) **1** *abbr* máx.

2 *n US Fam* **to the m.** *(totally)* a más no poder; **did you have a good time? – to the m.!** ¿te lo pasaste bien? – ¡a más no poder!

3 *adv (at the most)* como máximo; **it'll take three days m.** tardará *or Am* demorará como máximo tres días

4 *vt US Fam* **to m. an exam** ≃ sacar un sobresaliente

▸**max out 1** *vt sep* **to m. out one's credit card** llegar al límite de la tarjeta de crédito

2 *vi US Fam* **to m. out on chocolate/booze** pasarse con el chocolate/la bebida

maxi ['mæksɪ] **1** *n* **m. (skirt)** maxifalda *f*, falda *f*, *RP* pollera *f* larga

2 *adj* (**a**) *(skirt, coat)* maxi, largo(a) (**b**) *(package)* grande

maxilla [mæk'sɪlə] *n Anat & Zool* (**a**) *(of mammal)* maxilar *m* (**b**) *(of insect)* mandíbula *f*

maxim ['mæksɪm] *n* máxima *f*

maxima *pl of* **maximum**

maximal ['mæksɪməl] *adj* máximo(a)

maximization [mæksɪmaɪ'zeɪʃən] *n* maximización *f*

maximize ['mæksɪmaɪz] *vt* (**a**) *(profit, advantage, pleasure)* maximizar, elevar al máximo (**b**) *Comptr (window)* agrandar

maximum ['mæksɪməm] **1** *n* (*pl* **maxima** ['mæksɪmə]) (**a**) *(total possible)* máximo *m*; **to the m.** al máximo; **at the m.** como máximo (**b**) *(in snooker, darts)* máxima puntuación *f*

2 *adj* máximo(a); **to get the m. benefit (from)** sacar el máximo partido (de) ►► ***m. security prison*** cárcel *f* de máxima seguridad; ***m. speed*** velocidad *f* máxima

3 *adv* como máximo; **you can stay for two hours m.** te puedes quedar dos horas como máximo

maxi-single ['mæksɪsɪŋgəl] *n* maxi-single *m*

May [meɪ] *n* mayo *m*; **in M.** en mayo; **at the beginning/end of M.** a principios/finales de mayo; **during M.** en mayo; **in the middle of M.** a mediados de mayo; **each** *or* **every M.** todos los meses *or* cada mes de mayo; **last/next M.** el mayo pasado/próximo; **(on) the first/sixteenth of M.** el uno/dieciséis de mayo; **she was born on the 22nd M. 1953** nació el 22 de mayo de 1953 ►► ***M. beetle*** melolonta *f*; ***M. bug*** melolonta *f*; ***M. Day*** el Primero *or* Uno de Mayo; ***M. queen*** reina *f* de las fiestas *(del primero de mayo)*; ***M. tree*** espino *m* (albar)

MAY [meɪ] *v aux*

En las expresiones del apartado **(a)**, puede utilizarse **might** sin que se altere apenas el significado.

(*3rd person singular* **may**, *pt* **might** [maɪt]) **(a)** *(expressing possibility)* poder; **he m. return at any moment** puede volver de un momento a otro; **I m. tell you and I m. not** puede que te lo diga o puede que no, *RP* talvez te lo digo, talvez no; **will you tell them? – I m. (do)** ¿se lo dirás? – puede (que sí), *RP* ¿se lo vas a decir? – talvez (sí); **it m. be better to ask permission first** sería mejor pedir permiso primero; **you m. prefer to catch an earlier flight** si quiere puede tomar un vuelo anterior; **he m. have lost it** puede que lo haya perdido, puede haberlo perdido; **the reason m. never be discovered** puede *or* es posible que nunca se descubra la razón; *Formal* **it m. be worth mentioning the fact that...** cabe destacar que...; **it m. be that...** podría ser que...; **it m. well prove useful** puede que sirva; **that m. well be the case, but...** puede que sea el caso, pero...; **you m. well ask!** ¡eso quisiera saber yo!; **we m. as well go** ya puestos *or* ya que estamos, podríamos ir; **I m. as well tell you now, seeing as you'll find out soon anyway** no veo por qué no decírtelo ahora, de todas maneras te vas a enterar pronto; **shall we go? – we m. as well** ¿vamos? – bueno *or Esp* vale *or Méx* órale *or RP* dale; **I m. as well be talking to myself!** ¡es como si hablara con la pared!

(b) *Formal (be able or allowed to)* poder; **m. I borrow your pencil?** ¿me presta su lápiz?; **m. I come in? – of course you m.** ¿se puede? *or* ¿puedo pasar *or Col* seguir? – por supuesto que puede; **m. I have your name?** ¿me podría decir su nombre?; **m. I ask you how much you earn?** ¿le importaría decirme cuánto gana?; **how m. I help you, madam?** ¿en qué puedo ayudarla, señora?; **you m. leave now** ya puede retirarse; **only customers m. use the car park** el estacionamiento es sólo para los clientes; **I need quiet so that I m. think** necesito silencio para poder concentrarme; **the equation m. be solved as follows** la ecuación se puede resolver de la siguiente manera; **I m. add that I would never do such a thing myself** y me gustaría añadir que yo nunca haría nada así; **I'd like to say something, if I m.** me gustaría decir algo, si me lo permite/permiten; **if I m. say so** si me permite hacer una observación; **m. I?** *(when borrowing sth)* ¿me permite?

(c) *(expressing wishes, fears, purpose)* **m. she rest in peace** que en paz descanse; **m. the best man win!** ¡que gane el mejor!; **I fear you m. be right** me temo que tengas razón; **they work long hours so their children m. have a better future** trabajan mucho para que sus hijos tengan un futuro mejor

(d) *(conceding a fact)* **he m. be very rich, but I still don't like him** tendrá mucho dinero, pero sigue sin caerme bien; **you m. think this seems stupid, but...** te puede parecer estúpido, pero...; **whatever you m. say** digas lo que digas; **be that as it m., that's as m. be** en cualquier caso

Maya ['maɪə], **Mayan** ['maɪən] 1 *n* **(a)** *(person)* maya *mf* **(b)** *(language)* maya *m*

2 *adj* maya

maybe ['meɪbi:] 1 *adv* quizá(s), tal vez; **m. she won't accept** quizá no acepte; **I may do it but then again, m. I won't** tal vez lo haga o tal vez no; **m. not/so** quizá(s) no/sí

2 *n Fam* **I don't want any maybes** no me vengas con quizá sí quizá no

Mayday ['meɪdeɪ] *n Av Naut (distress signal)* SOS *m*, señal *f* de socorro; **M.!** ¡SOS!

mayflower ['meɪflaʊə(r)] *n* **(a)** *(flower)* flor *f* del espino **(b)** *US Hist* **the M.** el Mayflower

mayfly ['meɪflaɪ] *n* efímera *f*

mayhem ['meɪhem] *n* **(a)** *(uproar, disorder)* caos *m inv*; **it was absolute m. in that office** la oficina era un verdadero caos; **to create** *or* **cause m.** provocar el caos, alborotar **(b)** *US Law* mutilación *f* criminal

mayn't [meɪnt] = **may not**

mayo ['meɪəʊ] *n US Fam* mayonesa *f*, *Méx, RP* mayo *m*

mayonnaise [meɪə'neɪz] *n* mayonesa *f*

mayor ['meə(r)] *n* alcalde *m*

mayoral ['meərəl] *adj* del alcalde; **m. election** elecciones a la alcaldía

mayoralty ['meərəltɪ] *n* alcaldía *f*

mayoress ['meəres] *n* alcaldesa *f*

maypole ['meɪpəʊl] *n* mayo *m (poste)*

may've ['meɪəv] = **may have**

maze [meɪz] *n also Fig* laberinto *m*; **a m. of streets/lanes** un laberinto de calles/callejones

mazurka [mə'zɜ:kə] *n* mazurca *f*

MB **(a)** *Comptr* (*abbr* **megabyte**) MB **(b)** (*abbr* **Manitoba**) Manitoba

Mb *Comptr* (*abbr* **megabit**) Mb

MBA [embi:'eɪ] *n Univ* (*abbr* **Master of Business Administration**) MBA *m*, máster *m* en administración de empresas

MBE [embi:'i:] *n* (*abbr* **Member of the Order of the British Empire**) miembro *m* de la Orden del Imperio Británico

MBO [embi:'əʊ] (*pl* **MBOs**) *n Com* (*abbr* **management buyout**) = adquisición de una empresa por sus directivos

Mbps *Comptr* (*abbr* **megabytes per second**) Mbps

MBSc [embi:es'si:] *n* (*abbr* **Master of Business Science**) máster *m* en empresariales

MC [em'si:] *n* **(a)** (*abbr* **Master of Ceremonies**) maestro *m* de ceremonias **(b)** *Br* (*abbr* **Military Cross**) = medalla al valor **(c)** *US* (*abbr* **Member of Congress**) congresista *mf*, miembro *m* del congreso

MCC [emsi:'si:] *n Br* (*abbr* **Marylebone cricket club**) = organismo británico que regula el críquet

McCarthyism [mə'kɑ:θi:ɪzəm] *n* macartismo *m*

McCarthyite [mə'kɑ:θi:aɪt] 1 *n* macartista *mf*

2 *adj* macartista

McCoy [mə'kɔɪ] *n* IDIOM *Fam* **this caviar is the real M.** este caviar es el auténtico

Mcjob [mək'dʒɒb] *n US Fam* trabajo *m* basura *inv*

MCP [emsi:'pi:] *n* (*abbr* **male chauvinist pig**) *Fam* cerdo *m* machista

MD [em'di:] *n* **(a)** *Med* (*abbr* **Doctor of Medicine**) doctor(ora) *m,f* en medicina **(b)** *Com* (*abbr* **Managing Director**) director(ora) *m,f* gerente

Md (*abbr* **Maryland**) Maryland

MDF [emdi:'ef] *n* (*abbr* **medium density fibreboard**) MDF *f*

MDMA [emdi:em'eɪ] *n* (*abbr* **methylenedioxymethamphetamine**) MDMA *f*

MDS [emdi:'es] *n* (*abbr* **Master of Dental Surgery**) máster *m* en odontología

ME [em'i:] *n* **(a)** *Med* (*abbr* **myalgic encephalomyelitis**) encefalomielitis *f inv* miálgica **(b)** (*abbr* **Maine**) Maine

me [mi:, *unstressed* mɪ] *pron* **(a)** *(object)* me; **she hates me** me odia; **help me!** ¡ayúdame!; **she forgave my brother but not ME** perdonó a mi hermano, pero no a mí; **she gave me the book** me dio el libro; **lend it (to) me** préstamelo

(b) *(after preposition)* mí; **with me** conmigo; **she's older/bigger than me** es mayor/más grande que yo

(c) *(as complement of verb "to be")* yo; **it's me!** ¡soy yo!; **it's always me who pays** siempre soy yo quien paga

(d) *(in interjections)* **who, me?** ¿quién, yo?; **silly me!** ¡qué bobo soy!

(e) IDIOMS **now I'm going to show you the real me** te voy a mostrar mi verdadero yo *or* cómo soy de verdad; **is it just me or is it cold in here?** ¿soy yo o aquí hace frío?; *Fam* **this hairstyle isn't really me** este peinado no va *or RP* pega conmigo

mead [mi:d] *n* **(a)** *(drink)* aguamiel *f* **(b)** *Literary (meadow)* dehesa *f*

meadow ['medəʊ] *n* prado *m*, pradera *f* ►► ***m. grass*** poa *f* de los prados; ***m. pipit*** bisbita *f* (común); ***m. saffron*** cólquico *m*

meadowlark ['medəʊlɑ:k] *n* pradero *m*

meadowsweet ['medəʊswi:t] *n* reina *f* de los prados

meagre, *US* **meager** ['mi:gə(r)] *adj* exiguo(a), escaso(a); **I can't live on such a m. salary** no puedo sobrevivir con un salario tan precario

meagrely, *US* **meagerly** ['mi:gəlɪ] *adv* exiguamente, escasamente

meal[1] [mi:l] *n* comida *f*; **midday m.** comida, almuerzo; **evening m.** cena; **to have a m.** comer; **go to bed as soon as you've finished your m.** ve a la cama en cuanto acabes la comida; **children need three meals a day** los niños necesitan comer tres veces al día; **they've invited us round for a m.** nos han invitado a una comida; **have a nice m.!, enjoy your m.!** que aproveche, buen provecho; IDIOM **to make a m. of sth** *(make a fuss)* hacer de algo un mundo; *(take too long)* entretenerse un montón con algo ►► ***m. ticket*** *US (voucher)* vale *m* de comida; *Fam Fig (person)* hermanita *f* de la caridad; **he thought of being related to the president as a m. ticket for life** creyó que su parentesco con el presidente le iba a dar de comer de por vida

meal[2] *n (flour)* harina *f*

mealie ['mi:lɪ] *n SAfr* mazorca *f* de maíz; **mealies** maíz *m* ►► ***m. meal*** harina *f* de maíz

meals-on-wheels ['mi:lzɒn'wi:lz] *n Br* = servicio social de comidas gratuitas a domicilio para los ancianos y enfermos

mealtime ['mi:ltaɪm] *n* hora *f* de comer; **at mealtimes** a la hora de la comida

mealworm ['mi:lwɜ:m] *n* gusano *m* de la harina

mealy ['mi:lɪ] *adj* **(a)** *(floury)* harinoso(a) **(b)** *(pale)* pálido(a)

mealy-mouthed [mi:lɪ'maʊðd] *adj Pej* evasivo(a); **to be m.** andarse con rodeos; **don't be so m.!** ve al grano, no te andes con rodeos

mean[1] [mi:n] **1** *n (average)* media *f*; **arithmetic/geometric m.** media aritmética/geométrica; **to strike a m. (between sth and sth)** alcanzar el término medio (entre algo y algo)

2 *adj (average)* medio(a)

mean[2] *adj* **(a)** *(miserly)* tacaño(a); **he's m. with his money** es muy tacaño con su dinero

(b) *(nasty)* malo(a), mezquino(a); **to be m. to sb** ser malo(a) con alguien; **that was a m. thing to do/say** hacer/decir eso estuvo muy mal *or Esp* fatal *or Am* pésimo; **I feel m. not inviting him** he sido un odioso por no haberlo invitado; **she has a m. streak** a veces tiene muy mala uva; *US Fam* **he gets m. after a few drinks** cuando bebe un poco se pone de mala uva; **a m. trick** una jugarreta; **to play a m. trick on sb** jugarle una mala pasada a alguien

(c) *(poor)* **even the meanest intelligence would perceive that...** incluso el intelecto más mediocre se percataría de que...; **she's no m. photographer** es muy buena fotógrafa; **it was no m. feat** fue una gran proeza

(d) *(shabby)* sórdido(a), miserable; **m. slums** bajos fondos

(e) *Literary (of lower rank or class)* **of m. birth** de baja extracción social

(f) *Fam (good)* genial, *Esp* guay, *Andes, CAm, Carib, Méx* chévere, *RP* macanudo(a), *Méx* padre; **he plays a m. game of pool** juega al billar de vicio; **he makes a m. curry** hace un curry de chuparse los dedos

MEAN[3] *(pt & pp* **meant** [ment]) **1** *vt* **(a)** *(signify) (of word, event)* significar, querer decir; *(of person)* querer decir; **what does the word "tacky" m.?** ¿qué significa *or* qué quiere decir la palabra "tacky"?; **it doesn't m. anything** no quiere decir *or* no significa nada; **no means no** no es no; **what do you m. (by that)?** ¿qué quieres decir (con eso)?; **you know Tom? – you m. your sister's boyfriend?** ¿conoces a Tom? – ¿te refieres al novio de tu hermana?; **(do) you m. she won't even listen?** ¿quieres decir que ni siquiera te escucha?; **what do you m., you're not coming?** ¿qué dices, (que) no vas a venir?, *RP* ¿qué es eso de que no venís?; **how do you m.?** ¿qué quieres decir?; **it's unusual, (do) you know what I m.?** es extraño, ¿sabes?; **it really annoys me – I know what you m.** me molesta mucho – te entiendo; **they're an item, if you know** *or* **see what I m.** tienen una relación sentimental, ya me entiendes; **he's not very nice – I see what you m.!** no es muy simpático *or Esp* majo – ¡ya me doy cuenta!; **see what I m.? he never listens** ¿te das cuenta?, nunca escucha; **that's what I m., we need to be careful** precisamente, hay que tener cuidado; **this is Tim, I m. Tom** éste es Tim, digo Tom; **he was furious, and I m. really furious** estaba furioso, furioso pero de verdad; **I m., they could have said thank you!** ¡bien que podrían haber dado las gracias!

(b) *(speak sincerely)* hablar en serio; **I m. it** lo digo en serio; **you don't m. it!** ¡no lo dirás en serio!; **I m. what I say** hablo en serio

(c) *(be of importance)* significar (**to** para); **it means a lot to me** significa mucho para mí; **you m. everything to me** para mí lo eres todo; **the price means nothing to him** el precio no le preocupa; **the name doesn't m. anything to me** el nombre no me dice nada

(d) *(imply, involve)* significar, suponer; **this defeat means (that) he will not qualify** esta derrota supone su eliminación; **it would m. having to give up smoking** significaría tener que dejar de fumar

(e) *(intend)* **to m. to do sth** tener (la) intención de hacer algo; **I meant to tell her** tenía la intención de decírselo; **I didn't m. to upset you** no quería disgustarte; **I upset her without meaning to** la disgusté sin querer; **I've been meaning to phone you** quería llamarte, pensé en llamarte; **I don't m. to seem ungrateful, but...** no quiero parecer desagradecido, pero...; **I m. to succeed** me he propuesto triunfar; **you were meant to call me first** se suponía que primero me tenías que telefonear; **you weren't meant to see that** no tenías que haberlo visto, se suponía que no lo ibas a ver; **it was meant to be a secret** se suponía que era un secreto; **it wasn't meant to be funny** no lo he dicho para que te rías; **I suppose it was just meant to be** me imagino que tenía que pasar; **we didn't m. you to find out** no queríamos que te enteraras; **she meant you to have this ring** quería que este anillo fuera para ti; **they m. business** van en serio; **I'm sure they m. mischief** estoy seguro de que tienen malas intenciones; **I m. him no harm** no pretendo hacerle ningún daño; **she means well** hace las cosas con buena intención; **I didn't m. any harm by what I said** no pretendía herir con lo que dije; **it was meant as a joke/compliment** pretendía ser una broma/un cumplido; **the book isn't meant for children** no es un libro para niños; **we were meant for each other** estábamos hechos el uno para el otro

(f) *(consider)* **it's meant to be a good movie** al parecer la película está bien

2 *vi US* **to m. for sb to do sth** querer que alguien haga algo

meander [mɪ'ændə(r)] **1** *n* meandro *m*

2 *vi* **(a)** *(river, road)* serpentear **(b)** *(person)* vagar, callejear; **we meandered off into the night** comenzamos a callejear en la oscuridad de la noche

meandering [mɪ'ændərɪŋ] *adj* **(a)** *(speech)* que divaga **(b)** *(river)* con meandros

meanie, meany ['mi:nɪ] *n Fam* **(a)** *(selfish)* rata *mf, Méx* codo(a) *m,f, RP* roñoso(a) *m,f* **(b)** *(unpleasant)* malvado(a) *m,f*

meaning ['mi:nɪŋ] **1** *n* significado *m*, sentido *m*; **to understand sb's m.** entender lo que alguien quiere decir; *Fam* **if you get my m.** sabes por dónde voy, ¿no?, sabes lo que quiero decir, ¿no?; **what is the m. of this word?** ¿qué significa esta palabra?; **what's the m. of this?** *(expressing indignation)* ¿qué significa esto?; **loyalty? he doesn't know the m. of the word!** ¿lealtad? ¡pero si ni siquiera sabe lo que quiere decir!; **your success gives m. to what we're doing** tus buenos resultados dan razón de ser a lo que hacemos; **this building gives a new m. to the term "skyscraper"** este edificio le da un nuevo significado al término "rascacielos"; **the m. of life** el sentido de la vida

2 *adj (look)* de inteligencia

meaningful ['mi:nɪŋfʊl] *adj* **(a)** *(comprehensible, having meaning)* con sentido; **to be m.** tener sentido; **it no longer seemed m. to her** ya no parecía tener sentido para ella

(b) *(significant) (change, improvement)* significativo(a); **the experiment produced no m. results** el experimento no arrojó resultados significativos

(c) *(expressive) (gesture)* expresivo(a), intencionado(a); **a m. look/pause** una mirada/pausa intencionada *or* cargada de significado

(d) *(profound) (experience, relationship)* profundo(a), trascendente

meaningfully ['mi:nɪŋfʊlɪ] *adv* intencionadamente; **"they left together," she said m.** "se marcharon juntos", dijo intencionadamente

meaningless ['mi:nɪŋlɪs] *adj* **(a)** *(devoid of sense) (word, question)* sin sentido; **to be m.** no tener sentido **(b)** *(futile) (life)* sin sentido; *(violence)* gratuito(a)

meanly ['mi:nlɪ] *adv* **(a)** *(in miserly fashion)* con tacañería **(b)** *(nastily)* mezquinamente, ruinmente **(c)** *(shabbily)* sórdidamente, miserablemente

meanness ['mi:nnɪs] *n* **(a)** *(miserliness)* tacañería *f* **(b)** *(nastiness)* maldad *f* **(c)** *(shabbiness)* sordidez *f*, miseria *f*

means [mi:nz] **1** *n (method)* medio *m*; **he has no m. of support** no tiene ninguna forma de sustento; **there is no m. of escape** no hay forma de escapar; **we have no m. of letting him know** no tenemos manera *or* forma de decírselo; **to use every possible m. to do sth** utilizar cualquier medio para hacer algo; **a m. to an end** un medio para conseguir un (determinado) fin; **I obtained it by illegal m.** lo conseguí ilegalmente; **by m. of** mediante, por medio de; **they communicate by m. of signs** se comunican por signos; **by all m.** *(of course)* por supuesto; **it's not by any m. the best** no es el mejor de ninguna manera; **by no (manner of) m.** de ningún modo, en absoluto; **by some m. or other** de un modo u otro ►► ***m. of production*** medios *mpl* de producción; ***m. of transport*** medio *m* de transporte

2 *npl (income, resources)* medios *mpl*; **to have the m. to do sth** tener los medios para hacer algo; **the m. at our disposal** los medios que tenemos a nuestra disposición; **a man of m.** un hombre acaudalado *or* de posibles; **I live beyond/within my m.** vivo por encima de/de acuerdo con mis posibilidades ►► ***m. test*** *(for benefits)* estimación *f* de ingresos *(para la concesión de un subsidio)*

mean-spirited ['mi:n'spɪrɪtɪd] *adj* malintencionado(a)

means-test ['mi:nz'test] *vt* **all applicants are means-tested** se comprueban los recursos económicos de todos los solicitantes

meant *pt & pp of* **mean**

meantime ['mi:ntaɪm], **meanwhile** ['mi:nwaɪl] **1** *n* **in the m.** mientras tanto; **for the m.** por el momento
2 *adv* mientras tanto

meany = **meanie**

measles ['mi:zəlz] *n* sarampión *m*; **to have (the) m.** tener (el) sarampión

measly ['mi:zlɪ] *adj Fam* ridículo(a), irrisorio(a)

measurable ['meʒərəbəl] *adj* **(a)** *(rate, change, amount)* calculable, medible **(b)** *(noticeable, significant)* apreciable, sustancial; **we've made m. progress** hemos avanzado apreciablemente *or* sustancialmente

measurably ['meʒərəblɪ] *adv (noticeably, significantly)* apreciablemente, sustancialmente

measure ['meʒə(r)] **1** *n* **(a)** *(measurement, quantity)* medida *f*; **linear/square/cubic m.** medida de longitud/área/volumen; **she poured me a generous m. of gin** me sirvió una cantidad generosa de ginebra; IDIOM **to get the m. of sb** tomar la medida a alguien; **for good m.** por añadidura; **for good m., he called me a liar** no contento con ello, me llamó *or Am* dijo mentiroso
(b) *(standard amount)* medida *f*; **weights and measures** pesas y medidas; **to give short m.** *(in weight, volume)* quedarse corto(a)
(c) *(indication, means of estimating)* indicador *m*, índice *m*; **this was a m. of how serious the situation was** esto era una muestra *or* un indicador de la gravedad de la situación
(d) *(degree)* **a m. of** cierto grado de; **there was a m. of bravado in his words** había cierta fanfarronería en sus palabras; **beyond m.** increíblemente; **she has tried my patience beyond m.** ya ha acabado con mi paciencia; **she inspired fear and respect in equal m.** inspiraba miedo y respeto en igual medida *or* a partes iguales; **in full m.** completamente; **this is in large** *or* **no small m. due to...** esto se debe en gran medida a...; **in some m.** en cierta medida, hasta cierto punto
(e) *(instrument) (container)* medida *f*; *(ruler)* regla *f*; *(tape measure)* cinta *f* métrica; **a pint m.** una medida de una pinta
(f) *(action, step)* medida *f*; **to take measures** tomar medidas; **as a precautionary m.** como medida preventiva
(g) *Archaic or Hum (dance)* baile *m*
(h) *Lit (metre)* métrica *f*
(i) *US Mus* compás *m*
2 *vt* **(a)** *(take measurement of) (distance, size, temperature)* medir; **what does the door m.?** ¿cuánto mide la puerta?; **the circle measures 50 cm in diameter** la circunferencia tiene 50 cm de diámetro; **an earthquake measuring 6.2 on the Richter scale** un terremoto de intensidad 6,2 en la escala de Richter; **the tailor measured him for the suit** el sastre le tomó medidas para el traje; **the losses were measured in millions** las pérdidas ascendieron a varios millones; IDIOM **to m. one's length** caerse de bruces
(b) *(assess) (damage, impact)* evaluar; **to m. oneself** *or* **one's strength against sb** medir sus fuerzas con alguien; *Fig* **to m. one's words** medir las palabras
3 *vi* medir

> **False friend**: The Spanish noun **mesura** is not a translation for the English word **measure**. In Spanish **mesura** means "moderation", "courtesy" or "dignity".

▸ **measure off** *vt sep* **m. off 30 cm of string** extiende 30 cm de cuerda

▸ **measure out** *vt sep* **m. out a kilo of flour** tome *or* pese un kilo de harina; **he measured out a double gin** sirvió una ginebra doble

▸ **measure up 1** *vt sep (wood)* medir; **to m. sb up for a suit** tomar las medidas a alguien para un traje; *Fig* **he measured up his opponent** midió a su adversario (con la vista)
2 *vi* dar la talla, estar a la altura; **how is he measuring up?** ¿está dando la talla?; **to m. up to sth** *(expectations, standard)* estar a la altura de algo

measured ['meʒəd] *adj* **(a)** *(distance, length) Sport* **the record over a m. mile** el récord de la milla exacta **(b)** *(careful, deliberate) (movement, step)* medido(a), pausado(a); *(tone, response)* mesurado(a), *Esp* comedido(a)

measureless ['meʒəlɪs] *adj* inconmensurable

measurement ['meʒəmənt] *n* **(a)** *(quantity, length)* medida *f*; **he took my measurements** me tomó (las) medidas; **waist/hip m.** talla *or* medida de cintura/cadera **(b)** *(action)* medición *f*

measuring ['meʒərɪŋ] *n* ***m. instrument*** instrumento *m* de medida; ***m. jug*** recipiente *m* graduado; ***m. spoon*** cuchara *f* dosificadora; ***m. tape*** cinta *f* métrica

meat [mi:t] *n* **(a)** *(food)* carne *f*; *Br* **m. and two veg** = plato tradicional consistente en carne, patatas y alguna verdura; *Fig Hum* **she doesn't have much m. on her** tiene poca chicha ▸▸ ***m. hook*** garfio *m*; ***m. loaf*** = pastel de carne picada horneado en un molde; *Fam* ***m. market*** *(nightclub)* bar *m* de ligue *or RP* para el levante; ***m. paste*** = paté barato de carne; ***m. pie*** = empanada de carne picada; *Fam* ***m. rack:*** **that club's a real m. rack** en esa discoteca se liga por un tubo; ***m. slicer*** cortadora *f* de fiambres; *Fam* ***m. wagon*** *(ambulance)* ambulancia *f*
(b) *Fig (substantial content)* miga *f*, enjundia *f*; **there's not much m. in his report** su informe no tiene mucha miga
(c) IDIOMS **it was m. and drink to them** *(it was easy for them)* fue pan comido para ellos, les resultó facilísimo; *(they enjoyed it)* era algo que les entusiasmaba; *US Fam* **this is the m. and potatoes issue** éste es el tema fundamental

meatball ['mi:tbɔ:l] *n* **(a)** *Culin* albóndiga *f* **(b)** *US Fam (person)* imbécil *mf*

meat-eater ['mi:ti:tə(r)] *n (animal)* carnívoro(a) *m,f*; **we aren't big meat-eaters** no comemos mucha carne

meat-eating ['mi:ti:tɪŋ] *adj* carnívoro(a)

meatfly ['mi:tflaɪ] *n* mosca *f* de la carne, moscarda *f*

meathead ['mi:thed] *n US Fam* **he's a m.** es más bruto que un arado *or RP* que la miércoles

meatless ['mi:tlɪs] *adj* sin carne

meatpacking ['mi:tpækɪŋ] *n US* industria *f* cárnica

meatus [mɪ'eɪtəs] *n Anat* meato *m*; **auditory m.** meato auditivo; **urinary m.** meato urinario

meaty ['mi:tɪ] *adj* **(a)** *(taste, smell)* a carne; **a m. stew** un guiso con mucha carne **(b)** *(fleshy)* carnoso(a) **(c)** *(substantial) (book, film)* con mucha miga, sustancioso(a)

mebbe, mebby ['mebɪ] *Fam* = **maybe**

Mecca ['mekə] *n* **(a)** *Rel* La Meca **(b)** *(centre of attraction)* meca *f*; **the M. of country music** la meca de la música country; **it's a M. for book lovers** es una meca para los amantes de los libros

Meccano [mə'kɑ:nəʊ] *n* mecano *m*

mechanic [mɪ'kænɪk] *n* mecánico(a) *m,f*

mechanical [mɪ'kænɪkəl] *adj* **(a)** *(device, process, failure)* mecánico(a) ▸▸ *Tech* ***m. advantage*** ventaja *f* mecánica; *Tech* ***m. drawing*** dibujo *m* mecánico; ***m. engineer*** ingeniero(a) *m,f* industrial; ***m. engineering*** ingeniería *f* industrial; *US* ***m. pencil*** portaminas *m inv*, *Am* lapicero *m*, *Urug* lápiz *m* mecánico **(b)** *(machine-like)* mecánico(a); **a m. gesture** un gesto mecánico

mechanically [mɪ'kænɪklɪ] *adv* **(a)** *(by machine)* mecánicamente; **I'm not m. minded** no se me da bien la mecánica ▸▸ ***m. recovered meat*** carne *f* obtenida mediante separación mecánica **(b)** *(unthinkingly)* mecánicamente

mechanics [mɪ'kænɪks] **1** *n* **(a)** *(science)* mecánica *f* **(b)** *(working parts)* mecanismo *m*, mecánica *f*
2 *npl Fig* **the m. of the electoral system** la mecánica del sistema electoral

mechanism ['mekənɪzəm] *n* **(a)** *(of machine)* mecanismo *m* **(b)** *(process, procedure)* mecanismo *m*, procedimiento *m*

mechanistic [mekə'nɪstɪk] *adj* mecanicista

mechanization [mekənaɪ'zeɪʃən] *n (of production, agriculture)* mecanización *f*

mechanize ['mekənaɪz] *vt* **(a)** *(production, agriculture)* mecanizar **(b)** *Mil (motorize)* motorizar, mecanizar

mechanized ['mekənaɪzd] *adj* ***m. industry*** industria *f* mecanizada; ***m. troops*** tropas *fpl* mecanizadas

meconium [mɪ'kəʊnɪəm] *n Physiol* meconio *m*

MEd [e'med] *n Univ* (*abbr* **Master of Education**) *(title)* máster *m* en Pedagogía

Med [med] *n Br Fam* **the M.** el Mediterráneo

medal ['medəl] *n* **(a)** *(prize, award)* medalla *f*; **gold/silver/bronze m.** medalla de oro/plata/bronce; *Fig* **you deserve a m. for putting up with him** te mereces una medalla por aguantarlo **(b)** *(in golf)* medal play *m inv*

medalist *US* = **medallist**

medallion [mɪ'dæljən] *n* **(a)** *(jewellery)* medallón *m* ▸▸ *Br Fam Hum* ***m. man*** = cuarentón con la camisa abierta y pecho velludo, con un medallón al cuello que trata de ligar con jovencitas **(b)** *(of beef, fish)* medallón *m*

medallist, *US* **medalist** ['medəlɪst] *n* medallista *mf*; **gold/silver/bronze m.** medallista de oro/plata/bronce

medalplay ['medəlpleɪ] *n (in golf)* medal play *m inv*

meddle ['medəl] *vi* (**a**) *(interfere)* entrometerse (**in** en); **stop meddling in my affairs!** ¡deja de entrometerte en mis asuntos! (**b**) *(tamper)* **to m. with sth** enredar con algo

meddler ['medlə(r)] *n* entrometido(a) *m,f*

meddlesome ['medəlsəm] *adj* entrometido(a)

meddling ['medlɪŋ] **1** *adj* entrometido(a)
2 *n (action)* intromisión *f*

medevac ['medɪvæk] *n Mil* = operación de evacuación médica

media ['mi:dɪə] *n* (**a**) *(TV, press)* medios *mpl* de comunicación; **he works in the m.** trabaja para los medios de comunicación; **she knows how to handle the m.** sabe cómo arreglárselas con los medios de comunicación; **the m. follow** *or* **follows her everywhere** los medios de comunicación la siguen a todas partes ►► ***m. baron*** magnate *m* de la prensa; ***m. circus*** circo *m* mediático; ***m. coverage*** cobertura *f* informativa; ***m. event*** acontecimiento *m* mediático; ***m. mogul*** magnate *m* de la prensa; ***m. studies*** ciencias *fpl* de la información; ***m. tycoon*** magnate *m* de la prensa
(**b**) *pl of* **medium**

media-conscious ['mi:dɪəkɒnʃəs] *adj* **a m. politician** un político cuidadoso en su relación con los medios de comunicación

mediaeval, mediaevalism *etc* = **medieval, medievalism** *etc*

media-friendly ['mi:dɪə'frendlɪ] *adj* **to be m.** tratar bien a los medios de comunicación

medial ['mi:dɪəl] *adj Anat & Ling* medial

median ['mi:dɪən] **1** *n* (**a**) *Math* mediana *f* (**b**) *US Aut* **m. (strip)** mediana *f*, *Col, Méx* camellón *m*
2 *adj Math* mediano(a)

mediate ['mi:dɪeɪt] **1** *vt* (**a**) *(agreement, peace)* actuar como mediador en; *(dispute)* mediar en (**b**) *(communicate)* transmitir
2 *vi* mediar (**in/between** en/entre)

mediating ['mi:dɪeɪtɪŋ] *adj* mediador(ora)

mediation [mi:dɪ'eɪʃən] *n* (**a**) *(of agreement, dispute)* mediación *f*; **to go to m.** recurrir a una mediación (**b**) *(communication)* transmisión *f*

mediator ['mi:dɪeɪtə(r)] *n* mediador(ora) *m,f*

medic ['medɪk] *n Fam* (**a**) *(doctor)* médico(a) *m,f* (**b**) *(student)* estudiante *mf* de medicina

Medicaid ['medɪkeɪd] *n (in US)* = seguro médico estatal para personas con renta baja

medical ['medɪkəl] **1** *n (physical examination)* reconocimiento *m or* examen *m* médico; **to have a m.** someterse a *or* hacerse un examen médico; **to pass/fail a m.** pasar/no pasar un reconocimiento médico
2 *adj (record, treatment, profession)* médico(a); *(book, student, school)* de medicina ►► ***m. advice*** consejo *m* médico; ***m. attention*** asistencia *f* médica; ***m. certificate*** *(confirming state of health)* certificado *m* médico; *(excusing holder from work)* justificante *m* del médico; *Mil* ***m. corps*** cuerpo *m* médico; ***m. examination*** examen *m* médico, reconocimiento *m* médico; *US* ***m. examiner*** forense *mf*, médico(a) *m,f* forense; ***M. Faculty*** facultad *f* de medicina; ***m. history*** historial *m* clínico *or* médico, historia *f* clínica; ***m. insurance*** seguro *m* médico *or* de enfermedad; ***M. Officer*** médico(a) *mf* militar; ***m. practitioner*** facultativo(a) *m,f*, médico(a) *m,f*; ***the m. profession*** la profesión médica; ***m. report*** parte *m* médico

medically ['medɪklɪ] *adv* **m. interesting** interesante médicamente; **to be m. qualified** tener titulación médica; **they examined him m.** le hicieron un examen *or* chequeo médico

medicament [mə'dɪkəmənt] *n Formal* fármaco *m*

Medicare ['medɪkeə(r)] *n* (**a**) *(in US)* = seguro médico para ancianos y algunos discapacitados (**b**) *(in Australia)* = seguro médico estatal, ≃ *Esp* seguridad *f* social

medicate ['medɪkeɪt] *vt (patient)* medicar a

medicated ['medɪkeɪtɪd] *adj* medicinal

medication [medɪ'keɪʃən] *n* medicamento *m*, medicación *f*; **to increase/reduce sb's m.** aumentar/reducir la medicación a alguien; **to be on m.** tomar medicación

medicinal [mə'dɪsɪnəl] *adj* medicinal; **for m. purposes** con fines medicinales; *Hum* **it's just for m. purposes** *(when having an alcoholic drink)* me lo tomo con fines terapéuticos

medicinally [mə'dɪsɪnəlɪ] *adv* **to use a herb/substance m.** usar una planta/substancia con fines medicinales

medicine ['medɪsɪn] *n* (**a**) *(science)* medicina *f*; **to practise m.** ejercer la medicina; **to study m.** estudiar medicina
(**b**) *(drugs)* medicina *f*, medicamento *m*; IDIOM **to give sb a taste of his own m.** pagar a alguien con su misma moneda; IDIOM **to take one's m. like a man** apechugar sin rechistar ►► ***m. ball*** balón *m* medicinal; ***m. cabinet*** (armario *m* del) botiquín *m*; ***m. man*** *(traditional healer)* hechicero *m* (de la tribu), chamán *m*

medico ['medɪkəʊ] (*pl* **medicos**) *n Fam* médico(a) *m,f*

medico- ['medɪkəʊ] *prefix* médico-; **m.-political** médico-político(a)

medieval [medɪ'i:vəl] *adj* (**a**) *(of the Middle Ages)* medieval (**b**) *Fam (primitive, old-fashioned)* primitivo(a)

medievalism [medɪ'i:vəlɪzəm] *n* medievalismo *m*

medievalist [medɪ'i:vəlɪst] *n (scholar)* medievalista *mf*

mediocre [mi:dɪ'əʊkə(r)] *adj* mediocre

mediocrity [mi:dɪ'ɒkrɪtɪ] *n* (**a**) *(quality)* mediocridad *f* (**b**) *(person)* mediocridad *f*

meditate ['medɪteɪt] **1** *vt* meditar
2 *vi* (**a**) *(spiritually)* meditar (**b**) *(reflect)* reflexionar, meditar (**on** *or* **upon** sobre)

meditation [medɪ'teɪʃən] *n* (**a**) *(spiritual)* meditación *f* (**b**) *(reflection)* reflexión *f*, meditación *f*

meditative ['medɪtətɪv] *adj (person, mood)* meditativo(a), meditabundo(a); *(film, piece of music)* reflexivo(a)

meditatively ['medɪtətɪvlɪ] *adv* pensativamente

Mediterranean [medɪtə'reɪnɪən] **1** *n* **the M.** el Mediterráneo
2 *adj* mediterráneo(a); **the M. Sea** el (mar) Mediterráneo ►► ***the M. diet*** la dieta mediterránea; ***M. gull*** gaviota *f* cabecinegra

medium ['mi:dɪəm] **1** *n* (**a**) (*pl* **media** ['mi:dɪə] *or* **mediums**) *(means of expression, communication)* medio *m*; **through the m. of the press** a través de la prensa
(**b**) (*pl* **media**) *Phys (means of transmission)* medio *m*; **sound travels through the m. of air** el sonido se propaga por el aire
(**c**) (*pl* **media**) *Biol (environment)* medio *m* (ambiente); *(for growing bacteria)* caldo *m* de cultivo; **in its natural m.** en su medio natural
(**d**) (*pl* **media**) *Art* medio *m*
(**e**) *(in spiritualism)* médium *mf*
(**f**) *(middle course)* término *m* medio; **a happy m.** un término medio
(**g**) *(size)* mediano(a) *m,f*; **available in small, m. and large** disponible en talla pequeña, mediana y grande
2 *adj* medio(a); **of m. height** de estatura mediana; **in the m. term** a medio plazo; **m. dry** *(wine)* semiseco(a); *Culin* **m. rare** poco hecho(a) ►► *Br Rad* ***m. wave*** onda *f* media

medium-dated ['mi:dɪəm'deɪtɪd] *adj Fin (securities)* a medio plazo

medium-range ['mi:dɪəm'reɪndʒ] *adj (missile)* de medio alcance; **m. (weather) forecast** previsión meteorológica a medio plazo

medium-sized ['mi:dɪəm'saɪzd] *adj* mediano(a)

medium-term ['mi:dɪəm'tɜ:m] *adj* a medio plazo

medium-wave ['mi:dɪəm'weɪv] *adj* de onda media

medlar ['medlə(r)] *n (fruit, tree)* níspero *m*

medley ['medlɪ] *n* (**a**) *(mixture)* mezcla *f* (**b**) *Mus* popurrí *m* (**c**) *(in swimming)* estilos *mpl*; **the 200m medley** los 200 m estilos

medulla [me'dʌlə] *n* (**a**) *Anat (part of organ, structure)* médula *f*; **m. (oblongata)** bulbo *m* raquídeo, médula oblongada (**b**) *Bot* médula *f*

medusa [mə'dju:sə] *n* (**a**) *(jellyfish)* medusa *f* (**b**) *(mythical monster)* medusa *f*

meek [mi:k] *adj* manso(a), dócil; **to be m. and mild** ser manso(a) como un corderito

meekly ['mi:klɪ] *adv* dócilmente

meekness ['mi:knɪs] *n* docilidad *f*

meerkat ['mɪəkæt] *n* suricata *f*

meerschaum ['mɪəʃəm] *n* (**a**) *(mineral)* espuma *f* de mar, sepiolita *f* (**b**) *(pipe)* pipa *f* de espuma de mar

MEET [mi:t] (*pt & pp* **met** [met]) **1** *n (sports event)* encuentro *m*; *(in athletics)* reunión *f* atlética; *Br (fox hunt)* cacería *f* de zorros
2 *vt* (**a**) *(encounter) (by accident)* encontrar, encontrarse con; *(by arrangement)* encontrarse con, reunirse con; **m. me at six outside the station** nos vemos a las seis delante *or* en la puerta de la estación; **to m. sb in the street** encontrarse con alguien en la calle; **to arrange to m. sb** quedar con alguien; **to go to m. sb** ir a encontrarse con alguien; **to m. sb at the station** ir a buscar a alguien a la estación; **we're being met at the airport** nos vienen *or* van a buscar al aeropuerto; **to m. sb for lunch** quedar con alguien para comer, *Am* quedar de almorzar con alguien
(**b**) *(become acquainted with)* conocer; **m. Mr Jones** le presento al señor Jones; **have you met my husband?** ¿conoces a mi marido?; **haven't I met you somewhere before?** ¿no nos hemos visto antes en alguna parte?; **pleased** *or* **nice to m. you,** *US* **nice meeting you** encantado de conocerte/conocerlo

(c) *(in competition, battle)* enfrentarse a
(d) *(intercept, intersect)* unirse con, juntarse con; **where East meets West** donde se encuentran el Oriente y el Occidente; **his lips met hers** sus labios se fundieron en un beso; **his eyes met mine** nuestras miradas se encontraron; **I couldn't m. her eye** no me atrevía a mirarla a la cara
(e) *(satisfy) (demand, need, condition)* satisfacer; *(objection, criticism)* responder a; *(cost, expense)* cubrir; *(order)* servir, cumplir; *(obligations, target)* cumplir con; *(challenge)* estar a la altura de; **to m. a deadline** cumplir (con) un plazo
(f) *(encounter) (danger, difficulties)* encontrar, encontrarse con; **a remarkable sight met our eyes** nos topamos con una vista extraordinaria; **there's more to this than meets the eye** es más complicado de lo que parece; **to m. one's death** encontrar la muerte
3 *vi* (a) *(by accident)* encontrarse; *(by arrangement)* quedar, encontrarse (**with** con); **where shall we m.?** ¿dónde quedamos?; **shall we m. on Monday?** ¿quedamos el lunes?, *RP* ¿quedamos para el lunes?; **let's m. for lunch** quedemos para comer
(b) *(become acquainted)* conocerse; **I don't think we've met (before)** creo que no nos conocemos
(c) *(in competition, battle)* enfrentarse, encontrarse
(d) *(society, assembly)* reunirse; **the club meets every Tuesday** el club se reúne todos los martes
(e) *(intersect) (rivers, roads, continents)* encontrarse, unirse; **our eyes met** nuestras miradas se encontraron
(f) *(come into contact)* **their lips met** sus labios se encontraron; **the two trains met head on** los dos trenes chocaron de frente

▸**meet up** *vi* (a) *(by arrangement)* encontrarse, quedar (**with** con); **to m. up (with sb) for lunch** quedar (con alguien) para comer
(b) *(intersect) (rivers, roads)* encontrarse, unirse

▸**meet with** *vt insep* (a) *(danger, difficulty)* encontrarse con; *(success)* tener; *(accident)* sufrir; **the plan met with failure** el plan resultó un fracaso *or* fracasó; **to m. with refusal/approval** ser recibido(a) con rechazo/aprobación; **his arrival was met with jeers by the crowd** la multitud lo recibió con abucheos
(b) *esp US (by arrangement)* encontrarse con, reunirse con

---

meeting ['mi:tɪŋ] *n* (a) *(assembly) (of committee, delegates)* reunión *f*; **she's in a m.** está en una reunión; **to call a m.** convocar una reunión; **to hold a m.** celebrar una reunión; **to open/close the m.** comenzar/terminar la reunión; **the m. voted in favour of the measure** los reunidos votaron a favor de la medida
(b) *(encounter)* encuentro *m*; *Fig* **there's a m. of minds between them on this subject** en este asunto están de acuerdo
(c) *(prearranged)* reunión *f*, cita *f*; **I have a m. with the boss this morning** tengo una reunión con el jefe esta mañana ▸▸ ***m. place*** lugar *m or* punto *m* de encuentro; ***m. point*** punto *m* de encuentro *or* reunión; ***m. room*** salón *m* de sesiones
(d) *Br Sport* mitin *m*; **athletics m.** mitin de atletismo

meeting-house ['mi:tɪŋhaʊs] *n Rel* casa *f* de reunión

meetup ['mi:tʌp] *n Comptr* quedada *f*

meg [meg] *n Comptr Fam* mega *m*

mega ['megə] *Fam* 1 *adj (excellent)* genial, *Esp* guay, *Andes, CAm, Carib, Méx* chévere, *Méx* padrísimo, *RP* bárbaro(a), *Ven* arrecho(a); *(enormous)* gigantesco(a)
2 *adv (very)* **it's m. big** es supergigantesco(a)

mega- ['megə] *prefix Fam* super-, ultra-; **m.-famous** superfamoso(a), ultrafamoso(a); **he's m.-rich** es superrico, está forrado; **m.-trendy** supermoderno(a), ultramoderno(a)

megabit ['megəbɪt] *n Comptr* megabit *m*

megabucks ['megəbʌks] *npl Fam* una millonada, *Esp* un pastón, *Méx* un chingo de dinero, *RP* una ponchada de pesos

megabyte ['megəbaɪt] *n Comptr* megabyte *m*

megacycle ['megəsaɪkəl] *n* megaciclo *m*

megadeath ['megədeθ] *n* millón *m* de muertos

megaflop ['megəflɒp] *n* (a) *Comptr* megaflop *m* (b) *Fam (disaster)* desastre *m* absoluto

megahertz ['megəhɜ:ts] *n Elec* megahercio *m*

megalith ['megəlɪθ] *n* megalito *m*

megalomania [megələʊ'meɪnɪə] *n* megalomanía *f*

megalomaniac [megələʊ'meɪnɪæk] 1 *n* megalómano(a) *m,f*
2 *adj* megalómano(a)

megalopolis [megə'lɒpəlɪs] *n* megalópolis *f inv*

megalosaur ['megələsɔ:(r)], **megalosaurus** [megələ'sɔ:rəs] *n* megalosaurio *m*

megaphone ['megəfəʊn] *n* megáfono *m*

megastar ['megəstɑ:(r)] *n Fam* superestrella *f*

megastore ['megəstɔ:(r)] *n* macrotienda *f*

megaton ['megətʌn] *n* megatón *m*

megavolt ['megəvəʊlt] *n Elec* megavoltio *m*

megawatt ['megəwɒt] *n Elec* megavatio *m*

megilla(h) [mə'gɪlə] *n US Fam* **the whole m.** todo el rollo

meiosis [maɪ'əʊsɪs] (*pl* **meioses** [maɪ'əʊsi:z]) *n* (a) *Biol* meiosis *f inv* (b) *(in rhetoric)* lítote *f*, litote *f*

melamine ['meləmi:n] *n* melamina *f*

melancholia [melən'kəʊlɪə] *n Old-fashioned* melancolía *f*, depresión *f*

melancholic [melən'kɒlɪk] *adj* melancólico(a)

melancholy ['melənkəlɪ] 1 *n* melancolía *f*
2 *adj* melancólico(a)

Melanesia [melə'ni:ʒə] *n* Melanesia

Melanesian [melə'ni:ʒən] 1 *n* (a) *(person)* melanesio(a) *m,f* (b) *(language)* melanesio *m*
2 *adj* melanesio(a)

melange [meɪ'lɑ:nʒ] *n* mezcolanza *f*

melanin ['melənɪn] *n Physiol* melanina *f*

melanoma [melə'nəʊmə] *n Med* melanoma *m*

melatonin [melə'təʊnɪn] *n Physiol* melatonina *f*

Melba ['melbə] *n* ***M. sauce*** = salsa dulce elaborada con frambuesas; ***M. toast*** pan *m* tostado, biscote *m*

meld [meld] 1 *n (mixture)* mezcla *f*, combinación *f*
2 *vt* fusionar
3 *vi* fusionarse

mêlée ['meleɪ] *n* (a) *(excited crowd)* turba *f*, enjambre *m* (b) *(fight)* riña *f*, tumulto *m*

mellifluous [mə'lɪflʊəs] *adj Formal* melifluo(a)

mellophone ['meləfəʊn] *n* corno *m* tenor

mellow ['meləʊ] 1 *adj* (a) *(flavour)* delicado(a); *(wine)* añejo(a); *(voice, colour)* suave; *(light)* tenue (b) *(person, mood)* apacible, sosegado(a); **to become** *or* **grow m.** apaciguarse, sosegarse (c) *Fam (on drugs)* **to be m.** estar puesto(a)
2 *vt (of age, experience)* serenar, sosegar
3 *vi* (a) *(flavour)* ganar (con el tiempo); *(wine)* añejarse; *(voice, light)* suavizarse (b) *(person)* sosegarse

▸**mellow out** *vi Fam (relax)* relajarse

melodeon [mɪ'ləʊdɪən] *adj* melodeón *m*, = tipo de acordeón

melodic [mɪ'lɒdɪk] *adj* melódico(a)

melodious [mɪ'ləʊdɪəs] *adj* melodioso(a) ▸▸ ***m. warbler*** zarcero *m* común

melodiously [mɪ'ləʊdɪəslɪ] *adv* melodiosamente

melodrama ['melədrɑ:mə] *n* melodrama *m*

melodramatic [melədrə'mætɪk] *adj* melodramático(a); **don't be so m.!** ¡no te pongas tan melodramático!

melodramatically [melədrə'mætɪklɪ] *adv* melodramáticamente, con melodramatismo

melodramatics [melədrə'mætɪks] *npl* escenas *fpl*, teatro *m*

melodramatize [melə'dræmətaɪz] 1 *vt* melodramatizar
2 *vi* melodramatizar

melody ['melədɪ] *n* melodía *f*

melon ['melən] *n* (a) *(honeydew)* melón *m* (b) *(watermelon)* sandía *f* (c) *very Fam* **melons** *(breasts)* melones *mpl*, *Méx* chichís *fpl*, *RP* lolas *fpl*

melt [melt] 1 *vt* (a) *(snow, chocolate, metal)* derretir, fundir (b) *(sb's resistance)* vencer; **her expression melted my heart** la expresión de su rostro me ablandó *or* desarmó
2 *vi* (a) *(snow, chocolate, metal)* derretirse, fundirse; **it melts in the mouth** se funde en la boca; *Fig* **to m. into thin air** esfumarse (b) *(sb's resistance)* disiparse; **his heart melted** se ablandó (c) *(blend)* fundir; **he melted into the crowd** se perdió entre la multitud; **the green melts into the blue** el verde se funde con el azul
3 *n (sandwich)* **tuna m.** tostada de atún y queso fundido

▸**melt away** *vi* (a) *(snow)* derretirse (b) *(disappear) (crowd)* dispersarse, disgregarse; *(objections, opposition)* disiparse, desvanecerse

▸**melt down** *vt sep (metal, scrap)* fundir

meltdown ['meltdaʊn] *n* (a) *Phys (process)* = fusión accidental del núcleo de un reactor; *(leak)* fuga *f* radiactiva (b) *(disaster)* colapso *m*; **to go into m.** hundirse

melted ['meltɪd] *adj (cheese, chocolate)* fundido(a)

melting ['meltɪŋ] *adj* (**a**) *(ice, snow)* **we walked through the m. snow** caminamos por la nieve a medio derretir ►► ***m. point*** punto *m* de fusión (**b**) *(look)* **she gave him a m. look** lo desarmó con su mirada

melting-pot ['meltɪŋpɒt] *n* crisol *m*; **a m. of several cultures** un crisol de varias culturas; **the American m.** el crisol americano

meltwater ['meltwɔːtə(r)] *n* aguas *fpl* de deshielo

member ['membə(r)] **1** *n* (**a**) *(of family, group, classification)* miembro *m*, integrante *mf*; **it's a m. of the cat family** pertenece a la familia de los felinos; **a m. of the opposite sex** una persona del sexo opuesto; **a m. of the audience** un miembro de la audiencia; **a m. of the public** un miembro *or* integrante del público

(**b**) *(affiliate) (of club, society)* socio(a) *m,f*; *(of union, party)* afiliado(a) *m,f*, militante *mf*; **to become a m.** *(of club, society)* hacerse socio(a), ingresar; *(of union, party)* afiliarse, ingresar

(**c**) *Pol US* **M. of Congress** congresista, miembro del congreso; *Br* **M. of Parliament** diputado(a); **the M. (of Parliament) for Oxford** la diputada por Oxford

(**d**) *Math* elemento *m*

(**e**) *(limb, penis)* miembro *m*

2 *adj* **m. country/state** país/estado miembro

membership ['membəʃɪp] *n* (**a**) *(state of being a member) (of club)* calidad *f* de socio; *(of party, union)* afiliación *f*; **to apply for m.** solicitar el ingreso; **to renew one's m.** *(of club)* renovar el carné de socio; *(of party, union)* renovar la afiliación; **she resigned her m.** *(of club, party, union)* se dio de baja ►► ***m. card*** carné *m* de socio/afiliado; ***m. fee*** cuota *f* de socio/afiliado; ***m. list*** listado *m* de socios/afiliados

(**b**) *(members) (of club)* socios *mpl*; *(of union, party)* afiliación *f*, afiliados(as) *m,fpl*; **a large/small m.** un elevado/escaso número de socios/afiliados; **m. increased last year** el año pasado aumentó el número de socios/afiliados; **we have a m. of about 20** tenemos unos 20 socios/afiliados

membrane ['membreɪn] *n* membrana *f*

memento [mɪ'mentəʊ] (*pl* **mementos** *or* **mementoes**) *n* recuerdo *m*

memo ['meməʊ] (*pl* **memos**) *n* memorándum *m*; *(within office)* nota *f* ►► ***m. pad*** bloc *m* de notas

memoir ['memwɑː(r)] *n* (**a**) *(biography)* biografía *f*; **she's writing her memoirs** está escribiendo sus memorias (**b**) *(essay)* memoria *f*

memoirist ['memwɑːrɪst] *n* memorialista *mf*

memorabilia [memərə'bɪlɪə] *npl* **wartime m.** objetos *mpl* de la época de la guerra; **Elvis m.** recuerdos de Elvis

memorable ['memərəbəl] *adj* memorable; **there was nothing m. about the film** la película no tenía nada especial

memorably ['memərəblɪ] *adv* **as Reagan so m. said** como dicen las memorables palabras de Reagan

memorandum [memə'rændəm] (*pl* **memorandums** *or* **memoranda** [memə'rændə]) *n* (**a**) *(business communication)* memorándum *m*; *(within office)* nota *f* (**b**) *Pol* memorándum *m* ►► ***m. of agreement*** memoria *f* de un acuerdo (**c**) *Law* ***m. of association*** escritura *f* de constitución, estatutos *mpl* sociales

memorial [mɪ'mɔːrɪəl] **1** *n (monument)* monumento *m* conmemorativo; **to serve as a m. for** conmemorar

2 *adj (statue, festival, prize)* conmemorativo(a) ►► ***M. Day*** *(in US)* = día de los caídos en la guerra; ***m. service*** funeral *m*, misa *f* de difuntos

memorization [memərar'zeɪʃən] *n* memorización *f*

memorize ['meməraɪz] *vt* memorizar

memory ['memərɪ] *n* (**a**) *(faculty)* memoria *f*; **to have a good/bad m.** tener buena/mala memoria; **I've got a terrible m. for names/faces** tengo mala memoria para los nombres/las caras; **to have a short m.** ser olvidadizo(a); **if (my) m. serves me well** *or* **right** si la memoria no me engaña; **from m.** de memoria; **to commit sth to m.** memorizar algo; **there has been famine here within living m.** aquí todavía se recuerdan épocas de hambre; IDIOM **a m. like a sieve** una memoria de mosquito; IDIOM **the m. of an elephant** una memoria de elefante ►► ***m. loss*** pérdida *f* de memoria; ***m. span*** capacidad *f* de memorización *or* retención

(**b**) *(thing remembered)* recuerdo *m*; **good/bad memories (of sth)** buenos/malos recuerdos (de algo); **my earliest memories** mis primeros recuerdos; **to have no m. of sth** no recordar algo; **to keep sb's m. alive** mantener vivo el recuerdo de alguien; **in m. of** en memoria de; **to take a trip** *or* **stroll down m. lane** volver al pasado, rememorar el pasado

(**c**) *Comptr* memoria *f* ►► ***m. address*** dirección *f* de memoria; ***m. bank*** banco *m* de memoria; ***m. card*** tarjeta *f* de memoria; ***m. management*** gestión *f* de memoria; ***m. manager*** gestor *m* de memoria; ***m. mapping*** mapeado *m* de memoria; ***m. upgrade*** ampliación *f* de memoria

memory-intensive ['memərɪɪn'tensɪv] *adj Comptr (application)* que ocupa mucha memoria

memory-resident ['memərɪ'rezɪdənt] *adj Comptr* residente en memoria

memsahib ['memsɑːɪb] *n Hist (married European woman)* = en las colonias, mujer casada europea

men *pl of* **man**

menace ['menɪs] **1** *n* (**a**) *(threat)* amenaza *f*; **an air of m.** un aire amenazante (**b**) *(danger)* peligro *m*; *Fam* **that kid's a m.** este niño es un demonio

2 *vt* amenazar

menacing ['menəsɪŋ] *adj* amenazador(ora)

menacingly ['menəsɪŋlɪ] *adv* amenazadoramente

ménage [me'nɑːʒ] *n Literary* grupo *m* ►► ***m. à trois*** ménage à trois *m*

menagerie [mɪ'nædʒərɪ] *n* colección *f* de animales *(privada)*

menarche [me'nɑːkɪ] *n Physiol* menarquía *f*

mend [mend] **1** *n (repair)* remiendo *m*; *Fam* **she's on the m.** se está recuperando

2 *vt* (**a**) *(repair) (machine, vase, garment, shoes)* arreglar (**b**) *(improve, correct)* **to m. one's manners** portarse *or* comportarse mejor; **to m. matters** arreglar las cosas; **to m. one's ways** corregirse

3 *vi (broken bone)* soldarse; *(patient)* recuperarse; *Fam* **you'll soon m.** pronto te pondrás bien

mendacious [men'deɪʃəs] *adj Formal* mendaz

mendacity [men'dæsɪtɪ] *n Formal* mendacidad *f*

mendelevium [mendɪ'liːvɪəm] *n Chem* mendelevio *m*

mender ['mendə(r)] *n Br* **my shoes are at the m.'s** mis zapatos están en el zapatero

mendicant ['mendɪkənt] **1** *n* (**a**) *(monk)* mendicante *m* (**b**) *Literary (beggar)* pordiosero(a) *m,f*, mendigo(a) *m,f*

2 *adj* mendicante; **m. order** orden mendicante

mending ['mendɪŋ] *n (clothes being mended)* remiendos *mpl*; **I was doing some m.** estaba cosiendo

menfolk ['menfəʊk] *npl* **the m.** los hombres

menhir ['menhɪə(r)] *n* menhir *m*

menial ['miːnɪəl] **1** *n Pej* lacayo(a) *m,f*

2 *adj* ingrato(a), penoso(a)

meningeal [me'nɪndʒɪəl] *adj Anat* meníngeo(a)

meninges [me'nɪndʒiːz] *npl Anat* meninges *fpl*

meningitis [menɪn'dʒaɪtɪs] *n* meningitis *f inv*

meniscus [mə'nɪskəs] *n* (**a**) *Phys* menisco *m* (**b**) *Anat* menisco *m*

menopausal [menə'pɔːzəl] *adj* (**a**) *Med* menopáusico(a) (**b**) *Fam* menopáusico(a); **she's been a bit m. recently** últimamente está algo menopáusica

menopause ['menəpɔːz] *n* menopausia *f*

menorah [mə'nɔːrə] *n Rel* candelabro *m* de siete brazos, menorá *f*

menorrhagia [menə'reɪdʒɪə] *n Med* menorragia *f*

Mensa ['mensə] *n* Mensa, = asociación internacional para personas con un alto cociente intelectual

mensch [menʃ] *n US Fam* **he's a real m.** es buena gente, *Esp* es un tío legal

menses ['mensiːz] *npl Physiol* menstruo *m*, menstruación *f*

menstrual ['menstrʊəl] *adj* menstrual ►► ***m. cycle*** ciclo *m* menstrual

menstruate ['menstrʊeɪt] *vi* tener la menstruación, menstruar

menstruation [menstrʊ'eɪʃən] *n* menstruación *f*

mensuration [menʃə'reɪʃən] *n Tech* cálculo *m* de magnitudes

menswear ['menzweə(r)] *n* ropa *f* de caballero *or* hombre; **m. (department)** departamento *m or* sección *f* de caballeros

mental ['mentəl] *adj* (**a**) *(intellectual)* mental ►► *Psy* ***m. age*** edad *f* mental; ***m. effort*** esfuerzo *m* mental

(**b**) *(in the mind)* mental; **to make a m. note of sth/to do sth** tratar de acordarse de algo/de hacer algo ►► ***m. arithmetic*** cálculo *m* mental; ***m. block*** bloqueo *m* mental; **to have a m. block about sth** tener un bloqueo mental con algo; ***m. cruelty*** malos tratos *mpl* psicológicos; ***m. image*** imagen *f* mental; ***m. reservation*** reserva *f* mental

(**c**) *(psychiatric)* mental; **to have a m. breakdown** sufrir un ataque de enajenación mental ►► ***m. deficiency*** deficiencia *f* mental; *Law* ***m. disorder*** trastorno *m* psicológico; ***m. handicap*** deficiencia *f* mental, minusvalía *f* psíquica; ***m. health*** salud *f* mental; ***m. home*** hospital *m* psiquiátrico; ***m. illness*** enfermedad *f* mental; ***m. patient*** paciente *m* psiquiátrico; ***m. retardation*** retraso *m* mental

(**d**) *Br Fam (mad)* pirado(a), *CSur* rayado(a); **to be m.** estar pirado(a) *or CSur* rayado(a); **to go m.** *(go mad)* volverse loco(a); *(lose one's temper)* subirse por las paredes, *Méx* ponerse como agua para chocolate, *RP* ponerse como loco(a); **everyone was shouting and running about, it was m.!** todo el mundo gritaba y corría de un lado para el otro, era de locos

(**e**) *Br Fam (very good)* genial, *Esp* guay, *Andes, CAm, Carib, Méx* chévere, *Méx* padrísimo(a), *RP* bárbaro(a); **it was a m. party!** fue una fiesta genial

mentality [men'tælɪtɪ] *n* mentalidad *f*

mentally ['mentəlɪ] *adv* mentalmente; **to be m. disturbed** sufrir un trastorno mental; **to be m. handicapped** ser discapacitado(a) mental, tener una minusvalía psíquica; **to be m. ill** tener una enfermedad mental

menthol ['menθɒl] *n* mentol *m* ►► ***m. cigarettes*** cigarrillos *mpl* mentolados

mentholated ['menθəleɪtɪd] *adj* mentolado(a)

mention ['menʃən] **1** *n* mención *f*; **there's no m. of it in the papers** los diarios no lo mencionan; **it got a m. in the local paper** lo mencionaron en el diario local; **to make m. of sth** hacer mención de algo; **to make no m. of sth** omitir *or* no mencionar algo; **special m. should be made of all the people behind the scenes** hemos de hacer una mención especial para los que están entre bastidores; **at the m. of food, he looked up** al oír mencionar la comida, levantó los ojos

2 *vt* mencionar; **I'll m. it to him next time I see him** se lo mencionaré la próxima vez que lo vea; **it was mentioned as a possibility** se mencionó como posibilidad; **don't m. any names** no des nombres; **she failed to m. all the help we gave her** no mencionó toda la ayuda que le proporcionamos; **I should m. that it was dark at the time** cabe decir que en aquel momento era de noche; **to m. sth in passing** mencionar algo de pasada; **to m. sb in one's will** mencionar *or* incluir a alguien en el testamento; **for reasons too numerous/trivial to m.** por razones que son demasiado numerosas/triviales para mencionarlas; **not to m....** por no mencionar...; **now that you m. it** ahora que lo dices; **don't m. it!** ¡no hay de qué!

mentionable ['menʃənəbəl] *adj* **his name is no longer m. among them** su nombre es tabú entre ellos

mentor ['mentɔ:(r)] *n (adviser)* mentor(ora) *m,f*

mentoring ['mentərɪŋ] *n Com* = sistema por el cual un trabajador experimentado instruye y aconseja a otro u otros principiantes

menu ['menju:] *n* (**a**) *(list of dishes) (at restaurant)* carta *f*, menú *m*; *(for a particular meal)* menú *m*; **on the m.** en el menú; **all restaurants have taken it off the m.** ya no lo sirve ningún restaurante (**b**) *Comptr* menú *m* ►► ***m. bar*** barra *f* de menús; ***m. item*** ítem *m* del menú

menu-driven ['menju:drɪvən] *adj Comptr* a base de menús

meow [mjaʊ] **1** *vi* maullar

2 *exclam* ¡miau!

MEP [emi:'pi:] *n Br Pol* (*abbr* **Member of the European Parliament**) eurodiputado(a) *m,f*

Merc [mɜ:k] *n Fam* Mercedes *m inv*

mercantile ['mɜ:kəntaɪl] *adj* mercantil; **a m. nation** una nación de comerciantes ►► ***m. marine*** marina *f* mercante

mercantilism [mə'kæntɪlɪzəm] *n Hist* mercantilismo *m*

mercantilist [mə'kæntɪlɪst] *Hist* **1** *n* mercantilista *mf*

2 *adj* mercantilista

mercenary ['mɜ:sɪnərɪ] **1** *n* mercenario(a) *m,f*

2 *adj* mercenario(a); **he's very m.** es un mercenario

mercerized ['mɜ:səraɪzd] *adj* mercerizado(a)

merchandise ['mɜ:tʃəndaɪz] **1** *n* mercancías *fpl*, géneros *mpl*

2 *vt* comercializar

merchandiser ['mɜ:tʃəndaɪzə(r)] *n (person)* especialista *mf* en merchandising

merchandising ['mɜ:tʃəndaɪzɪŋ] *n Com* (**a**) *(activity)* merchandising *m*, promoción *f* (**b**) *(items)* artículos *mpl* de promoción *or* promocionales

merchant ['mɜ:tʃənt] *n* (**a**) *(trader)* comerciante *mf*; **wool m.** lanero(a); **wine m.** vinatero(a) ►► ***m. bank*** banco *m* mercantil *or* de negocios; *Br* ***m. banker*** banquero(a) *(en un banco mercantil o de negocios)*; ***m. marine*** marina *f* mercante; *Br* ***m. navy*** marina *f* mercante; ***m. seaman*** marino *m* mercante; ***m. ship*** buque *m or* barco *m* mercante

(**b**) *Br Fam Pej* **gossip m.** chismoso(a), *Esp* cotilla, *Méx* hocicón(ona); **rip-off** *or* **con m.** *Esp* timador(ora), *Col, RP* cagador(ora), *Méx* trinquetero(a); **he's a speed m.** *(fast driver)* va como un bólido

merchantable ['mɜ:tʃəntəbəl] *adj* comercializable, vendible; **of m. quality** de calidad comercializable

merchantman ['mɜ:tʃəntmən] *n (ship)* buque *m or* barco *m* mercante

merciful ['mɜ:sɪfʊl] *adj* compasivo(a), clemente; **to be m. (to** *or* **towards sb)** ser compasivo(a) *or* clemente (con alguien); **her death was a m. release** la muerte le llegó como una liberación

mercifully ['mɜ:sɪfʊlɪ] *adv* (**a**) *(showing mercy)* con compasión (**b**) *(fortunately)* afortunadamente

merciless ['mɜ:sɪlɪs] *adj* despiadado(a)

mercilessly ['mɜ:sɪləslɪ] *adv* sin compasión, despiadadamente; **the rain beat down m.** la lluvia martilleaba despiadadamente

mercurial [mɜ:'kjʊərɪəl] *adj (temperament, wit)* voluble, veleidoso(a)

mercuric [mɜ:'kjʊərɪk] *adj Chem* mercúrico(a)

mercurochrome® [mɜ:'kjʊərəkrəʊm] *n* mercurocromo *m*

Mercury ['mɜ:kjʊrɪ] *n (planet, god)* Mercurio *m*

mercury ['mɜ:kjʊrɪ] *n Chem* mercurio *m*

mercy ['mɜ:sɪ] **1** *n* (**a**) *(clemency)* compasión *f*, clemencia *f*; **to have m. on sb** tener compasión *or* apiadarse de alguien; **(have) m.!** ¡tenga compasión!; **she had** *or* **showed no m.** no tuvo *or* mostró compasión; **to beg for m.** suplicar clemencia; **to be at the m. of** estar *or* quedar a merced de; **to throw oneself on sb's m.** ponerse en manos de alguien ►► ***m. dash*** viaje *m* de urgencia; ***m. killing*** eutanasia *f*; ***m. mission*** misión *f* humanitaria

(**b**) *(blessing)* suerte *f*, fortuna *f*; **we should be thankful for small mercies** habría que dar gracias de que las cosas no vayan aún peor; *Fam* **it's a m. that she didn't find out** por suerte no se enteró; *Fam* **it's a m. (that) he died when he did** fue una suerte que muriese en aquel momento

2 *exclam Old-fashioned* ¡pardiez!

mere[1] [mɪə(r)] *adj* simple, mero(a); **it's a m. formality** es una simple *or* mera formalidad; **a m. 10 percent of the candidates passed the test** tan sólo un 10 por ciento de los aspirantes superaron la prueba; **the m. mention/presence of...** la sola *or* mera mención/presencia de...; **the m. thought of it disgusts her** le repugna la mera idea; **there was the merest hint of irony in his voice** en su voz había un matiz casi imperceptible de ironía

mere[2] *n Archaic or Literary* lago *m*

merely ['mɪəlɪ] *adv* simplemente, meramente; **she m. glanced at it** simplemente le echó un vistazo; **I mention this m. to draw attention to...** lo menciono simplemente para destacar que...; **I'm m. a beginner** no soy más que un principiante; **I was m. asking!** sólo era una pregunta

meretricious [merə'trɪʃəs] *adj Formal* vacuo(a), frívolo(a)

merganser [mə'gænsə(r)] *n* serreta *f* ►► ***red-breasted m.*** serreta *f* mediana

merge [mɜ:dʒ] **1** *vt* (**a**) *(companies, organizations)* fusionar (**b**) *Comptr (files)* fusionar, unir

2 *vi* (**a**) *(rivers, roads, traffic)* confluir; *(colours)* fundirse; *(voices)* confundirse; **where the sea and sky m.** donde el mar y el cielo se confunden; **to m. into the background** perderse de vista (**b**) *(companies, banks)* fusionarse

3 *n Comptr* fusión *f* ►► ***m. codes*** códigos *mpl* de fusión

merger ['mɜ:dʒə(r)] *n Com* fusión *f*; **the two companies are holding m. talks** las dos empresas negocian una fusión

meridian [mə'rɪdɪən] *n* (**a**) *Geog* meridiano *m* (**b**) *Astron* meridiano *m*

meringue [mə'ræŋ] *n Culin* merengue *m*

merino [mə'ri:nəʊ] **1** *n* (*pl* **merinos**) *(sheep)* (oveja *f*) merina *f*; *(wool)* lana *f* merina

2 *adj* merino(a)

merit ['merɪt] **1** *n (advantage, worth)* mérito *m*, ventaja *f*; **its great m. is its simplicity** su gran ventaja radica en su simplicidad; **the merits of peace** las ventajas de la paz; **the relative merits of theatre and cinema** las relativas virtudes del teatro y del cine; **to judge sth on its (own) merits** juzgar algo por sus (propios) méritos; **he got the job on his own merits** consiguió el empleo por méritos propios; **there's no m. in that** eso no tiene ningún mérito; **promotion is on** *or* **by m. alone** el ascenso se otorga exclusivamente en función de los méritos; **in order of m.** según los méritos ►► *US* ***m. system*** = sistema de contratación y ascenso por méritos

2 *vt* merecer, *Am* ameritar; **we hardly m. a mention in the report** apenas nos mencionan en el informe *or CAm, Méx* reporte

meritocracy [merɪ'tɒkrəsɪ] *n* meritocracia *f*

meritorious [merɪ'tɔ:rɪəs] *adj Formal* meritorio(a)

Merlin ['mɜ:lɪn] *pr n* **M. (the magician** *or* **wizard)** (el mago) Merlín

merlin ['mɜ:lɪn] *n* esmerejón *m*

mermaid ['mɜ:meɪd] *n* sirena *f*

merman ['mɜːmæn] *n* = ser fantástico con cabeza y torso de hombre y cola de pescado

merrily ['merɪlɪ] *adv* (**a**) *(happily)* alegremente (**b**) *(blithely)* con indiferencia

merriment ['merɪmənt] *n* diversión *f*; **it was the cause of much m. amongst her colleagues** causó la risa entre sus compañeros; **sounds of m. came from the garden** del jardín llegaban voces de felicidad

merry ['merɪ] *adj* (**a**) *(happy)* alegre; **to make m.** festejar; **M. Christmas!** ¡Feliz Navidad!; **the more the merrier** cuantos más, mejor; **eat, drink and be m.!** comed, bebed y sed felices (**b**) *Fam (slightly drunk)* alegre, *Esp* piripi

merry-go-round ['merɪgəʊraʊnd] *n* (**a**) *(amusement)* tiovivo *m*, carrusel *m*, *RP* calesita *f* (**b**) *(whirl)* torbellino *m*

merrymaker ['merɪmeɪkə(r)] *n* festero(a) *m,f*, juerguista *mf*

merrymaking ['merɪmeɪkɪŋ] *n* jolgorio *m*

mesa ['meɪsə] *n Geol* muela *f*

mescal [me'skæl] *n* mezcal *m*

mescalin(e) ['meskəlɪn] *n* mescalina f

mesentery ['mesəntərɪ] *n Anat* mesenterio *m*

mesh [meʃ] **1** *n* (**a**) *(of net, sieve)* malla *f*, red *f*; **a fine m.** una malla fina (**b**) *(fabric)* tela *f*, malla *f*; **wire m.** tela *or* malla metálica, alambrera; **nylon m.** malla de nailon (**c**) *(network)* entramado *m*; **a m. of lies/intrigue** un entramado de mentiras/intrigas (**d**) *(of gears)* engranaje *m*; **in m.** engranado(a)

2 *vt (gears)* engranar

3 *vi* (**a**) *(gears)* engranarse (**b**) *(proposals)* estar de acuerdo; *(ideas, characters)* encajar

▸**mesh with** *vt insep* encajar con

meshug(g)a [mə'ʃʊgə] *adj US Fam* chalado(a), *Esp* grillado(a)

mesmeric [mez'merɪk] *adj (performance, voice, beauty)* cautivador(ora); *(influence, motion)* hipnotizante

mesmerize ['mezməraɪz] *vt (of performance, voice, beauty)* cautivar; **he was mesmerized by the pendulum's motion** se quedó hipnotizado mirando el péndulo

mesmerizing ['mezməraɪzɪŋ] *adj* fascinante

Mesoamerica [miːsəʊə'merɪkə] *n* Mesoamérica

Mesoamerican [miːsəʊə'merɪkən] **1** *n* mesoamericano(a) *m,f*

2 *adj* mesoamericano(a)

mesocarp ['miːsəʊkɑːp] *n Bot* mesocarpio *m*

mesocephalic [miːsəʊsə'fælɪk] *adj Med* mesocéfalo(a)

Mesolithic [miːsəʊ'lɪθɪk] **1** *n* **the M. (period)** el Mesolítico

2 *adj* mesolítico(a)

mesomorph ['mesəʊmɔːf] *n* mesomorfo(a) *m,f*

meson ['miːzɒn] *n Phys* mesón *m*

Mesopotamia [mesəpə'teɪmɪə] *n* Mesopotamia

Mesopotamian [mesəpə'teɪmɪən] **1** *n* mesopotámico(a) *m,f*

2 *adj* mesopotámico(a)

mesosphere ['mesəʊsfɪə(r)] *n (of atmosphere)* mesosfera *f*

Mesozoic [mesəʊ'zəʊɪk] **1** *n* **the M.** el mesozoico

2 *adj* mesozoico(a)

mess [mes] **1** *n* (**a**) *(untidy state)* lío *m*, desorden *m*; *(dirty state)* guarrería *f*, porquería *f*; **what a m.!** *(untidy)* ¡menudo lío *or* desorden!; *(dirty)* ¡menuda porquería *or Esp* guarrería!; **clear up this m.!** *(make tidy)* pon todo en su sitio; *(make clean)* ¡limpia esta pocilga!; **the kitchen's a m.** la cocina está toda revuelta; **my hair is a m.!** *(untidy)* ¡tengo el pelo enmarañado *or* revuelto!; **you look a m.!** ¡vas hecho un desastre!; **to be in a m.** *(room, papers)* estar todo(a) revuelto(a); **he is in a terrible m.** *(dirty)* se ha puesto perdido; *(disorganized, depressed)* está totalmente destrozado; **the cooker is (in) a horrible m.** la cocina está guarrísima; **to make a m.** *(make things untidy)* desordenar todo; *(make things dirty)* ensuciar todo, ponerlo todo perdido

(**b**) *(muddle, chaos)* desastre *m*; **to make a m. of sth** *(bungle)* hacer algo desastrosamente; **he's making a m. of his life** está destrozando su vida; **he made a m. of the travel arrangements** metió la pata con los preparativos del viaje; **his life is a m.** su vida es un desastre; **this country is in a m.!** este país está patas arriba

(**c**) *Fam (predicament)* lío *m*, follón *m*; **to be in a m.** *(person)* estar en un lío *or* follón; **he's got himself into a bit of a m.** se metió en un lío *or* aprieto; **thanks for getting me out of that m.** gracias por sacarme de aquel lío *or* follón

(**d**) *(dirt)* porquería *f*; **the dog's done a m. on the carpet** el perro ha hecho caca en la alfombra

(**e**) *Mil* cantina *f*, comedor *m* ▸▸ *Br* ***m. tin*** plato *m* de campaña *or* del rancho

(**f**) *US Fam (lot)* montón *m*; **a whole m. of things** un montón de cosas

(**g**) **a m. of pottage** *(in Bible)* un plato de lentejas

2 *vt (dirty)* ensuciar

3 *vi* (**a**) *Br Fam* **no messing!** *(honestly)* ¡fuera coña! (**b**) *Fam (dog, cat)* hacer caca (**c**) *Mil* comer *(en el comedor)*

▸**mess about, mess around** *Fam* **1** *vt sep (treat badly)* maltratar; **I'm fed up with being messed about** *or* **around by men** estoy harta de que los hombres jueguen conmigo

2 *vi* (**a**) *(fool about, waste time)* hacer el tonto *or* indio; **stop messing about** *or* **around and listen to me!** deja de hacer el tonto *or* indio y préstame atención; **they don't m. about** *or* **around, do they?** *(they're quick, direct)* ¡ésos no pierden el tiempo!

(**b**) *(pass time)* **the children were messing about** *or* **around in the garden** los niños andaban enredando *or Am* dando vueltas en el jardín; **I spent the weekend messing about** *or* **around (in) the house** pasé el fin de semana sin dar golpe *or* haciendo el vago en casa; **he likes messing about** *or* **around in the garden** le gusta perder el tiempo en el jardín

(**c**) *(tinker)* **to m. about** *or* **around with sth** enredar *or Am* dar vueltas con algo; **don't m. about** *or* **around with my CD player** no enredes con mi compact disc, no me toquetees el compact disc; **to m. about** *or* **around with sb** *(annoy, treat badly)* jugar con alguien, dar la vara a alguien; *(sexually)* enrollarse *or* liarse con alguien

▸**mess up** **1** *vt sep Fam* (**a**) *(room)* desordenar (**b**) *(hair)* revolver; **stop it, you'll m. my hair up!** ¡para ya, que me vas a enredar el pelo! (**c**) *(plan)* fastidiar, estropear

2 *vi US Fam (bungle things)* pifiarla

▸**mess with** *vt insep* (**a**) *Fam (interfere)* **to m. with sth** enredar con algo (**b**) *Fam (provoke)* **to m. with sb** meterse con alguien

message ['mesɪdʒ] *n* (**a**) *(oral, written)* mensaje *m*; **to leave a m. for sb** dejar un recado *or Am* mensaje a *or* para alguien; **can you give her a m.?** ¿le puede dar un recado?; **would you like to leave a m.?, can I take a m.?** ¿quiere dejar algún recado?; **to get one's m. across** dejar claro lo que se quiere decir, explicarse claramente; *Fam* **to get the m.** enterarse; **to stay on m.** *(politician)* mantenerse dentro de la línea del partido; **m. received and understood** mensaje recibido

(**b**) *(of book, advert)* mensaje *m*

(**c**) *Comptr (e-mail)* mensaje *m* ▸▸ ***m. body*** cuerpo *m* del mensaje; ***m. box*** ventana *f* de diálogo

(**d**) *Irish, Scot* **to do the messages** hacer la compra

messenger ['mesɪndʒə(r)] *n* mensajero(a) *m,f* ▸▸ ***m. boy*** chico *m* de los recados; ***m. service*** *(courier)* (servicio *m* de) mensajería *f*

Messiah [mɪ'saɪə] *n Rel* Mesías *m inv*

messianic [mesɪ'ænɪk] *adj* mesiánico(a)

messily ['mesɪlɪ] *adv* (**a**) *(untidily)* desordenadamente; *(dirtily)* suciamente; **to eat m.** ponerse perdido(a) comiendo (**b**) *(unpleasantly)* **to end m.** *(of relationship)* terminar mal

messiness ['mesɪnɪs] *n* (**a**) *(of room) (untidiness)* desorden *m*; *(dirtiness)* suciedad *f* (**b**) *(unpleasant complications)* complicaciones *fpl*

Messrs ['mesɜːz] *npl* (*abbr* **Messieurs**) Sres., señores *mpl*

mess-up ['mesʌp] *n Fam* lío *m*, desastre *m*; **to make a m. of sth** pifiarla con algo; **there was a m. over the dates** la pifiaron con las fechas

messy ['mesɪ] *adj* (**a**) *(dirty)* sucio(a); **to be m.** *(place)* estar sucio(a); *(person)* ser sucio(a); **don't get all m.** no te vayas a manchar *or Esp* poner perdido(a); **he's a m. eater** no sabe comer

(**b**) *(untidy) (room)* desordenado(a); *(person)* desaliñado(a); *(hair)* revuelto(a); *(appearance)* desastroso(a); *(handwriting)* malo(a)

(**c**) *(unpleasantly complex)* complicado(a), desagradable; **to get m.** ponerse feo(a); **it was a very m. business** fue un asunto desagradable; **a m. divorce** un divorcio desagradable

Met [met] *n Fam* (**a**) *US* **the M.** = la ópera metropolitana de Nueva York (**b**) *US* **the M.** = el museo metropolitano de Nueva York (**c**) *Br* **the M.** = la policía metropolitana de Londres (**d**) *Br* **the M. Office** = el servicio nacional de meteorología, *Esp* ≃ el Instituto Nacional de Meteorología

met *pt & pp of* **meet**

metabolic [metə'bɒlɪk] *adj* metabólico(a) ▸▸ ***m. rate*** tasa *f* metabólica

metabolism [mə'tæbəlɪzəm] *n* metabolismo *m*

metabolize [mə'tæbəlaɪz] *vt* metabolizar

metacarpal [metə'kɑːpəl] *n Anat* **m. (bone)** (hueso *m*) metacarpiano *m*

metacarpus [metə'kɑːpəs] *n Anat* metacarpo *m*

metal ['metəl] **1** *n* **(a)** metal *m* ►► ***m. detector*** detector *m* de metales; ***m. fatigue*** fatiga *f* del metal; ***m. polish*** abrillantador *m* de metales **(b)** *(road surfacing)* **(road) m.** grava *f*
2 *adj* metálico(a), de metal; **a m. tube** un tubo metálico *or* de metal ►► ***m. wood*** *(golf club)* madera *f* metálica
3 *vt* (*pt & pp* **metalled,** *US* **metaled)** *(road)* pavimentar con grava

metalanguage ['metəlæŋgwɪdʒ] *n* metalenguaje *m*

metaled *US* = **metalled**

metalinguistic [metəlɪŋ'gwɪstɪk] *adj* metalingüístico(a)

metalled ['metəld] *adj Br (road)* de grava

metallic [mɪ'tælɪk] *adj* **(a)** *Chem (element, compound)* metálico(a) **(b)** *(sound, voice, taste)* metálico(a); *(paint)* metalizado(a)

metallography [metə'lɒgrəfɪ] *n* metalografía *f*

metalloide ['metəlɔɪd] *n* metaloide *m*

metallurgical [metə'lɜːdʒɪkəl] *adj* metalúrgico(a)

metallurgist [me'tælədʒɪst] *n* metalúrgico(a) *m,f*

metallurgy [me'tælədʒɪ] *n* metalurgia *f*

metalwork ['metəlwɜːk] *n* **(a)** *(craft)* trabajo *m* del metal, metalistería *f* **(b)** *(articles)* objetos *mpl* de metal

metalworker ['metəlwɜːke(r)] *n* trabajador(ora) *m,f* del metal

metamorphic [metə'mɔːfɪk] *adj Geol* metamórfico(a)

metamorphism [metə'mɔːfɪzəm] *n Geol* metamorfismo *m*

metamorphose [metə'mɔːfəʊz] *vi also Fig* metamorfosearse **(into** en)

metamorphosis [metə'mɔːfəsɪs] (*pl* **metamorphoses** [metə'mɔːfəsiːz]) *n* metamorfosis *f inv*

metaphor ['metəfə(r)] *n* metáfora *f*

metaphoric(al) [metə'fɒrɪk(əl)] *adj* metafórico(a)

metaphorically [metə'fɒrɪklɪ] *adv* metafóricamente; **m. speaking** metafóricamente hablando, hablando figuradamente

metaphysical [metə'fɪzɪkəl] *adj Phil* metafísico(a) ►► ***m. poetry*** poesía *f* metafísica

metaphysician [metəfɪ'zɪʃən] *n Phil* metafísico(a) *m,f*

metaphysics [metə'fɪzɪks] *n Phil* metafísica *f*

metastasis [me'tæstəsɪs] (*pl* **metastases** [me'tæstəsiːz]) *n Med* metástasis *f inv*

metastasize [me'tæstəsaɪz] *vi Med (cancerous tumour)* **the tumour metastasized** se produjo una metástasis a partir del tumor

metatarsal [metə'tɑːsəl] *n Anat* **m. (bone)** hueso *m* metatarsiano

metatarsus [metə'tɑːsəs] *n Anat* metatarso *m*

metatheory [metə'θɪərɪ] *n* metateoría *f*

metathesis [mɪ'tæθəsɪs] (*pl* **metatheses** [mɪ'tæθəsiːz]) *n Ling* metátesis *f inv*

mete [miːt]

► **mete out** *vt sep (punishment)* imponer; *(justice)* aplicar **(to** a)

meteor ['miːtɪə(r)] *n* meteoro *m*, bólido *m* ►► *Astron* ***m. shower*** lluvia *f* de estrellas *or* de meteoritos

meteoric [miːtɪ'ɒrɪk] *adj* **(a)** *Astron* meteórico(a) **(b)** *(rapid)* meteórico(a); **a m. rise** un ascenso meteórico

meteorite ['miːtɪəraɪt] *n* meteorito *m*

meteorological [miːtɪərə'lɒdʒɪkəl] *adj* meteorológico(a); **M. Office** = servicio nacional de meteorología, *Esp* ≃ Instituto *m* Nacional de Meteorología

meteorologist [miːtɪə'rɒlədʒɪst] *n* meteorólogo(a) *m,f*

meteorology [miːtɪə'rɒlədʒɪ] *n* meteorología *f*

meter ['miːtə(r)] **1** *n* **(a)** *(measuring device)* contador *m*; **(gas/electricity) m.** contador (del gas/de la electricidad); **to feed the m.** añadir monedas al contador ►► ***m. reading*** lectura *f* del contador **(b)** **(parking) m.** parquímetro *m*; **to feed the m.** añadir monedas al parquímetro ►► *US* ***m. maid*** = agente que pone multa por estacionamiento indebido **(c)** *US* = **metre**
2 *vt* **(a)** *(electricity, water, gas)* medir con contador; **our gas is metered** tenemos un contador para el gas **(b)** *(mail)* franquear

methacrylate [mɪ'θækrɪleɪt] *n* metacrilato *m*

methadone ['meθədəʊn] *n* metadona *f*

methamphetamine [meθæm'fetəmiːn] *n* metanfetamina *f*

methane ['miːθeɪn] *n Chem* metano *m*

methanol ['meθənɒl] *n Chem* metanol *m*

methinks [miː'θɪŋks] *adv Archaic or Hum* me parece a mí

method ['meθəd] *n* **(a)** *(means, procedure)* método *m*; **m. of payment** forma *or* modalidad de pago; **experimental methods** métodos experimentales **(b)** *(organization)* método *m*; **his work lacks m.** su trabajo carece de método; **there's m. in his madness** no está tan loco como parece **(c)** *Theat & Cin* **the M.** el Método *(de Stanislavski)* ►► ***m. acting*** interpretación *f* según el método de Stanislavski

methodical [mɪ'θɒdɪkəl] *adj* metódico(a)

methodically [mɪ'θɒdɪklɪ] *adv* metódicamente

Methodism ['meθədɪzəm] *n Rel* metodismo *m*

Methodist ['meθədɪst] *Rel* **1** *n* metodista *mf*
2 *adj* metodista

methodological [meθədə'lɒdʒɪkəl] *adj* metodológico(a)

methodologically [meθədə'lɒdʒɪklɪ] *adv* metodológicamente

methodology [meθə'dɒlədʒɪ] *n* metodología *f*

meths [meθs] *n Br Fam* alcohol *m* de quemar

Methuselah [mə'θuːzələ] *pr n* Matusalén; IDIOM **to be as old as M.** ser más viejo(a) que Matusalén

methyl ['meθɪl] *n* metilo *m* ►► ***m. alcohol*** alcohol *m* metílico; ***m. group*** grupo *m* metilo

methylated spirits ['meθɪleɪtɪd'spɪrɪts] *n Br* alcohol *m* desnaturalizado *(con metanol)*, alcohol *m* de quemar

methylene ['meθɪliːn] *n Chem* metileno *m* ►► ***m. blue*** azul *m* de metileno

meticulous [mɪ'tɪkjʊləs] *adj* meticuloso(a)

meticulously [mɪ'tɪkjʊləslɪ] *adv* meticulosamente

meticulousness [mɪ'tɪkjʊləsnɪs] *n* meticulosidad *f*

métier ['metɪeɪ] *n Literary* **(a)** *(profession)* oficio *m* **(b)** *(field of expertise)* terreno *m*

metonymy [mɪ'tɒnɪmɪ] *n Ling* metonimia *f*

metre[1], *US* **meter** ['miːtə(r)] *n (of poetry)* metro *m*

metre[2], *US* **meter** *n (measurement)* metro *m*

metric ['metrɪk] *adj (system)* métrico(a); **to go m.** cambiar al sistema métrico ►► ***m. system*** sistema *m* métrico; ***m. ton*** tonelada *f* métrica

metrical ['metrɪkəl] *adj (in poetry)* métrico(a)

metricate ['metrɪkeɪt] *vt* convertir al sistema métrico

metrication [metrɪ'keɪʃən] *n (of system)* conversión *f* al sistema métrico

metro ['metrəʊ] (*pl* **metros**) *n (underground railway)* metro *m*, *RP* subte *m*

metronome ['metrənəʊm] *n Mus* metrónomo *m*

metropolis [mɪ'trɒpəlɪs] *n* metrópolis *f inv*

metropolitan [metrə'pɒlɪtən] **1** *adj* **(a)** *(of a large city)* metropolitano(a); **the M. Police** la policía de Londres **(b)** *(mainland)* metropolitano(a); **m. France/Spain** la metrópoli francesa/española **(c)** *Rel* **m. bishop** obispo metropolitano
2 *n Rel* metropolitano *m*

mettle ['metəl] *n (courage)* coraje *m*; **you'll have to be on your m.** tendrás que dar el do de pecho; **she showed *or* proved her m.** demostró de lo que era capaz; **to put sb on their m.** espolear a alguien

mettlesome ['metəlsəm] *adj Literary* brioso(a)

MeV *Phys* (*abbr* **mega-electron-volt**) MeV, megaelectronvoltio *m*

mew [mjuː] **1** *n* maullido *m*
2 *vi* maullar

mewl [mjuːl] *vi (baby)* gimotear

mews [mjuːz] *n Br (backstreet)* = plazoleta o callejuela formada por antiguos establos convertidos en viviendas o garajes ►► ***m. cottage*** = antiguo establo reconvertido en apartamento de lujo

Mexican ['meksɪkən] **1** *n* mexicano(a) *m,f*, mejicano(a) *m,f*
2 *adj* mexicano(a), mejicano(a) ►► ***M. wave*** *(in stadium)* ola *f* (mexicana)

Mexican-American ['meksɪkənə'merɪkən] **1** *n* estadounidense *mf* de origen mexicano
2 *adj* estadounidense de origen mexicano

Mexico ['meksɪkəʊ] *n* México, Méjico ►► ***M. City*** Ciudad de México

mezzanine ['metsəniːn] *n* **(a)** *(in building)* **m. (floor)** entresuelo *m*, entreplanta *f* **(b)** *Br Theat* = espacio situado bajo el escenario **(c)** *US Theat* palco *m* de platea

mezzo-soprano ['metsəʊsə'prɑːnəʊ] (*pl* **mezzo-sopranos**) *n Mus* **(a)** *(singer)* mezzo-soprano *f* **(b)** *(voice)* mezzo-soprano *m*

mezzotint ['metsəʊtɪnt] *n Art* mezzo-tinto *m*

MF [em'ef] *Rad* (*abbr* **medium frequency**) frecuencia *f* media

MFA [emef'eɪ] *n US* (*abbr* **Master of Fine Arts**) máster *m* en bellas artes

mfrs (*abbr* **manufacturers**) fabricantes *mpl*

mg [em'dʒiː] *n* (*abbr* **milligram(s)**) mg

Mgr (**a**) *Rel* (*abbr* **monsignor**) Mons. (**b**) (*abbr* **manager**) (*of bank, company, hotel*) dir.; (*of shop, bar, restaurant*) encargado(a)

MHR [emeɪtʃ'ɑː(r)] *n Austr, US* (*abbr* **Member of the House of Representatives**) congresista *mf, Am* congresal *mf*

MHz *Elec* (*abbr* **megahertz**) Mhz

MI (*abbr* **Michigan**) Michigan

mi [miː] *n Mus* mi *m*

MI5 [emaɪ'faɪv] *n* (*abbr* **Military Intelligence Section 5**) = servicio británico de contraespionaje

MI6 [emaɪ'sɪks] *n* (*abbr* **Military Intelligence Section 6**) = servicio británico de espionaje exterior

MIA [emaɪ'eɪ] *US Mil* (*abbr* **missing in action**) **1** *n* desaparecido(a) *m,f* en combate
2 *adj* desaparecido(a) en combate

miaow [mɪ'aʊ] **1** *n* maullido *m*; **m.!** ¡miau!
2 *vi* maullar

miasma [mɪ'æzmə] *n Literary* (**a**) *(foul vapour)* miasma *m*, aire *m* mefítico (**b**) *(atmosphere)* estado *m* opresivo

mica ['maɪkə] *n* mica *f*

Micawberish [mɪ'kɔːbərɪʃ] *adj* iluso(a)

mice *pl of* **mouse**

Michael ['maɪkəl] *pr n* **Saint M.** san Miguel

Michaelmas ['mɪkəlməs] *n Rel* = festividad de San Miguel, el 29 de septiembre ►► ***M. daisy*** áster *m*; *Br Univ* ***M. term*** primer trimestre *m*

Michelin® ['mɪtʃəlɪn] *n* ***M. Guide*** guía *f* Michelín; ***the M. man*** el muñeco de Michelín

Michigan ['mɪʃɪgən] *n* Michigan

Michigander ['mɪʃɪgændə(r)] *n* persona *f* de Michigan

Mick [mɪk] *n Fam* = término generalmente ofensivo para referirse a los irlandeses

mick [mɪk], **mickey** ['mɪkɪ] *n Br Fam* **to take the m. (out of sb)** tomar el pelo (a alguien); **to take the m. out of sth** burlarse de algo

Mickey Finn ['mɪkɪ'fɪn] (*pl* **Mickey Finns**) *n Fam* = bebida alcohólica en la que alguien ha echado alguna droga

Mickey Mouse ['mɪkɪ'maus] *adj Fam Pej* de tres al cuarto, de pacotilla

micra *pl of* **micron**

micro ['maɪkrəʊ] (*pl* **micros**) *n* (**a**) *Comptr Esp* microordenador *m, Am* microcomputadora *f* (**b**) *Fam (microwave oven)* microondas *m inv*

micro- ['maɪkrəʊ] *prefix* micro-

microampere ['maɪkrəʊæmpɪə(r)] *n Phys* microamperio *m*

microbe ['maɪkrəʊb] *n* microbio *m*

microbial [maɪ'krəʊbɪəl] *adj* microbiano(a)

microbiological [maɪkrəʊbaɪə'lɒdʒɪkəl] *n* microbiológico(a)

microbiologist [maɪkrəʊbaɪ'ɒlədʒɪst] *n* microbiólogo(a) *m,f*

microbiology [maɪkrəʊbaɪ'ɒlədʒɪ] *n* microbiología *f*

microchip ['maɪkrəʊtʃɪp] *n Comptr* microchip *m*

microcircuit ['maɪkrəʊsɜːkɪt] *n Elec* microcircuito *m*

microcircuitry [maɪkrəʊ'sɜːkɪtrɪ] *n* microcircuitos *mpl*

microclimate ['maɪkrəʊklaɪmət] *n Biol* microclima *m*

microcomputer ['maɪkrəʊkəm'pjuːtə(r)] *n Comptr Esp* microordenador *m, Am* microcomputadora *f*

microcomputing ['maɪkrəʊkəm'pjuːtɪŋ] *n Comptr* microinformática *f*

microcosm ['maɪkrəʊkɒzəm] *n* microcosmos *m inv*, microcosmo *m*

microcredit ['maɪkrəʊkredɪt] *n Fin* microcrédito *m*

microdot ['maɪkrəʊdɒt] *n* (**a**) *(photograph)* microfotografía *f* (**b**) *(drug)* micropunto *m*

microeconomic ['maɪkrəʊiːkə'nɒmɪk] *adj* microeconómico(a)

microeconomics ['maɪkrəʊiːkə'nɒmɪks] *n* microeconomía *f*

microelectronic ['maɪkrəʊelek'trɒnɪk] *adj* microelectrónico(a)

microelectronics ['maɪkrəʊelek'trɒnɪks] *n* microelectrónica *f*

microfiche ['maɪkrəʊfiːʃ] *n* microficha *f* ►► ***m. reader*** lector *m* de microfichas

microfilm ['maɪkrəʊfɪlm] **1** *n* microfilm *m* ►► ***m. reader*** lector *m* de microfilms
2 *vt* microfilmar

microlight ['maɪkrəlaɪt] *n (light aircraft)* ultraligero *m*

micromanage ['maɪkrəʊmænɪdʒ] *vt* supervisar hasta el último detalle de

micromesh ['maɪkrəʊmeʃ] *n (hosiery)* malla *f* extrafina

micrometer[1] [maɪ'krɒmɪtə(r)] *n (tool)* micrómetro m

micrometre, *US* **micrometer**[2] ['maɪkrəʊmiːtə(r)] *n (measurement)* micrómetro m

micron ['maɪkrɒn] (*pl* **microns** *or* **micra** [-krə]) *n Formerly* micrón *m*, micra *f*

Micronesia [maɪkrə'niːzɪə] *n* Micronesia

Micronesian [maɪkrə'niːzɪən] **1** *n* (**a**) *(person)* micronesio(a) *m,f* (**b**) *(language group)* micronesio *m*
2 *adj* micronesio(a)

micronutrient ['maɪkrəʊ'njuːtrɪənt] *n Biol* oligoelemento *m*

micro-organism ['maɪkrəʊ'ɔːrgənɪzəm] *n* microorganismo *m*

microphone ['maɪkrəfəʊn] *n* micrófono *m*

microporous [maɪkrəʊ'pɒrəs] *adj* microporoso(a)

microprocessor ['maɪkrəʊ'prəʊsesə(r)] *n Comptr* microprocesador *m*

microscope ['maɪkrəskəʊp] *n* microscopio *m*; **to look at sth under the m.** observar algo al microscopio; *Fig* observar *or* estudiar algo con lupa

microscopic [maɪkrə'skɒpɪk] *adj* microscópico(a)

microscopically [maɪkrə'skɒpɪklɪ] *adv (to examine)* microscópicamente; **m. small** microscópicamente *or* infinitamente pequeño; **a m. small organism** un organismo microscópico

microscopy [maɪ'krɒskəpɪ] *n* microscopía *f*

microsecond ['maɪkrəʊsekənd] *n* microsegundo *m*

microsurgery [maɪkrəʊ'sɜːdʒərɪ] *n* microcirugía *f*

microtome ['maɪkrəʊtəʊm] *n* microtomo *m*

microwave ['maɪkrəʊweɪv] **1** *n* (**a**) *Phys* microonda *f*; **using m. technology** empleando la tecnología de microondas (**b**) **m. (oven)** (horno *m*) microondas *m inv*
2 *vt* cocinar en el microondas

microwaveable ['maɪkrəʊ'weɪvəbəl] *adj* **it's m.** se puede cocinar en el microondas

micturate ['mɪktjʊreɪt] *vi Formal (urinate)* miccionar

mid [mɪd] *adj* (**a**) *(middle)* **in m. ocean** en medio del océano; **in m. June** a mediados de junio; **he's in his m. fifties** tiene cincuenta años y pico, es un cincuentón; **she stopped in m. sentence** se detuvo a mitad de la frase (**b**) *(central)* **m. Wales** zona central de Gales ►► *Ling* ***m. vowels*** vocales *fpl* medias

'mid [mɪd] *prep Literary* = **amid**

midafternoon ['mɪdɑːftə'nuːn] *n* media tarde *f*; **a m. nap** una siesta de media tarde

midair [mɪd'eə(r)] **1** *n* **in m.** en el aire; *Fig* **to leave sth in m.** dejar algo en el aire
2 *adj (collision, explosion)* en pleno vuelo

Midas ['maɪdəs] *n Mythol* **King M.** el rey Midas; IDIOM **to have the M. touch** = ser como el rey Midas, que todo lo que toca se convierte en oro

mid-Atlantic ['mɪdət'læntɪk] *adj (accent)* = a medio camino entre el inglés británico y el americano

midbrain ['mɪdbreɪn] *n Anat* mesencéfalo *m*

midday ['mɪd'deɪ] *n* mediodía *m*; **at m.** a mediodía; **the m. heat/sun** el calor/sol del mediodía ►► ***m. meal*** comida *f*, almuerzo *m*

midden ['mɪdən] *n* (**a**) *Old-fashioned (dung heap)* estercolero *m*; *(rubbish heap)* montón *m* de basura (**b**) *Fam (mess)* pocilga *f*

MIDDLE ['mɪdəl] **1** *n* (**a**) *(with position)* medio *m*; **he was driving right down the m. of the road** conducía *or Am* manejaba justo por el medio de la carretera; **I'm the one in the m.** soy el del medio; **in the m. of the room** en medio de la habitación; **in the m. of the Atlantic** en medio del Atlántico; **in the m. of nowhere** en un lugar dejado de la mano de Dios, en el medio de la nada; *Fig* **to split sth down the m.** dividir algo por la mitad, *RP* partir algo a la mitad
(**b**) *(inside)* **the m. of the ball is made of cork** el interior de la pelota es de corcho; **it's not cooked in the m.** está crudo en el medio
(**c**) *(with time)* mitad *f*; **he was in the m. of an important conversation** estaba en mitad de una conversación importante; **in the m. of the day** en mitad del día; **in the m. of the month** a mediados de mes; **in the m. of the night** en plena noche, en mitad de la noche; **in the m. of summer** a mitad de verano, a mediados del verano; **in the m. of the week** a mitad de semana; **to be in the m. of doing sth** estar ocupado(a) haciendo algo
(**d**) *(waist)* cintura *f*
2 *adj (in the middle)* del medio; **I'll have the m. one of the three** tomaré el del medio, me quedo con el del medio; **I was the m. child of**

three fui el segundo de tres hermanos, yo era el hermano del medio; **she is in her m. thirties** tiene unos treinta y cinco años; **in the m. distance** a media distancia; IDIOM **to steer a m. course** *(in politics, diplomacy)* tomar la vía intermedia ►► ***m. age*** edad *f* madura, madurez *f*; *Hist* ***the M. Ages*** la Edad Media; ***M. America*** *Geog (in Central America)* Mesoamérica; *(in United States)* la llanura central; *Pol* los estadounidenses tradicionalistas y conservadores; *Mus* ***m. C*** do *m* central; ***the m. class(es)*** la clase media; *Anat* ***the m. ear*** el oído medio; ***the M. East*** Oriente *m* Medio; ***M. Eastern*** de Oriente Medio; *Pol* ***M. England*** la Inglaterra tradicionalista y conservadora; *Ling* ***M. English*** inglés *m* medio *(entre los años 1100 y 1500 aproximadamente)*; ***m. finger*** (dedo *m*) corazón *m or* mayor *m*; *Fam* ***m. finger salute*** = gesto obsceno que consiste en mostrar el dorso del dedo medio apuntando hacia arriba; *Pol* ***the m. ground*** el centro; **the mediator was unable to find any m. ground between the two parties** el mediador no consiguió hallar ningún terreno común entre las dos partes; ***m. management*** mandos *mpl* intermedios; ***m. manager*** mando *m* intermedio; ***m. name*** segundo nombre *m*; *Fam* **"generosity" isn't exactly his m. name!** ¡no destaca precisamente por su generosidad!; ***m. school*** *(in Britain)* = escuela para niños de ocho a doce años; *(in US)* = escuela para niños de once a catorce años; ***the M. West*** el Medio Oeste *m* (de Estados Unidos)

3 *vt Sport (ball)* golpear *or* conectar de lleno

---

middle-aged [mɪdəl'eɪdʒd] *adj* de mediana edad ►► ***m. spread*** la curva de la felicidad

middlebrow ['mɪdəlbraʊ] *adj (tastes, interests)* del público medio; **a m. novelist** un(a) novelista para el público medio

middle-class [mɪdəl'klɑːs] *adj* de clase media; **they've become terribly m.** se han aburguesado tremendamente

middle-distance ['mɪdəl'dɪstəns] *adj Sport (race)* de medio fondo ►► ***m. runner*** mediofondista *mf*; ***m. running*** medio fondo *m*

middle-income ['mɪdəl'ɪnkʌm] *adj (group, bracket)* de ingresos medios

middleman ['mɪdəlmæn] *n* intermediario *m*; **to cut out the m.** evitar a los intermediarios

middlemost ['mɪdəlməʊst], **midmost** ['mɪdməʊst] *adj (nearest the centre)* el/la más cercano(a) al centro

middle-of-the-road ['mɪdələvðə'rəʊd] *adj* **(a)** *(policy)* moderado(a) **(b)** *(music)* convencional

middle-sized ['mɪdəl'saɪzd] *adj* mediano(a)

middleweight ['mɪdəlweɪt] **1** *adj* del peso medio

2 *n* peso *m* medio

middling ['mɪdlɪŋ] *adj (performance, health)* regular; *(height, weight)* intermedio(a)

Middx (*abbr* **Middlesex**) Middlesex

Mideast ['mɪd'iːst] *n US* **the M.** Oriente Medio

midfield [mɪd'fiːld] *n (in soccer)* centro *m* del campo; **he plays in m.** juega de centrocampista ►► ***m. player*** centrocampista *mf*

midfielder [mɪd'fiːldə(r)] *n (in soccer)* centrocampista *mf*

midge [mɪdʒ] *n* mosquito *m (muy pequeño)*

midget ['mɪdʒɪt] **1** *n (small person)* enano(a) *m,f*

2 *adj* en miniatura

MIDI ['mɪdɪ] *Comptr* (*abbr* **musical instrument digital interface**) MIDI

midi ['mɪdɪ] *n* **(a)** *(coat)* abrigo *m* tres cuartos *or* midi; *(skirt)* falda *f* tres cuartos *or* midi **(b) m. system** *(stereo)* minicadena

midland ['mɪdlənd] *adj* (del) interior

Midlands ['mɪdləndz] *npl* **the M.** = la región central de Inglaterra

midlife ['mɪdlaɪf] *n* madurez *f*, edad *f* adulta; **in m.** en la madurez ►► ***m. crisis*** crisis *f inv* de los cuarenta

midmorning [mɪd'mɔːnɪŋ] *n* media mañana *f* ►► ***m. snack*** tentempié *m* a media mañana, *Col* onces *fpl*, *RP* colación *f*

midmost = **middlemost**

midnight ['mɪdnaɪt] *n* medianoche *f*; **at m.** a medianoche; IDIOM **to burn the m. oil** quedarse hasta muy tarde *(estudiando o trabajando)* ►► ***m. feast*** = comida que hacen los niños en la cama por la noche a escondidas; ***m. mass*** misa *f* del gallo; ***m. sun*** sol *m* de medianoche

midpoint ['mɪdpɔɪnt] *n* ecuador *m*

mid-range ['mɪd'reɪndʒ] *adj Com (computer, car)* de gama media

midriff ['mɪdrɪf] *n* diafragma *m*; **the short T-shirt exposed her m.** la camiseta corta le dejaba la barriga al aire

midrise ['mɪdraɪz] *adj US* **m. apartment block** edificio de pisos de altura media

midshipman ['mɪdʃɪpmən] *n* guardia *m* marina, guardiamarina *m*

midst [mɪdst] *n* **in the m. of** en medio de; **in our/their m.** entre nosotros/ellos; **in the m. of all this** *(these events)* en medio de todo esto

midstream [mɪd'striːm] *n* **in m.** por el centro del río; *Fig (when speaking)* en mitad del discurso; **to interrupt sb in m.** interrumpir a alguien en plena conversación

midsummer ['mɪdsʌmə(r)] *n* pleno verano *m*; **a m. night** una noche de (pleno) verano ►► ***M.('s) Day*** el 24 de junio, San Juan; ***m. madness*** la locura del verano

midterm ['mɪd'tɜːm] **1** *adj* **(a)** *Pol Br* ***m. by-election*** = elecciones parciales a mitad de legislatura; *US* ***m. elections*** = elecciones a mitad del mandato presidencial **(b)** *Sch & Univ* de mitad de trimestre ►► ***m. break*** = vacaciones de mitad de trimestre

2 *n US Sch & Univ* **midterms** exámenes a mitad de semestre

midtown ['mɪdtaʊn] *adj US* **a m. apartment** un apartamento *or Esp* piso no muy lejos del centro

midway ['mɪdweɪ] **1** *adj* medio(a); **the m. point** *(in time, space)* la mitad

2 *adv* **(a)** *(in space)* a mitad de camino, a medio camino **(b)** *(in time)* hacia la mitad; **she was m. through writing the first chapter** llevaba escrita la mitad del primer capítulo

midweek [mɪd'wiːk] **1** *adj* de entre semana; **m. show/flight** representación/vuelo de entre semana

2 *adv* a mediados de semana, entre semana

Midwest ['mɪd'west] *n* **the M.** el Medio Oeste (de Estados Unidos)

Midwestern [mɪd'westən] *adj* del Medio Oeste (de Estados Unidos)

midwife ['mɪdwaɪf] *n* comadrona *f* ►► ***m. toad*** sapo *m* partero

midwifery [mɪd'wɪfərɪ] *n* obstetricia *f*

midwinter ['mɪd'wɪntə(r)] *n* pleno invierno *m*

midyear ['mɪdjɪə(r)] **1** *n* **(a)** *(middle of year)* mediados *mpl* de año **(b)** *US (university exam)* **midyears** ≃ exámenes *mpl* parciales

2 *adj* de mediados de año, de mitad de año

mien [miːn] *n Literary (appearance, manner)* semblante *m*

miffed [mɪft] *adj Fam (offended)* mosqueado(a)

might[1] [maɪt] *n (strength)* fuerza *f*, poder *m*; **with all his m.** *(to work, push)* con todas sus fuerzas; **the full m. of the law** todo el peso de la ley; *Old-fashioned* **with m. and main** con todas sus/nuestras/*etc.* fuerzas; PROV **m. is right** quien tiene la fuerza tiene la razón

---

MIGHT[2] *v aux* **(a)** *(expressing possibility)* poder; **it m. be difficult** puede que sea *or* puede ser difícil; **I m. go if I feel like it** puede que vaya si tengo ganas; **it m. be better to ask permission first** sería mejor pedir permiso primero; **will you tell them? – I m. (do)** ¿se lo dirás? – puede (que sí) *or* puede ser; **he's the sort of person who m. do something like that** es el tipo de persona que haría algo así; **the reason m. never be discovered** puede *or* es posible que nunca se descubra la razón; **you m. want to read through this first** sería mejor que te leyeras esto primero; **I thought we m. go to the cinema** se me ha ocurrido *or* me ocurre que podríamos ir al cine; **you m. show a bit more respect!** ¡podrías ser más respetuoso!; **and who m. you be?** ¿y tú quién eres?; **it m. be that...** podría ser que...; **it m. well prove useful** puede que sirva, puede llegar a ser útil; **that m. well be the case, but...** puede que sea el caso, pero..., puede ser el caso, pero...; **you m. well ask!** ¡eso quisiera saber yo!; **she's sorry now, as well she m. be** ahora lo lamenta, y bien que debería; **we m. as well go** ya puestos *or* ya que estamos, podíamos ir; **shall we go? – we m. as well** ¿vamos? – bueno, *Esp* vale *or Méx* órale *or Arg* dale; **I m. as well tell you now, seeing as you'll find out soon anyway** no veo por qué no decírtelo ahora, de todas maneras te vas a enterar pronto; **I m. as well be talking to myself!** ¡es como si hablara con la pared!; **you m. have told me!** ¡me lo podrías haber dicho!, ¡habérmelo dicho!; **I m. have known that's what he'd say!** ¡debía haberme imaginado que diría algo así!

(b) *(as past form of* **may)** **I knew he m. be angry** ya sabía que se podía *esp Esp* enfadar *or esp Am* enojar; **I was afraid she m. have killed him** tenía miedo de que (ella) lo hubiera matado; **he said he m. be late** dijo que quizá se retrasaría; **she asked if she m. have a word with me** preguntó si podía hablar conmigo

(c) *Formal (asking for permission)* **m. I have a word with you?, I wonder if I m. have a word with you?** ¿podría hablar un momento con usted?; **m. I ask you how much you earn?** ¿le importaría decirme cuánto gana?; **and what, m. I ask, do you think you're doing?** ¿y se puede saber qué te crees que estás haciendo?; **I'd like to say something, if I m.** me gustaría decir algo, si me lo permite/permiten

(d) *(expressing purpose)* **they work long hours so their children m. have a better future** trabajan mucho para que sus hijos tengan un futuro mejor

(e) *(with concessions)* **she m. not be the prettiest girl in the world,**

but... no será la chica más bonita del mundo, pero...; **you m. think this seems stupid, but...** te puede parecer estúpido, pero...; **whatever you m. say** digas lo que digas

---

might-have-been ['maɪthəvbi:n] *n Fam* (**a**) *(opportunity)* **the might-have-beens** las ocasiones *orAm* chances perdidas, lo que podría haber sido (**b**) *(person)* promesa *mf* fallida

mightily ['maɪtɪlɪ] *adv* (**a**) *(powerfully)* con fuerza (**b**) *Fam* un montón; **we were m. impressed by his performance** su actuación nos impresionó un montón; **I was m. relieved** me quedé aliviadísimo

mightn't ['maɪtənt] = **might not**

might've ['maɪtəv] = **might have**

mighty ['maɪtɪ] **1** *adj* (**a**) *(powerful)* fuerte, poderoso(a) (**b**) *(large, imposing)* grandioso(a)

2 *adv US Fam* un montón, *Esp* cantidad; **m. fine** genial, *Esp* guay, *Andes, CAm, Carib, Méx* chévere, *Méx* padrísimo(a), *RP* bárbaro(a); **she looked m. pleased with herself** se la veía super satisfecha consigo misma

migraine ['mi:greɪn, 'maɪgreɪn] *n* migraña *f*

migrant ['maɪgrənt] **1** *n* (**a**) *(person) (in agriculture)* temporero(a) *m,f*; *(foreign)* emigrante *mf* (**b**) *(bird)* ave *f* migratoria (**c**) *Austr (immigrant)* inmigrante *mf*

2 *adj* (**a**) *(bird, animal)* migratorio(a) (**b**) *(person)* ***m. worker*** *(seasonal)* temporero(a) *m,f*; *(foreign)* trabajador(ora) *m,f* emigrante (**c**) *Austr (immigrant)* **m. accommodation** alojamiento para inmigrantes

migrate [maɪ'greɪt] *vi* (**a**) *(bird, animal)* emigrar, migrar; **to m. south** emigrar hacia el sur (**b**) *(person)* emigrar, migrar; **to m. towards the capital** emigrar a la capital

migration [maɪ'greɪʃən] *n* (**a**) *(of birds, animals)* emigración *f*, migración *f* (**b**) *(of people)* emigración *f*, migración *f*

migratory ['maɪgrətrɪ] *adj* migratorio(a)

mike [maɪk] *n Fam (microphone)* micro *m*

▸**mike up** *vt sep Fam* poner el micro a

mil [mɪl] *n Fam (millilitre)* mililitro *m*

milady [mɪ'leɪdɪ] *n Old-fashioned* señora *f*

Milan [mɪ'læn] *n* Milán

Milanese [mɪlə'ni:z] **1** *n* milanés(esa) *m,f*

2 *adj* milanés(esa)

milch [mɪltʃ] *adj (cattle)* de leche ▸▸ *Fig* ***m. cow*** gallina *f* de los huevos de oro

mild [maɪld] **1** *adj* (**a**) *(person, remark)* apacible, afable (**b**) *(not severe, strong) (punishment, illness, criticism)* leve; *(displeasure, amusement)* ligero(a); **a m. form of measles** una inflamación leve de sarampión ▸▸ ***m. steel*** acero *m* dulce (**c**) *(slight) (astonishment, amusement)* ligero(a) (**d**) *(food, sedative, laxative)* suave (**e**) *(climate, winter)* templado(a), suave

2 *n Br (beer)* = cerveza oscura con poco gas elaborada con poco lúpulo

mildew ['mɪldju:] **1** *n* (**a**) mildiú *m*, mildeu *m* (**b**) *(on paper, leather, food)* moho *m*

2 *vi* (**a**) *(plants)* cubrirse de mildiú *or* mildeu (**b**) *(paper, leather, food)* enmohecer(se)

mildewed ['mɪldju:d] *adj* (**a**) *(plants)* con mildiú *or* mildeu (**b**) *(paper, leather, food)* mohoso(a)

mildly ['maɪldlɪ] *adv* (**a**) *(to say)* con suavidad (**b**) *(moderately)* ligeramente; **to put it m.** por no decir algo peor

mild-mannered ['maɪld'mænəd] *adj* atento(a)

mildness ['maɪldnɪs] *n* (**a**) *(of person)* afabilidad *f* (**b**) *(of punishment, illness, criticism)* levedad *f* (**c**) *(of climate, weather)* suavidad *f*

mile [maɪl] *n* (**a**) *(distance)* milla *f (= 1,6 km)*; **miles per hour** millas por hora; **smaller cars do more miles to the** *or* **per gallon** los coches *orAm* carros *or RP* autos pequeños recorren más millas por galón; **he lives miles away** vive a kilómetros de distancia; **we're miles from the nearest town** estamos muy lejos del pueblo más cercano; **m. after** *or* **upon m. of...** kilómetros y kilómetros de...; **you can see for miles and miles** se alcanza a ver kilómetros de distancia

(**b**) *Fam* IDIOMS **to be miles away** *(be daydreaming)* estar en Babia; **to see** *or* **spot sth a m. off** ver algo a la legua; **miles better** muchísimo mejor; **it's miles more interesting** es muchísimo más interesante; **it was miles too easy** fue exageradamente fácil; **it sticks** *or* **stands out a m.** se ve a la legua; **you could see what was going to happen a m. off** se veía de lejos lo que iba a suceder; **someone not a million miles from us** alguien cercano a nosotros; **to go the extra m.** hacer un último esfuerzo

mileage ['maɪlɪdʒ] *n* (**a**) *(distance travelled)* millas *fpl* (recorridas), ≃ kilometraje *m*; **it's got a very high m.** ha hecho muchos kilómetros ▸▸ ***m. allowance*** ≃ (dieta *f* de) kilometraje *m*

(**b**) *(rate of fuel consumption)* consumo *m* (de combustible); **you get better m. with a small car** un coche *orAm* carro *or CSur* auto pequeño consume menos; IDIOM **to get a lot of m. out of sth** sacar mucho partido a algo

mileometer [maɪ'lɒmɪtə(r)] *n Br (in car)* ≃ cuentakilómetros *m inv*

milepost ['maɪlpəʊst] *n* mojón *m*

milestone ['maɪlstəʊn] *n* (**a**) *(on road)* mojón *m* (**b**) *Fig (in career, history)* hito *m*

milieu ['mi:ljɜ:] *n* entorno *m*, medio *m*

militancy ['mɪlɪtənsɪ] *n* militancia *f*

militant ['mɪlɪtənt] **1** *n* activista *mf*, militante *mf*

2 *adj* activista, beligerante

militaria [mɪlɪ'teərɪə] *npl* parafernalia *f* militar

militarily ['mɪlɪtərɪlɪ] *adv* militarmente

militarism ['mɪlɪtərɪzəm] *n* militarismo *m*

militarist ['mɪlɪtərɪst] *n* militarista *mf*

militaristic [mɪlɪtə'rɪstɪk] *adj* militarista

militarization [mɪlɪtəraɪ'zeɪʃən] *n* militarización *f*

militarize ['mɪlɪtəraɪz] *vt* militarizar

military ['mɪlɪtərɪ] **1** *n* **the m.** el ejército

2 *adj* militar; **a strong m. presence** una intensa presencia militar; **to be buried with full m. honours** ser enterrado(a) con todos los honores militares; **to plan sth with m. precision** planear algo con precisión milimétrica ▸▸ ***m. academy*** academia *f* militar; ***m. attaché*** agregado(a) *m,f* militar; ***m. man*** militar *m*; ***m. police*** policía *f* militar; ***m. policeman*** policía *m* militar; ***m. science*** arte *m or f* militar; ***m. service*** servicio *m* militar; ***m. training*** instrucción *f* militar

militate ['mɪlɪteɪt]

▸**militate against** *vt insep (fact, reason)* militar en contra de; **her temperament militates against her chances of being chosen for the job** su temperamento incide negativamente en las posibilidades que tiene de conseguir el trabajo

militia [mɪ'lɪʃə] *n* milicia *f*

militiaman [mɪ'lɪʃəmæn] *n* miliciano *m*

milk [mɪlk] **1** *n* leche *f*; **cow's/goat's m.** leche de vaca/cabra; **the m. of human kindness** el don de la amabilidad; IDIOM **it was all m. and water** era muy insulso(a) ▸▸ ***m. bottle*** botella *f* de leche; ***m. chocolate*** chocolate *m* con leche; ***m. churn*** lechera *f*; *Br* ***m. float*** = furgoneta eléctrica para el reparto de leche; ***m. jug*** jarra *f* de leche; ***m. of magnesia*** (leche *f* de) magnesia *f*; ***m. pudding*** = postre a base de arroz, tapioca o sémola de trigo cocidos en leche; ***m. round*** *(milk delivery)* = ruta de reparto de leche; *Br Fam (recruitment drive)* = visita anual de representantes de empresas a universidades para reclutar jóvenes con talento; ***m. run*** *(regular flight)* vuelo *m* de rutina; ***m. shake*** batido *m*; ***m. sugar*** lactosa *f*; ***m. teeth*** dentición *f* de leche *or* primaria; ***m. tooth*** diente *m* de leche

2 *vt* (**a**) *(cow, goat)* ordeñar (**b**) *(snake)* extraer el veneno a (**c**) *Fam (exploit)* **to m. sb dry** exprimir a alguien hasta la última gota; **they milked the story for all it was worth** le sacaron todo el jugo posible a la noticia

milk-and-water ['mɪlkənd'wɔ:tə(r)] *adj* insulso(a)

milker ['mɪlkə(r)] *n* (**a**) *(cow)* **a good m.** una buena vaca lechera (**b**) *(person)* ordeñador(ora) *m,f* (**c**) *(machine)* ordeñadora *f*

milking ['mɪlkɪŋ] *n* ordeño *m*; **to do the m.** ordeñar ▸▸ ***m. machine*** ordeñadora *f*; ***m. parlour*** establo *m* de ordeñar; ***m. shed*** establo *m* de ordeñar; ***m. stool*** taburete *m* para ordeñar

milkmaid ['mɪlkmeɪd] *n* lechera *f*

milkman ['mɪlkmən] *n* (**a**) *(who sells or delivers milk)* lechero *m* (**b**) *Br (who milks)* lechero *m*

milksop ['mɪlksɒp] *n (weak, effeminate man)* mariquita *m*

milk-white ['mɪlkwaɪt] *adj* pálido(a), blanco(a) como la nieve

milky ['mɪlkɪ] *adj* (**a**) *(containing too much milk)* con demasiada leche; *(containing a lot of milk)* con mucha leche (**b**) *(colour)* lechoso(a) ▸▸ ***the M. Way*** la Vía Láctea

mill [mɪl] **1** *n* (**a**) *(grinder) (for flour)* molino *m*; *(for coffee, pepper)* molinillo *m*; IDIOM *Fam* **to put sb through the m.** hacérselas pasar negras *or Esp* moradas a alguien (**b**) *(factory) (for textiles)* fábrica *f or* planta *f* textil; *(for paper)* fábrica *f* de papel, papelera *f*; **steel m.** acería ▸▸ ***m. hand*** obrero(a) *m,f*

2 *vt* (**a**) *(grain)* moler (**b**) *(metal)* fresar; **a coin with a milled edge** una moneda con cordoncillo (en el canto)

► **mill about, mill around** *vi (crowd)* pulular

millboard ['mɪlbɔːd] *n* cartón *m* gris

millenarian [mɪlə'neərɪən] **1** *n* milenario(a) *m,f*
2 *adj* milenario(a)

millennial [mɪ'lenɪəl] *adj* del milenio

millennium [mɪ'lenɪəm] (*pl* **millenniums** *or* **millennia** [mɪ'lenɪə]) *n* **(a)** *(thousand years)* milenio *m* **(b)** *Rel* **the m.** el milenio, = los mil años del reino de Cristo sobre la tierra antes del juicio final **(c)** *(year 2000)* año *m* 2000 ►► *Comptr* ***m. bug*** efecto *m* 2000

miller ['mɪlə(r)] *n* molinero(a) *m,f*

millesimal [mɪ'lesɪməl] *adj* milésimo(a)

millet ['mɪlɪt] *n* mijo *m*

milli- ['mɪlɪ] *prefix* mili-

millibar ['mɪlɪbɑː(r)] *n Met* milibar *m*

milligram(me) ['mɪlɪgræm] *n* miligramo *m*

millilitre, *US* **milliliter** ['mɪlɪliːtə(r)] *n* mililitro *m*

millimetre, *US* **millimeter** ['mɪlɪmiːtə(r)] *n* milímetro *m*

milliner ['mɪlɪnə(r)] *n* sombrerero(a) *m,f*

millinery ['mɪlɪnərɪ] *n* **(a)** *(hats)* sombreros *mpl (de mujer)* **(b)** *(craft)* fabricación *f* de sombreros de mujer

milling ['mɪlɪŋ] *n* **(a)** *(of grain)* molienda *f*, molido *m* **(b)** *(of metal)* fresado *m* **(c)** *(on coin)* cordoncillo *m*

million ['mɪljən] *n* millón *m*; **two m. men** dos millones de hombres; *Fam* **I've told him a m. times** se lo he dicho millones de veces; **thanks a m.!** ¡un millón de gracias!; **she's one in a m.** es única; **to look/feel like a m. dollars** estar/sentirse divino(a)

millionaire [mɪljə'neə(r)] *n* millonario(a) *m,f*; **he's a dollar m.** tiene millones de dólares; **a m. footballer** un futbolista millonario

millionairess [mɪljə'neərɪs] *n* millonaria *f*

million-selling ['mɪljənselɪŋ] *adj* **a m. record** un disco del que se han vendido un millón de copias; **a m. book** un libro del que se han vendido un millón de ejemplares

millionth ['mɪljənθ] **1** *n* **(a)** *(fraction)* millonésimo *m* **(b)** *(in series)* millonésimo(a) *m,f*
2 *adj* millonésimo(a)

millipede ['mɪlɪpiːd] *n* milpiés *m inv*

millisecond ['mɪlɪsekənd] *n* milisegundo *m*, milésima *f* de segundo

millivolt ['mɪlɪvɒlt] *n* milivoltio *m*

milliwatt ['mɪlɪwɒt] *n* milivatio *m*

millpond ['mɪlpɒnd] *n* presada *f*, cubo *m*; IDIOM **as calm as a m.** *(of water)* como una balsa de aceite, totalmente en calma

millrace ['mɪlreɪs] *n* **(a)** *(channel)* socaz *m*, caz *m* de molino **(b)** *(water)* corriente *f* que hace girar al molino, presada *f*

millstone ['mɪlstəʊn] *n* muela *f*, rueda *f* de molino; IDIOM **it's (like) a m. round my neck** es una cruz que llevo encima

millstream ['mɪlstriːm] *n* corriente *f* que hace girar al molino, presada *f*

millwheel ['mɪlwiːl] *n* rueda *f* hidráulica

milometer [maɪ'lɒmɪtə(r)] *n (in car)* ≃ cuentakilómetros *m inv*

milquetoast ['mɪlktəʊst] *n US Fam* pavo(a) *m,f*, pasmado(a) *m,f*

milt [mɪlt] *n* **(a)** *(fluid)* lecha *f* **(b)** *(organ)* lecha *f*

MIME [maɪm] *n Comptr* (*abbr* **Multipurpose Internet Mail Extensions**) (protocolo *m*) MIME *m*

mime [maɪm] **1** *n (performance)* mimo *m*, pantomima *f*; **to explain something in m.** explicar algo mediante mímica *or* gestos ►► ***m. artist*** mimo *m*
2 *vt* representar con gestos
3 *vi* hacer mimo *or* mímica

> **False friend**: The Spanish verb **mimar** is not a translation for the English word **mime**. In Spanish **mimar** means "to spoil, to pamper".

mimeograph ['mɪmɪəgrɑːf] **1** *n* **(a)** *(machine)* multicopista *f*, *Am* mimeógrafo *m* **(b)** *(text)* multicopia *f*
2 *vt* reproducir por multicopista, *Am* mimeografiar

mimesis [mɪ'miːsɪs] *n* **(a)** *Formal Lit* mimesis *f inv*, mímesis *f inv* **(b)** *Biol* mimetismo *m*

mimetic [mɪ'metɪk] *adj* **(a)** *Formal Lit* mimético(a) **(b)** *Biol* mimético(a)

mimic ['mɪmɪk] **1** *n* imitador(ora) *m,f*
2 *vt* (*pt & pp* **mimicked**) **(a)** *(person, voice)* imitar **(b)** *Biol* adoptar la apariencia de

mimicry ['mɪmɪkrɪ] *n* **(a)** *(imitation)* imitación *f* **(b)** *Biol* mimetismo *m*

mimosa [mɪ'məʊzə] (**mimosas** *or* **mimosae** [mɪ'məʊziː]) *n* mimosa *f* ►► ***m. thorn*** acacia *f* espinosa

Min **(a)** *Mus* (*abbr* **Minor**) menor **(b)** (*abbr* **Minister**) mtro(a). **(c)** (*abbr* **Ministry**) mtro.

min **(a)** (*abbr* **minute(s)**) min., minuto *m* **(b)** (*abbr* **minimum**) mín.

minaret [mɪnə'ret] *n* alminar *m*, minarete *m*

minatory ['mɪnətrɪ] *adj Formal* amenazador(ora), amenazante

mince [mɪns] **1** *n Br* carne *f Esp, RP* picada *or Am* molida ►► ***m. pie*** *(containing meat)* = especie de empanada de carne picada; *(containing fruit)* = pastel navideño a base de fruta escarchada, frutos secos y especias
2 *vt (chop up)* picar; IDIOM **she doesn't m. her words** no tiene pelos en la lengua
3 *vi (walk)* caminar con afectación

mincemeat ['mɪnsmiːt] *n* **(a)** *(meat)* carne *f Esp, RP* picada *or Am* molida; IDIOM *Fam* **to make m. of sb** hacer trizas *or Esp* picadillo *or RP* bolsa a alguien **(b)** *(fruit)* = relleno a base de fruta escarchada, frutos secos, especias, zumo de limón y grasa animal

mincer ['mɪnsə(r)] *n* picadora *f* (de carne)

mincing ['mɪnsɪŋ] *adj (walk, voice)* afectado(a)

MIND [maɪnd] **1** *n* **(a)** *(thoughts)* mente *f*; **I added it up in my m.** lo calculé mentalmente; **there is no doubt in my m. about it** no me queda la más mínima duda; **you can do it, it's all in the m.** todo es cosa de creérselo, la mente lo puede todo; **of course she doesn't hate you, it's all in your m.** claro que no te odia, son imaginaciones tuyas; **to be clear in one's m. about sth** tener algo clarísimo; **to see sth in one's m.'s eye** hacerse una imagen mental de algo; **it's a case of m. over matter** es un caso del poder de la mente; **her m. was on something else** tenía la cabeza en otro lado; **to bear** *or* **keep sth in m.** tener algo en cuenta; **to bring** *or* **call sth to m.** traer algo a la memoria; **say the first thing that comes into your m.** di lo primero que te venga a la cabeza *or* mente; **nothing comes** *or* **springs to m.** no se me ocurre nada; **I couldn't get it off** *or* **out of my m.** no podía quitármelo de la cabeza; **my m. went blank** me quedé en blanco; **it went completely** *or* **clean out of my m.** se me fue por completo de la cabeza; **to have sth on one's m.** tener algo en la cabeza; **do you have** *or* **is there something on your m.?** ¿te preocupa algo?; **it puts me in m. of...** me recuerda...; **to put sth/sb out of one's m.** olvidar algo/a alguien; **to put** *or* **set sb's m. at rest** tranquilizar a alguien; **to take sb's m. off sth** quitarle *or Am* sacarle a alguien algo de la cabeza, hacer que alguien olvide algo; **let us turn our minds to the question of funding** abordemos la cuestión de la financiación *or Am* del financiamiento ►► ***m. game*** *(in psychiatry)* juego *m* psicológico; *Fig* **to play m. games with sb** hacer la guerra psicológica a alguien
(b) *(opinion)* **to my m.** en mi opinión; **to be of one** *or* **like m., to be of the same m.** ser de la misma opinión; **to change sb's m. (about sth)** hacer cambiar de opinión a alguien (acerca de algo); **to change one's m. (about sth)** cambiar de opinión (acerca de algo); **to keep an open m. (about sth)** no formarse ideas preconcebidas (respecto a algo); **to speak one's m.** hablar sin rodeos; IDIOM *Fam* **I gave him a piece of my m.** le canté las cuarenta
(c) *(will, wants, intention)* **nothing could be further from my m.** nada más lejos de mis intenciones; **to be in two minds (about sth)** estar indeciso(a) (acerca de algo); **to have a m. of one's own** ser capaz de pensar *or* decidir por sí mismo(a); **this printer has a m. of its own** esta impresora hace lo que le da la gana *or* se le antoja; **I've a good m. to do it** me estoy planteando seriamente hacerlo, tengo en mente hacerlo; **I've half a m. to tell his parents** me entran *or* dan ganas de decírselo a sus padres; **to have sth/sb in m.** estar pensando en algo/alguien; **it's not quite what I had in m.** no es precisamente lo que me había imaginado; **to have it in m. to do sth** tener en mente hacer algo; **I bought it with you in m.** lo compré pensando en ti; **she knows her own m.** sabe bien lo que quiere; **to make up one's m., to make one's m. up** decidirse; **I have made up my m. to accept the job** he decidido aceptar el trabajo; **I can't make up my m. who to invite** no consigo decidir a quién invitar; **to set one's m. on sth/doing sth** meterse en la cabeza algo/hacer algo
(d) *(attention)* **your m. is not on the job** no estás concentrado en el trabajo; **my m. was wandering** mi mente divagaba; **to keep one's m. on sth** mantenerse concentrado(a) en algo; *US* **don't pay them any m.** no les hagas ningún caso; **I'm sure if you put** *or* **set your m. to it you could do it** estoy seguro de que podrías hacerlo si pusieses tus cinco sentidos (en ello)
(e) *(way of thinking)* mente *f*, mentalidad *f*; **to have the m. of a three-year-old** tener la mentalidad de un niño de tres años; **you've got a dirty/nasty m.!** ¡qué ideas más cochinas/desagradables tienes!; **to have a suspicious m.** tener una mente recelosa

(f) *(reason)* **to be/go out of one's m.** *(mad)* haber perdido/perder el juicio; **are you out of your m.?** ¿estás loco?; **to be out of one's m. with worry** estar preocupadísimo(a); *Fam* **to be bored out of one's m.** estar más aburrido(a) que una ostra; *Fam* **to be drunk/stoned out of one's m.** estar completamente borracho(a)/colocado(a); *Fam* **to be scared out of one's m.** estar muerto(a) de miedo; **no one in his right m....** nadie en su sano juicio...; **his m. is going** se está volviendo loco, se le va la cabeza

(g) *(intelligence)* **to have a quick m.** tener una mente despierta; **I'm doing the course to improve my m.** hago el curso para ampliar mis conocimientos

(h) *(person)* mente *f*; **one of the finest minds of this century** una de las mentes más insignes de este siglo

2 *vt* **(a)** *(pay attention to)* **m. you don't fall!** ¡ten cuidado no te caigas *or* no te vayas a caer!; **m. you're not late!** ¡ten cuidado de no llegar tarde!; **m. you don't forget anything** ten cuidado de no olvidarte nada; **m. where you're going!** ¡cuida *or* cuidado por dónde vas!; *Br Fam* **m. how you go!** ¡cuídate!; **m. your head!** ¡cuida *or* cuidado con la cabeza!; **m. the step!** ¡cuidado con el escalón!; **m. your language!** ¡vaya lenguaje!, ¡no digas palabrotas *or Esp* tacos!; **m. your manners!** ¡no seas maleducado!, ¡pórtate bien!; **you'll have to m. your p's and q's** tendrás que tener cuidado de no decir ninguna palabrota

(b) *(concern oneself with)* preocuparse de *or* por; **m. your own business!** ¡métete en tus asuntos!; **don't m. me, just carry on playing** como si no estuviera, tú sigue tocando; **never m. the distance/money** no te preocupes por la distancia/el dinero; **never m. her/what they say!** ¡no te preocupes por ella/por lo que digan!; **I don't even have enough money for a tie, never m. a suit!** no tengo dinero *or Am* plata para una corbata y mucho menos para un traje; **m. you, I've always thought that...** la verdad es que yo siempre he pensado que...; **he's a bit young, m. you** lo que pasa es que es un poco joven

(c) *(object to)* **I don't m. the cold** el frío no me importa *or* no me molesta; **do you like her? – I don't m. her** ¿te gusta? – no me disgusta; **he didn't m. that I hadn't phoned** no le importó que no lo hubiera llamado; **what I m. is...** lo que me molesta es...; **I don't m. what you do as long as you don't tell her** no me importa lo que hagas con tal de que no se lo digas a ella; **do you m. me smoking?** ¿le importa *or* molesta que fume?; **if you don't m. my asking** si no te importa que te lo pregunte; **I don't m. telling you I was furious** te puedo decir que estaba furioso; **would you m. not doing that?** ¿te importaría no hacer eso?; **I wouldn't m. a cup of tea** me gustaría tomar una taza de té; **I wouldn't m. a holiday in the Bahamas** no estarían mal *or* no me importarían unas vacaciones en las Bahamas

(d) *(look after) (children, house, shop)* cuidar; **would you m. my suitcases for me?** ¿le importaría cuidarme las maletas *or Méx* petacas *or Andes, RP* valijas?

(e) *Scot, Irish (remember)* acordarse de

3 *vi* **(a)** *(object)* **do you m.!** *(how dare you)* ¡te importa!, ¿cómo te atreves?; **do you m. if I smoke?** ¿le importa que fume?, ¿le molesta si fumo?; **do you m. if I switch the radio on?** ¿te importa *or* molesta si enciendo *or Am* prendo la radio?; **I don't m.** no me importa; **which do you prefer? – I don't m.** ¿cuál prefieres? – me da igual; **I don't m. if I do** *(accepting sth offered)* ¿por qué no?; **I'm quite capable of doing it on my own, if you don't m.!** ¡soy perfectamente capaz de hacerlo yo solito, gracias!

(b) *(trouble oneself)* **it's broken – never m.!** está roto – ¡es igual *or* no importa!; **never m., we'll try again later** no te preocupes, lo volveremos a intentar más tarde; **never m. about that now** olvídate de eso ahora; *Fam* **never you m.!** *(it's none of your business)* ¡no es asunto tuyo!

▸**mind out** *vi Br* tener cuidado; **m. out!** ¡cuidado!

▸**mind out for** *vt insep Br* **m. out for that dog!** ¡cuidado con ese perro!

mind-altering ['maɪndɔːltərɪŋ] *adj (drug)* psicotrópico(a), psicótropo(a)

mind-bending ['maɪndbendɪŋ] *adj Fam* **(a)** *(drug)* alucinógeno(a) **(b)** *(experience, event, film)* alucinante

mind-blowing ['maɪndbləʊɪŋ] *adj Fam* alucinante

mind-boggling ['maɪndbɒglɪŋ] *adj Fam* alucinante

minded ['maɪndɪd] *adj* **he is commercially/mechanically m.** se le da muy bien el comercio/la mecánica; *Formal* **if you were so m.** si te pusieras (a hacerlo); *Formal* **I'm not m. to do so** no siento la inclinación de hacerlo

minder ['maɪndə(r)] *n* **(a)** *Br Fam (bodyguard)* gorila *m*, *Méx* guarura *m* **(b)** *Fam (to supervise contact with media)* asesor(ora) *m,f* de imagen **(c)** **(baby *or* child) m.** niñero(a) *m,f*

mind-expanding ['maɪndɪkspændɪŋ] *adj (drug)* alucinógeno(a); *(experience)* revelador(ora)

mindful ['maɪndfʊl] *adj* **to be m. of sth** ser consciente de algo; **he is always m. of others** es muy considerado con los demás

mindless ['maɪndlɪs] *adj* **(a)** *(destruction, violence)* gratuito(a), absurdo(a) **(b)** *(task, job)* mecánico(a) **(c)** *(inane) (film, book)* insustancial, frívolo(a)

mindlessly ['maɪndlɪslɪ] *adv* **(a)** *(needlessly)* gratuitamente **(b)** *(stupidly)* tontamente

mind-numbing ['maɪndnʌmɪŋ] *adj Fam* embrutecedor(ora)

mind-numbingly ['maɪndnʌmɪŋlɪ] *adv Fam* **it was m. boring** fue desesperantemente aburrido(a)

mind-reader ['maɪndriːdə(r)] *n* adivinador(ora) *m,f* del pensamiento; *Fam Hum* **I'm not a m.!** ¡no soy adivino!

mind-reading ['maɪndriːdɪŋ] *n* adivinación *f* del pensamiento

mindset ['maɪndset] *n (fixed attitude)* mentalidad *f*

mine[1] [maɪn] **1** *n* **(a)** *(for coal, tin, diamonds)* mina *f*; **he went down the m.** *or* **mines at 14** a los catorce años comenzó a bajar a la mina; *Fig* **a m. of information** una mina *or* un filón de información ▸▸ ***m. owner*** minero(a) *m,f*, propietario(a) *m,f* de una mina; ***m. shaft*** pozo *m* de mina

(b) *(explosive device)* mina *f*; **to lay mines** colocar minas; **to clear a road of mines** limpiar una carretera de minas ▸▸ ***m. detector*** detector *m* de minas

2 *vt* **(a)** *(coal, gold)* extraer; **they m. coal in the area** extraen carbón en la zona **(b)** *(place explosive mines in) (land, sea)* minar, colocar minas en; **our ship was mined** nuestro barco colisionó contra una mina **(c)** *(undermine) (fortification, foundations)* minar *or* socavar los fundamentos de

3 *vi* **to m. for coal/gold** extraer carbón/oro

mine[2] *possessive pron* **(a)** *(singular)* el mío *m*, la mía *f*; *(plural)* los míos *mpl*, las mías *fpl*; **her house is big but m. is bigger** su casa es grande, pero la mía es mayor; **she didn't have a book so I gave her m.** como no tenía un libro le di el mío; **it must be one of m.** debe de ser uno de los míos; **it wasn't his fault, it was MINE** no fue culpa suya sino mía; **m. is the work they admire most** mi obra es la que más admiran

(b) *(used attributively) (singular)* mío(a); *(plural)* míos(as); **this book is m.** este libro es mío; **a friend of m.** un amigo mío; **that dog of m.** ese perro mío

minefield ['maɪnfiːld] *n* **(a)** *(containing mines)* campo *m* de minas **(b)** *Fig (in law, politics)* polvorín *m*

minehunter ['maɪnhʌntə(r)] *n (ship)* cazaminas *m inv*

minelayer ['maɪnleɪə(r)] *n (ship)* buque *m* minador

miner ['maɪnə(r)] *n* minero(a) *m,f* ▸▸ ***m.'s lamp*** lámpara *f* de minero

mineral ['mɪnərəl] *n* mineral *m*; **the m. kingdom** el reino mineral; **the country's m. resources** los recursos minerales del país ▸▸ ***m. deposits*** depósitos *mpl* minerales; ***m. oil*** *Br* aceite *m* mineral; *US* aceite *m* de parafina; ***m. ore*** mineral *m*; ***m. rights*** derechos *mpl* de explotación; ***m. water*** agua *f* mineral

mineralogist [mɪnə'rɒlədʒɪst] *n* mineralogista *mf*

mineralogy [mɪnə'rɒlədʒɪ] *n* mineralogía *f*

minestrone [mɪnə'strəʊnɪ] *n* **m. (soup)** (sopa *f*) minestrone *f*

minesweeper ['maɪnswiːpə(r)] *n (ship)* dragaminas *m inv*

mineworker ['maɪnwɜːkə(r)] *n* minero(a) *m,f*

Ming [mɪŋ] *adj Hist* de los Ming; **a M. vase** un jarrón Ming; **the M. dynasty** la dinastía de los Ming

minge [mɪndʒ] *n Br Vulg Esp* chocho *m*, *Méx* paloma *f*, *RP* concha *f*

mingle ['mɪŋgəl] **1** *vt* mezclar; **he mingled truth with lies** mezcló verdades y mentiras; **joy mingled with sadness** una mezcla de alegría y tristeza

2 *vi* **(a)** *(things)* mezclarse **(b)** *(person)* **to m. with the crowd** mezclarse con la multitud; **I don't like the people you m. with** no me gusta la gente con la que tratas; **I'm not very good at mingling** no se me da muy bien eso de hablar con unos y con otros; **excuse me, I must m.** perdonen, tengo que saludar a los otros invitados

mingy ['mɪndʒɪ] *adj Fam* **(a)** *(person)* roñica, agarrado(a) **(b)** *(sum, portion, amount)* miserable, roñoso(a)

Mini® ['mɪnɪ] *n (car)* Mini® *m*

mini ['mɪnɪ] *n* **(a)** *(miniskirt)* mini *f*, minifalda *f* **(b)** *Comptr Esp* miniordenador *m*, *Am* minicomputadora *f*

mini- ['mɪnɪ] *prefix* mini-

miniature ['mɪnɪtʃə(r)] **1** *n* (**a**) *(painting, copy, model)* miniatura *f*; **in m.** en miniatura (**b**) *(bottle)* botella *f* en miniatura

2 *adj* en miniatura; **a m. Eiffel Tower** una Torre Eiffel en miniatura ►► ***m. golf*** minigolf *m*; ***m. poodle*** caniche *m* enano; ***m. railway*** tren *m* en miniatura

miniaturist ['mɪnɪtʃərɪst] *n* miniaturista *mf*

miniaturize ['mɪnɪtʃəraɪz] *vt* miniaturizar

minibar ['mɪnɪbɑː(r)] *n* minibar *m*

minibreak ['mɪnɪbreɪk] *n Br* minivacaciones *fpl*

minibus ['mɪnɪbʌs] *n* microbús *m*

minicab ['mɪnɪkæb] *n Br* taxi *m (que sólo se puede pedir por teléfono)*

minicam ['mɪnɪkæm] *n* minicámara *f*

minicomputer ['mɪnɪkəm'pjuːtə(r)] *n Comptr Esp* miniordenador *m*, *Am* minicomputadora *f*

minicourse ['mɪnɪkɔːs] *n US* minicurso *m*

MiniDisc® ['mɪnɪdɪsk] *n Comptr* MiniDisc® *m*

minigolf ['mɪnɪgɒlf] *n* minigolf *m*

minim ['mɪnɪm] *n Br Mus* blanca *f*

minimal ['mɪnɪməl] *adj* mínimo(a) ►► *Med* ***m. invasive therapy*** terapia *f* no invasiva; *Ling* ***m. pair*** par *m* mínimo

minimalism ['mɪnɪməlɪzəm] *n (in art, music, design)* minimalismo *m*

minimalist ['mɪnɪməlɪst] **1** *n* minimalista *mf*; **when it came to government intervention, he was a m.** era partidario de que el gobierno interviniese lo menos posible

2 *adj* minimalista

minimalize ['mɪnɪməlaɪz] *vt* minimizar

minimally ['mɪnɪməlɪ] *adv* mínimamente; **the new system is only m. more efficient** el nuevo sistema sólo es ligeramente más eficaz ►► *Med* ***m. invasive therapy*** terapia *f* no invasiva

minimarket ['mɪnɪmɑːkɪt], **minimart** ['mɪnɪmɑːt] *n US* supermercado *m* pequeño

minimize ['mɪnɪmaɪz] *vt* (**a**) *(reduce) (risk, cost)* minimizar, reducir al mínimo (**b**) *(diminish) (importance, significance)* minimizar (**c**) *Comptr (window)* minimizar

minimum ['mɪnɪməm] **1** *n* mínimo *m*; **a m. of two years' experience** un mínimo de dos años de experiencia, dos años de experiencia como mínimo; **with the** *or* **a m. of fuss** con el mínimo de complicaciones; **to keep/reduce sth to a m.** mantener/reducir algo al mínimo; **as a m.** como mínimo, al menos; **at the (very) m. it will cost $2,000** como mínimo costará 2.000 dólares

2 *adj* mínimo(a) ►► *Fin* ***m. lending rate*** tipo *m* mínimo de interés, *Am* tasa *f* mínima de interés; ***m. wage*** salario *m* mínimo (interprofesional), sueldo *m* mínimo

mining ['maɪnɪŋ] *n* minería *f*; **a m. town** una localidad minera ►► ***m. area*** cuenca *f* minera; ***m. engineer*** ingeniero(a) *m,f* de minas; ***the m. industry*** el sector minero

minion ['mɪnjən] *n Pej* lacayo *m*, subordinado(a) *m,f*

minipill ['mɪnɪpɪl] *n* = píldora anticonceptiva sin estrógenos

mini-roundabout ['mɪnɪ'raʊndəbaʊt] *n Br* rotonda *f* pequeña

miniscule = **minuscule**

mini-series ['mɪnɪsɪəriːz] *n TV* miniserie *f*

miniskirt ['mɪnɪskɜːt] *n* minifalda *f*

minister ['mɪnɪstə(r)] **1** *n* (**a**) *Pol (in charge of department)* ministro(a) *m,f*; *(junior)* secretario(a) *m,f* de Estado ►► *Br* ***M. of the Crown*** ministro(a) *m,f*; *Br* ***M. of Defence*** ministro(a) *m,f* de Defensa; *Br* ***M. of Health*** ministro(a) *m,f* de Sanidad; *Br* ***M. of State*** Secretario(a) *m,f* de Estado; ***m. without portfolio*** ministro(a) *m,f* sin cartera

(**b**) *Rel* ministro *m*

2 *vi Formal* (**a**) *(provide care)* **to m. to sb** ocuparse de alguien; **to m. to sb's needs** atender las necesidades de alguien; **he ministered to the sick** procuraba atención *or* ayuda a los enfermos; **a ministering angel** un ángel de la guarda (**b**) *Rel* **to m. to** servir como ministro en

ministerial [mɪnɪ'stɪərɪəl] *adj Pol* ministerial; **to hold m. office** ostentar una cartera ministerial

ministrations [mɪnɪ'streɪʃənz] *npl Literary or Hum (help, service)* atenciones *fpl*, agasajos *mpl*

ministry ['mɪnɪstrɪ] *n* (**a**) *Pol* ministerio *m* ►► *Br* ***the M. of Defence*** el Ministerio de Defensa; *Br* ***the M. of Transport*** el Ministerio de Transportes (**b**) *Rel* **to enter the m.** hacerse sacerdote; **his years of m. in the slums** sus años de sacerdocio en los barrios marginales

mink [mɪŋk] *n* (**a**) *(animal)* visón *m* (**b**) *(fur)* **a m. (coat)** un abrigo de visón

minke (whale) ['mɪŋkɪ(weɪl)] *n* rorcual *m* aliblanco

Minn (*abbr* **Minnesota**) Minnesota

minneola [mɪnɪ'əʊlə] *n (citrus fruit)* = cítrico parecido a una naranja, híbrido de pomelo y mandarina

Minnesota [mɪnɪ'səʊtə] *n* Minnesota

minnow ['mɪnəʊ] *n* (**a**) *(fish)* alevín *m* (**b**) *Br (team, company)* comparsa *mf*

Minoan [mɪ'nəʊən] *Hist* **1** *n* minoico(a) *m,f*

2 *adj* minoico(a)

minor ['maɪnə(r)] **1** *n* (**a**) *Law* menor *mf* (de edad) (**b**) *US Univ* subespecialidad *f* (**c**) *US Sport* **the Minors** = ligas profesionales estadounidenses de béisbol de menor importancia que la liga nacional

2 *adj* (**a**) *(lesser)* menor ►► *Sport* ***m. league*** = liga profesional estadounidense de béisbol de menor importancia que la liga nacional; *Fig* **a m. league company** una empresa de segunda; *Rel* ***m. orders*** órdenes *fpl* menores; *Br* ***m. roads*** carreteras *fpl* secundarias

(**b**) *(not serious, unimportant) (injury, illness)* leve; *(role, problem)* menor; *(detail, repair)* pequeño(a); **of m. importance** de poca importancia ►► *Law* ***m. offence*** falta *f* culposa; *Med* ***m. operation*** operación *f* sencilla

(**c**) *(for emphasis)* **the movie is a m. classic** la película es casi un clásico; **it was a m. miracle that we weren't killed** fue casi un milagro que no nos mataran

(**d**) *Mus* menor; **in A m.** en la menor; **m. seventh/third** séptima/tercera menor ►► ***m. key*** tono *m* menor; ***m. mode*** modo *m* menor

(**e**) *Phil* ***m. premise*** premisa *f* menor

(**f**) *US Univ* **m. subject** subespecialidad

(**g**) *Br Sch* **Jones m.** el pequeño de los Jones

(**h**) *Astron* ***m. planet*** *(asteroid)* planeta *m* menor

(**i**) *(in cards)* **m. suit** palo menor

3 *vi US Univ* **to m. in sth** tener algo como asignatura optativa

Minorca [mɪ'nɔːkə] *n* Menorca

Minorcan [mɪ'nɔːkən] **1** *n* menorquín(ina) *m,f*

2 *adj* menorquín(ina)

minority [maɪ'nɒrɪtɪ] *n* (**a**) *(of total number)* minoría *f*; **to be in a** *or* **the m.** ser minoría; **I was in a m. of one** fui el único ►► *Fin* ***m. holding*** participación *f* minoritaria; *Fin* ***m. interest*** interés *m* minoritario; ***m. opinion*** opinión *f* de la minoría; *Fin* ***m. shareholder*** accionista *mf* minoritario(a); *US Fin* ***m. stockholder*** accionista *mf* minoritario(a)

(**b**) *(in vote)* minoría *f* ►► ***m. government*** gobierno *m* minoritario; *US Pol* ***m. leader*** líder *mf* de la oposición; ***m. party*** partido *m* minoritario; ***m. rule*** gobierno *m* de la minoría; *Law* ***m. verdict*** veredicto *m* por minoría

(**c**) *Law (age)* minoría *f* de edad

Minotaur ['maɪnətɔː(r)] *n Mythol* **the M.** el Minotauro

minster ['mɪnstə(r)] *n (large church)* catedral *f*

minstrel ['mɪnstrəl] *n* (**a**) *(in Middle Ages)* juglar *m* (**b**) *(with blackened face)* = actor con el rostro maquillado de negro ►► ***m. show*** = espectáculo teatral de variedades protagonizado por actores con el rostro maquillado de negro

mint[1] [mɪnt] *n* (**a**) *(plant)* menta *f* ►► ***m. julep*** = bebida a base de whisky con hielo, azúcar y hojas de menta; ***m. sauce*** salsa *f* de menta; ***m. tea*** *(herbal tea)* poleo *m* (**b**) *(sweet)* caramelo *m* de menta

mint[2] **1** *n* **the (Royal) M.** ≃ la Casa de la Moneda, *Esp* ≃ la Fábrica Nacional de Moneda y Timbre; *Fam* **to make a m.** montarse en el dólar, *Méx* llenarse de lana, *RP* llenarse de guita

2 *adj* nuevo(a), sin usar; **in m. condition** como nuevo(a)

3 *vt* (**a**) *(coins)* acuñar; *Fam* **he must be minting it** seguro que se está forrando, *Méx* seguro que se está pudriendo en dinero (**b**) *(word, expression)* acuñar

minty ['mɪntɪ] *adj (smell, taste)* a menta

minuet [mɪnjʊ'et] *n Mus* minué *m*, minueto *m*

minus ['maɪnəs] **1** *n* (**a**) *(sign)* (signo *m*) menos *m* (**b**) *(negative aspect)* desventaja *f*, aspecto *m* negativo

2 *adj* (**a**) *(quantity, number)* negativo(a) ►► ***m. sign*** signo *m* menos (**b**) *(aspect)* negativo(a); **the m. side** la parte negativa (**c**) *Sch* **B m.** notable bajo

3 *prep* (**a**) *(in arithmetic)* **ten m. eight leaves** *or* **equals two** diez menos ocho igual a dos; **m. 12** menos doce (**b**) *(in temperature)* **it's m. 12 degrees** hace 12 grados bajo cero (**c**) *Fam (without)* sin; **he managed to escape, but m. his luggage** consiguió escapar, pero sin el equipaje; **the chair was m. a leg** a la silla le faltaba una pata

minuscule, miniscule ['mɪnəskjuːl] *adj* minúsculo(a), diminuto(a)

minute[1] ['mɪnɪt] **1** *n* (**a**) *(sixty seconds)* minuto *m*; **for ten minutes** durante diez minutos; **I'll be ready in ten minutes** dentro de diez minutos estoy lista; **it's ten minutes to three** son las tres menos diez; **it's ten minutes past three** son las tres y diez; **it's only a few minutes' walk (from here)** es un paseo de pocos minutos; **he got there with**

only minutes to spare cuando llegó sólo le sobraban unos minutos; **they arrived within minutes of us** llegaron pocos minutos después de nosotros; **to observe a m.'s silence** guardar un minuto de silencio ▸▸ ***m. hand*** *(of watch)* minutero *m*; ***m. steak*** filete *m* muy fino
(**b**) *(short time)* minuto *m*, momento *m*; **I won't be a m.** no tardo *or Am* demoro ni un minuto; **have you got a m.?** ¿tienes un minuto *or* momento?; **just a m.** un momento; **wait a m.!** ¡espera un momento!; **it'll be ready in a m.** estará listo en un minuto *or* momento; **I've just popped in for a m.** sólo me quedaré un momento *or* un minuto; **not** *or* **never for one m.** ni por un momento *or* instante; **I don't have a m. to call my own** no tengo (ni) un minuto libre
(**c**) *(instant)* momento *m*; **he'll be here any m.** (**now**) llegará en cualquier momento; **at the m.** en este momento; **go downstairs this m.!** ¡baja ahora mismo!; **I'll talk to him the m. he arrives** en cuanto llegue hablaré con él; **the m. my back was turned, she...** en cuanto me di la vuelta, ella...; **one m. he says he's sorry, the next he's doing it again!** en un momento dice que lo siente y al minuto siguiente lo está haciendo de nuevo; **until/at the last m.** hasta/en el último momento; **I enjoyed/hated every m. of the film** la película me encantó/me pareció horrorosa de principio a fin; **there's not a** *or* **one m. to lose** no hay tiempo que perder
(**d**) *Geom* minuto *m*
(**e**) *(note)* nota *f*; **minutes** *(of meeting)* acta *f*, actas *fpl*; **to take the minutes** levantar las actas ▸▸ ***m. book*** libro *m* de actas
2 *vt* (**a**) *(make note of)* hacer constar en acta; **the meeting will be minuted** se levantará acta de la reunión (**b**) *(send note to)* notificar

minute[2] [maɪ'nju:t] *adj* (**a**) *(small)* diminuto(a), minúsculo(a); *(increase, improvement)* mínimo(a) (**b**) *(detailed) (examination)* minucioso(a); **in m. detail** con minucioso detalle

minutely [maɪ'nju:tlɪ] *adv (to examine, describe)* minuciosamente

minutiae [mɪ'nu:ʃɪaɪ] *npl Formal (small details)* pormenores *mpl*

minx [mɪŋks] *n Fam Hum* aprovechada *f*, fresca *f*

Miocene ['maɪəsi:n] *Geol* **1** *n* **the M.** el mioceno
2 *adj (era)* mioceno(a)

mips [mɪps] *n Comptr* (*abbr* **million instructions per second**) millón *m* de instrucciones por segundo

miracle ['mɪrəkəl] *n* milagro *m*; **to perform** *or* **work miracles** hacer milagros; **the m. of radio** el milagro de la radio; **by a** *or* **some m.** de milagro, milagrosamente; **it's a m. that...** es un milagro que... ▸▸ ***m. cure*** cura *f* milagrosa; ***m. play*** auto *m*; ***m. worker*** persona *f* que hace milagros; *Fam* **I'm not a m. worker you know!** ¡quién te has creído que soy yo!, crees que sé hacer milagros ¿o qué?

miraculous [mɪ'rækjʊləs] *adj* milagroso(a); *Ironic* **she made a m. recovery as soon as the weekend arrived** cuando llegó el fin de semana se recuperó como por arte de magia

miraculously [mɪ'rækjʊləslɪ] *adv* milagrosamente; **m., no one was hurt** milagrosamente nadie resultó herido

mirage ['mɪrɑ:ʒ] *n also Fig* espejismo *m*

Mirandize [mə'rændaɪz] *vt US* **to M. a suspect** leerle los derechos a un sospechoso

MIRAS ['məræs] *n Br Formerly* (*abbr* **Mortgage Interest Relief at Source**) = desgravación fiscal de intereses por adquisición o reforma de vivienda habitual

mire [maɪə(r)] **1** *n* lodo *m*, fango *m*
2 *vt* **they were mired in the legal complexities** estaban atrapados en un atolladero de complejidades legales

mirin ['mɪrɪn] *n Culin* mirin *m*, = variante dulce del sake

mirror ['mɪrə(r)] **1** *n* espejo *m*; *Fig* **to hold a m.** (**up**) **to sth** dar un fiel reflejo de algo; IDIOM **it's all done with mirrors** es un montaje ▸▸ ***m. image*** *(exact copy)* reflejo *m* exacto; *(reversed image)* imagen *f* invertida; *Comptr* ***m. site*** servidor *m* espejo; ***m. writing*** escritura *f* invertida
2 *vt* (**a**) *(reflect)* reflejar (**b**) *(imitate, reproduce)* ser un calco de

mirrorball ['mɪrəbɔ:l] *n* bola *f* de espejos *(en discoteca)*

mirrored ['mɪrəd] *adj (ceiling)* con espejo; **m. glasses** gafas de espejo

mirrorlike ['mɪrəlaɪk] *adj (sea, lake)* liso(a) como un espejo

mirth [mɜ:θ] *n Formal* regocijo *m*

mirthless ['mɜ:θlɪs] *adj* distante, frío(a)

mirthlessly ['mɜ:θlɪslɪ] *adv* distantemente, fríamente

MIS *n Comptr* (*abbr* **management information system**) sistema *m* de gestión de la información

misadventure [mɪsəd'ventʃə(r)] *n* (**a**) *(misfortune)* desventura *f* (**b**) *Law* **death by m.** muerte accidental

misaligned [mɪsə'laɪnd] *adj* desalineado(a)

misalliance [mɪsə'laɪəns] *n Formal (marriage)* matrimonio *m* desafortunado

misanthrope ['mɪzənθrəʊp] *n* misántropo(a) *m,f*

misanthropic [mɪzən'θrɒpɪk] *adj* misantrópico(a)

misanthropist [mɪ'zænθrəpɪst] *n* misántropo(a) *m,f*

misanthropy [mɪ'zænθrəpɪ] *n* misantropía *f*

misapply [mɪsə'plaɪ] *vt Formal* (**a**) *(law)* aplicar erróneamente (**b**) *(term)* utilizar erróneamente

misapprehend ['mɪsæprɪ'hend] *vt Formal* malinterpretar

misapprehension [mɪsæprɪ'henʃən] *n Formal* malentendido *m*, equívoco *m*; **to be (labouring) under a m.** albergar una falsa impresión

misappropriate [mɪsə'prəʊprɪeɪt] *vt Formal (for oneself)* apropiarse indebidamente de; *(for a wrong use)* malversar

misappropriation ['mɪsəprəʊprɪ'eɪʃən] *n Formal (for oneself)* apropiación *f* indebida; *(for a wrong use)* malversación *f* de fondos

misbegotten [mɪsbɪ'gɒtən] *adj* (**a**) *(plan, decision, idea)* desacertado(a), desafortunado(a) (**b**) *(person)* inútil (**c**) *Old-fashioned (child)* adulterino(a)

misbehave [mɪsbɪ'heɪv] *vi* portarse mal; *Fam Fig* **the washing machine has been misbehaving again** la lavadora vuelve a fallar

misbehaviour, *US* **misbehavior** [mɪsbɪ'heɪvjə(r)] *n* mala conducta *f*, mal comportamiento *m*

misc (*abbr* **miscellaneous**) varios

miscalculate [mɪs'kælkjʊleɪt] **1** *vt* calcular mal *or* erróneamente
2 *vi* calcular mal

miscalculation [mɪskælkjʊ'leɪʃən] *n* error *m* de cálculo

miscarriage [mɪs'kærɪdʒ] *n* (**a**) *Med* aborto *m* (natural *or* espontáneo); **to have a m.** abortar de forma natural (**b**) *Law* ***m. of justice*** error *m* judicial

miscarry [mɪs'kærɪ] *vi* (**a**) *(pregnant woman)* abortar de forma natural (**b**) *Formal (plan)* fracasar

miscast [mɪs'kɑ:st] *vt* **to m. an actor** dar a un actor un papel poco apropiado, dar a un actor un papel que no le va

miscegenation [mɪsɪdʒə'neɪʃən] *n Formal* mestizaje *m*

miscellaneous [mɪsə'leɪnɪəs] *adj* diverso(a), misceláneo(a); **m. expenses** gastos varios; **the file marked "m."** el archivo con la etiqueta "misceláneo"

miscellany [mɪ'selənɪ] *n* (**a**) *(mixture, assortment)* miscelánea *f* (**b**) *(anthology)* miscelánea *f*

mischance [mɪs'tʃɑ:ns] *n Formal* mala suerte *f*, desgracia *f*; **by m.** por desgracia

mischief ['mɪstʃɪf] *n* (**a**) *(naughtiness)* travesura *f*; **she looked at me with m. in her eyes** me miró con ojos traviesos *or* de diablillo; **to be full of m.** ser un/una travieso(a); **to get up to m.** hacer travesuras; **to keep sb out of m.** evitar que alguien haga de las suyas (**b**) *(trouble)* problemas *mpl*; **to make m. (for sb)** crear problemas (a alguien) (**c**) *Br Fam Hum (injury)* **to do oneself a m.** hacerse daño *or* pupa (**d**) *Fam Hum (child)* diablillo *m*

mischief-maker ['mɪstʃɪf'meɪkə(r)] *n* **she's a terrible m.** *(naughty)* es muy traviesa; *(nasty)* le encanta sembrar cizaña

mischievous ['mɪstʃɪvəs] *adj* (**a**) *(naughty) (child, look)* travieso(a) (**b**) *(malicious)* malicioso(a)

mischievously ['mɪstʃɪvəslɪ] *adv* (**a**) *(naughtily)* traviesamente; **he smiled m.** sonrió con gesto travieso (**b**) *(maliciously)* maliciosamente

mischievousness ['mɪstʃɪvəsnɪs] *n* (**a**) *(naughtiness)* travesuras *fpl* (**b**) *(nastiness)* malicia *f*

misconceived [mɪskən'si:vd] *adj* (**a**) *(mistaken)* erróneo(a), equivocado(a) (**b**) *(badly planned)* mal planteado(a)

misconception [mɪskən'sepʃən] *n* idea *f* equivocada *or* errónea; **it's a common m. that...** es un error muy común pensar que...; **a popular m.** una idea equivocada muy extendida

misconduct *Formal* **1** *n* [mɪs'kɒndʌkt] (**a**) *(misbehaviour)* conducta *f* poco ética; (**professional**) **m.** conducta *f* (profesional) poco ética (**b**) *(poor management)* mala gestión *f*
2 *vt* [mɪskən'dʌkt] *(mismanage)* administrar *or* gestionar mal

misconstruction [mɪskən'strʌkʃən] *n Formal* mala interpretación *f*; **to be open to m.** ser susceptible de malas interpretaciones

misconstrue [mɪskən'stru:] *vt Formal* malinterpretar

miscreant ['mɪskrɪənt] *n Formal* malhechor(ora) *m,f*

miscue ['mɪs'kju:] *vi* (**a**) *(in billiards, pool)* pifiar (**b**) *Theat* equivocarse en la réplica

misdate [mɪs'deɪt] *vt (letter)* poner la fecha equivocada a

misdeal [mɪs'di:l] (*pt & pp* **misdealt** [mɪs'delt]) **1** *vt* **to m. the cards** repartir mal las cartas
2 *vi* repartir mal *(en naipes)*
3 *n* mal reparto *m (en naipes)*

misdeed [mɪs'di:d] *n Formal* fechoría *f*

misdemeanour, *US* **misdemeanor** [mɪsdɪ'mi:nə(r)] *n* **(a)** *Law* falta *f* **(b)** *(minor act of misbehaviour)* fechoría *f*

misdiagnose [mɪsdaɪəg'nəʊz] *vt Med* diagnosticar erróneamente; *Fig* **to m. the situation** hacer un análisis erróneo *or* equivocado de la situación

misdiagnosis [mɪsdaɪəg'nəʊsɪs] *n Med* diagnóstico *m* erróneo

misdial [mɪs'daɪəl] (*pt & pp* **misdialled,** *US* **misdialed**) **1** *vt* equivocarse al marcar
2 *vi* equivocarse al marcar

misdirect [mɪsdɪ'rekt] *vt* **(a)** *(person)* dar indicaciones equivocadas a **(b)** *(misuse) (efforts, talents)* malgastar; **misdirected energy** energía mal utilizada **(c)** *(letter)* mandar a una dirección equivocada **(d)** *Law* **to m. the jury** dar instrucciones erróneas al jurado

misdirection [mɪsdɪ'rekʃən] *n* **(a)** *(of funds)* malversación *f* **(b)** *Law (of jury)* **his m. of the jury** el hecho de que diera instrucciones erróneas al jurado

miser ['maɪzə(r)] *n* avaro(a) *m,f*

miserable ['mɪzərəbəl] *adj* **(a)** *(unhappy)* deprimido(a); **to be m.** estar deprimido(a); **you look m.** te veo deprimido; **don't be so m.!** ¡alegra esa cara!, ¡anímate!; **to make sb m., to make sb's life m.** amargar la vida a alguien; IDIOM **to be as m. as sin** estar de lo más deprimido(a)
(b) *(unpleasant) (evening, weather, person)* desagradable; **to have a m. time** pasarlo *Esp* fatal *or Am* pésimo; IDIOM **to be as m. as sin** ser lo más desagradable
(c) *(poor)* **it was a m. performance** fue una actuación penosa; **a m. failure** *(plan, attempt)* un fracaso estrepitoso
(d) *(mean)* miserable; **I only got a m. £70** sólo me dieron 70 miserables libras

miserably ['mɪzərəblɪ] *adv* **(a)** *(unhappily)* tristemente **(b)** *(unpleasantly)* lamentablemente **(c)** *(poorly)* **I failed m.** tuve un fracaso estrepitoso **(d)** *(meanly)* **to be m. paid** cobrar una miseria

misericord [mɪ'zerɪkɔ:d] *n Rel (on seat)* misericordia *f*

miserliness ['maɪzəlɪnɪs] *n* avaricia *f*

miserly ['maɪzəlɪ] *adj* avariento(a); **a m. amount** una cantidad miserable

misery ['mɪzərɪ] *n* **(a)** *(unhappiness)* tristeza *f*, infelicidad *f*; **to make sb's life a m.** amargar la vida a alguien; **to put an animal out of its m.** terminar con los sufrimientos de un animal; *Hum* **put him out of his m.!** *(by telling him sth)* ¡acaba de una vez con sus sufrimientos! **(b)** *Br Fam (person)* amargado(a) *m,f*; **don't be such an old m.!** ¡deja de amargarnos!

> **False friend:** The Spanish noun **miseria** is not a translation for the English word **misery**. In Spanish **miseria** means "poverty", "meanness" or "hardship".

misery-guts ['mɪzərɪgʌts] *n Br Fam* amargado(a) *m,f*

misfield **1** *n* ['mɪsfi:ld] *(in baseball, cricket)* = fallo consistente en que a un jugador se le escape la pelota de las manos
2 *vi* [mɪs'fi:ld] *(in baseball, cricket)* **he misfielded** se le escapó la pelota de las manos

misfire [mɪs'faɪə(r)] *vi* **(a)** *(gun)* fallar **(b)** *(plan)* fallar; *(joke)* no hacer efecto

misfit ['mɪsfɪt] *n (person)* inadaptado(a) *m,f*; **a social m.** un(a) inadaptado(a) social; **she was always a m. at school** nunca encajó en la escuela

misfortune [mɪs'fɔ:tʃən] *n* **(a)** *(bad luck)* desgracia *f*; **allies** *or* **companions in m.** compañeros en el infortunio *or* en la desgracia; **I had the m. to meet him in Paris** tuve la desgracia de conocerlo en París **(b)** *(unfortunate event)* desgracia *f*; **he was plagued by misfortunes** le perseguían las desgracias

misgiving [mɪs'gɪvɪŋ] *n Formal* aprensión *f*; **to have misgivings (about sth)** sentir aprensión (ante algo); **she had misgivings about allowing them to go** dudaba si dejarlos ir, le daba cierta aprensión dejarlos ir

misgovern [mɪs'gʌvən] *vt* gobernar mal

misgovernment [mɪs'gʌvənmənt] *n* mala gestión *f (de un gobierno)*

misguidance [mɪs'gaɪdəns] *n* mala orientación *f*

misguided [mɪs'gaɪdɪd] *adj* **(a)** *(unwise) (person)* confundido(a), equivocado(a); *(advice, decision, attempt)* desacertado(a); **to be m.** *(person)* estar confundido(a) *or* equivocado(a); *(advice, decision, attempt)* ser desacertado(a) **(b)** *(misdirected) (energy, belief, idealism)* mal encaminado(a); **to be m.** *(energy, belief, idealism)* ir mal encaminado(a); **in the m. belief that...** creyendo erróneamente que...

misguidedly [mɪs'gaɪdɪdlɪ] *adv* erróneamente

mishandle [mɪs'hændəl] *vt* **(a)** *(device)* manejar mal **(b)** *(situation)* encauzar mal; **the case was mishandled from the outset** encauzaron el caso mal desde el principio **(c)** *(mistreat)* maltratar

mishap ['mɪshæp] *n* contratiempo *m*; **without m.** sin ningún contratiempo

mishear [mɪs'hɪə(r)] (*pt & pp* **misheard** [mɪs'hɜ:d]) **1** *vt* entender mal; **I misheard your name as "Joan"** entendí que tu nombre era "Joan"
2 *vi* entender mal

mishit *Sport* **1** *n* ['mɪshɪt] error *m*; **that was a serious m.** le ha dado mal a la pelota
2 *vt* [mɪs'hɪt] (*pt & pp* **mishit**) darle mal a; **he m. his drive** le salió mal el drive

mishmash ['mɪʃmæʃ] *n Fam* batiburrillo *m*, *Am* menjunge *m*

misinform [mɪsɪn'fɔ:m] *vt Formal* informar mal; **I think you have been misinformed** creo que le han informado mal

misinformation [mɪsɪnfə'meɪʃən] *n* falsa información *f*

misinterpret [mɪsɪn'tɜ:prɪt] *vt* malinterpretar; **this decision should not be misinterpreted as a sign of weakness** esta decisión no debe ser interpretada como una muestra de debilidad

misinterpretation [mɪsɪntɜ:prɪ'teɪʃən] *n* interpretación *f* errónea; **his words are open to m.** sus palabras se prestan a una mala interpretación

misjudge [mɪs'dʒʌdʒ] *vt* **(a)** *(distance, time, difficulty)* calcular mal **(b)** *(person, situation)* juzgar mal; **it appears I misjudged you** me parece que te he juzgado mal

misjudg(e)ment [mɪs'dʒʌdʒmənt] *n* error *m* de apreciación

miskey [mɪs'ki:] *vt Comptr* escribir mal

mislay [mɪs'leɪ] (*pt & pp* **mislaid** [mɪs'leɪd]) *vt* extraviar, perder

mislead [mɪs'li:d] (*pt & pp* **misled** [mɪs'led]) *vt* **they misled him into thinking that...** *(deliberately)* le hicieron creer que...; **we were misled into believing he was dead** creímos erróneamente que estaba muerto

misleading [mɪs'li:dɪŋ] *adj (deliberately)* engañoso(a); **m. advertising** publicidad engañosa; **the map is rather m.** este mapa es confuso

misleadingly [mɪs'li:dɪŋlɪ] *adv (deliberately)* engañosamente; **it's m. known as the White Park** se le conoce como "White Park", lo cual puede llevar a confusión

misled *pt & pp of* **mislead**

mismanage [mɪs'mænɪdʒ] *vt* administrar *or* gestionar mal

mismanagement [mɪs'mænɪdʒmənt] *n* mala administración *f*, mala gestión *f*

mismatch **1** *n* ['mɪsmætʃ] **(a)** *(clash)* **the colours are a m.** los colores no pegan *or* no combinan **(b)** *(in relationship)* **they are a bit of a m.** no pegan mucho uno con otro **(c)** *(in sport)* **the contest was a complete m.** fue un enfrentamiento completamente desigual
2 *vt* [mɪs'mætʃ] **(a)** **to be mismatched** *(colours, clothes)* combinar mal **(b)** *(in relationship)* **I've always thought they were mismatched** siempre me pareció que no estaban hechos el uno para el otro

misname [mɪs'neɪm] *vt* **to be misnamed** tener un nombre poco apropiado

misnomer [mɪs'nəʊmə(r)] *n (name)* nombre *m* poco apropiado; **to call it a democratic election is a complete m.** a esas elecciones no se las puede llamar democráticas

miso ['mi:səʊ] *n Culin* miso *m*

misogynist [mɪ'sɒdʒɪnɪst] *n* misógino(a) *m,f*

misogynistic [mɪsɒdʒɪ'nɪstɪk] *adj* misógino(a)

misogyny [mɪ'sɒdʒɪnɪ] *n* misoginia *f*

misplace [mɪs'pleɪs] *vt* **(a)** *(lose)* extraviar, perder **(b)** *(put in wrong place)* **you've misplaced it** no lo has puesto en su sitio; **she's utterly misplaced in social work** el trabajo social no es su sitio **(c)** *(trust, confidence)* depositar equivocadamente

misplaced ['mɪspleɪst] *adj* **we had a m. faith in his powers as a negotiator** habíamos depositado equivocadamente nuestra confianza en sus dotes de negociador; **your loyalty is m.** le estás siendo leal a quien no deberías

misprint ['mɪsprɪnt] *n* errata *f* (de imprenta)

misprision [mɪs'prɪʒən] *n Law* ocultación *f* de un delito

mispronounce [mɪsprə'naʊns] *vt* pronunciar mal

mispronunciation [mɪsprənʌnsɪ'eɪʃən] *n* pronunciación *f* incorrecta

misquotation [mɪskwəʊ'teɪʃən] *n* **(a)** *(quotation)* cita *f* errónea **(b)** *(action)* tergiversación *f*

misquote [mɪs'kwəʊt] *vt (person)* tergiversar las palabras de; *(words)* tergiversar

misread [mɪs'riːd] *(pt & pp* **misread** [mɪs'red]) *vt* (**a**) *(notice, timetable)* leer mal (**b**) *(misinterpret)* malinterpretar

misrepresent [mɪsreprɪ'zent] *vt (person)* tergiversar las palabras de; *(words, facts)* tergiversar

misrepresentation [mɪsreprɪzen'teɪʃən] *n* deformación *f*, tergiversación *f*; **that is a complete m. of the facts** es una deformación *or* tergiversación absoluta de los hechos

misrule [mɪs'ruːl] **1** *n* desgobierno *m*
2 *vt* gobernar mal

Miss[1] *(abbr* **Mississippi**) Misisipí

Miss[2] [mɪs] *n* señorita *f*; **M. Jones** la señorita Jones; **impudent little M.!** ¡señorita insolente! ▸▸ ***M. World*** Miss *f* Mundo

---

MISS [mɪs] **1** *n Esp* fallo *m*, *Am* falla *f*; *Fam* **I think I'll give the cake/film a m.** creo que voy a pasar de comer tarta/ver la película; PROV **he only lost by a second, but a m. is as good as a mile** perdió por un solo segundo, pero da lo mismo, un segundo o diez segundos, el caso es que perdió

2 *vt* (**a**) *(bus, train, chance)* perder; *(film, TV programme)* perderse; *(appointment)* faltar a; *(deadline)* no cumplir; **you've just missed him** se acaba de marchar; **to m. a class** perderse una clase; **you haven't missed much!** ¡no te has perdido mucho!; **don't m. it!** ¡no te lo pierdas!; **this movie is not to be missed** esta película es imprescindible; **I wouldn't m. it for anything** *or* **the world** no me lo perdería por nada del mundo; **to m. the cut** *(in golf)* no meterse en el corte; **to m. school** faltar a clase; IDIOM **to m. the boat** *or* **bus** perder el tren

(**b**) *(target)* no acertar en; *(shot, penalty) Esp* fallar, *Am* errar; *Fig* **her insults missed the mark** sus insultos no tuvieron ningún efecto

(**c**) *(not notice)* **I spotted a mistake that the others had missed** descubrí un error que los otros no habían visto; **you can't m. the house** la casa no tiene pérdida, es imposible pasar delante de la casa sin verla; **the boss doesn't m. much** *or* **a thing** al jefe no se le pasa *or* escapa nada; IDIOM **he doesn't m. a trick** no se le pasa una

(**d**) *(not hear, not understand) (question, remark)* no oír, perderse; *(joke)* no entender, *Esp* no coger; **to m. the point** no entender bien

(**e**) *(omit) (word, line)* saltarse; **you missed a comma here** te has saltado una coma aquí; **I've missed my period** no me ha venido el periodo *or* la regla

(**f**) *(avoid)* **the car just missed me** el coche *or Am* carro *or CSur* auto no me atropelló por poco; **I only just missed a tree** esquivé un árbol por muy poco; **my team just missed promotion** a mi equipo se le ha escapado el ascenso de las manos; **I often m. lunch** a menudo no como nada al mediodía; **if we leave early we'll m. the rush hour** si salimos temprano evitaremos la hora *Esp* punta *or Am* pico; **she just missed being killed** por poco se mata

(**g**) *(feel lack of)* echar de menos, *Am* extrañar; **I m. you** te echo de menos, *Am* te extraño; **I m. being able to get up whenever I wanted to** echo de menos *or Am* extraño levantarme a la hora que quiero; **what I m. most about the States is...** lo que más echo de menos *or Am* extraño de los Estados Unidos es...; **she will be sadly missed** la echaremos muchísimo de menos, *Am* la extrañaremos muchísimo; **we didn't m. her until the next day** no la echamos en falta hasta el día siguiente, no nos dimos cuenta que no estaba hasta el día siguiente

(**h**) *(lack)* **the table's missing one of its legs** a la mesa le falta una pata; **I'm missing two books from my collection** me faltan dos libros de mi colección

3 *vi* (**a**) *(miss target)* **his penalty missed** *Esp* falló el penalty, *Am* erró el penal; **he shot at me, but missed** me disparó, pero no me dio *or RP* le erró

(**b**) *(be absent)* **to be missing** faltar; **nothing is missing** no falta nada

(**c**) *Aut* fallar

▸ **miss off** *vt sep* **she missed me off the list** no me incluyó en la lista

▸ **miss out 1** *vt sep (omit)* pasar por alto, omitir; *Br* **have I missed anyone out?** ¿me he saltado a alguien?

2 *vi (not benefit)* **to m. out on sth** perderse algo; **she just missed out on a place in the finals** se perdió por muy poco un puesto en la fase final; **how come I always m. out?** ¿por qué salgo yo perdiendo siempre?

---

missal ['mɪsəl] *n Rel* misal *m*

missel thrush, mistle thrush ['mɪsəlθrʌʃ] *n* zorzal *m* charlo, cagaaceite *m*

misshape ['mɪsʃeɪp] *n* = chocolate, golosinas o galletas deformadas que se venden a precio económico

misshapen [mɪs'ʃeɪpən] *adj* deforme

missile ['mɪsaɪl, *US* 'mɪsəl] *n* (**a**) *(rocket)* misil *m* ▸▸ ***m. launcher*** lanzamisiles *m inv* (**b**) *(object thrown)* proyectil *m*

missing ['mɪsɪŋ] *adj* (**a**) *(lost)* perdido(a); *(absent)* ausente; **to be m.** *(person, thing)* faltar; **a young child has gone m.** se ha perdido un niño pequeño; **my wallet's gone m.** no sé dónde está mi cartera; **the table had one leg m.** a la mesa le falta una pata; **find the m. word** encontrar la palabra que falta ▸▸ ***m. link*** eslabón *m* perdido; ***m. person*** desaparecido(a) *m,f*; ***m. persons*** *(department)* registro *m* de personas desaparecidas

(**b**) *(in war)* desaparecido(a); **m. in action** desaparecido(a) en combate; **m. presumed dead** desaparecido(a) y dado(a) por muerto(a)

mission ['mɪʃən] *n* (**a**) *(task)* misión *f*; **a rescue m.** una misión de rescate; **she's found her m. in life** ha encontrado su misión en la vida; **m. accomplished** misión cumplida ▸▸ *Com* ***m. statement*** declaración *f* de (la) misión, misión *f*

(**b**) *Rel (campaign, building)* misión *f* ▸▸ ***m. station*** misión *f*

(**c**) *(delegation)* delegación *f*; **a Chinese trade m.** la delegación comercial china

(**d**) *US (permanent)* legación *f*

(**e**) *Mil & Astron* misión *f*; **he had flown 20 missions** ha volado *or* participado en veinte misiones ▸▸ ***m. control*** centro *m* de control

missionary ['mɪʃənərɪ] **1** *n* misionero(a) *m,f* ▸▸ ***m. position*** *(sexual)* postura *f* del misionero
2 *adj (work)* misionero(a); *(zeal)* apostólico(a)

missis = **missus**

Mississippi [mɪsɪ'sɪpɪ] *n* Misisipí; **the M. (River)** el (río) Misisipí

Mississippian [mɪsɪ'sɪpɪən] **1** *n* persona de Misisipí
2 *adj* de Misisipí

missive ['mɪsɪv] *n Formal* misiva *f*

Missouri [mɪ'zʊərɪ] *n* Misuri; **the M. (River)** el (río) Misuri

misspeak ['mɪs'spiːk] *(pt* **misspoke** [mɪs'spəʊk], *pp* **misspoken** [mɪs'spəʊkən]) *vi US* equivocarse al hablar

misspell ['mɪs'spel] *(pt & pp* **misspelt** ['mɪs'spelt]) *vt* escribir incorrectamente

misspelling ['mɪs'spelɪŋ] *n* falta *f* de ortografía; **"accomodation" is a common m. of "accommodation"** escribir "accomodation" por "accommodation" es un error muy común

misspelt *pt & pp of* **misspell**

misspend ['mɪs'spend] *(pt & pp* **misspent** [mɪ'spent]) *vt (money, talents)* malgastar

misspent ['mɪsspent] *adj* **a m. youth** una juventud malgastada *or* desaprovechada

misspoke *pt of* **misspeak**

misspoken *pp of* **misspeak**

missus, missis ['mɪsɪz] *n Br Fam (wife)* **the m.** la parienta, *Méx* la vieja, *RP* la doña

misstate ['mɪs'steɪt] *vt (unintentionally)* no explicar bien; *(deliberately)* tergiversar; **he deliberately misstated the facts** tergiversó deliberadamente los hechos

misstatement ['mɪs'steɪtmənt] *n* **when I said... that was a m.** cuando dije... me expliqué mal; **a deliberate m. of the facts** una tergiversación deliberada de los hechos

missy ['mɪsɪ] *n Fam Old-fashioned* jovencita *f*

mist [mɪst] *n* (**a**) *(fog)* neblina *f*; **sea m.** bruma; *Fig* **the mists of time** la noche de los tiempos (**b**) *(condensation)* vaho *m* (**c**) *(from spray)* nube *f*

▸ **mist over** *vi* (**a**) *(landscape)* quedar cubierto(a) por la neblina (**b**) *(mirror, eyes)* empañarse

▸ **mist up** *vi (mirror, glasses)* empañarse

mistakable, mistakeable [mɪs'teɪkəbəl] *adj* confundible (**for** por)

mistake [mɪs'teɪk] **1** *n* error *m*, equivocación *f*; **there must be some m.** tiene que haber un error; **to make a m.** equivocarse, cometer un error; **to make the m. of doing sth** cometer el error de hacer algo; **it's an easy m. to make** es un error fácil de cometer, es fácil equivocarse; **you're making a big mistake** cometes un grave error; **by m.** por error *or* equivocación; **sorry, my m.** lo siento, me he equivocado (yo); **make no m.** puedes estar seguro; *Fam* **this is hard work and no m.!** no cabe duda de que es un trabajo duro

2 *vt (pt* **mistook** [mɪs'tʊk], *pp* **mistaken** [mɪs'teɪkən]) (**a**) *(misunderstand)* interpretar mal; **I mistook her intentions** interpreté mal sus intenciones; **there's no mistaking what she means** lo ha dejado bien claro

(**b**) *(confuse)* confundir (**for** con); **I mistook him for someone else** lo confundí con otra persona; **I mistook his shyness for arrogance** creí que su timidez era arrogancia; **there's no mistaking a voice like that!** ¡esa voz es inconfundible!

mistakeable = **mistakable**

mistaken [mɪs'teɪkən] *adj (belief, impression)* equivocado(a), erróneo(a); **to be m.** *(person)* estar equivocado(a); **I was m. about the date** estaba en un error en cuanto a la fecha; **it was a case of m. identity** confundieron su identidad; **unless I'm very much m.,...** si no me equivoco,...; **he proposed to her in the m. belief that she loved him** se le declaró creyendo erróneamente que ella lo quería

mistakenly [mɪs'teɪkənlɪ] *adv* erróneamente; **they m. assumed that it would be easy** se equivocaron al suponer que sería fácil

Mister ['mɪstə(r)] *n* señor *m*; **M. Jones** el señor Jones; **hey M.!** ¡oiga, señor!

mistime [mɪs'taɪm] *vt* **to m. sth** hacer algo a destiempo; **to m. a counterattack** contraatacar a destiempo; **the launch of the new product has been badly mistimed** el producto no se lanzó en el momento propicio

mistiness ['mɪstɪnɪs] *n* **(a)** *(mist)* neblina *f* **(b)** *(condensation)* empañamiento *m*, condensación *f*

mistle thrush = **missel thrush**

mistletoe ['mɪsəltəʊ] *n* muérdago *m*

mistook *pt of* **mistake**

mistranslate [mɪstræns'leɪt] *vt* traducir erróneamente

mistranslation [mɪstræns'leɪʃən] *n* error *m* de traducción, mala traducción *f*

mistreat [mɪs'tri:t] *vt* maltratar

mistreatment [mɪs'tri:tmənt] *n* maltrato *m*, malos tratos *mpl*

mistress ['mɪstrɪs] *n* **(a)** *(of household, servants)* señora *f*, ama *f*; *(of dog)* dueña *f*; **the m. of the house** la señora de la casa; **to be one's own m.** ser dueña de sí misma; **to be m. of the situation** tener la situación controlada, estar al cargo de la situación

(b) *(woman teacher) (in primary school)* señorita *f*, maestra *f*; *(in secondary school)* profesora *f*; **French/geography m.** profesora de francés/geografía

(c) *(lover)* querida *f*, amante *f*; **he kept a m. for years** tuvo una querida *or* amante durante años

(d) *Old-fashioned (title)* **M. Bacon** la señora Bacon

mistrial [mɪs'traɪəl] *n Law* **(a)** *(because of flawed procedure)* juicio *m* nulo **(b)** *US (because jury cannot agree)* juicio *m* nulo *(por jurado en desacuerdo)*

mistrust [mɪs'trʌst] **1** *n* desconfianza *f*; **she has an instinctive m. of doctors** siente una desconfianza instintiva hacia los médicos

2 *vt (be suspicious of)* desconfiar de; *(doubt)* no confiar en; **he mistrusts his own abilities** no confía en sus propias habilidades

mistrustful [mɪs'trʌstfʊl] *adj* desconfiado(a); **to be m. of** desconfiar de

misty ['mɪstɪ] *adj* **(a)** *(place, weather)* neblinoso(a); *(at sea or seaside)* brumoso(a); **it's m.** hay niebla/bruma **(b)** *(window, mirror)* empañado(a); **her eyes were m. with tears** tenía los ojos empañados de lágrimas **(c)** *(form)* borroso(a) **(d)** *(like mist)* **a m. veil of cloud** un ligero velo de nubes; **m. blue** azul brumoso

mistype [mɪs'taɪp] *vt* mecanografiar *or* escribir mal

misunderstand [mɪsʌndə'stænd] (*pt & pp* **misunderstood** [mɪsʌndə'stʊd]) **1** *vt* **(a)** *(misinterpret)* entender mal; **don't m. me** no me malinterpretes; **your irony could be misunderstood** pueden interpretar mal tu ironía **(b)** *(misjudge)* malinterpretar; **he feels misunderstood** se siente incomprendido

2 *vi* entender mal; **if I have not misunderstood** si no lo he entendido mal

misunderstanding [mɪsʌndə'stændɪŋ] *n* **(a)** *(misconception)* malentendido *m*, confusión *f*; **there's been a m. about the time** ha habido un malentendido con la hora; **there seems to have been some m.** parece que ha habido un malentendido *or* una confusión; **the whole dispute hinges on a m.** toda la disputa se debe a un malentendido; **to clear up a m.** esclarecer *or* deshacer un malentendido

(b) *(disagreement)* desacuerdo *m*, diferencias *fpl*

misunderstood [mɪsʌndə'stʊd] **1** *pt & pp of* **misunderstand**

2 *adj* incomprendido(a); **a m. artist** un artista incomprendido

misuse 1 *n* [mɪs'ju:s] *(of power, one's position)* uso *m* indebido, abuso *m*; *(of word, phrase)* uso *m* incorrecto; *(of equipment)* uso *m* indebido; **m. of funds** uso indebido de fondos

2 *vt* [mɪs'ju:z] **(a)** *(power, one's position)* usar indebidamente, abusar; *(word, phrase)* usar sin propiedad; *(equipment, funds)* usar indebidamente **(b)** *(ill-treat)* explotar

MIT [emaɪ'ti:] *n (abbr* **Massachusetts Institute of Technology***)* MIT *m*

mite [maɪt] *n* **(a)** *(bug)* ácaro *m* **(b)** *Fam (child)* criatura *f*; **poor little m.!** ¡pobre criaturita! **(c)** *Fam (a little bit)* **it's a m. expensive** es un poquitín *or Esp* pelín caro

miter *US* = **mitre**

mitigate ['mɪtɪgeɪt] *vt Formal* **(a)** *(effect, suffering)* atenuar, mitigar; *(pain, anger, grief)* aliviar, mitigar **(b)** *Law* **mitigating circumstances** circunstancias atenuantes

mitigation [mɪtɪ'geɪʃən] *n Formal* **(a)** *(of effect, suffering)* atenuación *f*; *(of pain, anger, grief)* alivio *m* **(b)** *Law* **in m.** como atenuante; *also Fig* **it should be said in m. that...** como atenuante cabe decir que...

mitosis [maɪ'təʊsɪs] *n Biol* mitosis *f inv*

mitre, *US* miter ['maɪtə(r)] **1** *n* **(a)** *Rel* mitra *f* **(b)** *(joint)* ***m. box*** caja *f* de ingletes, inglete *m*; ***m. joint*** (ensambladura *f* a) inglete *m*

2 *vt (join)* unir *or* ensamblar a inglete

mitt [mɪt] *n* **(a)** *(mitten)* manopla *f*; *US* **(baseball) m.** guante *m* de béisbol **(b)** *Fam (hand)* **mitts** garras *fpl*, *Esp* zarpas *fpl*; **get your mitts off me!** ¡quítame las garras *or Esp* zarpas de encima!

mitten ['mɪtən] *n (glove)* manopla *f*; *(fingerless)* mitón *m*

mix [mɪks] **1** *n* **(a)** *(combination, blend)* mezcla *f*; **a fascinating m. of cultures** una mezcla fascinante de culturas; **he's got the right m. of talent for the team** tiene la combinación de talentos idónea para el equipo

(b) *(act of mixing)* **give the paint a (good) m.** mezcla (bien) la pintura

(c) *(in package)* preparado *m*; **a packet of soup m.** un sobre de sopa; **a packet of cake m.** un preparado para pastel instantáneo

(d) *Mus* mezcla *f*

2 *vt* **(a)** *(blend)* mezclar; **m. the sugar and** *or* **with the flour** mezcle el azúcar y *or* con la levadura; **m. the sugar into the batter** mezcle el azúcar con la pasta para rebozar

(b) *(combine)* mezclar; **you shouldn't m. your drinks** no deberías mezclar bebidas distintas; **to m. business with pleasure** mezclar el placer con los negocios; **to m. metaphors** hacerse un lío con las metáforas, confundir metáforas; *Br Fam* **to m. it with sb** *(fight)* darse de palos con alguien

(c) *(prepare) (cocktail, medicine, plaster)* preparar

(d) *Mus* mezclar

3 *vi* **(a)** *(blend)* mezclarse **(b)** *(combine well)* compaginar bien; **drinking and driving don't m.** beber y conducir *or Am* manejar no hacen buenas migas **(c)** *(socially)* relacionarse (**with** con); **she mixes well** se lleva bien *or* es muy abierta con todo el mundo; **he doesn't m. much** no es muy sociable

▸ **mix up** *vt sep* **(a)** *(ingredients)* mezclar

(b) *(confuse) (people, dates)* confundir; **I always m. her up with her sister** siempre la confundo con su hermana; **you've got the story completely mixed up** has confundido la historia por completo; **I get mixed up about which is which** nunca sé cuál es cuál, siempre los confundo; **I'm mixed up about how I feel about him** tengo sentimientos encontrados hacia él

(c) *(disorder) (papers, books)* revolver, desordenar

(d) *Fam (in situation, relationship)* **to be mixed up in sth** estar *or* andar metido(a) en algo; **I got mixed up in their quarrel** me vi metido en su pelea; **to get mixed up with sb** liarse con alguien

(e) *US Fam* **to m. it up** *(fight)* darse de palos con alguien

▸ **mix together** *vt sep* mezclar

mix-and-match ['mɪksən'mætʃ] *adj* **m. clothes** coordinados

mixed [mɪkst] *adj* **(a)** *(assorted)* variado(a); *Fam* **it was a m. bag** había de todo, había cosas buenas y malas ▸▸ *Econ* ***m. company*** empresa *f* mixta; ***m. economy*** economía *f* mixta; ***m. farming*** explotación *f* mixta; ***m. grill*** parrillada *f* mixta; *Art* ***m. media*** técnica *f* mixta; ***m. metaphor*** chascarrillo *m (mezclando frases hechas)*; ***m. salad*** ensalada *f* mixta

(b) *(for both sexes)* mixto(a); **it's not a joke that should be told in m. company** no es un chiste para contar delante de las damas; **of m. race** de raza mixta; **a m. neighbourhood** un barrio en el que conviven razas distintas ▸▸ ***m. doubles*** *(in tennis)* dobles *mpl* mixtos; ***m. marriage*** = matrimonio entre personas de distintas razas o religiones; *Br* ***m. school*** *(coeducational)* colegio *m* mixto

(c) *(ambivalent, not wholly positive)* **reaction to the proposal was m.** la propuesta recibió reacciones disímiles *or* diversas; **to have m. feelings (about sth)** tener sentimientos contradictorios (respecto a algo); IDIOM **it was a m. blessing** tuvo su lado bueno y su lado malo

(d) *Math* ***m. number*** número *m* mixto

mixed-ability ['mɪkstə'bɪlɪtɪ] *adj Br Sch* **a m. class** una clase con alumnos de distintos niveles de aptitud

mixed-media ['mɪkst'mi:dɪə] *adj Art* multimedia *inv;* **a m. work** un trabajo multimedia

mixed-up [mɪks'tʌp] *adj Fam (person)* desorientado(a), confuso(a); **she's a crazy m. kid** es una chica con un montón de problemas

mixer ['mɪksə(r)] *n* (a) *(machine for mixing) (for food)* batidora *f; (for cement)* hormigonera *f*
(b) *Cin & Mus (mixing desk)* mesa *f* de mezclas
(c) *(in drink)* refresco *m (para mezcla alcohólica)*
(d) *(person)* **to be a good m.** *(socially)* ser muy abierto(a) con la gente
(e) *Br* ***m. tap*** *(Esp* grifo *m or Chile, Col, Méx* llave *f or RP* canilla *f)* monomando *m*
(f) *US Univ Fam (party)* fiesta *f (para que se conozcan los nuevos estudiantes)*

mixing ['mɪksɪŋ] *n* ***m. bowl*** cuenco *m,* bol *m; Cin & Mus* ***m. desk*** mesa *f* de mezclas

mixture ['mɪkstʃə(r)] *n* (a) *(of different things)* mezcla *f;* **he's a strange m.** tiene cualidades contradictorias (b) *(medicine)* jarabe *m*

mix-up ['mɪksʌp] *n* confusión *f;* **there was a m. over the dates** hubo una confusión con las fechas

mizzenmast ['mɪzənmɑ:st] *n Naut* palo *m* de mesana

Mk (*abbr* **mark**) **M. II Jaguar** Jaguar II

mktg *Com* (*abbr* **marketing**) marketing *m*

ml (*abbr* **millilitre(s)**) ml

MLA [emel'eɪ] *n* (a) (*abbr* **Member of the Legislative Assembly**) *(in Australia, India, Canada, Northern Ireland)* miembro *mf* de la asamblea legislativa, diputado(a) *m,f* (b) (*abbr* **Modern Language Association**) Asociación *f* de Lenguas Modernas

MLitt [em'lɪt] *n* (*abbr* **Master of Letters**) Máster *m* en Letras

MLR [emel'ɑ:(r)] *n Fin* (*abbr* **minimum lending rate**) tipo *m* activo mínimo de interés, *Am* tasa *f* activa mínima de interés

M'lud [m'lʌd] *n Br* su señoría

mm (*abbr* **millimetre(s)**) mm

MMC [emem'si:] *n* (*abbr* **Monopolies and Mergers Commission**) = comisión británica antimonopolios

MMR [emem'ɑ:(r)] *n* (*abbr* **measles, mumps and rubella**) (vacuna *f*) triple vírica *f*

MMX [emem'eks] *n Comptr* (*abbr* **multimedia extensions**) MMX *m*

MN (*abbr* **Minnesota**) Minnesota

MNA [emen'eɪ] *n Can* (*abbr* **Member of the National Assembly**) *(in Quebec)* miembro *mf* de la asamblea nacional, diputado(a) *m,f*

mnemonic [nɪ'mɒnɪk] **1** *n* recurso *m* mnemotécnico; **mnemonics** mnemotecnia *f*
2 *adj* mnemotécnico(a), mnemónico(a)

MO [em'əʊ] *n* (a) (*abbr* **medical officer**) médico(a) *m,f* militar (b) (*abbr* **Missouri**) Misuri (c) (*abbr* **modus operandi**) modus operandi *m inv* (d) (*abbr* **money order**) transferencia *f,* giro *m*

mo [məʊ] *n Fam* segundo *m;* **half a mo!, just a mo!** ¡un segundito!

moan [məʊn] **1** *n* (a) *(sound)* gemido *m* (b) *(complaint)* queja *f;* **to have a m. (about sth)** quejarse (de algo)
2 *vi* (a) *(make sound)* gemir (b) *(complain)* quejarse (**about** de)

moaner ['məʊnə(r)] *n* quejica *mf, Am* quejoso(a) *m,f*

moaning ['məʊnɪŋ] **1** *n* (a) *(sound)* gemido *m* (b) *Fam (complaining)* quejas *fpl*
2 *adj* (a) *(groaning)* **a m. sound** un gemido (b) *Fam* ***m. minnie*** quejica *mf, Am* quejoso(a) *m,f*

moat [məʊt] *n* foso *m*

mob [mɒb] **1** *n* (a) *(crowd)* turba *f,* horda *f;* **we were faced with an angry m.** nos vimos frente a una multitud encolerizada ►► ***m. rule*** la ley de la calle (b) *Pej (common people)* **the m.** la plebe, la chusma (c) *Fam (bunch, clique)* camarilla *f,* pandilla *f;* **which m. were you in?** *(in armed forces)* ¿en qué cuerpo estabas? (d) *Fam* **the M.** *(the Mafia)* la Mafia
2 *vt* (*pt & pp* **mobbed**) (a) *(crowd round)* **to be mobbed by fans** ser asediado(a) por una multitud de admiradores (b) *(crowd)* **the streets were mobbed** las calles estaban abarrotadas

mob-cap ['mɒbkæp] *n* cofia *f*

mobile ['məʊbaɪl] **1** *n* (a) *(hanging ornament)* móvil *m* (b) *Fam (mobile phone)* móvil *m, Am* celular *m*
2 *adj* (a) *(not stationary)* móvil ►► ***m. home*** *(caravan)* caravana *f,* rulot *f, RP* casa *f* rodante; *Br* ***m. library*** bibliobús *m,* biblioteca *f* ambulante; ***m. phone*** teléfono *m* móvil, *Am* teléfono *m* celular
(b) *(able to move oneself)* **she's no longer very m.** ha perdido mucha movilidad; *Fam* **are you m.?** *(have you got a car?)* ¿tienes coche *or Am* carro *or CSur* auto?
(c) *(features, face)* expresivo(a)
(d) *(socially)* **to be (socially) m.** tener movilidad social

mobility [məʊ'bɪlɪtɪ] *n* movilidad *f;* **she has very little m. in her right arm** tiene poca movilidad en el brazo derecho; **social m.** movilidad social ►► ***m. allowance*** = subsidio para el transporte de minusválidos

mobilization [məʊbɪlaɪ'zeɪʃən] *n (of troops, support)* movilización *f*

mobilize ['məʊbɪlaɪz] **1** *vt (troops, support)* movilizar
2 *vi* movilizarse

Möbius strip ['mɜ:bɪəs'strɪp] *n* banda *f* de Möbius

mobster ['mɒbstə(r)] *n US Fam* gángster *m*

moccasin ['mɒkəsɪn] *n (shoe, slipper)* mocasín *m*

mocha ['mɒkə] **1** *n* (a) *(type of coffee)* (café *m*) moca *f* (b) *(flavour)* moca *f*
2 *adj (coffee, flavour)* de moca

mock [mɒk] **1** *adj* fingido(a), simulado(a); **m. surprise** sorpresa fingida ; **m. horror** horror fingido ►► ***m. battle*** simulacro *m* de batalla; *Br Sch* ***m. examination*** examen *m* de prueba
2 *vt* (a) *(ridicule)* burlarse de; *Hum* **don't m. the afflicted!** ¡no te rías de los desgraciados! (b) *Literary (frustrate)* malograr
3 *vi* burlarse; **don't m.!** ¡no te burles!
4 *n Br Fam (examination)* examen *m* de prueba *(sin valor evaluativo)*

► **mock up** *vt sep* hacer una reproducción *or* un modelo de tamaño real de

mockers ['mɒkəz] *npl Br Fam* **to put the m. on** fastidiar, *Esp* jorobar

mockery ['mɒkərɪ] *n* (a) *(ridicule)* burlas *fpl* (b) *(travesty)* farsa *f;* **the trial was a m. (of justice)** el juicio fue una farsa; **to make a m. of sth/sb** poner algo/a alguien en ridículo

mock-heroic ['mɒkhɪ'rəʊɪk] *adj (verse)* que satiriza la poesía épica

mocking ['mɒkɪŋ] *adj* burlón(ona)

mockingbird ['mɒkɪŋbɜ:d] *n* sinsonte *m*

mock-up ['mɒkʌp] *n* reproducción *f,* modelo *m (de tamaño natural)*

MOD [eməʊ'di:] *n Br* (*abbr* **Ministry of Defence**) Ministerio *m* de Defensa

mod [mɒd] *n Br Fam* mod *mf*

modal ['məʊdəl] *Gram* **1** *n* verbo *m* modal
2 *adj* ***m. auxiliary*** auxiliar modal; *Phil* ***m. logic*** lógica *f* modal; ***m. verb*** verbo *m* modal

modality [məʊ'dælɪtɪ] *n* (a) *Mus* modo *m* musical (b) *Gram & Phil* modalidad *f*

mod cons ['mɒd'kɒnz] *npl Br Fam* **with all m.** con todas las comodidades

mode [məʊd] *n* (a) *(manner)* **to be in holiday m.** tener la cabeza en las vacaciones ►► ***m. of behaviour*** forma *f* de comportarse; ***m. of life*** estilo *m* de vida; ***m. of transport*** medio *m* de transporte (b) *Comptr & Tech* modo *m;* **playback m.** función play (c) *Math* moda *f* (d) *Mus* modo *m*

model ['mɒdəl] **1** *n* (a) *(small version)* maqueta *f* ►► ***m. kit*** kit *m* de montaje; ***m. maker*** maquetista *mf;* ***m. making*** maquetismo *m*
(b) *(example)* modelo *m;* **this is our latest m.** éste es nuestro último modelo
(c) *(paragon)* modelo *m;* **a m. of politeness** un modelo de cortesía; **to take sb as one's m.** tomar a alguien como modelo
(d) *(person) (fashion model, for artist)* modelo *mf*
2 *adj* (a) *(miniature)* **m. aircraft** maqueta de avión (b) *(exemplary)* modelo *inv,* ejemplar; **m. pupil** alumno(a) modélico(a) *or* modelo
3 *vt* (*pt & pp* **modelled,** *US* **modeled**) (a) *(shape)* modelar
(b) *(design)* **the palace was modelled on Versailles** el palacio estaba construido en el estilo de Versalles; **to m. oneself on sb** seguir el ejemplo de alguien
(c) *(in fashion show)* **she models clothes** es modelo de moda *or* ropa; **Jacqueline is modelling a grey chinchilla coat** Jacqueline lleva un abrigo de chinchilla gris
(d) *Comptr* simular por *Esp* ordenador *or Am* computadora
4 *vi (artist's model)* posar; *(fashion model)* hacer *or* trabajar de modelo

modeller, *US* **modeler** ['mɒdələ(r)] *n (of model planes, boats)* maquetista *mf*

modelling, *US* **modeling** ['mɒdəlɪŋ] *n* **(a)** *(of model planes, boats)* modelismo *m* ►► ***m. clay*** arcilla *f* de modelar **(b)** *(in fashion show, for magazine)* trabajo *m* de modelo; **have you considered m. as a career?** ¿has considerado la posibilidad de ser modelo? ►► ***m. agency*** agencia *f* de modelos **(c)** *Comptr* modelado *m* **(d)** *Art* modelado *m*

modem ['məʊdem] *n Comptr* módem *m* ►► ***m. card*** tarjeta *f* de módem; ***m. port*** puerto *m* del módem

moderate ['mɒdərɪt] **1** *n Pol* moderado(a) *m,f*
2 *adj* **(a)** *(restrained, modest)* moderado(a); **the candidate holds m. views** el candidato mantiene opiniones moderadas; **to be a m. drinker** beber *or Am* tomar moderadamente **(b)** *(average)* medio(a) **(c)** *Met* ***m. breeze*** brisa *f* moderada; ***m. gale*** viento *m* fuerte
3 *vt* ['mɒdəreɪt] **(a)** *(make less extreme) (one's demands, zeal)* moderar **(b)** *(meeting, debate)* moderar **(c)** *Comptr* ***moderated list*** lista *f* moderada
4 *vi* **(a)** *(storm)* amainar; *(demands, zeal)* moderar(se) **(b)** *(at meeting)* moderar, hacer de moderador(ora)

moderately ['mɒdərɪtlɪ] *adv* **(a)** *(with moderation) (eat, drink)* moderadamente, con moderación **(b)** *(reasonably)* medianamente, moderadamente; **m. priced** a un precio moderado

moderation [mɒdə'reɪʃən] *n* moderación *f*; **in m.** con moderación; **taken in m. alcohol is not harmful** el alcohol no es perjudicial si se toma con moderación

moderator ['mɒdəreɪtə(r)] *n* **(a)** *(mediator)* mediador(ora) *m,f* **(b)** *Br Univ (in examination marking)* = persona encargada de comprobar que todos los examinadores siguen los mismos criterios **(c)** *Rel* moderador(ora) *m,f* **(d)** *Phys (in nuclear reactors)* moderador *m* **(e)** *Comptr (of discussion lists)* moderador(ora) *m,f*

modern ['mɒdən] **1** *adj* moderno(a); **in m. times** en la época moderna; **m. English/Greek** inglés/griego moderno ►► ***m. art*** arte *m* moderno; *Theat* ***m. dress*** indumentaria *f* moderna; ***m. languages*** lenguas *fpl* modernas; *Sport* ***m. pentathlon*** pentatlón *m* moderno
2 *n (person)* persona *f* de la época moderna

modern-day ['mɒdən'deɪ] *adj* actual, de hoy día

modernism ['mɒdənɪzəm] *n* modernismo *m*

modernist ['mɒdənɪst] **1** *n* modernista *mf*
2 *adj* modernista

modernistic [mɒdə'nɪstɪk] *adj* modernista

modernity [mɒ'dɜːnɪtɪ] *n* modernidad *f*

modernization [mɒdənaɪ'zeɪʃən] *n* modernización *f*

modernize ['mɒdənaɪz] **1** *vt* modernizar
2 *vi* modernizarse

modernizer ['mɒdənaɪzə(r)] *n* modernizador(ora) *m,f*

modest ['mɒdɪst] *adj* **(a)** *(not boastful)* modesto(a) **(b)** *(moderate) (requirement, increase)* modesto(a), moderado(a); **a m. salary** un sueldo *or* salario modesto **(c)** *(chaste)* recatado(a)

modestly ['mɒdɪstlɪ] *adv* **(a)** *(not boastfully)* modestamente **(b)** *(moderately)* moderadamente; **they live very m.** viven muy moderadamente **(c)** *(chastely)* recatadamente; **to dress m.** vestir recatadamente

modesty ['mɒdɪstɪ] *n* **(a)** *(humility)* modestia *f*; **in all m.** con toda modestia **(b)** *(moderation) (of requirement, increase)* modestia *f*, moderación *f* **(c)** *(chastity)* recato *m*, pudor *m*; **she lowered her gaze out of m.** bajó la vista por pudor

modicum ['mɒdɪkəm] *n Formal* **a m. of** un mínimo de

modification [mɒdɪfɪ'keɪʃən] *n* modificación *f*; **to make modifications to sth** hacer modificaciones en algo, modificar algo

modifier ['mɒdɪfaɪə(r)] *n* **(a)** *Gram* modificador *m* **(b)** *Comptr* ***m. key*** tecla *f* modificadora

modify ['mɒdɪfaɪ] *vt* **(a)** *(alter)* modificar **(b)** *(reduce) (demands)* moderar **(c)** *Gram* modificar

modish ['məʊdɪʃ] *adj* moderno(a), a la moda

modishly ['məʊdɪʃlɪ] *adv* a la moda

modular ['mɒdjʊlə(r)] *adj* por módulos ►► *Elec* ***m. construction*** construcción *f* por módulos; *Educ* ***a m. course*** un curso por módulos; ***m. furniture*** mobiliario *m* modular

modularity [mɒdjʊ'lærətɪ] *n* modularidad *f*

modulate ['mɒdjʊleɪt] **1** *vt* **(a)** *(voice)* modular **(b)** *Elec* modular
2 *vi Mus* **to m. to** modular a

modulation [mɒdjʊ'leɪʃən] *n* **(a)** *(of voice)* modulación *f* **(b)** *Elec* modulación *f*

modulator ['mɒdjʊleɪtə(r)] *n (device)* modulador *m*

module ['mɒdjuːl] *n* **(a)** *(unit)* módulo *m*; **lunar/command m.** *(in space travel)* módulo lunar/de mando **(b)** *Educ* módulo *m*

modus operandi ['məʊdəsɒpə'rændaɪ] *n Formal* modus *m* operandi

modus vivendi ['məʊdəsvɪ'vendaɪ] *n Formal* modus *m* vivendi

mofo ['məʊfəʊ] *n US very Fam* joputa *m*, japuta *f*

mog [mɒg], **moggie, moggy** ['mɒgɪ] *n Br Fam* minino(a) *m,f*

mogul[1] ['məʊgəl] **1** *n* **(a)** *Hist* Gran Mogol *m* **(b)** *(magnate)* magnate *m*
2 *adj Hist* mogol(ola)

mogul[2] *n Sport* bache *m*; **moguls** *(event)* esquí *m* de baches

mohair ['məʊheə(r)] *n* mohair *m* ►► ***m. sweater*** suéter *m or Esp* jersey *m or Col* saco *m or RP* pulóver *m* de mohair

Mohammed [məʊ'hæmɪd] *n* Mahoma

Mohammedan [mə'hæmɪdən] *Old-fashioned* **1** *n* mahometano(a) *m,f*
2 *adj* mahometano(a)

mohawk ['məʊhɔːk] *n* **(a)** *(in ice-skating)* = medio giro por el que la punta de la cuchilla de un patín se encuentra con la correspondiente del otro patín **(b)** *US (hairstyle)* cresta *f*, *RP* mohicano *m*

mohican [məʊ'hiːkən] *n* **(a)** *(North American Indian)* **M.** mohicano(a) *m,f*; *Fig* **the last of the Mohicans** el último Mohicano, el último de Filipinas **(b)** *Br (hairstyle)* cresta *f*

moire [mwɑː] *n Comptr, Phot & Typ* moiré *m*

moiré ['mwɑːreɪ] **1** *n* aguas *fpl*
2 *adj* con aguas

moist [mɔɪst] *adj (soil, skin, climate)* húmedo(a); *(cake)* esponjoso(a); **eyes m. with tears** ojos humedecidos por las lágrimas; **to grow m.** humedecerse

moisten ['mɔɪsən] *vt* humedecer; **she moistened her lips** se humedeció los labios

moistness ['mɔɪstnɪs] *n (of soil, skin, climate)* humedad *f*; *(of cake)* esponjosidad *f*

moisture ['mɔɪstʃə(r)] *n* vaho *m*, condensación *f*; **he wiped the m. from the window** limpió el vaho de los cristales ►► ***m. content*** grado *m or* contenido *m* de humedad

moisture-proof ['mɔɪstʃəpruːf] *adj (clothing, shoes)* impermeable; *(watch, container)* a prueba de humedad

moisturize ['mɔɪstʃəraɪz] *vt (skin)* hidratar

moisturizer ['mɔɪstʃəraɪzə(r)] *n* crema *f* hidratante

moisturizing ['mɔɪstʃəraɪzɪŋ] *adj* hidratante ►► ***m. cream*** crema *f* hidratante; ***m. lotion*** leche *f* hidratante

moke [məʊk] *n Fam* **(a)** *Br (donkey)* burro(a) *m,f*, jumento *m* **(b)** *Austr (horse)* jamelgo *m*

molar[1] ['məʊlə(r)] *n* muela *f*, molar *m*

molar[2] *adj Chem* molar ►► ***m. weight*** peso *m* molar

molarity [mə'lærɪtɪ] *n Chem* molaridad *f*

molasses [mə'læsɪz] *n* melaza *f*; IDIOM *US Fam* **to be as slow as m. (in winter)** ser muy lento(a), *Esp* ser más lento(a) que el caballo del malo

mold, molder *etc US* = **mould, moulder** *etc*

Moldavia [mɒl'deɪvɪə], **Moldova** [mɒl'dəʊvə] *n* Moldavia

Moldavian [mɒl'deɪvɪən], **Moldovan** [mɒl'dəʊvən] **1** *n* moldavo(a) *m,f*
2 *adj* moldavo(a)

mole[1] [məʊl] *n (birthmark)* lunar *m*

mole[2] *n* **(a)** *(animal)* topo *m* ►► ***m. cricket*** alacrán *m* cebollero, grillo *m* cebollero *or* real **(b)** *(spy)* topo *m*

mole[3] *n (breakwater)* malecón *m*

mole[4] *n Chem* mol *m*

molecular [mə'lekjʊlə(r)] *adj* molecular ►► ***m. biology*** biología *f* molecular; ***m. weight*** peso *m* molecular

molecule ['mɒlɪkjuːl] *n* molécula *f*

molehill ['məʊlhɪl] *n* topera *f*

moleskin ['məʊlskɪn] **1** *n* **(a)** *(fur)* piel *f* de topo **(b)** *(cotton fabric)* piel *f* de melocotón
2 *adj* de piel de melocotón

molest [mə'lest] *vt* **(a)** *(sexually)* abusar (sexualmente) de **(b)** *(pester)* importunar, molestar; *(more violently)* agredir

molestation [mɒle'steɪʃən] *n* **(a)** *(sexual)* abuso *m* sexual **(b)** *(pestering)* hostigamiento *m*; *(more violently)* agresión *f*

molester [mə'lestə(r)] *n* **(a)** *(sexual)* **child m.** corruptor(ora) *m,f* de menores, pederasta *mf* **(b)** *(pesterer)* **his molesters** los que le importunaban *or* molestaban; *(more violently)* sus agresores

moll [mɒl] *n Fam* **gangster's m.** amiguita *or Arg* mina *or Méx* vieja de un gángster

mollify ['mɒlɪfaɪ] *vt* apaciguar; **in a mollifying tone** con tono conciliador

mollusc, *US* **mollusk** ['mɒləsk] *n* molusco *m*

mollycoddle ['mɒlɪkɒdəl] *vt Fam* mimar

Molotov cocktail ['mɒlətɒf'kɒkteɪl] *n* cóctel *m* molotov

molt *US* = **moult**

molten ['məʊltən] *adj* fundido(a)

Moluccas [mə'lʌkəz] *npl* **the M.** las (islas) Molucas

molybdenum [mə'lɪbdəmən] *n Chem* molibdeno *m*

mom [mɒm] *n US Fam* mamá *f*, mami *f*; **m. and pop store** un negocio familiar

MOMA ['məʊmə] *n* (*abbr* **Museum of Modern Art**) Museo *m* de Arte Moderno *(de Nueva York)*

moment ['məʊmənt] *n* **(a)** *(instant, period of time)* momento *m*; **it was one of the worst moments of my life** fue uno de los peores momentos de mi vida; **her m. of glory** su momento de gloria; **at any m.** en cualquier momento; **any m. now** en cualquier momento; **at the m.** *(right now)* en este momento; *(these days)* actualmente; **at this m. in time** en estos momentos; **a m. ago** hace un momento; **at the last m.** en el último momento; **for the m.** por ahora, por el momento; **from that m. on** a partir de entonces *or* aquel momento; **in a m.** enseguida; **just a m.** *(wait a minute)* un momento; **wait a m.!, one m.!** ¡espera un momento!; **one m., please** *(on telephone)* aguarde un momento, por favor; **I haven't a m. to spare** no tengo ni un minuto; **tell him the m. he arrives** díselo en cuanto llegue; **without a m.'s hesitation** sin dudarlo un momento; **not** *or* **never for one m.** ni por un momento *or* instante; **the police arrived, and not a m. too soon!** la policía llegó, no precisamente sobrada de tiempo
(b) *(good parts, phases)* **he has his moments** tiene sus buenos golpes; **the book has its moments** el libro tiene sus (buenos) momentos
(c) *Formal (importance)* **of great/little m.** de mucha/poca importancia
(d) *Phys* ***m. of force*** momento *m* (de una fuerza); ***m. of inertia*** momento *m* de inercia
(e) IDIOMS **to live for the m.** vivir el presente; **the man of the m.** el hombre del momento; **the m. of truth** la hora de la verdad

momentarily [məʊmən'terɪlɪ] *adv* **(a)** *(for a moment)* durante un momento, momentáneamente **(b)** *US (shortly)* en un momento

momentary ['məʊməntərɪ] *adj* momentáneo(a); **there will be a m. delay** se retrasará brevemente

momentous [məʊ'mentəs] *adj* trascendental; **on this m. occasion** en esta ocasión tan significativa

momentousness [mə'mentəsnɪs] *n* trascendencia *f*, gran importancia *f*

momentum [məʊ'mentəm] *n* **(a)** *Phys* momento *m* (lineal) **(b)** *(impulse)* impulso *m*, ímpetu *m*; **to gather/lose m.** *(car, campaign)* cobrar/perder impulso; **they never got back that early m.** nunca recobraron el impulso *or* ímpetu inicial

momma ['mɒmə] *n US Fam* **(a)** *(mother)* mamá *f*, mami *f* **(b)** *(woman) Esp* tía *f*, *Am* tipa *f*

mommy ['mɒmɪ] *n US Fam* mamá *f*, mami *f*; IDIOM **to be on the m. track** estar ejerciendo de madre

Mon (*abbr* **Monday**) lun.

Monaco ['mɒnəkəʊ] *n* Mónaco

Mona Lisa ['məʊnə'li:zə] *n* **the M.** la Gioconda, (la) Mona Lisa; **she had a M. smile** tiene una sonrisa enigmática

monarch ['mɒnək] *n* monarca *mf* ▸▸ ***m. butterfly*** mariposa *f* monarca

monarchic(al) [mɒ'nɑ:kɪk(əl)] *adj* monárquico(a)

monarchism ['mɒnəkɪzəm] *n* monarquismo *m*

monarchist ['mɒnəkɪst] **1** *n* monárquico(a) *m,f*
2 *adj* monárquico(a)

monarchy ['mɒnəkɪ] *n* monarquía *f*

monastery ['mɒnəstrɪ] *n* monasterio *m*

monastic [mə'næstɪk] *adj* monástico(a)

monasticism [mə'næstɪsɪzəm] *n* **(a)** *(way of life)* monacato *m* **(b)** *(system)* monacato *m*

monaural [mɒ'nɔ:rəl] *adj* monoaural

Monday ['mʌndɪ] *n* lunes *m inv*; IDIOM *Fam* **that M. morning feeling** esa sensación de lunes por la mañana, *Andes, Méx* esas ganas de celebrar el San Lunes ▸▸ *US Fam* ***M. morning quarterback*** estratega *mf* de salón *(sobre todo el que comenta los resultados deportivos)*; *see also* **Saturday**

mondo [mɒndəʊ] *adv US Fam* super *inv*; **m. risky** super peligroso(a)

Monegasque [mɒnɪ'gæsk] **1** *n* monegasco(a) *m,f*
2 *adj* monegasco(a)

monetarism ['mʌnɪtərɪzəm] *n* monetarismo *m*

monetarist ['mʌnɪtərɪst] **1** *n* monetarista *mf*
2 *adj* monetarista ▸▸ ***m. theory*** monetarismo *m*

monetary ['mʌnɪtərɪ] *adj* monetario(a) ▸▸ ***m. crisis*** tormenta *f* monetaria; ***m. policy*** política *f* monetaria; ***M. Union*** Unión *f* Monetaria; ***m. unit*** unidad *f* monetaria

money ['mʌnɪ] *n* **(a)** *(cash, currency)* dinero *m*, *Am* plata *f*; **have you got any m. on you?** ¿llevas *or* tienes dinero?; **the job's boring but the m.'s good** el trabajo es aburrido pero está bien pagado; **to do sth for m.** hacer algo por dinero; **I got my m. back** *(I got reimbursed)* me devolvieron el dinero; *(I recovered my expenses)* recuperé el dinero; **to make m.** *(person)* ganar *or* hacer dinero; *(business)* dar dinero; **to put m. into sth** invertir dinero en algo; **to put up the m. for sth** poner el dinero para algo; **to be worth a lot of m.** *(thing)* valer mucho dinero; *(person)* tener mucho dinero; **the deal is worth a lot of m.** el contrato va a dar mucho dinero; **there's no m. in it** no es un buen negocio; **we really got our m.'s worth** desde luego, valía la pena pagar ese dinero; **it's m. well spent** es dinero bien empleado; **it's the best dictionary that m. can buy** es el mejor diccionario del mercado; **for my m.** para mí, en mi opinión; **your m. or your life!** ¡la bolsa o la vida!; **m. is no object** el dinero no es problema; *Sport* **to finish out of/in the m.** = no terminar/terminar entre los ganadores de un premio en metálico ▸▸ ***m. belt*** = cinturón donde se puede guardar el dinero; ***m. laundering*** blanqueo *m* de dinero; *Fin* ***m. market*** mercado *m* monetario; *Fam* ***the m. men*** los financieros; ***m. order*** transferencia *f*, giro *m*; *Br* ***m. spider*** = araña roja diminuta; *Econ* ***m. supply*** oferta *f or* masa *f* monetaria
(b) IDIOMS *Fam* **to be in the m.** haber ganado mucha plata, *Esp* haberse hecho con un montón de pasta, *Méx* haber hecho un chorro de lana, *RP* haber juntado un toco de guita; **to have m. to burn** tener dinero a espuertas, *Am* tener plata para tirar para arriba; **I'm not made of m.** no tengo un saco sin fondo; *Fam* **m. doesn't grow on trees!** el dinero no se encuentra así como así, *RP* ¡la plata no cae del cielo!; *Br Fam* **it was m. for old rope** *or* **for jam** era dinero fácil; **it's m. down the drain** es tirar el dinero; **to put one's m. where one's mouth is** hacer con el dinero lo que tanto se promete; **the Government must put its m. where its mouth is** el Gobierno debe demostrar con hechos lo que predica; *Fam* **to spend m. like water** gastar dinero a espuertas *or Am* a patadas; *US Fam* **on the m.** *(on time)* justo a tiempo; **to be on the m.** *(accurate)* dar en el clavo; **m. talks** el dinero es lo que cuenta; PROV **m. is the root of all evil** el dinero es la causa de todos los males

money-back ['mʌnɪ'bæk] *n* ***m. guarantee*** garantía *f* de devolución del dinero si el producto no es satisfactorio

moneybags ['mʌnɪbægz] *n Fam (person)* ricachón(ona) *m,f*; **lend us a fiver, m.** déjame cinco libras, tú que estás montado en el dólar

moneybox ['mʌnɪbɒks] *n Esp* hucha *f*, *esp Am* alcancía *f*

moneychanger ['mʌnɪtʃeɪndʒə(r)] *n* **(a)** *(person)* = empleado de una oficina de cambio de divisas **(b)** *US (machine)* máquina *f* de cambio

moneyed, monied ['mʌnɪd] *adj* adinerado(a), pudiente; **the m. classes** las clases adineradas *or* pudientes

money-grubber ['mʌnɪgrʌbə(r)] *n Fam* rácano(a) *m,f*, rata *mf*

money-grubbing ['mʌnɪgrʌbɪŋ] *adj Fam* rácano(a), rata

moneylender ['mʌnɪlendə(r)] *n* prestamista *mf*

moneymaker ['mʌnɪmeɪkə(r)] *n (business, product)* negocio *m* rentable

moneymaking ['mʌnɪmeɪkɪŋ] *adj* lucrativo(a); **it's another of his m. schemes** es otro de sus planes para enriquecerse

money-off ['mʌnɪ'ɒf] *adj (voucher)* de descuento; **a m. deal** una oferta

money-spinner ['mʌnɪspɪnə(r)] *n Br Fam* **a real m.** una mina (de oro)

mong [mɒŋ] *n Br Fam* subnormal *mf*

Mongol ['mɒŋgəl] *Hist* **1** *n* mongol(ola) *m,f*
2 *adj* mongol(ola)

mongol ['mɒŋgəl] *n Old-fashioned (person with Down's syndrome)* mongólico(a) *m,f*

Mongolia [mɒŋ'gəʊlɪə] *n* Mongolia; **Inner M.** Mongolia Interior; **Outer M.** Mongolia Exterior

Mongolian [mɒŋ'gəʊlɪən] **1** *n* mongol(ola) *m,f*
2 *adj* mongol(ola)

mongolism ['mɒŋgəlɪzəm] *n Old-fashioned (Down's syndrome)* mongolismo *m*

Mongoloid ['mɒŋgəlɔɪd] **1** *n* mongoloide *mf*
2 *adj* mongoloide

mongoloid ['mɒŋgəlɔɪd] *Old-fashioned* **1** *n (person with Down's syndrome)* mongólico(a) *m,f*
2 *adj* mongólico(a)

mongoose [mɒŋ'gu:s] *n* mangosta *f*

mongrel ['mʌŋgrəl] **1** *n* (**a**) *(dog)* perro *m* cruzado (**b**) *(hybrid)* híbrido *m*, cruce *m*
2 *adj (hybrid)* híbrido(a)

monied = **moneyed**

monies ['mʌnɪz] *npl Com Law* fondos *mpl*

moniker ['mɒnɪkə(r)] *n Fam* mote *m*, apodo *m*

monism ['mɒnɪzəm] *n Phil* monismo *m*

monist ['mɒnɪst] *n Phil* monista *mf*

monitor ['mɒnɪtə(r)] **1** *n* (**a**) *(supervisor)* supervisor(ora) *m,f* (**b**) *Med & Tech (device)* monitor *m* (**c**) *(screen) TV* pantalla *f*; *Comptr* monitor *m* (**d**) ***m. lizard*** varano *m*
2 *vt* (**a**) *(supervise, check)* controlar, hacer un seguimiento de; **this instrument monitors the pulse rate** este aparato controla el pulso (**b**) *(broadcasts, telephone conversation)* escuchar

monitoring ['mɒnɪtərɪŋ] *n* (**a**) *(supervision)* control *m*, seguimiento *m*, *Am* monitoreo *m* (**b**) *(of broadcasts, telephone conversation)* escuchas *fpl* ►► ***m. service*** = agencia que controla sistemáticamente las emisiones de radio y televisión procedentes del extranjero

monk [mʌŋk] *n* monje *m* ►► ***m. parakeet*** perico *m* monje; ***m. seal*** foca *f* monje

monkey ['mʌŋkɪ] *n* (**a**) *(animal)* mono *m* ►► *US* ***m. bars*** = en los parques, estructura de hierro o madera para que trepen los niños; *Br* ***m. nut*** cacahuete *m*, *Am* maní *m*, *CAm, Méx* cacahuate *m*; ***m. puzzle tree*** araucaria *f*; *Fam* ***m. suit*** traje *m* de etiqueta; *US* ***m. wrench*** llave *f* inglesa
(**b**) *Fam (naughty child)* diablillo *m*
(**c**) *Br Fam (£500)* = 500 libras
(**d**) IDIOMS **to make a m. out of sb** tomarle el pelo a alguien; *Br Fam* **I don't give a m.'s** me importa un pito; *US Fam* **to have a m. on one's back** *(be addicted to drugs)* ser yonqui, *RP* ser un(a) falopero(a) ►► *Fam* ***m. business*** tejemanejes *mpl*; *Br* ***m. tricks*** travesuras *fpl*

►**monkey about, monkey around** *vi Fam* (**a**) *(fool around)* hacer el indio (**with** con) (**b**) *(tamper)* **to m. about** *or* **around with sth** enredar con *or* toquetear algo

monkfish ['mʌŋkfɪʃ] *n* rape *m*

monkish ['mʌŋkɪʃ] *adj* monacal

mono ['mɒnəʊ] *n* **in m.** *(of sound recording)* en mono(aural)

monochromatic [mɒnəʊkrə'mætɪk] *adj (light)* monocromático(a)

monochrome ['mɒnəkrəʊm] **1** *n (technique)* monocromía *f*; **in m.** en blanco y negro; **to dream in m.** soñar en blanco y negro
2 *adj* (**a**) *Art & Comptr* monocromo(a), monocromático(a) (**b**) *Phot* en blanco y negro

monocle ['mɒnəkəl] *n* monóculo *m*

monocled ['mɒnəkəld] *adj* con monóculo

monocline ['mɒnəklaɪn] *n Geol* monoclinal *m*

monocotyledon [mɒnəʊkɒtɪ'li:dən] *n Bot* monocotiledónea *f*

monocotyledonous [mɒnəʊkɒtɪ'li:dənəs] *adj Bot* monocotiledóneo(a)

monoculture ['mɒnəʊkʌltʃə(r)] *n Agr* monocultivo *m*

monogamous [mɒ'nɒgəməs] *adj* monógamo(a)

monogamy [mɒ'nɒgəmɪ] *n* monogamia *f*

monoglot ['mɒnəglɒt] *n* = persona que habla un solo idioma

monogram ['mɒnəgræm] *n* monograma *m*

monogrammed ['mɒnəgræmd] *adj* con monograma

monograph ['mɒnəgræf] *n* monografía *f*

monohull ['mɒnəhʌl] *n* monocasco *m*

monokini ['mɒnəki:nɪ] *n* monobikini *m*, monokini *m*

monolingual [mɒnəʊ'lɪŋgwəl] *adj* monolingüe

monolith ['mɒnəlɪθ] *n* monolito *m*

monolithic [mɒnə'lɪθɪk] *adj* (**a**) *(monument, rock formation)* monolítico(a) (**b**) *(government, state)* monolítico(a)

monologue ['mɒnəlɒg] *n* monólogo *m*

monologist ['mɒnəlɒgɪst, mə'nɒlədʒɪst] *n* actor *m* de monólogos, actriz *f* de monólogos

monomania [mɒnəʊ'meɪnɪə] *n Psy* monomanía *f*

monomaniac [mɒnəʊ'meɪnɪæk] **1** *n* monomaníaco(a) *m,f*
2 *adj* monomaníaco(a)

monomer ['mɒnəmə(r)] *n Chem* monómero *m*

mononucleosis [mɒnəʊnju:klɪ'əʊsɪs] *n Med* mononucleosis *f inv* infecciosa

monophthong ['mɒnəfθɒŋ] *n Ling* monoptongo *m*

monoplane ['mɒnəʊpleɪn] *n* monoplano *m*

monopolist [mə'nɒpəlɪst] *n* monopolista *mf*

monopolistic [mənɒpə'lɪstɪk] *adj* monopolizador(ora)

monopolization [mənɒpəlaɪ'zeɪʃən] *n* (**a**) *(of market)* monopolización *f* (**b**) *(of conversation, attention)* monopolización *f*

monopolize [mə'nɒpəlaɪz] *vt* (**a**) *(market)* monopolizar (**b**) *(conversation, attention)* acaparar, monopolizar; **she monopolized him for the evening** lo acaparó *or* monopolizó toda la noche

Monopoly® [mə'nɒpəlɪ] *n* Monopoly® *m* ►► *Fam* ***M. money*** dinero *m* de juguete

monopoly [mə'nɒpəlɪ] *n* monopolio *m*; **to have a m. of** *or* **on sth** tener el monopolio *or* la exclusiva de algo; **no political party has a m. on morality** la moral no es exclusividad de ningún partido político; **state m.** monopolio estatal; **m. control** control exclusivo *or* monopolístico ►► ***the Monopolies and Mergers Commission*** Comisión *f* de Monopolios y Fusiones, = comité que vela por la defensa de la competencia en el Reino Unido

monorail ['mɒnəreɪl] *n* monorraíl *m*

monosaccharide [mɒnəʊ'sækəraɪd] *n Biochem* monosacárido *m*

monosemic [mɒnə'si:mɪk] *adj Ling* monosémico(a)

monoski ['mɒnəski:] *n* monoesquí *m*

monosodium glutamate ['mɒnəsəʊdɪəm'glu:təmeɪt] *n Culin* glutamato *m* monosódico

monospaced ['mɒnəʊspeɪst] *adj Comptr & Typ* monoespaciado(a)

monospacing [mɒnəʊ'speɪsɪŋ] *n Comptr & Typ* monoespaciado *m*

monosyllabic [mɒnəʊsɪ'læbɪk] *adj* (**a**) *(word)* monosílabo(a), monosilábico(a) (**b**) *(person, reply)* lacónico(a)

monosyllable [mɒnəʊ'sɪləbəl] *n* monosílabo *m*; **to answer in monosyllables** responder con monosílabos

monotheism ['mɒnəθiɪzəm] *n* monoteísmo *m*

monotheistic [mɒnəθɪ'ɪstɪk] *adj* monoteísta

monotone ['mɒnətəʊn] *n* tono *m* monótono; **to speak in a m.** hablar con voz monótona

monotonous [mə'nɒtənəs] *adj* monótono(a); **with m. regularity** con regularidad monótona

monotonously [mə'nɒtənəslɪ] *adv* monótonamente

monotony [mə'nɒtənɪ] *n* monotonía *f*; **to break the m.** romper la monotonía; **the m. of the landscape** la monotonía del paisaje

monotype ['mɒnətaɪp] *n Art* monotipo *m*

monounsaturated ['mɒnəʊʌn'sætjʊreɪtɪd] *adj* monoinsaturado(a)

monovalent ['mɒnəʊveɪlənt] *adj Chem* monovalente

monoxide [mə'nɒksaɪd] *n Chem* monóxido *m*

Monsignor [mɒn'si:njə(r)] *n* monseñor *m*

monsoon [mɒn'su:n] *n* monzón *m*; **the m. season** la estación del monzón

monster ['mɒnstə(r)] **1** *n* (**a**) *(beast, cruel person)* monstruo *m*
(**b**) *Fam (large person, thing)* **his last novel was a m.** su última novela era un tocho; **it's a m. of a machine** esa máquina es un mamotreto
2 *adj Fam (enormous)* monstruoso(a)

monstrosity [mɒn'strɒsɪtɪ] *n* monstruosidad *f*; **the town hall is a huge Victorian m.** el ayuntamiento es una enorme monstruosidad victoriana

monstrous ['mɒnstrəs] *adj* (**a**) *(appalling, repugnant)* monstruoso(a); **it is m. that...** es una monstruosidad que... (**b**) *(enormous)* descomunal

monstrously ['mɒnstrəslɪ] *adv* (**a**) *(appallingly)* monstruosamente (**b**) *(enormously)* **it was m. expensive** tenía un precio descomunal; **it was m. unfair** era una descomunal injusticia

mons veneris [mɒnz'venərɪs] *n Anat* monte *m* de Venus

Mont (*abbr* **Montana**) Montana

montage [mɒn'tɑ:ʒ] *n Cin & Phot* montaje *m*

Montagu's harrier ['mɒntəgju:z'hærɪə(r)] *n* aguilucho *m* cenizo

Montana [mɒn'tænə] *n* Montana

Mont Blanc ['mɒn'blɒnk] *n* Mont Blanc *m*

Monte Carlo ['mɒntɪ'kɑ:ləʊ] *n* Montecarlo

Montenegro [mɒntɪ'ni:grəʊ] *n* Montenegro

Montezuma [mɒntə'zu:mə] *pr n* Moctezuma ▸▸ *Fam Hum* ***M.'s revenge*** venganza *f* de Moctezuma, = diarrea sufrida por turistas especialmente en México

month [mʌnθ] *n* mes *m*; **in the m. of August** en el mes de agosto; **in the summer/winter months** en los meses de verano/invierno; **a m. ago** hace un mes; **a m. from now, in a m.'s time** en un mes, dentro de un mes; **a ten-m.-old baby** un niño de diez meses; **once a m.** una vez al mes; **(to earn) $2,000 a m.** (ganar) 2.000 dólares al mes; **we're paid by the m.** nos pagan mensualmente; *Fam* **he got six months** le cayeron seis meses (de cárcel); IDIOM *Euph* **is it that** *or* **your time of the m.?** *(menstruation)* ¿estás con el mes *or* la regla?; IDIOM *Fam* **never in a m. of Sundays** ni por casualidad

monthly ['mʌnθlɪ] **1** *n* **(a)** *(magazine)* revista *f* mensual **(b)** *Old-fashioned & Euph* **she's having her m.** *or* **monthlies** está con el mes
2 *adj* mensual ▸▸ ***m. instalment*** plazo *m* mensual; ***m. payment*** mensualidad *f*; ***m. statement*** *(from bank)* extracto *m* (bancario) mensual
3 *adv* mensualmente

Montreal [mɒntri:'ɔ:l] *n* Montreal

Montserrat [mɒntsə'ræt] *n* (la isla de) Monserrat

monument ['mɒnjʊmənt] *n* monumento *m*; IDIOM **it is a m. to human stupidity** es un monumento a la estupidez humana

monumental [mɒnjʊ'mentəl] *adj* **(a)** *(large, impressive)* monumental; **he's a m. bore** es un pelmazo insoportable; **of m. significance** de enorme trascendencia; **m. ignorance** ignorancia supina **(b)** *(sculpture, inscription)* monumental ▸▸ ***m. mason*** marmolista *mf*

moo [mu:] **1** *n* (*pl* **moos**) **(a)** *(animal sound)* mugido *m* **(b)** *Br Pej (woman)* **you silly m.!** ¡imbécil!
2 *vi* mugir
3 *exclam* ¡mu!

mooch [mu:tʃ] *Fam* **1** *vt* **(a)** *(cadge)* **to m. sth off sb** gorrear *or Esp, Méx* gorronear *or RP* garronear algo a alguien **(b)** *US (steal)* pispar, birlar
2 *vi* **(a)** *(wander aimlessly)* vagar, dar vueltas **(b)** *(cadge)* gorrear, *Esp, Méx* gorronear, *RP* garronear; **he's always mooching off** *or* **on people** siempre le está gorreando *or Esp, Méx* gorroneando *or RP* garroneando a la gente

▸ **mooch about, mooch around** *Fam* **1** *vt insep* **to m. about** *or* **around the house** dar vueltas *or* vagar por la casa
2 *vi* vagar, dar vueltas

moocher ['mu:tʃə(r)] *n US Fam* gorrero(a) *m,f*, *Esp, Méx* gorrón(ona) *m,f*, *RP* garronero(a) *m,f*

mood [mu:d] *n* **(a)** *(state of mind)* humor *m*; **the m. of the public/electorate** el sentir del gran público/del electorado; **to be in a good/bad m.** estar de buen/mal humor; **to be in a generous m.** sentirse generoso(a); **to be in the m. for reading/dancing** sentirse con ganas de leer/bailar; **I'm not in the m. (for...)** no estoy de humor (para...); **he's in no m. for jokes** no está de humor para chistes; **she can be quite funny when the m. takes her** cuando tiene el día es muy graciosa
(b) *(bad temper, sulk)* **to be in a m.** estar de mal humor; **she's in one of her moods** está otra vez de mal humor
(c) *(atmosphere)* ambiente *m*; **the m. is one of cautious optimism** el ambiente es de optimismo prudente ▸▸ ***m. music*** música *f* de ambiente
(d) *Gram* modo *m*

moodily ['mu:dɪlɪ] *adv* malhumoradamente

moodiness ['mu:dɪnɪs] *n* **(a)** *(sulkiness)* mal humor **(b)** *(changeability)* volubilidad *f*, cambios *mpl* de humor

moody ['mu:dɪ] *adj* **(a)** *(sulky)* malhumorado(a); **to be m.** *(permanently)* tener mal humor; *(temporarily)* estar malhumorado(a) *or* de mal humor **(b)** *(changeable)* voluble, variable

Moog (synthesizer)® ['mu:g('sɪnθəsaɪzə(r))] *n* moog *m*

moola(h) ['mu:lə] *n Fam Esp* pasta *f*, *Am* plata *f*, *Méx* lana *f*

mooli ['mu:lɪ] *n* (rábano *m*) daikon *m*, mooli *m*

moon [mu:n] **1** *n* **(a)** luna *f*; **the M.** la Luna ▸▸ ***m. buggy*** vehículo *m* lunar; ***m. landing*** alunizaje *m*; ***m. walk*** paseo *m* lunar **(b)** IDIOMS *Hum* **many moons ago** hace mucho tiempo, tiempo ha; *Fam* **to ask for the m.** pedir la luna; *Fam* **to promise sb the m.** prometer a alguien el oro y el moro; *Fam* **to be over the m.** estar encantado(a)
2 *vt Fam (show one's buttocks to)* enseñar el culo a
3 *vi Fam* **(a)** *(expose one's buttocks)* enseñar el culo **(b)** *(daydream)* **to m. (about** *or* **around)** *(lazily)* pasar el tiempo mirando a las musarañas; *(listlessly)* andar como alma en pena; **to m. over sb** suspirar por alguien, beber los vientos por alguien

moonbeam ['mu:nbi:m] *n* rayo *m* de luna

moon-faced ['mu:nfeɪst] *adj* con la cara redonda

Moonie ['mu:nɪ] *n Rel Fam* = seguidor(ora) de la secta Moon

moonless ['mu:nlɪs] *adj* sin luna

moonlight ['mu:nlaɪt] **1** *n* luz *f* de (la) luna; **in the m., by m.** a la luz de la luna; *Br Fam* **to do a m. flit** escaparse de noche
2 *vi Fam* **he's moonlighting for another company** trabaja de escondidas para otra compañía

moonlighter ['mu:nlaɪtə(r)] *n Fam* pluriempleado(a) *m,f*

moonlighting ['mu:nlaɪtɪŋ] *n Fam* pluriempleo *m*

moonlit ['mu:nlɪt] *adj* iluminado(a) por la luna; **a m. night** una noche de luna

moonscape ['mu:nskeɪp] *n* paisaje *m* lunar

moonshine ['mu:nʃaɪn] *n Fam* **(a)** *(nonsense)* sandeces *fpl* **(b)** *US (illegal alcohol)* = alcohol destilado ilegalmente

moonshiner ['mu:nʃaɪnə(r)] *n US Fam* = fabricante o contrabandista de alcohol ilegal

moonshot ['mu:nʃɒt] *n* lanzamiento *m* de un cohete lunar

moonstone ['mu:nstəʊn] *n Geol* labradorita *f*, piedra *f* de la luna

moonstruck ['mu:nstrʌk] *adj Fam* **(a)** *(dreamy, dazed)* alucinado(a) **(b)** *(mad)* loco(a), demente

moony ['mu:nɪ] *adj Fam (dreamy)* distraído(a)

Moor [mɔ:(r)] *n* moro(a) *m,f*

moor[1] [mɔ:(r)] *n (heath)* páramo *m*; **they went walking out on the moors** salieron a pasear por los páramos

moor[2] **1** *vt (ship)* atracar, amarrar
2 *vi* echar amarras, atracar

moorcock ['mɔ:kɒk] *n (black grouse)* gallo *m* lira; *(red grouse)* lagópodo *m* escocés

moorhen ['mɔ:hen] *n* **(a)** *(water bird)* polla *f* de agua **(b)** *(grouse) (black)* gallo *m* lira; *(red grouse)* lagópodo *m* escocés hembra

mooring ['mɔ:rɪŋ] *n* **(a)** *(place)* atracadero *m*, amarradero *m* ▸▸ ***m. buoy*** boya *f* de amarre, (boya *f* de) cuerpo *m* muerto; ***m. mast*** poste *m* de anclaje; ***m. ropes*** amarras *fpl* **(b)** *(ropes, chains)* **moorings** amarras *fpl*; IDIOM **to lose one's moorings** perder el norte

Moorish ['mɔ:rɪʃ] *adj (architecture)* árabe, musulmán(ana) *(en España)*; *(kingdom, troops)* árabe, moro(a); *(person, features)* moro(a)

moorland ['mɔ:lənd] *n* páramo *m*

moose [mu:s] (*pl* **moose**) *n* alce *m*

moot [mu:t] **1** *adj* **it's a m. point** es discutible
2 *vt (propose, suggest)* **it was mooted that...** se sugirió que...; **a change in the rules has been mooted** se ha propuesto *or* planteado un cambio en las normas
3 *n Univ (in law faculties)* discusión *f* de un caso práctico

mop [mɒp] **1** *n* **(a)** *(for floor) (implement)* fregona *f*, *Andes, CAm, Méx* trapeador *m*; **give the floor a quick m.** pásale la fregona al suelo en un momento **(b)** *(for dishes)* = utensilio para lavar los platos semejante a una fregona pequeña **(c)** *Fam* **a m. of hair** una mata de pelo
2 *vt* (*pt & pp* **mopped**) **to m. the floor** fregar el suelo, pasarle la fregona al suelo; **to m. one's brow** enjugarse la frente

▸ **mop up** *vt sep* **(a)** *(liquid)* limpiar, enjugar; **he used his bread to m. up the sauce** mojó (en) la salsa con el pan **(b)** *(enemy forces)* terminar con, limpiar

mopboard ['mɒpbɔ:rd] *n US* zócalo *m*, rodapié *m*

mope [məʊp] *Fam* **1** *n (bout of low spirits)* **to have a m.** estar (con la) depre
2 *vi* **to m. (about** *or* **around)** andar como alma en pena; **there's no use moping about** *or* **over it** de nada sirve andar lamentándose

moped ['məʊped] *n* ciclomotor *m*

moppet ['mɒpɪt] *n Fam* chavalín(ina) *m,f*, peque *mf*

mopping-up operation ['mɒpɪŋ'ʌpɒpə'reɪʃən] *n (of enemy forces)* operación *f* de limpieza

moquette [mɒ'ket] *n (fabric)* moqueta *f*

MOR [eməʊ'ɑ:(r)] *adj* (*abbr* **middle-of-the-road**) *(in music broadcasting)* convencional

moraine [mə'reɪn] *n Geol* morrena *f*

moral ['mɒrəl] **1** *n* **(a)** *(of story)* moraleja *f*; **what's the m. of the story?** ¿cuál es la moraleja? **(b)** **morals** *(ethics)* moral *f*, moralidad *f*; **he has no morals** es un inmoral, no tiene principios
2 *adj* moral; **it's a very m. story** es una historia muy didáctica; **we have a m. duty to help them** tenemos el deber moral de ayudarlos; **to give sb m. support** dar apoyo moral a alguien; **he is lacking in m. fibre** carece de solidez *or* talla moral ▸▸ ***the m. high ground*** la superioridad moral; ***the m. majority*** la mayoría moral; ***m. philosophy***

filosofía *f* moral; ***m. standards*** valores *mpl* morales; **he complains about the decline in m. standards** se queja de la decadencia moral; ***m. victory*** victoria *f* moral

morale [mɒ'rɑːl] *n* moral *f*; **his m. is very low/high** tiene la moral muy baja/alta; **to be good/bad for m.** ser bueno/malo para la moral; **she tried to raise their m.** trató de levantarles el ánimo *or* la moral; **the news sapped the troops' m.** la noticia mermó *or* minó la moral de las tropas ►► ***a m. booster*** una inyección de moral; **the president visited the front as a m. booster** el presidente se desplazó al frente para dar una inyección de moral

moralist ['mɒrəlɪst] *n* moralista *mf*

moralistic [mɒrə'lɪstɪk] *adj* moralista

morality [mə'rælɪtɪ] *n* **(a)** *(of person, decision)* moralidad *f* **(b)** *Lit* **m. (play)** moralidad *f*, auto *m* alegórico

moralize ['mɒrəlaɪz] *vi* moralizar; **as a writer he has a tendency to m. at length** como escritor tiende a moralizar en exceso *or* a dar largos discursos moralizantes

moralizing ['mɒrəlaɪzɪŋ] **1** *n* moralización *f*

2 *adj* moralizador(ora), moralizante

morally ['mɒrəlɪ] *adv* moralmente; **m. right/wrong** moralmente aceptable/inaceptable; **to be m. bound to do sth** tener el deber moral de hacer algo; **the parents are m. responsible** los padres son los responsables morales

morass [mə'ræs] *n* **(a)** *(marsh)* pantano *m*, cenagal *m* **(b)** *(of detail, despair)* marasmo *m*, laberinto *m*; **bogged down in a m. of rules and regulations** perdido en un mar *or* laberinto de normas y reglamentación

moratorium [mɒrə'tɔːrɪəm] *n* moratoria *f* (**on** en); **to declare a m. on sth** decretar *or* declarar una moratoria en algo

Moravia [mə'reɪvɪə] *n* Moravia

Moravian [mə'reɪvɪən] **1** *n* moravo(a) *m,f*

2 *adj* moravo(a)

moray ['mɒreɪ] *n* **m. (eel)** morena *f*

morbid ['mɔːbɪd] *adj* **(a)** *(curiosity, interest, thoughts)* morboso(a), malsano(a); **don't be so m.!** ¡no seas morboso! **(b)** *Med* mórbido(a), morboso(a) ►► ***m. anatomy*** anatomía *f* patológica

morbidity [mɔː'bɪdɪtɪ] *n* **(a)** *(of mind, idea)* morbosidad *f* **(b)** *Med* morbilidad *f*

morbidly ['mɔːbɪdlɪ] *adv* morbosamente

mordant ['mɔːdənt] *adj Formal (sarcasm, wit)* mordaz

MORE [mɔː(r)] *(comparative of* **many, much***)* **1** *pron* más; **there's no m.** ya no hay *or* queda más; **I've got two m.** tengo dos más; **do you want (any *or* some) m.?** ¿quieres más?; **he knows m. than you (do)** él sabe más que tú; **I've got m. than you think** tengo más de lo/los que piensas; **there are m. of us than of them** nosotros somos más que ellos; **we should see m. of each other** deberíamos vernos más; **it's just m. of the same** es más de lo mismo; **she's m. of a communist than a socialist** es más comunista que socialista; **there's m. to the game than just hitting a ball** el juego es mucho más que simplemente darle a la bola; **he's little m. than a cleaner** no es más que un limpiador; **she is eating m. and m.** cada vez come más; **that's what I expect from you, no m., no less** esto es lo que espero de ti, ni más ni menos; **let us say no m. about it** el asunto queda olvidado; **it's no m. than an hour long** no dura más de una hora; **a pay rise is no m. than I deserve** el aumento de sueldo me lo tengo bien merecido; **five hundred people or m.** por lo menos quinientas personas; **the m. I hear about this, the less I like it** cuanto más sé del asunto, menos me gusta; **bring plenty, the m. the better** trae muchos, cuantos más, mejor; **the m. the merrier** cuántos más, mejor; **what m. can I say?** ¿qué más puedo decir?; **what is m.** lo que es más

2 *adj* más; **m. water/children** más agua/niños; **m. than a hundred people** más de cien personas; **I've read m. books than you** he leído más libros que tú; **one m. week** una semana más; **is there any m. bread?** ¿hay *or* queda más pan?; **I have no m. money** no me queda (más) dinero; **to have some m. wine** tomar un poco más de vino; **there are two m. questions to go** quedan dos preguntas (más); **there are m. and m. accidents** cada vez hay más accidentes; **the m. matches you win, the m. points you get** cuantos más partidos ganas, más puntos recibes; *Br Fam* **m. fool you!** ¡peor para ti!

3 *adv* **(a)** *(to form comparative of adjective or adverb)* más; **m. interesting (than)** más interesante (que); **m. easily** más fácilmente; **she couldn't be m. wrong** no podía estar más equivocada; **their views are m. communist than socialist** sus ideas son más comunistas que socialistas; **it's m. than likely** es más que probable; **I would be m. than happy to help** estaría más que encantado en ayudar, *RP* estaría encantado de ayudar; **I was m. than a little annoyed to discover that...** me *esp Esp* enfadó *or esp Am* enojó muchísimo descubrir que...; **he became m. and m. drunk** cada vez estaba más borracho; **this made things all the m. difficult** esto *Esp* ponía *or Am* hacía las cosas aún más difíciles

(b) *(with verbs) (eat, exercise)* más; **I would think m. of her if...** tendría mejor opinión de ella si...; **I couldn't agree m.** estoy completamente de acuerdo; **I like her m. than I used to** me cae mejor que antes; **he was m. surprised than annoyed** más que molesto estaba sorprendido; **I'm m. than satisfied** estoy más que satisfecho; **that's m. like it!** ¡eso está mejor!; **m. or less** más o menos; **they m. or less accused me of lying!** ¡casi me acusaron de mentir!; **you've no m. been to Australia than I have** no has estado en Australia en tu vida; **(the) m.'s the pity** es una lástima

(c) *(in time)* **m. and m., people are choosing to work from home** cada vez hay más gente que elige trabajar desde su casa; **once m.** una vez más, otra vez; **twice m.** dos veces más; **he doesn't drink any m.** ha dejado la bebida; **do you drink? – not any m.** *Esp* ¿bebes? – ya no, *Am* ¿sigues tomando? – ya no; **shall we play some m.?** ¿jugamos un rato más?; **m. often than not** muchas veces; *Euph* **he is no m.** ha pasado a mejor vida

4 *exclam (at concert)* ¡otra!

---

moreish, morish ['mɔːrɪʃ] *adj Fam (food)* irresistible, adictivo(a); **these snacks are very m.** estos aperitivos son irresistibles *or* muy adictivos

morel [mə'rel] *n* colmenilla *f*, cagarria *f*

morello [mə'reləʊ] (*pl* **morellos**) *n* **m. (cherry)** guinda *f*

moreover [mɔː'rəʊvə(r)] *adv* además, (lo que) es más

mores ['mɔːreɪz] *npl Formal* costumbres *fpl*

morganatic [mɔːgə'nætɪk] *adj* morganático(a)

morgue [mɔːg] *n* depósito *m* de cadáveres, *esp Am* morgue *f*; *Fig* **this place is like a m.** este sitio parece un entierro

MORI ['mɔːrɪ] *n* (*abbr* **Market and Opinion Research Institute**) = empresa británica encargada de realizar sondeos de opinión ►► ***M. poll*** sondeo *m* de opinión *(realizado por MORI)*

moribund ['mɒrɪbʌnd] *adj* agonizante, moribundo(a)

morish = **moreish**

Mormon ['mɔːmən] *Rel* **1** *n* mormón(ona) *m,f*

2 *adj* mormón(ona)

Mormonism ['mɔːmənɪzəm] *n* mormonismo *m*

morn [mɔːn] *n Literary* mañana *f*

mornay ['mɔːneɪ] *n Culin* **cod/egg m.** bacalao/huevo en salsa Mornay

morning ['mɔːnɪŋ] **1** *n* **(a)** *(of day)* mañana *f*; **this m.** esta mañana; **tomorrow m.** mañana por la mañana; **yesterday m.** ayer por la mañana; **the next *or* following m., the m. after** la mañana siguiente; **on the m. of the next day, on the following m.** a la mañana siguiente; *Fam Hum* **the m. after (the night before)** la mañana de la resaca; **the previous m., the m. before** la mañana anterior; **all m.** toda la mañana; **every m.** todas las mañanas, cada mañana; **every Friday m.** todos los viernes por la mañana; **(early) in the m.** por la mañana (temprano); **see you in the m.!** ¡hasta mañana (por la mañana)!; **at eight o'clock in the m.** a las ocho de la mañana; **could I have the m. off?** ¿puedo tomarme la mañana libre?; **m., noon and night** (mañana,) día y noche; **from m. till night** todo el día; **she worked from m. till night** trabajaba de sol a sol; **on Wednesday m.** el miércoles por la mañana; **on Monday mornings** los lunes por la mañana; **on the m. of the twelfth** la mañana del (día) doce; **when I woke it was m.** cuando me desperté era de día; **I'm on mornings this week** esta semana estoy por la mañana *or* me toca de mañana; **good m.!** ¡buenos días!; *Fam* **m.!** ¡buenas! ►► ***m. coat*** chaqué *m*, *CSur* jaqué *m*; ***m. dress*** chaqué *m*; ***m. glory*** *(plant)* maravilla *f*; ***m. (news)paper*** diario *m* matinal *or* de la mañana; ***m. sickness*** náuseas *fpl* matutinas del embarazo; ***m. star*** lucero *m* del alba

(b) *Literary (beginning)* albores *mpl*, amanecer *m*; **in the m. of one's life** en los albores *or* el amanecer de su vida

2 *adj* matinal; **the m. rush hour** la hora *Esp* punta *or Am* pico de la mañana; **cancel the m. meeting** suspende la reunión de (por) la mañana; **my m. walk** mi paseo matutino

3 mornings *adv esp US* por las mañanas

morning-after pill ['mɔːnɪŋ'ɑːftəpɪl] *n* píldora *f* del día siguiente

Moroccan [mə'rɒkən] **1** *n* marroquí *mf*

2 *adj* marroquí

Morocco [mə'rɒkəʊ] *n* Marruecos

morocco [mə'rɒkəʊ] *n* **m. (leather)** tafilete *m*

moron ['mɔːrɒn] *n Fam* subnormal *mf*, *Am* zonzo(a) *m,f*

moronic [mə'rɒnɪk] *adj Fam (person)* subnormal, *Am* zonzo(a); *(expression, behaviour)* de subnormal, *Am* zonzo(a); **a m. comment** una memez

moronically [mə'rɒnɪklɪ] *adv Fam* estúpidamente

morose [mə'rəʊs] *adj* hosco(a), huraño(a)

> **False friend:** The Spanish word **moroso** is not a translation for the English word **morose**. In Spanish **moroso** means "defaulter, bad debtor".

morosely [mə'rəʊslɪ] *adv* malhumoradamente

morph [mɔːf] *Cin & Comptr* 1 *n* imagen *f* transformada por *Esp* ordenador *or Am* computadora
2 *vt* transformar *(con animación por ordenador o computadora)*
3 *vi* transformarse *(con animación por ordenador o computadora)*; **to m. into sth** transformarse en algo

morpheme ['mɔːfiːm] *n Ling* morfema *m*

morphemic [mɔː'fiːmɪk] *adj Ling* morfemático(a)

morphia ['mɔːfɪə] *n Old-fashioned* morfina *f*

morphine ['mɔːfiːn] *n* morfina *f*

morphing ['mɔːfɪŋ] *n Cin & Comptr* transformación *f (con animación por ordenador o computadora)*

morphological [mɔːfə'lɒdʒɪkəl] *adj Ling* morfológico(a)

morphology [mɔː'fɒlədʒɪ] *n Ling* morfología *f*

morris dancing ['mɒrɪs'dɑːnsɪŋ] *n* = baile tradicional inglés en el que varios personajes ataviados con cintas y cascabeles entrechocan unos palos

morrow ['mɒrəʊ] *n* (**a**) *Literary (next day)* día *m* siguiente; **with not a care for the m.** sin pensar en el mañana; **on the m.** mañana, al siguiente día (**b**) *Archaic or Literary (morning)* mañana *f*

Morse [mɔːs] *n* **in M.** en (código) morse ▸▸ ***M. code*** código *m* morse

morsel ['mɔːsəl] *n* pedacito *m*; **a choice** *or* **tasty m.** un bocado exquisito

mortal ['mɔːtəl] 1 *n* mortal *mf*; *Ironic* **he doesn't speak to mere mortals like us!** ¡no habla con los simples mortales como nosotros!
2 *adj* (**a**) *(not immortal)* mortal; **all men are m.** todos los hombres son mortales ▸▸ *Literary or Hum* ***m. coil:* to shuffle off this m. coil** irse al otro barrio; ***m. remains*** restos *mpl* mortales
(**b**) *(fatal) (wound, disease, injury)* mortal ▸▸ *Rel* ***m. sin*** pecado *m* mortal
(**c**) *(deadly) (enemy)* mortal; *(danger)* de muerte; **they were locked in m. combat** se enfrentaban en un combate a muerte
(**d**) *(very great)* **he lived in m. fear of being found out** vivía con un miedo atroz a ser descubierto

mortality [mɔː'tælɪtɪ] *n* (**a**) *(death rate)* mortalidad *f* ▸▸ ***m. rate*** tasa *f or* índice *m* de mortalidad (**b**) *(mortal state)* mortalidad *f*

mortally ['mɔːtəlɪ] *adv* (**a**) *(fatally)* mortalmente; **m. wounded** herido(a) de muerte (**b**) *(gravely)* **m. offended** ultrajado(a); **to be m. afraid (of sth/sb)** tener un miedo atroz (a algo/alguien)

mortar ['mɔːtə(r)] 1 *n* (**a**) *(in construction)* argamasa *f*, mortero *m* (**b**) *(for grinding)* mortero *m*, almirez *m*; **pass me the m. and pestle** pásame el mortero (**c**) *(weapon)* mortero *m* ▸▸ ***m. shell*** granada *f* de mortero
2 *vt* (**a**) *(in construction) (bricks)* fijar con argamasa; *(wall)* enlucir (con argamasa) (**b**) *(bombard)* bombardear con (fuego de) mortero

mortarboard ['mɔːtəbɔːd] *n* (**a**) *(in construction)* llana *f* (**b**) *(hat)* = sombrero en forma de cuadrado negro con una borla que cuelga, usado por los estudiantes en la ceremonia de graduación

mortgage ['mɔːgɪdʒ] 1 *n* hipoteca *f*, crédito *m* hipotecario; **a 25-year m.** una hipoteca a 25 años; **to take out a m. (on sth)** obtener una hipoteca (para algo); **to pay off a m.** pagar una hipoteca ▸▸ ***m. payments*** plazos *mpl* de la hipoteca; ***m. rate*** tipo *m* (de interés) hipotecario, *Am* tasa *f* de interés hipotecaria; ***m. repayments*** plazos *mpl* de la hipoteca
2 *vt (property, one's future)* hipotecar; **he mortgaged his happiness** hipotecó su felicidad

mortgageable ['mɔːgɪdʒəbəl] *adj* hipotecable

mortgagee [mɔːgɪ'dʒiː] *n Fin* acreedor(ora) *m,f* hipotecario(a)

mortgagor [mɔːgɪ'dʒɔː(r)] *n Fin* deudor(ora) *m,f* hipotecario(a)

mortice = **mortise**

mortician [mɔː'tɪʃən] *n US (undertaker)* encargado(a) *m,f* de funeraria

mortification [mɔːtɪfɪ'keɪʃən] *n* (**a**) *Rel* mortificación *f*; **m. of the flesh** mortificación de la carne (**b**) *(embarrassment)* bochorno *m*; **to my (eternal) m.** con gran bochorno por mi parte

mortify ['mɔːtɪfaɪ] *vt* (**a**) *Rel* mortificar; **to m. the flesh** mortificar la carne (**b**) *(embarrass)* **I was mortified** me sentí abochornado

mortifying ['mɔːtɪfaɪɪŋ] *adj* (**a**) *Rel* mortificante (**b**) *(embarrassing)* bochornoso(a)

mortise, mortice ['mɔːtɪs] 1 *n (in carpentry)* muesca *f*, mortaja *f* ▸▸ ***m. lock*** cerradura *f* embutida *or* de pestillo
2 *vt* mortajar, hacer una muesca *or* mortaja en; **to m. two beams together** juntar dos vigas con ensamblaje de espiga (y mortaja)

mortuary ['mɔːtjʊərɪ] *n* depósito *m* de cadáveres

Mosaic [məʊ'zeɪɪk] *adj* mosaico(a)

mosaic [məʊ'zeɪɪk] *n* (**a**) *(decorative work)* mosaico *m*; **m. floor** suelo de *or* en mosaico (**b**) *Bot* **m. (disease)** mosaico *m*

Moscow ['mɒskəʊ, *US* 'mɑːskaʊ] *n* Moscú

Moselle [məʊ'zel] *n* (**a**) *(river)* **the M.** el (río) Mosela (**b**) *(wine)* vino *m* de Mosela

Moses ['məʊzɪz] *pr n* Moisés ▸▸ ***M. basket*** moisés *m*, canastilla *f*

mosey ['məʊzɪ]

▸ **mosey along** *vi Fam* ir dando un paseo; **I'll just m. along to the bar** me iré dando un paseo hasta el bar; **I'll be moseying along now** *(leaving)* yo ya me marcho *or Esp, RP* me piro

▸ **mosey on down** *vi Fam* ir; **let's m. on down!** ¡vamos!, *Méx* ¡ándale!, *RP* ¡dale!

Moslem ['mɒzlem] 1 *n* musulmán(ana) *m,f*
2 *adj* musulmán(ana)

mosque [mɒsk] *n* mezquita *f*

mosquito [məs'kiːtəʊ] (*pl* **mosquitoes**) *n* mosquito *m*, *Am* zancudo *m* ▸▸ ***m. bite*** picadura *f* de mosquito; ***m. net*** mosquitera *f*, mosquitero *m*; ***m. repellent*** repelente *m* antimosquitos

moss [mɒs] *n* musgo *m* ▸▸ ***m. green*** verde *m* musgo

mossy ['mɒsɪ] *adj* cubierto(a) de musgo

MOST [məʊst] (*superlative of* **many, much**) 1 *pron* **of the calls we receive, m. are complaints** la mayoría de las llamadas que recibimos son quejas; **he is more interesting than m.** es más interesante que la mayoría; **he earns the m.** él es el que más (dinero) gana; **she got the m., as usual** como de costumbre, se llevó la parte más grande; **what's the m. you've ever paid for a hotel room?** ¿cuánto es lo máximo que has pagado por una habitación de hotel?; **the m. we can hope for is a draw** como máximo podemos aspirar a un empate; **m. of my friends** la mayoría de *or* casi todos mis amigos; **m. of us** la mayoría de nosotros; **m. of the time** la mayor parte del tiempo, casi todo el tiempo; **at m., at the (very) m.** como mucho; **to make the m. of an opportunity** aprovechar al máximo una oportunidad
2 *adj* (**a**) *(the majority of)* la mayoría de; **m. women** la mayoría de las mujeres; **m. whisky is made in Scotland** la mayor parte del whisky se hace en Escocia
(**b**) *(greatest amount of)* **he has (the) m. money** él es el que más dinero tiene; **how can we get (the) m. money?** ¿cómo podemos sacar el máximo dinero posible?; **to get the m. use out of sth** sacar el mayor partido a algo; **for the m. part, we get on** por lo general, nos llevamos bien; **the inhabitants are, for the m. part, Irish** los habitantes son, en su mayoría, irlandeses
3 *adv* (**a**) *(to form superlative of adjectives and adverbs)* **the m.** el/la más; **the m. beautiful woman** la mujer más bella; **the m. interesting book** el libro más interesante; **these are the m. expensive** éstos son los más caros; **the player m. likely to win** el jugador que tiene más probabilidades de ganar; **it operates m. efficiently when...** funciona óptimamente cuando...; **the question we get asked m. often** la pregunta que nos hacen más a menudo ▸▸ *US Sport* ***m. valuable player*** jugador(ora) *m,f* más destacado(a), mejor jugador(ora) *m,f*
(**b**) *(with verbs)* **the one who works m. is...** el/la que trabaja más es...; **who do you like m.?** ¿quién te cae mejor?; **what I want m.** lo que más deseo; **that's what worries me (the) m.** eso es lo que más me preocupa; **I liked the last song m. of all** la última canción fue la que más me gustó; **m. of all, I would like to thank my mother** por encima de todo, me gustaría dar las gracias a mi madre
(**c**) *(very)* muy, sumamente; **m. unhappy** muy desgraciado(a); **I'll m. certainly let you know** con toda seguridad te lo diré; **can I have a slice of cake? – m. certainly** ¿puedo servirme un trozo de pastel? – por supuesto que sí; **we will m. probably fail** es muy probable que *Esp* suspendamos *or Am* reprobemos; **m. unexpectedly** de manera totalmente inesperada
(**d**) *US Fam (almost)* casi; **I go there m. every day** voy ahí casi todos los días

most-favoured nation, *US* **most-favored nation** ['məʊst-'feɪvəd'neɪʃən] *n Econ* nación *f* más favorecida ▸▸ ***m. clause*** cláusula *f* de la nación más favorecida; ***m. status*** estatus *m inv* de nación más favorecida

mostly ['məʊstlɪ] *adv* (**a**) *(in the main)* principalmente, sobre todo; **it's m. sugar** tiene principalmente *or* sobre todo azúcar; **the soldiers were m. young men** los soldados eran principalmente *or* en su mayoría hombres jóvenes; **the story is m. true** la historia es casi toda cierta *or* en su mayor parte cierta
(**b**) *(most often)* casi siempre; **m. we stay in and watch TV** casi siempre nos quedamos en casa viendo la televisión

MOT [eməʊ'ti:] **1** *n Br Aut* = inspección técnica anual de vehículos de más de tres años, *Esp* ≃ ITV *f*, *RP* ≃ VTV *f* ▸▸ ***M. certificate*** certificado *m* de haber pasado la inspección técnica anual, *Esp* ≃ ITV *f*, *RP* ≃ VTV *f*; ***M. test*** = inspección técnica anual de vehículos de más de tres años, *Esp* ≃ ITV *f*, *RP* ≃ VTV *f*
2 *vt* (*pt & pp* **MOT'd** [eməʊ'ti:d]) **to have one's car MOT'd** llevar el automóvil a pasar la inspección técnica anual

mote [məʊt] *n Literary* mota *f*; **the m. in thy brother's eye** la paja en el ojo ajeno

motel [məʊ'tel] *n* motel *m*

motet [məʊ'tet] *n Mus* motete *m*

moth [mɒθ] *n* mariposa *f* nocturna; **(clothes) m.** polilla *f*

mothball ['mɒθbɔ:l] **1** *n* bola *f* de naftalina; *Fig* **to put a project in mothballs** aparcar un proyecto
2 *vt* (**a**) *(ship)* dejar en la reserva (**b**) *(project)* aparcar

moth-eaten ['mɒθi:tən] *adj* (**a**) *(clothing)* apolillado(a) (**b**) *Fam Fig (shabby)* cochambroso(a)

mother ['mʌðə(r)] **1** *n* (**a**) *(parent)* madre *f*; **m. of six** madre de seis hijos; *Pej* **a m.'s boy** un enmadrado, un niño *or RP* nené de mamá; **at one's m.'s knee** de pequeño(a), de pequeñito(a); **a m.'s love** el amor de madre *or* materno; *Br* **shall I be m.?** ¿sirvo el té?; IDIOM **the m. and father of sth: we had the m. and father of a row** *Esp* tuvimos una bronca de padre y muy señor mío *or* de aúpa, *Am* tuvimos un lío de padre y señor nuestro ▸▸ ***m. country*** madre patria *f*; ***M.'s Day*** día *m* de la madre; ***M. Earth*** la madre tierra; ***the M. of God*** *(Virgin Mary)* la madre de Dios; ***m. hen*** gallina *f* madre; IDIOM **she was fussing about like a m. hen** estaba metida en el papel de madre preocupada; ***m. lode*** *Min* filón *m* madre *or* principal; *Fig* filón *m*, mina *f*; ***M. Nature*** la madre naturaleza; *Hum* ***m.'s ruin*** ginebra *f*; *Mil* ***m. ship*** buque *m* nodriza; *Rel* ***M. Superior*** madre *f* superiora; ***m. tongue*** lengua *f* materna
(**b**) *US very Fam* cabrón(ona) *m,f*; **her boyfriend's a big m.** su novio es un cabrón *or* cabronazo; **I've got a m. of a hangover** tengo una resaca del carajo *or Esp* copón; **the m.'s broken down again** el cabrón (de él) ha vuelto a estropearse
(**c**) *Br (of trade union)* ***M. of Chapel*** delegada *f or Esp* enlace *f* sindical *(del sector editorial y de artes gráficas)*
2 *vt* mimar

motherboard ['mʌðəbɔ:d] *n Comptr* placa *f* madre

motherfucker ['mʌðəfʌkə(r)] *n Vulg* (**a**) *(person)* hijo(a) *m,f* de puta, *Méx* hijo(a) *m,f* de la chingada; **you m.!** ¡me cago en tu puta madre!, *Méx* ¡chinga tu madre!, *RP* ¡me cago en la puta que te parió! (**b**) *(thing)* **the m. won't start** el hijo de puta no arranca; **that was a m. of a meeting** fue una reunión muy jodida

motherfucking ['mʌðəfʌkɪŋ] *adj Vulg* puto(a), jodido(a); **that m. bastard!** ¡ese hijo de puta!; **open up or I'll kick the m. door in!** ¡abre o echo abajo la puta *or* jodida puerta!

motherhood ['mʌðəhʊd] *n* maternidad *f*

mothering ['mʌðərɪŋ] *n* maternidad *f*; **she's not confident about her m. skills** no confía en su capacidad para criar a un hijo ▸▸ *Br* ***M. Sunday*** el día de la madre

mother-in-law ['mʌðərɪnlɔ:] *n* suegra *f*

motherland ['mʌðəlænd] *n* tierra *f* natal

motherless ['mʌðəlɪs] *adj* huérfano(a) de madre, sin madre

motherly ['mʌðəlɪ] *adj* maternal

mother-of-pearl ['mʌðərəv'pɜ:l] *n* nácar *m*; **m. buttons** botones de nácar

mother-to-be ['mʌðətə'bi:] *n* futura madre *f*

mothproof ['mɒθpru:f] *adj (cloth)* resistente a las polillas

motif [məʊ'ti:f] *n (in music, design)* motivo *m*; *(in literature)* tema *m*

motion ['məʊʃən] **1** *n* (**a**) *(movement)* movimiento *m*; **with a swaying m. of the hips** con un balanceo de caderas; **to be in m.** estar en movimiento; **do not alight while the train is in m.** *(sign)* no se apeen mientras el tren esté en marcha; **to set sth in m.** *(machine, system)* poner algo en marcha *or* funcionamiento; IDIOM **to set the wheels in m.** poner las cosas en marcha; IDIOM **to go through the motions** hacer las cosas mecánicamente *or* por inercia ▸▸ *US* ***m. picture*** película *f*; ***m. sickness*** mareo *m (del viajero)*
(**b**) *(in meeting, debate)* moción *f*; **m. of censure/confidence** moción de censura/confianza; **to propose/second a m.** proponer/apoyar una moción; **the m. was carried/defeated** la moción fue aprobada/rechazada
(**c**) *Law (application)* petición *f*
(**d**) *Br Formal (of bowel)* deposición *f*, evacuación *f*; **to have** *or* **pass a m.** hacer de vientre, evacuar
2 *vt* **to m. sb to do sth** indicar a alguien (con un gesto) que haga algo; **to m. sb in/away/out** indicar a alguien que entre/se vaya/salga
3 *vi* **to m. to sb to do sth** indicar a alguien (con un gesto) que haga algo

motionless ['məʊʃənlɪs] *adj* inmóvil; **to remain m.** permanecer inmóvil

motivate ['məʊtɪveɪt] *vt* motivar; **how can I m. my pupils?** ¿cómo puedo motivar a mis alumnos?; **what motivated your choice?** ¿qué fue lo que motivó su elección?; **what motivated you to change your mind?** ¿qué te impulsó a cambiar de idea?

motivated ['məʊtɪveɪtɪd] *adj* motivado(a); **a highly m. young woman** una joven muy motivada; **a politically m. decision** una decisión por motivos políticos *or* con motivaciones políticas

motivating ['məʊtɪveɪtɪŋ] *adj* estimulante, alentador(ora)

motivation [məʊtɪ'veɪʃən] *n* motivación *f*; **the pupils lack m.** los alumnos están poco motivados, a los alumnos les falta motivación

motivational [məʊtɪ'veɪʃənəl] *adj* motivacional ▸▸ *Psy* ***m. research*** estudio *m* de la psicología del consumidor

motivator ['məʊtɪveɪtə(r)] *n* **he's a good m.** sabe motivar *or* estimular a la gente

motive ['məʊtɪv] **1** *n* (**a**) *(reason)* motivo *m*, razón *f*; **the motives for her behaviour** los motivos *or* las razones de su comportamiento; **my m. for asking is simple** la razón por la que pregunto es sencilla (**b**) *Law* móvil *m*
2 *adj* ***m. force*** fuerza *f* motriz; ***m. power*** energía *f* motriz

motiveless ['məʊtɪvlɪs] *adj* sin motivo; **an apparently m. murder** un asesinato sin motivo aparente

mot juste ['məʊ'ʒu:st] *n* **the m.** el término preciso *or* adecuado

motley ['mɒtlɪ] *adj* heterogéneo(a), abigarrado(a); *Pej* **a m. crew** una panda de lo más variopinto

motocross ['məʊtəkrɒs] *n* motocross *m*

motor ['məʊtə(r)] **1** *n* (**a**) *(engine)* motor *m* ▸▸ ***m. launch*** lancha *f* motora; ***m. vehicle*** vehículo *m* de motor
(**b**) *Br Fam (car)* coche *m*, *Am* carro *m*, *CSur* auto *m* ▸▸ ***m. car*** automóvil *m*; *Br* ***m. caravan*** autocaravana *f*, rulot *f*, *RP* casa *f* rodante; *US* ***m. court*** motel *m* (de carretera); ***m. home*** *(caravan)* autocaravana *f*, rulot *f*, *RP* casa *f* rodante; *US* ***m. hotel*** motel *m*; ***m. industry*** sector *m or* industria *f* automovilístico(a); *US* ***m. inn*** motel *m*; ***m. insurance*** seguro *m* de automóviles; *US* ***m. lodge*** motel *m*; ***m. race*** carrera *f* automovilística; ***m. racing*** carreras *fpl* de coches *or Am* carros *or RP* autos; ***m. show*** salón *m* del automóvil; ***the m. trade*** el sector de compraventa de automóviles
2 *vi* (**a**) *Old-fashioned (travel by car)* viajar en automóvil; **we motored up to London** fuimos hasta Londres en automóvil; **we motored across Europe** recorrimos Europa en automóvil (**b**) *Fam (move fast)* ir a toda mecha; **he was really motoring** iba a toda mecha
3 *adj Physiol (function, nerve)* motor(ora) ▸▸ *Med* ***m. neurone disease*** enfermedad *f* de la motoneurona *or* neurona motora

motorbike ['məʊtəbaɪk] *n* moto *f*

motorboat ['məʊtəbəʊt] *n* (lancha *f*) motora *f*

motorcade ['məʊtəkeɪd] *n* desfile *m* de coches *or Am* carros *or RP* autos

motorcycle ['məʊtəsaɪkəl] *n* motocicleta *f*, moto *f* ▸▸ *US Fam* ***m. cop*** policía *mf* motorizado(a), motorista *mf*; ***m. race*** carrera *f* de motos *or* motocicletas

motorcycling ['məʊtəsaɪklɪŋ] *n* motociclismo *m*, motorismo *m*

motorcyclist ['məʊtəsaɪklɪst] *n* motociclista *mf*, motorista *mf*

motoring ['məʊtərɪŋ] *n* automovilismo *m*; **school of m.** autoescuela ▸▸ *Br* ***m. offence*** infracción *f* de tráfico

motorist ['məʊtərɪst] *n* conductor(ora) *m,f*, automovilista *mf*

motorize ['məʊtəraɪz] *vt* motorizar

motorized ['məʊtəraɪzd] *adj* (**a**) *(vehicle, wheelchair)* motorizado(a), con motor (**b**) *Mil (troops, unit)* motorizado(a)

motorman ['məʊtəmən] *n US* conductor(ora) *m,f*

motormouth ['məʊtəmaʊθ] *n Fam (person)* charlatán(ana) *m,f*

motor-scooter ['məʊtəsku:tə(r)] *n* escúter *m*

motorway ['məʊtəweɪ] *n Br* autopista *f* ▸▸ ***m. pile-up*** colisión *f* múltiple en una autopista; ***m. services*** área *f* de servicios

Motown® ['məʊtaʊn] *n (pop music)* música *f* Motown

mottle ['mɒtəl] *vt (with blotches)* motear; *(with streaks)* vetear; **sunlight coming through the trees mottled the ground** la luz del sol salpicaba el suelo al pasar entre los árboles

mottled ['mɒtəld] *adj* (**a**) *(complexion)* con manchas rojizas (**b**) *(coat, surface) (with blotches)* moteado(a)

motto ['mɒtəʊ] (*pl* **mottoes**) *n* (**a**) *(maxim)* lema *m*; **the school m.** el lema del colegio; **"if you don't help yourself, no one else will": that's my m.** como yo digo *or* mi lema es: "si tú no te ayudas, nadie lo hará por ti" (**b**) *(in Christmas cracker) (joke)* chiste *m*; *(riddle)* acertijo *m*, adivinanza *f*

mould[1], *US* **mold** [məʊld] *n (fungus)* moho *m*

mould[2], *US* **mold** *n (soil)* mantillo *m*

mould[3], *US* **mold** **1** *n* (**a**) *(hollow form)* molde *m*; **cake m.** molde para pasteles; IDIOM **to break the m.** romper moldes *or* el molde; IDIOM **when they made him they broke the m.** como él no hay dos, después de hacerlo a él rompieron el molde

(**b**) *(moulded article)* molde *m*; **rice m.** molde de arroz

(**c**) *Fig (pattern)* **cast in the same m.** cortado(a) por el mismo patrón; **cast in a heroic m.** con madera *or* hechuras de héroe; *Fig* **a star in the John Wayne m.** un actor del estilo de John Wayne

(**d**) *Archit* moldura *f*

2 *vt* (**a**) *(shape) (plastic, metal)* moldear; **to m. sth in** *or* **from** *or* **out of clay** moldear algo con *or* en arcilla, modelar algo con *or* en arcilla; **moulded plastic chairs** sillas de plástico moldeado; **to m. sb into sth** modelar *or* educar a alguien para que se convierta en algo (**b**) *(influence) (person's character)* moldear; **they're trying to m. public opinion** tratan de moldear *or* dirigir la opinión pública

moulder, *US* **molder** ['məʊldə(r)] *vi* desmoronarse; **he's mouldering away in prison** se está pudriendo en la cárcel

moulding, *US* **molding** ['məʊldɪŋ] *n Archit* moldura *f*

mouldy, *US* **moldy** ['məʊldɪ] *adj* (**a**) *(covered with mould) (food)* mohoso(a); *(clothes)* lleno(a) de moho, apulgarado(a); **it smells m.** huele a humedad *or* a moho (**b**) *Br Fam (measly)* mísero(a), cochino(a)

Mouli® ['mu:lɪ] *n Br* picadora *f* (manual)

moult, *US* **molt** [məʊlt] **1** *vi (animal)* mudar el pelo; *(bird)* mudar el plumaje

2 *vt (hair, feathers)* mudar, pelechar; **the cat is moulting hairs all over the furniture** el gato está mudando *or* pelechando y deja pelos por todos los muebles

3 *n* muda *f*

mound [maʊnd] *n* (**a**) *(hill)* colina *f* (**b**) *(of earth, sand, rubble)* montículo *m* (**c**) *(heap)* montón *m*; *Fam* **he ate mounds of rice** comió montañas *or* un montón de arroz (**d**) *(in baseball)* montículo *m*

mount[1] [maʊnt] *n Literary* monte *m* ▸▸ ***M. Everest*** el Everest; ***M. Fuji*** el Fujiyama, el Monte Fuji; ***M. Sinai*** el Monte Sinaí

mount[2] **1** *n* (**a**) *(horse)* montura *f* (**b**) *(for painting, photograph)* paspartú *m*, soporte *m*; *(for colour slide)* marco *m*, montura *f*; *(for stamp in collection) (hinge)* charnela *f*, fijasellos *m inv*; *(pocket)* bolsillo *m* (**c**) *(for engine, gun)* soporte *m* (**d**) *(for object under microscope)* portaobjetos *m inv*, portaobjeto *m*

2 *vt* (**a**) *(ascend) (stairs, ladder)* subir

(**b**) *(get on) (bicycle, horse)* montar en, subirse a; **a truck mounted the pavement** un camión se subió a la acera

(**c**) *(painting, photograph) (in frame)* enmarcar, montar; *(on background)* poner paspartú a; **to m. stamps** pegar *or* fijar sellos *(en un álbum)*

(**d**) *(gun)* montar; **they mounted machine-guns on the roofs** montaron ametralladoras en los tejados

(**e**) *(organize, carry out)* montar; **to m. an exhibition** montar una exposición; **they mounted an attack on the party leadership** montaron *or* prepararon una ofensiva para hacerse con la jefatura del partido; *Mil* **to m. an offensive** realizar una ofensiva; *Mil* **to m. guard** montar guardia

(**f**) *(mate with)* montar, cubrir

(**g**) *Comptr* montar

3 *vi* (**a**) *(get onto horse)* montar, montarse (**b**) *(increase) (pressure, tension, panic)* aumentar, crecer; *(temperature, prices)* aumentar, subir; **her anger mounted** creció *or* aumentó su furia; **the number of cases was mounting** el número de casos iba en aumento

▸**mount up** *vi (cost, debts, bills)* acumularse

mountain ['maʊntɪn] *n* (**a**) *(large hill)* montaña *f*; **m. air** aire de la montaña; **m. pass** paso de montaña, puerto (de montaña); **m. stream** arroyo de montaña; **m. top** cumbre *f*, cima *f*; *Fig* **to move mountains** mover montañas; IDIOM **to make a m. out of a molehill** hacer una montaña de un grano de arena; PROV **if the m. won't go to Mohammed, Mohammed will have to go to the m.** si Mahoma no va a la montaña, la montaña irá a Mahoma ▸▸ ***m. ash*** serbal *m*; ***m. bike*** bicicleta *f* de montaña; ***m. climber*** montañero(a) *m,f*, alpinista *mf*, *Am* andinista *mf*; ***m. climbing*** montañismo *m*, alpinismo *m*, *Am* andinismo *m*; ***m. dew*** = alcohol destilado ilegalmente; ***m. goat*** *(in general)* cabra *f* montés; *(American variety)* rebeco *m* blanco, cabra *f* de las nieves *or* de las Montañas Rocosas; ***m. lion*** puma *m*; ***m. range*** cadena *f* montañosa, cordillera *f*; ***m. rescue team*** equipo *m* de rescate de montaña; ***m. sickness*** mal *m* de montaña; ***m. stage*** etapa *f* de montaña; *US* ***M. (Standard) Time*** = hora oficial en la zona de las Montañas Rocosas en los Estados Unidos

(**b**) *(heap, accumulation)* montaña *f*, montón *m*; **a m. of work** una montaña de trabajo; **the EU butter m.** las toneladas de excedentes de mantequilla de la Unión Europea

mountaineer [maʊntɪ'nɪə(r)] *n* montañero(a) *m,f*, alpinista *mf*, *Am* andinista *mf*

mountaineering [maʊntɪ'nɪərɪŋ] *n* montañismo *m*, alpinismo *m*, *Am* andinismo *m*

mountainous ['maʊntɪnəs] *adj* (**a**) *(region, landscape)* montañoso(a) (**b**) *(huge)* colosal, inmenso(a); **m. waves** olas colosales

mountainside ['maʊntɪnsaɪd] *n* ladera *f*; **a village perched on the m.** un pueblo enclavado en la ladera de la montaña

mountebank ['maʊntɪbæŋk] *n Literary* charlatán(ana) *m,f*

mounted ['maʊntɪd] *adj* montado(a) ▸▸ ***m. police*** policía *f* montada

Mountie, Mounty ['maʊntɪ] *n Fam (in Canada)* = agente de la policía montada del Canadá; **the Mounties** la policía montada del Canadá

mounting ['maʊntɪŋ] **1** *n (for engine, gun)* soporte *m*

2 *adj (cost, opposition, pressure, anxiety)* creciente; **there is m. evidence against her** cada vez hay más pruebas contra ella

Mounty = **Mountie**

mourn [mɔ:n] **1** *vt* llorar la muerte de; **there's no point mourning what might have been** de nada sirve lamentarse por lo que podría haber sido

2 *vi* **to m. for sb** llorar la muerte de alguien; **to m. over sth** lamentarse de algo; **he mourns over the loss of his son** llora la pérdida de su hijo

mourner ['mɔ:nə(r)] *n* doliente *mf*

mournful ['mɔ:nfʊl] *adj (person)* desconsolado(a), apesadumbrado(a); *(eyes, voice, mood)* apesadumbrado(a), entristecido(a); *(sound, place)* fúnebre, lúgubre; **a m. occasion** un triste *or* funesto acontecimiento

mournfully ['mɔ:nfʊlɪ] *adv* desconsoladamente, con pesadumbre

mourning ['mɔ:nɪŋ] *n* duelo *m*, luto *m*; **m. (clothes)** (ropa *f* de) luto *m*; **to be in m. (for sb)** guardar luto *or* estar de luto (por alguien); **to go into m.** ponerse de luto; **to come out of m.** dejar *or* quitarse el luto; **a day of m. was declared** se declaró un día de luto *or* duelo oficial

mouse [maʊs] **1** *n* (*pl* **mice** [maɪs]) (**a**) *(animal)* ratón *m* (**b**) *(person)* **to be a m.** ser poquita cosa (**c**) *Comptr Esp* ratón *m*, *Am* mouse *m* ▸▸ ***m. button*** botón *m* del *Esp* ratón *or Am* mouse; ***m. click*** clic *m* (del *Esp* ratón *or Am* mouse); ***m. mat*** alfombrilla *f*; ***m. pad*** alfombrilla *f*; ***m. port*** puerto *m* del *Esp* ratón *or Am* mouse

2 *vi (cat)* cazar ratones

mousehole ['maʊshəʊl] *n* ratonera *f*

mouser ['maʊsə(r)] *n (cat)* cazador(ora) *m,f* de ratones

mousetrap ['maʊstræp] *n* (**a**) *(device)* ratonera *f* (**b**) *Br Fam (cheese)* queso *m* corriente

mousey = **mousy**

moussaka [mu:'sɑ:kə] *n* musaka *f*

mousse [mu:s] *n* (**a**) *(food)* mousse *m o f*; **chocolate/lemon m.** mousse de chocolate/limón (**b**) *(for hair)* espuma *f*

moustache [mə'stæʃ], *US* **mustache** ['mʌstæʃ] *n* bigote *m*; **he's growing a m.** se está dejando bigote

moustached warbler [mə'stɑ:ʃt'wɔ:blə(r)] *n* carricerín *m* real

mousy, mousey ['maʊsɪ] *adj* (**a**) *(hair)* parduzco(a) (**b**) *(person, manner)* apocado(a), tímido(a)

mouth **1** *n* [maʊθ] (**a**) *(of person, animal)* boca *f*; **don't talk with your m. full!** ¡no hables con la boca llena!; **we have seven mouths to feed** tenemos siete bocas que alimentar; **he didn't open his m. once during the meeting** no abrió la boca durante toda la reunión; **he's incapable**

of keeping his m. shut es incapaz de tener la boca cerrada; *Fam* **keep your m. shut about this** no digas ni mu *or Esp* ni pío de esto ►► ***m. organ*** armónica *f*; ***m. ulcer*** llaga *f* en la boca

(b) *(of tunnel, bottle)* boca *f*

(c) *(of river)* desembocadura *f*

(d) IDIOMS *Fam* **he's all m.** todo lo hace de boquilla *or Méx* de dientes para afuera *or RP* de boca para afuera; *Br Fam* **he's all m. and trousers** se le va la fuerza por la boca; *Fam* **to have a big m.** ser un(a) bocazas *or Am* chusmo(a); **to be down in the m.** estar deprimido(a) *or* tristón(ona); **to put words into sb's m.** poner palabras en boca de alguien; *Fam* **he's always shooting his m. off** es un bocazas *or Am* chusmo(a); **me and my big m.!** ¡pero qué bocazas soy!; **out of the mouths of babes (and sucklings)...** los niños y los borrachos siempre dicen la verdad

2 *vt* [maʊð] (a) *(silently)* decir moviendo sólo los labios; **don't sing, just m. the words** no cantes, sólo mueve los labios (b) *(without sincerity)* decir mecánicamente; **to m. empty slogans** predicar eslóganes carentes de significado

► **mouth off** *vi Fam* (a) *(brag)* fanfarronear, *Esp* tirarse el moco (b) **to m. off at sb** *(insult)* gritarle a alguien (c) *(complain)* **to m. off about sth** quejarse de algo

mouthful [ˈmaʊθfʊl] *n* (a) *(of food)* bocado *m*; *(of drink)* trago *m*; **"I'll do it!" he said through a m. of pasta** "¡yo lo haré!", dijo él con la boca llena de pasta; **I couldn't eat another m.!** ¡no me cabía nada más *or* ni un bocado más!

(b) IDIOMS *Br Fam* **to give sb a m.** poner a alguien de vuelta y media; *Fam* **that's quite a m.!** *(of long name, word)* ¡qué *or Esp* menudo trabalenguas!; **his name's a bit of a m.** tiene un nombrecito impronunciable *or* que se las trae; *US* **you said a m.!** ¡qué razón tienes!, ¡y que lo digas!

mouthparts [ˈmaʊθpɑːts] *npl Zool* apéndices *mpl* bucales

mouthpiece [ˈmaʊθpiːs] *n* (a) *(of musical instrument)* boquilla *f*; *(of telephone)* micrófono *m* (b) *(of government, political party)* portavoz *mf*; *(newspaper, magazine)* portavoz *m*, órgano *m* de difusión (c) *US Fam (lawyer)* picapleitos *mf inv*

mouth-to-mouth [ˈmaʊθtəˈmaʊθ] *adj* ***m. resuscitation*** (respiración *f*) boca a boca *m*; **to give sb m. resuscitation** hacer el boca a boca a alguien

mouthwash [ˈmaʊθwɒʃ] *n* elixir *m* (bucal)

mouthwatering [ˈmaʊθwɔːtərɪŋ] *adj* apetitoso(a), tentador(ora); **a m. display of pastries** un surtido de apetitosos pasteles; **a m. prospect** una perspectiva muy tentadora

mouthy [ˈmaʊðɪ] *adj Fam Pej* (a) *(talkative)* parlanchín(ina), charlatán(ana) (b) *(boastful)* fanfarrón(ona)

movable, moveable [ˈmuːvəbəl] 1 *adj* móvil ►► *Rel* ***a m. feast*** una fiesta movible; *Law* ***m. property*** bienes *mpl* muebles

2 *n Law* **movables** bienes *mpl* muebles

MOVE [muːv] 1 *n* (a) *(motion)* movimiento *m*; **one m. and you're dead!** ¡un sólo movimiento y te mato!; **nobody make a m.!** ¡que nadie se mueva!; **to make a m. towards sth/sb** hacer amago de dirigirse hacia algo/alguien; *Fam* **if you like her, why don't you make a m. on her?** si te gusta, haz algo; **we must make a m.** *(leave)* debemos irnos; **on the m.** *(travelling)* de viaje; *(active, busy)* en marcha, en movimiento; **I've been on the m. all day** no he parado en todo el día; *Fam* **get a m. on!** ¡date prisa!, *Am* ¡apúrate!; *Fam* **we're going to have to get a m. on if we want to finish in time** tenemos que movernos si queremos terminar a tiempo; **to watch sb's every m.** vigilar a alguien muy de cerca

(b) *(action, step)* paso *m*; **that was a wise m.** ha sido una decisión muy acertada; **to make the first/next m.** dar el primer/siguiente paso; **they are making a m. to take over the company** se están preparando *or Am* alistando para absorber la compañía; *Fam* **to make a m. on sb** intentar seducir a alguien, *Esp* tirar los tejos a alguien, *RP* tirarse un lance con alguien

(c) *(from home)* mudanza *f*, traslado *m*; *(in job)* cambio *m*; **how did the m. go?** *(to new home)* ¿qué tal te fue la mudanza *or* el traslado?

(d) *(in board game)* movimiento *m*, jugada *f*; *(in sport)* jugada *f*; **(it's) your m.** te toca (jugar), tú mueves

2 *vt* (a) *(shift) (person, object, chesspiece)* mover; **m. your chair a bit closer** acerca la silla un poco; **we've moved the wardrobe into the other room** hemos puesto el armario en la otra habitación; **could you m. those bags out of the way?** ¿puedes quitar esas bolsas de en medio?; **we shall not be moved!** ¡no nos moverán!; **to m. house** mudarse de casa; **to m. jobs** *(within company, sector)* cambiar de trabajo; *Fam* **m. yourself** *or* **it, we're going to be late!** ¡muévete, que vamos a llegar tarde!

(b) *(transfer) (employee)* trasladar; **he has been moved to a high-security prison** ha sido trasladado a una prisión de máxima seguridad; **he asked to be moved to a room with a sea-view** pidió que le trasladaran a una habitación con vistas al mar

(c) *(postpone)* trasladar; **the meeting has been moved to next week** la reunión ha sido trasladada a la próxima semana, *RP* la reunión se postergó para la semana que viene

(d) *(influence)* **I won't be moved** no voy a cambiar de opinión; **what moved her to say such a thing?** ¿qué la habrá hecho decir algo así?; **I felt moved to protest** me sentí impulsado a protestar

(e) *(affect emotionally)* conmover; **to m. sb to anger** enfurecer a alguien; **to m. sb to tears** hacer llorar *or* saltar las lágrimas a alguien

(f) *(in debate) (resolution)* proponer, *Am* mocionar; **I m. that...** propongo que..., *Am* mociono que ...

(g) *Med* **to m. one's bowels** hacer de vientre

(h) *Fam (sell)* vender

3 *vi* (a) *(change position)* moverse; *(progress, advance)* avanzar; **don't m.!** ¡no te muevas!; **I can't m.!** *(I'm stuck)* ¡no puedo moverme!; **could you m., please?** ¿podría apartarse *or* correrse, por favor?; **it won't m. an inch** no se mueve ni a tiros, no hay quien lo mueva; **to m. closer** acercarse; **to m. into position** colocarse en posición; **to m. out of the way** *Esp* apartarse de en medio, *Am* salir del medio; **it was so crowded, you could hardly m.** había tanta gente que no podías ni moverte; *Fig* **you couldn't m. for tourists** había una cantidad enorme de turistas; *Fam* **come on, m.!** ¡venga *or Méx* ándale, muévete!, *RP* ¡dale, movete!; **let's get moving!** ¡en marcha!; **to get things moving** poner las cosas en marcha; **to m. with the times** adaptarse a los tiempos (que corren)

(b) *Fam (go fast)* correr; **this motorbike can really m.** esta moto corre lo suyo

(c) *(act)* moverse, actuar; **to m. to do sth** moverse *or* actuar para hacer algo; **they are moving to take over the company** se están preparando *or Am* alistando para absorber la compañía

(d) *(to new home, office)* mudarse; **to m. to another job** cambiar de trabajo; **to m. to the country** irse a vivir al campo

(e) *(socialize)* moverse; **he moves in exalted circles** se mueve por círculos elevados

(f) *(change opinion)* **I'm not going to m. on that point** no voy a cambiar de opinión en ese punto; **they have moved to the right** se han desplazado a la derecha

(g) *(in games)* mover; **you can't m. until you've thrown a six** no puedes mover hasta que tengas un seis

(h) *(in debate)* **to m. for sth** proponer algo

(i) *Formal (bowels)* **my bowels moved** hice de vientre

(j) *Fam (be sold)* venderse

► **move about, move around** 1 *vt sep (furniture)* mover; *(employee)* trasladar; **they're always moving the furniture around** siempre están cambiando los muebles de sitio; **I get moved about a lot in my job** me trasladan continuamente en mi trabajo

2 *vi* moverse; **I heard somebody moving about upstairs** oí a alguien trajinar arriba; **he moves around a lot** *(in job)* le trasladan continuamente en su trabajo

► **move ahead** *vi* (a) *(take lead)* adelantarse; **to m. ahead of sb** adelantarse a alguien (b) *(advance, progress)* avanzar

► **move along** 1 *vt sep (crowd)* dispersar; **he was moved along by the police** la policía lo echó de allí

2 *vi (make room)* echarse a un lado, correrse; **m. along!** *(on bench)* ¡apártate!, ¡córrete!; *(to crowd)* ¡apártense!, ¡muévanse!

► **move aside** *vi* (a) *(make room)* apartarse

(b) *(stand down)* retirarse

► **move away** 1 *vt sep* apartar, retirar

2 *vi* (a) *(from window, person)* apartarse, retirarse; *(car, train, procession)* partir; **we are moving away from the point** nos estamos apartando del asunto (b) *(from house)* mudarse; *(from area)* marcharse

► **move back** 1 *vt sep* (a) *(further away)* hacer retroceder; *(to former position)* devolver a su sitio; **could you m. that chair back a bit?** ¿podrías echar la silla hacia atrás un poco? (b) *(postpone)* aplazar (**to** a *or* hasta)

2 *vi (retreat)* retirarse; *(to former position)* volver; **m. back!** ¡atrás!; **we're moving back to the States** regresamos *or* volvemos a los Estados Unidos

► **move down** 1 *vi* (a) *(go to lower position)* bajar, descender; **they have moved down to seventh place** han retrocedido al séptimo puesto (b) *(make room)* echarse a un lado, correrse; **m. down!** ¡apártate!, ¡córrete!

2 *vt sep (from higher level, floor etc)* bajar

► **move forward** 1 *vt sep (meeting)* adelantar

2 *vi (person, car)* avanzar

▸ **move in** *vi* (a) *(take up residence)* instalarse, mudarse; **to m. in with sb** irse a vivir con alguien (b) *(intervene)* intervenir

▸ **move in on** *vt insep (prepare to attack)* avanzar sobre

▸ **move into** *vt insep* (a) *(house)* instalarse en (b) *(take over)* **to m. into second place/the lead** ponerse segundo/líder

▸ **move off** *vi (person)* marcharse, irse; *(car, train, procession)* partir

▸ **move on** 1 *vt sep (crowd)* dispersar; **he was moved on by the police** la policía lo echó de allí

2 *vi* (a) *(person, queue)* avanzar; **it's time we were moving on** es hora de marcharse; **time's moving on** no queda mucho tiempo; **things have moved on since then** las cosas han cambiado mucho desde entonces; **they have moved on to better** *or* **higher things** han pasado a ocuparse de cosas más importantes; **after five years in the same job I feel like moving on** tras cinco años en el mismo trabajo, me apetece cambiar

(b) *(change subject)* cambiar de tema; **to m. on to** pasar a (hablar de)

▸ **move out** *vi* (a) *(move house)* mudarse; **we have to m. out by Friday** tenemos que dejar la casa antes del viernes; **my boyfriend moved out last week** mi novio me dejó y se fue de casa la semana pasada (b) *Mil (troops)* retirarse

▸ **move over** *vi* (a) *(make room)* echarse a un lado, correrse; **m. over!** ¡apártate!, ¡córrete!; **she is moving over to make way for a younger leader** se está retirando para dejar el camino libre a un líder más joven (b) *(change)* **to m. over to a new system** pasar a un nuevo sistema

▸ **move towards** *vt insep (change over to)* **the party has moved towards the right** el partido se ha desplazado a la derecha; **more and more people are moving towards this view** más y más gente se está acercando a esta manera de pensar

▸ **move up** 1 *vi* (a) *(go to higher position)* subir, ascender; **they've moved up to third place** han subido *or* ascendido al tercer puesto, se han puesto terceros (b) *(make room)* echarse a un lado, correrse; **m. up!** ¡córrete! (c) *Mil (troops)* desplazarse al frente; **our batallion is moving up to the front** han llevado a otra división al frente

2 *vt sep* (a) *(in order to make room)* mover, correr (b) *(to higher level, floor etc)* subir; **he's been moved up a class** lo han cambiado a una clase superior (c) *Mil (troops)* desplazar *or* llevar al frente; **another division has been moved up** han desplazado *or* llevado a otra división al frente

---

moveable = **movable**

movement ['mu:vmənt] *n* (a) *(change of position, location)* movimiento *m*; **population/troop movements** movimientos de población/tropas; **free m. of people and goods** la libre circulación de personas y mercancías; **the armour made m. very difficult** la armadura dificultaba el movimiento; **she heard m. in the next room** oyó movimiento en la habitación contigua; **there was a general m. towards the bar** todo el mundo se dirigió *or* encaminó al bar

(b) *(gesture)* movimiento *m*; **all her movements were rapid and precise** todos sus movimientos eran rápidos y precisos

(c) **movements** *(activities)* movimientos *mpl*; **to watch sb's movements** seguir los movimientos de alguien; **I'm not sure what my movements are going to be over the next few weeks** no estoy seguro de qué voy a hacer en las próximas semanas

(d) *(organization, tendency)* movimiento *m*; **a liberation m.** un movimiento de liberación

(e) *(change, compromise)* movimiento *m*, cambio *m*; **there has been no m. on the issue of training** no se han registrado cambios de postura en el asunto de la formación; **there's a growing m. towards privatization** hay una tendencia generalizada hacia la privatización; **his speeches over the last year show a m. towards the right** sus discursos en este último año revelan cierta derechización; **the upward/downward m. of interest rates** la curva ascendente/descendente de los tipos de interés

(f) *(clock or watch mechanism)* mecanismo *m*

(g) *Mus* movimiento *m*

(h) *Formal* **(bowel) m.** evacuación *f* (del vientre); **to have a (bowel) m.** evacuar, hacer de vientre

mover ['mu:və(r)] *n* (a) *(physical)* **sloths are extraordinarily slow movers** los perezosos se desplazan con extraordinaria lentitud; **he's a beautiful m.** *(dancer, soccer player)* se mueve con mucha elegancia; *Fam* **he's a fast m.** no pierde el tiempo; **the movers and shakers** *(in politics)* los que mueven los hilos

(b) *(in debate)* ponente *mf*

(c) *US (removal man)* empleado(a) *m,f* de mudanzas; **the movers are coming tomorrow** los de la mudanza vienen mañana

movie ['mu:vɪ] *n* película *f*; **to go to the movies** ir al cine; **she's in the movies** es actriz de cine ▸▸ ***m. actor*** actor *m* de cine; ***m. actress*** actriz *f* de cine; ***m. camera*** *(professional)* cámara *f* cinematográfica *or* de cine; *(amateur)* tomavistas *m inv*; *US* ***m. house*** cine *m*; ***m. industry*** industria *f* cinematográfica *or* del cine; ***m. star*** estrella *f* de cine; *US* ***m. theater*** cine *m*

moviegoer ['mu:vɪgəʊə(r)] *n* **these scenes shocked many moviegoers** estas escenas sacudieron a muchos espectadores; **as regular moviegoers will know...** como los asiduos *or* aficionados al cine ya sabrán...; **she's not a regular m.** no va al cine con regularidad

moving ['mu:vɪŋ] 1 *n* **m. out** *(from house etc)* mudanza *f*, salida *f*; **m. in** *(into house etc)* mudanza *f*, entrada *f* ▸▸ *US* ***m. van*** camión *m* de mudanzas

2 *adj* (a) *(in motion) (train, vehicle)* en movimiento ▸▸ ***m. part*** pieza *f* móvil; *Old-fashioned Cin* ***m. picture*** película *f*; *Old-fashioned* ***m. staircase*** escalera *f* mecánica; ***m. target*** blanco *m* móvil; ***m. walkway*** pasillo *m* móvil *or* rodante (b) *(causing motion)* **the m. force** *or* **spirit** la fuerza impulsora (c) *(touching) (description, story)* conmovedor(ora)

movingly ['mu:vɪŋlɪ] *adv (to speak, write)* conmovedoramente

mow [məʊ] *vt (pp* **mown** [məʊn]) (a) *(lawn)* cortar (b) *(hay)* segar

▸ **mow down** *vt sep (slaughter)* segar la vida de

mower ['məʊə(r)] *n* (a) *(person)* segador(ora) *m,f* (b) *(machine) (for lawn)* cortadora *f* de césped, cortacésped *m or f*; *(for hay)* segadora *f*

mowing ['məʊɪŋ] *n* siega *f* ▸▸ ***m. machine*** segadora *f*

mown *pp of* **mow**

Mozambican [məʊzæm'bi:kən] 1 *n* mozambiqueño(a) *m,f*

2 *adj* mozambiqueño(a)

Mozambique [məʊzæm'bi:k] *n* Mozambique

mozzarella [mɒtsə'relə] *n* mozzarella *f*

MP [em'pi:] *n* (a) *Br Pol* (*abbr* **Member of Parliament**) diputado(a) *m,f*; **the M. for Finchley** el diputado por Finchley (b) *Mil* (*abbr* **Military Police**) policía *f* militar, PM *f*; **he was taken away by two MPs** se lo llevaron dos agentes de la policía militar (c) *Can* (*abbr* **Mounted Police**) policía *f* montada; **he was taken away by two MPs** se lo llevaron dos agentes de la policía montada

MP3 [empi:'θri:] *n Comptr* (*abbr* **MPEG1 Audio Layer**) MP3 *m*

MPEG ['empeg] *n Comptr* (*abbr* **Moving Pictures Expert Group**) MPEG *m*

mpg [empi:'dʒi:] *n Aut* (*abbr* **miles per gallon**) = consumo de un vehículo medido en millas por galón de combustible, ≃ litros *mpl* a los cien

mph [empi:'eɪtʃ] *n* (*abbr* **miles per hour**) millas *fpl* por hora

MPhil [em'fɪl] *n* (*abbr* **Master of Philosophy**) = curso de posgrado de dos años de duración, superior a un máster e inferior a un doctorado

MPV [empi:'vi:] *n* (*abbr* **multipurpose vehicle**) vehículo *m* polivalente

Mr ['mɪstə(r)] *n* (*abbr* **Mister**) Sr., señor *m*; **Mr Jones** el Sr. Jones; **Mr President** Señor Presidente; **Mr Bush and Mr Blair held a meeting last week** Bush y Blair se reunieron la semana pasada; IDIOM *Fam* **no more Mr Nice Guy!** ¡se acabó lo que se daba!, ¡hasta aquí hemos llegado! ▸▸ *Fam* ***Mr Big*** pope *m*, mandamás *m*; *Fam* ***Mr Fixit*** el que todo lo arregla, el experto en apagar fuegos; **so what did Mr Fixit have to say about our boiler, then?** bueno, ¿y qué dijo el chapuzas este de lo de la caldera?; ***Mr Right*** *(ideal man)* el hombre ideal

MRC [ema:'si:] *n* (*abbr* **Medical Research Council**) = organismo estatal británico que financia la investigación médica

MRCP [ema:si:'pi:] *n* (*abbr* **Member of the Royal College of Physicians**) = miembro del colegio británico de médicos

MRCS [ema:si:'es] *n* (*abbr* **Member of the Royal College of Surgeons**) = miembro del colegio británico de cirujanos

MRCVS [ema:si:vi:'es] *n* (*abbr* **Member of the Royal College of Veterinary Surgeons**) = miembro del colegio británico de veterinarios

MRI [ema:'raɪ] *n* (*abbr* **magnetic resonance imaging**) RM *f*

MRP [ema:'pi:] *n* (*abbr* **manufacturer's recommended price**) PVP *m* recomendado

Mrs ['mɪsɪz] *n* (*abbr* **Missus**) Sra., señora *f*; **M. Jones** la Sra. Jones

MS [em'es] *n* (a) (*abbr* **Mississippi**) Misisipi (b) (*abbr* **Master of Surgery**) máster *m or Am* maestría *f* en Cirugía (c) *US* (*abbr* **Master of Science**) máster *m or Am* maestría *f* en Ciencias; **Frederick Watson, M.** Frederick Watson, licenciado con máster en Ciencias (d) (*abbr* **multiple sclerosis**) esclerosis *f inv* múltiple (e) (*abbr* **manuscript**) ms., manuscrito *m*

Ms [mɪz] *n* Sra.; **M. Jones** la Sra. Jones

Ms es el equivalente femenino de **Mr**, y se utiliza para dirigirse a una mujer sin precisar su estado civil.

ms (*abbr* **milliseconds**) ms

MSc [emes'si:] *n Univ* (*abbr* **Master of Science**) máster *m orAm* maestría *f* en Ciencias; **to have an M. in chemistry** tener un máster en Química; **Fiona Watson, M.** Fiona Watson, licenciada con máster en Ciencias

MS-DOS® [emes'dɒs] *n Comptr* (*abbr* **Microsoft Disk Operating System**) MS-DOS® *m*

MSG [emes'dʒi:] *n Culin* (*abbr* **monosodium glutamate**) glutamato *m* monosódico

Msgr (*abbr* **Monsignor**) Mons.

MSP [emes'pi:] *n* (*abbr* **Member of the Scottish Parliament**) diputado(a) *m,f* del parlamento escocés

MST [emes'ti:] *n* (*abbr* **Mountain Standard Time**) = hora oficial en la zona de las Montañas Rocosas en los Estados Unidos

MT (*abbr* **Montana**) Montana

Mt (*abbr* **Mount**) monte *m*

MTB [emti:'bi:] *n Br* (*abbr* **motor torpedo boat**) lancha *f* torpedera

mth (*abbr* **month**) mes *m*

MTV [emti:'vi:] *n* (*abbr* **Music Television**) MTV *f*

MUCH [mʌtʃ] (*comparative* **more** [mɔ:(r)], *superlative* **most** [məʊst]) **1** *pron* mucho; **there is not m. left** no queda mucho; **it's not worth m.** no vale mucho, no tiene mucho valor; **m. has happened since you left** han pasado muchas cosas desde que te fuiste; **he's not m. to look at** no es precisamente *Esp* guapo *orAm* lindo; **we haven't seen m. of her lately** no la hemos visto mucho últimamente; **I don't think m. of him** no lo tengo en gran estima; **m. of the building was unharmed** una buena parte del edificio no sufrió daños; **it didn't come as m. of a surprise** no fue ninguna sorpresa; **she isn't m. of a singer** no es gran cosa como cantante; **m. of the time** una buena parte del tiempo; **in the end it cost as m. again** al final costó el doble; **twice as m.** el doble; **five times as m.** cinco veces más; **I thought/expected as m.** era lo que pensaba/me esperaba; **I don't like her and I told her as m.** no me gusta, y así se lo dije; **eat as m. as you like** come todo lo que quieras; **as m. as possible** todo lo posible; **it may cost as m. as £500** puede que cueste hasta 500 libras; **that is as m. as I am prepared to reveal** eso es todo lo que estoy dispuesto a revelar; **it was as m. as we could do to stand upright** apenas podíamos mantenernos en pie; **how m.?** ¿cuánto?; **how m. is this dress?** ¿cuánto cuesta *or* vale este vestido?; **do you have any money? – not m.** ¿tienes dinero? – no mucho; **there's nothing m. to see there** no hay mucho *or* gran cosa que ver allí; **he has drunk so m. that...** ha bebido *orAm* tomado tanto que...; **he left without so m. as saying goodbye** se marchó sin siquiera decir adiós; **if you so m. as look at her, I'll make you pay for it** si te atreves aunque sólo sea a mirarla, me las pagarás; **so m. for her promises of help!** ¡y me había prometido su ayuda!; **I haven't got that m.** no tengo tanto; **this m.** así; **I'll say this m. for him, he's very polite** tengo que admitir que es muy amable; **I've got too m.** tengo demasiado; **the suspense was too m. for me** el suspense era tal que no pude aguantarme; **you can have too m. of a good thing** también de lo bueno se cansa uno; **she made m. of the fact that...** le dio mucha importancia al hecho de que...; **that's not saying m.** no es que sea gran cosa; *Fam* **that's a bit m.!** ¡eso es pasarse!

2 *adj*

Normalmente, sólo se usa en estructuras comparativas, negativas e interrogativas, salvo en lenguaje formal.

mucho(a); **m. work still needs to be done** aún queda mucho trabajo por hacer; **after m. thought** tras mucho reflexionar; **as m. time as you like** tanto tiempo como quieras, todo el tiempo que quieras; **twice as m. money** el doble de dinero; **he earns three times as m. money as I do** gana tres veces más que yo; **how m. money?** ¿cuánto dinero?; **however m. money you have** por mucho dinero que tengas; **there isn't (very) m. traffic** no hay mucho tráfico; **I don't get m. chance to travel** no tengo muchas oportunidades de viajar; **so m. time** tanto tiempo; **we haven't got that m. time** no tenemos tanto tiempo; **add about this m. salt** añade un tanto así de sal

3 *adv* mucho; **I don't like it m., I don't m. like it** no me gusta mucho; **m. better/worse** mucho mejor/peor; **m. easier/harder** mucho más fácil/duro; **I'm not m. good at physics** *Esp* no se me da muy bien la física, *Am* no tengo facilidad para la física; **he is m. changed** ha cambiado mucho; **it is a m. debated issue** es un tema muy debatido; **I'd m. rather stay** yo ciertamente preferiría quedarme; **m. too good** demasiado bueno(a); **I've had m. too m. to drink** he bebido *orAm* tomado mucho más de la cuenta; **m. the best/largest** con mucho el mejor/más grande; **the two restaurants are m. the same** los dos restaurantes son muy parecidos; **m. to my astonishment** para mi estupefacción *or* asombro; **it was m. as I remembered it** era muy parecido a como lo recordaba; **m. as I like him, I don't really trust him** aunque me cae muy bien, no me fío de él; **m. as I'd like to, I can't go** por mucho que quiera, no puedo ir; **the result was m. as I expected** resultó más o menos como esperaba; **he can't even use a screwdriver, m. less fix the radio** ¡como va a arreglar la radio, si no sabe siquiera usar un destornillador!; **I don't go there as m. as I used to** ya no voy tanto por allí; **it is as m. an honour to me as a duty** para mí es tanto un honor como un deber; **how m. longer will you be?** ¿cuánto más vas a tardar *orAm* demorar?; **do you like it? – not m.** ¿te gusta? – no mucho; **don't shout so m.** no chilles tanto; **it's so m. better** es muchísimo mejor; **I'm not so m. upset as disappointed** estoy más decepcionado que *esp Esp* enfadado *or esp Am* enojado; **so m. the better/worse** tanto mejor/peor; **so m. so that...** tanto es así que...; **I don't go there that m.** no voy mucho por allí; **don't drink too m.** no bebas *orAm* tomes demasiado; **they charged me $10 too m.** me cobraron 10 dólares de más; **this is too m.!** ¡esto ya es el colmo!; **thank you very** *or* **so m.** muchas gracias; **I should very m. like to see them** me encantaría verlos

much- [mʌtʃ] *prefix* **m.-admired** admiradísimo(a); **m.-loved** muy querido(a), adorado(a); **m.-quoted** frecuentemente citado(a); **a m.-quoted line** una conocidísima cita

muchness ['mʌtʃnɪs] *n* IDIOM *Fam* **they're much of a m.** son prácticamente iguales

mucilage ['mju:sɪlɪdʒ] *n Bot* mucílago *m*

muck [mʌk] *n* **(a)** *(dirt)* mugre *f*, porquería *f*; PROV **where there's m. there's brass** será sucio y feo, pero hay dinero **(b)** *(manure)* estiércol *m*; *(of horse, cow)* boñigas *fpl*, bosta *f*; *(of dog)* caca *f* **(c)** *Fam (bad food)* bazofia *f*; *(worthless things)* basura *f*; **his book's a load of m.** su libro es una mierda **(d)** *Br Fam* **to make a m. of sth** *(bungle)* meter la pata con algo, *Esp* hacer algo fatal *or* de pena

▸ **muck about, muck around** *Br Fam* **1** *vt sep (treat badly)* traer a maltraer

2 *vi* **(a)** *(fool about, waste time)* hacer el tonto **(b)** *(tinker)* **to m. about** *or* **around with sth** enredar *orAm* dar vueltas con algo

▸ **muck in** *vi Br Fam (help)* arrimar el hombro, *Méx, RP* dar una mano

▸ **muck out** *vt sep (stable, byre, pigsty)* limpiar; *(cows, horses)* limpiar el establo a; *(pigs)* limpiar la pocilga a

▸ **muck up** *vt sep Fam* **(a)** *(make dirty)* ensuciar **(b)** *(spoil)* echar a perder

mucker ['mʌkə(r)] *n Br Fam Esp* colega *mf*, *Am* compadre *mf*

muckheap ['mʌkhi:p] *n (dungheap)* estercolero *m*

muck-raker ['mʌkreɪkə(r)] *n Fam (journalist)* = periodista que anda a la busca de escándalos

muck-raking ['mʌkreɪkɪŋ] *n Fam (in journalism)* búsqueda *f* del escándalo

muckspreader ['mʌkspredə(r)] *n* = máquina para extender el estiércol

muck-up ['mʌkʌp] *n Br Fam* **to make a m. of sth** meter la pata con algo; **you've made a right m. of those figures** menudo lío de cifras has armado

mucky ['mʌkɪ] *adj Fam* **(a)** *(filthy)* mugriento(a), asqueroso(a); **to get m.** ponerse hecho(a) una porquería *or* un asco; **she got her hands terribly m. changing the tyre** se llenó las manos de mugre *or* porquería cambiando la rueda; **don't come in here with m. boots on!** ¡aquí no pases con las botas llenas de barro!; *Br* **the weather was m.** hizo un tiempo asqueroso ▸▸ ***m. pup*** *or* ***puppy*** cochino(a) *m,f*

(b) *Br (pornographic)* porno *inv*

mucous ['mju:kəs] *adj* mucoso(a) ▸▸ *Anat* ***m. membrane*** mucosa *f*

mucus ['mju:kəs] *n* mocos *mpl*, mucosidad *f*

mud [mʌd] *n* barro *m*; **we got stuck in the m.** nos quedamos atascados en el barro; *Fig* **to throw** *or* **sling m. at sb** difamar *or* desacreditar a alguien; IDIOM **if you throw enough m. some of it is bound to stick** difama, que algo (siempre) queda; IDIOM *Br Fam Hum* **here's m. in your eye!** ¡a tu salud! ▸▸ ***m. flats*** marismas *fpl*; ***m. hut*** choza *f* de barro; ***m. wrestling*** lucha *f* libre en el barro

mudbank ['mʌdbæŋk] *n* barrizal *m*, cenagal *m*

mudbath ['mʌdbɑ:θ] *n* **(a)** *(for animal)* baño *m* de cieno *or* barro **(b)** *(medicinal)* baño *m* de arcilla

muddiness ['mʌdɪnɪs] *n* **(a)** *(dirtiness)* embarradura *f* **(b)** *(cloudiness) (of water)* turbiedad *f*; *(of colours)* terrosidad *f*, tono *m* terroso

muddle ['mʌdəl] **1** *n* lío *m*; **to be in a m.** *(things, person)* estar hecho(a) un lío; **all her belongings were in a m.** todas sus cosas estaban revueltas; **Peter was in a real m. over the holiday plans** Peter estaba hecho un lío con las vacaciones; **to get into a m.** *(things)* liarse; *(person)* hacerse un lío; **there was a m. over the dates** hubo un lío con las fechas

2 *vt* **(a)** *(put in disorder)* desordenar; *(mix up)* confundir; **the dates got muddled** hubo un lío de fechas *or* con las fechas **(b)** *(bewilder)* liar; **to get muddled** hacerse un lío; **now you've got me muddled** ya me has hecho un lío *or* liado

▸ **muddle along** *vi* ir tirando

▸ **muddle through** **1** *vt insep* arreglárselas en

2 *vi* arreglárselas; **we'll m. through somehow** ya nos las arreglaremos

▸ **muddle up** *vt sep* **(a)** *(put in disorder)* desordenar; *(mix up)* confundir **(b)** *(bewilder)* liar; **to get muddled up** hacerse un lío

muddled ['mʌdəld] *adj* confuso(a)

muddleheaded [mʌdəl'hedɪd] *adj Fam (person)* atolondrado(a); *(decision, plan)* descabellado(a)

muddy ['mʌdɪ] **1** *adj* **(a)** *(dirty) (path)* embarrado(a), enfangado(a); *(jacket, boots, hands)* lleno(a) de barro, embarrado(a) **(b)** *(cloudy) (water)* turbio(a); *(colour, complexion)* terroso(a)

2 *vt* manchar de barro; IDIOM **to m. the waters** enturbiar el asunto

mudflap ['mʌdflæp] *n Esp, RP* guardabarros *m inv*, *Andes, CAm, Carib* guardafango *m*, *Méx* salpicadera *f*

mudflat ['mʌdflæt] *n* marisma *f*

mudguard ['mʌdgɑːd] *n Br Esp, RP* guardabarros *m inv*, *Andes, CAm, Carib* guardafango *m*, *Méx* salpicadera *f*

mudhopper ['mʌdhɒpə(r)] *n* = tipo de gobio

mudpack ['mʌdpæk] *n* mascarilla *f* de barro

mudpuppy ['mʌdpʌpɪ] *n* = tipo de salamandra norteamericana

mudskipper ['mʌdskɪpə(r)] *n* = tipo de gobio

mudslinging ['mʌdslɪŋɪŋ] *n Fam* **the debate degenerated into m.** el debate degeneró en meras descalificaciones

muesli ['mjuːzlɪ] *n* muesli *m*

muezzin [mʊ'ezɪn] *n Rel* almuecín *m*, almuédano *m*

muff[1] [mʌf] *vt Fam (one's lines)* meter la pata en; *(catch)* fallar; *(chance, opportunity)* echar a perder

muff[2] *n (for hands)* manguito *m*

muff[3] *n Vulg (woman's genitals)* coño *m*, *Méx* paloma *f*, *RP* concha *f* ▸▸ ***m. diving*** lamida *f or* comida *f* de coño

muffin ['mʌfɪn] *n* **(a)** *Br (teacake)* tortita *f* **(b)** *US* ≃ magdalena *f*

muffle ['mʌfəl] *vt* **(a)** *(deaden sound of) (engine)* amortiguar el sonido de; *(footsteps)* amortiguar; *(oars, drums)* enfundar; **the silencer muffles engine noise** el silenciador amortigua el sonido del motor **(b)** *(cover)* **to m. oneself up** abrigarse bien

▸ **muffle up** *vi* abrigarse bien

muffled ['mʌfəld] *adj (sound, footstep)* apagado(a), sordo(a); *(oars, drums)* enfundado(a); **we could hear m. cries** se oían sollozos apagados; **there was a lot of m. laughter** hubo mucha risa contenida

muffler ['mʌflə(r)] *n* **(a)** *(scarf)* bufanda *f* **(b)** *US (of car)* silenciador *m*

Mufti ['mʌftɪ] *n Rel* muftí *m*

mufti ['mʌftɪ] *n Fam* **in m.** *(of soldier)* de paisano

mug [mʌg] **1** *n* **(a)** *(cup)* taza *f* alta; *(beer glass)* jarra *f* de cerveza, *CSur* chop *m* **(b)** *Fam (face)* jeta *f* ▸▸ ***m. shot*** foto *f* para ficha policial **(c)** *Br Fam (gullible person)* bobo(a) *m,f*, primo(a) *m,f*, *Am* zonzo(a) *m,f*; **it's a m.'s game** eso es cosa de tontos

2 *vt (pt & pp* **mugged**) *(attack)* atracar

3 *vi (grimace)* hacer muecas, poner caras raras

▸ **mug up** *Br Fam* **1** *vt sep (study)* matarse estudiando, *Esp* empollar, *RP* tragar

2 *vi* **to m. up on sth** matarse estudiando *or Esp* empollar *or RP* tragar algo

mugful ['mʌgfʊl] *n (of tea, coffee)* taza *f* alta *(contenido)*; *(of beer)* jarra *f* de cerveza, *CSur* chop *m*

mugger ['mʌgə(r)] *n* atracador(ora) *m,f*

mugging ['mʌgɪŋ] *n* atraco *m*; **he was the victim of a m.** fue víctima de un atraco en plena calle; **m. is on the increase** aumentan los atracos (en la calle)

muggins ['mʌgɪnz] *n Br Fam* **I suppose m. will have to do it!** ¡supongo que tendrá que hacerlo un servidor *or* mi menda, como siempre!; **m. (here) paid the bill as usual** el menda pagó la cuenta, como de costumbre

muggy ['mʌgɪ] *adj* bochornoso(a); **it's m.** hace mucho bochorno

mugwort ['mʌgwɜːt] *n* artemisa *f*

mugwump ['mʌgwʌmp] *n US* = persona con opiniones políticas independientes

Muhammad [mə'hæmɪd] *pr n* Mahoma

Muhammadan [mə'hæmɪdən] *Old-fashioned* **1** *n* mahometano(a) *m,f*

2 *adj* mahometano(a)

mujaheddin, mujahadeen [muːdʒɪhæ'diːn] *n* muyahidín *m inv*

mulatto [mjuː'lætəʊ] *(pl* **mulattos** *or* **mulattoes**) *Old-fashioned* **1** *n* mulato(a) *m,f*

2 *adj* mulato(a)

mulberry ['mʌlbərɪ] *n* **(a)** *(fruit)* mora *f* **(b)** *(tree)* **(white) m.** morera *f*; **(black) m.** moral *m* **(c)** *(colour)* morado *m*

mulch [mʌltʃ] **1** *n* mantillo *m*, *Col* capote *m*

2 *vt* cubrir con mantillo

mulct [mʌlkt] *Formal* **1** *n (fine)* sanción *f*, multa *f*

2 *vt* **(a)** *(fine)* sancionar, multar **(b)** *(defraud)* estafar; **to m. sb of sth** estafar algo a alguien

mule [mjuːl] *n* **(a)** *(animal)* mulo(a) *m,f* ▸▸ *US* ***m. skinner*** mulero(a) *m,f*; ***m. train*** recua *f or* reata *f* de mulas **(b)** *Fam (stubborn person)* mula *f* **(c)** *Fam (drug smuggler)* correo *m*, *RP* mula *f* **(d)** *(shoe)* babucha *f*; *(slipper)* pantufla *f*, chinela *f*

muleteer [mjuːlə'tɪə(r)] *n* mulero(a) *m,f*

mulish ['mjuːlɪʃ] *adj* tozudo(a), terco(a)

mull [mʌl] *vt (wine, beer)* = preparar en caliente con azúcar y especias

▸ **mull over** *vt sep (consider)* **to m. sth over** darle vueltas a algo

mullah ['mʊlə] *n* ulema *m*

mulled wine [mʌld'waɪn] *n* = vino con azúcar y especias que se toma caliente

mullet ['mʌlɪt] *n* **(a)** **(grey) m.** mújol *m*; **red m.** salmonete **(b)** *Fam (hairstyle)* = peinado largo por detrás, corto por los lados y con el flequillo medio de punta

mulligan ['mʌlɪgən] *n US* **m. (stew)** ≃ ropa *f* vieja

mulligatawny [mʌlɪgə'tɔːnɪ] *n* **m. (soup)** = sopa de carne al curry

mullion ['mʌljən] *n Archit* parteluz *m*

mullioned ['mʌljənd] *adj Archit (window)* de cuarterones

multi- ['mʌltɪ] *n* multi-

multi-access ['mʌltɪ'ækses] *adj Comptr* multiusuario *inv*, de acceso múltiple

multicast ['mʌltɪkɑːst] *n Comptr* multidireccionalidad *f*

multicellular ['mʌltɪ'seljʊlə(r)] *adj Biol* pluricelular

multicoloured, *US* **multicolored** ['mʌltɪ'kʌləd] *adj* multicolor

multicultural ['mʌltɪ'kʌltʃərəl] *adj* multicultural

multiculturalism ['mʌltɪ'kʌltʃərəlɪzəm] *n* multiculturalismo *m*

multidimensional ['mʌltɪdɪ'menʃənəl] *adj also Fig* multidimensional

multidirectional ['mʌltɪdɪ'rekʃənəl] *adj* multidireccional

multidisciplinary ['mʌltɪdɪsɪ'plɪnərɪ] *adj Educ* multidisciplinar

multiethnic ['mʌltɪ'eθnɪk] *adj* multiétnico(a)

multifaceted ['mʌltɪ'fæsɪtɪd] *adj* múltiple, con múltiples facetas

multifarious [mʌltɪ'feərɪəs] *adj Formal* múltiple

multiform ['mʌltɪfɔːm] *adj Formal* multiforme

multi-functional [mʌltɪ'fʌŋkʃənəl] *adj* multifuncional

multigrade ['mʌltɪgreɪd] *adj (oil)* multigrado *inv*

multigym ['mʌltɪdʒɪm] *n* = aparato para hacer varios ejercicios gimnásticos

multilateral [mʌltɪ'lætərəl] *adj* multilateral ▸▸ *Fin* ***m. agreement on investment*** acuerdo *m* multilateral de inversiones

multilateralism [mʌltɪ'lætərəlɪzəm] *n (economic)* multilateralismo *m*; *(on nuclear weapons)* disposición *f* al desarme nuclear multilateral

multilingual [mʌltɪ'lɪŋgwəl] *adj* **(a)** *(person)* polígloto(a) **(b)** *(dictionary, document)* multilingüe

multimedia [mʌltɪ'miːdɪə] **1** *n* multimedia *f*

2 *adj* multimedia *inv* ▸▸ ***m. computer*** *Esp* ordenador *m or Am* computadora *f* multimedia

multimillion [mʌltɪ'mɪljən] *adj* **a m. pound/dollar project** un proyecto multimillonario

multimillionaire ['mʌltɪ'mɪlɪəneə(r)] *n* multimillonario(a) *m,f*

multinational ['mʌltɪ'næʃənəl] **1** *n* multinacional *f*

2 *adj* multinacional ▸▸ ***m. corporation*** multinacional *f*

multiparous [mʌl'tɪpərəs] *adj Zool* multiparo(a)

multipartite [mʌltɪ'pɑːtaɪt] *adj Formal (multilateral)* multilateral

multiparty [mʌltɪ'pɑːtɪ] *adj* **m. democracy/system** democracia/sistema pluripartidista

multiple ['mʌltɪpəl] **1** *n* **(a)** *Math* múltiplo *m*; **in multiples of 100** en múltiplos de 100 **(b)** *Br Com (chain store)* cadena *f* (de tiendas)
2 *adj* múltiple; **he died of m. stab wounds** falleció a causa de múltiples cuchilladas ▸▸ ***m. birth*** parto *m* múltiple; *Comptr* ***m. mailboxes*** buzón *m* múltiple; ***m. personality*** personalidad *f* múltiple; *Math* ***m. regression*** regresión *f* múltiple; *Med* ***m. sclerosis*** esclerosis *f inv* múltiple; ***m. shop*** *or* ***store*** establecimiento *m (de una cadena de tiendas)*

multiple-choice ['mʌltɪpəl'tʃɔɪs] *adj* **m. exam/question** examen/pregunta (de) tipo test

multiple-journey ['mʌltɪpəl'dʒɜːnɪ] *adj* **m. ticket** *Esp* billete *or Am* boleto *or Am* pasaje de varios viajes

multiplex ['mʌltɪpleks] **1** *n* **(a)** *(cinema)* cine *m* multisalas *(en un centro comercial)* **(b)** *Tel* múltiplex *m inv*
2 *adj* **(a)** *(with several screens)* multisalas *inv* ▸▸ ***m. cinema*** cine *m* multisalas *(en un centro comercial)* **(b)** *Tel* múltiplex *inv*

multiplicand ['mʌltɪplɪkænd] *n Math* multiplicando *m*

multiplication [mʌltɪplɪ'keɪʃən] *n* multiplicación *f* ▸▸ ***m. sign*** signo *m* de multiplicar; ***m. table*** tabla *f* de multiplicar

multiplicity [mʌltɪ'plɪsɪtɪ] *n* multiplicidad *f*, diversidad *f*

multiplier ['mʌltɪplaɪə(r)] *n Math & Phys* multiplicador *m*

multiply ['mʌltɪplaɪ] **1** *vt* multiplicar (**by** por); **it will m. the costs by eight** multiplicará por ocho *or* octuplicará los costos *or Esp* costes
2 *vi (reproduce)* multiplicarse

multiprocessor [mʌltɪ'prəʊsesə(r)] *n Comptr* multiprocesador *m* ▸▸ ***m. system*** sistema *m* multiprocesador

multiprogramming [mʌltɪ'prəʊgræmɪŋ] *n Comptr* multiprogramación *f*

multipurpose ['mʌltɪ'pɜːpəs] *adj* multiuso *inv*

multiracial ['mʌltɪ'reɪʃəl] *adj* multirracial

multiscan ['mʌltɪ'skæn], **multiscanning** ['mʌltɪ'skænɪŋ] *n Comptr* multifrecuencia *f*

multiscreen ['mʌltɪ'skriːn] *adj* **m. cinema** multicine, (cine) multisalas

multiskilling ['mʌltɪ'skɪlɪŋ] *n Ind* polivalencia *f*

multi-stage ['mʌltɪsteɪdʒ] *adj* **(a)** *(process)* escalonado(a) **(b)** *Astron* ***m. rocket*** cohete *m* multietapa

multi-station ['mʌltɪ'steɪʃən] *adj Comptr* multipuesto *inv*

multistorey, *US* **multistory** ['mʌltɪ'stɔːrɪ] *adj* de varios pisos *or* plantas ▸▸ ***m. carpark*** estacionamiento *m or Esp* aparcamiento *m or Col* parqueadero *m* de varias plantas

multisyllabic ['mʌltɪsɪ'læbɪk] *adj* polisílabo(a)

multi-talented ['mʌltɪ'tæləntɪd] *adj* polivalente, de muy variadas dotes

multitasking ['mʌltɪ'tɑːskɪŋ] *n* **(a)** *Comptr* multitarea *f* **(b)** *Ind* movilidad *f* funcional

multi-terminal ['mʌltɪ'tɜːmɪnəl] *adj Comptr* multiterminal

multithreading ['mʌltɪ'θredɪŋ] *n Comptr* multiproceso *m*

multi-track ['mʌltɪ'træk] *adj* de pistas múltiples

multitude ['mʌltɪtjuːd] *n* **(a)** *(large number)* multitud *f*; **a m. of** multitud de; **to cover a m. of sins** esconder muchas cosas; **baggy clothes can cover** *or* **hide a m. of sins** la ropa holgada es una capa que todo lo tapa **(b)** *(crowd)* multitud *f*

multitudinous [mʌltɪ'tjuːdɪnəs] *adj Fam* multitudinario(a)

multi-user ['mʌltɪ'juːsə(r)] *adj Comptr* multiusuario *inv* ▸▸ ***m. system*** sistema *m* multiusuario

multivalent ['mʌltɪ'veɪlənt] *adj Chem* polivalente

multivitamin ['mʌltɪ'vɪtəmɪn] *n* complejo *m* vitamínico

mum [mʌm] *n Br* mamá *f*; **my m.** *(said by a child)* mi mamá; *(said by adult) Esp* mi madre *f*, *Am* mi mamá *f*; IDIOM **m.'s the word!** ¡de esto ni mu!

mumble ['mʌmbəl] **1** *n* murmullo *m*; **he replied in a m.** respondió entre dientes
2 *vt* mascullar, decir entre dientes; **to m. an apology** mascullar una disculpa
3 *vi* mascullar, hablar entre dientes; **he mumbled on for half an hour** se pasó media hora murmurando *or* mascullando

mumbo jumbo ['mʌmbəʊ'dʒʌmbəʊ] *n* **(a)** *(nonsense)* palabrería *f*, monsergas *fpl*; **as far as I'm concerned astrology is just a load of m.** para mí la astrología es todo palabrería **(b)** *(jargon)* jerigonza *f*, jerga *f*

mummer ['mʌmə(r)] *n Hist Theat* = actor que hacía mimo y solía aparecer enmascarado en el teatro popular tradicional

mummery ['mʌmərɪ] *n Pej Literary (ceremony)* fasto *m*

mummified ['mʌmɪfaɪd] *adj* momificado(a)

mummify ['mʌmɪfaɪ] *vt* momificar

mummy[1] ['mʌmɪ] *n Br Fam (mother)* mamá *f* ▸▸ ***m.'s boy*** enmadrado *m*, niño *m or RP* nene *m* de mamá

mummy[2] *n (embalmed body)* momia *f* ▸▸ ***m. sleeping bag*** saco *m* de dormir (tipo) momia

mumps [mʌmps] *n* paperas *fpl*; **to have (the) m.** tener paperas

mumsy ['mʌmsɪ] *Br Fam* **1** *n* mami *f*
2 *adj (maternal)* maternaloide

munch [mʌntʃ] **1** *vt* ronzar, mascar; **she munched her way through the whole packet** se zampó toda la bolsa
2 *vi* ronzar, masticar ruidosamente; **to m. on an apple** masticar una manzana; **he sat there munching away** estaba allí sentado sin parar de masticar; **she was munching away at some toast** mordisqueaba una tostada

Munchausen ['mʌntʃaʊzən] *n Med* ***M.('s) Syndrome*** síndrome *m* de Münchhausen; ***M.('s Syndrome) by proxy*** síndrome *m* de Münchhausen por poderes

munchies ['mʌntʃɪz] *npl Fam* **(a)** *(snacks)* cosillas *fpl* de picar, *Méx* antojitos *mpl* **(b)** *(desire to eat)* **to have the m.** tener un poquillo de hambre *or Esp* gusa

mundane [mʌn'deɪn] *adj (existence, details)* prosaico(a); *(task)* rutinario(a); *(event, comment)* banal, trivial

> **False friend**: The Spanish word **mundano** is not a translation for the English word **mundane**. In Spanish **mundano** means "worldly" or "high society".

mung bean ['mʌŋbiːn] *n* frijol *m or* judía *f* (de) mungo

Munich ['mjuːnɪk] *n* Múnich

municipal [mjuː'nɪsɪpəl] *adj* municipal

municipality [mjuːnɪsɪ'pælɪtɪ] *n* municipio *m*

munificence [mjuː'nɪfɪsəns] *n Literary* munificencia *f*

munificent [mjuː'nɪfɪsənt] *adj Literary* munificente, munífico(a)

munitions [mjuː'nɪʃənz] *npl* municiones *fpl*, armamento *m*; **m. dump/factory** depósito/fábrica de municiones; **she was a m. worker** trabajaba en una fábrica de municiones

muon ['mjuːɒn] *n Phys* muón *m*

mural ['mjʊərəl] *n* mural *m* ▸▸ ***m. painting*** (pintura *f*) mural *m*

muralist ['mjʊərəlɪst] *n* muralista *mf*

Murcian ['mɜːsɪən] **1** *n* murciano(a) *m,f*
2 *adj* murciano(a)

murder ['mɜːdə(r)] **1** *n* **(a)** *(killing)* asesinato *m*; **to commit m.** cometer un asesinato; **he's up on a m. charge** se le acusa de asesinato; IDIOM **she gets away with m.** se le consiente cualquier cosa ▸▸ ***m. case*** causa *f* de *or* juicio *m* por asesinato; ***m. inquiry*** investigación *f* de un asesinato; *US Law* ***m. one*** asesinato *m* en primer grado; ***m. weapon*** arma *f* homicida
(b) *Fam Fig (difficult task, experience)* tortura *f*; **the traffic was m.** el tráfico estaba imposible; **finding a parking place on a Saturday is m.** buscar estacionamiento *or Esp* aparcamiento el sábado es una tortura; **standing all day is m. on your feet** estar todo el día de pie *or Am* parado es una tortura para los pies
2 *vt* **(a)** *(kill)* asesinar; *Fam Fig* **I'll m. you (for that)!** ¡te voy a matar!; IDIOM *Fam* **I could m. a beer/pizza!** ¡me muero por una cerveza/pizza! **(b)** *Fig (ruin) (song, tune, language)* destrozar, estropear **(c)** *Fam (defeat)* dar una paliza a
3 *exclam* ¡al asesino!

murderer ['mɜːdərə(r)] *n* asesino(a) *m,f*

murderess ['mɜːdəres] *n* asesina *f*

murderous ['mɜːdərəs] *adj* **(a)** *(attack, hatred)* asesino(a); **he was in a m. mood when he got back** cuando volvió tenía un humor de perros; **to give sb a m. look** lanzarle a alguien una mirada asesina **(b)** *Fam (exhausting)* agotador(ora), matador(ora); *(hellish, unpleasant)* horroroso(a), atroz; **they kept up a m. pace** llevaban un ritmo endiablado

murderously ['mɜːdərəslɪ] *adv* (**a**) *(to attack)* con intención asesina; **he glared at them m.** les lanzó una mirada asesina (**b**) *(extremely)* tremendamente

murk [mɜːk] *n (darkness, fog)* tinieblas *fpl*; *(underwater)* turbulencia *f*

murkiness ['mɜːkɪnɪs] *n* (**a**) *(of weather, sky)* oscuridad *f*, tenebrosidad *f*; *(of liquid)* turbulencia *f* (**b**) *(of past)* turbulencia *f*

murky ['mɜːkɪ] *adj* (**a**) *(weather, sky)* oscuro(a), tenebroso(a); *(liquid)* turbio(a); **the m. depths of the pool** las oscuras *or* tenebrosas profundidades de la charca (**b**) *(details, past)* turbio(a), tenebroso(a); **a m. episode** un oscuro *or* tenebroso episodio

murmur ['mɜːmə(r)] **1** *n* (**a**) *(sound) (of conversation)* murmullo *m*; *Literary (of stream)* murmullo *m*, susurro *m*; **the distant m. of traffic** el rumor lejano del tráfico; **there wasn't a m.** no se oía ni una mosca (**b**) *(complaint)* queja *f*, protesta *f*; **there wasn't a m. of protest** no se alzó ni una sola voz de protesta; **to do sth without a m.** hacer algo sin rechistar
(**c**) *Med (of heart)* soplo *m* cardíaco, soplo *m* en el corazón
2 *vt* murmurar; **to m. excuses** murmurar alguna excusa
3 *vi* (**a**) *(make a sound) (people)* murmurar; *Literary (stream)* murmurar, susurrar (**b**) *(complain)* quejarse, protestar; **to m. at** *or* **against sth** quejarse *or* protestar de algo

Murphy bed ['mɜːfɪbed] *n US* cama *f* plegable, mueble *m* cama

Murphy's law ['mɜːfɪz'lɔː] *n Fam* la ley de Murphy, = aquello de que si algo puede ir mal, ten por seguro que lo hará

muscat ['mʌskæt] *n* (**a**) **m. (wine)** moscatel *m* (**b**) **m. (grape)** uva *f* de moscatel

muscatel [mʌskə'tel] *n* moscatel *m*

muscle ['mʌsəl] *n* (**a**) *Anat* músculo *m*; IDIOM **she didn't move a m.** no movió un solo músculo ▸▸ ***m. fibre*** fibra *f* muscular (**b**) *(influence, power)* fuerza *f*, poderío *m*; **it would give our campaign more m.** le daría mayor empuje a nuestra campaña; **political m.** pujanza política (**c**) *Fam (strong men)* tipos *mpl* musculosos *or Esp* cachas

▸ **muscle in** *vi Fam* meter la cuchara *or* las narices (**on** en), entrometerse (**on** en)

muscle-bound ['mʌsəlbaʊnd] *adj* exageradamente musculoso(a)

muscleman ['mʌsəlmæn] *n* forzudo *m*, hércules *m inv*

muscly ['mʌsəlɪ] *adj* musculoso(a)

muscovado [mʌskə'vɑːdəʊ] *n* **m. (sugar)** = azúcar de caña no refinada

Muscovite ['mʌskəvaɪt] **1** *n* moscovita *mf*
2 *adj* moscovita

Muscovy duck ['mʌskəvɪ'dʌk] *n* pato *m* almizclado

muscular ['mʌskjʊlə(r)] *adj* (**a**) *(tissue)* muscular ▸▸ *Med* ***m. dystrophy*** distrofia *f* muscular (**b**) *(person)* musculoso(a)

musculature ['mʌskjʊlətʃə(r)] *n* musculatura *f*

Muse [mjuːz] *n* musa *f*; **the (nine) Muses** las (nueve) musas

muse [mjuːz] **1** *vt* **"I wonder what happened to him," she mused** "¿qué habrá sido de él?" se preguntó
2 *vi* reflexionar, cavilar (**on** *or* **about** sobre)

museum [mjuː'zɪəm] *n* museo *m* ▸▸ *also Hum* ***m. piece*** pieza *f* de museo

mush[1] [mʌʃ] **1** *n* (**a**) *(pulp)* pasta *f*, puré *m* (**b**) *US (porridge)* gachas *fpl* de harina de maíz (**c**) *Fam Fig (sentimentality)* ñoñería *f*, sensiblería *f*
2 *exclam US* ¡andando!, ¡vamos!

mush[2] [mʊʃ] *n Br Fam* (**a**) *(face)* jeta *f* (**b**) *(term of address)* **oi, m.!** *Esp* ¡qué pasa, tío *or* tronco!, *Méx* ¡qué hay, güey!, *RP* ¡cuál es, che!

mushroom ['mʌʃrʊm] **1** *n Bot* hongo *m*, *Esp* seta *f*; *Culin (wild mushroom) Esp* seta *f*, *Am* hongo *m*; *(button mushroom)* champiñón *m* ▸▸ ***m. cloud*** hongo *m* atómico; ***m. omelette*** tortilla *f* de champiñones; ***m. soup*** crema *f* de champiñones
2 *vi* (**a**) *(gather mushrooms)* **to go mushrooming** ir a (re)coger setas (**b**) *(grow quickly)* crecer rápidamente; *(costs, prices)* dispararse; *(town)* expandirse rápidamente, extenderse rápidamente; *(houses, shops)* proliferar, surgir como hongos; **the conflict mushroomed into full-scale war** el conflicto derivó rápidamente en una guerra a gran escala

mushy ['mʌʃɪ] *adj* (**a**) *(pulpy)* blando(a), pastoso(a) ▸▸ *Br* ***m. peas*** puré *m* de *Esp* guisantes *or Am* arvejas *or Carib, Méx* chícharos (**b**) *Fam Fig (sentimental)* ñoño(a), sensiblero(a)

music ['mjuːzɪk] *n (art, sound)* música *f*; *(score)* partituras *fpl*; **to read m.** saber solfeo; **to set words to m.** poner música a la letra; IDIOM **those words were m. to her ears** esas palabras le sonaban a música celestial ▸▸ ***m. box*** caja *f* de música; *Br Old-fashioned* ***m. centre*** cadena *f or* equipo *m* de música; ***m. hall*** *(entertainment)* music-hall *m*; *(building)* teatro *m* de variedades; ***m. library*** discoteca *f*; ***the m. press*** la prensa musical; ***m. stand*** atril *m*; ***m. stool*** = taburete o banqueta para un músico; ***m. teacher*** profesor(ora) *m,f* de música; *Psy* ***m. therapy*** musicoterapia *f*

musical ['mjuːzɪkəl] **1** *n (show, film)* musical *m*
2 *adj* (**a**) *(evening, taste, composition)* musical ▸▸ *Br* ***m. box*** caja *f* de música; ***m. bumps*** = juego en el que los niños corren o bailan y el último en sentarse en el suelo cuando para la música, queda eliminado; ***m. chairs*** el juego de las sillas; *Fig* **to play m. chairs** andar constantemente cambiando de puesto; ***m. comedy*** comedia *f* musical; ***m. director*** director(ora) *m,f* musical; ***m. instrument*** instrumento *m* musical
(**b**) *(musically gifted)* con talento musical; **they are a m. family** en esa familia se les da bien la música; **I'm not very m.** la música no es lo mío
(**c**) *(tuneful, pleasant)* musical

musicality [mjuːzɪ'kælɪtɪ] *n* musicalidad *f*

musically ['mjuːzɪklɪ] *adv (to sing)* armoniosamente; **m., the band is reminiscent of...** la música del grupo recuerda a...; **m. gifted** con talento para la música

musician [mjuː'zɪʃən] *n* músico(a) *m,f*

musicianship [mjuː'zɪʃənʃɪp] *n* habilidad *f* musical

musicologist [mjuːzɪ'kɒlədʒɪst] *n* musicólogo(a) *m,f*

musicology [mjuːzɪ'kɒlədʒɪ] *n* musicología *f*

musings ['mjuːzɪŋz] *npl* reflexiones *fpl*, cavilaciones *fpl*

musk [mʌsk] *n* almizcle *m* ▸▸ ***m. deer*** almizclero *m*; ***m. ox*** buey *m* almizclero; ***m. rose*** rosa *f* almizcleña

musket ['mʌskɪt] *n* mosquete *m*

musketeer [mʌskɪ'tɪə(r)] *n* mosquetero *m*

muskiness ['mʌskɪnɪs] *n* almizcle *m*

muskrat ['mʌskræt], **musquash** ['mʌskwɒʃ] *n* (**a**) *(animal)* (rata *f*) almizclada *f* (**b**) *(fur)* piel *f* de (rata) almizclada

musky ['mʌskɪ] *adj* almizclado(a), almizcleño(a); **a m. smell** un olor a almizcle

Muslim ['mʌzlɪm, 'mʊzlɪm] **1** *n* musulmán(ana) *m,f*
2 *adj* musulmán(ana)

muslin ['mʌzlɪn] *n* muselina *f*

muso ['mjuːzəʊ] (*pl* **musos**) *n Fam* (**a**) *Br Pej* = músico al que le interesa demasiado la técnica (**b**) *Austr (musician)* músico(a) *m,f*; *(enthusiast)* fanático(a) *m,f* de la música

musquash = **muskrat**

muss [mʌs] *vt US Fam* **to m. (up)** *(hair)* revolver

mussel ['mʌsəl] *n* mejillón *m* ▸▸ ***m. bed*** vivero *m* de mejillones

MUST[1] [mʌst] **1** *n Fam* (**a**) *(necessity)* **to be a m.** ser imprescindible (**b**) *(thing not to be missed)* **this movie's a m.** esta película hay que verla *or* no hay que perdérsela
2 *modal aux v*

> El verbo **must** carece de infinitivo, de gerundio y de participio. En infinitivo o en participio se emplea la forma correspondiente de **have to**, por ejemplo: **I don't want to have to repeat that; they have always had to pay before.** En el inglés hablado, y en el escrito en estilo coloquial, la forma negativa **must not** se transforma en **mustn't**.

(**a**) *(expressing obligation)* tener que, deber; **you m. do it** tienes que hacerlo, debes hacerlo; **I m. lend you that book some time** tengo que dejarte ese libro un rato de éstos, tengo que pasarte ese libro en algún momento; **you m. be ready at four o'clock** tienes que estar listo a las cuatro; **you mustn't tell anyone** no se lo digas a nadie; **under no circumstances m. you tell her** en ningún caso se lo debes decir; **this plant m. be watered daily** esta planta hay que regarla todos los días; **this information mustn't be made public** no hay que hacer pública esta información; **it m. be remembered that...** debemos recordar que...; **m. you go? – yes, I m.** ¿seguro que tienes que ir? – sí, seguro; **I m. say** *or* **admit, I thought it was rather good** la verdad es que me pareció bastante bueno; **will you come with me? – if I m.** ¿vendrás conmigo? – si no queda más remedio; **take it if you m.** llévatelo *or Esp* cógelo si tanta falta te hace; **if you m. listen to that music, at least do it with headphones on!** ¡si de verdad tienes que escuchar esa música, al menos ponte auriculares!; **if you m. know** ya que insistes tanto; **m. you make such a racket?** ¿por qué tienes que armar tanto alboroto *or* jaleo *or Am* relajo?; *Fam* **it's a m. see movie!** ¡no te puedes perder esa película!; **a list of m. see websites** una lista de sitios web muy recomendados
(**b**) *(suggesting, inviting)* tener que; **you m. come and visit us** tienes que venir a vernos; **you m. listen to this record** tienes que escuchar este disco; **we m. go out for a drink sometime** tenemos que quedar algún día para tomar algo

(c) *(expressing probability)* deber de; **you m. be hungry** debes de tener hambre; **it m. be interesting working there** debe de ser interesante trabajar allí; **I m. have made a mistake** debo de haberme equivocado; **there m. have been at least 10,000 people there** debía de haber al menos 10.000 personas allí; **they mustn't have realized** no se deben de haber dado cuenta; **you m. have heard of Oasis!** ¡has tenido que oír hablar de Oasis!; **you m. be joking!** ¡no lo dirás en serio!; **you m. be mad** *or* **crazy!** ¿estás loco o qué?

must² *n* (**a**) *(for wine)* mosto *m* (**b**) *(mould)* moho *m*

mustache *US* = **moustache**

mustachioed [mə'stɑːʃɪəʊd] *adj* con bigotes, bigotudo(a)

mustang ['mʌstæŋ] *n* mustango *m*

mustard ['mʌstəd] **1** *n (plant, sauce)* mostaza *f*; IDIOM *Fam* **she couldn't cut the m.** no consiguió dar la talla ▸▸ ***m. and cress*** berros *mpl* y semillas de mostaza; ***m. gas*** gas *m* mostaza

2 *adj (colour)* mostaza *inv*

muster ['mʌstə(r)] **1** *n* IDIOM **it was good enough to pass m.** era pasable

2 *vt (gather)* reunir; **to m. troops** reunir *or* congregar tropas; **they were unable to m. enough support** no pudieron hacerse con *or* reunir el apoyo necesario; **to m. the energy/enthusiasm to do sth** reunir la energía necesaria/el entusiasmo necesario para hacer algo; **to m. one's courage** armarse de valor, hacer acopio de valor; **to m. one's strength** hacer acopio de fuerzas

3 *vi* reunirse, congregarse

▸**muster in** *vt sep US Mil* alistar

▸**muster out** *vt sep US Mil* licenciar

▸**muster up** *vt sep (energy, enthusiasm)* reunir; **to m. up one's courage** armarse de valor, hacer acopio de valor

must-have ['mʌst'hæv] *Fam* **1** *n* artículo *m* imprescindible

2 *adj* imprescindible

mustiness ['mʌstɪnɪs] *n (of room)* olor *m* a cerrado; *(of clothes)* olor *m* a humedad

mustn't ['mʌsənt] = **must not**

must've ['mʌstəv] = **must have**

musty ['mʌstɪ] *adj* (**a**) **to have a m. smell** *(room)* oler a cerrado; *(clothes)* oler a humedad (**b**) *(old-fashioned)* pasado(a) de moda, anticuado(a); **m. ideas** ideas rancias *or* anticuadas

mutability [mjuːtə'bɪlɪtɪ] *n Formal* mutabilidad *f*

mutable ['mjuːtəbəl] *adj Formal* mudable, mutable

mutagen ['mjuːtədʒən] *n Biol* (agente *m*) mutágeno *m*

mutant ['mjuːtənt] **1** *n* mutante *mf*

2 *adj* mutante *mf*

mutate [mjuː'teɪt] *vi Biol* mutarse (**into** en), transformarse (**into** en)

mutation [mjuː'teɪʃən] *n Biol* mutación *f*

mutatis mutandis [mjʊ'tɑːtɪsmjʊ'tændɪs] *adv Literary* mutatis mutandis

mute [mjuːt] **1** *n* (**a**) *(person)* mudo(a) *m,f* (**b**) *Mus* sordina *f*

2 *adj* (**a**) *(unable to speak)* mudo(a) (**b**) *(vowel, letter)* mudo(a) (**c**) *(silent) (person)* mudo(a); *(feeling)* mudo(a), callado(a); **to stand m.** permanecer mudo(a), callar (**d**) ***m. swan*** cisne *m* vulgar

3 *vt* (**a**) *Mus* poner sordina a (**b**) *(feelings)* refrenar, contener; *(colour)* suavizar, atenuar

muted ['mjuːtɪd] *adj* (**a**) *(sound)* apagado(a); *(voice)* débil, apagado(a); *(colour)* suave, apagado(a); *(protest, criticism)* débil; *(applause)* tibio(a); **to discuss sth in m. tones** discutir algo en voz baja (**b**) *Mus* con sordina

mutely ['mjʊːtlɪ] *adv (to stare, gaze)* en silencio

mutha ['mʌðə] *n US* = **mother** (**b**)

mutilate ['mjuːtɪleɪt] *vt* (**a**) *(person)* mutilar; *(face)* desfigurar; **his face was horribly mutilated in the crash** el accidente le dejó el rostro horriblemente desfigurado (**b**) *(text)* mutilar

mutilated ['mjuːtɪleɪtɪd] *adj (person)* mutilado(a); *(face)* desfigurado(a)

mutilation [mjuːtɪ'leɪʃən] *n* mutilación *f*

mutineer [mjuːtɪ'nɪə(r)] *n* amotinado(a) *m,f*

mutinous ['mjuːtɪnəs] *adj* (**a**) *(rebellious)* rebelde; **the inmates of the prison were m.** los reclusos pretendían amotinarse (**b**) *(taking part in mutiny)* amotinado(a)

mutiny ['mjuːtɪnɪ] **1** *n* motín *m*

2 *vi* amotinarse

mutt [mʌt] *n Fam* (**a**) *(dog)* chucho *m*, *RP* pichicho *m* (**b**) *(fool)* tarugo *m*, percebe *m*

mutter ['mʌtə(r)] **1** *n* (**a**) *(mumble)* murmullo *m*; **to speak in a m.** murmurar, hablar entre murmullos (**b**) *(grumble)* queja *f*, protesta *f*; **there were mutters of discontent** hubo débiles protestas

2 *vt* murmurar, mascullar; **he muttered a threat** lanzó una amenaza entre dientes

3 *vi* (**a**) *(mumble)* murmurar; **what are you muttering about?** ¿qué murmuras?; **to m. to oneself** murmurar para sí (**b**) *(grumble)* refunfuñar

mutton ['mʌtən] *n (meat of sheep)* carnero *m*; IDIOM *Fam* **m. dressed as lamb** = una mujer ya carroza con pintas de jovencita

muttonchops ['mʌtəntʃɒps], **mutton-chop whiskers** ['mʌtəntʃɒp'wɪskəz] *npl* = patillas que cubren gran parte de la mejilla

muttonhead ['mʌtənhed] *n Fam* pedazo *m* de animal

mutual ['mjuːtʃʊəl] *adj* (**a**) *(reciprocal) (admiration, help)* mutuo(a); **the feeling is m.** el sentimiento es mutuo; *Hum Fam* **a m. appreciation** *or* **admiration society** una sesión de palmaditas en la espalda

(**b**) *(shared)* común; **by m. agreement** *or* **consent** de mutuo acuerdo; **a m. friend** un amigo común; **a m. interest in art** un interés compartido por el arte

(**c**) *Fin US* ***m. fund*** fondo *m* de inversión mobiliaria; ***m. insurance company*** mutua *f* de seguros

mutually ['mjuːtʃʊəlɪ] *adv* (**a**) *(reciprocally)* mutuamente; **to be m. exclusive** excluirse mutuamente (**b**) *(by all)* por todos; **it was m. agreed to postpone the meeting** se decidió de común acuerdo posponer la reunión

Muzak® ['mjuːzæk] *n* música *f* de fondo, *Esp* hilo *m* musical, *RP* música *f* funcional

muzzle ['mʌzəl] **1** *n* (**a**) *(animal's snout)* hocico *m* (**b**) *(device for dog)* bozal *m* (**c**) *(of gun)* boca *f* ▸▸ ***m. velocity*** velocidad *f* inicial

2 *vt* (**a**) *(dog)* poner un bozal a (**b**) *(person, press)* amordazar

muzzle-loader ['mʌzəl'ləʊdə(r)] *n* = arma que se carga por la boca

muzzy ['mʌzɪ] *adj* (**a**) *(visually)* borroso(a), desdibujado(a) (**b**) *(mentally)* confuso(a); **my head feels a bit m.** me noto un poco mareado

MV *Elec* (*abbr* **megavolt**) MV *m*

MVP [emviː'piː] *n US Sport* (*abbr* **most valuable player**) jugador(ora) *m,f* más destacado(a), mejor jugador(ora) *m,f*

MW (**a**) *Rad* (*abbr* **Medium Wave**) OM (**b**) *Elec* (*abbr* **Megawatts**) MW

MY [maɪ] *possessive adj* (**a**) *(singular)* mi; *(plural)* mis; **my dog** mi perro; **my parents** mis padres; **my name is Paul** me llamo Paul; **it wasn't MY idea!** ¡no fue idea mía!; **they were upset at my mentioning it** les sentó *or* cayó mal que lo mencionara; **that wasn't my understanding** yo no lo entendí así

(**b**) *(for parts of body, clothes) (translated by definite article)* **my eyes are blue** tengo los ojos azules; **I hit my head** me di un golpe en la cabeza; **I washed my face** me lavé la cara; **I put my hands in my pockets** me metí las manos en los bolsillos *or CAm, Méx, Perú* las bolsas

(**c**) *(in exclamations)* **(oh) my!** ¡madre mía!, ¡Jesús!; **(oh) my God!** ¡Dios mío!

(**d**) *(in forms of address)* **my darling** querida; **my love** mi amor; **my dear fellow!** ¡mi querido amigo!; **my lady/lord** mi señora/señor

myalgia [maɪ'ældʒɪə] *n Med* mialgia *f*

myalgic encephalomyelitis [maɪ'ældʒɪkensefələʊmaɪə'laɪtɪs] *n Med* encefalomielitis *f inv* miálgica

Myanmar [maɪæn'mɑː(r)] *n (official name of Burma)* Myanmar

mycology [maɪ'kɒlədʒɪ] *n* micología *f*

myelin ['maɪəlɪn] *n Anat* mielina *f* ▸▸ ***m. sheath*** vaina *f* de mielina

myelitis [maɪə'laɪtɪs] *n Med* (**a**) *(of spinal cord)* mielitis *f inv* (**b**) *(of bone marrow)* osteomielitis *f inv*

mynah ['maɪnə] *n* **m. (bird)** miná *f*, = estornino hablador de la India

MYOB [emwaɪəʊ'biː] *Fam* (*abbr* **mind your own business**) ¿a ti qué te importa?

myocardial [maɪəʊ'kɑːdɪəl] *adj Med* de miocardio ▸▸ ***m. infarction*** infarto *m* de miocardio

myocarditis [maɪəʊkɑː'daɪtɪs] *n Med* miocarditis *f inv*

myocardium [maɪəʊ'kɑːdɪəm] *n Anat* miocardio *m*

myopia [maɪ'əʊpɪə] *n also Fig* miopía *f*

myopic [maɪ'ɒpɪk] *adj* miope; *Fig* corto(a) de miras

myriad ['mɪrɪəd] *Literary* **1** *n* miríada *f*, sinnúmero *m*

2 *adj* **there are m. examples** hay una miríada *or* un sinnúmero de ejemplos

myrrh [mɜː(r)] *n* mirra *f*

myrtle ['mɜːtəl] *n* mirto *m*, arrayán *m*

myself [maɪ'self] *pron* (**a**) *(reflexive)* me; **I hurt m.** me hice daño; **I introduced m.** me presenté; **I bought m. a jacket** me compré una chaqueta; **I could see m. reflected in the water** vi mi imagen reflejada *or* me vi reflejado en el agua; **I can't see m. going on holiday this year** no me veo yendo de vacaciones este año

(**b**) *(unaided, alone)* solo; **I can do it m.** (yo) lo puedo hacer solo; **I made the pattern m.** yo solo hice el diseño

(**c**) *(emphatic)* yo mismo(a); **I told her m.** se lo dije yo mismo; **I m. saw him leave** yo (mismo) lo vi salir con mis propios ojos; **though I say so m.** aunque sea yo quien lo diga; **I'm not a great fan of opera m.** yo no es que sea un gran amante de la ópera; **I'm a stranger here m.** yo también soy de fuera

(**d**) *(my usual self)* **I feel m. again** vuelvo a sentirme la de siempre; **I'm not quite m. today** me siento un poco raro hoy, *Esp* hoy no estoy muy allá

(**e**) *(after preposition)* mí; **I did it all by m.** lo hice yo mismo *or* yo solo; **I live by m.** vivo solo; **I was all by m.** estaba (completamente) solo; **I bought it for m.** lo compré para mí; **I realized I was talking to m.** me di cuenta de que estaba hablando solo; **"how unfair!" I thought to m.** "¡qué injusto!" pensé para mis adentros

(**f**) *(replacing 'me')* **the group included m. and Jim** en el grupo estábamos yo y Jim; **it is meant for people like m.** está pensado para gente como yo

mysterious [mɪs'tɪərɪəs] *adj* misterioso(a); **a m. smile** una sonrisa misteriosa *or* enigmática; **there's nothing m. about it** no tiene ningún misterio; **to be m. about sth** andarse con muchos misterios acerca de algo; **what are you two being so m. about?** ¿por qué andan los dos con tanto misterio?

mysteriously [mɪs'tɪərɪəslɪ] *adv* misteriosamente; **he smiled m.** sonrió de forma misteriosa *or* enigmática; **the money had m. disappeared** el dinero había desaparecido misteriosamente

mystery ['mɪstərɪ] **1** *n* (**a**) *(strange or unexplained event)* misterio *m*; **it's a m. to me** es un misterio para mí; **it's a m. to me why she came** no entiendo *or* comprendo por qué vino; **there's no m. about that** eso no tiene ningún misterio ►► ***m. tour*** = excursión organizada con un destino sorpresa

(**b**) *(strangeness)* misterio *m*; **she has a certain m. about her** la envuelve cierto aire de misterio

(**c**) *(story)* **m. (story)** novela *f* de intriga

(**d**) *Lit* ***m. play*** auto *m* sacramental

2 *adj (guest, prize)* sorpresa *inv*; *(benefactor, witness)* anónimo(a), desconocido(a)

mystic ['mɪstɪk] **1** *n* místico(a) *m,f*

2 *adj* místico(a)

mystical ['mɪstɪkəl] *adj* místico(a)

mysticism ['mɪstɪsɪzəm] *n* misticismo *m*

mystification [mɪstɪfɪ'keɪʃən] *n* (**a**) *(bewilderment)* estupefacción *f*, desconcierto *m* (**b**) *(deliberate confusion)* artimaña *f*, ardid *m*

mystify ['mɪstɪfaɪ] *vt* dejar estupefacto(a) *or* perplejo(a), desconcertar; **I was mystified** me quedé estupefacto

mystifying ['mɪstɪfaɪɪŋ] *adj* desconcertante

mystique [mɪs'ti:k] *n* aureola *f* de misterio

myth [mɪθ] *n* (**a**) *(traditional story)* mito *m* (**b**) *(fiction)* mito *m*; **the man behind the m.** el hombre que hay *or* se esconde tras el mito; **the m. of German invincibility** el mito de la invencible Alemania

mythical ['mɪθɪkəl] *adj* mítico(a)

mythological [mɪθə'lɒdʒɪkəl] *adj* mitológico(a)

mythologize [mɪ'θɒlədʒaɪz] *vt* mitificar

mythology [mɪ'θɒlədʒɪ] *n* mitología *f*; **Roman/Norse m.** mitología romana/nórdica; **the story has become part of Hollywood m.** la historia ha pasado a formar parte de la mitología *or* leyenda de Hollywood

mythomania [mɪθə'meɪnɪə] *n* mitomanía *f*

mythomaniac [mɪθə'meɪnɪæk] **1** *n* mitómano(a) *m,f*

2 *adj* mitómano(a)

mythopoeia [mɪθə'pi:ə] *n* creación *f* de mitos

mythopoeic [mɪθə'pi:ɪk], **mythopoetic** [mɪθəʊpəʊ'etɪk] *adj* de la creación de mitos

myxomatosis [mɪksəmə'təʊsɪs] *n* mixomatosis *f inv*

N, n

N, n [en] *n (letter)* N, n *f*

N (*abbr* **north**) N

'n', 'n [(ə)n] *conj Fam* y; **fish 'n' chips** pescado frito con *Esp* patatas *or Am* papas fritas

n/a (*abbr* **not applicable**) no corresponde

NAACP [eneɪeɪsiː'piː] *n* (*abbr* **National Association for the Advancement of Colored People**) = asociación estadounidense para la defensa de los derechos de la gente de color

NAAFI ['næfɪ] *n* (*abbr* **Navy, Army and Air Force Institutes**) (**a**) *(organization)* = servicio de tiendas y cantinas que abastecen a las fuerzas armadas británicas (**b**) *(shop, canteen)* = tienda/cantina que abastece a las fuerzas armadas británicas

naan, nan [nɑːn] *n* **n. (bread)** = clase de pan hindú en forma de hogaza aplanada

nab [næb] (*pt & pp* **nabbed**) *vt Fam* (**a**) *(catch, arrest)* pescar, pillar (**b**) *(steal)* birlar, afanar; *(take)* pillar; *(seat, parking place)* birlar

nabob ['neɪbɒb] *n* (**a**) *Hist* nabob *m* (**b**) *Fam (local worthy)* cacique *m*

nacelle [nə'sel] *n (of balloon)* barquilla *f*

nachos ['nætʃəʊz] *npl* nachos *mpl (con queso, salsa picante, etc.)*

nacre ['neɪkə(r)] *n* nácar *m*

nacreous ['neɪkrɪəs] *adj* nacarado(a)

nadir ['neɪdɪə(r)] *n* (**a**) *Astron* nadir *m* (**b**) *(lowest point)* peor momento *m*, nadir *m*; **to reach a n.** *(party, career)* tocar fondo

naff [næf] *adj Br Fam* (**a**) *(tasteless)* ordinario(a), *Esp* hortera, *Esp* cutre, *Chile* cuico(a), *RP* terraja; *(of poor quality)* pobre, *Esp* cutre, *RP* terraja; *(comment, behaviour)* de mal gusto (**b**) *(for emphasis)* **n. all** nada de nada; **I've got n. all money** estoy sin un centavo *or Esp* sin blanca

▸ **naff off** *vi Br Fam* **n. off!** ¡vete a paseo!, *Esp* ¡que te den!, *CSur* ¡andá a bañarte!

NAFTA ['næftə] *n* (*abbr* **North American Free Trade Agreement**) NAFTA *f*, TLC *m*

nag[1] [næg] *n Fam (horse)* rocín *m*, jamelgo *m*

nag[2] **1** *n (person)* pesado(a) *m,f*, latoso(a) *m,f*; **he's an awful n.** es pesadísimo

2 *vt* (*pt & pp* **nagged**) (**a**) *(pester)* fastidiar, dar la lata a; **she's always nagging him** no para de fastidiarlo *or* darle la lata; **to n. sb into doing sth** fastidiar *or* dar la lata a alguien para que haga algo (**b**) *(of doubt)* asaltar; **his conscience nagged him perpetually** le remordía la conciencia constantemente

3 *vi* (**a**) *(pester)* fastidiar, dar la lata; **to n. at sb to do sth** fastidiar *or* dar la lata a alguien para que haga algo (**b**) *(doubt)* persistir; **her conscience was nagging at her to go to the police** tenía remordimientos de conciencia que le impulsaban a acudir a la policía

nagging ['nægɪŋ] **1** *n* regañinas *fpl*; **I've had enough of your n.!** ¡estoy harto de que te pases la vida encima de mí!

2 *adj* (**a**) *(wife, husband)* gruñón(ona) (**b**) *(doubt, feeling, pain)* persistente

NAHT [eneɪeɪtʃ'tiː] *n* (*abbr* **National Association of Head Teachers**) = asociación de directores de centros escolares de Inglaterra y Gales

naiad ['naɪæd] *n Mythol* náyade *f*

nail [neɪl] **1** *n* (**a**) *(in carpentry)* clavo *m*; IDIOM **it was another n. in his coffin** aquello suponía un paso más hacia el desastre; IDIOM **to pay on the n.** pagar a tocateja; IDIOM **cash on the n.** dinero contante y sonante ▸▸ ***n. bomb*** = bomba de fabricación casera que contiene metralla y clavos; ***n. gun*** remachadora *f*, = aparato para clavar clavos; ***n. punch*** botador *m*, (punzón *m*) embutidor *m*

(**b**) *(of finger, toe)* uña *f*; **to do one's nails** hacerse las uñas ▸▸ ***n. clippers*** cortaúñas *m inv*; *US* ***n. enamel*** laca *f or* esmalte *m* de uñas; ***n. file*** lima *f* de uñas; ***n. polish*** laca *f or* esmalte *m* de uñas; ***n. polish remover*** quitaesmaltes *m inv*; ***n. scissors*** tijeras *fpl* de manicura; ***n. varnish*** laca *f or* esmalte *m* de uñas; ***n. varnish remover*** quitaesmaltes *m inv*

2 *vt* (**a**) *(in carpentry)* clavar; **n. the planks together** une las tablas con clavos; **he nailed the lid shut** fijó la tapa con clavos

(**b**) *Fam (catch, trap) (person)* pescar, pillar; **to n. sb for a crime** emplumar *or* empapelar a alguien por un delito

(**c**) *Fam (expose) (rumour)* probar la falsedad de; **to n. a lie** desterrar una falsedad

(**d**) *Fam (shoot)* acertar *(de un disparo)*; **I nailed his bodyguard** tumbé a su guardaespaldas de un solo tiro

(**e**) IDIOMS **he stood nailed to the spot** se quedó clavado; **she nailed her colours to the mast** dejó clara su postura

▸ **nail down** *vt sep* (**a**) *(fasten)* fijar con clavos; *Fam* **the burglars took everything that wasn't nailed down** nos limpiaron la casa, nos lo robaron todo (**b**) *Fam Fig (establish clearly)* **to n. sth down** aclarar algo; **to n. sb down to a date/price** hacer que alguien se comprometa a dar una fecha concreta/un precio concreto

▸ **nail up** *vt sep* (**a**) *(shut) (door, window)* condenar *(claveteando tablas)*; *(box)* tapar *or* cerrar con clavos (**b**) *(fix to wall, door) (picture, photo)* colgar *(con clavos)*; *(notice)* clavar

nail-bed ['neɪlbed] *n* lecho *m* de la uña

nail-biter ['neɪlbaɪtə(r)] *n* (**a**) *(person)* = persona que se muerde las uñas (**b**) *Fam (situation)* **the last race was a real n.** la última carrera fue de infarto *or* emocionantísima

nail-biting ['neɪlbaɪtɪŋ] *adj Fam (contest, finish)* de infarto, emocionantísimo(a); **after a n. few hours, the hostages were released** después de varias horas de tensa espera liberaron a los rehenes

nailbrush ['neɪlbrʌʃ] *n* cepillo *m* de uñas

naive, naïve [naɪ'iːv] *adj* ingenuo(a); **don't be so n.** ¡no seas ingenuo! ▸▸ ***n. art*** arte *m* naíf

naively, naïvely [naɪ'iːvlɪ] *adv* ingenuamente

naivety [naɪ'iːvətɪ], **naïveté** [naiːv'teɪ] *n* ingenuidad *f*

naked ['neɪkɪd] *adj* (**a**) *(unclothed)* desnudo(a); **to be n.** estar desnudo(a)

(**b**) *(bare) (tree)* desnudo(a), sin hojas; *(hillside, landscape)* pelado(a)

(**c**) *(undisguised) (truth, facts)* al desnudo, al descubierto; **n. aggression** agresión abierta *or* alevosa; **n. ambition** ambición manifiesta; **an expression of n. terror** una expresión de puro terror

(**d**) *(unprotected)* **a n. flame** una llama (sin protección); **a n. sword** una espada desenvainada

(**e**) *(unaided)* **visible to the n. eye** visible a simple vista

nakedly ['neɪkədlɪ] *adv* abiertamente, manifiestamente; **n. ambitious** de una ambición manifiesta

nakedness ['neɪkədnɪs] *n* desnudez *f*; **to cover one's n.** cubrirse las partes pudendas

Nam [nɑːm] *n US Fam* Vietnam

namby-pamby ['næmbɪ'pæmbɪ] *Fam* **1** *n* ñoño(a) *m,f*

2 *adj* ñoño(a); **a n. thing to say** una ñoñez

NAME [neɪm] **1** *n* (**a**) *(of person, thing)* nombre *m*; **my n. is...** me llamo...; **what's your n.?** ¿cómo te llamas?; **what's the n. of that lake?** ¿cómo se llama ese lago?; **my n.'s James** me llamo James; **the n.'s Bond** me llamo Bond; **what n. shall I say?** *(on phone)* ¿de parte de quién?, ¿quién lo llama?; **to go by** *or* **under the n. of** ser conocido(a) como; **to put one's n. down (for sth)** apuntarse (a algo); **to take sb's n.** *(note down)* anotar *or* tomar el nombre de alguien; *Sport (give booking)* mostrar una tarjeta amarilla a alguien; **to mention/know sb by n.** mencionar/conocer a alguien por su nombre; **a man by the n. of Lewis,** *US* **a man n. of Lewis** un hombre llamado Lewis; **in the n. of** en nombre de; **the account is in my husband's n.** la cuenta está a nombre de mi marido; **reserved in the n. of Fox** reservado a nombre de Fox; **in the n. of freedom** en nombre de la libertad; **in the n. of God** *or* **Heaven!, in God's** *or* **Heaven's n.!** ¡por el amor de Dios!; **what in**

God's *or* **Heaven's n. are you doing?** pero por el amor de Dios, ¿qué haces?; **he was president in all but n.** él era el presidente de hecho; **in n. only** sólo de nombre; **she writes under a different n.** escribe bajo pseudónimo; **to call sb names** insultar a alguien; **he hasn't got a penny to his n.** no tiene ni un centavo *or Esp* duro *or RP* peso; **to take sb's n. in vain** usar *or* tomar el nombre de alguien en vano; **a n. to conjure with** *(respected person)* un personaje de (muchas) campanillas; *(colourful name)* un nombre rimbombante; **survival is the n. of the game** lo que cuenta es sobrevivir; IDIOM *Fam* **his n. is mud** tiene muy mala prensa, *RP* está requemado; IDIOM **what's in a n.?** ¿qué importa el nombre? ►► ***n. day*** *(saint's day)* santo *m*; *Fin* día *m* de intercambio de nombres, día *m* de los boletos; ***n. part*** *(in film)* = personaje cuyo nombre da título a la película; ***n. tag*** chapa *f* (con el nombre)

(**b**) *(reputation)* nombre *m*, reputación *f*; **this kind of behaviour gives us a good/bad n.** este comportamiento nos da una buena/mala reputación; **she has a good/bad n.** tiene buena/mala fama; **to have a n. for prompt and efficient service** tener fama de ofrecer un servicio bueno y rápido; **he made his n. in the war** se hizo famoso en la guerra; **to make a n. for oneself (as)** hacerse un nombre (como) ►► ***n. brand*** marca *f* conocida

(**c**) *(famous person)* **a big n. in the theatre** una figura del teatro; **we need a n. to publicize the book** necesitamos a algún personaje conocido para dar publicidad al libro

2 *vt* (**a**) *(give name to)* poner nombre a; **they named her Paula** le pusieron *or* la llamaron Paula; **they named the new state Zimbabwe** llamaron al nuevo estado Zimbabwe; **I n. this ship Britannia** bautizo a este barco Britannia; **a man named Gerald** un hombre llamado Gerald; **to n. sb after** *or US* **for sb** poner a alguien el nombre de alguien; **the building is named the Lincoln Centre after** *or US* **for Abraham Lincoln** el edificio lleva el nombre de "Lincoln Centre" por Abraham Lincoln

(**b**) *(appoint)* nombrar; **she has been named as the new party leader** la han nombrado nueva líder del partido

(**c**) *(designate)* nombrar; **n. your price** di *or* pon un precio; **n. the place and I'll meet you there** tú di dónde, y nos veremos allí; **you n. it, we've got it** dígame qué busca, que seguro lo tenemos; **to n. the day** fijar la fecha de la boda

(**d**) *(identify)* **police have named the victim as...** la policía ha identificado a la víctima como...; **the journalist refused to n. his source** los periodistas se negaron a revelar el nombre de su fuente de información; **to n. but a few** por nombrar unos pocos; **to n. names** dar nombres concretos; **to n. and shame** nombrar y avergonzar

---

name-calling ['neɪmkɔːlɪŋ] *n* improperios *mpl*, insultos *mpl*

named [neɪmd] *adj* designado(a)

name-dropper ['neɪmdrɒpə(r)] *n Fam* **she's a terrible n.** se las da de conocer a muchos famosos

name-dropping ['neɪmdrɒpɪŋ] *n Fam* **there was a lot of n. in his speech** en el discurso se las daba de conocer a muchos famosos

nameless ['neɪmlɪs] *adj* (**a**) *(person)* anónimo(a); *Hum* **someone who shall remain n.** alguien que permanecerá en el anonimato (**b**) *(fear, regret)* indecible, indescriptible (**c**) *(atrocious) (crime, atrocity)* indecible, infame

namely ['neɪmlɪ] *adv* a saber, es decir

nameplate ['neɪmpleɪt] *n (on or beside door)* placa *f* (con (el) nombre)

namesake ['neɪmseɪk] *n* tocayo(a) *m,f*

nametape ['neɪmteɪp] *n* cinta *f* con el nombre

Namibia [nə'mɪbɪə] *n* Namibia

Namibian [nə'mɪbɪən] 1 *n* namibio(a) *m,f*
2 *adj* namibio(a)

nan[1] [næn] *n Br Fam (grandmother)* abuelita *f*, *Esp* yaya *f*

nan[2] = **naan**

nana ['nɑːnə] *n Fam* (**a**) *Br (banana)* plátano *m*, *RP* banana *f* (**b**) *Br Hum (idiot)* tonto(a) *m,f*, panoli *mf* (**c**) *Austr (head)* coco *m*; **to be off one's n.** estar mal del coco

nancy ['nænsɪ] *n very Fam* **n. (boy)** *(homosexual)* mariquita *m*, marica *m*; *(effeminate man)* mariposón *m*

nandrolone ['nændrələʊn] *n* nandrolona *f*

nanny ['nænɪ] *n* (**a**) *(nursemaid)* niñera *f*; IDIOM *Br* **the n. state** el estado protector (**b**) ***n. goat*** cabra *f*

nano- ['nænəʊ] *prefix* nano-

nanoengineering ['nænəʊendʒɪ'nɪərɪŋ] *n* nanoingeniería *f*

nanosecond ['nænəʊsekənd] *n Phys & Comptr* nanosegundo *m*

nanotechnology ['nænəʊtek'nɒlədʒɪ] *n* nanotecnología *f*

nap[1] [næp] 1 *n (sleep)* cabezada *f*, siesta *f*; **to take** *or* **have a n.** echar una cabezada *or* una siesta
2 *vi* (*pt & pp* **napped**) echar una cabezada *or* una siesta; IDIOM **they were caught napping** los *Esp* cogieron *or Am* agarraron desprevenidos

nap[2] *n (of cloth)* pelusa *f*, lanilla *f*; **against the n.** a contrapelo

nap[3] 1 *n (in horse racing)* favorito *m*
2 *vt* dar como favorito(a) a

napalm ['neɪpɑːm] 1 *n* napalm *m*
2 *vt (bomb)* bombardear con napalm; *(attack)* atacar con napalm

nape [neɪp] *n* **n. (of the neck)** nuca *f*

naphtha ['næfθə] *n* nafta *f*

naphthalene ['næfθəliːn] *n* naftalina *f*

napkin ['næpkɪn] *n* (**a**) **(table) n.** servilleta *f* ►► ***n. ring*** servilletero *m* *(aro)* (**b**) *US (sanitary towel)* compresa *f*, *Am* toalla *f* higiénica

Naples ['neɪpəlz] *n* Nápoles

Napoleon [nə'pəʊlɪən] *pr n* **N. (Bonaparte)** Napoleón (Bonaparte)

Napoleonic [nəpəʊlɪ'ɒnɪk] *adj* napoleónico(a); *Hist* **the N. Wars** las guerras napoleónicas

nappy ['næpɪ] 1 *n Br* pañal *m* ►► ***n. liner*** gasa *f*; ***n. rash*** escoceduras *fpl or* eritema *m* del pañal
2 *adj US* (**a**) *(fabric)* con pelusa (**b**) *(hair)* rizado(a), *Chile, Col* crespo(a), *Méx* quebrado(a), *RP* enrulado(a)

narc [nɑːk] *n US Fam* estupa *mf (agente de la brigada de estupefacientes)*

narcissi *pl of* **narcissus**

narcissism ['nɑːsɪsɪzəm] *n Psy & Fig* narcisismo *m*

narcissist ['nɑːsɪsɪst] *n* narcisista *mf*

narcissistic [nɑːsɪ'sɪstɪk] *adj* narcisista

narcissus [nɑː'sɪsəs] (*pl* **narcissi** [nɑː'sɪsaɪ]) *n* narciso *m*

narcolepsy ['nɑːkəlepsɪ] *n Med* narcolepsia *f*

narcosis [nɑː'kəʊsɪs] *n Med* narcosis *f inv*

narcoterrorism ['nɑːkəʊterərɪzəm] *n* narcoterrorismo *m*

narcotic [nɑː'kɒtɪk] 1 *n* (**a**) *(drug)* narcótico *m* (**b**) *US (illegal drug)* narcótico *m*, estupefaciente *m*; *US* **narcotics agent** agente *mf* (de la brigada) de estupefacientes
2 *adj* narcótico(a)

nark [nɑːk] *Br Fam* 1 *n* (**a**) *(informer)* soplón(ona) *m,f* (**b**) *(irritable person)* malaleche *mf*, picajoso(a) *m,f*
2 *vt (annoy)* mosquear
3 *vi* (**a**) *(inform)* **to n. on sb** delatar a alguien (**b**) *(gripe)* protestar, quejarse

narked [nɑːkt] *adj Br Fam* mosqueado(a)

narky ['nɑːkɪ] *adj Br Fam* **to be n.** *(by nature)* ser malaleche *or* picajoso(a); *(temporarily)* estar de mala leche *or* picajoso(a); **he's a n. git** es un susceptible

narrate [nə'reɪt] *vt* (**a**) *(relate) (story, event)* narrar, relatar (**b**) *(read commentary for)* narrar; **the movie was narrated by John Wayne** John Wayne era el narrador *or* ponía voz a la narración de la película

narration [nə'reɪʃən] *n* (**a**) *(story)* narración *f*, historia *f* (**b**) *(recounting)* narración *f* (**c**) *(of commentary)* comentario *m*, narración *f*

narrative ['nærətɪv] 1 *n (story)* narración *f*
2 *adj* narrativo(a); **the n. art** la narrativa, el arte narrativo

narrator [nə'reɪtə(r)] *n* (**a**) *(storyteller)* narrador(ora) *m,f* (**b**) *(of commentary)* narrador(ora) *m,f*

narrow ['nærəʊ] 1 *adj* (**a**) *(not wide) (street, passage, valley)* estrecho(a), angosto(a); *(skirt, shoe)* estrecho(a); **to grow** *or* **become n.** estrecharse, angostarse; **to have n. shoulders** ser estrecho(a) de espaldas, no tener hombros; **to have a n. face/waist** tener la cara/cintura estrecha ►► ***n. boat*** barcaza *f*; ***n. gauge*** vía *f* estrecha

(**b**) *(barely sufficient) (majority)* escaso(a); **it was a n. victory/defeat** fue una victoria/derrota por un estrecho *or* escaso margen; **to have a n. escape** *or* **squeak** librarse por muy poco *or* por los pelos; **by a n. margin** *(to win, lose)* por un estrecho *or* escaso margen; **to win/lose by the narrowest of margins** ganar/perder por un estrechísimo *or* escasísimo margen

(**c**) *(intolerant)* **to have a n. mind** ser estrecho(a) de miras; **to take a n. view of sth** enfocar algo desde un punto de vista muy limitado

(**d**) *(restricted) (sense, interpretation)* estricto(a); **in the narrowest sense** en el sentido más estricto

(**e**) *Formal (detailed)* **we were subjected to n. scrutiny** fuimos sometidos a un meticuloso *or* exhaustivo examen

2 *vt* (**a**) *(make narrow) (road)* estrechar; **to n. one's eyes** *(in suspicion, anger)* entornar los ojos *or* la mirada

(b) *(reduce) (majority)* acortar, reducir; **the Republicans have narrowed the gap between themselves and the Democrats** los republicanos han logrado reducir *or* acortar el margen que los separa de los demócratas; **the police have narrowed their search to a few streets** la policía ha acotado *or* reducido su búsqueda a unas cuantas calles

3 *vi* **(a)** *(become narrow) (road, space)* estrecharse; **the old man's eyes narrowed** los ojos del viejo se entrecerraron *or* se entornaron **(b)** *(be reduced) (majority)* acortarse, reducirse; **the gap between rich and poor has narrowed** se han acortado *or* reducido las diferencias entre pobres y ricos

4 narrows *npl (strait)* estrecho *m*

▶ **narrow down** **1** *vt sep* **(a)** *(limit) (choice, possibilities)* limitar, reducir **(b)** *(reduce) (majority, difference)* acortar, reducir

2 *vi* **the choice narrowed down to just two people** la elección se redujo a tan sólo dos personas

narrowcast ['nærəʊkɑːst] **1** *vt* retransmitir por cable

2 *vi* = hacer publicidad dirigida específicamente a un público determinado

narrow-gauge ['nærəʊgeɪdʒ] *adj* ***n. railway*** ferrocarril *m* de vía estrecha

narrowly ['nærəʊlɪ] *adv* **(a)** *(only just)* por poco; **he n. missed being run over** por poco lo atropellan **(b)** *(interpret)* estrictamente, al pie de la letra **(c)** *(closely)* detenidamente, atentamente

narrow-minded ['nærəʊ'maɪndɪd] *adj (person)* estrecho(a) de miras, cerrado(a); *(attitude, opinions)* cerrado(a)

narrow-mindedness ['nærəʊ'maɪndɪdnɪs] *n (of person)* estrechez *f* de miras, cerrazón *f*; *(of attitude, opinions)* cerrazón *f*

narrowness ['nærəʊnɪs] *n* **(a)** *(of street, passage, valley)* estrechez *f*; *(of skirt, shoe)* estrechez *f* **(b)** *(of majority)* escaso margen *m* **(c)** *(intolerance)* cerrazón *f* **(d)** *(of interpretation)* carácter *m* estricto, literalidad *f*

narwhal ['nɑːwəl] *n* narval *m*, unicornio *m* marino

nary ['neərɪ] *adv Fam* **there was n. a word of warning** ni una palabra de advertencia; **n. a one** ni uno

NASA ['næsə] *n* (*abbr* **National Aeronautics and Space Administration**) la NASA

nasal ['neɪzəl] **1** *adj* nasal; **to have a n. voice** tener la voz nasal ▸▸ *Anat* ***n. bone*** hueso *m* nasal; ***n. septum*** tabique *m* nasal, *Spec* septo *m* nasal

2 *n Ling* sonido *m* nasal

nasalize ['neɪzəlaɪz] *vt Ling* nasalizar

nasally ['neɪzəlɪ] *adv* **she speaks rather n.** tiene una forma de hablar muy nasal

nascent ['neɪsənt] *adj Formal (in early stages)* naciente, incipiente

Nasdaq ['næsdæk] *n St Exch* (*abbr* **National Association of Securities Dealers Automated Quotation**) (índice *m*) Nasdaq *m*

nastily ['nɑːstɪlɪ] *adv* **(a)** *(with malice)* con mala intención, desagradablemente **(b)** *(seriously)* **to fall n.** tener una mala caída

nastiness ['nɑːstɪnɪs] *n* **(a)** *(unpleasantness) (of taste, smell)* carácter *m* desagradable; *(of experience, atmosphere)* carácter *m* desagradable; **the n. of the weather** el pésimo estado del tiempo, la inclemencia del tiempo **(b)** *(of person, remark, behaviour)* mala intención *f*, maldad *f* **(c)** *(of injury, fall)* gravedad *f*

nasturtium [nə'stɜːʃəm] *n* capuchina *f*

nasty ['nɑːstɪ] **1** *adj* **(a)** *(unpleasant) (taste, smell)* desagradable, asqueroso(a); *(experience, shock, weather, atmosphere)* desagradable, horrible; *(book, film)* desagradable, repugnante; *(crime)* horrible, repugnante; **to give sb a n. fright** darle a alguien un susto tremendo *or* horrible; **it was a very n. moment** fue un momento muy desagradable; **to have a n. feeling that...** tener la desagradable sensación de que...; **he's got a n. habit of repeating everything you say to the boss** tiene la fea costumbre de contarle al jefe todo lo que dices; **to turn n.** *(situation, weather)* ponerse feo(a); **things started to turn really n.** la cosa se puso muy fea; IDIOM **to leave sb with a n. taste in the mouth** dejar a alguien con mal sabor de boca

(b) *(malicious) (person)* desagradable, malo(a); *(remark, rumour)* malintencionado(a); **what a n. man!** ¡qué hombre más desagradable *or* malo!; **he's got a n. temper** tiene muy mal genio; **you've got a n. mind!** ¡qué mal pensado eres!; **hiding her clothes was a really n. thing to do** esconderle la ropa fue una broma demasiado pesada; **to be n. to sb** portarse muy mal con alguien; **to turn n.** *(person)* ponerse desagradable; IDIOM *Br* **he's a n. piece of work** es un elemento de cuidado

(c) *(serious, dangerous) (road, junction)* muy peligroso(a); *(cold, blow)* fortísimo(a); **a n. accident** un accidente grave; **a n. cut** una herida muy fea; **a n. fall** una mala caída

(d) *(in children's language) (dragon, giant, wolf)* malo(a), malvado(a)

(e) *(ugly, in bad taste)* horrible, espantoso(a); **n. plastic flowers** horribles *or* espantosas flores de plástico

(f) *(difficult) (problem, question)* dificilísimo(a), peliagudo(a)

2 *n (person)* mala persona *f*

NASUWT [eneɪ'esjuːdʌbəljuː'tiː] *n* (*abbr* **National Association of Schoolmasters/Union of Women Teachers**) = sindicato británico de profesores de enseñanza secundaria

nat [næt] *n Br Fam* nacionalista *mf*

natatorium [neɪtə'tɔːrɪəm] *n US* piscina *f* cubierta

natch [nætʃ] *adv Fam* ¡pues claro!, ¡ya te digo!

nation ['neɪʃən] *n* **(a)** *(people)* nación *f*, pueblo *m*; **the British n.** el pueblo británico; **to address the n.** dirigirse a la nación ▸▸ ***N. of Islam*** Nación *f* del Islam **(b)** *(country)* nación *f*, país *m* ▸▸ ***n. state*** estado-nación *m*

national ['næʃənəl] **1** *n* **(a)** *(person)* ciudadano(a) *m,f*, súbdito(a) *m,f*; **all EU nationals** todos los ciudadanos de la Unión Europea **(b)** *(newspaper)* periódico *m* (de ámbito) nacional

2 *adj* nacional; **he became a n. hero** se convirtió en un héroe nacional; **a symbol of n. pride** un símbolo del orgullo nacional *or* patrio; **the n. newspapers** los periódicos de ámbito nacional; **it's not in the n. interest** no le interesa *or* conviene a la nación; **the case caused a n. outcry** el caso provocó indignación generalizada entre la ciudadanía; **on a n. scale** a escala nacional ▸▸ ***n. anthem*** himno *m* nacional; ***N. Audit Office*** ≃ Tribunal *m* de Cuentas; ***n. bank*** banco *m* nacional; *Tel* ***n. call*** llamada *f or Am* llamado *m* nacional; ***n. costume*** traje *m* típico; *Br* ***N. Curriculum*** programa *m* de estudios oficial; ***the n. debt*** la deuda pública; ***n. dress*** traje *m* típico; ***the N. Front*** el Frente Nacional, = partido racista de extrema derecha británico; ***n. government*** gobierno *m* nacional; ***the n. grid*** la red eléctrica nacional; *US* ***N. Guard*** Guardia *f* Nacional; ***N. Health Service*** = la sanidad pública británica; **to get treatment on the N. Health (Service)** recibir tratamiento a través de la seguridad social *or* sanidad pública; ***n. heritage*** patrimonio *m* nacional; *Econ* ***n. income*** renta *f* nacional; ***N. Insurance*** seguridad *f* social; *Br* ***N. Insurance contributions*** aportaciones *fpl or* cotizaciones *fpl* a la seguridad social; ***N. Insurance number*** número *m* de afiliación a la seguridad social; ***N. Liberation Front*** Frente *m* Nacional de Liberación, Frente *m* de Liberación Nacional; ***N. Lottery*** = lotería nacional británica, *Esp* ≃ lotería *f* primitiva, *RP* ≃ Quini 6 *f*; ***n. park*** parque *m* nacional; *US* ***N. Rifle Association*** = asociación estadounidense que se opone a cualquier restricción en el uso de armas de fuego; ***N. Savings Bank*** = caja de ahorros estatal británica; *Irish* ***N. School*** colegio *m* público; ***n. security*** seguridad *f* nacional; *US* ***N. Security Adviser*** asesor(ora) *m,f* en materia de seguridad nacional; *US* ***N. Security Council*** Consejo *m* de Seguridad Nacional; ***n. service*** *(in army)* servicio *m* militar; ***N. Socialism*** nacionalsocialismo *m*; ***N. Trust*** = organismo británico encargado de la conservación de edificios y parajes de especial interés, *Esp* ≃ Patrimonio *m* Nacional

nationalism ['næʃənəlɪzəm] *n* nacionalismo *m*

nationalist ['næʃənəlɪst] **1** *n* nacionalista *mf*

2 *adj* nacionalista

nationalistic [næʃənə'lɪstɪk] *adj* nacionalista

nationality [næʃə'nælɪtɪ] *n* nacionalidad *f*; **people of all nationalities** gente de todas las nacionalidades; **what n. are you?** ¿de qué nacionalidad eres?; **to take** *or* **adopt British n.** adquirir *or* adoptar la nacionalidad británica

nationalization [næʃənəlaɪ'zeɪʃən] *n* nacionalización *f*

nationalize ['næʃənəlaɪz] *vt* nacionalizar

nationalized ['næʃənəlaɪzd] *adj* nacionalizado(a)

nationally ['næʃənəlɪ] *adv* en el ámbito nacional; **to be n. renowned** ser conocido(a) en todo el país; **a n. recognized qualification** una titulación reconocida en todo el estado *or* país; **n., men still outnumber women in these sectors** a escala nacional, los hombres todavía superan en número a las mujeres en estos sectores

nationhood ['neɪʃənhʊd] *n* estatus *m inv* de nación; **a sense of n.** un sentimiento de patria; **to attain n.** constituirse en nación *or* estado

nationwide ['neɪʃənwaɪd] **1** *adj* de ámbito nacional; **a n. strike** una huelga a escala nacional; **a n. survey** una encuesta de ámbito nacional

2 *adv* en todo el país; **to be broadcast n.** ser transmitido(a) a todo el país

native ['neɪtɪv] **1** *n* **(a)** *(of country, town)* natural *mf*, nativo(a) *m,f*; **I am a n. of Edinburgh** soy natural de Edimburgo; **she speaks English like a n.** su inglés es perfecto

(b) *Old-fashioned (indigenous inhabitant)* nativo(a) *m,f,* indígena *mf; Hum* **the natives are getting restless** el patio se está revolucionando

(c) *(plant, animal)* especie *f* autóctona; **the koala is a n. of Australia** el koala es autóctono *or* originario de Australia; **this plant is a n. of southern Europe** esta planta es autóctona *or* originaria del sur de Europa

2 *adj* (a) *(of birth) (country)* natal; **he returned to his n. London** regresó a su Londres natal ►► ***n. land*** tierra *f* natal; ***n. language*** lengua *f* materna; ***n. speaker*** hablante *mf* nativo(a); **I'm not a n. speaker of Spanish** mi lengua materna no es el español

(b) *(by birth)* de nacimiento, nativo(a); **Portland honours its n. sons** Portland rinde honores a sus hijos predilectos ►► ***N. American*** indio(a) *m,f* americano(a)

(c) *(indigenous) (tribe, customs)* indígena, autóctono(a); *(costume)* típico(a) (del lugar); IDIOM *Fam* **to go n.** integrarse (en el país)

(d) *(innate) (ability)* natural, innato(a) ►► ***n. wit*** ingenio *m*

(e) *(plant, animal)* autóctono(a); **n. to India** autóctono(a) *or* originario(a) de la India

(f) *(ore, silver)* nativo(a)

native-born ['neɪtɪvbɔːn] *adj* de nacimiento, nativo(a)

nativism ['neɪtɪvɪzəm] *n Psy* innatismo *m*

nativist ['neɪtɪvɪst] *n Psy* innatista *mf*

Nativity [nə'tɪvɪtɪ] *n Rel* **the N.** la Natividad ►► ***N. play*** auto *m* navideño *or* de Navidad

Nato, NATO ['neɪtəʊ] *n* (*abbr* **North Atlantic Treaty Organization**) OTAN *f*

natter ['nætə(r)] *esp Br Fam* 1 *n* charla *f, CAm, Méx* plática *f*; **to have a n.** charlar, darle a la lengua, *CAm, Méx* platicar

2 *vi* charlar, darle a la lengua, *CAm, Méx* platicar; **what were they nattering about?** ¿de qué charlaban *or CAm, Méx* platicaban?

natterjack ['nætədʒæk] *n* **n. (toad)** sapo *m* corredor

nattily ['nætɪlɪ] *adv Fam* **n. dressed** de punta en blanco, muy bien vestido(a)

natty ['nætɪ] *adj Fam* (a) *(person, dress)* fino(a), elegante *(not Fam)*; **he's a n. dresser** va siempre de punta en blanco, es muy fino vistiendo (b) *(clever) (device)* ingenioso(a)

natural ['nætʃərəl] 1 *n* (a) *Fam (person)* **he's a n. as an actor** es un actor nato, tiene un talento natural como actor; **she's a n. for the job/part** el trabajo/papel le va que ni pintado (b) *Mus (note)* nota *f* natural; *(symbol)* becuadro *m*

2 *adj* (a) *(as created by nature) (colour, taste)* natural; **a n. harbour** un puerto natural, una ensenada; **in its n. state** en su estado natural; **the n. world** (el mundo de) la naturaleza; **death from n. causes** muerte natural ►► ***n. disaster*** catástrofe *f* natural; *Phys & Elec* ***n. frequency*** frecuencia *f* natural; ***n. gas*** gas *m* natural; ***n. history*** historia *f* natural; *Med* ***n. immunity*** inmunidad *f or* resistencia *f* natural; *Fig* **to have a n. immunity to sth** ser inmune a algo; *Old-fashioned* ***n. philosophy*** filosofía *f* natural; ***n. resources*** recursos *mpl* naturales; ***n. sciences*** ciencias *fpl* naturales; ***n. selection*** selección *f* natural

(b) *(not artificial) (wood, finish)* natural; **she's a n. redhead** es pelirroja natural; **to come to a n. break** llegar a una pausa obligada ►► ***n. childbirth*** parto *m* natural; ***n. family planning*** planificación *f* familiar natural, control *m* de natalidad por medios naturales; ***n. fibres*** fibras *fpl or* tejidos *mpl* naturales; ***n. language*** lenguaje *m* natural; *Comptr* ***n. language processing*** procesamiento *m* de lenguaje natural; ***n. light*** luz *f* natural; ***n. yoghurt*** yogur *m* natural

(c) *(normal, to be expected)* natural, lógico(a); **it's only n. that you should want to be here** es natural que quieras estar aquí; **one's** *or* **the n. reaction is to...** la reacción más normal es...; **as is (only) n.** como es natural *or* lógico ►► *Ind* ***n. wastage*** amortización *f* de puestos de trabajo por jubilación

(d) *(unaffected)* natural, espontáneo(a)

(e) *(innate) (talent)* natural, innato(a); **she's a n. organizer** es una organizadora nata, tiene una capacidad innata para organizar

(f) *(related by blood) (parents)* biológico(a); *Euph (child)* natural ►► ***n. mother*** madre *f* biológica

(g) *Law* ***n. justice*** justicia *f* natural; ***n. law*** derecho *m* natural

(h) *Math* ***n. number*** número *m* natural

(i) *Mus* natural; **G n.** sol natural

3 *adv Fam* **try to act n.!** ¡tú (haz) como si no pasara nada!

natural-born ['nætʃərəl'bɔːn] *adj* de nacimiento, nativo(a)

naturalism ['nætʃərəlɪzəm] *n* naturalismo *m*

naturalist ['nætʃərəlɪst] *n* naturalista *mf*

naturalistic ['nætʃərəlɪstɪk] *adj* naturalista

naturalization [nætʃərəlaɪ'zeɪʃən] *n* (a) *(of foreign person)* naturalización *f*, nacionalización *f*; *(of word)* adopción *f*, asimilación *f* ►► ***n. papers*** carta *f* de naturaleza (b) *(of plant, animal)* aclimatación *f*

naturalize ['nætʃərəlaɪz] 1 *vt* (a) *(person)* naturalizar, nacionalizar; *(word)* adoptar, asimilar; **to become naturalized** *(person)* naturalizarse, nacionalizarse (b) *(plant, animal)* aclimatar

2 *vi (plant, animal)* aclimatarse

naturalized ['nætʃərəlaɪzd] *adj* (a) *(person)* naturalizado(a), nacionalizado(a); *(word)* adoptado(a), asimilado(a) (b) *(plant, animal)* aclimatado(a)

naturally ['nætʃərəlɪ] *adv* (a) *(obviously, logically)* naturalmente; **she n. assumed that he was joking** naturalmente *or* como es natural, pensó que él estaba de broma; **n., this came as something of a shock** naturalmente, esto era toda una sorpresa; **were you pleased at the decision? – n.!** ¿te pareció bien la decisión? – ¡naturalmente (que sí)!

(b) *(in one's nature)* por naturaleza; **n. shy/lazy** tímido(a)/perezoso(a) por naturaleza; **to come n. to sb** ser innato(a) en alguien; *Ironic* **punctuality doesn't come n. to him** la puntualidad no es lo suyo

(c) *(unaffectedly)* con naturalidad; **you answered very n.** contestaste con mucha naturalidad

(d) *(in natural state)* en la naturaleza, en estado natural; **n. occurring microbes** microbios que se encuentran en la naturaleza

naturalness ['nætʃrəlnɪs] *n (unaffectedness)* naturalidad *f*

nature ['neɪtʃə(r)] *n* (a) *(the natural world)* la naturaleza; **N. can be cruel** la naturaleza puede ser cruel; **back to n.** de vuelta a la naturaleza; **to draw/paint from n.** dibujar/pintar del natural; **to go against n.** ir contra natura, ser antinatural; **to let n. take its course** dejar que la naturaleza siga su curso; **one of n.'s gentlemen** un caballero nato *or* de nacimiento ►► ***n. conservation*** conservación *f* de la naturaleza; ***n. lover*** amante *mf* de la naturaleza; ***the n./nurture debate*** el debate sobre lo que es innato y lo que es adquirido; ***n. reserve*** reserva *f* natural; ***n. study*** (estudio *m* de la) naturaleza *f*, ciencias *fpl* naturales; ***n. trail*** senda *f* natural, ruta *f* ecológica

(b) *(character) (of thing)* naturaleza *f*; *(of person)* naturaleza *f*, carácter *m*; **to have a jealous n.** tener un carácter celoso, ser celoso(a) por naturaleza; **it's not in her n.** no es su carácter, no es propio de ella; **it's not in her n. to complain** no es propio de ella quejarse, no es de las que se queja; **it's in the n. of things** las cosas son así; **to be shy by n.** ser tímido(a) por naturaleza; **war is by its very n. destructive** la guerra es por su propia naturaleza *or* de por sí destructiva

(c) *(sort)* género *m*, clase *f*; **problems of this n.** problemas de este género *or* esta naturaleza; **questions of a personal n.** cuestiones de índole *or* carácter personal; **do you sell chocolates or anything of that n.?** ¿tienen chocolatinas o algo por el estilo?; **something in the n. of a...** algo así como un/una...; *Formal* **what is the n. of your complaint?** ¿cuál es el motivo de su queja?

nature-loving ['neɪtʃəlʌvɪŋ] *adj* amante de la naturaleza

naturism ['neɪtʃərɪzəm] *n* naturismo *m*, nudismo *m*

naturist ['neɪtʃərɪst] *n* naturista *mf*

naturopath ['neɪtʃərəʊpæθ] *n* naturópata *mf*

naturopathy [neɪtʃə'rɒpəθɪ] *n* naturopatía *f*

Naugahyde® ['nɔːgəhaɪd] *n US* escay *m*

naught [nɔːt] 1 *n* (a) *Literary (nothing)* nada *f*; **his plans came to n.** sus planes (se) quedaron en nada (b) *US* = **nought**

2 *adv arch or Literary* **it matters n.** no importa en absoluto

naughtily ['nɔːtɪlɪ] *adv* (a) *(disobediently, mischievously)* traviesamente; **to behave n.** portarse mal (b) *(suggestively)* pícaramente, con picardía

naughtiness ['nɔːtɪnɪs] *n* (a) *(disobedience, mischievousness)* travesura *f* (b) *(sexual impropriety)* picardía *f*

naughty ['nɔːtɪ] *adj* (a) *(child)* malo(a), travieso(a); **it was n. of you not to tell me** *(said to adult)* ¡mira que no decírmelo!; **you n. boy!** *(to child)* ¡qué malo *or* travieso eres!; *(to adult)* ¡qué malo *or* pillín eres!

(b) *(word, picture, magazine)* picante ►► *Br Euph* ***n. bits*** partes *fpl* más picantes; ***the n. nineties*** *(1890s)* = el decenio de 1890, caracterizado por la vida alegre

Nauru ['naʊruː] *n* Nauru

nausea ['nɔːzɪə] *n* náuseas *fpl*; **to be overcome with n.** sentir auténticas náuseas

nauseate ['nɔːzɪeɪt] *vt* dar *or* provocar náuseas a; **the sight of blood nauseated him** cuando veía sangre le daban náuseas

nauseating ['nɔːzɪeɪtɪŋ] *adj* nauseabundo(a), repugnante; **the stench was n.** el hedor era nauseabundo *or* repugnante; **the very idea is n.** la sola idea es repugnante

nauseatingly ['nɔːzɪeɪtɪŋlɪ] *adv* repugnantemente; **she was n. smug** su engreimiento era repugnante

nauseous ['nɔːzɪəs, *US* 'nɔːʃəs] *adj* nauseabundo(a); **to feel n.** sentir *or* tener náuseas

nautical ['nɔːtɪkəl] *adj* náutico(a) ▸▸ ***n. mile*** milla *f* marina *or* náutica

nautilus ['nɔːtɪləs] *n* nautilo *m*

NAV [eneɪ'viː] *n Fin* (*abbr* **net asset value**) valor *m* activo neto

naval ['neɪvəl] *adj* naval ▸▸ ***n. architecture*** arquitectura *f or* ingeniería *f* naval; ***n. battle*** batalla *f* naval; ***n. engineer*** ingeniero(a) *m,f* naval; ***n. officer*** oficial *mf* de marina

Navarre [nə'vɑː(r)] *n* Navarra

Navarrese [nævɑː'riːz] *adj* navarro(a)

nave [neɪv] *n Archit* nave *f* central

navel ['neɪvəl] *n* ombligo *m*; IDIOM **to contemplate one's n.** mirarse el ombligo ▸▸ ***n. orange*** naranja *f* navelina

navel-gazing ['neɪvəlgeɪzɪŋ] *n* **to be guilty of n.** pecar de mirarse el ombligo

navigable ['nævɪgəbəl] *adj* **(a)** *(of river)* navegable **(b)** *(of ship)* apto(a) para la navegación; *(of balloon)* dirigible

navigate ['nævɪgeɪt] **1** *vt* **(a)** *(traverse) (seas)* surcar, navegar por; **to n. the Atlantic** navegar por *or* surcar el Atlántico; **this river is difficult to n.** es difícil navegar por este río

(b) *(direct) (ship, plane)* gobernar, pilotar; **he navigated the plane to the nearest airport** llevó *or* pilotó el avión hasta el aeropuerto más cercano; **she navigated us successfully through Bombay** *(in car)* consiguió llevarnos a través de Bombay conduciendo *or Am* manejando; **she navigated her way across the crowded room** se abrió paso por la abarrotada sala

(c) *Comptr* **to n. the Net** navegar por Internet

2 *vi* **(a)** *(in ship)* navegar; **to n. by the stars** navegar guiándose por las estrellas; **I'll drive if you n.** *(in car)* yo conduzco *or Am* manejo si tú haces de copiloto **(b)** *Comptr* navegar

navigation [nævɪ'geɪʃən] *n* **(a)** *(act, skill of navigating) (in ship)* navegación *f*; *(in plane)* pilotaje *m*, navegación *f*; *(in car)* función *f* de copiloto ▸▸ ***n. lights*** luces *fpl* de navegación **(b)** *(shipping)* navegación *f* **(c)** *Comptr (around website)* navegación *f* ▸▸ *Comptr* ***n. bar*** barra *f* de navegación

navigational [nævɪ'geɪʃənəl] *adj* **n. skill** aptitudes para la navegación ▸▸ ***n. aid*** ayuda *f* a la navegación; ***n. equipment*** equipo *m* de navegación

navigator ['nævɪgeɪtə(r)] *n* **(a)** *Naut* oficial *m* de derrota; *Av* piloto *m* navegante **(b)** *(in car)* copiloto *mf*

navvy ['nævɪ] *n Br* peón *m* caminero

navy ['neɪvɪ] **1** *n* **(a)** *(service)* armada *f*, marina *f* (de guerra); *(fleet)* armada *f* ▸▸ *US* ***n. yard*** astilleros *mpl* estatales **(b)** *(colour)* **n. (blue)** azul *m* marino

2 *adj* azul marino *inv*

navy-blue ['neɪvɪ'bluː] *adj* azul marino *inv*

nay [neɪ] **1** *n (in vote)* no *m*, voto *m* en contra; **the nays have it** son mayoría los votos en contra

2 *exclam Old-fashioned or Literary* no; **I ask not for another month, n. not even a fortnight** no pido otro mes, ni tan siquiera otras dos semanas; **I was asked, n. ordered to come** se me pidió, qué digo "pidió", se me ordenó que viniera; **for a few dollars, n. a few cents** por unos cuantos dólares, mejor dicho, unos cuantos centavos

naysayer ['neɪseɪə(r)] *n* persona *f* negativa

Nazarene ['næzəriːn] **1** *n* **the N.** el Nazareno

2 *adj* nazareno(a)

Nazareth ['næzərəθ] *n* Nazaret

Nazi ['nɑːtsɪ] **1** *n* nazi *mf*

2 *adj* nazi

Nazism ['nɑːtsɪzəm] *n* nazismo *m*

NB [en'biː] **(a)** (*abbr* **nota bene**) N.B. **(b)** (*abbr* **New Brunswick**) New Brunswick

NBA [enbiː'eɪ] *n* **(a)** *US* (*abbr* **National Basketball Association**) NBA *f* **(b)** *Br Formerly* (*abbr* **Net Book Agreement**) = acuerdo por el que la editorial fijaba el precio mínimo de los libros

NBC [enbiː'siː] *n* **(a)** *US* (*abbr* **National Broadcasting Company**) NBC *f* **(b)** *Mil* (*abbr* **nuclear, biological and chemical**) ***N. suit*** = traje que protege contra armas nucleares, biológicas y químicas; ***N. weapons*** armas nucleares, biológicas y químicas

NC **(a)** (*abbr* **no charge**) gratis **(b)** (*abbr* **North Carolina**) Carolina del Norte

NC-17 [en'siːsevən'tiːn] *adj US* para mayores de 17 años

NCCL [ensiːsiː'el] *n* (*abbr* **National Council for Civil Liberties**) = asociación británica para la defensa de los derechos civiles

NCO [ensiː'əʊ] (*pl* **NCOs**) *n Mil* (*abbr* **non-commissioned officer**) suboficial *mf*

NCVQ [ensiːviː'kjuː] *n* (*abbr* **National Council for Vocational Qualifications**) = organismo británico que regula los títulos de formación profesional

ND, NDak (*abbr* **North Dakota**) Dakota del Norte

NE **(a)** (*abbr* **Nebraska**) Nebraska **(b)** (*abbr* **north east**) NE

Neanderthal [nɪ'ændətɑːl] **1** *n Fam Fig (coarse person)* troglodita *mf*

2 *adj* **(a)** *(remains, artefacts)* Neandert(h)al; **N. man** el hombre de Neandert(h)al **(b)** *Fam Fig (attitude, behaviour)* cavernícola

neap [niːp] *n* **n. (tide)** marea *f* muerta

Neapolitan [niːə'pɒlɪtən] **1** *n* napolitano(a) *m,f*

2 *adj* napolitano(a) ▸▸ ***N. ice cream*** barra *f* de helado de chocolate, vainilla y fresa *or CSur* frutilla

NEAR [nɪə(r)] **1** *adj* **(a)** *(close)* cercano(a), próximo(a); **the n. bank of the lake** la orilla más cercana *or* próxima del lago; **a n. relative** un pariente cercano; **he was in a state of n. despair** estaba al borde de la desesperación; **the nearest shop is 10 miles away** la tienda más cercana *or* próxima está a 10 millas; **use maple syrup or the nearest equivalent** utilice jarabe de arce o lo más parecido que pueda encontrar; **in the n. future** en un futuro próximo *or* cercano; **to the nearest metre** en número redondo de metros; **what is the total, to the nearest hundred?** ¿cuál es el total, redondeándolo hasta la centena más cercana?; **$30 or nearest offer** 30 dólares negociables; **it was a n. thing** poco faltó; **it will be a n. thing which of the two wins** no está nada claro cuál de los dos va a ganar; **this is the nearest thing we have to a conference room** esto es lo más parecido que tenemos a una sala de reuniones ▸▸ *US* ***n. beer*** cerveza *f* sin alcohol; ***the N. East*** (el) Cercano Oriente, *Esp* (el) Oriente Próximo; *Comptr* ***n. letter quality*** calidad *f* (de impresión) casi de carta *or* próxima a la de carta; ***n. miss*** *(in plane, car)* incidente *m* (sin colisión); *(in factory)* = caso en el que casi se produce un accidente; **we were involved in a n. miss** no chocamos por muy poco; **it was a n. miss** *(narrow failure)* falló por poco

(b) *(left)* izquierdo(a); **the n. front wheel** la rueda delantera izquierda; **its n. hind leg** la pata trasera izquierda

2 *adv* **(a)** *(close)* cerca; **to be n. (to)** estar cerca (de); **to come nearer** acercarse; **the time is getting nearer when...** se acerca el momento en el que...; **n. at hand** *(thing)* a mano; *(event)* cercano(a); **it's not exactly what I wanted, but it's n. enough** no es exactamente lo que quería, pero casi casi; **it'll cost you £50 or n. enough, it'll cost you £50 or as n. as makes no difference** te costará 50 libras o algo así; **they were** *or* **came n. to giving up** estuvieron a punto de abandonar; **n. to despair** cercano(a) *or* próximo(a) a la desesperación; **n. to tears** a punto de (echarse a) llorar; **I came n. to insolvency** estuve a punto de declararme insolvente; **or as n. as makes no difference** o algo muy parecido; *Fam* **as n. as dammit** casi, casi; **they came from n. and far** vinieron de todas partes; **the shot was nowhere n.** el disparo salió totalmente desviado; **she's nowhere n. finished** le falta mucho para terminar; **it's nowhere n. as good** no es ni mucho menos tan bueno; **we have nowhere n. enough time** no tenemos el tiempo suficiente ni mucho menos

(b) *(almost)* casi; **a n. total failure** un fracaso casi absoluto

3 *prep* cerca de; **n. Miami/the town centre** cerca de Miami/del centro; **her birthday is n. Christmas** su cumpleaños cae por Navidad; **n. the end of the book** casi al final del libro; **we are n. the end of our holidays** se acerca el final de nuestras vacaciones; **don't come n. me** no te me acerques; **he came n. being run over** estuvo a punto de ser atropellado; **it's getting n. the time when...** se acerca el momento en el que...; **don't go n. the edge** no te acerques al precipicio; **don't let them n. my fax machine** no dejes que se acerquen a mi fax; **I'll let you know nearer the time** ya te lo haré saber cuando se acerque el momento; **the total was nearer $400** el total se acercó más a 400 dólares; **nobody comes anywhere n. her** *(in skill, performance)* nadie se le puede comparar; **they are no nearer a solution** no están más cerca de hallar una solución; **he's nowhere n. it!** *(with guess)* ¡no tiene ni idea!

4 *n* **my nearest and dearest** mis (parientes) más allegados

5 *vt* acercarse a; **we're nearing a time when everyone will be able to...** nos acercamos a una época en la que todos podremos...; **it is nearing completion** está casi terminado, falta poco para terminarlo; **he was nearing 70 when he got married** se acercaba a *or* le faltaba poco para los 70 años cuando se casó

6 *vi* acercarse

near- [nɪə(r)] *prefix* **n.-complete** casi completo(a); **n.-perfect** casi perfecto(a)

nearby 1 *adj* ['nɪəbaɪ] cercano(a); **we stopped at a n. post office** paramos en una oficina de correos cercana *or* que había cerca; **he threw it into a n. dustbin** lo tiró a un cubo de basura que había cerca *or* al lado
2 *adv* [nɪə'baɪ] cerca; **is there a station n.?** ¿hay una estación cerca?; **I live just n.** yo vivo muy cerca

near-death experience ['nɪə'deθɪks'pɪərɪəns] *n* = experiencia próxima a la muerte

nearly ['nɪəlɪ] *adv* **(a)** *(almost)* casi; **it's n. eight o'clock** son casi las ocho; **he's n. eighty** tiene casi ochenta años; **we're n. there** *(finished)* ya casi hemos terminado; *(at destination)* ya casi hemos llegado; **he very n. died** estuvo a punto de morir; **I n. fell** casi me caigo, por poco me caigo; **he was n. crying** *or* **in tears** estaba a punto de echarse a llorar; **I very n. didn't come** por poco no vengo
(b) *(with negative)* **we haven't got n. enough money/time** no tenemos dinero/tiempo suficiente ni de lejos; **it's not n. so beautiful as I remember** no es ni de lejos tan bonito como lo recuerdo; **he's not n. as important as he likes to think** no es ni mucho menos tan importante como se cree; **it's not n. as difficult as I thought** no es ni con mucho tan difícil como yo pensaba

nearly-new ['nɪəlɪ'nju:] *adj (clothes)* casi como nuevo(a)

nearness ['nɪənɪs] *n* **(a)** *(physical)* cercanía *f* **(b)** *(emotional)* confianza **(to** con)

nearside ['nɪəsaɪd] *Br Aut* 1 *n* lado *m* del copiloto
2 *adj* del lado del copiloto

near-sighted [nɪə'saɪtɪd] *adj* corto(a) de vista, miope

nearsightedness [nɪə'saɪtɪdnɪs] *n* miopía *f*

neat [ni:t] *adj* **(a)** *(person) (in habits)* ordenado(a); *(in appearance)* aseado(a), pulcro(a)
(b) *(tidy) (room, house)* pulcro(a), ordenado(a); *(garden)* muy cuidado(a); *(handwriting)* claro(a), nítido(a); *(exercise book)* bien presentado(a); **he's a n. worker** es un trabajador esmerado; **to do a n. job** hacer un trabajo con esmero; **she made a n. job of it** lo hizo con mucho esmero; **the surgeon made a n. job of those stitches** el cirujano se esmeró con la sutura; **to keep things n. and tidy** tener las cosas ordenaditas; IDIOM **to be as n. as a new pin** *(house, room)* estar como los chorros del oro; *(person)* ir de punta en blanco
(c) *(trim) (waist)* delgado(a); *(figure)* esbelto(a)
(d) *(skilful, well-formed) (solution)* certero(a), hábil; *(summary, explanation)* acertado(a), atinado(a); *(turn of phrase)* elegante; *(system, plan)* ingenioso(a); **that's a n. trick** es un buen truco
(e) *(whisky, vodka)* seco(a), solo(a); **to take** *or* **drink one's whisky n.** tomar el whisky seco *or* solo
(f) *US Fam (good)* genial, fenomenal; **that's a n. idea!** ¡qué buena idea!, ¡es una idea genial!; **what a n. outfit!** ¡qué vestido tan bonito *or Esp, Méx* chulo!

neaten ['ni:tən] *vt (make smart, tidy) (room, house, garden)* arreglar; **to n. sth (up)** arreglar algo; **go and n. your hair** ve y péinate, ve y arréglate el pelo; **to n. (up) the edges of sth** igualar los bordes de algo

neatly ['ni:tlɪ] *adv* **(a)** *(carefully)* cuidadosamente, con esmero; **put the papers n. on the desk** pon los papeles en la mesa bien ordenados; **to dress n.** ir bien vestido(a) *or* arreglado(a); **the desk fits n. into the corner of the room** la mesa cabe perfectamente en el rincón de la habitación
(b) *(skilfully)* **she n. avoided the subject** eludió hábilmente el tema; **that was n. put** estuvo muy elegante; **you got out of that very n.** saliste muy bien de ésa

neatness ['ni:tnɪs] *n* **(a)** *(of appearance)* pulcritud *f* **(b)** *(tidiness) (of room, house, garden)* pulcritud *f*; *(of work)* esmero *m*; *(of handwriting)* nitidez *f*; *(of exercise book)* buena presentación *f* **(c)** *(of solution)* acierto *m*, habilidad *f*; *(of explanation)* acierto *m*, tino *m*; *(of turn of phrase)* elegancia *f*; *(of system, plan)* ingenio *m*

Nebr (*abbr* **Nebraska**) Nebraska

nebula ['nebjʊlə] *n Astron* nebulosa *f*

nebulous ['nebjʊləs] *adj (vague)* nebuloso(a)

NEC [eni:'si:] *n* (*abbr* **National Executive Committee**) ejecutiva *f (de partido político)*

necessarily [nesɪ'serəlɪ] *adv* necesariamente; **it's not n. the case** no tiene por qué ser necesariamente así; **this will n. lead to major disruption** esto va a provocar inevitablemente un trastorno importante

necessary ['nesɪsərɪ] 1 *n Fam* **to do the n.** hacer lo necesario; **the n.** *(money) Esp* la pasta, *Am* la plata, *Méx* la lana; **the necessaries** *(food, money)* lo justo
2 *adj* **(a)** *(indispensable)* necesario(a), preciso(a); **he took the n. measures** tomó las medidas necesarias *or* precisas; **it is n. to remind them** hay que recordárselo; **it is n. for him to come** hace falta *or* es preciso que venga él; **is this visit really n.?** ¿es verdaderamente necesaria esta visita?; **it soon became n. to inform them** pronto fue necesario informarlos; **to do what is n.** hacer lo necesario; **he did no more than was n.** no hizo más que lo necesario, se limitó a hacer lo imprescindible; **I'll do everything n. to make her agree** haré lo que haga falta para que acceda; **to make it n. for sb to do sth** hacer necesario que alguien haga algo; **circumstances made it n. to delay our departure** las circunstancias exigían que retrasáramos nuestra partida; **if n.** si es preciso *or* necesario; **when(ever) n.** cuando sea necesario *or* preciso
(b) *(inevitable)* inevitable, necesario(a); **a n. evil** un mal necesario

necessitate [nɪ'sesɪteɪt] *vt Formal* hacer necesario(a) *or* preciso(a), precisar; **further complications may n. surgery** mayores complicaciones podrían hacer necesaria una intervención quirúrgica

necessitous [nɪ'sesɪtəs] *adj Formal (family, children)* necesitado(a); *(state)* de necesidad

necessity [nɪ'sesɪtɪ] *n* **(a)** *(need)* necesidad *f*; **I see no n. for that** no veo la necesidad de eso; **there is no n. for drastic measures** no son necesarias medidas drásticas; **there's no real n. for us to go** no hace verdadera falta que vayamos; **if the n. should arise** si hiciera falta; **in cases of absolute n.** en casos de extrema *or* absoluta necesidad; PROV **n. is the mother of invention** la necesidad aviva el ingenio
(b) *Formal (inevitability)* inevitabilidad *f*; **of n.** por fuerza, necesariamente
(c) necessities *(things needed)* necesidades *fpl*; **the basic** *or* **bare necessities of life** las necesidades básicas (de la vida); **a television is not one of life's necessities** un televisor no es una necesidad básica *or* no es imprescindible

neck [nek] 1 *n* **(a)** *(of person)* cuello *m*; *(of animal)* pescuezo *m*; **he threw his arms round her n.** le echó los brazos al cuello; **the cat had a collar round its n.** el gato llevaba collar
(b) *Culin* **n. of lamb/beef** cuello de cordero/vaca
(c) *(of dress)* cuello *m*; **high n.** *(of dress)* cuello alto; **low n.** *(of dress)* escote
(d) *(narrow part or extremity) (of bottle)* cuello *m*; *(of guitar)* mástil *m*; *(of violin)* mango *m*; *(of womb)* cuello *m*; *(of land)* istmo *m*
(e) *(in horse race)* **to win by a n.** ganar por una cabeza; **to finish n. and n.** llegar igualados(as); *Fig* **the two candidates are n. and n.** los dos candidatos van muy parejos *or* igualados
(f) *Br Fam (cheek)* cara *f*, caradura *f*; **she's got some n.!** ¡qué cara más dura tiene!, ¡qué caradura!
(g) IDIOMS *Fam* **he got it in the n.** *(was severely punished)* se le cayó el pelo; *Fam* **he's in it up to his n.** está metido hasta el cuello; **to be up to one's n. in work** estar hasta las cejas de trabajo; **to be up to one's n. in debt** estar hasta el cuello de deudas; **to be up to one's n. in trouble** estar hasta arriba de problemas; *Fam* **to risk one's n.** jugarse el pellejo; *Fam* **to stick one's n. out** *(take risk)* arriesgarse; *Fam* **what are you doing in this n. of the woods?** ¿qué haces tú por estos andurriales *or RP* pagos?; *Br Fam* **it's n. or nothing now** ahora nos jugamos el todo por el todo
2 *vi Fam (couple) Esp* morrear, *Am* manosearse

neckband ['nekbænd] *n (on garment)* tirilla *f*

neckerchief ['nekətʃi:f] *n* pañuelo *m* (para el cuello)

necking ['nekɪŋ] *n Fam* morreo *m*, *Am* manoseo *m*

necklace ['neklɪs] *n* collar *m*

necklet ['neklət] *n* gargantilla *f*

neckline ['neklaɪn] *n* escote *m*; **her dress had a low/plunging n.** era un vestido muy escotado/de escote pronunciado

necktie ['nektaɪ] *n US* corbata *f* ►► *Fam* ***n. party*** linchamiento *m*

neckwear ['nekweə(r)] *n* prendas *fpl* para el cuello

necromancer ['nekrəʊmænsə(r)] *n Formal* nigromante *mf*

necromancy ['nekrəʊmænsɪ] *n Formal* nigromancia *f*, necromancia *f*

necrophile ['nekrəfaɪl] 1 *n* necrófilo(a) *m,f*
2 *adj* necrófilo(a)

necrophilia [nekrə'fɪlɪə] *n* necrofilia *f*

necrophiliac [nekrə'fɪlɪæk] 1 *n* necrófilo(a) *m,f*
2 *adj* necrófilo(a)

necrophobia [nekrə'fəʊbɪə] *n* necrofobia *f*

necropolis [nə'krɒpəlɪs] *n* necrópolis *f inv*

necrosis [nə'krəʊsɪs] *n Med* necrosis *f inv*

nectar ['nektə(r)] *n also Fig* néctar *m*

nectarine ['nektəri:n] *n* nectarina *f*

nectary ['nektərɪ] *n Bot* nectario *m*

née [neɪ] *adj* de soltera; **Mrs Green, n. Bard** la Sra. Green, de soltera Bard

NEED [ni:d] **1** *n* **(a)** *(necessity)* necesidad *f* (**for** de); **I don't think there's any n. to worry** no creo que debamos preocuparnos; **there's no n. for us all to go** no hace falta que vayamos todos; **there is no n. to...** no hace falta...; **there's no n. to be so aggressive!** ¡no hace falta que seas tan agresivo!; **I feel the n. of some fresh air** necesito tomar el aire; **as the n. arises** cuando es necesario; **if n. be, in case of n.** si fuera necesario; **I don't want to do it, but needs must** no quiero hacerlo, pero no hay más remedio; **to be in n. of sth** necesitar algo; **the roof is badly in n. of repair** el tejado necesita urgentemente una reparación; **to have no n. of sth** no necesitar algo; **in time of n.** en los momentos de necesidad; **their n. is greater than mine** ellos están más necesitados que yo

(b) *(requirement)* necesidad *f*; **their needs can be easily satisfied** sus necesidades son fáciles de satisfacer; **to attend to sb's needs** atender las necesidades de alguien

(c) *(poverty)* necesidad *f*; **to be in n.** estar necesitado(a); **children in n.** niños necesitados

2 *vt* **(a)** *(require, have need of) (of person)* necesitar; **you'll n. to take more money** te hará falta más dinero; **I didn't n. to be reminded of it** no hizo falta que nadie me lo recordara; **you don't n. to be a genius to realize that...** no hace falta ser un genio para darse cuenta que...; **I n. you to give me your opinion on this matter** necesito saber tu opinión sobre el tema; **this work needs a lot of patience** este trabajo requiere mucha paciencia; **will I be needed next week?** ¿haré falta la próxima semana?, ¿me van a precisar la semana que viene?; **you only needed to ask** no tenías más que pedirlo; **one thing needs to be made clear** hay que dejar una cosa clara; **I don't n. you telling me what to do!** ¡no necesito que me digas lo que tengo que hacer!; *Ironic* **that's all I n.!** ¡sólo me faltaba eso!; **money? who needs it?** ¿a quién le hace falta el dinero?

(b) *(would benefit from)* **this soup needs a bit more pepper** a esta sopa le hace falta más pimienta; **the bathroom needs cleaning** hay que limpiar el baño; **his hair needs cutting** le hace falta un corte de pelo

(c) *(expressing obligation)* **to n. to do sth** tener que hacer algo; **I n. to ask the boss first** tengo que preguntárselo al jefe primero; **you n. to try harder** tienes que esforzarte más

3 *modal aux v*

Cuando se emplea como verbo modal sólo existe una forma, y los auxiliares **do/does** no se usan: **he need only worry about himself; need she go?; it needn't matter.**

you needn't worry, I'll be fine! ¡no te preocupes, no me va a pasar nada!; **you needn't wait** no hace falta que me esperes; **it needn't be too time-consuming** no tiene por qué llevar mucho tiempo, *Am* no tiene por qué demorar mucho rato; **you needn't have bothered** no tenías que haberte molestado; **it n. never have happened** no tenía que haber ocurrido; **what did she say? – n. you ask?** ¿qué dijo? – ¿qué iba a decir?; **I n. hardly say that he was most upset** no hace falta que diga que estaba muy disgustado; **n. I say more?** no hace falta decir más, ya se sabe

needful ['ni:dfʊl] **1** *n Fam* **to do the n.** hacer lo necesario; **have you got the n.?** *(money)* ¿tienes la *Esp* pasta *or Am* plata *or Méx* lana?

2 *adj Formal* preciso(a), necesario(a)

needle ['ni:dəl] **1** *n* **(a)** *(for sewing, knitting, crochet)* aguja *f*; *(of syringe)* aguja *f*; *(for record player)* aguja *f*; IDIOM **it's like looking for a n. in a haystack** es como buscar una aguja en un pajar ▸▸ ***n. bank*** centro *m* de intercambio de jeringuillas; ***n. exchange*** centro *m* de intercambio de jeringuillas; ***n. valve*** válvula *f* cónica *or* de aguja

(b) *(as indicator) (of compass, on dial)* aguja *f*

(c) *(of pine-tree)* aguja *f*

(d) *(rocky outcrop)* cresta *f* (rocosa)

(e) *(monument)* obelisco *m*

(f) *Fam* **to give sb the n.** *(annoy)* fastidiar a alguien; **to get the n.** pincharse, *Esp* picarse; **he gets a lot of n. for his religious beliefs** se meten mucho con él por sus creencias religiosas; *Br* **a bit of n. has crept into the match** el partido se ha ido calentando ▸▸ *Br* ***n. match*** *(in football)* partido *m* a muerte *or* con tintes revanchistas

2 *vt Fam (irritate)* pinchar, picar; **he's always needling her about her weight** anda siempre pinchándola con el peso; **they needled him into retaliating** lo picaron para que se desquitara

needlecord ['ni:dəlkɔ:d] *n* pana *f* (fina); **a n. suit** un traje de pana (fina)

needlecraft ['ni:dəlkrɑ:ft] *n* costura *f*

needlepoint ['ni:dəlpɔɪnt] *n* bordado *m*

needless ['ni:dlɪs] *adj* innecesario(a); **n. to say,...** ni que decir tiene que..., huelga decir que...

needlessly ['ni:dlɪslɪ] *adv* innecesariamente; **to be n. rude** ser grosero sin necesidad, ser innecesariamente grosero; **to suffer n.** sufrir innecesariamente *or* sin necesidad; **to die n.** morir sin razón

needlewoman ['ni:dəlwʊmən] *n* costurera *f*

needlework ['ni:dəlwɜ:k] *n* **(a)** *(sewing)* costura *f* **(b)** *(embroidery)* bordado *m*

needn't ['ni:dənt] = **need not**

need-to-know [ni:dtə'nəʊ] *adj* **information is given on a n. basis** se proporciona la información sólo a las personas que se considere que la necesitan

needy ['ni:dɪ] **1** *npl* **the n.** los necesitados

2 *adj (person)* necesitado(a); **to be n.** estar necesitado(a)

ne'er [neə(r)] *adv Literary* nunca, jamás

ne'er-do-well ['neədʊwel] **1** *n* inútil *mf*, bala *m* perdida

2 *adj* inútil; **my n. cousins** los inútiles de mis primos

nefarious [nɪ'feərɪəs] *adj Formal* infame

neg (*abbr* **negotiable**) negociable

negate [nɪ'geɪt] *vt Formal* **(a)** *(nullify) (work, effect, efforts)* anular, invalidar **(b)** *(deny)* negar

negation [nɪ'geɪʃən] *n Formal* **(a)** *(nullification)* anulación *f*, invalidación *f* **(b)** *(denial)* negación *f* **(c)** *Ling* negación *f*

negative ['negətɪv] **1** *n* **(a)** *Gram* negación *f*, forma *f* negativa; **in the n.** en forma negativa **(b)** *(answer)* negativa *f*; **to answer in the n.** contestar negativamente, dar una respuesta negativa **(c)** *Phot* negativo *m*

2 *adj* **(a)** *(answer)* negativo(a); *Med* **the test was n.** el resultado de la prueba fue negativo, la prueba dio (un resultado) negativo; **on the n. side** en el aspecto negativo

(b) *(defeatist, pessimistic) (person, philosophy)* negativo(a); **don't be so n.!** ¡no seas tan negativo!; **she's always so n. about my plans** siempre tiene una actitud muy negativa hacia mis proyectos ▸▸ ***n. feedback*** *(in circuit)* retroalimentación *f* negativa; *(critical response)* críticas *fpl*, mala respuesta *f*; *Psy* ***n. reinforcement*** refuerzo *m* negativo

(c) *Math & Elec* negativo(a) ▸▸ ***n. pole*** polo *m* negativo; ***n. sign*** *(minus)* signo *m* negativo

(d) *Fin* ***n. cash flow*** cash-flow *m or* flujo *m* de caja negativo; *Fin* ***n. equity*** = depreciación del valor de mercado de una propiedad por debajo de su valor en hipoteca

3 *vt* **(a)** *(nullify)* anular, invalidar **(b)** *(reject)* rechazar **(c)** *(deny)* negar

negatively ['negətɪvlɪ] *adv* **(a)** *(respond, think)* negativamente **(b)** *Elec & Phys* **n. charged** con carga negativa, cargado(a) negativamente

negativism ['negətɪvɪzəm] *n* negatividad *f*

neglect [nɪ'glekt] **1** *n* **(a)** *(lack of attention, care) (of garden, person, machine)* abandono *m*, descuido *m*; **to be in a state of n.** estar muy abandonado(a) *or* descuidado(a), estar en estado de abandono; **from** *or* **through n.** por negligencia; **many people fall ill through n.** mucha gente cae enferma por dejadez; **the roof fell in through n.** el tejado se hundió debido a su estado de abandono; **to fall into n.** quedar en estado de abandono

(b) *(disregard) (of duty, responsibilities)* incumplimiento *m*; **he was reprimanded for n. of duty** fue reprendido por incumplir *or* desatender sus funciones; **the n. of a few simple precautions** la omisión de unas sencillas medidas de precaución

2 *vt* **(a)** *(not care for) (child, one's health)* descuidar, desatender; *(sb's needs)* desatender; *(friend)* tener abandonado(a) a; *(building, garden)* descuidar, tener abandonado(a); **the house had been neglected for years** la casa llevaba años en estado de abandono; **he neglected his wife all evening** no hizo ningún caso a su mujer en toda la noche, tuvo a su mujer abandonada toda la noche; **to n. oneself** descuidarse, abandonarse; **to n. one's appearance** descuidar el aspecto

(b) *(ignore) (duty, responsibilities)* no cumplir con; *(post)* abandonar; *(one's work)* tener abandonado(a); **they n. elementary safety precautions** hacen caso omiso de *or* no observan las más elementales medidas de seguridad

(c) *Formal (omit, overlook)* **to n. to do sth** dejar de hacer algo; **they neglected to lock the door when they went out** olvidaron cerrar la puerta con llave al salir; **to n. to mention sth** omitir (mencionar) algo, no mencionar algo

neglected [nɪ'glektɪd] *adj* **(a)** *(uncared for) (garden, building)* abandonado(a), descuidado(a); *(appearance)* descuidado(a), dejado(a) **(b)** *(ignored)* olvidado(a); **a n. writer** un escritor poco reconocido; **to feel n.** sentirse abandonado(a) *or* marginado(a)

neglectful [nɪ'glektfʊl] *adj* descuidado(a), negligente; **to be n. of sth/sb** descuidar *or* desatender algo/a alguien; **to be n. of one's duty/responsibilities** no cumplir con el deber/las responsabilidades; **she's very n. of her appearance** es muy dejada, no cuida nada su aspecto

negligée ['neglɪʒeɪ] *n* salto *m* de cama, negligé *m*

negligence ['neglɪdʒəns] *n (inattention)* negligencia *f*, descuido *m*; *(of duties)* negligencia *f*, incumplimiento *m*; *(of rules)* incumplimiento *m*; **a moment of n. could lead to an accident** un momento de descuido *or* distracción podría provocar un accidente; **due to** *or* **through n.** por negligencia

negligent ['neglɪdʒənt] *adj* **(a)** *(neglectful)* negligente; **you have been n. in your duties** has actuado con negligencia en el cumplimiento de tus obligaciones **(b)** *(nonchalant) (attitude, manner)* despreocupado(a)

negligently ['neglɪdʒəntlɪ] *adv (neglectfully)* negligentemente

negligible ['neglɪdʒɪbəl] *adj* insignificante, nimio(a); **his poetry was n., but he was a gifted dramatist** su poesía era más bien desdeñable, pero era un dramaturgo muy dotado

negotiable [nɪ'gəʊʃəbəl] *adj* **(a)** *(to be mutually agreed) (demand, salary)* negociable; **salary n.** *(in job advert)* sueldo negociable; **not n.** *(demand)* no negociable, innegociable

(b) *(passable) (obstacle)* franqueable; **the path is easily n. on foot** el camino se puede recorrer fácilmente a pie; **not n.** *(obstacle)* infranqueable; *(path)* intransitable

(c) *Fin (exchangeable)* negociable ►► ***n. securities*** valores *mpl* negociables

negotiate [nɪ'gəʊʃɪeɪt] **1** *vt* **(a)** *(price, loan, treaty)* negociar (**with** con); **price to be negotiated** precio a convenir **(b)** *(obstacle)* salvar, franquear; **to n. a bend** tomar una curva

2 *vi* negociar (**with** con); **the unions will have to n. with the management for higher pay** los sindicatos deberán negociar con la patronal (para conseguir) un aumento salarial; **to n. for peace** negociar para conseguir la paz

negotiating [nɪ'gəʊʃɪeɪtɪŋ] *adj* negociador(ora); **to get back to the n. table** volver a la mesa de negociaciones

negotiation [nɪgəʊʃɪ'eɪʃən] *n* **(a)** *(discussion)* negociación *f*; **to enter into n.** *or* **negotiations (with sb)** entablar negociaciones (con alguien); **to be in n. with sb** estar en negociaciones *or* negociando con alguien; **under n.** en proceso de negociación; **negotiations** negociaciones; **pay/peace negotiations** negociaciones salariales/de paz **(b)** *(of obstacle)* franqueo *m*

negotiator [nɪ'gəʊʃɪeɪtə(r)] *n* negociador(ora) *m,f*

Negress ['ni:grɪs] *n Old-fashioned* negra *f*

Negro ['ni:grəʊ] *Old-fashioned* **1** *n* (*pl* **Negroes**) negro(a) *m,f*

2 *adj* negro(a) ►► ***N. spiritual*** *(song)* espiritual *m* negro

Negroid ['ni:grɔɪd] *adj* negroide

neigh [neɪ] **1** *n* relincho *m*

2 *vi* relinchar

neighbour, *US* **neighbor** ['neɪbə(r)] **1** *n* **(a)** *(person)* vecino(a) *m,f*; *(country)* (país *m*) vecino *m*; **what will the neighbours say?** ¿qué dirán *or* qué van a decir los vecinos?; **to be a good n.** ser un buen vecino **(b)** *(fellow man)* prójimo *m*, semejante *m*; *Rel* **love thy n. as thyself** ama a tu prójimo como a ti mismo

2 *vt* lindar con, ser colindante con

►**neighbour on** *vt insep (adjoin)* lindar con, ser colindante con; *(of country)* lindar con, limitar con

neighbourhood, *US* **neighborhood** ['neɪbəhʊd] *n* **(a)** *(district)* barrio *m*; *(people)* vecindario *m*, vecindad *f*; **I was in the n.** pasaba por aquí; **the whole n. is talking about it** todo el barrio *or* vecindario habla de ello ►► ***n. watch*** vigilancia *f* vecinal **(b)** *(vicinity)* cercanías *fpl*; **to live in the (immediate) n. of** vivir en las cercanías de; **a figure in the n. of £2,000** una cantidad que ronda las 2.000 libras

neighbouring, *US* **neighboring** ['neɪbərɪŋ] *adj (adjoining)* vecino(a), colindante; *(nearby)* cercano(a), vecino(a)

neighbourliness, *US* **neighborliness** ['neɪbəlɪnɪs] *n* **(good) n.** buena vecindad *f*

neighbourly, *US* **neighborly** ['neɪbəlɪ] *adj (person)* amable (con los vecinos); **to be n.** ser buen(a) vecino(a)

neither ['naɪðə(r), 'ni:ðə(r)] **1** *adv* **n.... nor** ni... ni; **I n. know nor care** ni lo sé ni me importa; **n. (the) one nor the other** ni uno ni otro; **it's n. one thing nor the other** no es ni una cosa ni (la) otra; **that's n. here nor there** eso no viene al caso; **n. do I** yo tampoco; *Fam* **me n.** yo tampoco; **I don't like it – n. do I** *or Fam* **me n.** no me gusta – a mí tampoco

2 *conj* **if you don't go, n. shall I** si tú no vas, yo tampoco; **the money wasn't available and n. were the facilities** no había ni dinero ni instalaciones

3 *adj* ninguno(a); **n. driver was injured** ninguno de los conductores resultó herido; **n. one of them has accepted** ninguno de ellos ha aceptado

4 *pron* ninguno(a); **n. of us/them** ninguno de nosotros/ellos; **which do you want? – n. (of them)** ¿cuál quieres? – ninguno; **n. of my brothers can come** no puede venir ninguno de mis hermanos

nelly ['nelɪ] *n Br Fam* **not on your n.!** ¡ni de broma!, *Esp* ¡ni hablar del peluquín!

nematode ['nemətəʊd] *n Zool* nematodo *m*

nem con ['nem'kɒn] *adv* por unanimidad

nemesis ['neməsɪs] *n Literary* verdugo *m*; **she saw the British press as her n.** veía a la prensa británica como su bestia negra; **he finally met his n.** finalmente se llevó su merecido

neo- ['ni:əʊ] *prefix* neo-

neocapitalism [ni:əʊ'kæpɪtəlɪzəm] *n* neocapitalismo *m*

neocapitalist [ni:əʊ'kæpɪtəlɪst] **1** *n* neocapitalista *mf*

2 *adj* neocapitalista

neoclassical [ni:əʊ'klæsɪkəl] *adj* neoclásico(a)

neoclassicism [ni:əʊ'klæsɪsɪzəm] *n* neoclasicismo *m*

neocolonial ['ni:əʊkə'ləʊnɪəl] *adj* neocolonial

neocolonialism ['ni:əʊkə'ləʊnɪəlɪzəm] *n* neocolonialismo *m*

neocolonialist ['ni:əʊkə'ləʊnɪəlɪst] **1** *adj* neocolonialista

2 *n* neocolonialista *mf*

neocortex ['ni:əʊ'kɔ:teks] *n Anat* neocórtex *m*

neodymium [ni:əʊ'dɪmɪəm] *n Chem* neodimio *m*

neofascism ['ni:əʊ'fæʃɪzəm] *n* neofascismo *m*

neofascist [nɪəʊ'fæʃɪst] **1** *n* neofascista *mf*

2 *adj* neofascista

neoliberalism ['ni:əʊ'lɪbərəlɪzəm] *n Econ* neoliberalismo *m*

Neolithic [ni:əʊ'lɪθɪk] **1** *adj* neolítico(a)

2 *n* **the N. (period)** el Neolítico

neologism [nɪ'ɒlədʒɪzəm] *n* neologismo *m*

neon ['ni:ɒn] *n Chem* neón *m* ►► ***n. light*** luz *f* de neón; ***n. sign*** letrero *m or* rótulo *m* de neón

neonatal ['ni:əʊ'neɪtəl] *adj* neonatal

neonate ['ni:əʊneɪt] *n Biol & Med* neonato *m*

neo-Nazi ['ni:əʊ'nɑ:tsɪ] **1** *n* neonazi *mf*

2 *adj* neonazi

neophyte ['nɪəʊfaɪt] *n Rel & Fig* neófito(a) *m,f*

neo-Platonic ['ni:əʊplə'tɒnɪk] *adj* neoplatónico(a)

Neoplatonism ['ni:əʊ'pleɪtənɪzəm] *n* neoplatonismo *m*

neoprene ['ni:əʊpri:n] *n* neopreno *m*

neorealism ['ni:əʊ'rɪəlɪzəm] *n Cin* neorrealismo *m*

neoteny [ni:'ɒtənɪ] *n Biol* neotenia *f*

Neozoic [ni:əʊ'zəʊɪk] **1** *n* **the N. (period)** el neozoico

2 *adj* neozoico(a)

Nepal [nɪ'pɔ:l] *n* Nepal

Nepalese [nepə'li:z], **Nepali** [ne'pɔ:lɪ] **1** *n* **(a)** *(person)* nepalés(esa) *m,f*, nepalí *mf* **(b)** *(language)* nepalés *m*, nepalí *m*

2 *adj* nepalés(esa), nepalí

nephew ['nefju:] *n* sobrino *m*

nephritic [nɪ'frɪtɪk] *adj Med* nefrítico(a)

nephritis [nɪ'fraɪtɪs] *n Med* nefritis *f inv*

nephrologist [nɪ'frɒlədʒɪst] *n Med* nefrólogo(a) *m,f*

nephrology [nɪ'frɒlədʒɪ] *n Med* nefrología *f*

nephron ['nefrɒn] *n Anat* nefrón *m*

ne plus ultra [neɪplʌs'ʌltrə] *n* no va más *m*

nepotism ['nepətɪzəm] *n* nepotismo *m*

Neptune ['neptju:n] *n (planet, god)* Neptuno *m*

neptunegrass ['neptju:ngrɑ:s] *n* posidonia *f*

neptunium [nep'tju:nɪəm] *n Chem* neptunio *m*

nerd [nɜ:d] *n Fam (unfashionable)* petardo(a) *m,f*, *RP* nerd *mf*; **a computer n.** un(a) tipo(a) obsesionado(a) con la informática

nerdy ['nɜ:dɪ] *adj Fam* de petardo(a) *or RP* nerd; **a n. type** un(a) petardo(a), *RP* un(a) nerd

Nero ['nɪərəʊ] *pr n* Nerón

nerve [nɜ:v] **1** *n* **(a)** *Anat* nervio *m* ►► ***n. cell*** neurona *f*; *Fig* ***n. centre*** *(of organization)* centro *m* neurálgico; ***n. ending*** terminación *f* nerviosa; ***n. fibre*** fibra *f* nerviosa; ***n. gas*** gas *m* nervioso; ***n. impulse*** impulso *m* nervioso; ***n. specialist*** neurólogo(a) *m,f*

(b) *Fam* **nerves** *(anxiety)* nervios *mpl*; **an attack of nerves** un ataque de nervios; **she gets on my nerves!** ¡me saca de quicio!; **her nerves were in a terrible state** tenía los nervios destrozados; **to live on one's nerves** ser un manojo de nervios, vivir en un estado de tensión constante

(c) *(courage)* coraje *m*, valor *m*; *(self-control)* sangre *f* fría; **to have nerves of steel** tener nervios de acero; **he didn't have the n. to say no** no tuvo el coraje *or* valor de decir que no; **it takes (some) n. to say no to him** hace falta valor para decirle que no; **his n. failed him** le faltó coraje/sangre fría; **to keep/lose one's n.** mantener/perder la calma; **to get up enough** *or* **the n. to do sth** armarse de valor para hacer algo, sacar arrestos para hacer algo

(d) *Fam (cheek)* cara *f* (dura), frescura *f*; **he had the n. to refuse** tuvo la cara de negarse; **what a n.!** ¡qué cara más dura!, ¡qué caradura!; **you've got a n.!** ¡qué cara tienes!; **you've got a n. coming here!** ¡hace falta tener cara *or* hay que tener cara para presentarse aquí!

(e) *(in leaf)* nervio *m*

2 *vt* **to n. oneself to do sth** templar los nervios para hacer algo; **to n. sb to do sth** templar los nervios a alguien para que haga algo

nerveless ['nɜːvlɪs] *adj* (a) *(lacking strength)* débil, flojo(a) (b) *(fearless)* sereno(a), tranquilo(a)

nerve-(w)racking ['nɜːvrækɪŋ] *adj* angustioso(a); **after a n. wait the result was announced** tras una tensa espera se anunció el resultado

nervous ['nɜːvəs] *adj* (a) *(apprehensive)* nervioso(a), inquieto(a); **to be n.** *(by nature)* ser nervioso(a); *(temporarily)* estar nervioso(a); **he is n. of Alsatians** le dan miedo los pastores alemanes; **he is n. of failure** tiene miedo al fracaso, lo asusta el fracaso; **he was n. about (doing) it** lo ponía nervioso (hacerlo); **the bank was n. about granting the loan** el banco era reacio *or* remiso a conceder el crédito; **you're making me n.** me estás poniendo nervioso; **not for those of a n. disposition** no apto para los que no están bien de los nervios; *Fam* **he's a n. wreck** es un manojo de nervios, está (mal) de los nervios

(b) *(of the nerve system)* ***n. breakdown*** crisis *f inv* nerviosa; **to have a n. breakdown** sufrir una crisis nerviosa; ***n. complaint*** molestia *f* nerviosa; ***n. disorder*** dolencia *f* nerviosa; ***n. energy*** nervio *m*; ***n. exhaustion*** agotamiento *m* nervioso; ***n. system*** sistema *m* nervioso; ***n. tension*** tensión *f* nerviosa

nervously ['nɜːvəslɪ] *adv* nerviosamente

nervousness ['nɜːvəsnɪs] *n (of speaker, performer)* nerviosismo *m*; **you could sense her n.** su nerviosismo era palpable

nervy ['nɜːvɪ] *adj Fam* (a) *(tense)* nervioso(a); **to be n.** estar nervioso(a) (b) *US (cheeky)* caradura, fresco(a) (c) *US (brave)* con agallas, valiente

nest [nest] 1 *n* (a) *(of bird, insects, snakes)* nido *m*; *(of ants)* hormiguero *m*; *(of wasps)* avispero *m*; *Fig* **to fly** *or* **leave the n.** dejar el nido, irse de casa ▸▸ *Fam* ***n. egg*** ahorrillos *mpl*; **I've got a nice little n. egg put by for when I retire** he juntado unos pocos ahorrillos para cuando me retire

(b) *Fig (of brigands)* nido *m*; *(for machine guns)* nido *m* (c) *(set)* **n. of tables** mesas nido

2 *vt Comptr & Ling* insertar

3 *vi* (a) *(bird)* anidar (b) *(fit together)* encajar(se)

nesting ['nestɪŋ] *n* **to go n.** ir a coger nidos ▸▸ ***n. box*** caja *f* nido; ***n. site*** lugar *m* de anidación

nestle ['nesəl] 1 *vt (baby)* **she nestled the baby against her chest** abrazó al bebé *or Andes* a la guagua *or RP* al nene contra su pecho

2 *vi* (a) *(person) (in comfortable place)* acomodarse; *(on a seat, chair)* arrellanarse; *(huddling, curled up)* acurrucarse; *(against sb)* recostarse, acurrucarse; **to n. up to sb** recostarse en alguien, acurrucarse contra alguien; **to n. down in bed** acurrucarse en la cama

(b) *(land, house)* estar enclavado(a); **a village nestling in a valley** una aldea enclavada al abrigo de un valle; **the ball was nestling in the branches of a tree** la pelota estaba atrapada entre las ramas

nestling ['neslɪŋ] *n (young bird)* polluelo *m*

Net [net] *n Fam Comptr (Internet)* **the N.** la Red ▸▸ ***N. user*** internauta *mf*, cibernauta *mf*

net[1] [net] 1 *n* (a) *(material)* red *f* ▸▸ ***n. curtain*** visillo *m*; ***n. stockings*** medias *fpl* de red *or* de malla

(b) *(for fishing)* red *f*; **(butterfly) n.** (red *f*) cazamariposas *m inv*

(c) *(in tennis, badminton)* **to come to the n.** subir a la red; **to put the ball in the (back of the) n.** *(in soccer)* introducir *or* alojar el balón en (el fondo de) la red; **to practise in the nets** *(in cricket)* practicar en el campo de entrenamiento ▸▸ ***n. cord*** cuerda *f* que sujeta la red; ***n. cord judge*** juez *mf* de red; ***n. game*** *or* ***play*** juego *m* cerca de la red

(d) *(for hair)* redecilla *f*

(e) *(network)* red *f*; **radio n.** cadena *or* red de emisoras

(f) *Fig (trap)* trampa *f*; **to fall into the n.** caer en la trampa *or* las redes; **to slip through the n.** *(mistake)* colarse; *(criminal)* escaparse

2 *vt* (*pt & pp* **netted**) (a) *(capture) (animals, criminals)* capturar, apresar; *(fish)* pescar, capturar; *(butterflies)* cazar, capturar; *Fig (drugs)* incautarse de; *(donations)* recoger; *(reward)* embolsarse (b) *Sport (goal)* marcar; **he netted his service** *(in tennis)* envió *or* lanzó su servicio contra la red (c) *(fruit tree)* cubrir con una red

3 *vi (score goal)* marcar

net[2] 1 *adj (income, price, profit, interest, weight)* neto(a); **to be a n. exporter/importer** ser un exportador/importador neto; **the n. result is...** el resultado neto es...; **n. of tax** después de impuestos ▸▸ *Fin* ***n. asset value*** valor *m* activo neto; *Br Formerly* ***N. Book Agreement*** = acuerdo por el que la editorial fijaba el precio mínimo de los libros; *Fin* ***n. book value*** valor *m* neto en libros; *Fin* ***n. loss*** pérdidas *fpl* netas; *Fin* ***n. present value*** valor *m* actual neto; *Fin* ***n. realizable value*** valor *m* neto de realización

2 *vt* (*pt & pp* **netted**) *(earn) (of person, company)* tener unos ingresos netos de; *(of sale)* suponer un ingreso neto de; **to n. £2,000** ganar 2.000 libras netas *or* limpias

netball ['netbɔːl] *n* nétbol *m*, = deporte femenino parecido al baloncesto

nethead ['nethed] *n Comptr Fam* **to be a n.** estar pirado(a) por Internet

nether ['neðə(r)] *adj Literary* bajo(a) ▸▸ ***n. regions*** *(of building, river)* parte *f* baja; *Hum (of person)* partes *fpl* pudendas; ***the n. world*** los infiernos

Netherlands ['neðələndz] *npl* **the N.** los Países Bajos

nethermost ['neðəməʊst] *adj Literary* inferior; **the n. depths of hell** las simas *or* profundidades del infierno

netiquette ['netɪket] *n Comptr* netiqueta *f*

netizen ['netɪzən] *n Comptr* ciudadano(a) *m,f* de la Red, ciuredano(a) *m,f*

netspeak ['netspiːk] *n Comptr* jerga *f* de Internet

netsuke ['netsuːkeɪ] *n* = figurilla tallada japonesa que se lleva como adorno colgada de la cadera

Nettie ['netɪ] *n Comptr Fam* ciudadano(a) *m,f* de la Red, ciuredano(a) *m,f*

netting ['netɪŋ] *n* red *f*, malla *f*; **put some n. over the window to stop flies getting in** pon una red *or* una malla en la ventana para que no pasen las moscas; **he bought some n. for curtains** compró tela de malla para unas cortinas; **the shot hit the n.** el disparo dio en la red

nettle ['netəl] 1 *n (plant)* ortiga *f*

2 *vt (irritate)* irritar, fastidiar

nettled ['netəld] *adj* irritado(a), molesto(a); **don't get n.** no te irrites

nettle-rash ['netəlræʃ] *n* urticaria *f*

network ['netwɜːk] 1 *n* (a) *(system)* red *f*; **road/rail/transport n.** red viaria/ferroviaria/de transportes; **distribution/sales n.** red de distribución/ventas (b) *TV* cadena *f* (c) *Comptr* red *f* ▸▸ ***n. administrator*** administrador(ora) *m,f* de red; ***n. card*** tarjeta *f* de red; ***n. computer*** *Esp* ordenador *m or Am* computadora *f* de red; ***n. traffic*** tráfico *m* en la red

2 *vt* (a) *TV (programme)* emitir en cadena (b) *Comptr (computers)* conectar en red

3 *vi (establish contacts)* establecer contactos

networking ['netwɜːkɪŋ] *n* (a) *Com* establecimiento *m* de contactos profesionales (b) *Comptr* conexión *f* en red; **to have n. capabilities** *(terminal)* poderse conectar a una red

neural ['njʊərəl] *adj Anat* neural ▸▸ *Comptr* ***n. network*** red *f* neuronal

neuralgia [njʊ'rældʒə] *n Med* neuralgia *f*

neuralgic [njʊ'rældʒɪk] *adj Med* neurálgico(a)

neurasthenia [njʊərəs'θiːnɪə] *n Med Old-fashioned* neurastenia *f*

neuritis [njʊ'raɪtɪs] *n Med* neuritis *f inv*

neuroanatomy ['njʊərəʊə'nætəmɪ] *n* neuroanatomía *f*

neurobiology ['njʊərəʊbaɪ'ɒlədʒɪ] *n* neurobiología *f*

neurolinguistic ['njʊərəʊlɪŋ'gwɪstɪk] *adj* neurolingüístico(a) ▸▸ ***n. programming*** programación *f* neurolingüística

neurolinguistics ['njʊərəʊlɪŋ'gwɪstɪks] *n* neurolingüística *f*

neurological [njʊərə'lɒdʒɪkəl] *adj* neurológico(a)

neurologist [njʊə'rɒlədʒɪst] *n* neurólogo(a) *m,f*

neurology [njʊə'rɒlədʒɪ] *n* neurología *f*

neuron ['njʊərɒn], **neurone** ['njʊərəʊn] *n Anat* neurona *f*

neuropath ['njʊərəpæθ] *n Med* neurópata *mf*

neuropathy [njʊə'rɒpəθɪ] *n Med* neuropatía *f*

neuropsychiatrist ['njʊərəʊsaɪ'kaɪətrɪst] *n* neuropsiquiatra *mf*

neuropsychiatry ['njʊərəʊsaɪ'kaɪətrɪ] *n* neuropsiquiatría *f*

neuropsychology ['njʊərəʊsaɪ'kɒlədʒɪ] *n* neuropsicología *f*

neuroscience [njʊərəʊ'saɪəns] *n* neurociencia *f*

neurosis [njʊ'rəʊsɪs] (*pl* **neuroses** [njʊ'rəʊsi:z]) *n* neurosis *f inv*

neurosurgeon ['njʊərəʊ'sɜ:dʒən] *n* neurocirujano(a) *m,f*

neurosurgery ['njʊərəʊ'sɜ:dʒərɪ] *n* neurocirugía *f*

neurotic [njʊ'rɒtɪk] **1** *n* **(a)** *Psy* neurótico(a) *m,f* **(b)** *(over-anxious person)* neurótico(a) *m,f*, paranoico(a) *m,f*
2 *adj* **(a)** *Psy* neurótico(a) **(b)** *(over-anxious)* neurótico(a), paranoico(a); **to be/get n. about sth** estar/ponerse neurótico(a) *or* paranoico(a) por algo

neurotically [njʊ'rɒtɪklɪ] *adv* de modo obsesivo; **to be n. obessed with sth/sb** estar paranoico con algo/alguien

neurotoxin [njʊərəʊ'tɒksɪn] *n* neurotoxina *f*

neurotransmitter ['njʊərəʊtrænz'mɪtə(r)] *n Physiol* neurotransmisor *m*

neuter ['nju:tə(r)] **1** *n Gram* (género *m*) neutro *m*; **in the n.** en la forma neutra, en (género) neutro
2 *adj* **(a)** *Gram* neutro(a) **(b)** *(animal)* castrado(a); *(insect, plant)* asexuado(a)
3 *vt (animal)* castrar

neutral ['nju:trəl] **1** *n* **(a)** *(country)* nación *f* neutral; **to be a n.** ser neutral **(b)** *Aut* **in n.** en punto muerto
2 *adj* **(a)** *Pol* neutral; **to remain n.** permanecer *or* mantenerse neutral **(b)** *Chem* neutro(a) **(c)** *Ling (vowel)* neutro(a) **(d)** *(uncommitted)* neutro(a); **I try to remain n. in these arguments** en estas discusiones trato de mantenerme neutral *or* al margen **(e)** *(colour)* neutro(a); **n. shoe polish** crema (de calzado) incolora

neutralism ['nju:trəlɪzəm] *n* neutralismo *m*

neutralist ['nju:trəlɪst] **1** *n* neutralista *mf*
2 *adj* neutralista

neutrality [nju:'trælɪtɪ] *n* neutralidad *f*

neutralization ['nju:trəlaɪ'zeɪʃən] *n* neutralización *f*

neutralize ['nju:trəlaɪz] *vt* **(a)** *Chem* neutralizar **(b)** *(effect, force)* neutralizar

neutrally ['nju:trəlɪ] *adv* **(a)** *(not taking sides)* de manera neutral **(b)** *(without emotion)* en tono neutro

neutrino [njʊ'tri:nəʊ] (*pl* **neutrinos**) *n Phys* neutrino *m*

neutron ['nju:trɒn] *n Phys* neutrón *m* ►► ***n. bomb*** bomba *f* de neutrones; ***n. star*** estrella *f* de neutrones

Nevada [nə'vɑ:də] *n* Nevada

NEVER ['nevə(r)] *adv* **(a)** *(at no time)* nunca; **I've n. been there** no he estado nunca (allí); **I've n. met him** no lo conozco de *or Méx, RP* para nada; **I'll n. trust them again** no confiaré en ellos nunca más; **I've n. been so angry** jamás había estado tan *esp Esp* enfadado *or esp Am* enojado; **n. in all my life had I seen such a thing** jamás en toda mi vida había visto algo así; **n. let them see that you're nervous** no les dejes saber en ningún momento que estás nervioso, *RP* nunca les demuestres que estás nervioso; *Fam* **do you know Joan Tomkins? – n. heard of her** ¿conoces a Joan Tomkins? – de nada *or Méx, RP* para nada; **the leader is under pressure as n. before** el líder está sufriendo más presiones que nunca; **n. again!** ¡nunca más!; *Formal* **n. before had I been so happy** nunca en mi vida había sido tan feliz; *Fam* **n. ever** nunca jamás; IDIOM **n. say die!** ¡ánimo!; **n. say n.** nunca digas nunca
(b) *(not)* **I n. expected this** jamás hubiera esperado esto; **I n. thought she'd carry out her threat** no podía imaginar que cumpliría su amenaza, jamás me hubiera imaginado que iba a cumplir su amenaza; **she n. said a word** no dijo ni una palabra; **I n. for a moment suspected them** no sospeché de ellos ni por un instante; *Fam* **he's n. eighteen!** ¡no puede tener dieciocho!; *Fam* **I asked her out – n.!** *or* **you n. did!** *Esp* le pedí salir *or Am* la invité a salir – ¡no fastidies *or Méx* híjole *or RP* no jodas!; **well I n.!** ¡no me digas!; **that will n. do!** ¡eso es intolerable!; **he n. even** *or* **so much as congratulated me** ni siquiera me felicitó; **n. fear** no te preocupes; **n. once did they suggest I was doing anything wrong** en ningún momento se quejaron de que estuviera haciéndolo mal

---

never-ending ['nevər'endɪŋ] *adj* interminable; **my problems seem to be n.** mis problemas no parecen tener fin; **a n. supply of funny stories** una fuente inagotable de historias divertidas; **housework is n.** las tareas de la casa no se acaban nunca

never-failing ['nevə'feɪlɪŋ] *adj (infallible)* inagotable

nevermore [nevə'mɔ:(r)] *adv Literary* nunca más

never-never [nevə'nevə(r)] *n* **(a)** *Br Fam* **to buy sth on the n.** comprar algo a plazos **(b)** ***N. land*** el País de Nunca Jamás; **you're living in n. land if you believe that...** vives en otro mundo *or* estás en la inopia, si crees que...

nevertheless [nevəðə'les], **nonetheless** [nʌnðə'les] *adv (however)* no obstante, sin embargo; *(despite everything)* de todas maneras, a pesar de todo; **a small, but n. significant increase** un aumento pequeño, pero sin embargo *or* no obstante significativo; **we shall continue n. and hope things get better** de todas maneras *or* a pesar de todo continuaremos y esperamos que las cosas mejoren; **she wasn't invited but she insisted on coming with us n.** no estaba invitada, pero a pesar de ello insistió en acompañarnos

---

NEW [nju:] **1** *adj* **(a)** *(not old, recent)* nuevo(a); **we need a n. dishwasher** nos hace falta otro lavavajillas *or* un lavavajillas nuevo; **to buy sth n.** comprar algo nuevo; **it costs $40 n.** nuevo, cuesta 40 dólares; **start on a n. sheet of paper** empieza en un papel limpio; **as good as n. (again)** *(clothing, carpet, appliance)* como nuevo(a); **I feel like a n. person since the operation** me siento como nuevo desde la operación; **have you seen the n. baby?** ¿ha visto al recién nacido?; **some call them the n. Beatles** algunos les llaman los nuevos Beatles; **I'm n. here** soy nuevo aquí; *Fam Fig* **the n. kid on the block** el nuevo; *Fam* **what's n.?** *(greeting)* ¿qué tal?, *CAm, Col, Méx, Ven* ¡qué hubo!; **what's n. in the world of fashion?** ¿cuáles son las novedades en el mundo de la moda?; *Ironic* **so what's n.?** ¿qué tiene de nuevo?; **that's nothing n.!** ¡no es ninguna novedad!; **this author is n. to me** no conocía a este autor; **she's n. to this work** es la primera vez que trabaja en esto; **everything's still very n. to me here** todo es muy nuevo todavía para mí; **to be n. to a town** ser nuevo(a) en *or* acabar de mudarse a una ciudad; IDIOM **to be like a n. pin** ser como los chorros del oro, *Urug* estar como un jaspe ►► ***n. arrival*** *(person)* recién llegado(a) *m,f*; *Fig* ***n. blood*** savia *f* nueva; ***n. boy*** *Sch* novato *m*; **he's the n. boy in the cabinet** es el nuevo en el *or* del gabinete; *Fig* ***n. face*** cara *f* nueva; ***n. girl*** *Sch* novata *f*; **she's the n. girl in the office** es la nueva en la *or* de la oficina; ***n. look*** nueva imagen *f*; ***n. man*** hombre *m* moderno *(que ayuda en casa, etc.)*; ***n. maths*** matemáticas *fpl* modernas; ***the n. media*** los nuevos medios; ***n. moon*** luna *f* nueva; *Br Old-fashioned* ***n. penny*** = nombre que se le dio al penique después de la conversión al sistema decimal; ***n. potatoes*** *Esp* patatas *fpl or Am* papas *fpl* tempranas *or* nuevas, *Andes* chauchas *fpl*; ***the n. rich*** los nuevos ricos; ***n. technology*** nueva tecnología *f*; ***n. town*** = ciudad satélite de nueva planta creada para descongestionar un núcleo urbano; *Med* ***n. variant CJD*** nueva variante *f* de ECJ
(b) *(in proper names)* ***N. Age*** New Age *f*, = movimiento que gira en torno a las ciencias ocultas, medicinas alternativas, religiones orientales, etc.; ***N. Age music*** música *f* New Age; ***N. Age traveller*** = persona que vive en una tienda o caravana sin lugar fijo de residencia y que lleva un estilo de vida contrario al de la sociedad convencional; ***N. Amsterdam*** Nueva Amsterdam; ***N. Brunswick*** New Brunswick; ***N. Caledonia*** Nueva Caledonia; ***N. Delhi*** Nueva Delhi; ***N. England*** Nueva Inglaterra; ***N. Guinea*** Nueva Guinea; ***N. Hampshire*** New Hampshire; *Formerly* ***the N. Hebrides*** las Nuevas Hébridas; ***N. Jersey*** Nueva Jersey; *Br Pol* ***N. Labour*** *(ideology)* el Nuevo Laborismo; *(party)* el Nuevo Partido Laborista; ***N. Mexico*** Nuevo México; ***N. Orleans*** Nueva Orleans; ***N. South Wales*** Nueva Gales del Sur; ***the N. Testament*** el Nuevo Testamento; ***the N. Wave*** *(in pop music, cinema)* la Nueva Ola; ***the N. World*** el Nuevo Mundo; ***the n. world order*** el nuevo orden mundial; ***N. Year*** año *m* nuevo; ***N. Year's Day*** día *m* de año nuevo; ***N. Year's Eve*** Nochevieja *f*, fin *m* de año; ***N. Year's resolutions*** = buenos propósitos para el año nuevo, resoluciones de año nuevo; ***N. York*** Nueva York; ***N. Yorker*** neoyorquino(a) *m,f*; ***N. Zealand*** Nueva Zelanda; ***N. Zealander*** neocelandés(esa) *m,f*, neozelandés(esa) *m,f*
2 *n* **the n.** lo nuevo

---

newbie ['nju:bɪ] *n Comptr Fam Pej* novato(a) *m,f*

newborn ['nju:bɔ:n] *adj* recién nacido(a); **n. baby** recién nacido

newcomer ['nju:kʌmə(r)] *n* **(a)** *(new arrival)* recién llegado(a) *m,f* (**to** a); **she's a n. to the town** acaba de llegar a la ciudad, es nueva en la ciudad **(b)** *(beginner)* principiante *mf* (**to** en); **a good book for newcomers to computing** un buen libro para los que se inician en la informática; **I'm a n. to all this** para mí todo esto es nuevo

newel ['nju:əl] *n (of spiral staircase)* alma *f*, espigón *m*; **n. (post)** *(of straight staircase)* pilar *m* de arranque *(de pasamanos)*

newfangled ['nju:fæŋgəld] *adj Pej* moderno(a); **I don't hold with those n. ideas** yo no comulgo con esas moderneces

new-found ['nju:faʊnd] *adj (friend)* nuevo(a); *(confidence, faith, freedom)* recién descubierto(a)

Newfoundland ['nju:fəndlænd] *n* (**a**) *(island)* Terranova (**b**) *(dog)* terranova *m*

newish ['nju:ɪʃ] *adj* tirando a nuevo(a), más bien nuevo(a)

new-laid ['nju:'leɪd] *adj* recién puesto(a)

new-look ['nju:'lʊk] *adj* nuevo(a), renovado(a)

newly ['nju:lɪ] *adv* recién; **n. painted/dug** recién pintado(a)/cavado(a); **a n. discovered galaxy** una galaxia descubierta recientemente; **their n. won independence** su recién obtenida independencia, la independencia que acaban de obtener ►► *Econ* ***n. industrialized country*** país *m* de reciente industrialización

newly-weds ['nju:lɪwedz] *npl* recién casados *mpl*

new-mown ['nju:'məʊn] *adj (grass, lawn)* recién cortado(a); *(hay)* recién segado(a)

newness ['nju:nɪs] *n* carácter *m* novedoso; **because of her n. to the job** por ser nueva en el trabajo

news [nju:z] *n* (**a**) *(information)* noticias *fpl*; **a piece of n.** una noticia; **good/bad n.** buenas/malas noticias; **that's good/bad n.** es una buena/mala noticia; **is there any more n. about the explosion?** ¿se sabe algo nuevo *or* hay alguna otra noticia sobre la explosión?; **I've just heard the n. that she has died** me acabo de enterar de que ha muerto; **to have n. of sb** tener noticia(s) de alguien, saber de alguien; **have you had** *or* **heard any n. of her?** ¿has sabido algo de ella?, ¿has tenido noticias de ella?; **what's your n.?** ¿qué hay de nuevo?, ¿qué novedades tienes?; **have I got n. for you!** ¡voy a darte una sorpresa!, ¡espera a oír esto!

(**b**) *(on TV)* telediario *m*, informativo *m*, *Am* noticiero *m*, *Andes, RP* noticioso *m*; *(on radio)* noticiario *m*, informativo *m*, *Am* noticiero *m*, *Andes, RP* noticioso *m*; **I heard it on the n.** lo escuché en las noticias; **the sports/financial n.** la información deportiva/económica, las noticias deportivas/de economía; **the nine o'clock n.** *(on TV, radio)* las noticias *or* el informativo de las nueve; **to be in the n.** ser noticia; **he's always in the n.** siempre es noticia, siempre sale en las noticias; **a city that is in the n. a lot these days** una ciudad que últimamente está muy de actualidad *or* sale mucho en las noticias ►► ***n. agency*** agencia *f* de noticias; ***n. blackout*** silencio *m* informativo, bloqueo *m* informativo; **to impose a n. blackout on sth** prohibir la cobertura informativa en torno a algo, imponer un bloqueo informativo en torno a algo; *US* ***n. in brief*** avance *m* informativo; ***n. bulletin*** boletín *m* de noticias; ***n. channel*** canal *m* de noticias, canal *m* informativo; ***n. conference*** rueda *f* de prensa; ***n. coverage*** cobertura *f* informativa; *Rad & TV* ***n. desk*** *(programme)* programa *m* de noticias; ***n. editor*** redactor(ora) *m,f* de informativos; ***n. gathering*** recopilación *f* de información; ***n. headlines*** resumen *m* *or* sumario *m* de las principales noticias, titulares *mpl*, *Méx, RP* encabezados *mpl*; ***n. item*** noticia *f*; ***n. magazine*** *(publication)* revista *f* de actualidad; *(on TV or radio)* programa *m* de actualidad; ***n. programme*** programa *m* de noticias; ***n. report*** crónica *f* (informativa), artículo *m*; ***n. service*** servicios *mpl* informativos; ***n. story*** noticia *f*; ***n. value*** interés *m* periodístico; ***n. vendor*** vendedor(ora) *m,f* de periódicos *or* diarios

(**c**) *Comptr* news *fpl*, grupos *mpl* de noticias ►► ***n. server*** servidor *m* de grupos de noticias

(**d**) IDIOMS *Fam* **he's bad n.** es un tipo de cuidado, no te traerá más que problemas; *Fam* **that's n. to me!** ¡(pues) ahora me entero!; PROV **no n. is good n.** si no hay noticias, es que todo va bien; PROV **bad n. travels fast** las malas noticias vuelan

newsagent ['nju:zeɪdʒənt] *n Br* vendedor(ora) *m,f* de periódicos; **n.'s (shop)** = tienda que vende prensa así como tabaco, chucherías e incluso artículos de papelería

newsboy ['nju:zbɔɪ] *n (in street)* vendedor *m* de periódicos callejero, *Andes, RP* canillita *mf*, *Col, Méx* voceador *m*; *(delivery boy)* repartidor *m* de periódicos, *Andes, RP* canillita *m*

newscast ['nju:zkɑ:st] *n US* noticias *fpl*

newscaster ['nju:zkɑ:stə(r)] *n US* locutor(ora) *m,f or* presentador(ora) *m,f* de informativos

newsdealer ['nju:zdi:lə(r)] *n US* vendedor(ora) *m,f* de periódicos

newsflash ['nju:zflæʃ] *n* noticia *f* de última hora *or* de alcance, flash *m* informativo

newsgroup ['nju:zgru:p] *n Comptr* grupo *m* de noticias

newshawk ['nju:zhɔ:k], **newshound** ['nju:zhaʊnd] *n Fam* gacetillero(a) *m,f*, reportero(a) *m,f*

newsletter ['nju:zletə(r)] *n* boletín *m* informativo

newsman ['nju:zmən] *n (reporter)* periodista *m*

newspaper ['nju:zpeɪpə(r)] *n* (**a**) *(publication)* periódico *m*; *(daily)* periódico *m*, diario *m*; **an evening n.** un (periódico *or* diario) vespertino ►► ***n. advertisement*** anuncio *m* de periódico; ***n. clipping*** *or* ***cutting*** recorte *m* de periódico; *US* ***n. of record*** = periódico considerado como la fuente de información más fiable de un país o ciudad; ***n. report*** artículo *m* periodístico; ***n. stand*** quiosco *m* (de periódicos); *(smaller)* puesto *m* de periódicos

(**b**) *(paper)* papel *m* de periódico; **wrapped in n.** envuelto(a) en papel de periódico

newspaperman ['nju:zpeɪpəmæn] *n* (**a**) *(reporter)* periodista *m* (**b**) *(proprietor)* propietario *m* de un periódico

newspaperwoman ['nju:zpeɪpəwʊmən] *n* (**a**) *(reporter)* periodista *f* (**b**) *(proprietor)* propietaria *f* de un periódico

newspeak ['nju:spi:k] *n* retórica *f* engañosa

newsprint ['nju:zprɪnt] *n* papel *m* de periódico; **I got my hands covered in n.** *(ink)* me manché las manos de tinta de periódico

newsreader ['nju:zri:də(r)] *n* (**a**) *Rad & TV* locutor(ora) *m,f or* presentador(ora) *m,f* de informativos (**b**) *Comptr* lector *m* de noticias

newsreel ['nju:zri:l] *n* noticiario *m* cinematográfico, ≃ nodo *m*

newsroom ['nju:zru:m] *n* (sala *f* de) redacción *f*

newssheet ['nju:zʃi:t] *n* boletín *m* informativo

newsvendor ['nju:zvendə(r)] *n (in street)* vendedor(ora) *m,f* de periódicos callejero(a)

newswoman ['nju:zwʊmən] *n (reporter)* periodista *f*

newsworthy ['nju:zwɜ:ðɪ] *adj* de interés periodístico; **political scandal is always n.** el escándalo político siempre es noticia

newsy ['nju:zɪ] *adj Fam* lleno(a) de noticias

newt [nju:t] *n* tritón *m*

newton ['nju:tən] *n Phys* newton *m*

Newtonian [nju:'təʊnɪən] *adj* newtoniano(a), de Newton

NEXT [nekst] **1** *adj* (**a**) *(in space)* siguiente; *(room, house, table)* de al lado; **n. door** (en la casa de) al lado; **I work n. door to her** trabajo en la oficina de al lado de la suya; *Fig* **the boy/girl n. door** un chico/una chica normal y corriente; *Br Fam* **n. door have got a new dog** los de al lado tienen un perro nuevo

(**b**) *(in time, order)* siguiente, próximo(a); **n. week** la próxima semana, la semana que viene; **n. month** el próximo mes, el mes que viene; **over the n. few months** durante los próximos meses; **n. Friday, Friday n.** el próximo viernes, el viernes que viene; **the n. chapter/page** el capítulo/la página siguiente; **the first one was red, the n. one was blue** el primero era rojo, el siguiente azul; **the n. one goes at five o'clock** el próximo *or* siguiente sale a las cinco; **(the) n. time I see him** la próxima vez que lo vea; **n. time, be more careful** la próxima vez ten más cuidado; **at the n. available opportunity** en la próxima oportunidad que se presente; **it's the n. station** es la próxima estación; **the n. turning on the right** el primer desvío a la derecha; **your name is n. on the list** tu nombre es el siguiente de la lista; **I enjoy a good laugh as much as the n. person, but...** me encanta reírme como al que más, pero...; **the n. size up/down** la siguiente talla más grande/más pequeña, *RP* el talle siguiente/anterior; **the n. world** el otro mundo; **some see him as the n. Elvis** algunos lo ven como el nuevo Elvis; **the n. thing I knew, I was in hospital** y después sólo sé que me desperté en el hospital; **who's n.?** ¿quién es el siguiente?, ¿a quién le toca?, *RP* ¿quién sigue?

2 *adv* (**a**) *(in space)* **to be n. to** estar al lado de; **n. to me** a mi lado; **I can't bear wool n. to my skin** no soporto el contacto de la lana (en la piel)

(**b**) *(in time, order)* después, luego; **what shall we do n.?** ¿qué hacemos ahora?; **what did you do n.?** ¿qué hiciste después *or* a continuación?; **whose turn is it n.?** ¿quién es el siguiente?, ¿a quién le toca?, *RP* ¿quién sigue?; **n., the news** a continuación, las noticias; **when shall we meet n.?** ¿cuándo nos volveremos a ver?; **when will you n. be in Texas?** ¿cuándo vas a volver por Tejas?; **she'll be asking me to give up my job n.!** ¡ya sólo falta que me pida que deje el trabajo!; **n. to the seaside I like the mountains best** después de la playa, lo que más me gusta es la montaña; **n. to her, he's a novice** al lado suyo, es un novato; **if we can't do that, the n. best thing would be to...** si eso no se puede hacer, siempre podríamos...; **I've never been there, but I've seen a video, which is the n. best thing** nunca he estado allí, aunque he visto un vídeo *or Am* video, que es lo más parecido; **who is the n. oldest/youngest after Mark?** ¿quién es el mayor/menor después de Mark?; **I'll take the n. largest** quiero el tamaño siguiente a este; **I got it for n. to nothing** lo compré por casi nada *or RP* por chirolas; **it's n. to impossible** es casi imposible; **in n. to no time** en un abrir y cerrar de ojos; *Hum* **what will they think of n.?** ¡qué se les ocurrirá ahora!

3 *pron* **the n.** el/la siguiente; **(the) n. to arrive was Carol** la siguiente en llegar fue Carol; **in my job, one day is much like the n.** en mi trabajo, todos los días son iguales; **n. please!** ¡el siguiente, por favor!; **your train is the n. but one** tu tren no es el siguiente, sino el otro; **the week after n.** la semana siguiente *or* que viene, no, la otra; **the year after n.** el año siguiente *or* que viene, no, el otro ►► ***n. of kin*** parientes *mpl or* familiares *mpl* más cercanos; **I'm his n. of kin** soy su pariente *or* familiar más cercano

next-day delivery ['neks'deɪdɪ'lɪvərɪ] *n Com* entrega *f* al día siguiente

next-door ['neks'dɔ:(r)] *adj* de al lado; **the n. garden** el jardín de al lado; **our** *or* **the n. neighbours** nuestros *or* los vecinos de al lado

nexus ['neksəs] *n Formal (complex)* entramado *m*, red *f*; **a n. of interests/activities** un entramado de intereses/actividades

NF [en'ef] *n* **(a)** *(abbr* **National Front**) Frente *m* Nacional, = partido fascista y racista británico **(b)** *(abbr* **Newfoundland**) Terranova

NFC [enef'si:] *n US (abbr* **National Football Conference**) = una de las conferencias que forman la NFL

NFL [enef'el] *n (abbr* **National Football League**) = una de las dos ligas nacionales de fútbol americano

Nfld *(abbr* **Newfoundland**) Terranova

NFS *(abbr* **not for sale**) no está a la venta

NFU [enef'ju:] *n (abbr* **National Farmers' Union**) = sindicato británico de agricultores

NG [en'dʒi:] *n US (abbr* **National Guard**) Guardia *f* Nacional

NGO [endʒi:'əʊ] *(pl* **NGOs**) *n (abbr* **non-governmental organization**) ONG *f*

NH *(abbr* **New Hampshire**) New Hampshire

NHL ['eneɪtʃel] *n (abbr* **National Hockey League**) = liga estadounidense de hockey sobre hielo

NHS [eneɪtʃ'es] *n (abbr* **National Health Service**) = la sanidad pública británica, *Esp* ≃ Insalud *m*

NI [en'aɪ] *n* **(a)** *(abbr* **Northern Ireland**) Irlanda del Norte **(b)** *Br (abbr* **National Insurance**) SS *f*

niacin ['naɪəsɪn] *n* niacina *f*

Niagara Falls [naɪ'ægrə'fɔ:lz] *npl* ***the N.*** las cataratas del Niágara

nib [nɪb] *n (of pen)* plumilla *f*

nibble ['nɪbəl] **1** *n* **(a)** *(small bite)* **to have a n. at sth** dar un mordisquito a *or* mordisquear algo **(b)** *Fam* **nibbles** *(snacks)* algo *m* de picar, *Méx* antojitos *mpl* **(c)** *(in angling)* **I've got a n.** han picado

2 *vt* mordisquear; **I'm not hungry, I'll just n. a piece of bread** no tengo hambre, sólo comeré un poquito de pan; **the fish nibbled the bait** el pez picó *or* mordió el anzuelo; **she nibbled his ear** le mordisqueó la oreja, le dio mordisquitos en la oreja

3 *vi* **she nibbled at her biscuit** mordisqueó la galleta; **the mice have nibbled through the wire** los ratones han roído el cable; **to n. at the bait** *(fish)* picar; *Fig* morder el anzuelo

nibs [nɪbz] *n Fam Hum* **his n.** su alteza, su señoría

NIC [enaɪ'si:] *n Econ (abbr* **newly industrialized country**) país *m* de reciente industrialización

nicad ['naɪkæd] *n* nicad *m*

Nicam ['naɪkæm] *n TV* Nicam *m*

Nicaragua [nɪkə'rægjʊə] *n* Nicaragua

Nicaraguan [nɪkə'rægjʊən] **1** *n* nicaragüense *mf*

2 *adj* nicaragüense

Nice [ni:s] *n* Niza

NICE [naɪs] *adj* **(a)** *(pleasant)* agradable; **shall we go to the beach? – yes, that would be n.** ¿vamos a la playa? – sí, estaría muy bien *or RP* sí, sería bárbaro; **it's n. to see you again** me alegro de verte de nuevo; **n. meeting** *or* **to meet you!** ¡encantado de conocerte!; **it's n. that we don't have to get up too early** está muy bien no tener que levantarnos demasiado temprano; **to have a n. time** pasarlo bien; **we had a n. holiday** pasamos unas vacaciones muy agradables; **have a n. day!** ¡adiós, buenos días!, ¡que pase un buen día!, *RP* ¡que lo pase bien!; *Fam* **(it's) n. work if you can get it** es *Esp* el chollo *or Méx* churro *or RP* curro del siglo; **to be** *or* **act as n. as pie** ser todo cumplidos; *Ironic* **that's a n. way to behave!** ¡*Esp* bonita *or Am* linda manera de comportarse!; *Br Fam* **n. one!** ¡olé!, ¡toma, qué bien!

(b) *(friendly)* simpático(a), *Esp* majo(a), *RP* dulce; **to be n. to sb** ser amable con alguien; **be n. to your sister!** ¡sé bueno(a) con tu hermana!; **it was n. of her to...** fue muy amable de su parte...; **how n. of you!** ¡qué detalle (de tu parte)!; **they were very n. about it** reaccionaron de manera muy comprensiva

(c) *(attractive) Esp* bonito(a), *Am* lindo(a); **you look really n.** estás muy *Esp* guapo *or Am* lindo; **that dress looks n. on you** ese vestido te queda muy bien; **the kitchen looks n.** la cocina tiene un aspecto sensacional *or* fantástico

(d) *(good)* bueno(a); **she's a n. person** es buena persona; **it's a n. part of town** es una parte buena de la ciudad; **this cheese is really n.** este queso está buenísimo; **that bread smells n.** ese pan huele bien; **n. shot!** ¡buen golpe!; *Ironic* **n. try!** ¡a mí no me engañas!; **n. work!** ¡bien hecho!; *Br Fam Ironic* **n. one!** ¡genial!, *CAm, Carib, Méx* ¡chévere!, *Méx* ¡padrísimo!, *RP* ¡bárbaro!

(e) *(well-mannered)* **it's not n. to pick your nose** es de mala educación meterse el dedo en la nariz; **n. girls don't do things like that** las niñas buenas no hacen esas cosas

(f) *(for emphasis)* **n. and easy** muy fácil; **take it n. and slowly** hazlo despacito y con calma; **I need a n. long rest** necesito un buen descanso; **a n. warm bath** un buen baño calentito

(g) *Formal (distinction, point)* sutil

nice-looking ['naɪslʊkɪŋ] *adj Esp* guapo(a), *Am* lindo(a)

nicely ['naɪslɪ] *adv* **(a)** *(politely) (to behave)* bien, correctamente; *(to ask)* con educación

(b) *(pleasantly)* agradablemente, amablemente; **she smiled at me n.** me sonrió amablemente

(c) *(well)* bien; **to be coming along n.** ir bien; **to be doing n.** ir bien; **we are doing n.** *(financially)* nos va bien, nos van bien las cosas; **this bag will do n.** esta bolsa valdrá *or* servirá; **n. done!** ¡muy bien!, ¡así se hace!; **n. put!** ¡bien dicho!, ¡así se habla!

(d) *(attractively) (decorated, arranged)* con gusto; **n. illustrated** con bonitas *or* lindas ilustraciones; **n. dressed** vestido(a) elegantemente *or* con gusto

(e) *Formal (exactly, subtly)* con precisión, con exactitud; **they judged the timing n.** calcularon muy bien *or* con precisión el tiempo

nicety ['naɪsɪtɪ] *n* **(a)** *(precision)* precisión *f*, exactitud *f*; **to a n.** con suma precisión *or* exactitud **(b)** *(subtlety, delicacy)* detalle *m*, sutileza *f*; **a distinction of some n.** una sutil distinción; **diplomatic niceties** protocolo diplomático; **legal niceties** sutilezas *or* detalles legales; **social niceties** cumplidos *mpl*, formalidades *fpl*

niche [ni:ʃ] *n* **(a)** *Archit* hornacina *f*, nicho *m* **(b)** *(place)* **to find/create a n. for oneself** encontrar/hacerse un hueco **(c)** *Com* **n. (market)** nicho *m* (de mercado)

Nicholas ['nɪkələs] *pr n* **Saint N.** san Nicolás

nick [nɪk] **1** *n* **(a)** *(cut) (in wood)* muesca *f*; *(on face)* corte *m* **(b)** *Br Fam (condition)* **in good/bad n.** en buen/mal estado; **he's in pretty good n. for his age** para la edad que tiene se conserva la mar de bien **(c)** *Br Fam (prison)* cárcel *f*, *Esp* trullo *m*, *Andes, RP* cana *f*, *Méx* bote *m* **(d)** *Br Fam (police station)* comisaría *f*; **down the n.** en/a comisaría **(e)** IDIOM **in the n. of time** justo a tiempo

2 *vt* **(a)** *(cut) (object)* hacer una muesca en; **to n. one's face** hacerse un corte en la cara, cortarse la cara **(b)** *Br Fam (arrest)* detener, trincar; **he got nicked (for stealing)** lo detuvieron *or* trincaron (por robar) **(c)** *Br Fam (steal)* afanar, *Esp* mangar

nickel ['nɪkəl] *n* **(a)** *Chem (metal)* níquel *m* ►► ***n. silver*** alpaca *f* **(b)** *US (coin)* moneda *f* de cinco centavos

nickel-and-dime ['nɪkələn'daɪm] *adj US* menor, de tres al cuarto ►► ***n. store*** = tienda en la que sólo se venden productos muy baratos

nickelodeon ['nɪkəl'əʊdɪən] *n US* **(a)** *(pianola)* pianola *f* **(b)** *(early cinema)* cinematógrafo *m*

nickel-plated ['nɪkəl'pleɪtɪd] *adj* niquelado(a)

nicker ['nɪkə(r)] *n Br Fam* **a hundred n.** cien libras *(esterlinas)*

nick-nack ['nɪk'næk] *n Fam* cachivache *m*, chisme *m*

nickname ['nɪkneɪm] **1** *n* apodo *m*, mote *m*

2 *vt* apodar; **he was nicknamed "Tank"** lo apodaron "Tank"

nicotine ['nɪkəti:n] *n* nicotina *f* ►► ***n. patch*** parche *m* de nicotina; ***n. poisoning*** tabaquismo *m*, intoxicación *f* por nicotina

niece [ni:s] *n* sobrina *f*

niff [nɪf] *Br Fam* **1** *n (bad smell)* tufo *m*, peste *f*; **what a n.!** ¡qué tufo *or* peste!

2 *vi (smell bad)* apestar, atufar

nifty ['nɪftɪ] *adj Fam* **(a)** *(clever) (idea, device)* ingenioso(a); **a n. little gadget** un cacharrillo de lo más ingenioso; **a n. piece of work** un trabajo la mar de apañado **(b)** *(agile) (person, footwork)* ágil **(c)** *(stylish)* coquetón(ona)

nigella [naɪ'dʒelə] *n* arañuela *f*

Niger ['naɪdʒə(r)] *n* **(a)** *(country)* Níger **(b)** *(river)* **the (River) N.** el (río) Níger

Nigeria [naɪ'dʒɪərɪə] *n* Nigeria

Nigerian [naɪ'dʒɪərɪən] **1** *n* nigeriano(a) *m,f*

2 *adj* nigeriano(a)

niggardly ['nɪgədlɪ] *adj* mísero(a)

nigger ['nɪgə(r)] *n very Fam* = término generalmente ofensivo para referirse a un negro, *RP* grone *m*; IDIOM *Br Old-fashioned* **a n. in the woodpile** un defecto oculto

niggle ['nɪgəl] 1 *n* (a) *(small criticism)* queja *f* (b) *(misgiving)* duda *f*
2 *vt (worry)* preocupar; **there's still something that is niggling me** todavía hay algo que me tiene preocupada
3 *vi* (a) *(be overfussy)* **to n. about details** ser muy quisquilloso(a) (b) *(worry)* **there's still something that is niggling (away) at me** todavía hay algo que me tiene preocupado (c) *(pester)* fastidiar, dar la lata; **to n. on at sb (about sth)** fastidiar *or* dar la lata a alguien (con algo)

niggling ['nɪglɪŋ] *adj* (a) *(details)* de poca monta, insignificante (b) *(annoying) (pain)* molesto(a); *(doubt)* inquietante

nigh [naɪ] 1 *adj Literary* próximo(a), cercano(a); **the hour is n. when all shall have to give account** se acerca *or* se aproxima la hora en que todos tendremos que rendir cuentas; **the end is n.!** ¡el final está próximo *or* cerca!
2 *adv* (a) *Literary* cerca; **for n. on thirty years** durante cerca de treinta años (b) **well n. impossible** *(almost)* casi *or* prácticamente imposible

night [naɪt] 1 *n* (a) *(between sunset and sunrise)* noche *f*; **at n.** por la noche; **late at n.** bien entrada la noche; **ten o'clock at n.** las diez de la noche; **all n. (long)** toda la noche; **by n.** de noche, por la noche; **during** *or* **in the n.** durante la noche, por la noche; **far** *or* **late into the n.** hasta altas horas de la noche, hasta bien entrada la noche; **last n.** anoche; **the n. before** la noche antes *or* anterior; **tomorrow n.** mañana por la noche; **on Thursday n.** el jueves por la noche; **good n.!** ¡buenas noches!; *Fam* **n., n.!** ¡hasta mañana!; **to work day and n.** *or* **n. and day** trabajar día y noche; **it went on n. after n.** continuó noche tras noche *or* una noche tras otra; **to turn n. into day** estar despierto(a) hasta las tantas ►► ***n. blindness*** ceguera *f* nocturna; ***n. clerk*** *(in hotel)* recepcionista *mf* de noche; *US* ***n. crawler*** lombriz *f* (de tierra); *US* ***n. depository*** cajero *m* nocturno; *Mil* ***n. fighter*** caza *m* nocturno; ***n. heron*** martinete *m*; ***n. light*** luz *f* tenue *(que queda encendida toda la noche)*; ***n. nurse*** enfermero(a) *m,f* de noche; *Fig* ***n. owl*** noctámbulo(a) *m,f*, trasnochador(ora) *m,f*; ***n. porter*** portero *m or* conserje *m* de noche; *Br* ***n. safe*** cajero *m* nocturno; ***n. school*** escuela *f* nocturna; ***n. shift*** turno *m* de noche; ***n. spot*** local *m* nocturno, discoteca *f*; *US* ***n. stand*** *or* ***table*** mesita *f or* mesilla *f* de noche, *RP* mesa *f* de luz, *Méx* buró *m*; ***n. vision:* to have good/bad n. vision** ver bien/mal de noche
(b) *(between going to bed and waking)* noche *f*; **to have a bad n.** pasar una mala noche; **to have an early/late n.** acostarse temprano/tarde; **what you need is a good n.'s sleep** lo que necesitas es dormir bien toda la noche
(c) *(evening's entertainment)* **Tuesday's our poker n.** los martes por la noche jugamos al póquer; **to have a n. out** salir por la noche; **to make a n. of it** salir toda la noche; **a n. on the town** *or* **the tiles** una noche de juerga *or Esp* marcha; *Hum* **the n. is (yet) young** la noche es joven
(d) *(darkness)* noche *f*; **he disappeared into the n.** desapareció en la oscuridad de la noche; **as n. was falling** a medida que iba cayendo la noche, a medida que anochecía
2 *adj (train, bus, flight, sky)* nocturno(a); **the n. air** el aire de la noche
3 *adv US* **nights** por las noches; **how can you sleep nights not knowing where he is?** ¿cómo puedes dormir por la noche sin saber dónde está?; **to work nights** trabajar de noche; **to lie awake nights** quedarse despierto(a) por la noche

night-bird ['naɪtbɜːd] *n* (a) *(bird)* ave *f* nocturna (b) *(person)* noctámbulo(a) *m,f*, trasnochador(ora) *m,f*

nightcap ['naɪtkæp] *n* (a) *(hat)* gorro *m* de dormir (b) *(drink)* copa *f* antes de acostarse

nightclass ['naɪtklæs] *n* clase *f* nocturna

nightclothes ['naɪtkləʊðz] *npl* ropa *f* de dormir

nightclub ['naɪtklʌb] *n* discoteca *f*

nightclubber ['naɪtklʌbə(r)] *n* discotequero(a) *m,f*

nightclubbing ['naɪtklʌbɪŋ] *n* **to go n.** ir de discotecas

nightdress ['naɪtdres] *n* camisón *m*

nightfall ['naɪtfɔːl] *n* anochecer *m*; **at n.** al anochecer; **we must get there by n.** debemos llegar allí antes del anochecer *or* de que anochezca

nightgown ['naɪtgaʊn] *n* camisón *m*

nighthawk ['naɪthɔːk] *n* (a) *(bird)* añapero *m* (b) *(person)* noctámbulo(a) *m,f*, trasnochador(ora) *m,f*

nightie ['naɪtɪ] *n Fam* camisón *m*

nightingale ['naɪtɪŋgeɪl] *n* ruiseñor *m*

nightjar ['naɪtdʒɑː(r)] *n (bird)* chotacabras *m inv* (gris) ►► ***red-necked n.*** chotacabras *m* pardo; ***standard-winged n.*** chotacabras *m* abanderado

nightlife ['naɪtlaɪf] *n* vida *f* nocturna, ambiente *m* nocturno; **what's the n. like round here?** ¿cómo es la vida nocturna aquí?

nightlong ['naɪtlɒŋ] *adj* **n. celebrations/vigil** fiesta/vigilia durante toda la noche

nightly ['naɪtlɪ] 1 *adj* **his n. stroll** su paseo de cada noche; **twice n. flights** dos vuelos cada noche
2 *adv* todas las noches

nightmare ['naɪtmeə(r)] *n also Fig* pesadilla *f*; **a n. vision/experience** una visión/experiencia espeluznante *or* de pesadilla; **to have a n.** tener una pesadilla; **to give sb nightmares** dar *or* producir pesadillas a alguien; **everybody's worst n.** la pesadilla de cualquiera, lo peor de lo peor; **the traffic was a n.!** ¡el tráfico estaba imposible!

nightmarish ['naɪtmeərɪʃ] *adj* de pesadilla

nightshade ['naɪtʃeɪd] *n* **black n.** hierba *f* mora; **deadly n.** belladona *f*; **woody n.** dulcamara *f*

nightshirt ['naɪtʃɜːt] *n* camisa *f* de dormir

night-soil ['naɪtsɔɪl] *n Old-fashioned* estiércol *m*

nightstick ['naɪtstɪk] *n US* porra *f*

night-time ['naɪttaɪm] 1 *n* noche *f*; **at n.** por la noche, durante la noche
2 *adj* nocturno(a)

nightwatchman [naɪt'wɒtʃmən] *n* vigilante *m* nocturno

nightwear ['naɪtweə(r)] *n* ropa *f* de dormir

nihilism ['naɪlɪzəm] *n* nihilismo *m*

nihilist ['naɪlɪst] *n* nihilista *mf*

nihilistic [naɪ'lɪstɪk] *adj* nihilista

Nikkei ['nɪkeɪ] *n Fin* **N. (index)** índice *m* Nikkei

nil [nɪl] 1 *n* cero *m*; *Br* **to win two/three n.** ganar (por) dos/tres a cero; *Med* **n. by mouth** *(sign)* debe permanecer en ayunas
2 *adj* nulo(a); **this has n. significance** esto no tiene importancia alguna *or* tiene una importancia nula

Nile [naɪl] *n* **the N.** el Nilo; **the Blue/White N.** el Nilo Azul/Blanco

nimble ['nɪmbəl] *adj (person, body)* ágil; *(mind)* ágil, despierto(a); **to be n. on one's feet** ser ágil; **to have n. feet** *(soccer player, boxer)* tener un buen juego de piernas

nimbly ['nɪmblɪ] *adv* con agilidad, ágilmente

nimbostratus [nɪmbəʊ'strɑːtəs] *n Met* nimbostrato *m*

nimbus ['nɪmbəs] *(pl* **nimbi** ['nɪmbaɪ] *or* **nimbuses)** *n* (a) *Met* nimbo *m* (b) *(halo)* nimbo *m*, halo *m*

NIMBY ['nɪmbɪ] *(abbr* **not in my back yard)** *Fam* 1 *n* = persona a la que le parece bien que exista algo mientras no le afecte
2 *adj* **N. attitude** = la actitud típica de la persona a la que le parece bien que exista algo mientras no le afecte

nincompoop ['nɪŋkəmpuːp] *n Fam* bobo(a) *m,f*, *Esp* percebe *mf*

nine [naɪn] 1 *n* nueve *m*; **the front/back n.** *(in golf)* los primeros/últimos nueve hoyos; **to dial** *Br* **999** *or US* **911** llamar al teléfono de emergencia, *Esp* ≃ llamar al 112; IDIOM *Fam* **to be dressed up to the nines** ir de punta en blanco
2 *adj* nueve; *Fig* **n. times out of ten** la mayoría de las veces; **n. day** *or* **days' wonder** flor de un día; IDIOM **to have n. lives** tener siete vidas (como los gatos); *see also* **eight**

ninefold ['naɪnfəʊld] 1 *adj* **there's been a n. increase in sales** las ventas se han multiplicado por nueve
2 *adv* por nueve

nine-hole ['naɪnhəʊl] *adj (golf course)* de nueve hoyos

ninepins ['naɪnpɪnz] *npl (game)* bolos *mpl (juego de nueve bolos)*; IDIOM **to go down** *or* **fall like n.** caer como chinches

nineteen [naɪn'tiːn] 1 *n* diecinueve *m*; IDIOM *Fam* **to talk n. to the dozen** hablar por los codos
2 *adj* diecinueve; *see also* **eight**

nineteenth [naɪn'tiːnθ] 1 *n* (a) *(fraction)* diecinueveavo *m*, diecinueveava parte *f* (b) *(in series)* decimonoveno(a) *m,f* (c) *(of month)* diecinueve *m*
2 *adj* decimonoveno(a); *Fam Hum* **the n. hole** *(of golf course)* el bar; *see also* **eleventh**

nineties ['naɪntiːz] *npl* **the n.** los (años) noventa; *see also* **eighties**

ninetieth ['naɪntɪɪθ] 1 *n* nonagésimo(a) *m,f*
2 *adj* nonagésimo(a)

nine-to-five ['naɪntə'faɪv] 1 *adj* **a n. job** un trabajo de oficina *(de nueve a cinco)*
2 *adv* **to work n.** trabajar de nueve a cinco, tener horario de oficina

ninety ['naɪntɪ] 1 *n* noventa *m*
2 *adj* noventa; **n.-nine times out of a hundred** el noventa y nueve por ciento de las veces; *see also* **eighty**

ninja ['nɪndʒə] *n* guerrero *m* ninja

ninjitsu [nɪn'dʒɪtsu:] *n Sport* ninjutsu *m*

ninny ['nɪnɪ] *n Fam* tonto(a) *m,f*

ninth [naɪnθ] 1 *n* **(a)** *(fraction)* noveno *m*, novena parte *f* **(b)** *(in series)* noveno(a) *m,f* **(c)** *(of month)* nueve *m*
2 *adj* noveno(a); *see also* **eighth**

niobium [naɪ'əʊbɪəm] *n Chem* niobio *m*

Nip [nɪp] *n Fam* = término ofensivo para referirse a los japoneses, *RP* ponja *mf*

nip [nɪp] 1 *n* **(a)** *(pinch)* pellizco *m*; *(with teeth)* bocado *m*, mordisquillo *m* **(b)** *(chill)* **there's a n. in the air** hace fresco **(c)** *Fam (of brandy, whisky)* copita *f*, *Esp* chupito *m* **(d)** *Fam* **he's had a n. and tuck done** *(cosmetic surgery)* se ha hecho la estética, *Méx, RP* se ha hecho cirugía; **it was n. and tuck right until the end** fueron muy igualados hasta el final
2 *vt (pt & pp* **nipped)** **(a)** *(pinch)* pellizcar; *(with teeth)* mordisquear; **she nipped her finger in the door** se pilló un dedo en *or* con la puerta; IDIOM *Fam* **to n. sth in the bud** cortar algo de raíz **(b)** *(of cold, frost)* **the cold nipped our ears** el frío nos cortaba las orejas; **the vines were nipped by the frost** el frío heló las vides, la helada quemó las vides
3 *vi* **(a)** *(try to bite)* **the dog nipped at my ankles** el perro me mordisqueaba los tobillos **(b)** *(sting)* escocer **(c)** *Br Fam (go)* **to n. (across** *or* **along** *or* **over) to the butcher's** ir un momento *or* acercarse a la carnicería; **to n. in and out of the traffic** sortear el tráfico

▸ **nip off** 1 *vt sep (cut off) (with scissors, shears)* cortar; *(with teeth, fingers)* arrancar
2 *vi Br Fam* irse

▸ **nip out** *vi Br Fam (go out)* salir (un momento); **I'll n. out and buy a paper** salgo un momento a comprar el periódico

▸ **nip round** *vi Br Fam* salir, ir

nipper ['nɪpə(r)] *n* **(a)** *(of crab, lobster)* pinza *f* **(b)** *Br Fam (child)* chavalín(ina) *m,f*, *CAm, Méx* chavalo(a) *m,f*, *RP* pibito(a) *m,f* **(c) nippers** *(tool)* pinzas *fpl*, tenazas *fpl*

nipple ['nɪpəl] *n* **(a)** *(female)* pezón *m*; *(male)* tetilla *f* **(b)** *US (on baby's bottle)* tetilla *f*, tetina *f* **(c)** *Tech (for greasing)* boquilla *f* de engrase, engrasador *m*

nippy ['nɪpɪ] *adj Fam* **(a)** *(cold)* fresco(a); **it's a bit n. today** hoy hace un poco de fresco **(b)** *(quick, agile) (person)* vivo(a), rápido(a); *(car, motorbike)* rápido(a); **the new Ford is very n. around town** el nuevo Ford es muy práctico para ir por la ciudad **(c)** *(flavour)* fuerte

nirvana [nɜ:'vɑ:nə] *n* nirvana *m*

nit [nɪt] *n* **(a)** *(insect)* piojo *m*; *(insect's egg)* liendre *f* **(b)** *Br Fam (person)* idiota *mf*, bobo(a) *m,f*

niter *US* = **nitre**

nit-pick ['nɪtpɪk] *vi Fam* poner peros *or Esp* pegas, ser un(a) quisquilloso(a); **I wish he wouldn't n. like that** ya podía dejar de ponerle peros *or Esp* pegas, ya podía ser un poco menos quisquilloso

nit-picker ['nɪtpɪkə(r)] *n Fam* quisquilloso(a) *m,f*

nit-picking ['nɪtpɪkɪŋ] *Fam* 1 *n* critiqueo *m* por nimiedades
2 *adj* quisquilloso(a)

nitrate ['naɪtreɪt] *n* nitrato *m*

nitre, *US* **niter** ['naɪtə(r)] *n Chem* nitro *m*

nitric ['naɪtrɪk] *adj* nítrico(a) ▸▸ ***n. acid*** ácido *m* nítrico; ***n. oxide*** óxido *m* nítrico

nitride ['naɪtraɪd] *n Chem* nitruro *m*

nitrite ['naɪtraɪt] *n Chem* nitrito *m*

nitro ['naɪtrəʊ] *n Fam* nitroglicerina *f*

nitrobenzene [naɪtrəʊ'benzi:n] *n* nitrobenceno *m*

nitrocellulose [naɪtrəʊ'seljʊləʊs] *n* nitrocelulosa *f*

nitrogen ['naɪtrədʒən] *n Chem* nitrógeno *m* ▸▸ ***n. cycle*** ciclo *m* del nitrógeno; ***n. dioxide*** dióxido *m* de nitrógeno

nitrogenous [naɪ'trɒdʒənəs] *adj* nitrogenado(a)

nitroglycerin(e) ['naɪtrəʊ'glɪsəri:n] *n* nitroglicerina *f*

nitrous ['naɪtrəs] *adj Chem* nitroso(a) ▸▸ ***n. oxide*** óxido *m* nitroso

nitty-gritty ['nɪtɪ'grɪtɪ] *n Fam* meollo *m*; **the n. of day-to-day work** la rutina del trabajo diario; **to get down to the n.** ir al grano, ir al meollo del asunto

nitwit ['nɪtwɪt] *n Fam* idiota *mf*, bobo(a) *m,f*

nix [nɪks] *US Fam* 1 *pron* nada (de nada)
2 *vt* **the boss nixed the idea** el jefe dijo que ni hablar
3 *exclam* ¡ni hablar!

NJ *(abbr* **New Jersey)** Nueva Jersey

NLF [enel'ef] *(abbr* **National Liberation Front)** *n* FNL *m*, FLN *m*

NLP [enel'pi:] *(abbr* **natural language processing)** procesamiento *m* de lenguaje natural

NLQ [enel'kju:] *n (abbr* **near letter quality)** calidad *f* (de impresión) casi de carta *or* próxima a la de carta

NM, NMex *(abbr* **New Mexico)** Nuevo México

NNE *(abbr* **north-northeast)** NNE

NNW *(abbr* **north-northwest)** NNO

No, no *(abbr* **number)** nº, núm.

NO [nəʊ] 1 *adv* **(a)** *(interjection)* no; **you're joking! – no, I'm not** ¡estás de broma! *or* ¡estás bromeando! – no, no lo estoy; **to say no** decir que no; **she won't take no for an answer** no para hasta salirse con la suya
(b) *(not)* no; **he's no cleverer than her** no es más listo que ella; **the film is no good** la película no es nada buena; **it is no small achievement** no deja de tener mérito; **it is of no great interest** no interesa mucho, *RP* no tiene demasiado interés; **no more/less than $100** no más/menos de 100 dólares; **$100, no more, no less** 100 dólares, ni más ni menos
2 *adj* **there is no bread** no hay pan; **a man with no qualifications** un hombre sin títulos; **no trees are to be found there** allí no se encuentra ningún árbol; **there's no hope of us winning** no hay posibilidad alguna de que ganemos; **it's no trouble** no es molestia; **he's no friend of mine** no es amigo mío; **I'm no expert** no soy ningún experto; **no two are the same** no hay dos iguales; **I am in no way surprised** no me sorprende en absoluto; **there's no denying it** no se puede negar; **there's no pleasing him** no hay forma de agradarle; **no dogs** *(sign)* perros no, no se admiten perros; **no smoking** *(sign)* prohibido fumar; *Fam* **no way!** ¡ni hablar!, *Esp* ¡de eso nada!, *Am* ¡para nada!
3 *n (pl* **noes)** **(a)** *(negative answer)* no *m*; **the answer was a clear no** la respuesta fue un claro no **(b)** *Pol* **ayes and noes** votos a favor y en contra

---

no-account ['nəʊə'kaʊnt] *adj US Fam* de tres al cuarto, de poca monta

no-brainer ['nəʊ'breɪnə(r)] *n US Fam* **it's a n.** es pan comido

Noah ['nəʊə] *pr n* Noé ▸▸ ***N.'s ark*** el arca *f* de Noé

nob [nɒb] *n Br Fam (rich person)* ricachón(ona) *m,f*, ricacho(a) *m,f*

no-ball ['nəʊ'bɔ:l] *n (in baseball, cricket)* lanzamiento *m* antirreglamentario

nobble ['nɒbəl] *vt Br Fam* **(a)** *(jury, witness) (with money)* comprar, untar, *Andes, RP* coimear, *CAm, Méx* dar la mordida a; *(with threats)* amedrentar, amenazar **(b)** *(horse)* drogar **(c)** *(attract attention of)* pillar, *Am* agarrar

Nobel ['nəʊbel] *n* ***N. laureate*** Premio *mf* Nobel; ***N. prize*** Premio *m* Nobel; ***N. prize winner*** Premio *mf* Nobel

nobelium [nəʊ'bi:lɪəm] *n Chem* nobelio *m*

nobility [nəʊ'bɪlɪtɪ] *n* **(a)** *(class)* nobleza *f* **(b)** *(of character)* nobleza *f*

noble ['nəʊbəl] 1 *n* noble *mf*
2 *adj* **(a)** *(birth, person)* noble **(b)** *(generous, distinguished) (sentiment, act, cause)* noble; **that's very n. of you** ¡qué generoso de tu parte!; **the n. art of...** el noble arte de... ▸▸ ***n. savage*** buen salvaje *m* **(c)** *(majestic) (building, sight)* grandioso(a), majestuoso(a) **(d)** *Chem* **n. gas** gas noble **(e)** *Culin* **n. rot** podredumbre noble

nobleman ['nəʊbəlmən] *n* noble *m*

noble-minded [nəʊbəl'maɪndɪd] *adj* noble

noblesse oblige [nəʊ'blesə'bli:ʒ] *n* nobleza obliga

noblewoman ['nəʊbəlwʊmən] *n* noble *f*

nobly ['nəʊblɪ] *adv* **(a)** *(by birth)* **n. born** de noble cuna **(b)** *(generously)* generosamente, noblemente; **she n. offered him the last one** en un acto de generosidad, ella le ofreció el último **(c)** *(majestically)* grandiosamente; **n. proportioned** de proporciones grandiosas

---

NOBODY ['nəʊbədɪ] 1 *n* **he's/she's a n.** es un/una don nadie
2 *pron* nadie; **n. spoke to me** nadie me dirigió la palabra; **is there n. here who knows the answer?** ¿no hay nadie aquí que sepa la respuesta?; **it's n. you would know** es alguien a quien no conoces; **n. with any sense would do it** nadie que tuviera dos dedos de frente lo haría; **n. else** nadie más; **if you don't have money, you're n.** si no

tienes dinero, no eres nadie; IDIOM **he is n.'s fool** no tiene un pelo de tonto; IDIOM **like n.'s business** *(very well)* como él solo/ella sola; **to run/work like n.'s business** correr/trabajar como un condenado

---

no-claim(s) ['nəʊ'kleɪm(z)] *n* ***n. bonus*** *or* ***discount*** descuento *m* por no siniestralidad

nocturnal [nɒk'tɜːnəl] *adj* nocturno(a) ►► ***n. emission*** *(wet dream)* polución *f* nocturna

nocturne ['nɒktɜːn] *n Mus* nocturno *m*

nod [nɒd] **1** *n* **(a)** *(greeting)* saludo *m (con la cabeza); (in agreement)* señal *f* de asentimiento *(con la cabeza);* **to give sb a n.** *(as signal)* hacer una señal con la cabeza a alguien; *(in assent)* decir a alguien que sí con la cabeza, asentir a alguien con la cabeza; *(in greeting)* saludar a alguien con la cabeza; **to give sth/sb the n.** dar el consentimiento para algo/a alguien; *Fig* **it was a n. in your direction** la indirecta iba dirigida a ti; **on the n.** sin ninguna discusión; PROV **a n. is as good as a wink (to a blind man)** a buen entendedor pocas palabras bastan

(b) *(sleep) Hum* **to be in the Land of N.** estar en brazos de Morfeo, estar soñando con los angelitos

2 *vt* (*pt & pp* **nodded**) **to n. one's head** *(in assent)* decir que sí *or* asentir con la cabeza; *(in greeting)* saludar con la cabeza; *(as signal)* hacer una señal con la cabeza; **to n. one's approval** dar la aprobación con una inclinación de cabeza

3 *vi* **(a)** *(as signal)* hacer una señal con la cabeza; *(in assent, approval)* decir que sí *or* asentir con la cabeza; *(in greeting)* saludar con la cabeza; **to n. in agreement** *or* **assent** decir que sí *or* asentir con la cabeza; **she nodded to him to start the film** le indicó con la cabeza que pusiera la película **(b)** *(doze)* dar cabezadas, cabecear **(c)** *(flowers)* agitarse, mecerse

►**nod off** *vi Fam* quedarse traspuesto(a), dormirse; **I must have nodded off** he debido de quedarme traspuesto *or* dormirme; **I kept nodding off during the chairman's speech** me pasé todo el discurso del presidente dando cabezadas *or* cabeceando

►**nod through** *vt sep* aprobar sumariamente

nodal ['nəʊdəl] *adj* nodal

nodding ['nɒdɪŋ] *adj* **to have a n. acquaintance with sth/sb** conocer un poco algo/a alguien; **to be on n. terms with sb** conocer a alguien lo suficiente como para saludarlo en la calle ►► *US Fam* ***n. donkey*** *(oil-pump)* = tipo de bomba para extraer petróleo

noddle ['nɒdəl] *n Br Fam* coco *m*, mollera *f*; **use your n.!** ¡usa la mollera un poco!, ¡piensa un poco!

noddy ['nɒdɪ] *adj Br* de tres al cuarto; **he's got a n. job** tiene un trabajo de poca monta

node [nəʊd] *n* **(a)** *Bot* nudo *m*, nódulo *m* **(b)** *Math & Comptr* nodo *m* **(c)** *Med* nodo *m*, nódulo *m* **(d)** *Ling* nudo *m*

nodular ['nɒdjʊlə(r)] *adj* nodular

nodule ['nɒdjuːl] *n* nódulo *m*

Noel, Noël [nəʊ'el] *n* Navidad *f*

no-fault ['nəʊ'fɔːlt] *adj Law* ***n. compensation*** seguro *m* a todo riesgo; ***n. divorce*** divorcio *m* de mutuo acuerdo

no-fly zone [nəʊ'flaɪzəʊn] *n* zona *f* de exclusión aérea

no-frills [nəʊ'frɪlz] *adj (airline, travel)* sin lujos, barato(a); *(insurance policy)* básico(a); *(service, wedding)* sencillo(a), sin florituras

noggin ['nɒgɪn] *n* **(a)** *Fam Old-fashioned (head)* coco *m* **(b)** *(measure)* chupito *m*

no-go ['nəʊ'gəʊ] **1** *adj* ***n. area*** zona *f* prohibida; **it's a (virtual) n. area for the police** la policía no se atreve a pisar esa zona *or* a poner los pies en esa zona

2 *adv* **it's n., I'm afraid** me temo que nada

no-good ['nəʊgʊd] *adj US Fam* inútil

Noh [nəʊ] *n Lit* (teatro *m*) no *m*

no-holds-barred ['nəʊ'həʊldz'bɑːd] *adj (report, documentary)* a fondo, sin restricciones

no-hoper [nəʊ'həʊpə(r)] *n Br Fam* inútil *mf*

nohow ['nəʊhaʊ] *adv US Fam* ¡ni hablar!

noirish ['nwɑːrɪʃ] *adj* con aires de cine negro

noise [nɔɪz] **1** *n* **(a)** *(sound, din)* ruido *m*; **what's that awful n.?** ¿qué es ese ruido tan horrible?; **I thought I heard a n. downstairs** me pareció oír un ruido abajo; **do you call that n. music?** ¿y a ese ruido lo llamas música?; **to make a n.** *(individual sound)* hacer un ruido; *(racket)* hacer ruido; **the clock is making a funny n.** el reloj hace un ruido raro; *Theat* **noises off** se oyen sonidos desde fuera de escena ►► ***n. level*** nivel *m* de ruido; ***n. pollution*** contaminación *f* acústica

(b) *Comptr & Tel* ruido *m*

(c) IDIOMS **they made a lot of n. about banning the march** habían anunciado a los cuatro vientos que prohibirían la marcha de protesta; **to make noises about doing sth** andar *or* ir diciendo que uno va a hacer algo; **to make encouraging/sympathetic noises** mostrarse favorable/comprensivo(a); **they're making all the right noises** *(they're saying the right things)* dicen todo lo que se supone que deben decir; *(I think they agree)* todo indica que están de acuerdo; **a big n.** un pez gordo; **he's a big n. in the theatre world** es un pez gordo del mundo del teatro; *Br Fam* **hold** *or* **shut your n.!** ¡cierra el pico!

2 *vt Formal* **rumours of his resignation are being noised abroad** corren rumores de que va a dimitir; **it's being noised about that the factory might close** se comenta por ahí que la fábrica podría cerrar

noiseless ['nɔɪzlɪs] *adj* silencioso(a)

noiselessly ['nɔɪzlɪslɪ] *adv* silenciosamente

noisemaker ['nɔɪzmeɪkə(r)] *n US (rattle)* carraca *f*, matraca *f*; *(trumpet)* bocina *f*, trompetón *m*

noisette [nwɑː'zet] *Culin n* **(a)** *(of lamb)* = rollo de carne de cordero **(b)** *(sweet)* bombón *m* de avellana

noisily ['nɔɪzɪlɪ] *adv* ruidosamente; **they were arguing n. outside** estaban fuera discutiendo a voz en grito; **do you have to do it so n.?** ¿es que tienes que armar tanto ruido?

noisiness ['nɔɪzɪnɪs] *n* ruido *m*; **I can't stand their n.** no soporto el ruido que arman, no soporto que armen tanto ruido

noisome ['nɔɪsəm] *adj Formal (unpleasant, offensive)* nocivo(a)

noisy ['nɔɪzɪ] *adj* ruidoso(a); **London was too n. for him** Londres era demasiado ruidosa para él; **my typewriter is very n.** mi máquina de escribir es muy ruidosa *or* hace mucho ruido; **it's very n. in here** aquí hay mucho ruido

no-jump ['nəʊdʒʌmp] *n (in long jump, triple jump)* salto *m* nulo

nomad ['nəʊmæd] **1** *n* nómada *mf*

2 *adj* nómada

nomadic [nəʊ'mædɪk] *adj* nómada

no-man's-land ['nəʊmænzlænd] *n also Fig* tierra *f* de nadie

nom de plume ['nɒmdə'pluːm] *n* seudónimo *m*, sobrenombre *m*

nomenclature [nəʊ'menklətʃə(r), *US* 'nəʊmənkleɪtʃə(r)] *n* nomenclatura *f*

nominal ['nɒmɪnəl] **1** *adj* **(a)** *(in name only)* nominal; **he was the n. president of the company** era el presidente nominal de la empresa

(b) *(token) (price, amount, rent)* simbólico(a) ►► *Law* ***n. damages*** daños *mpl* nominales *or* de poca consideración

(c) *Fin* ***n. accounts*** cuentas *fpl* generales de gastos; ***n. ledger*** libro *m* de ingresos y gastos; *St Exch* ***n. price*** *(of share)* precio *m* nominal, precio *m* de salida; ***n. value*** valor *m* nominal

(d) *Math* ***n. scale*** escala *f* nominal

(e) *Gram* nominal, sustantivo(a)

2 *n Gram* sintagma *m* nominal

nominalization [nɒmɪnəlaɪ'zeɪʃən] *n Gram* nominalización *f*, sustantivación *f*

nominalize ['nɒmɪnəlaɪz] *vt Gram* nominalizar, sustantivar

nominally ['nɒmɪnəlɪ] *adv* **(a)** *(in name only)* nominalmente, sólo de nombre **(b)** *(theoretically)* en teoría, teóricamente

nominate ['nɒmɪneɪt] *vt* **(a)** *(propose)* proponer; *(for award)* proponer como candidato(a), nominar; **to n. sb for a post** proponer a alguien (como candidato) para un puesto; **the film was nominated for an Oscar** la película fue nominada para un Óscar *or* candidata a un Óscar

(b) *(appoint)* nombrar, designar; **to n. sb to a post** nombrar *or* designar a alguien para un puesto

nomination [nɒmɪ'neɪʃən] *n* **(a)** *(proposal)* propuesta *f*; *(for an award)* candidatura *f*, nominación *f*; **who will get the Democratic n. (for president)?** ¿quién obtendrá la candidatura demócrata *or* será proclamado candidato demócrata a la presidencia?; **the film got three Oscar nominations** la película obtuvo tres nominaciones *or* candidaturas al Óscar **(b)** *(appointment)* nombramiento *m*, designación *f*

nominative ['nɒmɪnətɪv] *Gram* **1** *n* nominativo *m*

2 *adj* nominativo(a)

nominator ['nɒmɪneɪtə(r)] *n* = persona que propone una candidatura o realiza un nombramiento

nominee [nɒmɪ'niː] *n* **(a)** *(proposed)* candidato(a) *m,f* **(b)** *(appointed)* persona *f* nombrada

non- [nɒn] *prefix* no; **the n.-application of this rule** (el hecho de) no aplicar esta regla; **all n.-Spanish nationals** todos los ciudadanos no españoles; **his answers were n.-answers** sus respuestas no merecían ese nombre *or* no eran tales

non-abrasive ['nɒnə'breɪsɪv] *adj (substance, cleaner)* no abrasivo(a)

non-academic ['nɒnækə'demɪk] *adj* (**a**) *(staff)* no docente (**b**) *(course, subject)* no académico(a)
non-addictive ['nɒnə'dɪktɪv] *adj* que no crea adicción
nonagenarian ['nəʊnədʒə'neərɪən] **1** *n* nonagenario(a) *m,f*
2 *adj* nonagenario(a)
non-aggression ['nɒnə'greʃən] *adj Pol (pact, treaty)* de no agresión
non-alcoholic ['nɒnælkə'hɒlɪk] *adj* sin alcohol
nonaligned ['nɒnə'laɪnd] *adj Pol* no alineado(a)
nonalignment ['nɒnə'laɪnmənt] *n Pol* no alineamiento *m*
non-appearance ['nɒnə'pɪərəns] *n* (**a**) *(absence)* ausencia *f* (**b**) *Law* incomparecencia *f*
non-arrival ['nɒnə'raɪvəl] *n* **the n. of our guest/the merchandise** el hecho de que no llegara nuestro invitado/la mercancía
non-attendance ['nɒnə'tendəns] *n* ausencia *f*
non-attributable ['nɒnə'trɪbjʊtəbəl] *adj (briefing, remark)* anónimo(a); **on a n. basis** anónimamente
nonbeliever ['nɒnbɪ'li:və(r)] *n* no creyente *mf*
non-belligerent ['nɒnbə'lɪdʒərənt] **1** *n (country)* país *m* no beligerante
2 *adj* no beligerante
non-biological ['nɒnbaɪə'lɒdʒɪkəl] *adj (detergent)* sin acción biológica
nonce[1] ['nɒns] *n Literary or Hum* **for the n.** de momento, por el momento
nonce[2] *n Br very Fam* delincuente *m* sexual
nonce-word ['nɒnswɜ:d] *n* término *m* facticio
nonchalance ['nɒnʃələns, *US* nɒnʃə'lɑ:ns] *n (casualness)* despreocupación *f*; *(indifference)* indiferencia *f*
nonchalant ['nɒnʃələnt, *US* nɒnʃə'lɑ:nt] *adj (casual)* despreocupado(a); *(indifferent)* indiferente; **with a n. air** con aire despreocupado/indiferente; **with a n. shrug** encogiendo los hombros con indiferencia
nonchalantly ['nɒnʃələntlɪ, *US* nɒnʃə'lɑ:ntlɪ] *adv (casually)* con despreocupación; *(indifferently)* con indiferencia
non-Christian ['nɒn'krɪstʃən] **1** *n* no cristiano(a) *m,f*
2 *adj* no cristiano(a)
non-com ['nɒnkɒm] *n Mil Fam* suboficial *mf*
non-combatant [nɒn'kɒmbətənt] *Mil* **1** *n* no combatiente *mf*
2 *adj* no combatiente
non-commissioned officer ['nɒnkəmɪʃənd'ɒfɪsə(r)] *n Mil* suboficial *mf*
non-committal [nɒnkə'mɪtəl] *adj (answer)* evasivo(a); **to be n. (about)** responder con evasivas (acerca de)
non-compliance ['nɒnkəm'plaɪəns] *n Formal* incumplimiento *m* (**with** de)
non compos mentis ['nɒn'kɒmpəs'mentɪs] *adj Law* perturbado(a) mental; *Hum* **to be n.** estar atontado(a)
non-conductor [nɒnkən'dʌktə(r)] *n Elec* aislante *m*
nonconformist [nɒnkən'fɔ:mɪst] **1** *n* (**a**) *(maverick)* inconformista *mf* (**b**) *Br Rel* **N.** = miembro de una iglesia protestante escindida de la anglicana
2 *adj* (**a**) *(maverick)* inconformista (**b**) *Br Rel* **N.** = relativo a una iglesia protestante escindida de la anglicana
non-contributory ['nɒnkən'trɪbjʊtərɪ] *adj (pension scheme)* no contributivo(a)
non-controversial ['nɒnkɒntrə'vɜ:ʃəl] *adj* nada polémico(a); **I had expected my suggestion to be n.** no esperaba que mi sugerencia suscitara ninguna polémica
non-convertible ['nɒnkən'vɜ:təbəl] *adj (currency)* no convertible, inconvertible
non-co-operation ['nɒnkəʊɒpə'reɪʃən] *n* falta *f* de cooperación
non-custodial ['nɒnkə'stəʊdɪəl] *adj Law* ***n. sentence*** pena *f* que no implica privación de libertad
non-dairy ['nɒndeərɪ] *adj* no lácteo(a)
non-defining ['nɒndɪ'faɪnɪŋ] *adj Gram* ***n. relative clause*** oración *f* adjetiva explicativa
non-denominational ['nɒndɪnɒmɪ'neɪʃənəl] *adj* laico(a)
nondescript [*Br* 'nɒndɪskrɪpt, *US* nɒndɪ'skrɪpt] *adj (person, place, building)* anodino(a); *(taste)* indefinido(a)
nondirective ['nɒndə'rektɪv] *adj Psy* **n. therapy** (psico)terapia centrada en el cliente *or* no directiva
nondisclosure ['nɒndɪskləʊʒə(r)] *n Law (of evidence)* ocultación *f*
non-discriminatory ['nɒndɪs'krɪmɪnətərɪ] *adj* no discriminatorio(a)
non-drip ['nɒn'drɪp] *adj (paint)* que no gotea

NONE [nʌn] **1** *pron (not any)* nada; *(not one)* ninguno(a); **there was n. left** no quedaba nada; **there were n. left** no quedaba ninguno; **of all her novels, n. is better than this one** de todas sus novelas, ninguna es mejor que ésta; **n. of us/them** ninguno de nosotros/ellos; **n. of this concerns me** nada de esto me concierne; **he had n. of his brother's charm** no tenía ni mucho menos el encanto de su hermano; **I tried to help, but they would have n. of it** intenté ayudar, pero no querían saber nada; **she had a lot of luck, whereas I had n. at all** *or* **whatsoever** tuvo mucha suerte, y yo ninguna en absoluto; *Formal* **n. but his most devoted followers believed him** sólo sus seguidores más fervientes le creyeron; **it was n. other than the President** no era otro que el propio Presidente
2 *adv* **his answer left me n. the wiser** su respuesta no me aclaró nada; **I feel n. the worse for the experience** me siento perfectamente a pesar de la experiencia; **he's lost a couple of kilos but he's n. the worse for it** le ha sentado muy bien perder un par de kilos; **it was n. too easy** no fue nada fácil; **she was n. too happy about the situation** la situación no le hacía ninguna gracia; **n. too soon** justo a tiempo

non-elective ['nɒnɪ'lektɪv] *adj* no electivo(a)
nonentity [nɒ'nentɪtɪ] *n (insignificant person)* don nadie *mf*; *(useless person)* nulidad *f*
non-essential ['nɒnɪ'senʃəl] **1** *n* **non-essentials** lo accesorio
2 *adj* accesorio(a), prescindible
nonetheless = **nevertheless**
non-event ['nɒnɪ'vent] *n* chasco *m*; **the party turned out to be a bit of a n.** al final la fiesta no fue nada especial
non-executive director ['nɒnɪg'zekjʊtɪvdaɪ'rektə(r)] *n Com* director(ora) *m,f* no ejecutivo(a)
non-existence ['nɒnɪg'zɪstəns] *n* inexistencia *f*
non-existent ['nɒnɪg'zɪstənt] *adj* inexistente; **the n. safety procedures** las inexistentes normas de seguridad; **their contribution has been almost n.** su contribución ha sido prácticamente nula *or* inexistente
non-fat ['nɒnfæt] *adj (food)* sin grasa
non-fattening ['nɒn'fætnɪŋ] *adj* que no engorda
non-ferrous ['nɒn'ferəs] *adj (metals)* distinto(a) del hierro y el acero
non-fiction ['nɒn'fɪkʃən] *n* no ficción *f*; **I mostly read n.** la mayor parte de lo que leo no es literatura de ficción
non-fictional ['nɒn'fɪkʃənəl] *adj* **n. books** no ficción
non-figurative ['nɒn'fɪgjʊrətɪv] *adj Art* no figurativo(a)
non-finite ['nɒn'faɪnaɪt] *adj* (**a**) *(infinite)* infinito(a) (**b**) *Gram (verb)* no conjugado(a)
non-flammable ['nɒn'flæməbəl] *adj* incombustible, ininflamable
nong [nɒŋ] *n Austr Fam* estúpido(a) *m,f*, imbécil *mf*
non-governmental ['nɒngʌvən'mentəl] *adj* no gubernamental ►► ***n. organization*** ONG *f*, organización *f* no gubernamental
nonhuman ['nɒn'hju:mən] *adj* no humano(a)
noninfectious ['nɒnɪn'fekʃəs] *adj* no infeccioso(a)
non-interference ['nɒnɪntə'fɪərəns] *n* no intervención *f*
non-interlaced ['nɒnɪntə'leɪst] *adj Comptr (monitor)* no entrelazado(a)
non-intervention ['nɒnɪntə'venʃən] *n* no intervención *f*
non-invasive ['nɒnɪn'veɪsɪv] *adj Med* no invasivo(a)
non-judg(e)mental ['nɒndʒʌdʒ'mentəl] *adj* libre de prejuicios; **to try to be n.** tratar de dejar a un lado los prejuicios
non-juror ['nɒn'dʒʊərə(r)] *n Law* = persona que se niega a jurar lealtad
non-linear ['nɒn'lɪnɪə(r)] *adj Comptr (programming)* no lineal
nonmalignant ['nɒnmə'lɪgnənt] *adj* benigno(a)
non-member ['nɒn'membə(r)] *n* no miembro *mf*; *(of club)* no socio(a) *m,f*; *(of union, party)* no afiliado(a) *m,f*; **n. states** estados no miembros; **open to non-members** *(sign)* se permite el acceso a los no socios
non-native ['nɒn'neɪtɪv] *adj* no nativo(a); **n. speaker** hablante no nativo
non-negotiable ['nɒnnɪ'gəʊʃɪəbəl] *adj* no negociable; **these conditions are n.** estas condiciones no son negociables
non-nuclear ['nɒn'nju:klɪə(r)] *adj (war)* convencional; *(energy)* no nuclear; *(country)* sin armamento nuclear; **a n. defence policy** = una política de defensa que no incluye armas nucleares
no-no ['nəʊnəʊ] *n Fam* **asking him for more money is a definite n.** ni se te ocurra pedirle más dinero; **that's a n.** eso no se hace

no-nonsense [nəʊˈnɒnsəns] *adj (approach)* serio(a) y directo(a); *(implement, gadget)* práctico(a), funcional

nonpareil [nɒnpəˈreɪl] *n Literary (person)* persona *f* sin par *or* inigualable; *(thing)* cosa *f* sin par *or* inigualable; **the n. of literary novelists** el no va más de los novelistas serios

non-participating [ˈnɒnpɑːˈtɪsɪpeɪtɪŋ] *adj* (a) *(not taking part)* **n. members** los socios que no participan (b) *Fin (shares)* sin derecho a participación

non-partisan [nɒnˈpɑːtɪzæn] *adj* imparcial

non-party [ˈnɒnpɑːtɪ] *adj* independiente del partido

non-payment [nɒnˈpeɪmənt] *n* impago *m*

non-penetrative [ˈnɒnˈpenətrətɪv] *adj (sex)* sin penetración

non-persistent [ˈnɒnpəˈsɪstənt] *adj (pesticide)* (de acción) no permanente

non-person [ˈnɒnˈpɜːsən] *n* **politically, she became a n.** políticamente hablando, dejó de existir

nonplus [ˈnɒnˈplʌs] (*pt & pp Br* **nonplussed,** *US* **nonplused**) *vt* dejar perplejo(a) *or* anonadado(a) a

nonplussed [nɒnˈplʌst] *adj* perplejo(a), anonadado(a)

non-practising [ˈnɒnˈpræktɪsɪŋ] *adj* no practicante

non-productive [ˈnɒnprəˈdʌktɪv] *adj* improductivo(a)

non-profit(-making) [nɒnˈprɒfɪt(meɪkɪŋ)] *adj* sin ánimo de lucro

non-proliferation [ˈnɒnprəlɪfəˈreɪʃən] *n* no proliferación *f* ►► ***n. treaty*** tratado *m* de no proliferación

non-racist [nɒnˈreɪsɪst] *adj* no racista

non-refundable [ˈnɒnriːˈfʌndəbəl] *adj (deposit)* a fondo perdido, sin posibilidad de reembolso

non-renewable [ˈnɒnrɪˈnjuːəbəl] *adj* **n. resource/energy** recurso/energía no renovable

non-representational [ˈnɒnreprɪzenˈteɪʃənəl] *adj Art* no figurativo(a), no realista

non-resident [ˈnɒnˈrezɪdənt] *n* (a) *(of country)* no residente *mf* (b) *(of hotel)* **the dining room is open to non-residents** el comedor está abierto a clientes de fuera del hotel *or* al público en general

non-residential [ˈnɒnrezɪˈdenʃəl] *adj (course)* sin residencia ►► ***n. care*** asistencia *f or* atención *f* a domicilio

non-restrictive [nɒnrɪˈstrɪktɪv] *adj Gram (clause)* no restrictivo(a)

non-returnable [nɒnrɪˈtɜːnəbəl] *adj (bottle, container)* no retornable; *(deposit)* a fondo perdido, sin posibilidad de reembolso

non-scheduled [ˈnɒnˈʃedjuːld, *US* ˈnɒnˈskedjuːld] *adj (flight)* no regular; *(stop)* no programado(a) *or* previsto(a)

non-sectarian [ˈnɒnsekˈteərɪən] *adj* no sectario(a)

nonsense [ˈnɒnsəns] *n* (a) *(rubbish, absurdity)* tonterías *fpl*, disparates *mpl*; **n.!** ¡tonterías!; **a piece of n.** una tontería, un disparate; **to talk (a lot of) n.** decir (muchos) disparates; **you're talking n.!** ¡eso que dices es una tontería *or* un disparate!; **his accusations are utter n.** sus acusaciones son un completo disparate; **it's n. to say that things will never improve** es absurdo decir que las cosas no van a mejorar nunca; **what's all this n. about going to live in America?** ¿qué es esa tontería *or* qué tontería es ésa de irse a vivir a América?; **to make a n. of sth** *(rules)* poner en evidencia algo; *(attempt)* echar por tierra algo ►► ***n. verse*** poesía *f* absurda; ***n. word*** palabra *f* sin sentido

(b) *(foolishness, silly behaviour)* tonterías *fpl*; **stop this** *or* **no more of this n.!** ¡ya basta de tonterías!; **I've had enough of your n.!** ¡ya estoy harto de tus tonterías!; **she took no n. from her subordinates** no toleraba ninguna tontería de sus subordinados

nonsensical [nɒnˈsensɪkəl] *adj* absurdo(a), disparatado(a)

non sequitur [nɒnˈsekwɪtə(r)] *n* incongruencia *f*

non-sexist [ˈnɒnˈseksɪst] *adj* no sexista

non-skid [ˈnɒnskɪd], **non-slip** [ˈnɒnslɪp] *adj (surface)* antideslizante

non-smoker [ˈnɒnˈsməʊkə(r)] *n* no fumador(ora) *m,f*

non-smoking [ˈnɒnsməʊkɪŋ] *adj (area, carriage)* de no fumadores; **this is a n. flight** no está permitido fumar en este vuelo

non-specialist [ˈnɒnˈspeʃəlɪst] 1 *n* profano(a) *m,f*

2 *adj* no especializado(a)

non-specific [ˈnɒnspəˈsɪfɪk] *adj* (a) *(not precise)* amplio(a) (b) *Med* ***n. urethritis*** uretritis *f inv* no gonocócica

non-standard [ˈnɒnˈstændəd] *adj* (a) *Ling* no normativo(a) (b) *(product, size)* fuera de lo común

non-starter [ˈnɒnˈstɑːtə(r)] *n* (a) *Fam* **the project's a n.** es un proyecto inviable (b) *(horse)* caballo *m* inscrito y no presentado

non-stick [ˈnɒnˈstɪk] *adj* antiadherente

non-stop [ˈnɒnˈstɒp] 1 *adj (journey, flight)* directo(a), sin escalas; **they kept up a n. conversation** mantuvieron una conversación ininterrumpida *or* sin interrupciones

2 *adv (to talk, work)* sin parar, ininterrumpidamente; *(to fly)* directo

non-tariff barrier [ˈnɒnˈtærɪfˈbærɪə(r)] *n Econ* barrera *f* no arancelaria

non-taxable [ˈnɒnˈtæksəbəl] *adj* exento(a) de impuestos

non-threatening [ˈnɒnˈθretənɪŋ] *adj (manner, environment)* amistoso(a), no hostil

non-toxic [ˈnɒnˈtɒksɪk] *adj* atóxico(a), no tóxico(a)

non-transferable [ˈnɒntræns'fɜːrəbəl] *adj* intransferible

non-U [nɒnˈjuː] *adj Br Fam* **to be n.** *(expression, activity)* no ser de clase alta

non-union [nɒnˈjuːnɪən], **non-unionized** [ˈnɒnˈjuːnjənaɪzd] *adj* (a) *(worker, labour)* no sindicado(a) (b) *(firm, company)* = que no permite que sus trabajadores se afilien a ningún sindicato

non-verbal [nɒnˈvɜːbəl] *adj (communication)* no verbal

non-violence [nɒnˈvaɪələns] *n* no agresión *f*

non-violent [nɒnˈvaɪələnt] *adj* no violento(a)

non-vocational [ˈnɒnvəˈkeɪʃənəl] *adj* de carácter no profesional

non-voting [nɒnˈvəʊtɪŋ] *adj* (a) *(person) (not eligible)* sin derecho a voto; *(not exercising right)* abstencionista (b) *Fin (shares)* sin derecho a voto

non-white [nɒnˈwaɪt] 1 *n* = en Sudáfrica, durante el apartheid, persona de etnia diferente a la blanca

2 *adj* no blanco

noodle [ˈnuːdəl] *n* (a) *(pasta)* **noodles** tallarines *mpl (chinos)* ►► ***chicken n. soup*** sopa *f* de pollo con tallarines (b) *Br Fam (fool)* zoquete *m*, tarugo *m* (c) *US Fam (head)* coco *m*, mollera *f*

nook [nʊk] *n* (a) *(corner)* rincón *m*, recoveco *m*; **nooks and crannies** recovecos *mpl* (b) *Literary (secluded spot)* rincón *m*

nooky, nookie [ˈnʊkɪ] *n Fam Hum* marcha *f* para el cuerpo, ñacañaca *m*

noon [nuːn] *n* mediodía *m*; **at n.** al mediodía

noonday [ˈnuːndeɪ] *n* **the n. sun/heat** el sol/calor del mediodía

no one [ˈnəʊwʌn] *pron* = **nobody**

noontide [ˈnuːntaɪd] *n Literary* mediodía *m*

noontime [ˈnuːntaɪm] *n* mediodía *m*; **the n. traffic** el tráfico del mediodía *or* a mediodía

noose [nuːs] *n (loop)* nudo *m* corredizo; *(rope)* soga *f*; **the (hangman's) n.** la soga (del verdugo); IDIOM **to put one's head in a n., to put a n. around one's neck** meterse en la boca del lobo

NOP [enəʊˈpiː] *n* (*abbr* **National Opinion Polls** *or* **Poll**) = institución británica encargada de realizar sondeos de opinión

nope [nəʊp] *adv Fam* no

noplace [ˈnəʊpleɪs] *adv US* = **nowhere**

nor [nɔː(r)] 1 *conj (following* **neither, not***)* ni; **neither... n.** ni... ni; **I can offer you neither money n. assistance** no te puedo ofrecer ni dinero ni ayuda; **he neither drinks n. smokes** ni fuma ni bebe *orAm* toma; **n. do I** yo tampoco, ni yo

2 *adv* ni; **it's not the first time, n. will it be the last** no es la primera vez, ni será la última; **I don't like fish – n. do I** no me gusta el pescado – a mí tampoco *or* ni a mí; **I haven't read it, n. do I intend to** ni lo he leído, ni pienso hacerlo; **n. was that all...** y eso no fue todo...

nor' [nɔː(r)] *prefix* nor-

Nordic [ˈnɔːdɪk] *adj* nórdico(a) ►► ***N. skiing*** esquí *m* nórdico; ***N. track*** *(exercise)* = esquí realizado en un aparato gimnástico estático

Norf (*abbr* **Norfolk**) Norfolk

norm [nɔːm] *n* norma *f*; **social norms** costumbres *fpl* sociales; **to deviate from the n.** salirse de la norma; **to be a break from the n.** romper con la rutina ►► *Educ* ***n. referencing*** = comparación del nivel de un alumno con el de sus compañeros

normal [ˈnɔːməl] 1 *n* **above/below n.** *(temperature, rate)* por encima/por debajo de lo normal; **things quickly got back to n. after the strike** las cosas volvieron pronto a la normalidad después de la huelga; **he'll soon be back to n.** pronto se recuperará; **the situation has returned to n.** la situación se ha normalizado

2 *adj* (a) *(common, typical, standard)* normal; **a perfectly n. baby** un bebé perfectamente normal; **under n. conditions of use** en condiciones de uso normales; **it's n. to feel jealous** es normal sentir celos; **any n. person would have given up** cualquier otro habría abandonado

(b) *(habitual)* normal; **it's not n. for him to be so cheerful** no es normal que esté tan alegre; **at the n. time** a la hora habitual *or* acostumbrada, a la hora de siempre

(**c**) *Math (in statistics)* normal ►► ***n. distribution*** distribución *f* normal
(**d**) *Educ* ***n. school*** escuela *f* normal

normality [nɔːˈmælɪtɪ], *US* **normalcy** [ˈnɔːməlsɪ] *n* normalidad *f*; **everything returned to n.** todo volvió a la normalidad, todo se normalizó

normalization [nɔːməlaɪˈzeɪʃən] *n* normalización *f*

normalize [ˈnɔːməlaɪz] **1** *vt* normalizar
2 *vi* normalizarse

normally [ˈnɔːməlɪ] *adv* (**a**) *(in normal manner)* normalmente, con normalidad; **he's behaving n.** se comporta normalmente *or* con normalidad (**b**) *(ordinarily)* normalmente; **I n. get up at half past seven** normalmente me levanto a las siete y media

Norman [ˈnɔːmən] **1** *n* normando(a) *m,f*
2 *adj* normando(a) ►► *Hist* ***the N. Conquest*** la conquista normanda

Normandy [ˈnɔːməndɪ] *n* Normandía ►► *Hist* ***the N. landings*** el Desembarco de Normandía

normative [ˈnɔːmətɪv] *adj* normativo(a)

Norse [nɔːs] **1** *n (language)* nórdico *m*, lengua *f* nórdica *or* escandinava
2 *adj* nórdico(a), escandinavo(a)

Norseman [ˈnɔːsmən] *n* vikingo *m*

north [nɔːθ] **1** *n* norte *m*; **to the n. (of)** al norte (de); **the n. of Spain** el norte de España; **the wind is in** *or* **(coming) from the n.** el viento sopla del norte ►► ***the North–South divide*** *(in Britain)* la división *or* fractura Norte-Sur (en Gran Bretaña); *(in global economy)* la división Norte-Sur
2 *adj* (**a**) *(direction, side)* norte; **the n. coast** la costa norte *or* septentrional; **n. London** el norte de Londres ►► ***n. wind*** viento *m* del norte
(**b**) *(in names)* ***N. Africa*** África del Norte; ***N. African*** norteafricano(a) *m,f*; ***N. America*** Norteamérica, América del Norte; ***N. American*** norteamericano(a) *m,f*; ***N. American Free Trade Agreement*** Tratado *m* de Libre Comercio de América del Norte; ***N. Atlantic Treaty Organization*** Organización *f* del Tratado del Atlántico Norte; ***N. Carolina*** Carolina del Norte; ***the N. Country*** *Br* el norte de Inglaterra; *US* la zona nororiental de Norteamérica *(Alaska, Territorio del Yukón y Territorios del Noroeste)*; ***N. Dakota*** Dakota del Norte; ***N. Korea*** Corea del Norte; ***N. Korean*** norcoreano(a) *m,f*; ***the N. Pole*** el Polo Norte; ***the N. Sea*** el Mar del Norte; ***N. Star*** estrella *f* Polar
3 *adv* al norte; **it's (3 miles) n. of here** está (a 3 millas) al norte de aquí; **they live up n.** viven en el norte; **n. by east/by west** norte cuarta al nordeste/noroeste; **to face n.** *(person)* mirar hacia el norte; *(room)* estar orientado(a) *or* mirar al norte; **to go n.** ir hacia el norte

Northants [nɔːˈθænts] (*abbr* **Northamptonshire**) Northamptonshire

northbound [ˈnɔːθbaʊnd] *adj (train, traffic)* en dirección norte; **the n. carriageway** el carril que va hacia el norte

Northd (*abbr* **Northumberland**) Northumberland

northeast [nɔːθˈiːst] **1** *n* nordeste *m*, noreste *m*; **they live in the n.** viven al *or* en el nordeste *or* noreste
2 *adj (side)* nordeste, noreste ►► ***n. wind*** viento *m* del nordeste
3 *adv (to go, move)* hacia el nordeste; *(to be situated, face)* al nordeste

north-easter [nɔːθˈiːstə(r)] *n* viento *m* del nordeste

northeasterly [nɔːθˈiːstəlɪ] **1** *n (wind)* viento *m* del nordeste
2 *adj (direction)* nordeste ►► ***n. wind*** viento *m* del nordeste

northeastern [nɔːθˈiːstən] *adj (region)* del nordeste

northeastward [nɔːθˈiːstwəd] **1** *adj (direction)* nordeste, noreste; *(movement)* hacia el nordeste
2 *adv* hacia el nordeste, en dirección nordeste

northeastwardly [nɔːθˈiːstwədlɪ] **1** *adj (direction)* nordeste, noreste; *(movement)* hacia el nordeste
2 *adv* hacia el nordeste, en dirección nordeste

northeastwards [nɔːθˈiːstwədz] *adv* hacia el nordeste, en dirección nordeste

northerly [ˈnɔːðəlɪ] **1** *n (wind)* viento *m* del norte
2 *adj (direction)* norte; **the most n. point** el punto más septentrional ►► ***n. wind*** viento *m* del norte

northern [ˈnɔːðən] *adj (region, accent)* del norte, norteño(a); **n. Spain** el norte de España ►► ***n. fulmar*** fulmar *m* boreal; ***n. gannet*** alcatraz *m* atlántico ***n. hemisphere*** hemisferio *m* norte; ***N. Ireland*** Irlanda del Norte; ***N. Irish*** norirlandés(esa); ***n. lights*** aurora *f* boreal; ***n. oriole*** turpial *m* norteño; ***N. Territory*** Territorio *m* del Norte *(región australiana)*

northerner [ˈnɔːðənə(r)] *n* norteño(a) *m,f*; **I find that northerners are more friendly** encuentro a la gente del norte más simpática

northernmost [ˈnɔːðənməʊst] *adj* más septentrional, más al norte; **the n. island of the archipelago** la isla más septentrional del archipiélago

north-facing [ˈnɔːθˈfeɪsɪŋ] *adj* orientado(a) al norte

north-northeast [ˈnɔːθnɔːθˈiːst] *adv* en dirección nornordeste

north-northwest [ˈnɔːθnɔːθˈwest] *adv* en dirección nornoroeste

Northumb (*abbr* **Northumberland**) Northumberland

Northumbrian [nɔːˈθʌmbrɪən] **1** *n* persona *f* de Northumberland
2 *adj* de Northumberland

northward [ˈnɔːθwəd] **1** *adj* hacia el norte
2 *adv* hacia el norte

northwards [ˈnɔːθwədz] *adv* hacia el norte

northwest [nɔːθˈwest] **1** *n* noroeste *m*; **they live in the n.** viven en el *or* al noroeste
2 *adj (side)* noroeste ►► ***the N. Passage*** el paso *or* la ruta del Noroeste *(del Atlántico al Pacífico)*; ***the N. Territories*** los Territorios del Noroeste *(región canadiense)*; ***n. wind*** viento *m* del noroeste
3 *adv (to go, move)* hacia el noroeste; *(to be situated, face)* al noroeste

northwester [ˈnɔːθˈwestə(r)] *n* viento *m* del noroeste

northwesterly [nɔːθˈwestəlɪ] **1** *n (wind)* viento *m* del noroeste
2 *adj (direction)* noroeste ►► ***n. wind*** viento *m* del noroeste

northwestern [nɔːθˈwestən] *adj (region)* del noroeste

northwestward [nɔːθˈwestwəd] **1** *adj (direction)* noroeste; *(movement)* hacia el noroeste
2 *adv* hacia el noroeste, en dirección noroeste

northwestwardly [nɔːθˈwestwədlɪ] **1** *adj (direction)* noroeste; *(movement)* hacia el noroeste
2 *adv* hacia el noroeste, en dirección noroeste

northwestwards [nɔːθˈwestwədz] *adv* hacia el noroeste, en dirección noroeste

Norway [ˈnɔːweɪ] *n* Noruega ►► ***N. lobster*** cigala *f*

Norwegian [nɔːˈwiːdʒən] **1** *n* (**a**) *(person)* noruego(a) *m,f* (**b**) *(language)* noruego *m*
2 *adj* noruego(a)

Nos., nos. (*abbr* **numbers**) núms., n.

nose [nəʊz] **1** *n* (**a**) *(of person)* nariz *f*; **her n. is bleeding** está sangrando por la nariz; **your n. is running** tienes mocos, te moquea la nariz; **I punched him on** *or* **in the n.** le di un puñetazo en la nariz; **she's always got her n. in a book** siempre anda enfrascada en algún libro; **to blow one's n.** sonarse la nariz; **to hold one's n.** taparse la nariz; **to speak through one's n.** hablar con voz gangosa ►► *Fam* ***n. candy*** *(cocaine)* coca *f*, nieve *f*; ***n. drops*** gotas *fpl* para la nariz; *Fam* ***n. job:* to have a n. job** *(cosmetic surgery)* operarse la nariz; *Fam* ***n. rag*** pañuelo *m* de los mocos; ***n. ring*** *(on animal)* aro *m (en la nariz)*; *(on person) Esp* pendiente *m or Am* arete *m* de la nariz
(**b**) *(of animal)* hocico *m*; **the dog has a wet n.** el perro tiene el hocico húmedo; **the favourite won by a n.** *(in horseracing)* el favorito ganó en la misma línea *or* por muy poco; **I'll have £10 on the n.** apostaré 10 libras a ganador
(**c**) *(sense of smell)* olfato *m*; *Fig* **to have a n. for sth** tener olfato para algo; **she's got a (good) n. for a bargain** tiene (mucho) olfato para las gangas
(**d**) *(aroma) (of wine)* buqué *m*, bouquet *m*
(**e**) *(of vehicle, plane, missile)* parte *f* delantera, morro *m*; *(of ship)* proa *f*; *(of bullet)* cono *m*, punta *f*; **the traffic was n. to tail** había caravana ►► *Av* ***n. cone*** morro *m*; *Av* ***n. wheel*** rueda *f* delantera
(**f**) IDIOMS **it's right under your n.** lo tienes delante de las narices; **they stole it from under the nose(s) of the police** lo robaron delante de las narices de la policía; **you've got** *or* **hit it right on the n.** has dado en el clavo; **to cut off one's n. to spite one's face** tirar (uno) piedras contra su propio tejado; *Br* **to get up sb's n.** poner negro(a) a alguien; **to keep one's n. clean** no meterse en líos; *Fam* **keep your (big) n. out of my business!** ¡no metas la nariz *or* las narices en mis asuntos!; **to keep one's n. to the grindstone** dar el callo; **to keep sb's n. to the grindstone** hacer que alguien dé el callo; **they are leading them by the n.** les están manejando a su antojo; **to look down one's n. at sb** mirar a alguien por encima del hombro; **to look down one's n. at sth** hacer ascos a algo, tener algo en poco; **she paid through the n. for it** le costó un ojo de la cara; **to poke** *or* **stick one's n. into other people's business** meter las narices en los asuntos de otros; **to put sb's n. out of joint** hacerle un feo a alguien; **to turn one's n. up at sth** hacerle ascos a algo; **she walked by with her n. in the air** pasó con gesto engreído

2 *vt (push with nose)* **the dog nosed the door open** el perro abrió la puerta (empujando) con el hocico

3 *vi* (**a**) *(advance gradually)* **the car nosed out into the traffic** el coche *or Am* carro *or CSur* auto se fue incorporando al tráfico; **he nosed into the lead on the final stretch** poco a poco logró ponerse en cabeza en la recta final (**b**) *Fam (snoop)* **to n. into sth** husmear en algo, meter la nariz *or* las narices en algo

▸ **nose about, nose around** *vi Fam* husmear, curiosear; **two men came nosing about for information** llegaron dos hombres fisgoneando en busca de información; **I don't want them nosing about in here!** ¡no quiero que anden husmeando *or* curioseando por aquí!

▸ **nose out** *vt sep* (**a**) *(track down)* dar con; **he can n. out a bargain at an auction better than anyone** sabe como nadie olfatear una ganga en una subasta (**b**) *Fam (beat narrowly)* ganar por los pelos *or* por muy poco

nosebag ['nəʊzbæg] *n* morral *m*

noseband ['nəʊzbænd] *n* muserola *f*

nosebleed ['nəʊzbliːd] *n* hemorragia *f* nasal; **to have a n.** sangrar por la nariz

-nosed [nəʊzd] *suffix* **red-n.** con la nariz colorada

nose-dive ['nəʊzdaɪv] **1** *n* (**a**) *(of plane) Esp* picado *m*, *Am* picada *f*; **to take a n.** hacer *Esp* un picado *or Am* una picada (**b**) *(of prices, popularity)* caída *f* en *Esp* picado *or Am* picada; **to take a n.** caer en *Esp* picado *or Am* picada

2 *vi (plane)* hacer *Esp* un picado *or Am* una picada (**b**) *(prices, popularity)* caer en *Esp* picado *or Am* picada

nosegay ['nəʊzgeɪ] *n Literary* ramillete *m* de flores

nosepiece ['nəʊzpiːs] *n* (**a**) *(of bridle)* muserola *f* (**b**) *(of spectacles)* puente *m*

nosey, nosy ['nəʊzɪ] *adj Fam* entrometido(a); **I don't mean to be n., but...** no quisiera parecer entrometido *or* meterme donde no me llaman, pero... ▸▸ ***n. parker*** metomentodo *mf*

nosh [nɒʃ] *Br Fam* **1** *n (food) Esp* manduca *f*, *Méx, RP* papa *f*, *RP* morfi *m*

2 *vi (eat)* manducar, *Méx* echar papa, *RP* morfar

no-show [nəʊ'ʃəʊ] *n* (**a**) *(for flight)* pasajero *m* (con reserva) no presentado (**b**) *(at theatre)* reserva *f* no cubierta

nosh-up ['nɒʃʌp] *n Br Fam* comilona *f*

nosily ['nəʊzɪlɪ] *adv* **he n. asked how much she earned** el muy entrometido le preguntó cuánto ganaba

nosiness ['nəʊzɪnɪs] *n* entrometimiento *m*

no-smoking ['nəʊ'sməʊkɪŋ] *adj (carriage, area)* de *or* para no fumadores

nostalgia [nɒs'tældʒɪə] *n* nostalgia *f* (**for** de)

nostalgic [nɒs'tældʒɪk] *adj* nostálgico(a); **to be** *or* **feel n. for sth** tener *or* sentir nostalgia de algo

nostalgically [nɒs'tældʒɪklɪ] *adv* con nostalgia

nostril ['nɒstrɪl] *n* orificio *m* nasal, ventana *f* de la nariz

nostrum ['nɒstrəm] *n Literary* remedio *m* milagroso

nosy = **nosey**

NOT [nɒt] *adv*

En el inglés hablado, y en el escrito en estilo coloquial, **not** se contrae después de verbos modales y auxiliares.

no; **it's n. easy, it isn't easy** no es fácil; **it's n. unusual for this to happen** no es raro que ocurra esto; **n. me/him** yo/él no; **n. now/on Sundays** ahora/los domingos no; **I don't know** no sé; **it's terrible – no, it isn't!** es terrible – ¡no, no lo es!; **don't move!** ¡no te muevas!; **are you coming or n.?** ¿vienes o no?, *RP* ¿venís o no venís?; **whether she likes it or n.** le guste o no; **I think/hope n.** creo/espero que no; **are you going? – I'd rather n.** ¿vas? – preferiría no ir; **she asked me n. to tell him** me pidió que no se lo dijera; **you were wrong n. to tell him** hiciste mal en no decírselo; **you understand, don't you?** entiendes, ¿no?; **it's good, isn't it?** está bueno, ¿verdad? *or Esp* ¿a qué sí?; **n. her again!** ¡ella otra vez!, *Am* ¡otra vez (esta mujer)!; **n. wishing to cause an argument, he said nothing** como no deseaba provocar una discusión, no dijo nada; **it happened n. 10 metres away from where we are standing** ocurrió ni a 10 metros de donde estamos; *Fam* **I really liked her... n.!** me gustó mucho... ¡qué va!, *RP* me cayó muy bien... ¡nada que ver!; **you have one hour and n. a minute longer** tienes una hora, ni un minuto más; **n. at all** en absoluto; **it was n. at all funny** no tuvo nada de gracia, no fue nada gracioso; **thank you so much! – n. at all!** ¡muchísimas gracias! – ¡de nada! *or* ¡no hay de qué!; **n. always** no siempre; **n. any more** ya no; **n. even** ni siquiera; **n. one** *or* **a single person answered** ni una sola persona contestó; **n. only... but also...** no sólo... sino (que) también...; **n. that I minded** no es que me importara; **we missed the train, n. that I minded much** perdimos el tren, aunque no es que me importara mucho; **we lost, n. that it matters** perdimos, ¡pero qué más da! *or* ¡pero da lo mismo!; **n. yet** todavía no, aún no; *Br Fig Hum* **he is 86 n. out** tiene 86 años y aún le queda cuerda para rato

notable ['nəʊtəbəl] **1** *n (person)* persona *f* distinguida

2 *adj* notable; **to be n. for sth** destacar por algo; **it is n. that...** cabe resaltar que...; **with a few n. exceptions** con alguna que otra notable excepción

notably ['nəʊtəblɪ] *adv* (**a**) *(especially)* en particular, en especial (**b**) *(noticeably)* notablemente; **his name was n. absent from the list** notoriamente, su nombre no aparecía en la lista

notarize ['nəʊtəraɪz] *vt US Law (document)* autenticar, legalizar; **a notarized copy** una copia notarial *or* legalizada ante notario

notary ['nəʊtərɪ] *n Law* **n. (public)** notario(a) *m,f*, *Am* escribano(a) *m,f*

notation [nəʊ'teɪʃən] *n* (**a**) *(sign system)* notación *f*; **musical/mathematical n.** notación musical/matemática; **in binary n.** en sistema binario (**b**) *US (jotting)* anotación *f*

notch [nɒtʃ] **1** *n* (**a**) *(in stick)* muesca *f*; IDIOM **a n. on the bedpost** una conquista amorosa (**b**) *(grade, level)* punto *m*, grado *m*; **she's a n. above the rest** está por encima de los demás; **he's gone up a n. in my estimation** ha subido algún entero en mi estima, conmigo se ha apuntado un tanto (**c**) *US (gorge)* garganta *f*, desfiladero *m*

2 *vt (make cut in) (once)* hacer una muesca en; *(several times)* hacer muescas en

▸ **notch up** *vt sep (victory, sale)* apuntarse

note [nəʊt] **1** *n* (**a**) *(record)* nota *f*; **(lecture) notes** apuntes *mpl* de clase; **she spoke from/without notes** hablaba mirando/sin mirar las notas; **to take** *or* **make a n. of sth** tomar nota de algo, apuntar algo; **make a n. of everything you spend** apunta todo lo que gastes; **to take notes** *(of lecture, reading)* tomar notas; **to take n. of sth/sb** *(notice)* fijarse en algo/alguien; **I must make a (mental) n. to myself to ask her about it** tengo que acordarme de preguntárselo

(**b**) *(short letter)* nota *f*; **she left a n. to say she'd call back later** dejó una nota diciendo que volvería más tarde

(**c**) *(formal communication)* nota *f* (oficial); **the embassy sent a n. of protest** la embajada envió una nota (oficial) de protesta

(**d**) *(annotation, commentary) (handwritten)* nota *f*, anotación *f*; *(printed)* nota *f*; **editor's/translator's n.** nota del editor/traductor; **see n. 6** véase la nota número 6

(**e**) *(sound, tone)* tono *m*; *Fig (of doubt, anger)* nota *f*, tono *m*; **there was a n. of contempt in her voice** había un tono *or* deje de desprecio en su voz; **the meeting began on a promising n.** la reunión tuvo un comienzo prometedor; **on a lighter n.** pasando a cosas menos serias; **her speech struck a warning n.** su discurso dio un toque de atención; **the flowers add a n. of colour** las flores añaden una nota *or* un toque de color

(**f**) *(musical)* nota *f*; **to hit a high n.** *(in singing)* dar una nota alta

(**g**) *esp Br (banknote)* billete *m*; **a ten-pound n.** un billete de diez libras

2 *vt* (**a**) *(observe, notice)* notar; *(error, mistake)* advertir; *(fact, circumstance)* darse cuenta de; **we have noted several omissions** hemos advertido algunas omisiones; **he noted that the window was open** se dio cuenta de que la ventana estaba abierta; **please n. that...** tenga en cuenta que...; **please n. that payment is now due** permítanos informarle de que *or* recordarle que el plazo de pago ha vencido; **n. that she didn't actually refuse** fíjate que ella en ningún momento se negó

(**b**) *(write down)* anotar, apuntar; **all sales are noted in this book** en este libro se anotan *or* apuntan todas las ventas

(**c**) *(mention)* señalar; **as I noted earlier** como ya señalé antes

3 of note *adj (outstanding) (person)* destacado(a); *(thing, event)* destacable; **a writer of n.** un destacado *or* excepcional escritor; **a historian of some n.** un historiador de cierto renombre; **nothing of n. happened** no ocurrió nada destacable *or* nada digno de mención

▸ **note down** *vt sep* anotar, apuntar

notebook ['nəʊtbʊk] *n* (**a**) *(small)* libreta *f*; *(bigger)* cuaderno *m* (**b**) *Comptr* **n. (computer)** *Esp* ordenador *m or Am* computadora *f* portátil

notecase ['nəʊtkeɪs] *n Br Old-fashioned (wallet)* cartera *f*

noted ['nəʊtɪd] *adj* destacado(a); **a n. surgeon** un(a) destacado(a) cirujano(a); **to be n. for sth** destacar por algo; **a region n. for its lakes** una región conocida *or* famosa por sus lagos; **he's not n. for his subtlety** no destaca precisamente por su sutileza, lo que se dice sutil no es

notelet ['nəʊtlɪt] *n Br* = papel de cartas decorado y doblado en cuatro

notepad ['nəʊtpæd] *n* **(a)** *(paper)* libreta *f*, bloc *m* de notas **(b)** *Comptr* **n. (computer)** agenda *f* electrónica

notepaper ['nəʊtpeɪpə(r)] *n* papel *m* de carta

noteworthy ['nəʊtwɜːðɪ] *adj* destacable, digno(a) de mención; **a n. example of this trend** un ejemplo destacable de esta tendencia; **it is n. that...** cabe destacar que...

not-for-profit ['nɒtfər'prɒfɪt] *adj US* sin ánimo de lucro

NOTHING ['nʌθɪŋ] **1** *pron* nada; **n. new/remarkable** nada nuevo/especial; **n. happened** no pasó nada; **n. has been decided** no se ha decidido nada; **I have n. to do** no tengo nada que hacer; **I've had n. to eat** no he comido nada; **it's n. to worry about** no es para preocuparse; **n. you can do will make up for it** hagas lo que hagas no podrás compensarme; **say n. about it** no digas nada (de esto); **are you all right? – yes, it's n.** ¿estás bien? – sí, no es nada; **thank you very much – it was n.** muchísimas gracias – de nada *or* no hay de qué; **$1,000 is n. to her** para ella 1.000 dólares no son nada; **it's all or n. now** ahora es todo o nada; **there's n. clever about it** no tiene nada de inteligente; **to get angry/worried for** *or* **about n.** *esp Esp* enfadarse *or esp Am* enojarse/preocuparse por nada; **to do sth for n.** *(in vain)* hacer algo para nada; *(with no reason)* hacer algo porque sí; *(free of charge)* hacer algo gratis; **he has built up the firm from n.** ha construido la empresa partiendo de la nada; **you've caused me n. but trouble** no me has traído (nada) más que problemas; **buy n. but the best** compre sólo lo mejor; **n. else** nada más; **there is n. for it (but to...)** no hay más remedio (que...); **he was n. if not discreet** desde luego fue muy discreto; **there's n. in it** *(it's untrue)* es falso; **there's n. in it between the two models** los dos modelos se diferencian en muy poco; **there's n. like a nice steak!** ¡no hay nada como un buen filete!; **there is n. more to be said** no hay (nada) más que decir; **n. much** no mucho, poca cosa; **I said n. of the sort** yo no dije nada de eso; **as a pianist he has n. on his brother** como pianista, no tiene ni punto de comparación con su hermano; **to have n. to do with sth/sb** no tener nada que ver con algo/alguien; **that's n. to do with you** no tiene nada que ver contigo; **I want n. to do with it** no quiero tener nada que ver con eso; **to make n. of sth** *(achievement, result)* no dar importancia a algo; *(regrettable occurrence or event)* quitar importancia *or Esp* hierro a algo; **to say n. of...** por no hablar de...; **he thinks n. of spending $100 on drink** le parece normal gastarse 100 dólares en bebida; **think n. of it** *(response to thanks)* no hay de qué; *(response to apology)* olvídalo; *Fam* **can you lend me ten dollars? – n. doing** ¿me prestas diez dólares? – ¡ni soñando *or* soñar! *or Esp* ¡de eso nada! *or Méx* ¡ni un quinto! *or RP* ¡ni loco(a)!; IDIOM *Fam* **there's n. to it** no tiene ningún misterio

2 *n* **(a)** *(zero)* cero *m*; **we won three n.** ganamos (por) tres a cero **(b)** *(insignificant person)* cero *m* a la izquierda **(c)** *(trifle)* **a hundred dollars? – a mere n.!** ¿cien dólares? – ¡una bagatela!; **to come to n.** quedar en nada

3 *adv* **she looks n. like her sister** no se parece en nada a su hermana; **it was n. like as difficult as they said** no era ni mucho menos tan difícil como decían; **your behaviour was n. less than** *or* **short of disgraceful** tu comportamiento fue de lo más vergonzoso; **it was n. more than a scratch** no fue más que un pequeño rasguño

4 *adj Fam (worthless)* **it's a n. play!** la obra no vale para nada

nothingness ['nʌθɪŋnɪs] *n* nada *f*; **he stared out into the n.** miraba al vacío

NOTICE ['nəʊtɪs] **1** *n* **(a)** *(warning)* aviso *m*; **we require five days' n.** necesitamos que nos avisen con cinco días de antelación; **to give sb n. of sth** avisar a alguien de algo, notificar algo a alguien; **at a moment's n.** enseguida; **at short n.** en poco tiempo, con poca antelación; **until further n.** hasta nuevo aviso; **without (prior) n.** sin previo aviso

(b) *(attention)* **to attract n.** llamar la atención; **to bring sth to sb's n.** llamar la atención de alguien sobre algo; **it has come to my n. that...** ha llegado a mi conocimiento que...; **the fact escaped everyone's n.** el hecho pasó inadvertido para todo el mundo; **to take n. of sth/sb** prestar atención a algo/alguien; **to take no n. (of), not to take any n. (of)** no hacer caso (de)

(c) *(intent to terminate contract)* **to give** *or* **hand in one's n.** *(resign)* presentar la dimisión, despedirse; **to give sb their n.** *(make redundant)* despedir a alguien; **to give sb a month's n.** *(of redundancy)* comunicarle a alguien el despido con un mes de antelación; *(to move out)* darle a alguien un plazo de un mes para abandonar el inmueble; **you must give at least a month's n.** debes avisar con al menos un mes de antelación ►► ***n. period*** periodo *m or* plazo *m* de preaviso

(d) *(sign)* cartel *m*; **a n. was pinned to the door** había una nota en la puerta

(e) *(announcement in newspaper)* anuncio *m*

(f) *Theat* crítica *f*, reseña *f*

2 *vt (realize)* darse cuenta de; *(sense)* notar; *(observe)* fijarse en; **I noticed (that) he was uncomfortable** me di cuenta de que estaba incómodo; **have you noticed anything strange in her behaviour?** ¿has notado algo extraño en su comportamiento?; **I noticed a man yawning at the back** me fijé en un hombre al fondo que bostezaba; **did you n. her smiling?** ¿te diste cuenta de cómo sonreía?; **I noticed a gap in the fence** vi un hueco en la valla; **I n. you've dyed your hair** veo que te has teñido el pelo; **to do sth without being noticed** hacer algo sin que nadie se dé cuenta; **to be noticed, to get oneself noticed** llamar la atención

3 *vi* darse cuenta

> **False friend:** The Spanish noun **noticia** is not a translation for the English word **notice**. In Spanish **noticia** means "(piece of) news".

noticeable ['nəʊtɪsəbəl] *adj (change, difference, improvement, effect)* apreciable, notable; **barely n.** apenas perceptible; **the stain is barely n.** la mancha apenas se nota; **it was very n. that...** se notaba claramente que...

noticeably ['nəʊtɪsəblɪ] *adv* claramente, notablemente; **students did n. less well in these subjects** claramente, estas asignaturas se les daban peor a los alumnos; **to be n. absent** brillar por su ausencia; **n. absent from this list were...** entre las ausencias notables de la lista estaban...; **have things improved? – not n.** ¿han mejorado las cosas? – no de manera significativa

noticeboard ['nəʊtɪsbɔːd] *n Br* tablón *m* de anuncios

notifiable [nəʊtɪ'faɪəbəl] *adj (disease)* notificable

notification [nəʊtɪfɪ'keɪʃən] *n* notificación *f*; **to give sb n. of sth** notificar algo a alguien; **to receive n. (of sth)** recibir notificación *or* aviso (de algo)

notify ['nəʊtɪfaɪ] *vt* notificar; **to n. sb of sth** notificar algo a alguien; **why was I not notified of these changes?** ¿por qué no se me notificaron estos cambios?; **keep us notified of any change in your plans** manténganos informados *or* avísenos si cambia de planes; **the authorities have been notified** ya se ha informado *or CAm, Méx* reportado a las autoridades; **winners will be notified within ten days** los ganadores recibirán notificación en el plazo de diez días

notion ['nəʊʃən] **1** *n* **(a)** *(idea, concept)* idea *f*, noción *f*; **have you any n. of what it will cost?** ¿tienes idea de lo que puede costar?; **where did she get the n.** *or* **whatever gave her the n. that we don't like her?** ¿de dónde habrá sacado la idea de que nos cae mal?; **to have no n. of sth** no tener noción de algo; **I have no n. where they might be** no tengo ni idea de dónde pueden estar; **I have a n. that...** me parece que...; **I lost all n. of time** perdí por completo la noción del tiempo

(b) *(urge, whim)* **to have a n. to do sth** tener el capricho de hacer algo; **she had a n. to paint it red** le dio por pintarlo de rojo

2 notions *npl US (sewing materials)* cosas *fpl* de costura

notional ['nəʊʃənəl] *adj* **(a)** *(hypothetical) (sum, fee)* teórico(a), hipotético(a); **after a n. inspection, the goods were passed** tras una inspección de puro trámite, la mercancía pasó **(b)** *Ling* nocional, léxico(a)

notoriety [nəʊtə'raɪətɪ] *n* mala fama *f*; **this action gained** *or* **earned him some n.** este acto le dio *or* granjeó cierta mala fama

notorious [nəʊ'tɔːrɪəs] *adj Pej* famoso(a), célebre *(por algo negativo)*; **he's a n. liar** es famoso por sus mentiras; **she's n. for being late** tiene fama de impuntual; **a city n. for its slums** una ciudad tristemente famosa *or* con mala fama por sus barrios bajos

> **False friend:** The Spanish adjective **notorio** is not a translation for the English word **notorious**. In Spanish **notorio** means "widely-known" or "obvious".

notoriously [nəʊ'tɔːrɪəslɪ] *adv* **it is n. difficult/bad** es de sobra conocido lo difícil/malo que es; **the trains here are n. unreliable** aquí los trenes tienen fama de funcionar muy mal

no-trump(s) ['nəʊ'trʌmp(s)] *adv* sin triunfo

not-too-distant ['nɒttuː'dɪstənt] *adj* **in the n. future** en un futuro no muy lejano

Notts [nɒts] *(abbr* **Nottinghamshire***)* (condado *m* de) Nottinghamshire

notwithstanding [nɒtwɪθ'stændɪŋ] *Formal* 1 *prep* a pesar de, pese a; **n. the agreement** a pesar del acuerdo; **no liability will be accepted by the management, the agreement n.** a pesar de lo que estipule el contrato, la dirección no se responsabilizará
2 *adv* no obstante, sin embargo

nougat ['nu:gɑ:] *n* = tipo de turrón de textura similar a un caramelo de tofe, con frutos secos y frutas confitadas

nought, *US* **naught** [nɔ:t] *n* cero *m*; **n. point five** cero coma cinco; *Br* **noughts and crosses** *(game)* tres en raya *m*

noun [naʊn] *n Gram* sustantivo *m*, nombre *m*; **common/proper n.** nombre común/propio ►► ***n. clause*** cláusula *f or* oración *f* sustantiva; ***n. phrase*** sintagma *m* nominal

nourish ['nʌrɪʃ] *vt* **(a)** *(person, animal)* nutrir, alimentar; **to be well nourished** estar bien alimentado(a) **(b)** *(feeling, hope)* abrigar, albergar

nourishing ['nʌrɪʃɪŋ] *adj* nutritivo(a)

nourishment ['nʌrɪʃmənt] *n* **(a)** *(food)* alimentos *mpl*; **the patient has taken no n.** el paciente no ha tomado ningún alimento **(b)** *(nourishing quality)* alimento *m*; **it's full of/lacking in n.** tiene mucho/poco alimento

nous [naʊs] *n Br Fam (common sense)* seso *m*; **anyone with any n. would have seen what was happening** cualquiera con dos dedos de frente habría visto lo que estaba pasando; **to have the n. to do sth** tener vista para hacer algo

nouveau riche [nu:vəʊ'ri:ʃ] *Pej* 1 *n* (*pl* **nouveaux riches**) nuevo(a) rico(a) *m,f*
2 *adj* de nuevo rico

nouvelle cuisine ['nu:velkwɪ'zi:n] *n Culin* nouvelle cuisine *f*

Nov (*abbr* **noviembre**) nov.

nova ['nəʊvə] (*pl* **novae** ['nəʊvi:] *or* **novas**) *n Astron* nova *f*

Nova Scotia ['nəʊvə'skəʊʃə] *n* Nueva Escocia

Nova Scotian ['nəʊvə'skəʊʃən] 1 *n* persona *f* de Nueva Escocia
2 *adj* de Nueva Escocia

novel ['nɒvəl] 1 *n* novela *f*
2 *adj (original)* novedoso(a), original; **what a n. idea!** ¡qué idea tan original!

novelese [nɒvə'li:z] *n Pej* prosa *f* novelesca

novelette [nɒvə'let] *n Pej* novelucha *f*

novelettish [nɒvə'letɪʃ] *adj Pej* sentimentaloide

novelist ['nɒvəlɪst] *n* novelista *mf*

novella [nɒ'velə] (*pl* **novellas**) *n* novela *f* corta

novelty ['nɒvəltɪ] *n* **(a)** *(newness)* novedad *f*; **the n. will soon wear off** pronto dejará de ser una novedad; **it has a certain n. value** tiene un cierto atractivo por ser nuevo
(b) *(new thing)* novedad *f*; **as the only Chinese child, I was something of a n.** al ser el único niño chino, yo era la novedad; **now there's a n.!** ¡vaya *or* menuda novedad!
(c) *(cheap toy)* chuchería *f*; **n. jewellery** joyas de fantasía

November [nəʊ'vembə(r)] *n* noviembre *m*; *see also* **May**

novena [nəʊ'vi:nə] *n Rel* novena *f*

novice ['nɒvɪs] *n* **(a)** *(beginner)* principiante *mf*, novato(a) *m,f*; **I'm still a n. at golf/computing** soy todavía un principiante en el golf/la informática **(b)** *Rel* novicio(a) *m,f*

novitiate, noviciate [nə'vɪʃɪət] *n Rel* **(a)** *(period)* noviciado *m* **(b)** *(place)* noviciado *m*

Novocaine® ['nəʊvəkeɪn] *n* novocaína® *f*

NOW [naʊ] (*abbr* **National Organization for Women**) *n* = organización estadounidense que defiende los derechos de las mujeres

NOW [naʊ] 1 *adv* **(a)** *(at this moment)* ahora; *(these days)* hoy (en) día; **what shall we do n.?** ¿y ahora qué hacemos?; **n. is the time to...** ahora es el momento de...; **n.'s our chance** ésta es nuestra oportunidad *or* la nuestra; **n. you tell me!** ¡y me lo dices ahora!; **it's two years n. since his mother died** hace dos años que murió su madre; **he won't be long n.** no tardará mucho, *Am* no demorará mucho más; **and n. for some music** y a continuación, un poco de música; **any day n.** cualquier día de estos; **any minute n.** en cualquier momento; **they should have finished before n.** ya deberían haber acabado; **between n. and next week** entre ahora y la próxima semana; **he ought to be here by n.** ya debería haber llegado; **if she can't do it by n., she never will** si todavía no lo sabe hacer, no lo sabrá nunca; **n. and then** *or* **again** de vez en cuando; **that'll do for n.** por ahora *or* por el momento es suficiente; **in three days from n.** de aquí a tres días; **from n. on, as of n.** a partir de ahora; **I'm busy just n.** ahora mismo *or* en este momento estoy ocupado; **I saw her just n.** la acabo de ver; **right n.** ahora mismo; **up to** *or* **until n.** hasta ahora; *Fam* **it's n. or never** ahora o nunca
(b) *(referring to moment in past)* entonces; **n. it was time for them to leave** entonces fue el momento de marcharse
(c) *(introducing statement, question)* **n., there are two ways of interpreting this** ahora bien, lo podemos interpretar de dos maneras; **n., let me see...** bueno, vamos a ver...; **n., if I were you...** escucha, si yo estuviera en tu lugar...; **n. that was a good idea** esa sí que ha sido una buena idea; **n. what have I said about using bad language?** ¿y qué es lo que te tengo dicho sobre las palabrotas?; **n. why would she say a thing like that?** ¿pero por qué iba a decir algo así?; **come on, n., or we'll be late** venga, date prisa *orAm* apúrate o llegaremos tarde; **be careful, n.!** ten mucho cuidado, ¡eh!; **well n.** *or* **n. then, what's happened here?** vamos a ver, ¿qué ha pasado?
(d) *(as reproof)* **come n.!** *Esp* ¡venga, hombre/mujer!, *Am* ¡pero qué cosa!; **n., n., stop quarrelling!** *Esp* ¡hala, hala! *orAm* ¡bueno, bueno! ¡basta de peleas!
(e) *(when comforting)* **n., n., there's no need to cry** *Esp* venga, vamos, no llores, *Am* bueno, bueno, no llores
2 *conj* ahora que; **n. (that) I'm older I think differently** ahora que soy más viejo *orAm* grande, ya no pienso igual; **n. (that) you mention it** ahora que lo dices
3 *adj Fam* **(a)** *(current)* **the n. president** el presidente de ahora **(b)** *(fashionable)* **the n. place to go** el sitio de moda

nowadays ['naʊədeɪz] *adv* hoy (en) día, actualmente; **where's she working/living n.?** ¿dónde trabaja/vive actualmente *or* ahora?

noway ['nəʊweɪ], **noways** ['nəʊweɪz] *adv Fam* de ninguna manera

NOWHERE ['nəʊweə(r)] 1 *n* **there was n. to stay** no había dónde alojarse; **they have n. to live** no tienen dónde vivir; **an ambulance appeared from n.** una ambulancia apareció de la nada; **he came from n. to win the race** remontó desde atrás y ganó la carrera
2 *adv* en/a ningún lugar, en/a ninguna parte; **where did you hide it? – n.** ¿dónde lo has escondido? – en ninguna parte; **where did they send you? – n.** ¿adónde te mandaron? – a ninguna parte; **he was n. to be found** no lo encontrábamos por ninguna parte; **they were n. to be seen** no los veíamos por ninguna parte; **n. does the report mention her name** en ninguna parte del informe *or CAm, Méx* reporte se menciona su nombre; **n. is this more evident than in his written work** donde más se pone en evidencia esto es en su obra escrita; **n. else** en/a ningún otro lugar; **it's n. near the mall** no queda nada cerca del centro comercial; **it's n. near good enough** está lejos de ser aceptable; **the rest were n.** *(in contest)* los demás quedaron muy por detrás; **qualifications alone will get you n.** sólo con los estudios no irás a ninguna parte; **I'm getting n. with this essay** no estoy avanzando nada con este trabajo; *Fam* **we're getting n. fast** estamos perdiendo el tiempo; **you will go n. until I tell you to** tú no te mueves de ahí hasta que no te lo diga; *Fig* **we're going n.** así no vamos a ninguna parte

no-win ['nəʊ'wɪn] *adj* **a n. situation** un callejón sin salida

nowise ['nəʊwaɪz] *adv US* **in n.** de ninguna manera

nowt [naʊt] *pron Br Fam (nothing)* nada; PROV **there's n. so queer as folk** hay gente para todo

noxious ['nɒkʃəs] *adj Formal (gas, substance)* nocivo(a), pernicioso(a); *(influence)* pernicioso(a)

nozzle ['nɒzəl] *n (for hose, paint gun, vacuum cleaner)* boquilla *f*; *(of rocket)* tobera *f*

NP [en'pi:] **(a)** (*abbr* **new paragraph**) punto y aparte **(b)** (*abbr* **New Providence**) Nueva Providencia **(c)** (*abbr* **Notary Public**) notario(a) *m,f*, *Am* escribano(a) *m,f* **(d)** *Gram* (*abbr* **noun phrase**) SN

NPV [enpi:'vi:] *n Fin* (*abbr* **net present value**) VAN *m*

nr (*abbr* **near**) cerca de

NRA [enɑ:'reɪ] *n* (*abbr* **National Rifle Association**) = asociación estadounidense que se opone a cualquier restricción en el uso de armas de fuego

NRV [enɑ:'vi:] *n Fin* (*abbr* **net realizable value**) valor *m* neto de realización

NS [en'es] (*abbr* **Nova Scotia**) Nueva Escocia

NSC [enes'si:] *n US* (*abbr* **National Security Council**) Consejo *m* de Seguridad Nacional

NSPCC [enespi:si:'si:] *n Br* (*abbr* **National Society for the Prevention of Cruelty to Children**) = sociedad protectora de la infancia

NSU [enes'ju:] *n Med* (*abbr* **non-specific urethritis**) uretritis *f inv* no gonocócica

NSW (*abbr* **New South Wales**) Nueva Gales del Sur

NT [en'ti:] *n* (a) (*abbr* **National Trust**) = organismo estatal británico encargado de la conservación de edificios y parajes de especial interés, *Esp* ≃ Patrimonio *m* Nacional (b) (*abbr* **New Testament**) Nuevo Testamento (c) (*abbr* **Northern Territory**) Territorio *m* Septentrional

nth [enθ] *adj* (a) *Math* enésimo(a); **to the n. power** a la enésima potencia (b) *Fam (umpteenth)* enésimo(a); **for the n. time** por enésima vez; **to the n. degree** al máximo, a tope

nuance ['nju:ɒns] *n* matiz *m*

nuanced ['nju:ɒnst] *adj* sutil, rico(a) en matices

nub [nʌb] *n* (a) *(crux)* nudo *m*; **the n. of the matter** *or* **issue** el quid de la cuestión (b) *(small bump)* abolladura *f*

nubile ['nju:baɪl] *adj (attractive)* de buen ver

nuclear ['nju:klɪə(r)] *adj* (a) *Phys* nuclear ▸▸ ***n. energy*** energía *f* nuclear; ***n. fission*** fisión *f* nuclear; ***n. fuel*** combustible *m* nuclear; ***n. fusion*** fusión *f* nuclear; ***the n. industry*** la industria nuclear; ***n. physics*** física *f* nuclear; ***n. power*** energía *f* nuclear *or* atómica; ***n. power station*** central *f* nuclear; ***n. reaction*** reacción *f* nuclear; ***n. reactor*** reactor *m* nuclear; ***n. reprocessing*** reprocesamiento *m* nuclear; ***n. reprocessing plant*** planta *f or* central *f* de reprocesamiento nuclear; ***n. waste*** residuos *mpl* nucleares

(b) *Mil* nuclear; **to go n.** *(in war)* emplear armamento nuclear ▸▸ ***n. bomb*** bomba *f* nuclear; ***n. bunker*** refugio *m* antinuclear; ***n. capability*** capacidad *f* nuclear; ***n. disarmament*** desarme *m* nuclear; ***n. fallout*** lluvia *f* radiactiva; ***n. proliferation*** proliferación *f* nuclear; ***n. shelter*** refugio *m* antinuclear; ***n. submarine*** submarino *m* nuclear; ***n. test*** prueba *f* nuclear; ***n. umbrella*** paraguas *m inv* nuclear; ***n. war(fare)*** guerra *f* nuclear *or* atómica; ***n. warhead*** cabeza *f* nuclear; ***n. weapon*** arma *f* nuclear *or* atómica; ***n. winter*** invierno *m* nuclear

(c) ***n. family*** familia *f* nuclear

nuclear-free zone ['nju:klɪəfri:'zəʊn] *n* zona *f* desnuclearizada

nuclear-powered ['nju:klɪə'paʊəd] *adj* nuclear ▸▸ ***n. submarine*** submarino *m* nuclear

nuclease ['nju:klɪeɪz] *n Biochem* nucleasa *f*

nuclei *pl of* **nucleus**

nucleic [nju:'kli:ɪk] *adj* nucleico(a) ▸▸ ***n. acid*** ácido *m* nucleico

nucleon ['nju:klɪɒn] *n Phys* nucleón *m*

nucleus ['nju:klɪəs] (*pl* **nuclei** ['nju:klɪaɪ]) *n* (a) *Biol, Chem & Phys* núcleo *m* (b) *(core)* núcleo *m*; **they form the n. of the team** forman la base del equipo

nude [nju:d] **1** *n* (a) *(being nude)* desnudo *m*; **in the n.** desnudo(a) (b) *Art* desnudo *m*

2 *adj* desnudo(a); **to be n.** estar desnudo(a); **n. scenes** *(in film)* escenas de desnudo; **to sunbathe n.** tomar el sol desnudo(a)

nuddy ['nʌdɪ] *n Br Fam* **in the n.** en pelotas *or* cueros, *Méx* encuerado(a)

nudge [nʌdʒ] **1** *n* (a) *(push)* empujón *m*; *(with elbow)* codazo *m*; **to give sb a n.** *(push)* dar un ligero empujón a alguien; *(with elbow)* dar un leve codazo a alguien; *Br Fam Hum* **n. n., wink wink** ya me entiendes (b) *(encouragement)* empujón *m*; **he needs a n. in the right direction** necesita un empujoncito en la dirección adecuada

2 *vt* (a) *(push)* dar un ligero empujón a; *(with elbow)* dar un leve codazo a; **the truck nudged its way through the crowd** el camión avanzó a trompicones entre la multitud (b) *(encourage)* animar; **to n. sb's memory** refrescar la memoria a alguien (c) *(approach)* acercarse, rozar; **temperatures were nudging 40° C** las temperaturas rozaban los 40°C

3 *vi (move gradually)* avanzar lentamente

nudie ['nju:dɪ] *Fam* **1** *n (film)* película *f* con desnudos

2 *adj (film, magazine)* con *or* de desnudos; *(bathing)* en pelota(s) *or* cueros, *Méx* encuerado(a)

nudism ['nju:dɪzəm] *n (naturism)* nudismo *m*

nudist ['nju:dɪst] *n* nudista *mf* ▸▸ ***n. camp*** campamento *m*; ***n. colony*** colonia *f* nudista

nudity ['nju:dɪtɪ] *n* desnudez *f*

nugatory ['nju:gətərɪ] *adj Formal (trifling, insignificant)* fútil

nugget ['nʌgɪt] *n* (a) *(of gold)* pepita *f* (b) *Fig* **nuggets of wisdom** destellos de lucidez; **a few useful nuggets of information** unos cuantos datos útiles (c) *Culin* trozo *m*

nuisance ['nju:səns] *n* (a) *(annoying thing)* pesadez *f*, molestia *f*; **it's a n. having to commute every day** es un fastidio tener que desplazarse al trabajo todos los días; **what a n.!, that's a n.!** ¡qué contrariedad!; **the protests don't change anything but they have a certain n. value** las manifestaciones no cambian nada, pero sirven para molestar ▸▸ ***n. call*** llamada *f* (telefónica) molesta, *Am* llamado *m* (telefónico) molesto

(b) *(annoying person)* pesado(a) *m,f*; **to make a n. of oneself** fastidiar, dar la lata; **stop being a n.** no seas pesado

(c) *Law* **a public n.** afrenta pública

NUJ [enju:'dʒeɪ] *n* (*abbr* **National Union of Journalists**) = sindicato británico de periodistas

nuke [nju:k] *Fam* **1** *n* (a) *(weapon)* arma *f* nuclear (b) *US (power plant)* central *f or* planta *f* nuclear

2 *vt* (a) *(attack with nuclear weapons)* atacar con armas nucleares (b) *(cook in microwave)* cocinar en el microondas (c) *(defeat)* dar una paliza a

null [nʌl] *adj* (a) *Law (invalid)* nulo(a); **n. and void** nulo(a) (y sin valor); **the contract was rendered n. (and void)** el contrato quedó invalidado (b) *(insignificant)* insignificante; *(amounting to nothing)* irrisorio(a), ínfimo(a); **the effect of the embargo was n.** las repercusiones del embargo fueron ínfimas (c) *Math (set)* vacío(a) (d) *Comptr* ***n. modem cable*** cable *m* de módem nulo

nullification [nʌlɪfɪ'keɪʃən] *n* invalidación *f*

nullify ['nʌlɪfaɪ] *vt* (a) *Law (claim, contract)* anular, invalidar (b) *(advantage, effect)* neutralizar

nullity ['nʌlɪtɪ] *n* (a) *(worthlessness)* inutilidad *f* (b) *Law (invalidity)* nulidad *f*

NUM [enju:'em] *n* (*abbr* **National Union of Mineworkers**) = sindicato minero británico

numb [nʌm] **1** *adj* entumecido(a); **to be n.** estar entumecido(a); **to go n.** entumecerse; **my arm/foot/hand has gone n.** se me ha dormido el brazo/el pie/la mano; **n. with cold** entumecido(a) por el frío; **n. with fear** paralizado(a) por el miedo

2 *vt (of cold, grief)* entumecer; *(of terror)* paralizar; *(of drug)* adormecer, calmar; **she was numbed by her father's death** la muerte de su padre la dejó helada

NUMBER ['nʌmbə(r)] **1** *n* (a) *(figure)* número *m*; **I live at n. 40** vivo en el (número) 40; **the n. 5 (bus)** el (número) 5; **(telephone) n.** número *m* (de teléfono *or Am* telefónico); **I'm good at numbers** tengo facilidad para los números, se me dan bien los números *or* las cifras; IDIOM *Fam* **I've got your n.!** ¡te tengo fichado!; IDIOM *Fam* **his n.'s up** le ha llegado la hora, *RP* le toca el turno; IDIOM **to do sth by numbers** hacer algo mecánicamente ▸▸ ***n. one*** *(person, song)* número uno; *Fam* **to do a n. one** *(to urinate)* hacer pipí *or RP* pichí; *Fam* **to look after n. one** cuidarse sólo de los propios intereses; *Br* ***N. Ten*** = la residencia oficial del primer ministro británico; *Br* **there was no comment from N. Ten** el primer ministro no realizó ningún comentario; *Math* ***n. theory*** teoría *f* de números; ***n. two*** *(subordinate)* segundo *m* (de a bordo); *Fam* **to do a n. two** *(to defecate)* hacer caca

(b) *(quantity)* número *m*; **a large n. of** gran número de; **I have a small n. of queries** tengo unas pocas preguntas; **large numbers of people** grandes cantidades de gente; **what sort of numbers are you expecting?** ¿cuánta gente esperas?; **a n. of reasons** varias razones; **there are any n. of explanations** hay infinitas explicaciones; *Literary* **deaths beyond** *or* **without n.** innumerables *or* incontables muertes; **their supporters were present in small/great numbers** un pequeño/gran número de sus partidarios hizo acto de presencia; **we are twenty in n.** somos veinte; **their opponents are few in n.** sus adversarios son pocos

(c) *Br (of car)* matrícula *f* ▸▸ ***n. plate*** *(of car)* (placa *f* de la) matrícula *f*

(d) *(song)* tema *m*, canción *f*

(e) *Br (of magazine)* número *m*

(f) *(group)* **one of our n. was unable to continue** uno de los nuestros no pudo continuar

(g) *US* **numbers (game** *or* **racket)** lotería *f* ilegal

(h) *Fam (referring to dress, object)* **she was wearing a sexy little n.** llevaba un modelito bien sexy; **that car is a nice little n.** ¡vaya cochazo!, *Méx* ¡qué carro más padre!, *CSur* ¡flor de auto!; *Fam* **she's got a nice little n. there** *(situation)* ha conseguido un buen *Esp* chollo *or Méx* churro *or RP* curro

(i) *US Fam* **to do** *or* **to pull a n. on sb** timar a alguien

(j) *Gram* número *m*

2 *vt* (a) *(assign number to)* numerar; **the seats are numbered** los asientos están numerados

(b) *(include)* contar; **he numbers her among his friends** la cuenta entre sus amigos; **the society numbers several famous people among its members** la asociación cuenta con varios famosos entre sus miembros; **she is numbered among the greatest poets of her day** figura entre las grandes poetisas de su tiempo

(c) *(total)* **the dead numbered several thousand** había varios miles de muertos; **each team numbers six players** hay seis jugadores en cada equipo

(**d**) *(count)* contar; **his days are numbered** tiene los días contados
3 *vi* **she numbers among the great writers of the century** figura entre los grandes escritores de este siglo; **the crowd numbered in thousands** había miles de personas

> **Numbers**
> Los millares en inglés se marcan mediante una coma en lugar de un punto:
> **£3,234** 3.234 libras
> **$1,200,000** 1.200.000 dólares
> Por otra parte, los decimales comienzan con punto, a diferencia del español donde siguen a la coma:
> **5.3 seconds** 5,3 segundos

number-cruncher ['nʌmbəkrʌntʃə(r)] *n Fam Comptr* machacacifras *m or f inv*

number-crunching ['nʌmbəkrʌntʃɪŋ] *n Fam Comptr* cálculos *mpl* númericos largos y complicados

numbering ['nʌmbərɪŋ] *n* numeración *f*

numberless ['nʌmbəlɪs] *adj* (**a**) *(countless)* innumerables (**b**) *(without a number)* sin número

number-one ['nʌmbəwʌn] *adj* principal; **our n. priority is to...** nuestra principal prioridad es...; **our n. film star** nuestra estrella principal; **the n. hit in the charts** el número uno en las listas de éxitos

numbly ['nʌmlɪ] *adv (to answer, stare)* sin poder reaccionar

numbness ['nʌmnɪs] *n* (**a**) *(of fingers)* entumecimiento *m* (**b**) *(from grief)* aturdimiento *m*; *(from fear)* parálisis *f inv*

numbskull, numskull ['nʌmskʌl] *n Fam* idiota *mf*, majadero(a) *m,f*

numeracy ['nju:mərəsɪ] *n* conocimiento *m* de aritmética

numeral ['nju:mərəl] *n* número *m*; **in Roman/Arabic numerals** en números romanos/arábigos

numerate ['nju:mərət] *adj* **to be n.** tener un conocimiento básico de aritmética

numerator ['nju:məreɪtə(r)] *n Math* numerador *m*

numeric [nju:'merɪk] *adj* numérico(a) ►► *Comptr* ***n. keypad*** teclado *m* numérico

numerical [nju:'merɪkəl] *adj* numérico(a); **in n. order** en orden numérico ►► *Math* ***n. analysis*** análisis *m inv* numérico; *Comptr* ***n. control*** control *m* numérico; *Comptr* ***n. keypad*** teclado *m* numérico

numerically [nju:'merɪklɪ] *adv* en número, numéricamente; **n. superior** numéricamente superior

numerology [nju:mə'rɒlədʒɪ] *n* numerología *f*

numerous ['nju:mərəs] *adj* numeroso(a); **on n. occasions** en numerosas ocasiones; **they are too n. to mention** son incontables *or* innumerables

numismatics [nju:mɪz'mætɪks], **numismatology** [nju:mɪzmə'tɒlədʒɪ] *n* numismática *f*

numismatist [nju:'mɪzmətɪst] *n* numismático(a) *m,f*

numskull = **numbskull**

nun [nʌn] *n* monja *f*; **to become a n.** meterse monja

nunciature ['nʌnsɪətʃə(r)] *n* nunciatura *f*

nuncio ['nʌnsɪəʊ] (*pl* **nuncios**) *n* nuncio *m*

nunnery ['nʌnərɪ] *n* convento *m*

nuptial ['nʌpʃəl] *Literary or Hum* **1** *npl* **nuptials** nupcias *fpl*
2 *adj* nupcial

nurse [nɜ:s] **1** *n* (**a**) *(medical)* enfermera *f*; **(male) n.** enfermero *m* ►► *US* ***n.'s aide*** asistente *mf* de enfermería (**b**) *(looking after children)* niñera *f*
2 *vt* (**a**) *(through illness)* cuidar, atender; **she nursed him back to health** lo cuidó hasta que se restableció
(**b**) *(treat with care)* **he was nursing a bad hangover** estaba recuperándose de una resaca; **to n. one's pride** intentar recuperar el orgullo; **she nursed the boat back into harbour** pilotó con pericia el barco de vuelta al puerto
(**c**) *(suckle)* amamantar, dar de mamar a; **nursing mothers** madres lactantes
(**d**) *Fig (feeling, hope)* guardar, abrigar; **to n. a grievance** guardar rencor
(**e**) *(drink)* beber lentamente, saborear
3 *vi* (**a**) *(work as a nurse)* trabajar de enfermera (**b**) *(infant)* mamar, lactar

nursemaid ['nɜ:smeɪd], **nurserymaid** ['nɜ:sərɪmeɪd] *n* niñera *f*

nursery ['nɜ:sərɪ] *n* (**a**) *(for children) (establishment)* guardería *f*; *(room in house)* cuarto *m* de los niños ►► ***n. education*** educación *f* preescolar; *Br* ***n. nurse*** puericultora *f*; ***n. rhyme*** poema *m or* canción *f* infantil; ***n. school*** centro *m* de preescolar, parvulario *m* (**b**) *(for plants)* vivero *m*, semillero *m* (**c**) ***n. slopes*** *(in skiing)* pistas *fpl* para principiantes

nursery maid = **nursemaid**

nursing ['nɜ:sɪŋ] *n* (**a**) *(profession)* enfermería *f*; *(care given by a nurse)* cuidados *mpl*, atención *f* sanitaria ►► ***n. home*** *Br (where children are born)* maternidad *f*; *(for old people, war veterans)* residencia *f*; *Br* ***n. officer*** enfermera *f (que también realiza tareas administrativas)*; ***n. staff*** personal *m* sanitario
(**b**) *(breastfeeding)* ***n. bottle*** biberón *m*; ***n. bra*** sostén *m or Esp* sujetador *m or RP* corpiño *m* de lactancia

nurture ['nɜ:tʃə(r)] **1** *n (upbringing)* educación *f*
2 *vt* (**a**) *(children, plants)* nutrir, alimentar (**b**) *(plan, scheme)* alimentar

NUS [enju:'es] *n* (*abbr* **National Union of Students**) = sindicato británico de estudiantes

NUT [enju:'ti:] *n* (*abbr* **National Union of Teachers**) = sindicato británico de profesores

nut [nʌt] **1** *n* (**a**) *(food)* fruto *m* seco; *(walnut)* nuez *f*; *(peanut) Esp* cacahuete *m*, *Andes, Carib, RP* maní *m*, *CAm, Méx* cacahuate *m*; *(hazelnut)* avellana *f*; *(almond)* almendra *f*; *(cashew)* anacardo *m*; *(chestnut)* castaña *f*; *(pecan)* pacana *f*; *(pistachio)* pistacho *m*; *(Brazil nut)* coquito *m* del Brasil; **nuts and raisins** frutos secos; IDIOM **a hard** *or* **tough n.** *(person)* un hueso (duro de roer); IDIOM **a tough** *or* **hard n. to crack** *(problem)* un hueso duro de roer
(**b**) *Fam (head)* coco *m*; **to be off one's n.** estar mal de la azotea; **to go off one's n.** *(go mad)* volverse loco(a) *or Esp* majareta; *(get angry)* ponerse furioso(a); *Br* **he'll do his n. when he finds out!** ¡se va a cabrear *or RP* poner como loco cuando se entere!
(**c**) *Fam (mad person)* chiflado(a) *m,f*, chalado(a) *m,f*
(**d**) *Fam (enthusiast)* **a jazz/tennis n.** un(a) loco(a) del jazz/tenis
(**e**) *(for fastening bolt)* tuerca *f*; IDIOM **the nuts and bolts** *(of scheme, activity)* los aspectos prácticos; *(of subject)* el abecé
(**f**) *very Fam* **nuts** *(testicles)* huevos *mpl*, *Méx* albóndigas *fpl*
2 *vt Br Fam* dar un cabezazo a

nut-brown ['nʌtbraʊn] *adj (hair)* castaño(a); *(skin)* trigueño(a)

nutcase ['nʌtkeɪs] *n Fam* chalado(a) *m,f*

nutcracker ['nʌtkrækə(r)] *n* (**a**) *(device)* **nutcrackers** cascanueces *m inv*; **a pair of n.** un cascanueces (**b**) *(bird)* cascanueces *m inv*

nuthatch ['nʌthætʃ] *n (bird)* trepador *m* azul

nuthouse ['nʌthaʊs] *n Fam* manicomio *m*, loquero *m*

nutmeg ['nʌtmeg] **1** *n (nut, spice)* nuez *f* moscada; *(tree)* mirística *f*
2 *vt* **to n. sb** *(in soccer)* hacer el túnel a alguien

nutria ['nju:trɪə] *n* coipo *m*

nutrient ['nju:trɪənt] **1** *n* **nutrients** sustancias *fpl* nutritivas
2 *adj* nutritivo(a)

nutriment ['nju:trɪmənt] *n* nutriente *m*

nutrition [nju:'trɪʃən] *n* nutrición *f*; **high n. content** alto contenido nutritivo

nutritional [nju:'trɪʃənəl] *adj* nutritivo(a); **n. value** valor nutritivo

nutritionist [nju:'trɪʃənɪst] *n* nutricionista *mf*

nutritious [nju:'trɪʃəs] *adj* nutritivo(a), alimenticio(a)

nutritive ['nju:trətɪv] *adj* nutritivo(a)

nuts [nʌts] *Fam* **1** *adj (mad)* chiflado(a), *Esp* majara; **to be n.** estar chiflado(a) *or Esp* majara; **to go n.** *(go mad)* volverse loco(a) *or Esp* majareta; *(get angry)* volverse furioso(a); **to drive sb n.** poner histérico(a) a alguien; **to be n. about** *(be very keen on)* estar loco(a) por
2 *exclam (expressing irritation, annoyance)* ¡vaya!, *Col, RP* ¡miércoles!; **n. to that!** ¡de eso nada!

nutshell ['nʌtʃel] *n* cáscara *f* (de fruto seco); **in a n.** en una palabra; **to put it in a n.** por decirlo en una palabra

nutter ['nʌtə(r)] *n Br Fam (mad person)* chalado(a) *m,f*

nutty ['nʌtɪ] *adj* (**a**) *(in taste)* **to have a n. taste** saber a avellana/nuez/ *etc.* (**b**) *Fam (mad)* chiflado(a), chalado(a); **to be n. (about)** estar chiflado(a) *or* chalado(a) (por); IDIOM *Hum* **he is as n. as a fruitcake** le falta un tornillo, *Esp* está como una regadera, *Méx* está tumbado del burro

nuzzle ['nʌzəl] **1** *vt* (**a**) *(of dog, cat)* acariciar con el morro *or* hocico (**b**) *(of person)* acurrucarse contra
2 *vi* **to n. against sb** *(person)* acurrucarse contra alguien

NV (*abbr* **Nevada**) Nevada

NVQ [enviː'kjuː] *n* (*abbr* **National Vocational Qualification**) = en Inglaterra y Gales, título de formación profesional

NW (*abbr* **north west**) NO

NWT (*abbr* **Northwest Territories**) Territorios *mpl* del Noroeste

NY (*abbr* **New York**) Nueva York

NYC (*abbr* **New York City**) (ciudad *f* de) Nueva York

nylon ['naɪlɒn] **1** *n (textile)* nylon *m*, nailon *m*; **n. shirt/scarf** camisa/pañuelo de nailon
2 nylons *npl (stockings)* medias *fpl* de nylon; **a pair of nylons** unas medias de nylon

nymph [nɪmf] *n* (**a**) *Mythol* ninfa *f*; **water/wood n.** ninfa del agua/bosque (**b**) *Zool* ninfa *f*

nymphet ['nɪmfət] *n* ninfa *f*

nympho ['nɪmfəʊ] (*pl* **nymphos**) *n Fam* ninfómana *f*

nymphomania [nɪmfəʊ'meɪnɪə] *n* ninfomanía *f*

nymphomaniac [nɪmfəʊ'meɪnɪæk] *n* ninfómana *f*

NYSE [enwaɪes'iː] *n St Exch* (*abbr* **New York Stock Exchange**) Bolsa *f* de Nueva York

NZ (*abbr* **New Zealand**) Nueva Zelanda

O,o

O, o [əʊ] *n (letter)* O, o *f*

O [əʊ] *n* (**a**) *Br Formerly Sch* ***O. level*** = examen o diploma de una asignatura, de orientación académica, que se realizaba normalmente a los dieciséis años (**b**) *(zero)* cero *m* (**c**) *Med* **O. positive/negative** cero *m* positivo/negativo

o' [ə] *prep (of)* de

oaf [əʊf] *n* zopenco *m*, zoquete *m*

oafish ['əʊfɪʃ] *adj (clumsy, awkward)* torpe; *(loutish)* zafio(a), bruto(a)

oak [əʊk] *n (tree, wood)* roble *m*; **an o. forest** robledal

oak-apple ['əʊk'æpəl], **oak-gall** ['əʊk'gɔːl] *n* agalla *f* de roble

oaken ['əʊkən] *adj Literary* de roble

oakum ['əʊkəm] *n (rope)* estopa *f*

OAP [əʊeɪ'piː] *n Br* (*abbr* **old age pensioner**) pensionista *mf*, jubilado(a) *m,f*

oar [ɔː(r)] *n* (**a**) *(implement)* remo *m*; **to rest on one's oars** dejar de remar por un rato; *Fig* tomarse un descanso; IDIOM *Fam* **to stick** *or US* **put one's o. in** meter las narices (**b**) *(person)* remero(a) *m,f*

oarfish ['ɔːfɪʃ] *n* pez *m* remo

oarlock ['ɔːlɒk] *n US* escálamo *m*, tolete *m*

oarsman ['ɔːzmən] *n* remero *m*

oarsmanship ['ɔːzmənʃɪp] *n* habilidad *f* como remero(a)

oarswoman ['ɔːzwʊmən] *n* remera *f*

OAS [əʊeɪ'es] *n* (*abbr* **Organization of American States**) OEA *f*

oasis [əʊ'eɪsɪs] (*pl* **oases** [əʊ'eɪsiːz]) *n* oasis *m inv*; *Fig* **an o. of calm** un oasis de tranquilidad

oast-house ['əʊsthaʊs] *n* secadero *m*

oat [əʊt] **1** *n* (**a**) *(plant)* avena *f* ►► ***o. bran*** salvado *m* de avena (**b**) *(food)* **an o. biscuit** una galleta de avena

2 oats *npl* (**a**) *(food)* copos *mpl* de avena (**b**) IDIOMS *US Fam* **to be feeling one's oats** *(be full of energy)* estar en plena forma; *Br very Fam* **to get one's oats** echar el polvo de costumbre; *Br Fam* **to be off one's oats** *(have no appetite)* estar desganado(a)

oatcake ['əʊtkeɪk] *n* galleta *f* de avena

oath [əʊθ] *n* (**a**) *(pledge)* juramento *m*; **o. of allegiance** juramento de adhesión; **to take** *or* **swear an o.** prestar juramento, jurar; *Law* **on** *or* **under o.** bajo juramento; **she testified under o. that...** testificó bajo juramento que...; *Archaic* **it's true, on my o.!** ¡como hay Dios que eso es cierto! (**b**) *(swearword)* juramento *m*, palabrota *f*

oatmeal ['əʊtmiːl] **1** *n (flour)* harina *f* de avena; *US (flakes)* copos *mpl* de avena

2 *adj (colour)* pajizo(a)

OAU [əʊeɪ'juː] *n Formerly* (*abbr* **Organization of African Unity**) OUA *f*

ob. (*abbr* **obiit**) fallecido(a)

obbligato [ɒblɪ'gɑːtəʊ] *n Mus* obligado *m*

obduracy ['ɒbdjʊrəsɪ] *n Formal* tozudez *f*, obstinación *f*

obdurate ['ɒbdjʊrɪt] *adj Formal* obstinado(a); **to remain o.** permanecer inflexible

obdurately ['ɒbdjʊrɪtlɪ] *adv Formal (stubbornly)* obstinadamente; *(to resist)* inflexiblemente

OBE [əʊbiː'iː] *n* (*abbr* **Officer of the Order of the British Empire**) = título de miembro de la Orden del Imperio Británico, otorgado por servicios a la comunidad

obedience [ə'biːdɪəns] *n* obediencia *f*; **to show o. to sb** prestar obediencia a alguien; *Literary* **to owe o. to sb** deber obediencia a alguien; **in o. to** al dictado de

obedient [ə'biːdɪənt] *adj* obediente; **to be o. to sb** ser obediente a alguien; *Formal Old-fashioned* **your o. servant** *(in letters)* su seguro servidor

obediently [ə'biːdɪəntlɪ] *adv* obedientemente; **the dog sat down o.** el perro se sentó obediente

obeisance [əʊ'beɪsəns] *n Formal* (**a**) *(respect)* muestras *fpl* de respeto; **to make** *or* **pay o. (to sb)** mostrar respeto a alguien (**b**) *(bow)* reverencia *f*

obelisk ['ɒbəlɪsk] *n* obelisco *m*

obese [əʊ'biːs] *adj* obeso(a)

obesity [əʊ'biːsɪtɪ] *n* obesidad *f*

obey [ə'beɪ] **1** *vt (person, order)* obedecer; **to o. the law** obedecer las leyes; **he obeyed his instincts** obedeció a *or* siguió sus instintos; **the plane is no longer obeying the controls** el avión ya no responde a los controles

2 *vi* obedecer

obfuscate ['ɒbfəskeɪt] *vt Formal (issue)* enturbiar, oscurecer

obfuscation [ɒbfə'skeɪʃən] *n Formal* oscurecimiento *m*

obituarist [ə'bɪtʃʊərɪst] *n* escritor(ora) *m,f* de notas necrológicas

obituary [ə'bɪtʃʊərɪ] *n* nota *f* necrológica, necrología *f*; *Fig* **they are already writing her political o.** ya están certificando su defunción política ►► ***o. column*** sección *f* de necrológicas; ***o. notice*** nota necrológica

object **1** *n* ['ɒbdʒɪkt] (**a**) *(thing)* objeto *m*; **an unidentified o.** un objeto no identificado

(**b**) *(focus)* objeto *m*; **an o. of ridicule/interest** un objeto de burla/interés; **he was the o. of their admiration** él era el objeto de su admiración ►► ***o. lens*** *(of telescope)* lente *f* objetivo; ***o. lesson:*** **to give sb an o. lesson in sth** dar a alguien una lección magistral de algo

(**c**) *(purpose, aim)* objeto *m*, propósito *m*; **the real o. of his visit** el verdadero objeto *or* propósito de su visita; **with this o. in mind** *or* **in view** con la mente *or* vista puesta en este objetivo, con ese propósito; **the o. of the exercise is to...** el ejercicio tiene por objeto...

(**d**) *(obstacle)* **expense is no o.** el gasto no es ningún inconveniente

(**e**) *Gram* complemento *m*, objeto *m*; **direct/indirect o.** complemento *or* objeto directo/indirecto

(**f**) *Comptr* objeto *m* ►► ***o. language*** lenguaje *m* objeto

2 *vt* [əb'dʒekt] **to o. that...** objetar que...; **"that's unfair," she objected** "es injusto", objetó

3 *vi* (**a**) *(disapprove)* **why do you o. to all my friends?** ¿por qué pones peros *or Esp* pegas a todos mis amigos?; **I o. to doing that** me indigna tener que hacer eso; **I o. to that remark/being treated like this** me parece muy mal ese comentario/que me traten así; **he objects to her smoking** no quiere que fume

(**b**) *(express opposition)* oponerse (**to** a); **does anyone o.?** ¿alguna objeción?; **I o.!** ¡no estoy de acuerdo!; **I wouldn't o. to a cup of tea** no diría que no a una taza de té

(**c**) *Law* **to o. to a witness** impugnar un testigo

objection [əb'dʒekʃən] **1** *n* (**a**) *(protest, argument against)* objeción *f*, reparo *m*; **to make** *or* **raise objections** poner objeciones *or* reparos; **I see/have no o.** no veo/tengo ningún inconveniente; **I have no o. to his friends** no tengo nada en contra de sus amistades; **I have no o. to his coming** no me opongo a que venga

(**b**) *(reason for objecting)* inconveniente *m*, traba *f*; **the chief o. to his plan is its cost** el principal inconveniente de su plan es el costo *or Esp* coste

(**c**) *Law* protesta *f*; **o. sustained** se admite *or* acepta la protesta; **o. overruled** protesta denegada, no ha lugar

2 *exclam (in court)* ¡protesto!

objectionable [əb'dʒekʃənəbəl] *adj (behaviour)* reprobable; *(person)* desagradable; *(smell)* nauseabundo(a); *(language)* soez; **I find his views o.** sus opiniones me parecen inaceptables; **he made himself thoroughly o.** se puso muy desagradable

objectionably [əb'dʒekʃənəblɪ] *adv* de manera reprobable

objective [əb'dʒektɪv] **1** *n (aim, goal)* objetivo *m*; **to achieve** *or* **attain one's o.** conseguir *or* alcanzar el objetivo
2 *adj* **(a)** *(impartial)* objetivo(a); **an o. observer** un observador imparcial ►► *Educ* ***o. test*** examen *m* objetivo **(b)** *(real, observable)* objetivo(a); **o. reality** realidad observable **(c)** *Gram* acusativo(a); **the o. case** el caso acusativo

objectively [əb'dʒektɪvlɪ] *adv* objetivamente; **o. speaking...** en términos objetivos...

objectivity [ɒbdʒek'tɪvɪtɪ] *n* objetividad *f*

objector [ɒb'dʒektə(r)] *n* oponente *mf*, crítico(a) *m,f*; **are there many objectors to the proposal?** ¿se opone mucha gente a la propuesta?

object-oriented ['ɒbdʒɪkt'ɔːrɪentɪd] *adj Comptr* orientado(a) a objeto

objet ['ɒbʒeɪ] *n* ***o. d'art*** obra *f* de arte; ***o. trouvé*** cosa *f* encontrada

oblate ['ɒbleɪt] **1** *n Rel* oblato(a) *m,f*
2 *adj Geom* achatado(a)

obligate ['ɒblɪgeɪt] *vt* **(a)** *Formal (compel)* obligar; **to feel obligated to do sth** sentirse obligado(a) a hacer algo **(b)** *US Fin (funds, credits)* subscribir

obligation [ɒblɪ'geɪʃən] *n* obligación *f*; **family obligations** obligaciones familiares; **there's no o. (to do sth)** no hay obligación alguna (de hacer algo); **I did it out of a sense of o.** lo hice porque sentí que debía hacerlo; **it is my o. to inform you that...** me veo obligado a informarle de que...; **you are under no o. to reply** no tiene obligación de responder, puede negarse a responder; **to be under an o. to sb** tener una obligación para con alguien; **I am under a great o. to him** tengo una gran deuda con él; **to be under an o. to do sth** estar obligado(a) a hacer algo; **I don't want to put** *or* **place him under an o.** no quiero ponerlo en un compromiso; **to meet one's obligations** *(duty)* cumplir las obligaciones; *(financial commitments)* satisfacer las deudas

obligatory [ɒ'blɪgətərɪ] *adj* obligatorio(a); **attendance is o.** la asistencia es obligatoria; *Ironic* **the o. ovation** la ovación de rigor

oblige [ə'blaɪdʒ] **1** *vt* **(a)** *(compel)* obligar; **to be/feel obliged to do sth** estar/sentirse obligado(a) a hacer algo; **to o. sb to do sth** obligar a alguien a hacer algo; **you're not obliged to come** nadie te obliga a venir
(b) *(do a favour for)* hacer un favor a; **she obliged us with a song** nos obsequió con una canción; *Formal* **I would be obliged if you would refrain from smoking** le estaría muy agradecido si se abstuviese de fumar; *Formal* **could you o. me with a match?** ¿tendría la gentileza de darme lumbre?
(c) to be obliged to sb *(be grateful)* estarle agradecido(a) a alguien; **I would be obliged if you would...** te estaría muy agradecido si...; **much obliged** muy agradecido(a)
2 *vi* **always ready to o.!** ¡siempre a su disposición!; **I would be only too glad to o.** para mí sería un placer inmenso poder ayudar

obliging [ə'blaɪdʒɪŋ] *adj* atento(a); **it was very o. of him** fue muy considerado de su parte

obligingly [ə'blaɪdʒɪŋlɪ] *adv* amablemente

oblique [ə'bliːk] **1** *adj* **(a)** *(line, angle)* oblicuo(a) **(b)** *(reference, hint)* indirecto(a)
2 *n* barra *f* oblicua

obliquely [ə'bliːklɪ] *adv* **(a)** *(angled)* oblicuamente **(b)** *(indirectly) (to refer)* indirectamente; *(to glance)* de través

obliterate [ə'blɪtəreɪt] *vt* **(a)** *(erase) (figures, footprints, traces)* borrar; *Fig (the past, memories)* enterrar, borrar **(b)** *(destroy)* asolar, arrasar; **the town was all but obliterated during the war** la ciudad quedó prácticamente arrasada durante la guerra **(c)** *(cancel) (stamp)* matasellar

obliteration [əblɪtə'reɪʃən] *n* **(a)** *(erasure)* eliminación *f* **(b)** *(destruction)* destrucción *f* **(c)** *(of stamp)* matasellado *m*

oblivion [ə'blɪvɪən] *n* **(a)** *(being forgotten)* olvido *m*; **to fall** *or* **sink into o.** caer en el olvido; **to consign sth to o.** relegar algo al olvido; **to save sth/sb from o.** rescatar algo/a alguien del olvido **(b)** *(unconsciousness)* inconsciencia *f*; **he drank himself into o.** bebió *or Am* tomó hasta perder la consciencia

oblivious [ə'blɪvɪəs] *adj* inconsciente; **o. to the pain/to the risks** ajeno(a) al dolor/a los riesgos; **I was o. of** *or* **to what was going on** no era consciente de lo que estaba pasando; **he remained o. of the dangers** seguía sin darse cuenta del peligro

obliviously [ə'blɪvɪəslɪ] *adv* sin prestar atención

oblong ['ɒblɒŋ] **1** *n* rectángulo *m*
2 *adj* rectangular

obloquy ['ɒbləkwɪ] *n Formal* **(a)** *(abuse)* ultraje *m* **(b)** *(disgrace)* oprobio *m*

obnoxious [əb'nɒkʃəs] *adj (person, action)* repugnante; *(smell)* repulsivo(a)

obnoxiously [əb'nɒkʃəslɪ] *adv* de manera repugnante

obnoxiousness [əb'nɒkʃəsnɪs] *n* repugnancia *f*

oboe ['əʊbəʊ] *n* oboe *m*

oboist ['əʊbəʊɪst] *n* oboe *mf*

obscene [əb'siːn] *adj* **(a)** *(indecent)* obsceno(a); **an o. gesture** un gesto obsceno; **an o. publication** una publicación obscena **(b)** *Fam (unacceptable) (profits, prices)* escandaloso(a); **it's o. to earn so much money** es inmoral ganar tanto dinero

obscenely [əb'siːnlɪ] *adv* **(a)** *(indecently)* obscenamente **(b)** *Fam (unacceptably)* **o. rich** escandalosamente rico(a)

obscenity [əb'senɪtɪ] *n* **(a)** *(indecency)* obscenidad *f* **(b)** *(obscene word)* obscenidad *f* **(c)** *Fam (unacceptability)* **the o. of war** la inmoralidad de la guerra

obscurantism [ɒbskjʊə'ræntɪzəm] *n Formal* oscurantismo *m*

obscurantist [ɒbskjʊə'ræntɪst] *Formal* **1** *n* oscurantista *mf*
2 *adj* oscurantista

obscure [əb'skjʊə(r)] **1** *adj* **(a)** *(not clear) (remark, argument)* oscuro(a), enigmático(a); *(feeling, sensation)* vago(a), oscuro(a); *(background)* oscuro(a); **the meaning is rather o.** el significado es bastante oscuro; **for some o. reason he thought it would help** por alguna extraña razón, pensó que eso serviría de algo; *Formal* **of o. birth** de cuna plebeya
(b) *(little-known) (author, book)* oscuro(a); *(place)* poco conocido(a), perdido(a)
2 *vt* **(a)** *(hide from view)* ocultar; **that building obscures the view** ese edificio oculta la vista; **their view of the stage was obscured by a pillar** una columna les impedía ver el escenario **(b)** *(make unclear)* enturbiar, oscurecer; **to o. the facts/the issue** enturbiar los hechos/el asunto

obscurely [əb'skjʊəlɪ] *adv* **(a)** *(to feel, see)* vagamente **(b)** *(to speak)* confusamente

obscurity [əb'skjʊərɪtɪ] *n* **(a)** *(insignificance)* oscuridad *f*; **to rise from o. to fame** ascender del anonimato a la celebridad; **to fall into o.** caer en el anonimato **(b)** *(difficulty)* dificultad *f* **(c)** *(darkness)* oscuridad *f*

obsequies ['ɒbsəkwɪz] *npl Formal* exequias *f*

> **False friend**: The Spanish noun **obsequio** is not a translation for the English word **obsequies**. In Spanish **obsequio** means "gift, present".

obsequious [əb'siːkwɪəs] *adj* servil, rastrero(a)

obsequiously [əb'siːkwɪəslɪ] *adv* servilmente, rastreramente

obsequiousness [əb'siːkwɪəsnɪs] *n* servilismo *m*

observable [əb'zɜːvəbəl] *adj* apreciable; **such behaviour is also o. in humans** este comportamiento también se observa en los humanos

observance [əb'zɜːvəns] *n* **(a)** *(recognition) (of law, custom)* observancia *f*, acatamiento *m*; *(of anniversary)* celebración *f* **(b) religious observances** prácticas *fpl* religiosas

observant [əb'zɜːvənt] *adj* observador(ora); **how o. of him!** ¡qué observador es!

observation [ɒbzə'veɪʃən] *n* **(a)** *(act of observing)* observación *f*; *(by police)* vigilancia *f*; *also Med* **to keep sb under o.** tener a alguien en *or* bajo observación; **they are keeping the house under (close) o.** tienen la casa bajo (estrecha) vigilancia; **to escape o.** pasar inadvertido(a) ►► *Mil* ***o. aircraft*** avión *m* de observación; *Mil* ***o. balloon*** globo *m* de observación; *Rail* ***o. car*** = vagón con grandes ventanales; *Mil* ***o. post*** puesto *m* de observación; *Med* ***o. ward*** unidad *f* de observación
(b) *(perception)* perspicacia *f*; **to have great powers of o.** tener grandes dotes de perspicacia
(c) *(remark)* observación *f*, comentario *m*; **to make an o.** hacer una observación *or* un comentario

observational [ɒbzə'veɪʃənəl] *adj (work, techniques)* de observación; *(faculties, powers)* de perspicacia; *(data, research, study)* basado(a) en la observación

observatory [əb'zɜːvətərɪ] *n* observatorio *m*

observe [əb'zɜːv] **1** *vt* **(a)** *(watch)* observar; **the police are observing his movements** la policía está vigilando *or* siguiendo sus movimientos
(b) *(notice)* advertir; **did you o. anything unusual?** ¿advertiste algo extraño?
(c) *(comment, remark)* **to o. that...** señalar *or* observar que...; **"she seems worried," he observed** "parece preocupada", señaló
(d) *(law, customs)* observar, acatar; **to o. the Sabbath** guardar el descanso sabático; **to o. a minute's silence** guardar un minuto de silencio
2 *vi (watch)* observar, mirar

observer [əb'zɜːvə(r)] *n* observador(ora) *m,f*; **to the casual o.** para un ojo poco avezado; **he attended the talks as an o.** asistió a las charlas como observador; **political observers** observadores políticos

obsess [əb'ses] **1** *vt* obsesionar; **to be obsessed with** *or* **by sth/sb** estar obsesionado(a) con *or* por algo/alguien

2 *vi (be obsessive)* estar obsesionado(a) (**about** por *or* con)

obsession [əb'seʃən] *n* obsesión *f*; **his o. with death** su obsesión con la muerte; **to develop an o. about sth/sb** obsesionarse con algo/alguien; **it's becoming an o. with him** se está convirtiendo en su obsesión

obsessional [əb'seʃənəl] *adj* obsesivo(a); **to be o.** estar obsesionado(a) (**about** por *or* con); **to become o.** obsesionarse

obsessive [əb'sesɪv] **1** *n (person)* obseso(a) *m,f*

2 *adj* obsesivo(a); **to become o. about sth** obsesionarse con algo

obsessive-compulsive disorder [əb'sesɪvkəm'pʌlsɪvdɪs'ɔːdə(r)] *n Psy* trastorno *m* obsesivo-compulsivo

obsessively [əb'sesɪvlɪ] *adv* obsesivamente

obsidian [ɒb'sɪdɪən] *n Geol* obsidiana *f*

obsolescence [ɒbsə'lesəns] *n* obsolescencia *f*; **planned** *or* **built-in o.** = diseño de un producto de modo que quede obsoleto en poco tiempo

obsolescent [ɒbsə'lesənt] *adj* que se está quedando obsoleto(a)

obsolete ['ɒbsəliːt] **1** *adj* obsoleto(a); **to become o.** quedar obsoleto(a); **an o. word** un término en desuso

2 *vt* dejar obsoleto(a) *or* anticuado(a)

obstacle ['ɒbstəkəl] *n* obstáculo *m*; **what are the obstacles to free trade?** ¿cuáles son los obstáculos que impiden el libre comercio?; **age should be no o. to promotion** la edad no debería ser un impedimento para el ascenso; **to put obstacles in sb's way** ponerle a alguien obstáculos en el camino; **to overcome an o.** superar un obstáculo ►► *also Fig* ***o. course*** carrera *f* de obstáculos; ***o. race*** carrera *f* de obstáculos

obstetric(al) [ɒb'stetrɪk(əl)] *adj Med* obstétrico(a)

obstetrician [ɒbstə'trɪʃən] *n Med* obstetra *mf*, tocólogo(a) *m,f*

obstetrics [ɒb'stetrɪks] *n Med* obstetricia *f*, tocología *f*

obstinacy ['ɒbstɪnəsɪ] *n* (**a**) *(stubbornness, tenacity)* obstinación *f*, terquedad *f* (**b**) *(persistence)* persistencia *f*; **the o. of an infection** la persistencia de una infección

obstinate ['ɒbstɪnɪt] *adj* (**a**) *(stubborn, tenacious) (person)* obstinado(a), terco(a); *(resistance)* tenaz, obstinado(a); **an o. refusal** una obstinada negativa; **to be o. about sth** obstinarse en algo (**b**) *(persistent) (illness)* pertinaz; *(stain)* rebelde

obstinately ['ɒbstɪnɪtlɪ] *adv* obstinadamente

obstreperous [əb'strepərəs] *adj Formal or Hum* alborotado(a); **to get o. (about sth)** alborotarse (por algo)

obstruct [əb'strʌkt] *vt* (**a**) *(block) (road, passage, pipe)* obstruir, bloquear; *(vein, artery)* obstruir, bloquear; *(view)* impedir; **don't o. the exits** no bloqueen las salidas

(**b**) *(hinder) (progress, measures)* obstaculizar, entorpecer; *(traffic)* entorpecer; **I was arrested for obstructing a policeman in the course of his duty** me arrestaron por obstrucción a un policía en el cumplimiento de su deber; *Parl* **to o. a bill** entorpecer la aprobación de un proyecto de ley; *Law* **to o. the course of justice** obstaculizar *or* entorpecer la acción de la justicia (**c**) *Sport* obstruir

obstruction [əb'strʌkʃən] *n* (**a**) *(blockage) (in road, passage, pipe)* atasco *m*; *(in vein, artery)* obstrucción *f*; **to cause an o.** *(in road)* provocar un atasco (**b**) *(hindering)* obstrucción *f*; **a policy of o.** una política de obstrucción (**c**) *Sport* obstrucción *f* (**d**) *Av* ***o. lights*** luces *fpl* de obstrucción

obstructionism [əb'strʌkʃənɪzəm] *n* obstruccionismo *m*

obstructionist [əb'strʌkʃənɪst] **1** *n* obstruccionista *mf*

2 *adj* obstruccionista

obstructive [əb'strʌktɪv] *adj (behaviour, tactics)* obstruccionista; **to be o.** *(person)* poner impedimentos

obtain [əb'teɪn] **1** *vt (information, money)* obtener, conseguir; **to o. sth for sb** obtener *or* conseguir algo para alguien; **to o. sth from sb** obtener *or* conseguir algo de alguien; **the book may be obtained from the publisher** este libro se puede adquirir directamente del editor

2 *vi Formal (practice)* imperar; *(rule)* regir; **this custom still obtains in Europe** esta costumbre todavía se da en Europa; **the situation which currently obtains in Somalia** la situación que impera actualmente en Somalia

obtainable [əb'teɪnəbəl] *adj* **easily o.** fácilmente obtenible; **only o. on prescription** sólo disponible con receta médica; **o. from your local supermarket** de venta en todos los supermercados

obtrude [əb'truːd] **1** *vt (impose)* imponer (**on** a); **to o. itself** imponerse

2 *vi* (**a**) *(impose oneself)* imponerse (**b**) *(stick out)* sobresalir

obtrusion [əb'truːʒən] *n Formal* imposición *f*

obtrusive [əb'truːsɪv] *adj* (**a**) *(person)* entrometido(a); *(behaviour)* molesto(a); *(decor, advertising)* estridente (**b**) *(smell)* penetrante

obtrusively [əb'truːsɪvlɪ] *adv* **the background music was o. loud** la música de fondo estaba tan alta que molestaba

obtuse [əb'tjuːs] *adj* (**a**) *Math* obtuso(a) (**b**) *(person, mind)* obtuso(a), duro(a) de mollera; **you're being deliberately o.** no quieres entender

obverse ['ɒbvɜːs] **1** *n* (**a**) *(of coin, medal)* anverso *m* (**b**) *Formal* **the o. is sometimes true** a veces se da el caso contrario

2 *adj* **the o. side** *(of coin, medal)* el anverso; *(of opinion, argument)* la otra cara

obviate ['ɒbvɪeɪt] *vt Formal (difficulty, danger)* evitar; **this would o. the need to...** esto evitaría la necesidad de...

obvious ['ɒbvɪəs] **1** *n* **to state the o.** constatar lo evidente; **it would be stating the o. to say we were nervous** huelga decir que estábamos nerviosos

2 *adj* (**a**) *(evident)* obvio(a), evidente; **it's o. that he's wrong** es evidente que se equivoca; **it was o. that he was going to resign** era evidente que iba a dimitir; **the o. answer/choice/solution** la respuesta/elección/solución obvia; **an o. forgery** una falsificación patente; **her o. innocence/embarrassment** su evidente inocencia/rubor; **for o. reasons** por razones obvias; **an o. comparison would be with the French Revolution** una comparación lógica sería con la Revolución Francesa; **it was the o. thing to do** hacer eso era lo más lógico; **they made their displeasure very o.** mostraron *or* manifestaron claramente su disgusto; **there was a very o. stain in the middle** había una mancha muy llamativa en el medio

(**b**) *Pej (predictable)* predecible; **you were too o. about it** *(unsubtle)* fuiste muy poco sutil en ese asunto

obviously ['ɒbvɪəslɪ] *adv* (**a**) *(of course)* desde luego, por supuesto; **o. not** claro que no; **o. it hurt, but...** claro que me dolió, pero...

(**b**) *(evidently)* evidentemente; **she's o. not coming** evidentemente, no va a venir; **he o. got the wrong number** evidentemente, se equivocó de número; **she's o. not lying** está claro que no miente

(**c**) *(plainly, visibly)* manifiestamente; **if you must pick your nose, try not to do it o.** si tienes que hurgarte la nariz, intenta que no se note; **she made her point very o.** dejó patente su punto de vista

obviousness ['ɒbvɪəsnɪs] *n (of humour, ploy)* falta *f* de sutileza; **the o. of his displeasure** su evidente desagrado

OC [əʊ'siː] *n* (*abbr* **Officer Commanding**) oficial *mf* al mando

ocarina [ɒkə'riːnə] *n* ocarina *f*

OCAS [əʊsiːeɪ'es] (*abbr* **Organization of Central American States**) *n* ODECA *f*

occasion [ə'keɪʒən] **1** *n* (**a**) *(time)* ocasión *f*; **it wasn't a suitable o.** no era el momento adecuado; **on one o.** en una ocasión; **on several occasions** en varias ocasiones; **on that o.** en aquella ocasión; **on o.** *(occasionally)* en ocasiones

(**b**) *(event)* acontecimiento *m*; **his birthday is always a big o.** su cumpleaños es siempre un gran acontecimiento; **on great occasions** en las grandes ocasiones; **to have a sense of o.** saber comportarse en las grandes ocasiones; **on the o. of** con ocasión de

(**c**) *(opportunity)* ocasión *f*, oportunidad *f*; **on the first o.** a la primera oportunidad; **I'd like to take this o. to...** me gustaría aprovechar esta oportunidad para...; **if the o. arises, should the o. arise** si surge la oportunidad

(**d**) *Formal (cause)* motivo *m*; **her return was the o. for great rejoicing** su regreso fue motivo de gran júbilo; **to have o. to do sth** tener motivos para hacer algo; **there is no o. for worry** no hay por qué preocuparse; **o. for complaint** motivo de queja

2 *vt Formal (fear, surprise)* ocasionar, causar

occasional [ə'keɪʒənəl] *adj* (**a**) *(irregular, infrequent)* ocasional, esporádico(a); **he's an o. visitor/golfer** es un visitante/golfista ocasional; **I like an** *or* **the o. cigar** me gusta fumar un puro de vez en cuando; **she writes me the o. postcard** me escribe alguna que otra postal; **there will be o. showers** habrá chubascos ocasionales ►► ***o. table*** mesita *f* auxiliar

(**b**) *(music, verse)* para la ocasión

occasionally [ə'keɪʒənəlɪ] *adv* ocasionalmente, de vez en cuando; **I smoke only very o.** sólo fumo muy de vez en cuando

Occident ['ɒksɪdənt] *n* **the O.** (el) Occidente

occidental [ɒksɪ'dentəl] *adj* occidental

occipital [ɒk'sɪpɪtəl] *adj Anat* occipital ►► ***o. bone*** (hueso *m*) occipital *m*; ***o. lobe*** lóbulo *m* occipital

occiput ['ɒksɪpʌt] *n Anat* occipucio *m*

occlude [ə'kluːd] *vt* ocluir

occluded front [ə'kluːdɪd'frʌnt] *n Met* frente *m* ocluido

occult [ɒ'kʌlt, 'ɒkʌlt] **1** *n* **the o.** lo oculto
2 *adj* oculto(a)

occultism ['ɒkʌltɪzəm] *n* ocultismo *m*

occultist ['ɒkʌltɪst] *n* ocultista *mf*

occupancy ['ɒkjʊpənsɪ] *n* ocupación *f*; **period of o.** *(of house)* periodo de alquiler *or Méx* renta; *(of land)* periodo de arrendamiento; *(of post)* (periodo de) tenencia; **hotel o. levels** *or* **rates** niveles de ocupación hotelera

occupant ['ɒkjʊpənt] *n* **(a)** *(of house, flat, car)* ocupante *mf* **(b)** *(of job)* titular *mf*

occupation [ɒkjʊ'peɪʃən] *n* **(a)** *(profession)* profesión *f*, ocupación *f*; **what is his o.?** ¿a qué se dedica?; **I'm not an actor by o.** no soy actor de profesión
(b) *(pastime)* pasatiempo *m*; **the TV provides some o. for the children** la televisión proporciona entretenimiento a los niños
(c) *(of house, offices, land)* ocupación *f*; **during Mr Gray's o. of the premises** mientras el señor Gray ocupaba el inmueble; **the premises are ready for immediate o.** el inmueble está listo para que se instalen
(d) *(by enemy, strikers, protesters)* ocupación *f*; **army of o.** ejército *or* fuerzas de ocupación; **under o.** ocupado(a); *Hist* **the O.** = la ocupación nazi

occupational [ɒkjʊ'peɪʃənəl] *adj* profesional, laboral ►► ***o. disease*** enfermedad *f* profesional; ***o. hazard*** gaje *m* del oficio; *Br* ***o. pension*** pensión *f* de empleo *or* de empresa; *Br* ***o. pension scheme*** plan *m* de pensiones de empleo *or* de empresa; ***o. psychology*** psicología *f* del trabajo; ***o. therapy*** terapia *f* ocupacional

occupied ['ɒkjʊpaɪd] *adj* **(a)** *(house)* ocupado(a); **this seat is o.** este asiento está ocupado
(b) *(busy)* ocupado(a), atareado(a); **to be o. with sth** estar ocupado(a) con algo; **to be o. in** *or* **with doing sth** estar ocupado(a) haciendo algo; **to keep sb o.** tener ocupado(a) a alguien; **to keep oneself o.** mantenerse ocupado(a)
(c) *(by enemy, strikers, protesters)* ocupado(a); *Hist* **in o. France** en la Francia ocupada ►► ***the O. Territories*** los territorios ocupados

occupier ['ɒkjʊpaɪə(r)] *n Br (of house)* ocupante *mf*; **(to) the o.** *(on letter)* a la atención del ocupante

occupy ['ɒkjʊpaɪ] *vt* **(a)** *(house, room)* ocupar
(b) *(keep busy) (person, mind)* ocupar; **she occupies herself by doing crosswords** se distrae *or* se mantiene ocupada haciendo crucigramas; **find something to o. your mind** encuentra algo para tener la mente ocupada
(c) *(fill, take up) (time, space)* ocupar; **she occupies her time in studying** ocupa su tiempo estudiando, dedica su tiempo a estudiar; **the company occupies three floors** la empresa ocupa tres pisos; **the task occupied all her time** la tarea le ocupaba todo el tiempo; **how do you o. your evenings?** ¿a qué te dedicas por las noches?
(d) *(enemy country, factory)* ocupar, tomar; **occupying army** ejército de ocupación; **the students have occupied the library** los estudiantes han ocupado la biblioteca
(e) *(hold) (office, rank)* ocupar

occur [ə'kɜː(r)] *(pt & pp* **occurred***)* *vi* **(a)** *(event)* suceder, ocurrir; *(opportunity)* darse, surgir; *(vacancy)* surgir; *(accident)* tener lugar, producirse; **many changes have occurred since then** desde entonces se han producido muchos cambios; **misunderstandings often o. over the phone** a menudo se producen malentendidos hablando por teléfono; **if a difficulty/the opportunity occurs** si surge alguna dificultad/la oportunidad
(b) *(exist, be found)* aparecer, darse; **his name occurs several times in the report** su nombre aparece varias veces en el informe *or CAm, Méx* reporte; **the condition occurs mainly among older people** la enfermedad se da principalmente en los ancianos
(c) *(come to mind)* **when did the idea o. to you?** ¿cuándo se te ocurrió esa idea?; **it occurred to me later that he was lying** más tarde caí en la cuenta de que estaba mintiendo; **didn't it o. to you to call me?** ¿no se te ocurrió llamarme?; **it would never o. to me to use violence** nunca se me ocurriría usar la violencia

occurrence [ə'kʌrəns] *n* **(a)** *(event)* suceso *m*; **this was the first o. of its kind** fue la primera vez que se dio un fenómeno de estas características; **it's an everyday o.** sucede todos los días
(b) *Formal (incidence) (of disease)* incidencia *f*; **the increasing o. of racial attacks** el creciente número de ataques racistas; **to be of frequent o.** ocurrir con frecuencia; **of rare o.** infrecuente, inusitado(a)

> **False friend:** The Spanish noun **ocurrencia** is not a translation for the English word **occurrence**. In Spanish the main meanings of **ocurrencia** are "bright idea" and "witty remark".

ocean ['əʊʃən] *n* **(a)** *Geog* océano *m*; *US (sea)* mar *m* ►► ***o. bed*** fondo *m* oceánico; ***o. current*** corriente *f* marina *or* oceánica; ***o. floor*** fondo *m* oceánico; ***o. liner*** transatlántico *m* **(b)** *Fam* **oceans of** la mar de; **we've got oceans of time** tenemos tiempo de sobra

oceanfront ['əʊʃənfrʌnt] *US* **1** *n* primera línea *f* de playa
2 *adj* **an o. hotel** un hotel en primera línea de playa

ocean-going ['əʊʃəngəʊɪŋ] *adj (vessel)* marítimo(a)

Oceania [əʊʃɪ'eɪnɪə] *n* Oceanía

oceanic [əʊʃɪ'ænɪk] *adj* oceánico(a) ►► ***o. ridge*** dorsal *f* oceánica; ***o. trench*** fosa *f* abisal *or* marina

oceanographer [əʊʃə'nɒgrəfə(r)] *n* oceanógrafo(a) *m,f*

oceanographic(al) [əʊʃənə'græfɪk(əl)] *adj* oceanográfico(a)

oceanography [əʊʃə'nɒgrəfɪ] *n* oceanografía *f*

oceanology [əʊʃə'nɒlədʒɪ] *n* oceanología *f*

ocelot ['ɒsəlɒt] *n* ocelote *m*

oche ['ɒkɪ] *n (in darts)* línea *f* de tiro; **on** *or* **at the o.** en la línea de tiro

ochre, *US* **ocher** ['əʊkə(r)] **1** *n* ocre *m*; **red/yellow o.** ocre rojo/amarillo
2 *adj* ocre

ocker ['ɒkə(r)] *n Austr (boor)* = australiano rudo y sin educación

o'clock [ə'klɒk] *adv* **(a)** *(time)* **(it's) one o.** (es) la una; **(it's) two/three o.** (son) las dos/tres; **at four o.** a las cuatro; **after five o.** de a partir de las cinco; **before six o.** antes de las seis; **the 8 o. train** el tren de las ocho; **at twelve o.** *(midday)* al mediodía; *(midnight)* a medianoche
(b) *(position)* **enemy fighters at 7 o.** cazas enemigos en las siete

OCR [əʊsiː'ɑː(r)] *n Comptr* **(a)** (*abbr* **optical character reader**) lector *m* óptico de caracteres **(b)** (*abbr* **optical character recognition**) reconocimiento *m* óptico de caracteres

Oct (*abbr* **October**) oct.

octagon ['ɒktəgən] *n* octógono *m*, octágono *m*

octagonal [ɒk'tægənəl] *adj* octogonal, octagonal

octahedral [ɒktə'hiːdrəl] *adj* octaédrico(a)

octahedron [ɒktə'hiːdrən] *n* octaedro *m*

octane ['ɒkteɪn] *n Chem* octano *m* ►► ***o. number*** *or* ***rating*** octanaje *m*

octave ['ɒktɪv] *n* **(a)** *Mus* octava *f* **(b)** *Lit* octava *f*

octavo [ɒk'teɪvəʊ] (*pl* **octavos**) *n* octavo *m*

octet [ɒk'tet] *n* **(a)** *Mus* octeto *m* **(b)** *Lit* octava *f*

October [ɒk'təʊbə(r)] *n* octubre *m*; *see also* **May**

octogenarian [ɒktədʒɪ'neərɪən] **1** *n* octogenario(a) *m,f*
2 *adj* octogenario(a)

octopus ['ɒktəpəs] *n* pulpo *m*

ocular ['ɒkjʊlə(r)] *adj Anat* ocular

oculist ['ɒkjʊlɪst] *n* oculista *mf*

OD [əʊ'diː] (*abbr* **overdose**) *Fam* **1** *n* sobredosis *f inv*
2 *vi* (*pt & pp* **OD'd, OD'ed**) meterse una sobredosis *inv*; *Fig* **I think I've rather OD'd on pizza** creo que me he pasado con la pizza

ODA [əʊdiː'eɪ] *n* (*abbr* **Overseas Development Administration**) = organismo británico de ayuda al desarrollo en el tercer mundo

odalisque ['əʊdəlɪsk] *n* odalisca *f*

odd [ɒd] **1** *adj* **(a)** *(strange)* raro(a), extraño(a); **the o. thing is that the room was empty** lo extraño es que la habitación estaba vacía; **it felt o. seeing her again** fue raro volver a verla; **it's o. your not knowing about it** que no lo sepas es extraño; **it's an o. way of saying sorry** es una forma peculiar de pedir perdón; *Fam* **he's a bit o. in the head** es medio raro; **(well,) that's o.!, how o.!** ¡qué raro!, ¡qué extraño! ►► *Br Fam* ***an o. bod*** un(a) excéntrico(a) *m,f*, un(a) raro(a) *m,f*
(b) *(not even)* impar; **the o. pages of a book** las páginas impares de un libro ►► ***o. number*** (número *m*) impar *m*
(c) *(not matching)* **an o. sock** un calcetín desparejado; **to be the o. one out** ser el/la único(a) diferente; **I wasn't wearing black, so I was the odd one** *or* **man out** yo desentonaba porque no iba de negro; **to be the o. man/woman out** *(different)* ser el/la único(a) diferente
(d) *(occasional)* ocasional; **he has his o. moments of depression** se deprime de vez en cuando; **nobody visits, apart from the o. anthropologist** nadie viene, con excepción de algún que otro antropólogo; **I smoke the o. cigarette** me fumo un cigarrillo de cuando en cuando; **you've made the o. mistake** has cometido algún que otro error; **I only get the o. moment to myself** apenas tengo tiempo para mí; **at o. moments** muy raras veces ►► ***o. jobber*** = hombre que hace arreglos o apaños ocasionales; ***o. jobs*** chapuzas *fpl*, apaños *mpl*
2 *adv* **a hundred o. sheep** ciento y pico ovejas; **twenty o. pounds** veintitantas libras; **he must be forty o.** debe de tener cuarenta y tantos

oddball [ˈɒdbɔːl] *Fam* **1** *n* tipo(a) *m,f* excéntrico(a) *or* raro(a)
2 *adj* excéntrico(a), raro(a)

oddity [ˈɒdɪtɪ] *n* **(a)** *(strangeness)* rareza *f* **(b)** *(person)* bicho *m* raro; *(thing)* rareza *f*; **it's just one of his little oddities** no es más que otra de sus rarezas

odd-job man [ˈɒdˈdʒɒbmæn] *n* = hombre que hace arreglos o apaños ocasionales

odd-looking [ˈɒdˈlʊkɪŋ] *adj* extraño(a), raro(a)

oddly [ˈɒdlɪ] *adv* *(to behave, dress)* de manera extraña; **o. enough** aunque parezca raro

oddment [ˈɒdmənt] *n* **oddments** restos *mpl*

oddness [ˈɒdnɪs] *n* *(strangeness)* rareza *f*

odds [ɒdz] **1** *npl* **(a)** *(in betting)* apuestas *fpl*; **this horse has o. of seven to one** las apuestas para este caballo están en *or* son de siete a uno; *Br Fam* **to pay over the o. (for sth)** pagar más de lo que vale (por algo)
(b) *(probability)* probabilidades *fpl*; **what are the o. on his getting the job?** ¿qué posibilidades tiene de conseguir el empleo?; **the o. are that...** lo más probable es que...; **the o. are against him** tiene pocas posibilidades; **the o. are against a spring election** es poco probable que se convoquen elecciones para la primavera; **the o. are in his favour** tiene muchas posibilidades
(c) *(great difficulties)* **to succeed against the o.** triunfar a pesar de las dificultades; **against all the o.** contra todo pronóstico; **they won against overwhelming o.** a pesar de las enormes dificultades, ganaron *or* vencieron
(d) *Br Fam (difference)* **it makes no o. (either way)** da igual; **it makes no o. to me** me da igual; **it makes no o. what I say** lo que yo diga no importa; **what's the o.?** ¡qué más dará!
(e) *Fam* ***o. and ends*** *(miscellaneous objects)* cosillas *fpl* sueltas; **I made it out of o. and ends left over from the dress** lo hice con los retales que quedaron del vestido; **I've still a few o. and ends to do** aún tengo algunas cosillas sueltas que hacer; *Br* ***o. and sods*** *(miscellaneous objects)* cosillas *fpl* sueltas; **all sorts of o. and sods turn up at poetry readings** *(people)* a esos encuentros de poesía se presenta cualquier hijo de vecino
2 at odds *adj* **to be at o. with sb** *(disagree, be on bad terms)* estar enfrentado(a) con alguien (**over** por); **the minister is at o. with the government on this issue** en este tema el ministro tiene una posición opuesta a la del gobierno; **she's always been at o. with herself** nunca se ha sentido bien consigo misma; **that's at o. with what I was told** eso no se corresponde con lo que me dijeron; **the way she was dressed was completely at o. with her personality** estaba vestida de una manera que no iba con su personalidad

odds-on [ɒdzˈɒn] *adj* **(a)** *(horse)* **o. favourite** favorito(a) claro(a) *or* indiscutible **(b)** *Fam* **it's o. that...** es casi seguro que...

ode [əʊd] *n* oda *f*

Odin [ˈəʊdɪn] *n Mythol* Odín

odious [ˈəʊdɪəs] *adj* odioso(a), aborrecible

odium [ˈəʊdɪəm] *n* odio *m*, aborrecimiento *m*; **to bring o. upon sb** ocasionar la repulsa *or* el rechazo (de los demás) a una persona

odometer [əʊˈdɒmɪtə(r)] *n US (in car)* ≃ cuentakilómetros *m inv*

odor, odorless *US* = **odour, odourless**

odoriferous [əʊdəˈrɪfərəs] *adj Formal* aromático(a), fragante

odorous [ˈəʊdərəs] *adj Formal* **(a)** *(fragrant)* aromático(a), fragante **(b)** *(malodorous)* apestoso(a), maloliente

odour, *US* **odor** [ˈəʊdə(r)] *n* **(a)** *(smell)* olor *m*; IDIOM **to be in good/bad o. with sb** estar a bien/mal con alguien **(b)** *(unpleasant smell)* mal olor *m*, tufo *m* **(c)** *Rel* **o. of sanctity** olor *m* de la santidad

odourless, *US* **odorless** [ˈəʊdəlɪs] *adj* inodoro(a)

Odysseus [əˈdiːsɪəs] *n* Odiseo

Odyssey [ˈɒdɪsɪ] *n* odisea *f*; *Fig* **a spiritual O.** una odisea espiritual

OE [əʊˈiː] *n* (*abbr* **Old English**) inglés *m* antiguo

OECD [əʊiːsiːˈdiː] *n* (*abbr* **Organization for Economic Co-operation and Development**) OCDE *f*

oecumenical, oecumenism = **ecumenical, ecumenism**

oedema, *US* **edema** [ɪˈdiːmə] *n Med* edema *m*

Oedipal [ˈiːdɪpəl] *adj Psy* edípico(a)

Oedipus [ˈiːdɪpəs] *n Mythol* Edipo ▸▸ *Psy* ***O. complex*** complejo *m* de Edipo

o'er [ˈəʊə(r)] *prep & adv Literary* por

oesophagus, *US* **esophagus** [iːˈsɒfəgəs] (*pl* **oesophagi**, *US* **esophagi** [iːˈsɒfəgaɪ]) *n Anat* esófago *m*

oestrogen, *US* **estrogen** [ˈiːstrədʒen] *n Biol Chem* estrógeno *m*

oestrus, *US* **estrus** [ˈiːstrəs] *n Zool* estro *m*

OF [ɒv, *unstressed* əv] *prep* **(a)** *(indicating belonging)* de; **the husband of the Prime Minister** el marido de la primera ministra; **the back of the chair** el respaldo de la silla; **the poetry of Yeats** la poesía de Yeats; **the University of South Carolina** la Universidad de Carolina del Sur; **the King of Spain** el Rey de España; **now I've got a house of my own** ahora tengo casa propia; **a friend of mine** un amigo mío; **a habit of mine** una de mis manías; **those children of yours are a real nuisance** esos niños tuyos son un infierno *or Esp* incordio
(b) *(indicating characteristic)* de; **the size of the house** el tamaño de la casa; **the colour of blood/grass** el color de la sangre/la hierba; **the aim of the measures** el objetivo de las medidas; **a man of many charms** un hombre con muchos encantos; **a matter of great concern** un asunto de gran interés; **a girl of ten** una niña de diez años; **at the age of ten** a los diez años
(c) *(indicating amount)* de; **a kilo of apples** un kilo de manzanas; **a drop of 20 percent** una bajada del 20 por ciento; **there were four of us** éramos cuatro; **the two of us** los dos, nosotros dos; **how much of it do you want?** ¿cuánto quiere?
(d) *(containing)* de; **a bag of potatoes** una bolsa de *Esp* patatas *or Am* papas; **a bottle of wine** una botella de vino; **a cry of pain** un grito de dolor
(e) *(made with)* de; **a table (made) of wood** una mesa de madera; **what is it made of?** ¿de qué está hecho?
(f) *(forming part of)* de; **the top of the mountain** la cumbre de la montaña; **the bottom of the garden** el fondo del jardín; **part of the problem** parte del problema; **one of my uncles** uno de mis tíos; **journalist of the year** periodista del año
(g) *(indicating gap)* de; **within 10 metres of where we are standing** a no más de 10 metros de donde nos encontramos; **she came within a second of the record** se quedó a un segundo del récord
(h) *(with regard to)* de; **what do you know of this matter?** ¿qué sabes de este asunto?; **a map of London** un mapa de Londres; **south of Chicago** al sur de Chicago; **to dream of sth/sb** soñar con algo/alguien; **to speak of sb** hablar de alguien; **to think of sth/sb** pensar en algo/alguien; **to be proud/tired of** estar orgulloso(a)/cansado(a) de; **to be guilty/capable of** ser culpable/capaz de; **a fear of spiders** el miedo a las arañas; **the advantage of doing this** la ventaja de hacer esto
(i) *(indicating cause)* de; **she died of cholera** murió de cólera; **he told me of his own accord** me lo dijo de motu propio; **the results of this decision** los resultados de esta decisión
(j) *(commenting on behaviour)* **it was clever of her to do it** fue muy lista *or RP* viva en hacerlo; **it was very kind of you** fue muy amable de tu parte
(k) *(in comparisons)* de; **the best of them all** el mejor de todos ellos; **we are the best of friends** somos excelentes *or* muy buenos amigos; **of all my friends, I like her best** es la que más me gusta de todos mis amigos, de entre todos mis amigos, es con la que me llevo mejor; **he of all people should know that...** él más que nadie debería saber que...
(l) *(indicating removal)* **to deprive sb of sth** privar a alguien de algo; **to get rid of sth** deshacerse de algo
(m) *(indicating date)* de; **the 4th of October** el 4 de octubre; **the night of the disaster** la noche del desastre; **the financial crash of 1929** la crisis financiera de 1929
(n) *(during)* **of an evening** por la tarde; **my coach of several years** mi entrenador durante varios años *or* de varios años
(o) *US (indicating time)* **a quarter of one** la una menos cuarto
(p) *(indicating degree)* **it is more/less of a problem than we had expected** es un problema más/menos complicado de lo que esperábamos

ofay [əʊˈfeɪ] *n US very Fam* = término ofensivo del argot de los negros para referirse a un blanco

OFF [ɒf] **1** *prep* **(a)** *(away from)* **keep o. the grass** *(sign)* prohibido pisar el césped; **o. the coast** cerca de la costa; **10 miles o. the coast** a 10 millas de la costa; **o. the premises** fuera del establecimiento; **a street o. the main road** una calle que sale de la principal; **the kitchen is o. the living room** la cocina da al salón *or* living; **are we a long way o. finishing?** ¿nos queda *or* falta mucho para acabar?; **to be o. course** haber perdido el rumbo; **the shot was o. target** el disparo no dio en el blanco
(b) *(indicating removal from)* de; **the handle has come o. the saucepan** se ha desprendido el mango de la cacerola; **they cut the branch o. the tree** cortaron la rama del árbol; **to fall/jump o. sth** caerse/saltar de algo; **get your hands o. me!** ¡quítame *or Am* sácame las manos de encima!; **he took the lid o. the box** destapó la caja; *Fam* **she took my pencil o. me** me quitó *or Am* sacó el lápiz

(**c**) *(out of)* de; **to get o. a train/bus** bajarse de un tren/autobús
(**d**) *(with prices)* **20 percent/$5 o. the price** una rebaja del 20 por ciento/de 5 dólares; **20 percent/$5 o. the dress** un 20 por ciento/5 dólares de descuento en el vestido
(**e**) *(absent from)* **to be o. work/school** faltar al trabajo/colegio; **Jane's o. work today** Jane no viene hoy a trabajar; **to take a day o. work** tomarse un día de vacaciones
(**f**) *(from the direction of)* **a cool breeze o. the sea** una brisa fresca del mar
(**g**) *(not liking, not taking)* **she's been o. her food lately** últimamente no está comiendo bien *or* está sin apetito *or Esp* está desganada; **I'm o. the medicine now** ya no estoy tomando el medicamento; **I'm o. him at the moment** últimamente no me hace tanta gracia
(**h**) *Fam (from)* **to buy/borrow sth o. sb** comprar/pedir prestado algo a alguien; **I got some useful advice o. him** me dio algunos consejos útiles
(**i**) *(using)* **to live o. sth** vivir de algo; **it runs o. petrol** funciona con gasolina *or RP* nafta; **the lighting runs o. a generator** las luces funcionan con un generador
2 *adv* (**a**) *(away)* **5 miles o.** a 5 millas (de distancia); **the meeting is only two weeks o.** sólo quedan *or* faltan dos semanas para la reunión; **Washington/the meeting is a long way o.** todavía queda *or* falta mucho para Washington/la reunión; **to run o.** echar a correr, salir corriendo; **I must be o.** tengo que irme; **I'm o. to California** me voy a California; **o. you go!** ¡vamos!, ¡andando!; **it's o. to the right** es a la derecha
(**b**) *(indicating removal)* **the handle has come o.** se ha soltado el asa; **to cut sth o.** cortar algo; **to fall o.** caerse; **to jump o.** saltar; **he had his trousers o.** no llevaba pantalones; **to take o. one's coat** quitarse *or Am* sacarse el abrigo; **to take a player o.** sustituir a un jugador; **o. with his head!** ¡que le corten la cabeza!
(**c**) *(out)* **to get o.** bajarse
(**d**) *(indicating isolation)* **to close a street o.** cerrar una calle; **to cordon an area o.** acordonar un área
(**e**) *(indicating disconnection)* **turn the light/TV o.** apaga la luz/televisión; **turn the water/gas/tap o.** cierra el agua/el gas/*Esp* el grifo *or Chile, Col, Méx* la llave *or Carib* pluma *or RP* canilla
(**f**) *(with prices)* **20 percent/$5 o.** una rebaja del 20 por ciento/de 5 dólares
(**g**) *(away from work, school)* **take the day o.** tómate el día libre; **an afternoon o.** una tarde libre
(**h**) *(completely)* **to finish sth o.** acabar con algo; **to kill sth o.** acabar con algo, *RP* liquidar algo
3 *adj* (**a**) *(not functioning) (light, TV)* apagado(a); *(water, electricity, gas)* desconectado(a); *(tap)* cerrado(a); *Comptr (menu option)* desactivado(a); **in the "o." position** en la posición de apagado; **the o. button/switch** el botón/interruptor del apagado
(**b**) *(cancelled)* **the wedding is o.** se ha cancelado la boda; **the deal is o.** el acuerdo se ha roto; **the match is o.** han suspendido el partido; *Fam* **the soup is o.** no hay sopa; *Fam* **it's all o. between me and her** lo nuestro se ha acabado
(**c**) *(absent from work, school)* **to be o.** faltar; **Jane's o. today** Jane no viene hoy a trabajar/a clase
(**d**) *(food)* pasado(a); *(milk)* cortado(a); *(meat)* malo(a), *RP* estropeado(a); **this cheese is o.** este queso se ha echado a perder
(**e**) *(unsuccessful)* **you were o. with your calculations** te equivocaste en los cálculos; **to have an o. day** tener un mal día
(**f**) *(in tourism)* **the o. season** la temporada baja
(**g**) *(describing situation)* **to be well/badly o.** tener mucho/poco dinero; **how are you o. for money?** ¿qué tal vas *or* estás de dinero?; **we're pretty well o. for furniture** tenemos bastantes muebles; **you'd be better o. staying where you are** será mejor *or* más vale que te quedes donde estás; **we're better/worse o. than before** estamos mejor/peor que antes
(**h**) *Br (unacceptable)* **that comment was a bit o.** ese comentario estaba de más; **he was a bit o. with me** estuvo un poco distante conmigo; **that was a bit o. (of her)** eso estuvo un poco feo (de su parte)
4 *n Br (of race)* **the o.** la salida; *also Fig* **right from the o.** desde el primer momento
5 *vt US Fam (kill)* cargarse a
6 off and on *adv (intermittently)* intermitentemente; **how often do you see them? – o. and on** ¿los ves a menudo? – de vez en cuando; **they've been going out for six years o. and on** llevan seis años saliendo intermitentemente; **she is working o. and on as an actress** trabaja de actriz esporádicamente

---

off-air ['ɒf'eə(r)] **1** *adj* en circuito cerrado
2 *adv* en circuito cerrado

offal ['ɒfəl] *n* (**a**) *Culin* asaduras *fpl* (**b**) *(refuse)* basura *f*, desperdicios *mpl*

off-balance ['ɒf'bæləns] *adj* desacomodado(a), desprevenido(a); **her question caught me o.** su pregunta me tomó desprevenido *or* desacomodado

offbeat ['ɒf'bi:t] **1** *n Mus* tiempo *m* débil
2 *adj Fam (unconventional)* inusual, original

off-Broadway ['ɒf'brɔ:dweɪ] *adj US* = de las producciones teatrales fuera del circuito de Broadway

off-camera ['ɒf'kæmərə] **1** *adj* fuera de (la) cámara
2 *adv* fuera de (la) cámara

off-centre, *US* **off-center** [ɒf'sentə(r)] **1** *adj* (**a**) *(position)* descentrado(a); **the title is o.** el título no está centrado (**b**) *(eccentric)* excéntrico(a)
2 *adv* fuera del centro

off-chance ['ɒftʃɑ:ns] *n* **on the o.** por si acaso; **I asked her on the o. she might know something** le pregunté por si acaso sabía algo

off-colour, *US* **off-color** [ɒf'kʌlə(r)] *adj* (**a**) *(unwell)* indispuesto(a); **to be** *or* **feel o.** no sentirse muy bien, sentirse indispuesto(a); **to look o.** no tener muy buen aspecto (**b**) *(joke)* fuera de tono

offcut ['ɒfkʌt] *n (of wood)* recorte *m*; *(of cloth)* retal *m*; *(of carpet)* retazo *m*; *(of meat)* resto *m*

off-duty ['ɒf'dju:tɪ] *adj (soldier)* de permiso; *(policeman)* fuera de servicio

offence, *US* **offense** [ə'fens] *n* (**a**) *Law* delito *m*, infracción *f*; **it's his first o.** es su primer delito, es su primera infracción; **petty** *or* **minor o.** infracción leve; **to commit an o.** cometer un delito *or* una infracción; **a driving o.** una infracción de tráfico
(**b**) *(annoyance, displeasure)* ofensa *f*; **to cause** *or* **give o.** ofender; **to take o. (at)** sentirse ofendido(a) (por), ofenderse (por); **no o.!** no es mi intención ofender; **no o. intended – none taken** no quería ofenderte – no te preocupes; **the factory is an o. to the eye** es sumamente desagradable ver el aspecto de la fábrica; **it's an o. against good taste** es un insulto al buen gusto
(**c**) *Mil (attack)* ataque *m*, ofensiva *f*
(**d**) *Sport (attackers)* atacantes *mfpl*, línea *f* de ataque

offend [ə'fend] **1** *vt (person)* ofender; *(eyes, senses, reason)* dañar, herir; **the film contains scenes which may o. some viewers** la película contiene escenas que pueden ofender a algunos espectadores; **his behaviour offends my sense of fair play** su comportamiento atenta contra mi sentido del juego limpio
2 *vi* (**a**) *Law* delinquir; **he is liable to o. again** es probable que vuelva a delinquir (**b**) *(cause offence)* **I didn't mean to o.** *(the general public)* mi intención no fue ofender; *(you)* no quise ofenderte; **likely to o.** susceptible de ofender a alguien; **to o. against good taste** atentar contra el buen gusto

offended [ə'fendɪd] *adj (insulted)* ofendido(a); **he is easily o.** se ofende fácilmente, se ofende por nada; **to be** *or* **feel o. (at** *or* **by sth)** ofenderse *or* sentirse ofendido(a) (por algo); **don't be o. if I leave early** si me voy temprano no lo tomes a mal; **she was very o. when he didn't come to her party** se ofendió mucho porque no vino a la fiesta

offender [ə'fendə(r)] *n* (**a**) *Law* delincuente *mf*; **13 percent of convicted offenders return to crime** el 13 por ciento de los delincuentes condenados reincide (**b**) *(culprit)* culpable *mf*; **the chemical industry is the worst o.** la industria química es la principal responsable

offending [ə'fendɪŋ] *adj (causing a problem)* problemático(a); **the o. word was omitted** el término problemático se suprimió

offense *US* = **offence**

offensive [ə'fensɪv] **1** *n Mil & Fig* ofensiva *f*; **to take the o., to go on the o.** pasar a la ofensiva; **to be on the o.** estar en plena ofensiva; **a diplomatic/peace o.** una ofensiva diplomática/por la paz
2 *adj* (**a**) *(causing indignation, anger) (word, action, behaviour)* ofensivo(a); **to be o. to sb** mostrarse ofensivo(a) con alguien; **to find sth o.** encontrar algo ofensivo (**b**) *(disgusting) (smell)* asqueroso(a), repugnante (**c**) *(aggressive)* ofensivo(a); **they took immediate o. action** realizaron una inmediata acción ofensiva ►► ***o. weapon*** arma *f* ofensiva

offensively [ə'fensɪvlɪ] *adv* (**a**) *(insultingly)* de manera insultante *or* ofensiva (**b**) *(on the attack)* ofensivamente; **o., theirs is the stronger team** en el ataque, el equipo de ellos es el más fuerte

offensiveness [ə'fensɪvnɪs] *n* (**a**) *(of behaviour, remark)* lo ofensivo (**b**) *(of sight, smell)* lo repugnante, lo desagradable

offer ['ɒfə(r)] **1** *n* oferta *f*; **the o. still stands** la oferta sigue en pie; **we need somebody to help, any offers?** necesitamos que alguien ayude, ¿alguien se ofrece?; **to make sb an o. (for sth)** hacer a alguien una oferta (por algo); **make me an o.!** hazme una oferta, ¿cuánto me das?; **thanks for the o., but I can manage** gracias por tu ofrecimiento, pero puedo arreglármelas solo; **he turned down the o. of a free holiday**

declinó *or* rechazó la oferta de unas vacaciones gratuitas; **£500 or nearest o.** 500 libras negociables; **he wants £500 for it, but he's open to offers** pide 500 libras pero descarta otras ofertas; **on o.** *(reduced)* de oferta; *(available)* disponible; **the house is under o.** han hecho una oferta por la casa ►► ***o. of marriage*** proposición *f* de matrimonio; *St Exch* ***o. price*** precio *m* de oferta

2 *vt* **(a)** *(proffer)* ofrecer (**for** por); **to o. sb sth, to o. sth to sb** ofrecer algo a alguien; **to o. a suggestion/an opinion** hacer una sugerencia/dar una opinión; **may I o. a little advice?** ¿puedo darte un consejo?; **to o. to do sth** ofrecerse a hacer algo; **he offered her a chair/his arm** le ofreció una silla/su brazo; **can I o. you a drink?** ¿puedo ofrecerte un trago?, ¿te apetece un trago?; **nobody bothered to o. any explanation** nadie se molestó en dar explicaciones; **she offered to show him how to use the photocopier** le ofreció enseñarle a utilizar la fotocopiadora; *Law* **to o. a plea of guilty/innocent** declararse culpable/inocente

(b) *(provide)* ofrecer; **our proposal offers several advantages** nuestra propuesta ofrece diversas ventajas; **the job offers few prospects of promotion** el trabajo ofrece pocas perspectivas de ascender; **the area hasn't got much/has a lot to o.** el área tiene mucho/poco que ofrecer; **candidates may o. one of the following foreign languages** *(in exam)* los candidatos pueden elegir uno de los siguientes idiomas extranjeros

3 *vi* **don't say I didn't o.** no digas que no te lo ofrecí; **it was kind of you to o.** muchas gracias por tu ofrecimiento

► **offer up** *vt sep (prayers, sacrifice)* ofrecer

offering ['ɒfərɪŋ] *n* **(a)** *(gift, thing presented)* entrega *f*; **his latest o. is a novel set in Ireland** su último trabajo es una novela que se desarrolla en Irlanda **(b)** *Rel* ofrenda *f*

offertory ['ɒfətərɪ] *n Rel (collection)* colecta *f*; *(hymn)* ofertorio *m* ►► ***o. box*** cepillo *m*; ***o. plate*** plato *m* de las ofrendas

offhand [ɒf'hænd] 1 *adj* desconsiderado(a); **to be o. (with sb)** mostrarse desconsiderado(a) (con alguien)

2 *adv (immediately)* **I don't know o.** ahora mismo, no lo sé; **o. I'd say it'll take a week** a bote pronto me inclino a pensar que llevará una semana

offhanded [ɒf'hændɪd] *adj* desconsiderado(a)

offhandedly [ɒf'hændɪdlɪ] *adv (casually)* indiferentemente

offhandedness [ɒf'hændɪdnɪs] *n* desconsideración *f*

office ['ɒfɪs] *n* **(a)** *(place) (premises)* oficina *f*; *(room)* despacho *m*, oficina *f*; *(of lawyer)* despacho *m*, bufete *m*; *(of architect)* estudio *m*; *US (of doctor, dentist)* consulta *f*; **our office(s) in Lima, our Lima office(s)** nuestra sucursal de Lima; **he's out of the o. at the moment** en este momento no se encuentra en su despacho; **the whole o. is talking about it** toda la oficina está hablando de eso; **for o. use only** *(on form)* uso interno exclusivamente ►► ***o. automation*** ofimática *f*; ***o. block*** bloque *m* de oficinas; ***o. boy*** chico *m* de los recados *or RP* mandados; ***o. building*** bloque *m* de oficinas; ***o. equipment*** equipo *m* de oficina; ***o. girl*** chica *f* de los recados; ***o. hours*** horas *fpl or* horario *m* de oficina; **during/outside o. hours** en horario de oficina/fuera del horario de oficina; ***o. IT*** ofimática *f*; ***o. junior*** auxiliar *mf* de oficina; ***o. manager*** gerente *mf*; ***o. party*** fiesta *f* de la oficina; ***o. space*** espacio *m* físico para oficinas; ***o. stationery*** material *m* de oficina; ***o. work*** trabajo *m* de oficina; ***o. worker*** oficinista *mf*

(b) *(government department)* ***the O. of Fair Trading*** = organismo británico que vela por los intereses de los consumidores y regula las prácticas comerciales, ≃ Oficina *f* del Consumidor; ***the O. of Management and Budget*** = organismo que ayuda al presidente estadounidense a elaborar los presupuestos del estado

(c) *Pol (position)* cargo *m*; **to hold (high) o.** ocupar un (alto) cargo; **to run** *or* **stand for o.** presentarse al cargo; **to seek o.** aspirar a un cargo; **to take o.** tomar posesión de un cargo; **to be in o.** estar en el poder; **to leave o.** dejar el cargo; **to be out of o.** *(political party)* no estar (más) en el poder; **he's been out of o. for two years** *(politician)* hace dos años que dejó de ejercer el cargo

(d) *Formal* **I got the house through the good offices of Philip** conseguí la casa gracias a los buenos oficios de Philip

(e) *Rel* oficio *m*

office-bearer ['ɒfɪsbeərə(r)], **office-holder** ['ɒfɪshəʊldə(r)] *n* cargo *m*; **the previous o. was a woman** anteriormente ocupaba el cargo una mujer

officer ['ɒfɪsə(r)] 1 *n* **(a)** *(army)* oficial *mf* ►► ***o. of the day*** oficial *mf* de guardia; ***officers' mess*** cantina *f or* comedor *m* de oficiales; ***o. of the watch*** oficial *mf* de guardia **(b)** *(police)* agente *mf* **(c)** *(in local government, union)* delegado(a) *m,f* **(d)** *(of association, institution)* miembro *m* del comité ejecutivo

2 *vt Mil* comandar; **they were officered by inexperienced young men** estaban comandados por oficiales jóvenes sin experiencia

official [ə'fɪʃəl] 1 *n (representative)* representante *mf*; *(in public sector)* funcionario(a) *m,f*; *(in trade union)* representante *mf*; *Sport (referee)* árbitro *mf*, *Am* referí *mf*

2 *adj* oficial; **she was acting in her o. capacity** actuaba en el ejercicio de sus funciones; **his appointment will be made o. tomorrow** su nombramiento se hará oficial mañana; **is that o.?** ¿es oficial?; **it's o., they're getting a divorce** es oficial, se divorcian; **to go through o. channels** seguir los trámites necesarios ►► ***o. opening*** *(of factory, museum)* inauguración *f* oficial; *Com* ***o. receiver*** síndico *m*; *Br* ***O. Secrets Act*** ≃ ley *f* de secretos oficiales *or* de Estado; ***o. strike*** huelga *f* oficial

officialdom [ə'fɪʃəldəm] *n Pej (bureaucracy)* los funcionarios, la administración

officialese [əfɪʃə'li:z] *n Pej* jerga *f* administrativa

officially [ə'fɪʃəlɪ] *adv* oficialmente; **he has now been o. appointed** su nombramiento se ha hecho oficial; **we now have it o.** ahora está oficialmente confirmado; **o., he's at the dentist's** oficialmente, fue al dentista

officiate [ə'fɪʃɪeɪt] *vi* **(a)** *(act in official capacity)* oficiar; **to o. as** ejercer funciones de; **she officiated at the ceremony** ofició en la ceremonia; **the mayor will o. at the opening of the stadium** el alcalde presidirá la inauguración oficial del estadio **(b)** *Rel* oficiar (**at** en)

officious [ə'fɪʃəs] *adj (overzealous)* excesivamente celoso(a) *or* diligente; *(interfering)* entrometido(a)

> **False friend:** The Spanish adjective **oficioso** is not a translation for the English word **officious**. In Spanish **oficioso** means "unofficial".

officiously [ə'fɪʃəslɪ] *adv (overzealously)* con excesivo celo *or* excesiva diligencia; *(interferingly)* de manera entrometida

officiousness [ə'fɪʃəsnɪs] *n (overzealousness)* celo *m* excesivo, diligencia *f* excesiva; *(interfering manner)* carácter *m* entrometido

offie ['ɒfɪ] *n Br Fam* tienda *f* de bebidas alcohólicas *or* de licores

offing ['ɒfɪŋ] *n* **(to be) in the o.** (ser) inminente; **a confrontation had long been in the o.** el enfrentamiento era latente desde hacía tiempo

off-key ['ɒf'ki:] *Mus* 1 *adj* desafinado(a)

2 *adv* desafinadamente; **to play/sing o.** desafinar al tocar/al cantar

off-licence ['ɒflaɪsəns] *n Br* tienda *f* de bebidas alcohólicas *or* de licores

off-limits [ɒf'lɪmɪts] *adj (area)* prohibido(a); *Fig* **the subject is o.** es un tema prohibido

off-line, offline *Comptr* 1 *adj* ['ɒflaɪn] *(processing)* fuera de línea; *(printer)* desconectado(a); **to put the printer o.** desconectar la impresora ►► ***o. reader*** lector *m* off-line

2 *adv* [ɒf'laɪn] fuera de línea; **to go o.** desconectarse; **to work o.** trabajar sin estar conectado

off-load ['ɒf'ləʊd] *vt* **(a)** *(unload) (passengers)* hacer descender a; *(cargo)* descargar **(b)** *(dump) (surplus goods)* deshacerse de; **to o. sth onto sb** endosar algo a alguien; **to o. blame onto sb** descargar la culpa en alguien

off-message ['ɒf'mesɪdʒ] *adj Br Pol* **he's o.** no sigue la línea del partido

off-off-Broadway ['ɒfɒf'brɔ:dweɪ] *adj US* experimental

off-peak ['ɒf'pi:k] *adj (electricity, travel)* en horas valle; *(phone call)* en horas de tarifa reducida

offprint ['ɒfprɪnt] *n (article)* separata *f*

off-putting ['ɒfpʊtɪŋ] *adj Br* **(a)** *(unpleasant)* desagradable, molesto(a); **I find his manner rather o.** sus modales me resultan desagradables *or* molestos **(b)** *(distracting)* **I find that noise very o.** ese ruido me distrae mucho

off-ramp ['ɒfræmp] *n US* carril *m* de deceleración *or* de salida

off-road ['ɒfrəʊd] 1 *adj (driving)* fuera de pista; **an o. vehicle** un (vehículo) todoterreno

2 *adv (to drive, cycle)* a campo traviesa

off-sales ['ɒfseɪlz] *n Br* = venta de bebidas alcohólicas para llevar

off-screen ['ɒf'skri:n] *adj Cin & TV* **their o. relationship mirrored their love affair in the film** su relación detrás de la cámara era un reflejo de su aventura amorosa en la película

off-season ['ɒfsi:zən] 1 *adj (rate)* de temporada baja

2 *adv* en temporada baja

offset 1 *n* ['ɒfset] *Typ (process)* offset *m* ►► ***o. litho*** *or* ***lithography*** offset *m*

2 *vt* [ɒf'set] *(pt & pp* **offset***)* **(a)** *(make up for)* contrarrestar; **the advantages tend to o. the difficulties** la ventajas suelen contrarrestar los inconvenientes; **any wage increase will be o. by inflation**

cualquier aumento salarial se verá contrarrestado por la inflación; **to o. losses against tax** deducir (las) pérdidas de (los) impuestos (**b**) *Typ* imprimir en offset

offshoot ['ɒfʃu:t] *n* (**a**) *(of tree)* vástago *m* (**b**) *(of family)* rama *f*; *(of political party, artistic movement)* ramificación *f*; *(of company)* empresa *f* subsidiaria

offshore 1 *adv* [ɒf'ʃɔ:(r)] cerca de la costa
2 *adj* ['ɒfʃɔ:(r)] (**a**) *(island, shipping, waters)* cercano(a) a la costa; **o. fishing** pesca de bajura ►► ***o. oil rig*** plataforma *f* petrolífera *(en el mar)* (**b**) *(towards open sea) (current, direction)* mar adentro; *(wind)* de tierra, terral (**c**) *Fin (investment, company)* en paraíso fiscal ►► ***o. fund*** fondo *m* colocado en paraíso fiscal; ***o. investment*** inversión *f* en un paraíso fiscal

offside ['ɒfsaɪd] 1 *n Aut* lado *m* del conductor
2 *adj* (**a**) *Aut* del lado del conductor (**b**) [ɒf'saɪd] *(in soccer, rugby)* (en) fuera de juego ►► ***o. trap*** *(in soccer)* (trampa *f* del) fuera de juego *m*
3 *adv* [ɒf'saɪd] fuera de juego

off-site 1 *adj* ['ɒfsaɪt] de fuera, externo(a)
2 *adv* [ɒf'saɪt] externamente

offspring ['ɒfsprɪŋ] *npl* (**a**) *(young of an animal)* crías *fpl* (**b**) *(children)* hijos *mpl*, descendencia *f*

offstage *Theat* 1 *adv* [ɒf'steɪdʒ] fuera del escenario; **o., she was surprisingly reserved** fuera del escenario, ella era sorprendentemente reservada
2 *adj* ['ɒfsteɪdʒ] de fuera del escenario

off-stream ['ɒfstri:m] *adj (industrial plant)* **to go o.** dejar de funcionar; **to be o.** no estar en funcionamiento

off-street ['ɒf'stri:t] *adj* **o. parking** estacionamiento *or Esp* aparcamiento fuera de la vía pública

off-the-cuff [ɒfðə'kʌf] 1 *adj (remark)* improvisado(a), espontáneo(a)
2 *adv* improvisadamente, espontáneamente

off-the-peg [ɒfðə'peg] *adj esp Br (suit)* de confección

off-the-record [ɒfðə'rekɔ:d] *adj* extraoficial

off-the-shelf [ɒfðə'ʃelf] *adj (software, components)* estándar

off-the-shoulder [ɒfðə'ʃəʊldə(r)] *adj (woman's dress)* que deja los hombros al descubierto

off-the-wall [ɒfðə'wɔ:l] *adj Fam* estrafalario(a)

off-white ['ɒf'waɪt] 1 *n* tono *m* blancuzco, blanco *m* marfil
2 *adj* blancuzco(a)

off-year ['ɒfjɪə(r)] *n Pol* = año en que no hay elecciones presidenciales en Estados Unidos

OFGEM ['ɒfdʒem] *n* (*abbr* **Office of the Gas and Electricity Markets**) = organismo británico que regula los suministros de gas y energía eléctrica

OFSTED ['ɒfsted] *n* (*abbr* **Office for Standards in Education**) = organismo británico responsable de la supervisión del sistema educativo

OFT [əʊef'ti:] *n* (*abbr* **Office of Fair Trading**) = organismo británico que vela por los intereses de los consumidores y regula las prácticas comerciales, ≃ Oficina *f* del Consumidor

oft [ɒft] *adv Literary* a menudo

oft- [ɒft] *prefix* **o.-repeated** muy repetido(a); **o.-quoted** muy citado(a)

OFTEL ['ɒftel] *n* (*abbr* **Office of Telecommunications**) = organismo británico que regula las telecomunicaciones

often ['ɒfən, 'ɒftən] *adv* a menudo; **I've o. thought of leaving** he pensado a menudo en irme; **I don't see her very o.** no la veo muy a menudo; **we don't go there as o. as we used to** no vamos tanto como antes; **I go there as o. as possible** voy siempre que puedo; *Hum* **do you come here o.?** = expresión equivalente a "¿estudias o trabajas?"; **I o. wonder...** a menudo me pregunto...; **it's not o. you see that** eso no se ve a menudo; **it's not o. you get an offer like that** no todos los días te hacen una oferta como ésa; **twice as o. as before** el doble que antes; **how o.?** *(how many times)* ¿cuántas veces?; *(how frequently)* ¿cada cuánto (tiempo)?, ¿con qué frecuencia?; **all** *or* **only too o.** con demasiada frecuencia; **as o. as not** la mitad de las veces; **more o. than not** muchas veces; **every so o.** de vez en cuando, cada cierto tiempo

oftentimes ['ɒfəntaɪmz] *adv* (**a**) *Br Archaic* frecuentemente (**b**) *US* con frecuencia, a menudo

ofttimes ['ɒfttaɪmz] *adv Archaic or Literary* a menudo

OFWAT ['ɒfwɒt] *n Br* (*abbr* **Office of Water Services**) = organismo regulador del suministro de agua en Gran Bretaña

ogive ['əʊdʒaɪv] *n* (**a**) *Archit* ojiva *f* (**b**) *Math* ojiva *f*

ogle ['ɒgəl] *vt* **to o. sb** comerse a alguien con los ojos

ogre ['əʊgə(r)] *n also Fig* ogro *m*

ogreish ['əʊgərɪʃ] *adj (frightening)* **he's a bit o.** asusta un poco

ogress ['əʊgrɪs] *n (frightening woman)* ogro *m*

OH (*abbr* **Ohio**) Ohio

oh [əʊ] *exclam* (**a**) *(expressing surprise)* ¡oh!; **oh, what a surprise!** ¡eh! ¡qué sorpresa!; **oh no!** ¡oh, no!; **oh no, not again!** ¡oh, no, otra vez no!; **oh really?** ¿en serio?, ¡ah sí! (**b**) *(contradicting)* **oh no you don't!** ¡no, de ninguna manera!; **oh yes you will!** ¡por supuesto que sí! (**c**) *Literary (as vocative)* oh; **Oh God!** ¡oh, Dios!

Ohio [əʊ'haɪəʊ] *n* Ohio

ohm [əʊm] *n Elec* ohmio *m* ►► ***Ohm's law*** ley *f* de Ohm

ohmmeter ['əʊmmi:tə(r)] *n Elec* ohmímetro *m*

OHMS [əʊəɪtʃem'es] (*abbr* **On Her/His Majesty's Service**) = siglas que aparecen en documentos emitidos por el gobierno británico indicando su carácter oficial

oho [əʊ'həʊ] *exclam (expressing triumph, surprise)* ¡ajajá!

OHP [əʊeɪtʃ'pi:] *n* (*abbr* **overhead projector**) retroproyector *m*, proyector *m* de transparencias ►► ***O. slide*** transparencia *f*

oi [ɔɪ] *exclam Fam* ¡eh!; **oi, what do you think you're doing?** ¡eh, tú!, ¿qué te has creído que estás haciendo?

oik [ɔɪk] *n Br Fam* tipo(a) *m,f* vulgar

oil [ɔɪl] 1 *n* (**a**) *(for food)* aceite *m*; **sardines/tuna in o.** sardinas/atún en aceite ►► ***o. cake*** *(for livestock)* torta *f* de aceite; ***o. decanter*** aceitera *f*; ***o. palm*** palmera *f* de aceite; ***o. press*** molino *m* aceitero *or* de aceite
(**b**) *(lubricant)* aceite *m*; IDIOM **to pour o. on troubled waters** calmar los ánimos ►► ***o. change*** cambio *m* de aceite; *US Aut* ***o. pan*** cárter *m*; ***o. stain*** mancha *f* de aceite
(**c**) *(petroleum)* petróleo *m* ►► ***o. baron*** magnate *m* del petróleo; ***o. company*** compañía *f* petrolera; ***the o. crisis*** la crisis del petróleo; ***o. drum*** bidón *m* de petróleo; ***o. pipeline*** oleoducto *m*; ***o. platform*** plataforma *f* petrolífera; ***o. prospecting*** prospección *f* petrolífera; ***o. refinery*** refinería *f* de petróleo; ***o. reserves*** reservas *fpl* de petróleo *or* crudo; ***o. rig*** plataforma *f* petrolífera; ***o. slick*** marea *f* negra; ***o. spill*** derrame *m* petrolero *or* de petróleo; ***o. tanker*** *(ship)* petrolero *m*; *(vehicle)* camión *m* cisterna *(de petróleo)*; ***o. terminal*** estación *f* receptora de petróleo; ***o. well*** pozo *m* petrolífero *or* de petróleo; ***o. worker*** trabajador(ora) *m,f* del petróleo
(**d**) *(for lamp, stove)* aceite *m* ►► ***o. lamp*** lámpara *f* de aceite; ***o. stove*** estufa *f* de petróleo
(**e**) *(paint)* **to paint in oils** pintar al óleo ►► ***o. colour*** pintura *f* al óleo; ***o. paint*** pintura *f* al óleo; ***o. painting*** óleo *m*; IDIOM *Hum* **he's/she's no o. painting** no es ninguna belleza
2 *vt (machine, hinge)* engrasar, lubricar; *(wood)* dar aceite a; *Fig* **to o. the wheels** allanar el terreno

oilbird ['ɔɪlbɜ:d] *n* aceitero *m*, guácharo *m*

oil-burning ['ɔɪlbɜ:nɪŋ] *adj (stove)* de petróleo; *(lamp)* de aceite

oilcan ['ɔɪlkæn] *n* (**a**) *(for applying oil)* aceitera *f* (**b**) *(container)* lata *f* de aceite

oilcloth ['ɔɪlklɒθ] *n* hule *m*

oiled [ɔɪld] *adj* (**a**) *(machine, hinge)* engrasado(a), lubricado(a); *(wood, cloth)* aceitado(a), tratado(a) con aceite (**b**) *Fam* **(well) o.** *(drunk)* (bien) cargado(a)

oiler ['ɔɪlə(r)] *n (tanker)* petrolero *m*

oilfield ['ɔɪlfi:ld] *n* yacimiento *m* petrolífero, explotación *f* petrolífera

oil-fired ['ɔɪlfaɪəd] *adj* ***o. central heating*** calefacción *f* central de gasóleo

oiliness ['ɔɪlɪnɪs] *n* (**a**) *(of fish, food)* lo aceitoso (**b**) *(of person, manner)* lo empalagoso, zalamería *f*

oilman ['ɔɪlmæn] *n (owner)* petrolero *m*; *(worker)* trabajador *m* del petróleo

oil-producing ['ɔɪlprə'dju:sɪŋ] *adj* (**a**) *(country)* productor(a) de petróleo (**b**) *(plant, substance)* aceitero(a)

oil-rich ['ɔɪlrɪtʃ] *adj (countries)* con grandes reservas de crudo *or* petróleo

oilseed ['ɔɪlsi:d] *n* semilla *f* oleaginosa ►► ***o. rape*** colza *f*

oilskin ['ɔɪlskɪn] *n (fabric)* hule *m*; *(garment)* impermeable *m*

oilstone ['ɔɪlstəʊn] *n (for sharpening)* piedra *f* de afilar *or* afiladora

oily ['ɔɪlɪ] *adj* (**a**) *(hands, rag)* grasiento(a); *(skin, hair)* graso(a); *(food)* aceitoso(a), con aceite ►► ***o. fish*** pescado *m* azul (**b**) *Pej (manner)* empalagoso(a)

oink [ɔɪŋk] *vi (pig)* gruñir

ointment ['ɔɪntmənt] *n* ungüento *m*, pomada *f*

Oireachtas [ə'rɒχtəs] *n Pol* parlamento *m* de Irlanda

Oirish ['ɔɪrɪʃ] *adj Fam Hum* típicamente irlandés(esa)

OJ ['əʊdʒeɪ] *n US* (*abbr* **orange juice**) jugo *m or Esp* zumo *m* de naranja

OK[1] (*abbr* **Oklahoma**) Oklahoma

OK[2]**, OKAY** ['əʊ'keɪ] **1** *exclam* (**a**) *(expressing agreement)* de acuerdo, *Esp* vale, *Am* ok, *Méx* ándale; **we'll meet you at the station, OK?** nos vemos en la estación, ¿de acuerdo? *or Esp* ¿vale? *or Am* ¿ok? *or RP* ¿está bien?; **just calm down, OK?** cálmate, ¿quieres?; **OK, OK! I'll do it now** ¡bueno, de acuerdo *or Esp* vale *or Am* ok *or Méx* ándale *or RP* está bien!, ya lo hago

(**b**) *(introducing statement)* **OK, who wants to go first?** bueno *or Esp* venga, ¿quién quiere ir primero?; **OK, so he's not the cleverest person in the world** de acuerdo *or Esp* vale *or RP* está bien, no es la persona más inteligente del mundo

2 *adj* (**a**) *(in order, fine)* bien; **are you OK?** ¿estás bien?; **don't worry, I'll be OK** no te preocupes, me las arreglaré *or RP* me voy a arreglar; **sorry! – that's OK** ¡lo siento! – no ha sido nada *or* no es nada; **no, it is NOT OK!** no, no está bien

(**b**) *(acceptable)* **that's OK by** *or* **with me** (a mí) me parece bien; **is it OK by** *or* **with you if I wear shorts?** ¿te parece bien si llevo pantalón corto?, ¿te parece mal que me ponga pantalón corto?; **it's OK for you to come in now** ya puedes entrar; **is it OK to wear shorts?** ¿está bien si voy con pantalón corto?, ¿podré ir de pantalón corto?; **it was OK, but nothing special** no estuvo mal, pero nada del otro mundo

(**c**) *(understanding)* **she was OK about it** se lo tomó bastante bien

(**d**) *Fam (likeable)* **he's an OK sort of guy** es buena gente, es un tipo *Esp* legal *or Méx, RP* derecho

(**e**) **are we OK for time/money?** *(have enough)* ¿vamos bien de tiempo/dinero?; **are you OK for drinks?** ¿tienes de beber?

3 *adv* bien; **you did OK** hiciste bien

4 *n* **to get the OK** recibir el visto bueno; **to give (sb) the OK** dar permiso (a alguien)

5 *vt* (*pt & pp* **OK'd** *or* **okayed**) *Fam (proposal, plan)* dar el visto bueno a

okapi [əʊ'kɑːpɪ] (*pl* **okapis** *or* **okapi**) *n* okapi *m*

okay = **OK**

okey-doke ['əʊkɪ'dəʊk], **okey-dokey** ['əʊkɪ'dəʊkɪ] *exclam Fam* de acuerdo, *Esp* vale, *Arg* dale, *Méx* órale

Okie ['əʊkɪ] *n US Fam* = campesino de Oklahoma

Okla (*abbr* **Oklahoma**) Oklahoma

Oklahoma [əʊklə'həʊmə] *n* Oklahoma

okra ['ɒkrə, 'əʊkrə] *n* quingombó *m*, okra *f*

ol' [əʊl] *adj Fam* = **old**

OLD [əʊld] **1** *adj* (**a**) *(not young, not new) (person)* anciano(a), viejo(a); *(car, clothes, custom)* viejo(a); **an o. man** un anciano, un viejo; *Fam* **my o. man** *(husband)* mi *or* el pariente, *Méx* mi *or* el viejo, *RP* el don *or* el viejo; *(father)* mi *or* el viejo, *Méx* mi *or* el jefe; **an o. woman** una anciana, una vieja; *Fam* **my o. woman** *(wife)* mi *or* la parienta, *Méx* mi *or* la vieja, *RP* la patrona; *(mother)* mi *or* la vieja, *Méx* mi *or* la jefa; *Fam* **John's such an o. woman, he's always moaning** John es un quejica *or Am* quejoso, siempre protestando; *Fam* **my o. lady** *(wife)* mi señora; *(mother)* mi vieja; **o. people, o. folk(s)** los ancianos, las personas mayores; *Fam* **an o. boy** *(elderly man)* un viejecito, *RP* un viejito; *Fam* **an o. girl** *(elderly woman)* una viejecita, una viejita; *Fig* **to go over o. ground** volver sobre un asunto muy trillado; **to be an o. hand at sth** tener larga experiencia en algo; *Fam* **to be o. hat** estar muy visto(a), *Esp* estar más visto(a) que el tebeo; **the o. (part of) town** el casco antiguo *or* histórico *or* viejo; *Fig* **he's one of the o. school** es de la vieja escuela; IDIOM **it's the oldest trick in the book** es un truco muy viejo; IDIOM **to be as o. as the hills** *or* **as Methuselah** *(person)* ser más viejo(a) que Matusalén; *(thing)* ser del año de Maricastaña *or Esp* de la polca *or RP* de(l) ñaupa ►► ***o. age*** la vejez; *Br* ***o. age pension*** pensión *f* de jubilación; *Br* ***o. age pensioner*** jubilado(a) *m,f*, pensionista *mf*; ***the O. Bailey*** = tribunal superior de lo penal de Inglaterra; *Br Fam* ***the O. Bill*** la poli, *Esp* la pasma, *RP* la cana; *Br* ***an o. dear*** *(elderly woman)* una viejecita; *(mother)* madre *f*; ***O. English sheepdog*** bobtail *m*; ***O. Faithful*** = géiser en el parque nacional de Yellowstone; ***O. Glory*** *(US flag)* = la bandera estadounidense; *Fam* ***o. goat*** *(lecherous man)* viejo *m* verde; *Br* ***o. lag*** preso *m* viejo; ***an o. maid*** una vieja solterona; *Bot* ***o. man's beard*** clemátide *f*; ***o. master*** *(painter, painting)* gran clásico *m* de la pintura; ***o. people's home*** residencia *f* de ancianos, asilo *m* (de ancianos); ***the O. Testament*** el Antiguo Testamento; ***o. wives' tale*** cuento *m* de viejas; ***the O. World*** el Viejo Mundo; ***O. World monkey*** mono *m* del Viejo Mundo

(**b**) *(referring to person's age)* **how o. are you?** ¿cuántos años tienes?; **to be five years o.** tener cinco años; **at six years o.** a los seis años (de edad); **a two-year-o. (child)** un niño de dos años; **my older sister** mi hermana mayor; **our oldest daughter** nuestra hija mayor; **when you're older** cuando seas *Esp* mayor *or Am* grande; **you're o. enough to do that yourself** ya eres mayorcito para hacerlo tú mismo; **you're o. enough to know better!** ¡a tu edad no deberías hacer cosas así!; **she's o. enough to be his mother** podría ser su madre; **I must be getting o.!** ¡me estoy haciendo mayor!, ¡estoy envejeciendo!; **my older sister** my hermana mayor; **to grow** *or* **get older** hacerse mayor

(**c**) *(former) (school, job, girlfriend)* antiguo(a); **I bought some new glasses to replace my o. ones** he comprado gafas nuevas para reemplazar a las viejas; **in the o. days** antes, antiguamente; **I feel like my o. self again** me siento como nuevo; **for o. times' sake** por los viejos tiempos ►► ***o. boy*** *(of school)* antiguo alumno *m*, ex alumno *m*; ***o. boy network*** = red de contactos entre antiguos compañeros de los colegios privados y universidades más selectos; ***an o. flame*** un antiguo amor, *Am* un ex amor; ***o. girl*** *(of school)* antigua alumna *f*, ex alumna *f*; *Fig* ***o. school tie*** = ayuda mutua y enchufismo que se da entre los antiguos alumnos de una escuela privada

(**d**) *(long-standing)* **an o. friend (of mine)** un viejo amigo (mío); **o. habits die hard** es difícil abandonar las costumbres de toda una vida ►► ***the o. guard*** la vieja guardia

(**e**) *(off) (cheese)* echado(a) a perder; *(bread)* rancio(a), *RP* amanecido(a)

(**f**) *Ling* ***O. English*** inglés *m* antiguo

(**g**) *Fam (intensifier)* **any o. how** de cualquier manera; **any o. thing** cualquier cosa; **you'll feel better for a good o. cry** llora y ya verás cómo te sentirás mejor; **the same o. story** la misma historia de siempre; **you o. cow!** ¡qué bruja eres!

(**h**) *Fam (expressing affection)* **good o. Fred's made dinner for us!** ¡el bueno de Fred nos ha preparado la cena!; **poor o. Mary** la pobrecita Mary; *Old-fashioned* **o. fellow** *or* **boy** *or* **man** *(addressing sb)* muchacho; *Old-fashioned* **o. girl** *(addressing sb)* muchachita, señorita ►► *Fam* ***O. Harry*** *or* ***Nick*** *(the Devil) Esp* Pedro Botero, *Am* Mandinga

2 *n* **the o.** lo viejo; *Literary* **in days of o.** antaño; **I know her of o.** la conozco desde hace tiempo

3 *npl* **the o.** los ancianos, las personas mayores

olde [əʊld, 'əʊldɪ] *adj (in name of inn, shop)* de antaño; **Ye O. Tea Shoppe** La Casa de Té de Antaño

olden ['əʊldən] *adj Old-fashioned* **the o. days** *or* **times** los viejos tiempos

old-established ['əʊldɪs'tæblɪʃt] *adj* tradicional; **an o. tradition** una tradición muy arragaida; **an o. company** una empresa de larga trayectoria

olde-worlde ['əʊldɪ'wɜːldɪ] *adj Hum* de estilo antiguo

old-fashioned [əʊld'fæʃənd] **1** *adj* (**a**) *(outdated)* anticuado(a); **to be o.** *(person)* ser anticuado(a); **(you can) call me o. but...** (si quieres) llámame anticuado pero... (**b**) *(from former times)* tradicional, antiguo(a); **the o. way** a la antigua; *Fam Hum* **what you need is a good o. cup of tea** lo que necesitas es una buena taza de té de las de toda la vida

2 *n US* = cóctel hecho con whisky, fruta, azúcar, licor amargo y soda

oldie ['əʊldɪ] *n Fam* (**a**) *(song)* canción *f* antigua; *(movie)* película *f* antigua (**b**) *(person)* viejo(a) *m,f*, vejete *m*

old-growth ['əʊldgrəʊθ] *adj* **o. forest** bosque natural

oldish ['əʊldɪʃ] *adj* tirando a viejo(a), más bien viejo(a)

old-line ['əʊldlaɪn] *adj US* (**a**) *(firm)* tradicional, de larga trayectoria (**b**) *(conservative)* conservador(a)

oldster ['əʊldstə(r)] *n Fam* vejestorio *m*

old-style ['əʊldstaɪl] *adj (traditional)* tradicional

old-time ['əʊldtaɪm] *adj* de antaño

old-timer [əʊld'taɪmə(r)] *n Fam* (**a**) *(experienced person)* veterano(a) *m,f* (**b**) *US (form of address)* abuelo(a) *m,f*

old-world ['əʊld'wɜːld] *adj* (**a**) *(courtesy, charm)* del pasado, de antaño (**b**) *(of the Old World)* del viejo mundo

OLE [əʊel'iː] *n Comptr* (*abbr* **object linking and embedding**) OLE *m*

ole [əʊl] *adj Fam* = **old**

oleaginous [əʊlɪ'ædʒɪnəs] *adj* (**a**) *(substance)* oleaginoso(a) (**b**) *Pej (person)* demasiado obsequioso(a), servil

oleander [əʊlɪ'ændə(r)] *n* adelfa *f*, oleandro *m*

oleaster [əʊlɪ'æstə(r)] *n* árbol *m* de Bohemia *or* del Paraíso

olefin ['əʊlɪfɪn] *n Chem* olefina *f*

oleic acid [əʊ'liːɪk'æsɪd] *n Chem* ácido *m* oleico

olfactory [ɒl'fæktərɪ] *adj Anat* olfativo(a) ►► ***o. nerve*** nervio *m* olfatorio

oligarch ['ɒlɪgɑːk] *n* oligarca *mf*

oligarchic(al) [ɒlɪ'gɑːkɪk(əl)] *adj* oligárquico(a)

oligarchy ['ɒlɪgɑːkɪ] *n* oligarquía *f*

Oligocene ['ɒlɪgəʊsiːn] *Geol* **1** *n* **the O.** el oligoceno
2 *adj (era)* oligoceno(a)

oligopoly [ɒlɪ'gɒpəlɪ] *n Econ* oligopolio *m*

olivaceous [ɒlɪ'veɪʃəs] *adj* oliváceo(a), aceitunado(a) ▸▸ ***o. warbler*** zarcero *m* pálido

olive ['ɒlɪv] **1** *n* **(a)** *(fruit)* aceituna *f*, oliva *f* ▸▸ ***o. oil*** aceite *m* de oliva **(b)** *(tree)* olivo *m*; **o. (wood)** olivar *f*; IDIOM **to hold out the o. branch** hacer un gesto de paz ▸▸ ***o. grove*** olivar *m* **(c)** *(colour)* verde *m* oliva ▸▸ *US* ***o. drab*** = color gris verdoso de los uniformes militares
2 *adj (skin)* aceitunado(a); **o. (green)** verde oliva

olive-drab ['ɒlɪv'dræb] *adj* amarillo verdoso, caqui

olive-green ['ɒlɪv'griːn] *adj* verde oliva

Olympia [ə'lɪmpɪə] *n* Olimpia

Olympiad [ə'lɪmpɪæd] *n* Olimpiada *f*

Olympian [ə'lɪmpɪən] **1** *n* **(a)** *Mythol* dios(a) *m,f* del Olimpo **(b)** *Sport* atleta *mf* olímpico(a)
2 *adj also Fig* olímpico(a); **with O. disdain** con desdén olímpico; **an O. struggle** una lucha titánica

Olympic [ə'lɪmpɪk] **1** *npl* **the Olympics** las Olimpiadas, los Juegos Olímpicos
2 *adj* olímpico(a) ▸▸ ***the O. Games*** los Juegos Olímpicos; ***the O. torch*** la antorcha olímpica; ***O. village*** villa *f* olímpica

Olympic-size [ə'lɪmpɪksaɪz] *adj* **O. swimming pool** piscina *or Méx* alberca *or RP* pileta olímpica

Olympus [ə'lɪmpəs] *n* **(Mount) O.** el (monte) Olimpo

OM [əʊ'em] *n Br* (*abbr* **Order of Merit**) Orden *f* del Mérito

Oman [əʊ'mɑːn] *n* Omán

Omani [əʊ'mɑːnɪ] **1** *n* omaní *mf*
2 *adj* omaní

ombudsman ['ɒmbʊdzmən] *n* defensor(ora) *m,f* del pueblo

omelette, *US* **omelet** ['ɒmlɪt] *n* tortilla *f*, *Am* tortilla *f* francesa; **ham/cheese o.** tortilla de jamón/queso; PROV **you can't make an o. without breaking eggs** todo lo bueno tiene un precio que alguien tiene que pagar

omen ['əʊmen] *n* presagio *m*, augurio *m*; **a good/bad o.** un buen augurio/un mal presagio; **the omens aren't good** no son buenos augurios

omicron [əʊ'maɪkrən] *n* ómicron *f*

ominous ['ɒmɪnəs] *adj* siniestro(a); **an o. silence** un silencio siniestro; **an o.-looking sky** un cielo amenazador; **an emergency meeting... that sounds o.** una reunión de emergencia... eso no presagia nada bueno

ominously ['ɒmɪnəslɪ] *adv* siniestramente, amenazadoramente; **o., he agreed with everything I said** la mala señal fue que estuvo de acuerdo con todo lo que yo dije; **the deadline was drawing o. close** la fecha de entrega se acercaba amenazadoramente

omission [əʊ'mɪʃən] *n* omisión *f*; **their mistakes were sins of o.** sus errores fueron faltas *or* pecados de omisión

omit [əʊ'mɪt] (*pt & pp* **omitted**) *vt* **(a)** *(leave out)* omitir; **the garlic may be omitted** el ajo no es indispensable **(b)** *(fail)* **to o. to do sth** no hacer algo; **to o. to mention sth** no mencionar algo, omitir algo

omni- ['ɒmnɪ] *prefix* omni-

omnibus ['ɒmnɪbəs] *n* **(a)** *(book)* recopilación *f*, antología *f*; **an Edgar Allan Poe o.** una antología de Edgar Allan Poe ▸▸ ***o. edition*** *or* ***volume*** recopilación *f*, antología *f* **(b)** *TV & Rad* ***o. edition*** *or* ***programme*** = todos los capítulos de la semana de una serie seguidos **(c)** *Old-fashioned (bus)* ómnibus *m inv*

omnidirectional [ɒmnɪdɪ'rekʃənəl] *adj Tel (antenna, microphone)* omnidireccional

omnipotence [ɒm'nɪpətəns] *n* omnipotencia *f*

omnipotent [ɒm'nɪpətənt] **1** *n* **the O.** el Todopoderoso
2 *adj* omnipotente

omnipresence [ɒmnɪ'prezəns] *n* omnipresencia *f*

omnipresent [ɒmnɪ'prezənt] *adj* omnipresente

omniscience [ɒm'nɪsɪəns] *n* omnisciencia *f*

omniscient [ɒm'nɪsɪənt] *adj* omnisciente

omnivore ['ɒmnɪvɔː(r)] *n* omnívoro(a) *m,f*

omnivorous [ɒm'nɪvərəs] *adj* **(a)** *(animal)* omnívoro(a) **(b)** *Fig (reader)* insaciable, voraz

ON (*abbr* **Ontario**) Ontario

ON [ɒn] **1** *prep* **(a)** *(indicating position)* en; **on the table** encima de *or* sobre *or Am* arriba de la mesa, en la mesa; **on the second floor** en el segundo piso; **on the wall** en la pared; **on page 4** en la página 4; **on the right/left** a la derecha/izquierda; **a house on the river** una casa a la orilla del río; **they live on a farm** viven en una granja; **on the coast** en la costa; **what's on the menu?** ¿qué hay en el menú?; **they are currently on ten points** en este momento tienen diez puntos; **to be on one's knees** estar arrodillado(a)
(b) *(indicating direction, target)* **to fall on sth** caerse encima de *or* sobre *or Am* arriba de algo; **to get on a train/bus** subirse a un tren/autobús; **an attack on sb** un ataque contra alguien; **the effect on inflation** el efecto en la inflación; **a tax on alcohol** un impuesto sobre el *or Am* al alcohol; **the interest on a loan** el interés de un préstamo; **to be on course** seguir el rumbo; **the shot was on target** el disparo dio en el blanco; **all eyes were on her** todas las miradas estaban puestas en ella
(c) *(indicating method)* **on foot** a pie; **on horseback** a caballo; **we went there on the train/bus** fuimos en tren/autobús; **I'll arrive on the six o'clock train** llegaré en el tren de las seis; **to play sth on the guitar** tocar algo *Esp* a *or Am* en la guitarra; **to do sth on the computer** hacer algo en *Esp* el ordenador *or Am* la computadora; **on (the) television** en la televisión; **available on video/CD** disponible en *Esp* vídeo *or Am* video/CD; **call us on this number** llámenos a este número
(d) *(indicating time)* **on the 15th** el (día) 15; **on Sunday** el domingo; **on Tuesdays** los martes; **on Christmas Day** el día de Navidad, en Navidad; **on that occasion** en aquella *or* esa ocasión; **on the hour** *(every hour)* cada hora; **it's just on five o'clock** son las cinco en punto; **I met her on the way to the store** me la encontré camino de *or Am* a la tienda; **on completion of the test** una vez completada la prueba; **on our arrival** a nuestra llegada
(e) *(about)* sobre, acerca de; **a book on France** un libro sobre Francia; **now that we're on the subject** hablando del tema; **the police have nothing on them** la policía no los puede acusar de nada; **he's good on history** sabe mucho de historia
(f) *(introducing a gerund)* **on completing the test** después de terminar la prueba; **on arriving, we went straight to the hotel** al llegar, fuimos directamente al hotel
(g) *(indicating use, support)* **to live on £200 a week** vivir con 200 libras a la semana; **people on low incomes** la gente con bajos ingresos; **she's on $50,000 a year** gana 50.000 dólares al año; **it runs on electricity** funciona con electricidad; **to spend/waste money on sth** gastar/derrochar dinero en algo; **they were acting on reliable information** actuaban siguiendo información fiable *or Am* confiable; **I'm on antibiotics** estoy tomando antibióticos; **to be on drugs** tomar drogas; *Fam* **what's he on?** ¿qué le pasa?; **the drinks are on me** las bebidas corren de *or* por mi cuenta
(h) *(forming part of) (list, agenda)* en; **to be on a committee** formar parte de un comité; **we have two women on our team** tenemos dos mujeres en nuestro equipo; **who's side are you on?** ¿de qué lado estás?
(i) *(indicating process)* **on holiday** de vacaciones; **on sale** en venta; **I'm going on a course** voy a un curso; **fraud is on the increase** el fraude está aumentando
(j) *(referring to thing carried or worn)* **that dress looks good on you** ese vestido te sienta *or* queda bien; **I haven't got any money on me** no llevo nada de dinero encima, *Am* no tengo nada de plata encima; **she's got a gun on her** lleva una pistola
(k) *(compared to)* **unemployment is up/down on last year** el desempleo *or Am* la desocupación ha subido/bajado con respecto al año pasado
2 *adv* **(a)** *(functioning)* **turn the light/the TV on** enciende *or Am* prende la luz/la tele; **turn the water/gas on** abre el agua/el gas
(b) *(referring to clothes)* **she had a red dress on** llevaba *or* tenía puesto un vestido rojo; **to have nothing on** estar desnudo(a); **to put sth on** ponerse algo
(c) *(in time)* **earlier on** antes; **later on** más tarde; **from that day on** desde aquel día, a partir de aquel día; **two weeks on from the fall, she still hasn't recovered** dos semanas después de la caída, todavía no se ha recuperado
(d) *(in distance)* **2 miles (further) on we came across a river** 2 millas después llegamos a un río; **you go on ahead, we'll follow** sigue adelante, nosotros vamos detrás *or Am* atrás
(e) *(indicating position)* **climb/get on!** ¡sube!; **put the lid on** pon la tapa; **the lid wasn't on** estaba destapado; **tie it on firmly** átalo firmemente
(f) *(indicating continuation)* **to read/work on** seguir leyendo/trabajando; **he went on and on about it** no dejaba de hablar de ello; *Fam* **what are you on about?** ¿de qué estás hablando?, *Esp* ¿de qué vas?
(g) *(in phrases)* **I've been on at him to get it fixed** le he estado dando la lata para que lo arregle, *RP* le he estado encima para que lo

arreglara; *Fam* **to be on to sth** *(aware of)* estar enterado(a) *or* al tanto de algo; *Fam* **the police are on to us** la policía nos sigue la pista

3 *adj* (a) *(functioning) (light, television, engine)* encendido(a), *Am* prendido(a); *(water, gas, tap)* abierto(a); **put the brakes on** frena; **in the "on" position** en posición de encendido *or Am* prendido; **the on button/switch** el botón/interruptor del encendido

(b) *(taking place)* **what's on?** *(on TV)* ¿qué hay en la tele?, ¿qué están dando?; *(at cinema)* ¿qué película pasan *or* dan *or Esp* echan?; **is the meeting still on?** ¿sigue en pie lo de la reunión?; **when the war was on** en tiempos de la guerra; **I've got a lot on at the moment** *(am very busy)* ahora estoy muy ocupado; **I've got nothing on tomorrow** mañana estoy libre

(c) *(on duty, performing)* de servicio; **who's on this evening?** ¿quién está de servicio esta noche?; **I'm on in two minutes** entro en dos minutos

(d) *Br Fam (acceptable)* **it's not on** eso no está bien

(e) *(in betting)* **the odds are twenty to one on...** las apuestas están veinte a uno a que...

(f) *Fam* **fancy a game of chess? – you're on!** *(definitely)* ¿quieres jugar una partida de ajedrez? – ¡hecho!, *Esp* ¿te apetece una partida de ajedrez? – ¡hecho!

(g) *Br Fam* **to be on** *(menstruating)* tener la regla

4 **on and off** *adv (intermittently)* intermitentemente; **how often do you see them? – on and off** ¿lo ves a menudo? – de vez en cuando; **they've been going out for six years on and off** llevan seis años saliendo intermitentemente; **she is working on and off as an actress** trabaja de actriz esporádicamente

---

onager ['ɒnədʒə(r)] *n (wild ass)* onagro *m*

on-air ['ɒn'eə(r)] 1 *adj* en el aire
2 *adv* en el aire

onanism ['əʊnənɪzəm] *n* onanismo *m*

onanist ['əʊnənɪst] 1 *n* onanista *mf*
2 *adj* onanista

onanistic [əʊnə'nɪstɪk] *adj* onanístico(a)

onboard ['ɒnbɔːd] *adj* de a bordo ►► ***o. computer*** *Esp* ordenador *m or Am* computadora *f* de a bordo

ONC [əʊen'siː] *n* (*abbr* **Ordinary National Certificate**) = en Inglaterra y Gales, certificado de formación profesional

on-camera ['ɒn'kæmərə] 1 *adj* ante la cámara
2 *adv* ante la cámara

ONCE [wʌns] 1 *adv* (a) *(on one occasion)* una vez; **o. a week/a year** una vez a la semana/al año; **o. a fortnight** (una vez) cada dos semanas; **I've been there o. before** he estado allí una vez; **(every) o. in a while** de vez en cuando; **o. or twice** una o dos veces, un par de veces; **more than o.** más de una vez; **he's never o. said he was sorry** no ha pedido disculpas ni una sola vez; **o. more, o. again** otra vez, una vez más; **you've called me stupid o. too often** ya me has llamado estúpido demasiadas veces; **o. a liar always a liar** quien ha mentido seguirá mintiendo

(b) *(formerly)* una vez, en otro tiempo; **it's easier than it o. was** es más fácil de lo que solía serlo; **the o.-busy streets were now empty** las calles antaño ajetreadas ahora estaban vacías; **o. upon a time, there was a princess** érase una vez una princesa

2 *pron* **I've only seen her the o.** sólo la he visto una vez; **go on, just this o.** por favor *or Esp* venga *or Méx* ándale *or RP* dale, sólo una vez

3 *conj* una vez que; **o. you've finished** una vez que acabes; **o. he finishes, we can leave** cuando termine, nos podremos marchar; **o. he reached home, he immediately called the police** nada más llegar a casa *or RP* en cuanto llegó a su casa, llamó a la policía

4 **at once** *adv* (a) *(immediately)* inmediatamente, ahora mismo; **come here at o.!** ¡ven aquí inmediatamente *or* ahora mismo! (b) *(at the same time)* al mismo tiempo, a la vez; **it was at o. fascinating and terrifying** fascinaba y daba miedo al mismo tiempo *or* a la vez; **all at o.** *(suddenly)* de repente

5 **for once** *adv* para variar, por una vez; **I wish you'd pay attention for o.** podrías prestar atención, para variar

6 **once and for all** *adv* de una vez por todas

---

once-in-a-lifetime ['wʌnsɪnə'laɪftaɪm] *adj* irrepetible, único(a); **a o. opportunity** una ocasión única, una ocasión que sólo se presenta una vez en la vida

once-over ['wʌnsəʊvə(r)] *n Fam* (a) *(glance)* vistazo *m*; **to give sth the o.** dar un vistazo *or* repaso a algo; **to give sb the o.** mirar a alguien de arriba a abajo (b) *(clean)* **give the furniture a quick o. with a cloth** dale una repasadita a los muebles con un trapo (c) *(beating)* **to give sb the** *or* **a o.** dar una paliza a alguien

oncogene ['ɒŋkədʒiːn] *n* oncogén *m*

oncogenic [ɒŋkə'dʒenɪk] *adj* oncogénico(a)

oncological [ɒŋkə'lɒdʒɪkəl] *adj* oncológico(a)

oncologist [ɒŋ'kɒlədʒɪst] *n* oncólogo(a) *m,f*

oncology [ɒŋ'kɒlədʒɪ] *n* oncología *f*

oncoming ['ɒnkʌmɪŋ] *adj* (a) *(traffic)* en dirección contraria; **the o. vehicles** los vehículos en dirección contraria; **he stepped in front of an o. train** se puso delante de un tren que se aproximaba (b) *(year, season)* que se aproxima, que viene; **the o. generation of school-leavers** la próxima generación de alumnos que terminan la enseñanza secundaria (c) *Ind* **o. shift** turno entrante

oncosts ['ɒnkɒsts] *npl Com* costos *mpl or Esp* costes *mpl* fijos

OND [əʊen'diː] *n* (*abbr* **Ordinary National Diploma**) = en Inglaterra y Gales, certificado superior de formación profesional

---

ONE [wʌn] 1 *n* (a) *(number)* uno *m*; **a hundred and o.** ciento uno(a); **it is a fax, a phone and an answerphone all in o.** es fax, teléfono y contestador todo en uno; **they rose as o.** se levantaron todos a la vez, *Esp* se levantaron a una; **we are as o. on this issue** en este tema estamos plenamente de acuerdo; **to be at o. with sb** *(agree)* estar plenamente de acuerdo con alguien; **to be at o. with oneself** *(calm)* estar en paz con uno mismo; **the guests arrived in ones and twos** poco a poco fueron llegando los invitados; *Fam* **to be/get o. up on sb** estar/quedar por encima de alguien

(b) *(drink)* **to have o. for the road** tomar la última *or Esp* la espuela, *RP* tomar una para el camino; **I think he's had o. too many** *or Br Old-Fashioned* **o. over the eight** creo que lleva *or Esp* ha tomado una copa de más

(c) *Fam (blow)* **to sock** *or* **thump sb o.** dar *or Esp* arrear *or RP* encajar una a alguien

(d) *(joke)* **that's a good o.!** ¡qué bueno!; *Fam Ironic* **did you know I won the lottery? – oh yeah, that's a good o.!** ¿sabías que he ganado la lotería? – ¡sí, y yo me lo creo!; **did you hear the o. about...?** ¿has oído el (chiste) del...?

(e) *(question)* **that's a difficult o.!** ¡qué difícil!; **you'll have to work this o. out yourself** eso lo tienes que solucionar tú solo

(f) *Br Fam* **to go into o.** *(lose one's temper)* subirse por las paredes

(g) *very Fam* **to give sb o.** *(have sex)* tirarse a alguien

(h) *Br Fam (person)* **you are a o.!** ¡qué traviesillo *or* diablo eres!; **he's a right o., him!** ¡qué *or* menudo elemento!

(i) *Sport* **o. on o.** uno contra uno; **o. and o.** *(in basketball)* uno más uno

2 *pron* (a) *(identifying)* uno(a); **I've always wanted a yacht, but could never afford o.** siempre he querido un yate, pero nunca me lo he podido permitir; **could I have a different o.?** ¿me podría dar otro(a)?; **I don't like red ones** no me gustan los rojos; **there's only o. left** sólo queda uno; **this o.** éste(a); **that o.** ése(a), aquél(élla); **these ones** éstos(as); **those ones** ésos(as), aquéllos(as); **the o. I told you about** el/la que te dije; **the big o.** el/la grande; **the red o.** el/la rojo(a); **o. or two** *(a few)* algún(una) que otro(a); **the ones with the long sleeves** los/las de manga larga; **the o. that got away** *(of fish, goal, prize)* el/la que se escapó; **they are the ones who are responsible** ellos son los responsables; **which o. do you want?** ¿cuál quieres?; **which ones do you want?** ¿cuáles quieres?; **any o. except that o.** cualquiera menos ése/ésa; **the last but o.** el/la penúltimo(a)

(b) *(indefinite)* uno(a) *m,f*; **I haven't got a pencil, have you got o.?** no tengo lápiz, ¿tienes tú (uno)?; **o. of us will have to do it** uno de nosotros tendrá que hacerlo; **he is o. of us** es uno de los nuestros; **she is o. of the family** es de la familia; **o. of my friends** uno de mis amigos; **o. of these days** un día de estos; **their reaction was o. of panic** su reacción fue de pánico; **any o. of us** cualquiera de nosotros; **it is just o. of those things** son cosas que pasan; **o. after another** *or* **the other** uno tras otro; **o. at a time** de uno en uno, *Am* uno por uno; **o. by o.** de uno en uno, uno por uno; **o. or other of them will have to go** nos tendremos que desprender de uno de los dos

(c) *(particular person)* **to act like o. possessed** actuar como un(a) poseso(a); **I'm not o. to complain** yo no soy de los que se quejan; **she's a great o. for telling jokes** siempre está contando chistes; **he's not a great o. for parties** no le gustan *or Esp* van mucho las fiestas, no es muy fiestero; *Old-fashioned* **o. and all** todos; **they are o. and the same** son la misma cosa/persona

(d) *Formal (impersonal)* uno(a) *m,f*; **o. never knows** nunca se sabe; **if o. considers the long-term consequences** si tenemos en cuenta las consecuencias a largo plazo; **it is enough to make o. weep** basta para hacerlo llorar a uno; **to wash o.'s hands** lavarse las manos

3 *adj* (a) *(number)* un(a); **o. tea and two coffees** un té y dos cafés; **o. hundred** cien; **o. thousand** mil; **o. quarter** un cuarto; **chapter o.** capítulo primero; **page o.** primera página; **to be o. (year old)** tener un

año; **they live at number o.** viven en el número uno; **o. o'clock** la una; **come at o.** ven a la una; **o. or two people** una o dos personas, algunas personas; **for o. thing...** para empezar...
(b) *(indefinite)* **we should go there o. summer** tendríamos que ir un verano; **early o. day** un día temprano por la mañana; **o. day next week** un día de la próxima semana *or* de la semana que viene; **o. day, we shall be free** algún día seremos libres; *Formal* **his boss is o. James Bould** su jefe es un tal James Bould
(c) *(single)* un(a) único(a), un(a) solo(a); **he did it with o. end in mind** lo hizo con un solo propósito; **her o. worry** su única preocupación; **I only have the o. suit** sólo tengo un traje; **my o. and only suit** mi único traje; **the o. and only Sugar Ray Robinson!** ¡el inimitable Sugar Ray Robinson!; **they are o. and the same thing** son una *or* la misma cosa; **we'll manage o. way or another** nos las arreglaremos de una forma u otra; **they painted it all o. colour** lo pintaron de un solo color; *Fam* **it's all o. to me** me da igual; **as o. man** como un solo hombre
(d) *(only)* único(a); **he's the o. person I can rely on** es la única persona en la que puedo confiar
(e) *Fam (for emphasis)* **that's o. big problem you've got there** menudo problema tienes ahí
4 for one *adv* **I, for o., do not believe it** yo, por mi parte, no me lo creo; **I know that Eric for o. is against it** sé que, al menos, Eric está en contra

---

one-act ['wʌnækt] *adj* **o. play** obra (de teatro) de un solo acto

one-armed ['wʌnɑːmd] *adj* **(a)** *(person)* manco(a) **(b)** *Fam* ***o. bandit*** (máquina *f*) tragaperras *f inv, RP* tragamonedas *f inv*

one-dimensional ['wʌndaɪ'menʃənəl] *adj* **(a)** *Geom* unidimensional **(b)** *(character)* superficial

one-eyed ['wʌnaɪd] *adj* tuerto(a)

one-horse ['wʌnhɔːs] *adj Fig* **it's a o. race** sólo hay un ganador posible ►► *Fam* ***o. town*** pueblo *m* de mala muerte

oneiric [əʊ'naɪərɪk] *adj Literary* onírico(a)

one-legged [wʌn'legɪd] *adj* cojo(a)

one-liner [wʌn'laɪnə(r)] *n Fam (joke)* golpe *m*

one-man ['wʌnmæn] *adj (job)* individual, de una sola persona; **I'm a o. woman** soy mujer de un solo hombre ►► ***o. band*** *(musician)* hombre *m* orquesta; *Fam (business)* empresa *f* individual; ***o. show*** *(by artist)* exposición *f* de un único artista; *(by performer)* espectáculo *m* en solitario; *Fig* **this company/team is a o. show** el funcionamiento de esta empresa/de este equipo gira en torno a un solo hombre

oneness ['wʌnnɪs] *n* **a sense of o.** un sentido de unidad

one-night stand ['wʌnnaɪt'stænd] *n Fam* **(a)** *(of performer)* representación *f* única; *(of musician)* concierto *m* único **(b)** *(sexual encounter)* ligue *m or RP* levante *m* de una noche

one-off ['wʌnɒf] *Br* **1** *n Fam* **he's a complete o.** es un fuera de serie total; **it's a o.** *(object)* es una pieza única; **it was a o.** *(mistake, success)* fue una excepción *or* un hecho aislado
2 *adj (payment, order)* excepcional; **a o. job** un trabajo aislado

one-on-one ['wʌnɒn'wʌn] *US* **1** *adj (discussion)* cara a cara ►► ***o. tuition*** clases *fpl* particulares
2 *adv* **to go o. with sb** enfrentarse en un mano a mano con alguien

one-parent family ['wʌnpeərənt'fæmɪlɪ] *n* familia *f* monoparental

one-party ['wʌn'pɑːtɪ] *adj (state, system)* unipartidista

one-piece ['wʌn'piːs] **1** *n (swimsuit)* traje *m* de baño *or Esp* bañador *m or RP* malla *f* de una pieza
2 *adj* **(a) o. swimsuit** traje de baño *or Esp* bañador *or RP* malla de una pieza **(b)** *Tech (casting)* de una sola pieza

one-room ['wʌn'ruːm] *adj* de un (solo) ambiente

onerous ['əʊnərəs] *adj* oneroso(a)

oneself [wʌn'self] *pron* **(a)** *(reflexive)* **to look after o.** cuidarse; **to trust o.** confiar en uno(a) mismo(a); **to feel o. again** volver a sentirse el/la de siempre
(b) *(emphatic)* uno(a) mismo(a), uno(a) solo(a); **to tell sb sth o.** decirle algo a alguien uno(a) mismo(a)
(c) *(after preposition)* **to buy sth for o.** comprar algo para uno(a) mismo(a); **to do sth all by o.** hacer algo solo(a); **to live by o.** vivir solo(a); **to talk to o.** hablar solo(a); **to see (sth) for o.** ver (algo) uno(a) mismo(a)

one-sided [wʌn'saɪdɪd] *adj* **(a)** *(unequal)* desnivelado(a), desigual **(b)** *(biased)* parcial **(c)** *(not reciprocal)* unidireccional, unilateral; **our conversations tend to be pretty o.** nuestras conversaciones suelen ser bastante unidireccionales

one-sidedness [wʌn'saɪdɪdnɪs] *n* **(a)** *(unequal nature)* desigualdad *f* **(b)** *(bias)* parcialidad *f*

one-stop ['wʌnstɒp] *adj* ***o. shop*** *(service)* servicio *m* integral; **the o. shop for all your household needs** la tienda que ofrece todo lo que necesita para su hogar

one-time ['wʌntaɪm] *adj* antiguo(a); **her o. lover** su ex amante

one-to-one ['wʌntə'wʌn] *adj* **(a)** *(discussion)* cara a cara ►► ***o. tuition*** clases *fpl* particulares **(b)** *(correspondence)* de uno a uno; **there is a o. mapping between the two sets** hay una correspondencia idéntica entre los dos conjuntos

one-track ['wʌntræk] *adj (railway)* de una sola vía; IDIOM **to have a o. mind** *(be obsessed with one thing)* estar obsesionado(a) con una cosa, no pensar más que en una cosa; *(be obsessed with sex)* no pensar más que en el sexo

one-two [wʌn'tuː] *n* **(a)** *(in soccer, hockey)* pared *f*; **to play a o.** hacer la pared **(b)** *(in boxing)* izquierdazo *m* seguido de derechazo, (golpe *m*) izquierda derecha *m*

one-upmanship [wʌn'ʌpmənʃɪp] *n Fam* **it was pure o.** todo era por quedar por encima de los demás

one-way ['wʌnweɪ] *adj* **(a)** *(ticket)* de ida, sencillo(a); IDIOM **a o. ticket to disaster** un camino que conduce al desastre **(b)** *(street, traffic)* de sentido único; **he went the wrong way up a o. street** se metió en contradirección por una calle de sentido único, entró a contramano en una calle de mano única **(c)** *(mirror)* ***o. mirror*** espejo *m* espía

one-woman ['wʌnwʊmən] *adj (job)* individual, de una sola persona; **I'm a o. man** soy hombre de una sola mujer, soy un hombre fiel (a una sola mujer) ►► ***o. show*** *(by artist)* exposición *f* de una única artista; *(by performer)* espectáculo *m* en solitario; *Fig* **this company/team is a o. show** el funcionamiento de esta empresa/de este equipo gira en torno a una sola mujer

ongoing ['ɒngəʊɪŋ] *adj* continuo(a); **this is an o. situation** esta situación sigue pendiente; **the o. debate about the merits of the system** el continuo debate sobre las ventajas del sistema

onion ['ʌnjən] *n* cebolla *f*; IDIOM *Br Fam* **she knows her onions** sabe lo que se trae entre manos ►► ***o. dome*** cúpula *f* bizantina; ***o. rings*** aros *mpl* de cebolla; ***o. soup*** sopa *f* de cebolla

onionskin ['ʌnjənskɪn] *n* **o. (paper)** papel *m* cebolla

oniony ['ʌnjənɪ] *adj (in smell, taste)* a cebolla

on-line, online ['ɒn'laɪn] **1** *adj Comptr* on-line, en línea; **to be o.** *(person)* estar conectado(a) (a Internet); **the company went o. in November** *(have Internet presence)* la empresa comenzó a ofrecer sus servicios por Internet en noviembre; *(have Internet connection)* la empresa tiene acceso a Internet desde noviembre; **to put the printer o.** conectar la impresora ►► ***o. bank*** banco *m* on-line *or* en línea; ***o. banking*** banca *f* electrónica; ***o. gaming*** juegos *mpl* en línea *or* on-line; ***o. help*** ayuda *f* on-line *or* en línea; ***o. registration*** inscripción *f* on-line *or* en línea; ***o. retailer*** minorista *mf* on-line *or* por Internet; ***o. service*** servicio *m* on-line *or* en línea; ***o. shopping*** compras *fpl* on-line *or* por Internet
2 *adv* on-line, en línea; **to buy o.** comprar on-line *or* en línea; **to work o.** trabajar estando conectado(a)

onlooker ['ɒnlʊkə(r)] *n* curioso(a) *m,f*; **a crowd of onlookers** un montón de curiosos

---

ONLY ['əʊnlɪ] **1** *adj* único(a); **you're not the o. one** no eres el único; **the o. people left there** los únicos que quedan ahí; **the o. thing that worries me is...** lo único que me preocupa es...; **the o. thing is, I won't be there** lo único es que, no voy a estar allí ►► ***o. child*** hijo(a) *m,f* único(a)
2 *adv* **(a)** *(exclusively)* sólo, solamente; **there are o. two people I trust** sólo *or* solamente confío en dos personas
(b) *(just, merely)* sólo; **after all, it's o. money** al fin y al cabo es sólo dinero; **it's o. a suggestion** no es más que una sugerencia; **it's o. natural** es natural *or* normal; **it's o. to be expected** no es de sorprender; **it's o. me** (sólo) soy yo; **I saw her o. yesterday** la vi ayer mismo; **they left o. a few minutes ago** se han marchado tan sólo hace unos minutos, se fueron hace apenas unos minutos; **if you need help, you o. have to ask** si necesitas ayuda, no tienes más que pedirla; **I can o. assume they've got the wrong address** lo único que se me ocurre es que tengan la dirección equivocada; **I o. hope they don't find out** sólo espero que no lo descubran; **I o. wish you'd told me earlier** ¡ojalá me lo hubieras dicho antes!; **if you don't do it now, you'll o. have to do it later** si no lo haces ahora, lo tendrás que hacer después; **they travelled all that way, o. to be denied entry when they got there** hicieron todo ese viaje para que luego no los dejaran entrar
(c) *(to emphasize smallness of amount, number)* sólo, solamente; **it o. cost me $5** sólo *or* solamente me costó 5 dólares; **it o. took me half**

an hour sólo *or* solamente tardé media hora

(**d**) *(for emphasis) Fam* **she's o. gone and told her father!** ¡se le ha ocurrido contárselo a su padre!; **I shall be o. too pleased to come** me encantará acudir; **that's o. too true!** ¡qué *or* cuánta razón tienes!

3 *conj* sólo que, pero; **I would do it, o. I haven't the time** lo haría, sólo que no tengo tiempo; **have a go, o. be careful** inténtalo, pero con cuidado

4 only just *adv* (**a**) *(not long before)* **we had o. just arrived when...** acabábamos de llegar cuando... (**b**) *(barely)* **I o. just managed it** por poco no lo consigo; **we had o. just enough money** teníamos el dinero justo

5 not only *conj* **not o...., but also** no sólo..., sino también; **she's not o. smart, she's funny too** no sólo es inteligente, sino que también es graciosa

---

on-message ['ɒn'mesɪdʒ] *adj Br Pol* **she's very o.** sigue fielmente la línea del partido

o.n.o. [əʊen'əʊ] *adv Com* (*abbr* **or nearest offer**) **£300 o.** 300 libras negociables

on-off ['ɒn'ɒf] *adj* (**a**) *Elec* ***o. switch*** interruptor *m* (**b**) *(relationship)* intermitente

onomastic [ɒnə'mæstɪk] *adj* onomástico(a)

onomatopoeia [ɒnəmætə'pi:ə] *n* onomatopeya *f*

onomatopoeic [ɒnəmætə'pi:ɪk] *adj* onomatopéyico(a)

on-ramp ['ɒnræmp] *n US* carril *m* de aceleración *or* de incorporación

onrush ['ɒnrʌʃ] *n* (**a**) *(of emotions)* arrebato *m* (**b**) *(of people)* oleada *f*

onscreen [ɒn'skri:n] **1** *adj* (**a**) *Comptr (information, controls)* en pantalla ▸▸ ***o. help*** ayuda *f* en pantalla (**b**) *TV* televisivo(a); *Cin* cinematográfico(a); **she's nothing like her o. character** no tiene nada que ver con el personaje que representa (en la pantalla)

2 *adv Comptr (work) Esp* en el ordenador, *Am* en la computadora

onset ['ɒnset] *n* irrupción *f*; **the o. of a disease** el desencadenamiento *or* inicio de una enfermedad; **the o. of war** el estallido de la guerra

onshore **1** *adj* ['ɒnʃɔ:(r)] en tierra firme; **o. wind** viento del mar

2 *adv* [ɒn'ʃɔ:(r)] en tierra

onside [ɒn'saɪd] *adj (in soccer, rugby)* en posición correcta *or* reglamentaria

on-site ['ɒn'saɪt] **1** *adj* in situ ▸▸ ***o. guarantee*** garantía *f* in situ

2 *adv* in situ

onslaught ['ɒnslɔ:t] *n* acometida *f*

on-stage **1** *adj* ['ɒnsteɪdʒ] de escena

2 *adv* [ɒn'steɪdʒ] en escena

on-stream **1** *adj* ['ɒnstri:m] en funcionamiento

2 *adv* [ɒn'stri:m] **to come o.** ponerse en funcionamiento

Ont (*abbr* **Ontario**) Ontario

on-the-job ['ɒnðə'dʒɒb] *adj (training)* en el empleo; **he's got plenty of o. experience** tiene mucha experiencia laboral

on-the-spot ['ɒnðə'spɒt] *adj (decision)* en el acto; **an o. fine** una multa que se paga en el acto

onto ['ɒntʊ, *unstressed* 'ɒntə] *prep* (**a**) *(on)* sobre, encima de; **the room looks out o. a garden** la habitación da a un jardín; **let's move o. the next point** pasemos al punto siguiente; **to fall o. sth** caerse encima de algo; **to jump o. sth** saltar sobre algo

(**b**) *(in contact with)* **to get o. sb** ponerse en contacto con alguien; **she's been o. me about my poor marks** *(criticizing)* me ha estado sermoneando por mis malas notas

(**c**) *(on trail of)* **to be o. a good thing** habérselo montado bien; **I think the police are o. us** creo que la policía va *or* anda detrás de nosotros; **we're o. something big** estamos *or* andamos detrás de algo grande

ontogenic [ɒntəʊ'dʒi:nɪk] *adj Biol* ontogénico(a)

ontogeny [ɒn'tɒdʒənɪ] *n Biol* ontogenia *f*, ontogénesis *f*

ontological [ɒntə'lɒdʒɪkəl] *adj Phil* ontológico(a)

ontology [ɒn'tɒlədʒɪ] *n Phil* ontología *f*

onus ['əʊnəs] *n* responsabilidad *f*; **the o. is on you to make good the damage** la responsabilidad de corregir el daño hecho recae sobre usted; **the o. is on the government to resolve the problem** la resolución del problema es incumbencia del Gobierno ▸▸ *Law* ***o. of proof*** carga *f* de la prueba, onus probandi *m*

onward ['ɒnwəd] **1** *adj (motion)* hacia delante; **the o. journey** el viaje que sigue *or* continúa; **there is an o. flight to Chicago** hay un vuelo de conexión con Chicago

2 *adv* = **onwards**

onward(s) ['ɒnwəd(z)] *adv* **to go o.** avanzar, continuar hacia delante; **from tomorrow/now o.** a partir de mañana/ahora; **from this time o.** (de ahora) en adelante; **from her childhood o.** desde que era una niña; **o. and upwards!** ¡siempre hacia adelante!

onyx ['ɒnɪks] *n* ónice *m*

oodles ['u:dəlz] *npl Fam* **o. of time/money** una porrada *or Col* un jurgo *or Méx* un chorro *or RP* un toco de tiempo/dinero

ooh [u:] **1** *exclam* **o., that's lovely!** uy, ¡qué *Esp* bonito *or esp Am* lindo!; **o., is he really coming here?** ¡no me digas que viene!; **o., it's hot!** uf, ¡qué calor que hace!

2 *vi* **they were all oohing and aahing over her baby** estaban todos embelesados con su bebé

oomph [ʊmf] *n Fam* (**a**) *(energy)* garra *f*, *Esp* marcha *f* (**b**) *(sex appeal)* tirón *m or* atractivo *m* sexual

oophorectomy [əʊəfə'rektəmɪ] *n Med* ovariotomía *f*

oops [u:ps] *exclam* (**a**) *(to child)* ¡arriba!, *Esp* ¡aúpa! (**b**) *(after mistake)* ¡uy!, ¡oh!

oops-a-daisy ['u:psədeɪzɪ] *exclam Fam* ¡epa!

ooze [u:z] **1** *n* (**a**) *(mud)* fango *m* (**b**) *(flow)* flujo *m*

2 *vt* **the wound was oozing blood** la sangre salía de la herida lentamente; **the wound was oozing pus** la herida supuraba; **to o. charm** rezumar encanto; **to o. confidence** rebosar confianza

3 *vi* **the mud oozed up between her toes** el barro le brotaba lentamente por entre los dedos de los pies; **blood oozed from the wound** la herida rezumaba sangre; **to o. with confidence** rebosar confianza

op [ɒp] *n Fam (medical operation)* operación *f*

opacity [əʊ'pæsɪtɪ], **opaqueness** [əʊ'peɪknɪs] *n* (**a**) *(of material)* opacidad *f* (**b**) *(of meaning)* opacidad *f*, complicación *f*

opah ['əʊpə] *n* luna *f* real

opal ['əʊpəl] *n* ópalo *m*; **an o. brooch/ring** un broche/anillo de ópalo

opalescence [əʊpə'lesəns] *n* opalescencia *f*

opalescent [əʊpə'lesənt] *adj* opalescente

opaline ['əʊpəli:n] **1** *n* opalina *f*

2 *adj* opalino(a)

opaque [əʊ'peɪk] *adj* (**a**) *(glass)* opaco(a) ▸▸ *US* ***o. projector*** episcopio *m* (**b**) *(difficult to understand)* oscuro(a), poco claro(a)

opaqueness *n* = **opacity**

op art ['ɒp'ɑ:t], **optical art** ['ɒptɪkəl'ɑ:t] *n* op art *m*

op cit ['ɒp'sɪt] (*abbr* **opere citato**) op. cit.

OPEC ['əʊpek] *n* (*abbr* **Organization of Petroleum-Exporting Countries**) OPEP *f*; **the O. countries** los países de la OPEP

op-ed ['ɒped] *n US (in newspaper)* **an o. (piece)** un artículo de opinión, un artículo firmado; **the o. page** la sección de artículos de opinión

---

OPEN ['əʊpən] **1** *n* (**a**) **in the o.** *(outside)* al aire libre; *(not hidden)* a la vista; **to bring sth out into the o.** *(problem, disagreement)* sacar a relucir algo; **to come out into the o. about sth** desvelar algo

(**b**) *(sporting competition)* open *m*, abierto *m*; **the US/Australian O.** el Abierto USA/de Australia; **the French O.** el open *or* abierto de Francia

2 *adj* (**a**) *(not shut)* abierto(a); *(curtains)* corrido(a), abierto(a); **to be o.** estar abierto(a); **o. from nine to five** abierto(a) de nueve a cinco; **o. to the public** abierto(a) al público; **o. to traffic** abierto(a) al tráfico; **o. all night** abierto(a) toda la noche; **o. late** abierto(a) hasta tarde; *Fig* **to welcome sb with o. arms** recibir a alguien con los brazos abiertos ▸▸ *Comptr* ***o. architecture*** arquitectura *f* abierta; *Elec* ***o. circuit*** circuito *m* abierto; *Br* ***o. day*** jornada *f* de puertas abiertas; *US* ***o. house*** jornada *f* de puertas abiertas; *Br* **to keep o. house** tener las puertas siempre abiertas

(**b**) *(not enclosed, covered) (vehicle)* descubierto(a); **the hut was o. on three sides** la choza sólo tenía una pared; **in the o. air** al aire libre; **this motorbike will do 150 on the o. road** la moto alcanza los 240 en carretera ▸▸ ***o. carriage*** carruaje *m* descubierto; ***o. country*** campo *m* abierto; ***o. sandwich*** = una rebanada de pan con algo de comer encima; ***o. sea*** mar *m* abierto; ***o. spaces*** *(parks)* zonas *fpl or Am* áreas *fpl* verdes; **the wide o. spaces of Texas** las extensas llanuras de Tejas

(**c**) *(unrestricted) (competition, meeting, trial, society)* abierto(a); **club membership is o. to anyone** cualquiera puede hacerse socio del club; *Law* **in o. court** en juicio público, en vista pública ▸▸ ***o. bar*** barra *f* libre; ***o. invitation*** *(to guests)* invitación *f* permanente; *Fig (to thieves)* invitación *f* clara; *Econ* ***o. market*** mercado *m* libre; **to buy sth on the o. market** comprar algo en el mercado libre; ***o. relationship*** relación *f* abierta *or* liberal; ***o. season*** *(for hunting)* temporada *f* (de caza); *Fig* **to declare o. season on sth/sb** abrir la veda de *or* contra algo/alguien; ***o. ticket*** *Esp* billete *m or Am* boleto *m or Am* pasaje *m* abierto

(**d**) *(clear) (person, manner)* abierto(a); *(preference, dislike)* claro(a), manifiesto(a); **to be o. about sth** ser muy claro(a) *or* sincero(a) con respecto a algo; **to be o. with sb** ser franco(a) con alguien; **o. government is one of our priorities** la transparencia en el gobierno es una de nuestras prioridades ▸▸ ***o. letter*** *(in newspaper)* carta *f* abierta; ***o. secret*** secreto *m* a voces

(**e**) *(undecided)* abierto(a); **the championship is still o.** el campeonato todavía sigue abierto; **we left the date o.** no fijamos una fecha definitiva; **let's leave the matter o.** dejemos el asunto ahí pendiente de momento; **to keep an o. mind (on sth)** mantenerse libre de prejuicios (acerca de algo); **it's an o. question whether...** no está claro si... ▸▸ *Law* ***o. verdict*** *(at inquest)* = fallo del jurado en el que no se especifica la causa de la muerte

(**f**) *(unprotected) (flank)* desprotegido(a), franco(a); *Sport* **to miss an o. goal** fallar un gol a puerta vacía ▸▸ ***o. fire*** *or* ***fireplace*** chimenea *f*, hogar *m*; ***o. prison*** cárcel *f* de régimen abierto

(**g**) *(available, accessible)* **I'll keep this Friday o. for you** me reservaré el viernes para ti; **justice is o. to all** la justicia está al alcance de todos; **a career o. to very few** una profesión reservada a unos pocos; **two possibilities are o. to us** tenemos dos opciones ▸▸ ***o. forum*** tribuna *f* libre; *Educ* ***o. learning*** educación *f* abierta; *Comptr* ***o. source*** código *m* abierto; ***O. University*** = universidad a distancia británica, *Esp* ≃ UNED *f*

(**h**) *(blatant) (contempt, criticism)* manifiesto(a); *(conflict)* abierto(a); **they showed an o. disregard for the law** mostraban un manifiesto desprecio para con la ley

(**i**) *(exposed, susceptible)* **o. to the elements** expuesto(a) a las inclemencias del tiempo; **to be o. to abuse** ser susceptible de abuso; **to be o. to doubt** *or* **question** ser dudoso(a) *or* cuestionable; **to be o. to offers** estar abierto(a) a todo tipo de ofertas; **to be o. to ridicule** exponerse al ridículo *or* a quedar en ridículo; **to be o. to suggestions** estar abierto(a) a sugerencias ▸▸ *Med* ***o. fracture*** fractura *f* abierta; ***o. wound*** herida *f* abierta

(**j**) *(loose) (weave, mesh)* flojo(a)

(**k**) *Br (cheque)* abierto(a)

(**l**) *Ling* abierto(a)

3 *adv* **to cut sth o.** abrir algo de un corte; **the door flew o.** la puerta se abrió con violencia

4 *vt* (**a**) *(in general)* abrir; *(curtains)* correr; **to o. a hole in sth** abrir *or* practicar un agujero en algo; *Fig* **to o. the door to sth** abrir la puerta a algo; *Fig* **to o. sb's eyes** abrir los ojos a alguien, hacer ver las cosas a alguien; **he opened his heart to her** se sinceró con ella; **I shouldn't have opened my mouth** no debía haber abierto la boca

(**b**) *(begin) (talk, investigation, match)* comenzar, empezar; *(negotiations, conversation)* entablar, iniciar; **to o. fire (on sb)** hacer *or* abrir fuego (sobre alguien); **to o. the scoring** abrir el marcador; **to o. the bidding** *(in an auction)* abrir la puja

(**c**) *(set up) (new shop, business)* abrir; *(new museum, hospital)* inaugurar

5 *vi* (**a**) *(door, window, flower)* abrirse; **the window opens outwards** la ventana se abre hacia afuera; **to o. late** *(shop)* abrir hasta tarde; **o. wide!** *(at dentist's)* ¡abre bien la boca!

(**b**) *(begin) (talk, account, match)* comenzar, empezar; *(meeting, negotiations)* abrirse, dar comienzo; *(shares, currency)* abrir (**at** a); **the film opens next week** la película se estrena la semana que viene

(**c**) *(shop, bank)* abrir; **what time do you o. on Sundays?** ¿a qué hora abren los domingos?

▸ **open onto** *vt insep* dar a; **the kitchen opens onto the garden** la cocina da al jardín

▸ **open out** **1** *vt sep (sheet of paper)* abrir, desdoblar

2 *vi* (**a**) *(flower)* abrirse; *(view, prospects)* abrirse, extenderse; *(road, valley)* ensancharse, abrirse (**b**) *Br (speak frankly)* abrirse

▸ **open up** **1** *vt sep* (**a**) *(bag, gift, tomb)* abrir

(**b**) *(new shop, business)* abrir; *(new museum, hospital)* inaugurar

(**c**) *(remove restrictions on) (economy)* abrir; **to o. up opportunities for** abrir las puertas a, presentar nuevas oportunidades para

(**d**) *(establish) (lead, gap, advantage)* abrir

(**e**) *Fam (operate on)* abrir

2 *vi* (**a**) *(hole, crack, flower)* abrirse

(**b**) *(shopkeeper, new shop)* abrir; **this is the police, o. up!** ¡policía, abran la puerta!

(**c**) *(possibility, new market)* abrirse

(**d**) *(speak frankly)* abrirse, sincerarse; **he needs to o. up about his feelings** necesita sincerarse respecto a sus sentimientos

(**e**) *(start firing) (guns, troops)* abrir fuego

(**f**) *(become more exciting) (game)* abrirse

open-air [əʊpə'neə(r)] *adj (restaurant, market)* al aire libre; *(swimming pool)* al aire libre, descubierto(a) ▸▸ ***o. cinema*** cine *m* al aire libre; ***o. mass*** misa *f* de campaña

open-and-shut ['əʊpənən'ʃʌt] *adj* **an o. case** un caso elemental *or* claro

opencast ['əʊpən'kɑːst] *adj (mine)* a cielo abierto

open-door policy ['əʊpən'dɔːpɒlɪsɪ] *n* política *f* permisiva *or* de puertas abiertas

open-ended ['əʊpən'endɪd] *adj* (**a**) *(contract)* indefinido(a) (**b**) *(question)* abierto(a) (**c**) *(discussion)* sin restricciones

opener ['əʊpənə(r)] *n* (**a**) *(tool) (for tins)* abrelatas *m inv*; *(for bottles)* abridor *m*, abrebotellas *m inv* (**b**) *(initial action, statement)* comienzo *m*, introducción *f*; *(first song, act)* apertura *f*; *(first game)* primer partido *m*; **and that was just for openers** y eso fue sólo el principio (**c**) *(person) (in cards, games)* mano *f*; *(in cricket)* primer(a) bateador(ora) *m,f*

open-eyed ['əʊpən'aɪd] **1** *adj* con los ojos muy abiertos; **they watched in o. amazement** observaron con gran asombro

2 *adv* con los ojos muy abiertos

open-faced ['əʊpən'feɪst] *adj* (**a**) *(person)* inocente, cándido(a) (**b**) *US (sandwich)* **an o. sandwich with tuna** una rebanada de atún

open-handed ['əʊpən'hændɪd] *adj (generous)* generoso(a), desprendido(a)

open-hearted ['əʊpən'hɑːtɪd] *adj* franco(a), abierto(a)

open-heart surgery ['əʊpən'hɑːt'sɜːdʒərɪ] *n* cirugía *f* a corazón abierto

opening ['əʊpənɪŋ] **1** *n* (**a**) *(act of opening) (of play, new era)* principio *m*, comienzo *m*; *(of negotiations)* apertura *f*; *(of parliament)* sesión *f* inaugural

(**b**) *(of new museum, supermarket)* inauguración *f*

(**c**) *(gap)* abertura *f*, agujero *m*; **an o. in the clouds** un claro entre las nubes

(**d**) *(of cave, tunnel)* entrada *f*

(**e**) *US (in forest)* claro *m*

(**f**) *Law (speech by lawyer)* exposición *f* de los hechos

(**g**) *(opportunity)* oportunidad *f*; *(job)* (puesto *m*) vacante *f*; **they exploited an o. in the market** aprovecharon una oportunidad que ofrecía el mercado; **her remarks about health gave me the o. I needed** sus comentarios sobre la salud me dieron la oportunidad que necesitaba

2 *adj* ***o. bid*** *(in auction)* oferta *f* de apertura; *(in cards)* apuesta *f* inicial; ***o. ceremony*** ceremonia *f* inaugural *or* de apertura; ***o. gambit*** *(in chess)* gambito *m* de salida; *(in conversation, negotiation)* táctica *f* inicial; ***o. hours*** *(shop)* horario *m* comercial; *(tourist attraction)* horario *m* de visita; *(bank, office)* horario *m* de atención al público; ***o. night*** *(of play)* noche *f* del estreno; ***o. price*** *(of share)* precio *m* de apertura; ***o. speech*** *(in court case)* presentación *f* del caso; *Br* ***o. time*** *(of pub)* hora *f* de abrir

open-jaw ['əʊpən'dʒɔː] *adj* **o. ticket** *(returning to starting point)* = billete de ida y vuelta en el que el punto de origen del viaje de regreso no coincide con el de destino del viaje de ida; *(not returning to starting point)* = billete de ida y vuelta en el que el destino final no coincide con el lugar de origen

openly ['əʊpənlɪ] *adv* abiertamente; **to be o. contemptuous (of sth/sb)** mostrar un claro desprecio (por algo/alguien); **drugs are o. on sale** las drogas se venden abiertamente; **to weep o.** llorar abiertamente

open-minded [əʊpən'maɪndɪd] *adj* de mentalidad abierta; **my parents are pretty o. about sex** mis padres son bastante liberales en lo que respecta al sexo

open-mindedness [əʊpən'maɪndɪdnɪs] *n* mentalidad *f* abierta

open-mouthed [əʊpən'maʊðd] **1** *adv* boquiabierto(a)

2 *adj* boquiabierto(a); **he watched in o. astonishment** observaba boquiabierto

open-necked ['əʊpən'nekt] *adj (which doesn't fasten)* de cuello abierto; *(unfastened)* desabrochado(a)

openness ['əʊpənnɪs] *n* (**a**) *(frankness)* franqueza *f* (**b**) *(receptivity)* receptividad *f* (**c**) *(spaciousness)* amplitud *f*; **the mirror gives a feeling of o. to the room** el espejo da a la sala una sensación de amplitud (**d**) *(of terrain)* aspecto *m* descubierto

open-plan ['əʊpənplæn] *adj (office)* de planta abierta

open-skies ['əʊpən'skaɪz] *adj* **an o. policy** una política de cielos abiertos

open-toe(d) ['əʊpən'təʊ(d)] *adj* abierto(a), que deja los dedos al aire

open-top(ped) ['əʊpən'tɒp(t)] *adj (bus, carriage)* descubierto(a), sin techo

openwork ['əʊpənwɜːk] *n* calado *m*

opera ['ɒpərə] *n* ópera *f*; **she adores (the) o.** adora la ópera ►► ***o. buffa*** ópera *f* bufa; ***o. cloak*** capa *f*; ***o. glasses*** prismáticos *mpl*, gemelos *mpl (de teatro)*; ***o. hat*** sombrero *m* de copa plegable; ***o. house*** (teatro *m* de la) ópera *f*; ***o. singer*** cantante *mf* de ópera

operable ['ɒpərəbəl] *adj Med* operable

operagoer ['ɒprəgəʊə(r)] *n* **as regular operagoers will know...** como los asiduos *or* aficionados a la ópera ya sabrán...; **she's not a regular o.** no va a la ópera con regularidad

operand ['ɒpərænd] *n Math* operando *m*

operate ['ɒpəreɪt] **1** *vt* (**a**) *(machine)* manejar, hacer funcionar; *(brakes)* accionar; **a circuit-breaker operates the alarm** un disyuntor dispara la alarma; **to be operated by electricity** funcionar con electricidad

(**b**) *(service)* proporcionar; **they o. several casinos** manejan *or* regentan varios casinos; **they o. a protection racket in the area** manejan una red de extorsión en la zona

2 *vi* (**a**) *(machine)* funcionar; *(system, process)* operar, funcionar; **this is how colonialism operates** así opera *or* funciona el colonialismo; **the factory is operating at full capacity** la fábrica está funcionando *or* trabajando a capacidad plena

(**b**) *(be active) (company)* actuar, operar; **military patrols o. along the border** patrullas militares operan en la frontera; **many crooks o. in this part of town** en esta zona de la ciudad operan *or* actúan muchos sinvergüenzas; **we o. in most of the north of Scotland** desarrollamos nuestra actividad en la mayor parte del norte de Escocia; **the company operates out of Philadelphia** la empresa tiene su sede en Filadelfia; **this service operates only on Saturdays** este servicio sólo funciona los sábados

(**c**) *(produce an effect)* actuar; **the drug operates on the nervous system** la droga actúa sobre el sistema nervioso; **two elements o. in our favour** dos elementos actúan a nuestro favor

(**d**) *Formal (apply)* estar en vigor; **the rule doesn't o. in such cases** la norma no se aplica en estos casos; **those restrictions continue to o.** estas restricciones siguen en vigor

(**e**) *Med* operar; **to o. on sb (for)** operar a alguien (de); **to be operated on** ser operado(a); **he was operated on for cancer** lo operaron de cáncer; **we'll have to o.** tendremos que operar

operatic [ɒpə'rætɪk] **1** *adj (repertoire, role)* operístico(a) ►► ***o. society*** sociedad *f* operística

2 operatics *npl (amateur)* operística *f*

operating ['ɒpəreɪtɪŋ] *adj* (**a**) *(of business)* ***o. costs*** costos *mpl or Esp* costes *mpl* de explotación; ***o. loss*** pérdidas *fpl* de explotación; ***o. profit*** beneficios *mpl* de explotación; ***o. statement*** cuenta *f* de explotación (**b**) *Comptr* ***o. system*** sistema *m* operativo (**c**) *Med US* ***o. room*** quirófano *m*, sala *f* de operaciones; ***o. table*** mesa *f* de operaciones; *Br* ***o. theatre*** quirófano *m*, sala *f* de operaciones

operation [ɒpə'reɪʃən] *n* (**a**) *(functioning) (of machine, system, mine)* funcionamiento *m*; **to be in o.** estar funcionando

(**b**) *(management) (of firm, system)* gestión *f*; *(of machine)* manejo *m*; *(of mine)* explotación *f*

(**c**) *(act)* acción *f*, operación *f*; *Mil* operación *f*; **a police/rescue o.** una acción *or* operación policial/de rescate; **a firm's operations** las operaciones *or* actividades de una empresa; **O. Omega** Operación Omega ►► ***operations research*** = análisis de los procedimientos de producción y administración; ***operations room*** centro *m* de control

(**d**) *(company)* **she works for a mining o.** trabaja para una compañía minera

(**e**) *(of drug)* efecto *m*

(**f**) *(of law)* **to be in o.** *(apply)* estar en vigor; **to come into o.** *(law)* entrar en vigor

(**g**) *Med* operación *f*; **to have an o. (for sth)** operarse (de algo); **he had a heart/liver o.** lo operaron del corazón/hígado; **to perform an o. (on sb)** operar (a alguien)

(**h**) *Math* operación *f*

(**i**) *Comptr* operación *f*

operational [ɒpə'reɪʃənəl] *adj* (**a**) *(functional) (equipment, engine, system)* operativo(a); **it should be o. next year** debería entrar en funcionamiento el año que viene

(**b**) *(cost, requirements)* operativo(a); **to set up an o. base** establecer una base de operaciones; **there have been some o. difficulties** ha habido algunas dificultades operativas *or* de funcionamiento ►► ***o. research*** = análisis de los procedimientos de producción y administración

operative ['ɒpərətɪv] **1** *n Formal* (**a**) *(manual worker)* operario(a) *m,f* (**b**) *(spy)* agente *mf* secreto; *(detective)* detective *mf* privado

2 *adj (law, rule)* vigente; **to become o.** *(law)* entrar en vigor; **the system will soon be o.** el sistema pronto estará operativo *or* en funcionamiento; **the o. word** la palabra clave

operator ['ɒpəreɪtə(r)] *n* (**a**) *(of machine)* operario(a) *m,f*

(**b**) *Tel* **(switchboard) o.** telefonista *mf*, operador(ora) *m,f*

(**c**) *(of transport, lottery, mine)* operadorora *f*; **the o. of this service is Belfast Buses Ltd** este servicio lo proporciona Belfast Buses Ltd, Belfast Buses Ltd opera este servicio

(**d**) *(player)* **there are too many small operators in real estate** hay demasiadas empresas pequeñas en el sector inmobiliario; **an experienced political o.** un actor político con mucha experiencia; *Fam* **he's a pretty smooth o.** *(in business)* es un lince *or* un hacha para los negocios; *(with women)* se las lleva de calle

(**e**) *Math* operador *m*

operetta [ɒpə'retə] *n Mus* opereta *f*

ophthalmia [ɒf'θælmɪə] *n Med* oftalmía *f*

ophthalmic [ɒf'θælmɪk] *adj* ***o. nerve*** nervio *m* oftálmico; *Br* ***o. optician*** óptico(a) *m,f*

ophthalmological [ɒfθælmə'lɒdʒɪkəl] *adj Med* oftalmológico(a)

ophthalmologist [ɒfθæl'mɒlədʒɪst] *n Med* oftalmólogo(a) *m,f*

ophthalmology [ɒfθæl'mɒlədʒɪ] *n Med* oftalmología *f*

ophthalmoscope [ɒf'θælməskəʊp] *n Med* oftalmoscopio *m*

ophthalmoscopy [ɒfθæl'mɒskəpɪ] *n Med* oftalmoscopia *f*

opiate ['əʊpɪet] *n Med* opiáceo *m*

opine [əʊ'paɪn] *vt Formal or Literary* opinar

opinion [ə'pɪnjən] *n* (**a**) *(individual)* opinión *f*; **in my o.** en mi opinión; **in the o. of her teachers** según la opinión de sus maestros; **to be of the o. that...** ser de la opinión de que...; **to ask sb's o.** pedir la opinión de alguien; **I'd like your o.** me gustaría oír tu opinión; **to form an o. of sth/sb** formarse una opinión sobre algo/alguien; **to have a high/low o. of sb** tener (una) buena/mala opinión de alguien; **he has too high an o. of himself** tiene una opinión demasiado buena de sí mismo; **what is your o. of him?** ¿qué opinas de él?; **can you give us your o. on the festival?** ¿nos puedes dar tu opinión sobre el festival?

(**b**) *(collective)* **world/international o.** la opinión mundial/internacional; **o. is divided on this issue** en este tema las opiniones están divididas ►► ***o. former*** creador(ora) *m,f* de opinión; ***o. poll*** *or* ***survey*** sondeo *m or* encuesta *f* de opinión

(**c**) *Law* **it is the o. of the court that...** el tribunal considera que...

(**d**) *(professional advice)* opinión *f*, asesoramiento *m*; **to obtain a legal o.** obtener asesoramiento legal

opinionated [ə'pɪnjəneɪtɪd] *adj* dogmático(a); **to be o.** creer a toda costa que uno lleva la razón

opium ['əʊpɪəm] *n* opio *m* ►► ***o. addict*** adicto(a) *m,f* al opio; ***o. den*** fumadero *m* de opio; ***o. poppy*** adormidera *f*

opossum [ə'pɒsəm] *n* zarigüeya *f*

opp (*abbr* **opposite**) en la página opuesta

opponent [ə'pəʊnənt] *n* (**a**) *(in game, debate)* adversario(a) *m,f*, oponente *mf*; **(political) o.** *(democratic)* adversario(a) *m,f* político(a); *(of regime)* oponente *mf* político; **she has always been an o. of blood sports** siempre ha estado en contra de los deportes sangrientos (**b**) *(of policy, system)* opositor(ora) *m,f*

opportune ['ɒpətjuːn] *adj Formal* oportuno(a); **a very o. remark** un comentario muy oportuno; **is this an o. moment?** ¿es éste un momento oportuno?

opportunely ['ɒpətjuːnlɪ] *adv* oportunamente

opportunism [ɒpə'tjuːnɪzəm] *n* oportunismo *m*

opportunist [ɒpə'tjuːnɪst] **1** *n* oportunista *mf*

2 *adj* oportunista

opportunistic [ɒpətjʊ'nɪstɪk] *adj* oportunista ►► *Med* ***o. infection*** infección *f* oportunista

opportunity [ɒpə'tjuːnɪtɪ] *n* (**a**) *(chance)* oportunidad *f*, ocasión *f*; **to have an/the o. of doing sth** *or* **to do sth** tener una/la oportunidad *or* ocasión de hacer algo; **it would be an ideal o. to improve your French** sería una magnífica oportunidad *or* ocasión para mejorar tu francés; **to give sb an o. of doing sth** *or* **the o. to do sth** darle a alguien una *or* la oportunidad de hacer algo; **at every o.** a la mínima oportunidad; **at the first** *or* **earliest o.** a la primera oportunidad; **if I get an o.** si tengo ocasión *or* oportunidad; **should the o. present itself** *or* **arise** si se presentara *or* surgiera la oportunidad; **I took every o. of travelling** aproveché cada oportunidad *or* ocasión que tuve de viajar; **I'd like to take this o. to thank everyone** me gustaría aprovechar esta oportunidad *or* ocasión para agradecer a todos; **the o. of a lifetime** una oportunidad única en la vida

(**b**) *(prospect)* perspectiva *f*; **a job with opportunities** un trabajo con buenas perspectivas

(**c**) *Com* oportunidad *f* ▸▸ *Econ* ***o. cost*** costo *m or Esp* coste *m* de oportunidad

opposable [ə'pəʊzəbəl] *adj* **o. thumb** pulgar oponible

oppose [ə'pəʊz] *vt* (**a**) *(decision, plan, bill)* oponerse a; **the building of the road was opposed by most local people** la mayor parte de los residentes del lugar se oponía a la construcción de la carretera

(**b**) *(in contest, fight)* enfrentarse a; **to o. the motion** *(in formal debate)* oponerse a la moción

(**c**) *(contrast)* contraponer, contrastar; **the social sciences are often opposed to pure science** a menudo las ciencias sociales se contraponen a la ciencia pura

opposed [ə'pəʊzd] **1** *adj* **to be o. to sth** estar en contra de algo, oponerse a algo; **she is very much o. to the idea** se opone terminantemente a la idea; **his views are diametrically o. to mine** su perspectiva es diametralmente opuesta a la mía

2 as opposed to *prep* **we should act now as o. to waiting till later** deberíamos actuar ya en lugar de esperar más; **I'm referring to my real father as o. to my stepfather** me refiero a mi verdadero padre y no a mi padrastro

opposing [ə'pəʊzɪŋ] *adj* (**a**) *(army, team, party)* opuesto(a), contrario(a); **they're on o. sides** *(in sports, politics)* son adversarios; *(in war, battle)* están en bandos contrarios (**b**) *(contrasting) (views)* opuesto(a), contrario(a)

opposite ['ɒpəzɪt] **1** *n* **the o. of** lo contrario de; **what's the o. of "naive"?** ¿cuál es el contrario de "ingenuo"?; **she always does the o. of what she's told** siempre hace lo contrario *or* al revés de lo que se le dice; **Mary is the complete o. of her sister** Mary es todo el polo opuesto de su hermana; **I understood quite the o.** entendí todo lo contrario; **is she tall? – no, quite the o.** ¿es alta? – no, todo lo contrario; **opposites attract** los polos opuestos se atraen

2 *adj* (**a**) *(facing) (page, shore)* opuesto(a); **the o. side of the street** el otro lado de la calle

(**b**) *(opposing) (direction, position)* opuesto(a), contrario(a); *(team)* contrario(a); **the letter-box is at the o. end of the street** el buzón está en la otra punta de la calle; **we live at o. ends of the country** vivimos cada uno en un extremo del país; **in the o. direction** en dirección contraria

(**c**) *(contrary) (opinion, effect)* contrario(a); **his words had just the o. effect** sus palabras tuvieron el efecto contrario; **the o. sex** el sexo opuesto

(**d**) *(equivalent)* **my o. number** mi homólogo(a)

3 *adv* enfrente; **the house o.** la casa de enfrente; **the lady o.** la señora de enfrente *or* de delante; **they live just o.** viven justo enfrente

4 *prep* (**a**) *(across from)* enfrente de; **our houses are o. (to) each other** nuestras casas están una enfrente de otra; **we sat o. each other** nos sentamos el uno enfrente del otro; **put a cross o. the correct answer** coloque una cruz al lado de la respuesta correcta (**b**) *Cin & Theat* **to play o. sb** actuar junto a *or* como pareja de alguien

opposition [ɒpə'zɪʃən] *n* (**a**) *(resistance)* oposición *f*; **to meet with o.** encontrar oposición; **the army met with fierce o.** el ejército encontró una feroz resistencia; **the besieged city put up little o.** la ciudad tomada opuso muy poca resistencia

(**b**) *(opponents)* **the o.** *(in sport, politics)* los adversarios; *(in business)* la competencia

(**c**) *Pol* **the O.** la oposición; **to be in o.** estar en la oposición; **the O. benches** los escaños de la oposición

(**d**) *(contrast)* **to act in o. to** actuar en contra de

oppress [ə'pres] *vt* (**a**) *(treat cruelly)* oprimir (**b**) *(torment) (of anxiety, atmosphere)* agobiar, atormentar

oppressed [ə'prest] **1** *npl* **the o.** los oprimidos

2 *adj (people, nation)* oprimido(a)

oppression [ə'preʃən] *n* (**a**) *(of a people)* opresión *f*; **the o. of women** la opresión *or* el sometimiento de la mujer (**b**) *(of the mind)* agobio *m*, desasosiego *m*

oppressive [ə'presɪv] *adj* (**a**) *(law, regime)* opresor(ora), opresivo(a) (**b**) *(debt, situation)* opresivo(a), agobiante (**c**) *(weather, atmosphere)* agobiante; *(heat)* sofocante

oppressively [ə'presɪvlɪ] *adv* (**a**) *(hot)* **it was o. hot** hacía un calor agobiante (**b**) *(to govern)* opresivamente

oppressiveness [ə'presɪvnɪs] *n* (**a**) *(of law, regime)* opresión *f* (**b**) *(of debt, situation)* lo agobiante (**c**) *(of weather, atmosphere)* lo sofocante; **the o. of the heat** lo sofocante del calor

oppressor [ə'presə(r)] *n* opresor(ora) *m,f*

opprobrious [ə'prəʊbrɪəs] *adj Formal (scornful)* ignominioso(a), oprobioso(a)

opprobrium [ə'prəʊbrɪəm] *n Formal* oprobio *m*

opt [ɒpt] **1** *vt* **to o. to do sth** optar por hacer algo

2 *vi* **to o. for** optar por

▸ **opt in** *vi Br* unirse (**to** a), decidir participar (**to** en)

▸ **opt out** *vi* **to o. out of society** aislarse de la sociedad; **they opted out of the project** decidieron no participar en el proyecto; **you can't just o. out of paying bills** no puedes dejar de pagar las cuentas así porque sí

Optic® ['ɒptɪk] *n Br* medida *f (para botella)*

optic ['ɒptɪk] *adj* óptico(a) ▸▸ ***o. nerve*** nervio *m* óptico

optical ['ɒptɪkəl] *adj* (**a**) *(of the eye, sight)* óptico(a) ▸▸ *Phys* ***o. centre*** *(of lens)* centro *m* óptico; ***o. illusion*** ilusión *f* óptica, efecto *m* óptico

(**b**) *(of fibre optic technology)* ***o. cable*** cable *m* óptico; ***o. fibre*** fibra *f* óptica

(**c**) *Comptr* ***o. character reader*** lector *m* óptico de caracteres; ***o. character recognition*** reconocimiento *m* óptico de caracteres; ***o. disk*** disco *m* óptico; ***o. mouse*** *Esp* ratón *m or Am* mouse *m* óptico; ***o. resolution*** resolución *f* óptica; ***o. scanner*** lector *m* óptico

optical art = **op art**

optician [ɒp'tɪʃən] *n* óptico(a) *m,f*; **the o.'s** la óptica

optics ['ɒptɪks] *n (subject)* óptica *f*

optimal ['ɒptɪməl] *adj* óptimo(a)

optimally ['ɒptɪməlɪ] *adv* óptimamente

optimism ['ɒptɪmɪzəm] *n* optimismo *m*; **there are no grounds for o.** no hay motivos para ser optimista

optimist ['ɒptɪmɪst] *n* optimista *mf*

optimistic [ɒptɪ'mɪstɪk] *adj* optimista; **things are looking quite o.** las cosas parecen marchar bastante bien

optimistically [ɒptɪ'mɪstɪklɪ] *adv* con optimismo

optimization [ɒptɪmaɪ'zeɪʃən] *n* optimización *f*

optimize ['ɒptɪmaɪz] *vt* optimizar

optimizer ['ɒptɪmaɪzə(r)] *n Comptr* optimizador *m*

optimum ['ɒptɪməm] **1** *n* nivel *m* óptimo

2 *adj* óptimo(a)

option ['ɒpʃən] *n* (**a**) *(choice)* opción *f*; **to have the o. of doing sth** tener la opción de hacer algo; **to have no o. (but to do sth)** no tener otra opción *or* alternativa (más que hacer algo); **he didn't give me much o.** no me dio muchas opciones; **you leave me no o.** no me dejas opción; **a soft** *or* **easy o.** una opción cómoda *or* fácil; **to leave** *or* **keep one's options open** dejar abiertas varias opciones

(**b**) *(accessory)* extra *m*

(**c**) *Fin* opción *f*; **to take an o. on sth** adquirir una opción sobre *or* por algo ▸▸ ***options market*** mercado *m* de opciones; ***o. price*** precio *m* de opción; ***options trading*** negociación *f* de opciones

(**d**) *Sch Univ* (asignatura *f*) optativa *f*

(**e**) *Comptr* ***o. key*** tecla *f* de opción; ***options menu*** menú *m* de opciones

optional ['ɒpʃənəl] *adj* optativo(a); **power steering o.** dirección asistida opcional; **fancy dress is o.** el disfraz es optativo ▸▸ ***o. extras*** accesorios *mpl* opcionales; *Sch* ***o. subject*** asignatura *f* optativa

optionally ['ɒpʃənəlɪ] *adv* opcionalmente

optometrist [ɒp'tɒmətrɪst] *n Med* optometrista *mf*

optometry [ɒp'tɒmətrɪ] *n Med* optometría *f*

opt-out ['ɒptaʊt] **1** *n* autoexclusión *f*

2 *adj* ***o. clause*** claúsula *f* de exclusión *or* de no participación

opulence ['ɒpjʊləns] *n* opulencia *f*

opulent ['ɒpjʊlənt] *adj (lifestyle, decor)* opulento(a); *(figure)* exuberante

opulently ['ɒpjʊləntlɪ] *adv* con opulencia; **to live o.** vivir en la opulencia

opus ['əʊpəs] *(pl* **opuses** *or* **opera** ['ɒpərə]) *n* opus *m*; *Mus* **O. 42** opus 42

OR **1** (*abbr* **Oregon**) Oregón

2 *n* [əʊ'ɑː(r)] *US* (*abbr* **operating room**) quirófano *m*, sala *f* de operaciones

OR [ɔː(r), *unstressed* ə(r)] *conj* (**a**) *(in general)* o; *(before "o" or "ho")* u; **an hour or so** alrededor de una hora; **in a minute or two** en uno o dos minutos, en un par de minutos; **did she do it or not?** ¿lo hizo o no?; **do it or I'll tell the boss!** ¡hazlo o se lo digo al jefe!; **she must be better or she wouldn't be smiling** debe estar mejor, si no no sonreiría; **shut up! – or what?** ¡cállate! – si no, ¿qué?; **he was asleep... or**

was he? estaba dormido... ¿o no lo estaba?; **snow or no snow, she was determined to go** con nieve o sin ella, estaba decidida a ir
(**b**) *(with negative)* ni; **she didn't write or phone** no escribió ni llamó; **without affecting (either) the quality or the price** sin afectar (ni) a la calidad ni al precio; **I didn't mean to offend you or anything** no quise ofenderte ni mucho menos

---

oracle ['ɒrəkəl] *n* oráculo *m*; **to consult the o.** consultar el oráculo

oracular [ɒ'rækjʊlə(r)] *adj Formal* (**a**) *(of, like an oracle)* oracular (**b**) *(obscure)* misterioso(a); *(ambiguous)* ambiguo(a)

oracy ['ɒrəsɪ] *n* facultades *fpl* orales

oral ['ɔːrəl] **1** *n (exam)* (examen *m*) oral *m*
2 *adj* (**a**) *(spoken) (tradition, history, skills)* oral; *(agreement)* verbal ►► *Sch* ***o. examination*** examen *m* oral; ***o. history*** historia *f* oral; ***o. tradition*** tradición *f* oral (**b**) *(of mouth)* oral ►► ***o. contraceptive*** anticonceptivo *m* oral; ***o. hygiene*** higiene *f* bucal; *Med* ***o. rehydration therapy*** terapia *f* de rehidratación oral; ***o. sex*** sexo *m* oral (**c**) *Ling* oral

orality [ɒ'rælɪtɪ] *n* oralidad *f*

orally ['ɔːrəlɪ] *adv* (**a**) *(verbally)* oralmente (**b**) *(by mouth)* por vía oral, oralmente; **to take medicine o.** tomar un medicamento por vía oral

orange ['ɒrɪndʒ] **1** *n* (**a**) *(fruit)* naranja *f* ►► ***o. blossom*** (flor *f* de) azahar *m*; ***o. grove*** naranjal *m*; ***o. peel*** peladura *f* de naranja; *Fig* ***o. peel skin*** piel *m* de naranja; ***o. stick*** palito *m* de naranjo; ***o. tree*** naranjo *m*
(**b**) *(drink)* naranjada *f*; **vodka and o.** vodka con naranja ►► ***o. juice*** *Esp* zumo *m or Am* jugo *m* de naranja; ***o. pekoe*** = variedad de té de gran calidad; ***o. squash*** naranjada *f (sin gas)*
(**c**) *(colour)* naranja *m*
(**d**) *Pol* ***O. Lodge*** Logia *f* de Orange; ***O. Order*** Orden *f* de Orange
2 *adj (colour)* naranja, anaranjado(a)

orangeade [ɒrɪndʒ'eɪd] *n* naranjada *f*, refresco *m* de naranja

Orangeism ['ɒrɪndʒɪzəm] *n Pol* orangismo *m*

Orangeman ['ɒrɪndʒmən] *n Pol* orangista *m*

orangery ['ɒrɪndʒərɪ] *n* invernadero *m* de naranjos

Orangewoman ['ɒrɪndʒwʊmən] *n Pol* orangista *f*

orangey ['ɒrɪndʒɪ] *adj* (**a**) *(taste, smell)* a naranja (**b**) *(colour)* anaranjado(a)

orang-outan(g) [ə'ræŋə'tæŋ] *n* orangután *m*

orate [ɔː'reɪt] *vi Formal* perorar

oration [ɔː'reɪʃən] *n Formal* alocución *f*, discurso *m*

orator ['ɒrətə(r)] *n* orador(ora) *m,f*

oratorical [ɒrə'tɒrɪkəl] *adj* oratorio(a)

oratorio [ɒrə'tɔːrɪəʊ] (*pl* **oratorios**) *n Mus* oratorio *m*

oratory[1] ['ɒrətərɪ] *n (art of speaking)* oratoria *f*; **a superb piece of o.** un formidable ejemplo de oratoria

oratory[2] *n Rel (chapel)* oratorio *m*, capilla *f*

orb [ɔːb] *n* (**a**) *(of monarch)* orbe *f* (**b**) *Literary (sphere)* orbe *m*, esfera *f* (**c**) *Literary (sun, planet)* orbe *m* (**d**) *Literary (eye)* lucero *m*

orbit ['ɔːbɪt] **1** *n* (**a**) *(of planet)* órbita *f*; **in o.** en órbita; **to go into o.** entrar en órbita; *Fam Fig (get angry)* subirse por las paredes; **to put** *or* **send a satellite into o.** poner un satélite en órbita
(**b**) *(scope)* órbita *f*, ámbito *m*; **the countries within Washington's o.** los países que se encuentran dentro en la órbita de Washington
(**c**) *Phys (of electron)* órbita *f*
(**d**) *Anat (of eye)* órbita *f*
2 *vt* girar alrededor de
3 *vi* estar en órbita

orbital ['ɔːbɪtəl] **1** *n* (**a**) *Br (road)* carretera *f* de circunvalación (**b**) *Chem* orbital *m*
2 *adj* (**a**) *Astron* orbital ►► ***o. velocity*** velocidad *f* orbital (**b**) *Br (road)* de circunvalación (**c**) ***o. sander*** lijadora *f* orbital *or* de vibraciones

Orcadian [ɔː'keɪdɪən] **1** *n* persona de las islas Órcadas *(Escocia)*
2 *adj* de las islas Órcadas *(Escocia)*

orchard ['ɔːtʃəd] *n* huerto *m* (de frutales); **(apple) o.** huerto *m* de manzanos, manzanal *m*

orchestra ['ɔːkɪstrə] *n* (**a**) *(musicians)* orquesta *f* ►► *Theat* ***o. pit*** orquesta *f*, foso *m* (**b**) *US (in theatre)* platea *f*, patio *m* de butacas

orchestral [ɔː'kestrəl] *adj* orquestal; **an o. piece** una pieza orquestal *or* para orquesta

orchestrate ['ɔːkɪstreɪt] *vt* (**a**) *Mus* orquestar (**b**) *(organize)* orquestar; **an orchestrated campaign of slander** una orquestada campaña de difamación

orchestration [ɔːkə'streɪʃən] *n* (**a**) *Mus* orquestación *f* (**b**) *(organization)* orquestación *f*

orchid ['ɔːkɪd] *n* orquídea *f*

ordain [ɔː'deɪn] *vt* (**a**) *Formal (decree)* decretar, disponer; **fate ordained that we should meet** el destino dispuso que nos encontráramos; **it is ordained in the Bible** la Biblia dispone (**b**) *Rel (priest)* ordenar; **to be ordained (a priest)** ordenarse (sacerdote)

ordeal [ɔː'diːl] *n* (**a**) *(difficult experience)* calvario *m*; **to go through an o.** pasar por un calvario; **it was quite an o. for him** fue una prueba durísima para él; **I always find family Christmases an o.** para mí, las navidades en familia son un verdadero calvario (**b**) *Hist* ordalía *f*; **o. by fire** ordalía de fuego

---

ORDER ['ɔːdə(r)] **1** *n* (**a**) *(instruction)* orden *f*; **be quiet, and that's an o.!** ¡cállate, es una orden!; **my orders are to remain here** tengo órdenes de quedarme aquí; **to give sb an o.** dar una orden a alguien; **attack when I give the o.** ataquen cuando dé la orden; **to give orders that...** dar órdenes de que...; **to obey** *or* **follow orders** obedecer *or* cumplir órdenes; **I don't take orders from you/anyone** yo no acepto órdenes tuyas/de nadie; **by o. of, on the orders of** por orden de; **to be under orders (to do sth)** tener órdenes (de hacer algo); **orders are** *or* *Hum* **is orders** (las) órdenes son órdenes ►► *Mil* ***the o. of the day*** la orden del día
(**b**) *Com* pedido *m*; **to place an o. (with sb)** hacer un pedido (a alguien); **to have sth on o.** haber hecho un pedido de algo, haber encargado algo; **to make sth to o.** hacer algo por encargo ►► ***o. book*** libro *m* de pedidos; **our o. books are empty/full** no hay pedidos/hay muchos pedidos; ***o. form*** hoja *f* de pedido
(**c**) *(of food)* **a side o. of French fries** una porción de *Esp* patatas *or Am* papas fritas; **your o. will be ready in a minute** *(in restaurant)* su comida estará lista en un instante; **can I take your o. now?** ¿ya han decidido lo que van a comer *or Esp* tomar?, *Am* ¿puedo tomarles el pedido?
(**d**) *Fin* orden *f*; **pay to the o. of J. Black** páguese a J. Black
(**e**) *Law* orden *f*
(**f**) *(sequence)* orden *m*; **in o.** en orden; **in the right/wrong o.** bien/mal ordenado(a); **they have two boys and a girl, in that o.** tienen dos hijos y una hija más pequeña; **in chronological o.** por orden cronológico; **in o. of age/size** por orden de edad/tamaño; **in o. of preference** por orden de preferencia; **out of o.** desordenado(a) ►► *Parl* ***o. paper*** orden *m* del día; *Rel* ***o. of service*** orden *m* ritual *or* litúrgico
(**g**) *(tidiness)* orden *m*; **leave the room in good o.** deja la habitación bien limpia; *Fig* **to set one's own house in o.** poner (uno) orden en su vida
(**h**) *(system)* orden *m*; **this sort of thing seems to be the o. of the day** este tipo de cosas parece estar a la orden del día
(**i**) *(condition)* **in (good) working** *or* **running o.** en buen estado de funcionamiento; **your papers are in o.** tus papeles están en regla *or* orden; **to be out of o.** estar averiado(a), estar estropeado(a); **out of o.** *(sign)* no funciona
(**j**) *(peace, in meeting)* **o.!** ¡silencio, por favor!; **to restore/keep o.** restablecer/mantener el orden; **to keep sb in o.** mantener a alguien bajo control; **radical measures are in o.** se imponen medidas radicales; **I think a celebration is in o.** creo que se impone celebrarlo; **to rule a question out of o.** declarar improcedente una pregunta; *Fam* **that's out of o.!** ¡eso no está bien!, *Esp* ¡eso no es de recibo!; *Fam* **you're out of o.!** *(in the wrong)* ¡eso no está nada bien!; **to call sb to o.** llamar a alguien al orden; **he called the meeting to o.** llamó al orden a los asistentes
(**k**) *(degree)* orden *m*; **in** *or* **of the o. of** del orden de; **of the highest o.** de primer orden ►► ***o. of magnitude*** orden *f* de magnitud; **the cost is of the same o. of magnitude as last time** el costo es muy similar al de la última vez
(**l**) *Rel* orden *f*; **to take holy orders** ordenarse sacerdote
(**m**) *(official honour)* orden *f*; *Br* **the O. of the Garter** la Orden de la Jarretera ►► ***o. of knighthood*** orden *f* de caballería
(**n**) *(social class)* **the higher/lower orders** las capas altas/bajas de la sociedad
(**o**) *Bot & Zool* orden *m*
2 *vt* (**a**) *(instruct)* **to o. sb to do sth** mandar *or* ordenar a alguien hacer algo; **he ordered an immediate attack** ordenó un ataque inmediato; **"come here," she ordered** "ven aquí", ordenó; **to o. that sb do sth** mandar *or* pedir que alguien haga algo; *Law* **he was ordered to pay costs** el juez le ordenó pagar las costas
(**b**) *Com* pedir, encargar (**from** de); *(in restaurant)* pedir; *(taxi)* pedir, llamar; **to o. sth for sb, to o. sb sth** pedir algo para alguien
(**c**) *(arrange)* ordenar, poner en orden; **to o. sth according to size/age** ordenar algo de acuerdo con el tamaño/la edad; **to o. one's thoughts** poner las ideas en orden

3 *vi (in restaurant)* pedir; **are you ready to o.?** ¿han decidido qué van a pedir *or Esp* tomar?
4 in order that *conj Formal* para; **in o. that they understand** para que comprendan
5 in order to *conj* para; **in o. to do sth** para hacer algo; **in o. for us to succeed** para poder tener éxito
▸ **order about, order around** *vt sep* mangonear, no parar de dar órdenes a
▸ **order in** *vt sep* **(a)** *(supplies)* encargar **(b)** *(troops)* solicitar el envío de
▸ **order off** *vt sep Sport* expulsar
▸ **order out** *vt sep (tell to leave)* mandar salir

> En inglés culto o elevado, y especialmente en inglés americano, **order** puede ir seguido de **that** más un verbo en subjuntivo (ver el panel SUBJUNCTIVE):
> **he ordered that she stop talking to the press**
> *le ordenó que dejara de hablar con la prensa*
> Lo mismo también podría decirse de las formas siguientes:
> **he ordered that she should stop talking to the press**
> **he ordered her to stop talking to the press**

ordered ['ɔːdəd] *adj (organized)* ordenado(a); **an o. life** una vida ordenada
orderliness ['ɔːdəlɪnɪs] *n* **(a)** *(of room, desk)* orden *m* **(b)** *(of person, behaviour)* lo ordenado
orderly ['ɔːdəlɪ] **1** *n* **(a)** *(in hospital)* celador(ora) *m,f* **(b)** *Mil* ordenanza *mf* ▸▸ ***o. officer*** oficial *m* de guardia; ***o. room*** oficina *f* de cuartel
2 *adj (tidy, methodical)* ordenado(a); **he is very o. in his habits** tiene hábitos muy metódicos; **an o. retreat** una retirada ordenada; **in an o. fashion** de forma ordenada
ordinal ['ɔːdɪnəl] **1** *n* ordinal *m*
2 *adj* ordinal ▸▸ ***o. number*** número *m* ordinal; *Math* ***o. scale*** escala *f* ordinal
ordinance ['ɔːdɪnəns] *n Formal (decree)* ordenanza *f*, decreto *m*
ordinand ['ɔːdɪnænd] *n Rel* ordenando *m*
ordinarily ['ɔːdɪnərɪlɪ, *US* ɔːrdə'nerɪlɪ] *adv* normalmente; **o., she would be home by now** normalmente, a esta hora ya está en casa; **a more than o. gifted child** un niño con un talento por encima de lo normal
ordinariness ['ɔːdɪnərɪnɪs] *n* **(a)** *(normality)* normalidad *f* **(b)** *(mediocrity)* mediocridad *f*
ordinary ['ɔːdɪnərɪ] **1** *n* **(a)** *(commonplace)* **out of the o.** fuera de lo normal; **nothing out of the o. ever happens here** aquí nunca pasa nada raro **(b)** *Rel* **the O. of the mass** el ordinario de la misa
2 *adj* **(a)** *(normal, average)* normal; **an o. Englishman** un inglés medio; **she was just an o. tourist** no era más que una simple turista; **o. people** gente de la calle; **this is no o. coffee machine** es una máquina de café fuera de lo común; **in the o. course** *or* **run of events** si las cosas siguen su curso normal ▸▸ *Univ* ***o. degree*** = titulación universitaria inferior a una licenciatura; *Scot Formerly* ***O. grade*** = examen que se realizaba al final de la escolarización secundaria obligatoria; *Br Formerly* ***O. level*** = examen que se realizaba al final de la escolarización secundaria obligatoria; *Naut* ***o. seaman*** marinero *m*; *Br Fin* ***o. share*** acción *f* ordinaria
(b) *(mediocre)* común, mediocre; **I thought the food was a bit o.** la comida no me pareció nada especial; **a very o.-looking house/girl** una casa/una niña del montón
ordinate ['ɔːdɪnət] *n Math* ordenada *f*
ordination [ɔːdɪ'neɪʃən] *n Rel* ordenación *f*
ordnance ['ɔːdnəns] *n Mil (supplies)* pertrechos *mpl*; *(guns)* armamento *m* ▸▸ ***o. corps*** cuerpo *m* de pertrechos; ***o. factory*** fábrica *f or Am* planta *f* de armamento; *Br* ***O. Survey*** = instituto británico de cartografía; ***O. Survey map*** mapa *m (publicado por el Ordnance Survey)*
Ordovician [ɔːdəʊ'vɪʃɪən] *Geol* **1** *n* **the O.** el ordovícico
2 *adj (era)* ordovícico(a)
ordure ['ɔːdjʊə(r)] *n Literary* heces *fpl*, excremento *m*
ore [ɔː(r)] *n* mineral *m*; **iron/aluminium o.** mineral de hierro/aluminio
Ore(g) *(abbr* **Oregon***)* Oregón
oregano [ɒrɪ'gɑːnəʊ, *US* ə'regənəʊ] *n* orégano *m*
Oregon ['ɒrɪgən] *n* Oregón

Oreo ['ɔːrɪəʊ] *n US* **(a) O. (cookie)**® = galleta de chocolate con relleno de crema **(b)** *Fam Pej* **O. (cookie)** = persona negra que adopta la forma de pensar y el comportamiento de la clase media blanca
organ ['ɔːgən] *n* **(a)** *Anat* órgano *m*; **the organs of speech** los órganos del habla ▸▸ ***o. donor*** donante *mf* de órganos; ***o. transplant*** trasplante *m* de órganos
(b) *Euph* **(male) o., o. of generation** órgano *m* masculino, miembro *m* viril
(c) *(newspaper, journal)* órgano *m* (de difusión); **the official o. of the Party** el órgano oficial del partido
(d) *Mus* órgano *m* ▸▸ ***o. loft*** galería *f* del órgano; ***o. pipe*** tubo *m* de(l) órgano; ***o. stop*** registro *m* de órgano
organdie, *US* **organdy** ['ɔːgəndɪ] *n* organdí *m*
organ-grinder ['ɔːgəngraɪndə(r)] *n* organillero(a) *m,f*; IDIOM *Br Fam* **I want to speak to the o., not the monkey!** no quiero hablar con el mono sino con el que le da de comer
organic [ɔː'gænɪk] *adj* **(a)** *(disease, function)* orgánico(a) **(b)** *Chem* ***o. chemistry*** química *f* orgánica; ***o. compound*** compuesto *m* orgánico **(c)** *(farming, fruit, vegetable)* biológico(a), ecológico(a) ▸▸ ***o. fertilizer*** fertilizante *m or* abono *m* orgánico **(d)** *(structural)* orgánico(a); *(fundamental)* inherente, fundamental; **an o. part** una parte inherente; **o. change** cambio orgánico
organically [ɔː'gænɪklɪ] *adv* **(a)** *(constitutionally)* **there's nothing o. wrong (with him)** físicamente está en perfecto estado **(b)** *(farm, grow)* orgánicamente, biológicamente **(c)** *(structurally)* orgánicamente; *(fundamentally)* de forma inherente; **the two ideas are o. linked** las dos ideas se encuentran orgánicamente unidas
organism ['ɔːgənɪzəm] *n* organismo *m*
organist ['ɔːgənɪst] *n* organista *mf*
organization [ɔːgənaɪ'zeɪʃən] *n* **(a)** *(organizing)* organización *f*; **we need some o. around here** necesitamos un poco de organización; **to have a flair for o.** tener dotes para la organización
(b) *(association, official body)* organización *f*; **a political/charitable o.** una organización política/una institución de beneficencia ▸▸ ***o. chart*** organigrama *m*; ***o. man*** hombre *m* de empresa
(c) *(structure)* organización *f*, estructura *f*; **we are unhappy with the o. of the company** no estamos conformes con la estructura de la compañía
(d) *(in proper names)* ***O. for Economic Cooperation and Development*** Organización *f* para la Cooperación y el Desarrollo Económico; ***O. of Petroleum Exporting Countries*** Organización *f* de Países Exportadores de Petróleo; ***O. for Security and Cooperation in Europe*** Organización *f* para la Seguridad y Cooperación en Europa
organizational [ɔːgənaɪ'zeɪʃənəl] *adj* organizativo(a); **the conference turned out to be an o. nightmare** el congreso se convirtió en una pesadilla organizativa ▸▸ *Com* ***o. structure*** organigrama *m*
organize ['ɔːgənaɪz] **1** *vt* **(a)** *(arrange, bring about) (concert, party, outing)* organizar; **they organized accommodation for me** se encargaron de buscarme alojamiento; **she organized it so that we got in free** hizo que pudiéramos entrar gratis
(b) *(put in order)* **to o. people into groups** organizar a gente en grupos; **to o. one's thoughts** ordenar los pensamientos
(c) *(manage)* **he doesn't know how to o. himself** no sabe cómo organizarse; **I've learnt to o. my time better** he aprendido a organizar mejor mi tiempo
(d) *(into union)* sindicar
2 *vi (form union)* sindicarse
organized ['ɔːgənaɪzd] *adj* **(a)** *(arranged)* organizado(a); **to get o.** *(before a journey)* prepararse; **don't worry, it's all o.** no te preocupes, está todo organizado ▸▸ ***o. tour*** viaje *m* organizado **(b)** *(orderly, methodical)* organizado(a) **(c)** *(forming an organization)* ***o. crime*** crimen *m* organizado; ***o. labour*** trabajadores *mpl* sindicalizados, sindicalismo *m*
organizer ['ɔːgənaɪzə(r)] *n* **(a)** *(person)* organizador(ora) *m,f* **(b)** *(diary)* agenda *f* **(c)** *Comptr* organizador *m*
organza [ɔː'gænzə] *n* organza *f*
orgasm ['ɔːgæzəm] *n* orgasmo *m*; **to have an o.** tener un orgasmo; *Fam Fig* **they were having orgasms about the decor** estaban alucinados con la decoración
orgasmic [ɔː'gæzmɪk] *adj* orgásmico(a); *Fam Fig* **it was a positively o. experience** fue un verdadero alucine
orgiastic [ɔːdʒɪ'æstɪk] *adj* orgiástico(a)
orgy ['ɔːdʒɪ] *n* **(a)** *(wild party)* orgía *f*; **a drunken o.** una bacanal **(b)** *Fig* **an o. of shopping** una orgía de compras; **an o. of violence** una masacre

oriel ['ɔːrɪəl] *n Archit* **o. (window)** mirador *m*

orient ['ɔːrɪənt] **1** *n* **the O.** (el) Oriente
2 *vt* = **orientate**

oriental [ɔːrɪ'entəl] **1** *n Old-fashioned (person)* **an O.** un(a) oriental
2 *adj* oriental

Orientalist [ɔːrɪ'entəlɪst] *n* orientalista *mf*

orientate ['ɔːrɪənteɪt] *vt* orientar; **to o. oneself** orientarse

orientated = **oriented**

orientation [ɔːrɪən'teɪʃən] *n* orientación *f*; **she's found a new o. in life** ha encontrado un nuevo camino *or* norte en la vida ▸▸ ***o. course*** curso *m* orientativo

oriented ['ɔːrɪəntɪd], **orientated** ['ɔːrɪənteɪtɪd] *adj* orientado(a) (**towards** hacia); **our firm is very much o. towards the American market** nuestra empresa está muy orientada al mercado norteamericano

-oriented ['ɔːrɪəntɪd], **-orientated** ['ɔːrɪənteɪtɪd] *suffix* **ours is a money-o. society** la nuestra es una sociedad que asigna al dinero una importancia primordial; **she's very work-o.** el trabajo ocupa un lugar fundamental en su vida; **youth-o.** enfocado(a) hacia los jóvenes

orienteering [ɔːrɪən'tɪərɪŋ] *n* orientación *f (deporte de aventura)*

orifice ['ɒrɪfɪs] *n* orificio *m*

origami [ɒrɪ'gɑːmɪ] *n* papiroflexia *f*, origami *m*

origin ['ɒrɪdʒɪn] *n* (**a**) *(source) (of word, custom)* origen *m*; *(of river)* nacimiento *m*; **of unknown o.** de origen desconocido; **the present troubles have their o. in the proposed land reform** los problemas actuales tienen su origen en la reforma agrícola propuesta; **the song is Celtic in o.** la canción es de origen celta
(**b**) *(ancestry)* origen *m*; **country of o.** país de origen; **of Greek o.** de origen griego; **of humble/peasant origins** de origen humilde/campesino
(**c**) *Math* origen *m*

original [ə'rɪdʒɪnəl] **1** *n* (**a**) *(painting, document)* original *m*; **to read Tolstoy in the o.** leer a Tolstói en el idioma original (**b**) *(person)* **she's a real o.!** ¡es un tanto extravagante!
2 *adj* (**a**) *(initial)* original, originario(a); **the o. inhabitants/owners** los habitantes/dueños originarios; **my o. intention was to write the letter myself** mi intención original era escribir la carta yo mismo; **translated from the o. German** traducido(a) de la versión original en alemán
(**b**) *(innovative, unusual)* original; **she has an o. approach to child-rearing** tiene un enfoque muy original sobre cómo criar a los niños
(**c**) *(new) (play, writing)* original; **based on an o. idea by...** basado en una idea original de...
(**d**) *Rel* ***o. sin*** pecado *m* original

originality [ərɪdʒɪ'nælɪtɪ] *n* originalidad *f*

originally [ə'rɪdʒɪnəlɪ] *adv* (**a**) *(initially)* originariamente, en un principio; **where do you come from o.?** ¿cuál es tu lugar de origen?; **o., I had planned to go to Greece** originalmente había planeado ir a Grecia (**b**) *(in an innovative way)* originalmente, de forma original

originate [ə'rɪdʒɪneɪt] **1** *vt* crear, originar
2 *vi* (**a**) *(idea, rumour)* originarse; **to o. from** *(person)* proceder de; **where did the rumour o. (from)?** ¿dónde se originó el rumor?; **the cocaine originates from South America** la cocaína es originaria de América del Sur; **to o. in** *(river)* nacer en; *(custom)* proceder *or* surgir de (**b**) *US (flight, bus, train)* **to o. in** proceder de

originator [ə'rɪdʒɪneɪtə(r)] *n (of theory, technique)* inventor(ora) *m,f*; *(of rumour, trend)* iniciador(ora) *m,f*

oriole ['ɔːrɪəʊl] *n* (**a**) *(from Old World)* oropéndola *f* (**b**) *(from New World)* cazadora *f* ▸▸ ***o. blackbird*** maicero *m*

Orkney ['ɔːknɪ] *n* **the O. Islands, the Orkneys** las (Islas) Órcadas

Orlon® ['ɔːlɒn] *n* = tejido acrílico antiarrugas

ormolu ['ɔːməluː] *n* similor *m*; **an o. clock** un reloj de similor

ornament **1** *n* ['ɔːnəmənt] (**a**) *(decorative object)* adorno *m*; *Fig* **he would be an o. to any gathering** es una figura decorativa, no sirve para nada (**b**) *(decoration)* adorno *m*; **rich in o.** con mucha decoración, muy adornado(a) (**c**) *Mus* floritura *f*
2 *vt* ['ɔːnəment] *(room)* decorar; *(style)* adornar

ornamental [ɔːnə'mentəl] *adj* ornamental, decorativo(a); **purely o.** meramente decorativo(a)

ornamentation [ɔːnəmen'teɪʃən] *n* ornamentación *f*

ornate [ɔː'neɪt] *adj (building, surroundings)* ornamentado(a); *(style, decor)* recargado(a)

ornately [ɔː'neɪtlɪ] *adv* **o. decorated** muy ornamentado(a)

ornateness [ɔː'neɪtnɪs] *n (of building, surroundings)* lo ornamentado; *(of style, decor)* lo recargado

ornery ['ɔːnərɪ] *adj US Fam* gruñón(ona), cascarrabias *inv*

ornithological [ɔːnɪθə'lɒdʒɪkəl] *adj* ornitológico(a)

ornithologist [ɔːnɪ'θɒlədʒɪst] *n* ornitólogo(a) *m,f*

ornithology [ɔːnɪ'θɒlədʒɪ] *n* ornitología *f*

orogenesis [ɒrə'dʒenəsɪs] *n* orogénesis *f inv*

orogenic [ɒrə'dʒenɪk] *adj* orogénico(a)

orogeny [ɒ'rɒdʒənɪ] *n* orogenia *f*

orographic [ɒrə'græfɪk] *adj* orográfico(a)

orography [ɒ'rɒgrəfɪ] *n* orografía *f*

orotund ['ɒrətʌnd] *adj Formal (style)* pomposo(a); *(voice)* estentóreo(a)

orphan ['ɔːfən] **1** *n* (**a**) huérfano(a) *m,f*; **to be left an o.** quedar huérfano(a) (**b**) *Typ* línea *f* huérfana
2 *adj* **an o. child** un niño huérfano
3 *vt* **to be orphaned** quedar huérfano(a); **they were orphaned by the war** la guerra los dejó huérfanos

orphanage ['ɔːfənɪdʒ] *n* orfanato *m*

Orpheus ['ɔːfɪəs] *n Mythol* Orfeo

orrery ['ɒrərɪ] *n* planetario *m*

ORT [əʊɑː'tiː] *n Med* (*abbr* **oral rehydration therapy**) TRO *f*, terapia *f* de rehidratación oral

orthocentre ['ɔːθəʊsentə(r)] *n Geom* ortocentro *m*

orthoclase ['ɔːθəʊkleɪz] *n Geol* ortosa *f*

orthodontic [ɔːθə'dɒntɪk] *adj* ortodóntico(a); **o. specialist** ortodoncista

orthodontics [ɔːθə'dɒntɪks] *n* ortodoncia *f*

orthodontist [ɔːθə'dɒntɪst] *n* ortodontista *mf*

orthodox ['ɔːθədɒks] *adj* ortodoxo(a) ▸▸ ***O. Church*** Iglesia *f* Ortodoxa

orthodoxy ['ɔːθədɒksɪ] *n* ortodoxia *f*

orthogonal [ɔː'θɒgənəl] *adj Math* ortogonal ▸▸ ***o. projection*** proyección *f* ortogonal

orthography [ɔː'θɒgrəfɪ] *n* ortografía *f*

orthopaedic, *US* **orthopedic** [ɔːθə'piːdɪk] *adj Med* ortopédico(a) ▸▸ ***o. surgery*** cirugía *f* ortopédica

orthopaedics, *US* **orthopedics** [ɔːθə'piːdɪks] *n Med* ortopedia *f*

orthoptics [ɔː'θɒptɪks] *n* gimnasia *f* ocular

Orwellian [ɔː'welɪən] *adj* orwelliano(a)

oryx ['ɒrɪks] *n* oryx *m*

OS ['əʊ'es] *n* (**a**) (*abbr* **Ordnance Survey**) = servicio cartográfico nacional británico (**b**) *Comptr* (*abbr* **Operating System**) sistema *m* operativo

Oscar ['ɒskə(r)] *n* Oscar *m*

Oscar-winning ['ɒskəwɪnɪŋ] *adj (film, performance)* ganador(a) del Oscar; *Fam Fig* **she really put on an O. performance!** su actuación fue digna de un Oscar

OSCE [əʊessiː'iː] *n* (*abbr* **Organization for Security and Cooperation in Europe**) OSCE *f*

oscillate ['ɒsɪleɪt] *vi* (**a**) *Elec & Phys* oscilar (**b**) *(prices)* oscilar; **he oscillated between hope and despair** pasaba de la esperanza a la desesperación

oscillating ['ɒsɪleɪtɪŋ] *adj Elec* oscilatorio(a)

oscillator ['ɒsɪleɪtə(r)] *n Elec* oscilador *m*

oscillogram [ə'sɪləgræm] *n Phys* oscilograma *m*

oscillograph [ə'sɪləgræf] *n Phys* oscilógrafo *m*

oscilloscope [ə'sɪləskəʊp] *n Phys* osciloscopio *m*

osier ['əʊzɪə(r)] *n* (**a**) *(tree)* mimbrera *f* (**b**) *(branch)* mimbre *m*; ***o. basket*** canasta *f or* cesta *f* de mimbre

Oslo ['ɒzləʊ] *n* Oslo

osmium ['ɒzmɪəm] *n Chem* osmio *m*

osmosis [ɒz'məʊsɪs] *n* (**a**) *Chem* ósmosis *f inv*, osmosis *f inv* (**b**) *Fig* **to learn by o.** aprender por ósmosis

osmotic [ɒz'mɒtɪk] *adj* osmótico(a)

osprey ['ɒspreɪ] *n* águila *f* pescadora

osseous ['ɒsɪəs] *adj Anat* óseo(a)

ossification [ɒsɪfɪ'keɪʃən] *n* (**a**) *Anat* osificación *f* (**b**) *Fig (of person, system)* anquilosamiento *m*

ossify ['ɒsɪfaɪ] *vi* (**a**) *Anat* osificarse (**b**) *Fig (person, system)* anquilosarse

ossuary ['ɒsjʊərɪ] *n* osario *m*

osteitis [ɒstɪ'aɪtɪs] *n Med* osteítis *f inv*

ostensible [ɒs'tensɪbəl] *adj* aparente

> **False friend:** The Spanish adjective **ostensible** is not a translation for the English word **ostensible**. In Spanish **ostensible** means "obvious, evident".

ostensibly [ɒs'tensɪblɪ] *adv* aparentemente

> **False friend:** The Spanish adverb **ostensiblemente** is not a translation for the English word **ostensibly**. In Spanish **ostensiblemente** means "visibly, noticeably".

ostentation [ɒsten'teɪʃən] *n* ostentación *f*

ostentatious [ɒsten'teɪʃəs] *adj* ostentoso(a); **with o. distaste** con un mal gusto evidente

ostentatiously [ɒsten'teɪʃəslɪ] *adv* ostentosamente

osteoarthritis [ɒstɪəʊɑː'θraɪtɪs], **osteoarthrosis** ['ɒstɪəʊɑː'θrəʊsɪs] *n Med* osteoartritis *f inv*, artritis *f inv* ósea

osteomyelitis [ɒstɪəʊmaɪə'laɪtɪs] *n Med* osteomielitis *f*

osteopath ['ɒstɪəpæθ] *n Med* osteópata *mf*

osteopathy [ɒstɪ'ɒpəθɪ] *n Med* osteopatía *f*

osteoplasty ['ɒstɪəplæstɪ] *n Med* osteoplastia *f*

osteoporosis ['ɒstɪəʊpə'rəʊsɪs] *n Med* osteoporosis *f*

ostler ['ɒslə(r)] *n Hist* mozo *m* de cuadra

ostracism ['ɒstrəsɪzəm] *n* ostracismo *m*

ostracize ['ɒstrəsaɪz] *vt* aislar, condenar al ostracismo; **he was ostracized by his workmates** sus compañeros de trabajo le hacían el vacío *or* lo aislaban

ostrich ['ɒstrɪtʃ] *n* avestruz *m*

ostrich-like ['ɒstrɪtʃlaɪk] *Fig* **1** *adj* **to be o. about sth** adoptar la estrategia del avestruz en lo referente a algo

2 *adv* escondiendo la cabeza (como el avestruz)

OT [əʊ'tiː] *n* **(a)** (*abbr* **Old Testament**) Antiguo Testamento *m* **(b)** (*abbr* **occupational therapy**) terapia *f* ocupacional **(c)** (*abbr* **overtime**) horas *fpl* extra

OTC [əʊtiː'siː] *n* (*abbr* **Officers' Training Corps**) = unidad de adiestramiento de futuros oficiales del ejército británico provenientes de la universidad

OTE [əʊtiː'iː] *npl Mktg* (*abbr* **on target earnings**) beneficios *mpl* según los objetivos

OTHER ['ʌðə(r)] **1** *adj* otro(a); **the o. one** el otro/la otra; **bring some o. ones** trae otros; **the o. four** los otros cuatro; **o. people seem to like it** parece que a otros les gusta, a otra gente parece que le gusta; **o. people's property** propiedad ajena; **at all o. times** a cualquier otra hora; **any o. book but that one** cualquier otro libro menos ése; **are there any o. things you need doing?** ¿necesitas que te hagan alguna otra cosa?; **they didn't give us any o. details** no nos dieron más *or* mayores detalles; **the o. day** el otro día; **the o. week** hace unas semanas; **every o. day/week** cada dos días/semanas; **I work every o. day** trabajo un día sí, un día no; **you have no o. option** no te queda otra alternativa; **there's one o. thing I'd like to ask** hay una cosa más que querría preguntar; **some o. time** en otro momento; **somebody o. than me should do it** debería hacerlo alguien que no sea yo

2 *pron* **the o.** el otro/la otra; **the others** los otros/las otras; **some laughed, others wept** unos reían y otros lloraban; **you clean this one and I'll clean the others** tú limpia éste, yo limpiaré los otros *or* demás; **do we have any others?** ¿tenemos algún otro?, ¿tenemos alguno más?; **three died and one o. was injured** tres murieron y uno resultó herido; **one after the o.** uno tras otro; **one or o. of us will be there** alguno de nosotros estará allí; **somehow or o.** sea como sea, de la manera que sea; **somehow or o., we arrived on time** no sé como lo hicimos, pero llegamos a tiempo; **someone or o.** no sé quién, alguien; **some woman or o.** no sé qué mujer, una mujer; **something or o.** no sé qué, algo; **somewhere or o.** en algún sitio

3 *adv* **the colour's a bit odd, o. than that, it's perfect** el color es un poco raro, pero, por lo demás, es *or Esp* resulta perfecto; **candidates o. than those on the list** los candidatos que no aparezcan en la lista; **anywhere o. than there** en cualquier otro sitio menos ése; **nobody o. than you can do it** sólo tú puedes hacerlo; **she never speaks of him o. than admiringly** siempre habla de él con admiración

4 *n (in philosophy, psychology)* **the o.** el otro

otherness ['ʌðənɪs] *n Literary* otredad *f*

otherwise ['ʌðəwaɪz] **1** *adv* **(a)** *(differently)* de otra manera; **he could not do o.** no pudo hacer otra cosa; **it could hardly be o.** no podía ser de otra manera; **to think o.** pensar de otra manera; **I said it wasn't ready, but she thought o.** para mí no estaba listo pero ella no compartía mi opinión; **she claims to be innocent, but the facts indicate o.** ella alega inocencia pero los hechos dicen *or* indican otra cosa; **to be o. engaged** tener otros asuntos que resolver; **except where o. stated** excepto donde se indique lo contrario; **unless we inform you o.** a menos que le informemos en otro sentido, a menos que le digamos lo contrario

(b) *(apart from that)* por lo demás; **an o. excellent performance** fuera de eso, una actuación excelente; **o., things are fine** por lo demás *or* aparte de eso, las cosas van bien

(c) *(in other words)* en otras palabras; **Louis XIV, o. known as the Sun King** Luis XIV, también conocido como el Rey Sol

(d) *(in contrast, opposition)* **through diplomatic channels or o.** a través de canales diplomáticos o de cualquier otra índole; **it is of no importance, financial or o.** no tiene importancia alguna, ni financiera ni de ningún otro tipo

2 *conj* si no, de lo contrario; **you'd better phone your father, o. he'll worry** llama a tu padre para que no se preocupe

otherworldliness [ʌðə'wɜːldlɪnɪs] *n* **(a)** *(of person)* espiritualidad *f* **(b)** *(of religion, experience)* carácter *m* sobrenatural

other-worldly [ʌðə'wɜːldlɪ] *adj* **(a)** *(person)* espiritual **(b)** *(supernatural) (religion, experience)* sobrenatural

otiose ['əʊtɪəʊs] *adj Formal* superfluo(a), ocioso(a)

OTT [əʊtiː'tiː] *adj Br Fam* (*abbr* **over the top**) exagerado(a); **to be O.** pasarse un *Esp* pelín *or Méx* tantito *or RP* chiquitín; **he went completely O. when he heard what she'd said** cuando escuchó lo que ella había dicho se puso furioso *or* como loco

Ottawa ['ɒtəwə] *n* Ottawa

otter ['ɒtə(r)] *n* nutria *f*

Ottoman ['ɒtəmən] *Hist* **1** *n* otomano(a) *m,f*

2 *adj* otomano(a); **the O. Empire** el Imperio Otomano

ottoman ['ɒtəmən] *n (piece of furniture)* otomana *f*

OU [əʊ'juː] *n Br* (*abbr* **Open University**) = universidad a distancia británica, *Esp* ≃ UNED *f*

ouch [aʊtʃ] *exclam (expressing pain)* ¡ay!

OUGHT [ɔːt] *v aux* **(a)** *(expressing obligation, desirability)* deber, tener que; **you o. to tell her** tienes que *or* debes decírselo; **I o. to be going – yes, I suppose you o. (to)** tendría que irme ya – sí, me imagino; **he o. to be ashamed of himself** debería darle vergüenza, debería avergonzarse *or CAm, Carib, Col, Méx* apenarse; **you oughtn't to worry so much** no deberías preocuparte tanto; **I thought I o. to let you know about it** me pareció que deberías saberlo; **he had drunk more than he o. to** había bebido *or Am* tomado más de la cuenta; **this o. to have been done before** esto se tenía que haber hecho antes; **they o. not to have waited** no tenían que haber esperado

(b) *(expressing probability)* **they o. to be in Paris by now** a estas horas tendrían que estar ya en París; **they o. to win** deberían ganar; **you o. to be able to get $150 for the painting** deberías conseguir al menos 150 dólares por el cuadro; **this o. to be interesting** esto promete ser interesante; **there o. not to be any trouble getting hold of one** no deberíamos tener problemas para conseguir uno

oughta ['ɔːtə] *US Fam* = **ought to**

oughtn't ['ɔːtənt] = **ought not**

Ouija® board ['wiːdʒəbɔːd] *n* (tablero *m* de) ouija *f*

ounce[1] [aʊns] *n* **(a)** *(unit of weight)* onza *f (= 28,4 g)* **(b)** *US (fluid ounce)* onza *f* líquida *(= 29,6ml)* **(c)** IDIOMS **if you had an o. of sense** si tuvieras dos dedos de frente; **she hasn't an o. of decency** no tiene ni un ápice de decencia; **it took every o. of strength she had** le consumió hasta el último gramo de la energía que tenía

ounce[2] *n (animal)* pantera *f* de las nieves

OUR ['aʊə(r)] *possessive adj* **(a)** *(singular)* nuestro(a); *(plural)* nuestros(as); **o. dog** nuestro perro; **o. parents** nuestros padres; **o. names are Mary and Seamus** nos llamamos Mary y Seamus; **we went to o. house, not theirs** fuimos a nuestra casa, no a la de ellos; **it wasn't OUR idea!** ¡no fue idea nuestra!; **they were upset at o. mentioning it** les sentó *or* cayó muy mal que lo mencionáramos; **o. understanding was that we would share the cost** entendimos que el costo *or Esp* coste sería compartido

(b) *(for parts of body, clothes) (translated by definite article)* **o. eyes are the same colour** tenemos los ojos del mismo color; **we both hit o. heads** los dos nos golpeamos en la cabeza; **we washed o. faces** nos lavamos la cara; **we put o. hands in o. pockets** nos metimos las manos en los bolsillos *or CAm, Méx, Perú* las bolsas; **someone stole o. clothes** nos robaron la ropa

(c) *Br Fam (referring to member of family)* **o. Hilda** nuestra Hilda

ours ['aʊəz] *possessive pron* (**a**) *(singular)* el nuestro *m*, la nuestra *f*; *(plural)* los nuestros *mpl*, las nuestras *fpl*; **their house is big but o. is bigger** su casa es grande, pero la nuestra es mayor; **she didn't have a book so we gave her o.** como no tenía libro le dimos el nuestro; **it must be one of o.** debe ser uno de los nuestros; **it wasn't their fault, it was OURS** no fue culpa suya sino nuestra; **o. is the work they admire most** el trabajo que más admiran es el nuestro

(**b**) *(used attributively) (singular)* nuestro *m*, nuestra *f*; *(plural)* nuestros *mpl*, nuestras *fpl*; **this book is o.** este libro es nuestro; **a friend of o.** un amigo nuestro; **that wretched dog of o.** ese maldito perro que tenemos

ourselves [aʊə'selvz] *pron* (**a**) *(reflexive)* nos; **we both hurt o.** los dos nos hicimos daño; **we introduced o.** nos presentamos; **we bought o. a television** nos compramos un televisor; **we could see o. reflected in the water** podíamos vernos reflejados en el agua

(**b**) *(unaided, alone)* nososotros *mpl* solos, nosotras *fpl* solas; **we can do it o.** (nosotros) podemos hacerlo solos, podemos hacerlo nosotros solos; **we made the pattern o.** nosotros solos hicimos el diseño

(**c**) *(emphatic)* nosotros *mpl* mismos, nosotras *fpl* mismas; **we told them o.** se lo dijimos nosotros mismos; **we o. do not believe it** nosotros mismos no nos lo creemos; **though we say so o.** aunque nosotros mismos lo digamos

(**d**) *(our usual selves)* **we soon felt o. again** en breve volvimos a sentirnos los de siempre

(**e**) *(after preposition)* nosotros *mpl*, nosotras *fpl*; **we shouldn't talk about o.** no deberíamos hablar sobre nosotros; **we shared the money among o.** nos repartimos el dinero; **we did it all by o.** lo hicimos nosotros solos; **we live by o.** vivimos solos; **we were all by o.** estábamos nosotros solos; **we bought it for o.** la compramos para nosotros

(**f**) *(replacing 'us')* **the group included o. and the Wallaces** en el grupo estábamos nosotros y los Wallace; **it is meant for people like o.** es para gente como nosotros

oust [aʊst] *vt* desbancar; **to o. sb from his post** destituir a alguien, separar a alguien de su cargo

ouster ['aʊstə(r)] *n* (**a**) *Law (illicit)* expropiación *f* ilegal (**b**) *esp US (from job)* destitución *f*; *(from place)* expulsión *f*

OUT [aʊt] **1** *adv* (**a**) *(outside, not in, not at home)* fuera, afuera; **he's o.** está fuera *or* afuera; **I was only o. for a minute** sólo salí un momento; **she's waiting o. in the lobby** está esperando ahí fuera *or* afuera en el vestíbulo; **I saw them when I was o. doing the shopping** los vi cuando estaba haciendo la compra *orAm* las compras; **I haven't had an evening o. for ages** hace siglos que no salgo de *or Esp* por la *or Am* en la *orArg* a la noche; **o. here** aquí fuera *or* afuera; **it's cold o. (there)** hace frío (ahí) fuera *or* afuera; **it's good to see you o. and about again** *(after illness)* me alegro de verte rondar por ahí de nuevo; **to get o. and about** salir de casa, salir por ahí; **get o.!** ¡fuera!, ¡vete!, *RP* ¡andate!; **to go o.** salir; **to stay o. late** salir hasta muy tarde; **he stuck his head o.** sacó la cabeza

(**b**) *(of tide)* **the tide is o.** la marea está baja; **the tide is going o.** la marea está bajando

(**c**) *(far away)* **I spent a year o. in China** pasé un año en China; **o. at sea** en alta mar

(**d**) *(indicating removal)* **he took o. a gun** sacó una pistola; **the dentist pulled my tooth o.** el dentista me sacó un diente

(**e**) *(indicating distribution)* **to hand sth o.** repartir algo

(**f**) *(not concealed)* **to come o.** *(sun, flowers)* salir; *(secret)* descubrirse; *(homosexual)* declararse homosexual; *Fam* **come on, o. with it!** ¡vamos, cuéntamelo *or* larga!

(**g**) *(published)* **to bring sth o.** sacar algo; **to come o.** salir; **is her new book/record o.?** ¿ha salido su nuevo libro/disco?

(**h**) *(extinguished)* **turn the light o.** apaga la luz; **the fire went o.** el fuego se extinguió

(**i**) *(eliminated)* **to go o. (of a competition)** quedar eliminado (de una competición *orAm* competencia)

(**j**) *Fam (unconscious, asleep)* **I was** *or* **went o. like a light** caí redondo en la cama

(**k**) *(not working)* **to come o. (on strike)** declararse en huelga

(**l**) *Sport (not in field of play)* **o.!** *(in tennis)* ¡out!; **the umpire called the shot o.** el juez de silla dijo que la bola había salido

(**m**) *Sport (in baseball, cricket)* **to be o.** quedar eliminado(a); **the umpire gave him o.** el árbitro decidió que quedaba eliminado

(**n**) *Law* **the jury is o.** el jurado está deliberando

(**o**) *(loudly)* **to laugh o. loud** reírse a carcajadas

2 *adj* (**a**) *(extinguished) (fire, light)* apagado(a)

(**b**) *(not concealed)* **the sun is o.** ha salido el sol, hace sol; **the moon is o.** ha salido la luna, hay luna; **the tulips are o. early this year** los tulipanes han salido *or* florecido muy pronto este año; **the secret is o.** se ha desvelado el secreto; *Fam* **he's o.** *(openly gay)* es homosexual declarado

(**c**) *(available)* **her new book will be o. next week** la semana que viene sale su nuevo libro; **their new record is o. now** ya ha salido su nuevo disco

(**d**) *(not in fashion)* **flares are o.** *Esp* no se llevan los pantalones de campana, *Am* no se usan los pantalones acampanados; **existentialism is o.** el existencialismo ha pasado de moda

(**e**) *(eliminated)* **to be o. (of a competition)** estar eliminado(a) (de una *Esp* competición *orAm* competencia); **the Conservatives are o. (of power)** los conservadores ya no están en el poder

(**f**) *(not working)* **to be o. (on strike)** estar en huelga

(**g**) *Sport (injured)* **he was o. for six months with a knee injury** estuvo seis meses sin poder jugar por una lesión en la rodilla

(**h**) *(unconscious, asleep)* **to be o. cold** *(unconscious)* estar inconsciente; *Fam* **to be o. for the count** *(asleep)* estar roque *orAm* planchado(a)

(**i**) *(incorrect)* equivocado(a); **I was £50 o.** me equivocaba en 50 libras; **the calculations were o.** los cálculos no eran correctos

(**j**) *(unacceptable)* **going to the beach is o.** ir a la playa es imposible; **smoking at work is o.** no se permite fumar en el trabajo

(**k**) *(finished)* **before the week is o.** antes de que termine la semana

►► *Comptr* ***o. box*** buzón *m* de salida; ***o. tray*** bandeja *f* de trabajos terminados

(**l**) *(indicating intention)* **to be o. for money/a good time** ir en busca de dinero/diversión; **to be o. to do sth** pretender hacer algo; *Fam* **to be o. to get sb** ir detrás de alguien, *Esp* ir a por alguien

3 *prep Fam (through)* **to look o. the window** mirar por la ventana

4 *exclam* (**a**) *(leave)* ¡fuera!, ¡vete!, *RP* ¡andate! (**b**) *(on radio)* **(over and) o.!** (cambio y) corto

5 *vt Fam (homosexual)* revelar la homosexualidad de

6 *n Fam (excuse)* excusa *f*; **that will give you an o.** eso te servirá como excusa

7 out of *prep* (**a**) *(outside)* **to be o. of the country** estar fuera del país; **to get o. of bed** *Esp, Andes, RP* levantarse, *Carib, Méx* pararse; **to go o. of the office** salir de la oficina; **to throw sth o. of the window** tirar *orAndes, CAm, Carib, Méx* botar algo por la ventana; **to look o. of the window** mirar por la ventana

(**b**) *(away from)* **keep o. of direct sunlight** manténgase a resguardo de los rayos del sol; **to get sb o. of trouble** sacar a alguien de líos *or* de un problema; **to stay o. of trouble** no meterse en líos; **o. of danger** fuera de peligro; **o. of reach** fuera del alcance; **it's o. of sight** no está a la vista; *Fam* **o. of sight** *(wonderful)* genial; *Fam* **let's get o. of here!** ¡salgamos *or* vámonos de aquí!; *US Fam* **I'm o. of here!** ¡me largo!, *Esp* ¡me las piro!, *Méx, RP* ¡me rajo!

(**c**) *(indicating removal)* de; **to take sth o. of sth** sacar algo de algo

(**d**) *(lacking)* **I'm o. of cash/ideas** me he quedado sin dinero/ideas; **the supermarket was o. of bread** no quedaba pan en el supermercado; **we're o. of time** no nos queda tiempo

(**e**) *(from)* de; **to get sth o. of sth/sb** sacar algo de algo/a alguien; **we got a lot of enjoyment o. of it** nos divirtió muchísimo; **I copied it o. of a book** lo copié de un libro; **he built a hut o. of sticks** construyó una choza con palos; **it's made o. of plastic** está hecho de plástico; **she paid for it o. of her own money** lo pagó de *or* con su dinero

(**f**) *(in proportions)* de; **three days o. of four** tres días de cada cuatro; **twenty o. of twenty** *(mark)* veinte sobre *or* de veinte

(**g**) *(indicating reason)* por; **o. of friendship/curiosity** por amistad/curiosidad

(**h**) *(in phrases) Fam* **he's o. of it** *(dazed)* está atontado; *(drunk)* tiene *or Esp* lleva un pedo que no se tiene (en pie), *Méx* está tan pedo que no se tiene en pie; **to feel o. of it** *(excluded)* no sentirse integrado(a)

outa ['aʊtə] *Fam* = **out of**

outage ['aʊtɪdʒ] *n* (**a**) *(power cut)* apagón *m*, corte *m* de luz (**b**) *Com (missing goods)* faltante *m*

out-and-out [aʊtə'naʊt] *adj (villain, reactionary)* consumado(a), redomado(a); *(success, failure)* rotundo(a), absoluto(a); **that's o. madness!** ¡es una locura total!

out-argue [aʊt'ɑːgjuː] *vt* **she always out-argues me** siempre que discutimos me deja en evidencia

outback ['aʊtbæk] *n* **the o.** = el interior despoblado de Australia

outbid [aʊt'bɪd] (*pt & pp* **outbid**) *vt* **to o. sb (for sth)** pujar más que alguien (por algo)

outboard ['aʊtbɔːd] **1** *n (motor)* fueraborda *m*; *(boat)* fueraborda *f*

2 *adj* ***o. motor*** motor *m* (de) fueraborda

outbound ['aʊtbaʊnd] *adj (flight)* de ida; *(passengers)* en viaje de ida

outbreak ['aʊtbreɪk] *n (of epidemic, violence)* brote *m*; *(of war, conflict)* estallido *m*; *(of fire, strike)* comienzo *m*; **there's been an o. of flu** se ha desatado una epidemia de gripe

outbuilding ['aʊtbɪldɪŋ] *n* dependencia *f*

outburst ['aʊtbɜːst] *n* arrebato *m*, arranque *m*; **he apologized for his o.** se disculpó por su exabrupto; **outbursts of violence** estallidos de violencia

outcast ['aʊtkɑːst] *n* paria *mf*, marginado(a) *m,f*

outclass [aʊt'klɑːs] *vt* superar (ampliamente *or* cómodamente); **he was clearly outclassed by his opponent** fue superado cómodamente por su rival

outcome ['aʊtkʌm] *n* resultado *m*; **the o. of it all was that they never visited us again** como consecuencia, nunca más nos visitaron; **the desired o.** el resultado esperado

outcrop ['aʊtkrɒp] *n (of rock)* afloramiento *m*

outcry ['aʊtkraɪ] *n (protest)* protesta *f*; **the decision was greeted by a public o.** la decisión fue recibida con protestas generalizadas; **to raise an o. (against)** protestar (en contra de)

outdated [aʊt'deɪtɪd] *adj (ideas, attitude, equipment, methods)* anticuado(a); *(clothes)* pasado(a) de moda

outdid *pt of* **outdo**

outdistance [aʊt'dɪstəns] *vt* dejar atrás; **she was easily outdistanced by the Nigerian** la nigeriana la dejó atrás con suma facilidad

outdo [aʊt'duː] (*pt* **outdid** [aʊt'dɪd], *pp* **outdone** [aʊt'dʌn]) *vt (person)* superar, sobrepasar; **not to be outdone, she replied that...** para no ser menos, contestó que...

outdoor ['aʊtdɔː(r)] *adj* (**a**) *(open-air) (games, sports, work)* al aire libre ►► ***o. swimming pool*** piscina *f or Méx* alberca *f or RP* pileta *f* descubierta *or* al aire libre (**b**) **o. clothes** *(street clothes)* ropa de calle; *(outer garments)* prendas de llevar por encima; **o. shoes** calzado de calle (**c**) *(person, lifestyle)* **the o. life** la vida al aire libre; **she's an o. person** le gusta salir al aire libre

outdoors [aʊt'dɔːz] **1** *n* **the great o.** la naturaleza, el campo

2 *adv* fuera; **to go o.** salir fuera; **the scene takes place o.** la escena se desarrolla al aire libre; **the wedding will be held o.** la boda se celebrará al aire libre; **to sleep o.** dormir al raso

outer ['aʊtə(r)] *adj* (**a**) *(external)* externo(a), exterior; **o. garments** prendas de llevar por encima ►► ***o. door*** puerta *f* exterior; ***o. ear*** oído *m* externo

(**b**) *(peripheral)* periférico(a), exterior ►► ***the O. Hebrides*** las Hébridas Exteriores; ***o. London*** la periferia londinense; ***O. Mongolia*** Mongolia Exterior

(**c**) *(furthest) (limits)* más lejano(a) ►► ***o. planets*** planetas *fpl* exteriores; ***o. space*** el espacio exterior

outermost ['aʊtəməʊst] *adj* (**a**) *(closest to outside) (layer)* más exterior; **make sure the coloured side is o.** asegúrate de que la parte de color quede para afuera (**b**) *(most isolated)* más lejano(a), más remoto(a); **the o. planets of the galaxy** los planetas más lejanos *or* remotos de la galaxia

outerwear ['aʊtəweə(r)] *n* ropa *f* de llevar por encima

outface [aʊt'feɪs] *vt (confront)* hacer frente a

outfall ['aʊtfɔːl] *n* desembocadura *f*

outfield ['aʊtfiːld] *n (in baseball) (area)* extracampo *m*, jardín *m*; *(players)* exteriores *mpl*

outfielder ['aʊtfiːldə(r)] *n (in baseball)* jardinero(a) *m,f*

outfit ['aʊtfɪt] **1** *n* (**a**) *(clothes)* traje *m*; **a cowboy/nurse's o.** *(for child)* un disfraz de vaquero/enfermera; **she was wearing a new o.** llevaba un modelo nuevo (**b**) *(equipment)* equipo *m*; *(kit)* kit *m* (**c**) *Fam (organization, team)* equipo *m*; **he went over to a rival o.** se cambió de bando

2 *vt* (*pt & pp* **outfitted** ['aʊtfɪtɪd]) *(with equipment)* equipar

outfitter ['aʊtfɪtə(r)] *n* (**a**) *esp Br (for clothes)* sastre *m*; **gentleman's o.('s)** *(shop)* sastrería, tienda de confecciones de caballeros (**b**) *(for hunting equipment)* proveedor(ora) *m,f* de complementos y accesorios de caza

outflank [aʊt'flæŋk] *vt* (**a**) *Mil* sorprender por la espalda (**b**) *Fig (outmanoeuvre)* superar; **they outflanked their opponents on the right** *(of political party)* se hicieron todavía más de derechas que sus oponentes

outflow ['aʊtfləʊ] *n* (**a**) *(of liquid)* salida *f*, fuga *f* (**b**) *(outlet)* desagüe *m* (**c**) *(of capital, currency, population)* salida *f*

outfox [aʊt'fɒks] *vt* ser más astuto(a) que, burlar

outgoing [aʊt'gəʊɪŋ] *adj* (**a**) *(train, ship, plane)* saliente; *(telephone call)* saliente; *(mail, e-mail)* saliente (**b**) *(tide)* baja (**c**) *(government, minister)* saliente (**d**) *(sociable)* abierto(a), extrovertido(a)

outgoings ['aʊtgəʊɪŋz] *npl Br Fin* gastos *mpl*

outgrow [aʊt'grəʊ] (*pt* **outgrew** [aʊt'gruː], *pp* **outgrown** [aʊt'grəʊn]) *vt* (**a**) *(become too old for) (game, toys)* hacerse demasiado mayor para; **he has outgrown his protest phase** ya ha dejado atrás la fase de protestar; **he should have outgrown that habit by now** ya no tiene edad para esas cosas; **to have outgrown one's friends** tener ya poco en común *or* poco que ver con los amigos

(**b**) *(clothes)* **he's outgrown the shirt** se le ha quedado pequeña la camisa; **she has outgrown two pairs of shoes this year** este año le han quedado pequeños *or* chicos dos pares de zapatos

(**c**) *(grow faster than)* crecer más que; **he has outgrown most of his classmates** ha crecido más que casi todos sus compañeros de clase; **the world is outgrowing its resources** el mundo se está quedando sin recursos (naturales)

outgrowth ['aʊtgrəʊθ] *n (on tree)* excrecencia *f*, verruga *f*; *Fig (development)* ramificación *f*

outguess [aʊt'ges] *vt* anticiparse a

outgun [aʊt'gʌn] *vt* (*pt & pp* **outgunned** [aʊt'gʌnd]) superar en armamento; **we were outgunned** nos superaban en armamento

outhouse ['aʊthaʊs] *n* (**a**) *(building)* dependencia *f* (**b**) *US (outside toilet)* retrete *m* exterior

outing ['aʊtɪŋ] *n* (**a**) *(excursion)* excursión *f*; **to go on an o.** ir de excursión, hacer una salida (**b**) *(of horse)* **his first o. this season** su primera carrera esta temporada (**c**) *Fam (of homosexual)* = hecho de revelar la homosexualidad de alguien, generalmente un personaje célebre

outjump [aʊt'dʒʌmp] *vt (competitor)* superar en el salto a

outlandish [aʊt'lændɪʃ] *adj* estrafalario(a), extravagante

outlast [aʊt'lɑːst] *vt (person)* sobrevivir a; *(thing)* durar más que; **the theory has outlasted all its critics** la teoría ha sobrevivido a todos sus detractores

outlaw ['aʊtlɔː] **1** *n* proscrito(a) *m,f*

2 *vt (custom)* prohibir; *(organization)* ilegalizar

outlay ['aʊtleɪ] **1** *n (expense)* desembolso *m*; **to get back** *or* **recover one's o.** recuperar la inversión inicial

2 *vt* (*pt & pp* **outlaid** ['aʊtleɪd]) *(spend)* desembolsar

outlet ['aʊtlet] *n* (**a**) *(for water)* desagüe *m*; *(for steam)* salida *f* (**b**) *(for talents, energy)* válvula *f* de escape; **boxing was an o. for his frustration** el boxeo era una válvula de escape para sus frustraciones (**c**) *(shop)* punto *m* de venta; **we need more sales outlets in Japan** necesitamos más puntos de venta en Japón (**d**) *US (power point)* toma *f* de corriente

outline ['aʊtlaɪn] **1** *n* (**a**) *(shape)* silueta *f*, contorno *m*; *(drawing)* esbozo *m*, bosquejo *m* ►► ***o. drawing*** contorno *m*

(**b**) *(summary) (of play, novel)* resumen *m*; *(of plan, policy)* líneas *fpl* maestras; **a rough o.** *(of plan, proposal, article)* un esbozo, una idea aproximada; **she gave us an o. of what she planned to do** nos dio una idea aproximada de lo que pensaba hacer; **an o. of applied linguistics** una introducción a la lingüística aplicada; **in o.** a grandes rasgos ►► ***o. agreement*** preacuerdo *m*

(**c**) *Comptr* ***o. font*** fuente *f* de impresora *or* escalable

2 *vt* (**a**) *(shape)* perfilar; **the trees were outlined against the blue sky** los árboles se recortaban contra el cielo azul; **the figures are outlined in black** las figuras están bosquejadas en negro; **to o. one's eyes in black** hacerse la raya de negro (**b**) *(summarize) (plot of novel)* resumir; *(plan, policy)* exponer a grandes rasgos

outlive [aʊt'lɪv] *vt* sobrevivir a; **to have outlived its usefulness** *(machine, theory)* haber dejado de ser útil *or* de servir; **he'll o. us all at this rate** a este paso nos va a enterrar a todos nosotros

outlook ['aʊtlʊk] *n* (**a**) *(prospect)* perspectiva *f*; *(of weather)* previsión *f*; **the o. is gloomy** *(for economy)* las previsiones son muy malas; **the o. for March is cold and windy** la previsión (meteorológica) para marzo anuncia frío y viento

(**b**) *(attitude)* punto *m* de vista, visión *f*; **o. on life** visión de la vida; **she has a pessimistic o.** tiene una visión pesimista

(**c**) *(view) (from window)* vista *f*; **we have a pleasant o. onto a small park** tenemos una agradable vista a un pequeño parque

outlying ['aʊtlaɪɪŋ] *adj (remote) (area, village, province)* alejado(a), remoto(a); *(distant from centre) (urban area)* periférico(a)

outmanoeuvre, *US* **outmaneuver** [aʊtmə'nuːvə(r)] *vt Mil* superar a base de estrategia; *Fig* **we were outmanoeuvred by the opposition** la oposición desplegó una estrategia mejor que la nuestra

outmoded [aʊt'məʊdɪd] *adj* anticuado(a)

outnumber ['aʊt'nʌmbə(r)] *vt (the enemy)* superar en número; **we were outnumbered** eran más que nosotros; **women o. men by two to one** hay el doble de mujeres que de hombres

out-of-body experience ['aʊtəv'bɒdɪk'spɪərɪəns] *n* experiencia *f* extracorporal

out-of-court ['aʊtəv'kɔːt] *adj* **an o. settlement** un acuerdo

out-of-doors ['aʊtəv'dɔːz] *adv* fuera; **to sleep o.** dormir al raso

out-of-pocket expenses ['aʊtəv'pɒkɪtɪk'spensɪz] *npl* gastos *mpl* extras

out-of-the-way ['aʊtəvðə'weɪ] *adj* **(a)** *(remote)* apartado(a), remoto(a) **(b)** *(unusual)* fuera de lo común

out-of-town ['aʊtəv'taʊn] *adj (shopping centre, multiplex)* de las afueras de la ciudad

out-of-towner ['aʊtəv'taʊnə(r)] *n US Fam* forastero(a) *m,f*

out-of-work ['aʊtəv'wɜːk] *adj* sin trabajo, desempleado(a)

outpace [aʊt'peɪs] *vt* superar, dejar atrás; **demand has outpaced production** la demanda ha superado la producción

outpatient ['aʊtpeɪʃənt] *n* paciente *mf* externo(a) *or* ambulatorio(a); **he was being treated as an o.** hizo el tratamiento como paciente ambulatorio; **outpatients' (clinic** *or* **department)** clínica *f* ambulatoria, ambulatorio *m*

outperform ['aʊtpə'fɔːm] *vt* rendir más que, ofrecer un mejor rendimiento que

outplacement ['aʊtpleɪsmənt] *n Com* recolocación *f*, = asesoramiento dirigido a facilitar la recolocación de empleados, generalmente subvencionado por la empresa que los despide

outplay [aʊt'pleɪ] *vt* jugar mejor que

outpoint [aʊt'pɔɪnt] *vt (in boxing)* sumar más puntos que

outpost ['aʊtpəʊst] *n Mil* enclave *m*; *Fig* **the last o. of civilization** el último baluarte de la civilización

outpouring ['aʊtpɔːrɪŋ] *n (of affection)* efusión *f*; *(of frustration)* desahogo *m*; *(of ideas, creativity)* profusión *f*; **outpourings of grief** manifestaciones *fpl* exuberantes de dolor, lamentos *mpl*

output ['aʊtpʊt] **1** *n* **(a)** *(goods produced, author's work)* producción *f*; **he kept up this o. for several years** mantuvo este nivel de producción durante varios años

(b) *(of data, information)* información *f* producida ►► *Comptr* ***o. buffer*** memoria *f* intermedia de salida, búfer *m* de salida; *Comptr* ***o. device*** dispositivo *m* de salida

(c) *(of engine, generator)* potencia *f* (de salida); *(of amplifier)* potencia *f*

2 *vt (pt & pp* **output) (a)** *(goods)* producir **(b)** *Comptr (data)* producir; **to o. a file to the printer** enviar un archivo a la impresora

3 *vi Comptr* producir información

outrage ['aʊtreɪdʒ] **1** *n* **(a)** *(act)* ultraje *m*; **it's an o. against public decency** es un ultraje contra las buenas maneras; **three dead in bomb o.** tres muertos en atentado con bomba **(b)** *(scandal)* escándalo *m*; **it's an o.!** ¡es un escándalo! **(c)** *(indignation)* indignación *f*

2 *vt (make indignant)* indignar, ultrajar; **I am outraged** estoy indignado

outrageous [aʊt'reɪdʒəs] *adj* **(a)** *(cruelty)* atroz; *(price, behaviour)* escandaloso(a); *(claim, suggestion)* indignante, escandaloso(a); *(crime, attack)* atroz; **an o. violation of human rights** una violación escandalosa a los derechos humanos **(b)** *(clothes, haircut)* estrambótico(a), estrafalario(a)

outrageously [aʊt'reɪdʒəslɪ] *adv* **(a)** *(cruel)* espantosamente, terriblemente; *(to behave)* escandalosamente; **we have been treated o.** nos han tratado terriblemente mal; **to be o. expensive** tener un precio de escándalo **(b)** *(to dress)* estrambóticamente

outrageousness [aʊt'reɪdʒəsnɪs] *n* **(a)** *(unacceptable nature)* **the o. of her conduct** lo escandaloso de su comportamiento; **the o. of the proposal** lo indignante de la propuesta **(b)** *(of clothes, haircut)* **the o. of his appearance** su aspecto estrambótico

outran *pt of* **outrun**

outrank [aʊt'ræŋk] *vt* superar en rango a, estar por encima de; **he was outranked by most of those present** la mayoría de los allí presentes tenían cargos superiores al suyo

outré ['uːtreɪ] *adj Literary* estrambótico(a), estrafalario(a)

outreach 1 *vt* [aʊt'riːtʃ] *(exceed)* exceder, superar

2 *n* ['aʊtriːtʃ] ***o. worker*** = trabajador social que presta asistencia a personas que pudiendo necesitarla no la solicitan

outrider ['aʊtraɪdə(r)] *n* escolta *m*

outrigger ['aʊtrɪgə(r)] *n* **(a)** *(on boat)* balancín *m*, batanga *f* **(b)** *(boat)* barca *f* con batanga

outright 1 *adj* ['aʊtraɪt] **(a)** *(complete)* total, absoluto(a); **an o. failure** un fracaso total, un rotundo fracaso; **the proposal met with their o. opposition** la propuesta recibió su rotunda oposición; **the o. winner** el campeón absoluto **(b)** *(straightforward) (denial, refusal)* manifiesto(a); **her o. disapproval** su desaprobación manifiesta

2 *adv* [aʊt'raɪt] **(a)** *(completely) (to ban)* completamente, por completo; *(to own)* plenamente; *(to win)* claramente; **to buy sth o.** comprar algo (con) dinero en mano; **he was killed o.** murió en el acto; **I don't own the yacht o.** el yate no es del todo mío

(b) *(straightforwardly)* **I told him o. what I thought of him** le dije claramente lo que pensaba de él; **to refuse o.** negarse rotundamente

outrun [aʊt'rʌn] *(pt* **outran** [aʊt'ræn], *pp* **outrun)** *vt* **(a)** *(run faster than)* correr más rápido que **(b)** *(ability, energy, resources)* exceder; **our enthusiasm outran our financial resources** teníamos más entusiasmo que recursos financieros

outsell [aʊt'sel] *(pt & pp* **outsold** [aʊt'səʊld]) *vt* superar en ventas

outset ['aʊtset] *n* principio *m*; **at the o.** al principio; **from the o.** desde el principio

outshine [aʊt'ʃaɪn] *(pt & pp* **outshone** [aʊt'ʃɒn]) *vt* **(a)** *(shine brighter than)* brillar más que **(b)** *(surpass)* eclipsar; **he doesn't like being outshone** no le gusta ser eclipsado

OUTSIDE ['aʊtsaɪd, aʊt'saɪd] **1** *n (of book, building)* exterior *m*; **from the o.** desde fuera *orAm* afuera; **on the o.** *(externally)* por fuera *orAm* afuera; *Aut* **to overtake on the o.** *(in Britain)* adelantar por la derecha; *(in Europe, USA)* adelantar por la izquierda; **he overtook his rival on the o.** *(in race)* adelantó a su rival por fuera *or* por el exterior; **people on the o. do not understand** la gente de fuera *orAm* afuera no entiende; **at the o.** *(of estimate)* a lo sumo

2 *adj* **(a)** *(influence, world, toilet)* exterior; *(help, interest)* de fuera, del exterior; **we need an o. opinion** necesitamos la opinión de alguien de fuera *orAm* afuera; **the o. limit** el máximo, el tope ►► *Rad & TV* ***o. broadcast*** emisión *f* desde fuera del estudio; *Tel* ***o. call*** llamada *f orAm* llamado *m* (al exterior); ***o. half*** *(in rugby)* medio *m* apertura; ***o. lane*** *Aut (in Britain)* carril *m* de la derecha; *(in Europe, USA)* carril *m* de la izquierda; *Sport Esp* calle *f* de fuera, *Am* carril *m* de afuera; ***o. left*** *(in soccer)* extremo *m* izquierdo; *Tel* ***o. line*** línea *f* exterior; ***o. right*** *(in soccer)* extremo *m* derecho

(b) *(slight)* **there's an o. chance** existe una posibilidad remota

3 *adv* **(a)** *(out)* fuera; **to go/look o.** salir/mirar afuera; **from o.** desde fuera *orAm* afuera **(b)** *(outwardly)* **o., she appeared calm** por fuera estaba tranquila **(c)** *Fam (out of prison)* fuera de la cárcel *or Esp* de chirona *or Méx* del bote *or RP* de la cana

4 *prep* **(a)** *(physically)* fuera de; **once we were o. the door** cuando ya habíamos cruzado la puerta; **the village is just o. Liverpool** el pueblo está justo en las afueras de Liverpool; **I live 10 miles o. Detroit** vivo a 10 millas de Detroit; **she was wearing her blouse o. her trousers** llevaba la blusa por fuera de los pantalones; **nobody o. France has heard of him** fuera de Francia no se le conoce; **don't tell anybody o. this room** no se lo cuentes a nadie que no esté en esta habitación

(b) *(in front of)* delante; **they met o. the cathedral** se encontraron delante de la catedral; **I'll meet you o. the theatre** nos vemos a la entrada *or* en la puerta del teatro

(c) *(with time)* **o. office hours** fuera de horas de oficina; **his time was just o. the world record** su marca no batió el récord mundial por muy poco

(d) *(apart from)* aparte de; **o. a few friends** aparte de unos pocos amigos

5 outside of *prep* **(a)** *(to be, stay)* fuera de, *Am* afuera de; *(to look, run)* afuera de **(b)** *(apart from)* aparte de; **o. of a few friends** aparte de unos pocos amigos

---

outsider [aʊt'saɪdə(r)] *n* **(a)** *(from another city, company)* persona *f* de fuera; **I'd be glad to have an o.'s viewpoint** me encantaría escuchar la opinión de una persona de fuera **(b)** *(socially)* extraño(a) *m,f* **(c)** *(in election, race, competition)* **he's an o.** no figura entre los favoritos

outsize(d) ['aʊtsaɪz(d)] *adj* **(a)** *(clothes)* de talla especial **(b)** *(appetite, ego)* desmedido(a)

outskirts ['aʊtskɜːts] *npl (of city)* afueras *fpl*; **we live on the o. of Copenhagen** vivimos en las afueras de Copenhague

outsmart [aʊt'smɑːt] *vt* superar en astucia, burlar

outsold *pt & pp of* **outsell**

outsource ['aʊtsɔːs] *vt Com (contract out)* externalizar, subcontratar, *Am* tercerizar; **equipment maintenance was outsourced to another company** el servicio de mantenimiento de los equipos se subcontrató *o Am* tercerizó a otra empresa

outsourcing ['aʊtsɔːsɪŋ] *n Com* externalización *f*, subcontratación *f*, *Am* tercerización *f*, *Am* terciarización *f*

outspend [aʊt'spend] *(pt & pp* **outspent** [aʊt'spent]) *vt* gastar más que

outspoken [aʊt'spəʊkən] *adj* directo(a), abierto(a); **to be o.** ser directo(a) *or* abierto(a); **she was o. in her criticism of the project** fue muy directa en sus críticas al proyecto

outspokenness [aʊt'spəʊkənnɪs] *n* franqueza *f*

outspread [aʊt'spred] *adj (arms, legs, wings)* extendido(a); **an o. newspaper** un periódico desplegado; **with arms o.** con los brazos extendidos

outstanding [aʊt'stændɪŋ] *adj* **(a)** *(remarkable) (feature, incident)* notable, destacado(a); *(ability, performance, person)* excepcional; **she plays o. tennis** juega un tenis excepcional *or* excelente
(b) *(to be dealt with)* pendiente; **there is one o. matter** hay un asunto *or* tema pendiente; **there are still about 20 pages o.** aún quedan de 20 páginas
(c) *Fin (amount, invoice, debt)* pendiente
(d) *St Exch (shares)* en circulación

outstandingly [aʊt'stændɪŋlɪ] *adv* extraordinariamente

outstare [aʊt'steə(r)] *vt* hacer bajar la mirada a

outstation ['aʊtsteɪʃən] *n (in colony, isolated region)* puesto *m*

outstay [aʊt'steɪ] *vt* **to o. one's welcome** abusar de la hospitalidad, quedarse más tiempo del apropiado

outstretched [aʊt'stretʃt] *adj* extendido(a), estirado(a); **to lie o.** estar estirado(a); **with o. arms, with arms o.** con los brazos extendidos; **he put a coin in the beggar's o. hand** puso una moneda en la mano extendida del mendigo

outstrip [aʊt'strɪp] *(pt & pp* **outstripped***) vt* **(a)** *(overtake)* superar, tomar la delantera a **(b)** *(surpass)* superar, aventajar; **they outstripped all their rivals** aventajaron a todos sus rivales

outta ['aʊtə] *Fam* = **out of**

outtake ['aʊtteɪk] *n Cin & TV* toma *f* falsa

outvote [aʊt'vəʊt] *vt* ganar en una votación; **the Republicans were outvoted** los republicanos perdieron la votación; **we want to go to the beach, so you're outvoted** nosotros queremos ir a la playa, así que somos mayoría y te ganamos

outward ['aʊtwəd] **1** *adj* **(a)** *(journey, flight)* de ida; **to be o. bound** *(plane, train)* hacer el viaje de ida ►► *Br* ***O. Bound course*** curso *m* de aventura **(b)** *(external)* externo(a); **she showed no o. signs of fear** no mostraba señales externas de temor ►► *Econ* ***o. investment*** inversión *f* en el exterior
2 *adv* = **outwards**

outwardly ['aʊtwədlɪ] *adv* en apariencia, aparentemente; **the two vehicles are not o. different** externamente, los dos vehículos no difieren; **o. calm** aparentemente tranquilo(a)

outwards ['aʊtwədz] *adv* hacia fuera; **the door opens o.** la puerta se abre hacia fuera

outwear [aʊt'weə(r)] *(pt* **outwore** [aʊt'wɔː(r)], *pp* **outworn** [aʊt'wɔːn]) *vt* **it has outworn its usefulness** ha dejado de ser útil

outweigh [aʊt'weɪ] *vt* **(a)** *(be more important than)* tener más peso que; **the cost of the scheme far outweighs any possible benefits** el *Esp* coste *or Am* costo del proyecto pesa *or* gravita más que cualquier posible beneficio **(b)** *(weigh more than)* pesar más que

outwit [aʊt'wɪt] *(pt & pp* **outwitted***) vt* ser más astuto(a) que, burlar; **we've been outwitted** nos han engañado

outwore *pt of* **outwear**

outwork ['aʊtwɜːk] *n* **(a)** *Com (work at home)* trabajo *m* en *or* desde casa **(b)** *(fortification)* fortificación *f* exterior

outworker ['aʊtwɜːkə(r)] *n Com* trabajador(ora) *m,f* a domicilio *or* externo(a)

outworn [aʊt'wɔːn] *adj (theories, ideas)* anticuado(a)

ouzo ['uːzəʊ] *(pl* **ouzos***) n* ouzo *m*

ova *pl of* **ovum**

oval ['əʊvəl] **1** *n* óvalo *m*
2 *adj* oval, ovalado(a) ►► *US* ***the O. Office*** el despacho oval

ovarian [əʊ'veərɪən] *adj Anat* ovárico(a) ►► ***o. cancer*** cáncer *m* de ovario; ***o. cyst*** quiste *m* ovárico

ovary ['əʊvərɪ] *n Anat* ovario *m*

ovation [əʊ'veɪʃən] *n* ovación *f*; **the audience gave her a standing o.** el público puesto en pie le dedicó una calurosa ovación

oven ['ʌvən] *n* horno *m*; **electric/gas o.** horno eléctrico/de gas; **cook in a hot/medium o.** cocinar en el horno a temperatura alta/media; IDIOM **it's like an o. in here!** ¡esto es un horno! ►► ***o. gloves*** manoplas *fpl* de cocina

ovenbird ['ʌvənbɜːd] *n* hornero *m*

ovenproof ['ʌvənpruːf] *adj* refractario(a)

oven-ready ['ʌvənredɪ] *adj (meat)* listo(a) para hornear

ovenware ['ʌvənweə(r)] *n* accesorios *mpl* para el horno

OVER ['əʊvə(r)] **1** *n (in cricket)* = serie de seis lanzamientos realizados por el mismo jugador
2 *prep* **(a)** *(above, on top of)* sobre, encima de, *Am* arriba de; **a sign o. the door** un cartel en la puerta; **to put a blanket o. sb** cubrir a alguien con una manta; **he hung his coat o. the back of a chair** colgó su abrigo en el respaldo de una silla; **I'll do it o. the sink** lo haré en *Esp, Méx* el lavabo *or RP* la pileta *or Col* el lavamanos; **to pour sth o. sb** verter algo sobre alguien, *Am* volcar algo encima de alguien; **the dress won't go o. my head** este vestido no me entra por la cabeza; **to trip o. sth** tropezar con algo; **I couldn't hear her o. the noise** no la oía por el ruido; **all o. Spain** por toda España; **all o. the world** por todo el mundo; **directly o. our heads** justo encima *or* arriba de nosotros; IDIOM *Fam* **to be all o. sb** *(over-attentive)* estar encima de alguien (todo el tiempo), colmar de atenciones a alguien; IDIOM **the lecture was way o. my head** no entendí *or* me enteré de nada de la conferencia; IDIOM *Fam* **o. the top** *(excessive)* exagerado(a)
(b) *(across)* **to go o. the road** cruzar la calle; **she jumped o. the fence** saltó la cerca *or* valla; **to throw sth o. the wall** tirar *or* lanzar *or Andes, CAm, Carib, Méx* botar algo por encima de la tapia; **to read o. sb's shoulder** leer por encima del hombro de alguien; **the bridge o. the river** el puente sobre el río; **a view o. the valley** una vista panorámica del valle
(c) *(on the other side of)* **o. the border** al *or Am* del otro lado de la frontera; **o. the page** en el reverso de la página, *Am* del otro lado de la página; **to live o. the road** vivir al *or Am* del otro lado de la calle
(d) *(down from)* **to fall o. a cliff** caer por *or* desde un acantilado
(e) *(via)* **o. the phone/PA system** por teléfono/megafonía
(f) *(about)* **to fight o. sth** pelear por algo; **to laugh o. sth** reírse de algo; **we had trouble o. the tickets** tuvimos problemas con las entradas *or Am* los boletos; **to take a lot of time o. sth** entretenerse *or Am* demorarse mucho con algo
(g) *(with regard to)* **to have control/influence o. sth/sb** tener control/influencia sobre algo/alguien; **to have an advantage o. sth/sb** tener ventaja sobre algo/alguien; **a win o. our nearest rivals** una victoria sobre nuestros rivales más cercanos
(h) *(in excess of)* más de; **he's o. fifty** tiene más de cincuenta años; **children o. (the age of) five** los niños mayores de cinco años; **he's two o. par** *(in golf)* está dos sobre par; **the o.-sixties** los mayores de sesenta años; **we are** *or* **have gone o. the limit** nos hemos pasado del límite; **we value reliability o. price** valoramos la fiabilidad *or Am* confiabilidad más que el precio; **o. and above** además de, más allá de
(i) *(during)* durante; **o. Christmas/the weekend** durante la Navidad/el fin de semana; **to discuss sth o. lunch/a drink** hablar de algo durante la comida/tomando una copa; **o. the last three years** (durante) los tres últimos años; **o. time/the years** con el tiempo/los años
(j) *(recovered from)* **I'm o. the flu/the disappointment** ya se me ha pasado la gripe *or Méx* gripa/la desilusión; **I'm still not o. her** *(ex-girlfriend)* no consigo olvidarla
(k) *Math (divided by)* por
3 *adv* **(a)** *(across)* **o. here/there** aquí/allí, *Am* acá/allá; **to cross o.** *(the street)* cruzar; **he led me o. to the window** me llevó hasta la ventana; **he leaned o.** se inclinó; **pass that book o.** pásame *or* acércame ese libro; **I asked him o. (to my house)** lo invité a mi casa; **they live o. in France** viven en Francia; **o. to our correspondent in Nairobi** pasamos a nuestro corresponsal en Nairobi
(b) *(down)* **to bend o.** agacharse; **to fall o.** caerse; **to push sth o.** tirar algo, *CSur* voltear algo
(c) *(indicating change of position)* **to turn sth o.** dar la vuelta a algo, *Am* dar vuelta algo; **let's swap my table and your table o.** cambiemos tu mesa por la mía; **to change o. to a new system** cambiar a un nuevo sistema
(d) *(everywhere)* **the marks had been painted o.** las marcas habían sido cubiertas con pintura; **it was stained all o.** tenía manchas por todas partes; **I'm aching all o.** me duele todo el cuerpo; **that's her all o.** *(typical of her)* es típico de ella; **famous the world o.** famoso(a) en el mundo entero
(e) *(indicating repetition)* **three times o.** tres veces; *US* **I had to do it o.** tuve que volver a hacerlo; **o. and o. (again)** una y otra vez; **all o. again** otra vez desde el principio
(f) *(in excess)* **children of five and o.** niños mayores de cinco años; **scores of eight and o.** puntuaciones de ocho para arriba; **he's two o.** *(in golf)* está dos sobre par; **there was $5 (left) o.** sobraron *or* quedaron 5 dólares; *Fam* **I wasn't o. happy about it** no estaba demasiado contento
4 *adj (finished)* **it is (all) o.** (todo) ha terminado; **when all this is o.** cuando todo esto haya pasado; **the danger is o.** ha pasado el peligro; **to get sth o. (and done) with** terminar algo (de una vez por todas)
5 *exclam (on radio)* **o. (and out)** cambio (y corto)

over- ['əʊvə(r)] *prefix* **(a)** *(excessively)* **o.-exact** más que preciso(a) **(b)** *(more than)* **a club for the o.-fifties** un club para los mayores de cincuenta

overabundance [əʊvərə'bʌndəns] *n* sobreabundancia *f*, exceso *m*

overabundant [əʊvərə'bʌndənt] *adj* sobreabundante

overachieve [əʊvərə'tʃi:v] *vi* **the pressure to o.** la presión para rendir más de lo normal

overachiever [əʊvərə'tʃi:və(r)] *n* = persona que rinde más de lo normal

overact [əʊvər'ækt] *vi* sobreactuar

overacting [əʊvər'æktɪŋ] *n* sobreactuación *f*

overactive [əʊvər'æktɪv] *adj (person, imagination)* hiperactivo(a); **to have an o. thyroid** tener *or* sufrir de hipertiroidismo

overage ['əʊvərɪdʒ] *n US (surplus)* excedente *m*

over-age ['əʊvər'eɪdʒ] *adj (too old)* demasiado mayor

overall ['əʊvərɔ:l] **1** *adj (cost, amount)* total; *(measurement)* total; **the o. winner** *(in sport)* el ganador en la clasificación general; **this model was the o. winner** *(in product comparison)* en general, este modelo resultó ser el ganador; **my o. impression was...** mi impresión general fue...; **she has o. responsibility for sales** es la responsable global de ventas ►► *Econ* ***o. demand*** demanda *f* total; *Pol* ***o. majority*** mayoría *f* absoluta

2 *n Br (protective coat)* sobretodo *m*

3 *adv* [əʊvər'ɔ:l] en general; **England came third o.** Inglaterra quedó tercera en la clasificación general; **o., we've been quite successful** en términos generales, hemos andado muy bien

overalls ['əʊvərɔ:lz] *npl* **(a)** *Br (boiler suit)* mono *m* (de trabajo), *Am* overol *m* **(b)** *(with bib)* peto *m*, *CSur* mameluco *m*

overambitious [əʊvəræm'bɪʃəs] *adj* demasiado ambicioso(a), excesivamente ambicioso(a)

overanxious [əʊvər'æŋkʃəs] *adj* excesivamente preocupado(a); **he didn't seem o. to meet her** su cita con ella no parecía preocuparle demasiado

overarching [əʊvər'ɑ:tʃɪŋ] *adj* global

overarm ['əʊvərɑ:m] **1** *adj (ball)* = lanzado con el brazo en alto

2 *adv* **to throw a ball o.** lanzar una bola soltándola con el brazo en alto

overate *pt of* **overeat**

overawe [əʊvər'ɔ:] *vt* intimidar, cohibir; **to be overawed by sth/sb** quedarse anonadado(a) por algo/alguien; **don't be overawed by her reputation** no te dejes intimidar *or* amedrentar por su reputación

overbalance [əʊvə'bæləns] *vi* perder el equilibrio

overbearing [əʊvə'beərɪŋ] *adj* imperioso(a), despótico(a)

overblown [əʊvə'bləʊn] *adj* **(a)** *(prose, style)* ampuloso(a) **(b)** *(flower)* demasiado abierto(a)

overboard ['əʊvəbɔ:d] *adv* por la borda; **to fall o.** caer por la borda, caer al agua; **to jump o.** saltar por la borda *or* al agua; **to throw sth/sb o.** arrojar algo/a alguien por la borda; *Fig* deshacerse de algo/alguien; **man o.!** ¡hombre al agua!; IDIOM **to go o. (about)** entusiasmarse mucho (con); **don't go o. with the food** no te pases con la comida

overbook ['əʊvə'bʊk] **1** *vt (flight, hotel)* = aceptar un número de reservas mayor que el de plazas disponibles; **they've overbooked this flight** este vuelo tiene overbooking

2 *vi (airline, hotel)* hacer overbooking, = vender más plazas de las disponibles

overbooking [əʊvə'bʊkɪŋ] *n* overbooking *m*, = venta de más plazas de las disponibles

overburden [əʊvə'bɜ:dən] *vt (donkey)* sobrecargar; **to o. sb with work** agobiar a alguien de trabajo; **he is not overburdened with moral scruples** los escrúpulos morales no le quitan el sueño demasiado

overcame *pt of* **overcome**

overcapitalize ['əʊvə'kæpɪtəlaɪz] *vt Fin* sobrecapitalizar

overcast ['əʊvəkɑ:st] *adj (sky, day)* nublado(a); **to be o.** estar nublado(a)

overcautious [əʊvə'kɔ:ʃəs] *adj* demasiado cauteloso(a)

overcharge [əʊvə'tʃɑ:dʒ] **1** *vt* **(a)** *(for goods, services)* **to o. sb (for sth)** cobrar de más a alguien (por algo); **he overcharged me (by) £5** me cobró cinco libras de más **(b)** *Elec (battery)* sobrecargar **(c)** *(description, picture)* recargar; **the painting was overcharged with detail** la pintura estaba recargada de detalles

2 *vi* **to o. (for sth)** cobrar de más (por algo)

overcoat ['əʊvəkəʊt] *n* abrigo *m*

overcome [əʊvə'kʌm] (*pt* **overcame** [əʊvə'keɪm], *pp* **overcome**) **1** *vt* **(a)** *(defeat) (an opponent, one's fears)* vencer; *(problem, obstacle, shyness, prejudice)* superar

(b) *(debilitate, weaken)* hacer flaquear, debilitar; **she was o. by the fumes** los gases la hicieron flaquear

(c) *(overwhelm)* **I was o. by** *or* **with grief** el dolor me abrumaba; **I was quite o.** estaba totalmente abrumado, me embargaba la emoción

2 *vi* **we shall o.** venceremos

overcompensate [əʊvə'kɒmpenseɪt] *vi* **to o. for sth** compensar algo en exceso

overcompensation [əʊvəkɒmpən'seɪʃən] *n* sobrecompensación *f*

overcomplicate [əʊvə'kɒmplɪkeɪt] *vt* complicar en exceso

overconfidence [əʊvə'kɒnfɪdəns] *n* exceso *m* de confianza

overconfident [əʊvə'kɒnfɪdənt] *adj* demasiado confiado(a); **I was put off by his o. manner** su excesiva seguridad me sentó mal; **I'm not o. of our chances of winning** no estoy muy convencido de que podamos ganar

overconsumption [əʊvəkən'sʌmpʃən] *n* excesivo consumo *m*, consumo *m* en exceso

overcook [əʊvə'kʊk] *vt* **the vegetables have been overcooked** las verduras se pasaron de cocción

overcrowded [əʊvə'kraʊdəd] *adj (slum, prison)* abarrotado(a), masificado(a); *(room)* atestado(a); *(bus, train)* repleto(a); *(city, region)* superpoblado(a); **they live in very o. conditions** viven hacinados; **the problem of o. classrooms** el problema de la masificación de las aulas; **Paris is o. with tourists in summer** en verano, París está atestado *or* repleto de turistas; **the painting is o. with detail** la pintura está recargada de detalles

overcrowding [əʊvə'kraʊdɪŋ] *n (of slums, prisons)* hacinamiento *m*; *(of classrooms)* masificación *f*; *(on bus, train)* lo repleto; *(of city, region)* superpoblación *f*

overdeveloped [əʊvədɪ'veləpt] *adj* **(a)** *(physique)* hiperdesarrollado(a) **(b)** *Phot* sobrerrevelado(a)

overdo [əʊvə'du:] (*pt* **overdid** [əʊvə'dɪd], *pp* **overdone** [əʊvə'dʌn]) *vt* **(a)** *(exaggerate)* exagerar; **he rather overdoes the penniless student bit** exagera un poco con eso de que es un estudiante *Esp* sin un duro *or Am* sin un peso; **to o. it** *(work too hard)* trabajar demasiado; **I've been overdoing it recently** me he pasado un poco últimamente; *Ironic* **don't o. it!** ¡no te vayas a herniar!

(b) *(do or have too much of)* pasarse con; **to o. the salt/the make-up** pasarse con la sal/el maquillaje

overdone [əʊvə'dʌn] *adj* **(a)** *(exaggerated)* exagerado(a) **(b)** *(food)* demasiado hecho(a), pasado(a)

overdose ['əʊvədəʊs] **1** *n* sobredosis *f inv*; **to take an o.** tomar una sobredosis; *Fig Hum* **I've had an o. of culture today** hoy me he llevado una sobredosis de cultura

2 *vi (drugs)* tomar una sobredosis (**on** de); *Fig* **to o. on chocolate** darse un atracón de chocolate

overdraft ['əʊvədrɑ:ft] *n Fin (amount borrowed)* descubierto *m*, saldo *m* negativo *or* deudor; **to arrange an o.** acordar un (límite de) descubierto; **the bank gave me a £500 o.** el banco me autorizó un descubierto de 500 libras ►► ***o. facility*** servicio *m* de descubierto; ***o. limit*** línea *f* de descubierto

overdramatic [əʊvədrə'mætɪk] *adj* demasiado dramático(a)

overdraw [əʊvə'drɔ:] (*pt* **overdrew** [əʊvə'dru:], *pp* **overdrawn** [əʊvə'drɔ:n]) *vt* **(a)** *Fin (account)* girar en descubierto **(b)** *(exaggerate)* sobreactuar, exagerar

overdrawn [əʊvə'drɔ:n] *adj* **(a)** *Fin (account)* en descubierto; **to be $230 o.** tener un descubierto de 230 dólares **(b)** *(exaggerated)* sobreactuado(a)

overdressed [əʊvə'drest] *adj* demasiado trajeado(a)

overdrew *pt of* **overdraw**

overdrive ['əʊvədraɪv] *n (in car)* superdirecta *f*; IDIOM **to go into o.** entregarse a una actividad frenética

overdue [əʊvə'dju:] *adj* **to be o.** *(person, train, flight)* retrasarse, venir con retraso *or Am* demora; *(library book)* haber rebasado el plazo de préstamo *or Méx* prestamiento; **the bill/rent is o.** la factura/el pago del alquiler ha vencido; **this measure is long o.** esta medida debía haberse adoptado hace tiempo; **the motorbike is o. for a service** la moto ya tendría que haber pasado una revisión; **the baby was two weeks o.** el bebé venía con dos semanas de retraso

overeager [əʊvər'i:gə(r)] *adj (person)* demasiado entusiasta; *(look)* demasiado ávido(a); **to be o. to do sth** tener muchas ganas de hacer algo; **he is o. to help** tiene muchas ganas de ayudar; **I can't say I'm o. to go** no es que me muera de ganas de ir

overeat [əʊvər'iːt] (*pt* **overate** [əʊvər'et], *pp* **overeaten** [əʊvər'iːtən]) *vi* comer demasiado

overegg ['əʊvər'eg] *vt Br* IDIOM **to o. the pudding** cargar *or* recargar las tintas

overelaborate ['əʊverɪ'læbərət] *adj (dress, style)* recargado(a); *(scheme, description)* enrevesado(a); *(excuse)* rebuscado(a)

overemotional [əʊvərɪ'məʊʃənəl] *adj* embargado(a) por la emoción; **an o. speech** un discurso cargado de muchísima emoción; **he got o.** estaba embargado por la emoción

overemphasis [əʊvər'emfəsɪs] *n* énfasis *m* exagerado

overemphasize [əʊvər'emfəsaɪz] *vt* hacer excesivo hincapié en, recalcar en exceso; **I cannot o. the need for discretion** no me canso de recalcar que se requiere discreción

overenthusiastic [əʊvərɪnθjuːzɪ'æstɪk] *adj* excesivamente entusiasta

overestimate 1 *n* [əʊvər'estɪmət] **an o. of the time necessary** un cálculo que sobreestima el tiempo necesario

2 *vt* [əʊvər'estɪmeɪt] sobreestimar; **he overestimates his own importance** se cree demasiado importante

overexaggerate [əʊvərɪg'zædʒəreɪt] *vt* exagerar demasiado

overexcited [əʊvərɪk'saɪtɪd] *adj* demasiado emocionado(a) *or* entusiasmado(a); **to become** *or* **get o.** emocionarse *or* entusiasmarse más de la cuenta

overexcitement [əʊvərɪk'saɪtmənt] *n* emoción *f* excesiva, entusiasmo *m* excesivo

overexert [əʊvərɪg'zɜːt] *vt* **to o. oneself** hacer un esfuerzo excesivo; *Ironic* **don't o. yourself!** ¡no te vayas a herniar!

overexertion [əʊvərɪg'zɜːʃən] *n* esfuerzo *m* excesivo

overexpose [əʊvərɪks'pəʊz] *vt* (**a**) *Phot* sobreexponer (**b**) *(issue, public figure)* **to be overexposed** aparecer demasiado en los medios de comunicación

overexposure ['əʊvərɪks'pəʊʒə(r)] *n* (**a**) *(of film)* sobreexposición *f* (**b**) *(of issue, public figure)* **to suffer from o.** aparecer demasiado en los medios de comunicación

overextended [əʊvərɪks'tendɪd] *adj Fin* insolvente, con alto grado de pasivo

overfamiliar [əʊvəfə'mɪlɪə(r)] *adj* (**a**) *(too intimate, disrespectful)* confianzudo(a); **to be o. with sb** ser demasiado confianzudo(a) con alguien, tomarse demasiadas libertades con alguien (**b**) *(conversant)* **I'm not o. with the system** no estoy muy familiarizado con el sistema

overfish [əʊvə'fɪʃ] **1** *vt* sobreexplotar los recursos pesqueros de

2 *vi* sobreexplotar los recursos pesqueros

overfishing [əʊvə'fɪʃɪŋ] *n* sobrepesca *f*

overflew *pt of* **overfly**

overflow 1 *n* ['əʊvəfləʊ] (**a**) *(excess) (of population)* exceso *m* de población; *(of energy, emotion)* derroche *m*, desbordamiento *m* ►► ***o. meeting*** = reunión organizada para aquéllos que no pudieron asistir a la reunión principal por falta de espacio (**b**) *(flooding)* desbordamiento *m* (**c**) *(outlet)* **o. (pipe)** rebosadero *m*, desagüe *m* (**d**) *Comptr* desbordamiento *m*

2 *vt* [əʊvə'fləʊ] desbordar; **the river overflowed its banks** el río se desbordó

3 *vi* (**a**) *(river)* desbordarse (**onto** sobre); *(liquid, cup, bath)* rebosar; *(with people) (room, streets)* desbordarse; *(with objects) (box, wastebin)* desbordarse; **the crowd overflowed into the side streets** la multitud se desbordó hacia las calles laterales; **the glass is full to overflowing** el vaso está que rebalsa (**b**) *(with emotion)* **to o. with joy** estar rebosante de felicidad

overfly [əʊvə'flaɪ] (*pt* **overflew** [əʊvə'fluː], *pp* **overflown** [əʊvə'fləʊn]) *vt* sobrevolar

overfond [əʊvə'fɒnd] *adj* **he's rather o. of the sound of his own voice** le gusta demasiado el sonido de su propia voz; **I'm not o. of oranges** no soy muy fanático de las naranjas; **she's not o. of children** no le gustan mucho los niños

overfull [əʊvə'fʊl] *adj* repleto(a), saturado(a)

overgenerous ['əʊvə'dʒenərəs] *adj (person, act)* exageradamente generoso(a); *(portion, estimate)* demasiado generoso(a); **your estimate was rather o.** tus cálculos eran demasiado optimistas; **he hadn't exactly been o. with the wine** no había sido muy generoso *or* espléndido que digamos con el vino

overground 1 *adj* ['əʊvəgraʊnd] de superficie; **an o. rail link** un enlace ferroviario de superficie

2 *adv* [əʊvə'graʊnd] por la superficie

overgrown [əʊvə'grəʊn] *adj* **o. with weeds** *(garden)* invadido(a) por las malas hierbas; **the wall was o. with ivy** la pared estaba toda cubierta de hiedra; **he's like an o. schoolboy** es como un niño grande

overhang 1 *n* ['əʊvəhæŋ] *(of roof)* alero *m*, voladizo *m*; *(on mountain)* saliente *m*

2 *vt* [əʊvə'hæŋ] (*pt & pp* **overhung** [əʊvə'hʌŋ]) *(of balcony, rocks)* colgar sobre

3 *vi* sobresalir

overhanging ['əʊvəhæŋɪŋ] *adj (ledge, balcony)* sobresaliente; **we walked under the o. branches** caminamos bajo las crecidas ramas de los árboles

overhaul 1 *n* ['əʊvəhɔːl] *(of machine, policy)* revisión *f*; **the education system needs a complete o.** es necesario hacer una revisión exhaustiva del sistema educativo

2 *vt* [əʊvə'hɔːl] (**a**) *(machine, policy)* revisar (**b**) *(overtake)* adelantar

overhead ['əʊvəhed] **1** *adj (cable)* aéreo(a) ►► ***o. projector*** retroproyector *m*, proyector *m* de transparencias; ***o. shot*** *Cin & TV* toma *f* aérea; *(in tennis, badminton)* smash *m*

2 *adv* [əʊvə'hed] (por) arriba; **a plane flew o.** un avión sobrevoló nuestras cabezas

3 *n* (**a**) *US Com* = **overheads** (**b**) *(in tennis, badminton)* smash *m*

overheads ['əʊvəhedz] *npl Br Com* gastos *mpl* generales

overhear [əʊvə'hɪə(r)] (*pt & pp* **overheard** [əʊvə'hɜːd]) *vt* oír *or* escuchar casualmente; **she overheard them talking about her** les oyó hablar sobre ella; **I couldn't help overhearing what you were saying** no pude evitar oír lo que decías

overheat [əʊvə'hiːt] **1** *vt (oven, room)* calentar demasiado; *(economy)* recalentar

2 *vi (engine, economy)* recalentarse

overheated [əʊvə'hiːtɪd] *adj* (**a**) *(engine, economy)* recalentado(a) (**b**) *(argument, person)* acalorado(a), agitado(a); **to become** *or* **get o.** acalorarse, agitarse

overhung *pt & pp of* **overhang**

overimpressed [əʊvərɪm'prest] *adj* **she wasn't o. by the film** la película no la impresionó demasiado

overindulge [əʊvərɪn'dʌldʒ] **1** *vt* (**a**) *(person)* consentir (**b**) **to o. oneself** *(drink, eat to excess)* atiborrarse, empacharse; **she overindulges her taste for melodrama** hace un uso excesivo del melodrama

2 *vi* atiborrarse, empacharse

overindulgence [əʊvərɪn'dʌldʒəns] *n* (**a**) *(towards person)* indulgencia *f* excesiva (**b**) *(in food and drink)* exceso *m*; **a lifetime of o.** una vida de excesos

overindulgent ['əʊvərɪn'dʌldʒənt] *adj* (**a**) *(towards person)* demasiado indulgente (**b**) *(in food and drink)* **an o. weekend** un fin de semana de excesos

overjoyed [əʊvə'dʒɔɪd] *adj* contentísimo(a); **to be o. at** *or* **about sth** estar contentísimo(a) con algo; **he was o. to hear that they were coming** le encantó saber que venían

overkeen [əʊvə'kiːn] *adj* **he wasn't o. on her** no estaba demasiado interesado en ella; **he wasn't o. on the idea** la idea no le entusiasmaba demasiado

overkill ['əʊvəkɪl] *n* **there's a danger of o.** se corre el peligro de caer en el exceso; **media o.** cobertura informativa exagerada

overladen [əʊvə'leɪdən] *adj* sobrecargado(a)

overlaid *pt & pp of* **overlay**

overlain *pp of* **overlie**

overland 1 *adj* ['əʊvəlænd] terrestre; **the o. route** la ruta por tierra

2 *adv* [əʊvə'lænd] por tierra

overlap 1 *n* ['əʊvəlæp] (**a**) *(of planks, tiles)* superposición *f*, solapamiento *m* (**b**) *(between two areas of work, knowledge)* coincidencia *f* (**c**) *(in time)* coincidencia *f (parcial)*, solapamiento *m*

2 *vt* [əʊvə'læp] (*pt & pp* **overlapped**) superponerse a, solaparse con; **the edges/tiles o. each other** los bordes/los azulejos están superpuestos entre sí

3 *vi* (**a**) *(planks, tiles)* superponerse, solaparse (**with** con) (**b**) *(categories, theories)* tener puntos en común (**with** con); **my responsibilities o. with hers** mis responsabilidades coinciden en algunos puntos con las de ella (**c**) *(periods of time)* coincidir *(parcialmente)* (**with** con); **our visits overlapped** nuestras visitas coincidieron

overlapping [əʊvə'læpɪŋ] *adj (planks, tiles)* superpuestos(as); *(responsibilities, holidays)* coincidentes *(parcialmente)*

overlay 1 *n* ['əʊvəleɪ] (**a**) *(cover)* capa *f*, revestimiento *m* (**b**) *Fig (tinge)* nota *f*

2 *vt* [əʊvə'leɪ] (*pt & pp* **overlaid** [əʊvə'leɪd]) (**a**) *(cover)* recubrir, revestir (**with** de) (**b**) *Fig (tinge)* teñir (**with** de)

3 *pt of* **overlie**

overleaf [əʊvə'liːf] *adv* al dorso; **see o.** véase al dorso

overlie [əʊvə'laɪ] *vt* (*pt* **overlay** [əʊvə'leɪ], *pp* **overlain** [əʊvə'leɪn]) recubrir

overload 1 *n* ['əʊvələʊd] *Elec* sobrecarga *f*; *Fig* **an o. of information** un exceso de información
2 *vt* [əʊvə'ləʊd] **(a)** *(animal, vehicle)* sobrecargar; **she's overloaded with work** está sobrecargada de trabajo **(b)** *(electric circuit, engine, machine)* sobrecargar

overlong [əʊvə'lɒŋ] **1** *adj* demasiado largo(a)
2 *adv* demasiado largo(a); **we didn't have to wait o.** no tuvimos que esperar demasiado (tiempo)

overlook [əʊvə'lʊk] *vt* **(a)** *(look out over)* dar a; **the town is overlooked by the castle** el castillo domina la ciudad
(b) *(fail to notice)* pasar por alto, no darse cuenta de; **it's easy to o. the small print** es fácil pasar por alto la letra pequeña; **you've overlooked the fact that it's more expensive in summer** no te has dado cuenta de que es más caro durante el verano
(c) *(disregard)* pasar por alto, no tener en cuenta; **I'll o. it this time** esta vez lo pasaré por alto

overlord ['əʊvəlɔːd] *n Hist* señor *m* feudal

overly ['əʊvəlɪ] *adv* excesivamente, demasiado; **not o.** no excesivamente, no demasiado

overmanned [əʊvə'mænd] *adj Ind (factory, production line)* con exceso de empleados

overmanning [əʊvə'mænɪŋ] *n Ind* exceso *m* de empleados

overmatch *US Sport* **1** *n* ['əʊvəmætʃ] **(a)** *(superior opponent)* contrincante *mf* superior **(b)** *(unequal contest)* encuentro *m* desigual
2 *vt* [əʊvə'mætʃ] **(a)** *(be more than a match for)* ser superior a **(b)** *(match with superior opponent)* enfrentar a un(a) contrincante superior

overmuch [əʊvə'mʌtʃ] **1** *adj* excesivo(a)
2 *adv* en exceso

overnice [əʊvə'naɪs] *adj (distinction)* demasiado meticuloso(a) *or* puntilloso(a); **he wasn't o. about the means he used** no tenía problema en usar cualquier medio

overnight 1 *adv* [əʊvə'naɪt] **(a)** *(during the night)* durante la noche, de noche; **to stay o.** quedarse a pasar la noche; **the milk won't keep o.** la leche no se conservará *or* aguantará hasta mañana **(b)** *(suddenly)* de la noche a la mañana, de un día para otro; **her hair went grey o.** de un día para otro se llenó de canas
2 *adj* ['əʊvənaɪt] **(a)** *(for one night)* de una noche ►► ***o. bag*** bolso *m* *or* bolsa *f* de viaje; ***o. case*** maletín *m* de fin de semana; ***o. flight*** vuelo *m* nocturno; ***o. stay*** *Esp, Méx* estancia *f* *or Am* estadía *f* de una noche; **we had an o. stay in Paris** nos quedamos una noche en París; ***o. train*** tren *m* nocturno
(b) *(sudden)* repentino(a); **there has been an o. improvement in the situation** la situación mejoró repentinamente

overoptimism [əʊvər'ɒptɪmɪzəm] *n* optimismo *m* excesivo

overoptimistic [əʊvərɒptɪ'mɪstɪk] *adj* demasiado optimista; **I'm not o. about their chances** no soy muy optimista acerca de sus posibilidades

overpaid [əʊvə'peɪd] **1** *adj* **to be o.** ganar demasiado (dinero), estar demasiado bien pagado(a)
2 *pt & pp of* **overpay**

overparticular [əʊvəpə'tɪkjʊlə(r)] *adj* **he's not o. about hygiene/telling the truth** la higiene/decir la verdad no le preocupa demasiado

overpass ['əʊvəpɑːs] *n US* paso *m* elevado

overpay [əʊvə'peɪ] (*pt & pp* **overpaid** [əʊvə'peɪd]) *vt (employee)* pagar en exceso a, pagar de más a

overpayment [əʊvə'peɪmənt] *n (of taxes, employee)* pago *m* excesivo

overplay [əʊvə'pleɪ] *vt (exaggerate)* exagerar; IDIOM **to o. one's hand: he overplayed his hand** se le fue la mano

overpopulation [əʊvəpɒpjʊ'leɪʃən] *n* superpoblación *f*

overpower [əʊvə'paʊə(r)] *vt* **(a)** *(physically)* doblegar; **the prisoners quickly overpowered their guards** los prisioneros rápidamente sometieron a sus guardianes **(b)** *(of heat, smell)* aturdir; **I was overpowered by grief** el dolor me abrumaba; **they were overpowered by his charm** su encanto los cautivó

overpowering [əʊvə'paʊərɪŋ] *adj (emotion, heat)* tremendo(a), desmesurado(a); *(smell, taste)* fortísimo(a), intensísimo(a); *(desire)* irrefrenable, irreprimible; **I find him o.** me parece amedrantador

overprice [əʊvə'praɪs] *vt* dar un precio excesivo a

overpriced [əʊvə'praɪst] *adj* excesivamente caro(a)

overprint 1 *n* ['əʊvəprɪnt] *Typ* sobreimpresión *f*; *(on postage stamp)* sobrecarga *f*
2 *vt* [əʊvə'prɪnt] *Typ* sobreimprimir

overproduce [əʊvəprə'djuːs] **1** *vt* producir en exceso
2 *vi Econ* producir en exceso

overproduction [əʊvəprə'dʌkʃən] *n Econ* superproducción *f*

overprotective [əʊvəprə'tektɪv] *adj* sobreprotector(a)

overqualified [əʊvə'kwɒlɪfaɪd] *adj* **to be o. (for a job)** tener más títulos de los necesarios (para un trabajo)

overran *pt of* **overrun**

overrate [əʊvə'reɪt] *vt* sobrevalorar

overrated [əʊvə'reɪtɪd] *adj* sobrevalorado(a); **he is rather o. as a novelist** como novelista está sobrevalorado

overreach [əʊvə'riːtʃ] *vt* **to o. oneself** extralimitarse

overreact [əʊvərɪ'ækt] *vi* reaccionar exageradamente; **I thought she overreacted to the news** me pareció que había reaccionado de una manera exagerada ante la noticia

overreaction [əʊvərɪ'ækʃən] *n* reacción *f* exagerada *or* excesiva; **punching him was a bit of an o.** darle un puñetazo fue una reacción un tanto exagerada

override 1 *vt* [əʊvə'raɪd] (*pt* **overrode** [əʊvə'rəʊd], *pp* **overridden** [əʊvə'rɪdən]) **(a)** *(objections, wishes, regulations)* hacer caso omiso de; *(decision, order)* anular, desestimar **(b)** *(take precedence over)* anteponerse a **(c)** *Tech (controls)* neutralizar
2 *n* ['əʊvəraɪd] *Tech* neutralización *f*; **there's a manual o.** hay *or* existe un mecanismo de neutralización manual

overriding [əʊvə'raɪdɪŋ] *adj (importance)* primordial; *(belief, consideration, factor)* preponderante

overripe [əʊvə'raɪp] *adj* **(a)** *(fruit)* pasado(a), demasiado maduro(a); *(cheese)* rancio(a) **(b)** *Fam (language, humour)* pasado(a)

overrode *pt of* **override**

overrule [əʊvə'ruːl] *vt* **(a)** *(opinion)* desautorizar; **she was overruled by her boss** su jefe la desautorizó **(b)** *Law (decision)* anular, invalidar; *(objection)* denegar

overrun 1 *n* ['əʊvərʌn] **(a)** *(in time)* **the meeting had a ten-minute o.** la reunión duró diez minutos más de lo previsto **(b)** *Com* **(cost) o.** costos *mpl or Esp* costes *mpl* superiores a los previstos; **(production) o.** excedente *m*
2 *vt* [əʊvə'rʌn] (*pt* **overran** [əʊvə'ræn], *pp* **overrun**) **(a)** *(country)* invadir; *(defences)* atravesar
(b) *(infest)* **the house was o. with mice** los ratones habían invadido la casa; **the garden is o. with weeds** la maleza ha invadido el jardín
(c) *(allotted time)* rebasar, excederse de; **to o. a budget** salirse del presupuesto
(d) *(overshoot)* **the plane overran the runway** el avión se salió de la pista; **to o. a signal** saltarse una señal
3 *vi (exceed allotted time)* alargarse más de la cuenta, rebasar el tiempo previsto

oversaw *pt of* **oversee**

overscrupulous [əʊvə'skruːpjʊləs] *adj (morally)* excesivamente escrupuloso(a)

overseas 1 *adj* ['əʊvəsiːz] *(visitor)* extranjero(a); *(trade, debt)* exterior; *(travel)* al extranjero; **we need more o. markets for our goods** necesitamos más mercados exteriores para nuestros productos ►► ***o. possessions*** territorios *mpl* de ultramar
2 *adv* [əʊvə'siːz] fuera del país; **to live o.** vivir en el extranjero; **he's just come back from o.** acaba de volver al país

oversee [əʊvə'siː] (*pt* **oversaw** [əʊvə'sɔː], *pp* **overseen** [əʊvə'siːn]) *vt* supervisar

overseer ['əʊvəsɪə(r)] *n Old-fashioned* capataz(a) *m,f*

oversell [əʊvə'sel] (*pt & pp* **oversold** [əʊvə'səʊld]) *vt* **(a)** *(sell more than can be supplied)* **the concert had been oversold** vendieron entradas *or Am* boletos para el concierto por encima de la capacidad de la sala **(b)** *(overpromote)* exagerar las ventajas de

oversensitive [əʊvə'sensɪtɪv] *adj (to criticism)* susceptible; **you're being o.!** ¡no seas tan susceptible!

oversexed [əʊvə'sekst] *adj* obsesionado(a) con el sexo; **he's o.** es un obseso sexual

overshadow [əʊvə'ʃædəʊ] *vt* **(a)** *(person, success)* eclipsar **(b)** *(occasion)* deslucir

overshoe ['əʊvəʃuː] *n* chanclo *m*

overshoot [əʊvə'ʃuːt] (*pt & pp* **overshot** [əʊvə'ʃɒt]) *vt (platform, turning, target)* pasar (de largo); **to o. the runway** salirse de la pista

oversight ['əʊvəsaɪt] *n* **(a)** *(error)* descuido *m*, omisión *f*; **through** *or* **by** *or* **due to an o.** por descuido **(b)** *(supervision)* supervisión *f* ►► ***o. committee*** comisión *f* de control

oversimplification ['əʊvəsɪmplɪfɪ'keɪʃən] *n* simplificación *f* excesiva

oversimplify [əʊvəˈsɪmplɪfaɪ] *vt* simplificar en exceso

oversize(d) [ˈəʊvəsaɪz(d)] *adj* (**a**) *(very big)* enorme (**b**) *(too big)* descomunal

oversleep [əʊvəˈsliːp] *(pt & pp* **overslept** [əʊvəˈslept]) *vi* quedarse dormido(a)

oversleeve [ˈəʊvəsliːv] *n* manguito *m*

oversold *pt & pp of* **oversell**

overspend 1 *vt* [əʊvəˈspend] *(pt & pp* **overspent** [əʊvəˈspent]) **to o. one's budget** salirse del presupuesto
2 *vi* gastar de más; **to o. by $100** gastar cien dólares de más
3 *n* [ˈəʊvəspend] déficit *m* presupuestario

overspending [əʊvəˈspendɪŋ] *n* gasto *m* superior al previsto

overspill [ˈəʊvəspɪl] *n esp Br (of population)* exceso *m* de población *(urbana)*

overstaffed [əʊvəˈstɑːft] *adj* con exceso de personal; **the firm is o.** la compañía tiene un exceso de personal

overstaffing [əʊvəˈstɑːfɪŋ] *n* exceso *m* de personal

overstate [əʊvəˈsteɪt] *vt* exagerar; **I think he has overstated his case** me parece que ha exagerado un poco sus argumentos

overstatement [əʊvəˈsteɪtmənt] *n* exageración *f*

overstay [əʊvəˈsteɪ] *vt* **to o. one's welcome** abusar de la hospitalidad, quedarse más tiempo del apropiado

oversteer [əʊvəˈstɪə(r)] *vi (car)* girar demasiado

overstep [əʊvəˈstep] *(pt & pp* **overstepped**) *vt* traspasar, saltarse; IDIOM **to o. the mark** *(exceed one's powers)* pasarse de la raya

overstock [əʊvəˈstɒk] *vt (warehouse, shop)* **to be overstocked with sth** tener exceso (de existencias) de algo

overstretched [əʊvəˈstretʃt] *adj* **our resources are already o.** nuestros recursos no dan más de sí

overstrung [əʊvəˈstrʌŋ] *adj (person)* tenso(a)

oversubscribed [əʊvəsəbˈskraɪbd] *adj* **the school trip is o.** el número de inscritos en el viaje escolar excede la capacidad existente; *St Exch* **the share offer was (five times) o.** la demanda superó (en cinco veces) la oferta de venta de acciones

overt [əʊˈvɜːt] *adj* ostensible, manifiesto(a); **do you have to be so o. about it?** ¿tienes que mostrarlo tan a las claras?

overtake [əʊvəˈteɪk] *(pt* **overtook** [əʊvəˈtʊk], *pp* **overtaken** [əʊvəˈteɪkən]) 1 *vt* (**a**) *(pass beyond) (car)* adelantar; *(competitor in race)* rebasar; **China has overtaken France as the main exporter of these products** China ha arrebatado a Francia el primer lugar en la exportación de estos productos
(**b**) *(surprise)* **they had been overtaken by events** se habían visto superados por los acontecimientos
2 *vi Br (in car)* adelantar

overtax [əʊvəˈtæks] *vt* (**a**) *(overstrain)* exigir demasiado de; **to o. sb's patience** poner a prueba la paciencia de alguien; *Hum* **don't o. his brain!** no le exijas tanto que le va a salir humo de la cabeza (**b**) *(tax excessively)* gravar en exceso, cobrar más impuestos de los debidos

over-the-counter [ˈəʊvəðəˈkaʊntə(r)] 1 *adj (medicine)* sin receta
2 *adv* sin receta

overthrow 1 *n* [ˈəʊvəθrəʊ] derrocamiento *m*
2 *vt* [əʊvəˈθrəʊ] *(pt* **overthrew** [əʊvəˈθruː], *pp* **overthrown** [əʊvəˈθrəʊn]) derrocar

overtime [ˈəʊvətaɪm] 1 *n* (**a**) *(work)* horas *fpl* extraordinarias *or* extras; **to do o.** hacer horas extras ►► ***o. ban*** prohibición *f* de trabajar horas extras (**b**) *(overtime pay)* horas *fpl* extras; **to be paid o.** cobrar horas extra (**c**) *(in basketball, American football)* prórroga *f*; **the game has gone into o.** se está jugando tiempo adicional *or* la prórroga
2 *adv* (**a**) *Ind* **to work o.** hacer horas extras (**b**) *Fig* **your imagination is working o.** se te está disparando la imaginación

overtire [əʊvəˈtaɪə(r)] *vt (person)* agotar *or* cansar en exceso; **to o. oneself** agotarse en exceso

overtired [əʊvəˈtaɪəd] *adj* demasiado cansado(a), agotado(a)

overtly [əʊˈvɜːtlɪ] *adv* abiertamente, claramente

overtone [ˈəʊvətəʊn] *n* (**a**) *(of sadness, bitterness)* tinte *m*, matiz *m* (**b**) *Mus* armónico *m*

overtook *pt of* **overtake**

overture [ˈəʊvətjʊə(r)] *n* (**a**) *Mus* obertura *f* (**b**) *(proposal)* **to make overtures to sb** *(in business)* tener contactos con alguien; *(sexually)* hacer proposiciones a alguien; **diplomatic overtures** acercamientos *mpl* diplomáticos (**c**) *(prelude)* preludio *m*

overturn [əʊvəˈtɜːn] 1 *vt* (**a**) *(table, boat, car)* volcar (**b**) *(government)* derribar (**c**) *(legal decision)* rechazar
2 *vi (boat, car)* volcar

overuse 1 *n* [əʊvəˈjuːs] uso *m* excesivo, abuso *m*
2 *vt* [əʊvəˈjuːz] abusar de

overused [əʊvəˈjuːzd] *adj (expression, excuse)* muy usado(a) *or* viejo(a)

overvaluation [əʊvəvæljuːˈeɪʃən] *n (of currency, house, painting)* sobrevaloración *f*

overvalue [əʊvəˈvæljuː] *vt* (**a**) *(currency, house, painting)* sobrevalorar (**b**) *(person's abilities)* sobreestimar

overview [ˈəʊvəvjuː] *n* visión *f* general

overwater [əʊvəˈwɔːtə(r)] *vt (plant)* regar demasiado

overweening [əʊvəˈwiːnɪŋ] *adj (person)* arrogante; **o. pride** orgullo desmedido; **o. ambition** ambición desmesurada

overweight [əʊvəˈweɪt] *adj* (**a**) *(person)* con sobrepeso, con kilos de más; **to be o.** tener exceso de peso; **to be 10 kilos o.** tener 10 kilos de más (**b**) *(luggage, parcel)* **this suitcase is two kilos o.** esta maleta tiene un exceso de peso de dos kilos

overwhelm [əʊvəˈwelm] *vt* (**a**) *(defeat) (enemy, opponent)* arrollar
(**b**) *(with emotion)* abrumar; **to be overwhelmed with joy** no caber en sí de alegría; **overwhelmed by grief/with work** abrumado(a) por la pena/por el trabajo; **I was quite overwhelmed by his generosity** su generosidad me embargaba
(**c**) *(inundate)* inundar de, llenar de; **our switchboard has been overwhelmed by the number of calls** la cantidad de llamadas recibidas ha saturado *Esp* la centralita *or Am* el conmutador; **I'm completely overwhelmed with work** estoy abrumado por el trabajo

overwhelming [əʊvəˈwelmɪŋ] *adj* (**a**) *(massive) (defeat, majority)* arrollador(ora), aplastante; **in o. numbers** en cantidades abrumadoras (**b**) *(powerful) (need, desire)* acuciante; *(grief, joy)* irrefrenable; *(pressure)* abrumador(ora); **his friendliness is a bit o.** sus muestras de afecto son un tanto abrumadoras

overwhelmingly [əʊvəˈwelmɪŋlɪ] *adv* (**a**) *(massively) (to defeat)* arrolladoramente, aplastantemente; **to vote o. in favour of sth** aprobar algo por mayoría aplastante (**b**) *(as intensifier)* abrumadoramente, extremadamente

overwind [əʊvəˈwaɪnd] *(pt & pp* **overwound** [əʊvəˈwaʊnd]) *vt (clock, watch)* dar demasiada cuerda a

overwork [əʊvəˈwɜːk] 1 *n* exceso *m* de trabajo
2 *vt* (**a**) *(person)* hacer trabajar en exceso (**b**) *(expression)* **it's one of the most overworked phrases in the English language** es una de las frases más trilladas de la lengua inglesa
3 *vi* trabajar en exceso

overwound *pt & pp of* **overwind**

overwrite 1 *n* [ˈəʊvəraɪt] *Comptr* ***o. mode*** función *f* de "sobreescribir"
2 *vt* [əʊvəˈraɪt] (**a**) *(write on top)* sobreescribir (**b**) *Comptr (file, data)* sobreescribir
3 *vi* escribir con estilo recargado

overwritten [əʊvəˈrɪtən] *adj (book, passage)* recargado(a)

overwrought [əʊvəˈrɔːt] *adj* (**a**) *(person)* muy alterado(a), muy nervioso(a); **to get o. (about sth)** alterarse mucho (por algo) (**b**) *(style)* recargado(a)

overzealous [əʊvəˈzeləs] *adj* demasiado celoso(a)

Ovid [ˈɒvɪd] *pr n* Ovidio

oviduct [ˈɒvɪdʌkt] *n Anat & Zool* oviducto *m*

ovine [ˈəʊvaɪn] *adj* ovino(a)

oviparous [əʊˈvɪpərəs] *adj Zool* ovíparo(a)

ovipositor [əʊvɪˈpɒzɪtə(r)] *n Zool* órgano *m* ovipositor

ovoid [ˈəʊvɔɪd] *adj* ovoide

ovulate [ˈɒvjʊleɪt] *vi Biol* ovular

ovulation [ɒvjʊˈleɪʃən] *n Biol* ovulación *f*

ovum [ˈəʊvəm] *(pl* **ova** [ˈəʊvə]) *n Biol* óvulo *m*

ow [aʊ] *exclam* ¡ay!

owe [əʊ] 1 *vt* (**a**) *(money)* deber; **to o. sb sth, to o. sth to sb** deber algo a alguien; **how much** *or* **what do I o. (you) for the food?** ¿qué *or* cuánto te debo por la comida?; **I still o. you for the petrol** aún te debo dinero *or Am* plata por la gasolina; **how much do we still o. on the house?** ¿cuánto nos queda por pagar de la hipoteca?
(**b**) *(debt of obligation)* deber; **to o. sb an apology** deber disculpas a alguien; **I think you o. him an explanation** creo que le debes una disculpa; **to o. sb a favour** deberle a alguien un favor; **to o. it to oneself to do sth** tener(se) merecido hacer algo, *Am* ameritar hacer algo; **he thinks the world owes him a living** cree que la vida está en deuda con él; **I o. you one!** ¡te debo una! (**c**) *(can thank for)* deber; **I o. my life to you** te debo la vida; **he owes it all to his parents** se lo debe todo a sus padres; **her work owes much to Faulkner** su obra debe

mucho a Faulkner; **we o. this discovery to a lucky accident** debemos este descubrimiento a una casualidad; **to what do we o. the honour of your visit?** ¿a qué debemos el honor de tu visita?
2 *vi* deber

owing ['əʊɪŋ] 1 *adj (due)* **the money o. to me** el dinero que se me adeuda
2 **owing to** *prep (because of)* debido(a) a

owl [aʊl] *n* búho *m, CAm, Méx* tecolote *m;* **(barn) o.** lechuza *f* ▸▸ ***white-faced o.*** autillo *m* cariblanco

owlet ['aʊlɪt] *n* lechuza *f* joven

owlish ['aʊlɪʃ] *adj* **to look o.** tener aspecto de estudioso(a)

OWN [əʊn] 1 *adj* propio(a); **her o. money** su propio dinero; **I saw it with my o. eyes** lo vi con mis propios ojos; **I do my o. accounts** llevo mi propia contabilidad; **you'll have to clean your o. room** tendrás que limpiarte tú la habitación; **I can make my o. mind up** puedo decidirme por mí mismo, puedo decidir yo solo; **it's his o. fault** la culpa es toda suya; **my o. opinion is...** personalmente opino que...; **I'm my o. man** soy dueño de mí mismo; **in one's o. right** por derecho propio; **do it in your o. time** hazlo en tu tiempo libre; **do it your o. way, then!** ¡hazlo como prefieras!; *Br Com* **o. brand** *or* **label** del establecimiento ▸▸ *Br Com* ***o. brand product*** producto *m* de marca blanca; ***o. goal*** *(in soccer)* autogol *m*, gol *m* en propia meta *or Esp* puerta *or Am* propio arco, *RP* gol *m* en contra; *Fig* **to score an o. goal** meter la pata; *Br Com* ***o. label product*** producto *m* de marca blanca
2 *pron* **(a)** *(of possession)* **my o.** *(singular)* el/la mío(a); *(plural)* los/las míos(as); **your o.** *(singular)* el/la tuyo(a); *(plural)* los/las tuyos(as); **his/her/its o.** *(singular)* el/la suyo(a); *(plural)* los/las suyos(as); **our o.** *(singular)* el/la nuestro(a); *(plural)* los/las nuestros(as); **their o.** *(singular)* el/la suyo(a); *(plural)* los/las suyos(as); **it's my o.** es mío(a); **I have money of my o.** tengo dinero propio *or Am* mío; **a child of his o.** un hijo suyo; **she has a copy of her o.** tiene un ejemplar para ella; **I have enough problems of my o.** ya tengo yo suficientes problemas; **for reasons of his o.** por razones privadas; **he made that expression/part his o.** hizo suya esa expresión/suyo ese papel
(b) IDIOMS **to do sth (all) on one's o.** *(without company)* hacer algo solo(a); *(on one's own initiative)* hacer algo por cuenta propia; **I am (all) on my o.** estoy solo; **you're on your o.!** *(I won't support you)* ¡conmigo no cuentes!; **he has come into his o. since being promoted** desde que lo ascendieron ha demostrado su verdadera valía *or* sus verdaderas posibilidades; **to get one's o. back (on sb)** vengarse (de alguien), tomarse la revancha (contra alguien); **she managed to hold her o.** consiguió defenderse; **he looks after his o.** cuida de los suyos
3 *vt* **(a)** *(property)* poseer; **who owns this land?** ¿de quién es esta tierra?, ¿quién es el propietario de esta tierra?; **I o. two bicycles** tengo dos bicicletas; **do you o. your house or is it rented?** ¿la casa es tuya o la alquilas *or Méx* rentas?; **to be owned by sb** pertenecer a alguien; **he behaves as if he owns** *or* **acts like he owns the place** se comporta como si fuera el dueño
(b) *(admit) Old-fashioned* **to o. (that)...** reconocer que...
▸ **own to** *vt insep Old-fashioned* reconocer
▸ **own up** *vi (confess)* **to o. up (to sth)** confesar (algo)

owner ['əʊnə(r)] *n* dueño(a) *m,f*, propietario(a) *m,f*; **who is the o. of this jacket?** ¿quién es el dueño de esta chaqueta?, ¿de quién es esta chaqueta?; **cars parked here at owners' risk** *(sign)* estacionamiento *or Esp* aparcamiento permitido bajo responsabilidad del propietario

owner-occupier ['əʊnər'ɒkjʊpaɪə(r)] *n Br* propietario(a) *m,f* de la vivienda que habita

ownership ['əʊnəʃɪp] *n* propiedad *f*; **under new o.** *(sign)* nuevos propietarios; **to be in private/public o.** ser de propiedad privada/pública; **the o. of the land is contested** la propiedad de la tierra está en disputa; **change of o.** cambio de propietario *or* dueño

ownsome ['əʊnsəm], **owny-o** ['əʊnɪəʊ] *n Br Fam Hum* **(all) on one's o.** más sólo(a) que la una, más sólo(a) que Adán en el día de la madre

owt [aʊt] *pron Br Fam (anything)* algo; **he never said o.** nunca dijo nada; **is there o. the matter?** ¿qué pasa?

ox [ɒks] *(pl* **oxen** ['ɒksən]) *n* buey *m*

oxblood ['ɒksblʌd] 1 *n (colour)* granate *m*, color *m* vino
2 *adj* granate, color vino

oxbow ['ɒksbəʊ] *n Geog* **o. (lake)** = lago formado al quedar un meandro aislado del río

Oxbridge ['ɒksbrɪdʒ] *n* = las universidades de Oxford y Cambridge

oxen *pl of* **ox**

OXFAM ['ɒksfæm] *n Br* OXFAM, = organización caritativa benéfica de ayuda al desarrollo ▸▸ ***O. shop*** = tienda que vende objetos de segunda mano con fines benéficos

Oxford ['ɒksfəd] *n US* **O. (shoe)** zapato *m* de cordones

oxidant ['ɒksɪdənt] *n* **(a)** *Chem* oxidante *m* **(b)** *(in fuel)* oxidante *m*

oxidase ['ɒksɪdeɪz] *n Biochem* oxidasa *f*

oxidation [ɒksɪ'deɪʃən] *n Chem* oxidación *f*

oxidation-reduction [ɒksɪ'deɪʃənrɪ'dʌkʃən] *n Chem* oxidación-reducción *f*

oxide ['ɒksaɪd] *n Chem* óxido *m*

oxidization [ɒksɪdaɪ'zeɪʃən] *n Chem* oxidación *f*

oxidize ['ɒksɪdaɪz] *Chem* 1 *vt* oxidar
2 *vi* oxidarse

oxidizing agent ['ɒksɪdaɪzɪŋ'eɪdʒənt] *n Chem* agente *m* oxidante, oxidante *m*

oxlip ['ɒkslɪp] *n* primavera *f*, prímula *f*

Oxon. ['ɒksən] *n* **(a)** *(abbr* **Oxfordshire)** Oxfordshire **(b)** *(abbr* **Oxford)** *(in degree titles)* = abreviatura que indica que un título fue obtenido en la universidad de Oxford

oxtail ['ɒksteɪl] *n* rabo *m* de buey ▸▸ ***o. soup*** sopa *f* de rabo de buey

oxyacetylene ['ɒksɪə'setɪliːn] *n Chem* oxiacetileno *m* ▸▸ ***o. torch*** soplete *m* (oxiacetilénico)

oxygen ['ɒksɪdʒən] *n Chem* oxígeno *m* ▸▸ ***o. bar*** bar *m* de oxígeno; ***o. bottle*** *or* ***cylinder*** botella *f or* bombona *f* de oxígeno; ***o. mask*** mascara *f* de oxígeno; *Med* ***o. tent*** tienda *f or Am* carpa *f* de oxígeno

oxygenate ['ɒksɪdʒəneɪt] *vt Chem & Physiol* oxigenar

oxygenated ['ɒksɪdʒəneɪtɪd] *adj Chem & Physiol* oxigenado(a)

oxygenation [ɒksɪdʒə'neɪʃən] *n Chem & Physiol* oxigenación *f*

oxymoron [ɒksɪ'mɔːrɒn] *n* oxímoron *m*, = figura del lenguaje consistente en yuxtaponer dos palabras aparentemente contradictorias

oyez [əʊ'jes] *exclam Archaic* ¡atención!

oyster ['ɔɪstə(r)] *n* **(a)** *(shellfish)* ostra *f*; IDIOM **the world is your o.** el mundo es tuyo, te vas a comer el mundo ▸▸ ***o. bed*** criadero *m* de ostras; ***o. mushroom*** seta *f or Méx, CSur* hongo *m* de cardo **(b)** *(colour)* color *m* perla ▸▸ ***o. pink*** rosa *m* perla; ***o. white*** blanco *m* perla

oystercatcher ['ɔɪstəkætʃə(r)] *n (bird)* ostrero *m*

Oz [ɒz] *n Fam* Australia

oz *(abbr* **ounce(s))** onza(s) *f(pl)*

ozone ['əʊzəʊn] *n* **(a)** *(gas)* ozono *m* ▸▸ ***o. depletion*** degradación *f* de la capa de ozono; ***o. hole*** agujero *m* en la capa de ozono; ***o. layer*** capa *f* de ozono **(b)** *Fam (sea air)* aire *m* fresco

ozone-friendly ['əʊzəʊn'frendlɪ] *adj* no perjudicial para la capa de ozono

Ozzie ['ɒzɪ] *n Fam* australiano(a) *m*

P, p

P, p [piː] *n (letter)* P, p *f*; *Fam* **to mind one's P's and Q's** comportarse (con educación)

p [piː] *n Br* **(a)** (*abbr* **penny**) penique *m* **(b)** (*abbr* **pence**) peniques *mpl* **(c)** (*abbr* **page**) (*pl* **pp**) pág.

P45 ['piːfɔːtɪ'faɪv] *n Br* = impreso oficial que se entrega a la persona que deja un trabajo; IDIOM **to be handed one's P.** ser despedido(a)

PA [piː'eɪ] *n* **(a)** (*abbr* **public address**) megafonía *f*; **a message came over the PA (system)** dieron un mensaje por megafonía **(b)** *Com* (*abbr* **personal assistant**) secretario(a) *m,f* personal **(c)** (*abbr* **Pennsylvania**) Pensilvania

pa [pɑː] *n Fam (dad)* papá *m*

p.a. (*abbr* **per annum**) anual, al año

PAC [piːeɪ'siː] *n US Pol* (*abbr* **Political Action Committee**) = grupo de presión estadounidense para el apoyo de causas políticas

paca ['pɑːkə] *n* paca *m*

pace[1] [peɪs] **1** *n* **(a)** *(step)* paso *m*; **take two paces to the left** da dos pasos a la izquierda; **to put a horse through its paces** ejercitar un caballo; IDIOM **to put sb through his paces** poner a alguien a prueba; IDIOM **he showed his paces** demostró lo que es capaz de hacer
(b) *also Fig (speed)* ritmo *m*, paso *m*; **the slower p. of country life** el ritmo más lento de la vida del campo; **at a slow p.** lentamente; **at a fast p.** rápidamente; **do the test at your own p.** haz la prueba a tu propio ritmo; **to slacken/quicken one's p.** aflojar/aligerar *or* apurar el paso; **to force the p.** forzar el ritmo; **to keep p. with sb** seguir el ritmo de alguien; **our incomes haven't kept p. with inflation** nuestros ingresos no han aumentado al mismo ritmo que la inflación; **it's all happened so fast I can barely keep p. with it** todo ha sucedido tan rápido que apenas puedo seguirle el ritmo; **to set the p.** marcar el paso, imponer el ritmo; **to stand** *or* **take the p.** aguantar *or* seguir el ritmo ►► ***p. car*** *(in motor racing)* coche *m* de los jueces, *Arg* pace car *m*
2 *vt* **(a)** *(room, street)* caminar por; **the tiger paced its cage** el tigre recorría los límites de su jaula **(b)** *(regulate speed of)* regular el ritmo de; **the action is well paced** la trama tiene un buen ritmo; **to p. oneself** controlar el ritmo
3 *vi* caminar; **to p. up and down** caminar de un lado a otro

► **pace about** *vi* caminar de un lado a otro

► **pace off, pace out** *vt sep* medir a pasos

pace[2] ['pɑːtʃeɪ] *prep Formal* con el debido respeto a

pacemaker ['peɪsmeɪkə(r)] *n* **(a)** *Sport* liebre *f* **(b)** *(for heart)* marcapasos *m inv*

pacesetter ['peɪssetə(r)] *n* **(a)** *(in race)* liebre *f* **(b)** *Fig (in competitive field)* líder *mf*

pac(e)y ['peɪsɪ] *adj* rápido(a)

pachyderm ['pækɪdɜːm] *n* paquidermo *m*

Pacific [pə'sɪfɪk] **1** *n* **the P.** el Pacífico
2 *adj* ***the P. Ocean*** el océano Pacífico; ***the P. Rim*** = los países que bordean el Pacífico, sobre todo los asiáticos; *US* ***P. Standard Time*** = hora oficial de la costa del Pacífico en Estados Unidos

pacific [pə'sɪfɪk] *adj Formal* pacífico(a)

pacification [pæsɪfɪ'keɪʃən] *n* **(a)** *(of anger, person)* apaciguamiento *m* **(b)** *(of country)* pacificación *f*

pacifier ['pæsɪfaɪə(r)] *n US (for baby)* chupete *m*

pacifism ['pæsɪfɪzəm] *n* pacifismo *m*

pacifist ['pæsɪfɪst] **1** *n* pacifista *mf*
2 *adj* pacifista

pacify ['pæsɪfaɪ] *vt* **(a)** *(person, anger)* apaciguar **(b)** *(country)* pacificar

pack [pæk] **1** *n* **(a)** *(rucksack)* mochila *f*; *(on animal)* costal *m* ►► ***p. animal*** bestia *f* de carga; *Mil* ***p. drill*** ejercicio *m* con carga; IDIOM **no names, no p. drill** no voy a dar nombres
(b) *(small box) (of cigarettes)* paquete *m*; *Br* **a p. of washing powder** un paquete de jabón en polvo
(c) *(set of equipment)* equipo *m*; *(materials)* paquete *m*
(d) *Br (of playing cards)* baraja *f*
(e) *(group) (of thieves, photographers)* pandilla *f*; *(of cub scouts)* manada *f*; *(of runners, cyclists)* pelotón *m*; *(of wolves)* manada *f*; *(of hunting hounds)* jauría *f*; **a p. of fools** una panda de imbéciles; **a p. of lies** una sarta de mentiras ►► ***p. ice*** banco *m* de hielo
(f) *(in rugby)* delanteros *mpl*
(g) *(in snooker)* = grupo de bolas rojas agrupadas en forma de triángulo
2 *vt* **(a)** *(put into box)* empaquetar; *(items for sale)* envasar; *(in cotton wool, newspaper)* envolver; **the equipment is packed in polystyrene chips** el equipo está embalado con bolitas de poliestireno; **did you p. my toothbrush?** ¿metiste mi cepillo de dientes (en la maleta)?
(b) *(fill) (hole, box)* llenar (**with** de); **to p. one's suitcase** hacer la maleta *or Am* valija; *Fig* **to p. one's bags** *(leave)* hacer las maletas *or Am* valijas; **we're not packed** aún no hemos hecho las maletas *or Am* no hicimos las valijas
(c) *(crowd into) (of spectators, passengers)* atestar, abarrotar
(d) *(cram) (earth into hole)* meter; *(passengers into bus, train)* apiñar; **the book is packed with helpful information** el libro está repleto de información útil; *Fig* **we managed to p. a lot into a week's holiday** en una semana de vacaciones conseguimos hacer un montón de cosas; *Theat* **she packs the house every night** llena la sala todas las noches
(e) *(compress) (soil, snow)* apisonar
(f) *(rig)* **to p. a jury** influir indirectamente sobre las decisiones de un jurado; **to p. a meeting** llenar una sala de reuniones con los propios seguidores
(g) *(wield)* ejercer; **he packs a lot of influence in cabinet** ejerce una gran influencia en el gabinete; **to p. a punch** *(fighter, drink)* pegar duro
(h) *Fam* **to p. a gun** llevar una pistola
(i) *Comptr (database)* compactar
3 *vi* **(a)** *(prepare luggage)* hacer el equipaje; IDIOM *Fam* **to send sb packing** *(send away)* mandar a alguien a freír churros *or* a paseo **(b)** *(fit) (into container)* caber, entrar **(c)** *(cram)* **to p. into a room** apiñarse en una habitación; **we all packed into the van** nos apiñamos todos dentro de la camioneta

► **pack away 1** *vt sep* **(a)** *(tidy up)* guardar; *(bed)* guardar **(b)** *Fam (eat)* comer, *Arg* manducar; **he can really p. it away!** ¡cómo come *or Arg* lastra!
2 *vi (bed, table)* guardarse

► **pack down 1** *vt sep (soil, snow)* apisonar
2 *vi (in rugby)* formar *Esp* la melé *or Am* el scrum

► **pack in** *Fam* **1** *vt sep* **(a)** *(give up) (job, course)* dejar; **you should p. in smoking** deberías dejar de fumar *or Arg* cortar con el pucho; **p. it in!** *(stop complaining)* ¡deja de protestar *or* de dar la murga!
(b) *(cram in)* **I couldn't p. anything more in** no me entra nada más; **they packed in a lot of sightseeing on their short trip** metieron un montón de visitas turísticas en el corto viaje que hicieron; **we were packed in like sardines** estábamos como sardinas en lata; **to p. the crowds in** atraer a las masas; **the play is packing them in** la obra es un éxito de taquilla
2 *vi* **(a)** *(crowd in)* apiñarse **(b)** *Br (car, computer)* estropearse, *Esp* escacharrarse, *Méx* desconchinflarse, *RP* hacerse bolsa

► **pack off** *vt sep Fam (send)* mandar; **I packed the kids off to bed/school** mandé *or Arg* despaché a los chicos a la cama/a la escuela

► **pack out** *vt sep* abarrotar; **the event was completely packed out** el acto estaba abarrotado de gente

► **pack up 1** *vt sep* **(a)** *(suitcase, bags)* hacer **(b)** *(tidy up) (belongings, tools)* recoger
2 *vi Br* **(a)** *(before moving house)* embalar, preparar la mudanza; *(finish work)* dejarlo, parar de trabajar **(b)** *Fam (break down)* estropearse, *Esp* escacharrarse, *Méx* desconchinflarse, *RP* hacerse bolsa

package ['pækɪdʒ] **1** *n* **(a)** *(parcel)* paquete *m*; *US (packet)* paquete *m* ▸▸ *US* ***p. store*** tienda *f* de bebidas alcohólicas
(b) *(pay deal, contract)* paquete *m*; **a p. of measures** un paquete de medidas; **the p. includes private health insurance** el paquete incluye seguro médico privado ▸▸ *Com* ***p. deal*** acuerdo *m* global; ***p. holiday*** paquete *m* turístico, viaje *m* organizado; ***p. tour*** paquete *m* turístico, viaje *m* organizado
(c) *Comptr* **(software) p.** paquete *m* de software
2 *vt* **(a)** *(goods)* envasar **(b) to p. sb (as)** *(pop star, politician)* promover a alguien (como)

packaging ['pækɪdʒɪŋ] *n* **(a)** *(for transport, freight)* embalaje *m* **(b)** *(of product)* envasado *m* ▸▸ ***p. plant*** planta *f* de envase *or* envasadora **(c)** *(presentation)* imagen *f*, presentación *f*

packed [pækt] *adj* **(a)** *(crowded)* abarrotado(a); *Theat* **to play to a p. house** actuar en una sala abarrotada **(b)** *(wrapped)* ***p. lunch*** comida *f* preparada de casa *(para excursión, trabajo, colegio)*

packer ['pækə(r)] *n* empaquetador(ora) *m,f*, embalador(ora) *m,f*

packet ['pækɪt] *n* **(a)** *(of tea, cereal, cigarettes)* paquete *m*; *(of nuts, sweets)* bolsa *f* ▸▸ ***p. soup*** sopa *f* de sobre
(b) *Fam (lot of money)* **to make** *or* **earn a p.** ganar una millonada *or Méx* un chorro de lana *or RP* una ponchada de guita; **that'll cost a p.** costará un riñón
(c) *Naut* **p. (boat)** paquebote *m*
(d) *Comptr* paquete *m* ▸▸ ***p. switching*** conmutación *f* de paquetes
(e) *Fam (man's genitals) Esp* paquete *m*, *Méx* cosa *f*, *RP* bulto *m*

packhorse ['pækhɔːs] *n* caballo *m* de carga

packing ['pækɪŋ] *n* **(a)** *(of parcel)* envoltorio *m*; *(of commercial goods)* embalaje *m*; **to do one's p.** *(for trip)* hacer el equipaje; *(before moving house)* preparar las cosas para la mudanza ▸▸ ***p. list*** lista *f* de cosas para embalar **(b)** *(packing material)* embalaje *m* ▸▸ ***p. case*** cajón *m* **(c)** *US* ***p. house*** empresa *f* de productos cárnicos

pack-rat ['pækræt] *n* **(a)** *(animal)* = especie de rata norteamericana **(b)** *Fam (person)* **to be a p.** ser un(a) acaparador(ora)

packsaddle ['pæksædəl] *n* albarda *f*

packthread ['pækθred] *n* bramante *m*, hilo *m* de embalar

pact [pækt] *n* pacto *m*; **to make a p. with sb** hacer un pacto con alguien

pacy = **pacey**

pad [pæd] **1** *n* **(a)** *(for protection)* almohadilla *f*; *(of cotton wool)* tampón *m* **(b)** *(on dog's feet)* almohadilla *f* **(c)** *(for helicopters)* plataforma *f* **(d)** *(of paper)* **(writing) p.** bloc *m* **(e)** *(noise)* ruido *m* suave *or* apagado; **the p. of bare feet on marble** el sonido de unos pies descalzos caminando sobre el mármol **(f)** *Fam (home)* casa *f*, *Esp* choza *f*, *Esp* queli *f*
2 *vt* (*pt & pp* **padded**) **(a)** *(stuff)* acolchar, almohadillar (**with** con) **(b)** *(add bulk to) (speech, essay)* rellenar
3 *vi* **to p. about** caminar con suavidad; **he padded downstairs in his slippers** bajó las escaleras con suavidad, con sus pantuflas puestas; **the dog padded along beside the cyclist** el perro acompañaba con un suave andar al ciclista

▸ **pad out** *vt sep (speech, essay)* rellenar; **you can p. out the meal with rice** puedes acompañar la comida con arroz

padded ['pædɪd] *adj* **(a)** *(door, wall)* acolchado(a), almohadillado(a); *(envelope)* acolchado(a); *(jacket, material)* acolchado(a); *(bra)* con relleno; *(shoulders of jacket)* con hombreras ▸▸ ***p. cell*** celda *f* acolchada **(b)** *(fat)* **he's well p.** está bastante relleno

padding ['pædɪŋ] *n* **(a)** *(material)* relleno *m*; *(of cotton)* guata *f* **(b)** *Fig (in speech, essay)* paja *f*, relleno *m*; **use rice/pasta as p.** usa arroz/pasta de relleno

paddle ['pædəl] **1** *n* **(a)** *(for canoe)* remo *m*, canalete *m*; *(of paddle boat)* pala *f*; *(of waterwheel)* paleta *f* ▸▸ ***p. boat*** barco *m* (de vapor) de ruedas; ***p. steamer*** barco *m* (de vapor) de ruedas; ***p. wheel*** rueda *f* de paletas **(b)** *US (for table tennis)* pala *f* **(c)** *(walk in water)* **to go for** *or* **have a p.** dar un paseo por el agua *or* la orilla
2 *vt* **(a)** *(canoe)* remar en; IDIOM **to p. one's own canoe** arreglárselas solo(a) **(b)** *US Fam (spank)* dar una zurra a, *Arg* dar un chirlo a
3 *vi* **(a)** *(in canoe)* remar **(b)** *(duck)* nadar **(c)** *(walk in water)* dar un paseo chapoteando por el agua *or* la orilla

paddlefish ['pædəlfɪʃ] *n* pez *m* hoja

paddling pool ['pædlɪŋ'puːl] *n* **(a)** *(inflatable)* piscina *f or Méx* alberca *f or RP* pileta *f* hinchable **(b)** *(in park)* piscina *f or Méx* alberca *f or RP* pileta *f* para niños

paddock ['pædək] *n* **(a)** *(field)* cercado *m*, potrero *m* **(b)** *(at racecourse)* paddock *m* **(c)** *(at motor-racing circuit)* paddock *m*

Paddy ['pædɪ] *n Fam* = término a veces ofensivo para referirse a los irlandeses

paddy ['pædɪ] *n* **(a) p. (field)** *(rice field)* arrozal *m* **(b)** *US Fam* ***p. wagon*** *(police van)* furgón *m* policial, *Arg* celular *m* **(c)** *Br Fam (bad temper)* **to be in a p.** estar de malas pulgas

paddyfield warbler ['pædɪfiːld'wɔːblə(r)] *n* carricero *m* agrícola

padlock ['pædlɒk] **1** *n* candado *m*
2 *vt* cerrar con candado; **she padlocked her bicycle to a lamppost** ató con un candado su bicicleta a una farola

padre ['pɑːdreɪ] *n Fam (military chaplain)* capellán *m*

padsaw ['pædsɔː] *n* sierra *f* para cortar ángulos *(con el mango desmontable)*

paean, *US* **pean** ['piːən] *n Literary* panegírico *m*; **the movie received a p. of praise from the critics** la película recibió una lluvia de elogios *or* alabanzas de la crítica

paederast, *US* **pederast** ['pedəræst] *n Formal* pederasta *m*

paederasty, *US* **pederasty** ['pedəræstɪ] *n Formal* pederastía *f*

paediatric, *US* **pediatric** [piːdɪ'ætrɪk] *adj Med* pediátrico(a)

paediatrician, *US* **pediatrician** [piːdɪə'trɪʃən] *n Med* pediatra *mf*

paediatrics, *US* **pediatrics** [piːdɪ'ætrɪks] *n Med* pediatría *f*

paedophile, *US* **pedophile** ['piːdəfaɪl] *n* pedófilo(a) *m,f*

paedophilia, *US* **pedophilia** [piːdə'fɪlɪə] *n* pedofilia *f*

pagan ['peɪgən] **1** *n* pagano(a) *m,f*
2 *adj* pagano(a)

paganism ['peɪgənɪzəm] *n* paganismo *m*

page[1] [peɪdʒ] *n* página *f*; **on p. 6** en la página 6; *Fig* **a glorious p. in our history** una página gloriosa de nuestra historia; **the sports/business pages** *(in newspaper)* la sección de deportes/negocios ▸▸ *Comptr* ***p. break*** salto *m* de página; *Comptr* ***p. down key*** tecla *f* de avance de página; *Comptr* ***p. layout*** maquetación *f*; ***p. number*** número *m* de página; ***p. numbering*** numeración *f* de páginas, paginación *f*; *Comptr* ***p. preview*** previsualización *f*; *Comptr* ***p. setup*** ajuste *m* de página; *Br* ***p. three*** = página de los periódicos británicos sensacionalistas en la que aparece la foto de una chica atractiva medio desnuda; *Comptr* ***p. up key*** tecla *f* de retroceso de página

▸ **page down** *vi Comptr* desplazarse hacia abajo hasta la página siguiente

▸ **page up** *vi Comptr* desplazarse hacia arriba hasta la página anterior

page[2] **1** *n (servant, at wedding)* paje *m*; *(in hotel)* botones *m inv*; *US (in legislative body)* mensajero *m*
2 *vt (call) (by loudspeaker)* avisar por megafonía; *(by electronic device)* llamar por el buscapersonas *or Esp* busca *or Méx* localizador *or RP* radiomensaje; **paging Mrs Clark!** atención, Sra. Clark

pageant ['pædʒənt] *n (procession)* desfile *m*, procesión *f*; *(of historical events)* representación *f* de escenas históricas

pageantry ['pædʒəntrɪ] *n* pompa *f*, esplendor *m*

pageboy ['peɪdʒbɔɪ] *n* **(a)** *(servant, at wedding)* paje *m*; *(in hotel)* botones *m inv* **(b)** *(hairstyle)* **p. (haircut)** corte *m* estilo paje

pager ['peɪdʒə(r)] *n* buscapersonas *m inv*, *Esp* busca *m*, *Méx* localizador *m*, *RP* radiomensaje *m*

page-turner ['peɪdʒtɜːnə(r)] *n Fam* libro *m* absorbente

paginate ['pædʒɪneɪt] *vt Comptr* paginar

pagination [pædʒɪ'neɪʃən] *n Comptr* paginación *f*

pagoda [pə'gəʊdə] *n* pagoda *f*

pah [pɑː] *exclam* ¡bah!

paid [peɪd] **1** *adj* **(a)** *(person, work)* remunerado(a); **p. holidays** vacaciones pagadas; **to get p. sick/maternity leave** obtener la baja por enfermedad/maternidad **(b)** IDIOM *Fam* **to put p. to sb's chances/hopes** truncar las posibilidades/esperanzas de alguien; **well, that's put p. to that!** ¡entonces, eso lo echa por tierra!
2 *pt & pp of* **pay**

paid-up ['peɪdʌp] *adj* **(a)** *(member)* con las cuentas al día; *Fig* **he's a fully p. member of the awkward squad** es un tiquismiquis constante **(b)** *Fin (share)* liberado(a); **p. policy** póliza liberada *or* con prima; **p. (share) capital** capital liberado en acciones

pail [peɪl] *n (bucket)* cubo *m*, balde *m*

pailful ['peɪlfʊl] *n* **a p. of water** un cubo *or* balde de agua

pain [peɪn] **1** *n* **(a)** *(physical)* dolor *m*; **to cause sb p.** dolerle a alguien; **to be in p.** estar sufriendo; **to be in great p.** tener mucho dolor; **I have a p. in my leg** me duele una pierna; **to cry out in p.** gritar de dolor ▸▸ ***the p. barrier*** el umbral del dolor; ***p. relief*** tratamiento *m* del dolor; **aspirin for fast p. relief** aspirina para un rápido alivio del dolor
(b) *(mental, emotional)* sufrimiento *m*, pena *f*; **I can't bear the p. of losing her** no soporto el dolor de haberla perdido; **to cause sb p.** afligir *or* hacer sufrir a alguien; **he went through a lot of p. when his**

son left home sufrió mucho cuando su hijo se fue de casa

(c) *(trouble)* **to take pains to do sth, to be at great pains to do sth** tomarse muchas molestias para hacer algo; **she took great pains over her work** se esforzó mucho en su trabajo; **he went to great pains to help us** se esforzó mucho por ayudarnos; **for my pains** por mi esfuerzo

(d) *Formal* **on p. of death** so pena de muerte

(e) *Fam (annoying person, thing)* **he's a p. (in the neck)** es un plomazo *or* pelmazo *or Méx* sangrón; *US Fam* **to give sb a p. (in the neck)** dar la paliza a alguien; *Vulg* **it's a p. in the** *Br* **arse** *or US* **ass** es *Esp* un coñazo *or Méx* una chingadera *or RP* un embole; *Fam* **cooking can be a p.** a veces resulta un plomazo *or* una lata cocinar

2 *vt* afligir, apenar; **it pains me to say it, but...** me duele decirlo, pero...

pained [peɪnd] *adj (look, expression)* afligido(a), de pena

painful ['peɪnfʊl] *adj* **(a)** *(physically)* doloroso(a); *(part of body)* dolorido(a); **my burns are still p.** aún me duelen las quemaduras; **is it p. here?** ¿te duele aquí?; **these shoes are really p.** estos zapatos me hacen daño **(b)** *(mentally)* doloroso(a), penoso(a); **it's p. to watch them** resulta penoso mirarlos; **the p. truth** la dura realidad **(c)** *Fam (bad) (performance, singing)* malísimo(a), *Esp* de pena

painfully ['peɪnfʊlɪ] *adv* **(a)** *(to walk, move)* con dolor; **her head throbbed p.** le latía la cabeza con dolor; **she fell p.** tuvo una caída dolorosa **(b)** *Fig (obvious, clear)* tremendamente; **he's p. shy** es terriblemente tímido; **p. slowly** exasperantemente lento; **she's p. thin** es terriblemente flaca

painkiller ['peɪnkɪlə(r)] *n* analgésico *m*

painkilling ['peɪnkɪlɪŋ] *adj* analgésico(a)

painless ['peɪnlɪs] *adj* **(a)** *(not painful)* indoloro(a) **(b)** *Fig (easy)* fácil

painstaking ['peɪnzteɪkɪŋ] *adj (person, research)* meticuloso(a), concienzudo(a); *(care)* esmerado(a)

painstakingly ['peɪnzteɪkɪŋlɪ] *adv* meticulosamente, minuciosamente; **p. accurate work** un trabajo de una rigurosa exactitud

paint [peɪnt] 1 *n* pintura *f*; **oil/acrylic p.** pintura al óleo/acrílica; **a set** *or* **box of paints** un juego *or* una caja de pinturas; IDIOM *Hum* **it's as interesting as watching p. dry** es más aburrido que ver crecer la hierba ▸▸ ***p. gun*** pistola *f (para pintar)*; ***p. pot*** pote *m or* tarro *m* de pintura; *Comptr* ***p. program*** programa *m* de dibujo; ***p. remover*** decapante *m*; *Ind* ***p. shop*** taller *m* de pintura; ***p. stripper*** decapante *m*

2 *vt* **(a)** *(picture, person, room)* pintar; **the door was painted yellow** la puerta estaba pintada de amarillo; *Fam* **to p. one's face** *(put on make-up)* pintarse; **to p. one's nails** pintarse las uñas

(b) IDIOMS **to p. a favourable picture (of)** dar una visión favorable (de); **to p. a black picture of sth/sb** pintar algo/a alguien muy negro; **to p. everything in rosy colours** pintar todo color de rosa; **to p. the town red** irse de juerga; **to p. oneself into a corner** ponerse en una situación comprometida

3 *vi* pintar; **to p. in oils/watercolours** pintar al óleo/a la acuarela

▸ **paint over** *vt sep* tapar *or* cubrir con pintura

paintball ['peɪntbɔːl] *n* = juego bélico en el que los participantes se disparan pintura con pistolas de aire comprimido

paintbox ['peɪntbɒks] *n* caja *f* de acuarelas

paintbrush ['peɪntbrʌʃ] *n (of artist)* pincel *m*; *(of decorator)* brocha *f*

painted ['peɪntɪd] *adj* pintado(a) ▸▸ ***p. bunting*** verderón *m* pintado; ***the P. Desert*** el Desierto Pintado; ***p. lady*** *(butterfly)* vanesa *f* de la alcachofa

painter ['peɪntə(r)] *n* **(a)** *(artist)* pintor(ora) *m,f*; *(decorator)* pintor(ora) *m,f* (de brocha gorda); **p. and decorator** pintor(ora) *(que también empapela)* **(b)** *Naut (rope)* amarra *f*; **to cut the p.** soltar amarras

painterly ['peɪntəlɪ] *adj* de pintor

painting ['peɪntɪŋ] *n* **(a)** *(picture)* cuadro *m*, pintura *f* **(b)** *(activity)* pintura *f*; **p. and decorating** pintura y decoración

paintwork ['peɪntwɜːk] *n (of car, room)* pintura *f*

pair [peə(r)] 1 *n* **(a)** *(set of two) (of shoes, gloves)* par *m*; *(of people, animals, birds)* pareja *f*; **in pairs** *(of objects, people)* de dos en dos, por parejas; **I've only got one p. of hands!** ¡sólo tengo dos manos!; *Br Fam* **shut up, the p. of you!** *Esp* vosotros dos, ¡callaos!, *Am* ustedes dos, ¡cállense!; **they're a p. of idiots!** son un par de imbéciles! ▸▸ *Zool* ***p. bonding*** apareamiento *m*

(b) *(matching item)* par *m*; **where's the p. to this sock?** ¿dónde está el otro calcetín de este par?

(c) *(forming single item)* **a p. of glasses** unas gafas; **a p. of scissors** unas tijeras; **a p. of trousers** unos pantalones

(d) *(husband and wife)* pareja *f*

(e) *(in rowing)* par *m*

(f) *(in cards, dice)* pareja *f*

2 *vt (people, animals)* emparejar (**with** con)

3 *vi (animals, birds)* aparearse

▸ **pair off** 1 *vt sep (people)* emparejar; **he's trying to p. them off** *(in a relationship)* está haciendo de celestino

2 *vi (people)* ponerse en parejas

▸ **pair up** 1 *vt sep (socks)* formar pares de

2 *vi* hacer pareja, emparejarse (**with** con)

paisley ['peɪzlɪ] *adj Tex* de cachemir ▸▸ ***p. pattern*** estampado *m* de cachemira

pajama *US* = **pyjama**

pak choi ['pæk'tʃɔɪ] *n* col *f* china, repollo *m* chino

Paki ['pækɪ] *n Br very Fam (person)* = término generalmente ofensivo para referirse a los ciudadanos de origen pakistaní, indio o bangladeshí; **P. shop, P.'s** = tienda de alimentación perteneciente a un ciudadano de origen pakistaní, indio o bangladeshí

Paki-bashing ['pækɪ'bæʃɪŋ] *n Br very Fam* = ataques físicos o verbales contra ciudadanos de origen pakistaní, indio o bangladeshí

Pakistan [pɑːkɪ'stɑːn] *n* Paquistán

Pakistani [pɑːkɪ'stɑːnɪ] 1 *n* paquistaní *mf*

2 *adj* paquistaní

pakora [pə'kɔːrə] *n* = bola de verduras rebozada en harina que se sirve con salsa picante, típica de la comida india

PAL [pæl] *n TV* (*abbr* **phase alternation line**) (sistema *m*) PAL *m*

pal [pæl] *n Fam* **(a)** *(friend)* amiguete(a) *m,f*, *Esp* colega *mf*; **be a p. and fetch my coat** sé bueno y tráeme el abrigo **(b)** *(term of address)* **thanks, p.** gracias, *Esp* tío *or Am* compadre; **look here, p.!** ¡mira, *Esp* tío *or Am* compadre!; **watch where you're going, p.!** ¡fíjate por dónde andas, *Esp* tío *or Am* compadre!

▸ **pal up with** *vt insep Fam* hacerse amigo *or Esp* colega de

palace ['pælɪs] *n* **(a)** *(royal, president's)* palacio *m* ▸▸ *also Fig* ***p. coup*** golpe *m* de palacio; ***p. revolution*** revolución *f* de palacio **(b)** *Br* **the P.** *(Buckingham Palace)* el Palacio de Buckingham; **the P. of Westminster** el Palacio de Westminster

paladin ['pælədɪn] *n* paladín *m*

Palaeocene, *US* **Paleocene** ['pælɪəsiːn] *Geol* 1 *n* **the P.** el paleoceno

2 *adj* paleoceno(a)

palaeographer, *US* **paleographer** [pælɪ'ɒgrəfə(r)] *n* paleógrafo(a) *m,f*

palaeography, *US* **paleography** [pælɪ'ɒgrəfɪ] *n* paleografía *f*

palaeolithic, *US* **paleolithic** [pælɪə'lɪθɪk] *adj* paleolítico(a)

palaeontologist, *US* **paleontologist** [peɪlɪɒn'tɒlədʒɪst] *n* paleontólogo(a) *m,f*

palaeontology, *US* **paleontology** [peɪlɪɒn'tɒlədʒɪ] *n* paleontología *f*

Palaeozoic, *US* **Paleozoic** [pælɪə'zəʊɪk] *Geol* 1 *n* **the P.** el paleozoico

2 *adj* paleozoico(a)

palatable ['pælətəbəl] *adj* **(a)** *(food)* apetitoso(a) **(b)** *Fig (suggestion)* aceptable

palatal ['pælətəl] *adj* **(a)** *Anat* del paladar **(b)** *Ling* palatal

palatalize ['pælətəlaɪz] *vt Ling* palatalizar

palate ['pælɪt] *n* **(a)** *(in mouth)* paladar *m* **(b)** *(sense of taste)* paladar *m*

palatial [pə'leɪʃəl] *adj* suntuoso(a), señorial

palatinate [pə'lætɪnət] *n* palatinado *m*; *Hist* **the P.** el Palatinado

palatine ['pælətaɪn] *adj Hist* palatino(a)

palato-alveolar ['pælətəʊælvɪ'əʊlə(r)] *adj Ling* palato-alveolar

palaver [pə'lɑːvə(r)] *n Br Fam (fuss)* lío *m*, *Esp* follón *m*; **what a p.!** ¡vaya lío *or Esp* follón!

palazzo [pæ'lætsəʊ] *n* palacio *m (italiano)*; **p. pants, palazzos** palazo

pale[1] [peɪl] 1 *adj* **(a)** *(skin)* pálido(a); **to turn p. (with fright)** palidecer (de miedo); IDIOM **to be as p. as death** estar blanco(a) como el papel *or* la leche **(b)** *(colour)* claro(a); **a p. blue dress** un vestido azul pálido; *Fig* **a p. imitation of sth** una pálida imitación de algo ▸▸ *Br* ***p. ale*** = cerveza del tipo "bitter" pero más rubia

2 *vi (person)* palidecer; **our problems p. into insignificance beside hers** si los comparamos con los de ella, nuestros problemas son insignificantes

pale[2] *n (fence post)* estaca *f*; *(fence)* empalizada *f*, cerca *f*; IDIOM **to be** *or* **go beyond the p.** ser intolerable

paleface ['peɪlfeɪs] *n Hum Esp* rostro *m* pálido, *Am* carapálida *mf*

paleness ['peɪlnɪs] *n* palidez *f*

Paleocene, paleographer *etc US* = **Palaeocene, palaeographer** *etc*

Palestine [ˈpælɪstaɪn] *n* Palestina ▸▸ ***P. Liberation Organization*** Organización *f* para la Liberación de Palestina

Palestinian [pælɪˈstɪnɪən] **1** *n* palestino(a) *m,f*
2 *adj* palestino(a)

palette [ˈpælɪt] *n* **(a)** *Art* paleta *f* ▸▸ ***p. knife*** espátula *f* **(b)** *Comptr* paleta *f*

palfrey [ˈpɔːlfrɪ] *n* palafrén *m*

palimony [ˈpælɪmənɪ] *n Fam* pensión *f* alimenticia *(entre parejas de hecho)*

palimpsest [ˈpælɪmpsest] *n* palimpsesto *m*

palindrome [ˈpælɪndrəʊm] *n* palíndromo *m*

paling [ˈpeɪlɪŋ] *n (fence)* cerca *f*, estacada *f*; *(fence post)* estaca *f*, *RP* poste *m*

palisade [pælɪˈseɪd] *n* **(a)** *(fence)* empalizada *f* **(b)** *US* **palisades** *(cliffs)* acantilados *mpl*

pall^{1} [pɔːl] *n* **(a)** *(over coffin)* paño *m* mortuorio **(b)** *(coffin)* féretro *m* **(c)** *(of smoke)* cortina *f*, manto *m*; *(of darkness, gloom)* manto *m*; **a p. of silence hung over the room** un manto de silencio cubrió la sala

pall^{2} *vi (become uninteresting)* desvanecerse; **it began to p. on me** comenzó a cansarme

Palladian [pəˈleɪdɪən] *adj Archit* paladiano(a)

palladium [pəˈleɪdɪəm] *n Chem* paladio *m*

pallbearer [ˈpɔːlbeərə(r)] *n* portador(ora) *m,f* del féretro

pallet [ˈpælɪt] *n* **(a)** *(bed)* jergón *m* **(b)** *Ind (wooden platform)* palet *m*, palé *m*

palletization [pælɪtaɪˈzeɪʃən] *n Com* paletización *f*

palletize [ˈpælɪtaɪz] *vt Com* paletizar

palliasse [ˈpælɪæs] *n* jergón *m*

palliate [ˈpælɪeɪt] *vt* **(a)** *Med* paliar, mitigar **(b)** *Formal* paliar

palliative [ˈpælɪətɪv] **1** *n Med* paliativo *m*
2 *adj* paliativo(a); **her words had a p. effect** sus palabras tuvieron un efecto paliativo

pallid [ˈpælɪd] *adj* **(a)** *(pale)* pálido(a) **(b)** *(performance)* deslucido(a), pálido(a) **(c)** ***p. swift*** vencejo *m* pálido

pallor [ˈpælə(r)] *n* lividez *f*

pally [ˈpælɪ] *adj Fam* **to be p. with sb** comportarse amistosamente con alguien; **they're very p. all of a sudden** se han hecho muy amigos de repente

palm^{1} [pɑːm] *n* **(a)** *(plant)* **p. (tree)** palmera *f*; **p. grove** *or* **plantation** palmeral, plantación de palmeras ▸▸ ***p. court*** *(in hotel)* = salón decorado con palmeras donde toca una orquesta; ***p. oil*** aceite de palma; ***p. sugar*** panela *f*; ***p. wine*** = bebida alcohólica hecha a base de savia de palma fermentada
(b) *(branch)* **p. (leaf)** palma *f*; IDIOM **to carry off the p.** conseguir la victoria ▸▸ ***P. Sunday*** Domingo *m* de Ramos

palm^{2} **1** *n (of hand)* palma *f*; IDIOM **to have sb in the p. of one's hand** tener a alguien en el bolsillo
2 *vt (in conjuring)* hacer desaparecer

▸ **palm off** *vt sep* **to p. sth off on(to) sb** endilgar algo a alguien; **they tried to p. me off with a cheap imitation** intentaron colocarme una imitación barata; **he keeps palming me off with excuses** siempre se deshace de mí con excusas

palmetto [pælˈmetəʊ] *n* palma *f* enana

palmhouse [ˈpɑːmhaʊs] *n* = en un jardín botánico, invernadero para palmeras y otras plantas tropicales

palmist [ˈpɑːmɪst] *n* quiromántico(a) *m,f*

palmistry [ˈpɑːmɪstrɪ] *n* quiromancia *f*

palmitic acid [pælˈmɪtɪkˈæsɪd] *n Chem* ácido *m* palmítico

palmtop [ˈpɑːmtɒp] *n Comptr* palm(top) *m or f*, asistente *m* personal

palmy [ˈpɑːmɪ] *adj* próspero(a)

palomino [pæləˈmiːnəʊ] *n (horse)* = caballo alazán de crin y cola blancas

palooka [pəˈluːkə] *n US Fam* **(a)** *(clumsy person)* torpe *m* **(b)** *(stupid person)* imbécil *m* **(c)** *(boxer)* mal boxeador *m*

palpable [ˈpælpəbəl] *adj* **(a)** *(obvious)* palpable; **a p. lie** una mentira evidente **(b)** *Med* palpable

palpably [ˈpælpəblɪ] *adv* evidentemente; **p. obvious** muy evidente

palpate [pælˈpeɪt] *vt Med* explorar

palpitate [ˈpælpɪteɪt] *vi (heart)* palpitar; *Fig* **to p. with fear/excitement** estar estremecido(a) de miedo/emoción

palpitations [pælpɪˈteɪʃənz] *npl* palpitaciones *fpl*; *Hum* **I get p. whenever I see her** me da taquicardia cada vez que la veo

palsied [ˈpɔːlzɪd] *adj* **(a)** *(paralysed)* paralítico(a) **(b)** *Literary (trembling)* paralizado(a)

palsy^{1} [ˈpɔːlzɪ] *n Med* parálisis *f inv*

palsy^{2} [ˈpælzɪ] *adj Fam* **to be/get p. with sb** ser íntimo(a) de/intimar con alguien

paltry [ˈpɔːltrɪ] *adj (wage, sum)* miserable; **all this for a p. $100** todo esto por 100 miserables dólares; **a p. excuse** una pésima excusa

pampas [ˈpæmpəs] *npl* **the p.** la pampa, las pampas; **the P.** *(in Argentina)* la Pampa ▸▸ ***p. grass*** cortadera *f*

pamper [ˈpæmpə(r)] *vt (person)* mimar, consentir; **to p. oneself** darse lujos

pampered [ˈpæmpəd] *adj* mimado(a), consentido(a)

pamphlet [ˈpæmflɪt] *n (informative)* folleto *m*; *(controversial)* panfleto *m*

pamphleteer [pæmfləˈtɪə(r)] *n* panfletista *mf*

pamphleteering [pæmfləˈtɪərɪŋ] *n* panfletismo *m*, panfletarismo *m*

Pan [pæn] *n Mythol* Pan

pan^{1} [pæn] **1** *n* **(a)** *(for cooking)* cacerola *f*, cazuela *f*; *(frying pan)* sartén *f*; *US* **cake p.** molde para tartas **(b)** *(of scales)* platillo *m* **(c)** *(to search for gold, gems)* batea *f* **(d)** *Br (of lavatory)* taza *f*; IDIOM *Fam* **to go down the p.** echarse a perder, irse al carajo *or* al garete; **that's six months' work down the p.!** ¡seis meses de trabajo al carajo *or* al garete *or Arg* echados por la borda!
2 *vi* (*pt & pp* **panned**) **to p. for gold** extraer oro *(con cedazo)*
3 *vt (gravel)* cribar

pan^{2} (*pt & pp* **panned**) *vt Fam (criticize)* vapulear, *Esp* poner por los suelos

pan^{3} *Cin* **1** *n* **p. (shot)** plano *m* panorámico
2 *vi* (*pt & pp* **panned**) hacer un plano panorámico; **to p. left/right** rodar con un plano panorámico hacia la izquierda/derecha

▸ **pan out** *vi Fam (turn out)* salir; **let's see how things p. out** a ver cómo salen las cosas; **our strategy is not panning out** nuestra estrategia no está funcionando

pan- [pæn] *prefix* pan-; **P.-Asian** panasiático(a); **p.-sexual** pansexual

panacea [pænəˈsɪə] *n* panacea *f*

panache [pəˈnæʃ] *n* gracia *f*, garbo *m*

Pan-African [pænˈæfrɪkən] *adj* panafricano(a)

Panama [ˈpænəmɑː] *n* Panamá ▸▸ ***the P. Canal*** el canal de Panamá; ***P. City*** Ciudad de Panamá; ***P. hat*** (sombrero *m*) panamá *m*

Panamanian [pænəˈmeɪnɪən] **1** *n* panameño(a) *m,f*
2 *adj* panameño(a)

Pan-American [pænəˈmerɪkən] *adj* panamericano(a) ▸▸ ***the P. Games*** los Juegos Panamericanos; ***the P. Highway*** la autopista Panamericana

pan-Arab [pænˈærəb] *adj* panárabe

panatella [pænəˈtelə] *n* panatela *m*, = tipo de cigarro largo y delgado

pancake [ˈpænkeɪk] *n* **(a)** *(cake)* crepe *f*, torta *f* ▸▸ ***P. Day*** Martes *m inv* de Carnaval; ***p. race*** carrera *f* de crepes *or RP* panqueques; ***P. Tuesday*** Martes *m inv* de Carnaval **(b)** *(make-up)* **p. (make-up)** maquillaje *m* facial *(que se humedece antes de aplicar)* **(c)** *Av* ***p. landing*** = aterrizaje forzoso sobre el fuselaje del avión sin utilizar el tren de aterrizaje

panchromatic [pænkrəʊˈmætɪk] *adj Phot* pancromático(a)

pancreas [ˈpæŋkrɪəs] *n* páncreas *m inv*

pancreatic [pæŋkrɪˈætɪk] *adj* pancreático(a) ▸▸ ***p. juice*** jugo *m* pancreático

pancreatitis [pæŋkrɪəˈtaɪtəs] *n Med* pancreatitis *f inv*

panda [ˈpændə] *n* **(a)** *(bear)* (oso *m*) panda *m* **(b)** *Br* ***p. car*** coche *m or Am* carro *m or CSur* auto *m* patrulla

pandemic [pænˈdemɪk] *Med* **1** *n* pandemia *f*
2 *adj* pandémico(a)

pandemonium [pændɪˈməʊnɪəm] *n* **there was p., p. broke out** se armó un auténtico pandemónium; **the whole office is in p.** la oficina es un caos total; **to cause p.** sembrar el caos

pander [ˈpændə(r)] **1** *vi* **to p. to sb** complacer a alguien; **to p. to a vice/sb's whims** ceder a un vicio/consentirle los caprichos a alguien; **to p. to sb's views** someterse a la opinión de alguien; **these films p. to our worst instincts** estas películas apelan a nuestros peores instintos
2 *n Literary (pimp)* proxeneta *m*

Pandora's box [pænˈdɔːrəzˈbɒks] *n* la caja de Pandora; IDIOM **to open P.** abrir la caja de Pandora, destapar la caja de los truenos

pane [peɪn] *n* **p. (of glass)** hoja *f* de vidrio *or Esp* cristal

panegyric [pænə'dʒɪrɪk] *n Formal* panegírico *m*

panel ['pænəl] 1 *n* (a) *(on wall, of door)* panel *m* ▸▸ *Br* ***p. beater*** *(in car industry)* chapista *mf, Méx* hojalatero(a) *m,f;* ***p. heating*** calefacción *f* por paneles; *Br* ***p. pin*** espiga *f (clavo); US* ***p. truck*** furgoneta *f* de reparto
(b) *(of garment)* pieza *f*
(c) *(of switches, lights)* panel *m*, tablero *m*
(d) *Art (for picture)* tabla *f*
(e) *(at interview, of experts)* panel *m*, equipo *m*; **our p. for tonight's show** nuestros participantes en el programa de hoy ▸▸ ***p. discussion*** debate *m*, mesa *f* redonda; ***p. game*** concurso *m* por equipos
2 *vt (pt & pp* **panelled,** *US* **paneled)** *(wall)* revestir con paneles; **a panelled door** una puerta de paneles; **one wall was panelled in pine** una pared estaba revestida con paneles de pino

panelling, *US* **paneling** ['pænəlɪŋ] *n (on wall)* paneles *mpl*

panellist, *US* **panelist** ['pænəlɪst] *n (on radio, TV programme)* participante *mf (en un debate)*

pan-fry ['pæn'fraɪ] *vt* freír a la sartén

pang [pæŋ] *n (of hunger, jealousy)* punzada *f*; **pangs of conscience** *or* **guilt** remordimientos de conciencia; **he resigned without a p. of regret** renunció sin lamentarlo en absoluto; **I felt a p. of sadness** sentí una punzada de tristeza *or* dolor

pangolin [pæŋ'gəʊlɪn] *n* pangolín *m*

panhandle ['pænhændəl] *US* 1 *n (of state)* = península de forma estrecha y alargada unida a un territorio de mayor tamaño
2 *vt Fam* **to p. money from sb, to p. sb** mendigarle a alguien
3 *vi Fam (beg)* mendigar

panhandler ['pænhændlə(r)] *n US Fam* pordiosero(a) *m,f*

panic ['pænɪk] 1 *n* (a) *(alarm)* pánico *m*; **she phoned me up in a p.** me llamó toda histérica; **there's no need to get into a p. (over** *or* **about it)** no hace falta que te pongas tan nervioso (por ello); **the crowd was thrown into a p.** cundió el pánico entre la multitud; **the news started a p. on the stock exchange** la noticia causó el pánico en la bolsa; **let's not rush into p. measures** no tomemos ninguna medida producto del pánico; *Fam* **it was p. stations** cundió el pánico ▸▸ ***p. attack*** ataque *m* de pánico; ***p. button*** botón *m* de alarma; IDIOM *Fam* **to hit the p. button** volverse loco(a), ponerse histérico(a); *Fin* ***p. buying*** compra *f* provocada por el pánico; *Fin* ***p. selling*** venta *f* provocada por el pánico
(b) *Fam (rush)* apuro *m*, prisa *f*; **I was in a mad p. to get to the airport** iba totalmente desesperado por llegar al aeropuerto; **what's the p.?** ¿cuál es la prisa?
(c) *US Fam (funny thing)* **it was a p.!** ¡fue superdivertido!
2 *vt (pt & pp* **panicked)** infundir pánico a; **we were panicked into selling our shares** vendimos nuestras acciones provocados por el pánico
3 *vi* aterrorizarse; **she suddenly panicked** le entró el pánico de repente; **he's starting to p. about the wedding** está empezando a ponerse histérico por la boda *or RP* el casamiento; **don't p.!** ¡que no cunda el pánico!

panicky ['pænɪkɪ] *adj Fam (reaction)* de pánico; **she got p.** le entró el pánico

panicmonger ['pænɪkmʌŋgə(r)] *n* alarmista *mf*

panic-stricken ['pænɪkstrɪkən] *adj* aterrorizado(a); **to be p.** estar aterrorizado(a)

panjandrum [pæn'dʒændrəm] *n Hum* **finally Mr Wright, the great p. himself, deigned to appear** finalmente, el mismísimo Sr Wright se dignó a aparecer

pannier ['pænɪə(r)] *n (on animal, bicycle)* alforja *f*

panoply ['pænəplɪ] *n Formal* serie *f*, conjunto *m*; **there's a whole p. of options** hay toda una serie de opciones

panorama [pænə'rɑːmə] *n* panorama *m*

panoramic [pænə'ræmɪk] *adj* panorámico(a) ▸▸ ***p. camera*** cámara *f* panorámica; ***p. photograph*** fotografía *f* panorámica; ***p. view*** vista *f* panorámica

panpipes ['pænpaɪps] *npl Mus* zampoña *f*, flauta *f* de Pan

pansy ['pænzɪ] *n* (a) *(flower)* pensamiento *m* (b) *Fam Pej (effeminate man)* mariposón *m*; *(homosexual man)* maricón *m*

pant [pænt] 1 *vi* jadear; **he panted up the stairs** subió las escaleras jadeando; **to p. for breath** resollar *(intentando recobrar el aliento)*
2 *vt (say)* decir jadeando
3 *n (breath)* jadeo *m*

pantaloons [pæntə'luːnz] *npl* pantalones *mpl* anchos tipo bombachos *or Arg* bombacha

pantechnicon [pæn'teknɪkən] *n Br Old-fashioned* camión *m* de mudanzas (de gran tamaño)

pantheism ['pænθiːɪzəm] *n* panteísmo *m*

pantheist ['pænθiːɪst] *n* panteísta *mf*

pantheistic [pænθiː'ɪstɪk] *adj* panteísta

pantheon ['pænθɪən] *n also Fig* panteón *m*

panther ['pænθə(r)] *n* (a) *(leopard)* pantera *f* (b) *US (puma)* puma *m*

panties ['pæntɪz] *npl esp US Esp* bragas *fpl, Chile, Col, Méx* calzón *m*, calzones *mpl, Ecuad* follones *mpl*, calzonarios *mpl, RP* bombacha *f*; IDIOM *US Fam* **don't get your p. in a wad!** *(don't panic)* ¡no te pongas hecho un manojo de nervios!; *(don't get angry)* ¡no te salgas de tus casillas!

pantihose = **pantyhose**

pantile ['pæntaɪl] *n* teja *f* en forma de canalón

panto *Fam* = **pantomime**

pantograph ['pæntəgrɑːf] *n* pantógrafo *m*

pantomime ['pæntəmaɪm], *Fam* **panto** ['pæntəʊ] *n* = obra de teatro musical para niños típica del Reino Unido, que se representa en la época navideña ▸▸ ***p. dame*** = actor masculino que interpreta el principal papel femenino en una "pantomime"; ***p. horse*** caballo *m* de teatro

pantry ['pæntrɪ] *n* despensa *f*

pants [pænts] 1 *npl* (a) *Br (men's underwear)* calzoncillos *mpl, Chile* fundillos *mpl, Col* pantaloncillos *mpl, Méx* calzones *mpl, Méx* chones *mpl*; *(women's underwear) Esp* braga *f*, bragas *fpl, Chile, Col, Méx* calzones *mpl, Ecuad* follones *mpl*, calzonarios *mpl, RP* bombacha *f*
(b) *US (trousers)* **(pair of) p.** pantalones *mpl*; **p. leg** pierna de pantalón ▸▸ ***p. suit*** traje *m* pantalón
(c) IDIOMS *Fam* **to scare the p. off sb** hacer que a alguien le entre el canguelo *or Méx* mello *or RP* cuiqui; *US Fam* **she's the one who wears the p. (in that house)** ella es la que lleva los pantalones (en esa casa); *Fam* **he was caught with his p. down** lo agarraron con las manos en la masa, *Esp* lo pillaron en bragas
2 *adj Br Fam (of poor quality)* **to be p.** ser una porquería; **he's a nice guy but as a teacher he's just p.** es un buen tipo pero como maestro no vale nada

panty ['pæntɪ] *n* ***p. girdle*** faja *f* pantalón; ***p. liner*** protege-slips *m inv, RP, Ven* protector *m* diario

pantyhose, pantihose ['pæntɪhəʊz] *n US* medias *fpl*, pantis *mpl*

panzer ['pænzə(r)] *n* panzer *m*

Pap [pæp] *n US Med* ***P. smear*** citología *f*; ***P. test*** citología *f*

pap [pæp] *n* (a) *(mush)* papilla *f* (b) *Fam Pej (nonsense)* bobadas *fpl*

papa *n* (a) [pə'pɑː] *Br Old-fashioned* papá *m* (b) ['pɑːpə] *US* papá *m*, papi *m*

papacy ['peɪpəsɪ] *n* papado *m*

papal ['peɪpəl] *adj* papal ▸▸ ***p. bull*** bula *f* papal; ***p. encyclical*** encíclica *f* papal; ***p. nuncio*** nuncio *m* apostólico

paparazzo [pæpə'rætsəʊ] *(pl* **paparazzi** [pæpə'rætsiː]) *n* paparazzi *mf*

papaya [pə'paɪə], **papaw** ['pɔːpɔː] *n* (a) *(fruit)* papaya *f* (b) *(tree)* papayo *m*

paper ['peɪpə(r)] 1 *n* (a) *(material)* papel *m*; **a piece** *or* **sheet of p.** un papel; **I want to see it (written) down on p.** quiero verlo escrito; *Fig* **on p.** *(in theory)* sobre el papel ▸▸ ***p. aeroplane*** avión *m* de papel; ***p. bag*** bolsa *f* de papel; IDIOM *Fam* **he couldn't fight** *or* **punch his way out of a p. bag** es un debilucho; ***p. chains*** guirnalda *f* de papel; ***p. chase*** *(race)* = carrera a campo traviesa en la que un participante va tirando trozos de papel mientras el resto corre detrás de él; *Fig* **education has become a p. chase after qualifications** la enseñanza se ha convertido en una carrera por obtener títulos; ***p. cup*** vaso *m* de papel; ***p. fastener*** clip *m*, sujetapapeles *m inv*; *Comptr* ***p. feed*** alimentación *f* de papel; ***p. handkerchief*** pañuelo *m* de papel; ***p. hanger*** *(decorator)* empapelador(ora) *m,f*; *US Fam (counterfeiter)* falsificador(ora) *m,f*; *Fam* ***p. hankie*** kleenex *m*, pañuelo *m* de papel; ***the p. industry*** la industria del papel; *Comptr* ***p. jam*** atasco *m* de papel; ***p. mill*** fábrica *f or Am* planta *f* de papel, papelera *f*; ***p. money*** papel *m* moneda; ***p. plate*** plato *m* de papel; *Fin* ***p. profits*** ganancias *fpl* teóricas sobre el papel; ***p. shredder*** trituradora *f* de papel; *Pol* ***p. tiger*** tigre *m* de papel; ***p. tissue*** pañuelo *m* de papel; ***p. towel*** toallita *f* de papel; *Comptr* ***p. tray*** bandeja *f* de papel
(b) *(newspaper)* periódico *m*; **it's in all the morning papers** está todo en los periódicos *or* diarios de la mañana; **p. boy/girl** repartidor/repartidora de periódicos; **to have** *or* **do a p. round** hacer el reparto de periódicos a domicilio; *Br* **p. shop** ≃ quiosco de periódicos
(c) *(document)* **papers** papeles *mpl*, documentación *f*; **once you've got the necessary papers together** una vez que hayas reunido la

documentación necesaria; **the author's private papers** los documentos privados del autor
(**d**) *(examination)* prueba *f*
(**e**) *(scholarly study, report)* estudio *m*, trabajo *m*; **to read** *or* **give a p.** leer *or* presentar una ponencia
(**f**) *(wallpaper)* papel *m* para empapelar
2 *vt (wall, room)* empapelar

▸ **paper over** *vt sep* (**a**) *(with wallpaper)* empapelar (**b**) IDIOM **to p. over the cracks** poner parches

paperback ['peɪpəbæk] *n* libro *m or* edición *f* en rústica; **it's in p.** es una edición rústica *or* de tapas blandas *or* de bolsillo ▸▸ ***p. binding*** encuadernación *f* en rústica

paperclip ['peɪpəklɪp] 1 *n* clip *m*
2 *vt* enganchar con un clip

paperknife ['peɪpənaɪf] *n* abrecartas *m inv*

paperless ['peɪpəlɪs] *adj* informatizado(a), electrónico(a); **the p. office** la oficina completamente informatizada

paper-thin ['peɪpə'θɪn] *adj* muy fino(a)

paperweight ['peɪpəweɪt] *n* pisapapeles *m inv*

paperwork ['peɪpəwɜːk] *n* papeleo *m*; **to do the p.** hacer el papeleo

papery ['peɪpərɪ] *adj* apergaminado(a)

papier-mâché ['pæpjeɪ'mæʃeɪ] *n* cartón *m* piedra

papist ['peɪpɪst] *Fam Pej* 1 *n* papista *mf*
2 *adj* papista

papoose [pə'puːs] *n* bebé *m or* niño *m* indio norteamericano

pappy[1] ['pæpɪ] *adj* (**a**) *(mushy)* pastoso(a) (**b**) *(worthless)* trivial, barato(a)

pappy[2] *n US Fam* papi *m*, papá *m*

paprika ['pæprɪkə, pə'priːkə] *n* pimentón *m*, paprika *f*

Papuan ['pæpjʊən] 1 *n* papú *mf*, papúa *mf*
2 *adj* papú, papúa

Papua New Guinea ['pæpjʊənjuː'gɪnɪ] *n* Papúa Nueva Guinea

papyrus [pə'paɪrəs] *n* papiro *m*

par [pɑː(r)] 1 *n* (**a**) *(equality)* **to be on a p. with** estar al mismo nivel que; **the two systems are on a p.** los dos sistemas están al mismo nivel; **you can't put him on a p. with Mozart!** ¡no puedes compararlo con Mozart!
(**b**) *(normal, average)* promedio *m*; **to feel below p.** no encontrarse muy allá; **the film wasn't really up to p.** la película decepcionó un poco
(**c**) *(in golf)* par *m*; **a p.-three (hole)** un (hoyo de) par tres; **she was two under/over p.** estaba dos bajo/sobre par; **to break p.** romper el par; IDIOM **that's about p. for the course** lamentablemente, no se puede esperar otra cosa
(**d**) *Fin* **above p.** sobre la par; **below p.** bajo par ▸▸ ***p. of exchange*** tipo *m* de cambio; ***p. value*** valor *m* nominal
2 *vt (in golf)* **to p. a hole** hacer par en un hoyo

para ['pærə] *n Fam* (**a**) *(paragraph)* párrafo *m* (**b**) *Br (paratrooper)* paraca *m*

parable ['pærəbəl] *n* parábola *f*

parabola [pə'ræbələ] *n* parábola *f*

parabolic [pærə'bɒlɪk] *adj* parabólico(a) ▸▸ ***p. dish*** (antena *f*) parabólica *f*

paracetamol [pærə'siːtəmɒl] *n* paracetamol *m*

parachute ['pærəʃuːt] 1 *n* paracaídas *m inv*; **to drop sth/sb by p.** lanzar *or* tirar a algo/alguien en paracaídas ▸▸ ***p. jump*** salto *m* en paracaídas
2 *vt (person, supplies)* lanzar en paracaídas
3 *vi* saltar en paracaídas

parachuting ['pærəʃuːtɪŋ] *n* paracaidismo *m*; **to go p.** hacer paracaidismo

parachutist ['pærəʃuːtɪst] *n* paracaidista *mf*

parade [pə'reɪd] 1 *n* (**a**) *(procession)* desfile *m*; **on p.** *(troops)* en formación ▸▸ ***p. ground*** plaza *f* de armas (**b**) *(row)* **a p. of shops** una hilera de tiendas (**c**) *(show, ostentation)* ostentación *f*, alarde *m*; **a p. of force** una situación en la que se hace ostentación de fuerza
2 *vt* (**a**) *(troops)* hacer desfilar; **the prisoners were paraded through the streets** hicieron desfilar a los prisioneros por las calles (**b**) *(streets)* desfilar por (**c**) *(riches, knowledge)* ostentar
3 *vi* (**a**) *(troops)* desfilar; **supporters paraded through the streets** los seguidores desfilaron por las calles (**b**) *(strut)* **to p. about** *or* **around** andar pavoneándose; **he was parading up and down as if he owned the place** andaba de aquí para allí, exhibiéndose como si fuera el dueño del lugar

paradigm ['pærədaɪm] *n* paradigma *m*; **p. case** caso paradigmático; **there has been a p. shift in ideas about education** los paradigmas de la educación han cambiado

paradigmatic [pærədɪg'mætɪk] *adj* paradigmático(a)

paradisaical [pærədɪ'zaɪəkəl], **paradisiac** [pærə'dɪzɪæk] *adj Literary* paradisiaco(a), paradisíaco(a)

paradise ['pærədaɪs] *n* (**a**) *(heaven)* paraíso *m*; *(Eden)* el Paraíso (**b**) *Fig* **a whole week away from the kids was p.!** ¡toda una semana sin los niños fue una gloria *or* el paraíso!; **this river is a fisherman's p.** este río es el paraíso de los pescadores

paradisiac = **paradisaical**

paradox ['pærədɒks] *n* paradoja *f*

paradoxical [pærə'dɒksɪkəl] *adj* paradójico(a)

paradoxically [pærə'dɒksɪklɪ] *adv* paradójicamente

paraffin ['pærəfɪn] *n* queroseno *m* ▸▸ ***p. heater*** estufa *f* de petróleo; ***p. lamp*** lámpara *f* de queroseno; *Br* ***p. oil*** aceite *m* de parafina; ***p. stove*** cocina *f* de queroseno; ***p. wax*** parafina *f*

paraglider ['pærəglaɪdə(r)] *n* (**a**) *(person)* parapentista *mf* (**b**) *(parachute)* parapente *m*

paragliding ['pærəglaɪdɪŋ] *n* parapente *m*; **to go p.** ir a hacer parapente

paragon ['pærəgən] *n* dechado *m*; **a p. of virtue** un dechado de virtudes

paragraph ['pærəgrɑːf] 1 *n* (**a**) *(in writing)* párrafo *m*; **to start a new p.** comenzar un nuevo párrafo; **section A, p. 3 (of the contract)** sección A, párrafo 3 (del contrato) ▸▸ *Comptr* ***p. formatting*** formateo *m* de párrafos; *Comptr* ***p. mark*** marca *f* de párrafo, calderón *m* (**b**) *(short newspaper article)* artículo *m* corto
2 *vt* organizar en párrafos

Paraguay ['pærəgwaɪ] *n* Paraguay

Paraguayan [pærə'gwaɪən] 1 *n* paraguayo(a) *m,f*
2 *adj* paraguayo(a)

parakeet ['pærəkiːt] *n* periquito *m*

paralanguage ['pærəlæŋgwɪdʒ] *n Ling* paralenguaje *m*

paralegal [pærə'liːgəl] *n US* ayudante *mf* de un abogado, *RP* procurador(ora) *m,f*

paralinguistic [pærəlɪŋ'gwɪstɪk] *adj* paralingüístico(a)

paralinguistics [pærəlɪŋ'gwɪstɪks] *n* paralingüística *f*

parallax ['pærəlæks] *n Phys & Astron* paralaje *m*

parallel ['pærəlel] 1 *n* (**a**) *Math* (línea *f*) paralela *f*; *Fig* **in p.** *(at the same time)* paralelamente (**b**) *Geog* paralelo *m*; **the 48th p.** el paralelo 48 (**c**) *(analogy)* paralelismo *m*; **to draw a p. between two things** establecer un paralelismo entre dos cosas; **the disaster is without p.** el desastre no tiene paralelo (**d**) *Elec* paralelo *m*; **in p.** en paralelo
2 *adj* paralelo(a); **to be** *or* **run p. to sth** ser *or* ir paralelo(a) a algo ▸▸ ***p. bars*** barras *fpl* paralelas; *Elec* ***p. circuits*** circuitos *mpl* en paralelo; *Comptr* ***p. distributed processing*** procesamiento *m* en distribución paralela; *EU* ***p. importing*** importación *f* paralela; ***p. lines*** líneas *fpl* paralelas; ***p. parking*** estacionamiento *m* en paralelo; *Comptr* ***p. port*** puerto *m* paralelo; *Comptr* ***p. printer*** impresora *f* en paralelo; *Comptr* ***p. processing*** procesado *m* en paralelo; ***p. ruler*** regla *f* para trazar rectas paralelas; ***p. turn*** *(in skiing)* giro *m* en paralelo
3 *vt* (**a**) *(run parallel to)* ir paralelo(a) a (**b**) *(be similar to)* asemejarse a (**c**) *(equal)* igualar

parallelepiped [pærəlele'paɪped] *n Geom* paralelepípedo *m*

parallelism ['pærəlelɪzəm] *n* paralelismo *m*

parallelogram [pærə'leləgræm] *n Geom* paralelogramo *m*

paralogism ['pærələdʒɪzəm] *n* paralogismo *m*

Paralympic [pærə'lɪmpɪk] 1 *n* **the Paralympics** los parolímpicos
2 *adj* parolímpico(a)

paralyse, *US* **paralyze** ['pærəlaɪz] *vt* paralizar; **both his legs are paralysed, he's paralysed in both legs** tiene parálisis en ambas piernas; **to be paralysed by** *or* **with fear** estar paralizado(a) por el miedo

paralysis [pə'ræləsɪs] *n* parálisis *f inv*

paralytic [pærə'lɪtɪk] *adj* (**a**) *Med* paralítico(a) (**b**) *Br Fam (very drunk)* **to be p.** estar como una cuba *or Méx* hasta atrás

paralyze *US* = **paralyse**

paramedic [pærə'medɪk] *n* auxiliar *mf* sanitario(a)

paramedical [pærə'medɪkəl] *adj* auxiliar sanitario(a)

parameter [pə'ræmɪtə(r)] *n* parámetro *m*; **to set the parameters of sth** establecer los parámetros de algo ▸▸ *Comptr* ***p. RAM*** RAM *f* de parámetros

paramilitary [pærə'mɪlɪtrɪ] 1 *n* paramilitar *mf*
2 *adj* paramilitar

paramount ['pærəmaʊnt] *adj* primordial, vital; **it is of p. importance** es de capital *or* suma importancia; **the children's interests should be p.** los intereses de los niños deberían ser de capital *or* suma importancia

paramour ['pærəmɔː(r)] *n Literary* amante *mf*

Parana [pærə'nɑː] *n* **the P.** el Paraná

paranoia [pærə'nɔɪə] *n* paranoia *f*

paranoid ['pærənɔɪd], **paranoiac** [pærə'nɔɪæk] *adj* paranoico(a) (**about** por *or* con); *Fig* **he's p. about being cheated** la posibilidad de que lo timen lo tiene obsesionado

paranormal [pærə'nɔːməl] **1** *n* **the p.** lo paranormal
2 *adj* paranormal

parapenting ['pærəpentɪŋ] *n* parapente *m*

parapet ['pærəpet] *n* parapeto *m*

paraphernalia [pærəfə'neɪlɪə] *npl* parafernalia *f*

paraphrase ['pærəfreɪz] **1** *n* paráfrasis *f inv*
2 *vt* parafrasear

paraplegia [pærə'pliːdʒə] *n* paraplejia *f*

paraplegic [pærə'pliːdʒɪk] **1** *n* parapléjico(a) *m,f*
2 *adj* parapléjico(a)

parapsychological [pærəsaɪkə'lɒdʒɪkəl] *adj* parapsicológico(a)

parapsychologist [pærəsaɪ'kɒlədʒɪst] *n* parapsicólogo(a) *m,f*

parapsychology [pærəsaɪ'kɒlədʒɪ] *n* parapsicología *f*

Paraquat® ['pærəkwɒt] *n* = potente herbicida

parasailing ['pærəseɪlɪŋ] *n* = especie de parapente con esquís acuáticos y a remolque de una lancha motora

parascending ['pærəsendɪŋ] *n* parapente *m (a remolque de lancha motora)*

parasite ['pærəsaɪt] *n* (**a**) *(plant, animal)* parásito *m* (**b**) *(person)* parásito *m*

parasitic(al) [pærə'sɪtɪk(əl)] *adj also Fig* parásito(a); **p. disease** dolencia *or* enfermedad parasitaria

parasitism ['pærəsɪtɪzəm] *n* parasitismo *m*

parasitologist [pærəsaɪ'tɒlədʒɪst] *n* parasitólogo(a) *m,f*

parasitology [pærəsaɪ'tɒlədʒɪ] *n* parasitología *f*

parasitosis [pærəsɪ'təʊsɪs] *n* parasitosis *f*

parasol ['pærəsɒl] *n* sombrilla *f*

paratactic [pærə'tæktɪk] *adj Gram* paratáctico(a)

parataxis [pærə'tæksɪs] *n Gram* parataxis *f inv*

parathyroid [pærə'θaɪrɔɪd] *Anat* **1** *n* paratiroides *f inv*
2 *adj* paratiroideo(a)

paratrooper ['pærətruːpə(r)] *n* (soldado *m*) paracaidista *m*

paratroops ['pærətruːps] *npl* (tropas *fpl*) paracaidistas *mpl*

paratyphoid [pærə'taɪfɔɪd] *n* paratifoidea *f*

parboil ['pɑːbɔɪl] *vt* cocer a medias, sancochar

parcel ['pɑːsəl] **1** *n* (**a**) *(package)* paquete *m* ▸▸ ***p. bomb*** paquete *m* bomba; ***p. post*** (servicio *m* de) paquete *m* postal *or Andes, RP* encomienda *f*; *Aut* ***p. shelf*** estante *m* (**b**) *(of land)* parcela *f* (**c**) *Culin* paquete *m*
2 *vt* (*pt & pp* **parcelled**, *US* **parceled**) *(wrap up)* envolver, empaquetar

▸ **parcel out** *vt sep* (**a**) *(land)* parcelar (**b**) *(money)* dividir en lotes

▸ **parcel up** *vt sep (wrap up)* embalar, empaquetar

parch [pɑːtʃ] *vt* (**a**) *(dry up)* resecar (**b**) *Culin* tostar

parched [pɑːtʃt] *adj* (**a**) *(very dry)* reseco(a) (**b**) *Fam (very thirsty)* **I'm p.!** ¡me muero de sed!

Parcheesi® [pɑː'tʃiːzɪ] *n US* parchís *m*

parchment ['pɑːtʃmənt] *n* pergamino *m*

pardner ['pɑːrdnə(r)] *n US Fam* amigo(a) *m,f*, *Esp* colega *mf*

pardon ['pɑːdən] **1** *n* (**a**) *(forgiveness)* perdón *m*; **(I beg your) p.?** *(what did you say?)* ¿cómo dice?; **I beg your p.!** *(in apology)* ¡discúlpeme!; **this dish is revolting! – I beg your p., I made it myself!** este plato está asqueroso – ¡pero cómo te atreves, lo he hecho yo! (**b**) *Law* indulto *m*; **he was granted a p.** fue indultado
2 *vt* (**a**) *(action, person)* perdonar, excusar; **p. me?** *(what did you say?)* ¿cómo dice?; **p. me!** *(in apology)* ¡discúlpeme!; **this dish is revolting! – p. me, I made it myself!** este plato está asqueroso – ¡pero cómo te atreves, lo he hecho yo!; **p. me for asking, but...** discúlpeme que le pregunte pero...; *Ironic* **well p. me for breathing!** ¡usted me disculpe!; **you could be pardoned for thinking so** es entendible que lo creas *or* lo pienses
(**b**) *Law* indultar

pardonable ['pɑːdənəbəl] *adj (mistake, behaviour)* perdonable, excusable

pare [peə(r)] *vt* (**a**) *(fruit, vegetable)* pelar; **p. the rind off the cheese** quítale la corteza al queso (**b**) *(nails)* cortar (**c**) *(expenses)* recortar; **staff levels have already been pared to the bone** ya se han hecho recortes salvajes en la plantilla de personal

▸ **pare down** *vt sep (expenses)* recortar; **we've got to p. the report down to 50 pages** tenemos que recortar el informe hasta que queden sólo 50 páginas

parent ['peərənt] *n* (**a**) *(father)* padre *m*; *(mother)* madre *f*; **parents** padres; **when you first become a p.** la primera vez que eres padre; **Anne and Bob have become parents** Anne y Bob han tenido su primer hijo; **each p. should...** cada padre debería...; **if neither p. can...** si ninguno de los padres puede... ▸▸ ***parents' association*** asociación *f* de padres de alumnos; ***p.-teacher association*** = asociación de padres de alumnos y profesores, *Esp* ≃ APA *f*
(**b**) *(source)* **a cutting from the p. plant** madera del mismo leño; **one of the p. birds/seals** una de las aves/focas progenitoras; **our p. company** nuestra empresa matriz

> **False friend**: The Spanish noun **pariente** is not a translation for the English word **parent**. In Spanish **pariente** means "relation, relative".

parentage ['peərəntɪdʒ] *n* origen *m*, ascendencia *f*; **a child of unknown p.** un niño de padres desconocidos

parental [pə'rentəl] *adj* de los padres; **the p. home** la casa paterna

parenthesis [pə'renθəsɪs] (*pl* **parentheses** [pə'renθəsiːz]) *n* paréntesis *m inv*; **in parentheses** entre paréntesis

parenthetic(al) [pærən'θetɪk(əl)] *adj* parentético(a), entre paréntesis; *Gram* **p. clause** cláusula *or* oración parentética

parenthetically [pærən'θetɪklɪ] *adv Formal* parentéticamente

parenthood ['peərənthʊd] *n (fatherhood)* paternidad *f*; *(motherhood)* maternidad *f*; **the joys of p.** las satisfacciones que trae tener hijos

parenting ['peərəntɪŋ] *n* **a book on good p.** un libro sobre cómo ser buenos padres; **to learn p. skills** aprender a ser buenos padres

parentless ['peərəntlɪs] *adj* huérfano(a)

par excellence [pɑːr'eksəlɒns] *adv* por excelencia

parfait [pɑː'feɪ] *n Culin* = postre helado a base de nata, huevos y fruta

pariah [pə'raɪə] *n (person)* paria *mf*

parietal [pə'raɪətəl] *adj Anat* parietal ▸▸ ***p. bone*** parietal *m*; ***p. lobe*** lóbulo *m* parietal

paring ['peərɪŋ] *n* (**a**) *(activity) (of fruit, vegetables)* peladura *f*, mondadura *f*; *(of nails)* corte *m* ▸▸ ***p. knife*** cuchillo *m* de cocina (**b**) *(from fruit, vegetables)* cáscara *f*, monda *f*; *(from nails)* corte *m*

Paris ['pærɪs] *n* París

parish ['pærɪʃ] *n* (**a**) *Rel (area, parishioners)* parroquia *f*, feligresía *f* ▸▸ ***p. church*** parroquia *f*, iglesia *f* parroquial; ***p. clerk*** sacristán *m*; ***p. hall*** salón *m* parroquial; ***p. priest*** (cura *m*) párroco *m*; ***p. register*** registro *m* parroquial (**b**) *(administrative area)* parroquia *f*, distrito *m* ▸▸ ***p. council*** concejo *m*

parishioner [pə'rɪʃənə(r)] *n* feligrés(esa) *m,f*, parroquiano(a) *m,f*

parish-pump ['pærɪʃ'pʌmp] *adj Br Pej* provinciano(a); **p. politics** política provinciana

Parisian [pə'rɪzɪən, *US* pə'riːʒən] **1** *n* parisino(a) *m,f*, parisiense *mf*
2 *adj* parisino(a), parisiense

parity ['pærɪtɪ] *n* (**a**) *(equality)* igualdad *f*; *(of salaries)* equiparación *f*; **to achieve p. with** *(pay, output)* equipararse a (**b**) *Fin* paridad *f* ▸▸ ***p. of exchange*** paridad *f* de cambio (**c**) *Comptr* paridad *f* ▸▸ ***p. bit*** bit *m* de paridad; ***p. check*** prueba *f* de paridad

park [pɑːk] **1** *n* (**a**) *(green area)* parque *m* ▸▸ ***p. bench*** banco *m* público; *Br* ***p. keeper*** guarda *mf* del parque (**b**) *(private estate)* jardines *mpl* (**c**) *US (stadium)* estadio *m* (**d**) *Br Fam* **the p.** *(soccer pitch)* el campo, *Andes, RP* la cancha (**e**) *Aut (on automatic gearbox)* punto *m* muerto (**f**) *Mil (artillery, tanks)* parque *m*
2 *vt* (**a**) *(car)* estacionar, *Esp* aparcar; **he was parked by a fire hydrant** estaba estacionado *or Esp* aparcado al lado de una boca de incendios (**b**) *Fam (place) (person, box)* poner, tirar; **to p. oneself in front of the TV** apoltronarse *or Am* echarse enfrente de la televisión
3 *vi* estacionar, *Esp* aparcar, *Méx* estacionarse, *Col* parquearse

parka ['pɑːkə] *n* parka *f*

park-and-ride ['pɑːkən'raɪd] *n* = estacionamiento conectado con el centro de la ciudad por transporte público, *Esp* aparcamiento *m* disuasorio

parkie ['pɑːkɪ] *n Br Fam* guarda *mf* del parque

parkin ['pɑːkɪn] *n Br* = galleta de jengibre y avena

parking ['pɑːkɪŋ] *n* estacionamiento *m*, *Esp* aparcamiento *m*, *Col* parqueadero *m*; **p. is a problem in town** estacionar *or Esp* aparcar es un problema en la ciudad; **no p.** *(sign)* prohibido estacionar *or Esp* aparcar, estacionamiento prohibido ▸▸ ***p. attendant*** vigilante *mf* de estacionamiento *or Esp* aparcamiento; ***p. bay*** área *f* de estacionamiento *or Esp* aparcamiento *(señalizada)*; ***p. lights*** *(on car)* luces *fpl* de estacionamiento; *US* ***p. lot*** *Esp* aparcamiento *m*, *RP* playa *f* de estacionamiento, *Col* parqueadero *m*; ***p. meter*** parquímetro *m*; ***p. offence*** estacionamiento *m* indebido; ***p. place*** estacionamiento *m*, *Esp* aparcamiento *m*, sitio *m or* hueco *m* para estacionar; ***p. space*** estacionamiento *m*, *Esp* aparcamiento *m*, sitio *m or* hueco *m* para estacionar; ***p. ticket*** multa *f* de estacionamiento

Parkinson's disease ['pɑːkɪnsənzdɪ'ziːz] *n* (enfermedad *f* de) Parkinson *m*

parkland ['pɑːklænd] *n* zonas *fpl* verdes, parque *m*

parkway ['pɑːkweɪ] *n US* = carretera o avenida con árboles a los lados y en el medio

parky ['pɑːkɪ] *adj Br Fam* **it's a bit p.** hace un poco de fresquito

parlance ['pɑːləns] *n Formal* **in scientific/political p.** en la jerga científica/política; **in common p.** en el habla común

parlay ['pɑːlɪ] *US* **1** *n (bet)* = método que consiste en reinvertir de antemano lo que se ha ganado en otra apuesta

2 *vt* **(a)** *(winnings)* volver a apostar el dinero ganado en una apuesta **(b)** *Fig (money, talent, project)* convertir, transformar; **she parlayed the local newspapers into a press empire** a partir de los periódicos locales construyó un emporio periodístico

parley ['pɑːlɪ] **1** *n* negociación *f*

2 *vi* parlamentar (**with** con)

parleyvoo [pɑːlɪ'vuː] *Fam Hum* **1** *n (French language)* franchute *m*

2 *vi* **I don't p.** no hablo franchute

parliament ['pɑːləmənt] *n* **(a)** *(law-making body)* parlamento *m*; **in P.** en el Parlamento; **to go into P.** ser elegido(a) parlamentario(a) **(b)** *(period between elections)* legislatura *f*

parliamentarian [pɑːləmen'teərɪən] *n* **(a)** *(member)* parlamentario(a) *m,f* **(b)** *Hist* **P.** parlamentario(a) *m,f*

parliamentary [pɑːlə'mentərɪ] *adj* parlamentario(a) ▸▸ *Br* ***P. Commissioner (for Administration)*** ≃ defensor(ora) *m,f* del pueblo; ***p. democracy*** democracia *f* parlamentaria; ***p. immunity*** inmunidad *f or* inviolabilidad *f* parlamentaria; *Br* ***p. private secretary*** secretario *m* privado parlamentario; *Br* ***P. privilege*** inmunidad *f* parlamentaria; *Br* ***p. secretary*** secretario(a) *m,f* parlamentario(a)

parlour, *US* **parlor** ['pɑːlə(r)] *n* **(a)** *Old-fashioned (in house)* salón *m* ▸▸ ***p. game*** juego *m* de salón **(b)** *(shop)* **beauty p.** salón de belleza; **ice-cream p.** heladería **(c)** *US Rail* ***p. car*** coche *m or* vagón *m* de primera clase, *Arg* coche *m* superpullman

parlous ['pɑːləs] *adj Formal or Hum* **to be in a p. state** estar en un estado precario

Parma ['pɑːmə] *n* Parma ▸▸ ***P. ham*** jamón *m* de Parma; ***P. violet*** violeta *f* de Parma

Parmesan [pɑːmɪ'zæn, *US* pɑːmə'ʒɑːn] *n* **P. (cheese)** (queso *m*) parmesano *m*

Parnassus [pə'næsəs] *n (in mythology)* **(Mount) P.** el (Monte) Parnaso

parochial [pə'rəʊkɪəl] *adj* **(a)** *Rel* parroquial ▸▸ *US* ***p. school*** colegio *m* privado religioso, *Arg* ≃ colegio *m* parroquial **(b)** *Pej (narrow-minded)* provinciano(a), corto(a) de miras

parochialism [pə'rəʊkɪəlɪzəm] *n Pej (of mentality)* provincialismo *m*, estrechez *f* de miras

parodist ['pærədɪst] *n* parodista *mf*

parody ['pærədɪ] **1** *n* parodia *f* (**of** de)

2 *vt* parodiar

parole [pə'rəʊl] **1** *n* **(a)** *Law* libertad *f* condicional; **he's up for p. next year** el año próximo le corresponde la libertad condicional; **to be (out) on p.** estar en libertad condicional; **to break one's p.** quebrar la libertad condicional ▸▸ ***p. board*** junta *f* de libertad condicional; ***p. officer*** = asistente social que supervisa a un preso en libertad condicional y ante quien se presenta periódicamente

(b) *Ling* habla *f*

2 *vt Law* poner en libertad condicional

parolee [pərəʊ'liː] *n* convicto(a) *m,f* en libertad condicional

paroxysm ['pærəksɪzəm] *n* **(a)** *(of anger, guilt, jealousy)* arrebato *m*, ataque *m*; **to be in paroxysms of laughter** tener un ataque de risa **(b)** *Med (of disease)* paroxismo *m*, acceso *m* violento

parquet ['pɑːkeɪ] **1** *n* **(a)** *(on floor)* parqué *m*; **p. (floor)** (suelo *m* de) parqué **(b)** *US Theat* platea *f*

2 *vt* colocar parqué en

parricide ['pærɪsaɪd] *n* **(a)** *(crime)* parricidio *m* **(b)** *(person)* parricida *mf*

parrot ['pærət] **1** *n* **(a)** *(bird)* loro *m* **(b)** ***p. fish*** pez *m* papagayo

2 *vt* repetir como un loro

parrot-fashion ['pærətfæʃən] *adv (to repeat, learn)* como un loro

parry ['pærɪ] **1** *n (of blow, thrust)* parada *f*, desvío *m*

2 *vt* **(a)** *(blow, thrust)* parar, desviar **(b)** *(question)* esquivar, eludir

3 *vi (in fencing, boxing)* cubrirse, protegerse

parse [pɑːz] *vt* **(a)** *Gram (word)* analizar gramaticalmente **(b)** *Comptr & Ling (sentence)* analizar sintácticamente

parsec ['pɑːsek] *n Astron* pársec *m*

parser ['pɑːzə(r)] *n Comptr* analizador *m* sintáctico

parsimonious [pɑːsɪ'məʊnɪəs] *adj Formal (mean)* mezquino(a)

> **False friend**: The Spanish adjective **parsimonioso** is not a translation for the English word **parsimonious**. In Spanish **parsimonioso** means "unhurried, deliberate".

parsimoniously [pɑːsɪ'məʊnɪəslɪ] *adv Formal* con mezquindad

parsimony ['pɑːsɪmənɪ] *n Formal* mezquindad *f*

parsley ['pɑːslɪ] *n* perejil *m*

parsnip ['pɑːsnɪp] *n* pastinaca *f*, chirivía *f*; PROV **fine words butter no parsnips!** mucho te quiero perrito, pero pan poquito

parson ['pɑːsən] *n* párroco *m (protestante)* ▸▸ *Fam* ***p.'s nose*** rabadilla *f*

parsonage ['pɑːsənɪdʒ] *n* casa *f* parroquial

PART [pɑːt] **1** *n* **(a)** *(portion, element)* parte *f*; **the parts of the body** las partes del cuerpo; **the front p. of the aircraft** la parte delantera del avión; **p. two** *(of TV, radio series)* segunda parte; **p. of me still isn't sure** en parte todavía no estoy seguro; **good in parts** bueno(a) a ratos, *Am* bueno(a) de a ratos; **the difficult p. is remembering** lo difícil es acordarse; **the worst p. was when she started laughing** lo peor fue cuando empezó a reírse; **for the best** *or* **better p. of five years** durante casi cinco años; **the greater p. of the population** la mayor parte de la población; **to be** *or* **form p. of sth** ser *or* formar parte de algo; **it's all p. of growing up** forma parte del proceso de crecimiento; **it is p. and parcel of...** es parte integrante de...; **for the most p., we get on** por lo general, nos llevamos bien; **the visitors are, for the most p., Irish** los visitantes son, en su mayoría, irlandeses; **in p.** en parte; **in (a) large p.** en gran parte; IDIOM **to be like p. of the furniture** ser (como) parte del mobiliario ▸▸ ***p. of speech*** categoría *f* gramatical, parte *f* de la oración

(b) *(role)* papel *m*; **a man/woman of many parts** un hombre/una mujer con talento en muchos ámbitos; *Theat* **to play a p.** interpretar un papel; **to have** *or* **play a large p. in sth** tener un papel importante en algo; **we wish to play our full p. in the process** queremos participar plenamente en el proceso; **it played no p. in our decision** no influyó para nada en nuestra decisión; **he was jailed for his p. in the crime** fue encarcelado por su participación en el crimen; **to take p. (in sth)** participar *or* tomar parte (en algo); **to take sth in good p.** tomarse algo a bien; **I want no p. of** *or* **in it** no quiero tener nada que ver con eso; **to dress the p.** vestirse para la ocasión; **you really look the p. of the executive!** ¡*Esp* vas *or Am* estás hecho todo un ejecutivo!

(c) *(component) (of machine)* pieza *f*; **(spare) parts** recambios *mpl*, piezas *fpl* de recambio, *Méx* refacciones *fpl*, *Col, Cuba, RP* repuestos *mpl*

(d) *(area) (of country, town)* parte *f*; **in that p. of the world** en esa parte del mundo; **it's a dangerous p. of town** es un barrio peligroso; **in these parts** por aquí; **are you new to** *or* **in these parts?** ¿eres nuevo aquí?; **there will be rain in parts** lloverá en algunas partes

(e) *(side)* **to take sb's p.** tomar partido por *or* ponerse de parte de alguien; **for my p.** por mi parte; **on the p. of...** por parte de...; **it was a mistake on our p.** fue un error por *or Am* de nuestra parte

(f) *(measure)* parte *f*; **one p. rum to four parts water** una parte de ron por cada cuatro de agua; *Chem* **a concentration of six parts per million** una concentración de seis partes por millón

(g) *Mus* parte *f* ▸▸ ***p. song*** canto *m* polifónico

(h) *US (in hair)* raya *f*, *Col, Méx, Ven* carrera *f*

2 *adj* **in p. payment** como parte del pago; **they'll take your old one in p. exchange** aceptan el viejo como parte del pago ▸▸ ***p. owner*** copropietario(a) *m,f*

3 *adv* **she's p. Spanish** es medio española; **it's p. silk, p. cotton** es de seda y algodón; **the test is p. practical and p. theoretical** la prueba consta de una parte práctica y otra teórica

4 *vt* (a) *(move apart, open) (lips, branches, legs)* separar; *(curtains)* abrir, descorrer

(b) *(separate) (fighters, lovers)* separar; **he was parted from his wife during the war** la guerra lo separó de su mujer; **to p. company** separarse; *Fig* **here's where we p. company** aquí nos separamos; *Hum* **the handle finally parted company with the door** el picaporte acabó finalmente por abandonar la puerta

(c) *(hair)* **to p. one's hair** hacerse raya *or Col, Méx, Ven* carrera (en el pelo); **her hair is parted in the middle** lleva la raya al medio

5 *vi* (a) *(move apart) (lips, branches, legs, crowd)* separarse; *(curtains)* abrirse, descorrerse; **the clouds parted** las nubes se separaron

(b) *(leave one another)* separarse; **to p. (as) friends** quedar como amigos; **we parted on bad terms** acabamos mal

(c) *(break) (rope)* romperse

▸ **part with** *vt insep* desprenderse de; **he hates parting with his money** no soporta tener que desembolsar dinero

---

partake [pɑːˈteɪk] (*pt* **partook** [pɑːˈtʊk], *pp* **partaken** [pɑːˈteɪkən]) *vi Formal* (a) *(eat, drink)* **to p. of** compartir; **to p. of a meal** compartir una comida; **I no longer p.** *(don't drink)* ya no bebo; *Rel* **to p. of the Sacrament** compartir el Sacramento (b) *(participate)* **to p. in** *(event)* participar; *(joy, grief)* compartir (c) *(have quality)* **to p. of** participar de

parterre [pɑːˈteə(r)] *n* (a) *Br (flower garden)* parterre *m* (b) *US Theat* platea *f* ▸▸ ***p. box*** palco *m* de platea

parthenogenesis [pɑːθɪnəʊˈdʒenɪsɪs] *n Biol* partenogénesis *f inv*

Parthenon [ˈpɑːθɪnən] *n* **the P.** el Partenón

partial [ˈpɑːʃəl] *adj* (a) *(incomplete)* parcial; **a p. loss of hearing** una pérdida parcial de la audición; **the exhibition was only a p. success** la exhibición fue un éxito a medias ▸▸ *Astron* ***p. eclipse*** eclipse *m* parcial (b) *(biased)* parcial (c) *(fond)* **I'm quite p. to the odd glass of wine** no le hago ascos a un vaso de vino

partiality [pɑːʃɪˈælɪtɪ] *n* (a) *(bias)* parcialidad *f* (**towards** hacia) (b) *(fondness)* afición (**for** a)

partially [ˈpɑːʃəlɪ] *adv* (a) *(in part)* parcialmente; **p. sighted** con visión parcial (b) *(with bias)* parcialmente, con parcialidad

participant [pɑːˈtɪsɪpənt] 1 *n* participante *mf*

2 *adj* participante

participate [pɑːˈtɪsɪpeɪt] *vi* participar (**in** en)

participation [pɑːtɪsɪˈpeɪʃən] *n* participación *f* (**in** en); **they would welcome greater parental p.** recibirían muy bien una mayor participación de los padres

participatory [pɑːtɪsɪˈpeɪtərɪ] *adj* participativo(a)

participial [pɑːtɪˈsɪpɪəl] *adj Gram* de participio

participle [ˈpɑːtɪsɪpəl] *n Gram* participio *m*; **past p.** participio pasado *or* pasivo; **present p.** participio de presente *or* activo

particle [ˈpɑːtɪkəl] *n* (a) *(tiny piece)* partícula *f*; **there's not a p. of truth in the story** la historia no tiene nada de cierto (b) *Gram* partícula *f* (c) *Phys* partícula *f* ▸▸ ***p. accelerator*** acelerador *m* de partículas; ***p. beam*** haz *m* de partículas; ***p. physics*** física *f* de partículas

particoloured, *US* **particolored** [ˈpɑːtɪkʌləd] *adj* de varios colores

particular [pəˈtɪkjʊlə(r)] 1 *n* (a) *(detail)* detalle *m*, pormenor *m*; **alike in every p.** iguales en todos los aspectos; **to go into particulars** entrar en detalles; **to take down sb's particulars** tomar los datos de alguien; **for further particulars apply to...** para mayor información diríjase a... (b) *(specific)* **from the general to the p.** de lo general a lo particular

2 *adj* (a) *(specific)* específico(a); **do you have a p. day in mind?** ¿tienes en mente algún día en particular?; **which p. person did you have in mind?** ¿en quién pensabas en concreto?; **I haven't read that p. novel** no he leído esa novela concreta; **only that p. colour will do** sólo sirve ese color específico; **why did you insist on this p. one?** ¿por qué has insistido en ésta en particular?; **for no p. reason** por ninguna razón en particular *or* en especial; **we had no p. place to go** no teníamos ningún lugar en especial a dónde ir; **the problem is not p. to this region** no es un problema exclusivo de esta zona

(b) *(special)* especial; **he is a p. friend of mine** es un amigo mío muy querido; **to take p. care over sth** tener especial cuidado con algo

(c) *(exacting)* exigente; **to be p. about sth** ser exigente con algo; **it had to be pure silk, he was most p. about it** tenía que ser seda natural, sobre ese punto fue terminante; **I'm not p.** me da lo mismo; **he's not very p. about where his money comes from** no le importa mucho de dónde viene su dinero

3 **in particular** *adv (specifically)* en particular; **I didn't notice anything in p.** no noté nada de particular; **what did you do? – nothing in p.** ¿qué hiciste? – nada en particular

particularity [pətɪkjʊˈlærɪtɪ] *n* (a) *(special quality)* particularidad *f* (b) *(exacting nature)* lo particular, la singularidad (c) *(detailed nature) (of description)* lo detallado, lo pormenorizado

particularly [pəˈtɪkjʊləlɪ] *adv (especially)* particularmente, especialmente; **not p.** no especialmente; **it's cold here, p. at night** aquí hace frío, sobre todo por la noche; **I was surprised he wasn't there, p. as he'd received an official invitation** me sorprendió que no estuviera, en especial porque había recibido una invitación oficial

particulate [pəˈtɪkjʊlɪt] 1 *n* partícula *f*

2 *adj* de partículas

partied out [ˈpɑːtɪdaʊt] *adj Fam* harto(a) de fiestas

parting [ˈpɑːtɪŋ] 1 *n* (a) *(leave-taking)* despedida *f*; **they had come to the p. of the ways** había llegado la hora de despedirse *or* el momento de la despedida (b) *Br (in hair)* raya *f*; **centre/side p.** raya al medio/al lado

2 *adj (words, kiss)* de despedida; **her p. words** sus palabras de despedida ▸▸ ***p. shot*** = comentario hiriente a modo de despedida

partisan [ˈpɑːtɪzæn] 1 *n* (a) *(during 2nd World War)* partisano(a) *m,f* (b) *(supporter)* partidario(a) *m,f* (**of** de)

2 *adj (biased)* parcial

partition [pɑːˈtɪʃən] 1 *n* (a) *(in room)* tabique *m* ▸▸ ***p. wall*** tabique *m* (b) *(of country)* división *f*, partición *f* (c) *Comptr* partición *f*

2 *vt* (a) *(room)* dividir (b) *(country)* dividir (c) *Comptr (hard disk)* crear particiones en

▸ **partition off** *vt sep (room)* dividir con un tabique *or* con tabiques; **a small area had been partitioned off from the rest** habían delimitado con un tabique un pequeño sector

partitive [ˈpɑːtɪtɪv] *Gram* 1 *n* partitivo *m*

2 *adj* partitivo(a)

partly [ˈpɑːtlɪ] *adv* en parte; **p. by force, p. by persuasion** en parte por la fuerza, en parte a través de la persuasión; **she was only p. convinced** no estaba del todo convencida; **that's only p. true** sólo es verdad en parte

partner [ˈpɑːtnə(r)] 1 *n* (a) *(in company, project)* socio(a) *m,f*; **our European partners** nuestros socios europeos (b) *(in sports, for activity)* compañero(a) *m,f*; *(in dancing)* pareja *f* ▸▸ ***p. in crime*** cómplice *mf* (c) *(in couple)* compañero(a) *m,f*, pareja *f*

2 *vt* (a) *(in business)* asociar a (b) *(in games, in dancing)* hacer pareja con

partnership [ˈpɑːtnəʃɪp] *n* (a) *(cooperation)* **a p. between business and government** una colaboración entre la empresa y el gobierno; **the famous striking p.** la famosa pareja goleadora; **to work in p. with sb** trabajar conjuntamente *or* colaborar con alguien; **we work in p. with relief organizations** trabajamos conjuntamente con organizaciones humanitarias

(b) *(firm)* sociedad *f* colectiva *(en la que los socios comparten pérdidas y beneficios)*; **to enter** *or* **go into p. (with sb)** formar sociedad *or* asociarse (con alguien)

(c) *(position in firm)* **to offer sb a p. in the firm** ofrecer a alguien la posición de socio en la firma

partook *pt of* **partake**

part-owner [pɑːtˈəʊnə(r)] *n* copropietario(a) *m,f*

partridge [ˈpɑːtrɪdʒ] (*pl* **partridge** *or* **partridges**) *n* perdiz *f*; **red-legged p.** perdiz *f* roja

part-time [pɑːtˈtaɪm] 1 *adj* a tiempo parcial

2 *adv* a tiempo parcial

part-timer [pɑːtˈtaɪmə(r)] *n* trabajador(ora) *m,f* a tiempo parcial

parturition [pɑːtjʊˈrɪʃən] *n Med* parto *m*

partway [ˈpɑːtweɪ] *adv* **I'm p. through it** *(task)* ya llevo hecha una parte; *(book)* ya he leído parte; **p. through the year, she resigned** renunció ya entrado el año; **this will go p. towards covering the costs** esto sufragará parte de los gastos

partwork [ˈpɑːtwɜːk] *n* obra *f* en fascículos

party [ˈpɑːtɪ] 1 *n* (a) *(political)* partido *m*; **a p. member, a member of the p.** un miembro del partido; **he's just making a p. political point** está haciendo partidismo ▸▸ ***p. discipline*** *(in voting)* disciplina *f* de voto; ***the p. leadership*** los altos cargos del partido; ***p. line:*** **to follow** *or* **toe the p. line** seguir la línea del partido; ***the p. machine*** la maquinaria del partido; ***p. man*** hombre *m* de partido; *Br* ***p. political broadcast*** espacio *m* electoral *(no sólo antes de las elecciones)*; ***p. politics*** la política partidista, el partidismo

(b) *(celebration)* fiesta *f*; **to have** *or* **throw a p.** dar *or* celebrar una fiesta; *Fig* **the p.'s over** se acabó la fiesta; *Fam* **he's a p. animal** le gustan *or Esp* van las fiestas ▸▸ ***p. dress*** vestido *m* de fiesta; ***p. games*** juegos *mpl* de salón; *Br* ***p. piece*** numerito *m* habitual *(para entretener a la gente)*; *Fam* ***p. pooper*** aguafiestas *mf inv*

(c) *(group)* grupo *m*; **a wedding p.** los asistentes a una boda; **will you join our p.?** ¿querría sumarse a nuestro partido?; **a reservation for the Miller p.** una reserva para un grupo a nombre de Miller ►► *Tel* ***p. line*** línea *f* compartida, party-line *f*; ***p. wall*** *(in house)* pared *f* medianera

(d) *(participant)* & *Law* parte *f*; **the p. concerned** la parte interesada; **the parties to the contract** las partes contratantes; **to be a p. to** *(conversation)* participar en; *(crime)* ser cómplice de; *(conspiracy, enterprise)* formar parte de; **I would never be (a) p. to such a thing** nunca tomaría parte en algo semejante

(e) *(person)* persona *f*; **I understand a Spanish p. was involved** tengo entendido que había un español involucrado

2 *vi Fam (celebrate)* estar de fiesta *or* juerga; **I was out partying last night** anoche estuve de fiesta *or* juerga; **let's p.!** ¡que empiece la fiesta!

partygoer ['pɑːtɪgəʊə(r)] *n* **the streets were full of partygoers** las calles estaban llenas de gente que acudía a fiestas; **an inveterate p.** un fiestero empedernido

party-size ['pɑːtɪsaɪz] *adj (package)* de gran tamaño

parvenu ['pɑːvənuː] *Pej* 1 *n* advenedizo(a) *m,f*

2 *adj* advenedizo(a)

PASCAL ['pæskæl] *n Comptr* PASCAL *m*

pascal ['pæskəl] *n Phys* pascal *m* ►► ***P.'s triangle*** triángulo *m* de Pascal

paschal ['pæskəl] *adj* pascual ►► ***P. Lamb*** cordero *m* pascual

pasha ['pæʃə] *n* bajá *m*, pachá *m*

pashmina [pæʃ'miːnə] *n (garment)* pashmina *f*

Pashtun [pæʃ'tuːn] 1 *adj* pastún

2 *n* pastún *mf*

PASS [pɑːs] 1 *n* (a) *(permit)* pase *m*; **rail/bus p.** abono de tren/autobús

(b) *(in examination)* **to obtain** *or* **get a p.** aprobar ►► *Br* ***p. mark*** nota *f* mínima para aprobar; ***p. rate*** porcentaje *m* de aprobados

(c) *(in football, basketball, rugby)* pase *m*

(d) *(in tennis)* passing-shot *m*

(e) *(in bullfighting)* pase *m*

(f) *(in fencing)* pase *m*; **to make a p. at** dar un pase a

(g) *(by magician)* pase *m*

(h) *(fly-by)* **the aircraft made two low passes over the village** el avión pasó dos veces sobre el pueblo a baja altura

(i) *(through mountains)* paso *m*, puerto *m*

(j) *(revision)* **I found several mistakes on the first p.** encontré varios errores en la primera lectura

(k) *Fam (sexual advance)* **to make a p. at sb** intentar seducir a alguien, *Esp* tirar los tejos a alguien, *RP* tirarse un lance con alguien

(l) *(difficult situation)* **how did things come to such a p.?** ¿cómo se ha podido llegar a tan extrema situación?; **things have come to a pretty** *or* **fine** *or* **sorry p. when...** las cosas han llegado a un punto ridículo cuando...

2 *vt* (a) *(go past) (person, place)* pasar junto a; *(frontier, limit)* pasar; *(car, runner)* pasar, adelantar; *(unintentionally)* pasarse, saltarse; **I often p. him in the street** me cruzo con él a menudo en la calle; **I think we've passed their street already** creo que ya nos hemos pasado su calle; **if you p. a chemist's, get some aspirin** si pasas por una farmacia, compra aspirinas; **the ships passed each other in the fog** los barcos se cruzaron en la niebla; **this yoghurt has passed its sell-by date** este yogur ya ha caducado, *RP* este yogur ya está vencido

(b) *(exam, candidate, bill)* aprobar; **to p. sb fit (for)** declarar a alguien apto(a) (para); **to p. sth as fit (for)** declarar algo válido(a) (para)

(c) *(give)* pasar; **to p. sb sth, to p. sth to sb** pasarle algo a alguien; **p. me the salt, please** ¿me pasas la sal?; **p. the photocopies along** haz circular las fotocopias

(d) *(counterfeit money, stolen goods)* pasar

(e) *Sport (ball)* pasar

(f) *(spend) (time)* pasar; **we passed our time reading** pasamos el tiempo leyendo; **it passes the time** sirve para matar el tiempo; **to p. the time of day with sb** charlar *or CAm, Méx* platicar un rato con alguien

(g) *(move)* **p. the rope through the hole** pasa la cuerda por el agujero; **she passed a hand through her hair** se pasó la mano por el cabello; **he passed his hand over the deck of cards** pasó la mano por la baraja *or* el mazo de cartas

(h) *Formal (make)* **to p. comment on sth** hacer comentarios sobre algo; *Law* **to p. judgement on sb** juzgar a alguien; *Law* **to p. sentence** dictar sentencia

(i) *Formal (excrete)* **to p. blood** defecar heces con sangre; **to p. water** orinar; **to p. wind** ventosear, expulsar ventosidades

3 *vi* (a) *(go past)* pasar; *(overtake)* adelantar, pasar; **to let sb p., to allow sb to p.** dejar pasar a alguien; **I was just passing** pasaba por aquí; **the road was too narrow for two vehicles to p.** la carretera era demasiado estrecha para que pasaran dos vehículos; **to p. from one person to another** pasar de una persona a otra; **the plane is passing over Paris** el avión está sobrevolando París; **to p. unobserved** pasar desapercibido(a)

(b) *(go)* pasar; **she passed through the door/along the corridor** pasó por la puerta/el pasillo; **the rope passes through this hole** la cuerda pasa por este agujero; **alcohol passes rapidly into the bloodstream** el alcohol pasa rápidamente a la sangre; **a look of panic passed across her face** una expresión de pánico surcó su cara; **a glance passed between them** se intercambiaron una mirada; **his life passed before his eyes** su vida pasó delante de sus ojos

(c) *(time)* pasar, transcurrir

(d) *(go away, end)* pasar; **don't worry, the pain will soon p.** no te preocupes, el dolor se te pasará

(e) *(in exam)* aprobar; *(bill, proposal)* ser aprobado(a)

(f) *Sport* pasar

(g) *(change)* **to p. from one state to another** pasar de un estado a otro; **control of the company has passed to the receivers** el control de la compañía ha pasado a manos de los liquidadores; **the turn passes to the player on the left** el turno pasa al jugador de la izquierda

(h) *(fail to answer, take turn)* **p.!** *(when answering question, in cards)* ¡paso!; **he passed on four questions** dejó cuatro preguntas sin contestar; *Fam* **I think I'll p. on the salad** creo que no voy a comer ensalada

(i) *(take place)* **the party, if it ever comes to p., should be quite something** la fiesta va a ser impresionante, si de verdad se celebra; **harsh words passed between them** tuvieron palabras muy duras; *Literary* **it came to p. that...** aconteció que...

(j) *(go unchallenged)* pasar; **I thought the comment would annoy him, but he let it p.** pensé que le molestaría el comentario, pero no dijo nada

(k) *(be acceptable) (behaviour, repair job)* pasar; **in a dark suit you might just p.** con un traje oscuro podrías pasar

► **pass among** *vt insep (crowd)* pasear entre

► **pass around** *vt sep (food, documents)* pasar

► **pass as** *vt insep* pasar por; **don't try to p. as an expert** no intentes dártelas de experto

► **pass away** *vi Euph* fallecer

► **pass back** *vt sep* (a) *(give back)* devolver (b) *Rad & TV* **I'll now p. you back to the studio** devolvemos la conexión al estudio

► **pass by** 1 *vt insep (go past)* pasar delante de

2 *vt sep* **I feel that life is passing me by** siento que la vida se me está escurriendo de las manos

3 *vi (procession, countryside, time)* pasar

► **pass down** 1 *vt sep* (a) *(reach down)* pasar; **he passed me down my suitcase** me pasó la maleta (b) *(transmit) (knowledge, tradition)* pasar, transmitir; *(inheritance, disease)* pasar; **the songs were passed down from generation to generation** las canciones pasaron de generación en generación

2 *vi (knowledge, tradition, inheritance)* **the table passed down to me** yo heredé la mesa; **the custom has passed down to us from ancient times** la costumbre nos ha llegado de la antigüedad

► **pass for** *vt insep* pasar por; **he could p. for 35** podría pasar por una persona de 35

► **pass off** 1 *vt sep* **to p. sth off as sth** hacer pasar algo por algo; **to p. oneself off as** hacerse pasar por; **he tried to p. it off as a joke** intentó hacer ver que había sido una broma

2 *vi* (a) *(take place)* **everything passed off well** todo fue bien (b) *(end) (fever, fit)* pasar

► **pass on** 1 *vt sep (object)* pasar, hacer circular; *(news, information, tradition)* pasar, transmitir; *(genes)* transmitir; **he passed the disease on to me** me contagió la enfermedad; **the savings will be passed on to our customers** todo el ahorro revertirá en nuestros clientes; **please p. on my thanks to them** por favor, dales las gracias de mi parte; **we're meeting at 8, p. it on** quedamos a las 8, pásalo

2 *vi* (a) *(move on)* **to p. on to the next topic** pasar al siguiente tema (b) *Euph (die)* fallecer

► **pass out** 1 *vt sep (hand out)* repartir

2 *vi* (a) *(faint)* desvanecerse, desmayarse (b) *(military or police cadet)* graduarse

► **pass over** 1 *vt insep (ignore) (remark, detail)* pasar por alto

2 *vt sep* **to p. sb over (for promotion)** olvidar a alguien (para el ascenso)

▸**pass round** *vt sep* = **pass around**

▸**pass through 1** *vt insep (city, area, crisis)* pasar por; **the bullet passed through his shoulder** la bala le atravesó el hombro
2 *vi* **I was just passing through** pasaba por aquí

▸**pass up** *vt sep* **(a)** *(hand up)* pasar **(b)** *(opportunity)* dejar pasar

passable ['pɑːsəbəl] *adj* **(a)** *(adequate)* pasable; **he does a very p. impression of the boss** hace una imitación muy aceptable *or* bastante buena del jefe **(b)** *(road, bridge)* practicable, transitable

passably ['pɑːsəblɪ] *adv (adequately)* aceptablemente

passage ['pæsɪdʒ] *n* **(a)** *(passing)* paso *m*, avance *m*; **the trench did not block the p. of the tanks** la trinchera no frenó el paso *or* el avance de los tanques; **the p. of time** el paso *or* transcurso del tiempo
(b) *(way through)* paso *m*; **they cleared a p. through the crowd** se abrieron paso entre la multitud; *Formal* **to grant sb safe p.** otorgar a alguien un paso seguro
(c) *(journey)* viaje *m*, travesía *f*; **to work one's p.** *(on ship)* = costearse el pasaje trabajando durante la travesía
(d) *(corridor)* corredor *m*, pasillo *m*; *(alley)* pasaje *m*, callejón *m*; **a secret p.** un pasadizo secreto
(e) *Anat* conducto *m*
(f) *Pol (of bill)* discusión *f*; **the bill had an uninterrupted p. through parliament** el proyecto de ley fue discutido sin interrupción en el parlamento
(g) *(from book, piece of music)* pasaje *m*

passageway ['pæsɪdʒweɪ] *n (corridor)* corredor *m*, pasillo *m*; *(alley)* pasaje *m*, callejón *m*

passata [pə'sɑːtə] *n Culin* salsa *f* de tomate

passbook ['pɑːsbʊk] *n (bank book)* cartilla *f or* libreta *f* de banco

passé [pæ'seɪ] *adj* pasado(a) de moda

passenger ['pæsəndʒə(r)] *n* **(a)** *(in vehicle)* pasajero(a) *m,f*; **p. plane/ship/ferry** avión/barco/ferry de pasajeros ▸▸ ***p. list*** lista *f* de pasajeros; ***p. seat*** asiento *m* del pasajero **(b)** *Br Pej (worker, team member)* parásito *m*; **we can't carry passengers** no podemos aceptar parásitos **(c)** ***p. pigeon*** paloma *f* silvestre norteamericana

passer ['pɑːsə(r)] *n Sport* pasador(ora) *m,f*; **he's a good p. of the ball** es un buen pasador

passer-by ['pɑːsə'baɪ] (*pl* **passers-by** ['pɑːsəz'baɪ]) *n* transeúnte *mf*, viandante *mf*

passim ['pæsɪm] *adv* pássim

passing ['pɑːsɪŋ] **1** *n* **(a)** *(going past)* paso *m*; **in p.** de pasada ▸▸ *US* ***p. lane*** carril *m* para adelantamiento; ***p. place*** *(on road)* apartadero *m*
(b) *(of time)* paso *m*, transcurso *m*
(c) *(approval) (of bill, law)* aprobación *f*; *Fin (of accounts)* aprobación *f* ▸▸ *US* ***p. grade*** *(in examination)* nota *f* de aprobado
(d) *Sport* pases *mpl*; **a beautiful piece of p.** un hermoso pase
(e) *Euph (death)* fallecimiento *m* ▸▸ ***p. bell*** toque *m* de difuntos
2 *adj* **(a)** *(car)* que pasa; **she flagged down a p. taxi** hizo señas para que se detuviera un taxi que pasaba ▸▸ *Com* ***p. trade*** clientela *f* de paso
(b) *(casual, chance) (remark)* de pasada; **to have a p. acquaintance with sb** conocer ligeramente a alguien; **to bear a p. resemblance to sb** parecerse ligeramente a alguien
(c) *(whim, fancy)* pasajero(a)
(d) ***p. shot*** *(in tennis)* passing-shot *m*

passing-out parade ['pɑːsɪŋ'aʊtpəreɪd] *n* desfile *m* de graduación de cadetes

passion ['pæʃən] *n* **(a)** *(emotion, love)* pasión *f*; **she sings with great p.** canta con gran pasión; *Law* **crime of p.** crimen pasional ▸▸ ***p. flower*** pasionaria *f*; ***p. fruit*** granadilla *f*, fruta *f* de la pasión
(b) *(enthusiasm)* pasión *f*; **to have a p. for sth** sentir pasión por algo; **his latest p. is Faulkner** Faulkner es su nueva pasión
(c) *(anger, vehemence)* ira *f*; **in a fit of p.** *(anger)* en un arrebato de ira; **to be in a p. about sth** estar descontrolado(a) *or* fuera de sí por algo; **she hates him with a p.** lo odia con toda su alma
(d) *Rel* **the P. (of Christ)** la Pasión (de Cristo) ▸▸ ***P. play*** (representación *f* de la) Pasión *f*; ***P. Sunday*** Domingo *m* de Pascua

passionate ['pæʃənɪt] *adj* **(a)** *(lover, embrace)* apasionado(a); **to make p. love** hacer el amor apasionadamente
(b) *(speech, advocate)* vehemente, apasionado(a); **she's p. about fossils** es una apasionada de los fósiles; **she's p. about human rights** es una defensora apasionada de los derechos humanos; **he's p. in his commitment to peace** está vehementemente comprometido con la paz

passionately ['pæʃənɪtlɪ] *adv* **(a)** *(to love, kiss)* apasionadamente; **to be p. in love with sb** estar apasionadamente enamorado(a) de alguien **(b)** *(to believe)* vehementemente; **to be p. fond of (doing) sth** ser un(a) enamorado(a) de (hacer) algo; **she feels p. about capital punishment** la pena de muerte es un tema que le importa mucho; **to speak p. about sth** hablar con pasión sobre algo

passion-killer ['pæʃən'kɪlə(r)] *n Fam* **it was a real p.** mataba la pasión

passionless ['pæʃənlɪs] *adj* sin pasión

passive ['pæsɪv] **1** *n Gram* (voz *f*) pasiva *f*; **in the p.** en pasiva
2 *adj* pasivo(a) ▸▸ ***p. resistance*** resistencia *f* pasiva; ***p. smoker*** fumador(ora) *m,f* pasivo(a); ***p. smoking*** tabaquismo *m* pasivo; *Gram* ***p. voice*** voz *f* pasiva

passively ['pæsɪvlɪ] *adv* pasivamente

passiveness ['pæsɪvnɪs], **passivity** [pæ'sɪvɪtɪ] *n* pasividad *f*

passkey ['pɑːskiː] *n* llave *f* maestra

Passover ['pɑːsəʊvə(r)] *n Rel* Pascua *f* judía

passport ['pɑːspɔːt] *n* **(a)** *(document)* pasaporte *m*; **British p. holders** personas con pasaporte británico ▸▸ ***p. control*** control *m* de pasaportes; ***p. photo(graph)*** *(of typical size)* fotografía *f* de tamaño pasaporte; *(actual photo in passport)* fotografía *f* del pasaporte
(b) *Fig* **a p. to happiness** un pasaporte a la felicidad; **a degree is no longer a p. to a good job** un título universitario ya no garantiza un buen trabajo

pass-the-parcel ['pɑːsðə'pɑːsəl] *n Br* = juego infantil en el que, al son de la música, los participantes se pasan un paquete que van desenvolviendo paulatinamente hasta descubrir el regalo que contiene

password ['pɑːswɜːd] *n* **(a)** *Mil* contraseña *f* **(b)** *Comptr* contraseña *f* ▸▸ ***p. protection*** protección *f* por contraseña

password-protected ['pɑːswɜːdprə'tektɪd] *adj Comptr* protegido(a) por contraseña

PAST [pɑːst] **1** *n* pasado *m*; **in the p.** en el pasado; *Gram* en pasado; **to live in the p.** vivir en el pasado; **that's all in the p. now** ya ha quedado todo olvidado; **it is a thing of the p.** es (una) cosa del pasado; **politeness seems to have become a thing of the p.** la buena

PASSIVE

La voz pasiva es mucho más frecuente en inglés que en español. En inglés se usa cuando el centro de atención es la acción o los resultados de la misma y el agente de esa acción es desconocido, no tiene importancia o se puede deducir fácilmente. También es muy habitual en la descripción de procedimientos científicos y procesos técnicos. El equivalente en español es a menudo la forma impersonal o el sujeto "ellos":

she was given a scholarship *le dieron una beca*
he was shot while escaping *lo dispararon mientras escapaba*
they had been warned not to go there *ya se les había advertido que no fueran allí*
the mixture is heated in a copper vessel *se calienta la mezcla en un recipiente de cobre*

También se usa para resaltar el agente o el instrumento de la acción, con un sintagma preposicional tras el verbo:

we were defeated by a combination of fanaticism and sheer brute force *nos derrotó una combinación de fanatismo y fuerza bruta*
rusty patches can be cleaned with wire wool *las manchas de óxido se pueden limpiar con un estropajo de aluminio*

Toda una oración puede funcionar como sujeto de la acción, si el verbo en pasiva va precedido del sujeto gramatical **it**:

it was expected that major repairs would be needed *se esperaba que sería necesaria una obra importante*

educación parece que se ha convertido en algo del pasado; **he's a man with a p.** es un hombre con un pasado oscuro; **let's put the p. behind us** olvidemos el pasado

2 *adj* (a) *(former) (life, centuries)* pasado(a); **his p. misdemeanours** sus faltas del pasado; **a p. champion** un antiguo *or* ex campeón; **the p. mayors of the town** los antiguos alcaldes de la ciudad; **from p. experience** por experiencia; **those days are p.** esos días han pasado; **in times p.** en otros tiempos, en tiempos pasados; **to be a p. master at sth** ser un(a) maestro(a) consumado(a) en algo

(b) *(most recent)* último(a); **the p. week** la semana pasada, la última semana; **the p. twenty years** los últimos veinte años

(c) *Gram* **p. participle** participio pasado *or* pasivo; **p. perfect** pasado pluscuamperfecto; **the p. tense** el pasado

3 *prep* (a) *(beyond)* **a little/a mile p. the bridge** poco después/una milla después del puente; **to walk p. the house** pasar por delante de la casa; **he walked p. me without saying hello** pasó a mi lado sin saludarme; **once they were p. the checkpoint** una vez que habían pasado *or* superado el control; **she stared p. me at the mountains** miraba las montañas que había detrás de mí; **I didn't manage to get p. the first page** no conseguí pasar de la primera página; **it's p. all understanding** no hay quien lo entienda; **the yoghurt is p. its sell-by date** el yogur ya ha caducado, *RP* el yogur está vencido; **I'm p. the age when those things interest me** ya he superado la edad en que esas cosas me interesaban; **I'm p. caring** ya me trae sin cuidado, ya no me preocupa más; IDIOM *Fam* **to be p. it** estar para el arrastre, estar para tirar; IDIOM *Fam* **I wouldn't put it p. her** ella es muy capaz (de hacerlo)

(b) *(with time)* **it is p. four (o'clock)** son más de las cuatro; **it's p. my bedtime** ya debería estar acostado; **half p. four** las cuatro y media; **a quarter p. four** las cuatro y cuarto; **twenty p. four** las cuatro y veinte

4 *adv* **to walk** *or* **go p.** pasar (caminando); **three buses went p. without stopping** pasaron tres autobuses sin detenerse; **several weeks went p.** pasaron varias semanas; **to run p.** pasar corriendo; **one night about three years p.** una noche hace unos tres años; **I have to be there by half p.** tengo que estar allí a la media *or* a y media

---

pasta ['pæstə] *n* pasta *f* ▸▸ ***p. sauce*** salsa *f* para pasta

paste [peɪst] 1 *n* (a) *(smooth substance)* pasta *f*, crema *f* (b) *Br (sandwich spread)* **fish/meat p.** = paté barato de pescado/carne (c) *(glue) (for paper)* pegamento *m*; *(for wallpaper)* engrudo *m*, cola *f* (d) ***p. diamond*** *(imitation)* diamante *m* falso *or* de imitación

2 *vt* (a) *(glue)* pegar (b) *Comptr* pegar **(into/onto** en) (c) *Fam* **to get pasted** *(beaten up)* ser golpeado(a), *Arg* cobrar; *(defeated)* ser aplastado(a); *(criticized)* ser destrozado(a)

▸ **paste up** *vt sep* (a) *(poster, notice)* pegar (b) *Typ* armar

pasteboard ['peɪstbɔːd] *n* cartón *m*

pastel ['pæstəl] 1 *n* (a) *(crayon)* pastel *m*; **a portrait in pastels** un retrato al pastel (b) *(picture)* dibujo *m* al pastel

2 *adj* pastel; **p. pink** rosa pastel

pastern ['pæstɜːn] *n* cuartilla *f*

paste-up ['peɪstʌp] *n Typ* maqueta *f*

pasteurization [pɑːstjəraɪ'zeɪʃən] *n* pasteurización *f*

pasteurize ['pɑːstjəraɪz] *vt* pasteurizar; **pasteurized milk** leche pasteurizada

pastiche [pæ'stiːʃ] *n* pastiche *m*

pastille ['pæstɪl] *n* pastilla *f*; **cough pastilles** pastillas para la tos

pastime ['pɑːstaɪm] *n* pasatiempo *m*, afición *f*

pastiness ['peɪstɪnɪs] *n (of complexion)* palidez *f*

pasting ['peɪstɪŋ] *n Fam (beating, defeat)* paliza *f*; **to give sb a p.** dar una paliza a alguien; **we** *Br* **got** *or US* **took a p.** *(were beaten up)* nos dieron una paliza; *(were defeated)* nos dieron una paliza *or Esp* un repaso; **his new play was given a p. by the critics** su última obra se llevó un buen varapalo por parte de la crítica

pastor ['pɑːstə(r)] *n Rel* pastor *m*

pastoral ['pɑːstərəl] *adj* (a) *(rural)* pastoril, pastoral; **they are a p. people** son un pueblo de pastores (b) *(work, activities)* pastoral ▸▸ ***p. care*** tutoría y orientación *f* individual; *Rel* ***p. letter*** carta *f* pastoral (c) *Lit* **p. (poem)** poema *m* bucólico, égloga *f*

pastorale [pæstə'rɑːl] *n Mus* pastoral *m*

pastrami [pə'strɑːmɪ] *n* pastrami *m*, = embutido de ternera ahumado

pastry ['peɪstrɪ] *n* (a) *(dough)* masa *f* ▸▸ ***p. brush*** pincel *m* de repostería; ***p. case*** tartera *f*; ***p. cutter*** cortapasta *m* (b) *(cake)* pastel *m*; *Col, CSur* torta *f* ▸▸ ***p. cook*** pastelero(a) *m,f*

pasturage ['pɑːstjʊrɪdʒ] *n* pasto *m*

pasture ['pɑːstʃə(r)] 1 *n* (a) *(for animals)* pasto *m* (b) IDIOMS **to put sb out to p.** jubilar a alguien; **to move on to pastures new** ir en búsqueda *or* busca de nuevos horizontes

2 *vt (animal)* pastar

3 *vi* pastar

pasty[1] ['pæstɪ] *n Culin* empanadilla *f*

pasty[2] ['peɪstɪ] *adj* (a) *(face, complexion)* pálido(a), descolorido(a) (b) *(texture)* pastoso(a)

pasty-faced ['peɪstɪ'feɪst] *adj* pálido(a)

pat [pæt] 1 *n* (a) *(touch)* palmadita *f*; *Fig* **to give sb a p. on the back** dar a alguien unas palmaditas en la espalda; **to give oneself a p. on the back** felicitarse a uno mismo (b) *(of butter)* porción *f*

2 *adj* (a) *(glib) (answer, explanation)* fácil (b) *(in poker)* **a p. hand** una mano servida

3 *adv* (a) *(exactly)* **to know** *or* **have sth off p.** saber algo de memoria; **his answer came p.** respondió sin vacilar (b) *US* **to stand p.** *(on decision)* mantenerse en sus trece; *(in poker)* tener una mano servida, no necesitar cambiar ninguna carta

4 *vt* (*pt & pp* **patted**) *(tap)* **to p. sb on the head** dar palmaditas a alguien en la cabeza; *Fig* **to p. sb on the back** dar a alguien unas palmaditas en la espalda; **"sit here," he said, patting the place beside him** "siéntate aquí", dijo, golpeando suavemente el lugar junto al suyo; **she patted her hair** se acomodó el pelo con unos golpecitos

▸ **pat down** *vt sep (soil, sand)* aplastar con la mano

pat-a-cake ['pætəkeɪk] *n* **to play p.** ≃ hacer tortitas

Patagonia [pætə'gəʊnɪə] *n* la Patagonia ▸▸ ***P. cypress*** alerce *m* de Chile

Patagonian [pætə'gəʊnɪən] 1 *n* patagónico(a) *m,f*

2 *adj* patagónico(a)

patch [pætʃ] 1 *n* (a) *(of cloth)* remiendo *m*; *(on elbow)* codera *f*; **(eye) p.** parche *m* (en el ojo); IDIOM *Fam* **his last novel isn't a p. on the others** su última novela no le llega ni a la suela de los zapatos a las anteriores ▸▸ ***p. pocket*** bolsillo *m* de parche; *Med* ***p. test*** prueba *f* para determinar la existencia de alergia

(b) *(of colour, light, oil)* mancha *f*; *(of fog)* zona *f*; **a p. of blue sky** un claro; **there were damp patches on the ceiling** había manchas de humedad en el techo; **snow still lay in patches on the slopes** en las faldas de la montaña aún había manchas de nieve

(c) *(of land)* parcela *f*, terreno *m*; **cabbage/strawberry p.** parcela de repollo/fresas *or RP* frutillas

(d) *Br Fam (period)* racha *f*; **to be going through a bad** *or* **sticky** *or* **rough p.** estar pasando por un bache

(e) *Br (of prostitute, salesperson)* zona *f*; *Fam* **keep off my p.!** ¡fuera de mi territorio!

(f) *Comptr (for game, software)* parche *m*

2 *vt* (a) *(hole, garment)* remendar, poner un parche en; **his jeans were patched at the knees** sus vaqueros tenían parches en las rodillas (b) *Tel* **to p. sb through (to)** conectar a alguien (con)

▸ **patch together** *vt sep Fam* armar

▸ **patch up** *vt sep Fam* (a) *(mend)* remendar; *(wounded person)* hacer una cura *or Méx, RP* curación de urgencia a (b) *(marriage, friendship)* arreglar; **we've patched things up** *(after quarrel)* hemos hecho las paces

patchily ['pætʃɪlɪ] *adv* superficialmente, incompletamente; **we dealt with the period rather p.** vimos ese periodo de una manera bastante incompleta

patchouli [pə'tʃuːlɪ] *n* pachulí *m* ▸▸ ***p. oil*** esencia *f* de pachulí

patch-up ['pætʃʌp] *n Fam* arreglo *m* provisional

patchwork ['pætʃwɜːk] *n* (a) *(in sewing)* labor *f* de retazo, patchwork *m* ▸▸ ***p. quilt*** edredón *m* de retazos *or* de patchwork (b) *(of fields, ideas, policies)* mosaico *m*

patchy ['pætʃɪ] *adj* (a) *(uneven, irregular) (novel, economic recovery)* desigual; *(paintwork)* desparejo(a); *(rain)* irregular (b) *(evidence, knowledge)* incompleto(a)

pate [peɪt] *n Old-fashioned or Hum* calva *f*

pâté ['pæteɪ] *n* paté *m*

patella [pə'telə] (*pl* **patellae** [pə'teliː] *or* **patellas**) *n Anat* rótula *f*

paten ['pætn] *n Rel* patena *f*

patent ['pætənt, *Br* 'peɪtənt] 1 *n (on invention)* patente *f*; **to take out a p. on sth** patentar algo; *Com* **p. applied for, p. pending** patente solicitada, en espera de patente ▸▸ ***p. agent*** agente *mf* de patentes; ***p. holder*** titular *mf* de una patente; ***P. Office*** Registro *m* de la Propiedad Industrial, *Esp* ≃ Oficina *f* de Patentes y Marcas; ***p. rights*** propiedad *f* industrial

2 *adj* (a) *(patented)* patentado(a) ▸▸ ***p. leather*** charol *m*; ***p.***

medicine específico *m*, especialidad *f* farmacéutica **(b)** *(evident)* patente, evidente
3 *vt* patentar

patented ['pætəntɪd, *Br* 'peɪtəntɪd] *adj (product, procedure)* patentado(a)

patentee [pætən'tiː, *Br* peɪtən'tiː] *n* poseedor(ora) *m,f* de una patente

patently [*Br* 'peɪtəntlɪ, *US* 'pætəntlɪ] *adv* evidentemente, patentemente; **p. obvious** muy evidente

paterfamilias ['peɪtəfə'mɪlɪæs] (*pl* **patresfamilias** ['peɪtreɪsfə'mɪlɪæs]) *n Formal* páter *m inv* familias

paternal [pə'tɜːnəl] *adj* **(a)** *(fatherly) (feelings)* paternal; *(duty, responsibilities)* paterno(a) **(b)** *(related through father)* paterno(a); **p. grandfather** abuelo paterno

paternalism [pə'tɜːnəlɪzəm] *n (of government, management)* paternalismo *m*

paternalistic [pətɜːnə'lɪstɪk], **paternalist** [pə'tɜːnəlɪst] *adj* paternalista

paternally [pə'tɜːnəlɪ] *adv* paternalmente

paternity [pə'tɜːnɪtɪ] *n* paternidad *f* ►► ***p. leave*** baja *f* por paternidad; *Law* ***p. suit*** juicio *m* para determinar la paternidad; ***p. test*** prueba *f* de (la) paternidad

paternoster ['pætə'nɒstə(r)] *n (prayer)* padrenuestro *m*

path [pɑːθ] *n* **(a)** *(track)* camino *m*, sendero *m*; *Fig* **I don't think we want to go down that p.** no creo que debamos hacer eso
(b) *(way ahead or through) (of inquiry, to success)* vía *f*, camino *m*; **a tree blocked his p.** un árbol bloqueaba su camino; **he killed everyone in his p.** mató a todo el que encontró a su paso; **to cut** *or* **clear a p. through sth** abrirse camino a través de algo; **in the p. of an oncoming vehicle** en el camino de un vehículo que se aproxima
(c) *(trajectory) (of rocket, planet, bird)* trayectoria *f*; *(of moving body)* recorrido *m*; *(of ray of light)* trayectoria *f*; **their paths had crossed before** sus caminos ya se habían cruzado antes
(d) *Comptr* camino *m*, localización *f*

pathetic [pə'θetɪk] *adj* **(a)** *(feeble)* penoso(a); **you're p.!** ¡eres patético(a)!; **how p.!, it's p.!** ¡qué patético!, ¡es patético! **(b)** *(touching)* patético(a), conmovedor(ora); **it was p. to see how they lived** era patético *or* conmovedor ver cómo vivían ►► *Lit* ***the p. fallacy*** la falacia patética

pathetically [pə'θetɪklɪ] *adv* **(a)** *(feebly)* penosamente, lastimosamente; **that's a p. weak excuse** esa disculpa es patética; **p. bad** penoso(a) **(b)** *(touchingly)* patéticamente, conmovedoramente; **he was p. grateful for any kindness** agradecía de manera conmovedora cualquier gesto de amabilidad

pathfinder ['pɑːθfaɪndə(r)] *n* **(a)** *(explorer)* explorador(ora) *m,f* **(b)** *(aircraft)* = avión explorador que guía a los bombarderos

pathname ['pɑːθneɪm] *n Comptr* camino *m*, localización *f*

pathogen ['pæθədʒən] *n Med* patógeno *m*

pathogenesis [pæθə'dʒenɪsɪs] *n Med* patogénesis *f inv*

pathological [pæθə'lɒdʒɪkəl] *adj* patológico(a); **p. liar** mentiroso(a) patológico(a)

pathologically [pæθə'lɒdʒɪklɪ] *adv* patológicamente; **he's p. jealous** tiene celos patológicos

pathologist [pə'θɒlədʒɪst] *n (forensic scientist)* forense *mf*, médico(a) *m,f* forense

pathology [pə'θɒlədʒɪ] *n* patología *f*

pathos ['peɪθɒs] *n* patetismo *m*

pathway ['pɑːθweɪ] *n (path)* camino *m*

patience ['peɪʃəns] *n* **(a)** *(quality)* paciencia *f*; **to try** *or* **tax sb's p.** poner a prueba la paciencia de alguien; **to exhaust sb's p.** acabar con *or* agotar la paciencia de alguien; **to lose one's p. (with sb)** perder la paciencia (con alguien); **I've no p. with him** me exaspera; **he has no p. with children** no tiene paciencia con los niños; **my p. is wearing thin** se me está agotando *or* acabando la paciencia; **the p. of a saint** la paciencia de un santo; PROV **p. is a virtue** con paciencia se gana el cielo
(b) *Br (card game)* solitario *m*; **to play p.** hacer un solitario

patient ['peɪʃənt] **1** *n* paciente *mf*
2 *adj* paciente; **to be p. with sb** ser paciente con alguien, tener paciencia con alguien; **if you'll be p. a few moments longer** si es tan amable de aguardar unos instantes más

patiently ['peɪʃəntlɪ] *adv* pacientemente

patina ['pætɪnə] *n* **(a)** *(on bronze, copper, wood)* pátina *f* **(b)** *Fig (veneer)* pátina *f*

patio ['pætɪəʊ] (*pl* **patios**) *n* **(a)** *(paved area)* = área pavimentada contigua a una casa, utilizada para el esparcimiento o para comer al aire libre ►► ***p. doors*** puertas *fpl* del patio; ***p. furniture*** accesorios *mpl or* mobiliario *m* para patio **(b)** *(inner courtyard)* patio *m*

patois ['pætwɑː] *n (dialect)* dialecto *m*

patriarch ['peɪtrɪɑːk] *n* patriarca *m*

patriarchal [peɪtrɪ'ɑːkəl] *adj* patriarcal

patriarchy ['peɪtrɪɑːkɪ] *n* patriarcado *m*

patrician [pə'trɪʃən] **1** *n* patricio *m*
2 *adj* **(a)** *(upper-class)* patricio(a) **(b)** *(haughty)* altanero(a)

patricide ['pætrɪsaɪd] *n* **(a)** *(crime)* parricidio *m* **(b)** *(person)* parricida *mf*

Patrick ['pætrɪk] *pr n* **Saint P.** San Patricio

patrilineal [pætrɪ'lɪnɪəl] *adj* por línea paterna

patrimony ['pætrɪmənɪ] *n Formal* patrimonio *m*

patriot ['pætrɪət, 'peɪtrɪət] *n* patriota *mf*

patriotic [pætrɪ'ɒtɪk, peɪtrɪ'ɒtɪk] *adj* patriótico(a)

patriotically [pætrɪ'ɒtɪklɪ, peɪtrɪ'ɒtɪklɪ] *adv* patrióticamente

patriotism ['pætrɪətɪzəm, 'peɪtrɪətɪzəm] *n* patriotismo *m*

patrol [pə'trəʊl] **1** *n* **(a)** *(group)* patrulla *f* ►► ***p. leader*** líder *mf* de patrulla **(b)** *(task)* ronda *f*, patrulla *f*; **to be on p.** patrullar ►► ***p. boat*** patrullero *m*, (lancha *f*) patrullera *f*; ***p. car*** coche *m or Am* carro *m or CSur* auto *m* patrulla; *US, Austr* ***p. wagon*** furgón *m* celular *or* policial
2 *vt* (*pt & pp* **patrolled**) *(area, border)* patrullar
3 *vi* patrullar; **to p. up and down** ir y venir

patrolman [pə'trəʊlmæn] *n US* patrullero *m*, policía *m*

patrolwoman [pə'trəʊlwʊmən] *n US* patrullera *f*, policía *f*

patron ['peɪtrən] *n* **(a)** *(of artist)* mecenas *mf inv*; *(of charity)* patrocinador(ora) *m,f* ►► ***p. saint*** patrón(ona) *m,f*, santo(a) *m,f* patrón(ona) **(b)** *Formal (of restaurant, hotel, shop)* cliente(a) *m,f*; *(of theatre, cinema)* asistente *mf*; **patrons** el público

patronage ['pætrənɪdʒ] *n* **(a)** *(of arts)* mecenazgo *m*; *(of charity)* patrocinio *m*; **under the p. of...** bajo *or* con el patrocinio de... **(b)** *Formal (custom)* clientela *f* **(c)** *Pol Pej* clientelismo *m*; **political p.** clientelismo político

patronize ['pætrənaɪz] *vt* **(a)** *(treat condescendingly)* tratar con condescendencia *or* paternalismo **(b)** *Formal (restaurant, hotel, shop)* frecuentar **(c)** *(exhibition, play)* patrocinar

patronizing ['pætrənaɪzɪŋ] *adj* condescendiente, paternalista

patronizingly ['pætrənaɪzɪŋlɪ] *adv* con condescendencia

patronymic [pætrə'nɪmɪk] *n* patronímico *m*

patsy ['pætsɪ] *n US Fam* **(a)** *(gullible person)* pringado(a) *m,f* **(b)** *(scapegoat)* chivo *m* expiatorio

patter[1] ['pætə(r)] **1** *n* **(a)** *(of footsteps)* correteo *m*; *Hum* **are we going to be hearing the p. of tiny feet?** ¿estás pensando ser mamá? **(b)** *(of rain)* repiqueteo *m*
2 *vi* **(a)** *(person)* corretear; **he pattered along the corridor** pasó correteando por el pasillo **(b)** *(rain)* repiquetear, tamborilear

patter[2] *n Fam* **(a)** *(of salesman, entertainer)* labia *f* ►► *Br* ***p. merchant*** pico *m* de oro **(b)** *(of region)* jerga *f*

pattern ['pætən] **1** *n* **(a)** *(design)* dibujo *m*; *(on dress, cloth)* estampado *m*, dibujo *m*; *(on animal)* manchas *fpl* ►► ***p. book*** muestrario *m*
(b) *(arrangement, order) (of events)* evolución *f*; *(of behaviour)* pauta *f*; *(of shapes, colours)* diseño *m*
(c) *(in sewing, knitting)* patrón *m* ►► *Ind* ***p. maker*** fabricante *m* de modelos
(d) *(norm, regularity)* pauta *f*, norma *f*; **behaviour patterns in monkeys** patrones de conducta de los monos; **the p. of TV viewing in the average household** los hábitos televisivos de una familia tipo; **to set a p.** marcar la pauta; **a p. was beginning to emerge** comenzaba a aflorar un modelo de comportamiento; **the evening followed the usual p.** la noche transcurrió como de costumbre; **to follow a set p.** seguir una conducta establecida
2 *vt* **(a)** *(mark) (fabric)* estampar **(b)** *(model)* **to p. sth on sth** imitar algo tomando algo como modelo; **their quality control is patterned on Japanese methods** su control de calidad está basado en métodos japoneses

patterned ['pætənd] *adj* estampado(a)

patty ['pætɪ] *n* **(a)** *US (burger)* hamburguesa *f* **(b)** *(meat pie)* empanadilla *f* de carne

paucity ['pɔːsɪtɪ] *n Formal* penuria *f*

Paul [pɔːl] *pr n* **Saint P.** San Pablo

paunch [pɔːntʃ] *n* barriga *f*, panza *f*, *Chile* guata *f*; **to have a p.** tener barriga

pauper ['pɔːpə(r)] *n* indigente *mf* ▸▸ ***p.'s grave*** fosa *f* común

pauperization [pɔːpəraɪ'zeɪʃən] *n* pauperización *f*, empobrecimiento *m*

pauperize ['pɔːpəraɪz] *vt* depauperar, empobrecer

pause [pɔːz] **1** *n* (**a**) *(in conversation)* pausa *f*; *(rest)* pausa *f*, descanso *m*; **without a p.** sin pausa; **there was a long p. before she answered** hubo una larga pausa antes de que respondiera; **to give sb p. (for thought)** dar que pensar a alguien ▸▸ ***p. button*** botón *m* de pausa (**b**) *Mus* pausa *f*

2 *vi (when working)* parar, descansar; *(when speaking)* hacer una pausa; **she paused on the doorstep** se detuvo brevemente en la entrada; **I signed it without pausing to read the details** lo firmé sin detenerme a leer los detalles; **to p. for breath** hacer una pausa *or* detenerse para tomar aliento

pave [peɪv] *vt (in general)* pavimentar; *(with slabs)* enlosar; *(with cobbles)* adoquinar, empedrar; *(with bricks)* enladrillar; IDIOM **they thought the streets were paved with gold** creían que ataban a los perros con longanizas; IDIOM **to p. the way for sth/sb** preparar el terreno para algo/alguien

pavement ['peɪvmənt] *n* (**a**) *Br (beside road)* acera *f*, *CSur* vereda *f*, *CAm, Méx* banqueta *f* ▸▸ ***p. artist*** = dibujante que pinta con tiza sobre la acera; ***p. cafe*** café *m* con terraza (**b**) *US (roadway)* calzada *f*

pavilion [pə'vɪlɪən] *n* (**a**) *(building, tent)* pabellón *m*; **the Japanese p. at the exhibition** el pabellón japonés en la exhibición (**b**) *(at cricket ground)* = edificio adyacente a un campo de críquet en el que se encuentran los vestuarios y el bar

paving ['peɪvɪŋ] *n (surface)* pavimento *m*; *(slabs)* enlosado *m*; *(cobbles)* adoquinado *m* ▸▸ ***p. stone*** losa *f*

pavlova [pæv'ləʊvə] *n Culin* = pastel de nata, merengue y fruta

Pavlovian [pæv'ləʊvɪən] *adj Psy* pavloviano(a)

paw [pɔː] **1** *n* (**a**) *(of cat, lion, bear)* garra *f*, pata *f*; *(of dog)* pata *f* (**b**) *Fam (hand)* mano *f*, *Arg* pata *f*; **keep your (big) paws off!** ¡no se toca!

2 *vt* (**a**) *(of animal)* tocar con la pata; **to p. the ground** piafar (**b**) *(of person)* **to p. sb** manosear *or* sobar a alguien

3 *vi* **to p. at sth** dar zarpazos a algo; **to p. at sb** manosear *or* sobar a alguien

pawl [pɔːl] *n Tech* trinquete *m*

pawn[1] [pɔːn] **1** *n* **to put sth in p.** empeñar algo; **I got my watch out of p.** desempeñé mi reloj ▸▸ ***p. ticket*** resguardo *m* de la casa de empeños

2 *vt* empeñar

pawn[2] *n (chesspiece)* peón *m*; *Fig* títere *m*

pawnbroker ['pɔːnbrəʊkə(r)] *n* prestamista *mf (de casa de empeños)*

pawnshop ['pɔːnʃɒp] *n* casa *f* de empeños

pawpaw = **papaya**

pax [pæks] *exclam Br Old-fashioned* ¡basta!

PAY [peɪ] **1** *n* sueldo *m*, paga *f*; **the p.'s good/bad** el sueldo es bueno/malo; **to be in sb's p.** estar a sueldo de alguien ▸▸ ***p. award*** aumento *m* de sueldo; *Br* ***p. bed*** = en un hospital público, cama de pago reservada a un paciente con seguro privado; *Br* ***p. cheque*** *or US* ***check*** cheque *m* del sueldo; ***p. claim*** reivindicación *f* salarial; ***p. cut*** recorte *m* salarial; *US* ***p. envelope*** sobre *m* de la paga; ***p. formula*** fórmula *f* para calcular las subidas salariales; ***p. freeze*** congelación *f* salarial; ***p. increase*** aumento *m* de sueldo; *Br* ***p. packet*** sobre *m* de la paga; *Br Fig* **the boss takes home a large p. packet** el jefe tiene un salario muy grande; ***p. rise*** aumento *m* de sueldo; ***p. slip*** nómina *f (documento)*; *US* ***p. station*** cabina *f*, teléfono *m* público; ***p. talks*** negociación *f* salarial; ***p. TV*** televisión *f* de pago

2 *vt* (*pt & pp* **paid** [peɪd]) (**a**) *(person, money, bill)* pagar; **to p. sb sth** pagarle algo a alguien; **to p. sb for sth** pagarle a alguien por algo; **I paid £5 for it** me costó 5 libras; **to p. sb to do sth** pagar a alguien para que haga algo; **to be well/badly paid** estar bien/mal pagado(a); **we get paid monthly** cobramos mensualmente; **to p. cash** pagar en efectivo; **the account pays interest** la cuenta da intereses; **interest is paid quarterly** los intereses se abonan trimestralmente; **to p. money into sb's account** *Esp* ingresar *or Am* depositar dinero en la cuenta de alguien; *Fam* **p. the man his money!** ¡págale lo que le debes!; **they've paid their debt to society** ya han pagado su deuda con la sociedad; **I wouldn't do it if you paid me** no lo haría ni aunque me pagarás; **he insisted on paying his own way** se empeñó en pagarlo de su propio dinero *or* costeárselo él mismo; IDIOM *Fam* **you pays your money and you takes your choice** es a gusto del consumidor

(**b**) *(give)* **to p. attention** prestar atención; **to p. sb a compliment** hacerle un cumplido a alguien; *Old-fashioned* **to p. court to sb** cortejar a alguien; **to p. homage to sb** rendir homenaje a alguien; **she paid her respects to the President** presentó sus respetos al presidente; **to p. sb a visit** hacer una visita a alguien

(**c**) *(profit)* **it will p. you to do it** te va a resultar rentable *or Am* redituable

3 *vi* (**a**) *(give payment)* pagar; **who's paying?** ¿quién paga?; **how would you like to p.?** ¿cómo lo va a pagar?; **they p. well** pagan bien; **the job pays well** el trabajo está bien pagado; **to p. in cash** pagar en efectivo; **to p. by cheque** pagar con un cheque; **to p. for sth** pagar algo; **my parents paid for me to go to Florida** mis padres me pagaron el viaje a Florida; **the printer soon paid for itself** la impresora se rentabilizó rápidamente, *RP* en poco tiempo desquité lo que pagué por la impresora; **I paid good money for that!** ¡he pagado mucho dinero por eso!; IDIOM **to p. through the nose** pagar un ojo de la cara *or Esp* un riñón

(**b**) *(be profitable)* **the business didn't p.** el negocio no fue rentable; **Brazil made their superiority p.** Brasil hizo valer su superioridad; **it pays to be honest** conviene ser honrado, ser honrado compensa; **it doesn't p. to tell lies** no compensa decir mentiras

(**c**) *(suffer)* **you'll p. for this!** ¡ésta me la pagas!, ¡me las pagarás!; **he paid (dearly) for his mistake** pagó (caro) su error

▸ **pay back** *vt sep (person)* devolver el dinero a; *(money)* devolver; *(loan)* amortizar; *Fig* **to p. sth back with interest** devolver *or* pagar algo con creces; **I'll p. you back for this!** *(take revenge on)* ¡me las pagarás por esto!

▸ **pay in** *vt sep (cheque, money) Esp* ingresar, *Am* depositar

▸ **pay into 1** *vt sep (money)* **I'd like to p. this cheque into my account** quiero *Esp* ingresar *or Am* depositar este cheque en mi cuenta

2 *vt insep* **to p. into a pension scheme** hacer aportaciones a un plan de pensiones

▸ **pay off 1** *vt sep* (**a**) *(debt)* saldar, liquidar; *(mortgage)* amortizar, redimir (**b**) *(worker)* hacer el finiquito a; *Fam* **to p. sb off** *(bribe)* sobornar *or* untar a alguien, *Méx* dar una mordida a alguien, *RP* coimear a alguien

2 *vi (efforts)* dar fruto; *(risk)* valer la pena

▸ **pay out 1** *vt sep* (**a**) *(money)* gastar (**b**) (*pt* **payed**) *(rope)* soltar poco a poco

2 *vi* pagar

▸ **pay over** *vt sep* pagar

▸ **pay up** *vi* pagar

---

payable ['peɪəbəl] *adj* pagadero(a); **p. in advance** pagadero(a) por adelantado; **the interest p. on the loan** los intereses que se pagan sobre el préstamo; **to make a cheque p. to sb** extender un cheque a favor de alguien

pay-and-display ['peɪəndɪs'pleɪ] *adj Br* **p. car park** estacionamiento *or Esp* aparcamiento de pago *(en el que hay que colocar el justificante de pago en la ventanilla)*

pay-as-you-earn ['peɪəzjʊ'ɜːn] *n* retención *f* en nómina del impuesto sobre la renta, *Esp* ≃ Impuesto *m* sobre el Rendimiento del Trabajo Personal

pay-as-you-view ['peɪəzjʊ'vjuː] **1** *n* pago *m* por visión

2 *adj* **on a p. basis** en un sistema de pago por visión

payback ['peɪbæk] *n* (**a**) *Fin* recuperación *f*, reembolso *m* ▸▸ ***p. period*** periodo *m* de amortización *or* reembolso (**b**) *US Fam (revenge)* venganza *f*, revancha *f*

payday ['peɪdeɪ] *n* día *m* de pago

pay-dirt ['peɪdɜːt] *n US also Fig* **to hit** *or* **strike p.** hallar un filón

PAYE [piːeɪwaɪ'iː] *n* (*abbr* **pay-as-you-earn**) retención *f* en nómina del impuesto sobre la renta, *Esp* ≃ Impuesto *m* sobre el Rendimiento del Trabajo Personal

payee [peɪ'iː] *n* beneficiario(a) *m,f*

payer ['peɪə(r)] *n (of debts, of cheque)* pagador(ora) *m,f*

paying ['peɪɪŋ] *adj* (**a**) *(who pays)* que paga; **p. guest** huésped de pago (**b**) *(profitable)* **it's not a p. proposition** no es una propuesta interesante

paying-in ['peɪɪŋ'ɪn] *adj Br* ***p. book*** talonario *m* de pagos *or* depósitos; ***p. slip*** talón *m* de pago, *RP* boleta *f* de depósito

payload ['peɪləʊd] *n* (**a**) *(of vehicle, spacecraft)* carga *f* útil (**b**) *(of missile)* carga *f* explosiva

paymaster ['peɪmɑːstə(r)] *n* oficial *m* pagador; **the World Bank acts as p. of the project** el Banco Mundial financia el proyecto; **the terrorists' p.** la mano negra que financia a los terroristas ▸▸ ***P. General*** *Br* =

funcionario encargado del pago de sueldos y pensiones a los funcionarios públicos; *US* = funcionario encargado del pago de sueldos al personal de las Fuerzas Armadas

payment ['peɪmənt] *n* (a) *(act of paying)* pago *m*; **they offered their services without p.** ofrecieron sus servicios sin cobrar nada; **to give/receive sth in p. (for sth)** dar/recibir algo en pago (por algo); **to present a bill for p.** presentar una factura; **to stop p. on a cheque** revocar un cheque; **on p. of £100** previo pago de 100 libras; **p. by instalments** pago a plazos; **p. in full** liquidación
(b) *(amount paid)* pago *m*; **48 monthly payments** 48 pagos *or RP* cuotas mensuales; **to make a p.** efectuar un pago
(c) *(reward, compensation)* recompensa *f*, compensación *f*

pay-off ['peɪɒf] *n* (a) *(act of paying off)* cancelación *f*, liquidación *f* (b) *Fam (bribe)* soborno *m*, *Méx* mordida *f*, *RP* coima *f* (c) *Fam (reward)* compensación *f* (d) *Fam (consequence)* consecuencia *f*

payola [peɪ'əʊlə] *n US Fam* = soborno, especialmente a un presentador radiofónico para que promocione un disco determinado

payout ['peɪaʊt] *n* pago *m*, desembolso *m*

pay-per-view ['peɪpə'vju:] **1** *n* pago *m* por visión
2 *adj* **p. channel** canal de pago por visión; **p. television** televisión de pago

payphone ['peɪfəʊn] *n* cabina *f*, teléfono *m* público

payroll ['peɪrəʊl] *n Com* (a) *(list)* plantilla *f*, nómina *f (de empleados)*; **to be on the p.** estar en plantilla *or* nómina (b) *(wages)* nómina *f*, salario *m*

PB ['pi:'bi:] *n Sport* (*abbr* **personal best**) mejor marca *f* personal

PBS [pi:bi:'es] *n* (*abbr* **Public Broadcasting Service**) = canal estadounidense público de televisión, con información no comercial y educativa

PC ['pi:'si:] **1** *n* (a) (*abbr* **personal computer**) PC *m* (b) *Br* (*abbr* **Police Constable**) agente *mf* de policía
2 *adj* (*abbr* **politically correct**) políticamente correcto(a)

pc (*abbr* **postcard**) (tarjeta *f*) postal *f*

PC-compatible ['pi:si:kəm'pætəbəl] *adj* compatible PC

PCI [pi:si:'aɪ] *n Comptr* (*abbr* **peripheral component interconnect**) PCI

pcm *Br* (*abbr* **per calendar month**) por mes

PCMCIA [pi:si:'emsi:aɪ'eɪ] *n Comptr* (*abbr* **Personal Computer Memory Card International Association**) PCMCIA

PD [pi:'di:] *n US* (*abbr* **Police Department**) Departamento *m* de Policía

pd (a) (*abbr* **paid**) pagado(a) (b) *Phys* (*abbr* **potential difference**) diferencia *f* de potencial

PDA [pi:di:'eɪ] *n Comptr* (*abbr* **personal digital assistant**) PDA *m*, asistente *m* personal

PDF [pi:di:'ef] *n Comptr* (*abbr* **portable document format**) PDF

PDQ [pi:di:'kju:] *adv Fam* (*abbr* **pretty damn quick**) por la vía rápida, rapidito

PE ['pi:'i:] *n Sch* (*abbr* **physical education**) educación *f* física

pea [pi:] *n Esp* guisante *m*, *Am* arveja *f*, *Carib, Méx* chícharo *m*; IDIOM **like two peas in a pod** como dos gotas de agua ▸▸ ***p. green*** verde *m* manzana; ***p. jacket*** chaquetón *m* marinero; ***p. soup*** = sopa espesa hecha con guisantes secos

peace [pi:s] *n* (a) *(absence of war, conflict)* paz *f*; **in time of p.** en tiempos de paz; **at p.** en paz; **I come in p.** vengo en son de paz; **to make (one's) p. with sb** hacer las paces con alguien; **give p. a chance** denle una oportunidad a la paz ▸▸ ***p. camp*** campamento *m* por la paz; ***p. campaigner*** pacifista *mf*; ***P. Corps*** = organización gubernamental estadounidense de ayuda al desarrollo con cooperantes sobre el terreno; ***p. dividend*** = dinero sobrante como resultado de la reducción del gasto militar en época de paz; ***p. movement*** movimiento *m* pacifista; ***p. negotiations*** negociaciones *fpl* de paz; ***p. offensive*** ofensiva *f* de paz; ***p. offering*** oferta *f* de paz; ***p. pipe*** *(of Native American)* pipa *f* de la paz; ***p. process*** proceso *m* de paz; ***the p. sign*** *(made with fingers)* el signo de la paz *(la 'v' formada con los dedos)*; ***p. studies*** estudios *mpl* sobre la paz; ***p. symbol*** símbolo *m* de la paz; ***p. talks*** conversaciones *fpl* de paz; ***p. treaty*** tratado *m* de paz
(b) *(calm)* paz *f*; **at p.** en paz; **the countryside was at p. after a busy day** después de un día ajetreado, la campiña estaba en calma; **to be at p. with oneself/the world** estar en paz con uno mismo/con el mundo; **we haven't had a moment's p. all morning** no hemos tenido un momento de tranquilidad en toda la mañana; **he'll give you no p. until you pay him** no te dejará tranquilo hasta que no le pagues; **to hold** *or* **keep one's p.** guardar silencio; **p. and quiet** paz y tranquilidad; **for the sake of p. and quiet** para tener la fiesta en paz; **all I want is a bit of p. and quiet** todo lo que quiero es un poco de tranquilidad; **p. of mind** tranquilidad de espíritu, sosiego; *Rel* **p. be with you!** la paz sea con *Esp* vosotros *or Am* ustedes
(c) *(treaty)* paz *f*; **they wanted to sign a separate p. with the invaders** querían firmar una paz por separado con los invasores
(d) *Law* **to keep/disturb the p.** mantener/alterar el orden (público)

peaceable ['pi:səbəl] *adj* (a) *(peace-loving) (nation, person)* pacífico(a) (b) *(calm) (atmosphere, demonstration)* pacífico(a)

peaceably ['pi:səblɪ] *adv* de forma pacífica

peaceful ['pi:sfʊl] *adj* (a) *(non-violent)* pacífico(a); **we are a p. nation** somos una nación pacífica; **the p. uses of nuclear energy** los usos pacíficos de la energía nuclear ▸▸ ***p. coexistence*** coexistencia *f* pacífica (b) *(calm)* tranquilo(a), sosegado(a); **it's so p. in the country!** ¡en el campo hay tanta tranquilidad!; **he had a p. death** tuvo una muerte serena

peacefully ['pi:sfʊlɪ] *adv* (a) *(without violence)* pacíficamente; **the rally went off p.** la concentración se desarrolló pacíficamente (b) *(calmly)* tranquilamente; **he died p. in the end** tuvo una muerte serena; **p., at home** *(in death notice)* descansa en paz

peacefulness ['pi:sfʊlnɪs] *n* (a) *(absence of violence)* paz *f* (b) *(calmness)* tranquilidad *f*

peacekeeper ['pi:ski:pə(r)] *n* (a) *(soldier)* soldado *m* de las fuerzas de pacificación (b) *(country, organization)* fuerza *f* de pacificación

peacekeeping ['pi:ski:pɪŋ] *n* mantenimiento *m* de la paz, pacificación *f*; **UN p. troops** fuerzas *fpl* de pacificación de la ONU, cascos *mpl* azules ▸▸ ***p. forces*** fuerzas *fpl* de pacificación *or* interposición

peace-loving ['pi:slʌvɪŋ] *adj* amante de la paz

peacemaker ['pi:smeɪkə(r)] *n* pacificador(ora) *m,f*, conciliador(ora) *m,f*; **blessed are the peacemakers** *(Bible quotation)* benditos son los pacificadores

peacenik ['pi:snɪk] *n Fam Pej* pacifista *mf*

peacetime ['pi:staɪm] *n* tiempo *m* de paz

peach [pi:tʃ] **1** *n* (a) *(fruit)* melocotón *m*, *Am* durazno *m*; *(tree)* melocotonero *m*, *Am* duraznero *m*; IDIOM **she has a peaches and cream complexion** tiene un cutis de seda ▸▸ ***p. brandy*** licor *m* de melocotón *or Am* durazno; ***p. melba*** copa *f* Melba, = postre a base de melocotón, helado de vainilla y jarabe de frambuesa; ***p. tree*** melocotonero *m*, *Am* duraznero *m*
(b) *(colour)* melocotón *m*, *Am* durazno *m*
(c) *Fam (something very good)* **she's a p.** es un bombón; **that goal was a p.** fue un golazo
2 *adj (colour)* melocotón, *Am* durazno

▸**peach on** *vi Fam Old-fashioned* **to p. on sb** *(betray)* traicionar a alguien, *Esp* chivarse de alguien

peachy ['pi:tʃɪ] *adj* (a) *(complexion)* de seda (b) *US Fam (excellent)* estupendo(a), *Andes, CAm, Carib, Méx* chévere, *Méx* padre, *RP* bárbaro(a); **everything's p.!** ¡todo va de perlas *or* de maravilla!

peacoat ['pi:kəʊt] *n* chaquetón *m* marinero

peacock ['pi:kɒk] *n* pavo *m* real; IDIOM **he was strutting about like a p.** andaba pavoneándose ▸▸ ***p. blue*** azul *m* eléctrico; ***p. butterfly*** pavón *m*

peacock-blue ['pi:kɒk'blu:] *adj* azul eléctrico

peafowl ['pi:faʊl] *n* pavo(a) *m,f* real

pea-green ['pi:'gri:n] *adj* verde claro

peahen ['pi:hen] *n* pava *f* real

peak [pi:k] **1** *n* (a) *(summit of mountain)* cima *f*, cumbre *f*; *(mountain)* pico *m*
(b) *(pointed part) (of roof)* arista *f*; **beat the egg whites until they form peaks** bate las claras hasta que se formen picos
(c) *(high point) (of price, inflation, success)* punto *m* máximo, (máximo) apogeo *m*; *(on graph)* pico *m*; **emigration was at its p. in the 1890s** la emigración alcanzó su punto máximo en la década de 1890; **the party was at its p.** la fiesta estaba en su mejor momento; **sales have reached a new p.** las ventas han alcanzado un nuevo máximo
(d) *(of cap)* visera *f*
2 *adj* **in p. condition** en condiciones óptimas ▸▸ ***p. hour*** *(of traffic)* hora *f* punta; *(of electricity, gas)* hora *f* de mayor consumo; *(of TV watching)* hora *f* de mayor audiencia; ***p. load*** *(of electricity)* carga *f* máxima, pico *m* de carga; ***p. period*** horas *fpl* punta; ***p. rate*** tarifa *f* máxima; ***p. season*** temporada *f* alta; ***p. viewing times*** horas *fpl* de mayor audiencia
3 *vi* (a) *(production, inflation, popularity)* alcanzar el punto máximo (b) *(athlete)* alcanzar la mejor forma

peaked cap ['pi:kt'kæp] *n* gorra *f* de plato

peaky ['pi:kɪ] *adj Br Fam* pachucho(a), *Am* flojo(a)

peal [pi:l] **1** *n* (**a**) *(sound) (of bells)* repique *m*; **p. of thunder** trueno; **peals of laughter** risotadas, carcajadas (**b**) *(set of bells)* carillón *m*
2 *vt (bells)* repicar
3 *vi (bells)* repicar; *(thunder)* tronar, retumbar; *(laughter)* resonar

▸ **peal out** *vi (bells)* repicar

pean *US* = **paean**

peanut ['pi:nʌt] *n* (**a**) *(nut)* cacahuete *m*, *Andes, Carib, RP* maní *m*, *CAm, Méx* cacahuate *m* ▸▸ ***p. butter*** mantequilla *f or* crema *f* de cacahuete *or Andes, Carib, Ven* maní *or CAm, Méx* cacahuate; ***p. oil*** aceite *m* de cacahuete *or Andes, Carib, RP* maní *or CAm, Méx* cacahuate (**b**) *Fam Fig* **peanuts** *(small sum of money)* calderilla *f*; **to earn peanuts** ganar una miseria

peapod ['pi:pɒd] *n* vaina *f* de *Esp* guisante *or Am* arveja *or Méx* chícharo

pear [peə(r)] *n (fruit)* pera *f*; *(tree)* peral *m* ▸▸ ***p. drop*** *(boiled sweet)* caramelo *m* de pera; *(shape)* forma *f* de pera; ***p. tree*** peral *m*

pearl [pɜ:l] *n* (**a**) *(jewel)* perla *f*; *Fig* **pearls of dew** perlas de rocío; IDIOM **it was like casting pearls before swine** era como echar margaritas a los cerdos ▸▸ ***p. diver*** pescador(ora) *m,f* de perlas; *Br* ***p. grey***, *US* ***p. gray*** gris *m* perla; ***p. necklace*** collar *m* de perlas; ***p. oyster*** ostra *f* perlífera, madreperla *f*
(**b**) *(mother-of-pearl)* nácar *m*, madreperla *f* ▸▸ ***p. button*** botón *m* nacarado
(**c**) *(precious, beautiful thing)* perla *f*; **Hong Kong, p. of the East** Hong Kong, la perla de oriente; **pearls of wisdom** perlas de sabiduría
(**d**) *Culin* ***p. barley*** cebada *f* perlada

pearl-grey, *US* **pearl-gray** ['pɜ:l'greɪ] *adj* gris perla

pearl-handled ['pɜ:l'hændəld] *adj* con mango de perlas

pearlized ['pɜ:laɪzd] *adj* nacarado(a)

pearly ['pɜ:lɪ] *adj* perlado(a) ▸▸ ***the P. Gates*** las puertas del cielo

pear-shaped ['peəʃeɪpt] *adj* (**a**) *(figure)* en forma de pera (**b**) IDIOM *Br Fam* **to go p.** irse a paseo *or Col, Méx* al piso *or RP* en banda

peasant ['pezənt] *n* (**a**) *(country person)* campesino(a) *m,f*; **p. farmer** pequeño(a) agricultor(ora) (**b**) *Pej (uncultured person)* cateto(a) *m,f*, *Esp* paleto(a) *m,f*

peasantry ['pezəntrɪ] *n* campesinado *m*

peashooter ['pi:ʃu:tə(r)] *n* cerbatana *f*

pea-souper [pi:'su:pə(r)] *n Br Old-fashioned (fog)* niebla *f* espesa y amarillenta

peat [pi:t] *n* turba *f* ▸▸ ***p. bog*** turbera *f*; ***p. moss*** musgo *m* de pantano

peaty ['pi:tɪ] *adj (soil)* rico(a) en turba; *(smell, taste)* a turba; *(whisky)* con sabor a turba

pebble ['pebəl] *n* (**a**) *(stone)* guijarro *m*; IDIOM **he's not the only p. on the beach** con él no se acaba el mundo ▸▸ ***p. beach*** playa *f* pedregosa (**b**) *(lens)* cristal *m* de roca ▸▸ *Fam* ***p. glasses*** gafas *fpl* de culo de botella

pebbledash ['pebəldæʃ] *Br* **1** *n* enguijarrado *m (mampostería)*
2 *vt* revestir con enguijarrado

pebbly ['peblɪ], **pebbled** ['pebəld] *adj* pedregoso(a)

pecan [*Br* 'pi:kən, *US* pɪ'kæn] *n* pacana *f* ▸▸ ***p. pie*** tarta *f* de pacana; ***p. tree*** pacana *f*

peccadillo [pekə'dɪləʊ] (*pl* **peccadillos** *or* **peccadilloes**) *n* desliz *m*

peccary ['pekərɪ] *n* pecarí *m*

peck [pek] **1** *n* (**a**) *(of bird)* picotazo *m* (**b**) *Fam (kiss)* besito *m*; **to give sb a p. on the cheek** dar un besito a alguien en la mejilla (**c**) *(measure)* = medida para granos y legumbres que equivale a nueve litros
2 *vt* (**a**) *(of bird)* picotear, picar; **to p. at sth** picotear algo (**b**) *Fam (kiss)* **to p. sb on the cheek** dar un besito a alguien en la mejilla

▸ **peck at** *vt insep* **to p. at one's food** comer sin ganas

pecker ['pekə(r)] *n Fam* (**a**) *Br (spirits)* **keep your p. up!** ¡ánimo! (**b**) *US (penis)* pito *m*, cola *f*

pecking order ['pekɪŋ'ɔ:də(r)] *n (of people)* jerarquía *f*

peckish ['pekɪʃ] *adj Br Fam* **to be** *or* **feel p.** tener un poco de hambre *or Esp* gusa

pecs [peks] *npl Fam (pectoral muscles)* pectorales *mpl*

pectin ['pektɪn] *n Chem* pectina *f*

pectineus [pek'tɪnɪəs] *n Anat* pectíneo *m*

pectoral ['pektərəl] *Anat* **1** *n* **pectorals** pectorales *mpl*
2 *adj* pectoral ▸▸ ***p. cross*** pectoral *m*; ***p. fin*** aleta *f* pectoral; ***p. muscle*** músculo *m* pectoral

peculiar [pɪ'kju:lɪə(r)] *adj* (**a**) *(strange)* raro(a); **how p.!** ¡qué raro!; **she is a little p.** es un poco rara; **to feel p.** *(unwell)* sentirse mal (**b**) *(particular)* **p. to** característico(a) *or* peculiar de; **this species is p. to Spain** es una especie autóctona de España; **a detail of p. significance** un detalle de singular relevancia

peculiarity [pɪkju:lɪ'ærɪtɪ] *n* (**a**) *(strangeness)* rareza *f*; **we all have our little peculiarities** todos tenemos nuestras rarezas (**b**) *(unusual characteristic)* peculiaridad *f*

peculiarly [pɪ'kju:lɪəlɪ] *adv* (**a**) *(strangely)* extrañamente (**b**) *(especially)* particularmente; **a p. Spanish institution/obsession** una institución/obsesión típicamente española

pecuniary [pɪ'kju:nɪərɪ] *adj Formal* pecuniario(a)

pedagogic(al) [pedə'gɒdʒɪk(əl)] *adj* pedagógico(a)

pedagogue ['pedəgɒg] *n Formal or Old-fashioned* pedagogo(a) *m,f*

pedagogy ['pedəgɒdʒɪ] *n* pedagogía *f*

pedal ['pedəl] **1** *n* pedal *m*; **clutch/brake p.** pedal del embrague/del freno; **loud p.** *(of piano)* pedal fuerte; **soft p.** *(of piano)* sordina ▸▸ ***p. bin*** cubo *m or Am* bote *m* (de basura) con pedal; ***p. boat*** patín *m*; ***p. car*** cochecito *m* de pedales
2 *vt* (*pt & pp* **pedalled**, *US* **pedaled**) **to p. a bicycle** dar pedales a la bicicleta
3 *vi* pedalear

pedalo ['pedələʊ] (*pl* **pedalos**) *n* patín *m*

pedant ['pedənt] *n* puntilloso(a) *m,f*

pedantic [pɪ'dæntɪk] *adj* puntilloso(a)

pedantically [pɪ'dæntɪklɪ] *adv* puntillosamente

pedantry ['pedəntrɪ] *n* puntillosidad *f*, meticulosidad *f* exagerada

peddle ['pedəl] *vt* (**a**) *(goods)* vender de puerta en puerta (**b**) *(ideas, theories)* propagar (**c**) *(illegally)* **to p. drugs** traficar con drogas

peddler ['pedlə(r)] *n* (**a**) *(of goods)* vendedor(ora) *m,f* ambulante, mercachifle *mf* (**b**) *(of ideas, theories)* propagador(ora) *m,f* (**c**) *(of drugs)* pequeño(a) traficante *mf*

pederast, pederasty *US* = **paederast, paederasty**

pedestal ['pedɪstəl] *n* (**a**) *(base)* pedestal *m* ▸▸ ***p. desk*** escritorio *m* con pie central (**b**) IDIOMS **to put sb on a p.** poner a alguien en un pedestal; **to knock sb off his/her p.** sacudir los cimientos de alguien

pedestrian [pɪ'destrɪən] **1** *n* peatón(ona) *m,f*; **pedestrians only** *(sign)* sólo para peatones ▸▸ *US* ***p. crossing*** paso *m* de peatones; ***p. precinct*** zona *f* peatonal
2 *adj (unimaginative)* prosaico(a), pedestre

pedestrianize [pɪ'destrɪənaɪz] *vt* **to p. a road** hacer peatonal una calle; **pedestrianized streets** calles peatonales

pediatric, pediatrician *etc US* = **paediatric, paediatrician** *etc*

pedicab ['pedɪkæb] *n* taxi *m* triciclo

pedicure ['pedɪkjʊə(r)] *n* pedicura *f*; **to have a p.** hacerse la pedicura

pedigree ['pedɪgri:] **1** *n* (**a**) *(descent) (of animal)* pedigrí *m*; *(of person)* linaje *m* (**b**) *(document)* pedigrí *m*, *Arg* pedigrée *m* (**c**) *(background) (of person)* linaje *m*; **his p. as a democrat is open to question** su pedigrí democrático es discutible
2 *adj (bull, cat, dog)* de raza; *(horse)* con pedigrí

pediment ['pedɪmənt] *n Archit* frontón *m*

pedlar ['pedlə(r)] *n Br* vendedor(ora) *m,f* ambulante, mercachifle *mf*

pedometer [pɪ'dɒmɪtə(r)] *n* podómetro *m*, cuentapasos *m inv*

pedophile, pedophilia *US* = **paedophile, paedophilia**

pee [pi:] *Fam* **1** *n* pis *m*; **to have a p.** hacer pis
2 *vt* **to p. oneself** *or* **(in) one's pants** hacerse pis *or* mearse en los pantalones; **to p. oneself (laughing)** mearse (de risa)
3 *vi* hacer pis

peek [pi:k] **1** *n* vistazo *m*, ojeada *f*; **to take** *or* **have a p. (at sth)** echar un vistazo *or* una ojeada (a algo)
2 *vi* echar un vistazo *or* una ojeada (**at** a); **someone was peeking through the keyhole** alguien espiaba a través de la cerradura; **no peeking!** ¡sin espiar!

peekaboo ['pi:kəbu:] **1** *exclam* ¡cucú!
2 *n (game)* = juego en el que una persona se tapa el rostro con las manos y lo descubre de repente diciendo cucú, normalmente para hacer reír a un bebé
3 *adj (garment) (see-through)* transparente; *(with holes)* calado(a)

peel [pi:l] **1** *n (on fruit, vegetable)* piel *f*; *(after peeling)* monda *f*, peladura *f*; **add a twist of lemon p.** agrega un trocito de cáscara de limón
2 *vt (fruit, vegetable, twig)* pelar; *(bark)* descortezar; IDIOM **to keep one's eyes peeled** tener los ojos bien abiertos
3 *vi (paint)* levantarse; *(wallpaper)* despegarse; *(sunburnt skin, person)* pelarse; **I'm peeling all over** me estoy pelando todo

▸ **peel away** *vt sep (label, wallpaper)* despegar

▸ **peel back** *vt sep (label, wallpaper)* quitar, despegar; **p. back the plastic backing** despegue la base de plástico

▸ **peel off** 1 *vt sep* **(a)** *(skin of fruit, vegetable)* pelar; *(label, film)* despegar **(b)** *(one's clothes)* quitarse, despojarse de, *Am* sacarse
2 *vi* **(a)** *(paint)* levantarse; *(sunburnt skin)* pelarse **(b)** *(turn away)* salirse de la formación; **two aircraft peeled off from the main group** dos de los aparatos abandonaron la formación

peeler ['pi:lə(r)] *n* **(a)** *(for potatoes) Esp* pelapatatas *m inv, Am* pelapapas *m inv* **(b)** *Irish Fam (policeman)* pasma *mf, RP* cana *mf*

peeling ['pi:lɪŋ] *n* **(a)** *(of skin)* descamación *f* **(b) peelings** *(of potato, carrot)* mondas *fpl*, peladuras *fpl*

peep[1] [pi:p] 1 *n (furtive glance)* vistazo *m*, ojeada *f*; **to have** *or* **take a p. (at sth)** echar un vistazo *or* una ojeada (a algo)
2 *vi* **(a)** *(glance)* echar una ojeada **(at** a); **to p. through the keyhole** mirar *or* espiar por el ojo de la cerradura; **no peeping!** ¡sin espiar! **(b)** *(emerge)* asomar

▸ **peep out** *vi (be visible)* asomar; **the moon peeped out through the clouds** la luna se asomaba entre las nubes; **to p. out from behind sth** asomar por detrás de algo

peep[2] 1 *n (sound)* pitido *m*; *Fam* **I don't want to hear another p. out of you** no quiero volver a oírte decir ni pío; **one more p. out of you and you've had it!** ¡como vuelva a escucharte sabrás lo que es bueno!; *Fam* **any news from him? – not a p.!** ¿alguna noticia de él? – nada en absoluto
2 *vi (bird)* piar

peepers ['pi:pəz] *npl Fam (eyes)* ojos *mpl*

peephole ['pi:phəʊl] *n* mirilla *f*

Peeping Tom ['pi:pɪŋ'tɒm] *n Fam* mirón(ona) *m,f*

peepshow ['pi:pʃəʊ] *n* **(a)** *(device)* mundonuevo *m* **(b)** *(live entertainment)* peepshow *m*

peer[1] [pɪə(r)] *n* **(a)** *(equal)* igual *m*; **a jury of one's peers** un jurado compuesto por los pares *or* iguales de uno; **as a negotiator she has no p.** como negociadora no tiene iguales; *Formal* **without p.** sin igual, sin par; **he started smoking because of p. (group) pressure** empezó a fumar por influencia de la gente de su entorno; **his p. group** sus pares ▸▸ ***p. review*** crítica *f* de pares
(b) *(noble)* par *m*

peer[2] *vi* **to p. at sth/sb** mirar con concentración algo/a alguien; **to p. over a wall** atisbar por encima de un muro; **to p. out** asomarse

peerage ['pɪərɪdʒ] *n* **(a)** *(rank)* título *m* de par; **he was given a p.** *or* **raised to the p.** le concedieron el título de lord **(b)** *(body of peers)* **the p.** los pares **(c)** *(book)* nobiliario *m*

peeress [pɪə'res] *n* paresa *f*

peerless ['pɪəlɪs] *adj Literary* sin igual, sin par

peeve [pi:v] *Fam* 1 *vt* fastidiar
2 *n* manía *f*, locura *f*

peeved [pi:vd] *adj Fam* cabreado(a), mosqueado(a); **to be p. about sth** estar fastidiado(a) *or* molesto(a) por algo

peevish ['pi:vɪʃ] *adj* irritable, malhumorado(a); **in a p. mood** de mal humor

peewee ['pi:wi:] *adj US* diminuto(a)

peewit ['pi:wɪt] *n* avefría *f*

peg [peg] 1 *n* **(a)** *(for coat, hat)* colgador *m*; **to buy clothes off the p.** comprar ropa prêt-à-porter
(b) *(pin for fastening)* clavija *f*; *Br* **(clothes) p.** pinza *f*; **(tent) p.** clavija *f*, estaca *f* ▸▸ ***p. board*** *(for keeping score)* = marcador formado por un tablero en el que se insertan clavijas; *Fam* ***p. leg*** *(wooden leg)* pata *f* de palo
(c) *(in mountaineering)* clavija *f*
(d) *(on string instrument)* clavija *f*
(e) IDIOMS **to use sth as a p. to hang an argument on** utilizar algo como pretexto para elaborar una teoría; **she's gone down a p. (or two) in my estimation** la aprecio bastante menos; **to take sb down a p. (or two)** bajarle a alguien los humos
2 *vt (pt & pp* **pegged) (a)** *(fasten)* **to p. sth in place** fijar algo con clavijas; **to p. a tent** fijar una tienda de campaña con clavijas; **to p. the washing on the line** tender la ropa (con pinzas)
(b) *(prices)* fijar; **to p. sth to the rate of inflation** ajustar algo al índice de inflación; **export earnings are pegged to the exchange rate** los ingresos por exportaciones están determinados por la tasa de cambio
(c) *US Fam (classify)* ordenar

▸ **peg away** *vi Fam* **to p. away (at sth)** *Esp* currar *or Méx, Perú, Ven* chambear *or RP* laburar sin parar (en algo)

▸ **peg down** *vt sep (fasten down)* fijar, sujetar

▸ **peg out** 1 *vt sep* **(a)** *(hang out) (washing)* tender **(b)** *(mark out with pegs)* delimitar con estacas
2 *vi Fam (die)* estirar la pata, *Méx* petatearse

Pegasus ['pegəsəs] *n Mythol* Pegaso

PEI *(abbr* **Prince Edward Island)** Isla *f* Príncipe Eduardo

pejorative [pɪ'dʒɒrətɪv] *adj* peyorativo(a)

pejoratively [pɪ'dʒɒrətɪvlɪ] *adv* de manera peyorativa

peke [pi:k] *n Fam* pequinés *m*

Pekinese [pi:kɪ'ni:z], **Pekingese** [pi:kɪŋ'i:z] *n* (perro *m*) pequinés *m*

Peking [pi:'kɪŋ] *n* Pekín ▸▸ ***P. duck*** pato *m* al estilo de Pekín

pelican ['pelɪkən] *n* **(a)** *(bird)* pelícano *m* **(b)** *Br* **p. crossing** = paso de peatones con semáforo accionado mediante botón

pellagra [pə'lægrə] *n Med* pelagra *f*

pellet ['pelɪt] *n* **(a)** *(of paper, bread, clay)* bolita *f* **(b)** *(for gun)* perdigón *m* **(c)** *(from animal) (regurgitated food)* bola *f*; *(excrement)* excremento *m (en forma de bola)*

pell-mell ['pel'mel] *adv (to pile, throw)* desordenadamente; **the crowd ran p. into the square** la multitud entró en la plaza corriendo en tropel

pellucid [pe'lu:sɪd] *adj* **(a)** *(water)* cristalino(a) **(b)** *(prose, style)* diáfano(a)

pelmet ['pelmɪt] *n* **(a)** *(of wood)* galería *f (para cortinas)* **(b)** *(of cloth)* cenefa *f*

Peloponnese [peləpə'ni:z] *n* **the P.** el Peloponeso

pelota [pə'lɒtə] *n* cesta *f* punta ▸▸ ***p. player*** pelotari *mf*

peloton ['pelətɒn] *n (in cycling)* pelotón *m*

pelt[1] [pelt] *n (animal skin)* piel *f*, pellejo *m*

pelt[2] 1 *n* **at full p.** a toda velocidad
2 *vt* lanzar, arrojar; **to p. sb with stones** lanzar a alguien una lluvia de piedras, apedrear a alguien
3 *vi* **(a)** *Fam (rain)* **it was pelting down** *or* **with rain** llovía a cántaros; **I changed the tyre in the pelting rain** cambié la rueda bajo una lluvia torrencial **(b)** *(go fast)* ir disparado(a); **he came pelting along the corridor** venía disparado por el pasillo

pelvic ['pelvɪk] *adj* pélvico(a) ▸▸ *Zool* ***p. fin*** aleta *f* pélvica; *Anat* ***p. girdle*** anillo *m* pélvico; *Med* ***p. inflammatory disease*** enfermedad *f* inflamatoria pélvica

pelvis ['pelvɪs] *n* pelvis *f inv*

pen[1] [pen] 1 *n (fountain pen)* pluma *f* (estilográfica); *(ballpoint)* bolígrafo *m*, *Chile* lápiz *m* (de pasta), *Col, Ecuad, Ven* esferográfica *f*, *Méx* pluma *f*, *RP* birome *m*; **another novel from the p. of John Irving** otra novela de la pluma de John Irving; **she lives by her p.** se gana la vida con la pluma; **to put p. to paper** ponerse a escribir; PROV **the p. is mightier than the sword** la palabra es más fuerte que el fusil ▸▸ ***p. friend*** amigo(a) *m,f* por correspondencia; ***p. light*** linterna *f* (en forma de bolígrafo); ***p. name*** seudónimo *m*; ***p. nib*** punta *f* del bolígrafo; ***p. pal*** amigo(a) *m,f* por correspondencia; *Pej* ***p. pusher*** *(clerk)* chupatintas *m inv*
2 *vt (pt & pp* **penned)** escribir

pen[2] *n* **(a)** *(for sheep)* redil *m*; *(for cattle)* corral *m* **(b) (submarine) p.** muelle para submarinos

▸ **pen in, pen up** *vt sep (animals, people)* encerrar

pen[3] *n (female swan)* cisne *m* hembra

pen[4] *n US Fam (prison) Esp* trullo *m*, *Andes, Col, RP* cana *f*, *Méx* bote *m*

pen[5] *n Br Fam (penalty)* penalti *m*

penal ['pi:nəl] *adj* penal; **p. levels of taxation** impuestos draconianos ▸▸ ***p. code*** código *m* penal; ***p. colony*** colonia *f* penitenciaria; ***p. institution*** establecimiento *m* penitenciario; ***p. servitude*** trabajos *mpl* forzados

penalize ['pi:nəlaɪz] *vt* **(a)** *(punish)* penalizar; **poor handwriting will be penalized** se penalizará por mala caligrafía; **to p. sb for doing sth** penalizar a alguien por hacer algo **(b)** *(disadvantage)* perjudicar; **the new tax penalizes large families** el nuevo impuesto perjudica a las familias numerosas

penalty ['penəltɪ] *n* **(a)** *(punishment) (fine)* sanción *f*; *(for serious crime)* pena *f*, castigo *m*; **to impose a p. on sb** imponer un castigo a alguien; **on** *or* **under p. of death** so pena de muerte; **p. for improper use: £50** *(sign)* multa por uso indebido: 50 libras ▸▸ *Com* ***p. clause*** cláusula *f* de penalización
(b) *Fig (unpleasant consequence)* **to pay the p.** pagar las consecuencias; **that's the p. for being famous** ése es el precio de la fama
(c) *Sport (in soccer, hockey)* penalti *m*, penalty *m*, *Am* penal *m*; *(in*

rugby) golpe *m* de castigo; *(loss of time, points)* penalización *f*; **to take a p.** *(in soccer, hockey)* lanzar un penalti; *(in rugby)* lanzar un golpe de castigo; **to award a p.** *(in soccer, hockey)* conceder un penalti; *(in rugby)* conceder un golpe de castigo; **to score (from) a p.** *(in soccer, hockey)* anotar desde el punto de penalti; *(in rugby)* anotar con un golpe de castigo; **to win on penalties** ganar en los penaltis ►► ***p. area*** área *f* de castigo; ***p. bench*** *(in ice hockey)* banquillo *m* de castigo; ***p. box*** *(in soccer)* área *f* de castigo; ***p. corner*** *(in field hockey)* penalti *m or Am* penal *m* córner; ***p. goal*** gol *m* de penalti; ***p. kick*** (lanzamiento *m* de) penalti *m or Am* penal *m*; ***p. shoot-out*** lanzamiento *m or* tanda *f* de penaltis *or Am* penales; ***p. shot*** *(in ice hockey)* (lanzamiento *m* de) penalti *m or Am* penal *m*; ***p. spot*** *(in soccer)* punto *m* de penalti *or Am* penal; ***p. stroke*** *(in golf)* golpe *m* de penalización; *(in field hockey)* (lanzamiento *m* de) penalti *m or Am* penal *m*

penance ['penəns] *n Rel & Fig* penitencia *f*; **to do p. (for sth)** hacer penitencia (por algo); **to do sth as a p.** hacer algo como penitencia

pen-and-ink ['penənd'ɪŋk] *adj (drawing)* a pluma

pence *pl of* **penny**

penchant ['pɒŋʃɒŋ] *n Formal* inclinación *f*, propensión *f*; **to have a p. for (doing) sth** tener propensión a (hacer) algo

pencil ['pensəl] **1** *n* **(a)** *(for writing, make-up)* lápiz *m* ►► ***p. box*** caja *f* de lápices; ***p. case*** plumier *m*; ***p. drawing*** dibujo *m* a lápiz; ***p. lead*** grafito *m* (para lápices); *US Pej* ***p. pusher*** *(clerk)* chupatintas *m inv*; ***p. sharpener*** sacapuntas *m inv* **(b)** *(narrow beam)* **a p. of light** un hilo de luz **(c)** ***p. skirt*** falda *f* de tubo

2 *vt* (*pt & pp* **pencilled**, *US* **penciled**) *(draw)* dibujar a lápiz; *(write)* redactar *(con lápiz)*; **question marks were pencilled in the margin** había signos de interrogación anotados a lápiz en el margen; **to p. one's eyebrows** maquillarse las cejas

► **pencil in** *vt sep (provisionally decide)* apuntar provisionalmente

pendant ['pendənt] *n* **(a)** *(necklace)* colgante *m* **(b)** *(piece of jewellery) (on necklace)* pendiente *m*; **p. earrings** *Esp* pendientes *or Am* aretes largos

pending ['pendɪŋ] **1** *adj (unresolved)* pendiente; **a p. court case** un juicio pendiente de resolución; **to be p.** estar pendiente ►► ***p. tray*** bandeja *f* de asuntos pendientes

2 *prep* a la espera de; **p. the outcome** a la espera del resultado

penduline tit ['pendjʊlaɪn'tɪt] *n* pájaro *m* moscón

pendulous ['pendjʊləs] *adj Literary* colgante

pendulum ['pendjʊləm] *n* péndulo *m*; *Fig* **the p. of fashion has swung back to a sixties look** el vaivén de la moda nos ha traído de nuevo a los sesenta ►► ***p. clock*** reloj *m* de péndulo

penetrate ['penɪtreɪt] **1** *vt* **(a)** *(pierce) (object, body, wall)* penetrar **(b)** *(find way into or through) (jungle, area)* penetrar en, adentrarse en; *(of sound, light)* atravesar; **the cold wind penetrated her clothing** el frío viento le penetraba la ropa; *Com* **to p. a market** introducirse en un mercado

(c) *(infiltrate) (enemy, rival group)* infiltrarse en

(d) *(see through) (darkness, disguise)* ver a través de; *(mystery)* esclarecer, dilucidar; **to p. sb's thoughts** leer los pensamientos de alguien

(e) *(sexually)* penetrar

2 *vi* **(a)** *(break through)* penetrar; **the troops penetrated deep into enemy territory** las tropas se adentraron en territorio enemigo **(b)** *(ideas, beliefs)* extenderse; **the custom has not penetrated to this part of the country** la costumbre no se ha extendido a esta parte del país **(c)** *(sink in)* calar

penetrating ['penɪtreɪtɪŋ] *adj* **(a)** *(sound, voice, cold)* penetrante **(b)** *(mind, insight)* perspicaz, penetrante; **she had p. eyes** tenía una mirada penetrante

penetratingly ['penɪtreɪtɪŋlɪ] *adv* **(a)** *(loudly) (to scream, shout)* ensordecedoramente **(b)** *(acutely)* perspicazmente

penetration [penɪ'treɪʃən] *n* **(a)** *(entry)* penetración *f* **(b)** *(of mind)* perspicacia *f*, penetración *f* **(c)** *(sexual)* penetración *f*

penetrative ['penɪtrətɪv] *adj (sex)* con penetración

penguin ['peŋgwɪn] *n* pingüino *m* ►► *Fam Hum* ***p. suit*** chaqué *m*

penicillin [penɪ'sɪlɪn] *n* penicilina *f*

peninsula [pə'nɪnsjʊlə] *n* península *f*

peninsular [pə'nɪnsjʊlə(r)] *adj* peninsular ►► ***p. Spanish*** español *m* peninsular; *Hist* ***the P. War*** la Guerra de la Independencia (española)

penis ['pi:nɪs] (*pl* **penises** ['pi:nɪsɪz]) *n* pene *m* ►► *Psy* ***p. envy*** envidia *f* del pene

penitence ['penɪtəns] *n* arrepentimiento *m*

penitent ['penɪtənt] **1** *n* penitente *mf*

2 *adj* arrepentido(a)

penitential [penɪ'tenʃəl] *adj* penitencial

penitentiary [penɪ'tenʃərɪ] *n US* prisión *f*, cárcel *f*

penitently ['penɪtəntlɪ] *adv* arrepentidamente

penknife ['pennaɪf] *n* navaja *f*, cortaplumas *m inv*

penmanship ['penmənʃɪp] *n* caligrafía *f*

pennant ['penənt] *n* **(a)** *(small flag)* banderín *m* **(b)** *Naut* grímpola *f* **(c)** *US Sport* **to win the p.** ganar el título

penniless ['penɪlɪs] *adj* **to be p.** estar sin un centavo *or Esp* duro; **the stock market crash left him p.** el hundimiento del mercado de valores lo dejó en la ruina

Pennines ['penaɪnz] *npl* **the P.** los montes Peninos

pennon ['penən] *n* **(a)** *(flag)* pendón *m* **(b)** *Naut* grímpola *f*

Pennsylvania [pensɪl'veɪnɪə] *n* Pensilvania

penny ['penɪ] *n* **(a)** *Br (coin)* (*pl* **pence** [pens]) penique *m*; **a ten/fifty pence piece** una moneda de diez/cincuenta peniques; **it was worth every p.** valía (realmente) la pena *(el precio pagado)*; **it didn't cost them a p.** no les costó ni un centavo *or Esp* duro; **every p. counts** toda ayuda es necesaria, por pequeña que sea ►► *Fam* ***p. dreadful*** *(cheap novel)* novela *f* barata, novelucha *f*; ***p. farthing*** velocípedo *m*; ***p. pinching*** tacañería *f*; ***p. whistle*** flautín *m*

(b) *US (cent)* centavo *m* ►► ***p. arcade*** salón *m* recreativo

(c) IDIOMS **they haven't a p. to their name** no tienen ni una perra gorda *or Esp* ni un duro; **I don't have two pennies to rub together** estoy sin un *Esp* duro *or Am* centavo; **pennies from heaven** dinero llovido del cielo; **in for a p., in for a pound** de perdidos al río; **she didn't get the joke at first, but then the p. dropped** al principio no entendió el chiste, pero más tarde cayó; **they're two** *or* **ten a p.** los hay a patadas; **a p. for your thoughts** dime en qué estás pensando; **he keeps turning up like a bad p.** no hay forma de perderlo de vista *or* de quitárselo de encima; PROV *Br* **take care of the pennies and the pounds will take care of themselves** si tienes cuidado con los gastos ordinarios, ya verás cómo ahorras; PROV **p. wise, pound foolish** de nada sirve ahorrar en las pequeñas cosas si luego se derrocha en las grandes

penny-ante ['penɪæntɪ] *adj US Fam* de poca monta, insignificante

penny-pinching ['penɪpɪntʃɪŋ] *Fam* **1** *n* tacañería *f*

2 *adj (person)* agarrado(a), tacaño(a); *(ways, habits)* mezquino(a)

pennyroyal [penɪ'rɔɪəl] *n (medicinal plant)* poleo *m*

pennywort ['penɪwɜ:t] *n* = planta de la familia de las crasuláceas de hojas redondas

pennyworth ['penəθ] *n Old-fashioned* penique *m*; IDIOM *Br Fam* **she put in her (two) p.** aportó su opinión

penologist [pi:'nɒlədʒɪst] *n* criminólogo(a) *m,f*

penology [pi:'nɒlədʒɪ] *n* criminología *f*

pension ['penʃən] *n* **(a)** *(payment)* pensión *f*; **company/state p.** pensión de la empresa/del estado; **to be on a p.** cobrar una pensión; **to draw a p.** cobrar una pensión ►► ***p. book*** libreta *f* de pensión; ***p. fund*** fondo *m* de pensiones; ***p. plan*** plan *m* de pensiones; ***p. scheme*** plan *m* de jubilación *or* de pensiones **(b)** *(small hotel)* pensión *f*

► **pension off** *vt sep* jubilar

pensionable ['penʃənəbəl] *adj* **(a)** *(person)* con derecho a cobrar pensión; **of p. age** en edad de jubilación **(b)** *(job)* con derecho a cobrar pensión

pensioner ['penʃənə(r)] *n* pensionista *mf*

pensive ['pensɪv] *adj* pensativo(a); **to be p.** *or* **in a p. mood** estar pensativo(a)

pensively ['pensɪvlɪ] *adv* pensativamente

pentagon ['pentəgən] *n* **(a)** *(shape)* pentágono *m* **(b)** **the P.** *(building, Ministry of Defense)* el Pentágono

pentagonal [pen'tægənəl] *adj* pentagonal

pentagram ['pentəgræm] *n* estrella *f* de cinco puntas

pentahedron [pentə'hi:drən] (*pl* **pentahedrons** *or* **pentahedra** [pentə'hi:drə]) *n Geom* pentaedro *m*

pentameter [pen'tæmɪtə(r)] *n* pentámetro *m*

Pentateuch ['pentətju:k] *n Rel* **the P.** el Pentateuco

pentathlete [pen'tæθli:t] *n* pentatleta *mf*

pentathlon [pen'tæθlən] *n* pentatlón *m*

Pentecost ['pentɪkɒst] *n Rel* Pentecostés *m*

Pentecostal [pentɪ'kɒstəl] *adj Rel* pentecostal

Pentecostalist [pentɪ'kɒstəlɪst] **1** *n* pentecostalista *mf*

2 *adj* pentecostalista

penthouse ['penthaʊs] *n* ático *m* ▸▸ ***p. suite*** suite *f* en el ático

Pentium® ['pentɪəm] *n Comptr* Pentium® *m*

pent-up [pent'ʌp] *adj* contenido(a), acumulado(a); **to get rid of p. energy** liberar la energía acumulada

penultimate [pe'nʌltɪmɪt] *adj* penúltimo(a)

penumbra [pɪ'nʌmbrə] (*pl* **penumbras** *or* **penumbrae** [pɪ'nʌmbri:]) *n* penumbra *f*

penurious [pə'njʊərɪəs] *adj Formal* (**a**) *(poor)* indigente (**b**) *(stingy)* mezquino(a), tacaño(a)

penury ['penjʊrɪ] *n Formal* miseria *f*, penuria *f*

peon ['pi:ən] *n* (**a**) *(in Latin America)* peón *m* agrícola, bracero *m* (**b**) *US Fam (worker)* obrero(a) *m,f*

peony ['pi:ənɪ] *n* peonía *f*

PEOPLE ['pi:pəl] **1** *npl* (**a**) *(plural of* **person***) (as group)* gente *f*; *(as individuals)* personas *fpl*; **many p. think that...** mucha gente piensa que..., muchos piensan que...; **most p.** la mayoría de la gente; **other p.** otros; **rich/poor/blind p.** los ricos/pobres/ciegos; **disabled p.** los discapacitados; **old p.** las personas de la tercera edad, *Esp* las personas mayores; **young p.** los jóvenes; **there were five p. in the room** había cinco personas en la habitación; **the p. next door** la gente *or* los de al lado; **he's one of those p. who...** es una de esas personas que...; **p. often mistake me for my brother** a menudo me confunden con mi hermano, la gente a menudo me confunde con mi hermano; **what will p. think?** ¿qué va a pensar la gente?, *Esp* ¿qué pensará la gente?; **p. say that...** se dice que...; **I'm surprised that you, of all p., should say such a thing** me sorprende que precisamente tú digas algo así; **who should appear but Jim, of all p.!** ¿quién apareció sino el mismísimo Jim?; **I don't know, some p.!** ¡es que hay cada uno(a) por ahí!; **to have p. skills** tener aptitud para tratar con la gente; **she's a real p. person** le gusta mucho el trato con la gente; *Fam* **right, p., let's get started!** bueno, todo el mundo, vamos a empezar, *Esp* venga gentes, ¡en marcha! ▸▸ ***p. carrier*** monovolumen *m*; ***p. mover*** *(car)* monovolumen *m*; *(automatic train)* servicio *m* de conexión; *(moving pavement)* cinta *f* transportadora (de personas)

(**b**) *(citizens)* pueblo *m*, ciudadanía *f*; **the common p.** la gente corriente *or* común; **a man of the p.** un hombre del pueblo; *Br* **to go to the p.** *(call elections)* convocar elecciones ▸▸ *Pol* ***p.'s democracy*** democracia *f* popular; *Pol* ***p.'s front*** frente *m* popular; ***p. power*** poder *m* popular; ***p.'s republic*** república *f* popular; **the P.'s Republic of China** la República Popular China

(**c**) *(employed in a specified job)* **I'll call the electricity/gas p. tomorrow** mañana llamo a los de la electricidad/los del gas; **the President's financial p.** los consejeros financieros del presidente

(**d**) *Fam (family)* **my/his p.** mi/su gente

2 *n (nation)* pueblo *m*; **the Scottish p.** el pueblo escocés; **the indigenous peoples of Polynesia** los pueblos indígenas de Polinesia

3 *vt* poblar; **to be peopled by** *or* **with** estar poblado(a) de; **the monsters that p. his dreams** los monstruos que pueblan sus sueños

---

PEP [pep] *n Br Fin* (*abbr* **personal equity plan**) = plan personal de inversión en valores de renta variable fiscalmente incentivado por el Gobierno

pep [pep] *n Fam* ánimo *m*, energía *f*; **she gave us a p. talk** nos dirigió unas palabras de ánimo ▸▸ ***p. pill*** estimulante *m*

▸ **pep up** (*pt & pp* **pepped**) *vt sep Fam* (**a**) *(person, event)* animar; **a cup of tea will soon p. you up** una taza de té y te sentirás mejor en un momento (**b**) *(dish)* alegrar

peperoni = **pepperoni**

pepper ['pepə(r)] **1** *n* (**a**) *(spice)* pimienta *f*; **black/white p.** pimienta negra/blanca ▸▸ ***p. mill*** molinillo *m* de pimienta; *Br* ***p. pot*** pimentero *m*; *US* ***p. shaker*** pimentero *m* (**b**) *(vegetable)* pimiento *m*, *Méx* chile *m*, *RP* ají *m*, *Col, Ven* pimentón *m*; **green/red/yellow p.** pimiento verde/rojo/amarillo

2 *vt* (**a**) *(in cooking)* sazonar con pimienta (**b**) *(sprinkle)* **her text was peppered with quotations** su texto estaba salpicado de citas; **they peppered their conversation with obscenities** salpicaron la conversación de obscenidades; **to p. sth with bullets** acribillar a balazos algo

pepper-and-salt ['pepərənd'sɔ:lt] *adj (flecked)* moteado(a) y entrecano(a)

pepperbox ['pepəbɒks] *n US* pimentero *m*

peppercorn ['pepəkɔ:n] *n* grano *m* de pimienta ▸▸ *Br* ***p. rent*** alquiler *m or* arrendamiento *m* (por un precio) simbólico

peppermint ['pepəmɪnt] *n* (**a**) *(plant)* hierbabuena *f* ▸▸ ***p. tea*** infusión *f* de hierbabuena (**b**) *(flavour)* menta *f* (**c**) *(sweet)* caramelo *m* de menta ▸▸ ***p. cream*** bombón *m* relleno de menta

pe(p)peroni [pepə'rəʊnɪ] *n* pepperoni *m*, = especie de chorizo picante

peppery ['pepərɪ] *adj* (**a**) *(spicy)* **to be too p.** tener demasiada pimienta (**b**) *(irritable)* picajoso(a), irascible

peppy ['pepɪ] *adj Fam (person)* jovial, vivaracho(a)

peptic ['peptɪk] *adj Med* péptico(a) ▸▸ ***p. ulcer*** úlcera *f* péptica

peptide ['peptaɪd] *n Biochem* péptido *m*

per [pɜ:(r)] *prep* (**a**) *(in rates)* por; **p. day** al día, por día; **p. head** por persona; **100 km p. hour** 100 kms por hora; **p. annum** al año, por año; **p. capita** per cápita (**b**) *Formal (according to)* **as p. your instructions** según sus instrucciones; **as p. usual** como de costumbre

peradventure [pərəd'ventʃə(r)] *adv Archaic or Hum* por ventura

perambulation [pəræmbjʊ'leɪʃən] *n Literary or Hum (stroll)* paseo *m*

perambulator [pə'ræmbjʊleɪtə(r)] *n Old-fashioned* cochecito *m* de bebé

perceivable [pə'si:vəbəl] *adj (noticeable)* apreciable, perceptible

perceive [pə'si:v] *vt* (**a**) *(notice) (sound, light, smell)* percibir; *(difference)* apreciar, distinguir; **he was unable to p. colours** era incapaz de distinguir los colores (**b**) *(understand) (truth, importance)* apreciar, entender (**c**) *(view)* **to p. sth/sb as...** ver *or* juzgar algo/a alguien como...

perceived [pə'si:vd] *adj (injustice, benefit)* patente, evidente

per cent, percent [pə'sent] **1** *n* porcentaje *m*, tanto *m* por ciento; **forty p. of women** el cuarenta por ciento de las mujeres; **a ten p. increase** un aumento del diez por ciento; **a nine p. interest rate** una tasa de interés del nueve por ciento; IDIOM **everyone's giving one hundred p.** *(working as hard as possible)* todo el mundo está dando todo lo que tiene

2 *adv* por ciento; **it's fifty p. cotton** es cincuenta por ciento algodón; **I'm ninety-nine p. certain** estoy prácticamente seguro

percentage [pə'sentɪdʒ] *n* (**a**) *(proportion)* porcentaje *m*, tanto *m* por ciento; **in a high/tiny p. of cases** en la gran mayoría/minoría de los casos; **to express sth as a p.** expresar algo en forma de porcentaje ▸▸ ***p. increase*** incremento *m* porcentual; ***p. point*** punto *m* porcentual; ***p. sign*** signo *m* porcentual

(**b**) *(share of profits, investment)* tanto *m* por ciento; **to receive a p. on all sales** percibir un tanto por ciento de todas las ventas

(**c**) *US Fam (advantage)* **there's no p. in it** no vale la pena

percentile [pə'sentaɪl] *n (in statistics)* percentil *m*

perceptible [pə'septɪbəl] *adj* perceptible

perceptibly [pə'septɪblɪ] *adv* perceptiblemente

perception [pə'sepʃən] *n* (**a**) *(with senses)* percepción *f*; **visual/aural p.** capacidad visual/auditiva; **the organs of p.** los órganos sensoriales (**b**) *(of difference, importance, facts)* apreciación *f*; **the general public's p. of the police** la valoración de la policía por parte de la opinión pública (**c**) *(discernment)* perspicacia *f*

perceptive [pə'septɪv] *adj (person)* atinado(a), perspicaz; *(remark)* atinado(a), certero(a)

perceptively [pə'septɪvlɪ] *adv* atinadamente, perspicazmente

perceptiveness [pə'septɪvnɪs] *n* perspicacia *f*

perceptual [pə'septjʊəl] *adj* sensorial

perch[1] [pɜ:tʃ] **1** *n* (**a**) *(for bird)* percha *f* (**b**) *Fam (seat, position)* atalaya *f* (**c**) IDIOMS *Fam* **to knock sb off his p.** bajarle los humos a alguien; *Hum* **to fall** *or* **drop off one's p.** irse al otro barrio

2 *vt* **she perched herself on the edge of the table** se sentó en el borde de la mesa; **she was perched on a stool/on the arm of the chair** estaba encaramada sobre un taburete/el brazo del sillón; **a castle perched on a hill** un castillo alzado en lo alto de un monte; **with his glasses perched on the end of his nose** con las gafas sostenidas en la punta de la nariz

3 *vi (bird)* posarse; **he perched on the edge of the table** *(person)* se sentó en el borde de la mesa

perch[2] *n (fish)* perca *f*

perch[3] *n (linear measure)* = antigua medida de longitud equivalente a 5,029 metros

perchance [pə'tʃɑ:ns] *adv Old-fashioned (possibly)* acaso, por alguna casualidad; *Hum* **that wouldn't, p., be the five pounds you owe me?** ¿no serán ésas, por ventura, las cinco libras que me debes?

percipient [pə'sɪpɪənt] *adj (perceptive)* atinado(a), perspicaz

percolate ['pɜ:kəleɪt] **1** *vt (coffee)* hacer *(con cafetera)*; **percolated coffee** café de cafetera

2 *vi* (**a**) *(liquid)* filtrarse; **toxic chemicals had percolated through the soil** se habían filtrado productos tóxicos a través del suelo (**b**) *(ideas, news)* difundirse; **the news gradually percolated through the organization** la noticia se difundió *or* propagó gradualmente por la organización (**c**) *US Fam (be excited)* bullir

percolator ['pɜːkəleɪtə(r)] *n* cafetera *f* eléctrica

percuss [pə'kʌs] *vt Med* percutir

percussion [pə'kʌʃən] *n* (**a**) *Mus* percusión *f*; **Jane Stowell on p.** a la percusión, Jane Stowell ▸▸ ***p. instruments*** instrumentos *mpl* de percusión (**b**) ***p. cap*** cápsula *f* fulminante

percussionist [pə'kʌʃənɪst] *n Mus* percusionista *mf*

perdition [pə'dɪʃən] *n Literary (damnation)* perdición *f*

peregrination [perɪgrɪ'neɪʃən] *n Literary or Hum* peregrinación *f*

peregrine falcon ['perɪgrɪn'fɔːlkən] *n* halcón *m* peregrino

peremptorily [pə'remptərəlɪ] *adv* imperiosamente

peremptory [pə'remptərɪ] *adj (person, manner, voice)* imperioso(a); *(command)* perentorio(a)

perennial [pə'renɪəl] **1** *n Bot* planta *f* perenne

2 *adj* (**a**) *(plant)* (de hoja) perenne (**b**) *(problems, beauty)* eterno(a); **a p. subject of debate** un eterno tema de debate

perennially [pə'renɪəlɪ] *adv (everlastingly)* eternamente; *(recurrently, continually)* invariablemente

perfect ['pɜːfɪkt] **1** *adj* (**a**) *(excellent, flawless)* perfecto(a); **it was a p. day** *(weather)* hizo un día estupendo; *(activities)* fue un día perfecto; **her English is p.** habla un inglés perfecto; **no one's p.** nadie es perfecto; **to be in p. condition** *(engine, appliance)* estar en óptimas condiciones; *(teeth, hair, product)* estar en perfecto estado; **in p. health** en perfecto estado de salud

(**b**) *(complete)* **it makes p. sense** es del todo razonable; **you have a p. right to be here** tienes todo el derecho del mundo a estar aquí; **he's a p. stranger to me** no lo conozco de nada; **he's a p. fool** es un perfecto idiota; **he's a p. gentleman** es un perfecto caballero

(**c**) *(fitting, right) (example, gift, opportunity)* ideal, perfecto(a); **Tuesday/seven o'clock would be p.** el martes/a las 7 sería ideal; **that colour is p. on you** ese color te sienta de maravilla

(**d**) *Gram* perfecto(a); **future p.** futuro perfecto; **past p.** pretérito pluscuamperfecto ▸▸ ***p. participle*** participio *m* de pretérito

(**e**) *Mus* **to have p. pitch** tener una entonación perfecta ▸▸ ***p. fifth*** quinta *f*; ***p. fourth*** cuarta *f*; ***p. interval*** intervalo *m* perfecto

(**f**) *Math* ***p. number*** número *m* perfecto

2 *n Gram* pretérito *m* perfecto

3 *vt* [pə'fekt] perfeccionar

perfectibility [pəfektə'bɪlɪtɪ] *n* perfectibilidad *f*

perfectible [pə'fektəbəl] *adj* perfectible, perfeccionable

perfection [pə'fekʃən] *n* (**a**) *(quality)* perfección *f*; **to attain p.** alcanzar la perfección; **to p.** *(cooking, task)* a la perfección (**b**) *(perfecting)* perfeccionamiento *m*

perfectionism [pə'fekʃənɪzəm] *n* perfeccionismo *m*

perfectionist [pə'fekʃənɪst] *n* perfeccionista *mf*

perfective [pə'fektɪv] *adj Gram* perfectivo(a)

perfectly ['pɜːfɪktlɪ] *adv* (**a**) *(faultlessly)* perfectamente; **he speaks English p.** habla inglés perfectamente; **it fits p.** se ajusta perfectamente; **p. formed** perfectamente formado(a)

(**b**) *(absolutely)* **it's p. all right** no pasa absolutamente nada; **it's p. clear to me that...** tengo clarísimo que...; **to be p. frank** *or* **honest with you...** para serte totalmente sincero...; **it's a p. good raincoat** es un impermeable estupendo; **it's p. idiotic** es completamente estúpido; **it's p. obvious** resulta totalmente evidente; **she's p. right** tiene toda la razón; **you know p. well I can't go** sabes perfectamente que no puedo ir

perfidious [pə'fɪdɪəs] *adj Literary* pérfido(a) ▸▸ ***p. Albion*** la pérfida Albión

perfidiously [pə'fɪdɪəslɪ] *adv Literary* pérfidamente

perfidy ['pɜːfɪdɪ] *n Literary* perfidia *f*

perforate ['pɜːfəreɪt] *vt* perforar

perforated ['pɜːfəreɪtɪd] *adj* perforado(a) ▸▸ *Med* ***p. eardrum*** tímpano *m* perforado; ***p. line*** línea *f* perforada; *Comptr* ***p. paper*** papel *m* perforado; *Med* ***p. ulcer*** úlcera *f* perforada

perforation [pɜːfə'reɪʃən] *n (hole, on stamp)* perforación *f*; **tear along the perforations** separar por la línea perforada

perforce [pə'fɔːs] *adv Old-fashioned or Literary* forzosamente, por fuerza

perform [pə'fɔːm] **1** *vt* (**a**) *(carry out) (task, miracle, manoeuvre)* realizar, efectuar; *(calculation)* realizar; *(ritual)* realizar, llevar a cabo; *(function, one's duty)* cumplir; **the robot can p. complex movements** el robot puede realizar movimientos complejos; **to p. an operation** *(surgery)* practicar *or* realizar una operación; **the agency performs a vital service** la agencia presta un servicio esencial

(**b**) *(play)* representar; *(ballet, opera)* interpretar; *(role)* interpretar; *(piece of music)* interpretar, ejecutar

2 *vi* (**a**) *(in job, situation, sports team, athlete)* rendir; **he'd never spoken in public before, but he performed well** era la primera vez que hablaba en público, pero lo hizo muy bien; **how does she p. under pressure?** ¿cómo se desenvuelve bajo presión?; **I couldn't p.** *(sexually)* no pude consumar el acto sexual

(**b**) *(actor, comedian)* actuar; *(musician)* tocar; *(dancer)* actuar; *(singer)* interpretar, cantar; **the Berlin Philharmonic is performing tonight** la Filarmónica de Berlín ofrecerá un concierto esta noche

(**c**) *(company, business)* rendir; *(shares)* comportarse

(**d**) *(machine, car)* funcionar, comportarse

performance [pə'fɔːməns] *n* (**a**) *(of task, manoeuvre)* realización *f*, ejecución *f*; *(of ritual)* celebración *f*; *(of duty)* cumplimiento *m* ▸▸ ***p. appraisal*** evaluación *f* del rendimiento; ***p. art*** = expresión artística en la que se combinan diferentes disciplinas como teatro, música, escultura o fotografía

(**b**) *(of sportsperson, team, politician)* actuación *f*; *(of pupil)* comportamiento *m*; **to put on** *or* **up a good p.** hacer buen papel

(**c**) *(rendition) (by actor, musician, dancer)* actuación *f*; **he gave an excellent p. in the role of Othello** ofreció una actuación excelente en el papel de Otelo

(**d**) *(of play)* representación *f*; *(ballet, opera)* actuación *f*; *(of musical piece)* interpretación *f*, ejecución *f*; *(in cinema)* sesión *f*

(**e**) *(of economy, currency, shares)* comportamiento *m*; *(of company, business)* rendimiento *m*

(**f**) *(of machine, car)* prestaciones *fpl*, rendimiento *m* ▸▸ ***p. car*** coche *m or Am* carro *m or CSur* auto *m* de alto rendimiento

(**g**) *Fam (fuss)* **to make a p. (about sth)** armar un escándalo *or Esp* montar una escena (por algo); **it's such a p. getting a visa!** conseguir el visado es toda una operación; **what a p.!** ¡vaya actuación!

(**h**) *Ling* realización *f*

performance-related [pə'fɔːmənsrɪ'leɪtɪd] *adj* según el rendimiento

performative [pə'fɔːmətɪv] *adj Ling & Phil* performativo(a)

performer [pə'fɔːmə(r)] *n (actor, dancer, musician)* intérprete *mf*; **she's a very capable p.** es muy capaz; **the new coupé is a useful p. around town** el nuevo cupé se comporta muy bien en ciudad; **our shares are amongst the top performers** nuestras acciones están entre las de mayor rentabilidad; **he has been a consistent p.** *(in sport)* ha sido muy regular en su rendimiento

performing [pə'fɔːmɪŋ] *adj (dog, seal)* amaestrado(a) ▸▸ ***p. arts*** artes *fpl* interpretativas; ***p. rights*** derechos *mpl* de interpretación

perfume **1** *n* ['pɜːfjuːm] (**a**) *(of flowers)* aroma *m*, fragancia *f* (**b**) *(for person)* perfume *m* ▸▸ ***p. counter*** sección *f* de perfumería

2 *vt* [pə'fjuːm] perfumar

perfumed ['pɜːfjuːmd] *adj* perfumado(a)

perfumery [pə'fjuːmərɪ] *n* perfumería *f*

perfunctorily [pə'fʌŋktərɪlɪ] *adv (to glance, smile)* rutinariamente, superficialmente; *(to examine)* superficialmente; *(to apologize)* indiferentemente

perfunctory [pə'fʌŋktərɪ] *adj (glance, smile)* rutinario(a), superficial; *(letter, instructions, examination)* somero(a); *(apology)* indiferente; **he greeted me with a p. nod** me saludó con un gesto indiferente

pergola ['pɜːgələ] *n* pérgola *f*

PERHAPS [pə'hæps] *adv* (**a**) *(maybe)* quizá, quizás, tal vez, *Am* talvez; **p. so/not** quizá sí/no; **p. she'll come** quizá venga

(**b**) *(about)* aproximadamente; **there were p. 500 people there** había aproximadamente *or* como 500 personas

(**c**) *Formal (in polite requests, suggestions)* **p. you'd like a glass of water?** ¿querría un vaso de agua?; **I thought p. you might like to have dinner with us** ¿le gustaría quedarse a cenar con nosotros?; **p. you could try that bit again** ¿por qué no intentas esa parte otra vez?

---

pericarditis [perɪkɑː'daɪtɪs] *n Med* pericarditis *f inv*

pericardium [perɪ'kɑːdɪəm] (*pl* **pericardia** [perɪ'kɑːdɪə]) *n Anat* pericardio *m*

peril ['perɪl] *n* peligro *m*, riesgo *m*; **in p. of her life** a riesgo de (perder) su vida; **at your p.** por tu cuenta y riesgo

perilous ['perɪləs] *adj* peligroso(a)

perilously ['perɪləslɪ] *adv* peligrosamente; **we came p. close to a collision** estuvimos en un tris de chocar

perimeter [pə'rɪmɪtə(r)] *n* perímetro *m* ▸▸ ***p. fence*** valla *f* exterior

perinatal [perɪ'neɪtəl] *adj Med* perinatal

perineum [perɪ'niːəm] *n Anat* perineo *m*, periné *m*

period ['pɪərɪəd] *n* (a) *(stretch of time)* periodo *m*, período *m*; **for a p. of three months** durante un periodo de tres meses; **within the agreed p.** dentro del plazo acordado; **sunny periods** intervalos de sol
(b) *(phase)* etapa *f*, fase *f*; **he's going through a difficult p.** está pasando una mala racha; **at that p. in her life** en aquella etapa de su vida; **his cubist/jazz p.** su etapa cubista/de jazz
(c) *(historical age)* época *f*, periodo *m*; **a p. of colonial expansion** una época de expansión colonial; **the Elizabethan/Jacobean p.** la época Isabelina/Jacobea; **the play has a definite p. flavour** es una obra muy de la época ▸▸ *TV* ***p. drama*** drama *m* (televisivo) de época; ***p. dress*** traje *m* de época; ***p. features*** *(in house)* detalles *mpl* de época; ***p. furniture*** muebles *mpl* de época; ***p. piece*** pieza *f* de época
(d) *Geol* era *f*; **the Jurassic/Cretaceous p.** la era jurásica/cretácea
(e) *Sch* clase *f*; **a French p.** una clase de francés
(f) *(menstruation)* periodo *m*, regla *f*; **my periods have stopped** ya no me viene la regla; **to have one's p.** tener el periodo *or* la regla ▸▸ ***p. pains*** dolores *mpl* menstruales
(g) *US (punctuation mark)* punto *m*; **I'm not going, p.** no voy, y punto
(h) *(sentence)* oración *f*
(i) *(of basketball, ice hockey game)* tiempo *m*
(j) *Com* ***p. of grace*** periodo *m* de prosperidad
(k) *Astron* ***p. of rotation*** periodo *m* de rotación
(l) *Chem (in periodic table)* periodo *m*

periodic [pɪərɪ'ɒdɪk] *adj* (a) *(occasional)* periódico(a) (b) *Math* ***p. function*** función *f* periódica (c) *Chem* ***p. table*** tabla *f* periódica

periodical [pɪərɪ'ɒdɪkəl] 1 *n* publicación *f* periódica, boletín *m*
2 *adj* (a) *(occasional)* periódico(a) (b) *(publication)* periódico(a)

> **False friend:** The Spanish noun **periódico** is not a translation for the English noun **periodical**. In Spanish **periódico** means "newspaper".

periodically [pɪərɪ'ɒdɪklɪ] *adv* periódicamente

periodicity [pɪərɪə'dɪsətɪ] *n* periodicidad *f*

periodontics [perɪə'dɒntɪks] *n* periodontología *f*

periodontitis [perɪədɒn'taɪtɪs] *n Med* periodontitis *f inv*

periosteum [perɪ'ɒstɪəm] *n Anat* periostio *m*

peripatetic [perɪpə'tetɪk] *adj* (a) *(itinerant)* ambulante, itinerante (b) *(teacher)* que trabaja en varios centros

peripheral [pə'rɪfərəl] 1 *n Comptr* periférico *m*
2 *adj (area, vision)* periférico(a); *(issue, importance)* secundario(a) ▸▸ *Comptr* ***p. device*** (dispositivo *m*) periférico *m*; *Med* ***p. vision*** visión *f* periférica

periphery [pə'rɪfərɪ] *n* periferia *f*; **on the p. of society** al margen de la sociedad

periphrasis [pə'rɪfrəsɪs] (*pl* **periphrases** [pə'rɪfrəsi:z]) *n* perífrasis *f inv*

periphrastic [perɪ'fræstɪk] *adj* perifrástico(a)

periscope ['perɪskəʊp] *n* periscopio *m*; **up p.!** ¡arriba el periscopio!

perish ['perɪʃ] 1 *vi* (a) *Literary (person)* perecer; **p. the thought!** ¡Dios no lo quiera! (b) *(rubber, leather)* estropearse; *(food)* pudrirse
2 *vt (rubber, leather)* estropear

perishable ['perɪʃəbəl] 1 *n* **perishables** productos *mpl* perecederos
2 *adj* perecedero(a)

perished ['perɪʃt] *adj Br Fam* **I'm p.** *(very cold)* ¡hace una rasca que me muero!

perisher ['perɪʃə(r)] *n Br Fam (mischievous child)* bribón(ona) *m,f*, diablillo(a) *m,f*

perishing ['perɪʃɪŋ] *adj Fam* (a) *(very cold)* **it's p.** ¡hace un frío que pela! (b) *Old-fashioned (as expletive)* endiablado(a); **what a p. nuisance!** ¡qué contrariedad!

peristalsis [perɪ'stælsɪs] *n Physiol* peristaltismo *m*

peritoneal [perɪtə'ni:əl] *adj Anat* peritoneal

peritoneum [perɪtə'ni:əm] *n Anat* peritoneo *m*

peritonitis [perɪtə'naɪtɪs] *n Med* peritonitis *f inv*

periwig ['perɪwɪg] *n* peluquín *m*

periwinkle ['perɪwɪŋkəl] *n* (a) *Bot* vinca *f*, vincapervinca *f* (b) *Zool* bígaro *m*

perjure ['pɜ:dʒə(r)] *vt Law* **to p. oneself** perjurar

perjured ['pɜ:dʒəd] *adj Law (witness)* perjuro(a); **p. evidence** pruebas falsas

perjurer ['pɜ:dʒərə(r)] *n Law* perjuro(a) *m,f*

perjury ['pɜ:dʒərɪ] *n Law* perjurio *m*; **to commit p.** cometer perjurio

perk[1] [pɜ:k] *n Fam* ventaja *f*; **cheap air travel is one of the perks of his job** una de las ventajas de su trabajo son los vuelos baratos

perk[2] 1 *vt (coffee)* hacer
2 *vi* hacerse

▸ **perk up** *Fam* 1 *vt sep* animar, levantar el ánimo a
2 *vi* (a) *(cheer up)* animarse; **he perked up in the afternoon** por la tarde se animó (b) *(ears, head)* erguirse

perkily ['pɜ:kɪlɪ] *adv Fam* animadamente

perkiness ['pɜ:kɪnɪs] *n Fam* alborozo *m*

perky ['pɜ:kɪ] *adj Fam* animado(a); **to be p.** estar animado(a)

perm [pɜ:m] 1 *n* (a) *(hairdo)* permanente *f*; **to have a p.** llevar una permanente (b) *(in football pools)* combinación *f* fija
2 *vt* **to have one's hair permed** hacerse la permanente

permaculture ['pɜ:məkʌltʃə(r)] *n* = sistema natural de agricultura

permafrost ['pɜ:məfrɒst] *n Geol* permafrost *m*

permanence ['pɜ:mənəns] *n* permanencia *f*

permanency ['pɜ:mənənsɪ] *n (of quality)* permanencia *f*; *(of colour)* permanencia *f*

permanent ['pɜ:mənənt] 1 *adj* permanente; *(employee, job)* fijo(a); **no p. damage was caused** no se produjeron daños irreparables; **she has taken up p. residence abroad** se ha establecido en el extranjero de manera permanente; **on a p. basis** de manera definitiva ▸▸ ***p. address*** domicilio *m* fijo, residencia *f* habitual; ***p. contract*** contrato *m* fijo *or* indefinido; ***p. ink*** tinta *f* indeleble; ***p. magnet*** imán *m* permanente; ***p. press*** = tratamiento químico que convierte las ropas en inarrugables; *Br* ***P. Secretary*** Secretario(a) *m,f* Permanente *(alto cargo del funcionariado británico)*; *Comptr* ***p. storage*** almacenamiento *m* permanente; ***p. tooth*** diente *m* definitivo; *Br* ***P. Undersecretary*** Subsecretario(a) *m,f* Permanente *(alto cargo del funcionariado británico)*; ***p. wave*** *(hairdo)* permanente *f*; *Br Rail* ***p. way*** vía *f* del ferrocarril
2 *n US (in hair)* permanente *f*

permanently ['pɜ:mənəntlɪ] *adv* (a) *(constantly)* constantemente; **he's p. drunk** está siempre borracho (b) *(indefinitely)* para siempre; **they came to live here p.** vinieron a vivir aquí para siempre

permanent-press ['pɜ:mənənt'pres] *adj* **p. trousers/skirt** pantalón/falda inarrugable

permanganate [pə'mæŋgəneɪt] *n Chem* permanganato *m*

permeability [pɜ:mɪə'bɪlətɪ] *n* permeabilidad *f*

permeable ['pɜ:mɪəbəl] *adj* permeable

permeate ['pɜ:mɪeɪt] 1 *vt* (a) *(of gas, smell)* inundar; *(of liquid)* impregnar (b) *(of ideas, feelings)* impregnar; **the atmosphere of gloom which permeates his novels** la atmósfera triste que impregna sus novelas
2 *vi* **to p. through sth** *(gas, smell)* inundar algo; *(liquid)* filtrarse a través de algo; *(fear, suspicion)* extenderse por algo

Permian ['pɜ:mɪən] *Geol* 1 *n* **the P.** el pérmico
2 *adj* pérmico(a)

permissible [pə'mɪsɪbəl] *adj* (a) *(allowed)* admisible, permisible (b) *(tolerable) (behaviour)* tolerable; **a p. degree of error** un margen de error permisible

permission [pə'mɪʃən] *n* permiso *m*; **to ask for p. to do sth** pedir permiso para hacer algo; **to give sb p. to do sth** dar a alguien permiso para hacer algo; **to have p. to do sth** tener permiso para hacer algo; **with your p.** con (su) permiso; **photos published by kind p. of Larousse** fotos publicadas por gentileza de Larousse; **you need written p. to work at home** necesitas permiso por escrito para trabajar en casa

permissive [pə'mɪsɪv] *adj* permisivo(a); **the p. society** la sociedad permisiva

permissiveness [pə'mɪsɪvnɪs] *n* permisividad *f*

permit 1 *n* ['pɜ:mɪt] *(for fishing, imports, exports)* licencia *f*; *(for parking, work, residence)* permiso *m*; **p. holders only** *(sign)* estacionamiento reservado
2 *vt* [pə'mɪt] (*pt & pp* **permitted**) (a) *(allow)* permitir; **to p. sb to do sth** permitir a alguien hacer algo; **I won't p. it!** ¡no lo pienso permitir!; **he permits far too much rudeness from his children** les tolera demasiada grosería a sus hijos; *Formal* **p. me to inform you that...** me permito informarlo de que...; **smoking is not permitted** no se permite fumar
(b) *Formal* **to p. of sth** *(give scope for)* permitir algo
3 *vi* **weather permitting** si el tiempo lo permite; **if time permits** si hay tiempo; **if our budget permits** si el presupuesto lo permite

permitted [pə'mɪtɪd] *adj* permitido(a)

permutate ['pɜ:mjʊteɪt] *vt* permutar

permutation [pɜ:mjʊ'teɪʃən] *n* permutación *f*

pernicious [pəˈnɪʃəs] *adj* pernicioso(a) ▸▸ *Med* ***p. anaemia*** anemia *f* perniciosa

pernickety [pəˈnɪkɪtɪ], *US* **persnickety** [pəˈsnɪkɪtɪ] *adj Fam* (**a**) *(person)* quisquilloso(a); **to be p. about one's food** ser un tiquismiquis con la comida; **she's very p. about punctuality** es muy maniática con la puntualidad (**b**) *(task)* engorroso(a)

peroration [perəˈreɪʃən] *n Formal* (**a**) *(summing up)* peroración *f* (**b**) *(long speech)* perorata *f*

peroxide [pəˈrɒksaɪd] **1** *n Chem* peróxido *m* ▸▸ ***p. blonde*** *(woman)* rubia *f* oxigenada *or Esp* de bote

2 *vt (hair)* teñir de rubio oxigenado

perpendicular [pɜːpənˈdɪkjʊlə(r)] **1** *n* perpendicular *f*

2 *adj* (**a**) *(line)* perpendicular (**to** a); **the line AB is p. to the line CD** la línea AB es perpendicular a la CD (**b**) *Archit* **the P.** = estilo de arquitectura gótica inglesa, típica de los siglos XIV y XV

perpetrate [ˈpɜːpɪtreɪt] *vt Formal (crime, deception)* perpetrar

perpetrator [ˈpɜːpɪtreɪtə(r)] *n Formal* autor(ora) *m,f*; **the p. of the crime** el autor del delito

perpetual [pəˈpetjʊəl] *adj* continuo(a), constante ▸▸ ***p. calendar*** calendario *m* perpetuo; ***p. check*** *(in chess)* jaque *m* continuo; ***p. motion*** movimiento *m* continuo

perpetually [pəˈpetjʊəlɪ] *adv* (**a**) *(eternally)* perpetuamente (**b**) *(constantly)* continuamente, constantemente

perpetuate [pəˈpetjʊeɪt] *vt Formal* perpetuar

perpetuation [pəpetjʊˈeɪʃən] *n Formal* perpetuación *f*

perpetuity [pɜːpɪˈtjuːɪtɪ] *n Formal* **in p.** a perpetuidad

Perpignan [ˈpɜːpɪnjɒn] *n* Perpiñán

perplex [pəˈpleks] *vt* dejar perplejo(a)

perplexed [pəˈplekst] *adj* perplejo(a); **I'm p. about what to do** estoy confuso sobre qué hacer

perplexedly [pəˈpleksɪdlɪ] *adv* perplejamente, con perplejidad

perplexing [pəˈpleksɪŋ] *adj* desconcertante

perplexity [pəˈpleksɪtɪ] *n* perplejidad *f*, desconcierto *m*

perquisite [ˈpɜːkwɪzɪt] *n Formal* ventaja *f* extra

perry [ˈperɪ] *n* = bebida alcohólica hecha con zumo de pera fermentado

per se [ˈpɜːˈseɪ] *adv* en sí, per se

persecute [ˈpɜːsɪkjuːt] *vt* (**a**) *(for political, religious reasons)* perseguir; **she was persecuted for her beliefs** fue perseguida por sus creencias (**b**) *(harass)* acosar, atormentar

persecution [pɜːsɪˈkjuːʃən] *n* persecución *f* ▸▸ *Psy* ***p. complex*** manía *f* persecutoria

persecutor [ˈpɜːsɪkjuːtə(r)] *n* perseguidor(ora) *m,f*

Perseus [ˈpɜːsɪəs] *n Mythol* Perseo

perseverance [pɜːsɪˈvɪərəns] *n* perseverancia *f*

persevere [pɜːsɪˈvɪə(r)] *vi* perseverar (**with** en); **I persevered until it worked** no desistí hasta que funcionó; **to p. in one's efforts** perseverar uno en su intento; **to p. in doing sth** seguir haciendo algo con perseverancia

persevering [pɜːsɪˈvɪərɪŋ] *adj* perseverante

Persia [ˈpɜːʒə] *n Formerly* Persia

Persian [ˈpɜːʒən] **1** *n* (**a**) *(person)* persa *mf* (**b**) *(language)* persa *m*

2 *adj* persa ▸▸ ***P. blinds*** persianas *fpl*; ***P. carpet*** alfombra *f* persa; ***P. cat*** gato *m* persa; ***the P. Gulf*** el Golfo Pérsico; ***P. lamb*** caracul *m*

persiflage [pɜːsɪˈflɑːʒ] *n Literary* facecia *f*

persimmon [pəˈsɪmən] *n* caqui *m (fruta)*

persist [pəˈsɪst] *vi* (**a**) *(person)* persistir, perseverar; **to p. in doing sth** empeñarse en hacer algo; **to p. in one's belief that...** empeñarse en creer que...; **to p. in one's efforts (to do sth)** no cejar en el empeño (de hacer algo) (**b**) *(fog, pain, belief, rumours)* persistir; **rain will p. in the north** continuará la lluvia en el norte; **if the fever persists** si continúa la fiebre

persistence [pəˈsɪstəns] *n* (**a**) *(of person)* empeño *m*, persistencia *f* (**b**) *(of pain, belief, rumours)* persistencia *f* ▸▸ *Physiol* ***p. of vision*** persistencia *f* retiniana

persistent [pəˈsɪstənt] *adj* (**a**) *(person)* persistente, insistente; **his p. refusal to cooperate** su reiterada falta de cooperación; **you must be more p. in your efforts** deberías ser más constante en tu trabajo ▸▸ ***p. offender*** delincuente *mf* habitual, reincidente *mf*

(**b**) *(rain, pain)* persistente, pertinaz; *(doubts, rumours)* persistente ▸▸ *Med* ***p. vegetative state*** estado *m* vegetativo permanente

persistently [pəˈsɪstəntlɪ] *adv (constantly)* constantemente; *(repeatedly)* repetidamente, una y otra vez

persnickety *US* = **pernickety**

person [ˈpɜːsən] (*pl* **people** [ˈpiːpəl], *Formal* **persons**) *n* (**a**) *(individual)* persona *f*; **a young p.** *(female)* una joven; *(male)* un joven; **in p.** en persona; **he's a very unpleasant p.** es un tipo muy desagradable; **he's just the p. we need** es justo la persona que necesitamos; **she's nice enough as a p., but...** como persona es bastante agradable, pero...; **I'm not the p. to ask, try Mr Green** yo no soy la persona adecuada, pregúntale al Sr. Green; **he's not that sort of p.** no es de esa clase de persona; *Fam* **are you a cat p. or a dog p.?** ¿qué prefieres, los perros o los gatos?; **the Royal Family, in the p. of Queen Elizabeth** la Familia Real, encarnada por (la figura de) la reina Isabel; *Law* **by a p. or persons unknown** por uno o varios desconocidos

(**b**) *Formal (body)* **to have sth on** *or* **about one's p.** llevar algo encima

(**c**) *Gram* persona *f*; **the first/second/third p. singular** la primera/segunda/tercera persona del singular; **in the first/second/third p.** en primera/segunda/tercera persona

(**d**) *Rel* persona *f*

persona [pəˈsəʊnə] (*pl* **personas** *or* **personae** [pəˈsəʊniː]) *n* **her public p.** su imagen pública; **he adopts the p. of a war veteran** adopta el personaje de un veterano de guerra; **to be p. non grata** ser persona no grata; **to declare sb p. non grata** declarar a alguien persona no grata

personable [ˈpɜːsənəbəl] *adj* agradable

personage [ˈpɜːsənɪdʒ] *n* personaje *m*

personal [ˈpɜːsənəl] **1** *adj* (**a**) *(individual) (experience, belief)* personal; **she tries to give her work a p. touch** trata de darle un toque personal a su trabajo; **my p. opinion is that he drowned** mi opinión personal es que se ahogó ▸▸ *Fin* ***p. allowance*** dietas *fpl*; ***p. assistant*** *(person)* secretario(a) *m,f* personal; *Comptr* asistente *m* personal; ***p. best*** *(in sport)* plusmarca *f* (personal), récord *m* personal; ***p. growth*** desarrollo *m* personal; ***p. identification number*** número *m* secreto, PIN *m*

(**b**) *(in person)* en persona; **under the p. supervision of the author** bajo la supervisión del propio autor; **to make a p. appearance** hacer acto de presencia; **p. callers welcome** *(in advertisement)* se atienden llamadas de particulares

(**c**) *(for one's own use)* personal; **to be careless about one's p. appearance** no cuidar uno su apariencia; **this is for my p. use** esto es de uso personal ▸▸ *Comptr* ***p. computer*** *Esp* ordenador *m or Am* computadora *f* personal; *Comptr* ***p. computing*** informática *f* personal; *Comptr* ***p. digital assistant*** asistente *m* personal; ***p. effects*** efectos *mpl* personales; *Br Fin* ***p. equity plan*** = plan personal de inversión en valores de renta variable fiscalmente incentivado por el Gobierno; *Comptr* ***p. home page*** página *f* personal; ***p. loan*** préstamo *m or* crédito *m or Méx* prestamiento *m* personal; ***p. organizer*** agenda *f*; *Comptr* agenda *f* electrónica; ***p. pension plan*** plan *m* personal de jubilación; *Law* ***p. property*** bienes *mpl* muebles; ***p. shopper*** asistente(a) *m,f* de compras; ***p. stereo*** walkman® *m*; ***p. trainer*** preparador(ora) *m,f* físico(a) personal

(**d**) *(private) (message, letter)* personal; **p. (and private)** *(on letter)* personal y privado; **for p. reasons** por motivos personales; **I'd like to see her on a p. matter** me gustaría hablar con ella de un asunto personal ▸▸ ***p. ad*** *(in newspaper, magazine)* anuncio *m* personal (por palabras); ***p. column*** *(in newspaper, magazine)* sección *f* de anuncios personales *or* de contactos

(**e**) *(intimate) (feelings, reasons, life)* personal; **he's a p. friend of the president** es amigo personal del presidente

(**f**) *(offensive)* **there's no need to be so p.!** ¡no hace falta que hagamos tantas referencias personales!; **don't be p., don't make p. remarks** no hagas comentarios de índole personal; **it's nothing p. but...** no es nada personal, pero...

(**g**) *(bodily)* ***p. foul*** *(in basketball)* (falta *f*) personal *f*; ***p. hygiene*** aseo *m* personal; *Law* ***p. injury*** lesiones *fpl*, daños *mpl* corporales

(**h**) *Gram* ***p. pronoun*** pronombre *m* personal

2 *n US (advert)* anuncio *m* en la sección de contactos

personality [pɜːsəˈnælɪtɪ] *n* (**a**) *(character)* personalidad *f*; **to have a lot of p.** tener mucha personalidad; **he's got no p.** no tiene personalidad

(**b**) *(famous person)* personalidad *f*; **sports/media p.** un famoso del mundo del deporte/de la comunicación ▸▸ ***p. cult*** culto *m* a la personalidad

(**c**) *Psy* personalidad *f* ▸▸ ***p. disorder*** trastorno *m* de la personalidad; ***p. questionnaire*** test *m* de personalidad; ***p. quiz*** test *m* de personalidad

personalize [ˈpɜːsənəlaɪz] *vt* (**a**) *(object, luggage, software)* personalizar (**b**) *(argument, idea)* personalizar; **I don't want to p. the issue** no quiero hacer de este asunto una cuestión personal

personalized ['pɜːsənəlaɪzd] *adj* personalizado(a); **p. stationery** artículos de papelería con membrete

personally ['pɜːsənəlɪ] *adv* (**a**) *(individually)* **I was talking about the whole team, not you p.** me refería a todo el equipo, no a ti en particular; **don't take it p.** no te lo tomes como algo personal; **I will hold you p. responsible if she gets hurt** si se hace daño te pediré cuentas a ti personalmente
(**b**) *(in person) (to visit, talk to, know)* en persona; **I was not p. involved in the project** yo no estuve metido personalmente en el proyecto; **deliver the letter to the director p.** entrega la carta al director en persona; **I'll see to it p.** me encargaré personalmente de ello
(**c**) *(in my opinion)* personalmente; **p., I think...** personalmente, creo...

personification [pəsɒnɪfɪ'keɪʃən] *n* personificación *f*; **to be the p. of meanness** ser la tacañería personificada

personify [pə'sɒnɪfaɪ] *vt* personificar; **he is evil personified** es la maldad personificada

personnel [pɜːsə'nel] *n* (**a**) *(staff)* personal *m*; **p. (department)** departamento *m* de personal ►► ***p. management*** gestión *f* de personal; ***p. manager*** director(ora) *m,f or* jefe(a) *m,f* de personal (**b**) *Mil (troops)* tropas *fpl* ►► ***p. carrier*** transporte *m* de tropas

person-to-person ['pɜːsəntə'pɜːsən] **1** *adv* **I'd like to speak to her p.** querría hablar con ella en persona
2 *adj Tel* **p. call** llamada de persona a persona

perspective [pə'spektɪv] **1** *n* (**a**) *Art* perspectiva *f*; **to draw sth in p.** dibujar algo en perspectiva; **the houses are out of p.** las casas no están en perspectiva
(**b**) *(viewpoint)* perspectiva *f*; **it gives you a different p. on the problem** da un nuevo enfoque al problema
(**c**) *(proportion)* **to see things in p.** ver las cosas con perspectiva; **to put sth into p.** poner algo con perspectiva; **to get sth out of p.** sacar algo de quicio
(**d**) *Formal (view, vista)* perspectiva *f*
2 *adj (drawing)* en perspectiva

Perspex® ['pɜːspeks] *n* perspex® *m*, plexiglás® *m*

perspicacious [pɜːspɪ'keɪʃəs] *adj Formal* perspicaz

perspicacity [pɜːspɪ'kæsɪtɪ] *n Formal* perspicacia *f*

perspicuity [pɜːspɪ'kjuːɪtɪ] *n Formal* perspicuidad *f*

perspicuous [pə'spɪkjʊəs] *adj Formal* perspicuo(a)

perspiration [pɜːspɪ'reɪʃən] *n* (**a**) *(substance)* sudor *m*; **bathed in** *or* **dripping with p.** bañado(a) *or* empapado(a) en sudor (**b**) *(act)* transpiración *f*

perspire [pə'spaɪə(r)] *vi* transpirar, sudar; **she was perspiring freely** *or* **heavily** estaba transpirando copiosamente

persuadable [pə'sweɪdəbəl] *adj* **they weren't easily p.** no se dejaban convencer fácilmente

persuade [pə'sweɪd] *vt* persuadir, convencer; **he's easily persuaded** se le persuade *or* convence muy fácilmente; **he would not be persuaded** no se convencía; **to p. sb to do sth** persuadir *or* convencer a alguien para que haga algo; **to p. sb not to do sth** disuadir a alguien de que haga algo; **to p. sb of sth** persuadir *or* convencer a alguien de algo; **she persuaded herself that everything would work out** se convenció a sí misma de que todo saldría bien; **I let myself be persuaded into coming** me dejé convencer y vine; **I'm not persuaded that he's right** no estoy convencido de que tenga razón; *Formal* **I was persuaded of her innocence** me convencieron de su inocencia; **she finally persuaded the lawnmower to start** finalmente convenció al cortacésped para que arrancara

persuasion [pə'sweɪʒən] *n* (**a**) *(act, ability)* persuasión *f*; **I wouldn't need much p. to give it up** no necesitan insistirme mucho para que lo deje; **to be open to p.** estar dispuesto(a) a reconsiderar algo; **powers of p.** poder de persuasión
(**b**) *(beliefs)* convicciones *fpl*; **regardless of their political p., they must be appalled by this news** independientemente de sus convicciones políticas, esta noticia debe haberlos destrozado; **they're not of our p.** no comparten nuestras creencias

persuasive [pə'sweɪzɪv] *adj (person, argument, manner)* persuasivo(a); **she has considerable p. powers** tiene buenos poderes de persuasión

persuasively [pə'sweɪzɪvlɪ] *adv* persuasivamente

persuasiveness [pə'sweɪzɪvnəs] *n (of person, argument)* persuasión *f*

pert [pɜːt] *adj* (**a**) *(cheeky)* pizpireta (**b**) *(stylishly neat) (hat)* coqueto(a) (**c**) *(nose, bottom)* respingón(ona); *(breasts)* turgente

pertain [pə'teɪn] *vi* (**a**) *(apply)* corresponder (**b**) *Formal* **to p. to** *(be relevant to)* concernir a; *(belong to)* pertenecer a

pertinacious [pɜːtɪ'neɪʃəs] *adj Formal* pertinaz

pertinaciously [pɜːtɪ'neɪʃəslɪ] *adv Formal* pertinazmente

pertinacity [pɜːtɪ'næsɪtɪ] *n Formal* pertinacia *f*

pertinence ['pɜːtɪnəns] *n Formal* pertinencia *f*

pertinent ['pɜːtɪnənt] *adj Formal* pertinente; **a very p. question** una pregunta muy pertinente; **to be p. to** concernir a

pertinently ['pɜːtɪnəntlɪ] *adv Formal* pertinentemente

pertly ['pɜːtlɪ] *adv (to reply)* con descaro, atrevidamente

pertness ['pɜːtnɪs] *n* (**a**) *(of reply, manner)* descaro *m*, atrevimiento *m* (**b**) *(of dress)* lo coqueto (**c**) *(of nose, bottom)* lo respingón; *(of breasts)* lo turgente

perturb [pə'tɜːb] *vt* inquietar, desconcertar

perturbation [pɜːtə'beɪʃn] *n* (**a**) *Formal (anxiety)* perturbación *f*, inquietud *f* (**b**) *Astron* perturbación *f*

perturbed [pə'tɜːbd] *adj* inquieto(a), desconcertado(a); **I was p. to hear that...** me inquietó escuchar que...

perturbing [pə'tɜːbɪŋ] *adj* inquietante, perturbador(ora)

Peru [pə'ruː] *n* Perú

perusal [pə'ruːzəl] *n Formal* lectura *f*; **he left the document for her p.** dejó el documento para que ella lo analizara; **on further p....** en un análisis más profundo...

peruse [pə'ruːz] *vt* (**a**) *(read carefully)* leer con detenimiento (**b**) *(read quickly)* ojear

Peruvian [pə'ruːvɪən] **1** *n* peruano(a) *m,f*
2 *adj* peruano(a)

perv [pɜːv] *n Br Fam* pervertido(a) *m,f* (sexual)

pervade [pə'veɪd] *vt* impregnar; **the fundamental error that pervades their philosophy** el error fundamental que impregna su filosofía; **a feeling of mistrust pervaded their relationship** una sensación de desconfianza impregnaba su relación

pervasive [pə'veɪsɪv] *adj (smell)* penetrante; *(influence)* poderoso(a); **the p. influence of television** la omnipresente influencia de la televisión; **a p. atmosphere of pessimism** una atmósfera cargada de pesimismo

perverse [pə'vɜːs] *adj* (**a**) *(contrary, wilful)* **he felt a p. urge to refuse** sintió la perversa necesidad de negarse; **he's just being p.** simplemente está llevando la contraria; **she takes a p. delight in causing harm to others** siente un placer malsano haciendo daño a otros (**b**) *(sexually deviant)* pervertido(a)

perversely [pə'vɜːslɪ] *adv* (**a**) *(paradoxically)* **p. enough, I quite enjoyed it** paradójicamente *or* aunque parezca extraño, me gustó (**b**) *(contrarily)* **she p. refused me the money** se negó a prestarme el dinero por llevarme la contraria

perverseness [pə'vɜːsnɪs] *n (contrariness, wilfulness)* obstinación *f*, desobediencia *f*

perversion [*Br* pə'vɜːʃən, *US* pə'vɜːrʒən] *n* (**a**) *(sexual)* perversión *f* (**b**) *(distortion) (of the truth)* deformación *f*, tergiversación *f*; *(of justice)* distorsión *f*, corrupción *f*; *Law* **p. of the course of justice** obstaculización del curso de la justicia

perversity [pə'vɜːsɪtɪ] *n* (**a**) *(sexual)* perversión *f* (**b**) *(contrariness, wilfulness)* obstinación *f*, desobediencia *f*; **he refused to let me do it out of p.** se negó a dejarme hacerlo por pura mala idea

pervert 1 *n* ['pɜːvɜːt] **(sexual) p.** pervertido(a) *m,f* (sexual)
2 *vt* [pə'vɜːt] (**a**) *(corrupt)* pervertir (**b**) *(distort)* tergiversar; *Law* **to p. the course of justice** obstaculizar el curso de la justicia

perverted [pə'vɜːtɪd] *adj* pervertido(a)

pervy ['pɜːvɪ] *adj Br Fam* pervertido(a)

peseta [pə'seɪtə] *n Formerly* peseta *f*

pesky ['peskɪ] *adj US Fam* plomo(a), latoso(a), *Méx* sangrón(ona), *RP* hinchón(ona); **p. weather!** ¡qué tiempo más plomo!

peso ['peɪsəʊ] (*pl* **pesos**) *n* peso *m*

pessary ['pesərɪ] *n Med* pesario *m*

pessimism ['pesɪmɪzəm] *n* pesimismo *m*

pessimist ['pesɪmɪst] *n* pesimista *mf*

pessimistic [pesɪ'mɪstɪk] *adj* pesimista; **I feel very p. about her chances of getting the job** soy pesimista sobre las posibilidades que tiene de conseguir el empleo

pessimistically [pesɪ'mɪstɪklɪ] *adv* con pesimismo

pest [pest] *n* (**a**) *(vermin, insects)* plaga *f* ►► ***p. control*** métodos *mpl* para combatir las plagas (**b**) *Fam (nuisance)* plomazo *m*, *Esp* latazo *m*

pester ['pestə(r)] *vt* molestar, *Esp* incordiar; **they're always pestering me for money** siempre me están incordiando pidiéndome dinero; **to p. sb with questions** acosar *or* acribillar a alguien con preguntas; **to**

p. sb to do sth *Esp* incordiar a alguien para que haga algo; **she pestered me into helping them** consiguió que les ayudara a base de darme la lata

pesticide ['pestɪsaɪd] *n* pesticida *m*

pestiferous [pe'stɪfərəs] *adj Literary (unhealthy)* pestilente

pestilence ['pestɪləns] *n Literary* pestilencia *f*, peste *f*

pestilential [pestɪ'lenʃəl] *adj Fam (annoying)* cargante

pestle ['pesəl] *n* mano *f* del mortero

pesto ['pestəʊ] *n* pesto *m*

PET [pet] (*abbr* **positron emission tomography**) ***P. scan*** PET *m*

pet [pet] **1** *n* (**a**) *(animal)* animal *m* doméstico *or* de compañía; **sorry, no pets** no se admiten mascotas ▸▸ ***p. food*** comida *f* para animales domésticos; ***p. shop*** pajarería *f* (**b**) *(favourite)* **mother's/teacher's p.** preferido(a) de mamá/del profesor (**c**) *Fam (term of endearment)* **my p.!** ¡mi tesoro!; **be a p. and close the door** sé buena y cierra la puerta (**d**) *Fam (temper)* **to be in a p.** estar enojado(a)

2 *adj* (**a**) *(bird, animal)* de mascota (**b**) *Fam (favourite) (project, theory)* favorito(a), preferido(a); **his p. subject** *or* **topic** su tema favorito *or* preferido; **my p. hate** *or US* **peeve** lo que más odio (**c**) *Fam* ***p. name*** *(diminutive)* apelativo *m or* nombre *m* cariñoso

3 *vt (pt & pp* **petted**) (**a**) *(stroke, pat) (person, dog)* acariciar (**b**) *Fam (caress sexually)* meter mano a, *Arg* apretar

4 *vi Fam (sexually) Esp* darse *or* pegarse el lote, *Am* manosearse

petal ['petəl] *n* pétalo *m*

petard [pə'tɑːd] *n* IDIOM **he was hoist with** *or* **by his own p.** le salió el tiro por la culata

Pete [piːt] *n* IDIOM *Fam* **for P.'s sake** ¡por Dios!, ¡por el amor de Dios!

Peter ['piːtə(r)] *pr n* **Saint P.** san Pedro; **Saint P.'s (basilica)** la Basílica de san Pedro; **P. the Great** Pedro el Grande

peter ['piːtə(r)] *n US Fam (penis)* pilila *f*, pito *m*

▸ **peter out** *vi (path, stream)* extinguirse, desaparecer; *(funds, supplies)* ir agotándose; *(conversation)* ir decayendo; *(enthusiasm)* ir decayendo *or* declinando

Peter Pan ['piːtə'pæn] *n Fig* Peter Pan *m*, niño *m* grande ▸▸ ***P. collar*** = cuello de camisa plano y con los bordes redondeados

pethidine ['peθɪdiːn] *n* petidina *f*

petit bourgeois ['petɪ'bʊəʒwɑː] **1** *n* pequeñoburgués(esa) *m,f*

2 *adj* pequeñoburgués(esa)

petite [pə'tiːt] *adj* menudo(a)

petit four ['petɪ'fɔː] (*pl* **petits fours** ['petɪ'fɔːz]) *n* petit four *m*, *Arg* masa *f* fina

petition [pə'tɪʃən] **1** *n* (**a**) *(with signatures)* petición *f* de firmas recogidas; **to sign a p.** firmar una petición (**b**) *(formal request)* petición *f*, súplica *f*, *Am* pedido *m* (**c**) *Law* **p. for a divorce** demanda de divorcio

2 *vt (court, sovereign)* presentar una petición *or Am* un pedido a

3 *vi* (**a**) *(with signatures)* presentar una petición (**b**) *(formally request)* **to p. for sth** solicitar algo; **to p. against sth** presentar una petición en contra de algo (**c**) *Law* **to p. for divorce** presentar una demanda de divorcio

petitioner [pə'tɪʃənə(r)] *n* (**a**) *(signer of petition)* peticionario(a) *m,f* (**b**) *(person making formal request)* peticionario(a) *m,f* (**c**) *Law (in divorce)* demandante *mf*

petits pois ['petɪ'pwɑː] *npl* guisantes finos *mpl*, *Am* arvejas *fpl* finas, *Méx* chicharitos *mpl*

Petrarch ['petrɑːk] *pr n* Petrarca

Petrarchan [pə'trɑːkən] *adj* petrarcano(a), de Petrarca

petrel ['petrəl] *n* petrel *m*

Petri dish ['petrɪdɪʃ] *n Biol* placa *f* de Petri

petrified ['petrɪfaɪd] *adj* (**a**) *Geol* petrificado(a) ▸▸ ***p. forest*** bosque *m* petrificado (**b**) *(terrified)* paralizado(a), muerto(a) de miedo

petrify ['petrɪfaɪ] *vt* (**a**) *Geol* petrificar (**b**) *(with fear)* petrificar, paralizar

petrifying ['petrɪfaɪɪŋ] *adj (frightening)* aterrador(ora)

petrochemical [petrəʊ'kemɪkəl] **1** *n* **petrochemicals** productos *mpl* petroquímicos

2 *adj* petroquímico(a)

petrocurrency ['petrəʊkʌrənsɪ] *n Fin* petrodivisa *f*

petrodollar ['petrəʊdɒlə(r)] *n Fin* petrodólar *m*

petrol ['petrəl] *n Br* gasolina *f*, *RP* nafta *f* ▸▸ ***p. blue*** azul *m* petróleo; ***p. bomb*** cóctel *m* Molotov; ***p. can*** lata *f* de gasolina *or RP* nafta; ***p. engine*** motor *m* de gasolina *or RP* nafta; *Br* ***p. gauge*** indicador *m* de nivel de gasolina; ***p. pump*** surtidor *m* de gasolina *or RP* nafta; **prices at the p. pump have risen** ha subido el precio de la gasolina en el surtidor; ***p. station*** gasolinera *f*, estación *f* de servicio, *Andes* grifo *m*; ***p. tank*** depósito *m* de la gasolina *or RP* de la nafta *or* del combustible; ***p. tanker*** *(lorry)* camión *m* cisterna; *(ship)* petrolero *m*

> **False friend**: The Spanish noun **petróleo** is not a translation for the English word **petrol**. In Spanish **petróleo** means "oil, petroleum".

petrolatum [petrə'leɪtəm] *n US* vaselina *f*

petrol-bomb ['petrəlbɒm] *vt* arrojar cócteles Molotov contra

petroleum [pə'trəʊlɪəm] *n* petróleo *m*; **p. company** compañía petrolera; **p. industry** industria del petróleo ▸▸ ***p. jelly*** vaselina *f*

petticoat ['petɪkəʊt] *n* (**a**) *(from waist down)* enaguas *fpl* (**b**) *(full-length)* combinación *f* (**c**) *Pej* ***p. government*** = gobierno sobre el que una o varias mujeres ejercen una fuerte influencia

pettifogging ['petɪfɒgɪŋ] *adj (person)* puntilloso(a); *(details)* insignificante

pettily ['petɪlɪ] *adv* mezquinamente

pettiness ['petɪnɪs] *n* (**a**) *(unimportance)* insignificancia *f* (**b**) *(small-mindedness)* mezquindad *f*

petting ['petɪŋ] *n* (**a**) *Fam (sexual) Esp* magreo *m*, *Am* manoseo *m*, *RP* franeleo *m* (**b**) *US* ***p. zoo*** = parque zoológico en el que los niños pueden acariciar y dar de comer a los animales

pettish ['petɪʃ] *adj* irritable, malhumorado(a)

petty ['petɪ] *adj* (**a**) *(unimportant)* insignificante ▸▸ ***p. bourgeois*** pequeñoburgués(esa) *m,f*; ***p. cash*** caja *f* para gastos menores; ***p. crime*** delitos *mpl* menores; *US Law* ***p. larceny*** = delito de latrocinio por un valor inferior a los 500 dólares; *Naut* ***p. officer*** suboficial *mf* de marina; ***p. thief*** ladronzuelo(a) *m,f*, ratero(a) *m,f* (**b**) *(small-minded)* mezquino(a); **don't be so p.!** ¡no seas tan mezquino!

petty-minded ['petɪ'maɪndɪd] *adj* mezquino(a)

petty-mindedness ['petɪ'maɪndɪdnɪs] *n* mezquindad *f*

petulance ['petjʊləns] *n* **a fit of p.** una rabieta

petulant ['petjʊlənt] *adj (person)* caprichoso(a); **with a p. gesture** con un gesto de niño caprichoso

> **False friend**: The Spanish adjective **petulante** is not a translation for the English word **petulant**. In Spanish **petulante** means "opinionated, arrogant".

petulantly ['petjʊləntlɪ] *adv* malhumoradamente

petunia [pɪ'tjuːnɪə] *n* petunia *f*

pew [pjuː] *n* banco *m (en iglesia)*; *Br Fam Hum* **take a p.!** ¡siéntate!

pewter ['pjuːtə(r)] *n* peltre *m*

peyote [peɪ'əʊtɪ] *n* peyote *m*

PFC [piːef'siː] (*abbr* **private first class**) *n US* = rango del ejército de los Estados Unidos que se encuentra entre soldado raso y cabo

PFI [piːef'aɪ] *n Br* (*abbr* **private finance initiative**) = contrato entre un consorcio privado y la administración local por el que el primero construye, por ejemplo, una escuela o un hospital y se encarga de su funcionamiento a cambio de mantener su titularidad y percibir un alquiler de la administración

PFLP [piːefel'piː] *n* (*abbr* **Popular Front for the Liberation of Palestine**) FPLP *f*

PG [piː'dʒiː] *n Cin* (*abbr* **parental guidance**) = película para todos los públicos aunque se recomienda que los menores vayan acompañados de un adulto

PG-13 [piː'dʒiːθɜː'tiːn] *n US Cin* = película para todos los públicos aunque se recomienda que los menores de trece años vayan acompañados de un adulto

PGA [piːdʒiː'eɪ] *n* (*abbr* **Professional Golfers' Association**) PGA *f*

PGCE [piːdʒiːsiː'iː] *n Br Educ* (*abbr* **postgraduate certificate of education**) = diploma para licenciados que capacita para ejercer en la enseñanza pública, *Esp* ≃ C.A.P. *m*

pH [piː'eɪtʃ] *n Chem* pH *m*; **a pH of 9** un pH 9

phagocyte ['fægəsaɪt] *n Biol* fagocito *m*

phalangeal [fə'lændʒɪəl] *adj Anat* falangiano(a)

phalanges *pl of* **phalanx**

Phalangist [fə'lændʒɪst] **1** *n* falangista *mf*

2 *adj* falangista

phalanx ['fælæŋks] *n* (**a**) *Mil Hist* falange *f* (**b**) *(of officials, journalists)* pelotón *m* (**c**) *Anat* (*pl* **phalanges** [fə'lændʒiːz]) falange *f*; **second p.** falangina; **third p.** falangeta

phalarope ['fælərəʊp] *n* falaropo *m*

phallic ['fælɪk] *adj* fálico(a) ▸▸ ***p. symbol*** símbolo *m* fálico

phallocentric [fæləʊ'sentrɪk] *adj* falocéntrico(a)

phallus ['fæləs] *n* falo *m*

Phanerozoic [fænərə'zəʊɪk] *Geol* **1** *n* **the P.** el fanerozoico
2 *adj (era)* fanerozoico(a)

phantasm ['fæntæzəm] *n* fantasma *m*, espectro *m*

phantasmagoria [fæntæzmə'gɔːrɪə] *n* fantasmagoría *f*

phantasmagoric(al) [fæntæzmə'gɒrɪk(əl)] *adj* fantasmagórico(a)

phantom ['fæntəm] *n* **(a)** *(ghost)* fantasma *m* **(b)** *(illusion)* fantasía *f* **(c)** *Med* ***p. limb*** miembro *m* fantasma; ***p. pregnancy*** embarazo *m* psicológico

Pharaoh ['feərəʊ] *n* faraón *m*

pharisaic(al) [færɪ'seɪɪk(əl)] *adj* farisaico(a)

Pharisee ['færɪsiː] *n* **(a)** *Rel* fariseo(a) *m,f* **(b)** *(hypocrite)* fariseo(a) *m,f*

pharmaceutical [fɑːmə'sjuːtɪkəl] **1** *n* **pharmaceuticals** productos *mpl* farmacéuticos; **the p. industry** la industria farmacéutica
2 *adj* farmacéutico(a)

pharmacist ['fɑːməsɪst] *n* farmacéutico(a) *m,f*

pharmacological [fɑːməkə'lɒdʒɪkəl] *adj* farmacológico(a)

pharmacologist [fɑːmə'kɒlədʒɪst] *n* farmacólogo(a) *m,f*

pharmacology [fɑːmə'kɒlədʒɪ] *n* farmacología *f*

pharmacopoeia, *US* **pharmacopeia** [fɑːməkə'piːə] *n Pharm* farmacopea *f*

pharmacy ['fɑːməsɪ] *n* **(a)** *(science)* farmacia *f*, farmacéutica *f* **(b)** *(dispensary, shop)* farmacia *f*

pharyngitis [færɪn'dʒaɪtɪs] *n Med* faringitis *f inv*

pharynx ['færɪŋks] (*pl* **pharynxes** *or* **pharynges** [fæ'rɪndʒiːz]) *n* faringe *f*

phase [feɪz] **1** *n* **(a)** *(stage)* fase *f*, etapa *f*; **it's just a p. (he's going through)** ya se le pasará **(b)** *(coordination)* **in p. (with)** sincronizado(a) (con); **out of p. (with)** desfasado(a) (con respecto a) **(c)** *Astron (of moon)* fase *f* **(d)** *Chem & Elec* fase *f*
2 *vt* **(a)** *(schedule)* realizar por etapas **(b)** *(synchronize)* sincronizar

▸**phase in** *vt sep* introducir gradualmente *or* escalonadamente

▸**phase out** *vt sep* eliminar gradualmente *or* escalonadamente

phased [feɪzd] *adj (in stages)* gradual, escalonado(a)

phase-out ['feɪzaʊt] *n* eliminación *f* progresiva

phat [fæt] *adj Fam* total

phatic ['fætɪk] *adj Ling* fático(a)

PhD [piːeɪtʃ'diː] *n Univ* (*abbr* **Doctor of Philosophy**) *(person)* doctor(ora) *m,f*; *(degree)* doctorado *m*; **P. thesis** tesis doctoral

pheasant ['fezənt] *n* faisán *m*

phenobarbital [fiːnəʊ'bɑːbɪtəl], **phenobarbitone** [fiːnəʊ'bɑːbɪtəʊn] *n Pharm* fenobarbital *m*

phenol ['fiːnɒl] *n* fenol *m*

phenomena *pl of* **phenomenon**

phenomenal [fɪ'nɒmɪnəl] *adj* extraordinario(a)

phenomenally [fɪ'nɒmɪnəlɪ] *adv* extraordinariamente

phenomenological [fɪnɒmɪnə'lɒdʒɪkəl] *adj Phil* fenomenológico(a)

phenomenology [fɪnɒmɪ'nɒlədʒɪ] *n Phil* fenomenología *f*

phenomenon [fɪ'nɒmɪnən] (*pl* **phenomena** [fɪ'nɒmɪnə]) *n* fenómeno *m*

phenotype ['fiːnətaɪp] *n Biol* fenotipo *m*

phenyl ['fiːnəl] *n* fenilo *m*

pheromone ['ferəməʊn] *n* feromona *f*

phew [fjuː] *exclam* ¡uf!

phi [faɪ] *n (Greek letter)* fi *f*

phial ['faɪəl] *n* ampolla *f*, vial *m*

Phi Beta Kappa ['faɪbiːtə'kæpə] *n* = sociedad estadounidense de universitarios que se han distinguido en sus estudios

Philadelphia [fɪlə'delfɪə] *n* Filadelfia

Philadelphian [fɪlə'delfɪən] **1** *n* persona de Filadelfia
2 *adj* de Filadelfia

philander [fɪ'lændə(r)] *vi Pej* ir detrás de las mujeres

philanderer [fɪ'lændərə(r)] *n Pej* mujeriego *m*

philandering [fɪ'lændərɪŋ] *Pej* **1** *n* líos *mpl* amorosos
2 *adj* mujeriego(a)

philanthropic [fɪlən'θrɒpɪk] *adj* filantrópico(a)

philanthropist [fɪ'lænθrəpɪst] *n* filántropo(a) *m,f*

philanthropy [fɪ'lænθrəpɪ] *n* filantropía *f*

philatelist [fɪ'lætəlɪst] *n* filatelista *mf*

philately [fɪ'lætəlɪ] *n* filatelia *f*

-phile [faɪl] *suffix* -filo; **Russophile** rusófilo(a)

philharmonic [fɪlə'mɒnɪk] *Mus* **1** *n* filarmónica *f*
2 *adj* filarmónico(a)

-philia ['fɪlɪə] *suffix* -filia; **Russophilia** rusofilia

Philip ['fɪlɪp] *pr n* **P. I/II** Felipe I/II

philippic [fɪ'lɪpɪk] *n* filípica *f*, diatriba *f*

Philippines ['fɪlɪpiːnz] *npl* **the P.** las Filipinas

philistine ['fɪlɪstaɪn] **1** *n* **(a)** *(uncultured person)* inculto(a) *m,f*, ignorante *mf* **(b)** *Hist* **the Philistines** los filisteos
2 *adj* inculto(a), ignorante

philistinism ['fɪlɪstɪnɪzəm] *n* incultura *f*, ignorancia *f*

Phillips ['fɪlɪps] *n* ***P. screw***® tornillo *m* de cabeza en cruz; ***P. screwdriver***® destornillador *m orAm* desatornillador *m* de cruz

philological [fɪlə'lɒdʒɪkəl] *adj* filológico(a)

philologist [fɪ'lɒlədʒɪst] *n* filólogo(a) *m,f*

philology [fɪ'lɒlədʒɪ] *n* filología *f*

philosopher [fɪ'lɒsəfə(r)] *n* filósofo(a) *m,f* ►► ***p.'s stone*** piedra *f* filosofal

philosophic(al) [fɪlə'sɒfɪk(əl)] *adj* **(a)** *(writings, argument)* filosófico(a) **(b)** *(calm, resigned) (person, attitude)* filosófico(a); **to be p. about sth** tomarse algo con filosofía

philosophically [fɪlə'sɒfɪklɪ] *adv* **(a)** *(to argue)* filosóficamente **(b)** *(calmly, dispassionately)* con filosofía

philosophize [fɪ'lɒsəfaɪz] *vi* filosofar (**about** acerca de)

philosophy [fɪ'lɒsəfɪ] *n* filosofía *f*; *Fam* **my p. is...** mi filosofía es...; *Fig* **we share the same p. of life** compartimos la misma filosofía de vida

phiz [fɪz], **phizog** ['fɪzɒg] *n Br Fam* cara *f*, jeta *f*

phlebitis [flə'baɪtɪs] *n Med* flebitis *f inv*

phlegm [flem] *n* **(a)** *(mucus)* flema *f* **(b)** *(composure)* flema *f*

phlegmatic [fleg'mætɪk] *adj* flemático(a)

phlegmatically [fleg'mætɪklɪ] *adv* flemáticamente

phlox [flɒks] *n Bot* polemonio *m*

Phnom Penh [pnɒm'pen] *n* Phnom Penh

-phobe [fəʊb] *suffix* -fobo; **Russophobe** rusófobo(a)

-phobia ['fəʊbɪə] *suffix* -fobia; **Russophobia** rusofobia

phobia ['fəʊbɪə] *n* fobia *f*; **I have a p. about spiders/heights** le tengo fobia a las arañas/alturas

phobic ['fəʊbɪk] *adj* **she's a bit p. about spiders** le tiene fobia a las arañas

Phoebus ['fiːbəs] *n Mythol* Febo

Phoenicia [fə'niːʃə] *n Hist* Fenicia

Phoenician [fə'niːʃən] *Hist* **1** *n* **(a)** *(person)* fenicio(a) *m,f* **(b)** *(language)* fenicio *m*
2 *adj* fenicio(a)

phoenix ['fiːnɪks] *n* fénix *m inv*; IDIOM **to rise like a p. (from the ashes)** renacer de las propias cenizas como el ave fénix

phonation [fəʊ'neɪʃən] *n* fonación *f*

phone [fəʊn] **1** *n* teléfono *m*; **to be on the p.** *(talking)* estar al teléfono; *(have a telephone)* tener teléfono; **you're wanted on the p.** te llaman; **to give sb a p.** llamar a alguien (por teléfono); **to get sb on the p.** contactar con alguien por teléfono; **could you get the p., please?** ¿podrías atender (el teléfono) por favor?; **to get on the p. to sb** llamar a alguien por teléfono; **to discuss sth on** *or* **over the p.** discutir algo por teléfono; **it can all be arranged over the p.** se puede arreglar todo por teléfono ►► ***p. bill*** factura *f* del teléfono; ***p. book*** guía *f* telefónica *or* de teléfonos, *Am* directorio *m* de teléfonos; ***p. booth*** cabina *f* telefónica; *Br* ***p. box*** cabina *f* telefónica; ***p. call*** llamada *f* telefónica, *Am* llamado *m* telefónico; ***p. number*** número *m* de teléfono
2 *vt* **to p. sb** telefonear a alguien, llamar a alguien (por teléfono); **to p. home** llamar a casa (por teléfono); **to p. Paris** llamar a París; **can you p. me the answer?** ¿me puedes pasar la respuesta por teléfono?
3 *vi* telefonear, llamar (por teléfono); **to p. for a plumber/a taxi** llamar a un fontanero/taxi

▸**phone around** *vi* hacer algunas llamadas *orAm* llamados

▸**phone in 1** *vt* **(a)** *(answer, report)* llamar, telefonear **(b)** *Fam Hum* **to p. in one's performance** hacer la actuación mecánica de siempre
2 *vi* **(a)** *(to radio programme)* llamar **(b)** *(to work)* llamar; **I phoned in sick** llamé al trabajo para decir que estaba enfermo

▸**phone up 1** *vt sep* llamar, telefonear
2 *vi* llamar, telefonear

phonecard ['fəʊnkɑːd] *n* tarjeta *f* telefónica

phoned-in ['fəʊndɪn] *adj Fam Hum (performance)* mecánico(a)

phone-in ['fəʊnɪn] *n Rad & TV* **p. (programme)** = programa con llamadas de los televidentes/oyentes

phoneme ['fəʊni:m] *n* fonema *m*

phonemic [fə'ni:mɪk] *adj* fonémico(a)

phonemics [fə'ni:mɪks] *n* fonemática *f*

phonetic [fə'netɪk] *adj* fonético(a) ►► ***p. alphabet*** alfabeto *m* fonético; ***p. transcription*** transcripción *f* fonética

phonetically [fə'netɪklɪ] *adv* fonéticamente

phonetician [fəʊnə'tɪʃən] *n* fonetista *mf*

phonetics [fə'netɪks] *n* fonética *f*

phoney, *US* **phony** ['fəʊnɪ] *Fam* **1** *n* (*pl* **phoneys,** *US* **phonies**) (**a**) *(person)* falso(a) *m,f*, farsante *mf* (**b**) *(fake object)* falsificación *f*
2 *adj* falso(a); **his story sounds p.** su historia no es nada convincente

phonic ['fəʊnɪk] *adj* fónico(a)

phonics ['fɒnɪks] *npl Educ* = método de aprender a leer a través de la asociación de las letras con su fonética

phoniness ['fəʊnɪnɪs] *n Fam* falsedad *f*

phonograph ['fəʊnəgrɑ:f] *n* (**a**) *US Old-fashioned* gramófono *m* (**b**) *(early form of gramophone)* fonógrafo *m*

phonological [fəʊnə'lɒdʒɪkəl] *adj* fonológico(a)

phonologist [fə'nɒlədʒɪst] *n* fonólogo(a) *m,f*

phonology [fə'nɒlədʒɪ] *n* fonología *f*

phony *US* = **phoney**

phooey ['fu:ɪ] *exclam Fam* ¡bah!, *Esp* ¡qué va!

phosgene ['fɒsdʒi:n] *n* fosgeno *m*

phosphate ['fɒsfeɪt] *n* fosfato *m*

phosphor ['fɒsfə(r)] *n* fósforo *m*

phosphoresce [fɒsfə'res] *vi* fosforescer

phosphorescence [fɒsfə'resəns] *n* fosforescencia *f*

phosphorescent [fɒsfə'resənt] *adj* fosforescente

phosphoric [fɒs'fɒrɪk] *adj* fosfórico(a) ►► ***p. acid*** ácido *m* fosfórico

phosphorous ['fɒsfərəs] *adj* fosforoso(a)

phosphorus ['fɒsfərəs] *n Chem* fósforo *m*

photo ['fəʊtəʊ] (*pl* **photos**) *n* foto *f*; **to take good photos** tomar buenas fotos; **to take a good p.** *(be photogenic)* salir bien en las fotos ►► ***p. album*** álbum *m* de fotos; ***p. call*** = sesión fotográfica con la prensa; *Comptr* ***p. CD*** photo CD *m*; ***p. finish*** *(in race)* foto-finish *f*, fotofinis *f*; *Fig* **the election is going to be a p. finish** la elección será sumamente reñida; ***p. opportunity*** = ocasión de aparecer fotografiado dando una buena imagen; ***p. realism*** fotorrealismo *m*; ***p. retouching*** retocado *m* fotográfico

photoactive [fəʊtəʊ'æktɪv] *adj (organism, substance)* fotoactivo(a), fotosensible

photobooth ['fəʊtəʊbu:ð] *n* fotomatón *m*

photocell ['fəʊtəʊsel] *n* célula *f* fotoeléctrica

photochemical [fəʊtəʊ'kemɪkəl] *adj* fotoquímico(a)

photocomposition [fəʊtəʊkɒmpə'zɪʃən] *n Typ* fotocomposición *f*

photoconductive [fəʊtəʊkən'dʌktɪv] *adj Elec* fotoconductor(ora)

photoconductivity [fəʊtəʊkɒndʌk'tɪvɪtɪ] *n Elec* fotoconductividad *f*

photoconductor [fəʊtəʊkən'dʌktə(r)] *n Elec* fotoconductor *m*

photocopier ['fəʊtəkɒpɪə(r)] *n* fotocopiadora *f*

photocopy ['fəʊtəkɒpɪ] **1** *n* fotocopia *f*; **to take** *or* **make a p. of sth** hacer una fotocopia de algo
2 *vt* fotocopiar

photocopying ['fəʊtəʊkɒpɪɪŋ] *n* fotocopiado *m*; **there's some p. to do** hay que hacer algunas fotocopias

photodegradable [fəʊtəʊdi:'greɪdəbəl] *adj* fotodegradable

photoelectric [fəʊtəʊɪ'lektrɪk] *adj* fotoeléctrico(a) ►► ***p. cell*** célula *f* fotoeléctrica; *Phys* ***p. effect*** efecto *m* fotoeléctrico

photoengraving ['fəʊtəʊɪn'greɪvɪŋ] *n* fotograbado *m*

Photofit® ['fəʊtəʊfɪt] *n* **P. (picture)** retrato *m* robot *(elaborado con fotografías)*

photogenic [fəʊtə'dʒenɪk] *adj* fotogénico(a)

photograph ['fəʊtəgrɑ:f] **1** *n* fotografía *f*; **to take sb's p.** sacarle una fotografía a alguien; **to have one's p. taken** sacarse una fotografía; **she takes a good p.** *(is photogenic)* sale bien en las fotos ►► ***p. album*** álbum *m* de fotografías
2 *vt* fotografiar
3 *vi* **to p. well** salir bien

photographer [fə'tɒgrəfə(r)] *n* fotógrafo(a) *m,f*; **I'm not much of a p.** no soy muy buen fotógrafo

photographic [fəʊtə'græfɪk] *adj (film, laboratory)* fotográfico(a); **to have a p. memory** tener memoria fotográfica

photographically [fəʊtə'græfɪklɪ] *adv* fotográficamente

photography [fə'tɒgrəfɪ] *n* fotografía *f*; **a p. course/magazine** un curso/una revista de fotografía

photogravure [fəʊtəʊgrə'vʊə(r)] *n* huecograbado *m*

photojournalism [fəʊtəʊ'dʒɜ:nəlɪzəm] *n* periodismo *m* gráfico

photojournalist [fəʊtəʊ'dʒɜ:nəlɪst] *n* periodista *mf* gráfico(a)

photolithography [fəʊtəʊlɪ'θɒgrəfɪ] *n* fotolitografía *f*

photoluminescence [fəʊtəʊlu:mɪ'nesəns] *n* fotoluminiscencia *f*

photomontage [fəʊtəʊmɒn'tɑ:ʒ] *n* fotomontaje *m*

photon ['fəʊtɒn] *n Phys* fotón *m*

photonovel ['fəʊtənɒvəl] *n* fotonovela *f*

photo-offset ['fəʊtəʊ'ɒfset] *n* offset *m*

photorealism [fəʊtəʊ'rɪəlɪzəm] *n Art* fotorrealismo *m*

photosensitive [fəʊtəʊ'sensɪtɪv] *adj* fotosensible

photosetter ['fəʊtəʊsetə(r)] *n* filmadora *f*

Photostat® ['fəʊtəstæt] *n* (fotocopia *f* de) fotostato *m*

photostat ['fəʊtəstæt] *vt* fotocopiar

photosynthesis [fəʊtəʊ'sɪnθɪsɪs] *n Bot* fotosíntesis *f inv*

photosynthesize [fəʊtəʊ'sɪnθɪsaɪz] *vt Bot* fotosintetizar

phototypesetter [fəʊtəʊ'taɪpsetə(r)] *n Typ* (**a**) *(machine)* fotocomponedora *f* (**b**) *(person)* fotocomponedor(ora) *m,f*

photovoltaic [fəʊtəʊvɒl'teɪɪk] *adj* fotovoltaico(a) ►► ***p. cell*** célula *f* fotovoltaica

phrasal verb ['freɪzəl'vɜ:b] *n Gram* verbo *m* con partícula *(preposición o adverbio)*

phrase [freɪz] **1** *n* (**a**) *(expression)* frase *f*; *Ling* **noun/verb p.** frase nominal/verbal ►► ***p. book*** manual *m or* guía *f* de conversación (**b**) *Mus* frase *f*
2 *vt* (**a**) *(express, word)* expresar; **he phrased it very elegantly** lo dijo de una manera muy elegante (**b**) *Mus* frasear

phraseology [freɪzɪ'ɒlədʒɪ] *n* fraseología *f*

phrasing ['freɪzɪŋ] *n* (**a**) *(expressing)* expresión *f* (**b**) *Mus* fraseo *m*

phreaker ['fri:kə(r)] *n* = persona que manipula las líneas telefónicas para obtener llamadas gratis

phreaking ['fri:kɪŋ] *n* **(phone) p.** = manipulación de las líneas telefónicas para obtener llamadas gratis

phrenologist [frə'nɒlədʒɪst] *n* frenólogo(a) *m,f*

phrenology [frə'nɒlədʒɪ] *n* frenología *f*

phut [fʌt] *adv Br Fam* **to go p.** *(machine)* estropearse, *Esp* escacharrarse, *Am* joderse; *(plans)* irse al garete *or Col, Méx* piso *or RP* diablo

phylactery [fɪ'læktərɪ] *n Rel* filacteria *f*

phyllo ['fi:ləʊ] *n* **p. (pastry)** hojaldre *m* griego

phylloxera [fɪ'lɒksərə] *n* filoxera *f*

phylogeny [faɪ'lɒdʒənɪ] *n* filogenia *f*

phylum ['faɪləm] *n Biol & Zool* fílum *m*, tipo *m*

Phys Ed ['fɪz'ed] *n Educ* (*abbr* **physical education**) educación *f* física

physical ['fɪzɪkəl] **1** *n (examination)* chequeo *m*, examen *m or* reconocimiento *m* médico
2 *adj* (**a**) *(bodily)* físico(a); **a p. examination** un examen físico ►► ***p. education*** educación *f* física; ***p. exercise*** ejercicios *mpl* físicos; ***p. fitness*** buena forma *f* física; ***p. handicap*** defecto *m* físico; *Br Fam* ***p. jerks*** gimnasia *f*, ejercicios *mpl* físicos; ***p. therapy*** fisioterapia *f*; ***p. training*** *(in school)* educación *f* física; *(in army)* preparación *f* física; ***a p. wreck*** un desastre, una ruina
(**b**) *(natural, material) (forces, presence)* físico(a), material; *(manifestation, universe)* físico(a); **to be a p. impossibility** ser una imposibilidad física *or* material; **the p. features of the desert** las características físicas del desierto ►► ***p. anthropology*** antropología *f* física; ***p. chemistry*** química *f* física; ***p. geography*** geografía *f* física; ***p. sciences*** ciencias *fpl* físicas
(**c**) *(involving bodily contact)* físico(a); **rugby is a very p. sport** el rugby es un deporte en el que hay mucho contacto físico; **we had to get a bit p. to persuade him** tuvimos que ponernos un tanto firmes para convencerlo

physicality [fɪzɪ'kælɪtɪ] *n* **the p. of this sport** el carácter físico de este deporte

physically ['fɪzɪklɪ] *adv* físicamente; **p. fit** en buena forma física; **p. handicapped** discapacitado(a) físico(a); *Euph* **p. challenged** con necesidades físicas especiales

physician [fɪˈzɪʃən] *n Formal* médico(a) *m,f* ►► *US* ***p. assistant*** médico(a) *m,f* auxiliar

physicist [ˈfɪzɪsɪst] *n* físico(a) *m,f*

physics [ˈfɪzɪks] *n* física *f*

physio [ˈfɪzɪəʊ] *n Fam* (**a**) *(treatment)* fisioterapia *f* (**b**) *(person)* fisio *mf*, fisioterapeuta *mf*

physiognomy [fɪzɪˈɒnəmɪ] *n Formal* (**a**) *(facial features)* fisonomía *f*, fisionomía *f* (**b**) *(of place)* fisonomía *f*, fisionomía *f*

physiological [fɪzɪəˈlɒdʒɪkəl] *adj* fisiológico(a)

physiologist [fɪzɪˈɒlədʒɪst] *n* fisiólogo(a) *m,f*

physiology [fɪzɪˈɒlədʒɪ] *n* fisiología *f*

physiotherapist [fɪzɪəʊˈθerəpɪst] *n* fisioterapeuta *mf*

physiotherapy [fɪzɪəʊˈθerəpɪ] *n* fisioterapia *f*

physique [fɪˈziːk] *n* físico *m*

phytochemistry [ˈfaɪtəʊˈkemɪstrɪ] *n* fitoquímica *f*

PI [piːˈaɪ] *n* (**a**) *US* (*abbr* **private investigator**) investigador(ora) *m,f* privado(a) (**b**) *Law* (*abbr* **personal injury**) lesiones *fpl*, daños *mpl* corporales

pi [paɪ] *n Math* pi *m*

pianissimo [pɪəˈnɪsɪməʊ] *Mus* 1 *n* pianissimo *m*
2 *adv* pianissimo

pianist [ˈpɪənɪst] *n* pianista *mf*

piano [pɪˈænəʊ] 1 *n* (*pl* **pianos**) piano *m* ►► ***p. accordion*** acordeón *m*; ***p. bar*** piano bar *m*; ***p. concerto*** concierto *m* para piano y orquesta; ***p. stool*** escabel *m*, taburete *m* de piano; ***p. tuner*** afinador(ora) *m,f* de pianos
2 *adj Mus* de piano
3 *adv Mus* piano

pianoforte [pɪænəʊˈfɔːteɪ] *n Formal* pianoforte *m*

Pianola® [pɪənˈəʊlə] *n* pianola *f*

piazza [piːˈætsə] *n* (**a**) *(Italian)* piazza *f* (**b**) *Br (covered walkway)* galería *f* (**c**) *US (verandah)* porche *m*

pibroch [ˈpiːbrɒk] *n* = variaciones marciales o fúnebres para gaita escocesa

pic [pɪk] (*pl* **pics** *or* **pix** [pɪks]) *n Fam* foto *f*

pica [ˈpaɪkə] *n Typ* pica *f*

picador [ˈpɪkədɔː(r)] *n* picador(ora) *m,f*

picaresque [piːkəˈresk] *adj Lit* picaresco(a)

picayune [pɪkəˈjuːn] *adj US Fam* insignificante

piccalilli [pɪkəˈlɪlɪ] *n* = salsa agridulce a base de trocitos de verdura y mostaza

piccaninny [ˈpɪkənɪnɪ] *n Pej* (**a**) *US (black child)* = término ofensivo para referirse a un niño negro (**b**) *Austr (aboriginal child)* = término ofensivo para referirse a un niño aborigen

piccolo [ˈpɪkələʊ] (*pl* **piccolos**) *n* flautín *m*, piccolo *m*

piccy [ˈpɪkɪ] *n Br Fam* foto *f*

PICK [pɪk] 1 *n* (**a**) *(tool)* pico *m*
(**b**) *US (plectrum)* púa *f*
(**c**) *(choice)* **we had first p.** nos dejaron elegir primero *or* los primeros; **we had our p. of seats** pudimos elegir nuestros asientos; **take your p.** escoge *or* elije a tu gusto
(**d**) *(best)* **the p. of the bunch** *or US* **litter** el/la mejor de todos(as)
2 *vt* (**a**) *(choose)* escoger, elegir; *(team)* seleccionar; **to p. sb for a team** seleccionar a alguien para un equipo; **to p. a fight with sb** buscar pelea con alguien; **to p. one's way: she picked her way through the crowd** pasó por entre la multitud con dificultad; **he picked his way across the minefield** cruzó el campo minado con extremo cuidado; **it's not easy to p. a winner** no es fácil pronosticar un ganador
(**b**) *(remove) (flowers, fruit)* recoger, *Esp* coger; **p. your own strawberries** *(sign)* = cartel al borde de la carretera que identifica un campo al que la gente puede ir a recoger sus propias fresas pagando; **to p. a spot/a scab** arrancarse un grano/una costra; *Fig* **to p. sb's pocket** robar algo del bolsillo de alguien, *RP* punguear a alguien
(**c**) *(open)* **to p. a lock** forzar una cerradura
(**d**) *(clean)* **to p. one's nose** meterse el dedo en *or* hurgarse la nariz; **to p. one's teeth** escarbarse los dientes; **the dog picked the bone clean** el perro dejó el hueso limpio; **to p. sth/sb to pieces** poner algo/a alguien por los suelos; IDIOM **to p. sb's brains** aprovecharse de los conocimientos de alguien; **can I p. your brains?** a ver si tú me puedes ayudar
(**e**) *(make)* **she picked a hole in her sweater** se hizo un agujero *or Esp* punto en el suéter (tirando); IDIOM **to p. holes in sth** *(in argument, theory)* sacar fallos a algo, *Am* encontrar fallas a algo
(**f**) *Mus* **to p. a guitar** puntear
3 *vi* **we can't afford to p. and choose** no podemos permitirnos elegir

► **pick at** *vt insep* (**a**) *(scab, spot)* rascarse; *(loose flake of paint)* arrancar (**b**) *(eat without enthusiasm)* **she picked at her food** picoteó su comida con desgana (**c**) *(criticize pettily)* poner por los suelos a

► **pick off** *vt sep* (**a**) *(remove)* **I picked my briefcase off the chair** recogí mi maletín de la silla; **he picked the hairs off his trousers** quitó *or Am* sacó los pelos de sus pantalones uno a uno (**b**) *(of gunman, sniper)* ir abatiendo (uno por uno)

► **pick on** *vt insep* (**a**) *(bully)* meterse con; **I got picked on at school** se metían conmigo en el colegio; **p. on somebody your own size!** ¡no seas *Esp* abusón *or Am* abusador! (**b**) *(choose)* elegir

► **pick out** *vt sep* (**a**) *(remove)* quitar, *Am* sacar; **she picked the splinter out of her finger** se arrancó la astilla del dedo
(**b**) *(select)* elegir, escoger; **he picked out the centre forward with his pass** metió un pase preciso al delantero centro
(**c**) *(recognize)* reconocer
(**d**) *(identify)* **he picked out three key moments that had turned the course of the election** resaltó tres momentos clave que habían decidido la elección; **they picked him out as a future leader** lo identificaron como futuro líder; **the headlights picked out a figure** las luces largas cayeron sobre una figura
(**e**) *(write)* **her name was picked out in gold** su nombre estaba escrito en letras de oro
(**f**) *(a tune)* sacar

► **pick over** *vt insep (select best from)* seleccionar (lo mejor de)

► **pick up** 1 *vt sep* (**a**) *(lift up)* recoger, *Esp* coger; **see if you can p. up this box** a ver si puedes levantar esta caja; **to p. up the phone** descolgar el teléfono; **if you need my help, just p. up the phone** si necesitas mi ayuda, llámame; **p. up a leaflet at our new store** recoja un folleto en nuestra nueva tienda; **she picked the puppy up by the scruff of the neck** levantó al cachorro por el cogote; **to p. oneself up** *(after fall)* levantarse; *(after defeat)* recuperarse; *also Fig* **to p. up the bill** *or* **tab** pagar la cuenta; IDIOM **to p. up the pieces** empezar de nuevo *(tras un fracaso)*; IDIOM **to p. up the threads of a discussion** retomar el hilo de una discusión
(**b**) *(collect)* recoger; *(arrest)* detener; **I'll p. you up at eight** pasaré a buscarte a las ocho; **I never p. up hitchhikers** nunca recojo *or Esp* cojo a gente haciendo autoestop; **to p. up survivors** rescatar supervivientes
(**c**) *(learn) (language, skill)* aprender; *(habit)* adquirir, *Esp* coger; **I picked up some useful tips from him** aprendí algunos trucos útiles de él
(**d**) *(obtain) (bargain, votes, information)* conseguir; *(medal, points, money)* ganar; *(disease, virus)* contraer; **I picked this radio up for £10** conseguí esta radio por 10 libras; **to p. up speed** cobrar *or* ganar velocidad
(**e**) *(radio station)* sintonizar; *(message, signal)* captar, recibir
(**f**) *(notice)* percatarse de
(**g**) *(discussion)* reanudar; *(theme, point)* retomar
(**h**) *(make better)* **that will p. you up** eso te reconfortará
(**i**) *Fam* **to p. sb up** *(as sexual partner)* ligarse *or RP* levantar a alguien
2 *vi* (**a**) *(improve)* mejorar; **business is picking up** el negocio se va animando; **his spirits** *or* **he picked up when he heard the news** se animó al oír las noticias (**b**) *(increase) (wind)* aumentar; *(speed, tempo)* incrementarse; *(prices)* subir (**c**) *(continue)* **let's p. up where we left off** vamos a seguir por donde estábamos

► **pick up on** 1 *vt insep* (**a**) *(continue to discuss)* retomar (**b**) *(notice)* darse cuenta de
2 *vt sep Br (correct)* **to p. sb up on sth** corregir algo a alguien

pickaback = **piggyback**

pickaxe, *US* **pickax** [ˈpɪkæks] *n* pico *m*

picker [ˈpɪkə(r)] *n (of fruit, tea)* recolector(ora) *m,f*

picket [ˈpɪkɪt] 1 *n* (**a**) *(in strike) (group)* piquete *m*; *(individual)* miembro *m* de un piquete ►► ***p. line*** piquete *m*; **to be** *or* **stand on a p. line** estar en un piquete; **to cross a p. line** atravesar *or* cruzar un piquete (**b**) *(stake)* estaca *f* ►► ***p. fence*** cerca *f*, estacada *f* (**c**) *Mil* piquete *m*
2 *vt (during strike)* hacer piquetes en
3 *vi* hacer piquetes

picketing [ˈpɪkətɪŋ] *n* **there is heavy p. at the factory gates** hay un gran piquete en la entrada de la fábrica

pickings [ˈpɪkɪŋz] *npl* (**a**) *(booty)* botín *m*; **rich** *or* **easy p.** pingües beneficios (**b**) *(leftovers)* restos *mpl*

pickle ['pɪkəl] **1** *n* **(a)** *Br (sauce)* = salsa agridulce a base de trocitos de fruta y verduras **(b) pickles** *(vegetables in vinegar)* variantes *mpl*, encurtidos *mpl* **(c)** *US (cucumber)* pepinillos *mpl* en vinagre **(d)** *(liquid)* escabeche *m* **(e)** *Fam (difficult situation)* **to be in a bit of a p.** estar metido(a) en un buen lío
2 *vt* encurtir

pickled ['pɪkəld] *adj* **(a)** *(food)* **p. cabbage** col en vinagre; **p. herrings** arenques en escabeche; **p. onions** cebolletas en vinagre; **p. walnuts** nueces en vinagre **(b)** *Fam (drunk)* como una cuba

picklock ['pɪklɒk] *n* **(a)** *(person)* ladrón(ona) *m,f* de ganzúa **(b)** *(tool)* ganzúa *f*

pick-me-up ['pɪkmɪʌp] *n Fam* reconstituyente *m*, tónico *m*

pick-'n'-mix ['pɪkən'mɪks] *Br* **1** *n (sweets, cheese)* = surtido seleccionado por el cliente
2 *adj* surtido(a); *Fig* **a p. approach** un enfoque arbitrario

pickpocket ['pɪkpɒkɪt] *n* carterista *mf*

pick-up ['pɪkʌp] **1** *n* **(a)** *Br* **p. (arm)** *(on record player)* brazo *m* del tocadiscos
(b) *(vehicle)* **p. (truck)** camioneta *f*
(c) *(for goods, passengers)* **the truck made several pick-ups on the way** el camión se detuvo varias veces en el camino para cargar mercancías/pasajeros ►► ***p. point*** *(for goods, passengers)* lugar *m* de recogida
(d) *(on guitar)* pastilla *f*
(e) *Fam (improvement)* recuperación *f*; **we're hoping for a p. in sales** esperamos que haya una recuperación en las ventas
(f) *US (acceleration)* aceleración *f*; **it has good p.** tiene buena aceleración
(g) *Fam (sexual partner)* ligue *m*, *RP, Ven* levante *m*
2 *adj US (impromptu)* improvisado(a), espontáneo(a)

picky ['pɪkɪ] *adj Fam* exigente, escrupuloso(a); **she's really p. about her food** es muy exigente con la comida

pick-your-own ['pɪkjər'əʊn] *adj* = que se pueden ir a recoger pagando

picnic ['pɪknɪk] **1** *n* picnic *m*, comida *f* campestre; **to go on** *or* **for a p.** ir de picnic; **we took a p. lunch** llevamos el almuerzo; IDIOM *Fam* **it's no p.** no es moco de pavo, se las trae ►► ***p. area*** zona *f* de picnic; ***p. basket*** cesta *f* de merienda; ***p. hamper*** cesta *f* de merienda; ***p. site*** zona *f* de picnic
2 *vi (pt & pp* **picnicked***)* ir de picnic

picnicker ['pɪknɪkə(r)] *n* excursionista *mf*

Pict [pɪkt] *n Hist* picto(a) *m,f*

pictogram ['pɪktəgræm], **pictograph** ['pɪktəgrɑːf] *n* pictograma *m*, pictografía *f*

pictorial [pɪk'tɔːrɪəl] **1** *n (magazine)* revista *f* ilustrada
2 *adj* gráfico(a), ilustrado(a)

pictorially [pɪk'tɔːrɪəlɪ] *adv* con imágenes *or* ilustraciones

picture ['pɪktʃə(r)] **1** *n* **(a)** *(painting)* cuadro *m*, pintura *f*; *(drawing)* dibujo *m*; *(in book)* ilustración *f*; *(photograph)* fotografía *f*; **to draw/paint a p. (of sth/sb)** hacer un dibujo/pintar un cuadro (de algo/alguien); **to take a p. of sb, to take sb's p.** tomar una fotografía de alguien, tomarle a alguien una fotografía ►► ***p. book*** libro *m* ilustrado; ***p. card*** figura *f (naipe)*; ***p. frame*** marco *m*; ***p. gallery*** pinacoteca *f*; ***p. library*** archivo *m* fotográfico; ***p. postcard*** postal *f*; ***p. rail*** moldura *f* para colgar cuadros; ***p. researcher*** = persona encargada de buscar fotografías para anuncios publicitarios, publicaciones, etc.; ***p. restorer*** restaurador(ora) *m,f* de cuadros; ***p. window*** ventanal *m*
(b) *(image) (on TV, in mind)* imagen *f*; **we can't get a good p. here** aquí no nos llega una buena imagen
(c) *(impression, overview)* **the political/economic p.** el panorama político/económico; **this book gives a totally different p. of medieval life** este libro presenta una imagen completamente diferente de la vida medieval; **the p. he painted was a depressing one** el panorama que describió fue deprimente; **they have a distorted p. of the truth** tienen una imagen distorsionada de los hechos
(d) *Fam (movie)* película *f*; *Br* **to go to the pictures** ir al cine ►► *Br Old-fashioned* ***p. house*** cinematógrafo *m*; *Br Old-fashioned* ***p. palace*** cinematógrafo *m*
(e) IDIOMS **he's the p. of health** es la viva imagen de la salud; **his face was a p.** puso una cara digna de verse; **are you still seeing Jim? – no, he's out of the p. now** ¿sigues saliendo con Jim? – no, ya es historia; **she hates being left out of the p.** odia quedar al margen; **to put sb in the p.** poner a alguien al tanto *or* en situación; *Fam* **I get the p.** ya veo, ya entiendo
2 *vt* **(a)** *(imagine)* imaginarse; **I can't p. him as a teacher** no me lo imagino (trabajando) de profesor; **just p. the scene** imagínate la escena **(b)** *(represent, portray)* retratar; **the headmaster, pictured here on the left...** el director, que aparece aquí a la izquierda...

picture-perfect ['pɪktʃə'pɜːfɪkt] *adj US (flawless)* impecable, perfecto(a)

picture-postcard ['pɪktʃə'pəʊstkɑːd] *adj* de postal

picturesque [pɪktʃə'resk] *adj* pintoresco(a)

picturesquely [pɪktʃə'resklɪ] *adv* pintorescamente

piddle ['pɪdəl] *Fam* **1** *n* **to have a p.** hacer pis
2 *vi* hacer pis

► **piddle about, piddle around** *vi Fam* perder el tiempo

piddling ['pɪdəlɪŋ] *adj Fam* insignificante; **she sold it for a p. 20 dollars** lo vendió por 20 míseros dólares

pidgin ['pɪdʒɪn] *n* pidgin *m* ►► ***p. English*** inglés *m* pidgin

pie [paɪ] *n* **(a)** *(of meat, fish)* empanada *f*, pastel *m*, *Col, CSur* torta *f*; *(of fruit)* tarta *f* ►► ***p. chart*** gráfico *m* circular *or* de sectores; ***p. diagram*** gráfico *m* circular *or* de sectores **(b)** IDIOMS *Fam* **p. in the sky** castillos en el aire; **everyone wants a piece of the p.** todo el mundo quiere tomar parte

piebald ['paɪbɔːld] **1** *n (horse)* picazo *m*
2 *adj* picazo(a)

PIECE [piːs] *n* **(a)** *(of paper, meat, cake)* trozo *m*, pedazo *m*; **a p. of advice** un consejo; **a p. of carelessness** un descuido; **a p. of clothing** una prenda (de vestir); **this barometer is a delicate p. of equipment** este barómetro es un instrumento delicado; **a p. of evidence** una evidencia; **a p. of fruit** una fruta; **a p. of furniture** un mueble; **a p. of information** una información; **a p. of jewellery** una joya; **a p. of land** un terreno; **that was a p. of (good) luck!** ¡fue (una) suerte!; **a p. of legislation** una ley; **a p. of luggage** un bulto (de equipaje); **a p. of news** una noticia; **what an amazing p. of skill!** ¡qué habilidad!; **a p. of software** un software; **a p. of toast** una tostada; **a p. of work** un trabajo; IDIOM *Fam* **you really are a p. of work!** ¡eres de lo que no hay!; **this novel is a fascinating p. of writing** esta novela es una obra fascinante; **a four-p. band** una formación con cuatro instrumentos; **a 24-p. canteen of cutlery** una cubertería de 24 piezas; **they took the radio apart p. by p.** desmontaron la radio pieza a pieza; **to put sth together p. by p.** recomponer algo pieza a pieza; **the vase arrived (all) in one p.** el jarrón llegó intacto; **to be still in one p.** *(person)* estar sano(a) y salvo(a); **to be in pieces** *(broken)* estar destrozado(a); *(unassembled)* estar desmontado(a); **to break sth into pieces** romper algo en pedazos; **they are all of a p.** están cortados por el mismo patrón; **to come** *or* **fall to pieces** caerse a pedazos; *Fig* **that jumper is falling to pieces!** ese suéter *or Esp* jersey *or Col* saco *or RP* pulóver se cae a pedazos; **to take sth to pieces** desmontar algo; **to tear sth to pieces** hacer trizas algo; *Fig* **to tear** *or* **pull sth/sb to pieces** *(criticize)* hacer trizas algo/a alguien; IDIOM **to go to pieces** *(of person)* derrumbarse; IDIOM **to want a p. of the action** querer un pedazo del pastel; IDIOM **to want a p. of sb: now he's successful, everyone wants a p. of him** ahora que ha tenido éxito, todo el mundo quiere algo de él; *US Fam* **do you want a p. of me?** ¿me tienes ganas?; IDIOM **it was a p. of cake** *(very easy)* estaba tirado *or* chupado, *RP* fue un boleto; IDIOM *Br very Fam* **it was a p. of piss** *(very easy)* estaba tirado *or Esp* mamado, *RP* fue un boleto; IDIOM **to give sb a p. of one's mind** cantar las cuarenta a alguien; IDIOM **he said his p.** dijo lo que pensaba ►► ***p. rate*** *(pay)* tarifa *f* a destajo
(b) *(in games, of jigsaw puzzle)* pieza *f*; *(in dominoes, draughts, checkers)* ficha *f*
(c) *(coin)* **five/fifty pence p.** moneda de cinco/cincuenta peniques; *Formerly* **pieces of eight** ocho reales
(d) *(work of art)* pieza *f*
(e) *(newspaper article)* artículo *m*; *(television report)* información *f*; *(music)* pieza *f*
(f) *(of artillery)* pieza *f*; *Fam (gun)* pipa *f*, *Am* fierro *m*
(g) *US (distance)* **it's a p. from here** está a una buena tirada de aquí
(h) *Fam (girl)* **she's a nice** *or* **tasty p.** está para comérsela

► **piece together** *vt sep (parts)* montar; *(broken object)* recomponer; *(facts)* reconstruir; *(evidence)* componer

---

pièce de résistance [pɪ'esdərə'zɪstɔːns] *n* plato *m* fuerte

piecemeal ['piːsmiːl] **1** *adj* deslavazado(a), poco sistemático(a)
2 *adv* deslavazadamente, desordenadamente

piecework ['piːswɜːk] *n Ind* (trabajo *m* a) destajo *m*; **to be on p.** estar trabajando a destajo

piecrust ['paɪkrʌst] *n* = masa o pasta que recubre un pastel

pied [paɪd] *adj* de varios colores, moteado(a); **the P. Piper (of Hamelin)** el flautista de Hamelín ►► ***p. flycatcher*** papamoscas *m* cerrojillo

pied-à-terre ['pjeɪdæ'teə(r)] *n* = segunda vivienda, a menudo en una ciudad o un país diferente

Piedmont ['pi:dmənt] *n* Piamonte *m*

pie-eyed ['paɪ'aɪd] *adj Fam* como una cuba, trompa; **to get p.** *Esp, RP* agarrar una curda, *Méx* ponerse una buena peda

pier [pɪə(r)] *n* (**a**) *(landing stage)* muelle *m*, embarcadero *m* (**b**) *(with seaside amusements)* malecón *m* (**c**) *(of bridge)* pilar *m*

pierce [pɪəs] *vt* (**a**) *(make hole in)* perforar; **to p. a hole in sth** hacer un agujero en algo; **the knife/bullet pierced her lung** el cuchillo/la bala le perforó un pulmón; **to have one's ears pierced** hacerse agujeros en las orejas; **to have one's navel pierced** hacerse un piercing en el ombligo, hacerse un agujero en el ombligo *(para ponerse un pendiente)*; *Fig* **his words pierced my heart** sus palabras me rompieron el corazón
(**b**) *(of sound, light)* atravesar; **the lights were unable to p. the fog** las luces no conseguían atravesar la niebla
(**c**) *(penetrate) (defence, barrier)* penetrar en

pierced [pɪəst] *adj* **to have p. ears** tener orejas con la perforación hecha

piercing ['pɪəsɪŋ] *adj (voice, sound, look)* penetrante; *(wind)* cortante

piercingly ['pɪəsɪŋlɪ] *adv* de manera penetrante; **she looked at me p.** me miró penetrantemente

pierhead ['pɪəhed] *n* cabecera *f* de muelle

Pierrot ['pɪərəʊ] *n* pierrot *m*

pietà [pɪ'eɪtɑ:] *n Art* piedad *f*

pietism ['paɪətɪzəm] *n* devoción *f*, piedad *f*

piety ['paɪətɪ] *n* piedad *f*

piezoelectric ['pi:zəʊɪ'lektrɪk] *adj* piezoeléctrico(a)

piezoelectricity ['pi:zəʊɪlek'trɪsətɪ] *n* piezoelectricidad *f*

piffle ['pɪfəl] *n Fam* tonterías *fpl*, bobadas *fpl*

piffling ['pɪfəlɪŋ] *adj Fam (amount, excuse)* ridículo(a); *(mistake)* insignificante

pig [pɪg] **1** *n* (**a**) *(animal)* cerdo *m*, puerco *m*, *Am* chancho *m* ►► ***p.'s trotters*** manitas *fpl* de cerdo
(**b**) *Fam (greedy person)* comilón(ona) *m,f*, glotón(ona) *m,f*, *Am* chancho(a) *m,f*; *(unpleasant person)* cerdo(a) *m,f*, asqueroso(a) *m,f*, *Am* chancho(a) *m,f*; **the dirty p.!** ¡el muy cerdo!; **what a selfish p.!** ¡que tragón!
(**c**) *very Fam (policeman) Esp* madero *m*, *Andes* paco *m*, *Col* tombo *m*, *Méx* tamarindo *m*, *RP* cana *m*
(**d**) *Br Fam (unpleasant task, thing)* rollazo *m*, *RP* embole *m*; **cleaning the oven is a p. of a job** limpiar el horno es un rollazo *or RP* embole bárbaro; **the desk was a p. to move** fue dificilísimo mover el escritorio
(**e**) *Ind* ***p. iron*** arrabio *m*, hierro *m* en lingotes
(**f**) IDIOMS **to live like pigs** vivir como cerdos; *US* **to be like a p. in mud** *or very Fam* **shit** estar más contento(a) que unas castañuelas, *CSur* estar como chancho en el barro; *Fam* **to buy a p. in a poke** recibir gato por liebre; **to make a p. of oneself** ponerse las botas de comida; *Br Fam* **to make a p.'s ear of sth** hacer un desaguisado *or Méx* desmadre *or RP* despelote con algo; *Fam* **a p. of a job** una auténtica faena; *US Fam* **in a p.'s eye!** ¡jamás!; **pigs might fly!** ¡que te crees tú eso!, *Esp* ¡y yo soy la reina de los mares!, *Méx* ¡y yo soy el presidente de la República!, *RP* ¡y yo soy Gardel!
2 *vt (pt & pp* **pigged***) Fam* **to p. oneself (on)** ponerse las botas (comiendo)

► **pig out** *vi Fam* **to p. out (on)** ponerse las botas (comiendo)

pigeon ['pɪdʒən] *n* (**a**) *(bird)* paloma *f* ►► ***p. fancier*** colombófilo(a) *m,f*; ***p. loft*** palomar *m*; ***p. post*** correo *m* por paloma mensajera (**b**) *Br Fam (business)* **it's not my p.** no es asunto mío; **that's their p. now** ahora es problema de ellos

pigeon-breasted ['pɪdʒən'brestɪd], **pigeon-chested** ['pɪdʒən'tʃestɪd] *adj* = con el pecho estrecho y salido

pigeonhole ['pɪdʒənhəʊl] **1** *n* casillero *m*, casilla *f*; IDIOM **he tends to put people in pigeonholes** tiende a encasillar a las personas
2 *vt* (**a**) *(classify)* encasillar; **they pigeonholed me as a feminist** me catalogaron de feminista (**b**) *(postpone)* postergar

pigeon-toed ['pɪdʒən'təʊd] *adj* con las puntas de los pies para dentro

piggery ['pɪgərɪ] *n* (**a**) *(pig farm)* granja *f* porcina (**b**) *Fam (dirty, untidy place)* pocilga *f*, *Méx* mugrero *m*, *RP* chiquero *m* (**c**) *Fam (greed)* glotonería *f*

piggish ['pɪgɪʃ] *adj Fam* (**a**) *(dirty, untidy)* cochino(a), cerdo(a), *Am* chancho(a) (**b**) *(greedy)* glotón(ona)

piggy ['pɪgɪ] *Fam* **1** *n* cerdito(a) *m,f*, *Am* chanchito(a) *m,f* ►► ***p. bank*** = alcancía en forma de cerdito, *CSur* chanchita *f*
2 *adj* **p. eyes** ojillos de cerdo

piggyback ['pɪgɪbæk], **pickaback** ['pɪkəbæk] **1** *n* **to give sb a p.** llevar a alguien a cuestas
2 *adv* **to ride** *or* **be carried p.** ir *or* ser llevado a caballo *or Arg* caballito

piggy-in-the-middle = **pig-in-the-middle**

pigheaded ['pɪg'hedɪd] *adj* tozudo(a), testarudo(a)

pigheadedly ['pɪg'hedɪdlɪ] *adv* tozudamente, testarudamente

pigheadedness ['pɪg'hedɪdnɪs] *n* tozudez *f*, testarudez *f*

pig-in-the-middle ['pɪgɪnðə'mɪdəl], **piggy-in-the-middle** ['pɪgɪɪnðə'mɪdəl] *n (game)* = juego en el que dos niños se arrojan una pelota y el tercero, que está entre ambos, intenta atraparla, *Arg* ≃ loco *m*; IDIOM **to feel like p.** sentirse como el tercero en discordia

piglet ['pɪglɪt] *n* cochinillo *m*, cerdito *m*

pigmeat ['pɪgmi:t] *n* carne *m* de cerdo

pigment ['pɪgmənt] **1** *n* pigmento *m*
2 *vt* pigmentar

pigmentation [pɪgmən'teɪʃən] *n* pigmentación *f*

pigmy ['pɪgmɪ] *n* pigmeo(a) *m,f*

pigpen ['pɪgpen] *n US also Fig* pocilga *f*

pigskin ['pɪgskɪn] **1** *n* (**a**) *(material)* piel *m* de cerdo *or* puerco *or Am* chancho (**b**) *US Fam (football)* balón *m* (de fútbol americano)
2 *adj* de piel de cerdo *or* puerco *or Am* chancho

pigsty ['pɪgstaɪ] *n also Fig* pocilga *f*; **this place is a p.!** ¡esto es una pocilga!

pigswill ['pɪgswɪl] *n Br* bazofia *f*

pigtail ['pɪgteɪl] *n (plaited)* trenza *f*; *(loose)* coleta *f*

pig-ugly ['pɪg'ʌglɪ] *adj Br Fam* espantoso(a), horrible

pike[1] [paɪk] *n (weapon)* pica *f*

pike[2] *n (fish)* lucio *m*

pike[3] *n (in diving)* carpa *f*

pike[4] *n US (road)* autopista *f* de peaje; IDIOM **to come down the p.** acercarse

pikestaff ['paɪkstɑ:f] *n* IDIOM *Fam* **it's as plain as a p.** está más claro que el agua

pilaf(f) = **pilau**

pilaster [pɪ'læstə(r)] *n Archit* pilastra *f*

Pilate ['paɪlət] *pr n* **(Pontius) P.** (Poncio) Pilatos

pilau [pɪ'laʊ], **pilaf(f)** ['pɪlæf] *n* = plato de arroz especiado ►► ***p. rice*** = arroz de colores especiado servido como acompañamiento

pilchard ['pɪltʃəd] *n* sardina *f*

pile [paɪl] **1** *n* (**a**) *(heap)* pila *f*, montón *m*; **to put in(to) a p., to make a p. of** apilar; **she left her clothes/records in a p. on the floor** dejó su ropa amontonada/sus discos amontonados en el suelo; *Fam Fig* **to be at the top/bottom of the p.** estar en lo más alto/bajo de la escala
(**b**) *Fam (lots)* **to have piles of** *or* **a p. of work to do** tener un montón de trabajo que hacer; **to have piles of money** tener un montón de dinero *or RP* guita
(**c**) *Fam (fortune)* **she made her p. in property** se forró *or Méx* se llenó de lana *or RP* se llenó de guita con el negocio inmobiliario
(**d**) *(of carpet)* pelo *m*
(**e**) *Phys* **(atomic) p.** pila *f* atómica
(**f**) *Elec* pila *f*
(**g**) *Formal or Hum (building)* mansión *f*
(**h**) *(column, pillar)* pilar *m*
2 *vt* apilar; **he piled more coal on the fire** echó más carbón al fuego; **they piled food onto my plate** me llenaron el plato de comida; **the table was piled high with papers** la mesa estaba cubierta de torres de papeles; **she wears her hair piled high on her head** lleva el pelo recogido en un moño alto

► **pile in** *vi Fam* (**a**) *(enter)* meterse atropelladamente; **p. in!** *(into car)* ¡arriba! (**b**) *(join fight)* **once the first punch was thrown we all piled in** cuando voló el primer puñetazo, todos nos metimos

► **pile into** *vt insep Fam* (**a**) *(get into)* meterse atropelladamente en (**b**) *(crash)* estrellarse contra; **the two cars piled into each other** los dos coches se estrellaron uno contra el otro (**c**) *(attack)* arremeter contra

► **pile off** *vi Fam* salir atropelladamente

► **pile on 1** *vi (onto bus, train)* subir atropelladamente

2 *vt sep* incrementar, aumentar; **to p. on the pressure** aumentar la presión al máximo; IDIOM *Fam* **to p. it on thick** *(exaggerate)* cargar las tintas

▸ **pile out** *vi Fam* salir atropelladamente

▸ **pile up** 1 *vt sep* (**a**) *(objects)* apilar, amontonar (**b**) *(debts)* acumular, amontonar
2 *vi* (**a**) *(dirty clothes, work)* amontonarse, apilarse (**b**) *(debts, evidence)* acumularse, amontonarse (**c**) *(crash)* chocar en cadena

pile-driver ['paɪldraɪvə(r)] *n (machine)* martinete *m*

piles [paɪlz] *npl (haemorrhoids)* almorranas *fpl*

pile-up ['paɪlʌp] *n (of cars)* colisión *f* múltiple

pilfer ['pɪlfə(r)] 1 *vt* hurtar, *Esp* sisar
2 *vi* hurtar, *Esp* sisar

pilferage ['pɪlfərɪdʒ] *n* hurto *m*; **the percentage lost through p.** el porcentaje perdido por robo

pilgrim ['pɪlgrɪm] *n* peregrino(a) *m,f*; **the P. Fathers** = el primer grupo de puritanos ingleses que llegó a América

pilgrimage ['pɪlgrɪmɪdʒ] *n* peregrinación *f*, peregrinaje *m*; **to go on** *or* **make a p.** hacer una peregrinación

pill [pɪl] *n* (**a**) *(medicine)* pastilla *f*, píldora *f*; IDIOM **to sugar** *or* **sweeten the p. (for sb)** dorar la píldora (a alguien) (**b**) *(contraceptive)* **the p.** la píldora; **to be on the p.** tomar la píldora; **to go on the p.** empezar a tomar la píldora

pillage ['pɪlɪdʒ] 1 *n* pillaje *m*, saqueo *m*
2 *vt* saquear
3 *vi* saquear

pillar ['pɪlə(r)] *n* (**a**) *(of building)* pilar *m*; IDIOM **from p. to post** de la Ceca a la Meca; IDIOM **to be a p. of strength** ser como una roca ▸▸ *Br* ***p. box*** buzón *m* (de correos)
(**b**) *(of rock, fire, smoke, water)* columna *f*; **a p. of salt** *(in bible)* una estatua de sal
(**c**) *(respected member)* **a p. of society/the Church** uno de los pilares de la sociedad/la Iglesia

pillar-box red ['pɪləbɒks'red] *n Br* rojo *m* vivo

pillbox ['pɪlbɒks] *n* (**a**) *(for pills)* cajita *f* para pastillas (**b**) *Mil* fortín *m* (**c**) *(hat)* **p. (hat)** sombrero *m* sin alas

pillion ['pɪljən] 1 *n* **p. (seat)** asiento *m* trasero; **p. passenger** *or* **rider** pasajero de atrás
2 *adv* **to ride p.** ir de paquete

pillock ['pɪlək] *n Br very Fam Esp* gilipollas *mf inv*, *Am* pendejo(a) *m,f*

pillory ['pɪlərɪ] 1 *n* picota *f*
2 *vt (ridicule)* poner en la picota

pillow ['pɪləʊ] 1 *n* almohada *f* ▸▸ ***p. fight*** guerra *f* de almohadas; ***p. talk*** secretos *mpl or* conversaciones *fpl* de alcoba
2 *vt (rest)* apoyar, recostar

pillow-biter ['pɪləʊ'baɪtə(r)] *n very Fam Pej* maricón *m*, *Esp* bujarrón *m*, *Méx* tortillón *m*, *RP* tragasables *m inv*

pillowcase ['pɪləʊkeɪs], **pillowslip** ['pɪləʊslɪp] *n* funda *f* de almohada

pill-popper ['pɪlpɒpə(r)] *n Fam* = consumidor habitual de pastillas sedantes o estimulantes, *Esp* pastillero(a) *m,f*

pilot ['paɪlət] 1 *n* (**a**) *(of plane, ship)* piloto *mf* ▸▸ *Br* ***p. officer*** alférez *m* (**b**) *(experimental) TV* **p. (programme)** programa *m* piloto; **p. scheme/study** proyecto/estudio piloto (**c**) *(fish)* ***p. fish*** pez *m* piloto; ***p. whale*** ballena *f* piloto (**d**) *(in oven, heater)* **p. (light)** piloto *m*
2 *vt* (**a**) *(plane, ship)* pilotar (**b**) *(guide)* dirigir, conducir; **she piloted the bill through parliament** logró que la ley fuera aprobada en el parlamento (**c**) *(test)* poner a prueba

pilotless ['paɪlətlɪs] *adj (automatic)* sin piloto

Pils(e)ner ['pɪlznə(r)] *n* Pils(e)ner *f*

pimento [pɪ'mentəʊ] *n* (**a**) *(allspice)* pimienta *f* inglesa (**b**) *(sweet pepper)* pimiento *m* morrón, *Méx* chile *m*, *RP* ají *m*, *Col, Ven* pimentón *m*

pi-meson ['paɪ'mi:zɒn] *n Phys* mesón *m* pi

pimiento [pɪ'mjentəʊ] *n (sweet pepper)* pimiento *m* morrón, *Méx* chile *m*, *RP* ají *m*, *Col, Ven* pimentón *m*

pimp [pɪmp] 1 *n* proxeneta *m*, *Esp* chulo *m*, *RP* cafiolo *m*
2 *vi* **to p. for sb** ser el proxeneta de alguien

pimpernel ['pɪmpənel] *n* pimpinela *f*

pimple ['pɪmpəl] *n* grano *m*

pimply ['pɪmplɪ] *adj* lleno(a) de granos

PIN [pɪn] *n* (*abbr* **personal identification number**) **P. (number)** PIN *m*

pin [pɪn] 1 *n* (**a**) *(with point) (for sewing)* alfiler *m*; *(hairpin)* horquilla *f*; *Fam* **pins and needles** hormigueo; **(safety) p.** *(for fastening clothes)* imperdible *m*, *Am* alfiler *m* de gancho, *CAm, Méx* seguro *m*; IDIOM **you could have heard a p. drop** se oía el vuelo de una mosca ▸▸ ***p. money*** dinero *m* extra
(**b**) *(bolt)* clavija *f*; **(firing) p.** percutor *m*
(**c**) *(peg)* pata *f*
(**d**) *(brooch, badge)* pin *m*
(**e**) *Med (for broken bone)* clavo *m*
(**f**) *Br Elec (of wall plug)* clavija *f*; *Comptr (on cable)* pin *m*; **two/three p. plug** enchufe de dos/tres clavijas
(**g**) *(of grenade)* seguro *m*
(**h**) *Fam* **pins** *(legs)* patas *fpl*
(**i**) *(in golf)* **the p.** el banderín; **the p. position** la posición del banderín
(**j**) *(in bowling, skittles)* bolo *m*
2 *vt* (*pt & pp* **pinned**) (**a**) *(fasten) (with pin)* clavar; **there was a sign pinned to the door** había un aviso clavado en la puerta; **she had a brooch pinned to her jacket** tenía un broche prendido en la chaqueta; **to p. the blame on sb** cargar la culpa a alguien; **they can't p. anything on me** no me pueden acusar de nada; **he pinned his hopes on them** puso *or* cifró sus esperanzas en ellos
(**b**) *(hold still)* sujetar, atrapar; **she was pinned under a boulder** estaba atrapada bajo una roca; **they pinned his arms behind his back** le sujetaron los brazos en la espalda; **to p. sb against** *or* **to a wall** atrapar a alguien contra una pared; **to p. sb to the ground** sujetar a alguien contra el suelo
(**c**) *(in chess)* clavar

▸ **pin back** *vt sep* (**a**) *(in operation)* **to have one's ears pinned back** operarse de las orejas (**b**) *Br Fam* **to p. one's ears back** *(listen carefully)* prestar atención

▸ **pin down** *vt sep* (**a**) *(with pin or pins)* sujetar con alfileres
(**b**) *(immobilize, trap)* atrapar, sujetar; **his legs were pinned down by the fallen tree** sus piernas quedaron atrapadas por el árbol caído
(**c**) *(identify)* identificar
(**d**) *(force to be definite)* obligar a definirse; **we tried to p. him down to a date** intentamos que se comprometiera a dar una fecha; **she doesn't want to be pinned down about future policy** no quiere verse obligada a hablar de futuras políticas

▸ **pin together** *vt sep* unir con alfileres

▸ **pin up** *vt sep* (**a**) *(notice)* clavar, colocar (**b**) *(hair)* recoger; *(hem)* prender con alfileres

piña colada ['pi:nəkə'lɑ:də] *n* piña *f* colada

pinafore ['pɪnəfɔ:(r)] *n* (**a**) *(apron)* delantal *m* (**b**) **p. (dress)** *Esp* pichi *m*, *CSur, Méx* jumper *m*

pinaster [paɪ'næstə(r)] *n* pino *m* marítimo

pinball ['pɪnbɔ:l] *n* **to play p.** jugar a la máquina *or* al flíper ▸▸ ***p. machine*** máquina *f* de bolas, flíper *m*

pince-nez ['pæns'neɪ] *npl* quevedos *mpl*

pincer ['pɪnsə(r)] *n* (**a**) *(of crab, insect)* pinza *f* (**b**) *Mil* ***p. movement*** movimiento *m* de tenaza

pincers ['pɪnsəz] *npl (tool)* tenazas *fpl*

pinch [pɪntʃ] 1 *n* (**a**) *(action)* pellizco *m*; **to give sb a p.** dar un pellizco a alguien (**b**) *(small amount)* pizca *f*, pellizco *m* (**c**) IDIOMS **to feel the p.** pasar estrecheces; *Br* **at** *or US* **in a p.** si fuera necesario; **to take sth with a p. of salt** no tomarse algo muy en serio, no dar demasiado crédito a algo
2 *vt* (**a**) *(nip)* pellizcar; **he pinched her cheek** le pellizcó la mejilla; **I had to p. myself to make sure I wasn't dreaming** tuve que pellizcarme para estar seguro de que no estaba soñando; **these shoes p. my feet** estos zapatos me aprietan (**b**) *esp Br Fam (steal)* afanar, *Esp* levantar (**c**) *Fam (arrest)* arrestar, llevar
3 *vi* (**a**) *(shoes)* apretar (**b**) *(economize)* **to p. and scrape** apretarse el cinturón

> **False friend:** The Spanish verb **pinchar** is not a translation for the English word **pinch**. In Spanish the main meanings of **pinchar** are "to prick" and "to pierce".

pinched [pɪntʃt] *adj* (**a**) *(features)* demacrado(a) (**b**) *(lacking)* **to be p. for time/money/space** tener muy poco tiempo/dinero/espacio

pinch-hit ['pɪntʃ'hɪt] *vi US* (**a**) *(in baseball)* = sustituir a un bateador en un momento decisivo del partido (**b**) *Fig (substitute)* **to p. for sb** sustituir a alguien *(en una emergencia)*

pinch-hitter ['pɪntʃ'hɪtə(r)] *n US* bateador(ora) *m,f* de emergencia

pincushion ['pɪnkʊʃən] *n* acerico *m*, alfiletero *m*

pine[1] [paɪn] *n (tree, wood)* pino *m*; **a p. table** una mesa de pino ▸▸ ***p. cone*** piña *f*; ***p. forest*** pinar *m*; ***p. kernel*** piñón *m*; ***p. marten*** marta *f*; ***p. needle*** aguja *f* de pino; ***p. nut*** piñón *m*; ***p. tree*** pino *m*

pine² *vi* **to p. for sth/sb** echar de menos *or* añorar algo/a alguien, *Am* extrañar algo/a alguien

▸ **pine away** *vi* consumirse de pena

pineal gland ['pɪnɪəl'glænd] *adj Anat* glándula *f* pineal

pineapple ['paɪnæpəl] *n* piña *f*, *RP* ananá *m* ▸▸ ***p. chunks*** rodajas *fpl* de piña

pinewood ['paɪnwʊd] *n* (**a**) *(group of trees)* pinar *m*, bosque *m* de pinos (**b**) *(wood)* madera *f* de pino

PING [pɪŋ] *n Comptr* (*abbr* **Packet Internet groper**) PING *m*

ping [pɪŋ] **1** *n* sonido *m* metálico
 2 *vi* (**a**) *(make pinging sound)* sonar (**b**) *US (car engine)* golpetear

pinger ['pɪŋə(r)] *n (timer)* reloj *m* alarma *(utilizado en la cocina)*

ping-pong ['pɪŋpɒŋ] *n* pimpón *m*, ping-pong *m*; **p. ball/table** pelota/ mesa de pimpón *or* ping pong

pinhead ['pɪnhed] *n* (**a**) *(of pin)* cabeza *f* de alfiler (**b**) *Fam (stupid person)* estúpido(a) *m,f*, majadero(a) *m,f*

pinhole ['pɪnhəʊl] *n* agujero *m* muy pequeño ▸▸ ***p. camera*** cámara *f* de apertura diminuta sin lente

pinion ['pɪnjən] **1** *n* (**a**) *(cogwheel)* piñón *m* (**b**) *Literary (wing)* ala *f*
 2 *vt* (**a**) *(restrain)* inmovilizar, sujetar; **to p. sb to the ground** inmovilizar a alguien en el suelo (**b**) *(bird)* cortarle las alas a

pink [pɪŋk] **1** *n* (**a**) *(color)* rosa *m*; IDIOM *Fam* **to be in the p. (of health)** *(be well)* estar como una rosa (**b**) *(flower)* clavel *m*
 2 *adj* (**a**) *(in colour)* rosa; **to turn p.** *(material, flower)* volverse rosado(a); *(person) (with pleasure, anger, embarrassment)* sonrojarse; IDIOM *Fam Hum* **he was seeing p. elephants** estaba tan borracho que veía alucinaciones ▸▸ ***p. champagne*** champagne *m* rosado; *US* ***p. dollar*** = el poder adquisitivo de los homosexuales; ***p. gin*** pink gin *m*, ginebra *f* con angostura; *Br* ***the p. pound*** = el poder adquisitivo de los homosexuales; *US Fam* ***p. slip:*** **to get a p. slip** ser despedido(a)
 (**b**) *Fam (left-wing)* rojeras, *Arg* medio(a) zurdo(a)
 3 *vt (to cut)* cortar con tijera dentada
 4 *vi Br (car engine)* golpear, golpetear

pink-collar ['pɪŋk'kɒlə(r)] *adj US Fam (job, worker)* de mujer, femenino(a)

pinkeye ['pɪŋkaɪ] *n US* conjuntivitis *f inv*

pinkie, pinky ['pɪŋkɪ] *n US, Scot* (dedo *m*) meñique *m*

pinking shears ['pɪŋkɪŋ'ʃɪəz] *npl* tijeras *fpl* dentadas

pinkish ['pɪŋkɪʃ] *adj* (**a**) *(in colour)* tirando a rosa (**b**) *Fam (left-wing)* rojeras

pinko ['pɪŋkəʊ] *Fam Pej* **1** *n* socialista *mf* de pacotilla *or Esp* descafeinado(a)
 2 *adj* socialista de pacotilla *or Esp* descafeinado(a)

pinky = **pinkie**

pinnace ['pɪnɪs] *n Naut* pequeño bote *m* a motor

pinnacle ['pɪnəkəl] *n* (**a**) *(of mountain)* cima *f*, cumbre *f* (**b**) *(of fame, career)* cima *f*, cumbre *f* (**c**) *Archit* pináculo *m*

pinnate ['pɪneɪt] *adj Bot* pinada

pinny ['pɪnɪ] *n Br Fam* delantal *m*

pinochle ['piːnʌkl] *n* pinacle *m*

pinole [pɪ'nəʊleɪ] *n* harina *f* de maíz tostado

pinpoint ['pɪnpɔɪnt] **1** *vt* (**a**) *(identify)* señalar, precisar (**b**) *(locate)* localizar
 2 *n* **a p. of light** un minúsculo punto de luz
 3 *adj* **with p. accuracy** con precisión milimétrica

pinprick ['pɪnprɪk] *n* (**a**) *(puncture)* pinchazo *m*; **a p. of light** un agujerito de luz (**b**) *(irritation)* molestia *f*, incomodidad *f*

pinstripe ['pɪnstraɪp] **1** *n* (**a**) *(stripe)* raya *f* fina (**b**) *(material)* tela *f* milrayas
 2 *adj* de milrayas ▸▸ ***p. suit*** (traje *m*) milrayas *m inv*

pinstriped ['pɪnstraɪpt] *adj* de milrayas

pint [paɪnt] *n* (**a**) *(measurement)* pinta *f (UK = 0,57 litros; US = 0,47 litros)* (**b**) *Br* **a p. (of beer)** una pinta (de cerveza); **I'm going for a p.** voy a tomarme una cerveza

pinta ['paɪntə] *n Br Fam* pinta *f* de leche

pintail ['pɪnteɪl] *n* ánade *m* rabudo

pintle ['pɪntəl] *n Tech* (**a**) *(bolt, pin)* perno *m*, pata *f* (**b**) *(in oil engine)* aguja *f*

pinto ['pɪntəʊ] **1** *n* caballo *m* pinto
 2 *adj* pinto(a) ▸▸ ***p. bean*** alubia *f or Esp* judía *f* pinta, *Am* frijol *m or CSur* poroto *m* pinto

pint-size(d) ['paɪntsaɪz(d)] *adj Fam* diminuto(a), pequeñajo(a)

pin-up ['pɪnʌp] *n Fam* (**a**) *(poster)* = póster de actriz, actor, cantante o modelo atractivo(a) (**b**) *(person)* = actriz, actor, cantante o modelo considerado(a) atractivo(a)

pinwheel ['pɪnwiːl] *n* (**a**) *US (toy windmill)* molinillo *m* (**b**) *(firework)* girándula *f*

Pinyin ['pɪn'jɪn] *n Ling* pinyin *m*

pion ['paɪɒn] *n Phys* pión *m*

pioneer [paɪə'nɪə(r)] **1** *n* (**a**) *(explorer, settler)* pionero(a) *m,f* (**b**) *(of technique, activity)* pionero(a) *m,f* (**c**) *Mil* zapador(ora) *m,f*
 2 *vt* **to p. research in nuclear physics** liderar la investigación en física nuclear; **the town is pioneering a job-creation scheme** la ciudad es la pionera en la aplicación de un plan de creación de empleo; **the technique was pioneered in this hospital** esta técnica fue implementada por primera vez en este hospital

pioneering [paɪə'nɪərɪŋ] *adj* pionero(a); **in p. days** en el tiempo de los colonizadores

pious ['paɪəs] *adj* (**a**) *(religious)* pío(a), piadoso(a) (**b**) *Pej (sanctimonious)* mojigato(a) (**c**) *(unrealistic)* **a p. hope** una vana ilusión

piously ['paɪəslɪ] *adv* (**a**) *(religiously)* piadosamente (**b**) *Pej (sanctimoniously)* hipócritamente, con tono moralista (**c**) *(unrealistic)* vanamente

piousness ['paɪəsnɪs] *n (religiousness)* religiosidad *f*

pip [pɪp] **1** *n* (**a**) *(of fruit)* pepita *f* (**b**) *(on playing card, dice, domino)* punto *m* (**c**) *Br (on uniform)* estrella *f* (**d**) *Br (sound)* **the pips** *(on radio)* las señales horarias; *(on public telephone)* la señal *or* los tonos de fin de llamada *or Am* llamado (**e**) IDIOM *Br Fam Old-fashioned* **it gives me the p.!** ¡me saca de quicio!
 2 *vt* (*pt & pp* **pipped**) *Br Fam (beat)* superar; **he was pipped at the post** lo superaron en el último momento

pipe [paɪp] **1** *n* (**a**) *(tube)* tubería *f*; **the pipes have frozen** las cañerías se han congelado ▸▸ ***p. bomb*** granada *f* casera
 (**b**) *(musical instrument)* flauta *f*; *(on organ)* cañón *m*, tubo *m*; **the pipes** *(bagpipes)* la gaita ▸▸ ***p. band*** grupo *m* de gaiteros
 (**c**) *(boatswain's whistle)* pito *m*
 (**d**) *(for smoking)* pipa *f*; **to smoke a p.** *(as habit)* fumar en pipa; *(on one occasion)* fumarse una pipa; IDIOM *Fam* **put that in your p. and smoke it!** *Esp* ¡toma del frasco, Carrasco!, *Am* ¡tómate esa! ▸▸ ***p. cleaner*** desatascador *m*; ***p. dream*** sueño *m* imposible; ***p. of peace*** pipa *f* de la paz; ***p. rack*** = mueble para poner las pipas; ***p. tobacco*** tabaco *m* de pipa
 (**e**) *(symbol)* pleca *f* interrumpida
 (**f**) *Geol* **(volcanic) p.** piedra *f* de pipa (volcánica)
 2 *vt* (**a**) *(water, oil)* conducir mediante tuberías; **to p. coolant through a system** hacer circular refrigerante a través de un sistema; *Fam* **piped music** música ambiental, hilo musical, *RP* música funcional
 (**b**) *(tune)* tocar; **to p. sb in/out** *(on bagpipes)* acompañar la entrada/salida de alguien con el sonido de la gaita
 (**c**) *Naut (order)* **to p. sb aboard** tocar el silbato cuando alguien sube a bordo
 (**d**) *(say)* decir con voz aflautada
 (**e**) *(clothing)* ribetear
 (**f**) *(icing, potato)* poner con manga de repostería
 3 *vi (on simple pipe)* tocar la flauta; *(on bagpipes)* tocar la gaita

▸ **pipe down** *vi Fam* cerrar el pico, callarse; **p. down!** ¡cierra el pico!

▸ **pipe up** *vi* **"I want to go too!" he piped up** "yo también quiero ir", saltó

pipeclay ['paɪpkleɪ] *n* greda *f*

pipefish ['paɪpfɪʃ] *n* aguja *f* de mar

pipeline ['paɪplaɪn] *n* (**a**) *(for water, gas)* tubería *f*, conducto *m*; **oil p.** oleoducto (**b**) IDIOMS **there are several projects in the p.** hay en preparación varios proyectos; **changes are in the p. for next year** se están preparando cambios para el año próximo

piper ['paɪpə(r)] *n (bagpipe player)* gaitero(a) *m,f*; PROV **he who pays the p. calls the tune** el que paga, manda

pipette, *US* **pipet** [pɪ'pet] *n* pipeta *f*

piping ['paɪpɪŋ] **1** *n* (**a**) *(pipes)* tuberías *fpl*, tubos *mpl*; **a piece of copper p.** una cañería de cobre (**b**) *(sound of bagpipes)* (sonido *m* de) gaitas *fpl* (**c**) *(on uniform)* ribetes *mpl* (**d**) *(on cake)* decoración *f* hecha con manga pastelera ▸▸ ***p. bag*** manga *f* (pastelera)
 2 *adj (sound)* agudo(a); **a p. voice** una voz de pito
 3 *adv* **p. hot** caliente, calentito(a)

pipistrelle [pɪpɪ'strel] *n* murciélago *m* enano

pipit ['pɪpɪt] *n* bisbita *m or f*; **red-throated p.** bisbita *m or f* gorgirrojo

pippin ['pɪpɪn] *n* = manzana parecida a la reineta

pip-pip ['pɪp'pɪp] *exclam Br Fam Old-fashioned (goodbye)* ¡adiós!, ¡chao!

pipsqueak ['pɪpskwi:k] *n Fam* pelagatos *mf inv*

piquancy ['pi:kənsɪ] *n* **(a)** *(of taste)* sabor *m* picante, fuerza *f* **(b)** *(intriguing nature)* **the p. of the situation** la gracia *or* lo sabroso de la situación

piquant ['pi:kənt] *adj* **(a)** *(tasty, spicy)* picante, fuerte **(b)** *(intriguing)* sabroso(a)

pique [pi:k] **1** *n* rabia *f*; **in a fit of p.** en una rabieta
2 *vt* **(a)** *(irritate)* molestar **(b)** *(arouse, intrigue)* despertar; **their curiosity was piqued by his remarks** sus comentarios les despertaron la curiosidad

piqued [pi:kt] *adj (resentful)* resentido(a)

piquet [pɪ'ket] *n* piquet *m*

piracy ['paɪrəsɪ] *n* **(a)** *(of vessel)* piratería *f* **(b)** *(of copyright material)* piratería *f*

piranha [pɪ'rɑ:nə] *n* piraña *f*

pirate ['paɪrət] **1** *n* **(a)** *(of vessel)* pirata *mf* **(b)** *(of copyright material)* pirata *mf* ►► ***p. edition*** edición *f* pirata; ***p. radio*** radio *f* pirata
2 *vt* piratear

pirated ['paɪrətɪd] *adj* pirateado(a)

piratical [paɪ'rætɪkəl] *adj Fig* **to be p.** *(person)* comportarse como un pirata

pirouette [pɪrʊ'et] **1** *n* pirueta *f*
2 *vi* hacer piruetas

Pisa ['pi:zə] *n* Pisa

Piscean ['paɪsɪən] **1** *n* **to be a P.** ser Piscis
2 *adj* de Piscis

Pisces ['paɪsi:z] *n (sign of zodiac)* Piscis *m inv*; **to be (a) P.** ser Piscis

pisciculture ['pɪsɪkʌltʃə(r)] *n* piscicultura *f*

piss [pɪs] *very Fam* **1** *n* **(a)** *(urine)* meada *f*; **to have** *or* **take a p.** mear, echar una meada; IDIOM *US* **to be full of p. and vinegar** estar lleno(a) de energía
(b) *Br* **to take the p. out of sth/sb** *(mock)* burlarse *or Esp* cachondearse de algo/alguien; **are you taking the p.?** ¿me estás tomando el pelo?, *Esp* ¿te estás quedando conmigo?
(c) *Br* **to go on the p.** *(go drinking)* salir de copas
(d) *(worthless thing)* **the movie/book was p.** la película/el libro era una mierda; **this beer is p.** esta cerveza es una mierda
2 *vt* **to p. oneself** *or Br* **one's pants** mearse encima, mearse en los pantalones; *Fig* **to p. oneself laughing** mearse de risa
3 *vi* **(a)** *(urinate)* mear **(b)** IDIOMS **we're pissing into the wind** esto es una pérdida de tiempo que te cagas *or Méx* de la madre *or RP* de cagarse; **it's pissing with rain** está lloviendo que te cagas *or Méx* duro, *RP* caen soretes de punta; **to p. all over sb** *(defeat)* dar una paliza a alguien, *RP* romperle el culo a alguien; **to p. on sth from a great height** pasarse algo por la entrepierna
4 *adv* **it was p. poor** era una mierda; *Br* **p. easy** chupado(a), *Esp* mamado(a)

► **piss about, piss around** **1** *vi very Fam* **(a)** *(behave foolishly)* hacer el *Esp* gilipollas *or Am* pendejo; **don't p. about** *or* **around with my stuff** no hagas el gilipollas *or RP* boludeces con mis cosas **(b)** *(waste time)* tocarse los huevos
2 *vt sep* tomar el pelo a

► **piss away** *vt sep very Fam* **to p. sth away** *(winnings, inheritance)* liquidarse algo

► **piss down** *vi very Fam* **it's pissing down (with rain)** está lloviendo *Esp* que te cagas *or Méx* duro, *RP* caen soretes de punta

► **piss off** *very Fam* **1** *vt sep (annoy)* joder, cabrear, *Méx* fregar; **to be pissed off (with)** estar cabreado(a) (con), *Méx* estar enchilado(a) (con)
2 *vi (go away)* largarse; **p. off!** ¡vete a la mierda *or* al carajo *or Méx* a la chingada!

piss-ant ['pɪsænt] *adj very Fam (insignificant)* diminuto(a)

piss-artist ['pɪsɑ:tɪst] *n Br very Fam* **(a)** *(drunk)* borrachuzo(a) *m,f*, *Am* borrachón(ona) *m,f* **(b)** *(useless person)* puto(a) inútil *m,f*

pissed [pɪst] *adj very Fam* **(a)** *Br (drunk)* pedo, *Esp* ciego(a), *Col* caído(a), *Méx* ahogado(a), *RP* en pedo; **to be p.** estar pedo; **to get p.** agarrarse un pedo *or Col* una perra, *Méx* traer un cuete; IDIOM **to be as p. as a fart** *or* **newt, to be p. out of one's head** *or* **mind** *Esp* llevar una mierda como un piano, *Méx* traer un cuete de nevero, *RP* tener una curda de caerse
(b) *US (angry)* cabreado(a); **to be p. (with sth/sb)** estar cabreado(a) (con algo/alguien)

pisser ['pɪsə(r)] *n very Fam* **(a)** *(annoying situation)* **what a p.!** ¡qué putada!, *Col, RP* ¡qué cagada!, *Méx* ¡es una chingadera!
(b) *US (good thing)* **to be a p.** ser genial *or Esp* cojonudo(a) *or Méx* chingón(ona)
(c) *US (annoying person) Esp* borde *mf*, *Méx* sangrón(ona) *m,f*, *RP* pesado(a) *m,f*
(d) *(toilet)* meadero *m*, *Esp* meódromo *m*
(e) *US (penis)* verga *f*, *Esp* picha *f*, *Chile* pico *m*, *Méx* pájaro *m*, *RP* pija *f*; IDIOM **to pull sb's p.** tomar el pelo a alguien, *Arg* tomar a alguien para la chacota

pisshead ['pɪshed] *n very Fam* **(a)** *Br (drunkard)* borrachuzo(a) *m,f*, *Am* borrachón(ona) *m,f* **(b)** *US (unpleasant person) Esp* capullo(a) *m,f*, *Am* pendejo(a) *m,f*

pisshole ['pɪshəʊl] *n very Fam* **his eyes were like two pissholes in the snow** tenía los ojos de sueño

piss-poor ['pɪs'pʊə(r)] *adj very Fam* mierdero(a)

piss-take ['pɪsteɪk] *n Br very Fam* vacilada *f*, *RP* joda *f*; **this is a p., isn't it?** me estás vacilando *or RP* jodiendo, ¿no?; **the movie is a p. of...** la película se burla *or Esp* se cachondea *or RP* se caga de risa de...

piss-up ['pɪsʌp] *n Br very Fam* **to have a p.** *Esp* ponerse ciegos a privar, *Col* agarrarse una perra, *Méx* ponerse una buena peda, *RP* ponerse requete en pedo; IDIOM *Hum* **he couldn't organize a p. in a brewery** es un inútil de tomo y lomo, *Col* es nulo(a), *Méx* es un desmadre, *RP* es más inútil que la mierda

pistachio [pɪ'stæʃɪəʊ] (*pl* **pistachios**) *n* **(a)** *(nut)* pistacho *m* **(b)** *(tree)* alfóncigo *m*, pistachero *m* **(c)** *(colour)* verde *m* pistacho

piste [pi:st] *n (ski slope)* pista *f*

pistil ['pɪstɪl] *n Bot* pistilo *m*

pistol ['pɪstəl] *n (gun)* pistola *f* ►► ***p. grip*** *(on camera)* empuñadura *f*, asidero *m*; ***p. shot*** disparo *m* (de pistola), pistoletazo *m*

pistol-whip ['pɪstəl'wɪp] *vt* golpear con una pistola a

piston ['pɪstən] *n* émbolo *m*, pistón *m* ►► ***p. ring*** anillo *m* de émbolo *or* pistón; ***p. rod*** barra *f or* biela *f* del pistón

pit[1] [pɪt] **1** *n* **(a)** *(hole in ground)* hoyo *m*; **to dig a p.** cavar un hoyo; **the news hit him in the p. of his stomach** la noticia le dolió en lo más profundo
(b) *(coal mine)* mina *f*; **to go down the p.** *(work as miner)* trabajar en la mina ►► ***p. bull (terrier)*** pitbull terrier *m*; ***p. pony*** = tipo de poni que antiguamente hacía de animal de carga en las minas británicas; ***p. prop*** soporte *m* de mina
(c) *US Fam* **it's/he's the pits!** ¡es de ponerse a llorar!, ¡es penoso!
(d) *Theat* foso *m* (de la orquesta)
(e) the pits *(in motor racing)* los boxes ►► ***p. stop*** *(in motor race)* parada *f* en boxes; *US (in journey)* parada *f*; **to make a p. stop** entrar en boxes
(f) *(indentation) (on metal, glass)* marca *f*; *(on skin)* picadura *f* ►► ***p. viper*** crótalo *m*
(g) *Fam (untidy place)* selva *f*
(h) *Br Fam (bed)* sobre *m*, cama *f*
(i) *Literary (hell)* **the p. (of hell)** el abismo
2 *vt (mark)* marcar, picar

pit[2] **1** *n (of cherry)* hueso *m*, pipo *m*, *RP* carozo *m*; *US (of peach, plum)* hueso *m*, *RP* carozo *m*
2 *vt (cherry, olive)* deshuesar

pit[3] (*pt & pp* **pitted**) *vt* **to p. sb against sb** enfrentar a alguien con alguien; **to p. oneself against sb** enfrentarse con alguien; **she pitted her wits against them** midió su ingenio con el de ellos

pita bread = **pitta bread**

pit-a-pat ['pɪtə'pæt], **pitter-patter** ['pɪtə'pætə(r)] **1** *n (of rain)* tamborileo *m*, repiqueteo *m*; *(of feet, heart)* golpeteo *m*
2 *adv* **to go p.** *(rain)* repiquetear; *(feet, heart)* golpetear

pitch[1] [pɪtʃ] *n (tar)* brea *f*

pitch[2] **1** *n* **(a)** *esp Br (for sport)* campo *m*
(b) *Br (for market stall)* puesto *m*
(c) *Mus (of note)* tono *m*; **to rise/fall in p.** subir/bajar de tono ►► ***p. pipes*** diapasón *m*
(d) *(level, degree)* punto *m*, nivel *m*; **a high p. of excitement was reached** se llegó un punto de mucha excitación; **to reach such a p. that...** llegar a tal punto que...
(e) *(talk)* **(sales) p.** charla *f* para vender
(f) *(slope) (of roof, ceiling)* pendiente *f*
(g) *(movement) (of boat, aircraft)* cabezada *f*
(h) *(in baseball)* lanzamiento *m*
(i) *(in golf)* golpe *m* corto y bombeado ►► ***p. and putt*** = campo de golf de pequeño tamaño a cuyos hoyos se puede llegar en un solo golpe
(j) *(in climbing)* inclinación *f*

2 *vt* **(a)** *(throw)* lanzar; *Fig* **she found herself pitched into the political arena** se vio lanzada a la arena política
(b) *(in baseball)* lanzar, pichear; **he pitched a great game last night** anoche picheó muy bien
(c) *(in golf)* **to p. the ball onto the green** poner la pelota en el green con un golpe corto
(d) *Mus (tune, one's voice)* dar; **I can't p. my voice any higher** mi voz no da más alto
(e) *(aim)* **our new model is pitched to appeal to executives** nuestro nuevo modelo está diseñado para atraer a ejecutivos; **he pitched the talk at the right level** le imprimió a la charla *or CAm, Méx* plática el tono *or* nivel apropiado
(f) *(set up) (tent, camp)* montar
3 *vi* **(a)** *(ship, plane)* cabecear, tambalearse
(b) *(fall over)* caerse; **the passengers pitched forwards/backwards** los pasajeros se cayeron hacia delante/atrás
(c) *(in baseball)* lanzar la pelota, pichear; IDIOM *US Fam* **she's still in there pitching** aún no se ha dado por vencida
(d) *(land) (ball)* caer
(e) *(in golf)* **to p. out of the rough** sacar la pelota del rough con un golpe corto; **she pitched to within four feet of the hole** lanzó la pelota a poco más de un metro del hoyo
(f) *(slope) (roof)* inclinarse
(g) *(for contract)* pujar (**for** por)

▸ **pitch in** *vi* **(a)** *(start work)* ponerse a trabajar **(b)** *(lend a hand)* colaborar, echar una mano

▸ **pitch into** *vt insep* **(a)** *(attack)* arremeter contra **(b)** *(work, food)* abalanzarse sobre, atacar

pitch[3] *n Comptr & Typ* grado *m* de inclinación, pitch *m*

pitch-black [ˈpɪtʃˈblæk], **pitch-dark** [ˈpɪtʃˈdɑːk] *adj* como la boca del lobo, muy oscuro(a)

pitchblende [ˈpɪtʃblend] *n* pechblenda *f*, pecblenda *f*

pitch-dark = **pitch-black**

pitched [pɪtʃt] *adj* **(a)** *(sloping)* en pendiente **(b)** *(all-out)* **p. battle** batalla campal

pitcher[1] [ˈpɪtʃə(r)] *n (jug)* jarra *f*; *(large and made of clay)* cántaro *m*; PROV **little pitchers have big ears** los niños entienden más de lo que parece ▸▸ ***p. plant*** sarracenia *f*

pitcher[2] *n US (in baseball)* pícher *mf*, pítcher *mf*, lanzador(ora) *m,f* ▸▸ ***p.'s plate*** plataforma *f* de lanzamiento

pitchfork [ˈpɪtʃfɔːk] **1** *n* horca *f*
2 *vt* **(a)** *(hay)* mover con la horca **(b)** *(person)* obligar, forzar; **she was pitchforked into the job** la obligaron *or* forzaron a hacerse cargo del puesto

pitching wedge [ˈpɪtʃɪŋwedʒ] *n (golf club)* wedge *m* para rough

pitchpine [ˈpɪtʃpaɪn] *n* pino *m* de tea

piteous [ˈpɪtɪəs] *adj Formal* penoso(a), patético(a)

piteously [ˈpɪtɪəslɪ] *adv Formal* lastimeramente

pitfall [ˈpɪtfɔːl] *n (danger)* peligro *m*, riesgo *m*; **he avoided the obvious pitfalls in the translation** evitó las trampas obvias de la traducción

pith [pɪθ] *n* **(a)** *(of citrus fruit)* piel *f* blanca **(b)** *(in plant stem)* médula *f* ▸▸ ***p. helmet*** *(for tropics)* salacot *m* **(c)** *(of argument, idea)* meollo *m* **(d)** *(force)* fuerza *f*, vigor *m*

pithead [ˈpɪthed] *n* bocamina *f* ▸▸ ***p. ballot*** = votación realizada a la entrada de la mina

pithily [ˈpɪθɪlɪ] *adv* concisamente, sucintamente

pithiness [ˈpɪθɪnɪs] *n* carácter *m* apropiado y conciso

pithy [ˈpɪθɪ] *adj* **(a)** *(style, story)* apropiado(a) y conciso(a) **(b)** *(plant stem)* meduloso(a)

pitiable [ˈpɪtɪəbəl] *adj* **(a)** *(arousing pity)* lastimero(a), miserable **(b)** *(deplorable)* lamentable, deplorable

pitiful [ˈpɪtɪfʊl] *adj* **(a)** *(arousing pity)* lastimoso(a); **it was a p. sight** fue una escena lastimosa **(b)** *(deplorable)* lamentable, deplorable; **they're paid a p. wage** reciben un sueldo *or* salario miserable

pitifully [ˈpɪtɪfʊlɪ] *adv* **(a)** *(arousing pity)* lastimosamente **(b)** *(deplorably)* deplorablemente, lamentablemente

pitiless [ˈpɪtɪlɪs] *adj* despiadado(a)

pitilessly [ˈpɪtɪlɪslɪ] *adv* despiadadamente

piton [ˈpiːtɒn] *n* pitón *m*

pit(t)a bread [ˈpɪtəbred] *n* pan *m* (de) pitta, = pan hindú sin levadura

pittance [ˈpɪtəns] *n* miseria *f*; **to work for a p.** trabajar por una miseria

pitted [ˈpɪtɪd] *adj* **(a)** *(skin, metal)* picado(a) **(b)** *(cherries, dates, olives)* sin hueso

pitter-patter = **pit-a-pat**

pituitary gland [pɪˈtjuːɪtərɪˈglænd] *n Anat* hipófisis *f inv*, glándula *f* pituitaria

pity [ˈpɪtɪ] **1** *n* **(a)** *(compassion)* piedad *f*, compasión *f*; **the sight moved him to p.** la escena hizo que se compadeciera; **to take** *or* **have p. (on sb)** apiadarse *or* compadecerse (de alguien); **to feel p. for sb** sentir compasión *or* pena por alguien; **to show no p.** no mostrar compasión; **out of p.** por compasión; **for p.'s sake!** ¡por el amor de Dios!
(b) *(misfortune)* **it's a p. that...** es una lástima *or* una pena que...; **it seems a p. not to finish the bottle** es una pena no terminar la botella; **what a p.!** ¡qué pena!, ¡qué lástima!; **more's the p.** por desgracia
2 *vt* compadecer; **they are greatly to be pitied** son dignos de compasión *or* lástima; **I p. you if she ever finds out!** si se llega a enterar, ¡te compadezco!

pitying [ˈpɪtɪɪŋ] *adj* **(a)** *(compassionate)* compasivo(a) **(b)** *(scathing)* mordaz, cáustico(a)

pityingly [ˈpɪtɪɪŋlɪ] *adv* compasivamente, con compasión

Pius [ˈpaɪəs] *pr n* **P. I/II** Pío I/II

pivot [ˈpɪvət] **1** *n* **(a)** *(of turning mechanism)* eje *m*, pivote *m* **(b)** *(key person)* eje *m*
2 *vi* **(a)** *(turning mechanism)* pivotar (**on** sobre); **p. on your left foot** gira sobre tu pie izquierdo **(b)** *(plan, plot)* girar (**on** *or* **around** en torno a); **his life pivots around his family** su vida gira en torno a su familia
3 *vt* hacer girar; **the platform is pivoted at the base to allow it to move** la plataforma gira en la base para permitir el movimiento

pivotal [ˈpɪvətəl] *adj* crucial

pixel [ˈpɪksəl] *n Comptr* píxel *m*

pixelated [ˈpɪksəleɪtɪd] *adj Comptr (image)* pixelado(a)

pixelize [ˈpɪksəlaɪz] *vt TV (to hide identity)* = preservar la identidad de una persona pixelando su rostro

pixie [ˈpɪksɪ] *n* duende *m* ▸▸ ***p. boots*** botas *fpl* de duende; ***p. hat*** sombrero *m* de duende

pixi(l)lated [ˈpɪksɪleɪtɪd] *adj US Fam (drunk) Esp, Méx* pedo *inv*, *Col* caído(a), *Méx* cuete, *RP* en pedo

pizazz = **pizzazz**

pizza [ˈpiːtsə] *n* pizza *f* ▸▸ ***p. base*** base *f* de pizza; *Fam Pej* ***p. face*** cara de paella *mf*, granudo(a) *m,f*; ***p. parlour*** pizzería *f*

piz(z)azz, pzazz [pɪˈzæz] *n Fam* vitalidad *f*, energía *f*

pizzeria [piːtsəˈrɪə] *n* pizzería *f*

pizzicato [pɪtsɪˈkɑːtəʊ] *Mus* **1** *adj* pizzicato
2 *adv* **this passage is played p.** este pasaje es un pizzicato

PJs [ˈpiːdʒeɪz] *npl Fam* pijama *m*, *Am* piyama *m or f*

Pk (*abbr* **Park**) parque *m*

pkg (*abbr* **package**) paquete *m*

pkt (*abbr* **packet**) paquete *m*

pkwy *US* (*abbr* **parkway**) = carretera o avenida con árboles a los lados y en el medio

Pl (*abbr* **Place**) C/

placard [ˈplækɑːd] **1** *n (carried)* pancarta *f*; *(on wall)* cartel *m*, letrero *m*
2 *vt* **(a)** *(wall, town)* cubrir con carteles, empapelar **(b)** *(advertise)* anunciar con carteles

placate [pləˈkeɪt] *vt* aplacar

placatory [pləˈkeɪtərɪ] *adj* apaciguador(ora)

PLACE [pleɪs] **1** *n* **(a)** *(location)* lugar *m*, sitio *m*; **to move from one p. to another** ir *or Am* andar de un lugar a otro; **a good p. to meet people** un buen sitio para conocer (a) gente; **I'm looking for a p. to live** estoy buscando casa; **can you recommend a p. to eat?** ¿me puedes recomendar un restaurante?; **the whole p. went up in flames** ardió todo; IDIOM *Fam* **to shout** *or* **scream the p. down** gritar como un/una loco(a); **this is no p. for you** éste no es lugar para ti; **this isn't the p. to discuss the matter** éste no es el lugar más indicado para hablar del tema; **I can't be in two places at once!** ¡no puedo estar en dos sitios a la vez!; **she has worked all over the p.** ha trabajado en mil sitios; **the paint went all over the p.** la pintura se esparció *or* desparramó por todas partes; *Fig* **his explanation was all over the p.** su explicación fue muy confusa *or Esp* liosa *or CSur* entreverada; *Fam* **my hair is all over the p.** tengo *or* llevo el pelo hecho un desastre; *Fam* **at the interview he was all over the p.** en la entrevista no dio pie con bola *or Esp* una a derechas; **the path is muddy in places** el camino tiene algunos tramos embarrados; **the movie was funny in places** la película tenía trozos divertidos; IDIOM **there's a time and a p. for everything** cada cosa a su tiempo; IDIOM **a p. in the sun** una posición privilegiada; IDIOM *Fam* **to go places** *(be successful)* llegar lejos; PROV **there's no p. like home** no hay nada como estar en casa ▸▸ ***p. of birth*** lugar *m* de nacimiento; ***p. of death*** lugar *m* de defunción; ***p. of interest*** lugar *m* de interés; ***p. kick*** *(in rugby)* puntapié *m* colocado; ***p. name*** topónimo *m*; ***p. of residence*** lugar *m* de residencia; ***p. of work*** lugar *m* de trabajo; ***p. of worship*** templo *m*

(**b**) *(in street names)* calle *f*

(**c**) *(position) (of person)* puesto *m*; *(of thing)* sitio *m*; *(at university, on course)* lugar *m*, *Esp* plaza *f*; **to find a p. for sb** *(job)* encontrar colocación *or* trabajo a alguien; **to get a p. at university** obtener un lugar *or Esp* una plaza en la universidad; **to keep one's p. (in the team)** mantener el puesto (en el equipo); **you have a special p. in my heart** ocupas un lugar muy especial en mi corazón; **such people have no p. in our party** en nuestro partido no hay sitio para gente así; **it is not my p. to comment** no me corresponde a mí hacer comentarios; *US* **in p.** *(run, jump)* en el sitio; **make sure that everything is in p.** asegúrate de que todo está en su sitio; **to hold sth in p.** sujetar algo; **the arrangements are all in p.** los preparativos están finalizados; **push the lever till it clicks into p.** empuja la palanca hasta que llegue a hacer clic; **in p. of** *(instead of)* en lugar de; **I went in his p.** fui en su lugar; **I don't know what I'd do in her p.** no sé lo que haría yo en su lugar; **put yourself in my p.** ponte en mi lugar; *also Fig* **out of p.** *(person, remark)* fuera de lugar; **he had lost his p.** *(in book)* había perdido la página por la que iba; **to take p.** tener lugar; **to take the p. of sth/sb** ocupar el lugar de algo/alguien; **nobody can take her p.** es irreemplazable; **she took her p. at the head of the organization** ocupó su lugar al frente de la organización; IDIOM **to put sb in their p.** poner a alguien en su sitio; IDIOM **everything fell** *or* **clicked into p.** *(I saw the light)* todo tenía lógica; *(everything went well)* todo salió a la perfección

(**d**) *(home)* casa *f*; *(business premises)* oficina *f*; *(restaurant)* restaurante *m*; **a little p. in the country** una casita en el campo; **your p. or mine?** ¿en tu casa o en la mía?

(**e**) *(seat)* sitio *m*, asiento *m*; **there are a few places left on the next flight** quedan algunas plazas en el próximo vuelo; **to keep** *or* **save sb's p. in a** *Br* **queue** *or US* **line** guardarle a alguien el lugar *or* sitio en una cola; **to set** *or* **lay an extra p. at table** poner un cubierto *or* servicio más en la mesa; **he showed us to our places** nos llevó a nuestros asientos *or Am* lugares; **please take your places** tomen asiento, por favor; **to change places with sb** cambiarle el sitio a alguien, cambiar de lugar con alguien; *Fig* cambiarse por alguien, ponerse en el lugar de alguien ▸▸ ***p. card*** tarjeta *f* con el nombre *(en banquete, recepción)*; ***p. mat*** mantel *m* individual; ***p. setting*** cubierto *m*

(**f**) *(in competition)* puesto *m*, lugar *m*; **to get** *or* **take second/third p.** *(in race)* llegar en segundo/tercer lugar; **her job always takes second p. to her family** su trabajo siempre ocupa un segundo plano con respecto a su familia; **in first/second p.** en primer/segundo lugar; **in the first/second p....** *(giving list)* en primer/segundo lugar...; **I don't know why they gave him the job in the first p.** no sé cómo se les ocurrió darle el trabajo

(**g**) *Math* **to three decimal places** con tres (cifras) decimales, *Am* hasta tres decimales

(**h**) *US (in adverbial phrases)* **no p.** ningún sitio; **I'm not going any p.** no voy a ningún sitio; **I've looked every p.** he mirado en todos los sitios

(**i**) *Br Parl* **in another p.** *(said in House of Commons)* en la Cámara Alta; *(said in House of Lords)* en la Cámara Baja

2 *vt* (**a**) *(put)* colocar, poner; **to p. an advertisement in a newspaper** poner un anuncio *or Am* aviso en un periódico; **to p. a bet (on sth)** hacer una apuesta (por algo); **p. your bets!** *(in casino)* ¡hagan juego!; **to p. a contract with sb** conceder un contrato a alguien; **to p. sb in a difficult position** poner a alguien en un compromiso; **to p. emphasis on sth** poner énfasis en algo; **to p. importance on sth** conceder importancia a algo; **to p. an order (with sb)** hacer un pedido (a alguien); **we p. your safety above** *or* **before all else** para nosotros su seguridad es lo primero; **to p. sb under pressure** presionar a alguien

(**b**) *(position)* **the house is well placed** la casa está bien situada *or Am* localizada; **to be well placed to do sth** estar en una buena posición *or* bien situado para hacer algo; **you are better placed to judge than I am** tú estás en una posición mejor para juzgarlo que yo; **how are you placed for money at the moment?** ¿cómo andas de dinero ahora?

(**c**) *(find a job for)* colocar

(**d**) *(classify)* situar, colocar; **he was placed third** se clasificó en tercer lugar; **the Broncos are currently placed second** los Broncos van actualmente en segundo lugar; **I would p. her amongst the best writers of our time** yo diría que está entre los mejores escritores de nuestra época; **to be placed** *(in horseracing)* llegar colocado(a), *RP* llegar placé

(**e**) *(identify)* **I know his face but I can't p. him** conozco su cara, pero no sé de qué *or* de dónde

(**f**) *Fin (shares)* colocar

3 *vi (in horseracing)* llegar colocado(a), *RP* llegar placé

---

placebo [plə'si:bəʊ] *(pl* **placebos***)* *n also Fig* placebo *m* ▸▸ ***p. effect*** efecto *m* placebo

placeman ['pleɪsmæn] *n Pej* arribista *mf*

placement ['pleɪsmənt] *n* (**a**) *(putting)* colocación *f* (**b**) *(for trainee, student)* colocación *f* en prácticas ▸▸ *US Educ* ***p. test*** examen *m* de nivel

placenta [plə'sentə] *(pl* **placentas** *or* **placentae** [plə'senti:]) *n* placenta *f*

placid ['plæsɪd] *adj* plácido(a)

placidity [plə'sɪdɪtɪ], **placidness** ['plæsɪdnɪs] *n* placidez *f*

placidly ['plæsɪdlɪ] *adv* plácidamente

placing ['pleɪsɪŋ] *n* (**a**) *(act of putting)* colocación *f* (**b**) *(situation, position)* ubicación *f*, posición *f*

plagiarism ['pleɪdʒərɪzəm] *n* plagio *m*

plagiarist ['pleɪdʒərɪst] *n* plagiario(a) *m,f*

plagiarize ['pleɪdʒəraɪz] **1** *vt* plagiar; **to p. sth from sb** plagiar algo de alguien

2 *vi* cometer plagio

plague [pleɪg] **1** *n* (**a**) *(disease)* peste *f* (**b**) *(of insects, frogs)* plaga *f*; *Fig* **there's been a p. of burglaries here recently** últimamente, los robos en casas en esta zona se han convertido en una plaga (**c**) IDIOMS **to avoid sb like the p.** huir de alguien como de la peste; *Literary* **a p. on both your houses!** ¡que la justicia no beneficie a nadie!

2 *vt* (**a**) *(of person)* molestar, fastidiar; **to p. sb with questions** asediar a alguien a *or* con preguntas

(**b**) *(annoy, afflict)* **this problem has been plaguing him for some time** este problema lleva fastidiándole un buen tiempo; **the project was plagued with technical difficulties** el proyecto estaba plagado de dificultades técnicas; **the region is plagued by floods** la región es asolada por las inundaciones

plaice [pleɪs] *(pl* **plaice***)* *n (fish)* solla *f*, platija *f*

plaid [plæd, pleɪd] **1** *n* (**a**) *(fabric)* tela *f* escocesa (**b**) *(worn over shoulder)* banda *f* escocesa de lana

2 *adj* escocés(esa), con cuadros escoceses

plain [pleɪn] **1** *n* (**a**) *(flat land)* llanura *f* ▸▸ *Hist* ***the Plains Indians*** los Indios de las Llanuras (**b**) *(in knitting)* punto *m* del derecho

2 *adj* (**a**) *(clear, unambiguous)* claro(a); **a p. answer** una respuesta directa *or* clara; **in p. English** en lenguaje llano; **I'll be quite p. with you** voy a ser claro con usted; **to make sth p. to sb** dejar claro algo a alguien; **he made it p. to us that he wasn't interested** nos dejó muy claro que no le interesaba; **to make oneself p.** explicarse, hablar claro; IDIOM *Fam* **it's as p. as the nose on your face** *or* **as a pikestaff** está más claro que el agua ▸▸ ***p. language*** lenguaje *m* llano; ***p. speaking*** franqueza *f*; ***the p. truth*** la verdad pura y simple

(**b**) *(not patterned, unmarked)* liso(a); **under p. cover, in a p. envelope** en un sobre liso; **p. paper** *(unheaded)* papel sin membrete; *(unruled)* papel liso

(**c**) *(simple, not fancy) (style, garment, food)* sencillo(a); **she was just p. Sally Walker then** en ese entonces era Sally Walker, a secas; **in p. clothes** *(policeman)* de paisano; IDIOM **it was p. sailing** fue pan comido ▸▸ ***p. man:*** **a p. man's guide to personal finance** una guía sobre las finanzas personales para la persona de la calle

(**d**) *(without added ingredients)* ***p. chocolate*** chocolate *m* amargo; ***p. flour*** harina *f* sin levadura; ***p. omelette*** tortilla *f* (a la) francesa

(**e**) *Fam (downright)* **that's just p. foolishness** es pura tontería

(**f**) *(not beautiful)* falto(a) de atractivo ▸▸ *Fam* ***a p. Jane*** un patito feo

(**g**) *(in knitting)* **one p., one purl** uno del derecho, uno del revés

3 *adv* (**a**) *(clearly)* claramente; **you couldn't have put it any plainer** no podías haberlo dejado más claro (**b**) *US Fam (utterly)* totalmente, completamente; **I just p. forgot!** ¡me olvidé por completo!

plainchant ['pleɪntʃɑ:nt] *n Mus* canto *m* llano

plain-clothed ['pleɪnkləʊðd], **plain-clothes** ['pleɪnkləʊðz] *adj (police)* de paisano

plainclothesman [pleɪn'kləʊðzmən] *n US* policía *m* de paisano

plainly ['pleɪnlɪ] *adv* (**a**) *(in a clear manner)* claramente; **to speak p.** hablar con franqueza (**b**) *(distinctly) (to remember, hear)* claramente, con claridad (**c**) *(simply) (to live, dress)* con sencillez (**d**) *(obviously)* claramente; **p., that won't be possible now** está claro que eso ya no va a ser posible

plainness ['pleɪnnɪs] *n* (**a**) *(of style, expression, food)* sencillez *f* (**b**) *(of looks)* falta *f* de atractivo

plain-paper ['pleɪn'peɪpə(r)] *adj (fax, printer)* de papel común
plainsman ['pleɪnzmən] *n* habitante *m* de la llanura
plainsong ['pleɪnsɒŋ] *n Mus* canto *m* llano
plain-spoken ['pleɪn'spəʊkən] *adj* franco(a), directo(a)
plaintiff ['pleɪntɪf] *n Law* demandante *mf*
plaintive ['pleɪntɪv] *adj* lastimero(a)
plaintively ['pleɪntɪvlɪ] *adv* lastimosamente
plait [plæt] **1** *n* (**a**) *(of hair, ribbon, straw)* trenza *f* (**b**) *Br (loaf)* pan *m* en forma de trenza
2 *vt* trenzar
plaited ['plætɪd] *adj (hair)* trenzado(a); **p. loaf** pan en forma de trenza
plan [plæn] **1** *n* (**a**) *(proposal, intention)* plan *m*; **I've thought of a p.** tengo un plan; **a change of p.** un cambio de planes; **everything went according to p.** todo fue según lo previsto; **the best p. would be to...** lo mejor sería...; **the p. is to meet up at John's** la idea es encontrarnos en casa de John; **what are your plans for the summer?** ¿qué planes tienes para el verano?; **to have other plans** tener otras cosas que hacer; **to draw up** *or* **make a p.** hacer un plan; **to make plans** hacer planes; **we had made plans to stay at a hotel** habíamos hecho planes de quedarnos en el hotel; **to put a p. into effect** *or* **operation** poner un plan en marcha; IDIOM **we'll have to try** *or* **use p. B** tendremos que intentar recurrir al plan B ►► ***p. of action*** plan *m* de acción
(**b**) *(diagram, map) (of building, town)* plano *m*; **I'll draw you a p. of the office** te haré un mapa *or* croquis de la oficina
(**c**) *(outline) (of essay, book)* esquema *m*
2 *vt (pt & pp* **planned**) (**a**) *(arrange)* planear, planificar; **p. your time carefully** planifica bien tu tiempo; **they're planning a surprise for you** te están preparando una sorpresa; **the Pope's visit is planned for March** la visita del Papa está prevista para marzo; **it all went as planned** todo fue según lo previsto
(**b**) *(intend)* planear; **to p. to do sth** planear hacer algo
(**c**) *(design) (building, town)* proyectar; *(economy)* planificar; *(essay, book, lesson)* preparar
3 *vi* hacer planes; **to p. ahead** hacer planes con anticipación
► **plan for** *vt insep* planear, planificar; **to p. for the future** hacer planes para el futuro; **we didn't p. for this many people** no previmos tanta gente; **you can't p. for every eventuality** es imposible prever todas las eventualidades
► **plan on** *vt insep* (**a**) *(intend)* planear, pensar; **I'm not planning on doing anything tonight** no tengo nada planeado para esta noche (**b**) *(expect)* planear; **we hadn't planned on it raining** no habíamos contado con que lloviera; **don't p. on it** no cuentes con ello; **I'm planning on it** cuento con ello
► **plan out** *vt sep* planificar
planar ['pleɪnə(r)] *adj Geom* del plano
Planck's constant ['plæŋks'kɒnstənt] *n Phys* constante *f* de Planck
plane[1] [pleɪn] *n* (**a**) *Archit, Art & Geom (surface)* plano *m*; **vertical/horizontal p.** plano vertical/horizontal ►► *Geom* ***p. angle*** ángulo *m* plano *or* rectilíneo (**b**) *(level, degree)* nivel *m*; **she's on a different p. (from the rest of us)** está a un nivel superior (al nuestro)
plane[2] **1** *n (aircraft)* avión *m*; **by p.** en avión; **on the p.** en el avión; **it's just a short p. ride** es un viaje muy corto en avión ►► ***p. crash*** accidente *m* de aviación *or* aéreo; ***p. ticket*** *Esp* billete *m or Am* boleto *m or Am* pasaje *m* de avión
2 *vt (transport by plane)* transportar en avión
3 *vi (glide)* planear
plane[3] **1** *n (tool)* cepillo *m*
2 *vt* cepillar
► **plane down** *vt sep* aplanar *(con cepillo)*
► **plane off** *vt sep* alisar *(con cepillo)*
plane[4] *n* **p. (tree)** plátano *m*
planet ['plænɪt] *n* planeta *m*; *Fam* **he's on a different p.** está tocado del ala
planetarium [plænɪ'teərɪəm] *(pl* **planetariums** *or* **planetaria** [plænɪ'teərɪə]) *n* planetario *m*
planetary ['plænɪtərɪ] *adj* (**a**) *(motion, orbit)* planetario(a) (**b**) *Tech (gear)* planetario(a)
plangent ['plændʒənt] *adj Literary* (**a**) *(ringing)* plañidero(a), quejumbroso(a) (**b**) *(sad)* triste, consternado(a)
plank [plæŋk] *n* (**a**) *(of wood)* tablón *m*; **to walk the p.** = caminar por un tablón colocado sobre la borda hasta caer al mar (**b**) *(central element)* punto *m* central
► **plank down** *vt sep (put down heavily)* dejar caer pesadamente
planking ['plæŋkɪŋ] *n* entablado *m*, entarimado *m*
plankton ['plæŋktən] *n* plancton *m*
planned [plænd] *adj* (**a**) *(intended)* planeado(a); **news of the p. sale was leaked to the press** la noticia de la venta que se planeaba se filtró a la prensa (**b**) *Econ* ***p. economy*** economía *f* planificada; *Com* ***p. obsolescence*** depreciación *f or* obsolescencia *f* prevista
planner ['plænə(r)] *n* (**a**) *(of project, scheme)* encargado(a) *m,f* de la planificación (**b**) *(town planner)* urbanista *mf* (**c**) *(in diary, on wall)* organizador *m* de actividades
planning ['plænɪŋ] *n* (**a**) *(of project, scheme)* planificación *f*; **it's still at the p. stage** aún está en fase de estudio (**b**) *(town planning)* urbanismo *m* ►► *Br* ***p. permission*** licencia *f* de obras
plant [plɑːnt] **1** *n* (**a**) *(living thing)* planta *f* ►► ***p. food*** alimento *m* para plantas; ***p. life*** flora *f*; ***p. pot*** maceta *f*, tiesto *m*
(**b**) *Ind (equipment)* maquinaria *f*; *(factory)* fábrica *f*, planta *f* ►► ***p. hire*** alquiler *m* de equipo; ***p. maintenance*** mantenimiento *m* de la planta
(**c**) *Fam (person) (in audience)* compinche *m*; *(undercover agent)* topo *m*
(**d**) *Fam (false evidence)* **the drugs found in his house were a p.** habían colocado las drogas en su casa para incriminarle
(**e**) *(in snooker, pool)* tiro *m* combinado, combinación *f*
2 *vt* (**a**) *(tree, flower)* plantar; *(crops, field)* sembrar (**with** con); **to p. an idea/a doubt in sb's mind** inculcar una idea/sembrar(le) una duda a alguien
(**b**) *(place) (bomb)* colocar; *Fam* **the police planted the evidence (on him)** la policía colocó (en él) las pruebas que lo incriminaban
(**c**) *Fam (place firmly)* **she planted herself in the doorway** se plantó en la entrada
(**d**) *Br (offload)* **don't try and p. the blame on me!** ¡no intentes cargarme con la culpa!, ¡no intentes echarme la culpa a mí!; **they planted their kids on us for the weekend** nos encajaron a sus hijos todo el fin de semana
(**e**) *Fam (give) (punch, kiss)* dar, plantar
► **plant out** *vt sep* trasplantar
plantain ['plæntɪn] *n* (**a**) *(wild plant)* llantén *m* (**b**) *(similar to banana) (fruit)* plátano *m*, *RP* banana *f*; *(tree)* platanero *m*
plantation [plæn'teɪʃən] *n* (**a**) *(estate)* plantación *f* (**b**) *Hist (colony)* colonia *f*, asentamiento *m*
planter ['plɑːntə(r)] *n* (**a**) *(person)* plantador(ora) *m,f* ►► ***p.'s punch*** = ponche de ron y frutas con hielo molido (**b**) *(machine)* sembradora *f* (**c**) *(flowerpot holder)* macetero *m*
plaque [plæk] *n* (**a**) *(bronze, marble)* placa *f* (**b**) *(on teeth)* placa *f* dental, placa *f* bacteriana
plash [plæʃ] *Literary* **1** *n* salpicadura *f*
2 *vi* salpicar
plasma ['plæzmə] *n* (**a**) *Med* plasma *m* (**b**) *Phys* plasma *m* ►► *Comptr* ***p. display*** pantalla *f* de plasma; *Comptr* ***p. screen*** pantalla *f* de plasma; ***p. TV*** televisor *m* con pantalla de plasma
plaster ['plɑːstə(r)] **1** *n* (**a**) *(on wall, ceiling)* yeso *m*, enlucido *m* (**b**) *(for plaster casts)* **to put a leg in p.** escayolar una pierna ►► ***p. cast*** escayola *f*; ***p. of Paris*** escayola *f*; *Fig* ***p. saint*** mojigato(a) *m,f* (**c**) *Br* **(sticking) p.** tirita *f*, *Am* curita *f*
2 *vt* (**a**) *(wall)* enyesar, enlucir
(**b**) *(cover)* cubrir (**with** de); **plastered with mud** embarrado(a), cubierto(a) de barro; **she had plastered make-up on her face, her face was plastered with make-up** tenía la cara llena de maquillaje; **his name was plastered over the front pages** su nombre aparecía en los titulares *or Méx, RP* encabezados de todas las portadas
(**c**) *(make stick)* pegar; **he tried to p. his hair down with oil** intentó aplastar su pelo con gomina
(**d**) *Fam (defeat heavily)* aplastar, darle una paliza a
► **plaster over, plaster up** *vt sep (hole, crack)* rellenar con yeso
plasterboard ['plɑːstəbɔːd] *n* pladur® *m*
plastered ['plæstəd] *adj Fam (drunk)* trompa; **to be/get p.** estar/ponerse trompa
plasterer ['plɑːstərə(r)] *n* enlucidor(ora) *m,f*, enyesador(ora) *m,f*
plastering ['plɑːstərɪŋ] *n* enlucido *m*, enyesado *m*
plasterwork ['plɑːstəwɜːk] *n* enlucido *m*, enyesado *m*
plastic ['plæstɪk] **1** *n* (**a**) *(material)* plástico *m* (**b**) *Fam (credit cards)* plástico *m*; **to put sth on the p.** comprar algo con tarjeta de crédito; **do you take p.?** ¿se puede pagar con plástico?
2 *adj* (**a**) *(bag)* de plástico ►► ***p. bullet*** bala *f* de plástico; ***p. cup*** vaso *m* de plástico; ***p. explosive*** (explosivo *m*) plástico *m*; ***p. wrap*** plástico *m* transparente *(para envolver alimentos)*
(**b**) *(malleable)* plástico(a), maleable
(**c**) *Art* ***p. arts*** artes *fpl* plásticas

(**d**) *Med* ***p. surgeon*** cirujano(a) *m,f* plástico(a); ***p. surgery*** cirugía *f* plástica; **she had p. surgery on her nose** se hizo la (cirugía) plástica en la nariz

(**e**) *Fam Pej (artificial)* de plástico; **the p. rubbish they call bread** esa basura de plástico que llaman pan

Plasticine® ['plæstɪsi:n] *n* plastilina® *f*

plasticity [plæs'tɪsɪtɪ] *n (of material)* plasticidad *f*; *Fig (of mind)* ductilidad *f*, adaptabilidad *f*

plate [pleɪt] **1** *n* (**a**) *(for food)* plato *m*; **he ate a huge p. of spaghetti** se comió un plato enorme de espaguetis; IDIOM *Fam* **she's got a lot on her p.** tiene un montón de cosas entre manos; IDIOM *Fam* **to hand sth to sb on a p.** poner algo en bandeja a alguien ►► ***p. rack*** escurreplatos *m inv*

(**b**) *(for church offering)* platillo *m*

(**c**) *(sheet of metal, glass, plastic)* placa *f*; **he has a metal p. in his thigh** tiene una placa de metal en el muslo ►► ***p. glass*** vidrio *m* para cristaleras

(**d**) *(on car)* matrícula *f*, placa *f*

(**e**) *(on cooker)* plato *m*

(**f**) *Typ (for printing, engraving)* plancha *f*; *(illustration)* lámina *f*, ilustración *f*

(**g**) *Phot* placa *f*

(**h**) *Geol* placa *f* ►► ***p. tectonics*** tectónica *f* de placas

(**i**) *(dishes, cutlery)* vajilla *f*

(**j**) *(coating)* **gold p.** oro chapado; **silver p.** plata chapada

(**k**) *(denture)* dentadura *f* postiza

(**l**) *(in baseball) (for batter)* base *f* meta; IDIOM *US* **to step up to the p.** dar la cara

2 *vt (with gold)* dorar; *(with silver)* platear; *(with metal plates)* enchapar; *(with armour plate)* blindar

plateau ['plætəʊ] *n Geog* meseta *f*; *Fig* **to reach a p.** *(career, economy)* estabilizarse

plateful ['pleɪtfʊl] *n* plato *m*; **to eat sth by the p.** comer platos de algo

plate-glass ['pleɪt'glɑ:s] *adj* de vidrio en planchas

platelet ['pleɪtlət] *n Biol* plaqueta *f*

platen ['plætən] *n* (**a**) *(of typewriter)* rodillo *m* (**b**) *(of printing press)* platina *f* (**c**) *(of machine tool)* mesa *f*, placa *f* gruesa

platform ['plætfɔ:m] *n* (**a**) *(raised flat surface)* plataforma *f*; **(oil) p.** plataforma *f* petrolífera ►► *Comptr* ***p. game*** juego *m* de plataformas; ***p. shoes*** zapatos *mpl* de plataforma; ***p. soles*** suelas *fpl* de plataforma

(**b**) *(at train station)* andén *m*; *(track)* vía *f*; **the train at p. 4** el tren en la vía 4

(**c**) *(at meeting)* tribuna *f*; *Fig (place to express one's views)* plataforma *f*; **she refused to share a p. with her rival** se negó a compartir una plataforma con su rival

(**d**) *Br (on bus)* plataforma *f*

(**e**) *(political programme)* programa *m*

(**f**) *Comptr* plataforma *f*

platform-independent ['plætfɔ:mɪndɪ'pendənt] *adj Comptr* que funciona en cualquier plataforma

platform-soled ['plætfɔ:m'səʊld] *adj* con plataforma

plating ['pleɪtɪŋ] *n* (**a**) *(protective)* blindaje *m* (**b**) *(coating with metal) (in gold, silver)* enchapado *m*

platinum ['plætɪnəm] *n* (**a**) *Chem* platino *m* (**b**) *Mus* **to go p.** *(album) (in Britain)* vender más de 300.000 copias; *(in US)* vender más de 1.000.000 copias ►► ***p. disc*** disco *m* de platino (**c**) *(colour)* platino *m* ►► ***p. blonde*** rubia *f* platino

platinum-blond(e) ['plætɪnəm'blɒnd] *adj* rubio(a) platinado(a) *or* platino; **p. hair** pelo rubio platino

platitude ['plætɪtju:d] *n* tópico *m*, trivialidad *f*

platitudinous [plætɪ'tju:dɪnəs] *adj Formal* de Perogrullo

Plato ['pleɪtəʊ] *pr n* Platón

platonic [plə'tɒnɪk] *adj* (**a**) *Phil* **P.** platónico(a) (**b**) *(love, relationship)* platónico(a)

Platonism ['pleɪtənɪzəm] *n Phil* platonismo *m*

Platonist ['pleɪtənɪst] *n* platonista *mf*

platoon [plə'tu:n] *n Mil* sección *f*

platter ['plætə(r)] *n* (**a**) *(serving plate)* fuente *f* (**b**) *(on menu)* **salad/seafood p.** fuente de ensalada/marisco (**c**) *US Fam* plástico *m*, disco *m*

platypus ['plætɪpəs] *n* ornitorrinco *m*

plaudits ['plɔ:dɪts] *npl Formal* aplausos *mpl*, alabanzas *fpl*

plausibility [plɔ:zɪ'bɪlɪtɪ] *n* plausibilidad *f*; **the plot is lacking in p.** el argumento carece de credibilidad

plausible ['plɔ:zəbəl] *adj (excuse, argument)* plausible; **he's a very p. liar** sus mentiras son muy convincentes

plausibly ['plɔ:zɪblɪ] *adv* plausiblemente; **he argued his case very p.** defendió su caso muy plausiblemente

PLAY [pleɪ] **1** *n* (**a**) *(drama)* obra *f* (de teatro); **to be in a p.** actuar en una obra; **a radio/television p.** una obra para la radio/televisión

(**b**) *(recreation)* juego *m*; **we don't get much time for p.** no nos queda mucho tiempo para jugar; **at p.** jugando; IDIOM **to make great p. of sth** sacarle mucho jugo a algo ►► ***p. on words*** juego *m* de palabras

(**c**) *(in sport) (move)* juego *m*, jugada *f*; **p. began at one o'clock** el juego comenzó a la una; **that was great p. by France** ha sido una gran jugada de Francia; **a set p.** una jugada preparada; **an offensive p.** *(in American football)* una jugada ofensiva; **in p.** en juego; **out of p.** fuera del campo; IDIOM **to come** *or* **be brought into p.** entrar en juego; IDIOM **to make a p. for sth** tratar de conseguir algo; IDIOM **to make a p. for sb** tirar los tejos a alguien

(**d**) *(activity, interaction)* **the result of a complex p. of forces** el resultado de una compleja interacción de fuerzas; **I like the p. of light and shadow in his photographs** me gusta el juego de luces y sombras en sus fotografías

(**e**) *Fam (attention, interest)* **her speech is getting a lot of p. in the media** se está hablando mucho de su discurso en los medios

(**f**) *Tech* juego *m*; *Fig* **to give** *or* **allow sth full p.** dar rienda suelta a algo

2 *vt* (**a**) *(match)* jugar; *(sport, game)* jugar a; *(opponent)* jugar contra; **to p. tennis/chess** jugar al tenis/ajedrez; **to p. sb at sth** jugar contra alguien a algo; **to p. centre forward** jugar de delantero centro *or Am* centro delantero *or Am* centro forward; **to p. a card** jugar una carta; **she played her ace** sacó el as; *Fig* jugó su mejor baza; **to p. a shot** *(in snooker, pool)* dar un golpe, hacer un tiro; **he decided not to p. Sanders** decidió no sacar a Sanders; **fifteen points plays twenty** quince a veinte; **to p. the ball back to the keeper/into the box** retrasar la pelota al portero *or Am* arquero/al área; **to p. ball (with sb)** *(cooperate)* cooperar (con alguien); IDIOM **to p. the field: he knew that if he got married he'd have to stop playing the field** sabía que si se casaba tendría que dejar de acostarse con quien quisiera; IDIOM **p. your cards right and you could get promoted** si juegas bien tus cartas, puedes conseguir un ascenso

(**b**) *(of children) (game)* jugar; **to p. doctors and nurses** jugar a médicos y enfermeras, *Am* jugar a los doctores; **to p. a joke** *or* **a trick on sb** gastarle *or RP* hacerle una broma a alguien; IDIOM **to p. the game** jugar limpio; IDIOM **stop playing games!** ¡basta ya de juegos!; IDIOM **my eyes must be playing tricks on me** debo estar viendo visiones

(**c**) *(in play, movie)* interpretar; **to p. Macbeth** interpretar a Macbeth; **to p. it cool** aparentar calma; *Fig* **to p. it straight** jugar limpio; *Fig* **to p. the fool** hacer el tonto; *Fig* **to p. God** hacer de Dios; **don't p. the innocent with me!** ¡no te hagas el tonto conmigo!; *Fig* **to p. an important part (in sth)** desempeñar un papel importante (en algo); *Fig* **to p. no part in sth** *(person)* no tomar parte en algo; *(thing, feeling)* no tener nada que ver con algo

(**d**) *(perform at)* actuar en; **they played Broadway last year** actuaron en Broadway el año pasado

(**e**) *(musical instrument, note, piece)* tocar; *(record, CD, tape)* poner; **this station plays mainly rock** esta emisora pone *or RP* pasa sobre todo rock

(**f**) *(speculate on)* **to p. the Stock Exchange** jugar a la bolsa

(**g**) *(direct) (beam, nozzle)* dirigir; **he played his torch over the cave walls** paseó la linterna por los muros de la cueva

3 *vi* (**a**) *(children)* jugar; *(animals)* retozar; **to p. with sth** *(pen, hair, food)* juguetear con algo; **to p. with an idea** darle vueltas a una idea; **we have $500/two days to p. with** tenemos 500 dólares/dos días a nuestra disposición; *Euph* **to p. with oneself** *(masturbate)* tocarse; IDIOM **to p. with fire** jugar con fuego

(**b**) *(sportsperson)* jugar; *also Fig* **to p. fair/dirty** jugar limpio/sucio; **he plays at quarterback** juega de quarterback; **can't you see he's just playing with you?** ¿no ves que está jugando contigo?; **to p. against sb** jugar contra alguien; **she plays for the Jets** juega en los Jets; **to p. for money** jugar por dinero; *Fig* **to p. safe** ir a lo seguro, no arriesgarse; IDIOM **to p. for time** intentar ganar tiempo; IDIOM **to p. into sb's hands** hacerle el juego a alguien, facilitarle las cosas a alguien

(**c**) *(musical instrument)* sonar; *(musician)* tocar; **I heard a guitar playing** oía tocar una guitarra; **the stereo/radio was playing full blast** el estéreo/la radio sonaba a todo volumen

(**d**) *(actor)* actuar; *(pop group)* tocar; *(movie)* exhibirse; *(play)* representarse; **the show played to a full house** el espectáculo se representó en una sala abarrotada; **what's playing at the Odeon?** ¿qué ponen en el Odeon?; **to p. dead** hacerse el muerto; IDIOM **to p. hard to get** hacerse de rogar, hacerse el difícil (**e**) *(move) (sunlight)* reverberar (**on** *or* **over** en *or* sobre); **a smile played across** *or* **on** *or* **over his lips** en sus labios se dibujó una sonrisa

▸ **play about, play around** *vi (mess about)* juguetear, jugar; **stop playing about** *or* **around!** ¡deja de enredar!; **to p. around with an idea/a possibility** dar vueltas a una idea/una posibilidad; *Fam* **he's been playing around with another woman** ha tenido un lío con otra mujer

▸ **play along** *vi* seguir la corriente (**with** a)

▸ **play at** *vt insep* (**a**) *(of children)* **to p. at doctors and nurses** jugar a médicos y enfermeras; *Fam Fig* **what's she playing at?** ¿a qué juega? (**b**) *(dabble at)* **he's only playing at being a poet** sólo juega a ser poeta

▸ **play back** *vt sep* **to p. back a recording** reproducir una grabación

▸ **play down** *vt sep* restar importancia a

▸ **play off** 1 *vt sep* **she played her two enemies off against each other** enfrentó a sus dos enemigos entre sí
2 *vi Sport* **the two teams will p. off for third place** los dos equipos disputarán un partido por el tercer puesto

▸ **play on** 1 *vt insep (exploit) (feelings, fears)* aprovecharse de; **the waiting began to p. on my nerves** la espera me empezó a afectar los nervios
2 *vi (continue to play) (musician)* seguir tocando; *(sportsperson)* seguir jugando

▸ **play out** *vt sep* (**a**) *(act out) (one's fantasies)* hacer real; **the drama being played out before them** el drama que se desarrolla ante sus ojos (**b**) *(use up)* **Finland played out the last ten minutes** Finlandia dejó pasar el tiempo durante los últimos diez minutos; **to be (all) played out** estar agotado(a) *or* exhausto(a)

▸ **play up** 1 *vt sep (exaggerate)* exagerar
2 *vi* (**a**) *Br Fam (car, child, injury)* dar guerra (**b**) *Pej* **to p. up to sb** *(flatter)* adular a alguien

---

playable ['pleɪəbəl] *adj* (**a**) *(pitch, surface)* en condiciones para jugar; *(golf ball)* en condiciones de ser golpeada (**b**) *(game)* **a very p. computer game** un juego de *Esp* ordenador *or Am* computadora que se disfruta jugando

play-act ['pleɪækt] *vi (pretend, act frivolously)* hacer teatro

play-acting ['pleɪæktɪŋ] *n* teatro *m*, cuento *m*

playback ['pleɪbæk] *n* reproducción *f* ▸▸ ***p. head*** cabeza *f* reproductora

playbill ['pleɪbɪl] *n Theat* cartel *m or Am* afiche *m* anunciador

playboy ['pleɪbɔɪ] *n* vividor *m*, playboy *m*

play-by-play ['pleɪbaɪ'pleɪ] *adj* (**a**) *(commentary)* jugada a jugada (**b**) *(detailed)* pormenorizado(a)

Play-Doh® ['pleɪdəʊ] *n* = pasta de modelar

player ['pleɪə(r)] *n* (**a**) *(of game, sport)* jugador(ora) *m,f*; **are you a bridge/poker p.?** ¿juegas al bridge/al póker?
(**b**) *(musician)* intérprete *mf*; **she's a gifted piano/guitar p.** es una pianista/guitarrista con talento ▸▸ ***p. piano*** pianola *f*
(**c**) *Old-fashioned (actor)* actor *m*, actriz *f*, intérprete *mf*
(**d**) *Fig (influential person, company)* principal protagonista *mf*; **the major players in the bond market** los principales protagonistas en el mercado de los bonos

playfellow ['pleɪfeləʊ] *n Old-fashioned* compañero(a) *m,f* de juego

playful ['pleɪfʊl] *adj* (**a**) *(person, animal)* juguetón(ona); **to be in a p. mood** estar con ganas de jugar (**b**) *(remark, suggestion)* de *or* en broma

playfully ['pleɪfʊlɪ] *adv* (**a**) *(to smile, push)* juguetonamente (**b**) *(to remark, suggest)* en broma

playfulness ['pleɪfʊlnɪs] *n (of smile, remark, suggestion)* carácter *m* juguetón

playgoer ['pleɪgəʊə(r)] *n* asistente *mf* a una obra de teatro

playground ['pleɪgraʊnd] *n* (**a**) *(at school)* patio *m* de recreo (**b**) *(in park)* parque *m* infantil; *Fig* **the islands are a p. for the rich** las islas son el lugar de diversión de los ricos

playgroup ['pleɪgruːp] *n* escuela *f* infantil, guardería *f*

playhouse ['pleɪhaʊs] *n* (**a**) *(theatre)* teatro *m* (**b**) *(for children)* = casita de juguete del tamaño de un niño

playing ['pleɪɪŋ] *n* **the pianist's p. was excellent** la actuación del pianista fue excelente ▸▸ ***p. card*** carta *f*, naipe *m*; ***p. field*** campo *m* de juego

playlet ['pleɪlɪt] *n* obra *f* breve

playlist ['pleɪlɪst] *n Rad* = lista predeterminada de canciones que se emite en un programa de radio

playmaker ['pleɪmeɪkə(r)] *n Sport* creador *m* de juego

playmate ['pleɪmeɪt] *n* compañero(a) *m,f* de juegos

play-off ['pleɪɒf] *n Sport* (**a**) *(single game)* (partido *m* de) desempate *m* (**b**) *(series of games)* play-off *m*

playpen ['pleɪpen] *n* parque *m*, corral *m*

playroom ['pleɪruːm] *n* cuarto *m* de juegos

playschool ['pleɪskuːl] *n Br* escuela *f* infantil, guardería *f*

plaything ['pleɪθɪŋ] *n also Fig* juguete *m*

playtime ['pleɪtaɪm] *n (at school)* recreo *m*; **at p.** en el recreo

playwright ['pleɪraɪt] *n* dramaturgo(a) *m,f*, autor(ora) *m,f* teatral

plaza ['plɑːzə] *n US (shopping centre)* centro *m* comercial

PLC, plc [piːel'siː] *n Br Com* (*abbr* **public limited company**) ≃ S.A.

plea [pliː] *n* (**a**) *(appeal)* petición *f*, súplica *f*, *Am* pedido *m*; **they ignored his pleas for help** ignoraron su petición de auxilio; **to make a p. for sth** suplicar algo
(**b**) *(excuse)* excusa *f*; **his p. of ill health didn't fool anyone** no engañó a nadie con la excusa de que estaba enfermo; **on the p. that...** alegando que...
(**c**) *Law* declaración *f*; **to enter a p. of guilty/not guilty** declararse culpable/inocente ▸▸ *US* ***p. bargaining*** = negociación extrajudicial entre el abogado y el fiscal por la que el acusado se declara culpable de un delito menos grave

plead [pliːd] (*US, Scot pt & pp* **pled**) 1 *vt* (**a**) *(beg)* suplicar, implorar; **"please let me go," he pleaded** "por favor, déjenme ir", suplicó *or* imploró
(**b**) *Law* **to p. sb's case** *(lawyer)* defender a alguien; *Fig* **who will p. our cause to the government?** ¿quién defenderá nuestra causa ante el gobierno?; **to p. insanity/self-defence** alegar demencia/defensa propia
(**c**) *(give as excuse)* **to p. ignorance** alegar desconocimiento; **she pleaded a prior engagement** alegó tener un compromiso previo
2 *vi* (**a**) *(appeal, beg)* suplicar, implorar; **to p. for forgiveness** suplicar *or* implorar perdón; **to p. with sb (to do sth)** implorar a alguien (que haga algo); **he pleaded with them for more time** les imploró que le concedieran más tiempo
(**b**) *Law* **how do you p.?** ¿cómo se declara?; **to p. guilty/not guilty** declararse culpable/inocente; **he pleaded guilty to the charge of theft** se declaró culpable del cargo de robo

> En inglés culto o elevado, y especialmente en inglés americano, **plead** puede ir seguido de **that** más un verbo en subjuntivo (ver el panel SUBJUNCTIVE):
> **he pleaded that they be given more time**
> *imploró que les concedieran más tiempo*
> Lo mismo también podría decirse del siguiente modo:
> **he pleaded that they should be given more time**

pleading ['pliːdɪŋ] 1 *n* (**a**) *(entreaty)* ruegos *mpl*, súplicas *fpl* (**b**) *Law* **pleadings** alegatos *mpl*, alegaciones *fpl*
2 *adj* suplicante

pleadingly ['pliːdɪŋlɪ] *adv (to look, ask)* suplicantemente

pleasant ['plezənt] *adj* (**a**) *(enjoyable) (place, weather)* agradable; *(surprise)* grato(a), agradable; **thank you for a most p. evening** les agradecemos mucho una velada tan agradable; **the account of the trial does not make p. reading** la lectura de los detalles del juicio no es muy agradable; **p. dreams!** ¡felices sueños!
(**b**) *(friendly) (person, attitude, smile)* agradable, simpático(a); **she was always very p. to us** con nosotros siempre fue muy simpática

pleasantly ['plezəntlɪ] *adv* (**a**) *(attractively)* de forma agradable *or* atractiva; **the room was p. arranged** la sala estaba arreglada de una forma muy agradable (**b**) *(enjoyably)* placenteramente, agradablemente; **to be p. surprised** estar gratamente sorprendido(a) (**c**) *(in a friendly way) (to smile, behave)* con simpatía

pleasantness ['plezəntnɪs] *n* (**a**) *(attractiveness)* atractivo *m* (**b**) *(enjoyableness)* amenidad *f*, lo placentero (**c**) *(friendliness)* simpatía *f*

pleasantry ['plezəntrɪ] *n* (**a**) *(joke)* comentario *m* gracioso (**b**) *(polite remarks)* **to exchange pleasantries** intercambiar cumplidos

---

PLEASE [pliːz] 1 *adv* por favor; **could you pass the salt, p.?** ¿me pasas la sal, por favor?; **p. don't cry** no llores, por favor; **p. don't interrupt!** ¡no interrumpas!; **p. sit down** tome asiento, por favor; **p. tell me...** dime..., *RP* decime...; **p. let them arrive safely!** ¡por favor, que lleguen sanos y salvos!; **will you p. be quiet!** ¡te quieres callar de una vez!, ¡cállate de una vez!; **p., Miss, I know!** ¡señorita?, ¡yo lo sé!; **may I? – p. do** ¿puedo? – por favor *or* no faltaba más; **(yes,) p.!** ¡sí!; **(oh) p.!** *(in indignation, disgust)* ¡habrase visto!
2 *vt (give pleasure to)* complacer, agradar; **you can't p. everybody**

no se puede complacer a todo el mundo; **to be easy/hard to p.** ser fácil/difícil de complacer; **p. God!** ¡ojalá!; **we pleased ourselves** hicimos lo que nos dio la gana; **p. yourself!** ¡como quieras!

3 *vi* (a) *(like)* **he does as he pleases** hace lo que quiere; **do as you p.** haz lo que quieras; **in she walked, as cool as you p.** entró como quien no quiere la cosa; **this way, if you p.** por aquí, por favor; **and then, if you p., he blamed me for it!** ¡y luego, por si fuera poco, me echó la culpa a mí!

(b) *(give pleasure)* agradar, complacer; **we aim to p.** nuestro objetivo es su satisfacción; **to be eager to p.** estar ansioso(a) por agradar

4 *n* **without so much as a p. or thank you** sin ni tan siquiera dar las gracias

---

pleased [pli:zd] *adj (happy)* contento(a); **to be p. (at** *or* **about sth)** estar contento(a) (por algo); **to be p. with sth/sb** *(satisfied)* estar satisfecho(a) *or* contento(a) con algo/alguien; **to be p. to do sth** alegrarse de hacer algo; **she would be only too p. to help us** le encantaría ayudarnos; *Formal* **Mr and Mrs Adams are p. to announce...** el Sr. y la Sra. Adams se complacen en anunciar...; **to be p. for sb** alegrarse por alguien; **they were none too p. when I told them** cuando se lo conté no les hizo ninguna gracia; **he's very p. with himself** está muy satisfecho *or* pagado de sí mismo; **p. to meet you** encantado(a) (de conocerle); **I'm p. to say that...** tengo el gusto de comunicarles que...; IDIOM **he was as p. as Punch** estaba encantado de la vida

pleasing ['pli:zɪŋ] *adj* agradable, grato(a); **the news of his engagement was p. to his parents** su compromiso fue una grata noticia para sus padres

pleasingly ['pli:zɪŋlɪ] *adv* agradablemente, gratamente

pleasurable ['pleʒərəbəl] *adj* agradable, grato(a)

pleasurably ['pleʒərəblɪ] *adv* agradablemente, placenteramente

pleasure ['pleʒə(r)] **1** *n* (a) *(enjoyment, contentment)* placer *m*; **to write/to paint for p.** escribir/pintar por placer; **are you here on business or for p.?** ¿estás aquí en viaje de negocios o de placer?; **the pleasures of camping** los placeres del cámping; **it's one of my few pleasures** es uno de mis pocos placeres; **it gave me great p.** fue un auténtico placer para mí; **to take** *or* **find p. in (doing) sth** disfrutar (haciendo) algo ►► ***p. boat*** barco *m* de recreo; *Psy* ***the p. principle*** el principio del placer; ***p. trip*** viaje *m* de placer

(b) *(in polite expressions)* **with p.!** con (mucho) gusto; **(it's) my p.!** *(replying to thanks)* ¡no hay de qué!; **it's a great p. (to meet you)** es un gran placer (conocerle); **it gives me great p. to introduce...** tengo el grandísimo placer de presentar a...; *Formal* **I haven't had the p. of meeting her** no he tenido el placer de conocerla; *Formal* **I am delighted to have had the p.** estoy encantado de haber tenido el gusto; *Formal* **I have p. in informing you that...** tengo el gusto de *or* me complace informarles de que...; *Formal* **may I have the p. (of this dance)?** ¿me concede el honor (de esta pieza)?; *Formal* **would you do me the p. of having lunch with me?** ¿me concedería el placer de compartir el almuerzo conmigo?; *Formal* **Mr and Mrs Evans request the p. of your company at their son's wedding** el Sr. y la Sra. Evans tienen el placer de invitar a Ud. a la celebración del matrimonio de su hijo

(c) *(will)* voluntad *f*; **at sb's p.** según disponga alguien; **they are appointed at the chairman's p.** son nombrados directamente por el presidente; *Br Law* **to be detained at** *or* **during Her Majesty's p.** ser encarcelado(a) a discreción del Estado

(d) *Old-fashioned or Literary (sexual gratification)* **he took his p. of her** saciaba su necesidad con ella

2 *vt Old-fashioned or Literary (give pleasure to)* deleitar a; *(sexually)* satisfacer a

pleasure-seeker ['pleʒə'si:kə(r)] *n* buscador(ora) *m,f* de placer

pleasure-seeking ['pleʒə'si:kɪŋ] *adj* en busca de placer

pleat [pli:t] **1** *n (in sewing)* pliegue *m*

2 *vt* plisar

pleated ['pli:tɪd] *adj (skirt)* plisado(a) ►► ***p. trousers*** pantalón *m* de pinzas

pleb [pleb] *n* (a) *Br Fam Pej* ordinario(a) *m,f*; **the plebs** la plebe; **you p.!** ¡qué ordinario!, *Arg* ¡qué grasa! (b) *Hist* **the plebs** la plebe

plebby ['plebɪ] *adj Br Fam Pej* ordinario(a), *Arg* grasa

plebeian [plə'bi:ən] **1** *n* (a) *(lower class person)* plebeyo(a) *m,f* (b) *Hist* plebeyo(a) *m,f*

2 *adj* (a) *(of the lower classes)* obrero(a) (b) *Pej (vulgar, unsophisticated)* ordinario(a) (c) *Hist* plebeyo(a)

plebiscite ['plebɪsɪt] *n* plebiscito *m*; **to hold a p.** celebrar un plebiscito

plectrum ['plektrəm] (*pl* **plectrums** *or* **plectra** ['plektrə]) *n Mus* púa *f*, plectro *m*

pled *US, Scot pt & pp of* **plead**

pledge [pledʒ] **1** *n* (a) *(promise)* promesa *f*; **thousands of people phoned in with pledges of money** miles de personas llamaron ofreciendo donar dinero; **I am under a p. of secrecy** prometí guardar silencio; **to fulfil** *or* **keep a p.** cumplir *or* mantener una promesa; **to make a p.** hacer una promesa; IDIOM **to take** *or* **sign the p.** jurar no beber *or Am* tomar alcohol ►► ***the P. of Allegiance*** la Jura de la Bandera *(en colegios estadounidenses)*

(b) *(security, collateral)* garantía *f*, aval *m*; **in p.** en garantía

(c) *(token)* prenda *f*; **as a p. of our sincerity** como prenda de nuestra sinceridad

(d) *Formal (toast)* brindis *m inv*; **let us drink a p. to their success** hagamos un brindis por su éxito

(e) *US Univ* = estudiante que ha sido aceptado como miembro de una fraternidad o asociación estudiantil pero que aún no ha sido iniciado

2 *vt* (a) *(promise)* prometer; **to p. money** *(in radio, television appeal)* prometer hacer un donativo (de dinero); **they have pledged £500 to the relief fund** se han comprometido a donar 500 libras al fondo de ayuda; **she pledged never to see him again** *(to herself)* se prometió no volver a verlo nunca más; *(to sb else)* prometió que no lo volvería a ver nunca más; *Literary* **her heart is pledged to another** su corazón le pertenece a otra persona

(b) *Formal (commit)* comprometerse a; **to p. one's word** empeñar la palabra; **to p. one's support** comprometerse a brindar apoyo; **to p. one's allegiance to the king** jurar fidelidad al rey; **I am pledged to secrecy** he hecho la promesa de guardar silencio; **to p. oneself to do sth** comprometerse a hacer algo

(c) *(offer as security)* ofrecer en garantía *or* como prenda; *(pawn)* empeñar

(d) *Formal (toast)* brindar

(e) *US Univ* = aceptar a un estudiante como miembro de una fraternidad o asociación estudiantil

Pleiades ['plaɪədi:z] *npl Astron* **the P.** las Pléyades

Pleistocene ['plaɪstəsi:n] *Geol* **1** *n* **the P.** el pleistoceno

2 *adj* pleistoceno(a)

plenary ['pli:nərɪ] **1** *n (at conference)* plenaria *f*

2 *adj* plenario(a) ►► ***p. assembly*** asamblea *f* plenaria; *Rel* ***p. indulgence*** indulgencia *f* plenaria; ***p. powers*** plenos poderes *mpl*; ***p. session*** *(at conference)* plenaria *f*; **to meet in p. session** reunirse en sesión plenaria

plenipotentiary [plenɪpə'tenʃərɪ] **1** *n* embajador(ora) *m,f* plenipotenciario(a)

2 *adj* plenipotenciario(a)

plenitude ['plenɪtju:d] *n Literary (abundance)* profusión *f*

plenteous ['plentjəs] *adj Literary* copioso(a), abundante

plentiful ['plentɪfʊl] *adj* abundante; **in p. supply** en abundancia

plentifully ['plentɪfʊlɪ] *adv* copiosamente, abundantemente

plenty ['plentɪ] **1** *n* abundancia *f*; **the years of p.** los años de la abundancia; **land of p.** tierra de la abundancia

2 *pron* (a) *(enough)* suficiente; **that's p.** es (más que) suficiente; **$20 should be p.** 20 dólares tendrían que ser suficientes; **they have p. to live on** tienen recursos más que suficientes para vivir; **to arrive in p. of time** llegar con tiempo de sobra

(b) *(a great deal)* **p. of time/money** mucho tiempo/dinero; **p. of food** mucha comida; **p. of books** muchos libros; **there'll be p. of other opportunities** no faltarán oportunidades; **there's still p. to be done** aún queda mucho por hacer; **we see p. of Ray and Janet** vemos a Ray y Janet con mucha frecuencia; **we need hot water, and p. of it!** necesitamos agua caliente, ¡y mucha *or* en cantidad!

3 *adv Fam* **it's p. big enough** es grande más que de sobra; **this beer's great! – there's p. more where that came from** ¡esta cerveza está genial! – pues tenemos mucha más; *US* **he sure talks p.** desde luego sí que habla sin parar

4 **in plenty** *adv* en abundancia

plenum ['pli:nəm] *n* (a) *(meeting)* sesión *f* plenaria (b) *Phys* plenum *m*

pleonasm ['pli:ənæzəm] *n* pleonasmo *m*

pleonastic [plɪə'næstɪk] *adj* pleonástico(a)

plesiosaur ['pli:sɪəsɔ:(r)] *n* plesiosaurio *m*

plethora ['pleθərə] *n Formal* plétora *f*

pleura ['plʊərə] (*pl* **pleurae** ['plʊəri:]) *n Anat* pleura *f*

pleural ['plʊərəl] *adj Anat* pleural ►► ***p. membrane*** pleura *f*

pleurisy ['plʊərɪsɪ] *n* pleuresía *f*; **to have p.** tener pleuresía

Plexiglas® ['pleksɪglɑ:s] *n US* plexiglás® *m*

plexus ['pleksəs] *n Anat* plexo *m*; **brachial p.** plexo braquial; **sacral p.** plexo sacro

pliability [plaɪə'bɪlɪtɪ], **pliancy** ['plaɪənsɪ] *n* (**a**) *(of material)* maleabilidad *f* (**b**) *(of person)* flexibilidad *f*, ductilidad *f*

pliable ['plaɪəbəl], **pliant** ['plaɪənt] *adj* (**a**) *(material)* flexible (**b**) *(person)* acomodaticio(a)

pliancy = **pliability**

pliant = **pliable**

pliers ['plaɪəz] *npl* alicates *mpl*; **a pair of p.** unos alicates

plight[1] [plaɪt] *n* situación *f* grave *or* difícil; **the p. of the young homeless** la difícil situación de los jóvenes que no tienen un lugar donde vivir; **to be in a sad** *or* **sorry p.** estar en una situación penosa

plight[2] *vt Old-fashioned or Formal* **to p. one's troth to sb** dar palabra de matrimonio a alguien; **to p. one's word** empeñar la palabra

Plimsoll ['plɪmsəl] *n Naut* ***P. line*** línea *f* de máxima carga; ***P. mark*** línea *f* de máxima carga

plimsoll ['plɪmsəl] *n Br (shoe)* playera *f*

plink [plɪŋk] **1** *n* tintineo *m*

2 *vi* tintinear

plinth [plɪnθ] *n* pedestal *m*

Pliocene ['plaɪəsiːn] *Geol* **1** *n* **the P.** el plioceno

2 *adj* plioceno(a)

PLO [piːel'əʊ] *n* (*abbr* **Palestine Liberation Organization**) OLP *f*

plod [plɒd] **1** *n* (**a**) *(walk)* caminata *f*; *(pace)* paso *m* lento y cansino; *Fig* **the movie/book is a bit of a p.** la película/el libro es un poco lenta/lento (**b**) *Br Fam (police officer)* poli *mf*, *RP* cana *f*, *Arg* yuta *f*

2 *vi* (*pt & pp* **plodded**) (**a**) *(walk)* caminar con paso lento; **to p. on** seguir caminando *(con lentitud o esfuerzo)*

(**b**) *(work)* **to p. (away)** trabajar pacientemente; **he'd been plodding along in the same job for years** había estado trabajando laboriosamente en el mismo empleo durante años; **I'm plodding through a rather boring book just now** en este momento estoy lidiando con un libro bastante aburrido

plodder ['plɒdə(r)] *n* = persona mediocre pero voluntariosa en el trabajo

plodding ['plɒdɪŋ] *adj (walk, rhythm, style)* lento(a) y cansino(a); *(worker)* laborioso(a) pero lento(a)

plonk[1] [plɒŋk] *esp Br* **1** *n (sound)* golpe *m* (seco), ruido *m* (sordo)

2 *vt Fam* **to p. sth down** dejar *or* poner algo de golpe; **to p. oneself down in an armchair** dejarse caer (de golpe) en una butaca

3 *vi* **to p. away on the piano** aporrear el piano

plonk[2] *n Br Fam (cheap wine)* vino *m* peleón *or RP* cualunque

plonker ['plɒŋkə(r)] *n Br very Fam* (**a**) *(idiot) Esp* gilipollas *mf inv*, *Am* pendejo(a) *m,f* (**b**) *(penis)* verga *f*, *Esp* picha *f*, *Chile* pico *m*, *Méx* pájaro *m*, *RP* pija *f*

plop [plɒp] **1** *n* glu(p) *m*, = sonido de algo al hundirse en un líquido

2 *adv* **to go p.** hacer glu(p)

3 *vt* (*pt & pp* **plopped**) *(put)* poner

4 *vi* caer haciendo glu(p)

plosion ['pləʊʒən] *n Ling* explosión *f*

plosive ['pləʊsɪv] *Ling* **1** *n* oclusiva *f*

2 *adj* oclusivo(a)

plot [plɒt] **1** *n* (**a**) *(conspiracy)* trama *f*, complot *m* (**b**) *(of play, novel)* trama *f*, argumento *m*; IDIOM **the p. thickens** el asunto se complica (**c**) *(land)* terreno *m*; **(vegetable) p.** huerta *f*, huerto *m* (**d**) *US (graph)* gráfico *m*

2 *vt* (*pt & pp* **plotted**) (**a**) *(plan)* tramar, planear; **to p. (to do) sth** tramar *or* planear (hacer) algo; **to p. sb's downfall** tramar *or* planear la caída de alguien

(**b**) *(play, novel)* trazar el argumento de; **the novel is well/poorly plotted** la novela tiene un buen/mal argumento

(**c**) *(draw) (curve)* trazar; *(progress, development)* representar; **to p. a course** planear *or* trazar una ruta (en el mapa)

3 *vi (conspire)* confabularse, conspirar (**against** contra)

plotless ['plɒtlɪs] *adj* sin argumento

plotter ['plɒtə(r)] *n* (**a**) *(conspirator)* conspirador(ora) *m,f* (**b**) *Comptr* plóter *m*, plotter *m*

plotting ['plɒtɪŋ] *n (conspiring)* tramas *fpl*, complots *mpl*

plough, *US* **plow** [plaʊ] **1** *n* (**a**) *(tool)* arado *m*; **large areas of land have gone under the p.** grandes extensiones de suelo han sido aradas; *Fig* **to put one's hand to the p.** ponerse a trabajar ▸▸ ***p. horse*** caballo *m* de tiro (**b**) *(constellation)* **the Plough** la Osa Mayor

2 *vt* (**a**) *(field, furrow)* arar, labrar; IDIOM **to p. a lonely furrow** trabajar en solitario (**b**) *Fig (invest)* **to p. profits back into a company** reinvertir beneficios en una empresa (**c**) *Br Sch Old-fashioned Fam* **to p. an exam** *Esp* suspender *or Am* reprobar un examen

3 *vi* (**a**) *(farmer)* arar, labrar (**b**) *Br Sch Old-fashioned Fam* **I ploughed** *Esp* he suspendido, *Arg* he rebotado

▸ **plough in,** *US* **plow in** *vt sep Agr (earth, crops, stubble)* arar

▸ **plough into,** *US* **plow into** *vt insep* (**a**) *(of vehicle)* estrellarse contra (**b**) *(attack) (physically)* embestir, arremeter contra; *(verbally)* arremeter contra

▸ **plough on,** *US* **plow on** *vi* avanzar con dificultad (**with** con); **as negotiations p. on** mientras las negociaciones avanzan con gran dificultad

▸ **plough through,** *US* **plow through** **1** *vt insep* (**a**) *(move laboriously)* **to p. through the snow** avanzar con dificultad en la nieve; **the ship ploughed through the waves** el barco se abría camino entre las olas (**b**) *(progress laboriously)* **to p. through sth** *(work, reading)* tomarse el trabajo de hacer algo; **I've still got all this to p. through** aún tengo que hacer todo esto

2 *vt sep* **to p. one's way through sth** avanzar en algo con dificultad

▸ **plough up,** *US* **plow up** *vt sep (field)* roturar; **the park had been ploughed up by vehicles** los vehículos dejaron el parque lleno de surcos

ploughboy, *US* **plowboy** ['plaʊbɔɪ] *n* mozo(a) *m,f* de labranza

ploughland, *US* **plowland** ['plaʊlænd] *n* tierra *f* de labranza *or* cultivo

ploughman, *US* **plowman** ['plaʊmən] *n* labrador *m* ▸▸ *Br* ***p.'s lunch*** = almuerzo a base de pan, queso, ensalada y encurtidos

ploughshare, *US* **plowshare** ['plaʊʃeə(r)] *n* ancla *f* de arado

plover ['plʌvə(r)] *n* chorlito *m*

plow, plowboy *etc US* = **plough, ploughboy** *etc*

ploy [plɔɪ] *n* estratagema *f*

pluck [plʌk] **1** *n (courage)* coraje *m*, valor *m*; **it takes p. to do that** hacer eso requiere valor

2 *vt* (**a**) *(pick) (flower)* arrancar; *(fruit)* arrancar, *Arg* sacar; **to p. one's eyebrows** depilarse las cejas

(**b**) *(pull)* arrancar, quitar; **they were plucked from danger by a helicopter** un helicóptero les sacó del peligro; **to p. sb from obscurity** sacar a alguien del anonimato; **these figures have been plucked from the air** estas cifras han salido de la nada

(**c**) *(chicken)* desplumar; *(feathers)* arrancar

(**d**) *(instrument)* tocar; *(string)* rasguear, puntear; **to p. a guitar** puntear (a la guitarra)

3 *vi* **to p. at sb's sleeve** tirar a alguien de la manga; **she was plucking at (the strings of) her guitar** estaba rasgando las cuerdas de su guitarra

▸ **pluck out** *vt sep (feathers, eyes)* arrancar; **he was plucked out of obscurity** salió del anonimato

▸ **pluck up** *vt sep* (**a**) *(uproot)* arrancar (**b**) IDIOMS **I plucked up my courage** me armé de valor; **to p. up the courage to do sth** armarse de valor para hacer algo

pluckily ['plʌkɪlɪ] *adv* valientemente

pluckiness ['plʌkɪnɪs] *n* valor *m*, coraje *m*

plucky ['plʌkɪ] *adj* valiente

plug [plʌg] **1** *n* (**a**) *(for sink, bath, barrel, pipe)* tapón *m*

(**b**) *(electrical)* enchufe *m*; *Aut* **(spark) p.** bujía *f*; IDIOM *Fam* **to pull the p. on sth** dejar de apoyar algo

(**c**) *(of tobacco)* rollo *m* (de tabaco de mascar)

(**d**) *(for fixing screws)* tarugo *m*

(**e**) *Geol* **(volcanic) p.** masa cilíndrica de lava solidificada

(**f**) *Fam (of toilet)* cadena *f*; **to pull the p.** tirar la cadena

(**g**) *Fam (publicity)* publicidad *f*; **to give sth a p.** hacer publicidad de *or* promocionar algo

2 *vt* (*pt & pp* **plugged**) (**a**) *(block)* tapar, taponar; **to p. a leak** tapar una fuga; IDIOM **to p. a loophole (in the law)** cerrar un vacío legal (**b**) *Fam (promote)* hacer publicidad de, promocionar (**c**) *Fam (shoot)* disparar (**d**) *Comptr* **p. and play** conectar y funcionar, enchufar y usar

▸ **plug away** *vi Fam* trabajar con tesón (**at** en)

▸ **plug in** *vt sep* enchufar

▸ **plug into** **1** *vt sep (connect)* **to p. sth into sth** conectar algo a algo

2 *vt insep* (**a**) *(connect)* **the TV plugs into that socket** la tele se enchufa en aquella toma *or* aquel enchufe; *Fig* **to p. into a computer network** conectarse a una red informática (**b**) *(be in touch with)* estar en contacto con

▸ **plug up** *vt sep* taponar

plug-and-play ['plʌgən'pleɪ] *adj Comptr* para enchufar y usar

plugboard ['plʌgbɔːd] *n Comptr & Tel* tablero *m* de contacto

plughole ['plʌghəʊl] *n* desagüe *m*; IDIOM *Fam* **to go down the p.** echarse a perder

plug-in ['plʌgɪn] *n Comptr* plug-in *m*, dispositivo *m* opcional, programa *m* auxiliar *or* complementario

plug-ugly ['plʌg'ʌglɪ] *Fam* **1** *adj* **to be p.** ser un coco
2 *n US (ruffian)* matón *m*

plum [plʌm] **1** *n* **(a)** *(fruit)* ciruela *f*; IDIOM *Br* **to have a p. in one's mouth** hablar engoladamente, = tener acento de clase alta ►► *Br* ***p. duff*** = pudín con pasas y otras frutas típico de Navidad; *Br* ***p. pudding*** = pudín con pasas y otras frutas típico de Navidad; ***p. sauce*** salsa *f* de ciruela; ***p. tomato*** tomate *m* de pera; ***p. tree*** ciruelo *m*
(b) *(colour)* color *m* ciruela
(c) *Fam (choice specimen)* perla *f*
2 *adj* **(a)** *(colour)* morado(a) **(b)** *Fam (very good)* **a p. job** un *Esp* chollo *or Méx* churro (de trabajo), *RP* un laburazo

plumage ['plu:mɪdʒ] *n* plumaje *m*

plumb [plʌm] **1** *n* **p. (line)** plomada *f*; **out of p.** torcido(a) ►► ***p. bob*** plomada *f*
2 *adv Fam* **(a)** *(exactly)* de lleno, directamente; **p. in the centre** en todo *or* justo en el centro **(b)** *US (utterly, completely)* totalmente, completamente; **he's p. crazy** está totalmente *or* completamente loco
3 *vt* **(a)** *(sea)* sondar; *Fig* **to p. the depths of** abismarse *or* sumergirse en las profundidades de **(b)** *(test for verticality)* aplomar

► **plumb in** *vt sep Br* **to p. in a washing machine** conectar una lavadora *or RP* un lavarropas

plumbago [plʌm'beɪgəʊ] *(pl* **plumbagos***) n* **(a)** *(plant)* plumbaginácea *f* **(b)** *(graphite)* plombagina *f*

plumber ['plʌmə(r)] *n* fontanero(a) *m,f*, *Méx, RP, Ven* plomero(a) *m,f* ►► *US* ***p.'s friend*** desatascador *m*; ***p.'s helper*** desatascador *m*

plumbing ['plʌmɪŋ] *n* **(a)** *(job)* fontanería *f*, *Am* plomería *f* **(b)** *(system)* cañerías *fpl* **(c)** *Euph (uro-genital system)* cañerías *fpl*

plume [plu:m] **1** *n* **(a)** *(single feather)* pluma *f*; *(on hat, helmet)* penacho *m* **(b)** *(of smoke)* nube *f*, penacho *m*
2 *vt* **(a)** *(preen)* limpiar con el pico **(b)** **to p. oneself on sth** *(take pride in)* congratularse *or* enorgullecerse de algo

plummet ['plʌmɪt] **1** *n* **(a)** *(angler's weight)* plomada *f* **(b)** *(plumb line)* plomada *f*
2 *vi* **(a)** *(plunge, dive)* desplomarse, caer *Esp* en picado *or Am* en picada **(b)** *(drop) (price, amount, temperature)* desplomarse, caer *Esp* en picado *or Am* en picada; **educational standards have plummeted** los niveles educativos han caído *Esp* en picado *or Am* en picada

plummy ['plʌmɪ] *adj Fam (voice, accent)* engolado(a) *(propio de la clase alta británica)*

plump [plʌmp] **1** *adj (person, arms, face)* rechoncho(a); *(peach, turkey)* gordo(a); **a p. wallet** una billetera gorda
2 *adv* **(a)** *(heavily)* pesadamente, con fuerza **(b)** *(directly)* directamente
3 *vt* **(a)** *(pillow, cushion)* ahuecar **(b)** *(drop)* **to p. oneself into an armchair** dejarse caer en una butaca

► **plump down** *vt sep* dejar *or* poner de golpe; **she plumped herself down on the sofa** se dejó caer en el sofá

► **plump for** *vt insep Fam (choose)* decidirse por

► **plump up** *vt sep (cushion, pillow)* ahuecar

plumpness ['plʌmpnɪs] *n (of person)* rechonchez *f*; *(of peach, turkey)* gordura *f*; **to be inclined to p.** tener tendencia a la gordura

plunder ['plʌndə(r)] **1** *n* **(a)** *(action)* saqueo *m*, pillaje *m* **(b)** *(loot)* botín *m*
2 *vt (place)* saquear, expoliar; *(object)* robar; *Fig (bookshelves, fridge)* saquear

plunge [plʌndʒ] **1** *n* **(a)** *(dive)* zambullida *f*; **prices have taken a p.** los precios se han desplomado *or* han caído *Esp* en picado *or Am* en picada; IDIOM *Fam* **to take the p.** *(take major step)* lanzarse; *(get married)* dar el paso (decisivo) **(b)** *(of share values, prices)* desplome *m*; *(of temperature)* descenso *m* brusco
2 *vt* sumergir (**into** en); **p. the tomatoes into boiling water** sumerja los tomates en agua hirviendo; **he plunged his hands into his pockets** hundió las manos en los bolsillos; **to p. a knife into sb's back** hundir a alguien un cuchillo en la espalda; **the office was plunged into darkness** la oficina quedó a oscuras; **to p. sb into despair** sumir a alguien en la desesperación
3 *vi* **(a)** *(dive, fall)* caer (**into** en); **the lorry plunged over the cliff** el camión cayó por el precipicio; **she plunged to her death** murió tras caer al vacío **(b)** *(share values, prices)* desplomarse; *(temperature)* descender bruscamente **(c)** *(neckline)* acentuarse **(d)** *(engage oneself in)* meterse; **he plunged into a long and complicated story** se metió en una larga y compleja historia

► **plunge in** *vi* meterse de cabeza, lanzarse

plunger ['plʌndʒə(r)] *n* **(a)** *(of syringe, coffee-maker, detonator)* émbolo *m* **(b)** *(for clearing sink)* desatascador *m*

plunging ['plʌndʒɪŋ] *adj* **a p. neckline** un escote pronunciado; **p. prices** precios que se desploman

PLURALS

El plural de las palabras extranjeras en inglés
Hay una serie de palabras en inglés que tienen dos plurales distintos. Uno de ellos está basado en el plural de la lengua de la que provienen (normalmente latín o griego) y otro sigue las normas de la formación del plural en inglés:

Singular	Plural culto	Plural normal
antenna	**antennae** (latín)	**antennas**
automaton	**automata** (griego)	**automatons**
cherub	**cherubim** (hebreo)	**cherubs**
focus	**foci** (latín)	**focuses**
memorandum	**memoranda** (griego)	**memorandums**
tempo	**tempi** (italiano)	**tempos**

La primera de estas formas suele usarse sobre todo en contextos especializados o técnicos, aunque hay quien la usa de forma general e incluso critica el plural formado siguiendo las reglas generales del inglés. En general, a medida que se usa más una palabra extranjera en inglés, se tiende más a utilizar el plural regular. Por ejemplo **agenda** se ha convertido en una palabra de uso corriente en singular (con **agendas** como plural), aunque en un principio era el plural de la palabra latina "agendum" (que significa "cosa que se ha de hacer"). Sin embargo, hay casos en los que no se ha alcanzado un consenso sobre si la palabra se ha asimilado ya al inglés o no. Por ejemplo, para la mayoría de los hablantes de inglés **data** es un sustantivo incontable, por lo que *un dato* sería **a piece of data** o **an item of data**. Pero para otros sigue siendo el plural de **datum**, como en latín, si bien es cierto que fuera del campo de la filosofía **datum** no es de uso frecuente. No obstante, en contextos científicos **data** sigue considerándose plural:

such data are difficult to interpret *tales datos son difíciles de interpretar*

De la misma forma, **media** es siempre el plural de **medium** en el campo de las ciencias de la naturaleza, pero actualmente se usa a menudo como sustantivo incontable cuando significa "prensa, radio y televisión", aunque para muchos siga siendo plural:

the media was/were there in force *los medios se habían presentado allí en gran número*

A veces se crean falsos plurales irregulares por creer erróneamente en un posible origen latino de la palabra. Por ejemplo hay quien usa **octopi** como plural de **octopus** (siguiendo el modelo latino de **cactus/cacti**), cuando en realidad la forma **octopuses** no es incorrecta ya que **octopus** viene del griego.

plunk [plʌŋk] *Fam* **1** *n (sound)* rasgueo *m*, punteo *m*
2 *vt* (**a**) *(put down)* tirar, poner (**b**) *(guitar, banjo)* rasguear, puntear
3 *vi* **he was plunking away at the piano** estaba aporreando el piano
▸ **plunk down** *vt sep* **he plunked himself down on the sofa** se dejó caer en el sofá

pluperfect ['plu:'pɜ:fɪkt] *Gram* **1** *n* pluscuamperfecto *m*
2 *adj* pluscuamperfecto(a)

plural ['plʊərəl] **1** *n Gram* plural *m*; **in the p.** en plural
2 *adj* (**a**) *Gram* plural (**b**) *Pol* ***p. society*** sociedad *f* plural

pluralism ['plʊərəlɪzəm] *n* pluralismo *m*

pluralist ['plʊərəlɪst] **1** *n* pluralista *mf*
2 *adj* pluralista

pluralistic [plʊərə'lɪstɪk] *adj (society)* plural; *(views)* pluralista

plurality [plʊə'rælɪtɪ] *n* (**a**) *(variety)* pluralidad *f* (**b**) *US* **a p. of** la mayoría relativa de

pluralize ['plʊərəlaɪz] *vt Gram* poner en plural

plus [plʌs] **1** *n* (*pl* **plusses** ['plʌsɪz]) (**a**) *(sign)* **p. (sign)** signo *m* más ▸▸ *Comptr* ***p. key*** tecla *f* de suma (**b**) *(advantage)* ventaja *f*
2 *adj* (**a**) *(positive)* **on the p. side, the bicycle is light** esta bicicleta tiene la ventaja de ser ligera (**b**) *(over, more than)* **fifteen p.** de quince para arriba, más de quince; *Fam* **we're looking for somebody with talent p.** buscamos a alguien con mucho talento; **I got a C p.** saqué un aprobado alto (**c**) ***p. fours*** *(trousers)* (pantalones *mpl*) bombachos *mpl*
3 *prep* más; **seven p. nine** siete más nueve; **$97 p. tax** 97 dólares más impuestos; **two floors p. an attic** dos pisos y una buhardilla
4 *conj Fam* además, encima; **he's stupid, p. he's ugly** es un imbécil y además *or* encima es feo

plush [plʌʃ] **1** *n Tex* felpa *f*
2 *adj Fam* lujoso(a), *Esp* muy puesto(a)

Pluto ['plu:təʊ] *n* (**a**) *(planet)* Plutón (**b**) *(god)* Plutón

plutocracy [plu:'tɒkrəsɪ] *n* plutocracia *f*

plutocrat ['plu:təkræt] *n* (**a**) *Pol* plutócrata *mf* (**b**) *Pej (wealthy person)* ricachón(ona) *m,f*

plutocratic [plu:tə'krætɪk] *adj* plutocrático(a)

plutonium [plu:'təʊnɪəm] *n Chem* plutonio *m*

pluvial ['plu:vjəl] *adj* pluvial

pluviometer [plu:vɪ'ɒmɪtə(r)] *n* pluviómetro *m*

ply[1] [plaɪ] *n* (**a**) *(thickness)* **three-p.** *(wood, paper handkerchief)* de tres capas; *(wool)* de tres hebras (**b**) *Fam (plywood)* aglomerado *m*

ply[2] **1** *vt* (**a**) *(exercise)* **to p. one's trade** ejercer su oficio (**b**) *(supply in excess)* **to p. sb with questions** acribillar a alguien a preguntas; **to p. sb with drink** ofrecer bebida insistentemente a alguien (**c**) *(use) (tool)* usar, manejar; *(needle)* manejar (**d**) *(travel) (river, ocean)* navegar, surcar
2 *vi* **to p. for hire** *(taxi)* circular despacio en busca de pasajeros; **to p. between** *(ferry, plane)* cubrir la ruta entre

plywood ['plaɪwʊd] *n* contrachapado *m*

PM [pi:'em] *n* (*abbr* **Prime Minister**) primer(era) ministro(a) *m,f*

p.m. [pi:'em] *adv* (*abbr* **post meridiem**) p.m.; **6 p.m.** las 6 de la tarde

PMS [pi:em'es] *n* (*abbr* **premenstrual syndrome**) síndrome *m* premenstrual

PMT [pi:em'ti:] *n* (*abbr* **premenstrual tension**) tensión *f* premenstrual

pneumatic [nju:'mætɪk] *adj* (**a**) *(containing air)* neumático(a) ▸▸ ***p.*** *Br* ***tyre*** *or US* ***tire*** neumático *m* (**b**) *(operated by air)* ***p. drill*** martillo *m* neumático; ***p. pump*** bomba *f* neumática (**c**) *Fam (woman, figure)* con buenas curvas, bien provisto(a)

pneumatically [nju:'mætɪklɪ] *adv* neumáticamente

pneumatics [nju:'mætɪks] *n* neumática *f*

pneumoconiosis [nju:məkəʊnɪ'əʊsɪs] *n Med* neumoconiosis *f inv*

pneumonia [nju:'məʊnɪə] *n* pulmonía *f*, neumonía *f*

PO [pi:'əʊ] *n* (**a**) (*abbr* **Post Office**) oficina *f* de correos ▸▸ ***PO Box*** apartado *m* de correos, *CAm, Carib, Méx* casilla *f* postal, *Andes, RP* casilla *f* de correos, *Col* apartado *m* aéreo (**b**) *Br* (*abbr* **postal order**) giro *m* postal (**c**) *Naut* (*abbr* **petty officer**) suboficial *mf* de marina

po [pəʊ] (*pl* **pos**) *n Br Fam* orinal *m*, *Am* bacinica *f*

poach[1] [pəʊtʃ] *vt Culin (eggs)* escalfar; *(fish)* cocer; **poached eggs** huevos escalfados

poach[2] **1** *vt* (**a**) *(catch illegally)* **to p. fish/game** pescar/cazar furtivamente (**b**) *(steal) (idea, employee)* robar
2 *vi* **to p. for game** cazar furtivamente; **to p. for salmon** pescar salmón furtivamente; **you're poaching on my territory** te estás metiendo en mi territorio

poacher ['pəʊtʃə(r)] *n (hunter) (of game)* cazador *m* furtivo; *(of fish)* pescador *m* furtivo

poaching ['pəʊtʃɪŋ] *n* (**a**) *(cooking)* escalfado *m* (**b**) *(illegal hunting)* caza *f* furtiva; *(illegal fishing)* pesca *f* furtiva

po' boy ['pəʊbɔɪ] *n US* = sandwich grande típico de Nueva Orleans

pochard ['pəʊtʃəd] *n* porrón *m*; **red-crested p.** pato *m* colorado

pock = **pockmark**

pocked = **pockmarked**

pocket ['pɒkɪt] **1** *n* (**a**) *(in trousers, jacket)* bolsillo *m*, *CAm, Méx, Perú* bolsa *f*; **p. comb/mirror** peine/espejo de bolsillo; **to go through sb's pockets** buscar en los bolsillos de alguien; IDIOM **to be in each other's pockets** no separarse ni para ir al baño; IDIOM **to have sb in one's p.** tener a alguien metido en el bolsillo; IDIOM **we thought we had the deal in our p.** pensábamos que ya teníamos el acuerdo en el bolsillo; IDIOM *Fam Hum* **to play p.** *Br* **billiards** *or US* **pool** tocarse las pelotas ▸▸ ***p. calculator*** calculadora *f* de bolsillo; ***p. edition*** edición *f* de bolsillo; ***p. money*** *(for buying things)* dinero *m* para gastos; *(given by parents)* paga *f*, propina *f*; *US Pol* ***p. veto*** = veto indirecto que puede aplicar el presidente al no firmar un decreto dentro del plazo establecido de diez días; ***p. watch*** reloj *m* de bolsillo
(**b**) *(referring to financial means)* **he doesn't like putting his hand in his p.** no es de los que mete la mano en el bolsillo con facilidad; **prices to suit every p.** precios para todos los bolsillos; **I paid for the presents out of my own p.** pagué los regalos de mi propio bolsillo; **to be in p.** tener dinero en el bolsillo; **to be out of p.** haber perdido dinero; IDIOM **to line one's pockets** llenarse los bolsillos, forrarse
(**c**) *(of air, gas)* bolsa *f*; *(of resistance, rebellion)* foco *m*
(**d**) *Naut* ***p. battleship*** acorazado *m* de bolsillo
(**e**) *(in snooker, pool)* agujero *m*, tronera *f*
2 *vt* (**a**) *(put in pocket)* meter en el bolsillo; IDIOM **to p. one's pride** meterse el orgullo en el bolsillo (**b**) *Fam (steal)* afanar, *Esp* embolsarse (**c**) *(in snooker, pool)* meter

pocketbook ['pɒkɪtbʊk] *n US* (**a**) *(wallet)* cartera *f* (**b**) *(handbag) Esp* bolso *m*, *Col, CSur* cartera *f*, *Méx* bolsa *f*

pocketful ['pɒkɪtfʊl] *n* **he had a p. of coins** tenía el bolsillo lleno de monedas

pocketknife ['pɒkɪtnaɪf] *n* navaja *f*, cortaplumas *m inv*

pocket-size(d) ['pɒkɪtsaɪz(d)] *adj* (**a**) *(book, revolver)* de bolsillo (**b**) *(tiny)* pequeño(a), de bolsillo

pockmark ['pɒkmɑ:k], **pock** [pɒk] **1** *n* (**a**) *(on skin)* marca *f* de viruela (**b**) *(on surface)* marca *f*
2 *vt* (**a**) *(skin)* marcar (**b**) *(surface)* marcar

pockmarked ['pɒkmɑ:kt], **pocked** [pɒkt] *adj* (**a**) *(face)* picado(a) (de viruelas) (**b**) *(surface)* acribillado(a)

POD [pi:əʊ'di:] *n* (*abbr* **pay on delivery**) pago *m* contra reembolso

PO'd ['pi:'əʊd] *adj US Fam* cabreado(a), *Arg* caliente

pod [pɒd] *n* (**a**) *(of plant)* vaina *f* (**b**) *(of aircraft)* tanque *m*; *(of spacecraft)* módulo *m*

podgy ['pɒdʒɪ] *adj Br* regordete(a)

podiatrist [pə'daɪətrɪst] *n US* podólogo(a) *m,f*

podiatry [pə'daɪətrɪ] *n US* podología *f*

podium ['pəʊdɪəm] (*pl* **podiums** *or* **podia** ['pəʊdɪə]) *n* podio *m*

poem ['pəʊɪm] *n* poema *m*

poesy ['pəʊɪzɪ] *n Archaic or Literary* poesía *f*

poet ['pəʊɪt] *n (male)* poeta *m*; *(female)* poetisa *f*, poeta *f* ▸▸ ***p. laureate*** = en el Reino Unido, poeta de la corte encargado de escribir poemas para ocasiones oficiales

poetaster [pəʊɪ'tæstə(r)] *n Pej* poetastro(a) *m,f*

poetess [pəʊɪ'tes] *n Old-fashioned* poetisa *f*

poetic [pəʊ'etɪk] *adj* poético(a); **he gets quite p. when he's enthusiastic** cuando se entusiasma con algo se pone muy poético ▸▸ ***p. justice:*** **it was p. justice that she should be replaced by someone she herself had sacked** fue una ironía del destino que la reemplazaran por alguien a quien ella había despedido anteriormente; ***p. licence*** licencia *f* poética

poetical [pəʊ'etɪkəl] *adj* poético(a)

poetically [pəʊ'etɪklɪ] *adv* de manera poética, poéticamente

poetics [pəʊ'etɪks] *n* poética *f*

poetry ['pəʊɪtrɪ] *n* poesía *f*; **p. in motion** poesía en movimiento ▸▸ ***p. reading*** recital *m* de poesía

po-faced ['pəʊfeɪst] *adj Fam* (**a**) *(person)* **she was wearing a p. expression** tenía cara de pocos amigos (**b**) *(reaction, attitude)* demasiado(a) serio(a)

pogo ['pəʊgəʊ] **1** *n* **p. *stick*** = palo provisto de un muelle para dar saltos
2 *vi (dance)* = bailar dando saltos y cabezazos imaginarios

pogrom ['pɒgrɒm] *n* pogromo *m*

poignancy ['pɔɪnjənsɪ] *n* patetismo *m*, lo conmovedor

poignant ['pɔɪnjənt] *adj* patético(a), conmovedor(ora)

poignantly ['pɔɪnjəntlɪ] *adv* de modo conmovedor

poinsettia [pɔɪn'setɪə] *n* poinsettia *f*, flor *f* de Pascua

POINT [pɔɪnt] **1** *n* **(a)** *(in space)* punto *m*; **a straight line between two points** una línea recta entre dos puntos; **at that p. you'll see a church on the left** a esa altura verás una iglesia a la izquierda; **the terrorists claim they can strike at any p. in the country** los terroristas aseguran que pueden atentar en cualquier parte del país; **the bus service to Dayton and points west** el servicio de autobús a Dayton y otras localidades más al oeste ▸▸ *Ling* ***p. of articulation*** punto *m* de articulación; ***p. of contact*** punto *m* de contacto; *Com* ***p. of sale*** punto *m* de venta
(b) *(stage, moment)* instante *m*, momento *m*; **at one p. everything went dark** en un momento determinado se oscureció todo; **at some p.** en algún momento; **at this p. in time** a esta altura, *Esp* en este preciso instante; **at that** *or* **this p. the phone rang** en ese instante sonó el teléfono; **at the p. of death** en el momento de la muerte; **we've gone beyond the p. where negotiations are possible** hemos llegado a un punto en el que ya no es posible la negociación; **by that p., I was too tired to move** para entonces yo ya estaba muy cansado para moverme; **the regime is on the p. of collapse** el régimen está a punto de caer; **to be on the p. of doing sth** estar a punto de hacer algo; **to drive sb to the p. of despair** llevar a alguien hasta *or* a la desesperación; **outspoken to the p. of rudeness** franco hasta lindar con la grosería; **up to a p.** hasta cierto punto; **when it comes to the p....** a la hora de la verdad...; **I/it got to the p. where I didn't know what I was doing** llegó un momento en el que ya no sabía lo que estaba haciendo; **we've reached the p. of no return** ya no nos podemos echar atrás, *RP* llegamos al punto desde donde no hay más retorno
(c) *(in argument, discussion)* punto *m*; **she has** *or* **she's got a p.** no le falta razón; **on that p. we disagree** en ese punto no estamos de acuerdo; **he made several interesting points** hizo varias observaciones *or* puntualizaciones muy interesantes; **you've made your p.!** ¡ya nos hemos enterado!, *RP* sí, sí, ya entendimos; **this proves my p.** esto prueba *or* confirma lo que digo; **I can see her p.** no le falta razón; **I take your p.** estoy de acuerdo con lo que dices; **p. taken!** ¡de acuerdo!, ¡tienes razón!; **that's ridiculous! – my p. exactly** ¡es ridículo! – precisamente lo que decía yo; **they don't arrive till eight – that's a p.** no llegan hasta las ocho – es verdad; **in p. of fact** en realidad; **not to put too fine a p. on it...** hablando en plata... ▸▸ ***a p. of grammar*** una cuestión gramatical; ***p. of honour*** cuestión *f* de honor; ***p. of order*** cuestión *f* de procedimiento *or* de forma; ***p. of principle*** cuestión *f* de principio; ***p. of reference*** punto *m* de referencia; ***p. of view*** punto *m* de vista
(d) *(most important thing)* **the p. is...** la cuestión es que...; **won't she be surprised? – that's the whole p.** ¿no se sorprenderá? – de eso se trata; **that's not the p.** no es esa la cuestión; **that's beside the p.** eso no viene al caso; **her remarks were very much to the p.** sus comentarios fueron muy pertinentes *or* venían al caso; **where is he, and more to the p., who is he?** ¿dónde está y, lo que es más importante, quién es?; **to come** *or* **get to the p.** ir al grano; **we're getting away from** *or* **off the p.** nos estamos desviando del tema; **I didn't get the p. of the joke** no entendí el chiste; **to keep** *or* **stick to the p.** no divagar, no irse por las ramas; **to make a p. of doing sth** preocuparse de *or* procurar hacer algo
(e) *(aspect, characteristic)* aspecto *m*; **it has its good points** tiene sus cosas buenas; **it's my weak/strong p.** es mi punto fuerte/débil
(f) *(purpose)* **there is no** *or* **little p. (in) waiting any longer** no vale la pena seguir esperando; **the p. of the game is to get rid of all your cards** el objetivo del juego es deshacerse de todas las cartas; **I can't see the p. in continuing** no veo para qué vamos a continuar; **what's the p.?** ¿para qué?; **what's the p. of** *or* **in doing that?** ¿qué sentido tiene hacer eso?, *Esp* ¿qué se consigue haciendo eso?
(g) *(in game, exam)* punto *m*; *(on stock market)* entero *m*, punto *m*; **to win on points** ganar por puntos ▸▸ ***points competition*** *(in cycling)* clasificación *f* por puntos *or* de la regularidad
(h) *(mark, dot)* punto *m*; **a p. of light** un punto de luz; **three** *or* **ellipsis points** puntos suspensivos
(i) *Math* **(decimal) p.** coma *f* (decimal); **three p. five** tres coma cinco
(j) *(on compass)* punto *m*; **the family were scattered to all points of the compass** la familia se haya esparcida por los cuatro puntos cardinales
(k) *(of needle, pencil, sword)* punta *f*; **to end in a p.** acabar en punta; **a star with five points** una estrella de cinco puntas
(l) *(of land)* punta *f*, cabo *m*
(m) *Typ* punto *m* ▸▸ ***p. size*** tamaño *m*
(n) *esp Br (electric socket)* toma *f* de corriente, *Am* toma *f* de contacto
(o) *Aut* **points** platinos *mpl*
(p) *Br* **to be on point(s) duty** *(policeman)* estar dirigiendo el tráfico con los brazos
(q) *Rail* **points** agujas *fpl*
(r) *(in basketball)* ***p. guard*** base *mf*
(s) **points** *(ballet shoes)* puntas *fpl*
2 *vt* **(a)** *(aim)* dirigir; **to p. a gun at sb** apuntar con un arma a alguien; **to p. one's finger at sb** señalar a alguien con el dedo; IDIOM **to p. the finger at sb** *(accuse)* señalar a alguien (con el dedo); **he pointed the boat out to sea** puso proa al mar; **he pointed us in the direction of his office** nos señaló dónde quedaba su oficina, nos indicó la dirección de su oficina; **if anybody asks about money, just p. them in my direction** si alguien hace alguna pregunta sobre dinero, envíamelo a mí; *Fam* **just p. me in the right direction** *(show how to do)* basta con que me digas cómo hacerlo más o menos, *RP* alcanza con que me encamines
(b) *(indicate)* **to p. the way** indicar el camino; *Fig* indicar el rumbo a seguir; **to p. the moral that...** demostrar el principio de que...
(c) *Constr* rellenar las juntas de
(d) *(in ballet)* **to p. one's toes** bailar en puntas
3 *vi* **(a)** *(physically)* **to p. north/left** señalar al norte/a la izquierda; **make sure your fingers are pointing down** asegúrate de que tus dedos señalan hacia abajo; **it's rude to p.** es de mala educación señalar con el dedo; **to p. at sth/sb** *(with finger)* señalar algo/a alguien; **the rifle was pointing straight at me** el rifle me apuntaba directamente; **the signpost points up the hill** la señal indica la cima de la montaña; **the telescopes were all pointing in the same direction** todos los telescopios estaban enfocados *or* orientados en la misma dirección; **the hour hand is pointing to ten** *Esp* la manecilla horaria *or Am* el horario indica las diez; **to be pointing towards sth** estar mirando *or* apuntando hacia algo
(b) *(indicate)* **he pointed to this issue as the key to their success** señaló esta cuestión como la clave de su éxito; **this points to the fact that...** esto nos lleva al hecho de que...; **everything points to a Labour victory** todo indica una victoria laborista; **all the evidence points to suicide** todas las pruebas sugieren que se trata de un suicidio
(c) *(dog)* señalar

▸ **point out** *vt sep (error)* hacer notar, indicar; *(fact)* recalcar; *(dangers, risks)* señalar; **to p. sth/sb out (to sb)** *(with finger)* señalar algo/a alguien (a alguien); **to p. out to sb the advantages of sth** mostrar a alguien las ventajas de algo; **I pointed out that there was a serious flaw in the plan** advertí que había un grave fallo en el plan; **might I p. out that...?** ¿puedo hacer notar que...?

▸ **point up** *vt sep (highlight)* subrayar

point-and-shoot ['pɔɪntən'ʃuːt] *adj (camera)* totalmente automático(a)

point-blank ['pɔɪnt'blæŋk] **1** *adj* **(a)** *(shot)* a quemarropa; **at p. range** a bocajarro, a quemarropa **(b)** *(direct) (refusal, denial)* rotundo(a), tajante
2 *adv* **(a)** *(to fire)* a bocajarro, a quemarropa **(b)** *(directly)* **he asked me p. whether...** me preguntó de sopetón si...; **to deny sth p.** negar algo en redondo; **to refuse p.** negarse en redondo *or* de plano

point-by-point ['pɔɪntbaɪ'pɔɪnt] *adj* puntualizado(a)

pointed ['pɔɪntɪd] *adj* **(a)** *(sharp)* puntiagudo(a) **(b)** *(meaningful) (remark)* intencionado(a); *(look)* significativo(a) **(c)** *(marked)* evidente; **with p. indifference** con evidente indiferencia

pointedly ['pɔɪntɪdlɪ] *adv* **(a)** *(meaningfully)* intencionadamente, con intención; **"well I certainly won't be late," she said p.** "yo por lo menos no llegaré tarde", dijo lanzando una indirecta **(b)** *(markedly)* evidentemente; **she p. ignored me all evening** me ignoró deliberadamente toda la noche

pointer ['pɔɪntə(r)] *n* **(a)** *(stick)* puntero *m* **(b)** *(on dial)* aguja *f* **(c)** *(indication, sign)* indicador *m*, pista *f* **(d)** *Fam (advice)* indicación *f* **(e)** *(dog)* perro *m* de muestra, pointer *m* **(f)** *Comptr* puntero *m*

pointillism ['pɔɪntɪlɪzəm] *n Art* puntillismo *m*

pointing ['pɔɪntɪŋ] *n* **(a)** *(act, job)* sellado *m or* llenado *m* de juntas **(b)** *(cement work)* rejuntado *m*

pointless ['pɔɪntlɪs] *adj* sin sentido; **to be p.** no tener sentido; **it's p. trying to convince him** es inútil intentar convencerlo

point-of-sale ['pɔɪntəv'seɪl] *adj* ***p. advertising*** publicidad *f* en los puntos de venta

pointsman ['pɔɪntsmən] *n Br Rail* guardagujas *m inv*

point-to-point ['pɔɪnttə'pɔɪnt] *n* (**a**) *(horse race) Br* = carrera de caballos por el campo señalizada con banderines (**b**) *Comptr* **p. *protocol*** protocolo *m* punto a punto

pointy-head ['pɔɪntɪhed] *n US Pej* cerebrito *m*

pointy-headed ['pɔɪntɪ'hedɪd] *adj US Pej* intelectualoide

poise [pɔɪz] **1** *n* (**a**) *(physical)* equilibrio *m*; **to recover one's p.** recobrar el equilibrio (**b**) *(composure)* compostura *f*, aplomo *m*

2 *vt (balance)* acomodar, colocar; **she poised herself on the arm of my chair** se acomodó en el brazo de mi silla

poised [pɔɪzd] *adj* (**a**) *(composed)* sereno(a) (**b**) *(ready)* **her hand was p. over the telephone** tenía la mano lista, sobre el teléfono; **to be p. to do sth** estar listo(a) para hacer algo (**c**) *(balanced)* **he was p. between life and death** estaba entre la vida y la muerte; **to be p. on the brink of sth** estar al borde de algo

poison ['pɔɪzən] **1** *n* (**a**) *(chemical, of reptile)* veneno *m* ►► ***p. gas*** gas *m* tóxico; ***p. ivy*** zumaque *m* venenoso; ***p. pen letter*** anónimo *m* malicioso; *Fam Com* **p. *pill*** *(action)* = actuación defensiva contra una OPA hostil; *(clause in contract)* = cláusula para prevenir una OPA hostil; ***p. sumach*** zumaque *m* venenoso

(**b**) IDIOMS *Fam* **he's absolute p.!** es un cerdo asqueroso; **they hate each other like p.** se odian a muerte; *Fam Hum* **what's your p.?** ¿qué tomas?

2 *vt* (**a**) *(person, food) (intentionally)* envenenar; *(accidentally)* intoxicar (**b**) *(pollute)* contaminar (**c**) IDIOMS **his arrival poisoned the atmosphere** su llegada estropeó el ambiente; **to p. sb's mind (against sb)** enemistar *or* encizañar a alguien (con alguien)

poisoned ['pɔɪzənd] *adj* envenenado(a) ►► ***p. chalice*** caramelo *m* muy amargo, = algo que parece una pera en dulce pero no lo es

poisoner ['pɔɪzənə(r)] *n* envenenador(ora) *m,f*

poisoning ['pɔɪzənɪŋ] *n* (**a**) *(of person, food) (intentional)* envenenamiento *m*; *(accidental)* intoxicación *f*; **to die of p.** *(intentional)* morir envenenado(a); *(accidental)* morir por intoxicación (**b**) *(pollution)* contaminación *f*

poisonous ['pɔɪzənəs] *adj* (**a**) *(toxic) (snake, plant, mushroom)* venenoso(a); *(chemical, fumes)* tóxico(a) (**b**) *(vicious) (remark, atmosphere)* envenenado(a), emponzoñado(a); *(rumour, doctrine)* nocivo(a), dañino(a); **he's got a p. tongue** tiene una lengua viperina

poke [pəʊk] **1** *n* (**a**) *(jab)* golpe *m (con la punta de un objeto)*; **she gave him a p. with her umbrella** le dio con la punta del paraguas; **give the fire a p.** atiza un poco el fuego; IDIOM *Hum* **it's better than a p. in the eye with a sharp stick** podía haber sido mucho peor

(**b**) *US Fam (punch)* puñetazo *m*, *Arg* piña *f*; **he's asking for a p. in the nose!** se está buscando un puñetazo *or Arg* una piña

(**c**) *very Fam (sexual intercourse)* **to have a p.** echar un polvo *or* casquete *or Cuba* palo

(**d**) *Scot, US (bag)* bolsa *f* de papel

2 *vt* (**a**) *(jab)* **to p. sb with one's finger/a stick** dar a alguien con la punta del dedo/de un palo; **to p. sb in the ribs** *(with elbow)* dar a alguien un codazo en las costillas; **to p. a hole in sth** hacer un agujero en algo; **to p. the fire** atizar el fuego; IDIOM **to p. fun at sth/sb** reírse de algo/alguien

(**b**) *(insert)* **she poked her finger/knife into the tart** hundió el dedo/cuchillo en la tarta; **to p. one's head round a door** asomar la cabeza por una puerta; IDIOM **to p. one's nose into other people's business** meter las narices en asuntos ajenos

(**c**) *US Fam (punch)* pegar un puñetazo *or Arg* una piña a; **I poked him in the nose** le pegué un puñetazo *or Arg* una piña en la nariz

(**d**) *very Fam (have sex with)* tirarse a

3 *vi* **to p. at sth (with one's finger/a stick)** dar un golpe a algo (con la punta del dedo/de un palo)

► **poke about, poke around** *vi (search)* rebuscar; *(be nosy)* fisgonear, fisgar

► **poke along** *vi US* ir a paso de tortuga

► **poke out 1** *vt sep* **to p. one's head out (of) the window** asomar la cabeza por la ventana; **to p. one's tongue out** sacar la lengua; **be careful! you nearly poked my eye out!** ¡ten cuidado! ¡casi me sacas un ojo!

2 *vi (protrude)* asomar, sobresalir

poker[1] ['pəʊkə(r)] *n (for fire)* atizador *m*

poker[2] *n (card game)* póquer *m*, póker *m* ►► ***p. dice*** dados *mpl* de póquer; ***p. face*** cara *f* de póquer

poker-faced ['pəʊkəfeɪst] *adj* con cara de póquer

pokerwork ['pəʊkəwɜːk] *n Br (technique)* pirograbado *m*; *(decoration)* pirograbado *m*

pokey ['pəʊkɪ] **1** *n US Fam (prison) Esp* chirona *f*, *Andes, RP* cana *f*, *Méx* bote *m*

2 *adj* = **poky**

poky ['pəʊkɪ] *adj Fam* enano(a), minúsculo(a); **a p. room** un cuchitril, un cuartucho

pol [pɒl] *n US Fam* político(a) *m,f*

Polack ['pəʊlæk] *n US Fam* = término generalmente ofensivo para referirse a los polacos

Poland ['pəʊlənd] *n* Polonia

polar ['pəʊlə(r)] *adj* (**a**) *Geog* polar ►► ***p. bear*** oso *m* polar *or* blanco; ***p. circle*** círculo *m* polar (**b**) *Math* ***p. co-ordinates*** coordenadas *fpl* polares (**c**) *(completely different)* **p. opposites** polos opuestos

polarity [pə'lærɪtɪ] *n* (**a**) *Geog* polaridad *f* (**b**) *Phys* polaridad *f* (**c**) *(division)* polaridad *f*

polarization [pəʊləraɪ'zeɪʃən] *n* polarización *f*

polarize ['pəʊləraɪz] **1** *vt* polarizar

2 *vi* polarizarse

polarizing ['pəʊləraɪzɪŋ] *adj Phot* **p. filter** filtro polarizador

Polaroid® ['pəʊlərɔɪd] *n* (**a**) *(camera)* polaroid® *f* (**b**) *(photo)* foto *f* instantánea (**c**) **Polaroids** *(sunglasses)* gafas de sol Polaroid

polder ['pəʊldə(r)] *n* pólder *m*

Pole [pəʊl] *n* polaco(a) *m,f*

pole[1] [pəʊl] **1** *n* (**a**) *(for supporting)* poste *m*; *(for jumping, punting)* pértiga *f*; *(for flag, tent)* mástil *m*; *(for skier)* bastón *m*; *(of stretcher)* palo *m*; *(for phonelines)* poste *m*; *(in fire station)* barra *f* de descenso; IDIOM *Fam* **to drive sb up the p.** hacer que alguien se suba por las paredes ►► ***p. vault*** salto *m* con pértiga, *Am* salto *m* con garrocha; ***p. vaulter*** saltador(ora) *m,f* con pértiga, pertiguista *mf*

(**b**) *(in motor racing)* pole-position *f*, = puesto en la primera línea de salida; **to be on p.** estar en la pole-position; **to be in p. position** *(in motor racing)* estar en la pole-position; *Fig* estar en una posición excelente

(**c**) *(unit of measure)* = antigua medida de longitud equivalente a 5,029 metros

(**d**) *very Fam (penis)* pito *m*

2 *vt (punt)* impulsar

pole[2] *n* (**a**) *(of planet)* polo *m*; **North/South P.** Polo Norte/Sur; IDIOM **to be poles apart** estar en polos opuestos ►► ***P. Star*** estrella *f* polar (**b**) *(of magnet)* polo *m*

poleaxe, *US* **poleax** ['pəʊlæks] **1** *n* (**a**) *(weapon)* hacha *f* de guerra (**b**) *(for slaughter)* hacha *f*

2 *vt (physically)* noquear, tumbar de un golpe; *(emotionally)* dejar anonadado(a)

polecat ['pəʊlkæt] *n* (**a**) *(like weasel)* turón *m* (**b**) *US (skunk)* mofeta *f*

polemic [pə'lemɪk] *n* (**a**) *(controversy)* polémica *f*; **I don't want to indulge in polemics** no quiero entrar en polémica (**b**) *(speech, article)* diatriba *f*

polemic(al) [pə'lemɪk(əl)] *adj* polémico(a)

polemicist [pə'lemɪsɪst] *n* polemista *mf*

polenta [pə'lentə] *n* polenta *f*

police [pə'liːs] **1** *npl* **the p.** la policía; **200 p.** 200 policías; **he's in the p.** es policía; **there was a heavy p. presence** había una gran presencia policial; **all p. leave was cancelled** todos los permisos de los policías fueron suspendidos ►► *US* ***p. academy*** academia *f* de policía; ***p. car*** coche *m or Am* carro *m or CSur* auto *m* de policía; ***p. cell*** calabozo *m*; ***p. chief*** jefe *m* de policía; *US* ***p. commissioner*** = ciudadano que preside un consejo civil encargado de supervisar la actuación de la policía; *Br* ***P. Complaints Authority*** = organismo que investiga las quejas contra la policía en Inglaterra y Gales; *Br* ***p. constable*** (agente *mf* de) policía *mf*; *Br* ***p. court*** juzgado *m* de primera instancia; ***p. custody*** custodia *f* policial; **to be in p. custody** estar bajo custodia policial; **to be taken into p. custody** ser detenido(a); *US* ***p. department*** jefatura *f* de policía; ***p. dog*** perro *m* policía; ***p. escort*** escolta *f* policial; *Br* ***the P. Federation*** = organización profesional de la policía; ***p. force*** policía *f*, cuerpo *m* de policía; *Br* ***p. inspector*** inspector(ora) *m,f* de policía; *US* ***p. line*** cordón *m* policial; ***p. officer*** (agente *mf* de) policía *mf*; *US* ***p. precinct*** *(division)* distrito *m* policial; *(police station)* comisaría *f* de policía; ***p. procedural*** *(novel, movie)* = novela o película que describe una investigación policial; ***p. record*** *(history)* antecedentes *mpl* policiales; *(document)* ficha *f* policial; ***p. state*** estado *m* policial; ***p. station*** comisaría *f* de policía; ***p. van*** coche *m or Am* carro *m* celular, *RP* jaula *f* de policía; *US* ***p. wagon*** coche *m or Am* carro *m* celular, *RP* jaula *f* de policía

2 *vt* (**a**) *(keep secure)* vigilar, custodiar; **the streets are not properly policed these days** no hay suficientes policías en la calle hoy en día;

the match was heavily policed en el partido había una fuerte presencia policial
(**b**) *(supervise)* vigilar, supervisar; **prices are policed by consumer associations** los precios son supervisados por las asociaciones de consumidores
(**c**) *US (clean) (military camp)* limpiar

policeman [pəˈliːsmən] *n* policía *m*

policewoman [pəˈliːswʊmən] *n* (mujer *f*) policía *f*

policing [pəˈliːsɪŋ] *n* (**a**) *(by police)* mantenimiento *m* del orden; **the p. of the match/demonstration was inadequate** la actuación policial durante el partido/la manifestación dejó bastante que desear (**b**) *(supervision)* control *m*, supervisión *f*; **the p. of these regulations** el control de estas normas

policy [ˈpɒlɪsɪ] *n* (**a**) *(of government, in business)* política *f*; **foreign/domestic p.** política exterior/nacional *or* interna; **the government's economic p.** la política económica del gobierno; **it's a matter of p.** es una cuestión de política; **this is in line with company p.** esto se encuadra dentro de la política de la empresa ►► ***p. maker*** responsable *m* político; ***p. paper*** documento *m* normativo; ***p. statement*** declaración *f* de principios; ***p. unit*** = grupo de funcionarios encargados de ofrecer información y análisis a los responsables políticos; *Pol Pej* ***p. wonk*** tecnócrata *mf*
(**b**) *(personal principle, rule of action)* política *f*; **her p. has been always to tell the truth** su política ha sido decir siempre la verdad; **it's (a) good/bad p.** es/no es conveniente
(**c**) *Fin* **(insurance) p.** póliza *f* (de seguros); **to take out a p.** hacerse un seguro

policyholder [ˈpɒlɪsɪhəʊldə(r)] *n* asegurado(a) *m,f*

polio [ˈpəʊlɪəʊ] *n* poliomielitis *f inv*, polio *f*; **to have p.** tener polio ►► ***p. vaccine*** vacuna *f* de la poliomielitis *or* de la polio

poliomyelitis [ˈpəʊlɪəʊmaɪəˈlaɪtɪs] *n Med* poliomielitis *f inv*

Polish [ˈpəʊlɪʃ] **1** *n (language)* polaco *m*
2 *adj* polaco(a)

polish [ˈpɒlɪʃ] **1** *n* (**a**) *(finish, shine)* brillo *m*; **to put a p. on sth** hacer que algo brille; **his shoes have lost their p.** sus zapatos necesitan betún
(**b**) *(act of polishing)* **the brass could do with a p.** al latón le vendría bien que le sacaran el brillo *or Am* una lustrada; **to give sth a p.** dar *or* sacar brillo a algo
(**c**) *(for shoes)* betún *m*, crema *f* (para calzado); *(for furniture, floors)* cera *f*; *(for metal)* limpiametales *m inv*; *(for car)* cera *f*; *(for nails)* esmalte *m*, laca *f*
(**d**) *(refinement)* refinamiento *m*; **his performance lacks p.** le hace falta refinar su actuación; **his writing lacks p.** lo que escribe no tiene brillo *or* refinamiento
2 *vt* (**a**) *(shoes)* dar brillo a, limpiar; *(furniture, floor)* encerar; *(wood, stone)* pulir; *(metal)* limpiar; *(car)* encerar; *(nails)* pintar (**b**) *(rice)* pulir (**c**) *(improve)* pulir

► **polish off** *vt sep Fam (food)* zamparse; *(drink)* cepillarse, *Esp* pimplarse, *RP* mandarse; *(work, opponent)* acabar con, *Esp* cepillarse

► **polish up 1** *vt sep* (**a**) *(shine)* sacar brillo a (**b**) *Fig (skill, language)* pulir, perfeccionar
2 *vi* **brass polishes up well** al latón se le saca el brillo muy fácilmente, *Am* el latón se lustra muy fácil

polished [ˈpɒlɪʃt] *adj* (**a**) *(shiny) (wood, metal, stone)* pulido(a); *(shoes)* brillante, limpio(a); *(floor)* encerado(a) (**b**) *(rice)* pulido(a) (**c**) *(refined) (manners)* refinado(a); *(performance)* pulido(a); *(style)* acabado(a), pulido(a)

polisher [ˈpɒlɪʃə(r)] *n* (**a**) *(person)* lustrador(ora) *m,f* (**b**) *(machine)* pulidora *f*

Politburo [ˈpɒlɪtbjʊrəʊ] *n (of communist state)* Politburó *m*

polite [pəˈlaɪt] *adj* (**a**) *(well-mannered)* educado(a), cortés; **to be p. to sb** ser amable *or* educado(a) con alguien; **he's only being p., he's only saying that to be p.** lo dice por educación; **it's not p. to...** no es de buena educación...; **to make p. conversation** mantener una conversación por cortesía *or* intentando ser agradable (**b**) *(refined)* **in p. society** entre gente educada

politely [pəˈlaɪtlɪ] *adv* educadamente, cortésmente

politeness [pəˈlaɪtnɪs] *n* educación *f*, cortesía *f*; **to do sth out of p.** hacer algo por cortesía

politic [ˈpɒlɪtɪk] *adj Formal* prudente; **it would not be p. to refuse** no sería muy conveniente no aceptar

political [pəˈlɪtɪkəl] *adj* (**a**) *(relating to politics)* político(a); **man is a p. animal** el hombre es un animal político; **it was a p. decision** fue una decisión política ►► ***p. asylum*** asilo *m* político; ***p. correctness*** lo políticamente correcto; ***p. corruption*** corrupción *f* política; *Old-fashioned* ***p. economy*** economía *f* política; ***p. editor*** redactor(ora) *m,f or* director(ora) *m,f* de la sección política; ***p. geography*** geografía *f* política; ***p. prisoner*** preso(a) *m,f* político(a); ***p. science*** ciencias *fpl* políticas, politología *f*; ***p. scientist*** politólogo(a) *m,f*
(**b**) *(interested in politics)* **he's always been very p.** siempre le ha interesado mucho la política; **he isn't very p.** no le va mucho la política
(**c**) *(involving factions)* político(a); **things are getting far too p. in the office** en la oficina están comenzando a aparecer demasiadas divisiones internas

politically [pəˈlɪtɪklɪ] *adv* políticamente; **to be p. aware** tener conciencia política; **p. correct** políticamente correcto(a); **p. motivated** por motivos políticos

politician [pɒlɪˈtɪʃən] *n* político(a) *m,f*

politicization [pəlɪtɪsaɪˈzeɪʃən] *n* politización *f*

politicize [pəˈlɪtɪsaɪz] *vt* politizar; **the whole issue has become highly politicized** el tema ha sido totalmente politizado

politicking [ˈpɒlɪtɪkɪŋ] *n Pej* politiqueo *m*

politico [pəˈlɪtɪkəʊ] (*pl* **politicos** *or* **politicoes**) *n Fam Pej* politicastro(a) *m,f*

politics [ˈpɒlɪtɪks] **1** *n* (**a**) *(activity, profession)* política *f*; **to go into p.** meterse en política; **local/national p.** la política local/nacional (**b**) *(subject)* ciencias *fpl* políticas; **she studied p. at university** estudió ciencias políticas en la facultad
2 *npl* (**a**) *(views)* ideas *fpl* políticas; **what exactly are her p.?** ¿qué ideas políticas tiene?; **his p. are right of centre** políticamente es de centroderecha (**b**) *(scheming)* politiqueo *m*; **office p.** intrigas de oficina

polity [ˈpɒlɪtɪ] *n Formal* (**a**) *(body)* administración *f* (**b**) *(form of government)* sistema *m* de gobierno

polka [ˈpɒlkə] **1** *n* polca *f*
2 *vi* (*pt & pp* **polkaed**) bailar la polca

polka dot [ˈpɒlkədɒt] *n* lunar *m*

polka-dot [ˈpɒlkədɒt] *adj* de lunares ►► *Sport* ***the p. jersey*** el maillot de lunares

poll[1] [pəʊl] **1** *n* (**a**) *(elections)* votación *f*; **to go to the polls** acudir a las urnas; **the party is likely to be defeated at the polls** es muy probable que el partido sea derrotado en las urnas
(**b**) *(votes cast)* participación *f* electoral; **there was an unexpectedly heavy p.** la participación electoral fue sorprendentemente alta; **the ecology candidate got 3 percent of the p.** el candidato de ecología obtuvo el 3 por ciento de los votos
(**c**) *(survey) (of voting intentions)* sondeo *m* electoral; **(opinion) p.** sondeo *m or* encuesta *f* (de opinión); **to carry out** *or* **conduct a p. on** *or* **about sth** realizar una encuesta *or* un sondeo de opinión sobre algo
(**d**) *(count, census)* encuesta *f*
(**e**) *Br* ***p. tax*** = impuesto directo, individual y de tarifa única
2 *vt* (**a**) *(votes)* obtener; **the Greens polled 14 percent of the vote** los verdes obtuvieron el 14 por ciento de los votos (**b**) *(people)* sondear; **most of those polled were in favour of the plan** la mayor parte de los encuestados se manifestó a favor del plan (**c**) *Comptr (terminal)* interrogar
3 *vi* (**a**) *(cast one's vote)* votar (**b**) *(receive votes)* **the party polled well** al partido le fue bien en las elecciones

poll[2] *vt (tree)* podar; *(cattle)* descornar

pollack [ˈpɒlək] *n* gado *m*

pollard [ˈpɒləd] **1** *n (tree)* árbol *m* desmochado; *(cattle)* animal *m* descornado
2 *vt (tree)* desmochar; *(cattle)* descornar

pollen [ˈpɒlən] *n* polen *m* ►► ***p. count*** concentración *f* de polen en el aire; ***p. sac*** saco *m* polínico

pollinate [ˈpɒlɪneɪt] *vt* polinizar

pollination [pɒlɪˈneɪʃən] *n* polinización *f*

polling [ˈpəʊlɪŋ] *n* (**a**) *(voting)* votación *f*; **p. takes place every five years** las elecciones se celebran cada cinco años; **p. is up on last year** la participación electoral es superior a la del año pasado ►► ***p. booth*** cabina *f* electoral; ***p. day*** jornada *f* electoral; ***p. station*** colegio *m* electoral (**b**) *(for opinion poll)* sondeo *m*, encuesta *f*

polliwog, pollywog [ˈpɒlɪwɒg] *n US Fam* renacuajo *m*

pollster [ˈpəʊlstə(r)] *n* encuestador(ora) *m,f*

pollutant [pəˈluːtənt] *n* (sustancia *f*) contaminante *m*

pollute [pəˈluːt] *vt* (**a**) *(environment, river, atmosphere)* contaminar (**b**) *(language, mind)* contaminar

polluted [pəˈluːtɪd] *adj US Fam (drunk)* como una cuba

polluter [pəˈluːtə(r)] *n (company)* empresa *f* contaminante; *(industry)* industria *f* contaminante; **the p. pays** quien contamina, paga

pollution [pəˈluːʃən] *n* (**a**) *(of environment, river, atmosphere)* contaminación *f* (**b**) *(pollutants)* contaminación *f* (**c**) *(of language, mind)* contaminación *f*

Pollyanna [pɒlɪˈænə] *n US* **she's a real P.** es ingenuamente optimista

pollywog = **polliwog**

polo [ˈpəʊləʊ] *n (sport)* polo *m* ►► *Br* **p. neck (sweater)** suéter *m or Esp* jersey *m or Col* saco *m or RP* pulóver *m* de cuello alto *or* de cisne; **p. shirt** polo *m*, *Méx* playera *f*, *RP* chomba *f*; **p. stick** bastón *m* de polo

polonium [pəˈləʊnɪəm] *n Chem* polonio *m*

poltergeist [ˈpɒltəgaɪst] *n* espíritu *m or* fuerza *f* paranormal, poltergeist *m*

poltroon [pɒlˈtruːn] *n Old-fashioned* cobarde *mf*

poly [ˈpɒlɪ] *n Br Fam Formerly (polytechnic)* (escuela *f*) politécnica *f*

polyamide [pɒlɪˈæmaɪd] *n Chem* poliamida *f*

polyandrous [pɒlɪˈændrəs] *adj* poliandro(a)

polyandry [ˈpɒlɪændrɪ] *n* poliandria *f*

polyanthus [pɒlɪˈænθəs] (*pl* **polyanthuses**) *n* = variedad híbrida de prímula

poly bag [ˈpɒlɪˈbæg] *n Br Fam* bolsa *f* de plástico

polycarbonate [ˈpɒlɪˈkɑːbənət] *n Chem* policarbonato *m*

polychrome [ˈpɒlɪkrəʊm] *adj Art (multicoloured)* polícromo(a), policromo(a)

polyester [ˈpɒlɪestə(r)] *n* poliéster *m*

polyethylene [pɒlɪˈeθəliːn] *n US* polietileno *m*

Polyfilla® [ˈpɒlɪfɪlə(r)] *n* masilla *f*

polygamous [pəˈlɪgəməs] *adj* polígamo(a)

polygamy [pəˈlɪgəmɪ] *n* poligamia *f*

polyglot [ˈpɒlɪglɒt] **1** *n* políglota(a) *m,f*
2 *adj* políglota(a)

polygon [ˈpɒlɪgən] *n* polígono *m*

polygonal [pəˈlɪgənəl] *adj* poligonal

polygraph [ˈpɒlɪgrɑːf] *n (lie detector)* detector *m* de mentiras; **to take a p. test** pasar por el detector de mentiras

polyhedral [pɒlɪˈhiːdrəl] *adj* poliédrico(a)

polyhedron [pɒlɪˈhiːdrən] (*pl* **polyhedrons** *or* **polyhedra** [pɒlɪˈhiːdrə]) *n* poliedro *m*

polymath [ˈpɒlɪmæθ] *n* erudito(a) *m,f*

polymer [ˈpɒlɪmə(r)] *n Chem* polímero *m*

polymerization [pɒlɪməraɪˈzeɪʃən] *n* polimerización *f*

polymerize [ˈpɒlɪməraɪz] *vt Chem* polimerizar

polymorph [ˈpɒlɪmɔːf] *n* polimorfo *m*

polymorphic [pɒlɪˈmɔːfɪk], **polymorphous** [pɒlɪˈmɔːfəs] *adj* polimorfo(a)

Polynesia [pɒlɪˈniːzɪə] *n* Polinesia

Polynesian [pɒlɪˈniːzɪən] **1** *n* polinesio(a) *m,f*
2 *adj* polinesio(a)

polynomial [pɒlɪˈnəʊmɪəl] *Math* **1** *n* polinomio *m*
2 *adj* polinómico(a)

polyp [ˈpɒlɪp] *n Med* pólipo *m*

polyphonic [pɒlɪˈfɒnɪk] *adj Mus* polifónico(a)

polyphony [pəˈlɪfənɪ] *n Mus* polifonía *f*

polypropylene [pɒlɪˈprəʊpəliːn], **polypropene** [pɒlɪˈprəʊpiːn] *n Chem* polipropileno *m*

polysaccharide [pɒlɪˈsækəraɪd] *n Biochem* polisacárido *m*

polysemous [pəˈlɪsɪməs] *adj Ling* polisémico(a)

polysemy [pəˈlɪsɪmɪ] *n Ling* polisemia *f*

polystyrene [pɒlɪˈstaɪriːn] *n* poliestireno *m* ►► **p. cement** pegamento *m* para poliestireno; **p. tiles** baldosas *fpl* de poliestireno

polysyllabic [pɒlɪsɪˈlæbɪk] *adj* polisílabo(a)

polysyllable [ˈpɒlɪsɪləbəl] *n* polisílabo *m*

polytechnic [pɒlɪˈteknɪk] *n Br Formerly* (escuela *f*) politécnica *f*

polytheism [ˈpɒlɪθiːɪzəm] *n* politeísmo *m*

polytheistic [pɒlɪθiːˈɪstɪk] *adj* politeísta

polythene [ˈpɒlɪθiːn] *n Br* polietileno *m* ►► **p. bag** bolsa *f* de plástico

polyunsaturated [pɒlɪʌnˈsætjʊreɪtɪd] *adj* poliinsaturado(a)

polyurethane [pɒlɪˈjʊərɪθeɪn] *n* poliuretano *m* ►► **p. foam** espuma *f* de poliuretano

polyvalent [pɒlɪˈveɪlənt] *adj Chem* polivalente

polyvinyl chloride [ˈpɒlɪvaɪnəlˈklɔːraɪd] *n Chem* cloruro *m* de polivinilo

pom = **pommie**

pomade [pəˈmeɪd] **1** *n* pomada *f*
2 *vt* pasar pomada por

pomander [pəˈmændə(r)] *n* bola *f* perfumada

pomarine [ˈpɒməraɪn] *n* **p. skua** págalo *m* pomarino

pomegranate [ˈpɒmɪgrænɪt] *n (fruit)* granada *f*; **p. (tree)** granado *m*

pomelo [ˈpɒmɪləʊ] (*pl* **pomelos**) *n* pomelo *m*

pommel [ˈpɒməl] *n* (**a**) *(on saddle)* perilla *f* (**b**) *(on sword)* pomo *m* (**c**) **p. horse** *(in gymnastics)* caballo *m* con arcos

pommie, pommy [ˈpɒmɪ] *n Austr Fam* = término a veces ofensivo para referirse a los ingleses

Po-Mo [ˈpəʊˈməʊ] *adj Fam* (*abbr* **post-modern**) posmo

pomp [pɒmp] *n* pompa *f*, boato *m*; **p. and circumstance** pompa y circunstancia

Pompeii [pɒmˈpeɪ] *n* Pompeya

pompom [ˈpɒmpɒm], **pompon** [ˈpɒmpɒn] *n (on hat)* pompón *m*

pom-pom [ˈpɒmpɒm] *n Mil (gun)* cañón *m* antiaéreo

pomposity [pɒmˈpɒsɪtɪ], **pompousness** [ˈpɒmpəsnɪs] *n (of person)* pretenciosidad *f*, pedantería *f*; *(of language, remark)* grandilocuencia *f*; *(of language, remark, style, speech)* pomposidad *f*

pompous [ˈpɒmpəs] *adj (person)* pretencioso(a), pedante; *(language, remark)* grandilocuente; *(style, speech)* pomposo(a)

pompously [ˈpɒmpəslɪ] *adv* pomposamente

pompousness = **pomposity**

ponce [pɒns] *n Br Fam* (**a**) *(effeminate man)* maricón *m*, marica *m* (**b**) *(pimp)* proxeneta *m*, *Esp* chulo *m*, *RP* cafiolo *m*

►**ponce about, ponce around** *vi Br Fam* (**a**) *(waste time)* perder el tiempo (**b**) *(effeminate man)* hacer el mariquita

poncho [ˈpɒntʃəʊ] (*pl* **ponchos**) *n* poncho *m*

poncy [ˈpɒnsɪ] *adj Br Fam* de mariquita

pond [pɒnd] *n (man-made)* estanque *m*; *(natural)* laguna *f*; *Fam* **the P.** *(the Atlantic)* el charco ►► **p. life** fauna *f* de laguna

ponder [ˈpɒndə(r)] **1** *vt* considerar; **I sat down and pondered what to do** me senté a pensar qué iba a hacer; **to p. the meaning of life** meditar sobre el sentido de la vida
2 *vi* **to p. over** *or* **on sth** reflexionar sobre algo

ponderous [ˈpɒndərəs] *adj (person, movement)* pesado(a), cansino(a); *(progress)* ralentizado(a), muy lento(a); *(piece of writing)* cargante, pesado(a)

ponderously [ˈpɒndərəslɪ] *adv (to move)* pesadamente, cansinamente; *(to express oneself)* torpemente

pondskater [ˈpɒndskeɪtə(r)] *n Br* zapatero *m*

pondweed [ˈpɒndwiːd] *n* planta *f* acuática

pone [pəʊn] *n US* **p. (bread)** pan *m* de maíz, *Am* arepa *f*

pong [pɒŋ] *Br Fam* **1** *n (unpleasant smell)* mal olor *m*; *(stink)* tufo *m*, peste *f*
2 *vi (smell unpleasant)* oler mal; *(stink)* apestar; **the room still pongs of cigarettes** la sala aún huele a tabaco

pongy [ˈpɒŋɪ] *adj Br Fam (unpleasant)* que huele mal; *(stinking)* apestoso(a)

pontiff [ˈpɒntɪf] *n* pontífice *m*

pontifical [pɒnˈtɪfɪkəl] *adj* (**a**) *Rel* pontificio(a), pontifical (**b**) *(pompous)* pomposo(a)

pontificate[1] [pɒnˈtɪfɪkət] *n Rel* pontificado *m*

pontificate[2] [pɒnˈtɪfɪkeɪt] *vi* pontificar (**about** sobre)

pontoon[1] [pɒnˈtuːn] *n (float)* pontón *m* ►► **p. bridge** puente *m* de pontones

pontoon[2] *n Br (card game)* veintiuna *f*

pony [ˈpəʊnɪ] *n* (**a**) *(small horse)* poni *m*; **to go p. trekking** hacer recorridos en poni (**b**) *Fam (glass)* copita *f* (**c**) *Br Fam (£25)* veinticinco libras *fpl* (**d**) *US Fam (crib) Esp, Ven* chuleta *f*, *Arg* machete *m*, *Chile* torpedo *m*, *Col, Méx* acordeón *m*, *Perú* comprimido *m*, *Urug* trencito *m*

ponytail [ˈpəʊnɪteɪl] *n (hairstyle)* coleta *f*; **she wears her hair in a p.** lleva una coleta

poo [puː] *Fam* **1** *n* (*pl* **poos**) (**a**) *(excrement)* caca *f*; **to do** *or Br* **have a p.** hacer caca (**b**) *Br (worthless things)* **it's a load of p.** es una caca
2 *vi* hacer(se) caca

pooch [puːtʃ] *n Fam* chucho *m*

poodle [ˈpuːdəl] *n* caniche *m*; IDIOM **to be sb's p.** ser el perrito faldero de alguien

poof[1] [pʊf], **poofter** [ˈpʊftə(r)] *n Br Fam* maricón *m*, marica *m*

poof[2] *exclam* ¡plin!

poofy [ˈpʊfɪ] *adj Br Fam Pej* amariconado(a)

pooh[1] [puː] *exclam (at a smell)* ¡puaj!; *(scornful)* ¡bah!

pooh[2] = **poo**

pooh-pooh [ˈpuːˈpuː] *vt* **to p. a suggestion** despreciar una sugerencia

pool[1] [puːl] *n* (**a**) *(pond)* charca *f*; **(swimming) p.** piscina *f*, *Méx* alberca *f*, *RP* pileta *f* ►► ***p. party*** fiesta *f* piscinera, *Arg* pileta party *f* (**b**) *(puddle, of blood)* charco *m*; **a p. of light** un potente haz de luz

pool[2] **1** *n* (**a**) *(group)* grupo *m* (**b**) *(common supply) (of money)* fondo *m* común; *(of company cars)* flota *f*; *(of ideas, talent)* cúmulo *m*, reserva *f*

2 *vt (ideas, resources)* poner en común; *(efforts)* aunar; *(capital, profits)* juntar

pool[3] *n (game)* billar *m* americano, pool *m*; *Br* **to have a game of p.,** *US* **to shoot p.** jugar al billar americano *or* pool ►► ***p. cue*** taco *m* de billar americano *or* pool; ***p. table*** mesa *f* de billar americano *or* pool

poolroom [ˈpuːlruːm] *n* sala *f* de billar americano *or* pool

pools [puːlz] *npl Br* **the p.** las quinielas, *Arg* el Prode, *Col, CRica* el totogol; **to do the (football) p.** jugar a las quinielas *or Arg* al Prode *or Col, CRica* al totogol; **to win the (football) p.** ganar a las quinielas *or Arg* al Prode *or Col, CRica* al totogol ►► ***p. coupon*** boleto *m* de quinielas, *Arg* boleta *f* del Prode

poontang [ˈpuːntæŋ] *n US Vulg (woman's genitals) Esp* conejo *m*, *Col* cuca *f*, *Méx* paloma *f*, *RP* concha *f*, *Ven* cuchara *f*; **he hasn't had any p. for months** hace meses que no moja el churro *or Méx* que no se chinga a nadie

poop[1] [puːp] *n Naut* toldilla *f* ►► ***p. deck*** toldilla *f*

poop[2] *n US Fam* **1** *n (faeces)* cacas *fpl*; **to take a p.** hacer caca

2 *vi* hacer(se) caca

► **poop out** *US Fam* **1** *vt sep (exhaust)* destrozar, *Arg* matar

2 *vi (give up)* abandonar

pooped [puːpt] *adj esp US Fam* hecho(a) migas *or* polvo

poop-scoop [ˈpuːpˈskuːp], **pooper-scooper** [ˈpuːpəˈskuːpə(r)] *n Fam* = instrumento para recoger los excrementos caninos de zonas públicas

---

POOR [pɔː(r)] **1** *npl* **the p.** los pobres

2 *adj* (**a**) *(not rich)* pobre; **to be p. in sth** *(lacking)* carecer de algo; **a p. man/woman** un/una pobre; **the abacus is the p. man's calculator** el ábaco es la calculadora de los pobres; IDIOM **to be as p. as a church mouse** ser más pobre que las ratas ►► ***p. box*** cepillo *m*, *Am* alcancía *f*; *Hist* ***p. law*** ley *f* de asistencia a los pobres; *Fig* ***p. relation*** pariente *m* pobre; ***p. White*** = persona pobre de raza blanca

(**b**) *(inferior)* malo(a), pobre; *(chances, reward)* escaso(a); *(soil)* pobre; **the light is p.** hay poca luz; **to have p. eyesight** tener mal la vista, tener mala vista; **to have p. hearing** no tener buen oído; **to have a p. memory** tener mala memoria; **to have a p. understanding of the basic principles** no comprender bien los principios básicos; **there was a very p. turnout** hubo pocos asistentes; **the match took place in p. light** el partido se celebró con poca luz; **to be p. at physics** no ser bueno(a) en física; **I'm a p. tennis player** soy bastante malo jugando al tenis, *Esp* se me da bastante mal el tenis, *Am* no tengo nada de facilidad para el tenis; **to be a p. sailor** marearse siempre en los barcos, ser marinero de agua dulce; **to be a p. loser** ser un(a) mal(a) perdedor(ora); **to be in p. health** estar mal de salud; **she has very p. taste in clothes** no tiene buen gusto vistiendo; **in p. taste** de mal gusto; **her family comes a p. second to her job** su trabajo es mucho más importante que su familia

(**c**) *(expressing pity)* pobre; **p. creature** *or* **thing!** ¡pobrecito(a)!; **p. (old) Tim!** ¡pobre Tim!; **p. you!** ¡pobrecito(a)!; **p. me!** ¡pobre de mí!

(**d**) *Sch (mark)* ≃ insuficiente

---

poorhouse [ˈpɔːhaʊs] *n Hist* asilo *m* para pobres; **you'll have us in the p. if you carry on like this!** ¡como sigas así vamos a acabar en la ruina!

poorly [ˈpʊəlɪ] **1** *adv* mal; **p. dressed** mal vestido(a); **p. lit** mal iluminado(a); **to be p. off** ser pobre; **the city is p. off for cinemas** la ciudad no tiene muchos cines; **to think p. of sb** no tener un buen concepto de alguien

2 *adj Fam* enfermo(a); **to be p.** estar enfermo(a)

poor-mouth [ˈpʊəmaʊθ] *vt US Fam* menospreciar, criticar

POP *Comptr* (**a**) (*abbr* **post office protocol**) (protocolo *m*) POP *m* (**b**) (*abbr* **point of presence**) punto *m* de acceso *or* conexión

pop. (*abbr* **population**) población *f*

pop[1] [pɒp] **1** *n (music)* (música *f*) pop *m*

2 *adj* (**a**) *(singer, song)* pop ►► ***p. art*** pop-art *m*, arte *m* pop; ***p. concert*** concierto *m* pop; ***p. group*** grupo *m* (de música) pop; ***p. music*** música *f* pop; ***p. star*** estrella *f* del pop (**b**) *(popularized)* popular

pop[2] *n US (father)* papá *m*

pop[3] **1** *n* (**a**) *(sound)* pequeño estallido *m*; **we heard a p.** oímos un pequeño estallido (**b**) *Fam (fizzy drink)* gaseosa *f* (**c**) *Fam* **the dinner is 15 dollars a p.** la cena cuesta 15 dólares por cabeza

2 *vt (pt & pp* **popped**) (**a**) *(burst)* hacer explotar

(**b**) *Fam (put quickly)* **to p. sth into a drawer** poner *or* echar algo en un cajón; **to p. one's head out of the window** asomar la cabeza por la ventana; **to p. pills** consumir pastillas; *US* **let's p. a few beers** abramos unas cervecitas

(**c**) *Fam (shoot)* acabar con, *Esp* cargarse a *(con arma de fuego)*

(**d**) *Fam Old-fashioned (pawn)* empeñar

(**e**) IDIOMS *Br Hum* **to p. one's clogs** estirar la pata, irse al otro barrio; **he decided to p. the question** decidió pedirle que se casara con él

3 *vi* (**a**) *(burst)* estallar, explotar; *(cork)* saltar; **my ears popped** se me destaponaron los oídos; **to p. open** *(box, bag)* abrir; *(buttons)* saltar

(**b**) *(ears)* destaparse; **his eyes almost popped out of his head in surprise** casi se le salen los ojos de las órbitas de la sorpresa

(**c**) *Fam (go quickly)* **to p. into town** pasar por el pueblo; **we popped over to France for the weekend** el fin de semana hicimos una escapada a Francia

► **pop in** *vi Fam* pasarse un momento *(por casa de alguien)*; **p. in on your way home** pasa un momento de camino a casa

► **pop off** *vi Fam* (**a**) *(leave)* largarse; **he popped off home to get his tennis things** se largó a casa a buscar las cosas de tenis (**b**) *(die)* estirar la pata, *Esp* irse al otro barrio, *Méx* patatearse

► **pop out** *vi Fam (go out)* salir; **she's just popped out to the shops** acaba de salir a hacer unas compras

► **pop up** *vi Fam* (**a**) *(go upstairs)* subir; **p. up to see me sometime** sube a verme en algún momento (**b**) *(crop up)* aparecer; **his name seems to p. up everywhere** que su nombre aparece por todas partes

popcorn [ˈpɒpkɔːn] *n* palomitas *fpl* de maíz, *RP* pochoclo *m*

pope [pəʊp] *n* (**a**) *(in Catholic Church)* papa *m*; **P. Pius XI** el Papa Pío XI; IDIOM *Fam Hum* **is the P. Catholic?** ¡claro que sí! ►► ***p.'s nose*** rabadilla *f* (**b**) *(in Eastern Orthodox Church)* pope *m*

popemobile [ˈpəʊpməbiːl] *n Fam* papamóvil *m*

popery [ˈpəʊpərɪ] *n Pej* papismo *m*

pop-eyed [ˈpɒpaɪd] *adj Fam* de ojos saltones; **to stare p. at sth** mirar algo con los ojos desorbitados

popgun [ˈpɒpgʌn] *n* pistola *f* de juguete *(con corchos)*

popinjay [ˈpɒpɪndʒeɪ] *n Old-fashioned or Literary* presumido(a) *m,f*

popish [ˈpəʊpɪʃ] *adj Pej* papista

poplar [ˈpɒplə(r)] *n* álamo *m*

poplin [ˈpɒplɪn] *n (cloth)* popelina *f*, popelín *m*; **a p. shirt** una camisa de popelina

poppadom, poppadum [ˈpɒpədəm] *n* = crepe fina, frita o a la parrilla, que se sirve con platos de la comida india

popper [ˈpɒpə(r)] *n Fam* (**a**) *Br (fastener)* automático *m*, corchete *m* (**b**) *US (for popcorn)* = recipiente utilizado para hacer palomitas de maíz (**c**) *(drug)* = cápsula de nitrato de amilo

poppet [ˈpɒpɪt] *n* (**a**) *Br Fam* **she's a p.** es una ricura; **my p.!** ¡mi tesoro!, ¡mi vida! (**b**) *Tech* **p. (valve)** válvula *f* de vástago

poppy [ˈpɒpɪ] *n* amapola *f* ►► ***p. seed*** semilla *f* de amapola

poppycock [ˈpɒpɪkɒk] *n Fam Old-fashioned (nonsense) Esp* majaderías *fpl*, *Am* zonceras *fpl*

Popsicle® [ˈpɒpsɪkəl] *n US* polo *m*, *Am* paleta *f* helada, *Arg* palito *m* de agua

pop socks [ˈpɒpsɒks] *npl Br* medias *fpl* de nylon *(que cubren hasta la rodilla)*

pop-top [ˈpɒptɒp] *n US* anilla *f (de lata)* ►► ***p. can*** lata *f* de anilla

populace [ˈpɒpjʊləs] *n Formal* **the p.** el pueblo; **the entire p. of the town** el pueblo al completo; **panic spread among the p.** el pánico cundió entre la población

popular [ˈpɒpjʊlə(r)] *adj* (**a**) *(well-liked)* popular; **you won't make yourself very p. doing that** no va a sentar nada bien que hagas eso; **she is p. with her colleagues** cae bien a sus compañeros; **it's very p. with the customers** se vende mucho; **I'm not going to be very p. when they find out it's my fault!** cuando descubran que fue mi culpa, me van a querer matar

(**b**) *(chosen by many) (excuse, answer, reason)* frecuente; *(choice,*

product, restaurant, resort) popular; **DVDs are a p. present** los DVDs son un regalo que se lleva mucho
(**c**) *(non-intellectual, non-specialist) (newspapers, TV programmes)* de masas ▸▸ ***p. culture*** acervo *m* popular; ***p. science*** divulgación *f* científica
(**d**) *(general, widespread)* **by p. demand** a petición *orAm* pedido popular *or* del público; **contrary to p. belief** en contra de lo que comúnmente se cree; **a p. misconception** una idea equivocada generalizada; **it's an idea that enjoys great p. support** es una idea que goza de gran apoyo popular ▸▸ ***p. wisdom*** sabiduría *f* popular
(**e**) *(of or for the people)* del pueblo, popular; **after weeks of p. unrest** después de semanas de malestar popular; **quality goods at p. prices** productos de calidad a precios económicos; **he won the p. vote** ganó el voto popular ▸▸ *Pol* ***p. front*** frente *m* popular

popularity [pɒpjʊˈlærɪtɪ] *n* popularidad *f*; **to grow/decline in p.** ganar/perder popularidad; **to come high/low in the p. stakes** estar arriba/abajo en la escala de popularidad ▸▸ ***p. rating*** índice *m* de popularidad

popularization [pɒpjʊlәraɪˈzeɪʃәn] *n* popularización *f*

popularize [ˈpɒpjʊlәraɪz] *vt* (**a**) *(make popular)* popularizar; **a sport popularized by television** un deporte que ha sido popularizado por la televisión (**b**) *(make easy to understand)* divulgar

popularizer [ˈpɒpjʊlәraɪzә(r)] *n (of fashion, ideas)* popularizador(ora) *m,f*

popularly [ˈpɒpjʊlәlɪ] *adv* comúnmente, popularmente; **he was p. known as "the King"** se le conocía popularmente por "el Rey"; **it is p. believed that...** casi todo el mundo cree que...

populate [ˈpɒpjʊleɪt] *vt* poblar; **sparsely populated** *(region)* poco poblado(a)

population [pɒpjʊˈleɪʃәn] *n* población *f*; **the whole p. is in mourning** todo la población está de luto; **the white p. of South Africa** la población blanca de Sudáfrica; **the prison p.** la población carcelaria; **the beaver p. is declining** la población de castores está disminuyendo ▸▸ ***p.*** *Br* ***centre*** *or US* ***center*** núcleo *m* de población; ***p. density*** densidad *f* de población; ***p. explosion*** explosión *f* demográfica; ***p. figures*** cifras *fpl* de población; ***p. growth*** crecimiento *m* de la población

populism [ˈpɒpjʊlɪzәm] *n* populismo *m*

populist [ˈpɒpjʊlɪst] **1** *n* populista *mf*
2 *adj* populista

populous [ˈpɒpjʊlәs] *adj* populoso(a)

pop-up [ˈpɒpʌp] *adj* (**a**) *(book)* desplegable (**b**) *(toaster)* automático(a) (**c**) *Comptr (menu)* desplegable

porbeagle [ˈpɔːbiːgәl] *n* **p. (shark)** marrajo *m* de Cornualles

porcelain [ˈpɔːsәlɪn] *n* porcelana *f* ▸▸ ***p. ware*** porcelana *f*

porch [pɔːtʃ] *n* (**a**) *Br (entrance)* zaguán *m* (**b**) *US (veranda)* porche *m*

porcine [ˈpɔːsaɪn] *adj* porcino(a)

porcini [pɔːˈtʃiːnɪ] *n* **p. (mushroom)** *Esp* seta *f or Am* hongo *m* porcini

porcupine [ˈpɔːkjʊpaɪn] *n* puerco *m* espín

pore [pɔː(r)] *n* poro *m*

▸ **pore over** *vt insep* estudiar con detenimiento

pork [pɔːk] **1** *n* (carne *f* de) cerdo *m or* puerco *m or Am* chancho *m* ▸▸ *US Fam* ***p. barrel politics*** = política de adjudicación de contratas estatales que benefician a la zona del que las concede; ***p. butcher*** chacinero(a) *m,f*; ***p. chop*** chuleta *f* de cerdo; ***p. pie*** empanada *f* de carne de cerdo *or* puerco; *US* ***p. rinds*** cortezas *fpl* de cerdo; *Br* ***p. scratchings*** cortezas *fpl* de cerdo; *Vulg* ***p. sword*** *(penis) Esp* polla *f*, *Am* verga *f*, *Chile* pico *m*, *Méx* pito *m*, *RP* pija *f*, *Ven* pinga *f*
2 *vt Vulg (have sex with)* tirarse a

porker [ˈpɔːkә(r)] *n* (**a**) *(pig)* cerdo *m* cebón (**b**) *Fam (person)* gordinflón(ona) *m,f*

porkpie hat [ˈpɔːkpaɪˈhæt] *n* sombrero *m* de copa baja

porky [ˈpɔːkɪ] *Fam* **1** *n Br* **p. (pie)** *(lie)* mentira *f*, trola *f*, *Col* carreta *f*, *Méx* chisme *m*, *RP* bolazo *m*; **to tell porkies** decir mentiras, meter trolas, *Am* contar cuentos, *RP* bolacear
2 *adj (fat)* rechoncho(a)

porn [pɔːn] *n Fam* porno *m* ▸▸ ***p. shop*** tienda *f* porno; *Br* ***the p. squad*** la brigada de moralidad

porno [ˈpɔːnәʊ] *adj Fam* porno

pornographer [pɔːˈnɒgrәfә(r)] *n* pornógrafo(a) *m,f*

pornographic [pɔːnәˈgræfɪk] *adj* pornográfico(a)

pornography [pɔːˈnɒgrәfɪ] *n* pornografía *f*

porosity [pɔːˈrɒsɪtɪ] *n* porosidad *f*

porous [ˈpɔːrәs] *adj* poroso(a)

porphyry [ˈpɔːfɪrɪ] *n Geol* pórfiro *m*

porpoise [ˈpɔːpәs] *n* marsopa *f*

porridge [ˈpɒrɪdʒ] *n* (**a**) *(cereal)* gachas *fpl* de avena ▸▸ ***p. oats*** copos *mpl* de avena (**b**) *Br Fam* **to do p.** *(serve prison sentence)* estar a la sombra

porringer [ˈpɒrɪndʒә(r)] *n* escudilla *f*

port¹ [pɔːt] *n* (**a**) *(harbour, town)* puerto *m*; **to come** *or* **put into p.** entrar a puerto; **we left p. before dawn** zarpamos antes del amanecer; **in p.** en puerto; PROV **any p. in a storm** en casos extremos, se olvidan los remilgos ▸▸ ***p. of arrival*** puerto *m* de llegada; ***p. authority*** autoridad *f* portuaria; ***p. of call*** escala *f*; *Fig* parada *f*; ***p. charges*** tasas *fpl* portuarias; ***p. of departure*** puerto *m* de salida; ***p. dues*** tasas *fpl* portuarias; ***p. of entry*** puerto *m* de entrada; ***p. of registry*** puerto *m* de matrícula
(**b**) *(in proper names)* ***P. Moresby*** Port Moresby; ***P. of Spain*** Puerto España

port² **1** *n Naut (left-hand side)* babor *m*; **the ship was listing to p.** el barco escoraba a babor; **ship to p.!** ¡barco a babor!
2 *vt* (**a**) *Naut* **p. the helm!** ¡virar a babor! (**b**) *Mil* cruzar; **p. arms!** ¡presenten armas!

port³ *n (drink)* (vino *m* de) oporto *m*

port⁴ *n* (**a**) *(window) (on ship, plane)* portilla *f* (**b**) *(for loading)* porta *f* (**c**) *Comptr* puerto *m*

portability [pɔːtәˈbɪlɪtɪ] *n* (**a**) *(transportability)* transportabilidad *f* (**b**) *Comptr (of program, software)* portabilidad *f* (**c**) *(of mortgage, pension)* portabilidad *f*, transferibilidad *f*

portable [ˈpɔːtәbәl] **1** *adj* (**a**) *(easy to transport)* portátil; **p. TV (set)** televisor portátil (**b**) *Comptr (program, software)* portátil (**c**) *(mortgage, pension)* portátil, transferible
2 *n (typewriter)* máquina *f* de escribir portátil; *(TV)* televisor *m* portátil; *(computer)* portátil *m*

portacrib [ˈpɔːtәkrɪb] *n US* moisés *m*, capazo *m*

portage [ˈpɔːtɪdʒ] *n Com (transport, cost)* porte *m*

Portakabin® [ˈpɔːtәkæbɪn] *n Br* caseta *f* prefabricada, barracón *m*

portal [ˈpɔːtәl] **1** *n* (**a**) *Formal (entrance)* pórtico *m* (**b**) *Comptr (web page)* portal *m*
2 *adj Anat* ***p. vein*** (vena *f*) porta *f*

Portaloo® [ˈpɔːtәluː] *n* sanitarios retretes *mpl* portátiles

Port-au-Prince [ˈpɔːtәʊˈpræns] *n* Puerto Príncipe

portcullis [pɔːtˈkʌlɪs] *n* rastrillo *m (reja)*

portend [pɔːˈtend] *vt Formal* augurar

portent [ˈpɔːtent] *n Formal* (**a**) *(omen)* augurio *m* (**b**) *(marvel, wonder)* maravilla *f*

portentous [pɔːˈtentәs] *adj Formal* (**a**) *(ominous) (words, dream)* premonitorio(a); **a p. decision** una decisión que trajo/traerá importantes consecuencias (**b**) *(momentous) (event)* trascendental (**c**) *(pompously solemn)* solemne, pomposo(a)

porter¹ [ˈpɔːtә(r)] *n* (**a**) *(at station)* mozo *m* de equipaje (**b**) *esp Br (doorkeeper) (at hotel)* portero(a) *m,f*, conserje *mf*; *(in block of flats)* portero(a) *m,f*; *(in university, college)* bedel *mf* (**c**) *(in hospital)* celador(ora) *m,f* (**d**) *US (on train)* mozo *m*

porter² *n (beer)* = tipo de cerveza negra

porterhouse steak [ˈpɔːtәhaʊsˈsteɪk] *n* filete *m or RP* bife *m* de ternera de primera

portfolio [pɔːtˈfәʊlɪәʊ] (*pl* **portfolios**) *n* (**a**) *(case) (for documents, drawings)* cartera *f* (**b**) *(of person's work)* carpeta *f* (**c**) *Fin (of shares)* cartera *f* (de valores) ▸▸ ***p. management*** gestión *f* de cartera (**d**) *Pol* cartera *f*; **the Defence/Health p.** la cartera de Defensa/Sanidad

porthole [ˈpɔːthәʊl] *n Naut* portilla *f*, ojo *m* de buey

portico [ˈpɔːtɪkәʊ] (*pl* **porticos** *or* **porticoes**) *n Archit* pórtico *m*

portion [ˈpɔːʃәn] *n* (**a**) *(part, section)* parte *f*; **this p. to be given up** *(on ticket)* esta parte debe ser entregada
(**b**) *(share)* parte *f*, porción *f*; **three portions of flour to one p. of sugar** tres partes de harina por cada parte de azúcar
(**c**) *(of food)* ración *f*, porción *f*
(**d**) *Literary (fate)* destino *m*; **it fell to my p. to break the news to her** fue mi destino tener que darle la noticia a ella
(**e**) *(dowry) Old-fashioned* **(marriage) p.** dote *f*

▸ **portion out** *vt sep* repartir

portliness [ˈpɔːtlɪnɪs] *n* corpulencia *f*

portly [ˈpɔːtlɪ] *adj* corpulento(a)

portmanteau [pɔːtˈmæntәʊ] (*pl* **portmanteaus** *or* **portmanteaux** [pɔːtˈmæntәʊz]) *n Old-fashioned* portamanteo *m* ▸▸ ***p. word*** = término compuesto por la fusión de dos palabras

portrait ['pɔːtreɪt] *n* (**a**) *also Fig (picture)* retrato *m*; **he had his p. painted** le pintaron su retrato; **a vivid p. of 18th century society** un fiel retrato de la sociedad del siglo 18 ►► ***p. gallery*** galería *f* de retratos; ***p. painter*** retratista *mf* (**b**) *Comptr* **p. (orientation)** formato *m or* orientación *f* vertical

portraitist ['pɔːtrətɪst] *n* retratista *mf*

portraiture ['pɔːtrɪtʃə(r)] *n* retrato *m*

portray [pɔː'treɪ] *vt* (**a**) *(of painting, writer, book)* retratar, describir; **he portrayed King John as a scoundrel** retrató al rey John como a un sinvergüenza; **in the film the soldiers are portrayed as monsters** en la película, los soldados aparecen como monstruos (**b**) *(of actor)* interpretar (el papel de)

portrayal [pɔː'treɪəl] *n* (**a**) *(description)* descripción *f*, representación *f* (**b**) *(by actor)* interpretación *f*

Portugal ['pɔːtjʊgəl] *n* Portugal

Portuguese [pɔːtjʊ'giːz] **1** *n* (**a**) (*pl* **Portuguese**) *(person)* portugués(esa) *m,f* (**b**) *(language)* portugués *m*

2 *adj* portugués(esa) ►► ***P. man-of-war*** *(jellyfish)* = tipo de medusa venenosa

Port-wine stain ['pɔːt'waɪnsteɪn] *n (birthmark)* mancha *f* de nacimiento de color rojo oscuro

POS [piːəʊ'es] *n Com* (*abbr* **point of sale**) punto *m* de venta

pose [pəʊz] **1** *n* (**a**) *(position)* postura *f*, posición *f*; **to take up** *or* **strike a p.** adoptar una postura (**b**) *Pej (affectation)* pose *f*; **it's just a p.** no es más que una pose

2 *vt (present) (problem, question)* plantear; *(danger, threat)* suponer

3 *vi* (**a**) *(for portrait)* posar; **to p. for a photograph/an artist** posar para una fotografía/un artista (**b**) *Pej (behave affectedly)* tomar *or* hacer poses (**c**) *(pretend to be)* **to p. as** hacerse pasar por

Poseidon [pə'saɪdən] *n Mythol* Poseidón

poser ['pəʊzə(r)] *n Fam* (**a**) *Br Pej (affected person)* presumido(a) *m,f* (**b**) *(difficult question)* rompecabezas *m inv*

poseur [pəʊ'zɜː(r)] *n Pej (affected person)* presumido(a) *m,f*

posh [pɒʃ] *Br Fam* **1** *adj (person, accent) Esp* pijo(a), *Méx* fresa, *RP* (con)cheto(a), *Ven* sifrino(a); *(restaurant, area, clothes)* elegante; *(car, house)* de lujo; **he moves in some very p. circles** se mueve en algunos círculos muy elegantes

2 *adv* **to talk p.** hablar con acento *Esp* pijo *or Méx* como una fresa *or RP* como un concheto

►**posh up** *vt sep Fam* arreglar

posit ['pɒzɪt] *vt Formal (assume, suggest)* postular

position [pə'zɪʃən] **1** *n* (**a**) *(physical posture)* posición *f*; **in a horizontal/vertical p.** en posición horizontal/vertical; **in a sitting p.** sentado(a); **in a standing p.** de pie, *Am* parado(a); **in the on/off p.** *(switch, lever)* (en la posición de) encendido *or Am* prendido/apagado

(**b**) *(place)* posición *f*, lugar *m*; **remember the p. of the cards** recuerden la posición de las cartas; **to change** *or* **shift p.** cambiar de lugar; **to jockey** *or* **jostle** *or* **manoeuvre for p.** luchar *or* maniobrar por conseguir la posición; *Fig* luchar por un lugar; **to put sth in** *or* **into p.** poner algo en posición; **in p.** en su sitio; **out of p.** fuera de su sitio

(**c**) *(post, appointed place) (of player, actor, soldier)* posición *f*; **he can play in any p.** puede jugar en cualquier posición; **to defend a p.** *(in battle)* defender una posición; **take up your positions!, get into p.!** *(actors, dancers)* ¡cada uno a su lugar!; *(soldiers)* ¡a sus puestos!

(**d**) *(rank) (in table, scale)* posición *f*; **they're in tenth p.** *(in race, league)* están décimos *or* en la décima posición; *(in hierarchy)* están en la décima posición; **she is concerned about her social p.** le preocupa su posición social

(**e**) *(situation)* posición *f*, situación *f*; **the p. as I see it is this...** según lo veo yo, ésta es la situación...; **to be in a strong p.** estar en una buena posición; **it's an awkward p. to be in** es una situación bastante incómoda; **our financial p. is improving** nuestra situación financiera está mejorando; **put yourself in my p.** ponte en mi lugar *or* situación; **to be in a p. to do sth** estar en condiciones de hacer algo; **to be in no p. to do sth** no estar en condiciones de hacer algo

(**f**) *(opinion, standpoint)* postura *f*, posición *f*; **to take up a p. on sth** tomar *or* asumir una posición respecto de algo; **to change** *or* **shift p.** cambiar de posición ►► ***p. paper*** = documento en el que se analiza un asunto y se hacen recomendaciones generales

(**g**) *Formal (job)* puesto *m*; **a p. of responsibility** un puesto de responsabilidad

(**h**) *(in bank, post office)* ***p. closed*** *(sign)* puesto *m* cerrado

2 *vt* (**a**) *(place) (object)* colocar, situar; *(troops)* apostar; **the school is positioned near a dangerous crossroads** la escuela está ubicada cerca de un cruce peligroso; **to p. oneself** colocarse, situarse; **to be well/poorly positioned to do sth** estar en una buena/mala posición para hacer algo (**b**) *Com (product)* posicionar

positioning [pə'zɪʃənɪŋ] *n Com* posicionamiento *m*

positive ['pɒzɪtɪv] *adj* (**a**) *(affirmative) (answer)* afirmativo(a); *Med* **the test was p.** la prueba ha dado positivo; **on the p. side** como aspecto positivo

(**b**) *(constructive) (person, philosophy)* positivo(a); **haven't you got any p. suggestions?** ¿no tienes ninguna idea constructiva que aportar?; **she has a very p. approach to the problem** aborda el problema con un enfoque muy positivo; **I'm feeling more p. about my life now** ahora me siento un poco más optimista ►► *Br* ***p. discrimination*** discriminación *f* positiva; ***p. feedback*** *(constructive response)* reacciones *fpl* positivas; *Psy* ***p. reinforcement*** refuerzo *m* positivo; ***p. thinking*** actitud *f* positiva; *Br* ***p. vetting*** *(security check)* = investigación completa a la que es sometido un aspirante a un cargo público relacionado con la seguridad nacional

(**c**) *(definite) (evidence, proof)* concluyente; *(progress)* decidido(a); *(advantage, benefit)* seguro(a)

(**d**) *(certain)* (completamente) seguro(a); **to be p. about sth** estar completamente seguro de algo; **are you absolutely sure? – yes, p.** ¿estás completamente seguro? – sí, sin ninguna duda

(**e**) *(for emphasis)* **it was a p. disgrace/nightmare** fue una verdadera desgracia/pesadilla; **it would be a p. pleasure** sería un verdadero placer

(**f**) *Math* positivo(a)

(**g**) *Elec (charge, electrode, pole)* positivo(a) ►► ***p. feedback*** *(in circuit)* retroalimentación *f* positiva

(**h**) *Phot* **p. print** copia positiva

positively ['pɒzɪtɪvlɪ] *adv* (**a**) *(affirmatively) (to answer)* afirmativamente

(**b**) *(constructively) (to think, react)* positivamente; **people have responded quite p. to our suggestions** la gente ha respondido muy positivamente a nuestras sugerencias

(**c**) *(definitely)* **it has yet to be p. identified** todavía no se ha hecho una identificación definitiva

(**d**) *(for emphasis)* verdaderamente, realmente; **smiling? – she was p. beaming!** ¿sonriendo? – ¡tenía una sonrisa verdaderamente radiante!; **this is p. ridiculous!** ¡esto es totalmente ridículo!; *Fam* **p. not** de ninguna manera

(**e**) *Elec & Phys* **p. charged** con carga positiva, cargado(a) positivamente

positivism ['pɒzɪtɪvɪzəm] *n Phil* positivismo *m*

positivist ['pɒzɪtɪvɪst] **1** *n* positivista *mf*

2 *adj* positivista

positron ['pɒzɪtrɒn] *n Phys* positrón *m* ►► *Med* ***p. emission tomography*** tomografía *f* por emisión de positrones

poss [pɒs] *adj Fam* **as soon as p.** en cuanto pueda

posse ['pɒsɪ] *n* (**a**) *(to catch criminal)* partida *f or* cuadrilla *f* (de persecución) (**b**) *(group)* banda *f*, cuadrilla *f*; **a p. of fans were soon in hot pursuit** un grupo de fans se puso a perseguirlo de inmediato

possess [pə'zes] *vt* (**a**) *(property, quality, faculty)* poseer; **she possesses a clear understanding of the subject** posee una clara comprensión del tema

(**b**) *(dominate, overcome)* **he was completely possessed by the idea of going to India** estaba obsesionado con la idea de ir a la India; **what possessed you to do that?** ¿qué te impulsó a hacer eso?

(**c**) *Formal or Literary* **to p. oneself of sth** armarse *or* hacerse de algo; **to be possessed of** *(quality)* poseer

possessed [pə'zest] *adj* (**a**) *(dominated, overcome)* **p. by fear/rage** embargado(a) por el miedo/la rabia (**b**) *(demonically)* **to be p. (by demons)** estar poseído(a) (por demonios); IDIOM **like one p.** como un poseso

possession [pə'zeʃən] *n* (**a**) *(thing possessed)* posesión *f*; **the jade vases are our most precious possessions** los jarrones de jade son los objetos más valiosos que tenemos; **foreign** *or* **overseas possessions** *(colonies)* posesiones coloniales

(**b**) *(ownership)* posesión *f*; **the file is no longer in my p.** el archivo ya no está en posesión mía; **how did this come into your p.?** ¿cómo te hiciste con esto?; **certain documents have come into my p.** me han llegado ciertos documentos; **to gain** *or* **acquire p. of sth** adquirir algo; **to take p. of sth** *(by force)* tomar posesión de algo; **in full p. of his senses** *or* **faculties** en plena posesión de sus facultades (mentales); PROV **p. is nine tenths** *or* **points of the law** = en caso de duda, el que tiene algo en su poder es su dueño

(**c**) *(by evil spirit)* posesión *f*

(**d**) *Law (of illegal thing)* **p. (of drugs)** tenencia *f* de drogas; **he was**

found in p. of a flick-knife, a flick-knife was found in his p. se lo encontró en posesión de una navaja automática
(**e**) *Law (of property)* posesión *f*; **to take p.** tomar posesión
(**f**) *Sport* posesión *f* de la pelota; **to be in** *or* **have p. (of the ball)** estar en *or* tener posesión de la pelota

possessive [pə'zesɪv] **1** *n Gram* posesivo *m*
2 *adj* (**a**) *Gram* posesivo(a); **p. adjective/pronoun** adjetivo/pronombre posesivo (**b**) *(parent, lover)* posesivo(a); **to be p. of** *or* **about sth/sb** ser posesivo(a) con algo/alguien

possessively [pə'zesɪvlɪ] *adv* de manera posesiva, posesivamente; **she clung p. to her father's hand** se aferraba posesivamente a la mano de su padre

possessor [pə'zesə(r)] *n* poseedor(ora) *m,f*; **I found myself the p. of an old mansion** de pronto me encontré como el poseedor de una vieja mansión

posset ['pɒsɪt] **1** *n (drink)* = bebida caliente de leche con vino o cerveza
2 *vi (baby)* regurgitar

possibility [pɒsɪ'bɪlɪtɪ] *n* (**a**) *(chance)* posibilidad *f*; **the p. of a settlement is fading fast** las posibilidades de un acuerdo se están desvaneciendo; **to be within/outside the bounds of p.** entrar/no entrar dentro de lo posible; **there's a p. that we might be delayed** es posible que nos retrasemos; **there's no p. of that happening** no hay posibilidades de que eso suceda; **is there any p. that you could help me?** ¿le importaría ayudarme?
(**b**) *(possible choice)* posibilidad *f*; **one p. would be to...** una posibilidad sería...; **she's still a p. for the job** sigue siendo una posible candidata para el puesto
(**c**) *(possible event, outcome)* posibilidad *f*; **that is a distinct p.** es una posibilidad real; **to allow for all possibilities** prepararse para cualquier eventualidad; **the possibilities are endless!** las posibilidades son infinitas; **this house has possibilities** esta casa tiene potencial; **the job has a lot of possibilities** el trabajo tiene mucho potencial

possible ['pɒsɪbəl] **1** *n* (**a**) *(activity)* **diplomacy is the art of the p.** la diplomacia es el arte de lo posible (**b**) *(choice) (for job)* candidato(a) *m,f* posible; **we looked at ten houses, of which two were possibles** visitamos diez casas, de las cuales dos son posibles candidatas
2 *adj* (**a**) *(which can be done)* posible; **if (at all) p.** si es posible; **would it be p. for you to...?** ¿te importaría...?; **to make sth p.** hacer posible algo; **as far as p.** *(within one's competence)* en la medida de lo posible; *(at maximum distance)* tan lejos como sea posible; **as little as p.** lo menos posible; **as long as p.** todo el tiempo que sea posible; **as much as p.** cuanto sea posible; **I want you to try, as much as p., to behave** quiero que, en la medida de lo posible, intentes portarte bien; **I visit her as often as p.** la visito siempre que puedo; **as soon as p.** cuanto antes; **whenever/wherever p.** cuando/donde sea posible
(**b**) *(conceivable, imaginable)* posible; **what p. benefit can we get from it?** ¿en qué podría beneficiarnos?; **it seems barely p.** parece muy poco posible; **the best/worst p. result** el mejor/peor resultado posible; **the best of all p. worlds** lo mejor que podría pasar; **it is p. that he will come** es posible que venga; **anything's p.** todo es posible
(**c**) *(potential)* posible; **p. risks/consequences** posibles riesgos/consecuencias

possibly ['pɒsɪblɪ] *adv* (**a**) *(perhaps)* posiblemente; **will you go? – p.** ¿irás? – puede *or* quizá; **p. not** puede que no
(**b**) *(for emphasis)* **I can't p. do it** me resulta de todo punto imposible hacerlo; **I'll do all I p. can** haré todo lo que esté en mi mano; **how could you p. do such a thing?** ¿cómo se te ocurrió hacer semejante cosa?; **that can't p. be true!** ¡es imposible que sea verdad!; **what could he p. mean?** ¿qué querrá decir?; **could you p. help me?** ¿te importaría ayudarme?; **I couldn't p. accept your offer** me es imposible aceptar tu ofrecimiento

possum ['pɒsəm] *n* (**a**) *US (opossum)* zarigüeya *f*; IDIOM *Fam* **to play p.** *(pretend to be asleep)* hacerse el/la dormido(a); *(pretend to know nothing)* hacerse el/la sueco(a) (**b**) *Austr (marsupial)* falangero *m*

post[1] [pəʊst] **1** *n* (**a**) *(wooden stake)* poste *m*; **the near/far p.** *(of goal)* el poste más cercano/lejano; **his horse was beaten at the p.** a su caballo le ganaron en la llegada (**b**) *(job)* puesto *m*; **to take up a p.** ocupar un puesto (**c**) *(military position, station)* puesto *m*; **to be/die at one's p.** estar/morir al pie del cañón ▸▸ *US **p. exchange*** = tienda en una base militar
2 *vt* (**a**) *(station)* apostar; **they posted men all around the house** apostaron hombres alrededor de la casa (**b**) *Br (assign)* destinar

post[2] *vt* (**a**) *(affix)* poner, pegar; **p. no bills** *(sign)* prohibido fijar carteles (**b**) *(publish) (banns, names)* hacer público, anunciar; *(on bulletin board)* anunciar, pegar; *Comptr* enviar a; **he has been posted (as) missing** lo han dado por desaparecido (**c**) *US* **to p. bail (for sb)** pagar una fianza (de alguien) (**d**) *Fin* anotar, contabilizar; **to p. an entry** hacer *or* contabilizar un movimiento

post[3] *esp Br* **1** *n (mail)* correo *m*; **by p.** por correo; **the first p.** el correo de (primera hora de) la mañana; **it came in this morning's p.** llegó en el correo de esta mañana; **has the p. come?** ¿ha venido *or* llegado el correo?; **was there any p. (for me)?** ¿había alguna carta (para mí)?; **to miss the p.** llegar tarde para la recogida del correo; **will we still catch the p.?** ¿llegaremos a tiempo para la recogida del correo?; **can you take these letters to the p.?** ¿podrías llevar estas cartas al correo?; **it's in the p.** ha sido enviado por correo ▸▸ ***the P. Office*** *(service) Esp* Correos *m inv, Am* Correo *m*; ***p. office*** oficina *f* de correos; *US* = juego infantil en el que un niño hace de cartero que entrega una carta y a cambio recibe un beso; ***p. office box*** apartado *m* postal *or* de correos; ***p. office savings account*** = cuenta postal de ahorros
2 *vt* (**a**) *(letter) (send by post)* enviar *or* mandar (por correo); *(put in box)* poner en el buzón (**b**) *Fam (inform)* **I'll keep you posted** te tendré al tanto

▸ **post on** *vt sep (letters)* enviar a nombre de

▸ **post up** *vt sep (notice)* pegar

postage ['pəʊstɪdʒ] *n* franqueo *m*; **what's the p. on this parcel?** ¿cuánto cuesta el franqueo para este paquete?; **p. paid** franqueo pagado ▸▸ *US **p. and handling*** gastos *mpl* de envío; *US **p. meter*** máquina *f* de franqueo; *Br **p. and packing*** gastos *mpl* de envío; ***p. stamp*** sello *m* (de correos), *Am* estampilla *f*

postal ['pəʊstəl] *adj* (**a**) *(charge, service)* postal ▸▸ *Br **p. code*** código *m* postal; ***p. district*** distrito *m* postal; *Br **p. order*** giro *m* postal; *US **the P. Service*** *Esp* Correos *m inv, Am* Correo *m*; ***p. strike*** huelga *f* postal; ***p. vote*** voto *m* por correo (**b**) *US Fam* **to go p.** volverse loco(a) *or Esp* majara, *CSur* rayarse, *Méx* zafarse

postbag ['pəʊstbæg] *n Br* (**a**) *(bag)* saca *f* de correos (**b**) *(letters)* correspondencia *f*, cartas *fpl*; **we've got a full p. this morning** esta mañana hemos recibido una gran cantidad de cartas

postbox ['pəʊstbɒks] *n Br* buzón *m* (de correos)

postbus ['pəʊstbʌs] *n Br* = furgoneta utilizada para repartir el correo y transportar viajeros, especialmente en áreas rurales

postcard ['pəʊstkɑːd] *n* (tarjeta *f*) postal *f*

postcode ['pəʊstkəʊd] *n Br* código *m* postal

postdate ['pəʊst'deɪt] *vt* (**a**) *(cheque)* extender con fecha posterior (**b**) *(happen after)* **this event postdates the tragedy by several years** este acontecimiento tuvo lugar varios años después de la tragedia

postdoctoral [pəʊst'dɒktərəl] *adj* pos(t)doctoral

poster ['pəʊstə(r)] *n (for advertising)* cartel *m*, póster *m*, *Am* afiche *m*; *(of painting, pop group)* póster *m* ▸▸ ***p. art*** arte *m* del cartel *or* póster *or Am* afiche; ***p. colour*** témpera *f*; ***p. paint*** témpera *f*

poste restante ['pəʊstre'stɒnt] *n Br* lista *f* de correos, *Am* poste *m* restante

posterior [pɒs'tɪərɪə(r)] **1** *n Hum (buttocks)* trasero *m*, posaderas *fpl*
2 *adj Anat & Zool* posterior

posterity [pɒs'terɪtɪ] *n* posteridad *f*; **for p.** para la posteridad

posterization [pəʊstəraɪ'zeɪʃən] *n Comptr* posterización *f*

post-feminism [pəʊst'femɪnɪzəm] *n* pos(t)feminismo *m*

post-feminist [pəʊst'femɪnɪst] **1** *n* pos(t)feminista *mf*
2 *adj* pos(t)feminista

post-free ['pəʊst'friː], **post-paid** ['pəʊst'peɪd] **1** *adj* con el franqueo pagado
2 *adv* libre de gastos de envío

postgraduate ['pəʊst'grædjʊɪt], *Fam* **postgrad** ['pəʊst'græd] **1** *n* estudiante *mf* de posgrado
2 *adj* de posgrado ▸▸ ***p. studies*** estudios *mpl* de posgrado

posthaste ['pəʊst'heɪst] *adv* a toda prisa

postholder ['pəʊsthəʊldə(r)] *n* persona *f* que ocupa un puesto

posthouse ['pəʊst'haʊs] *n Hist* casa *f* de postas

posthumous ['pɒstjʊməs] *adj* póstumo(a)

posthumously ['pɒstjʊməslɪ] *adv* póstumamente

postie ['pəʊstɪ] *n Fam (postman)* cartero(a) *m,f*

postimpressionism ['pəʊstɪm'preʃənɪzəm] *n* postimpresionismo *m*

postimpressionist ['pəʊstɪm'preʃənɪst] **1** *n* postimpresionista *mf*
2 *adj* postimpresionista

post-industrial ['pəʊstɪn'dʌstrɪəl] *adj* postindustrial ▸▸ ***p. society*** sociedad *f* postindustrial

posting ['pəʊstɪŋ] *n* destino *m*

Post-it® ['pəʊstɪt] *n* **P. (note)** post-it® *m*

postman ['pəʊstmən] *n Br* cartero *m* ►► ***p.'s knock*** = juego infantil en el que un niño hace de cartero que entrega una carta y a cambio recibe un beso

postmark ['pəʊstmɑːk] **1** *n* matasellos *m inv*

2 *vt* **the letter is postmarked Phoenix** la carta lleva un matasellos de Phoenix

postmaster ['pəʊstmɑːstə(r)] *n* **(a)** *(in post office)* funcionario *m* de correos **(b)** *Pol* ***P. General*** ≃ Director(ora) *m,f* General de Correos **(c)** *Comptr* postmaster *m*, jefe *m* de correos

post meridiem ['pəʊstmə'rɪdɪəm] *adv Formal (in afternoon, evening)* postmeridiano(a)

postmillennial [pəʊstmɪ'lenɪəl] *adj* pos(t)milenario(a)

postmistress ['pəʊstmɪstrɪs] *n* funcionaria *f* de correos

post-modern [pəʊst'mɒdən] *adj* posmoderno(a)

post-modernism [pəʊst'mɒdənɪzəm] *n* posmodernismo *m*

post-modernist [pəʊst'mɒdənɪst] **1** *n* posmoderno(a) *m,f*

2 *adj* posmoderno(a)

post-modernity [pəʊstmə'dɜːnɪtɪ] *n* posmodernidad *f*

postmortem [pəʊst'mɔːtəm] *n* **(a)** *Med* autopsia *f* ►► ***p. examination*** autopsia *f* **(b)** *Fig (retrospective analysis)* análisis *m* retrospectivo; **they held a p. on the game** una vez concluido, hicieron un análisis del partido

postnatal ['pəʊst'neɪtəl] *adj Med* posparto, puerperal ►► ***p. depression*** depresión *f* puerperal *or* posparto

post-operative ['pəʊst'ɒpərətɪv] *adj Med* pos(t)operatorio(a)

post-paid *US* = **post-free**

postpartum ['pəʊst'pɑːtəm] *n Med* posparto *m*

postpone [pəs'pəʊn] *vt* aplazar, posponer

postponement [pəs'pəʊnmənt] *n* aplazamiento *m*

postprandial ['pəʊst'prændɪəl] *adj Formal or Hum* **I like to take a p. nap** después de comer me gusta echarme una siesta

post-production ['pəʊstprə'dʌkʃən] *n Cin* postproducción *f*

PostScript® ['pəʊstskrɪpt] *n Comptr* PostScript® *m* ►► ***P. font*** fuente *f* PostScript®

postscript ['pəʊstskrɪpt] *n* **(a)** *(in letter)* posdata *f*; **by way of p.** como posdata **(b)** *(in book)* epílogo *m*; *Fig (additional events)* colofón *m*

post-structuralism [pəʊs'strʌktʃərəlɪzəm] *n* postestructuralismo *m*

post-structuralist [pəʊs'strʌktʃərəlɪst] **1** *n* postestructuralista *mf*

2 *adj* postestructuralista

postsynchronization ['pəʊstsɪŋkrənaɪ'zeɪʃən] *n Cin* postsincronización *f*

post-traumatic stress disorder ['pəʊsttrɔː'mætɪk'stresdɪs'ɔːdə(r)] *n Med* síndrome *m* de estrés postraumático

postulant ['pɒstjʊlənt] *n Rel* postulante *mf*

postulate **1** *n* ['pɒstjʊlət] postulado *m*

2 *vt* ['pɒstjʊleɪt] **(a)** *(hypothesize)* postular **(b)** *(take as granted)* presuponer

postural ['pɒstʃərəl] *adj* de la postura

posture ['pɒstʃə(r)] **1** *n* **(a)** *(body position)* postura *f* **(b)** *(poise)* postura *f*; **to have good/bad p.** tener (una) buena/mala postura **(c)** *(attitude)* postura *f*

2 *vi* tomar *or* hacer poses

posturing ['pɒstʃərɪŋ] *n Pej* pose *f*

postviral syndrome ['pəʊst'vaɪrəl'sɪndrəʊm] *n Med* síndrome *m* posviral *or* posvírico

postvocalic [pəʊstvə'kælɪk] *adj Ling* postvocálico(a)

postwar ['pəʊst'wɔː(r)] *adj* de posguerra; **the p. period** la posguerra

posy ['pəʊzɪ] *n* ramillete *m*, ramo *m*

pot [pɒt] **1** *n* **(a)** *(container)* bote *m*; **a p. of paint/mustard** un bote de pintura/mostaza

(b) *(for plant)* **(plant) p.** maceta *f*, tiesto *m* ►► ***p. marigold*** caléndula *f*, maravilla *f*; ***p. plant*** planta *f* de interior

(c) *(for cooking)* cacerola *f*, olla *f*; **pots and pans** cazos y ollas ►► ***p. roast*** estofado *m or Andes, Méx* ahogado *m* de carne

(d) *(pottery object)* vasija *f*; **to throw a p.** hacer una vasija

(e) *(for tea)* tetera *f*; *(for coffee)* cafetera *f*; **I'd like a p. of tea** quiero una tetera

(f) *(in gambling)* bote *m*

(g) *(in snooker, pool)* billa *f*

(h) *Fam (marijuana)* maría *f*

(i) *US (kitty)* fondo *m* común

(j) *Fam (belly)* barriga *f*, panza *f*, *Chile* guata *f*

(k) *Br Fam* **to take a p. (shot) at sth/sb** pegarle un tiro a algo/a alguien a la buena de Dios

(l) IDIOMS *Fam* **pots of money** montones de dinero; *Fam* **to go to p.** irse al garete, *Am* irse al diablo; *Fam* **to take p. luck** aceptar lo que haya; *very Fam* **he hasn't got a p. to piss in** no tiene ni un maldito centavo *or Esp* un puto duro *or Méx* ni un quinto *or RP* un mango partido al medio; **that's the p. calling the kettle black** mira quién fue a hablar; PROV **a watched p. never boils** el que espera desespera

2 *vt* (*pt & pp* **potted**) **(a)** *(butter, meat)* envasar **(b)** *(plant)* plantar (en tiesto) **(c)** *(in snooker, pool)* meter **(d)** *Br (shoot)* cazar

3 *vi (do pottery)* hacer cerámica

potable ['pəʊtəbəl] *adj Literary or Hum* potable

potash ['pɒtæʃ] *n* potasa *f*

potassium [pə'tæsɪəm] *n Chem* potasio *m* ►► ***p. chloride*** cloruro *m* potásico

potato [pə'teɪtəʊ] (*pl* **potatoes**) *n Esp* patata *f*, *Am* papa *f* ►► ***p. blight*** añublo *m* de la *Esp* patata *or Am* papa; ***p.*** *Br* ***crisps*** *or US* ***chips*** *Esp* patatas *or Am* papas fritas *(de bolsa)*; ***p. peeler*** *Esp* pelapatatas *m inv*, *Am* pelapapas *m inv*; ***p. salad*** ensalada *f* de *Esp* patatas *or Am* papas; ***p. scone*** = bollo pequeño, redondo y bastante seco, hecho de patatas

potbellied ['pɒtbelɪd] *adj* **(a)** *(person) (from over-eating)* barrigón(ona); *(from malnourishment)* con el vientre hinchado **(b) p. stove** estufa con panza

potbelly ['pɒtbelɪ] *n (stomach)* barriga *f*, panza *f*, *Chile* guata *f*; **he's getting** *or* **developing a p.** está echando barriga, *Arg* se está quedando con panza

potboiler ['pɒtbɔɪlə(r)] *n Pej (book)* producto *m* puramente comercial

potbound ['pɒtbaʊnd] *adj (plant)* de maceta

poteen [pɒ'tʃiːn] *n* = whisky destilado ilegalmente en Irlanda

potency ['pəʊtənsɪ] *n* **(a)** *(sexual)* potencia *f* **(b)** *(of charm, message, influence)* fuerza *f* **(c)** *(of drink, drug)* fuerza *f*

potent ['pəʊtənt] *adj* **(a)** *(sexually)* potente **(b)** *(charm, message, influence)* fuerte; *(argument)* contundente **(c)** *(drink, drug)* fuerte; **it's p. stuff, this rum!** ¡este ron sí que es fuerte!

potentate ['pəʊtənteɪt] *n* soberano *m* absoluto

potential [pə'tenʃəl] **1** *n* **(a)** *(promise) (of person)* potencial *m*; *(of discovery, situation, place)* potencial *m*, posibilidades *fpl*; **to have p.** tener potencial; **she has the p. to succeed** tiene lo necesario para triunfar; **she failed to fulfil her p.** no llegó a explotar todo su potencial; **p. for good/evil** potencial de hacer el bien/el mal **(b)** *Elec* potencial *m*

2 *adj* **(a)** *(possible)* potencial; **they're p. criminals** son delincuentes en potencia; **we mustn't discourage p. investors** no debemos desalentar a potenciales inversores **(b)** *Elec* ***p. difference*** diferencia *f* de potencial; *Phys* ***p. energy*** energía *f* potencial

potentiality [pətenʃɪ'ælɪtɪ] *n* potencial *m*

potentially [pə'tenʃəlɪ] *adv* en potencia; **p. lethal poisons** venenos que son potencialmente letales; **p., this idea might revolutionize the industry** potencialmente, esta idea podría revolucionar el sector

potentiometer [pətenʃɪ'ɒmɪtə(r)] *n Elec* potenciómetro *m*

pothead ['pɒthed] *n Fam* porrero(a) *m,f*, porreta *mf*

pot-herb [*Br* 'pɒthɜːb, *US* 'pɒtɜːb] *n* hierba *f* aromática

pot-hole ['pɒthəʊl] *n* **(a)** *(cave)* cueva *f* **(b)** *(in road)* bache *m*

pot-holer ['pɒthəʊlə(r)] *n* espeleólogo(a) *m,f*

pot-holing ['pɒthəʊlɪŋ] *n* espeleología *f*; **to go p.** hacer espeleología

pot-hook ['pɒthʊk] *n (in fireplace)* gancho *m*

potion ['pəʊʃən] *n* poción *f*

potlatch ['pɒtlætʃ] *n* **(a)** *(among Native Americans)* = fiesta que celebran algunas tribus indígenas norteamericanas durante la que los participantes se intercambian suntuosos regalos **(b)** *US Fam* fiesta *f*

pot-luck ['pɒt'lʌk] *adj US Fam* **p. dinner/party** = cena/fiesta en la que cada uno de los invitados acude con un plato

potpie ['pɒtpaɪ] *n US* = plato consistente en carne y verdura cubierto de pasta y hervido u horneado en una olla

potpourri [pəʊpʊ'riː] *n (of flowers, music)* popurrí *m*

potsherd ['pɒtʃɜːd], **potshard** ['pɒtʃɑːd] *n* trozo *m* de cerámica

pottage ['pɒtɪdʒ] *n* potaje *m*

potted ['pɒtɪd] *adj* **(a)** *(food)* en conserva; **p. meat** paté de carne; **p. shrimps** gambas en conserva **(b)** *(plant)* en maceta *or* tiesto **(c)** *(condensed)* **a p. version** una versión condensada; **a p. history of the Second World War** una historia resumida de la Segunda Guerra Mundial

potter[1] ['pɒtə(r)] *n* alfarero(a) *m,f*, ceramista *mf* ►► *US* ***p.'s field*** cementerio *m* de pobres; ***p.'s wheel*** torno *m* (de alfarero)

potter[2] *vi Br* **after lunch, I'll p. down to the post office** después del almuerzo me acercaré hasta correos; **I might p. along to the library later** tal vez vaya a la biblioteca más tarde

▸ **potter about, potter around** *Br Fam* **1** *vi* entretenerse; **he spent the morning pottering about** *or* **around in the garden** ha estado toda la mañana entretenido *or* ocupado en el jardín
2 *vt insep* **I like to spend Sunday pottering about** *or* **around the house/garden** me gusta pasar los domingos de aquí para allá en la casa/el jardín

pottery ['pɒtərɪ] *n* (**a**) *(art)* alfarería *f* (**b**) *(place)* alfarería *f* (**c**) *(objects)* cerámica *f*, alfarería *f*

potting-shed ['pɒtɪŋʃed] *n Br* cobertizo *m (en el jardín)*

Pott's fracture ['pɒts'fræktʃə(r)] *n Med* fractura *f* de Pott

potty[1] ['pɒtɪ] *n Fam* orinal *m*

potty[2] *adj Br Fam (mad)* pirado(a), *Col* corrido(a), *CSur* rayado(a), *Méx* zafado(a); **to be p.** estar pirado(a) *or Col* corrido(a) *or CSur* rayado(a) *or Méx* zafado(a); **to go p.** volverse loco(a) *or Esp* majara, *CSur* rayarse, *Méx* zafarse; **you're driving me p.** me estás volviendo loco; **to be p. about sth/sb** estar loco(a) por algo/alguien

potty-mouthed ['pɒtɪmaʊðd] *adj US Fam* malhablado(a)

potty-train ['pɒtɪtreɪn] *vt* enseñar a usar el orinal a

potty-trained ['pɒtɪtreɪnd] *adj* **he/she is p.** ya no necesita pañales

potty-training ['pɒtɪtreɪnɪŋ] *n* = proceso de enseñar a un niño a usar el orinal

pouch [paʊtʃ] *n* (**a**) *(for money)* saquito *m*; *(for tobacco)* petaca *f*; *(for ammunition)* cebador *m* (**b**) *(of marsupial)* marsupio *m*; *(in cheeks)* bolsa *f* (**c**) *US (mailbag)* valija *f*

pouf(fe) [pu:f] *n* puf *m*

poulterer ['pəʊltərə(r)] *n* pollero(a) *m,f*

poultice ['pəʊltɪs] *n* cataplasma *f*

poultry ['pəʊltrɪ] *n* (**a**) *(birds)* aves *fpl* de corral ▸▸ ***p. farm*** granja *f* avícola; ***p. farmer*** avicultor(ora) *m,f* (**b**) *(meat)* carne *f* de ave *or* pollería

pounce [paʊns] **1** *vi (attack)* abalanzarse (**on** sobre)
2 *n* salto *m*; **with a sudden p.** con un salto repentino

▸ **pounce on, pounce upon** *vt insep* (**a**) *(of animal, bird, police)* caer sobre; **he was quick to p. on the defender's mistake** se aprovechó rápidamente del error del defensor (**b**) *(in criticism)* **they p. on your slightest mistake** no pierden la oportunidad de criticar tus errores más pequeños (**c**) *(seize) (opportunity)* aprovechar

pound[1] [paʊnd] *n* (**a**) *(unit of weight)* libra *f (= 0,454 kg)*; **three p.** *or* **pounds of apples** tres libras de manzanas; **to sell sth by the p.** vender algo por libras; **two dollars a p.** dos dólares la libra; IDIOM **he's determined to get** *or* **have his p. of flesh** está decidido a conseguir a toda costa lo que es suyo ▸▸ ***p. cake*** pastel *m* con pasas
(**b**) *(British currency)* libra *f* (esterlina) ▸▸ ***p. coin*** moneda *f* de una libra; ***p. shop*** = tienda en la que todo se vende a una libra, *Esp* ≃ todo a cien; ***p. sign*** símbolo *m* de la libra; ***p. sterling*** libra *f* esterlina
(**c**) *US* ***p. sign*** = el símbolo '#'; *(on telephone)* almohadilla *f*, numeral *m*

pound[2] *n* (**a**) *(for dogs)* perrera *f* (**b**) *(for cars)* depósito *m*

pound[3] **1** *vt* (**a**) *(crush)* machacar; **to p. sth to pieces** destrozar algo a golpes; IDIOM *US Fam* **to tell sb to go p. salt** mandar a alguien al cuerno (**b**) *(hammer, hit)* golpear; **the waves pounded the rocks/boat** las olas golpeaban contra las rocas/el bote (**c**) *(with artillery)* bombardear incesantemente (**d**) *(walk) (corridor)* caminar por; **to p. the** *Br* **streets** *or US* **pavement** caminar *or* andar por las calles; **to p. the beat** *(policeman)* salir de ronda
2 *vi* (**a**) *(hammer) (waves)* golpear (**on** *or* **against** en *or* contra); **to p. at** *or* **on sth** aporrear algo; **the rain was pounding on the roof** la lluvia golpeaba en *or* contra el techo
(**b**) *(rhythmically) (drum)* redoblar; *(heart)* palpitar; **my head is pounding** tengo la cabeza a punto de estallar
(**c**) *(more heavily)* **he heard their feet pounding above** escuchó el retumbar de sus pasos en el apartamento *or Esp* piso de arriba

▸ **pound away** *vi* (**a**) *(on typewriter, piano, drums)* aporrear (**b**) *(with artillery)* **to p. away at the enemy lines** bombardear incesantemente las líneas enemigas

▸ **pound down** *vt sep* (**a**) *(crush)* moler, triturar (**b**) *(flatten) (earth)* allanar

▸ **pound out** *vt sep Br* (**a**) *(rhythm, tune)* tocar vigorosamente (**b**) *(letter, book)* escribir

poundage ['paʊndɪdʒ] *n* (**a**) *(charge)* = impuesto cobrado por libra de peso (**b**) *(weight)* peso *m* en libras

-pounder ['paʊndə(r)] *suffix* **a fifteen-p.** *(fish)* un ejemplar de quince libras; **a six/twenty-five-p.** *(gun)* una pieza de 6/25 libras

pounding ['paʊndɪŋ] *n* (**a**) *(beating)* **to give sb a p.** dar una buena tunda a alguien; **the city centre took a p. from the enemy artillery** el centro de la ciudad fue bombardeado ferozmente por la artillería enemiga; **the play took a real p. from the critics** la obra fue masacrada por la crítica; **the dollar took a severe p. last week** el dólar recibió un duro revés la semana pasada
(**b**) *(sound) (of artillery)* martilleo *m*; *(of heart)* palpitaciones *fpl*; *(of waves, fist)* golpes *mpl*

pour [pɔ:(r)] **1** *vt* (**a**) *(liquid)* verter (**into** en); **we poured the water/wine down the sink** tiramos el agua/vino por el fregadero *or RP* la pileta; **to p. sb a drink/some tea** servir una bebida/té a alguien; **p. yourself a drink** sírvete un trago
(**b**) *(invest)* **to p. money into a project** invertir un dineral en un proyecto; **he poured all his energy into the project** puso toda su energía en el proyecto
(**c**) IDIOMS **to p. cold water on sth** echar agua fría sobre algo; **to p. scorn on sth/sb** hablar de algo/alguien con desdén; **she looked as if she'd been poured into her jeans** parecía que se había puesto los vaqueros con calzador
2 *vi* (**a**) *(liquid, light, smoke)* brotar, fluir (**from** *or* **out of** de); **tears poured down her face** le brotaban las lágrimas; **blood poured from the wound** brotaba sangre de la herida; **it's pouring (with rain)** llueve a cántaros; **sweat was pouring off him** le chorreaba el sudor
(**b**) *(people)* salir en masa (**from** *or* **out of** de); **tourists were pouring into the palace** oleadas de turistas entraban al palacio; **reporters p. into Cannes for the festival** los periodistas llegan a Cannes en masa para el festival
(**c**) *(teapot, jug)* **to p. well/badly** verter bien/mal

▸ **pour away** *vt sep (throw out)* tirar

▸ **pour down** *vi (rain)* llover a cántaros

▸ **pour forth** *vi Literary* (**a**) *(light, water)* emanar (**b**) *(people)* salir en masa (**c**) *(be produced)* **hundreds of pamphlets poured forth from the presses** las imprentas producían cientos de panfletos; **he opened his mouth and a stream of insults poured forth** abrió la boca y dejó salir una catarata de insultos

▸ **pour in** **1** *vt sep (liquid)* verter
2 *vi* (**a**) *(liquid, light, smoke)* entrar a raudales (**b**) *(people, letters)* llegar a raudales; **offers of help poured in from all sides** llegó una avalancha de ayuda proveniente de todas partes

▸ **pour out** **1** *vt sep* (**a**) *(liquid)* sacar; *(drink)* servir (**b**) *(anger, grief)* desahogar; **he poured out his heart to me** se desahogó conmigo
2 *vi* (**a**) *(liquid, light, smoke)* salirse (**b**) *(people)* salir a raudales

pourer ['pɔ:rə(r)] *n* **this teapot isn't a good p.** esta tetera no vierte *or* sirve bien

pouring ['pɔ:rɪŋ] *adj* (**a**) *(rain)* torrencial (**b**) *(cream)* líquido(a); **the sauce should be of p. consistency** la salsa no debe ser muy espesa

poussin ['pu:sæn] *n* pollito *m*

pout [paʊt] **1** *n (of annoyance)* mohín *m*; *(seductive)* mueca *f* seductora (con los labios)
2 *vi (in annoyance)* hacer un mohín; *(seductively)* fruncir los labios con aire seductor

pouter ['paʊtə(r)] *n (bird)* paloma *f* buchona

POV [pi:əʊ'vi:] *n TV & Cin* (*abbr* **point of view**) punto *m* de vista

poverty ['pɒvətɪ] *n* (**a**) *(financial)* pobreza *f*; **to live in p.** vivir en la pobreza ▸▸ ***p. line*** umbral *m* de pobreza; **to be living on/below the p. line** vivir en/debajo del umbral de la pobreza; ***p. trap*** = situación del que gana menos trabajando que desempleado, porque sus ingresos superan por poco el nivel mínimo a partir del cual hay que pagar impuestos
(**b**) *(shortage) (of ideas, imagination)* escasez *f*, pobreza *f*
(**c**) *(of soil)* pobreza *f*

poverty-stricken ['pɒvətɪstrɪkən] *adj* empobrecido(a)

POW [pi:əʊ'dʌbəlju:] *n* (*abbr* **prisoner of war**) prisionero(a) *m,f* de guerra ▸▸ ***P. camp*** campo *m* de prisioneros de guerra

pow [paʊ] *exclam* ¡paf!

powder ['paʊdə(r)] **1** *n* (**a**) *(dust, fine grains)* polvo *m* ▸▸ ***p. blue*** azul *m* pastel
(**b**) *(gunpowder)* pólvora *f*; IDIOM **to keep one's p. dry** mantenerse a la espera ▸▸ ***p. burn*** marca *f* de pólvora; ***p. horn*** cuerno *m* de pólvora; ***p. keg*** barril *m* de pólvora; *Fig* polvorín *m*
(**c**) *(cosmetic)* (**face**) **p.** polvos *mpl* ▸▸ ***p. compact*** polvera *f*; ***p. puff*** borla *f*; ***p. room*** *(toilet)* baño *m or Esp* servicios *mpl or CSur* toilette *m* de señoras

(**d**) *(medicine)* polvo *m*; IDIOM *US Fam* **to take a p.** *(disappear)* poner los pies en polvorosa

(**e**) **p. (snow)** nieve *f* en polvo

2 *vt* (**a**) *(crush, pulverize)* pulverizar, hacer polvo (**b**) *(cover with powder)* **to p. sth with sugar** espolvorear azúcar sobre algo; **to p. one's face** empolvarse la cara; IDIOM *Euph* **to p. one's nose** ir al tocador

powder-blue ['paʊdə'blu:] *adj* azul pastel

powdered ['paʊdəd] *adj* (**a**) *(milk)* en polvo; *(coffee)* en polvo, instantáneo(a) ►► *US* ***p. sugar*** azúcar *m Esp, Méx* glas *or Esp* de lustre *or Chile* flor *or Col* pulverizado *or RP* impalpable (**b**) *(face, wig)* empolvado(a)

powdery ['paʊdərɪ] *adj* (**a**) *(covered in powder)* polvoriento(a), lleno(a) de polvo (**b**) *(substance)* arenoso(a), como polvo (**c**) *(snow)* en polvo

POWER ['paʊə(r)] 1 *n* (**a**) *(authority, control)* poder *m* (**over** sobre); **to be in/out of p.** estar/no estar en el poder; **to come to p.** subir *or* llegar al poder; **to fall from p.** perder el poder, caer; **to seize** *or* **take p.** tomar el poder; **to be in sb's p.** estar en poder de alguien; **he had them in his p.** los tenía en su poder; **to fall into sb's p.** caer en poder de alguien; **to have p. of life and death over sb** tener poder para decidir sobre la vida de alguien, tener poder de vida y muerte sobre alguien ►► ***p. base*** bastión *m* de popularidad; ***p. block*** grupo *m* de poder; ***p. breakfast*** desayuno *m* de trabajo; ***p. broker*** persona *f* con mucha influencia política; ***p. dressing*** = estilo de vestir utilizado por mujeres ejecutivas y que transmite profesionalidad y seguridad; ***p. forward*** *(in basketball)* ala-pívot *mf*; ***p. games*** maniobras *fpl* por el poder; ***p. lunch*** almuerzo *m* de trabajo; ***p. play*** *(in ice hockey)* situación *f* de superioridad numérica; ***p. politics*** política *f* de fuerza; ***p. structure*** estructura *f* de poder; ***p. struggle*** lucha *f* por el poder; *Comptr* ***p. user*** usuario(a) *m,f* experto(a); ***p. vacuum*** vacío *m* de poder; ***p. yoga*** yoga *m* deportivo

(**b**) *(official right)* poder *m*; **the government has granted us new powers** el gobierno nos ha concedido nuevas competencias; **the council has the p. to grant licences** el ayuntamiento tiene la competencia para conceder permisos; **he has the p. to fire employees from their job** tiene autoridad para despedir empleados; **it is not in** *or* **within my p. to do it** no está dentro de mis atribuciones hacerlo ►► *Law* ***p. of attorney*** poder *m* (notarial)

(**c**) *(capacity)* capacidad *f*, facultad *f*; **the p. of reason** el uso de razón; **the p. of speech** la facultad del habla; **powers of concentration** capacidad de concentración; **powers of persuasion** poder de persuasión; **her powers are failing** está perdiendo facultades; **to have the p. to do sth** tener la facultad de hacer algo; **it is beyond my p.** no está en mi mano, no depende de mí; **she did everything in her p. to help** hizo todo lo posible por ayudar, *Esp* hizo todo lo que estuvo en su mano para ayudar; **it is within her p. to win the match** ganar el partido está dentro de sus posibilidades; **to be at the height** *or* **peak of one's powers** estar en plena forma, estar en el auge de su carrera

(**d**) *(physical strength)* fuerza *f*; **I underestimated the p. of the explosion** subestimé la fuerza de la explosión; IDIOM *Fam* **more p. to your elbow!** ¡bien hecho!

(**e**) *(powerful person)* autoridad *f*; *(powerful group, nation)* potencia *f*; **the great powers** las grandes potencias; **to be a p. in the land** tener mucho peso; **no p. on earth will persuade me to go** nada en el mundo me va a convencer de que vaya; IDIOM **the powers that be** las autoridades; IDIOM *Literary* **the powers of darkness** las fuerzas del mal; IDIOM **the p. behind the throne** el/la que maneja los hilos

(**f**) *(electricity)* electricidad *f*; *(energy)* energía *f*; **the engine requires a lot of p.** el motor consume mucha energía; **p. is provided by batteries** funciona con pilas, *RP* funciona a pila; **to turn the p. on/off** conectar *or Esp* dar/cortar la corriente; **at full p.** a toda potencia; **wind p.** energía eólica; **the ship completed the journey under its own p.** el barco completó el viaje impulsado por sus motores ►► *Aut* ***p. brakes*** servofreno *m*, *Am* frenos *mpl* hidráulicos; ***p. cut*** apagón *m*; ***p. dive*** *(of aircraft)* descenso *m* en *Esp* picado *or Am* picada *(con el motor al máximo)*; ***p. drill*** taladro *m* eléctrico; ***p. failure*** corte *m* de corriente *or* del fluido eléctrico; ***p. lines*** cables *mpl* del tendido eléctrico; *US* ***p. outage*** apagón *m*; ***p. pack*** unidad *f* de alimentación; ***p. plant*** central *f or Andes, RP* usina *f* eléctrica; *esp Br* ***p. point*** toma *f* de corriente, *Am* toma *f* de contacto; ***p. shower*** ducha *f* de chorro a presión; ***p. station*** central *f or Andes, RP* usina *f* eléctrica; *Aut* ***p. steering*** *Esp* dirección *f* asistida, *Esp* servodirección *f*, *Am* dirección *f* hidráulica; ***p. strike*** huelga *f* de los trabajadores del sector energético; ***p. supply*** *(for city, building)* suministro *m* eléctrico; *(for machine)* fuente *f* de alimentación; ***p. supply unit*** alimentador *m* de corriente; ***p. switch*** interruptor *m* de corriente; ***p. tool*** herramienta *f* eléctrica; ***p. unit*** alimentador *m* de corriente; ***p. worker*** trabajador(ora) *m,f* del sector energético

(**g**) *Math* potencia *f*; **three to the p. of ten** tres elevado a diez

(**h**) *(of lens)* potencia *f*

(**i**) *Fam (a lot)* **that'll do you a p. of good** eso te sentará estupendamente *or* de maravilla, *RP* esto te va a hacer muy bien

2 *vt (provide with power)* propulsar; **a plane powered by two engines** un avión propulsado por dos motores; **the vehicle is powered by a diesel engine** el vehículo tiene un motor diesel

3 *vi (move powerfully)* **the athlete powered ahead of her rivals** la atleta se escapó de sus rivales de un tirón; **she powered through the work** despachó el trabajo con diligencia, *Esp* le cundió mucho el trabajo

► **power down** *Comptr* 1 *vt sep* apagar

2 *vi* apagarse

► **power up** *Comptr* 1 *vt sep* encender, *Am* prender

2 *vi* encenderse, *Am* prenderse

power-assisted steering ['paʊərəsɪstɪd-'stɪərɪŋ] *n Aut* dirección *f* asistida, servodirección *f*

powerboat ['paʊəbəʊt] *n* motonave *f (de gran cilindrada)* ►► ***p. racing*** carreras *fpl* de motoras, motonáutica *f*

-powered ['paʊəd] *suffix* **steam-p.** de *or* a vapor, accionado(a) por vapor de agua; **wind-p.** de viento, alimentado(a) por el viento

powerful ['paʊəfʊl] 1 *adj (country, politician)* poderoso(a); *(muscles, engine, voice)* potente; *(kick)* fuerte, poderoso(a); *(imagination)* fértil; *(drug, smell)* fuerte; *(speech, image, scene)* conmovedor(ora); *(argument, incentive)* poderoso(a), convincente

2 *adv Br Fam* muy

powerfully ['paʊəfʊlɪ] *adv* (**a**) *(with great strength)* con fuerza; **a p. built man** un hombre muy fornido (**b**) *(to argue)* convincentemente; *(to speak)* de forma conmovedora

powerhouse ['paʊəhaʊs] *n* (**a**) *Elec* central *f or Andes, RP* usina *f* eléctrica (**b**) *(person)* generador(ora) *m,f*; *(place)* polo *m* generador; **the economic p. of Germany** el motor de la economía alemana

powerless ['paʊəlɪs] *adj* impotente; **our arguments were p. in the face of such conviction** nuestros argumentos carecían de vigor frente a semejante convicción; **to feel p.** sentirse impotente; **to be p. to react** no tener capacidad para reaccionar, no ser capaz de reaccionar

powerlessly ['paʊəlɪslɪ] *adv* sin poder hacer nada; **I watched p. as they were led away** observé sin poder hacer nada mientras se los llevaban

powerlessness ['paʊəlɪsnɪs] *n* impotencia *f*

power-on key ['paʊər'ɒnki:] *n Comptr* tecla *f* de encendido

power-sharing ['paʊəʃeərɪŋ] *n Pol* reparto *m* del poder

powwow ['paʊwaʊ] 1 *n* (**a**) *(of Native Americans)* asamblea *f* (**b**) *Fam (meeting, discussion)* reunión *f*; **to have** *or* **hold a p.** tener una reunión

2 *vi Fam (talk)* conversar

pox [pɒks] *n Br Fam* **the p.** *(syphilis)* la sífilis; *Old-fashioned or Literary* **a p. on...!** ¡maldita sea...!

poxy ['pɒksɪ] *adj Br Fam* **all I got for Christmas was a p. box of chocolates** todo lo que me regalaron para Navidad fue una mísera caja de bombones; **you can keep your p. flowers!** ¡te puedes meter las flores donde te quepan!

p & p [pi:ən'pi:] *n Br* (*abbr* **postage and packing**) gastos *mpl* de envío

pp 1 (**a**) (*abbr* **pages**) págs. (**b**) *Mus* (*abbr* **pianissimo**) pp. (**c**) *Br Com (on behalf of)* p.p.

2 *vt* [pi:'pi:] *Br Com* **could you pp those letters for me?** ¿podrías firmar estas cartas en mi nombre?

ppm (*abbr* **parts per million**) p.p.m.

PPP [pi:pi:'pi:] *n Comptr* (*abbr* **point-to-point protocol**) PPP *m*

PPS [pi:pi:'es] *n Br* (*abbr* **Parliamentary Private Secretary**) Secretario(a) *m,f* Privado(a) Parlamentario(a)

PPV [pi:pi:'vi:] *n* (*abbr* **pay-per-view**) pago *m* por visión

PR [pi:'ɑ:(r)] *n* (**a**) (*abbr* **public relations**) relaciones *fpl* públicas ►► ***P. company*** asesor *m* de imagen y comunicación (**b**) *Pol* (*abbr* **proportional representation**) representación *f* proporcional (**c**) (*abbr* **Puerto Rico**) Puerto Rico

practicability [præktɪkə'bɪlɪtɪ] *n (feasibility)* viabilidad *f*

practicable ['præktɪkəbəl] *adj* (**a**) *(feasible)* factible, viable; **as far as is p.** en la medida de lo posible (**b**) *(road)* transitable

practical ['præktɪkəl] 1 *n (lesson)* (clase *f*) práctica *f*; *(exam)* examen *m* práctico

2 *adj* (**a**) *(convenient, efficient)* práctico(a)

(**b**) *(sensible, commonsense) (person, mind, suggestion)* práctico(a); **he's very p.** es muy práctico; **now, be p., we can't afford a holiday** sé

realista, en este momento no podemos permitirnos ir de vacaciones
(c) *(not theoretical) (training, experience)* práctico(a); **for all p. purposes** a efectos prácticos ►► *US* ***p. nurse*** enfermero(a) *m,f* auxiliar
(d) *(virtual)* **it's a p. certainty** es prácticamente seguro; **it's a p. impossibility** es prácticamente imposible
(e) ***p. joke*** broma *f*; **to play a p. joke on sb** gastar una broma a alguien; ***p. joker*** bromista *mf*

practicality [præktɪˈkælɪtɪ] *n* (a) *(of suggestion, plan)* viabilidad *f* (b) **practicalities** *(practical issues)* aspectos *mpl* prácticos

practically [ˈpræktɪklɪ] *adv* (a) *(sensibly)* sensatamente; **she very p. suggested telephoning home** sugirió sensatamente que llamáramos a casa; **to be p. dressed** estar vestido(a) de manera muy práctica
(b) *(through practice)* con la práctica
(c) *(almost, virtually)* prácticamente; **there has been p. no snow** casi no ha nevado; **p. the whole of the audience** casi todo el público; **we're p. there** casi estamos allí, casi llegamos
(d) *(in practice)* en la práctica; **p. speaking** prácticamente hablando

practical-minded [ˈpræktɪkəlˈmaɪndɪd] *adj* con sentido práctico; **he's the p. one** él es el que tiene un sentido práctico

practice [ˈpræktɪs] **1** *n* (a) *(exercise, training)* práctica *f*; *(in sport)* entrenamiento *m*; **I've had a lot of p. at** *or* **in doing that** tengo mucha práctica en eso; **it'll be good p. for your interview** será una buena práctica para tu entrevista; **to be in p.** estar en buena forma; **to be out of p.** estar desentrenado(a); **I'm getting out of p.** estoy perdiendo la forma; PROV **p. makes perfect** se aprende a base de práctica ►► ***p. ground*** *(in golf)* campo *m* de práctica; ***p. match*** partido *m* de entrenamiento
(b) *(training session)* práctica *f*; *(rehearsal)* ensayo *m*
(c) *(practical application)* práctica *f*; **in p.** en la práctica; **to put an idea into p.** poner en práctica una idea
(d) *(custom)* práctica *f*; **tribal/religious practices** prácticas tribales/religiosas; **to be good/bad p.** ser una buena/mala costumbre; **to make a p. of doing sth** tener por costumbre hacer algo; **it's the usual p.** es el procedimiento habitual; **it's normal p. among most shopkeepers** es una práctica habitual entre la mayoría de los comerciantes; **it's standard p. to make a written request** lo habitual es formular una petición por escrito
(e) *(of profession)* ejercicio *m*, práctica *f*; **to be in p. as a doctor/lawyer** ejercer como médico/abogado; **to go into** *or* **set up p. as a doctor/lawyer** comenzar a ejercer como médico/abogado
(f) *(business)* **medical p.** *(place)* consulta médica, consultorio médico; *(group of doctors)* = grupo de médicos que comparten un consultorio; **legal p.** *(place, legal firm)* bufete de abogados; **he has a country p.** ejerce en el campo
2 *vt US* = **practise**
3 *vi US* = **practise**

practiced, practicing *US* = **practised, practising**

practise, *US* **practice** [ˈpræktɪs] **1** *vt* (a) *(musical instrument, language)* practicar; *(musical piece)* ensayar; **can I p. my Spanish on you?** ¿puedo practicar español contigo?; **to p. one's serve** practicar el servicio (b) *(medicine, law)* ejercer (c) *(religion, custom)* practicar; IDIOM **to p. what one preaches** predicar con el ejemplo (d) *(inflict)* infligir, aplicar (e) *(magic)* practicar
2 *vi* (a) *(musician)* practicar; *(sportsperson)* entrenar; **to p. on the guitar** practicar con la guitarra (b) *(doctor, lawyer)* ejercer (**as** de *or* como)

practised, *US* **practiced** [ˈpræktɪst] *adj* experto(a) (**at** en); **a p. liar** un mentiroso consumado; **with a p. hand** con una mano *or* ayuda experta; **to be p. in the arts of seduction/deception** ser un experto en el arte de la seducción/en el engaño

practising, *US* **practicing** [ˈpræktɪsɪŋ] *adj* (a) *(doctor, lawyer)* en ejercicio, en activo (b) *(religious believer)* practicante (c) *(homosexual)* activo(a)

practitioner [prækˈtɪʃənə(r)] *n (of art, profession, skill)* profesional *mf*; **(medical) p.** facultativo(a) *m,f*, médico(a) *m,f*

praesidium = **presidium**

praetorian guard [priːˈtɔːrɪənˈgɑːd] *n Hist* guardia *f* pretoriana

pragmatic [prægˈmætɪk] *adj* pragmático(a)

pragmatically [prægˈmætɪklɪ] *adv* pragmáticamente, de manera pragmática

pragmatics [prægˈmætɪks] *n Ling* pragmática *f*

pragmatism [ˈprægmətɪzəm] *n* pragmatismo *m*

pragmatist [ˈprægmətɪst] *n* pragmático(a) *m,f*

Prague [prɑːg] *n* Praga

prairie [ˈpreərɪ] *n* pradera *f*; **the P.** *or* **Prairies** *(in US)* la Pradera ►► ***p. chicken*** gallo *m* de las praderas; ***p. dog*** perro *m* de las praderas; ***p. oyster*** *(alcoholic drink)* = bebida hecha con yema de huevo cruda, salsa inglesa, sal y pimienta que se utiliza para aliviar la resaca; *(testicle)* criadilla *f*; ***p. wolf*** coyote *m*

praise [preɪz] **1** *n* (a) *(compliments)* elogios *mpl*, alabanzas *fpl*; **to be full of p. for sth/sb** no tener más que elogios *or* alabanzas para algo/alguien; **in p. of** en alabanza de; **to sing the praises of** prodigar alabanzas a; **I have nothing but p. for him** no tengo más que elogios para él; **her film has received high p. from the critics** los críticos han elogiado mucho su película; **it is beyond p.** no alcanzan las palabras para elogiarlo
(b) *Rel* alabanza *f*; **hymn** *or* **song of p.** himno *or* canción de alabanza; **to give p. to the Lord** alabar al Señor; **p. (be to) the Lord!** ¡alabado sea el Señor!; **p. be!** ¡alabado sea Dios!
2 *vt* (a) *(compliment)* elogiar, alabar; **to p. sb to the skies** poner a alguien por las nubes (b) *Rel* alabar; **to p. God** alabar a Dios; **p. the Lord!** ¡alabad al Señor!

praiseworthiness [ˈpreɪzwɜːðɪnɪs] *n* lo encomiable, lo loable

praiseworthy [ˈpreɪzwɜːðɪ] *adj* encomiable, loable

praline [ˈprɑːliːn] *n* praliné *m*

pram [præm] *n Br* cochecito *m* de niño

prance [prɑːns] *vi* (a) *(horse)* encabritarse (b) *(person)* dar brincos, brincar; **to p. in/out** entrar/salir dando brincos

► **prance around, prance about** **1** *vt insep* dar brincos por
2 *vi* dar brincos *or* brincar de un lado a otro

prang [præŋ] *Br Fam Old-fashioned* **1** *n* **to have a p.** *Esp* darse una castaña con el coche, *Méx* darse un madrazo con el carro, *CSur* hacerse bolsa con el auto
2 *vt* **I pranged my car** *Esp* me di castaña con el coche, *Méx* me di un madrazo con el carro, *CSur* me hice bolsa con el auto

prank [præŋk] *n* broma *f* (pesada), jugarreta *f*; **to play a p. on sb** gastarle una broma a alguien

prankster [ˈpræŋkstə(r)] *n* bromista *mf*

prat [præt] *n Br Fam* soplagaitas *mf inv*

► **prat about, prat around** *vi Fam* (a) *(act foolishly)* hacer el tonto (b) *(waste time)* rascarse la barriga, *Andes* huevear

prate [preɪt] *vi Formal* perorar (**about** sobre)

pratfall [ˈprætfɔːl] *n US Fam* (a) *(fall)* tropezón *m*, batacazo *m* (b) *(failure)* revés *m*, trompazo *m*

pratincole [ˈprætɪŋkəʊl] *n* canastera *f*

prattle [ˈprætəl] **1** *n* parloteo *m*
2 *vi* parlotear (**about** de *or* acerca de); **she prattles away** *or* **on about her children for hours** se pone a hablar de los niños y no para

prawn [prɔːn] *n* gamba *f*, *Am* camarón *m* ►► ***p. cocktail*** cóctel *m* de gambas; *Br* ***p. cracker*** corteza *f* de gambas, = especie de corteza ligera y crujiente con sabor a marisco

praxis [ˈpræksɪs] (*pl* **praxes** [ˈpræksiːz]) *n* praxis *f inv*

pray [preɪ] **1** *vi* rezar, orar; **to p. over sb's grave** rezar en la tumba de alguien; **to p. to God** rezar a Dios; **to p. for sth/sb** rezar por algo/alguien; **to p. for sb's soul** rezar por el alma de alguien; *Fig* **to p. for good weather/rain** rezar para que haga buen tiempo/llueva; **she's past praying for** *(will die)* no hay nada que se pueda hacer por ella
2 *vt Formal* (a) *(ask)* **I p. God I am mistaken** a Dios ruego estar equivocado; **I just p. he doesn't come back** sólo ruego que no vuelva (b) *(in imperatives)* **p. come in** entre, por favor; **and why, p., was that?** ¿y por qué, si se puede saber?

> En inglés culto o elevado, y especialmente en inglés americano, **pray** puede ir seguido de **that** más un verbo en subjuntivo (ver el panel SUBJUNCTIVE):
> **I only pray that he arrive on time!**
> *¡sólo ruego que llegue a tiempo!*
> Lo mismo también podría decirse del siguiente modo:
> **I only pray that he arrives on time!**

prayer [preə(r)] *n* oración *f*; **Morning P.** maitines; **Evening P.** vísperas; **to say one's prayers** rezar (las oraciones); **to say a p.** rezar una oración; **to be at p.** estar orando; **her prayers had been answered** sus súplicas habían sido atendidas; **remember me in your prayers** tenme presente en tus plegarias; IDIOM *Fam* **he doesn't have a p.** *(has no chance)* no tiene ninguna posibilidad, no tiene nada que hacer ►► ***p. beads*** rosario *m*; ***p. book*** devocionario *m*; ***p. mat*** = esterilla que utilizan los musulmanes para el rezo; ***p. meeting*** = reunión de creyentes, generalmente protestantes, para rezar en grupo; ***p. rug*** = esterilla que utilizan los musulmanes para el rezo; *Rel* ***p. wheel*** rodillo *m* de oraciones *(utilizado por los budistas del Tíbet para rezar)*

prayerful ['preəfʊl] *adj* devoto(a)

praying mantis ['preɪɪŋ'mæntɪs] *n* mantis *f inv* religiosa

pre- [pri:] *prefix* pre-; **a p.-match talk** una charla antes del partido; **p.-exam nerves** los nervios que preceden al examen; **p.-Christian** precristiano(a)

preach [pri:tʃ] **1** *vt* **(a)** *Rel* predicar; **to p. the gospel** predicar el Evangelio; **to p. a sermon** dar un sermón **(b)** *(recommend)* preconizar; **she preaches austerity and lives in luxury** preconiza austeridad y vive en el lujo

2 *vi* **(a)** *(give sermon)* predicar; IDIOM **you're preaching to the converted** estás evangelizando en un convento **(b)** *Pej (give advice)* sermonear; **stop preaching at me!** ¡deja ya de sermonearme!

preacher ['pri:tʃə(r)] *n* **(a)** *(sermon giver)* predicador(ora) *m,f* **(b)** *US (clergyman)* pastor(ora) *m,f*

preaching ['pri:tʃɪŋ] *n (of clergy, guru)* prédica *f*; **to follow sb's preachings** seguir las prédicas de alguien

preachy ['pri:tʃɪ] *adj Fam* moralista

preamble ['pri:æmbəl] *n Formal (to speech, law)* preámbulo *m*

prearrange [pri:ə'reɪndʒ] *vt* organizar *or* acordar de antemano

prearranged [pri:ə'reɪndʒd] *adj* organizado(a) *or* acordado(a) de antemano; **at a p. time/place** en un momento/lugar acordado

prebendary ['prebəndrɪ] *n* prebendado *m*

Precambrian [pri:'kæmbrɪən] *Geol* **1** *n* **the P.** el precámbrico

2 *adj* precámbrico(a)

precancerous [pri:'kænsərəs] *adj* precanceroso(a)

precarious [prɪ'keərɪəs] *adj* precario(a); **to make a p. living** apenas llegar a fin de mes

precariously [prɪ'keərɪəslɪ] *adv* precariamente; **p. balanced** *(object, situation)* en equilibrio precario

precariousness [prɪ'keərɪəsnɪs] *n* precariedad *f*

precast [pri:'kɑ:st] *adj (concrete)* prefabricado(a)

precaution [prɪ'kɔ:ʃən] *n* precaución *f*; **to take precautions** tomar precauciones; *Euph (use contraceptive)* usar anticonceptivos; **she took the p. of informing her solicitor** tomó la precaución de informar a su abogado; **as a p.** como (medida de) precaución

precautionary [prɪ'kɔ:ʃənərɪ] *adj* preventivo(a); **as a p. measure** como medida preventiva

precede [prɪ'si:d] *vt* **(a)** *(in time, space)* preceder a; **in the weeks preceding her departure** durante las semanas previas a su partida **(b)** *(in importance, rank)* preceder a **(c)** *(preface)* preceder

precedence ['presɪdəns] *n* **(a)** *(priority)* prioridad *f*, precedencia *f*; **to take p. over** tener prioridad sobre **(b)** *(in rank, status)* precedencia *f*; **in order of p.** por orden de precedencia; **to have** *or* **take p. over sb** tener precedencia sobre alguien

precedent ['presɪdənt] *n* precedente *m*; **a (legal) p.** un precedente legal; **to create** *or* **set a p.** sentar (un) precedente; **to follow a p.** basarse en un precedente; **to break with p.** romper con los precedentes; **without p.** sin precedentes

preceding [prɪ'si:dɪŋ] *adj* precedente, anterior

precept ['pri:sept] *n Formal* precepto *m*

preceptorial [pri:sep'tɔ:rɪəl] *n US Univ* = curso universitario en el que se asignan pequeños grupos de alumnos a un profesor quien, en su calidad de tutor, se reúne con ellos periódicamente para dirigirlos en sus estudios y lecturas

precinct ['pri:sɪŋkt] *n* **(a)** *Br (area)* **(shopping) p.** zona *f* comercial; **within the castle precincts** dentro del recinto del castillo **(b)** *(boundary)* **within the precincts of** dentro de los límites de; **the question falls within the precincts of philosophy** la cuestión pertenece al terreno de la filosofía **(c)** *US (administrative, police division)* distrito *m*; *(police station)* comisaría *f* (de policía)

> **False friend**: The Spanish noun **precinto** is not a translation for the English word **precinct**. In Spanish **precinto** means "seal" or "sealing (off)".

preciosity [presɪ'ɒsɪtɪ] *n Formal* amaneramiento *m*, afectación *f*

precious ['preʃəs] **1** *n (term of endearment)* **my p.!** ¡mi cielo!

2 *adj* **(a)** *(valuable)* precioso(a), valioso(a); *(secret, possession)* preciado(a); **this photo is very p. to me** esta foto tiene mucho valor para mí; **my time with her is p.** el tiempo que paso con ella es muy importante para mí; **the ambulance lost p. minutes in a traffic jam** la ambulancia perdió valiosos minutos en un embotellamiento ►► ***p. metal*** metal *m* precioso; ***p. stone*** piedra *f* preciosa

(b) *(affected)* afectado(a)

(c) *Fam (expressing irritation)* **you and your p. books!** ¡tú y tus dichosos libros!

3 *adv Fam (for emphasis)* **p. little** poquísimo(a); **p. few** poquísimos(as)

preciousness ['preʃəsnɪs] *n* **(a)** *(value)* lo precioso **(b)** *(affectedness)* afectación *f*, amaneramiento *m*

precipice ['presɪpɪs] *n* precipicio *m*; *Fig* **this crisis has taken us to the edge of a p.** esta crisis nos ha llevado al borde del precipicio

precipitant [prɪ'sɪpɪtənt] *adj (action, decision, remark)* precipitado(a)

precipitate [prɪ'sɪpɪtɪt] **1** *n Chem* precipitado *m*

2 *adj* **(a)** *Formal (hasty)* precipitado(a); **to be p.** precipitarse **(b)** *(steep)* pronunciado(a), abrupto(a)

3 *vt* [prɪ'sɪpɪteɪt] **(a)** *(hasten)* precipitar **(b)** *(throw)* arrojar

4 *vi* **(a)** *Chem* precipitar **(b)** *Met* condensarse

precipitately [prɪ'sɪpɪtɪtlɪ] *adv Formal* precipitadamente

precipitation [prɪsɪpɪ'teɪʃən] *n* **(a)** *Met* precipitaciones *fpl*; **annual p.** pluviosidad anual **(b)** *Chem* precipitación *f*

precipitous [prɪ'sɪpɪtəs] *adj* **(a)** *(steep) (rise, incline)* empinado(a); *(fall, descent)* en *Esp* picado *or Am* picada **(b)** *Formal (hasty)* precipitado(a); **to be p.** precipitarse

precipitously [prɪ'sɪpɪtəslɪ] *adv* **(a)** *(steeply)* abruptamente, pronunciadamente **(b)** *Formal (hastily)* precipitadamente

précis ['preɪsi:] **1** *n* (*pl* **précis** ['preɪsi:z]) resumen *m*; **to write a p. of sth** escribir un resumen de algo

2 *vt* resumir

precise [prɪ'saɪs] *adj* **(a)** *(exact)* preciso(a); **to be p.** para ser exactos; **he was very p. in his description** dio una descripción muy precisa; **at the p. moment when...** en el preciso momento en que... **(b)** *(meticulous)* meticuloso(a)

precisely [prɪ'saɪslɪ] *adv* precisamente; **at six (o'clock) p.** a las seis en punto; **that's p. why I'm not going** precisamente por eso no voy; **she speaks very p.** habla de manera muy precisa; **p.!** ¡exactamente!; **what, p., do you mean?** ¿qué quieres decir exactamente?

precision [prɪ'sɪʒən] *n* precisión *f*; **with great p.** con gran precisión ►► *Mil* ***p. bombing*** bombardeo *m* de precisión; ***p. engineering*** ingeniería *f* de precisión; ***p. instrument*** instrumento *m* de precisión

precision-made [prɪ'sɪʒən'meɪd] *adj* de precisión

preclinical [prɪ'klɪnɪkəl] *adj Med* **(a)** *(training)* preclínico(a) **(b)** *(disease)* preclínico(a)

preclude [prɪ'klu:d] *vt Formal* excluir; **to p. sb from doing sth, to p. sb's doing sth** impedir a alguien hacer algo

precocious [prɪ'kəʊʃəs] *adj* precoz

precociousness [prɪ'kəʊʃəsnɪs], **precocity** [prɪ'kɒsɪtɪ] *n* precocidad *f*

precognition [pri:kɒg'nɪʃən] *n* precognición *f*

pre-Columbian ['pri:kə'lʌmbɪən] *adj* precolombino(a)

preconceived [pri:kən'si:vd] *adj (idea)* preconcebido(a)

preconception [pri:kən'sepʃən] *n* idea *f* preconcebida; *(prejudice)* prejuicio *m*; **to free oneself from all preconceptions** abandonar toda idea preconcebida

precondition [pri:kən'dɪʃən] *n* condición *f* previa

precooked [pri:'kʊkt] *adj* precocinado(a)

precursor [prɪ'kɜ:sə(r)] *n Formal* precursor(ora) *m,f* (**to** *or* **of** de)

precut ['pri:'kʌt] *adj* precortado(a)

predate [pri:'deɪt] *vt* **(a)** *(precede)* preceder a, anteceder a **(b)** *(put earlier date on)* antedatar

predator ['predətə(r)] *n (animal, bird)* predador(ora) *m,f*, depredador(ora) *m,f*; *(person)* aprovechado(a) *m,f*, buitre *mf*

predatory ['predətərɪ] *adj (animal, bird)* predador(ora), depredador(ora); *(person)* aprovechado(a); *(instinct)* predador(ora) ►► *Com* ***p. pricing*** fijación *f* de precios desleales

predecease [pri:dɪ'si:s] *vt Law* premorir

predecessor ['pri:dɪsesə(r)] *n* predecesor(ora) *m,f*

predestination [pri:destɪ'neɪʃən] *n* predestinación *f*

predestine [pri:'destɪn] *vt* predestinar; **to be predestined to do sth** estar predestinado(a) a hacer algo

predetermine [pri:dɪ'tɜ:mɪn] *vt* predeterminar

predetermined [pri:dɪ'tɜ:mɪnd] *adj* predeterminado(a); **at a p. date/place** en una fecha predeterminada/un lugar predeterminado

predicament [prɪ'dɪkəmənt] *n* (**a**) *(unpleasant situation)* aprieto *m*, apuro *m*; **to be in an awkward p.** estar en un brete (**b**) *(difficult choice)* dilema *m*, conflicto *m*

> **False friend:** The Spanish noun **predicamento** is not a translation for the English word **predicament**. In Spanish **predicamento** means "esteem, regard".

predicate **1** *n* ['predɪkət] (**a**) *Gram* predicado *m* (**b**) *Phil* predicado *m* ►► ***p. calculus*** cálculo *m* predicativo
2 *vt* ['predɪkeɪt] *Formal* (**a**) *(state)* afirmar (**b**) *(base)* **to be predicated on sth** fundarse *or* basarse en algo (**c**) *Phil* **to p. a quality of sth** atribuir una cualidad a algo

predicative ['predɪkətɪv] *n* (**a**) *Phil* predicativo(a) (**b**) *Gram (adjective)* atributivo(a), predicativo(a)

predict [prɪ'dɪkt] *vt* predecir, pronosticar; **rain is predicted for the weekend** está prevista lluvia para todo el fin de semana

predictability [prɪdɪktə'bɪlɪtɪ] *n* predicibilidad *f*

predictable [prɪ'dɪktəbəl] *adj* (**a**) *(foreseeable)* predecible, previsible (**b**) *(unoriginal)* poco original; *Fam* **you're so p.!** ¡siempre estás con lo mismo!

predictably [prɪ'dɪktəblɪ] *adv* previsiblemente; **p., he arrived an hour late** como era de prever, llegó con una hora de retraso *or Am* demora; **the evening proceeded entirely p.** la velada continuó muy predeciblemente

prediction [prɪ'dɪkʃən] *n* predicción *f*, pronóstico *m*

predictive [prɪ'dɪktɪv] *adj* indicador(ora), profético(a)

predictor [prɪ'dɪktə(r)] *n (indicator)* indicador *m*

predigested [pri:daɪ'dʒestɪd] *adj (information)* simplificado(a)

predilection [predɪ'lekʃən] *n Formal (liking)* predilección *f* (**for** por)

predispose [pri:dɪs'pəʊz] *vt* predisponer; **I was not predisposed to believe her** no estaba predispuesto a creerla

predisposition [pri:dɪspə'zɪʃən] *n* predisposición *f* (**to** *or* **towards** a)

predominance [prɪ'dɒmɪnəns] *n* predominio *m*; **there is a p. of women in the profession** en esta profesión existe un predominio femenino

predominant [prɪ'dɒmɪnənt] *adj* predominante; **the p. mood was one of resignation** predominaba un clima de resignación

predominantly [prɪ'dɒmɪnəntlɪ] *adv* predominantemente; **the population is p. English-speaking** la mayoría de la población es de habla inglesa

predominate [prɪ'dɒmɪneɪt] *vi* (**a**) *(be greater in number)* predominar (**b**) *(prevail)* preponderar, reinar

pre-eclampsia [pri:ɪ'klæmpsɪə] *n Med* preeclampsia *f*

pre-embryo ['pri:'embrɪəʊ] *n Med* preembrión *m*

preemie ['pri:mɪ] *n US Fam (premature baby)* bebé *m* prematuro

pre-eminence [pri:'emɪnəns] *n* preeminencia *f*; **to achieve p. in the field** lograr destacar en el campo

pre-eminent [pri:'emɪnənt] *adj* preeminente

pre-eminently [pri:'emɪnəntlɪ] *adv (mainly)* sobre todo, por encima de todo; **the reasons are p. economic** las razones son, sobre todo *or* por encima de todo, económicas

pre-empt [pri:'empt] **1** *vt* (**a**) *(person, decision)* adelantarse a; **he was pre-empted by a rival** se le adelantó uno de sus rivales (**b**) *esp US Law (land, property)* = ocupar con el objetivo de conseguir el derecho de compra
2 *vi (in bridge)* hacer una apertura preventiva

pre-emptive [pri:'emptɪv] *adj* ***p. bid*** *Fin* licitación *f or* oferta *f* preferente; *(in bridge)* apuesta *f* preventiva; *Comptr* ***p. multitasking*** multitarea *f* preferencial; *Mil* ***p. strike*** ataque *m* preventivo

preen [pri:n] **1** *vt* (**a**) *(of bird) (plumage)* limpiar con el pico; **to p. itself** atusarse las plumas (**b**) *(of person)* **to p. oneself** acicalarse; *Fig* **to p. oneself on sth** enorgullecerse *or* congratularse de algo
2 *vi* (**a**) *(bird)* atusarse las plumas (**b**) *(person)* mostrar satisfacción

pre-established [pri:ɪs'tæblɪʃt] *adj* preestablecido(a)

pre-exist [pri:ɪg'zɪst] *vt* preexistir

pre-existence [pri:ɪg'zɪstəns] *n* preexistencia *f*

pre-existent [pri:ɪg'zɪstənt], **pre-existing** [pri:ɪg'zɪstɪŋ] *adj* preexistente

prefab ['pri:fæb] *n Fam (house)* casa *f* prefabricada

prefabricate [pri:'fæbrɪkeɪt] *vt* prefabricar

prefabricated [pri:'fæbrɪkeɪtɪd] *adj* prefabricado(a)

preface ['prefɪs] **1** *n (of book)* prefacio *m*, prólogo *m*; *(to speech)* preámbulo *m*; **this incident was the p. to all-out war** este incidente fue el preámbulo de una guerra total
2 *vt (book)* prologar; **she prefaced her speech with an anecdote** abrió su discurso con una anécdota; **the events that prefaced the crisis** los hechos que prologaron la crisis

prefatory ['prefətərɪ] *adj Formal* introductorio(a)

prefect ['pri:fekt] *n* (**a**) *Sch* monitor(ora) *m,f* (**b**) *(administrator)* prefecto *m* ►► ***the P. of Police*** el prefecto de policía (**c**) *(in ancient Rome)* prefecto *m*

prefecture ['pri:fektʃə(r)] *n (administrative district)* prefectura *f*

prefer [prɪ'fɜ:(r)] (*pt & pp* **preferred**) *vt* (**a**) *(favour)* preferir; **I much p. his first film** prefiero mucho más su primera película, *Arg* prefiero lejos su primera película; **she prefers living** *or* **to live alone** prefiere vivir sola; **I p. wine to beer** prefiero el vino a la cerveza; **I p. her to her sister** me cae mejor ella que su hermana; **he prefers to walk rather than take the bus** prefiere caminar a tomar el autobús; **I would p. to stay at home** preferiría quedarme en casa; **he'd p. you not to come** preferiría que no vinieras; **we'd p. it if you weren't there** preferiríamos que no estuvieras allí; **do you mind if I smoke? – I'd p. (it) if you didn't** ¿te importa si fumo? – preferiría que no lo hicieras
(**b**) *Law* **to p. charges (against sb)** presentar cargos (contra alguien)
(**c**) *Formal (appoint)* nombrar

> En inglés culto o elevado, y especialmente en inglés americano, **prefer** puede ir seguido de **that** más un verbo en subjuntivo (ver el panel SUBJUNCTIVE):
> **he prefers that his name not be mentioned in the press**
> *prefiere que no se mencione su nombre en la prensa*
> Lo mismo también podría decirse del siguiente modo:
> **he prefers his name not to be mentioned in the press**

preferable ['prefərəbəl] *adj* preferible; **it is p. to book seats** es preferible reservar asientos

preferably ['prefərəblɪ] *adv* preferiblemente; **come tomorrow, p. in the evening** ven mañana, preferentemente por la noche; **would you like to make the presentations? – p. not** ¿te gustaría hacer las presentaciones? – si fuera posible preferiría no hacerlas

preference ['prefərəns] *n* (**a**) *(greater liking)* preferencia *f*; **to have** *or* **show a p. for sth** tener *or* mostrar preferencia por algo; **his p. is for Mozart** su preferencia es por Mozart; **I have no p.** me da lo mismo; **to express a p.** expresar una preferencia
(**b**) *(precedence)* **to give sth/sb p., to give p. to sth/sb** dar preferencia a algo/alguien; **married women will be given p.** se dará preferencia a las mujeres casadas; **in p. to...** antes que..., en lugar de...; **in order of p.** por orden de preferencia
(**c**) *Comptr* **preferences** preferencias *fpl*
(**d**) *Br St Exch* ***p. shares*** acciones *fpl* preferentes *or* privilegiadas

preferential [prefə'renʃəl] *adj* preferente; **to give sb p. treatment** dar tratamiento preferencial a alguien ►► ***p. creditor*** acreedor(ora) *m,f* preferente; ***p. interest rate*** interés *m* preferencial; ***p. voting*** = sistema electoral en el que los votantes eligen candidatos por orden de preferencia

preferment [prɪ'fɜ:mənt] *n Formal* ascenso *m* ►► *US St Exch* ***p. stock*** acciones *fpl* preferentes *or* privilegiadas

preferred [prɪ'fɜ:d] *adj* preferido(a)

prefigure [pri:'fɪgə(r)] *vt* (**a**) *(foreshadow)* prefigurar (**b**) *(foresee)* imaginar

prefix ['pri:fɪks] **1** *n* prefijo *m*
2 *vt* anteponer; **telephone numbers prefixed with the code 0800** números de teléfono con el prefijo 0800; **she prefixed her speech with some explanatory remarks** antes de comenzar su discurso hizo unas aclaraciones

pre-flight ['pri:flaɪt] *adj* previo(a) al vuelo

pre-formatted [pri:'fɔ:mætɪd] *adj Comptr* preformateado(a)

prefrontal ['pri:'frʌntəl] *adj Anat* prefrontal

pregame ['pri:geɪm] *adj* previo(a) al partido

preggers ['pregəz] *adj Br Fam* **to be p.** estar con bombo

pregnancy ['pregnənsɪ] *n (of woman)* embarazo *m*; *(of animals)* preñez *f* ►► ***p. test*** prueba *f* de embarazo

pregnant ['pregnənt] *adj* (**a**) *(woman)* embarazada; *(animal)* preñada; **to be p.** *(woman)* estar embarazada; *(animal)* estar preñada; **to get** *or* **become** *or* **fall p.** quedar embarazada; **to get sb p.** embarazar a alguien; **she's three months p.** está (embarazada) de tres meses; **she**

was p. with her third child estaba embarazada de su tercer hijo (**b**) *Literary* **to be p. with** *(situation, remark)* estar preñado(a) *or* cargado(a) de; **a p. silence** un silencio significativo

preheat ['pri:'hi:t] *vt* precalentar

prehensile [pri:'hensaıl] *adj* prensil

prehistoric ['pri:hıs'tɒrık] *adj* (**a**) *(man, remains)* prehistórico(a) (**b**) *Fam (old-fashioned)* prehistórico(a)

prehistory [pri:'hıstərı] *n* prehistoria *f*

pre-ignition ['pri:ıg'nıʃən] *n Aut* preencendido *m*

pre-industrial ['pri:ın'dʌstrıəl] *adj* preindustrial

pre-installed ['pri:ın'stɔ:ld] *adj Comptr* preinstalado(a)

prejudge [pri:'dʒʌdʒ] *vt* prejuzgar

prejudice ['predʒʊdıs] **1** *n* (**a**) *(bias)* prejuicio *m*; **to have a p. in favour of/against** tener prejuicios a favor de/en contra de; **I have no p. either way** cualquier opción me parece bien; **he's full of p.** tiene muchos prejuicios; **he's without p.** no tiene prejuicios; **racial p.** prejuicio racial (**b**) *Formal* **to the p. of** en perjuicio de; *Law* **without p. to** sin perjuicio *or* menoscabo de

2 *vt* (**a**) *(bias)* predisponer (**against/in favour of** en contra de/a favor de) (**b**) *(harm)* perjudicar

prejudiced ['predʒʊdıst] *adj* con prejuicios; **to be p.** tener prejuicios; **to be p. against/in favour of** estar predispuesto(a) en contra de/a favor de

prejudicial [predʒʊ'dıʃəl] *adj* perjudicial (**to** para); **this decision is p. to world peace** esta decisión pone en peligro la paz mundial

prelapsarian [pri:læp'seərıən] *adj* previo(a) al pecado original

prelate ['prelət] *n Rel* prelado *m*

preliminary [prı'lımınərı] **1** *n* preludio *m*; **as a p. to...** como preludio a...; **preliminaries** *(to investigation, meeting, of competition)* preliminares *mpl*; **let's dispense with the preliminaries** saltémonos las introducciones

2 *adj* preliminar; *Formal* **p. to departure, p. to leaving** antes de la partida, antes de partir

prelims ['pri:lımz] *npl* (**a**) *Br Univ* exámenes *mpl* preliminares (**b**) *Typ* introducción *f*

prelude ['prelju:d] *n* (**a**) *(introdution)* preludio *m* (**to** de *or* a) (**b**) *Mus* preludio *m*

premarital [pri:'mærıtəl] *adj* prematrimonial ►► ***p. sex*** relaciones *fpl* prematrimoniales

prematch ['pri:mætʃ] *adj* previo(a) al partido

premature ['premətjʊə(r)] *adj* (**a**) *(birth, child)* prematuro(a); **three months p.** tres meses prematuro(a) (**b**) *(death, judgment)* prematuro(a); *Fam* **you're being a bit p.!** ¡te estás adelantando un poco! ►► ***p. ejaculation*** eyaculación *f* precoz

prematurely ['premətjʊəlı] *adv* prematuramente; **to be p. senile/bald** quedarse senil/calvo prematuramente

premed ['pri:med] *Fam* **1** *n* (**a**) *Educ (student)* = estudiante que se prepara para el ingreso en la Facultad de Medicina; *(studies)* = estudios de preparación para la carrera de Medicina (**b**) *Med (medication)* premedicación *f*

2 *adj (studies)* = preparatorio para el ingreso en la Facultad de Medicina

premedical [pri:'medıkəl] *adj (studies)* = preparatorio para el ingreso en la Facultad de Medicina; *(student)* = que se prepara para el ingreso en la Facultad de Medicina

premedication ['pri:medı'keıʃən] *n Med* premedicación *f*

premeditated [pri:'medıteıtıd] *adj* premeditado(a)

premeditation ['pri:medı'teıʃən] *n* premeditación *f*; **with/without p.** con/sin premeditación

premenstrual [pri:'menstrʊəl] *adj* **to be p.** tener tensión premenstrual ►► *Med* ***p. syndrome*** síndrome *m* premenstrual; ***p. tension*** tensión *f* premenstrual

premier ['premıə(r)] **1** *n (prime minister)* jefe(a) *m,f* del Gobierno, primer(era) ministro(a) *m,f*

2 *adj* (**a**) *(leading)* primero(a) (**b**) *Br* ***the P. League*** *(top soccer division)* la (Liga de) Primera División

premiere ['premıeə(r)] **1** *n (of play, movie)* estreno *m*; **the movie's London/television p.** el estreno de Londres/televisivo de la película

2 *vt* estrenar

3 *vi* estrenarse

premiership ['premıəʃıp] *n* (**a**) *Pol (period)* mandato *m (del Primer Ministro)*; *(position)* cargo *m* de Primer Ministro (**b**) *Br* **the P.** *(top soccer division)* la (Liga de) Primera División

pre-millennial ['pri:mı'lenıəl] *adj* ancestral, premilenario(a)

premise ['premıs] **1** *n (of argument, theory)* premisa *f*; **on the p. that...** sobre la premisa de que...

2 *vt* **to be premised on...** partir del supuesto *or* de la premisa de que...

premises ['premısız] *npl (of factory)* instalaciones *fpl*; *(of shop)* local *m*, locales *mpl*; *(of office)* oficina *f*; **business p.** locales comerciales; **on/off the p.** dentro/fuera del establecimiento; **to see sb off the p.** sacar a alguien del establecimiento

premium ['pri:mıəm] *n* (**a**) *Fin (for insurance)* prima *f*

(**b**) *(additional sum)* recargo *m*; **to sell sth at a p.** vender algo por encima de su valor ►► ***p. bond*** = bono numerado emitido por el Gobierno británico, cuyo comprador entra en un sorteo mensual de premios en metálico otorgados informáticamente al azar

(**c**) IDIOMS **to be at a p.** *(be scarce)* estar muy cotizado(a); **to put a p. on sth** conceder una importancia especial a algo

(**d**) *US (fuel)* gasolina *f* súper

premolar ['pri:'məʊlə(r)] *Anat* **1** *n* premolar *m*

2 *adj* **p. tooth** premolar

premonition [pri:mə'nıʃən] *n* presentimiento *m*, premonición *f*; **I had a p. of my death** tuve el presentimiento de que iba a morir; **to have a p. that...** tener el presentimiento de que...

prenatal [pri:'neıtəl] *adj* prenatal

prenup ['pri:nʌp] *n US Fam* acuerdo *m* prenupcial

prenuptial ['pri:'nʌpʃəl] *adj* prenupcial ►► ***p. agreement*** acuerdo *m* prenupcial

preoccupation [pri:ɒkjʊ'peıʃən] *n* preocupación *f* (**with** por); **our main p. is safety** para nosotros la seguridad es lo primero; **his obsessive p. with physical fitness** su obsesión con la forma física

preoccupied [pri:'ɒkjʊpaıd] *adj* (**a**) *(worried)* preocupado(a); **to be p. with** *or* **by sth** estar preocupado(a) por algo (**b**) *(lost in thought)* ensimismado(a); **she was too p. with her work to spare a thought for me** estaba demasiado metida en su trabajo como para pensar en mí

preoccupy [pri:'ɒkjʊpaı] *vt* preocupar; **such thoughts as these p. my waking hours** este tipo de pensamientos me dan vueltas en la cabeza todo el día

preordain [pri:ɔ:'deın] *vt* predestinar

prep [prep] *Fam* **1** *n* (**a**) *Br (schoolwork)* deberes *mpl*; *(study period)* estudio *m* ►► ***p. school*** = colegio privado para alumnos de entre 7 y 13 años (**b**) *US* **p. (school)** = escuela privada de enseñanza secundaria y preparación para estudios superiores

2 *vt US Med (for operation)* preparar

3 *vi US* = acudir a un prep school

prepackaged [pri:'pækıdʒd], **prepacked** [pri:'pækt] *adj* empaquetado(a)

prepaid [pri:'peıd] *adj (envelope)* franqueado(a), con franqueo pagado

preparation [prepə'reıʃən] *n* (**a**) *(act of preparing)* preparación *f*; **in p. for sth** en preparación para algo; **to be in p.** estar en preparación; **the dish/event requires careful p.** el plato/evento requiere una cuidadosa preparación (**b**) *(for event)* **preparations** preparativos *mpl*; **to make preparations for sth** hacer preparativos para algo (**c**) *(medicine)* preparado *m*

preparatory [prı'pærətərı] *adj* (**a**) *(work, measure, stage)* preparatorio(a) (**b**) *Formal* **p. to (doing) sth** antes de (hacer) algo (**c**) ***p. school*** *Br* = colegio privado para alumnos de entre 7 y 13 años; *US* = escuela privada de enseñanza secundaria y preparación para estudios superiores

prepare [prı'peə(r)] **1** *vt* (**a**) *(make ready)* preparar; **to p. oneself for sth** prepararse *or Am* alistarse para algo; **you'd better p. yourself for some bad news** prepárate para recibir malas noticias

(**b**) *(make)* preparar, hacer; **to p. a meal for sb** prepararle *or* hacerle una comida a alguien; **to p. a surprise for sb** prepararle una sorpresa a alguien; **prepared from the finest ingredients** preparada con los ingredientes de mejor calidad

2 *vi* prepararse, *Am* alistarse (**for** para); **to p. to do sth** prepararse *or Am* alistarse para hacer algo; **p. for the worst!** ¡prepárate para lo peor!

prepared [prı'peəd] *adj* (**a**) *(willing)* **to be p. to do sth** estar dispuesto(a) a hacer algo; **he was not p. to lie for her** no estaba dispuesto a mentir por ella

(**b**) *(ready)* **to be p. for sth** estar preparado(a) para algo; **be p. for a surprise** prepárate para recibir una sorpresa; **to be p. for anything** estar preparado(a) para cualquier cosa; **be p.** *(Scout's motto)* siempre listos

(**c**) *(made in advance)* **a p. statement** una declaración preparada (de antemano)

preparedness [prɪ'peərɪdnɪs] *n* preparación *f*

prepay ['pri:'peɪ] (*pt & pp* **prepaid** ['pri:'peɪd]) *vt* pagar por adelantado

prepayment [pri:'peɪmənt] *n* pago *m* (por) adelantado

preponderance [prɪ'pɒndərəns] *n Formal* preponderancia *f*, predominio *m*

preponderantly [prɪ'pɒndərəntlɪ] *adv Formal* preponderantemente, predominantemente

preposition [prepə'zɪʃən] *n* preposición *f*

prepositional [prepə'zɪʃənəl] *adj* preposicional ▸▸ ***p. phrase*** frase *f* preposicional

prepossessing ['pri:pə'zesɪŋ] *adj* atractivo(a), agradable; **her manner is not very p.** tiene una forma de ser bastante desagradable

preposterous [prɪ'pɒstərəs] *adj* absurdo(a), ridículo(a); **that's a p. idea/suggestion!** ¡qué idea/sugerencia más absurda *or* ridícula!

preposterously [prɪ'pɒstərəslɪ] *adv* absurdamente, ridículamente; **it was p. easy** fue ridículamente sencillo

preppy ['prepɪ] *US Fam* **1** *n Esp* pijo(a) *m,f*, *Méx* fresa *mf*, *RP* (con)cheto(a) *m,f*, *Ven* sifrino(a) *m,f*
2 *adj Esp* pijo(a), *Méx* fresa, *RP* (con)cheto(a), *Ven* sifrino(a)

preprandial ['pri:'prændɪəl] *adj Literary or Hum* **a p. drink** un aperitivo

prepress ['pri:'pres] *n Typ* preimpresión *f*

preproduction [pri:prə'dʌkʃən] *n Cin* preproducción *f*; **the film is in p.** la película está en preproducción

preprogrammed ['pri:'prəʊgræmd] *adj Comptr* preprogramado(a); **humans are p. to behave in certain ways** los seres humanos estamos preprogramados para comportarnos de determinada forma

prepubescent ['pri:pju:'besənt] *adj* preadolescente

prepuce ['pri:pju:s] *n Anat* prepucio *m*

prequel ['pri:kwəl] *n Cin* = película o libro que desarrolla una historia o se refiere a eventos que preceden a otros contenidos en una obra ya existente

Pre-Raphaelite [prɪ'ræfəlaɪt] **1** *n* prerrafaelista *mf*
2 *adj* prerrafaelista; **she has gorgeous P. hair** tiene un hermoso cabello prerrafaelista

prerecorded ['pri:rɪ'kɔ:dɪd] *adj (cassette, TV programme)* pregrabado(a)

prerequisite ['pri:'rekwɪzɪt] **1** *n* requisito *m* previo (**of/for** para)
2 *adj* indispensable, esencial; **a p. condition** una condición indispensable

prerogative [prɪ'rɒgətɪv] *n* prerrogativa *f*; **to exercise one's p.** hacer uso de las prerrogativas que uno tiene; **that's your p.** estás en tu derecho

Pres. (*abbr* **president**) presidente(a) *m,f*

presage ['presɪdʒ] *Literary* **1** *n* presagio *m*
2 *vt* presagiar

Presbyterian [prezbɪ'tɪərɪən] **1** *n* presbiteriano(a) *m,f*
2 *adj* presbiteriano(a)

Presbyterianism ['prezbɪ'tɪərɪənɪzəm] *n* presbiterianismo *m*

presbytery ['prezbɪt(ə)rɪ] *n* (**a**) *(court)* presbiterio *m* (**b**) *(part of church)* presbiterio *m* (**c**) *(house)* casa *f* parroquial

preschool ['pri:'sku:l] **1** *n US* jardín *m* de infancia
2 *adj* preescolar ▸▸ ***p. education*** educación *f* preescolar

preschooler ['pri:'sku:lə(r)] *n US* niño(a) *m,f* en edad preescolar

prescience ['presɪəns] *n Formal* presciencia *f*

prescient ['presɪənt] *adj Formal* profético(a)

prescribe [prɪ'skraɪb] *vt* (**a**) *(medicine)* recetar; **do not exceed the prescribed dose** *(on medicine label)* no exceder la dosis prescripta (**b**) *(punishment, solution)* prescribir; **in the prescribed manner** de la forma prescrita; **prescribed reading** lectura obligatoria

prescription [prɪ'skrɪpʃən] *n* (**a**) *(for medicine)* receta *f*; **the doctor wrote out a p. for her** el médico le hizo una receta; **to make up a p. for sb** preparar una receta para alguien; **available only on p.** sólo con receta médica ▸▸ ***p. charge*** precio *m* de un medicamento con receta; ***p. drug*** droga *f* genérica; ***p. glasses*** gafas *fpl* graduadas
(**b**) *(recommendation)* receta *f*; **what's your p. for a happy life?** ¿cuál es tu receta para una vida feliz?

prescriptive [prɪ'skrɪptɪv] *adj* (**a**) *(authoritative)* preceptivo(a) (**b**) *Gram* normativo(a)

prescriptivism [prɪ'skrɪptɪvɪzəm] *n* (**a**) *Gram* normativismo *m* (**b**) *Phil* normativismo *m*

preselect ['pri:sə'lekt] *vt (tracks, channels)* preseleccionar

preselection [pri:sɪ'lekʃən] *n* preselección *f*

presence ['prezəns] *n* (**a**) *(attendance)* presencia *f*; **in the p. of** en presencia de; **don't say anything about it in his p.** delante de él no digas nada al respecto; **your p. is requested at Saturday's meeting** se requiere su presencia en la reunión del sábado; *Formal* **to be admitted to the p. of sb** ser admitido(a) ante alguien; **she made her p. felt** hizo sentir su presencia; **p. of mind** presencia de ánimo; **to have the p. of mind to do sth** tener la sensatez de hacer algo
(**b**) *(number of people present)* presencia *f*; **the police maintained a discreet p.** había una discreta presencia policial; **they maintain a strong military p. in the area** mantienen una fuerte presencia militar en la zona
(**c**) *(impressiveness)* **to have p.** tener mucha presencia
(**d**) *(supernatural entity)* espíritu *m*

PRESENT PERFECT/PAST SIMPLE

El pretérito indefinido es el tiempo más usado en inglés para referise a una acción ya acabada o a una situación del pasado, especialmente cuando se narra o explica algo. El pretérito perfecto se usa para referirse a hechos pasados que son aún relevantes en el presente porque ocurrieron en un periodo de tiempo que aún no ha finalizado:

they've just found out what really happened *acaban de enterarse de lo que ocurrió en realidad*
I've waited years for a chance like this! *¡llevo años esperando una oportunidad como esta!*
I've never eaten caviar *nunca he comido caviar*
we've seen all of your films! *¡hemos visto todas sus películas!*

Se puede hacer hincapié en la relevancia que la acción tiene aún en el presente con los adverbios **yet** y **already**. Estos adverbios se usan con el pretérito perfecto en inglés británico; en inglés americano se pueden usar también con el indefinido:

have you finished yet? (*US* **did you finish yet?**) *¿has terminado ya?*
they've already seen that one (*US* **they already saw that one**) *esa ya la han visto*

El uso del indefinido con **just** para referirse a un pasado muy reciente, que tradicionalmente se consideraba un uso americano, es cada vez más frecuente en inglés británico:

he just left *acaba de irse*

Pero a pesar de todo, en inglés británico el pretérito perfecto está aún muy asociado a la relevancia que tenga la acción en el presente. Por ejemplo, las oraciones siguientes pueden oírse tanto en inglés británico como americano:

did you ever go skiing?
have you ever been skiing?

Sin embargo, en inglés británico la primera pregunta implica que se habla de un tiempo pasado en el que se tuvo la oportunidad o intención de esquiar, como si la pregunta pudiera continuar: "cuando vivías en Italia" o "cuando te interesaba el deporte en tu juventud", mientras que la segunda sería una pregunta general sobre si alguna vez se ha esquiado.

present[1] ['prezənt] **1** *n* (**a**) *(in time)* **the p.** el presente; **at p.** *(now)* en estos momentos; *(these days)* actualmente; **for the p.** de momento, por el momento; **to live only for the p.** vivir el presente; **up to the p.** hasta la fecha, hasta ahora (**b**) *Gram* **in the p.** en presente (**c**) *Law* **by these presents** por el presente documento

2 *adj* (**a**) *(in attendance)* presente; **to be p.** estar presente; **to be p. at sth** estar presente en *or* presenciar algo; **how many were p.?** ¿cuántos estaban presentes?; **no women were p.** no había mujeres; **this chemical is not p. in the atmosphere** este compuesto químico no se encuentra *or* se halla en la atmósfera; **those p.** los presentes; **p. company excepted, of course** con excepción de esta compañía, por supuesto

(**b**) *(current)* actual; **the p. day** el día de hoy; **at the p. time** *or* **moment** en estos momentos; **in the p. case** en este caso; **given (the) p. circumstances** en vista de las circunstancias actuales; *Formal* **in the p. writer's opinion** en opinión de quien escribe

(**c**) *Gram* ***p. participle*** participio *m* de presente *or* activo; ***p. perfect*** pretérito *m* perfecto; ***the p. tense*** el (tiempo) presente

present[2] **1** *n* ['prezənt] *(gift)* regalo *m*; **to give sb a p.** regalar algo a alguien; **we gave her a pony as a p.** le dimos un poni de regalo, le regalamos un poni; **it's for a p.** *(in shop)* es para regalo; **to make sb a p. of sth** regalar algo a alguien; **birthday/Christmas p.** regalo de cumpleaños/Navidad

2 *vt* [prɪ'zent] (**a**) *(put forward)* presentar; *Formal (apologies, compliments)* presentar; **I wish to p. my complaint in person** deseo formular *or* presentar mi queja personalmente; **he presented his case very well** presentó muy bien el caso; **the essay is well presented** el ensayo está muy bien presentado; **he's trying to p. himself in a different light** está intentando cambiar su imagen; **if the opportunity presents itself** si se presenta la ocasión; *Parl* **to p. a bill** presentar un proyecto de ley

(**b**) *(confront)* **to p. sb with a challenge** ser un desafío para alguien; **I'd never been presented with a problem like this before** nunca se me había presentado un problema como éste

(**c**) *(be, constitute) (problem, difficulty)* representar, constituir; **this presents an ideal opportunity** esto es *or* constituye una oportunidad ideal

(**d**) *(give)* entregar; **to p. sth to sb, to p. sb with sth** *(gift)* regalar algo a alguien; *(award, certificate)* otorgar *or* entregar algo a alguien; **she presented him with a daughter** le dio una hija

(**e**) *(show) (passport, ticket)* presentar, mostrar; **you must p. proof of ownership** debes presentar el título de propiedad

(**f**) *Formal (introduce)* presentar; **to p. sb to sb** presentarle alguien a alguien; **allow me to p. Mr Jones** permítanme presentarles al Sr Jones; **to be presented at Court** ser presentado(a) ante la Corte

(**g**) *Formal* **to p. oneself** *(arrive, go)* presentarse; **you will p. yourself in my office at five o'clock** se presentará en mi oficina a las cinco

(**h**) *(play, production)* **Columbia Pictures presents...** Columbia Pictures presenta...; **presenting Sarah Brown as the Queen** presentando a Sarah Brown en el papel de la Reina

(**i**) *(radio or TV show)* conducir

(**j**) *Mil* **p. arms!** ¡presenten armas!

3 *vi Med* **the patient presented with flu symptoms** el paciente presentaba síntomas de gripe

presentable [prɪ'zentəbəl] *adj* presentable; **do I look p.?** ¿estoy presentable?; **to make oneself p.** ponerse presentable

presentation [prezən'teɪʃən] *n* (**a**) *(putting forward) (of ideas, facts)* presentación *f*; **he made a very clear p. of the case** presentó el caso con suma claridad

(**b**) *(of gift, award)* entrega *f*; **p. (ceremony)** ceremonia *f* de entrega; **to make a p. to sb** *(give present)* hacer (entrega de) un obsequio a alguien; *(give award)* otorgar *or* entregar un premio a alguien ▸▸ ***p. copy*** copia *f* obsequio; ***p. pack*** envase *m* promocional

(**c**) *(formal talk)* presentación *f*, exposición *f*; **to give a p.** hacer una exposición, dar una charla *(con la ayuda de gráficos, diapositivas, etc)*

(**d**) **on p. of** *(passport, coupon)* con la presentación de, presentando

(**e**) *(manner of presenting)* presentación *f*; **she lost marks for poor p.** le bajaron puntos por mala presentación ▸▸ *Comptr* ***p. graphics*** gráficos *mpl* para presentaciones; *Comptr* ***p. graphics program*** programa *m* de presentaciones

(**f**) *Med (of foetus)* presentación *f*

present-day ['prezənt'deɪ] *adj* actual, de hoy en día

presenter [prɪ'zentə(r)] *n (on radio, TV)* presentador(ora) *m,f*

presentiment [prɪ'zentɪmənt] *n Formal* premonición *f*, presentimiento *m*

presently ['prezəntlɪ] *adv* (**a**) *(soon)* pronto; *(soon afterwards)* poco después; **I'll be with you p.** estaré con usted dentro de poco; **p., she got up and left** poco (tiempo) después, se levantó y se fue (**b**) *(now)* actualmente, en estos momentos; **she's p. working on a new novel** actualmente *or* en estos momentos está trabajando en una nueva novela

preservation [prezə'veɪʃən] *n* (**a**) *(maintenance)* conservación *f*, mantenimiento *m* (**b**) *(protection) (of species, building)* conservación *f*, protección *f* ▸▸ *Br* ***p. order*** orden *f* de conservación *(de un monumento o edificio de valor histórico-artístico)*

preservative [prɪ'zɜːvətɪv] **1** *n* conservante *m*; **contains no artificial preservatives** *(on food label)* no posee conservantes artificiales

2 *adj* conservante

preserve [prɪ'zɜːv] **1** *n* (**a**) *(jam)* confitura *f*, mermelada *f*; **preserves** conservas (**b**) *(in hunting)* coto *m* de caza (**c**) *(area of dominance)* territorio *m*; **cruises are still the p. of the rich** los viajes en crucero siguen siendo un privilegio exclusivo de los ricos; **engineering is no longer a male p.** la ingeniería ya no es un reducto masculino

2 *vt* (**a**) *(maintain)* conservar, mantener; **to be well preserved** *(building, specimen)* estar bien conservado(a); *Hum (person)* conservarse bien; **they tried to p. some semblance of normality** intentaron mantener una cierta apariencia de normalidad

(**b**) *(leather, wood)* conservar

(**c**) *(fruit)* confitar, poner en conserva; *(vegetable)* poner *or* hacer *or* preparar en conserva

(**d**) *(protect)* conservar, proteger (**from** de); **saints p. us!** ¡que Dios nos proteja *or* ampare!

preset ['priː'set] **1** *vt* programar

2 *adj* preprogramado(a)

preshrunk ['priː'ʃrʌŋk] *adj* lavado(a) previamente

preside [prɪ'zaɪd] *vi* presidir; **to p. at** *or* **over a meeting** presidir una reunión; **he presided over the decline of the empire** él estuvo al mando durante el declive del imperio

presidency ['prezɪdənsɪ] *n* presidencia *f*; **during his p.** durante su presidencia; **to assume the p.** asumir la presidencia

president ['prezɪdənt] *n* (**a**) *(of state)* presidente(a) *m,f* (**b**) *(of company, bank)* presidente(a) *m,f* (**c**) *(of organization, club)* presidente(a) *m,f* ▸▸ *Br* **P. of the Board of Trade** Ministro(a) *m,f* de Industria y Comercio

president-elect ['prezɪdəntɪ'lekt] *n* presidente(a) *m,f* electo(a)

presidential [prezɪ'denʃəl] *adj* presidencial; **p. hopeful** persona con aspiraciones presidenciales

presiding [prɪ'zaɪdɪŋ] *adj* ***p. judge*** juez *m* presidente de la sala; *Br* ***p. officer*** *(at polling station)* presidente(a) *m,f* de mesa

presidium, praesidium [prɪ'zɪdɪəm] *n* presidium *m*

presoak ['priː'səʊk] **1** *vt (dried fruit)* poner en remojo; *(clothes)* preenjuagar

2 *n* preenjuague *m*

PRESS [pres] **1** *n* (**a**) *(act of pushing)* **give it a p.** *(push it)* aprieta, apriétalo; *(iron it)* plánchalo; **he gave my hand a p.** me apretó la mano; **at the p. of a button...** al pulsar un botón...; **in the p. to get out we became separated** con tanta gente tratando de salir acabamos separándonos ▸▸ *Hist* ***p. gang*** = grupo de marineros que se encargaba de reclutar por la fuerza a gente para la Armada; ***p. stud*** automático *m*, corchete *m*

(**b**) *(newspapers)* **the p.** la prensa; **the national/local p.** la prensa nacional/local; **the p. were there** la prensa estaba presente; **to get** *or* **have a good/bad p.** tener buena/mala prensa ▸▸ ***p. agency*** agencia *f* de noticia, agencia *f* de prensa; ***p. agent*** agente *mf* de prensa; ***p. attaché*** jefe(a) *m,f* de prensa; ***p. baron*** magnate *mf* de la prensa; ***p. box*** tribuna *f* de prensa *or* periodistas; ***p. campaign*** campaña *f* mediática; ***p. card*** carné *m* de periodista; *US* ***p. clipping*** recorte *m* de prensa; ***p. conference*** rueda *f or* conferencia *f* de prensa; ***the p. corps*** los periodistas acreditados; ***p. coverage*** cobertura *f* periodística; *Br* ***p. cutting*** recorte *m* de prensa; ***p. department*** servicio *m* de prensa; ***p. gallery*** tribuna *f* de prensa; ***p. kit*** carpeta *f or* dossier *m* de prensa; ***p. office*** oficina *f* de prensa; ***p. officer*** jefe(a) *m,f* de prensa; ***p. pack*** carpeta *f or* dossier *m* de prensa; ***p. pass*** pase *m or* acreditación *f* de prensa; ***p. photographer*** reportero(a) *m,f* gráfico(a); ***p. release*** comunicado *m or* nota *f* de prensa; ***p. report*** información *f*, noticia *f*; ***p. reporter*** reportero(a) *m,f*; *US* ***p. run*** tirada *f*, *Am* tiraje *m*; ***p. secretary*** secretario(a) *m,f* de prensa

(**c**) *(machine) (industrial, for winemaking)* prensa *f*; **(printing) p.** imprenta *f*; **to go to p.** *(newspaper)* entrar en prensa ▸▸ *Typ* ***p. proof*** prueba *f* de imprenta

(**d**) *(publishing house)* editorial *f*

(**e**) *(cupboard)* alacena *f (con puerta)*

(**f**) *(in basketball)* presión *f*; **full court p.** presión a toda la cancha

(**g**) *(in weightlifting)* levantamiento *m* con apoyo

2 *vt* (**a**) *(push) (button, switch)* apretar; *(into clay, cement)* presionar (**into** sobre); **they pressed their faces against the window** apretaron sus caras contra la ventana; **she pressed herself against the wall** se echó *or* se arrimó contra la pared; **to p. sth down** apretar algo hacia abajo; **he pressed the note into my hand** me puso el billete en la mano; **to p. sth shut** cerrar algo apretando; **to p. one's way through a crowd** abrirse camino a empujones por entre la multitud

(**b**) *(squeeze)* apretar; *(juice, lemon)* exprimir; *(grapes, olives, flowers)* prensar; **he pressed her arm** le apretó el brazo; **she pressed the book to her chest** apretó el libro contra el pecho; IDIOM *Hum* **to p. the flesh** *(politician)* darse un baño de multitudes

(**c**) *(iron)* planchar

(**d**) *(manufacture) (record, CD)* estampar, prensar; *(component)* prensar

(**e**) *(pressurize)* presionar; **to p. sb to do sth** presionar a alguien para que haga algo; **the interviewer pressed her on the issue** el entrevistador insistió en el tema; **don't let yourself be pressed into going** no dejes que te presionen para que vayas; **to be (hard) pressed for time/money** estar apurado(a) de tiempo/dinero; **you'll be be hard pressed to do that** te resultará muy difícil hacer eso

(**f**) *(force)* **to p. sth on sb** obligar a alguien a aceptar algo; **to p. one's attentions on sb** prodigar excesivas atenciones a alguien; **he pressed home his advantage** sacó el máximo partido a su ventaja; **I've had to p. my old bike into service, because the new one's broken** he tenido que rescatar mi vieja bici, porque la nueva está estropeada

(**g**) *(insist on)* **he pressed his case for the reforms** defendió vigorosamente sus argumentos a favor de las reformas; **I've decided not to p. charges** a pesar de todo, he decidido no presentar cargos; **I don't want to p. the point, but...** no quiero insistir más, pero...

3 *vi* (**a**) *(push)* empujar; **p. twice, then wait** aprieta dos veces, y espera; **to p. down on sth** apretar algo; **he pressed (down) on the accelerator** pisó el acelerador; **the rucksack pressed on his shoulders** la mochila hacía presión sobre sus hombros; *Fig* **her problems pressed on her mind** los problemas le pesaban en la conciencia

(**b**) *(insist)* **he pressed hard to get the grant** insistió denodadamente para que le dieran la beca; **time is pressing!** el tiempo apremia

(**c**) *(crowd, surge)* apelotonarse (**against** contra); **they pressed forward to get a better view** se apelotonaron hacia delante para ver mejor; **to p. through a crowd** abrirse camino a empujones por entre la multitud

▸ **press ahead** = **press on**

▸ **press for** *vt insep (demand)* exigir

▸ **press on** *vi* seguir adelante (**with** con)

---

pressed [prest] *adj (flower)* prensado(a) ▸▸ ***p. steel*** acero *m* prensado

press-gang ['presgæŋ] *vt* (**a**) *(force)* **to p. sb into doing sth** forzar a alguien a hacer algo (**b**) *Hist* grupo *m or* patrulla *f* de reclutamiento

pressie ['prezɪ] *n Br Fam* regalito *m*

pressing ['presɪŋ] **1** *n* (**a**) *(of grapes, olives)* prensado *m* (**b**) *(of record)* prensado *m* (**c**) *(insistence)* insistencia *f*

2 *adj* (**a**) *(urgent)* apremiante (**b**) *(insistent)* insistente

pressman ['presmən] *n* (**a**) *Br* periodista *m* (**b**) *(printer)* impresor(ora) *m,f*

pressroom ['presrʊm] *n* (**a**) *(for printing press)* taller *m* de prensas (**b**) *(for journalists)* sala *f* de prensa

press-up ['presʌp] *n Br (exercise)* fondo *m*, flexión *f* (de brazos); **to do press-ups** hacer fondos

pressure ['preʃə(r)] **1** *n* (**a**) *(physical)* presión *f*; **a p. of 20 kilogrammes to the square centimetre** una presión de 20 kilos por centímetro cuadrado; **to put p. on sth** aplicar presión sobre algo ▸▸ ***p. cooker*** olla *f* a presión, olla *f* exprés; ***p. gauge*** manómetro *m*; *Med* ***p. point*** punto *m* de presión; ***p. sore*** úlcera *f* de decúbito

(**b**) *Met* **area of high/low p.** área de altas/bajas presiones

(**c**) *(persuasive, oppressive force)* presión *f*; **there's no p., don't come if you don't want to** no hay ningún tipo de obligación, si no quieres, no vengas; **there's a lot of p. on her to succeed** se siente muy presionada para triunfar; **to be under p. (to do sth)** estar presionado(a) (para hacer algo); **to put p. on sb (to do sth)** presionar a alguien (para que haga algo); **to bring p. to bear on sb (to do sth)** ejercer presión sobre alguien (para que haga algo); **to come under heavy** *or* **sustained p.** estar sometido(a) a mucha presión *or* presión continua ▸▸ ***p. group*** grupo *m* de presión

(**d**) *(stress)* **the pressures of running a large company** la presión *or* tensión que supone dirigir una gran compañía; **I'm under a lot of p. at work at the moment** estoy muy presionado en el trabajo en estos momentos; **to work under p.** trabajar bajo presión; **he's obviously feeling the p.** es evidente que la presión a la que está sometido se está dejando notar; **he pleaded p. of work** argumentó que tenía mucha presión en el trabajo

2 *vt* **to p. sb to do sth** presionar a alguien para que haga algo

pressure-cook ['preʃəkʊk] *vt* cocinar en olla a presión

pressurize ['preʃəraɪz] *vt* (**a**) *Tech (container)* presurizar (**b**) *(person)* **to p. sb (into doing sth)** presionar a alguien (para que haga algo)

pressurized ['preʃəraɪzd] *adj Tech (liquid, gas)* presurizado(a) ▸▸ ***p. cabin*** *(in aircraft)* cabina *f* presurizada; ***p. water reactor*** reactor *m* de agua presurizada

presswoman ['preswʊmən] *n Br* periodista *f*

prestidigitation [prestɪdɪdʒɪ'teɪʃən] *n* prestidigitación *f*

prestige [pres'tiːʒ] *n* prestigio *m* ▸▸ ***p. value*** valor *m* que otorga el prestigio

prestigious [pres'tɪdʒəs] *adj* prestigioso(a)

pre-stressed ['priː'strest] *adj (concrete)* pretensado(a)

presumable [prɪ'zjuːməbəl] *adj* presumible

presumably [prɪ'zjuːməblɪ] *adv* presumiblemente, según cabe suponer; **p. she'll come** cabe suponer que vendrá; **have they left? – p.** ¿se han ido? – supongo que sí

presume [prɪ'zjuːm] **1** *vt* (**a**) *(suppose)* suponer; **I p. so** supongo (que sí); **Mr Dobson, I p.?** si no me equivoco usted debe ser el Sr. Dobson (**b**) *(be so bold)* **to p. to do sth** tomarse la libertad de hacer algo; **I wouldn't p. so far as to...** yo no me tomaría semejante libertad como para... (**c**) *(presuppose)* presuponer

2 *vi (be cheeky)* **I don't want to p., but...** no querría parecer demasiado atrevido, pero...; **I don't want to p. on** *or* **upon you** no quiero abusar de su generosidad

presumed [prɪ'zjuːmd] *adj* **20 people are missing, p. dead** han desaparecido 20 personas, por cuyas vidas se teme; **everyone is p. innocent until proven guilty** todo el mundo es inocente hasta que no se demuestre lo contrario

> **False friend**: The Spanish adjective **presumido** is not a translation for the English word **presumed**. In Spanish **presumido** means "show-offish" or "vain".

presumption [prɪ'zʌmpʃən] *n* (**a**) *(assumption)* suposición *f*, supuesto *m*; **the p. is that he was drowned** se supone que se ahogó; *Law* **p. of innocence** presunción de inocencia (**b**) *(arrogance)* atrevimiento *m*, osadía *f*; **she had the p. to suggest I was lying** tuvo el atrevimiento de sugerir que yo mentía

presumptive [prɪ'zʌmptɪv] *adj (heir)* presunto(a)

presumptuous [prɪ'zʌmptjʊəs] *adj* impertinente; **I don't want to be p., but...** no quiero ser impertinente, pero...

> **False friend**: The Spanish adjective **presuntuoso** is not a translation for the English word **presumptuous**. In Spanish **presuntuoso** means "conceited" or "pretentious".

presumptuously [prɪ'zʌmptjʊəslɪ] *adv* con impertinencia, impertinentemente; **she p. assumed that...** supuso impertinentemente que...

presumptuousness [prɪ'zʌmptjʊəsnɪs] *n* impertinencia *f*

> **False friend**: The Spanish noun **presuntuosidad** is not a translation for the English word **presumptuousness**. In Spanish **presuntuosidad** means "conceit".

presuppose ['priːsə'pəʊz] *vt* presuponer

presupposition [priːsʌpə'zɪʃən] *n* supuesto *m*, suposición *f*

pre-tax ['priː'tæks] *adj* antes de impuestos, bruto(a) ▸▸ ***p. profits*** beneficios *mpl* antes de impuestos *or* brutos

pre-teen ['priː'tiːn] **1** *n US* preadolescente *mf*

2 *adj (sizes, fashions)* preadolescente; *(problems)* de la pubertad, preadolescente

pretence, *US* **pretense** [prɪ'tens] *n* (**a**) *(false display)* fingimiento *m*; **he says... but it's all** *or* **only (a) p.** dice que... pero es pura fachada; **a p. of democracy/impartiality** una pretensión democrática/de imparcialidad; **to make a p. of doing sth** aparentar hacer algo; **he made no p. of his scepticism** no trató de ocultar su escepticismo

(**b**) *(pretext)* pretexto *m*; **under** *or* **on the p. of doing sth** con *or* bajo el pretexto de hacer algo; **he criticizes her on the slightest p.** la critica con cualquier pretexto

(**c**) *(claim)* pretensión *f*; **she hasn't the slightest p. of culture** carece de cualquier noción de cultura; **he makes no p. to musical taste** no se las da de tener gusto musical

pretend [prɪ'tend] **1** *vt* **(a)** *(feign)* fingir, simular; **to p. to be ill** hacerse el/la enfermo(a); **to p. to do sth** fingir hacer algo; **they pretended not to see** *or* **to have seen us** fingieron no vernos *or* habernos visto
(b) *(act as if)* **they pretended (that) nothing had happened** hicieron como si no hubiera pasado nada; **we'll p. it never happened, shall we?** como si no hubiera ocurrido, ¿de acuerdo?; **I'll p. I didn't hear that** voy a hacer de cuenta que no te escuché; **she pretends that everything is all right** actúa como si no pasara nada; **it's no use pretending things will improve** no tiene sentido actuar como si las cosas fueran a mejorar
(c) *(claim)* pretender; **I don't p. to be an expert on the matter...** no pretendo ser un experto en el tema...
2 *vi* **(a)** *(put on an act)* fingir **(b)** *(lay claim)* **to p. to sth** pretender tener algo; **I don't p. to great knowledge on the matter** no pretendo saber mucho del asunto; *Hist* **to p. to the throne** aspirar al trono
3 *adj Fam* de mentira; **p. money** dinero de mentira; **a p. slap** un amago de bofetada; **it was only p.!** ¡era una mentira!

pretender [prɪ'tendə(r)] *n (to throne)* pretendiente *mf*

pretense *US* = **pretence**

pretension [prɪ'tenʃən] *n* **(a)** *(claim)* pretensión *f*; **to have pretensions to sth** tener pretensiones de algo; **I make no pretensions to expert knowledge** no tengo pretensiones de poseer un conocimiento especializado **(b)** *(pretentiousness)* pretenciosidad *f*

pretentious [prɪ'tenʃəs] *adj* pretencioso(a)

pretentiously [prɪ'tenʃəslɪ] *adv* pretenciosamente

pretentiousness [prɪ'tenʃəsnəs] *n* pretenciosidad *f*

preterite, *US* **preterit** ['pretərɪt] **1** *n Gram* **the p.** el pretérito
2 *adj* pretérito(a)

preterm ['pri:'tɜ:m] *Med* **1** *adj* prematuro(a)
2 *adv* prematuramente

preternatural [pri:tə'nætʃərəl] *adj Formal (uncanny)* sobrenatural

preternaturally ['pri:tə'nætʃərəlɪ] *adv Formal* sobrenaturalmente; **p. gifted** con dotes sobrenaturales

pretext ['pri:tekst] *n* pretexto *m*; **under** *or* **on the p. of doing sth** con el pretexto de hacer algo

prettify ['prɪtɪfaɪ] *vt* embellecer; **to p. oneself** acicalarse, embellecerse

prettily ['prɪtɪlɪ] *adv (decorated, arranged)* de forma bonita *or* linda; **she smiled p.** lanzó una bonita *or* linda sonrisa; **she sang very p.** cantó muy bien

prettiness ['prɪtɪnɪs] *n* lo bonito; **she had a certain p.** era bastante guapa *or Am* linda

pretty ['prɪtɪ] **1** *adj* **(a)** *(person, thing, smile)* bonito(a), *Am* lindo(a); **who's a p. boy?** *(to parrot)* ¡hola, lorito!; **it's not enough to make p. speeches** no alcanza con dar discursos bonitos *or Am* lindos
(b) IDIOMS *Fam* **I'm not just a p. face, you know!** ¡soy algo más que una cara bonita *or Am* linda!; *Old-fashioned* **things have come to a p. pass when...** mal van las cosas cuando...; **it's not a p. sight** es un espectáculo lamentable; **to cost a p. penny** costar un buen pellizco *or* pico; **to be as p. as a picture** ser precioso(a) *or* lindísimo(a)
2 *adv (fairly)* bastante; **you did p. well for a beginner** para ser un principiante lo hiciste bastante bien; *Fam* **p. much** *or* **well** *or* **nearly** *(almost)* casi casi, prácticamente; **they're p. much the same** son poco más o menos lo mismo; **we've got a p. good idea who did it** tenemos una idea bastante clara de quién lo hizo
3 *n Fam Old-fashioned (girl, animal)* belleza *f*; **come here, my p.** ven aquí, belleza

▸ **pretty up** *vt sep* arreglar

pretty-boy ['prɪtɪbɔɪ] *adj* **his p. good looks** su aspecto de niño guapo *or Am* lindo

pretty-pretty ['prɪtɪ'prɪtɪ] *adj Fam Pej* muy bonito(a)

pretzel ['pretzəl] *n* palito *m* salado *(alargado o en forma de 8)*

prevail [prɪ'veɪl] *vi* **(a)** *(be successful)* prevalecer (**over** *or* **against** sobre); **let us hope that justice prevails** esperemos que se imponga la justicia; **luckily, common sense prevailed** por suerte, prevaleció la cordura *or* el sentido común **(b)** *(predominate)* predominar; **in the conditions which now p.** en las circunstancias actuales

▸ **prevail on, prevail upon** *vt insep Formal* **to p. (up)on sb to do sth** convencer a alguien para que haga algo; **he was not to be prevailed (up)on** no era fácil convencerlo

prevailing [prɪ'veɪlɪŋ] *adj* **(a)** *(wind)* dominante, predominante **(b)** *(dominant) (belief, opinion, fashion)* predominante **(c)** *(current)* actual

prevalence ['prevələns] *n* **(a)** *(dominance)* predominio *m*; **the p. of these beliefs can only do harm** el predominio de estas creencias sólo puede ocasionar daños **(b)** *(widespread existence)* preponderancia *f*; **the p. of rented property surprised him** la preponderancia de propiedades en alquiler lo sorprendió

prevalent ['prevələnt] *adj* **(a)** *(dominant)* predominante **(b)** *(widespread)* preponderante, frecuente; **to become p.** convertirse en algo preponderante *or* frecuente

prevaricate [prɪ'værɪkeɪt] *vi* dar rodeos, andar con evasivas; **stop prevaricating!** ¡deja ya de dar rodeos *or* andar con evasivas!

> **False friend:** The Spanish verb **prevaricar** is not a translation for the English word **prevaricate**. In Spanish **prevaricar** means "to pervert the course of justice".

prevarication [prɪværɪ'keɪʃən] *n* rodeos *mpl*, evasivas *fpl*

prevent [prɪ'vent] *vt (accident, catastrophe, scandal)* evitar, impedir; *(illness)* prevenir; **to p. sb (from) doing sth** evitar *or* impedir que alguien haga algo; **to p. sth from happening** evitar *or* impedir que pase algo; **they couldn't p. his departure** no pudieron evitar que se fuera; **she opened the parcel before I could p. her** abrió el paquete antes de que pudiera evitarlo

preventable [prɪ'ventəbəl] *adj* evitable; **a p. disease** una enfermedad prevenible

preventative = **preventive**

prevention [prɪ'venʃən] *n* prevención *f*; PROV **p. is better than cure** más vale prevenir que curar

preventive, [prɪ'ventɪv], **preventative** [prɪ'ventətɪv] **1** *n* **(a)** *(measure)* medida *f* preventiva; **as a p. (against)** como medida preventiva (contra) **(b)** *(medicine)* medicina *f* preventiva
2 *adj* **to take p. measures** tomar medidas preventivas ▸▸ ***p. custody*** prisión *f* preventiva; ***p. detention*** detención *f* preventiva *or* cautelar; ***p. medicine*** medicina *f* preventiva

preverbal ['pri:'vɜ:bəl] *adj* **(a)** *(infant)* **p. communication** comunicación preverbal **(b)** *Gram* antes del verbo

preview ['pri:vju:] **1** *n* **(a)** *(of play, movie)* preestreno *m*; *(of exhibition)* preapertura *f*; *Fig* **can you give us a p. of what to expect?** ¿puedes anticiparnos qué es lo que podemos esperar? **(b)** *(of TV programme)* avance *m* **(c)** *US Cin (trailer)* avance *m*, tráiler *m*, *Arg* cola *f* **(d)** *Comptr* previsualización *f*
2 *vt* **(a)** *(play, movie) (put on)* hacer el preestreno de; *(see)* asistir al preestreno de; **the movie was previewed** hubo un preestreno de la película **(b)** *(TV programmes)* reseñar por anticipado **(c)** *Comptr* previsualizar

previous ['pri:vɪəs] **1** *adj* **(a)** *(prior) (experience, appointment)* previo(a); *(attempt, page)* anterior; **on p. occasions** en ocasiones anteriores *or* previas; **I have a p. engagement** tengo un compromiso previo ▸▸ *Law* ***p. convictions*** antecedentes *mpl* penales
(b) *(former)* anterior, previo(a); **my p. house** mi última casa; **the p. owner** el dueño anterior; **in a p. life** en una vida anterior
(c) *(with days and dates)* anterior, pasado(a); **the p. day** el día anterior; **the p. Monday/June** el lunes/junio pasado
(d) *Fam (hasty)* precipitado(a); **aren't you being a little p.?** ¿no estás precipitándote un poco?
2 *adv* **p. to** con anterioridad a; **the two months p. to your arrival** los dos meses anteriores a tu llegada

previously ['pri:vɪəslɪ] *adv* **(a)** *(in the past)* anteriormente; **three days p.** tres días antes; **p., the country was under British rule** anteriormente, el país se encontraba bajo dominio británico; *US TV* **p., on "ER"** en episodios anteriores de "Urgencias" **(b)** *(already)* ya; **we've met p.** ya nos conocíamos

prevocalic ['pri:və'kælɪk] *adj Ling* prevocálico(a)

prevue ['pri:vju:] *n US Cin (trailer)* avance *m*, tráiler *m*, *Arg* cola *f*

prewar ['pri:'wɔ:(r)] *adj* de preguerra

pre-wash ['pri:wɒʃ] *n (on washing cycle)* prelavado *m*

prey [preɪ] *n* presa *f*; *Fig* **to be a p. to** ser presa de; **to be (a) p. to doubts/nightmares** ser presa de las dudas/pesadillas; **to fall p. to** caer *or* ser víctima de

▸ **prey on, prey upon** *vt insep* **(a)** *(of animal)* alimentarse de **(b)** *(of opportunist)* aprovecharse de; **something is preying on his mind** está atormentado por algo

prez [prez] *n US Fam* presi *mf*

prezzie ['prezɪ] *n Br Fam* regalito *m*

priapism ['praɪəpɪzəm] *n Med* priapismo *m*

PRICE [praɪs] **1** *n* (**a**) *(amount charged)* precio *m*; *(of shares)* cotización *f*; **what p. is it?** ¿cuánto vale?, ¿qué precio tiene?; **it's the same p. as the other make, but has more features** cuesta lo mismo que el de la otra marca, pero tiene más *Esp* opciones *or Am* opcionales; **prices start at £200** desde 200 libras; **tickets vary in p.** hay entradas *or Am* boletos de diferentes precios; **to rise/fall in p.** subir/bajar de precio; **prices are rising/falling** los precios están subiendo/bajando; **it's gone up/down in p.** ha subido/bajado de precio; **if the p. is right** si el precio es el adecuado; **he'd buy it if the p. were right** lo compraría al precio adecuado; **that's my p., take it or leave it** ése es el precio, lo tomas o lo dejas; **we can get it for you, but at** *or* **for a p.** te lo podemos conseguir, pero te saldrá caro; **they managed to win, but at a p.** consiguieron ganar, pero a un precio muy alto; **at any p.** a toda costa; **not at any p.** por nada del mundo; **they won, but at what p.?** ganaron, ¿pero a qué precio?; **I paid $50 for it and it was cheap at the p.** me costó 50 dólares, estaba tirado; *Fig* **everyone has his p.** todos tenemos un precio; *Fig* **to pay the p. (for sth)** pagar el precio (de algo); *Fig* **he paid a heavy p. for his mistake** pagó un precio muy caro por su error; *Fig* **it's too high a p. (to pay)** es un precio demasiado alto *or* caro; *Fig* **it's a small p. to pay for our freedom** supone poco a cambio de nuestra libertad; **to put a p. on sth** poner precio a algo; *Fig* **you cannot put a p. on human life** la vida humana no tiene precio; *Fig* **to put** *or* **set a p. on sb's head** poner precio a la cabeza de alguien; *Fam* **what p. a Conservative victory now?** ¿quién da un centavo por una victoria conservadora?; *Fam* **what p. patriotism now?** ¿de qué ha servido tanto patriotismo? ►► ***p. controls*** controles *mpl* de precios; ***p. cut*** reducción *f* de precios; ***p. freeze*** congelación *f* de precios; ***p. increase*** subida *f* de precios; ***p. index*** índice *m* de precios; ***p. list*** lista *f* de precios; ***p. range*** escala *f* de precios; **that's outside my p. range** eso no está a mi alcance, eso está fuera de mi alcance; ***p. tag*** etiqueta *f* del precio; *Fig* **the player has a p. tag of over $5 million** el jugador se cotiza por más de 5 millones de dólares; ***p. war*** guerra *f* de precios

(**b**) *(in betting)* apuestas *fpl*; **what p. can you give me on Red Rocket?** ¿cómo están las apuestas con respecto a *or* para Red Rocket?

2 *vt* (**a**) *(decide cost of)* poner precio a; *(shares)* valorar; **the product is competitively priced** el producto tiene un precio competitivo; **we need to p. our products more aggressively** tenemos que disminuir sensiblemente el precio de nuestros productos, *Esp* tenemos que poner precios más agresivos a nuestros productos; **the toy is priced at £10** el precio del juguete es de 10 libras; **to p. sb out of the market** sacar a alguien del mercado bajando los precios; **to p. oneself out of the market** perder mercado *or* ventas por pedir precios demasiado elevados

(**b**) *(put price tag on)* ponerle el precio a

(**c**) *(compare prices of)* comparar los precios de

► **price down** *vt sep Br* rebajar

► **price up** *vt sep Br* encarecer, subir el precio de

price-conscious ['praɪs'kɒnʃəs] *adj* que busca buenos precios

price-cutting ['praɪs'kʌtɪŋ] *n Com* reducción *f* de precios

-priced [praɪst] *suffix* **high-p.** caro(a); **low-p.** barato(a)

price-earnings ratio ['praɪs'ɜːnɪŋz'reɪʃɪəʊ] *n St Exch* relación *f* precio-beneficio

price-fixing ['praɪs'fɪksɪŋ] *n Com* fijación *f* de precios

priceless ['praɪslɪs] *adj* (**a**) *(invaluable)* de valor incalculable (**b**) *Fam (funny)* graciosísimo(a)

price-sensitive ['praɪs'sensɪtɪv] *adj Com* **p. information** = información que puede afectar el valor de las acciones de la compañía

pricey ['praɪsɪ] *adj Fam* carillo(a)

prick [prɪk] **1** *n* (**a**) *(of needle, insect, thorn)* pinchazo *m*; *(mark)* agujero *m*; *Fig* **pricks of conscience** remordimientos de conciencia

(**b**) *Vulg (penis) Esp* polla *f*, picha *f*, *Am* verga *f*, *Chile* pico *m*, *Chile* penca *f*, *Méx* pito *m*, *RP* pija *f*, *Ven* pinga *f*

(**c**) *Vulg (person) Esp* gilipollas *mf inv*, *Am* pendejo(a) *m,f*, *RP* forro *m*; **stop making such a p. of yourself!** *Esp* ¡deja de ser tan gilipollas!, *Am* ¡no seas tan pendejo!, *RP* ¡pero qué forro que sos!

2 *vt* (**a**) *(make holes in)* pinchar; **to p. a hole in sth** hacer un agujero en algo; **to p. one's finger** pincharse el dedo; **the thorns pricked their legs** las espinas les pinchaban las piernas; *Fam* **to p. the bubble** deshacer el encanto (**b**) *(irritate)* irritar; **it pricked my conscience** me remordió la conciencia

3 *vi* (**a**) *(needle, thorn)* **the injection pricked a little, but it wasn't really painful** la inyección pinchó un poquito pero no fue nada dolorosa (**b**) *(be irritated)* irritarse

► **prick out** *vt sep (seedlings)* transplantar

► **prick up 1** *vt sep* **to p. up one's ears** *(dog)* aguzar las orejas; *(person)* aguzar el oído *or* los oídos

2 *vi (ears)* levantarse, *Am* pararse

pricking ['prɪkɪŋ] **1** *n (sensation)* ardor *m*; **the prickings of conscience** los remordimientos de conciencia

2 *adj* de ardor

prickle ['prɪkəl] **1** *n* (**a**) *(of hedgehog)* púa *f*; *(of plant)* espina *f*, pincho *m* (**b**) *(sensation)* hormigueo *m*

2 *vt (irritate)* irritar

3 *vi (skin)* hormiguear

prickly ['prɪklɪ] *adj* (**a**) *(animal)* cubierto(a) de púas; *(plant)* espinoso(a); *(beard)* que pincha; *(fabric, pullover)* que pica ►► ***p. pear*** *(cactus)* chumbera *f*, higuera *f* chumba, nopal *m*; *(fruit)* higo *m* chumbo, *Am* tuna *f*

(**b**) *(sensation)* hormigueante ►► ***p. heat*** = erupción cutánea producida por el calor

(**c**) *Fam (irritable) (person)* irritable, quisquilloso(a)

(**d**) *Fam (tricky) (subject, problem) Esp* chungo(a), *Am* jodido(a)

pricktease(r) ['prɪktiːz(ə(r))] *n Vulg Esp* calientapollas *f inv*, *Col, Ven* calientahuevos *f inv*, *RP* calientapija *f*

pride [praɪd] **1** *n* (**a**) *(satisfaction)* orgullo *m*; **to take p. in sth** enorgullecerse de algo; **to take (a) p. in one's appearance** tomarse muy en serio el cuidado del aspecto personal; **he takes no p. in his work** no se toma en serio su trabajo

(**b**) *(self-esteem)* amor *m* propio; **he has no p.** no tiene amor propio; **I have my p.!** ¡yo también tengo mi orgullo *or* amor propio!; **her p. was hurt** su orgullo fue lastimado

(**c**) *Pej (vanity)* soberbia *f*, orgullo *m*; **the sin of p.** el pecado de vanidad; PROV **p. comes** *or* **goes before a fall** a muchos les pierde el orgullo

(**d**) *(person, thing)* **he is the p. of the family** es el orgullo de la familia; **the p. of my collection** la joya de mi colección; **she's his p. and joy** ella es su mayor orgullo; **to have** *or* **take p. of place** ocupar el lugar preferente

(**e**) *(of lions)* manada *f*

2 *vt* **to p. oneself (up)on sth** enorgullecerse de algo

priest [priːst] *n* sacerdote *m*; **a Buddhist p.** un sacerdote budista

priestcraft ['priːstkrɑːft] *n Pej (influence)* clericalismo *m*

priestess [priːs'tes] *n* sacerdotisa *f*

priesthood ['priːsthʊd] *n* (**a**) *(office)* sacerdocio *m*; **to enter the p.** ordenarse sacerdote (**b**) *(body)* **the p.** el clero

priestly ['priːstlɪ] *adj* sacerdotal

prig [prɪg] *n* puritano(a) *m,f*, mojigato(a) *m,f*; **don't be such a p.!** ¡no seas tan puritano *or* mojigato!

priggish ['prɪgɪʃ] *adj* puritano(a), mojigato(a)

priggishness ['prɪgɪʃnɪs] *n* puritanismo *m*, mojigatería *f*

prim [prɪm] *adj* (**a**) *(prudish)* **p. (and proper)** remilgado(a) (**b**) *(neat, precise)* muy cuidado(a)

prima ballerina ['priːməbælə'riːnə] *n* primera bailarina *f*

primacy ['praɪməsɪ] *n* (**a**) *Formal (preeminence)* primacía *f*; *Ling* **the p. of speech** la primacía del habla (**b**) *Rel* primacía *f*

prima donna [priːmə'dɒnə] *n* (**a**) *(in opera)* primadona *f* (**b**) *(difficult person)* **to behave like a p.** actuar como un divo

primaeval = **primeval**

prima facie ['praɪmə'feɪʃiː] **1** *adj Law* ***p. case*** caso *m* prima facie; ***p. evidence*** prueba *f* suficiente a primera vista

2 *adv* a primera vista

primal ['praɪməl] *adj* (**a**) *(original)* primario(a) ►► ***p. scream*** llanto *m* del recién nacido; ***p. (scream) therapy*** terapia *f* de la angustia del nacimiento (**b**) *(fundamental)* primordial

primarily [praɪ'merɪlɪ] *adv* principalmente; **we're not p. concerned with that issue** esa cuestión no es lo que más nos preocupa

primary ['praɪmərɪ] **1** *n* (**a**) *Br (school)* escuela *f* primaria; **he's in p. one/four** está en primero/cuarto de primaria (**b**) *(in US election)* elecciones *fpl* primarias

2 *adj* (**a**) *(main)* principal; **our p. duty** nuestra tarea principal; **our p. objective** nuestro principal objetivo ►► *Ling* ***p. accent*** acento *m* primario; *Elec* ***p. cell*** pila *f*; ***p. colours*** colores *mpl* primarios; ***p. feather*** pluma *f* primaria; ***p. health care*** atención *f* médica primaria; *Zool* ***p. sexual characteristics*** características *fpl* primarias sexuales; *Ling* ***p. stress*** acento *m* primario

(**b**) *Educ (initial)* ***p. education*** educación *f* primaria; ***p. school*** escuela *f* primaria; ***p. school teacher*** maestro(a) *m,f* de escuela primaria

(**c**) *Econ* primario(a)

primate ['praɪmeɪt] *n* (**a**) *(animal)* primate *m* (**b**) *Rel* primado *m*

prime [praɪm] **1** *n* (**a**) *(best time)* **the p. of life** la flor de la vida; **she was in her p.** estaba en sus mejores años; **when Romantic poetry was in its p.** cuando la poesía romántica estaba en su apogeo; **she is past her**

p. su mejor momento ha pasado; **to be cut off in one's p.** *(die prematurely)* morir en la flor de la vida *or* edad; *Hum* **I don't want to cut you off in your p., but your time is up** no querría interrumpirte el discurso, pero se te ha acabado el tiempo

(**b**) *Math (prime number)* número *m* primo

(**c**) *Rel* prima *f*

2 *adj* (**a**) *(principal)* principal, primordial; *(importance)* capital ►► *Econ* ***p. cost*** costo *m or Esp* coste *m* básico de producción, precio *m* de costo; *Econ* ***p. (lending) rate*** tipo *m* preferencial *or* básico, *Am* tasa *f* preferencial *or* básica; ***p. minister*** primer(era) ministro(a) *m,f*; ***p. ministership*** *or* ***ministry*** mandato *m* de primer ministro; ***p. mover*** alma *f* máter, promotor(ora) *m,f*; *Math* ***p. number*** número *m* primo; ***p. time*** *(on TV)* franja *f* (horaria) de máxima audiencia

(**b**) *(excellent)* óptimo(a), excelente; **a p. example (of)** un ejemplo palmario (de) ►► ***p. quality*** calidad *f* suprema; *US* ***p. rib*** costilla *f* de primera calidad

(**c**) *Fin* ***p. (lending) rate*** tasa *f* preferencial (para préstamos)

3 *vt* (**a**) *(prepare) (engine, pump)* cebar; **to p. sb with drink** preparar a alguien dándole algo de beber (**b**) *(provide with information)* **to p. sb for sth** preparar *or* instruir a alguien para algo (**c**) *(surface)* imprimar

prime-ministerial ['praɪmɪnɪ'stɪərɪəl] *adj* de primer ministro, *f* de primera ministra

primer[1] ['praɪmə(r)] *n* (**a**) *(paint)* tapaporos *m inv* (**b**) *(for explosive)* cebo *m*

primer[2] *n (textbook)* texto *m* elemental

prime-time ['praɪm'taɪm] *adj (TV programme, advertising)* en la franja horaria de mayor audiencia

primeval [praɪ'mi:vəl] *adj* primigenio(a), primitivo(a) ►► ***p. forests*** bosques *mpl* vírgenes

priming ['praɪmɪŋ] *n* (**a**) *(of surface)* imprimación *f*, base *f* (**b**) *(of engine, pump)* cebadura *f*

primitive ['prɪmɪtɪv] **1** *n* (**a**) *(primitive person)* primitivo(a) *m,f* (**b**) *(artist)* primitivista *mf*

2 *adj* (**a**) *(culture, people)* primitivo(a) (**b**) *(rudimentary)* rudimentario(a)

primitively ['prɪmɪtɪvlɪ] *adv (to live)* primitivamente; *(constructed, equipped)* rudimentariamente

primitivism ['prɪmɪtɪvɪzəm] *n Art* primitivismo *m*

primly ['prɪmlɪ] *adv* con remilgo, remilgadamente

primness ['prɪmnɪs] *n* remilgo *m*, lo formal y correcto

primogeniture [praɪməʊ'dʒenɪtʃə(r)] *n* primogenitura *f*

primordial [praɪ'mɔ:dɪəl] *adj* primigenio(a), primitivo(a) ►► ***p. soup*** sustancia *f* primigenia

primp [prɪmp] **1** *vt* **to p. oneself** acicalarse

2 *vi* acicalarse

primrose ['prɪmrəʊz] *n (plant)* primavera *f*; IDIOM **the p. path** = camino aparentemente de rosas que lleva a la perdición ►► ***p. yellow*** amarillo *m* claro

primula ['prɪmjʊlə] *n* prímula *f*

Primus® **(stove)** ['praɪməs('stəʊv)] *n* infiernillo *m*, camping gas *m inv*, *Am* primus *m inv*

prince [prɪns] *n* príncipe *m* ►► ***P. Charming*** príncipe *m* azul; ***p. consort*** príncipe *m* consorte; ***P. of Darkness*** *(Satan)* príncipe *m* de las tinieblas; ***P. of Peace*** *(Messiah)* Príncipe *m* de la paz; ***p. regent*** príncipe *m* regente; ***the P. of Wales*** el Príncipe de Gales

princedom ['prɪnsdəm] *n* principado *m*

princeling ['prɪnslɪŋ] *n Pej* principito *m*

princely ['prɪnslɪ] *adj (splendid)* magnífico(a); *also Ironic* **a p. sum** una bonita suma

princess ['prɪnses] *n* princesa *f* ►► *Br* ***the P. Royal*** = hija mayor del monarca

principal ['prɪnsɪpəl] **1** *n* (**a**) *(of school)* director(ora) *m,f*; *(of university)* rector(ora) *m,f* (**b**) *Theat* primera figura *f* (**c**) *Law (employer of agent)* principal *mf*, mandante *mf* (**d**) *Fin (sum)* principal *m*

2 *adj* (**a**) *(main)* principal (**b**) *(violin, oboe)* primero(a) (**c**) *Gram* ***p. clause*** oración *f* principal; ***p. parts*** formas *fpl* principales (**d**) *Br* ***p. boy*** *(in pantomime)* = papel de joven héroe representado por una actriz

principality [prɪnsɪ'pælɪtɪ] *n* principado *m*; **the P.** *(Wales)* Gales

principally ['prɪnsɪplɪ] *adv* principalmente

principle ['prɪnsɪpəl] *n* (**a**) *(for behaviour)* principio *m*; **on p.** por principios; **as a matter of p.** por una cuestión de principios; **a matter** *or* **question of p.** una cuestión de principios; **a person of p.** una persona de principios; **he has no principles** carece de principios; **it's the p. of the thing that matters to me** lo que me importa es el principio; **it's against my principles (to do sth)** va en contra de mis principios (hacer algo); **she makes it a p. never to criticize others** tiene como principio nunca criticar a otros

(**b**) *(fundamental law)* principio *m*; **to go back to first principles** volver a los principios básicos

(**c**) *(theory)* principio *m*; **in p.** en principio; **to reach an agreement in p.** llegar a un acuerdo de principio; **machines that work on the same p.** máquinas que funcionan según el mismo principio; **we acted on the p. that everybody knew** actuamos partiendo de la base que todos lo sabían

principled ['prɪnsɪpəld] *adj (person, behaviour)* ejemplar, de grandes principios; **to take a p. stand** asumir una posición fundada *or* basada en principios

print [prɪnt] **1** *n* (**a**) *(of fingers, feet)* huella *f*; **the thief left his prints all over the door handle** el ladrón dejó sus huellas en el picaporte

(**b**) *(printed matter)* **in p.** publicado(a); **out of p., no longer in p.** agotado(a); **to appear in p.** aparecer impreso(a); **to get into p.** *(novel)* ser publicado(a); **his unguarded comments got into p.** sus imprudentes comentarios fueron publicados ►► ***p. run*** *(of books, newspapers)* tirada *f*, *Am* tiraje *m*; ***p. shop*** imprenta *f*; ***the p. unions*** los sindicatos de las artes gráficas

(**c**) *(printed characters)* caracteres *mpl*, letra *f*; *(text)* texto *m*; **in large/bold p.** en letra grande/negrita

(**d**) *(in photography)* copia *f*

(**e**) *Art (engraving)* grabado *m*; *(reproduction)* reproducción *f*

(**f**) *(textile)* estampado *m*

(**g**) *Comptr* ***p. buffer*** buffer *m* de impresión; ***p. head*** cabezal *m* de impresión; ***p. job*** *(file)* trabajo *m* de impresión; ***p. merge*** fusión *f* de códigos; ***p. preview*** presentación *f* preliminar; ***p. quality*** calidad *f* de impresión; ***p. queue*** cola *f* de impresión; ***p. screen key*** tecla *f* de impresión de pantalla; ***p. speed*** velocidad *f* de impresión

2 *adj (dress)* estampado(a)

3 *vt* (**a**) *(mark)* marcar; **the mark of a man's foot was printed in the wet sand** en la arena mojada había la marca de un pie de hombre; **the image had printed itself on her memory** se le quedó la imagen grabada en la memoria

(**b**) *(book)* imprimir; *(newspaper)* publicar; *(money)* emitir; **printed in Mexico** impreso en Méjico

(**c**) *(write clearly)* escribir claramente *(con las letras separadas)*

(**d**) *(in photography)* **to p. a negative** sacar copias de un negativo

(**e**) *(fabric)* estampar

(**f**) *Comptr (documento)* imprimir; **to p. (sth) to disk** copiar (algo) a disco

4 *vi* (**a**) *(book, newspaper)* imprimirse; **the book is now printing** el libro está en imprenta (**b**) *(write clearly)* escribir con claridad (**c**) *(negative)* **to p. well** salir bien (**d**) *Comptr (document)* imprimirse; *(printer)* imprimir

► **print off** *vt sep* imprimir

► **print out** *vt sep* imprimir

printable ['prɪntəbəl] *adj* (**a**) *(able to be printed)* que se puede imprimir (**b**) *(fit to print)* publicable

printed ['prɪntɪd] *adj* impreso(a); **p. cotton** algodón impreso; **the p. word** la letra impresa ►► *Elec* ***p. circuit*** circuito *m* impreso; *Elec* ***p. circuit board*** placa *f* de circuito impreso; ***p. matter*** impresos *mpl*

printer ['prɪntə(r)] *n* (**a**) *(person)* impresor(ora) *m,f*; **it's at the p.'s** está en imprenta ►► ***p.'s devil*** aprendiz(iza) *m,f* de imprenta *or* de tipógrafo; ***p.'s error*** error *m* de imprenta; ***p.'s ink*** tinta *f* de imprenta

(**b**) *(machine)* impresora *f*

(**c**) *Comptr* impresora *f* ►► ***p. driver*** controlador *m* de impresora; ***p. paper*** papel *m* de impresora; ***p. port*** puerto *m* de la impresora; ***p. ribbon*** cinta *f* de impresora; ***p. server*** servidor *m* de impresora; ***p. speed*** velocidad *f* de impresión

printing ['prɪntɪŋ] *n* (**a**) *(process, action)* impresión *f* ►► ***p. error*** errata *f* (de imprenta); ***p. house*** imprenta *f*; ***p. press*** imprenta *f* (**b**) *(copies printed)* tirada *f*; **first/second p.** primera/segunda impresión (**c**) *(industry)* imprenta *f*, artes *fpl* gráficas (**d**) *(handwriting)* letra *f* de imprenta

printmaker ['prɪntmeɪkə(r)] *n (of prints)* grabador(ora) *m,f*

printout ['prɪntaʊt] *n Comptr* copia *f* impresa

prion ['praɪɒn] *n Biol* prión *m*

prior[1] ['praɪə(r)] **1** *adj* (**a**) *(earlier)* previo(a); **to have a p. engagement** tener un compromiso previo; **to have p. knowledge of sth** tener conocimiento previo de algo; **without p. notice/warning** sin aviso previo/advertencia previa ►► *US Law* ***p. restraint*** restricción *f* previa (**b**) *(more important)* **to have a p. claim to** *or* **on sth** tener un derecho mayor a *or* sobre algo

2 *adv* **p. to** con anterioridad a; **p. to his winning/appointment** antes de ganar/ser nombrado

prior[2] n Rel prior m

prioress [praɪə'res] n Rel priora f

prioritize [praɪ'ɒrɪtaɪz] 1 vt (a) (give priority to) dar prioridad a (b) (arrange according to priority) priorizar, dar un orden de prioridad a
2 vi (evaluate priorities) priorizar

priority [praɪ'ɒrɪtɪ] n (a) (precedence) prioridad f; to give p. to dar prioridad a; to have or take p. (over sth/sb) tener prioridad (sobre algo/alguien); drivers on the main road have p. los conductores que circulan por la carretera principal tienen prioridad; to do sth as a (matter of) p. hacer algo como prioridad; in order of p. por orden de prioridad ►► p. booking reserva f preferencial; US p. mail = servicio postal de entrega rápida para envíos ligeros
(b) (important aim) our main p. is safety para nosotros la seguridad es lo primero; it's not a p. no es (una) prioridad; we need to get our priorities right tenemos que establecer un orden de prioridades; you should get your priorities right! ¡tienes que darte cuenta de lo que es verdaderamente importante!; the library came high/low on the list of priorities la biblioteca ocupaba uno de los primeros/últimos lugares en la lista de prioridades

priory ['praɪərɪ] n Rel priorato m

prise, US prize [praɪz], US **pry** [praɪ] vt she managed to p. her leg free logró extraer la pierna; to p. sth off arrancar algo; to p. sth open forzar algo; to p. sth out of sb (secret, truth) arrancarle algo a alguien

prism ['prɪzəm] n prisma m

prismatic [prɪz'mætɪk] adj (binoculars) prismático(a) ►► p. compass brújula f de reflexión or prisma

prison ['prɪzən] n cárcel f, prisión f; p. food la comida de la cárcel; p. conditions las condiciones carcelarias; to be in p. estar en la cárcel or en prisión; he's been in or to p. ha estado preso or en prisión; he went to p., he was sent to or put in p. lo encarcelaron; to sentence sb to three years in p. sentenciar a alguien a tres años en prisión; Fig the marriage had become a p. for her su matrimonio se había convertido en una prisión ►► p. camp campo m de prisioneros; p. cell celda f; Br p. governor director(ora) m,f de una prisión; p. officer funcionario(a) m,f de prisiones; p. reform reforma f carcelaria or penitenciaria; p. sentence pena f de reclusión or de cárcel; the p. system el sistema penitenciario; p. visitor = voluntario que se ofrece a visitar a presos que no reciban visitas de parientes o amigos; p. warder carcelero(a) m,f; p. yard patio m de la cárcel

prisoner ['prɪzənə(r)] n (a) (in jail) recluso(a) m,f ►► Pol p. of conscience preso(a) m,f de conciencia
(b) (captive) prisionero(a) m,f; Fig she became a p. of her own fears se convirtió en prisionera de sus propios temores; to hold/take sb p. tener/hacer prisionero(a) a alguien; to take no prisoners (in war) no tomar prisioneros; Fig (in debate, contest) no andarse con chiquitas ►► p. of war prisionero(a) m,f de guerra
(c) Law the p. at the bar el acusado/la acusada

prissy ['prɪsɪ] adj Fam remilgado(a)

pristine ['prɪsti:n] adj (a) (immaculate) prístino(a), inmaculado(a); in p. condition en estado impecable or inmaculado (b) (original) prístino(a)

prithee ['prɪðɪ] exclam Archaic ¡se lo ruego!

privacy ['prɪvəsɪ, 'praɪvəsɪ] n (a) (seclusion) intimidad f, privacidad f; in the p. of one's own home en la intimidad del hogar; there is no p. here aquí no hay privacidad (b) (private life) vida f privada; I value my p. valoro mi privacidad or vida privada ►► p. law (against press intrusion) ley f de protección de la intimidad

private ['praɪvɪt] 1 n (a) in p. (not public) en privado (b) p. (soldier) soldado m raso; P. Murdoch! ¡soldado Murdoch!
2 adj (a) (personal) privado(a), personal; (on envelope) personal; for p. reasons por motivos personales; in a p. capacity a título personal; it's a p. joke es un chiste privado ►► p. life vida f privada; Parl p. member's bill = proyecto de ley propuesto de forma independiente por un diputado; p. tuition clases fpl particulares
(b) (confidential, secret) privado(a); a p. conversation una conversación privada; p. and confidential privado(a) y confidencial; can we go somewhere p.? ¿podemos ir a un lugar donde estemos a solas?; can I tell the others? – no, it's p. ¿les puedo contar a los demás? – no, es confidencial
(c) (for personal use) particular; for your p. use para su uso particular ►► a p. house una casa particular; p. income rentas fpl; p. lessons clases fpl particulares; Tel p. line línea f privada; p. means rentas fpl; p. office oficina f particular; p. secretary secretario(a) m,f personal
(d) (not state-run) privado(a); Br to go p. (for health care) acudir a la sanidad privada ►► p. company empresa f privada (que no cotiza en bolsa); p. detective detective mf privado(a); p. education enseñanza f privada; p. enterprise la empresa or iniciativa privada; Fam p. eye sabueso(a) m,f; Br p. finance initiative = contrato entre un consorcio privado y la administración local por el que el primero construye, por ejemplo, una escuela o un hospital y se encarga de su funcionamiento a cambio de mantener su titularidad y percibir un alquiler de la administración; p. healthcare sanidad f privada; p. international law derecho m internacional privado; p. investigator investigador(ora) m,f privado(a); p. limited company sociedad f (de responsabilidad) limitada; p. patient paciente mf privado(a); p. pension pensión f privada; p. practice: to be in p. practice (doctor) ejercer la medicina privada; p. school colegio m privado; Econ p. sector sector m privado
(e) (not for the public) particular, privado(a); (on door) privado; a p. citizen un(a) ciudadano(a) común; it was a p. funeral fue un funeral privado; a p. party una fiesta particular or privada ►► p. property propiedad f privada; (sign) coto m privado; p. road carretera f particular; p. view or viewing (of exhibition) visita f privada (antes de la inauguración)
3 in private adv (confidentially) en privado; (in private life) en la intimidad; (personally) personalmente

privateer [praɪvɪ'tɪə(r)] n Hist (a) (ship) corsario m (b) (commander) corsario m

privately ['praɪvɪtlɪ] adv (a) (personally) en privado (b) (confidentially, secretly) en privado; p., he was plotting against her secretamente conspiraba contra ella (c) (as a private individual) como un(a) ciudadano(a) común (d) (not publicly) p. owned en manos privadas; she was p. educated (at school) fue a un colegio privado; (with tutor) aprendió con profesores particulares; Br I had it done p. (treatment at doctor's, dentist's) me lo hice en una consulta privada

private parts ['praɪvɪt'pɑ:ts], **privates** ['praɪvɪts] npl Fam Euph partes fpl pudendas or íntimas

private-sector ['praɪvɪt'sektə(r)] adj (company, pay, bosses) del sector privado

privation [praɪ'veɪʃən] n Formal privación f; to suffer real p. sufrir verdaderas privaciones

privatization [praɪvɪtaɪ'zeɪʃən] n privatización f

privatize ['praɪvɪtaɪz] vt privatizar

privet ['prɪvɪt] n alheña f ►► p. hedge seto m de alheñas

privilege ['prɪvɪlɪdʒ] 1 n (a) (right, advantage) privilegio m (b) (unfair advantage) a struggle against p. una lucha contra los privilegios (c) (honour) privilegio m; it is my p. to introduce to you... tengo el privilegio de presentarles a...
2 vt (a) (honour) to be privileged to do sth tener el privilegio de hacer algo (b) (give greater importance to) privilegiar

privileged ['prɪvɪlɪdʒd] adj (a) (person) privilegiado(a); only a p. few were invited sólo unos pocos privilegiados fueron invitados (b) (document, information) confidencial

privy ['prɪvɪ] 1 n Old-fashioned (toilet) retrete m, excusado m
2 adj (a) Formal to be p. to sth estar enterado(a) de algo (b) Br Pol the P. Council el consejo privado del monarca, = grupo formado principalmente por ministros y antiguos ministros del gabinete que asesora al monarca; P. Councillor consejero(a) m,f del monarca; P. Purse presupuesto m para los gastos del monarca

prize[1] [praɪz] 1 n (a) (award) premio m; to award a p. to sb otorgarle or darle un premio a alguien; to win first p. ganar el primer premio ►► p. day día m de la entrega de premios (en colegio)
(b) (in game, lottery) premio m; to win first p. ganar el primer premio; IDIOM (there are) no prizes for guessing who did it es evidente quién lo hizo ►► p. draw rifa f; p. money (dinero m del) premio m; he won p. money of £60,000 ganó un premio en metálico de 60.000 libras
(c) (ship) presa f
2 adj (a) (prizewinning) (bull, entry) premiado(a) (b) (excellent) perfecto(a), excelente; Fam he's a p. fool no es más idiota porque no se entrena, es un idiota de campeonato (c) (valuable, cherished) preciado(a), valorado(a); it's my p. possession es mi posesión más preciada
3 vt (value) apreciar; original editions are highly prized las ediciones originales están muy cotizadas

prize[2] US = prise

prizefight ['praɪzfaɪt] n combate m profesional de boxeo

prizefighter ['praɪzfaɪtə(r)] n boxeador m profesional

prizegiving ['praɪzgɪvɪŋ] n (at school) entrega f de premios

prizewinner ['praɪzwɪnə(r)] n premiado(a) m,f

prizewinning ['praɪzwɪnɪŋ] adj (novel, entry, contestant) premiado(a), galardonado(a); (ticket, number) premiado(a)

pro[1] [prəʊ] *Fam* **1** *n* (*pl* **pros**) (**a**) *(professional)* profesional *mf*, *Méx* profesionista *mf* (**b**) *(prostitute)* profesional *mf*
2 *adj US* profesional ►► ***p. football*** fútbol *m* americano profesional

pro[2] **1** *n* (*pl* **pros**) **the pros and cons** los pros y los contras
2 *prep* **to be p. sth** estar a favor de algo

pro- *prefix (in favour of)* pro-; **p.-Europe** proeuropeo(a); **they were p.-Stalin** eran proestalinistas

proactive [prəʊ'æktɪv] *adj* **to be p.** tomar la iniciativa

pro-am ['prəʊ'æm] *n Sport* = torneo informal en el que se enfrentan profesionales y aficionados

prob [prɒb] *n Fam* lío *m*, problemita *m*; *Br* **no probs!** *(of course)* cómo no; *(not at all)* no hay de qué

probabilism ['prɒbəbɪlɪzəm] *n Phil* probabilismo *m*

probability [prɒbə'bɪlɪtɪ] *n* (**a**) *(likelihood)* probabilidad *f*; **the p. is that he won't come** es muy probable que no venga; **in all p.** con toda probabilidad (**b**) *Math* probabilidad *f* ►► ***p. theory*** cálculo *m* de probabilidades

probable ['prɒbəbəl] **1** *adj* probable; **the p. cause/time of death** la posible causa/la hora probable de su muerte ►► *Law* ***p. cause*** causa *f* razonable *or* presunta
2 *n* candidato(a) *m,f*

probably ['prɒbəblɪ] *adv* probablemente; **she's p. left already** probablemente ya se ha ido; **p. not** probablemente no

proband ['prəʊbænd] *n US Med* caso *m* control *or* testigo

probate ['prəʊbeɪt] *Law* **1** *n* validación *f* de un testamento, certificado *m* de testamentaría
2 *vt US (will)* legalizar, autenticar

probation [prə'beɪʃən] *n* (**a**) *Law* condena *f* condicional, suspension *f* de la ejecución de la pena; **on p.** en condena condicional ►► ***p. officer*** = asistente social que ayuda y supervisa a un preso que cumple una condena condicional (**b**) *(in job)* periodo *m* de prueba; **on p.** a prueba

probationary [prə'beɪʃənərɪ] *adj* de prueba

probationer [prə'beɪʃənə(r)] *n (in job)* empleado(a) *m,f* en periodo de prueba

probe [prəʊb] **1** *n* (**a**) *(instrument)* sonda *f* (**b**) **(space) p.** sonda *f* espacial (**c**) *Fam (enquiry)* investigación *f*
2 *vt* (**a**) *Med* sondar (**b**) *(sound out) (person, motive, reasons)* tantear, sondear (**c**) *(investigate)* investigar; **to p. the mysteries of the mind** explorar los misterios de la mente
3 *vi* investigar; **the police are probing for clues** la policía está buscando pistas; **to p. into** *(past, private life)* escarbar en

probing ['prəʊbɪŋ] *adj (look, mind)* perspicaz, profundo(a); **after hours of p. questioning** después de un interrogatorio a fondo que duró horas

probity ['prəʊbɪtɪ] *n Formal* probidad *f*

problem ['prɒbləm] *n* problema *m*; **a maths p.** un problema de matemáticas; **a technical/financial p.** un problema técnico/financiero; **the housing/drugs p.** el problema de la vivienda/de las drogas; **to have a drink/drug/weight p.** tener un problema con la bebida/las drogas/el peso; **he's a p.** es problemático; **I don't want to be a p.** no quiero molestar; **he's got problems with the police** tiene problemas con la policía; **money isn't a p.** el dinero no es problema; **what's the p.?** ¿qué (te) pasa?, ¿cuál es el problema?; **what seems to be the p.?** ¿cuál es el problema?; **what's your p.?** ¿qué te pasa?; **that's your p.** ése es tu problema; **your p. is that you don't listen** tu problema es que no escuchas; *Fam* **have you got a p. with that?** ¿hay algún problema con eso?; *Fam* **and I thought I had problems!** comparado con esto, lo mío no es nada; *Fam* **no p.!** ¡no hay problema! ►► ***p. area*** *(in town)* zona *f* problemática; *(in project)* asunto *m* problemático; ***p. child*** niño(a) *m,f* problemático(a) *or* difícil; ***p. page*** consultorio *m* sentimental; *Lit* ***p. play*** obra *f* de tesis

problematic(al) [prɒblɪ'mætɪk(əl)] *adj* problemático(a)

problem-solving ['prɒbləmsɒlvɪŋ] **1** *n* resolución *f* de problemas
2 *adj* **p. test** prueba de resolución de problemas; **p. skills** habilidades para la resolución de problemas; **p. ability** habilidad para resolver problemas

pro bono [prəʊ'bəʊnəʊ] *adj US (lawyer)* que trabaja sin cobrar; *(legal work)* por el que no se cobra

proboscis [prə'bɒsɪs] (*pl* **proboscises** [prə'bɒsɪsiːz] *or* **proboscides** [prə'bɒsɪdiːz]) *n Zool* trompa *f* ►► ***p. monkey*** mono *m* narigudo, násico *m*

procaine ['prəʊkeɪn] *n Med* procaína *f*

procedural [prə'siːdʒərəl] *adj* de procedimiento

procedure [prə'siːdʒə(r)] *n* (**a**) *(process)* procedimiento *m*; **applying for a grant is a simple p.** la solicitud de una beca es un trámite sencillo; **the normal p. is to...** lo que se hace normalmente es... (**b**) *Comptr* procedimiento *m*

proceed [prə'siːd] **1** *vt* **to p. to do sth** proceder a hacer algo, ponerse a hacer algo
2 *vi* (**a**) *Formal (move)* avanzar; **she proceeded on her way** siguió su camino; **I was proceeding along the street...** caminaba por la calle...; **please p. to the nearest exit** les rogamos se dirijan a la salida más próxima
(**b**) *(go on)* proseguir, continuar; **the road proceeds along the coast** la carretera se extiende a lo largo de la costa; **to p. with sth** seguir adelante con algo; **to p. with caution** proceder con cautela; **how should I p.?** ¿qué debo hacer a continuación?; **let's p. to item 32** pasemos al punto 32
(**c**) *Comptr (in dialog box)* continuar
(**d**) *(originate)* **to p. from** proceder de; **smells proceeding from the kitchen** olores provenientes de la cocina
(**e**) *(happen)* llevarse a cabo, tener lugar; **is the meeting proceeding according to plan?** ¿la reunión se está llevando a cabo según lo previsto?
(**f**) *Law* **to p. with charges against sb** presentar cargos contra alguien

►**proceed against** *vt insep Law* **to p. against sb** procesar *or* demandar a alguien

proceedings [prə'siːdɪŋz] *npl* (**a**) *(events)* acto *m*; **p. were coming to a close** el acto llegaba a su fin; **p. were interrupted by...** el acto se vio interrumpido por... (**b**) *Law* proceso *m*, pleito *m*; **to start** *or* **institute p. against sb** entablar un pleito contra alguien (**c**) *(of conference, learned society)* actas *fpl*

proceeds ['prəʊsiːdz] *npl* recaudación *f*; **I was able to retire on the p.** las ganancias me permitieron retirarme; **all p. will go to charity** todo lo recaudado será destinado a obras de beneficencia

process[1] ['prəʊses] **1** *n* (**a**) *(series of events, operation)* proceso *m*; **by a p. of elimination** por eliminación; **to be in the p. of doing sth** estar haciendo algo; **they're in the p. of getting a divorce** están en medio del divorcio; **in the p. of time** con el tiempo; **he failed, and lost all his money in the p.** al fracasar, perdió todo su dinero
(**b**) *(industrial, chemical)* proceso *m* ►► *Typ* ***p. colours*** cuatricromía *f*
(**c**) *Law (summons)* citación *f*
(**d**) *Anat* protuberancia *f*
2 *vt* (**a**) *(raw material, waste, information)* procesar (**b**) *(request, application, cheque)* tramitar, procesar (**c**) *(film)* revelar (**d**) **processed food** alimentos manipulados *or* procesados ►► ***processed*** *or US* ***p. cheese*** queso *m* fundido

process[2] [prə'ses] *vi Formal (walk in procession)* desfilar

processing ['prəʊsesɪŋ] *n* (**a**) *(of raw material, waste, information)* procesamiento *m* (**b**) *(of request, application, cheque)* tramitación *f*, procesamiento *m* (**c**) *(of photographs)* revelado *m* (**d**) *Comptr* proceso *m* ►► ***p. language*** lenguaje *m* de programación; ***p. speed*** velocidad *f* de proceso; ***p. time*** tiempo *m* de procesamiento

procession [prə'seʃən] *n* procesión *f*; **I've had a p. of people through my office all day** hoy tuve una procesión de gente en la oficina; **in p.** en fila

processional [prə'seʃənəl] **1** *n (hymn)* procesionario *m*
2 *adj* procesional

processor ['prəʊsesə(r)] *n* (**a**) *(in kitchen)* **(food) p.** robot *m* (de cocina) (**b**) *Comptr* procesador *m* ►► ***p. speed*** velocidad *f* del procesador

process-server ['prəʊses'sɜːvə(r)] *n Law* persona *f* encargada de notificar las citaciones

pro-choice ['prəʊ'tʃɔɪs] *adj* = en favor del derecho de la mujer a decidir en materia de aborto

proclaim [prə'kleɪm] *vt* (**a**) *(one's innocence, guilt)* proclamar (**b**) *(declare)* proclamar, declarar; **to p. a state of emergency** declarar el estado de emergencia; **he proclaimed himself emperor** se autoproclamó emperador (**c**) *(reveal)* revelar

proclamation [prɒklə'meɪʃən] *n* proclamación *f*; **to issue** *or* **make a p.** emitir *or* hacer una proclama *or* proclamación

proclivity [prə'klɪvɪtɪ] *n Formal* propensión *f*, proclividad *f* (**for** a); **sexual proclivities** tendencias *or* inclinaciones sexuales

proconsul [prəʊ'kɒnsəl] *n Hist* procónsul

procrastinate [prəʊ'kræstɪneɪt] *vi Formal* andarse con dilaciones, retrasar las cosas

procrastination [prəʊkræstɪ'neɪʃən] *n Formal* dilaciones *fpl*, demora *f*; PROV **p. is the thief of time** no dejes para mañana lo que puedes hacer hoy

procrastinator [prəʊ'kræstɪneɪtə(r)] *n* persona *f* que se anda con dilaciones

procreate ['prəʊkrɪeɪt] *Formal* **1** *vt* procrear
2 *vi* reproducirse, procrear

procreation [prəʊkrɪ'eɪʃən] *n Formal* procreación *f*

Procrustean [prəʊ'krʌstɪən] *adj Literary* procusteano(a), inflexible, duro(a)

proctologist [prɒk'tɒlədʒɪst] *n Med* proctólogo(a) *m,f*

proctology [prɒk'tɒlədʒɪ] *n Med* proctología *f*

proctor ['prɒktə(r)] **1** *n* (**a**) *Br (disciplinary officer)* = en una universidad, persona encargada de velar por la disciplina (**b**) *US (invigilator)* vigilante *mf (en examen)*
2 *vt US* vigilar
3 *vi US* vigilar

procurable [prə'kjʊərəbəl] *adj* **these goods are p. only from an overseas supplier** estas mercancías sólo se pueden obtener a través de un proveedor en el extranjero; **it is no longer p.** ya no se consigue

procurator ['prɒkjʊreɪtə(r)] *n* (**a**) *Law* procurador *m* ►► *Scot* ***p. fiscal*** fiscal *mf* (del Estado) (**b**) *Hist* procurador *m*

procure [prə'kjʊə(r)] **1** *vt* (**a**) *Formal (obtain)* obtener, conseguir; *(buy)* adquirir, conseguir; **to p. sth for sb** procurarle algo a alguien; **to p. sth for oneself** hacerse con algo (**b**) *Law (for sex)* **he was convicted of procuring women for immoral purposes** fue condenado por proxenetismo
2 *vi Law* dedicarse al proxenetismo

procurement [prə'kjʊəmənt] *n Formal (obtaining)* obtención *f*; *(buying)* adquisición *f*

procurer [prə'kjʊərə(r)] *n Old-fashioned or Literary* proxeneta *mf*

procuress [prə'kjʊərɪs] *n Old-fashioned or Literary* proxeneta *f*

Prod [prɒd], **Proddy** ['prɒdɪ] *Fam Pej* **1** *n* protestante *mf*
2 *adj* protestante

prod [prɒd] **1** *n* (**a**) *(poke)* **I gave her a p. with my elbow** le di un codazo; **she gave him a p. to see if he was awake** le dio un empujoncito para ver si estaba despierto; **he gave the sausages a p. with his fork** pinchó las salchichas con el tenedor; **he gave the bundle a p. with his stick** tocó el bulto con el bastón
(**b**) *(encouragement)* **he needs a p.** necesita que lo espoleen
(**c**) *(for cattle)* picana *f*
2 *vt (pt & pp* **prodded**) (**a**) *(poke) (with stick, finger)* tocar; *(with fork)* pinchar; **he was prodding me with his elbow** me daba unos codazos (**b**) *(encourage)* **to p. sb into doing sth** espolear a alguien para que haga algo

► **prod at** *vt insep* tocar ligeramente

prodigal ['prɒdɪgəl] **1** *n* hijo(a) *m,f* pródigo(a)
2 *adj* pródigo(a); **to be p. with** *or* **of sth** ser pródigo(a) con algo; **he'd been rather p. with the salt, and the dish was almost inedible** se había excedido con la sal y la comida estaba intragable ►► ***p. son*** hijo *m* pródigo

prodigious [prə'dɪdʒəs] *adj (feat, talent)* prodigioso(a); **p. quantities/amounts** ingentes *or* enormes cantidades; **a p. reader** un ávido lector

prodigiously [prə'dɪdʒəslɪ] *adv* **she was p. talented** tenía un talento prodigioso; **she was p. well-read** era sumamente culta

prodigy ['prɒdɪdʒɪ] *n* (**a**) *(person)* prodigio *m*; **child** *or* **infant p.** niño(a) prodigio (**b**) *(marvel)* prodigio *m*

produce 1 *n* ['prɒdju:s] *(food)* productos *mpl* del campo; **agricultural/dairy p.** productos agrícolas/lácteos; **p. of Spain** producto de España
2 *vt* [prə'dju:s] (**a**) *(manufacture, make) (food, goods)* producir
(**b**) *(yield) (minerals, crops)* producir, dar; *(interest, profit)* dar, devengar; **halogen lamps p. a lot of light** las lámparas halógenas dan mucha luz
(**c**) *(bring out) (book, record)* sacar, editar; *(publish)* publicar; **he hasn't produced a new painting for over a year now** hace más de un año que no pinta nada nuevo
(**d**) *(give birth to)* tener
(**e**) *(secrete) (saliva, sweat)* secretar
(**f**) *(bring about) (effect, reaction)* producir, provocar; *(situation)* generar; **the team has produced some good results/some surprises this season** el equipo ha generado algunos buenos resultados/provocado algunas sorpresas esta temporada
(**g**) *(present, show) (ticket, passport)* presentar, mostrar; *(documents)* presentar; *(gun, rabbit)* sacar; **she produced a £10 note** sacó un billete de 10 libras; **to p. a witness** presentar un testigo; **they produced some excellent arguments** esgrimieron algunos argumentos excelentes
(**h**) *(play)* montar; *(movie, radio, TV programme)* producir
3 *vi* (**a**) *(yield) (factory, mine)* producir (**b**) *(on movie, play, radio or TV programme)* producir

producer [prə'dju:sə(r)] *n* (**a**) *(of crops, goods)* productor(ora) *m,f*; **the country is a major p. of coffee** *or* **coffee p.** el país es uno de los principales productores de café ►► ***p. gas*** gas *m* pobre; *Econ* ***p. goods*** bienes *mpl* de producción (**b**) *(of movie, play, radio or TV programme)* productor(ora) *m,f*

product ['prɒdʌkt] *n* (**a**) *(manufacture)* producto *m* ►► ***p. awareness*** conocimiento *m* del producto; *Com* ***p. development*** desarrollo *m* del producto; ***p. liability*** responsabilidad *f* civil; ***p. liability insurance*** seguro *m* de responsabilidad civil; ***p. life-cycle*** ciclo *m* de vida del producto; ***p. manager*** jefe(a) *m,f* de producto; ***p. placement*** = práctica por la que empresas pagan a las productoras para que sus productos aparezcan en sus películas o programas
(**b**) *(result)* resultado *m*, producto *m*; **that's the p. of a lively imagination** es el producto de una imaginación muy fértil; **she was a p. of her age** fue el producto de su época
(**c**) *Math* producto *m*

production [prə'dʌkʃən] *n* (**a**) *Ind (manufacture)* producción *f*; **the workers have halted p.** los obreros han detenido la producción; **to go into p.** empezar a fabricarse; **it went out of p. years ago** hace años que dejó de fabricarse ►► ***p. capacity*** capacidad *f* de producción; ***p. costs*** costos *mpl or Esp* costes *mpl* de producción; ***p. line*** cadena *f* de producción; ***p. manager*** jefe(a) *m,f* de producción; ***p. platform*** plataforma *f* (de extracción); ***p. process*** proceso *m* de producción; ***p. target*** objetivo *m* de producción
(**b**) *(amount produced)* producción *f*; **an increase/fall in p.** un incremento/una caída de la producción
(**c**) *(of document, ticket)* presentación *f*; **on p. of one's passport** al presentar el pasaporte
(**d**) *(play)* montaje *m*; *(movie, radio or TV programme)* producción *f*; IDIOM *Fam* **to make a (big) p. out of sth** hacer un escándalo por algo ►► ***p. company*** compañía *f* productora; ***p. designer*** diseñador(ora) *m,f* de producción; ***p. manager*** jefe(a) *m,f* de producción; ***p. values:*** **a film with high/low p. values** una película con muy buena producción/una producción pobre

productive [prə'dʌktɪv] *adj* (**a**) *(activity, land, imagination)* productivo(a); *Formal* **to be p. of** ser generador(ora) de (**b**) *(useful)* productivo(a); **our visit/meeting has been very p.** nuestra visita/reunión ha sido muy productiva (**c**) *Econ* productivo(a), de producción; **the p. forces** las fuerzas productivas (**d**) *Ling* productivo(a)

productively [prə'dʌktɪvlɪ] *adv* de manera productiva *or* provechosa; **to use one's time p.** aprovechar bien el tiempo

productivity [prɒdʌk'tɪvɪtɪ] *n Ind* productividad *f*; **p. is up/down** ha aumentado/disminuido la productividad ►► ***p. agreement*** acuerdo *m* sobre productividad; ***p. bonus*** plus *m* de productividad; ***p. drive*** campaña *f* de productividad

Prof *Br* (*abbr* **Professor**) catedrático(a) *m,f*

prof [prɒf] *n Br Fam* profe *mf*

profanation [prɒfə'neɪʃən] *n Rel* profanación *f*

profane [prə'feɪn] **1** *adj* (**a**) *(language)* blasfemo(a) (**b**) *Rel (secular)* profano(a)
2 *vt* profanar

profanity [prə'fænɪtɪ] *n* (**a**) *(oath)* blasfemia *f* (**b**) *(blasphemous nature)* grosería *f*

profess [prə'fes] *vt* (**a**) *(declare)* manifestar; **to p. oneself satisfied/baffled** declararse satisfecho(a)/confuso(a); **to p. an opinion/a belief** profesar una opinión/creencia (**b**) *(claim)* proclamar; **he professes to be a socialist** se dice socialista; **I don't p. to be an expert, but...** no pretendo ser un experto, pero... (**c**) *Rel (faith)* profesar

professed [prə'fest] *adj* (**a**) *(self-declared)* declarado(a); **that is my p. aim** ése es mi objetivo declarado (**b**) *(pretended)* supuesto(a), pretendido(a) (**c**) *Rel* profeso(a)

professedly [prə'fesɪdlɪ] *adv* (**a**) *(avowedly)* declaradamente, confesamente (**b**) *(allegedly)* supuestamente

profession [prə'feʃən] *n* (**a**) *(occupation)* profesión *f*; **the professions** las profesiones liberales; **by p.** de profesión; *Hum* **the oldest p. (in the world)** el oficio más viejo del mundo
(**b**) *(body)* profesión *f*; **there are those in the p. who think that...** hay en la profesión quienes piensan que...; **the teaching p.** el profesorado
(**c**) *Formal (declaration)* manifestación *f*
(**d**) *Rel* ***p. of faith*** profesión *f* de fe

professional [prəˈfeʃənəl] **1** *n* profesional *mf, Méx* profesionista *mf*; **leave it to the professionals** déjalo en manos de profesionales; **a golf/rugby p.** un golfista/jugador de rugby profesional
2 *adj* **(a)** *(relating to a profession)* profesional; **p. person wanted for house share** *(in advertisement)* se busca profesional para compartir casa; **to take a p. interest in sth** interesarse profesionalmente en algo ▸▸ ***p. association*** asociación *f* profesional; *Fin* ***p. indemnity insurance*** seguro *m* de indemnización profesional
(b) *(as career, full-time)* profesional; *(soldier)* de carrera; *(army)* profesional; *Fig Hum* **he's a p. drunk** es un borracho profesional
(c) *(not amateur)* profesional; **to turn** *or* **go p.** *(sportsperson)* hacerse profesional *or Méx* profesionista ▸▸ ***p. foul*** falta *f* técnica
(d) *(competent, qualified)* profesional; **they made a very p. job of the repair** hicieron la reparación excelente; **his work is not up to p. standards** su trabajo no tiene un nivel profesional; **she is very p. in her approach** tiene un enfoque muy profesional; **to take p. advice on sth** pedir asesoramiento sobre algo a un profesional *or Méx* profesionista; *Euph* **I think she needs p. help** creo que necesita asistencia *or* ayuda profesional ▸▸ ***p. misconduct*** violación *f* de la ética profesional

professionalism [prəˈfeʃənəlɪzəm] *n* **(a)** *(professional approach)* profesionalidad *f* **(b)** *(in sports)* profesionalismo *m*

professionally [prəˈfeʃənəlɪ] *adv* **(a)** *(referring to job)* **she acts/sings p.** es actriz/cantante profesional; **he plays tennis p.** juega al tenis como profesional; **I've only ever met her p.** sólo la conozco como profesional; **she's a p. qualified doctor** es una médica titulada
(b) *(competently)* de forma *or* manera profesional
(c) *(by professional)* **to get a job done p.** encargar un trabajo a un profesional *or Méx* profesionista

professor [prəˈfesə(r)] *n Univ* **(a)** *Br* catedrático(a) *m,f*; **the p. of sociology** el catedrático de sociología **(b)** *US* profesor(ora) *m,f*; **a p. of sociology, a sociology p.** una profesora de sociología

professorial [prɒfəˈsɔːrɪəl] *adj* profesoral

professorship [prəˈfesəʃɪp] *n Br* cátedra *f*

proffer [ˈprɒfə(r)] *vt Formal (advice)* brindar; *(opinion)* ofrecer, dar; *(thanks)* dar; *(hand, object)* tender; **we all proffered our excuses to her** todos le ofrecimos nuestras disculpas

proficiency [prəˈfɪʃənsɪ] *n* competencia *f* (**in** *or* **at** en); **p. in driving is essential** es esencial ser un conductor competente

proficient [prəˈfɪʃənt] *adj* competente (**in** *or* **at** en); **to be p. in German** dominar el alemán; **to be a p. liar** ser un buen mentiroso

proficiently [prəˈfɪʃəntlɪ] *adv* competentemente

profile [ˈprəʊfaɪl] **1** *n* **(a)** *(side view, outline)* perfil *m*; **in p.** de perfil
(b) *(image)* perfil *m*; **to have the right p. for the job** tener el perfil perfecto para el puesto; **to have a high p.** estar en el candelero; **to keep a low p.** mantenerse en un segundo plano; **to raise the p. of an organization** potenciar la imagen de una organización
(c) *(description)* retrato *m*; **psychiatrists came up with a p. of the killer** los psiquiatras aportaron un perfil del asesino
2 *vt* **(a)** *(write profile of)* retratar; **she was profiled in a recent TV programme** en un reciente programa televisivo presentaron su perfil biográfico **(b)** *(show in profile)* **he was profiled against the wall** su imagen se perfilaba contra la pared

profit [ˈprɒfɪt] **1** *n* **(a)** *(of company, on deal)* beneficio *m*; **profits were down/up this year** los beneficios han caído/subido este año; **at a p.** *(to sell, operate)* con beneficios; **I don't do it for p.** no lo hago por dinero; **to be in p.** tener beneficios; **to move into p.** pasar a tener beneficios; **to make a p. (out of sth)** obtener *or* sacar beneficios (de algo); **we made a £200 p. on the sale** ganamos 200 libras con la venta; **to show a p.** arrojar beneficios ▸▸ *Com* ***p. centre*** centro *m* de beneficios; *Fin* ***p. and loss account*** cuenta *f* de pérdidas y ganancias; *Fin* ***p. margin*** margen *m* de beneficios; ***the p. motive*** el lucro; ***p. sharing*** reparto *m* de beneficios; ***p. squeeze*** reducción *f* de los márgenes de beneficio; ***p. taking*** realización *f* de beneficios
(b) *(advantage)* provecho *m*; **to gain p. from sth** obtener beneficios de algo; **to turn sth to one's p.** utilizar algo en beneficio propio; **what p. is there in it for us?** ¿y nosotros qué beneficio sacamos de ello?
2 *vi* **to p. by** *or* **from** sacar provecho de; **you could well p. by being more careful** te vendría bastante bien ser un poco más cuidadoso

profitability [prɒfɪtəˈbɪlɪtɪ] *n* rentabilidad *f*; **to restore a company to p.** devolverle la rentabilidad a una compañía

profitable [ˈprɒfɪtəbəl] *adj* **(a)** *(company, deal)* rentable **(b)** *(experience)* provechoso(a)

profitably [ˈprɒfɪtəblɪ] *adv* **(a)** *(to trade, operate)* con beneficios; **we sold it very p.** su venta nos reportó muy buenas ganancias **(b)** *(to use one's time)* provechosamente

profiteer [prɒfɪˈtɪə(r)] *Pej* **1** *n* especulador(ora) *m,f*
2 *vi* especular

profiteering [prɒfɪˈtɪərɪŋ] *n Pej* especulación *f*

profiterole [prəˈfɪtərəʊl] *n* profiterol *m*

profitless [ˈprɒfɪtlɪs] *adj* infructuoso(a), improductivo(a)

profit-making [ˈprɒfɪtmeɪkɪŋ] *adj* **(a)** *(aiming to make profit)* con fines de lucro **(b)** *(profitable)* lucrativo(a)

profligacy [ˈprɒflɪgəsɪ] *n Formal* **(a)** *(wastefulness)* **his p. shocked us** su manera de derrochar dinero nos escandalizó **(b)** *(dissoluteness)* licencia *f*, disolución *f*

profligate [ˈprɒflɪgət] *Formal* **1** *adj* **(a)** *(wasteful)* derrochador(ora); **the p. use of natural resources** el uso irresponsable de los recursos naturales **(b)** *(dissolute)* disoluto(a), licencioso(a)
2 *n* **(a)** *(spendthrift)* derrochador(ora) *m,f*, despilfarrador(ora) *m,f* **(b)** *(dissolute person)* libertino(a) *m,f*, licencioso(a) *m,f*

pro-form [ˈprəʊfɔːm] *n Ling* proforma *f*

pro forma [ˈprəʊˈfɔːmə] *adj* pro forma; **p. invoice** factura pro forma *or* proforma

profound [prəˈfaʊnd] *adj* profundo(a)

profoundly [prəˈfaʊndlɪ] *adv* profundamente; **we disagree p. on the issue** estamos en profundo desacuerdo con respecto al tema; **he's p. deaf** tiene sordera total

profundity [prəˈfʌndɪtɪ] *n* **(a)** *(of thought)* profundidad *f* **(b)** *(remark, thought)* observación *f* profunda

profuse [prəˈfjuːs] *adj* **(a)** *(fulsome)* profuso(a); **he offered p. apologies/thanks** se prodigó en disculpas/agradecimientos; **to be p. in one's praise/compliments** prodigarse en elogios/halagos **(b)** *(copious)* profuso(a), copioso(a)

profusely [prəˈfjuːslɪ] *adv* **(a)** *(to apologize, thank)* cumplidamente; **to praise sb p.** halagar profusamente a alguien **(b)** *(to sweat, bleed)* profusamente

profusion [prəˈfjuːʒən] *n* profusión *f*; **in p.** en abundancia *or* profusión

prog [prɒg] *n TV & Rad Fam* programa *m*

progenitor [prəʊˈdʒenɪtə(r)] *n Formal* **(a)** *(ancestor)* progenitor(ora) *m,f* **(b)** *(originator)* creador(ora) *m,f*, precursor(ora) *m,f*

progeny [ˈprɒdʒɪnɪ] *n Formal* progenie *f*, prole *f*

progesterone [prəʊˈdʒestərəʊn] *n Biochem* progesterona *f*

prognosis [prɒgˈnəʊsɪs] (*pl* **prognoses** [prɒgˈnəʊsiːz]) *n* **(a)** *Med* pronóstico *m* **(b)** *(prediction)* pronóstico *m*; **the p. is for an increase next year** el pronóstico es que habrá un incremento el próximo año

prognosticate [prɒgˈnɒstɪkeɪt] *Formal* **1** *vt* pronosticar
2 *vi* hacer pronósticos

prognostication [prɒgnɒstɪˈkeɪʃən] *n Formal* pronóstico *m*

program[1] [ˈprəʊgræm] *n Comptr* programa *m* ▸▸ ***p. error*** error *m* de programa; ***p. file*** archivo *m* de programa; ***p. language*** lenguaje *m* de programación

program[2] *US* = **programme**

programed, programer *etc US* = **programmed, programmer** *etc*

programmable, *US* **programable** [prəʊˈgræməbəl] *adj* programable ▸▸ ***p. calculator*** calculadora *f* programable

programme, *US* **program** [ˈprəʊgræm] **1** *n* **(a)** *(on TV, radio) (broadcast)* programa *m*; **an arts/current affairs p.** un programa de *or* sobre arte/de actualidad; **to change p.** *(station)* cambiar de canal ▸▸ ***p. controller*** director(ora) *m,f* de programación
(b) *(of washing machine)* programa *m*
(c) *(of political party)* programa *m*
(d) *(for play)* programa *m* ▸▸ ***p. notes*** comentarios *mpl* del programa; ***p. seller*** vendedor(ora) *m,f* de programas
(e) *(schedule of events)* programa *m*; **what's the p. for today?** ¿qué programa tenemos para hoy? ▸▸ ***p. of study*** programa *m* de trabajo *(de estudiante)*
(f) *Mus* ***p. music*** música *f* de programa
2 *vt* (*pt & pp* **programmed** *or US* **programed**) **(a)** *(computer, robot)* programar; **to p. sth to do sth** programar algo para que haga algo; **to be programmed** *or US* **programed to do sth** estar programado(a) para hacer algo **(b)** *(event)* programar
3 *vi Comptr* programar; **to p. in assembly language** programar en ensamblador

programmed, *US* **programed** [ˈprəʊgræmd] *n Educ* ***p. instruction*** enseñanza *f* programada; *Educ* ***p. learning*** enseñanza *f* programada

programmer, *US* **programer** [ˈprəʊgræmə(r)] *n* **(a)** *TV & Rad* programador(ora) *m,f* **(b)** *Comptr* programador(ora) *m,f*

programming, *US* **programing** ['prəʊgræmɪŋ] *n* (a) *TV & Rad* programación *f* (b) *Comptr* programación *f* ►► ***p. error*** error *m* de programación; ***p. language*** lenguaje *m* de programación

progress 1 *n* ['prəʊgres] (a) *(improvement)* progreso *m*; **to make p. (in sth)** hacer progresos (en algo); **to make good p.** *(in journey, process, studies, recovery)* avanzar bastante; **it was slow p.** se avanzaba poco; **you can't stop p.** no puedes detener el progreso; *Ironic* **that's p. for you!** ¡ahí tienes el progreso!
(b) *(development) (of events, plan, disease)* progreso *m*; **roadworks are in p. between exits 11 and 12** el tramo entre la salida 11 y la 12 está en obras; **the meeting is already in p.** la reunión ya ha comenzado; **meeting in p.** *(on sign)* reunión: no molestar; **exam in p.** *(on sign)* silencio, examen; **service in p.** *(in cathedral)* se está celebrando un oficio; **a p. report on the project** un informe *or CAm, Méx* reporte sobre la marcha del proyecto ►► *Com* ***p. payment*** pago *m* parcial
(c) *(movement)* avance *m*; **I followed the ship's p. down the river** seguía el avance del barco río abajo
(d) *Br Hist (royal journey)* viaje *m* del monarca
2 *vi* [prə'gres] (a) *(making headway)* progresar; **she's progressing in her studies** está avanzando en sus estudios; **the talks are progressing well** las conversaciones están bien encaminadas; **the patient is progressing satisfactorily** el paciente evoluciona satisfactoriamente
(b) *(moving forward)* avanzar; **as the day progressed** conforme avanzaba el día; **I never progressed beyond the first lesson** nunca pude llegar más allá de la primera clase *or* lección
3 *vt Com (advance)* avanzar

progression [prə'greʃən] *n* (a) *(advance)* progresión *f*, evolución *f*; **a natural/logical p. (from)** un paso natural/lógico (de *or* desde) (b) *(series)* progresión *f* (c) *Math & Mus* progresión *f*

progressive [prə'gresɪv] 1 *n* (a) *(forward-looking person)* progresista *mf* (b) *Gram* tiempo *m* continuo
2 *adj* (a) *(increasing)* progresivo(a) ►► ***p. disease*** enfermedad *f* degenerativa; ***p. income tax*** impuesto *m* de renta progresivo (b) *(forward-looking)* progresista ►► ***p. education*** educación *f* progresista; ***p. jazz*** jazz *m* progresivo (c) *(dance)* progresivo(a)

progressively [prə'gresɪvlɪ] *adv* (a) *(continuously)* progresivamente; **the situation got p. worse** la situación se puso cada vez peor (b) *(in a forward-looking way)* de manera progresista

prohibit [prə'hɪbɪt] *vt* (a) *(forbid)* prohibir; **to p. sb from doing sth** prohibir a alguien que haga algo; **smoking prohibited** *(sign)* prohibido fumar; **it is prohibited by law** lo prohíbe la ley; **prohibited area** *(sign)* prohibido el acceso (b) *(prevent)* impedir

prohibition [prəʊɪ'bɪʃən] *n* (a) *(ban)* prohibición *f*; **there is a p. on the sale of such goods** la venta de este tipo de productos está prohibida (b) *Hist* **P.** la Ley Seca

prohibitionist [prəʊɪ'bɪʃənɪst] *n* prohibicionista *mf*

prohibitive [prə'hɪbɪtɪv] *adj (cost)* prohibitivo(a)

prohibitively [prə'hɪbɪtɪvlɪ] *adv* **p. expensive** de precio prohibitivo

project 1 *n* ['prɒdʒekt] (a) *(undertaking, plan)* proyecto *m* ►► *Com* ***p. manager*** jefe(a) *m,f* de proyecto (b) *(at school, university)* trabajo *m* (c) *US (housing)* = urbanización con viviendas de protección oficial
2 *vt* [prə'dʒekt] (a) *(movie, image)* proyectar
(b) *(plan, predict)* proyectar, planear; **inflation is projected to fall** se prevé que baje la inflación; **projected income** ingresos previstos
(c) *(propel)* proyectar; **to p. one's voice** proyectar la voz
(d) *(convey) (image)* proyectar; **to p. one's personality** proyectar la personalidad de uno; **he tries to p. himself as a great humanist** intenta proyectar *or* transmitir una imagen de gran humanista
(e) *Psy* **to p. sth onto sth/sb** proyectar algo en algo/alguien
(f) *Geom* proyectar
3 *vi* (a) *(protrude)* sobresalir, proyectarse (b) *(as personality)* **she doesn't p. well** no se proyecta bien (c) *(with voice)* **to learn to p.** aprender a proyectarse

projected [prə'dʒektɪd] *adj* (a) *(planned)* proyectado(a) (b) *(forecast)* proyectado(a)

projectile [prə'dʒektaɪl] *n* proyectil *m* ►► *Med* ***p. vomiting*** vómito *m* en escopetazo

projecting [prə'dʒektɪŋ] *adj (roof, balcony)* saliente

projection [prə'dʒekʃən] *n* (a) *(of movie, image)* proyección *f* ►► *Cin* ***p. room*** sala *f* de proyección (b) *(prediction)* estimación *f*, pronóstico *m* (c) *(protruding part)* proyección *f*, saliente *m* (d) *Psy* proyección *f* (e) *(in mapmaking)* proyección *f*

projectionist [prə'dʒekʃənɪst] *n* proyeccionista *mf*

projector [prə'dʒektə(r)] *n* proyector *m*

prokaryote [prəʊ'kærɪɒt] *n Biol* procariota *f*

prolactin [prəʊ'læktɪn] *n Med* prolactina *f*

prolapse ['prəʊlæps] *n Med* prolapso *m*; **p. of the uterus** prolapso de útero

prolapsed [prəʊ'læpst] *adj Med* **a p. uterus** un prolapso de útero

prole [prəʊl] *n Fam Pej* proletario(a) *m,f*

> **False friend:** The Spanish noun **prole** is not a translation for the English word **prole**. In Spanish **prole** means "offspring".

prolegomenon [prəʊle'gɒmɪnən] *(pl* **prolegomena** [prəʊle'gɒmɪnə]*)* *n* prolegómeno *m*

prolepsis [prəʊ'lepsɪs] *(pl* **prolepses** [prəʊ'lepsiːz]*)* *n Lit* prolepsis *f inv*

proletarian [prəʊlɪ'teərɪən] 1 *n* proletario(a) *m,f*
2 *adj* proletario(a)

proletariat [prəʊlɪ'teərɪət] *n* proletariado *m*

pro-life ['prəʊ'laɪf] *adj* pro vida, antiabortista

pro-lifer ['prəʊ'laɪfə(r)] *n Fam* antiabortista *mf*

proliferate [prə'lɪfəreɪt] *vi* proliferar

proliferation [prəlɪfə'reɪʃən] *n* (a) *(rapid increase)* proliferación *f* (b) *(large amount or number)* proliferación *f*

prolific [prə'lɪfɪk] *adj* prolífico(a)

prolix ['prəʊlɪks] *adj Formal* prolijo(a)

prolixity [prəʊ'lɪksɪtɪ] *n Formal* prolijidad *f*

prologue, *US* **prolog** ['prəʊlɒg] *n* (a) *(introduction)* prólogo *m* (to de); **her arrival was the p. to yet another row** su llegada fue el prólogo a una nueva pelea (b) *(in cycling)* prólogo *m*

prolong [prə'lɒŋ] *vt* prolongar; **I don't want to p. the agony** no quiero prolongar la agonía

prolongation [prəʊlɒŋ'geɪʃən] *n (of life, time)* prolongación *f*

prolonged [prə'lɒŋd] *adj* prolongado(a)

prom [prɒm] *n Fam* (a) *Br (at seaside)* paseo *m* marítimo
(b) *Br (concert)* = concierto sinfónico en el que parte del público está de pie
(c) *US (school dance)* baile *m* de fin de curso ►► ***p. queen*** reina *f* del baile

promenade ['prɒmənɑːd] 1 *n* (a) *Br (at seaside)* paseo *m* marítimo (b) *Br* ***p. concert*** = concierto sinfónico en el que parte del público está de pie (c) **p. deck** *(on ship)* cubierta de paseo (d) *US (school dance)* baile *m* de fin de curso
2 *vi* (a) *(walk)* pasear (b) *(in dancing)* hacer el paso militar

promenader [prɒmə'nɑːdə(r)] *n Br* asistente *mf* a un concierto al aire libre

Prometheus [prə'miːθɪəs] *n Mythol* Prometeo

promethium [prə'miːθɪəm] *n Chem* prometio *m*

prominence ['prɒmɪnəns] *n* (a) *(of land, physical feature)* prominencia *f* (b) *(of issue, person)* relevancia *f*, importancia *f*; **to give sth p., to give p. to sth** destacar algo; **to come to p.** empezar a descollar *or* sobresalir; **to occupy a position of some p.** ocupar un puesto de cierto relieve (c) *Astron* protuberancia *f*

prominent ['prɒmɪnənt] *adj* (a) *(projecting)* prominente (b) *(conspicuous)* visible, destacado(a) (c) *(important)* renombrado(a), prominente; **she was p. in the world of the arts** era una figura prominente en el mundo de las artes; **to play a p. part** *or* **role in sth** desempeñar un papel destacado en algo

prominently ['prɒmɪnentlɪ] *adv* (a) *(conspicuously)* visiblemente; **the medal was p. displayed** la medalla estaba exhibida muy visiblemente (b) *(importantly)* **to figure p. in sth** tener un papel relevante *or* destacar en algo

promiscuity [prɒmɪs'kjuːɪtɪ], **promiscuousness** [prə'mɪskjʊəsnɪs] *n* promiscuidad *f*

promiscuous [prə'mɪskjʊəs] *adj (sexually)* promiscuo(a)

promiscuously [prə'mɪskjʊəslɪ] *adv* promiscuamente

promise ['prɒmɪs] 1 *n* (a) *(pledge)* promesa *f*; **a p. of help** una promesa de ayuda; **to make a p.** hacer la promesa; **I'll try, but I can't make (you) any promises** lo intentaré, pero no te prometo nada; **to keep/break one's p.** mantener/romper la promesa; **I kept** *or* **held him to his p.** le hice cumplir su promesa; **to hold out the p. of sth to sb** prometerle algo a alguien; **...and that's a p.!** ¡...se lo garantizamos!; **a p. is a p.** una promesa es una promesa; *Fam* **promises, promises!** sí, sí, ¡promesas!
(b) *(potential)* buenas perspectivas *fpl*; **an artist/sportsman of p.** un artista/deportista que promete; **to show p.** ser prometedor(ora); **she never fulfilled her early p.** nunca llegó tan lejos como parecía prometer
2 *vt* (a) *(pledge)* prometer; **to p. to do sth** prometer hacer algo; **to p. sth to sb, to p. sb sth** prometerle algo a alguien; **I'll try, but I can't p.**

(you) anything lo intentaré, pero no te prometo nada; **it won't be easy, I can p. you** no será fácil, te lo puedo asegurar; **he promised me he'd do it** me prometió que lo haría; **I've been promising myself a holiday for months** hace meses que llevo prometiéndome unas vacaciones

(**b**) *(be potentially)* prometer; **it promises to be hot** promete hacer calor

(**c**) *(in marriage)* **she was promised to the King's son at birth** fue prometida al hijo del rey al nacer

3 *vi* (**a**) *(pledge)* **but he promised!** ¡lo prometió!; **(do you) p.? – yes, I p.** ¿lo prometes? – sí, lo prometo; **they came early, as promised** llegaron pronto, tal y como habían prometido (**b**) *(show potential)* **to p. well** prometer

promised land ['prɒmɪst'lænd] *n* (**a**) *Rel* **the P.** la Tierra Prometida (**b**) *(ideal world)* meca *f*

promising ['prɒmɪsɪŋ] *adj* (**a**) *(full of potential)* prometedor(ora) (**b**) *(encouraging)* alentador(ora); **she got off to a p. start** tuvo un comienzo alentador

promisingly ['prɒmɪsɪŋlɪ] *adv* de manera prometedora; **things started p. enough** todo comenzó de manera bastante prometedora

promissory note ['prɒmɪsərɪ'nəʊt] *n Fin* pagaré *m*

promo ['prəʊməʊ] *Fam* **1** *n (short video) Esp* vídeo *m or Am* video *m* promocional

2 *adj (video, leaflet)* promocional

promontory ['prɒməntərɪ] *n* promontorio *m*

promote [prə'məʊt] *vt* (**a**) *(raise in rank)* ascender; **to be promoted** *(officer, employee)* ser ascendido(a); **she's been promoted to regional manager** ha sido ascendida a gerente regional

(**b**) **to be promoted** *(sports team)* ascender, subir

(**c**) *(encourage, stimulate)* fomentar, promover; **to p. sb's interests** favorecer los intereses de alguien; **to p. economic growth** promover el crecimiento económico

(**d**) *(product)* promocionar; **she's in England to p. her new record** está en Inglaterra promocionando su último disco

(**e**) *(organize) (boxing match, show)* organizar

(**f**) *(in chess)* convertir

promoter [prə'məʊtə(r)] *n* (**a**) *(of theory, cause, scheme)* promotor(ora) *m,f* (**b**) *(of product)* promotor(ora) *m,f* (**c**) *(of boxing match)* promotor(ora) *m,f*; *(of show)* organizador(ora) *m,f*

promotion [prə'məʊʃən] *n* (**a**) *(of employee, officer, sports team)* ascenso *m*; **to get p.** ser ascendido(a); **he has no prospects of p.** no tiene perspectivas de un ascenso (**b**) *(encouragement, stimulus)* fomento *m*; **the p. of a good working atmosphere** el fomento de una buena atmósfera de trabajo (**c**) *(of product, plan)* promoción *f*; **this week's p.** la oferta de la semana

promotional [prə'məʊʃənəl] *adj (literature, campaign, offer)* promocional; *(T shirt)* publicitario(a)

prompt [prɒmpt] **1** *n* (**a**) *(for actor)* **to give an actor a p.** dar el pie a un actor (**b**) *Comptr (short phrase)* mensaje *m* (al usuario); **return to the C:\ p.** volver a C:\ (**c**) *Com* ***p. note*** aviso *m*, *Arg* resumen *m*

2 *adj* (**a**) *(swift)* rápido(a); **to be p. in doing sth** *or* **to do sth** hacer algo con prontitud; **you should give this matter p. attention** deberías encargarte de este tema lo antes posible ►► ***p. payment*** pronto pago *m* (**b**) *(punctual)* puntual

3 *adv* **at three o'clock p.** a las tres en punto

4 *vt* (**a**) *(cause)* provocar, suscitar; **the scandal prompted his resignation** el escándalo provocó su renuncia; **to p. sb to do sth** provocar que alguien haga algo, impulsar a alguien a hacer algo; **I felt prompted to intervene** sentí que tenía que intervenir (**b**) *(actor, speaker)* apuntar (**c**) *(encourage) (interviewee)* ayudar a seguir

promptbook ['prɒmptbʊk] *n Theat* libreto *m* del apuntador

prompter ['prɒmptə(r)] *n Theat* apuntador(ora) *m,f* ►► ***p.'s box*** concha *f* del apuntador

prompting ['prɒmptɪŋ] *n (persuasion)* persuasión *f*, insistencia *f*; **to do sth at sb's p.** acceder a hacer algo ante la insistencia de alguien; **he ignored the promptings of his conscience** no hizo caso de los dictados de su conciencia; **she needed no p. when asked her opinion** no hubo que insistirle mucho para que diera su opinión

promptly ['prɒmptlɪ] *adv* (**a**) *(rapidly)* sin demora (**b**) *(punctually)* con puntualidad; **he always leaves p. at 5 o'clock** siempre se va a las cinco en punto (**c**) *(immediately)* inmediatamente; **I p. forgot what I was meant to do** me olvidé de inmediato lo que iba a hacer

promptness ['prɒmptnɪs] *n* (**a**) *(speed)* rapidez *f* (**b**) *(punctuality)* puntualidad *f*

promulgate ['prɒmʊlgeɪt] *vt Formal* (**a**) *(new law)* promulgar (**b**) *(belief, idea, opinion)* promulgar, propagar

promulgation [prɒmʊl'geɪʃən] *n Formal* (**a**) *(of decree, law)* promulgación *f* (**b**) *(of belief, idea, opinion)* promulgación *f*, propagación *f*

pronation [preʊ'neɪʃən] *n Anat* pronación *f*

pronator [preʊ'neɪtə(r)] *Anat* **1** *adj* pronador(ora)

2 *n* músculo *m* pronador

prone [prəʊn] *adj* (**a**) *(inclined)* **to be p. to (do) sth** ser propenso(a) a (hacer) algo; **p. to a disease** propenso(a) a enfermarse (**b**) *(lying face down)* boca abajo; **in a p. position** boca abajo

proneness ['prəʊnnɪs] *n* propensión *f*

prong [prɒŋ] *n* (**a**) *(of fork)* diente *m* (**b**) *(of attack, argument)* flanco *m*

-pronged [prɒŋgd] (**a**) *suffix* **three-p.** *(fork)* con tres dientes (**b**) **two-p.** *(attack)* desde dos flancos

pronghorn ['prɒŋhɔːn] *n US* antílope *m* americano

pronominal [prə'nɒmɪnəl] *adj Gram* pronominal

pronominally [prə'nɒmɪnəlɪ] *adv* pronominalmente

pronoun ['prəʊnaʊn] *n Gram* pronombre *m*

pronounce [prə'naʊns] **1** *vt* (**a**) *(word)* pronunciar; **how is it pronounced?** ¿cómo se pronuncia?; **this letter is not pronounced** esta letra no se pronuncia

(**b**) *Formal (declare) (opinion)* manifestar; **to p. that...** manifestar que...; **to p. oneself for/against sth** pronunciarse a favor de/en contra de algo; **to p. oneself satisfied** manifestarse satisfecho(a); **he was pronounced dead** fue declarado muerto; **I now p. you man and wife** *(in marriage service)* los declaro marido y mujer

(**c**) *Law* **to p. sentence** dictar sentencia; **he was pronounced innocent** fue declarado inocente

2 *vi* **to p. on** *or* **upon** pronunciarse sobre; **to p. for/against sb** emitir un dictamen a favor de/en contra de alguien

pronounceable [prə'naʊnsəbəl] *adj* pronunciable

pronounced [prə'naʊnst] *adj* pronunciado(a), acusado(a); **he walks with a p. limp** tiene una cojera bastante pronunciada

pronouncement [prə'naʊnsmənt] *n Formal* declaración *f*, manifestación *f*

pronto ['prɒntəʊ] *adv Fam* enseguida, ya

pronunciation [prənʌnsɪ'eɪʃən] *n* pronunciación *f*; **his Spanish p. is good** tiene una buena pronunciación en español

proof [pruːf] **1** *n* (**a**) *(evidence)* prueba *f*; **that's no p.!** eso no prueba nada; **she cited several cases in p. of her argument** citó diversos casos para probar su argumento; **to give** *or* **show p. of sth** probar *or* dar pruebas de algo; **to put sth to the p.** poner algo a prueba; **by way of p.** como prueba; PROV **the p. of the pudding is in the eating** el movimiento se demuestra caminando *or Esp* andando ►► ***p. of delivery*** acuse *m* de recibo; ***p. of identity*** documento *m* de identidad; ***p. of payment*** comprobante *m* de pago; ***p. positive*** prueba *f* concluyente; ***p. of postage*** comprobante *m* de envío; ***p. of purchase*** tíquet *m or* justificante *m* de compra

(**b**) *Typ* prueba *f*; **at the p. stage** en la fase de prueba

(**c**) *(of alcohol)* graduación *f* alcohólica; **40 degrees p.** una graduación (alcohólica) de 40 grados ►► ***p. spirit*** = mezcla de alcohol y agua con un porcentaje de alcohol fijo (*Br* 57,10 y *US* 50 por ciento) que sirve como base para medir la graduación de las bebidas alcohólicas

2 *adj (resistant)* **to be p. against sth** ser resistente a algo

3 *vt* (**a**) *(against weather)* impermeabilizar (**b**) *Typ (proofread)* corregir pruebas de

proofread ['pruːfriːd] *Typ* **1** *vt* corregir pruebas de

2 *vi* corregir pruebas

proofreader ['pruːfriːdə(r)] *n Typ* corrector(ora) *m,f* de pruebas

proofreading ['pruːfriːdɪŋ] *n Typ* corrección *f* de pruebas

prop [prɒp] **1** *n* (**a**) *(physical support)* puntal *m*; *(for washing line)* palo *m*; *(emotional support)* apoyo *m*, sostén *m*; **he uses alcohol as a p.** se apoya en el alcohol (**b**) *(in theatre)* accesorio *m*; **props** atrezo (**c**) *(in rugby)* **p. (forward)** pilar *m* (**d**) *Av Fam* hélice *f*

2 *vt* (*pt & pp* **propped**) apoyar (**against** contra); **p. yourself** *or* **your back against these cushions** recuéstate sobre estos almohadones; **I propped the door open with a chair** utilicé una silla para mantener la puerta abierta

► **prop up** *vt sep* (**a**) *(support) (building, tunnel)* apuntalar; *(plant)* apuntalar, *Arg* poner guías a; **to p. sth up against sth** apoyar algo contra *or* en algo (**b**) *(economy, regime)* apoyar; **the government stepped in to p. up the pound** el gobierno intervino para apuntalar la libra

prop. (*abbr* **proprietor**) propietario(a)

propaganda [prɒpə'gændə] *n* propaganda *f*; **a p. campaign/film** una campaña/película propagandística; **it's all just p.** es pura propaganda

propagandist [prɒpə'gændɪst] **1** *n* propagandista *mf*
2 *adj* propagandístico(a), panfletario(a)

propagandize [prɒpə'gændaɪz] *vi* hacer propaganda (**for** *or* **in favour of** a favor de)

propagate ['prɒpəgeɪt] **1** *vt* (**a**) *(plant, species)* propagar (**b**) *(theory, ideas)* propagar (**c**) *Phys (light, sound)* propagar
2 *vi (plant)* propagarse

propagation [prɒpə'geɪʃən] *n* (**a**) *(of plant, species)* propagación *f* (**b**) *(of theory, ideas)* propagación *f*, difusión *f* (**c**) *Phys (of light, sound)* propagación *f*

propagator ['prɒpəgeɪtə(r)] *n* (**a**) *(for seedlings)* propagador(ora) *m,f* (**b**) *(of theory, ideas)* propulsor(ora) *m,f*, impulsor(ora) *m,f*

propane ['prəʊpeɪn] *n Chem* propano *m*

propanol ['prəʊpənɒl] *n Chem* propanol *m*

propel [prə'pel] (*pt & pp* **propelled**) *vt* propulsar; **the force of the explosion propelled the debris hundreds of feet into the air** la onda expansiva lanzó escombros a decenas de metros de altura; **to p. sth/sb along** propulsar algo/a alguien; **propelled by ambition** impulsado(a) por la ambición; **he was propelled into the position of manager** fue empujado a la posición de jefe

propellant, propellent [prə'pelənt] *n* (**a**) *(for rocket)* propulsante *m*, combustible *m* (**b**) *(for aerosol)* propelente *m*

propeller [prə'pelə(r)] *n* hélice *f*

propelling pencil [prə'pelɪŋ'pensəl] *n Br* portaminas *m inv*

propene ['prəʊpi:n] *n Chem* propileno *m*

propensity [prə'pensɪtɪ] *n Formal* tendencia *f*, propensión *f*; **to have a p. to do sth/for sth** tener tendencia *or* propensión a hacer algo/a algo

PROPER ['prɒpə(r)] **1** *adj* (**a**) *(real)* verdadero(a); **he isn't a p. doctor** no es médico de verdad; **to get oneself a p. job** conseguir un trabajo serio; **I need a p. holiday** necesito unas vacaciones de verdad; **a p. meal** una comida en condiciones; **to get a p. night's sleep** dormir bien toda la noche; **we're still not in New York p.** todavía no estamos en Nueva York propiamente dicha ►► *Math* ***p. fraction*** fracción *f* propia; *Gram* ***p. name*** nombre *m* propio; *Gram* ***p. noun*** nombre *m* propio
(**b**) *(appropriate)* adecuado(a); **I like everything to be in its p. place** me gusta que todo esté en su sitio; **we will give this matter the p. consideration** daremos a este asunto la atención debida; **you must go through the p. channels** has de seguir los cauces apropiados; **I don't have the p. tools** no tengo las herramientas adecuadas
(**c**) *(polite, socially acceptable)* correcto(a); **it's not p. for young ladies to speak like that** no está *or RP* queda bien que las jóvenes hablen así; **it's only p. that they should pay you compensation** es normal que te paguen una indemnización
(**d**) *(characteristic)* **p. to** propio(a) de
(**e**) *Br Fam (for emphasis)* **we're in a p. mess** estamos en un buen lío; **he's a p. fool** es un perfecto idiota, es un idiota de tomo y lomo; **she's a p. little madam** es una auténtica señoritinga
2 *adv Br Fam* (**a**) *Hum (correctly)* **to talk p.** hablar como Dios manda (**b**) *(completely)* **you've ruined it good and p.** *Esp* la has hecho buena, *Méx* metiste las cuatro, *RP* metiste la pata hasta el cuadril

properly ['prɒpəlɪ] *adv* (**a**) *(correctly)* correctamente, bien; **the lid isn't on p.** la tapa no está bien puesta; **do it p. this time!** ¡esta vez hazlo bien *or* como Dios manda!; **he quite p. refused** se negó con toda razón; **she's not a nurse, p. speaking** hablando en propiedad, no es una enfermera
(**b**) *(appropriately, suitably)* apropiadamente; **I haven't thanked you p.** no te he dado las gracias como corresponde; **I'm not p. dressed** *(for weather, activity)* no estoy vestida adecuadamente; **I haven't slept p. in weeks** hace semanas que no duermo bien
(**c**) *(politely, socially acceptably)* correctamente; **eat p.!** ¡come bien *or* como corresponde!
(**d**) *Br Fam (as intensifier)* **they were p. told off** recibieron una seria reprimenda

propertied ['prɒpətɪd] *adj* adinerado(a), acaudalado(a)

property ['prɒpətɪ] *n* (**a**) *(possessions)* propiedad *f*; **it's my p.** es mío, me pertenece; **this book is the p. of Tony Simpson** este libro es propiedad de *or* pertenece a Tony Simpson; **you shouldn't steal other people's p.** no deberías robar la propiedad ajena; **government/personal p.** bienes públicos/personales; **literary/intellectual p.** propiedad literaria/intelectual
(**b**) *(land)* propiedades *fpl*; *(real estate)* bienes *mpl* inmuebles; **we're investing our money in p.** estamos invirtiendo (nuestro dinero) en tierras; **a man of p.** una persona que tiene muchos bienes ►► ***p. developer*** promotor(ora) *m,f* inmobiliario(a); ***p. ladder:*** **to get a foot on the p. ladder** comprar la primera propiedad; ***p. market*** mercado *m* inmobiliario; ***p. speculation*** especulación *f* en bienes inmuebles; ***p. tax*** impuesto *m* sobre la propiedad inmobiliaria
(**c**) *(plot of land)* terreno *m*, parcela *f*; *(house)* inmueble *m*; *(building)* inmueble *m*; **to be on sb's p.** estar en propiedad de alguien; **get off my p.!** ¡sal de mi propiedad!
(**d**) *(quality)* propiedad *f*; **what are the chemical properties of cobalt?** ¿cuáles son las propiedades químicas del cobalto?
(**e**) *Theat* ***p. man*** encargado *m* de atrezo; ***p. mistress*** encargada *f* de atrezo

prophecy ['prɒfɪsɪ] *n* profecía *f*

prophesy ['prɒfɪsaɪ] **1** *vt* profetizar; **scaremongers prophesied the end of the world** los alarmistas presagiaron el fin del mundo
2 *vi* profetizar

prophet ['prɒfɪt] *n* profeta *m*; **the P.** *(in Islam)* el Profeta; **a p. of doom** un(a) agorero(a)

prophetess ['prɒfɪtes] *n* profetisa *f*

prophetic [prə'fetɪk] *adj* profético(a)

prophetically [prə'fetɪklɪ] *adv* proféticamente

prophylactic [prɒfɪ'læktɪk] *Med* **1** *n Formal* (**a**) *(drug)* profiláctico *m* (**b**) *(condom)* preservativo *m*, profiláctico *m*
2 *adj* profiláctico(a)

prophylaxis [prɒfɪ'læksɪs] *n* profilaxis *f inv*

propinquity [prə'pɪŋkwɪtɪ] *n Formal* (**a**) *(in space, time)* propincuidad *f* (**b**) *(in kinship)* parentesco *m*

propitiate [prə'pɪʃɪeɪt] *vt Formal* propiciar; **to p. the gods** ganar el favor de los dioses

propitiation [prəpɪʃɪ'eɪʃən] *n Formal* propiciación *f*

propitious [prə'pɪʃəs] *adj Formal* propicio(a)

propitiously [prə'pɪʃəslɪ] *adv Formal* de una manera propicia

proponent [prə'pəʊnənt] *n* partidario(a) *m,f*, defensor(ora) *m,f*

proportion [prə'pɔ:ʃən] **1** *n* (**a**) *(ratio)* proporción *f*; **in the p. of 6 parts water to 1 part concentrate** en una proporción de 6 partes de agua por cada parte de concentrado; **in p. to...** en proporción a...; **in direct/inverse p. to sth** en proporción directa/inversa a algo; **the payment is out of all p. to the work involved** lo que se paga no es proporcional al trabajo que supone
(**b**) *(perspective)* perspectiva *f*; **to lose all sense of p.** perder el sentido de la medida; **in p.** proporcionado(a); **you must try to see things in p.** intenta ver las cosas en perspectiva; **out of p.** desproporcionado(a); **to get sth out of p.** exagerar algo; **they have got** *or* **blown the problem out of (all) p.** han exagerado mucho el problema
(**c**) *(part, amount)* proporción *f*, parte *f*; **a large/small p. of the profits** una pequeña/gran parte de los beneficios; **what p. of your income do you spend on food?** de lo que ganas, ¿cuánto gastas en comida?
(**d**) **proportions** *(dimensions)* proporciones *fpl*; **a ship of vast proportions** un barco de enormes proporciones; **the problem has assumed worrying proportions** el problema ha cobrado una envergadura sumamente preocupante
2 *vt* **to p. one's expenditure to one's resources** ajustar los gastos personales a los recursos con los que se cuenta; **well proportioned** proporcionado(a)

proportional [prə'pɔ:ʃənəl] *adj* (**a**) *(in proportion)* proporcional (**to** a) (**b**) *Pol* ***p. representation*** representación *f* proporcional (**c**) *Comptr* ***p. spacing*** espaciado *m* proporcional, monoespaciado *m*

proportionally [prə'pɔ:ʃənəlɪ] *adv* proporcionalmente; **they spend p. more on research than we do** proporcionalmente, gastan más en investigación que nosotros

proportionate [prə'pɔ:ʃənɪt] *adj Formal* proporcional (**to** a)

proportionately [prə'pɔ:ʃənɪtlɪ] *adv* proporcionalmente

proposal [prə'pəʊzəl] *n* (**a**) *(offer)* propuesta *f*; **to make/accept a p.** hacer/aceptar una propuesta; **p. (of marriage)** propuesta *f or* proposición *f* de matrimonio (**b**) *(plan)* proyecto *m*

propose [prə'pəʊz] **1** *vt* (**a**) *(suggest)* proponer; **to p. to do sth, to p. doing sth** proponer hacer algo; **and what do you p. we do about this?** ¿qué propones que hagamos al respecto?; **it was proposed that we stay a few days longer** se propuso que nos quedáramos unos días más
(**b**) *(intend)* **to p. to do sth** proponerse hacer algo; **I don't p. to spend any more time on this** no tengo la intención de perder más tiempo con esto; **what do you p. to do about this?** ¿y tú qué propones hacer (al respecto)?
(**c**) *(present) (policy, resolution)* proponer; **to p. sb for** *or* **as sth**

(post, job) proponer a alguien para *or* como algo; **to p. a motion/an amendment** *(in debate)* proponer una moción/una enmienda; **to p. a toast** proponer un brindis

2 *vi* **(a)** *(offer marriage)* **he proposed to her** le pidió que se casara con él **(b)** PROV **man proposes, God disposes** el hombre propone y Dios dispone

> En inglés culto o elevado, y especialmente en inglés americano, **propose** puede ir seguido de **that** más un verbo en subjuntivo (ver el panel SUBJUNCTIVE):
> **we propose that she remain with her family**
> *proponemos que permanezca con su familia*
> Lo mismo también podría decirse de las formas siguientes:
> **we propose that she remains with her family**
> **we propose that she should remain with her family**

proposed [prəˈpəʊzd] *adj* propuesto(a)

proposer [prəˈpəʊzə(r)] *n (of motion)* impulsor(ora) *m,f; (of candidate, member)* proponente *mf*

proposition [prɒpəˈzɪʃən] **1** *n* **(a)** *(offer, suggestion)* propuesta *f*
(b) *(task)* empresa *f*, asunto *m*; **that's quite a p.** es toda una empresa
(c) *(available choice)* opción *f*; **it's an attractive p.** es una opción interesante; *Fam* **it's not a paying p.** no es rentable
(d) *(offer of sex)* proposición *f*; **to make sb a p.** hacerle una proposición a alguien
(e) *(in logic, argument)* proposición *f*
(f) *US (in referendum)* propuesta *f*
2 *vt* hacer proposiciones a

propositional [prɒpəˈzɪʃənəl] *adj Phil* proposicional ►► ***p. calculus*** cálculo *m* proposicional

propound [prəˈpaʊnd] *vt Formal* exponer

proprietary [prəˈpraɪɪtərɪ] *adj* **(a)** *(air, attitude)* de propietario(a) **(b)** *Com (brand, process)* registrado(a) ►► ***p. name*** nombre *m* comercial; ***p. rights*** derechos *mpl* de propiedad **(c)** *US (hospital, clinic)* privado(a)

proprietor [prəˈpraɪətə(r)] *n* propietario(a) *m,f*

proprietorial [prəpraɪəˈtɔːrɪəl] *adj (air, attitude)* de propietario(a); **he's very p. about the fax machine** actúa como si el fax fuese de él

proprietress [prəˈpraɪətrɪs] *n* propietaria *f*

propriety [prəˈpraɪətɪ] *n* **(a)** *(decorum)* decoro *m*; **to behave with p.** comportarse con decoro **(b) the proprieties** *(etiquette)* las convenciones

propulsion [prəˈpʌlʃən] *n* propulsión *f*

pro rata [ˈprəʊˈrɑːtə] **1** *adj* prorrateado(a)
2 *adv* de forma prorrateada

prorate [ˈprəʊreɪt] *vt US* prorratear

prorogation [prəʊrəˈgeɪʃən] *n (of parliament, assembly)* prorrogación *f*

prorogue [prəˈrəʊg] *vt (parliament, assembly)* prorrogar

prosaic [prəʊˈzeɪɪk] *adj* prosaico(a)

prosaically [prəʊˈzeɪɪklɪ] *adv* prosaicamente

proscenium [prəˈsiːnɪəm] *n Theat* **p. (arch)** proscenio *m*

prosciutto [prɒˈʃuːtəʊ] *n* prosciutto *m (embutido italiano)*

proscribe [prəˈskraɪb] *vt* proscribir, excluir

proscription [prəˈskrɪpʃən] *n* proscripción *f*

prose [prəʊz] *n* **(a)** *(not poetry)* prosa *f* ►► ***p. poem*** poema *m* en prosa; ***p. style*** estilo *m* prosístico **(b)** *(translation in exam)* (prueba *f* de) traducción *f* inversa

prosecutable [prɒsɪˈkjuːtəbəl] *adj* procesable

prosecute [ˈprɒsɪkjuːt] **1** *vt* **(a)** *Law (case, prisoner)* procesar; **to p. sb for sth** procesar a alguien por algo; **trespassers will be prosecuted** *(sign)* prohibido el paso (bajo sanción) **(b)** *Formal (continue) (enquiry, war)* proseguir con
2 *vi Law* **(a)** *(lawyer)* ejercer de acusación **(b)** *(plaintiff)* **I've decided not to p.** he decidido no abrir un procedimiento judicial

prosecuting attorney [ˈprɒsɪkjuːtɪŋəˈtɜːnɪ] *n US* fiscal *m*

prosecution [prɒsɪˈkjuːʃən] *n* **(a)** *Law (proceedings)* proceso *m*, juicio *m*; **to bring a p. (against sb)** interponer una demanda (contra alguien), iniciar una acción judicial (contra alguien); **to be liable to p.** estar sujeto(a) a una acción judicial
(b) *Law (accusing side)* **the p.** la acusación; **p. witness, witness for the p.** testigo de cargo
(c) *Formal (of enquiry, war)* prosecución *f*; **in the p. of his duties** en la prosecución de sus tareas

prosecutor [ˈprɒsɪkjuːtə(r)] *n Law* fiscal *mf*; **(public) p.** fiscal *mf* (del Estado)

proselyte [ˈprɒsəlaɪt] *n Rel* prosélito(a) *m,f*

proselytize [ˈprɒsəlɪtaɪz] *Rel & Fig* **1** *vt* hacer proselitismo entre
2 *vi* hacer proselitismo

prosodic [prəˈsɒdɪk] *adj* prosódico(a)

prosody [ˈprɒsədɪ] *n Lit & Ling* prosodia *f*

prospect 1 *n* [ˈprɒspekt] **(a)** *(likelihood)* posibilidad *f*; **there is very little p. of it** es muy poco probable; **there is no p. of agreement** no hay posibilidad *or* perspectivas de acuerdo; **we had given up all p. of hearing from you** pensábamos que ya no íbamos a tener noticias tuyas
(b) *(impending event, situation)* perspectiva *f*; **I don't relish the p. of working for him** la perspectiva de trabajar para él no me hace ninguna gracia; **to have sth in p.** tener la perspectiva de algo
(c) *(outlook, chance of success)* **the prospects for the automobile industry** las perspectivas para la industria del automóvil; **what are the weather prospects for tomorrow?** ¿cuál es el pronóstico del tiempo para mañana?; **future prospects** perspectivas de futuro; **a job with prospects** un trabajo con buenas perspectivas (de futuro)
(d) *(person) (player)* promesa *f*; *Com (potential customer)* cliente *mf* potencial
(e) *Formal (view)* vista *f*, panorámica *f*
2 *vt* [prəˈspekt] *(area, land)* explorar
3 *vi* **to p. for gold** hacer prospecciones en búsqueda *or* busca de oro

prospective [prəˈspektɪv] *adj* **(a)** *(future)* futuro(a) **(b)** *(potential)* posible, potencial

prospector [prəˈspektə(r)] *n* **oil/gold p.** buscador(ora) de petróleo/oro

prospectus [prəˈspektəs] *n* **(a)** *(for university, company)* folleto *m* informativo, prospecto *m* **(b)** *Fin (for share issue)* folleto *m or* prospecto *m* de emisión

prosper [ˈprɒspə(r)] *vi* prosperar

prosperity [prɒsˈperɪtɪ] *n* prosperidad *f*

prosperous [ˈprɒspərəs] *adj* próspero(a)

prosperously [ˈprɒspərəslɪ] *adv* prósperamente

prostaglandin [prɒstəˈglændɪn] *n Med* prostaglandina *f*

prostate [ˈprɒsteɪt] *n Anat* **p. (gland)** próstata *f*

prosthesis [prɒsˈθiːsɪs] (*pl* **prostheses** [prɒsˈθiːsiːz]) *n* prótesis *f inv*

prosthetic [prɒsˈθetɪk] *adj* artificial ►► ***p. limb*** prótesis *f*

prosthetics [prɒsˈθetɪks] *n* protética *f*

prostitute [ˈprɒstɪtjuːt] **1** *n* prostituta *f*; **male p.** prostituto
2 *vt also Fig* **to p. oneself** prostituirse; **to p. one's talent** prostituir *or* vender el talento de uno

prostitution [prɒstɪˈtjuːʃən] *n* prostitución *f*

prostrate 1 *adj* [ˈprɒstreɪt] **(a)** *(lying down)* postrado(a), tendido(a) boca abajo; **to lie p. before sb** yacer postrado(a) ante alguien **(b)** *(overcome)* **p. with grief/exhaustion** postrado(a) por el dolor/agotamiento
2 *vt* [prəˈstreɪt] **to p. oneself (before)** postrarse (ante); **to be prostrated by illness** estar postrado(a) por una enfermedad

prostration [prɒˈstreɪʃən] *n* **(a)** *(lying down)* postración *f* **(b)** *(exhaustion)* postración *f*; **the country was in a state of economic p.** el país se encontraba en un estado de postración económica

prosy [ˈprəʊzɪ] *adj (speech, text)* aburrido(a)

protactinium [prəʊtækˈtɪnɪəm] *n Chem* protactinio *m*

protagonist [prəˈtægənɪst] *n* **(a)** *(main character)* protagonista *mf* **(b)** *(of idea, theory)* abanderado(a) *m,f*, promotor(ora) *m,f*

protean [ˈprəʊtɪən] *adj Literary* proteico(a)

protease [ˈprəʊtɪeɪz] *n Biochem* proteasa *f* ►► ***p. inhibitor*** inhibidor *m* de la proteasa

protect [prəˈtekt] *vt* proteger (**from** *or* **against** de *or* contra); **she protected her eyes from the sun** se protegió los ojos del sol; **to p. oneself from sth** protegerse de algo; **a protected species** una especie protegida

► **protect against** *vt insep* proteger contra

protection [prəˈtekʃən] *n* protección *f* (**from** *or* **against** contra); **to be under sb's p.** estar bajo la protección de alguien; **a society for the p. of birds** una sociedad para la protección de las aves ►► ***p. factor*** *(of suntan lotion)* factor *m* de protección; ***p. money*** extorsión *f or* impuesto *m (a cambio de protección)*; ***p. racket*** red *f* de extorsión

protectionism [prəˈtekʃənɪzəm] *n Econ* proteccionismo *m*

protectionist [prəˈtekʃənɪst] *Econ* **1** *n* proteccionista *mf*
2 *adj* proteccionista

protective [prə'tektɪv] *adj* (**a**) *(material, clothing, measure)* protector(ora) ▸▸ ***p. custody*** detención *f* cautelar *(para protección del detenido)*; ***p. markings*** coloración *f* defensiva; ***p. seal*** precinto *m* de garantía (**b**) *(person, attitude)* protector(ora); **to be p. (towards** *or* **of sb)** tener una actitud protectora (hacia alguien); **to be p. of one's interests** proteger *or* cuidar los intereses propios

protectively [prə'tektɪvlɪ] *adv (to behave, act)* de manera protectora

protectiveness [prə'tektɪvnɪs] *n* lo protector

protector [prə'tektə(r)] *n* (**a**) *(device)* protector *m* (**b**) *(person)* protector(ora) *m,f* (**c**) *(regent)* regente *mf*

protectorate [prə'tektərət] *n* protectorado *m*

protectress [prə'tektrɪs] *n* protectora *f*

protégé(e) ['prɒtəʒeɪ] *n* protegido(a) *m,f*

protein ['prəʊti:n] *n* proteína *f*

pro tem ['prəʊ'tem] **1** *adv* por ahora, por el momento
2 *adj* interino(a)

Proterozoic [prəʊtərəʊ'zəʊɪk] *Geol* **1** *n* **the P.** el Proterozoico
2 *adj (era)* proterozoico(a)

protest 1 *n* ['prəʊtest] (**a**) *(objection)* protesta *f*; **to make a p. (against** *or* **about sth)** protestar (contra *or* por algo); **to register** *or* **lodge a p. (with sb)** presentar una queja (ante alguien); **to do sth under p.** hacer algo de mal grado; **she resigned in p.** dimitió en señal de protesta; **without p.** sin protestar ▸▸ ***p. march*** marcha *f* de protesta; ***p. song*** canción *f* protesta; ***p. vote*** voto *m* de castigo
(**b**) *(demonstration)* protesta *f*; **to stage a p.** hacer una manifestación de protesta
2 *vt* [prə'test] (**a**) *US (protest against)* protestar en contra de (**b**) *(one's innocence, love)* declarar, manifestar; **to p. that...** declarar *or* manifestar que...
3 *vi* protestar (**about/against** por/en contra de); **to p. to sb** presentar una protesta ante alguien; *Formal* **I must p. in the strongest terms about...** me veo obligado a presentar mi protesta más enérgica por...

Protestant ['prɒtɪstənt] **1** *n* protestante *mf*
2 *adj* protestante

Protestantism ['prɒtɪstəntɪzəm] *n* protestantismo *m*

protestation [prɒtes'teɪʃən] *n Formal* proclamación *f*

protester [prə'testə(r)] *n* manifestante *mf*; **anti-nuclear/peace p.** manifestante antinuclear/pacifista

proto- ['prəʊtəʊ] *prefix* proto-

protocol ['prəʊtəkɒl] *n also Comptr* protocolo *m*

proton ['prəʊtɒn] *n Phys* protón *m*

protoplasm ['prəʊtəplæzəm] *n Biol* protoplasma *m*

prototype ['prəʊtətaɪp] *n* prototipo *m*

prototypical [prəʊtə'tɪpɪkəl] *adj* prototípico(a)

protozoan, protozoon [prəʊtə'zəʊən] *n Zool* protozoo *m*

protract [prə'trækt] *vt (prolong)* prolongar

protracted [prə'træktɪd] *adj* prolongado(a)

protractor [prə'træktə(r)] *n Geom* transportador *m*

protrude [prə'tru:d] *vi* sobresalir (**from** de); **the promontory protrudes into the sea** el promontorio se prolonga *or* proyecta hacia el mar

protruding [prə'tru:dɪŋ] *adj* (**a**) *(ledge)* saliente (**b**) *(jaw, teeth, chin, belly)* prominente; *(eyes)* saltón(ona)

protrusion [prə'tru:ʒən] *n Formal (lump)* protuberancia *f*

protuberance [prə'tju:bərəns] *n Formal* protuberancia *f*

protuberant [prə'tju:bərənt] *adj Formal* protuberante

proud [praʊd] **1** *adj* (**a**) *(pleased, satisfied)* orgulloso(a); **they are now the p. parents of a daughter** son ahora los orgullosos padres de una niña; **to be p. of sb/(having done) sth** estar orgulloso(a) de alguien/(haber hecho) algo; **it's nothing to be p. of!** ¡no es para estar orgulloso!; **to be p. of oneself** sentirse orgulloso(a) de uno(a) mismo(a); *Ironic* **I hope you're p. of yourself!** ¡espero que estés orgulloso!; **to be p. to do sth** estar orgulloso(a) de hacer algo; **we are p. to present this award to...** tenemos el orgullo de entregar esta distinción a...; **a p. moment** un momento de gran satisfacción; **it was her proudest possession** era su mayor orgullo
(**b**) *(arrogant)* orgulloso(a), soberbio(a); **she was too p. to accept** su orgullo no le permitió aceptar; **I'll take any job, I'm not p.** no tengo problemas en aceptar cualquier empleo; IDIOM **to be as p. as a peacock** estar orgullosísimo(a)
(**c**) *(majestic)* majestuoso(a), soberbio(a)
(**d**) *Br (protruding)* **to be** *or* **stand p. of sth** sobresalir por encima de algo; **it's a few millimetres p.** sobresale algunos milímetros
2 *adv* **you've done us p.** lo has hecho muy bien; **to do oneself p.** hacerlo muy bien

proudly ['praʊdlɪ] *adv* (**a**) *(with satisfaction)* orgullosamente, con orgullo (**b**) *(arrogantly)* con soberbia (**c**) *(majestically)* majestuosamente, soberbiamente

Proustian ['pru:stɪən] *adj* proustiano(a)

provable, proveable ['pru:vəbəl] *adj* demostrable

prove [pru:v] (*pp* **proven** ['pru:vən, 'prəʊvən] *or* **proved**) **1** *vt* (**a**) *(demonstrate)* demostrar, probar; **the autopsy proved that it was suicide** la autopsia probó que fue un suicidio; **she quickly proved herself indispensable** en poco tiempo demostró que era indispensable; **to p. sb wrong/guilty** demostrar que alguien está equivocado(a)/es culpable; **to do sth to p. a point** hacer algo para demostrar algo; **that proves my point** eso prueba lo que digo; **she wanted a chance to p. herself** quería una oportunidad para demostrar su valía
(**b**) *(test)* probar; **to p. oneself** probarse
(**c**) *US Law (will)* homologar, hacer público
2 *vi* (**a**) *(turn out)* resultar; **to p. (to be) correct** resultar (ser) correcto(a); **if that proves to be the case** si eso resulta ser así; **it has proved impossible to find him** ha sido imposible hallarlo (**b**) *(dough)* subir, fermentar

proven ['pru:vən, 'prəʊvən] *adj* (**a**) *(tested)* probado(a), comprobado(a) (**b**) *Scot Law* **not p.** = veredicto intermedio entre culpable e inocente que implica que el acusado probablemente es culpable pero que esto no ha podido probarse

provenance ['prɒvənəns] *n Formal* procedencia *f*, origen *m*

Provençal [prɒvɒn'sɑ:l] **1** *n (language)* provenzal *m*
2 *adj* provenzal

Provence [prə'vɒns] *n* Provenza

provender ['prɒvəndə(r)] *n* (**a**) *(fodder)* forraje *m* (**b**) *Formal (food)* alimento *m*

proverb ['prɒvɜ:b] *n* refrán *m*, proverbio *m*; **(the Book of) Proverbs** (el Libro de los) Proverbios

proverbial [prə'vɜ:bɪəl] *adj* proverbial; **a p. expression** una frase proverbial; **they showed none of the Scots' p. meanness** no exhibieron la proverbial tacañería escocesa; **this decision was the p. straw which broke the camel's back** esa decisión fue la proverbial gota que colmó el vaso

proverbially [prə'vɜ:bɪəlɪ] *adv* proverbialmente

provide [prə'vaɪd] **1** *vt* (**a**) *(supply)* suministrar, proporcionar; *(service, support)* prestar, proporcionar; **to p. sb with sth, to p. sth for sb** suministrar *or* proporcionar algo a alguien; **food will be provided** se proporcionará comida; **this factory will p. 500 new jobs** la fábrica creará 500 nuevos puestos de trabajo; **the plane is provided with eight emergency exits** el avión está provisto de *or* cuenta con ocho salidas de emergencia; **write the answers in the spaces provided** escriba las respuestas en los espacios disponibles
(**b**) *(offer, afford)* ofrecer, dar; **the trees p. shade in summer** los árboles dan sombra en verano; **this provides an ideal opportunity to...** ésta es *or* constituye una oportunidad ideal para...
(**c**) *Formal (stipulate)* establecer
2 *vi* **the Lord will p.** el Señor proveerá

▸ **provide against** *vt insep (danger, possibility)* prepararse *or Am* alistarse para

▸ **provide for** *vt insep* (**a**) *(support)* mantener; **I have a family to p. for** tengo una familia que mantener
(**b**) *(make provisions for)* **I think we've provided for every eventuality** creo que hemos tomado medidas para hacer frente a cualquier eventualidad; **they hadn't provided for the drop in demand** no habían tomado las medidas necesarias ante una eventual caída de la demanda; **he left his family well provided for** dejó a su familia el futuro asegurado
(**c**) *Formal (allow for) (of law, clause)* prever

provided [prə'vaɪdɪd] *conj* **p. (that)** siempre que, a condición de que

providence ['prɒvɪdəns] *n* (**a**) *(fate)* providencia *f*; **P. smiled on us** la providencia nos sonrió (**b**) *(foresight, thrift)* previsión *f*

provident ['prɒvɪdənt] *adj (foresighted, thrifty)* previsor(ora)

providential [prɒvɪ'denʃəl] *adj Formal* providencial

providentially [prɒvɪ'denʃəlɪ] *adv Formal* providencialmente

providently ['prɒvɪdəntlɪ] *adv* previsoramente

provider [prə'vaɪdə(r)] *n* proveedor(ora) *m,f*; **she's the family's sole p.** es el único sostén de la familia

providing [prə'vaɪdɪŋ] *conj* **p. (that)** siempre que, a condición de que

province ['prɒvɪns] *n* (**a**) *(of country)* provincia *f*; **in the provinces** en provincias (**b**) *(domain)* terreno *m*, campo *m* de acción; **that isn't my p.** no es mi área; **politics was once the sole p. of men** hace tiempo, la política era el territorio exclusivo del hombre (**c**) *Rel* provincia *f*

provincial [prə'vɪnʃəl] **1** *n* (**a**) *(from provinces)* provinciano(a) *m,f* (**b**) *Rel* provincial *mf*
2 *adj* (**a**) *(of a province)* provincial (**b**) *(not of the capital)* provinciano(a) (**c**) *Pej (parochial)* provinciano(a)

provincialism [prə'vɪnʃəlɪzəm] *n* provincianismo *m*

proving-ground ['pru:vɪŋ'graʊnd] *n* campo *m* de pruebas

provision [prə'vɪʒən] **1** *n* (**a**) **provisions** *(supplies)* provisiones *fpl* (**b**) *(supplying) (of money, water, supplies, food)* suministro *m*, abastecimiento *m*; *(of services)* prestación *f*; **social service p. has been cut again** han vuelto a recortar las prestaciones sociales; **the p. of new jobs** la oferta de nuevos puestos de trabajo
(**c**) *(allowance)* **to make p. for sth** prever algo, tener en cuenta algo; **the law makes no p. for a case of this kind** la ley no contempla un caso de este tipo
(**d**) *(arrangement)* **to make provisions for one's family/the future** hacer previsiones para la familia/el futuro
(**e**) *(in treaty, contract)* estipulación *f*, disposición *f*; **under the provisions of the UN charter/his will** según lo estipulado en la carta de las Naciones Unidas/su testamento; *Law* **notwithstanding any p. to the contrary** no obstante la existencia de cualquier disposición en contrario
2 *vt Formal (supply)* abastecer

provisional [prə'vɪʒənəl] **1** *adj* provisional, *Am* provisorio(a) ►► *Br* ***p. driving licence*** = permiso de conducir provisional que recibe un conductor en prácticas; ***the P. IRA*** el IRA provisional
2 *n* miembro *m* del IRA provisional; **the Provisionals** el IRA provisional

provisionally [prə'vɪʒənəlɪ] *adv* provisionalmente

proviso [prə'vaɪzəʊ] (*pl* **provisos,** *US* **provisoes**) *n* condición *f*; **with the p. that...** a condición de que...; **they accept, with one p.** aceptan pero con una condición

Provo ['prəʊvəʊ] *n Fam* miembro *m* del IRA provisional

provocateur [prɒ'vɒkətɜ:(r)] *n* agitador(ora) *m,f*

provocation [prɒvə'keɪʃən] *n* provocación *f*; **at the slightest p.** a la menor provocación; **without p.** sin mediar provocación

provocative [prə'vɒkətɪv] *adj* (**a**) *(trouble-making, polemical)* provocador(ora); **she just said that to be p.** sólo lo dijo para provocar (**b**) *(sexually)* provocativo(a)

provocatively [prə'vɒkətɪvlɪ] *adv* (**a**) *(provokingly)* provocadoramente (**b**) *(enticingly)* provocativamente

provoke [prə'vəʊk] *vt* (**a**) *(try to make angry)* provocar; **he's easily provoked** se *esp Esp* enfada *or esp Am* enoja por nada, salta por nada; **to p. sb to anger** provocar la ira de alguien; **to p. sb into doing sth** empujar a alguien a hacer algo
(**b**) *(give rise to) (criticism)* provocar; *(interest, debate)* despertar, suscitar; **to p. a reaction** provocar una reacción; **the revelations provoked a public outcry** las revelaciones provocaron protestas generalizadas

provoking [prə'vəʊkɪŋ] *adj (irritating)* irritante, enojoso(a)

provost ['prɒvəst] *n* (**a**) *Br Univ (head of college)* decano(a) *m,f* (**b**) *Scot (mayor)* alcalde(esa) *m,f* (**c**) *Rel* deán *m* (**d**) *Mil* ***p. guard*** policía *m* militar; ***p. marshal*** jefe *m* de la policía militar

prow [praʊ] *n (of ship)* proa *f*

prowess ['praʊɪs] *n (skill)* proezas *fpl*; **he showed great p. on the sports field** demostró un muy elevado nivel deportivo; **sexual p.** potencia sexual

prowl [praʊl] **1** *n* **to be on the p.** *(person, animal)* merodear; **to be on the p. for sth** ir a la caza de algo; **to go for a** *or* **on the p.** *(person, animal)* salir a merodear ►► *US* ***p. car*** coche *m or Am* carro *m or CSur* auto *m* patrulla
2 *vt (streets, area)* merodear por
3 *vi* merodear

prowler ['praʊle(r)] *n* merodeador(ora) *m,f*

proxemics [prɒk'si:mɪks] *n* prosémica *f*

proximal ['prɒksɪməl] *n Anat* proximal *m*

proximity [prɒk'sɪmɪtɪ] *n* cercanía *f*, proximidad *f*; **its p. to the capital/the shops** su cercanía a la capital/a las tiendas; **in close p. to** muy cerca de ►► ***p. fuse*** espoleta *f* de proximidad; ***p. talks*** = situación en la que las partes implicadas en una disputa se encuentran en diferentes oficinas dentro de un mismo edificio con el propósito de poder llegar a desarrollar conversaciones cara a cara

proxy ['prɒksɪ] *n* (**a**) *(person)* apoderado(a) *m,f* (**b**) *(power)* poder *m*; **to vote by p.** votar por poderes; **to marry by p.** casarse por poder (**c**) *Comptr* proxy *m*, servidor *m* caché ►► ***p. server*** servidor *m* proxy

Prozac® ['prəʊzæk] *n* Prozac® *m*

prude [pru:d] *n* mojigato(a) *m,f*; **don't be such a p.!** ¡no seas tan mojigato(a)!

prudence ['pru:dəns] *n* prudencia *f*

prudent ['pru:dənt] *adj* prudente

prudently ['pru:dəntlɪ] *adv* prudentemente

prudery ['pru:dərɪ] *n* mojigatería *f*

prudish ['pru:dɪʃ] *adj* mojigato(a), pacato(a)

prudishness ['pru:dɪʃnɪs] *n* mojigatería *f*

prune[1] [pru:n] *n* (**a**) *(fruit)* ciruela *f* pasa; IDIOM *Fam* **to look like an old p.** parecer una pasa *or Arg* pasa de uva (**b**) *Br Fam (fool)* tonto(a) *m,f*

prune[2] *vt* (**a**) *(bush, tree)* podar (**b**) *(article, budget)* recortar; **to p. (back** *or* **down) expenditure** recortar *or* reducir el gasto

pruning ['pru:nɪŋ] *n* (**a**) *(of bush, tree)* poda *f* ►► ***p. hook*** podadera *f*; ***p. knife*** podadera *f* (**b**) *(of article, budget, staff)* recorte *m*, reducción *f*

prurience ['prʊərɪəns] *n Formal* lascivia *f*

prurient ['prʊərɪənt] *adj Formal* procaz, lascivo(a)

prurigo [prʊə'raɪgəʊ] *n Med* prurigo *m*

pruritus [prʊə'raɪtɪs] *n Med* prurito *m*

Prussia ['prʌʃə] *n* Prusia

Prussian ['prʌʃən] **1** *n* prusiano(a) *m,f*
2 *adj* prusiano(a) ►► ***P. blue*** azul *m* de Prusia

prussic acid ['prʌsɪk'æsɪd] *n Chem* ácido *m* prúsico

pry[1] [praɪ] *vi* entrometerse, husmear; **I didn't mean to p.** no fue mi intención meterme en tus asuntos; **to p. into sth** entrometerse en algo

pry[2] *US* = **prise**

prying ['praɪɪŋ] *adj* entrometido(a); **p. eyes** ojos fisgones

PS [pi:'es] *n* (*abbr* **postscript**) P.D.

psalm [sɑ:m] *n* salmo *m*; **(the Book of) Psalms** (el Libro de los) Salmos

psalmist ['sɑ:mɪst] *n* salmista *mf*

psalter ['sɔ:ltə(r)] *n* salterio *m*

psaltery ['sɔ:ltərɪ] *n Mus* salterio *m*

PSB [pi:es'bi:] *n* (*abbr* **public-service broadcasting**) servicio *m* público de radiodifusión

PSBR [pi:esbi:'ɑ:(r)] *n Br Econ* (*abbr* **public sector borrowing requirement**) necesidades *fpl* de endeudamiento del sector público

psephologist [se'fɒlədʒɪst] *n* analista *mf* electoral

psephology [se'fɒlədʒɪ] *n* análisis *m inv* de los resultados electorales

pseud [sju:d] *n Br Fam* pretencioso(a) *m,f*

pseudo ['sju:dəʊ] *adj Fam (kindness, interest)* fingido(a), falso(a)

pseudo- ['sju:dəʊ] *prefix* seudo-, pseudo-

pseudointellectual ['sju:dəʊɪntə'lektjʊəl] **1** *n* pseudointelectual *mf*
2 *adj* pseudointelectual

pseudonym ['sju:dənɪm] *n* seudónimo *m*

pseudonymous [sju:'dɒnɪməs] *adj* bajo seudónimo

pseudy ['sju:dɪ] *adj Br Fam* intelectualoide

pshaw [(p)ʃɔ:] *exclam Old-fashioned or Hum* ¡pamplinas!

psi (*abbr* **pounds per square inch**) libras por pulgada cuadrada

psittacosis [sɪtə'kəʊsɪs] *n Med* psitacosis *f inv*

PSNI [pi:esen'aɪ] *n* (*abbr* **Police Service of Northern Ireland**) = cuerpo de policía de Irlanda del Norte

psoas ['səʊæs] *n Anat* psoas *m inv*

psoriasis [sə'raɪəsɪs] *n* soriasis *f*

psst [pst] *exclam* chis

PST [pi:es'ti:] *n US* (*abbr* **Pacific Standard Time**) = hora oficial de la costa del Pacífico en Estados Unidos

PSV [pi:es'vi:] *n Br* (*abbr* **public-service vehicle**) vehículo *m* público

psych(e) [saɪk] *vt Fam* **to p. (out)** *(unnerve)* poner nervioso(a) a

► **psych(e) out** *vt sep Fam (sense)* entender, *Arg* cazar la onda de

► **psych(e) up** *vt sep Fam* **to p. sb up** mentalizar a alguien; **to p. oneself up (for sth)** mentalizarse (para algo)

psyche ['saɪkɪ] *n* psique *f*, psiquis *f inv*

psychedelia [saɪkə'di:lɪə] *npl* psicodelia *f*

psychedelic [saɪkə'delɪk] *adj* psicodélico(a)

psychiatric [saɪkɪ'ætrɪk] *adj* psiquiátrico(a) ▸▸ ***p. hospital*** sanatorio *m* psiquiátrico

psychiatrist [saɪ'kaɪətrɪst] *n* psiquiatra *mf*

psychiatry [saɪ'kaɪətrɪ] *n* psiquiatría *f*

psychic ['saɪkɪk] **1** *n* médium *mf inv*
2 *adj (phenomena, experiences)* paranormal, extrasensorial; *(person)* vidente; **to be p., to have p. powers** tener poderes paranormales; *Fam* **I'm not p.!** ¡no soy un adivino!

psycho ['saɪkəʊ] (*pl* **psychos**) *n Fam (crazy person)* psicópata *mf*

psychoactive ['saɪkəʊ'æktɪv] *adj* psicotrópico(a)

psychoanalyse, *US* **psychoanalyze** ['saɪkəʊ'ænəlaɪz] *vt* psicoanalizar

psychoanalysis ['saɪkəʊə'nælɪsɪs] *n* psicoanálisis *m inv*; **to undergo p.** hacer psicoanálisis *or Arg* terapia; **he spent five years in p.** hizo cinco años de psicoanálisis

psychoanalyst ['saɪkəʊ'ænəlɪst] *n* psicoanalista *mf*

psychoanalytic(al) ['saɪkəʊænə'lɪtɪk(əl)] *adj* psicoanalítico(a)

psychoanalyze *US* = **psychoanalyse**

psychobabble ['saɪkəʊbæbəl] *n Fam* frases *fpl* vacías pseudopsicológicas

psychodrama ['saɪkəʊdrɑːmə] *n Psy* psicodrama *m*

psychokinesis [saɪkəʊkɪ'niːsɪs] *n* psicoquinesia *f*

psycholinguistic ['saɪkəʊlɪŋ'gwɪstɪk] *adj* psicolingüístico(a)

psycholinguistics ['saɪkəʊlɪŋ'gwɪstɪks] *n* psicolingüística *f*

psychological ['saɪkə'lɒdʒɪkəl] *adj* psicológico(a) ▸▸ ***p. block:*** **I have a p. block about driving** conducir me produce un bloqueo psicológico; ***p. moment*** momento *m* psicológico; ***p. warfare*** guerra *f* psicológica

psychologically ['saɪkə'lɒdʒɪklɪ] *adv* psicológicamente; **inflation has fallen below the p. important 5 percent level** la inflación ha caído por debajo del nivel psicológicamente importante del 5 por ciento

psychologist [saɪ'kɒlədʒɪst] *n* psicólogo(a) *m,f*

psychology [saɪ'kɒlədʒɪ] *n* (**a**) *(discipline)* psicología *f* (**b**) *(mental processes)* psicología *f*; **I understand her p. better than most people** comprendo mejor que nadie su forma de pensar (**c**) *(for influencing people)* psicología *f*; **it would be good/bad p. to tell them** sería/no sería muy acertado decírselo

psychometric ['saɪkə'metrɪk] *adj* **p. test** prueba psicométrica

psychometrics [saɪkəʊ'metrɪks] *n* psicometría *f*

psychomotor ['saɪkəʊ'məʊtə(r)] *adj* psicomotor

psychopath ['saɪkəʊpæθ] *n* psicópata *mf*

psychopathic ['saɪkəʊ'pæθɪk] *adj* psicopático(a)

psychopathology ['saɪkəʊpə'θɒlədʒɪ] *n* psicopatología *f*

psychopathy [saɪ'kɒpəθɪ] *n* psicopatía *f*

psychopharmacology ['saɪkəʊfɑːmə'kɒlədʒɪ] *n* psicofarmacología *f*

psychosexual ['saɪkəʊ'sekʃʊəl] *adj* psicosexual

psychosis [saɪ'kəʊsɪs] (*pl* **psychoses** [saɪ'kəʊsiːz]) *n* psicosis *f inv*

psychosocial ['saɪkəʊ'səʊʃəl] *adj* psicosocial

psychosomatic ['saɪkəʊsə'mætɪk] *adj* psicosomático(a)

psychotherapeutic ['saɪkəʊθerə'pjuːtɪk] *adj* psicoterapeuta

psychotherapist ['saɪkəʊ'θerəpɪst] *n* psicoterapeuta *mf*

psychotherapy ['saɪkəʊ'θerəpɪ] *n* psicoterapia *f*

psychotic [saɪ'kɒtɪk] **1** *n* psicótico(a) *m,f*
2 *adj* psicótico(a)

psychotropic [saɪkəʊ'trɒpɪk] *adj* psicotrópico(a) ▸▸ ***p. drug*** psicofármaco *m*

PT [piː'tiː] *n* (*abbr* **physical training**) educación *f* física

pt (*abbr* **pint**) pinta *f*

PTA [piːtiː'eɪ] *n Sch* (*abbr* **Parent-Teacher Association**) = asociación de padres de alumnos y profesores, ≃ APA *f*

ptarmigan ['tɑːmɪgən] *n* perdiz *f* nival, lagópodo *m* alpino

PT boat [piː'tiːbəʊt] *n US* lancha *f* torpedera

Pte *Br Mil* (*abbr* **private**) soldado *m* raso

pterodactyl [terə'dæktɪl] *n* pterodáctilo *m*

PTO [piːtiː'əʊ] (*abbr* **please turn over**) sigue

Ptolemaic [tɒlə'meɪɪk] *adj* tolemaico(a), tolomaico(a); **the P. system** el sistema tolemaico *or* tolomaico

Ptolemy ['tɒləmɪ] *pr n* Tolomeo

ptomaine [təʊ'meɪn] *n Chem* ptomaína *f*

ptyalin ['taɪəlɪn] *n Biol* tialina *f*, ptialina *f*

PU ['piː'juː] *exclam US Fam* ¡uf!

pub [pʌb] *n Br* pub *m*, = típico bar de las Islas Británicas donde a veces se sirve comida además de bebidas alcohólicas ▸▸ *Fam* ***p. crawl:*** **to go on a p.** ir de copas; *Fam* ***p. grub*** comida *f* de pub; ***p. quiz*** = concurso de preguntas y respuestas que se celebra regularmente en algunos pubs británicos y en el que participan varios equipos

pube [pjuːb] *n Fam* pelo *m* púbico

puberty ['pjuːbətɪ] *n* pubertad *f*; **to reach p.** alcanzar la pubertad

pubes [pjuːbz] *npl* (**a**) *(area)* pubis *m inv* (**b**) *Fam (hair)* vello *m* púbico

pubescent [pjuː'besənt] *adj* pubescente

pubic ['pjuːbɪk] *adj* púbico(a), pubiano(a) ▸▸ ***p. bone*** hueso *m* púbico *or* pubiano; ***p. hair*** vello *m* púbico *or* pubiano; ***p. louse*** ladilla *f*

pubis ['pjuːbɪs] *n Anat* pubis *m inv*

public ['pʌblɪk] **1** *n* **the (general) p.** el público en general, el gran público; **the film-going p.** el público que acude al cine; **the viewing p.** los telespectadores; **in p.** en público
2 *adj* (**a**) *(of, for people in general)* público(a); **p. awareness of the problem has increased** el público en general tiene cada vez más conciencia del problema; **the bill has wide p. support** el proyecto cuenta con un gran apoyo popular; **in the p. interest** en favor del interés general; **p. interest in the matter was flagging** el interés del público por el asunto iba decayendo; IDIOM **to be in the p. eye** estar expuesto(a) a la opinión pública ▸▸ ***p. address system*** (sistema *m* de) megafonía *f*; *Br* ***p. bar*** = en ciertos "pubs" y hoteles, bar de decoración más sencilla que la del "lounge bar"; *Br* ***p. call box*** cabina *f* telefónica; *Br* ***p. convenience*** servicios *mpl or Esp* aseos *mpl* públicos; ***p. enemy*** enemigo(a) *m,f* público(a); ***p. enemy number one*** el enemigo público número uno; ***p. footpath*** sendero *m or* camino *m* público; ***the p. gallery*** *(in Parliament)* la tribuna de invitados *or* del público; ***p. holiday*** día *m* festivo, *Am* día *m* feriado; *Br* ***p. house*** = típico bar de las Islas Británicas donde a veces se sirve comida además de bebidas alcohólicas; ***p. image*** imagen *f* pública; *Br* ***p. lavatory*** servicios *mpl or Esp* aseos *mpl* públicos; *Br* ***p. lending right*** = derechos que recibe un autor cada vez que una obra suya es prestada en una biblioteca pública; ***p. library*** biblioteca *f* pública; ***p. nuisance*** *Law* alteración *f* del orden público; *Fam (annoying person)* pesado(a) *m,f*, petardo(a) *m,f*; ***p. opinion*** la opinión pública; ***p. opinion poll*** sondeo *m or* encuesta *f* de opinión pública; ***p. relations*** relaciones *fpl* públicas; **it's all just a p. relations exercise** es sólo una operación de relaciones públicas; ***p. relations officer*** encargado(a) *m,f* de relaciones públicas; ***p. safety*** seguridad *f* ciudadana; ***p. school*** *Br* colegio *m* privado; *US* colegio *m* público; ***p. transport*** transporte *m* público; *Com* ***p. utility*** (empresa *f* de) servicio *m* público
(**b**) *(of the state, local authorities)* público(a); **at p. expense** con dinero público ▸▸ *US* ***p. assistance*** ayudas *fpl* estatales; ***p. body*** ente *m or* organismo *m* estatal; *US Law* ***p. defender*** abogado(a) *m,f* de oficio; *Com* ***p. enterprise*** empresa *f* pública; ***p. examination*** examen *m* abierto; ***p. expenditure*** gasto *m* público; ***p. funds*** fondos *mpl* públicos; ***p. health*** salud *f* pública; *Br Formerly* ***p. health inspector*** inspector(ora) *m,f* de sanidad; ***p. international law*** derecho *m* internacional público; ***p. office*** cargo *m* público; **to hold p. office** tener un cargo público; ***p. ownership*** propiedad *f* pública; ***p. property*** bienes *mpl* públicos; *Law* ***p. prosecutor*** fiscal *mf* (del Estado); *Br* ***the p. purse*** el erario *or* tesoro público; ***P. Record Office*** = oficina británica de registros públicos; ***p. sector*** sector *m* público; ***p. sector firm*** empresa *f* pública; ***p. servant*** funcionario(a) *m,f*; ***p. service*** *(public administration)* administración *f* pública; *(amenity)* servicio *f* público; **our organization performs a p. service** nuestra organización presta un servicio público; ***p. services*** servicios *mpl* públicos; ***p. spending*** gasto *m* público; ***p. works*** obras *fpl* públicas
(**c**) *(not secret, restricted)* público(a); **let's talk somewhere less p.** vamos a hablar a algún sitio más privado; **to go p. with sth** *(reveal information)* revelar públicamente algo; **to make sth p.** hacer público(a) algo; **to make a p. appearance** hacer *or* efectuar una aparición pública; **it's p. knowledge that...** todo el mundo sabe que...; **it created a p. scandal** generó un escándalo público ▸▸ *US* ***p. access television*** = sistema de televisión que permite a sus usuarios emitir sus propios programas; *also Comptr* ***p. domain*** dominio *m* público; **to be in the p. domain** ser del dominio público; *Comptr* ***p. domain software*** software *m* de dominio público; ***a p. figure*** un hombre público; ***p. hearing*** audiencia *f* pública; ***p. inquiry*** investigación *f (de puertas abiertas)*; ***p. life*** la vida pública; **the contrast between his p. and his private life** el contraste existente entre su vida pública y su vida privada; ***p. room*** *(in hotel, institution)* recepción *f*; ***p. speaking*** oratoria *f*
(**d**) *Com* **to go p.** *(company)* pasar a cotizar en Bolsa ▸▸ ***p. (limited) company*** sociedad *f* anónima

publican ['pʌblɪkən] *n* (a) *Br* = dueño/encargado de un "pub" (b) *Hist (tax collector)* publicano *m*

publication [pʌblɪ'keɪʃən] *n* publicación *f*; **this isn't for p.** esto no es oficial; **on p.** en el momento de la publicación ▸▸ ***p. date*** fecha *f* de publicación

publicist ['pʌblɪsɪst] *n (press agent)* publicista *mf*

publicity [pʌb'lɪsɪtɪ] *n* (a) *(interest, exposure)* publicidad *f*; **to get** *or* **attract a lot of p.** conseguir mucha publicidad, despertar mucho interés; PROV **there's no such thing as bad p.** no hay publicidad que no sirva ▸▸ ***p. stunt*** artimaña *f* publicitaria

(b) *(advertising material, activity)* publicidad *f* ▸▸ ***p. campaign*** campaña *f* publicitaria *or* de publicidad; ***p. manager*** gerente *m* de publicidad; *Cin* ***p. still*** foto *f* publicitaria

publicize ['pʌblɪsaɪz] *vt* (a) *(make known)* dar a conocer; **a much publicized dispute** un enfrentamiento muy aireado por los medios de comunicación (b) *(advertise)* dar publicidad a; **the festival was well publicized** se hizo buena publicidad del festival

public-liability insurance ['pʌblɪklaɪə'bɪlɪtɪɪn'ʃʊərəns] *n Br* seguro *m* de responsabilidad civil

publicly ['pʌblɪklɪ] *adv* (a) *(in public)* públicamente; **it is not yet p. available** todavía no está a la disposición del público (b) *(by the State)* **p. owned** de titularidad pública

public-service ['pʌblɪk'sɜːvɪs] *adj* ***p. broadcasting*** servicio *m* público de radiodifusión; *US* ***p. corporation*** empresa *f* privada de servicios públicos; *Br* ***p. vehicle*** vehículo *m* de transporte público

public-spirited ['pʌblɪk'spɪrɪtɪd] *adj* cívico(a)

publish ['pʌblɪʃ] **1** *vt* (a) *(book, newspaper, web page)* publicar; **the magazine is published quarterly** la revista es de publicación trimestral (b) *(announce publicly)* proclamar a los cuatro vientos (c) *Law* **to p. a libel** publicar una difamación *or* un libelo

2 *vi* publicar; IDIOM **p. and be damned!: we're going to p. and be damned** vamos a publicar sin importarnos las consecuencias

publishable ['pʌblɪʃəbl] *adj* publicable

publisher ['pʌblɪʃə(r)] *n* (a) *(person)* editor(ora) *m,f* (b) *(company)* editorial *f* ▸▸ ***p.'s reader*** lector(ora) *m,f* de manuscritos (c) *US (newspaper owner)* propietario(a) *m,f* de (un) periódico

publishing ['pʌblɪʃɪŋ] *n* industria *f* editorial ▸▸ ***p. company*** editorial *f*; ***p. house*** editorial *f*

puce [pjuːs] **1** *n* morado *m*

2 *adj* morado(a)

puck [pʌk] *n (in ice hockey)* disco *m*, puck *m*

pucker ['pʌkə(r)] **1** *vt (face)* arrugar; *(forehead, fabric, collar)* fruncir, arrugar; **to p. one's lips** fruncir los labios

2 *vi (face, forehead)* arrugarse; *(lips)* fruncirse

3 *n (crease)* arruga *f*, frunce *m*

▸ **pucker up** *vi Fam (for kiss)* fruncir los labios

puckish ['pʌkɪʃ] *adj* pícaro(a)

pud [pʊd] *n Br Fam* (a) *(dessert)* postre *m*; **what's for p.?** ¿qué hay de postre? (b) *(dish) (sweet)* budín *m*, pudín *m*; *(savoury)* pastel *m*, *Col, CSur* torta *f*

pudding ['pʊdɪŋ] *n* (a) *Br (dessert)* postre *m*; **what's for p.?** ¿qué hay de postre? (b) *(dish) (sweet)* budín *m*, pudín *m*; *(savoury)* pastel *m*, *Col, CSur* torta *f* ▸▸ ***p. basin*** bol *m*; ***p. basin haircut*** corte *m* de pelo estilo tazón; ***p. bowl*** bol *m*; ***p. rice*** arroz *m* de grano fino (c) IDIOM *Br Fam Hum* **to be in the p. club** estar con bombo (d) *Geol* ***p. stone*** pudinga *f*

puddle ['pʌdəl] *n* charco *m*; *Fam* **the dog's made a p. on the carpet** el perro ha orinado en la alfombra

puddling ['pʌdlɪŋ] *n (of iron)* pudelación *f*

pudenda [pjuː'dendə] *npl Formal* partes *fpl* pudendas

pudgy ['pʌdʒɪ] *adj* rechoncho(a), regordete(a)

puerile ['pjʊəraɪl] *adj Pej* pueril, infantil

puerility [pjʊə'rɪlətɪ] *n Pej* puerilidad *f*, infantilismo *m*

puerperal [pjuː'ɜːpərəl] *adj Med* puerperal ▸▸ ***p. fever*** fiebre *f* puerperal; ***p. psychosis*** psicosis *f* puerperal

Puerto Rican ['pweətəʊ'riːkən] **1** *n* portorriqueño(a) *m,f*, puertorriqueño(a) *m,f*

2 *adj* portorriqueño(a), puertorriqueño(a)

Puerto Rico ['pweətəʊ'riːkəʊ] *n* Puerto Rico

puff [pʌf] **1** *n* (a) *(of breath)* bocanada *f*; *Br Fam* **to be out of p.** resoplar, estar sin aliento

(b) *(of air)* soplo *m*; *(of smoke)* nube *f*; IDIOM **all our plans went up in a p. of smoke** todos nuestros planes se quedaron en agua de borrajas

(c) *(of cigarette)* chupada *f*, *Esp* calada *f*, *Am* pitada *f*; **to have** *or* **take a p. (on** *or* **at)** dar una chupada *or Esp* calada *or Am* pitada (a)

(d) *(sound) (of train)* pitido *m*

(e) *(for make-up)* **(powder) p.** borla *f* (de maquillaje)

(f) *US (eiderdown)* edredón *m*

(g) *Fam (free publicity)* **to give sth a p.** hacer publicidad a algo (gratuitamente), hacer propaganda (gratuita) de algo

(h) *Br Fam (homosexual)* maricón *m*, marica *m*

(i) *Culin* pastelito *m or* dulce *m* de hojaldre ▸▸ *US* ***p. paste*** hojaldre *m*; ***p. pastry*** hojaldre *m* (j) *Zool* ***p. adder*** = especie de víbora silbadora africana

2 *vt* (a) *(pant)* **"I can't go on," he puffed** "no puedo seguir", resopló (b) *(emit)* **to p. (out) smoke/steam** echar humo/vapor; **to p. smoke into sb's face** echar una bocanada de humo a la cara de alguien (c) *(cigar, pipe)* dar chupadas *or Esp* caladas *or Am* pitadas a (d) *(swell) (sail, parachute)* inflar

3 *vi* (a) *(person)* resoplar, jadear (b) *(smoke, steam)* salir (c) *(smoke)* **to p. on** *or* **at a cigarette/pipe** dar chupadas *or Esp* caladas *or Am* pitadas a un cigarrillo/una pipa (d) **to p. along** *(steam engine)* avanzar echando humo

▸ **puff out** *vt sep* (a) *(inflate) (cheeks, chest)* inflar, hinchar; **the pigeon puffed out its feathers** la paloma erizó las plumas (b) *Br Fam (exhaust)* **I'm puffed (out)!** ¡estoy muerto!, ¡estoy rendido!

▸ **puff up** *vt sep (cheeks)* inflar, hinchar; **her eyes were puffed up** tenía los ojos hinchados; IDIOM **he was puffed up with pride** no cabía en sí de orgullo

Puffa jacket® ['pʌfə'dʒækɪt] *n* chaqueta *f* de rapero

puffball ['pʌfbɔːl] *n* (a) *(fungus)* bejín *m*, pedo *m* de lobo (b) ***p. skirt*** falda *f or RP* pollera *f* abullonada

puffed [pʌft] *adj* (a) *(rice, wheat)* inflado(a) (b) *(clothing)* ***p. sleeves*** mangas *fpl* abullonadas

puffed-up ['pʌft'ʌp] *adj* (a) *(inflated, swollen)* hinchado(a) (b) *(arrogant)* engreído(a)

puffer ['pʌfə(r)] *n* (a) **p. (fish)** pez *m* globo (b) *Br Fam (train)* tren *m* de vapor (c) *Scot Fam (boat)* barca *f* de vapor

puffin ['pʌfɪn] *n* frailecillo *m*

puffiness ['pʌfɪnɪs] *n* hinchazón *f*

puff-puff ['pʌfpʌf] *n Fam (in baby talk) (train)* chucuchú *m*

puffy ['pʌfɪ] *adj* hinchado(a)

pug [pʌg] *n (dog)* doguillo *m* ▸▸ ***p. nose*** *(of person)* nariz *f* de cerdito

pugilism ['pjuːdʒɪlɪzəm] *n Formal* pugilismo *m*

pugilist ['pjuːdʒɪlɪst] *n Formal* púgil *m*

pugnacious [pʌg'neɪʃəs] *adj Formal* pugnaz

pugnaciously [pʌg'neɪʃəslɪ] *adv Formal* combativamente

pugnacity [pʌg'næsɪtɪ] *n Formal* pugnacidad *f*

pug-nosed ['pʌg'nəʊzd] *adj (person)* con nariz de cerdito

puke [pjuːk] *Fam* **1** *n* papa *f*, vomitona *f*

2 *vt* devolver

3 *vi* echar la papa, devolver; **you make me p.!** ¡me das asco!

▸ **puke up 1** *vt sep* vomitar, devolver

2 *vi* vomitar, devolver

pukey ['pjuːkɪ] *adj Fam* vomitivo(a)

pukka ['pʌkə] *adj Br Fam* (a) *(posh)* de clase alta (b) *(genuine, proper)* como Dios manda (c) *(excellent)* de primera

pulchritude ['pʌlkrɪtjuːd] *n Literary* belleza *f*, hermosura *f*

Pulitzer ['pʊlɪtsər] *n* **the P. (prize)** el (premio) Pulitzer

PULL [pʊl] **1** *n* (a) *(act of pulling)* tirón *m*, *Andes, CAm, Carib, Méx* jalón *m*; *(of water current)* fuerza *f*; **to give sth a p.** dar un tirón *or Andes, CAm, Carib, Méx* jalón a algo; **he felt a p. at** *or* **on his sleeve** notó que le tiraban de la manga; **the Earth's gravitational p.** la atracción gravitatoria de la Tierra; **the p. of the current** la fuerza de la corriente

(b) *(on curtains, blinds)* cordón *m*, cuerda *f*

(c) *(drink)* **to take a p. at a bottle** echar un trago de una botella

(d) *(on cigarette, pipe)* chupada *f*, *Esp* calada *f*, *Am* pitada *f*; **to take a p. at** *or* **on** *(drink, bottle)* dar un trago a; *(cigarette, pipe)* dar una chupada *or Esp* calada a

(e) *(climb, effort)* **it was a long p. to the summit** quedaba un largo ascenso hasta la cima; **it's going to be a long uphill p. to make the firm profitable** se nos va a hacer muy cuesta arriba conseguir que la empresa sea rentable

(f) *Fam (influence)* influencia *f*, peso *m*; **to have a lot of p.** ser muy influyente, ser de peso

(g) *Fam (attraction)* tirón *m*, *RP* arrastre *m*; **the p. of city life** la atracción *or* el tirón de la vida urbana (**h**) *Br Fam (sexually)* **to be on the p.** estar de ligue *or RP, Ven* de levante

2 *vt* (**a**) *(tug)* tirar de; *(drag)* arrastrar; *(gun trigger)* apretar; **she pulled my hair** me tiró del pelo; **they pulled the box across the floor** arrastraron la caja por el suelo; **to p. sth/sb away from sth** apartar algo/a alguien de algo; **they pulled him free of the wreckage** lo sacaron de entre los hierros retorcidos; **p. the table nearer the door** acerca la mesa a la puerta; **to p. sth open/shut** abrir/cerrar algo de un tirón *or Andes, CAm, Carib, Méx* jalón; **to p. the curtains** *or US* **drapes** descorrer las cortinas; **to p. a lever** tirar de *or* accionar una palanca; **to p. a rope tight** tensar una cuerda; **to p. a knot tight** apretar un nudo; *also Fig* **to p. sth to bits** *or* **pieces** hacer algo añicos

(**b**) *(attract)* atraer; **to p. the crowds** atraer a las masas, arrastrar multitudes

(**c**) *(extract) (tooth, cork)* sacar; **she pulled a book off the shelf** tomó *or Esp* cogió *or Am* agarró un libro de la estantería; **to p. a pint** tirar *or* servir una cerveza (de barril); **to p. a gun on sb** sacar una pistola *or* un revólver y apuntar a alguien

(**d**) *(injure)* **to p. a muscle** sufrir un tirón en un músculo

(**e**) *Fam (withdraw)* retirar

(**f**) *Br Fam (sexually)* ligarse a, *RP, Ven* levantarse a

(**g**) IDIOMS *Fam* **to p. a bank job** atracar un banco; **to p. a face** hacer una mueca; *Fam* **to p. sb's leg** tomarle el pelo a alguien; *US Fam* **to p. the pin** jubilarse; *Br Fam* **to p. the plug on sth** acabar con algo; **he didn't p. his punches** no tuvo pelos en la lengua, se despachó a gusto; **she pulled rank on him** le recordó quién mandaba (allí); **to p. strings** mover hilos; *Fam* **talking to her is like pulling teeth** hay que sacarle las cosas con sacacorchos; **she's not pulling her weight** no arrima el hombro (como los demás); *Fam* **to p. a fast one on sb** hacer una jugarreta *or* engañar a alguien; *Fam* **what is he trying to p.?** ¿qué es lo que busca?; **p. the other one (it's got bells on)!** ¡no me vengas con ésas!, *Esp* ¡a otro perro con ese hueso!, *Méx* ¡no mames!

3 *vi* (**a**) *(tug)* tirar, *Andes, CAm, Carib, Méx* jalar (**at** *or* **on** de); **P.** *(sign)* tirar, tire, *Andes, CAm, Carib, Méx* jalar, jale

(**b**) *(move)* **to p. clear of sth** dejar algo atrás; **to p. to the right/left** desviarse hacia la derecha/izquierda; **the steering pulls to the right** la dirección se desvía hacia la derecha; **to p. to a halt** *or* **stop** ir parándose *or* deteniéndose

(**c**) *(row)* **to p. for shore** remar hacia la orilla

(**d**) *Fam (exert influence, give support)* **the head of personnel is pulling for you** el jefe de personal te está echando un cable

(**e**) *Br Fam (sexually)* ligar, *RP, Ven* levantar

▸**pull about** *vt sep (handle roughly)* zarandear, maltratar

▸**pull ahead** *vi (in race, election)* tomar la delantera, ponerse en cabeza; **he pulled ahead of his opponents** se adelantó a sus adversarios

▸**pull apart 1** *vt sep* (**a**) *(separate)* separar (**b**) *also Fig (tear to pieces)* hacer trizas

2 *vi (furniture, parts)* desmontarse; **the shelves simply p. apart** las estanterías se desmontan sin herramientas

▸**pull at** *vt insep (cigarette, pipe)* dar una chupada *or Esp* calada *or Am* pitada a; *(bottle)* dar un (buen) trago a

▸**pull away 1** *vi (from station)* alejarse; *(from kerb, embrace)* apartarse; **he pulled away from the rest of the field** se fue escapando del resto de participantes

2 *vt sep* apartar

▸**pull back 1** *vt sep (curtains)* descorrer; *(troops)* retirar; **p. the lever back** acciona la palanca

2 *vi (person)* echarse atrás; *(troops)* retirarse; *Fig* **to p. back from doing sth** echarse atrás a la hora de hacer algo

▸**pull down** *vt sep* (**a**) *(blinds)* bajar; *Comptr (menu)* desplegar; **p. down your trousers** bájate los pantalones (**b**) *(demolish)* demoler, derribar (**c**) *US Fam (earn)* sacar

▸**pull in 1** *vt sep* (**a**) *(rope, fishing line)* recoger; **to p. sb in** *(into building, car)* hacer entrar a alguien; **she pulled him in and he nearly drowned** lo metió en el agua tirando de él y casi se ahoga; **to p. sb in for questioning** detener a alguien para interrogarlo; **to p. one's stomach in** meter barriga (**b**) *Fam (money)* sacar (**c**) *(attract)* atraer

2 *vi (car)* pararse a un lado; *(train, bus)* llegar

▸**pull into** *vt insep (of train)* llegar a; **we pulled into an empty parking space** estacionamos *or Esp* aparcamos en un espacio libre

▸**pull off 1** *vt sep* (**a**) *(remove)* quitar, *Am* sacar; **she pulled the covers off the bed** quitó *or Am* sacó la cubierta de la cama; **she pulled off her T-shirt** se quitó *or Am* se sacó la camiseta (**b**) *Fam (succeed in doing)* conseguir; **he pulled it off** lo consiguió (**c**) *Vulg (masturbate)* hacer una *or Am* la paja a; **to p. oneself off** hacerse una *or Am* la paja

2 *vi (leave main road)* desviarse; *(stop)* parar

▸**pull on 1** *vt insep (cigarette, pipe)* dar una chupada *or Esp* calada *o Am* pitada a

2 *vt sep (clothes)* **she pulled on her T-shirt** se puso la camiseta

▸**pull out 1** *vt sep (remove)* sacar; *(tooth)* sacar, arrancar; *(drawer)* abrir; *(troops)* retirar; **he pulled a page out of his notebook** arrancó una página de su libreta; **she pulled herself out of the pool** salió de la piscina impulsándose con los brazos; **to p. the country out of recession** sacar al país de la recesión; IDIOM **they pulled a surprise victory out of the bag** *or* **hat** se sacaron de la manga una sorprendente victoria

2 *vi* (**a**) *(train)* salir; **a taxi pulled out in front of us** un taxi se metió justo delante de nosotros; **he pulled out into the stream of traffic** se incorporó al tráfico; **to p. out of a dive** salir de *Esp* un picado *or Am* una picada; *Fig* **we're pulling out of the recession** estamos superando la recesión (**b**) *(from race, agreement)* retirarse (**of** de); **British troops are pulling out of the region** las tropas británicas se están retirando de la región (**c**) *(extend)* **the table pulls out** la mesa se abre; **the sofa pulls out into a bed** el sofá se convierte en una cama

▸**pull over 1** *vt sep* (**a**) *(draw closer)* acercar; **the police pulled me over** me paró la policía (**b**) *(make fall)* tirar

2 *vi (driver)* parar en *Esp* el arcén *or Chile* la berma *or Méx* el acotamiento *or RP* la banquina *or Ven* el hombrillo

▸**pull round** *Br* **1** *vt sep (revive)* reanimar

2 *vi (regain consciousness)* recuperar la consciencia; *(recover)* reponerse

▸**pull through 1** *vt insep (recover from) (illness)* recuperarse de; *(crisis)* superar

2 *vt sep (help to recover)* **my friends pulled me through (the divorce)** mis amigos me ayudaron a recuperarme (del divorcio)

3 *vi (recover) (from illness)* recuperarse; *(from crisis)* salir adelante

▸**pull to** *vt sep (door, gate)* cerrar

▸**pull together 1** *vt sep (facts, ideas)* reunir; **to p. oneself together** serenarse; **p. yourself together!** ¡cálmate!

2 *vi* juntar esfuerzos

▸**pull up 1** *vt sep* (**a**) *(move closer) (chair)* acercar

(**b**) *(draw upwards)* **they pulled the boat up onto the beach** tiraron de la barca hasta dejarla en la playa; **he pulled his trousers up** se subió los pantalones; **he pulled himself up the rope** subió por la cuerda; IDIOM **to p. one's socks up** espabilar

(**c**) *(stop)* **to p. sb up (short)** parar a alguien en seco

(**d**) *(weeds)* arrancar, quitar, *Am* sacar; *(floorboards)* levantar, quitar, *Am* sacar

(**e**) *Fam (criticize)* regañar, reñir, *Am* rezongar (**over** *or* **on** por)

(**f**) *Fam (improve) (score, average)* hacer subir

2 *vi* (**a**) *(stop) (car)* parar; *(athlete, horse)* abandonar; **to p. up short** detenerse de repente (**b**) *(draw level)* **the police pulled up alongside them** la policía se puso a su altura

---

pullback ['pʊlbæk] *n Mil* retirada *f*

pull-down menu ['pʊldaʊn'menju:] *n Comptr* menú *m* desplegable

pullet ['pʊlɪt] *n* polla *f*, gallina *f* joven

pulley ['pʊlɪ] *n* polea *f*, motón *m* ▸▸ ***p. block*** polea *f*

pull-in ['pʊlɪn] *n Br (café)* café-restaurante *m* de carretera

pulling power ['pʊlɪŋ'paʊə(r)] *n Fam (of star, attraction)* gancho *m*; *Br (sexual)* tirón *m* sexual, *RP* arrastre *m*

Pullman ['pʊlmən] *n Rail* ***P. (car)*** coche *m* pullman

pull-off ['pʊlɒf] *n US Aut* área *f* de descanso

pull-out ['pʊlaʊt] *n* (**a**) *(in newspaper, magazine)* suplemento *m* (**b**) *(withdrawal)* retirada *f*

pullover ['pʊləʊvə(r)] *n* suéter *m*, *Esp* jersey *m*, *Col* saco *m*, *RP* pulóver *m*

pullulate ['pʌljʊleɪt] *vi Literary (teem)* pulular, abundar

pull-up ['pʊlʌp] *n (exercise)* flexión *f (colgando de una barra con los brazos)*

pulmonary ['pʌlmənərɪ] *adj Anat* pulmonar ▸▸ ***p. artery*** arteria *f* pulmonar; ***p. oedema*** edema *m* pulmonar; ***p. vein*** vena *f* pulmonar

pulp [pʌlp] **1** *n* (**a**) *(of fruit)* pulpa *f*, carne *f* (**b**) *(for paper)* pulpa *f*, pasta *f* (**c**) *(in tooth)* pulpa *f* (**d**) *(mush)* **to reduce sth to (a) p.** reducir algo a (una) pasta; *Fam* **to beat sb to a p.** hacer picadillo *or* papilla a alguien (**e**) *(cheap fiction)* **p. (fiction)** literatura *f* barata *or* de baja estofa, novelas *fpl* de tiros; **p. (magazine)** revista *f* barata, revistucha *f*

2 *vt* (**a**) *(crush) (fruit, vegetables)* triturar (**b**) *(remove pulp from) (fruit)* extraer la pulpa de (**c**) *(books)* hacer pasta de papel con; **all copies had to be pulped** todas los ejemplares tuvieron que ser destruidas

pulpit ['pʊlpɪt] *n* púlpito *m*

pulpy ['pʌlpɪ] *adj* (**a**) *(fruit, tissue)* carnoso(a) (**b**) *Pej (novel, magazine)* malo(a)

pulsar ['pʌlsɑː(r)] *n Astron* púlsar *m*

pulsate [pʌl'seɪt] *vi* (**a**) *(throb) (heart)* palpitar; *(music, room)* vibrar; **pulsating rhythms** ritmos palpitantes (**b**) *(light)* brillar intermitentemente

pulsation [pʌl'seɪʃən] *n* pulsación *f*

pulse[1] [pʌls] **1** *n* (**a**) *(of blood)* pulso *m*; **her p. (rate) is a hundred** su pulso está en cien; **his p. quickened when he saw her** se le aceleró el pulso al verla; **to feel** *or* **take sb's p.** tomar el pulso a alguien; IDIOM **to have one's finger on the p.** estar al corriente de lo que pasa (**b**) *(of light, sound)* impulso *m* (**c**) *(bustle, life)* ritmo *m*
2 *vi* (**a**) *(blood, vein)* latir (**b**) *(throb) (music, room)* vibrar

pulse[2] *n (pea, bean, lentil)* legumbre *f*

pulse[3] *n Tel* pulso *m*

pulverize ['pʌlvəraɪz] *vt* pulverizar; *Fam Fig* **to p. sb** *(beat up, defeat heavily)* dar una paliza a alguien

puma ['pjuːmə] *n* puma *m*, león *m* americano

pumice ['pʌmɪs] *n* **p. (stone)** piedra *f* pómez

pummel ['pʌməl] *(pt & pp* **pummelled,** *US* **pummeled)** *vt* aporrear

pump[1] [pʌmp] *n* (**a**) *(flat shoe)* zapato *m* de salón (**b**) *(ballet shoe)* zapatilla *f* de ballet (**c**) *Br (plimsoll)* playera *f*

pump[2] **1** *n* (**a**) *(for liquid, gas, air)* bomba *f* (**b**) *(at petrol station)* surtidor *m* ►► ***p. attendant*** = encargado(a) de los surtidores de una gasolinera
2 *vt* (**a**) *(liquid, gas, air)* bombear; **to p. water into sth** introducir agua en algo bombeando; **to p. water out of sth** sacar agua de algo bombeando; **to p. sb's stomach** hacer un lavado de estómago a alguien; *Fig* **to p. money into sth** inyectar una gran cantidad de dinero en algo; *Fig* **to p. bullets into sth/sb** acribillar a balazos algo/a alguien
(**b**) *(move back and forth)* **p. the brakes or they'll lock** pisa el freno repetidamente para que no se bloquee; **p. the handle to get it started** mueve la palanca de arriba abajo para que arranque
(**c**) IDIOMS *Fam* **to p. sb for information** sonsacar a alguien; **to p. sb's hand** dar un enérgico apretón de manos a alguien; *Fam* **to p. iron** *(do weightlifting)* hacer pesas
3 *vi* (**a**) *(heart, machine)* bombear (**b**) *(liquid)* brotar

► **pump out** *vt sep (music, information)* emitir

► **pump up** *vt sep* (**a**) *(tyre)* inflar (**b**) *Fam (volume)* subir (**c**) *US Fam (excite)* **to be all pumped up** estar entusiasmado(a)

pump-action shotgun ['pʌmpækʃən'ʃɒtgʌn] *n* escopeta *f* (de) corredera

pumpernickel ['pʌmpənɪkəl] *n* pan *m* integral de centeno

pumpkin ['pʌmpkɪn] *n* calabaza *f*, *Andes, RP* zapallo *m*, *Col, Carib* auyama *f*

pumpkinseed ['pʌmpkɪnsiːd] *n* (**a**) *(seed)* semilla *f* de calabaza *or Andes, RP* zapallo *or Col, Carib* auyama (**b**) *(fish)* perca *f* sol

pun [pʌn] **1** *n* juego *m* de palabras
2 *vi* hacer un juego de palabras

Punch [pʌntʃ] *n* (**a**) *Theat* polichinela *f* (**b**) **(Mr) P.** = personaje principal del espectáculo de títeres, caracterizado por su joroba y por golpear a todo el mundo con una cachiporra ►► ***P. and Judy show*** = espectáculo de títeres de la cachiporra representado en una feria o junto al mar

punch[1] [pʌntʃ] **1** *n* (**a**) *(blow)* puñetazo *m*; IDIOM **he didn't pull his punches** no tuvo pelos en la lengua, se despachó a gusto (**b**) *(tool)* punzón *m*; **(ticket) p.** canceladora *f* (**c**) *(energy)* garra *f* ►► ***p. line*** *(of joke)* final *m* del chiste, golpe *m*; **he had forgotten the p. line** había olvidado cómo acababa el chiste
2 *vt* (**a**) *(hit)* dar *or* pegar un puñetazo a; **to p. sb in the face/on the nose** pegarle a alguien un puñetazo en la cara/en la nariz (**b**) *(perforate) (metal)* perforar; *(ticket)* picar ►► *Comptr* ***punched card*** tarjeta *f* perforada

► **punch in 1** *vt sep* (**a**) *(enter) (figures, data)* introducir (**b**) *Fam (knock in)* **I'll p. your face in!** ¡te voy a partir la cara!; **he almost punched my teeth in** casi me hizo tragar los dientes (de un puñetazo)
2 *vi US (at work)* fichar *or Am* marcar tarjeta (a la entrada)

► **punch out 1** *vt sep* (**a**) *(cut out) (form, pattern)* perforar (**b**) *US Fam (beat up)* dar una tunda *or* paliza a
2 *vi US (at work)* fichar *or Am* marcar tarjeta (a la salida)

punch[2] *n (drink)* ponche *m* ►► ***p. bowl*** ponchera *f*

punch-bag ['pʌntʃbæg], *US* **punching bag** ['pʌntʃɪŋbæg] *n also Fig* saco *m* (de boxeo)

punchball ['pʌntʃbɔːl] *n* (**a**) *Br (equipment)* punching-ball *m* (**b**) *US (game)* = versión simplificada del béisbol que se juega generalmente en la calle con una pelota de tenis y sin bate

punch-drunk ['pʌntʃdrʌŋk] *adj (dazed)* aturdido(a); *(boxer)* sonado(a)

punching bag *US* = **punch-bag**

punching ball ['pʌntʃɪŋbɔːl] *n US* punching-ball *m*

punch-up ['pʌntʃʌp] *n Fam* pelea *f*; **they had a p.** se pelearon

punchy ['pʌntʃɪ] *adj Fam* (**a**) *(snappy)* con garra (**b**) *(dazed)* aturdido(a)

punctilious [pʌŋk'tɪlɪəs] *adj* puntilloso(a)

punctiliously [pʌŋk'tɪlɪəslɪ] *adv* de manera puntillosa

punctual ['pʌŋktjʊəl] *adj* puntual; **he's always p.** siempre es puntual

punctuality [pʌŋktjʊ'ælɪtɪ] *n* puntualidad *f*

punctually ['pʌŋktjʊəlɪ] *adv* puntualmente

punctuate ['pʌŋktjʊeɪt] **1** *vt* (**a**) *(sentence, writing)* puntuar (**b**) *Fig* **he punctuated his speech with anecdotes** salpicó su discurso de anécdotas; **her speech was punctuated with applause** su discurso se vio interrumpido en ocasiones por aplausos
2 *vi* puntuar

punctuation [pʌŋktjʊ'eɪʃən] *n* puntuación *f* ►► ***p. mark*** signo *m* de puntuación

puncture ['pʌŋktʃə(r)] **1** *n* (**a**) *(in tyre, ball)* pinchazo *m*, *Guat, Méx* ponchadura *f*; **to have a p.** tener un pinchazo *or Guat, Méx* una ponchadura ►► ***p. repair kit*** equipo *m* para reparar pinchazos *or Guat, Méx* ponchaduras (**b**) *(in skin)* punción *f* (**c**) *(in metal)* perforación *f*
2 *vt* (**a**) *(tyre, ball)* pinchar, *Guat, Méx* ponchar (**b**) *(metal, lung)* perforar (**c**) *(blister, abscess)* punzar (**d**) *(deflate) (pride, self-esteem)* minar, herir en; **to p. sb's ego** herir el ego de alguien

pundit ['pʌndɪt] *n* experto(a) *m,f*

pungency ['pʌndʒənsɪ] *n* (**a**) *(of smell, taste)* acritud *f* (**b**) *(of wit)* mordacidad *f*

pungent ['pʌndʒənt] *adj* (**a**) *(smell, taste)* acre (**b**) *(style, wit)* mordaz

puniness ['pjuːnɪnɪs] *n* debilidad *f*

punish ['pʌnɪʃ] *vt* (**a**) *(person, crime)* castigar; **to p. sb for doing sth** castigar a alguien por hacer algo (**b**) *Fam (opponent, enemy)* castigar; *(engine)* castigar, maltratar

punishable ['pʌnɪʃəbəl] *adj* punible; **this offence is p. by death** este delito es castigado con la pena de muerte

punishing ['pʌnɪʃɪŋ] **1** *n Fam* **to take a p.** *(opponent, enemy)* recibir una paliza
2 *adj (test, schedule)* penoso(a), exigente; *(climb, pace)* agotador(ora)

punishment ['pʌnɪʃmənt] *n* (**a**) *(for crime)* castigo *m*; **to make the p. fit the crime** hacer que el castigo guarde proporción con el delito; IDIOM **to take one's p. like a man** comportarse como un hombre
(**b**) *Fam (harsh treatment)* **to take a lot of p.** *(boxer)* recibir una paliza; *(clothing, furniture, equipment)* aguantar mucho trote; **the city took heavy p. from the enemy artillery** la artillería enemiga castigó duramente la ciudad

punitive ['pjuːnɪtɪv] *adj* (**a**) *(military expedition)* de castigo, punitivo(a) (**b**) *(rate of taxation, interest)* punitivo(a), gravoso(a); *Law (damages)* punitivos

Punjab ['pʌndʒɑːb] *n* **the P.** el Punyab

Punjabi [pʌn'dʒɑːbɪ] **1** *n* (**a**) *(person)* punyabí *mf* (**b**) *(language)* punyabí *m*
2 *adj* punyabí

punk [pʌŋk] **1** *n* (**a**) *(person)* **p. (rocker)** punk *mf*, punki *mf* (**b**) *(music)* **p. (rock)** (música *f*) punk *m* (**c**) *US Fam (contemptible person)* desgraciado(a) *m,f*; *(hoodlum)* vándalo(a) *m,f*, *Esp* gamberro(a) *m,f*, *RP* atorrante(a) *m,f*
2 *adj* (**a**) *(music, fashion, haircut)* punk *inv* (**b**) *US Fam (inferior)* pésimo(a), *Esp* fatal (**c**) *US Fam (ill)* **he's feeling kind of p.** anda medio mal

punky ['pʌŋkɪ] *adj* punki, punky

punnet ['pʌnɪt] *n Br* cestita *f (para fresas, bayas, etc)*

punt[1] [pʌnt] **1** *n* batea *f (impulsada con pértiga)* ►► ***p. pole*** pértiga *f (para bateas)*
2 *vi* **to go punting** pasear en batea *(por un río)*

punt[2] *n (in American football, rugby)* patada *f* larga de volea ►► ***p. return*** *(in American football)* = carrera de un jugador del equipo contrario tras capturar un "punt"

punt[3] [pʊnt] *n Formerly (Irish currency)* libra *f* irlandesa

punter ['pʌntə(r)] *n Br Fam* (**a**) *(gambler)* apostante *mf* (**b**) *(customer)* cliente *mf*; **the punters** *(the public)* el personal, el público; *(regulars in bar)* los parroquianos; **the average p.** *(man-in-the-street)* el tipo de la calle, *Esp* un tío normal (**c**) *(prostitute's client)* cliente *m*

puny ['pju:nɪ] *adj* (**a**) *(person, arm, leg)* enclenque, raquítico(a) (**b**) *(attempt, defence)* lamentable, penoso(a)

pup [pʌp] **1** *n* (**a**) *(of dog)* cachorro *m*; **to be in p.** *(bitch)* estar preñada; IDIOM *Fam* **to sell sb a p.** darle a alguien gato por liebre (**b**) *(of seal)* cría *f* (**c**) *Br Fam (youth)* mocoso(a) *m,f*; **you cheeky young p.!** ¡mocoso atrevido!
2 *vi* parir

pupa ['pju:pə] *(pl* **pupae** ['pju:pi:] *or* **pupas)** *n Zool* pupa *f*

pupate [pju:'peɪt] *vi Zool* transformarse en crisálida

pupil[1] ['pju:pəl] *n (student)* alumno(a) *m,f*; *(of painter, musician)* discípulo(a) *m,f*

pupil[2] *n (of eye)* pupila *f*

pupillage ['pju:pɪlɪdʒ] *n Br Law* pasantía *f*

puppet ['pʌpɪt] *n* (**a**) *(doll) (gen)* títere *m*; *(with strings)* marioneta *f*, títere *m* ►► ***p. show*** (espectáculo *m* de) guiñol *m* (**b**) *(person)* títere *m*, marioneta *f* ►► ***p. government*** gobierno *m* títere

puppeteer [pʌpɪ'tɪə(r)] *n* titiritero(a) *m,f*, marionetista *mf*

puppetry ['pʌpɪtrɪ] *n* arte *m* del titiritero *or* marionetista; **they use p. to communicate health information** usan marionetas para informar sobre la salud

puppy ['pʌpɪ] *n* (**a**) *(young dog)* cachorro *m* (**b**) *Br Fam (youth)* mocoso(a) *m,f* ►► ***p. fat*** obesidad *f* infantil; *Fam* ***p. love*** amor *m* de adolescente

purblind ['pɜ:blaɪnd] *adj Literary* (**a**) *(poorly sighted)* casi ciego(a) (**b**) *(obtuse)* miope

purchase ['pɜ:tʃɪs] *Formal* **1** *n* (**a**) *(action, thing bought)* compra *f*, adquisición *f*; **to make a p.** hacer una compra ►► *Com* ***p. ledger*** libro *m* de compras proveedores; *Com* ***p. order*** orden *f* de compra; ***p. price*** precio *m* de compra; ***p. tax*** impuesto *m* sobre la compra (**b**) *(grip)* **to get a p. on sth** agarrarse *or* asirse a algo
2 *vt* comprar, adquirir; **to p. sth from sb** comprar algo a alguien; **to p. sth for sb** comprar algo a *or* para alguien; **to p. sb sth** comprar algo a *or* para alguien

purchaser ['pɜ:tʃəsə(r)] *n* comprador(ora) *m,f*

purchasing ['pɜ:tʃəsɪŋ] *n* (**a**) *(act)* compra *f*, adquisición *f* ►► ***p. manager*** jefe(a) *m,f* de compras; ***p. power*** poder *m* adquisitivo, capacidad *f* adquisitiva (**b**) **p. (department)** departamento *m* de compras

purdah ['pɜ:də] *n* purdah *m or f*, = práctica de mantener a las mujeres alejadas del contacto con los hombres; *Fig* **to go into p.** *(politician)* recluirse

pure [pjʊə(r)] *adj* (**a**) *(unmixed, untainted)* puro(a); **p. air/water** aire puro/agua pura; **the p. tones of the flute** los tonos puros *or* limpios de la flauta ►► ***p. silk*** seda *f* natural; ***p. wool*** pura lana *f* virgen
(**b**) *(chaste)* puro(a); IDIOM **to be p. as the driven snow** ser puro(a) y virginal
(**c**) *(science, research)* puro(a) ►► ***p. mathematics*** matemáticas *fpl* puras
(**d**) *(as intensifier)* **by p. chance** por pura casualidad; **it's the truth, p. and simple** es la verdad, pura y dura

pure-bred ['pjʊəbred] *adj (dog)* de raza; *(horse)* purasangre

puree, purée ['pjʊəreɪ] **1** *n* puré *m*
2 *vt* hacer puré; **pureed carrots** puré de zanahoria

purely ['pjʊəlɪ] *adv* puramente; **a p. professional relationship** una relación estrictamente *or* puramente profesional; **p. by chance** por pura casualidad; **p. and simply** simple y llanamente

pureness ['pjʊənɪs] *n* pureza *f*

purgative ['pɜ:gətɪv] **1** *n* purgante *m*
2 *adj* purgante

purgatorial [pɜ:gə'tɔ:rɪəl] *adj* (**a**) *Rel* del purgatorio (**b**) *Fam (very unpleasant)* espantoso(a)

purgatory ['pɜ:gətərɪ] *n Rel* purgatorio *m*; *Fig* **these meetings are absolute p.!** estas reuniones son un suplicio

purge [pɜ:dʒ] **1** *n* (**a**) *(of bowels)* purga *f* (**b**) *Pol* purga *f*
2 *vt* (**a**) *(bowels)* purgar (**b**) *Pol (party, organization)* purgar; *(undesirable elements)* eliminar (**c**) *(free, rid)* librar; **p. your mind of such morbid ideas** libra tu mente de esas ideas tan morbosas; *Rel* **to p. oneself of** *or* **from sin** librarse del pecado

purification [pjʊərɪfɪ'keɪʃən] *n (of oil, mind)* purificación *f*; *(of water, blood)* depuración *f* ►► ***p. plant*** planta *f* depuradora

purifier ['pjʊərɪfaɪə(r)] *n (of water)* depurador *m*; *(of air)* purificador *m*

purify ['pjʊərɪfaɪ] *vt (oil, mind)* purificar; *(water, blood)* depurar

purism ['pjʊərɪzəm] *n* purismo *m*

purist ['pjʊərɪst] *n* purista *mf*

puritan ['pjʊərɪtən] **1** *n* (**a**) *(strict person)* puritano(a) *m,f* (**b**) *Hist* **the Puritans** los puritanos
2 *adj* (**a**) *(strict)* puritano(a) (**b**) *Hist* **P.** puritano(a)

puritanical [pjʊərɪ'tænɪkəl] *adj* puritano(a)

puritanism ['pjʊərɪtənɪzəm] *n* (**a**) *(strictness)* puritanismo *m* (**b**) *Hist* **P.** puritanismo *m*

purity ['pjʊərɪtɪ] *n* (**a**) *(freedom from taint)* pureza *f* (**b**) *(chasteness)* pureza *f*

purl [pɜ:l] **1** *n* punto *m* del revés
2 *vi* hacer punto del revés; **knit one, p. one** haz uno del derecho y uno del revés

purlieus ['pɜ:lju:z] *npl Literary or Formal* inmediaciones *fpl*

purloin [pɜ:'lɔɪn] *vt Formal* sustraer

purple ['pɜ:pəl] **1** *n* (**a**) *(colour)* morado *m*, púrpura *m* (**b**) *Rel* **the p.** la púrpura
2 *adj* morado(a); **to turn** *or* **go p.** *(with embarrassment, anger)* enrojecer ►► *Mil* ***P. Heart*** = medalla concedida a los heridos estadounidenses en combate; *Br Fam* ***p. heart*** *(amphetamine)* anfeta *f*; ***p. heron*** garza *f* imperial; ***p. martin*** avión *m* purpúreo; ***a p. patch*** *(of prose)* un trozo sobreelaborado; **to go through a p. patch** *(be lucky)* estar en racha; ***p. prose*** prosa *f* recargada; ***p. sandpiper*** correlimos *m inv* oscuro

purplish ['pɜ:pəlɪʃ] *adj* púrpureo(a), violáceo(a)

purport *Formal* **1** *n* ['pɜ:pɔ:t] sentido *m*, significado *m*
2 *vt* [pə'pɔ:t] **to p. to be sth** pretender *or* afirmar ser algo

purported [pə'pɔ:tɪd] *adj Formal* pretendido(a), supuesto(a)

purportedly [pə'pɔ:tɪdlɪ] *adv Formal* supuestamente

purpose ['pɜ:pəs] **1** *n* (**a**) *(object, aim)* propósito *m*, objeto *m*; **what is the p. of your visit?** ¿cuál es el objeto de su visita?; **to have a p. in life** tener un objetivo en la vida; **to do sth with a p. in mind** *or* **for a p.** hacer algo con un propósito *or* un objetivo en mente; **on p.** adrede, a propósito; **her remarks were very much to the p.** sus comentarios fueron muy pertinentes; **they have a real sense of p.** saben lo que quieren (conseguir); **to give sb a sense of p.** dar a alguien un sentido de la vida
(**b**) *(use)* finalidad *f*; **to serve a p.** tener una utilidad *or* finalidad; **to serve no p.** no servir para nada; **to serve sb's purpose(s)** ser útil a alguien; **once she had served her p. they abandoned her** cuando dejó de serles útil, la abandonaron; **once it has served its p.** una vez que ha cumplido su finalidad; **to suit sb's purpose(s)** venir bien a alguien; **it's ideal for our purposes** nos viene perfectamente; **for all practical purposes** a efectos prácticos; **$5,000 will be enough for present purposes** 5.000 dólares serán suficientes para los fines actuales; **for tax/military purposes** con fines fiscales/militares; **the money will be put** *or* **used to good p.** el dinero será bien utilizado; **to be to no p.** ser en vano; **for the purposes of the present discussion...** para este debate...
(**c**) *(determination)* determinación *f*
2 *vt Literary* **to p. to do sth** *or* **doing sth** disponer hacer algo

purpose-built ['pɜ:pəs'bɪlt] *adj* construido(a) al efecto; **a p. conference centre** un centro de congresos construido especialmente pare ese uso

purposeful ['pɜ:pəsfʊl] *adj* decidido(a)

purposefully ['pɜ:pəsfʊlɪ] *adv (determinedly)* resueltamente

purposeless ['pɜ:pəslɪs] *adj (life)* sin objetivo; *(act, violence)* gratuito(a)

purposely ['pɜ:pəslɪ] *adv* adrede, a propósito

purposive ['pɜ:pəsɪv] *adj Formal* intencional

purr [pɜ:(r)] **1** *n* (**a**) *(of cat)* ronroneo *m*; *(of engine)* zumbido *m* (**b**) *(of machine)* rumor *m*, zumbido *m*
2 *vt* susurrar sensualmente
3 *vi (cat)* ronronear; *(engine)* hacer un zumbido

purse [pɜ:s] **1** *n* (**a**) *Br (for coins)* monedero *m*; **the public p.** el erario público; IDIOM **to hold** *or* **control the p. strings** llevar las riendas del gasto; IDIOM **to loosen/tighten the p. strings** aumentar/ajustar el presupuesto (**b**) *US (handbag) Esp* bolso *m*, *Col, CSur* cartera *f*, *Méx* bolsa *f* (**c**) *(prize money for boxing contest)* premio *m* (**d**) ***p. seine*** *(fishing net)* red *f* de cerco
2 *vt* **to p. one's lips** fruncir los labios

purser ['pɜ:sə(r)] *n Naut* sobrecargo *m*

pursuance [pə'sju:əns] *n Formal* **he was injured in p. of his duty** resultó herido durante el cumplimiento de su deber

pursuant to [pə'sjʊəntʊ] *prep Formal* (a) *(following)* **events p. this occurrence** los acontecimientos que sucedieron a este suceso (b) *Law (in accordance with)* de conformidad con

pursue [pə'sju:] *vt* (a) *(chase) (person, animal)* perseguir; *Literary* **she was pursued by bad luck/ill health** la perseguía la mala suerte/la enfermedad
(b) *(search for) (pleasure, knowledge, happiness)* buscar; **we are all pursuing the same goals** todos perseguimos los mismos objetivos
(c) *(continue with) (studies, enquiry)* proseguir, continuar con; *(course of action, policy)* seguir; **if I may p. that line of argument...** si se me permite continuar con ese argumento...
(d) *(profession)* ejercer; **to p. a career in law/journalism** dedicarse al derecho/periodismo

pursuer [pə'sju:ə(r)] *n* perseguidor(ora) *m,f*

pursuit [pə'sju:t] *n* (a) *(of person, animal)* persecución *f*; **he came with two policemen in hot p.** venía con dos policías pisándole los talones
(b) *(of pleasure, knowledge, happiness)* búsqueda *f*; **to be in p. of** ir en búsqueda *or* busca de
(c) *(activity)* ocupación *f*; **(leisure) pursuits** aficiones *fpl*
(d) *Sport (in cycling, winter sports)* persecución *f*; **individual/team p.** persecución individual/por equipos

purulent ['pjʊərələnt] *adj Med* purulento(a)

purvey [pə'veɪ] *vt Formal* (a) *(goods)* proveer, abastecer; **to p. sth to sb** proveer *or* abastecer a alguien de algo (b) *(lies, rumours)* difundir

purveyor [pə'veɪə(r)] *n Formal* (a) *(supplier)* proveedor(ora) *m,f*; **purveyors of jam to HM the Queen** proveedores de mermelada de su Majestad la Reina (b) *(of gossip, lies)* generador *m*, fuente *f*

purview ['pɜ:vju:] *n Formal* ámbito *m*; **to be within/outside the p. of** estar dentro/fuera del ámbito de

pus [pʌs] *n* pus *m*

PUSH [pʊʃ] **1** *n* (a) *(act of pushing)* empujón *m*, *CAm, Méx* aventón *m*; **at the p. of a button** con sólo apretar un botón; **to give sth/sb a p.** dar un empujón a algo/alguien; **we need to give him a little p.** *(encouragement)* tenemos que darle un empujoncito; **shall I give you a p. start?** ¿te ayudo a arrancar empujando?; IDIOM *Br Fam* **to give sb the p.** *(employee)* poner a alguien de patitas en la calle; *(lover)* dejar a alguien; **he got the p.** *(employee)* lo pusieron de patitas en la calle; *(lover)* su pareja lo dejó; IDIOM *Fam* **when** *or* **if p. comes to shove..., if it comes to the p....** como último recurso... ►► *Comptr* ***p. technology*** tecnología *f* informativa por suscripción
(b) *(campaign)* campaña *f*; *Mil* ofensiva *f*; **sales p.** campaña de ventas; **to give a product a p.** promocionar un producto; **we are making a p. into the European market** estamos apostando fuerte por el *or Am* al mercado europeo; **to make a p. for sth** tratar de conseguir algo
(c) *(drive, dynamism)* empuje *m*
(d) *Fam (struggle)* **it'll be a p. for us to finish by Friday** va a haber que darse prisa *or* apurarse para terminar el viernes; **at a p.** apurando mucho
2 *vt* (a) *(shove)* empujar; *(button)* apretar, pulsar; **they pushed the box across the floor** empujaron la caja por el suelo; **p. the rod into the hole** inserta presionando la barra en el agujero, *Am* mete la barra por el agujero; **she pushed me into the water** me empujó *or CAm, Méx* aventó al agua; **p. the table nearer the door** empuja la mesa hacia la puerta; **we pushed the car off the road** apartamos el coche de la carretera empujando, *Am* empujamos el carro para afuera de la carretera; **to p. the door open/shut** *or* **to** abrir/cerrar la puerta empujándola *or* de un empujón; **to p. sb out of the way** apartar a alguien de un empujón *or CAm, Méx* aventón; **to p. one's way through the crowd** abrirse paso a empujones entre la multitud; *Fig* **to p. sth to the back of one's mind** tratar de no pensar en algo
(b) *(strain, tax)* **he pushed himself to the limit of his endurance** se esforzó hasta el límite de su resistencia; **don't p. yourself too hard** no te pases con el esfuerzo; *Ironic* cuidado no te vayas a cansar; **our Spanish lecturer always pushed us hard** nuestro profesor de español siempre nos apretaba mucho; *Fam* **a great democrat? that's pushing it a bit!** ¿un gran demócrata? ¡eso es pasarse un poco *or Esp* pelín!; **to p. one's luck, to p. it** tentar a la suerte; *Fam* **don't p. your luck!, don't p. it!** *(said in annoyance)* ¡no me busques!, *Esp* ¡no me busques las cosquillas!, *RP* ¡no me torees!; **to be pushed (for time)** estar apurado(a) *or RP* corto(a) de tiempo; **we'll be pushed** *or* **pushing it to finish by Friday** vamos a tener que darnos prisa para acabar el viernes, vamos a tener que apurarnos para terminar el viernes
(c) *(pressurize, force)* **to p. sb to do sth** empujar a alguien a hacer algo, *Am* incitar a alguien para que haga algo; **to p. sb into doing sth** forzar a alguien a hacer algo; **they've been pushing the government for more funds** han estado presionando al gobierno para conseguir más fondos; **to p. prices up/down** hacer subir/bajar los precios; **when pushed, she admitted accepting the money** cuando la presionaron, admitió haber aceptado el dinero
(d) *(promote) (goods)* promocionar; *(theory)* defender
(e) *Fam (drugs)* pasar, trapichear con, *RP* transar
(f) *Fam (be approaching)* **he's pushing sixty** ronda los sesenta; **we were pushing 100 km/h** íbamos casi a 100 km/h
3 *vi* (a) *(shove)* empujar; **to p. at sth** empujar algo; **P.** *(sign)* empuje, empuje; IDIOM **she's pushing at an open door** lo tiene medio hecho
(b) *(move forward)* avanzar (a empujones); **the troops are pushing southwards** las tropas avanzan hacia el sur; **she pushed in front of me** se me coló; **he pushed past me** me adelantó *or RP* pasó a empujones; **we pushed through the crowd** nos abrimos paso a empujones entre la multitud
(c) *(in childbirth)* empujar

► **push about** *vt sep Fam (bully)* abusar de; **don't let him p. you about** no dejes que abuse de ti

► **push ahead** *vi* seguir adelante (**with** con)

► **push along 1** *vt sep (trolley, pram)* empujar
2 *vi Fam (leave)* largarse, *Esp, RP* pirarse

► **push around** *vt sep* = **push about**

► **push aside** *vt sep (person, object)* apartar (de un empujón); *Fig (reject)* dejar a un lado; **we can't just p. these issues aside** no podemos dejar a un lado estos temas

► **push away** *vt sep* apartar

► **push back** *vt sep* (a) *(frontiers, boundaries)* ampliar (b) *(repulse)* hacer retroceder a

► **push down** *vt sep* (a) *(lever)* bajar, tirar de; **she pushed the clothes down in the bag** apretujó la ropa en la bolsa (b) *(knock over)* derribar

► **push for** *vt insep (demand)* reclamar; **we are pushing for the proposed bypass to be abandoned** estamos haciendo campaña para que sea abandonado el proyecto de circunvalación

► **push forward 1** *vt sep* (a) *(frontiers, boundaries)* ampliar
(b) *(promote)* **to p. oneself forward** hacerse valer
2 *vi* empujar hacia delante

► **push in 1** *vt sep* (a) *(knife)* hundir; *(button)* apretar; *(disk)* insertar, meter
(b) *(shove)* **they pushed me in** *(into water)* me tiraron al agua (de un empujón); *(into room)* me metieron de un empujón
(c) *(break down) (door, window)* tirar *or* echar abajo
2 *vi (in queue)* colarse

► **push off 1** *vt sep* (a) *(knock off)* tirar de; **I was pushed off the committee** me echaron del comité (b) *(boat)* desatracar
2 *vi* (a) *(swimmer, in boat)* impulsarse (b) *Fam (leave)* largarse; **p. off!** ¡lárgate!, ¡fuera!

► **push on 1** *vi (continue)* seguir, continuar; **to p. on with sth** seguir adelante con algo; **let's p. on to the capital** sigamos hasta la capital
2 *vt sep (urge on)* alentar, animar

► **push out 1** *vt sep* (a) *(person, object)* sacar empujando (b) *(oust) (from job, market)* echar, expulsar
2 *vi (appear) (roots, leaves, flowers)* salir

► **push over** *vt sep* (a) *(pass)* acercar (b) *(knock over)* derribar; **a big boy pushed me over at school** un niño mayor me tiró al suelo en el colegio

► **push through 1** *vt sep* (a) *(deal, reform)* **they pushed the deal through** aceleraron el cierre del trato; **the reform was pushed through** tramitaron la reforma con carácter de urgencia (b) *(thrust) (needle)* pasar; **she pushed her way through the crowd** se abrió camino por entre la multitud
2 *vi (get through)* avanzar

► **push up 1** *vt sep* (a) *(push upwards) (handle, lever)* levantar (b) *(increase) (costs, taxes)* hacer subir
2 *vi (flowers, weeds)* brotar

push-bike ['pʊʃbaɪk] *n Br Fam* bici *f*, bicicleta *f*

push-broom ['pʊʃbru:m] *n US* escoba *f*

push-button ['pʊʃbʌtən] *adj* de teclas, de botones ►► ***p. warfare*** guerra *f* a distancia

pushcart ['pʊʃkɑ:t] *n US* carretilla *f*

pushchair ['pʊʃtʃeə(r)] *n Br (for baby)* silla *f* de paseo *or* de niño

pusher ['pʊʃə(r)] *n Fam* **(drug) p.** camello *m*, *Am* dealer *m*

pushiness ['pʊʃɪnɪs] *n Fam* (a) *(ambitiousness)* arribismo *m* (b) *(forwardness)* agresividad *f*

pushing ['pʊʃɪŋ] *n* **no p.!** ¡sin empujar!; **there was a lot of p. and shoving** hubo muchos empujones

pushover ['pʊʃəʊvə(r)] *n Fam* **it's a p.** es pan comido; **he's no p.** *(in contest)* no se deja vencer fácilmente; **I'm a p. (for)** no sé decir que no (a)

pushpin ['pʊʃpɪn] *n US* alfiler *m* (de cabeza redonda)

push-pull ['pʊʃ'pʊl] *adj Elec (amplifier, circuit)* en contrafase, push-pull

push-start ['pʊʃ'stɑːt] **1** *n (to car)* **we'll have to give it a p.** tendremos que arrancar(lo) empujando
2 *vt* arrancar empujando

push-up ['pʊʃʌp] *n* fondo *m*, flexión *f* (de brazos)

pushy ['pʊʃɪ] *adj Fam* **(a)** *Pej (ambitious)* arribista; **p. parents** padres con demasiadas ambiciones para sus hijos **(b)** *(self-assertive)* agresivo(a)

pusillanimity [pjuːsɪlə'nɪmətɪ] *n Formal* pusilanimidad *f*

pusillanimous [pjuːsɪ'lænɪməs] *adj Formal* pusilánime

puss [pʊs] *n Fam* **(a)** *(cat)* gatito *m*, minino *m* ▸▸ ***P. in Boots*** el gato con botas **(b)** *(face)* jeta *f*

pussy ['pʊsɪ] *n* **(a)** *Fam* **p. (cat)** gatito *m*, minino *m* ▸▸ ***p. willow*** sauce *m* blanco **(b)** *Vulg (woman's genitals) Esp* conejo *m*, *Col* cuca *f*, *Méx* paloma *f*, *RP* concha *f*, *Ven* cuchara *f*; **he hasn't had any p. for months** hace meses que no moja el churro *or Méx* que no se chinga a nadie **(c)** *Fam (weak, cowardly man)* mariquita *m*

pussyfoot ['pʊsɪfʊt] *vi Fam* **to p. around** *or* **about** andarse con rodeos

pussy-whipped ['pʊsɪwɪpt] *adj US very Fam* calzonazos *inv*, *Am* calzonudo(a)

pustule ['pʌstjʊl] *n* pústula *f*

PUT [pʊt] *(pt & pp* **put**) **1** *vt* **(a)** *(place)* poner; *(carefully)* colocar; **p. your coat in the bedroom** pon tu abrigo en el dormitorio *or Am* el cuarto *or CAm, Col, Méx* la recámara; **p. the knife to the right of the fork** coloca el cuchillo a la derecha del tenedor; **to p. one's arms around sth** rodear algo con los brazos, abrazar algo; **to p. one's arms around sb** abrazar a alguien; **to p. sth in** *or* **into sth** meter algo en algo; **to p. money into an account** *Esp* ingresar *or Am* depositar dinero en una cuenta; **he p. his hands over his eyes** se cubrió *or* tapó los ojos con las manos; **she p. her head round the door** asomó la cabeza por la puerta; **p. your arm through the hole** mete el brazo por el agujero; **p. those tables closer together** junta más esas mesas; **we p. the chairs (up) against the wall** arrimamos las sillas a la pared; **we'll p. them on the train** los pondremos en el tren; **to p. a man on the Moon** mandar *or* llevar un hombre a la Luna; **to p. the ball out of play** sacar la pelota fuera *or Am* afuera del campo; **to p. the ball in the back of the net** marcar (un gol); **to p. a limit on sth** poner un límite a algo; *Fam Br* **p. it there!**, *US* **put 'er there!** *(shake hands)* ¡choca esos cinco!, ¡chócala!; *Fig* **to p. oneself into sb's hands** ponerse en manos de alguien; *Fig* **p. yourself in my position** *or* **place** ponte en mi lugar; *Fam Fig* **I didn't know where to p. myself** no sabía dónde meterme
(b) *(cause to be)* **to p. sb's health at risk** poner la salud de alguien en peligro; **to p. sb in charge** poner a alguien al mando; **to p. sb in a difficult position** poner a alguien en una posición difícil; **to p. sb in a good mood** poner a alguien de buen humor; **a small error p. the final figure out by over a million** un pequeño error resultó en una equivocación de más de un millón en la cifra final; **to p. sb under pressure** presionar a alguien
(c) *(attribute)* **he p. his faith in them/it** puso su fe en ellos/ello *or* eso; **to p. a tax on sth** gravar algo con un impuesto; **he p. a value of $40,000 on it** le atribuyó un valor de 40.000 dólares, lo evaluó en 40.000 dólares; **we can't p. a figure on the final cost** no sabemos cuál será exactamente el costo *or Esp* coste final; **it's putting a strain on our relationship** está creando tensiones en nuestra relación; **I know the name, but I can't p. a face to it** conozco el nombre, pero no consigo recordar su cara
(d) *(present, suggest)* **I'll p. it to the boss and see what he says** se lo propondré al jefe, a ver qué le parece; **to p. a proposal to sb/before a committee** presentar una propuesta a alguien/ante un comité; **to p. a question to sb** plantear una pregunta a alguien; **I p. it to you that...** *(in court case)* ¿no es cierto que...?
(e) *(devote)* **I've p. a lot of effort into this piece of work** me he esforzado mucho con este trabajo; **to p. a lot of money into sth** invertir mucho dinero en algo; **I've p. a lot of thought into this proposal** he reflexionado sobre esta propuesta muy detenidamente; **to p. a lot of work into sth** trabajar intensamente en algo; **we've p. a lot into this project** hemos dedicado un gran esfuerzo a este proyecto
(f) *(bet)* **to p. money on a horse** apostar a un caballo; *Fig* **I wouldn't p. money on it!** ¡yo no (me) apostaría nada!
(g) *(write)* poner; **p. it in your diary** escríbelo *or* ponlo en tu agenda; **she p. her name to the document** firmó el documento
(h) *(express)* **to p. sth well/badly** expresar algo bien/mal; **how shall I p. it?** ¿cómo lo diría?; **if you p. it like that, I can hardly say no** si me lo planteas así, no puedo decir que no; **I couldn't have p. it better myself** nadie lo hubiera dicho mejor; **to p. it bluntly** hablando claro; **to p. it mildly** por no decir otra cosa; **to p. it another way...** por decirlo de otra manera...; **let me p. it this way, he's not exactly intelligent** no es precisamente inteligente *or* no es muy inteligente que digamos; **to p. sth into words** expresar algo con palabras; **as Proudhon p. it, property is theft** como dijo Proudhon, la propiedad es un robo
(i) *(estimate, consider)* calcular (**at** en); **I would p. her age at forty** yo diría que tiene unos cuarenta años; **I'd p. him among the five best sprinters of all time** yo lo incluiría entre los cinco mejores esprinters de todos los tiempos; **she always puts her children first** para ella sus niños son lo primero
(j) *Sport* **to p. the shot** lanzar peso
(k) *St Exch* ***p. option*** opción *f* de venta
2 *vi* **to p. to sea** zarpar

▸ **put about 1** *vt sep* **(a)** *(rumour)* difundir; **to p. it about that...** difundir el rumor de que... **(b)** *(boat)* virar **(c)** *Br Fam* **he puts it about, he puts himself about** *(has several sexual partners)* es un pendón *or Méx* cascolino *or RP* picaflor
2 *vi (ship)* cambiar de rumbo

▸ **put across** *vt sep* **(a)** *(message, idea)* transmitir, hacer llegar; **to p. oneself across well/badly** hacerse entender bien/mal **(b)** *Br Fam* **don't try putting anything across on me!** no trates de jugármela

▸ **put aside** *vt sep* **(a)** *(reserve)* apartar; **I p. an hour aside each day for reading** dejo una hora diaria para la lectura; **we'll p. it aside for you** *(in shop)* se lo dejamos apartado **(b)** *(save) (money)* ahorrar **(c)** *(problem, differences, fact)* dejar a un lado

▸ **put away** *vt sep* **(a)** *(tidy away)* ordenar, recoger; **p. your money/wallet away** guarda tu dinero/cartera **(b)** *(save) (money)* ahorrar **(c)** *Fam (in prison, mental hospital) (person)* encerrar **(d)** *Fam (eat, drink)* tragarse; **he can really p. it away!** ¡cómo traga! **(e)** *Fam (score) (penalty)* convertir

▸ **put back 1** *vt sep* **(a)** *(replace)* devolver a su sitio **(b)** *(postpone)* aplazar, posponer; *(clock)* retrasar, atrasar; *(schedule)* retrasar; IDIOM **that puts the clock back ten years** esto nos devuelve a la misma situación de hace diez años
2 *vi Naut* **to p. back (to port)** regresar (a puerto)

▸ **put behind** *vt sep* **I've p. my disappointment behind me** he superado mi decepción

▸ **put by** *vt sep (save)* ahorrar

▸ **put down 1** *vt sep* **(a)** *(set down)* dejar; *(phone, receiver)* colgar; **she p. the child down and he ran off** puso al niño en el suelo y se marchó corriendo; **she p. the phone down on me** me colgó; **I couldn't p. the book down** no me podía despegar del libro; **p. that down!** ¡suelta eso!; **p. me down!** ¡suéltame!
(b) *(drop off) (passenger)* dejar
(c) *(aircraft)* **he managed to p. the plane down on the beach** se las apañó para aterrizar en la playa
(d) *(put to bed) (baby)* acostar
(e) *(reduce) (prices, interest rates)* bajar
(f) *(revolt, opposition)* reprimir, ahogar
(g) *(write)* poner por escrito; **to p. sth down in writing** poner algo por escrito; **I can p. it down as expenses** lo puedo hacer constar como gastos; *Parl* **to p. down a motion** presentar una moción; **to p. sb** *or* **sb's name down for sth** apuntar a alguien a algo; **to p. one's name** *or* **oneself down for sth** apuntarse a *or* inscribirse en algo; **p. me down for $5** apúntame 5 dólares, apunta que yo pago 5 dólares; IDIOM **they've p. me down as a troublemaker** me han catalogado como alborotador
(h) *(pay) (deposit)* dejar
(i) *(attribute)* **to p. sth down to sth** achacar *or* atribuir algo a algo; **we'll just have to p. it down to experience** por lo menos nos queda la experiencia
(j) *(animal)* sacrificar; **to have a cat/dog p. down** sacrificar a un gato/perro
(k) *(criticize)* **to p. sb down** dejar a alguien en mal lugar; **to p. oneself down** menospreciarse
(l) *(wine)* dejar envejecer
2 *vi (aircraft)* aterrizar

▸ **put forth** *vt insep* **(a)** *Literary (shoots, leaves)* echar **(b)** *Formal (idea, theory, proposal)* presentar

▸ **put forward** *vt sep* **(a)** *(plan, theory, candidate)* proponer; *(proposal)* presentar; *(suggestion)* hacer; **to p. oneself forward as a candidate** presentarse como candidato(a) **(b)** *(clock, time of meeting)* adelantar

▸ **put in** 1 *vt sep* (**a**) *(install)* poner, instalar
(**b**) *(present) (claim, protest)* presentar; **to p. in a request for sth** solicitar algo; **to p. in an application for a job** presentar una solicitud para un empleo; **to p. in a (good) word for sb** decir algo en favor de alguien
(**c**) *(devote) (time, work)* invertir, dedicar (**on** en); **I've been putting in a lot of overtime** he hecho muchas horas extras; **I p. in a few hours' revision yesterday** ayer le dediqué unas cuantas horas a la revisión; **to p. in a full day's work** trabajar una jornada completa
(**d**) *(include)* incluir en; **should we p. this word in?** ¿incluimos esta palabra?
(**e**) *(add, expand)* añadir
(**f**) *(appoint)* nombrar
(**g**) *(interject)* interponer; **"her name was Alice," the woman p. in** "se llamaba Alice", interrumpió la mujer
2 *vi (ship)* atracar, hacer escala (**at** en)

▸ **put in for** *vt insep (apply for) (exam)* apuntarse a; *(job, pay rise)* solicitar

▸ **put off** *vt sep* (**a**) *(postpone)* aplazar, posponer; **to p. off cleaning the bathroom** dejar la limpieza del baño para más tarde
(**b**) *(make wait)* tener esperando; **can we p. her off until tomorrow?** ¿podemos hacer que espere hasta mañana?; **it's no good trying to p. me off with excuses** conmigo las excusas no funcionan
(**c**) *(cause to dislike)* desagradar, resultar desagradable a; **that meal p. me off seafood** después de aquella comida dejó de gustarme el marisco
(**d**) *(distract)* distraer; **to p. sb off their work** distraer a alguien de su trabajo; IDIOM **to p. sb off their stride** *or* **stroke** cortar el ritmo *or* desconcentrar a alguien
(**e**) *(discourage)* **to p. sb off doing sth** quitarle *or Am* sacarle a alguien las ganas de hacer algo; **we were p. off by the price** el precio nos desanimó; **my parents' example p. me off marriage** el ejemplo de mis padres me ha quitado *or Am* sacado las ganas de casarme; **don't be p. off by the dish's appearance** no dejes que el aspecto del plato te quite las ganas
(**f**) *(drop off)* dejar

▸ **put on** *vt sep* (**a**) *(clothes)* ponerse; **he p. his trousers on** se puso el pantalón; **to p. on one's make-up** ponerse el maquillaje, maquillarse
(**b**) *(light, TV, heating)* encender, *Am* prender; *(music, videotape)* poner; *(brakes)* echar; **to p. the kettle on** poner el agua a hervir *(en el hervidor de agua)*; **p. the carrots on** empieza a cocinar las zanahorias
(**c**) *(add)* **to p. 5 pence on the price of a bottle of wine** subir 5 peniques el precio de una botella de vino; **to p. on speed** acelerar; **to p. on weight** engordar; **to p. years on sb** hacer más viejo(a) *or* mayor a alguien
(**d**) *(play, show)* representar, hacer; *(meal)* preparar; *(bus, transport)* organizar
(**e**) *(feign)* **he's not really hurt, he's just putting it on** no está lesionado, está fingiendo; **to p. on an accent** poner *or* simular un acento; **to p. on an act** fingir; **he p. on a silly voice** puso una vocecilla tonta
(**f**) *(on telephone)* **if Mr Wilson's there could you p. him on please?** si está el señor Wilson, ¿podría decirle que se ponga, por favor?
(**g**) *US Fam (tease)* **you're putting me on!** ¡me estás tomando el pelo!

▸ **put onto** *vt sep (inform about)* **to p. sb onto sth/sb** dirigir a alguien a algo/alguien; **what first p. you onto the butler, detective Smith?** ¿qué le puso sobre la pista del mayordomo, detective Smith?

▸ **put out** 1 *vt sep* (**a**) *(fire, light, cigarette)* apagar
(**b**) *(place outside) (washing, rubbish, cat)* sacar; **we p. some food out for the birds** sacamos algo de comida para los pájaros; *Fig* **to p. sth out of one's mind** quitarse *or Am* sacarse algo de la cabeza
(**c**) *(extend)* **to p. out one's hand** tender la mano; **to p. one's tongue out** sacar la lengua
(**d**) *(arrange for use)* dejar preparado(a); **he p. out his clothes for the next day** preparó su ropa para el día siguiente
(**e**) *(report, statement, warning)* emitir
(**f**) *(subcontract)* subcontratar
(**g**) *(eliminate) (from competition)* eliminar (**of** de)
(**h**) *(in baseball)* eliminar
(**i**) *(make unconscious)* dormir
(**j**) *(annoy)* **to be p. out** estar disgustado(a)
(**k**) *(inconvenience)* molestar; **to p. oneself out (for sb)** molestarse (por alguien)
(**l**) *(dislocate)* **to p. one's shoulder/knee out** dislocarse el hombro/la rodilla; **I've p. my back out** tengo una luxación en la espalda
(**m**) *(remove)* **to p. sb's eye out** sacarle el ojo a alguien
(**n**) *(sprout) (shoots, leaves)* echar
2 *vi* (**a**) *(ship)* hacerse a la mar, zarpar (**b**) *US very Fam (have sex willingly)* acostarse, meterse en la cama (**for** con)

▸ **put over** *vt sep* (**a**) = **put across** (**b**) IDIOM *Fam* **to p. one over on sb** timar *or Esp* pegársela *or RP* pasar a alguien

▸ **put through** *vt sep* (**a**) *(on phone)* **to p. sb through to sb** poner *or* pasar a alguien con alguien; **p. the call through to my office** páseme la llamada a mi despacho (**b**) *(subject to)* **to p. sb through sth** someter a alguien a algo; **he has p. her through hell** le ha hecho pasar las de Caín (**c**) *(pay for)* **to p. sb through school** pagarle a alguien el colegio (**d**) *(carry through, conclude)* concluir; **we finally p. through the necessary reforms** finalmente concluimos las reformas necesarias

▸ **put to** *vt sep* **we don't wish to p. you to any trouble** no deseamos importunarte; **to p. sth to a vote** someter algo a voto; **we p. them to work sweeping the floor** les pusimos a trabajar barriendo el suelo

▸ **put together** *vt sep* (**a**) *(assemble) (machine, furniture)* montar; *(file, report, meal, team)* confeccionar; *(plan, strategy)* elaborar, preparar; **you'll never p. that vase back together again** no conseguirás recomponer ese jarrón; **we're trying to p. together enough evidence to convict him** estamos tratando de reunir las pruebas necesarias para condenarlo (**b**) *(combine) (colours, ingredients)* mezclar; **she's more intelligent than the rest of them p. together** ella es más lista que todos los demás juntos

▸ **put towards** *vt sep* **here's some money for you to p. towards a new bike** aquí tienes algo de dinero para la nueva bici

▸ **put under** *vt sep (with drug, injection)* dormir

▸ **put up** 1 *vt sep* (**a**) *(erect) (ladder)* situar; *(tent)* montar; *(building, barricade, fence)* levantar, construir; *(statue)* erigir, poner
(**b**) *(affix) (painting, notice, curtains)* colocar, poner; **they've already p. up the Christmas decorations** ya han colocado los adornos de Navidad; **to p. up the shutters** bajar *or* cerrar las persianas
(**c**) *(raise) (umbrella)* abrir; *(hood)* poner; *(flag)* izar; **he p. his collar up** se subió el cuello; **to p. up one's hand** levantar la mano; **to p. one's hair up** recogerse el pelo; **p. your hands up!** ¡arriba las manos!; *Fam* **p. 'em up!** *(fists)* ¡defiéndete!
(**d**) *(increase) (prices, interest rates)* subir, aumentar
(**e**) *(provide accommodation for)* alojar; **could you p. me up for the night?** ¿podría dormir en tu casa esta noche?
(**f**) *(provide) (money)* aportar; *(candidate)* presentar; **to p. a child up for adoption** ofrecer un niño en adopción; **he p. up a good case for abstention** defendió la abstención con un planteamiento sólido; **to p. sth up for sale** poner algo a la venta; **to p. up a fight** *or* **struggle** ofrecer resistencia
(**g**) *(send up) (rocket, satellite)* lanzar
2 *vi* (**a**) *(stay)* alojarse (**b**) IDIOM *Fam* **p. up or shut up!** ¡más hechos y menos palabras!

▸ **put upon** *vt insep* **to feel p. upon** sentirse utilizado(a)

▸ **put up to** *vt sep* **to p. sb up to doing sth** animar a alguien a hacer algo

▸ **put up with** *vt insep* aguantar, soportar

---

putative ['pju:tətɪv] *adj Formal* presunto(a), supuesto(a); *Law (father)* putativo(a)

put-down ['pʊtdaʊn] *n Fam* pulla *f*, corte *m*

put-on ['pʊtɒn] 1 *n Fam* (**a**) *(pretence)* cuento *m*, farsa *f*, comedia *f*; **it's just a p.** es puro cuento; **is that one of your put-ons?** ¿me estás tomando el pelo *or Esp, Carib, Méx* vacilando? (**b**) *(hoax)* tomadura *f* de pelo, vacilada *f*
2 *adj* fingido(a), simulado(a)

putrefaction [pju:trɪ'fækʃən] *n* putrefacción *f*

putrefy ['pju:trɪfaɪ] *vi* pudrirse

putrescence [pju:'tresəns] *n Formal* putrescencia *f*

putrescent [pju:'tresənt] *adj* putrefacto(a), pútrido(a)

putrid ['pju:trɪd] *adj* (**a**) *(rotting)* putrefacto(a), pútrido(a); **a p. smell** un olor pútrido (**b**) *Fam (very bad)* pésimo(a), *Esp* infumable

putsch [pʊtʃ] *n* pronunciamiento *m* (militar)

putt [pʌt] 1 *n (in golf)* putt *m*, golpe *m* con el putt(er); **to hole** *or* **sink a p.** embocar un putt; **to line up a p.** alinear un putt; **to miss a p.** fallar un putt
2 *vt* golpear con el putt(er), patear
3 *vi (in golf)* golpear con el putt(er), patear

puttee ['pʌti:] *n* polaina *f*

putter ['pʌtə(r)] *n* (**a**) *(golf club)* putt(er) *m* (**b**) *(player)* **I'm a terrible p.** soy muy malo con el putt(er)

▸ **putter about, putter around** *US Fam* 1 *vi* entretenerse; **he spent the morning puttering about** *or* **around in the garden** ha estado toda la mañana entretenido *or* ocupado en el jardín
2 *vt insep* **I like to spend Sunday puttering about** *or* **around the**

house/garden me gusta pasar los domingos de aquí para allá en la casa/el jardín

putting ['pʌtɪŋ] *n* golpes *mpl* con el putt ►► ***p. green*** *(on golf course)* = terreno para practicar el putt; *Br (for entertainment)* = área de césped de pequeñas dimensiones abierta al público para jugar al golf con un putter

putty ['pʌtɪ] **1** *n* masilla *f*; IDIOM **he's p. in her hands** hace lo que quiere con él ►► ***p. knife*** espátula *f* para masilla
2 *vt* poner masilla en

put-up job ['pʊtʌp'dʒɒb] *n Fam* pufo *m*, apaño *m*

put-upon ['pʊtəpɒn] *adj* **to feel p.** sentirse utilizado(a); **a p. expression** una expresión de mártir

puzzle ['pʌzəl] **1** *n* **(a)** *(game)* rompecabezas *m inv*; *(mental)* acertijo *m* ►► ***p. book*** libro *m* de pasatiempos **(b)** *(mystery)* enigma *m*; **how he escaped remains a p.** cómo escapó sigue siendo un enigma
2 *vt (person)* dejar perplejo(a), desconcertar; **you p. me, Mr Cox** me deja perplejo, Sr Cox; **don't p. your head over** *or* **about it** no le des más vueltas

► **puzzle out** *vt sep (reason, cause)* explicarse; **I'm still trying to p. out how/why he did it** todavía estoy intentando explicarme cómo/porqué lo hizo; **I was never able to p. her out** nunca pude entenderla

► **puzzle over** *vt insep* dar vueltas a; **ithat'll give you something to p. over!** eso te dará en qué pensar

puzzled ['pʌzəld] *adj* perplejo(a), desconcertado(a); **to look p.** tener cara de perplejidad *or* desconcierto; **the public are puzzled** el público está desconcertado

puzzlement ['pʌzəlmənt] *n* perplejidad *f*, desconcierto *m*; **to look at sb in p.** mirar a alguien con desconcierto

puzzler ['pʌzlə(r)] *n* **(a)** *(person)* = persona aficionada a los rompecabezas, crucigramas, etc. **(b)** *(mystery, problem)* enigma *m*, misterio *m*

puzzling ['pʌzəlɪŋ] *adj* desconcertante

PVC [pi:vi:'si:] *n* (*abbr* **polyvinyl chloride**) PVC *m*

PVS [pi:vi:'es] *n Med* (*abbr* **permanent vegetative state**) estado *m* vegetativo profundo

Pvt. (*abbr* **private**) soldado *m* raso

PW *Br* (*abbr* **policewoman**) mujer *f* policía

pw *adv* (*abbr* **per week**) a la semana, por semana

PWA [pi:dʌbəlju:'eɪ] *n* (*abbr* **person with AIDS**) enfermo(a) *m,f* de sida

PWR [pi:dʌbəlju:'ɑ:(r)] *n* (*abbr* **pressurized-water reactor**) RAP *m*, reactor *m* de agua a presión

PX *n* (*abbr* **post exchange**) *US Mil* cooperativa *f* militar, economato *m* militar

pygmy ['pɪgmɪ] *n* **(a)** *(tribesman)* **P.** pigmeo(a) *m,f* **(b)** ***p. hippopotamus*** hipopótamo *m* enano; ***p. owl*** mochuelo *m* chico **(c)** *(insignificant person)* pigmeo(a) *m,f*, enano(a) *m,f*; **they're political pygmies** son políticos sin importancia

pyjama, *US* **pajama** [pə'dʒɑ:mə] *n* **pyjamas** pijama *m*, *Am* piyama *m or f*; **a pair of pyjamas** un pijama *or Am* piyama ►► ***p. bottom(s)*** pantalón *or* pantalones del pijama *or Am* piyama; ***p. case*** bolsa *f* para pijamas *or Am* piyamas; ***p. jacket*** camiseta *f* del pijama *or Am* piyama; ***p. party*** = fiesta en la que un grupo de amigas se queda a dormir en casa de otra, *Am* pijama *f or m* party, *Méx* pijamada *f*; ***p. top*** camiseta del pijama *or Am* piyama; ***p. trousers*** pantalón *m* del pijama *or Am* piyama

pylon ['paɪlɒn] *n* torre *f* (de alta tensión)

pylorus [paɪ'lɔ:rəs] *n Anat* píloro *m*

Pyongyang ['pjɒŋ'jæŋ] *n* Pyonyang

pyorrhea, *Br* **pyorrhoea** [paɪə'rɪə] *n Med* piorrea *f*

pyramid ['pɪrəmɪd] *n* pirámide *f* ►► ***p. selling*** venta *f* piramidal

pyramidal [pɪ'ræmɪdəl] *adj* piramidal

pyre ['paɪə(r)] *n* pira *f*

Pyrenean [pɪrə'nɪən] *adj* pirenaico(a) ►► ***P. desman*** desmán *m* del Pirineo; ***P. Mastiff*** mastín *m* del Pirineo

Pyrenees [pɪrə'ni:z] *npl* **the P.** los Pirineos

Pyrex® ['paɪreks] *n* pyrex® *m* ►► ***P. dish*** fuente *f* de pyrex®

pyrites [paɪ'raɪti:z] *n Geol* pirita *f*; **iron p.** pirita amarilla *or* de hierro

pyromania [paɪrə'meɪnɪə] *n* piromanía *f*

pyromaniac [paɪrə'meɪnɪæk] *n* pirómano(a) *m,f*

pyrotechnics [paɪrə'teknɪks] **1** *n (science)* pirotecnia *f*
2 *npl* **(a)** *(fireworks display)* fuegos *mpl* artificiales **(b)** *(in speech, writing)* malabarismos *mpl*, virguerías *fpl*

Pyrrhic ['pɪrɪk] *n* ***P. victory*** victoria *f* pírrica

Pythagoras [paɪ'θægərəs] *n pr* Pitágoras ►► ***P.'s theorem*** teorema *m* de Pitágoras

Pythagorean [paɪθægə'ri:ən] **1** *n* pitagórico(a) *m,f*
2 *adj* pitagórico(a)

python ['paɪθən] *n* (serpiente *f*) pitón *m or f*

Pythonesque [paɪθən'esk] *adj* como de Monty Python

pzazz = **pizzazz**

Q, q

Q, q [kjuː] *n (letter)* Q, q *f*

Q (**a**) (*abbr* **Queen**) *(in chess)* D (**b**) **Q and A (session)** (sesión de) preguntas y respuestas

q (*abbr* **quart**) cuarto *m* de galón

Qatar [kæ'tɑː(r)] *n* Qatar

Qatari [kæ'tɑːrɪ] **1** *n* persona de Qatar
2 *adj* de Qatar

QC [kjuː'siː] *n Br Law* (*abbr* **Queen's Counsel**) = título honorífico que la Reina concede a algunos abogados eminentes

QED [kjuːiː'diː] (*abbr* **quod erat demonstrandum**) QED

QM [kjuː'em] *n Mil* (*abbr* **quartermaster**) oficial *m* de intendencia

QMG [kjuːem'dʒiː] *n Mil* (*abbr* **Quartermaster-General**) intendente *mf* general

qr (*abbr* **quarter**) cuarto *m*

qt (**a**) (*abbr* **quart**) cuarto *m* de galón (**b**) (*abbr* **quantity**) cantidad *f*

q.t. [kjuː'tiː] *n Fam* **to do sth on the q.t.** hacer algo a escondidas *or Esp* a la chita callando

Q-tip® ['kjuːtɪp] *n US* bastoncillo *m* (de algodón)

qtly (*abbr* **quarterly**) trimestralmente

qty *Com* (*abbr* **quantity**) cantidad *f*

Qu. (*abbr* **Quebec**) Quebec

qua [kwɑː] *prep Formal* **money q. money has no interest for him** el dinero por sí mismo no le interesa

quack¹ [kwæk] **1** *n (of duck)* graznido *m*
2 *vi (duck)* graznar

quack² *n* (**a**) *Br, Austr Pej or Hum (doctor)* matasanos *m inv* (**b**) *(unqualified)* curandero(a) *m,f*

quackery ['kwækərɪ] *n* curanderismo *m*

quad [kwɒd] **1** *n* (**a**) *Fam (of school, college)* patio *m* (**b**) *Fam (child)* cuatrillizo(a) *m,f* (**c**) ***q. bike*** moto *f* de rally *(con tres ruedas gruesas)*
2 *adj Fam* cuadrafónico(a)

quadrangle ['kwɒdræŋgəl] *n* (**a**) *(shape)* cuadrilátero *m*, cuadrángulo *m* (**b**) *(of school, college)* patio *m*

quadrangular [kwɒ'dræŋgjʊlə(r)] *adj* cuadrangular

quadrant ['kwɒdrənt] *n* (**a**) *Geom* cuadrante *m* (**b**) *Astron & Naut* cuadrante *m*

quadraphonic [kwɒdrə'fɒnɪk] *adj* cuadrafónico(a)

quadratic [kwɒ'drætɪk] *Math* **1** *n* ecuación *f* de segundo grado, (ecuación *f*) cuadrática *f*
2 *adj* cuadrático(a); **q. equation** ecuación de segundo grado, ecuación cuadrática

quadrennial [kwə'drenɪəl] *adj* cuatrienal

quadriceps ['kwɒdrɪseps] *n Anat* cuádriceps *m inv*

quadrilateral [kwɒdrɪ'lætərəl] **1** *n* cuadrilátero *m*
2 *adj* cuadrilátero(a)

quadrille [kwə'drɪl] *n* (**a**) *(dance)* = baile para cuatro parejas, en cinco o seis movimientos (**b**) *(music)* = música para el "quadrille"

quadrillion [kwə'drɪlɪən] *n Br* (10^{24}) cuatrillón *m*; *US* (10^{15}) mil billones *mpl*

quadripartite [kwɒdrɪ'pɑːtaɪt] *adj* cuatripartito(a)

quadriplegia [kwɒdrɪ'pliːdʒɪə] *n* tetraplejía *f*

quadriplegic [kwɒdrɪ'pliːdʒɪk] **1** *n* tetrapléjico(a) *m,f*
2 *adj* tetrapléjico(a)

quadruped ['kwɒdrʊped] *n* cuadrúpedo *m*

quadruple [kwɒ'druːpəl] **1** *adj* cuádruple, cuádruplo(a) ►► *Mus* ***q. time*** compás *m* de cuatro por cuatro
2 *vt* cuadruplicar
3 *vi* cuadruplicarse

quadruplet ['kwɒdrʊplɪt] *n* cuatrillizo(a) *m,f*

quadruplicate [kwɒ'druːplɪkət] **1** *adj* cuadruplicado(a)
2 *n* **in q.** por cuadruplicado
3 *vt* [kwɒ'druːplɪkeɪt] (**a**) *(multiply by four)* cuadruplicar (**b**) *(make four copies of)* cuadruplicar

quaff [kwɒf] *vt Literary* trasegar, ingerir a grandes tragos

quagmire ['kwægmaɪə(r)] *n* (**a**) *(bog)* barrizal *m*, lodazal *m* (**b**) *(difficult situation)* atolladero *m*

quahog ['kwɑːhɒg] *n US* mercenaria *f*, almeja *f* americana

quail¹ [kweɪl] (*pl* **quail**) *n (bird)* codorniz *f*

quail² *vi (person)* amedrentarse, amilanarse (**at** *or* **before** ante)

quaint [kweɪnt] *adj* (**a**) *(picturesque)* pintoresco(a) (**b**) *(old-fashioned)* anticuado(a) (**c**) *(odd)* singular, extraño(a)

quaintly ['kweɪntlɪ] *adv* (**a**) *(in a picturesque way)* pintorescamente (**b**) *(in an old-fashioned way)* de forma anticuada; **she was q. dressed** iba vestida a la antigua (**c**) *(oddly)* singularmente, extrañamente

quaintness ['kweɪntnɪs] *n* (**a**) *(picturesqueness)* lo pintoresco (**b**) *(old-fashioned charm)* encanto *m* anticuado (**c**) *(oddness)* lo singular *or* extraño

quake [kweɪk] **1** *n Fam (earthquake)* terremoto *m*
2 *vi* temblar, estremecerse; IDIOM **to q. in one's boots** estar muerto(a) de miedo

Quaker ['kweɪkə(r)] *n Rel* cuáquero(a) *m,f*

Quakerism ['kweɪkərɪzəm] *n* cuaquerismo *m*

qualification [kwɒlɪfɪ'keɪʃən] *n* (**a**) *(diploma)* titulación *f*; **he left school with no qualifications** se fue del colegio sin obtener ninguna titulación; **academic qualifications** títulos académicos; **professional qualifications** cualificaciones profesionales
(**b**) *(requirement)* requisito *m*; **one of the qualifications for this job is a sense of humour** uno de los requisitos para este puesto es tener sentido del humor
(**c**) *(completion of studies)* **after q.** después de obtener el título
(**d**) *(modification)* reserva *f*; **they accepted the idea with some/without q.** aceptaron la idea con/sin reservas
(**e**) *(for competition)* clasificación *f*

qualified ['kwɒlɪfaɪd] *adj* (**a**) *(having diploma)* titulado(a); **to be q. to do sth** tener el título necesario para hacer algo; **our staff are highly q.** nuestro personal está altamente cualificado; **applications are invited from suitably q. persons** sólo se aceptarán solicitudes de personas debidamente cualificadas
(**b**) *(competent)* capaz, capacitado(a); **to be q. to do sth** estar capacitado(a) para hacer algo; **I don't feel q. to discuss such matters** no me siento capacitado para abordar temas de este tipo
(**c**) *(modified)* limitado(a), parcial; **their plan met with q. acceptance** su plan fue aceptado pero con ciertas salvedades ►► *Pol* ***q. majority*** mayoría *f* cualificada; *Pol* ***q. majority voting*** votación *f* por mayoría cualificada

qualifier ['kwɒlɪfaɪə(r)] *n* (**a**) *(person, team)* clasificado(a) *m,f*; *(match)* partido *m* de clasificación, eliminatoria *f* (**b**) *Gram* calificador *m*, modificador *m*

qualify ['kwɒlɪfaɪ] **1** *vt* (**a**) *(make competent)* **to q. sb for sth/to do sth** capacitar a alguien para algo/para hacer algo; **what qualifies him to talk about French politics?** ¿qué autoridad tiene para hablar de política francesa? (**b**) *(modify)* matizar; **they qualified their acceptance of the plan** aceptaron el plan con algunas salvedades (**c**) *Gram* modificar
2 *vi* (**a**) *(complete studies)* **to q. as a doctor** obtener el título de médico(a); **only 10 percent of the students go on to q.** sólo el 10 por ciento de los alumnos termina la carrera *or Am* llega a recibirse (**b**) *(be eligible)* **to q. for sth** tener derecho a algo; *Fig* **it hardly qualifies as a mountain** difícilmente podría decirse que es una montaña (**c**) *(in competition)* clasificarse (**for** para)

qualifying ['kwɒlɪfaɪɪŋ] *adj* (**a**) *(round, game)* eliminatorio(a); *(team)* clasificado(a) (**b**) *(exam)* de ingreso; *(candidate)* aceptado(a) (**c**) *(modifying)* **a q. statement** una matización

qualitative ['kwɒlɪtətɪv] *adj* cualitativo(a) ►► ***q. analysis*** análisis *m* cualitativo

qualitatively ['kwɒlɪtətɪvlɪ] *adv* cualitativamente

quality ['kwɒlɪtɪ] *n* **1** (**a**) *(standard)* calidad *f*; **of good/poor q.** de buena/mala calidad; **q. of life** calidad de vida ►► ***q. control*** control *m* de calidad; *Ind* ***q. controller*** responsable *mf* del control de calidad
(**b**) *(excellence)* calidad *f*; **q. matters more than quantity** la calidad es más importante que la cantidad ►► *Ind* ***q. circle*** círculo *m* de calidad
(**c**) *(characteristic, feature)* cualidad *f*; **these tyres have superior road-holding qualities** estos neumáticos tienen mejor agarre *or* adherencia
(**d**) *(tone) (of voice, sound)* timbre *m*
(**e**) *(in phonetics)* calidad *f*
(**f**) *Br Fam (newspaper)* periódico *m* serio
(**g**) *Old-fashioned (high social status)* clase *f*; **a gentleman of q.** un caballero con clase
2 *adj (product)* de calidad ►► *Br* ***q. newspapers*** prensa *f* no sensacionalista; ***q. time*** = tiempo que uno reserva para disfrutar de la pareja, la familia, los amigos, etc., y alejarse de las preocupaciones laborales y domésticas

qualm [kwɑːm] *n* escrúpulo *m*, reparo *m*; **to have no qualms about doing sth** no tener ningún escrúpulo *or* reparo en hacer algo

quandary ['kwɒndərɪ] *n* dilema *m*; **to be in a q. (about sth)** estar en un dilema (sobre algo)

quango ['kwæŋgəʊ] (*pl* **quangos**) *n Br Pol* (*abbr* **quasi-autonomous non-governmental organization**) = organismo público semiindependiente

quanta *pl of* **quantum**

quantifiable [kwɒntɪ'faɪəbəl] *adj* cuantificable

quantification [kwɒntɪfɪ'keɪʃən] *n* cuantificación *f*

quantifier ['kwɒntɪfaɪə(r)] *n* (**a**) *Math* cuantificador *m* (**b**) *Gram* cuantificador *m* (**c**) *Phil* cuantificador *m*

quantify ['kwɒntɪfaɪ] *vt* cuantificar; **it is hard to q. the damage** es difícil cuantificar el daño

quantitative ['kwɒntɪtətɪv] *adj* cuantitativo(a) ►► ***q. analysis*** análisis *m* cuantitativo

quantitatively ['kwɒntɪtətɪvlɪ] *adv* cuantitativamente

quantity ['kwɒntɪtɪ] *n* (**a**) *(amount)* cantidad *f*; **in q.** en grandes cantidades ►► ***q. surveyor*** estimador(ora) *m,f*, medidor(ora) *m,f (en obra)* (**b**) *Math* cantidad *f* (**c**) *(of syllable, vowel)* cantidad *f*

quantum ['kwɒntəm] (*pl* **quanta** ['kwɒntə]) *n* (**a**) *Phys* cuanto *m* ►► *Fig* ***q. jump*** paso *m* de gigante; ***q. leap*** paso *m* de gigante; ***q. mechanics*** mecánica *f* cuántica; ***q. physics*** física *f* cuántica; ***q. theory*** teoría *f* cuántica (**b**) *Formal* cuantía *f*

quarantine ['kwɒrəntiːn] **1** *n* cuarentena *f*; **to be in q.** estar en cuarentena; **they put the town under q.** pusieron al pueblo en cuarentena
2 *vt* poner en cuarentena

quark [kwɑːk] *n Phys* quark *m*

quarrel ['kwɒrəl] **1** *n* (**a**) *(argument)* pelea *f*, discusión *f*; **to have a q.** pelearse; **to pick a q. with sb** buscar pelea con alguien; **are you trying to start a q.?** ¿buscas pelea? (**b**) *(disagreement)* discrepancia *f*, desacuerdo *m*; **I have no q. with you/her proposal** no tengo nada en contra tuya/de su propuesta; **my only q. with the plan is its cost** mi único reparo con el plan es su costo
2 *vi* (*pt & pp* **quarrelled**, *US* **quarreled**) (**a**) *(argue)* pelearse, discutir (**with/about** *or* **over** con/por); **let's not q. about or over it** no discutamos por esto; **they're always quarrelling over money** siempre se están peleando por dinero
(**b**) *(disagree)* **to q. with sth** discrepar de algo; **I can't q. with that** estoy de acuerdo

quarrelling, *US* **quarreling** ['kwɒrəlɪŋ] *n* peleas *fpl*, discusiones *fpl*

quarrelsome ['kwɒrəlsəm] *adj* peleón(ona)

quarry[1] ['kwɒrɪ] *n* (**a**) *(prey)* presa *f* (**b**) *Fig* presa *f*

quarry[2] **1** *n (for stone)* cantera *f*
2 *vt (hill)* excavar; *(stone)* extraer; *Fig* **innumerable film plots have been quarried from his plays** innumerables argumentos de películas se han inspirado en sus piezas teatrales
3 *vi* explotar una cantera

quarryman ['kwɒrɪmæn] *n* cantero *m*

quart [kwɔːt] *n (liquid measurement)* cuarto *m* de galón *(UK = 1,136 litros; US = 0,946 litros)*; PROV *Br* **you can't get** *or* **put** *or* **fit a q. into a pint pot** lo que no puede ser, no puede ser, y además es imposible

quarter ['kwɔːtə(r)] **1** *n* (**a**) *(fraction, of orange, of moon)* cuarto *m*; **he ate a q. of the cake** se comió una *or* la cuarta parte del pastel; **we've only done a q. of the work** sólo hemos hecho una cuarta parte del trabajo; **a q. of a century** un cuarto de siglo; **during the first q. of the century** durante el primer cuarto de siglo; **a q. of an hour** un cuarto de hora; **a q. of a pound** un cuarto de libra *(= 113,5 grs)*; **three quarters** tres cuartos; **three quarters of all women** las tres cuartas partes de las mujeres; **three and a q. (litres)** tres (litros) y cuarto; **the bottle was still a q. full** quedaba aún un cuarto de botella; **it's a q. empty** le falta un cuarto; **it's three quarters empty** le faltan tres cuartos
(**b**) *(in telling time)* **it's/at a q. to** *or US* **of six** son/a las seis menos cuarto; **it's a q. to** son menos cuarto; **it's/at a q. past** *or US* **after six** son/a las seis y cuarto; **it's a q. past** son y cuarto
(**c**) *(three-month period)* trimestre *m*; **published every q.** publicado(a) trimestralmente ►► *Br* ***q. day*** = día del trimestre en el que se paga el alquiler
(**d**) *(area of city)* barrio *m*, zona *f*; **the residential/industrial q.** el barrio *or* la zona residencial/industrial
(**e**) *(part of butchered animal)* cuarto *m*
(**f**) *(phase of moon)* cuarto *m*; **the moon is in the first/last q.** la luna está en cuarto creciente/menguante
(**g**) *Naut (direction)* **the wind is in the port/starboard q.** el viento sopla de babor/estribor
(**h**) *(group)* **in some quarters** en algunos círculos; **in well-informed quarters** en círculos bien informados; **help came from an unexpected q.** la ayuda llegó de donde menos se esperaba; **donations poured in from all quarters** llegaban donaciones de todos lados
(**i**) **quarters** *(lodgings)* alojamiento *m*; **she took up quarters in central London** se alojó en el centro de Londres; *Mil* **officer quarters** residencia de oficiales
(**j**) *(mercy)* **to give no q.** no dar cuartel; **there was no q. given or asked** ni se dio ni se pidió cuartel
(**k**) *US (coin)* cuarto *m* de dólar
(**l**) *Sport* ***q. final*** *(match)* enfrentamiento *m* de cuartos de final; ***the q. finals*** los cuartos de final
(**m**) *(in basketball, ice hockey)* cuarto *m*
(**n**) *US Mus* ***q. note*** negra *f*
2 *adj* **a q. hour/century/pound** un cuarto de hora/siglo/libra ►► ***q. pounder*** = hamburguesa que pesa aproximadamente un cuarto de libra
3 *vt* (**a**) *(divide into four)* dividir en cuatro partes (**b**) *Mil (troops)* acantonar, alojar (**c**) *Hist (prisoner)* descuartizar

quarterback ['kwɔːtəbæk] **1** *n US* quarterback *m (en fútbol americano, jugador que dirige el ataque), Méx* mariscal *m* de campo
2 *vt US* (**a**) *(football team)* **he quarterbacked the Marlins to three Superbowls** como quarterback, condujo a los Marlins a tres Superbowls (**b**) *(enterprise)* dirigir

quarterdeck ['kwɔːtədek] *n (of ship)* alcázar *m*, cubierta *f* de popa

quarter-finalist ['kwɔːtə'faɪnəlɪst] *n* cuartofinalista *mf*

quarterlight ['kwɔːtəlaɪt] *n Aut (window)* ventanilla *f* triangular

quarterly ['kwɔːtəlɪ] **1** *n* publicación *f* trimestral
2 *adj* trimestral
3 *adv* trimestralmente

quartermaster ['kwɔːtəmɑːstə(r)] *n Mil* oficial *m* de intendencia

quarterstaff ['kwɔːtəstɑːf] *n Hist* pica *f*

quartet [kwɔː'tet] *n* (**a**) *Mus (players, piece of music)* cuarteto *m* (**b**) *(group of four people)* cuarteto *m*

quartile ['kwɔːtaɪl] *n (in statistics)* cuartil *m*

quarto ['kwɔːtəʊ] **1** *n* (*pl* **quartos**) pliego *m* en cuarto
2 *adj (volume)* en cuarto; **a q. sheet** una cuartilla

quartz [kwɔːts] *n* cuarzo *m* ►► ***q. clock*** reloj *m* de cuarzo; ***q. crystal*** cristal *m* de cuarzo; ***q. watch*** reloj *m* de cuarzo

quartz-halogen ['kwɔːts'hælədʒən] *adj* de cuarzo halógeno

quasar ['kweɪzɑː(r)] *n Astron* cuásar *m*, quasar *m*

quash [kwɒʃ] *vt* (**a**) *(revolt)* sofocar; *(objection)* acallar; **their creativity is quashed at an early age** se reprime su creatividad a temprana edad (**b**) *Law (sentence, verdict)* revocar, anular

quasi- ['kweɪzaɪ] *prefix* cuasi-

quatercentenary [kwætəsen'tiːnərɪ] *n* cuarto centenario *m*

Quaternary [kwɒ'tɜːnərɪ] *Geol* **1** *n* **the Q.** el cuaternario
2 *adj* cuaternario(a)

quatrain ['kwɒtreɪn] *n Lit* cuarteto *m*

quattrocento [kwætrəʊ'tʃentəʊ] *n Art* quattrocento *m*

quaver ['kweɪvə(r)] **1** *n* (**a**) *Mus* corchea *f* (**b**) *(in voice)* temblor *m*
2 *vi (voice)* temblar

quavering ['kweɪvərɪŋ], **quavery** ['kweɪvərɪ] *adj* temblante, trémulo(a)

quay [kiː] *n* muelle *m*

quayside ['kiːsaɪd] *n* muelle *m*

Que (*abbr* **Quebec**) Quebec

queasiness ['kwiːzɪnɪs] *n* (**a**) *(nausea)* mareo *m*, náuseas *fpl* (**b**) *(uneasiness)* incomodidad *f*

queasy ['kwiːzɪ] *adj* (**a**) *(nauseous)* mareado(a); **to feel q.** estar mareado(a), tener náuseas; **the very sight of meat makes her feel q.** con sólo ver carne tiene náuseas (**b**) *(uneasy)* intranquilo(a)

Quebec [kwɪ'bek] *n* (provincia *f* de) Quebec ▸▸ ***Q. City*** Quebec (capital)

Quebec(k)er [kwɪ'bekə(r)], **Quebecois** (*pl* **Quebecois**) [kebe'kwɑː] *n* persona de Quebec

queen [kwiːn] **1** *n* (**a**) *(of country)* reina *f*; **she was q. to Charles II** fue la reina consorte de Charles II ▸▸ ***q. bee*** abeja *f* reina; IDIOM **she's q. bee** es la que corta el bacalao *or* dirige el cotarro; ***the Queen's English*** el inglés estándar; ***the Q. Mother*** *or Fam* ***Mum*** la reina madre; *Br Parl* ***the Queen's Speech*** = discurso inaugural que pronuncia la reina en su apertura anual del parlamento; *Br Mil* ***Queen's Regulations*** reglamento *m* militar
(**b**) *Br Law* ***Q.'s Bench (Division)*** = una de las tres secciones del Tribunal Supremo; ***Q.'s Counsel*** = abogado de alto rango; ***Q.'s evidence:*** **to turn Q.'s evidence** = inculpar a un cómplice ante un tribunal a cambio de recibir un trato indulgente
(**c**) *(in cards, chess)* dama *f*, reina *f*; **the q. of clubs/hearts** la reina de tréboles /corazones
(**d**) *Fam Pej (homosexual)* marica *m*, maricón *m*
2 *vt* (**a**) *(put on airs)* **to q. it over sb** ser una marimandona con alguien (**b**) *(in chess)* **to q. a pawn** convertir un peón en reina

queenly ['kwiːnlɪ] *adj (grace, bearing)* de reina

Queensberry Rules ['kwiːnzbərɪ'ruːlz] *npl* (**a**) *(in boxing)* reglamento *m* (**b**) *Fig* reglamento *m*

queen-size(d) ['kwiːnsaɪz(d)] *adj (bed)* grande

queer ['kwɪə(r)] **1** *n Fam Pej (male homosexual)* marica *m*, maricón *m*
2 *adj* (**a**) *(strange)* raro(a), extraño(a); IDIOM *Fam Old-fashioned* **to be in q. street** estar con la soga *or Esp* el agua al cuello; *Fam* **a q. fish** un bicho raro (**b**) *(suspicious)* raro(a), sospechoso(a) (**c**) *Fam (unwell)* **to feel q.** encontrarse mal; **to come over** *or* **to be taken q.** ponerse malo(a) (**d**) *Fam Pej (homosexual)* marica, maricón(ona); **q. poetry/cinema** poesía/cine gay
3 *vt Fam* **to q. sb's pitch** aguarle la fiesta a alguien; *US* **to q. the act** fastidiarla

queer-basher ['kwɪəbæʃə(r)] *n Br Fam* = persona que agrede a los homosexuales

queer-bashing ['kwɪəbæʃɪŋ] *n Br Fam* = ataques físicos o verbales contra homosexuales

queerly ['kwɪəlɪ] *adv (oddly)* extrañamente; **to look at sb q.** mirar extrañado(a) a alguien

queerness ['kwɪənɪs] *n* (**a**) *(strangeness)* extrañeza *f* (**b**) *(queasiness)* mareo *m*, náusea *f*

quell [kwel] *vt* (**a**) *(revolt)* sofocar (**b**) *(passion)* apagar (**c**) *(allay) (pain)* mitigar; *(doubt, worry, fears)* disipar

quench [kwentʃ] *vt* (**a**) *(thirst)* apagar (**b**) *(fire)* apagar (**c**) *(enthusiasm, desire)* aplacar (**d**) *(metal)* enfriar

querulous ['kwer(j)ʊləs] *adj* lastimero(a), quejumbroso(a)

querulously ['kwer(j)ʊləslɪ] *adv* lastimeramente, quejumbrosamente

query ['kwɪərɪ] **1** *n* (**a**) *(question, doubt)* duda *f*, pregunta *f*; *(on phone line, to expert, at information desk)* consulta *f*; **I have a q.** tengo una duda *or* pregunta; **she accepted my explanations without (a) q.** aceptó mis explicaciones sin preguntar nada; **to raise a q. about sth** *(call into question)* poner en duda algo
(**b**) *Br (question mark)* signo *m* de interrogación ▸▸ *US* ***q. mark*** signo *m* de interrogación
2 *vt* (**a**) *(express doubt about) (invoice)* pedir explicaciones sobre; *(decision)* cuestionar; **to q. if** *or* **whether...** poner en duda si...
(**b**) *(ask)* preguntar; **"how much is it?" she queried** "¿cuánto es?", preguntó
(**c**) *US (consult)* **he queried some eminent authors for advice** acudió a autores de renombre en busca de consejo
(**d**) *Comptr (database)* consultar ▸▸ ***q. language*** lenguaje *m* de consulta (estructurado)

querying ['kwɪərɪɪŋ] *adj* dubitativo(a)

quest [kwest] *Literary* **1** *n* búsqueda *f* (for de); **her q. for justice** su búsqueda de justicia; **to go** *or* **be in q. of sth** ir en busca de algo
2 *vi* **to q. after** *or* **for sth** ir en busca de algo, buscar algo

QUESTION ['kwestʃən] **1** *n* (**a**) *(interrogation)* pregunta *f*; **to ask (sb) a q.** hacer una pregunta (a alguien); **we'll send you a refund, no questions asked** le reembolsaremos, sin ningún compromiso; **how will we pay for it? – good q.!** ¿cómo lo vamos a pagar? – ¡buena pregunta!; **the q. is/remains, can we trust them?** la cuestión es/sigue siendo, ¿podemos confiar en ellos?; **to carry out orders without q.** ejecutar órdenes sin preguntar ▸▸ ***q. mark*** signo *m* de interrogación; *Fig* **there is a q. mark against her reliability** su *Esp* fiabilidad *or Am* confiabilidad está en duda; *Fig* **a q. mark hangs over the future of the project** el futuro del proyecto está en el aire; *Br* ***q. master*** *(in quiz game)* presentador(ora) *m,f (de un concurso)*; *Gram* ***q. tag*** = pregunta corta de confirmación, question tag *f*; *Br Parl* ***q. time*** = sesión semanal de control parlamentario en la que los ministros responden a las preguntas de los diputados
(**b**) *(doubt)* duda *f*; **there is no q. about it** no cabe duda (al respecto); **there is no q. that...** no cabe duda alguna (de) que...; **to call sth into q.** poner algo en duda; **beyond q.** *(irrefutably)* fuera de (toda) duda; *(undoubtedly)* sin duda; **her commitment is in q.** su compromiso está en duda; **to be open to q.** ser cuestionable; **without q.** *(undoubtedly)* sin duda
(**c**) *(matter)* cuestión *f*; **the Irish q.** el problema irlandés; **it is a q. of keeping your concentration** se trata de mantener la concentración; **it's only a q. of time** sólo es cuestión de tiempo; **the matter/person in q.** el asunto/ individuo en cuestión
(**d**) *(possibility)* **there is no q. of our agreeing to that** en ningún caso vamos a aceptar eso; **that's out of the q.!** ¡de eso ni hablar!
2 *vt* (**a**) *(ask questions to)* preguntar; *(for inquiry)* interrogar; *(for survey)* encuestar; **she was questioned on her views** *(in interview)* le pidieron su opinión
(**b**) *(cast doubt on)* cuestionar, poner en duda; **I would q. the wisdom of that course of action** yo pondría en duda la oportunidad de esa táctica

questionable ['kwestʃənəbəl] *adj* (**a**) *(doubtful)* cuestionable, dudoso(a); **it is q. whether she knew** no está muy claro si ella lo sabía; **to be in q. taste** ser de un gusto más que dudoso (**b**) *(suspicious, disreputable) (motives, behaviour)* cuestionable, dudoso(a)

questioner ['kwestʃənə(r)] *n* interrogador(ora) *m,f*; **our next q. is from Belfast** *(on discussion programme)* la siguiente pregunta nos la hace una persona de Belfast

questioning ['kwestʃənɪŋ] **1** *n (interrogation)* interrogatorio *m*; **he was held for q. by the police** la policía lo detuvo para interrogarlo
2 *adj (look, mind)* inquisitivo(a)

questioningly ['kwestʃənɪŋlɪ] *adv* inquisitivamente

questionnaire [kwestʃə'neə(r)] *n* cuestionario *m*

queue [kjuː] **1** *n* (**a**) *Br (line)* cola *f*; **they were standing in a q.** estaban haciendo cola; **I was first in the q.** yo era el primero en la cola; **to form a q.** hacer cola; **to jump the q.** colarse (**b**) *Comptr* cola *f*
2 *vt Comptr* poner en cola
3 *vi Br* hacer cola; **we had to q. for tickets** tuvimos que hacer cola para comprar las entradas

▸ **queue up** *vi Br* hacer cola

queue-jump ['kjuːdʒʌmp] *vi Br* colarse, saltarse la cola

queue-jumper ['kjuːdʒʌmpə(r)] *n Br* = persona que no respeta su turno en una cola o lista de espera

queue-jumping ['kjuːdʒʌmpɪŋ] *n Br* **q. is considered impolite** el colarse *or* saltarse la cola es considerado una falta de educación

quibble ['kwɪbəl] **1** *n* objeción *f or Esp* pega *f* insignificante; **I have one small q.** tengo una pequeña objeción
2 *vi* poner peros *or Esp* pegas (**about** *or* **over** a); **to q. over details** poner peros *or Esp* pegas a detalles mínimos; **let's not q.** no vamos a discutir por una tontería

quibbler ['kwɪbələ(r)] *n* quisquilloso(a) *m,f*

quibbling ['kwɪbəlɪŋ] *n* peros *mpl*, *Esp* pegas *fpl*

quiche [kiːʃ] *n* quiche *m or f* ▸▸ ***q. lorraine*** quiche *m or f* de tocino *or Esp* beicon y queso

QUICK [kwɪk] **1** *n* **to bite one's nails to the q.** morderse las uñas hasta hacerse daño *or* lastimarse; *Archaic or Literary* **the q. and the dead** los vivos y los muertos; IDIOM **to cut sb to the q.** herir a alguien en lo más profundo
2 *adj* (**a**) *(rapid)* rápido(a); **to have a q. bath** darse un baño rápido; **to have a q. drink** tomarse algo rápidamente; **can I have a q. word with you?** ¿podríamos hablar un momento?; **to be a q. learner** aprender

rápidamente; **there is little prospect of a q. solution** es improbable que se halle una pronta solución; **to have a q. temper** tener un genio muy vivo; **q. thinking** rapidez mental; **that was q.!** ¡qué rápido!; **q., the train's about to leave!** ¡corre *or* rápido, que el tren va a salir!; **be q.!** ¡date prisa!, *Am* ¡apúrate!; **...and be q. about it** ...y rapidito; **three buses went by in q. succession** tres autobuses pasaron rápidamente uno detrás del otro; **to be q. to do sth** no tardar *or Am* demorar en hacer algo; **to be q. to criticize** apresurarse a criticar; **to be q. off the mark** *(to act)* no perder el tiempo; *(to understand)* ser muy espabilado(a) *or* despabilado(a); **the solution is just a q. fix** la solución es sólo un arreglo rápido, esto es sólo una solución de emergencia; *Mil* **q. march!** ¡paso ligero!; *Fam* **to have a q. one** *(drink)* tomar una copa rápida; *(sex)* echar uno rápido

(**b**) *(clever) (person)* listo(a), despierto(a), *RP* vivo(a); *(mind)* despierto(a)

3 *adv Fam (to run, talk, think)* rápido; IDIOM **as q. as a flash** en un suspiro, como una exhalación

quick-acting ['kwɪk'æktɪŋ] *adj (mechanism, medication)* de acción rápida

quick-change artist ['kwɪk'tʃeɪndʒɑːtɪst] *n Theat* transformista *mf*; *Fig* chaquetero(a) *m,f*

quicken ['kwɪkən] 1 *vt* (**a**) *(make faster)* acelerar; **to q. one's pace** *or* **step** apretar *or* acelerar el paso (**b**) *(imagination, appetite)* estimular; *(interest)* despertar

2 *vi* (**a**) *(pace)* acelerarse; **his pulse quickened** se le aceleró el pulso (**b**) *(imagination)* estimularse; *(interest)* despertarse (**c**) *Literary (baby in womb)* empezar a moverse

quickening ['kwɪkənɪŋ] 1 *n Literary (of baby)* primeros movimientos *mpl*

2 *adj* cada vez más acelerado(a)

quickfire ['kwɪkfaɪə(r)] *adj (repartee, questions)* rápido(a)

quick-freeze ['kwɪk'friːz] *vt* congelar rápidamente

quickie ['kwɪkɪ] *Fam* 1 *n (question)* pregunta *f* rápida; **to have a q.** *(drink)* tomar una copa rápida; *(sex)* echar uno rápido

2 *adj* **q. divorce** divorcio por la vía rápida

quicklime ['kwɪklaɪm] *n* cal *f* viva

quickly ['kwɪklɪ] *adv* rápidamente, rápido, deprisa; **come as q. as possible** ven en cuanto puedas; **I q. realized that...** enseguida me di cuenta de que...; **she q. lost interest in the subject** enseguida perdió interés en el tema

quickness ['kwɪknɪs] *n* (**a**) *(speed)* rapidez *f* (**b**) *(of mind)* agudeza *f* (**c**) *(hastiness)* **his q. of temper** el genio tan vivo que tiene

quick-release ['kwɪkrə'liːs] *adj (wheel, mechanism)* abre-fácil

quicksand ['kwɪksænd] *n* arenas *fpl* movedizas

quicksilver ['kwɪksɪlvə(r)] 1 *n Old-fashioned (mercury)* azogue *m*

2 *adj (mind, tongue)* imprevisible

quickstep ['kwɪkstep] *n* = baile de salón de pasos rápidos

quick-tempered ['kwɪk'tempəd] *adj* irascible; **to be q.** tener un genio muy vivo

quick-witted ['kwɪk'wɪtɪd] *adj (intelligent)* agudo(a)

quick-wittedness ['kwɪk'wɪtədnɪs] *n (intelligence)* agudeza *f*

quid[1] [kwɪd] *(pl* **quid**) *n Br Fam (pound)* libra *f*; IDIOM *Fam* **to be quids in** *(financially)* salir ganando; *(be lucky)* estar de suerte

quid[2] *n (of tobacco)* pedazo *m*, trozo *m*

quiddity ['kwɪdətɪ] *n* (**a**) *Phil* esencia *f* (**b**) *(trifling detail)* minucia *f*

quid pro quo ['kwɪdprəʊ'kwəʊ] *n* compensación *f*; **what was the q. for her silence?** ¿cuál fue la contrapartida de su silencio?

quiescence [kwɪ'esəns] *n Literary* inactividad *f*, pasividad *f*

quiescent [kwɪ'esənt] *adj Literary* inactivo(a), pasivo(a)

QUIET ['kwaɪət] 1 *n (silence)* silencio *m*; *(peacefulness)* tranquilidad *f*; **the q. of the countryside** la paz del campo; **q. please!** ¡silencio, por favor!; IDIOM *Fam* **to do sth on the q.** hacer algo a escondidas *or* bajo cuerda *or Esp* a la chita callando

2 *adj* (**a**) *(not loud) (music)* tranquilo(a); *(voice)* bajo(a); *(engine, machine)* silencioso(a); **it was very q. in the church** no se oía ni un ruido en la iglesia; **be q.!** ¡cállate!; **please be as q. as possible** procura no hacer ruido, por favor; **you're very q. today!** ¡estás muy callado hoy!; **she was a q. child** era una niña muy callada; **they went q.** se callaron; **to keep q.** *(make no noise)* no hacer ruido; *(say nothing)* estar callado(a), callarse; **to keep q. about sth** guardar silencio *or* no decir nada sobre algo; **to keep sb q.** hacer callar a alguien; **to keep sth q.** mantener algo en secreto; IDIOM **to be as q. as a mouse** *(person)* no hacer ni un ruido; IDIOM **it was as q. as the grave** había un silencio sepulcral

(**b**) *(discreet)* discreto(a); *(confidence, determination)* contenido(a); **to have a q. laugh at sth/sb** reírse para sus adentros de algo/alguien; **I'm going to have to have a q. word with him about his behaviour** voy a tener que discutir con él en privado su comportamiento; *(irony, optimism)* contenido(a)

(**c**) *(peaceful) (village, evening)* tranquilo(a); **a q. wedding** una boda íntima *or* discreta; **anything for a q. life** lo que sea con tal de que me dejen en paz; **we had a q. Christmas** pasamos una Navidad tranquila; **she had a q. night** *(sick person)* pasó una noche tranquila; *Hum* **all q. on the western front** sin moros en la costa

(**d**) *(business, market)* inactivo(a), poco animado(a)

3 *vt* = **quieten**

▸ **quiet down** = **quieten down**

quieten ['kwaɪətən] 1 *vt (child, audience, conscience)* calmar, tranquilizar; *(doubts, fears)* disipar

2 *vi (child)* calmarse; *(music)* apagarse

▸ **quieten down** 1 *vt sep (make silent)* hacer callar; *(make calm)* tranquilizar, calmar

2 *vi (become silent)* callarse; *(become calm)* calmarse, tranquilizarse; **the meeting gradually quietened down** poco a poco la reunión se fue calmando; **he's quietened down a lot since he got married** es mucho más moderado desde que se casó

quietism ['kwaɪətɪzəm] *n* (**a**) *Rel* quietismo *m* (**b**) *(passivity)* quietismo *m*, pasividad *f*

quietist ['kwaɪətɪst] 1 *n Rel* quietista *mf*

2 *adj* quietista, pasivo(a)

quietly ['kwaɪətlɪ] *adv* (**a**) *(silently)* silenciosamente, sin hacer ruido; **they were talking q.** hablaban en voz baja; **sit q.** siéntate y no hagas ruido

(**b**) *(discreetly)* discretamente; **he q. removed their names from the list** borró sus nombres discretamente de la lista; **they got married q.** se casaron en la intimidad

(**c**) *(calmly)* tranquilamente, apaciblemente; **a q. flowing river** un río que fluye apaciblemente; **to be q. determined** estar interiormente resuelto(a); **to be q. confident** estar íntimamente convencido(a)

quietness ['kwaɪətnɪs] *n* (**a**) *(silence)* silencio *m*; **the q. of her voice** el tono quedo de su voz (**b**) *(calmness, tranquillity)* calma *f*, tranquilidad *f* (**c**) *(of colour, style)* discreción *f*

quietude ['kwaɪətjuːd] *n Literary* placidez *f*

quietus [kwaɪ'iːtəs] *n Literary (death)* óbito *m*; **to give sth its q.** firmar el acta de defunción de algo

quiff [kwɪf] *n Br (of hair)* tupé *m*

quill [kwɪl] *n* (**a**) *(feather)* pluma *f*; *(shaft of feather)* cañón *m* (**b**) **q. (pen)** pluma *f* (**c**) *(of porcupine)* púa *f*

quilt [kwɪlt] 1 *n (thin bedcover)* edredón *m*; *(duvet)* edredón *m* (nórdico) ▸▸ ***q. cover*** funda *f* de edredón

2 *vt* acolchar

quilted ['kwɪltɪd] *adj (jacket, toilet paper)* acolchado(a)

quilting ['kwɪltɪŋ] *n* (**a**) *(material)* acolchado *m* (**b**) *(activity)* acolchado *m* ▸▸ *US* ***q. bee*** *or* **party** = reunión de amigas en una casa para coser un edredón

quim [kwɪm] *n Br Vulg* chocho *m*

quin [kwɪn] *n Br Fam* quintillizo(a) *m,f*

quince [kwɪns] *n* membrillo *m* ▸▸ ***q. jelly*** dulce *m* de membrillo

quincentenary ['kwɪnsen'tiːnərɪ], *US* **quincentennial** ['kwɪnsen'tenɪəl] 1 *n* quinto centenario *m*

2 *adj* quingentésimo(a)

quinidine ['kwɪnɪdaɪn] *n* quinidina *f*

quinine ['kwɪniːn] *n* quinina *f*

quinquennial [kwɪŋ'kwenɪəl] *adj* quinquenal

quinsy ['kwɪnzɪ] *n Med* angina *f*

quint [kwɪnt] *n US Fam* quintillizo(a) *m,f*

quintessence [kwɪn'tesəns] *n Formal* quintaesencia *f*; **she's the q. of Parisian glamour** es la quintaesencia del glamour parisino

quintessential [kwɪntɪ'senʃəl] *adj Formal* arquetípico(a), prototípico(a); **he's the q. Englishman** es el inglés por antonomasia, es la quintaesencia de lo inglés

quintessentially [kwɪntɪ'senʃəlɪ] *adv Formal* **he's q. Australian** es el australiano por antonomasia, es la quintaesencia de lo australiano

quintet [kwɪn'tet] *n* quinteto *m*

quintillion [kwɪn'tɪljən] *n Br* (10^{30}) quintillón *m*; *US* (10^{18}) trillón *m*

quintuple [kwɪn'tjuːpəl] 1 *adj* quíntuple

2 *vt* quintuplicar

3 *vi* quintuplicarse

quintuplet [kwɪnˈtjuːplɪt] *n* quintillizo(a) *m,f*

quip [kwɪp] **1** *n* broma *f*, chiste *m*; **to make a q.** hacer un chiste
2 *vi* (*pt & pp* **quipped**) bromear; **"only if I'm asked nicely," he quipped** "sólo si me lo piden amablemente", bromeó

quire [ˈkwaɪə(r)] *n* mano *m* (de papel)

quirk [kwɜːk] *n* **(a)** *(of character)* manía *f*; **it's one of the program's little quirks** es una de las manías que tiene este programa **(b)** *(of fate, nature)* capricho *m*; **by a q. of fate** por un capricho del destino

quirky [ˈkwɜːkɪ] *adj* peculiar

quirt [kwɜːrt] *n US* fusta *f*

quisling [ˈkwɪzlɪŋ] *n* traidor(ora) *m,f*

quit [kwɪt] **1** *vt* (*pt & pp* **quit** *or* **quitted**) **(a)** *(leave) (person, place)* abandonar, dejar; **to q. one's job** dejar el trabajo **(b)** *esp US (stop)* **to q. doing sth** dejar de hacer algo; **q. stalling and answer the question!** ¡déjate de rodeos y contesta a la pregunta!; *Fam* **q. it!** ¡déjalo ya! **(c)** *Comptr (application)* salir de
2 *vi* **(a)** *(leave)* irse; **to receive notice to q.** *(tenant)* recibir notificación de desalojo **(b)** *(give up)* abandonar; **you shouldn't q. so easily** no te rindas tan fácilmente; **I q.!** ¡me rindo! **(c)** *(resign)* dimitir; **I q.!** ¡me retiro! **(d)** *Comptr* salir
3 *adj* **to be q. of** haberse librado *or* deshecho de

> **False friend**: The Spanish verb **quitar** is not a translation for the English word **quit**. In Spanish the main meanings of **quitar** are "to remove", "to take off" or "to take away".

QUITE [kwaɪt] *adv* **(a)** *(entirely)* completamente, totalmente; **I q. agree** estoy completamente *or* totalmente de acuerdo; **I q. understand** lo entiendo perfectamente; **I can q. confidently say that...** puedo decir con toda confianza que...; **I'd be q. happy to lend a hand** me encantaría ayudar; **to be q. honest..., q. honestly...** para ser sincero(a)...; **q. the opposite** todo lo contrario; **you know q. well what I mean!** ¡sabes muy bien lo que quiero decir!; **if you've q. finished...** si es que has acabado ya...; **that's q. another matter!** eso es harina de otro costal; **not q. a month ago** no hace ni siquiera un mes; **that's not q. true** no es del todo cierto; **I'm not q. ready/sure** no estoy del todo listo/seguro; **it's not q. what I wanted** no es exactamente lo que yo quería; **it wasn't q. as easy as last time** no fue tan fácil como la última vez; **I can't q. see what you mean** no alcanzo a ver qué quieres decir, no veo bien qué es lo que quieres decir; **I didn't q. know how to react** no supe muy bien cómo reaccionar; **there's nothing q. like a hot bath** no hay nada como un baño caliente; **q. (so)!** ¡efectivamente!; **that's q. all right** *(it doesn't matter)* no importa; *(you're welcome)* no hay de qué; **q. apart from the fact that...** sin mencionar el hecho de que...; **q. enough** más que suficiente; **that's q. enough of that!** ¡ya es más que suficiente!; **she was sacked, and q. rightly too!** la echaron, ¡y con razón!
(b) *(fairly)* bastante; **q. recently** hace muy poco; **she's q. a good singer** es una cantante bastante buena; **I q. like him** me cae bastante bien; **q. a few** *or* **a lot of problems** bastantes problemas; **q. a lot of wine** bastante vino; **for q. a while** durante mucho tiempo; **we travelled q. some distance before finding help** tuvimos que recorrer una gran distancia hasta encontrar ayuda
(c) *(for emphasis)* **it was q. a surprise** fue toda una sorpresa; **it's been q. a** *or* **some day!** ¡menudo día!, *RP* ¡qué día!; **that movie is q. something** ¡menuda película!, *RP* ¡qué película!; **it was q. the best pizza I have ever had** ha sido la pizza más deliciosa que he comido nunca *or* en mi vida; **he's q. the gentleman** es todo un caballero

Quito [ˈkiːtəʊ] *n* Quito

quits [kwɪts] *adj* **to be q. (with sb)** estar en paz (con alguien); **now we're q.** ahora estamos en paz; **let's call it q.** vamos a dejarlo así

quitter [ˈkwɪtə(r)] *n Fam* **I'm no q.!** ¡no soy de los que abandonan!

quiver[1] [ˈkwɪvə(r)] *n (for arrows)* carcaj *m*, aljaba *f*

quiver[2] **1** *n (tremble)* estremecimiento *m*; **a q. of fear went down my spine** un escalofrío *or* estremecimiento me recorrió la espalda; **he had a q. in his voice** le temblaba la voz
2 *vi (tremble) (person)* estremecerse (**with** de); *(lips, voice)* temblar (**with** de); **to q. with fear/rage** estremecerse de miedo/ira

quivering [ˈkwɪvərɪŋ] *adj* tembloroso(a), trémulo(a); **he was a q. wreck** era un manojo de nervios

qui vive [ˈkiːˈviːv] *n* **to be on the q.** estar alerta, estar ojo avizor

quixotic [kwɪkˈsɒtɪk] *adj* quijotesco(a)

quixotically [kwɪkˈsɒtɪklɪ] *adv* quijotescamente

quiz [kwɪz] **1** *n* (*pl* **quizzes**) **(a)** *(competition, game)* concurso *m*; **q. (show)** programa *m* concurso **(b)** *US (test)* examen *m*, control *m*
2 *vt* (*pt & pp* **quizzed**) **(a)** *(question)* interrogar (**about** sobre) **(b)** *US (test)* examinar

quizmaster [ˈkwɪzmɑːstə(r)] *n* presentador(ora) *m,f (de un concurso)*

quizzical [ˈkwɪzɪkəl] *adj (look, air)* de duda burlona; **to give sb a q. look** echarle a alguien una mirada de duda burlona

quizzically [ˈkwɪzɪklɪ] *adv* con aire de duda burlona

quoin [kɔɪn] *n (cornerstone)* piedra *f* angular; *(keystone)* clave *f*

quoit [kwɔɪt] *n* herrón *m*, aro *m*; **quoits** *(game)* juego *m* de los aros

quorate [ˈkwɔːreɪt] *adj Br* **are we q.?** ¿hay quórum?

Quorn® [kwɔːn] *n* = tipo de proteína vegetal utilizada como sustituto de la carne

quorum [ˈkwɔːrəm] *n* quórum *m inv*; **to have a q.** tener quórum

quota [ˈkwəʊtə] *n* **(a)** *(limited quantity)* cuota *f*; **they operate a q. system** se rigen por un sistema de cuotas **(b)** *(share)* cupo *m*, cuota *f*; **I've had my q. of bad luck** ya he tenido mi cuota de mala suerte

quotable [ˈkwəʊtəbəl] *adj (remark, writer, book)* que se presta a ser citado(a); **the press find him very q.** con frecuencia aparecen citas suyas en la prensa; **what he said is not q. in a family newspaper** sus declaraciones no se pueden reproducir en un periódico leído por toda la familia

quotation [kwəʊˈteɪʃən] *n* **(a)** *(from author)* cita *f* ►► ***q. marks*** comillas *fpl*; *Fam* **our friend, in q. marks** nuestro amigo, entre comillas **(b)** *Com (for work)* presupuesto *m* **(c)** *St Exch* cotización *f*

quote [kwəʊt] **1** *n Fam* **(a)** *(from author)* cita *f*; **is that an actual q.?** ¿son palabras textuales? **(b) quotes** *(quotation marks)* comillas *fpl*; **in quotes** entre comillas **(c)** *Com (for work)* presupuesto *m*
2 *vt* **(a)** *(author, passage)* citar; **he was quoted as saying that...** se le atribuye haber dicho que...; **she was quoted as denying the allegation** se asegura que negó la acusación; **don't q. me on that** *(I'm not sure)* no estoy seguro; *(don't say I've said it)* no digas que he dicho eso; **in reply please q. this number** en su contestación por favor indique este número
(b) *Com (price)* dar un presupuesto de; **he quoted me a price of £100** me dio un presupuesto de 100 libras, fijó un precio de 100 libras
(c) *St Exch* cotizar; **gold prices were quoted at £500** el oro se cotizó a 500 libras; **quoted company** empresa cotizada en Bolsa
3 *vi (cite)* **to q. from Yeats** citar a Yeats; **q. unquote** entre comillas; **and I q....** y cito textualmente...

quoteworthy [ˈkwəʊtwɜːðɪ] *adj* digno(a) de ser citado(a)

quoth [kwəʊθ] *vt Old-fashioned or Hum* **q. I/she/they** fueron mis/sus/sus palabras

quotidian [kwəʊˈtɪdɪən] *adj Formal (commonplace)* cotidiano(a)

quotient [ˈkwəʊʃənt] *n Math* cociente *m*

q.v. [kjuːˈviː] *Formal* (*abbr* **quod vide**) véase

qwerty [ˈkwɜːtɪ] *adj (keyboard)* qwerty

R, r

R, r [ɑː(r)] *n (letter)* R, r *f*; *Fam* **the three R's** = lectura, escritura y aritmética

R *US* **(a)** *Pol* (*abbr* **Republican**) republicano(a) **(b)** *Cin* (*abbr* **restricted**) no recomendado(a) para menores

RA [ɑːˈreɪ] *n* (*abbr* **Royal Academician**) = miembro de la Real Academia de las Bellas Artes británica

RAAF [ræf] *n* (*abbr* **Royal Australian Air Force**) fuerzas *fpl* aéreas australianas

rabbet [ˈræbɪt] *n (groove)* rebaje *m*

rabbi [ˈræbaɪ] *n Rel* rabino *m*

rabbinate [ˈræbɪnɪt] *n* **(a)** *(post)* rabinato *m* **(b)** *(body)* rabinato *m*

rabbinic(al) [rəˈbɪnɪk(əl)] *adj* rabínico(a)

rabbit [ˈræbɪt] **1** *n* conejo *m*; **to produce a r. out of a hat** sacar un conejo de la chistera; IDIOM **to go at it like rabbits** darle como locos ►► *Fam* ***r. food*** = término despectivo para referirse a la ensalada y verdura; ***r. hole*** madriguera *f*; ***r. hutch*** conejera *f*; *Br Fam (cramped accommodation)* caja *f* de cerillas; ***r. punch*** colleja *f*, golpe *m* en la nuca; ***r. warren*** red *f* de madrigueras; *Fig* laberinto *m*

2 *vi* **(a)** *(hunt)* **to go rabbiting** ir a cazar conejos **(b)** *Br Fam (chatter)* parlotear, *Esp* cascar

►**rabbit on** *vi Br Fam* parlotear, *Esp* cascar

rabble [ˈræbəl] *n* **(a)** *(disorderly mob)* muchedumbre *f* **(b)** *Pej* **the r.** *(lower classes)* la chusma, el populacho

rabble-rouser [ˈræbəlˈraʊzə(r)] *n* agitador(ora) *m,f* (de masas)

rabble-rousing [ˈræbəlˈraʊzɪŋ] *adj* agitador(ora)

Rabelaisian [ræbəˈleɪzɪən] *adj* rabelesiano(a)

rabid [ˈræbɪd] *adj* **(a)** *(animal)* rabioso(a) **(b)** *(person, emotion)* furibundo(a)

rabidly [ˈræbɪdlɪ] *adv* **he's r. nationalistic** es un nacionalista furibundo

rabies [ˈreɪbiːz] *n* rabia *f*

RAC [ɑːreɪˈsiː] *n* (*abbr* **Royal Automobile Club**) = organización británica de ayuda al automovilista, *Esp* ≃ RACE *m*, *Arg* ≃ ACA *m*

raccoon [rəˈkuːn] *n* mapache *m*; **a r. coat** un abrigo de piel de mapache

race[1] [reɪs] **1** *n* **(a)** *(contest)* carrera *f*; **the hundred metres r.** los cien metros lisos; **the r. for the Presidency** la carrera por la presidencia; *Fig* **the r. is on (to)** ha comenzado la carrera (para); IDIOM **a r. against time** *or* **the clock** una carrera contra reloj

(b) **the races** *(horseraces)* las carreras; **a day at the races** un día en las carreras ►► ***r. meeting*** concurso *m* de carreras de caballos

(c) *(current, in sea)* corriente *f*

2 *vt* **(a)** *(athlete)* correr con *or* contra; **I'll r. you home!** ¡te echo una carrera hasta casa!

(b) *(rush)* **the casualties were raced to hospital** llevaron a los heridos al hospital a toda prisa

(c) *(put into race)* **to r. horses** tener caballos de carreras; **to r. pigeons** hacer carreras de palomas

(d) *Aut* **to r. the engine** acelerar el motor

3 *vi* **(a)** *(athlete, horse)* correr, competir; **his horse will be racing at Ascot** su caballo va a correr en Ascot; **the drivers were racing against each other** los conductores estaban a ver quién iba más deprisa

(b) *(move quickly)* correr; **to r. in/out** entrar/salir corriendo; **to r. down the street** correr calle abajo; **to r. by** *(time)* pasar volando; **a thousand ideas raced through her mind** se le ocurrieron mil ideas; **the competition is racing ahead of us** la competencia se nos adelanta

(c) *(engine)* acelerarse; *(pulse, heart)* palpitar aceleradamente

►**race about, race around** *vi* dar vueltas de un lado a otro

race[2] *n (of people, animals)* raza *f*; **the human r.** la raza humana; *Old-fashioned* **the Spanish r.** la raza hispánica; *Fig* **the r. of shopkeepers** la raza especial que son los tenderos ►► ***r. hatred*** odio *m* racial; ***r. relations*** relaciones *fpl* interraciales; ***r. riot*** disturbio *m* racial

racecard [ˈreɪskɑːd] *n* programa *m* de carreras

racecourse [ˈreɪskɔːs] *n* **(a)** *(for horses)* hipódromo *m* **(b)** *US (for cars, motorbikes)* circuito *m*; *(for runners, cycles)* pista *f*

racegoer [ˈreɪsgəʊə(r)] *n* aficionado(a) *m,f* a las carreras (de caballos)

racehorse [ˈreɪshɔːs] *n* caballo *m* de carreras

racer [ˈreɪsə(r)] *n* **(a)** *(person)* corredor(ora) *m,f* **(b)** *(bicycle)* bicicleta *f* de carreras **(c)** *US (snake)* (serpiente *f*) corredora *f*

racetrack [ˈreɪstræk] *n* **(a)** *(for athletes)* pista *f*; *(for cars)* circuito *m* **(b)** *US (for horses)* hipódromo *m*

raceway [ˈreɪsweɪ] *n US* **(a)** *(channel for water)* acequia *f*, canal *m* **(b)** *(for wiring)* canal *m* **(c)** *(for horseracing)* hipódromo *m*

racial [ˈreɪʃəl] *adj* racial ►► ***r. discrimination*** discriminación *f* racial; *US* ***r. profiling*** = acciones policiales instigadas por consideraciones raciales, no por la observación de un comportamiento sospechoso; ***r. purity*** limpieza *f* de sangre

racialism [ˈreɪʃəlɪzəm] *n* racismo *m*

racialist [ˈreɪʃəlɪst] **1** *n* racista *mf*

2 *adj* racista

racially [ˈreɪʃəlɪ] *adv* racialmente; **a r. motivated attack** una agresión racista; **r. prejudiced** con prejuicios raciales

raciness [ˈreɪsɪnɪs] *n* **(a)** *(liveliness)* viveza *f* **(b)** *(suggestiveness)* atrevimiento *m*

racing [ˈreɪsɪŋ] **1** *n (of horses)* carreras *fpl*

2 *adj* ***r. bicycle*** bicicleta *f* de carreras; ***r. car*** coche *m* or *Am* carro *m* or *CSur* auto *m* de carreras; ***r. colours*** colores *mpl* de la cuadra; ***r. driver*** piloto *mf* de carreras; ***r. pigeon*** paloma *f* (mensajera) de carreras

racism [ˈreɪsɪzəm] *n* racismo *m*

racist [ˈreɪsɪst] **1** *n* racista *mf*

2 *adj* racista

rack [ræk] **1** *n* **(a)** *(for display, storage) (for bottles)* botellero *m*; *(for plates)* escurreplatos *m inv*; *(for magazines)* revistero *m*; *(for goods in shop)* expositor *m*; *(for luggage)* portaequipajes *m inv*; *(on bicycle)* cesta *f*; **(clothes) r.** perchero *m*; **to buy a suit off the r.** comprar un traje hecho

(b) *Tech* **r. and pinion** engranaje de piñón y cremallera ►► ***r. (and pinion) railway*** ferrocarril *m* de cremallera

(c) *(for torture)* potro *m*; IDIOM **to be on the r.** estar contra las cuerdas; IDIOM **to put sb on the r.** poner a alguien contra las cuerdas

(d) *Culin* **r. of lamb** costillar de cordero

(e) *Fam (bust)* pechera *f*

(f) IDIOM **to go to r. and ruin** venirse abajo

2 *vt (torment)* torturar, atormentar; **racked by guilt** atormentado(a) por la culpa; **to be racked with pain** estar atormentado(a) por el dolor; **to r. one's brains** devanarse los sesos

►**rack off** *vi Austr Fam* largarse; **r. off!** ¡vete a paseo!

►**rack up** *vt insep (points, victories)* acumular

racket[1] [ˈrækɪt] *n* **(a)** *(for tennis)* raqueta *f* ►► ***r. press*** tensor *m* de raquetas **(b)** **rackets** *(game)* = juego parecido al squash que disputan dos o cuatro jugadores y que se juega en una pista de mayores dimensiones **(c)** *(snowshoe)* raqueta *f*

racket[2] *n* **(a)** *Fam (noise)* estruendo *m*, jaleo *m*; **to make a r.** armar alboroto *or* jaleo; **turn that r. off!** ¡quita ese ruido! **(b)** *(criminal activity)* negocio *m* mafioso; **drug r.** red de tráfico de drogas **(c)** *Fam (job)* trabajo *m*, *Esp* curro *m*, *RP* laburo *m*; **is she still in the teaching/publishing r.?** ¿está todavía en el mundillo de la enseñanza/editorial?

racketeer [rækɪˈtɪə(r)] *n* mafioso(a) *m,f*, persona *f* envuelta en negocios sucios

racketeering [rækɪˈtɪərɪŋ] *n* negocios *mpl* mafiosos

rack-rent [ˈrækrent] **1** *n* alquiler *m* abusivo

2 *vt* alquilar a precios abusivos

raconteur [rækɒn'tɜ:(r)] *n* **he's a skilful r.** tiene una gran habilidad para contar anécdotas

racquet ['rækɪt] *n (for tennis)* raqueta *f*

racquetball ['rækətbɔ:l] *n US* = especie de frontenis

racy ['reɪsɪ] *adj* (**a**) *(lively)* vívido(a) (**b**) *(risqué)* atrevido(a)

rad [ræd] **1** *n Phys* rad *m*

2 *adj US Fam* genial

RADA ['rɑ:də] *n* (*abbr* **Royal Academy of Dramatic Art**) = academia británica de arte dramático

radar ['reɪdɑ:(r)] *n* radar *m* ►► ***r. beacon*** baliza *f* de radar; ***r. gun*** radar *m* de velocidad; ***r. operator*** operador(ora) *m,f* de radar; ***r. screen*** pantalla *f* de radar; ***r. trap*** control *m* de velocidad por radar

raddled ['rædəld] *adj* demacrado(a)

radial ['reɪdɪəl] **1** *n (tyre)* neumático *m or Col, Méx* llanta *f or Arg* goma *f* (de cubierta) radial

2 *adj* (**a**) *Tech & Math* radial ►► ***r. engine*** motor *m* radial *or* en estrella; ***r. symmetry*** simetría *f* radial (**b**) *Anat (artery, nerve)* radial

radial-ply ['reɪdɪəl'plaɪ] *adj (tyre)* de cubierta radial

radian ['reɪdɪən] *n Geom* radián *m*

radiance ['reɪdɪəns], **radiancy** ['reɪdɪənsɪ] *n* (**a**) *(of light)* resplandor *m*; *(of person, smile)* esplendor *m* (**b**) *Phys* radiancia *f*

radiant ['reɪdɪənt] *adj* (**a**) *(light, person, smile)* radiante, resplandeciente (**b**) *Phys* ***r. energy*** energía *f* radiante; ***r. heat*** calor *m* radiante (**c**) ***r. heating*** *(in building)* calefacción *f* radiante

radiantly ['reɪdjəntlɪ] *adv (to shine, glow)* radiantemente; **r. beautiful** de una belleza radiante; **she was smiling r.** tenía una sonrisa radiante

radiate ['reɪdɪeɪt] **1** *vt (heat, light)* irradiar; *Fig (happiness, enthusiasm)* irradiar; *(health)* rebosar

2 *vi* irradiar (**from** de); **heat radiates from the centre** el calor irradia del centro; **the roads which r. from Chicago** las carreteras que irradian de Chicago

radiation [reɪdɪ'eɪʃən] *n* (**a**) *(energy radiated)* radiación *f* ►► ***r. sickness*** síndrome *m* producido por la radiación; ***r. therapy*** terapia *f* de radiación (**b**) *(act of radiating)* irradiación *f*

radiator ['reɪdɪeɪtə(r)] *n* (**a**) *(heater)* radiador *m* ►► ***r. key*** llave *f* del radiador (**b**) *(in car engine)* radiador *m* ►► ***r. grille*** rejilla *f* del radiador

radical ['rædɪkəl] **1** *n* (**a**) *(person)* radical *mf* (**b**) *Ling* radical *m* (**c**) *Math* radical *m* (**d**) *Chem* radical *m*

2 *adj* (**a**) *(policy, solution)* radical; **he adopted a r. new approach to the problem** le dio al problema un enfoque nuevo y radical ►► ***r. chic*** estética *f* progre (**b**) *Fam* genial

radicalism ['rædɪkəlɪzəm] *n* radicalismo *m*

radicalize ['rædɪkəlaɪz] *vt* radicalizar

radically ['rædɪklɪ] *adv* radicalmente

radicchio [ræ'di:kɪəʊ] *n* achicoria *f* morada *(para ensaladas)*

radicle ['rædɪkəl] *n Bot* radícula *f*

radii *pl of* **radius**

radio ['reɪdɪəʊ] **1** *n* (*pl* **radios**) (**a**) *(apparatus)* radio *f*; **to turn the r. on/off** encender/apagar la radio; **there was something about it on the r.** hablaron de eso en la radio

(**b**) *(system, industry)* radio *f*; **to work in r.** trabajar en la radio; **by r.** por radio ►► ***r. alarm (clock)*** radio(-reloj) despertador *m*; ***r. astronomy*** radioastronomía *f*; ***r. beacon*** radiofaro *m*, radiobaliza *f*; ***r. beam*** haz *m* radioeléctrico; ***r. broadcast*** retransmisión *f* por radio; *Comptr* ***r. button*** botón *m* de tipo radio; ***r. cassette (player)*** radiocasete *m*; ***r. cassette (recorder)*** radiocasete *m*; ***r. compass*** radiocompás *m*; ***r. frequency*** radiofrecuencia *f*; *Fam* ***r. ham*** radioaficionado(a) *m,f*; ***r. microphone*** micrófono *m* inalámbrico; ***r. operator*** radiooperador(ora) *m,f*; ***r. programme*** programa *m* radiofónico; ***r. receiver*** radiorreceptor *m*; *Astron* ***r. source*** radiofuente *f*, fuente *f* de radio; ***r. star*** radiofuente *f*, fuente *f* de radio; ***r. station*** emisora *f* de radio; ***r. telescope*** radiotelescopio *m*; ***r. transmitter*** radiotransmisor *m*; ***r. wave*** onda *f* de radio

2 *vt (information)* transmitir por radio; *(person)* comunicar por radio con

3 *vi* **to r. for help** pedir ayuda por radio

radioactive ['reɪdɪəʊ'æktɪv] *adj* radiactivo(a) ►► ***r. decay*** desintegración *f* radiactiva; ***r. fallout*** lluvia *f* radiactiva; ***r. waste*** vertidos *mpl* radiactivos

radioactivity ['reɪdɪəʊæk'tɪvɪtɪ] *n* radiactividad *f*

radiobiology ['reɪdɪəʊbaɪ'ɒlədʒɪ] *n* radiobiología *f*

radiocarbon ['reɪdɪəʊ'kɑ:bən] *n* radiocarbono *m* ►► ***r. dating*** datación *f* por carbono 14

radiochemistry ['reɪdɪəʊ'kemɪstrɪ] *n* radioquímica *f*

radio-controlled ['reɪdɪəʊkən'trəʊld] *adj* teledirigido(a)

radiogram ['reɪdɪəʊgræm] *n* (**a**) *Br Old-fashioned* radiogramola *f* (**b**) *(message)* radiograma *m* (**c**) *(X-ray image)* radiografía *f*

radiograph ['reɪdɪəʊgrɑ:f] *n* radiografía *f*

radiographer [reɪdɪ'ɒgrəfə(r)] *n* técnico(a) *m,f* de rayos X

radiography [reɪdɪ'ɒgrəfɪ] *n* radiografía *f*

radioisotope ['reɪdɪəʊ'aɪsətəʊp] *n* radioisótopo *m*

radiologist [reɪdɪ'ɒlədʒɪst] *n* radiólogo(a) *m,f*

radiology [reɪdɪ'ɒlədʒɪ] *n* radiología *f*

radiometer [reɪdɪ'ɒmɪtə(r)] *n* radiómetro *m*

radio-pager ['reɪdɪəʊ'peɪdʒə(r)] *n* buscapersonas *m inv*, *Esp* busca *m*, *Méx* localizador *m*, *RP* radiomensaje *m*

radioscopy [reɪdɪ'ɒskəpɪ] *n* radioscopia *f*

radiosensitive ['reɪdɪəʊ'sensɪtɪv] *adj* radiosensible

radiosonde ['reɪdɪəʊsɒnd] *n* radiosonda *f*

radiotelegraphy ['reɪdɪəʊtə'legrəfɪ] *n* radiotelegrafía *f*

radiotelephone ['reɪdɪəʊ'teləfəʊn] *n* radioteléfono *m*

radiotelephony ['reɪdɪəʊtə'lefənɪ] *n* radiotelefonía *f*

radiotherapist ['reɪdɪəʊ'θerəpɪst] *n* radioterapeuta *mf*

radiotherapy ['reɪdɪəʊ'θerəpɪ] *n* radioterapia *f*

radish ['rædɪʃ] *n* rábano *m*

radium ['reɪdɪəm] *n Chem* radio *m*

radius ['reɪdɪəs] (*pl* **radii** ['reɪdɪaɪ]) *n* (**a**) *Geom* radio *m* (**b**) *(limit)* radio *m*; **within a r. of** en un radio de (**c**) *Anat* radio *m*

radon ['reɪdɒn] *n Chem* radón *m*

RAF [ɑ:reɪ'ef] *n* (*abbr* **Royal Air Force**) RAF *f*

raffia ['ræfɪə] *n* rafia *f*

raffish ['ræfɪʃ] *adj* pícaro(a)

raffle ['ræfəl] **1** *n* rifa *f* ►► ***r. ticket*** boleto *m* de rifa

2 *vt* rifar; **to r. sth off** rifar algo

raft [rɑ:ft] *n* (**a**) *(vessel)* balsa *f* (**b**) *Fam (large amount)* montón *m*; **we got rafts** *or* **a r. of mail on that subject** recibimos un montón de correo sobre ese tema

rafter ['rɑ:ftə(r)] *n* viga *f* (de tejado); **the rafters** las vigas

rafting ['rɑ:ftɪŋ] *n* rafting *m*; **to go r.** hacer rafting

rag[1] [ræg] *n* (**a**) *(piece of cloth)* trapo *m*; IDIOM *Br Fam* **to lose one's r.** perder los estribos; IDIOM *very Fam* **to be on the r.**, *US* **to have the r. on** estar con el mes; IDIOM *Fam* **to feel like a wet r.** *or US* **a dish r.** estar para el arrastre ►► ***r. doll*** muñeca *f* de trapo

(**b**) *(shred, scrap)* jirón *m*; **torn to rags** hecho(a) jirones

(**c**) **rags** *(clothes)* harapos *mpl*; IDIOM **to go from rags to riches** salir de la miseria y pasar a la riqueza; **it's a rags-to-riches story** es la historia del pobre que se hizo rico ►► *Fam* ***the r. trade*** la industria de la moda

(**d**) *Fam Pej (newspaper)* periodicucho *m*; **the local r.** el periodicucho local

(**e**) *Mus* rag *m*

rag[2] *Br Old-fashioned* **1** *n (prank)* broma *f* ►► *Univ* ***r. mag*** = revista universitaria que se vende, durante la semana designada para ese fin, para recolectar dinero para obras de caridad; *Univ* ***r. week*** = semana en que los estudiantes colectan dinero para obras de caridad

2 *vt* (*pt & pp* **ragged**) *(tease)* tomar el pelo a

ragamuffin ['rægəmʌfɪn] *n* golfillo(a) *m,f*, pilluelo(a) *m,f*

rag-and-bone man ['rægən'bəʊnmæn] *n Br* trapero(a) *m,f*

ragbag ['rægbæg] *n* batiburrillo *m*; **a r. of ideas** un batiburrillo de ideas

rage [reɪdʒ] **1** *n* (**a**) *(fury)* cólera *f*, ira *f*; **a fit of r.** un arrebato *or* ataque de ira; **to be in a r.** estar hecho(a) una furia; **to fly into a r.** ponerse hecho(a) una furia (**b**) *Fam (fashion)* **to be all the r.** *(music, style)* hacer furor

2 *vi* (**a**) *(be furious)* **to r. about sth** despotricar contra algo; **to r. against** *or* **at sth/sb** encolerizarse con algo/alguien

(**b**) *(sea, storm)* bramar; **while the battle was raging in the valley** mientras la batalla encarnizada continuaba en el valle; **the epidemic/fire raged throughout the city** la epidemia/el fuego se extendió con furia por la ciudad; **the controversy still rages** la polémica todavía colea

ragga ['rægə] *n Mus* ragga *m*

ragged ['rægɪd] *adj* (**a**) *(tattered) (clothes)* raído(a); *(person)* andrajoso(a); IDIOM *Fam* **to run sb r.** desriñonar a alguien; IDIOM *Fam* **she had run herself r.** se había quedado molida

(**b**) *(uneven) (edge, coastline)* irregular; **they formed a r. line** formaban una línea irregular
(**c**) *Typ* **r. right/left** no justificado(a) a la derecha/izquierda

raggedy ['rægɪdɪ] *adj Fam* hecho(a) un guiñapo

ragging ['rægɪŋ] *n Br* burlas *fpl*, tomaduras *fpl* de pelo; **to give sb a r.** tomar el pelo a alguien

raggle-taggle ['rægəltægəl] *adj Br Fam* zarrapastroso(a)

raghead ['ræghed] *n US Fam Pej Esp* moro(a) *m,f*, *Andes, CSur, Ven* turco(a) *m,f*

raging ['reɪdʒɪŋ] *adj* (**a**) *(person)* furioso(a); **to be in a r. temper** estar hecho(a) una furia (**b**) *(sea)* embravecido(a), encrespado(a); *(storm)* enfurecido(a); *(fire)* pavoroso(a); *(fever, thirst, headache)* atroz

raglan ['ræglən] *adj (sleeve, coat)* ranglan

ragman ['rægmən] *n US* trapero(a) *m,f*

ragout [ræ'gu:] *n* ragout *m*

ragtag ['rægtæg] *adj* desordenado(a) y variopinto(a); **the r. and bobtail** la chusma

ragtime ['rægtaɪm] *n* ragtime *m*

ragworm ['rægwɜ:m] *n Br* = gusano utilizado como cebo

ragwort ['rægwɜ:t] *n* hierba *f* cana

raid [reɪd] **1** *n* (**a**) *(by robbers)* atraco *m* (**b**) *(by army)* incursión *f* (**c**) *(by police)* redada *f*; **a drugs r.** una redada antidrogas
2 *vt* (**a**) *(of robbers)* atracar; **somebody's raided my locker** me han desvalijado la taquilla; **to r. the fridge** saquear la nevera (**b**) *(of army)* hacer una incursión en; **raiding party** grupo de ataque (**c**) *(of police)* hacer una redada en

raider ['reɪdə(r)] *n* (**a**) *(criminal)* atracador(ora) *m,f* (**b**) *(soldier, boat, plane)* comando *m* de ataque (**c**) *St Exch* tiburón *m*

rail[1] [reɪl] *n* (**a**) *(of stairway, balcony, bridge)* baranda *f*, *Esp* barandilla *f*; **(towel) r.** toallero *m*
(**b**) *(train system)* ferrocarril *m*, tren *m*; *(track)* riel *m*, raíl *m*; **by r.** en tren; IDIOM *Br* **to go off the rails** *(person, economy)* desencaminarse, perder el norte; IDIOM **to get sth/sb back on the rails** volver a encarrilar algo/a alguien ►► ***r. bridge*** puente *m* ferroviario; ***r. journey*** viaje *m* en tren; ***r. network*** red *f* ferroviaria; ***r. strike*** huelga *f* ferroviaria *or* de trenes; ***r. ticket*** *Esp* billete *m or Am* boleto *m or Am* pasaje *m* de tren; ***r. travel*** los viajes en tren
(**c**) **the rails** *(in horse racing)* la valla interior; **to be coming up on the rails** *(racehorse)* avanzar por el interior; *Fig* acercarse rápidamente

► **rail in, rail off** *vt sep* cercar

rail[2] *vi Formal* protestar encolerizado(a); **to r. at** *or* **against sth** protestar encolerizado(a) contra algo

rail[3] *n (bird)* ***water r.*** rascón *m*

railcar ['reɪlkɑ:(r)] *n* (**a**) *(self-propelled)* automotor *m* (**b**) *US (carriage)* vagón *m*

railcard ['reɪlkɑ:d] *n Br* = tarjeta para obtener billetes de tren con descuento

railhead ['reɪlhed] *n* (**a**) *(terminus)* final *m* de trayecto (**b**) *(of railway being built)* cabeza *f* de línea

railing ['reɪlɪŋ] *n* (**a**) *(horizontal barrier)* valla *f* (**b**) *(metal post)* reja *f*; **railings** *(fence)* verja *f*

raillery ['reɪlərɪ] *n Formal* mofas *fpl*

railroad ['reɪlrəʊd] **1** *n US* = **railway**
2 *vt* (**a**) *Fam (coerce)* **to r. sb into doing sth** avasallar a alguien para que haga algo; **to r. a bill through Parliament** utilizar el rodillo parlamentario para que se apruebe un proyecto de ley (**b**) *US Fam (convict) (by false charges)* condenar injustamente; *(hastily)* condenar precipitadamente (**c**) *US (transport)* enviar por ferrocarril

railroader ['reɪlrəʊdə(r)] *n US* ferroviario(a) *m,f*

railway ['reɪlweɪ], *US* **railroad** ['reɪlrəʊd] *n (system)* (red *f* de) ferrocarril *m*; *(track)* vía *f* férrea ►► ***r. accident*** accidente *m* ferroviario; ***r. bridge*** puente *m* ferroviario; *US* ***r. car*** vagón *m* (de tren); *Br* ***r. carriage*** vagón *m* (de tren); ***r. crossing*** paso *m* a nivel; ***r. line*** *(track)* vía *f* (férrea); *(route)* línea *f* de tren; ***r. network*** red *f* ferroviaria; ***r. station*** estación *f* de tren *or* de ferrocarril; ***r. strike*** huelga *f* ferroviaria *or* de trenes; ***r. system*** red *f* ferroviaria; ***r. ticket*** *Esp* billete *m or Am* boleto *m or Am* pasaje *m* de tren; ***r. track*** vía *f* (férrea)

railwayman ['reɪlweɪmən] *n Br, Can* ferroviario *m*

raiment ['reɪmənt] *n Literary* vestimenta *f*, atuendo *m*

rain [reɪn] **1** *n* lluvia *f*; **we've had a lot of r. recently** hemos tenido mucha lluvia últimamente; **come in out of the r.** entra, que te estás mojando; **in the r.** bajo la lluvia; **it looks like r.** parece que va a llover; **the rains** las lluvias; **come r. or shine** *(whatever the weather)* llueva o truene; *(whatever the circumstances)* sea como sea, pase lo que pase ►► *US* ***r. check*** *(at sporting event)* = entrada para asistir más tarde a un encuentro suspendido por la lluvia; *Fam* **I'll take a r. check on that** lo dejaré para otra vez; ***r. cloud*** nube *f* de lluvia, nubarrón *m*; ***r. dance*** danza *f* de la lluvia; ***r. water*** agua *f* de lluvia
2 *vt* **to r. blows/gifts on sb** hacer llover los golpes/los regalos sobre alguien
3 *vi* llover; **it's raining** está lloviendo; **arrows rained from the sky** llovían flechas del cielo; IDIOM *Fam* **it's raining cats and dogs** está lloviendo a cántaros *or* a mares; PROV *Br* **it never rains but it pours,** *US* **when it rains, it pours** las desgracias nunca vienen solas

► **rain down 1** *vt sep (projectiles, blows)* lanzar una lluvia de
2 *vi* llover

► **rain off,** *US* **rain out** *vt sep* **the game was rained off** *or US* **out** el partido se suspendió por la lluvia

rainbow ['reɪnbəʊ] *n* arco *m* iris; **all the colours of the r.** todos los colores del arco iris ►► ***r. coalition*** = coalición de partidos minoritarios; ***r. trout*** trucha *f* arco iris

rainbow-coloured ['reɪnbəʊ'kʌləd] *adj* con los colores del arco iris

raincoat ['reɪnkəʊt] *n* impermeable *m*

raindrop ['reɪndrɒp] *n* gota *f* de lluvia

rainfall ['reɪnfɔ:l] *n* (**a**) *(amount of rain)* pluviosidad *f* (**b**) *(shower)* aguacero *m*

rainforest ['reɪnfɒrɪst] *n* selva *f* tropical

rain-gauge ['reɪn'geɪdʒ] *n* pluviómetro *m*

rain-maker ['reɪnmeɪkə(r)] *n* (**a**) *(in tribal society)* = persona que afirma poder traer la lluvia (**b**) *Fam Com* empleado(a) *m,f* altamente productivo(a)

rainproof ['reɪnpru:f] **1** *adj* impermeable
2 *vt* impermeabilizar

rainstick ['reɪnstɪk] *n* palo *m* de lluvia

rainstorm ['reɪnstɔ:m] *n* aguacero *m*

rainwear ['reɪnweə(r)] *n* ropa *f* para la lluvia

rainy ['reɪnɪ] *adj* lluvioso(a); **the r. season** la estación de las lluvias; IDIOM **to save sth for a r. day** guardar algo para cuando haga falta

raise [reɪz] **1** *n US (pay increase)* aumento *m* (de sueldo)
2 *vt* (**a**) *(lift)* levantar; *(flag)* izar; *(blind, theatre curtain)* levantar, subir; **to r. one's hand** *(to volunteer, ask question)* levantar la mano; **to r. one's eyes** levantar la vista; **to r. one's glass to one's lips** llevarse el vaso a los labios; **she raised herself to her full height** se irguió cual alta era; *also Fig* **to r. one's hat to sb** quitarse *or Am* sacarse el sombrero ante alguien; IDIOM **the audience raised the roof** *(in theatre)* el teatro (literalmente) se vino abajo
(**b**) *(increase) (price, rent, salary)* aumentar, subir; **to r. one's voice** alzar *or* levantar la voz; *Fig* **to r. the temperature of a dispute** caldear un conflicto; IDIOM **to r. the stakes** forzar la situación
(**c**) *(boost, improve) (standard)* aumentar, elevar; *(awareness)* aumentar; **I don't want to r. your hopes** no quisiera darte falsas esperanzas; **to r. sb's spirits** levantar el ánimo de alguien
(**d**) *(bring up) (problem, subject)* plantear; *(objection)* hacer; **to r. sth with sb** plantear algo a alguien, sacar a colación algo ante alguien
(**e**) *(provoke) (smile, laugh)* provocar; *(fears, doubts)* sembrar; *(blister)* levantar; **to r. the alarm** dar la voz de alarma
(**f**) *(promote)* ascender; **the Queen raised him to the peerage** la reina le otorgó un título nobiliario
(**g**) *(collect together) (money, funds)* reunir, recaudar; *(taxes)* recaudar; *(support)* recabar; *(army)* reclutar; **we have raised over a million signatures** hemos recogido más de un millón de firmas
(**h**) *(children, cattle)* criar; *(crops)* cultivar; **I was raised in the countryside** me crié en el campo; **to r. a family** sacar adelante una familia
(**i**) *(blockade, embargo, siege)* levantar
(**j**) *(statue)* erigir (**to** a)
(**k**) *(resurrect)* **to r. sb from the dead** resucitar a alguien; **to r. the dead** resucitar a los muertos; IDIOM **to r. Cain** *or* **hell** *(being rowdy)* armar bronca; *(when annoyed)* poner el grito en el cielo
(**l**) *(contact)* contactar con
(**m**) *(in cards)* subir; **I'll r. you $5** (te) subo 5 dólares
(**n**) *(dough, bread)* hacer subir
(**o**) *Math* **to r. a number to the power of n** elevar un número a la enésima potencia
3 *vi (in cards)* subir

raised [reɪzd] *adj* (**a**) *(elevated) (ground, platform)* elevado(a) ►► *Geog* ***r. beach*** cantil *m* (**b**) *(embossed)* con relieve (**c**) *US Culin* hecho(a) con levadura

raisin ['reɪzən] *n* (uva *f*) pasa *f*

raising ['reɪzɪŋ] n (a) (lifting) (of curtain) subida f; (of flag) izamiento m (b) (increase) (of prices, rents, salaries) aumento m; **r. of the school-leaving age** prolongación de la escolaridad (c) (improvement) (of standards, awareness) aumento m (d) Culin **r. agent** gasificante m

raison d'être ['reɪzɒn'detrə] n razón f de ser

raita [raɪ'iːtə] n raita f, = salsa india a base de yogur con pepino rallado, menta y especias

Raj [rɑːʒ] n Hist **the (British) R.** el Imperio británico en la India

rajah ['rɑːdʒə] n Hist rajá m

rake [reɪk] 1 n (a) (garden tool) rastrillo m (b) Old-fashioned (dissolute man) crápula m, calavera m (c) Theat pendiente f (d) (of mast, funnel) inclinación f

2 vt (a) (leaves, soil) rastrillar; IDIOM **to r. one's memory** escarbar en la memoria (b) (scan) escudriñar; **a searchlight raked the darkness** un foco barría la oscuridad (c) (shoot at) (enemy lines) barrer

▶ **rake about, rake around** vi (search) **to r. about** or **around for sth** rebuscar algo

▶ **rake in** vt sep Fam (money) amasar; **she's raking it in!** ¡se está forrando!, Méx ¡se está llenando de lana!

▶ **rake off** vt sep Fam (money) llevarse

▶ **rake over** vt sep (a) (soil, lawn, path) rastrillar (b) (subject, the past) remover; IDIOM **to r. over the ashes of sth** remover las cenizas de algo

▶ **rake up** vt sep (a) (leaves, grass cuttings) rastrillar (b) (dredge up) remover, escarbar en; **to r. up sb's past** sacar a relucir el pasado de alguien

raked [reɪkt] adj (inclined) inclinado(a)

rake-off ['reɪkɒf] n Fam tajada f, comisión f

rakish ['reɪkɪʃ] adj (a) (dissolute) licencioso(a), disoluto(a) (b) (charm, smile) desenvuelto(a); **to wear one's hat at a r. angle** llevar el sombrero ladeado con un aire de desenfado

rakishly ['reɪkɪʃlɪ] adv (to smile, laugh) con desenfado, con desenvoltura

rakishness ['reɪkɪʃnɪs] n (of smile, laugh) desenfado m, desenvoltura f

rally ['rælɪ] 1 n (a) (protest gathering) concentración f (de protesta) (b) (recovery) (in battle, game) recuperación f; (of prices, shares) recuperación f, repunte m; **after a late r. the stock market closed up half a point** tras un repunte de última hora, la bolsa cerró con una subida de medio punto

(c) (in tennis, badminton) intercambio m de golpes, peloteo m

(d) (car race) rally m ▶▶ **r. driver** piloto mf de rallys

2 vt (a) (gather) (supporters) reunir; (support) reunir, recabar (b) (troops) reagrupar (c) (cause to recover) **to r. sb's spirits** elevar el ánimo a alguien

3 vi (a) (assemble, gather) agruparse; **to r. to sb's defence** salir en defensa de alguien (b) (troops) reagruparse (c) (recover) (person) recobrar ánimos or bríos; (team, patient) recuperarse; (currency, share prices) recuperarse, repuntar (d) (in tennis, badminton) pelotear (e) (in car race) correr en rallies

▶ **rally round** 1 vt insep arropar, prestar su apoyo a

2 vi **all her family rallied round** toda su familia la arropó or le prestó su apoyo

rallycross ['rælɪkrɒs] n Sport autocross m inv

rallying ['rælɪɪŋ] n Sport carreras fpl de rallys; **to go r.** hacer carreras de rallys

rallying-cry ['rælɪɪŋ'kraɪ] n consigna f, grito m de guerra

rallying-point ['rælɪɪŋ'pɔɪnt] n punto m de encuentro

ralph [rælf] vi Fam (vomit) echar la pota

RAM [ræm] n (a) Comptr (abbr **random access memory**) (memoria f) RAM f ▶▶ **R. cache** RAM f caché; **R. disk** disco m RAM (b) (abbr **Royal Academy of Music**) = conservatorio nacional de música de Londres

ram [ræm] 1 n (a) (animal) carnero m (b) (piston) pistón m (c) Hist (on ship) espolón m; **(battering) r.** ariete m

2 vt (pt & pp **rammed**) (a) (crash into) embestir; **he rammed the trolley into my ankles** me embistió con el carrito y me dio en los tobillos

(b) (force into place) embutir, insertar con fuerza; **he rammed the papers into his bag** embutió los papeles en la bolsa; **she rammed the nail into the wood** hundió el clavo con fuerza en la madera; **in order to r. home the point** para dejarlo bien claro; IDIOM Fam **she's always ramming her views down my throat** siempre está tratando de inculcarme a la fuerza sus ideas

3 vi **to r. into sth** chocar contra algo

Ramadan ['ræmədæn] n Rel ramadán m

ramble ['ræmbəl] 1 n (walk) excursión f, caminata f; **to go for a r.** ir de excursión

2 vi (a) (walk) ir de excursión, hacer senderismo (b) (digress) divagar (c) (plant) crecer sin control (d) (path, stream) serpentear

▶ **ramble on** vi divagar; **to r. on about sth** divagar sobre algo; **what's he rambling on about now?** ¿sobre qué está divagando ahora?

rambler ['ræmblə(r)] n (a) (walker) excursionista mf, senderista mf (b) (rose bush) rosal m trepador

rambling ['ræmblɪŋ] 1 n (a) (walking) **to go r.** ir de excursión, hacer senderismo (b) **ramblings** (words) divagaciones fpl, digresiones fpl; **the ramblings of old age** las divagaciones de la vejez

2 adj (a) (letter, speech) inconexo(a) (b) (house) laberíntico(a) (c) **r. rose** (plant) rosal m trepador

rambunctious [ræm'bʌnkʃəs] adj Fam bullicioso(a)

RAMC [ɑːreɪem'siː] n (abbr **Royal Army Medical Corps**) = cuerpo médico del ejército de tierra británico

ramekin, ramequin ['ræmɪkɪn] n (a) (container) cazuelita f individual (para cocinar al horno) (b) (baked savoury) = plato a base de queso y huevos, que se prepara al horno en una cazuelita individual

ramification [ræmɪfɪ'keɪʃən] n (a) (consequence) ramificación f (b) (branching) ramificación f

ramjet ['ræmdʒet] n estatorreactor m

ramp [ræmp] n (a) (to ease access) rampa f (b) (to plane, ship) escalerilla f (c) US (to join freeway) carril m de incorporación or aceleración; (to exit freeway) carril m de salida or deceleración (d) Br (on road) resalto m (de moderación de velocidad)

rampage 1 n ['ræmpeɪdʒ] **to go on the r.** ir arrasando con todo; **to be on the r.** estar desmandado(a)

2 vi [ræm'peɪdʒ] pasar arrasando; **to r. about** ir en desbandada

rampant ['ræmpənt] adj (a) (unrestrained) (corruption, disease) incontrolado(a); (growth) incontrolado(a), desenfrenado(a); (inflation) galopante (b) (in heraldry) rampante; **a lion r.** un león rampante

rampart ['ræmpɑːt] n (wall) muralla f; (earthwork) terraplén m

ram-raiding ['ræm'reɪdɪŋ] n Br alunizaje m, = robo en una tienda embistiendo contra el escaparate con un vehículo

ramrod ['ræmrɒd] n (for rifle) baqueta f; Fig **r. straight** con la espalda recta; IDIOM **to stand as stiff as a r.** estar más tieso(a) que un palo

ramshackle ['ræmʃækəl] adj destartalado(a)

ran pt of **run**

ranch [rɑːntʃ] 1 n rancho m ▶▶ US **r. dressing** = aderezo para ensalada con leche y mayonesa; **r. hand** peón(ona) m,f, jornalero(a) m,f; **r. house** (on ranch) casa f (en un rancho); (bungalow) bungalow m

2 vt **to r. cattle** criar ganado

3 vi dedicarse a la cría de ganado or a la ganadería

rancher ['rɑːntʃə(r)] n ranchero(a) m,f

ranching ['rɑːntʃɪŋ] n cría f de ganado; **cattle r.** cría de ganado vacuno or bovino, ganadería; **chicken r.** cría de pollos, avicultura

rancid ['rænsɪd] adj rancio(a); **to go** or **turn r.** ponerse rancio(a)

rancor US = **rancour**

rancorous ['ræŋkərəs] adj (person) rencoroso(a); (debate, dispute) agrio(a); (atmosphere) hostil

rancour, US rancor ['ræŋkə(r)] n acritud f, resentimiento m

rand [rænd] n rand m

random ['rændəm] 1 n **at r.** al azar; **to lash out at r.** lanzar golpes a voleo or a diestro y siniestro

2 adj (choice) hecho(a) al azar; (sample) aleatorio(a); **I just made a r. guess** lo intenté adivinar a voleo; **a r. selection of people were asked if...** preguntaron a un grupo de gente escogida al azar si... ▶▶ Comptr **r. access memory** memoria f de acceso aleatorio; **r. number** número m al azar; **r. sampling** muestreo m aleatorio; Math **r. variable** variable f aleatoria

randomized ['rændəmaɪzd] adj (sample, number) aleatorio(a)

randomly ['rændəmlɪ] adv al azar

randy ['rændɪ] adj Fam caliente, Esp, Méx cachondo(a); **to feel r.** estar caliente or Esp, Méx cachondo(a); **to get r.** ponerse caliente or Esp, Méx cachondo(a)

rang pt of **ring**[2]

range [reɪndʒ] 1 n (a) (reach) (of weapon, telescope, hearing) alcance m; (of ship, plane) autonomía f; **out of r.** fuera del alcance; **within** or **in r.** al alcance

(b) (distance) distancia f; **it can kill a man at a r. of 800 metres** puede matar a una distancia de 800 metros

(c) (variety) **the r. of possibilities is almost infinite** el abanico de posibilidades es prácticamente ilimitado; **there is a wide r. of temperatures in these parts** hay una gran variación de temperaturas en esta zona; **we talked on a wide r. of topics** hablamos de muchos temas diferentes; **it provoked a wide r. of reactions** provocó toda clase de reacciones; **it's out of our (price) r.** se sale de lo que podemos gastar

(**d**) *Com (of products)* gama *f*; **this model is the top/bottom of the r.** éste es un modelo alto/bajo de gama; **the new autumn r.** *(of clothes)* la nueva línea de otoño

(**e**) *(extent, scope) (of instrument, voice)* registro *m*; *(of knowledge)* amplitud *f*; *(of research)* ámbito *m*; **that is beyond the r. of the present inquiry** eso se sale del ámbito de esta investigación

(**f**) *(of hills, mountains)* cordillera *f*

(**g**) *US (prairie)* prado *m*

(**h**) *(practice area)* (**shooting**) **r.** campo *m* de tiro; **missile r.** campo de tiro de misiles

(**i**) *(cooker)* fogón *m*, cocina *f or Col, Méx, Ven* estufa *f* de carbón

(**j**) *Biol (habitat)* medio *m*

2 *vt* (**a**) *(arrange in row) (troops, books)* alinear; **the desks are ranged in threes** las mesas están alineadas de tres en tres (**b**) *(join, ally)* **to r. oneself with/against sb** alinearse con/en contra de alguien (**c**) *(travel)* recorrer (**d**) *Typ* **to r. a text left/right** justificar un texto a la izquierda/derecha

3 *vi* (**a**) *(vary)* **ages ranging from ten to ninety** edades comprendidas entre los diez y los noventa años; **during the summer temperatures r. from 21 to 30 degrees** durante el verano las temperaturas oscilan entre los 21 y los 30 grados

(**b**) **to r. over** *(include)* abarcar, comprender; **our conversation ranged over a large number of topics** nuestra conversación abarcó un gran número de temas

(**c**) *(roam)* viajar sin rumbo fijo; **to r. over** recorrer

rangefinder ['reɪndʒfaɪndə(r)] *n* telémetro *m*

ranger ['reɪndʒə(r)] *n* (**a**) *(in forest)* guardabosques *mf inv* (**b**) *US (lawman)* policía *mf* (**c**) *US Mil* comando *m*

Rangoon [ræn'gu:n] *n* Rangún

rangy ['reɪndʒɪ] *adj (person)* larguirucho(a)

rank[1] [ræŋk] **1** *n* (**a**) *(status)* rango *m*; **promoted to the r. of colonel** ascendido(a) al rango de coronel; **the r. of manager** el rango de gerente

(**b**) *(quality)* fila *f*, línea *f*; **players of** *or* **in the first** *or* **top r.** jugadores de primera fila

(**c**) *(row)* fila *f*

(**d**) *(on chessboard)* fila *f*

(**e**) *Mil* **the ranks** la tropa; **he had served in the ranks** había estado en el ejército como soldado raso; **the r. and file** *(in army)* la tropa; *(of political party, union)* las bases; **to come up through** *or* **rise from the ranks** ascender de soldado a oficial

(**f**) *(numbers)* **to join the ranks of the unemployed/the opposition** pasar a engrosar las filas del desempleo *or Esp* paro/de la oposición

(**g**) *Br* (**taxi**) **r.** parada *f* de taxis

(**h**) IDIOMS **to break ranks (with)** desmarcarse (de); **to close ranks** cerrar filas; **to pull r.: she pulled r. on him** le recordó quién mandaba (allí)

2 *vt* (**a**) *(rate, classify)* clasificar (**among** entre *or* dentro de); **to r. sth/sb as** catalogar algo/a alguien como; **he is ranked among the best contemporary writers** está catalogado como uno de los mejores escritores contemporáneos; **I r. this as one of our finest performances** considero que ésta es una de nuestras mejores actuaciones

(**b**) *(arrange)* disponer

(**c**) *US (outrank)* ser de rango superior a

3 *vi* figurar (**among** entre *or* dentro de); **to r. above/below sb** tener un rango superior/inferior al de alguien; **that ranks as one of the best movies I've seen** es una de las mejores películas que he visto; **this ranks as a major disaster** esto constituye un desastre de primer orden; **he hardly ranks as an expert** apenas se le puede considerar un experto

rank[2] *adj* (**a**) *(foul-smelling)* pestilente; **it smells r.** huele que apesta (**b**) *(absolute)* total; **it's a r. injustice** es una injusticia que clama al cielo; **she's a r. outsider** no es más que una comparsa, no tiene muchas posibilidades (**c**) *Br Fam (worthless)* birrioso(a) (**d**) *Literary (profuse) (vegetation, weeds)* frondoso(a)

rank-and-file ['ræŋkən'faɪl] *adj* de las bases

ranker ['ræŋkə(r)] *n Br Mil (ordinary soldier)* soldado *mf* raso; *(officer)* = oficial que empezó como soldado raso

ranking ['ræŋkɪŋ] **1** *n (classification)* clasificación *f*

2 *adj US (senior)* de más alto rango

rankle ['ræŋkəl] *vi* doler, escocer; **to r. with sb** dolerle *or* escocerle a alguien; **their refusal to help rankles (with her)** le duele que se nieguen a ayudarla

ransack ['rænsæk] *vt* (**a**) *(search) (house, desk)* revolver; **he ransacked the wardrobe for his tie** revolvió todo el armario buscando la corbata (**b**) *(plunder) (shop, town)* saquear

ransom ['rænsəm] **1** *n* rescate *m*; **to hold sb to r.** pedir un rescate por alguien; *Fig* **the strikers are holding the country to r.** los huelguistas tienen al país a su merced; *Fig* **to be held to r. by sb** estar a merced de alguien ►► ***r. demand*** petición *f or Am* pedido *m* de rescate; ***r. note*** nota *f* pidiendo el rescate

2 *vt* pagar el rescate de

rant [rænt] *Fam* **1** *n* sermoneo *m*

2 *vi* despotricar (**about/at** sobre/contra); **to r. and rave (about sth/at sb)** poner el grito en el cielo (por algo/ante alguien)

ranting ['ræntɪŋ] **1** *n* sermoneos *mpl*

2 *adj* sermoneante

RAOC [ɑ:reɪəʊ'si:] *n (abbr* **Royal Army Ordnance Corps**) cuerpo *m* de artillería del ejército de tierra británico

rap [ræp] **1** *n* (**a**) *(sharp blow)* golpe *m*; **I heard a r. at the door** oí un golpe en la puerta; IDIOM **to give sb a r. over the knuckles** echar *Esp* un rapapolvo *or Méx* un buen regaño *or RP* un buen reto a alguien; IDIOM *Br Fam* **I don't care** *or* **give a r.!** ¡me importa un bledo!

(**b**) *Fam (blame, punishment)* **to take the r. for sth** pagar el pato por algo

(**c**) *US Fam (legal charge)* acusación *f*; **he's up on a murder/drugs r.** está acusado de asesinato/tráfico de drogas ►► ***r. sheet*** ficha *f* con los antecedentes penales

(**d**) *US Fam (chat)* charla *f*, *CAm, Méx* plática *f*; **we had a r. session about it** tuvimos una charla *or CAm, Méx* plática sobre eso

(**e**) *(music)* rap *m*; **r. music/artist** música/artista de rap

2 *vt* (*pt & pp* **rapped**) (**a**) *(strike)* dar un golpe a; IDIOM **to r. sb's knuckles, to r. sb over the knuckles** echar *Esp* un rapapolvo *or Méx* un buen regaño *or RP* un buen reto a alguien (**b**) *(in newspaper headlines)* atacar

3 *vi* (**a**) *(knock)* golpear (**b**) *US (chat)* charlar, *CAm, Méx* platicar (**c**) *Mus* rapear

►**rap out** *vt sep* (**a**) *(say sharply)* espetar (**b**) *(tap out)* **to r. out a message** dar un mensaje con golpecitos

rapacious [rə'peɪʃəs] *adj (person)* rapaz; *(appetite)* voraz

rapaciousness [rə'peɪʃəsnɪs], **rapacity** [rə'pæsɪtɪ] *n (of person)* rapacidad *f*; *(of appetite)* voracidad *f*

rape[1] [reɪp] **1** *n* (**a**) *(crime)* violación *f*; **to commit r.** cometer una violación (**b**) *(spoiling) (of countryside, environment)* destrucción *f* (**c**) *Archaic (abduction)* rapto *m*

2 *vt* (**a**) *(person)* violar (**b**) *(countryside, environment)* destruir

rape[2] *n* (**a**) *(crop)* colza *f* (**b**) *(remains of grapes)* hollejo *m*, orujo *m*

rapeseed ['reɪpsi:d] *n* semilla *f* de colza ►► ***r. oil*** aceite *m* de colza

rapid ['ræpɪd] *adj* rápido(a); **in r. succession** en rápida sucesión ►► *Physiol* ***r. eye movement*** movimientos *mpl* oculares rápidos; ***r. fire*** tiro *m* rápido; ***r. reaction force*** fuerza *f* de intervención rápida; *US* ***r. transit*** transporte *m* urbano rápido

rapid-fire ['ræpɪd'faɪə(r)] *adj* (**a**) *(weapon)* de tiro rápido (**b**) *(questions, repartee)* a toda velocidad

rapidity [rə'pɪdɪtɪ] *n* rapidez *f*, celeridad *f*

rapidly ['ræpɪdlɪ] *adv* rápidamente

rapids ['ræpɪdz] *npl (in river)* rápidos *mpl*

rapier ['reɪpɪə(r)] *n* estoque *m* ►► ***r. thrust*** estocada *f*; ***r. wit*** ingenio *m* vivaz

rapist ['reɪpɪst] *n* violador(ora) *m,f*

rappel [rə'pel] **1** *n* rápel *m*

2 *vi* hacer rápel

rappelling [rə'pelɪŋ] *n* rápel *m*

rapper ['ræpə(r)] *n (singer)* rapero(a) *m,f*

rapport [ræ'pɔ:(r)] *n* relación *f*; **I need to improve my r. with the class** necesito mejorar la relación que tengo con la clase; **to have a good r. (with sb)** entenderse *or* llevarse muy bien (con alguien); **there was an instant r. between them** se entendieron desde el primer momento

rapprochement [ræ'prɒʃmɒŋ] *n Formal* acercamiento *m*

rapscallion [ræp'skælɪən] *n Old-fashioned* pillastre *mf*, bribón(ona) *m,f*

rapt [ræpt] *adj (attention, look)* extasiado(a); **the clown held the children r.** el payaso tenía a los niños extasiados; **to be r. in contemplation** estar absorto(a) en la contemplación

raptor ['ræptə(r)] *n (bird)* rapaz *f*

rapture ['ræptʃə(r)] *n* gozo *m*; **to be in raptures** estar encantado(a); **to go into raptures over sth** deshacerse en alabanzas a algo

rapturous ['ræptʃərəs] *adj (cries, applause)* arrebatado(a); *(reception, welcome)* clamoroso(a)

rapturously ['ræptʃərəslɪ] *adv (to praise, applaud)* con entusiasmo; **to watch r.** mirar extasiado(a)

ra-ra skirt ['rɑːrɑː'skɜːt] *n Br* = falda corta con volantes, que estuvo de moda en los años 80

rare [reə(r)] *adj* **(a)** *(uncommon)* raro(a); **a r. example of an intact Roman mosaic** un raro ejemplo de un mosaico romano intacto; **a r. stamp** un sello difícil de encontrar; **a r. antique** un objeto antiguo de gran valor; **it's r. to see such things nowadays** es raro ver esas cosas hoy en día; **on r. occasions** en contadas ocasiones; **on the r. occasions when I've seen him drunk** las raras veces en que lo he visto borracho; **to have a r. gift for sth** tener un raro don para algo
(b) *(excellent)* estupendo(a), de fábula; **we had a r. old time** nos lo pasamos de fábula
(c) *(steak)* poco hecho(a)
(d) *Chem* ***r. earth*** tierra *f* rara

rarebit ['reəbɪt] *n* **(Welsh) r.** tostada *f* de queso fundido

rarefied ['reərɪfaɪd] *adj* **(a)** *(air, gas)* rarificado(a), enrarecido(a) **(b)** *(atmosphere, ideas)* exclusivista, encopetado(a)

rarefy ['reərɪfaɪ] **1** *vt* enrarecer
2 *vi* enrarecerse

rarely ['reəlɪ] *adv* raras veces, raramente; **r. have I** *or* **I have r. met anyone like him** raras veces he conocido a alguien como él

rareness ['reənəs] *n (scarcity)* rareza *f*

raring ['reərɪŋ] *adj* **to be r. to do sth** estar deseando hacer algo; **to be r. to go** estar deseando empezar

rarity ['reərɪtɪ] *n* **(a)** *(uncommon person, thing)* rareza *f*; **to be/become a r.** ser/convertirse en una rareza *or* un caso especial **(b)** *(scarcity)* rareza *f* ►► ***r. value*** rareza *f*

rascal ['rɑːskəl] *n* **(a)** *(child)* pillo(a) *m,f* **(b)** *Old-fashioned or Hum (scoundrel)* bribón(ona) *m,f*

rascally ['rɑːskəlɪ] *adj (person, deed)* sinvergüenza

rash[1] [ræʃ] *n* **(a)** *(on skin)* erupción *f*, sarpullido *m* **(b)** *(of complaints, letters)* racha *f*; **a r. of strikes** una racha de huelgas; **last summer's r. of air disasters** la racha de desastres aéreos del verano pasado

rash[2] *adj (person)* impulsivo(a), precipitado(a); *(action, remark)* imprudente, precipitado(a); **it was r. of her to walk out** actuó de manera precipitada al marcharse así; **don't make any r. promises!** ¡no hagas promesas precipitadas!; **I bought it in a r. moment** lo compré de forma impulsiva

rasher ['ræʃə(r)] *n* **r. (of bacon)** loncha *f* de tocino *or Esp* beicon

rashly ['ræʃlɪ] *adv* impulsivamente, precipitadamente; **I rather r. offered to drive her home** me ofrecí, un poco impulsivamente, a llevarla a casa

rashness ['ræʃnɪs] *n* precipitación *f*, impetuosidad *f*

rasp [rɑːsp] **1** *n* **(a)** *(tool)* lima *f* gruesa, escofina *f* **(b)** *(sound)* chirrido *m*; **the r. in his voice** su voz áspera
2 *vt* **(a)** *(scrape, file)* raspar; **the cat rasped its tongue over my face** el gato me raspó la cara con la lengua **(b)** *(say hoarsely)* decir con voz áspera

raspberry ['rɑːzbərɪ] *n* **(a)** *(fruit)* frambuesa *f*; *(plant)* frambueso *m* ►► ***r. jam*** mermelada *f* de frambuesa **(b)** *Fam (noise)* **to blow a r. at sb** hacer una pedorreta a alguien

rasping ['rɑːspɪŋ] *adj* áspero(a)

Rasta ['ræstə] *Fam* **1** *n* rasta *mf*
2 *adj* rasta

Rastafarian [ræstə'feərɪən] **1** *n* rastafari *mf*
2 *adj* rastafari

Rastafarianism [ræstə'feərɪənɪzəm] *n* rastafarismo *m*

raster ['ræstə(r)] *n Comptr* trama *f*

rasterize ['ræstəraɪz] *vt Comptr* rasterizar

rat [ræt] **1** *n* **(a)** *(animal)* rata *f* ►► ***r. poison*** matarratas *m inv*, raticida *m*; ***r. trap*** ratonera *f*, trampa *f* para ratas
(b) *Fam (scoundrel)* miserable *mf*, canalla *mf*
(c) *US Fam (informer)* soplón(ona) *m,f*, *Esp* chivato(a) *m,f*
(d) *Br Fam* **rats!** *(exclamation of irritation)* ¡mecachis!
(e) IDIOMS **to be caught like a r. in a trap** caer en una vil trampa; **to get out of the r. race** huir de la lucha frenética por escalar peldaños en la sociedad; *US very Fam* **I don't give a r.'s ass** me importa un huevo, *Esp* me la suda; **it's like rats leaving a sinking ship in this company** todo el mundo está abandonando esta empresa antes de que se vaya a pique ►► *Br* ***r. run*** = calle de zona residencial que algunos conductores utilizan para evitar los atascos en la carretera principal; *Br* ***rats' tails*** greñas *fpl*
2 *vi* (*pt & pp* **ratted**) **(a)** *(hunt rats)* **to go ratting** ir a cazar ratas **(b)** *Fam (inform)* cantar; **to r. on sb** delatar a alguien **(c)** *Fam (go back on)* **they ratted on our deal** pasaron del trato

ratable value = **rateable value**

rat-arsed ['rætɑːst] *adj Br very Fam Esp, Méx* pedo *inv*, *Col* caído(a), *RP* en pedo; **to get r.** agarrarse un pedo

rat-a-tat-tat ['rætətæt'tæt] *n* golpeteo *m*; **he went r. on the door** llamó golpeteando a la puerta

ratatouille [rætə'tuːiː] *n* pisto *m*

ratbag ['rætbæg] *n Br Fam* miserable *mf*, *Esp* borde *mf*

rat-catcher ['rætkætʃə(r)] *n* cazador(ora) *m,f* de ratas

ratchet ['rætʃɪt] *n* trinquete *m*; **r. (wheel)** rueda *f* de trinquete; *Fig* **this had a r. effect on prices** eso disparó los precios ►► ***r. screwdriver*** destornillador *m or Am* desatornillador *m* de trinquete; ***r. wrench*** llave *f* de trinquete

► **ratchet up** *vt sep (increase)* hacer subir, incrementar

rate [reɪt] **1** *n* **(a)** *(of inflation, crime, divorce, unemployment)* índice *m*, tasa *f*; *(of interest)* tipo *m*, *Am* tasa *f* ►► *Fin* ***r. of exchange*** (tipo *m or Am* tasa *f* de) cambio *m*; *Fin* ***r. of return*** tasa *f* de rentabilidad; ***r. of taxation*** tipo *m* impositivo
(b) *(speed)* ritmo *m*; **at this r.** a este paso; **at the r. we're going** *or* **at this r. we'll never get there** al paso que llevamos *or* a este paso, no vamos a llegar nunca; **she shot past at a terrific r.** pasó de largo a una velocidad de vértigo; IDIOM **at a r. of knots** a toda velocidad ►► ***r. of climb*** *(in plane)* velocidad *f* de ascenso
(c) *(price, charge)* tarifa *f*; **his rates have gone up** ha subido sus tarifas; **to strike for higher rates of pay** hacer huelga en demanda de aumentos salariales; **postal** *or* **postage r.** tarifa postal; **standard/reduced r.** tarifa normal/reducida
(d) *Br Formerly* **rates** *(local tax)* contribución *f* municipal; **(business) rates** contribución *f* municipal *(para empresas)*
2 *vt* **(a)** *(classify)* clasificar (**among** entre *or* dentro de); **to r. sth/sb as** catalogar algo/a alguien como; **to r. sth/sb highly** tener una buena opinión de algo/alguien; **to r. sth/sb on a scale of one to ten** valorar algo/a alguien en una escala del uno al diez
(b) *(deserve)* merecer; **that performance should r. him third place** esa actuación debería valerle el tercer puesto; **to r. a mention** ser digno(a) de mención
(c) *Fam (regard as good)* valorar mucho; **I don't r. him as an actor** no lo considero muy buen actor; **I don't really r. their chances** no les doy muchas posibilidades
(d) *Br (fix rateable value of)* tasar
(e) *(scold)* reprender
3 *vi (be regarded, ranked)* **he rates among the top ten of all time** está entre los diez mejores de todos los tiempos; **this rates as one of my favourite ever movies** es una de mis películas favoritas de todos los tiempos; **he rates highly in my estimation** lo tengo en gran estima
4 at any rate *adv (anyway)* en cualquier caso; *(at least)* por lo menos

rateable value ['reɪtəbəl'væljuː] *n Br* ≃ valor *m* catastral

rated ['reɪtɪd] *adj Tech (load, speed, voltage)* recomendado(a), indicado(a)

ratepayer ['reɪtpeɪə(r)] *n Br Formerly* contribuyente *mf (de impuestos municipales)*

ratfink ['rætfɪŋk] *n US Fam* miserable *mf*, canalla *mf*

RATHER ['rɑːðə(r)] *adv* **(a)** *(preferably)* **I'd r. stay** preferiría *or* prefiero quedarme; **I'd r. not go** preferiría *or* prefiero no ir; **I'd r. you didn't mention it** preferiría que no lo mencionaras; **are you coming for a walk? – I'd r. not** ¿vienes a dar un paseo? – no, gracias; **I'd r. die than ask her a favour** antes morirme que pedirle un favor; **would you r. go to Scotland?** ¿prefieres ir a Escocia?; **I would r. that you came too** preferiría que tú también vinieses; **r. you than me!** ¡no quisiera estar en tu lugar!
(b) *(quite)* bastante; *(very)* muy; **it's r. difficult** es bastante difícil; **this soup is r. good** esta sopa está muy buena *or* buenísima; **I r. liked it** me gustó mucho; **I r. doubt it** lo dudo mucho; **she r. cheekily asked me my age** la descarada me preguntó qué edad tenía; **I had r. a lot to drink** bebí *or Am* tomé más de la cuenta; **that was r. an unfair question** fue una pregunta bastante injusta; **it's r. a pity they couldn't come** es una auténtica pena que no pudieran venir, *RP* es realmente una lástima que no hayan podido venir; **it's r. too warm for me** hace demasiado calor para mi gusto; **did you like it? – r.!** ¿te gustó? – ¡ya lo creo!
(c) *(more exactly)* más bien; **he seemed tired or, r., bored** parecía

cansado o, más bien, aburrido; **I'd say it's blue r. than green** yo diría que es más azul que verde

(**d**) *(instead of)* **r. than him** en vez *or* lugar de él; **r. than staying** en vez *or* lugar de quedarse; **r. than wait any longer I set off on foot** para no tener que esperar más me marché caminando; **it proved to be a male r. than a female** resultó ser un macho y no una hembra

---

ratification [rætɪfɪ'keɪʃən] *n* ratificación *f*

ratify ['rætɪfaɪ] *vt* ratificar

rating ['reɪtɪŋ] *n* (**a**) *(classification)* puesto *m*, clasificación *f*; *(of movie)* clasificación *f* ►► ***r. scale*** *(in market research)* escala *f* (de puntuación) (**b**) **the ratings** *(for TV, radio)* los índices de audiencia; **to be high in the ratings** tener altos índices de audiencia; **the ratings battle** *or* **war** la batalla *or* guerra por la audiencia (**c**) *Br (ordinary seaman)* marinero *m*

ratio ['reɪʃɪəʊ] (*pl* **ratios**) *n* proporción *f*; **in a r. of four to one** en una proporción de cuatro a uno; **the teacher-student r. is 1 to 10** la proporción profesor-alumno es de 1 a 10 ►► *Math* ***r. scale*** escala *f* de razón

ratiocination ['rætɪɒsɪ'neɪʃən] *n Formal* reflexión *f*

ration ['ræʃən, *US* 'reɪʃən] **1** *n* (**a**) *(allocated amount)* ración *f*; **he was put on short/double rations** le redujeron/doblaron la ración; **I've had my r. of television for today** ya he tenido mi dosis de televisión por hoy ►► ***r. book*** cartilla *f* de racionamiento; ***r. card*** cartilla *f or* tarjeta *f* de racionamiento (**b**) **rations** *(food)* rancho *m*

2 *vt* (**a**) *(food, supplies)* racionar; **he rationed them to three a day** les redujo la ración a tres al día; **I've rationed myself to five cigarettes a day** me he prohibido fumar más de cinco cigarrillos al día (**b**) *(funds)* recortar

► **ration out** *vt sep* racionar

rational ['ræʃənəl] *adj* (**a**) *(capable of reason)* racional; **a r. being** un animal racional (**b**) *(sensible)* racional; **it seemed like the r. thing to do** hacer eso parecía lo más lógico; **he wasn't being very r. about it** no se comportaba de modo muy racional (**c**) *(sane)* lúcido(a) (**d**) *Math* ***r. number*** número *m* racional

rationale [ræʃə'nɑːl] *n* lógica *f*, razones *fpl*; **what is the r. for** *or* **behind their decision?** ¿cómo han razonado su decisión?

rationalism ['ræʃənəlɪzəm] *n* racionalismo *m*

rationalist ['ræʃənəlɪst] **1** *n* racionalista *mf*

2 *adj* racionalista

rationalistic [ræʃənə'lɪstɪk] *adj* racionalista

rationality [ræʃə'nælɪtɪ] *n* racionalidad *f*

rationalization [ræʃənəlaɪ'zeɪʃən] *n* (**a**) *(explanation)* racionalización *f* (**b**) *(of company, industry)* racionalización *f*, reconversión *f*

rationalize ['ræʃənəlaɪz] *vt* (**a**) *(explain)* racionalizar (**b**) *(company, industry)* racionalizar, reconvertir

rationally ['ræʃənəlɪ] *adv* (**a**) *(sensibly)* racionalmente (**b**) *(sanely)* lúcidamente

rationing ['ræʃənɪŋ] *n* (**a**) *(of food, supplies)* racionamiento *m* (**b**) *(of funds)* **banks are warning of mortgage r.** los bancos advierten de un posible racionamiento de créditos hipotecarios

ratpack ['rætpæk] *n Pej (press)* reporteros *mpl* de la prensa del corazón

rattan [rə'tæn] *n (material)* ratán *m*; **r. furniture** muebles de ratán

rattle ['rætəl] **1** *n* (**a**) *(for baby)* sonajero *m*; *(for sports fan)* matraca *f*; *(of rattlesnake)* cascabel *m* (**b**) *(noise) (of train)* traqueteo *m*; *(of car, engine)* petardeo *m*; *(of gunfire)* tableteo *m*; *(of chains)* crujido *m*; *(of glass, coins, keys)* tintineo *m*; *(of door, window, hailstones)* golpeteo *m*

2 *vt* (**a**) *(box)* agitar; *(chains, keys)* hacer entrechocar; *(door, window)* sacudir; IDIOM *Fam* **who rattled your cage?** ¿qué mosca te ha picado? (**b**) *Fam (make nervous)* **to be rattled by sth** quedar desconcertado(a) por algo; **don't get rattled!** ¡no hagas caso!

3 *vi (train)* traquetear; *(car, engine)* petardear; *(gun)* tabletear; *(chains)* crujir; *(glass, coins, keys)* tintinear; *(door, window, hailstones)* golpetear; **the explosion made the windows r.** la explosión sacudió las ventanas; **somebody was rattling at the door** alguien estaba golpeteando la puerta

► **rattle about, rattle around** *vi* **there was something rattling about** *or* **around inside the box** algo hacía ruido en el interior de la caja; *Fig* **you'll be rattling about** *or* **around in that big old house!** ¡te vas a perder en esa casona!

► **rattle off** *vt sep Fam (say quickly)* soltar de un tirón; *(write quickly)* garabatear

► **rattle on** *vi Fam* parlotear, *Esp* cascar

► **rattle through** *vt insep Fam (work, book, meeting)* despachar, terminar rápidamente

rattler ['rætlə(r)] *n US Fam* serpiente *f* de cascabel

rattlesnake ['rætəlsneɪk] *n* serpiente *f* de cascabel

rattling ['rætlɪŋ] **1** *n (noise) (of train)* traqueteo *m*; *(of car, engine)* petardeo *m*; *(of gunfire)* tableteo *m*; *(of chains)* crujido *m*; *(of glass, coins, keys)* tintineo *m*; *(of door, window, hailstones)* golpeteo *m*

2 *adj (fast)* **at a r. pace** a una velocidad de vértigo

3 *adv Fam Old-fashioned (as intensifier)* **a r. good read** un libro muy entretenido

ratty ['rætɪ] *adj Fam* (**a**) *(annoyed)* mosqueado(a); *(irritable)* susceptible, picajoso(a); **don't get r.!** ¡no te mosquees! (**b**) *US (shabby)* raído(a)

raucous ['rɔːkəs] *adj (voice, laughter, cry)* estridente; *(crowd)* ruidoso(a); **things got a bit r. as the evening wore on** la escandalera aumentaba a medida que avanzaba la tarde

raucously ['rɔːkəslɪ] *adv* estridentemente

raunchiness ['rɔːntʃɪnɪs] *n* tono *m* picante

raunchy ['rɔːntʃɪ] *adj Fam* (**a**) *(sexy) (lyrics, movie, novel)* picante, caliente; *(dress, dance)* atrevido(a), provocativo(a) (**b**) *US (slovenly)* descuidado(a), desastrado(a)

ravage ['rævɪdʒ] **1** *vt (countryside, city)* arrasar, asolar; **the city had been ravaged by war** la ciudad había sido arrasada *or* asolada por la guerra; **his face was ravaged by illness** la enfermedad había hecho estragos en su cara

2 **ravages** *npl* estragos *mpl*; **the ravages of time** los estragos del tiempo

rave [reɪv] **1** *n* (**a**) *(praise)* elogio *m* (**b**) *(party)* macrofiesta *f* (tecno)

2 *adj* **r. notice** *or* **review** *(for play)* crítica entusiasta

3 *vi* (**a**) *(deliriously)* desvariar (**b**) *Fam (enthusiastically)* **to r. about sth/sb** deshacerse en elogios sobre algo/alguien (**c**) *(angrily)* despotricar (**at** contra)

► **rave up** *vt sep Br Fam* **to r. it up** meterle caña

ravel ['rævəl] (*pt & pp* **ravelled**, *US* **raveled**) **1** *vt* (**a**) *(entangle)* enredar, enmarañar (**b**) **to r. sth out** *(untangle)* desenredar *or* desenmarañar algo

2 *vi (fray)* deshilacharse

raven ['reɪvən] **1** *n (bird)* cuervo *m*

2 *adj (colour)* azabache

raven-haired ['reɪvənheəd] *adj Literary* de pelo (negro) azabache

ravening ['rævənɪŋ] *adj* voraz

ravenous ['rævənəs] *adj (animal, person)* hambriento(a); **to be r.** tener un hambre canina

ravenously ['rævənəslɪ] *adv* con gran apetito; **to be r. hungry** tener un hambre canina

raver ['reɪvə(r)] *n Br Fam* (**a**) *(who goes to lots of parties)* juerguista *mf*, *Am* parrandero(a) *m,f* (**b**) *(who goes to raves) Esp* aficionado(a) *m,f* al bakalao, *Am* raver *mf*

rave-up ['reɪvʌp] *n Br Fam* juerga *f*, farra *f*, *Am* pachanga *f*; **to have a r.** ir de juerga *or* farra *or Am* pachanga

ravine [rə'viːn] *n* barranco *m*

raving ['reɪvɪŋ] **1** *adj* (**a**) *(delirious)* **to be r. mad** estar como una cabra; **a r. lunatic** un loco de atar (**b**) *(success)* clamoroso(a); *(beauty)* arrebatador(ora)

2 *n* desvarío *m*; **the ravings of a madman** los desvaríos de un loco

ravioli [rævɪ'əʊlɪ] *npl* raviolis *mpl*

ravish ['rævɪʃ] *vt* (**a**) *Literary (delight)* deslumbrar, cautivar (**b**) *Old-fashioned (rape)* forzar, violar

ravishing ['rævɪʃɪŋ] *adj* deslumbrante, cautivador(ora); **she's a r. beauty** es de una belleza deslumbrante

ravishingly ['rævɪʃɪŋlɪ] *adv* **r. beautiful** de una belleza deslumbrante

raw [rɔː] **1** *adj* (**a**) *(uncooked)* crudo(a); **to be r.** *(meat, vegetables)* estar crudo(a); IDIOM *Austr Fam* **don't come the r. prawn with me** no intentes jugármela

(**b**) *(unprocessed) (silk, milk)* crudo(a); *(cotton)* en rama; *(sugar)* sin refinar; *(sewage)* sin depurar; *(data, statistics)* sin procesar; **r. edge** *(of material)* borde cortado ►► ***r. materials*** materias *fpl* primas; **her failed marriage provided the r. material for her novel** su fracaso matrimonial le proporcionó la materia prima para su novela

(**c**) *(inexperienced)* **a r. recruit** un(a) novato(a)

(**d**) *(sore) (skin)* enrojecido(a) e irritado(a); *(wound, blister)* en carne viva; IDIOM **to get a r. deal** ser tratado(a) injustamente; IDIOM **to touch a r. nerve** tocar la fibra sensible; **my nerves are r.** tengo los nervios a flor de piel

(**e**) *(emotion, power, energy)* puro(a) y duro(a)

(**f**) *(weather)* crudo(a); **a r. February night** una cruda noche de febrero; **a r. wind** un viento cortante

(**g**) *Art* **r. sienna/umber** siena/ocre crudo

2 *n* **in the r.** *(not treated, toned down)* en toda su crudeza; *(naked)* desnudo(a); IDIOM **to touch sb on the r.** tocar la fibra sensible de alguien

rawhide ['rɔːhaɪd] **1** *n* (**a**) *(skin)* cuero *m* crudo *or* sin curtir (**b**) *(whip)* látigo *m* de cuero

2 *adj* de cuero crudo *or* sin curtir

Rawlplug® ['rɔːlplʌg] *n* taco *m*

rawness ['rɔːnɪs] *n* (**a**) *(inexperience)* inexperiencia *f*, bisoñez *f* (**b**) *(soreness) (of skin, wound)* irritación *f* (**c**) *(of emotion)* fuerza *f* (**d**) *(of weather)* rigor *m*

ray[1] [reɪ] *n* (**a**) *(of light, sun)* rayo *m*; **a r. of sunlight** un rayo de sol (**b**) *(glimmer)* **a r. of hope** un rayo de esperanza; IDIOM **she's a r. of sunshine** irradia alegría (**c**) *Mus* re *m*

ray[2] *n (fish)* raya *f*

ray-gun ['reɪgʌn] *n* pistola *f* de rayos

rayon ['reɪɒn] *n (fabric)* rayón *m*

raze [reɪz] *vt* arrasar; **to r. sth to the ground** arrasar totalmente algo

razor ['reɪzə(r)] *n (cut-throat)* navaja *f* barbera, navaja *f* de afeitar; *(electric)* maquinilla *f* de afeitar, maquinilla *f* eléctrica; *(safety, disposable)* maquinilla *f* (de afeitar); IDIOM **to be on a r.'s edge** pender de un hilo ►► ***r. blade*** cuchilla *f* *or RP* hoja *f* de afeitar; ***r. cut*** = corte de pelo hecho a navaja; ***r. wire*** = alambre con trozos afilados de metal, parecido al alambre de púas

razorback ['reɪzəbæk] *n* (**a**) *(whale)* rorcual *m* común (**b**) *US (pig)* = especie de jabalí que habita en el sudeste de los EE.UU.

razorbill ['reɪzəbɪl] *n* alca *f* común

razor-sharp ['reɪzə'ʃɑːp] *adj* (**a**) *(knife)* muy afilado(a) (**b**) *Fig (person, intelligence)* agudo(a); *(wit)* afilado(a)

razor-shell ['reɪzəʃel] *n* navaja *f (molusco)*

razz [ræz] *vt US Fam (mock)* burlarse de

razzle ['ræzəl] *n Br Fam* **to go (out) on the r.** irse de parranda

razzle-dazzle ['ræzəl'dæzəl], **razzmatazz** ['ræzmətæz] *n Fam* parafernalia *f*

R & B ['ɑːrən'biː] *n* (*abbr* **rhythm and blues**) rhythm and blues *m*

RC [ɑː'siː] (*abbr* **Roman Catholic**) **1** *n* católico(a) *m,f* romano(a)

2 *adj* católico(a) romano(a)

RCAF [ɑːsiːeɪ'ef] *n* (*abbr* **Royal Canadian Air Force**) fuerzas *fpl* aéreas canadienses

RCMP [ɑːsiːem'piː] *n* (*abbr* **Royal Canadian Mounted Police**) Policía *f* Montada del Canadá

RCN [ɑːsiː'en] *n* (*abbr* **Royal Canadian Navy**) fuerzas *fpl* navales canadienses

RCP [ɑːsiː'piː] *n* (*abbr* **Royal College of Physicians**) = colegio profesional de los médicos británicos

RCS [ɑːsiː'es] *n* (*abbr* **Royal College of Surgeons**) = colegio profesional de los cirujanos británicos

RCVS [ɑːsiːviː'es] *n* (*abbr* **Royal College of Veterinary Surgeons**) = colegio profesional de los cirujanos veterinarios británicos

R & D ['ɑːrən'diː] *n Com* (*abbr* **research and development**) I+D *m*

Rd (*abbr* **Road**) C/

RDA [ɑːdiː'eɪ] *n* (*abbr* **recommended daily allowance**) cantidad *f* diaria recomendada

RE [ɑːr'iː] *n Br* (**a**) (*abbr* **Religious Education**) (asignatura *f* de) religión *f* (**b**) (*abbr* **Royal Engineers**) = cuerpo de ingenieros del ejército británico

re[1] [riː] *prep* con referencia a; **re your letter...** con referencia a *or* en relación con su carta...; **re: 2001 sales figures** REF: cifras de ventas de 2001

re[2] [reɪ] *n Mus* re *m*

reabsorb [riːəb'sɔːb] *vt* reabsorber

REACH [riːtʃ] **1** *n* (**a**) *(accessibility)* alcance *m*; **beyond the r. of** fuera del alcance de; **out of r.** fuera del alcance, inalcanzable; **the title is now out of** *or* **beyond his r.** el título ha quedado fuera de su alcance; **within r.** al alcance; **within arm's r.** al alcance de la mano; **within easy r. of the shops** a poca distancia de las tiendas; **within everyone's r.** *(affordable by all)* al alcance de todos los bolsillos; **do not leave within r. of children** *(label)* no dejar al alcance de los niños; **nuclear physics is beyond my r.** la física nuclear es demasiado complicada para mí; **we came within r. of victory** estuvimos a punto de ganar

(**b**) *(of boxer)* alcance *m*

(**c**) *(area)* **the upper/lower reaches of a river** el curso alto/bajo de un río; **the further reaches of the empire** los últimos confines del imperio; **the outer reaches of the galaxy** los confines de la galaxia

2 *vt* (**a**) *(manage to touch)* alcanzar; **her hair reached her waist** el pelo le llegaba a la cintura; **can you r. the top shelf?** ¿llegas a la estantería de arriba?; **his feet don't r. the floor** sus pies no tocan el suelo; **the water reached my knees** el agua me llegaba hasta las rodillas

(**b**) *(arrive at) (destination, final, conclusion, decision)* llegar a; *(agreement, stage, level)* alcanzar, llegar a; **the news didn't r. him** no le llegó la noticia; **answers must r. us by next Friday** las respuestas deben llegarnos no más tarde del próximo viernes *or* a más tardar el próximo viernes; **I've reached the point where I no longer care** he llegado a un punto en el que ya no me importa nada; **to r. the age of 80** llegar a los 80

(**c**) *(contact) (by phone)* contactar con *orAm* a; **you can always r. me at this number** en este número estoy siempre localizable; **to r. a wider audience** llegar a un público más amplio

(**d**) *(pass)* alcanzar; **r. me down that vase** bájame ese jarrón; **r. me up that box** alcánzame esa caja

3 *vi* (**a**) *(person)* **I can't r.** no llego, no alcanzo; **she reached across and took the money** *Esp* alargó la mano y cogió el dinero, *Am* estiró la mano y agarró la plata; **he reached across the table for the mustard** alcanzó la mostaza desde el otro lado de la mesa; **r. down and touch your toes** agáchate y tócate la punta de los pies; **he reached into the bag** metió la mano en la bolsa; **r. up as high as you can** estírate todo lo que puedas

(**b**) *(extend) (forest, property)* extenderse; **the noise/his voice reached them** oían el ruido/su voz; **the water reached up to** *or* **as far as my waist** el agua me llegaba a la cintura; **it won't r.** no llega; **her skirt reached down to her ankles** la falda le llegaba hasta las rodillas

► **reach for** *vt insep* (tratar de) alcanzar; **he reached for his wallet** fue a sacar su cartera; IDIOM **to r. for the sky** *or* **the stars** apuntar a lo más alto

► **reach out 1** *vt sep* **she reached a hand out** extendió la mano

2 *vi* (**a**) *(try to grasp)* **r. out with your arms** extiende los brazos; **to r. out for sth** extender el brazo para agarrar *or Esp* coger algo

(**b**) *(try to communicate)* **to r. out to sb** intentar echar un cable a alguien; **to r. out to sb for help** dirigirse a alguien buscando ayuda

---

reachable ['riːtʃəbəl] *adj* (**a**) *(place, person)* accesible (**b**) *(contactable)* contactable

reach-me-downs ['riːtʃmɪdaʊnz] *npl Br Fam* **he wore his brother's r.** llevaba ropa heredada de su hermano

react [rɪ'ækt] *vi* reaccionar (**against/to** contra/ante); **the patient is reacting well to the treatment** el paciente reacciona bien al tratamiento; **to r. with sth** *(chemical)* reaccionar con algo

reactance [rɪ'æktəns] *n Elec* reactancia *f*

reactant [rɪ'æktənt] *n Chem* reactivo *m*

reaction [rɪ'ækʃən] *n* (**a**) *(response)* reacción *f*; **what was her r.?** ¿cuál fue su reacción?; **her work is a r. against abstract art** su obra es una reacción al arte abstracto; **public r. has been mixed** la opinión pública ha tenido diferentes reacciones ►► ***r. engine*** motor *m* a reacción; ***r. motor*** motor *m* a reacción; ***r. time*** tiempo *m* de reacción

(**b**) *(reflex)* reacción *f*; **alcohol slows down your reactions** el alcohol reduce la capacidad de reacción

(**c**) *Pol* reacción *f*; **the forces of r.** las fuerzas reaccionarias

reactionary [rɪ'ækʃənərɪ] **1** *n* reaccionario(a) *m,f*

2 *adj* reaccionario(a)

reactivate [rɪ'æktɪveɪt] *vt* reactivar

reactive [rɪ'æktɪv] *adj* reactivo(a)

reactor [rɪ'æktə(r)] *n* reactor *m*

READ [riːd] **1** *n* **to give sth a r. through** leer algo, darle una leída a algo; **to have a quiet r. (of sth)** leer (algo) tranquilamente; **can I have a r. of your paper?** ¿me dejas echarle un vistazo al periódico?; **this book's a good r.** este libro se lee muy bien *or* es muy entretenido ►► ***r. head*** *(of video, tape recorder)* cabeza *f* lectora

2 *vt* (*pt & pp* **read** [red]) (**a**) *(book, letter, electricity meter)* leer; **this magazine is widely r.** esta revista la leen muchas personas, ésta es una revista muy leída; **to r. Italian** leer en italiano; **to r. music** leer música; **I can't r. her writing** no entiendo su letra; **r. me a story** léeme un cuento; **she r. herself to sleep** se quedó dormida leyendo; IDIOM **to take sth as r.** dar por hecho *or* por sentado algo

(**b**) *(say aloud) (letter, poem)* leer (en voz alta)

(**c**) *(of dial, thermometer)* marcar; **the sign reads "No Entry"** el letrero dice "prohibida la entrada"

(d) *(interpret)* interpretar; **it can be r. in two ways** tiene una doble lectura; **in paragraph two, r. "fit" for "fat"** en el párrafo segundo, donde dice "fit" debe decir "fat"; **the defender r. the pass and intercepted it** el defensor se anticipó al pase y lo interceptó; **to r. the future** adivinar el futuro; **to r. sb's lips** leer los labios a alguien; IDIOM **r. my lips** presta atención, escúchame bien; **to r. sb's mind** *or* **thoughts** adivinar los pensamientos a alguien; **to r. sb's palm** leer la mano a alguien; IDIOM **she can r. me like a book** me conoce muy bien; IDIOM *Br* **to r. the runes** leer el futuro

(e) *(understand)* **do you r. me?** *(on radio)* ¿me recibes?; *Fam Fig* ¿está claro?; **reading you loud and clear** te recibo alto y claro

(f) *(correct) (proofs)* corregir, *Am* revisar

(g) *Br Univ (study)* estudiar

(h) *Comptr* leer; **this computer only reads double-density disks** *Esp* este ordenador *or Am* esta computadora sólo lee discos de doble densidad

3 *vi* (a) *(person)* leer; **I r. about it in the paper** lo leí en el periódico; **to r. aloud** leer en alto *or* en voz alta; **she r. to him from a book** le leyó de un libro; *Fig* **to r. between the lines** leer entre líneas

(b) *(text, notice)* decir; **to r. well/badly** estar bien/mal escrito(a); **the statement reads as follows...** la declaración dice *or* reza lo siguiente...; **the table reads from left to right** la tabla se lee de izquierda a derecha; **the text reads like a translation** el escrito parece una traducción

(c) *(student)* **to r. for a degree** cursar una licenciatura

▸**read back** *vt sep (dictated letter)* volver a leer

▸**read into** *vt sep* **I wouldn't r. too much into his comments** yo no le daría demasiada importancia a sus comentarios

▸**read off** *vt sep* (a) *(read out loud)* leer (en voz alta) (b) *(from table, instrument)* leer

▸**read on** *vi* continuar leyendo

▸**read out** *vt sep* (a) *(read out loud)* leer (en voz alta) (b) *US (expel)* expulsar

▸**read over, read through** *vt sep* leer; **r. your answers over** *or* **through before you hand the test in** repasen sus respuestas antes de entregar la prueba

▸**read up on** *vt insep* empaparse de, leer mucho sobre

---

readability [riːdəˈbɪlɪtɪ] *n* (a) *(of writer, style)* amenidad *f* (b) *(of handwriting)* legibilidad *f* (c) *Comptr* legibilidad *f*

readable [ˈriːdəbəl] *adj* (a) *(book)* ameno(a) (b) *(handwriting)* legible

readdress [riːəˈdres] *vt* (a) *(letter)* cambiar la dirección de (b) *Comptr* redireccionar

reader [ˈriːdə(r)] *n* (a) *(of book, text)* lector(ora) *m,f*; **I'm not much of a r.** no me gusta mucho la lectura; **I'm a fast/slow r.** leo rápido/despacio

(b) *(reading book)* libro *m* de lectura; **German r.** libro de lectura en alemán

(c) *(anthology)* antología *f*

(d) *Br Univ* = profesor entre el rango de catedrático y el de profesor titular

(e) *US Univ* ayudante *mf*

(f) *Rel* = persona que tiene potestad para encargarse de ciertos oficios religiosos, sin incluir la eucaristía

(g) *Comptr* lector *m*

readership [ˈriːdəʃɪp] *n* (a) *(of publication)* lectores *mpl*; **this magazine has a large r.** esta revista tiene muchos lectores (b) *Br Univ* = cargo entre el rango de catedrático y el de profesor titular (c) *US Univ* ayudantía *f*

readily [ˈredɪlɪ] *adv* (a) *(willingly)* de buena gana, de buen grado; **I would r. help if I had the time** ayudaría de buen grado si tuviera tiempo (b) *(easily)* fácilmente; **r. understandable ideas** ideas fáciles de entender; **our products are r. available** nuestros productos se pueden conseguir fácilmente

readiness [ˈredɪnɪs] *n* (a) *(willingness)* disposición *f*; **I was pleased by their r. to help** me agradó su disposición a ayudar (b) *(preparedness)* preparación *f*; **in r. for** en preparación para, a la espera de; **to be/remain in r. for sth** estar/continuar preparado(a) para algo; **to be in (a state of) constant r.** estar siempre listo(a) para cualquier eventualidad

reading [ˈriːdɪŋ] *n* (a) *(action, pastime)* lectura *f*; **I have a lot of r. to catch up on** tengo muchas lecturas pendientes; **I have a r. knowledge of Italian** entiendo el italiano escrito; **a person of wide r.** una persona leída; **the r. public** el público lector ▸▸ ***r. ability*** capacidad *f* de lectura; ***r. age*** nivel *m* de lectura; **she has a r. age of 11** tiene un nivel de lectura propio de un niño de 11 años; ***r. glasses*** gafas *fpl* para leer; ***r. list*** lista *f* de lecturas; ***r. material*** (material *m* de) lectura *f*, lecturas *fpl*; ***r. matter*** lectura *f*; ***r. room*** *(in library)* sala *f* de lectura

(b) *(reading material)* lectura *f*; **some light r.** una lectura ligera; **his memoirs should make (for) interesting r.** será interesante leer sus memorias

(c) *(recital)* lectura *f*; **the r. of the will** la lectura del testamento

(d) *Pol* **to give a bill its first/second r.** dar primera/segunda lectura a un proyecto de ley

(e) *(measurement)* lectura *f*; **the r. on the dial was wrong** lo que indicaba el cuadrante estaba mal; **to take a r. from the gas meter** leer el contador del gas

(f) *(interpretation)* interpretación *f*, lectura *f*; **a new r. of "The Waste Land"** una nueva lectura de "La tierra baldía"; **what's your r. of the situation?** ¿cómo interpretas la situación?

(g) *(variant)* variante *f*

reading-book [ˈriːdɪŋbʊk] *n* libro *m* de lectura

reading-desk [ˈriːdɪŋdesk] *n* mesa *f* para leer

reading-lamp [ˈriːdɪŋlæmp] *n* lámpara *f* para leer

reading-light [ˈriːdɪŋlaɪt] *n* luz *f* de lectura

readjust [riːəˈdʒʌst] 1 *vt* (a) *(readapt)* **to r. oneself** readaptarse (b) *(alter)* reajustar

2 *vi* readaptarse (**to** a)

readjustment [riːəˈdʒʌstmənt] *n* (a) *(readaptation)* readaptación *f* (b) *(alteration)* reajuste *m*

readme file [ˈriːdmiːˈfaɪl] *n Comptr* (documento *m*) léeme *m*

readmission [ˈriːədˈmɪʃən] *n (to political party)* readmisión *f*; *(to hospital)* reingreso *m*; **no r.** *(on ticket)* esta entrada no permite el reingreso al local

readmit [riːədˈmɪt] *vt* readmitir (**to** en)

read-only [ˈriːdˈəʊnlɪ] *adj Comptr* **to make a file r.** hacer que un archivo sea sólo de lectura ▸▸ ***r. file*** archivo *m* de sólo lectura; ***r. memory*** memoria *f* de sólo lectura

read-out [ˈriːdaʊt] *n Comptr* visualización *f*

readvertise [riːˈædvətaɪz] 1 *vt* **to r. a post** volver a anunciar un puesto

2 *vi* volver a anunciar el puesto

readvertisement [ˈriːədˈvɜːtɪsmənt] *n* segundo anuncio *m*; **this is a r.** *(in advert)* segundo anuncio de esta oferta de empleo

read-write [ˈriːdˈraɪt] *n Comptr* ***r. head*** cabeza *f* lectora/grabadora; ***r. memory*** memoria *f* de lectura/escritura

ready [ˈredɪ] 1 *n* (a) **at the r.** *(prepared)* preparado(a) (b) *Br Fam* **readies** *(cash)* dinero *m* contante y sonante

2 *adj* (a) *(prepared)* listo(a), preparado(a) (**for** para); **to be r. (to do sth)** estar listo(a) *or* preparado(a) (para hacer algo); **to be r. and waiting** estar ya listo(a) *or* preparado(a); **he's not r. for such responsibility** no está preparado para tanta responsabilidad; **are you r. to order?** ¿desea pedir ya?; **we were r. to give up** estuvimos a punto de darnos por vencidos; **to get (oneself) r.** *(prepared)* prepararse, *Am* alistarse; *(smarten up)* arreglarse; **to get the children r.** arreglar a los niños; **to get sth r.** preparar algo; **to get r. to do sth** prepararse *or Am* alistarse para hacer algo; **to get r. for bed** prepararse para ir a la cama; *Literary* **to make r. (for sth/sb)** poner a punto (para algo/alguien); **(we're) r. when you are** cuando quieras; **dinner's r.!** la cena está lista, ¡a cenar!; **r. for use** *or* **to use** listo(a) para ser usado(a); **r., steady, go!** preparados, listos, ¡ya!

(b) *(willing)* dispuesto(a); **to be r. to do sth** estar dispuesto(a) a hacer algo; **they are always r. to find fault** siempre están buscando algo que criticar; **you know me, I'm r. for anything** ya me conoces, estoy dispuesto a todo

(c) *(easily accessible)* **a r. market for our products** un mercado abierto a nuestros productos; **I don't have one r. to hand** no tengo ninguno a mano ▸▸ ***r. cash*** dinero *m* en efectivo; *Fam* ***r. money*** dinero *m* contante y sonante; ***r. reckoner*** baremo *m*

(d) *(quick)* **he had a r. answer to all my questions** tenía una respuesta pronta a todas mis preguntas; **to have a r. wit** ser muy ingenioso(a); **you're always a bit too r. with advice** enseguida te pones a dar consejos; **he's very r. with his fists** enseguida se lía a puñetazos; **don't be too r. to condemn him** no lo juzgues a la ligera

(e) *(likely)* **she looks r. to explode** va a estallar de un momento a otro; **I'm r. to collapse!** ¡voy a caer rendido de un momento a otro!

3 *vt (prepare)* preparar; **to r. oneself for action** prepararse *or Am* alistarse para la acción

ready-cooked [ˈredɪˈkʊkt] *adj* precocinado(a)

ready-made [ˈredɪˈmeɪd] *adj* (a) *(clothes, curtains)* confeccionado(a), hecho(a); **r. food** platos precocinados (b) *(excuse, solution. explanation)* perfecto(a); **a r. phrase** una frase hecha

ready-mix ['redımıks] *adj (cake)* = en sobre, ya listo para cocinar; *(concrete)* premezclado(a)

ready-salted ['redı'sɔːltıd] *adj Br (crisps)* con sal

ready-to-wear ['redıtə'weə(r)] *adj* de confección

reaffirm [riːə'fɜːm] *vt* reafirmar

reaffirmation [riːæfə'meıʃən] *n* reafirmación *f*

reafforest [riːə'fɒrıst] *vt Br* reforestar

reafforestation ['riːəfɒrı'steıʃən] *n Br* reforestación *f*, repoblación *f* forestal

reagent [riː'eıdʒənt] *n Chem* reactivo *m*

REAL [rıəl] **1** *adj* **(a)** *(genuine) (danger, fear, effort)* real; *(gold, leather)* auténtico(a); **r. flowers** flores naturales; **the r. reason** el verdadero motivo; **a r. friend** un amigo de verdad; **I don't know his r. name** no sé su verdadero nombre; **we have no r. cause for concern** no tenemos realmente motivos para preocuparnos; **that's what I call a r. cup of tea!** eso es una taza de té como Dios manda; **she never showed them her r. self** nunca les reveló su auténtica personalidad; **he has shown r. determination** ha mostrado verdadera determinación; **our first r. opportunity** nuestra primera oportunidad real; **the pizzas you get here are nothing like the r. thing** las pizzas de aquí no se parecen en nada a las auténticas; **this time it's the r. thing** esta vez va de verdad; *Hum* **r. men don't drink shandy** los hombres de pelo en pecho no beben *or Am* toman cerveza con gaseosa; **for r.** de verdad; IDIOM *Fam Pej* **is he for r.?** ¿qué le pasa a éste?, *Esp* ¿de qué va éste? ►► ***r. ale*** = cerveza de malta de elaboración tradicional y con presión natural; *Math* ***r. number*** número *m* real; *Sport* ***r. tennis*** = versión primitiva del tenis que se juega en una pista con paredes

(b) *(actual)* real; **the r. problem is how to make it profitable** el problema central es cómo hacer que sea rentable; **the threat is a very r. one** se trata de una seria amenaza; **the r. world** el mundo real; **in r. life** en la vida real; *Econ* **in r. terms** en términos reales; **what does that mean in r. terms?** ¿qué significado tiene a efectos prácticos? ►► ***r. estate*** bienes *mpl* inmuebles; *US* ***r. estate agent*** agente *mf* inmobiliario(a); ***r. estate developer*** *Esp* promotor(ora) *m,f* inmobiliario, *Am* constructor(ora) *m,f*; *US* ***r. property*** bienes *mpl* inmuebles

(c) *Comptr* ***r. time*** tiempo *m* real; ***r. time chat*** charla *f* en tiempo real; ***r. time clock*** reloj *m* de tiempo real

(d) *(for emphasis)* auténtico(a), verdadero(a); **it's a r. gem of a novel** es una auténtica joya de novela; *very Fam* **a r. bastard** un verdadero hijo de puta; **a r. disaster** un perfecto desastre; **a r. idiot** un tonto de remate, *RP* el rey de los bobos; **you've been a r. help** nos has ayudado mucho

(e) *Fam (realistic)* **get r.!** *Esp* ¡espabila!, *Méx* ¡despabílate!, *RP* ¡despertate!

2 *adv US Fam (very)* muy; **it's r. good** es superbueno(a); **you were r. lucky** tuviste muchísima suerte

3 *n Phil* **the r.** lo real

realign [riːə'laın] *vt* **(a)** *(wheels)* realinear **(b)** *(party, policy)* realinear

realignment [riːə'laınmənt] *n* **(a)** *(of wheels)* realineación *f* **(b)** *(of party, policy)* realineamiento *m*

realism ['rıəlızəm] *n* realismo *m*

realist ['rıəlıst] **1** *n* realista *mf*; **I'm a r. in these matters** en estas cuestiones soy bastante realista

2 *adj* realista

realistic [rıə'lıstık] *adj* **(a)** *(sensible, practical)* realista; **let's be r. about this** seamos realistas acerca de esto **(b)** *(lifelike)* realista

realistically [rıə'lıstıklı] *adv* **(a)** *(sensibly, practically)* de forma realista; **r. (speaking)** para ser realistas, siendo realistas; **they can't r. expect us to do all this on our own** si son realistas no pueden esperar que hagamos todo esto solos **(b)** *(like life)* con realismo, de manera realista

reality [rı'ælıtı] *n* realidad *f*; **the realities of living in today's world** la realidad de la vida en el mundo de hoy; **to become (a) r.** hacerse realidad; **to face r.** enfrentarse a la realidad; **it was a r. check for him** le hizo volver a la realidad; **in r.** en realidad ►► ***r. TV*** la televisión de los reality-shows

realizable ['rıəlaızəbəl] *adj* **(a)** *(achievable)* realizable, alcanzable **(b)** *Fin (assets)* realizable

realization [rıəlaı'zeıʃən] *n* **(a)** *(awareness)* **this r. frightened her** al darse cuenta se asustó; **the r. of what he meant was slow in coming** tardó *or Am* demoró en darse cuenta de lo que quería decir **(b)** *(of ambition, dream)* realización *f* **(c)** *Fin (of assets)* realización *f*

realize ['rıəlaız] **1** *vt* **(a)** *(be or become aware of)* darse cuenta de; **I didn't r. how late it was** no me di cuenta de lo tarde que era; **it made me r. what a fool I had been** me hizo darme cuenta de lo tonto que había sido; **I r. he's busy, but...** ya sé que está ocupado, pero...

(b) *(ambition, dream)* realizar, hacer realidad; **she's finally realized her full potential** por fin ha alcanzado su potencial pleno; **our fears were realized** nuestros temores se vieron confirmados

(c) *Fin (profit)* obtener, sacar; *(asset)* realizar, liquidar; **how much did they r. on the sale?** ¿cuánto obtuvieron por la venta?

2 *vi* **I'm sorry, I didn't r.** lo siento, no me di cuenta

real-life ['rıəllaıf] *adj* de la vida real; **his r. wife** su mujer en la vida real; **this never happens in r. situations** esto nunca sucede en la vida real

reallocate [riː'æləkeıt] *vt (funds, resources, tasks)* reasignar

REALLY ['rıəlı] *adv* **(a)** *(truly)* de verdad; **did they r. fire her?** ¿de verdad que la despidieron?, ¿en serio la despidieron?; **r.?** ¿de verdad?,¿en serio?; **you don't r. expect me to believe you, do you?** no esperarás que te vaya a creer, ¿no?, *RP* no pretenderás que te crea, ¿no?

(b) *(very)* realmente, verdaderamente; **r. good** buenísimo(a); **is it good? – not r.** ¿es bueno? – la verdad (es) que no

(c) *(actually)* **she's r. my sister** en realidad es mi hermana; **it was quite good, r.** estaba muy bueno, de verdad; **this is r. not all that bad** *Esp* esto no está pero que nada mal, *Am* esto no está nada mal; **do you want to go? – I suppose I do r.** ¿quieres ir? – pues la verdad es que sí

(d) *(softening negative statements)* **it doesn't r. matter** no tiene demasiada importancia; **you weren't to know, but you shouldn't r. be here** aunque no lo sabías, no tendrías que haber venido

(e) *(in exclamations)* **oh, r., don't be so childish!** ¡por favor, no seas tan infantil!; **well r., that's no way to behave!** ¡desde luego no es manera de comportarse!, *Am* ¡realmente, ésa no es manera de comportarse!

realm [relm] *n* **(a)** *(kingdom)* reino *m* **(b)** *(field)* ámbito *m*, dominio *m*; **the r. of the supernatural** el mundo de lo sobrenatural; **within/beyond the realms of possibility** dentro de/fuera de lo posible

realpolitik [reıælpɒlı'tık] *n Pol* realpolitik *f*

real-time ['rıəl'taım] *adj Comptr* en tiempo real ►► ***r. strategy game*** juego *m* de estrategia en tiempo real

realtor ['rıəltə(r)] *n US* agente *mf* inmobiliario(a)

realty ['rıəltı] *n US* bienes *mpl* inmuebles

ream [riːm] **1** *n (of paper)* resma *f*; *Fig* **reams of** montones de; *Fam* **to write reams** escribir a porrillo

2 *vt* **(a)** *Tech (hole)* escariar **(b)** *US (lemon)* exprimir **(c)** *US Fam (scold)* echar una reprimenda *or Esp* una bronca a alguien, dar *Méx* una jalada *or RP* un rezongo a alguien **(d)** *US Fam (swindle)* timar

►**ream out** *vt sep US Fam (scold)* echar una reprimenda *or Esp* una bronca a alguien, dar *Méx* una jalada *or RP* un rezongo a alguien

reamer ['riːmə(r)] *n* **(a)** *(tool)* escariador *m* **(b)** *US (lemon squeezer)* exprimidor *m*

reanimate [riː'ænımeıt] *vt* reanimar

reap [riːp] **1** *vt* **(a)** *(harvest)* segar; IDIOM **to r. what one has sown** recoger lo que se ha sembrado **(b)** *(obtain)* **to r. the benefits (of)** cosechar los beneficios (de); **she reaped a rich reward** recogió los frutos

2 *vi* segar

reaper ['riːpə(r)] *n* **(a)** *(machine)* segadora *f* **(b)** *(person)* segador(ora) *m,f*; *Literary* **the (Grim) R.** la dama de la guadaña

reappear [riːə'pıə(r)] *vi* reaparecer; **my pen eventually reappeared** al final mi bolígrafo volvió a aparecer

reappearance [riːə'pıərəns] *n* reaparición *f*

reapply [riːə'plaı] **1** *vt (cream, lotion)* reaplicar

2 *vi (for job)* volver a presentar solicitud, volver a presentarse; **previous applicants need not r.** no se aceptarán solicitudes de candidatos rechazados anteriormente

reappoint [riːə'pɔınt] *vt* volver a nombrar

reappointment [riːə'pɔıntmənt] *n* **since her r. as minister for the arts** desde su nuevo nombramiento como ministra de arte y cultura

reappraisal [riːə'preızəl] *n* revaluación *f*

reappraise [riːə'preız] *vt* reconsiderar

rear[1] [rıə(r)] **1** *n* **(a)** *(back part)* parte *f* trasera; **at the r. of** *(inside)* al fondo de; *(behind)* detrás de; **in the r.** detrás, en la parte de atrás; **they attacked them from the r.** los atacaron por detrás **(b)** *(of military column)* retaguardia *f*; **to bring up the r.** *(in military column)* cerrar la marcha; *(in race)* ser el farolillo rojo **(c)** *Fam (buttocks)* trasero *m*

2 *adj* trasero(a) ►► ***r. admiral*** contralmirante *m*; ***r. entrance*** puerta *f* trasera; ***r. gunner*** artillero *m* trasero; *US* ***r. lamps*** *(of car)* luces *fpl* traseras; ***r. legs*** *(of animal)* patas *fpl* traseras; ***r. lights*** *(of car)* luces *fpl* traseras; ***r. window*** *(of car)* luneta *f*, ventana *f* trasera

rear[2] *vt* (**a**) *(child, livestock)* criar (**b**) *(one's head)* levantar; **fascism has reared its ugly head** ha vuelto a asomar el fantasma del fascismo

▶ **rear up** *vi* (**a**) *(horse)* encabritarse (**b**) *(mountain, skyscraper)* alzarse

rear-end ['rɪərend] **1** *n Fam* trasero *m*
2 *vt esp US (drive into back of)* chocar contra la parte trasera de

rear-engined [rɪər'endʒɪnd] *adj* con propulsión trasera

rearguard ['rɪəgɑːd] *n Mil* retaguardia *f*; IDIOM **to fight a r. action** emprender un último intento a la desesperada

rearm [riː'ɑːm] **1** *vt* rearmar
2 *vi* rearmarse

rearmament [riː'ɑːməmənt] *n* rearme *m*

rearmost ['rɪəməʊst] *adj* último(a)

rearrange [riːə'reɪndʒ] *vt* (**a**) *(arrange differently) (books, furniture)* reordenar; *(apartment, room)* redistribuir; **the layout of the house had been totally rearranged** habían cambiado totalmente la distribución de la casa
(**b**) *(put back in place)* volver a colocar; **she rearranged her hair** se arregló el pelo
(**c**) *(reschedule) (date, time)* cambiar; **we'll have to r. our schedule** tendremos que reorganizar el programa

rearrangement [riːə'reɪndʒmənt] *n (of date, time)* cambio *m*

rear-view mirror ['rɪəvjuː'mɪrə(r)] *n* (espejo *m*) retrovisor *m*

rearward ['rɪəwəd] **1** *adj (part, end)* posterior, de atrás; *(motion)* hacia atrás
2 *adv* hacia atrás

rearwards ['rɪəwədz] *adv* hacia atrás

rear-wheel drive ['rɪəwiːl'draɪv] *n* tracción *f* trasera

REASON ['riːzən] **1** *n* (**a**) *(cause, motive)* razón *f*, motivo *m* (**for** de); **that's no r. for giving up!** ¡eso no es motivo para darse por vencido!; **she gave no r. for her absence** no explicó su ausencia; **what is the r. for his absence?** ¿cuál es el motivo de que no haya acudido?; **she's my r. for living** es mi razón de ser; **I (can) see no r. for disagreeing** *or* **to disagree** no veo ningún motivo para discrepar; **the r. (that) I'm telling you** la razón por la que te lo cuento; **the r. why they lost** la razón por la que perdieron; **I don't know the r. why** no sé por qué; **I did it for a r.** lo hice por algo; **for reasons of health** por razones de salud; **for reasons of state** por razones de Estado; *Ironic* **for reasons best known to himself** por razones que a mí se me escapan; **for no good r.** sin ninguna razón; **for no particular r.** sin *or* por ningún motivo en especial; **for one r. or another** por un motivo u otro; **but that's the only r. I came!** ésa es la única razón por la que he venido; **give me one good r. why I should!** ¿y por qué razón debería hacerlo?; **I have/there is r. to believe that...** tengo/existen motivos para pensar que...; **I have (good** *or* **every) r. to trust him** tengo (buenos) motivos para confiar en él; **we've no r. not to believe her** no tenemos motivos para no creerle; **why did you do it? – I have my reasons** ¿por qué lo hiciste? – tengo mis razones; **all the more r. to tell him now** razón de más para decírselo ahora; *Formal* **by r. of** en virtud de; *Fam* **why did you say that? – no r.** ¿por qué dijiste eso? – por decir; **with (good) r.** con razón
(**b**) *(sanity, common sense)* razón *f*; **to listen to r., to see r.** atender a razones, *Am* atender razones; **to lose one's r.** perder la razón; **it stands to r.** es lógico *or* evidente; **within r.** dentro de lo razonable
(**c**) *(rationality)* razón *f*; **man has the power of r.** el hombre tiene el don de la razón
2 *vt* **to r. that...** *(argue)* argumentar que...; *(deduce)* deducir que...
3 *vi* razonar (**about** sobre); **to r. with sb** razonar con alguien; **there's no reasoning with her** es imposible razonar con ella; IDIOM **ours is not to r. why** nosotros ni pinchamos ni cortamos

▶ **reason out** *vt sep (puzzle, problem)* resolver; **let's try to r. out why...** intentemos encontrar una explicación de por qué...

reasonable ['riːzənəbəl] *adj* (**a**) *(fair, sensible)* razonable; **be r.!** ¡sé razonable!; **they were r. in their demands** sus reivindicaciones fueron razonables; **a r. doubt** una duda razonable
(**b**) *(moderate)* razonable; **he has a r. chance (of doing it)** tiene bastantes posibilidades (de hacerlo)
(**c**) *(inexpensive)* razonable; **that restaurant is very r.** ese restaurante está muy bien de precio
(**d**) *(acceptable)* aceptable, razonable; **we've had quite a r. day** hemos tenido un día bastante aceptable; **the weather/meal was r.** el tiempo/la comida fue aceptable

reasonableness ['riːzənəbəlnɪs] *n* (**a**) *(of person, behaviour)* sensatez *f* (**b**) *(of price)* moderación *f*

reasonably ['riːzənəblɪ] *adv* (**a**) *(to behave, act)* razonablemente; **r. priced at $100** al razonable precio de 100 dólares; **you can't r. expect them to believe that** no es razonable esperar que se vayan a creer eso (**b**) *(quite, fairly)* bastante, razonablemente; **the quality is r. good** es de una calidad razonable

reasoned ['riːzənd] *adj (argument, discussion)* razonado(a)

reasoning ['riːzənɪŋ] *n (thinking)* razonamiento *m*; **the r. behind the decision** las razones de la decisión

reassemble [riːə'sembəl] **1** *vt* (**a**) *(people)* reagrupar (**b**) *(machine)* volver a montar *or* ensamblar
2 *vi (people)* reagruparse; **Parliament will r. in September** el Parlamento se volverá a reunir en septiembre

reassembly ['riːə'semblɪ] *n* (**a**) *(of group)* reagrupamiento *m* (**b**) *(of machine)* reensamblaje *m*

reassert ['riːə'sɜːt] *vt (authority)* reafirmar, volver a imponer; **her distrust of men reasserted itself** se reafirmó su desconfianza de los hombres

reassess [riːə'ses] *vt* (**a**) *(policy, situation)* replantearse (**b**) *Fin (property)* volver a tasar

reassessment ['riːə'sesmənt] *n* (**a**) *(of policy, situation)* replanteamiento *m* (**b**) *Fin (of property)* nueva tasación *f*, retasación *f*

reassign [riːə'saɪn] *vt (employee)* destinar (**to** a); *(work, project)* reasignar (**to** a)

reassume [riːə'sjuːm] *vt (one's duties)* reasumir

reassurance [riːə'ʃʊərəns] *n* (**a**) *(comfort)* tranquilidad *f*; **he found r. in her determination to succeed** le tranquilizó el que estuviera tan dispuesta a triunfar (**b**) *(guarantee)* garantía *f*; **the government has given us reassurances that...** el gobierno nos ha dado garantías de que...; **my reassurances failed to allay their fears** mis intentos de calmar sus temores no surtieron efecto

reassure [riːə'ʃʊə(r)] *vt* (**a**) *(put at ease)* confortar, tranquilizar; **to feel reassured** sentirse más tranquilo(a); **he reassured them that he would be there** les aseguró que estaría allí (**b**) *Fin* reasegurar

reassuring [riːə'ʃʊərɪŋ] *adj* tranquilizador(ora), confortante; **it's r. to know he's with them** tranquiliza *or* conforta saber que está con ellos

reassuringly [riːə'ʃʊərɪŋlɪ] *adv* de modo tranquilizador; **a r. solid keyboard** un teclado bien sólido; **the procedure is r. simple** el procedimiento es de una sencillez tranquilizadora

reawake [riːə'weɪk] *vi* volver a despertarse

reawaken [riːə'weɪkən] **1** *vt (sleeper, interest, curiosity)* volver a despertar
2 *vi (person)* volver a despertarse

reawakening [riːə'weɪkənɪŋ] *n (of sleeper)* nuevo despertar *m*; *(of interest, curiosity)* renacimiento *m*; **the r. of national pride** el rebrote del orgullo nacionalista

rebarbative [rɪ'bɑːbətɪv] *adj Formal* execrable

rebate[1] ['riːbeɪt] *n* (**a**) *(refund)* devolución *f*, reembolso *m* (**b**) *(discount)* bonificación *f*

rebate[2] *n (groove, step)* rebaje *m*

rebel 1 *n* ['rebəl] rebelde *mf*; **r. MPs helped defeat the government's bill** parlamentarios rebeldes ayudaron a que no prosperara el proyecto de ley del gobierno ▸▸ ***r. leader*** cabecilla *mf* rebelde *or* de la rebelión
2 *vi* [rɪ'bel] (*pt & pp* **rebelled**) rebelarse (**against** contra); *Hum* **my stomach rebels at the very thought** se me revuelve el estómago solo de pensarlo

rebellion [rɪ'beljən] *n* rebelión *f*; **to rise (up) in r. against sth/sb** alzarse en rebelión contra algo/alguien; **in open r.** en abierta rebelión

rebellious [rɪ'beljəs] *adj* (**a**) *(in revolt) (troops, populace)* rebelde; **a r. act** un acto de rebeldía (**b**) *(difficult to control) (behaviour, child)* rebelde

rebelliousness [rɪ'beljəsnɪs] *n* (**a**) *(of troops, populace)* rebeldía *f* (**b**) *(of behaviour, child)* rebeldía *f*

rebirth ['riː'bɜːθ] *n (renewal)* resurgimiento *m*

reboot [riː'buːt] *Comptr* **1** *vt* reinicializar
2 *vi* reinicializar(se)

rebore ['riːbɔː(r)] **1** *vt* rectificar
2 *n* rectificado *m*

reborn [riː'bɔːn] *adj* **to be r.** renacer; **I feel r.** me siento como si hubiera vuelto a nacer

rebound 1 *n* ['riːbaʊnd] (**a**) *(of ball)* rebote *m*; **to catch a ball on the r.** atrapar un balón en el rebote; **defensive/offensive r.** *(in basketball)* rebote defensivo/ofensivo
(**b**) IDIOMS **to be on the r.** *(after relationship)* estar recuperándose de una decepción amorosa; *(after setback)* estar recuperándose de un

traspiés; **she married him on the r.** se casó con él cuando todavía estaba recuperándose de una decepción amorosa

2 *vi* [rɪ'baʊnd] (**a**) *(ball)* rebotar; **the ball rebounded against the wall/into the road** el balón rebotó contra la pared/en la carretera (**b**) *Fig* **to r. on sb** *(joke, lie)* volverse en contra de alguien (**c**) *(recover)* recuperarse

rebuff [rɪ'bʌf] **1** *n (slight)* desaire *m*, desplante *m*; *(rejection)* rechazo *m*; **to meet with** *or* **suffer a r.** *(person, suggestion)* ser rechazado(a)

2 *vt (slight)* desairar; *(reject)* rechazar

rebuild [riː'bɪld] (*pt & pp* **rebuilt** [riː'bɪlt]) **1** *vt* (**a**) *(building, town, economy)* reconstruir (**b**) *(company, relationship, life)* reconstruir; **we must r. confidence in industry** debemos restaurar la confianza en la industria

2 *vi* reedificar, reconstruir

rebuilding [riː'bɪldɪŋ] *n (of building, town, economy)* reconstrucción *f*

rebuke [rɪ'bjuːk] **1** *n* reprensión *f*, reprimenda *f*

2 *vt* reprender (**for** por); **to r. sb for doing/having done sth** reprender a alguien por hacer/haber hecho algo

rebus ['riːbəs] *n* jeroglífico *m*

rebut [rɪ'bʌt] (*pt & pp* **rebutted**) *vt* refutar

rebuttal [rɪ'bʌtəl] *n* refutación *f*

rec [rek] *n Fam* (**a**) *Br* **r. (ground)** recinto *m* deportivo (**b**) *US Sch (break)* recreo *m*; **r. room** *(in home)* sala de juegos

recalcitrance [rɪ'kælsɪtrəns] *n* carácter *m* recalcitrante

recalcitrant [rɪ'kælsɪtrənt] *adj* recalcitrante

recall **1** *n* ['riːkɔːl] (**a**) *(memory)* memoria *f*; **lost beyond r.** perdido(a) irremisiblemente; **total/instant r.** memoria prodigiosa/instantánea

(**b**) *(of goods)* retirada *f* del mercado; *(of library book)* reclamación *f*; *(of ambassador, troops)* retirada *f* ▸▸ ***r. slip*** *(from library)* solicitud *f* de reclamación

(**c**) *Br Pol (of parliament)* convocatoria *f* extraordinaria (fuera del periodo de sesiones)

(**d**) *US Pol (of official)* = retirada de un cargo político o judicial por votación tras una petición popular

(**e**) ***r. button*** *(on telephone)* botón *m* de rellamada

2 *vt* [rɪ'kɔːl] (**a**) *(remember)* recordar; **to r. doing sth** recordar haber hecho algo; **as far as I can r.** que yo recuerde; **as you may r.** como recordarás

(**b**) *(evoke)* evocar, hacer recordar

(**c**) *(summon back) (defective goods)* retirar del mercado; *(library book)* reclamar; *(ambassador, troops)* retirar; **the sound of the telephone recalled her to the present** el sonido del teléfono la trajo de vuelta al presente

(**d**) *Br Pol* **to r. Parliament** convocar un pleno extraordinario del Parlamento (fuera del periodo de sesiones)

(**e**) *Sport (player)* volver a llamar

recant [rɪ'kænt] **1** *vt (opinion)* retractarse de

2 *vi* (**a**) *(change opinion)* retractarse (**b**) *Rel* abjurar

recantation [riːkæn'teɪʃən] *n* (**a**) *(of opinion, statement)* retractación *f* (**b**) *(of religion)* abjuración *f*

recap ['riːkæp] **1** *n* (**a**) *(summary)* recapitulación *f*, resumen *m* (**b**) *US, Austr (tyre)* neumático *m* recauchutado, *Col, Méx* llanta *f or Arg* goma *f* recauchutada

2 *vt* (*pt & pp* **recapped**) (**a**) *(summarize)* recapitular, resumir (**b**) *US, Austr (tyre)* recauchutar

3 *vi* recapitular, resumir; **to r.,...** para recapitular *or* resumir,...

recapitulate [riːkə'pɪtjʊleɪt] **1** *vt* (**a**) *Formal (summarize)* recapitular (**b**) *Mus (theme)* repetir (**c**) *Biol* recapitular

2 *vi Formal* recapitular; **so, to r.,...** de modo que, para recapitular,...

recapitulation [riːkəpɪtjʊ'leɪʃən] *n* (**a**) *Formal (summary)* recapitulación *f* (**b**) *Mus (of theme)* repetición *f* (**c**) *Biol* recapitulación *f*

recapture [riː'kæptʃə(r)] **1** *n (of escapee)* nueva captura *f*; *(of animal)* nueva captura *f*; *(of town, territory)* nueva toma *f*; **he escaped r. for nearly a year** no lo volvieron a capturar hasta pasado casi un año

2 *vt* (**a**) *(escapee)* volver a capturar *or* apresar; *(animal)* volver a capturar; *(town, territory)* volver a tomar (**b**) *(memory, atmosphere)* recuperar; *(one's youth)* revivir

recast ['riː'kɑːst] (*pt & pp* **recast**) *vt* (**a**) *(redraft)* readaptar, reescribir (**b**) *(play, movie)* cambiar el reparto de; *(actor)* dar un nuevo papel a; **he was r. in the role of Prospero** le dieron un nuevo papel, el de Próspero (**c**) *(statue, bell)* refundir

recce ['rekɪ] *Br Fam Mil* **1** *n* reconocimiento *m*; **to go on a r.** hacer un reconocimiento

2 *vt* (*pt & pp* **recced** *or* **recceed**) hacer un reconocimiento de

recede [rɪ'siːd] *vi* (**a**) *(move away) (tide, coastline)* retroceder; **to r. into the past** perderse en el pasado (**b**) *(fade) (hopes, fears, danger)* desvanecerse; **as memories of the past r.** a medida que se desvanecen los recuerdos del pasado (**c**) *(hairline)* **his hair has started to r.** le están empezando a salir entradas

receding [rɪ'siːdɪŋ] *adj* **to have a r. chin** tener la barbilla hundida; **to have a r. hairline** tener entradas

receipt [rɪ'siːt] **1** *n* (**a**) *(act of receiving)* recibo *m*; **to acknowledge r. of sth** acusar recibo de algo; *Formal* **I am in r. of the goods** se me ha hecho entrega de la mercancía, la mercancía obra en mi poder; **on r. of** a la recepción de (**b**) *(proof of payment) (for service)* recibo *m*; *(for purchase)* ticket *m or* tiquet *m* (de compra), justificante *m* de compra (**c**) **receipts** *(at box office)* recaudación *f*

2 *vt* (**a**) *(mark as paid)* indicar como pagado(a) (**b**) *US (give a receipt for)* entregar un recibo por

receivable [rɪ'siːvəbəl] *Com* **1** *adj* a *or* por cobrar

2 **receivables** *npl (accounts due)* cuentas *fpl* pendientes de cobro, cuentas *fpl* por cobrar

receive [rɪ'siːv] **1** *vt* (**a**) *(be given, get) (gift, letter, blow)* recibir; *(salary, damages)* cobrar; *(insults, injuries)* sufrir; **we received your letter on Monday** recibimos tu carta el lunes; **he received (a sentence of) five years** le condenaron a cinco años; **he received a fine** le pusieron una multa; **I never received payment** no me pagaron; **to r. treatment** *(for injuries, disease)* recibir tratamiento; **he received dreadful treatment** lo trataron de forma inhumana; **received with thanks** *(on receipt)* recibí conforme

(**b**) *(radio or television signal)* recibir; **do you r. me?** ¿me recibes?; **I'm receiving you loud and clear** te recibo alto y claro

(**c**) *(greet, welcome)* recibir; **it was well/badly received** *(movie, proposal)* fue bien/mal acogido(a), tuvo un buen/mal recibimiento; **how was the news received?** ¿cómo cayó la noticia?; **to r. sb into the Church** recibir a alguien en el seno de la Iglesia

(**d**) *Law* **to r. stolen goods** receptar bienes robados

(**e**) *Formal (accommodate)* recibir; **holes were drilled to r. the pegs** se taladraron agujeros para recibir las alcayatas

2 *vi* (**a**) PROV **it is better to give than to r.** más vale dar que recibir (**b**) *(in tennis)* restar (**c**) *Formal Old-fashioned (have guests)* recibir (**d**) *Law* receptar bienes robados

received [rɪ'siːvd] *adj (idea, opinion)* común, aceptado(a) ▸▸ ***R. Pronunciation*** pronunciación *f* estándar *(del inglés)*; ***the r. wisdom*** la creencia popular

receiver [rɪ'siːvə(r)] *n* (**a**) *(of stolen goods)* perista *mf*; *Law* receptador(ora) *m,f* (**b**) *(of telephone)* auricular *m*, *RP, Ven* tubo *m*; **to pick up** *or* **lift the r.** descolgar el teléfono; **to replace the r.** colgar el teléfono (**c**) *(radio set)* receptor *m* (**d**) *Fin* **to call in the receivers** ser intervenido(a) (**e**) *(in tennis)* jugador(ora) *m,f* al resto; *(in American football)* receptor *m*, receiver *m*

receiver-general [rɪ'siːvə'dʒenərəl] (*pl* **receivers-general**) *n US, Can* recaudador(ora) *m,f* general

receivership [rɪ'siːvəʃɪp] *n Fin* **to go into r.** ser intervenido(a)

receiving [rɪ'siːvɪŋ] **1** *n (of stolen goods)* receptación *f*

2 *adj* IDIOM *Fam* **to be on the r. end of sth** ser el blanco de algo; **if it was you on the receiving end of her sarcasm** si tuvieras tú que aguantar su sarcasmo

recent ['riːsənt] *adj* reciente; **in r. months** en los últimos meses; **in r. times** en los últimos tiempos; **her most r. novel** su última *or* su más reciente novela

recently ['riːsəntlɪ] *adv* recientemente, hace poco; **as r. as yesterday** ayer sin ir más lejos; **this was still happening as r. as the 1950s** esto todavía ocurría en los años 50, sin ir más lejos; **until quite r.** hasta hace muy poco; **not r.** últimamente no

recentness ['riːsəntnɪs] *n* carácter *m* reciente

receptacle [rɪ'septəkəl] *n Formal* (**a**) *(container)* receptáculo *m* (**b**) *Bot* receptáculo *m*

reception [rɪ'sepʃən] *n* (**a**) *(welcome) (of guests, new members)* recibimiento *m*; *(of announcement, new movie)* recibimiento *m*, acogida *f*; **to get a warm r.** ser acogido(a) calurosamente; **to get a cool** *or* **frosty r.** ser acogido(a) con frialdad ▸▸ *Br* ***r. centre*** centro *m* de acogida; *Br* ***r. class*** primer curso *m* de primaria; ***r. committee*** comité *m* de bienvenida; *Med* ***r. order*** *(in mental hospital)* = orden de ingresar a un paciente en un hospital psiquiátrico; *Br* ***r. room*** *(in house)* sala *f* de estar, salón *m*

(**b**) *(party)* recepción *f*; **to hold a r.** ofrecer una recepción; **(wedding) r.** banquete *m* de boda *or Andes* matrimonio *or RP* casamiento ▸▸ ***r. room*** *(in hotel)* sala *f* de recepciones

(**c**) *(in hotel)* **r. (desk)** recepción *f*; **at r.** en recepción ▸▸ *US* ***r. clerk***

recepcionista *mf*
(**d**) *(of radio, TV programme)* recepción *f*
(**e**) *US Sport (of ball)* recepción *f*

receptionist [rɪ'sepʃənɪst] *n* recepcionista *mf*

receptive [rɪ'septɪv] *adj* receptivo(a); **he's not very r. to suggestions** no es muy abierto a las sugerencias

receptiveness [rɪ'septɪvnɪs], **receptivity** [ri:sep'tɪvɪtɪ] *n* receptividad *f*

receptor [rɪ'septə(r)] *n Physiol* receptor *m*

recess ['ri:ses] **1** *n* (**a**) *(in wall) (gen)* hueco *m (for statue)* nicho *m*, hornacina *f*; *(in bedroom)* alcoba *f*
(**b**) *(of mind, past, memory)* recoveco *m*; **in the innermost recesses of the soul** en los recovecos más oscuros del alma
(**c**) *(of Parliament)* periodo *m* vacacional; **Parliament is in r.** las sesiones del Parlamento están suspendidas por vacaciones
(**d**) *(in trial)* descanso *m*, receso *m*; *US* **the court went into r.** el tribunal levantó la sesión
(**e**) *US Sch (between classes)* recreo *m*
2 *vt (lighting, switch)* empotrar
3 *vi US* (**a**) *(legislature)* suspender las sesiones, entrar en receso (**b**) *(court)* levantar la sesión; **the court recessed until Friday** el juicio se suspendió hasta el viernes

recessed ['ri:sest] *adj (door, window, bookshelves, lighting)* empotrado(a)

recession [rɪ'seʃən] *n Econ* recesión *f*; **the economy is in r.** la economía está en recesión

recessional [rɪ'seʃənəl] **1** *n (hymn)* = himno que se canta al retirarse el celebrante
2 *adj Econ* recesivo(a)

recessionary [rɪ'seʃənərɪ] *adj Econ* recesivo(a)

recessive [rɪ'sesɪv] *adj Biol (gene)* recesivo(a)

recharge [ri:'tʃɑ:dʒ] **1** *vt (battery)* recargar; *Fig* **to r. one's batteries** recargar las baterías
2 *vi (battery)* recargarse

rechargeable [ri:'tʃɑ:dʒəbəl] *adj* recargable

recherché [rə'ʃeəʃeɪ] *adj Formal* rebuscado(a)

rechip [ri:'tʃɪp] *vt (mobile phone)* cambiar el chip de

recidivism [rɪ'sɪdɪvɪzəm] *n Law* reincidencia *f*

recidivist [rɪ'sɪdɪvɪst] *Law* **1** *n* reincidente *mf*
2 *adj* reincidente

recipe ['resɪpɪ] *n also Fig* receta *f*; **a r. for paella, a paella r.** una receta para preparar *or* cocinar paella; **a r. for disaster/success** la receta para el desastre/el éxito; **his r. for long life is...** su secreto para vivir muchos años es... ►► ***r. book*** recetario *m* (de cocina); ***r. card*** ficha *f* de cocina

recipient [rɪ'sɪpɪənt] *n* (**a**) *(of gift, letter)* destinatario(a) *m,f*; *(of award, honour)* receptor(ora) *m,f*; **he was the proud r. of a gold watch** tuvo el orgullo de recibir un reloj de oro (**b**) *Med (of transplant)* receptor(ora) *m,f*

> **False friend:** The Spanish noun **recipiente** is not a translation for the English word **recipient**. In Spanish **recipiente** means "container".

reciprocal [rɪ'sɪprəkəl] **1** *n Math* recíproca *f*
2 *adj* recíproco(a); **the feeling was not r.** el sentimiento no era mutuo

reciprocate [rɪ'sɪprəkeɪt] **1** *vt (favour, invitation)* corresponder a; *(attack)* responder a; **to r. sb's kindness** corresponder a la amabilidad de alguien; **his feelings for her were not reciprocated** sus sentimientos por ella no eran correspondidos
2 *vi (return an invitation)* devolver la invitación; *(return a blow)* devolver el golpe; *(return a compliment)* devolver el cumplido; *(return an insult)* devolver el insulto; **to r. with sth** corresponder con algo

reciprocating [rɪ'sɪprəkeɪtɪŋ] *adj Tech* ***r. engine*** motor *m* alternativo

reciprocation [rɪsɪprə'keɪʃən] *n* **in r. for** como respuesta a

reciprocity [resɪ'prɒsɪtɪ] *n Formal* reciprocidad *f*

recital [rɪ'saɪtəl] *n* (**a**) *(of poetry, music)* recital *m*; **to give a r.** dar *or* ofrecer un recital (**b**) *(of facts)* perorata *f*

recitation [resɪ'teɪʃən] *n (of poem)* recitación *f*

recitative [resɪtə'ti:v] *n Mus* recitativo *m*

recite [rɪ'saɪt] **1** *vt* (**a**) *(poem)* recitar (**b**) *(complaints, details)* enumerar
2 *vi* recitar

reckless ['reklɪs] *adj (decision, behaviour, person)* imprudente; *(driving)* temerario(a); **it would be r. to ignore the danger** sería imprudente no hacer caso del peligro ►► ***r. driver*** conductor(ora) *m,f* temerario(a)

recklessly ['reklɪslɪ] *adv (to decide, behave)* imprudentemente; *(to drive)* de modo temerario; **to spend r.** gastar de forma imprudente

recklessness ['reklɪsnɪs] *n (of decision, behaviour)* imprudencia *f*; *(of driving)* temeridad *f*

reckon ['rekən] **1** *vt* (**a**) *(consider)* considerar; **he is reckoned to be...** está considerado como...; *Fam* **I don't r. her chances much** no le doy muchas posibilidades
(**b**) *(calculate)* calcular; **I r. it will take two hours** calculo que llevará dos horas; **they had reckoned to make more profit from the venture** habían contado con sacar un mayor beneficio del negocio
(**c**) *Fam (think)* **to r. (that)** creer que; **I r. this omelette is ready** creo que esta tortilla ya está lista; **it's all over now, I r.** creo que todo ha terminado; **what do you r.?** ¿qué opinas?, ¿qué te parece?
2 *vi* calcular; **reckoning from today** contando desde hoy

►**reckon in** *vt sep Br* incluir

►**reckon on** *vt insep* (**a**) *(rely on)* contar con; **don't r. on it** no cuentes con ello; **you can always r. on him making a mess of things** con él ya se sabe que lo puede liar todo (**b**) *(expect)* contar con; **you should r. on there being about thirty people there** cuenta con que haya unas treinta personas; **I hadn't reckoned on that extra cost** no había contado con ese gasto extra

►**reckon up 1** *vt sep (figures, cost)* calcular; **to r. up a bill** calcular el importe de una factura
2 *vi* **to r. up with sb** saldar cuentas con alguien

►**reckon with** *vt insep* contar con; **she's someone to be reckoned with** es una mujer de armas tomar; **we had to r. with some stiff opposition** tuvimos que vérnoslas con una fuerte oposición

►**reckon without** *vt insep* **to r. without sth/sb** no tener en cuenta algo/a alguien; **he had reckoned without his rivals** no había tenido en cuenta a sus rivales

reckoning ['rekənɪŋ] *n* (**a**) *(calculation)* cálculo *m*; **you're way out in your r.** te has equivocado totalmente en tus cálculos; **by my r.** según mis cálculos; IDIOM **to come into the r.** contar (**b**) *(estimation, opinion)* juicio *m*, opinión *f*; **by** *or* **on any r. she's a fine pianist** no se puede negar que es una pianista excelente (**c**) *(settling of debts, scores)* **day of r.** día del juicio final

reclaim [rɪ'kleɪm] *vt* (**a**) *(lost property, baggage)* recoger; **you'll be able to r. your expenses at the end of the conference** al terminar el congreso puedes pedir que te devuelvan los gastos
(**b**) *(waste materials)* recuperar; **to r. land from the sea** ganar terreno al mar
(**c**) *(sinner, drunkard)* enderezar
(**d**) *(rehabilitate) (term, word)* recuperar; **the word "queer" has been reclaimed by the gay community** la comunidad gay ha hecho suya la palabra "queer"

reclamation [reklə'meɪʃən] *n* (**a**) *(of lost property, baggage)* recogida *f*; **new legislation governing payment and r. of tax** nueva legislación que regula el pago y la devolución de impuestos (**b**) *(of waste materials)* recuperación *f*; **land r. project** proyecto para ganar terreno al mar (**c**) *(of sinner, drunkard)* enderezamiento *m* (**d**) *(of term, word)* recuperación *f*

reclassify [ri:'klæsɪfaɪ] *vt* reclasificar

recline [rɪ'klaɪn] **1** *vt* (**a**) *(head)* apoyar (**b**) *(seat)* reclinar
2 *vi* reclinarse; **he was reclining on the sofa** estaba reclinado en el sofá

recliner [rɪ'klaɪnə(r)] *n (chair)* silla *f* reclinable; *(armchair)* sillón *m* reclinable

reclining [rɪ'klaɪnɪŋ] *adj* **in a r. position** reclinado(a) ►► ***r. seat*** asiento *m* reclinable

recluse [rɪ'klu:s] *n* solitario(a) *m,f*; **she's a bit of a r.** vive un poco recluida

> **False friend:** The Spanish noun **recluso** is not a translation for the English word **recluse**. In Spanish **recluso** means "prisoner".

reclusive [rɪ'klu:sɪv] *adj* solitario(a), retraído(a)

recognition [rekəg'nɪʃən] *n* (**a**) *(identification)* reconocimiento *m*; **she disguised her voice to avoid r.** cambió la voz para que no la reconocieran; **to have changed beyond** *or* **out of all r.** estar irreconocible
(**b**) *(acknowledgement, appreciation)* reconocimiento *m*; **his play received little r.** su obra pasó desapercibida; **he has achieved worldwide r.** ha conseguido el reconocimiento mundial; **there is**

growing r. of the problem hay una creciente concienciación sobre el problema; **in r. of** en reconocimiento a
(**c**) *(of state, organization, trade union)* reconocimiento *m*; **to withhold r. from a country** negarse a reconocer un país

recognizable [rekəg'naɪzəbəl] *adj* reconocible (**as** como); **barely r.** apenas reconocible; **his style was instantly r.** tenía un estilo reconocible fácilmente

recognizably [rekəg'naɪzəblɪ] *adv* claramente; **the place was not r. different** el lugar apenas había cambiado

recognizance [rɪ'kɒgnɪzəns] *n Law* **to be released on one's own recognizances** ser puesto(a) en libertad bajo palabra

recognize ['rekəgnaɪz] *vt* (**a**) *(identify)* reconocer (**b**) *(acknowledge, appreciate)* reconocer; **I r. (that) I may have been mistaken** reconozco que me he podido confundir; **the scale of the disaster has finally been recognized** por fin se reconoce la magnitud del desastre (**c**) *(state, organization, qualification)* reconocer (**d**) *US (in debate)* conceder la palabra a

recognized ['rekəgnaɪzd] *adj (government, state, method)* reconocido(a); *(qualification)* homologado(a); **to be a r. authority (on sth)** ser una autoridad reconocida (en algo)

recoil 1 *n* ['ri:kɔɪl] *(of gun)* retroceso *m*
2 *vi* [rɪ'kɔɪl] (**a**) *(gun)* retroceder (**b**) *(person)* retroceder; **to r. in terror/horror** retroceder aterrorizado(a)/horrorizado(a); **to r. from (doing) sth** retroceder ante la idea de (hacer) algo

recollect [rekə'lekt] **1** *vt* (**a**) *(remember)* recordar; **I don't r. having asked her** no recuerdo haberle preguntado a ella (**b**) *(recover)* **to r. oneself** recobrar la compostura
2 *vi* recordar; **as far as I can r.** que yo recuerde

recollection [rekə'lekʃən] *n* recuerdo *m*; **I have no r. of having said that** no recuerdo haber dicho eso; **to the best of my r.** en lo que alcanzo a recordar

> **False friend**: The Spanish noun **recolección** is not a translation for the English word **recollection**. In Spanish **recolección** means "harvest" or "collection".

recombinant [ri:'kɒmbɪnənt] *adj Biol* ***r. DNA*** ADN *m* preparado en laboratorio

recommence [ri:kə'mens] *Formal* **1** *vt* reanudar
2 *vi* volver a comenzar

recommend [rekə'mend] *vt* (**a**) *(speak in favour of, praise)* recomendar; **to r. sth to sb** recomendar algo a alguien; **she recommended him for the job** ella lo recomendó para el puesto; **the proposal has a lot to r. it** la propuesta presenta muchas ventajas; **recommended reading** lectura recomendada; **recommended** *(in review, listings)* recomendado(a)
(**b**) *(advise)* recomendar, aconsejar; **to r. sb to do sth** recomendar a alguien hacer algo; **it is not to be recommended** no es nada recomendable; *Com* **recommended (retail) price** precio de venta al público recomendado
(**c**) *Formal or Literary (entrust)* encomendar; **to r. one's soul to God** encomendar su alma a Dios

> En inglés culto o elevado, y especialmente en inglés americano, **recommend** puede ir seguido de **that** más un verbo en subjuntivo (ver panel SUBJUNCTIVE):
> **I wouldn't recommend that he see her again**
> *no le recomiendo que la vuelva a ver*
> Lo mismo también podría decirse del siguiente modo:
> **I wouldn't recommend that he should see her again**

recommendable [rekə'mendəbəl] *adj* recomendable

recommendation [rekəmen'deɪʃən] *n* recomendación *f*; **my r. is that...** mi recomendación es que...; **to make a r. that** recomendar que; **on my/her r.** por recomendación mía/suya

recommittal [ri:kə'mɪtəl] *n US Pol* devolución *f* al comité parlamentario

recompense ['rekəmpens] **1** *n* (**a**) *(reward)* recompensa *f*; **in r. for** como recompensa por (**b**) *(compensation)* compensación *f*, indemnización *f*
2 *vt* recompensar (**for** por)

recon ['ri:kɒn] *n US Mil* reconocimiento *m*

reconcilable [rekən'saɪləbəl] *adj (opinions, accounts)* conciliable; *(people)* reconciliable

reconcile ['rekənsaɪl] *vt* (**a**) *(people)* reconciliar; **to be reconciled with sb** reconciliarse con alguien; **Peter and Jane were reconciled at last** Peter y Jane por fin se reconciliaron
(**b**) *(resign)* **to be reconciled to sth** estar resignado(a) a algo; **she had reconciled herself to the idea of going** se había resignado a la idea de ir
(**c**) *(facts, differences, opinions)* conciliar; **you cannot r. morality with politics** no se puede conciliar la moral con la política
(**d**) *Acct (figures, accounts)* cuadrar

reconciliation [rekənsɪlɪ'eɪʃən] *n* (**a**) *(of people)* reconciliación *f*; **to bring about a r. between...** promover una reconciliación entre... (**b**) *(of differences, opinions)* conciliación *f* (**c**) *Acct (of figures, accounts)* conciliación *f*

recondite ['rekəndaɪt] *adj Formal (information, knowledge)* abstruso(a)

recondition ['ri:kən'dɪʃən] *vt (TV, washing machine)* reparar

reconditioned ['ri:kən'dɪʃənd] *adj (TV, washing machine)* reparado(a)

reconfigure ['ri:kən'fɪgə(r)] *vt Comptr* reconfigurar

reconnaissance [rɪ'kɒnɪsəns] *n Mil* reconocimiento *m*; **to be on r.** estar haciendo un reconocimiento ►► ***r. flight*** vuelo *m* de reconocimiento

reconnect ['ri:kə'nekt] *vt (water, electricity supply)* reconectar; **the operator reconnected us** *(during an interrupted telephone call)* el operador reestableció la conexión

reconnection [ri:kə'nekʃən] *n (of water, electricity supply)* reconexión *f* ►► *Tel* ***r. charge*** *(for disconnected telephone)* tarifa *f* de reconexión

reconnoitre, *US* **reconnoiter** [rekə'nɔɪtə(r)] *Mil* **1** *vt* reconocer
2 *vi* hacer un reconocimiento

reconquer ['ri:'kɒŋkə(r)] *vt* reconquistar

reconquest ['ri:'kɒŋkwest] *n* reconquista *f*

reconsider ['ri:kən'sɪdə(r)] **1** *vt* reconsiderar
2 *vi* recapacitar; **I advise you to r.** te aconsejo que recapacites

reconsideration ['ri:kənsɪdə'reɪʃən] *n* reconsideración *f*; **on r., the problem seemed simpler** tras reconsiderarlo, el problema parecía más sencillo

reconstitute ['ri:'kɒnstɪtju:t] *vt* (**a**) *(organization, committee)* reconstituir (**b**) *(dried food)* rehidratar

reconstruct ['ri:kən'strʌkt] *vt* (**a**) *(building, part of body, economy)* reconstruir; **to r. one's life** reconstruir su vida (**b**) *(events, crime)* reconstruir

reconstruction ['ri:kən'strʌkʃən] *n* (**a**) *(of building, part of body, economy)* reconstrucción *f* (**b**) *(of events, crime)* reconstrucción *f*

reconstructive ['ri:kən'strʌktɪv] *adj Med* ***r. surgery*** cirugía *f* reconstructiva

reconvene ['ri:kən'vi:n] **1** *vt* volver a convocar
2 *vi* volver a reunirse

record ['rekɔ:d] **1** *n* (**a**) *(account)* **there is no r. of their visit** no hay constancia de su visita; **do you have any r. of the transaction?** ¿tiene algún documento de la transacción?; **according to our records...** de acuerdo con nuestros datos...; **to keep a r. of sth** llevar nota de algo; *(more officially)* llevar un registro de algo; **to put sth on r.** dejar constancia (escrita) de algo; **we have it on r. that...** tenemos constancia de que...; **the coldest winter on r.** *or* **since records began** el invierno más frío del que se tiene constancia; **to be on r. as saying that...** haber declarado públicamente que...; **off the r.** *(to say)* confidencialmente; **I want these remarks to be off the r.** estos comentarios deben quedar en la confidencialidad; **(just) for the r.** para que conste; **for your records** para su información; **to put** *or* **set the r. straight** poner las cosas en claro *or* en su sitio ►► ***r. card*** ficha *f*; ***r. office*** (oficina *f* del) registro *m*
(**b**) *(personal history)* historial *m*; **they have a r. of breaking their promises** no es la primera vez que rompen una promesa; **she has an excellent attendance r.** su nivel de asistencia a clase es excelente; **service** *or* **army r.** hoja de servicios
(**c**) *(of criminal)* antecedentes *mpl* (penales); **to have a r.** tener antecedentes (penales)
(**d**) *(past results) (of team, athlete)* resultados *mpl*; **the government's r. on unemployment** la actuación del gobierno en la lucha contra el desempleo; **to have a good/bad safety r.** tener un buen/mal historial en materia de seguridad; **academic r.** expediente académico
(**e**) *(musical)* disco *m*; **to make** *or* **cut a r.** grabar un disco ►► ***r. company*** compañía *f* discográfica, casa *f* discográfica; ***r. deck*** plato *m*; ***r. label*** sello *m* discográfico; ***r. library*** *(personal, public)* discoteca *f*; ***r. player*** tocadiscos *m inv*; ***r. producer*** productor(ora) *m,f* discográfico(a); ***r. token*** vale *m* canjeable por discos
(**f**) *(best performance)* récord *m*; **the world/200 m r.** el récord mundial/de los 200 m.; **to set a r.** establecer un récord; **to hold the r.**

tener el récord; **to break** *or* **beat the r.** batir el récord ►► ***r. breaker*** *(man)* plusmarquista *m*, recordman *m*; *(woman)* plusmarquista *f*
(**g**) *Comptr (in database)* registro *m*
2 *adj (score, time)* récord *inv*; **a r. number of spectators** una cifra récord de espectadores; **today saw r. temperatures of...** las temperaturas han alcanzado hoy el nivel histórico de...; **to reach r. levels** alcanzar un nivel histórico *or* sin precedentes; **unemployment is at a r. high/low** el desempleo *orAm* la desocupación ha alcanzado un máximo/mínimo histórico
3 *vt* [rɪ'kɔːd] (**a**) *(on video, cassette)* grabar; **they're recording their new album** están grabando su nuevo álbum
(**b**) *(write down)* anotar; **your objection has been recorded** queda constancia de su protesta; **Napoleon's reply is not recorded** la respuesta de Napoleón no está documentada
(**c**) *(attest, give account of)* dar testimonio de; **history records that 30,000 soldiers took part** la historia da testimonio de la participación de 30.000 soldados; **a photograph was taken to r. the event** se hizo una fotografía para dejar constancia del acontecimiento
(**d**) *(register)* registrar; **temperatures of 50° were recorded** se registraron temperaturas de 50°
(**e**) *Sport (score, time)* obtener, hacer
4 *vi (machine)* grabar

record-breaking ['rekɔːd'breɪkɪŋ] *adj* récord; **to have r. sales** batir todos los récords de ventas

recorded [rɪ'kɔːdɪd] *adj* (**a**) *(message, tape, programme)* grabado(a) (**b**) *(documented)* documentado(a); **throughout r. history** a lo largo del periodo histórico del que se tienen documentos escritos ►► *Br* ***r. delivery*** correo *m* certificado

recorder [rɪ'kɔːdə(r)] *n* (**a**) *(machine)* (**tape**) **r.** grabadora *f*, magnetófono *m*; (**video**) **r.** (grabadora *f* de) vídeo *m orAm* video *m* (**b**) *(musical instrument)* flauta *f* (dulce), flauta *f* de pico

record-holder ['rekɔːd'həʊldə(r)] *n (man)* plusmarquista *m*, recordman *m*; *(woman)* plusmarquista *f*

recording [rɪ'kɔːdɪŋ] *n* (**a**) *(on tape, video)* grabación *f* ►► ***r. artist*** artista *mf* de grabación; *Comptr* ***r. head*** cabeza *f* magnética grabadora; ***r. studio*** estudio *m* de grabación (**b**) *Rel* ***the R. Angel*** = ángel que anota nuestras buenas y malas acciones

recork ['riː'kɔːk] *vt* volver a poner el corcho a

re-count 1 *n* ['riːkaʊnt] *(in election)* segundo recuento *m*; **to demand a r.** exigir un segundo recuento
2 *vt* ['riː'kaʊnt] *(count again)* volver a contar, volver a hacer un recuento de

recount [rɪ'kaʊnt] *vt (relate)* relatar

recoup [rɪ'kuːp] *vt (energies, investment, costs)* recuperar; *(losses)* resarcirse de

recourse [rɪ'kɔːs] *n* recurso *m*; **to have r. to** recurrir a; **without r. to** sin recurrir a

re-cover ['riː'kʌvə(r)] *vt (sofa, book)* recubrir

recover [rɪ'kʌvə(r)] 1 *vt* (**a**) *(reclaim) (property, loan, deposit)* recuperar
(**b**) *(get back) (strength, health, senses)* recobrar, recuperar; **to r. one's breath** recobrar *or* recuperar el aliento; **to r. one's calm** recobrar *or* recuperar la calma; **to r. consciousness** recobrar *or* recuperar el conocimiento; **to r. lost ground** recobrar *or* recuperar (el) terreno perdido
(**c**) *(retrieve)* rescatar, recuperar; **50 bodies have been recovered** se han rescatado 50 cadáveres
(**d**) *Law* **to r. damages** conseguir una indemnización
(**e**) *Comptr* recuperar
2 *vi* (**a**) *(from illness, setback)* recuperarse (**from** de) (**b**) *(economy, market, currency)* recuperarse

recoverable [rɪ'kʌvərəbəl] *adj* recuperable

recovery [rɪ'kʌvərɪ] *n* (**a**) *(of lost object)* recuperación *f*; **the r. of his sight changed his life** su vida cambió cuando recobró la vista
(**b**) *(from illness, setback)* recuperación *f*; **to make a r.** recuperarse; **to be on the way** *or* **road to r.** estar en vías *or* camino de recuperación; **he is past** *or* **beyond (hope of) r.** *(patient)* no tiene (posibilidades de) recuperación ►► ***r. position*** posición *f* de recuperación; ***r. room*** sala *f* de recuperación
(**c**) *(of economy, market, currency)* recuperación *f*
(**d**) *(retrieval)* rescate *m*, recuperación *f* ►► *Br* ***r. vehicle*** (vehículo *m*) grúa *f*
(**e**) *Law (of damages)* (obtención *f* de) indemnización *f*
(**f**) *Comptr* recuperación *f*

re-create ['riːkrɪ'eɪt] *vt* recrear

re-creation ['riːkrɪ'eɪʃən] *n (of event, scene)* recreación *f*

recreation [rekrɪ'eɪʃən] *n* (**a**) *(leisure)* ocio *m*, esparcimiento *m*; **to do sth for r.** hacer algo como pasatiempo ►► ***r. centre*** polideportivo *m*; *Br* ***r. ground*** recinto *m* deportivo; ***r. room*** *(in school, hospital)* sala *f* de recreo; *(in hotel)* sala *f* de juegos; *US (at home)* sala *f* de juegos (**b**) *Sch (break)* recreo *m*

recreational [rekrɪ'eɪʃənəl] *adj (activities, facilities)* recreativo(a) ►► ***r. drug*** = droga de consumo esporádico y por diversión; *US, Can* ***r. vehicle*** autocaravana *f*, casa *f* caravana

recriminate [rɪ'krɪmɪneɪt] *vi Formal* **to r. against sb** recriminar a alguien

recrimination [rɪkrɪmɪ'neɪʃən] *n* recriminación *f*, reproche *m*

recriminatory [rɪ'krɪmɪnətərɪ] *adj* recriminatorio(a)

recrudescence ['riːkruː'desəns] *n Formal* recrudecimiento *m*

recruit [rɪ'kruːt] 1 *n* (**a**) *(soldier)* recluta *mf* (**b**) *(new employee)* nuevo(a) empleado(a) *m,f*; *(new member)* nuevo miembro *m*; **our latest/newest r. will be starting work on Monday** el nuevo empleado empieza a trabajar el lunes
2 *vt* (**a**) *(soldier)* reclutar (**into** para) (**b**) *(employee)* contratar; *(member)* enrolar, reclutar

recruiting [rɪ'kruːtɪŋ] *n* reclutamiento *m* ►► ***r. officer*** oficial *mf* encargado(a) del reclutamiento; ***r. sergeant*** sargento *mf* encargado del reclutamiento

recruitment [rɪ'kruːtmənt] *n* (**a**) *(of soldier)* reclutamiento *m* ►► ***r. campaign*** campaña *f* de reclutamiento (**b**) *(of employee)* contratación *f*; *(of new member)* enrolamiento *m*, reclutamiento *m* ►► ***r. agency*** agencia *f* de contratación; ***r. campaign, r. drive*** *(of organization, party)* campaña *f* de reclutamiento

rectal ['rektəl] *adj Med* rectal; **r. examination** examen rectal

rectangle ['rektæŋgəl] *n* rectángulo *m*

rectangular [rek'tæŋgjʊlə(r)] *adj* rectangular

rectifiable [rektɪ'faɪəbəl] *adj* rectificable

rectification [rektɪfɪ'keɪʃən] *n* rectificación *f*; **to publish a r.** publicar una rectificación

rectify ['rektɪfaɪ] *vt* rectificar

rectilinear [rektɪ'lɪnɪə(r)], **rectilineal** [rektɪ'lɪnɪəl] *adj* rectilíneo(a)

rectitude ['rektɪtjuːd] *n Formal* rectitud *f*, integridad *f*

recto ['rektəʊ] *n Typ* recto *m*

rector ['rektə(r)] *n* (**a**) *Rel (protestant, catholic)* rector(ora) *m,f* (**b**) *Scot Univ* representante *mf* de los estudiantes *(que no es un alumno, sino una figura pública)* (**c**) *Scot (headmaster)* director(ora) *m,f*

rectory ['rektərɪ] *n Rel* rectoría *f*

rectum ['rektəm] *n Anat* recto *m*

recumbent [rɪ'kʌmbənt] *adj Formal (pose, figure)* recostado(a); *(statue)* yacente

recuperate [rɪ'kuːpəreɪt] 1 *vt (one's strength, money)* recuperar
2 *vi (person)* recuperarse (**from** de)

recuperation [rɪkuːpə'reɪʃən] *n* (**a**) *(from illness)* recuperación *f* (**b**) *(of materials, money)* recuperación *f*

recuperative [rɪ'kuːpərətɪv] *adj (rest)* reparador(ora); *(powers)* de recuperación

recur [rɪ'kɜː(r)] (*pt & pp* **recurred**) *vi* (**a**) *(occur again) (event, problem)* repetirse; *(illness)* reaparecer (**b**) *(reappear) (theme, image)* repetirse (**c**) *Math* repetirse hasta el infinito

> **False friend:** The Spanish verb **recurrir** is not a translation for the English word **recur**. In Spanish **recurrir** means "to appeal (against)", "to turn (to)" or "resort (to)".

recurrence [rɪ'kʌrəns] *n (of event, problem)* repetición *f*; *(of illness)* reaparición *f*; **there must be no r. of such behaviour** ese comportamiento no debe repetirse; **has there been any r. of the symptoms?** ¿han vuelto a aparecer los síntomas?

recurrent [rɪ'kʌrənt] *adj* recurrente; **it's a r. problem** es un problema recurrente

recurring [rɪ'kɜːrɪŋ] *adj* (**a**) *(problem)* recurrente; **a r. nightmare** una pesadilla recurrente (**b**) *Math* **six point six r.** seis coma seis periodo *or* periódico (puro)

recursion [rɪ'kɜːʃən] *n Math & Ling* recursión *f*

recursive [rɪ'kɜːsɪv] *adj Math & Ling* recursivo(a)

recusant ['rekjʊzənt] *Hist* 1 *n* inconverso(a) *m,f*
2 *adj* inconverso(a)

recyclable [riː'saɪkləbəl] *adj* reciclable

recycle [riːˈsaɪkəl] **1** *vt* reciclar; **recycled paper/glass** papel/vidrio reciclado ▸▸ *Comptr* ***r. bin*** papelera *f* de reciclaje
2 *vi* reciclar

recycling [riːˈsaɪklɪŋ] *n* reciclaje *m*, reciclado *m* ▸▸ ***r. plant*** planta *f* de reciclaje

red [red] **1** *n* **(a)** *(colour)* rojo *m*; **dressed in r.** vestido(a) de rojo; IDIOM *Fam* **to see r.** *(become angry)* ponerse hecho(a) una furia **(b)** *(wine)* tinto *m* **(c)** *Fam (communist)* rojo(a) *m,f*; IDIOM **to see reds under the bed** ver rojos por todas partes **(d)** *(deficit)* **to be in the r.** estar en números rojos; **to go into/get out of the r.** entrar en/salir de números rojos
2 *adj* **(a)** *(colour)* rojo(a); **to have r. hair** ser pelirrojo(a); **to turn** *or* **go r.** *(sky, leaves)* ponerse rojo; *(person)* ponerse colorado(a) *or* rojo(a); **wait till the lights turn r.** espera a que el semáforo se ponga en rojo; **r. with anger/shame** rojo(a) de ira/vergüenza; **to be r. in the face** *(after effort, anger)* estar rojo(a), tener la cara roja; *(with embarrassment)* estar colorado(a) *or* sonrojado(a); *(permanently)* ser sonrosado(a); **there will be some r. faces on the Opposition benches** a más de uno en los bancos de la oposición se le subirán los colores ▸▸ ***r. admiral*** *(butterfly)* vanesa *f* atalanta; ***r. alert*** alerta *f* roja; **to be on r. alert** estar en alerta roja; ***r. ant*** hormiga *f* roja; ***r. blood cell*** glóbulo *m* rojo; ***r. cabbage*** lombarda *f*; ***r. card*** tarjeta *f* roja; **to be shown the r. card** ser expulsado(a) del campo; *Physiol* ***r. corpuscle*** glóbulo *m* rojo, hematíe *m*; ***r. deer*** ciervo *m*; *US Fam* ***r. devil*** cápsula *f* de secobarbital; *Astron* ***r. dwarf*** enana *f* roja; ***r. flag*** *(danger signal)* bandera *f* roja; ***r. fox*** zorro *m* rojo; *Astron* ***r. giant*** estrella *f* gigante; ***r. grouse*** lagópodo *m* escocés; ***r. heat:*** **to bring sth to (a) r. heat** calentar algo hasta ponerlo al rojo vivo; *Fig* ***r. herring*** *(distraction)* señuelo *m (para desviar la atención)*; *(misleading clue)* pista *f* falsa; *Old-fashioned* ***R. Indian*** (indio(a) *m,f*) piel roja *mf*; ***r. kite*** *(bird)* milano *m* real; ***r. lead*** minio *m*; ***r. light*** *(road signal)* semáforo *m* (en) rojo; **to go through a r. light** saltarse un semáforo en rojo; ***r. light district*** barrio *m* chino; ***r. meat*** carne *f* roja; ***r. mullet*** salmonete *m*; ***r. pepper*** *(vegetable)* pimiento *m* rojo *or* morrón; *(spice)* cayena *f*; ***r. setter*** setter *mf* irlandés(esa); ***r. snapper*** pargo *m* colorado; ***r. squirrel*** ardilla *f* roja; ***r. tape*** burocracia *f*, papeleo *m* (burocrático); **to cut through the r. tape** evitar la burocracia *or* el papeleo; ***r. wine*** vino *m* tinto
(b) *Fam (Communist)* rojo(a) ▸▸ *Formerly* ***the R. Army*** el Ejército Rojo; ***the R. Flag*** la Bandera roja *(himno)*; ***r. China*** la China comunista
(c) *(in proper names)* ***the R. Crescent*** la Media Luna Roja; ***the R. Cross*** la Cruz Roja; ***R. Ensign*** = pabellón de la marina mercante británica; *Br* ***R. Nose Day*** = día en que se adquieren narices rojas de payaso para recaudar fondos con fines benéficos; ***the R. Planet*** el planeta rojo; ***(Little) R. Riding Hood*** Caperucita *f* Roja; ***the R. Sea*** el Mar Rojo; ***R. Square*** la Plaza Roja
(d) IDIOMS **to be as r. as a beetroot** estar más rojo que un tomate *or Méx* jitomate; **to be as r. as a lobster** *(with sunburn)* estar como un cangrejo; **to roll out the r. carpet for sb** recibir a alguien con todos los honores; *US Fam* **I don't have a r. cent** estoy sin un centavo *or Esp* sin blanca; *US Fam* **it's not worth a r. cent** no vale un pimiento; *US* **to go into r. ink** entrar en números rojos; **to take a r. pen to sth** *(edit)* enmendar algo; *(delete)* borrar algo; **mentioning her name to him was like a r. rag to a bull** la sola mención de su nombre le ponía hecho una furia; PROV **r. sky at night, shepherd's delight(, r. sky in the morning, shepherd's warning)** = un atardecer rojo es signo de buen tiempo (y un rojo por la mañana es signo de mal tiempo)

red-blooded [ˈredˈblʌdɪd] *adj* **a r. male** un macho de pelo en pecho

redbreast [ˈredbrest] *n* petirrojo *m*

redbrick [ˈredbrɪk] *adj (building)* de ladrillo rojo; **r. university** = por oposición a Oxford y Cambridge, universidad construida en alguna gran urbe británica, aparte de Londres, a finales del XIX o principios del XX

red-cap [ˈredkæp] *n* **(a)** *Br Mil* policía *m* militar **(b)** *US Rail (porter)* maletero *m*, mozo *m* de equipajes

red-carpet [ˈredˈkɑːpɪt] *adj* **to give sb the r. treatment** tratar a alguien con todos los honores

redcoat [ˈredkəʊt] *n* **(a)** *Hist (British soldier)* casaca *m* roja **(b)** *Br (in holiday camp)* animador(ora) *m,f*

redcurrant [ˈredkʌrənt] *n* grosella *f* (roja)

redden [ˈredən] **1** *vt* enrojecer
2 *vi (sky)* ponerse rojo(a); *(person)* ponerse colorado(a)

reddish [ˈredɪʃ] *adj (light, colour)* rojizo(a)

redecorate [riːˈdekəreɪt] **1** *vt (repaint)* pintar de nuevo; *(repaper)* empapelar de nuevo
2 *vi (repaint)* pintar de nuevo la casa/habitación/*etc*; *(repaper)* empapelar de nuevo la casa/habitación/*etc*.

redecoration [riːdekəˈreɪʃən] *n* **the r. of the house took them three months** *(painting)* tardaron tres meses en volver a pintar la casa; *(wallpapering)* tardaron tres meses en volver a empapelar la casa

redeem [rɪˈdiːm] *vt* **(a)** *(pawned item)* desempeñar
(b) *(gift token, coupon)* canjear; *(bond)* amortizar; *(share)* rescatar; **to r. a mortgage** amortizar una hipoteca
(c) *(promise)* cumplir
(d) *(save) (situation, honour)* salvar; *Rel (sinner, humankind)* redimir; *Fig* **he redeemed himself by scoring the equalizer** subsanó su error al marcar el gol del empate
(e) *(make up for) (mistake, failure)* compensar

redeemable [rɪˈdiːməbəl] *adj* **(a)** *(bond)* amortizable; *(share)* rescatable; **not r. for cash** *(stamps, vouchers)* no canjeable por dinero **(b)** *(sin, crime)* expiable; *(sinner)* redimible

Redeemer [rɪˈdiːmə(r)] *n Rel* **the R.** el Redentor

redeeming [rɪˈdiːmɪŋ] *adj* **his one r. feature** lo único que le salva; **he has no r. features** no se salva por ningún lado, no tiene nada que lo salve

redefine [ˈriːdɪfaɪn] *vt* redefinir

redemption [rɪˈdempʃən] *n* **(a)** *(from pawn)* desempeño *m*
(b) *(of gift token, coupon)* canjeo *m*; *(of bond, mortgage)* amortización *f*; *(of share)* rescate *m*
(c) *(of promise)* cumplimiento *m*
(d) *(saving) (of situation, honour)* salvación *f*; *Rel* redención *f*; *also Fig* **to be beyond** *or* **past r.** no tener salvación; *Fig* **this setback proved to be his r.** este traspiés resultó ser su salvación
(e) *(making up for) (mistake, failure)* compensación *f*

redemptive [rɪˈdemptɪv] *adj Formal* redentor(ora)

redeploy [riːdɪˈplɔɪ] *vt (troops)* redesplegar; *(resources, workers)* redistribuir, reorganizar

redeployment [riːdɪˈplɔɪmənt] *n (of troops)* redespliegue *m*; *(of resources, workers)* redistribución *f*, reorganización *f*

redesign [riːdɪˈzaɪn] **1** *n* rediseño *m*
2 *vt* rediseñar

redevelop [riːdɪˈveləp] *vt (land, area)* reconvertir

redevelopment [riːdɪˈveləpmənt] *n (of land, area)* reconversión *f*

red-eye [ˈredaɪ] *n* **(a)** *Phot* ojos *mpl* rojos **(b)** *US Fam (whisky)* whisky *m* de poca calidad **(c)** *US Fam (overnight flight)* vuelo *m* nocturno

red-eyed [ˈredˈaɪd] *adj* **to be r.** tener los ojos rojos

red-faced [ˈredˈfeɪst] *adj (naturally)* sonrosado(a); *(with anger)* sulfurado(a); *(with embarrassment)* ruborizado(a)

red-haired [ˈredˈheəd] *adj* pelirrojo(a)

red-handed [ˈredˈhændɪd] *adj* IDIOM **he was caught r.** lo *Esp* cogieron *or Am* agarraron con las manos en la masa

redhead [ˈredhed] *n* pelirrojo(a) *m,f*

redheaded [redˈhedɪd] *adj* pelirrojo(a)

red-hot [ˈredˈhɒt] **1** *adj* **(a)** *(very hot)* al rojo vivo, candente; **careful! the plates are r.** ¡cuidado! los platos están ardiendo
(b) *(passion, anger)* ardiente
(c) *Fam* **to be r. (on sth)** *(very good)* ser un genio (para algo), *Esp, Méx* ser un hacha (en algo); *(enthusiastic)* ser un fanático(a) (de algo)
(d) *Fam (news, information)* de candente actualidad
(e) *Fam (tip, favourite)* infalible
(f) ***r. poker*** *(plant)* = tipo de lilácea
2 *n US Fam (hot dog)* perrito *m* caliente

redial [riːˈdaɪəl] *Tel* **1** *n* [ˈriːdaɪəl] **r. (feature)** (botón *m* de) rellamada *f*
2 *vt (number)* volver a marcar *or Andes, RP* discar (el número)
3 *vi* volver a marcar *or Andes, RP* discar (el número)

redid *pt of* **redo**

redirect [riːdɪˈrekt, riːdaɪˈrekt] *vt* **(a)** *(letter)* reexpedir **(b)** *(plane, traffic)* desviar; *Fig* **to r. one's energies (towards sth)** reorientar los esfuerzos (hacia algo)

redirection [riːdɪˈrekʃən, riːdaɪˈrekʃən] *n* **(a)** *(of letter)* reexpedición *f* **(b)** *(of plane, traffic)* desvío *m*

rediscover [riːdɪsˈkʌvə(r)] *vt* redescubrir

rediscovery [riːdɪˈskʌvərɪ] *n* redescubrimiento *m*

redistribute [riːˈdɪstrɪbjuːt] *vt* redistribuir

redistribution [riːdɪstrɪˈbjuːʃən] *n* redistribución *f*

red-letter day [ˈredˈletədeɪ] *n* jornada *f* memorable, día *m* señalado

redline ['redlaɪn] *vi US Fin* = no conceder hipotecas o seguros en barrios marginales

redneck ['rednek] *n US Pej* = sureño racista y reaccionario, de baja extracción social; **a r. politician** un(a) político(a) racista y reaccionario(a)

redness ['rednɪs] *n* rojez *f*

redo [riː'duː] (*pt* **redid** [riː'dɪd], *pp* **redone** [riː'dʌn]) *vt* rehacer

redolent ['redələnt] *adj Literary* **to be r. of** *(smell of)* oler a; *(be suggestive of)* tener reminiscencias de

redone *pp of* **redo**

redouble [riː'dʌbəl] **1** *vt* (**a**) *(in intensity)* redoblar; **to r. one's efforts** redoblar los esfuerzos (**b**) *(in bridge)* redoblar
2 *vi (in bridge)* redoblar

redoubt [rɪ'daʊt] *n Mil (fortification)* reducto *m*; *Fig* **the last r. of clerical reaction** el último reducto de reacción clerical

redoubtable [rɪ'daʊtəbəl] *adj (opponent)* temible

redound [rɪ'daʊnd] *vi Formal* **to r. to sb's advantage** redundar en beneficio de alguien; **to r. to sb's credit** redundar en un mayor prestigio de alguien

redox ['riːdɒks] *n Chem* ***r. reaction*** reacción *f* rédox

red-pencil ['red'pensɪl] *vt* (**a**) *(correct)* marcar en rojo (**b**) *(censor)* censurar

redpoll ['redpɒl] *n* pardillo *m* sizerín

redraft [riː'drɑːft] *vt* redactar de nuevo, reescribir

redraw [riː'drɔː] *vt* (**a**) *(boundary, border)* volver a dibujar (**b**) *Comptr* redibujar

redress [rɪ'dres] **1** *n (of grievance)* reparación *f*; **to seek r. (for sth)** exigir reparación (por algo); **there is no r. if you lose your money** si pierdes el dinero no tiene arreglo
2 *vt (injustice, grievance)* reparar; **to r. the balance** restablecer el equilibrio

redshank ['redʃæŋk] *n* archibebe *m* común

redshift ['redʃɪft] *n Astron* corrimiento *m* hacia el rojo

redskin ['redskɪn] *n Old-fashioned* piel roja *mf*

redstart ['redstɑːt] *n* colirrojo *m* real

reduce [rɪ'djuːs] **1** *vt* (**a**) *(make smaller, lower)* reducir, disminuir; **to r. speed** reducir la velocidad; **I reduced my sugar consumption by half** he reducido mi consumo de azúcar a la mitad
(**b**) *(make cheaper) (price, product)* rebajar; *(cost, tax)* reducir
(**c**) *(bring to a certain state)* **to r. sth to ashes/dust** reducir algo a cenizas/polvo; **to r. sb to silence/poverty** abocar a alguien al silencio/a la miseria; **his words reduced her to tears** sus palabras le hicieron llorar; **we were reduced to helpless laughter** nos hizo desternillarnos de risa; **to be reduced to doing sth** no tener más remedio que hacer algo, verse obligado(a) a hacer algo
(**d**) *(simplify)* **to r. sth to the simplest terms** reducir algo a los términos más sencillos
(**e**) *Culin* **to r. a sauce** reducir una salsa
(**f**) *Math* **to r. a fraction to a common denominator** reducir una fracción a un común denominador
(**g**) *Mil* **to r. an officer to the ranks** degradar un oficial a soldado
2 *vi* (**a**) *Culin (sauce, stock)* reducirse (**b**) *(slim)* adelgazar

reduced [rɪ'djuːst] *adj* (**a**) *(smaller)* reducido(a); **on a r. scale** a escala reducida; **a r. service** *(because of strike, emergency)* un servicio reducido (**b**) *(cheaper)* **at r. prices** a precios reducidos; **r. to clear** *(on label)* rebajado(a) por liquidación (**c**) *Formal* **to live in r. circumstances** haber venido a menos

reducible [rɪ'djuːsɪbəl] *adj* reducible

reducing agent [rɪ'djuːsɪŋ'eɪdʒənt] *n Chem* agente *m* reductor

reductase [rɪ'dʌkteɪz] *n Biochem* reductasa *f*

reductio ad absurdum [rɪ'dʌktɪəʊædəb'sɜːdəm] *n* reducción *f* al absurdo

reduction [rɪ'dʌkʃən] *n* (**a**) *(in number, size)* reducción *f*, disminución *f*
(**b**) *(of price, product)* rebaja *f*; **to make a 5 percent r. on sth** hacer una rebaja *or* un descuento del 5 por ciento en algo; **I'll give you a r.** *(on purchase)* le haré un descuento; **big reductions** *(sale notice)* grandes rebajas
(**c**) *(bringing to a certain state) (to ashes, dust)* reducción *f*
(**d**) *(simplification)* reducción *f*
(**e**) *Math* reducción *f*
(**f**) *Mil* degradación *f*

reductionism [rɪ'dʌkʃənɪzəm] *n* reduccionismo *m*

reductionist [rɪ'dʌkʃənɪst] **1** *n* reduccionista *mf*
2 *adj* reduccionista

reductive [rɪ'dʌktɪv] *adj* reductor(ora)

redundancy [rɪ'dʌndənsɪ] *n* (**a**) *Br (dismissal)* despido *m (por reducción de plantilla)* ▸▸ ***r. notice*** notificación *f* de despido; ***r. pay*** indemnización *f* por despido (**b**) *(superfluousness)* redundancia *f* (**c**) *Ling* redundancia *f*

redundant [rɪ'dʌndənt] *adj* (**a**) *Br Ind* **to make sb r.** despedir a alguien; **to be made r.** ser despedido(a) (**b**) *(superfluous)* superfluo(a), innecesario(a); *(words, information)* redundante; **recent changes have made much of this chapter r.** los recientes cambios han hecho que gran parte de este capítulo sea superfluo *or* innecesario

reduplication [riːdjuːplɪ'keɪʃən] *n* (**a**) *(doubling)* reduplicación *f* (**b**) *Ling* reduplicación *f*

redwing ['redwɪŋ] *n* zorzal *m* alirrojo

redwood ['redwʊd] *n* secuoya *f*, secoya *f*

re-echo ['riː'ekəʊ] **1** *vt* reproducir
2 *vi* resonar

reed [riːd] *n* (**a**) *(plant)* caña *f*; IDIOM **he's a broken r.** está acabado (**b**) *Mus (of instrument)* lengüeta *f* ▸▸ ***r. instrument*** instrumento *m* de lengüeta (**c**) ***r. bunting*** escribano *m* palustre; ***r. warbler*** carricero *m* común

re-educate [riː'edjʊkeɪt] *vt* reeducar

re-education [riːedjʊ'keɪʃən] *n* reeducación *f*

reedy ['riːdɪ] *adj* (**a**) *(place)* cubierto(a) de juncos (**b**) *(sound, voice)* agudo(a), chillón(ona)

reef[1] [riːf] *n (coral, rock)* arrecife *m*; **to hit a r.** *(ship)* chocar contra un arrecife

reef[2] *Naut* **1** *n* ***r. knot*** nudo *m* de envergue *or* de rizos
2 *vt (sail)* rizar

reef[3] *n (in gold mine)* filón *m*

reefer ['riːfə(r)] *n* (**a**) *(clothing)* **r. (jacket)** chaquetón *m* (**b**) *Old-fashioned Fam (cannabis cigarette)* porro *m*

reek [riːk] **1** *n* peste *f*, tufo *m*
2 *vi* apestar (**of** a); **to r. of cheap perfume** apestar a perfume barato; *Fig* **the whole affair reeks of corruption** todo el asunto apesta a corrupción

reel [riːl] **1** *n* (**a**) *(for tape, cable, fishing line, hose)* carrete *m*, bobina *f*; *(for fishing line)* carrete *m*; *Br (for thread)* carrete *m* (**b**) *(of cinema film)* rollo *m*; **at the end of the third r.** al final del tercer rollo (**c**) *(dance, music)* = melodía y baile escocés o irlandés de ritmo muy vivo
2 *vi* (**a**) *(sway)* tambalearse; **a drunk came reeling downstairs** un borracho bajó las escaleras tambaleándose (**b**) *(whirl)* dar vueltas; **my head is reeling** me da vueltas la cabeza (**c**) *(recoil)* **to r. (back)** retroceder; **they were still reeling from the shock** todavía no se habían recuperado del impacto

▸ **reel in** *vt sep (fishing line, fish)* sacar (enrollando el carrete)

▸ **reel off** *vt sep (names, statistics)* soltar de un tirón

re-elect ['riːɪ'lekt] *vt* reelegir

re-election ['riːɪ'lekʃən] *n* reelección *f*; **to stand** *or* **run for r.** presentarse a la reelección

reeling ['riːlɪŋ] *adj (gait)* tambaleante

reel-to-reel ['riːltə'riːl] *adj (tape recorder)* de cinta abierta

re-embark ['riːɪm'bɑːk] **1** *vt (passengers)* reembarcar
2 *vi* reembarcar; **to r. on sth** *(project)* reembarcarse en algo

re-emerge ['riːɪ'mɜːdʒ] *vi (from water, room, hiding)* reaparecer, salir; **he has re-emerged as a major contender** ha reaparecido como un candidato de primera fila

re-emergence ['riːɪ'mɜːdʒəns] *n (from water, room, hiding)* reaparición *f*, salida *f*; **the r. of this problem in recent years** la reaparición de este problema en los últimos años

re-employ ['riːɪm'plɔɪ] *vt (workers)* volver a emplear

re-enact ['riːɪ'nækt] *vt (crime, battle)* reconstruir

re-enactment ['riːɪ'næktmənt] *n (of crime, battle)* reconstrucción *f*

re-engage ['riːɪn'geɪdʒ] **1** *vt* (**a**) *(employee)* volver a contratar (**b**) *(troops)* volver a enfrentarse con (**c**) *(cog, gear)* volver a engranar; **to r. the clutch** volver a embragar
2 *vi* (**a**) *(troops)* volver a entablar combate (**b**) *(cog, gear)* volver a engranar

re-enter ['riː'entə(r)] **1** *vt* (**a**) *(room, country)* volver a entrar en; **to r. the job market** reinsertarse en el *or* reincorporarse al mercado de trabajo (**b**) *Comptr (data)* reintroducir
2 *vi* volver a entrar; **to r. for an examination** volver a examinarse

re-entry ['riː'entrɪ] *n* reingreso *m*

re-equip [ˈriːɪˈkwɪp] 1 *vt* reequipar
2 *vi* reequiparse

re-establish [ˈriːɪˈstæblɪʃ] *vt* (**a**) *(order, practice)* restablecer (**b**) *(person)* **to r. oneself** *or* **one's position** volver a establecerse

re-establishment [ˈriːɪˈstæblɪʃmənt] *n* (**a**) *(of order, practice)* restablecimiento *m* (**b**) *(of person)* **her r. as team leader** su reintegración como jefe de equipo

re-evaluate [ˈriːɪˈvæljʊeɪt] *vt* reevaluar

re-evaluation [ˈriːɪvæljʊˈeɪʃən] *n* reevaluación *f*

reeve [riːv] *n* (**a**) *Br Hist (in town)* corregidor *m*; *(in manor)* capataz *m* (**b**) *Can* presidente(a) *m,f* del concejo local

re-examination [ˈriːɪgˈzæmɪneɪʃən] *n* (**a**) *(of question, case)* reexamen *m*; *(of student)* nuevo examen *m* (**b**) *Law (of witness)* segundo interrogatorio *m*

re-examine [ˈriːɪgˈzæmɪn] *vt* (**a**) *(question, case)* reexaminar; *(student)* volver a examinar (**b**) *Law (witness)* interrogar por segunda vez

ref[1] (*abbr* **reference**) ref.; **your r.** S/Ref.; **our r.** N/Ref.; **r. number** n ref., número de referencia

ref[2] *n Fam (referee)* árbitro(a) *m,f*

reface [ˈriːˈfeɪs] *vt (wall)* cambiar el revestimiento de

refashion [ˈriːˈfæʃən] *vt* reconvertir

refectory [rɪˈfektərɪ] *n* (**a**) *(at university, school)* comedor *m* (**b**) *(in monastery)* refectorio *m*

refer [rɪˈfɜː(r)] (*pt & pp* **referred**) *vt* (**a**) *(submit, pass on)* remitir; **the reader is referred to Thompson's book for further examples** para más ejemplos, el lector deberá remitirse al libro de Thompson; **to r. a matter to sb** remitir un asunto a alguien; **to r. a patient to a specialist** enviar a un paciente al especialista; **to r. a case to a higher court** remitir el caso a instancias superiores; *Fin* **r. to drawer** *(on cheque)* devolver al librador

(**b**) *Med* **the pain may be referred to another part of the body** el dolor puede estar referido a otra parte del cuerpo ►► ***referred pain*** dolor *m* referido

(**c**) *Br Univ (student) Esp* suspender, *Am* reprobar; *(thesis)* devolver *(para que se revise)*

► **refer back** *vt sep (case, patient)* volver a enviar

► **refer to** *vt insep* (**a**) *(consult) (person, notes, instructions)* consultar; **I shall have to r. to my manager** necesito consultar a mi jefe

(**b**) *(allude to, mention)* referirse a; **who are you referring to?** ¿a quién te estás refiriendo?; **he keeps referring to me as Dr Rayburn** siempre se refiere a mí como Dr Rayburn; **referred to as...** conocido(a) como...; **he never refers to the matter** nunca hace referencia al asunto; *Formal* **I r. to your letter of 27 March** con referencia a su carta fechada el 27 de marzo

(**c**) *(relate to)* **the numbers r. to notes at the back of the book** los números remiten a notas al final del libro

(**d**) *(apply to)* referirse a, aplicarse a; **these measures only r. to taxpayers** estas medidas sólo se aplican a los contribuyentes

referee [refəˈriː] 1 *n* (**a**) *(in sport)* árbitro(a) *m,f* (**b**) *Br (for job)* **please give the names of two referees** por favor dé los nombres de dos personas que puedan proporcionar referencias suyas; **you can give my name as a r.** puedes dar mi nombre para referencias
2 *vt* arbitrar; **he refereed the game well** arbitró bien el partido
3 *vi* arbitrar

reference [ˈrefərəns] 1 *n* (**a**) *(consultation)* consulta *f*; *(source)* referencia *f*; **without r. to me** sin consultarme; **for r. only** *(book)* para consulta en sala; **to keep sth for future r.** guardar algo para su posterior consulta; **for future r., please note...** para su información en el futuro, recuerde... ►► ***r. book*** libro *m* de consulta; ***r. library*** biblioteca *f* de consulta; ***r. point, point of r.*** punto *m* de referencia; ***r. work*** obra *f* de consulta

(**b**) *(allusion)* referencia *f*; **it's a biblical r.** es una referencia bíblica; **to make a r. to sth** hacer referencia a algo; **with r. to...** con referencia a...; **a talk on the environment with particular r. to...** una conferencia sobre el medio ambiente con especial atención a...

(**c**) *(footnote, cross-reference)* remisión *f*

(**d**) *Br (from employer)* informe *m*, referencia *f*; **to take up references** comprobar referencias

(**e**) *(remit)* competencia *f*, atribuciones *fpl*; **the question is outside the tribunal's r.** la cuestión queda fuera del ámbito de competencia de este tribunal

(**f**) *Com* referencia *f*; **quote this r.** indique esta referencia ►► ***r. number*** número *m* de referencia

(**g**) *Ling & Phil* referencia *f*

2 *vt* (**a**) *(refer to)* hacer referencia a (**b**) *(quotation)* indicar la procedencia de; *(thesis)* dar la bibliografía de

referendum [refəˈrendəm] *n* referéndum *m*; **to hold a r.** celebrar un referéndum

referent [ˈrefərənt] *n Ling & Phil* referente *m*

referral [rɪˈfɜːrəl] *n* (**a**) *(passing on)* remisión *f*; **the r. of the case to a higher court** la remisión del caso a un tribunal superior; **ask for a r. to a specialist** pide que te manden al especialista (**b**) *(allusion)* alusión *f* (**c**) *Univ (of thesis)* devolución *f* para revisión

refill 1 *n* [ˈriːfɪl] (**a**) *(for notebook, pen)* recambio *m*; *(for propelling pencil)* mina *f* (**b**) *(of drink)* **would you like a r.?** ¿quieres que te vuelva a llenar?
2 *vt* [riːˈfɪl] (**a**) *(lighter, pen)* recargar (**b**) *(glass)* volver a llenar

refillable [riːˈfɪləbəl] *adj* recargable

refinance [ˈriːˈfaɪnæns] *vt* refinanciar

refinancing [riːˈfaɪnænsɪŋ] *n Fin* refinanciación *f*

refine [rɪˈfaɪn] *vt* (**a**) *(sugar, petroleum)* refinar (**b**) *(technique, machine)* perfeccionar

► **refine on, refine upon** *vt insep* perfeccionar

refined [rɪˈfaɪnd] *adj* (**a**) *(sugar, petroleum)* refinado(a) (**b**) *(person, taste)* refinado(a), sofisticado(a)

refinement [rɪˈfaɪnmənt] *n* (**a**) *(of oil, sugar)* refinación *f*, refinamiento *m* (**b**) *(of manners, taste, person)* refinamiento *m*; **a person of r.** una persona refinada (**c**) *(of technique)* sofisticación *f* (**d**) *(improvement)* **to make refinements to sth** perfeccionar algo

refiner [rɪˈfaɪnə(r)] *n (of oil, sugar)* refinadora *f*

refinery [rɪˈfaɪnərɪ] *n* refinería *f*

refit [riːˈfɪt] 1 *n* [ˈriːfɪt] *(of ship)* reparación *f*; **the yacht is under r.** el yate está en reparación
2 *vt* (*pt & pp* **refitted**) *(ship)* reparar
3 *vi (ship)* estar en reparación

reflag [riːˈflæg] *vt (ship)* cambiar de bandera

reflate [riːˈfleɪt] *vt* (**a**) *(ball, tyre)* volver a inflar (**b**) *Econ* reflacionar

reflation [riːˈfleɪʃən] *n Econ* reflación *f*

reflationary [riːˈfleɪʃənərɪ] *adj Econ* reflacionario(a)

reflect [rɪˈflekt] 1 *vt* (**a**) *(image, light, sound, heat)* reflejar; **to be reflected** reflejarse; **she saw herself reflected in the window** se vio reflejada en la ventana; *Fig* **to bask** *or* **bathe in reflected glory** disfrutar de la gloria ajena

(**b**) *(have as a consequence)* **the behaviour of a few reflects discredit on us all** el comportamiento de unos pocos nos desprestigia a todos

(**c**) *(attitude, mood, personality)* reflejar; **this lack of direction is reflected in the sales figures** la falta de dirección se refleja en las cifras de ventas; **the graph reflects population movements** el gráfico refleja movimientos de población

(**d**) *(think)* **to r. that...** considerar que...; **Peter might know, she reflected** quizá Peter lo sepa, pensó

2 *vi* (**a**) *(light, image, sound, heat)* reflejarse (**b**) *(think)* reflexionar (**on** sobre); **after reflecting for a while...** tras un rato de reflexión...

► **reflect on, reflect upon** *vt insep* **how is that going to r. on the company?** ¿cómo va a repercutir eso en la empresa?; **to r. well/badly on sb** dejar en buen/mal lugar a alguien; **this will r. badly upon the company** esto perjudicará a la imagen de la empresa

reflecting [rɪˈflektɪŋ] *adj Astron* ***r. telescope*** telescopio *m* reflector

reflection, *Br* **reflexion** [rɪˈflekʃən] *n* (**a**) *(reflected image)* reflejo *m*

(**b**) *(representation)* **an accurate r. of the situation** un fiel reflejo de la situación; **the result was not a fair r. of the game** el resultado no refleja con justicia el partido

(**c**) *(negative indication)* **the termination of the project is no r. on your own performance** la cancelación del proyecto no significa que tú no lo hayas hecho bien; **this case is a poor r. on today's youth** este caso no dice mucho de la juventud actual

(**d**) *(thought)* reflexión *f*; **after some r. I changed my mind** después de reflexionar, cambié de opinión; **on r.** después de pensarlo; **reflections on the current crisis** *(book title)* reflexiones sobre la crisis actual

reflective [rɪˈflektɪv] *adj* (**a**) *(material, surface)* reflectante (**b**) *(person, mood)* reflexivo(a)

reflectively [rɪˈflektɪvlɪ] *adv (thoughtfully)* reflexivamente, con reflexión

reflector [rɪˈflektə(r)] *n* (**a**) *(of light, heat, sound)* reflector *m* (**b**) *(on bicycle, vehicle)* reflectante *m*, catadióptrico *m*

reflex [ˈriːfleks] 1 *n* reflejo *m*; **to have good reflexes** tener buenos reflejos; **to test sb's reflexes** poner a prueba los reflejos de alguien
2 *adj* reflejo(a) ►► ***r. action*** acto *m* reflejo; *Geom* ***r. angle*** ángulo *m* cóncavo; ***r. camera*** (cámara *f*) réflex *f inv*

reflexion *Br* = **reflection**

reflexive [rɪ'fleksɪv] *adj Gram (pronoun)* reflexivo(a) ►► ***r. verb*** verbo *m* reflexivo

reflexively [rɪ'fleksɪvlɪ] *adv Gram* reflexivamente

reflexology ['ri:fleks'ɒlədʒɪ] *n* reflexología *f*

refloat [ri:'fləʊt] *vt* (**a**) *(ship)* reflotar, sacar a flote (**b**) *Fin (company)* reflotar, sacar a flote

reflux ['ri:flʌks] *n Chem* reflujo *m*

refocus ['ri:'fəʊkəs] (*pt & pp* **refocused** *or* **refocussed**) *vt (projector, camera)* reenfocar; **it has refocused attention on the problem** ha vuelto a centrar la atención en el problema

reforest [ri:'fɒrɪst] *vt* reforestar

reforestation [ri:fɒrɪ'steɪʃən] *n* reforestación *f*, repoblación *f* forestal

re-form ['ri:'fɔ:m] **1** *vt (organization, pop group)* volver a formar
2 *vi (organization, pop group)* volver a formarse

reform [rɪ'fɔ:m] **1** *n* reforma *f* ►► *Br Formerly* ***r. school*** reformatorio *m*
2 *vt* (**a**) *(improve) (law, system, institution)* reformar (**b**) *(person)* reformar
3 *vi* reformarse

reformat ['ri:'fɔ:mæt] (*pt & pp* **reformatted**) *vt Comptr (disk)* volver a formatear

reformation [refə'meɪʃən] *n* (**a**) *(of law, system, institution)* reforma *f* (**b**) *(of person)* reforma *f* (**c**) *Hist* **the R.** la Reforma

reformatory [rɪ'fɔ:mətərɪ] *n* reformatorio *m*

reformed [rɪ'fɔ:md] *adj* (**a**) *(person)* reformado(a); **he's a r. character** se ha reformado completamente (**b**) *Rel (Christian, Jewish)* reformista; **the R. Church** la Iglesia Reformista

reformer [rɪ'fɔ:mə(r)] *n* reformador(ora) *m,f*

reformism [rɪ'fɔ:mɪzəm] *n* reformismo *m*

reformist [rɪ'fɔ:mɪst] **1** *n* reformista *mf*
2 *adj* reformista

reformulate [ri:'fɔ:mjʊleɪt] *vt* volver a formular

refract [rɪ'frækt] **1** *vt (light)* refractar
2 *vi* refractarse

refracting [rɪ'fræktɪŋ] *adj Astron* ***r. telescope*** telescopio *m* de refracción

refraction [rɪ'frækʃən] *n Phys* refracción *f*

refractive index [rɪ'fræktɪv'ɪndeks] *n Phys* índice *m* de refracción

refractory [rɪ'fræktərɪ] *adj* (**a**) *Formal (person)* obstinado(a), rebelde; *(animal)* desobediente (**b**) *Med (disease)* intratable (**c**) *Tech (material)* refractario(a)

refrain [rɪ'freɪn] **1** *n (musical)* estribillo *m*; *Fig (repeated comment)* cantinela *f*
2 *vi* abstenerse (**from** de); **to r. from comment** abstenerse de hacer comentarios; **please r. from talking/smoking** *(sign)* se ruega guardar silencio/no fumar

> **False friend:** The most common sense of the English noun **refrain** is not translated by the Spanish word **refrán**. In Spanish **refrán** means "proverb, saying".

re-freeze ['ri:'fri:z] *vt* volver a congelar

refresh [rɪ'freʃ] **1** *vt* (**a**) *(freshen, revive)* refrescar; **to r. oneself** refrescarse; **to r. one's memory** refrescar la memoria; **to r. sb's glass** *(top up)* llenarle el vaso a alguien (**b**) *Comptr* refrescar
2 *n Comptr* refresco *m* ►► ***r. rate*** velocidad *f* de refresco

refresher [rɪ'freʃə(r)] *n* (**a**) *(drink)* refresco *m* (**b**) *Educ* ***r. course*** cursillo *m* de reciclaje

refreshing [rɪ'freʃɪŋ] *adj* (**a**) *(cooling) (breeze, drink)* refrescante (**b**) *(reinvigorating) (bath, cup of tea)* reconfortante; *(sleep, holiday)* reparador(ora) (**c**) *(pleasingly novel) (honesty, simplicity)* alentador(ora), reconfortante; **it makes a r. change to hear a politician being honest** qué gusto ver a un político honrado para variar

refreshingly [rɪ'freʃɪŋlɪ] *adv* **he's r. honest** da gusto su honradez; **it's r. different** es un cambio agradable

refreshment [rɪ'freʃmənt] *n* (**a**) *(of body, mind)* descanso *m* (**b**) **refreshments** *(food and drink)* refrigerio *m*; **refreshments will be served** se servirá un refrigerio

refried beans ['ri:fraɪd'bi:nz] *npl* frijoles *mpl* refritos

refrigerant [rɪ'frɪdʒərənt] *n Tech* refrigerante *m*

refrigerate [rɪ'frɪdʒəreɪt] *vt* refrigerar, conservar en (la) nevera *or Esp* (el) frigorífico *or Méx* (el) refrigerador *or RP* (la) heladera; **keep refrigerated** *(on packet)* mantener refrigerado(a) ►► ***refrigerated lorry*** camión *m* frigorífico

refrigeration [rɪfrɪdʒə'reɪʃən] *n* refrigeración *f*; **keep under r.** manténgase en la nevera *or* el *Esp* frigorífico *or Méx* refrigerador *or RP* la heladera

refrigerator [rɪ'frɪdʒəreɪtə(r)] *n (domestic)* nevera *f*, *Esp* frigorífico *m*, *RP* heladera *f*, *Méx* refrigerador *m*; *(industrial)* cámara *f* frigorífica; **r. ship/lorry** buque/camión frigorífico

refuel [ri:'fjʊəl] **1** *vt (ship, aircraft)* repostar combustible a; *Fig* **to r. speculation** alimentar especulaciones
2 *vi* (**a**) *(ship, aircraft)* repostar (**b**) *Hum (eat, drink)* repostar

refuelling [ri:'fjʊəlɪŋ] *n* repostaje *m*; **r. plane/ship** avión/barco nodriza ►► ***r. stop*** escala *f* técnica *or* de repostaje

refuge ['refju:dʒ] *n* (**a**) *(shelter)* refugio *m*; **(women's) r.** centro *m* de acogida (para mujeres maltratadas) (**b**) *(protection) (from danger, weather)* refugio *m*, cobijo *m*; **a place of r.** un refugio; **God is my r.** Dios es mi refugio; **to seek r.** buscar refugio; **to take r.** refugiarse (**c**) *Br (for crossing road)* refugio *m*, isleta *f*

refugee [refju:'dʒi:] *n* refugiado(a) *m,f* ►► ***r. camp*** campo *m* de refugiados; ***r. status*** condición *f or* estatuto *m* de refugiado

refulgent [rɪ'fʌldʒənt] *adj Literary* refulgente

refund **1** *n* ['ri:fʌnd] reembolso *m*; **to ask for a r.** pedir una devolución del importe; **to get** *or* **obtain a r.** recibir la devolución del importe; **no refunds will be given** no se admiten devoluciones
2 *vt* [ri:'fʌnd] reembolsar; **to r. sth to sb** reembolsar algo a alguien; **they refunded me the postage** me reembolsaron los gastos de envío

refundable [ri:'fʌndəbəl] *adj* reembolsable

refurbish [ri:'fɜ:bɪʃ] *vt (room, restaurant)* remodelar, renovar

refurbishment [rɪ'fɜ:bɪʃmənt] *n* remodelación *f*, renovación *f*

refurnish [ri:'fɜ:nɪʃ] *vt (house)* renovar el mobiliario de

refusal [rɪ'fju:zəl] *n* (**a**) *(of request, suggestion)* negativa *f*; **we don't understand their r. to compromise** no entendemos por qué se niegan a transigir; **to give a flat r.** negarse rotundamente; **to meet with a r.** *(offer)* ser rechazado(a); *(person)* recibir una negativa; IDIOM **to have first r. (on sth)** tener primera opción de compra (sobre algo)
(**b**) *(in showjumping) (of horse)* **that's its third r.** ha rehusado por tercera vez

refuse[1] ['refju:s] *n (rubbish)* basura *f*; **no r.** *(sign)* prohibido tirar basura ►► ***r. collection*** recogida *f* de basuras; ***r. collector*** basurero(a) *m,f*; ***r. disposal*** eliminación *f* de basuras; ***r. dump*** vertedero *m* (de basuras)

refuse[2] [rɪ'fju:z] **1** *vt* (**a**) *(turn down) (invitation, offer, request)* rechazar, rehusar; **to r. to do sth** negarse a hacer algo; **the bike refuses to start** la moto no quiere arrancar; **the offer was too good to r.** la oferta era demasiado buena como para rechazarla; **she refused him** *(would not marry him)* lo rechazó
(**b**) *(deny) (visa, loan)* denegar; **to r. sb sth** denegar algo a alguien; **we were refused permission to leave** nos denegaron el permiso para salir; **he was refused entry** le negaron la entrada; **I don't see how we can r. them** no veo cómo vamos a decirles que no
(**c**) *(of horse)* **to r. a jump** rehusar ante un obstáculo
2 *vi (person)* negarse; *(horse)* rehusar

refus(e)nik [rɪ'fju:znɪk] *n* = persona que, por convicciones morales, se niega a acatar una ley o cooperar con un organismo

refutable ['refjʊtəbəl] *adj* refutable

refutation [refjʊ'teɪʃən] *n* refutación *f*

refute [rɪ'fju:t] *vt* (**a**) *(argument, theory)* refutar (**b**) *(allegation)* desmentir, negar

reg [redʒ] *Br Fam* (*abbr* **registration**) matrícula *f*; **an S-r. Jaguar** un Jaguar con matrícula S

regain [rɪ'geɪn] *vt* (**a**) *(get back) (territory, strength, composure)* recuperar; **to r. one's balance** recuperar el equilibrio; **to r. consciousness** recobrar el conocimiento; **to r. the lead** *(in contest)* volver a ponerse en cabeza; **to r. possession of sth** volver a tomar posesión de algo (**b**) *Formal (reach again) (shore, seat)* volver a alcanzar

regal ['ri:gəl] *adj* regio(a)

regale [rɪ'geɪl] *vt* divertir, entretener (**with** con)

regalia [rɪ'geɪlɪə] *npl* galas *fpl*; **in full r.** *(judge, general)* con traje de gala; *Hum* con sus mejores galas, todo(a) emperifollado(a)

> **False friend:** The Spanish noun **regalía** is not a translation for the English word **regalia**. In Spanish **regalía** means "royal prerogative".

regally ['ri:gəlɪ] *adv* con majestuosidad, de modo majestuoso

regard [rɪ'gɑ:d] **1** *n Formal* (**a**) *(admiration)* admiración *f*, estima *f*; **to have great r. for sth/sb** tener en gran estima algo/a alguien; **to hold sb in high/low r.** tener mucha/poca estima a alguien
(**b**) *(consideration)* consideración *f*; **having r. to his age** en consideración

a su edad; **out of r. for** por consideración hacia; **without r. to** *(safety, rules)* sin (ninguna) consideración por; *(gender, race)* independientemente de; **he has no r. for my feelings** no le importa nada lo que siento; **don't pay any r. to what she says** no hagas caso de lo que diga

(c) *(connection)* **in this r.** en este sentido; **in all regards** en todos los sentidos *or* aspectos; **with r. to** en cuanto a, con respecto a

(d) **regards** *(good wishes)* saludos *mpl*, *CAm, Col, Ecuad* saludes *fpl*; **give her my regards** salúdala de mi parte; **she sends (them) her regards** les manda recuerdos

2 *vt* (a) *(admire, respect)* **I r. him highly** tengo un alto concepto de él; **they are highly regarded** están muy bien considerados

(b) *(consider)* **to r. sth/sb as...** considerar algo/a alguien...; **it's not what I would r. as an emergency** yo eso no lo consideraría una emergencia; **he regards himself as an expert** se considera un experto; **to r. sth/sb with suspicion** tener recelo de algo/alguien; **to r. sth with horror** contemplar algo con terror; **she is regarded with respect** le tienen respeto

(c) *(concern)* concernir; **as regards...** en cuanto a..., con respecto a...

regarding [rɪ'gɑːdɪŋ] *prep* en cuanto a, con respecto a

regardless [rɪ'gɑːdlɪs] *adv* (a) *(despite everything)* a pesar de todo; **they carried on r.** a pesar de todo, continuaron (b) **r. of** *(without considering)* **r. of the danger** sin tener en cuenta el peligro; **r. of the expense** cueste lo que cueste; **I'm going to do it, r. of what they say** voy a hacerlo, digan lo que digan

regatta [rɪ'gætə] *n* regata *f*

regency ['riːdʒənsɪ] *n* regencia *f*

Regency ['riːdʒənsɪ] *adj* **R. furniture** muebles estilo regencia

regenerate [riː'dʒenəreɪt] **1** *vt (urban area)* regenerar

2 *vi Biol* regenerarse

regeneration [riːdʒenə'reɪʃən] *n* (a) *(of urban area)* regeneración *f* (b) *Biol (of tail, organ)* regeneración *f*

regent ['riːdʒənt] *n* (a) *Hist* regente *mf* (b) *US Univ* miembro *mf* del equipo rectoral

reggae ['regeɪ] *n Mus* reggae *m*

regicide ['redʒɪsaɪd] *n* (a) *(act)* regicidio *m* (b) *(person)* regicida *mf*

regime [reɪ'ʒiːm] *n (government)* régimen *m*; **under the present r.** *(government)* bajo el régimen actual; *(system)* en el sistema actual

regimen ['redʒɪmən] *n* régimen *m*

regiment ['redʒɪmənt] **1** *n (in army)* regimiento *m*

2 *vt* someter a severa disciplina

regimental [redʒɪ'mentəl] *adj (band, flag)* de regimiento ►► ***r. sergeant major*** sargento *mf* primero *(encargado de la administración y la disciplina de la tropa)*

regimentals [redʒɪ'mentəlz] *npl* **in full r.** con el uniforme completo

regimentation [redʒɪmen'teɪʃən] *n* severa disciplina *f*

regimented ['redʒɪmentɪd] *adj (strict)* disciplinado(a); **a r. lifestyle** una (clase de) vida muy estricta

Regina [rɪ'dʒaɪnə] *n Br* **Victoria R.** Reina Victoria; *Law* **R. vs Gibson** la corona contra Gibson

region ['riːdʒən] *n* (a) *(of country)* región *f*; **the Chicago r.** la región de Chicago; *Br* **in the regions** en las provincias (b) *(of body)* región *f*; **in the lower back r.** en la región sacrolumbar (c) *(of knowledge, sentiments)* ámbito *m*, campo *m* (d) **in the r. of** *(approximately)* alrededor de, del orden de

regional ['riːdʒənəl] *adj* regional ►► ***r. development*** desarrollo *m* regional; ***r. planning*** ordenación *f* del territorio *or* territorial

regionalism ['riːdʒənəlɪzəm] *n* (a) *(local patriotism)* regionalismo *m* (b) *(word, phrase)* regionalismo *m*

regionalist ['riːdʒənəlɪst] **1** *n* regionalista *mf*

2 *adj* regionalista

regionally ['riːdʒənəlɪ] *adv* regionalmente, por regiones

register ['redʒɪstə(r)] **1** *n* (a) *(record)* registro *m*; *Sch* **to call** *or* **take the r.** pasar lista ►► ***r. of births, marriages and deaths*** registro *m* civil; *Br* ***r. office*** registro *m* civil; ***r. of shipping*** registro *m* de embarque; ***r. of voters*** censo *m* electoral (b) **(cash) r.** caja *f* registradora (c) *Mus* registro *m* (d) *Ling* registro *m*

2 *vt* (a) *(record) (member)* inscribir; *(student, vehicle)* matricular; *(birth, marriage, death)* registrar; *(trademark, software)* registrar; *(complaint, protest)* presentar; **wind speeds as high as 100mph have been registered in parts of the country** en algunas regiones del país se han registrado vientos con una intensidad de hasta 160 km/h

(b) *(show) (temperature, speed)* registrar; *(astonishment, displeasure)* denotar, mostrar

(c) *(realize) (fact, problem)* darse cuenta de, enterarse de; **they still haven't registered (the fact) that they lost** aún no se han enterado de que han perdido

(d) *(achieve) (progress)* realizar

(e) *(parcel, letter)* certificar

3 *vi* (a) *(for course)* matricularse; *(at hotel)* inscribirse, registrarse; *(voter)* inscribirse (en el censo); **foreign nationals must r. with the police** los extranjeros deben inscribirse en los registros de la policía; *Br* **to r. with a GP** inscribirse como paciente de un médico

(b) *Fam (fact)* **it didn't r. (with him)** no se enteró; **I daresay you told me, but it obviously didn't r.** juraría que me lo dijiste pero es obvio que ni me enteré

(c) *(instrument)* registrar; **is the barometer registering** ¿funciona el barómetro?

registered ['redʒɪstɜːd] *adj Fin* ***r. capital*** capital *m* social; *Br* ***R. General Nurse*** enfermero(a) *m,f* diplomado(a), *Esp* ≃ ATS *mf*; *Br* ***r. letter*** carta *f* certificada *(con derecho a indemnización)*; *US* ***r. mail*** correo *m* certificado *(con derecho a indemnización)*; *Br Com* ***r. office*** domicilio *m* social; *Br* ***r. post*** correo *m* certificado *(con derecho a indemnización)*; ***r. trademark*** marca *f* registrada; *Comptr* ***r. user*** usuario(a) *m,f* registrado(a)

registrar ['redʒɪstrɑː(r)] *n* (a) *(record keeper)* registrador(ora) *m,f* (b) *Univ* secretario(a) *m,f* (c) *Br (in hospital)* doctor(ora) *m,f*, médico(a) *m,f*

registration [redʒɪ'streɪʃən] *n* (a) *(of student, vehicle)* matriculación *f*; *(of voter)* inscripción *f* (en el censo); *(of birth, death, marriage)* registro *m*; *(of trademark, software)* registro *m*; **when does r. start?** *(for university, evening classes)* ¿cuándo comienza la matriculación? ►► *Br Aut* ***r. document*** permiso *m* de circulación; ***r. fee*** *(for course)* matrícula *f*; *(for competition)* cuota *f* de inscripción; ***r. number*** *(of vehicle)* (número *m* de) matrícula *f*; *Austr* ***r. plate*** *(on car)* (placa *f* de la) matrícula *f*

(b) *Br Sch* hora *f* de pasar lista

(c) *Comptr* ***r. card*** tarjeta *f* de registro; ***r. number*** número *m* de registro

registry ['redʒɪstrɪ] *n* (a) *(office)* registro *m* ►► *Br* ***r. office*** registro *m* civil (b) *(of ship)* abanderamiento *m*; **a ship of Japanese r.** un barco de bandera japonesa

regress [rɪ'gres] *vi* involucionar, sufrir una regresión; **to r. to childhood** hacer una regresión a la infancia

> **False friend**: The most common sense of the English verb **to regress** is not translated by the Spanish word **regresar**. In Spanish **regresar** means "to go back, to return".

regression [rɪ'greʃən] *n* (a) *(to childhood)* regresión *f* (b) *(in statistics)* regresión *f* ►► ***r. towards the mean*** regresión *f* a la media

regressive [rɪ'gresɪv] *adj* (a) *(tendency)* regresivo(a) (b) *(taxation)* regresivo(a)

regret [rɪ'gret] **1** *n* (a) *(sadness)* tristeza *f*; *(remorse)* arrepentimiento *m*; **I have no regrets** no me arrepiento de nada; **my biggest r. is that...** lo que más lamento es que...; **my only r. is that I didn't resign earlier** lo único que lamento es no haber renunciado antes; **do you have any regrets about what you did?** ¿te arrepientes de lo que has hecho?; **there was a note of r. in her voice** había un tono de remordimiento en su voz; **he expressed his regrets about her son's death** le transmitió su pesar por la muerte de su hijo; **it is with great r. that I have to inform you that...** me da mucho pesar tener que informarle de que...; **much to my r....** muy a mi pesar...

(b) *(apology)* **she sent her regrets** mandó sus disculpas *or* excusas

2 *vt* (*pt & pp* **regretted**) (a) *(error, decision)* sentir, lamentar; **to r. doing** *or* **having done sth** arrepentirse de *or* lamentar haber hecho algo; *Formal* **it is to be regretted that...** es de lamentar que...; **I r. to say I will be unable to attend** lamento decirles que no podré asistir; **I r. to say our efforts were unsuccessful** lamentablemente nuestros esfuerzos no tuvieron éxito; **you won't r. it** no te arrepentirás; **you'll live to r. this!** ¡te arrepentirás!

(b) *Formal (in official apologies)* **the management regrets any inconvenience caused** la dirección lamenta las molestias causadas; **I r. to (have to) inform you that...** siento (tener que) comunicarle que...

> Hay una serie de verbos en inglés que pueden ir seguidos tanto como de infinitivo como de gerundio sin que apenas cambie su significado; por ejemplo **begin**, **bother**, **continue**, **hate**, **like** o **try**. Sin embargo, **regret** es uno de los pocos verbos en los que existe una clara diferencia entre ambas opciones:
>
> **I regret to say they were proved right**
> *lamento decir que resultaron tener razón*
> **I regret having told him the truth**
> *me arrepiento de haberle dicho la verdad*

regretful [rɪ'gretfʊl] *adj (sad)* apesadumbrado(a), pesaroso(a); *(remorseful)* arrepentido(a); **to be** *or* **feel r. about sth** *(sad)* estar *or* sentirse apesadumbrado(a) por algo; *(remorseful)* sentirse arrepentido(a) por algo

regretfully [rɪ'gretfʊlɪ] *adv (sadly)* tristemente, con tristeza; *(remorsefully)* con arrepentimiento; **I r. have to decline your offer** lamento tener que declinar su oferta

regrettable [rɪ'gretəbəl] *adj* lamentable; **it is most r. that you were not informed** es verdaderamente lamentable que no haya sido informado

regrettably [rɪ'gretəblɪ] *adv (unfortunately)* lamentablemente; **a joke in r. poor taste** un chiste de un lamentable mal gusto

regroup [riː'gruːp] **1** *vt* reagrupar
2 *vi* reagruparse

regt (*abbr* **regiment**) regto.

regular ['regjʊlə(r)] **1** *n* (**a**) *(customer) (in bar, restaurant)* habitual *mf*, parroquiano(a) *m,f*; *(in shop)* cliente *mf* habitual (**b**) *(contributor, player)* **she's a r. on our column** es una habitual columnista (nuestra); **he's a r. in the team** juega normalmente (**c**) *(soldier)* regular *m* (**d**) *US Pol (loyal party member)* = militante que sigue la línea oficial del partido (**e**) *US (petrol)* súper *f*
2 *adj* (**a**) *(evenly spaced) (breathing, pulse)* regular; **to be r.** ser regular; **to have a r. income** tener ingresos regulares; **on a r. basis** con regularidad, regularmente; **at r. intervals** a intervalos regulares; IDIOM **as r. as clockwork** como un reloj, con una regularidad cronométrica
(**b**) *(frequent) (meetings, bus service)* frecuente; **it's a r. occurrence** sucede frecuentemente
(**c**) *(normal) (brand, supplier, customer, listener)* habitual; **who is your r. doctor?** ¿quién es tu médico de cabecera?
(**d**) *(even) (features)* regular; *(teeth)* parejo(a)
(**e**) *(bowel movements, menstruation)* regular; **it keeps you r.** *(not constipated)* evita el estreñimiento
(**f**) *(of medium size)* normal, mediano(a)
(**g**) *(army, soldier)* profesional
(**h**) *(clergy)* regular
(**i**) *US Pol (loyal to party line)* fiel a la línea del partido
(**j**) *Fam (for emphasis)* verdadero(a), auténtico(a); **a r. mess** un verdadero *or* auténtico desastre
(**k**) *US Fam (decent)* **a r. guy** *Esp* un tío legal, *Am* un tipo derecho
(**l**) *Gram (verb)* regular
(**m**) *Geom (figure)* regular

regularity [regjʊ'lærɪtɪ] *n* regularidad *f*; **with unfailing r.** con una regularidad impecable

regularize ['regjʊləraɪz] *vt* regularizar

regularly ['regjʊləlɪ] *adv* (**a**) *(at equal intervals)* regularmente (**b**) *(frequently)* a menudo, frecuentemente (**c**) *Gram* de forma regular

regulate ['regjʊleɪt] *vt* (**a**) *(adjust) (expenditure, machine, voltage)* regular (**b**) *(supervise by legislation)* regular; **hitherto the industry has regulated itself** hasta ahora, la industria se ha regulado a sí misma

regulating ['regjʊleɪtɪŋ] *adj* (**a**) *(knob, valve)* regulador(ora); *(mechanism)* regulador(ora), de regulación (**b**) *(body)* regulador(ora), de regulación

regulation [regjʊ'leɪʃən] **1** *n* (**a**) *(adjustment) (of expenditure, machine, voltage)* regulación
(**b**) *(supervision by law) (of industry, food additives)* regulación *f*
(**c**) *(rule)* regla *f*, norma *f*; **regulations** reglamento *m*, normas *fpl*; **it's contrary to** *or* **against (the) regulations** va contra las normas; **it complies with EU regulations** cumple con las normas de la EU; **safety/building regulations** normas de seguridad/de construcción
2 *adj (size, dress)* reglamentario(a)

regulator ['regjʊleɪtə(r)] *n* (**a**) *(device)* regulador *m* (**b**) *(regulatory body)* organismo *m* regulador

regulatory [regjʊ'leɪtərɪ] *adj* regulador(ora)

regulo ['regjʊləʊ] *n Br* = posición del mando de la temperatura en un horno de gas; **cook at** *or* **on r. 4** ≃ cocínese a una temperatura de 180°C

regurgitate [rɪ'gɜːdʒɪteɪt] *vt* (**a**) *(food)* regurgitar (**b**) *(facts)* vomitar

rehab ['riːhæb] *n Fam* rehabilitación *f*; **to be in r.** estar rehabilitándose ►► ***r. centre*** centro *m* de rehabilitación

rehabilitate [riːhə'bɪlɪteɪt] *vt* (**a**) *(convict, former addict)* rehabilitar (**b**) *(disgraced person, reputation)* rehabilitar (**c**) *(area, building)* rehabilitar, renovar

rehabilitation [riːhəbɪlɪ'teɪʃən] *n* (**a**) *(of convict, former addict)* rehabilitación *f* ►► ***r. centre*** centro *m* de rehabilitación (**b**) *(of disgraced person, reputation)* rehabilitación *f* (**c**) *(of area, building)* rehabilitación *f*, renovación *f*

rehash *Fam Pej* **1** *n* ['riːhæʃ] refrito *m*; **it was a r. of her first novel** fue un refrito de su primera novela
2 *vt* [riː'hæʃ] hacer un refrito con

rehearing ['riː'hɪərɪŋ] *n Law* = revisión de una causa judicial

rehearsal [rɪ'hɜːsəl] *n* (**a**) *(practice) (of play, music, speech)* ensayo *m*; **to have** *or* **hold a r.** hacer un ensayo; **the play is currently in r.** están ensayando la obra ►► ***r. space*** local *m* de ensayo (**b**) *(recitation, repetition)* repetición *f*

rehearse [rɪ'hɜːs] **1** *vt* (**a**) *(practise) (play, music, speech)* ensayar; *(actors, singers, orchestra)* ensayar (**b**) *(recite, repeat)* repetir
2 *vi* ensayar

reheat ['riː'hiːt] *vt* recalentar

re-heel [riː'hiːl] *vt* cambiar las tapas a

rehouse ['riː'haʊz] *vt* realojar

rehydration [riːhaɪ'dreɪʃən] *n* (**a**) *Phys* rehidratación *f* (**b**) *Med* rehidratación *f*

reification ['reɪɪfɪ'keɪʃən] *n* materialización *f*

reify ['reɪɪfaɪ] *vt* materializar, convertir en realidad

reign [reɪn] **1** *n* reinado *m*; **in** *or* **under the r. of** durante el reinado de; **r. of terror** régimen de terror
2 *vi* reinar (**over** sobre); **to r. supreme** *(champion, style)* imperar; **they reigned supreme over the Sixties pop scene** fueron los dueños de la escena pop durante los años 60

reigning ['reɪnɪŋ] *adj* (**a**) *(monarch)* reinante (**b**) *(champion)* actual (**c**) *(predominant) (attitude, idea)* imperante, predominante

reignite [riːɪg'naɪt] *vt* reencender

reimburse [riːɪm'bɜːs] *vt* reintegrar, reembolsar; **to r. sb for sth** reintegrar *or* reembolsar algo a alguien; **I was fully reimbursed** me reintegraron *or* reembolsaron todos los gastos

reimbursement [riːɪm'bɜːsmənt] *n* reembolso *m*

reimpose [riːɪm'pəʊz] *vt* imponer de nuevo

rein [reɪn] *n* (**a**) *(for horse)* rienda *f*; **reins** *(for horse, child)* arnés *m*; *Fig* **the reins of government** las riendas del gobierno
(**b**) IDIOMS **to hand over the reins (to sb)** ceder las riendas (a alguien); **to give sb free r. to do sth** dar carta blanca a alguien para hacer algo; **to give free r. to one's imagination** dar rienda suelta a la imaginación; **to keep a tight r. on sth** controlar algo de cerca; **to keep a tight r. on sb** atar corto a alguien

► **rein back** *vt sep (horse)* detener, frenar

► **rein in** *vt sep* (**a**) *(horse)* frenar (**b**) *(emotions)* controlar; *(inflation)* controlar

reincarnate **1** *vt* [riːɪn'kɑːneɪt] **to be reincarnated (as)** reencarnarse (en)
2 *adj* [riːɪn'kɑːnɪt] reencarnado(a); **he danced like Nijinsky r.** bailó como si fuera la reencarnación de Nijinski

reincarnation [riːɪnkɑː'neɪʃən] *n* reencarnación *f*

reindeer ['reɪndɪə(r)] *n* reno *m*

reinfect [riːɪn'fekt] *vt* reinfectar, infectar de nuevo

reinfection [riːɪn'fekʃən] *n* reinfección *f*

reinforce [riːɪn'fɔːs] *vt* (**a**) *(wall, structure)* reforzar ►► ***reinforced concrete*** hormigón *m* or *Am* concreto *m* armado (**b**) *(army)* reforzar (**c**) *(emphasize)* reforzar, reafirmar (**d**) *Psy* reforzar

reinforcement [riːɪn'fɔːsmənt] *n* (**a**) *(of wall, structure)* refuerzo *m* (**b**) **reinforcements** *(for army)* refuerzos *mpl* (**c**) *(emphasis)* refuerzo *m* (**d**) *Psy* refuerzo *m*

reinitialize [riːɪ'nɪʃəlaɪz] *vt Comptr* reinicializar

reinsert [riːɪn'sɜːt] *vt* volver a introducir

reinstall [riːɪn'stɔːl] *vt Comptr* reinstalar

reinstate [riːɪn'steɪt] *vt* (**a**) *(person in job)* restituir (en el puesto) (**b**) *(clause)* reincorporar; *(law, practice)* reinstaurar

reinstatement [riːɪn'steɪtmənt] *n* (**a**) *(of person in job)* reincorporación *f*, rehabilitación *f* (**b**) *(of clause, law, practice)* reinstauración *f*

reinsurance [riːɪn'ʃʊərəns] *n* reaseguro *m*

reinsure [riːɪn'ʃʊə(r)] *vt* reasegurar

reintegrate [riː'ɪntɪgreɪt] *vt (into society)* reintegrar

reintegration [riːɪntə'greɪʃən] *n* reintegración *f*; *(into society)* reinserción *f* (social)

reinterpret [riːɪn'tɜːprɪt] *vt* reinterpretar

reinterpretation [riːɪntɜːprɪ'teɪʃən] *n* reinterpretación *f*

reintroduce [riːɪntrəˈdjuːs] *vt* reintroducir; **to r. an animal to the wild** reintroducir un animal en su hábitat natural, devolver a un animal a su hábitat natural

reinvent [riːɪnˈvent] *vt* IDIOM **to r. the wheel** reinventar la rueda, = perder el tiempo haciendo algo que ya está hecho

reinvest [riːɪnˈvest] *vt* reinvertir

reissue [riːˈɪʃuː] 1 *n* (a) *(of book, record)* reedición *f* (b) *(of bank note, stamp)* nueva emisión *f*

2 *vt* (a) *(book, record)* reeditar (b) *(bank note, stamp)* emitir de nuevo

reiterate [riːˈɪtəreɪt] *vt Formal* reiterar

reiteration [riːɪtəˈreɪʃən] *n Formal* reiteración *f*

reject 1 *n* [ˈriːdʒekt] (a) *(object)* artículo *m* con tara *or* defectuoso (b) *Fam Pej (person)* desecho *m*

2 *vt* [rɪˈdʒekt] (a) *(spurn)* rechazar; **to feel rejected** sentirse rechazado(a); **the machine keeps rejecting this coin** la máquina me sigue devolviendo esta moneda (b) *Med (transplanted tissue, organ)* rechazar

rejection [rɪˈdʒekʃən] *n* (a) *(spurning)* rechazo *m*; **to meet with r.** ser rechazado(a); **to be afraid of r.** *(emotional)* tener miedo al rechazo *or* a ser rechazado(a) ►► ***r. letter*** *(from publisher, employer)* carta *f* con respuesta negativa (b) *Med (of tissue, organ)* rechazo *m*

rejig [riːˈdʒɪg] *vt Br* (a) *(reequip)* reequipar (b) *(reorganize, alter)* modificar

rejoice [rɪˈdʒɔɪs] *vi* alegrarse (**at** *or* **over** por *or* de)

► **rejoice in** *vt insep* (a) *(good fortune)* alegrarse con, regocijarse con (b) *Hum (have)* **she rejoices in the name of...** tiene el divertido nombre de...

rejoicing [rɪˈdʒɔɪsɪŋ] *n* regocijo *m*, alegría *f*; **it was the occasion of much r.** fue una ocasión llena de alegría

rejoin [riːˈdʒɔɪn] *vt* (a) *(go back to)* reunirse con; **to r. one's regiment** reincorporarse al regimento (b) *(join again) (party, firm)* reincorporarse a; **the road rejoins the highway just outside town** la carretera vuelve a enlazar con la autopista justo al otro lado de la ciudad (c) *(retort)* replicar

rejoinder [rɪˈdʒɔɪndə(r)] *n* réplica *f*

rejuvenate [rɪˈdʒuːvɪneɪt] *vt* rejuvenecer

rejuvenating [rɪˈdʒuːvɪneɪtɪŋ] *adj* rejuvenecedor(ora) ►► ***r. cream*** crema *f* rejuvenecedora

rejuvenation [rɪdʒuːvɪˈneɪʃən] *n* rejuvenecimiento *m*

rekindle [riːˈkɪndəl] 1 *vt (fire)* volver a prender; *(enthusiasm, hope)* reavivar

2 *vi (fire)* volver a prenderse; *(feelings)* reavivar

relapse *Med* 1 *n* [ˈriːlæps] recaída *f*; **to have a r.** tener *or* sufrir una recaída

2 *vi* [rɪˈlæps] recaer, sufrir una recaída; **to r. into unconsciousness/a coma** volver a perder el conocimiento/a entrar en coma; *Fig* **they relapsed into silence** volvieron a callarse

relate [rɪˈleɪt] 1 *vt* (a) *(narrate)* relatar, narrar; **strange to r.,...** aunque parezca mentira... (b) *(connect) (two facts, ideas)* relacionar; **we can r. this episode to a previous scene in the novel** se puede relacionar este episodio con una escena previa de la novela

2 *vi* (a) *(connect) (idea, event)* **I don't see how the two ideas r.** no veo cuál es la relación entre las dos ideas; **to r. to sth** *(be relevant to)* estar relacionado(a) con algo; **questions relating to expenditure** las cuestiones relacionadas con los gastos

(b) *(have relationship, interact)* **she doesn't r. to other children very well** no tiene muy buena relación con los demás niños

(c) **to r. to sth** *(understand)* comprender *or* entender algo; **we can all r. to that** todos nos podemos identificar con eso

related [rɪˈleɪtɪd] *adj* (a) *(of same family)* **are they r.?** ¿están emparentados(as)?; **to be r. to** *(person)* ser pariente de; *(language)* estar emparentado(a) con; **they are related on his father's side** son parientes por parte de su padre; **to be r. by marriage** ser pariente político; **an animal r. to the weasel** un animal que tiene cierto parentesco con la comadreja

(b) *(linked)* relacionado(a); **problems r. to smoking** problemas relacionados *or* asociados con el tabaco; **the two events are not r.** los dos hechos no guardan relación

-related [rɪˈleɪtɪd] *suffix* **business-r. activities** actividades de carácter empresarial; **defence-r. industries** industrias relacionadas con la defensa

relation [rɪˈleɪʃən] *n* (a) *(relative)* pariente *mf*; **he's a distant r. (of mine)** es un pariente lejano (mío); **she is no r. of mine** no es pariente mía

(b) *(kinship)* parentesco *m*; **what r. is he to you?** ¿qué parentesco tiene contigo?

(c) *(connection)* relación *f*; **to have** *or* **bear no r. to** no guardar relación con; **in r. to salary** en relación con el *or* con relación al sueldo

(d) **relations** *(diplomatic, personal links)* relaciones *fpl*; **to enter into relations with** comenzar a tener relaciones con; **to break off/re-establish relations with** romper/restablecer relaciones con; **to have friendly relations with** tener relaciones de amistad con; *Formal* **to have (sexual) relations with** tener relaciones (sexuales) con

(e) *Formal (narration)* relación *f*, relato *m*

relational [rɪˈleɪʃənəl] *adj Comptr* ***r. database*** base *f* de datos relacional

relationship [rɪˈleɪʃənʃɪp] *n* (a) *(between people, countries)* relación *f*; **our r. is purely a business one** nuestra relación es estrictamente de negocios; **to have a good/bad r. with sb** llevarse bien/mal con alguien

(b) *(sexual)* relación *f*; **I'm already in a r.** tengo pareja; **to have a r. (with sb)** tener una relación (con alguien)

(c) *(connection)* relación *f*

(d) *(kinship)* parentesco *m*; **what is your exact r. to her?** ¿cuál es exactamente tu parentesco con ella?

relative [ˈrelətɪv] 1 *n (person)* pariente *mf*; **she is my only living r.** ella es el único pariente vivo que me queda *or* que tengo

2 *adj* (a) *(comparative)* relativo(a); **to live in r. comfort** vivir con cierta *or* relativa comodidad; **the r. qualities of the two candidates** las respectivas cualidades de los dos canditatos; **r. to** *(compared with)* en comparación con; **taxation should be r. to income** los impuestos deben guardar relación con los ingresos

(b) *(not absolute)* relativo(a) ►► *Br* ***r. majority*** mayoría *f* relativa

(c) *Gram (pronoun)* relativo(a) ►► ***r. clause*** oración *f* de relativo

(d) *Phys* ***r. density*** peso *m* específico

relatively [ˈrelətɪvlɪ] *adv* relativamente; **r. difficult/safe** relativamente difícil/seguro(a); **r. speaking,...** hablando en términos relativos...

relativism [ˈrelətɪvɪzəm] *n Phil* relativismo *m*

relativist [ˈrelətɪvɪst] 1 *n* relativista *mf*

2 *adj* relativista

relativistic [relətɪˈvɪstɪk] *adj* relativista

relativity [reləˈtɪvɪtɪ] *n Phys* relatividad *f*

relativize [ˈrelətɪvaɪz] *vt* relativizar

relaunch [riːˈlɔːntʃ] 1 *n* relanzamiento *m*

2 *vt* relanzar

relax [rɪˈlæks] 1 *vt* (a) *(person)* relajar (b) *(muscles, discipline, restrictions, laws)* relajar; **to r. one's hold** *or* **grip** dejar de apretar; **to r. one's grip on sth** *(country, party, business)* aflojar las riendas de algo

2 *vi* (a) *(person)* relajarse; **I won't be able to r. till I know it's over** no podré tranquilizarme *or* relajarme hasta que sepa que ha terminado; **r.!** *(calm down)* ¡tranquilízate!; **to r. in one's efforts** cejar en el esfuerzo (b) *(muscles, discipline)* relajarse; **his face relaxed into a smile** al distenderse, su rostro dibujó una sonrisa

relaxant [rɪˈlæksənt] *n* relajante *m*

relaxation [riːlækˈseɪʃən] *n* (a) *(of person)* relajación *f*; **he plays golf for r.** juega al golf para relajarse; **a form of r.** una forma de relajarse ►► ***r. therapy*** terapia *f* de relajación (b) *(of muscles, discipline, restrictions, laws)* relajación *f*

relaxed [rɪˈlækst] *adj (atmosphere, person)* relajado(a); **to feel/look r.** estar/parecer relajado(a); **he was very r. about changing the date** no le importó nada cambiar la fecha

relaxing [rɪˈlæksɪŋ] *adj* relajante; **she finds gardening r.** la jardinería le parece relajante

relay 1 *n* [ˈriːleɪ] (a) *(of workers)* relevo *m*, turno *m*; *(horses)* posta *f*; **to work in relays** trabajar por turnos (b) *Rad & TV* ***r. station*** repetidor *m* (c) *Elec* relé *m* (d) **r. (race)** carrera *f* de relevos

2 *vt* [rɪˈleɪ] (a) *Rad & TV* retransmitir (b) *(information)* pasar

re-lay [ˈriːˈleɪ] *vt (carpet)* recolocar

release [rɪˈliːs] 1 *n* (a) *(of prisoner, captive)* liberación *f*; **r. on parole/bail** libertad condicional/bajo fianza

(b) *(from care, worry)* alivio *m*; *(from obligation, promise)* liberación *f*; *(from pain, suffering)* liberación *f*, alivio *m*

(c) *(letting go) (of handle, brake)* liberación *f*; *(of bomb)* lanzamiento *m*

(d) *(issue) (of book, record)* publicación *f*; *(of movie)* estreno *m*; *(of software)* versión *f*; **new releases** *(records)* novedades (discográficas); **to be on general r.** *(movie)* estar en cartel

(e) *(of information)* comunicado *m*

(f) *(of gas, energy)* emisión *f*

(**g**) *(of funds)* liberación *f*
(**h**) *(lever, safety catch)* liberador *m*
2 *vt* (**a**) *(prisoner, captive, animal)* liberar, soltar; **to be released on bail/parole** ser liberado(a) bajo fianza/ser puesto(a) en libertad condicional; **to r. sb's hand** soltar la mano a alguien
(**b**) *(from care, worry)* librar, liberar; **to r. sb from an obligation/a promise** liberar a alguien de una obligación/una promesa; **to r. sb from a debt** eximir a alguien de una deuda
(**c**) *(handle, catch)* soltar, liberar; *(balloon, bomb, brake)* soltar; **to r. the clutch** soltar el embrague; **to r. the shutter** disparar el obturador; **he released his grip on my hand** me soltó la mano
(**d**) *(issue) (book, record)* publicar; *(movie)* estrenar; **to be released** *(software)* salir a la venta; *(movie)* estrenarse
(**e**) *(make public) (statement, news, information)* hacer público(a)
(**f**) *(gas, fumes, heat, light, energy)* desprender, emitir; **the explosion released chemicals into the river** la explosión contaminó el río con productos químicos
(**g**) *(funds)* liberar

relegate ['relɪgeɪt] *vt* (**a**) *(consign)* relegar; **we relegated the old bed to the spare room** relegamos la cama vieja a la habitación de huéspedes (**b**) *Br Sport* **United were relegated** el United bajó de categoría *or* descendió

relegation [relɪ'geɪʃən] *n* (**a**) *(of person, issue)* relegación *f* (**b**) *Br Sport (of team)* descenso *m*

relent [rɪ'lent] *vi* (**a**) *(person)* ceder; **he finally relented and let us go** finalmente cedió y nos dejó ir (**b**) *(storm, wind)* amainar

relentless [rɪ'lentlɪs] *adj* implacable; **she was r. in her search for the truth** no cesaba en su búsqueda de la verdad

relentlessly [rɪ'lentlɪslɪ] *adv* implacablemente; **the rain beat down r.** la lluvia caía inexorablemente

relevance ['reləvəns] *n* pertinencia *f*; **to have no r. to sth** no tener nada que ver con algo; **what is the r. of this to the matter under discussion?** ¿qué tiene que ver esto con lo que se está discutiendo?; **many students fail to see the practical r. of such courses** muchos alumnos no se dan cuenta de la importancia práctica de tales cursos

relevant ['reləvənt] *adj* pertinente; **to be r. (to sth)** tener que ver (con algo); **that's not r.** eso no viene al caso; **she doesn't have much r. experience** no tiene mucha experiencia pertinente; **the r. chapters** los capítulos correspondientes; **the r. facts** los hechos que vienen al caso; **the r. authorities** la autoridad competente; **her ideas are still r. today** sus ideas siguen teniendo vigencia

> **False friend:** The Spanish adjective **relevante** is not a translation for the English word **relevant**. In Spanish **relevante** means "outstanding, important".

reliability [rɪlaɪə'bɪlɪtɪ] *n* (**a**) *(of employee)* responsabilidad *f*; *(of witness, evidence, information)* fiabilidad *f*, *Am* confiabilidad *f* (**b**) *(of clock, engine, vehicle)* fiabilidad *f*, *Am* confiabilidad *f*

reliable [rɪ'laɪəbəl] *adj* (**a**) *(employee)* responsable; *(witness)* fiable, *Am* confiable; *(evidence, information)* fidedigno(a), fiable, *Am* confiable; **my memory isn't r.** no puedo confiar en mi memoria, no me puedo fiar de mi memoria; **from a r. source** de fuentes fidedignas (**b**) *(clock, engine, vehicle)* fiable, *Am* confiable

reliably [rɪ'laɪəblɪ] *adv* **to be r. informed that...** saber de buena fuente que...; **the engine performs r. in all weathers** el motor demuestra fiabilidad *or Am* confiabilidad en todas las condiciones climáticas

reliance [rɪ'laɪəns] *n* (**a**) *(dependence)* dependencia *f* (**on** de) (**b**) *(trust)* confianza *f* (**on** en); **to place r. on sth/sb** depositar la confianza en algo/alguien

reliant [rɪ'laɪənt] *adj* **to be r. on** depender de; **we are heavily r. on their advice/funding** dependemos mucho de su asesoramiento/financiamiento

relic ['relɪk] *n* (**a**) *(reminder of past, remnant)* reliquia *f*; **the last surviving r. of** la última reliquia que queda de; *Hum* **their TV is an old r.** su televisor es una verdadera reliquia (**b**) *Rel* reliquia *f*

relief [rɪ'li:f] *n* (**a**) *(alleviation)* alivio *m*; **it offers r. from pain** alivia el dolor; **to bring r. to sb** aliviar a alguien; **it came as a r.** fue un alivio; **to provide some light r.** *(humour)* poner la nota cómica; **that's** *or* **what a r.!** ¡qué alivio!; **much to my r., to my great r.** para alivio mío; **it was a r. to know they were safe** fue un alivio saber que estaban a salvo ►► ***r. road*** vía *m* de descongestión
(**b**) *(aid)* ayuda *f*, auxilio *m*; **to send r. to third world countries** enviar ayuda a países del tercer mundo ►► ***r. agency*** organización *f* de ayuda humanitaria *(que trabaja sobre el terreno)*; ***r. convoy*** convoy *m* de ayuda humanitaria; ***r. fund*** fondo *m* de ayuda; ***r. worker*** trabajador(ora) *m,f* de ayuda humanitaria
(**c**) *US (state benefit)* **to be on r.** cobrar un subsidio
(**d**) *(replacement)* relevo *m* ►► ***r. driver*** conductor(ora) *m,f* de relevo; *US* ***r. pitcher*** lanzador(ora) *m,f* sustituto(a)
(**e**) *(of besieged city, troops)* liberación *f*
(**f**) *Art* relieve *m*; **high/low r.** alto/bajo relieve; **in r.** en relieve; *Fig* **to throw** *or* **bring sth into r.** poner algo de relieve
(**g**) *Geog* relieve *m*; **an area of low r.** una zona con poco relieve ►► ***r. map*** mapa *m* de relieve

relieve [rɪ'li:v] *vt* (**a**) *(alleviate) (pain, anxiety, problem)* aliviar; *(tension, boredom)* atenuar, mitigar; **we were greatly relieved by the news** la noticia nos tranquilizó mucho; **the darkness of the room was relieved only by the firelight** sólo el fuego daba un poco de luz a la oscuridad de la sala; **they relieved the monotony of the wait by playing cards** hicieron la espera menos monótona jugando a cartas
(**b**) *(replace)* relevar
(**c**) *(liberate) (besieged city, troops)* liberar
(**d**) *(take away)* **to r. sb of a burden/obligation** quitar a alguien una carga/obligación; *Formal* **can I r. you of your suitcase?** ¿quiere que le lleve la maleta?; *Formal* **he was relieved of his post** *or* **duties** fue apartado de su puesto; *Hum* **somebody relieved me of my wallet** alguien me afanó la cartera
(**e**) *Euph* **he relieved himself** hizo sus necesidades

relieved [rɪ'li:vd] *adj (sigh, laugh)* de alivio; **to feel relieved** sentirse aliviado(a)

religion [rɪ'lɪdʒən] *n* (**a**) *(faith)* religión *f*; **it's against my r.** va contra mis principios religiosos; *Fam* **to get r.** volverse creyente (**b**) *(obsession)* obsesión *f*; IDIOM **to make a r. of sth** hacer de algo una forma de vida

religiosity [rɪlɪdʒɪ'ɒsətɪ] *n* religiosidad *f*

religious [rɪ'lɪdʒəs] **1** *adj* (**a**) *(authority, ceremony, art)* religioso(a) ►► ***r. education*** *(subject)* (asignatura *f* de) religión *f*; ***r. instruction*** instrucción *f* religiosa; ***r. order*** orden *f* religiosa (**b**) *(devout)* religioso(a) (**c**) *(scrupulous)* escrupuloso(a), meticuloso(a); **to do sth with r. care** hacer algo con un cuidado extremo
2 *n (monk, nun)* religioso(a) *m,f*

religiously [rɪ'lɪdʒəslɪ] *adv* (**a**) *(in a religious manner)* religiosamente (**b**) *(scrupulously)* religiosamente, escrupulosamente

reline [ri:'laɪn] *vt (garment)* forrar de nuevo; *(picture)* colocar una nueva tela de soporte a; **to r. the brakes** cambiar el revestimiento *or* forro de los frenos

relinquish [rɪ'lɪŋkwɪʃ] *vt (claim, responsibility, rights)* renunciar a; *(hope, power)* abandonar; *(property)* renunciar a; **to r. the throne to sb** ceder el trono a alguien; **to r. one's hold** *or* **grip on sth** *(let go)* soltar algo; **she refused to r. her hold** *or* **grip on the party** se negó a abandonar su control sobre el partido

reliquary ['relɪkwərɪ] *n* relicario *m*

relish ['relɪʃ] **1** *n* (**a**) *(pleasure)* deleite *m*, goce *m*; **to do sth with r.** hacer algo con gran deleite; **he has lost his r. for reading** leer ha dejado de parecerle placentero (**b**) *(pickle)* salsa *f* condimentada
2 *vt* gozar con, deleitarse en; **I bet he's relishing this moment** me imagino que estará disfrutando de este momento; **I didn't r. the idea** no me entusiasmaba la idea

relive [ri:'lɪv] *vt* revivir

reload [ri:'ləʊd] **1** *vt (gun, camera)* volver a cargar; *(ship, software)* recargar, volver a cargar
2 *vi (person with firearm)* volver a cargar el arma; *(photographer)* cambiar el carrete; *(gun, software)* recargarse

relocate [ri:ləʊ'keɪt] **1** *vt* (**a**) *(move)* trasladar; **the facilities were relocated to Scotland** trasladaron las instalaciones a Escocia (**b**) *(find)* localizar de nuevo
2 *vi* mudarse, trasladarse (**to** a)

relocation [ri:ləʊ'keɪʃən] *n* traslado *m* ►► ***r. allowance*** *(for employee)* suplemento *m* por traslado; ***r. expenses*** *(for employee)* gastos *mpl* de traslado

reluctance [rɪ'lʌktəns] *n* resistencia *f*, reticencia *f*; **to do sth with r.** hacer algo a regañadientes; **she expressed some r. to get involved** se mostró algo reticente *or* reacia a involucrarse; **his r. to admit the truth** su reticencia a admitir la verdad

reluctant [rɪ'lʌktənt] *adj* reacio(a), reticente; **she gave a r. smile** sonrió forzadamente; **he was a r. sex symbol** no estaba muy contento con su rol de sex symbol; **to be r. to do sth** ser reacio(a) a hacer algo

reluctantly [rɪ'lʌktəntlɪ] *adv* de mala gana; **to do sth r.** hacer algo de mala gana

rely [rɪ'laɪ]

► **rely on, rely upon** *vt insep* (**a**) *(count on)* contar con; **I'm relying on you to do it** cuento con que vas a hacerlo; **we were relying on the weather being good** contábamos con que hiciera buen tiempo; *Ironic* you can r. on them to get things wrong puedes estar seguro de que la pifiarán; she can't be relied on no se puede contar con ella; he can never be relied on to keep a secret no esperes que guarde un secreto (b) *(be dependent on)* depender de; he relies on his family for everything depende de su familia para todo; I r. on my daughter to drive me to the shops dependo de mi hija para que me lleve a hacer las compras; the plan relies too much on luck el plan depende demasiado de la suerte

REM [ɑːriː'em] *n* (*abbr* **rapid eye movement**) (fase *f*) REM *m* ►► ***R. sleep*** sueño *m* REM *or* paradójico

remain [rɪ'meɪn] *vi* (a) *(stay behind)* quedarse; **she remained at her desk** se quedó en su mesa; **he remained behind after the meeting** se quedó allí después de la reunión

(b) *(be left)* quedar; **much remains to be discussed** aún queda mucho por discutir; **it remains to be seen** queda *or* está por ver; **the fact remains that...** el hecho es que...; **all that remained to be done was to say goodbye** sólo faltaba *or* quedaba decir adiós; **it only remains for me to thank you** sólo me queda agradecerte

(c) *(continue to be)* seguir siendo; **to r. seated** quedarse sentado(a); **I r. unconvinced** sigo sin convencerme; **the weather remains unsettled** el tiempo continúa inestable; **the crime remains unsolved** el crimen aún no ha sido esclarecido *or* resuelto; **to r. silent** permanecer callado(a); **to r. a problem** continuar siendo un problema; **the result remains in doubt** todavía no se sabe cuál va a ser el resultado; **let things r. as they are** dejemos las cosas como están; **to r. faithful to** permanecer fiel a; *Formal* **I r., yours faithfully...** le saluda muy atentamente...

remainder [rɪ'meɪndə(r)] **1** *n* (a) *(leftover)* resto *m*; **for the r. of his life** (por) el resto de su vida; **she spent the r. on sweets** gastó lo que quedaba *or* sobraba en dulces (b) *Math* resto *m* (c) *(unsold book)* saldos *mpl*

2 *vt (books)* liquidar

remaindered [rɪ'meɪndəd] *adj* **r. books** libros de saldo

remaining [rɪ'meɪnɪŋ] *adj* restante; **it's our only r. hope** es la única esperanza que nos queda

remains [rɪ'meɪnz] *npl* (a) *(of meal)* sobras *fpl*, restos *mpl*; *(of civilization, fortune)* restos *mpl*; *(of old building)* ruinas *fpl* (b) *(of person)* restos *mpl* (mortales); **human r.** restos humanos (c) *Old-fashioned* **(literary) r.** obras *fpl* póstumas

remake 1 *vt* [riː'meɪk] *(movie)* hacer una nueva versión de; *Fig* **he remade himself in the image of his hero** se reinventó a imagen de su ídolo

2 *n* ['riːmeɪk] *(of movie)* nueva versión *f*

remand [rɪ'mɑːnd] **1** *n Law* **to be on r.** *(in custody)* estar en prisión preventiva; **to be out on r.** estar en libertad bajo fianza ►► *Br* ***r. centre*** centro *m* de preventivos; ***r. home*** = centro de reclusión para delincuentes juveniles a la espera de juicio; ***r. prisoner*** preso(a) *m,f* preventivo(a)

2 *vt Law* **to r. sb in custody** poner a alguien en prisión preventiva; **to r. sb on bail** dejar a alguien en libertad bajo fianza

remark [rɪ'mɑːk] **1** *n* (a) *(comment)* comentario *m*; **to make** *or* **pass a r.** hacer un comentario; **she made the r. that no one really knew the truth** apuntó que nadie en realidad sabía la verdad; **to let sth pass without r.** dejar que algo pase desapercibido

(b) *Formal (notice)* **worthy of r.** digno(a) de destacar; **his behaviour did not escape r.** su comportamiento no pasó desapercibido

2 *vt* (a) *(comment)* comentar, observar; **to r. (up)on sth** comentar *or* observar algo; **he remarked on the lateness of the hour** comentó que era muy tarde (b) *Formal (notice)* observar; **it may be remarked that...** puede observarse que...

> **False friend**: The Spanish verb **remarcar** is not a translation for the English word **remark**. In Spanish **remarcar** means "to underline, to stress".

remarkable [rɪ'mɑːkəbəl] *adj (impressive)* extraordinario(a), excepcional; *(surprising)* insólito(a), sorprendente; **they are r. for their bright plumage** destacan por su plumaje brillante

remarkably [rɪ'mɑːkəblɪ] *adv (impressively)* extraordinariamente, excepcionalmente; *(surprisingly)* insólitamente, sorprendentemente; **she was looking r. well** tenía un aspecto estupendo; **r., most of the crew survived** insólitamente, gran parte de la tripulación sobrevivió

remarriage [riː'mærɪdʒ] *n* segundo matrimonio *m*, segundas nupcias *fpl*

remarry [riː'mærɪ] **1** *vt (first spouse)* volver a casarse con, contraer segundas nupcias con

2 *vi* volver a casarse, contraer segundas nupcias

remaster [riː'mɑːstə(r)] *vt (album)* remasterizar

rematch ['riːmætʃ] *n Sport* revancha *f*

REME ['riːmiː] *n Br* (*abbr* **Royal Electrical and Mechanical Engineers**) = sección de ingenieros electromecánicos del ejército de Tierra británico

remediable [rɪ'miːdɪəbəl] *adj* remediable; **the fault is easily r.** *Esp* el fallo *or Am* la falla se puede arreglar fácilmente

remedial [rɪ'miːdɪəl] *adj* (a) *(action, measures)* correctivo(a); **to take r. action** tomar medidas correctivas (b) *(classes)* de refuerzo; **she teaches r. maths** da clases de refuerzo de matemáticas ►► ***r. education*** enseñanza *f* de refuerzo; ***r. teacher*** = profesor especializado en enseñanza de refuerzo (c) *Med (treatment)* rehabilitador(ora), de rehabilitación

remedy ['remɪdɪ] **1** *n* (a) *(cure)* remedio *m*; **to find a r. for sth** encontrar el remedio para algo; **it's past** *or* **beyond r.** ya no tiene remedio (b) *Br Law* remedio *m*, satisfacción *f*

2 *vt* poner remedio a, remediar; **the situation cannot be remedied** la situación no tiene remedio

REMEMBER [rɪ'membə(r)] **1** *vt* (a) *(recall)* recordar, acordarse de; **to r. (that)...** recordar que...; **don't you r. me?** ¿no te acuerdas de mí?; **I'll r. his name in a minute** su nombre me vendrá enseguida a la memoria; **we have nothing to r. him by** no tenemos nada que nos lo recuerde; **to r. doing sth** recordar haber hecho algo, acordarse de haber hecho algo; **I r. them saying something about a party** me acuerdo de que *or* recuerdo que mencionaron una fiesta; **to r. to do sth** acordarse de hacer algo; **r. to lock the door** no te olvides de cerrar *or Am* trancar la puerta; **a night to r.** una noche inolvidable; **I r. her as an awkward teenager** la recuerdo como una adolescente difícil; **he will be remembered for his good humour** se lo recordará por su buen humor; **r. where you are/who you're talking to!** no olvides dónde estás/con quién estás hablando; **he remembered himself just in time** se contuvo justo a tiempo; **let us r. them in our prayers** recemos por ellos

(b) *(give greetings from)* **r. me to your father** dale recuerdos a tu padre de mi parte

(c) *(give gift)* **they remembered me on my birthday** me dieron un regalo de cumpleaños, *Esp* me dieron un regalo por mi cumpleaños; **she remembered me in her will** me dejó algo en su testamento

(d) *(commemorate)* recordar

2 *vi* recordar, acordarse; **who's Mary? – Mary, you r., my brother's wife** ¿quién es Mary? – Mary, ¿(no) te acuerdas?, la esposa de mi hermano *or Esp* Mary, sí, hombre, la mujer de mi hermano; **as far as I r.** por lo que yo recuerdo, por lo que yo me acuerdo; **it has been like that for as long as I can r.** desde que lo conozco siempre ha sido así, *Am* ha sido así desde que tengo memoria; **if I r. correctly** si mal no recuerdo

> Hay una serie de verbos en inglés que pueden ir seguidos tanto como de infinitivo como de gerundio sin que apenas cambie su significado; por ejemplo **begin**, **bother**, **continue**, **hate**, **like** o **try**. Sin embargo, **remember** es uno de los pocos verbos en los que existe una clara diferencia entre ambas opciones:
> **I remembered to buy the fish on the way home**
> *me acordé de comprar el pescado de camino a casa*
> **she remembers leaving the party, but nothing after that**
> *se acuerda de haberse marchado de la fiesta, pero de nada más después de eso*

remembrance [rɪ'membrəns] *n Formal (memory)* recuerdo *m*; **I have no r. of it** no lo recuerdo; **in r. of** en recuerdo *or* conmemoración de; **r. service, service of r.** *(for war dead)* oficio por los caídos; *(for recently deceased person)* oficio de difuntos ►► *Br* ***R. Day, R. Sunday*** día *m* de homenaje a los caídos *(en las guerras mundiales)*

remind [rɪ'maɪnd] *vt* recordar (**of** a); **could you r. me about my appointment?** ¿me podrías recordar la cita?; **she reminds me of my sister** me recuerda a mi hermana; **they reminded him of the rules** le recordaron las normas; **do I need to r. you how important this meeting is?** ¿es que tengo que recordarte lo importante que es esta reunión?; **I'm glad you reminded me** me alegro de que me lo hayas recordado; **she reminded herself that he was still very young** se recordó a sí misma que él era todavía muy joven; **to r. sb to do sth** recordar a alguien que haga algo; **that reminds me... did you get the cheese?** a propósito *or* ahora que recuerdo... ¿has comprado el queso?; **passengers are reminded that the duty-free shop will close in five minutes** se recuerda a los señores pasajeros que el duty-free cerrará sus puertas en cinco minutos

reminder [rɪˈmaɪndə(r)] *n* aviso *m*; **it serves as a useful r.** sirve de recordatorio; **his bad leg was a constant r. of the accident** su pierna mala le recordaba constantemente el accidente; **the exhibition is a stark** *or* **grim r. of the horrors of war** la exposición es un crudo recordatorio de los horrores de la guerra; **to give/send sb a r. (to do sth)** dar/enviar a alguien un recordatorio (para que haga algo)

reminisce [remɪˈnɪs] *vi* rememorar; **to r. about sth** rememorar algo

reminiscence [remɪˈnɪsəns] *n* rememoración *f*, remembranza *f*; **we listened to his reminiscences of the war** escuchamos sus remembranzas de la guerra

reminiscent [remɪˈnɪsənt] *adj* (**a**) *(suggestive)* **to be r. of** evocar, tener reminiscencias de; **in a voice r. of her mother's** con una voz que recordaba a la de su madre; **parts of the book are r. of Proust** algunas partes del libro recuerdan a Proust (**b**) *(nostalgic) (smile, mood)* nostálgico(a)

remiss [rɪˈmɪs] *adj Formal* negligente, descuidado(a); **he is r. in his duties** desempeña sus funciones con negligencia; **it was very r. of him** fue muy descuidado por su parte

remission [rɪˈmɪʃən] *n* (**a**) *Law* reducción *f* de la pena (**b**) *(of disease)* **to be in r.** haber remitido (**c**) *(of sins)* remisión *f*

remit [rɪˈmɪt] **1** *n* [ˈriːmɪt] cometido *m*; **our r. is to...** nuestro cometido es...; **that goes beyond/comes within our r.** eso está fuera de/dentro de nuestro ámbito de actuación

2 *vt* (*pt & pp* **remitted**) (**a**) *(dispense with)* dispensar, eximir; **his exam fees were remitted** lo eximieron del pago del derecho de examen

(**b**) *(send) (money)* remitir, girar

(**c**) *Law (cancel)* perdonar, condonar; **his sentence was remitted by five years** le redujeron la pena cinco años

(**d**) *Law (transfer)* **to r. a case to a lower court** remitir un caso a un tribunal inferior

(**e**) *(sins)* perdonar

3 *vi (fever, disease)* remitir

remittance [rɪˈmɪtəns] *n Fin* giro *m*, envío *m* de dinero ►► ***r. advice*** aviso *m* de pago

remittent [rɪˈmɪtənt] *adj Med (fever)* remitente

remix *Mus* **1** *n* [ˈriːmɪks] remezcla *f*

2 *vt* [riːˈmɪks] volver a mezclar

remnant [ˈremnənt] *n* (**a**) *(of banquet, building)* resto *m*; **the remnants of his fortune** los restos de su fortuna; **the remnants of the army straggled home** lo que quedaba del ejército fue regresando poco a poco (**b**) *(of civilization, dignity)* vestigio *m* (**c**) *(of cloth)* retal *m*

remodel [ˈriːˈmɒdəl] (*Br pt & pp* **remodelled,** *US pt & pp* **remodeled**) *vt (building, facade)* remodelar

remold *US* = **remould**

remonstrance [rɪˈmɒnstrəns] *n Formal (protest)* protesta *f*

remonstrate [ˈremənstreɪt] *vi Formal* quejarse, protestar; **to r. with sb** tratar de hacer entrar en razón a alguien; **she remonstrated with him over his decision** trató de convencerle de que cambiara su decisión

remora [ˈremərə] *n* rémora *f*

remorse [rɪˈmɔːs] *n* remordimientos *mpl*; **he was filled with r. at what he had done** los remordimientos por lo que había hecho lo abrumaban; **to feel r.** tener remordimientos; **to show no r.** no mostrar remordimientos; **in a fit of r.** en un ataque de culpa; **without r.** sin remordimientos

remorseful [rɪˈmɔːsfʊl] *adj* lleno(a) de remordimientos; **to be r.** tener remordimientos

remorsefully [rɪˈmɔːsfʊlɪ] *adv* con remordimiento

remorseless [rɪˈmɔːslɪs] *adj* (**a**) *(merciless)* despiadado(a) (**b**) *(relentless)* implacable; **he was r. in the demands that he made on his employees** era implacable en lo que les exigía a sus empleados

remorselessly [rɪˈmɔːslɪslɪ] *adv* (**a**) *(mercilessly)* despiadadamente (**b**) *(relentlessly)* implacablemente

remortgage [riːˈmɔːgɪdʒ] *vt (house, property)* volver a hipotecar

remote [rɪˈməʊt] **1** *n (for TV)* mando *m* a distancia, telemando *m*

2 *adj* (**a**) *(far-off) (time, place)* remoto(a), lejano(a); *(ancestor)* lejano(a); **in the r. future/past** en un futuro/pasado remoto; **in the remotest parts of the continent** en las regiones más remotas del continente; **his plays are r. from everyday life** sus obras no tienen nada que ver con la vida cotidiana

(**b**) *(aloof)* distante

(**c**) *(slight) (chance, possibility)* remoto(a); **it's a r. possibility** es una posibilidad muy remota; **I haven't the remotest idea** no tengo ni la más remota idea

(**d**) *(controlled from a distance) (computer terminal)* remoto(a) ►► ***r. access*** *(to computer, answering machine)* acceso *m* remoto; ***r. control*** *(for TV, video)* mando *m* a distancia, telemando *m*; *(for gate, robot)* control *m* remoto; **it's guided by r. control** se mueve por control remoto; ***r. handling equipment*** *(in nuclear engineering)* equipo *m* para el manejo a distancia; *Astron* ***r. sensing*** detección *f* a distancia

remote-controlled [rɪˈməʊtkənˈtrəʊld] *adj* teledirigido(a)

remotely [rɪˈməʊtlɪ] *adv* (**a**) *(distantly)* remotamente, lejanamente; **the two subjects are only very r. linked** existe sólo una muy lejana relación entre los dos temas (**b**) *(slightly)* remotamente; **not r.** ni remotamente, ni de lejos

remoteness [rɪˈməʊtnɪs] *n* (**a**) *(in space)* lejanía *f*, lo remoto; *(in time)* lo remoto, lo distante (**b**) *(aloofness) (of person)* distanciamiento *m*

remould, *US* **remold** **1** *vt* [riːˈməʊld] (**a**) *(person, character)* volver a amoldar (**b**) *Br (tyre)* recauchutar

2 *n* [ˈriːməʊld] *Br Aut* neumático *m* recauchutado, *Col, Méx* llanta *f or Arg* goma *f* recauchutada

remount [riːˈmaʊnt] **1** *vt* (**a**) *(horse, bicycle)* volver a subir a (**b**) *(picture)* volver a enmarcar; *(jewel)* volver a engastar

2 *vi (on horse, bicycle)* volver a subirse *or* montarse

removable [rɪˈmuːvəbəl] *adj (hood, handle)* de quita y pon; **this stain is r.** esta mancha se va ►► *Comptr* ***r. hard disk*** disco *m* duro extraíble *or* removible

removal [rɪˈmuːvəl] *n* (**a**) *(taking away) (of structure, object)* retirada *f*; *(of organ, tumour)* extirpación *f*; *(of stain, wart)* eliminación *f*; **it makes the r. of make-up easier** hace que desmaquillarse sea más fácil

(**b**) *(of politician, official)* destitución *f*; **r. from office** destitución *or Andes, RP* remoción del cargo

(**c**) *(taking off) (of garment, covering, tyre)* **after r. of the bandage** después de quitarse la venda; **it makes r. of the tyre easier** hace que quitar la rueda sea más fácil

(**d**) *(suppression) (of clause, paragraph, word)* supresión *f*, eliminación *f*; *(of control, doubt, threat)* eliminación *f*; *(of suspicion)* eliminación *f*; *(of fear)* eliminación *f*, supresión *f*

(**e**) *(moving house)* mudanza *f*; *(change of residence)* traslado *m*, mudanza *f* ►► ***r. man*** empleado *m* de la compañía de mudanzas, *Arg* hombre *m* de la mudanza; ***r. van*** camión *m* de mudanzas

remove [rɪˈmuːv] **1** *n Formal* **they're at one r. from an agreement** están a un paso de alcanzar un acuerdo; **her account is (at) several removes from the truth** su versión dista bastante de la verdad; **to experience sth at one r.** experimentar algo indirectamente

2 *vt* (**a**) *(take away) (thing)* quitar, retirar, *Am* sacar; *(wart)* eliminar; *(tumour, organ)* extirpar; *(stain)* quitar, *Am* sacar; *(make-up)* quitar; *Comptr (file)* eliminar; **to r. hair from one's legs** *(with wax)* depilarse las piernas; *(with razor)* afeitarse las piernas; **the chairs were removed to the attic** se llevaron las sillas al desván *or* altillo

(**b**) *(person) (politician, official)* destituir; **his opponents had him removed from office** sus oponentes consiguieron su destitución; **to r. a child from school** no llevar más a un niño al colegio; **she was removed to hospital** fue trasladada al hospital; *Formal* **she removed herself to her room** se retiró a sus aposentos; **police removed the demonstrators from the hall** la policía sacó a los manifestantes de la sala; **the judge ordered her to be removed from the court** el juez ordenó su expulsión de la sala

(**c**) *(take off) (bandage, covering, tyre)* quitar, *Am* sacar; **to r. one's coat** quitarse *or Am* sacarse el abrigo

(**d**) *(suppress) (clause, paragraph, word)* suprimir; *(doubt)* despejar; *(control, threat, suspicion)* eliminar; *(fear)* eliminar, suprimir; **all obstacles have been removed** todos los obstáculos han sido eliminados; **I hope this removes your objection** espero que ahora te des por satisfecho; **to r. sb's name from a list** eliminar *or* quitar el nombre de alguien de una lista

(**e**) *Euph (kill)* eliminar; **I want him removed** quiero que lo eliminen

3 *vi Formal (firm, premises, family)* mudarse, trasladarse

removed [rɪˈmuːvd] *adj* **to be far r. from sth** estar muy lejos de algo; **what you say is not far r. from the truth** lo que dices no está muy lejos de la verdad; **first cousin once/twice r.** primo(a) segundo(a)/tercero(a)

remover [rɪˈmuːvə(r)] *n* (**a**) *(liquid)* **paint r.** decapante; **nail varnish r.** quitaesmaltes (**b**) **(furniture) removers** *(people)* empleados *mpl* de mudanzas; *(firm)* (empresa *f* de) mudanzas *fpl*

remunerate [rɪˈmjuːnəreɪt] *vt Formal* remunerar, retribuir

remuneration [rɪmjuːnəˈreɪʃən] *n Formal* remuneración *f*, retribución *f* ►► ***r. package*** paquete *m* de beneficios

remunerative [rɪˈmjuːnərətɪv] *adj Formal* bien remunerado(a); **it's not very r.** no está muy bien remunerado

renaissance [rɪ'neɪsəns] *n* (**a**) *(renewal of interest, activity)* renacimiento *m*; **a r. in the arts** un renacimiento de las artes (**b**) *Hist* **the R.** el Renacimiento ►► ***r. man*** hombre *m* de muchos talentos

renal ['ri:nəl] *adj Anat* renal ►► *Med* ***r. colic*** cólico *m* nefrítico *or* renal

rename [ri:'neɪm] *vt* (**a**) *(person, street)* cambiar el nombre a (**b**) *Comptr (file)* cambiar el nombre a

renascent [rɪ'næsənt] *adj* renovado(a)

renationalization [ri:næʃənəlaɪ'zeɪʃən] *n* renacionalización *f*

renationalize [ri:'næʃənəlaɪz] *vt* renacionalizar

rend [rend] (*pt & pp* **rent** [rent]) *vt Literary* (**a**) *(tear)* desgarrar; **the country was rent by civil war** el país quedó destrozado por la guerra civil; **the party was rent apart by this dispute** la disputa provocó la ruptura del partido; **their cries rent the air** sus llantos desgarraron el aire; IDIOM **to r. sb's heart** destrozar el corazón de alguien

(**b**) *(wrench)* arrancar; **the child was rent from its mother's arms** arrancaron al niño de los brazos de su madre

render ['rendə(r)] *vt* (**a**) *Formal (give)* **to r. homage to sb** rendir homenaje a alguien; **to r. thanks to sb** dar las gracias a alguien; **to r. sb a service** prestar un servicio a alguien; **for services rendered** por los servicios prestados; IDIOM **r. unto Caesar the things that are Caesar's** al César lo que es del César

(**b**) *(cause to be)* dejar; **the news rendered her speechless** la noticia la dejó sin habla; **a misprint rendered the text incomprehensible** un error de imprenta hizo que el texto fuera inentendible; **to r. sth harmless** hacer que algo resulte inofensivo(a); **to r. sth useless** inutilizar algo

(**c**) *(submit) (bill, account)* presentar

(**d**) *(translate)* traducir; **to r. sth into French** traducir *or* vertir algo al francés

(**e**) *(perform) (song, piece of music)* interpretar

(**f**) *(convey, portray) (scene, atmosphere)* describir, retratar

(**g**) *(fat)* derretir; *(carcass)* desgrasar

(**h**) *Constr* revestir, cubrir

(**i**) *Comptr (image)* renderizar

►**render down** *vt sep (fat)* derretir

►**render up** *vt sep (yield)* entregar

renderer ['rendərə(r)] *n (of carcasses)* transformador(ora) *m,f*

rendering ['rendərɪŋ] *n* (**a**) *(translation)* traducción *f* (**b**) *(performance) (of song, piece of music)* interpretación *f* (**c**) *(of carcasses)* transformación *f* ►► ***r. plant*** planta *f* procesadora (**d**) *Constr (coat of plaster)* enlucido *m* (**e**) *Comptr (of image)* renderizado *m*

rendezvous ['rɒndɪvu:] **1** *n* (*pl* **rendezvous** ['rɒndɪvu:z]) *(meeting)* cita *f*; *(meeting place)* lugar *m* de encuentro; **to arrange a r. with sb** concertar un encuentro con alguien

2 *vi* encontrarse, reunirse (**with** con)

rendition [ren'dɪʃən] *n* interpretación *f*; **to give a r. of sth** interpretar algo

> **False friend**: The Spanish noun **rendición** is not a translation for the English word **rendition**. In Spanish **rendición** means "surrender".

renegade ['renɪgeɪd] **1** *n* renegado(a) *m,f*

2 *adj* renegado(a)

renege [rɪ'neɪg] *vi* (**a**) *Formal* **to r. on a promise** incumplir una promesa (**b**) *(in cards)* renunciar

renegotiate [ri:nɪ'gəʊʃɪeɪt] **1** *vt* renegociar

2 *vi* renegociar

renegotiation ['ri:nɪgəʊʃɪ'eɪʃən] *n* renegociación *f*

renew [rɪ'nju:] *vt* (**a**) *(passport, membership, library book, contract, subscription)* renovar (**b**) *(repeat) (attempts, calls, attacks)* reanudar; *(promise, request, threat)* reiterar (**c**) *(relations, friendship)* reanudar; **to r. one's acquaintance with sb** reanudar una relación con alguien (**d**) *(replace) (brakes, tyres)* renovar, cambiar; **to r. one's wardrobe** renovar el vestuario

renewable [rɪ'nju:əbəl] *adj (lease, contract)* renovable ►► ***r. energy source*** fuente *f* de energía renovable; ***r. resource*** recurso *m* renovable

renewal [rɪ'nju:əl] *n* (**a**) *(of passport, membership, library book, contract, subscription)* renovación *f* (**b**) *(of attempts, calls, attacks)* reanudación *f*; *(of promise, request, threat)* reiteración *f* (**c**) *(of relations, friendship)* reanudación *f* (**d**) *(spiritual, moral)* renovación *f*

renewed [rɪ'nju:d] *adj (vigour, interest, enthusiasm)* renovado(a); **r. outbreaks of rioting** renovados focos de disturbios; **there have been r. calls for his resignation** se ha vuelto a pedir su dimisión

rennet ['renɪt] *n Culin* cuajo *m*

renounce [rɪ'naʊns] *vt (claim, title, nationality, religion, belief, behaviour)* renunciar a; *Rel* **to r. Satan and all his works** renunciar al demonio y sus obras

renovate ['renəveɪt] *vt (house)* renovar, reformar; *(painting, monument)* restaurar

renovation [renə'veɪʃən] *n* (**a**) *(of building)* reformas *fpl*, renovación *f*; **closed for renovation(s)** *(notice in shop window)* cerrado por reformas; **to carry out renovations** realizar reformas (**b**) *(of painting, monument)* restauración *f*

renown [rɪ'naʊn] *n* fama *f*, renombre *m*; **a man of great r.** un hombre de mucha fama *or* de mucho renombre; **to win r.** adquirir fama (**as/for** como/por)

renowned [rɪ'naʊnd] *adj* célebre, renombrado(a); **here he painted his r. Mona Lisa** aquí pintó su célebre Mona Lisa; **an internationally r. expert** un experto reconocido mundialmente; **to be r. for sth** ser célebre *or* muy conocido(a) por algo

rent[1] [rent] **1** *n (on property)* alquiler *m*; **for r.** *(house)* en alquiler; *(sign)* se alquila; **how much r. do you pay?** ¿cuánto pagas de alquiler? ►► ***r. allowance*** complemento *m* para el alquiler; ***r. book*** = libro que registra la fecha y el pago del alquiler por un inquilino; *Br Fam* ***r. boy*** *(male prostitute)* puto *m*, chapero *m*; ***r. collector*** cobrador(ora) *m,f* del alquiler; ***r. rebate*** subsidio *m* de alquiler; ***r. strike*** = forma de protesta por la que los inquilinos dejan de pagar el alquiler; ***r. tribunal*** tribunal *m* de alquileres

2 *vt (house, video, car)* alquilar (**to/from** a); **we r. our offices from the local government** alquilamos nuestras oficinas al gobierno local; **he rented one of his houses to us** nos alquiló una de sus casas

3 *vi* (**a**) *(tenant)* estar de alquiler; **he doesn't own the house, he rents** no es dueño de la casa, está de alquiler (**b**) *US (property)* **it rents for $600 a month** se alquila por 600 dólares al mes

►**rent out** *vt sep* alquilar

rent[2] **1** *n (tear) (in clothing)* rasgadura *f*; *(in clouds)* claro *m*

2 *pt & pp of* **rend**

rent-a-mob ['rentə'mɒb] *n Br Fam (protestors)* agitadores *mpl* violentos

rental ['rentəl] *n* (**a**) *(hire) (of house, video, car)* alquiler *m* ►► ***r. agreement*** contrato *m* de alquiler; ***r. car*** coche *m or Am* carro *m or CSur* auto *m* de alquiler; ***r. with option to buy*** alquiler *m* con opción a compra (**b**) *(payment) (for house, video, car, telephone)* alquiler *m* (**c**) *US (property)* vivienda *f* de alquiler; *(vehicle)* vehículo *m* de alquiler

rented ['rentɪd] *adj* alquilado(a), de alquiler; **we live in r. accommodation** estamos en una vivienda de alquiler

rent-free ['rent'fri:] **1** *adj* exento(a) del pago de alquiler

2 *adv* sin pagar alquiler

rent-roll ['rent'rəʊl] *n Br (register)* registro *m* de alquileres; *(income)* ingresos *mpl* por alquiler

renumber ['ri:'nʌmbə(r)] *vt* renumerar

renunciation [rɪnʌnsɪ'eɪʃən] *n (of claim, title, nationality, religion)* renuncia *f*; *(of belief, behaviour)* rechazo *m*

reoccupy [ri:'ɒkjʊpaɪ] *vt* ocupar de nuevo

reopen [ri:'əʊpən] **1** *vt* (**a**) *(door, wound, shop, theatre, frontier)* reabrir, volver a abrir; IDIOM **to r. old wounds** abrir viejas heridas (**b**) *(investigation)* reabrir; *(talks)* reanudar

2 *vi* (**a**) *(door, wound, frontier)* reabrirse; *(shop, theatre)* volver a abrir; **school reopens on 21 August** las clases se reanudan el 21 de agosto

(**b**) *(investigation)* reabrirse; *(talks)* reanudarse

reopening [ri:'əʊpənɪŋ] *n* (**a**) *(of shop, theatre)* reapertura *f* (**b**) *(of investigation)* reapertura *f*; *(of negotiations)* reanudación *f*

reorder **1** *vt* [ri:'ɔ:də(r)] (**a**) *Com* pedir de nuevo (**b**) *(rearrange)* reorganizar

2 *n* ['ri:ɔ:də(r)] *Com* nuevo pedido *m*

reorganization [ri:ɔ:gənaɪ'zeɪʃən] *n* reorganización *f*

reorganize [ri:'ɔ:gənaɪz] **1** *vt* reorganizar

2 *vi* reorganizarse

reorient(ate) [ri:'ɔ:rɪənt(eɪt)] *vt* reorientar

reorientation [ri:ɔ:rɪən'teɪʃən] *n* reorientación *f*

Rep *US* (**a**) (*abbr* **Representative**) diputado(a), representante (**b**) (*abbr* **Republican**) republicano(a)

rep [rep] *n Fam* (**a**) *(salesman)* representante *mf*, comercial *mf* (**b**) *Br Theat* teatro *m* de repertorio; **to be** *or* **work in r.** estar *or* trabajar en una compañía de repertorio ►► ***r. company*** compañía *f* de repertorio (**c**) *US (reputation)* reputación *f*, nombre *m*

repackage [riːˈpækɪdʒ] *vt* (**a**) *(goods)* reempaquetar, reembalar (**b**) *(renew image of)* renovar la imagen de; **they tried to r. the product for the teenage market** intentaron dar una nueva imagen al producto, dirigida al mercado adolescente

repaginate [riːˈpædʒɪneɪt] *vt Comptr* repaginar

repaint [riːˈpeɪnt] *vt* repintar

repair [rɪˈpeə(r)] **1** *n* (**a**) *(mending) (of watch, car, machine)* reparación *f*, *(of roof)* reparación *f*, arreglo *m*; *(of shoes, clothes, road)* arreglo *m*; **to be beyond r.** no poderse arreglar; **to be under r.** estar en reparación; **to do a r. job on sth** hacer un arreglo a algo; **closed for repairs** *(sign)* cerrado por reparaciones; **repairs done while you wait** *(sign)* reparaciones en el acto ►► ***r. kit*** kit *m* de reparación; ***r. shop*** taller *m* (de reparaciones)
(**b**) *(condition)* **to be in good/bad r.** estar en buen/mal estado; **the road is in a terrible state of r.** la carretera está en muy mal estado
2 *vt* (**a**) *(mend) (watch, car, machine)* reparar; *(roof)* arreglar, reparar; *(shoes, clothes, road)* arreglar (**b**) *(make amends for)* reparar
3 *vi Formal or Hum* **to r. to** retirarse a

repairable [rɪˈpeərəbəl] *adj* reparable

repairman [rɪˈpeəmæn] *n* técnico *m*

reparation [repəˈreɪʃən] *n* (**a**) *Formal (compensation)* compensación *f*, reparación *f*; **to make r. for sth** compensar por algo (**b**) *(after war)* **reparations** indemnizaciones *fpl* (de guerra)

repartee [repɑːˈtiː] *n* intercambio *m* de comentarios ingeniosos; **we were amused by his witty r.** encontramos sus ingeniosas réplicas muy divertidas

repast [rɪˈpɑːst] *n Literary* colación *f*, comida *f*

repatriate [riːˈpætrɪeɪt] *vt* (**a**) *(person)* repatriar (**b**) *(profits)* repatriar

repatriation [riːpætrɪˈeɪʃən] *n* (**a**) *(of person)* repatriación *f* (**b**) *(of profits)* repatriación *f*

repay [riːˈpeɪ] (*pt & pp* **repaid** [riːˈpeɪd]) *vt* (**a**) *(debt)* pagar, saldar; *(money)* devolver; *(loan)* amortizar; *(person)* pagar
(**b**) *(return) (person for kindness, help)* recompensar; *(kindness, loyalty)* pagar; **to r. good for evil** pagar el mal con el bien
(**c**) *(reward) (efforts, help)* recompensar; **to be repaid for one's efforts/persistence** ser recompensado(a) por el esfuerzo/la persistencia; **the issue will r. further study** el tema merece un mayor análisis

repayable [riːˈpeɪəbəl] *adj (loan)* pagadero(a), a devolver (**over** en); *(debt)* amortizable

repayment [riːˈpeɪmənt] *n* (**a**) *(of debt, person)* pago *m*; *(of money)* devolución *f*; *(of loan)* amortización *f*; **repayments can be spread over twelve months** los pagos *or* las cuotas pueden repartirse en doce meses ►► ***r. mortgage*** préstamo *m* hipotecario *(con amortización periódica del capital)*; ***r. plan*** plan *m* de amortización (**b**) *(of favour)* devolución *f*

repeal [rɪˈpiːl] **1** *n (of law, regulation)* revocación *f*
2 *vt (law, regulation)* derogar, abrogar

repeat [rɪˈpiːt] **1** *n* (**a**) *(of event)* repetición *f*; **we don't want a r. of what happened last year** no queremos que se repita lo del año pasado ►► ***r. offender*** reincidente *mf*; *Com* ***r. order:*** **the success of a business depends on r. orders** el éxito de un negocio depende de la renovación de pedidos; ***r. performance*** *(of play, opera)* repetición *f*; *Fig* **we don't want a r. performance of last year's chaos** no queremos una repetición del caos del año pasado; ***r. prescription*** = receta que permite obtener un medicamento regularmente sin tener que volver al médico
(**b**) *(of TV or radio programme)* repetición *f*, reposición *f*
(**c**) *Mus (passage)* repetición *f*; *(sign)* repetición *f*
2 *vt* (**a**) *(say again)* repetir; **to r. oneself** repetirse; **don't r. this, but...** no se lo cuentes a nadie, pero...
(**b**) *(do again)* repetir; **I wouldn't like to r. the experience** no me gustaría repetir la experiencia; **it's history repeating itself** la historia se repite; **the pattern repeats itself** *(in decorative design)* el motivo se repite; *(in events)* el patrón *or* modelo se repite
(**c**) *(TV or radio programme)* repetir, volver a pasar
(**d**) *Com (order)* **to r. an order** volver a hacer un pedido, renovar un pedido
(**e**) *Educ (course, year)* repetir
3 *vi* (**a**) *(say again)* repetir; **I r., I have never heard of him** repito, nunca lo he oído nombrar; **I shall never, r. never, go there again** jamás, repito, volveré allí; **r. after me** repite después de mí (**b**) *(food)* repetir; **the garlic repeated on me** el ajo me repetía (**c**) *Math (recur)* repetirse (**d**) *US Pol* = votar más de una vez en unas mismas elecciones

repeatable [rɪˈpiːtəbəl] *adj* repetible; **what he said is not r.** lo que dijo no se puede repetir

repeated [rɪˈpiːtɪd] *adj (action, effort)* repetido(a); *(question, accusation, threat)* reiterado(a)

repeatedly [rɪˈpiːtɪdlɪ] *adv* repetidas veces, repetidamente; **you have been told r. not to play by the canal** se te ha repetido hasta el cansancio que no juegues cerca del canal

repeater [rɪˈpiːtə(r)] *n* (**a**) *(clock)* reloj *m* de repetición; *(alarm)* alarma *f* de repetición (**b**) *(gun)* fusil *m* de repetición (**c**) *Educ* repetidor(ora) *m,f* (**d**) *Elec* repetidor *m*

repechage [ˈrepəʃɑːʒ] *n (in rowing, fencing)* repesca *f*

repel [rɪˈpel] (*pt & pp* **repelled**) *vt* (**a**) *(drive back) (attacker, advance)* repeler; **a spray that repels greenfly** un espray que repele los pulgones; **to r. moisture** evitar la condensación (**b**) *(disgust)* repeler, repugnar; **the sight of blood repelled him** le repugnó ver sangre; **I was repelled by their behaviour** su comportamiento me repugnaba (**c**) *(of magnet)* repeler

repellent [rɪˈpelənt] **1** *n (for insects)* repelente *m* (antiinsectos)
2 *adj* repelente; **to find sth/sb r.** encontrar algo sumamente desagradable/a alguien repelente

repent [rɪˈpent] **1** *vt* arrepentirse de
2 *vi* arrepentirse (**of** de)

repentance [rɪˈpentəns] *n* arrepentimiento *m*

repentant [rɪˈpentənt] *adj* arrepentido(a); **to be r.** (**of** *or* **for**) estar arrepentido(a) (de)

repercussion [riːpəˈkʌʃən] *n* repercusión *f*; **to have repercussions for** *or* **on** tener repercusiones en *or* sobre

repertoire [ˈrepətwɑː(r)] *n also Fig* repertorio *m*; **to have a wide/limited r.** tener un amplio repertorio/repertorio limitado

repertory [ˈrepətərɪ] *n* **to be** *or* **work in r.** trabajar en una compañía de repertorio ►► *Theat* ***r. company*** compañía *f* de repertorio; ***r. theatre*** teatro *m* de repertorio

repetition [repɪˈtɪʃən] *n* (**a**) *(of words)* repetición *f*; **it bears r.** vale la pena repetirlo (**b**) *(of action)* repetición *f*; **I don't want any r. of this disgraceful behaviour** no quiero que este comportamiento vergonzoso se repita

repetitious [repɪˈtɪʃəs] *adj* repetitivo(a)

repetitive [rɪˈpetɪtɪv] *adj (style, job)* repetitivo(a) ►► ***r. strain*** *or* ***stress injury*** lesión *f* por esfuerzo *or* movimiento repetitivo

repetitiveness [rɪˈpetɪtɪvnɪs] *n* lo reiterativo, lo repetitivo

rephrase [riːˈfreɪz] *vt* reformular, expresar de forma diferente; **I think I should r. that** creo que será mejor que lo exprese de otra forma *or* en otros términos

replace [rɪˈpleɪs] *vt* (**a**) *(put back)* volver a colocar; **to r. the receiver** colgar (el teléfono) (**b**) *(substitute for)* sustituir, reemplazar (**with** *or* **by** por); *(battery, tyre, broken part)* (re)cambiar; *(lost, damaged item)* reponer, restituir; **she replaced him as head of department** lo reemplazó *or* sustituyó en el puesto de jefe del departamento (**c**) *Comptr* **r. all** *(command)* reemplazar todos

replaceable [rɪˈpleɪsəbəl] *adj* reemplazable, sustituible; **he/it is easily r.** es fácil de reemplazar *or* sustituir

replacement [rɪˈpleɪsmənt] *n* (**a**) *(act of putting back)* devolución *f*
(**b**) *(act of substituting)* sustitución *f*; *(of battery, tyre, broken part)* (re)cambio *m* ►► *Fin* ***r. cost*** costo *m or Esp* coste *m* de reposición; ***r. parts*** piezas *fpl* de recambio; *Fin* ***r. value*** valor *m* de reposición
(**c**) *(thing replaced) (because lost, damaged)* repuesto *m*; *(because worn out)* recambio *m*; **they sent me a r.** me enviaron otro *or* uno nuevo
(**d**) *Med* **r. hip/knee** cadera/rodilla (articulación) ortopédica
(**e**) *(for person)* sustituto(a) *m,f*; **we are looking for a r. for our secretary** estamos buscando una sustituta *or* un reemplazo para nuestra secretaria ►► ***r. teacher*** (profesor(ora) *m,f*) sustituto(a) *m,f*

replant [riːˈplɑːnt] *vt* replantar

replay 1 *n* [ˈriːpleɪ] *(of game)* repetición *f* (del partido); (*Br* **action** *or US* **instant**) **r.** *(on TV)* repetición *f* (de la jugada)
2 *vt* [riːˈpleɪ] *(game)* jugar de nuevo; *(piece of film, music)* repetir, volver a poner *or* pasar

replenish [riːˈplenɪʃ] *vt (cup, tank)* rellenar; **to r. one's supplies** surtirse de provisiones; **she kept his glass replenished** se aseguró de que tuviera el vaso lleno en todo momento

replenishment [rɪˈplenɪʃmənt] *n Formal (of cup, tank)* rellenado *m*; **r. of supplies** reabastecimiento

replete [rɪˈpliːt] *adj Formal* repleto(a) (**with** de)

repletion [rɪˈpliːʃən] *n Formal* saciedad *f*, hartazgo *m*; **to eat to r.** comer hasta la saciedad

replica [ˈreplɪkə] *n* réplica *f*; **a r. handgun** una pistola de imitación

replicate ['replɪkeɪt] **1** *vt* reproducir; **to r. an experiment** reproducir un experimento; **the gene can r. itself** el gen puede *or* tiene la capacidad de autoreproducirse
2 *vi (gene)* reproducirse

False friend: The Spanish verb **replicar** is not a translation for the English word **replicate**. In Spanish **replicar** means "to answer, to retort".

reply [rɪ'plaɪ] **1** *n* respuesta *f*, contestación *f*; **he made no r.** no respondió; **his r. to that was to march out of the room** su forma de contestar fue abandonar la habitación; **in r.** en *or* como respuesta; **to say sth in r. (to sth/sb)** decir algo en respuesta (a algo/alguien); **there was no r.** *(to telephone)* no contestaban, no había nadie ►► ***r. slip*** cupón *m* de respuesta
2 *vt (answer)* contestar, responder; **"I don't know," she replied** "no sé", contestó *or* respondió
3 *vi* responder, contestar; **to r. to a letter** contestar a una carta; **have you replied to their offer?** ¿has dado una respuesta a su oferta?

reply-paid [rɪ'plaɪpeɪd] *adj Br (envelope)* con franqueo pagado

repo ['ri:pəʊ] *n US Fam (of property)* = ejecución de una hipoteca por parte de un banco ►► ***r. man*** = persona encargada de llevar a cabo el embargo de los bienes en cuestión por impago

repoint [ri:'pɔɪnt] *vt Constr* reapuntalar

repopulate [ri:'pɒpjuleɪt] *vt* repoblar

report [rɪ'pɔ:t] **1** *n* **(a)** *(account, review)* informe *m*, *Andes, CAm, Méx, Ven* reporte *m* (**on** sobre); **to draw up** *or* **make a r. on sth** preparar *or* hacer un informe sobre algo; **there are reports that...** según algunas informaciones...; **according to the latest reports...** de acuerdo con las últimas informaciones...; **financial r.** informe financiero ►► *Parl* ***r. stage*** = en el parlamento británico, momento en el que un proyecto de ley enmendado por un comité vuelve a la Cámara antes de su tercera y última lectura
(b) *(in newspaper, on radio, television) (short)* información *f*; *(long)* reportaje *m*; **according to a r. in "The Times"...** según una información aparecida en "The Times"...; **here is a r. from Tina Church** el siguiente es un reportaje de Tina Church; **weather r.** información meteorológica; **reports are coming in of an earthquake in China** nos llegan noticias sobre un terremoto en China
(c) *Sch Br* **(school) r.** boletín *m* de evaluación, *RP* carné *m* de notas *or* calificaciones ►► *US* ***r. card*** boletín *m* de evaluación, *RP* carné *m* de notas *or* calificaciones
(d) *Law (of court proceedings)* acta *f*; **law reports** compilación de decisiones judiciales
(e) *(sound)* estallido *m*, explosión *f*
(f) *Formal (repute)* reputación *f*; **of good r.** de buena reputación; **I only know it by r.** sólo lo conozco de oídas
2 *vt* **(a)** *(news, fact)* informar de; *(debate, speech)* informar (acerca) de; *(profits, losses, discovery)* anunciar, *CAm, Méx* reportar de; *(accident, theft, crime)* dar parte de; **our correspondent reports that enemy troops have entered the city** nuestro corresponsal nos informa de que las tropas enemigas han entrado en la ciudad; **there is nothing to r.** no hay novedades; **the incident was reported in the local press** la prensa local informó del incidente; **it is reported that the Prime Minister is about to resign, the Prime Minister is reported to be about to resign** se ha informado de la inminente dimisión del primer ministro; **he is reported to have left the country** se tienen noticias de que ha abandonado el país; **to r. the position of a ship** informar sobre *or* dar parte de la posición de un barco; **to r. sth to sb** informar a alguien de algo; **she reported her findings to him** le informó de sus hallazgos; **to r. sb missing** denunciar la desaparición de alguien
(b) *(complain about)* denunciar; **to r. sb to the police** denunciar a alguien a la policía; **the school reported the boy's rudeness to his parents** la escuela informó a los padres del niño sobre su falta de respeto
(c) *(present)* **to r. oneself for duty** presentarse al trabajo
3 *vi* **(a)** *(give account)* informar (**on** sobre); *(committee)* presentar sus conclusiones; **she reported to her boss** informó a su jefe
(b) *(journalist)* informar, *CAm, Méx* reportar (**on/from** sobre/desde); **this is Mandy Martin, reporting from Moscow for CBS** les habla Mandy Martin, informando *or CAm, Méx* reportando desde Moscú para la CBS; **he reports for the BBC** trabaja de reportero para la BBC
(c) *(be in hierarchy)* **to r. to sb** estar bajo las órdenes de alguien; **who do you r. to?** ¿quién es tu superior?
(d) *(present oneself)* presentarse (**to** en); **to r. for duty** *(arrive at work)* presentarse al trabajo; **he reported sick** informó que estaba enfermo

► **report back** *vi* **(a)** *(give account)* presentar un informe *or Andes, CAm, Méx, Ven* reporte (**to** a); **can you r. back on what was discussed?** ¿podrías presentar un informe sobre lo conversado? **(b)** *(return)* volver (**to** a)

► **report out** *vt sep US Pol (bill)* = devolver a la cámara legislativa para su debate y votación

reportage [repɔ:'tɑ:ʒ] *n Journ* reportaje *m*

reported [rɪ'pɔ:tɪd] *adj* **there have been several r. sightings** se tienen noticias de varios avistamientos; **what was their last r. position?** ¿cuál era su última posición conocida? ►► *Gram* ***r. speech*** el estilo indirecto

reportedly [rɪ'pɔ:tɪdlɪ] *adv* según se dice, al parecer; **he is r. resident in Paris** según se dice *or* al parecer, reside en París

reporter [rɪ'pɔ:tə(r)] *n* **(a)** *(for newspaper)* reportero(a) *m,f*, periodista *mf*; *(in radio, TV)* locutor(ora) *m,f* **(b)** *(scribe) (in court)* relator(ora) *m,f*; *(in parliament)* taquígrafo(a) *m,f*

reporting [rɪ'pɔ:tɪŋ] *n* cobertura *f* (informativa); **she is noted for her objective r.** es conocida por la objetividad de sus coberturas, es conocida por su objetividad a la hora de cubrir una noticia; *Law* **r. restrictions were not lifted** no se levantó el secreto de sumario

repose [rɪ'pəʊz] *Formal* **1** *n* reposo *m*; **in r.** en reposo; *Rel* **to pray for the r. of a soul** rezar por un alma, rezar para que alguien descanse en paz
2 *vt* **(a)** *(head, limb)* reposar, apoyar **(b)** *(confidence, trust)* depositar
3 *vi* **(a)** *(rest) (person)* reposar; *(head, limb)* descansar; *(the dead)* descansar **(b)** *(be founded) (belief, theory)* fundarse, basarse

reposition [ri:pə'zɪʃən] *vt* **(a)** *(move)* desplazar, mover; **she repositioned herself nearer the door** se puso más cerca de la puerta **(b)** *(product, party)* reposicionar

repository [rɪ'pɒzɪtərɪ] *n* **(a)** *(for books, furniture)* depósito *m* **(b)** *(of knowledge)* arsenal *m*, depositario(a) *m,f*

repossess [ri:pə'zes] *vt* recobrar, recuperar; **our house has been repossessed** el banco ha ejecutado la hipoteca de nuestra casa

repossession [ri:pə'zeʃən] *n (of property)* = ejecución de una hipoteca por parte de un banco ►► ***r. order*** orden *f* de ejecución de una hipoteca

repot [ri:'pɒt] *vt (plant)* cambiar de maceta, trasplantar

reprehend [reprɪ'hend] *vt (person)* reprender; *(conduct, attitude)* condenar

reprehensible [reprɪ'hensɪbəl] *adj* censurable, recriminable

reprehensibly [reprɪ'hensɪblɪ] *adv* de un modo censurable *or* recriminable

represent [reprɪ'zent] *vt* **(a)** *(symbolize)* representar; **the statue represents peace** la estatua representa la libertad
(b) *(describe, depict)* presentar, describir; **the play represents him as a superstitious fool** la obra lo presenta como a un tonto supersticioso
(c) *(be representative for) (president, voters, union members)* representar; **who is representing the plaintiff?** ¿quién representa al demandante?; **to r. a company** representar a una empresa; **the voice of women is not represented on the committee** la voz femenina no está representada en el comité
(d) *(in numbers)* **his early work is poorly represented in the exhibition** sus primeras obras no tienen mucha presencia en la exposición; **foreign students are well represented in the university** en la universidad hay un buen número de estudiantes extranjeros
(e) *(be, constitute)* representar, constituir; **this represents a great improvement** esto representa *or* constituye una gran mejora; **the book represents five years' work** el libro representa cinco años de trabajo
(f) *Formal (express, explain)* presentar, expresar; **they represented their grievances to the director** presentaron *or* expresaron sus quejas al director
(g) *Theat (of actor)* representar, hacer el papel de

re-present ['ri:prɪ'zent] *vt Fin* volver a presentar

representation [reprɪzen'teɪʃən] *n* **(a)** *(of facts)* representación *f*; **that isn't a fair r. of their point of view** no están presentando fielmente su punto de vista, están tergiversando su punto de vista
(b) *(in parliament, on committee)* representación *f*
(c) *Formal* **to make representations (to sb)** *(complain)* presentar una protesta (ante alguien); *(intervene)* intervenir, hacer una exposición (ante alguien); **she made representations to the committee on behalf of the charity** intervino ante el comité en representación de la organización benéfica

representational [reprɪzen'teɪʃənəl] *adj Art* figurativo(a)

representative [reprɪ'zentətɪv] **1** *n* **(a)** *(of company, on committee)* representante *mf*; **(sales) r.** representante *mf or* agente *mf* de ventas, vendedor(ora) *m,f* **(b)** *US Pol* representante *mf*, diputado(a) *m,f*
2 *adj* representativo(a) **(of** de**)** ►► *Pol* ***r. assembly*** asamblea *f* representativa

repress [rɪ'pres] *vt* reprimir; **I repressed the urge to laugh** contuve *or* reprimí las ganas de reír

repressed [rɪ'prest] *adj* **to be r.** estar reprimido(a); **she had a very r. adolescence** en su adolescencia fue una muchacha muy reprimida

repression [rɪ'preʃən] *n* represión *f*

repressive [rɪ'presɪv] *adj* represivo(a)

repressiveness [rɪ'presɪvnɪs] *n* lo represivo

reprieve [rɪ'pri:v] **1** *n* **(a)** *Law* suspensión *f* (de la pena); **he was given a r.** se le suspendió la pena **(b)** *(of project, company)* **to win a r.** salvarse de momento; **this is a r. for the government** es un balón de oxígeno para el gobierno
2 *vt* **(a)** *Law* **he was reprieved** se le suspendió la pena **(b)** *(project, company)* salvar de momento

reprimand ['reprɪmɑ:nd] **1** *n* reprimenda *f*
2 *vt* reprender

reprint [ri:'prɪnt] **1** *n* ['ri:prɪnt] reimpresión *f*; **her novel is in its tenth r.** su novela ya tiene diez reimpresiones
2 *vt* reimprimir
3 *vi (book)* reimprimirse

reprisal [rɪ'praɪzəl] *n* represalia *f*; **a r. raid** un ataque en represalia; **to take reprisals (against)** tomar represalias (contra); **as a** *or* **in r. for** en represalia por

reprise [rɪ'pri:z] *n Mus* repetición *f*

repro ['ri:prəʊ] *n Fam* reproducción *f*; **r. Victorian furniture** reproducciones de muebles victorianos

reproach [rɪ'prəʊtʃ] **1** *n* reproche *m*; **in a tone of r.** en tono de reproche; **to heap reproaches on sb** avasallar a alguien con reproches; **to be a r. to** representar una deshonra para; **beyond** *or* **above r.** irreprochable, intachable
2 *vt* hacer reproches a; **to r. sb for (doing) sth** reprochar (el haber hecho) algo a alguien; **to r. oneself for** *or* **with sth** reprocharse algo; **to r. sb with having done sth** reprochar a alguien que haya hecho algo

reproachful [rɪ'prəʊtʃfʊl] *adj (tone, look)* de reproche

reproachfully [rɪ'prəʊtʃfʊlɪ] *adv* de manera reprobatoria

reprobate ['reprəbeɪt] *n Formal* granujilla *mf*, tunante *mf*

reprocess [ri:'prəʊses] *vt* reprocesar, volver a tratar

reprocessing [ri:'prəʊsesɪŋ] *n* reprocesado *m* ►► ***r. plant*** planta *f* de reprocesado

reproduce [ri:prə'dju:s] **1** *vt* reproducir
2 *vi* **(a)** *Biol* reproducirse **(b)** *(photocopier)* copiarse; **this picture will r. well** las copias de esta fotografía quedarán muy bien

reproduction [ri:prə'dʌkʃən] *n* **(a)** *Biol* reproducción *f* **(b)** *(of painting, document)* reproducción *f* ►► ***r. furniture*** reproducciones *fpl* de muebles antiguos

reproductive [ri:prə'dʌktɪv] *adj Biol* reproductor(ora) ►► ***r. organs*** órganos *mpl* reproductores; ***r. system*** sistema *m* reproductor

reprogram [ri:'prəʊgræm] *vt* reprogramar

reprogrammable [ri:prəʊ'græməbəl] *adj* reprogramable

reprographics [reprə'græfɪks], **reprography** [rɪ'prɒgrəfɪ] *n* reprografía *f*

reproof [rɪ'pru:f] *n Formal* reprobación *f*, desaprobación *f*

reproval [rɪ'pru:vəl] *n* desaprobación *f*

reprove [rɪ'pru:v] *vt Formal* recriminar, reprobar; **he was reproved for his conduct** le recriminaron su conducta

reproving [rɪ'pru:vɪŋ] *adj Formal* de reprobación, reprobatorio(a)

reprovingly [rɪ'pru:vɪŋlɪ] *adv* de manera reprobatoria

reptile ['reptaɪl] *n* **(a)** *(creature)* reptil *m* ►► ***r. house*** casa *f* de los reptiles **(b)** *(person)* víbora *f*

reptilian ['reptɪlɪən] *adj* **(a)** *(species, characteristic)* reptiliano(a) **(b)** *(leer)* de reptil

republic [rɪ'pʌblɪk] *n* república *f* ►► ***the R. of Ireland*** la República de Irlanda; ***the R. of South Africa*** la República de Sudáfrica

Republican [rɪ'pʌblɪkən] *Pol* **1** *n* **(a)** *US* republicano(a) *m,f*; **the Republicans** *(party)* los republicanos, el partido republicano **(b)** *(in Northern Ireland)* republicano(a) *m,f*
2 *adj* **(a)** *US* republicano(a) **(b)** *(in Northern Ireland)* republicano(a)

republican [rɪ'pʌblɪkən] **1** *n* republicano(a) *m,f*
2 *adj* republicano(a)

republicanism [rɪ'pʌblɪkənɪzəm] *n* republicanismo *m*

republication [ri:pʌblɪ'keɪʃən] *n (of book)* reedición *f*

republish [ri:'pʌblɪʃ] *vt (book)* volver a publicar *or* editar

repudiate [rɪ'pju:dɪeɪt] *vt Formal* **(a)** *(reject) (offer)* rechazar; *(rumour, remark)* desmentir **(b)** *(refuse to honour) (agreement)* denunciar, repudiar; *(debt)* negarse a reconocer **(c)** *(disown) (spouse, friend)* repudiar

repudiation [rɪpju:dɪ'eɪʃən] *n Formal* **(a)** *(rejection) (of offer)* rechazo *m*; *(of rumour, remark)* desmentido *m* **(b)** *(refusal to honour) (of agreement)* denuncia *f*; *(of debt)* negativa *f* a reconocer **(c)** *(disowning) (of spouse, friend)* repudio *m*

repugnance [rɪ'pʌgnəns] *n* repugnancia *f* **(for** por)

repugnant [rɪ'pʌgnənt] *adj* repugnante; **I find the idea r.** la idea me repugna, creo que es una idea repugnante

repulse [rɪ'pʌls] **1** *n (of attack)* rechazo *m*
2 *vt (army, attack)* rechazar; **I am repulsed by your heartlessness** me repulsa tu crueldad

repulsion [rɪ'pʌlʃən] *n* **(a)** *(disgust)* repulsión *f* **(b)** *Phys* repulsión *f*

repulsive [rɪ'pʌlsɪv] *adj* repulsivo(a)

repulsively [rɪ'pʌlsɪvlɪ] *adv* de manera repulsiva

repulsiveness [rɪ'pʌlsɪvnɪs] *n (disgusting quality)* repulsión *f*, repugnancia *f*

repurchase [ri:'pɜ:tʃɪs] **1** *n* recompra *f* ►► *Fin* ***r. agreement*** acuerdo *m* de recompra
2 *vt* recomprar

reputable ['repjʊtəbəl] *adj* reputado(a), acreditado(a)

reputation [repjʊ'teɪʃən] *n (of person, shop)* reputación *f*; **to have a good/bad r.** tener buena/mala reputación *or* fama; **to have a r. for frankness** tener fama de franco(a); **to know sb by r.** conocer a alguien de oídas; **his r. had gone before him** le precedió su reputación; **they lived up to their r.** hicieron honor a su reputación; *Old-fashioned* **to ruin a girl's r.** deshonrar a una joven

repute [rɪ'pju:t] **1** *n Formal* reputación *f*, fama *f*; **I only know her by r.** sólo la conozco de nombre; **of r.** de renombre *or* gran reputación; **to be of good/ill r.** tener buena/mala reputación; **to be held in high r.** estar muy bien considerado(a)
2 *vt* **to be reputed to be wealthy/a genius** tener fama de rico(a)/de ser un genio

reputed [rɪ'pju:tɪd] *adj* presunto(a), supuesto(a); **the r. author of the work** el supuesto autor de la obra

reputedly [rɪ'pju:tɪdlɪ] *adv* según parece, según se dice; **he is, at least r., the best lawyer in the country** es, al menos en la opinión de la gente, el mejor abogado del país

request [rɪ'kwest] **1** *n* **(a)** *(demand, appeal)* petición *f*, solicitud *f*, *Am* pedido *m*; **any last requests?** ¿cuál es su última voluntad?; **to make a r. (for sth)** hacer una petición *orAm* un pedido (de algo); **I did it at** *or* **on her r.** lo hice a instancias de ella; **available on r.** disponible mediante solicitud; **by popular r.** a petición *orAm* pedido del público ►► ***r. stop*** *(for bus)* parada *f* discrecional
(b) *(song)* canción *f* solicitada ►► ***r. programme*** *(on radio)* = programa al que se puede llamar para solicitar que pongan una canción determinada
2 *vt* pedir, solicitar; **to r. sb to do sth** pedir *or* solicitar a alguien que haga algo; *Formal* **to r. sth of sb** pedir *or* solicitar algo a alguien; **passengers are requested not to smoke** se ruega a los señores pasajeros se abstengan de fumar; *Formal* **Mr and Mrs Booth r. the pleasure of your company** al Sr. y la Sra. Booth les complacería poder contar con vuestra grata presencia; **as requested** como se solicitaba

> En inglés culto o elevado, y especialmente en inglés americano, **request** puede ir seguido de **that** más un verbo en subjuntivo (ver el panel SUBJUNCTIVE):
> **she requested that he not be given the information**
> *solicitó que no se le diera la información*
> Lo mismo también podría decirse del siguiente modo:
> **she requested that he should not be given the information**

requiem ['rekwɪəm] *n* **(a)** *Rel* **r. (mass)** misa *f* de difuntos **(b)** *Mus* réquiem *m*

require [rɪ'kwaɪə(r)] *vt* **(a)** *(need)* necesitar; **it requires considerable skill (to)** se necesita *or* requiere una habilidad considerable (para); **is that all you r.?** ¿es eso todo lo que necesitas?; **as required** según sea necesario; **if required** si es necesario; **when required** cuando sea necesario; *Formal* **your presence is urgently required** su presencia se requiere con urgencia (**b**) *(demand)* requerir; **we r. complete cooperation** requerimos cooperación plena; **to r. sb to do sth** requerir a alguien que haga algo; **to r. sth of sb** requerir *or* pedir algo a alguien; **you are required to wear a seat belt** es obligatorio llevar puesto el cinturón de seguridad; **it is required that you begin work at 8 am** su horario de trabajo comienza a las 8 de la mañana; **formal dress required** *(on invitation)* vestimenta formal

required [rɪ'kwaɪəd] *adj* (**a**) *(necessary, compulsory)* necesario(a) ►► ***r. reading*** lectura *f* obligatoria (**b**) *(stipulated)* **in** *or* **by the r. time** en el tiempo estipulado; **to reach the r. standard** alcanzar el nivel necesario *or* requerido

requirement [rɪ'kwaɪəmənt] *n* (**a**) *(demand)* requisito *m*; **to meet sb's requirements** cumplir con los requisitos de alguien (**b**) *(necessity)* requisito *m*; **energy requirements** necesidades energéticas (**c**) *(condition, prerequisite)* requisito *m*; **she doesn't fulfil the requirements for the job** no cumple con los requisitos para el puesto

> **False friend**: The Spanish noun **requerimiento** is not a translation for the English word **requirement**. In Spanish **requerimiento** means "request".

requisite ['rekwɪzɪt] *Formal* **1** *n* (**a**) *(prerequisite)* requisito *m* (**b**) **requisites** *(objects)* accesorios *mpl*, artículos *mpl*

2 *adj* necesario(a), requerido(a); **without the r. care** sin el debido cuidado

requisition [rekwɪ'zɪʃən] **1** *n (request)* pedido *m*, solicitud *f*; *(enforced)* requisa *f*

2 *vt (supplies) (to request)* requerir; *(to take over)* requisar; **my taxi was requisitioned by the army** el ejército me requisó el taxi

requital [rɪ'kwaɪtəl] *n Formal* **in r. of** *or* **for sth** *(as reward)* como retribución por algo; *(in retaliation)* en represalia por algo

requite [rɪ'kwaɪt] *vt (kindness, insult)* resarcir; **to r. sb's love** corresponder el amor de alguien

re-read ['riː'riːd] *vt* releer

reredos ['rɪədɒs] *n Archit* retablo *m*

rerelease ['riːrɪ'liːs] **1** *n (movie)* reestreno *m*; *(record)* relanzamiento *m*

2 *vt (movie)* reestrenar; *(record)* relanzar

reroute [riː'ruːt] *vt* desviar

rerun **1** *n* ['riːrʌn] (**a**) *(of race)* repetición *f* (**b**) *(on TV)* reposición *f*; *US* **to be in reruns** estar de nuevo en pantalla, ser repuesto(a) (**c**) *(of situation, conflict)* repetición *f*

2 *vt* [riː'rʌn] (**a**) *(race)* repetir (**b**) *(TV programme)* reponer (**c**) *Comptr* volver a ejecutar

resale ['riːseɪl] *n* reventa *f*; **not for r.** prohibida la venta ►► *Com* ***r. price maintenance*** = sistema de fijación de precios mínimos por parte de los fabricantes; ***r. value*** valor *m* de reventa

rescale [riː'skeɪl] *vt US* reajustar

reschedule [riː'skedʒuːl, *Br* riː'ʃedjuːl] *vt* (**a**) *(meeting, flight)* volver a programar; *(plan, order)* reprogramar (**b**) *(debt)* renegociar

rescind [rɪ'sɪnd] *vt Formal (law)* derogar; *(order)* cancelar; *(contract)* rescindir

rescore [riː'skɔː(r)] *vt Mus* reescribir

rescue ['reskjuː] **1** *n* rescate *m*; **r. was impossible** el rescate fue imposible; **r. mission/operation** expedición/operación de rescate *or* de salvamento; **to come** *or* **go to sb's r.** acudir al rescate de alguien; **to be beyond r.** ser irrecuperable ►► *Fin* ***r. package*** medidas *fpl* de rescate; ***r. services*** servicios *mpl* de salvamento; ***r. worker*** integrante *mf* de un equipo de rescate

2 *vt* rescatar; **to r. sb from sth** rescatar a alguien de algo; **to r. sb from financial ruin** salvar a alguien de la ruina; **thanks for rescuing me from that awful bore** te agradezco que me hayas rescatado de ese plomo *or* plomazo; **I rescued this picture from the trash** rescaté esta fotografía de la basura

rescuer ['reskjuːə(r)] *n* salvador(ora) *m,f*

resealable [riː'siːləbəl] *adj* **r. envelopes/packs** sobres/paquetes que se pueden volver a cerrar

research [rɪ'sɜːtʃ] **1** *n* investigación *f*; **an excellent piece of r.** un excelente trabajo de investigación; **r. has shown that...** las investigaciones han demostrado que...; **to do r. into sth** investigar algo; **more r. is needed into the subject** hace falta investigar el tema con mayor profundidad ►► ***r. assistant*** ayudante *mf* de investigación; ***r. budget*** presupuesto *m* de investigación; ***r. and development*** investigación *f* y desarrollo; ***r. fellow*** becario(a) *m,f* investigador(ora); ***r. laboratory*** laboratorio *m* de investigación; ***r. student*** = estudiante de posgrado que se dedica a la investigación; ***r. tool*** herramienta *f* de investigación

2 *vt* investigar; **a well researched book** un libro muy bien documentado

3 *vi* investigar; **to r. into sth** investigar algo

researcher [rɪ'sɜːtʃə(r)] *n* investigador(ora) *m,f*

resell [riː'sel] *vt* revender, volver a vender

resemblance [rɪ'zembləns] *n* parecido *m*, similitud *f*; **to bear a r. to sth/sb** guardar parecido con algo/alguien; **the brothers show a strong family r.** los hermanos tienen un gran parecido; **any r. to persons living or dead is purely coincidental** cualquier parecido con personajes de la vida real es mera coincidencia

resemble [rɪ'zembəl] *vt* parecerse a; **they r. each other greatly** se parecen mucho, guardan un gran parecido

resent [rɪ'zent] *vt* **to r. sb** guardar rencor a alguien; **I r. his interference** me parece mal que se entrometa; **I r. that!** ¡eso no me parece nada bien!; **they obviously resented my presence** evidentemente, les molestaba mi presencia; **she resented the fact that they never invited her** le sentaba muy mal que nunca la invitaran; **I r. being treated like an idiot** me molesta que me traten como a un imbécil

resentful [rɪ'zentfʊl] *adj (look, silence)* lleno(a) de rencor; **to be** *or* **feel r. of sth/sb** sentirse molesto(a) por algo/con alguien; **to be r. of sb's achievements** tener envidia de los logros de alguien

resentment [rɪ'zentmənt] *n* resentimiento *m*; **to feel r. towards sb** sentirse molesto(a) con alguien

reservation [rezə'veɪʃən] *n* (**a**) *(booking)* reserva *f*, *Am* reservación *f*; **to make a r.** hacer una reserva; **I have a r.** *(at hotel)* tengo una reserva ►► ***r. desk*** mostrador *m* de reservas

(**b**) *(doubt)* reserva *f*; **to have reservations about sth** tener reservas acerca de algo; **to accept sth with some reservations** aceptar algo con algunas reservas; **without r.** sin reservas

(**c**) *(for native Americans)* reserva *f* india

reserve [rɪ'zɜːv] **1** *n* (**a**) *(supply)* reserva *f*; **he has great reserves of energy** tiene mucha energía; **to have** *or* **keep sth in r.** reservar algo, tener algo reservado(a); **he drew on his reserves** echó mano de sus reservas ►► ***r. tank*** *(for fuel)* depósito *m or* tanque *m* de reserva

(**b**) *Sport (second-team player)* jugador(ora) *m,f* del filial; *(substitute)* reserva *mf*; **to play for the reserves** jugar en el filial; **the r. quarterback** el quarterback suplente

(**c**) *Mil* **the reserves** la reserva; **to call up the r.** *or* **reserves** llamar a la reserva ►► *US* ***R. Officer Training Corps*** = unidad de formación de futuros oficiales compuesta por estudiantes universitarios becados por el ejército

(**d**) *(for birds, game)* reserva *f*; **game r.** coto de caza; **nature r.** reserva natural

(**e**) *(reticence)* reserva *f*; **to break through sb's r.** superar las reticencias de alguien; **without r.** sin reservas

(**f**) *(doubt, qualification)* **without r.** sin reservas

(**g**) *(at auction)* **r. (price)** precio *m* mínimo

(**h**) *Fin* ***r. bank*** = uno de los doce bancos que forman la Reserva Federal estadounidense; ***r. capital*** capital *m* de reserva; ***r. currency*** divisa *f* de reserva; ***r. fund*** fondo *m* de reserva

2 *vt* (**a**) *(retain, keep back)* reservar; **to r. one's strength** ahorrar *or* reservar fuerzas; **to r. the right to do sth** reservarse el derecho a hacer algo; **to r. judgement (on sth)** reservarse la opinión (sobre algo) (**b**) *(book)* reservar; **these seats are reserved for VIPs** estos asientos están reservados para las personalidades *or* los VIPs

reserved [rɪ'zɜːvd] *adj* (**a**) *(shy)* reservado(a) (**b**) *(room, seat)* reservado(a) (**c**) *Comptr* ***r. character*** carácter *m* reservado

reservist [rɪ'zɜːvɪst] *n Mil* reservista *mf*

reservoir ['rezəvwɑː(r)] *n* (**a**) *(lake)* embalse *m*, pantano *m* (**b**) *(of strength, courage)* reserva *f*, cúmulo *m*; **they had built up a r. of goodwill among the population** se habían granjeado la buena voluntad de gran parte de la población

reset [riː'set] (*pt & pp* **reset**) **1** *n Comptr* ***r. button, r. switch*** botón *m* para reinicializar

2 *vt* (**a**) *(watch)* ajustar; *(counter)* poner a cero; *(alarm)* reprogramar; *(alarm clock)* poner, programar (**b**) *(jewel)* volver a engastar (**c**) *Med (bone)* volver a colocar en su sitio (**d**) *Comptr* reinicializar (**e**) *Typ* recomponer

resettle [riː'setəl] **1** *vt (refugees)* reasentar; *(territory)* repoblar

2 *vi* mudarse, trasladarse (**in** a)

resettlement ['riː'setəlmənt] *n (of refugees)* reasentamiento *m*; *(of territory)* repoblamiento *m*

reshape [riː'ʃeɪp] *vt (plans, future)* rehacer, reorganizar; *(party, industry)* reestructurar, remodelar

reshuffle 1 *n* ['ri:ʃʌfəl] *Pol* **(Cabinet) r.** reajuste *m or* remodelación *f* del Gabinete (ministerial)

2 *vt* [ri:'ʃʌfəl] **(a)** *Pol (cabinet)* reorganizar **(b)** *(cards)* volver a barajar

reside [rɪ'zaɪd] *vi* **(a)** *(person)* residir **(b)** *(power, quality)* **to r. in** *or* **with** residir en, radicar en; **the problem resides in the fact that...** el problema reside *or* radica en que...

residence ['rezɪdəns] *n* **(a)** *(stay)* residencia *f*; **she took up r. in London** fijó su residencia en Londres; **place of r.** lugar de residencia; **to be in r.** *(monarch)* encontrarse en la residencia real *or* en palacio; **writer/poet in r.** escritor(ora)/poeta residente ►► ***r. permit*** permiso *m* de residencia

(b) *Formal (home)* residencia *f*; **Lord Bellamy's r.** la residencia de Lord Bellamy; *Hum* **the Hancock r.** la residencia de los Hancock

(c) *Univ Br* **(hall of) r.**, *US* **r. hall** residencia *f* universitaria, *Esp* colegio *m* mayor

residency ['rezɪdənsɪ] *n* **(a)** *(stay)* residencia *f* **(b)** *US Med (period)* = periodo de prácticas para conseguir el título de especialista **(c)** *Mus (engagement)* = acuerdo para tocar durante cierto periodo en un lugar determinado

resident ['rezɪdənt] 1 *n* **(a)** *(of country, street)* residente *mf*; *(of hotel)* residente *mf*, huésped *mf*; **residents only** *(in street)* sólo para residentes; *(in hotel)* exclusivo para huéspedes *or* clientes ►► ***residents' association*** asociación *f* de vecinos **(b)** *US Med* = médico que realiza el periodo de prácticas para conseguir el título de especialista

2 *adj* **(a)** *(living)* residente; **to be r. in Seattle** residir en Seattle; **you have to be r. during the week** tienes que residir allí los días de entre semana ►► *US* ***r. alien*** extranjero(a) *m,f* residente *or* con permiso de residencia

(b) *(on staff)* **our r. interpreter/pianist** nuestro intérprete/pianista habitual; **he's our r. expert on football** él es el experto en fútbol de la casa

(c) *Comptr* residente ►► ***r. font*** fuente *f* residente

residential [rezɪ'denʃəl] *adj* residencial ►► ***r. area*** zona *f* residencial; ***r. care*** = cuidados en residencias o en pisos protegidos

residual [rɪ'zɪdjʊəl] 1 *adj* residual ►► *Law* ***r. estate*** heredad *f* residual *or* residuaria

2 *n* **(a)** *Math* residuo *m* **(b)** *Cin & TV* **residuals** *(repeat fees)* derechos *mpl* de retransmisión *or* redifusión *(para actores, músicos, etc.)*

residuary legatee [rɪ'zɪdjʊərɪlegə'ti:] *n Law* heredero(a) *m,f* universal

residue ['rezɪdju:] *n* **(a)** *(remainder)* resto *m*, residuo *m* **(b)** *Chem* residuo *m* **(c)** *Law (of estate)* remanente *f* del patrimonio

resign [rɪ'zaɪn] 1 *vt* **(a)** *(give up) (job, position)* dimitir de, renunciar a; **I resigned my voting rights to the chairman** le cedí mi derecho a voto al presidente **(b)** *(reconcile)* **to r. oneself to (doing) sth** resignarse a (hacer) algo

2 *vi* **(a)** *(from post)* dimitir (**from** de), renunciar (**from** a); **he has resigned as Prime Minister** ha dimitido de primer ministro **(b)** *(in chess)* abandonar

resignation [rezɪg'neɪʃən] *n* **(a)** *(from job)* dimisión *f*, renuncia *f*; **to hand in** *or Formal* **tender one's r.** presentar la dimisión **(b)** *(attitude)* resignación *f*

resigned [rɪ'zaɪnd] *adj* resignado(a); **a r. look/smile** una mirada/sonrisa de resignación; **to be r. to sth** estar resignado(a) a algo

resignedly [rɪ'zaɪnɪdlɪ] *adv* con resignación

resilience [rɪ'zɪlɪəns] *n* **(a)** *(of material, metal)* elasticidad *f* **(b)** *(of person)* capacidad *f* de recuperación

resilient [rɪ'zɪlɪənt] *adj* **(a)** *(material, metal)* elástico(a) **(b)** *(person, economy)* **to be r.** tener capacidad de recuperación; **the economy is proving remarkably r.** la economía está demostrando una gran capacidad de recuperación

resin ['rezɪn] *n* resina *f*

resinous ['rezɪnəs] *adj* resinoso(a)

resist [rɪ'zɪst] 1 *vt* resistir; **it's hard to r. his charm** es difícil resistirse a su encanto; *Law* **to r. arrest** resistirse a la autoridad; **I couldn't r. telling him** no pude resistir la tentación de decírselo; **I can't r. chocolates** los bombones me resultan irresistibles

2 *vi* resistir

resistance [rɪ'zɪstəns] *n* **(a)** *(opposition)* resistencia *f*; **to put up** *or* **offer r.** oponer *or* ofrecer resistencia; **to meet with no r.** no encontrar resistencia; **her r. to infection is low** tiene bajas defensas inmunológicas; IDIOM **to take the line of least r.** tomar el camino más fácil

(b) *Hist & Pol* resistencia *f*; **the R.** la Resistencia ►► ***r. fighter*** miembro *mf* de la resistencia

(c) *Elec* resistencia *f*

(d) *Phys* **air/wind r.** resistencia del aire/viento

resistant [rɪ'zɪstənt] *adj* **to be r. to sth** *(change, suggestion)* mostrarse remiso(a) a aceptar algo, mostrar resistencia a algo; *(disease)* ser resistente a algo

-resistant [rɪ'zɪstənt] *suffix* anti; **rust-r.** antioxidante; **stain-r.** antimanchas

resistible [rɪ'zɪstɪbəl] *adj* resistible; **I find his supposed charm highly r.** su supuesto encanto no me impresiona en lo más mínimo

resistor [rɪ'zɪstə(r)] *n Elec* resistencia *f*

resit *Br* 1 *n* ['ri:sɪt] repesca *f*; **how many resits do you have?** ¿cuántas veces puedes presentarte?

2 *vt* [ri:'sɪt] *(pt & pp* **resat** [ri:'sæt]*) (exam, driving test)* presentarse de nuevo a

resize [ri:'saɪz] *vt Comptr (window)* cambiar de tamaño

resole [ri:'səʊl] *vt* cambiar la suela a

resolute ['rezəlu:t] *adj* resuelto(a), decidido(a); **to be r. in one's efforts** realizar denodados esfuerzos

resolutely ['rezəlu:tlɪ] *adv* con resolución, resueltamente

resoluteness ['rezəlu:tnɪs] *n* resolución *f*, determinación *f*

resolution [rezə'lu:ʃən] *n* **(a)** *(decision) (of individual)* resolución *f*, determinación *f*; **she made a r. to stop smoking** se propuso firmemente dejar de fumar, se prometió a sí misma que iba a dejar de fumar; **to be full of good resolutions** rebosar buenas intenciones

(b) *(decision) (of committee)* resolución *f*; **to pass/adopt/reject a r.** aprobar/adoptar/rechazar una resolución; **to put a r. to the meeting** presentar una moción a la asamblea

(c) *(firmness)* resolución *f*, decisión *f*; **to speak/act with r.** hablar/actuar con decisión

(d) *(solution)* resolución *f*, solución *f*

(e) *(of TV, microscope)* resolución *f*; **high r. screen** pantalla de alta resolución

(f) *Comptr* resolución *f*

resolvable [rɪ'zɒlvəbəl] *adj* soluble

resolve [rɪ'zɒlv] 1 *n* **(a)** *(determination)* determinación *f*; **it only strengthened our r.** sólo sirvió para incrementar nuestra determinación **(b)** *(decision)* decisión *f*, determinación *f*; **to make a firm r. to do sth** resolver firmemente hacer algo

2 *vt* **(a)** *(decide)* **to r. to do sth** resolver hacer algo; **it was resolved that...** se decidió que... **(b)** *(solve)* resolver, solucionar; **have you resolved your difficulties yet?** ¿ya has resuelto *or* solucionado tus problemas? **(c)** *(break down, separate)* dividir, descomponer

3 *vi* **(a)** *(decide)* **to r. on/against doing sth** tomar la resolución de hacer/no hacer algo **(b)** *(break down, separate)* dividirse

resolved [rɪ'zɒlvd] *adj* resuelto(a) (**to** a); **I was firmly r. to go** estaba resuelto *or* decidido a ir

resonance ['rezənəns] *n (of voice, cavity)* resonancia *f*

resonant ['rezənənt] *adj (voice, cavity)* resonante

resonate ['rezəneɪt] *vi* resonar; **the valley resonated with their cries** sus gritos resonaban en el valle

resonator ['rezəneɪtə(r)] *n* resonador *m*

resorption [rɪ'sɔ:pʃən] *n Med* resorción *f*

resort [rɪ'zɔ:t] *n* **(a)** *(recourse)* recurso *m*; **to have r. to sth** recurrir a algo; **without r. to threats** sin (necesidad de) recurrir a amenazas; **as a last r.** como último recurso; **in the last r.** en última instancia; **flight was the only r. left to me** *or* **my only r.** el único recurso que me quedaba era huir

(b) *(holiday place)* centro *m* turístico, lugar *m* de vacaciones; **a ski r.** una estación de esquí

(c) *(haunt, hang-out)* refugio *m*

> **False friend**: The Spanish noun **resorte** is not a translation for the English word **resort**. In Spanish **resorte** means "spring" or "means".

► **resort to** *vt insep* **(a)** *(violence, sarcasm)* recurrir a; **to r. to doing sth** recurrir a hacer algo **(b)** *Literary or Hum (place)* acudir a

resound [rɪ'zaʊnd] *vi* **(a)** *(voice, explosion)* resonar, retumbar; **the trumpet resounded through the barracks** la trompeta resonó en el cuartel

(b) *(hall, cave, hills, room)* retumbar, resonar; **the stadium resounded with applause** los aplausos resonaban en el estadio, el estadio resonaba con aplausos

(c) *(spread) (rumour, fame)* propagarse; **the declaration resounded throughout the country** la declaración se propagó por todo el país

resounding [rɪ'zaʊndɪŋ] *adj* **(a)** *(crash)* estruendoso(a); *(applause)* sonoro(a), clamoroso(a) **(b)** *(success, failure)* clamoroso(a), sonado(a)

resoundingly [rɪ'zaʊndɪŋlɪ] *adv (to defeat)* rotundamente, de manera rotunda; **to be r. successful** tener un éxito rotundo

resource [rɪ'zɔːs] **1** *n* (**a**) *(asset)* recurso *m*; **there's a limit to the resources we can invest** hay un límite para los recursos que podemos invertir; **natural/energy resources** recursos naturales/energéticos ►► ***r. management*** gestión *f* de recursos

(**b**) *(human capacity)* recurso *m*; **the task called for all my resources of tact** para hacerlo tuve que usar el mayor tacto posible; **to be left to one's own resources** tener que arreglárselas solo(a)

(**c**) *(ingenuity)* recursos *mpl*; **a man of r.** un hombre con recursos

2 *vt (project)* financiar

resourceful [rɪ'zɔːsfʊl] *adj* ingenioso(a), lleno(a) de recursos; **that was very r. of you** ¡qué ingenioso!, ¡eso es tener recursos!

resourcefulness [rɪ'zɔːsfʊlnɪs] *n* recursos *mpl*, inventiva *f*

respect [rɪ'spekt] **1** *n* (**a**) *(admiration, esteem)* respeto *m*; **to have r. for sth/sb** respetar algo/a alguien; **she is held in great r. by her colleagues** sus compañeros la respetan mucho; **you have to get** *or* **to gain the children's r.** tienes que ganarte el respeto de los niños; **I have lost all r. for her** le he perdido todo el respeto

(**b**) *(consideration, politeness)* respeto *m*; **show a little r.!** ¡muestra un poco de respeto!; **they have no r. for public property** no respetan la propiedad pública; **out of r. for...** por respeto hacia...; **to treat mountains with r.** respetar la montaña; **with all due r....** con el debido respeto...

(**c**) **respects** *(salutations)* respetos *mpl*; **give my respects to your father** preséntale mis respetos a tu padre; **to pay one's respects to sb** presentar los respetos a alguien; **to pay one's last respects** decir el último adiós

(**d**) *(compliance) (with rules, customs)* respeto *m*, cumplimiento *m*; **his strict r. of the letter of the law** su estricto respeto *or* cumplimiento de la ley

(**e**) *(aspect)* sentido *m*, aspecto *m*; **in some/certain respects** en algunos/ciertos aspectos; **in all respects, in every r.** en todos los sentidos; **with r. to, in r. of** con respecto a

2 *vt* (**a**) *(admire, esteem)* respetar; **I r. him for his efficiency** su eficiencia me inspira respeto (**b**) *(comply with) (rules, customs)* respetar; **to r. sb's wishes** respetar los deseos de alguien

respectability [rɪspektə'bɪlɪtɪ] *n* respetabilidad *f*

respectable [rɪ'spektəbəl] *adj* (**a**) *(honourable, decent)* respetable; **I'm a r. married woman!** ¡soy una mujer casada decente!; **that's not done in r. society** eso no se hace entre *or* delante de gente decente; **I'm not r., YOU answer the door** no estoy visible *or* presentable, contesta tú la puerta

(**b**) *(fairly large)* considerable, respetable; *(fairly good)* decente; **I play a r. game of golf** juego al golf bastante decentemente; **he left a r. tip** dejó una buena propina

respectably [rɪ'spektəblɪ] *adv* (**a**) *(in a respectable manner)* respetablemente (**b**) *(fairly well)* decentemente, pasablemente

respected [rɪ'spektɪd] *adj* respetado(a); **she's a highly r. researcher** es una investigadora muy respetada

respecter [rɪ'spektə(r)] *n* **she is no r. of tradition** las tradiciones le traen sin cuidado; IDIOM **death is no r. of persons** la muerte no hace distinciones

respectful [rɪ'spektfʊl] *adj* respetuoso(a)

respectfully [rɪ'spektfʊlɪ] *adv* respetuosamente; *Old-fashioned* **(I remain,) yours r.** *(at end of letter)* quedo a su entera disposición

respecting [rɪ'spektɪŋ] *prep Formal* con respecto a, en cuanto a

respective [rɪ'spektɪv] *adj* respectivo(a)

respectively [rɪ'spektɪvlɪ] *adv* respectivamente

respiration [respɪ'reɪʃən] *n* respiración *f*

respirator ['respɪreɪtə(r)] *n Med* respirador *m*; **to be on a r.** estar conectado(a) a un respirador artificial

respiratory [rɪ'spɪrɪtərɪ] *adj Anat* respiratorio(a) ►► ***r. failure*** *Esp* fallo *m or Am* falla *f* respiratorio(a); ***r. tract*** vías *fpl* respiratorias

respire [rɪ'spaɪə(r)] *Biol* **1** *vt (air)* respirar

2 *vi (plant, animal)* respirar

respite ['respaɪt] *n* (**a**) *(pause, rest)* respiro *m*, tregua *f*; **there wasn't a moment's r. from the noise** el ruido no daba ni un minuto de tregua; **to work without r.** trabajar sin tregua; **they gave her no r.** no le concedieron un momento de respiro, no le dieron cuartel ►► ***r. care*** = servicio de sustitución para que las personas que cuidan de sus familiares ancianos o discapacitados puedan realizar un descanso

(**b**) *(delay)* prórroga *f*; *(stay of execution)* aplazamiento *m*

resplendence [rɪ'splendəns] *n Literary (splendour)* esplendor *m*

resplendent [rɪ'splendənt] *adj* resplandeciente; **to be r.** estar resplandeciente; **Joe arrived, r. in his new suit** Joe llegó resplandeciente con su nuevo traje

respond [rɪ'spɒnd] **1** *vi* (**a**) *(answer)* responder; **to r. to a request** responder *or* contestar a una solicitud *or Am* un pedido; **she responded with a smile** respondió con una sonrisa

(**b**) *(react)* responder, reaccionar (**to** a); **he doesn't r. well to criticism** no reacciona muy bien a las críticas; **the steering is slow to r.** la dirección tarda en responder

(**c**) *Med* **to r. to treatment** responder al tratamiento

2 *vt* **"who cares?" he responded angrily** "¿qué importa?", respondió enojado

respondent [rɪ'spɒndənt] *n* (**a**) *Law* demandado(a) *m,f* (**b**) *(to questionnaire)* encuestado(a) *m,f*

response [rɪ'spɒns] *n* (**a**) *(answer)* respuesta *f*; **have you had any r. to your request/letter yet?** ¿has recibido alguna respuesta a tu pedido/carta?; **she gave** *or* **made no r.** no respondió; **he smiled in r.** contestó con una sonrisa; **in r. to your question/letter** en respuesta a su pregunta/carta

(**b**) *(reaction)* respuesta *f*, reacción *f*; **their proposals met with a favourable/lukewarm r.** sus propuestas encontraron una respuesta favorable/una tibia respuesta; **r. from the public was disappointing** la respuesta *or* reacción del público no fue la que se esperaba; **in r. to** en respuesta a ►► ***r. rate*** *(to questionnaire)* tasa *f* de respuesta; ***r. time*** *(of emergency services)* tiempo *m* de reacción; *Comptr* tiempo *m* de respuesta

(**c**) *Rel* responsorio *m*

(**d**) *(in bridge)* respuesta *f*

responsibility [rɪspɒnsɪ'bɪlɪtɪ] *n* (**a**) *(control, authority)* responsabilidad *f*; **to have r. for sth** ser responsable de algo; **a position of great r.** un puesto de gran responsabilidad; **can he handle all that r.?** ¿puede manejar semejante responsabilidad?; **he authorized it on his own r.** lo autorizó bajo su propia responsabilidad

(**b**) *(accountability)* responsabilidad *f* (**for** de); **he has no sense of r.** carece de cualquier sentido de la responsabilidad; **to take** *or* **accept (full) r. for sth** asumir (toda) la responsabilidad de algo; **the management accepts no r. for lost or stolen items** *(sign)* la gerencia *or* dirección no acepta responsabilidad por artículos perdidos o robados; **to claim r. for sth** *(bombing, assassination)* reivindicar algo

(**c**) *(duty)* responsabilidad *f*; **answering the phone is his r., not mine** contestar el teléfono le corresponde a él, no a mí; **children are a big r.** los niños son una gran responsabilidad; **responsibilities include product development** las responsabilidades incluyen el desarrollo de producto; **to have a r. to sb** tener una responsabilidad frente a *or* ante alguien

responsible [rɪ'spɒnsɪbəl] *adj* (**a**) *(trustworthy, sensible)* responsable; **it wasn't very r. of him** no fue muy responsable de su parte

(**b**) *(carrying responsibility)* **a r. job** *or* **post** *or* **position** un puesto de responsabilidad

(**c**) *(answerable, accountable)* responsable (**to** ante); **to be r. for** ser responsable de; **who's r. for this mess?** ¿quién es el responsable de este desastre?; **stop making that noise or I won't be r. for my actions!** ¡deja ya de hacer ese ruido o no respondo por mis actos!; **I can't be r. for what happens** no me hago responsable de lo que pueda pasar; **to hold sb r.** considerar a alguien responsable

responsibly [rɪ'spɒnsɪblɪ] *adv* de manera responsable

responsive [rɪ'spɒnsɪv] *adj* (**a**) *(person)* receptivo(a); **the play found a r. audience** la obra fue muy bien recibida por el público; **to be r.** *(to criticism, praise, idea, suggestion)* ser receptivo(a), responder bien; *(willing to participate)* demostrar interés; **to be r. to treatment** responder (bien) al tratamiento

(**b**) *(brakes, controls)* sensible; **the industry is not r. to market signals** el sector no se muestra receptivo ante las señales del mercado

responsiveness [rɪ'spɒnsɪvnɪs] *n* (**a**) *(of person)* receptividad *f* (**b**) *(of brakes, controls)* sensibilidad *f*

respray **1** *n* ['riːspreɪ] *(of car)* **it needs a r.** necesita que lo vuelvan a pintar *(con pistola)*

2 *vt* [riː'spreɪ] *(car)* volver a pintar *(con pistola)*

REST[1] [rest] **1** *n* (**a**) *(repose)* descanso *m*; **to have** *or* **take a r.** descansar, tomarse un descanso; **try to get some r.** trata de reposar; **I need a good night's r. tonight** necesito dormir bien esta noche; **I need a r. from work** necesito descansar del trabajo; **to be at r.** *(not moving)* estar en reposo; *Euph (dead)* descansar en paz; **to put** *or* **set sb's mind at r.** tranquilizar a alguien; **to come to r.** detenerse; *Formal* **to lay sb to r.** *(bury)* dar sepultura a alguien; **to put** *or* **lay sth to r.** *(rumour, speculation)* acabar con algo; **he gave them no r. until they consented** no los dejó en paz hasta que cedieron; **you'd better**

give the skiing a r. mejor que dejes de esquiar durante una temporada; *Fam* **give it a r., will you!** ¿quieres parar de una vez?, *RP* ¡parala de una buena vez! ►► *US* ***r. area*** área *f* de descanso; ***r. cure*** cura *f* de reposo; ***r. day*** día *m* de descanso; ***r. home*** residencia *f* de ancianos; *US Mil* ***r. and recuperation*** permiso *m*; *US* ***r. room*** baño *m*, *Esp* servicios *mpl*, *CSur* toilette *m*; *US* ***r. stop*** área *f* de descanso; **to make a r. stop** hacer una parada de descanso

(**b**) *(support)* soporte *m*, apoyo *m*; *(in snooker)* = utensilio para reposar el taco de billar en los tiros largos

(**c**) *Mus (pause)* silencio *m*

2 *vt* (**a**) *(cause to repose)* descansar; **to r. one's eyes/legs** descansar los ojos/las piernas; **the manager is resting the captain for this game** el entrenador no va a sacar al capitán en este partido para que descanse; *Law* **I r. my case** la defensa no tiene nada más que alegar *or* da por concluidos sus alegatos; *Fig (that proves my point)* ¿qué decía yo?; **God r. his soul!** ¡Dios lo tenga en su gloria!

(**b**) *(lean)* apoyar (**on/against** en/contra); **she rested her elbows on the table** puso los codos en la mesa

3 *vi* (**a**) *(relax)* descansar; **I won't r. until...** no descansaré hasta...; *Euph or Hum* **to be resting** *(actor)* estar ocioso(a)

(**b**) *(lean, be supported)* **the spade was resting against the wall** la pala estaba apoyada *or Méx* recargada contra la pared; **she was resting on her broom** descansaba apoyada en la escoba; **her elbows were resting on the table** sus codos descansaban sobre la mesa

(**c**) *(remain)* **there the matter rests** así ha quedado la cosa; **we have decided to let the matter r.** hemos decidido pasar por alto el asunto; **I won't let it r. at that** esto no va a quedar así; **their fate rests in our hands** tenemos sus destinos en nuestras manos; **r. assured (that)** puedes estar seguro(a) (de que); **you can r. easy** puedes estar tranquilo, quédate tranquilo

(**d**) *Formal (be buried)* descansar; **r. in peace** *(on gravestone)* descanse en paz; **Mr Lamont, may he r. in peace** el Señor Lamont, que en paz descanse

(**e**) *Law* **the defence rests** la defensa ha concluido

(**f**) *Agr (lie fallow)* estar en barbecho

► **rest on** 1 *vt insep* (**a**) *(of structure, argument, belief)* descansar en *or* sobre, apoyarse en *or* sobre; *(of success, future)* depender de (**b**) *(of gaze)* posarse sobre

2 *vt sep (argument, theory)* apoyar en, basar en; *(one's hopes, confidence)* depositar en

► **rest up** *vi Fam* descansar

► **rest with** *vt insep (of decision, responsibility)* corresponder a; *(of hopes, prospects)* recaer en

---

rest[2] *n* **the r.** *(remainder)* el resto; *(others)* el resto, los demás; **the r. of us/them** los demás; **the r. of the time they watch television** el resto del tiempo miran la televisión; **what are you going to do for the r. of the day?** ¿qué vas a hacer en lo que queda de día?; **(as) for the r.** *(otherwise)* por lo demás; *Fam* **and all the r. of it** y todo lo demás, y todo eso; **the r. is history** el resto es (ya) historia

restart [riː'stɑːt] 1 *vt* (**a**) *(activity)* reanudar, empezar de nuevo; *(engine, mechanism)* (volver a) poner en marcha (**b**) *Comptr* reiniciar

2 *vi* (**a**) *(activity)* reanudarse, empezar de nuevo; *(engine, mechanism)* (volver a) poner en marcha (**b**) *Comptr* reiniciarse

3 *n* ['riːstɑːt] (**a**) *(of engine, mechanism)* reencendido *m* (**b**) *Comptr* rearranque *m*, reencendido *m*; **warm/cold r.** rearranque en caliente/frío

restate [riː'steɪt] *vt* (**a**) *(position, argument)* reafirmar (**b**) *(formulate differently) (problem)* reformular, replantear

restatement [riː'steɪtmənt] *n* (**a**) *(repetition) (of position, argument)* reafirmación *f*, repetición *f* (**b**) *(different formulation)* reformulación *f*

restaurant ['restrɒnt] *n* restaurante *m* ►► *Br* ***r. car*** *(in train)* coche *m or* vagón *m* restaurante

restaurateur [restərə'tɜː(r)] *n* restaurador(ora) *m,f*

rested ['restɪd] *adj* descansado(a); **to feel r.** estar *or* sentirse descansado(a)

restful ['restfʊl] *adj* tranquilo(a), reposado(a); **it's very r. on the eyes** relaja mucho los ojos

resting-place ['restɪŋpleɪs] *n* **her final** *or* **last r.** su última morada

restitution [restɪ'tjuːʃən] *n* (**a**) *Formal (compensation)* restitución *f*; **to make r. to sb for sth** restituir a alguien algo (**b**) *Law* restitución *f*, devolución *f*

restive ['restɪv] *adj* inquieto(a), nervioso(a); **to become r.** inquietarse, ponerse nervioso(a)

restively ['restɪvlɪ] *adv* con inquietud

restless ['restlɪs] *adj* (**a**) *(fidgety, nervous)* inquieto(a), agitado(a); **I get r. after a few days in the country** después de unos días en el campo comienzo a inquietarme; **the audience was growing r.** el público comenzaba a impacientarse (**b**) *(dissatisfied)* descontento(a); **her r. mind** su mente inquieta (**c**) *(giving no rest)* **I've had a r. night** he pasado una noche agitada

restlessly ['restlɪslɪ] *adv* (**a**) *(nervously)* nerviosamente; **she paced r. up and down** caminaba impacientemente de aquí para allá (**b**) *(sleeplessly)* **she tossed r. all night** dio vueltas toda la noche sin poder dormir

restlessness ['restlɪsnɪs] *n (fidgeting, nervousness)* inquietud *f*, agitación *f*; **the audience was showing signs of r.** el público comenzaba a dar muestras de impaciencia

restock [riː'stɒk] *vt* (**a**) *(shop, shelf, freezer)* reabastecer, reaprovisionar (**b**) *(lake)* repoblar

restoration [restə'reɪʃən] *n* (**a**) *(repairing) (of building, furniture, painting)* restauración *f*

(**b**) *(re-establishment) (of communications, peace, law and order)* restablecimiento *m*; *(of monarchy)* restauración *f* ►► ***R. Comedy*** comedia *f* de la Restauración, = género dramático del periodo de la Restauración (a partir de 1660) que trata sobre todo de las costumbres libertinas de la clase alta inglesa

(**c**) *(of lost property, fortune)* restitución *f*

restorative [rɪ'stɔːrətɪv] 1 *n* reconstituyente *m*

2 *adj* reconstituyente

restore [rɪ'stɔː(r)] *vt* (**a**) *(repair) (building, furniture, painting)* restaurar; **to r. sth to its former glory** devolver a algo su gloria pasada

(**b**) *(re-establish) (communications, peace, law and order)* restablecer; *(monarchy)* restaurar; *(confidence)* devolver; **to r. public confidence in sth** restaurar la confianza pública en algo; **it restored my faith in human nature** me devolvió la fe en la naturaleza humana; **if the reform government is restored to power** si el gobierno reformista es restaurado en el poder; **she managed to r. the company to profitability** logró devolverle la rentabilidad a la compañía; **to r. sb's sight/hearing** devolver la vista/la audición a alguien; **to r. sb to health/strength** devolver la salud/la fuerza a alguien

(**c**) *(property, fortune)* restituir

(**d**) *Comptr (files)* restaurar

restorer [rɪ'stɔːrə(r)] *n (of building, furniture, painting)* restaurador(ora) *m,f*

restrain [rɪ'streɪn] *vt (person, crowd, dog, one's curiosity)* contener; *(passions, anger)* reprimir, dominar; **it took four policemen to r. him** hicieron falta cuatro policías para poder reducirlo; **I had to r. an impulse to laugh out loud** tuve que contener una carcajada; **to r. sb from doing sth** impedir a alguien que haga algo; **to r. oneself** contenerse, controlarse

restrained [rɪ'streɪnd] *adj* (**a**) *(person)* comedido(a); *(response, emotion)* contenido(a) (**b**) *(colour, style)* sobrio(a)

restraint [rɪ'streɪnt] *n* (**a**) *(moderation)* dominio *m* de sí mismo(a), comedimiento *m*; **he showed remarkable r.** se mostró muy comedido; **to urge r.** pedir moderación

(**b**) *(restriction)* restricción *f*, limitación *f*; **to put a r. on sb** imponer limitaciones a alguien; **to keep sb under r.** tener reducido(a) a alguien; **to place sb under r.** reducir a alguien; **without r.** sin restricciones ►► *Com* ***r. of trade*** restricción *f* comercial

(**c**) *(control)* restricción *f*; **a policy of price/wage r.** una política de control de precios/moderación salarial

(**d**) **restraints** *(for criminal, patient)* correas *fpl*

restrict [rɪ'strɪkt] *vt (person, access, movement)* restringir, limitar; *(freedom)* coartar, restringir; **airlines r. the amount of luggage you can take** las compañías aéreas limitan la cantidad de equipaje con que se puede viajar; **fog is restricting visibility** la niebla está reduciendo la visibilidad; **to r. sth/sb to sth** limitar algo/a alguien a algo; **to r. oneself to...** limitarse a...

restricted [rɪ'strɪktɪd] *adj* (**a**) *(access, opportunities)* restringido(a), limitado(a); **the choice is too r.** hay muy pocas opciones; **to be on a r. diet** hacer una dieta restringida ►► ***r. area*** *(out of bounds)* zona *f* de acceso restringido; *Br Aut (with parking restrictions)* zona *f* de *Esp* aparcamiento *or Am* estacionamiento restringido; *(with speed limit)* zona *f* con límite de velocidad; ***r. document*** documento *m* confidencial

(**b**) *(narrow) (ideas, outlook)* limitado(a), cerrado(a)

(**c**) *US (movie)* no recomendado(a) para menores

restriction [rɪ'strɪkʃən] *n* restricción *f*, limitación *f*; **speed restrictions** límites de velocidad; **weight restrictions** restricciones *or* límites de peso; **they will accept no r. of their liberty** no aceptarán restricciones sobre su libertad; **there are no restrictions on how much you can**

buy no hay ninguna restricción sobre la cantidad de productos que te dejan comprar; **to put** *or* **place** *or* **impose restrictions on sth** poner trabas a algo; **without r.** sin restricciones

restrictive [rɪ'strɪktɪv] *adj* restrictivo(a) ►► *Gram* ***r. clause*** oración *f* relativa especificativa *or* determinativa; *Ind* ***r. practices*** prácticas *fpl* restrictivas

restring [riː'strɪŋ] *vt* (*pt & pp* **restrung**) *(bow)* cambiar la cuerda a; *(musical instrument, tennis racket)* encordar; *(beads, pearls)* reenhebrar

restructure [riː'strʌktʃə(r)] *vt (company, economy)* reestructurar, reconvertir; *(text, argument)* reestructurar; *Fin (debt)* refinanciar, reestructurar

restructuring [riː'strʌktʃərɪŋ] *n (of company, economy)* reestructuración *f*, reconversión *f*; *(of text, argument)* reestructuración *f*; *Fin (of debt)* refinanciamiento *m*, reestructuración *f*

restrung *pt & pp of* **restring**

restyle ['riː'staɪl] *vt (car)* rediseñar, cambiar el diseño de; *(hair, clothes)* cambiar el estilo de; *(magazine)* cambiar el aspecto *or* diseño de

result [rɪ'zʌlt] **1** *n* (**a**) *(consequence)* resultado *m*; **with disastrous results** con pésimos resultados; **this paint gives excellent results** esta pintura da un resultado excelente; **it was all the r. of a misunderstanding** fue fruto de un malentendido; **as a r.** por lo tanto; **as a r. of these changes** como consecuencia *or* resultado de estos cambios; **the r. is that...** el caso es que...; **with the r. that...** y como resultado...

(**b**) *(success)* resultado *m*; **to yield** *or* **show results** dar resultado; **to get results** obtener resultados; *Br Sport* **to get/need a r.** obtener/necesitar un buen resultado

(**c**) *(of match, exam, election)* resultado *m*

(**d**) *Fin* **the company's results are down on last year** las ganancias de la compañía fueron inferiores a las del año pasado

2 *vi* resultar; **a price rise would inevitably r.** el resultado inevitable sería una subida *or CSur* suba de precios; **the resulting protests** las protestas que se generaron; **to r. from** resultar de, ser ocasionado(a) por; **to r. in sth** tener algo como resultado, ocasionar algo

resultant [rɪ'zʌltənt] **1** *n Math & Phys* resultante *f*

2 *adj* resultante

resume [rɪ'zjuːm] **1** *vt (relations, work, talks, journey)* reanudar; **he resumes his post on Monday** volverá a su puesto el lunes; *Formal* **kindly r. your seats** tengan la amabilidad de regresar a sus asientos; **she resumed her maiden name** retomó su nombre de soltera

2 *vi* continuar, reanudarse; **the meeting will r. after lunch** la reunión continuará *or* se reanudará después de la comida *or* del almuerzo

> **False friend**: The most common senses of the English verb **resume** are not translated by the Spanish word **resumir**. In Spanish **resumir** means "to summarize" or "to sum up".

résumé ['rezjʊmeɪ] *n* (**a**) *(summary)* resumen *m*; **to give a r. of sth** hacer un resumen de algo (**b**) *US (curriculum vitae)* currículum (vitae) *m*

resumption [rɪ'zʌmpʃən] *n* reanudación *f*

resurface [riː'sɜːfɪs] **1** *vt (road)* rehacer el firme de

2 *vi* (**a**) *(submarine)* volver a la superficie (**b**) *(reappear) (person, rumour)* reaparecer; **the stolen jewels resurfaced in Australia** las joyas robadas aparecieron en Australia

resurgence [rɪ'sɜːdʒəns] *n* resurgimiento *m*

resurgent [rɪ'sɜːdʒənt] *adj* renaciente, resurgente

resurrect [rezə'rekt] *vt (the dead, fashion, argument)* resucitar; **they've resurrected this old tradition** han resucitado esta vieja costumbre; **the minister succeeded in resurrecting his career** el ministro logró resucitar su carrera

resurrection [rezə'rekʃən] *n* (**a**) *(of conflict, accusation)* reavivamiento *m* (**b**) *Rel* **the R.** la Resurrección

resuscitate [rɪ'sʌsɪteɪt] *vt* (**a**) *(person)* resucitar (**b**) *(scheme, career)* resucitar

resuscitation [rɪsʌsɪ'teɪʃən] *n* (**a**) *(of person)* resucitación *f* (**b**) *(of scheme, career)* vuelta *f or* retorno *m* a la vida

retail ['riːteɪl] **1** *n Com (selling, trade)* venta *f* al por menor, *Am* menoreo *m* ►► ***r. outlet*** punto *m* de venta; *Br* ***r. park*** = complejo comercial formado por diferentes tiendas y almacenes grandes; ***r. price*** precio *m* de venta (al público); *Br Econ* ***r. price index*** índice *m* de precios al consumo; *Hum* ***r. therapy:*** **there's nothing like a bit of r. therapy** no hay mejor terapia que irse de compras; ***the r. trade*** los minoristas

2 *adv* al (por) menor, al detalle

3 *vt* (**a**) *(goods)* vender al por menor (**b**) *(gossip)* contar

4 *vi* **it retails at** *or* **for $995** su precio de venta al público es 995 dólares

retailer ['riːteɪlə(r)] *n Com* minorista *mf*

retain [rɪ'teɪn] *vt* (**a**) *(keep)* conservar; *(heat)* retener, conservar; **the village has retained its charm** la aldea ha conservado su encanto (**b**) *(hold in place)* sujetar (**c**) *(remember)* retener; **I just can't r. dates** nunca recuerdo *or* retengo las fechas (**d**) *(lawyer, consultant)* contratar; **to r. sb's services** contratar los servicios de alguien

retained [rɪ'teɪnd] *adj Fin* ***r. earnings*** ganancias *fpl* acumuladas

retainer [rɪ'teɪnə(r)] *n* (**a**) *(fee)* anticipo *m* (**b**) *(servant)* criado(a) *m,f* (de toda la vida)

retaining wall [rɪ'teɪnɪŋ'wɔːl] *n* muro *m* de contención

retake 1 *n* ['riːteɪk] (**a**) *(of exam)* repesca *f*; **how many retakes did you have?** ¿cuántas veces tuviste que presentarte? (**b**) *Cin (of scene)* nueva toma *f*; **to do a r.** repetir una toma

2 *vt* [riː'teɪk] (**a**) *(exam)* volver a presentarse a (**b**) *(town, fortress)* volver a tomar, recuperar (**c**) *Cin (scene)* volver a rodar

retaliate [rɪ'tælɪeɪt] *vi* responder, tomar represalias; **we will r. if attacked** si nos atacan tomaremos represalias; **the player was sent off for retaliating** el jugador fue expulsado por haber reaccionado (con una agresión)

retaliation [rɪtælɪ'eɪʃən] *n* represalias *fpl*; **in r. (for sth)** como represalia (por algo)

retaliatory [rɪ'tælɪətərɪ] *adj* como *or* en represalia; **a r. attack** un ataque en represalia

retard 1 *n* ['riːtɑːd] *US Fam* retrasado(a) *m,f*

2 *vt* [rɪ'tɑːd] *(delay)* retrasar, demorar

retardant [rɪ'tɑːdənt] **1** *n* retardador *m*

2 *adj* retardador(ora), retardante

retarded [rɪ'tɑːdɪd] *Old-fashioned* **1** *n* **the (mentally) r.** los retrasados (mentales)

2 *adj* **to be (mentally) r.** ser retrasado(a) mental

retch [retʃ] *vi* tener arcadas; **we could hear him retching** oímos cómo le daban arcadas

retching ['retʃɪŋ] *n* arcadas *fpl*

retd (*abbr* **retired**) retirado(a)

retell [riː'tel] *vt* volver a contar

retelling [riː'telɪŋ] *n* **the story gained in the r.** la historia se enriqueció al volver a contarla

retention [rɪ'tenʃən] *n* (**a**) *(of custom, practice)* conservación *f*, preservación *f* (**b**) *(of fact, impression)* retención *f* (**c**) *(memory)* retención *f* (**d**) *Med* **fluid/urine r.** retención de líquidos/orina

retentive [rɪ'tentɪv] *adj (memory, person)* retentivo(a)

rethink 1 *n* ['riːθɪŋk] **to have a r. (about sth)** hacerse un replanteamiento (de algo); **we need a complete r. of our strategy** necesitamos hacer un replanteamiento completo de nuestra estrategia

2 *vt* [riː'θɪŋk] (*pt & pp* **rethought** [riː'θɔːt]) replantear(se)

reticence ['retɪsəns] *n* reticencia *f*

reticent ['retɪsənt] *adj* reservado(a) (**about** sobre)

> **False friend**: The Spanish adjective **reticente** is not a translation for the English word **reticent**. In Spanish **reticente** means "reluctant" or "full of insinuation".

reticle ['retɪkəl] *n* retícula *f*

reticulate [rɪ'tɪkjʊlət] *adj* reticular

reticule ['retɪkjuːl] *n* (**a**) *Hist (bag)* ridículo *m* (**b**) *(on optical instrument)* retículo *m*

reticulum [rɪ'tɪkjʊləm] *n* (**a**) *(network)* retículo *m* (**b**) *Zool* retículo *m*

retina ['retɪnə] *n Anat* retina *f*

retinal ['retɪnəl] *adj* retinal ►► *Med* ***r. detachment*** desprendimiento *m* de retina

retinue ['retɪnjuː] *n* comitiva *f*, séquito *m*

retire [rɪ'taɪə(r)] **1** *vt* (**a**) *(employee)* jubilar (**b**) *(troops)* replegar, retirar (**c**) *Fin (coins, bonds, shares)* amortizar

2 *vi* (**a**) *(employee)* jubilarse; **they retired to the south of France** se jubilaron y se fueron a vivir al sur de Francia; **to r. from boxing/politics** retirarse del boxeo/de la política

(**b**) *(withdraw)* retirarse; **the jury retired to consider its verdict** el jurado se retiró a discutir el veredicto; *Formal* **shall we r. to the lounge?** ¿pasamos a la sala?

(**c**) *(troops)* replegarse, retirarse

(**d**) *(from match, competition)* retirarse; **to r. hurt** retirarse lesionado(a), abandonar lesionado(a) el campo de juego
(**e**) *Formal or Hum (to bed)* retirarse (a descansar)

retired [rɪ'taɪəd] *adj* (**a**) *(from job)* jubilado(a); *(from military)* retirado(a); **to be r.** *(from job)* estar jubilado(a); *Mil* **to put sb on the r. list** poner a alguien en la lista de retirados del servicio activo (**b**) *(secluded)* apartado(a); **he led a r. life after leaving politics** tras dejar la política llevó una vida discreta

retiree [rɪtaɪə'ri:] *n US* jubilado(a) *m,f*

retirement [rɪ'taɪəmənt] *n* (**a**) *(from job)* jubilación *f*; **to take early r.** tomar la jubilación anticipada; **he came out of r.** salió de su retiro; **(of) r. age** (en) edad de jubilación ▸▸ ***r. community*** complejo *m* residencial para jubilados; ***r. home*** residencia *f* de ancianos; ***r. pension*** pensión *f* de jubilación; *US* ***r. plan*** plan *m* de jubilación
(**b**) *(seclusion)* retiro *m*
(**c**) *(of troops)* repliegue *m*, retirada *f*
(**d**) *(from match, competition)* retirada *f*

retiring [rɪ'taɪərɪŋ] *adj* (**a**) *(reserved)* retraído(a), reservado(a) (**b**) *(employee)* saliente *(por jubilación)*, que se jubila; *(officeholder)* saliente

retool ['ri:'tu:l] **1** *vt* (**a**) *Ind* reequipar; **to r. a factory for armaments production** reconvertir una fábrica para la producción de armamento (**b**) *US (reorganize)* reorganizar
2 *vi* (**a**) *Ind* reequiparse (**b**) *US (reorganize)* reorganizarse

retort [rɪ'tɔ:t] **1** *n* (**a**) *(answer)* réplica *f* (**b**) *Chem* retorta *f*
2 *vt* replicar
3 *vi* replicar

retouch [ri:'tʌtʃ] *vt (photograph, painting)* retocar

retrace [ri:'treɪs] *vt* (**a**) *(go back over) (route)* desandar; **they retraced their steps** volvieron sobre sus pasos (**b**) *(reconstitute) (past events, sb's movements)* reconstruir

retract [rɪ'trækt] **1** *vt* (**a**) *(statement, offer, promise)* retractarse de, revocar (**b**) *(claws)* retraer; *(undercarriage)* replegar
2 *vi* (**a**) *(person)* retractarse (**b**) *(claws)* retraerse; *(undercarriage)* replegarse

retractable [rɪ'træktəbəl] *adj (antenna, tip of instrument)* retráctil; *(undercarriage)* replegable

retractile [rɪ'træktaɪl] *adj* retráctil

retraction [rɪ'trækʃən] *n (of statement, offer)* retractación *f*; **to publish a r.** *(newspaper)* publicar una retractación

retrain [ri:'treɪn] **1** *vt (employee)* reciclar
2 *vi (employee)* reciclarse (**as** como)

retraining [ri:'treɪnɪŋ] *n* reciclaje *m* profesional

retread ['ri:tred] **1** *n Aut* neumático *m* recauchutado, *Col, Méx* llanta *f or Arg* goma *f* recauchutada
2 *vt* recauchutar

retreat [rɪ'tri:t] **1** *n* (**a**) *(withdrawal)* retirada *f*; **nationalism is in r.** el nacionalismo está retrocediendo; **this is a r. from the unions' original position** esto constituye una marcha atrás respecto a la posición inicial de los sindicatos
(**b**) *(of troops, army)* retirada *f*; **the r. from Moscow** la retirada de Moscú; **they were forced into r.** se vieron obligados a replegarse; **to beat a r.** batirse en retirada; IDIOM **she beat a hasty r.** salió zumbando
(**c**) *(place)* retiro *m*, refugio *m*; **a weekend r.** un refugio de fin de semana
(**d**) *Rel* retiro *m* espiritual, ejercicios *mpl* espirituales; **to go on** *or* **into r.** ir de ejercicios espirituales
2 *vi* (**a**) *(withdraw)* retirarse; **management was forced to r. on this point** la gerencia se vio obligada a ceder en este punto; **he retreated into a world of his own** se encerró en su propio mundo (**b**) *(troops, army)* replegarse, retirarse (**c**) *(flood waters)* bajar

retrench [rɪ'trentʃ] *vi Formal (financially)* reducir gastos

retrenchment [rɪ'trentʃmənt] *n Formal* reducción *f* de gastos

retrial ['ri:'traɪəl] *n Law* nuevo juicio *m*

retribution [retrɪ'bju:ʃən] *n* represalias *fpl*; **it is divine r.** es el castigo divino; **in r. (for)** en represalia (por)

> **False friend:** The Spanish noun **retribución** is not a translation for the English word **retribution**. In Spanish **retribución** means "payment" or "reward".

retributive [rɪ'trɪbjʊtɪv] *adj (involving punishment)* punitivo(a)

retrievable [rɪ'tri:vəbəl] *adj* (**a**) *(object)* recuperable; **once it had fallen from the ledge, the ball was no longer r.** cuando la pelota cayó de la cornisa, fue imposible de recuperarla (**b**) *(situation)* remediable (**c**) *Comptr (data)* recuperable

retrieval [rɪ'tri:vəl] *n* (**a**) *(of object)* recuperación *f* (**b**) *(salvation)* **the situation is beyond r.** la situación es irremediable (**c**) *Comptr (of data)* recuperación *f*

retrieve [rɪ'tri:v] **1** *vt* (**a**) *(object)* recuperar; **I retrieved my bag from the lost property office** recuperé mi cartera en la oficina de objetos perdidos (**b**) *(of dog) (ball, stick)* buscar; *(game bird)* cobrar (**c**) *(situation)* salvar (**d**) *Comptr (data)* recuperar
2 *vi (hunting dog)* **I taught it to r.** le he enseñado a cobrar piezas

retriever [rɪ'tri:və(r)] *n (dog)* perro *m* cobrador

retro ['retrəʊ] *adj* retro ▸▸ ***r. chic*** estilo *m* retro

retroactive [retrəʊ'æktɪv] *adj* retroactivo(a); **the increase is r. to last January** el aumento se aplicará con efecto retroactivo a enero pasado

retroactively [retrəʊ'æktɪvlɪ] *adv* retroactivamente

retrofit ['retrəʊfɪt] *vt* reequipar

retroflex ['retrəʊfleks] *adj Ling* retroflexo(a)

retrograde ['retrəgreɪd] *adj (movement, step)* retrógrado(a)

retrogression [retrə'greʃən] *n Formal* retroceso *m*

retrogressive [retrə'gresɪv] *adj Formal* retrógrado(a)

retrospect ['retrəspekt] *n* **in r.** restrospectivamente, en retrospectiva

retrospection [retrə'spekʃən] *n* retrospección *f*

retrospective [retrə'spektɪv] **1** *n (exhibition, movie season)* retrospectiva *f*
2 *adj* retrospectivo(a)

retrospectively [retrə'spektɪvlɪ] *adv* retrospectivamente

retroussé [rə'tru:seɪ] *adj* respingón(ona)

retrovirus ['retrəʊvaɪrəs] *n Med* retrovirus *m inv*

retry [ri:'traɪ] **1** *vt Law* volver a procesar a
2 *vi Comptr* reintentar

retsina [ret'si:nə] *n* retsina *m*

retune [ri:'tju:n] **1** *vt (radio)* volver a sintonizar, resintonizar
2 *vi (radio)* **to r. to medium wave** volver a sintonizar *or* resintonizar onda media

RETURN [rɪ'tɜ:n] **1** *n* (**a**) *(coming or going back) (of person, peace, season)* vuelta *f*, regreso *m*; **a r. to normal** un regreso a la normalidad; **the strikers' r. to work** la vuelta al trabajo de los huelguistas; **on my r.** a mi vuelta *or* regreso; **by r. of post,** *US* **by r. mail** a vuelta de correo ▸▸ ***r. journey*** viaje *m* de vuelta; ***r. match*** partido *m* de vuelta
(**b**) *Br (for train, plane)* **r. (ticket)** *Esp* billete *m or Am* pasaje *m or Am* boleto *m* de ida y vuelta
(**c**) *(giving back) (of goods)* devolución *f*; **returns** *(goods taken back, theatre tickets)* devoluciones *fpl*
(**d**) *(in tennis)* **r. (of serve)** resto *m*
(**e**) *(exchange)* **in r. (for)** a cambio (de)
(**f**) *Fin (profit)* rendimiento *m*; **r. on investment** rendimiento de las inversiones; **to bring a good r.** proporcionar buenos dividendos
(**g**) *(for income tax)* (formulario *m* de la) declaración *f* de la renta
(**h**) *Comptr* **r. (key)** (tecla *f* de) retorno *m*
(**i**) *(greeting)* **many happy returns of the day!** ¡muchas felicidades!, ¡feliz cumpleaños!
(**j**) *(in election)* **returns** resultados *mpl*
2 *vt* (**a**) *(give or send back)* devolver; **to r. sth to its place** volver a poner algo en su lugar, devolver *or Andes, CAm, Carib, Méx* regresar algo a su sitio; **r. to sender** *(on letter)* devolver al remitente; **to r. service** *(in tennis)* restar, devolver el servicio
(**b**) *(do in exchange)* **to r. sb's call** devolver una llamada a alguien, *Am* llamar a alguien en respuesta a su llamado; **to r. a compliment/favour** devolver *or RP* retribuir un cumplido/favor; **he ordered them to r. fire** les ordenó abrir fuego en respuesta a los disparos; **to r. sb's love** corresponder al amor de alguien; **she returned my look** me devolvió la mirada; **he returned my visit** me devolvió *or RP* retribuyó la visita
(**c**) *Law* **to r. a verdict of guilty/not guilty** pronunciar un veredicto de culpable/inocente
(**d**) *Br (elect)* elegir (**as** como)
(**e**) *Com & Fin (profit)* rendir, proporcionar; *(interest)* devengar
(**f**) *(reply)* replicar, reponer
3 *vi* (**a**) *(come or go back)* volver, regresar; **to r. home** volver a casa; **to r. to work** volver al trabajo; **she returned to her reading** volvió a lo que estaba leyendo; **he soon returned to his old ways** al poco tiempo volvió a las andadas; **to r. to consciousness** recobrar la consciencia; **let's r. to the subject** volvamos al tema; **the situation has returned to normal** la situación ha vuelto a la normalidad
(**b**) *(start again) (fears, fever, good weather)* volver; **his old feelings**

for her returned recuperó el cariño hacia ella; **the tumour has returned** el tumor ha vuelto a desarrollarse
(c) *(in tennis)* restar

---

returnable [rɪ'tɜːnəbəl] *adj (bottle)* retornable; **sale items are not r.** no se admite la devolución de artículos rebajados

returning officer [rɪ'tɜːnɪŋ'ɒfɪsə(r)] *n Br Pol* = funcionario encargado de organizar las elecciones al Parlamento en su circunscripción electoral y que anuncia oficialmente los resultados de éstas

reuben ['ruːbɪn] *n US* **r. (sandwich)** = sandwich tostado de pan de centeno relleno de "corned beef", queso suizo y chucrut

reunification [riːjuːnɪfɪ'keɪʃən] *n* reunificación *f*

reunify [riː'juːnɪfaɪ] *vt* reunificar

reunion [riː'juːnɪən] *n* reencuentro *m*, reunión *f*; **a family r.** una reunión familiar; **a class r.** un reencuentro de ex compañeros de clase; **r. celebration/dinner** fiesta/cena de reencuentro

reunite [riːjʊ'naɪt] **1** *vt* reunir; **to be reunited (with sb)** reencontrarse *or* volver a reunirse (con alguien)
2 *vi* reunirse

re-up [riː'ʌp] *vi US Fam (re-enlist)* reengancharse

reusable [riː'juːzəbəl] *adj* reutilizable

reuse [riː'juːz] *vt* volver a utilizar, reutilizar

Rev *Rel (abbr* **Reverend)** **R. Gray** el reverendo Gray

rev [rev] *Aut* **1** *n* **the engine was doing 5,000 revs** el motor iba a 5.000 revoluciones (por minuto) ▸▸ ***r. counter*** cuentarrevoluciones *m inv*
2 *vt (pt & pp* **revved)** **to r. the engine** revolucionar *or* acelerar el motor
3 *vi* acelerarse

▸**rev up** **1** *vt sep (engine)* acelerar, revolucionar
2 *vi* (**a**) *(driver)* acelerar; *(engine)* acelerarse, subir de revoluciones (**b**) *(preparing)* prepararse, calentar motores; **the town is revving up for its annual fair** el pueblo ya está calentando motores para su feria anual

revaluate *US* = **revalue**

revaluation [riːvæljʊ'eɪʃən] *n* (**a**) *(of currency)* revalorización *f* (**b**) *(of property)* revaloración *f* (**c**) *(of reputation, importance, artist)* revaloración *f*, reconsideración *f*

revalue [riː'væljuː], *US* **revaluate** [riː'væljʊeɪt] *vt* (**a**) *(currency)* revalorizar (**b**) *(property)* revalorar, volver a valorar (**c**) *(reputation, importance, artist)* reconsiderar, revalorar

revamp [riː'væmp] *Fam* **1** *n* renovación *f*; **to give sth a r.** renovar algo
2 *vt* renovar

revanchism [rɪ'væntʃɪzəm] *n* revanchismo *m*

revanchist [rɪ'væntʃɪst] **1** *n* revanchista *mf*
2 *adj* revanchista

Revd *Rel (abbr* **Reverend)** **R. Green** el reverendo Green

reveal [rɪ'viːl] *vt* (**a**) *(disclose, divulge)* revelar; **to r. a secret** revelar un secreto; **it has been revealed that...** se ha dado a conocer que...; **all will be revealed in the concluding episode** todo se desvelará en el episodio final
(**b**) *(show)* revelar, mostrar; **she removed the veil to r. her face** se quitó el velo para descubrir su rostro; **he tried hard not to r. his true feelings** hizo un gran esfuerzo por no demostrar lo que de verdad sentía; **a medical examination revealed two cracked ribs** un examen clínico reveló dos costillas fracturadas

revealed [rɪ'viːld] *adj* revelado(a)

revealing [rɪ'viːlɪŋ] *adj* (**a**) *(sign, comment)* revelador(ora) (**b**) *(dress)* insinuante

revealingly [rɪ'viːlɪŋlɪ] *adv (significantly)* significativamente; **r., not one of them speaks a foreign language** es significativo que ninguno (de ellos) hable otro idioma

reveille [*Br* rɪ'vælɪ, *US* 'revəlɪ] *n Mil* (toque *m* de) diana *f*

revel ['revəl] **1** *vi (pt & pp* **revelled,** *US* **reveled)** (**a**) *(bask, wallow)* **to r. in sth** deleitarse con algo; **to r. in one's freedom** disfrutar plenamente de la libertad (**b**) *(make merry)* estar de juerga
2 revels *npl* farra *f*

revelation [revə'leɪʃən] *n* revelación *f*; **her singing was a r. to me** para mí fue una revelación, no sabía que cantaba tan bien; **(the Book of) Revelations** el Apocalipsis

revelatory [revə'leɪtərɪ] *adj* revelador(ora)

reveller, *US* **reveler** ['revələ(r)] *n* juerguista *mf*

revelry ['revəlrɪ] *n* jolgorio *m*

revenge [rɪ'vendʒ] **1** *n* venganza *f*; **to take r. (on sb)** vengarse (de alguien); **to get** *or* **take one's r.** vengarse; **to do sth out of r.** hacer algo por venganza; **to do sth in r. (for sth)** hacer algo como venganza (por algo); PROV **r. is sweet** la venganza es un placer de dioses
2 *vt* **to be revenged** vengarse; **to r. oneself on sb** vengarse de alguien

revengeful [rɪ'vendʒfʊl] *adj* vengativo(a)

revenue ['revənjuː] *n Fin* ingresos *mpl* ▸▸ ***r. bond*** obligación *f* pagadera mediante ingresos fiscales; ***r. expenditure*** gastos *mpl* operativos *or* corrientes; ***r. stamp*** timbre *m* fiscal

reverb ['riːvɜːb] *n Mus Fam* eco *m*; **r. (unit)** cámara *f* de eco

reverberate [rɪ'vɜːbəreɪt] *vi* (**a**) *(sound)* reverberar; **the stadium reverberated with applause** el estadio resonaba con los aplausos (**b**) *(news, rumour)* repercutir; **the scandal reverberated through the country** el escándalo tuvo repercusiones en todo el país

reverberation [rɪvɜːbə'reɪʃən] *n* (**a**) *(of sound)* reverberación *f* (**b**) *(of news, rumour)* repercusión *f*

revere [rɪ'vɪə(r)] *vt* reverenciar, venerar; **she was a much revered figure** era una figura muy venerada

reverence ['revərəns] *n* (**a**) *(respect)* reverencia *f*, veneración *f*; **they hold her in r.** la veneran (**b**) *(term of address)* **Your R.** Su Reverencia; **His R. the Archbishop** Su Excelencia el Reverendísimo Arzobispo (**c**) *(bow)* reverencia *f*

Reverend ['revərənd] *n Rel* reverendo *m*; **Right R.** Reverendísimo ▸▸ ***R. Mother*** Reverenda Madre *f*

reverent ['revərənt] *adj* reverente

reverential [revə'renʃəl] *adj* reverente

reverently ['revərəntlɪ] *adv* con reverencia

reverie ['revərɪ] *n* ensoñación *f*

revers [rɪ'vɪə(r)] *(pl* **revers** [rɪ'vɪəz]) *n* solapa *f*

reversal [rɪ'vɜːsəl] *n* (**a**) *(of opinion, policy, roles)* inversión *f* (**b**) *Law (of decision)* revocación *f* (**c**) *(setback)* **r. of fortune** revés de la fortuna; **to suffer a r.** sufrir un revés (**d**) *Phot* ***r. film*** película *f* reversible

reverse [rɪ'vɜːs] **1** *n* (**a**) *(opposite)* **the r.** lo contrario; **quite the r.!** ¡todo lo contrario!; **in r.** al revés; **go through the steps of the process in r.** haz el proceso inverso (**b**) *(other side) (of coin, medal)* reverso *m*; *(of fabric)* revés *m*; *(of sheet of paper)* dorso *m* (**c**) *(defeat, misfortune)* revés *m* (**d**) *Aut (gear)* marcha *f* atrás; **in r.** marcha atrás; **the vehicle was in r.** el vehículo tenía puesta la marcha atrás; **he put the vehicle into r.** puso el vehículo en marcha atrás
2 *adj* (**a**) *(opposite, contrary)* contrario(a), inverso(a); **in r. order** en orden inverso ▸▸ ***r. discrimination*** discriminación *f* inversa; *Ind* ***r. engineering*** = práctica de desmontar un producto de la competencia para ver cómo está diseñado; ***r. lay-up*** *(in basketball)* canasta *f* a aro pasado; *Comptr* ***r. slash*** barra *f* oblicua invertida; *Fin* ***r. takeover*** absorción *f* inversa; *Biol* ***r. transcriptase*** transcriptasa *f* inversa; *Comptr* ***r. video*** vídeo *m or Am* video *m* inverso
(**b**) *(back)* **the r. side** *(of fabric)* el revés; *(of sheet of paper)* el dorso
(**c**) *(turned around)* invertido(a); **a r. image** una imagen invertida
(**d**) *Aut* ***r. gear*** marcha *f* atrás
3 *vt* (**a**) *(order, situation, trend)* invertir; *(process, decline)* invertir; **this should r. the effects of the drug** esto debería revertir los efectos de la droga; **the roles are reversed** se han invertido los papeles
(**b**) *(decision)* revertir, revocar; **the unions have reversed their policy** los sindicatos han hecho un giro de 180 grados en su política
(**c**) *(cause to go backwards) (vehicle)* poner en marcha atrás; *(machine)* invertir; **this lever reverses the belt** esta palanca invierte la dirección de la cinta; **she reversed the car into the road** salió a la carretera marcha atrás; **he reversed the taxi into a lamppost** estrelló el taxi contra una farola dando marcha atrás
(**d**) *Br* **to r. the charges** *(for phone call)* llamar a cobro revertido
(**e**) *(garment)* **the jacket can be reversed** es una chaqueta reversible
4 *vi (car, driver)* dar marcha atrás; **the driver in front reversed into me** el conductor que estaba delante de mí me golpeó dando marcha atrás

reverse-charge call [rɪ'vɜːstʃɑːdʒ'kɔːl] *n Br* llamada *f or Am* llamado *m* a cobro revertido

reversi [rɪ'vɜːsɪ] *n* reversi *m*

reversible [rɪ'vɜːsəbəl] *adj* (**a**) *(jacket)* reversible (**b**) *(decree, decision)* revocable; *(surgery)* reversible; **the decision is not r.** la decisión es irrevocable (**c**) *Chem* ***r. reaction*** reacción *f* reversible

reversing light [rɪ'vɜːsɪŋlaɪt] *n Br* luz *f* de marcha atrás

reversion [rɪ'vɜːʃən] *n* (**a**) *(to former state, habit)* vuelta *f* (**b**) *Law* reversión *f* (**c**) *Biol* **r. to type** regresión al tipo original; *Fig* **this was a not unexpected r. to type** era la predecible vuelta a las andadas

reversionary bonus [rɪ'vɜːʃənərɪ'bəʊnəs] *n Fin* bonificación *f* diferida

revert [rɪ'vɜːt] *vi* (**a**) *(return)* volver; **they reverted to barbarism** regresaron a la barbarie; **the land has reverted to a wild meadow** el terreno se ha vuelto a convertir en una pradera (**b**) *Law (property)* revertir (**c**) *Biol* **to r. to type** hacer una regresión; *Fig* **he soon reverted to type** pronto volvió a su antiguo ser

revetment [rɪ'vetmənt] *n* revestimiento *m*

review [rɪ'vjuː] **1** *n* (**a**) *(of policy, situation)* revisión *f*; **the case is coming up for r.** el caso va a ser revisado; **all our prices are subject to r.** todos nuestros precios están sujetos a cambio; **to be under r.** estar siendo revisado(a) ►► ***r. body*** comisión *f* de estudio
(**b**) *Law (of case)* revisión *f*
(**c**) *(survey)* repaso *m*; **she gave us a brief r. of the situation** nos hizo un resumen rápido de la situación; **a r. of the year** un repaso del año
(**d**) *(of book, play, movie)* crítica *f*, reseña *f*; **the play got good/bad reviews** la obra recibió buenas/malas críticas ►► ***r. copy*** ejemplar *m* para la prensa
(**e**) *(magazine)* revista *f*; *(radio, TV programme)* crítica *f*, reseña *f*
(**f**) *Mil* revista *f*; **to pass troops in r.** pasar revista a las tropas
(**g**) *Theat* revista *f*
(**h**) *US (revision)* repaso *m*, revisión *f*
2 *vt* (**a**) *(policy, situation)* revisar; *(progress)* analizar, examinar; **they should r. their security arrangements** deberían revisar su sistema de seguridad
(**b**) *Law (case)* revisar
(**c**) *(book, play, movie)* hacer una crítica de, reseñar
(**d**) *(go back over)* hacer una revisión de; **we shall be reviewing the events of the past year** haremos una revisión de los hechos más destacados del año pasado; **she quickly reviewed her notes before the speech** antes del discurso, revisó rápidamente sus notas
(**e**) *Mil (troops)* pasar revista a
(**f**) *US (revise)* repasar
3 *vi* (**a**) *(write reviews)* **he reviews for "The Times"** escribe críticas para "The Times" (**b**) *US (revise for exam, test)* repasar

reviewer [rɪ'vjuːə(r)] *n (of book, play, movie)* crítico(a) *m,f*

revile [rɪ'vaɪl] *vt Formal* denigrar, vilipendiar; **our much reviled education system** nuestro muy vilipendiado sistema educativo

revise [rɪ'vaɪz] **1** *vt* (**a**) *(text, policy, offer)* revisar; **to r. one's opinion of sb** cambiar de opinión sobre alguien; **to r. sth upwards/downwards** subir/bajar algo; **to r. a price upwards/downwards** revisar *or* corregir el precio al alza/a la baja (**b**) *Br (for exam) (subject, notes)* repasar
2 *vi Br (for exam)* repasar (**for** para)

revised [rɪ'vaɪzd] *adj* (**a**) *(figures, estimate)* revisado(a), corregido(a) (**b**) *(edition)* revisado(a)

reviser [rɪ'vaɪzə(r)] *n* revisor(ora) *m,f*

revision [rɪ'vɪʒən] *n* (**a**) *(of text, policy, offer)* revisión *f* (**b**) *(correction)* corrección *f* (**c**) *(revised edition)* edición *f* revisada (**d**) *Br (for exam)* repaso *m*; **to do some r.** repasar

revisionism [rɪ'vɪʒənɪzəm] *n Pol* revisionismo *m*

revisionist [rɪ'vɪʒənɪst] *Pol* **1** *n* revisionista *mf*
2 *adj* revisionista

revisit [riː'vɪzɪt] *vt* volver a visitar; **"War and Peace" revisited** "Guerra y Paz" revisitado

revitalize [riː'vaɪtəlaɪz] *vt* reanimar, revitalizar; **to r. the economy** reactivar la economía

revival [rɪ'vaɪvəl] *n* (**a**) *(of person)* reanimación *f*; **all attempts at r. failed** los intentos por reanimarla no funcionaron
(**b**) *(of industry)* reactivación *f*
(**c**) *(of hope, interest)* resurgimiento *m*
(**d**) *(of custom, fashion)* resurgimiento *m*; **they would like to see a r. of Victorian values** les gustaría que hubiera un resurgimiento de los valores victorianos
(**e**) *(of play)* reposición *f*, nuevo montaje *m*
(**f**) **(religious) r.** renacimiento *m*

revivalism [rɪ'vaɪvəlɪzəm] *n Rel* evangelismo *m*

revivalist [rɪ'vaɪvəlɪst] *Rel* **1** *n* evangelista *mf*
2 *adj* evangelista; **a r. meeting** un encuentro evangelista

revive [rɪ'vaɪv] **1** *vt* (**a**) *(person)* reanimar; **this will r. you!** *(drink)* esto te reanimará
(**b**) *(industry)* reactivar; **a plan to r. the city centre** un plan para reactivar el centro de la ciudad; **this role could r. his flagging career** este papel daría nuevo vigor a su carrera, actualmente en decadencia
(**c**) *(hopes, interest)* resucitar
(**d**) *(custom, fashion)* hacer resurgir; **prewar styles have been revived** han resurgido los estilos anteriores a la guerra
(**e**) *(play)* reponer
2 *vi* (**a**) *(person)* reanimarse (**b**) *(industry)* reactivarse (**c**) *(hopes, interest)* renacer, volver a cobrar fuerza (**d**) *(custom, fashion)* revivir

revivify [riː'vɪvɪfaɪ] *vt Formal* revivificar

revocation [revə'keɪʃən] *n Formal* revocación *f*

revoke [rɪ'vəʊk] **1** *vt Formal (law)* derogar; *(decision, privilege)* revocar
2 *vi (in cards)* renunciar

revolt [rɪ'vəʊlt] **1** *n* rebelión *f*; **to be in r.** rebelarse; **the peasants rose up in r.** los campesinos se alzaron en revuelta
2 *vt (disgust)* repugnar; **the very thought revolts me** sólo pensarlo me repugna; **to be revolted by sth** sentir asco por algo
3 *vi (rebel)* rebelarse (**against** contra)

revolting [rɪ'vəʊltɪŋ] *adj (disgusting)* repugnante, asqueroso(a); **the food was r.** la comida estaba asquerosa; **don't be r.!** ¡no hagas guarradas!

revoltingly [rɪ'vəʊltɪŋlɪ] *adv (disgustingly)* asquerosamente, repugnantemente

revolution [revə'luːʃən] *n* (**a**) *(radical change)* revolución *f*; **a r. in information technology** una revolución en tecnología de la información (**b**) *(turn)* revolución *f*, giro *m*; **100 revolutions per minute** 100 revoluciones por minuto

revolutionary [revə'luːʃənərɪ] **1** *n* revolucionario(a) *m,f*
2 *adj* revolucionario(a); **such a suggestion was r. in those days** en aquellos tiempos ese tipo de ideas era revolucionario

revolutionize [revə'luːʃənaɪz] *vt* revolucionar; **these changes will r. the industry** estos cambios revolucionarán el sector

revolve [rɪ'vɒlv] **1** *vi* (**a**) *(rotate)* girar (**around** en torno a); *Fig* **these ideas revolved in her mind** estas ideas le daban vueltas en la cabeza (**b**) *(centre, focus)* **to r. round** *or* **around sth** girar en torno *or* alrededor de algo
2 *vt* (**a**) *(rotate)* girar (**b**) *Formal (ponder)* considerar

> **False friend:** The Spanish verb **revolver** is not a translation for the English word **revolve**. In Spanish **revolver** means "to stir", "to mix", "to turn upside down" or "to upset".

revolver [rɪ'vɒlvə(r)] *n* revólver *m*

revolving [rɪ'vɒlvɪŋ] *adj* giratorio(a) ►► *Fin* ***r. credit*** crédito *m* renovable automáticamente, crédito *m* rotativo; ***r. door*** puerta *f* giratoria; *Fin* ***r. fund*** fondo *m* rotativo

revue [rɪ'vjuː] *n Theat* revista *f*

revulsion [rɪ'vʌlʃən] *n* repugnancia *f*; **she turned away in r.** se dio media vuelta asqueada

reward [rɪ'wɔːd] **1** *n* recompensa *f*; **they're offering a $500 r.** ofrecen una recompensa de 500 dólares; **as a r.** como recompensa; **I do everything for him, and what do I get in r.?** hago todo por él y ¿de qué forma *or* cómo me agradece?
2 *vt* recompensar (**with** con); **our patience has finally been rewarded** finalmente, nuestra paciencia se ha visto recompensada; **the book rewards closer attention** el libro resulta más provechoso si se lee atentamente

rewarding [rɪ'wɔːdɪŋ] *adj* gratificante; **the conference was most r.** el congreso resultó muy provechoso; **financially r.** bien remunerado(a)

rewind [riː'waɪnd] **1** *vt* (*pt & pp* **rewound** [riː'waʊnd]) *(tape, film)* rebobinar
2 *vi* rebobinarse
3 *n* ['riːwaɪnd] rebobinado *m* ►► ***r. button*** botón *m* de rebobinado

rewire [riː'waɪə(r)] *vt (house)* renovar la instalación eléctrica de

reword [riː'wɜːd] *vt* reformular, expresar de otra manera

rework [riː'wɜːk] *vt (idea, text)* rehacer, reelaborar; **his last novel reworks the same theme** su última novela vuelve a abordar el mismo tema

reworking [riː'wɜːkɪŋ] *n (of idea, text)* adaptación *f*; **the movie is a r. of the Faust legend** la película es una adaptación de la leyenda de Fausto

rewound *pt & pp of* **rewind**

rewritable [riː'raɪtəbəl] *adj Comptr (media)* regrabable

rewrite **1** *n* ['riːraɪt] *Cin (of script)* nueva versión *f* ►► *Ling* ***r. rule*** regla *f* de la reescritura
2 *vt* [riː'raɪt] (*pt* **rewrote** [riː'rəʊt], *pp* **rewritten** [riː'rɪtən]) reescribir; **to r. history** reescribir la historia

Rex [reks] *n Br* **Edward/George R.** el Rey Eduardo/Jorge; *Law* **R. vs Gibson** la Corona contra Gibson

Reykjavik ['rekjəvɪk] *n* Reikiavik

rezone [riː'zəʊn] *vt US* recalificar

RFC [ɑːref'siː] *n* (*abbr* **Rugby Football Club**) club *m* de rugby

RFD *US* (*abbr* **rural free delivery**) entrega *f* rural gratuita

RFU [ɑːref'juː] *n* (*abbr* **Rugby Football Union**) = federación inglesa de "rugby union"

RGB [ɑːdʒiː'biː] *adj Comptr* (*abbr* **red, green and blue**) RGB; **an R. display** un monitor RGB

RGN [ɑːdʒiː'en] *n Br Formerly* (*abbr* **Registered General Nurse**) enfermero(a) *m,f* diplomado(a), *Esp* ATS *mf*

Rgt (*abbr* **regiment**) regimiento

Rh [ɑːr'eɪtʃ] *n* (*abbr* **Rhesus**) Rh *m* ►► ***R. factor*** factor *m* Rh

rhapsodic(al) [ræp'sɒdɪk(əl)] *adj (prose, description)* enardecido(a)

rhapsodize ['ræpsədaɪz] *vi* deshacerse en elogios (**over** *or* **about** sobre)

rhapsody ['ræpsədɪ] *n* (**a**) *Mus* rapsodia *f* (**b**) **to go into rhapsodies over sth** *(enthuse about)* deshacerse en elogios sobre algo; **to send sb into rhapsodies** extasiar a alguien

rhea ['riːə] *n* ñandú *m*

rheme [riːm] *n Ling* rema *f*

Rhenish ['riːnɪʃ] **1** *n* renano(a) *m,f*
2 *adj* renano(a); **R. Wine** vino del Rin

rhenium ['riːnɪəm] *n Chem* renio *m*

rheology [rɪ'ɒlədʒɪ] *n Phys* reología *f*

rheostat ['riːəʊstæt] *n* reóstato *m*

rhesus ['riːsəs] *n* (**a**) *Med* **r. negative/positive** Rh negativo/positivo ►► ***r. factor*** factor *m* Rh (**b**) *(animal)* ***r. monkey*** mono *m* rhesus, macaco *m* (de la India)

rhetoric ['retərɪk] *n* (**a**) *(art of speaking)* retórica *f* (**b**) *Pej (bombast)* retórica *f*; **it's just empty r.** es pura retórica

rhetorical [rɪ'tɒrɪkəl] *adj* retórico(a); **her writing contains many a r. flourish** su texto tiene una gran cantidad de florituras retóricas ►► ***r. question*** pregunta *f* retórica

rhetorically [rɪ'tɒrɪklɪ] *adv* retóricamente

rhetorician [retə'rɪʃən] *n* (**a**) *(teacher of rhetoric)* profesor(ora) *m,f* de retórica (**b**) *Pej (who uses over-elaborate language)* retórico(a) *m,f*

rheum [ruːm] *n* legaña *f*

rheumatic [ruː'mætɪk] *adj Med* reumático(a) ►► ***r. fever*** fiebre *f* reumática

rheumaticky [ruː'mætɪkɪ] *adj Fam* reumático(a)

rheumatics [ruː'mætɪks] *npl Fam* reúma *m*; **to have** *or* **suffer from r.** sufrir de *or* tener reúma

rheumatism ['ruːmətɪzəm] *n* reumatismo *m*, reúma *m*

rheumatoid arthritis ['ruːmətɔɪd'ɑːθraɪtɪs] *n Med* artritis *f inv* reumatoide

rheumatologist [ruːmə'tɒlədʒɪst] *n* reumatólogo(a) *m,f*

rheumatology [ruːmə'tɒlədʒɪ] *n* reumatología *f*

rheumy ['ruːmɪ] *adj (eyes)* legañoso(a)

Rhine [raɪn] *n* **the R.** el Rin

Rhineland ['raɪnlænd] *n* **the R.** Renania

rhinestone ['raɪnstəʊn] *n* diamante *m* de imitación

rhino ['raɪnəʊ] (*pl* **rhinos**) *n Fam* rinoceronte *m*

rhinoceros [raɪ'nɒsərəs] *n* rinoceronte *m*

rhinoplasty ['raɪnəʊplæstɪ] *n* rinoplastia *f*

rhizome ['raɪzəʊm] *n Bot* rizoma *m*

Rhode Island ['rəʊd'aɪlənd] *n* Rhode Island

Rhodes [rəʊdz] *n* Rodas

Rhodesia [rəʊ'diːʒə] *n Formerly* Rodesia

Rhodesian [rəʊ'diːʒən] *Formerly* **1** *n* rodesiano(a) *m,f*
2 *adj* rodesiano(a)

rhodium ['rəʊdɪəm] *n Chem* rodio *m*

rhododendron [rəʊdə'dendrən] *n* rododendro *m*

rhomb = **rhombus**

rhombic ['rɒmbɪk] *adj* rómbico(a)

rhomboid ['rɒmbɔɪd] **1** *n* romboide *m*
2 *adj* romboidal, romboideo(a)

rhomboidal [rɒm'bɔɪdəl] *adj* romboidal, romboideo(a)

rhomb(us) ['rɒmb(əs)] *n* rombo *m*

rhonchus ['rɒŋkəs] *n Med* ronquido *m*

Rhone [rəʊn] *n* **the R.** el Ródano

rhubarb ['ruːbɑːb] *n* (**a**) *(plant)* ruibarbo *m* ►► ***r. jam*** confitura *f* de ruibarbo (**b**) *Br Theat* **r., r.** *(simulating conversation)* bla, bla, bla (**c**) *US Fam Old-fashioned (squabble)* pelotera *f*

rhyme [raɪm] **1** *n* (**a**) *(sound, word)* rima *f*; **give me a r. for "mash"** dime algo que rime con "mash"; **to find a r. for sth** buscar una palabra que rime con algo; IDIOM **without r. or reason** sin venir a cuento (**b**) *(verse, poem)* rima *f*; **to speak in r.** hablar en verso; **I've made up a r. about you** escribí un poema sobre ti ►► ***r. scheme*** rima *f*
2 *vt* rimar; **you can't r. "lost" with "host"** "lost" no rima con "host"
3 *vi* rimar (**with** con); **what rhymes with "orange"?** ¿qué rima con "orange"?

rhymester ['raɪmstə(r)] *n Pej* rimador(ora) *m,f*

rhyming ['raɪmɪŋ] *adj Lit* ***r. couplet*** pareado *m (en rima)*; ***r. slang*** = argot originario del este de Londres

rhythm ['rɪðəm] *n* ritmo *m*; **she's got (a sense of) r.** tiene (sentido del) ritmo ►► ***r. and blues*** rhythm and blues *m*; ***r. guitar*** guitarra *f* rítmica; ***r. method*** *(of contraception)* método *m* (de) Ogino; ***r. section*** sección *f* rítmica

rhythmic(al) ['rɪðmɪk(əl)] *adj* rítmico(a)

rhythmically ['rɪðmɪklɪ] *adv* rítmicamente, con ritmo

rhythmic gymnastics ['rɪðmɪkdʒɪm'næstɪks] *n* gimnasia *f* rítmica

RI (*abbr* **Rhode Island**) Rhode Island

rial [riː'ɑːl] *n* rial *m*

rib [rɪb] **1** *n* (**a**) *(of person, animal)* costilla *f*; **to poke** *or* **dig sb in the ribs** dar a alguien un codazo en las costillas (**b**) *Culin* costilla *f* (**c**) *(of umbrella)* varilla *f*; *(of leaf, aircraft or insect wing)* nervadura *f*; *(of ship's hull)* cuaderna *f*, costilla *f* (**d**) *Archit* nervio *m* (**e**) *(in knitting)* punto *m* elástico
2 *vt* (*pt & pp* **ribbed**) *Fam (tease)* tomar el pelo a
3 *vi (in knitting)* hacer punto elástico

RIBA [ɑːraɪbiː'eɪ] *n* (*abbr* **Royal Institute of British Architects**) = colegio profesional de los arquitectos británicos

ribald ['rɪbəld, 'raɪbəld] *adj (joke, song)* procaz

ribaldry ['rɪbəldrɪ] *n* picardía *f*

riband, ribband ['rɪbənd] *n* (**a**) *(award)* galardón *m* (**b**) *Old-fashioned (in hair)* cinta *f*

ribbed [rɪbd] *adj* (**a**) *(pullover)* acanalado(a); *(condom)* estriado(a) (**b**) *Archit (vault)* de crucería

ribbing ['rɪbɪŋ] *n* (**a**) *(on pullover)* cordoncillos *mpl* (**b**) *Fam (teasing)* tomadura *f* de pelo; **to give sb a r.** tomar el pelo a alguien

ribbon ['rɪbən] *n* (**a**) *(for hair)* cinta *f*; *(on parcel)* lazo *m*, cinta *f*; IDIOM **his clothes had been cut** *or* **torn to ribbons** su ropa estaba hecha jirones ►► ***r. microphone*** micrófono *m* de cinta
(**b**) *(on medal)* cinta *f*; *(of order)* galón *m*
(**c**) *(for typewriter)* cinta *f*
(**d**) *(narrow strip) (of land)* franja *f*, faja *f*; **a r. of road across the desert** una carretera que cruza el desierto como una cinta ►► ***r. development*** = desarrollo urbano a ambos lados de una carretera

ribcage ['rɪbkeɪdʒ] *n* caja *f* torácica

rib-eye ['rɪbaɪ] *n* **r. (steak)** bistec *m* de lomo

riboflavin ['raɪbəʊ'fleɪvɪn], **riboflavine** ['raɪbəʊfleɪviːn] *n* riboflavina *f*

ribonucleic acid ['raɪbəʊnjʊ'kleɪɪk'æsɪd] *n* ácido *m* ribonucleico

rib-tickler ['rɪbtɪklə(r)] *n Fam* **it's a real r.** es desternillante

rib-tickling ['rɪbtɪklɪŋ] *adj Fam* desternillante

rice [raɪs] **1** *n* arroz *m* ►► ***r. bowl*** *(bowl)* cuenco *m* de arroz; *(region)* zona *f* arrocera; ***r. field*** arrozal *m*; ***r. paddy*** arrozal *m*; ***r. paper*** papel *m* de arroz; ***r. pudding*** arroz *m* con leche; ***r. wine*** vino *m* de arroz
2 *vt US (potatoes)* pasar por el pasapuré

ricer ['raɪsə(r)] *n US* pasapuré *m*

rich [rɪtʃ] **1** *n* (**a**) *(wealthy people)* **the r.** los ricos (**b**) *(wealth)* **riches** riquezas *fpl*
2 *adj* (**a**) *(wealthy) (person, country)* rico(a); **to become** *or* **get r.** hacerse rico(a); **the r. part of town** la zona de clase alta de la ciudad; **I'm a hundred pounds richer** soy cien libras más rico
(**b**) *(luxurious) (furnishings, decor)* suntuoso(a), opulento(a)
(**c**) *(fertile) (soil)* fértil; **a r. imagination** una fértil imaginación
(**d**) *(abundant) (harvest, supply)* abundante; **to be r. in...** ser rico(a) en...; *Fig* **a r. seam** un filón abundante; IDIOM **there are r. pickings to be had** se pueden conseguir suculentas ganancias
(**e**) *(culture, traditions)* rico(a)
(**f**) *(food)* **avoid r. foods** evita alimentos con alto contenido graso; **this dessert is very r.** este postre llena mucho; **it's delicious but a bit too r. for me** está delicioso pero me resulta un tanto empalagoso
(**g**) *(colour, smell)* intenso(a)

(**h**) *(voice, tone)* sonoro(a)
(**i**) *Fam (cheeky)* **that's a bit r. (coming from you)!** ¡mira quién habla *or Esp* quién fue a hablar!

-rich [rɪtʃ] *suffix* **a target-r. environment** una zona con numerosos objetivos; **vitamin-r. foods** alimentos ricos en vitaminas

Richard ['rɪtʃəd] *pr n* **R. the Lionheart** Ricardo Corazón de León

richly ['rɪtʃlɪ] *adv* (**a**) *(furnished, decorated)* lujosamente (**b**) *(fully)* **r. deserved** merecidísimo(a); **he was r. rewarded** le pagaron muy generosamente (**c**) *(abundantly)* profusamente; **r. illustrated** profusamente ilustrado(a) (**d**) *(vividly)* **r. coloured** con colores muy intensos; **r. scented** muy perfumado(a)

richness ['rɪtʃnɪs] *n* (**a**) *(wealth) (of person, country)* riqueza *f*
(**b**) *(luxuriousness) (of furnishings, decor)* suntuosidad *f*, opulencia *f*
(**c**) *(fertility) (of soil)* fertilidad *f*; **the r. of her imagination** la fertilidad de su imaginación
(**d**) *(abundance) (of harvest, supply)* abundancia *f*; **an amazing r. of detail** una increíble riqueza de detalles
(**e**) *(of culture, traditions)* riqueza *f*
(**f**) *(of food)* **the r. of the food gave him indigestion** la comida llenaba tanto que acabó por empacharse
(**g**) *(of colour, smell)* intensidad *f*
(**h**) *(of voice, tone)* sonoridad *f*

Richter Scale ['rɪktə'skeɪl] *n* escala *f* de Richter; **it measured six on the R.** tuvo una intensidad seis en la escala de Richter

rick[1] [rɪk] **1** *n (of hay, straw)* almiar *m*
2 *vt* almiarar

rick[2] *vt esp Br* **to r. one's neck** torcerse el cuello; **to r. one's back** hacerse daño en la espalda

rickets ['rɪkɪts] *npl Med* raquitismo *m*

rickety ['rɪkɪtɪ] *adj Fam (furniture, staircase)* desvencijado(a); *(alliance, alibi)* precario(a)

rickshaw ['rɪkʃɔː] *n* rickshaw *m*, = calesa oriental tirada por una persona o por una bicicleta o motocicleta

ricochet ['rɪkəʃeɪ] **1** *n* bala *f* rebotada
2 *vi* (*pt* **ricochetted** ['rɪkəʃeɪd]) rebotar (**off** de)

ricotta [rɪ'kɒtə] *n* **r. (cheese)** (queso *m*) ricotta *m*, = queso blanco italiano de vaca u oveja

rictus ['rɪktəs] *n* (**a**) *(of bird)* rictus *m*, apertura *f* del pico (**b**) *(of person)* rictus *m*

rid [rɪd] (*pt & pp* **rid**) *vt* **to r. sb of sth** librar a alguien de algo; **to r. oneself of sth, to get r. of sth** deshacerse de algo; **we haven't been able to get r. of the house** no hemos podido deshacernos de la casa; **I can't seem to get r. of this cold** parece que no puedo quitarme este resfriado *or Andes, RP* resfrío de encima; **I thought we were never going to get r. of them!** *(guests)* ¡pensé no nos íbamos a poder librar de ellos!; **I don't want a child... you'll have to get r. of it** yo no quiero un hijo, tendrás que deshacerte de él; **to be r. of sth/sb** estar libre de algo/alguien; **you're well r. of him** estás mejor sin él

riddance ['rɪdəns] *n Fam* **he's gone, and good r. (to bad rubbish)!** se ha ido, ¡y ya iba siendo hora!

ridden ['rɪdən] **1** *pp of* **ride**
2 *adj* **to be r. with** *or* **by guilt** estar atormentado(a) por el sentimiento de culpa

-ridden ['rɪdən] *suffix* **flea-r.** infectado(a) de pulgas; **a disease-r. town** una población azotada por las enfermedades

riddle[1] ['rɪdəl] **1** *n* (**a**) *(puzzle)* acertijo *m*, adivinanza *f*; **to ask sb a r.** decir una adivinanza a alguien (**b**) *(mystery)* enigma *m*; **to talk** *or* **speak in riddles** hablar en clave
2 *vt (pierce)* **to r. sb with bullets** acribillar a alguien a balazos; **riddled with mistakes** plagado(a) de errores; **his body is riddled with cancer** tiene el cuerpo consumido por el cáncer; **the department is riddled with corruption** el departamento es un antro de corrupción

riddle[2] **1** *n (sieve)* criba *f*
2 *vt (sift)* cribar

RIDE [raɪd] **1** *n* (**a**) *(on bicycle, in car, on horse)* paseo *m*; **to give sb a r.** *(in car)* llevar a alguien (en coche), *CAm, Méx* dar aventón *or Col* chance *or Cuba* botella *or Perú* una jalada *or Ven* cola a alguien; **he gave the child a r. on his back** llevó al niño a hombros *or RP* babucha; **to go for a r.** ir a dar una vuelta (en coche/en bicicleta/a caballo); **can I have a r. on your horse/bike?** ¿me dejas dar una vuelta en tu caballo/moto?; **she was very tired after the bus r. from Puebla** estaba muy cansada después del viaje en autobús desde Puebla; **it's a ten minute train r. to work** se tarda *or Am* demora diez minutos en llegar al trabajo en tren, *RP* son diez minutos en tren hasta el trabajo; **it's only a short r. away (in the car)** está a poca distancia (en coche); **this type of suspension gives a smoother r.** este tipo de amortiguación proporciona una conducción más cómoda *or Am* un manejo más cómodo; *US (lift in car)* **I have a r. coming** me van a llevar en coche *or Am* carro *or CSur* auto; **don't accept rides from strangers** no te montes *or* subas en el coche *or Am* carro *or CSur* auto de extraños
(**b**) *(attraction at funfair) Esp* atracción *f*, *Am* juego *m*; **it's $1 a r.** vale un dólar por viaje
(**c**) *Vulg (sex) Esp* polvo *m*, *Méx* acostón *m*, *Cuba* palo *m*; **she's a good r.** *(sexual partner) Esp* folla *or Am* coge *or Méx* chinga genial
(**d**) IDIOMS **I just went along for the r.** me apunté por hacer algo; **she was given a rough r.** *(by interviewer, critics)* se las hicieron pasar negras *or Esp* moradas; **to take sb for a r.** *(deceive)* engañar a alguien como a un chino, tomar a alguien el pelo, *RP* venderle un buzón a alguien; *US (kill)* dar un paseo a alguien
2 *vt* (*pt* **rode** [rəʊd], *pp* **ridden** ['rɪdən]) (**a**) *(horse, vehicle)* **to r. a horse/a bicycle** *Esp* montar *or Am* andar a caballo/en bicicleta; **he was riding a black horse** montaba un caballo negro, *Am* estaba andando en un caballo negro; **he let me r. his bike** me dejó *Esp* montar *or Am* andar en su bici; **she rode her bike into town** fue a la ciudad en bici; **we rode twenty miles today** *(on horse)* hoy hemos cabalgado veinte millas; *(on bike)* hoy hemos recorrido veinte millas; *US* **to r. the bus/train** viajar en autobús/tren; **he rode the chairlift to the top of the slope** subió en el telesilla hasta el principio de la pista; **when the Sioux rode the prairies** cuando los sioux cabalgaban por las llanuras; *Fig* **the candidate is riding a surge of popularity** el candidato flota en una nube de popularidad; *also Fig* **to r. the storm** aguantar el temporal; *US* **I'll r. you home** *(give a lift to)* te llevo a casa; *US* **to r. sb out of town** *(drive out)* expulsar a alguien del pueblo; **to r. a good race** *(jockey)* hacer una buena carrera; **he has ridden ninety winners this season** *(jockey)* ha ganado noventa carreras esta temporada; **the winner was ridden by Willie Carson** Willie Carson montaba al ganador; **we watched the surfers riding the waves** vimos cómo los surfistas se mantenían sobre las olas *or Esp* la cresta de la ola
(**b**) *(punch, blow)* amortiguar
(**c**) *US Fam* **to r. sb** *(nag)* dar la lata a alguien; *(tease)* tomar el pelo a alguien
(**d**) *Vulg (have sex with)* tirarse a, *Esp* follarse a, *Am* cogerse a, *Méx* chingarse a
3 *vi* (**a**) *(on horse, in vehicle)* **can you r.?** *(on horse, bicycle) Esp* ¿sabes montar?, *Am* ¿sabes andar?; **to r. on a horse/bicycle** *Esp* montar a caballo/en bicicleta, *Am* andar a caballo/en bicicleta; **I rode into town** fui a la ciudad en bicicleta/a caballo; **we rode there in a taxi** fuimos allí en taxi; **we rode home on the bus** volvimos a casa en autobús; **they rode past us** *(on horseback)* pasaron cabalgando delante de nosotros, iban a caballo y nos pasaron; *(on bicycle)* pasaron delante de nosotros, iban en bicicleta y nos pasaron; **she was riding in the back seat** iba en el asiento de atrás; **have you ever ridden in a rickshaw?** ¿has ido *or* te has montado alguna vez en un rickshaw?
(**b**) *US (in elevator)* **to r. down** bajar; **to r. up** subir
(**c**) *(float, sail)* **to r. with the current** dejarse llevar por la corriente; **to r. at anchor** estar anclado(a)
(**d**) IDIOMS **to be riding for a fall** ir camino del *or Am* al desastre; **they are riding high** atraviesan un buen momento; **he is riding on a wave of popularity** se halla *or RP* está en la cresta de la ola; **to let sth r.** dejar pasar algo

▸ **ride down** *vt sep* (**a**) *(trample)* atropellar
(**b**) *(catch up with)* cazar

▸ **ride off** *vi (on horse, bicycle)* marcharse

▸ **ride on** *vt insep (depend on)* depender de; **I have several thousand pounds riding on that horse** tengo varios miles de libras apostadas en ese caballo; **there's a lot riding on this match** en este partido hay mucho en juego

▸ **ride out** *vt sep (problem, crisis)* soportar, aguantar; **to r. out the storm** capear el temporal

▸ **ride up** *vi (clothing)* subirse

---

rider ['raɪdə(r)] *n* (**a**) *(on horse) (man)* jinete *m*; *(woman)* amazona *f*; *(on bicycle)* ciclista *mf*; *(on motorbike)* motorista *mf*
(**b**) *(to document, treaty)* cláusula *f* adicional; **he agrees, but with the r. that he won't have to pay for it** acepta, pero con la condición de no hacerse cargo del costo *or Esp* coste; **I'd like to add a r. to what my colleague said** me gustaría hacer una salvedad respecto de lo que mi colega ha dicho
(**c**) *Br Law (jury recommendation)* = recomendación hecha por un jurado que complementa al veredicto, en la que, por ejemplo, se aconseja una condena menos severa

riderless ['raɪdəlɪs] *adj (horse)* sin jinete

ridership [ˈraɪdəʃɪp] *n US* número *m* de usuarios *or* viajeros *(en un transporte público)*

ridge [rɪdʒ] *n* **(a)** *(of mountain)* cresta *f* **(b)** *(of roof)* caballete *m*, cumbrera *f* **(c)** *(on surface)* rugosidad *f*; *(in ploughed field)* caballón *m*; **the wet sand formed ridges** la arena mojada formaba pequeños montículos ►► ***r. tent*** tienda *f* (de campaña) canadiense **(d)** *Met* **r. of high pressure** cuña anticiclónica

ridged [rɪdʒd] *adj* rugoso(a)

ridgepole [ˈrɪdʒpəʊl] *n (of roof)* cumbrera *f*; *(of tent)* barra *f* superior

ridge-tile [ˈrɪdʒtaɪl] *n* cobija *f*, teja *f* de caballete

ridgetree [ˈrɪdʒtriː] *n (of roof)* cumbrera *f*

ridgeway [ˈrɪdʒweɪ] *n Br* = camino por la cresta de una montaña

ridicule [ˈrɪdɪkjuːl] **1** *n* burlas *fpl*, mofa *f*; **to hold sth/sb up to r.** burlarse *or* mofarse de algo/alguien; **to lay oneself open to r.** exponerse al ridículo; **to be an object of r.** ser el centro de las burlas

2 *vt* burlarse de, mofarse de

ridiculous [rɪˈdɪkjʊləs] **1** *adj* ridículo(a); **you look r. in that hat** ese sombrero te queda ridículo; **£500? don't be r.!** ¿500 libras? ¡no seas ridículo!; **to make sb look r.** poner en ridículo *or* ridiculizar a alguien; **to make oneself r.** hacer el ridículo

2 *n* **to verge on the r.** rozar lo ridículo

ridiculously [rɪˈdɪkjʊləslɪ] *adv* **to behave/dress r.** comportarse/vestir de forma ridícula; **it was r. slow/cheap** fue ridículo lo lento/barato que era

ridiculousness [rɪˈdɪkjʊləsnɪs] *n* lo ridículo

riding[1] [ˈraɪdɪŋ] *n* equitación *f*, monta *f*; **to go r.** ir a montar (a caballo) ►► ***r. boots*** botas *fpl* de montar; ***r. breeches*** pantalón *m* de montar; ***r. crop*** fusta *f*; ***r. habit*** ropa *f* de montar *(para mujeres)*; ***r. school*** escuela *f* hípica *or* de equitación; ***r. whip*** fusta *f*

riding[2] *n (in Canada, New Zealand)* distrito *m* electoral

rife [raɪf] *adj* **(a)** *(widespread)* **to be r.** reinar, imperar; **corruption is r.** impera la corrupción, la corrupción es moneda corriente **(b)** *(full)* plagado(a) (**with** de); **the text is r. with errors** el texto está plagado de errores; **the office is r. with rumour** en la oficina los rumores están a la orden del día; **the city was r. with disease** la enfermedad asolaba la ciudad

riff [rɪf] *n Mus* riff *m*, = breve pasaje que se repite varias veces

riffle [ˈrɪfəl] *vt* **(a)** *(magazine, pages)* pasar rápidamente **(b)** *(cards)* = barajar con dos montones de naipes intercalando las cartas

►**riffle through** *vt insep* pasar rápidamente

riff-raff [ˈrɪfræf] *n* gentuza *f*

rifle[1] [ˈraɪfəl] **1** *n* **(a)** *(gun)* rifle *m*, fusil *m* ►► ***r. range*** *(place)* campo *m* de tiro; *(distance)* alcance *m* (de un rifle); ***r. shot*** disparo *m* de rifle **(b)** *(groove)* estría *f* **(c)** *TV & Rad* ***r. mike*** micrófono *m* direccional

2 *vt (gun barrel)* estriar

rifle[2] *vt* **(a)** *(search) (house, office)* revolver *(en busca de algo)*; *(pockets, drawer)* rebuscar en **(b)** *(rob)* robar; **they rifled the safe** desvalijaron la caja fuerte

►**rifle through** *vt insep* rebuscar en

rifleman [ˈraɪfəlmən] *n* fusilero *m*

rifling [ˈraɪflɪŋ] *n (in gun barrel)* estriado *m*

rift [rɪft] *n* **(a)** *(gap) (in earth, rock)* grieta *f*, brecha *f*; **a r. in the clouds** un claro en las nubes ►► *Geol* ***r. valley*** = valle formado entre dos grietas paralelas **(b)** *(in relationship)* desavenencia *f*; *(in political party)* escisión *f*; **there is a deep r. between them** están muy distanciados

rig [rɪg] **1** *n* **(a)** *(of ship)* aparejo *m* **(b)** **(oil) r.** *(on land)* torre *f* de perforación (petrolífera); *(at sea)* plataforma *f* petrolífera **(c)** *Fam (equipment)* bártulos *mpl*, aparejos *mpl* **(d)** *Fam (outfit)* **have you seen the r. he's wearing?** ¿has visto la vestimenta que me lleva? **(e)** *US Fam (truck)* camión *m*

2 *vt* (*pt & pp* **rigged**) **(a)** *(ship)* aparejar **(b)** *Fam (election, boxing match, race)* amañar; **to r. a jury** manipular al jurado

►**rig out** *vt sep Fam* **(a)** *(clothe)* vestir; **to be rigged out in...** ir ataviado(a) con... **(b)** *(equip)* equipar

►**rig up** *vt sep* improvisar, *Esp* apañar

rigger [ˈrɪgə(r)] *n (on oil rig)* = operario cuya tarea es montar plataformas petroleras

rigging [ˈrɪgɪŋ] *n* **(a)** *Naut* jarcias *fpl*, cordaje *m* **(b)** *Fam (of election, boxing match, race)* amaño *m*

RIGHT [raɪt] **1** *n* **(a)** *(morality)* el bien; **to know r. from wrong** distinguir lo que está bien de lo que está mal; **to be in the r.** tener razón; **I don't wish to discuss the rights and wrongs of the decision** no quiero discutir la conveniencia de la decisión; **to put** *or* **set things to rights** poner las cosas en orden

(b) *(entitlement)* derecho *m*; **r. of assembly/asylum** derecho de reunión/asilo; **the r. to vote** el derecho al voto; **women's rights** los derechos de la mujer; **what gives you the r. to tell me what to do?** ¿con qué derecho me dices lo que tengo que hacer?; **to have the r. to do sth** tener derecho a hacer algo; **you have a r. to your opinion, but...** puedes opinar lo que quieras, pero...; **you have every r. to be angry** tienes todo el derecho del mundo a estar *esp Esp* enfadado *or esp Am* enojado; **you have no r. to demand this of us** no tienes derecho a pedirnos esto; **to be within one's rights to do sth** tener todo el derecho a hacer algo; **it is mine as of r.** *or* **by r.** es mío por derecho propio; **by r. of her position as chairwoman** en su condición de presidenta; **by rights, I should have first choice** en justicia, debería ser yo el primero en elegir; **to be famous in one's own r.** ser famoso(a) por méritos propios *or* por derecho propio ►► ***r. to reply*** derecho *m* de réplica *or* respuesta; ***r. of way*** *(on land)* derecho *m* de paso; *(on road)* prioridad *f*

(c) **rights** *(of book)* derechos (**of** *or* **to** de); **all rights reserved** todos los derechos reservados

(d) *(right-hand side)* derecha *f*; **she's second from the r.** es la segunda por la derecha *or RP* empezando de la derecha; **on** *or* **to the r. (of)** a la derecha (de); **on my r.** a mi derecha; **the one on the r.** el/la de la derecha; **turn to the r.** gira a la derecha; **to make** *or* **take a r.** girar a la derecha

(e) *Pol* **the r.** la derecha; **she is further to the r. than her husband** es más de derechas que su marido

(f) *(in boxing)* **a r. to the jaw** un derechazo en la mandíbula

(g) *Fin* ***rights issue*** emisión *f* con derechos de suscripción preferente

2 *adj* **(a)** *(correct)* correcto(a); **you take sugar, don't you? – yes, that's r.** con azúcar, ¿no? – sí; **I'm going to get promoted – is that r.?** me van a ascender – ¿ah, sí?; **that was the r. thing to do** eso es lo que había que hacer; **am I going in the r. direction?** ¿voy en *or Esp* por la dirección correcta?; **are you sure that's the r. time?** ¿seguro que es ésa la hora?; **my watch is r.** mi reloj va *or Am* marcha *or RP* anda bien; **you're not doing it the r. way** no lo estás haciendo bien; **put your sweater on the r. way round** ponte el suéter del *or Am* al derecho; **this soup is just r.** esta sopa está perfecta; **to be r.** *(person)* tener razón; **you were r. about them, they turned out to be dishonest** tenías razón, resultaron ser deshonestos; **it was r. of you** *or* **you were r. not to say anything** hiciste bien en no decir nada; **you're r. to be angry** tienes derecho a estar *esp Esp* enfadado *or esp Am* enojado; **am I r. in thinking that...?** ¿me equivoco al pensar que...?; **r. you are!** ¡de acuerdo!; **how r. you are!** tienes toda la razón; *Fam* **too r.!** ¡ya lo creo!; **r., I see what you mean** ya, entiendo lo que quieres decir; **you do want to come, r.?** quieres venir, ¿verdad?; **I'll ring you tomorrow, r.?** te llamaré mañana, ¿de acuerdo *or Esp* vale *or Méx* órale *or RP* está bien?; **and I'm saying you still owe me £10, r.!** ¿me entiendes cuando te digo que todavía me debes diez libras?; *Fam* **this man comes in, r., and gets out a gun** entra un tipo, ¿sabes? *or Esp* ¿vale?, y saca una pistola; **I can't seem to get anything r.** parece que no hago nada bien; **you got the answer/sum r.** has acertado en la respuesta/suma; IDIOM **to be on the r. lines** ir bien encaminado(a); **to put sb r. (on sth)** sacar a alguien de su error (sobre algo) ►► ***r. side*** *(of material)* cara *f* anterior *or* de arriba; IDIOM **to stay on the r. side of sb** seguir a buenas con alguien, *RP* mantenerse en buenos términos con alguien; IDIOM **to stay on the r. side of the law** no meterse en problemas con la justicia

(b) *(morally good)* **it's not r.** no está bien; **I don't think capital punishment is r.** creo que la pena capital es un error; **it is only r. (and proper) that...** es de justicia que...; **to do the r. thing** hacer lo (que es) debido

(c) *(appropriate) (place, time, action)* apropiado(a); **those curtains are just r. for the bedroom** esas cortinas son perfectas para el dormitorio; **we are r. for each other** estamos hechos el uno para el otro; **teaching isn't r. for you** no estás hecho para la docencia; **the r. person for the job** la persona indicada para el trabajo; **I can't find the r. word** no doy con la palabra adecuada; **to wait for the r. moment** esperar el momento oportuno; **if the price is r.** si el precio es el adecuado; **to know the r. people** tener buenos contactos; **to be in the r. place at the r. time** estar en el lugar y en el momento adecuados

(d) *(well, in good order)* **I'm not feeling quite r.** no me siento muy bien; **something isn't r. with the engine** a este motor le pasa algo; **no one in their r. mind...** nadie en su sano juicio...; **you'll be (as) r. as rain in a couple of days** en un par de días te volverás a encontrar de maravilla, *RP* en un par de días te vas a volver a sentir perfecto; **we'll have** *or* **put you r. in no time** *(make you better)* esto te lo curamos en seguida; **to put sth/things r.** arreglar algo/las cosas; **he's not quite r. in the head** no está muy bien de la cabeza

(e) *Br Fam (as intensifier)* **I felt a r. fool** me sentí como un tonto de remate *or RP* como el rey de los bobos; **he's a r. clever so-and-so** ¡qué listo está hecho el tipo *or Esp* tío!; **the place was in a r. mess** el lugar estaba todo patas arriba *or Am* para arriba; **she's a r. one!** ¡mira que es tonta!

(f) *(right-hand)* derecho(a); **on the r. side** a la derecha; **to take a r. turn** girar a la derecha; IDIOM **I would have given my r. arm to be there** habría dado lo que fuera por estar allí ►► *Comptr* ***r. arrow*** flecha *f* derecha; *Comptr* ***r. arrow key*** tecla *f* de flecha derecha; ***r. back*** lateral *m* derecho; ***r. field*** *(in baseball)* extracampo *m or* exterior *m* derecho; ***r. fielder*** *(in baseball)* exterior *m* derecho; ***r. hand*** mano *f* derecha; ***r. hook*** *(in boxing)* gancho *m* de derecha; *Sport* ***r. wing*** *(place)* banda *f* derecha; *(player) (in rugby)* ala *m* derecho; *Pol* ***the r. wing*** la derecha

(g) *Math* ***r. angle*** ángulo *m* recto; **the two lines are at r. angles (to each other)** las dos líneas forman un ángulo recto; *US* ***r. triangle*** triángulo *m* rectángulo

(h) *Zool* ***r. whale*** ballena *f* franca *or* vasca

3 *adv* (a) *(straight)* directamente; **he drove r. into the wall** chocó de frente *or* directamente contra la pared; **they walked r. past us** pasaron justo delante de nosotros; **the bike drove r. through the roadblock** la moto cruzó por en medio del control de carretera

(b) *(immediately)* **r. after/before we had arrived** justo antes/después de que llegáramos; **r. away** en seguida, inmediatamente, *CAm, Méx* ahorita, *Chile* al tiro; **I'll be r. back** vuelvo en seguida; **r. now** ahora mismo; *Fam* **let me say r. off that...** déjame decir de entrada que...; **r. then** justo entonces

(c) *(completely)* **it tore her arm r. off** le arrancó el brazo de cuajo; **he turned r. round** se dio media vuelta, *RP* se dio vuelta; **the bullet went r. through his arm** la bala le atravesó el brazo; **his shoes were worn r. through** tenía los zapatos raídos del todo; **to go r. up to sb** acercarse hasta donde está alguien; **fill the glass r. up to the top** *Esp* llena el vaso justo hasta el borde, *Am* llena el vaso bien hasta el borde; **r. at the top/back** arriba/detrás del todo; *Fig* **to be r. behind sb** *(support)* apoyar plenamente a alguien; **we're r. out of beer** nos hemos quedado sin nada de cerveza

(d) *(exactly)* **r. here/there** aquí/ahí mismo; **r. behind/in the middle** justo detrás *or Am* atrás/en medio; **I stepped r. in it** *(puddle, dog dirt)* lo/la pisé de lleno; *Fig (said the wrong thing)* metí la pata hasta el fondo; **to have sb r. where one wants them** tener a alguien en sus manos; *Fam* **r. on!** *(excellent!)* *Esp* ¡qué guay!, *Andes, CAm, Carib, Méx* ¡qué chévere!, *Col* ¡qué tenaz!, *Méx* ¡qué padre!, *RP* ¡qué bárbaro!

(e) *(correctly) (to answer, guess)* correctamente, bien; **I can never do anything r.** nunca me sale nada bien; **the door doesn't shut r.** la puerta no cierra bien; **the lid isn't on r.** la tapa no está bien puesta; **the roast is done just r.** el asado está hecho en su punto; **it doesn't look quite r.** hay algo que no está del todo bien; **to understand/remember r.** entender/recordar bien

(f) *(well)* **I'm sure it'll all come r. for you** estoy seguro de que todo te saldrá bien; **to do r. by sb** portarse bien con alguien; **things have/haven't gone r. for us** las cosas nos han/no nos han ido bien; **to see sb r.** asegurar el futuro de alguien; **it was a mistake, r. enough** fue un error, ciertamente

(g) *(to look, turn)* a la derecha; **take the first/second r.** toma *or Esp* gira por la primera/la segunda a la derecha; **the party is moving further r.** el partido está girando aún más hacia la derecha; **a r. of centre party** un partido de centro derecha; IDIOM **r., left and centre** por todas partes

(h) *Br Fam (for emphasis)* **I was r. angry** estaba superenfadado; **it's a r. cold day** hoy hace un frío terrible *or* que pela

(i) *(in titles)* **the R. Honourable** = en el Reino Unido, tratamiento formal aplicado a ministros y ex ministros del gobierno y a ciertos miembros de la aristocracia, ≃ su señoría; **the R. Honourable Edward Heath, M.P.** ≃ su Señoría, Edward Heath; **the R. Reverend Henry Watson** el Reverendísimo Henry Watson

4 *vt* (a) *(put upright) (boat, car)* enderezar, poner derecho(a); **the boat righted itself** el barco se enderezó (b) *(redress) (situation)* corregir, rectificar; **the problem won't just r. itself** el problema no se va a solucionar por sí mismo; **to r. a wrong** terminar con una injusticia

5 *exclam* (a) *(expressing agreement)* **you go first – r.!** tú primero – ¡de acuerdo *or Esp* vale *or Méx* órale *or RP* está bien! (b) *(to attract attention, when ready to begin)* **r., let's start!** *Esp* ¡venga, comencemos!, *Am* ¡bueno, vamos a empezar!

---

right-angled ['raɪtæŋgəld] *adj (triangle)* rectángulo(a); *(corner, bend)* en ángulo recto

right-click ['raɪt'klɪk] 1 *vt* hacer click con el botón derecho en
2 *vi* hacer click con el botón derecho

righteous ['raɪtʃəs] *adj* (a) *(person)* virtuoso(a), justo(a); **there's no need to sound so r.!** ¡no te pongas ahora a dar lecciones de ética! (b) *(indignation, anger)* justificado(a) (c) *US Fam (genuine)* genuino(a); *(excellent)* alucinante

righteously ['raɪtʃəslɪ] *adv (virtuously)* virtuosamente

righteousness ['raɪtʃəsnɪs] *n* honradez *f*, rectitud *f*

rightful ['raɪtfʊl] *adj (owner, heir)* legítimo(a); **he was given his r. share** le entregaron lo que se merecía

rightfully ['raɪtfʊlɪ] *adv* **it is r. mine** me pertenece por legítimo derecho; **...and r. so** ...y con razón

right-hand ['raɪthænd] *adj* **a r. bend** una curva a la derecha; **on the r. side** a la derecha; **in the top/bottom r. corner** en el ángulo superior/inferior derecho; IDIOM **to be sb's r. man** ser la mano derecha de alguien ►► *Aut* ***r. drive*** *(vehicle)* vehículo *m* con el volante a la derecha

right-handed ['raɪt'hændɪd] 1 *adj* (a) *(person)* diestro(a); **to be r.** ser diestro(a) (b) *(punch)* **a r. punch** un derechazo (c) *(tool, golf club)* para diestros; **a r. screw** un tornillo que ajusta en el sentido de las agujas del reloj
2 *adv* con la mano derecha

right-hander ['raɪt'hændə(r)] *n (person)* diestro(a) *m,f*

rightist ['raɪtɪst] 1 *n* derechista *mf*
2 *adj* derechista

rightly ['raɪtlɪ] *adv* (a) *(exactly, correctly)* correctamente; **if I remember r., Walter wasn't there** si no recuerdo mal, Walter no estaba allí; **as Jenkins so r. points out...** como Jenkins (muy) bien señala...; **I don't r. know why...** no sé muy bien por qué... (b) *(justifiably)* **r. or wrongly** para bien o para mal; **...and r. so** ...y con razón; **he was r. angry** se *esp Esp* enfadó *or esp Am* enojó y con razón

right-minded ['raɪt'maɪndɪd], **right-thinking** ['raɪt'θɪŋkɪŋ] *adj* **any r. person would have done the same** cualquier persona de bien hubiera hecho lo mismo

righto = **right-oh**

right-of-centre ['raɪtəv'sentə(r)] *adj Pol* de centro derecha

right-oh, righto ['raɪtəʊ] *exclam Fam Esp* ¡vale!, *Arg* ¡dale!, *Méx* ¡órale!

right-on ['raɪt'ɒn] *adj Fam* (a) *(socially aware)* progre (b) *(fashionable)* de moda

rightsizing ['raɪtsaɪzɪŋ] *n Com* racionalización *f*

right-thinking = **right-minded**

right-to-life ['raɪttə'laɪf] *adj* antiaborto *inv*, pro vida *inv*

right-to-lifer ['raɪttə'laɪfə(r)] *n Fam* antiabortista *mf*

right-to-work ['raɪttə'wɜːk] *adj* (a) *US (law, state)* = que prohíbe exigir la afiliación sindical de los trabajadores para contratarlos (b) *Br (anti-unemployment)* **a r. march** una manifestación para exigir puestos de trabajo

rightward ['raɪtwəd] 1 *adj* derechista; **the r. drift of the party** la paulatina derechización del partido
2 *adv* hacia la derecha

rightwards ['raɪtwədz] *adv* hacia la derecha

right-wing ['raɪt'wɪŋ] *adj Pol* derechista, de derechas

right-winger ['raɪt'wɪŋə(r)] *n* (a) *Pol* derechista *mf* (b) *(in soccer)* extremo *mf* derecho(a)

rigid ['rɪdʒɪd] *adj* (a) *(structure, material)* rígido(a); **he was r. with fear** estaba paralizado por el miedo; **they were shocked r. by this revelation** la revelación los dejó de piedra; *Br Fam* **to be bored r.** aburrirse como una ostra (b) *(approach, mentality)* rígido(a), inflexible; *(discipline)* estricto(a); *(timetable, schedule)* inflexible; **she's very r. in her ideas** es de ideas muy rígidas

rigidity [rɪ'dʒɪdɪtɪ] *n* (a) *(of structure, material)* rigidez *f* (b) *(of approach, mentality)* rigidez *f*, inflexibilidad *f*

rigidly ['rɪdʒɪdlɪ] *adv* (a) *(stiffly, erectly)* rígidamente (b) *(uncompromisingly)* inflexiblemente

rigmarole ['rɪgmərəʊl] *n Fam* (a) *(process)* engorro *m*, *Esp* latazo *m* (b) *(speech)* rollo *m*, galimatías *m inv*

rigor *US* = **rigour**

rigor mortis ['rɪgə'mɔːtɪs] *n Med* rigidez *f* cadavérica, rigor *m* mortis

rigorous ['rɪgərəs] *adj* riguroso(a)

rigorously ['rɪgərəslɪ] *adv* rigurosamente

rigour, *US* **rigor** ['rɪgə(r)] *n* rigor *m*; **the rigours of army life** los rigores de la vida militar; **the full r. of the law** todo el peso de la ley

rig-out ['rɪgaʊt] *n Br Fam (outfit)* **have you seen the r. he's wearing?** ¿has visto la vestimenta que me lleva?

rile [raɪl] *vt Fam (annoy)* fastidiar, irritar, *Am* enojar; **don't get riled!** ¡no te enfades *or* mosquees!

Riley ['raɪlɪ] *n* IDIOM *Fam* **to lead** *or* **live the life of R.** vivir como un rey *or Esp* como un rajá

rill [rɪl] *n (brook)* arroyuelo *m*

rim [rɪm] **1** *n* (**a**) *(of cup, bowl)* borde *m* (**b**) *(of wheel)* llanta *f* (**c**) *(of spectacles)* montura *f (sin incluir las patillas)* (**d**) *(of dirt)* cerco *m*, borde *m* (de suciedad); **there was a r. around the bath** había un borde de suciedad en la bañera

2 *vt* bordear

rime [raɪm] *n (frost)* escarcha *f*

rimless ['rɪmlɪs] *adj (spectacles)* sin montura *(pero con patillas)*

-rimmed [rɪmd] *suffix* **gold/steel-r.** *(spectacles)* con montura dorada/de metal, *RP* con armazón dorado/de metal; **to have red-r. eyes** tener los ojos inyectados en sangre

rind [raɪnd] *n (of fruit)* cáscara *f*; *(of cheese, bacon)* corteza *f*

ring[1] [rɪŋ] **1** *n* (**a**) *(for finger)* anillo *m*; *(with gem)* sortija *f*; *(plain metal band)* aro *m*; *(in nose, ear)* aro *m*, *Esp* pendiente *m* ►► ***r. finger*** (dedo *m*) anular *m*

(**b**) *(round object) (for can of drink, bird, curtains)* anilla *f*; **(rubber) r.** *(for swimmer)* flotador *m*; **the rings** *(in gymnastics)* las anillas ►► ***r. binder*** archivador *m or* carpeta *f* de anillas, *RP* biblioratο *m*

(**c**) *(surrounding planet)* anillo *m*

(**d**) *(circular arrangement) (of people, chairs)* corro *m*, círculo *m*; **to stand in a r.** estar en un círculo; **she looked round the r. of faces** miró a los rostros que la rodeaban ►► *Elec* ***r. circuit*** circuito *m* anular *or* de anillo; *Comptr* ***r. network*** red *f* en anillo

(**e**) *Chem* anillo *m*

(**f**) *(circular shape) (stain)* cerco *m*; *(in tree trunk)* anillo *m*; **to have rings under one's eyes** tener ojeras; IDIOM **to run rings round sb** darle mil vueltas a alguien ►► *Br* ***r. road*** carretera *f* de circunvalación, ronda *f* (de circunvalación)

(**g**) *(on stove)* fuego *m*

(**h**) *(for boxing, wrestling)* cuadrilátero *m*, ring *m*

(**i**) *(at circus)* pista *f*

(**j**) *(of spies, criminals)* red *f*

2 *vt* (**a**) *(surround)* rodear; **a lake ringed with trees** un lago rodeado de árboles (**b**) *(draw circle around)* poner un círculo alrededor de; **r. the right answer** rodee la respuesta correcta (**c**) *(bird)* anillar; *(bull, pig)* colocar un aro a

ring[2] **1** *n* (**a**) *(sound) (of doorbell, phone, bike)* timbre *m*; *(of small bell)* tintineo *m*; **there was a r. at the door** sonó el timbre de la puerta; **the r. of their voices in the empty warehouse** el sonido de sus voces en el depósito vacío

(**b**) *(distinctive sound)* **to have a r. of truth** ser verosímil; **the name has a familiar r. to it** el nombre me suena; **that excuse has a familiar r.!** esa excusa me suena de algo; **his name has a sinister r. to it** su nombre suena siniestro

(**c**) *Br Fam (phone call)* **to give sb a r.** dar un telefonazo *or RP* tubazo a alguien

2 *vt* (*pt* **rang** [ræŋ], *pp* **rung** [rʌŋ]) (**a**) *(bell, alarm)* hacer sonar; **the church clock rings the hours** el reloj de la iglesia marca las horas; IDIOM **that rings a bell** *(sounds familiar)* eso me suena; IDIOM **to r. the changes** hacer combinaciones (**b**) *Br (on phone)* llamar (por teléfono) a, telefonear a

3 *vi* (**a**) *(bell, telephone)* sonar; *(alarm)* sonar; **to r. at the door** llamar al timbre de la puerta; **to r. for the maid** llamar a la sirvienta; **you rang, Sir?** ¿llamaba el señor?

(**b**) *Br (on phone)* llamar (por teléfono), telefonear; **to r. for a doctor** llamar a un doctor; **to r. for help** llamar para pedir ayuda

(**c**) *(resonate) (street, room)* resonar; **their laughter rang through the house** sus risas resonaban en toda la casa; **my ears were ringing** me zumbaban los oídos; **my ears are still ringing with their laughter, their laughter still rings in my ears** su risa aún resuena en mis oídos; **to r. hollow** *(promise, boast)* ser poco convincente; *Fig* **to r. true/false** tener pinta de ser verdad/mentira

► **ring back** *Br* **1** *vt sep (on phone)* llamar más tarde a

2 *vi* devolver la llamada *or Am* el llamado; **he said he'd r. back later** dijo que volvería a llamar más tarde

► **ring down** *vt sep Theat* **to r. down the curtain** bajar el telón; *Fig* **to r. down the curtain on sth** poner punto y final a algo

► **ring in 1** *vi Br (to radio, TV show)* llamar; **I rang in sick** llamé para avisar de que estaba enfermo

2 *vt sep* **to r. the New Year in** recibir el año nuevo

► **ring off** *Br vi (on phone)* colgar

► **ring out 1** *vi (voice, shout, bell)* resonar

2 *vt sep* **to r. out the old year** despedir el año viejo; **r. out the old, r. in the new** despidamos lo viejo y demos la bienvenida a lo nuevo

► **ring round** *vt insep Br* llamar, telefonear

► **ring up** *vt sep* (**a**) *Br (on phone)* llamar (por teléfono) a, telefonear a (**b**) *(on cash register)* teclear; **the concert rang up a profit of...** el concierto recaudó unos beneficios de...

(**c**) *Theat* **to r. up the curtain** levantar el telón; *Fig* **this apparently trivial incident rang up the curtain on a decade of bloody war** este incidente, aparentemente insignificante, marcó el inicio de una década de sangrienta guerra

ring-a-ring-a-roses ['rɪŋə'rɪŋə'rəʊzɪz] *n* ≃ el corro de la patata, *CSur* ≃ la ronda; **to play r.** ≃ jugar al corro de la patata, *CSur* ≃ jugar a la ronda

ringbolt ['rɪŋbəʊlt] *n* cáncamo *m* de argolla

ring-bound ['rɪŋbaʊnd] *adj (notebook, file)* con anillas, anillado(a)

ringdove ['rɪŋdʌv] *n* paloma *f* torcaz

ringed plover ['rɪŋd'plʌvə(r)] *n* chorlitejo *m* grande ►► ***little r.*** chorlitejo *m* chico

ringer ['rɪŋə(r)] *n* (**a**) *(of bells)* campanero(a) *m,f* (**b**) *Fam (double)* **to be a dead r. for sb** ser el vivo retrato de alguien (**c**) *US Fam (horse)* = caballo que es inscrito en una carrera bajo un falso nombre para elevar el valor de las apuestas (**d**) *Austr Fam (expert)* experto(a) *m,f*

ring-fence ['rɪŋ'fens] **1** *n (round field)* cerca *f (que rodea una propiedad)*

2 *vt Br Fin* proteger

ringing ['rɪŋɪŋ] **1** *n* (**a**) *(of doorbell, phone)* timbre *m*; *(alarm)* sonido *m*; *(of church bells)* repique *m*, tañido *m* (**b**) *(in ears)* zumbido *m*

2 *adj* (**a**) *(noise)* resonante, sonoro(a); **in r. tones** con sonoridad (**b**) *(wholehearted)* incondicional, sin reservas (**c**) *Br* ***r. tone*** *(on telephone)* señal *f* de llamada

ringleader ['rɪŋli:də(r)] *n* cabecilla *mf*

ringlet ['rɪŋlɪt] *n* tirabuzón *m*; **to wear one's hair in ringlets** llevar tirabuzones

ringmaster ['rɪŋmɑ:stə(r)] *n* director *m* de circo

ring-necked ['rɪŋnekt] *adj (bird, snake)* de collar

ring-pull ['rɪŋpʊl] *n Br* anilla *f (de lata)* ►► ***r. can*** lata *f* de anilla

ringside ['rɪŋsaɪd] *n* **at the r.** al lado del cuadrilátero; **a r. seat** *(in boxing)* un asiento de primera fila; *(close view)* una visión muy cercana

ring-tailed lemur ['rɪŋteɪld'li:mə(r)] *n* lemur *m* de cola anillada

ringworm ['rɪŋwɜ:m] *n* tiña *f*

rink [rɪŋk] *n* (**a**) *(for ice-skating)* pista *f* de patinaje *or* de hielo; *(for rollerskating)* pista *f* de patinaje (**b**) *(in bowling green)* calle *f* (**c**) *(bowls, curling team)* equipo *m (que juega en una calle)*

rinky-dink ['rɪŋkɪdɪŋk] *adj US Fam* (**a**) *(cheap)* ordinario(a), *Esp* cutre, *Méx* naco(a), *RP* groncho(a) (**b**) *(small-time)* de poca importancia *or Esp* monta

rinse [rɪns] **1** *n* (**a**) *(clean, wash)* enjuague *m*, *Esp* aclarado *m*; **to give sth a r.** enjuagar *or Esp* aclarar algo; **put the washing machine on r.** pon la lavadora en enjuague *or* aclarado (**b**) *(hair tint)* reflejos *mpl*

2 *vt (clothes, dishes)* enjuagar, *Esp* aclarar; **to r. one's hands/mouth** enjuagarse las manos/la boca

► **rinse down** *vt sep Fam* **he rinsed the meal down with a glass of wine** regó la comida con un vaso de vino

► **rinse out 1** *vt sep (cup)* enjuagar; *(clothes)* enjuagar, *Esp* aclarar; **to r. the soap out of the clothes** enjuagar (el jabón de) la ropa; **to r. out one's mouth** enjuagarse la boca; IDIOM **go and r. your mouth out (with soapy water)!** ¡ve a lavarte la boca con jabón!

2 *vi (stain, dye)* **it'll r. out easily** saldrá fácilmente al enjuagarlo *or Esp* aclararlo

Rio (de Janeiro) ['ri:əʊ(dɪdʒə'neərəʊ)] *n* Río de Janeiro

Rio Grande ['ri:əʊ'grændɪ] *n* **the R.** el Río Bravo

riot ['raɪət] **1** *n* (**a**) *(uprising)* disturbio *m*; **a group of youths ran r.** un grupo de jóvenes provocó disturbios ►► *Hist* ***the R. Act*** = ley que permitía a las fuerzas de orden dispersar una manifestación por la fuerza; *Fam* **to read sb the r. act** poner los puntos sobre las íes a alguien, *Esp* leerle la cartilla a alguien; ***r. gear*** equipo *m or* material *m* antidisturbios; ***r. police*** policía *f* antidisturbios; ***r. shield*** escudo *m* antidisturbios; ***r. squad*** brigada *f* antidisturbios

(**b**) *(profusion)* **a r. of colour** una explosión de colores

(**c**) *Fam (amusing person, thing)* **he's a complete r.** es divertidísimo, *Esp* es una juerga total; **the party was a r.** la fiesta fue divertidísima *or Esp* una juerga total

(**d**) IDIOM **to run r.: the children ran r. while their parents were away** los niños se desmandaron cuando no estaban sus padres; **her**

imagination was running r. su imaginación se había desbocado; **the garden is running r.** el jardín está hecho un desastre *or* una selva
2 *vi (prisoners)* amotinarse; **in order to prevent the crowd from rioting** para evitar que estallaran disturbios

rioter ['raɪətə(r)] *n* alborotador(ora) *m,f*

rioting ['raɪətɪŋ] *n* disturbios *mpl*; **r. has broken out in the city** han estallado disturbios en la ciudad

riotous ['raɪətəs] *adj* **(a)** *(behaviour)* descontrolado(a); *(mob)* descontrolado(a), exaltado(a) ►► *Law* ***r. assembly*** alteración *f* del orden público **(b)** *Fam (party, occasion, living)* desenfrenado(a); **bursts of r. laughter** estallidos de risa descontrolada; **a r. success** un éxito arrasador

riotously ['raɪətəslɪ] *adv* **r. funny** de morirse de risa

RIP [ɑːraɪ'piː] (*abbr* **Rest In Peace**) R.I.P., Q.E.P.D.

rip [rɪp] 1 *n (in cloth, paper)* desgarrón *m*, rasgadura *f*
2 *vt* (*pt & pp* **ripped**) **(a)** *(cloth, paper)* rasgar; **to r. sth to pieces** *or* **shreds** *(cloth, paper)* hacer jirones algo; *(performance, argument)* hacer añicos algo **(b)** *(snatch)* arrebatar; **she ripped the book from my hands** me arrebató el libro de las manos
3 *vi* **(a)** *(cloth, paper)* rasgarse **(b)** *Fam (go fast)* ir a toda velocidad *or Esp* pastilla; **a motorbike ripped past** una moto pasó a toda velocidad *or Esp* pastilla; **to let r.** *(while driving)* pisar a fondo; *(in performance)* darlo todo, entregarse; *(fart)* echarse un pedo; **let it r.!** ¡que comience la diversión *or* fiesta!; **to let r. (at sb)** *(shout)* poner el grito en el cielo (a alguien)

► **rip apart** *vt sep* destrozar; **the scandal ripped the party apart** el escándalo hizo añicos el partido

► **rip off** *vt sep* **(a)** *(tear)* arrancar; **he ripped off his shirt** se desembarazó de su camisa **(b)** *Fam (swindle) (person)* timar **(c)** *Fam (steal)* birlar; **that sketch was ripped off from another comedian** ese sketch está fusilado de otro humorista; **she ripped them off for millions** les birló millones

► **rip open** *vt sep* abrir de un tirón

► **rip out** *vt sep* arrancar

► **rip through** *vt insep* **(a)** *(of explosion, fire)* arrasar; **the explosion ripped through the building** la explosión arrasó el edificio **(b)** *(complete quickly)* hacer rápidamente; **we ripped through the work in no time** terminamos el trabajo rápidamente

► **rip up** *vt sep* **(a)** *(letter)* hacer pedazos **(b)** *(annul) (contract, treaty)* anular **(c)** *(road, pavement)* destrozar

riparian [rɪ'peərɪən] *adj Formal (plant, wildlife)* ribereño(a)

ripcord ['rɪpkɔːd] *n* cable *m* de apertura manual

ripe [raɪp] *adj* **(a)** *(fruit)* maduro(a); *(cheese)* curado(a); **to be r.** *(fruit)* estar maduro(a); IDIOM **to live to a r. old age** vivir hasta una edad avanzada
(b) *(ready)* **this area is r. for development** esta zona está lista *or* preparada para ser urbanizada; **the time is r. for...** es el momento ideal *or* idóneo para...; **the time is not yet r.** todavía no es el momento (adecuado)
(c) *(full) (lips)* carnoso(a); *(breasts)* turgente
(d) *(pungent) (smell)* acre, fuerte
(e) *Fam (language, humour)* subido(a) de tono, atrevido(a)

ripen ['raɪpən] 1 *vt* hacer madurar
2 *vi* madurar

ripeness ['raɪpnɪs] *n* **(a)** *(of fruit)* madurez *f* **(b)** *Fam (of language)* atrevimiento *m*

rip-off ['rɪpɒf] *n Fam* **(a)** *(swindle)* timo *m*, robo *m*; **what a r.!** ¡menudo robo! **(b)** *(theft)* robo *m*; **it's a r. of a French play** es una fusilada de una obra francesa

riposte [rɪ'pɒst] 1 *n* **(a)** *(reply)* réplica *f* **(b)** *(in fencing)* estocada *f* de contragolpe
2 *vi* replicar

ripped [rɪpt] *adj US Fam (drunk, on drugs)* colocado(a), *Esp* ciego(a); *very Fam* **to be r. to the tits** llevar un buen colocón

ripper ['rɪpə(r)] 1 *n (murderer)* destripador(ora) *m,f*
2 *adj Austr Fam (excellent)* alucinante

ripping ['rɪpɪŋ] *adj Old-fashioned* **we had a r. (good) time** lo pasamos bomba; *Fam* **a r. yarn** una historia muy entretenida

ripple ['rɪpəl] 1 *n* **(a)** *(small wave) (on water)* onda *f*, ondulación *f*; *(on wheatfield, in sand)* ondulación *f*
(b) *(sound) (of water, conversation)* murmullo *m*; *(of applause)* murmullo *m*; **a r. of laughter ran through the audience** las risas recorrían la audiencia como una ola
(c) *(of excitement)* asomo *m*
(d) *(repercussion)* repercusión *f*; **her resignation hardly caused a r.** su dimisión apenas tuvo repercusiones ►► ***r. effect*** reacción *f* en cadena
(e) *(ice-cream)* = helado de vainilla con vetas de jarabe de frambuesa o de otros sabores
(f) *Elec (in current)* ondulación *f*
2 *vi* **(a)** *(undulate) (water)* ondular; *(wheatfield, hair)* ondularse; **moonlight rippled on the surface of the lake** la luz de la luna se reflejaba en la superficie ondulada del lago; **rippling muscles** músculos marcados **(b)** *(murmur) (water)* murmurar; *(laughter, applause)* extenderse **(c)** *(have repercussions)* tener repercusiones
3 *vt (water, lake)* ondular

rip-roaring ['rɪprɔːrɪŋ] *adj Fam* **(a)** *(success)* apoteósico(a) **(b)** *(story)* lleno(a) de acción

ripsaw ['rɪpsɔː] *n* sierra *f* de cortar al hilo *or* de hender

ripsnorter ['rɪpsnɔːtə(r)] *n Fam* **a r. of a movie** una película alucinante

riptide ['rɪptaɪd] *n* corriente *f* turbulenta

RISC [rɪsk] *n Comptr* (*abbr* **reduced instruction set computer**) ***R. processor*** procesador *m* RISC

rise [raɪz] 1 *n* **(a)** *(ascent)* ascenso *m*; *(of theatre curtain)* subida *f*; **the r. and fall of the tide** la subida y la bajada de la marea
(b) *(increase) (in price, temperature, pressure, number)* aumento *m*, subida *f* (**in** de); **to be on the r.** ir en aumento
(c) *Br* **(pay) r.** aumento *m* (de sueldo); **to ask for/be given a r.** pedir/recibir un aumento
(d) *(of leader, party)* ascenso *m*; **her r. to power/fame** su ascenso *or* acceso al poder/a la fama; **the r. and fall** *(of empire, politician)* el ascenso y la caída, el esplendor y la decadencia
(e) *(of phenomenon, practice)* ascenso *m*; **to give r. to sth** dar pie a algo
(f) *Fam* **to take** *or* **get a r. out of sb** conseguir mosquear a alguien
(g) *(in ground)* cuesta *f*
2 *vi* (*pt* **rose** [rəʊz], *pp* **risen** ['rɪzən]) **(a)** *(get up)* levantarse; **to r. early/late** levantarse temprano/tarde; **they rose from their seats** se levantaron de sus asientos; **to r. to one's feet** ponerse de pie, levantarse, *Am* pararse; **the horse rose on its hind legs** el caballo se levantó sobre las patas posteriores; **to r. from the dead** *or* **grave** resucitar de entre los muertos; *Fam* **r. and shine!** ¡arriba!; IDIOM **to r. from the ashes** surgir de las cenizas
(b) *(move upwards) (smoke, balloon)* ascender, subir; *Theat (curtain)* subir; *(sun, moon)* salir; *(road, ground)* subir, elevarse; *(tide, river level)* subir; **his eyebrows rose in surprise** levantó las cejas sorprendido; **the colour rose in** *or* **to her cheeks** se sonrojó; **a murmur rose from the crowd** la multitud murmuraba; **to r. to the surface** *(swimmer, whale, body)* salir *or* subir a la superficie; IDIOM **to r. to the bait** morder el anzuelo
(c) *(increase) (temperature, price, pressure, number)* aumentar, subir; *(standards, hope)* aumentar; *(wind)* arreciar; *(voice)* elevarse, subir; *(barometer)* subir; **to r. in price/number** aumentar el precio/la cantidad; **my spirits rose** se me levantó el ánimo
(d) *(mountains, buildings)* elevarse, alzarse; **the trees rose above our heads** los árboles se elevaban por sobre nuestras cabezas; **an entire city has risen in what was wasteland thirty years ago** una ciudad entera se ha alzado en lo que hace treinta años era un descampado
(e) *(dough)* fermentar, subir; *(soufflé)* subir
(f) *(socially, professionally)* ascender; **she rose to the position of personnel manager** ascendió a jefa de personal; **to r. in society** ascender en la sociedad; **to r. from the ranks** ascender de soldado raso; **to r. in sb's esteem** ganarse la estima de alguien; **to r. to the challenge** *or* **occasion** estar a la altura de las circunstancias; **to r. to fame** alcanzar la fama; **to r. to power** ascender *or* acceder al poder
(g) *(adjourn) (parliament, court)* levantarse
(h) *(revolt)* levantarse (**against** contra); **to r. in revolt** levantarse, alzarse; **to r. in arms** levantarse en armas; **to r. in protest (against sth)** alzarse en protesta (contra algo)
(i) *(react angrily)* **to r. to a remark** responder a una provocación
(j) *(have source) (river)* nacer

► **rise above** *vt insep* **(a)** *(be higher than)* levantarse por encima de
(b) *(be heard over)* **a cry rose above the sound of the waves** se oyó un grito entre el sonido del oleaje
(c) *(problem, criticism)* remontar, superar; **he rose above his limitations** superó sus limitaciones; **she didn't let him annoy her, she just rose above it** no dejó que la molestara, estuvo por encima de ello

► **rise up** *vi* **(a)** *(move upwards) (smoke, balloon)* ascender, subir; *(road, ground, waters)* subir, elevarse; *(in society)* ascender; **to r. up from one's chair** levantarse de la silla

(b) *(revolt)* levantarse (**against** contra); **to r. up in arms** levantarse en armas; **to r. up in protest (against sth)** alzarse en protesta (contra algo)
(c) *(appear)* aparecer, surgir; **a shadowy figure rose up out of the mist** una figura imprecisa apareció de entre la niebla

risen ['rɪzən] **1** *pp of* **rise**
2 *adj Rel* resucitado(a); **Christ is r.** Cristo ha resucitado

riser ['raɪzə(r)] *n* **(a)** *(person)* **an early r.** un(a) madrugador(ora); **a late r.** un(a) dormilón(ona) **(b)** *(of stairs)* contrahuella *f* **(c)** *(for water, gas)* tubo *m* de subida

risible ['rɪzɪbəl] *adj Formal* risible

rising ['raɪzɪŋ] **1** *n (revolt)* revuelta *f*, levantamiento *m*
2 *adj* **(a)** *(sun)* naciente; *(tide, water level)* creciente; *(ground)* ascendente ►► *Br* ***r. damp*** humedad *f (que asciende por las paredes)* **(b)** *(prices, temperature, pressure, number)* ascendente, en aumento; *(emotion)* creciente **(c)** *(artist, politician)* en alza ►► ***r. star*** valor *m* en alza, estrella *f* en ciernes
3 *adv Br Fam* **she's r. forty** roza los cuarenta ►► ***r. fives*** niños *mpl* a punto de cumplir cinco años

risk [rɪsk] **1** *n* **(a)** *(danger)* riesgo *m*, peligro *m*; **it's too big a r.** es un riesgo demasiado grande; **it's not worth the r.** no vale la pena arriesgarse; **is there any r. of him making another blunder?** ¿se corre el riesgo de que cometa otro error garrafal?; **there's no r. of that happening** es muy poco probable que eso suceda; **at r.** en peligro; **at great r. to himself** con gran peligro para su integridad física; **to be at r.** *(child)* estar en *or* correr peligro; **to put** *or* **place sth at r.** poner algo en peligro; **at the r. of...** a riesgo de...; **to run the r. of...** correr el riesgo de...; **to take risks** arriesgarse, correr riesgos; **that's a r. we'll have to take** es un riesgo que tendremos que correr; **you do so at your own r.** lo haces bajo tu propia responsabilidad; **cars may be parked here at the owner's r.** *(sign)* se permite estacionar bajo la responsabilidad del propietario del vehículo ►► ***r. assessment*** evaluación *f* de riesgos; *Fin* ***r. capital*** capital *m* (de) riesgo; *Med* ***r. factor*** factor *m* riesgo; ***r. management*** gestión *f* de riesgos
(b) *(source of danger)* peligro *m*; **it's a health r.** es un peligro para la salud
(c) *Fin (in insurance)* riesgo *m*; **to be a good/bad r.** constituir un bajo/alto riesgo
2 *vt* **(a)** *(endanger) (future, money, reputation)* arriesgar; *(health)* poner en peligro; *(life)* poner en peligro, arriesgar; **they decided to r. everything on a last desperate gamble** a la desesperada, decidieron arriesgar todo a una última carta; IDIOM **to r. one's neck** jugarse el cuello; IDIOM **to r. life and limb** jugarse el cuello; *Hum* **you r. life and limb every day as a primary teacher** los profesores de primaria se juegan el cuello *or* ponen en peligro su integridad física a diario
(b) *(run risk of)* **we can't r. it** no podemos correr ese riesgo; **I think I'll r. it** creo que correré el riesgo; **you're risking an accident when you drive so fast** conduciendo *or Am* manejando tan rápido te arriesgas a tener un accidente; **to r. defeat** correr el riesgo de *or* arriesgarse a ser derrotado(a)

riskiness ['rɪskɪnɪs] *n* riesgo *m*, peligro *m*

risk-taking ['rɪskteɪkɪŋ] *n* **there's too much r. going on** se corren demasiados riesgos

risky ['rɪskɪ] *adj* arriesgado(a); **it's a r. business** es un asunto arriesgado *or* peligroso

risotto [rɪ'zɒtəʊ] (*pl* **risottos**) *n* risotto *m*

risqué [rɪs'keɪ] *adj (humour)* atrevido(a), subido(a) de tono

rissole ['rɪsəʊl] *n* = pequeña masa frita, generalmente redonda, de carne o verduras

rite [raɪt] *n* **(a)** *Rel* rito *m*; **the last rites** la extremaunción **(b)** *(ceremony)* ***r. of passage*** trámite *m* iniciático en la vida

ritual ['rɪtjʊəl] **1** *n* ritual *m*; **his nightly r. of locking the doors** su ritual de todas las noches de cerrar todas las puertas con llave; **it's become a bit of a r.** se ha convertido en una especie de ritual
2 *adj* ritual; **there was r. condemnation of him in the press** recibió la consabida *or* automática condena de parte de la prensa

ritualistic [rɪtjʊə'lɪstɪk] *adj (following a pattern)* ritual; *Rel* ritualista

ritualism ['rɪtʃʊəlɪzəm] *n* ritualismo *m*

ritualist ['rɪtʃʊəlɪst] *n* ritualista *mf*

ritualistic [rɪtʃʊə'lɪstɪk] *adj* ritualista

ritually ['rɪtjʊəlɪ] *adv* de modo ritual

ritz [rɪts] *n US Fam* **to put on the r.** tirar la casa por la ventana

ritzy ['rɪtsɪ] *adj Fam* lujoso(a)

rival ['raɪvəl] **1** *n* rival *mf*; **rivals in business/love** rivales en los negocios/el amor
2 *adj* rival; **a r. company** una empresa rival *or* de la competencia
3 *vt* (*pt & pp* **rivalled**, *US* **rivaled**) rivalizar con; **it rivals anything to be seen in Paris** no tiene nada que envidiarle a lo que puedas ver en París; **the scenery rivals the Grand Canyon** el paisaje no tiene nada que envidiar al Gran Cañón; **New York cannot r. London for historic interest** Nueva York no le hace sombra a Londres en cuanto al patrimonio histórico

rivalry ['raɪvəlrɪ] *n* rivalidad *f*; **there's a lot of r. between the two brothers** entre los dos hermanos existe una gran rivalidad

riven ['rɪvən] *adj* dividido(a), escindido(a); **the party was r. by deep ideological divisions** el partido estaba dividido *or* escindido por profundas diferencias ideológicas

river ['rɪvə(r)] *n* **(a)** *(waterway)* río *m*; **we sailed up/down the r.** navegamos río arriba/abajo; **up/down r. (from)** río arriba/abajo (desde); *US Fam* **to be up the r.** *(in prison)* estar en *Esp* chirona *or Andes, RP* la cana *or Méx* el bote ►► ***r. basin*** cuenca *f* fluvial; *Med* ***r. blindness*** ceguera *f* de río; ***r. port*** puerto *m* fluvial; ***r. system*** red *f* hidrográfica; ***r. traffic*** tráfico *m* fluvial
(b) *(of mud, lava)* río *m*; **a r. of blood** un río de sangre

riverbank ['rɪvəbæŋk] *n* orilla *f or* margen *m* del río

riverbed ['rɪvəbed] *n* lecho *m* (del río)

riverine ['rɪvəraɪn] *adj* ribereño(a)

River Plate ['rɪvə'pleɪt] *n* Río de la Plata

riverside ['rɪvəsaɪd] **1** *n* ribera *f*, orilla *f* (del río)
2 *adj* ribereño(a) *(de un río)*; **r. villa** mansión a la orilla del río

rivet ['rɪvɪt] **1** *n* remache *m* ►► ***r. gun*** (pistola *f*) remachadora *f*
2 *vt* **(a)** *(fasten with rivet)* remachar **(b)** *Fig (fascinate)* **to be absolutely riveted** estar completamente fascinado(a); **to be riveted to the spot** quedarse clavado(a); **the children were riveted to the TV** los niños estaban pegados a la tele

riveter ['rɪvɪtə(r)] *n* **(a)** *(person)* remachador(ora) *m,f* **(b)** *(machine)* remachadora *f*

riveting ['rɪvɪtɪŋ] *adj (fascinating)* fascinante

Riviera [rɪvɪ:'eərə] *n* **the R.** la Riviera

rivulet ['rɪvjʊlət] *n* **(a)** *(small river)* arroyuelo *m* **(b)** *(of blood, sweat)* hilo *m*

Riyadh ['ri:æd] *n* Riad

riyal [rɪ'jæl] *n (unit of currency)* riyal *m*

rly (*abbr* **railway**) F.C., ferrocarril

RM [ɑ:r'em] (*abbr* **Royal Marines**) = infantería de marina británica

RMT [ɑ:rem'ti:] *n* (*abbr* **National Union of Rail, Maritime and Transport Workers**) = sindicato británico de trabajadores del sector de transportes

RN [ɑ:r'en] **(a)** (*abbr* **Royal Navy**) armada *f* británica **(b)** (*abbr* **registered nurse**) enfermero(a) *m,f* diplomado(a)

RNA [ɑ:ren'eɪ] *n Biol* (*abbr* **ribonucleic acid**) ARN *m*

RNIB [ɑ:renaɪ'bi:] *n* (*abbr* **Royal National Institute for the Blind**) = asociación británica de ayuda a los ciegos, *Esp* ≃ ONCE *f*

RNLI [ɑ:renel'aɪ] *n* (*abbr* **Royal National Lifeboat Institution**) = organización británica de voluntarios para operaciones marítimas de salvamento

RNR [ɑ:ren'ɑ:(r)] *n Formerly* (*abbr* **Royal Naval Reserve**) = reserva de la marina británica

RNVR [ɑ:renvi:'ɑ:(r)] *n Formerly* (*abbr* **Royal Naval Volunteer Reserve**) = reserva de voluntarios de la marina británica

RNZAF [ɑ:renzedeɪ'ef] *n* (*abbr* **Royal New Zealand Air Force**) fuerza(s) *f(pl)* aérea(s) neozelandesa(s)

RNZN [ɑ:renzed'en] *n* (*abbr* **Royal New Zealand Navy**) marina *f* neozelandesa

roach [rəʊtʃ] *n* **(a)** *(fish)* rubio *m*, rutilo *m* **(b)** *US Fam (cockroach)* cucaracha *f*; *Chile* barata *f* ►► ***r. motel***® trampa *f* para cucarachas **(c)** *Fam (for cannabis cigarette)* colilla *f* de porro ►► ***r. clip*** pinza *f* para porros

road [rəʊd] *n* **(a)** *(in general)* carretera *f*; *(in town)* calle *f*; *(path, track)* camino *m*; **the London road** la carretera a *or* de Londres; **is this the (right) r. for** *or* **to Liverpool?** ¿es ésta la carretera (que va) a Liverpool?, ¿voy bien por aquí a Liverpool?; **they live across** *or* **over the r. (from us)** viven al otro lado de la calle, viven enfrente (de nosotros); **she was standing in the middle of the r.** estaba parada en medio de la carretera; **by r.** por carretera; **to be off the r.** *(vehicle)* estar averiado(a); **down** *or* **up the r.** un poco más lejos, por *or* en la misma calle; **after three hours on the r.** después de tres horas en la carretera *or* de camino; **to be on the r.** *(salesman)* estar de viaje (de ventas); *(pop group)* estar de gira; **we've been on the r. since 6 o'clock this morning** llevamos viajando *or* en carretera desde las 6 de la mañana; **he shouldn't be on the r.** él no está en condiciones de *Esp* conducir *orAm* manejar; **that vehicle shouldn't be on the r.** ese vehículo no está en condiciones de circular; *Br* **the price on the r.** el precio final del vehículo; **to take to the r.** *(driver)* salir de viaje, ponerse en camino; *(tramp)* ponerse a vagar sin rumbo fijo; *also Fig* **somewhere along the r.** en algún punto *or* momento; IDIOM *Fam* **let's have one for the r.** vamos a tomar la última *or* la espuela; PROV **all roads lead to Rome** todos los caminos llevan a Roma; PROV **the r. to hell is paved with good intentions** con la intención no basta ►► ***r. accident*** accidente *m* de circulación *or* tráfico; ***r. atlas*** guía *f* de carreteras; ***r. bridge*** puente *m (de carretera)*; ***r. conditions*** estado *m* de las carreteras; *Br* ***r. fund licence*** pegatina *f* del impuesto de circulación; ***r. haulage*** transporte *m* por carretera; ***r. haulier*** compañía *f* de transporte por carretera, transportista *m (por carretera)*; *Fam* ***r. kill*** animal *m* muerto por un vehículo; ***r. manager*** mánager *mf or* organizador(ora) *m,f* de una gira; ***r. map*** mapa *m* de carreteras; ***r. metal*** grava *f*, *Arg* tosca *f*; ***r. movie*** = película en la que los protagonistas emprenden un viaje largo por carretera; ***r. network*** red *f* viaria *or* de carreteras; ***r. pricing*** = práctica de cobrar a los conductores por el uso de algunas carreteras con mucho tráfico en momentos determinados; ***r. race*** *(in cycling)* carrera *f* en ruta *or* de fondo en carretera; ***r. racing*** *(in cycling)* ciclismo *m* en ruta, fondo *m* en carretera; ***r. rage*** violencia *f* al volante *or* en carretera; ***r. repairs*** obras *fpl*; ***r. roller*** apisonadora *f*; ***r. safety*** seguridad *f* en carretera, seguridad *f* vial; ***r. sense*** buen instinto *m* en la carretera; ***r. show*** = programa, torneo, exhibición, etc. itinerantes; ***r. sign*** señal *f* de tráfico *or* circulación; ***r. tax*** impuesto *m* de circulación; *Br* ***r. tax disc*** pegatina *f* del impuesto de circulación; ***r. test*** prueba *f* en carretera; ***r. traffic*** tráfico *m or* tránsito *m* rodado; ***r. transport*** transporte *m* por carretera; *US* ***r. warrior*** = hombre de negocios que viaja mucho

(**b**) *(route)* **we don't want to go down that r.** no queremos tomar ese camino; **down the r.** *(in the future)* en el futuro; **a few years down the r.** dentro de unos años; **to be on the r. to recovery/success** estar en vías de recuperación/de alcanzar el éxito; **he is on the r. to an early death** va camino de morir joven; **to be on the right r.** ir por (el) buen camino; **to come to the end of the r.** *(of relationship)* acabar

(**c**) *Br Fam (way)* **you're in my r.!** *(I can't pass)* ¡no me dejas pasar!; *(I can't see)* ¡no me dejas ver!; **get out of my r.** *or* **the r.** quítate de en medio, aparta

(**d**) *Br Fam* **any r.** de todos modos

(**e**) *Naut* **roads** fondeadero *m*

roadbed ['rəʊdbed] *n* (**a**) *(of road)* firme *m* (**b**) *Rail* balasto *m*

roadblock ['rəʊdblɒk] *n* control *m* de carretera

roadbuilding ['rəʊdbɪldɪŋ] *n* construcción *f* de carreteras; **r. programme** plan de obras viales

road-hog ['rəʊdhɒg] *n Fam* conductor(ora) *m,f* temerario(a), loco(a) *m,f* del volante

roadholding ['rəʊdhəʊldɪŋ] *n Aut* agarre *m*, adherencia *f*

roadhouse ['rəʊdhaʊs] *n Old-fashioned* = taberna o bar al lado de la carretera

roadie ['rəʊdɪ] *n Fam* roadie *m*, = persona encargada del montaje del escenario y el equipo musical de un grupo en gira

roadrunner ['rəʊdrʌnə(r)] *n* correcaminos *m inv*

roadside ['rəʊdsaɪd] *n* borde *m* de la carretera; **r. bar/hotel** bar/hotel de carretera; **r. repairs** reparaciones en carretera

roadstead ['rəʊdsted] *n Naut* fondeadero *m*

roadster ['rəʊdstə(r)] *n* (**a**) *Old-fashioned (car)* deportivo *m* descapotable de dos plazas (**b**) *(bicycle)* bicicleta *f* de paseo

road-test ['rəʊdtest] *vt (car)* probar en carretera; *(computer)* probar el rendimiento de

roadtrip ['rəʊdtrɪp] *n US* viaje *m* largo por carretera

road-user ['rəʊdju:zə(r)] *n Br* usuario(a) *m,f* de la vía pública

roadway ['rəʊdweɪ] *n* calzada *f*

roadwork ['rəʊdwɜ:k] *n (by boxer, athlete)* trote *m* por carretera *(para entrenar)*; **to do r.** salir a correr

roadworks ['rəʊdwɜ:ks] *npl* obras *fpl*

roadworthiness ['rəʊdwɜ:ðɪnɪs] *n* = condición de estar en condiciones de circular; **certificate of r.** = certificado de estar en condiciones de circular

roadworthy ['rəʊdwɜ:ðɪ] *adj (vehicle)* en condiciones de circular

roam [rəʊm] **1** *vt (streets, the world)* vagar por, recorrer; **to r. the seven seas** recorrer *or* surcar los siete mares

2 *vi* (**a**) *(wander)* **to r. (about** *or* **around)** vagar; **he allowed his imagination/his thoughts to r.** dejó volar (a) su imaginación/su mente (**b**) *Tel (mobile phone user)* usar el (teléfono) móvil en el extranjero, hacer uso del servicio de roaming *or* itinerancia (internacional)

roan [rəʊn] **1** *n* caballo *m* ruano

2 *adj* ruano(a)

roar [rɔ:(r)] **1** *n (of person)* grito *m*, rugido *m*; *(of lion, tiger)* rugido *m*; *(of elephant, bull)* bramido *m*; *(of crowd)* rugido *m*, clamor *m*; *(of sea, wind)* rugido *m*, bramido *m*; *(of thunder, storm, engine)* estruendo *m*, rugido *m*; *(of fire, furnace)* rugido *m*; *(of traffic, guns)* estruendo *m*; **to give a r.** *(person)* vociferar, rugir; *(lion)* dar un rugido, rugir; **roars of laughter** fuertes carcajadas

2 *vt* gritar; **the sergeant roared (out) an order to the men** el sargento dio una orden a sus hombres vociferando; **the crowd roared their delight** la multitud gritó *or* rugió entusiasmada; **they roared their team on** *(encouraged)* daban gritos de ánimo a su equipo

3 *vi* (**a**) *(make loud noise) (person)* vociferar, rugir; *(lion, tiger)* rugir; *(elephant, bull)* bramar; *(crowd)* gritar, rugir; *(sea, wind, storm)* rugir, bramar; *(thunder, guns)* retumbar; *(fire, furnace)* rugir; *(traffic)* hacer mucho ruido, armar gran estruendo; *(engine)* rugir; **to r. with laughter** reírse a carcajadas; **to r. with pain** rugir de dolor

(**b**) *(move loudly)* **to r. past** pasar con gran estruendo; **he roared up to us on his motorbike** se nos acercó con gran estruendo en su motocicleta

roaring ['rɔ:rɪŋ] **1** *adj* **a r. fire** un fuego muy vivo; **the shop was doing a r. trade** el negocio iba viento en popa; **they did a r. trade in pancakes** vendían las crepes como rosquillas; **it was a r. success** fue un éxito clamoroso ►► *Hist* ***the R. Twenties*** los locos años 20; ***the R. Forties*** = zona marítima de fuertes vientos entre las latitudes 40 y 50

2 *adv Fam* **r. drunk** como una cuba, borracho(a) perdido(a)

roast [rəʊst] **1** *n* (**a**) *(piece of meat)* asado *m*, carne *f* asada (al horno); **a pork r., a r. of pork** una porción de cerdo asado *or* de asado de cerdo (**b**) *US (barbecue)* barbacoa *f* (al aire libre), *Col, CSur* asado *m*

2 *adj* asado(a); **r. beef** rosbif, asado de vaca; **r. lamb** cordero asado, asado de cordero; **r. chestnuts** castañas asadas; **r. potatoes** *Esp* patatas *orAm* papas asadas; **medium/high r. coffee** café de tueste natural/torrefacto

3 *vt* (**a**) *(meat)* asar; *(nuts, coffee)* tostar (**b**) *Fam (by sun, fire)* abrasar, achicharrar; **thousands of tourists roasting themselves in the sun** miles de turistas tostándose al sol (**c**) *Fam (criticize)* desollar (**d**) *US Fam (tease)* burlarse de, reírse de

4 *vi* (**a**) *(meat)* asarse (**b**) *Fam (person)* achicharrarse, asarse de calor; **we spent a week roasting in the sun** pasamos una semana tostándonos al sol

roaster ['rəʊstə(r)] *n* (**a**) *(dish)* fuente *f* para asar (**b**) *(bird)* pieza *f* para asar

roasting ['rəʊstɪŋ] **1** *n* (**a**) *(of meat)* asado *m* (al horno) ►► *US* ***r. pan*** fuente *f* para asar, *CSur* asadera *f*; *Br* ***r. tin*** fuente *f* para asar, *CSur* asadera *f*

(**b**) *Fam* **to give sb a r.** *(tell off)* echar una bronca *or Esp* un broncazo a alguien; *(criticize)* poner a parir a alguien, *Méx* viborear a alguien, *RP* dejar por el piso a alguien; **to get a r.** *(telling-off)* llevarse una bronca *or Esp* un broncazo; *(criticism)* ser vapuleado(a)

2 *adj* **r.(-hot)** abrasador(ora), achicharrante; **it's r. in here** aquí te achicharras; **I'm r.!** ¡me aso de calor!, ¡qué calor!

rob [rɒb] *(pt & pp* **robbed**) *vt* (**a**) *(steal from) (person, bank)* atracar; *(house)* robar; **I've been robbed!** ¡me han robado!; **to r. sb of sth** robar algo a alguien; IDIOM **to r. Peter to pay Paul** desnudar a un santo para vestir a otro (**b**) *(deprive)* **to r. sb of sth** privar a alguien de algo, quitarle algo a alguien; *Fam* **we were robbed!** *(after team's defeat)* ¡nos han robado!, ¡fue un robo!

robber ['rɒbə(r)] *n (of bank, shop)* atracador(ora) *m,f*; *(of house)* ladrón(ona) *m,f* ►► ***r. baron*** *(in middle ages)* = señor feudal que asaltaba a los viajeros que atravesaban sus dominios; *US (ruthless capitalist)* = capitalista explotador y sin escrúpulos de finales del siglo XIX en Estados Unidos

robbery ['rɒbərɪ] *n (of bank, shop)* atraco *m*; *(of house)* robo *m*; *Fam* **the prices are nothing short of r.!** ¡estos precios son un robo!

robe [rəʊb] **1** *n* (**a**) *(ceremonial) (of priest)* sotana *f*; *(of judge)* toga *f* (**b**) *esp US (dressing gown)* bata *f*, batín *m*

2 *vt (dress)* vestir; **robed in red** vestido(a) de rojo

3 *vi (judge)* ponerse la toga

robin ['rɒbɪn] *n* **r. (redbreast)** petirrojo *m*

robot ['rəʊbɒt] *n* robot *m*

robotic [rəʊ'bɒtɪk] *adj* de robot

robotics [rəʊ'bɒtɪks] *n* robótica *f*

robot-like ['rəʊbɒtlaɪk] *adj* de robot

robust [rəʊ'bʌst] *adj* (**a**) *(person)* robusto(a); *(health)* vigoroso(a), de hierro; *(appetite)* fuerte (**b**) *(material, suitcase)* resistente; *(structure, economy)* sólido(a), fuerte (**c**) *(defence, speech)* enérgico(a) (**d**) *(humour)* directo(a) (**e**) *(wine)* con cuerpo

robustly [rəʊ'bʌstlɪ] *adv* (**a**) *(built, constructed)* sólidamente (**b**) *(to defend)* enérgicamente

robustness [rəʊ'bʌstnɪs] *n* (**a**) *(of person)* robustez *f*; *(of health)* vigor *m*; *(of appetite)* fuerza *f* (**b**) *(of material)* resistencia *f*; *(of structure, economy)* solidez *f* (**c**) *(of defence)* energía *f*, vigor *m* (**d**) *(of humour)* carácter *m* saludable (**e**) *(of wine)* cuerpo *m*

rock [rɒk] **1** *n* (**a**) *(substance)* roca *f*; IDIOM **to be a r.: she was an absolute r. during the crisis** durante la crisis se mantuvo con la mayor entereza; IDIOM **to be r. solid** *(support, morale)* ser inquebrantable ►► ***r. climber*** escalador(ora) *m,f*; ***r. climbing*** escalada *f*; **to go r. climbing** ir a escalar; ***r. crystal*** cristal *m* de roca, *Spec* cuarzo *m* hialino; ***r. face*** pared *f* (de roca); ***r. formation*** formación *f* rocosa

(**b**) *(large stone, boulder)* roca *f*; *US (stone)* piedra *f*; **on the rocks** *(whisky)* con hielo; **to run onto the rocks** *(ship)* encallar; *(project)* irse a pique, fracasar; IDIOM **to be on the rocks** *(marriage, company)* estar al borde del naufragio; IDIOM **to reach** *or* **hit r. bottom** tocar fondo; IDIOM **to be between a r. and a hard place** estar entre la espada y la pared ►► *Br* ***r. bun*** *or* ***cake*** = bizcocho duro por el exterior hecho con frutas secas; ***r. dove*** paloma *f* bravía; ***r. garden*** jardín *m* de rocalla; ***r. lobster*** langosta *f*; ***r. pigeon*** paloma *f* bravía; ***r. pipit*** bisbita *m* ribereño costero; ***r. plant*** = planta alpina que crece en la roca; ***r. pool*** charca *f* (en las rocas de la playa); ***r. salmon*** lija *f*, pintarroja *f*; ***r. salt*** sal *f* gema; ***r. sparrow*** gorrión *m* chillón; ***r. wool*** lana *f* mineral

(**c**) **the R. (of Gibraltar)** el Peñón (de Gibraltar)

(**d**) *Fam (diamond)* pedrusco *m*, diamante *m*

(**e**) *Br (sweet)* = caramelo de menta en forma de barra que se vende sobre todo en localidades costeras y lleva dentro el nombre del lugar impreso

(**f**) *(rocking motion)* **to give sth a r.** mecer algo

(**g**) *(music)* rock *m* ►► ***r. concert*** concierto *m* de rock; ***r. group*** grupo *m* de rock; ***r. music*** música *f* rock; ***r. opera*** ópera *f* rock; ***r. and roll*** rock and roll *m*; ***r. singer*** cantante *mf* de rock; ***r. star*** estrella *f* de(l) rock

(**h**) *Fam (cocaine)* farlopa *f*; *(crack)* crack *m*

(**i**) *very Fam* **rocks** *(testicles)* huevos *mpl*; IDIOM **to get one's rocks off** *(have sex)* mojar; *(have orgasm)* correrse, irse; *(enjoy oneself)* disfrutar como un(a) cerdo(a); **to get one's rocks off doing sth** disfrutar como un(a) cerdo(a) haciendo algo

2 *vt* (**a**) *(swing to and fro) (boat, chair)* mecer, balancear; **to r. a baby to sleep** mecer *or* acunar a un niño hasta dormirlo, dormir a un niño meciéndolo; IDIOM **to r. the boat** *(create problems)* complicar el asunto (**b**) *(shake) (building)* sacudir; **the country was rocked by these revelations** estas revelaciones conmocionaron al país

3 *vi* (**a**) *(sway)* mecerse, balancearse; *(building)* estremecerse; **to r. (backwards and forwards) in one's chair** mecerse en la silla; **to r. with laughter** reírse a carcajadas; **he rocked on his heels when he heard the news** cuando escuchó la noticia se le aflojaron las piernas

(**b**) *(play music)* tocar rock; *(dance)* bailar rock; *Fam* **the party was really rocking** la fiesta estaba supermovida

rockabilly ['rɒkəbɪlɪ] *n* rockabilly *m*

rock-bottom ['rɒkbɒtəm] *adj (price)* mínimo(a)

rocker ['rɒkə(r)] *n* (**a**) *(of cradle, chair)* arco *m*; IDIOM *Fam* **she's off her r.** le falta un tornillo; IDIOM *Fam* **to go off one's r.** *(go mad)* volverse loco(a) *or Esp* majara; *(lose one's temper)* ponerse hecho(a) una furia (**b**) *(chair)* mecedora *f* (**c**) *Elec* ***r. switch*** conmutador *m* basculante (**d**) *(musician, fan)* roquero(a) *m,f*

rockery ['rɒkərɪ] *n (in garden)* jardín *m* de rocalla

rocket[1] ['rɒkɪt] **1** *n* (**a**) *(weapon, vehicle)* cohete *m*; **to fire** *or* **launch a r.** disparar *or* lanzar un cohete ►► ***r. engine*** motor *m* (de) cohete; ***r. fuel*** combustible *m* para cohetes; *Fam (wine)* vinazo *m*, vino *m* peleón; ***r. launcher*** lanzacohetes *m inv*; ***r. motor*** motor *m* de cohete *or* de reacción; ***r. range*** campo *m* de tiro para cohetes

(**b**) *(signal, firework)* cohete *m*

(**c**) IDIOMS *Br Fam* **to give sb a r.** *(reprimand)* echar una bronca *or Esp* un broncazo a alguien; *Br Fam* **to get a r.** llevarse una bronca *or Esp* un broncazo; **it isn't r. science** no se trata de descubrir América; **she's no r. scientist** no es una lumbrera

2 *vi (prices)* dispararse, subir como la espuma; **to r. to fame** hacerse famoso(a) de la noche a la mañana; **the group rocketed up the charts** el grupo saltó de la noche a la mañana a los primeros puestos de las listas de éxitos; **the bike rocketed down the road** la moto iba como un rayo *or* cohete por la carretera

3 *vt* (**a**) *(missile)* lanzar; *(astronaut)* enviar al espacio; **the spacecraft was rocketed to the moon** la nave fue lanzada a la luna (**b**) *(record, singer)* lanzar (a la fama); **the record rocketed the group into the top ten** el disco aupó a la banda a un puesto entre los diez primeros de las listas de éxitos

rocket[2] *n (salad plant)* oruga *f*, roqueta *f*

rocketing ['rɒkɪtɪŋ] *adj (prices, costs)* disparados(as), que suben como la espuma; *(inflation)* galopante

rocketry ['rɒkɪtrɪ] *n (science)* cohetería *f*

rockfall ['rɒkfɔːl] *n* desprendimiento *m* (de piedras)

rockfish ['rɒkfɪʃ] *n* lija *f*, pintarroja *f*

rock-hard ['rɒk'hɑːd] *adj* duro(a) como una piedra

rock-hopper ['rɒkhɒpə(r)] *n* **r. (penguin)** pingüino *m* de penacho amarillo

Rockies ['rɒkɪz] *npl* **the R.** las Rocosas

rockily ['rɒkɪlɪ] *adv* de manera inestable *or* poco firme

rocking ['rɒkɪŋ] *adj (motion)* de balanceo, de vaivén ►► ***r. chair*** mecedora *f*; ***r. horse*** caballo *m* de balancín

rockrose ['rɒkrəʊz] *n* jara *f*, jaguarzo *m*

rockslide ['rɒkslaɪd] *n* desprendimiento *m* (de rocas)

rock-solid ['rɒk'sɒlɪd] *adj (support)* firme, inquebrantable; **a r. majority** una amplia *or* sólida mayoría

rock-steady ['rɒk'stedɪ] *adj (hand)* firme

rocky ['rɒkɪ] *adj* (**a**) *(path, soil)* pedregoso(a) ►► ***R. Mountain goat*** rebeco *m* blanco, cabra *f* de las nieves *or* de las Montañas Rocosas; ***the R. Mountains*** las Montañas Rocosas

(**b**) *(unstable) (marriage, relationship, economy)* inestable; **to go through a r. patch** pasar una mala racha, atravesar un bache; **things got off to a r. start** las cosas tuvieron un comienzo incierto, no se comenzó con buen pie

rococo [rə'kəʊkəʊ] **1** *n* rococó *m*

2 *adj* rococó

rod [rɒd] **1** *n* (**a**) *(wooden)* vara *f*; *(metal)* barra *f*; IDIOM **to rule with a r. of iron** gobernar con mano de hierro; IDIOM **to make a r. for one's own back** cavarse la propia tumba

(**b**) *(of uranium)* barra *f*

(**c**) *(symbol of office)* bastón *m* de mando; *(of king, emperor)* cetro *m*

(**d**) *(for fishing)* caña *f* (de pescar)

(**e**) *(for surveying)* vara *f* (de medir), jalón *m*

(**f**) *(in engine)* barra *f* de transmisión

(**g**) *Anat (in retina)* bastoncillo *m*

(**h**) *(linear measure)* = antigua medida de longitud equivalente a 5,029 metros

(**i**) *US Fam (gun)* pipa *f*, *Am* fierro *m*

(**j**) *Fam (car)* coche *m* trucado

(**k**) *very Fam (penis)* verga *f*, *Esp* picha *f*, *Chile* pico *m*, *Méx* pájaro *m*, *RP* pija *f*

2 *vt (drain)* desatascar con una varilla

rode *pt of* **ride**

rodent ['rəʊdənt] *n* roedor *m*

rodeo ['rəʊdɪəʊ] *n* rodeo *m*

rodomontade [rɒdəmɒn'tɑːd] *n Literary* fanfarronada *f*

roe[1] [rəʊ] *n* **r. (deer)** corzo *m*

roe[2] *n (of fish)* huevas *fpl*

roebuck ['rəʊbʌk] *n* corzo *m* (macho)

rogation [rəʊ'geɪʃən] *n Rel* rogativa *f* ►► ***R. Days*** rogativas *fpl* de la Ascensión

roger[1] ['rɒdʒə(r)] *exclam (in radio message)* ¡recibido!

roger[2] *vt Br very Fam* tirarse a, *Am* cogerse a, *Méx* chingarse a

rogue [rəʊg] **1** *n* (**a**) *(dishonest)* granuja *mf*, bribón(ona) *m,f*; *Fam* **a rogues' gallery** *(police photographs of known criminals)* un archivo de delincuentes fichados (**b**) *(mischievous)* truhán(ana) *m,f*, pícaro(a) *m,f*

2 *adj* (**a**) *(animal)* solitario(a), apartado(a) de la manada ►► ***r. elephant*** elefante *m* solitario (**b**) *(deviant)* que va a su aire ►► ***r. gene*** gen *m* defectuoso *or* aberrante; ***r. state*** estado *m* delincuente; ***r. trader*** *(on stockmarket)* agente *m* de bolsa sin escrúpulos; *(builder, plumber)* pirata *mf*, chapucero(a) *m,f*

roguery ['rəʊgərɪ] *n* granujadas *fpl*

roguish ['rəʊgɪʃ] *adj (smile, look)* pícaro(a), picarón(ona)

roguishly ['rəʊgɪʃlɪ] *adv (to smile, wink)* con picardía

ROI (*abbr* **Republic of Ireland**) República *f* de Irlanda

roil [rɔɪl] *US* **1** *vt* (**a**) *(annoy)* irritar, enojar (**b**) *(liquid)* enturbiar, agitar

2 *vi (water)* agitarse

roisterer ['rɔɪstərə(r)] *n* jaranero(a) *m,f*

roisterous ['rɔɪstərəs] *adj* bullicioso(a), jaranero(a)

ROK (*abbr* **Republic of Korea**) República *f* de Corea

role [rəʊl] *n* (**a**) *Cin, Theat* papel *m*; **a starring r.** un papel estelar *or* principal; **a supporting r.** un papel secundario *or* de reparto (**b**) *(function)* papel *m*; **to play an important r.** desempeñar un papel importante; **to have a r. in life** tener un papel *or* una misión en la vida ▸▸ ***r. model*** ejemplo *m*, modelo *m* a seguir; ***r. reversal*** cambio *m* de papeles

role-play ['rəʊlpleɪ] **1** *n (in training, therapy)* dramatización *f* improvisada, juego *m* de roles; *(in language classes)* role-play *m*

2 *vt (situation)* representar de manera imaginaria; *(interview)* hacer un simulacro de

role-playing ['rəʊlpleɪɪŋ] *n (in training, therapy)* dramatización *f* improvisada, juego *m* de roles ▸▸ ***r. game*** juego *m* de rol

rolf [rɒlf] *vi US Fam* hacer rolfing, hacer masajes del método Rolf

roll [rəʊl] **1** *n* (**a**) *(of paper, cloth, film)* rollo *m*; *(of carpet, wallpaper)* rollo *m*; *(of fat, flesh) Esp* michelín *m*, *Méx* llanta *f*, *RP* rollo *m*; *(of banknotes)* fajo *m*; **it's sold by the r.** se vende por rollos; **a r. of tools** un manojo de herramientas

(**b**) *(bread)* panecillo *m*, *Méx* bolillo *m*; **ham/cheese r.** *Esp* bocadillo *or Am* sándwich de jamón/queso

(**c**) *(noise) (of drum)* redoble *m*; *(of thunder)* retumbo *m*

(**d**) *(movement) (of ship, plane)* balanceo *m*; **a r. of the dice** una tirada de dados

(**e**) *(list)* lista *f*; **to be on the r.** *(of club)* ser socio(a); *Br Sch* estar matriculado(a); **to call the r.** pasar lista ▸▸ *Mil* ***r. of honour*** = lista de los caídos en la guerra

(**f**) *US Fam (ecstasy pill)* éxtasis *m inv*, *Esp* equis *m inv*, *Esp* X *m inv*

(**g**) IDIOMS *Fam* **to be on a r.** llevar una buena racha; *Fam* **to have a r. in the hay** echar un polvo *or* casquete, *RP* fifar

2 *vt* (**a**) *(ball)* hacer rodar; *(dice)* tirar, lanzar; **to r. sth along the ground** hacer rodar algo por el suelo; **the dog rolled itself in the mud** el perro se revolcó en el barro

(**b**) *(flatten) (road, lawn)* apisonar; *(metal)* laminar; *(pastry, dough)* extender, estirar

(**c**) *(form into a ball, cylinder) (cigarette)* liar; **to r. yarn into a ball** hacer un ovillo de hilo; **the animal rolled itself into a ball** el animal se hizo un ovillo *or* una bola; **she rolled the clay into a long snake** hizo una larga serpiente con la arcilla; **to r. sth in** *or* **between one's fingers** enrollar algo con los dedos; **he rolled his sleeves above his elbows** se remangó la camisa por encima de *or Am* arriba de los codos; *Br* **he rolls his own** se hace los suyos; *Fig* **a brother, friend and teacher, (all) rolled into one** un hermano, amigo y profesor, todo en uno

(**d**) *(pronounce strongly)* **to r. one's r's** marcar las erres al hablar

(**e**) *(move in circular motion)* **to r. one's eyes** *(in mock despair, in fright)* poner los ojos en blanco; **to r. one's hips/shoulders** menear las caderas/los hombros de manera sensual

(**f**) *(start working) (movie camera, printing press)* poner en marcha *or* en funcionamiento; **r. the cameras!** ¡se rueda!

3 *vi* (**a**) *(move) (ball)* rodar; **to r. in the mud** *(animal, person)* revolcarse en el fango *or* barro; **the ball rolled down the stairs** la pelota cayó rodando por las escaleras, la pelota rodó escaleras abajo; **the boulders rolled down the mountainside** las grandes rocas caían (rodando) por la ladera; **the bus rolled into the yard** el autobús entró en el patio; **the taxi rolled to a halt** el taxi se detuvo suavemente; **tears rolled down his face** le caían lágrimas por las mejillas; **sweat rolled off her back** el sudor le caía *or* le corría por la espalda

(**b**) *(drums)* redoblar; *(thunder)* retumbar; **the organ music rolled through the corridors** la música de órgano retumbaba en los pasillos

(**c**) *(ship, plane)* balancearse

(**d**) *(start working) (movie camera)* comenzar a rodar; *(printing press)* entrar en funcionamiento; **the credits started to r.** *(in movie)* comenzaron a aparecer los créditos (en la pantalla)

(**e**) *US Fam* **to be rolling** ir colocado(a) *or* llevar un colocón de éxtasis, estar dado vuelta

(**f**) IDIOMS **to get** *or* **start things rolling** empezar la cosa; **OK, we're ready to r.!** bueno, estamos listos; **he had them rolling in the aisles** se morían de risa con él; **heads will r.** van a rodar cabezas; *Fam* **to be rolling in money** *or* **in it** nadar en la abundancia, *Esp* estar montado(a) en el dólar; **let the good times r.!** ¡por los buenos tiempos!

▸**roll about, roll around** *vi* revolcarse; IDIOM **she had them rolling about** se morían de risa con ella

▸**roll along** *vi* (**a**) *(river)* pasar, correr; *(car)* avanzar (**b**) *(project)* avanzar, progresar

▸**roll around** = **roll about**

▸**roll away** **1** *vt sep (stone)* hacer rodar; *(map, carpet)* enrollar y guardar

2 *vi (car, clouds)* alejarse, perderse; **the hills rolled away into the distance** las colinas se perdían en la distancia; **all my troubles seemed to r. away** fue como si todos mis problemas se disiparan

▸**roll back** **1** *vt sep* (**a**) *(carpet)* enrollar; *(blankets)* doblar; **to r. back the enemy** hacer retroceder al enemigo; **to r. back the frontiers of the state** reducir el papel (intervencionista) del estado; **to r. back the years** retrotraerse en el tiempo (**b**) *US (prices)* reducir

2 *vi (waves)* retroceder; *(memories)* resurgir, regresar

▸**roll by** *vi (car, time)* pasar

▸**roll down** *vt sep (blind, sleeves, car window)* bajar

▸**roll in** *vi* (**a**) *(waves)* avanzar (**b**) *(arrive)* aparecer, llegar; **they finally rolled in at 3 a.m.** al final aparecieron a las 3 de la mañana (**c**) *Fam (pour in) (money)* llover; *(crowds)* venir en masa; **offers of help are rolling in** llueven los ofrecimientos de ayuda

▸**roll off** **1** *vi (fall)* caer(se) rodando

2 *vt insep* **to r. off the presses** salir de la imprenta

▸**roll on** **1** *vt sep* (**a**) *(paint)* pasar *or* aplicar con un rodillo; *(deodorant)* aplicar *(con la bola)* (**b**) *(stockings)* poner(se) *(enrollando)*

2 *vi (time, weeks)* pasar; IDIOM *Br Fam* **r. on Friday/Christmas!** ¡que llegue el viernes/la Navidad!

▸**roll out** **1** *vt sep* (**a**) *(flatten) (map, carpet)* desenrollar; *(pastry)* extender *or* estirar con el rodillo (**b**) *(produce) (goods)* producir, sacar (**c**) *(extend) (new scheme, production)* ampliar

2 *vi* **to r. out of bed** *(person)* salir de la cama, levantarse

▸**roll over** **1** *vt sep* (**a**) *(turn over)* dar la vuelta (**b**) *Fam (defeat)* barrer

2 *vi (several times)* dar vueltas; *(once) (person)* darse la vuelta; *(car)* dar una vuelta (de campana)

▸**roll past** **1** *vt insep (of car, procession)* pasar por

2 *vi (car, time)* pasar

▸**roll up** **1** *vt sep (map, carpet)* enrollar; *(trousers)* remangar, arremangar; *(blind, car window)* subir; **to r. sth up in paper** envolver algo con papel; **to r. up one's sleeves** remangarse *or* arremangarse la camisa; *Fig* poner toda la carne en el asador

2 *vi* (**a**) *(map, carpet, paper)* enrollarse; **it's rolling up at the edges** se está abarquillando *or* doblando por los bordes; **to r. up into a ball** hacerse un ovillo *or* una bola (**b**) *Fam (arrive)* llegar; *Old-fashioned* **r. up!, r. up!** ¡vengan todos!, ¡pasen y vean!

rollback ['rəʊlbæk] *n US (of prices)* reducción *f*

roll-bar ['rəʊlbɑː(r)] *n* barra *f* antivuelco

roll-call ['rəʊlkɔːl] *n* acto *m* de pasar lista; **to take (a** *or* **the) r.** pasar lista

rolled [rəʊld] *adj* **r. gold** metal laminado en oro; **r. oats** copos de avena

rolled-up ['rəʊldʌp] *adj (sleeves, trousers)* remangado(a), arremangado(a); *(umbrella)* cerrado(a); *(newspaper)* enrollado(a)

Roller ['rəʊlə(r)] *n Br Fam* Rolls (Royce)® *m inv*

roller ['rəʊlə(r)] *n* (**a**) *(for paint, garden, in machine)* rodillo *m* ▸▸ ***r. blind*** persiana *f* (de tela) enrollable; ***r. hockey*** hockey *m* sobre patines; ***r. skates*** patines *mpl* (de ruedas); ***r. towel*** toalla *f* de rodillo

(**b**) *(for hair)* rulo *m*, *Chile* tubo *m*, *RP* rulero *m*; **to put rollers in (one's hair), to put one's hair in rollers** ponerse (los) rulos *or Chile* tubos *or RP* ruleros

(**c**) *(wave)* ola *f* grande

(**d**) *(bird)* carraca *f*

roller-bearing ['rəʊlə'beərɪŋ] *n* cojinete *m* de rodillos

rollerblades ['rəʊləbleɪdz] *npl* patines *mpl* en línea

rollerblading ['rəʊləbleɪdɪŋ] *n* patinaje *m (con patines en línea)*; **to go r.** ir a patinar *(con patines en línea)*

rollercoaster ['rəʊləkəʊstə(r)] *n* montaña *f* rusa; *Fig* **it's been a r. (of a) year for the economy** ha sido un año lleno de altibajos en la economía

roller-skate ['rəʊləskeɪt] *vi* patinar (sobre ruedas)

roller-skater ['rəʊləskeɪtə(r)] *n* patinador(ora) *m,f (sobre ruedas)*

roller-skating ['rəʊləskeɪtɪŋ] *n* patinaje *m* (sobre ruedas); **to go r.** ir a patinar (sobre ruedas)

rollicking ['rɒlɪkɪŋ] *Fam* **1** *n Br* **to give sb a r.** echar una reprimenda *or Esp* una bronca a alguien, dar *Méx* una jalada *or RP* un rezongo a alguien

2 *adv* **a r. good read** un libro divertidísimo; **to get r. drunk** agarrarse un buen pedo *or* una buena cogorza

rolling ['rəʊlɪŋ] **1** *adj* (**a**) *(undulating) (hills, fields)* ondulado(a); *(sea, waves)* ondulante; **to have a r. gait** tambalearse al andar; *Culin* **bring to a r. boil** hacer que rompa el hervor, hacer que hierva a borbotones

(**b**) *(moving)* que rueda; IDIOM **to be a r. stone** ser un ave de paso, tener alma de viajero(a); PROV **a r. stone gathers no moss** piedra movediza nunca moho cobija ▸▸ *Rail* ***r. stock*** material *m* móvil *or* rodante

(**c**) *(for flattening)* ***r. mill*** *(for steel) (machine)* laminador *m*, laminadora *f*; *(factory)* planta *f* de laminación; ***r. pin*** rodillo *m* (de cocina)
(**d**) *(thunder)* retumbante
(**e**) *Br* ***r. tobacco*** tabaco *m* de liar
(**f**) *(progressive)* gradual, progresivo(a); **a r. plan for development** un plan de desarrollo escalonado; **r. strikes** una sucesión creciente de paros
2 *n (of boat)* balanceo *m*
3 *adv Br Fam* **to be r. drunk** no tenerse en pie de la borrachera, estar borracho(a) como una cuba

rollmop ['rəʊlmɒp] *n* **r. (herring)** filete *m* de arenque en escabeche

rollneck ['rəʊlnek] *adj (sweater)* de cuello vuelto, de cuello de cisne

roll-on ['rəʊlɒn] **1** *n* (**a**) *(deodorant)* desodorante *m* de bola (**b**) *(corset)* faja *f*
2 *adj* **r. (deodorant)** desodorante *m* de bola

roll-on roll-off ferry [rəʊl'ɒnrəʊl'ɒf'ferɪ] *n* transbordador *m or* ferry *m* de carga horizontal *or* rodada, ro-ro *m*

roll-over ['rəʊləʊvə(r)] *n (in UK national lottery)* bote *m* acumulado; **r. week** = semana en la que hay bote acumulado

Rolls [rəʊlz] *n Br Fam* Rolls (Royce)® *m inv*

roll-top desk ['rəʊltɒp'desk] *n* buró *m*

roll-up ['rəʊlʌp] *n Br Fam (cigarette)* pitillo *m* (liado a mano)

roly-poly ['rəʊlɪ'pəʊlɪ] *adj Fam (plump)* rechoncho(a) ►► ***r. pudding*** = dulce compuesto de mermelada y masa pastelera enrolladas

ROM [rɒm] *n Comptr* (*abbr* **read only memory**) (memoria *f*) ROM *f*

romaine [rəʊ'meɪn] *n US* **r. (lettuce)** lechuga *f* romana

Roman ['rəʊmən] **1** *n* romano(a) *m,f*
2 *adj* romano(a) ►► ***R. alphabet*** alfabeto *m* latino; ***R. candle*** = tipo de fuego artificial; *Rel* ***R. Catholic*** católico(a) *m,f* (romano(a)); ***R. Catholic Church*** Iglesia *f* católica (romana); ***R. Catholicism*** catolicismo *m*; ***R. Empire*** Imperio *m* Romano; ***R. law*** derecho *m* romano; ***R. nose*** nariz *f* aguileña; ***R. numerals*** números *mpl* romanos, numeración *f* romana; ***R. road*** calzada *f* romana

roman ['rəʊmən] *n Typ* (letra *f*) redonda *f or* redondilla *f*

romance [rə'mæns, 'rəʊmæns] **1** *n* (**a**) *(love)* romanticismo *m*, amor *m* romántico; **r. is in the air** hay una atmósfera romántica, se respira romanticismo
(**b**) *(love affair)* romance *m*, aventura *f* (amorosa); **to have a r. with sb** tener un romance con alguien; **a summer r.** un amor de verano
(**c**) *(charm)* encanto *m*; **the r. soon wore off** el encanto pronto se disipó
(**d**) *(book)* novela *f* rosa *or* romántica; *(movie)* película *f* romántica *or* de amor
(**e**) *Lit* romance *m*, libro *m* de caballerías
(**f**) *Ling* ***R. languages*** lenguas *fpl* romance *or* románicas
2 *vt (person)* galantear, seducir
3 *vi* soñar, fantasear

Romanesque [rəʊmə'nesk] **1** *n* románico *m*
2 *adj* románico(a)

Romania [rə'meɪnɪə] *n* Rumanía

Romanian [rə'meɪnɪən] **1** *n* (**a**) *(person)* rumano(a) *m,f* (**b**) *(language)* rumano *m*
2 *adj* rumano(a)

Romansch [rə'mænʃ] **1** *n* romanche *m*
2 *adj* del romanche, retorrománico(a)

romantic [rə'mæntɪk] **1** *n* romántico(a) *m,f*; **he's an incurable r.** es un romántico incorregible
2 *adj* (**a**) *(amorous, sentimental)* romántico(a); **to be/feel r.** ser/estar romántico (**b**) *(unrealistic)* idealizado(a), romántico(a); **she had some r. notion about helping the poor** tenía una idea un tanto romántica acerca de ayudar a los pobres (**c**) *Lit & Mus* **R. poetry/music** poesía/música romántica

romantically [rə'mæntɪklɪ] *adv* de manera romántica; **to be r. involved with sb** tener un romance con alguien

romanticism [rə'mæntɪsɪzəm] *n* (**a**) *(of person, scene)* romanticismo *m* (**b**) **R.** *(in art, literature, music)* romanticismo *m*

romanticize [rə'mæntɪsaɪz] **1** *vt (idea, incident)* idealizar; **to r. war** rodear la guerra de un halo romántico
2 *vi* idealizar (las cosas)

Romany ['rəʊmənɪ] **1** *n* (**a**) *(person)* romaní *mf*, gitano(a) *m,f* (**b**) *(language)* romaní *m*; *(in Spain)* caló *m*
2 *adj* romaní, gitano(a)

Rome [rəʊm] *n* (**a**) *(city)* Roma; PROV **all roads lead to R.** todos los caminos conducen a Roma; PROV **R. wasn't built in a day** Zamora no se ganó en una hora; PROV **when in R., (do as the Romans do)** (allá) donde fueres haz lo que vieres (**b**) *Rel* **(the Church of) R.** (la iglesia de) Roma, la Iglesia católica romana; **to go over to R.** venderse a Roma, convertirse al catolicismo

Romeo ['rəʊmɪəʊ] *n* (**a**) *(in Shakespeare)* Romeo; **R. and Juliet** Romeo y Julieta (**b**) *(lover)* donjuán *m*, casanova *m*

romp [rɒmp] **1** *n* **to have a r.** *(frolic)* juguetear; *(have sex)* darse un revolcón; **the play is an enjoyable r.** la obra es un divertimiento agradable
2 *vi* **to r. (about** *or* **around)** juguetear; **to r. through an examination** sacar un examen con toda facilidad; **to r. home** *(in election, race)* vencer con un amplio margen *or* una amplia ventaja

romper ['rɒmpə(r)] *n* **r. suit, rompers** pelele *m*

rondo ['rɒndəʊ] *n Mus* rondó *m*

roo [ru:] *n Austr Fam* canguro *m* ►► ***r. bars*** = barras protectoras de metal para casos de choque con animales

rood [ru:d] *n* (**a**) *(cross)* crucifijo *m*, cruz *f* ►► ***r. screen*** trascoro *m* *(entre el coro y la nave central)* (**b**) *Br (square measure)* cuarto *m* de acre *(= 0,10 hectáreas)*

roof [ru:f] **1** *n* (**a**) *(of building)* tejado *m*; *(of tunnel, cave)* techo *m*; **to have a r. over one's head** tener un techo *or* sitio donde dormir; **I won't have this behaviour under my r.** no toleraré semejante comportamiento en mi casa; **to live under one** *or* **the same r.** vivir bajo el mismo techo; *Fig* **the r. of the world** el techo del mundo; IDIOM *Fam* **to go through the r.** *(inflation, prices)* ponerse por las nubes; IDIOM **to go through** *or* **hit the r.** *(person)* subirse por las paredes ►► ***r. garden*** azotea *f* con jardín, azotea *f* ajardinada
(**b**) *(of car)* techo *m* ►► *Aut* ***r. rack*** baca *f*
(**c**) **the r. of the mouth** el paladar, el cielo de la boca
2 *vt* techar, cubrir; **roofed with corrugated iron** con techo de chapa ondulada

► **roof in, roof over** *vt sep* techar, poner (un) techo a

roofer ['ru:fə(r)] *n* techador *m*

roofing ['ru:fɪŋ] *n* (**a**) *(material)* ***r. felt*** fieltro *m* impermeable para techos; ***r. material*** *(for making roofs)* techumbre *f*; *(for covering roofs)* revestimiento *m* de tejados (**b**) *(activity)* **a r. firm** una empresa constructora (y reparadora) de tejados

rooftop ['ru:ftɒp] *n (in general)* tejado *m*; *(flat roof)* azotea *f*; **a chase over the rooftops** una persecución por los tejados/las azoteas; IDIOM **to shout** *or* **proclaim sth from the rooftops** proclamar algo a los cuatro vientos

rooinek ['rɔɪnek] *n SAfr Fam Pej* = término utilizado por afrikáners para referirse a los británicos o a los sudafricanos de origen inglés

rook [rʊk] **1** *n* (**a**) *(bird)* grajo(a) *m,f* (**b**) *(in chess)* torre *f*
2 *vt Fam (swindle)* timar

rookery ['rʊkərɪ] *n* (**a**) *(of rooks)* colonia *f* de grajos (**b**) *(of seals, penguins)* colonia *f*

rookie ['rʊkɪ] *n US Fam* novato(a) *m,f*; **a r. cop** un poli novato, *Arg* un pichón de rati

ROOM [ru:m] *n* (**a**) *(in house)* habitación *f*, cuarto *m*; *(in hotel)* habitación *f*; *(bedroom)* dormitorio *m*, *Am* cuarto *m*, *CAm, Col, Méx* recámara *f*; *(large, public)* sala *f*; **double/single r.** habitación doble/individual; **the r. went silent** se hizo el silencio en la habitación; **r. to let** *or* **rent** *(sign)* se alquila habitación ►► ***r. and board*** pensión *f* completa; *US* ***r. clerk*** recepcionista *mf* (de hotel); ***r. divider*** tabique *m*; ***r. number*** número *m* de habitación; ***r. service*** servicio *m* de habitaciones; ***r. temperature*** temperatura *f* ambiente
(**b**) *(space)* espacio *m*, sitio *m*, *Am* lugar *m*, *Andes* campo *m*; **there's no r.** no hay sitio *or Am* lugar *or Andes* campo; **there's plenty of r.** hay sitio de sobra; **it takes up too much r.** ocupa demasiado sitio *or* lugar; **is there r. for one more?** ¿cabe uno más?; **will there be enough r. for all of us?** *(in vehicle, house)* ¿cabremos todos?, ¿habrá sitio para todos?; **to make r. (for sb)** hacer sitio *or Am* lugar *or Andes* campo (para *or* a alguien); **we must leave him r. to develop his own interests** debemos dejarlo que persiga libremente sus intereses, tenemos que dejarle espacio para que se dedique a lo que le interesa; **we have no r. for people like him in our organization** en esta organización no cabe gente como él; **there's no r. for doubt** no hay lugar a dudas; **there is r. for improvement** se puede mejorar; **we have no r. for manoeuvre** no tenemos margen de maniobra; IDIOM *Fam* **there isn't enough r. to swing a cat in here** aquí no cabe ni un alfiler

► **room together** *vi US* compartir habitación *or* cuarto

► **room with** *vt insep US* compartir alojamiento con

-roomed [ru:md] *suffix* **two/three/four-r.** de dos/tres/cuatro habitaciones

roomer ['ru:mə(r)] *n US* huésped *mf*, huéspeda *f*

roomette [ruː'met] *n US* compartimento *m or* departamento *m* de coche cama

roomful ['ruːmfʊl] *n* **a r. of furniture** una habitación llena de muebles; **a r. of people** una sala llena *or* repleta de gente

roomie ['ruːmɪ] *n US Fam* compañero(a) *m,f* de cuarto *or* habitación

roominess ['ruːmɪnɪs] *n (of house, office, car)* espaciosidad *f*, amplitud *f*; *(of suitcase, bag, clothes)* amplitud *f*

rooming house ['ruːmɪŋhaʊs] *n US* casa *f* de huéspedes, pensión *f*

roommate ['ruːmmeɪt] *n* compañero(a) *m,f* de cuarto *or* habitación

roomy ['ruːmɪ] *adj (house, office, car)* espacioso(a), amplio(a); *(suitcase, bag, clothes)* amplio(a)

roost [ruːst] **1** *n* percha *f*, palo *m*

2 *vi* estar posado(a) *(para dormir)*; IDIOM **his actions have come home to r.** ahora está sufriendo las consecuencias de sus actos

rooster ['ruːstə(r)] *n esp US* gallo *m*

root [ruːt] **1** *n* **(a)** *(of plant)* raíz *f*; **to pull sth up by the roots** arrancar algo de raíz; **to take r.** *(plant, idea)* arraigar; *also Fig* **to put down roots** echar raíces; IDIOM **they destroyed the party r. and branch** destrozaron el partido por completo ►► *US* ***r. beer*** = bebida gaseosa sin alcohol elaborada con extractos de plantas; ***r. crops*** tubérculos *mpl* (comestibles); ***r. vegetables*** tubérculos *mpl*

(b) *(of tooth, hair, nail)* raíz *f*; **to touch up one's roots** *(person with dyed hair)* retocarse las raíces ►► ***r. canal surgery*** endodoncia *f*; ***r. canal work*** endodoncia *f*

(c) *(of word)* raíz *f*

(d) *(origin)* raíz *f*; **the conflict has its roots in the past** el conflicto hunde sus raíces en el pasado; **he has no real roots** no tiene raíces, es un desarraigado; **she is searching for her roots** está buscando sus raíces; **to get back to one's roots** volver a las raíces; **the r. cause of sth** la verdadera causa de algo; **the r. of all evil** el origen de todo mal; **to get at** *or* **to the r. of sth** llegar a la raíz de algo ►► ***roots music*** música *f* con raíces

(e) *Math* raíz *f*

(f) *Comptr* ***r. directory*** directorio *m* raíz

2 *vt* **it is rooted in...** tiene sus raíces en...; **to be rooted to the spot** quedarse de una pieza

3 *vi* **to r. about** *or* **around (for sth)** *(search)* rebuscar (algo); **I found her rooting through my desk** la pesqué hurgando en mi escritorio

► **root for** *vt insep (support)* apoyar; **we'll all be rooting for you** vamos a estar todos apoyándote *or* alentándote

► **root out** *vt sep (racism, crime)* cortar de raíz

► **root up** *vt sep* arrancar de raíz

rooted ['ruːtɪd] *adj (belief, habits)* enraizado(a), arraigado(a); **deeply r. superstitions** supersticiones profundamente enraizadas *or* arraigadas

rootless ['ruːtlɪs] *adj* desarraigado(a)

rootsy ['ruːtsɪ] *adj Fam* folkie, folk

rope [rəʊp] **1** *n* **(a)** *(thick, for hanging)* soga *f*; *(thinner)* cuerda *f*; *Naut* cabo *m*, maroma *f*; **to bring back the r.** reinstaurar la pena de muerte ►► ***r. ladder*** escalera *f* de cuerda; ***r. maker*** cordelero(a) *m,f*, soguero(a) *m,f*

(b) *(of pearls)* sarta *f*; *(of onions)* ristra *f*

(c) IDIOMS **to be on the ropes** estar contra las cuerdas; **to have sb on the ropes** tener a alguien contra las cuerdas; **to know the ropes** saber de qué va el asunto; **to learn the ropes** ponerse al tanto *(con un trabajo)*; **to show sb the ropes** poner a alguien al tanto; **to give sb plenty of r.** dar gran libertad de movimientos a alguien; **give them enough r. and they'll hang themselves** déjalos hacer, ya verás cómo se cavan su propia tumba

2 *vt* **(a)** *(fasten)* atar **(to** a); **they roped themselves together** *(for climbing)* se encordaron **(b)** *US (cattle, horses)* atrapar con el lazo, *CSur* lacear

> **False friend**: The Spanish noun **ropa** is not a translation for the English word **rope**. In Spanish **ropa** means "clothes".

► **rope in** *vt sep Fam* **to r. sb in (to doing sth)** liar *or* enganchar a alguien (para hacer algo); **he got himself roped in to be chairman** lo engancharon para que fuera presidente

► **rope off** *vt sep* acordonar

► **rope up** *vi (climbers)* encordarse, hacer una cordada

rop(e)y ['rəʊpɪ] *adj Fam* **(a)** *(unreliable)* flojo(a) **(b)** *(ill)* pachucho(a), *Am* flojo(a); **to feel a bit r.** no sentirse muy allá

Roquefort ['rɒkəfɔː(r)] *n* (queso *m*) roquefort *m*

ro-ro ferry ['rəʊrəʊ'ferɪ] *n* transbordador *m*, ferry *m* (con trasbordo horizontal)

rorqual ['rɔːkwəl] *n* rorcual *m*

Rorschach test ['rɔːʃæk'test] *n* prueba *f or* test *m* de Rorschach

rosary ['rəʊzərɪ] *n Rel* rosario *m*; **to say the** *or* **one's r.** rezar el rosario

rose [rəʊz] **1** *n* **(a)** *(flower)* rosa *f*; **r. (bush)** rosal *m* ►► ***r. bed*** macizo *m* de rosas; ***r. garden*** rosaleda *f*, jardín *m* de rosas, *Méx, CSur* rosedal *m*; ***r. grower*** cultivador(ora) *m,f* de rosas; ***r. quartz*** cuarzo *m* rosa *or* rosado; *Archit* ***r. window*** rosetón *m*

(b) *(on watering can, shower)* alcachofa *f*

(c) *(on ceiling)* rosetón *m* (de techo)

(d) IDIOMS **life is not a bed of roses, life is not all roses** la vida no es un lecho *or* camino de rosas; **to come up roses** salir a pedir de boca; **he always comes up smelling of roses** de todo sale bien parado; **that holiday put the roses back in his cheeks** esas vacaciones le han devuelto el buen color

2 *adj (colour)* rosa

3 *pt of* **rise**

rosé ['rəʊzeɪ] *n (wine)* rosado *m*

roseate ['rəʊzɪət] *adj Literary* rosáceo(a)

rosebud ['rəʊzbʌd] *n* capullo *m* de rosa; **r. lips** labios bien definidos

rose-coloured ['rəʊzkʌləd], **rose-tinted** ['rəʊztɪntɪd] *adj* rosado(a), color de rosa; IDIOM **to see things through r. glasses** *or* **spectacles** ver las cosas de color de rosa

rosehip ['rəʊzhɪp] *n* escaramujo *m*

rosemary ['rəʊzmərɪ] *n* romero *m*

rose-tinted = **rose-coloured**

rosette [rəʊ'zet] *n* **(a)** *(badge of party, team)* escarapela *f* **(b)** *Archit (carving)* rosetón *m*

rose-water ['rəʊzwɔːtə(r)] *n* agua *f* de rosas

rosewood ['rəʊzwʊd] *n* palo *m* de rosa

Rosh Hashana(h) ['rɒʃhə'ʃɑːnə] *n* = el Año Nuevo judío

Rosicrucian ['rəʊzɪ'kruːʃən] **1** *n* rosacruz *mf*

2 *adj* rosacruz, de la (orden de la) Rosacruz

rosin ['rɒzɪn] **1** *n* colofonia *f*, colofonía *f*

2 *vt* frotar con colofonia

RoSPA ['rɒspə] *n* (*abbr* **Royal Society for the Prevention of Accidents**) = organización británica para la prevención de accidentes

roster ['rɒstə(r)] **1** *n (list)* lista *f*; *(of duties)* lista *f* de turnos

2 *vt* apuntar en la lista de turnos, asignar turno a; **he's rostered to do the washing up** le toca a él lavar los platos

rostrum ['rɒstrəm] *n* estrado *m*, tribuna *f*; **to take the r.** subir al estrado *or* a la tribuna ►► *Cin & TV* ***r. camera*** cámara *f* truca, truca *f* de animación

> **False friend**: The Spanish noun **rostro** is not a translation for the English word **rostrum**. In Spanish **rostro** means "face".

rosy ['rəʊzɪ] *adj* **(a)** *(pink)* rosa, rosado(a); *(cheeks, complexion)* sonrosado(a) **(b)** *(future)* (de) color de rosa; IDIOM **to paint a r. picture of sth** pintar algo (de) color de rosa

rot [rɒt] **1** *n* **(a)** *(in house, wood)* podredumbre *f*; *(in fruit, vegetable)* parte *f* podrida, putrefacción *f*

(b) *(in society)* degradación *f*, degeneración *f*; IDIOM **the r. has set in** el mal ha empezado a arraigar; IDIOM **to stop the r.** impedir que la situación siga degenerando

(c) *Br Fam (nonsense)* sandeces *fpl*, *Am* pendejadas *fpl*; **don't talk r.!** ¡no digas sandeces *or Am* pendejadas!; **what r.!** ¡menuda sandez *or Am* pendejada!

2 *vt* (*pt & pp* **rotted**) pudrir; **sugar rots your teeth** el azúcar produce caries; *Fam* **too much TV rots your brain** ver mucha tele te acaba atontando

3 *vi (fruit, vegetable, wood)* pudrirse; *(body)* descomponerse; **to r. in prison** pudrirse en la cárcel; *Fam* **let them r.!** ¡que se pudran!

► **rot away** **1** *vt sep* corroer, destruir

2 *vi (fabric)* deshacerse; *(wood, rubber, leaves)* pudrirse; *(flesh)* descomponerse

► **rot down** *vi (compost material)* descomponerse

rota ['rəʊtə] *n Br* horario *m* con los turnos; **we have a r. for the housework** nos turnamos para hacer las tareas de la casa

Rotarian [rəʊ'teərɪən] **1** *n* rotario(a) *m,f*

2 *adj* rotario(a)

rotary ['rəʊtərɪ] **1** *n US (roundabout)* rotonda *f*

2 *adj (movement)* rotatorio(a), giratorio(a) ►► ***R. Club*** Club *m* de Rotarios, Rotary Club *m*; ***r. engine*** motor *m* rotativo; ***r. pump*** bomba *f* rotativa

rotate [rəʊ'teɪt] **1** *vt* (**a**) *(turn)* hacer girar (**b**) *(alternate) (duties, crops)* alternar
2 *vi* (**a**) *(turn)* girar (**b**) *(in job)* turnarse, rotar; **the presidency rotates every two years among the members** los miembros se turnan para ocupar la presidencia cada dos años

rotating [rəʊ'teɪtɪŋ] *adj* (**a**) *(turning)* giratorio(a) (**b**) *(alternating)* **on a r. basis** en forma rotativa *or* rotatoria

rotation [rəʊ'teɪʃən] *n* (**a**) *(circular movement)* rotación *f*; **rotations per minute** rotaciones por minuto (**b**) *(alternation) (of duties, crops)* rotación *f*; *(in job)* rotación *f*, alternancia *f*; **by** *or* **in r.** por turno (rotatorio) (**c**) *(in volleyball)* rotación *f*

rotational [rə'teɪʃənəl] *adj (axis)* de rotación; *(inertia)* rotacional

Rotavator® ['rəʊtəveɪtə(r)] *n Br* motocultor *m*

ROTC [ɑːrəʊtiː'siː] *n US* (*abbr* **Reserve Officers' Training Corps**) = unidad de formación de futuros oficiales compuesta por estudiantes universitarios becados por el ejército

rote [rəʊt] *n* **to learn sth by r.** aprender algo de memoria *or* de corrido ▸▸ ***r. learning*** aprendizaje *m* memorístico

rotgut ['rɒtgʌt] *n Fam (drink)* matarratas *m inv*

rotisserie [rəʊ'tɪsərɪ] *n (spit)* asador *m*

rotogravure [rəʊtəgrə'vjʊə(r)] *n* huecograbado *m*

rotor ['rəʊtə(r)] *n* rotor *m*

Rotovator® ['rəʊtəveɪtə(r)], *US* **Rototiller**® ['rəʊtətɪlə(r)] *n* motocultor *m*

rotproof ['rɒtpruːf] *adj* imputrescible, incorrompible

rotten ['rɒtən] *adj* (**a**) *(wood, egg, fruit)* podrido(a); *(tooth)* picado(a), cariado(a); **to be r.** estar podrido(a); **to go r.** pudrirse; **to smell r.** oler a podrido; IDIOM **he's a r. apple** *or* **the r. apple in the barrel** es una manzana podrida
(**b**) *(corrupt)* degenerado(a), corrompido(a); **to be r. through and through** *or* **to the core** estar totalmente corrompido(a)
(**c**) *Fam (bad, of poor quality)* malísimo(a), pésimo(a); **I always get the r. jobs!** ¡siempre me tocan los peores trabajos!; **he's a r. cook** cocina *Esp* fatal *or Esp* de pena *or Am* pésimo; **we had a r. time** lo pasamos *Esp* fatal *or Esp* de pena *or Am* pésimo; **what r. luck!** ¡qué mala pata!
(**d**) *Fam (unkind)* **that was a r. thing to do/say!** ¡eso fue una canallada!; **to be r. to sb** comportarse como un canalla con alguien; **a r. trick** una canallada, *Andes, RP* una guachada
(**e**) *Fam* **I feel r.** *(ill)* me siento *Esp* fatal *or Am* pésimo; **you look r.** *Esp* se te ve fatal, *Am* te ves muy mal *or* pésimo; **I feel r. about what happened** *(sorry)* siento en el alma lo que pasó, me sabe muy mal lo que pasó
(**f**) *(in indignation)* maldito(a); **keep your r. (old) sweets!** ¡no me interesan tus malditos dulces!

rottenly ['rɒtənlɪ] *adv Fam Esp* fatal, *Esp* de pena, *Am* pésimo

rotter ['rɒtə(r)] *n Br Fam Old-fashioned* truhán(ana) *m,f*, bribón(ona) *m,f*

rotting ['rɒtɪŋ] *adj* podrido(a), que se está pudriendo

Rottweiler ['rɒtwaɪlə(r)] *n* (**a**) *(dog)* rotweiller *m* (**b**) *Fig Hum (fierce person)* bestia *f* parda, dóberman *m*

rotund [rəʊ'tʌnd] *adj* (**a**) *(shape)* redondeado(a) (**b**) *(person) (plump)* orondo(a), rollizo(a)

rotunda [rə'tʌndə] *n Archit* rotonda *f*

rotundity [rəʊ'tʌndɪtɪ] *n (of person)* gordura *f*

rouble, *US* **ruble** ['ruːbəl] *n (Russian currency)* rublo *m*

roué ['ruːeɪ] *n* crápula *m*, calavera *m*

rouge [ruːʒ] **1** *n* colorete *m*
2 *vt* ponerse colorete en

ROUGH [rʌf] **1** *n* (**a**) *(in golf)* rough *m*
(**b**) *Fam Old-fashioned (hooligan)* matón *m*
(**c**) *(difficulty)* IDIOM **to take the r. with the smooth** estar a las duras y a las maduras, *Am* estar para las buenas y las malas
(**d**) *Fam* **a bit of r.** *(person)* un macho, un hombre de pelo en pecho; *(sexual activity)* un poco de sexo fuerte
2 *adj* (**a**) *(surface, skin, cloth)* áspero(a); *(terrain)* accidentado(a); IDIOM *Br Old-fashioned* **to give sb the r. side of one's tongue** echar una buena reprimenda a alguien
(**b**) *(unrefined) (manners, speech)* tosco(a); **a r. shelter** un refugio improvisado; IDIOM **she is a r. diamond** *or US* **a diamond in the r.** vale mucho, aunque no tenga muchos modales ▸▸ *Fam* ***r. trade*** *(violent)* = joven prostituto homosexual de tendencias violentas; *(working-class)* homosexual *m* proletario
(**c**) *(violent, not gentle) (person)* bruto(a); *(game)* duro(a); *(weather)* borrascoso(a); *Fig* **the bill had a r. passage through the House** el proyecto de ley ha pasado por dificultades en el parlamento; **to receive r. treatment** ser maltratado(a); **it's a r. area** es una zona peligrosa; **a r. crossing** *or* **passage** una travesía muy movida; **they were r. with** *or* **on the new recruits** tuvieron mano dura con los nuevos reclutas; **r. sea(s)** mar brava, mar embravecido
(**d**) *(harsh) (voice)* ronco(a); *(wine)* peleón(ona), cabezón(ona); *(alcoholic spirits)* de garrafa; **the engine sounds r.** el motor hace un ruido ronco
(**e**) *(difficult, tough)* **it was r. on her** fue muy duro para ella; **I'm going through a r. patch** estoy pasando un bache malo, *RP* estoy pasando por una mala racha; **to give sb a r. time** *or* **ride** *(treat harshly)* hacerle pasar un mal rato a alguien, *Esp* hacérselas pasar canutas a alguien; *(criticize)* poner como un trapo a alguien, *RP* bajarle el hacha a alguien; **we've had a r. time of it recently** lo hemos pasado muy mal últimamente; **to have a r. life** tener una vida dura; **we got a r. deal** recibimos un trato injusto ▸▸ ***r. justice*** justicia *f* sumaria; ***r. luck*** mala suerte *f*
(**f**) *(approximate) (calculation, estimate)* aproximado(a); **r. draft** borrador; **at a r. guess** a ojo (de buen cubero); **these indicators serve as a r. guide to the state of the economy** estos indicadores nos dan una idea aproximada de la situación económica; **I've got a r. idea of what he wants** tengo una vaga idea de *or* sé más o menos lo que quiere; **r. sketch** bosquejo ▸▸ ***r. paper*** papel *m* (de) borrador
(**g**) *Fam (ill)* **to feel r.** sentirse mal; **to look r.** tener mal aspecto
3 *adv* **to play r.** jugar duro; *Fam* **to sleep r.** dormir a la intemperie *or Esp* al raso
4 *vt Fam* **we had to r. it** nos las arreglamos *or Esp* apañamos como pudimos
5 **in rough** *adv (in preliminary form)* en borrador

▸**rough in** *vt sep* bosquejar, esbozar

▸**rough out** *vt sep (drawing)* bosquejar, esbozar; *(ideas, plan)* esbozar

▸**rough up** *vt sep Fam* **to r. sb up** dar a alguien una paliza

roughage ['rʌfɪdʒ] *n* fibra *f*

rough-and-ready ['rʌfən'redɪ] *adj* (**a**) *(makeshift) (structure, apparatus)* rudimentario(a); *(work)* improvisado(a); *(methods)* rudimentario(a) (**b**) *(person)* basto(a), tosco(a)

rough-and-tumble ['rʌfən'tʌmbəl] *n* riña *f*, rifirrafe *m*; **the r. of politics** la brega de la política

roughcast ['rʌfkɑːst] **1** *n* argamasa *f* basta, mortero *m* grueso
2 *vt* enlucir con argamasa basta *or* mortero grueso

roughen ['rʌfən] **1** *vt (surface)* raspar; *(hands)* poner áspero(a)
2 *vi* (**a**) *(surface)* ponerse áspero(a) (**b**) *(sea)* picarse, embravecerse

rough-hewn ['rʌf'hjuːn] *adj (stone)* labrado(a) toscamente; *(facial features)* tosco(a)

roughhouse ['rʌfhaʊs] *Fam* **1** *n* bronca *f*, trifulca *f*
2 *vt US* tratar a lo bruto *(generalmente en broma)*
3 *vi US* armar jaleo, *RP* hacer quilombo

roughly ['rʌflɪ] *adv* (**a**) *(violently)* brutalmente; **to treat sb r.** tratar a alguien con brutalidad
(**b**) *(harshly)* bruscamente, con aspereza; **he answered her very r.** le contestó muy bruscamente *or* con mucha aspereza
(**c**) *(crudely)* toscamente, groseramente; **to sketch sth r.** bosquejar *or* esbozar algo de una manera muy esquemática; **the dress is r. stitched** las costuras del vestido son muy toscas *or* groseras
(**d**) *(approximately)* aproximadamente, más o menos; **they live in r. the same area** viven aproximadamente *or* más o menos en la misma zona; **it was r. five o'clock** eran más o menos las cinco; **she told me r. how to get there** me dijo más o menos cómo llegar; **r. speaking** aproximadamente

roughneck ['rʌfnek] *n Fam* (**a**) *(tough)* matón *m*, duro *m* (**b**) *(oil worker)* = trabajador en una explotación petrolífera

roughness ['rʌfnɪs] *n* (**a**) *(of surface, skin)* aspereza *f*; *(of terrain)* irregularidad *f*, carácter *m* accidentado (**b**) *(of manner)* tosquedad *f*; *(of speech)* brusquedad *f* (**c**) *(violent behaviour)* agresividad *f*, brutalidad *f* (**d**) *(of sea)* agitación *f*

roughrider ['rʌfraɪdə(r)] *n US (horse breaker)* domador(ora) *m,f* de caballos

roughshod ['rʌfʃɒd] *adv* IDIOM **to ride r. over sth** pisotear algo

rough-spoken ['rʌf'spəʊkən] *adj* malhablado(a)

rough-stuff ['rʌfstʌf] *n Fam* comportamiento *m* violento

roulade [rʊ'lɑːd] *n Culin* rollo *m or RP* arrollado *m* de carne

roulette [ruː'let] *n (game)* ruleta *f*; **to play r.** jugar a la ruleta ▸▸ ***r. table*** mesa *f* de ruleta; ***r. wheel*** ruleta *f*

Roumania = **Romania**

Roumanian = **Romanian**

ROUND [raʊnd] 1 *n* (**a**) *(stage of tournament)* vuelta *f*, ronda *f* (eliminatoria); *(in boxing)* asalto *m*, round *m*; *(of golf)* recorrido *m* (del campo); **the first r. of the elections** la primera vuelta de las elecciones; **to have a r. of 65** *(in golf)* hacer un recorrido en 65 golpes; **shall we play a r. of golf?** ¿jugamos un partido de golf?

(**b**) *Br (of bread)* **a r. of sandwiches** un sándwich *(cortado en dos o en cuatro)*; **a r. of toast** una tostada

(**c**) *(of talks, visits)* ronda *f*; *(of drinks)* ronda *f*, *Am* vuelta *f*; *(in cards)* mano *f*; **it's my r.** me toca pagar esta ronda *or Am* vuelta; **her life is one long r. of parties** su vida es una sucesión de fiestas; **a r. of applause** una ovación, *Am* una salva de palmas; **a r. of applause for our special guest!** ¡un aplauso para nuestro invitado especial!

(**d**) *(of doctor)* **to do one's rounds** *(visit patients at home)* hacer las visitas (a los pacientes); *(in hospital)* hacer la ronda de visitas en sala; **to do a paper/milk r.** repartir el periódico/la leche; **to do one's r.** *(milkman, paper boy)* hacer el reparto; **I did the rounds of the local museums** hice un recorrido *or Am* una recorrida por los museos locales; **one of the rumours doing the rounds** uno de los rumores que corren; **the daily r.** *(of tasks)* las tareas cotidianas

(**e**) *(circular shape)* rodaja *f*

(**f**) *Mil (bullet)* bala *f*

(**g**) *Mus* canon *m*

(**h**) *Theat* **theatre in the r.** teatro circular

2 *adj* (**a**) *(in shape)* redondo(a); *(cheeks)* redondeado(a); **their eyes were r. with excitement** tenían los ojos como platos; **to have r. shoulders** tener las espaldas cargadas, ser ancho(a) de espalda ►► ***r. arch*** arco *m* de medio punto; ***r. robin*** *(letter)* escrito (colectivo) *m* de protesta; *(competition)* liguilla *f*, torneo *m (de todos contra todos)*; *Hist* ***the R. Table*** la Mesa Redonda; ***r. table (conference)*** mesa *f* redonda; *US* ***r. trip*** viaje *m* de ida y vuelta

(**b**) *(number)* redondo(a); **a r. dozen** una docena justa; **in r. figures** en números redondos

3 *adv* (**a**) *(surrounding)* alrededor; **there were trees all r.** había árboles por todos lados; **all (the) year r.** durante todo el año; **all r., it was a good result** en conjunto, fue un buen resultado

(**b**) *(indicating position, order)* **to change** *or* **move the furniture r.** cambiar los muebles de sitio *or* lugar; **to be the wrong/right way r.** *(sweater)* estar del *or Am* al revés/del *or Am* al derecho; **to do sth the right/wrong way r.** hacer algo bien/al revés; **the other way r.** al revés

(**c**) *(indicating circular motion)* **to go r. (and r.)** dar vueltas; **to look r.** mirar alrededor; **to turn r.** darse la vuelta, *Am* darse vuelta; **turn the steering wheel all** *or* **right the way r.** gira el volante a tope; **it was easier the second time r.** fue más fácil la segunda vez

(**d**) *(to other side)* **we went r. to the back** fuimos a la parte de atrás

(**e**) *(by indirect route)* **we had to take the long way r.** tuvimos que ir dando un rodeo

(**f**) *(to all parts)* **to look r.** mirar por todas partes *or* todos lados; **to travel/walk r.** viajar/caminar por ahí

(**g**) *(to several people)* **to pass sth r.** pasar algo

(**h**) *(to sb's house)* **come r. some time** pásate por casa un día de éstos; **to go r. to sb's house** ir a casa de alguien; **to invite sb r.** invitar a alguien a casa

(**i**) *(in circumference)* **it's 5 metres r.** tiene 5 metros de circunferencia

(**j**) *(approximately)* **r. about** alrededor de, aproximadamente; **r. (about) midday** a eso del mediodía; **it cost somewhere r. £30** costó algo así como 30 libras, *RP* costó alrededor de 30 libras

4 *prep* (**a**) *(surrounding)* alrededor de; **r. the table** en torno a la mesa, alrededor de la mesa; **the countryside r. the city is lovely** las zonas de campo que rodean la ciudad son preciosas; **they tied the rope r. me** me ataron con la cuerda; **he put a blanket r. her legs** le cubrió las piernas con una manta; **he put his arm r. her shoulders/waist** le rodeó los hombros/la cintura con el brazo; **she wears a scarf r. her neck** lleva una bufanda al cuello; **I measure 65 cm r. the waist** mido 65 cm de cintura; **there are trees all r. the lake** el lago está rodeado de árboles

(**b**) *(indicating position)* **the garden is r. the back** el jardín está (en la parte de) atrás; **it's just r. the corner** está a la vuelta de la esquina, *RP* queda a la vuelta; **r. here** por aquí

(**c**) *(indicating circular motion)* alrededor de; **to go r. an obstacle** rodear un obstáculo; **the Earth goes r. the Sun** la Tierra gira alrededor del Sol; **to go r. the corner** doblar la esquina; **to sail r. the world** circunnavegar el mundo; **we drove r. and r. the lake** dimos varias vueltas al lago; **I can't find a way r. the problem** no encuentro una solución al problema

(**d**) *(to all parts of)* **to look/walk r. the room** mirar/caminar por toda la habitación; **to travel r. the world/Europe** viajar por todo el mundo/por Europa

(**e**) *Br Fam (to)* **come r. our house some time** pásate por nuestra casa un rato de éstos, *RP* pasá por casa en algún momento; **to go r. sb's house/the pub** ir a casa de alguien/al pub

5 *vt* (**a**) *(make round)* redondear

(**b**) *(move round) (obstacle)* rodear; *(corner)* doblar

► **round down** *vt sep (figures)* redondear a la baja; **he rounded it down to $500** lo dejó en 500 dólares

► **round off** 1 *vt sep* (**a**) *(corners, edges)* redondear (**b**) *(conclude)* rematar, concluir (**c**) *(number)* redondear

2 *vi (conclude)* rematar, concluir

► **round on** *vt insep* (**a**) *(attack)* atacar (**b**) *(criticize)* revolverse contra

► **round out** *vt sep (make complete)* completar

► **round up** *vt sep* (**a**) *(cattle)* recoger; *(children)* reunir; *(criminals, suspects)* detener (**b**) *(figures)* redondear al alza; **I'll r. it up to $500** lo dejamos en 500 dólares

---

roundabout ['raʊndəbaʊt] 1 *Br n* (**a**) *(at fairground)* tiovivo *m*, carrusel *m*, *RP* calesita *f* (**b**) *(for cars)* rotonda *f*, *Esp* glorieta *f*

2 *adj (approach, route)* indirecto(a); **to hear of sth in a r. way** enterarse de algo indirectamente; **to lead up to a question in a r. way** preguntar algo después de un largo preámbulo

rounded ['raʊndɪd] *adj* (**a**) *(in shape)* redondeado(a) (**b**) *(balanced) (personality)* formado(a); *(education)* completo(a) (**c**) *Ling (vowel)* labializado(a)

roundelay ['raʊndɪleɪ] *n (song)* rondel *m*, tonada *f* simple

rounders ['raʊndəz] *n Br* = juego similar al béisbol

round-eyed ['raʊndaɪd] *adj (surprised)* atónito(a), con los ojos muy abiertos *or* como platos

Roundhead ['raʊndhed] *n Hist* cabeza *mf* redonda, = seguidor de Oliver Cromwell en la guerra civil inglesa del siglo XVII

roundhouse ['raʊndhaʊs] *n* (**a**) *Rail* depósito-taller *m* de locomotoras (con rotonda giratoria) (**b**) *Naut* chupeta *f* (**c**) *Fam (punch)* gancho *m*

roundly ['raʊndlɪ] *adv (to praise)* de forma entusiasta; *(to condemn)* rotundamente, con rotundidad; **they were r. beaten** recibieron una soberana paliza

roundness ['raʊndnɪs] *n (shape)* redondez *f*

round-shouldered ['raʊnd'ʃəʊldəd] *adj* cargado(a) de espaldas

round-table ['raʊndteɪbəl] *adj* **r. discussion** mesa redonda; **r. negotiations** mesa de negociaciones

round-the-clock ['raʊndðə'klɒk] 1 *adj* continuo(a), de 24 horas

2 *adv* (durante) las 24 horas del día

round-trip ['raʊnd'trɪp] *adj US (ticket)* de ida y vuelta

round-up ['raʊndʌp] *n* (**a**) *(of criminals)* redada *f* (**b**) *(on TV, radio)* resumen *m*

roundworm ['raʊndwɜːm] *n* lombriz *f* intestinal

rouse [raʊz] *vt* (**a**) *(person) (from sleep)* despertar; *(make more active)* incitar; **he was roused from his thoughts by the doorbell** el sonido del timbre lo devolvió a la realidad; **to r. oneself (to do sth)** animarse (a hacer algo); **to r. sb to action** empujar a alguien a la acción; **to r. sb to anger** encolerizar a alguien; **to r. sb from their apathy** despertar *or* sacar a alguien de su apatía; **now she's roused, sparks will fly** ahora que está alterada, pueden saltar chispas

(**b**) *(provoke) (interest, suspicion)* despertar, suscitar; *(hope)* alentar

rousing ['raʊzɪŋ] *adj (music, speech)* estimulante; *(welcome, send-off, cheers)* entusiasta

roust [raʊst] *vt* (**a**) *(rouse)* **to r. sb (out) from bed** arrancar *or* sacar a alguien de la cama (**b**) *(harass)* dar la lata a (**c**) *(arrest)* detener

roustabout ['raʊstəbaʊt] *n* (**a**) *(on oil rig)* obrero(a) *m,f or* operario(a) *m,f* (de plataforma petrolífera) (**b**) *Austr* peón *m (agropecuario)*

rout [raʊt] 1 *n (defeat)* derrota *f* aplastante; *(flight)* huída *f* despavorida

2 *vt (army) (defeat)* aplastar; *(put to flight)* hacer huir en desbandada; **they were routed 5-0** encajaron un aplastante 5 a 0

3 *vi (animal)* hozar, hocicar

► **rout about** *vi* buscar

► **rout out** *vt sep* (**a**) *(find)* encontrar, sacar (**b**) *(remove, force out)* forzar a salir; **they routed out their enemies** buscaron a sus enemigos hasta sacarlos de su escondite

route [ruːt, *US* raʊt] 1 *n* (**a**) *(of traveller)* ruta *f*, itinerario *m*; *(of plane, ship)* ruta *f*; *(of parade)* itinerario *m*; *(to failure, success)* camino *m*, vía *f* (**to** hacia); **all routes** *(road sign)* todas direcciones ►► ***r. map*** mapa *m* de las carreteras principales; ***r. march*** marcha *f* de entrenamiento

(**b**) *(for buses)* **bus r.** línea de autobús; **are they near a bus r.?** ¿les queda cerca algún autobús?

(**c**) *US (main road)* carretera *f* general *or* principal; **R. 66** la carretera *or* ruta 66

(**d**) *US (for deliveries)* recorrido *m or* itinerario *m* (de reparto); **he's got a paper r.** hace un reparto de periódicos

2 *vt* conducir, dirigir; **the train was routed through Birmingham** hicieron pasar el tren por Birmingham; **during the building work, the buses are routed along the sidestreets** durante las obras, los autobuses son desviados por calles adyacentes

router ['ru:tə(r)] *n Comptr* router *m*, direccionador *m*

routine [ru:'ti:n] 1 *n* (**a**) *(habit)* rutina *f*; **the daily r.** la rutina diaria; **it has become a regular r.** se ha convertido en una rutina, se ha hecho costumbre (**b**) *(of performer, comedian)* número *m*; IDIOM *Fam* **don't give me that r.** no me vengas con ese cuento (**c**) *Comptr* rutina *f*

2 *adj* (**a**) *(ordinary, unremarkable)* de rutina, rutinario(a); **it's just r.** es sólo rutina; **r. enquiries** investigación rutinaria (**b**) *(dull)* rutinario(a), monótono(a)

routinely [ru:'ti:nlɪ] *adv* habitualmente, por sistema

roux [ru:] (*pl* **roux** [ru:z]) *n Culin* roux *m*, = espesante de salsas a base de harina y mantequilla

rove [rəʊv] 1 *vt* vagar por, recorrer

2 *vi* vagar; **his eyes roved around the room** sus ojos recorrieron la habitación

rover ['rəʊvə(r)] *n (wanderer)* trotamundos *mf inv*

roving ['rəʊvɪŋ] *adj* **r. ambassador** embajador(ora) itinerante; **r. reporter** periodista ambulante; **he has a r. commission** su encargo no se limita a una zona determinada; IDIOM *Fam Pej* **to have a r. eye** ser un ligón/una ligona

row[1] [rəʊ] *n* (**a**) *(line) (of trees, houses, chairs)* hilera *f*, fila *f*; *(of cars)* fila *f*; *(of people) (next to one another)* hilera *f*; *(behind one another)* fila *f*; **in a r.** en hilera, en fila; **they sat/stood in a r.** estaban sentados/de pie en fila ►► *US* ***r. house*** casa *f* adosada

(**b**) *(of seats)* fila *f*; **in the front r.** en primera fila

(**c**) *(in rugby)* **the front/second/back r.** la primera/segunda/última línea

(**d**) *Br (in street names)* calle *f*; **56 Henderson R.** Henderson Row, (número) 56

(**e**) *(succession)* **two Sundays in a r.** dos domingos seguidos; **for the third time in a r.** por tercera vez consecutiva

(**f**) *(in knitting)* vuelta *f*

(**g**) *Comptr (in spreadsheet)* fila *f*

row[2] [rəʊ] 1 *n (in boat)* paseo *m* en barca; **to go for a r.** darse un paseo en barca

2 *vt* **to r. a boat** llevar una barca remando; **he rowed us across the river** nos llevó al otro lado del río en barca

3 *vi* remar; **to r. across a lake** cruzar un lago remando *or* a remo

row[3] [raʊ] 1 *n* (**a**) *(noise)* jaleo *m*, alboroto *m*; *(protest)* escándalo *m*; **to make a r.** *(be noisy)* armar mucho jaleo; *(protest)* armar un escándalo; **stop that r.!** ¡basta de alborotar! (**b**) *(quarrel)* bronca *f*, trifulca *f*; **to have a r. (with sb)** tener una bronca (con alguien)

2 *vi* discutir

rowan ['raʊən] *n (fruit)* serba *f*; **r. (tree)** serbal *m*

rowboat ['rəʊbəʊt] *n US* bote *m or* barca *f* de remos

rowdiness ['raʊdɪnɪs] *n* alboroto *m*, escándalo *m*

rowdy ['raʊdɪ] 1 *n* alborotador(ora) *m,f*

2 *adj (noisy)* ruidoso(a), escandaloso(a); *(disorderly)* alborotador(ora); **things got r. towards the end** al final hubo bronca

rower ['rəʊə(r)] *n* remero(a) *m,f*

rowing ['rəʊɪŋ] *n* remo *m*; **to go r.** ir a remar ►► *esp Br* ***r. boat*** bote *m or* barca *f* de remos; ***r. machine*** banco *m* de remo

rowlock ['rɒlək] *n* escálamo *m*, tolete *m*

royal ['rɔɪəl] 1 *n Fam* miembro *m* de la familia real; **the Royals** la Familia Real

2 *adj* (**a**) *(of the monarch)* real; **His/Her R. Highness** Su Alteza Real ►► ***the R. Academy*** la Real Academia de Bellas Artes británica; *Br Parl* ***r. assent*** = sanción real de una ley, tras ser aprobada ésta por el parlamento; ***r. blue*** azul *m* real *(intenso y más claro que el marino)*; ***r. charter:*** **by r. charter** mediante cédula real; ***r. commission*** = comisión de investigación nombrada por la corona a petición del parlamento; ***the R. Family*** la Familia Real, la Casa Real; ***r. flush*** *(in cards)* escalera *f* real; ***r. icing*** = glaseado duro y blanco de azúcar en polvo y clara de huevo; ***r. jelly*** jalea *f* real; ***the R. Mail*** el servicio de correos británico; ***the R. Mint*** ≃ la Casa de la Moneda, *Esp* ≃ la Fábrica Nacional de Moneda y Timbre; ***the R. Navy*** la armada británica; ***r. palm*** palma *f or* palmera *f* real, palmiche *m*; ***r. prerogative*** prerrogativa *f* real; ***the R. Society*** la Real Academia de Ciencias británica; ***r. standard*** = estandarte con el escudo de armas de la corona; ***r. tennis*** = versión primitiva del tenis que se juega en una pista con paredes; ***r. warrant*** = autorización oficial a un pequeño comerciante para suministrar productos a la casa real; ***the r. we*** el plural mayestático

(**b**) *(splendid)* soberbio(a), magnífico(a); **they gave us a (right) r. welcome** nos dispensaron un soberbio recibimiento; **to be in r. spirits** sentirse magníficamente *or* espléndidamente

royalism ['rɔɪəlɪzəm] *n* monarquismo *m*, adhesión *f* a la monarquía

royalist ['rɔɪəlɪst] 1 *n* monárquico(a) *m,f*

2 *adj* monárquico(a)

royally ['rɔɪəlɪ] *adv (to entertain, welcome)* con magnificencia

royalty ['rɔɪəltɪ] *n* (**a**) *(rank, class)* realeza *f*; **a hotel patronized by r.** un hotel frecuentado por la realeza; **we were treated like r.** nos trataron como a reyes; **is he r.?** ¿es de la realeza?

(**b**) **royalties** *(for author, singer)* derechos *mpl* de autor, royalties *mpl*, *Spec* regalías *fpl*; *(for patent)* derechos *mpl* de patente, royalties *mpl*, *Spec* regalías *fpl*; **he is paid a 10 percent r.** le pagan un 10 por ciento en concepto de derechos de autor

rozzer ['rɒzə(r)] *n Br Fam Esp* madero *m*, *Col* tombo *m*, *Méx* tamarindo *m*, *RP* cana *m*

RP [ɑ:'pi:] *n Ling* (*abbr* **received pronunciation**) pronunciación *f* estándar *(del inglés británico)*

RPI [ɑ:pi:'aɪ] *n Br Econ* (*abbr* **retail price index**) IPC *m*, Índice *m* de Precios al Consumo

RPM [ɑ:pi:'em] *n Econ* (*abbr* **resale price maintenance**) mantenimiento *m or* fijación *f* del precio de venta al público

rpm [ɑ:pi:'em] *n Aut* (*abbr* **revolutions per minute**) rpm

R & R ['ɑ:rən'ɑ:(r)] *n US Mil* (*abbr* **rest and recreation**) permiso *m*

RRP *Com* (*abbr* **recommended retail price**) P.V.P. *m* recomendado

RS [ɑ:'res] *n* (*abbr* **Royal Society**) = academia británica de las ciencias

RSA [ɑ:res'eɪ] *n* (**a**) (*abbr* **Republic of South Africa**) República *f* de Sudáfrica (**b**) (*abbr* **Royal Society of Arts**) = sociedad británica para el fomento de las artes y el comercio

RSC [ɑ:res'si:] *n* (*abbr* **Royal Shakespeare Company**) = prestigiosa compañía británica de teatro que se especializa en la representación de obras de Shakespeare

RSI [ɑ:res'aɪ] *n* (*abbr* **repetitive strain** *or* **stress injury**) lesión *f* por esfuerzo *or* movimiento repetitivo

RSM [ɑ:res'em] *n* (*abbr* **regimental sergeant major**) sargento *mf* primero de regimiento

RSPB [ɑ:respi:'bi:] *n Br* (*abbr* **Royal Society for the Protection of Birds**) = sociedad protectora de las aves, *Esp* ≃ SEO *f*

RSPCA [ɑ:respi:si:'eɪ] *n Br* (*abbr* **Royal Society for the Prevention of Cruelty to Animals**) ≃ Sociedad *f* Protectora de Animales

RSPCC [ɑ:respi:si:'si:] *n Br* (*abbr* **Royal Society for the Prevention of Cruelty to Children**) = sociedad protectora de la infancia

RSVP [ɑ:resvi:'pi:] (*abbr* **répondez s'il vous plaît**) *(on invitation)* se ruega contestación

RTE [ɑ:ti:'i:] *n* (*abbr* **Radio Telefis Eirann**) = radiotelevisión de la República de Irlanda

RTF [ɑ:ti:'ef] *n Comptr* (*abbr* **rich text format**) RTF

Rt Hon *Parl* (*abbr* **Right Honourable**) = en el Reino Unido, tratamiento formal aplicado a ministros y ex ministros del gobierno y a ciertos miembros de la aristocracia, ≃ su señoría

Rt Rev (*abbr* **Right Reverend**) Reverendísimo

RU (*abbr* **Rugby Union**) rugby *m* (a quince)

rub [rʌb] 1 *n* (**a**) **to give sth a r.** *(polish)* frotar algo; **give yourself a r. with the towel** sécate con la toalla; **can you give my back a r.?** *(massage)* ¿me puedes hacer un masaje en la espalda? (**b**) IDIOMS **there's the r.!** ¡ahí está el problema!; **to get the r. of the green** tener el santo de cara

2 *vt* (*pt & pp* **rubbed**) (**a**) *(hands, surface)* frotar; **these shoes r. my heels** estos zapatos me rozan los talones; **to r. one's hands together** frotarse las manos; **to r. one's eyes** restregarse los ojos; **r. your chest with this** frótate esto en el pecho; **she rubbed herself dry with a towel** se secó con una toalla; IDIOM **to r. shoulders with sb** codearse con alguien

(**b**) *(lotion, ointment)* frotar, poner *or* dar (frotando); **r. this ointment on your chest** ponte *or* date esta pomada en el pecho

3 *vi* (**a**) *(person, animal)* **to r. against sth/sb** restregarse contra algo/alguien, rozarse con algo/alguien (**b**) *(straps, shoes)* rozar (**against** contra)

► **rub along** *vi Fam* (**a**) *(manage)* arreglarse, defenderse, *Esp* apañarse (**b**) *(get on)* llevarse bien, congeniar (**with** con)

▸ **rub away** 1 *vt sep* quitar frotando; **the inscription has been rubbed away** se ha borrado la inscripción
2 *vi* quitarse *or* salir frotando

▸ **rub down** *vt sep* (**a**) *(horse)* almohazar; *(person)* secar frotando (**b**) *(with sandpaper) (wall, door)* lijar

▸ **rub in** *vt sep* (**a**) *(lotion, polish)* aplicar frotando; **r. the butter into the mixture** añada mantequilla a la mezcla, rebozándolo todo bien con las manos (**b**) IDIOMS *Fam* **there's no need to r. it in!** ¡no tienes por qué restregármelo por las narices!; *Fam* **to r. sb's nose in it** pasárselo *or* restregárselo a alguien por las narices

▸ **rub off** 1 *vt sep (dirt, stains)* limpiar, eliminar *(frotando)*; *(writing)* borrar
2 *vi* borrarse; **the newspaper ink rubbed off on the cushions** la tinta del periódico ha manchado los almohadones; *Fig* **to r. off on sb** *(manners, enthusiasm)* influir en *or* contagiarse a alguien

▸ **rub on** *vt sep* aplicar frotando

▸ **rub out** *vt sep* 1 (**a**) *(erase)* borrar (**b**) *US Fam (murder)* acabar con, liquidar, cepillarse a
2 *vi (mark, stain)* quitarse *or* salir frotando

▸ **rub up** 1 *vt sep (polish)* sacar brillo a, lustrar; IDIOM *Fam* **to r. sb up the wrong way** sacar de quicio a alguien
2 *vi (animal, person)* restregarse (**against** contra), rozarse (**against** con)

rubber[1] ['rʌbə(r)] *n* (**a**) *(substance) (finished product)* goma *f*, *Am* hule *m*; *(raw material)* caucho *m* ▸▸ ***r. ball*** pelota *f* de goma; ***r. band*** goma *f* (elástica); ***r. bullet*** bala *f* de goma; ***r. cement*** = adhesivo hecho con goma disuelta; *Fam* ***r. cheque*** cheque *m* sin fondos; *US Fam* ***the r. chicken circuit*** = campaña a base de recepciones locales para captar fondos o influir en la opinión pública; ***r. dinghy*** lancha *f* neumática; ***r. gloves*** guantes *mpl* de goma; *Old-fashioned Euph* ***r. goods*** gomas *fpl* higiénicas, condones *mpl*; ***r. plant*** ficus *m inv*; ***r. plantation*** plantación *f* de caucho; ***r. planter*** cauchero *m*; ***r. ring*** *(swimming aid)* flotador *m*; ***r. stamp*** tampón *m* (de goma), sello *m* (de caucho); ***r. tree*** (árbol *m* del) caucho *m*
(**b**) *Br (eraser)* goma *f* (de borrar); *(for blackboards)* borrador *m*
(**c**) *Fam (condom)* goma *f*, *Méx* impermeable *m*, *RP* forro *m*
(**d**) *US* **rubbers** *(boots)* botas *fpl* de goma

rubber[2] *n (in bridge, whist)* rubber *m*, = partida al mejor de tres o cinco juegos

rubberize ['rʌbəraɪz] *vt* engomar, impregnar con una capa de goma

rubberneck ['rʌbənek] *Fam* 1 *n* (**a**) *(at scene of accident)* curioso(a) *m,f*, mirón(ona) *m,f* (**b**) *(tourist)* turista *mf* que todo lo mira
2 *vi* (**a**) *(at scene of accident)* curiosear (**b**) *(tourist)* no parar de mirarlo todo

rubber-stamp ['rʌbə'stæmp] *vt* (**a**) *(document)* sellar (**b**) *Fig (approve)* dar el visto bueno a

rubbery ['rʌbərɪ] *adj (meat)* correoso(a); **it feels r.** parece de goma (al tacto)

rubbing ['rʌbɪŋ] *n* (**a**) *(image)* = dibujo o impresión que se obtiene al frotar con carbón, ceras, etc. un papel que cubre una superficie labrada (**b**) *US* ***r. alcohol*** alcohol *m* para friegas

rubbish ['rʌbɪʃ] 1 *n* (**a**) *(refuse)* basura *f*; IDIOM **to throw sth/sb on the r. heap** desahuciar algo/a alguien ▸▸ *Br* ***r. bin*** cubo *m or Am* bote *m* de (la) basura; ***r. collection*** recogida *f* de basuras; ***r. dump*** vertedero *m* (de basura); *Br* ***r. tip*** vertedero *m* (de basura)
(**b**) *(junk)* basura *f*; **shall I keep this stuff? – no, it's just r.** ¿guardo esto? – no, eso es para tirar; **it's amazing how much r. one accumulates over the years** es increíble la cantidad de porquerías que uno acumula con los años
(**c**) *Fam (nonsense)* tonterías *fpl*, bobadas *fpl*; **to talk r.** decir tonterías; **that book is a load of r.** ese libro es una porquería *or* una basura; **what r.!** ¡qué tontería!; **what a load of (old) r.!** ¡qué sarta de tonterías!
2 *adj Fam (worthless)* **that was a r. film/meal** fue una basura de película/cena
3 *vt Br Fam (book, plan)* poner por los suelos; **he always rubbishes my ideas** siempre tira por tierra lo que se me ocurre
4 *exclam Fam (expressing disagreement)* ¡qué tontería!, ¡tonterías!

rubbishy ['rʌbɪʃɪ] *adj Fam* de pésima calidad, *Esp* cutre

rubble ['rʌbəl] *n* (**a**) *(ruins)* escombros *mpl*; **the building was reduced to (a heap of) r.** el edificio quedó reducido a (un montón de) escombros (**b**) *(for roadmaking, building)* grava *f*, *Arg* cascote *m*

rubblework ['rʌbəlwɜːk] *n Archit* mampostería *f* concertada

rub-down ['rʌbdaʊn] *n (of person)* fricción *f*, friega *f*; *(of horse)* almohazado *m*, cepillado *m*

rube [ruːb] *n US Fam* palurdo(a) *m,f*, *Esp* paleto(a) *m,f*, *Col, Méx* indio(a) *m,f*, *RP* pajuerano(a) *m,f*

Rube Goldberg ['ruːb'gəʊldbɜːg] *adj US* complicadísimo(a); **a R. invention** un invento increíble *or Esp* del tebeo

rubella [ruː'belə] *n Med* rubeola *f*

rubeola [ruː'biːələ] *n Med* sarampión *m*

Rubicon ['ruːbɪkɒn] *n* IDIOM **to cross the R.** cruzar el Rubicón

rubicund ['ruːbɪkʌnd] *adj Literary* rubicundo(a)

rubidium [ruː'bɪdɪəm] *n Chem* rubidio *m*

ruble *US* = **rouble**

rubric ['ruːbrɪk] *n* (**a**) *(set of instructions)* directrices *fpl*, normas *fpl* (**b**) *Rel* rúbrica *f*

ruby ['ruːbɪ] 1 *n* rubí *m*; **a r. necklace** un collar de rubíes ▸▸ ***r. port*** oporto *m* ruby, = oporto joven de color rubí; ***r. wedding*** cuadragésimo aniversario *m* de boda *or Andes* matrimonio *or RP* casamiento
2 *adj (colour)* rojo(a) intenso(a) *or* rubí; **r. (red) lips** labios color rubí ▸▸ ***r. port*** oporto *m* rubí

RUC [ɑːjuː'siː] *n Formerly* (*abbr* **Royal Ulster Constabulary**) = la policía de Irlanda del Norte

ruched [ruːʃt] *adj* fruncido(a)

ruck[1] [rʌk] 1 *n* (**a**) *(in rugby)* melé *f* espontánea, ruck *m* (**b**) *(fight) Br Fam* **there was a bit of a r. after the match** hubo una trifulca después del partido (**c**) *(masses)* **the (common) r.** la gente corriente, el común de los mortales
2 *vi (in rugby)* formar una melé espontánea *or* un ruck

ruck[2] *n (in cloth)* arruga *f*

▸ **ruck up** *vi (sheet, dress)* arrugarse

rucksack ['rʌksæk] *n* mochila *f*, macuto *m*

ruckus ['rʌkəs] *n Fam* jaleo *m*, *Esp* follón *m*, *RP* quilombo *m*; **to make a r.** armar jaleo, *Esp* montar un follón, *RP* armar un quilombo; **to cause a r.** *(news)* armar la de San Quintín *or* la gorda

ructions ['rʌkʃənz] *npl Fam* bronca *f*, jaleo *m*; **there'll be r.** se va a armar la gorda

rudder ['rʌdə(r)] *n (on boat, plane)* timón *m*

rudderless ['rʌdəlɪs] *adj (boat, government)* sin timón

ruddiness ['rʌdɪnɪs] *n* rubicundez *f*

ruddy ['rʌdɪ] 1 *adj* (**a**) *(complexion)* rubicundo(a); *(sky)* rojizo(a), arrebolado(a) (**b**) *Br Old-fashioned Fam (damned)* condenado(a); **the r. fool!** ¡el/la muy estúpido(a)! (**c**) ***r. duck*** malvasía *f* canela
2 *adv Br Old-fashioned Fam (for emphasis)* condenadamente; **you look r. ridiculous** qué bochorno da verte, estás absolutamente ridículo

rude [ruːd] *adj* (**a**) *(impolite)* maleducado(a); **he was very r. about my new dress** hizo unos comentarios muy descorteses acerca de mi nuevo vestido; **to be r. to sb** faltar al respeto a alguien; **it's r. to pick your nose** meterse el dedo en la nariz es de mala educación
(**b**) *esp Br (indecent)* grosero(a), ordinario(a); **to make a r. gesture** hacer un gesto grosero *or* obsceno; **a r. joke** un chiste verde; **r. words** palabras malsonantes, groserías
(**c**) *(rudimentary)* tosco(a), rudimentario(a)
(**d**) *(unpleasant) (shock, surprise)* duro(a); **to receive a r. awakening** llevarse un palo *or* una desagradable sorpresa
(**e**) *(vigorous)* **to be in r. health** estar rebosante de salud

rudely ['ruːdlɪ] *adv* (**a**) *(impolitely)* maleducadamente
(**b**) *esp Br (indecently)* groseramente; **to gesture r.** hacer gestos groseros
(**c**) *(rudimentarily)* toscamente, rudimentariamente
(**d**) *(unpleasantly)* bruscamente, violentamente; **to be r. awakened** ser despertado(a) bruscamente; **they were r. awakened to the difficulties which such an operation entails** de pronto se estremecieron al darse cuenta de las dificultades que conlleva una operación de ese tipo

rudeness ['ruːdnɪs] *n* (**a**) *(impoliteness)* mala educación *f*; *(obscenity)* grosería *f* (**b**) *esp Br (indecency) (of joke, story)* ordinariez *f*, mal gusto *m* (**c**) *(rudimentary nature)* tosquedad *f*, carácter *m* rudimentario

rudimentary [ruːdɪ'mentərɪ] *adj* rudimentario(a); **to have a r. grasp of sth** tener unas nociones muy básicas de algo; **I speak r. Chinese** hablo un poquito de chino

rudiments ['ruːdɪmənts] *npl* rudimentos *mpl*, fundamentos *mpl*

rue[1] [ruː] *vt Formal* lamentar; **I lived to r. my words** me arrepentí toda la vida de lo que había dicho; **I r. the day I met him** en qué mala hora lo conocí

rue[2] *n (plant)* ruda *f*

rueful ['ruːfʊl] *adj* arrepentido(a) y apesadumbrado(a)

ruefully ['ru:fəlɪ] *adv* con arrepentimiento y pesar

ruefulness ['ru:fʊlnɪs] *n (of smile, tone)* pesar *m*, desconsuelo *m*

ruff[1] [rʌf] *n* (**a**) *(on costume)* golilla *f* (**b**) *(on bird, animal)* collar *m*, collarín *m* (**c**) *(bird)* combatiente *m*

ruff[2] **1** *n (in cards)* fallada *f*
2 *vt* matar, fallar a

ruffian ['rʌfiən] *n Old-fashioned* rufián *m*

ruffle ['rʌfəl] **1** *n* (**a**) *(frill)* volante *m*, *RP, Ven* volado *m* (**b**) *(ripple)* onda *f*, ondulación *f*
2 *vt (disturb) (water surface)* rizar; *(hair)* despeinar; **to r. sb's composure** hacer perder la calma a alguien; IDIOM **to r. sb's feathers** hacer *esp Esp* enfadar *or esp Am* enojar a alguien

ruffled ['rʌfəld] *adj* **the decision caused a few r. feathers** la decisión molestó a unos cuantos; **to smoothe sb's r. feathers** tranquilizar a alguien

rug [rʌg] *n* (**a**) *(carpet)* alfombra *f*; IDIOM **to pull the r. from under sb's feet** dejar a alguien en la estacada ►► *Fam* ***r. rat*** renacuajo(a) *m,f* (**b**) *(blanket)* manta *f* (**c**) *Fam (hairpiece)* peluquín *m*

rugby ['rʌgbɪ] *n* rugby *m* ►► ***r. ball*** pelota *f or* balón *m* de rugby; ***r. football*** *(game)* rugby *m*; ***r. league*** rugby *m* a trece; ***r. player*** jugador(ora) *m,f* de rugby; ***r. shirt*** camiseta *f* de rugby; ***r. tackle*** placaje *m*, *Am* tackle *m*; ***r. union*** rugby *m* (a quince)

rugby-tackle ['rʌgbɪ'tækəl] *vt* **to r. sb** hacer un placaje a alguien, atrapar a alguien por las piernas, *Am* tacklear alguien

rugged ['rʌgɪd] *adj* (**a**) *(ground, country)* irregular, accidentado(a); *(region, coastline)* abrupto(a), escarpado(a) (**b**) *(facial features)* recio(a); **his r. good looks** su atractivo aspecto de tipo duro *or* recio (**c**) *(manner)* rudo(a), tosco(a) (**d**) *(clothing, equipment, vehicle)* resistente

ruggedness ['rʌgɪdnɪs] *n* (**a**) *(of countryside, region)* irregularidad *f*; *(of coastline)* carácter *m* abrupto *or* escarpado; **the r. of the terrain** lo escarpado del terreno (**b**) *(of features, face)* reciedumbre *f*, dureza *f* (**c**) *(of manner)* rudeza *f*, tosquedad *f* (**d**) *(of clothing, equipment, vehicle)* resistencia *f*

ruggedly ['rʌgɪdlɪ] *adv* **r. handsome** de tosca belleza

rugger ['rʌgə(r)] *n Br Fam (rugby)* rugby *m*

ruin ['ru:ɪn] **1** *n* (**a**) *(remains)* ruina *f*; **the ruins of an old castle** las ruinas de un viejo castillo; **to fall into ruin(s)** quedar en ruinas; **to lie in ruins** *(building)* estar en ruinas; *(plans, career)* quedar arruinado(a)
(**b**) *(destruction)* ruina *f*; **it will be the r. of him** será su ruina; **to go to r.** *(economy, country)* ir a la ruina; *(person)* ir a la ruina
(**c**) *(bankruptcy)* ruina *f*, bancarrota *f*; **r. is staring us in the face** estamos a punto de perderlo todo
2 *vt* (**a**) *(spoil) (party, dress, surprise, plans)* arruinar, estropear; *(health, career, life)* arruinar, destruir; **to r. one's health/eyesight** arruinarse la salud/la vista; **to r. sb's chances of doing sth** echar por tierra las posibilidades de alguien de hacer algo; **the meal is ruined** se ha echado a perder la comida; **tourism has ruined the town** el turismo ha echado a perder la ciudad
(**b**) *(bankrupt)* arruinar, llevar a la bancarrota; **we're ruined** estamos arruinados; **they were ruined in the Wall Street Crash** se arruinaron con el crac de Wall Street

ruination [ru:ɪ'neɪʃən] *n* ruina *f*; **it will be the r. of us** será nuestra ruina

ruined ['ru:ɪnd] *adj (building, city)* en ruinas; *(career, reputation, health)* arruinado(a)

ruinous ['ru:ɪnəs] *adj (expense)* ruinoso(a); **in a r. condition** en un estado ruinoso

ruinously ['ru:ɪnəslɪ] *adv* **r. expensive** extraordinariamente caro

rule [ru:l] **1** *n* (**a**) *(regulation)* regla *f*, norma *f*; **the rules of chess/grammar** las reglas del ajedrez/gramaticales; **rules and regulations** normativa, reglamento; **it's against the rules** va contra las normas; **as a r. of thumb** por regla general; *Ind* **to work to r.** hacer huelga de celo ►► ***r. book*** reglamento *m*; IDIOM **to go by** *or* **stick to the r. book** seguir las normas establecidas; IDIOM **to throw away the r. book** romper con las normas, romper esquemas; *Math* ***r. of three*** regla *f* de tres
(**b**) *(principle)* regla *f*, norma *f*; **to make it a r. to do sth** tener por costumbre *or* norma hacer algo
(**c**) *(normal state of affairs)* norma *f*, costumbre *f*; **tipping is the r. here** aquí se acostumbra a dar propina; **the exception rather than the r.** la excepción y no la norma; **as a r.** normalmente, por regla general
(**d**) *(government)* gobierno *m*; **under British r.** bajo dominio *or* gobierno británico; **the r. of law** el imperio de la ley
(**e**) *(for measuring)* regla *f*
(**f**) *Typ (line)* renglón *m*, raya *f*
(**g**) *Rel (for monks)* regla *f*; **the R. of St Benedict** la Regla de San Benito
2 *vt* (**a**) *(govern) (country, people)* gobernar; *(emotions, instincts)* controlar; **if I ruled the world** si yo gobernara el mundo
(**b**) *(dominate) (of person, emotion)* dominar, ejercer control sobre; **don't let him r. your life** no dejes que gobierne *or* controle tu vida; **their lives are ruled by fear** el miedo domina sus vidas; IDIOM **to r. the roost** llevar la voz cantante, *Esp* cortar el bacalao
(**c**) *(decide, decree)* decretar, determinar; **the referee ruled the ball out** el árbitro dictaminó que el balón había salido del terreno de juego; **the court ruled that he should have custody of the children** el juzgado determinó que él debía recibir la custodia de los niños
(**d**) *(paper)* rayar; **ruled paper** papel rayado *or* pautado
3 *vi* (**a**) *(monarch)* reinar; **he ruled over a vast kingdom** fue el soberano de un inmenso reino; *Fam* **Chelsea r. (OK)!** ¡viva el Chelsea!
(**b**) *(prevail)* predominar, prevalecer; **chaos rules outside the capital** fuera de la capital reina el caos; **the philosophy currently ruling in the party** la filosofía que actualmente predomina en el partido
(**c**) *(judge)* decidir, fallar; **to r. on a dispute** emitir dictamen en una disputa; **to r. in favour of/against sb** fallar a favor de/en contra de alguien

> En inglés culto o elevado, y especialmente en inglés americano, **rule** puede ir seguido de **that** más un verbo en subjuntivo (ver el panel SUBJUNCTIVE):
> **the court ruled that the charges be dismissed**
> *el juzgado determinó que se retiraran los cargos*
> Lo mismo también podría decirse del siguiente modo:
> **the court ruled that the charges should be dismissed**

► **rule off** *vt sep* marcar con una regla

► **rule out** *vt sep (possibility, suggestion, suspect)* descartar, excluir; **she cannot be ruled out of the inquiry** no puede quedar excluida de la investigación, no se puede dejar de investigarla; **the injury rules him out for Saturday's game** la lesión lo deja fuera del partido del sábado

ruler ['ru:lə(r)] *n* (**a**) *(of country)* gobernante *mf* (**b**) *(for measuring)* regla *f*

ruling ['ru:lɪŋ] **1** *n (of judge, umpire)* fallo *m*, decisión *f*; **to give** *or* **hand down a r. in favour of/against sb** dar un fallo a favor/en contra de alguien, fallar a favor/en contra de alguien
2 *adj* (**a**) *(party)* gobernante, en el poder; **the sport's r. body** el organismo que dirige este deporte; **the r. classes** las clases dirigentes (**b**) *(passion, consideration)* predominante, primordial

rum[1] [rʌm] *n (drink)* ron *m* ►► *Br* ***r. baba*** (bizcocho *m*) borracho *m* de ron

rum[2] *adj Br Fam (strange)* raro(a); **I was feeling a bit r.** me sentía un poco raro *or* extraño; **it's a r. do** qué cosa más rara, qué raro

Rumania = **Romania**

Rumanian = **Romanian**

rumba ['rʌmbə] **1** *n* rumba *f*
2 *vi* bailar la rumba

rumble ['rʌmbəl] **1** *n* (**a**) *(noise) (of thunder, gunfire)* rugido *m*, retumbo *m*; *(of cart)* fragor *m*, estrépito *m*; *(of stomach)* gruñido *m*; **rumbles of discontent** murmullos de insatisfacción ►► ***r. strip*** banda *f* sonora *(en carretera)* (**b**) *US Fam (fight)* riña *f* callejera (**c**) *US* ***r. seat*** tra(n)sportín *m* trasero (exterior)
2 *vt Br Fam (see through)* descubrir (el juego a), pillar; **we've been rumbled** nos han pillado *or Esp* cogido *or Am* agarrado
3 *vi* (**a**) *(thunder, guns)* retumbar; *(stomach)* gruñir; **to r. past** pasar rugiendo (**b**) *US Fam (fight)* pelearse

► **rumble on** *vi (person)* hablar largo y tendido, extenderse; *(conversation, debate)* prolongarse; **the dispute rumbled on** el conflicto se prolongó

rumbling ['rʌmblɪŋ] **1** *n* **there were rumblings of discontent among the workers** los trabajadores comenzaban a mostrar su descontento
2 *adj* **a r. noise** un ruido sordo

rumbustious [rʌm'bʌstjəs] *adj Br Fam* bullicioso(a)

ruminant ['ru:mɪnənt] **1** *n Zool* rumiante *m*
2 *adj (person, look, mood)* pensativo(a), meditabundo(a)

ruminate ['ru:mɪneɪt] **1** *vi* (**a**) *Zool (animal)* rumiar (**b**) *Formal (person)* **to r. about** *or* **on sth** meditar acerca de algo, rumiar algo
2 *vt* (**a**) *Zool (of animal)* rumiar (**b**) *Formal (of person)* meditar, rumiar

ruminative ['ru:mɪnətɪv] *adj* pensativo(a), meditabundo(a)

rummage ['rʌmɪdʒ] **1** *n* (**a**) *(search)* **to have a r. through** *or* **in sth** hurgar *or* rebuscar en algo; **I had a quick r. in his pockets** revisé rápidamente sus bolsillos (**b**) *US (jumble)* cosas *fpl* usadas ►► *US* ***r. sale*** *(in store)* liquidación *f* de saldos; *(for charity)* mercadillo *m or* rastrillo *m* benéfico
2 *vi* **he rummaged through my suitcase** rebuscó en *or* revolvió mi maleta *orAm* valija; **to r. about** *or* **around** hurgar, rebuscar

rummy ['rʌmɪ] *n* (**a**) *(card game)* = juego de cartas en el que cada jugador debe conseguir grupos de tres o más cartas (**b**) *US Fam (drunk)* borrachín(ina) *m,f*

rumour, *US* **rumor** ['ru:mə(r)] **1** *n* rumor *m*; **r. has it that...** según los rumores,...; **there's a r. going round that...** corren rumores de que..., se rumorea que...
2 *vt* **it is rumoured that...** se rumorea que...; **he is rumoured to be ill** se rumorea que está enfermo; **so it was rumoured** ése es el rumor que circulaba

rumoured, *US* **rumored** ['ru:məd] *adj* rumoreado(a); **the table was sold for a r. $2m** se rumorea que la mesa se vendió por 2 millones de dólares

rump [rʌmp] *n* (**a**) *(of animal)* cuartos *mpl* traseros ►► ***r. steak*** filete *m* de lomo (**b**) *Fam (of person)* trasero *m* (**c**) *(of political party, assembly)* resto *m (tras escisión)*; **the organization was reduced to a r.** la organización quedó reducida a su mínima expresión ►► ***r. state*** = estado que ha quedado reducido a una porción de lo que era

rumple ['rʌmpəl] *vt (crease)* arrugar; *(hair)* despeinar

rumpus ['rʌmpəs] *n Fam (noise)* jaleo *m*, bronca *f*, *Esp* follón *m*; **to kick up** *or* **cause** *or* **make a r.** armar un jaleo *or* una bronca *or Esp* un follón ►► *US* ***r. room*** cuarto *m* de juegos

rumpy-pumpy ['rʌmpɪ'pʌmpɪ] *n Br Fam Hum* ñacañaca *m*; **to have a bit of r.** hacer ñacañaca

RUN [rʌn] **1** *n* (**a**) *(act of running)* carrera *f*, corrida *f*; **to go for a r.** ir a correr; **a charity r.** una carrera benéfica; **I took the dog for a r. in the park** saqué al perro a que corriese por el parque; **to break into a r.** echar a correr; *Sport* **to make a r.** pegarse una carrera *or* corrida; *Fam* **to make a r. for it** salir corriendo *or Esp* por piernas; **at a r.** corriendo, *RP* a las corridas; **to be on the r.** *(prisoner, suspect)* estar fugado(a) *or* en fuga; IDIOM **we've got them on the r.** los tenemos contra las cuerdas; IDIOM **to give sb the r. of the house** poner la casa a disposición de alguien; IDIOM **to give sb a r. for their money** hacer sudar (la camiseta) a alguien; **she has been an international for ten years, so she's had a good r. for her money** ha sido internacional durante diez años, no se puede quejar
(**b**) *(journey) (to bomb, to get supplies)* misión *f*; *(for pleasure)* vuelta *f*; **the Oaktown to Newport r.** el trayecto de Oaktown a Newport; **I do the school r. in the morning** yo llevo a los niños al colegio por la mañana; **to go for a r.** ir a dar una vuelta (en coche)
(**c**) *Com (of book)* tirada *f*; *(of product)* partida *f*, tanda *f*
(**d**) *(sequence, series)* serie *f*; *(in cards)* escalera *f*; **the play had a six-month r.** la obra estuvo en cartel seis meses; **a r. of good/bad luck** una racha de buena/mala suerte; **a r. of six straight wins** una serie *or* racha de seis victorias consecutivas; **in the long r.** a la larga, a largo plazo; **in the short r.** a corto plazo
(**e**) *(pattern, tendency)* **to score against the r. of play** marcar cuando el otro equipo domina el partido; **the general** *or* **usual r. of sth** la típica clase de algo; **in the ordinary r. of events** *or* **things** en condiciones normales; **she's well above the average** *or* **ordinary r. of students** está muy por encima de la media de los demás estudiantes
(**f**) *Fin (on bank, stock exchange)* retirada *f* masiva de fondos; **a r. on the dollar** una fuerte presión sobre el dólar, una venta apresurada de dólares; **there has been a r. on hosepipes because of the hot weather** ha habido una gran demanda de mangueras debido al calor
(**g**) *(bid) (in election)* candidatura *f*; **his r. for the presidency** su candidatura a la presidencia
(**h**) *(in baseball, cricket)* carrera *f*
(**i**) *(in stocking)* carrera *f*
(**j**) *(on skiing, bobsleigh course)* pista *f*; *(individual descent)* descenso *m*
(**k**) *(for chickens, rabbits)* corral *m*
(**l**) *Mus* carrerilla *f*
2 *vt* (*pt* **ran** [ræn], *pp* **run**) (**a**) *(distance)* correr, recorrer; **to r. a race** *(compete in)* correr (en) una carrera; **to r. a good/bad race** hacer una buena/mala carrera; **the race will be r. tomorrow** la carrera se disputará mañana; **we are running three horses in the next race** tenemos tres caballos en la próxima carrera; **to r. an errand** hacer un recado *or RP* mandado; **to allow things to r. their course** dejar que las cosas sigan su curso; **to r. sb close** quedarse a un paso de vencer a alguien; IDIOM **she'd r. a mile if I asked her out** si le pidiera salir saldría escopeteada *or Esp* por piernas; IDIOM *Fam* **we were r. off our feet** no tuvimos ni un momento de descanso
(**b**) *(drive)* **to r. sb to the airport** llevar a alguien al aeropuerto, dar *CAm, Méx* aventón *or Col* chance *or Cuba* botella *or Ven* una cola *or Perú* una jalada a alguien hasta el aeropuerto
(**c**) *(smuggle) (drugs, arms)* pasar de contrabando
(**d**) *(operate) (machine, engine)* hacer funcionar; *(tape, video)* poner; *(test, experiment)* hacer, realizar, *Esp* efectuar; *Comptr (program)* ejecutar; **it's expensive to r.** consume mucho; **you can r. it off solar energy/the mains** funciona con energía solar/electricidad; **I can't afford to r. two cars** no puedo permitirme mantener dos coches; **they are running extra buses today** hoy han puesto *or* sacado autobuses adicionales
(**e**) *(manage) (business, hotel)* dirigir, llevar; *(country)* gobernar; *(course, seminar)* organizar; **the postal service is r. by the state** el correo es un servicio estatal; **the hotel is very well r.** el servicio en este hotel es muy bueno; **stop trying to r. my life for me!** ¡deja de dirigir mi vida!; IDIOM **who's running the show?** ¿quién está a cargo de esto?
(**f**) *(pass) (cables, pipes)* hacer pasar; **I ran my finger down the list** pasé el dedo por la lista, recorrí la lista con el dedo; **to r. one's fingers over sth** pasar la mano por algo, *Esp* acariciar algo; **he ran his fingers through his hair** se pasó los dedos por los cabellos; **she ran her eye over the page** echó una ojeada a la página
(**g**) *(water)* dejar correr; **to r. a bath** preparar un baño; **r. some water over that cut** deja correr agua por ese corte
(**h**) *(suffer from)* **to r. a fever** *or* **temperature** tener fiebre; **to r. a deficit** tener déficit
(**i**) *(article, story, advertisement) (in newspaper)* publicar; **the ten o'clock news ran a story about child pornography** el telediario *or Am* noticiero de las diez mostró un reportaje sobre pornografía infantil
(**j**) *(chase, force)* **they were r. out of town** los expulsaron *or* echaron de la ciudad; **he tried to r. me off the road!** ¡trató de echarme *or* sacarme de la carretera!
(**k**) *(go through) (blockade)* eludir; *US (red light)* saltarse
(**l**) *(enter for election)* presentar; **they're running a candidate in every constituency** presentan a un candidato en todas las circunscripciones
(**m**) *(expose oneself to)* **to r. the risk of...** correr el riesgo de...; **you r. the risk of a heavy fine** te expones a una multa considerable
3 *vi* (**a**) *(person)* correr; **to r. about** *or* **around** correr de acá para allá; **I'll just r. across** *or* **over** *or* **round to the shop** voy en un momento a la tienda, voy hasta la tienda de una corrida; **to r. after sb** correr detrás *orAm* atrás de alguien; *Fam* **he's always running after women** siempre va detrás de las tías *or Méx* de las faldas, *RP* está siempre atrás de alguna pollera; **r. and fetch your sister** corre y trae a tu hermana; **he ran at her with a knife** corrió hacia ella con un cuchillo; **we ran back to the house** volvimos corriendo a la casa; **to r. down/up the street** bajar/subir la calle corriendo; **to r. for help** correr en busca de ayuda; **we had to r. for the bus** tuvimos que correr para alcanzar *or Esp* coger el autobús; **to r. in/out** entrar/salir corriendo; **to r. up to sb** correr hacia alguien; **don't come running to me when it all goes wrong!** ¡no me vengas corriendo cuando las cosas vayan mal!; IDIOM **to r. like the wind** correr como una flecha *or* una bala; IDIOM **to be running scared** haber perdido los papeles; PROV **it's no good trying to r. before you can walk** de nada vale empezar la casa por el tejado
(**b**) *(flee)* escapar corriendo; **he's always running around with other women** siempre tiene líos con otras mujeres; **you can't just keep running from your past** no puedes huir de tu pasado constantemente; **r. for it!, r. for your lives!** ¡corre!, *Esp* ¡huye!, *Am* ¡sálvese quien pueda!
(**c**) *(compete) (athlete)* correr; *(horse)* salir, correr; **I've decided to r. against her for the presidency** he decidido disputarle la presidencia; **to r. for Parliament/president** presentarse a las elecciones parlamentarias/presidenciales
(**d**) *(flow)* correr; **to leave the tap running** *Esp* dejar el grifo abierto, dejar la *Chile, Col, Méx* llave *or Carib* pluma *or RP* canilla abierta; **my eyes were running** me lloraban los ojos; **my nose is running** me moquea *or RP* chorrea la nariz, tengo mocos; **a trickle of blood ran down his leg** un hilo de sangre bajaba por su pierna; **the river runs into a lake** el río desemboca en un lago; **my back was running with sweat** me corría el sudor por la espalda; **my blood ran cold** se me heló la sangre en las venas
(**e**) *(pass) (road, railway)* ir; **the line runs along the coast** la línea de tren discurre paralela a la costa; **a fence runs around the garden** una cerca rodea el jardín; **we keep this part well oiled so it runs backwards and forwards smoothly** mantenemos esta pieza bien lubricada para que se mueva sin problemas; **a murmur ran through the**

crowd se extendió un murmullo entre la multitud; **a shiver ran through her** sintió un escalofrío; **that song keeps running through my head** no se me va esa canción de la cabeza; **this theme runs through all of her novels** este tema está presente en todas sus novelas

(**f**) *(last, extend) (contract, lease)* durar; *(play)* estar en cartel; **the controversy looks set to r. and r.** parece que la polémica va a durar bastante tiempo; **it runs in the family** es cosa de familia

(**g**) *(bus, train)* circular; **a bus runs into town every half hour** hay un autobús al centro cada media hora; **to be running late** *(bus, person)* ir con retraso, *Am* estar atrasado *or* demorado(a); **the trains are running on time** los trenes circulan puntuales, los trenes están circulando *Am* a horario *or RP* en hora

(**h**) *(operate) (machine)* funcionar (**on** con); **the engine's running** el motor está en marcha; **we left the program running** dejamos el programa en marcha; **to r. off the mains** funcionar conectado(a) a la red; **the software won't r. on this machine** el programa no funciona en *Esp* este ordenador *or Am* esta computadora; **do not interrupt the program while it is running** no interrumpa el programa mientras se está ejecutando; **things are running smoothly/according to plan** las cosas marchan bien/tal y como estaba planeado

(**i**) *(become)* **the river had r. dry** el río se había secado; **feelings** *or* **tempers are running high** los ánimos están revueltos; **supplies are running low** se están agotando las reservas; **he was running short of time** se le estaba acabando el tiempo

(**j**) *(be)* **the poem runs as follows** el poema dice así; **unemployment is running at 10 percent** el desempleo *or Am* la desocupación está en el 10 por ciento; **their hatred of each other runs deep** se odian profundamente

(**k**) *(colour, dye)* desteñir; *(paint, make-up)* correrse

(**l**) *(get damaged)* **my stocking has r.** *Esp* me he hecho una carrera en la media, *Am* se me corrió la media

▶ **run across** *vt insep (meet by chance)* encontrarse con

▶ **run along** *vi* **r. along, now, little girl** ¡ya puedes marchar, niña!; **it's getting late, I must be running along** se hace tarde, tengo que irme

▶ **run away** *vi* (**a**) *(flee)* echar a correr, salir corriendo; **I'll be with you in a minute, don't r. away** estoy contigo en un momento, no te vayas; **to r. away from sth/sb** escaparse *or* huir de algo/alguien; **to r. away from one's responsibilities** eludir las responsabilidades; **to r. away from home** escaparse de casa; *Fig* **to r. away from the facts** no querer ver los hechos

(**b**) *(elope)* fugarse *(para casarse)*

▶ **run away with** *vt insep* (**a**) *(win easily)* ganar fácilmente (**b**) *(take over)* **don't let your imagination r. away with you** no te dejes llevar por la imaginación (**c**) *(steal)* llevarse (**d**) *(get) Fig* **don't r. away with the idea that...** no vayas a pensar que...

▶ **run back 1** *vi* (**a**) *(review)* **to r. back over sth** repasar algo

2 *vt sep* (**a**) *(drive back)* acompañar, llevar *(en vehículo)* (**b**) *(rewind) (tape, film)* rebobinar

▶ **run by, run past** *vt sep* **to r. an idea by sb** proponer una idea a alguien; **could you r. that by me one more time?** ¿me lo podrías repetir otra vez?

▶ **run down 1** *vt sep* (**a**) *(in car)* atropellar (**b**) *(find)* localizar, encontrar (**c**) *(criticize)* menospreciar, criticar; **stop running yourself down all the time** deja ya de subestimarte constantemente (**d**) *(reduce) (production, stocks)* reducir, disminuir; *(industry, factory)* desmantelar

2 *vi (battery)* agotarse; *(clock)* pararse

▶ **run in** *vt sep* (**a**) *Fam (arrest)* detener (**b**) *(engine)* rodar (**c**) *(in rugby) (try)* marcar

▶ **run into** *vt insep* (**a**) *(collide with)* chocar con *or* contra (**b**) *(meet by chance)* encontrarse con (**c**) *(get into) (difficulties)* tropezar con; **to r. into debt** endeudarse (**d**) *(merge with) (of colours, memories)* mezclarse con (**e**) *(amount to)* ascender a

▶ **run off 1** *vt sep* (**a**) *(make a copy of) (print)* tirar; *(photocopy)* sacar; *(write quickly)* escribir rápidamente; *(copies) (on printer)* tirar; *(on photocopier)* sacar (**b**) *(excess weight)* quemar *(corriendo)* (**c**) *(liquid)* sacar

2 *vi* (**a**) *(flee)* echar a correr, salir corriendo; **to r. off with the cash** escapar con el dinero; **to r. off with sb** escaparse con alguien (**b**) *(liquid)* correr

▶ **run on 1** *vt Typ* unir al párrafo contiguo

2 *vi* (**a**) *(meeting)* continuar; **the play ran on for hours** la obra se prolongó horas y horas (**b**) *Fam (talk a lot)* hablar sin parar (**c**) *Typ* unir párrafos, hacer punto y seguido

▶ **run out 1** *vi* (**a**) *(lease, contract)* vencer, cumplirse; *(passport, licence)* caducar

(**b**) *(money, supplies)* agotarse; **do you have any disks? – no, we've r. out** ¿tienes algún disquete? – no, se nos han acabado; **to r. out of sth** quedarse sin algo; **we've r. out of time** se nos ha acabado el tiempo; **I'm running out of patience** estoy perdiendo la paciencia; IDIOM **to r. out of steam** *(person)* quedarse sin fuerzas; *(project)* perder empuje

2 *vt sep (cable, rope)* soltar

▶ **run out on** *vt insep* abandonar

▶ **run over 1** *vt sep (in car)* atropellar; **I nearly got run over** casi me atropellan

2 *vt insep (rehearse, check)* ensayar, repasar; *(repeat)* repasar; **he ran the idea over in his mind** le dio vueltas a la idea en la cabeza

3 *vi* (**a**) *(run late) (meeting, TV programme)* durar demasiado; **we've already r. over by half an hour** ya nos hemos excedido media hora (**b**) *(overflow)* desbordarse, rebosar; *Literary or Hum* **my cup runneth over** estoy rebosante de alegría

▶ **run past** *vt sep* = **run by**

▶ **run through 1** *vt insep* (**a**) *(rehearse, check)* ensayar, repasar; *(repeat)* repasar (**b**) *(spend quickly)* despilfarrar

2 *vt sep Literary (with sword)* atravesar

▶ **run to** *vt insep* (**a**) *Br (be able to afford)* poder permitirse; **I'm afraid we don't r. to that kind of thing** me temo que el dinero no nos da para algo así (**b**) *(amount to)* ascender a (**c**) IDIOM **to r. to fat** ponerse fofo(a)

▶ **run up** *vt sep* (**a**) *(debts)* acumular; **she ran up a huge bill at the jeweller's** gastó una enorme cantidad de dinero en la joyería (**b**) *(flag)* izar (**c**) *(clothes)* hacerse, coser

▶ **run up against** *vt insep (opposition, problems)* tropezar con

---

runabout ['rʌnəbaʊt] *n Fam (automobile)* coche *m or Am* carro *m or CSur* auto *m* pequeño

run-around ['rʌnəraʊnd] *n Fam* **to give sb the r.** enredar *or* liar a alguien

runaway ['rʌnəweɪ] **1** *n* (**a**) *(slave, teenager)* fugitivo(a) *m,f* (**b**) *(horse)* caballo *m* desbocado

2 *adj* (**a**) *(prisoner, slave)* fugitivo(a) (**b**) *(out of control) (horse)* desbocado(a); *(train, lorry)* incontrolado(a), fuera de control; *(inflation)* galopante (**c**) *(victory, success)* apabullante, arrollador(ora); **a r. bestseller** un éxito de ventas arrollador

run-down [rʌn'daʊn] *adj* (**a**) *(building)* en malas condiciones; *(part of town)* en decadencia (**b**) *(person)* **to be r.** estar débil; **I'm feeling a bit r.** me siento un poco flojo, no me encuentro demasiado bien (**c**) *(battery)* agotado(a)

rundown ['rʌndaʊn] *n* (**a**) *(reduction)* reducción *f*; **the r. of the coal industry** el progresivo desmantelamiento de la industria del carbón (**b**) *(summary)* resumen *m*, informe *m*, *CAm, Méx* reporte *m*; **to give sb a r. (on sth)** poner a alguien al tanto (de algo)

rune [ru:n] *n* runa *f*

rung [rʌŋ] **1** *n (of ladder)* peldaño *m*, escalón *m*; *Fig* **the bottom r.** *(in organization)* el escalón más bajo; IDIOM **it's the first r. on the ladder** es el primer paso

2 *pp of* **ring**[2]

runic ['ru:nɪk] *adj* rúnico(a)

run-in ['rʌnɪn] *n* (**a**) *Fam (argument)* **to have a r. with sb** tener una pelea *or* una riña con alguien (**b**) *(of race, championship)* periodo *m* previo, fase *f* previa; **the r. to the election** el preámbulo de *or* el periodo previo a las elecciones

runnel ['rʌnəl] *n* arroyuelo *m*

runner ['rʌnə(r)] *n* (**a**) *(athlete)* corredor(ora) *m,f*; **he's a good/fast r.** es un buen corredor/un corredor rápido

(**b**) *(messenger)* mensajero(a) *m,f*, recadero(a) *m,f*

(**c**) *Br* ***r. bean*** *Esp* judía *f* verde, *Bol, RP* chaucha *f*, *Chile* poroto *m* verde, *Col* habichuela *f*, *Méx* ejote *m*

(**d**) *(for drawer)* guía *f*

(**e**) *(on sleigh)* patín *m*; *(on skate)* cuchilla *f*

(**f**) *(carpet)* alfombra *f* estrecha *(para pasillos, escaleras)*; *(for table)* tapete *m*

(**g**) *(on plant)* rama *f* rastrera, *Spec* estolón *m*

(**h**) *Br Fam* **to do a r.** salir corriendo *or Esp* por piernas

runner-up [rʌnər'ʌp] (*pl* **runners-up**) *n* subcampeón(ona) *m,f*; **there will be ten prizes for the runners-up** habrá (diez) premios para los diez mejores después del ganador

running ['rʌnɪŋ] **1** *n* (**a**) *(activity)* **I don't like r.** no me gusta correr; **to go r.** ir a correr; **no r.** *(sign)* prohibido correr ▸▸ ***r. back*** *(in American football)* running back *m*; ***r. shoe*** zapatilla *f* deportiva; ***r. track*** pista *f* (de atletismo)

(**b**) *(competition, race)* **to be out of/in the r.** no tener/tener posibilidades de ganar; **to make all the r.** *(in contest)* ocupar el primer puesto desde el principio; *(in relationship)* llevar siempre la iniciativa ►► *US Pol* ***r. mate*** candidato(a) *m,f* a la vicepresidencia

(c) *(of train)* **we apologize for the late r. of this train** pedimos disculpas por la demora de este tren

(d) *(operation) (of machine, car)* funcionamiento *m* ►► ***r. costs*** *(for business)* gastos *mpl* corrientes; *(for car, machine)* costos *mpl or* gastos *mpl* de mantenimiento; ***r. lights*** *(of car)* luces *fpl* de posición; *(of ship)* luces *fpl* de navegación

(e) *(management) (of hotel, restaurant)* dirección *f*, gestión *f*; **she leaves the day-to-day r. of the department to her assistant** delega la gestión cotidiana del departamento en su ayudante

2 *adj* (a) *(at a run) (person, animal)* que corre ►► ***r. jump*** salto *m* con carrerilla; IDIOM *Fam* **he told them to take a r. jump (*US* at the moon)** los mandó a freír espárragos

(b) *(continuous) (battle, feud)* continuo(a), constante; **they have a r. battle about housework** tienen una pelea constante *or* permanente por las tareas del hogar ►► ***r. commentary*** comentario *m* en directo; ***r. head*** *(in book)* título *m* de página, folio *m*; ***r. joke*** *(of perfomer)* chiste *m* de repertorio; *(among group of people)* chiste *m* habitual; ***r. stitch*** bastilla *f*, dobladillo *m*; ***r. title*** *(in book)* título *m* de página, folio *m*; ***r. total*** total *m* actualizado

(c) *(flowing) (tap)* abierto(a) ►► ***r. sore*** llaga *f* supurante; *Br Fig* **the issue has become a r. sore between them** la cuestión se ha convertido en una herida abierta entre ellos; ***r. water*** *(water supply)* agua *f* corriente; *(in stream, river)* agua *f* que corre

(d) *(operating)* **to be up and r.** estar en funcionamiento ►► ***r. order*** *(of show, ceremony)* programa *m*; **in r. order** *(vehicle)* en condiciones de *or* para circular; ***r. repairs*** arreglos *mpl* (momentáneos)

3 *adv (consecutively)* de manera consecutiva; **three years r.** tres años consecutivos *or* seguidos

running-board ['rʌnɪŋbɔːd] *n Aut* estribo *m*

runny ['rʌnɪ] *adj* (a) *(sauce, custard)* demasiado líquido(a); *(honey)* fluido(a); *(egg, yolk)* poco hecho(a), líquido(a) (b) *(nose)* **to have a r. nose** tener mocos, moquear

run-off ['rʌnɒf] *n* (a) *(to decide game)* desempate *m (partido, carrera)* (b) *Pol* **r. (election)** segunda vuelta *f* (c) *(water)* (agua *f* de) escorrentía *f*

run-of-the-mill ['rʌnəvðə'mɪl] *adj* corriente y moliente

run-on ['rʌnɒn] *n (in printed matter)* texto *m* seguido *or* corrido

run-proof ['rʌnpruːf], **run-resist** ['rʌnrɪ'zɪst] *adj (stocking, tights)* indesmallable, *RP* indemallable

runs [rʌnz] *npl Fam* **the r.** *(diarrhoea)* cagalera *f*, *Méx* el chorro, *RP* cagadera *f*; **he got the r.** le entró cagalera *or Méx* el chorro *or RP* cagadera

runt [rʌnt] *n* (a) *(of litter)* cachorro *m* más pequeño (b) *Fam (weak person)* canijo(a) *m,f*, pigmeo(a) *m,f*

run-through ['rʌnθruː] *n* (a) *(rehearsal)* ensayo *m*; **to have a r.** hacer un ensayo (b) *(review)* repaso *m*

run-time ['rʌntaɪm] *n Comptr* periodo *m or* tiempo *m* de ejecución ►► ***r. error*** error *m* de periodo de ejecución; ***r. version*** versión *f* run-time, = versión limitada de un programa de apoyo que acompaña a una aplicación

run-up ['rʌnʌp] *n* (a) *(before jump)* carrerilla *f* (b) *(before event)* periodo *m* previo (**to** a)

runway ['rʌnweɪ] *n* (a) *(for take-off)* pista *f* de despegue *or Am* decolaje; *(for landing)* pista *f* de aterrizaje ►► ***r. lights*** balizas *fpl* (b) *(in long jump, pole vault)* pista *f* de aceleración

rupee [ruː'piː] *n (Indian currency)* rupia *f*

rupture ['rʌptʃə(r)] 1 *n* (a) *(breaking)* ruptura *f* (b) *Med* hernia *f*

2 *vt* (a) *(relations, container)* romper (b) *Med (blood vessel, appendix, spleen)* reventar; **to r. oneself** herniarse

3 *vi* (a) *(container, pipeline)* romperse (b) *Med (blood vessel, appendix)* reventar(se)

rural ['rʊərəl] *adj* rural

Ruritania [rʊərɪ'teɪnɪə] *n* Ruritania *(país ficticio)*

Ruritanian [rʊərɪ'teɪnɪən] *adj* ruritano(a) *(de un país ficticio)*

ruse [ruːz] *n* artimaña *f*, ardid *m*

rush[1] [rʌʃ] *n (plant)* **rushes** juncos *mpl* ►► ***r. light*** vela *f* de junco; ***r. mat** or **matting*** estera *f or* esterilla *f* (de junco)

rush[2] 1 *n* (a) *(hurry)* prisa *f*, *Am* apuro *m*, *Col* afán *m*; **there was a r. to get things finished** había prisa *or Am* apuro *or Col* afán *m* por terminar las cosas; **it'll be a bit of a r., but we should make it** habrá que darse prisa *or Am* apurarse *or Col* afanarse, pero llegaremos a tiempo; **to be in a r.** tener prisa, *Am* estar apurado(a); **to do sth in a r.** hacer algo a toda prisa *or* con prisa(s) *or Am* con apuro *or Col* con afán; **there's no r.** no hay prisa *or Am* apuro; **what's the r.?** ¿qué prisa *or Am* apuro *or Col* afán tienes? ►► ***r. job*** *(done too quickly)* trabajo *m* hecho a toda prisa *or* velocidad; **it's a r. job for Japan** es un trabajo urgente para Japón

(b) *(run, stampede)* avalancha *f*, desbandada *f*; **there was a r. for the door** todos corrieron *or* se precipitaron hacia la puerta; **I lost it in the r.** lo perdí en medio de aquel alboroto; **to make a r. for sth** apresurarse a alcanzar algo; **to make a r. at sb** abalanzarse hacia alguien

(c) *(busy period)* periodo *m* álgido *or* de máxima actividad, pico *m*; **the six o'clock r.** la hora *Esp* punta *or Am* pico de las seis; **I try to avoid the lunchtime/holiday r.** trato de evitar las aglomeraciones de la hora del almuerzo/la temporada de vacaciones ►► ***r. hour*** *Esp* hora *f* punta, *Am* hora *f* pico

(d) *(surge) (of air)* ráfaga *f*; *(of water)* chorro *m*; *(of requests)* ola *f*; **I couldn't hear them above the r. of water** el ruido del (chorro de) agua no me dejaba oírlos; IDIOM **a r. of blood to the head** un arrebato (de locura)

(e) *(demand)* demanda *f*; **there's been a r. on sugar** ha habido una fuerte demanda de azúcar

(f) *Cin* **rushes** primeras pruebas *fpl*

(g) *US Univ* = periodo en que asociaciones y clubes de estudiantes universitarios tratan de captar nuevos miembros

(h) *Fam (after taking drugs)* subidón *m*; **I got a real r. from that coffee** ese café me ha puesto a cien

2 *vt* (a) *(do quickly) (task)* realizar a toda prisa *or* apresuradamente; **don't r. your food** no comas tan rápido; **they rushed the first act, I thought** me pareció que hicieron demasiado rápido *or Am* apuraron *or Col* afanaron el primer acto; IDIOM **to r. one's fences** actuar a la ligera, apresurarse

(b) *(cause to hurry) (person)* apresurar; **don't r. me!** ¡no me metas prisa!, *Am* ¡no me apures!; **to r. sb into doing sth** meter prisa *or Am* apurar a alguien para que haga algo; **don't be rushed into signing** no dejes que te metan prisa *or Am* no te dejes apurar para firmar; **to be rushed off one's feet** no tener un momento de descanso

(c) *(transport quickly)* llevar apresuradamente; **she was rushed to hospital** la llevaron al hospital a toda prisa; **they rushed a first aid team to the site** enviaron rápidamente un equipo de primeros auxilios al lugar del hecho; **please r. me your new catalogue** agradeceré me hagan llegar cuanto antes una copia de su nuevo catálogo

(d) *(attack)* arremeter contra; **a group of prisoners rushed the guards** un grupo de prisioneros arremetió contra los guardas

(e) *US Fam (court)* cortejar

(f) *US Univ* intentar captar como miembro *(para asociación o club de estudiantes)*

3 *vi* (a) *(move fast)* correr, precipitarse; **I rushed home after work** después del trabajo me fui corriendo a casa; **people rushed out of the blazing house** la gente salía corriendo *or* a toda prisa de la casa en llamas; **the dog rushed at me** el perro se precipitó hacia *or* se abalanzó sobre mí; **passers-by rushed to help the injured man** los que pasaban por allí acudieron rápidamente a auxiliar al herido; **he rushed past/over/up** pasó/fue/acudió a toda velocidad

(b) *(hurry)* apresurarse, *Am* apurarse; **I must r.** (me voy, que) tengo mucha prisa *or Am* estoy muy apurado; **there's no need to r.** no hay por qué apresurarse; **his friends rushed to defend him in the press** sus amigos se apresuraron a defenderlo en la prensa

(c) *(act overhastily)* precipitarse; **now don't r. into anything** bueno, piénsalo y no te precipites; **to r. into a decision** tomar una decisión precipitada *or* apresurada, precipitarse al tomar una decisión; **she rushed into marriage** se casó demasiado apresuradamente

(d) *(surge) (air, liquid)* salir/pasar con fuerza; **the cold water rushed over her bare feet** el agua helada corría sobre sus pies descalzos; **I could hear the wind rushing through the trees** oía el viento soplando con fuerza entre los árboles; **the blood rushed to his cheeks** *or* **face** se le subieron los colores; **the blood rushed to her head** le hirvió la sangre, le dio un arrebato (de ira)

(e) *(in American football)* **he rushed for 9 yards** hizo una carrera de 9 yardas; **he rushed for 139 yards in the game** hizo un total de 139 yardas (de carrera) durante el partido

▸ **rush about, rush around** *vi* trajinar (de acá para allá)

▸ **rush in** *vi* (a) *(enter)* entrar apresuradamente *or* a toda prisa (b) *(decide overhastily)* tomar una decisión precipitada *or* apresurada

▸ **rush off** *vi (flee)* irse corriendo

▸ **rush out** 1 *vt sep (book, new product)* sacar apresuradamente *or* a toda prisa

2 *vi (exit)* salir apresuradamente

▸ **rush through** 1 *vt sep* **to r. a bill/decision through** aprobar un proyecto de ley/tomar una decisión apresuradamente *or* a toda prisa

2 *vt insep (book, meal, work)* despachar con rapidez; **he rushed through his speech and left immediately** dio su discurso a toda prisa y se fue de inmediato

rushed [rʌʃt] *adj (work, meal)* apresurado(a), *Am* apurado(a); **a r. decision** una decisión precipitada *or* apresurada

rush-hour ['rʌʃaʊə(r)] *adj (crowds, traffic) Esp* de (la) hora punta, *Am* de (la) hora pico

rusk [rʌsk] *n* = galleta dura y crujiente para niños que comienzan a masticar

russet ['rʌsɪt] **1** *n* (**a**) *(colour)* castaño *m* rojizo (**b**) *(apple)* manzana *f* russet

2 *adj* rojizo(a)

Russia ['rʌʃə] *n* Rusia

Russian ['rʌʃən] **1** *n* (**a**) *(person)* ruso(a) *m,f* (**b**) *(language)* ruso *m* ▸▸ ***R. class/teacher*** clase *f*/profesor(ora) *m,f* de ruso

2 *adj* ruso(a) ▸▸ ***R. doll*** muñeca *f* rusa; ***the R. Federation*** la Federación Rusa; ***R. roulette*** ruleta *f* rusa; ***R. salad*** ensaladilla *f* rusa

Russification [rʌsɪfɪ'keɪʃən] *n* rusificación *f*

Russki, Russky ['rʌskɪ] *n Fam* = término a veces ofensivo para referirse a los rusos

Russo- ['rʌsəʊ] *prefix* ruso-; **R.-Chinese relations** relaciones rusochinas

Russophile ['rʌsəʊfaɪl] **1** *n* rusófilo(a) *m,f*

2 *adj* rusófilo(a)

Russophobe ['rʌsəʊfəʊb] **1** *n* rusófobo(a) *m,f*

2 *adj* rusófobo(a)

rust [rʌst] **1** *n* (**a**) *(on metal)* óxido *m*, herrumbre *f* ▸▸ ***the R. Belt*** = región del noreste de Estados Unidos con una alta concentración de industria pesada en declive (**b**) *(on plant)* roya *f* (**c**) *(colour)* color *m* óxido *or* teja, marrón *m* rojizo

2 *adj (colour)* color óxido *or* teja *inv*, marrón rojizo(a)

3 *vi* oxidarse; **the door had rusted through** la puerta se había oxidado por completo

4 *vt* oxidar

▸ **rust away** *vi* oxidarse poco a poco

▸ **rust up** *vi* oxidarse por completo

rust-bucket ['rʌstbʌkɪt] *n Fam (car)* chatarra *f* ambulante, *Méx* arnero *m*

rusted ['rʌstɪd] *adj* oxidado(a)

rustic ['rʌstɪk] **1** *n* campesino(a) *m,f*, pueblerino(a) *m,f*

2 *adj* rústico(a)

rusticate ['rʌstɪkeɪt] *vt Br Univ (student)* expulsar temporalmente, *Am* suspender

rusticity [rʌs'tɪsɪtɪ] *n* rusticidad *f*

rustiness ['rʌstɪnɪs] *n* (**a**) *(of metal)* óxido *m*, herrumbre *f* (**b**) *(lack of fluency, practice) (of person)* falta *f* de práctica, anquilosamiento *m*; **the r. of my French** la falta de práctica que tengo en francés, lo olvidado que tengo el francés

rusting ['rʌstɪŋ] *adj* oxidado(a)

rustle[1] ['rʌsəl] **1** *n (of leaves)* susurro *m*; *(of paper)* crujido *m*; *(of clothing)* roce *m*

2 *vt (leaves)* hacer susurrar; *(paper)* hacer crujir

3 *vi (leaves)* susurrar; *(paper)* crujir; **her dress rustled** su vestido produjo un ruido al rozarse

rustle[2] *vt (cattle)* robar

▸ **rustle up** *vt sep Fam (meal, snack)* improvisar, *Esp* apañar; **to r. up support** reunir apoyo

rustler ['rʌslə(r)] *n (cattle thief)* cuatrero(a) *m,f*, ladrón(ona) *m,f* de ganado

rustling ['rʌslɪŋ] *n* (**a**) *(of cattle)* robo *m* (**b**) = **rustle**[1]

rustproof ['rʌstpruːf] **1** *adj* inoxidable

2 *vt* tratar con (un) antioxidante

rusty ['rʌstɪ] *adj* (**a**) *(metal)* oxidado(a), herrumbroso(a) (**b**) *(colour)* color óxido *or* teja *inv*, marrón rojizo(a) (**c**) *(lacking fluency, practice) (person)* falto(a) de práctica, anquilosado(a); **my playing is very r.** hace mucho que no juego; **my French is a bit r.** tengo el francés un poco olvidado (**d**) ***r. nail*** *(cocktail)* rusty nail *m*, = cóctel que lleva mitad de whisky escocés y mitad de Drambuie®

rut[1] [rʌt] **1** *n* (**a**) *(in road)* rodada *f* (**b**) IDIOMS **to be in a r.** *(routine)* estar estancado(a); **to get into a r.** estancarse

2 *vt (ground)* hacer surcos en; **the track had been deeply rutted by tractors** los tractores habían dejado profundas rodadas en el camino

rut[2] **1** *n (of stag)* celo *m*, berrea *f*; **in r.** en celo

2 *vi (pt & pp* **rutted**) *(stag)* estar en celo

rutabaga [ruːtə'beɪgə] *n US* nabo *m* sueco

Ruthenia [ruː'θiːnɪə] *n* Rutenia, Ucrania Subcarpática

Ruthenian [ruː'θiːnɪən] **1** *n* ruteno(a) *m,f*

2 *adj* ruteno(a)

ruthenium [ruː'θiːnɪəm] *n Chem* rutenio *m*

ruthless ['ruːθlɪs] *adj (person, act)* despiadado(a); *(criticism)* despiadado(a), implacable; **to be r. in enforcing the law** aplicar la ley de manera implacable *or* inflexible; **he was r. in shortening the text** no tuvo el menor reparo a la hora de acortar el texto; **she's quite r. when she's determined to get her way** es capaz de lo que sea con tal de conseguir lo que se propone; **with r. efficiency** con rigurosa eficacia

ruthlessly ['ruːθlɪslɪ] *adv* despiadadamente; **r. efficient** con rigurosa eficacia

ruthlessness ['ruːθlɪsnɪs] *n* crueldad *f*

rutted ['rʌtɪd] *adj* con surcos; **a badly r. road** una carretera llena de grandes surcos *or* rodadas

rutting ['rʌtɪŋ] *n* ***r. season*** época *f* de celo

RV [ɑː'viː] *n US* (*abbr* **recreational vehicle**) autocaravana *f*, casa *f or* coche *m* caravana

Rwanda [rə'wændə] *n* (**a**) *(country)* Ruanda (**b**) *(language)* kinyarwanda *m*, kinyaruanda *m*

Rwandan [rə'wændən] **1** *n* ruandés(esa) *m,f*

2 *adj* ruandés(esa)

Ryder Cup ['raɪdə'kʌp] *n* **the R.** *(in golf)* la Ryder Cup

rye [raɪ] *n* (**a**) *(cereal)* centeno *m* (**b**) **r. (whiskey)** whisky *m* de centeno (**c**) **r. (bread)** pan *m* de centeno

rye-grass ['raɪgrɑːs] *n* ballico *m*, césped *m* inglé

S, s

S, s [es] *n* (**a**) *(letter)* S, s *f* (**b**) (*abbr* **south**) S (**c**) (*abbr* **small**) *(on clothes label)* S, s

SA (**a**) (*abbr* **South Africa**) Sudáfrica (**b**) (*abbr* **South America**) Sudamérica

Saar [sɑː(r)] *n* **the S.** el Sarre

Saarland [ˈsɑːlænd] *n* Sarre *m*

Sabbatarian [sæbəˈteərɪən] **1** *n* sabatario(a) *m,f*
2 *adj* sabatario(a)

Sabbath [ˈsæbəθ] *n (Jewish)* Sabbat *m*, sábado *m* judío; *(Christian)* domingo *m*; **to observe the S.** *(Jew)* respetar el Sabbat; *(Christian)* respetar el domingo; **(witches') S.** aquelarre *m* ▸▸ ***S. day observance*** cumplimiento *m* del descanso sabático/dominical

sabbatical [səˈbætɪkəl] **1** *n* (**a**) *Univ* **to be on s.** estar en excedencia; **to take a s.** tomarse un periodo sabático (**b**) *(long break)* año *m or* periodo *m* sabático; **to take a s.** tomarse un periodo sabático
2 *adj Univ* ***s. term*** trimestre *m* sabático *or* de excedencia; ***s. year*** año *m* sabático *or* de excedencia

saber *US* = **sabre**

sable [ˈseɪbəl] **1** *n* (**a**) *(animal)* marta *f* cebellina (**b**) *(fur)* marta *f*; **s. coat** abrigo de marta (**c**) *Literary (black)* negro *m* azabache
2 *adj Literary (black)* prieto(a), negro(a)

sabot [ˈsæbəʊ] *n (shoe)* zueco *m*

sabotage [ˈsæbətɑːʒ] **1** *n* sabotaje *m*
2 *vt* sabotear

saboteur [sæbəˈtɜː(r)] *n* saboteador(ora) *m,f*

sabra [ˈsæbrə] *n US Fam* israelita *mf*

sabre, *US* **saber** [ˈseɪbə(r)] *n* sable *m*

sabre-rattling, *US* **saber-rattling** [ˈseɪbərætlɪŋ] *n Fig* **the president's remarks were mere s.** los comentarios del presidente fueron sólo una bravuconada

sabre-toothed tiger *n* [ˈseɪbətuːθtˈtaɪgə(r)] tigre *m* dientes de sable

sac [sæk] *n* (**a**) *Anat* bolsa *f*, saco *m*; **ink s.** *(of squid)* bolsa de tinta (**b**) *Bot* saco *m*

saccharide [ˈsækəraɪd] *n Chem* sacárido *m*

saccharin [ˈsækərɪn] *n* sacarina *f*

saccharine [ˈsækərɪn] *adj* (**a**) *Pej (smile, movie)* empalagoso(a) (**b**) *Chem* sacarino(a)

sacerdotal [sæsəˈdəʊtəl] *adj* sacerdotal

sachet [ˈsæʃeɪ] *n* sobrecito *m*

sack[1] [sæk] **1** *n* (**a**) *(for coal, flour, potatoes)* saco *m* ▸▸ ***s. race*** carrera *f* de sacos *or RP* embolsados (**b**) *US (for groceries)* bolsa *f* (**c**) *Fam (bed)* **to hit the s.** *(go to bed)* meterse en el sobre, *Esp* irse a la piltra; **to be good in the s.** montárselo bien en la cama, *Am* coger como los dioses (**d**) *Fam (dismissal)* **to give sb the s.** echar *or* despedir a alguien; **he got the s.** lo echaron *or* despidieron
2 *vt* (**a**) *Fam (dismiss from job)* echar, despedir (**b**) *(put in sacks)* embolsar, meter en sacos

▸**sack out** *vi US Fam* meterse al sobre

sack[2] **1** *n (plundering)* saqueo *m*
2 *vt (town)* saquear

sack[3] **1** *n (in American football)* = placaje al quarterback para evitar que dé un pase
2 *vt (in American football)* = placar (al quarterback) para evitar que dé un pase

sackbut [ˈsækbʌt] *n* sacabuche *m*

sackcloth [ˈsækklɒθ] *n* arpillera *f*, tela *f* de saco; *Rel* **to wear s. and ashes** llevar túnica de penitente; IDIOM **to be wearing s. and ashes** *(express remorse)* entonar el mea culpa

sackful [ˈsækfʊl], **sackload** [ˈsækləʊd] *n* saco *m* (lleno *or* entero); **we've been getting letters by the s.** hemos estado recibiendo toneladas de cartas

sacking[1] [ˈsækɪŋ] *n* (**a**) *(textile)* arpillera *f*, tela *f* de saco (**b**) *Fam (dismissal)* despido *m*

sacking[2] *n (plundering)* saqueo *m*

sackload = **sackful**

sacra *pl of* **sacrum**

sacral [ˈseɪkrəl] *adj Anat* sacro(a)

sacrament [ˈsækrəmənt] *n Rel* sacramento *m*; **the Blessed** *or* **Holy S.** el Santísimo Sacramento; **to receive the sacraments** recibir los sacramentos; **to take the sacraments** tomar los sacramentos

sacramental [sækrəˈmentəl] *adj Rel* sacramental

sacred [ˈseɪkrɪd] *adj* (**a**) *(holy) (place, book)* sagrado(a); **s. to the memory of...** consagrado(a) a la memoria de... ▸▸ ***the S. Heart*** el Sagrado Corazón
(**b**) *(solemn) (duty, vow)* solemne
(**c**) *(highly respected) (animal, human life)* sagrado(a) IDIOM **to be a s. cow** ser sacrosanto(a) ▸▸ ***s. ibis*** ibis *m* sagrado
(**d**) *(too important to change)* sagrado(a); **is nothing s.?** ¿es que ya no se respeta nada?
(**e**) *(connected with religion) (music)* sacro(a); *(writings)* sagrado(a)

sacredness [ˈseɪkrɪdnɪs] *n* (**a**) *(holiness)* santidad *f* (**b**) *(solemness)* solemnidad *f* (**c**) *(respectedness)* carácter *m* sagrado

sacrifice [ˈsækrɪfaɪs] **1** *n* (**a**) *(offering)* sacrificio *m*; **human s.** sacrificio humano (**b**) *(act of giving up)* sacrificio *m*; **to make sacrifices (for sb)** sacrificarse (por alguien); **to make the supreme s.** *(give one's life)* hacer el sacrificio supremo (**c**) *(in baseball)* sacrificio *m* ▸▸ *US* ***s. fly*** fly *m* de sacrificio; ***s. hit*** batazo *m* de sacrificio
2 *vt* (**a**) *(give as offering)* sacrificar; **to s. oneself (for sb)** sacrificarse (por alguien) (**b**) *(give up)* sacrificar; **to s. sth for sb** sacrificar algo por alguien; **we cannot afford to s. quality to quantity** no podemos permitirnos sacrificar la calidad por la cantidad (**c**) *(in chess)* sacrificar

sacrificial [sækrɪˈfɪʃəl] *adj (rite, dagger)* de sacrificio ▸▸ ***s. bunt*** *(in baseball)* batazo *m* de sacrificio; *Fig* ***s. lamb*** chivo *m* expiatorio; *Fig* ***s. victim*** chivo *m* expiatorio

sacrilege [ˈsækrɪlɪdʒ] *n also Fig* sacrilegio *m*; **it's s. to drink whisky with lemonade** beber whisky con gaseosa es un sacrilegio

sacrilegious [sækrɪˈlɪdʒəs] *adj also Fig* sacrílego(a)

sacristan [ˈsækrɪstən] *n Rel* sacristán *m*

sacristy [ˈsækrɪstɪ] *n* sacristía *f*

sacroiliac [sækrəʊˈɪlɪæk] *Anat* **1** *n* región *m* sacroilíaca
2 *adj* sacroilíaco(a)

sacrosanct [ˈsækrəʊsæŋkt] *adj also Fig* sacrosanto(a)

sacrum [ˈseɪkrəm] (*pl* **sacra** [ˈseikrə]) *n Anat* sacro *m*

SAD [sæd] *n Med* (*abbr* **Seasonal Affective Disorder**) trastorno *m* afectivo estacional

sad [sæd] *adj* (**a**) *(unhappy)* triste; **to feel s.** sentirse *or* estar triste; **to become s.** entristecerse; **to make sb s.** entristecer a alguien; **I shall be s. to see you leave** me entristecerá verte partir; **to be s. at heart** estar apesadumbrado(a) *or* afligido(a); **he came through the experience a sadder but wiser man** fue una experiencia triste para él, pero aprendió mucho de ella
(**b**) *(depressing) (film, news, loss)* triste; **the s. fact is he's incompetent** la triste realidad es que es incompetente; **but s. to say it didn't last long** desafortunadamente, no duró mucho; **she came to a s. end** tuvo un triste final
(**c**) *(deplorable)* lamentable; **it's a s. state of affairs when this sort of thing can go unpunished** es lamentable que este tipo de cosas no sea castigado; **a s. reflection on modern society** una reflexión desesperanzada sobre la sociedad moderna; **it's a s. day when you can no longer walk the streets at night in safety** es lamentable que ya no se pueda caminar sin peligro de noche por la calle

(d) *Fam Pej (pathetic)* lamentable, penoso(a); **she's a s. case** es un caso patético; *very Fam* **he's a s. bastard!** ¡es un desgraciado!, *Esp* ¡es un capullo integral!; *US* **s. sack** mamarracho(a)

sadden ['sædən] *vt* entristecer

saddle ['sædəl] 1 *n* (a) *(on horse)* silla *f* (de montar); *(on bicycle)* sillín *m*; **in the s.** a caballo; **this is the tenth race he has won with Dettori in the s.** es la décima carrera que gana con Dettori llevando las riendas IDIOM **to be in the s.** *(be in charge)* llevar las riendas; **to be s. sore** tener rozaduras de montar a caballo; **now she's back in the s. again** ha vuelto a tomar las riendas ►► ***s. soap*** = jabón aceitoso que se emplea para conservar el cuero; ***s. stitch*** *(in needlework)* pespunte *m*

(b) *Culin (of lamb, mutton)* silla *f*; *(of hare)* rabadilla *f*

(c) *Geog* collado *m*

2 *vt* (a) *(horse)* ensillar

(b) *Fam (lumber)* **to s. sb with sth** encajar *or Esp, Méx* encasquetar algo a alguien; **I always get saddled with doing the nasty jobs** siempre me encajan *or Esp, Méx* encasquetan a mí los trabajos más desagradables; **she was saddled with the children for the whole weekend** le encajaron *or Esp, Méx* encasquetaron los niños todo el fin de semana; **I don't want to s. myself with any more work** no quiero cargarme con más trabajo

►**saddle up** 1 *vi (rider)* ensillar

2 *vt sep (horse)* ensillar

saddlebacked ['sædlbækt] *adj (horse)* ensillado(a)

saddlebag ['sædəlbæg] *n (for horse)* alforja *f*; *(for bicycle)* cartera *f*

saddlecloth ['sædəlklɒθ] *n* sudadero *m*

saddler ['sædlə(r)] *n* guarnicionero(a) *m,f*, talabartero(a) *m,f*

saddlery ['sædlərɪ] *n* (a) *(trade)* talabartería *f* (b) *(goods)* arreos *mpl*

sadism ['seɪdɪzəm] *n* sadismo *m*

sadist ['seɪdɪst] *n* sádico(a) *m,f*

sadistic [sə'dɪstɪk] *adj* sádico(a)

sadistically [sə'dɪstɪklɪ] *adv* con sadismo, de manera sádica

sadly ['sædlɪ] *adv* (a) *(unhappily) (reply, smile)* tristemente

(b) *(regrettably)* desgraciadamente, por desgracia; **s., this is so** así es, por desgracia; **s., no one has come forward to claim the child** desgraciadamente *or* por desgracia, nadie ha salido reclamando al niño

(c) *(badly)* terriblemente, por completo; **compassion is s. lacking in our society** la compasión es algo de lo que nuestra sociedad carece por completo; **you're s. mistaken** estás muy equivocado(a); **he is s. missed** lo echamos mucho de menos, *Am* lo extrañamos mucho

sadness ['sædnɪs] *n* tristeza *f*

sado-masochism ['seɪdəʊ'mæsəkɪzəm] *n* sadomasoquismo *m*

sado-masochist ['seɪdəʊ'mæsəkɪst] *n* sadomasoquista *mf*

sado-masochistic ['seɪdəʊmæsə'kɪstɪk] *adj* sadomasoquista

SAE [eseɪ'iː] *n Br* (*abbr* **stamped addressed envelope**) sobre *m* franqueado con la dirección del remitente

safari [sə'fɑːrɪ] *n* safari *m*; **to be on s.** estar de safari; **to go on s.** ir de safari ►► ***s. jacket*** sahariana *f*; ***s. park*** safari park *m*; ***s. suit*** traje *m* de safari

safe [seɪf] 1 *n (for money)* caja *f* fuerte

2 *adj* (a) *(not dangerous) (activity, car, building, chemical)* seguro(a); **the staircase doesn't look very s.** la escalera no parece muy segura; **this part of town isn't s. at night** este barrio no es seguro de noche; **is it s. to swim here?** ¿se puede nadar (sin peligro) aquí?; **the water is perfectly s. to drink** el agua se puede beber sin problemas; **at a s. distance** a una distancia prudencial; **emissions should be kept within s. limits** el nivel de emisiones debe mantenerse dentro de límites seguros; **the bomb has been made s.** la bomba ha sido desactivada

(b) *(protected, not in danger)* seguro(a); **I don't feel s. alone at night** no me siento segura estando sola de noche; **you're s. now that I'm with you** ahora que estoy contigo estás segura; **the money's s. in the bank** el dinero está seguro en el banco; **your secret is s. with me** tu secreto muere conmigo; **s. from attack/suspicion** a salvo de cualquier ataque/sospecha

(c) *(unharmed)* ileso(a), sano(a) y salvo(a); **to come home s.** llegar a casa sano y salvo; **the money will be paid upon their s. return** el dinero será entregado una vez que regresen sanos y salvos; **to wish sb a s. journey** desear a alguien un feliz viaje *or* un viaje sin percances; **(have a) s. journey!** ¡(que tengas un) buen viaje!; **to grant sb s. passage** otorgar a alguien un salvoconducto; **s. and sound** sano(a) y salvo(a); PROV **better s. than sorry** más vale prevenir (que curar)

(d) *(secure) (place)* seguro(a); **to keep sth s.** guardar algo en lugar seguro ►► ***s. haven*** refugio *m* seguro; ***s. house*** piso *m* franco

(e) *(not risky) (investment)* seguro(a); *(option, topic of conversation)* prudente; *(estimate)* prudente, conservador(a); **it is s. to say that...** se puede decir sin temor a equivocarse que...; **it's a pretty s. assumption** *or* **bet that...** es prácticamente seguro que...; **the steak's a s. bet** el filete seguro que está bueno; **he's a s. bet for the title** puedes apostar que ganará el título; **to be on the s. side** para mayor seguridad, para ir sobre seguro; IDIOM **as s. as houses** completamente seguro(a) ►► ***s. period*** *(to avoid conception)* días *mpl* seguros, días *mpl* no fértiles; ***s. seat*** *(in parliament)* escaño *m* seguro; ***s. sex*** sexo *m* seguro *or* sin riesgo

(f) *(reliable) (driver)* seguro(a); **in s. hands** en buenas manos; **he's a s. pair of hands** *(manager, minister)* es sumamente competente

3 *adv* **to play (it) s.** ser precavido(a)

4 *exclam Br Fam (excellent)* ¡buenísimo!, *Esp* ¡guay!

safe-breaker ['seɪf'breɪkə(r)], **safe-cracker** ['seɪf'krækə(r)] *n* ladrón(ona) *m,f* de cajas fuertes

safe-conduct ['seɪf'kɒndʌkt] *n* salvoconducto *m*

safe-cracker = **safe-breaker**

safe-deposit ['seɪfdɪ'pɒzɪt] *n* cámara *f* acorazada ►► ***s. box*** caja *f* de seguridad

safeguard ['seɪfgɑːd] 1 *n* salvaguardia *f*, garantía *f*; **as a s. against abuse of the rules** como garantía contra un eventual abuso de las normas

2 *vt (sb's interests, rights)* salvaguardar; **to s. sth/sb against sth** salvaguardar a algo/alguien de algo

3 *vi* **to s. against sth** salvaguardarse *or* protegerse de algo

safekeeping ['seɪf'kiːpɪŋ] *n* **in s.** bajo custodia; **the money is in their s.** guardan el dinero en un lugar seguro; **he gave it to her for s.** se lo dio para que lo guardara en lugar seguro

safely ['seɪflɪ] *adv* (a) *(without danger)* sin riesgos; **an area where women can s. go out at night** una zona en la que las mujeres pueden salir solas de noche

(b) *(without incident)* **once the hostages have been s. returned** una vez que los rehenes hayan sido liberados sanos y salvos; **to arrive s.** *(person)* llegar sano(a) y salvo(a); *(parcel)* llegar sin daños; *(ship)* llegar a buen puerto; **once we're s. home** cuando estemos tranquilos en casa; **once I'm s. on the other side...** una vez que esté sano y salvo al otro lado...; **now that we're s. through to the next round** ahora que pasamos sin problema alguno a la ronda siguiente

(c) *(securely)* **I've put the money away s.** he guardado el dinero a buen recaudo; **the kids are s. tucked up in bed** los niños están bien arropaditos en la cama; **once he is s. behind bars** una vez que esté a buen recaudo entre rejas

(d) *(carefully)* **drive s.!** ¡conduce *or Am* maneja con cuidado!

(e) *(without risk)* con seguridad; **we can s. let her do it** podemos dejar que lo haga sin ninguna preocupación

(f) *(with certainty)* con certeza; **I can s. say that...** puedo decir sin temor a equivocarme que...; **we can s. assume he won't be back soon** podemos estar seguros de que tardará en volver

safeness ['seɪfnɪs] *n* (a) *(absence of danger)* seguridad *f*; **a feeling of s.** una sensación de seguridad (b) *(of bridge, nuclear power, electrical appliances)* seguridad *f*

safety ['seɪftɪ] *n* (a) *(prevention of danger)* seguridad *f*; **s. in the workplace** seguridad en el trabajo; **road s.** seguridad en carretera, seguridad vial; **there are fears for the s. of the hostages** se teme por la seguridad de los rehenes; **she's very s. conscious** tiene muy en cuenta la seguridad; **for s.'s sake** para mayor seguridad; **s. first!** ¡la seguridad es lo primero!; **the team decided to adopt a s. first approach** el equipo decidió no correr riesgos innecesarios; PROV **there's s. in numbers** en compañía está uno más seguro ►► ***s. belt*** cinturón *m* de seguridad; ***s. catch*** *(on gun)* seguro *m*; ***s. chain*** *(on door)* cadena *f*; *(on bracelet)* cadenita *f* de seguridad; *Theat* ***s. curtain*** telón *m* de seguridad; *Tech* ***s. factor*** factor *m* de seguridad; ***s. feature*** componente *m* de seguridad; ***s. glass*** vidrio *m* de seguridad; ***s. helmet*** casco *m* de seguridad; *US* ***s. island*** isleta *f*; ***s. lamp*** *(of miner)* lámpara *f* de seguridad; ***s. matches*** fósforos *mpl or Esp* cerillas *fpl or Am* cerillos *mpl* de seguridad; ***s. measures*** medidas *fpl* de seguridad; ***s. net*** *(in circus)* red *f* (de seguridad); *Fig* red *f* asistencial (del Estado); *Fig* **to fall through the s. net** quedar excluido(a) de la red asistencial; ***s. officer*** = persona a cargo de la seguridad en el lugar donde se desarrollan actividades peligrosas para la salud o los trabajadores; ***s. pin*** imperdible *m*, *Am* alfiler *m* de gancho, *CAm, Méx* seguro *m*; ***s. razor*** maquinilla *f* de afeitar; *also Fig* ***s. valve*** válvula *f* de escape

(b) *(absence of danger) (of activity, car, building, chemical)* seguridad *f*

(c) *(safe place)* lugar *m* seguro; **the injured were helped to s.** llevaron a los heridos a un lugar seguro; **he ran for s.** corrió a refugiarse; **to reach s.** alcanzar un lugar seguro

(d) *(in American football)* safety *m*

(e) *(in snooker)* ►► ***s. shot*** tiro *m* defensivo, = tiro cuya intención no es colar una bola en la tronera sino dejar una posición complicada al contrincante

saffron [ˈsæfrən] **1** *n* **(a)** *Bot & Culin* azafrán *m* **(b)** *(colour)* azafrán *m*
2 *adj* **(a)** *(colour)* (de color) azafrán **(b)** *Culin* ►► ***s. rice*** arroz *m* con azafrán

sag [sæg] *(pt & pp* **sagged***)* **1** *vi* **(a)** *(roof, bridge)* hundirse, ceder; *(flesh, rope)* colgar; **the bed sags in the middle** la cama se hunde en medio; **the branches sagged under the weight of the fruit** las ramas cedían bajo el peso de las frutas; **her shoulders sagged in dejection** tenía los hombros caídos por el desánimo **(b)** *(confidence, support)* decaer; *(prices, stocks, demand)* caer; **their spirits sagged** sus ánimos flaqueaban
2 *n (in mattress, ceiling)* combadura *f*

saga [ˈsɑːgə] *n (story)* saga *f*; *Fig* **a s. of corruption** una historia interminable de corrupción

sagacious [səˈgeɪʃəs] *adj Formal* **(a)** *(person)* sagaz **(b)** *(remark)* sagaz, astuto(a)

sagacity [səˈgæsɪtɪ] *n Formal* **(a)** *(of person)* sagacidad *f* **(b)** *(of remark)* sagacidad *f*, astucia *f*

sage[1] [seɪdʒ] **1** *n (wise person)* sabio(a) *m,f*
2 *adj (person, conduct)* sabio(a)

sage[2] *n* **(a)** *(herb)* salvia *f*; **s. and onion stuffing** relleno de salvia y cebolla **(b)** *(colour)* ***s. (green)*** salvia *m* verde

sagebrush [ˈseɪdʒbrʌʃ] *n* artemisa *f*

sagely [ˈseɪdʒlɪ] *adj* con sabiduría, sabiamente

saggy [ˈsægɪ] *adj (mattress)* hundido(a); *(bottom)* flácido(a), fofo(a); *(breasts)* caído(a)

Sagittarian [sædʒɪˈteərɪən] *Astrol* **1** *n* **to be a S.** ser Sagitario
2 *adj* de Sagitario, *Am* sagitariano(a)

Sagittarius [sædʒɪˈteərɪəs] *n* **(a)** *(sign of zodiac)* Sagitario *m*; **to be (a) S.** ser Sagitario **(b)** *(constellation)* Sagitario *m*

sago [ˈseɪgəʊ] *n* (fécula *f* de) sagú *m* ►► ***s. palm*** sagú *m*

Sahara [səˈhɑːrə] *n* **the S. (Desert)** el (desierto del) Sáhara

Saharan [səˈhɑːrən] *adj Geog* sahariano(a)

sahib [ˈsɑːɪb] *n* señor *m*; **Jones s.** señor Jones

said[1] *pt & pp of* **say**

said[2] *adj Formal* **the s. Howard Riley** el mencionado Howard Riley; **the s. articles** los mencionados artículos

Saigon [saɪˈgɒn] *n* Saigón

sail [seɪl] **1** *n* **(a)** *(on boat)* vela *f*; **to set s. (for)** *(boat)* zarpar (con rumbo a); *(person)* partir (en dirección a); *Naut* **in full s., with all sails set** con las velas desplegadas; *Naut* **to be under s.** ir a toda vela **(b)** *(journey)* **to go for a s.** hacer una excursión en velero; **it's a few hours' s. from here** está a unas pocas horas de navegación de aquí **(c)** *(of windmill)* aspa *f*
2 *vt* **(a)** *(boat)* gobernar; **she sailed the boat into port** llevó el bote hasta el puerto **(b)** *(the Pacific, the Atlantic, the world)* navegar por; *Literary* **to s. the seven seas** surcar los siete mares
3 *vi* **(a)** *(ship, person)* navegar; **the boat sailed up the river** el bote navegó río arriba; **it took us three days to s. to the next island** nos tomó tres días navegar hasta la próxima isla; **are you flying or sailing?** ¿vas en avión o en barco?; **they sailed around the Mediterranean** navegaron por el Mediterráneo; **to s. round a cape** circunnavegar un cabo; IDIOM **to s. close to the wind** adentrarse en terreno peligroso
(b) *(start voyage) (ship)* zarpar; *(person)* partir
(c) *(glide)* **she sailed into the room** entró en la habitación con un aire de elegancia; **the clouds sailed by** las nubes avanzaban suavemente; **a sports car sailed past me** me pasó un deportivo con suma facilidad; **his book sailed out of the window** su libro salió volando por la ventana; *Fam* **to s. through an examination** pasar un examen con mucha facilidad *or Esp* con la gorra *or RP* de taquito

► **sail into** *vt insep Fam (attack verbally)* arremeter contra

sailboard [ˈseɪlbɔːd] *n* tabla *f* de windsurf

sailboarder [ˈseɪlbɔːdə(r)] *n* windsurfista *mf*

sailboarding [ˈseɪlbɔːdɪŋ] *n* windsurf *m*

sailboat [ˈseɪlbəʊt] *n US* velero *m*

sailcloth [ˈseɪlklɒθ] *n* lona *f*

sailfish [ˈseɪlfɪʃ] *n* pez *m* vela

sailing [ˈseɪlɪŋ] *n* **(a)** *(activity)* (navegación *f* a) vela *f*; **to go s.** ir a navegar ►► *Br* ***s. boat*** (barco *m*) velero *m*; ***s. ship*** barco *m* de vela **(b)** *(departure)* salida *f*; **we're going on the 12 o'clock s.** nos vamos en el barco de las doce

sailor [ˈseɪlə(r)] *n (crew member)* marinero *m*; *Sport* navegante *mf*; **to be a good/bad s.** soportar bien/mal los viajes por mar ►► ***s. hat*** gorra *f* marinera; ***s. suit*** traje *m* de marinero *(de niño)*

sailplane [ˈseɪlpleɪn] *n* planeador *m*

saint [seɪnt]

> **santa** is used for female saints, and **san** is used for male saints except in the case of Domingo, Tomás, Tomé and Toribio, where **santo** is used instead: Santa Teresa, San Pablo, Santo Domingo

n **(a)** *Rel* santo(a) *m,f*; **All Saints' (Day)** día *m* de Todos los Santos ►► ***S. Bernard*** *(dog)* San Bernardo *m*; ***s.'s day*** onomástica *f*, santo *m*; ***S. Helena*** *(island)* Santa Elena; ***S. John the Baptist*** San Juan Bautista; ***S. John's wort*** hierba *f* de San Juan; ***S. Kitts and Nevis*** *(island group)* San Cristóbal y Nevis; ***S. Lucia*** *(island)* Santa Lucía; ***S. Vincent and the Grenadines*** *(island group)* San Vicente y las Granadinas; *Med* ***S. Vitus's dance*** baile *m* de San Vito
(b) *(good person)* santo(a) *m,f*; **she's an absolute s.** es una santa; **I'm no s.** no soy ningún santo

sainthood [ˈseɪnthʊd] *n* santidad *f*

saintlike [ˈseɪntlaɪk] *adj* de santo(a)

saintly [ˈseɪntlɪ] *adj* **(a)** *(person, life, virtue)* santo(a) **(b)** *(smile, air)* angelical

sake[1] [seɪk] *n* **for the s. of sb, for sb's s.** por (el bien de) alguien; **I didn't do it for your s.** no lo hice por ti; **I did it for my own s.** lo hice por mi propio bien; **they decided not to divorce for the s. of the children** decidieron no divorciarse por el bien de los niños; **for all our sakes, tell no one** por el bien de todos, no se lo cuentes a nadie; **for God's** *or* **goodness'** *or* **heaven's** *or* **Christ's** *or* **pity's s.** por (el amor de) Dios; **for the s. of peace** para que haya paz; **for old times' s.** por los viejos tiempos; **for Pete's s.!** *(expresses annoyance)* ¡caramba!; **this is talking for talking's s.** *or* **for the s. of it** es hablar por hablar; **art for art's s.** el arte por el arte; **for the s. of argument, let's assume it costs £100** pongamos por caso que cuesta 100 libras

sake[2] [ˈsɑːkɪ] *n (drink)* sake *m*

sal [sæl] *n Chem* sal *f* ►► ***s. ammoniac*** sal *f* amónica

salaam [səˈlɑːm] **1** *n* zalema *f*
2 *vi* saludar haciendo una zalema *or* reverencia
3 *exclam* ¡salve!

salacious [səˈleɪʃəs] *adj* salaz

salaciousness [səˈleɪʃəsnɪs] *n* salacidad *f*, lascivia *f*

salad [ˈsæləd] *n* ensalada *f* ►► ***s. bar*** *(restaurant)* bar *m* de ensaladas; *(area)* mostrador *m* de ensaladas; ***s. bowl*** ensaladera *f*; *Br* ***s. cream*** = especie de mayonesa un poco dulce para ensaladas; ***s. days*** tiempos *mpl* mozos; ***s. dressing*** aderezo *m or Esp* aliño *m* para la ensalada; ***s. spinner*** escurridor *m* de lechuga

salamander [ˈsæləmændə(r)] *n* salamandra *f*

salami [səˈlɑːmɪ] *n* salami *m*, *Am* salame *m*; *Fam Hum* **to play hide the s.** *(have sex)* echar un casquete

salami-slice [səˈlɑːmɪslaɪs] *vt Fig* recortar gradualmente

salaried [ˈsælərɪd] *adj* asalariado(a); **a s. employee** un asalariado

salary [ˈsælərɪ] *n* salario *m*, sueldo *m*; **s. cut/review** reducción/revisión salarial; **I have to bring up a family on a teacher's s.** tengo que educar una familia con el sueldo de un profesor ►► ***s. earner*** asalariado(a) *m,f*; ***s. grade*** nivel *m or* grado *m* salarial; ***s. scale*** escala *f* salarial

salchow [ˈsælkəʊ] *n (in ice skating)* salko *m*; **double/triple s.** doble/triple salko

sale [seɪl] *n* **(a)** *(action of selling)* venta *f*; **to make a s.** realizar una venta, vender algo; **for s.** *(available)* en venta; *(sign)* se vende; **that article is not for s.** ese artículo no está a la venta; **to put sth up for s.** poner algo en venta; **on s.** a la venta; **on s. at a supermarket near you** a la venta en su supermercado más próximo; **to go on s.** salir *or* ponerse a la venta; **s. or return** venta en depósito; **we bought the goods on a s. or return basis** compramos la mercancía con la condición de que podíamos devolver lo que no se vendiera ►► ***s. price*** precio *m* de venta; *Br* ***sales assistant*** dependiente(a) *m,f*; ***sales brochure*** folleto *m* promocional; ***sales conference*** conferencia *f* de ventas; ***sales department*** departamento *m* de ventas; ***sales director*** director(ora) *m,f* de ventas; ***sales drive*** promoción *f* de ventas; ***sales executive*** ejecutivo(a) *m,f* de ventas; ***sales force*** personal *m* de ventas; ***sales manager*** jefe(a) *m,f* de ventas; ***sales office*** oficina *f* de ventas; ***sales outlet*** punto *m* de venta; ***sales pitch*** estrategia *f* de ventas; ***sales promotion*** promoción *f* de ventas; ***sales representative*** *or Fam* ***rep*** (representante *mf*) comercial *mf*; *US* ***sales slip*** recibo *m*; ***sales talk*** charla *f* de ventas; ***sales team*** equipo *m* de ventas; ***s. of work*** mercadillo *m* benéfico (de artesanía)
(b) sales *(turnover)* ventas *fpl* ►► ***sales figures*** cifra *f* de ventas;

sales forecast previsión *f* de ventas; ***sales target*** objetivo *m* de ventas; ***sales tax*** impuesto *m* de venta

(c) *(auction)* subasta *f*; **book s.** mercadillo de libros

(d) *(with reduced prices)* rebajas *fpl*; **the sales** las rebajas; **there's a s. on at Woolworths** están de rebajas en Woolworths; **this offer does not apply to s. items** *or* **goods** esta promoción no incluye a los productos de oferta ►► ***s. price*** precio *m* rebajado

(e) *(department)* **he works in sales** trabaja en el departamento de ventas

saleable ['seɪləbəl] *adj* vendible

saleroom ['seɪlru:m], *US* **salesroom** ['seɪlzru:m] *n (for auctions)* sala *f* de subastas

salesclerk ['seɪlzklз:k] *n US* dependiente(a) *m,f*, vendedor(ora) *m,f*

salesgirl ['seɪlzgз:l] *n* dependienta *f*

salesman ['seɪlzmən] *n (for company)* comercial *m*, vendedor *m*; *(in shop)* dependiente *m*, vendedor *m*

salesmanship ['seɪlzmənʃɪp] *n* habilidad *f* para vender; **high-pressure** *or* **aggressive s.** técnica de ventas agresiva

salesperson ['seɪlzpз:sən] *n (for company)* comercial *mf*, vendedor(ora) *m,f*; *(in shop)* dependiente(a) *m,f*, vendedor(ora) *m,f*

salesroom *US* = **saleroom**

saleswoman ['seɪlzwʊmən] *n (for company)* comercial *f*, vendedora *f*; *(in shop)* dependienta *f*, vendedora *f*

salicin, salicine ['sælɪsɪn] *n Pharm* salicina *f*

salicylic [sælɪ'sɪlɪk] *adj Chem* salicílico(a) ►► ***s. acid*** ácido *m* salicílico

salient ['seɪlɪənt] *adj (feature, fault)* relevante, sobresaliente; **s. points** puntos más sobresalientes

saline ['seɪlaɪn] **1** *adj* salino(a) ►► *Med* ***s. drip*** gota a gota *m* de suero (fisiológico); ***s. solution*** solución *f* salina, suero *m* fisiológico

2 *n Med (salt solution)* solución *f* salina, suero *m* fisiológico

salinity [sə'lɪnətɪ] *n* salinidad *f*

saliva [sə'laɪvə] *n* saliva *f*

salivary [sə'laɪvərɪ] *adj* salival, salivar ►► ***s. gland*** glándula *f* salivar *or* salival

salivate ['sælɪveɪt] *vi* salivar, segregar saliva; *Fig* **he was salivating over the prospect of meeting her** se le hacía la boca agua pensando en que iba a verla

salivation [sælɪ'veɪʃən] *n* salivación *f*

sallow ['sæləʊ] *adj (complexion)* amarillento(a)

sallowness ['sæləʊnɪs] *n (of complexion)* aspecto *m* amarillento

sally ['sælɪ] *n* (a) *Mil* misión *f*, incursión *f* (b) *(excursion)* salida *f*, excursión *f*; **his first s. into travel writing** su primera incursión como escritor en la literatura de viajes

► **sally forth** *(pt & pp* **sallied**) *vi Literary* partir con determinación

Sally Army [sælɪ'ɑ:mɪ] *n Br Fam (Salvation Army)* Ejército *m* de Salvación

salmon ['sæmən] *(pl* **salmon**) **1** *n* (a) *(fish)* salmón *m* ►► ***s. farm*** criadero *m* de salmones; ***s. ladder*** *or* ***leap*** salmonera *f (rampa)*; ***s. steak*** filete *m* de salmón; ***s. trout*** trucha *f* asalmonada (b) *(colour)* **s. (pink)** color *m* salmón

2 *adj (colour)* salmón

salmonella [sælmə'nelə] *n (bacteria)* salmonella *f*; *(illness)* salmonelosis *f inv* ►► ***s. poisoning*** intoxicación *f* por salmonella

salon ['sælɒn] *n* **(beauty) s.** salón *m* de belleza; **(hairdressing) s.** (salón *m* de) peluquería *f*

Salonika [sə'lɒnɪkə] *n* Salónica, Tesalónica

saloon [sə'lu:n] *n* (a) *(room)* sala *f*, salón *m* (b) *US (bar)* bar *m* (c) *Br (in pub, hotel)* **s. (bar)** = en ciertos "pubs" y hoteles, bar más caro y elegante que el resto (d) *Br* **s. (car)** turismo *m*; **a four-door s.** una berlina

salopettes [sælə'pets] *npl* pantalones *mpl* de esquí

salsa ['sælsə] *n* (a) *(music, dance)* salsa *f* (b) *(food)* salsa *f* picante *or* brava

salsify ['sælsɪfɪ] *n* salsifí *m*

SALT [sɔ:lt] *n (abbr* **Strategic Arms Limitation Talks**) SALT *fpl*

salt [sɔ:lt] **1** *n* (a) *(substance)* sal *f*; **there's too much s. in the soup** la sopa tiene demasiada sal; **(bath) salts** sales de baño ►► *US* ***s. box*** *(house)* = casa colonial de Nueva Inglaterra de dos pisos; ***s. flat*** salina *f*; ***s. lake*** lago *m* salado; ***s. lick*** *(place)* salegar *m*; ***s. marsh*** salar *m*; ***s. mine*** mina *f* de sal, salina *f*; ***s. pan*** salina *f*; *US* ***s. shaker*** salero *m*

(b) *Chem* sal *f*

(c) *Fam (sailor)* **an old s.** un lobo de mar

(d) IDIOMS **to take a story with a pinch** *or* **grain of s.** no creerse del todo una historia; **no journalist worth his s....** ningún periodista que se precie...; **to rub s. in sb's wounds** removerle la herida a alguien; **the fifth goal was just rubbing s. into the wound** el quinto gol no hizo más que hurgar en la herida; **the s. of the earth** la sal de la tierra

2 *adj (taste)* salado(a); *(air)* salobre ►► ***s. beef*** salazón *f* de ternera; ***s. cod*** bacalao *m* (salado); ***s. pork*** tocino *m*, panceta *f*; ***s. water*** agua *f* salada

3 *vt* (a) *(food)* salar (b) *(roads)* esparcir sal en

► **salt away** *vt sep (money)* ahorrar *or* guardar en secreto

► **salt down** *vt sep (food)* salar

saltcellar ['sɔ:ltselə(r)] *n* salero *m*

salted ['sɔ:ltɪd] *adj* (a) *(preserved)* en salazón (b) *(flavoured)* salado(a), con sal

salt-free ['sɔ:lt'fri:] *adj* sin sal

saltiness ['sɔ:ltɪnɪs] *n* (a) *(of food)* sabor *m* salado (b) *(salinity)* salinidad *f*

saltire ['sɔ:ltaɪə(r)] *n* cruz *f or* aspa *f* de San Andrés, sotuer *m*

saltpetre, *US* **saltpeter** [sɔ:lt'pi:tə(r)] *n* salitre *m*

saltwater ['sɔ:ltwɔ:tə(r)] *adj* ***s. fish*** pez *m* de agua salada; ***s. lake*** lago *m* de agua salada

saltworks ['sɔ:ltwз:ks] *n* salinas *fpl*, refinería *f* de sal

saltwort ['sɔ:ltwз:t] *n Bot* caramillo *m*, *RP* cardo *m* ruso

salty ['sɔ:ltɪ] *adj* (a) *(taste, food)* salado(a) (b) *Old-fashioned (joke, wit)* picante

salubrious [sə'lu:brɪəs] *adj Formal* (a) *(respectable)* acomodado(a), respetable (b) *(hygienic)* salubre

salubriousness [sə'lu:brɪəsnɪs] *n Formal* (a) *(respectability)* respetabilidad *f* (b) *(hygiene)* salubridad *f*

saluki [sə'lu:kɪ] *n* saluki *m*

salutary ['sæljʊtərɪ] *adj* saludable; **to have a s. effect on sb** tener un efecto saludable sobre alguien

salutation [sæljʊ'teɪʃən] *n Formal* (a) *(greeting)* salutación *f*, saludo *m* (b) *(in letter)* encabezamiento *m*

salute [sə'lu:t] **1** *n* (a) *(with hand)* saludo *m*; **to give sb a s.** saludar a alguien; **to take the s.** pasar revista a las tropas (en desfile) (b) *(with guns)* **(to fire) a ten gun s.** (disparar) una salva de diez cañonazos (c) *(tribute)* homenaje *m* (**to** a)

2 *vt* (a) *(with hand)* saludar; **to s. the flag** saludar la bandera (b) *(pay tribute to) (person)* homenajear; *(achievements)* rendir homenaje a

3 *vi* saludar

Salvadoran [sælvə'dɔ:rən], **Salvadorean** [sælvə'dɔ:rɪən] **1** *n* salvadoreño(a) *m,f*

2 *adj* salvadoreño(a)

salvage ['sælvɪdʒ] **1** *n* (a) *(of ship)* rescate *m*, salvamento *m*; *(of waste material)* recuperación *f* ►► ***s. operation*** operación *f* de rescate *or* salvamento; ***s. vessel*** buque *m* de salvamento (b) *(objects salvaged)* material *m* rescatado (c) *(fee)* derechos *mpl* de salvamento

2 *vt* (a) *(vessel, cargo, belongings)* salvar, rescatar; *(waste material)* recuperar; **a counter salvaged from an old butcher's shop** un mostrador rescatado de una antigua carnicería

(b) *(marriage, reputation, career)* salvar, rescatar; **she managed to s. her self-respect** logró mantener a flote su dignidad; **the team managed to s. a draw** el equipo consiguió salvar un empate; **his inspired suggestion salvaged the situation** su muy inspirada sugerencia salvó la situación

salvageable ['sælvɪdʒəbəl] *adj* (a) *(vessel, cargo, belongings, waste material)* recuperable (b) *(marriage, reputation, career)* salvable

salvation [sæl'veɪʃən] *n* (a) *Rel* salvación *f* ►► ***S. Army*** Ejército *m* de Salvación (b) *(deliverance)* salvación *f*; **this thermos flask was my s. when I was stuck up the mountain** este termo fue mi salvación cuando me quedé atrapado en la montaña

salvationist [sæl'veɪʃənɪst] *n* (a) *(member of evangelical sect)* evangelista *mf* (b) *(member of Salvation Army)* salvacionista *mf*

salve [sælv] **1** *n* (a) *(ointment)* ungüento *m*, bálsamo *m* (b) *(relief)* alivio *m*; **I sent her the chocolates as a s. to my conscience** le envié chocolates para aliviar mi conciencia

2 *vt* **to s. one's conscience** descargar la conciencia

salver ['sælvə(r)] *n (tray)* bandeja *f*, fuente *f*; **a silver s.** una bandeja de plata

salvo ['sælvəʊ] *(pl* **salvos** *or* **salvoes**) *n* (a) *Mil* salva *f* (b) *(of applause, laughter, insults)* salva *f*; **in her opening s., she criticized the government's record on health** comenzó criticando la gestión del gobierno en materia de salud

SAM [sæm] *n (abbr* **surface-to-air missile**) SAM *m*

Samaritan [sə'mærɪtən] *n (helpful person)* samaritano(a) *m,f*; **I wish you'd stop being such a good S.** me gustaría que dejaras de obrar como el buen samaritano; **the Good S.** el Buen Samaritano; **the Samaritans** los Samaritanos, *Esp* ≃ el Teléfono de la Esperanza

samarium [sə'meərɪəm] *n Chem* samario *m*

samba ['sæmbə] **1** *n (music, dance)* samba *f*
2 *vi* bailar la samba, sambar

sambo ['sæmbəʊ] *n Br very Fam Old-fashioned* (**a**) *(black person)* negro(a) *m,f* (**b**) *(form of address to black person)* negro(a) *m,f*

SAME [seɪm] **1** *adj* **the s. man** el mismo hombre; **the s. woman** la misma mujer; **the s. children** los mismos niños; **the s. one** el mismo, la misma; **are they the s. people who robbed you?** ¿son los (mismos) que te robaron?; **would you do the s. thing for me?** ¿harías lo mismo por mí?; **she's the s. old Susan** es la Susan de siempre; **at the s. time** *(simultaneously)* al mismo tiempo; *(nevertheless)* sin embargo; **in the s. way** *(likewise)* del mismo modo, de igual forma; **the** *or* **that very s. day** el *or* ese mismo día; **it all amounts** *or* **comes to the s. thing** todo viene a ser lo mismo; **I feel the s. way about it** yo pienso lo mismo; **to go the s. way** ir por el mismo camino; *Fam* **s. difference!** ¡igual da!
2 *pron* **the s.** lo mismo; **the two vases are exactly the s.** los dos jarrones son idénticos; **I would have done the s.** yo hubiera hecho lo mismo; **how do you feel? – the s.** ¿cómo te encuentras? – igual; **the s. is true of..., the s. holds for...** lo mismo vale para...; **it's the s. everywhere** es igual en todas partes; **he's the s. as ever** es el mismo de siempre; **the house isn't the s. without her** la casa no es la misma sin ella; **he had an accident and he's never been the s. since** sufrió un accidente y desde entonces no ha vuelto a ser el mismo; **things will never be the s. again** las cosas no volverán a ser igual *or* lo mismo; **both words are spelt the s.** las dos palabras se escriben igual; **to think/taste the s.** pensar/saber igual; **they say we look the s.** dicen que nos parecemos; *Formal* **construction of one oak table and delivery of s.** construcción de una mesa de roble y entrega de la misma; **men are all the s.!** ¡todos los hombres son iguales!; **it's all the s. to me** me da igual *or* lo mismo; **if it's all the s. to you** si no te importa; **all the s.** *(nevertheless)* de todas maneras; **we are hoping for more of the s.** esperamos más de lo mismo; **the two are much the s.** se parecen bastante; **they are one and the s.** *(thing)* son una sola cosa; *(person)* son la misma persona; *Fam* **(the) s. again?** *(in pub)* ¿(otra de) lo mismo?; *Fam* **s. here!** *(I agree)* estoy de acuerdo; *(I did the same thing)* yo también; *Fam* **(the) s. to you!** ¡lo mismo digo!; **are you Mr Jackson? – yes, the very s.** ¿usted es Mr Jackson? – el mismísimo
3 *adv Fam (alike)* igual; **I need affection, s. as anybody else** necesito cariño, como todo el mundo; **s. as ever** como siempre

same-day ['seɪmdeɪ] *adj Com* ***s. delivery*** entrega *f* en el día

sameness ['seɪmnɪs] *n* (**a**) *(similarity)* similaridad *f*, parecido *m* (**b**) *(tedium)* monotonía *f*

same-sex ['seɪm'seks] *adj* homosexual

samey ['seɪmɪ] *adj Fam* monótono(a); **their songs are a bit s.** sus canciones suenan todas muy parecidas

samisen ['sæmɪsen] *n Mus* samisén *m*

samizdat ['sæmɪzdæt] *n* publicación *f* clandestina

Samoa [sə'məʊə] *n* Samoa

Samoan [sə'məʊən] **1** *n* (**a**) *(person)* samoano(a) *m,f* (**b**) *(language)* samoano *m*
2 *adj* samoano(a)

samosa [sə'məʊsə] *n* samosa *f*, = empanadilla de carne o verduras de la cocina india

samovar ['sæməvɑː(r)] *n* samovar *m*

Samoyed [sə'mɔɪəd] (*pl* **Samoyed** *or* **Samoyeds**) *n (dog)* samoyedo *mf*

sampan ['sæmpæn] *n* sampán *m*

samphire ['sæmfaɪə(r)] *n* **(rock) s.** hinojo *m* marino

sample ['sɑːmpəl] **1** *n* (**a**) *(of blood, urine, soil)* muestra *f*; **a water/rock s.** una muestra de agua/roca; **to take a s.** tomar una muestra
(**b**) *(of product)* muestra *f*; **a free s.** una muestra gratuita; **a s. bottle/pack** una botella/un paquete de muestra ▸▸ ***s. size*** tamaño *m* muestral
(**c**) *(example)* ejemplo *m*, muestra *f*; **please bring a s. of your work** por favor, traiga una muestra de su trabajo; **a s. question from last year's exam paper** una pregunta de muestra del examen del año pasado
(**d**) *(in statistics)* muestra *f*; **a representative s. of the population** una muestra representativa de la población
(**e**) *Mus* muestra *f*
2 *vt* (**a**) *(rock, water, soil)* tomar muestras de (**b**) *(food)* probar (**c**) *(experience)* probar; **I had never sampled the delights of Lebanese cuisine** nunca había probado las delicias de la cocina libanesa (**d**) *(public opinion)* sondear (**e**) *Mus* samplear

sampler ['sɑːmplə(r)] *n* (**a**) *(selection of samples)* muestra *f*, selección *f* (**b**) *(embroidery)* dechado *m* (**c**) *Mus* sampler *m*

sampling ['sɑːmplɪŋ] *n* (**a**) *(of rock, water, soil)* toma *f* de muestras, muestreo *m* (**b**) *(in statistical research)* muestreo *m* ▸▸ ***s. error*** error *m* de muestreo (**c**) *Mus* sampleado *m*

Samson ['sæmsən] *pr n* Sansón

samurai ['sæmʊraɪ] (*pl* **inv**) **1** *n* samurái *m*
2 *adj* de samurái

San Andreas Fault ['sænæn'dreɪəs'fɔːlt] *n Geol* **the S.** la falla de San Andrés

sanatorium [sænə'tɔːrɪəm], *US* **sanitarium** [sænɪ'teərɪəm] (*pl* **sanatoriums** *or* **sanatoria** [sænə'tɔːrɪə], *US* **sanitariums** *or* **sanitaria** [sænɪ'teərɪə]) *n* sanatorio *m*

sancta *pl of* **sanctum**

sanctification [sæŋktɪfɪ'keɪʃən] *n* santificación *f*

sanctify ['sæŋ(k)tɪfaɪ] *vt* santificar

sanctimonious [sæŋ(k)tɪ'məʊnɪəs] *adj* mojigato(a)

sanctimoniously [sæŋ(k)tɪ'məʊnɪəslɪ] *adv* con mojigatería

sanctimoniousness [sæŋktɪ'məʊnjəsnɪs], **sanctimony** ['sæŋ(k)tɪmənɪ] *n* mojigatería *f*

sanction ['sæŋ(k)ʃən] **1** *n* (**a**) *(penalty)* sanción *f*; **(economic) sanctions** sanciones *fpl* económicas; **to impose (economic) sanctions on a country** imponer sanciones (económicas) a un país ▸▸ ***sanctions busting:*** **the firm was accused of sanctions busting** acusaron a la empresa de violar las sanciones (**b**) *Formal (consent)* sanción *f*; **it hasn't yet been given official s.** aún no ha recibido sanción oficial
2 *vt Formal* (**a**) *(authorize)* sancionar, autorizar (**b**) *(approve) (behaviour)* sancionar

sanctity ['sæŋ(k)tɪtɪ] *n (of life)* carácter *m* sagrado; *(of home)* santidad *f*; **the s. of marriage** la inviolabilidad del matrimonio

sanctuary ['sæŋ(k)tjʊərɪ] *n* (**a**) *Rel* santuario *m* (**b**) *(for fugitive, refugee)* asilo *m*, refugio *m*; **to seek s.** buscar refugio; **to take s.** refugiarse (**c**) *(for birds, wildlife)* santuario *m*; **a wildlife s.** una reserva natural

sanctum ['sæŋktəm] (*pl* **sancta** ['sæŋktə] *or* **sanctums**) *n* (**a**) *(holy place)* lugar *m* sagrado, sagrario *m* (**b**) *(private place)* **inner s.** sanctasanctórum *m*

sand [sænd] **1** *n* arena *f*; **the sands** *(beach)* la playa; **miles of golden sands** kilómetros de playas doradas; **the sands (of time) are running out for us** se nos está acabando el tiempo; ▸▸ ***s. dune*** duna *f*; ***s. eel*** caduchón *m*; ***s. flea*** *(sandhopper)* pulga *f* de mar; ***s. martin*** avión *m* zapador *(ave)*; *US* ***s. trap*** *(in golf)* búnker *m*; ***s. wedge*** *(in golf)* wedge *m* para arena; ***s. yacht*** triciclo *m* a vela
2 *vt* (**a**) *(smooth with sandpaper)* lijar (**b**) *(cover with sand)* enarenar

▸**sand down** *vt sep (wood)* lijar

sandal ['sændəl] *n* sandalia *f*, *Andes, CAm* ojota *f*, *Méx* guarache *m*

sandalwood ['sændəlwʊd] *n* (**a**) *(tree)* sándalo *m* (**b**) *(wood)* (madera *f* de) sándalo *m*

sandbag ['sændbæg] **1** *n* saco *m* terrero, saco *m* de arena, *RP* bolsa *f* de arena
2 *vt* (*pt & pp* **sandbagged**) proteger con sacos terreros

sandbank ['sændbæŋk] *n* banco *m* de arena

sandbar ['sændbɑː(r)] *n (of river)* bajío *m*, barra *f*

sandblast ['sændblɑːst] *vt* limpiar con chorro de arena

sandblaster ['sændblɑːstə(r)] *n* limpiadora *f* de chorro de arena

sandbox ['sændbɒks] *n* (**a**) *US (for children)* recinto *m* de arena (**b**) *Rail* arenero *m*

sandboy ['sændbɔɪ] *n* IDIOM *Br* **as happy as a s.** como un niño con zapatos nuevos

sandcastle ['sændkɑːsəl] *n* castillo *m* de arena

sander ['sændə(r)] *n (device)* acuchillador(ora) *m,f* de suelos

sanderling ['sændəlɪŋ] *n* correlimos *m inv* tridáctilo

sandfly ['sændflaɪ] *n* jején *m*

sandgrouse ['sændgraʊs] *n* ganga *f*

sandhill crane ['sændhɪl'kreɪn] *n* grulla *f* canadiense

sandhopper ['sændhɒpə(r)] *n* pulga *f* de mar

sandiness ['sændɪnɪs] *n* arenosidad *f*

sanding ['sændɪŋ] *n* (**a**) *(of wood, plaster)* lijado *m*, pulido *m* (**b**) *(of roads)* enarenado *m*

sandlot ['sændlɒt] *US* **1** *n* = solar abandonado utilizado para jugar a béisbol y otros deportes
2 *adj (amateur)* amateur, aficionado(a)

sandman ['sændmæn] *n* **the s.** *(in folklore)* = personaje de cuento que hace dormir a los niños

sandpaper ['sændpeɪpə(r)] **1** *n* (papel *m* de) lija *f*
2 *vt* lijar

sandpiper ['sændpaɪpə(r)] *n* andarríos *m inv* chico; **common s.** andarríos chico; **curlew s.** correlimos zarapitín; **purple s.** correlimos oscuro

sandpit ['sændpɪt] *n Br (for children)* recinto *m* de arena

sandshoe ['sændʃu:] *n Br, Austr* playera *f*

sandstone ['sændstəʊn] *n* arenisca *f*

sandstorm ['sændstɔ:m] *n* tormenta *f* de arena

sandwich ['sændwɪtʃ] **1** *n* **(a)** *(with sliced bread)* sándwich *m*; *(with French bread) Esp* bocadillo *m*, *Am* sándwich *m*, *CSur* sándwiche *m*, *Col* sánduche *m*, *Méx* torta *f*; IDIOM *Br Fam Hum* **to be one s.** *or* **a few sandwiches short of a picnic** estar mal de la azotea, *Esp* tener algún tornillo de menos ►► *Br* ***s. bar*** sandwichería *f*; ***s. board*** cartelón *m (de hombre anuncio)*; ***s.(-board) man*** hombre *m* anuncio; ***s. box*** fiambrera *f*, tartera *f*, *Am* vianda *f*; *Educ* ***s. course*** curso *m* de formación en alternancia, = curso que combina la formación teórica con la práctica laboral; ***s. filling*** relleno *m*; ***S. Islands*** Islas *fpl* Sandwich; ***s. tern*** charrán *m* patinegro; ***s. toaster*** sandwichera *f*, *RP* carlitera *f*
(b) *Br (cake)* **a sponge s.** un bizcochuelo relleno con mermelada y crema
2 *vt* intercalar; **I was sandwiched between two buses** quedé atrapado entre dos autobuses; **I'll try to s. you between the last two appointments** te intentaré hacer un hueco entre mis dos últimas citas

sandworm ['sændwɜ:m] *n* lombriz *f* arenera

sandy ['sændɪ] *adj* **(a)** *(earth, beach)* arenoso(a) **(b)** *(covered in sand) (clothes, feet)* lleno(a) de arena **(c)** *(hair)* rubio(a) rojizo(a)

sane [seɪn] *adj* **(a)** *(not mad)* cuerdo(a); **how do you manage to stay s. in this environment?** ¿cómo haces para no volverte loco en este ambiente? **(b)** *(sensible)* juicioso(a)

> **False friend**: The Spanish adjective **sano** is not a translation for the English word **sane**. In Spanish **sano** means "healthy", "sound" or "intact".

sanely ['seɪnlɪ] *adv (sensibly)* sensatamente

San Franciscan ['sænfrən'sɪskən] **1** *n* persona de San Francisco
2 *adj* de San Francisco

San Francisco ['sænfrən'sɪskəʊ] *n* San Francisco

sang *pt of* **sing**

sangfroid ['sɒŋ'frwɑ:] *n* sangre *f* fría

sangria [sæŋ'grɪə] *n* sangría *f*

sanguinary ['sæŋgwɪnərɪ] *adj Literary (murderer, tyrant, battle)* sanguinario(a)

sanguine ['sæŋgwɪn] *adj Formal* **(a)** *(optimistic)* optimista; **he was s. about the company's prospects** confiaba plenamente en las perspectivas de la empresa **(b)** *Literary (ruddy) (complexion)* sanguíneo(a)

sanitarium *US* = **sanatorium**

sanitary ['sænɪtərɪ] *adj* **(a)** *(clean)* higiénico(a); **the kitchen didn't look very s.** la cocina no parecía muy higiénica
(b) *(relating to hygiene)* sanitario(a) ►► ***s. disposal bag*** bolsa *f* para desechos sanitarios; ***s. engineer*** ingeniero(a) *m,f* sanitario(a); ***s. engineering*** ingeniería *f* civil de salud pública *or* de saneamiento; ***s. inspector*** inspector(ora) *m,f* de sanidad; *US* ***s. napkin***, *Br* ***s. towel*** compresa *f*, *Am* toalla *f* higiénica

sanitation [sænɪ'teɪʃən] *n* **(a)** *(public health)* salud *f* pública, salubridad *f* **(b)** *(waste removal systems)* saneamiento *m* ►► *US* ***s. worker*** recolector(ora) *m,f* de residuos, basurero(a) *m,f*

sanitize ['sænɪtaɪz] *vt* **(a)** *(document, biography)* mutilar, meter la tijera a; **a sanitized account of events** un relato de los hechos demasiado aséptico **(b)** *(disinfect)* desinfectar

sanity ['sænɪtɪ] *n* **(a)** *(mental health)* cordura *f*; **to keep one's s.** no perder el juicio *or* la razón, mantener la cordura; **to lose one's s.** perder el juicio **(b)** *(good sense)* sensatez *f*; **in the end, s. prevailed** al final predominó la sensatez

> **False friend**: The Spanish noun **sanidad** is not a translation for the English word **sanity**. In Spanish **sanidad** means "health" or "health service".

sank *pt of* **sink**

San Marino ['sænmə'ri:nəʊ] *n* San Marino

San Salvador ['sæn'sælvədɔ:(r)] *n* San Salvador

sanserif [sæn'serɪf], **sans serif** *Typ n* sans serif *m*

Sanskrit ['sænskrɪt] **1** *n* sánscrito *m*
2 *adj* sánscrito(a)

Santa (Claus) ['sæntə('klɔ:z)] *n* Papá *m* Noel

Santiago [sæntɪ'ɑ:gəʊ] *n* Santiago de Chile

Santo Domingo ['sæntəʊdə'mɪŋgəʊ] *n* Santo Domingo

santonin ['sæntənɪn] *n Chem* santonina *f*

Sao Paulo [saʊ'paʊləʊ] *n* São Paulo, *RP* San Pablo

Sao Tomé and Principe ['saʊtə'meɪən'prɪnsɪpeɪ] *n* Santo Tomé y Príncipe

sap[1] [sæp] *n (of plant)* savia *f*

sap[2] *n Fam (gullible person)* papanatas *mf inv*, *Esp* pardillo(a) *m,f*; **you s.!** ¡papanatas!

sap[3] *US Fam* **1** *n (cosh)* cachiporra *f*
2 *vt (cosh)* golpear con una cachiporra

sap[4] *(pt & pp* **sapped)** **1** *n (trench)* zanja *f*, trinchera *f*
2 *vt* **(a)** *Mil* cavar **(b)** *(undermine)* minar, debilitar; **the fever has sapped (him of) his strength** la fiebre lo ha debilitado mucho

sapele [sə'pi:lɪ] *n* **(a)** *(tree)* sapeli *m* **(b)** *(wood)* sapeli *m*

saphead ['sæphed] *n US Fam* bobo(a) *m,f*, *Esp* memo(a) *m,f*

sapient ['seɪpjənt] *adj Formal* sapiente

sapling ['sæplɪŋ] *n* pimpollo *m*, árbol *m* joven

sapodilla [sæpə'dɪlə] *n* **(a)** *(tree)* zapote *m* **(b)** *(fruit)* zapote *m*

saponin ['sæpənɪn] *n Chem* saponina *f*

sapper ['sæpə(r)] *n Mil* zapador(ora) *m,f*

Sapphic ['sæfɪk] *adj Literary (lesbian)* sáfico(a)

sapphire ['sæfaɪə(r)] **1** *n* **(a)** *(precious stone)* zafiro *m*; **a s. ring** un anillo de zafiro **(b)** *(colour)* azul *m* zafiro
2 *adj (colour)* zafiro ►► ***s. blue*** azul *m* zafiro

sappy ['sæpɪ] *adj US Fam* **(a)** *(stupid)* bobo(a), *Esp* memo(a) **(b)** *(corny)* cursi, sensiblero(a)

saraband(e) ['særəbænd] *n* zarabanda *f*

Saracen ['særəsən] **1** *n* sarraceno(a) *m,f*
2 *adj* sarraceno(a)

Saragossa [særə'gɒsə] *n* Zaragoza

Sarajevo [særə'jeɪveʊ] *n* Sarajevo

Saran wrap® [sə'ræn'ræp] *n US* plástico *m* transparente *(para envolver alimentos)*

sarcasm ['sɑ:kæzəm] *n* sarcasmo *m*

sarcastic [sɑ:'kæstɪk] *adj* sarcástico(a)

sarcastically [sɑ:'kæstɪklɪ] *adv* sarcásticamente

sarcoma [sɑ:'kəʊmə] *(pl* **sarcomas** *or* **sarcomata** [sɑ:'kəʊmətə]) *n Med* sarcoma *m*

sarcophagus [sɑ:'kɒfəgəs] *(pl* **sarcophagi** [sɑ:'kɒfəgaɪ]) *n* sarcófago *m*

sardine [sɑ:'di:n] *n* sardina *f*; IDIOM **we were packed in like sardines** íbamos como sardinas en lata

Sardinia [sɑ:'dɪnɪə] *n* Cerdeña

Sardinian [sɑ:'dɪnɪən] **1** *n* **(a)** *(person)* sardo(a) *m,f* **(b)** *(language)* sardo *m*
2 *adj* sardo(a)

sardonic [sɑ:'dɒnɪk] *adj* sardónico(a)

sardonically [sɑ:'dɒnɪklɪ] *adv* sardónicamente

Sargasso Sea [sɑ:'gæsəʊ'si:] *n* **the S.** el mar de los Sargazos

sarge [sɑ:dʒ] *n Fam* sargento *mf*

sari ['sɑ:rɪ] *n* sari *m*

sarky ['sɑ:kɪ] *adj Br Fam* socarrón(ona), sarcástico(a); **don't you get s. with me!** no te hagas el sarcástico conmigo

sarnie ['sɑ:nɪ] *n Br Fam (with sliced bread)* sándwich *m*; *(with French bread) Esp* bocata *m*, *Am* sándwich *m*

sarong [sə'rɒŋ] *n* sarong *m*, pareo *m*

sarsaparilla [sɑ:spə'rɪlə] *n* **(a)** *(plant)* zarzaparrilla *f* **(b)** *(drink)* zarzaparrilla *f*

sartorial [sɑ:'tɔ:rɪəl] *adj Formal* del vestir; **s. elegance** elegancia en el vestir

sartorius [sɑ:'tɔ:rɪəs] *n Anat* sartorio *m*

SAS [eseɪ'es] *n (abbr* **Special Air Service)** = comando de operaciones especiales del ejército británico, *Esp* ≃ GEO *m*

SASE [eseɪes'i:] *n US (abbr* **self-addressed stamped envelope)** sobre *m* franqueado con la dirección del remitente

sash [sæʃ] *n* **(a)** *(on dress)* faja *f*, fajín *m* **(b)** *(on uniform)* banda *f* **(c)** *(of window)* marco *m* ►► ***s. cord*** cordón *m (de las ventanas de guillotina)*; ***s. window*** ventana *f* de guillotina

sashay ['sæʃeɪ] *vi Fam* caminar pavoneándose; **she sashayed down the catwalk** recorrió la pasarela pavonéandose; **she sashayed out of the room** abandonó la sala pavoneándose

Sask *(abbr* **Saskatchewan**) Saskatchewan

Saskatchewan [sæs'kætʃɪwən] *n* Saskatchewan

sasquatch ['sæskwɒtʃ] *n* el abominable hombre de las nieves *(en Estados Unidos y Canadá)*

sass [sæs] *US Fam* **1** *n* frescura *f*, impertinencia *f*
2 *vt* venir con impertinencias a; **don't you s. me!** ¡a ver cómo me hablas!

sassaby ['sæsəbɪ] *n Zool* antílope *m* sasabi

sassafras ['sæsəfræs] *n* sasafrás *m* ►► ***s. oil*** aceite *m* de sasafrás

Sassenach ['sæsənæk] *n Scot* = término generalmente peyorativo para referirse a un inglés

sassy ['sæsɪ] *adj US Fam* **(a)** *(cheeky)* fresco(a), impertinente **(b)** *(in style)* que da la nota, muy llamativo(a); **that's one s. pair of shoes you've got there** con esos zapatos sí que vas dando la nota

SAT *n* **(a)** [sæt] *Br* (*abbr* **standard assessment task**) = tarea de la que se examina a un alumno para determinar si ha alcanzado el nivel de conocimientos correspondiente a su edad **(b)** [eseɪ'tiː] *US* (*abbr* **Scholastic Aptitude Test**) = examen que realizan al final de la enseñanza secundaria los alumnos que quieren ir a la universidad

Sat (*abbr* **Saturday**) sáb.

sat *pt & pp of* **sit**

Satan ['seɪtən] *n* Satanás *m*, Satán *m*

satanic [sə'tænɪk] *adj* satánico(a)

Satanism ['seɪtənɪzəm] *n* satanismo *m*

Satanist ['seɪtənɪst] *n* practicante *mf* del satanismo

satay ['sæteɪ] *n Culin* = plato del sudeste asiático que consiste en pinchos con tiras de carne de vaca o de pollo marinada servidos con una salsa picante de cacahuete; **chicken s.** pollo "satay" ►► ***s. sauce*** salsa *f* "satay"

satchel ['sætʃəl] *n* cartera *f (de colegial)*

sate [seɪt] *vt Formal* saciar; **to be sated (with sth)** estar saciado(a) (de algo)

sateen [sæ'tiːn] *n* satén *m*

satellite ['sætəlaɪt] *n* **(a)** *(device)* satélite *m*; **(tele)communications s.** satélite de (tele)comunicaciones; **meteorological** *or* **weather s.** satélite meteorológico; **broadcast live by s.** transmitido en directo vía satélite ►► ***s. broadcasting*** emisión *f* vía satélite; ***s. dish*** (antena *f*) parabólica *f*; ***s. link*** conexión *f* vía satélite; ***s. picture*** *(photograph)* imagen *f* de satélite; *(in weather forecast)* imagen *f* del satélite; ***s. television*** *or* ***TV*** televisión *f* por *or* vía satélite
(b) *(planet)* satélite *m*
(c) *(dependency)* **s. (state)** estado *m* satélite; **s. (town)** ciudad *f* satélite

satiate ['seɪʃɪeɪt] *vt Formal* saciar; **to be satiated (with sth)** estar saciado(a) (de algo)

satiation [seɪʃɪ'eɪʃən] *n Formal* saciedad *f*; **to the point of s.** hasta la saciedad

satin ['sætɪn] *n (cloth)* satén *m*, raso *m*; **her skin was as smooth as s.** su piel era suave como la seda ►► ***s. finish*** *(of paper, paint)* (acabado *m*) satinado *m*; ***s. pyjamas*** pijama *m* *or Am* piyama *m* *or f* de raso; ***s. sheets*** sábanas *fpl* de raso

satinwood ['sætɪnwʊd] *n* **(a)** *(tree)* satín *m* **(b)** *(wood)* satín *m*

satiny ['sætɪnɪ] *adj* satinado(a)

satire ['sætaɪə(r)] *n* sátira *f* (**on** de)

satirical [sə'tɪrɪkəl] *adj* satírico(a)

satirically [sə'tɪrɪklɪ] *adv* satíricamente

satirist ['sætɪrɪst] *n* escritor(ora) *m,f* de sátiras

satirize ['sætɪraɪz] *vt* satirizar

satisfaction [sætɪs'fækʃən] *n* **(a)** *(pleasure)* satisfacción *f* (**with** con); **he expressed his s. at the way things had turned out** expresó su satisfacción por la forma en la que había salido todo; **is everything to your s.?** ¿está todo en orden?; **the plan was agreed to everyone's s.** el plan fue aprobado con la conformidad de todos; **it must be proved to the s. of the court** las pruebas que se presenten deben convencer al tribunal; **it gives me great s. to know that...** me satisface enormemente saber que...; **to have the s. of doing sth** tener la satisfacción de hacer algo; *Com* **s. guaranteed, or your money back** si no queda satisfecho le devolvemos su dinero
(b) *(pleasing thing)* satisfacción *f*, placer *m*; **life's little satisfactions** los pequeños placeres de la vida
(c) *(of condition)* cumplimiento *m*; *(of curiosity, hunger)* satisfacción *f*; **the s. of the union's demands** la satisfacción de las reivindicaciones sindicales
(d) *(of debt)* satisfacción *f*, saldo *m*
(e) *Old-fashioned (redress)* **to demand s.** exigir una satisfacción

satisfactorily [sætɪs'fæktrɪlɪ] *adv* satisfactoriamente

satisfactory [sætɪs'fæktərɪ] *adj (result, standard, condition)* satisfactorio(a); **their progress is no more than s.** su progreso es apenas satisfactorio; *Sch* **I got "s." for my work** saqué un aprobado en el trabajo

satisfied ['sætɪsfaɪd] *adj* **(a)** *(pleased)* satisfecho(a); **to be s. (with)** estar satisfecho(a) (con); **she gave a s. sigh** dio un suspiro de satisfacción; **there goes another s. customer** ahí va otro cliente satisfecho; **are you s. now you've made her cry?** ¿estás contento ahora que la has hecho llorar?; **they'll have to be s. with what they've got** tendrán que contentarse con lo que han conseguido; *Ironic* **not s. with that she then broke the other chair** no contenta con eso, rompió la otra silla
(b) *(convinced)* **I am s. that he is telling the truth** estoy convencido de que dice la verdad; **I'm s. of his sincerity** estoy plenamente seguro de su sinceridad

satisfy ['sætɪsfaɪ] *vt* **(a)** *(please)* satisfacer; **to s. the examiners** aprobar el examen
(b) *(condition, demand)* satisfacer, cumplir; *(curiosity)* satisfacer; **to s. one's hunger/thirst** satisfacer el hambre/la sed
(c) *(debt)* satisfacer, saldar
(d) *(convince)* convencer; **she failed to s. me that she was up to the job** no logró convencerme de que podía realizar el trabajo; **I satisfied myself that all the windows were closed** me aseguré de que todas las ventanas estuvieran cerradas

satisfying ['sætɪsfaɪɪŋ] *adj* **(a)** *(job)* gratificante; *(result)* satisfactorio(a) **(b)** *(meal)* sustancioso(a), que llena; **it makes a s. snack** es un tentempié sustancioso

satisfyingly ['sætɪsfaɪɪŋlɪ] *adv* satisfactoriamente

satrap ['sætrəp] *n* **(a)** *(in Persia)* sátrapa *m* **(b)** *(despotic local ruler)* sátrapa *m*

satsuma [sæt'suːmə] *n (fruit)* satsuma *f*

saturate ['sætʃəreɪt] *vt* **(a)** *(soak)* empapar (**with** de *or* en); *Fam (person) Esp* calar hasta los huesos, *Am* hacer sopa **(b)** *(swamp)* saturar (**with** de); **modern advertising saturates us with images of a glossy lifestyle** la publicidad moderna nos satura con imágenes de un estilo de vida reluciente; **to s. the market** saturar el mercado **(c)** *Chem* saturar

saturated ['sætʃəreɪtɪd] *adj* **(a)** *(soaked)* empapado(a) (**with** de *or* en); *Fam (person) Esp* calado(a) hasta los huesos, *Am* hecho(a) sopa **(b)** *(swamped) (market)* saturado(a) (**with** de) **(c)** *Chem* ***s. fats*** grasas *fpl* saturadas; ***s. solution*** disolución *f* saturada

saturation [sætʃə'reɪʃən] *n* **(a)** *(soaking)* empapamiento *m* **(b)** *(of market)* saturación *f*; **to reach s. point** llegar al punto de saturación ►► *Mil* ***s. bombing*** bombardeo *m* intensivo; *Journ* ***s. coverage*** cobertura *f* informativa exhaustiva **(c)** *Chem* saturación *f* ►► ***s. point*** punto *m* de saturación

Saturday ['sætədɪ] *n* sábado *m*; **this S.** este sábado; **on S.** el sábado; **on S. morning/night** el sábado por la mañana/noche; **on S. afternoon/evening** el sábado por la tarde/noche; **on Saturdays** los sábados; **every S.** todos los sábados; **every other S.** cada dos sábados, un sábado sí y otro no; **last S.** el sábado pasado; **the S. before last** hace dos sábados; **next S.** el sábado que viene; **the S. after next, a week on S., S. week** dentro de dos sábados, del sábado en ocho días; **the following S.** el sábado siguiente; **S.'s paper** el periódico del sábado; **the S. movie** la película del sábado ►► ***S. job*** trabajo *m* de sábados; **I've got a S. job** tengo un trabajo de sábados; *US Fam* ***S. night special*** *(gun)* pistola *f* barata

Saturn ['sætɜːn] *n* **(a)** *(planet)* Saturno **(b)** *(god)* Saturno

saturnalia [sætə'neɪljə] *n* saturnal *f*, orgía *f*

saturnine ['sætənaɪn] *adj (gloomy)* taciturno(a)

satyr ['sætə(r)] *n (in Greek mythology)* sátiro *m*

sauce [sɔːs] *n* **(a)** *(for food)* salsa *f*; **tomato/cheese s.** salsa de tomate *or Méx* jitomate/de queso; **chocolate s.** chocolate líquido; PROV **what's s. for the goose is s. for the gander** lo que es bueno para uno lo es también para el otro ►► ***s. boat*** salsera *f*
(b) *Br Fam (impudence)* descaro *m*; **that's enough of your s.!** ¡no seas tan caradura!

(**c**) *Br Fam (alcohol)* bebida *f*, *Esp* priva *f*, *Méx* chupe *m*, *RP* chupi *m*; **to hit the s.** darle a la bebida; **to be on the s.** estar bebiendo de nuevo; **to be off the s.** no estar bebiendo

sauced [sɔːst] *adj Br Fam (drunk)* como una cuba, *Esp, RP* mamado(a), *Col* caído(a) (de la perra), *Méx* ahogado(a)

saucepan [ˈsɔːspən] *n* cazo *m*

saucer [ˈsɔːsə(r)] *n* platillo *m*

saucily [ˈsɔːsɪlɪ] *adv* (**a**) *(impertinently)* descaradamente, con mucha cara dura (**b**) *(provocatively)* con picardía, en tono picante

sauciness [ˈsɔːsɪnɪs] *n* (**a**) *(impertinence)* descaro *m*, cara *f* dura (**b**) *(provocativeness)* picardía *f*

saucy [ˈsɔːsɪ] *adj* (**a**) *(impertinent)* descarado(a) (**b**) *(risqué)* picante, subido(a) de tono

Saudi [ˈsaʊdɪ] **1** *n* (**a**) *(person)* saudí *mf* (**b**) *Fam (country)* Arabia Saudí
2 *adj* saudí

Saudi Arabia [ˈsaʊdɪəˈreɪbɪə] *n* Arabia Saudí

Saudi Arabian [ˈsaʊdɪəˈreɪbɪən] **1** *n* saudí *mf*
2 *adj* saudí

sauerkraut [ˈsaʊəkraʊt] *n* chucrut *m*

sauna [ˈsɔːnə] *n* (**a**) *(activity)* sauna *f*, *Am* sauna *m or f*; **to go for** *or* **have a s.** meterse en la sauna (**b**) *(place)* sauna *f*, *Am* sauna *m or f*; *Fam* **it's like a s. in here!** ¡esto es una sauna!

saunter [ˈsɔːntə(r)] **1** *n* paseo *m (con aire desenfadado)*; **we went for a s. along the river** fuimos a dar un paseo por el río
2 *vi* **to s. (along)** pasear (con aire desenfadado); **to s. up to sb** acercarse a alguien con aire despreocupado; **she sauntered in, half an hour late** entró como si tal cosa *or Arg* como si nada, con media hora de retraso

saurian [ˈsɔːrɪən] **1** *n* saurio *m*
2 *adj* de saurio

saury [ˈsɔːrɪ] *n* paparda *f*

sausage [ˈsɒsɪdʒ] *n* (**a**) *(raw)* salchicha *f*; *(cured)* = chorizo, salchichón u otro tipo de embutidos ►► *Fam* ***s. dog*** perro *m* salchicha; ***s. machine*** máquina *f* de hacer salchichas; ***s. meat*** carne *f* picada *(utilizada para rellenar salchichas)*; *Br* ***s. roll*** salchicha *f* envuelta en hojaldre (**b**) *Br Fam Hum (penis)* salchicha *f* (**c**) IDIOMS *Br Fam* **not a s.** *(nothing)* nada de nada; *Br Hum* **you silly s.!** ¡mira que eres tontorrón(ona)!

sauté [ˈsəʊteɪ] *Culin* **1** *adj* salteado(a); **s. potatoes** *Esp* patatas *or Am* papas salteadas
2 *vt* saltear

savable [ˈseɪvəbəl] *adj* salvable, recuperable

savage [ˈsævɪdʒ] **1** *n Old-fashioned* salvaje *mf*; *Fig* **the fans behaved like savages** los seguidores se comportaron como salvajes
2 *adj* (**a**) *(animal, person)* salvaje (**b**) *(attack, blow, cuts)* salvaje, brutal; *(criticism)* virulento(a) (**c**) *Old-fashioned (primitive) (tribe, people)* primitivo(a)
3 *vt* (**a**) *(attack physically)* atacar salvajemente; **she was savaged by a dog** fue atacada salvajemente por un perro (**b**) *(criticize)* criticar con saña *or* virulencia; **they were savaged by the press** la prensa los criticó con saña *or* virulencia

savagely [ˈsævɪdʒlɪ] *adv* (**a**) *(to beat, attack)* salvajemente (**b**) *(to criticize)* con saña *or* virulencia

savagery [ˈsævɪdʒərɪ] *n* (**a**) *(of attack, blow, cuts)* salvajismo *m*, brutalidad *f*; *(of criticism)* saña *f*, virulencia *f* (**b**) *Old-fashioned (primitiveness)* **the tribe still lives in s.** la tribu aún vive en condiciones primitivas

savanna(h) [səˈvænə] *n* sabana *f*

save[1] [seɪv] *prep Formal (except)* salvo, a excepción de; **we'd thought of every possibility s. one** habíamos considerado todas las posibilidades con excepción de una; **s. for the fact we lost, it was a great match** si no tenemos en cuenta que perdimos, fue un partido estupendo; **she was utterly alone, s. for one good friend** estaba completamente sola a excepción de una buena amiga

save[2] **1** *vt* (**a**) *(rescue) (person, marriage, job)* salvar (**from** de); **to s. a species from extinction** salvar una especie de la extinción; **the doctors managed to s. her eyesight** los doctores lograron salvarle la vista; **to s. sb's life** salvarle la vida a alguien; **we can but try to s. him from himself** lo que debemos hacer es tratar de ayudarlo para que no se destruya a sí mismo; **saved by the bell!** ¡me salvó la campana!; **to s. the situation** *or* **day** salvar la situación; **to s. one's soul** salvar el alma; **God s. the King/Queen!** ¡Dios salve al Rey/a la Reina!; IDIOM *Fam* **she can't sing to s. her life** no tiene ni idea de cantar; IDIOM *Fam* **to s. one's bacon** *or* **neck** *or* **skin** salvar el pellejo
(**b**) *(help to avoid)* **it saved me a lot of trouble** me ahorró muchos problemas; **this has saved him a great deal of expense** esto le ha ahorrado un montón de dinero; **thanks, you've saved me a trip** gracias, me ahorraste un viaje; **to s. sb from falling/drowning** evitar que alguien se caiga/ahogue; **he saved me from making a terrible mistake** evitó que cometiera un terrible error; **this will s. us having to do it again** esto nos evitará *or* ahorrará tener que hacerlo de nuevo
(**c**) *Sport* **to s. a shot/penalty** parar un disparo/penalty
(**d**) *(keep for future)* guardar; *(money)* ahorrar; **my mum always used to s. old jars** mi mamá solía guardar frascos viejos; **I'm saving stamps for the appeal** estoy juntando sellos para la campaña; **I s. £100 a month in a special account** ahorro 100 libras al mes en una cuenta especial; **how much money have you got saved?** ¿cuánto dinero tienes ahorrado?; **to s. oneself for sth** reservarse para algo; **I am saving my strength** estoy ahorrando fuerzas; **I'll s. you a seat** te guardaré un asiento *or* lugar; **I always s. the cherry till last** siempre dejo la cereza para el final; **he saved the best till last, scoring a hat-trick in the last ten minutes** guardó lo mejor para el final y marcó tres goles en los últimos diez minutos; *Fam* **s. your breath!** ¡no te esfuerces!, ¡ahórrate las palabras!; *Fam* **s. the sympathy!** ¡puedes ahorrarte tu compasión!, ¡no necesito que me compadezcan!
(**e**) *Comptr* guardar; *(on screen)* archivar, guardar; **s. as** guardar como; **to s. sth to disk** guardar algo en disco; **click on "s."** haga click en "guardar"
(**f**) *(not waste) (time, money, space, work)* ahorrar; **I saved £10 by buying it there** me ahorré 10 libras por comprarlo ahí; **their advice saved me a fortune** su asesoramiento me hizo ahorrar una fortuna
(**g**) *Rel* redimir, salvar; **have you been saved?** ¿te has salvado?; **to s. sb's soul** salvar el alma de alguien
2 *vi* (**a**) *(not waste money)* ahorrar; **s. on heating costs by insulating your house** aísle su casa y ahorre en calefacción
(**b**) *(put money aside)* ahorrar; **to s. for sth** ahorrar para algo; *Br Fin* **a s. as you earn scheme** un plan de ahorro mediante descuentos en la nómina
(**c**) *Comptr* guardar cambios
(**d**) *(goalkeeper)* realizar una parada (**from** a tiro de); **the goalkeeper saved with his legs** el guardametas hizo una parada con las piernas
3 *n (of goalkeeper)* parada *f*; **to make a s.** hacer una parada

► **save up 1** *vt sep* ahorrar (**for** para)
2 *vi* ahorrar (**for** para)

saveloy [ˈsævəlɔɪ] *n* salchicha *f* de cerdo ahumada

-saver [-ˈseɪvə] *suffix* **it's a real money-s.** sale bastante más barato; **the loan was an absolute life-s. for me** el préstamo fue mi salvación

saver [ˈseɪvə(r)] *n* (**a**) *Fin* ahorrador(ora) *m,f*, *RP* ahorrista *mf*; **regular savers will benefit from this scheme** aquellos que ahorran regularmente se beneficiarán de este plan; **small savers** pequeños ahorradores (**b**) *(cheap ticket) Esp* billete *m or Am* boleto *m or Am* pasaje *m* económico; *Br Rail (standard ticket)* = billete en segunda clase de lunes a jueves

-saving [-ˈseɪvɪŋ] *suffix* **energy-s.** *(device)* que ahorra energía, de bajo consumo; **time-s.** que ahorra tiempo

saving[1] [ˈseɪvɪŋ] **1** *n* (**a**) *(economy)* ahorro *m*; **to make savings** ahorrar, economizar; **we made a s. of $20 on the usual price** lo compramos 20 dólares más barato de lo que cuesta normalmente; **we are offering huge savings on all our stock** estamos ofreciendo grandes descuentos en todos nuestros productos
(**b**) *Fin* **savings** ahorros *mpl*; **she lived off her savings** vivía de sus ahorros; **I spent my life savings on a trip to Hawaii** gasté los ahorros de toda una vida en un viaje a Hawai ►► ***savings account*** cuenta *f* de ahorros; ***savings bank*** ≃ caja *f* de ahorros; *US* ***savings bond*** bono *m* de ahorro; ***savings book*** cartilla *f* (de ahorros); ***savings certificate*** certificado *m* de ahorro; *US* ***savings and loan association*** ≃ caja *f* de ahorros; ***savings plan*** plan *m* de ahorro
2 *adj* **her s. grace** lo único que le salva; **the film has one s. grace** hay un elemento que salva la película

saving[2] *prep Formal (except for)* con excepción de

saviour, *US* **savior** [ˈseɪvjə(r)] *n* salvador(ora) *m,f*; *Rel* **the Saviour** el Salvador

savoir-faire [ˈsævwɑːˈfeə(r)] *n* savoir faire *m*

savor, savorless *etc US* = **savour, savourless** *etc*

savory [ˈseɪvərɪ] *n* (**a**) *Bot* ajedrea *f* (**b**) *US* = **savoury**

savour, *US* **savor** [ˈseɪvə(r)] **1** *n* (**a**) *(taste)* sabor *m* (**b**) *(interest, charm)* encanto *m*
2 *vt (food, experience)* saborear
3 *vi* **to s. of** oler a

savourless, *US* **savorless** [ˈseɪvəlɪs] *adj* (**a**) *(food)* sin sabor, insípido(a) (**b**) *(experience)* soso(a), insulso(a)

savoury, *US* **savory** ['seɪvərɪ] 1 *adj* (a) *(food) (appetizing)* sabroso(a); *(not sweet)* salado(a) (b) *(wholesome)* **not a very s. subject** un tema no muy edificante; **he's not a very s. individual** no es nada honesto
2 **savouries** *npl* salados *mpl*

Savoy [sə'vɔɪ] *n* Saboya

savoy [sə'vɔɪ] *n* **s. (cabbage)** col *f* rizada *or* de Milán, *CSur* repollo *m* rizado *or* de Milán

savvy ['sævɪ] 1 *n Fam (common sense)* seso *m*, sentido *m* común; *(know-how)* conocimentos *mpl*
2 *vi Old-fashioned* **he's not our sort of person, s.?** no es de nuestro estilo, ¿comprendes?
3 *adj Fam (shrewd)* espabilado(a)

saw[1] *pt of* **see**

saw[2] 1 *n (tool)* sierra *f*; *(with one handle)* serrucho *m*
2 *vt* (*pp* **sawn** [sɔːn] *or* **sawed**) serrar, cortar; **he sawed the table in half** serró *or* cortó la mesa por la mitad; **to s. a tree down** talar un árbol con una sierra IDIOM *Fam* **to s. logs** *or US* **wood** roncar
3 *vi* serrar, cortar; **she sawed through the branch** serró la rama

▶ **saw off** *vt sep* serrar, cortar

▶ **saw up** *vt sep* serrar *or* cortar en trozos

saw[3] *n (saying)* dicho *m*

sawbill ['sɔːbɪl] *n Zool* serreta *f*

sawbones ['sɔːbəʊnz] *n Fam Pej* matasanos *mf inv*

sawbuck ['sɔːbʌk] *n US Fam* billete *m* de diez dólares

sawdust ['sɔːdʌst] *n* serrín *m*

sawed-off [sɔːd'ɒf] *adj US* (a) *Fam Hum (short)* canijo(a), retaco(a) (b) ***s. shotgun*** escopeta *f* de cañones recortados, recortada *f*

sawfish ['sɔːfɪʃ] *n* pez *m* sierra

sawgrass ['sɔːgrɑːs] *n* masiega *f*

sawhorse ['sɔːhɔːs] *n* borriquete *m*, borriqueta *f*

sawmill ['sɔːmɪl] *n* aserradero *m*, serrería *f*

sawn *pp of* **saw**

sawn-off shotgun ['sɔːnɒf'ʃɒtgʌn] *n Br* escopeta *f* de cañones recortados, recortada *f*

sawyer ['sɔːjə(r)] *n* aserrador(ora) *m,f*

sax [sæks] *n Fam (saxophone)* saxo *m*

saxhorn ['sækshɔːn] *n Mus* bombardino *m*

saxifrage ['sæksɪfreɪdʒ] *n Bot* saxífraga *f*

Saxon ['sæksən] 1 *n* (a) *(member of Germanic people)* sajón(ona) *m,f* (b) *(person from Saxony)* sajón(ona) *m,f* (c) *(language)* sajón *m*
2 *adj* (a) *(of Germanic people)* sajón(ona) (b) *(of Saxony)* sajón(ona)

Saxony ['sæksənɪ] *n* Sajonia

saxophone ['sæksəfəʊn] *n* saxofón *m* ▸▸ ***s. player*** saxofonista *mf*

saxophonist [sæk'sɒfənɪst] *n* saxofonista *mf*

SAY [seɪ] 1 *n* **he wasn't allowed to have his s.** no le dejaron expresar su opinión; **I had no s. in the matter** no tuve ni voz ni voto en el asunto; **we had little s. in the matter** nuestra opinión apenas contó
2 *vt* (*pt & pp* **said** [sed]) (a) *(of person)* decir; **to s. sth to sb** decir algo a alguien; **to s. sth to oneself** decirse algo; **let's s. no more about it** no se hable más; **s. what you think** di lo que piensas; **s. what you mean** dilo claramente; *US* **s. what?** ¿que cómo?; **"good morning," she said** "buenos días", dijo; **he said (that) you were here** dijo que estabas aquí; **to s. mass** decir misa; **to s. a prayer** rezar una oración; **that's a strange thing to s.** qué cosa más extraña dice/dices/*etc*; **that's not saying much** eso es decir muy poca cosa; **he didn't s. a word** no dijo nada; **to s. goodbye (to sb)** despedirse (de alguien); **to s. hello (to sb)** saludar (a alguien); **because I s. so!** ¡porque lo digo yo!; **if you s. so** si tú lo dices; **and so s. all of us** y estamos todos de acuerdo; **well said!** ¡bien dicho!; **this salad's rather good, though I s. so myself** modestia aparte, esta ensalada está bien buena; **she said yes/no** dijo que sí/que no; **to s. no/yes to an offer** rechazar/aceptar una oferta; **I wouldn't s. no to a cup of tea** me tomaría un té; *Fam* **what would you s. to a drink?** ¿te gustaría tomar algo?, *¿Esp* te apetece *or Carib, Col, Méx* te provoca *or Méx* se te antoja tomar algo?; *Fam* **what do you s. we go for a drink?** ¿qué tal si vamos a tomar algo?; *Fam* **we could go there together, what do you s.?** ¿y qué tal si vamos juntos?; **I s. we don't tell them** yo voto que no se lo digamos; **what can I s.?** ¿qué quieres que diga?; **s. what you like, you can't beat a Mercedes** yo lo tengo muy claro, no hay nada mejor que un Mercedes; **who shall I s. is calling?** ¿quién le llama?, ¿de parte de quién?; **you can't do that? – says who?** no puedes hacer eso – ¿quién lo dice?; **I can't s. I like her** no puedo decir que me guste; **don't s. you've forgotten already!** ¡no me digas que ya te has olvidado!; **it was very good, I must s.** tengo que confesar que estuvo muy bien; **well this is a fine time to arrive, I must s.!** ¡qué horas de llegar son éstas!; **it wasn't, shall I** *or* **we s., totally unintentional** no fue, cómo te lo diría, sin querer; *Fam* **that wasn't very clever of me – you said it!** no tenía que haber hecho eso – ¡tú lo has dicho!; **that says it all!** eso lo dice todo; **to s. sth about sth/sb** decir algo de algo/alguien; **it says a lot about her that...** dice mucho de ella que...; **to s. sth again** repetir algo; **you can s. that again!** ¡y que lo digas!; **I'd never s. a word against her** nunca hablaría mal de ella; **there's a lot to be said for...** hay mucho que decir a favor de...; **it says a lot for/doesn't s. much for their courage that...** dice/no dice mucho de su valor que...; **you're honest, I'll s. that for you** eres honrado, eso sí *or* eso hay que reconocerlo; **what have you got to s. for yourself?** ¿qué tienes que decir a tu favor?; **he didn't have a lot to s. for himself** no tenía nada interesante que decir; **he said to be there by nine** dijo que estuviéramos allí a las nueve; **need I s. more?** está claro ¿no?; **s. no more** no me digas más; **having said that,...** dicho esto,...; **it would be unwise, not to s. dangerous** sería imprudente, por no decir peligroso; **that's not to s. I'm against the idea** lo que no quiere decir que esté en contra de la idea; **when all is said and done** a fin de cuentas, al fin y al cabo
(b) *(of text, sign)* decir, poner; *(of law, rules, newspaper)* decir; *(of meter)* marcar; **my watch says four o'clock** mi reloj marca las cuatro; **it says "shake well"** dice "agítese bien"
(c) *(allege)* **they s. (that)..., it is said (that)...** dicen que..., se dice que...; **he is said to be a good tennis player** dicen que es un buen tenista; **so they s.** eso dicen; **you know what they s.,...** sabes lo que se dice,...; **I've heard it said that...** he oído que...; **some might s. she's too young** puede que algunos piensen que es demasiado joven
(d) *(tell)* **it is difficult to s. when/where/which...** es difícil decir cuándo/dónde/cuál...; **there's no saying what might happen if they find out** como se enteren se va a armar una buena; **who can s. when he'll come?** ¿quién sabe cuándo vendrá?; **who's to s. she hasn't got one already?** ¿cómo sabemos que no tiene uno ya?
(e) *(think)* decir; **I s. (that) they'll lose** yo digo que perderán; **to look at them, you wouldn't s. they were a day over forty** a primera vista nadie diría que tienen más de cuarenta años
(f) *(decide)* **it's (not) for him to s.** (no) le corresponde a él decidir
(g) *(in hypothetical statements)* **(let's) s. I believe you...** supongamos que te creo...; **if I had, (let's) s., £100,000** si yo tuviera, digamos, 100.000 libras; **countries such as Germany, s., or France** países como Alemania, por poner un caso *or* ejemplo, o Francia; **come tomorrow, s. after lunch** ven mañana, digamos que después de la comida
3 *vi* **I'm not saying** no te lo digo; **when will he be back? – he didn't s.** ¿cuándo volverá? – no lo dijo; **which is best? – I couldn't s.** ¿cuál es el mejor? – no te sabría decir; **as they s., as people s.** como se dice, como dice la gente; **I s.!** *(expressing surprise)* ¡caramba!; *Old-fashioned (to attract attention)* ¡oiga!; **I'll s.!** ¡ya lo creo!; **I mean to s.!** ¡habrase visto!; **that is to s.** esto es; **who can s.?** ¿quién sabe?; *Fam* **you don't s.!** ¡no me digas!
4 *exclam US* **s., why don't we go for a drink?** ¡eh!, ¿por qué no vamos a tomar algo?; **s., thanks!** ¡gracias, hombre/mujer!

SAYE [eseɪwaɪ'iː] *n Br* (*abbr* **save-as-you-earn**) = plan de ahorro mediante descuentos en la nómina

saying ['seɪɪŋ] *n* dicho *m*; **as the s. goes** como dice el refrán

say-so ['seɪsəʊ] *n* (a) *(authorization)* visto *m* bueno, aprobación *f*; **with my s.** con mi visto bueno *or* aprobación (b) *(assertion)* **I won't believe it just on his s.** me niego a creerlo sólo porque él lo diga

S-bend ['esbend] *n Br (in pipe)* sifón *m*

SBU [esbiː'juː] *n* (*abbr* **strategic business unit**) unidad *f* estratégica de negocio

SC (a) (*abbr* **South Carolina**) Carolina del Sur (b) *US* (*abbr* **supreme court**) Tribunal *m* Supremo, *Am* Corte *f* Suprema

S/C (*abbr* **self-contained**) independiente

scab [skæb] 1 *n* (a) *(on skin)* costra *f*, postilla *f* (b) *(animal disease)* sarna *f* (c) *Fam Pej (strikebreaker)* esquirol *m*, *Am* rompehuelgas *mf inv*, *RP* carnero *m*
2 *vi Fam Pej (work as a strikebreaker)* trabajar saboteando huelgas

scabbard ['skæbəd] *n* vaina *f*

scabby ['skæbɪ] *adj* (a) *(skin) (of person)* lleno(a) de costras (b) *(animal)* sarnoso(a) (c) *Br Fam (worthless)* asqueroso(a)

scabies ['skeɪbiːz] *n* sarna *f* ▸▸ ***s. mite*** arador *m* de la sarna

scabious ['skeɪbɪəs] *n Bot* escabiosa *f*

scabrous ['skeɪbrəs] *adj Formal* (a) *(skin)* áspero(a) (b) *(humour)* escabroso(a)

scads [skædz] *npl US Fam* **s. (of)** un montón (de), una porrada (de)

scaffold ['skæfəld] *n* (**a**) *(outside building)* andamio *m* (**b**) *(for execution)* patíbulo *m*; **to go to the s.** ir al patíbulo

scaffolder ['skæfəldə(r)] *n* montador(ora) *m,f* de andamios

scaffolding ['skæfəldɪŋ] *n* andamiaje *m*

scag, skag [skæg] *n Fam* (**a**) *(heroin)* caballo *m*, *Esp* jaco *m* (**b**) *US (ugly woman)* foca *f*, *RP* escracho *m*

scalable ['skeɪləbəl] *adj Comptr* ***s. font*** fuente *f* escalable

scalar ['skeɪlə(r)] *adj Math* escalar

scalawag *US* = **scallywag**

scald [skɔːld] **1** *n* escaldadura *f*

2 *vt* (**a**) *(hands, skin)* escaldar; **I scalded myself with the milk** me quemé con la leche; **the hot tea scalded my tongue** el té me quemó la lengua (**b**) *(tomatoes)* escaldar; *(milk)* calentar sin que llegue a hervir (**c**) *(sterilize)* esterilizar

scalding ['skɔːldɪŋ] *adj* **to be s. (hot)** estar ardiendo, quemar

scale[1] [skeɪl] **1** *n* (**a**) *(on fish, reptile)* escama *f*; IDIOM **the scales fell from her eyes** se le cayó la venda de los ojos (**b**) *(in pipes, kettle)* incrustación *f* (de cal); *(on teeth)* sarro *m* (**c**) *(of paint, plaster, rust)* escama *f*

2 *vt* (**a**) *(fish)* escamar, descamar (**b**) *(teeth)* limpiar, quitar *orAm* sacar el sarro a; *(boiler, pipe)* desincrustar

3 *vi (paint, rust)* descascararse; *(skin)* pelarse

scale[2] *n* (**a**) *(for measuring, of pay rates)* escala *f*; **the social s.** la escala social; **on a s. of one to ten** en una escala de uno a diez ▸▸ ***s. of charges*** lista *f* de precios *or* honorarios

(**b**) *(of problem, changes)* escala *f*, magnitud *f*; **the s. of the devastation** la escala *or* magnitud de la devastación; **on a large/small s.** a gran/pequeña escala; **this will affect us on a global s.** esto nos afectará a escala global; **they had never previously suffered losses on this s.** nunca antes habían sufrido pérdidas de esta escala *or* magnitud

(**c**) *(of map, drawing)* escala *f*; **the map is on a s. of 1 cm to 1 km** el mapa está en una escala de 1 cm equivalente a 1 km; **it is drawn to s.** está dibujado *or* hecho a escala; **the drawing is out of s.** *or* **is not to s.** el dibujo no está hecho a escala ▸▸ ***s. drawing*** dibujo *m* a escala; ***s. model*** modelo *m* a escala, maqueta *f*

(**d**) *Mus* escala *f*; **to practise** *or* **to do one's scales** practicar *or* hacer las escalas

(**e**) **scales** *(for weighing)* balanza *f*; **a pair** *or* **set of (kitchen) scales** una balanza (de cocina); **(bathroom) scales** báscula (de baño)

(**f**) *(scale pan)* platillo *m*

▸ **scale down** *vt sep* (**a**) *(reduce in size)* reducir

(**b**) *(demands, expectations)* reducir; *(production)* disminuir; *(search)* reducir la intensidad de

▸ **scale up** *vt sep* (**a**) *(increase in size)* aumentar, agrandar

(**b**) *(prices, demands)* aumentar

scale[3] *vt (climb)* escalar

scalene ['skeɪliːn] *adj Geom* escaleno(a)

scallion ['skælɪən] *n US* (**a**) *(spring onion)* cebolleta *f* (**b**) *(shallot)* escalonia *f*

scallop, scollop ['skæləp, 'skɒləp] **1** *n* (**a**) *(shellfish)* vieira *f*; *(shell)* concha *f* (de peregrino) (**b**) *(in sewing)* festón *m*

2 *vt* (**a**) *(in sewing)* festonear (**b**) *Culin* gratinar

scalloped ['skɒləpt] *adj* (**a**) *(fabric)* festoneado(a) (**b**) *Culin* **s. potatoes** *Esp* patatas *orAm* papas gratinadas

scallywag ['skælɪwæg], *US* **scalawag** ['skæləwæg] *n Fam* granuja *mf*, sinvergüenza *mf*; **you little s.!** *(child)* ¡pillín!

scalp [skælp] **1** *n* (**a**) *(skin of head)* cuero *m* cabelludo; *(as war trophy)* cabellera *f*; *Fig* **the opposition were baying for the minister's s.** la oposición pedía a gritos la cabeza del ministro (**b**) *(victory)* **the local team claimed another important s. this weekend** el equipo local logró otra importante victoria este fin de semana

2 *vt* (**a**) *(in war)* cortar la cabellera a; *Fig* **she'll s. you when she finds out!** cuando se entere te cortará la cabeza (**b**) *Hum (of hairdresser)* pelar (**c**) *US Fam (tickets, securities)* revender

scalpel ['skælpəl] *n Med* bisturí *m*

scalper ['skælpə(r)] *n US Fam (of tickets, securities)* revendedor(ora) *m, f*

scaly ['skeɪlɪ] *adj* (**a**) *(fish)* con escamas; *(skin)* escamoso(a) (**b**) *(kettle, pipe)* con sarro

scam [skæm] **1** *n Fam* chanchullo *m*, pufo *m*

2 *vt* timar

scamp [skæmp] *n (rascal)* granuja *mf*; **you little s.!** *(child)* ¡pillín!

scamper ['skæmpə(r)] *vi (child)* ir dando brincos; *(animal)* correr dando saltitos; **the kids scampered up the stairs** los niños subieron las escaleras a saltos; **the squirrel scampered up the tree** la ardilla subió rápidamente al árbol dando saltitos

▸ **scamper away, scamper off** *vi (child)* salir dando brincos; *(animal)* alejarse *or* irse corriendo dando saltitos

scampi ['skæmpɪ] *n* (**a**) *(as food)* gambas *fpl* rebozadas (**b**) *(in sea)* cigala *f*

scan [skæn] **1** *vt* (*pt & pp* **scanned**) (**a**) *(examine closely) (face, crowd)* escrutar, escudriñar; *(the horizon)* otear, escudriñar

(**b**) *(read quickly)* echar una ojeada a; **he scans the local papers for bargains** ojea los periódicos locales en busca de gangas

(**c**) *Med* hacer un escáner a; *(in pregnancy)* hacer una ecografía a

(**d**) *(glance at) (newspaper, list)* ojear

(**e**) *(of radar, searchlight)* explorar

(**f**) *Comptr* escanear

(**g**) *Lit* escandir

2 *vi Lit* **this line doesn't s.** este verso no está bien medido

3 *n* (**a**) *Med* escáner *m*; *(in pregnancy)* ecografía *f*; **to have a s.** tener un escáner/hacerse una ecografía (**b**) *Comptr* escaneo *m* (**c**) *(of radar)* exploración *f*

▸ **scan in** *vt sep Comptr* escanear

scandal ['skændəl] *n* (**a**) *(outrage)* escándalo *m*; **sex/financial/political s.** escándalo sexual/financiero/político; **it's a s.!** ¡es un escándalo!; **to create** *or* **cause a s.** provocar *or* ocasionar un escándalo (**b**) *(gossip)* chismorreo *m*, *Esp* cotilleo *m*; **here's a juicy bit of s.** tengo un cotilleo muy jugoso

scandalize ['skændəlaɪz] *vt* escandalizar; **he was scandalized by what she said** se escandalizó por lo que dijo ella

scandalmonger ['skændəlmʌŋgə(r)] *n* murmurador(ora) *m,f*

scandalous ['skændələs] *adj* (**a**) *(conduct)* escandaloso(a); **it's absolutely s. that they should be allowed to get away with it!** ¡es escandaloso que se salgan con la suya! (**b**) *(price)* escandaloso(a)

scandalously ['skændələslɪ] *adv* (**a**) *(to behave)* escandalosamente (**b**) *(extremely)* **s. expensive** escandalosamente caro(a)

Scandinavia [skændɪ'neɪvɪə] *n* Escandinavia

Scandinavian [skændɪ'neɪvɪən] **1** *n* escandinavo(a) *m,f*

2 *adj* escandinavo(a)

scandium ['skændɪəm] *n Chem* escandio *m*

scanner ['skænə(r)] *n* (**a**) *Comptr* escáner *m* (**b**) *Med* escáner *m*; *(ultrasound)* ecógrafo *m*

scanning ['skænɪŋ] *n Comptr* escaneo *m*; **this fax can also be used for scanning** este fax también sirve para escanear ▸▸ ***s. electron microscope*** microscopio *m* electrónico de escaneo

scansion ['skænʃən] *n Lit* escansión *f*

scant [skænt] *adj* escaso(a); **to pay s. attention to sth/sb** prestar *or* dar muy poca atención a algo/alguien; **they showed s. regard for our feelings** nuestros sentimientos no parecieron importarles mucho; **a s. teaspoonful** una cucharadita de té escasa

scantily ['skæntɪlɪ] *adv (furnished, populated)* apenas; **s. clad** *or* **dressed** ligero(a) de ropa

scanty ['skæntɪ] *adj (clothing)* exiguo(a); *(information)* escaso(a); *(meal)* frugal; *(audience)* pobre; *(praise)* escaso(a)

scapegoat ['skeɪpgəʊt] *n* chivo *m* expiatorio

scaphoid ['skæfɔɪd] *Anat* **1** *n* escafoides *m inv*

2 *adj* escafoides

scapula ['skæpjʊlə] (*pl* **scapulae** ['skæpjʊliː] *or* **scapulas**) *n Anat* escápula *f*

scar [skɑː(r)] **1** *n* (**a**) *(from wound, surgery)* cicatriz *f*; *(from acne, smallpox)* marca *f* ▸▸ ***s. tissue*** tejido *m* cicatrizal (**b**) *(emotional)* cicatriz *f*, huella *f*; **he will carry the scars of this defeat for years to come** esta derrota le marcará durante años (**c**) *(on land)* huella *f*; **the mine was an ugly s. on the landscape** la mina había dejado una horrible cicatriz en el paisaje (**d**) *Br (rocky outcrop)* peñasco *m*

2 *vt* (*pt & pp* **scarred**) (**a**) *(skin, face) (of wound, surgery)* dejar cicatrices en; *(of acne, smallpox)* marcar, dejar marcas en; **his hands were badly scarred** tenía las manos llenas de cicatrices (**b**) *(emotionally)* marcar; **to be scarred for life** quedar marcado(a) de por vida (**c**) *(land, countryside)* marcar; **a war-scarred country** un país marcado por la guerra

3 *vi (wound)* cicatrizar

scarab ['skærəb] *n* **s. (beetle)** escarabajo *m*

scarce ['skeəs] 1 *adj* escaso(a); **sugar is s. at the moment** en este momento escasea el azúcar; **work of this quality is becoming ever scarcer** es cada vez más difícil encontrar un trabajo de esta calidad; IDIOM *Fam* **to make oneself s.** esfumarse, poner (los) pies en polvorosa
2 *adv Literary* apenas

scarcely ['skeəslɪ] *adv* apenas; **she could s. speak** apenas podía hablar; **I know s. any of those people** no conozco a casi ninguna de esas personas; **he has s. any hair left** apenas le quedan unos pelos; **s. ever/anyone** casi nunca/nadie; **s. had I begun to speak when...** apenas había empezado a hablar cuando..., no había hecho más que empezar a hablar cuando...; **it is s. likely that...** es muy improbable que...; **I could s. tell his mother, now could I!** ¿cómo se lo iba a contar a su madre?; **I s. know where to begin** no sé muy bien por dónde empezar

scarcity ['skeəsɪtɪ], **scarceness** ['skeəsnɪs] *n* escasez *f*; **the book has a high s. value** el libro tiene un gran valor debido a su rareza

scare ['skeə(r)] 1 *n* (**a**) *(fright)* susto *m*; **we had a bit of a s.** nos dimos *or* pegamos un buen susto; **you gave me an awful s.** me has dado un susto tremendo (**b**) *(widespread alarm)* alarma *f*; **a safety/pollution s.** una alarma (social) por razones de seguridad/contaminación; **a bomb s.** una amenaza de bomba; **to use s. tactics (on sb)** amedrentar (a alguien) ►► ***s. story*** historia *f* alarmista
2 *vt* asustar; **you scared me!** ¡qué susto me has dado!; *Fam* **to s. the hell** *or* **the life** *or* **the living daylights** *or* **the wits out of sb** pegarle un susto de muerte a alguien; *Vulg* **to s. sb shitless** hacer cagarse de miedo a alguien, *Esp* acojonar a alguien, *Méx* sacar un pedo a alguien, *RP* hacer que alguien se cague hasta las patas; **the film scared me stiff!** la película me hizo morirme de miedo
3 *vi* asustarse; **I don't s. easily** no me asusto fácilmente

►**scare away, scare off** *vt sep* ahuyentar

►**scare up** *vt sep US Fam (meal)* improvisar

scarecrow ['skeəkrəʊ] *n* (**a**) *(for birds)* espantapájaros *m inv* (**b**) *Fam (badly dressed person)* espantajo *m* (**c**) *Fam (very thin person)* fideo *m*

scared [skeəd] *adj* asustado(a); **to be s.** estar asustado(a); **to be s. of** tener miedo de; **I'm s. of spiders** me dan miedo las arañas; **don't be s. of me** no me temas, no me tengas miedo; **to be s. to do sth** tener miedo de hacer algo; *Fam* **I was s. out of my wits!** ¡tenía muchísimo miedo!; *Vulg* **to be s. shitless** estar cagado(a) de miedo, *Esp* estar acojonado(a), *RP* tener un cagazo de la puta madre; **to be s. stiff, to be s. to death** estar muerto(a) de miedo

scaredy cat ['skeədɪkæt] *n Br Fam* gallina *mf*, *Esp* miedica *mf*

scaremonger ['skeəmʌŋgə(r)] *n* alarmista *mf*

scaremongering ['skeəmʌŋgərɪŋ] *n* alarmismo *m*

scarf[1] [skɑːf] (*pl* **scarves** [skɑːvz]) *n* *(woollen)* bufanda *f*; *(of silk, for head)* pañuelo *m*

scarf[2] [skɑːf] *vt US Fam* **to s. (down)** *(eat)* zamparse

scarify ['skærɪfaɪ] *vt* (**a**) *Med* escarificar (**b**) *Agr* escarificar (**c**) *Literary (criticize severely)* criticar con severidad

scarily ['skeərɪlɪ] *adv (unnervingly)* estremecedoramente; **we came s. close to being killed** estuvimos terriblemente cerca de que nos mataran

scarlet ['skɑːlɪt] 1 *n* (color *m*) escarlata *m*
2 *adj* escarlata; **to go** *or* **turn s.** *(with anger, embarrassment)* ponerse colorado(a) ►► ***s. fever*** escarlatina *f*; *Bot* ***s. pimpernel*** muraje *m*; ***s. rosefinch*** camachuelo *m* carminoso; *Old-fashioned* ***s. woman*** mujer *f* pública

scarp [skɑːp] *n* escarpadura *f*, escarpa *f*

scarper ['skɑːpə(r)] *vi Br Fam* largarse, *Esp* darse el piro, *Am* rajarse; **go on, s.!** ¡vamos, largo!

SCART [skɑːt] *n Elec* euroconector *m* ►► ***S. cable*** cable *m* (de) euroconector; ***S. plug*** enchufe *m* (de) euroconector; ***S. socket*** entrada *f* de euroconector

scary ['skeərɪ] *adj Fam (noise, situation)* aterrador(ora), espantoso(a); *(movie, book)* de miedo, de terror; *(coincidence)* estremecedor(ora), espeluznante; *Hum* **they're so in love with each other it's s.** están tan enamorados que da miedo

scat[1] [skæt] *exclam Fam* ¡lárgate!, ¡largo!

scat[2] *n Mus* = estilo de jazz en el que se improvisan letras sin sentido

scathing ['skeɪðɪŋ] *adj (remark, sarcasm)* mordaz, cáustico(a); **she was s. about the security arrangements** criticó con mordacidad las medidas de seguridad; **to give sb a s. look** lanzarle a alguien una mirada cáustica

scathingly ['skeɪðɪŋlɪ] *adv (to remark, speak)* con mordacidad

scatological [skætə'lɒdʒɪkəl] *adj* escatológico(a)

scatology [skæ'tɒlədʒɪ] *n* escatología *f*

scatter ['skætə(r)] 1 *vt* (**a**) *(disperse) (clouds, demonstrators)* dispersar; **my family are scattered all round the country** tengo a la familia dispersa *or* desperdigada *or* repartida por todo el país
(**b**) *(strew) (corn, seed)* esparcir; **to s. crumbs/papers all over the place** dejar todo lleno *or* sembrado de migas/papeles ►► ***s. cushion*** cojín *m*; *Math* ***s. diagram*** diagrama *m* de dispersión; ***s. gun*** escopeta *f*
(**c**) *Phys (light)* dispersar
2 *vi* (**a**) *(crowd, clouds)* dispersarse; **the birds scattered as soon as the cat approached** en cuanto apareció el gato los pájaros se dispersaron rápidamente (**b**) *(be strewn)* **the beads scattered all over the floor** las cuentas se esparcieron *or* se desparramaron por el suelo
3 *n* **a s. of farms on the hillside** algunas granjas dispersas en la ladera de la colina

scatterbrain ['skætəbreɪn] *n Fam* cabeza *mf* de chorlito, despistado(a) *m,f*

scatterbrained ['skætəbreɪnd] *adj Fam* atolondrado(a), despistado(a)

scattered ['skætəd] *adj (dispersed) (villages, houses)* disperso(a); *(applause, fighting)* aislado(a); **there will be s. showers** habrá chubascos aislados

scattering ['skætərɪŋ] *n* **a s. of followers** algunas seguidores aislados; **there was a s. of farms** había algunas granjas dispersas

scatty ['skætɪ] *adj Br Fam* atolondrado(a), despistado(a)

scaup [skɔːp] *n* porrón *m* bastardo

scavenge ['skævɪndʒ] 1 *vt (material, metals)* rebuscar (entre los desperdicios); **he managed to s. a meal** consiguió rescatar algo para comer
2 *vi* **to s. for sth** rebuscar algo entre los desperdicios; **to s. in the dustbins** rebuscar en los cubos de basura

scavenger ['skævɪndʒə(r)] *n* (**a**) *(animal)* (animal *m*) carroñero *m* (**b**) *(person)* = persona que vive de lo que puede rescatar de la basura, *Arg* ciruja *mf*

scenario [sɪ'nɑːrɪəʊ] (*pl* **scenarios**) *n* (**a**) *(of movie)* argumento *m* (**b**) *(situation)* situación *f* hipotética; **a likely s. is...** puede muy bien ocurrir que...

> **False friend**: In the contexts of films and the theatre, the Spanish word **escenario** is not a translation for the English word **scenario**. In Spanish **escenario** means "stage", "setting" or "scene".

scene [siːn] *n* (**a**) *Theat & Cin* escena *f*; **Act IV, S. 2** acto cuarto, escena segunda; **the murder s.** la escena del crimen; IDIOM **to set the s.** describir la escena; **this decision set the s. for a major confrontation** esta decisión abonó el terreno para un enfrentamiento muy serio
(**b**) *(image, situation)* escena *f*; **a touching/terrifying s.** una escena conmovedora/aterradora; **a s. of devastation** una escena de destrucción; **there were some nasty scenes at the match** en el partido se produjeron algunas escenas desagradables; **I can picture the s.** me puedo imaginar la escena
(**c**) *Theat (scenery)* decorado *m*; IDIOM **behind the scenes** entre bastidores ►► ***s. change*** cambio *m* de decorado; ***s. painter*** pintor(ora) *m,f* de decorados; ***s. shifter*** tramoyista *mf*
(**d**) *(place, spot)* escenario *m*; **the s. of the crime/accident** el escenario *or* lugar del crimen/accidente; **a change of s. would do him good** un cambio de aires le vendría bien; **the police were soon on the s.** la policía no tardó en llegar al lugar de los hechos; **to arrive** *or* **come on the s.** aparecer (en escena)
(**e**) *Art* escena *f*
(**f**) *(fuss)* **to make a s.** hacer una escena, *Esp* montar un número; **to have a s. with sb** tener una escena con alguien
(**g**) *(world)* **the music s.** la movida musical; **the drug s.** el mundo de la droga; **the political/sporting s.** el panorama político/deportivo; *Fam* **it's not my s.** no me gusta *or Esp* va mucho; **the s.** *(gay milieu)* el ambiente (gay)

scenery ['siːnərɪ] *n* (**a**) *(in play)* decorado *m* (**b**) *(landscape)* paisaje *m*; *Fam* **you need a change of s.** necesitas un cambio de aires

> **False friend**: The Spanish word **escenario** is not a translation for the English word **scenery**. In Spanish **escenario** means "stage", "setting" or "scene".

scenic ['siːnɪk] *adj* (**a**) *(picturesque)* pintoresco(a); **an area of great s. beauty** una zona de gran belleza escénica ►► ***s. railway*** *(train)* tren *m* turístico; ***s. route*** ruta *f* turística; *Hum* **we came by the s. route** *(we got lost)* nos perdimos (**b**) *Theat* de decorados

scent [sent] 1 *n* (**a**) *(smell)* aroma *m* (**b**) *(perfume)* perfume *m* (**c**) *(in hunting)* rastro *m*; **to pick up the s.** detectar el rastro; **to be on the s. of** seguir el rastro de; **to lose the s.** perder el rastro; **he threw his**

pursuers off the s. despistó a sus perseguidores
2 *vt* (**a**) *(smell)* olfatear, localizar el rastro de (**b**) *(sense)* **to s. danger** olerse *or* barruntar el peligro; **to s. victory** intuir una victoria; **the president's critics could s. blood** los críticos del presidentes olían su sangre (**c**) *(perfume)* perfumar

scented ['sentɪd] *adj (fragrant)* perfumado(a)

scepter *US* = **sceptre**

sceptic, *US* **skeptic** ['skeptɪk] *n* escéptico(a) *m,f*

sceptical, *US* **skeptical** ['skeptɪkəl] *adj* escéptico(a)

sceptically, *US* **skeptically** ['skeptɪklɪ] *adv* escépticamente, con escepticismo

scepticism, *US* **skepticism** ['skeptɪsɪzəm] *n* escepticismo *m*

sceptre, *US* **scepter** ['septə(r)] *n* cetro *m*

schadenfreude ['ʃɑːdənfrɔɪdə] *n* **he experienced a degree of s. at his enemy's demise** la muerte de su enemigo le produjo cierto regocijo

schedule ['ʃedjuːl, *US* 'skedjuːl] 1 *n* (**a**) *(plan)* programa *m*, plan *m*; **to arrive/depart on s.** *(train, bus)* llegar/salir a la hora; **the train is currently on s.** en este momento el tren circula según el horario previsto; **the work was completed on s.** el trabajo se terminó en el plazo pactado *or* previsto; **we are currently running ten minutes behind/ ahead of s.** *(on train, plane)* ahora mismo tenemos diez minutos de atraso/adelanto con respecto al horario previsto; **we are ahead of/ behind s. with the project** llevamos el proyecto con adelanto/retraso con respecto a la planificación; **they have fallen behind s. with the work** se han atrasado con el trabajo; **everything went according to s.** todo fue según las previsiones; **I have a very busy s. this week** esta semana tengo una agenda muy intensa; **I work to a very tight s.** tengo que cumplir unos plazos muy estrictos
(**b**) *Com (list of prices)* lista *f or* catálogo *m* de precios
(**c**) *US (timetable)* horario *m*
(**d**) *Law (to law, articles of association)* anexo *m*, apéndice *m*
2 *vt* programar; **a meeting has been scheduled for 4.00 pm** se ha programado *or* fijado una reunión para las 4 de la tarde; **we're scheduled to arrive at 21.45** está previsto que lleguemos a las 21:45; **she wasn't scheduled to arrive until Sunday** no estaba previsto que llegara antes del domingo; **which day is the film scheduled for?** ¿para cuándo está programada la película?; **I'm only scheduled to speak for ten minutes** sólo tengo diez minutos para hablar; **the building is scheduled for demolition** está programada la demolición del edificio; **could you s. a meeting with my lawyer for me?** ¿podría concertarme una reunión con mi abogado?

scheduled ['ʃedjuːld, *US* 'skedjuːld] *adj (services)* programado(a); **at the s. time** a la hora prevista; *TV* **we announce a change to our s. programmes** anunciamos un cambio en nuestra programación habitual; **its s. time of departure is 7.30** su salida está programada para las 7:30 ►► ***s. flight*** vuelo *m* regular

scheduler ['ʃedjuːlə(r), *US* 'skedjuːlə(r)] *n* (**a**) *Comptr* software *m* de planificación (de proyectos) (**b**) *TV* responsable *mf* de la programación

scheduling ['ʃedjuːlɪŋ, *US* 'skedjuːlɪŋ] *n* (**a**) *(of events, meetings)* programación *f*, planificación *f* (**b**) *TV* programación *f*

schema ['skiːmə] (*pl* **schemata** [-mətə]) *n* (**a**) *(diagram)* esquema *m* (**b**) *Psy* esquema *m*

schematic [skɪ'mætɪk] *adj* esquemático(a)

schematically [skɪ'mætɪklɪ] *adv* esquemáticamente

scheme [skiːm] 1 *n* (**a**) *(arrangement, system)* sistema *m*, método *m*; **in the (greater) s. of things** desde una perspectiva general, en un plano global; **where does he fit into the s. of things?** ¿qué lugar ocupará exactamente?
(**b**) *(plan)* plan *m*, proyecto *m*; *(plot)* intriga *f*; **a s. to get rich quick** un plan para hacerse rico rápidamente; **government unemployment schemes** programas *or* planes gubernamentales para el desempleo
2 *vi* intrigar; **they schemed against the general** conspiraron contra el general

schemer ['skiːmə(r)] *n* intrigante *mf*

scheming ['skiːmɪŋ] 1 *n* intrigas *fpl*
2 *adj* intrigante

scherzo ['skeətsəʊ] *n Mus* scherzo *m*

schilling ['ʃɪlɪŋ] *n Formerly (Austrian currency)* chelín *m* (austriaco)

schism ['s(k)ɪzəm] *n* cisma *m*

schismatic [s(k)ɪz'mætɪk] 1 *n* cismático(a) *m,f*
2 *adj* cismático(a)

schist [ʃɪst] *n Geol* esquisto *m*

schizo ['skɪtsəʊ] *Fam* 1 *n* esquizo *mf*
2 *adj* esquizo

schizoid ['skɪtsɔɪd] 1 *n* esquizoide *mf*
2 *adj* esquizoide

schizophrenia [skɪtsə'friːnɪə] *n* esquizofrenia *f*

schizophrenic [skɪtsə'frenɪk] 1 *n* esquizofrénico(a) *m,f*
2 *adj* esquizofrénico(a)

schlemiel [ʃlə'miːl] *n US Fam* pelagatos *mf inv*, desgraciado(a) *m,f*

schlep(p) [ʃlep] *Fam* 1 *n* (**a**) *(journey)* caminata *f* (**b**) *US (person)* besugo(a) *m,f*, *Arg* ganso(a) *m,f*
2 *vt (carry)* acarrear
3 *vi (walk)* **to s. home** pegarse una caminata hasta casa; **I had to s. to the corner store** arrastré mis huesos hasta la tienda de la esquina

schlock [ʃlɒk] *US Fam* 1 *n (worthless things)* porquerías *fpl*
2 *adj (worthless)* de porquería

schlong [ʃlɒŋ] *n US very Fam* verga *f*, cimbel *m*

schmaltz [ʃmɔːlts] *n Fam* ñoñería *f*, sensiblería *f*

schmaltzy ['ʃmɔːltsɪ] *adj Fam* sensiblero(a), *Esp* ñoño(a)

schmo [ʃməʊ] *n US Fam (useless person)* lelo(a) *m,f*, *Esp* memo(a) *m,f*, *RP* boludo(a) *m,f*

schmooze [ʃmuːz] *vi Fam* chismorrear, *Esp* cotillear, *Am* chismear

schmuck [ʃmʌk] *n US Fam* lelo(a) *m,f*

schnap(p)s [ʃnæps] *n* schnapps *m inv*

schnauzer ['ʃnaʊtsə(r)] *n (dog)* schnauzer *m*

schnitzel ['ʃnɪtsəl] *n* filete *m* de ternera; **Wiener s.** filete de ternera a la milanesa

schnook [ʃnʊk] *n US Fam* bobo(a) *m,f*

schnozz [ʃnɒz], **schnozzle** ['ʃnɒzəl] *n US Fam* napia *f*, napias *fpl*

scholar ['skɒlə(r)] *n* (**a**) *(learned person)* erudito(a) *m,f*; *(expert)* especialista *mf*; **an Egyptian s.** un egiptólogo; **a Latin s.** un latinista; **I'm not much of a s.** no tengo una gran formación académica (**b**) *(award holder)* becario(a) *m,f*

scholarly ['skɒləlɪ] *adj* (**a**) *(person, article, work)* erudito(a) (**b**) *(approach)* científico(a), académico(a)

scholarship ['skɒləʃɪp] *n* (**a**) *Educ (grant)* beca *f* ►► ***s. holder, s. student*** becario(a) *m,f* (**b**) *(learning)* erudición *f*

scholastic [skə'læstɪk] 1 *n* escolástico(a) *m,f*
2 *adj* (**a**) *Formal (academic)* académico(a) (**b**) *Phil* escolástico(a)

scholasticism [skə'læstɪsɪzəm] *n* escolasticismo *m*

school[1] [skuːl] 1 *n* (**a**) *(for children) (up to 14)* colegio *m*, escuela *f*; *(from 14 to 18)* instituto *m*; **to go to s.** ir al colegio; **what did you do at s. today?** ¿qué has hecho hoy en clase?; **I went to** *or* **was at s. with him** fuimos juntos al colegio; **our youngest son is still at s.** nuestro hijo más pequeño aún está en la escuela; **we go back to s. next week** la semana que viene volvemos a clase; **there is no s. tomorrow** mañana no hay colegio *or* clase; **when does s. start?** ¿cuándo empiezan las clases?; **what are you doing after s.?** ¿qué vas a hacer después de clase?; **I was kept behind after s.** me hicieron quedarme después de clase; **she left s. at sixteen** dejó de estudiar a los dieciséis; **the whole s. is invited** está invitado todo el colegio; **of s. age** en edad escolar; IDIOM **she went to the s. of hard knocks** estudió en la escuela de la vida; **the s. of life** la escuela de la vida ►► *Br* ***s. board*** consejo *m* escolar; ***s. book*** libro *m* de texto (escolar); ***s. buildings*** edificios *mpl* del colegio; ***s. bus*** autobús *m* escolar; ***s. day*** *(hours in school)* jornada *f* escolar; **on school days** en días de colegio; ***s. dinners*** almuerzo *m* escolar; ***s. district*** distrito *m* escolar; ***s. fees*** cuota *f* del colegio; ***s. friend*** amigo(a) *m,f* del colegio; ***s. holidays*** vacaciones *f* escolares; ***s. hours*** horas *fpl* de clase; ***s. leaver*** = alumno que ha finalizado sus estudios; ***s. magazine*** revista *f* del colegio; ***s. meals*** almuerzo *m* escolar; ***s. report*** libro *m* de escolaridad; *Br* ***s. run:* to do the s. run** *(morning)* llevar a los niños al colegio; *(evening)* recoger a los niños del colegio; ***s. trip*** excursión *f* escolar; ***s. uniform*** uniforme *m* escolar; *US* ***s. yard*** patio *m* de recreo; ***s. year*** año *m* escolar *or* académico
(**b**) *(for driving, languages etc) (private)* academia *f* ►► ***s. of dance, dancing s.*** escuela *f or* academia *f* de baile
(**c**) *US (college, university)* universidad *f*
(**d**) *(university department)* facultad *f*; **the Business S.** la Facultad de Empresariales; **she's at law s.** está estudiando derecho ►► ***s. of art, art s.*** escuela *f* de bellas artes
(**e**) *(of artists, thinkers)* escuela *f*; **s. of thought** corriente *or* escuela de pensamiento; IDIOM **he's one of the old s.** es de la vieja escuela
2 *vt* (**a**) *(educate)* educar (**b**) *(train) (child, mind)* instruir, adiestrar; **to s. sb in sth** instruir a alguien en algo; **she is well schooled in diplomacy** está bien instruida en la diplomacia

school[2] *n (of fish)* banco *m*

schoolbag ['skuːlbæg] *n* cartera *f*

schoolboy ['sku:lbɔɪ] *n* colegial *m*; **as every s. knows** como es de todos sabido ►► ***s. humour*** humor *m* de niños

schoolchild ['sku:ltʃaɪld] *n* colegial(ala) *m,f*

schooldays ['sku:ldeɪz] *npl* años *mpl* de colegio

schoolfellow ['sku:lfeləʊ] *n* compañero(a) *m,f* de colegio

schoolgirl ['sku:lgɜ:l] *n* colegiala *f* ►► ***s. crush:*** **she had the usual s. crush on the gym teacher** se enamoró como una colegiala del profesor de gimnasia

schoolhouse ['sku:lhaʊs] *n* colegio *m*, escuela *f*

schooling ['sku:lɪŋ] *n* enseñanza *f or* educación *f* escolar; **I have had no formal s.** no he recibido educación formal

schoolkid ['sku:lkɪd] *n Fam* escolar *mf*; **stop behaving like an overgrown s.!** ¡deja de comportarte como un niño!

schoolmarm ['sku:lmɑ:m] *n Fam* maestra *f*

schoolmarmish ['sku:lmɑ:mɪʃ] *adj Fam* **she's very s.** parece una institutriz de las de antes

schoolmaster ['sku:lmɑ:stə(r)] *n Formal (primary)* maestro *m*; *(secondary)* profesor *m*

schoolmate ['sku:lmeɪt] *n* compañero(a) *m,f* de colegio

schoolmistress ['sku:lmɪstrɪs] *n Formal (primary)* maestra *f*; *(secondary)* profesora *f*

schoolroom ['sku:lru:m] *n* aula *f*, clase *f*

schoolteacher ['sku:lti:tʃə(r)] *n (primary)* maestro(a) *m,f*; *(secondary)* profesor(ora) *m,f*

schoolteaching ['sku:lti:tʃɪŋ] *n* enseñanza *f*

schoolwork ['sku:lwɜ:k] *n* trabajo *m* escolar

schooner ['sku:nə(r)] *n* **(a)** *(ship)* goleta *f* **(b)** *(glass) (for sherry)* copa *f*; *(for beer)* jarra *f*

schuss [ʃʊs] **1** *n (in skiing)* descenso *m* en línea recta
2 *vi (in skiing)* descender en línea recta

schwa [ʃwɑ:] *n Ling* schwa *f*, = sonido vocálico central átono

sciatic [saɪ'ætɪk] *adj Anat* ciático(a) ►► ***s. nerve*** nervio *m* ciático

sciatica [saɪ'ætɪkə] *n Med* ciática *f*

science ['saɪəns] *n* ciencia *f*; *Educ* **she's good at s.** se le dan bien las ciencias; **forecasting the stock market is not an exact s.** el pronóstico de los vaivenes de la bolsa no es una ciencia exacta ►► ***s. class*** clase *f* de ciencias; ***s. fiction*** ciencia *f* ficción; ***s. park*** parque *m* tecnológico universitario; ***s. teacher*** profesor(ora) *m,f* de ciencias

scientific [saɪən'tɪfɪk] *adj* científico(a)

scientifically [saɪən'tɪfɪklɪ] *adv* científicamente; **to be s. minded** tener inclinaciones científicas

scientist ['saɪəntɪst] *n* científico(a) *m,f*

Scientologist [saɪən'tɒlədʒɪst] *n* cientólogo(a) *m, f*

Scientology® [saɪən'tɒlədʒɪ] *n* cienciología *f*

sci-fi ['saɪfaɪ] *Fam* **1** *n* ciencia *f* ficción
2 *adj* de ciencia ficción

Scilly ['sɪlɪ] *n* **the S. Isles, the Scillies** las Islas Scilly *or* Sorlingas

scimitar ['sɪmɪtə(r)] *n* cimitarra *f*

scintilla [sɪn'tɪlə] *n Formal* atisbo *m*; **there is not a s. of proof that...** no existe el menor atisbo de prueba de que...

scintillate ['sɪntɪleɪt] *vi* **(a)** *(sparkle) (give off sparks)* chispear; *(shine brightly)* centellear **(b) to s. with wit** tener un ingenio chispeante

scintillating ['sɪntɪleɪtɪŋ] *adj (conversation, wit)* chispeante; *(performance)* brillante

scion ['saɪən] *n* **(a)** *Bot* púa *f*, esqueje *m* **(b)** *Formal (offspring)* vástago *m*, descendiente *mf*

Scipio ['skɪpɪəʊ] *pr n* Escipión

scissors ['sɪzəz] *npl* **(a)** *(for cutting)* tijeras *fpl*; **a pair of s.** unas tijeras ►► ***s. kick*** *(in soccer) (overhead)* tijereta *f*, chilena *f*; *(in swimming)* patada *f* con tijera **(b)** *(in wrestling)* **s. (hold)** (llave *f*) tijera *f* **(c)** *(in athletics)* **s. (jump)** (salto *m* de) tijera *f* **(d)** *(in rugby)* tijera *f*

sclera ['sklɪərə] *n Anat* esclerótica *f*

sclerosis [sklə'rəʊsɪs] *n Med* esclerosis *f inv*

sclerotic [sklə'rɒtɪk] **1** *n* esclerótica *f*
2 *adj Med* esclerótico(a)

scoff [skɒf] **1** *vt Fam (eat)* zamparse; **he scoffed the whole packet** se zampó todo el paquete
2 *vi (mock)* burlarse, mofarse (**at** de); **you may s., but it really can be done** tú búrlate lo que quieras, pero se puede hacer

scoffer ['skɒfə(r)] *n* burlón(ona) *m,f*

scofflaw ['skɒflɔ:] *n US* = persona que no respeta las normas o leyes, en especial las de tráfico o las del consumo de alcohol

scold [skəʊld] *vt* reñir, regañar (**for** por)

scolding ['skəʊldɪŋ] **1** *n* regañina *f*; **to give sb a s. (for doing sth)** regañar a alguien (por haber hecho algo), echar una regañina a alguien (por haber hecho algo)
2 *adj (tone)* severo(a)

scollop = **scallop**

sconce [skɒns] *n (for candlestick)* candelabro *m* de pared; *(for electric light)* aplique *m*

scone [skɒn, skəʊn] *n* = bollo redondo y bastante seco, dulce o salado, que a veces contiene pasas

scooby ['sku:bɪ] *n Br Fam* **he hasn't got a s.** *(is incompetent, ignorant, inexperienced)* no tiene ni la más remota idea

scoop [sku:p] **1** *n* **(a)** *(utensil) (for flour, mashed potato)* paleta *f*; *(for ice cream)* pinzas *fpl* de cuchara; *(for sugar)* cucharilla *f* plana **(b)** *(portion) (of ice cream)* bola *f*; *(of mashed potato, flour)* cucharada *f* **(c)** *Journ* primicia *f*; **to get** *or* **to make a s.** conseguir una primicia **(d)** *Br Fam (profit)* ganancia *f*; **to make a s.** forrarse, *RP* juntar la guita a paladas
2 *vt* **(a)** *(pick up)* **s. the ice-cream into a dish** pon el helado en un plato con la cuchara; **she scooped the papers into her case** recogió como pudo los papeles con sus brazos y los metió en el maletín **(b)** *Journ* **to s. a story** obtener una primicia; **they scooped the other newspapers** obtuvieron la primicia por delante del resto de los periódicos **(c)** *(win) (prize)* llevarse

► **scoop out** *vt sep* **(a)** *(take) (with hands)* sacar con las manos; *(with spoon)* sacar con cuchara
(b) *(hollow out) (hole)* excavar; **s. out the flesh from the grapefruit** quítale la pulpa al pomelo

► **scoop up** *vt sep (with spoon)* tomar una cucharada de; **he scooped up the papers in his arms** recogió los papeles como pudo entre sus brazos

scoopful ['sku:pfʊl] *n (of ice cream)* bola *f*; *(of mashed potato, flour)* cucharada *f*

scoot [sku:t] *vi Fam* **to s. (off** *or* **away)** salir disparado(a); **the boat scooted over the water** la lancha se deslizaba rápidamente sobre el agua; **s.!** ¡lárgate!

scooter ['sku:tə(r)] *n* **(a)** *(propelled by foot)* patinete *m* **(b) (motor) s.** escúter *m*, Vespa® *f*

scope [skəʊp] **1** *n* **(a)** *(extent)* ámbito *m*, alcance *m*; **does the matter fall within the s. of the law?** ¿se encuadra esta cuestión dentro del ámbito de la ley?; **it is beyond the s. of this study** está fuera del alcance de este estudio; **the book is too narrow in s.** el libro tiene una cobertura muy limitada
(b) *(opportunity)* margen *m*, posibilidades *fpl*; **there's s. for improvement** hay margen para mejorar, se puede mejorar; **to give s. for...** *(interpretation, explanation)* permitir (la posibilidad de)...; **the job gave him full/little s. to demonstrate his talents** el puesto le dio amplias/escasas posibilidades de demostrar sus aptitudes; **to give free s. to one's imagination** dar rienda suelta a la imaginación **(c)** *Fam (telescope)* telescopio *m*
2 *vt US Fam (look at)* mirar

► **scope out** *vt sep US Fam* mirar

scops owl ['skɒpsaʊl] *n* autillo *m*

scorch [skɔ:tʃ] **1** *n* **s. (mark)** (marca *f* de) quemadura *f*
2 *vt* chamuscar; **I scorched my shirt** quemé la camisa con la plancha; **the sun scorched the grass** el sol quemó la hierba
3 *vi* **(a)** *(food)* chamuscarse **(b)** *Fam (move quickly)* **he scorched across the turf** cruzó la hierba a toda velocidad *or Esp* pastilla; **we were scorching along at over 100 mph** íbamos disparados a más de 100 millas por hora

scorched [skɔ:tʃt] *adj* chamuscado(a) ►► ***s. earth policy*** *(of retreating army)* política *f* de tierra quemada

scorcher ['skɔ:tʃə(r)] *n Fam* **(a)** *(hot day)* **tomorrow will be a real s.** mañana hará un calor abrasador, *Arg RP* mañana va a ser un horno **(b)** *(something powerful, fast etc)* **the shot was a s.** el disparo fue un verdadero cañonazo; **she's a real s.** está buenísima

scorching ['skɔ:tʃɪŋ] *adj* **(a)** *(weather, surface)* abrasador(ora); **this tea/the sand is s.** este té/la arena está que arde; **it's s. (hot)** hace un calor abrasador **(b)** *(criticism)* durísimo(a) **(c)** *(powerful, fast, etc)* **a s. shot** un cañonazo; **a s. run** una carrera imparable

score [skɔ:(r)] **1** *n* **(a)** *(total) (in sport)* resultado *m*; *(in quiz)* puntuación *f*; **the s. was five-nil at half time** en el descanso el marcador era 5-0; **the s. is 5-2 in the second set** van 5-2 en el segundo set; **there was still no s.** no se había movido el marcador; **what's the s.?** *(in game)* ¿cómo van?; *Fam Fig (what's the situation)* ¿qué pasa?; **what was the (final) s.?** ¿cuál fue el resultado (final)?; **to keep (the) s.** llevar el

tanteo; IDIOM *Fam* **to know the s.** conocer el percal ▸▸ ***s. draw*** *(in football)* empate *m* con goles
(**b**) *(in rugby) (try or goal)* tanto *m*
(**c**) *(line)* arañazo *m*
(**d**) *(quarrel)* **to have a s. to settle with sb** tener una cuenta que saldar con alguien
(**e**) *(reason, grounds)* **don't worry on that s.** no te preocupes en ese aspecto; **on that s. alone** sólo por eso; **he deserved to be rejected on more than one s.** merecía ser rechazado por más de un motivo
(**f**) *Mus* partitura *f*; *(for movie)* banda *f* sonora original; **piano/vocal s.** partitura para piano/voces
(**g**) *Old-fashioned (twenty)* **a s.** una veintena; **three s. and ten** setenta; *Fam* **there were scores of people there** *(a lot)* había un montón de gente allí
2 *vt* (**a**) *(in sport) (goal, try)* marcar; *(point, run)* anotar; *Fig (success, victory)* apuntarse; **to s. a basket** *(in basketball)* encestar; **to s. a hit** *(hit target)* hacer blanco; *Fig (person, movie)* acertar; *Fig* **to s. points off sb** *(in debate)* anotarse puntos a costa de alguien
(**b**) *(in exam, quiz)* sacar; **I scored 65 percent in the exam** saqué 65 sobre 100 en el examen; **each correct answer scores ten points** cada respuesta correcta vale diez puntos
(**c**) *(cut line in) (paper, wood, ground)* marcar; *(pastry, meat)* hacer cortes en; **she scored her name on a tree** grabó su nombre en un árbol; **a face scored with lines** una cara llena de arrugas
(**d**) *(symphony, opera)* componer; *(movie)* escribir la música para
(**e**) *Fam (buy)* **to s. drugs** conseguir *or Esp* pillar droga
3 *vi* (**a**) *(get a goal, point, try)* marcar; *(get a basket)* encestar
(**b**) *(in quiz)* **he scored well in the first round** sacó una buena puntuación en la primera ronda
(**c**) *(keep the score)* llevar el tanteo
(**d**) *(have the advantage)* **her proposal scores on cost** el punto fuerte de su propuesta son los costos; **that's where their plan scores over ours** en eso su plan se lleva la palma sobre el nuestro
(**e**) *Fam (sexually)* ligar; **to s. with sb** ligarse *or RP, Ven* levantarse a alguien
(**f**) *Fam (buy drugs)* conseguir *or Esp* pillar droga

▸ **score off** *vt sep (delete)* tachar; **her name has been scored off the list** su nombre ha sido eliminado de la lista

▸ **score out, score through** *vt sep (delete)* tachar

scoreboard ['skɔːbɔːd] *n* marcador *m*

scorecard ['skɔːkɑːd] *n* tarjeta *f*

scorekeeper ['skɔːkiːpə(r)] *n* encargado(a) *m,f* del marcador

score-line ['skɔːlaɪn] *n Sport* marcador *m*

scorer ['skɔːrə(r)] *n* (**a**) *(player) (in soccer, hockey)* goleador(ora) *m,f*; *(in basketball, American football, rugby)* anotador(ora) *m,f*; **Beckham was the s.** Beckham marcó el gol; **the team's top s.** el máximo goleador/anotador del equipo (**b**) *(score keeper)* encargado(a) *m,f* del marcador

scoresheet ['skɔːʃiːt] *n* planilla *f*; **to get on the s.** *(score)* marcar

scoring ['skɔːrɪŋ] *n* (**a**) *(of goals, tries)* **to open the s.** abrir el marcador (**b**) *(scorekeeping)* **I'm not very good at s.** no se me da muy bien llevar el marcador (**c**) *(orchestration)* orquestación *f*

scorn [skɔːn] 1 *n* desprecio *m*, desdén *m*; **to pour s. on sth/sb** hablar de algo/alguien con desdén
2 *vt* despreciar, desdeñar; **to s. to do sth** no dignarse a hacer algo

scornful ['skɔːnfʊl] *adj* despreciativo(a), desdeñoso(a); **to be s. of sth** despreciar *or* desdeñar algo

scornfully ['skɔːnfʊlɪ] *adv* con desdén, con aire despreciativo

Scorpio ['skɔːpɪəʊ] *n* (**a**) *(sign of zodiac)* Escorpio *m*, Escorpión *m*; **to be (a) S.** ser Escorpio *or* Escorpión (**b**) *(constellation)* Escorpio *m*, Escorpión *m*

scorpion ['skɔːpɪən] *n* escorpión *m*, alacrán *m* ▸▸ ***s. fish*** diablo *m* marino; ***s. fly*** mosca *f* escorpión

Scot [skɒt] *n* escocés(esa) *m,f*

Scotch [skɒtʃ] 1 *n (whisky)* whisky *m* escocés
2 *adj* escocés(esa) ▸▸ ***S. broth*** = caldo típico escocés; ***S. egg*** = bola de fiambre frita y rebozada con un huevo duro en el centro; ***S. mist*** bruma *f*; ***S. pancake*** torta *f* gruesa y esponjosa; ***S. pine*** pino *m* silvestre; *US* ***S. tape***® cinta *f* adhesiva, *Esp* celo *m*, *CAm, Méx* Durex® *m*; ***S. terrier*** terrier *m* escocés; ***S. whisky*** whisky *m* escocés

scotch [skɒtʃ] *vt (rumour)* desmentir; *(plan, attempt)* arruinar, frustrar

scoter ['skəʊtə(r)] *n* ***common s.*** negrón *m* común; ***velvet s.*** negrón *m* especulado

scot-free ['skɒt'friː] *adj Fam* **to get off s.** quedar impune

Scotland ['skɒtlənd] *n* Escocia ▸▸ ***S. Yard*** Scotland Yard

Scots [skɒts] 1 *n (dialect)* = variedad escocesa del inglés
2 *adj* escocés(esa) ▸▸ ***S. pine*** pino *m* albar

Scotsman ['skɒtsmən] *n* escocés *m*

Scotswoman ['skɒtswʊmən] *n* escocesa *f*

Scottie (dog) ['skɒtɪ('dɒg)] *n Fam* terrier *m* escocés

Scottish ['skɒtɪʃ] *adj* escocés(esa) ▸▸ ***S. gaelic*** (gaélico *m)* escocés *m*; ***S. terrier*** terrier *m* escocés

scoundrel ['skaʊndrəl] *n* (**a**) *(wicked person)* bellaco(a) *m,f*, canalla *mf* (**b**) *Fam (rascal)* sinvergüenzón(ona) *m,f*, granujilla *mf*

scour ['skaʊə(r)] *vt* (**a**) *(pot, surface)* restregar (**b**) *(search) (area)* peinar; *(house)* registrar, rebuscar en (**c**) *(erode)* erosionar

▸ **scour about** *vi Br* **to s. about for sth** buscar algo por todas partes

▸ **scour out** *vt sep (pot)* restregar

scourer ['skaʊərə(r)] *n* estropajo *m*

scourge [skɜːdʒ] 1 *n* (**a**) *(bane)* azote *m*; **the s. of war** el azote de la guerra (**b**) *(person)* azote *m* (**c**) *(whip)* azote *m*
2 *vt* (**a**) *(afflict)* azotar (**b**) *(whip)* azotar

scouring pad ['skaʊərɪŋpæd] *n* estropajo *m*

scouring powder ['skaʊərɪŋpaʊdə(r)] *n* polvo *m* limpiador

Scouse [skaʊs] *Fam* 1 *n* (**a**) *(dialect)* dialecto *m* de Liverpool (**b**) *(person)* persona de Liverpool
2 *adj* de Liverpool

Scouser ['skaʊsə(r)] *n Fam* persona de Liverpool

scout [skaʊt] 1 *n* (**a**) *Mil (person)* explorador(ora) *m,f*; *(ship, aircraft)* nave *f* de reconocimiento ▸▸ ***s. car*** vehículo *m* de reconocimiento (**b**) **(boy) s.** boy-scout *m*, escultista *m*; *US* **(girl) s.** scout *f*, escultista *f* ▸▸ ***the s. movement*** el movimiento scout (**c**) *Sport* ojeador(ora) *m,f*; **(talent) s.** cazatalentos *mf inv* (**d**) *(action)* **to have a s. around (for sth)** buscar (algo)
2 *vi* **to s. ahead** reconocer el terreno; **to s. around (for sth)** buscar (algo); **to s. for talent** ir a la caza de talentos

▸ **scout out** *vt insep* inspeccionar

scoutmaster ['skaʊtmɑːstə(r)] *n* jefe *m* de exploradores *or* boy-scouts

scow [skaʊ] *n* barcaza *f*

scowl [skaʊl] 1 *n* **to give sb a s.** mirar a alguien con cara de *esp Esp* enfado *or esp Am* enojo
2 *vi* fruncir el ceño, poner cara de *esp Esp* enfado *or esp Am* enojo; **she scowled at me** me frunció el ceño, me miró con *esp Esp* enfado *or esp Am* enojo

scowling ['skaʊlɪŋ] *adj (look)* severo(a)

scrabble ['skræbəl] *vi* **she was scrabbling for a handhold on the cliff face** buscaba con desesperación un punto al que agarrarse en la pared del precipicio; **to s. about** *or* **around for sth** buscar algo a tientas

scrag [skræg] 1 *n* **s. (end)** pescuezo *m*
2 *vt (pt & pp* **scragged***) (grab by the neck)* agarrar del cuello

scraggy ['skrægɪ] *adj (thin)* raquítico(a), esquelético(a)

scram [skræm] *(pt & pp* **scrammed***) vi Fam* largarse, *Esp, RP* pirarse; **s.!** ¡fuera!, ¡largo!

scramble ['skræmbəl] 1 *n* (**a**) *(rush)* desbandada *f*; *(struggle)* lucha *f* **(for** por); **there was a mad s. for seats** se desató una lucha frenética por conseguir un asiento; **it was a short s. to the top** para alcanzar la cumbre había que trepar un poco; **there was a s. for jobs when the factory opened** cuando la fábrica abrió se generó un alboroto tremendo por conseguir empleo (**b**) *(motorcycle rally)* carrera *f* de motocross
2 *vt* (**a**) *(cook)* **to s. some eggs** hacer unos huevos revueltos (**b**) *Tel (signal)* codificar (**c**) *(jumble)* mezclar; IDIOM *Fam* **all the alcohol has scrambled his brain** tanto alcohol lo ha dejado hecho un idiota (**d**) *Sport* **the defender managed to s. the ball away** el defensa consiguió despejar la pelota como pudo
3 *vi* (**a**) *(move)* **he scrambled to his feet** se puso de pie como pudo; **to s. up/down a hill** trepar por/bajar una colina con dificultad (**b**) *(struggle, fight)* **to s. for sth** luchar por algo (**c**) *(on motorcycle)* **to go scrambling** salir a hacer motocross (**d**) *Mil* despegar con urgencia

scrambled eggs ['skræmbəld'egz] *npl* huevos *mpl* revueltos

scrambler ['skræmblə(r)] *n Tel* distorsionador *m* (de frecuencias), scrambler *m*

scrambling ['skræmblɪŋ] *n* (**a**) *(sport)* motocross *m* (**b**) *(in rock climbing)* ascenso *m* trepando

scran [skræn] *n Br Fam* papeo *m*, *RP* morfi *m*

scrap[1] [skræp] 1 *n* (**a**) *(of material, paper)* trozo *m*; *(of information, conversation)* fragmento *m*; **to tear sth into scraps** hacer trizas algo; **scraps** *(of food)* sobras *fpl*; **they didn't have a s. of evidence** no tenían ni un indicio; **there isn't a s. of truth in what she says** no hay ni rastro de verdad en lo que dice; **what I say won't make a s. of difference** lo que yo diga no importará lo más mínimo; **he hasn't done a s. of work all day** *Esp* no ha dado (ni) golpe en todo el día, *Am* no movió un dedo en todo el día ►► ***s. paper*** papel *m* usado

(**b**) *(metal)* **s. (metal)** chatarra *f*; **to sell sth for s.** vender algo para chatarra ►► ***s. dealer*** chatarrero(a) *m,f*; ***s. iron*** chatarra *f*; ***s. merchant*** chatarrero(a) *m,f*; ***s. value*** valor *m* como chatarra

2 *vt* (*pt & pp* **scrapped**) (**a**) *(car)* mandar a la chatarra; *(submarine, missile)* desmantelar; *(machinery)* desguazar (**b**) *(project, idea)* descartar, abandonar; **I scrapped the first version of the script** descarté la primera versión del guión

scrap[2] *Fam* **1** *n (fight)* bronca *f*, pelea *f*; **to have** *or* **get into a s. (with sb)** pelearse (con alguien)

2 *vi* (*pt & pp* **scrapped**) *(fight)* pelearse; **he scrapped for every point** peleó cada punto

scrapbook ['skræpbʊk] *n* (**a**) *(for cuttings)* álbum *m* de recortes (**b**) *Comptr* apuntador *m*

scrape [skreɪp] **1** *n* (**a**) *(action)* rascada *f*; **to give sth a s.** rascar algo (**b**) *(mark)* arañazo *m*; *(on skin)* arañazo *m*, rasguño *m* (**c**) *(sound)* chirrido *m* (**d**) *Fam (adventure)* aventura *f*, lío *m*; **to get into a s.** meterse en un lío *or* fregado; **to get sb out of a s.** sacar a alguien de un lío

2 *vt* (**a**) *(scratch) (paint, wood, side of car)* rayar, arañar; **to s. one's knee** arañarse *or* rasguñarse la rodilla; **to s. a hole in the ground** excavar un hoyo en el suelo; **the plane just scraped the surface of the water** el avión apenas rozó la superficie del agua

(**b**) *(clean) (dirt, wallpaper)* rascar; *(vegetables)* raspar; **to s. the paint off the door** rascar la pintura de la puerta; **to s. the mud off one's shoes** rascar el barro de los zapatos; **to s. one's plate clean** rebañar el plato; IDIOM **to s. the bottom of the barrel** tener que recurrir a lo peor; **you took him on? you must really be scraping the bottom of the barrel!** ¿lo has contratado? ¡debes estar desesperado!

(**c**) *(drag)* **don't s. the chair across the floor like that** no arrastres así la silla por el suelo

(**d**) *(barely obtain)* **I just s. a living** me gano la vida como puedo; **to s. a pass** *(in exam)* aprobar por los pelos; **we scraped a draw** arañamos un empate

3 *vi* (**a**) *(rub)* rascar, raspar; **branches that s. against the shutters** ramas que rozan contra las persianas

(**b**) *(make sound)* chirriar; **she was scraping away on her fiddle** rascaba el violín con un sonido chirriante

(**c**) *(barely manage)* **to s. home** *(in contest)* ganar a duras penas; **to s. into college** entrar en la universidad por los pelos; **the ambulance just scraped past** la ambulancia consiguió pasar por los pelos

►**scrape along** *vi (financially)* arreglárselas

►**scrape back** *vt sep* **she had her hair scraped back** tenía el cabello bien peinado hacia atrás

►**scrape by** *vi (financially)* arregárselas; **she scrapes by on £150 a month** se las arregla con 150 libras por mes

►**scrape in** *vi (in election)* ganar por un pelo

►**scrape off** *vt sep* rascar, raspar

►**scrape out** *vt sep (saucepan)* restregar; *(residue)* limpiar

►**scrape through 1** *vt insep* (**a**) *(exam)* aprobar por los pelos (**b**) *(doorway, gap)* pasar por los pelos por

2 *vi* (**a**) *(in exam)* aprobar por los pelos, sacar un aprobado pelado (**b**) *(through doorway, gap)* pasar por los pelos

►**scrape together** *vt sep (money, resources)* reunir a duras penas; *(support)* conseguir a duras penas

►**scrape up** *vt sep* (**a**) *(into pile) (leaves, stones)* apilar (**b**) *(money, resources)* reunir a duras penas; *(support)* conseguir a duras penas

scraper ['skreɪpə(r)] *n* (**a**) *(tool)* rasqueta *f* (**b**) *(for muddy shoes)* limpiabarros *m inv*

scrapheap ['skræphiːp] *n* montón *m* de chatarra; IDIOM **she is scared of finding herself on the s.** tiene pánico de no conseguir nunca más un empleo; **that idea has been thrown on the s.** la idea ha sido descartada; **he was thrown on the s. at the age of forty-five** a los cuarenta y cinco años le pusieron punto final a su vida laboral

scrapie ['skreɪpɪ] *n* escrapie *m*, tembladera *f*

scraping ['skreɪpɪŋ] **1** *n (thin layer)* **toast with a s. of butter** tostadas con un poquito de mantequilla untada

2 scrapings *npl (food)* sobras *fpl*; *(from paint, wood)* raspaduras *fpl*

scrapper ['skræpə(r)] *n Br Fam (resilient person)* luchador(ora) *m,f*

scrappy ['skræpɪ] *adj (knowledge, performance)* rudimentario(a)

scrapyard ['skræpjɑːd] *n* desguace *m*, cementerio *m* de automóviles

scratch [skrætʃ] **1** *n* (**a**) *(on skin, furniture)* arañazo *m*, rasguño *m*; *(on glass, record)* raya *f*; **it's just a s.** no es más que un rasguño *or* arañazo; **he came out of it without a s.** salió sin un rasguño

(**b**) *(action)* **to give one's nose a s.** rascarse la nariz; **the dog was having a good s.** el perro se estaba rascando con ganas

(**c**) *(sound)* rasgueo *m*

(**d**) *(in golf)* scratch *m*; **to play off s.** jugar sin scratch

(**e**) *US Fam (money)* pasta *f*, *Am* plata *f*, *RP* guita *f*

(**f**) IDIOMS **she built the business up from s.** construyó el negocio partiendo de cero; **I learnt Italian from s. in six months** aprendí italiano a partir de cero en seis meses; **to start from s.** partir de cero; **to be** *or* **come up to s.** dar la talla; **to bring** *or* **get sth/sb up to s.** poner algo/a alguien a punto

2 *adj* (**a**) *(meal, team)* improvisado(a), de circunstancias (**b**) *(for notes)* *US* ***s. pad*** bloc *m* de notas; ***s. paper*** papel *m* usado (**c**) *(in golf)* **a s. player** un jugador que tiene scratch

3 *vt* (**a**) *(damage) (skin, furniture)* arañar; *(glass, record)* rayar; **she scratched her hand on the brambles** se rascó la mano con las zarzas; **he was badly scratched** quedó lleno de arañazos; **he scratched his name on the card** garabateó su nombre en la tarjeta; IDIOM **we've only scratched the surface of the problem** no hemos hecho más que empezar a tratar el problema

(**b**) *(rub) (itch, rash)* rascar; **to s. oneself** rascarse; **to s. one's nose** rascarse la nariz; **I'm scratching my head looking for a solution** me sale humo de la cabeza de tanto buscar una solución; IDIOM **you s. my back and I'll s. yours** hoy por ti y mañana por mí

(**c**) *(of bird, animal) (ground)* arañar

(**d**) *(cancel) (meeting, match)* suspender; *(sentence, paragraph)* eliminar; **to s. sb's name from a list** quitar *or Am* sacar a alguien de una lista; **to s. sb from a team** sacar a alguien de un equipo

4 *vi* (**a**) *(to relieve itch) (person, animal)* rascarse (**b**) *(thorns)* picar; *(new clothes)* rascar, raspar (**c**) *(animal)* **the dog was scratching at the door** el perro estaba arañando la puerta (**d**) *(withdraw from competition)* retirarse

►**scratch about, scratch around** *vi* **to s. about** *or* **around for ideas** buscar desesperadamente ideas

►**scratch off** *vt sep* raspar

►**scratch out** *vt sep (number, name)* tachar; **to s. sb's eyes out** arrancarle a alguien los ojos

scratchcard ['skrætʃkɑːd] *n* tarjeta *f* de rasca y gana, *Arg* ≃ raspadita *f*

scratching ['skrætʃɪŋ] **1** *n (DJ technique)* scratching *m*

2 scratchings *npl Br* **(pork) scratchings** cortezas *fpl* de cerdo, chicharrones *mpl*

scratchy ['skrætʃɪ] *adj* (**a**) *(garment, towel)* áspero(a) (**b**) *(record)* con muchos arañazos (**c**) *(noisy) (pen)* que hace ruido al escribir

scrawl [skrɔːl] **1** *n* garabatos *mpl*; **her signature is just a s.** su firma es sólo un garabato

2 *vt* garabatear

3 *vi* hacer garabatos

scrawly ['skrɔːlɪ] *adj* garabateado(a)

scrawny ['skrɔːnɪ] *adj (person, neck, cat, chicken)* esquelético(a), raquítico(a)

scream [skriːm] **1** *n* (**a**) *(of person)* grito *m*, chillido *m*; *(of bird, monkey)* chillido *m*; **to let out** *or* **give a s.** soltar un grito; **screams of laughter** carcajadas *fpl* (**b**) *(of tyres)* chirrido *m*; *(of siren)* aullido *m* (**c**) *Fam (good fun)* **it was a s.** fue para morirse de risa *or Esp* para mondarse; **he's a s.** es la monda; **you look a s. in that hat!** ¡ese sombrero te queda supergracioso!

2 *vt* gritar; **she screamed herself hoarse** se quedó ronca de tanto gritar; **to s. abuse (at sb)** lanzar improperios *or* insultos (a alguien); **the headlines screamed "guilty"** los titulares *or Méx, RP* encabezados clamaban "culpable"

3 *vi* (**a**) *(shout) (person, baby)* gritar, chillar; *(bird, monkey)* chillar; **stop screaming at me!** ¡deja ya de gritarme!; **to s. in pain** gritar de dolor; **to s. with laughter** reírse a carcajadas (**b**) *(tyres)* chirriar; *(siren)* aullar; **the jets screamed overhead** los reactores pasaron con estruendo; **to s. past** *(car, train)* pasar estruendosamente a toda velocidad

►**scream out** *vi* gritar, chillar; **to s. out in pain** gritar de dolor; *Fig* **to be screaming out for sth** pedir algo a gritos

screamer ['skriːmə(r)] *n Br Fam (powerful shot)* cañonazo *m*

screaming ['skriːmɪŋ] **1** *n* gritos *mpl*, chillidos *mpl*

2 *adj* **a s. baby** un niño berreando

screamingly ['skriːmɪŋlɪ] *adv Fam* **s. funny** *Esp* para mondarse de risa, *Am* chistosísimo(a)

scree [skriː] *n* pedruscos *mpl*

screech [skriːtʃ] **1** *n* **(a)** *(of bird, person, monkey)* chillido *m*; **a s. of laughter** una carcajada; **a s. of rage** un grito de furia; **a s. of pain** un alarido de dolor ►► ***s. owl*** autillo *m* americano **(b)** *(of tyres, brakes)* chirrido *m*; *(of siren)* aullido *m*
2 *vt* chillar; **to s. an order** dar una orden con un chillido
3 *vi* **(a)** *(bird, person, monkey)* chillar; **to s. with laughter** soltar una resonante carcajada; **to s. with pain** chillar de dolor **(b)** *(brakes)* chirriar, rechinar; **the taxi screeched to a halt** el taxi se detuvo chirriando

screeds [skriːdz] *npl* **he has written s. on this subject** ha escrito páginas y páginas sobre la materia

screen [skriːn] **1** *n* **(a)** *(of TV, cinema, computer)* pantalla *f*; **the big/small s.** la gran/pequeña pantalla; **on s.** en pantalla; *Comptr* **to work on s.** trabajar en pantalla; **the book was adapted for the s.** se hizo una adaptación del libro para la pantalla ►► ***s. actor*** actor *m* de cine; ***s. actress*** actriz *f* de cine; ***s. adaptation*** adaptación *f* para la pantalla; *Comptr* ***s. capture*** captura *f* de pantalla; *Comptr* ***s. dump*** pantallazo *m*, captura *f* de pantalla; *Comptr* ***s. font*** fuente *f* de pantalla; *Comptr* ***s. memory*** memoria *f* en pantalla; *Comptr* ***s. shot*** pantallazo *m*, captura *f* de pantalla; *Cin* ***s. test*** prueba *f* (de cámara)
(b) *(barrier)* mampara *f*; *(folding)* biombo *m*; *(in front of fire)* rejilla *f*; *(over window)* mosquitero *m*; **the rooms are divided by sliding screens** las habitaciones están divididas por tabiques corredizos ►► *US* ***s. door*** puerta *f* con mosquitero; ***s. printing*** serigrafía *f*, serigrafiado *m*
(c) *(for hiding)* **a s. of trees** una fila de árboles; **the shop was just a s. for her criminal activities** la tienda era sólo una pantalla para ocultar sus actividades delictivas
(d) *(sieve)* criba *f*
(e) *(in basketball)* bloqueo *m*
2 *vt* **(a)** *(show) (movie)* proyectar; *(TV programme)* emitir
(b) *(protect)* proteger; **he screened his eyes from the sun with his hand** se protegió los ojos del sol con la mano; **to s. sth from view** ocultar algo a la vista
(c) *(check) (staff, applicants)* examinar, controlar; *(samples)* comprobar (**for** en busca de); *(information)* filtrar; **to s. women for breast cancer** realizar controles a mujeres para la detección del cáncer de mama
(d) *(sieve) (coal, grain)* cribar

►**screen off** *vt sep* separar (con mampara) (**from** de)

►**screen out** *vt sep* **(a)** *(rays, light)* bloquear, no permitir el paso de **(b)** *(person)* descartar, eliminar

screening ['skriːnɪŋ] *n* **(a)** *(of movie)* proyección *f*; *(of TV programme)* emisión *f*; **first s.** estreno **(b)** *(of staff, applicants)* examen *m*, control *m*; *(of samples)* comprobación *f*; **a cancer s. programme** un programa para la detección del cáncer de mama

screenplay ['skriːnpleɪ] *n Cin* guión *m*

screensaver ['skriːnseɪvə(r)] *n Comptr* salvapantallas *m inv*

screenwriter ['skriːnraɪtə(r)] *n Cin* guionista *mf*

screw [skruː] **1** *n* **(a)** *(for fixing)* tornillo *m*; IDIOM *Fam* **she's got a s. loose** le falta un tornillo; IDIOM *Fam* **to put the screws on sb** apretar las clavijas a alguien; IDIOM **to turn the s.** apretar las clavijas ►► ***s. top*** *(of bottle, jar)* tapón *m* de rosca
(b) *(turn)* vuelta *f*; **give it a couple more screws** dale un par de vueltas más
(c) *(propeller)* hélice *f*
(d) *Br Fam (prison officer)* carcelero *m*, *Esp* boqueras *m inv*
(e) *Vulg (sexual intercourse)* polvo *m*, *Cuba* palo *m*; **to have a s.** echar un polvo *or Cuba* palo, *Am* coger; **to be a good s.** *(person) Esp* follar *or Am* coger de puta madre
(f) *Br Fam Old-fashioned (salary)* **he's on a good s.** *Esp* gana una pasta gansa, *Am* gana una buena plata
(g) *(in snooker, pool)* retroceso *m*; **s. shot** retroceso
2 *vt* **(a)** *(fix)* atornillar (**on** *or* **onto** a); **to s. two things together** juntar dos cosas atornillándolas; **to s. the lid on a bottle** poner la tapa de rosca en una botella; **s. the board down tight** atornilla bien la tabla
(b) *(crumple)* **I screwed the letter into a ball** hice una pelota con la carta; **to s. one's face into a smile** sonreír forzadamente
(c) *Vulg (have sex with) Esp* follar, *Am* coger
(d) *very Fam (for emphasis)* **go and s. yourself!** ¡vete a la mierda!, *Esp* ¡vete a tomar por culo!, *Méx* ¡vete a la chingada!; **s. you!** *Esp* ¡que te den por culo!, *Méx* ¡vete a la chingada!; *RP* ¡andate a la puta que te parió!; **s. the expense!** ¡a la mierda con el gasto!
(e) *Fam (cheat)* timar, tangar; **to s. money out of sb** desplumar a alguien, *Esp, RP* sacarle la guita a alguien; *Fam* **they'll s. you for every penny you've got** van a sacarte hasta el último centavo
(f) *(in snooker, pool)* imprimir un efecto bajo a
3 *vi Vulg (have sex)* joder, *Esp* follar, *Am* coger

►**screw around 1** *vt sep Fam* **to s. sb around** *(treat badly)* tratar a alguien a patadas; *(waste time of)* traer a alguien al retortero
2 *vi* **(a)** *Fam (act foolishly)* hacer tonterías, *RP* hacer boludeces; *(waste time)* rascarla, *RP* boludear **(b)** *Vulg (be promiscuous) Esp* follar *or Am* coger con todo el mundo

►**screw on 1** *vt sep* **(a)** *(with screw)* atornillar **(b)** *(lid, top)* enroscar; IDIOM *Fam* **he's got his head screwed on** tiene la cabeza en su sitio
2 *vi* **(a)** *(using screws)* **it screws on to the wall** se atornilla a la pared **(b)** *(lid, top)* enroscarse

►**screw up 1** *vt sep* **(a)** *(make small)* **to s. up a piece of paper** arrugar un trozo de papel; **she screwed up her eyes** apretó los ojos; **to s. up one's face** contraer *or* arrugar la cara; **to s. up one's courage** armarse de valor
(b) *Fam (spoil)* jorobar; **you've really gone and screwed everything up now!** ¡ahora sí que has jorobado todo!
(c) *Fam (damage psychologically)* **his parents really screwed him up** sus padres lo dejaron bien tarado
2 *vi Fam (fail)* **don't s. up this time** esta vez no vayas a jorobarla

screwball ['skruːbɔːl] *US Fam* **1** *n* **(a)** *(person)* cabeza *mf* loca, *RP* tiro *m* al aire **(b)** *(in baseball)* tirabuzón *m*, lanzamiento *m* de tornillo
2 *adj* chiflado(a) ►► ***s. comedy*** comedia *f* disparatada

screwdriver ['skruːdraɪvə(r)] *n* **(a)** *(tool)* destornillador *m*, *Am* desatornillador *m* **(b)** *(drink)* destornillador *m*

screwed [skruːd] *adj Fam (in trouble)* **we're s.** la hemos fastidiado

screwed-up ['skruːd'ʌp] *adj Fam* tarado(a); **he's one s. kid** ese niño está bien tarado

screw-loose ['skruːluːs] *adj US Fam* chiflado(a), pirado(a)

screw-on ['skruːɒn] *adj* de rosca

screw-top ['skruːtɒp] **1** *n* tapón *m* de rosca
2 *adj* (con tapón) de rosca

screw-up ['skruːʌp] *n Fam* **(a)** *(mess, failure)* metedura *f or Am* metida *f* de pata, cagada *f* **(b)** *(person)* negado(a) *m,f*

screwy ['skruːɪ] *adj US Fam (person)* rarísimo(a); *(idea)* descabellado(a)

scribble ['skrɪbəl] **1** *n* garabatos *mpl*; **I can't read this s.** no entiendo estos garabatos
2 *vt* **to s. sth (down)** garabatear algo; **she scribbled a few lines to her sister** le garabateó unas líneas a su hermana
3 *vi* hacer garabatos

scribbler ['skrɪblə(r)] *n Pej* escritor(ora) *m,f* de poca monta

scribbling ['skrɪblɪŋ] *n* **scribblings** *Fam (inferior writings)* garabatos *mpl* ►► ***s. pad*** bloc *m* de borrador

scribe [skraɪb] *n* escribano(a) *m,f*, amanuense *mf*

scrimmage ['skrɪmɪdʒ] **1** *n* **(a)** *(fight)* tumulto *m*, alboroto *m* **(b)** *(in American football)* scrimmage *m*
2 *vi (in American football)* hacer un scrimmage

scrimp [skrɪmp] *vi* **to s. (and save)** economizar, hacer economías; **she scrimps on food** ahorra mucho en comida

scrip [skrɪp] *n* **(a)** *St Exch* vale *m* canjeable ►► ***s. issue*** emisión *m* de acciones liberadas **(b)** *Fam (prescription)* receta *f*

script [skrɪpt] **1** *n* **(a)** *(for play, movie)* guión *m*; IDIOM **to forget to read the s.: the Lakers forgot to read the s. and won easily** los Lakers echaron por tierra las esperanzas de algunos y ganaron con facilidad ►► ***s. editor*** responsable *mf* del guión; ***s. girl*** script *f* **(b)** *(in exam)* ejercicio *m* (escrito), examen *m* **(c)** *(handwriting)* caligrafía *f*, letra *f*; *(alphabet)* alfabeto *m* **(d)** *(typeface)* **in italic s.** en cursiva **(e)** *Comptr* script *m*
2 *vt (play, movie)* escribir el guión de

scripted ['skrɪptɪd] *adj (speech, interview, remarks)* escrito(a) de antemano

scriptural ['skrɪptʃərəl] *adj* bíblico(a)

Scripture ['skrɪptʃə(r)] *n* **(a)** *(holy books)* **(Holy) S., the Scriptures** la Sagrada Escritura **(b)** *(subject)* religión *f*

scriptwriter ['skrɪptraɪtə(r)] *n TV & Cin* guionista *mf*

scrofula ['skrɒfjʊlə] *n Old-fashioned Med* escrófula *f*

scroll [skrəʊl] **1** *n* **(a)** *(of paper, parchment)* rollo *m*; *(manuscript)* manuscrito *m*, rollo *m*; *(as award)* pergamino *m* **(b)** *Archit* voluta *f* **(c)** *Comptr* ***s. arrow*** flecha *f* de desplazamiento; ***s. bar*** barra *f* de desplazamiento; ***s. lock (key)*** (tecla *f* de) bloqueo *m* de desplazamiento
2 *vi Comptr* desplazarse por la pantalla *(de arriba a abajo o de un lado a otro)*

►**scroll down** *vi Comptr* bajar

►**scroll through** *vt insep Comptr* bajar, recorrer

▸**scroll up** *Comptr* 1 *vt* **to s. up a page** subir a la página anterior
2 *vi* subir

scrolling ['skrəʊlɪŋ] *n Comptr* desplazamiento *m* por la pantalla

Scrooge [skru:dʒ] *n Fam (miser)* tacaño(a) *m,f*, roñoso(a) *m,f*

scrote [skrəʊt] *n Br very Fam (person)* cabrón(ona) *m,f*

scrotum ['skrəʊtəm] *n* escroto *m*

scrounge [skraʊndʒ] *Fam* 1 *n* **to be on the s.** andar gorreando *or Esp, Méx* gorroneando *or RP* garroneando
2 *vt* **to s. sth from** *or* **off sb** gorrear *or Esp, Méx* gorronear *or RP* garronear algo a alguien; **could I s. a lift from someone?** ¿me podría llevar alguien?
3 *vi* gorrear, *Esp, Méx* gorronear, *RP* garronear; **to s. off sb** vivir a costa de alguien, *Esp, Méx* vivir de alguien por la gorra; **to s. around for sth** andar buscando algo

scrounger ['skraʊndʒə(r)] *n Fam* gorrero(a) *m,f*, *Esp, Méx* gorrón(ona) *m,f*, *RP* garronero(a) *m,f*

scrounging ['skraʊndʒɪŋ] *n Fam Esp, Méx* gorronería *f*, *RP* garronería *f*

scrub [skrʌb] 1 *n* (**a**) *(bushes)* maleza *f*, matorral *m* (**b**) *(wash)* **to give the floor a (good) s.** darle una (buena) fregada al suelo; **can you give my back a s.?** ¿podrías frotarme la espalda? (**c**) *(for skin)* limpiador *m* cutáneo, leche *f or* crema *f* limpiadora (**d**) *US Sport (team)* equipo *m* reserva; *(player)* reserva *mf*
2 *vt* (*pt & pp* **scrubbed**) (**a**) *(floor, pots)* fregar; *(face, back)* refregar; **to s. one's hands** lavarse bien las manos; **to s. sth clean** fregar algo hasta que quede limpio(a) (**b**) *Fam (cancel)* suspender; **s. that last remark, it's not a good idea** olvida esa última observación, no es una buena idea (**c**) *(drop) (from team)* echar

▸**scrub down** *vt sep (wall, paintwork)* limpiar frotando

▸**scrub out** *vt sep (dirt, stain)* quitar con un cepillo; *(bucket, pan, cell)* fregar

▸**scrub up** *vi Med* lavarse *(antes de entrar al quirófano)*

scrubber ['skrʌbə(r)] *n* (**a**) *(for dishes)* estropajo *m* (**b**) *Br very Fam (woman)* fulana *f*, putón *m* (verbenero)

scrubbing brush ['skrʌbɪŋ'brʌʃ] *n* cepillo *m* de fregar

scrubby ['skrʌbɪ] *adj* (**a**) *(land)* cubierto(a) de maleza (**b**) *(tree, vegetation)* achaparrado(a)

scrubland ['skrʌblænd] *n* monte *m* bajo, matorral *m*

scruff [skrʌf] *n* (**a**) *(of neck)* **to grab sb by the s. of the neck** agarrar a alguien del cogote (**b**) *Fam (unkempt person)* andrajoso(a) *m,f*, zarrapastroso(a) *m,f*

scruffily ['skrʌfɪlɪ] *adv* **to be s. dressed** vestir andrajosamente *or* con desaliño

scruffiness ['skrʌfɪnɪs] *n (of dress, appearance)* desaliño *m*, descuido *m*; *(of building, area)* abandono *m*; *(of handwriting)* desorden *m*

scruffy ['skrʌfɪ] *adj (person)* desaliñado(a), zarrapastroso(a); *(clothes)* andrajoso(a); *(building, area)* abandonado(a); *(handwriting)* desordenado(a)

scrum [skrʌm] *n (in rugby) Esp* melé *f*, *Am* scrum *f*; *Fig* **there was a s. at the door** hubo apretujones en la puerta ▸▸ ***s. half*** *Esp* medio (de) melé *mf*, *Am* medio scrum *mf*

▸**scrum down** *vi* hacer *Esp* una melé *or Am* un scrum; **s. down!** ¡formación!

scrum-cap ['skrʌmkæp] *n* protector *m* para las orejas

scrummage ['skrʌmɪdʒ] 1 *n (in rugby) Esp* melé *f*, *Am* scrum *m*
2 *vi* disputar *Esp* la melé *or Am* el scrum

scrummy ['skrʌmɪ] *adj Br Fam (food)* riquísimo(a), para chuparse los dedos; **he's so s.!** ¡está buenísimo *or Méx* padrísimo!, *Esp* ¡está para parar un tren!

scrumptious ['skrʌm(p)ʃəs] *adj Fam (food)* riquísimo(a), de chuparse los dedos

scrumpy ['skrʌmpɪ] *n* = sidra seca y fuerte que se elabora en el sudoeste de Inglaterra

scrunch [skrʌn(t)ʃ] 1 *vt* (**a**) *(paper)* estrujar; *(can)* aplastar (**b**) *(biscuit, apple, snow, gravel)* hacer crujir
2 *vi (make sound)* crujir

▸**scrunch up** *vt sep (paper)* estrujar; **he scrunched up his face in disgust** arrugó la cara con asco

scrunch-dry ['skrʌntʃdraɪ] *vt* peinar con secador a mano

scrunchie ['skrʌntʃɪ] *n (for hair)* coletero *m*

scruple ['skru:pəl] 1 *n* escrúpulo *m*; **to have no scruples (about doing sth)** no tener escrúpulos (en hacer algo)
2 *vi* **not to s. to do sth** no tener escrúpulos en hacer algo

scrupulous ['skru:pjʊləs] *adj* escrupuloso(a); **they're very s. about punctuality** son muy escrupulosos con la puntualidad

scrupulously ['skru:pjʊləslɪ] *adv* escrupulosamente; **s. clean** impecable

scrupulousness ['skru:pjʊləsnɪs] *n* escrupulosidad *f*

scrutineer [skru:tɪ'nɪə(r)] *n Pol* escrutador(ora) *m,f*

scrutinize ['skru:tɪnaɪz] *vt (document, votes)* escrutar; *(face, painting)* examinar

scrutiny ['skru:tɪnɪ] *n (of document, votes)* escrutinio *m*; *(of face, painting)* examen *m*; **to be under s.** ser objeto de un examen meticuloso; **to come under s.** ser cuidadosamente examinado(a); **her work does not stand up to close s.** un análisis riguroso de su trabajo pone en evidencia sus debilidades

SCSI ['skʌzɪ] *n Comptr* (*abbr* **small computer system interface**) SCSI *m* ▸▸ ***S. address*** dirección *f* SCSI; ***S. chain*** cadena *f* SCSI

scuba ['sku:bə] *n* ***s. diver*** submarinista *mf* buceador(ora) *m,f (con botellas de oxígeno)*; ***s. diving*** buceo *m*, submarinismo *m*; **to go s. diving** hacer submarinismo

scud [skʌd] *vi* deslizarse rápidamente; **the clouds scudded across the sky** las nubes se deslizaban vertiginosamente por el cielo; **two boats scudded across the lake** dos lanchas surcaban con rapidez el lago

scuff [skʌf] 1 *n* ***s. (mark)*** rozadura *f*, rasguño *m*
2 *vt* (**a**) *(damage)* rozar; **she had scuffed her shoes** se había hecho unas rozaduras en los zapatos (**b**) *(drag)* **to s. one's feet** arrastrar los pies

scuffle ['skʌfəl] 1 *n* riña *f*, reyerta *f*
2 *vi* reñir, pelear; **demonstrators scuffled with the police** los manifestantes se enfrentaron con la policía

scull [skʌl] 1 *n* (**a**) *(oar)* espadilla *f*; **single/double sculls** *(event)* scull individual/doble (**b**) *(boat)* scull *m*
2 *vt* hacer avanzar remando con espadillas
3 *vi* remar con espadillas

scullery ['skʌlərɪ] *n Br* fregadero *m*, trascocina *f* ▸▸ ***s. maid*** fregona *f*

sculpt [skʌlpt] 1 *vt* esculpir
2 *vi* esculpir

sculptor ['skʌlptə(r)] *n* escultor(ora) *m,f*

sculptress ['skʌlptrɪs] *n* escultora *f*

sculptural ['skʌlptʃərəl] *adj* escultórico(a)

sculpture ['skʌlptʃə(r)] 1 *n* (**a**) *(art)* escultura *f* (**b**) *(object)* escultura *f* ▸▸ ***s. park*** jardín *m* de esculturas
2 *vt* esculpir; **she has finely sculptured features** tiene unos rasgos esculturales
3 *vi* esculpir

sculptured ['skʌlptʃəd] *adj (statue, model)* esculpido(a); *(hair)* bien moldeado(a); *(features)* torneado(a)

scum [skʌm] *n* (**a**) *(layer of dirt)* capa *f* de suciedad; *(froth)* espuma *f* (**b**) *Fam (worthless people)* escoria *f*; **he's/they're just s.** no es/son más que escoria; **the s. of the earth** la escoria de la sociedad (**c**) *US Vulg (semen)* leche *f*, *Esp* lefa *f*

scumbag [skʌmbæg] *n very Fam* (**a**) *(person)* cerdo(a) *m,f*, mamón(ona) *m,f* (**b**) *US (condom)* goma *f*, *Arg* forro *m*

scummy ['skʌmɪ] *adj* (**a**) *Fam (dirty, worthless)* asqueroso(a) (**b**) *(liquid)* cubierto(a) de porquería

scupper ['skʌpə(r)] 1 *n Naut* imbornal *m*
2 *vt* (**a**) *(ship)* hundir (**b**) *(project)* hundir; **we're completely scuppered unless we can find the cash** si no conseguimos el dinero estamos acabados

scurf [skɜ:f] *n (dandruff)* caspa *f*

scurrilous ['skʌrɪləs] *adj* injurioso(a), calumnioso(a)

scurrilously ['skʌrɪləslɪ] *adv* injuriosamente, calumniosamente

scurry ['skʌrɪ] 1 *n (sound) (of feet)* correteo *m*
2 *vi (person)* correr apresuradamente; *(mouse, beetle)* correr rápidamente; **all the animals were scurrying for shelter** todos los animales corrían en busca de refugio

▸**scurry away, scurry off** *vi* escabullirse

scurvy ['skɜ:vɪ] 1 *n Med* escorbuto *m*
2 *adj (trick)* ruin, vil

scut [skʌt] *n (of rabbit, hare)* colita *f*, rabo *m*

scutcheon ['skʌtʃən] *n (shield)* escudo *m* de armas, blasón *m*

scuttle[1] ['skʌtəl] 1 *n* **(coal) s.** cajón *m* para el carbón
2 *vt* (**a**) *(ship)* hundir (**b**) *(plan)* hundir; *(hopes)* arruinar, frustrar

scuttle[2] *vi (run)* corretear; **a cockroach scuttled across the floor** una cucaracha correteó por el suelo

▸**scuttle away, scuttle off** *vi (person)* escabullirse; *(animal)* huir rápidamente

scuzzy ['skʌzɪ] *adj US Fam* asqueroso(a), *Esp* guarrísimo(a)

scythe [saɪð] **1** *n* guadaña *f*

2 *vt* segar

scything ['saɪðɪŋ] *adj* **a s. tackle** una segada

Scylla ['sɪlə] *n Mythol* **S. and Charybdis** Escila y Caribdis

SD, S Dak (*abbr* **South Dakota**) Dakota del Sur

SDI [esdiː'aɪ] *n* (*abbr* **Strategic Defence Initiative**) Iniciativa *f* de Defensa Estratégica

SDLP [esdiːel'piː] *n Br* (*abbr* **Social Democratic and Labour Party**) = partido norirlandés que propugna la reintegración en la República de Irlanda por medios pacíficos

SDRAM [es'diːræm] *n Comptr* (*abbr* **synchronous dynamic random access memory**) (memoria *f*) SDRAM *f*

SE (*abbr* **south east**) SE

SEA [esiː'eɪ] *n* (*abbr* **Single European Act**) Acta *f* Única Europea

sea [siː] *n* **(a)** *(body of water)* mar *m or f (note that the feminine is used in literary language, by people such as fishermen with a close connection with the sea, and in some idiomatic expressions)*; **by the s.** junto al mar; **to go by s.** ir en barco; **to go to s.** *(become a sailor)* enrolarse de marinero; **to put to s.** zarpar, hacerse a la mar; **to be at s.** estar en la mar; **we've been at s. for two weeks** llevamos dos semanas navegando; **life at s.** la vida en el mar; **the bedroom looks out to s.** la habitación da al mar; **the little boat was swept** *or* **washed out to s.** el bote fue arrastrado mar adentro; **heavy** *or* **rough seas** mar gruesa; **on the high seas, out at s.** en alta mar; IDIOM **to be all at s.: when it comes to computers, I'm all at s.** no tengo ni idea de informática; **he's been all at sea since his wife left him** desde que su mujer lo dejó anda muy perdido ▸▸ ***s. air*** aire *m* del mar; ***s. anemone*** anémona *f* de mar; ***s. bass*** lubina *f*; ***s. battle*** batalla *f* naval; ***s. bed*** fondo *m* del mar, lecho *m* marino; ***s. bird*** ave *f* marina; ***s. bream*** besugo *m*; ***s. breeze*** brisa *f* marina; ***s. captain*** capitán *m* de la marina mercante; ***s. change*** *(radical change)* cambio *m* profundo *or* radical; ***s. cow*** manatí *m*, vaca *f* marina; ***s. crossing:* Calais is just a 40 minute s. crossing from Dover** Calais está a 40 minutos de navegación de Dover; ***s. cucumber*** holoturia *f*; *Fam* ***s. dog*** *(sailor)* lobo *m* de mar; ***s. eagle*** águila *f* pescadora; ***s. elephant*** elefante *m* marino; ***s. floor*** lecho *m* del mar; ***s. grass*** césped *m* marino; ***s. green*** verde *m* mar; ***s. kale*** col *f* marina; *Naut* ***s. lane*** ruta *f* marítima; ***s. legs:* to find** *or* **to get one's s. legs** dejar de marearse; ***s. level*** nivel *m* del mar; **above/below s. level** sobre/bajo el nivel del mar; ***s. lion*** león *m* marino; *Scot* ***s. loch*** ría *f* de agua salada; ***s. mist*** bruma *f*; ***s. monster*** monstruo *m* marino; ***s. otter*** nutria *f* de mar; ***s. power*** *(country)* potencia *f* naval; ***s. salt*** sal *f* marina; ***S. Scout*** scout *m* marino; ***s. serpent*** serpiente *f* marina; ***s. shanty*** canción *f* de marineros; ***s. slug*** babosa *f* de mar; ***s. snail*** caracol *m* marino; ***s. snake*** serpiente *f* marina; ***S. of Tranquility*** *(on the Moon)* Mar *m* de la Tranquilidad; ***s. trout*** trucha *f* de mar; ***s. urchin*** erizo *m* de mar; ***s. view*** vistas *fpl* al mar; ***s. voyage*** travesía *f*, viaje *m* por mar; ***s. wall*** malecón *m*

(b) *(large quantity) (of blood, mud, people, faces)* mar *m*

seaboard ['siːbɔːd] *n* litoral *m*, costa *f*

seaborne ['siːbɔːn] *adj (invasion, troops)* naval; *(goods)* transportado(a) por mar

seafarer ['siːfeərə(r)] *n* marino(a) *m,f*, marinero(a) *m,f*

seafaring ['siːfeərɪŋ] *adj (nation)* marinero(a); *(days, life)* en el mar

seafood ['siːfuːd] *n* marisco *m*, *Am* mariscos *mpl* ▸▸ ***s. platter*** mariscada *f*, fuente *f* de marisco; ***s. restaurant*** marisquería *f*

seafront ['siːfrʌnt] *n* paseo *m* marítimo; **a s. hotel** un hotel frente al mar

seagoing ['siːgəʊɪŋ] *adj* **(a)** *(nation)* marinero(a); *(days, life)* en el mar **(b)** *(vessel)* de alta mar, de altura

seagull ['siːgʌl] *n* gaviota *f*

seahorse ['siːhɔːs] *n* hipocampo *m*, caballito *m* de mar

seal[1] [siːl] *n (animal)* foca *f*

seal[2] **1** *n* **(a)** *(stamp)* sello *m*; **to give one's s. of approval to sth** dar el visto bueno a algo; **to set the s. on sth** *(alliance, friendship, defeat)* sellar algo; *(fate)* determinar algo **(b)** *(on machine, pipes, connection)* junta *f*; *(on bottle, box, letter)* precinto *m*; *(on lid of jar)* aro *m*; *(on fridge, washing machine, window)* burlete *m*

2 *vt* **(a)** *(with official seal)* sellar; **sealed with a kiss** sellado(a) con un beso **(b)** *(close) (envelope, frontier)* cerrar; *(with wax)* lacrar **(c)** *(jar)* cerrar herméticamente; *(joint)* sellar; *(door)* colocar burletes a; *(house)* precintar; *(wood)* sellar con tapaporos; **it is sealed in an airtight jar** está guardado en un frasco hermético; **my lips are sealed** soy una tumba **(d)** *(fate)* determinar; *(result, victory)* sentenciar; *(deal)* cerrar

▸ **seal in** *vt sep (flavour)* conservar

▸ **seal off** *vt sep (road, entrance)* cerrar, cortar; **the street had been sealed off** la calle había sido cerrada *or* cortada por la policía

▸ **seal up** *vt sep* **(a)** *(house, container)* precintar; *(window, door)* colocar burletes a; *(hole)* rellenar, tapar **(b)** *(envelope)* cerrar

sealant ['siːlənt] *n* sellador *m* (de junturas)

sealer ['siːlə(r)] *n* **(a)** *(hunter)* cazador(ora) *m,f* de focas **(b)** *(ship)* barco *m* para la caza de focas **(c)** *(paint, varnish)* sellador *m*

sealing ['siːlɪŋ] *n (hunting of seals)* caza *f* de focas

sealing-wax ['siːlɪŋ'wæks] *n* lacre *m*

sealskin ['siːlskɪn] *n* piel *f* de foca ▸▸ ***s. coat/hat*** abrigo *m*/gorro *m* de (piel de) foca

seam [siːm] **1** *n* **(a)** *(of garment)* costura *f*; *(in metalwork)* unión *f*, juntura *f*; **to be coming apart at the seams** *(clothing)* estar descosiéndose; *(plan, organization)* estar desmoronándose **(b)** *(of coal)* filón *m*, veta *f*

2 *vt (garment)* coser; *(plastic, metal, wood)* juntar

seaman ['siːmən] *n* **(a)** *(sailor)* marino *m* **(b)** *(in US Navy)* marinero *m* de primera

seamanlike ['siːmənlaɪk] *adj* de buen marinero

seamanship ['siːmənʃɪp] *n* **(a)** *(art)* navegación *f* **(b)** *(of person)* habilidad *f* para la navegación

seamless ['siːmlɪs] *adj* **(a)** *(stocking)* sin costura; *(metal tube)* de una pieza **(b)** *(transition, changeover)* perfecto(a)

seamlessly ['siːmlɪslɪ] *adv* a la perfección

seamstress ['siːmstrɪs] *n* costurera *f*

seamy ['siːmɪ] *adj* sórdido(a)

seance ['seɪɒns] *n* sesión *f* de espiritismo

seaplane ['siːpleɪn] *n* hidroavión *m*

seaport ['siːpɔːt] *n* puerto *m* de mar

sear [sɪə(r)] *vt* **(a)** *(skin)* quemar, abrasar; *(meat, fish)* brasear, dorar (a fuego vivo); **the image was seared on his memory** la imagen le quedó grabada a fuego en la memoria **(b)** *(wither)* marchitar

▸ **sear through** *vt insep (metal, wall)* cortar con calor; **the pain seared through her** el dolor la atravesaba

search [sɜːtʃ] **1** *n* **(a)** *(hunt)* búsqueda *f* (**for** de); **to be in s. of** ir en búsqueda *or* busca de; **he went in s. of food** fue a buscar comida; **to make a s. of the area** rastrear la zona; **a s. and rescue operation** una operación de búsqueda y rescate ▸▸ ***s. party*** equipo *m* de búsqueda

(b) *(by police, customs)* registro *m*; **the police made a thorough s. of the offices** la policía registró minuciosamente las oficinas ▸▸ ***s. warrant*** orden *f* de registro

(c) *Comptr* búsqueda *f*; **to do a s.** hacer una búsqueda; **to do a s. for sth** buscar algo ▸▸ ***s. engine*** *(for Web)* motor *m or* página *f* de búsqueda; ***s. time*** tiempo *m* de búsqueda

2 *vt* **(a)** *(person, place, bags)* registrar (**for** en búsqueda de); *(records)* revisar, examinar; *(conscience)* examinar; **s. your memory and see if you can remember her name** haz memoria a ver si consigues recordar su nombre; **we've searched the whole house for the keys** hemos revisado toda la casa buscando las llaves; **she searched her bag for a comb** buscó un peine en el bolso; **the spectators were searched before they were let in** registraron a los espectadores antes de dejarlos entrar; **I searched her face for some sign of emotion** busqué en su rostro alguna señal de que sentía algo; IDIOM *Fam* **s. me!** ¡ni idea!, ¡yo qué sé!

(b) *Comptr* **to s. for a file in a directory** buscar un archivo en un directorio

3 *vi* **(a)** *(hunt)* buscar; **to s. for sth** buscar algo; **to s. after the truth** buscar la verdad **(b)** *Comptr* **s. and replace** buscar y reemplazar

▸ **search out** *vt sep* **(a)** *(look for)* intentar encontrar a **(b)** *(find)* encontrar, descubrir

▸ **search through** *vt insep (drawer, pockets, case, documents)* buscar en; *(records)* examinar, revisar

searcher ['sɜːtʃə(r)] *n (for missing person)* miembro *m* del equipo de búsqueda; **he was a s. after truth** buscaba la verdad

searching ['sɜːtʃɪŋ] *adj* **(a)** *(question)* penetrante; *(exam)* exigente **(b)** *(gaze)* escrutador(ora); *(look)* penetrante, inquisidor(ora)

searchingly ['sɜːtʃɪŋlɪ] *adv* **(a)** *(to question)* de manera incisiva **(b)** *(to stare)* con mirada escrutadora

searchlight ['sɜːtʃlaɪt] *n* reflector *m*

searing ['sɪərɪŋ] *adj* **(a)** *(pain)* punzante; *(heat)* abrasador(ora) **(b)** *(criticism, indictment)* incisivo(a) **(c)** *(very fast)* **a s. run** una carrera imparable

seascape ['siːskeɪp] *n Art* marina *f*

seashell ['siːʃel] *n* concha *f* (marina)

seashore ['si:ʃɔ:(r)] *n* orilla *f* del mar; **on the s.** a la orilla del mar, junto al mar
seasick ['si:sɪk] *adj* **to be s.** estar mareado(a); **to get s.** marearse
seasickness ['si:sɪknɪs] *n* mareo *m (en barco)*; **she suffers from s.** se marea en los barcos
seaside ['si:saɪd] *n* playa *f*; **we spent the afternoon at the s.** pasamos la tarde en la playa; **we live by** *or* **at the s.** vivimos al lado de *or* en la playa; **a s. holiday** vacaciones en el mar ▸▸ ***s. resort*** centro *m* turístico costero; ***s. town*** pueblo *m* costero *or* de la costa
season[1] ['si:zən] *n* (**a**) *(period of year)* estación *f*; **S.'s Greetings** Felices Fiestas
(**b**) *(for sport, plants, activity)* temporada *f*; **the tourist s.** la temporada turística; **the holiday s.** las vacaciones; *Br* **the football s.** la temporada de fútbol; **the raspberry s.** la época de las frambuesas; **the Christmas s.** las Navidades; **in s.** *(of food)* en temporada; *(of animal)* en celo; **out of s.** *(of food)* fuera de temporada; **the high/low s.** *(for tourism)* la temporada alta/baja ▸▸ ***s. ticket*** abono *m*; ***s. ticket holder*** titular *mf* de un abono, abonado(a) *m,f*
(**c**) *(of movies)* ciclo *m*; *(for show, actor)* temporada *f*
season[2] *vt* (**a**) *(food)* condimentar, sazonar; *(with salt and pepper)* salpimentar; **s. to taste** condimentar a gusto (**b**) *(wood)* curar (**c**) *(intersperse)* **his speech was seasoned with witty remarks** intercaló comentarios ingeniosos en su discurso
seasonable ['si:zənəbəl] *adj* (**a**) *(appropriate to season)* **s. weather** tiempo propio de la época (**b**) *(help, advice)* oportuno(a)
seasonal ['si:zənəl] *adj (changes)* estacional; *(work, crop)* de temporada ▸▸ ***s. adjustment*** fluctuación *f or* ajuste *m* estacional; *Med* ***s. affective disorder*** trastorno *m* afectivo estacional; ***seasonal unemployment*** desempleo *m* estacional; ***s. worker*** temporero(a) *m,f*, trabajador(ora) *m,f* temporero(a)
seasonally ['si:zənəlɪ] *adv* **s. adjusted figures** cifras corregidas estacionalmente
seasoned ['si:zənd] *adj* (**a**) *(food)* condimentado(a), sazonado(a) (**b**) *(wood)* curado(a) (**c**) *(person)* experimentado(a); **a s. soldier** un soldado veterano
seasoning ['si:zənɪŋ] *n* (**a**) *Culin* condimento *m* (**b**) *(of wood)* curación *f*
seat [si:t] **1** *n* (**a**) *(chair) (on bus, train, plane)* asiento *m*; *(on bicycle)* asiento *m*, sillín *m*; *(in theatre, cinema)* butaca *f*; *(in stadium)* localidad *f*, asiento *m*; **there are no seats left for tonight's screening** no quedan asientos para la proyección de esta noche; **to have** *or* **take a s.** tomar asiento, sentarse; *Formal* **please take your seats for dinner** tengan a bien sentarse para disfrutar de la cena; **please stay in your seats** por favor, permanezcan en sus asientos ▸▸ ***s. belt*** cinturón *m* de seguridad
(**b**) *(part) (of chair, toilet)* asiento *m*; *(of trousers)* parte *f* del trasero; IDIOM **to do sth by the s. of one's pants** hacer algo intuitivamente
(**c**) *(in legislature)* escaño *m*; **he kept/lost his s.** perdió/mantuvo su escaño
(**d**) *Br (constituency)* circunscripción *f* electoral
(**e**) *(on committee)* lugar *m*, puesto *m*; **to have a s. on the board** ser miembro del consejo de administración
(**f**) *(centre) (of government)* sede *f*; *(of disease, infection)* foco *m*; **a s. of learning** un centro de enseñanza
(**g**) *Euph (buttocks)* trasero *m*
(**h**) *(manor)* (**country**) **s.** *(of aristocrat)* casa *f* de campo
2 *vt* (**a**) *(cause to sit)* sentar; **to remain seated** permanecer sentado(a); *Formal* **please be seated** por favor, tome asiento (**b**) *(accommodate)* **the bus seats thirty** el autobús tiene capacidad *or* cabida para treinta pasajeros sentados; **this table seats twelve** en esta mesa caben doce personas (**c**) *(valve)* asentar
seatback ['si:tbæk] *n* respaldo *m* del asiento
-seater [-'si:tə(r)] *suffix* **it's a two/four-s.** *(car)* es de dos/cuatro asientos
seating ['si:tɪŋ] *n (seats)* asientos *mpl*; **there's s. for 300 in the hall** el salón tiene capacidad para 300 personas ▸▸ ***s. accommodation*** asientos *mpl*; ***s. capacity*** *(of cinema, stadium)* aforo *m (de personas sentadas)*; *(on bus, plane)* número *m* de plazas (sentadas); ***s. plan*** *(in theatre)* plano *m* de ubicación de los asientos; *(at table)* plano *m* de ubicación de los comensales
seatwork ['si:twɜ:k] *n US* actividad *f* de pupitre
seaward ['si:wʊd] *adj* **in a s. direction** en dirección al mar; **there was a strong s. wind** soplaba un viento fuerte del mar
seaward(s) ['si:wəd(z)] *adv* hacia el mar
seawater ['si:wɔ:tə(r)] *n* agua *f* de mar
seaway ['si:weɪ] *n* ruta *f* marítima
seaweed ['si:wi:d] *n* algas *fpl* marinas; **a piece of s.** un alga
seaworthiness ['si:wɜ:ðɪnɪs] *n* condiciones *fpl* para la navegación
seaworthy ['si:wɜ:ðɪ] *adj (ship)* en condiciones de navegar
sebaceous [sɪ'beɪʃəs] *adj Biol* sebáceo(a) ▸▸ *Anat* ***s. gland*** glándula *f* sebácea
SEC [esi:'si:] *n* (*abbr* **Securities and Exchange Commission**) = comisión del mercado de valores estadounidense
sec **1** (*abbr* **seconds**) s.
2 *n* [sek] *Fam (moment)* **just a s.!** ¡un momentín!
SECAM ['si:kæm] *n* (*abbr* **séquentiel couleur à mémoire**) SECAM *m*
secant ['si:kənt] *n Geom* secante *f*
secateurs [sekə'tɜ:z] *npl* podadera *f*, tijeras *fpl* de podar
secede [sɪ'si:d] *vi* escindirse, separarse (**from** de)
secession [sɪ'seʃən] *n* secesión *f*, escisión *f*
secessionist [sɪ'seʃənɪst] **1** *n* secesionista *mf*
2 *adj* secesionista
seclude [sɪ'klu:d] *vt* retirar, apartar; **to s. oneself (from)** aislarse (de)
secluded [sɪ'klu:dɪd] *adj (place)* apartado(a), retirado(a); *(life)* solitario(a)
seclusion [sɪ'klu:ʒən] *n* (**a**) *(state)* retiro *m*; **to live in s.** vivir recluido(a) (**b**) *(act)* reclusión *f*
second[1] ['sekənd] *n* (**a**) *(unit of time)* segundo *m* ▸▸ ***s. hand*** *(of clock)* segundero *m* (**b**) *(moment)* segundo *m*, momento *m*; **I won't be a s.** no tardo *or Am* demoro nada; **I'll be with you in a s.** estaré contigo en un segundo *or* momento; **just** *or* **half a s.** un segundo, un momento (**c**) *Math* segundo *m*

SECOND[2] **1** *n* (**a**) *(in series)* segundo(a) *m,f*; **she was s.** quedó (en) segunda (posición); ▸▸ ***s. in command*** segundo de a bordo; *Mil* ***s. strike*** respuesta *f* nuclear
(**b**) *(of month)* **the s. of May** el dos de mayo; **we're leaving on the s.** nos marchamos el (día) dos
(**c**) *Com* **seconds** *(defective goods)* artículos *mpl* defectuosos
(**d**) *Sport* **seconds** *(second team)* segundo equipo *m*
(**e**) *(in duel)* padrino *m*; *(in boxing)* cuidador(ora) *m,f*; **seconds out, round three!** ¡segundos fuera, tercer asalto!
(**f**) *Br Univ* **to get an upper s.** *(in degree)* = licenciarse con la segunda nota más alta en la escala de calificaciones; **to get a lower s.** *(in degree)* = licenciarse con una nota media
(**g**) *(second gear)* segunda *f*; **in s.** en segunda
(**h**) *Fam* **anyone for seconds?** *(at meal)* ¿alguien quiere repetir?
(**i**) *Mus* segunda *f*
2 *adj* segundo(a); **the 2nd century** *(written)* el siglo II; *(spoken)* el siglo dos *or* segundo; **Philip the Second** *(written)* Felipe II; *(spoken)* Felipe segundo; **twenty-s.** vigésimo segundo(a), vigésimosegundo(a); **would you like a s. helping?** ¿quieres repetir?; **this is your s. offence** es la segunda vez que cometes un delito; **and in the s. place...** *(in demonstration, argument)* y en segundo lugar...; **I don't want to have to tell you a s. time** no me gustaría tener que decírtelo otra vez; **a s. Picasso** un nuevo Picasso; **every s. child** uno de cada dos niños; **to be s. to none** no tener rival; **s. only to...** sólo superado(a) por...; **on s. thoughts** pensándolo bien; **to have s. thoughts (about sth)** tener alguna duda (sobre algo); **to do sth without a s. thought** hacer algo sin pensárselo dos veces; **lying is s. nature to her** las mentiras le salen automáticamente, mentir es algo natural en ella; *Fig* **to take s. place (to sb)** quedar por debajo (de alguien); IDIOM **she got her s. wind** le entraron energías renovadas, se recuperó; IDIOM **to play s. fiddle to sb** hacer de comparsa de alguien ▸▸ ***s. ballot*** segunda *f* votación; ***s. base*** *(in baseball) (place)* segunda base *f*; *(player)* segunda base *mf*; ***s. chamber*** *(in parliament)* cámara *f* alta; ***s. chance*** segunda oportunidad *f*; *Euph* ***s. childhood*** senilidad *f*; ***s. class*** *(on train)* segunda *f* (clase); *(for mail)* = en el Reino Unido, tarifa postal de segunda clase, más barata y lenta que la primera; *Rel* ***the S. Coming*** el Segundo Advenimiento; ***s. cousin*** primo(a) *m,f* segundo(a); ***s. eleven*** *(in soccer, cricket)* segundo equipo *m*; ***s. floor*** *Br* segundo piso *m*; *US* primer piso *m*; *Aut* ***s. gear*** segunda *f* (marcha); *Sport* ***s. half*** segunda parte *f*; ***s. home*** segunda vivienda *f*; **France is my s. home** Francia es mi segundo hogar; ***s. language*** segunda lengua *f*; ***s. leg*** *(return match)* partido *m* de vuelta; *Mil* ***s. lieutenant*** alférez *mf*; ***s. name*** apellido *m*; ***s. opinion*** segunda opinión *f*; *Gram* ***s. person*** segunda persona *f*; **in the s. person** en segunda persona; ***s. row*** *(in rugby)* segunda línea *f*; ***s. row forward*** *(in rugby)* segunda línea *f* de delanteros; ***s. sight*** clarividencia *f*; *Mil* ***s. strike*** respuesta *f* nuclear; *Sport* ***s. team*** segundo equipo *m*; *Cin* ***s. unit*** segunda unidad *f*; ***S. Vatican Council*** concilio *m* Vaticano II; ***s. violin*** segundo violín *m*; ***the S. World War*** la Segunda Guerra Mundial; ***s. year*** *(at school, university)* segundo curso *m*; *(pupil, student)* estudiante *mf* de segundo curso

3 *adv* (**a**) *(in order)* **to come s.** *(in race, contest)* quedar segundo(a); **his job comes s. to his family** su familia le importa más que su trabajo; **you go s.!** ¡tú segundo! (**b**) *(with superlative)* **he's the s. oldest player** sólo hay un jugador mayor que él; **the s. largest city in the world** la segunda ciudad más grande del mundo (**c**) *(secondly)* **first, I don't want to and s., I can't** en primer lugar, no quiero, y en segundo (lugar), no puedo

second[3] *vt (motion, speaker)* secundar; **I'll s. that!** ¡apoyo la moción!

second[4] [sɪ'kɒnd] *vt (officer, employee)* trasladar temporalmente; **to be seconded** ser trasladado(a)

secondary ['sekəndərɪ] *adj* (**a**) *(less important)* secundario(a); **to be s. to sth** ser menos importante que algo; **this issue is of s. importance** este asunto es de importancia secundaria ►► *Geol* ***s. era*** secundario *m*; ***s. glazing*** doble ventana *f*; *Br* ***s. picketing*** = piquete que actúa contra una compañía que sigue trabajando con la compañía cuyos trabajadores están en huelga; ***s. road*** carretera *f* secundaria; *Gram* ***s. stress*** acento *m* secundario
(**b**) *Educ (teacher, student)* de enseñanza secundaria ►► ***s. education*** enseñanza *f* secundaria; *Br Formerly* ***s. modern (school)*** = instituto de enseñanza secundaria con énfasis en conocimientos técnicos; ***s. school*** instituto *m (de enseñanza secundaria)*; ***s. school teacher*** profesor(ora) *m,f* de enseñanza secundaria
(**c**) *(industry)* manufacturero(a) (**d**) *Med* secundario(a)

second-best ['sekənd'best] 1 *n* segunda opción *f*; **to be content with s.** conformarse con una segunda opción; **he would never be more than s.** nunca sería más que un segundón
2 *adj* **my s. suit** mi segundo mejor traje
3 *adv* **to come off s.** caer derrotado(a)

second-class ['sekənd'klɑ:s] 1 *adj* (**a**) *Br (ticket, carriage)* de segunda (clase)
(**b**) *(postage)* ***s. mail*** = en el Reino Unido, servicio postal de segunda clase, más barato y lento que la primera clase; ***s. stamp*** = en el Reino Unido, sello *or Am* estampilla correspondiente a la tarifa postal de segunda clase
(**c**) *Br Univ (degree)* = con la segunda o tercera calificación posible; **to get an upper s. degree** = licenciarse con la segunda nota más alta en la escala de calificaciones; **to get a lower s. degree** = licenciarse con una nota media
(**d**) *(inferior)* de segunda ►► ***s. citizen*** ciudadano(a) *m,f* de segunda (clase)
2 *adv* (**a**) *Br (on train)* **to travel s.** viajar en segunda (**b**) *(for mail)* **to send a letter s.** enviar una carta utilizando la tarifa postal de segunda clase

second-degree ['sekənddɪ'gri:] *adj* (**a**) *Med (burns)* de segundo grado (**b**) *US Law (murder)* en segundo grado, sin premeditación

seconder ['sekəndə(r)] *n* **the s. of a motion** la persona que secunda una moción

second-generation ['sekənddʒenə'reɪʃən] *adj* (**a**) *(immigrant)* de segunda generación (**b**) *(computer)* de segunda generación

second-guess ['sekənd'ges] *vt* (**a**) *(predict)* predecir, anticiparse a (**b**) *esp US (criticize after the event)* criticar a posteriori

second-hand ['sekənd'hænd] 1 *adj* (**a**) *(car, clothes, book)* usado(a), de segunda mano ►► ***s. bookshop*** *or* ***bookstore*** librería *f* de lance *or* de ocasión; ***s. shop*** tienda *f* de artículos usados *or* de segunda mano (**b**) *(news, information)* de segunda mano
2 *adv* (**a**) *(buy)* de segunda mano (**b**) *(indirectly)* **to hear news s.** enterarse de una noticia a través de terceros

secondly ['sekəndlɪ] *adv* en segundo lugar

secondment [sɪ'kɒndmənt] *n* **to be on s. (to)** estar trasladado(a) temporalmente (a); *(in civil service, government department)* estar en comisión de servicios (en)

second-rate ['sekənd'reɪt] *adj* de segunda (categoría)

second-string ['sekənd'strɪŋ] *adj* suplente, reserva

secrecy ['si:krɪsɪ] *n* confidencialidad *f*; **in s.** en secreto; **I was told in the strictest s.** me lo contaron con total confidencialidad; **to swear sb to s.** hacer jurar a alguien que guardará el secreto; *Rel* **the s. of the confessional** el secreto de confesión

secret ['si:krɪt] 1 *n* (**a**) *(information kept hidden)* secreto *m*; **to unlock the secrets of nature** desentrañar los secretos de la naturaleza; **to do sth in s.** hacer algo en secreto; **it's no s. that she doesn't like him** no es ningún secreto que a ella él no le gusta; **I have no secrets from her** con ella no tengo secretos; **can you keep a s.?** ¿sabes *or* puedes guardar un secreto?; **to let sb into a s.** revelar *or* contar un secreto a alguien; **she makes no s. of her hatred of him** no oculta su odio por él; **this information must remain a s.** esta información debe permanecer en secreto
(**b**) *(explanation)* secreto *m*, clave *f*; **the s. of her success** el secreto *or* la clave de su éxito
2 *adj* secreto(a); **you have a s. admirer** tienes un admirador secreto; **to keep sth s. from sb** ocultar algo a alguien ►► ***s. agent*** agente *mf* secreto(a); ***s. ballot*** voto *m* secreto; ***s. police*** policía *f* secreta; ***the S. Service*** los servicios secretos; *also Fig* ***s. weapon*** arma *f* secreta

secretaire [sekrɪ'teə(r)] *n* cómoda *f*, bureau *m*, *Arg* secretaire *m*

secretarial [sekrə'teərɪəl] *adj (work)* administrativo(a) ►► ***s. college*** escuela *f* de secretariado; ***s. course*** curso *m* de secretariado; ***s. skills*** técnicas *fpl* de secretaria

secretariat [sekrə'teərɪət] *n Pol* secretaría *f*

secretary ['sekrətərɪ] *n* (**a**) *(in office)* secretario(a) *m,f* (**b**) *Pol* ministro(a) *m,f* ►► *US* ***S. of State*** secretario(a) *m,f* de Estado; *Br* ***the S. of State for Employment*** el ministro de Trabajo; *Br* ***the S. of State for Transport*** el ministro de Transportes (**c**) *Zool* ***s. bird*** secretario *m*

secretary-general ['sekrətərɪ'dʒenərəl] *n Pol* secretario(a) *m,f* general

secrete [sɪ'kri:t] *vt* (**a**) *(discharge)* secretar, segregar (**b**) *Formal (hide)* ocultar

secretion [sɪ'kri:ʃən] *n* (**a**) *(discharge)* secreción *f* (**b**) *Formal (act of hiding)* ocultamiento *m*

secretive ['si:krɪtɪv] *adj* reservado(a); **to be s. about sth** ser reservado(a) respecto a algo

secretively ['si:krɪtɪvlɪ] *adv (to behave)* muy en secreto

secretiveness ['si:krɪtɪvnɪs] *n* reserva *f*, hermetismo *m*

secretly ['si:krɪtlɪ] *adv* en secreto; **I s. agreed with her** aunque no lo dijera, yo estaba de acuerdo con ella

sect [sekt] *n* secta *f*

sectarian [sek'teərɪən] *adj* sectario(a)

sectarianism [sek'teərɪənɪzəm] *n* sectarismo *m*

section ['sekʃən] 1 *n* (**a**) *(part)* sección *f*; *(of book, exam)* parte *f*; *(of road)* tramo *m*; *(of orange)* gajo *m*; **s. B, paragraph 2** *(in report)* sección B, párrafo 2; **the sports s.** *(of newspaper)* la sección de deportes; *Mus* **the brass/string s.** la sección de metal/cuerda; **the shelves come in easy-to-assemble sections** los estantes vienen en partes de fácil montaje; **all sections of society** todos los sectores de la sociedad
(**b**) *(department)* sección *f*; **the children's s.** *(in shop, library)* la sección de niños
(**c**) *Geom* sección *f*
(**d**) *Med* sección *f*
(**e**) *Mil* pelotón *m*
2 *vt* (**a**) *(cut)* seccionar (**b**) *Br (place in psychiatric hospital)* internar en un psiquiátrico

► **section off** *vt sep (of police)* acordonar

sectional ['sekʃənəl] *adj* (**a**) *(interests)* particular; *(rivalries)* entre facciones (**b**) *Geom* **a s. drawing** una sección, un corte (**c**) *(furniture)* modular

sector ['sektə(r)] *n* (**a**) *(part)* sector *m*; **whole sectors of society live below the poverty line** sectores enteros de la sociedad se encuentran por debajo del umbral de la pobreza (**b**) *Econ* sector *m*; **public/private s.** sector público/privado (**c**) *Comptr* sector *m* (**d**) *Mil* sector *m* (**e**) *Geom* sector *m*

sectoral ['sektərəl] *adj Econ* sectorial

secular ['sekjʊlə(r)] *adj* (**a**) *(history, art)* secular; *(music)* profano(a); *(education)* laico(a) (**b**) *(life, priest)* seglar

secularism ['sekjʊlərɪzəm] *n* secularismo *m*, laicismo *m*

secularize, -ise ['sekjʊləraɪz] *vt* secularizar

secure [sɪ'kjʊə(r)] 1 *adj* (**a**) *(free from anxiety)* seguro(a); **to be financially s.** tener seguridad económica; **s. in the knowledge that...** con la conciencia tranquila sabiendo que...
(**b**) *(safe) (investment, place, borders)* seguro(a) ►► *Comptr* ***s. electronic transaction*** transacción *f* electrónica segura; *Comptr* ***s. server*** servidor *m* seguro; *Br* ***s. unit*** *(for offenders)* = en una cárcel o centro de detención, unidad dotada de medidas de seguridad especiales
(**c**) *(assured) (future, victory)* asegurado(a); **the third goal meant victory was s.** el tercer gol aseguró la victoria
(**d**) *(firm) (foothold)* seguro(a); *(foundations)* firme, seguro(a); **all the windows are s.** todas las ventanas están bien cerradas; **to make sth s.** asegurar algo
2 *vt* (**a**) *(make safe) (area)* proteger; **we did everything we could to s. the boat against** *or* **from the storm** hicimos todo lo posible por poner el bote a salvo de la tormenta
(**b**) *(guarantee) (future, victory)* asegurar

(c) *(fasten) (load)* asegurar, afianzar; *(door, window)* cerrar bien; **s. the ladder against the wall first** asegura primero la escalera contra la pared
(d) *(obtain) (support, promise, loan)* conseguir; *(majority)* conseguir; **to s. sb's release** lograr la liberación de alguien
(e) *(debt, loan)* garantizar

secured [sɪ'kjʊəd] *adj (debt, loan)* garantizado(a) ►► ***s. bond*** bono *m* hipotecario *or* con garantía

securely [sɪ'kjʊəlɪ] *adv* (a) *(safely)* a buen recaudo (b) *(firmly)* firmemente; **the door was s. fastened** la puerta estaba firmemente cerrada; **make sure your seatbelts are s. fastened** asegúrense de que los cinturones de seguridad estén bien abrochados

> **False friend:** The Spanish adverb **seguramente** is not a translation for the English word **securely**. In Spanish **seguramente** means "probably".

securitization [sɪkjʊərɪtaɪ'zeɪʃən] *n St Exch* titulización *f*

security [sɪ'kjʊərɪtɪ] *n* (a) *(safety)* seguridad *f*; **terrorism is a threat to national s.** el terrorismo representa una amenaza para la seguridad nacional ►► ***S. Council*** Consejo *m* de Seguridad; ***s. risk*** peligro *m* para la seguridad del Estado *(persona)*
(b) *(police measures, protection)* seguridad *f*; **there was tight s. for the President's visit** para la visita del presidente se extremaron las medidas de seguridad ►► ***s. alarm*** alarma *f (de seguridad)*; ***s. alert*** alerta *f* de seguridad; ***s. firm*** empresa *f* de seguridad; ***s. forces*** fuerzas *fpl* de seguridad, fuerzas *fpl* del orden (público); ***s. guard*** guarda *mf* jurado(a); ***s. leak*** filtración *f* de información secreta; ***s. measures*** medidas *fpl* de seguridad; ***s. officer*** agente *mf* de seguridad; ***s. system*** sistema *m* de seguridad
(c) *(department)* (departamento *m* de) seguridad *f*; **please call s.** por favor, llame a seguridad
(d) *(emotional, financial, in job)* seguridad *f*, tranquilidad *f* ►► ***s. blanket*** = objeto que proporciona sensación de seguridad a un niño; ***s. of tenure*** *(in employment)* seguridad *f* en el cargo; *(in residence)* seguridad *f* de posesión
(e) *Fin (for loan)* garantía *f*, aval *m*; **to stand s. for sb** avalar a alguien
(f) *Fin* **securities** valores *mpl* ►► ***Securities and Exchange Commission*** = comisión del mercado de valores estadounidense; ***securities market*** mercado *m* de valores
(g) *Comptr* ***s. certificate*** certificado *m* de seguridad; *Comptr* ***s. level*** nivel *m* de seguridad

secy (*abbr* **secretary**) secretario(a) *m,f*

sedan [sɪ'dæn] *n* (a) *US Aut* turismo *m* (b) *Hist* ***s. (chair)*** silla *f* de manos

sedate [sɪ'deɪt] 1 *adj* sosegado(a), tranquilo(a)
2 *vt* sedar; **he's heavily sedated** le han administrado un sedante muy fuerte

sedately [sɪ'deɪtlɪ] *adv* sosegadamente

sedation [sɪ'deɪʃən] *n* sedación *f*; **under s.** sedado(a)

sedative ['sedətɪv] 1 *n* sedante *m*
2 *adj* sedante

sedentary ['sedəntrɪ] *adj* sedentario(a)

sedge [sedʒ] *n Bot* juncia *f* ►► ***s. warbler*** carricerín *m*

sediment ['sedɪmənt] *n* (a) *(of wine)* poso *m*; *(in tank)* sedimento *m* (b) *Geol* sedimento *m*

sedimentary [sedɪ'mentərɪ] *adj Geol* sedimentario(a)

sedimentation [sedɪmen'teɪʃən] *n* sedimentación *f*

sedition [sɪ'dɪʃən] *n* sedición *f*

seditious [sɪ'dɪʃəs] *adj* sedicioso(a)

seduce [sɪ'dju:s] *vt* (a) *(sexually)* seducir (b) *(attract)* seducir, atraer; **to s. sb into doing sth** inducir a alguien a hacer algo; **he was seduced by the large salary** lo que lo sedujo *or* atrajo fue el altísimo sueldo; **she was seduced away from the company** la sedujeron para que dejara la empresa

seducer [sɪ'dju:sə(r)] *n* seductor(ora) *m,f*

seduction [sɪ'dʌkʃən] *n* (a) *(sexual)* seducción *f* (b) *(attraction)* atractivo *m*

seductive [sɪ'dʌktɪv] *adj (person, smile, dress)* seductor(ora); **a s. offer** una oferta tentadora

seductively [sɪ'dʌktɪvlɪ] *adv* seductoramente

seductiveness [sɪ'dʌktɪvnɪs] *n (of person, smile)* poder *m* de seducción; *(of offer)* lo atrayente, lo tentador

seductress [sɪ'dʌktrɪs] *n* seductora *f*

sedulous ['sedjʊləs] *adj Formal* diligente, afanoso(a)

sedulously ['sedjʊləslɪ] *adv Formal* con diligencia *or* aplicación

see[1] [si:] *n Rel* sede *f* (episcopal)

SEE[2] (*pt* **saw** [sɔ:], *pp* **seen** [si:n]) 1 *vt* (a) *(with eyes, perceive)* ver; **to s. sb do** *or* **doing sth** ver a alguien hacer algo; **I saw the train leave at six thirty** vi salir el tren a las seis y media; **did you s. that programme last night?** ¿viste anoche ese programa?; **you were seen near the scene of the crime** te vieron cerca del escenario del crimen; **I don't want to be seen in her company** no quiero que me vean en compañía suya; **there wasn't a single tree to be seen** no se veía ni un solo árbol; **children should be seen and not heard** los niños tienen que estarse callados; **we don't want to be seen to be giving in to their demands** no queremos que parezca que cedemos a sus demandas; **now s. what you've done!** ¡mira lo que has hecho!; **I s. you've got a new motorbike** ya he visto que tienes una moto nueva; **I could s. she'd been crying** vi que había llorado; **to s. the sights** hacer turismo; **s. page 50** ver *or* véase pág. 50; **s. above/below** véase más arriba/más abajo; *Fam* **you ain't seen nothing yet!** ¡y esto no es nada!; **to be seeing things** *(hallucinate)* ver visiones; **it has to be seen to be believed** hay que verlo para creerlo; **I could s. it coming** lo veía *or* se veía venir; *Fam* **he must have seen you coming** *(he tricked you)* te debe haber visto la cara, *Esp* te ha debido camelar; **he's a very straightforward person, what you s. is what you get** es una persona muy directa, no engaña; **when will we s. an end to this conflict?** ¿cuándo veremos el final de este conflicto?; **to s. the future** ver el futuro; **to s. sense** *or* **reason** atender a razones; **I can't s. any** *or* **the sense in continuing this discussion** creo que no tiene sentido continuar esta discusión; **I can't s. a way out of this problem** no le veo solución a este problema; **could you s. your way (clear) to lending me the money?** ¿crees que podrías prestarme el dinero?; IDIOM **to s. the back** *or* **last of sth/sb** perder algo/a alguien de vista
(b) *(understand)* ver, entender; **I don't s. the joke** no le veo la gracia; **I s. what you mean** ya veo lo que quieres decir; **I don't s. the need for...** no veo qué necesidad hay de...; **I don't s. the point** no creo que tenga sentido; **they think it's great, but I don't s. it, myself** dicen que es genial, pero no acabo de ver por qué; **I don't s. why not** no veo por qué no; **now I can s. her for what she really is** ahora veo lo que realmente es
(c) *(consider, interpret)* ver; **as I s. it** tal como lo veo yo; **this is how I s. it** yo lo veo así; **we s. things differently** *(from you)* vemos las cosas desde otra óptica; *(from each other)* vemos las cosas desde una óptica diferente; **we don't s. them as a threat** no los consideramos una amenaza; **I don't s. myself as clever** no me considero inteligente; **his behaviour must be seen against a background of abuse** hay que ver su comportamiento en el contexto de los abusos que ha sufrido
(d) *(envisage, imagine)* creer, imaginarse; **what do you s. happening next?** ¿qué crees que ocurrirá a continuación?; **I can't s. them/myself accepting this** no creo que vayan/vaya a aceptar esto; **I can't s. you as a boxer** no te imagino como *or* de boxeador; **she just couldn't s. herself as a wife and mother** no se veía en el papel de esposa y de madre
(e) *(find out)* **go and s. who's at the door** ve a ver quién está llamando; **I'll s. how it goes** ya veré cómo me va; **I'll s. what I can do** veré qué puedo hacer; **let's s. what happens if...** veamos qué ocurre si...; **it remains to be seen whether...** está por ver si...
(f) *(like)* **I don't know what you s. in her** no sé qué ves en ella
(g) *(make sure)* **I shall s. (to it) that he comes** me encargaré de que venga; **s. (to it) that you don't miss the train!** ¡asegúrate de no perder el tren!; *Fam* **he'll s. you (all) right** él te echará una mano
(h) *(meet) (person)* ver; *(doctor, solicitor)* ver, visitar; **I'm seeing Bill tomorrow** mañana voy a ver a Bill; **he's too ill to s. anyone** está demasiado enfermo como para recibir visitas; **do you still s. the Browns?** ¿todavía ves a los Brown?; **I want to s. the manager** *(in shop)* quiero ver al encargado; **to s. sb about sth** ver a alguien para hablar de algo; **they've been seeing a lot of each other lately** se han visto mucho últimamente; **s. you (later)!, I'll be seeing you!** ¡hasta luego!; **s. you soon!** ¡hasta pronto!; **s. you tomorrow!** ¡hasta mañana!
(i) *(have relationship with)* salir con
(j) *(escort, accompany)* acompañar; **to s. sb home/to the door** acompañar a alguien a casa/a la puerta; **to s. sb across the road** cruzar la calle con alguien
(k) *(witness)* **1945 saw the end of the war** la guerra finalizó en 1945; **these years saw many changes** estos años fueron testigos de muchos cambios; **most recruits never s. active service** la mayor parte de los reclutas nunca llegan al servicio activo; **I never thought I'd s. the day when...** nunca creí que vería el día en que... **I've seen it all before** estoy curado de espanto
(l) *(inspect)* ver; **can I s. your ticket, sir?** ¿me enseña su billete *orAm* boleto, por favor?
(m) *(in cards)* ver; **I'll s. you** las veo; **I'll s. your ten dollars and raise you twenty** veo tus diez dólares y subo veinte

2 *vi* (a) *(with eyes)* ver; **to s. in the dark** ver en la oscuridad; **as far as the eye can s.** hasta donde alcanza la vista; **for all to s.** a la vista de todos; **s., I told you!** ¡ves, ya te lo dije!; **s. for yourself** míralo tú mismo; **you can s. for yourself how easy it is** ya verás tú mismo qué fácil es; **so I s.** ya lo veo; **we shall s.** ya veremos

(b) *(understand)* entender, ver; **as far as I can s.** a mi entender; **ah, I s.!** ¡ah, ya veo!; **I won't be able to come – I s.** no podré venir – ya veo; **I'm diabetic, you s.** soy diabético, ¿sabes? *Fam* **I don't want any trouble, s.?** no quiero líos, ¿entendido?; *Old-fashioned Fam* **now s. here, young man!** vamos a ver, jovencito

(c) *(examine, consider)* **let me s., let's s.** veamos, vamos a ver; **can we go to the beach? – we'll s.** ¿podemos ir a la playa? – ya veremos; *Fam* **s.! I told you he wouldn't let us down** ¡lo ves! te dije que no nos defraudaría

(d) *(find out)* **I'll go and s.** voy a ver; **I'll s. if anyone knows** voy a ver si alguien lo sabe; **I'll get my own back, you'll s.!** ¡ya me desquitaré, ya verás!

► **see about** *vt insep* (a) *(deal with)* encargarse *or* ocuparse de; **they're sending someone to s. about the gas** han enviado a alguien para que mire lo del gas

(b) *(consider)* ver, pensar; **we'll have to s. about getting a new TV** tendremos que plantearnos comprar un nuevo televisor; *Fam* **we'll (soon) s. about that!** ¡eso está por ver!

► **see around** 1 *vt insep (have a look around)* recorrer, ver

2 *vt sep* **I haven't been introduced to her, but I've seen her around** no me la han presentado, aunque la he visto por ahí; *Fam* **(I'll) s. you around!** ¡nos vemos!

► **see in** 1 *vt sep (escort inside)* acompañar adentro; **to s. the New Year in** recibir el Año Nuevo

2 *vi* ver el interior; **we couldn't s. in** no se podía ver lo que había dentro

► **see off** *vt sep* (a) *(say goodbye to)* despedir (b) *(chase away)* ahuyentar; *(in fight)* deshacerse de (c) *(defeat)* derrotar; *(challenge, threat)* superar

► **see out** *vt sep* (a) *(escort to door)* acompañar a la puerta; **I'll s. myself out** ya conozco el camino (de salida), gracias

(b) *(survive)* aguantar; **it is unlikely that they will s. the year out** es muy poco probable que aguanten todo el año; **he'll s. us all out!** ¡nos sobrevivirá a todos!, ¡nos enterrará a todos!

► **see over, see round** *vt insep (view)* visitar, examinar

► **see through** 1 *vt sep* (a) *(project)* **to s. sth through** participar en algo hasta el final

(b) *(help, sustain)* **to s. sb through sth** ayudar a alguien a pasar algo; **£20 should s. me through (to Monday)** con 20 libras me las apañaré (hasta el lunes)

2 *vt insep (not be deceived by) (person)* ver las intenciones de; **I can s. through your lies** tus mentiras no me engañan; **I saw through their little game** me percaté de lo que estaban tramando

► **see to** *vt insep (deal with)* ocuparse de; *(customer)* atender a; **to get sth seen to** hacer que alguien se ocupe de algo; **you should get that leg seen to** deberías ir a que te vieran la pierna; **I'll s. to it that you're not disturbed** me aseguraré *or* encargaré de que nadie te moleste

---

seed [si:d] 1 *n* (a) *(for sowing)* semilla *f*; *(of fruit)* pepita *f*; **the price of s.** el precio de las semillas; **to go** *or* **run to s.** *(plant)* granar; *(person)* venirse abajo, abandonarse ►► ***s. corn*** simiente *f* de trigo; *Fig* inversión *f* de futuro; ***s. merchant*** vendedor *m* de semillas; ***s. money*** capital *m* inicial; ***s. pearl*** aljófar *m*; ***s. pod*** vaina *f*; ***s. potatoes*** *Esp* patatas *fpl* or*Am* papas *fpl* de siembra; ***s. tray*** semillero *m*, germinador *m*

(b) *(of doubt, suspicion, rebellion)* germen *m*; **to sow (the) seeds of discord/doubt** sembrar la discordia/duda

(c) *Sport (in tournament)* cabeza *mf* de serie; **the top s.** el primer cabeza de serie

(d) *Literary (semen)* semilla *f*, semen *m*

(e) *Literary (offspring)* simiente *m*

2 *vt* (a) *(lawn, field)* sembrar (**with** de) (b) *(remove seeds from)* despepitar (c) *Sport (in tournament)* **seeded players/teams** jugadores/equipos seleccionados como cabezas de serie; **he's seeded 5** es el cabeza de serie número 5 (d) *(clouds)* dispersar

3 *vi (plant)* dar semilla, granar

seedbed ['si:dbed] *n* semillero *m*

seedcake ['si:dkeɪk] *n* tarta *f* de carvis

seediness ['si:dɪnɪs] *n (of person, appearance, hotel)* lo zarrapastroso; *(of hotel)* lo cochambroso

seedless ['si:dlɪs] *adj* sin pepitas

seedling ['si:dlɪŋ] *n* plantón *m*

seedy ['si:dɪ] *adj* (a) *(shabby) (person, appearance)* zarrapastroso(a); *(hotel)* cochambroso(a); *(area)* abandonado(a), sórdido(a) (b) *Fam (unwell)* **to feel s.** estar malo(a) *or* pachucho(a) *or Col* maluco(a)

seeing ['si:ɪŋ] 1 *n* IDIOM **s. is believing** ver para creer

2 *conj Fam* **s. that** *or* **as** *or* **how...** en vista de que..., ya que...; **s. it's so simple, why don't you do it yourself?** ya que es tan sencillo, ¿por qué no lo haces tú mismo?

seeing-eye dog ['si:ɪŋaɪ'dɒg] *n US* perro *m* lazarillo

seeing-to ['si:ɪŋtu:] *n Br Fam* **to give sb a good s.** *(beat up)* dar una buena paliza a alguien; *(have sex with)* acostarse con alguien, cepillarse a alguien

seek [si:k] (*pt & pp* **sought** [sɔ:t]) 1 *vt* (a) *(look for) (thing lost, job, solution)* buscar; *(friendship, promotion, approval)* buscar; **to s. one's fortune** buscar fortuna; **he sought revenge on them** buscaba vengarse de ellos; **we sought shelter in a shop doorway** nos guarecimos en la puerta de una tienda

(b) *(request)* **to s. sth from sb** pedir algo a alguien; **to s. sb's help/advice** pedir ayuda/consejo a alguien

(c) *(try)* **to s. to do sth** procurar hacer algo

(d) *(move towards)* buscar

(e) *Comptr* ***s. time*** tiempo *m* de búsqueda

2 *vi* buscar; **to s. after sth** ir en busca de algo

► **seek out** *vt sep (person, enemy)* ir en búsqueda *or* busca de; **he's all right, but I wouldn't s. him out** *or* **s. out his company** no me cae mal pero tampoco me muero por verlo

seeker ['si:kə(r)] *n* buscador(ora) *m,f*

SEEM [si:m] *vi* parecer; **to s. (to be) tired** parecer cansado(a); **she seemed tired to me** me pareció que estaba cansada; **do what seems best** haz lo que te parezca mejor; **it doesn't s. right** no me parece bien; **he seemed like** *or* **as if he no longer cared** parecía que no le preocupara ya nada; **it seemed like a dream** parecía un sueño; **it seems like yesterday that...** parece que fue ayer cuando...; **I s. to have dropped your vase** creo que he tirado tu jarrón; **I s. to remember that...** creo recordar que...; **I s. to have been chosen to do it** parece que me han elegido a mí para hacerlo; **I can't s. to get it right** no consigo que me salga bien; **I know how this must s., but...** ya sé lo que te va a parecer, pero...; **funny as it may s....** aunque parezca extraño...; **he is not all he seems** no es lo que parece; **it seems (that** *or* **as if)..., it would s. (that** *or* **as if)...** parece que...; **it seems likely that...** parece probable que...; **it seems to me that...** me parece que...; **it seems** *or* **would s. so/not** parece que sí/no; **she's resigning, or so it seems** va a dimitir, o eso parece; **there seems** *or* **would s. to be a problem** tengo la impresión de que hay un problema; **what seems to be the problem?** dígame, ¿cuál es el problema?

---

seeming ['si:mɪŋ] *adj* aparente

seemingly ['si:mɪŋlɪ] *adv* aparentemente; **s. so/not** aparentemente sí/no

seemliness ['si:mlɪnɪs] *n Formal* corrección *f*

seemly ['si:mlɪ] *adj Formal* correcto(a), apropiado(a)

seen *pp of* **see**

seep [si:p] *vi* **to s. into sth** filtrarse en algo; **water was seeping through the cracks in the floor** el agua se filtraba por las grietas del piso

► **seep away** *vi* irse apagando *or* agotando

► **seep out** *vi* (a) *(blood, liquid)* brotar, manar; *(gas, smoke)* emanar (b) *(information, secret)* filtrarse

seepage ['si:pɪdʒ] *n* filtración *f*

seer [sɪə(r)] *n Literary* adivino(a) *m,f*, profeta *m*

seersucker ['sɪəsʌkə(r)] *n* sirsaca *f*

seesaw ['si:sɔ:] 1 *n* balancín *m*, subibaja *m*; **a s. motion** un balanceo *or* vaivén

2 *vi (prices, mood)* fluctuar

seethe [si:ð] *vi* (a) *(liquid)* borbotar (b) *(person)* **to s. (with anger)** estar a punto de estallar (de cólera) (c) *(teem)* bullir; **the streets seethed with shoppers** las calles bullían *or* eran un hervidero de gente haciendo compras

seething ['si:ðɪŋ] *adj* (a) *(angry)* furioso(a), colérico(a); **to be s. (with anger)** estar a punto de estallar (de cólera) (b) *(teeming)* **a s. mass of people** un hervidero de gente

see-through ['si:θru:] *adj* transparente

segment 1 *n* ['segmənt] *(of circle, worm)* segmento *m*; *(of orange, grapefruit)* gajo *m*; *(of society, economy, organization)* sector *m*

2 *vt* [seg'ment] *(circle, market)* segmentar; *(orange, grapefruit)* desgajar

segmentation [segmen'teɪʃən] *n Econ* segmentación *f*

segmented [seg'mentɪd] *adj Econ* segmentado(a)

segregate ['segrɪgeɪt] *vt (separate)* segregar (**from** de); *(keep apart)* separar; **he went to a school where the sexes were segregated** iba a una escuela en la que los niños estaban separados de las niñas

segregated ['segrɪgeɪtɪd] *adj (school, beach)* segregado(a)

segregation [segrɪ'geɪʃən] *n* segregación *f*

segregationist [segrɪ'geɪʃənɪst] **1** *n* segregacionista *mf*
2 *adj* segregacionista

segue ['segweɪ] **1** *n* (**a**) *Mus* enlace *m* (**into** con) (**b**) *(transition)* transición *f* (**into** hacia)
2 *vi* (**a**) *Mus* **to s. into sth** enlazar con algo (**b**) *(merge)* **our honeymoon seemed to s. into a whole month of parties** después de la luna de miel pasamos sin solución de continuidad a un mes entero de fiestas

Seine [seɪn] *n* **the (River) S.** el (río) Sena

seine [seɪn] *n* ***s. (net)*** red *f* de arrastre

seismic ['saɪzmɪk] *adj* (**a**) *Geol* sísmico(a) (**b**) *(change, proportions)* dramático(a)

seismograph ['saɪzməgræf] *n* sismógrafo *m*

seismography [saɪz'mɒgrəfɪ] *n* sismografía *f*

seismologist [saɪz'mɒlədʒɪst] *n* sismólogo(a) *m,f*

seismology [saɪz'mɒlədʒɪ] *n* sismología *f*

seize [siːz] *vt* (**a**) *(grab)* agarrar, *Esp* coger; **my mother seized me by the arm** mi madre me agarró del brazo; **to s. hold of sth** agarrar algo
(**b**) *(take for oneself) (city, territory, power)* tomar; *(hostage)* tomar; **to s. control of sth** tomar el control de algo
(**c**) *(drugs, stolen goods)* incautarse de
(**d**) *(arrest) (terrorist, smuggler)* arrestar, detener
(**e**) *(make the most of)* **to s. the opportunity of doing sth** aprovechar la oportunidad de hacer algo
(**f**) *(overcome)* apoderarse de; **we were seized with panic/fright** fuimos presa del pánico/miedo; **I was seized with the desire to go to Mexico** me entraron unas ganas tremendas de ir a México

► **seize on, seize upon** *vt insep (opportunity, excuse, mistake)* aprovecharse de; *(idea)* aferrarse a

► **seize up** *vi (engine, machine)* atascarse; *(back, knees)* agarrotarse; *(traffic)* detenerse, paralizarse

seizure ['siːʒə(r)] *n* (**a**) *(of land, city, power)* toma *f*; *(of hostage)* toma *f* (**b**) *(of property, goods)* incautación *f*; **a large drugs s.** la incautación de un enorme alijo de drogas
(**c**) *Med* ataque *m*; **to have a s.** sufrir un ataque

seldom ['seldəm] *adv* rara vez, raras veces; **he s., if ever, visits his mother** muy raras veces visita a su madre; *Formal* **s. have I been so worried** rara vez he estado tan preocupado

select [sɪ'lekt] **1** *adj* (**a**) *(elite) (restaurant, club, neighbourhood)* selecto(a); **a s. few** unos cuantos escogidos ►► *Br Parl* ***s. committee*** comisión *f* parlamentaria (**b**) *(in quality) (goods, wines)* selecto(a)
2 *vt* (**a**) *(choose) (team, person)* seleccionar; *(gift, wine, record)* escoger, elegir (**b**) *Comptr* seleccionar

selected [sɪ'lektɪd] *adj* seleccionado(a); **s. items at half price** algunos artículos a mitad de precio; **s. works** obras escogidas

selection [sɪ'lekʃən] *n* (**a**) *(act of choosing) (of team, person)* selección *f*; *(of gift, wine, record)* elección *f*; **to make a s.** realizar una selección; **make your s. from among the books on the bottom shelf** elija de entre los libros que hay del estante de abajo ►► ***s. box*** *(of chocolate bars)* surtido *m* (**b**) *(range)* gama *f* (**c**) *(thing chosen)* elección *f* (**d**) *(of stories, poems)* colección *f*, selección *f*

selective [sɪ'lektɪv] *adj* selectivo(a); *(school)* con examen de ingreso; **to be s. (about sth)** ser selectivo(a) (con algo); **you should be more s. in your choice of friends** tendrías que ser un poco más selectivo con los amigos que eliges ►► ***s. breeding*** cultivo *m* selectivo, cría *f* selectiva

selectively [sɪ'lektɪvlɪ] *adv* con un criterio selectivo

selectivity [sɪlek'tɪvətɪ] *n* (**a**) *(elitism)* elitismo *m* (**b**) *Elec* selectividad *f*

selector [sɪ'lektə(r)] *n* (**a**) *(of team)* miembro *m* del comité seleccionador (**b**) *Tel* selector *m*

selenite ['selənaɪt] *n* selenita *f*

selenium [sɪ'liːnɪəm] *n Chem* selenio *m*

self [self] (*pl* **selves** [selvz]) *n* (**a**) *(personality)* **he's back to his old** *or* **usual s. again** ha vuelto a ser él mismo; **she is a shadow of her former s.** no es ni sombra de lo que era; **she was her usual cheerful s.** se mostró alegre como siempre; **they began to reveal their true selves** comenzaron a mostrarse tal cual eran; **could I ask your good s. to sit here** ¿puedo pedirle que tenga la gentileza de sentarse aquí?
(**b**) *Psy* **the s.** el yo, el ser
(**c**) *(self-interest)* **all she thinks of is s., s., s.** sólo piensa en sí misma

self- [self] *prefix* (**a**) *(of oneself)* **s.-admiration** vanidad *f*, presunción *f* (**b**) *(by oneself)* auto-; **s.-financing** que se autofinancia (**c**) *(automatic)* auto-; **s.-lubricating** autolubricante

self-abasement ['selfə'beɪsmənt] *n* autohumillación *f*, autodegradación *f*

self-abnegation ['selfæbnə'geɪʃən] *n* abnegación *f*

self-absorbed ['selfəb'zɔːbd] *adj* ensimismado(a)

self-abuse ['selfə'bjuːs] *n Pej (masturbation)* masturbación *f*

self-addressed envelope ['selfə'drest'envələʊp] *n* sobre *m* dirigido a uno mismo

self-adhesive ['selfəd'hiːsɪv] *adj* autoadhesivo(a)

self-advertisement ['selfəd'vɜːtɪsmənt] *n* autopromoción *f*

self-advocacy ['self'ædvəkəsɪ] *n (of disabled people)* autoafirmación *f*

self-aggrandizement ['selfə'grændɪzmənt] *n Formal* exaltación *f* de sí mismo(a)

self-analysis ['selfə'næləsɪs] *n* autoanálisis *m inv*

self-apparent *adj* ['selfə'pærənt] obvio(a), evidente

self-appointed ['selfə'pɔɪntɪd] *adj* autodesignado(a), autoproclamado(a)

self-appraisal ['selfə'preɪzəl] *n* autoevaluación *f*

self-approving ['selfə'pruːvɪŋ] *adj* autocomplaciente

self-assembly ['selfə'semblɪ] **1** *n* automontaje *m*
2 *adj (furniture)* para armar uno mismo

self-assertive ['selfə'sɜːtɪv] *adj* **you need to be more s.** deberías tener más confianza en ti mismo

self-assertiveness ['selfə'sɜːtɪvnɪs] *n* **you need to show more s.** deberías mostrar más confianza en ti mismo; **a course in s.** un curso de autoafirmación

self-assessment ['selfə'sesmənt] *n* (**a**) *(self-evaluation)* autoevaluación *f* (**b**) *Br (of tax liabilities)* autoliquidación *f* tributaria

self-assurance ['selfə'ʃʊərəns] *n* seguridad *f* de sí mismo(a), confianza *f* en sí mismo(a)

self-assured ['selfə'ʃʊəd] *adj* seguro(a) de sí mismo(a); **to be s.** estar seguro(a) de sí mismo(a)

self-awareness ['selfə'weənɪs] *n* conocimiento *m* de sí mismo(a)

self-belief ['selfbɪ'liːf] *n* confianza *f* en sí mismo(a)

self-catering ['self'keɪtərɪŋ] *adj (holiday, accommodation)* sin servicio de comidas

self-censorship ['self'sensəʃɪp] *n* autocensura *f*

self-centred, *US* **self-centered** ['self'sentəd] *adj* egoísta

self-coloured, *US* **self-colored** ['self'kʌləd] *adj (of one colour)* de un solo color

self-command ['selfkə'mɑːnd] *n* autocontrol *m*, dominio *m* de sí mismo(a)

self-complacent ['selfkəm'pleɪsənt] *adj* autocomplaciente

self-composed ['selfkəm'pəʊzd] *adj* sereno(a)

self-composure ['selfkəm'pəʊʒə(r)] *n* compostura *f*

self-conceited ['selfkən'siːtɪd] *adj* engreído(a), presuntuoso(a)

self-confessed ['selfkən'fest] *adj* confeso(a)

self-confidence ['self'kɒnfɪdəns] *n* confianza *f* en sí mismo(a)

self-confident ['self'kɒnfɪdənt] *adj* lleno(a) de confianza en sí mismo(a)

self-confidently ['self'kɒnfɪdəntlɪ] *adv* con gran confianza *or* seguridad

self-congratulatory ['self'kəngrætjʊ'leɪtərɪ] *adj* de autosatisfacción

self-conscious ['self'kɒnʃəs] *adj* (**a**) *(embarrassed)* cohibido(a) (**about** por); **he's very s. about his red hair** está muy acomplejado por ser pelirrojo (**b**) *(affected)* afectado(a)

self-consciously ['self'kɒnʃəslɪ] *adv* (**a**) *(with embarrassment)* con inhibición, tímidamente (**b**) *(affectedly)* afectadamente, con afectación

self-contained ['selfkən'teɪnd] *adj* (**a**) *(person)* independiente (**b**) *(apartment)* independiente

self-contempt ['selfkən'tempt] *n* desprecio *m* por uno mismo

self-contradiction ['selfkɒntrə'dɪkʃən] *n* contrasentido *m*, contradicción *f*

self-contradictory ['selfkɒntrə'dɪktərɪ] *adj* contradictorio(a)

self-control ['selfkən'trəʊl] *n* autocontrol *m*; **to lose/regain one's s.** perder/recuperar el control de uno mismo

self-controlled ['selfkən'trəʊld] *adj* controlado(a)

self-critical ['self'krɪtɪkəl] *adj* autocrítico(a)

self-criticism ['self'krɪtɪsɪzəm] *n* autocrítica *f*

self-deception ['selfdɪ'sepʃən] *n* autoengaño *m*

self-defeating ['selfdɪ'fi:tɪŋ] *adj* contraproducente

self-defence, *US* **self-defense** ['selfdɪ'fens] *n* **(a)** *(judo, karate etc)* defensa *f* personal **(b)** *(non-violent action)* defensa *f* propia; **to act in s.** actuar en defensa propia

self-delusion ['selfdɪ'lu:ʒən] *n* autoengaño *m*

self-denial ['selfdɪ'naɪəl] *n* abnegación *f*

self-deprecating ['self'deprɪkeɪtɪŋ] *adj* **he's famous for his s. humour** siempre se ríe de sí mismo

self-destruct ['selfdɪ'strʌkt] **1** *vi* autodestruirse
2 *adj* IDIOM **to press the s. button** estropearla

self-destruction ['selfdɪ'strʌkʃən] *n* autodestrucción *f*

self-destructive ['selfdɪs'trʌktɪv] *adj* autodestructivo(a)

self-determination ['selfdɪtɜ:mɪ'neɪʃən] *n* autodeterminación *f*

self-discipline ['self'dɪsɪplɪn] *n* autodisciplina *f*

self-disciplined ['self'dɪsɪplɪnd] *adj* autodisciplinado(a)

self-doubt ['self'daʊt] *n* falta *f* de confianza (en uno mismo)

self-drive ['self'draɪv] *adj* sin conductor

self-educated ['self'edjʊkeɪtɪd] *adj* autodidacta

self-effacing ['selfɪ'feɪsɪŋ] *adj* modesto(a), humilde

self-employed ['selfɪm'plɔɪd] **1** *adj* autónomo(a) ▸▸ ***s. person*** trabajador(ora) *m,f* autónomo(a) *or* por cuenta propia
2 *npl* **the s.** los autónomos

self-employment ['selfɪm'plɔɪmənt] *n* autoempleo *m*, trabajo *m* por cuenta propia

self-esteem ['selfɪ'sti:m] *n* **to have high/low s.** tener mucho/poco amor propio, tener mucha/poca autoestima

self-evident ['self'evɪdənt] *adj* evidente, obvio(a)

self-examination ['selfɪgzæmɪ'neɪʃən] *n* **(a)** *(of conscience)* autoexamen *m* **(b)** *(of breasts, testicles)* autoexamen *m*

self-explanatory ['selfɪk'splænɪtərɪ] *adj* **to be s.** estar muy claro(a), hablar por sí mismo(a)

self-expression ['selfɪk'spreʃən] *n* autoexpresión *f*

self-extracting ['selfɪk'stræktɪŋ] *adj Comptr (archive)* autodescomprimible

self-fulfilling ['selffʊl'fɪlɪŋ] *adj (prophecy, prediction)* que se autorrealiza

self-fulfilment, *US* **self-fulfillment** ['selffʊl'fɪlmənt] *n* realización *f* personal

self-governing ['self'gʌvənɪŋ] *adj* autónomo(a)

self-government ['self'gʌvəmənt] *n* autogobierno *m*, autonomía *f*

self-help ['self'help] *n* autoayuda *f* ▸▸ ***s. book*** manual *m* de autoayuda; ***s. group*** grupo *m* de apoyo

self-image ['self'ɪmɪdʒ] *n* imagen *f* de sí mismo(a)

self-importance ['selfɪm'pɔ:təns] *n* engreimiento *m*, presunción *f*

self-important ['selfɪm'pɔ:tənt] *adj* engreído(a), presuntuoso(a)

self-importantly ['selfɪm'pɔ:təntlɪ] *adv* presuntuosamente, con engreimiento

self-imposed ['selfɪm'pəʊzd] *adj (prohibition, restriction)* autoimpuesto(a); *(exile, silence)* voluntario(a)

self-improvement ['selfɪm'pru:vmənt] *n* autosuperación *f*

self-induced ['selfɪn'dju:st] *adj (hysteria, illness)* provocado(a) por uno mismo

self-induction coil ['selfɪn'dʌkʃən'kɔɪl] *n Elec* bobina *f* de autoinducción

self-indulgence ['selfɪn'dʌldʒəns] *n* **(a)** *(quality)* autocomplacencia *f* **(b)** *(luxury)* lujo *m*

self-indulgent ['selfɪn'dʌldʒənt] *adj* autocomplaciente

self-inflicted ['selfɪn'flɪktɪd] *adj* autoinfligido(a)

self-interest ['self'ɪntrest] *n* interés *m* propio

self-interested ['self'ɪntrestɪd] *adj* egoísta

selfish ['selfɪʃ] *adj* egoísta

selfishly ['selfɪʃlɪ] *adv* egoístamente, con egoísmo

selfishness ['selfɪʃnɪs] *n* egoísmo *m*

self-justification ['selfdʒʌstɪfɪ'keɪʃən] *n* autojustificación *f*

self-knowledge ['self'nɒlɪdʒ] *n* conocimiento *m* de sí mismo(a)

selfless ['selflɪs] *adj* desinteresado(a), desprendido(a)

selflessly ['selflɪslɪ] *adv* desinteresadamente, de manera desinteresada

selflessness ['selflɪsnɪs] *n* desinterés *m*, generosidad *f*

self-loathing ['self'ləʊðɪŋ] *n* desprecio *m* por uno mismo

self-made man ['selfmeɪd'mæn] *n* hombre *m* hecho a sí mismo

self-mockery ['self'mɒkərɪ] *n* burla *f* de uno mismo

self-motivated ['self'məʊtɪveɪtɪd] *adj* automotivado(a)

self-mutilation ['selfmjʊtɪ'leɪʃən] *n* automutilación *f*

self-obsessed ['selfəb'sest] *adj* egocéntrico(a)

self-opinionated ['selfə'pɪnjəneɪtɪd] *adj* **to be s.** querer llevar la razón siempre

self-perpetuating ['selfpə'petʃʊeɪtɪŋ] *adj* que se autoperpetúa

self-pity ['self'pɪtɪ] *n* autocompasión *f*

self-pitying ['self'pɪtɪɪŋ] *adj* autocompasivo(a)

self-pollination ['selfpɒlɪ'neɪʃən] *n Bot* autopolinización *f*

self-portrait ['self'pɔ:treɪt] *n* autorretrato *m*

self-possessed ['selfpə'zest] *adj* sereno(a), dueño(a) de sí mismo(a)

self-possession ['selfpə'zeʃən] *n* serenidad *f*, autocontrol *m*

self-preservation ['selfprezə'veɪʃən] *n* propia conservación *f*; **instinct for s.** instinto de conservación

self-proclaimed ['selfprə'kleɪmd] *adj* autoproclamado(a)

self-propelled ['selfprə'peld] *adj* autopropulsado(a)

self-publicist ['self'pʌblɪsɪst] *n* persona *f* que se autopromociona; **he's a very accomplished s.** es un rey de la autopromoción

self-raising flour ['selfreɪzɪŋ'flaʊə(r)], *US* **self-rising flour** ['selfraɪzɪŋ'flaʊə(r)] *n Esp* harina *f* con levadura, *Am* harina *f* con polvos de hornear, *RP* harina *f* leudante

self-realization ['selfrɪəlaɪ'zeɪʃən] *n* realización *f* personal

self-referential ['selfrefə'renʃəl] *adj* sobre *or* acerca de uno mismo, lleno(a) de referencias personales; **his style is very s.** su estilo se caracteriza por la presencia constante de referencias personales

self-regard ['selfrɪ'gɑ:d] *n* autoestima *f*

self-regulating ['self'regjʊleɪtɪŋ] *adj* **(a)** *(authority, organization)* autorregulado(a) **(b)** *(temperature)* autorregulado(a)

self-regulation ['selfregjʊ'leɪʃən] *n (of authority, organization)* autorregulación *f*

self-reliance ['selfrɪ'laɪəns] *n* autosuficiencia *f*

self-reliant ['selfrɪ'laɪənt] *adj* autosuficiente

self-replicating ['self'replɪkeɪtɪŋ] *adj* que se autorreproduce

self-respect ['selfrɪ'spekt] *n* amor *m* propio, dignidad *f*

self-respecting ['selfrɪ'spektɪŋ] *adj* con dignidad; **no s. person would ever...** nadie con un mínimo de dignidad...; **as any s. baseball fan knows...** como todo aficionado al béisbol que se precie sabe...

self-restraint ['selfrɪs'treɪnt] *n* autodominio *m*, autocontrol *m*

self-righteous ['self'raɪtʃəs] *adj* santurrón(ona)

self-righteousness ['self'raɪtʃəsnɪs] *n* santurronería *f*

self-rising flour *US* = **self-raising flour**

self-rule ['self'ru:l] *n* autonomía *f*

self-sacrifice ['self'sækrɪfaɪs] *n* abnegación *f*

self-sacrificing ['self'sækrɪfaɪsɪŋ] *adj* abnegado(a)

selfsame ['selfseɪm] *adj* mismísimo(a)

self-satisfaction ['selfsætɪs'fækʃən] *n* autocomplacencia *f*, aires *mpl* de suficiencia

self-satisfied ['self'sætɪsfaɪd] *adj* satisfecho(a) *or* pagado(a) de sí mismo(a); **to be s.** estar satisfecho(a) *or* pagado(a) de sí mismo(a)

self-sealing ['self'si:lɪŋ] *adj (envelope)* autoadhesivo(a)

self-seeking ['self'si:kɪŋ] *adj* egoísta, interesado(a)

self-service ['self'sɜ:vɪs] **1** *n* autoservicio *m*
2 *adj (shop)* autoservicio ▸▸ ***s. restaurant*** autoservicio *m*

self-serving ['self'sɜ:vɪŋ] *adj* egoísta, interesado(a)

self-starter ['self'stɑ:tə(r)] *n (person)* persona *f* con iniciativa

self-styled ['self'staɪld] *adj (president, king)* autoproclamado(a); *(philosopher, expert)* pretendido(a), sedicente

self-sufficiency ['selfsə'fɪʃənsɪ] *n (economic)* autosuficiencia *f*; *(emotional)* independencia *f*

self-sufficient ['selfsə'fɪʃənt] *adj (economically)* autosuficiente; *(emotionally)* independiente; **our country is s. in coal** nuestro país se autoabastece de carbón

self-supporting ['selfsə'pɔ:tɪŋ] *adj (financially)* económicamente independiente

self-taught ['self'tɔːt] *adj* autodidacto(a)

self-test ['self'test] *Comptr* **1** *n* autotest *m*
2 *vi* efectuar un autotest

self-willed ['self'wɪld] *adj* obstinado(a)

self-winding ['self'waɪndɪŋ] *adj (watch)* de cuerda automática

sell [sel] (*pt & pp* **sold** [səʊld]) **1** *vt* (**a**) *(goods, property)* vender (**for** por); **to s. sb sth, to s. sth to sb** vender algo a alguien; **he sold me his bike for $500** me vendió su moto por 500 dólares; **I was sold a faulty washing machine** me vendieron una lavadora que era defectuosa; **the book sold 50,000 copies** el libro vendió 50.000 ejemplares; **scandal sells newspapers** las noticias escandalosas venden bien; **to s. sth at a loss/profit** vender algo con pérdida/ganancia; **they s. the cassettes at £3 each** venden cassettes a 3 libras cada uno; **she was sold into prostitution** la vendieron a un proxeneta; **s. by 05.12.03.** *(on food packaging)* fecha límite de venta: 05.12.03; **sold** *(sign)* vendido(a)
(**b**) *(promote)* vender; **to s. sb an idea** vender una idea a alguien; **she tried to s. me some story about running out of petrol** intentó venderme el cuento de que se había quedado sin gasolina; **to be sold on sth** estar convencido(a) de que algo es una buena idea; **he doesn't s. himself very well** no se sabe vender
(**c**) IDIOMS **to s. one's body** *or* **oneself** vender el cuerpo, venderse; *Fam Hum* **he'd s. his own grandmother for a pint of beer** vendería a su madre por una cerveza; **to s. one's soul (to the devil)** vender el alma (al diablo); **to s. sb down the river** traicionar *or* vender a alguien; *Fam* **to s. sb short** *(cheat)* engañar a alguien; **to s. oneself short** infravalorarse, subestimarse
2 *vi* (**a**) *(person, shop)* vender (**b**) *(product)* venderse (**for** por; **at** a); IDIOM **to s. like hot cakes** venderse como rosquillas

▸ **sell off** *vt sep (property, stock)* liquidar; *(shares)* vender; *(industry)* privatizar

▸ **sell on** *vt sep* revender

▸ **sell out 1** *vt sep* (**a**) **the concert is sold out** *(no tickets remain)* no quedan entradas *or Am* boletos para el concierto; **we are sold out of champagne** se nos ha agotado el champán; **sold out** *(sign)* agotadas las localidades, no hay localidades *or* entradas *or Am* boletos (**b**) *(betray)* vender, traicionar
2 *vi* (**a**) *(sell all tickets)* **they have sold out of tickets** se han agotado las entradas *or Am* los boletos; **the concert has sold out** no quedan entradas *or Am* boletos para el concierto (**b**) *(betray beliefs)* venderse (**c**) *(sell business)* liquidar el negocio; **he sold out to some Japanese investors** les vendió el negocio a unos inversores japoneses

▸ **sell up 1** *vt sep (business)* vender, liquidar
2 *vi (sell home, business)* venderlo todo

sell-by date ['selbaɪ'deɪt] *n Com* fecha *f* límite de venta

seller ['selə(r)] *n* (**a**) *(person)* vendedor(ora) *m,f* ▸▸ *Econ* ***sellers' market*** mercado *m* de vendedores (**b**) *(product)* **these shoes are good/poor sellers** estos zapatos se venden muy bien/mal; **it's one of our biggest sellers** es uno de los que más vendemos

selling ['selɪŋ] *n* venta *f* ▸▸ ***s. point*** ventaja *f (de un producto)*; ***s. price*** precio *m* de venta

sell-off ['selɒf] *n (of state-owned company)* privatización *f*; *(of stocks, shares)* liquidación *f*

Sellotape® ['seləteɪp] *Br* **1** *n* cinta *f* adhesiva, *Esp* celo *m*, *CAm, Méx* Durex® *m*
2 *vt* pegar con cinta adhesiva *or Esp* celo *or CAm, Méx* Durex®

sellout ['selaʊt] *n* (**a**) *(play, concert)* lleno *m*; **the match was a s.** se vendieron todas las entradas para el partido (**b**) *(betrayal)* traición *f*

sell-through ['sel'θruː] *n Com* venta *f* (al por menor)

Seltzer ['seltsə(r)] *n* **S. (water)** agua *f* de Seltz

selves *pl of* **self**

semantic [sɪ'mæntɪk] *adj* semántico(a)

semantically [sɪ'mæntɪklɪ] *adv* semánticamente

semantics [sɪ'mæntɪks] *n* semántica *f*; *Fig* **let's not worry about s.** dejemos a un lado los matices

semaphore ['seməfɔː(r)] *n* (**a**) *(code)* código *m* alfabético de banderas (**b**) *(device)* semáforo *m*

semblance ['sembləns] *n* apariencia *f*; **the s. of a smile** un atisbo *or* asomo de sonrisa; **to maintain some s. of dignity** mantener cierto asomo de dignidad

semen ['siːmen] *n* semen *m*

semester [sɪ'mestə(r)] *n Univ* semestre *m*

semi ['semɪ] *n Fam* (**a**) *Br* (*abbr* **semi-detached house**) chalet *m* pareado *or* semiadosado (**b**) *US* (*abbr* **semitrailer**) semirremolque *m* (**c**) (*abbr* **semifinal**) semifinal *f*

semi- ['semɪ, *US* 'semaɪ] *prefix (partly)* semi-; **s.-civilized** semicivilizado(a)

semi-arid ['semɪ'ærɪd] *adj* semiárido(a)

semiautomatic ['semɪɔːtə'mætɪk] **1** *n* semiautomática *f*
2 *adj* semiautomático(a)

semibreve ['semɪbriːv] *n Br Mus* redonda *f*

semicircle ['semɪsɜːkəl] *n* semicírculo *m*

semicircular ['semɪ'sɜːkjʊlə(r)] *adj* semicircular ▸▸ *Anat* ***s. canal*** conducto *m* semicircular

semicolon ['semɪ'kəʊlən] *n* punto *m* y coma

semiconductor ['semɪkən'dʌktə(r)] *n Elec* semiconductor *m*

semiconscious ['semɪ'kɒnʃəs] *adj* semiconsciente

semidarkness ['semɪ'dɑːknɪs] *n* **in s.** en la penumbra

semi-detached ['semɪdɪ'tætʃt] **1** *n (house)* chalet *m* pareado *or* semiadosado
2 *adj* pareado(a), semiadosado(a)

semifinal ['semɪ'faɪnəl] *n* semifinal *f*

semifinalist ['semɪ'faɪnəlɪst] *n* semifinalista *mf*

semi-finished ['semɪ'fɪnɪʃt] *adj (goods)* semiacabado(a), semielaborado(a)

semiliterate ['semɪ'lɪtərət] *adj* semialfabetizado(a)

semimembranosus ['semɪmembrə'nəʊsəs] *n Anat* semimembranoso *m*

seminal ['semɪnəl] *adj* (**a**) *(very important)* trascendental, fundamental (**b**) *(fluid, duct)* seminal

seminar ['semɪnɑː(r)] *n* seminario *m*

seminarian [semɪ'neərɪən], **seminarist** ['semɪnərɪst] *n* seminarista *m*

seminary ['semɪnərɪ] *n* seminario *m*

semiofficial ['semɪə'fɪʃəl] *adj* semioficial

semiology [semɪ'ɒlədʒɪ] *n* semiología *f*

semiotics [semɪ'ɒtɪks] *n* semiótica *f*

semi-permeable ['semɪ'pɜːmɪəbəl] *adj* ***s. membrane*** membrana *f* semipermeable

semi-precious ['semɪ'preʃəs] *adj* ***s. stone*** piedra *f* semipreciosa

semi-professional ['semɪprə'feʃənəl] *Sport* **1** *n* semiprofesional *mf*
2 *adj* semiprofesional

semiquaver ['semɪkweɪvə(r)] *n Br Mus* semicorchea *f*

semi-retirement ['semɪrɪ'taɪəmənt] *n* jubilación *f* parcial

semi-rough ['semɪ'rʌf] *n (in golf)* semi-rough *m*

semi-skilled ['semɪ'skɪld] *adj* semicualificado(a)

semi-skimmed [semɪskɪmd] *adj (milk)* semidesnatado(a), semidescremado(a)

Semite ['siːmaɪt] *n* semita *mf*

semitendinosus ['semɪtendɪ'nəʊsəs] *n Anat* semitendinoso *m*

Semitic [sɪ'mɪtɪk] *adj* semita, semítico(a)

semitone ['semɪtəʊn] *n Br Mus* semitono *m*

semitrailer ['semɪtreɪlə(r)] *n US* semirremolque *m*

semi-tropical ['semɪ'trɒpɪkəl] *adj* subtropical

semivowel ['semɪvaʊəl] *n* semivocal *f*

semolina [semə'liːnə] *n* (**a**) *(grain)* sémola *f* (**b**) *(dessert)* ***s. (pudding)*** = postre elaborado con sémola y leche

Sen. (*abbr* **Senator**) senador(ora) *m,f*

senate ['senɪt] *n* (**a**) *Pol* **the S.** el Senado (**b**) *Univ* rectorado *m*

senator ['senətə(r)] *n* senador(ora) *m,f*

senatorial [senə'tɔːrɪəl] *adj* senatorial, de senador

SEND [send] (*pt & pp* **sent** [sent]) **1** *vt* (**a**) *(letter, message, person)* mandar, enviar; *(transmission, signal)* enviar; **to s. sb sth, to s. sth to sb** enviar algo a alguien; **s. her my love** dale un abrazo de mi parte; **she sends (you) her love** *or* **regards** te manda recuerdos; **to s. sb for sth** enviar a alguien a por algo; **to s. sb on an errand/a course** mandar a alguien a (hacer) un recado/curso; **he was sent to bed/his room** lo mandaron a la cama/a su habitación; **to s. sb home** mandar a alguien a casa; **to s. sb to prison** enviar a alguien a la cárcel; **to s. word to sb (that...)** avisar *or* informar a alguien (de que...)
(**b**) *(expressing cause)* **to s. sth/sb flying** mandar *or* lanzar algo/a alguien por los aires; **the explosion sent us running for cover** la explosión nos obligó a correr a ponernos a cubierto; **it sends me crazy** me vuelve loco; **the news sent share prices down/up** la noticia hizo bajar/subir el precio de las acciones; **it sent a shiver down my spine** me produjo *or* dio escalofríos; **that sent him into a rage** aquello lo puso hecho una furia; **that sent him into fits of laughter** aquello le provocó un ataque de risa; **to s. sb to sleep** hacer que alguien se duerma

(c) *Fam Old-fashioned (thrill)* pirrar; **his voice really sends me** su voz me pirra de verdad

2 *vi* (a) *(send word)* **she sent to say she'd be late** avisó diciendo que llegaría tarde

(b) *(for information, equipment)* **we sent to Madrid for a copy** pedimos un ejemplar a Madrid

▸ **send away** 1 *vt sep* **to s. sb away** mandar *or* decir a alguien que se marche; **to s. a radio away to be repaired** mandar una radio a arreglar; **the children were sent away to school** enviaron a los niños al colegio

2 *vi* **to s. away for sth** pedir algo por correo

▸ **send back** *vt sep (purchase, order of food)* devolver; **we sent her back to fetch a coat** le pedimos que regresara para buscar un abrigo

▸ **send down** *vt sep* (a) *(person, lift)* mandar, enviar; **they sent me down to the cellar** me enviaron al sótano

(b) *(cause to fall) (prices, temperature)* hacer bajar

(c) *Br Univ (expel)* expulsar

(d) *Br Fam (send to prison)* encarcelar, *Esp* enchironar, *Andes, Col, RP* mandar en cana, *Méx* mandar al bote

▸ **send for** *vt insep* (a) *(help, supplies)* mandar traer; *(doctor)* llamar; **I was sent for by the boss** el jefe mandó que me llamaran

(b) *(request by post)* pedir, encargar

▸ **send forth** *vt insep Literary* (a) *(person)* mandar

(b) *(emit) (light, smoke, noises)* emitir; *(smell, sparks)* desprender

▸ **send in** *vt sep* (a) *(application, troops, supplies)* enviar

(b) *(tell to enter)* hacer entrar *or* pasar

▸ **send off** 1 *vt sep* (a) *(letter, order, person)* mandar, enviar

(b) *Sport* expulsar

(c) *(to sleep)* **to s. sb off (to sleep)** dormir a alguien

2 *vi* **to s. off (to sb) for sth** pedir algo (a alguien) por correo

▸ **send on** *vt sep* (a) *(forward) (mail)* remitir, reexpedir; **we had our belongings sent on ahead** enviamos nuestras pertenencias a nuestro destino antes de partir

(b) *(person)* **they sent us on ahead** *or* **in front** nos dijeron que fuéramos nosotros (por) delante

(c) *(pass on after use)* enviar

(d) *Sport (substitute)* sacar

▸ **send out** 1 *vt sep* (a) *(letters, invitations)* mandar, enviar; *(radio signals, light, heat)* emitir; *(shoots)* echar; *(search party)* enviar

(b) *(tell to leave room)* echar, expulsar

2 *vi* **to s. out for sth** pedir que traigan algo

▸ **send round** *vt sep (message, parcel, repairman)* mandar, enviar; **they sent a taxi round for us** nos mandaron *or* enviaron un taxi

▸ **send up** *vt sep* (a) *(upstairs)* **s. him up** hágalo subir; **I had a pizza sent up to my room** pedí que me subieran una pizza a la habitación

(b) *(emit) (smoke)* enviar, emitir

(c) *(raise) (price, pressure, temperature)* hacer subir

(d) *(send into sky)* lanzar

(e) *US Fam (to prison)* encarcelar, *Esp* enchironar, *Andes, Col, RP* mandar en cana, *Méx* mandar al bote

(f) *Br Fam (parody)* parodiar, remedar

---

sender ['sendə(r)] *n* remitente *mf*

sending-off ['sendɪŋ'ɒf] *n Sport* expulsión *f*

send-off ['send'ɒf] *n Fam* despedida *f*

send-up ['sendʌp] *n Br Fam* parodia *f*, remedo *m*

Senegal [senɪ'gɔːl] *n* Senegal

Senegalese [senɪgə'liːz] 1 *n* senegalés(esa) *m,f*

2 *adj* senegalés(esa)

senile ['siːnaɪl] *adj* senil; **she's going s.** se está poniendo senil; **he's gone s.** está senil, chochea ▸▸ *Med* ***s. dementia*** demencia *f* senil

senility [sɪ'nɪlɪtɪ] *n* senilidad *f*

senior ['siːnjə(r)] 1 *n* (a) *(in age)* **to be sb's s.** ser mayor que alguien; **she is three years his s.** ella es tres años mayor que él

(b) *(in rank)* **to be sb's s.** ser el superior de alguien

(c) *(student)* estudiante *mf* de último curso

(d) *US (senior citizen)* persona *f* de la tercera edad

2 *adj* (a) *(in age)* mayor; **he's two years s. to me** es dos años mayor que yo; **Thomas Smith, S.** Thomas Smith, padre ▸▸ ***s. citizen*** persona *f* de la tercera edad

(b) *(in rank, position)* superior; **she holds a s. position in the company** ocupa un cargo de responsabilidad en la empresa ▸▸ ***s. executive*** alto(a) ejecutivo(a) *m,f*; *Br Univ* ***s. lecturer*** profesor(ora) *m,f* titular; ***s. management*** altos directivos *mpl*; ***s. officer*** oficial *m* superior; ***s. partner*** *(in company)* socio *m* principal

(c) *(longer-serving)* **the s. members of staff** los miembros más antiguos de la plantilla; **he's s. to me** tiene más antigüedad que yo

(d) *Sch* de los últimos cursos ▸▸ *US* ***s. high school*** colegio *m or Esp* instituto *m* de enseñanza secundaria *(16-18 años)*; *Br* ***s. school*** colegio *m or Esp* instituto *m* de enseñanza secundaria

seniority [siːnɪ'ɒrɪtɪ] *n* (a) *(in age, length of service)* antigüedad *f*; **he became chairman by virtue of s.** lo nombraron presidente debido a su antigüedad (b) *(in rank)* rango *m*, categoría *f*

senna ['senə] *n* (a) *(plant)* sena *f* (b) *(laxative)* diasén *m*

sensation [sen'seɪʃən] *n* (a) *(feeling)* sensación *f*; **burning s.** quemazón; **the cold made me lose all s. in my hands** el frío me hizo perder la sensibilidad en las manos; **I had the s. of falling** tenía la sensación de que me caía (b) *(excitement)* **to be a s.** ser todo un éxito; **to cause a s.** causar sensación

sensational [sen'seɪʃənəl] *adj* (a) *(exaggerated)* tremendista, sensacionalista (b) *(causing a sensation)* sensacional (c) *(excellent)* sensacional

sensationalism [sen'seɪʃənəlɪzəm] *n* sensacionalismo *m*

sensationalist [sen'seɪʃənəlɪst] *adj* sensacionalista

sensationalize [sen'seɪʃənəlaɪz] *vt* dar una visión sensacionalista de

sensationally [sen'seɪʃənəlɪ] *adv* (a) *(exaggeratedly)* con sensacionalismo (b) *(causing a sensation)* **s., the champion was defeated** para asombro de todos, el campeón perdió (c) *(excellently)* de maravilla, estupendamente (d) *(extremely)* increíblemente; **s. successful** de tremendo éxito

sense [sens] 1 *n* (a) *(physical faculty)* sentido *m*; **s. of smell/hearing** sentido del olfato/oído; **to come to one's senses** *(recover consciousness)* recobrar el conocimiento *or* sentido; *(see reason)* entrar en razón ▸▸ ***s. organ*** órgano *m* sensorial

(b) *(notion)* sentido *m*; **business s.** vista para los negocios; **dress s.** gusto en el vestir; **to lose all s. of time** perder la noción del tiempo; **he has an overdeveloped s. of his own importance** se cree mucho más importante de lo que es ▸▸ ***s. of direction*** sentido *m* de la orientación; *Fig* **to lose one's s. of direction** perder el rumbo; ***s. of duty*** sentido *m* del deber; ***s. of humour*** sentido *m* del humor; ***s. of the ridiculous*** sentido *m* del ridículo

(c) *(feeling)* sensación *f*; **a s. of achievement** la sensación de haber logrado algo; **a s. of occasion** la sensación de gran acontecimiento; **the light colours give a s. of space** los colores claros dan una sensación de amplitud

(d) *(rationality, common sense)* sensatez *f*, buen juicio *m*; **good s.** buen juicio; **there's a lot of s. in what she says** lo que dice tiene mucho sentido; **to have the (good) s. to do sth** ser lo suficientemente sensato(a) como para hacer algo; **I hope you'll have more s. than to tell her** espero que seas lo suficientemente sensato como para no contárselo; **he talked a lot of s.** estaba cargado de razón; **to make (no) s.** (no) tener sentido; **it makes good political/business s.** en términos políticos/de negocios tiene mucho sentido; **it makes more s. to do this first** es más lógico hacer esto primero; **she wasn't making any s.** lo que decía no tenía ningún sentido; **are you out of your senses?, have you taken leave of your senses?** ¿has perdido el juicio?; **to bring sb to their senses** *(cause to see reason)* hacer entrar en razón a alguien

(e) *(point)* sentido *m*; **there's no s. in staying** no tiene sentido quedarse; **what's** *or* **where's the s. in that?** ¿qué sentido tiene?

(f) *(meaning)* sentido *m*; **to make s. of sth** entender algo; **in a s.** en cierto sentido; **I think we have, in a very real s., tackled the problem** creo que hemos abordado muy en serio el problema; **in every s. (of the word)** en el sentido pleno (del término); **in more senses than one** en más de un sentido; **in no s.** de ninguna de las maneras, en modo alguno; **in the s. that...** en el sentido de que...; **in the strictest s. of the word** en el más puro sentido de la palabra

(g) *(impression)* impresión *f*, sensación *f*; **what was your s. of their mood?** ¿de qué humor te ha parecido que estaban?

2 *vt* (a) *(of person)* notar, percibir; **to s. that...** tener la sensación de que...; **I sensed as much** ya me di cuenta; **I sensed her meaning** entendí lo que quería decir (b) *(of machine)* detectar

senseless ['senslɪs] *adj* (a) *(unconscious)* inconsciente; **to beat** *or* **knock sb s.** golpear a alguien hasta dejarle inconsciente (b) *(pointless)* absurdo(a); **it's s. trying to persuade her** no tiene sentido intentar convencerla

senselessly ['senslɪslɪ] *adv (pointlessly)* de forma absurda, sin sentido

senselessness ['senslɪsnɪs] *n (pointlessness)* sinsentido *m*, falta *f* de sentido

sensibility [sensɪ'bɪlɪtɪ] 1 *n (of artist)* sensibilidad *f*

2 **sensibilities** *npl* sensibilidad *f*; **to offend sb's sensibilities** herir la sensibilidad de alguien

sensible ['sensɪbəl] *adj* (**a**) *(rational) (person, decision)* sensato(a); **the s. thing to do** lo sensato; **be s.!** ¡sé sensato! (**b**) *(practical) (clothes, shoes)* práctico(a) (**c**) *Formal (aware)* **to be s. of sth** ser consciente de algo (**d**) *Formal (notable) (change, quantity, difference)* considerable

False friend: The Spanish adjective **sensible** is not a translation for the English word **sensible**. In Spanish **sensible** means "sensitive" or "significant".

sensibly ['sensɪblɪ] *adv* (**a**) *(rationally)* sensatamente (**b**) *(practically) (dressed)* cómodamente, de manera práctica

sensitive ['sensɪtɪv] *adj* (**a**) *(physically) (person, skin, film, instrument)* sensible; **to be s. to sth** ser sensible a algo
(**b**) *(emotionally aware)* sensible (**to** a); **to be s. to sb's needs** tener sensibilidad frente a las necesidades de alguien
(**c**) *(tactful)* delicado(a), cuidadoso(a)
(**d**) *(touchy)* susceptible; **he's very s. about his hair** le molesta mucho que le hablen del pelo, es muy susceptible con el tema de su pelo
(**e**) *(issue, subject)* delicado(a), polémico(a); *(information, document)* confidencial
(**f**) ***s. plant*** mimosa *f* púdica *or* vergonzosa

sensitively ['sensɪtɪvlɪ] *adv (tactfully)* con delicadeza, con tacto

sensitivity [sensɪ'tɪvɪtɪ] *n* (**a**) *(physical) (of person, skin, film, instrument)* sensibilidad *f* (**b**) *(emotional awareness)* sensibilidad *f* (**c**) *(tact)* tacto *m* (**d**) *(touchiness)* susceptibilidad *f* (**e**) *(of issue, subject)* carácter *m* polémico; *(of information, document)* confidencialidad *f*

sensitize ['sensɪtaɪz] *vt* (**a**) *(make aware)* sensibilizar (**to** acerca de *or* ante) (**b**) *(photographic film)* sensibilizar

sensor ['sensə(r)] *n* sensor *m*

sensory ['sensərɪ] *adj* sensorial ►► ***s. deprivation*** privación *f* sensorial; ***s. organs*** órganos *mpl* sensoriales

sensual ['sensjʊəl] *adj* sensual

sensuality [sensjʊ'ælɪtɪ] *n* sensualidad *f*

sensually ['sensjʊəlɪ] *adv* sensualmente

sensuous ['sensjʊəs] *adj* sensual

sensuousness ['sensjʊəsnɪs] *n* sensualidad *f*

sent *pt & pp of* **send**

sentence ['sentəns] **1** *n* (**a**) *Gram* oración *f*, frase *f* ►► ***s. structure*** estructura *f* de la oración (**b**) *Law* sentencia *f*; **to pass s. (on)** dictar sentencia (contra); **she was given a two-year s. for fraud** la condenaron a dos años (de cárcel) por estafa; **to be under s. of death** estar condenado(a) a muerte
2 *vt Law* condenar, sentenciar (**to** a); **he was sentenced to three years' imprisonment** lo condenaron a tres años de cárcel

sententious [sen'tenʃəs] *adj Formal* sentencioso(a)

sententiously [sen'tenʃəslɪ] *adv* sentenciosamente; **he spoke s. on the subject** habló del tema en un tono sentencioso

sentient ['sentɪənt] *adj* sensitivo(a), sensible

sentiment ['sentɪmənt] *n* (**a**) *(opinion)* parecer *m*; **public s.** el sentir popular; **they should be shot! – my sentiments exactly** ¡deberían ser fusilados! - pienso exactamente lo mismo (**b**) *(feeling)* sentimiento *m* (**c**) *(sentimentality)* sentimentalismo *m*

sentimental [sentɪ'mentəl] *adj* (**a**) *(overemotional)* sentimental (**b**) *(relating to emotions)* sentimental; **the photos have s. value** las fotos guardan *or* tienen un valor sentimental

sentimentalist [sentɪ'mentəlɪst] *n* sentimental *mf*

sentimentality [sentɪmen'tælɪtɪ] *n* sentimentalismo *m*

sentimentalize [sentɪ'mɒntəlaɪz] *vt* tratar con sentimentalismo; **one often tends to s. one's childhood memories** uno tiende a menudo a ponerse sentimental con los recuerdos de infancia

sentimentally [sentɪ'mentəlɪ] *adv* (**a**) *(overemotionally)* sentimentalmente (**b**) *(emotionally)* **to be s. attached to sb** tener una relación sentimental con alguien; **to be s. attached to sth** tener cariño a algo

sentinel ['sentɪnel] *n Literary (sentry)* centinela *m*; *Fig* guardián(ana) *m,f*

sentry ['sentrɪ] *n Mil* centinela *m*; **to be on s. duty** estar de guardia ►► ***s. box*** garita *f*; ***s. post*** puesto *m* de vigilancia

Seoul [səʊl] *n* Seúl

Sep (*abbr* **September**) sep.

sepal ['sepəl] *n Bot* sépalo *m*

separable ['sepərəbəl] *adj* separable

separate **1** *adj* ['sepərət] (**a**) *(independent) (parts, box, room)* separado(a); **the canteen is s. from the main building** la cantina está separada del edificio principal; **fish and meat should be kept s.** hay que guardar la carne y el pescado por separado; **she likes to keep her home life s. from the office** no le gusta mezclar su vida privada con la oficina; **to lead s. lives** vivir separados(as); *also Fig* **they went their s. ways** siguieron cada uno su camino
(**b**) *(different) (occasion, attempt, category)* distinto(a); *(organization)* independiente; **we asked for s. receipts** pedimos cuentas separadas; **use a s. piece of paper for the title** utiliza otro trozo de papel para el título; **the two issues are quite s.** son dos cuestiones bien distintas
2 *vt* ['sepəreɪt] (**a**) *(move apart)* separar (**from** de); **the last three coaches will be separated from the rest of the train** los últimos tres vagones serán separados del resto del tren
(**b**) *(keep apart)* separar (**from** de); **the seriously ill were separated from the other patients** los que estaban gravemente enfermos fueron separados del resto de los pacientes
(**c**) *(distinguish)* distinguir (**from** de); **the records can be separated into four categories** los discos pueden agruparse en cuatro categorías
3 *vi* (**a**) *(move apart)* separarse (**from** de); **they separated after the meeting** después de la reunión se separaron (**b**) *(split up) (couple)* separarse; **the party separated into various factions** el partido se escindió en varias facciones (**c**) *(liquids)* disgregarse
4 separates *npl (clothes)* = prendas femeninas que se venden por separado y se combinan entre sí

► **separate out** **1** *vt sep (individuals, elements)* separar; *(reasons)* distinguir
2 *vi (elements, liquids)* disgregarse

► **separate up** *vt sep* dividir

separated ['sepəreɪtɪd] *adj* separado(a); **he is s. from his wife** está separado de su mujer

separately ['sepərətlɪ] *adv* (**a**) *(apart)* por separado; **to live s.** vivir separados(as) (**b**) *(individually)* por separado; **can we pay s.?** ¿podemos pagar por separado?; **they don't sell yogurts s.** no venden yogures sueltos

separation [sepə'reɪʃən] *n* (**a**) *(division)* separación *f* (**b**) *(of couple)* separación *f*

separatism ['sepərətɪzəm] *n Pol* separatismo *m*

separatist ['sepərətɪst] **1** *n Pol* separatista *mf*
2 *adj* separatista

separator ['sepəreɪtə(r)] *n* separador *m*

Sephardi [se'fɑːdiː] (*pl* **Sephardim** [-dɪm]) *n (person)* sefardí *mf*

Sephardic [se'fɑːdɪk] *adj* sefardí, sefardita

sepia ['siːpɪə] *n (colour)* (color *m*) sepia *m*; **s. photograph** fotografía *f* en color sepia

sepsis ['sepsɪs] *n Med* sepsis *f inv*

Sept (*abbr* **September**) sep.

September [sep'tembə(r)] *n* septiembre *m*; *see also* **May**

septet [sep'tet] *n Mus* septeto *m*

septic ['septɪk] *adj* séptico(a); **to go** *or* **become s.** infectarse ►► ***s. tank*** fosa *f* séptica

septicaemia, *US* **septicemia** [septɪ'siːmɪə] *n Med* septicemia *f*

septuagenarian [septʊədʒə'neərɪən] **1** *n* septuagenario(a) *m,f*
2 *adj* septuagenario(a)

septum ['septəm] *n Anat* septo *m*, septum *m*

septuplet ['septjʊplet] *n* (**a**) *(baby)* septillizo(a) *m,f* (**b**) *Mus* septillo *m*

sepulchral [sə'pʌlkrəl] *adj Literary* sepulcral

sepulchre, *US* **sepulcher** ['sepəlkə(r)] *n Literary* sepulcro *m*

sequel ['siːkwəl] *n* (**a**) *(book, movie)* continuación *f* (**to** de) (**b**) *(following event)* secuela *f*; **as a s. to this event** como consecuencia de este hecho

sequence ['siːkwəns] **1** *n* (**a**) *(order)* sucesión *f*, secuencia *f*; **the s. of events** la secuencia de los hechos *or* acontecimientos; **in s.** en sucesión *or* orden; **numbered in s.** ordenados(as) numéricamente; **in historical s.** en orden cronológico; **out of s.** desordenado(a) (**b**) *(of numbers, events)* serie *f* (**c**) *(in movie)* secuencia *f* (**d**) *Mus* secuencia *f* (**e**) *(in cards)* escalera *f* (**f**) *Biol & Chem* secuencia *f*
2 *vt Biol & Chem* secuenciar

sequencer ['siːkwənsə(r)] *n Mus* secuenciador *m*

sequencing ['siːkwənsɪŋ] *n Biol & Chem* secuenciación *f*

sequential [sɪ'kwenʃəl] *adj* secuencial ►► *Comptr* ***s. access*** acceso *m* secuencial

sequentially [sɪ'kwenʃəlɪ] *adv* secuencialmente

sequester [sɪ'kwestə(r)] *vt* (**a**) *Formal (shut away)* aislar (**b**) *Law (goods, property)* embargar

sequestrate ['siːkwəstreɪt] *vt Law* embargar

sequestration [si:kwə'streɪʃən] *n Law* embargo *m*
sequin ['si:kwɪn] *n* lentejuela *f*
sequined ['si:kwɪnd] *adj* de lentejuelas
sequoia [sɪ'kwɔɪə] *n* sec(u)oya *f*
seraglio [se'rɑ:lɪəʊ] (*pl* **seraglios**) *n* serrallo *m*
serape [sə'rɑ:pɪ] *n* capote *m* de monte, *RP* poncho *m*
seraph ['serəf] (*pl* **seraphs** *or* **seraphim** ['serəfɪm]) *n* serafín *m*
seraphic [se'ræfɪk] *adj Literary* seráfico(a)
Serb ['sɜ:b] **1** *n* serbio(a) *m,f*
2 *adj* serbio(a)
Serbia ['sɜ:bɪə] *n* Serbia
Serbian ['sɜ:bɪən] **1** *n* (**a**) *(person)* serbio(a) *m,f* (**b**) *(dialect)* serbio *m*
2 *adj* serbio(a)
Serbo-Croat ['sɜ:bəʊ'krəʊæt], **Serbo-Croatian** ['sɜ:bəʊkrəʊ'eɪʃən] **1** *n (language)* serbocroata *m*
2 *adj* serbocroata
serenade [serə'neɪd] **1** *n* serenata *f*
2 *vt* dar una serenata a
serendipitous [serən'dɪpɪtəs] *adj* **a s. discovery** una serendipidad
serendipity [serən'dɪpɪtɪ] *n* serendipidad *f*
serene [sə'ri:n] *adj* sereno(a)
serenely [sə'ri:nlɪ] *adv (to answer, smile)* con serenidad; **she was s. unaware of what was going on** estaba completamente tranquila inconsciente de lo que sucedía
serenity [sə'renɪtɪ] *n* serenidad *f*
serf [sɜ:f] *n Hist* siervo(a) *m,f* (de la gleba)
serfdom ['sɜ:fdəm] *n Hist* servidumbre *f*
serge [sɜ:dʒ] **1** *n* sarga *f*
2 *adj (cloth, trousers, suit)* de sarga
sergeant ['sɑ:dʒənt] *n* (**a**) *Mil* sargento *mf* (**b**) *(in police)* ≃ oficial *mf* de policía
sergeant-at-arms ['sɑ:dʒəntæt'ɑ:mz] *n* = funcionario que se encarga de mantener el orden en el parlamento británico
sergeant-major ['sɑ:dʒənt'meɪdʒə(r)] *n Mil* sargento *mf* primero
serial ['sɪərɪəl] **1** *n* (**a**) *(in magazine)* novela *f* por entregas, folletín *m*; **published in s. form** publicado(a) por entregas ►► ***s. rights*** derechos *mpl* de publicación por entregas (**b**) *(on TV)* serial *m*
2 *adj* (**a**) *(in series)* en serie ►► ***s. killer*** asesino(a) *m,f* en serie; ***s. killing*** asesinato *m* en serie; ***s. monogamy*** monogamia *f* en serie; ***s. number*** número *m* de serie (**b**) *Comptr* ***s. access*** acceso *m* en serie; ***s. cable*** cable *m* de serie; ***s. device*** periférico *m* en serie; ***s. interface*** interfaz *f* de serie; ***s. port*** puerto *m* (en) serie; ***s. printer*** impresora *f* en serie
serialization [sɪərɪəlaɪ'zeɪʃən] *n* (**a**) *(in newspaper, magazine)* publicación *f* por entregas (**b**) *(on TV)* serialización *f*, adaptación *f* al formato de serie
serialize ['sɪərɪəlaɪz] *vt* (**a**) *(in newspaper, magazine)* publicar por entregas (**b**) *(on TV)* emitir en forma de serie; **the novel is being serialized in six parts** la novela va a ser emitida en seis partes
sericulture [sɪərɪ'kʌltʃə(r)] *n* sericultura *f*
series ['sɪəri:z] *n* (**a**) *(sequence)* serie *f*; **to make a s. of mistakes** cometer toda una serie de errores (**b**) *(on TV)* serie *f*; *(on radio)* serial *m* (**c**) *(of books, stamps, coins)* serie *f* (**d**) *(in baseball, rugby, cricket)* serie *f* (de encuentros); *(of lectures, films)* ciclo *m* (**e**) *Elec* **connected in s.** conectado(a) en serie (**f**) *Math* serie *f*
serif ['serɪf] *n Typ* serif *m*
serin ['serɪn] *n* verdecillo *m*
serine ['seri:n] *n Biol & Chem* serina *f*
serious ['sɪərɪəs] *adj* (**a**) *(not frivolous) (person, newspaper, subject, occasion)* serio(a); **to be s. about doing sth** estar decidido(a) a hacer algo; **to be s. about sb** *(boyfriend, girlfriend)* ir en serio con alguien; **are you s.?** ¿lo dices en serio?; **it's no joke, I'm quite s.** no es broma, lo digo muy en serio; **you can't be s.!** ¡estás de broma!, ¿no lo dirás en serio?; **it wasn't a s. suggestion** no lo decía en serio; **the s. student of astronomy** el estudiante serio de astronomía; **she's a s. actress** es una actriz seria
(**b**) *(thoughtful) (expression, tone, consideration)* serio(a); **don't look so s.** no estés tan serio
(**c**) *(grave) (situation, problem)* serio(a), grave; *(injury, mistake)* grave; **a s. crime** un delito grave; **doctors described his condition as s.** los médicos informaron que su estado era grave ►► *Br* ***s. crime squad*** = departamento de la policía que se ocupa de los delitos peligrosos
(**d**) *Fam (for emphasis)* **we're talking s. money here** estamos hablando de mucho dinero; **we did some s. drinking last night** anoche bebimos de lo lindo *or Esp* a base de bien; **that is one s. computer** esa sí que es una computadora
seriously ['sɪərɪəslɪ] *adv* (**a**) *(in earnest)* seriamente, en serio; **think about it s.** piénsalo seriamente; **to take sth/sb s.** tomar algo/a alguien en serio; **to take oneself too s.** tomarse demasiado en serio; **are you s. suggesting we sell it?** ¿de verdad sugieres venderlo?; **you don't s. think I did it on purpose, do you?** no pensarás de verdad que lo hice adrede, ¿no?; **s. though, what are you going to do?** ahora en serio, ¿qué vas a hacer?
(**b**) *(gravely)* seriamente, gravemente; *(injured)* gravemente; **s. ill** seriamente *or* gravemente enfermo(a); **you are s. mistaken** estás muy equivocado
(**c**) *Fam (very)* **he's s. gorgeous** está buenísimo; **she's getting s. fat** se está poniendo supergorda; **he was s. drunk** estaba borracho a más no poder; **he's s. rich** está forrado
serious-minded ['sɪərɪəs'maɪndɪd] *adj* serio(a), sensato(a)
seriousness ['sɪərɪəsnɪs] *n* (**a**) *(earnestness)* seriedad *f*; **in all s.** con toda seriedad, de lo más serio(a) (**b**) *(gravity)* seriedad *f*, gravedad *f*; *(of injury, mistake)* gravedad *f*
sermon ['sɜ:mən] *n* (**a**) *Rel* sermón *m*; **the S. on the Mount** el Sermón de la Montaña (**b**) *(lecture)* sermón *m*; **he gave me a s. on the evils of drink** me soltó un sermón sobre los males de la bebida
sermonize ['sɜ:mənaɪz] *vi* soltar un sermón, sermonear
serology [sɪə'rɒlədʒɪ] *n* serología *f*
seropositive ['sɪərəʊ'pɒzɪtɪv] *adj* seropositivo(a)
serotonin [sɪərə'təʊnɪn] *n* serotonina *f*
serous ['sɪərəs] *adj* seroso(a)
serpent ['sɜ:pənt] *n Literary* sierpe *f*, serpiente *f*
serpentine ['sɜ:pəntaɪn] *adj Literary* serpenteante, serpentino(a)
SERPS [sɜ:ps] *n Br* (*abbr* **State Earnings Related Pension Scheme**) = sistema público de pensiones contributivas
serrated [sə'reɪtɪd] *adj* dentado(a)
serried ['serɪd] *adj Literary* **s. ranks** filas cerradas
serum ['sɪərəm] *n Med* suero *m*
servant ['sɜ:vənt] *n* (**a**) *(in household)* criado(a) *m,f*, sirviente(a) *m,f*; *Formal Old-fashioned* **your most obedient s.** *(in correspondence)* su seguro servidor ►► ***s. girl*** sirvienta *f*, criada *f*; ***servants' quarters*** habitaciones *fpl* del servicio (**b**) *(of leader, country)* servidor(ora) *m,f*

SERVE [sɜ:v] **1** *n (in tennis)* servicio *m*, saque *m*; **(it's) your s.!** ¡tú sacas!; **to break s.** romper el servicio; **to hold one's s.** mantener el servicio; **first/second s.** primer/segundo servicio
2 *vt* (**a**) *(be faithful to) (master, cause)* servir, estar al servicio de; *(one's country)* servir a; **to s. one's own interests** actuar en interés propio; IDIOM **to s. two masters** nadar entre dos aguas
(**b**) *(be useful to)* servir; **it serves me as an office** me sirve de oficina; **what function does it s.?** ¿qué función tiene?; **it would s. your interests not to say anything** te convendría no decir nada; **it doesn't s. my purpose(s)** no me sirve; **it serves no useful purpose** no sirve para nada; **it has served me well** me ha hecho un buen servicio; **if my memory serves me right** si mal no recuerdo; IDIOM **it serves her right!** ¡se lo merece!, ¡lo tiene bien merecido!
(**c**) *(complete) (prison sentence, term of office)* cumplir; *(apprenticeship)* realizar, hacer
(**d**) *(customer)* atender; **are you being served?** *(in shop)* ¿le están atendiendo?; *(in pub)* ¿te sirven?
(**e**) *(meal, drink)* servir; **to s. lunch/dinner** servir el almuerzo/la cena; **breakfast is served in the restaurant** el desayuno se sirve en el restaurante; *Formal & Hum* **dinner is served!** ¡la cena está en la mesa!; **the buffet car serves a selection of sandwiches** en el vagón restaurante se sirve una selección de *Esp* bocadillos *or Am* sandwiches; **serves four** *(on packet)* contiene cuatro raciones; *(in recipe)* para cuatro personas
(**f**) *(provide for)* **the power station will s. an area of 500 square miles** la central abastecerá de *or* suministrará electricidad a un área de 500 millas cuadradas; **the city is served by two airports** la ciudad cuenta con dos aeropuertos
(**g**) *Law* **to s. notice on sb that...** comunicar oficialmente a alguien que...; **to s. sb with a summons, to s. a summons on sb** citar a alguien
(**h**) *(in tennis) (ace)* servir; *(double fault)* hacer
3 *vi* (**a**) *(carry out duty)* servir (**as** como); **he served in the army/in Bosnia** sirvió en el ejército/en Bosnia; **to s. in a government/on a committee** ser miembro de un gobierno/una comisión; **I served under him during the war** serví bajo sus órdenes durante la guerra
(**b**) *(be used)* **to s. as...** servir de...; **to s. as an example** servir de

ejemplo; **that serves to explain her behaviour** eso explica su comportamiento; **this stone will s. to keep the door open** estará piedra servirá para dejar la puerta abierta

(**c**) *(in shop)* atender, despachar

(**d**) *(with food, drink)* servir; **to s. at table** servir mesas; **s. chilled** *(on wine)* sírvase bien frío

(**e**) *(in tennis)* servir, sacar; **Hingis to s.!** ¡al servicio, Hingis!; **to s. for the match** servir para ganar (el partido)

(**f**) *Rel* hacer de monaguillo

► **serve out** *vt sep* (**a**) *(sentence, notice)* cumplir

(**b**) *(food)* servir

(**c**) *(in tennis)* **she broke her opponent and served out the match** rompió el servicio de su rival y conservó el suyo para ganar el partido

► **serve up** *vt sep (food)* servir; *Fig* ofrecer

server ['sɜːvə(r)] *n* (**a**) *(in tennis, badminton, squash)* jugador(ora) *m,f* al servicio; **she's a powerful s.** tiene un servicio muy potente (**b**) *Comptr* servidor *m* (**c**) *(utensil)* cubierto *m* para servir (**d**) *(tray)* bandeja *f* (**e**) *Rel* monaguillo *m*

servery ['sɜːvərɪ] *n* mostrador *m* de autoservicio

SERVICE ['sɜːvɪs] **1** *n* (**a**) *(work) (with army, firm)* servicio *m*; **to be at sb's s.** estar al servicio de alguien; **Dan Berry, at your s.** Dan Berry, a su disposición; **bonuses depend on length of s.** los pluses dependen de la antigüedad; **in the s. of one's country** al servicio de la patria; *Formal* **to do sb a s.** hacer un favor a alguien; **he offered his services** ofreció sus servicios; **for services rendered** por los servicios prestados ►► *Mil* ***s. stripe*** galón *m* de servicio

(**b**) *(use)* **this suitcase has given me good s.** esta maleta me ha durado mucho tiempo; **to come into s.** *(system, equipment)* entrar en servicio; **to be in s.** *(ship, plane, machine)* estar en funcionamiento; **to be out of s.** *(machine)* estar fuera de servicio; *Formal* **to be of s. to sb** serle a alguien de utilidad; **to do s. as** hacer las veces de

(**c**) *(in shop, restaurant)* servicio *m*; **when are we going to get some s. round here?** ¿nos atienden o no?; **s. is included** el servicio está incluido; **s. not included** servicio no incluido ►► ***s. charge*** (tarifa *f* por) servicio *m*

(**d**) *(provided by business, organization)* servicio *m*; **we offer a photocopying s.** ofrecemos un servicio de copistería; **a bus s. will operate between Newcastle and Durham** un autobús funcionará entre Newcastle y Durham ►► ***s. bureau*** servicio *m* de filmación; ***s. entrance*** entrada *f* de servicio; ***s. industry*** industria *f* de servicios; *Br* ***s. lift*** montacargas *m inv*; ***s. road*** vía *f* de servicio; ***s. sector*** sector *m* servicios; ***s. stairs*** escalera *f* de servicio *(en hotel)*

(**e**) *Comptr* ***s. provider*** proveedor *m* de servicios

(**f**) *(system)* **postal/air/train s.** servicios postales/aéreos/de ferrocarril

(**g**) *(maintenance)* revisión *f* ►► ***s. area,*** *Br* ***services*** *(on motorway)* área *f* de servicio; ***s. engineer*** ténico(a) *m,f* de mantenimiento; ***s. station*** estación *f* de servicio

(**h**) *Rel* oficio *m*, servicio *m*

(**i**) *(set)* **tea/dinner s.** servicio de té/mesa

(**j**) *(in tennis, badminton, squash)* servicio *m*, saque *m*; **first/second s.** primer/segundo servicio; **he lost three s. games in a row** perdió el servicio tres veces consecutivas ►► ***s. box*** *(in squash)* cuadro *m* de saque; ***s. break*** rotura *f* del servicio; ***s. fault*** falta *f* de saque; ***s. line*** línea *f* de saque *or* servicio

(**k**) *Old-fashioned (of servant)* **to be in s.** estar de sirviente(a); **to go into s.** entrar a servir

(**l**) *Mil* **the services** las fuerzas armadas ►► ***s. corps*** intendencia *f* militar

(**m**) *Law (of summons, writ)* notificación *f* (judicial)

2 *vt* (**a**) *(car, computer, TV)* revisar

(**b**) *(loan, debt)* amortizar los intereses de

(**c**) *(of bull, stallion)* cubrir a

serviceable ['sɜːvɪsəbəl] *adj* (**a**) *(in working order)* en buen uso (**b**) *(useful)* útil, práctico(a) (**c**) *(durable)* duradero(a)

serviceman ['sɜːvɪsmən] *n Mil* militar *m*

servicewoman ['sɜːvɪswʊmən] *n Mil* militar *f*

servicing ['sɜːvɪsɪŋ] *n* (**a**) *(of heating, car)* revisión *f* (**b**) *(of loan, debt)* servicio *m*

serviette [sɜːvɪ'et] *n Br* servilleta *f* ►► ***s. ring*** servilletero *m*

servile ['sɜːvaɪl] *adj* servil

servility [sɜː'vɪlətɪ] *n* servilismo *m*

serving ['sɜːvɪŋ] *n (portion)* ración *f* ►► ***s. dish*** fuente *f*; ***s. hatch*** ventanilla *f* (de cocina); ***s. spoon*** cuchara *f* de servir

servitude ['sɜːvɪtjuːd] *n* esclavitud *f*

servo ['sɜːvəʊ] **1** *n* (*pl* **servos**) *Fam (servomechanism)* servomecanismo *m*

2 *adj Aut* ***s. brake*** servofreno *m*

servo-assisted ['sɜːvəʊə'sɪstɪd] *adj* servoasistido(a)

servomechanism ['sɜːvəʊ'mekənɪzəm] *n* servomecanismo *m*

servomotor ['sɜːvəʊ'məʊtə(r)] *n* servomotor *m*

sesame[1] ['sesəmɪ] *n (plant)* ajonjolí *m*, sésamo *m* ►► ***s. oil*** aceite *m* de sésamo *or* de ajonjolí; ***s. seeds*** (semillas *fpl* de) sésamo *m*

sesame[2] *exclam* **open s.!** ¡ábrete, Sésamo!

sesh [seʃ] *n Br Fam* **a drinking s.** una reunión para privar

session ['seʃən] *n* (**a**) *(period of activity)* sesión *f*; **a discussion s.** una sesión de debate; *Fam* **a drinking s.** una juerga, una borrachera

(**b**) *(meeting)* reunión *f*; **to be in s.** estar reunido(a); **the House is not in s. during the summer** la cámara no se reúne durante el verano; **to go into secret s.** pasar a celebrarse a puertas cerradas

(**c**) *Sch & Univ (term)* trimestre *m*; *(year)* curso *m*

(**d**) *Mus* ***s. musician*** músico *m* de sesión

SET[1] [set] **1** *n* (**a**) *(of keys, tools, furniture, pans, tyres)* juego *m*; *(of problems, rules, symptoms)* conjunto *m*; *(of stamps, picture cards, books)* serie *f*, colección *f*; **a chemistry s.** un juego de química; **a train s.** un tren eléctrico de juguete *(con vías, etc.)*; **a s. of cutlery** una cubertería, un juego de cubiertos; **a s. of table/bed linen** un juego de mantelería/cama; **a s. of teeth** una dentadura; **they have a different s. of values** tienen una escala de valores diferente; **they make a s.** forman parte del mismo juego; **in another s. of circumstances, things might have gone very differently** en otras circunstancias, las cosas habrían sido diferentes

(**b**) *(of people)* grupo *m*, círculo *m*; **the literary s.** los literatos

(**c**) *Sch* **top/bottom s.** = grupo de los alumnos más/menos aventajados en cada asignatura a los que se enseña por separado

(**d**) *(TV, radio)* aparato *m*, receptor *m*; **television s.** televisor, (aparato de) televisión

(**e**) *Theat & TV (scenery)* decorado *m*; *TV & Cin (filming area)* plató *m*; **on s.** en el plató ►► ***s. designer*** escenógrafo(a)

(**f**) *(in tennis)* set *m*, manga *f* ►► ***s. point*** punto *m* de set

(**g**) *Mus (performance)* **they played a thirty-minute s.** tocaron durante treinta minutos

(**h**) *(in hairdressing)* **shampoo and s.** lavar y marcar

(**i**) *(posture)* **the s. of sb's shoulders** la postura de los hombros

(**j**) *Math* conjunto *m* ►► ***s. square*** *(with angles of 45, 45 and 90°)* escuadra *f*; *(with angles of 30, 60 and 90°)* cartabón *m*

(**k**) *(direction) (of wind, current)* dirección *f*

2 *adj* (**a**) *(fixed) (ideas, price)* fijo(a); **we have to finish by a s. time** tenemos que acabar a una hora determinada; **with no s. purpose** sin motivo aparente; **to be s. in one's ways** tener hábitos fijos ►► ***s. expression*** frase *f* hecha; ***s. lunch*** menú *m* (del día); ***s. meal*** menú *m* del día, *Am* comida *f* corrida *or* corriente; ***s. phrase*** frase *f* hecha; ***s. piece*** *(in play, movie)* = escena clásica e impactante; *(in sport)* jugada *f* ensayada (a balón parado); *Sch* ***s. text*** lectura *f* obligatoria

(**b**) *(ready)* **to be (all) s. for sth/to do sth** estar preparado(a) para algo/para hacer algo; **she is s. to become the first woman president** va camino de convertirse en la primera presidenta; **the good weather is s. to continue** va a continuar el buen tiempo; **to get s. to do sth** prepararse *or Am* alistarse para hacer algo

(**c**) *(determined)* **to be (dead) s. against sth** oponerse totalmente a algo; **to be (dead) s. on doing sth** estar empeñado(a) en hacer algo

3 *vt* (*pt & pp* **set**) (**a**) *(place)* colocar; **to s. sth before sb** *(dish, glass)* poner algo delante de alguien; *(proposal, plan)* presentar algo a alguien; **to s. a trap (for sb)** tender una trampa (a alguien)

(**b**) *(situate)* **the house is s. in a picturesque valley** la casa se encuentra *or* está situada en un valle pintoresco; **his eyes are s. too close together** tiene los ojos demasiado juntos; **the movie is s. in New Orleans/against a background of the war** la película transcurre *or* se desarrolla en Nueva Orleans/durante la guerra

(**c**) *(establish) (date, limit, price, target, standards)* fijar (**at/for** a/para); *(record)* establecer; *(trend)* imponer; *(precedent)* sentar; **to s. an example (to sb)** dar ejemplo (a alguien); **to s. the mood** crear el ambiente; **the judge s. bail at $1,000** el juez decretó una fianza de 1.000 dólares; **to s. a value on sth** poner precio *or* asignar un valor a algo

(**d**) *(fix in position)* fijar; **stakes had been s. in the ground** habían fijado estacas en el suelo; *Comput* **to s. the margins** ajustar los márgenes; **her face was s. in determination** su rostro estaba lleno de determinación; **to s. one's jaw** apretar la mandíbula

(**e**) *(assign) (task)* dar, asignar; *(problem)* poner, plantear; *(exam)* poner; **to s. sb a challenge** desafiar a alguien; *Sch* **to s. an essay** mandar (hacer) un trabajo (**f**) *(adjust, prepare) (watch, clock)* poner en hora; *(controls, dial)* poner (**to** en); *(stage)* preparar; **we had s. ourselves to resist** estábamos decididos a resistir; **s. the alarm clock for 8 a.m.** pon el despertador a las ocho; **the alarm is s. for 2.30** la alarma está puesta para las 2.30; **to s. the table** poner la mesa

(**g**) *(cause to start)* **to s. sb on the road to recovery** hacer que alguien comience a recuperarse; **they s. us to work on the project immediately** nos pusieron a trabajar en el proyecto inmediatamente; **her performance s. people talking** su actuación dio que hablar (a la gente); **that s. me thinking** eso me hizo pensar; **the noise s. the dogs barking** el ruido hizo ladrar a los perros; **he s. the machine going** puso en marcha la máquina

(**h**) *(cause to be)* **to s. sth alight** *or* **on fire** prender fuego a algo; **to s. sb free** dejar libre *or* poner en libertad a alguien; **to s. sth right** *(mistake)* enmendar algo

(**i**) *(jewel)* engastar; **a brooch s. with emeralds** un broche con esmeraldas engastadas *or* incrustadas

(**j**) *(poem)* **to s. sth to music** poner música a algo

(**k**) *Med (bone, fracture)* recomponer

(**l**) *(in hairdressing)* **to have one's hair s.** marcarse el pelo

(**m**) *Typ* componer

(**n**) *(solidify) (jelly)* cuajar; *(concrete)* endurecer

4 *vi* (**a**) *(sun, moon)* ponerse; **we saw the sun setting** vimos la puesta de sol (**b**) *(become firm) (jelly)* cuajar; *(concrete, glue)* endurecerse; *(broken bone)* soldarse; **her features had s. in an expression of determination** una expresión de determinación había endurecido sus facciones (**c**) *(begin)* **to s. to work** comenzar a trabajar

▶ **set about** *vt insep* (**a**) *(task, job)* emprender; *(problem, situation)* abordar; **to s. about doing sth** empezar a hacer algo (**b**) *(attack)* atacar

▶ **set against** *vt sep* (**a**) *(cause to oppose)* **to s. sb against sb** enemistar a alguien con alguien; **she has s. herself against it** se opone rotundamente a ello

(**b**) *(compare)* **to s. sth against sth** comparar algo con algo

(**c**) *(deduct)* **to s. expenses against tax** deducir gastos de los impuestos

▶ **set apart** *vt sep* (**a**) *(place separately)* apartar

(**b**) *(distinguish)* distinguir (**from** de)

▶ **set aside** *vt sep* (**a**) *(leave) (task, matter, differences)* dejar a un lado (**b**) *(save) (money)* ahorrar; *(time)* reservar; **I've s. tomorrow aside for house hunting** me he reservado mañana para ir a buscar casa (**c**) *(overturn) (decision, conviction)* anular (**d**) *EU (land)* retirar

▶ **set back** *vt sep* (**a**) *(withdraw)* **the house is s. back from the road** la casa está apartada de la carretera

(**b**) *(delay)* retrasar

(**c**) *(hinder)* **the defeat s. back their chances of victory** la derrota disminuyó sus oportunidades de ganar; **the scandal has s. back the modernization of the party by several years** el escándalo ha retrasado la modernización del partido varios años

(**d**) *Fam (cost)* **that suit must have s. you back (a bit)** ese traje te debe haber costado un ojo de la cara; **how much did that television s. you back?** ¿por cuánto te salió ese televisor?

▶ **set down** *vt sep* (**a**) *(put down) (object)* dejar; *(passenger)* dejar (bajar) (**b**) *(land) (plane)* aterrizar (**c**) *(stipulate)* **the rules are s. down in this document** las normas están recogidas en este documento; **to s. sth down in writing** poner algo por escrito

▶ **set forth** **1** *vt sep Formal (explain)* exponer

2 *vi Literary (depart)* partir, ponerse en camino

▶ **set in** *vi (fog, winter)* instalarse; *(night)* caer; *(mood, infection)* arraigar; **panic s. in** *(began)* el pánico sobrevino; *(lasted)* el pánico se instauró

▶ **set off** **1** *vt sep* (**a**) *(alarm)* activar; *(bomb)* hacer explotar; *(argument, chain of events)* desencadenar; **don't s. him off on that subject** no le saques ese tema que no parará de hablar; **what I said just s. her off again** *(laughing, in anger)* lo que le dije le hizo explotar otra vez

(**b**) *(enhance) (colour, feature)* realzar

(**c**) *Fin (offset)* **some of these expenses can be s. off against tax** algunos de estos gastos los podemos deducir de impuestos

2 *vi (depart)* salir (**for** hacia)

▶ **set on** *vt sep* (**a**) *(cause to attack)* **I'll s. my dog on you!** ¡te soltaré a mi perro!

(**b**) *(cause to follow)* **to s. the police on sb's tracks** *or* **trail** poner a la policía sobre la pista de alguien

▶ **set out** **1** *vt sep (arrange)* disponer; *(ideas, details)* exponer; **the information is s. out in the table below** la información se muestra en la tabla de abajo IDIOM **to s. out one's stall: the candidates s. out their stall during the debate** los candidatos expusieron sus planteamientos durante el debate

2 *vi* (**a**) *(depart)* salir (**for** hacia) (**b**) *(begin) (in job, task)* empezar, comenzar (**c**) *(intend)* **to s. out to do sth** pretender hacer algo

▶ **set to** *vi* (**a**) *(start working)* empezar *or* ponerse a trabajar (**b**) *Fam (start arguing, start fighting)* meterse *or Esp* enzarzarse en una pelea

▶ **set up** **1** *vt sep* (**a**) *(erect) (statue)* erigir; *(tent, barrier)* montar

(**b**) *(organize, start up) (meeting, group)* organizar; *(system, company)* establecer; *(hospital, school)* fundar, abrir; *(republic)* instaurar; *(inquiry)* abrir; *(fund)* crear; **to s. up camp** *(pitch tents)* poner el campamento; *Fam Fig (take up residence) Esp* poner la tienda, *Am* instalarse; **to s. up house** *or* **home** instalarse; **to s. up shop** montar un negocio; **to s. up a dialogue** establecer un diálogo; **to s. up a chant** ponerse a corear

(**c**) *(financially, in business) (person)* **he set his son up in a dry-cleaning business** le ha montado a su hijo un negocio de lavado en seco; **she s. herself up as a consultant** se estableció como asesora

(**d**) *(prepare) (game, equipment, experiment)* preparar; **he s. the chessboard up** colocó las piezas en el tablero de ajedrez

(**e**) *(provide)* **we were well s. up with food for the journey** teníamos comida de sobra para el viaje; **I can s. you up with a girlfriend of mine** te puedo conseguir una cita con una amiga; **they are s. up for life** tienen el porvenir asegurado

(**f**) *Fam (frame)* **I've been s. up!** ¡me han tendido una trampa!; **he was s. up as the fall guy** lo usaron de chivo expiatorio

(**g**) *(restore energy to)* animar; **have a brandy, that'll s. you up** tómate un brandy, verás como te anima; **that meal should s. you up for the journey!** ¡esa comida te preparará para el viaje!

(**h**) *Typ (text)* componer

2 *vi* (**a**) *(establish oneself)* establecerse (**as** de *or* como); **to s. up in business** montar un negocio; **to s. up on one's own** *(business)* ponerse por cuenta propia; *(home)* irse a vivir solo(a) (**b**) *(prepare equipment)* prepararse, *Am* alistarse

▶ **set upon** *vt insep (attack)* atacar

---

set[2] *n (of badger)* tejonera *f*

set-aside ['setəsaɪd] *n EU* retirada *f or* abandono *m* de tierras

setback ['setbæk] *n* contratiempo *m*, revés *m*; **to suffer a s.** sufrir un revés

settee [se'tiː] *n* sofá *m*

setter[1] ['setə(r)] *n (dog)* setter *m*

setter[2] *n* (**a**) *(of test, quiz, crossword)* autor *m* (**b**) *(of jewels)* engarzador(ora) *m,f*, montador(ora) *m,f* (**c**) *(typesetter)* tipógrafo(a) *m,f*

setting ['setɪŋ] **1** *n* (**a**) *(of story, festival)* escenario *m*, marco *m*; **they photographed the foxes in their natural s.** fotografiaron a los zorros en su escenario natural; **the film has Connemara as its s.** el film está ambientado en Connemara

(**b**) *(of sun)* puesta *f*

(**c**) *(on machine)* posición *f*; **highest s.** máximo; **lowest s.** mínimo

(**d**) *(of jewel)* engarce *m*, engaste *m*

(**e**) ***s. lotion*** *(for hair)* fijador *m*

(**f**) *(of fracture)* soldadura *f*

(**g**) *(at table)* cubiertos *mpl*

(**h**) *Comptr* **settings** configuración *f*

(**i**) *Mus* arreglo *m*

2 *adj (sun, star)* poniente

settle ['setəl] **1** *vt* (**a**) *(put in place)* colocar, poner; **to s. one's feet in the stirrups** acomodar el pie en el estribo; **she had settled herself in an armchair** se había instalado cómodamente en un sillón; **to s. the children for the night** acostar a los niños

(**b**) *(calm) (nerves)* calmar; *(doubts)* disipar; **I took something to s. my stomach** tomé algo que me asentara el estómago

(**c**) *(decide) (day, venue, price)* fijar; **it has been settled that...** se ha acordado que...; **nothing is settled yet** aún no se ha decidido nada; **you must s. that among yourselves** eso es algo que deben acordar entre ustedes; **that's settled, then!** ¡entonces, ya está (decidido)!; **that settles it, the party's tomorrow!** ¡no se hable más! la fiesta se hace mañana; **that settles it, he's fired** ésta es la gota que colma el vaso, está despedido

(**d**) *(problem, dispute, differences)* resolver; **questions not yet settled** asuntos pendientes; **she settled her affairs** resolvió sus asuntos; *Law* **to s. a matter out of court** llegar a un acuerdo extrajudicial

(**e**) *(pay) (account, debt)* liquidar, saldar; *(claim)* satisfacer

(**f**) *(colonize)* colonizar

(**g**) *Law (money, allowance, estate)* legar; **to s. an annuity on sb** otorgar una anualidad a alguien

2 *vi* (**a**) *(bird, insect, dust)* posarse (**on** en *or* sobre); *(sediment)* depositarse; *(snow)* cuajar; *(liquid, beer)* reposar; **her gaze settled on the book** su mirada se posó en el libro; **an eerie calm settled over the village** una extraña calma descendió sobre el pueblo

(**b**) *(get comfortable) (in bed, new home)* ponerse cómodo(a), acomodarse; **to s. into an armchair** instalarse en un sillón
(**c**) *(road, wall, foundations)* asentarse; **contents may s. during transport** *(on packaging)* el contenido puede acumularse en el fondo del paquete durante el transporte
(**d**) *(go to live) (person, family)* asentarse (**in** en)
(**e**) *(calm down) (nerves)* calmarse, tranquilizarse; *(stomach)* asentarse; *(crowd, situation)* apaciguarse, tranquilizarse; **the weather is settling** el tiempo se está estabilizando
(**f**) *(reach agreement)* llegar a un acuerdo; *Law* **to s. (out of court)** llegar a un acuerdo extrajudicial
(**g**) *(pay up)* saldar cuentas, ajustar cuentas; **to s. with sb** saldar *or* ajustar cuentas con alguien

▸ **settle back** *vi* acomodarse, arrellanarse

▸ **settle down** 1 *vt sep* (**a**) *(make comfortable)* acomodar; **she settled the baby down for the night** acostó al niño (**b**) *(make calm)* calmar, tranquilizar
2 *vi* (**a**) *(make oneself comfortable)* acomodarse, instalarse; **we settled down to wait** nos instalamos a esperar; **to s. down to work** concentrarse en el trabajo
(**b**) *(become established)* establecerse; **it took the children some weeks to s. down in their new school** a los niños les llevó algunas semanas adaptarse a su nueva escuela
(**c**) *(adopt regular life)* sentar la cabeza; **he's not someone you could imagine settling down with** no es alguien con quien te puedas imaginar haciendo una vida juntos
(**d**) *(calm down) (situation, excitement, person)* tranquilizarse, calmarse; **s. down, children!** ¡tranquilos, niños!

▸ **settle for** *vt insep (accept)* conformarse con; **I insist on the best quality, I never s. for (anything) less** yo busco la mejor calidad, nunca me conformo con menos

▸ **settle in** *vi (in new job, school)* adaptarse, aclimatarse; *(in new house)* instalarse

▸ **settle into** *vt insep (new job, school)* adaptarse *or* aclimatarse a; *(new house)* instalarse en; *(routine)* acomodarse a; **he has settled into a nice rhythm** ha encontrado un buen ritmo

▸ **settle on** *vt insep* (**a**) *(decide on, choose)* decidirse por (**b**) *(reach agreement on)* ponerse de acuerdo sobre

▸ **settle up** *vi (pay bill)* pagar; **can we s. up?** la cuenta, por favor; **to s. up with sb** pagar a alguien

settled ['setəld] *adj* (**a**) *(stable)* estable; *(team)* estable; **it took me a while to get s. in my new home** me tomó un tiempo acomodarme en mi nueva casa (**b**) *(weather)* estable (**c**) *(colonized)* poblado(a)

settlement ['setəlmənt] *n* (**a**) *(agreement)* acuerdo *m*; **to reach a s.** llegar a un acuerdo
(**b**) *(of problem, dispute)* resolución *f*
(**c**) *(of account, debt)* liquidación *f*; **I enclose a cheque in s. of your account** adjunto un cheque como liquidación de la cuenta
(**d**) *(financial gift, dowry)* legado *m*; **to make a s. on sb** hacer un legado a alguien
(**e**) *(town, village) (recently built)* asentamiento *m*; *(in isolated area)* poblado *m*
(**f**) *(of people in a country)* asentamiento *m*; *(colonization)* colonización *f*

settler ['setlə(r)] *n* colono *m*

settling ['setlɪŋ] *n* (**a**) *(of contents)* **there may be some s. of contents** el contenido puede acumularse en el fondo del paquete (**b**) *(of argument, dispute)* resolución *f* ▸▸ ***s. of scores*** ajuste *m* de cuentas (**c**) *(of debt)* liquidación *f*, saldo *m*

settling-in ['setlɪŋ'ɪn] *n* ***s. allowance*** gastos *mpl* de desplazamiento

set-to ['set'tu:] *(pl* **set-tos**) *n Br Fam (argument, fight)* pelea *f*, trifulca *f*; **to have a s. (with sb)** tener una trifulca *or RP* agarrada (con alguien)

set-top box ['settɒp'bɒks] *n TV* descodificador *m*

set-up ['setʌp] *n* (**a**) *Fam (organization, arragement)* sistema *m*, montaje *m*; **the project manager explained the s. to me** el director del proyecto me explicó cómo funcionan las cosas; **it's an odd s.** *(marriage, relationship)* es un arreglo extraño
(**b**) *Fam (trap, trick)* montaje *m*, trampa *f*
(**c**) *Comptr* ***s. CD-ROM*** CD-ROM *m* de instalación; ***s. charge*** cuota *f* de conexión; ***s. fee*** cuota *f* de conexión; ***s. program*** programa *m* de configuración

seven ['sevən] 1 *n* (**a**) *(number)* siete *m* (**b**) *(in rugby)* **sevens** rugby *m* a siete, *RP* sevens *mpl*
2 *adj* siete ▸▸ *Rel* ***the s. deadly sins*** los siete pecados capitales; ***the S. Wonders of the World*** las siete maravillas del mundo; *see also* **eight**

sevenfold ['sevənfəʊld] 1 *adj* septuplicado(a); **there was a s. increase in price** el precio se multiplicó por siete
2 *adv* por siete, siete veces

seven-inch ['sevənɪntʃ] *n* **s. (single)** single *m or* sencillo *m (de vinilo)*

seventeen [sevən'ti:n] 1 *n* diecisiete *m*
2 *adj* diecisiete; *see also* **eight**

seventeenth [sevən'ti:nθ] 1 *n* (**a**) *(fraction)* diecisieteavo *m*, decimoséptima parte *f* (**b**) *(in series)* decimoséptimo(a) *m,f* (**c**) *(of month)* diecisiete *m*
2 *adj* decimoséptimo(a); *see also* **eleventh**

seventh ['sevənθ] 1 *n* (**a**) *(fraction)* séptimo *m*, séptima parte *f* (**b**) *(in series)* séptimo(a) *m,f* (**c**) *(of month)* siete *m*
2 *adj* séptimo(a); IDIOM **to be in s. heaven** estar en el séptimo cielo ▸▸ ***S. Day Adventist*** adventista *mf* del Séptimo Día; *see also* **eighth**

seventies ['sevənti:z] *npl* **the s.** los (años) setenta; *see also* **eighties**

seventieth ['sevəntɪɪθ] 1 *n* septuagésimo(a) *m,f*
2 *adj* septuagésimo(a)

seventy ['sevəntɪ] 1 *n* setenta *m*
2 *adj* setenta; *see also* **eighty**

seventy-eight ['sevəntɪ'eɪt] *n (record)* disco *m* de 78 r.p.m.

seven-year itch ['sevənjɪə'ɪtʃ] *n Hum* comezón *f* del séptimo año

sever ['sevə(r)] 1 *vt* (**a**) *(rope, limb)* cortar; **a severed head** una cabeza cortada (**b**) *(relationship, contact)* cortar
2 *vi* cortarse

several ['sevərəl] 1 *adj* (**a**) *(in number)* varios(as); **s. thousand dollars** varios miles de dólares (**b**) *(separate)* **they went their s. ways** cada uno fue por su camino
2 *pron* varios(as) *m,fpl*; **s. of us/them** varios de nosotros/ellos; **there are s. of them** hay *or* existen varios

severally ['sevrəlɪ] *adv Formal* por separado, individualmente

severance ['sevərəns] *n* ruptura *f* ▸▸ *Ind* ***s. pay*** indemnización *f* por despido

severe [sɪ'vɪə(r)] *adj* (**a**) *(harsh) (person, punishment, criticism)* severo(a); **I gave them a s. telling-off** les di una severa reprimenda
(**b**) *(weather)* severo(a); *(winter)* duro(a), severo(a); *(frost)* intenso(a)
(**c**) *(intense) (pain, storm, pressure, depression)* fuerte, intenso(a); *(competition)* duro(a); **it will be a s. test of our capabilities** será una dura prueba de nuestras aptitudes
(**d**) *(serious) (illness, handicap, problem)* grave; *(losses)* serio(a), grave; *(blow)* duro(a); *(shortage)* grande, serio(a); **I've got s. toothache** tengo un dolor de muelas terrible
(**e**) *(austere) (style, architecture)* sobrio(a), austero(a)

severely [sə'vɪəlɪ] *adv* (**a**) *(harshly)* con severidad
(**b**) *(seriously) (injured, ill)* gravemente; *(damaged, limited, reduced)* seriamente; **to be s. disabled** tener una discapacidad grave; **the vehicle's roadholding was s. tested by the conditions** las condiciones existentes fueron una dura prueba para la adherencia del vehículo; **his patience was s. tested** su paciencia sufrió una dura prueba
(**c**) *(austerely)* con sobriedad, con austeridad

severity [sɪ'verɪtɪ] *n* (**a**) *(harshness) (of person, punishment, criticism)* severidad *f* (**b**) *(of weather)* severidad *f*; *(of winter)* dureza *f*, severidad *f* (**c**) *(intensity) (of pain, storm, pressure, depression)* intensidad *f* (**d**) *(seriousness) (of illness, handicap, problem)* gravedad *f*; *(of losses)* seriedad *f*, gravedad *f*; *(of blow)* dureza *f*; *(of shortage)* seriedad *f* (**e**) *(austerity) (of style, architecture)* sobriedad *f*, austeridad *f*

Seville [se'vɪl] *n* Sevilla ▸▸ ***S. orange*** naranja *f* agria *or* amarga

sew [səʊ] (*pp* **sewn** [səʊn]) 1 *vt* coser; **to s. a button on a shirt** coser un botón en una camisa; **you'll have to s. the pieces together again** tendrás que volver a coser las piezas
2 *vi* coser

▸ **sew up** *vt sep* (**a**) *(hole)* zurcir, coser; *(wound)* coser, suturar (**b**) *Fam (clinch)* **it's all sewn up** está todo arreglado; **they've got the election all sewn up** ya tienen la elección en el bolsillo

sewage ['su:ɪdʒ] *n* aguas *fpl* residuales ▸▸ ***s. disposal*** depuración *f* de aguas residuales; ***s. farm*** depuradora *f*; ***s. system*** alcantarillado *m*; ***s. works*** depuradora *f*

sewer ['su:ə(r)] *n (pipe)* alcantarilla *f*, cloaca *f*; **main s.** colector; IDIOM **he's got a mind like a s.** tiene una mente sucia

sewerage ['su:ərɪdʒ] *n (system)* alcantarillado *m*, cloacas *fpl*

sewermouth ['sʊərmaʊθ] *n US Fam* soez *mf*

sewing ['səʊɪŋ] *n* (**a**) *(activity)* costura *f*; **to do some s.** coser un rato ▸▸ ***s. basket*** costurero *m*, cesta *f* de la costura; ***s. kit*** equipo *m* de costura; ***s. machine*** máquina *f* de coser; ***s. needle*** aguja *f* de coser (**b**) *(items)* labor *m*, costura *f*

sewn *pp of* **sew**

sex [seks] **1** *n* **(a)** *(intercourse)* sexo *m*; **to have s.** tener relaciones sexuales; **to have s. with sb** hacer el amor con alguien, acostarse con alguien; **that film contains too much s.** esa película tiene demasiado sexo ►► ***the s. act*** el acto sexual; ***s. addict*** adicto(a) *m,f* al sexo, sexoadicto(a) *m,f*; ***s. aid*** artículo *m* erótico; ***s. appeal*** atractivo *m* sexual; ***s. attack*** agresión *f* sexual; *Fam* ***s. bomb:* to be a s. bomb** ser puro sexo, estar como para parar un tren; ***s. drive*** impulso *m or* deseo *m or* apetito *m* sexual; **to have a low/high s. drive** tener una libido alta/baja; ***s. education*** educación *f* sexual; *Fam* ***s. god*** dios *m* del sexo; *Fam* ***s. goddess*** diosa *f* del sexo; ***s. hormone*** hormona *f* sexual; ***the s. industry*** la industria del sexo; ***s. kitten*** gatita *f*; ***s. life*** vida *f* sexual; *Fam* ***s. machine*** máquina *f* sexual; ***s. maniac*** obseso(a) *m,f* (sexual); ***s. object*** objeto *m* sexual; ***s. offender*** autor(ora) *m,f* de un delito sexual; ***s. organ*** órgano *m* sexual; ***s. scandal*** escándalo *m* sexual; ***s. scene*** escena *f* de sexo; ***s. shop*** sex-shop *f*; ***s. symbol*** símbolo *m* sexual, sex symbol *mf*; ***s. therapist*** terapeuta *mf* sexual; ***s. therapy*** terapia *f* sexual; ***s. tourism*** turismo *m* sexual
(b) *(gender)* sexo *m*; **the war between the sexes** la guerra de (los) sexos; **we do not discriminate according to s.** no discriminamos según el sexo ►► ***s. change*** cambio *m* de sexo; **to have a s. change (operation)** hacerse un cambio de sexo, cambiarse el sexo; ***s. chromosome*** cromosoma *m* sexual; ***s. discrimination*** discriminación *f* sexual
2 *vt (animal)* sexar

sexagenarian [seksədʒɪ'neərɪən] **1** *n* sexagenario(a) *m,f*
2 *adj* sexagenario(a)

sex-crazed [seks'kreɪzd] *adj* obsesionado(a) por el sexo

sexed [sekst] *adj* **to be highly s.** tener un gran apetito sexual *or* una libido muy fuerte

sexily ['seksɪlɪ] *adv* de forma sexy, muy sensualmente

sexiness ['seksɪnɪs] *n* atractivo *m* sexual, sensualidad *f*

sexism ['seksɪzəm] *n* sexismo *m*

sexist ['seksɪst] **1** *n* sexista *mf*
2 *adj* sexista

sexless ['sekslɪs] *adj* **(a)** *Biol* asexuado(a) **(b)** *(person) (sexually unattractive)* asexuado(a)

sex-mad ['seks'mæd] *adj Fam* loco(a) por el sexo

sexologist [sek'sɒlədʒɪst] *n* sexólogo(a) *m,f*

sexology [sek'sɒlədʒɪ] *n* sexología *f*

sexploitation [seksplɔɪ'teɪʃən] *n* explotación *f* sexual

sexpot ['sekspɒt] *n Fam* tipo(a) *m,f* muy sexy

sex-starved ['seksstɑːvd] *adj Fam* hambriento(a) de sexo, con ganas de sexo

sextant ['sekstənt] *n Naut* sextante *m*

sextet [seks'tet] *n Mus* sexteto *m*

sexton ['sekstən] *n Rel* sacristán *m*

sextuplet ['sekstjʊplət] *n* **(a)** *(baby)* sextillizo(a) *m,f* **(b)** *Mus* seisillo *m*, sextillo *m*

sexual ['seksjʊəl] *adj* **(a)** *(relating to intercourse, desire)* sexual ►► ***s. abuse*** abusos *mpl* deshonestos, abuso *m* sexual; ***the s. act*** el acto sexual; ***s. assault*** agresión *f* sexual; *Fam* ***s. athlete*** atleta *mf* sexual; ***s. attraction*** atracción *f* sexual; ***s. harassment*** acoso *m* sexual; ***s. intercourse*** relaciones *fpl* sexuales, el acto sexual; ***s. orientation*** orientación *f* sexual; ***s. partner*** compañero(a) *m,f* sexual; ***s. prowess*** potencia *f* sexual; ***s. reproduction*** reproducción *f* sexual; ***s. relations*** trato *m* carnal; ***s. relationship*** relación *f* sexual; ***the s. revolution*** la revolución sexual
(b) *(relating to gender)* sexual ►► ***s. discrimination*** discriminación *f* sexual; ***s. equality*** igualdad *f* de sexos; ***s. politics*** política *f* de los sexos

sexuality [seksjʊ'ælɪtɪ] *n* sexualidad *f*

sexually ['seksjʊəlɪ] *adv* sexualmente; **s. abused** víctima de abusos deshonestos; **s. explicit** con sexo explícito; **to be s. active** estar teniendo relaciones sexuales ►► ***s. transmitted disease*** enfermedad *f* de transmisión sexual

sexy ['seksɪ] *adj* **(a)** *(sexually attractive) (person)* sexy **(b)** *(sexually arousing) (clothes, talk)* sexy **(c)** *(sexually aroused)* **to feel s.** estar caliente *or Esp, Méx* cachondo(a) **(d)** *Fam (car, idea, object)* excitante

Seychelles [seɪ'ʃelz] *npl* **the S.** las (islas) Seychelles

SF [es'ef] (*abbr* **science fiction**) ciencia *f* ficción

SFA [ese'feɪ] *n* (*abbr* **Scottish Football Association**) = federación escocesa de fútbol

sforzando [sfɔːt'sændəʊ] *adv Mus* sforzando

sfx [esef'eks] *n* (*abbr* **special effects**) efectos *mpl* especiales

SGML [esdʒiːem'el] *n Comptr* (*abbr* **Standard Generalized Markup Language**) SGML *m*

Sgt *Mil* (*abbr* **Sergeant**) sargento *mf*

sh [ʃ] *exclam* ¡chsss!, ¡shis(t)!

shabbily ['ʃæbɪlɪ] *adv* **(a)** *(dressed)* desaliñadamente, desastradamente; *(furnished)* cochambrosamente **(b)** *(to behave)* ruinmente, con mezquindad; **he was treated very s.** lo trataron muy mal *or Esp* fatal

shabbiness ['ʃæbɪnɪs] *n* **(a)** *(of clothing)* aspecto *m* raído *or* desgastado; *(of appearance)* desaliño *m*; *(of furniture, house)* aspecto *m* cochambroso **(b)** *(of conduct, treatment)* ruindad *f*, mezquindad *f*

shabby ['ʃæbɪ] *adj* **(a)** *(clothing)* raído(a), desgastado(a); *(appearance)* desaliñado(a), desastrado(a); *(furniture, house)* cochambroso(a) **(b)** *(conduct, behaviour)* ruin, mezquino(a); **a s. trick** una mala jugada *or* pasada **(c)** *(excuse)* pobre

shack [ʃæk] *n* casucha *f*, *Esp* chabola *f*, *CSur, Ven* rancho *m*

▶ **shack up** *vi Fam* **to s. up with sb** arrejuntarse *or* vivir arrejuntado(a) con alguien; **they've shacked up together** se han arrejuntado

shackle ['ʃækəl] **1** *n* **shackles** *(fetters)* grilletes *mpl*; **to free oneself from the shackles of convention** escapar de los convencionalismos
2 *vt* **(a)** *(prisoner)* poner grilletes a; **he was shackled to the post** estaba encadenado al puesto **(b)** *(constrain)* atar, constreñir; **to be shackled by convention** ser prisionero(a) de los convencionalismos

shad [ʃæd] *n* sábalo *m*

shade [ʃeɪd] **1** *n* **(a)** *(shadow)* sombra *f*; **in the s.** a la sombra; **these trees give plenty of s.** estos árboles dan mucha sombra; **shades of 1968...** *(reminders)* esto recuerda a 1968...; IDIOM **to put sb in the s.** hacer sombra *or* eclipsar a alguien
(b) *(lampshade)* pantalla *f* (de lámpara); *(eyeshade)* visera *f*; *US (blind)* persiana *f*
(c) *(nuance) (of colour)* tono *m*, tonalidad *f*; *(of opinion, meaning)* matiz *m*; *Comptr* sombreado *m*; **an attractive s. of blue** un tono azul atractivo; **all shades of political opinion were represented** toda la opinión política estaba representada ►► *Comptr* ***shades of grey*** tonos *mpl* de gris
(d) *Art* sombra *f*
(e) **a s.** *(slightly)* un poquito, una pizca; **a s. better/longer** ligeramente mejor/más largo(a)
(f) *Literary (ghost)* espíritu *m*, fantasma *m*
(g) *Fam* **shades** *(sunglasses)* gafas *fpl orAm* anteojos *mpl* de sol
2 *vt* **(a)** *(protect from sun)* proteger del sol; **she shaded her eyes from the sun with her hand** se protegió los ojos del sol con la mano **(b)** *(drawing)* sombrear **(c)** *(win narrowly)* ganar por escaso margen; **we just shaded it** ganamos por muy poco
3 *vi (merge)* **the blue shades into purple** el azul se va haciendo púrpura

▶ **shade in** *vt sep (part of drawing)* sombrear

▶ **shade off** *vi* matizarse; **the film shades off into a conventional romance** la película se va decantando hacia los terrenos del romanticismo más convencional

shaded ['ʃeɪdɪd] *adj* **(a)** *(in the shade) (path, ground)* sombreado(a) **(b)** *(coloured in) (drawing, area on diagram)* sombreado(a)

shadiness ['ʃeɪdɪnɪs] *n* **(a)** *(of garden, lane)* sombra *f* **(b)** *(of person)* deshonestidad *f*; *(of behaviour, transaction)* lo turbio, lo oscuro

shading ['ʃeɪdɪŋ] *n (on drawing, map)* sombreado *m*

shadow ['ʃædəʊ] **1** *n* **(a)** *(dark area)* sombra *f*; **to cast a s.** proyectar una sombra; **in the s. (of)** a la sombra (de); **to have shadows under one's eyes** tener ojeras; **the s. of suspicion fell on them** la sombra de la sospecha cayó sobre ellos; **he follows me everywhere like a s.** me sigue a todos lados como una sombra; IDIOM **the news cast a s. over the occasion** la noticia vino a ensombrecer el acto; IDIOM **she's a s. of her former self** es apenas una sombra de lo que era; IDIOM **to live in sb's shadow** vivir a la sombra de alguien ►► *Econ* ***s. economy*** economía *f* sumergida; *Comptr* ***s. printing*** impresión *f* subordinada; ***s. puppet*** sombra *f* chinesca
(b) *(slightest bit)* **without a s. of (a) doubt** sin sombra de duda
(c) *(detective)* **he managed to lose his s.** consiguió escabullirse de la persona que lo seguía; **I want a s. put on him** quiero que lo sigan a sol y sombra
(d) *Med (on lung)* mancha *f*
2 *adj Br Pol* ***S. Cabinet*** gabinete *m* en la sombra; ***S. Minister*** = político de la oposición encargado de una cartera específica
3 *vt* **(a)** *(follow)* seguir **(b)** *Literary (darken)* oscurecer

shadow-box ['ʃædəʊbɒks] *vi* practicar boxeo con la propia sombra

shadow-boxing ['ʃædəʊbɒksɪŋ] *n Sport* boxeo *m* con la propia sombra; *Fig* **a lot of s. went on between them** los dos se tanteaban para ver cómo reaccionaba el otro

shadowy [ˈʃædəʊɪ] *adj* (**a**) *(vague)* vago(a), impreciso(a); **a s. form** una figura en la oscuridad (**b**) *(dark)* oscuro(a), sombrío(a) (**c**) *(mysterious)* **a s. figure** una oscura *or* misteriosa figura

shady [ˈʃeɪdɪ] *adj* (**a**) *(garden, lane)* sombreado(a), umbrío(a); **I'd rather sit somewhere s.** preferiría sentarme a la sombra (**b**) *Fam (suspicious) (person)* sospechoso(a), siniestro(a); *(transaction)* turbio(a), oscuro(a)

shaft [ʃɑːft] **1** *n* (**a**) *(of spear)* asta *f*, vara *f*; *(of golf club)* vara *f*, barra *f*; *(of tool, axe)* mango *m*; *(of feather)* cañón *m*; *(of bone)* caña *f*; *(of cart)* vara *f* (**b**) *(of mine)* pozo *m*; *(for elevator)* hueco *m* (**c**) *(of light)* rayo *m* (**d**) *(in engine, machine)* eje *m* (**e**) *US Fam* **to give sb the s.** *(cheat)* timar a alguien; **he got the s.** le timaron

2 *vt* (**a**) *Br Vulg (have sex with)* tirarse, *Esp* follarse, *Am* cogerse, *Méx* chingar; **if he finds out, we're shafted** si se entera, la cagamos (**b**) *Fam (cheat)* timar, *Am* joder; **to get shafted** salir mal parado(a)

shag[1] [ʃæg] *n (tobacco)* picadura *f*

shag[2] *n (bird)* cormorán *m* moñudo

shag[3] *adj (made of long wool)* **a s. carpet** una alfombra peluda

shag[4] **1** *n Br very Fam (sexual intercourse)* **to have a s.** *Esp, Arg* echar un polvo, *Am* coger; **to be a good s.** *(person)* ser bueno(a) en la cama (**b**) *Br very Fam (boring task) Esp* coñazo *m*, *Col* jartera *f*, *Méx, Ven* aguaje *m*, *RP* plomazo *m*

2 *vt* (*pt & pp* **shagged**) (**a**) *Vulg (have sexual intercourse with) Esp, Arg* echar un polvo a, *Esp* follar, *Am* cogerse a (**b**) *US (in baseball) (fetch)* recoger

3 *vi Br Vulg (have sexual intercourse) Esp, Arg* echar un polvo, *Esp* follar, *Am* coger

shaggable [ˈʃægəbəl] *adj Br Vulg* sexy, *Esp* follable; *Am* cogible

shagged (out) [ˈʃægd(ˈaʊt)] *adj Br very Fam* reventado(a), hecho(a) polvo *or Méx* camotes

shagger [ˈʃægə(r)] *n Br Vulg* cabrón(ona) *m,f*

shaggy [ˈʃægɪ] *adj* (**a**) *(hairy)* peludo(a); *(dog)* lanudo(a) ►► *Fam* ***s. dog story*** chiste *m* interminable *(con final flojo)* (**b**) *(carpet, rug)* peludo(a)

shah [ʃɑː] *n* sha *m*

shake [ʃeɪk] **1** *n* (**a**) *(action)* sacudida *f*; **give my hand a s.** dame un apretón de manos; **give the bottle a good s.** agita bien la botella; **have another s. of the dice** sacude de nuevo los dados; **a s. of the head** *(to say no)* un movimiento negativo de la cabeza; *(with resignation)* un gesto de resignación con la cabeza; **with a s. in his voice** con la voz temblorosa; *Fam* **he got/has got the shakes** le entró/tiene el tembleque; IDIOM *Fam* **in two shakes (of a lamb's tail)** en un abrir y cerrar de ojos, *Arg* al toque; IDIOM *Fam* **to be no great shakes** no ser gran cosa; **he's no great shakes at painting** *or* **as a painter** no es gran cosa pintando *or* como pintor

(**b**) *(drink)* **(milk) s.** batido *m*

(**c**) *US Fam (deal)* **he'll give you a fair s.** te dará un trato justo

2 *vt* (*pt* **shook** [ʃʊk], *pp* **shaken** [ˈʃeɪkən]) (**a**) *(person, duster)* sacudir; *(branch, box, bottle)* agitar; *(building)* sacudir, hacer temblar; *(dice)* menear, agitar; **she shook me by the shoulders** me sacudió por los hombros; **she shook the crumbs off her clothes** se sacudió las migas de la ropa; **they shook the apples from the tree** sacudieron el árbol para que cayeran las manzanas; **to s. vinegar onto sth** echarle chorritos de vinagre a algo; **s. well before use** *(on packaging)* agítese bien antes de usar; **the dog shook itself dry** el perro se sacudió para secarse; **they shook themselves free** se liberaron dando sacudidas; **to s. one's fist/a stick at sb** amenazar a alguien con el puño/un palo; **to s. hands with sb** estrechar *or* dar la mano a alguien; **they shook hands** se dieron la mano; **to s. hands on a deal** sellar un trato con un apretón de manos; **to s. one's head** *(to say no)* negar con la cabeza; *(in disbelief)* hacer un gesto de incredulidad con la cabeza; *Fam* **s. a leg!** *(hurry up)* ¡muévete!, ¡date prisa!, *Am* ¡apúrate!

(**b**) *(shock emotionally)* afectar, perturbar; *(of news, revelations)* conmocionar; **I felt shaken after the fall** la caída me dejó conmocionado; **the team was shaken by the early goal** el gol tan temprano desconcertó al equipo; **to s. sb's faith** quebrantar la fe de alguien

3 *vi* (**a**) *(person, building, voice)* temblar; *(leaves, branches)* agitarse; **to s. with fear/rage** temblar de miedo/rabia; **to s. with laughter** retorcerse de risa; IDIOM **to be shaking like a jelly** *or* **leaf** temblar como un flan (**b**) *Fam (shake hands)* **to s. on it** cerrar el trato con un apretón de manos; **let's s. on it!** ¡choca esos cinco!, ¡venga esa mano!

►**shake down** **1** *vt sep US Fam* (**a**) *(search)* cachear (**b**) *(extort money from)* sacar dinero a; **they shook her down for $10,000** le sacaron 10.000 dólares

2 *vi Fam* (**a**) *(go to bed)* **they had to s. down on the floor for the night** tuvieron que dormir en el suelo esa noche (**b**) *(adapt) (to new situation, job)* adaptarse, acostumbrarse

►**shake off** *vt sep* (**a**) *(sand, snow, water)* sacudir (**b**) *(illness, depression)* salir de, quitarse *or Am* sacarse de encima; *(pursuer)* librarse de

►**shake out** *vt sep (tablecloth, rug, bag)* sacudir; **he shook the sand out of his shoes** se sacudió la arena de los zapatos

►**shake up** *vt sep* (**a**) *(upset)* trastornar; **they were badly shaken up after the accident** después del accidente quedaron muy conmocionados (**b**) *(reorganize) (system)* reorganizar; *Fam* **you need to s. your ideas up!** tienes que ponerte las pilas

shakedown [ˈʃeɪkdaʊn] *n* (**a**) *US Fam (search)* cacheo *m* (**b**) *US Fam (extortion)* chantaje *m* (**c**) *Fam (of ship, plane) (test)* prueba *f* (**d**) *Fam (bed)* catre *m*

shaken *pp of* **shake**

shake-out [ˈʃeɪkaʊt] *n* reestructuración *f*

shaker [ˈʃeɪkə(r)] *n (for salt)* salero *m*; *(for pepper)* pimentero *m*; *(for sugar)* azucarero *m*; *(for cocktails)* coctelera *f*; *(for dice)* cubilete *m*

Shakespearean, Shakespearian [ʃeɪksˈpɪərɪən] *adj* shakespeariano(a)

shake-up [ˈʃeɪkʌp] *n (reorganization)* reorganización *f*

shakily [ˈʃeɪkɪlɪ] *adv* (**a**) *(to walk, write, speak)* temblorosamente (**b**) *(uncertainly)* con poca firmeza; **the novel starts rather s., but improves later on** la novela empieza un tanto floja pero después mejora

shakiness [ˈʃeɪkɪnɪs] *n* (**a**) *(of table, ladder)* inestabilidad *f*; *(of handwriting, voice, hand)* temblor *m* (**b**) *(of health, position)* debilidad *f*; *(of government)* inestabilidad *f, debilidad f*; *(of team, defence, argument)* debilidad *f*, fragilidad *f*

shaky [ˈʃeɪkɪ] *adj* (**a**) *(table, ladder)* inestable, inseguro(a); *(handwriting, voice)* tembloroso(a); *(hand)* tembloroso(a), trémulo(a)

(**b**) *(health, position)* débil, precario(a); *(government)* inestable, débil; *(team, defence, argument)* flojo(a); **I'm feeling a bit s.** no estoy muy allá; **to get off to a s. start** comenzar con mal pie, tener un comienzo flojo; **her memory is a bit s.** su memoria es un poco frágil; **his English is s.** habla un inglés precario

shale [ʃeɪl] *n (rock)* esquisto *m* ►► ***s. oil*** aceite *m* de esquisto

---

SHALL [ʃæl, *unstressed* ʃəl] *modal aux v* (**a**) *(with first person) (expressing intentions, promises, predictions)* **I s. be there if I can** si puedo, estaré allí; **I shan't say this more than once** esto no lo voy a repetir; **we s. take note of your comments** tendremos en cuenta sus comentarios; **you s. have your wish** tendrás lo que deseas; **I want to meet her – you s.** quiero conocerla – lo harás; **I s. look forward to seeing you again** estoy deseando volver a verle; **as we s. see** como veremos

(**b**) *Formal (with 2nd and 3rd person) (expressing determination)* **you s. pay for this!** ¡me las pagarás *or* vas a pagar!; **we s. overcome!** ¡venceremos!; **we s. not be moved!** ¡no nos moverán!; **they s. not pass** ¡no pasarán!

(**c**) *(in suggestions, offers)* **s. I open the window?** ¿abro la ventana?; **s. I make some coffee?** ¿preparo café?; **I'll put it here, s. I?** lo pongo aquí, ¿te parece?; **let's go, s. we?** vámonos, ¿te parece?

(**d**) *(indicating rule)* **all members s. be entitled to vote** todos los socios tendrán derecho al voto; **the term "company property" s. be understood to include...** se entiende que el término "propiedad de la empresa" comprende...

---

shallot [ʃəˈlɒt] *n* chalota *f*

shallow [ˈʃæləʊ] **1** *n* **shallows** bajío *m*

2 *adj* (**a**) *(water)* poco profundo(a); *(dish)* llano(a); *(grave)* poco profundo(a); **the s. end** *(of swimming pool)* la parte poco profunda (**b**) *(breathing)* superficial (**c**) *(person, mind, conversation, argument)* superficial, poco profundo(a)

shallowness [ˈʃæləʊnɪs] *n* (**a**) *(of water)* poca profundidad *f* (**b**) *(of breathing)* superficialidad *f* (**c**) *(of person, mind, conversation, argument)* superficialidad *f*

shalt [ʃælt] *(2nd person singular of* **shall**) *Archaic & Rel* **thou s. not steal** no robarás

sham [ʃæm] **1** *n* (**a**) *(trial, election)* farsa *f*; **her illness is a s.** su enfermedad es puro teatro *or* cuento (**b**) *(person)* farsante *mf*

2 *adj (illness, emotion)* fingido(a); **a s. election was held** se celebraron unas elecciones que fueron una farsa

3 *vt* (*pt & pp* **shammed**) *(feign)* fingir, simular

4 *vi* fingir

shaman [ˈʃeɪmən] *n* chamán *m*

shamanism [ˈʃeɪmənɪzəm] *n* chamanismo *m*

shamateur [ˈʃæmətɜ:(r)] *n Fam* = jugador que, siendo teóricamente aficionado, gana mucho dinero a través de contratos con patrocinadores y similares

shamble [ˈʃæmbəl] *vi* **to s. along** caminar arrastrando los pies

shambles [ˈʃæmbəlz] *n* desastre *m*, desorden *m*; **this place is a s.!** ¡esto es un desorden!; **what a s.!** ¡qué desastre!; **the party's election campaign was a s.** la campaña electoral del partido fue un desastre

shambling [ˈʃæmblɪŋ] *adj* **he has a s. gait** camina arrastrando los pies

shambolic [ʃæmˈbɒlɪk] *adj Fam* desastroso(a)

shame [ʃeɪm] **1** *n* (**a**) *(disgrace, guilt)* vergüenza *f*, *Andes, CAm, Carib, Méx* pena *f*; **to my s.** para mi vergüenza; **she hung her head in s.** bajó *or* agachó la cabeza avergonzada *or Andes, CAm, Carib, Méx* apenada; **to have no (sense of) s.** no tener vergüenza; **the s. of it!** ¡qué vergüenza!; **s. on you!** ¡debería darte vergüenza!; **to bring s. on sb** traer la deshonra a alguien, deshonrar a alguien; **she works so hard, she puts you to s.** trabaja tanto que realmente te deja mal parado

(**b**) *(pity)* pena *f*; **it's a s. Matt can't be here** qué pena que *or* es una pena que Matt no pueda estar aquí; **it would be a s. to miss it** sería una pena perdérselo; **what a s.!** ¡qué pena!

2 *vt* (**a**) *(cause to feel ashamed)* avergonzar, *Andes, CAm, Carib, Méx* apenar; **it shames me to admit it** me avergüenza *or* da vergüenza admitirlo; **to s. sb into doing sth** avergonzar a alguien para que haga algo (**b**) *(bring shame on)* deshonrar, dejar en mal lugar

shamefaced [ˈʃeɪmˈfeɪst] *adj* avergonzado(a), *Andes, CAm, Carib, Méx* apenado(a)

shamefacedly [ʃeɪmˈfeɪsɪdlɪ] *adv* con vergüenza; *Andes, CAm, Carib, Méx* con pena

shameful [ˈʃeɪmfʊl] *adj* vergonzoso(a); **it's s. the way young people behave these days** es vergonzoso cómo se comportan los jóvenes hoy en día

shamefully [ˈʃeɪmfəlɪ] *adv* vergonzosamente; **she has been treated s.** ha sido tratada de una manera vergonzosa; **he was s. ignorant about the issue** tenía una ignorancia vergonzosa sobre el tema

shameless [ˈʃeɪmlɪs] *adj* desvergonzado(a); **he is s. about doing it** no le da ninguna vergüenza *or CAm, Carib, Col, Méx* pena hacerlo

shamelessly [ˈʃeɪmlɪslɪ] *adv* con desvergüenza, con descaro

shamelessness [ˈʃeɪmlɪsnɪs] *n* falta *f* de vergüenza, desvergüenza *f*

shaming [ˈʃeɪmɪŋ] *adj* vergonzoso(a), bochornoso(a)

shammy [ˈʃæmɪ] *n* **s. (leather)** gamuza *f*

shampoo [ʃæmˈpu:] **1** *n* champú *m*; **a s. and set** un lavado y marcado

2 *vt (carpet)* limpiar con champú; **to s. one's hair** lavarse el pelo con champú

shamrock [ˈʃæmrɒk] *n* trébol *m*

shamus [ˈʃeɪməs] *n US Fam (private detective)* detective *mf* privado

shandy [ˈʃændɪ] *n Br* cerveza *f* con gaseosa, *Esp* clara *f*

Shanghai [ʃæŋˈhaɪ] *n* Shanghai

shanghai [ˈʃæŋhaɪ] *vt Fam* (**a**) *Naut (kidnap)* = embarcar a alguien por la fuerza o emborrachándole (**b**) *(force)* **to s. sb into (doing) sth** obligar a alguien a (hacer) algo por la fuerza

Shangri-La [ʃæŋgrɪˈlɑ:] *n* el paraíso terrenal

shank [ʃæŋk] **1** *n* (**a**) *(of person)* espinilla *f*; *(of horse)* caña *f*; *(of lamb, beef)* pierna *f* (deshuesada) (**b**) *(of chisel, drill bit)* pala *f*; *(of screw, bolt)* vástago *m*, caña *f*; *(of key)* tija *f*; *(of anchor)* caña *f* (**c**) *US Fam (knife)* pincho *m*, *Arg* punta *f*

2 *vt US Fam (stab)* apuñalar, *Arg* clavar una punta a

Shanks's pony [ˈʃæŋksɪzˈpəʊnɪ], *US* **Shanks's mare** [ˈʃæŋksɪzˈmeə(r)] *n Fam* **to go by S.** ir a pata, ir en el coche de San Fernando (un poquito a pie y otro poquito andando)

shan't [ʃɑ:nt] = **shall not**

shanty[1] [ˈʃæntɪ] *n (hut)* casucha *f*, *Esp* chabola *f*, *CSur, Ven* rancho *m* ►► ***s. town*** *Esp* barrio *m* de chabolas, *Am* barriada *f*, *Andes* pueblo *m* joven, *Arg* villa *f* miseria, *Carib* ranchería *f*, *Chile* callampa *f*, *Méx* ciudad *f* perdida, *Urug* cantegril *m*

shanty[2], *US* **chant(e)y** *n (song)* saloma *f* (marinera)

shape [ʃeɪp] **1** *n* (**a**) *(physical form)* forma *f*; **what s. is it?** ¿qué forma tiene?; **to be the same s. as...** tener la misma forma que...; **the room was hexagonal in s.** la habitación tenía forma hexagonal; **in the s. of a T** en forma de T; **they come in all shapes and sizes** los hay de todo los tipos y tamaños; **he bent the wire into s.** le dio forma al alambre; **my hat was knocked out of s.** se me abolló el sombrero; **my pullover has lost its s.** se me ha deformado el suéter

(**b**) *(figure, silhouette)* silueta *f*, forma *f*; **vague shapes could be seen in the mist** en la niebla se podían divisar unas vagas formas *or* siluetas

(**c**) *(abstract form)* perfil *m*, forma *f*; **it's the s. of things to come** es lo que nos espera; **to take s.** *(plan)* tomar forma

(**d**) *(guise)* **they won't accept change in any s. or form** no aceptarán absolutamente ningún tipo de cambio; **in the s. of...** en forma de...; **help eventually arrived in the s. of her parents** al final la ayuda llegó a través de sus padres

(**e**) *(condition)* **to be in good/bad s.** *(person)* estar/no estar en forma; *(company, economy)* estar en buenas/malas condiciones; **she was in pretty bad s.** *(very ill, badly injured)* estaba muy mal; **to get into/keep in s.** *(person)* ponerse/mantenerse en forma; **you're in no s. to go hiking** no estás en forma como para hacer senderismo; **to be out of s.** no estar en forma; **the economy is in poor s. at the moment** la economía está bastante mal en estos momentos

(**f**) *(mould)* molde *m*

2 *vt* (**a**) *(clay)* modelar, moldear; *(wood)* tallar; **to be shaped like sth** tener forma de algo; **she shaped the clay into rectangular blocks** hizo bloques rectangulares con la arcilla (**b**) *(character, attitude)* moldear, modelar; *(events)* dar forma a; **these events will s. our country's future** estos acontecimientos darán forma al *or* forjarán el futuro de nuestro país

3 *vi Sport* **he shaped as if to shoot** hizo como que iba a tirar

► **shape up** *vi* (**a**) *(progress)* **how is she shaping up in her new job?** ¿qué tal se está adaptando a su nuevo trabajo?; **he is shaping up well** va haciendo progresos; **it's shaping up to be a close contest** se está perfilando una contienda muy reñida (**b**) *(improve oneself)* enmendarse; **you'd better s. up, young man!** ¡será mejor que te espabiles, jovencito! (**c**) *(get fit)* recuperar la forma

-shaped [-ʃeɪpt] *suffix* **crescent/heart-s.** con forma de media luna/corazón

shapeless [ˈʃeɪplɪs] *adj* informe

shapelessness [ˈʃeɪplɪsnɪs] *n* falta *f* de forma

shapeliness [ˈʃeɪplɪnɪs] *n (of legs, figure)* forma *f* proporcionada

shapely [ˈʃeɪplɪ] *adj (legs, figure)* esbelto(a), torneado(a); **she's very s.** tiene muy buen tipo

shard [ʃɑ:d] *n (of pottery)* fragmento *m*; *(of glass)* esquirla *f*

share [ʃeə(r)] **1** *n* (**a**) *(portion)* parte *f* (**in** de); *(of market)* cuota *f*; **how much does my s. come to?** ¿cuánto me corresponde?; **divided into equal shares** dividido(a) en *or* a partes iguales; **to have a s. in sth** participar en algo; **he doesn't do his s.** no hace lo que le corresponde; **she had a s. in his downfall** tuvo que ver con su caída; **you've had your (fair) s. of problems/luck** has tenido bastantes problemas/bastante suerte; **he's come in for his (full) s. of criticism** ha sido muy criticado; *Fam* **to go shares on sth** ir a medias en algo

(**b**) *Fin (stock)* acción *f* ►► ***s. capital*** capital *m* social; ***s. certificate*** título *m* de acción; ***s. dealing*** compraventa *f* de acciones; ***s. index*** índice *m* bursátil, índice *m* de cotización; ***s. issue*** emisión *f* de acciones; ***s. market*** mercado *m* de acciones; ***s. option*** opción *f* sobre acciones; ***s. option scheme*** plan *m* de opción sobre acciones; ***s. ownership*** titularidad *f* de acciones; **an increase in s. ownership** un aumento en el número de personas que tienen acciones; ***s. price*** cotización *f*

(**c**) *(stake)* participación *f*; **I have a 10 percent s. in a villa in Spain** tengo una participación del 10 por ciento en una villa en España

2 *vt* (**a**) *(divide)* dividir, repartir; *(money, food, chores, blame)* compartir; **he shared the chocolate among the children** repartió *or* dividió el chocolate entre los niños

(**b**) *(use jointly) (tools, flat, bed)* compartir; **I shared a taxi home with her** volvimos juntos a casa en un taxi

(**c**) *(have in common) (interest, opinion, characteristic, heritage)* compartir; **we s. the same name** nos llamamos igual, somos tocayos; **we s. a passion for opera** nos une la pasión por la ópera

(**d**) *(tell) (experience, impressions, secrets)* compartir; **to s. a joke (with sb)** contar un chiste (a alguien)

3 *vi* compartir; **to s. in sth** participar de algo; **s. and s. alike!** ¡hay que compartir las cosas!

► **share out** *vt sep* repartir

sharecropper [ˈʃeəkrɒpə(r)] *n* aparcero(a) *m,f*

shared [ʃeəd] *adj* compartido(a), común

shareholder [ˈʃeəhəʊldə(r)] *n Fin* accionista *mf*; **the shareholders** el accionariado, los accionistas ►► ***s. economy*** = concepto neoliberal de la economía en el que las personas son accionistas y las compañías son sociedades anónimas; ***shareholders' meeting*** junta *f* (general) de accionistas

shareholding [ˈʃeəhəʊldɪŋ] *n Fin* participación *f* accionarial

share-out [ˈʃeəraʊt] *n* reparto *m*

shareware [ˈʃeəweə(r)] *n Comptr* shareware *m*

shark [ʃɑ:k] *n* (**a**) *(fish)* tiburón *m* (**b**) *(ruthless person)* buitre *mf*

sharkskin [ˈʃɑ:kskɪn] *n (leather)* piel *f* de tiburón

sharon fruit [ˈʃærənˈfru:t] *n* caqui *m*

sharp [ʃɑːp] 1 *n Mus* sostenido *m*
2 *adj* (**a**) *(knife, point, features, edge, teeth)* afilado(a), *Am* filoso(a); *(needle, pencil, thorn)* puntiagudo(a); **to be s.** *(knife)* estar afilado(a); **use a s. knife/pencil** use un cuchillo filoso/lápiz afilado; IDIOM **to be at the s. end of sth** tener que enfrentarse cara a cara con algo; **the men and women at the s. end** las personas que están en la línea de fuego; IDIOM *Hum* **he isn't the sharpest knife in the drawer** *or* **tool in the box** no es precisamente una lumbrera
(**b**) *(angle, bend)* cerrado(a); *(rise, fall, change)* pronunciado(a)
(**c**) *(outline, focus, photograph, TV picture)* nítido(a); *(contrast)* acusado(a), fuerte
(**d**) *(keen) (eyesight, hearing)* agudo(a); **to have a s. eye for a bargain** tener buen ojo para las oportunidades; **we'll have to keep a s. eye on them so they don't escape** tendremos que vigilarlos de cerca para que no se escapen; **keep a s. lookout for any mistakes** revisa muy bien para que no haya errores
(**e**) *(in intellect) (person)* agudo(a), despierto(a); **that was a pretty s. move** fue una decisión muy astuta
(**f**) *(unscrupulous) (trading, lawyer)* sin escrúpulos; **s. practice** tejemanejes, triquiñuelas
(**g**) *(harsh) (retort, words, person)* mordaz, seco(a); *(criticism)* severo(a), duro(a); **a s. tongue** una lengua afilada *or* viperina
(**h**) *(rap, blow)* seco(a); *(shock)* breve y severo(a)
(**i**) *(quick, brisk) (reflex, pace)* rápido(a); **be s. (about it)!** ¡(hazlo) rápido!
(**j**) *(taste, sauce)* ácido(a)
(**k**) *(sound, pain)* agudo(a)
(**l**) *(wind, frost)* fuerte, intenso(a)
(**m**) *(fashionable) (suit)* fino(a), elegante; **to be a s. dresser** ser muy fino(a) vistiendo
(**n**) *Mus* sostenido(a); **C s.** do sostenido; **to be s.** *(violinist)* desafinar, tocar demasiado alto; *(singer)* desafinar, cantar demasiado alto
3 *adv* (**a**) *(punctually)* en punto; **at four o'clock s.** a las cuatro en punto (**b**) *(immediately)* **the road turns s. left** la ruta dobla abruptamente a la izquierda; **turn s. left when you get to the traffic lights** en cuanto llegues al semáforo dobla a la izquierda (**c**) *(sing, play)* fuera de tono, demasiado alto (**d**) IDIOMS *Fam* **look s.!** ¡espabila!, ¡despabílate!; **to pull up s.** detenerse en seco

sharpen [ˈʃɑːpən] 1 *vt* (**a**) *(knife, tool)* afilar; *(claws)* afilar; *(pencil)* sacar punta a (**b**) *(pain, desire)* agudizar, acentuar; *(appetite)* abrir; *(resolve)* acentuar; *(contrast)* incrementar, aumentar; **to s. one's wits** agudizar el ingenio
2 *vi (pain, desire)* agudizarse, acentuarse; *(appetite)* abrirse; *(resolve)* acentuarse; *(contrast)* incrementarse, aumentarse

▸**sharpen up** 1 *vt sep* pulir
2 *vi* mejorar

sharpener [ˈʃɑːpnə(r)] *n (for knife)* afilador *m*; *(for pencil)* sacapuntas *m inv*, afilalápices *m inv*

sharper [ˈʃɑːpə(r)] *n (con man in general)* estafador(ora) *m,f*; *(card sharp)* tahúr(ura) *m,f*

sharp-eyed [ˈʃɑːpaɪd] *adj* observador(ora)

sharpish [ˈʃɑːpɪʃ] *adv Br Fam* rapidito

sharply [ˈʃɑːplɪ] *adv* (**a**) **s. pointed** *(knife, needle)* puntiagudo(a); *(pencil)* afilado(a); *(features)* pronunciado(a), anguloso(a)
(**b**) *(to contrast)* acusadamente; **to bring sth s. into focus** enfocar algo nítidamente
(**c**) *(to curve, turn)* abruptamente; *(to brake)* en seco; *(to rise, fall, change)* pronunciadamente; **the car took the bend too s.** el auto tomó la curva muy cerrada
(**d**) *(harshly)* ásperamente; *(speak, reply)* secamente; *(criticize)* severamente, duramente
(**e**) *(quickly)* rápidamente
(**f**) *(rap, hit)* con fuerza

sharpness [ˈʃɑːpnɪs] *n* (**a**) *(of knife, point)* lo afilado; *(of thorn, needle)* lo puntiagudo; *(of point, features)* agudeza *f*
(**b**) *(of angle, bend)* lo pronunciado, lo cerrado; *(of rise, fall, change)* lo pronunciado
(**c**) *(of outline, focus, photograph, TV picture)* nitidez *f*; *(of contrast)* lo marcado
(**d**) *(of hearing, sight)* agudeza *f*
(**e**) *(of intellect)* agudeza *f*
(**f**) *(harshness)* brusquedad *f*; *(of retort, words, person)* mordacidad *f*; *(of criticism)* severidad *f*; dureza *f*
(**g**) *(of rap, blow)* fuerza *f*
(**h**) *(quickness, briskness) (of reflex, pace)* rapidez *f*
(**i**) *(of taste, sauce)* intensidad *f*
(**j**) *(of pain, sound)* agudeza *f*
(**k**) *(of wind)* intensidad *f*

sharpshooter [ˈʃɑːpʃuːtə(r)] *n* tirador(ora) *m,f* de élite

sharp-sighted [ˈʃɑːpˈsaɪtɪd] *adj* (**a**) *(with good eyes)* con ojos de lince (**b**) *(observant)* observador(ora)

sharp-tongued [ˈʃɑːpˈtʌŋd] *adj* mordaz

sharp-witted [ˈʃɑːpˈwɪtɪd] *adj* agudo(a)

shat *pt & pp of* **shit**

shatter [ˈʃætə(r)] 1 *vt* (**a**) *(glass, bone)* hacer añicos (**b**) *(hopes, dreams, confidence)* echar por tierra; *(silence)* romper; *(health, nerves)* destrozar; *(record)* pulverizar; **they were shattered by the news** la noticia los destrozó
2 *vi (glass, windscreen)* hacerse añicos

shattered [ˈʃætəd] *adj Fam* (**a**) *(devastated)* **to be s.** quedarse destrozado(a) (**b**) *Br (exhausted)* **to be s.** estar rendido(a), *Méx* estar camotes

shattering [ˈʃætərɪŋ] *adj* (**a**) *(blow, defeat, news)* demoledor(ora), devastador(ora) (**b**) *Fam (exhausting)* agotador(ora), matador(ora)

shatterproof [ˈʃætəpruːf] *adj* inastillable

shave [ʃeɪv] 1 *n* afeitado *m*; **to have a s.** afeitarse; **to give sb a s.** afeitar a alguien; IDIOM **that was a close s.!** ¡ha faltado un pelo!
2 *vt* (**a**) *(face, legs)* afeitar; **to s. one's face** afeitarse; **to s. one's legs** afeitarse las piernas (**b**) *(wood)* cepillar (**c**) *(graze) (of bullet, ball)* rozar, pasar rozando
3 *vi* afeitarse

▸**shave off** *vt sep* (**a**) *(cut off)* **he shaved his beard off** se afeitó la barba; **can you s. some cheese off for me to try?** ¿puedes cortarme una rodaja finísima de queso (para que la pruebe)? (**b**) *(deduct)* recortar; **she has shaved a hundredth of a second off the world record** ha rebajado el récord del mundo en una centésima de segundo

shaven [ˈʃeɪvən] *adj* afeitado(a)

shaver [ˈʃeɪvə(r)] *n* maquinilla *f* (de afeitar) eléctrica ▸▸ ***s.*** *Br* ***point*** *or US* ***outlet*** enchufe *m* para la maquinilla de afeitar

shaving [ˈʃeɪvɪŋ] *n* (**a**) *(for removing hair)* ***s. brush*** brocha *f* de afeitar; ***s. cream*** crema *f* de afeitar; ***s. foam*** espuma *f* de afeitar; ***s. mirror*** espejo *m* de afeitar; ***s. stick*** barra *f* de jabón para afeitar (**b**) *(piece of wood, metal)* viruta *f*; *(of chocolate)* rayadura *f*

shawl [ʃɔːl] *n* chal *m*, *Am* rebozo *m*

shawm [ʃɔːm] *n Mus* chirimía *f*

SHE [ʃiː] 1 *pron* ella *(usually omitted in Spanish, except for contrast)*; **she's Scottish** es escocesa; **SHE hasn't got it!** ¡ella no lo tiene!; **she's quite old for a cat** para ser una gata es bastante mayor; **she's a beautiful ship** es un barco precioso; **s. likes red wine** le gusta el vino tinto; **who's s.?** *(pointing at sb)* ¿quién es ésa?
2 *n* **it's a s.** *(of animal)* es hembra

---

sheaf [ʃiːf] (*pl* **sheaves** [ʃiːvz]) *n (of wheat)* gavilla *f*; *(of arrows)* haz *m*; *(of papers)* manojo *m*

shear [ʃɪə(r)] (*pp* **shorn** [ʃɔːn] *or* **sheared**) 1 *vt* (**a**) *(sheep)* esquilar; **her blonde locks had been shorn** le habían cortado sus cabellos rubios; **he was shorn of all real power** le quitaron todo el poder (**b**) *(metal)* romper
2 *vi* (**a**) *(break)* romperse (**b**) *(cut)* **to s. through sth** atravesar *or* cortar algo

▸**shear off** *vi* romperse, quebrarse

shearer [ˈʃɪərə(r)] *n (person)* esquilador(ora) *m,f*

shearing [ˈʃɪərɪŋməˈʃiːn] *n* esquila *f*

shears [ˈʃɪəz] *npl (for garden)* tijeras *fpl* de podar *(grandes)*; *(for sheep)* tijeras *fpl* de esquilar

shearwater [ˈʃɪəwɔːtə(r)] *n* pardela *f* ▸▸ ***Manx s.*** pardela *f* pichoneta

sheath [ʃiːθ] *n* (**a**) *(for knife)* funda *f*; *(for sword)* vaina *f* ▸▸ ***s. dress*** vestido *m* tubo; ***s. knife*** cuchillo *m* de monte (**b**) *(for cable)* cubierta *f* (**c**) *(contraceptive)* condón *m* (**d**) *Bot, Anat & Zool* vaina *f*

sheathe [ʃiːð] *vt* (**a**) *(sword, dagger)* envainar (**b**) *(cables)* recubrir, revestir (**in** de)

sheathing [ˈʃiːðɪŋ] *n (of cable)* cubierta *f*

shebang [ʃəˈbæŋ] *n Fam* **the whole s.** todo, toda la pesca

shebeen [ʃɪˈbiːn] *n Irish, Scot, SAfr* bar *m* ilegal

she'd [ʃiːd] = **she had, she would**

shed[1] [ʃed] *n* (**a**) *(in garden)* cobertizo *m*; *(lean-to)* cobertizo *m* (**b**) *(in factory)* nave *f*, *Andes, Carib, RP* galpón *m*

shed[2] (*pt & pp* **shed**) *vt* (**a**) *(leaves)* perder; *(clothes)* quitarse; **to s. its skin** *(snake)* mudar la piel; **to s. weight** perder peso; **a lorry has s. its load on the motorway** un camión ha perdido su carga por la autopista (**b**) *(tears, blood)* derramar (**c**) *(workers)* despedir; *(inhibitions)* liberarse de (**d**) *(emit) (smell)* despedir; *Fig* **to s. light on sth** arrojar luz sobre algo

shedload [ˈʃedləʊd] *n Br Fam* montón *m*, *Esp* mogollón *m*; **they sold them by the s** vendieron montones *or Esp* mogollón

sheen [ʃiːn] *n* lustre *m*, brillo *m*

sheep [ʃiːp] (*pl* **sheep**) *n* (**a**) *(animal)* oveja *f* ▸▸ ***s. farmer*** criador(ora) *m,f* de ovejas; ***s. farming*** ganadería *f* ovina; ***s. station*** granja *f* para la cría de ovejas (**b**) IDIOMS **they followed her like s.** la seguían como borregos; **I may as well be hung for a s. as a lamb** de perdidos al río; **to separate the s. from the goats** separar las churras de las merinas; *Old-fashioned* **to make s.'s eyes at sb** mirar a alguien amorosamente

sheep-dip [ˈʃiːpdɪp] *n (liquid)* desinfectante *m* para ovejas

sheepdog [ˈʃiːpdɒg] *n* perro *m* pastor ▸▸ ***s. trials*** = competición en la que los perros ovejeros tienen que demostrar su habilidad conduciendo las ovejas

sheepfold [ˈʃiːpfəʊld] *n* redil *m*

sheepish [ˈʃiːpɪʃ] *adj* avergonzado(a), azarado(a)

sheepishly [ˈʃiːpɪʃlɪ] *adv* tímidamente

sheepshank [ˈʃiːpʃæŋk] *n* pierna *f or* pernil *m* de cordero

sheepskin [ˈʃiːpskɪn] *n* (**a**) *(textile)* piel *f* de oveja ▸▸ ***s. jacket*** zamarra *f* (**b**) *US Fam (diploma)* diploma *m*

sheer [ʃɪə(r)] *adj* (**a**) *(pure, total)* puro(a), verdadero(a); **it's s. madness** es una verdadera locura; **by s. accident** *or* **chance** por pura casualidad; **I achieved it by s. hard work** lo conseguí a costa de mucho esfuerzo; **we did it out of s. desperation** lo hicimos por pura desesperación; **the s. boredom of her job drove her mad** la extrema monotonía de su trabajo la volvió loca *or* hizo enloquecer; **I was impressed by the s. size of the building** la sola magnitud del edificio me dejó impresionado

(**b**) *(steep)* empinado(a), escarpado(a); **it's a s. 50 metre drop** hay una caída de 50 metros

(**c**) *(stockings, fabric)* fino(a), transparente

▸ **sheer away** *vi (ship)* desviarse; **to s. away from a subject** desviarse de un tema

▸ **sheer off** *vi (ship)* desviarse; **when he saw us, he sheered off in the opposite direction** al vernos se desvió en la dirección opuesta

sheet [ʃiːt] *n* (**a**) *(on bed)* sábana *f*; *(tarpaulin)* lona *f*; *Fam* **what's he like between the sheets?** ¿qué tal es en la cama?

(**b**) *(of paper)* hoja *f*; *(of stamps)* plancha *f* ▸▸ *Comptr* ***s. feeder*** alimentador *m* de hojas sueltas; ***s. music*** partituras *fpl* sueltas

(**c**) *(newspaper)* periódico *m*

(**d**) *(of glass)* hoja *f*; *(of metal, plastic)* lámina *f* ▸▸ ***s. metal*** chapa *f* (de metal)

(**e**) *(of ice)* capa *f*; *(of flame)* cortina *f*; **the rain came down in sheets** llovía a cántaros ▸▸ ***s. ice*** *(on road)* hielo *m* en capas; ***s. lightning*** relámpagos *mpl* (difusos)

(**f**) *Naut* escota *f*; IDIOM *Fam* **to be three sheets to the wind** estar como una cuba *or Esp, RP* mamado(a) *or Col* caído(a) (de la perra) *or Méx* ahogado(a) ▸▸ ***s. anchor*** *(of ship)* ancla *f* de la esperanza; *Fig* tabla *f* de salvación

sheetfeed [ˈʃiːtfiːd] *n Comptr* alimentador *m* de hojas sueltas

sheeting [ˈʃiːtɪŋ] *n (of metal)* láminas *fpl*, chapas *fpl*; *(of plastic)* laminado *m*

sheik(h) [ʃeɪk] *n* jeque *m*

sheik(h)dom [ˈʃeɪkdəm] *n* dominios *mpl* de un jeque

sheila [ˈʃiːlə] *n Austr, NZ Fam Esp* tía *f*, *Am* tipa *f*, *RP* mina *f*

shekel [ˈʃekəl] *n* (**a**) *(Israeli currency)* shekel *m* (**b**) *Fam* **shekels** *(money) Esp* pasta *f*, *Am* plata *f*

shelduck [ˈʃeldʌk] *n* tarro *f* blanco

shelf [ʃelf] (*pl* **shelves** [ʃelvz]) *n* (**a**) *(in cupboard, bookcase)* estante *m*, balda *f*; *(in oven)* parrilla *f*; *(in fridge)* estante *m*; **(set of) shelves** estantería *f*; **this software can be bought off the s.** este software se puede adquirir en versión estándar; IDIOM **to be left on the s.** quedarse para vestir santos ▸▸ *Com* ***s. life*** *(of goods)* vida *f* útil, vida *f* en estantería *or* expositor; **to have a short s. life** *(ideas, pop groups)* tener una vida corta; ***s. space*** espacio *m* de exposición

(**b**) *(on cliff, rock face)* plataforma *f*, saliente *m*; *(under sea)* plataforma *f* submarina

shell [ʃel] **1** *n* (**a**) *(of snail, oyster, on beach)* concha *f*; *(of lobster, crab, tortoise)* caparazón *m*; *(of egg, nut)* cáscara *f*; IDIOM **she soon came out of her s.** rápidamente salió de su concha *or* caparazón; **he crawled** *or* **went back into his s.** volvió a meterse en su caparazón ▸▸ *US* ***s. game*** *(game)* = truco que originalmente se hacía con tres cáscaras de nuez y un objeto pequeño en el que los apostadores debían adivinar debajo de cuál de las cáscaras se encontraba el objeto; ***s. suit*** *Esp* chándal *m or Méx* pants *mpl or RP* jogging *m* de nylon

(**b**) *(of building)* esqueleto *m*, armazón *m or f*; *(of car, machine)* armazón *m*, estructura *f*; *(of ship)* casco *m*

(**c**) *(bomb)* proyectil *m*; *US (cartridge)* cartucho *m*

(**d**) *Comptr* shell *m*

(**e**) *Culin* base *f*

2 *vt* (**a**) *(nuts, eggs)* pelar; *(peas)* desgranar; *(prawns)* pelar; *(oyster)* quitarle la concha a (**b**) *(bombard)* atacar con fuego de artillería

▸ **shell out** *Fam* **1** *vt sep (money)* poner, *Esp* apoquinar

2 *vi* poner, *Esp* apoquinar; **to s. out for sth** pagar algo

she'll [ʃiːl] = **she will, she shall**

shellac [ˈʃelæk] **1** *n* **s. (varnish)** laca *f*

2 *vt* (*pt & pp* **shellacked**) (**a**) *(varnish)* laquear (**b**) *US Fam (defeat)* dar una paliza a

shellacking [ʃəˈlækɪŋ] *n US Fam* (**a**) *(defeat)* paliza *f*; **to give sb a s.** dar una paliza a alguien (**b**) *(beating)* paliza *f*; **to give sb a s.** dar una paliza a alguien

shellfire [ˈʃelfaɪə(r)] *n* fuego *m* de artillería; **to be under s.** ser bombardeado(a), estar *or* encontrarse bajo fuego de artillería

shellfish [ˈʃelfɪʃ] *n* (**a**) *(crustacean)* crustáceo *m*; *(mollusc)* molusco *m* (**b**) *(food)* marisco *m*

shelling [ˈʃelɪŋ] *n* ataque *m* de artillería

shellproof [ˈʃelpruːf] *adj* a prueba de bombas

shell-shock [ˈʃelʃɒk] *n* neurosis *f inv* de guerra

shell-shocked [ˈʃelʃɒkt] *adj (soldier)* que sufre neurosis de guerra; *Fig* **to feel s.** sentirse traumatizado(a)

shelter [ˈʃeltə(r)] **1** *n* (**a**) *(protection)* refugio *m*; **to take s. (from)** refugiarse (de); **we ran for s.** corrimos a refugiarnos; **where can we find s.?** ¿dónde podemos refugiarnos? (**b**) *(accommodation)* **to give sb s.** dar refugio *or* cobijo a alguien (**c**) *(construction)* refugio *m*; *(for homeless people, battered wives)* refugio *m*

2 *vt* (**a**) *((protect) (from rain, sun, bombs)* resguardar, proteger (**from** de); *(from blame, suspicion)* proteger (**from** de) (**b**) *(fugitive, refugee)* proteger, acoger

3 *vi* resguardarse, refugiarse (**from** de)

sheltered [ˈʃeltəd] *adj (position, garden, waters)* resguardado(a); **he had a s. childhood** fue un niño muy protegido ▸▸ *Br* ***s. accommodation*** *or* ***housing*** = hogares con atención especial para ancianos

shelve [ʃelv] **1** *vt (postpone)* aparcar, posponer

2 *vi (ground)* descender

shelves *pl of* **shelf**

shelving [ˈʃelvɪŋ] *n (shelves)* estanterías *fpl*

shenanigans [ʃɪˈnænɪgənz] *npl Fam* (**a**) *(pranks)* travesuras *fpl* (**b**) *(underhand behaviour)* chanchullos *mpl*, tejemanejes *mpl*

shepherd [ˈʃepəd] **1** *n* pastor *m* ▸▸ ***s. boy*** niño *m* pastor; ***s.'s pie*** = pastel de carne picada y puré de *Esp* patatas *or Am* papas; ***s.'s purse*** *(plant)* bolsa *f* de pastor, pan *m* y quesillo

2 *vt* (**a**) *(sheep)* pastorear (**b**) *(people)* dirigir; **to s. sb out of a room** conducir a alguien fuera de una habitación; **we were shepherded round the museum in under an hour** nos hicieron recorrer todo el museo en menos de una hora

shepherdess [ʃepəˈdes] *n* pastora *f*

sherbet [ˈʃɜːbət] *n* (**a**) *Br (powder)* = dulce consistente en polvos efervescentes (**b**) *US (sorbet)* sorbete *m*

sheriff [ˈʃerɪf] *n* (**a**) *(in US)* sheriff *m* (**b**) *Law (in England and Wales)* = representante de la Corona (**c**) *Law (in Scotland)* ≃ juez *mf* de primera instancia ▸▸ ***s. court*** ≃ juzgado *m or* tribunal *m* de primera instancia

Sherpa [ˈʃɜːpə] *n* sherpa *mf*

sherry [ˈʃerɪ] *n* jerez *m* ▸▸ ***s. glass*** copa *f* de jerez

she's [ʃiːz] = **she is, she has**

Shetland [ˈʃetlənd] *n* **the S. Islands, the S. Isles, the Shetlands** las Islas Shetland ▸▸ ***S. pony*** pony *m* de Shetland; ***S. wool*** lana *f* shetland

shh [ʃ] *exclam* ¡chis!

Shia(h) [ˈʃiːə] **1** *n* (**a**) *(religion)* chiísmo *m* (**b**) *(Shiite)* **S. (Muslim)** chiíta *mf*

2 *adj* chiíta

shiatsu [ʃiːˈætsuː] *n* shiatsu *m*

shibboleth [ˈʃɪbəleθ] *n* consigna *f*, rasgo *m* distintivo

shield [ʃiːld] **1** *n* (**a**) *(of knight, in heraldry)* escudo *m* (**b**) *(police badge)* placa *f* (**c**) *(trophy)* placa *f* (**d**) *(protective device)* placa *f* protectora (**e**) *Fig (protection)* protección *f*

2 *vt (protect)* proteger (**from** de); **to s. one's eyes** protegerse los ojos

shift [ʃɪft] **1** *n* (**a**) *(change)* cambio *m*; **there was a light s. in the wind** el viento cambió ligeramente de dirección; **there was a sudden s. in public opinion** hubo un repentino cambio en la opinión pública; **there's been a s. towards holidaying abroad** ahora hay una nueva tendencia a irse de vacaciones al extranjero; **a s. in meaning** un cambio de significado; **a s. to the right/left** *(in politics)* un desplazamiento hacia la derecha/izquierda

(**b**) *Ind* turno *m*; **to work (in) shifts** trabajar por turnos; **she works long shifts** trabaja turnos largos; **when does** *or* **do the morning s. arrive?** ¿a qué hora llegan los del turno de la mañana? ▸▸ ***s. pattern*** esquema *m* de turnos; ***s. worker*** trabajador(ora) *m,f* por turnos

(**c**) *(turn)* turno *m*; **to do sth in shifts** hacer algo por turnos

(**d**) *(dress)* vestido *m* recto; *Old-fashioned (woman's slip)* enagua *f*

(**e**) *US Aut* ***s. (stick)*** (palanca *f* de) cambios *mpl*

(**f**) *Comptr* **press s.** presionar la tecla de mayúsculas ▸▸ ***s. key*** tecla *f* de mayúsculas

(**g**) IDIOM *Fam* **get a s. on!** *(hurry up)* ¡muévete!

2 *vt* (**a**) *(move)* mover; *(scenery)* cambiar; **help me s. the bed nearer the window** ayúdame a mover la cama más cerca de la ventana; *Fam* **s. yourself!** *(move)* ¡apártate!, ¡quita *or Am* saca de en medio!; *(hurry up)* ¡date prisa!, *Esp* ¡aligera!, *Am* ¡apúrate!

(**b**) *(transfer)* **to s. allegiance** cambiar de bando; **the latest developments have shifted attention away from this area** los últimos acontecimientos han desplazado el foco de atención a otras áreas; **we're trying to s. the balance towards exports** estamos intentando redireccionar nuestras actividades hacia las exportaciones; **to s. the blame onto sb** transferir la culpa a a alguien; **he shifted his weight onto his right leg** pasó el peso de su cuerpo a la pierna derecha

(**c**) *(remove) (stain)* eliminar

(**d**) *US Aut* **to s. gears** cambiar de marcha

(**e**) *Fam (sell)* vender

(**f**) *Fam (eat, drink)* cepillarse; **hurry up and s. that beer!** ¡vamos, cepíllate esa cerveza!, *Arg* ¡dale, mandate esa cerveza!

3 *vi* (**a**) *(move)* moverse; **he shifted onto his side** se puso de lado; **she kept shifting uneasily from one foot to the other** nerviosa, cambiaba todo el tiempo su pie de apoyo; *Fam* **come on, s.!** *(get out of the way)* vamos, ¡fuera!

(**b**) *(change)* cambiar; *(wind)* cambiar de dirección; **attention has shifted away from this issue** la atención ya no está centrada en este tema; **the consensus is shifting towards banning the substance** hay cada vez más consenso para prohibir la sustancia

(**c**) *(stain)* irse

(**d**) *US Aut* cambiar de marcha; **to s. into fourth (gear)** meter la cuarta

(**e**) *Fam (move quickly)* ir a toda mecha; **this bike can really s.!** ¡esta moto va a toda mecha!

(**f**) **to s. for oneself** *(cope)* arreglárselas *or Esp* apañárselas solo(a)

▸ **shift over, shift up** *vi Br* correrse, hacerse a un lado

shiftily [ˈʃɪftɪlɪ] *adv (to behave, loiter)* de forma sospechosa; *(to look)* evasivamente

shiftless [ˈʃɪftlɪs] *adj* holgazán(ana)

shiftlessness [ˈʃɪftlɪsnɪs] *n* holgazanería *f*

shiftwork [ˈʃɪftwɜːk] *n Ind* trabajo *m* por turnos

shifty [ˈʃɪftɪ] *adj (person)* sospechoso(a); *(look, eyes)* evasivo(a)

shi(i)take [ʃɪˈtækɪ] *n* ***s. mushroom*** shitake *m*

Shiite [ˈʃiːaɪt] **1** *n* chiíta *mf*

2 *adj* chiíta

shillelagh [ʃɪˈleɪlɪ] *n* cachiporra *f*

shilling [ˈʃɪlɪŋ] *n* chelín *m*; *Old-fashioned* **to take the (King's** *or* **Queen's) s.** alistarse en el ejército

shilly-shally [ˈʃɪlɪˈʃælɪ] *vi Fam Pej* **stop shilly-shallying around!** ¡deja ya de darle vueltas!

shilly-shallying [ʃɪlɪˈʃælɪɪŋ] *n Fam Pej* **after a lot of s. they eventually came to an agreement** después de darle muchas vueltas llegaron a un acuerdo

shim [ʃɪm] *n* calce *m*, cuña *f*

shimmer [ˈʃɪmə(r)] **1** *n* brillo *m* trémulo

2 *vi* rielar

shimmering [ˈʃɪmərɪŋ] *adj* con brillo trémulo; **a dress of s. silk** un vestido de seda con un delicado brillo

shimmy [ˈʃɪmɪ] *n* (**a**) *(dance)* shimmy *m* (**b**) *Sport (sidestep)* amago *m* (**c**) *Aut* vibraciones *fpl*

shin [ʃɪn] **1** *n* (**a**) *Anat* espinilla *f*, *RP* canilla *f* ▸▸ ***s. guard*** espinillera *f*; ***s. pad*** espinillera *f*, *RP* canillera *f* (**b**) *(of beef)* jarrete *m*, *Arg* pata *f*

2 *vi (pt & pp* **shinned**) *(climb)* **to s. up/down a tree** trepar a/bajar de un árbol

shinbone [ˈʃɪnbəʊn] *n* tibia *f*

shindig [ˈʃɪndɪg], **shindy** [ˈʃɪndɪ] *n Fam* (**a**) *(party)* fiestón *m*, *RP* fiestichola *f* (**b**) *(din)* jaleo *m*, lío *m*, *Esp* follón *m* ; **to kick up a s.** armar un jaleo *or* lío *or Esp* follón

shine [ʃaɪn] **1** *n* (**a**) *(polish)* brillo *m*, lustre *m*; **to give one's shoes a s.** sacar brillo a los zapatos; IDIOM **to take the s. off sth** empañar *or* deslucir algo; IDIOM *Fam* **to take a s. to sb** tomar cariño a alguien (**b**) *US very Fam (black person)* = término ofensivo para referirse a una persona negra

2 *vt (pt & pp* **shone** [ʃɒn]) (**a**) *(light)* **to s. a torch on sth/sb** enfocar una linterna hacia algo/alguien; **to s. a light on sth** alumbrar algo; **don't s. that lamp in my eyes** no me apuntes con esa lámpara (**b**) *(pt & pp* **shined** [ʃaɪnd]) *(polish)* sacar brillo a

3 *vi* (**a**) *(glow)* brillar; **the sun was shining in my eyes** me daba el sol en los ojos; **there was a light shining in the window** una luz brillaba en la ventana; **her face shone with joy** estaba resplandeciente de alegría (**b**) *(do well)* destacar (**at** en)

▸ **shine through** *vi* (**a**) *(light)* filtrarse (**b**) *(courage, skill, generosity)* destacarse, brillar

shiner [ˈʃaɪnə(r)] *n Fam (black eye)* ojo *m* morado *or Esp* a la virulé

shingle [ˈʃɪŋgəl] *n* (**a**) *(wooden tile)* teja *f* de madera (**b**) *(pebbles)* guijarros *mpl* (**c**) *US (nameplate)* placa *f* con el nombre; IDIOM **to hang out one's s.** abrir un consultorio/despacho/*etc.* (**d**) *(haircut)* corte *m* a lo garçon

shingles [ˈʃɪŋgəlz] *n (disease)* herpes *m inv* (zoster); **to have s.** tener un herpes (zoster)

shingly [ˈʃɪŋglɪ] *adj (beach)* de guijarros

shininess [ˈʃaɪnɪnɪs] *n* brillo *m*

shining [ˈʃaɪnɪŋ] *adj (glass, metal, shoes, eyes)* brillante, reluciente; *(face)* brillante, lustroso(a); *Fig* **a s. example (of)** un ejemplo señero *or* brillante (de)

shinny [ˈʃɪnɪ] *vi (pt & pp* **shinnied**) *US (climb)* **to s. up/down a tree** trepar a/bajar de un árbol

Shinto [ˈʃɪntəʊ] *n* sintoísmo *m*

shinty [ˈʃɪntɪ] *n* = deporte similar al hockey sobre hierba

shiny [ˈʃaɪnɪ] *adj* brillante, reluciente; **he has a s. nose** tiene la nariz lustrosa; **her jacket is s. at the elbows** los codos de la chaqueta le brillan del desgaste

ship [ʃɪp] **1** *n* (**a**) *(boat)* barco *m*, buque *m*; **to go by s.** ir en barco; **on (board) s.** a bordo (de la embarcación); **the ship's company** la tripulación; *Fig* **the s. of the desert** *(camel)* el camello ▸▸ ***s. broker*** agente *mf* marítimo(a) (**b**) *(spaceship)* nave *f* (**c**) IDIOMS **when my s. comes in** cuando me haga rico(a); **like ships that pass in the night** como aves de paso, como extraños

2 *vt (pt & pp* **shipped**) (**a**) *Com (deliver) (goods, order)* despachar (**b**) *(send by sea)* enviar por barco (**c**) *(take on board)* cargar (**d**) *Naut* **to s. oars** levantar los remos; **to s. water** hacer agua (**e**) *Sport (concede)* **the team has been shipping goals all season** la defensa ha encajado innumerables goles toda esta temporada

3 *vi Com (goods, order)* ser enviado(a)

▸ **ship off** *vt sep Fam* mandar

▸ **ship out** *vt sep (goods, belongings)* enviar por barco; *(troops)* transportar por barco

shipboard [ˈʃɪpbɔːd] *n Naut* **on s.** a bordo

shipbuilder [ˈʃɪpbɪldə(r)] *n* constructor *m* naval *or* de buques

shipbuilding [ˈʃɪpbɪldɪŋ] *n* construcción *f* naval; **the s. industry** la industria naval

shipload [ˈʃɪpləʊd] *n* cargamento *m*, carga *f*; *Fig* **by the s.** a montones

shipmate [ˈʃɪpmeɪt] *n Naut* compañero *m* de tripulación

shipment [ˈʃɪpmənt] *n* (**a**) *(goods sent)* cargamento *m*; **an illegal arms s.** un cargamento ilegal de armas (**b**) *(sending of goods)* despacho *m*, envío *m*

shipowner [ˈʃɪpəʊnə(r)] *n* armador(ora) *m,f*, naviero(a) *m,f*

shipper [ˈʃɪpə(r)] *n* consignador(ora) *m,f*

shipping [ˈʃɪpɪŋ] *n* (**a**) *(ships)* navíos *mpl*, buques *mpl*; *Rad* **"attention all s."** "atención a todas las embarcaciones" ▸▸ ***s. agent*** *(person)* agente *mf* marítimo(a), consignatario(a) *m,f*; *(company)* compañía *f* naviera; ***s. company*** compañía *f* naviera; ***s. forecast*** parte *m* marítimo; ***s. lane*** ruta *f* de navegación; ***s. line*** naviera *f* (**b**) *(of goods)* flete *m*, envío *m* ▸▸ ***s. clerk*** expedidor(ora) *m,f*; ***s. documents*** documentos *mpl* de embarque

shipshape [ˈʃɪpʃeɪp] *adj* ordenado(a), en perfecto orden; **let's try to get this place s.** vamos a ordenar bien este sitio

shipwreck [ˈʃɪprek] **1** *n* (**a**) *(disaster at sea)* naufragio *m* (**b**) *(wrecked ship)* barco *m* naufragado

2 *vt* **to be shipwrecked** naufragar; **they were shipwrecked on a desert island** después del naufragio, quedaron varados en una isla desierta

shipwrecked [ˈʃɪprekt] *adj* náufrago(a); **a s. woman** una náufraga

shipwright [ˈʃɪpraɪt] *n Naut* carpintero *m* de ribera

shipyard [ˈʃɪpjɑːd] *n* astillero *m*

shire [ˈʃaɪə(r)] *n* (**a**) *(county)* condado *m*; **the s. counties, the Shires** los condados del centro de Inglaterra (**b**) *(animal)* ***s. (horse)*** (caballo *m*) percherón *m*

shirk [ʃɜːk] **1** *vt (obligation, task)* eludir

2 *vi (avoid work)* gandulear

shirker [ˈʃɜːkə(r)] *n Fam* vago(a) *m,f*, gandul(ula) *m,f*, *Méx* flojo(a) *m,f*, *RP* vagoneta *mf*

shirt [ʃɜːt] *n* (**a**) *(item of clothing)* camisa *f* ►► *US* ***s. jacket*** camisa *f* chaqueta (**b**) IDIOMS *Fam* **keep your s. on!** ¡no te sulfures!; **I wouldn't bet** *or* **put my s. on it** no pondría la mano en el fuego; **to have the s. off sb's back** quitarle *orAm* sacarle a alguien hasta la camisa; **to lose one's s.** perder hasta la camisa

shirtcollar [ˈʃɜːtkɒlə(r)] *n* cuello *m* de (la) camisa

shirt-dress [ˈʃɜːtdres] *n* blusa *f*, *RP* chemisier *f*

shirtfront [ˈʃɜːtfrʌnt] *n* pechera *f*

shirtless [ˈʃɜːtlɪs] *adj* sin camisa, descamisado(a)

shirt-lifter [ˈʃɜːtlɪftə(r)] *n Br Fam Pej* marica *m*

shirtmaker [ˈʃɜːtmeɪkə(r)] *n* camisero(a) *m,f*

shirtsleeves [ˈʃɜːtsliːvz] *npl* **to be in (one's) s.** estar en mangas de camisa

shirt-tail [ˈʃɜːtteɪl] *n* faldón *m* de la camisa

shirtwaister [ˈʃɜːtweɪstə(r)] *n* blusa *f*, *RP* chemisier *f*

shirty [ˈʃɜːtɪ] *adj Br Fam* **to be s.** estar mosqueado(a) *or* de mala uva; **to get s. (with sb)** mosquearse (con alguien)

shish kebab [ˈʃɪʃkəˈbæb] *n* kebab *m*, pincho *m* moruno

shit [ʃɪt] *Vulg* **1** *n* (**a**) *(excrement)* mierda *f*; **to** *Br* **have** *or US* **take a s.** cagar; **to have the shits** tener cagalera *or RP* cagadera, *Méx* estar suelto(a)

(**b**) *(nonsense) Esp* gilipolleces *fpl*, *Am* pendejadas *fpl*, *RP* pelotudeces *fpl*; **that's a load of s.!** *Esp* ¡qué gilipollez!, *RP* ¡es una boludez tremenda!; **he's full of s.** no dice más que *Esp* gilipolleces *or Am* pendejadas; **don't give me that s.!** no me vengas con esas *Esp* gilipolleces *orAm* pendejadas; **I hate it when he starts on his anarchy s.** *Esp* lo odio cuando comienza con sus gilipolleces anarquistas, *RP* me embola cuando empieza con esa boludez del anarquismo; **to talk s.** decir *Esp* gilipolleces *orAm* pendejadas; **no s.?** ¡no jodas!, ¿en serio?

(**c**) *(worthless, unpleasant things)* mierda *f*, porquería *f*; **to be a load of s.**, *US* **to be the shits** ser una mierda; **clear all that s. off your desk** quita toda esa porquería de tu mesa; **I can't eat this s.** esta mierda es incomible

(**d**) *(unfair treatment)* **to give sb s.** tratar de culo a alguien, *RP* tener cagando a alguien; **don't take any s. from him!** no permitas que te dé por culo *or RP* que te cague; **I don't need this s.!** ¡no me toques los huevos!

(**e**) *(nasty person)* cabrón(ona) *m,f*, hijo(a) *m,f* de puta; **he's been a real s. to her** ha sido un verdadero hijo de puta con ella

(**f**) *(cannabis)* chocolate *m*, *Esp* mierda *f*; *(heroin)* caballo *m*

(**g**) IDIOMS **to treat sb like s.** tratar a alguien de puta pena; **to feel like s.** *(ill)* sentirse de puta pena *or Méx* de la chingada *or RP* para la mierda; **he's in the s.** está jodidísimo, *Esp* tiene un marrón que te cagas; **you've really dropped us in the s.** nos has jodido bien; **he doesn't give a s.** le importa un huevo; **who gives a s.?** ¿a quién cojones le importa?; **I can't see s.** no veo una mierda *or Esp* un pijo; **he doesn't do s.** se está tocando los huevos constantemente; **to beat** *or* **kick** *or* **knock the s. out of sb** inflar a alguien a hostias; **to bore the s. out of sb** aburrir muchísimo a alguien, *Arg* embolar a alguien al mango; **to scare the s. out of sb** hacer cagarse de miedo a alguien, *Esp* acojonar a alguien, *Méx* sacar un pedo a alguien, *RP* hacer que alguien se cague hasta las patas; **when the s. hits the fan** cuando la cosa se pone fea *or Esp* chunga; **to get one's s. together** ponerse las pilas; **to be up s. creek (without a paddle)** ir muy mal *or* de puto culo; **tough s.!** ¡te jodes!, *Esp* ¡jódete y baila!; **eat s. (and die)!** ¡vete bien a la mierda! *Arg* ¡andate a la concha de tu madre!; **s. happens** hay que joderse y aguantarse

2 *adj (bad)* de mierda; **it's a s. film** es una mierda de película; **he's a s. driver** conduce de puta pena, *RP* maneja como el culo; **to feel s.** *(ill, guilty)* sentirse de puta pena *or Méx* de la chingada *or RP* para la mierda; **I had a really s. time** lo pasé de puta pena *or Méx* de la chingada *or RP* para la mierda

3 *adv* **to be s. out of luck** estar muy jodido(a), *Arg* estar hecho mierda

4 *vt (pt & pp* **shitted** *or* **shat** [ʃæt]) (**a**) **to s. oneself** *(defecate)* cagarse (encima); *(be scared)* cagarse *or Esp* jiñarse de miedo; IDIOM **to s. a brick** *or* **bricks** cagarse de miedo (**b**) *US* **to s. sb** *(lie to, deceive)* mentir *or RP* joder a alguien

5 *vi* (**a**) *(defecate)* cagar; IDIOM **s. or get off the pot** decídete de una maldita vez (**b**) **to s. on sb** *(treat badly)* joder a alguien (**c**) *US (react with anger, surprise)* cabrearse, *Arg* ponerse del tomate

6 *exclam* ¡mierda!, *RP* ¡la puta!

shitake = **shiitake**

shit-ass [ˈʃɪtæs] *n US Vulg (person)* hijo(a) de puta *m,f*, cerdo(a) *m,f*

shit-can [ˈʃɪtkæn] *vt US Vulg (discard, abandon)* tirar *or* mandar a la mierda

shite [ʃaɪt] *Br Vulg* **1** *n* (**a**) *(excrement)* mierda *f*

(**b**) *(nonsense) Esp* gilipolleces *fpl*, *Am* pendejadas *fpl*, *RP* pelotudeces *fpl*; **he's full of s.** no dice más que *Esp* gilipolleces *orAm* pendejadas; **to talk s.** decir *Esp* gilipolleces *orAm* pendejadas; **that's (a load of) s.!** eso es una *Esp* gilipollez *orAm* pendejada

(**c**) *(worthless, unpleasant things)* mierda *f*, porquería *f*; **to be a load of s.** ser una mierda; **clear all that s. off your desk** quita toda esa porquería de tu mesa; **I can't eat this s.** esta mierda está incomible

(**d**) *(nasty person)* cabrón(ona) *m,f*, hijo(a) *m,f* de puta

2 *adj (bad)* de mierda; **it's a s. film** es una mierda de película; **he's a s. driver** conduce de puta pena, *RP* maneja como el culo; **to feel s.** *(ill, guilty)* sentirse de puta pena *or Méx* de la chingada *or RP* para la mierda; **I had a really s. time** lo pasé de puta pena *or Méx* de la chingada *or RP* para la mierda

3 *exclam* ¡mierda!, *RP* ¡la puta!

shit-faced [ˈʃɪtfeɪst] *adj Vulg* (**a**) *(drunk)* **to be s.** estar *Esp* pedo *or Méx* ahogado(a) *or RP* en pedo; **to get s.** ponerse *Esp* pedo *or Méx* ahogado(a) *or RP* en pedo (**b**) *(on drugs)* **to be s.** estar colocado(a) *or Esp* pedo *or Col* trabado(a) *or RP* falopeado(a); **to get s.** ponerse *Esp* pedo *or Col* trabado(a), *RP* falopearse

shit-for-brains [ˈʃɪtfəbreɪnz] *n Vulg Esp* gilipollas *mf inv*, *Am* pendejo(a) *m,f*

shithead [ˈʃɪthed] *n Vulg* hijo(a) *m,f* de puta, cabrón(ona) *m,f*, *Méx* hijo(a) *m,f* de la chingada

shit-heel [ˈʃɪthiːl] *n US Vulg (person)* cabrón(ona) *m,f*, *Arg* forro(a) *m,f*

shithole [ˈʃɪthəʊl] *n Vulg (dirty place)* mierda *f*; **this town's a complete s.** este pueblo es una mierda

shit-hot [ˈʃɪthɒt] *adj Vulg Esp* cojonudo(a), *Esp* acojonante, *Méx* chingón(ona)

shithouse [ˈʃɪthaʊs] *n Vulg (toilet)* cagódromo *m*

shit-kicker [ˈʃɪtkɪkə(r)] *n US Vulg (farmhand)* peón *m*; *(rustic)* pueblerino(a) *m,f*

shitless [ˈʃɪtlɪs] *adj Vulg* **to scare sb s.** hacer cagarse de miedo a alguien, *Esp* acojonar a alguien, *Méx* sacar un pedo a alguien, *RP* hacer que alguien se cague hasta las patas; **to be scared s.** estar cagado(a) de miedo, *Esp* estar acojonado(a); **he's scared s. of her brother** su hermano lo tiene cagado de miedo *or Esp* acojonado, *RP* le tiene un cagazo bárbaro a su hermano; **to be bored s.** estar más aburrido(a) que la hostia

shitload [ˈʃɪtləʊd] *n Vulg* **he bought a (whole) s. of** *or* **shitloads of books** compró una porrada *or Esp* un huevo *or Méx* un chingo de libros

shit-scared [ˈʃɪtˈskeəd] *adj Vulg* **to be s.** estar cagado(a) de miedo, *Esp* estar acojonado(a)

shit-stirrer [ˈʃɪtstɜːrə(r)] *n Vulg* camorrero(a) *m,f*, *Esp* follonero(a) *m,f*, *Méx* buscarriñas *mf inv*

shitty [ˈʃɪtɪ] *adj Vulg (weather, job, hotel)* de mierda, *Esp* chungo(a), *RP* chotísimo(a); *(behaviour, remark)* muy cabrón(ona); **that was a s. thing of him to do/say** eso que hizo/dijo fue una cabronada *or* putada; **to feel s.** sentirse de puta pena *or Méx* de la chingada *or RP* para la mierda

shiv [ʃɪv] *US Fam* **1** *n (knife)* cuchillo *m*

2 *vt (stab)* acuchillar a

shiver [ˈʃɪvə(r)] **1** *n (of cold, fear, fever, excitement)* escalofrío *m*; **to give sb the shivers** poner los pelos de punta a alguien; **it sent shivers down my spine** me produjo *or* dio escalofríos

2 *vi (with cold, fever)* tiritar (**with** de); *(with fear)* temblar (**with** de); *(with excitement)* estremecerse (**with** de)

shivery [ˈʃɪvərɪ] *adj (cold)* tembloroso(a); *(feverish)* con escalofríos

shoal [ʃəʊl] *n* (**a**) *(of fish)* banco *m* (**b**) *(of people)* manada *f* (**c**) *(sandbank)* banco *m* de arena

shoat [ʃəʊt] *n* lechón *m* destetado

shock[1] [ʃɒk] *n* **a s. of hair** una mata de pelo, una pelambrera

shock[2] 1 *n* (**a**) *(surprise)* susto *m*; *(emotional blow)* conmoción *f*; **a s. to the system** un palo enorme; **I got** *or* **it gave me a real s. when...** me quedé de piedra cuando...; **you gave me a s.!** ¡qué susto me has dado!; **the party is still in s. after its election defeat** el partido aún está conmocionado tras la derrota electoral; **they're in for a s.** se van a llevar una tremenda sorpresa; **to come as a s./as no s. (to sb)** suponer/no suponer una gran sorpresa (para alguien); *Fam Hum* **s. horror!** ¡qué horror! ▸▸ ***s. defeat*** derrota *f* inesperada; *US Fam* ***s. jock*** = presentador de programa de radio que busca impactar o generar polémica de manera deliberada; ***s. tactics*** *(in campaign)* tácticas *fpl* sensacionalistas

(**b**) *(impact)* sacudida *f*; *(of earthquake)* temblor *m* ▸▸ ***s. absorber*** amortiguador *m*; *Mil* ***s. troops*** tropas *fpl* de choque; ***s. wave*** onda *f* expansiva *or* de choque; **the news sent s. waves through the scientific community** la noticia sacudió a la comunidad científica

(**c**) *(electric)* calambrazo *m*, descarga *f* (eléctrica); **to get a s.** recibir una descarga ▸▸ ***s. therapy*** *or* ***treatment*** terapia *f* de electrochoque

(**d**) *Med* shock *m*; **to be in (a state of) s., to be suffering from s.** estar en estado de shock; **to go into s.** sufrir un shock

(**e**) *Fam (shock absorber)* amortiguador *m*

2 *vt* (**a**) *(surprise)* dejar boquiabierto(a); *(upset)* conmocionar; *(startle)* dar un susto a; **I was shocked to hear that she had left** me quedé impresionada cuando oí que se había ido; **she was deeply shocked by her daughter's death** quedó conmocionada por la muerte de su hija; **to s. sb into doing sth** amedrentar a alguien para que haga algo; **the news reports shocked them out of their apathy** las noticias los despertaron de su apatía

(**b**) *(scandalize)* escandalizar; **he's easily shocked** se escandaliza por nada

3 *vi* escandalizar

shockable ['ʃɒkəbəl] *adj* **he's easily/not easily s.** se impresiona/no se impresiona con facilidad

shocked [ʃɒkt] *adj* (**a**) *(surprised)* sorprendido(a); *(upset)* conmocionado(a); **a s. meeting was told of the takeover** los reunidos se quedaron conmocionados cuando supieron la noticia de la absorción; **they listened in s. silence to the news of her death** escucharon en dolido silencio la noticia de su muerte (**b**) *(scandalized)* escandalizado(a)

shocker ['ʃɒkə(r)] *n Fam* (**a**) *(surprise)* bombazo *m*, escándalo *m* (**b**) *(very bad thing)* desastre *m* (**c**) *Hum (naughty child)* **you little s.!** ¡pequeño granuja!, *Arg* ¡atorrante!

shocking ['ʃɒkɪŋ] *adj* (**a**) *(scandalous) (prices, behaviour)* escandaloso(a) (**b**) *(horrifying) (crime, truth)* horripilante, espeluznante (**c**) *(very bad) (film, actor, performance)* pésimo(a); *(cough)* espantoso(a); *(weather)* de perros; *(pain)* insoportable; **his room is in a s. state** su habitación está en un estado penoso (**d**) *(garish)* **s. pink** rosa chillón

shockingly ['ʃɒkɪŋlɪ] *adv* (**a**) *(extremely) (bad)* espantosamente, terriblemente; *(expensive)* escandalosamente (**b**) *(extremely badly)* terriblemente mal

shockproof ['ʃɒkpru:f] *adj (watch)* antichoque

shod *pt & pp of* **shoe**

shoddily ['ʃɒdɪlɪ] *adv* (**a**) *(made, built)* chapuceramente (**b**) *(to behave, treat)* de un modo pésimo

shoddiness ['ʃɒdɪnɪs] *n* (**a**) *(of goods)* mala calidad *f*; *(of workmanship)* lo chapucero (**b**) *(of conduct, treatment)* lo pésimo

shoddy ['ʃɒdɪ] 1 *adj* (**a**) *(goods)* de mala calidad; *(workmanship)* chapucero(a) (**b**) *(conduct, treatment)* pésimo(a)

2 *n (wool)* lana *f* regenerada

shoe [ʃu:] 1 *n* (**a**) *(for person)* zapato *m*; **a pair of shoes** unos zapatos, un par de zapatos; **the s. section** *(of a shop)* la sección de zapatería; **he wasn't wearing any shoes, he didn't have any shoes on** iba descalzo; IDIOM **I wouldn't like to be in his shoes** no me gustaría estar en su pellejo; IDIOM **put yourself in my shoes** ponte en mi lugar; IDIOM **to step into** *or* **to fill sb's shoes** pasar a ocupar el lugar de alguien ▸▸ ***s. box*** caja *f* de zapatos; ***s. cream*** betún *m*; ***the s. industry*** la industria *or* el sector del calzado; ***s. leather:*** **I wore out a lot of s. leather looking for it** gasté muchos zapatos buscándolo; ***s. polish*** betún *m*; ***s. shop*** zapatería *f*; ***s. size*** número *m* de zapato; **what s. size do you take?** ¿qué número calza?; ***s. tree*** horma *f*

(**b**) *(horseshoe)* herradura *f*

(**c**) *(of brake)* zapata *f*

2 *vt* (*pt & pp* **shod** [ʃɒd]) (**a**) *(horse)* herrar (**b**) *Literary (person)* **John was shod in sandals** John calzaba sandalias

shoeblack ['ʃu:blæk] *n Old-fashioned* limpiabotas *mf inv*, lustrabotas *mf inv*

shoebrush ['ʃu:brʌʃ] *n* cepillo *m (para zapatos)*

shoehorn ['ʃu:hɔ:n] *n* calzador *m*

shoelace ['ʃu:leɪs] *n* cordón *m* (de zapato); **to tie one's shoelaces** atarse (los cordones de) los zapatos

shoemaker ['ʃu:meɪkə(r)] *n* zapatero(a) *m,f*

shoe-polishing machine ['ʃu:pɒlɪʃɪŋməʃi:n] *n* máquina *f* para limpiar zapatos

shoeshine ['ʃu:ʃaɪn] *n* (**a**) *(action)* **could I get a s.?** ¿me podría sacar brillo a los zapatos? (**b**) *US (person)* limpiabotas *mf inv*

shoestring ['ʃu:strɪŋ] *n* (**a**) IDIOM *Fam* **on a s.** *(cheaply)* con cuatro perras, sin mucha *Am* plata *or Méx* lana, *RP* con dos mangos (**b**) *US* cordón *m* (de zapato)

shone *pt & pp of* **shine**

shoo [ʃu:] 1 *exclam* ¡fuera!

2 *vt* **she shooed the children out of the kitchen** echó a los niños de la cocina

▸ **shoo away, shoo off** *vt sep* espantar

shoo-in ['ʃu:ɪn] *n US Fam* **he was a s. for the leadership election** tenía asegurada la elección como líder

shook *pt of* **shake**

shook-up [ʃʊk'ʌp] *adj Fam* conmocionado(a)

shoot [ʃu:t] 1 *n* (**a**) *(of plant)* retoño *m*, vástago *m* (**b**) *(hunting party)* cacería *f*; *(land)* coto *m* de caza (**c**) *(for photos)* sesión *f* fotográfica; *(for movie)* rodaje *m*

2 (*pt & pp* **shot** [ʃɒt]) *vt* (**a**) *(fire) (bullet, gun)* disparar; *(arrow)* lanzar, tirar; *(missile)* lanzar; **to s. a glance at sb** lanzar una mirada a alguien; **to s. questions at sb** acribillar a alguien a preguntas; IDIOM *Vulg* **to s. one's load** *or* **wad** *(ejaculate)* correrse

(**b**) **to s. sb** *(wound)* disparar a alguien; *(kill)* matar de un tiro a alguien; *(execute)* fusilar a alguien; **she was shot in the back, they shot her in the back** la dispararon por la espalda; **he was shot through the heart** una bala le atravesó el corazón; **a man was shot dead yesterday** ayer asesinaron a un hombre de un balazo; **if you try to escape you will be shot** si intentas escapar te dispararán; **to s. oneself** pegarse un tiro; *Fam Hum* **you'll get me shot** vas a hacer que me la cargue; IDIOM **to s. oneself in the foot** tirar (uno) piedras contra su propio tejado; IDIOM *Fam* **to s. one's mouth off** dar la nota *or Esp* el cante

(**c**) *(hunt)* **to s. rabbits/birds** cazar conejos/aves

(**d**) *(send)* arrojar, despedir; **the explosion shot debris high into the air** la explosión arrojó desechos por el aire

(**e**) *(movie, TV programme)* rodar

(**f**) *(pass rapidly)* **to s. the rapids** salvar *or* atravesar los rápidos; **to s. the lights** *(in car)* saltarse el semáforo

(**g**) *(play)* **to s. dice/pool** jugar a los dados/al billar americano

(**h**) *(score) (goal)* marcar; *(basket)* anotar; **to s. 70** *(in golf)* hacer el recorrido en 70 golpes

(**i**) *Fam (drugs)* pincharse, *Esp* chutarse

(**j**) *US Fam* **to s. the breeze** *or* **the bull** *(chat)* estar de cháchara *or Esp* palique *or Méx* plática

3 *vi* (**a**) *(with gun)* disparar (**at** a); **stop or I'll s.!** ¡alto o disparo!; **to s. to kill** disparar a matar; **to s. on sight** disparar sin contemplaciones

(**b**) *(hunt)* cazar; **to go shooting** ir de cacería

(**c**) *(in soccer)* tirar, chutar; **to s. at goal** tirar a gol *or Am* al arco *or Esp* a puerta

(**d**) *(move rapidly)* ir a escape, ir como una exhalación; **the bus was shooting along** el autobús iba a toda velocidad; **he shot into/out of the house** entró en/salió de la casa como una exhalación; **she shot out of her seat** se levantó de su asiento como una exhalación; **the pain shot up his left side** le daban punzadas de dolor en el costado izquierdo; **the record shot straight to number three** el disco salió catapultado hasta el número tres de las listas

(**e**) *(movie)* rodar; **s.!** ¡se rueda!

(**f**) *(plant)* brotar; *(seed)* germinar

(**g**) *Fam* **can I ask you now? – s.!** ¿puedo preguntar ahora? – ¡desembucha! *or Esp* ¡dispara! *or RP* ¡largá!

4 *exclam US Fam* ¡miércoles!, ¡mecachis!, *Méx* ¡chin!

▸ **shoot back** *vi* (**a**) *(fire back)* responder con disparos (**b**) *(return quickly)* regresar rápidamente

▸ **shoot down** *vt sep* (**a**) *(person)* abatir (a tiros) (**b**) *(plane, pilot)* derribar (**c**) *(argument)* echar por tierra

▸ **shoot off** *vi* (**a**) *(leave quickly)* salir a escape (**b**) *Vulg (ejaculate)* correrse, *RP, Ven* acabar

▸ **shoot out** 1 *vt sep* (**a**) *(extend quickly)* sacar rápidamente; **she shot out a hand** extendió rápidamente una mano (**b**) **to s. it out with**

sb *(gunman)* emprenderla a tiros con alguien; *(in argument, debate)* resolverlo a tiros con alguien

2 *vi (emerge quickly)* salir rápidamente; **the taxi shot out in front of us** el taxi apareció de repente frente a nosotros

▸ **shoot through** *vi Br Fam* largarse corriendo

▸ **shoot up 1** *vt sep Fam* **(a)** *(drugs)* pincharse, *Esp* chutarse **(b)** *(saloon, town)* tirotear

2 *vi* **(a)** *(plants, children)* crecer mucho; *(buildings)* levantarse con rapidez **(b)** *(hand)* levantarse rápidamente **(c)** *(rocket)* elevarse a gran velocidad; *(flame, geyser)* levantarse **(d)** *(prices, inflation)* dispararse **(e)** *Fam (inject drugs)* pincharse, *Esp* chutarse

shoot-'em-up ['ʃu:təmʌp] *n (computer game)* = videojuego violento en el que se dispara al enemigo; *(movie)* = película con mucha violencia y muchos tiroteos

shooter ['ʃu:tə(r)] *n Fam (gun)* pipa *f*, *Am* fierro *m*

shooting ['ʃu:tɪŋ] **1** *n* **(a)** *(exchange of gunfire)* tiros *mpl*; **I heard what sounded like s.** me pareció escuchar tiros; **a s. war** una guerra real ▸▸ ***s. incident*** ataque *m* con disparos; *Fam* ***s. iron*** arma *f* de fuego

(b) *(incident)* ataque *m* con disparos; *(killing)* asesinato *m* (con arma de fuego)

(c) *(sport) (at targets)* tiro *m* al blanco; *(at birds, animals)* caza *f* ▸▸ ***s. gallery*** *(at fairground)* galería *f* de tiro al blanco; *Fam (for drug taking)* picadero *m*; ***s. range*** campo *m* de tiro; ***s. stick*** bastón *m* asiento

(d) *(of movie, TV programme)* rodaje *m*

2 *adj* **(a)** *(pain)* punzante **(b)** *(in basketball)* ***s. guard*** escolta *mf* **(c)** *Astron* ***s. star*** estrella *f* fugaz

shooting-match ['ʃu:tɪŋmætʃ] *n Fam* **the whole s.** todo, toda la pesca

shoot-out ['ʃu:taʊt] *n* **(a)** *(gunfight)* tiroteo *m* **(b)** *(in soccer)* **penalty s.** lanzamiento *or* tanda de penaltis *or Am* penales

shop [ʃɒp] **1** *n* **(a)** *(for goods)* tienda *f*; **the fruit s.** la frutería; **she's gone out to the shops** ha salido a comprar; **the new book should reach the shops in July** el nuevo libro debería estar en las librerías *or* a la venta en julio ▸▸ ***s. assistant*** dependiente(a) *m,f*; ***s. window*** escaparate *m*, *Am* vidriera *f*, *Chile, Col, Méx* vitrina *f*

(b) *Fam* **to do a s.** *(do shopping)* hacer la compra

(c) *(workshop)* taller *m*; *Ind* **the s. floor** *(manual workers)* los trabajadores a pie de máquina; **there is unrest on the s. floor** hay malestar en la línea de producción ▸▸ ***s. steward*** delegado(a) *m,f* sindical

(d) *US Sch* taller *m* de manualidades

(e) IDIOMS *Fam* **all over the s.: she got paint all over the s.** tenía pintura por todas partes; **their defence was all over the s.** la defensa del equipo no daba pie con bola; **the government's defence policy is all over the s.** la política de defensa del gobierno es caótica; *Fam* **to set up s. (as)** montar un negocio (de); **he's set up s. as a freelance translator** ahora trabaja como traductor autónomo *or* freelance; *Fam* **to talk s.** hablar del trabajo *or Esp* del curro *or Méx* de la chamba *or RP* del laburo

2 *vt (pt & pp* **shopped***) Br Fam (betray) Esp* chivarse de, *Col* sapear, *Méx* soplar, *RP* mandar al frente a

3 *vi* comprar, hacer compra(s); **I always s. at the local supermarket** siempre compro en el supermercado del vecindario; **to go shopping** ir de compras; **to s.** *or* **go shopping for sth** ir a comprar algo

▸ **shop around** *vi* comparar precios (en diferentes establecimientos); **our company is shopping around for new premises** nuestra empresa está buscando un nuevo local y está comparando precios; **always s. around for the best deal** mira siempre en varios sitios hasta que encuentres la mejor oferta

shopaholic [ʃɒpə'hɒlɪk] *n Fam* consumista *mf*

shopfitter ['ʃɒpfɪtə(r)] *n Br* diseñador(ora) *m,f* de locales comerciales

shopfront ['ʃɒpfrʌnt] *n Br* fachada *f* de una tienda

shopgirl ['ʃɒpgɜ:l] *n* dependienta *f*

shopkeeper ['ʃɒpki:pə(r)] *n* tendero(a) *m,f*; **small shopkeepers** los pequeños comerciantes

shoplift ['ʃɒplɪft] **1** *vt* **he got arrested for shoplifting a mobile phone** lo detuvieron por robar un móvil en una tienda

2 *vi* robar en las tiendas

shoplifter ['ʃɒplɪftə(r)] *n* ratero(a) *m,f (en comercios)*

shoplifting ['ʃɒplɪftɪŋ] *n* hurtos *mpl (en comercios)*

shopper ['ʃɒpə(r)] *n* comprador(ora) *m,f*; **for the convenience of shoppers** *(sign in shop)* para comodidad de nuestros clientes

shopping ['ʃɒpɪŋ] *n* **(a)** *(activity)* compra *f*, *Am* compras *fpl*; **to do the s.** hacer la compra *or Am* las compras; **to do a bit of s.** hacer algunas compras; **this area is good for s.** en esta zona hay muy buenas tiendas ▸▸ ***s. arcade*** galería *f* comercial; ***s. bag*** bolsa *f* de la compra; ***s. basket*** *(in shop, for Internet shopping)* cesta *f* de la compra; *US* ***s. cart*** *(in shop, for Internet shopping)* carrito *m* (de la compra); ***s. centre*** centro *m* comercial; *TV* ***s. channel*** canal *m* de compras, teletienda *f*; ***s. day:*** **there are only three s. days to Christmas** sólo quedan tres días para hacer las compras antes de Navidad; ***s. list*** lista *f* de la compra; *US* ***s. mall*** centro *m* comercial; ***s. precinct*** área *f* comercial; ***s. street*** calle *f* comercial; ***s. trip*** *(visit to shop)* salida *f* de compras; *(organised shopping excursion)* excursión *f* de compras; ***s. trolley*** *Br (in shop)* carrito *m* (de la compra); *(for taking shopping home)* carro *m* de la compra

(b) *(purchases)* compras *fpl*; **where shall I put the s.?** ¿dónde dejo la compra?

shop-soiled ['ʃɒpsɔɪld] *adj* deteriorado(a)

shopwalker ['ʃɒpwɔ:kə(r)] *n Br* jefe(a) *m,f* de taller

shop-worn ['ʃɒpwɔ:n] *adj* **(a)** *US (goods)* deteriorado(a) **(b)** *(cliché)* trillado(a), manido(a)

shore [ʃɔ:(r)] *n* **(a)** *(of sea, lake)* orilla *f*; **on the s. of a lake** a la orilla de un lago; **on s.** en tierra; **to go on s.** *(from ship)* bajar a tierra ▸▸ *US Culin* ***s. dinner*** mariscada *f*; ***s. lark*** alondra *f* cornuda; ***s. leave*** permiso *m* en tierra **(b)** *Literary* **shores** *(country)* tierras *fpl*; **he was one of the first Europeans to set foot on these shores** fue uno de los primeros europeos en pisar estas tierras

▸ **shore up** *vt sep also Fig* apuntalar

shorebird ['ʃɔ:bɜ:d] *n (ave f)* zancuda *f*

shoreline ['ʃɔ:laɪn] *n* costa *f*

shorewards ['ʃɔ:wədz] *adv* en dirección a la costa

shorn *pp of* **shear**

SHORT [ʃɔ:t] **1** *n* **(a)** *(short movie)* corto *m*, cortometraje *m*

(b) *Br (drink)* copa *f*

(c) *Fam (short circuit)* cortocircuito *m*

2 *adj* **(a)** *(in length, distance)* corto(a); *(person)* bajo(a), *Méx* chaparro(a), *RP* petiso(a); **it's a s. distance away** está a poca distancia; **it's a s. walk away** está a poca distancia a pie; **it's shorter this way** es más corto por aquí; **to be s. in the leg/arms** *(suit)* quedar corto de piernas/brazos; **A S. History of Spain** *(book title)* Breve historia de España; **Bill is s. for William** Bill es el diminutivo de William; **they call me Bill for s.** me llaman Bill para abreviar; **he's s. of the green** *(in golf)* se ha quedado a poca distancia del green; **to be 10 feet s. of the target** quedarse a 10 pies del blanco; **to have a s. temper** *or* **fuse** tener el genio muy vivo; **a s. back and sides, please** bien corto de atrás y de los lados; IDIOM *Fam* **to have sb by the s. hairs** *or Br* **the s. and curlies** tener a alguien en un puño *or* bien agarrado(a); IDIOM **to draw** *or* **get the s. straw** cargar con el muerto ▸▸ ***s. corner*** *(in hockey)* penalty *m* córner; *Br* ***s. drink*** copa *f*; ***s. game*** *(in golf)* juego *m* corto; ***s. story*** cuento *m*; ***s. ton*** tonelada *f* (aproximada) *(= 907 kilos)* ***s. trousers*** pantalón *m* corto; **that was when I was still in s. trousers** esto sucedió cuando yo todavía usaba pantalones cortos; *Rad* ***s. wave*** onda *f* corta

(b) *(in time)* corto(a), breve; **the s. answer is "no"** en pocas palabras, la respuesta es "no"; **for a few s. days** durante unos pocos días; **the days are getting shorter** los días se están haciendo más cortos; **he gave a s. laugh** soltó una carcajada breve; **s. and sweet** conciso(a) y al grano; **s. sharp shock** castigo ejemplar; **a s. time** *or* **while ago** hace muy poco; **at s. notice** en poco tiempo, con poca antelación; **in s.** en resumen, en pocas palabras; **in s. order** inmediatamente; **in the s. term** *or* **run** a corto plazo; *Br* **to be on s. time** trabajar con jornada reducida; **to make s. work of sth/sb** dar buena cuenta de algo/alguien

(c) *(abrupt)* seco(a); **to be s. with sb** ser seco(a) con alguien

(d) *(insufficient, lacking)* escaso(a); **time/money is s.** hay poco tiempo/dinero; **the change was 50 pence s.** faltaban 50 peniques en la vuelta *or Am* el vuelto; **we're 50 pence s.** nos faltan 50 peniques; *Br Fam* **I'm a bit s. today** *(lacking money)* hoy estoy *or* ando escaso de dinero; **to be in s. supply** *(money, water)* escasear; **to be s. of** estar *or* andar escaso(a) de; **to be s. of breath** *(from running)* estar sin aliento; *(a condition)* tener dificultades respiratorias; **it's little** *or* **not far s. of...** *(almost)* le falta poco para ser...; **it was little s. of miraculous that she survived** fue poco menos que un milagro que sobreviviera; **he's not far s. of forty** está *or* anda cerca de los cuarenta, tiene cerca de cuarenta años; **it's nothing s. of disgraceful!** ¡es absolutamente indignante!; **their team is s. on pace** su equipo carece de velocidad; IDIOM *Fam Hum* **he's a few sandwiches s. of a picnic** es un poco duro de mollera

(e) *Elec* ***s. circuit*** cortocircuito *m*

(f) *Ling* breve, corto(a)

(g) *Fin & St Exch* corto(a), al descubierto

(h) *(pastry)* quebrado(a)

(**i**) *(in betting)* **they're giving s. odds** pagan las apuestas muy bajas

3 *adv* (**a**) *(suddenly)* **to bring** *or* **pull sb up s.** dejar paralizado(a) a alguien; **to stop s.** pararse en seco

(**b**) *(in length, duration)* **to cut sth/sb s.** *(interrupt)* interrumpir algo/a alguien; **they stopped s. of...** no llegaron a...

(**c**) *(without)* **to go s.** pasar privaciones; **to go s. of sth** pasar sin algo

(**d**) *(expressing insufficiency)* **to fall s.** quedarse corto(a); **to fall s. of** *(target, standard, expectations)* no alcanzar; **we are running s. of coffee** se nos está terminando el café; **time is running s.** se nos está acabando el tiempo; **I was taken** *or* **caught s.** me entraron muchas ganas de ir al cuarto de baño

(**e**) *St Exch* **to buy/sell s.** comprar corto/vender al descubierto

4 *vt Fam (short-circuit)* provocar un cortocircuito en

5 *vi Fam (short-circuit)* tener un cortocircuito

6 short of *prep* **s. of sacking her, there's little we can do** salvo que la despidamos, no podemos hacer mucho más; **he would do anything s. of stealing** sería capaz de cualquier cosa excepto *or* salvo robar

---

shortage ['ʃɔːtɪdʒ] *n* escasez *f*; **petrol/food s.** escasez de gasolina *or RP* nafta/alimentos; **he has no s. of ideas** no le faltan ideas; **there's no s. of good restaurants in this town** en esta ciudad no faltan buenos restaurantes

shortarse ['ʃɔːtɑːs] *n Br very Fam* retaco *m*, *Méx* chaparrito(a) *m,f*, *RP* retacón(ona) *m,f*

shortbread ['ʃɔːtbred] *n* = especie de galleta elaborada con mantequilla, ≃ mantecada *f*

shortcake ['ʃɔːtkeɪk] *n* (**a**) *Br (biscuit)* = especie de galleta elaborada con mantequilla, ≃ mantecada *f* (**b**) *US (cake)* = bizcocho que generalmente lleva fruta y nata batida

short-change ['ʃɔːt'(t)ʃeɪndʒ] *vt* (**a**) *(in shop)* devolver de menos a (**b**) *(cheat)* timar, estafar

short-circuit ['ʃɔːt'sɜːkɪt] **1** *vt* (**a**) *(electrically)* producir un cortocircuito en (**b**) *Fig (bypass)* saltarse

2 *vi* tener un cortocircuito

shortcode ['ʃɔːtkəʊd] *n Tel* código *m* de marcado abreviado ►► ***s. dialling*** marcado *m* abreviado

shortcoming ['ʃɔːtkʌmɪŋ] *n* defecto *m*

shortcrust pastry ['ʃɔːtkrʌst'peɪstrɪ] *n* pasta *f* quebrada

shortcut ['ʃɔːtkʌt] *n* (**a**) *(quicker route)* atajo *m*; **to take a s.** tomar un atajo (**b**) *(quicker method)* atajo *m*; **there is no s. to mastering the piano** no existen fórmulas mágicas para aprender a tocar bien el piano (**c**) *Comptr* atajo *m* ►► ***s. key*** tecla *f* de atajo

short-dated ['ʃɔːt'deɪtɪd] *adj Fin (securities)* a corto plazo

short-eared owl ['ʃɔːtɪəd'aʊl] *n* lechuza *f* campestre

shorten ['ʃɔːtən] **1** *vt* (**a**) *(skirt, text)* acortar; **the name Kenneth is often shortened to Ken** a menudo se usa Ken en lugar de Kenneth para acortar (**b**) *(visit, task)* abreviar; **we had to s. our journey** tuvimos que acortar el viaje; **the new trains will s. the journey time to London** los nuevos trenes reducirán el tiempo de viaje a Londres (**c**) *Culin (pastry)* agregarle mantequilla a

2 *vi* acortarse; **the odds on her winning have shortened considerably** las posibilidades que tiene de ganar son ahora mucho mayores

shortening ['ʃɔːtnɪŋ] *n Culin* = grasa vegetal o animal utilizada en las masas de pastelería

shortfall ['ʃɔːtfɔːl] *n (of money)* déficit *m*; **a s. in teachers was expected** se preveía que habría una escasez de profesores

short-grain ['ʃɔːtgreɪn] *adj* ***s. rice*** arroz *m* de grano corto

shorthaired ['ʃɔːtheəd] *adj* de pelo corto

shorthand ['ʃɔːthænd] *n* taquigrafía *f*; **to take s.** taquigrafiar; **to take notes in s.** tomar notas taquigráficas; *Fig* **it's s. for...** es una forma breve de referirse a... ►► ***s. typing*** taquimecanografía *f*; ***s. typist*** taquimecanógrafo(a) *m,f*

short-handed [ʃɔːt'hændɪd] *adj* falto(a) de personal; **we're very s. at the moment** en este momento nos falta (mucho) personal

short-haul ['ʃɔːthɔːl] *adj (flight, aircraft)* de corto recorrido

shorthorn [ʃɔːt] *n* (vaca *f*) shorthorn *f*, (vaca *f* de) Durham *f*

shortie = **shorty**

shortish ['ʃɔːtɪʃ] *adj* (**a**) *(in length)* cortito(a) (**b**) *(in height)* bajito(a) (**c**) *(in time)* cortito(a)

shortlist ['ʃɔːtlɪst] **1** *n* **the s. of novels for the Booker prize** la lista de las novelas preseleccionadas para el premio Booker; **I've been trying to decide which dictionary to buy, and I've drawn up a s. of three** he estado pensando qué diccionario comprar y he hecho una preselección de tres

2 *vt* preseleccionar; **to be shortlisted (for sth)** estar preseleccionado(a) (para algo)

short-lived ['ʃɔːt'lɪvd] *adj (success, rejoicing)* pasajero(a), fugaz; *(animal)* de corta vida **their celebrations were s.** sus festejos duraron poco

shortly ['ʃɔːtlɪ] *adv* (**a**) *(soon)* en seguida, pronto; **s. after(wards)/before** poco después/antes; **I'll join you s.** enseguida estaré con ustedes; **President Smith who was s. to be** *or* **would s. be re-elected** el presidente Smith, quien poco tiempo después sería reelecto (**b**) *(abruptly)* secamente, bruscamente

shortness ['ʃɔːtnɪs] *n* (**a**) *(in length)* escasa *f* longitud; *(in time)* brevedad *f* (**b**) *(lack)* **s. of breath** falta *f* de aliento (**c**) *(of manner)* sequedad *f*

short-order cook ['ʃɔːtɔːdə'kʊk] *n* = cocinero que prepara platos rápidos *or RP* minutas

short-range ['ʃɔːtreɪndʒ] *adj* (**a**) *(missile)* de corto alcance; *(vehicle, aircraft)* de poca autonomía (**b**) *(prediction, outlook)* a corto plazo

shorts [ʃɔːts] *npl* (**a**) *(short trousers)* pantalones *mpl* cortos; *US Fam* **eat my shorts!** ¡toma castaña! (**b**) IDIOM *Fam* **to have the s.** *(have little money)* estar sin un chavo

short-sheet ['ʃɔːt'ʃiːt] *vt US* **to s. sb's bed** hacer la petaca a alguien

short-sighted ['ʃɔːt'saɪtɪd] *adj* (**a**) *Med (person, gaze)* miope, corto(a) de vista (**b**) *(ill-considered) (attitude, policy, person)* corto(a) de miras

short-sightedly [ʃɔːt'saɪtɪdlɪ] *adv* (**a**) *(to peer)* con ojos de miope (**b**) *(to act)* sin visión, sin amplitud de miras

short-sightedness ['ʃɔːt'saɪtɪdnɪs] *n* (**a**) *Med (of person, gaze)* miopía *f* (**b**) *(ill-considered nature) (of attitude, policy, person)* estrechez *f* de miras

short-sleeved ['ʃɔːt'sliːvd] *adj* de manga corta

short-staffed ['ʃɔːt'stɑːft] *adj* falto(a) de personal; **we're very s. at the moment** en este momento nos falta (mucho) personal

short-stay ['ʃɔːtsteɪ] *adj (car park)* para estancias breves

shortstop ['ʃɔːtstɒp] *n US (in baseball)* shortstop *m*, = jugador que intenta interceptar bolas entre la segunda y tercera base

short-tempered ['ʃɔːt'tempəd] *adj (reply)* con mal genio; **he's a very s. person** tiene muy mal genio; **you're rather s. today** hoy estás de mal genio

short-term ['ʃɔːttɜːm] *adj (solution, prospects, loan, memory)* a corto plazo ►► ***s. bond*** bono *m* de caja; ***s. contract*** contrato *m* temporal

short-termism [ʃɔːt'tɜːmɪzəm] *n* soluciones *fpl* a corto plazo

short-time ['ʃɔːttaɪm] *adj Br* **to be on s. working** trabajar una jornada reducida

short-track speed skating [ʃɔːttræk'spiːdskeɪtɪŋ] *n* patinaje *m* de velocidad en pista corta

short-wave ['ʃɔːtweɪv] *adj (radio, programme, broadcasting)* de onda corta

short-winded ['ʃɔːt'wɪndɪd] *adj* **to be s.** ser corto(a) de resuello, tener pocos pulmones

shorty, shortie ['ʃɔːtɪ] *n Fam* retaco(a) *m,f*, canijo(a) *m,f*, *Méx* chaparrito(a) *m,f*, *RP* retacón(ona) *m,f*

shot [ʃɒt] **1** *n* (**a**) *(act of firing, sound)* tiro *m*, disparo *m*; **to fire a s.** disparar; **to fire several shots** hacer varios disparos; IDIOM **a s. across the bows** un disparo de advertencia; IDIOM **my answer was a s. in the dark** respondí al azar *or* a ciegas; IDIOM **to call the shots** dirigir el cotarro; IDIOM **like a s.: when he saw me he was off like a s.** en cuanto me vio salió disparado; **would you marry him? – like a s.!** ¿te casarías con él? – ¡ahora mismo!

(**b**) *(marksman)* **he is a good/bad s.** es un buen/mal tirador

(**c**) *(shotgun pellets)* perdigones *mpl*

(**d**) *(in sports) (in soccer)* tiro *m*, chut(e) *m*; *(in hockey)* tiro *m*; *(in basketball)* tiro *m*, lanzamiento *m*; *(in golf, pool, tennis)* golpe *m*; *(in darts)* lanzamiento *m*; **two shots ahead/behind** *(in golf)* dos golpes por encima/debajo; **good s.!** ¡buen golpe!; **it's your s.** *(in pool, golf, darts)* es tu turno; **his first s. at goal hit the post** su primer tiro a puerta dio en el poste

(**e**) *(in athletics)* **to put the s.** lanzar peso *or Am* bala ►► ***s. put*** lanzamiento *m* de peso *orAm* de bala

(**f**) *(photograph)* foto *f*; *(of movie, TV programme)* toma *f*; **in/out of s.** en/fuera de pantalla

(**g**) *Fam (injection)* inyección *f*; **to get one's shots** *(before holiday)* ponerse las vacunas; IDIOM **a s. in the arm** un balón de oxígeno

(**h**) *(attempt)* intento *m*, intentona *f*; **to have a s. at (doing) sth** intentar (hacer) algo; **I'll give it a s.** probaré, lo intentaré; **you won't get**

another s. no tendrás una segunda oportunidad; **to give sth one's best s.** intentar algo esforzándose al máximo

(i) *(in betting)* **this horse is a 3-1 s. (for the race)** las apuestas están 3-1 a favor de este caballo (en esta carrera)

(j) *(drink)* chupito *m*, dedal *m* ►► **s. glass** vaso *m* para chupitos

2 *pt & pp of* **shoot**

3 *adj* (a) *Br Fam (rid)* **to get s. of sth/sb** quitarse *or Am* sacarse algo/a alguien de encima; **I can't wait to be s. of this house** estoy ansioso por deshacerme de esta casa

(b) *(fabric)* **s. silk** seda tornasolada

(c) *(permeated)* **her dress was red s. through with gold** su vestido era rojo con un jaspeado dorado; **the book is s. through with humour** el humor está presente a lo largo de todo el libro

(d) *esp US Fam (worn out) (person)* agotado(a), rendido(a); *(tyres, brakes)* hecho(a) trizas; **my nerves were s. (to pieces)** tenía los nervios destrozados

shotgun ['ʃɒtgʌn] *n (weapon)* escopeta *f*; *Fam* **to have a s. wedding** casarse por haber metido la pata, *Esp* casarse de penalti, *RP* casarse de apuro

shot-putter ['ʃɒtpʊtə(r)] *n* lanzador(ora) *m,f* de peso

SHOULD [ʃʊd, *unstressed* ʃəd] *modal aux v* (a) *(expressing obligations, recommendations, instructions)* **you s. do it at once** deberías hacerlo inmediatamente; **you shouldn't laugh at him** no deberías reírte de él; **you s. have come earlier** deberías haber venido antes; **he shouldn't have told them** no debería habérselo dicho; **you s. read the instructions carefully** lea detenidamente las instrucciones; **s. I open the window?** ¿abro la ventana?; **shall I tell her? – I (don't) think you s.** ¿se lo digo? – creo que (no) deberías; **don't do that! – why shouldn't I?** no hagas eso – ¿y por qué no?; **I'm very embarrassed – and so you s. be!** estoy muy avergonzado *or Andes, CAm, Carib, Méx* apenado – ¡deberías estarlo!; **everything is as it s. be** todo va como debería; **you s. have seen the expression on his face!** ¡tendrías que haber visto la cara que puso!; **a present?, oh you shouldn't have!** ¿un regalo? ¡no tenías que haberte molestado!

(b) *(expressing probability)* **the weather s. improve from now on** a partir de ahora, el tiempo debería mejorar; **the movie s. be good** la película promete ser buena; **she s. have arrived by this time** a estas horas ya debe de haber llegado; **can I come? – I s. think so** ¿puedo ir? – no veo por qué no; **I s. know!** ¡me lo dices a mí!

(c) *(in exclamations, in rhetorical questions)* **why s. you suspect me?** ¿por qué habrías de sospechar de mí?; **who s. I meet but Martin!** y ¿a quién me encontré? ¡a Martin!; **how s. I know?** ¿y cómo quieres que lo sepa?; **I s. hope so!** ¡eso espero!; **I didn't go in – I s. think not!** no entré – ¡faltaría más!; **he apologized – I s. think so, too!** se disculpó – ¡es lo mínimo que podía hacer!; **I s. be so lucky!** ¡ojalá!

(d) *(in subordinate clauses)* **he ordered that they s. be released** ordenó que los liberaran; **she insisted that he s. wear his hair short** insistió en que llevase el pelo corto; **it's funny (that) you s. say that** tiene gracia que digas eso

(e) *(in conditional clauses)* **if he s. come** *or Formal* **s. he come, let me know** si viene, avísame; **if you s. have any difficulty, phone this number** si tuviera algún problema, llame a este número

(f) *(expressing opinions, preferences)* **I s. like a drink** me gustaría *or Esp* me apetecería tomar algo; **we s. want to know if there was anything seriously wrong** si algo va muy mal, nos gustaría saberlo; **we s. have told you earlier if we'd known** te lo habríamos dicho antes si lo hubiéramos sabido; **I s. demand compensation (if I were you)** yo (en tu lugar) pediría una indemnización; **I shouldn't worry** yo no me preocuparía; **I s. imagine he was rather angry!** ¡me imagino que estaría bastante *esp Esp* enfadado *or esp Am* enojado!; **I s. have thought you'd have realized that by now** pensaba que a estas alturas ya te habrías dado cuenta de eso; **I shouldn't be surprised if…** no me sorprendería que…

shoulder ['ʃəʊldə(r)] 1 *n* (a) *(of person, garment)* hombro *m*; **s. to s.** hombro con hombro; **you can carry it over your s.** puedes llevarlo al hombro; **I looked over my s.** miré por encima del hombro; *Fig* **the responsibility fell on her shoulders** sobre ella recayó la responsabilidad; *Fig* **a weight had been lifted from his shoulders** le habían quitado *or Am* sacado un peso de encima ►► ***s. bag*** bolsa *f* de bandolera; ***s. blade*** omóplato *m*; ***s. charge*** *(in ice hockey, rugby)* carga *f*; ***s. pad*** hombrera *f*; ***s. strap*** *(of garment)* tirante *m*, *CSur* bretel *m*; *(of bag)* correa *f*

(b) *(of meat)* paletilla *f*

(c) *(along road) Esp* arcén *m*, *Méx* acotamiento *m*, *RP* banquina *f*, *Ven* hombrillo *m*

(d) IDIOMS **I just needed a s. to cry on** necesitaba a alguien a quien agarrar de paño de lágrimas; **to be looking over one's s.** estar inquieto(a); **to put one's s. to the wheel** arrimar el hombro; **(to give it to sb) straight from the s.** (decírselo a alguien) sin rodeos

2 *vt* (a) *(push)* **to s. one's way through the crowd** abrirse paso a empujones entre la multitud; **to s. sb aside** apartar a alguien de un empujón (del hombro) (b) *(put on shoulder)* echarse al hombro; **to s. arms** echar las armas al hombro (c) *(responsibility, blame)* asumir

shoulder-charge ['ʃəʊldətʃɑːdʒ] *vt* empujar con el hombro

shoulder-high ['ʃəʊldəhaɪ] 1 *adj* **we pushed through the s. grass** avanzamos por entre la hierba que nos llegaba hasta los hombros

2 *adv* **to carry sb s.** llevar a alguien en hombros

shoulder-length ['ʃəʊldəleŋθ] *adj (hair)* hasta los hombros

shouldn't ['ʃʊdnt] = **should not**

should've ['ʃʊdəv] = **should have**

shout [ʃaʊt] 1 *n* (a) *(cry)* grito *m*; **shouts of laughter** carcajadas *fpl*; **give me a s. when you're leaving** avísame cuando te vayas (b) *Fam (chance)* **to be in with a s. of qualifying** tener todavía posibilidades de clasificarse (c) *Br Fam (turn to buy round of drinks)* **it's my s.** ésta me toca a mí

2 *vt* gritar; **to s. sth at sb** gritarle algo a alguien; **he shouted me a warning** me lanzó un grito de aviso; **to s. insults at sb** insultar a alguien a gritos; **they shouted themselves hoarse** gritaron hasta quedarse roncos

3 *vi* gritar; **to s. at sb** gritar a alguien; **don't s. at me!** ¡no me grites!; **they were shouting at each other** discutían a gritos; **to s. for help** gritar pidiendo ayuda; **he shouted to her to be careful** le gritó que tuviera cuidado; *Fig* **it's nothing to s. about** no es nada del otro mundo; *Fig* **to have something to s. about** tener algo que celebrar

► **shout down** *vt sep* **the minister was shouted down by the crowd** la multitud impidió con sus gritos que el ministro hablara

► **shout out** 1 *vt sep* gritar

2 *vi* gritar, pegar gritos

shouting ['ʃaʊtɪŋ] *n* griterío *m*, gritos *mpl*; **we were within s. distance of the lifeguard** estábamos en un sitio desde el cual nos podía oír el socorrista; **the debate ended up as a s. match** el debate acabó a grito pelado; **it's all over bar the s.** es asunto concluido

shove [ʃʌv] 1 *n* empujón *m*; **to give sth/sb a s.** dar un empujón a algo/alguien; IDIOM **to give sb the s.** cortar con alguien; IDIOM **he got the s.** su pareja lo dejó

2 *vt* (a) *(push)* empujar; **we shoved all the furniture up against the walls** corrimos todos los muebles contra las paredes; **to s. sth in/out** meter/sacar algo a empujones; **to s. sb out of the way** apartar a alguien a empujones (b) *(insert, put)* poner, meter; **s. it in the drawer** ponlo *or* mételo en el cajón; IDIOM *Vulg* **s. it up your** *Br* **arse** *or US* **ass!** vete a tomar por culo, *Arg* ¡metételo en el culo *or* horto!; IDIOM *very Fam* **you can s. it!** ¡mételo donde te quepa!

3 *vi* empujar; **to s. past** pasar a empujones; **stop shoving!** ¡deja *or* para ya de empujar!

► **shove about, shove around** *vt sep Fam (bully)* abusar de

► **shove off** *vi* (a) *Fam (leave)* largarse; **s. off!** ¡lárgate!, *Esp* ¡largo! (b) *(in boat)* alejarse de la orilla

► **shove over, shove up** *vi Fam (make room)* correrse, hacerse a un lado

shove-halfpenny ['ʃʌv'heɪpnɪ] *n Br* = juego que consiste en impulsar con la mano monedas sobre un panel con zonas delineadas

shovel ['ʃʌvəl] 1 *n* pala *f*

2 *vt (pt & pp* **shovelled**, *US* **shoveled**) echar a paladas; **to s. snow off the path** quitar *or Am* sacar la nieve del camino a paladas *or* con la pala; **to s. food into one's mouth** atiborrarse de comida; *Fam* **don't s. your food down!** ¡no comas tan a lo bruto!

shoveler ['ʃʌvələ(r)] *n* cuchara *f* común, pato *m* cuchara

shovelful ['ʃʌvəlfʊl] *n* palada *f*

SHOW [ʃəʊ] 1 *n* (a) *(exhibition)* exposición *f*; **to be on s.** exhibirse, estar expuesto(a); **to put sth on s.** exponer algo ►► ***s. Br flat*** *or US* ***apartment*** apartamento *m or Esp* piso *m or Arg* departamento *m* piloto; ***s. house*** casa *f* piloto; ***s. jumper*** jinete *m*/amazona *f* de pruebas de saltos; ***s. jumping*** prueba *f* de saltos (de equitación)

(b) *(concert, play)* espectáculo *m*; *(on TV, radio)* programa *m*; *Fam Old-fashioned* **good s.!** *(well done)* ¡bien hecho!; **they put on a good s.** *(did their best)* hicieron un buen papel; **it's a pretty poor s. when your own mother forgets your birthday** es triste que tu propia madre se olvide de tu cumpleaños; *Fam* **it's up to you, it's your s.** depende de ti, tú mandas; IDIOM **to run the s.** dirigir el cotarro; IDIOM **the s. must go on** ¡tenemos que continuar a pesar de todo!; IDIOM *Fam* **let's get this s. on the road!** ¡en marcha!, ¡vamos allá! ►► ***s. business*** el mundo del espectáculo; ***s. business personality*** personalidad *f* del

(mundo del) espectáculo; ***s. girl*** corista *f*; **s. stopper:** IDIOM *Fam* **it was a real s. stopper** fue una auténtica sensación
(**c**) *(act of showing)* demostración *f*; **a s. of unity** una demostración de unidad; **a s. of hands** una votación a mano alzada
(**d**) *(pretence)* **it's all s.** es pura fachada; **to do sth for s.** hacer algo por alardear; **all those flashing lights are just for s.** todas esas lucecitas están de decoración; **they made** *or* **put on a s. of being interested** hicieron un gran esfuerzo por parecer interesados ►► *Pej* ***s. trial*** juicio *m* ejemplarizante
2 *vt* (*pp* **shown** [ʃəʊn]) (**a**) *(display) (passport, ticket)* mostrar, enseñar; *(picture)* exponer, exhibir; *(courage, talent, knowledge)* mostrar, demostrar; **to s. sb sth, to s. sth to sb** enseñar *or* mostrar algo a alguien; **the photo shows them leaving the hotel** en la foto están saliendo del hotel; **he has shown some improvement** ha mejorado algo; **to s. a taste for sth** mostrarse interesado(a) en algo; **the invader showed no mercy** el invasor no mostró compasión; **the audience began to s. signs of restlessness** el público comenzaba a mostrarse impaciente; **to s. a profit/loss** registrar *or* arrojar beneficios/pérdidas; **you're showing your age** estás hecho un carcamal; **he won't s. his face here again** no volverá a dejarse ver por aquí; **this is all we've got to s. for our hard work** esto es todo lo que tenemos después de trabajar tanto; **they had nothing to s. for all their work** trabajaron mucho para nada; **to s. oneself** dejarse ver; IDIOM **to s. one's cards** *or* **one's hand** mostrar las verdaderas intenciones
(**b**) *(indicate)* mostrar; *(time, temperature)* indicar, señalar; **to s. sb the way** mostrar a alguien el camino; **the worst affected areas are shown in red** las áreas más afectadas aparecen en rojo
(**c**) *(reveal)* **his expression showed his embarrassment** su rostro revelaba su vergüenza *or Am* pena; **she never shows any emotion** nunca muestra sus sentimientos; **this carpet shows the dirt** el polvo se nota mucho en esta alfombra
(**d**) *(prove, demonstrate)* mostrar, demostrar; **this shows him to be a liar** esto demuestra lo mentiroso que es; **to s. oneself to be...** demostrar ser...; **it just goes to s. that..., it just shows that...** eso viene a demostrar que...
(**e**) *(teach)* enseñar; **to s. sb how to do sth** enseñar a alguien a hacer algo; **I'll s. you, just you wait!** ¡tú espera, que te vas a enterar!; *Fam* **that'll s. them!** ¡eso les enseñará!
(**f**) *(movie)* proyectar; *(TV programme)* emitir, poner; **they are showing a Clint Eastwood movie tonight** esta noche ponen *or* echan una película de Clint Eastwood; **as shown on TV** anunciado(a) en TV
(**g**) *(escort, lead)* **to s. sb to the door** acompañar a alguien a la puerta; **to s. sb to their room** llevar a alguien a su habitación
(**h**) *(enter in competition) (dog, cat)* presentar en competición *or Am* competencia
3 *vi* (**a**) *(be visible)* notarse; **he didn't let his confusion s.** no dejó que se notara su confusión; **I've never done this before – it shows** nunca había hecho esto antes – ya se nota; **I'm nervous – it doesn't s.** estoy nerviosa – no lo parece; *Fam* **ah well, it just** *or* **all goes to s.!** ¡para que veas!
(**b**) *(movie)* **what's showing this week?** ¿qué ponen *or* echan esta semana?; **now showing at the Odeon** *(on poster)* en pantalla en el cine Odeon
(**c**) *Fam (arrive)* aparecer
► **show around** *vt sep* = **show round**
► **show in** *vt sep (escort in)* acompañar hasta dentro; **s. him in** hágale entrar *or* pasar
► **show off** 1 *vt sep* (**a**) *(show proudly)* **he was showing off his new motorbike** iba alardeando de moto nueva; **to s. off one's knowledge** alardear *or* hacer alarde de conocimientos
(**b**) *(complement)* realzar
2 *vi* alardear, fanfarronear; **stop showing off!** ¡deja de alardear!
► **show out** *vt sep (escort out)* acompañar hasta la puerta; **I'll s. myself out** no hace falta que me acompañe a la puerta
► **show over** *vt sep* guiar por
► **show round** *vt sep* **let me s. you round** déjame que te enseñe el lugar/la casa/*etc.*; **to s. sb round the town/house** enseñarle la ciudad/casa a alguien
► **show through** 1 *vt insep* transparentarse por; **her knickers showed through her dress** las bragas se le transparentaban por el vestido; **his nervousness showed through his cocky exterior** su apariencia de gallito dejaba ver cierto nerviosismo
2 *vi also Fig* transparentarse
► **show up** 1 *vt sep* (**a**) *(reveal)* descubrir, poner al descubierto; **the report showed him up for the coward he is** el informe puso al descubierto lo cobarde que es
(**b**) *(embarrass)* poner en evidencia
(**c**) *(escort upstairs)* acompañar hasta arriba; **s. him up** hágale subir
2 *vi* (**a**) *(stand out)* notarse; **the marks s. up under infra-red light** la luz infrarroja revela las marcas
(**b**) *Fam (arrive)* aparecer, presentarse

show-and-tell [ʃəʊən'tel] *n US* = ejercicio escolar en que un alumno lleva a la clase un objeto de su elección y habla sobre él
showbiz ['ʃəʊbɪz] *n Fam* mundo *m* del espectáculo ►► ***s. personality*** personalidad *f* del (mundo del) espectáculo
showboat ['ʃəʊbəʊt] *esp US Fam* 1 *n (show-off)* fanfarrón(ona) *m,f*, *Esp* fantasma *mf*
2 *vi (show off)* fanfarronear
showcase ['ʃəʊkeɪs] 1 *n* (**a**) *(for displaying objects)* vitrina *f* (**b**) *(for talents, work)* escaparate *m*
2 *vt* exhibir, servir de escaparate a
showdown ['ʃəʊdaʊn] *n* enfrentamiento *m* (cara a cara)
shower ['ʃaʊə(r)] 1 *n* (**a**) *(for washing)* ducha *f*, *Col, Méx, Ven* regadera *f*; **to have** *or* **take a s.** ducharse, darse una ducha; **I'm in the s.!** ¡me estoy duchando! ►► ***s. cap*** gorro *m* de baño *or* ducha; ***s. curtain*** cortinas *fpl* de ducha; ***s. gel*** gel *m* de baño; ***s. head*** alcachofa *f* (de ducha); ***s. unit*** ducha *f*
(**b**) *(of rain)* chubasco *m*, chaparrón *m*; **snow s.** nevisca
(**c**) *(of stones, bullets, sparks, insults)* lluvia *f*
(**d**) *Br Fam (group)* **what a s.!** ¡qué pandilla!, *Esp* ¡menuda cuadrilla!; **you lazy s.!** *Esp* ¡(h)atajo *or Méx* bola *or Méx, RP* manga de vagos!
(**e**) *US (party)* = fiesta celebrada en honor a una persona que se va a casar o que va tener un bebé, y a la que todos los invitados traen un regalo
2 *vt* **to s. sb with sth, to s. sth on sb** *(liquid, sparks)* regar a alguien de algo; *(gifts, praise)* colmar a alguien de algo; **to s. sb with kisses** llenar a alguien de besos de arriba abajo
3 *vi* (**a**) *(pour)* llover, caer (**b**) *(take a shower)* ducharse
► **shower down** *vi (rocks, sparks, compliments, insults)* llover
showerproof ['ʃaʊəpruːf] *adj* impermeable
showery ['ʃaʊərɪ] *adj* lluvioso(a); **it will be a s. day tomorrow** mañana lloverá durante todo el día
showgirl ['ʃəʊgɜːl] *n* chica *f* de revista
showground ['ʃəʊgraʊnd] *n* recinto *m* de ferial
showily ['ʃəʊɪlɪ] *adv* llamativamente, ostentosamente
showiness ['ʃəʊɪnɪs] *n* lo llamativo, ostentosidad *f*
showing ['ʃəʊɪŋ] *n* (**a**) *(exhibition)* exposición *f*, muestra *f* (**b**) *(of movie)* pase *m*, proyección *f* (**c**) *(performance)* actuación *f*; **on this s....** ante esta actuación...
showman ['ʃəʊmən] *n* (**a**) *(circus manager)* director *m* de circo (**b**) *(entertaining person)* showman *m*
showmanship ['ʃəʊmənʃɪp] *n* espectacularidad *f*
show-me ['ʃəʊ'miː] *adj US Fam (attitude)* de desconfianza
shown *pp of* **show**
show-off ['ʃəʊɒf] *n Fam* fanfarrón(ona) *m,f*, *Esp* fantasma *mf*
showpiece ['ʃəʊpiːs] *n* (**a**) *(of collection)* pieza *f* principal (**b**) *(model)* modelo *m*
showplace ['ʃəʊpleɪs] *n* atracción *f* turística
showring ['ʃəʊrɪŋ] *n (at equestrian event)* pista *f* de saltos
showroom ['ʃəʊruːm] *n* sala *f* de exposición; **in s. condition** como nuevo(a)
show-stopping ['ʃəʊstɒpɪŋ] *adj* sensacional, soberbio(a)
showy ['ʃəʊɪ] *adj* llamativo(a), ostentoso(a)
shrank *pt of* **shrink**
shrapnel ['ʃræpnəl] *n* metralla *f*; **a piece of s.** un trozo de metralla ►► ***s. wound*** herida *f* de metralla
shred [ʃred] 1 *n* (**a**) *(of paper, fabric)* pedazo *m*; **in shreds** *(clothes)* hecho(a) pedazos; *Fig* **his reputation/confidence was in shreds** su reputación/confianza estaba hecha pedazos *or* trizas; *also Fig* **to tear sth to shreds** hacer pedazos *or* trizas algo; *Fig* **to tear sb to shreds** hacer pedazos *or* trizas a alguien (**b**) *(of truth, decency)* pizca *f*; **there isn't a s. of evidence** no hay ni rastro de pruebas
2 *vt* (*pt & pp* **shredded**) (**a**) *(documents)* triturar (**b**) *(food)* cortar en tiras
shredded ['ʃredɪd] *adj US Fam (drunk)* **to be s.** estar *Esp* bolinga *or Méx* ahogado(a) *or RP* en pedo; **to get s.** ponerse *Esp* bolinga *or Méx* ahogado(a) *or RP* en pedo
shredder ['ʃredə(r)] *n (for paper)* trituradora *f* (de documentos)
shrew [ʃruː] *n* (**a**) *(animal)* musaraña *f* (**b**) *Pej (nagging woman)* bruja *f*

shrewd [ʃruːd] *adj (person)* astuto(a); *(decision)* astuto(a), inteligente; *(decision, investment, guess)* inteligente; **he's a s. businessman** es un hombre de negocios astuto; **she's a s. judge of character** tiene buen ojo con la gente; **I had a s. suspicion that they were up to something** estaba convencido de que tramaban algo

shrewdly [ˈʃruːdlɪ] *adv* astutamente

shrewdness [ˈʃruːdnɪs] *n (of person)* astucia *f*; *(of decision)* astucia *f*, inteligencia *f*; *(of investment)* inteligencia *f*, astucia *f*

shrewish [ˈʃruːrɪʃ] *adj Pej* cascarrabias, regañón(ona)

shriek [ʃriːk] **1** *n* chillido *m*, alarido *m*; **shrieks of joy** chillidos de alegría; **shrieks of laughter** carcajadas; **to give a s.** soltar un chillido *or* alarido

2 *vt* chillar; **to s. abuse at sb** lanzar insultos contra alguien

3 *vi* chillar; **to s. at sb** dar un chillido a alguien; **to s. with pain** chillar de dolor; **to s. with laughter** reírse a carcajadas

shrift [ʃrɪft] *n* **to give sb/sth short s.** prestar escasa atención a alguien/algo; **to get short s. (from sb)** recibir escasa atención (de alguien)

shrike [ʃraɪk] *n* alcaudón *m*; **great grey s.** alcaudón real; **red-backed s.** alcaudón dorsirrojo

shrill [ʃrɪl] *adj* (**a**) *(voice, tone)* estridente, agudo(a); *(whistle)* chirriante (**b**) *(criticism)* vociferante, estridente

shrillness [ˈʃrɪlnɪs] *n* (**a**) *(of voice, tone)* estridencia *f*, agudeza *f*; *(of whistle)* chirrido *m* (**b**) *(of criticism)* estridencia *f*

shrilly [ˈʃrɪlɪ] *adv* con estridencia, estridentemente

shrimp [ʃrɪmp] *n* (**a**) *Br (small crustacean)* camarón *m*, quisquilla *f* (**b**) *US (prawn)* gamba *f* ▸▸ ***s. cocktail*** cóctel *m* de gambas (**c**) *Fam (small person)* retaco *m*, renacuajo(a) *m,f*, *Méx* chaparrito(a) *m,f*, *RP* retacón(ona) *m,f*

shrimping [ˈʃrɪmpɪŋ] *n* (**a**) *(fishing)* **to go s.** ir a pescar camarones/gambas (**b**) *Fam (toe-sucking)* = práctica sexual que implica lamerle los dedos de los pies a la pareja

shrine [ʃraɪn] *n* (**a**) *(place of worship)* santuario *m* (**to** en honor a) (**b**) *(tomb)* sepulcro *m* (**c**) *(of famous person, event)* santuario *m* (**to** en honor a) (**d**) *(container for relics)* relicario *m*

shrink [ʃrɪŋk] **1** *n Fam (psychiatrist)* psiquiatra *mf*

2 *vt* (*pt* **shrank** [ʃræŋk], *pp* **shrunk** [ʃrʌŋk]) encoger

3 *vi* (**a**) *(fabric)* encoger(se); *(wood)* contraerse; *(meat)* encogerse; **to s. in the wash** encoger(se) al lavar

(**b**) *(income, budget, size)* reducirse, disminuir; *(economy)* contraerse; *(numbers, amount)* decrecer; **my savings have shrunk (away) to nothing** mis ahorros se han quedado en nada

(**c**) *(person)* encoger

(**d**) *(move back)* **to s. from sth** retroceder ante algo; **to s. back in horror** retroceder horrorizado(a)

(**e**) *(shy away)* **she shrank from the thought of meeting him again** se encogía de miedo de pensar que lo vería otra vez; **to s. from doing sth** no atreverse a hacer algo

shrinkage [ˈʃrɪŋkɪdʒ] *n* (**a**) *(of material)* encogimiento *m* (**b**) *(in sales, profits)* reducción *f* (**c**) *Com (through pilferage)* pérdidas *fpl* por robo; *(through damage)* pérdidas *fpl* por daños

shrinking [ˈʃrɪŋkɪŋ] *adj Fam* **he's no s. violet** no se corta un pelo

shrink-wrap [ˈʃrɪŋkˈræp] **1** *n* envoltura *f* de plástico (de polietileno) adherente

2 *vt* envolver con plástico (de polietileno) adherente

shrink-wrapped [ˈʃrɪŋkˈræpt] *adj* empaquetado(a) con plástico (de polietileno) adherente

shrivel [ˈʃrɪvəl] (*pt & pp* **shrivelled**, *US* **shriveled**) **1** *vt (flower)* marchitar; *(leaf, crops)* secar; *(fruit, vegetables)* arrugar, secar; *(skin)* ajar, arrugar; **a shrivelled old woman** una vieja arrugada

2 *vi (flower)* marchitarse; *(leaf, crops)* secarse; *(fruit, vegetables)* arrugarse, secarse; *(skin)* ajarse, arrugarse

▸ **shrivel up** *vi (flower)* marchitarse; *(leaf, crops)* secarse; *(fruit, vegetables)* arrugarse, secarse

shroud [ʃraʊd] **1** *n* (**a**) *(for body)* mortaja *f*, sudario *m* (**b**) *(of mystery)* halo *m*; **a s. of secrecy surrounds the project** el proyecto está rodeado de un gran secreto (**c**) *Naut* obenquillo *m*

2 *vt* (**a**) *(body)* amortajar (**b**) *(obscure)* envolver; **to be shrouded in sth** estar envuelto(a) en algo; **the town was shrouded in mist/darkness** la ciudad estaba envuelta en la niebla/sumida en la oscuridad; **its origins are shrouded in mystery** sus orígenes están rodeados de misterio

Shrovetide [ˈʃrəʊvtaɪd] *n* carnestolendas *fpl*

Shrove Tuesday [ˈʃrəʊvˈtjuːzdɪ] *n* Martes *m inv* de Carnaval

shrub [ʃrʌb] *n* arbusto *m*

shrubbery [ˈʃrʌbərɪ] *n* (**a**) *(in garden)* arbustos *mpl* (**b**) *(scrubland)* maleza *f*, matorrales *mpl*

shrug [ʃrʌg] **1** *n (of shoulders)* encogimiento *m* de hombros; **to give a s.** encogerse de hombros

2 *vt* (*pt & pp* **shrugged**) **to s. one's shoulders** encogerse de hombros

3 *vi* encogerse de hombros

▸ **shrug off** *vt sep (failure, problems)* quitar *or* restar importancia a

shrunk *pp of* **shrink**

shrunken [ˈʃrʌŋkən] *adj* encogido(a); **s. with age** *(person)* encogido(a) con los años

shtook, shtuck [ʃtʊk] *n Br Fam* **to be in s.** estar metido(a) en un lío

shtoom [ʃtʊm] *adj Br Fam* **to keep s.** no decir ni mu

shuck [ʃʌk] *US* **1** *n Fam (trick)* engaño *m*

2 *vt* (**a**) *(corn)* descascarillar; *(peas)* pelar; *(oysters)* quitar la concha a, desbullar (**b**) *(trick)* engañar (**c**) **to s. (off)** *(bad habit)* abandonar; **to s. (off) one's clothes** quitarse la ropa; **the snake shucked (off) its skin** la serpiente mudó la piel

3 *vi* **to s. (and jive)** *(act foolishly)* hacerse el/la tonto(a); *(speak misleadingly, bluff)* contar cuentos

shucks [ʃʌks] *exclam US* ¡vaya por Dios!, ¡caramba!

shudder [ˈʃʌdə(r)] **1** *n* (**a**) *(of person) (with fear, pleasure)* estremecimiento *m*; *(with cold)* escalofrío *m*; **to give a s.** estremecerse; *Fam* **it gives me the shudders** me pone los pelos de punta; **it sent a s. through me** hizo que me estremeciera, hizo que me diera un escalofrío (**b**) *(of engine, vehicle)* **to give a s.** dar una sacudida

2 *vi* (**a**) *(person) (with fear, pleasure)* estremecerse (**with** de); *(with cold)* tiritar (**with** de); *(with pain)* tener escalofríos (**with** por); **I s. to think what...** tiemblo *or* me dan escalofríos sólo de pensar qué... (**b**) *(engine, vehicle)* dar una sacudida; *(machinery)* dar sacudidas; *(building)* temblar; **the bus shuddered to a halt** el autobús dio una sacudida y se paró

shuffle [ˈʃʌfəl] **1** *n* (**a**) *(of feet)* **to walk with a s.** caminar arrastrando los pies (**b**) *(of cards)* **to give the cards a s.** barajar *or* mezclar las cartas (**c**) *(of Cabinet)* remodelación *f*

2 *vt* (**a**) *(cards)* barajar; *(dominoes)* mover; *(papers)* revolver (**b**) *(rearrange) (cabinet)* remodelar; *(defence)* reordenar (**c**) *(drag)* **to s. one's feet** *(when walking)* arrastrar los pies; *(with embarrassment)* mover nerviosamente los pies de un lado a otro

3 *vi* (**a**) *(when walking)* arrastrar los pies; **to s. out/in** salir/entrar arrastrando los pies; **to s. from one foot to the other** mover nerviosamente los pies de un lado a otro (**b**) *(fidget)* **the children were shuffling in their seats** los niños no se estaban quietos en sus asientos (**c**) *(in cards)* barajar

▸ **shuffle off** **1** *vt sep* sacudirse; **to s. off responsibility for sth onto sb else** sacudir la responsabilidad de algo a otro

2 *vi* alejarse arrastrando los pies

shuffling [ˈʃʌflɪŋ] *adj (gait)* arrastrando los pies

shufty, shufti [ˈʃʊftɪ] *n Br Fam* **to have** *or* **take a s. (at)** echar un ojo (a)

shun [ʃʌn] (*pt & pp* **shunned**) *vt* rehuir, evitar; **they were shunned by decent society** la sociedad bien pensante les daba la espalda

shunt [ʃʌnt] **1** *n* (**a**) *Elec* derivación *f* (**b**) *Rail* cambio *m* de vías (**c**) *Fam (in motor racing)* colisión *f*, *Esp* enganchada *f*

2 *vt* (**a**) *(train, carriages)* cambiar de vía (**b**) *(move)* **we were shunted into another room** nos metieron en otra habitación; **they were shunted about from one prison to another** los llevaban de una cárcel a otra; **they shunted him off to the Fresno office** lo mandaron a la oficina de Fresno

3 *vi (travel)* **I spent the day shunting back and forth between the two offices** me tuvieron todo el día de una oficina a otra

shunter [ˈʃʌntə(r)] *n* locomotora *f* de arrastre

shush [ʃʊʃ] **1** *vt* hacer callar

2 *exclam* ¡chis!, ¡sssh!

SHUT [ʃʌt] **1** *adj* cerrado(a); **to be s.** estar cerrado(a); **the door banged s.** la puerta se cerró de un portazo; **she slammed the door s.** cerró la puerta de un portazo

2 *vt* (*pt & pp* **shut**) cerrar; **to s. the door on sb** *or* **in sb's face** dar a alguien con la puerta en las narices; **s. your eyes** cierra los ojos; **to s. one's finger in the door** pillarse un dedo con la puerta; *Fam* **s. your mouth** *or* **face** *or* **gob!, s. it!** ¡cierra el pico!

3 *vi (door)* cerrarse; *(shop)* cerrar

▸ **shut away** *vt sep* encerrar; **to s. oneself away** encerrarse

▸ **shut down** **1** *vt sep* (**a**) *(close) (shop, factory)* cerrar (por completo); *(production)* suspender

(**b**) *(switch off) (engine, machine)* apagar

(c) *Sport (mark closely)* marcar de cerca
2 *vi* (a) *(shop, factory)* cerrar (por completo)
(b) *(computer)* apagarse

▸ **shut in** *vt sep (confine)* encerrar; **he s. himself in in his room** se encerró en su habitación; **to feel s. in** sentirse encerrado(a); **the village is s. in by hills** el pueblo queda recluido entre colinas

▸ **shut off** 1 *vt sep* (a) *(electricity, water, funds, flow of arms)* cortar; *(engine, machine)* apagar
(b) *(block) (road, exit)* cortar; **the new building shuts off all our sunlight** el nuevo edificio nos tapa toda la luz del sol
(c) *(isolate)* aislar; **to s. oneself off (from)** aislarse (de)
2 *vi (engine, machine)* apagarse

▸ **shut out** *vt sep* (a) *(exclude) (person)* excluir; *(light, view)* tapar; *(memory, thought)* bloquear; **I couldn't s. out the noise** no conseguía hacer que el ruido no me distrajera; **she keeps shutting me out and won't let me help** se cierra sin dejar que la ayude
(b) *(keep outside)* dejar fuera; **we had to s. the children out of the kitchen** tuvimos que cerrar la puerta de la cocina para que no entraran los niños; **to s. oneself out** quedarse fuera sin llaves
(c) *(prevent from scoring)* dejar a cero

▸ **shut up** 1 *vt sep* (a) *(confine)* encerrar; **to s. oneself up** encerrarse
(b) *(close)* cerrar; *also Fig* **to s. up shop** cerrar el negocio
(c) *Fam (silence)* hacer callar; **that s. him up!** ¡eso le hizo callarse!
2 *vi* (a) *Fam (be quiet)* callarse; **s. up!** ¡cállate!; **I wish you'd s. up about your holiday!** ¡deja de dar la lata con tus vacaciones!
(b) *(close shop)* cerrar

---

shutdown ['ʃʌtdaʊn] *n* (a) *(of factory)* cierre *m* (b) *Comptr* apagado *m*

shuteye ['ʃʌtaɪ] *n Fam* **to get some s.** echar un sueñecito *or* una cabezadita

shut-in ['ʃʌtɪn] *US* 1 *adj* encerrado(a)
2 *n* = discapacitado o enfermo confinado en su casa

shut-off ['ʃʌtɒf] *n (device)* válvula *f* de cierre; *Elec* interruptor *m*

shutout ['ʃʌtaʊt] *n Sport* **he has had 6 shutouts in the last 10 games** ha conseguido mantener su portería imbatida en 6 de los últimos 10 partidos

shutter ['ʃʌtə(r)] *n* (a) *(on window)* contraventana *f*; *(of shop)* persiana *f*; **to put up the shutters** *(of shop)* cerrar (b) *(of camera)* obturador *m* ▸▸ ***s. release*** disparador *m*; ***s. speed*** tiempo *m* de exposición

shuttered ['ʃʌtəd] *adj (with shutters fitted)* con contraventanas; *(with shutters closed)* con las persianas cerradas

shuttle ['ʃʌtəl] 1 *n* (a) *(of loom, sewing machine)* lanzadera *f* (b) *(train, bus)* servicio *m* de conexión; *(plane)* avión *m (de puente aéreo)* ▸▸ ***s. bus*** autobús *m* directo; ***s. diplomacy*** mediación *f* internacional; ***s. service*** *(of trains, buses)* servicio *m* de conexión; *(para distancias cortas)*; *(of planes)* puente *m* aéreo (c) *(space vehicle)* transbordador *m or* lanzadera *f* espacial (d) *(in badminton)* volante *m*
2 *vt* trasladar; **to s. sb back and forth** trasladar a alguien de acá para allá
3 *vi* **to s. between A and B** ir y venir entre A y B

shuttlecock ['ʃʌtəlkɒk] *n* volante *m*

shy [ʃaɪ] 1 *adj* (a) *(timid) (person, smile)* tímido(a); *(animal, bird)* asustadizo(a); **I felt s. about asking her for money** me daba vergüenza pedirle dinero; **to be s. of sb** ser vergonzoso(a) con alguien; **most people are s. of speaking in public** a la mayoría de la gente le da vergüenza hablar en público; **don't be s. of asking for more** que no te dé vergüenza pedir más; **they're not s. of letting you know how they feel** no tienen ningún reparo en decir lo que sienten (b) *US Fam (lacking)* escaso(a), corto(a) (**of** de); **we're still a few dollars s. of the cost** aún nos faltan unos dólares para cubrir el costo; **I'm a couple of months s. of the minimum age** no llego a la edad mínima por un par de meses
2 *n (throw)* tirada *f*; **to have** *or* **take a s. at sth** intentar dar a algo
3 *vi* (a) *(horse)* asustarse (**at** de) (b) *(have throw)* apuntar (**at** a)
4 *vt* apuntar con (**at** a)

▸ **shy away** *vi* **to s. away from doing sth** no atreverse a hacer algo; **to s. away from sth** eludir algo

shyly ['ʃaɪlɪ] *adv* tímidamente, con timidez

shyness ['ʃaɪnɪs] *n (of person, smile)* timidez *f*; *(of animal, bird)* miedo *m*

shyster ['ʃaɪstə(r)] *n Fam (politician, businessman)* sinvergüenza *mf*; **s. (lawyer)** picapleitos *mf inv*, *Am* abogado(a) *m,f* buscapleitos

SI [es'aɪ] (a) (*abbr* **Système International (d'Unités)**) SI *m* ▸▸ ***S. system*** sistema *m* internacional de unidades; ***S. unit*** unidad *f* del SI (b) (*abbr* **stroke index**) *(in golf)* índice *m* de golpes

Siam [saɪ'æm] *n Formerly* Siam

Siamese [saɪə'mi:z] 1 *n* (*pl* **Siamese**) (a) *(person)* siamés(esa) *m,f* (b) *(language)* siamés *m* (c) *(cat)* (gato *m*) siamés *m*
2 *adj* siamés(esa) ▸▸ ***S. cat*** gato *m* siamés; ***S. twins*** (hermanos(as) *m,fpl*) siameses(esas) *m,fpl*; *Fam Fig* **they're like S. twins, those two!** ¡esos dos van siempre de la mano!

SIB [esaɪ'bi:] *n* (*abbr* **Securities and Investments Board**) = comisión del mercado de valores londinense

Siberia [saɪ'bɪərɪə] *n* Siberia

Siberian [saɪ'bɪərɪən] 1 *n* siberiano(a) *m,f*
2 *adj* siberiano(a)

sibilance ['sɪbɪləns] *n* sibilancia *f*

sibilant ['sɪbɪlənt] 1 *n* sibilante *f*
2 *adj* sibilante

sibling ['sɪblɪŋ] *n (brother)* hermano *m*; *(sister)* hermana *f*; **all his siblings** todos sus hermanos ▸▸ ***s. rivalry*** rivalidad *f* entre hermanos

sibyl ['sɪbɪl] *n* sibila *f*

sic[1] [sɪk] *adv* sic

sic[2] *vt* (a) *(attack)* atacar; **s. 'em, Simba!** ¡ataca, Simba! (b) *US (incite)* **he tried to s. his dog on us** trató de echarnos al perro encima

Sicilian [sɪ'sɪlɪən] 1 *n (person)* siciliano(a) *m,f*
2 *adj* siciliano(a)

Sicily ['sɪsɪlɪ] *n* Sicilia

sick [sɪk] 1 *n Br Fam (vomit)* vómito *m*, devuelto *m*
2 *npl* **the s.** los enfermos
3 *adj* (a) *(ill)* enfermo(a); **they care for s. people** cuidan a los enfermos; **to be s.** estar enfermo(a); *US* **to fall s., to get** *or* **take s.** ponerse enfermo(a); **my secretary is off s.** mi secretaria está de baja (por enfermedad); *Fig* **it makes me s.!** ¡me pone enfermo!; *Fig* **to be s. with fear/worry** haberse puesto enfermo(a) de miedo/preocupación; *Fig* **to be worried s.** estar muerto(a) de preocupación; *US Fam* **you're so good at it you make me look s.!** ¡lo haces tan bien que a mí me dejas fatal!; IDIOM **I was s. as a dog** *(was ill)* me puse malísimo ▸▸ ***s. bay*** enfermería *f*; ***s. building syndrome*** síndrome *m* del edificio enfermo, = trastorno que se suele dar entre oficinistas que trabajan en edificios con mala ventilación; ***s. leave*** baja *f* por enfermedad; ***s. note*** certificado *m* de baja (por enfermedad); ***s. pay*** paga *f* por enfermedad
(b) *(nauseous)* **I feel s.** *(about to vomit)* voy a vomitar *or* devolver; *(unwell in stomach)* estoy mareado; **to be s.** *(vomit)* vomitar, devolver; **I get s. at the sight of blood** ver sangre me da náuseas; **oysters make me s.** las ostras me sientan mal; **to make oneself s.** *(deliberately)* provocarse el vómito; **you're going to make yourself s.!** *(eating)* ¡te vas a empachar!; IDIOM **I was s. as a dog** *(vomited)* vomité hasta la primera papilla
(c) *(disgusted)* **it makes me s.!** ¡me pone enfermo!; **you make me s.!** ¡me pones enfermo!; **he's off to the Bahamas on business again – makes you s., doesn't it?** otra vez se va a las Bahamas en viaje de negocios, ¿no te pone enfermo?; **she felt s. (to her stomach)** se le revolvía el estómago
(d) *(fed up)* **to be s. of sth/sb** estar harto(a) de algo/alguien; **he was s. of living alone** estaba harto de vivir solo; **to grow s. of sth** hartarse de algo; *Fam* **to be s. (and tired)** *or* **s. to death of sth/sb** estar hasta la coronilla de algo/alguien; *Fam* **to be s. of the sight of sth/sb** estar hasta las narices *or Méx* manitas de algo/alguien
(e) *(unhappy, disappointed)* **to feel s. about sth** sentir mucha angustia por algo; **to be/feel s. at heart** estar/sentirse destrozado(a); IDIOM *Br Fam* **to be (as) s. as a parrot** haberse llevado un chasco tremendo
(f) *(cruel) (humour, joke)* morboso(a), macabro(a); *(person)* retorcido(a); **to have a s. mind** tener una mente retorcida, ser retorcido(a)

▸ **sick up** *vt sep Br Fam (vomit)* devolver, vomitar

sickbag ['sɪkbæg] *n* bolsa *f* para el mareo; *Br Fam Fig* **pass the s.!** ¡me dan ganas de vomitar!

sickbed ['sɪkbed] *n* lecho *m* de convaleciente

sicken ['sɪkən] 1 *vt* (a) *(disgust)* poner enfermo(a) (b) *(make ill)* (hacer) enfermar
2 *vi* (a) *(become ill)* ponerse enfermo(a), enfermar; *Br* **to be sickening for something** estar empezando a ponerse enfermo(a) (b) *(grow tired of, become disgusted with)* **to s. of sth** hartarse de algo

sickening ['sɪknɪŋ] *adj* (a) *(nauseating)* repugnante; **a s. thud/crash** un golpe/estruendo horripilante (b) *(disgusting)* **it's s. the way the refugees are treated** me pone enfermo la manera en que tratan a los refugiados; *Fam Hum* **she's so talented it's s.!** tiene tanto talento que da asco

sickeningly ['sɪknɪŋlɪ] *adv* asquerosamente; *Fam Hum* **s., she won all the prizes** qué asco, ganó todos los premios; *Fam Hum* **she's s. successful** tiene tanto éxito que da asco

sickie ['sɪkɪ] *n Br, Austr Fam* **to take** *or* **throw a s.** llamar al trabajo fingiendo que está uno enfermo(a)

sickle ['sɪkəl] *n* hoz *f*

sickle-cell anaemia ['sɪkəlselə'ni:mɪə] *n* anemia *f* (de célula) falciforme

sickly ['sɪklɪ] *adj* (**a**) *(person, complexion)* enfermizo(a); *(plant)* marchito(a); *(colour, light)* pálido(a), desvaído(a); *(smile)* falso(a) (**b**) *(taste, sentiment)* empalagoso(a); **s. sweet** empalagoso(a), dulzarrón(ona)

sick-making ['sɪkmeɪkɪŋ] *adj Br Fam* asqueroso(a)

sickness ['sɪknɪs] *n* (**a**) *(illness)* enfermedad *f*; **in s. and in health** en la salud y en la enfermedad ►► ***s. benefit*** subsidio *m* por enfermedad (**b**) *(nausea)* mareo *m*; *(vomiting)* vómito *m*

sicko ['sɪkəʊ] *n Fam* pirado(a) *m,f* peligroso(a)

sick-out ['sɪkaʊt] *n US* = forma de huelga en la que los trabajadores se dan de baja por enfermedad

sickroom ['sɪkru:m] *n* habitación *f* del enfermo

SIDE [saɪd] **1** *n* (**a**) *(of person)* costado *m*; *(of animal)* ijada *f*; **a s. of pork** medio cerdo *or* puerco *orAm* chancho; **at** *or* **by sb's s.** al lado de alguien; **the dog never left her s.** el perro nunca se apartó de ella; **she was lying on her s.** estaba acostada de lado; **he kept his arms at his sides** no separaba los brazos de los costados; **s. by s.** uno(a) al lado del/de la otro(a); **to live/work s. by s.** vivir/trabajar juntos(as)

(**b**) *(part) (of house, box, triangle, square)* lado *m*; *(of river)* orilla *f*, margen *m or f*; *(of road)* borde *m*, margen *m or f*; *(of mountain)* ladera *f*; *(of cave, stomach)* pared *f*; **on the south s. (of the city)** en la parte sur (de la ciudad); **I sat on the s. of the bed** me senté en el borde de la cama; **lay the barrel on its s.** coloque el barril de costado; **her hair is cut short at the sides** lleva el pelo corto por los lados; **there's a door at the s.** hay una puerta lateral; **they live on the other s. of the country/world** viven en el otro lado del país/mundo; *Sport* **his shot hit the s. netting** su disparo dio en la parte de fuera de la red ►► ***s. door*** puerta *f* lateral; ***s. entrance*** entrada *f* lateral; ***s. view*** vista *f* lateral; ***s. whiskers*** patillas *fpl*

(**c**) *(of record, sheet of paper, piece of material, coin)* cara *f*; **on the other s. of the page** en la otra cara *or* carilla de la hoja; **I've written ten sides** he escrito diez caras *or* carillas; **grill for three minutes on each s.** áselo tres minutos por cada lado; **this s. up** *(on packaging)* este lado arriba; IDIOM **the other s. of the coin** la otra cara de la moneda

(**d**) *(adjacent area)* lado *m*; **the left-hand s.** la izquierda; **the right-hand s.** la derecha; **at** *or* **by the s. of** al lado de; **on this/that s. (of)** a este/ese lado (de); **on the other s. (of sth)** al otro lado (de algo); **on all sides, on every s.** por todos (los) lados; **on both sides, on either s.** a ambos lados; **to stand on** *or* **to one s.** mantenerse al margen; **the vehicle was hit from the s.** el vehículo fue embestido por el costado; **from all sides, from every s.** desde todas partes; **to move from s. to s.** moverse de un lado a otro; **a hamburger with salad on the s.** una hamburguesa con ensalada de acompañamiento ►► ***s. aisle*** pasillo *m* lateral; ***s. chapel*** capilla *f* lateral; ***s. dish*** plato *m* de acompañamiento *or* guarnición; *Archit* ***s. elevation*** vista *f* lateral; ***s. order*** ración *f (como acompañamiento)*; ***s. plate*** platito *m* para el pan; ***s. salad*** ensalada *f* de acompañamiento *or* guarnición

(**e**) *(of situation, argument, personality)* lado *m*, aspecto *m*; **he showed us his nasty s.** nos enseñó su lado desagradable; **I kept my s. of the bargain** yo cumplí mi parte del trato; **to hear** *or* **look at both sides of the question** considerar las dos caras de una situación; **let's hear her s. of the story** escuchemos su versión de la historia; **I could see the funny s. of the situation** vi el lado divertido de la situación; **she's very good at the practical s. of things** es muy buena con el aspecto práctico de las cosas; **to look on the bright/gloomy s. (of things)** mirar el lado positivo/negativo (de las cosas); **on the positive s....** como aspecto positivo...

(**f**) *(in game)* equipo *m*; *(in dispute)* parte *f*, bando *m*; **to be on sb's s.** *(defending)* estar de parte de alguien; *(in game)* estar en el equipo de alguien; **he's on our s.** está de nuestro lado; **whose s. are you on, anyway?** ¿y tú, de parte de quién estás?; **we need to get them on our s.** necesitamos ponerlos de nuestro lado; **we have time/youth on our s.** el tiempo/la juventud está de nuestra parte *or* nuestro lado; **to change sides, to go over to the other s.** cambiar de bando; **to take sb's s.** ponerse del lado *or* de parte de alguien; **to take sides** tomar partido; *also Fig* **he let the s. down** dejó en mal lugar a los suyos

(**g**) *Br TV* lado *m*; **what's on the other s.?** ¿qué echan por el otro canal?

(**h**) *(secondary part)* ***s. effects*** efectos *mpl* secundarios; ***s. issue*** cuestión *f* secundaria; ***s. road*** carretera *f* secundaria; ***s. street*** bocacalle *f*

(**i**) *(in pool, snooker) (spin)* = efecto que se consigue golpeando un lado de la bola

(**j**) *Br Fam (arrogance, presumption)* **there's no s. to him** no tiene doblez

(**k**) *US (side order)* acompañamiento *m*, guarnición *f*; **with a s. of fries** con acompañamiento *or* guarnición de *Esp* patatas *orAm* papas fritas

(**l**) IDIOMS **on his mother's s.** *(of family)* por línea materna; **it's a bit on the expensive/long s.** es un poco caro/largo; **he does a bit of gardening on the s.** hace algunos trabajos extras de jardinería; **I make a bit of money on the s. by baby-sitting** me saco un dinero extra cuidando niños; *Fam* **to have a bit on the s.** tener un lío (amoroso); **to be on the right/wrong s. of forty** no llegar a/pasar de los cuarenta; **don't get on the wrong s. of the law** no te metas en líos con la justicia; **to get on the right s. of sb** caer en gracia a alguien, complacer a alguien; **to get on the wrong s. of sb** ganarse la antipatía de alguien, ponerse a mal con alguien; **to keep** *or* **stay on the right s. of sb** no llevarle la contraria a alguien; *esp US* **to live on the right/wrong s. of the tracks** vivir en la zona rica/pobre de la ciudad; **to put sth to one s.** *(money)* apartar algo; *(matter, differences)* dejar algo a un lado; **to take sb to one s.** llevar a alguien aparte; **this s. of Christmas** antes de las Navidades; **they do the best paella this s. of Spain** preparan la mejor paella que se puede comer fuera de España; **this s. of the grave** en vida

2 *vi* **to s. with/against sb** ponerse del lado de/en contra de alguien

sidearm ['saɪdɑ:m] *n* = arma blanca o de fuego que se puede transportar colgada del cinturón o del hombro

sideboard ['saɪdbɔ:d] *n* aparador *m*

sideburns ['saɪdbɜ:nz], *Br* **sideboards** ['saɪdbɔ:dz] *npl* patillas *fpl*

sidecar ['saɪdkɑ:(r)] *n* sidecar *m*

-sided [-'saɪdɪd] *suffix* **three/many-s.** de tres/múltiples caras; **a steep-s. valley** un valle de laderas escarpadas

side-impact bar [saɪd'ɪmpækt'bɑ:(r)] *n Aut* barra *f* de protección lateral

sidekick ['saɪdkɪk] *n Fam* compinche *mf*

sidelight ['saɪdlaɪt] *n* (**a**) *Aut* luz *f* de posición (**b**) *(information)* detalle *m* incidental

sideline ['saɪdlaɪn] **1** *n* (**a**) *(of football pitch)* línea *f* de banda; *(of rugby pitch)* lateral *m*; **her injury kept her on the sidelines all season** la lesión la tuvo en el banquillo toda la temporada; IDIOM **to sit on the sidelines** quedarse al margen; IDIOM **to watch from the sidelines** mirar desde la barrera (**b**) *Com (business)* negocio *m* subsidiario; *(job)* segundo empleo *m*

2 *vt* **the player was sidelined through injury** el jugador se quedó en el banquillo por culpa de una lesión; **the project has been sidelined** el proyecto ha sido aplazado

sidelong ['saɪdlɒŋ] *adj (glance)* de reojo, de soslayo

side-on ['saɪd'ɒn] **1** *adv* de lado

2 *adj (colisión)* lateral; *(photo)* de perfil

sidereal [saɪ'dɪərɪəl] *adj Astron* sideral, sidéreo(a) ►► ***s. year*** año *m* sideral

side-saddle ['saɪdsædəl] **1** *n* jamugas *fpl*, silla *f* de amazona

2 *adv* **to ride s.** montar a mujeriegas

sideshow ['saɪdʃəʊ] *n* (**a**) *(at fair)* barraca *f* (de feria) (**b**) *(less important activity)* cuestión *f* menor *or* secundaria

sideslip ['saɪdslɪp] *(pt & pp* **sideslipped**) **1** *n Av* deslizamiento *m* lateral

2 *vi (in skiing)* deslizarse de lado

sidespin ['saɪdspɪn] *n* efecto *m* lateral

side-splitting ['saɪdsplɪtɪŋ] *adj Fam* desternillante, divertidísimo(a)

sidesplittingly ['saɪdsplɪtɪŋlɪ] *adv Fam* **s. funny** desternillante, divertidísimo(a)

sidestep ['saɪdstep] **1** *n Sport* regate *m*, quiebro *m*

2 *vt (pt & pp* **sidestepped**) (**a**) *(tackle)* esquivar, evitar; *(player)* regatear (**b**) *(question)* soslayar, eludir

3 *vi* (**a**) *(in boxing)* esquivar (**b**) *(in dancing)* dar un paso a un lado

sidestroke ['saɪdstrəʊk] *n* brazada *f* de costado; **to swim** *or* **do s.** nadar de lado

sideswipe ['saɪdswaɪp] **1** *n* **to take a s. at sth/sb** *(criticize)* meterse de pasada con algo/alguien

2 *vt US* rozar el lateral de

sidetrack ['saɪdtræk] **1** *vt (person)* distraer; *(enquiry, investigation)* desviar; **we got sidetracked** nos distrajimos

2 *n US Rail* apartadero *m*; *(connected at only one end to main track)* vía *f* muerta

sidewalk ['saɪdwɔːk] *n US* acera *f, CSur* vereda *f, CAm, Méx* banqueta *f* ►► *US* ***s. artist*** = dibujante que pinta con tiza sobre la acera; *US* ***s. cafe*** café *m* con terraza

sidewall ['saɪdwɔːl] *n (of tyre)* flanco *m*

sidewards ['saɪdwədz] *adv* de lado

sideways ['saɪdweɪz] **1** *adj (movement)* lateral; *(glance)* de reojo; **the job is a s. move** el puesto es de la misma categoría
2 *adv (glance)* de reojo; *(lean, walk)* de lado; **to step s.** hacerse a un lado; **I was thrown s.** me caí de lado; **it only goes in s.** sólo entra de lado

sideways-on ['saɪdweɪz'ɒn] *adv* de lado

sidewinder ['saɪdwaɪndə(r)] *n US Fam (rattlesnake)* serpiente *f* de cascabel cornuda, crótalo *m* cornudo

siding ['saɪdɪŋ] *n (on railway)* apartadero *m*; *(connected at only one end to main track)* vía *f* muerta

sidle ['saɪdəl] *vi* **to s. in/out** entrar/salir sigilosamente; **to s. up to sb** acercarse tímidamente a alguien

Sidon [saɪdən] *n* Sidón

SIDS [sɪdz] *n* (*abbr* **sudden infant death syndrome**) muerte *f* súbita infantil

siege [siːdʒ] *n* asedio *m*, sitio *m*; **to lay s. to a town** sitiar una ciudad; **they laid s. to their opponents' goal** asediaron la portería contraria; **under s.** sitiado(a) ►► ***s. mentality*** mentalidad *f* defensiva; ***s. warfare*** guerra *f* de asedio

sienna ['siːenə] **1** *n (colour)* siena *m*
2 *adj* siena

Sierra Leone [siː'erəliː'əʊn] *n* Sierra Leona

Sierra Leonean [siː'erəliː'əʊnɪən] **1** *n* sierraleonés(esa) *m,f*
2 *adj* sierraleonés(esa), de Sierra Leona

siesta [sɪ'estə] *n* siesta *f*; **to have** *or* **take a s.** echar(se) una siesta

sieve [sɪv] **1** *n (with coarse mesh)* criba *f*, cedazo *m*; *(with fine mesh)* tamiz *m*; *(in kitchen)* colador *m*; IDIOM *Fam* **to have a memory** *or* **mind like a s.** tener una memoria pésima *or* de mosquito
2 *vt (with coarse mesh)* cribar, cerner; *(with fine mesh)* tamizar; *(in kitchen)* colar

sift [sɪft] **1** *vt* **(a)** *(flour, sugar)* colar; *(soil)* cribar; **s. a little cocoa powder over the cake** espolvorear un poco de cacao sobre el pastel con ayuda del colador **(b)** *(evidence)* examinar a fondo
2 *vi (search)* **to s. through sth** examinar algo cuidadosamente

► **sift out** *vt sep* **(a)** *(remove) (lumps)* separar con el colador; *(debris)* separar con la criba **(b)** *(distinguish)* seleccionar

sigh [saɪ] **1** *n* suspiro *m*; **to give** *or* **heave a s.** dar *or* exhalar un suspiro, suspirar; **I gave** *or* **heaved a s. of relief** suspiré aliviado, di un suspiro de alivio
2 *vi* **(a)** *(person)* suspirar; **to s. with** *or* **in relief** suspirar aliviado(a), dar un suspiro de alivio; **to s. for** *or* **over sth/sb** suspirar por algo/alguien **(b)** *(wind)* susurrar
3 *vt* decir suspirando

sight [saɪt] **1** *n* **(a)** *(faculty)* vista *f*; **to have good/bad s.** tener buena/mala vista; **to lose one's s.** perder la vista
(b) *(act of seeing)* **it was my first s. of the Pacific** era la primera vez que veía el Pacífico; **he fainted at the s. of the blood** se desmayó al ver la sangre; **to catch s. of sth/sb** ver algo/a alguien; **to lose s. of sth/sb** perder de vista algo/a alguien; **we mustn't lose s. of the fact that ...** no debemos perder de vista el hecho de que...; **I can't stand the s. of blood** no soporto ver la sangre; **I hate** *or* **can't stand the s. of him** no lo puedo ni ver; **to shoot sb on s.** disparar contra alguien en cuanto se lo ve; **to know sb by s.** conocer a alguien de vista; **he can play music at** *or US* **by s.** es capaz de tocar a simple vista; **to buy sth s. unseen** comprar algo a ciegas ►► *Fin* ***s. bill*** letra *f* a la vista; *Fin* ***s. draft*** giro *m* a la vista; ***s. gag*** gag *m* visual
(c) *(range of vision)* **the plane was still in s.** todavía se divisaba el avión; **there wasn't a taxi in s.** no había ningún taxi a la vista; **there's still no end in s. to the conflict** aún no se divisa un final para el conflicto; **to come into s.** aparecer; **to be within s. (of)** *(able to see)* estar a la vista (de); *(of victory, the end)* estar a un paso (de); *also Fig* **to keep sth/sb in s.** no perder de vista algo/a alguien; **I watched her until she was out of s.** la estuve mirando hasta que la perdí de vista; **to keep out of s.** no dejarse ver; **to keep sth out of s.** quitar algo de la vista; **she never lets him out of her s.** no lo pierde de vista; **to put sth out of s.** quitar algo de la vista; **(get) out of my s.!** ¡fuera de mi vista!; **get that dog out of my s.!** ¡quita ese perro de mi vista!; PROV **out of s., out of mind** ojos que no ven, corazón que no siente
(d) *(spectacle)* espectáculo *m*; **a familiar/rare s.** algo habitual/singular; **the waterfalls are a s. worth seeing** las cataratas son un espectáculo digno de ver; **it was not a pretty s.** era un espectáculo bochornoso; IDIOM *Fam* **you're/it's a s. for sore eyes!** ¡dichosos los ojos que te/lo ven!
(e) *Fam (mess)* **the kitchen was a s.!** ¡la cocina era una guarrada!; **you look a s.!** ¡mira cómo te has puesto!; *(ridiculous)* ¡qué facha *or* pinta que tienes!
(f) *(tourist attraction)* lugar *m* de interés; **the sights** los lugares de interés; **to see/show sb the sights** visitar/enseñar a alguien los lugares de interés
(g) *(of instrument)* visor *m*; *(of gun)* mira *f*, punto *m* de mira; *Fig* **to have sth/sb in one's sights** tener algo/a alguien en el punto de mira; *Fig* **to have** *or* **set one's sights on sth/sb** tener las miras puestas en algo/alguien; *Fig* **to lower one's sights** bajar el listón
(h) *Fam (for emphasis)* **a (damn) s. longer/harder** muchísimo más largo/duro; **he's a s. too modest** se pasa de modesto
2 *vt* **(a)** *(see)* avistar, ver **(b)** *(gun) (aim)* apuntar; *(adjust sights of)* ajustar la mira de

sighted ['saɪtɪd] **1** *npl* **the s.** las personas sin discapacidades visuales
2 *adj (person)* sin discapacidades visuales

sighting ['saɪtɪŋ] *n* avistamiento *m*; **several sightings have been reported** se ha informado de varios avistamientos

sightless ['saɪtlɪs] *adj* ciego(a)

sightly ['saɪtlɪ] *adj* **that power station isn't very s.** esa central eléctrica es horrible *or* muy fea

sight-read ['saɪtriːd] (*pt & pp* **sight-read** ['saɪtred]) **1** *vt* repentizar
2 *vi* repentizar

sight-reading ['saɪtriːdɪŋ] *n Mus* repentización *f*

sightseeing ['saɪtsiːɪŋ] *n* visitas *fpl* turísticas; **to go s., to do some s.** hacer turismo ►► ***s. tour*** visita *f* guiada por los lugares de interés

sightseer ['saɪtsiːə(r)] *n* turista *mf*

sigma ['sɪgmə] *n* sigma *f*

sign [saɪn] **1** *n* **(a)** *(gesture)* seña *f*, señal *f*; **to make a s. to sb** hacer una seña *or* senal a alguien; **she made a s. for me to enter** me hizo una seña *or* señal para que entrara; **to make the s. of the cross** santiguarse, hacer la señal de la cruz; **when I give the s., run** cuando te haga la señal, corre ►► ***s. language*** *(for the deaf)* lenguaje *m* por señas *or* de signos; **using s. language, he managed to ask for food** haciendo uso de las señas consiguió pedir algo de comer
(b) *(indication)* indicio *m*, señal *f*; **a red sunset is a s. of fair weather** una puesta de sol rojiza es indicio *or* señal de buen tiempo; **it's a sure s. that...** es un indicio inequívoco de que...; **a good/bad s.** una buena/mala señal; **as a s. of respect** como señal de respeto; **at the first s. of danger, he disappears** a la primera señal de peligro, desaparece; **a s. of the times** un signo de los tiempos que corren; **there's no s. of an improvement** no hay indicios de mejoría; **there is no s. of him/it** no hay ni rastro de él/ello; **is there any s. of Amy yet?** ¿se ha sabido algo de Amy ya?; **there's no s. of her changing her mind** nada hace pensar que vaya a cambiar de idea; **he gave no s. of having heard** no dio muestras de haberlo oído; **since then, he's given no s. of life** desde entonces no ha dado señales de vida; **all the signs are that...** todo parece indicar que...; **the situation is showing signs of improvement** la situación muestra indicios de mejora; **the equipment showed signs of having been used** el equipo tenía aspecto de haber sido utilizado
(c) *(notice)* cartel *m*; *(of pub, shop)* letrero *m*, rótulo *m*; *(on road)* señal *f* (de tráfico); *(in demonstration)* pancarta *f*; **follow the signs for baggage reclaim** sigue las indicaciones para la zona de recogida de equipaje ►► ***s. painter*** *(for pubs, shops)* rotulista *mf*
(d) *(symbol)* signo *m*; **plus/minus s.** signo más/menos
(e) *(of zodiac)* signo *m*; **what s. are you?** ¿de qué signo eres? ►► ***s. of the zodiac*** signo *m* del zodíaco
2 *vt* **(a)** *(write signature on)* firmar; **to s. one's name** firmar; **I s. myself Jo Davies** firmo como Jo Davies; **a signed photo** una foto autografiada; *US* **do you want to s. this to your room?** ¿desea que se le cargue esto a la habitación?; **the deal will be signed and sealed tomorrow** el trato será firmado y sellado mañana **(b)** *(in sign language)* indicar (con señas) **(c)** *(in sport)* fichar; *(of record company)* fichar, contratar
3 *vi* **(a)** *(write signature)* firmar; **s. here, please** firme aquí, por favor **(b)** *(in sport)* fichar (**for** por); *(to record company)* fichar (**to** por), firmar contrato (**to** con) **(c)** *(make gesture)* **she signed for** *or* **to him to come over** le hizo señas para que se acercara **(d)** *(use sign language)* utilizar el lenguaje por señas

► **sign away** *vt sep (rights, land, power)* renunciar a; **I felt I was signing away my freedom** sentía que estaba renunciando a mi libertad

► **sign for** *vt insep (delivery, equipment)* firmar el acuse de recibo de

► **sign in** **1** *vt sep (guest)* meter en el registro

2 *vi (in hotel)* firmar en el libro de registro; *(in factory)* firmar a la entrada

► **sign off** *vi* (**a**) *(radio, TV presenter)* despedir la emisión (**b**) *(close letter)* despedirse, terminar

► **sign on** *Br* 1 *vi* (**a**) *Fam (for unemployment benefit) (initially)* = registrarse para recibir el seguro de desempleo, *Esp* apuntarse al paro; *(regularly)* ir a sellar (**b**) *(enrol)* apuntarse a
2 *vt sep (student, participant)* apuntar

► **sign out** 1 *vt sep* **to s. sth out** *(book, equipment)* registrar *or* consignar el préstamo de algo; **he signed himself out** *(hospital patient)* se fue sin esperar el alta
2 *vi* firmar a la salida

► **sign over** *vt sep (property, rights)* traspasar

► **sign up** 1 *vt sep (soldier)* reclutar; *(employee)* contratar; *(in sport)* fichar; *(of record company)* fichar, contratar
2 *vi* (**a**) *(for course)* apuntarse (**for** a) (**b**) *(soldier)* alistarse

signal ['sɪgnəl] 1 *n* (**a**) *(indication)* señal *f*; **to give sb the s. to do sth** dar a alguien la señal de hacer algo; IDIOM **to send the wrong signals** dar una impresión equivocada ►► ***s. flare*** bengala *f*; ***s. rocket*** cohete *m* de señales (**b**) *Rail* señal *f* ►► ***s. box*** sala *f* de agujas, puesto *m* de señales (**c**) *Rad, Tel & TV* señal *f*
2 *adj Formal (success, failure)* significativo(a); **you showed a s. lack of tact** mostraste una notable falta de tacto
3 *vt* (*pt & pp* **signalled**, *US* **signaled**) (**a**) *(indicate)* indicar (mediante señales) a; **to s. sb to do sth** hacerle una señal a alguien de *or* para que haga algo; **he signalled his approval** dio su aprobación (mediante una señal); **the cyclist signalled a left turn** el ciclista indicó que iba a girar a la izquierda
(**b**) *(be sign of)* señalar, indicar; **this announcement signals a major change in policy** este anuncio marca *or* indica un importante cambio de política
4 *vi* (**a**) *(gesture)* **s. to me if you need help** hazme una seña si necesitas ayuda; **she signalled for the bill** pidió la cuenta con una seña *or* haciendo señas; **to s. to sb to do sth** hacerle una señal a alguien de *or* para que haga algo (**b**) *Aut (with indicator)* señalizar, poner el intermitente; *(with arm)* señalizar

signaller ['sɪgnələ(r)] *n Rail* guardavía *m*

signalling, *US* **signaling** ['sɪgnəlɪŋ] *n Rail* señalización *f* ►► ***s. failure*** *Esp* fallo *m or Am* falla *f* en el sistema de señales

signally ['sɪgnəlɪ] *adv* evidentemente; **they s. failed to do this** está clarísimo que no lo hicieron

signalman ['sɪgnəlmən] *n Rail* guardavía *m*

signal-to-noise ratio ['sɪgnəltə'nɔɪz'reɪʃɪəʊ] *n Elec* relación *f* señal-ruido

signatory ['sɪgnətərɪ] *n* signatario(a) *m,f*, firmante *mf*; **Namibia is a s. to** *or* **of the treaty** Namibia es uno de los signatarios *or* firmantes del tratado

signature ['sɪgnətʃə(r)] *n* (**a**) *(name)* firma *f*; **he put his s. to the document** puso su firma al documento, firmó el documento ►► ***s. tune*** *(of radio, TV programme)* sintonía *f* (**b**) *Typ* pliego *m* (**c**) *Comptr (on e-mail)* firma *f*

signboard ['saɪnbɔːd] *n* letrero *m*

signet ring ['sɪgnɪt'rɪŋ] *n* sello *m (sortija)*

significance [sɪg'nɪfɪkəns] *n* (**a**) *(importance)* importancia *f*; **of no/great s.** de ninguna/gran importancia; **what happened? – nothing of any s.** ¿qué pasó? – nada importante ►► *Math* ***s. test*** contraste *m* (de hipótesis), test *m* de hipótesis (**b**) *(meaning)* significado *m*

significant [sɪg'nɪfɪkənt] *adj* (**a**) *(important)* importante; *Math* **...to two s. digits** *or* **figures** ...redondeándolo a dos decimales ►► ***s. other*** media naranja *f* (**b**) *(meaningful)* significativo(a)

significantly [sɪg'nɪfɪkəntlɪ] *adv* (**a**) *(appreciably)* sensiblemente; **unemployment figures are not s. lower** el número de desempleados no ha descendido significativamente (**b**) *(meaningfully)* significativamente; **s., no one mentioned it** es significativo que nadie lo mencionara

signifier ['sɪgnɪfaɪə(r)] *n Ling & Phil* significante *m*

signify ['sɪgnɪfaɪ] 1 *vt* (**a**) *(indicate)* señalar; *(constitute)* suponer, representar (**b**) *(mean)* significar
2 *vi US Fam* llevar a cabo un duelo verbal

signing ['saɪnɪŋ] *n* (**a**) *(of document)* firma *f* (**b**) *(sign language)* uso *m* del lenguaje por señas (**c**) *Sport (transfer, player)* fichaje *m*

signpost ['saɪnpəʊst] 1 *n* (**a**) *(giving directions)* señal *f* (**b**) *(indication)* indicación *f*
2 *vt* (**a**) *(place, route)* señalizar; **the village is clearly signposted** el pueblo tiene muy buena señalización (**b**) *(indicate)* señalar

signwriter ['saɪnraɪtə(r)] *n* rotulista *mf*

Sikh [siːk] 1 *n* sij *mf*
2 *adj* sij

Sikhism ['siːkɪzəm] *n* sijismo *m*, religión *f* sij

silage ['saɪlɪdʒ] *n* forraje *m*

silence ['saɪləns] 1 *n* silencio *m*; **to listen/watch in s.** escuchar/observar en silencio; **to call for s.** pedir silencio; **to observe a minute's s.** guardar un minuto de silencio; **s.!** ¡silencio!; **s. in court!** ¡silencio en la sala!; **what's my s. worth to you?** ¿cuánto estás dispuesto a pagar por mi silencio?; PROV **s. is golden** en boca cerrada no entran moscas
2 *vt* (**a**) *(make quiet) (person)* acallar, hacer callar; *(guns)* silenciar (**b**) *(opposition)* hacer callar; *(conscience, rumours, complaints)* acallar; **to s. one's critics** silenciar *or* acallar a los críticos

silencer ['saɪlənsə(r)] *n* (**a**) *(on gun)* silenciador *m* (**b**) *Br (on car)* silenciador *m*

silent ['saɪlənt] 1 *adj* (**a**) *(place, movements)* silencioso(a); **to be s.** *(not talk)* estar callado(a); **please be s.** por favor, permanezcan en silencio; **he was s. for a moment** permaneció en silencio un momento; **to fall s.** quedarse en silencio; **to remain** *or* **keep s.** permanecer callado(a), guardar silencio; **you have the right to remain s.** tiene derecho a guardar silencio *or* permanecer en silencio; IDIOM **as s. as the grave** como una tumba ►► ***s. movie*** *or Br* ***film*** película *f* muda; ***s. movies*** *or Br* ***films*** el cine mudo; ***the s. majority*** la mayoría silenciosa; *Rel* ***s. order*** orden *f* silenciosa; *Bus* ***s. partner*** socio(a) *m,f* capitalista; ***s. protest*** protesta *f* silenciosa
(**b**) *(taciturn)* callado(a); **she's rather s.** es muy callada
(**c**) *(unspoken) (prayer, emotion, reproach)* silencioso(a)
(**d**) *(not pronounced) (letter)* mudo(a)
2 *n Cin* **the silents** el cine mudo

silently ['saɪləntlɪ] *adv* (**a**) *(not speaking)* en silencio (**b**) *(without noise)* sin hacer ruido, silenciosamente

Silesia [saɪ'liːʒɪə] *n* Silesia

silex ['saɪleks] *n* sílex *m*

silhouette [sɪluː'et] 1 *n* silueta *f*; **he could just see the church in s.** sólo podía ver la silueta de la iglesia
2 *vt* **she was silhouetted against the light** la luz dibujaba su silueta, su silueta se recortaba al trasluz

silhouettist [sɪlʊ(ː)'etɪst] *n* = profesional que corta siluetas

silica ['sɪlɪkə] *n* sílice *f* ►► ***s. gel*** gel *m* de sílice

silicate ['sɪlɪkeɪt] *n* silicato *m*

siliceous, silicious [sɪ'lɪʃəs] *adj* silíceo(a)

silicic [sɪ'lɪsɪk] *adj Chem* ***s. acid*** ácido *m* silícico

silicious = **siliceous**

silicon ['sɪlɪkən] *n Chem* silicio *m* ►► ***s. carbide*** carburo *m* silícico; ***s. chip*** chip *m* de silicio; ***S. Valley*** Silicon Valley

silicone ['sɪlɪkəʊn] *n* silicona *f* ►► ***s. implant*** implante *m* de silicona

silicosis [sɪlɪ'kəʊsɪs] *n* silicosis *f inv*

silk [sɪlk] *n* (**a**) *(material)* seda *f*; **a s. shirt/tie** una camisa/corbata de seda; PROV **you can't make a s. purse out of a sow's ear** no se puede pedir peras al olmo, aunque la mona se vista de seda, mona se queda ►► ***s. industry*** industria *f* de la seda; ***s. merchant*** mercader *m* de la seda; ***s. screen printing*** serigrafía *f*
(**b**) **silks** *(of jockey)* colores *mpl (de una cuadra)*
(**c**) *Br Law (barrister)* abogado(a) *m,f* de alto rango; **to take s.** = ser nombrado(a) abogado(a) de alto rango de la corona

silken ['sɪlkən] *adj Literary* (**a**) *(material)* de seda (**b**) *(skin, hair)* sedoso(a) (**c**) *(voice)* aterciopelado(a)

silkiness ['sɪlkɪnɪs] *n* (**a**) *(of material)* sedosidad *f* (**b**) *(of skin, hair)* tacto *m* sedoso (**c**) *(of voice)* melosidad *f*

silkworm ['sɪlkwɜːm] *n* gusano *m* de (la) seda

silky ['sɪlkɪ] *adj* (**a**) *(material)* sedoso(a) (**b**) *(skin, hair)* sedoso(a) (**c**) *(voice)* meloso(a) (**d**) *Sport* **he demonstrated his s. ball skills** demostró la maestría y dulzura con la que controla la pelota

sill [sɪl] *n* (**a**) *(of window)* alféizar *m* (**b**) *Aut* umbral *m*

silliness ['sɪlɪnɪs] *n* tontería *f*, estupidez *f*; **stop this s.!** ¡ya basta de tonterías!

silly ['sɪlɪ] 1 *adj* tonto(a), estúpido(a); **you s. idiot!** ¡qué imbécil eres!; **not there, you s. man!** ¡ahí no, tonto!; **how s. of me!, s. me!** ¡qué tonto soy!; **it's s. to worry** es una tontería preocuparse; **now you're just being s.!** ¡no seas tonto!; **the s. thing is that...** lo más ridículo es que...; **to make sb look s.** poner a alguien en ridículo; **to say/do something s.** decir/hacer una tontería; **that was a s. thing to say/do** fue una tontería decir/hacer eso; **there was a new manager every week, it was** *or* **things were getting s.** cada semana había un jefe nuevo, era ridículo; **to laugh/worry oneself s.** morirse de la risa/de

preocupación; **he drank himself s.** se puso como una cuba; **to knock sb s.** dejar a alguien atontado(a) de un mamporro ▸▸ ***the s. season*** = periodo estival en el que los periódicos suplen la ausencia de noticias de índole política con información más o menos banal
2 *n Fam* tonto(a) *m,f*

silly-billy ['sɪlɪ'bɪlɪ] *n Fam* tonto(a) *m,f* de capirote

silo ['saɪləʊ] (*pl* **silos**) *n* silo *m*

silt [sɪlt] *n* limo *m*, sedimentos *mpl* fluviales

▸ **silt up** 1 *vi* encenagarse
2 *vt sep* encenagar

Silurian [saɪ'lʊərɪən] *adj* silúrico(a)

silver ['sɪlvə(r)] 1 *n* (**a**) *(metal)* plata *f* ▸▸ ***s. disc*** disco *m* de plata; *Br* ***s. foil*** *(kitchen foil)* papel *m* de plata; ***s. gilt*** plata *f* dorada; ***s. iodide*** yoduro *m* de plata; ***s. mine*** mina *f* de plata; ***s. nitrate*** nitrato *m* de plata; *Br* ***s. paper*** papel *m* de plata; ***s. plate*** *(coating)* baño *m* de plata; *(articles)* objetos *mpl* plateados; ***the s. screen*** la pantalla grande; ***s. service*** servicio *m* de guante blanco
(**b**) *Br (coins)* monedas *fpl* plateadas *(de entre 5 y 50 peniques)*
(**c**) *(silverware)* (objetos *mpl* de) plata *f*
(**d**) *(colour)* plata *f*
(**e**) *Sport* **s. (medal)** medalla *f* de plata
2 *adj* (**a**) *(made of silver)* de plata (**b**) *(in colour)* **s.(-coloured)** plateado(a) ▸▸ ***s. birch*** abedul *m* blanco; ***s. fir*** abeto *m* blanco; ***s. fox*** zorro *m* plateado (**c**) *(twenty-fifth anniversary)* **s. jubilee** vigésimo quinto aniversario; **s. wedding** bodas de plata
3 *adv* **to go s.** *(record)* convertirse en disco de plata
4 *vt (metal)* platear, dar un baño de plata a; *(mirror)* azogar

silverfish ['sɪlvəfɪʃ] *n (insect)* lepisma *f*

silver-haired [sɪlvə'heəd] *adj* con el pelo blanco

silver-grey [sɪlvə'greɪ] *adj* gris plata

silver-plate [sɪlvə'pleɪt] *vt* dar un baño de plata a

silver-plated [sɪlvə'pleɪtɪd] *adj* con baño de plata

silverside ['sɪlvəsaɪd] *n Br* babilla *f*

silverskin ['sɪlvəskɪn] *adj* ***s. onion*** cebollino *m*

silversmith ['sɪlvəsmɪθ] *n* platero(a) *m,f*

silver-tongued [sɪlvə'tʌŋd] *adj* de pico de oro

silverware ['sɪlvəweə(r)] *n* (objetos *mpl* de) plata *f*, vajilla *f* de plata

silverweed ['sɪlvəwiːd] *n* argentina *f*

silverwork ['sɪlvəwɜːk] *n* (trabajo *m* de) platería *f*

silvery ['sɪlvərɪ] *adj* (**a**) *(in colour)* plateado(a); *(hair)* canoso(a) (**b**) *(sound)* argentino(a)

silviculture ['sɪlvɪkʌltʃə(r)] *n* silvicultura *f*

SIM [sɪm] *n* (*abbr* **subscriber identity module**) ***S. card*** *(in mobile phone)* tarjeta *f* SIM

simian ['sɪmɪən] 1 *n* simio *m*
2 *adj* simiesco(a)

similar ['sɪmɪlə(r)] *adj* (**a**) *(showing resemblance)* parecido(a), similar (**to** a); **to be s. to sth/sb** ser parecido(a) *or* parecerse a algo/alguien; **s. in appearance/size (to)** de parecido aspecto/tamaño (a) (**b**) *Geom* semejante

similarity [sɪmɪ'lærɪtɪ] *n* (**a**) *(resemblance)* parecido *m*, similitud *f* (**to** a); **that's where the s. ends** hasta ahí llega el parecido (**b**) **similarities** *(features in common)* rasgos *mpl* comunes; **our similarities are more important than our differences** los rasgos que tenemos en común son más importantes que las diferencias

similarly ['sɪmɪləlɪ] *adv* (**a**) *(in a like way)* de forma similar (**b**) *(to the same extent)* igualmente; **we found ourselves s. puzzled** todos nos quedamos igual de perplejos (**c**) *(likewise)* igualmente, del mismo modo

simile ['sɪmɪlɪ] *n* símil *m*

similitude [sɪ'mɪlɪtjuːd] *n Formal* similitud *f*

SIMM [sɪm] *n Comptr* (*abbr* **single in-line memory module**) SIMM *m*

simmer ['sɪmə(r)] 1 *n* **at a s.** a fuego lento
2 *vt* cocer a fuego lento
3 *vi* (**a**) *(liquid)* cocerse a fuego lento (**b**) *(revolt, discontent)* estar a punto de explotar; **she was simmering with rage** estaba a punto de explotar de rabia

▸ **simmer down** *vi* calmarse, tranquilizarse; *Fam* **s. down!** ¡cálmate!

simmering ['sɪmərɪŋ] *adj* a punto de explotar

simnel cake ['sɪmnəlkeɪk] *n Br* = bizcocho tradicional de la Cuaresma, hecho con frutas y mazapán

simp [sɪmp] *n US Fam* simplón(ona) *m,f*

simpatico [sɪm'pætɪkəʊ] *adj US (like-minded)* parecido(a)

simper ['sɪmpə(r)] 1 *n* sonrisa *f* afectada
2 *vt* decir con una sonrisa afectada
3 *vi* sonreír con afectación

simperingly ['sɪmpərɪŋlɪ] *adv* con una sonrisa afectada

simple ['sɪmpəl] *adj* (**a**) *(uncomplicated) (task, reasons, operation)* sencillo(a); **it would be simpler to do it myself** sería más sencillo que lo hiciera yo mismo; **it's a s. question of telling the truth** se trata simplemente de decir la verdad; **I want a s. "yes" or "no"** no quiero más que un "sí" o un "no"; **I did it for the s. reason that I had no choice** lo hice por la sencilla razón de que no tenía elección; **keep it s.** *(explanation, meal, design)* que sea sencillo(a), no te compliques la vida; **it's as s. as that** es así de sencillo; **it's s. to use** es muy fácil de usar, es de fácil manejo; **in s. terms** sencillamente; **at its simplest...** básicamente..., esencialmente...; **the s. truth** la pura verdad
(**b**) *(unsophisticated) (person, dress, meal, wedding)* sencillo(a); **s. country folk** gente sencilla del campo
(**c**) *(naive)* inocente, cándido(a); **he's a bit s.** es un poco simplón
(**d**) *(unintelligent)* simple
(**e**) *(not compound) Math* ***s. equation*** ecuación *f* de primer grado; *Math* ***s. fraction*** fracción *f* ordinaria; *Med* ***s. fracture*** fractura *f* simple; *Fin* ***s. interest*** interés *m* simple; ***s. majority*** mayoría *f* simple; *Gram* ***s. past*** pretérito *m* indefinido; *Gram* ***s. sentence*** oración *f* simple; *Gram* ***s. tense*** tiempo *m* simple; *Mus* ***s. tone*** tono *m* puro

simple-hearted ['sɪmpəl'hɑːtɪd] *adj (person)* ingenuo(a), cándido(a)

simple-minded ['sɪmpəl'maɪndɪd] *adj (person)* simplón(ona); *(ideas, belief)* ingenuo(a)

simpleton ['sɪmpəltən] *n* simplón(ona) *m,f*

simplicity [sɪm'plɪsɪtɪ] *n* (**a**) *(easiness)* sencillez *f*; **it's s. itself** es de lo más sencillo (**b**) *(unsophisticated nature) (of person, dress, meal, wedding)* sencillez *f* (**c**) *(naivety)* inocencia *f*, candidez *f*

simplification [sɪmplɪfɪ'keɪʃən] *n* simplificación *f*

simplified ['sɪmplɪfaɪd] *adj* simplificado(a)

simplify ['sɪmplɪfaɪ] *vt* simplificar

simplistic [sɪm'plɪstɪk] *adj* simplista

simplistically [sɪm'plɪstɪklɪ] *adv* simplísticamente

simply ['sɪmplɪ] *adv* (**a**) *(in uncomplicated manner)* con sencillez; **to express oneself s.** expresarse de forma sencilla *or* simple; **put quite s., it's a disaster** para que me entiendan, es un desastre
(**b**) *(absolutely)* sencillamente; **I s. adore pizzas!** ¡las pizzas es que me encantan de verdad!; **she's s. marvellous** es sencillamente maravillosa; **I s. HAVE to see him!** ¡sencillamente tengo que verlo!; **you s. must go and see it!** ¡no te lo pierdas por nada del mundo!; **this behaviour is quite s. unacceptable** este comportamiento es sencillamente inaceptable
(**c**) *(just)* sólo; **it's s. a question of time** sólo es una cuestión de tiempo; **she s. had to snap her fingers and...** sólo con chasquear los dedos...; **we s. can't go on like this** así es imposible seguir; **s. add water and cook for five minutes** simplemente añade agua y dejar hervir durante cinco minutos

simulate ['sɪmjʊleɪt] *vt* simular

simulated ['sɪmjʊleɪtɪd] *adj* (**a**) *(leather, marble, fur)* de imitación (**b**) *(surprise, anger)* fingido(a), simulado(a); **a s. battle** una simulación de una batalla

simulation [sɪmjʊ'leɪʃən] *n* simulación *f* ▸▸ *Comptr* ***s. model*** modelo *m* de simulación

simulator ['sɪmjʊleɪtə(r)] *n* simulador *m*

simulcast [[*Br* 'sɪməlkɑːst, *US* 'saɪməlkæst] *vt* retransmitir simultáneamente

simultaneity [sɪməltə'nɪətɪ] *n* simultaneidad *f*

simultaneous [sɪməl'teɪnɪəs] *adj* simultáneo(a) ▸▸ ***s. broadcast*** retransmisión *f* simultánea; ***s. interpreting*** interpretación *f* simultánea; ***s. translation*** traducción *f* simultánea

simultaneously [sɪməl'teɪnɪəslɪ] *adv* simultáneamente

sin [sɪn] 1 *n* pecado *m*; *Fig* **a s. of omission** una falta por omisión; *Old-fashioned or Hum* **to be living in s.** vivir en pecado; *Fam* **it would be a s. to...** sería un pecado...; *Hum* **for my sins** para mi desgracia ▸▸ ***s. bin*** *(in hockey, rugby league)* banquillo *m* de castigo
2 *vi* (*pt & pp* **sinned**) pecar

▸ **sin against** *vt insep Rel* pecar contra; *Fig (principle, rule)* traicionar; **more sinned against than sinning** más víctima que villano

Sinai ['saɪnaɪ] *n (region)* Sinaí *m*; **the S. (Desert)** el (desierto del) Sinaí; **(Mount) S.** el (monte) Sinaí

sin-bin ['sɪnbɪn] *vt (in hockey, rugby league)* mandar al banquillo de castigo

since [sɪns] 1 *prep* desde; **s. his death** desde su muerte; **s. June/1993** desde junio/1993; **s. then** desde entonces; **that was in 1966, s. when the law has been altered** eso fue en 1966, desde entonces la ley ha cambiado; **s. when have you been in charge?** ¿desde cuándo mandas tú aquí?

2 *adv* desde entonces; **I have s. changed my mind** de entonces a ahora he cambiado de opinión; **long s.** hace mucho; **she left not long s.** no hace mucho que se fue

3 *conj* **(a)** *(in time)* desde que; **it's a long time s. I saw her** ha pasado mucho tiempo desde que la vi; **it's a year s. she died** murió hace ya un año; **it's been ages s. we've gone to a play** hace siglos que no vamos a una obra de teatro; **s. leaving New York, I…** desde que me vine de Nueva York, yo…

(b) *(because)* ya que; **I'll do it s. it's you that's asking** lo haré porque eres tú quien me lo pide; **how much do you weigh? – 70 kilos, s. you ask** ¿cuánto pesas? – ya que lo preguntas, te diré que 70 kilos

sincere [sɪn'sɪə(r)] *adj* sincero(a); **please accept my s. apologies** le ruego que acepte mis sinceras disculpas; **it is my s. belief that war can be avoided** creo sinceramente que la guerra puede evitarse

sincerely [sɪn'sɪəlɪ] *adv* sinceramente; **I'm s. sorry** lo siento en el alma; **I s. hope so!** ¡así lo espero!; **Yours s.** *(ending letter)* Atentamente

sincerity [sɪn'serɪtɪ] *n* sinceridad *f*; **in all s.** con toda sinceridad; **I do not doubt your s., but…** no dudo de su sinceridad, pero…

sine [saɪn] *n Math* seno *m* ▸▸ ***s. wave*** onda *f* pura *or* sinusoidal

sinecure ['saɪnɪkjʊə(r)] *n* sinecura *f*

sine qua non ['sɪnɪkwɑː'nɒn] *n Formal* condición *f* sine qua non

sinew ['sɪnjuː] *n* **(a)** *(of person)* tendón *m*; *(in meat)* nervio *m*; *Fig* **I will resist with every s. of my body** resistiré con todas mis fuerzas **(b)** *Literary (source of strength)* pilar *m*

sinewy ['sɪnjuːɪ] *adj (person, muscles)* fibroso(a); *(hands, neck)* nervudo(a); *(meat)* duro(a), con mucho nervio

sinful ['sɪnfʊl] *adj* **(a)** *(person)* pecador(ora); *(act, thought, life)* pecaminoso(a); **a s. man** un hombre pecador **(b)** *(waste)* escandaloso(a); **such waste is downright s.!** ¡tanto derroche es un verdadero escándalo!

sinfulness ['sɪnfʊlnɪs] *n (of behaviour, act)* lo pecaminoso; **a life of s.** una vida pecaminosa

sing [sɪŋ] *(pt* **sang** [sæŋ], *pp* **sung** [sʌŋ]) 1 *vt (song)* cantar; **to s. sb to sleep** arrullar a alguien; **who sings tenor?** ¿quién tiene voz de tenor?; **to s. sth's/sb's praises** cantar las excelencias de algo/alguien; **to s. one's own praises** alabarse a uno mismo

2 *vi* **(a)** *(person, bird)* cantar **(b)** *(kettle)* pitar; **the noise made my ears s.** me zumbaban los oídos con el ruido **(c)** *Literary* **to s. of** *(recount)* trovar, cantar **(d)** *Fam (confess, inform)* cantar

▸**sing along** *vi* cantar a coro **(with/to** con/siguiendo)

▸**sing out** *vi (sing loudly)* cantar en voz alta; *Fam* **when you're ready, s. out** cuando estés listo, péganos un grito

▸**sing up** *vi* cantar más fuerte

singalong ['sɪŋəlɒŋ] *n* canto *m* a coro, coros *mpl*; **to have a s.** cantar a coro

Singapore [sɪŋə'pɔː(r)] *n* Singapur

Singaporean [sɪŋə'pɔːrɪən] 1 *n* singapurense *mf*

2 *adj* singapurense

singe [sɪndʒ] 1 *vt* chamuscar; **she singed her eyebrows** se chamuscó las cejas

2 *n* ***s. (mark)*** quemadura *f*

singer ['sɪŋə(r)] *n* cantante *mf*; **I'm a terrible s.** canto muy mal ▸▸ ***s. songwriter*** cantautor(ora) *m,f*

Singhalese = **Sinhalese**

singing ['sɪŋɪŋ] *n* **(a)** *(of person, bird)* canto *m*; **his s. is awful** canta muy mal; **the s. went on until dawn** los cantos continuaron hasta el amanecer; **we left after the s. of the national anthem** nos fuimos después de que se entonara el himno nacional; **to have a fine s. voice** tener una excelente voz ▸▸ ***s. lessons*** clases *fpl* de canto **(b)** *(of kettle)* pitido *m*, silbido *m*; *(in ears)* pitido *m*, zumbido *m*

single ['sɪŋgəl] 1 *n* **(a)** *(record)* sencillo *m*, single *m*

(b) *Br (ticket) Esp* billete *m or Am* boleto *m or Am* pasaje *m* sencillo *or* de ida

(c) *(hotel room)* habitación *f* sencilla *or* individual

(d) *(in baseball, cricket)* carrera *f*

(e) *(money) (pound note)* billete *m* de una libra; *(pound coin)* moneda *f* de una libra; *(dollar bill)* billete *m* de un dólar

(f) *Sport* **singles** (modalidad *f* de) individuales *mpl*; **the men's/ladies' singles** los individuales masculinos/femeninos ▸▸ ***singles champion*** campeón(ona) *m,f* individual

(g) **singles** *(unattached people)* gente *f* sin pareja ▸▸ ***singles bar*** *or* ***club*** bar *m* de encuentros; ***s. night*** noche *f* de solteros

2 *adj* **(a)** *(just one)* solo(a); **the report comes in a s. volume** el informe se presenta en un solo *or* único volumen; **he gave her a s. red rose** le dio una (sola) rosa roja; **every s. day** todos los días; **not a s. one** ni uno(a) solo(a); **I can't think of one s. reason why I should do it** no se me ocurre ni una sola *or* ninguna razón por la que deba hacerlo; **I couldn't think of a s. thing to say** no se me ocurrió absolutamente nada que decir; **I haven't seen a s. soul** no he visto ni un alma; **don't say a s. word** no digas ni una (sola) palabra; **it's the s. most important decision of my life** es la decisión más importante de mi vida ▸▸ *Fin* ***s. currency*** moneda *f* única; *EU* ***the S. European Act*** el Acta Única Europea; *Econ* ***s. (European) market*** mercado *m* único (europeo)

(b) *(individual, considered separately)* **we sell s. items at a higher price per unit** vendemos los artículos sueltos a un precio unitario superior; **in any s. year, sales average ten million** en cualquier año, las ventas alcanzan una media de diez millones ▸▸ ***s. combat*** combate *m* individual

(c) *(not double)* **in s. figures** por debajo de diez; **in s. file** en fila india ▸▸ ***s. bed*** cama *f* individual; ***s. cream*** *Esp* nata *f or Am* crema *f* de leche; *Br Univ* ***s. honours*** licenciatura *f* en una sola especialidad; ***s. malt (whisky)*** whisky *m* puro de malta; ***s. occupancy rate*** tarifa *f* de ocupación individual; *Typ* ***s. quotes*** comillas *fpl* simples; ***s. room*** habitación *f* sencilla *or* individual; ***s. room supplement*** suplemento *m* por habitación sencilla *or* individual; ***s. sheet*** sábana *f* individual, sábana *f* para cama individual; *Typ* ***s. spacing*** espacio *m* simple; ***s. transferable vote*** voto *m* personal transferible (por listas); ***s. yellow line*** *(on road)* = línea continua de color amarillo próxima al bordillo que indica la prohibición total de estacionamiento entre las 8 de la mañana y las 4.30 de la tarde entre semana

(d) *(not married)* soltero(a); **a s. woman** una soltera ▸▸ ***s. mother*** madre *f* soltera; ***s. parent*** padre *m*/madre *f* soltero(a); ***s. parent family*** familia *f* monoparental

(e) *Br (ticket)* sencillo(a), de ida; *(fare)* de ida

▸**single out** *vt sep* señalar, distinguir; **to s. sb out for blame/criticism** culpar/criticar a alguien en particular; **she was singled out for special praise** fue distinguida con una mención especial

single-breasted ['sɪŋgəl'brestɪd] *adj (jacket, suit)* recto(a), no cruzado(a)

single-celled ['sɪŋgəl'seld] *adj Biol* unicelular

single-decker ['sɪŋgəl'dekə(r)] *n (bus)* autobús *m* de un piso

single-density ['sɪŋgəl'densɪtɪ] *adj Comptr* de densidad sencilla

single-engined ['sɪŋgəl'endʒɪnd] *adj (plane)* de un solo motor

single-entry ['sɪŋgəl'entrɪ] *adj* ***s. bookkeeping*** contabilidad *f* por partida simple

single-figure ['sɪŋgəl'fɪgə(r)] *adj* de una cifra

single-handed ['sɪŋgəl'hændɪd] 1 *adj* **(a)** *(unaided) (voyage)* en solitario; *(achievement)* sin ayuda (de nadie) **(b)** *Sport (backhand)* a una mano

2 *adv (sail)* en solitario; *(transform, defeat)* sin ayuda (de nadie)

single-handedly ['sɪŋgəl'hændɪdlɪ] *adv (to transform, defeat)* sin ayuda (de nadie)

single-income ['sɪŋgəl'ɪnkəm] *adj (family, couple)* con una única *or* sola fuente de ingresos

single-lane ['sɪŋgəl'leɪn] *adj (traffic)* por un solo carril

single-lens ['sɪŋgəl'lenz] *adj* ***s. camera*** cámara *f* de un solo objetivo

single-masted ['sɪŋgəl'mɑːstɪd] *adj* de un solo palo

single-minded ['sɪŋgəl'maɪndɪd] *adj* resuelto(a), determinado(a)

single-mindedly ['sɪŋgəl'maɪndɪdlɪ] *adv* con determinación, con empeño

single-mindedness ['sɪŋgəl'maɪndɪdnɪs] *n* resolución *f*, determinación *f*

single-seater ['sɪŋgəl'siːtə(r)] *n (plane)* avión *m* monoplaza

single-sex school ['sɪŋgəl'seks'skuːl] *n (for girls)* colegio *m* para niñas; *(for boys)* colegio *m* para niños

single-spaced ['sɪŋgəl'speɪst] *adj Typ* a un (solo) espacio

singlet ['sɪŋglɪt] *n Br* camiseta *f* (de tirantes *or Am* breteles)

singleton ['sɪŋgəltən] *n (in bridge)* semifallo *m*

single-track ['sɪŋgəl'træk] *adj* ***s. railway*** vía *f* única; *Br* ***s. road*** carretera *f or* camino *m* de un solo carril

singly ['sɪŋglɪ] *adv* **(a)** *(one at a time)* individualmente, uno(a) por uno(a) **(b)** *(individually) (packaged)* individualmente, por separado

singsong ['sɪŋsɒŋ] 1 *n* (a) *(voice, tone)* **he spoke in a s.** habló con voz cantarina (b) *Br (singing session)* **to have a s.** reunirse para cantar
2 *adj (voice, tone)* cantarín(ina)

singular ['sɪŋgjələ(r)] 1 *n Gram* singular *m*; **in the s.** en singular
2 *adj* (a) *Gram* singular (b) *Formal (remarkable)* singular, excepcional

singularity [sɪŋgjə'lærɪtɪ] *n* (a) *Astron* singularidad *f* (b) *Formal (strangeness)* singularidad *f* (c) *Formal (characterisitic)* particularidad *f*, singularidad *f*

singularly ['sɪŋgjələlɪ] *adv* singularmente, excepcionalmente; **I was s. unimpressed** no me impresionó lo más mínimo

Sinhalese [sɪnhə'li:z], **Singhalese** [sɪŋhə'li:z] 1 *n* (a) *(person)* cingalés(esa) *m,f* (b) *(language)* cingalés *m*
2 *adj* cingalés(esa)

sinister ['sɪnɪstə(r)] *adj* siniestro(a)

sink[1] [sɪŋk] 1 *n* (a) *(in kitchen)* fregadero *m* ►► ***s. tidy*** organizador *m* para el fregadero; ***s. unit*** módulo *m* or mueble *m* fregadero (b) *(in bathroom)* lavabo *m*, *Am* lavamanos *m inv*
2 *adj Br* ***s. estate*** urbanización *f* muy pobre

sink[2] (*pt* **sank** [sæŋk], *pp* **sunk** [sʌŋk]) 1 *vt* (a) *(ship, submarine)* hundir
(b) *(well)* cavar; *(shaft)* excavar
(c) *(plunge) (knife)* hundir, clavar; **to s. one's teeth into sth** clavar *or* hincar el diente a algo; **they're sinking the piles for the jetty** están enterrando en el suelo los pilares para el embarcadero; **to s. money into a project** invertir mucho dinero en un proyecto
(d) *(cause to fail)* hundir, hacer fracasar; *Fam* **to be sunk** *(in trouble)* estar perdido(a)
(e) *Br Fam (drink)* **to s. a pint** *Esp* pimplarse *or Am* tomarse una pinta (de cerveza)
(f) *Sport (ball, putt, pot)* meter; *(basket)* encestar
(g) *(forget)* **they sank their differences** dejaron a un lado *or* enterraron sus diferencias
(h) *(immerse)* **to be sunk in thought** estar abstraído(a)
2 *vi* (a) *(in water, mud)* hundirse; **the bottle sank slowly to the bottom of the pool** la botella se hundió lentamente hasta el fondo de la piscina; **at each step, I sank up to my knees in water** a cada paso que daba, me sumergía en el agua hasta las rodillas; *also Fig* **to s. without trace** hundirse *or* desaparecer sin dejar rastro; IDIOM **to s. like a stone** hundirse con rapidez; IDIOM **he's sinking fast** se está yendo por momentos; IDIOM **to be left to s. or swim** estar abandonado(a) a su suerte; IDIOM **it was a case of s. or swim** no quedaba otra alternativa que pelear o morir
(b) *(drop) (water, level)* descender; *(sun, moon)* ocultarse; **as I climbed, the valley sank out of sight** a medida que ascendía, el valle desaparecía de mi vista; **her voice sank to a whisper** su voz se redujo a un susurro; **to s. into despair** sumirse en la desesperación; **to s. into oblivion** sumirse en el olvido; **to s. into sb's memory** quedar grabado(a) en la memoria de alguien
(c) *(sag, slump)* **to s. to the ground** ir cayendo al suelo; **to s. to one's knees** hincarse de rodillas; **to s. into an armchair** hundirse en un sillón; **to s. into a deep sleep** sumirse en un sueño profundo; **her heart sank** se le cayó el alma a los pies; **his spirits sank** se desanimó
(d) *(decrease) (currency, rate, temperature)* desplomarse; **the euro has sunk to a new low** el euro ha alcanzado un nuevo mínimo
(e) *(morally)* **he has sunk in my estimation** ha perdido gran parte de mi estima; **how could you s. so low?** ¿cómo pudiste caer tan bajo?
(f) *(penetrate) (knife, arrow, teeth)* hundirse, clavarse

► **sink in** *vi* (a) *(liquid, cream, varnish)* penetrar, calar (b) *(information)* calar; **it hasn't sunk in yet** todavía no lo he *or* lo tengo asumido; **I paused to let my words s. in** hice una pausa para que los oyentes pudieran asimilar mis palabras

sinker ['sɪŋkə(r)] *n* (a) *(for fishing)* plomo *m*, plomada *f* (b) *US Fam (doughnut)* donut *m*

sinking ['sɪŋkɪŋ] 1 *n* (a) *(of ship)* hundimiento *m* (b) *(of well)* excavación *f*, perforación *f*; *(of shaft)* excavación *f*, profundización *f* (c) *Fin* ***s. fund*** fondo *m* de amortización
2 *adj* **with a s. heart** con creciente desánimo; **to get that s. feeling** empezar a preocuparse

sinner ['sɪnə(r)] *n* pecador(ora) *m,f*

Sinn Féin [ʃɪn'feɪn] *n* Sinn Fein *m*

Sino- ['saɪnəʊ] *prefix* chino-; **the S.-Japanese War** la guerra chino-japonesa

Sinologist [saɪ'nɒlədʒɪst] *n* sinólogo(a) *m,f*

Sinology [saɪ'nɒlədʒɪ] *n* sinología *f*

sintered ['sɪntəd] *adj* de metal en polvo

sinuous ['sɪnjʊəs] *adj* sinuoso(a)

sinus ['saɪnəs] *n* seno *m* (nasal) ►► ***s. infection*** sinusitis *f inv*

sinusitis [saɪnə'saɪtɪs] *n* sinusitis *f inv*

Sioux [su:] 1 *n (person)* sioux *mf inv*
2 *adj* sioux

sip [sɪp] 1 *n* sorbo *m*; **to take a s. (of sth)** dar un sorbo (a algo)
2 *vt* (*pt & pp* **sipped**) sorber, beber a sorbos
3 *vi* **she sipped at her drink** bebió un sorbo a su bebida

siphon ['saɪfən] 1 *n* sifón *m*
2 *vt (liquid, petrol)* sacar con sifón (**into** a)

► **siphon off** *vt sep* (a) *(liquid)* sacar con sifón (b) *(money, supplies, traffic)* desviar

sir [sɜ:(r)] *n* (a) *(form of address)* señor *m*; *(to teacher)* profesor *m*; **yes, s.!** *(to military officer)* ¡sí, mi teniente/capitán/coronel/*etc*!; *Fam* **pass me those books – yes, s.!** pásame esos libros – ¡sí, señor! *or* ¡lo que usted diga *or* mande!; *Fam* **did you win? – yes s.!** ¿ganaste? – ¡sí señor!
(b) *(in letters)* **Dear S.** Estimado señor, Muy señor mío; **Dear Sirs** Estimados señores, Muy señores míos; **S.** *(in letter to newspaper)* Señor Director
(c) *(title)* **S. Cedric** sir Cedric *(título nobiliario masculino)*

sire ['saɪə(r)] 1 *n* (a) *(of animal)* padre *m* (b) *Old-fashioned (address to sovereign)* señor *m*, majestad *m*
2 *vt* (a) *(horse)* ser el padre de (b) *Old-fashioned or Hum (person)* engendrar

siren ['saɪrən] *n* (a) *(alarm)* sirena *f* (b) *(in mythology)* sirena *f*; *Fig* **who can resist the s. call of fame and wealth?** ¿quién puede resistirse a la seductora llamada de la fama y el dinero?

Sirius ['sɪrɪəs] *n* Sirio

sirloin ['sɜ:lɔɪn] *n* **s. (steak)** lomo *m*

sirocco [sɪ'rɒkəʊ] *n* siroco *m*

sirree [sɜ:'ri:] *exclam US Fam* **yes/no s.!** ¡sí/no, señor!

sis [sɪs] *n Fam* hermanita *f*, *RP* her *f*

sisal ['saɪzəl] *n (plant)* pita *f*; *(material)* sisal *m* ►► ***s. grass*** pita *f*

siskin ['sɪskɪn] *n* lugano *m*

sissy ['sɪsɪ] 1 *n Fam (cowardly male)* blandengue *m*, gallina *m*; *(effeminate male)* mariquita *m*
2 *adj (cowardly)* cobardica, blandengue; *(effeminate)* afeminado(a), amariposado(a)

sister ['sɪstə(r)] *n* (a) *(sibling)* hermana *f* ►► *US* ***s. city*** ciudad *f* hermanada; ***s. company*** empresa *f* asociada; ***s. organization*** organización *f* hermana; ***s. ship*** buque *m* gemelo
(b) *(nun)* hermana *f*; **s. Teresa** sor Teresa, la hermana Teresa; **the Sisters of Mercy** las hermanas de la Caridad
(c) *(nurse)* enfermera *f* jefe
(d) *US Fam (fellow black woman)* hermana *f* (negra)
(e) *Fam (fellow feminist)* hermana *f* (feminista)
(f) *US Fam (term of address for woman)* amiga *f*, hermana *f*

sisterhood ['sɪstəhʊd] *n* (a) *(community of nuns)* hermandad *f*, congregación *f* (b) *(solidarity)* hermandad *f* (entre mujeres)

sister-in-law ['sɪstərɪn'lɔ:] (*pl* **sisters-in-law**) *n* cuñada *f*

sisterly ['sɪstəlɪ] *adj* de hermana

Sistine ['sɪsti:n] *n* **the S. Chapel** la Capilla Sixtina

SIT [sɪt] (*pt & pp* **sat** [sæt]) 1 *vt* (a) *(seat)* **to s. a child on one's knee** sentar a un niño en el regazo; **she sat me next to her** me sentó al lado de ella *or* a su lado; **the table sits ten** es una mesa de *or* para diez; **the main dining room sits 200 people** en el comedor principal caben 200 personas
(b) *Br (exam)* presentarse a
2 *vi* (a) *(person) (be seated)* estar sentado(a); *(sit down)* sentarse; **s.!** *(to dog)* ¡siéntate!; **where would you like me to s.?, where shall I s.?** ¿dónde quiere que me siente?, ¿dónde me siento?; **he sits in front of the television all day** se pasa todo el día sentado delante del televisor; **are you sitting comfortably?** ¿estás sentado cómodamente?; **s. still!** ¡quédate ahí sentado y no te muevas!; **he was sitting at his desk** estaba sentado en su mesa; **there was a bird sitting on the wall** había un pájaro posado en el muro; **don't just s. there!** ¡no te quedes ahí (sentado) sin hacer nada!; **the thought sat uneasily on my conscience** la idea me remordía la conciencia; IDIOM **to s. on one's hands** quedarse de brazos cruzados; IDIOM *Fam* **to be sitting pretty** estar en una situación ventajosa; IDIOM **to s. tight: s. tight and wait till I get back** no te muevas y espera a que vuelva; **we've been advised to s. tight for the time being** nos han recomendado que por el momento no hagamos nada
(b) *(assembly, court)* reunirse; **the committee is currently sitting** la comisión está reunida en estos momentos

(**c**) *Pol* **to s. in parliament** ser diputado(a); **to s. for Finchley** ser diputado(a) por Finchley, representar a Finchley

(**d**) *(object)* **to be sitting on the radiator** estar encima del radiador; **I found the book sitting on the shelf** encontré el libro en la estantería; **the house sits on top of a hill** la casa se encuentra en lo alto de una colina; **a tank was sitting in the middle of the road** había un tanque en medio de la carretera; **the letter sat unopened** la carta se quedó cerrada

(**e**) *(as artist's model)* posar (**for** para)

(**f**) *(baby-sit)* cuidar a los niños, *Esp* hacer de canguro

(**g**) *(hen)* **the hen is sitting (on its eggs)** la gallina está empollando (los huevos)

(**h**) *(be suited)* **the jacket sits very well on you** la chaqueta *or Am* el saco te sienta muy bien; **my comments didn't s. well with them** mis comentarios no les cayeron *or* sentaron muy bien

(**i**) *Literary* **the wind sits in the east** el viento sopla del este

(**j**) *Br (be candidate)* **to s. for an exam** presentarse a un examen

▸ **sit about, sit around** *vi (be lazy)* gandulear, holgazanear; **I've been sitting about** *or* **around waiting for ages** llevo *or Méx, Ven* tengo una eternidad esperando aquí sentado

▸ **sit back** *vi* (**a**) *(lean back)* **to s. back in one's chair** recostarse en la silla (**b**) *(relax)* relajarse, ponerse cómodo(a); *(not intervene)* quedarse de brazos cruzados

▸ **sit by** *vi* quedarse de brazos cruzados

▸ **sit down** 1 *vt sep* **to s. sb down** sentar a alguien; *Fam* **s. yourself down!** ¡siéntate!

2 *vi* sentarse; **to be sitting down** estar sentado(a); **we need to s. down together and find a compromise** tenemos que sentarnos y llegar a un acuerdo; **I was just sitting down to work when the phone rang** estaba a punto de sentarme a trabajar cuando sonó el teléfono; **to s. down to table** sentarse a la mesa

▸ **sit in** *vi* (**a**) *(at meeting, in class)* estar presente (**on** en) *(como observador)* (**b**) *(protest)* hacer una sentada

▸ **sit in for** *vt insep* reemplazar a

▸ **sit on** *vt insep* (**a**) *(be member of) (committee, jury, board)* formar parte de

(**b**) *(not deal with)* no tocar; **we have decided to s. on the results for a while** hemos decidido no revelar por ahora los resultados

(**c**) *Sport* **they mustn't s. on their one-goal lead** ahora que ganan por un gol, no deben dormirse en los laureles

(**d**) *Fam (repress)* hacer la vida imposible a

(**e**) *Fam (of food)* **that meal is sitting on my stomach** tengo el estómago pesado con esa comida

▸ **sit out** 1 *vt sep* (**a**) *(not participate in)* saltarse; **I think I'll s. the next one out** *(dance)* creo que en el siguiente baile voy a descansar; *(in cards)* creo que no jugaré la siguiente

(**b**) *(put up with)* aguantar hasta el final

2 *vi (in garden)* sentarse fuera

▸ **sit through** *vt insep* aguantar; **we sat through dinner in silence** nos pasamos toda la cena (sentados) en silencio

▸ **sit up** 1 *vt sep (help to sitting position)* incorporar

2 *vi* (**a**) *(straighten one's back)* sentarse derecho(a); *(from lying position)* incorporarse; **she was sitting up in bed reading** leía sentada en la cama; **s. up straight!** ¡siéntate derecho!; *Fig* **to make sb s. up (and take notice)** hacer reaccionar a alguien

(**b**) *(not go to bed)* **to s. up (late)** quedarse levantado(a) hasta tarde; **don't bother sitting up for me** no me esperes despierto; **I'll s. up with her until the fever passes** velaré junto a ella hasta que se le pase la fiebre

---

sitar ['sɪtɑː(r)] *n Mus* sitar *m*

sitcom ['sɪtkɒm] *n TV* telecomedia *f* (de situación), comedia *f* de situación

sit-down ['sɪtdaʊn] 1 *n Fam (rest)* **I could do with a bit of a s.** me vendría bien un pequeño descanso

2 *adj* (**a**) *(meal)* a la mesa (**b**) *(strike)* de brazos caídos

site [saɪt] 1 *n* (**a**) *(position)* lugar *m*; *(of monument, building, complex)* emplazamiento *m*; **this forest has been the s. of several battles** este bosque ha sido escenario de diversas batallas; **on the s. of** en el emplazamiento de ▸▸ ***S. of Special Scientific Interest*** Sitio *m* de Especial Interés Científico

(**b**) *(of construction)* **(building) s.** obra *f*; **he is responsible for safety on s.** es el responsable de la seguridad a pie de obra

(**c**) *(archaeological)* yacimiento *m*

(**d**) *Comptr* sitio *m* ▸▸ ***s. map*** mapa *m* del sitio

2 *vt* emplazar, ubicar; **to be sited** estar situado(a)

sit-in ['sɪtɪn] *n (protest)* sentada *f*; *(strike)* encierro *m*

sitter ['sɪtə(r)] *n* (**a**) *(babysitter) Esp* canguro *mf*, *Am* babysitter *mf* (**b**) *Art (model)* modelo *mf* (**c**) *Sport (easy chance)* ocasión *f* fácil; **to miss a s.** *(in soccer)* fallar un gol cantado (**d**) *Br Fam (in horseracing)* gran favorito *m*

sitting ['sɪtɪŋ] 1 *n (of committee, for portrait)* sesión *f*; *(for meal)* turno *m*; **at one s.** de una sentada ▸▸ ***S. Bull*** Toro *m* Sentado; *Br* ***s. room*** *(in house)* salón *m*, sala *f* de estar

2 *adj* (**a**) *(seated)* sentado(a); **make sure you are in the s. position** no olvide que debe estar sentado(a); IDIOM *Fam* **to be a s. duck** *or* **target** ser un blanco fácil (**b**) *(current) Parl* **the s. member (for)** el/la actual representante (por) ▸▸ ***s. tenant*** inquilino(a) *m,f* titular *or* legal

situate ['sɪtjʊeɪt] *vt* situar, ubicar

situated ['sɪtjʊeɪtɪd] *adj* (**a**) *(physically)* situado(a); **the house is conveniently s. for the shops** la casa está situada a muy poca distancia de las tiendas; **the island is strategically s.** la isla tiene un emplazamiento estratégico (**b**) *(circumstantially)* **he's well s. to know what's going on** está en un buen sitio para enterarse de lo que pasa

situation [sɪtjʊ'eɪʃən] *n* (**a**) *(circumstances)* situación *f*; **what would you do in my s.?** ¿qué harías tú en mi caso *or* lugar?; **a crisis s.** una situación de crisis; **it won't work in a classroom s.** no funcionará llevado al ámbito de la clase; *Fam* **what's** *or* **how's the coffee s.?** ¿cómo *or* qué tal estamos *or* andamos de café? ▸▸ ***s. comedy*** *(on TV)* telecomedia *f* (de situación); *Phil* ***s. ethics*** ética *f* circunstancial *or* situacionista

(**b**) *(job)* colocación *f*; **situations vacant/wanted** *(in newspaper)* ofertas *fpl*/demandas *fpl* de empleo

(**c**) *(location)* situación *f*, ubicación *f*

sit-up ['sɪtʌp] *n* **to do sit-ups** hacer abdominales

six [sɪks] 1 *n* (**a**) *(number)* seis *m*

(**b**) *(in ice hockey) (team)* equipo *m*

(**c**) *(in cricket)* = seis carreras que se otorgan al bateador cuando éste envía la pelota directamente fuera del perímetro del campo marcado por la cuerda

(**d**) IDIOMS *Fam* **it's s. of one and half a dozen of the other** viene a ser lo mismo; *Fam* **to be at sixes and sevens** estar hecho(a) un lío; **to give sb s. of the best** propinar a alguien seis buenos azotes; *Br Fam* **to knock sb for s.** hacer polvo *or* picadillo a alguien

2 *adj* seis; IDIOM *Fam* **to be s. feet under** estar bajo tierra ▸▸ ***the S. Nations (Championship)*** *(in rugby)* el (Torneo de las) Seis Naciones; *see also* **eight**

sixer ['sɪksə(r)] *n Br (of Brownies, Cubs)* = jefe de un grupo de seis scouts

six-figure ['sɪks'fɪgə(r)] *adj* **a s. sum** una cantidad (de dinero) de seis cifras

sixfold ['sɪksfəʊld] 1 *adj* sextuplicado(a), séxtuplo(a)

2 *adv* por seis, seis veces; **the population has increased s.** la población se ha sextuplicado

six-footer [sɪks'fʊtə(r)] *n Fam (person)* **both her sons are six-footers** sus dos hijos rebasan el metro ochenta de estatura

six-pack ['sɪkspæk] *n* (**a**) *(of beer)* paquete *m or* pack *m* de seis cervezas (**b**) *Fam (stomach muscles) (of man)* abdominales *mpl*

sixpence ['sɪkspəns] *n Br Formerly* (moneda *f* de) seis peniques *mpl*; **it can turn on a s.** *(of car)* da la vuelta en una baldosa, tiene un ángulo de giro muy pequeño

six-shooter ['sɪksʃuːtə(r)] *n* revólver *m (de seis disparos)*

sixteen [sɪks'tiːn] 1 *n* dieciséis *m*

2 *adj* dieciséis; *see also* **eight**

sixteenth [sɪks'tiːnθ] 1 *n* (**a**) *(fraction)* dieciseisavo *m*, decimosexta parte *f* ▸▸ *US Mus* ***s. note*** semicorchea *f* (**b**) *(in series)* decimosexto(a) *m,f* (**c**) *(of month)* dieciséis *m*

2 *adj* decimosexto(a); *see also* **eleventh**

sixth [sɪksθ] 1 *n* (**a**) *(fraction)* sexto *m*, sexta parte *f* (**b**) *(in series)* sexto(a) *m,f* (**c**) *(of month)* seis *m* (**d**) *Mus* sexta *f*

2 *adj* sexto(a); *Br Sch* **the s. form** = los dos últimos cursos del bachillerato británico previos a los estudios superiores ▸▸ *Br Sch* ***s. former*** = estudiante de los dos últimos cursos del bachillerato británico; *Br Sch* ***s. form college*** = centro de enseñanza secundaria para alumnos a partir de 16 años que cursan sus dos últimos años de bachillerato; ***s. sense*** sexto sentido *m*; *see also* **eighth**

sixthly ['sɪkθlɪ] *adv* en sexto lugar

sixties ['sɪkstiːz] *npl* **the s.** los (años) sesenta; *see also* **eighties**

sixtieth ['sɪkstɪɪθ] 1 *n* sexagésimo(a) *m,f*

2 *adj* sexagésimo(a)

sixty ['sɪkstɪ] 1 *n* sesenta *m*

2 *adj* sesenta; *see also* **eighty**

sixty-four thousand dollar question ['sɪkstɪfɔː'θaʊzənddɒlə-'kwestʃən] *n Fam* pregunta *f* del millón (de dólares)
sixty-nine ['sɪkstɪ'naɪn] *n Fam (sexual position)* sesenta y nueve *m*
six-yard box [sɪks'jɑːdbɒks] *n (in soccer)* área *f* pequeña *or* chica
sizable = **sizeable**
size [saɪz] **1** *n* (**a**) *(of place, object)* tamaño *m*; *(of person)* talla *f*, tamaño *m*; *(of problem, undertaking)* envergadura *f*, dimensiones *fpl*; *Comptr (of file)* tamaño *m*; *Typ (of font)* tamaño *m*; **the two rooms are the same s.** las dos habitaciones son igual de grandes *or* del mismo tamaño; **what s. is the sofa?** ¿qué dimensiones tiene el sofá?; **it's the s. of an apple** es del tamaño de una manzana; **this box is half/twice the s. of the other one** esta caja mide la mitad/el doble de la otra; **it's a city of some s.** es una ciudad de dimensiones considerables; **we weren't expecting a crowd of this s.** no contábamos con tamaña multitud; **it is one cubic metre in s.** mide un metro cúbico; **the budget will have to double in s.** el presupuesto deberá duplicarse; **look at the s. of that carrot!** ¡mira el tamaño de esa zanahoria!; *Fam* **that's about the s. of it** así están las cosas
(**b**) *(of clothes)* talla *f*; *(of shoes)* número *m*; **what s. do you take?, what s. are you?** *(of clothes)* ¿qué talla usas *or* gastas?; *(of shoes)* ¿qué número calzas?; **s. 10 shoes** ≃ zapatos del número 44; **it's a couple of sizes too big for me** *(dress)* me queda dos tallas grande, me sobran dos tallas; **to try sth (on) for s.** probarse algo para ver qué tal queda de talla
(**c**) *(glue) (for leather, textiles)* apresto *m*; *(for paper, plaster)* cola *f*
2 *vt* (**a**) *(sort)* clasificar según el tamaño (**b**) *(glue) (leather, textiles)* aprestar; *(paper, plaster)* encolar (**c**) *Comptr* cambiar de tamaño
▸**size up** *vt sep (situation)* calibrar; *(person)* calar; **we all waited outside, sizing each other up** todos esperamos fuera, cada uno intentando adivinar lo que el otro podía dar de sí
sizeable, sizable ['saɪzəbəl] *adj (piece, box, car, town)* bastante grande; *(sum, income, crowd, error, majority)* considerable
-sized [-saɪzd] *suffix* **a fair-s. crowd** una nutrida multitud
sizzle ['sɪzəl] **1** *n* crepitación *f*
2 *vi* crepitar
sizzler ['sɪzlə(r)] *n Fam (hot day)* **tomorrow's going to be a s.** mañana va a hacer un calor achicharrante
sizzling ['sɪzlɪŋ] *adj* (**a**) *(sputtering)* chisporroteante (**b**) *Fam (hot) (day)* achicharrante, abrasador(ora) (**c**) *Fam (very good) (shot)* impresionante
sjambok ['ʃæmbɒk] *n* = látigo sudafricano de piel de rinoceronte o hipopótamo
SK (*abbr* **Saskatchewan**) Saskatchewan
ska [skɑː] *n Mus* ska *m*
skag = **scag**
skank [skæŋk] *n US Fam* coco *m*, *Esp* feto *m* (malayo), *Am* bagre *m*
skat [skæt] *n* = juego de cartas parecido al tresillo
skate[1] [skeɪt] *n (fish)* raya *f*
skate[2] **1** *n (with blade, rollers)* patín *m*; IDIOM *Fam* **to get** *or* **put one's skates on** *(hurry)* ponerse las pilas, aligerar
2 *vi* (**a**) *Sport* patinar; *Fig* **to s. (a)round an issue** eludir una cuestión; **to be skating on thin ice** pisar un terreno peligroso (**b**) *(slide) (pen, plate)* deslizarse
▸**skate over** *vt insep (deal with superficially)* tocar muy por encima
skateboard ['skeɪtbɔːd] **1** *n* monopatín *m*, *RP* skate *m* ▸▸ ***s. park*** pista *f* para monopatines
2 *vi* deslizarse sobre un monopatín; **to go s.** ir a montar en monopatín
skateboarder ['skeɪtbɔːdə(r)] *n* patinador(ora) *m,f (en monopatín)*
skateboarding ['skeɪtbɔːdɪŋ] *n* patinaje *m* en monopatín
skater ['skeɪtə(r)] *n* patinador(ora) *m,f*
skating ['skeɪtɪŋ] *n (on ice)* patinaje *m* (sobre hielo); *(on skates)* patinaje *m* (sobre ruedas); **to go s.** ir a patinar ▸▸ ***s. rink*** pista *f* de patinaje
skedaddle [skɪ'dædəl] *vi Fam* esfumarse, *Esp* darse el piro
skeet [skiːt] *n Sport* skeet *m*, = modalidad del tiro al plato
skeg [skeg] *n (on yacht)* talón *m* de quilla; *(on surfboard)* aleta *f*
skein [skeɪn] *n* madeja *f*
skeletal ['skelɪtəl] *adj* (**a**) *Anat* óseo(a) (**b**) *(thin) (person, body)* esquelético(a) (**c**) *(presentation, report)* sucinto(a), escueto(a)
skeleton ['skelɪtən] *n* (**a**) *(of person)* esqueleto *m*; **he was little more than a s.** era poco más que un saco de huesos, estaba prácticamente en los huesos; IDIOM **a s. in the cupboard** *or* **closet** un secreto vergonzante ▸▸ ***s. crew*** tripulación *f* mínima; ***s. key*** llave *f* maestra; ***s. service*** servicios *mpl* mínimos; ***s. staff*** personal *m* mínimo
(**b**) *(of building)* esqueleto *m*, estructura *f*
(**c**) *(outline) (of book, report, strategy)* esqueleto *m*, esquema *m*
skeptic, skeptical *etc US* = **sceptic, sceptical** *etc*
sketch [sketʃ] **1** *n* (**a**) *(drawing)* esbozo *m*, bosquejo *m* ▸▸ ***s. map*** esquema *m*, croquis *m inv*; ***s. pad*** bloc *m* de dibujo (**b**) *(description)* esbozo *m*, bosquejo *m* (**c**) *(on stage, TV)* episodio *m*, sketch *m*
2 *vt* (**a**) *(draw)* esbozar (**b**) *(describe)* esbozar
3 *vi* hacer bocetos
▸**sketch in** *vt sep* (**a**) *(details, main points)* exponer, aclarar (**b**) *(draw)* esbozar, bosquejar
▸**sketch out** *vt sep (plan)* hacer un esquema de
sketchbook ['sketʃbʊk] *n* cuaderno *m* de dibujo
sketchily ['sketʃɪlɪ] *adv* someramente, superficialmente
sketching ['sketʃɪŋ] *n* dibujo *m*; **I prefer s. to painting** prefiero dibujar a pintar ▸▸ ***s. block*** cuaderno *m or* bloc *m* de dibujo
sketchy ['sketʃɪ] *adj (knowledge)* somero(a), básico(a); *(account, treatment)* esquemático(a), superficial; *(details, information)* incompleto(a), fragmentario(a); *(memories)* vago(a), impreciso(a)
skew [skjuː] **1** *n* **on the s.** ladeado(a), torcido(a)
2 *vt (distort)* distorsionar
3 *vi* desplazarse en sentido oblicuo; **the truck skewed across the intersection** el camión invadió el cruce deslizándose en sentido oblicuo
4 *adj* (**a**) *(crooked) (picture)* torcido(a) (**b**) *(in statistics)* sesgado(a); **s. distribution** distribución asimétrica
skewbald ['skjuːbɔːld] **1** *n* caballo *m* pío
2 *adj* pío(a)
skewed [skjuːd] *adj (distorted)* sesgado(a)
skewer ['skjuːə(r)] **1** *n* brocheta *f*
2 *vt* (**a**) *(meat)* ensartar, espetar (**b**) *(person)* ensartar
skew-whiff ['skjuː'wɪf] *Br Fam* **1** *adj* torcido(a)
2 *adv* de lado
ski [skiː] **1** *n (for person)* esquí *m*; *(of plane, vehicle)* esquí *m*; **a pair of skis** unos esquís ▸▸ ***s. boots*** botas *fpl* de esquí; *US Fam* ***s. bum*** fanático(a) *m,f* del esquí; ***s. instructor*** monitor(ora) *m,f* de esquí; ***s. jump*** *(ramp)* trampolín *m* de saltos de esquí; *(event, activity)* saltos *mpl* de esquí; ***s. jumper*** saltador(ora) *m,f* de esquí; ***s. jumping*** esquí *m* de saltos, saltos *mpl* de esquí; ***s. lift*** remonte *m*; ***s. mask*** pasamontañas *m inv*; ***s. pants*** pantalones *mpl* de esquí; ***s. pole*** bastón *m* de esquí; ***s. resort*** estación *f* de esquí; ***s. run*** pista *f* de esquí; ***s. slope*** pista *f* de esquí; ***s. stick*** bastón *m* de esquí; ***s. suit*** traje *m* de esquí; ***s. tow*** telearrastre *m*
2 *vi* (*pt & pp* **skied**) esquiar; **they skied down the slope** bajaron esquiando por la pista
skid [skɪd] **1** *n* (**a**) *(of car)* patinazo *m*; **to go into a s.** patinar ▸▸ *Br Fam* ***s. lid*** casco *m* de moto; ***s. mark*** *(on road)* marca *f* de neumáticos; *Fam (on underwear)* palomino *m*; ***s. pan*** pista *f* de (prácticas de) derrapaje
(**b**) *(on plane, helicopter)* patín *m*
(**c**) IDIOMS *Fam* **to put the skids under sth/sb** ocasionar la ruina de algo/alguien; *Fam* **to be on the skids** estar yéndose a pique; *US Fam* **to hit the skids** *(company, sales, prices)* venirse abajo; *US Fam* **to be on s. row** pordiosear, vivir en la indigencia
2 *vi* (*pt & pp* **skidded**) patinar; **to s. off the road** salirse de la carretera patinando; **the truck skidded to a halt** el camión fue patinando hasta que se paró; **his glasses went skidding across the table** sus gafas resbalaron por encima de la mesa
skidoo [skɪ'duː] *n* motoesquí *m or f*
skidpan ['skɪdpæn] *n Br* pista *f* de pruebas deslizante
skidproof ['skɪdpruːf] *adj* antideslizante
skier ['skiːə(r)] *n* esquiador(ora) *m,f*
skiff [skɪf] *n* esquife *m*
skiffle ['skɪfəl] *n Br* = estilo musical popular en los años cincuenta
skiing ['skiːɪŋ] *n* esquí *m*; **to go s.** ir a esquiar ▸▸ ***s. holiday*** vacaciones *fpl* de esquí; ***s. instructor*** monitor(ora) *m,f* de esquí
skilful, *US* **skillful** ['skɪlfʊl] *adj* hábil; **she's very s. with the scissors** es muy habilidosa con las tijeras
skilfully, *US* **skillfully** ['skɪlfʊlɪ] *adv* hábilmente
skilfulness, *US* **skillfullness** ['skɪlfʊlnɪs] *n* habilidad *f*
skill [skɪl] *n* (**a**) *(ability)* destreza *f*, habilidad *f*; *(talent)* talento *m*, aptitud *f*; **the footballer has tremendous s.** el futbolista es muy habilidoso; **a display of s.** un despliegue *or* una demostración de habilidad; **his s. as a mediator was crucial** su capacidad mediadora fue crucial; **he showed little s. at this task** demostró tener pocas aptitudes para esta tarea

(**b**) *(technique)* técnica *f*, capacidad *f*; **there's a (special) s. to it** requiere (cierta) técnica; **to improve sb's language/communication skills** mejorar la capacidad lingüística/de communicación de alguien; **she has poor reading skills** no se le da muy bien la lectura; **she has poor social skills** no es muy sociable; **footballers practising their skills** futbolistas ensayando sus habilidades con el balón

skilled [skɪld] *adj* (**a**) *(able, good) (driver, negotiator)* experto(a), hábil; *(work)* especializado(a); **she's s. in resolving such problems** se le da muy bien resolver ese tipo de problemas (**b**) *Ind (labour, jobs)* especializado(a), cualificado(a) ►► ***s. worker*** trabajador(ora) *m,f* cualificado(a)

skillet ['skɪlɪt] *n* (**a**) *US (frying-pan)* sartén *f* (**b**) *Br (long-handled pot)* cazo *m*, cacerola *f*

skillful, skillfully *US* = **skilful, skilfully**

skim [skɪm] *(pt & pp* **skimmed**) **1** *vt* (**a**) *(milk) Esp* quitar la nata a, *Am* sacar la crema a; *(soup)* espumar

(**b**) *(remove)* **to s. the froth from** *or* **off a glass of beer** quitarle la espuma a una cerveza

(**c**) *(surface)* rozar apenas; **the seagull skimmed the waves** la gaviota voló a ras de las olas, la gaviota voló rozando *or* acariciando las olas; *Fig* **we've only skimmed the surface** *(of topic)* sólo hemos abordado el asunto muy por encima

(**d**) *(throw)* **to s. stones (on the water)** hacer cabrillas *or* la rana (en el agua)

(**e**) *(text)* ojear, echar una ojeada a

2 *vi* **to s. along** *or* **over the ground** pasar rozando el suelo

► **skim off** *vt sep* (**a**) *(fat, cream)* retirar; *Fig* **the accounts department skims off the best recruits** el departamento de contabilidad se reserva los mejores fichajes (**b**) *(money)* quedarse con

► **skim over** *vt insep (letter, report)* echar una ojeada *or* un vistazo a

► **skim through** *vt insep (novel, document)* echar una ojeada a

skimmed milk ['skɪmd'mɪlk], *US* **skim milk** ['skɪm'mɪlk] *n* leche *f* desnatada *or* descremada

skimmer ['skɪmə(r)] *n* (**a**) *(bird)* picotijera *m*, rayador *m* (**b**) *(kitchen utensil)* espumadera *f*

skimp [skɪmp] **1** *vt* escatimar

2 *vi* **to s. on sth** escatimar algo

skimpily ['skɪmpɪlɪ] *adv* **s. dressed** ligero(a) de ropa; **a s. furnished apartment** un apartamento escasamente amueblado; **the book deals rather s. with the economic background** el libro trata de manera un tanto superficial el trasfondo económico

skimpy ['skɪmpɪ] *adj* (**a**) *(meal)* exiguo(a), escaso(a); *(praise, thanks, details)* parco(a) (**b**) *(clothes)* exiguo(a)

skin [skɪn] **1** *n* (**a**) *(of person, animal)* piel *f*; **she has beautiful s.** tiene una piel muy bonita, tiene un cutis muy bonito; **to have dark/fair s.** tener la piel oscura *or* morena/clara *or* blanca; **I always wear cotton next to my s.** siempre llevo tejidos de algodón en contacto con la piel ►► ***s. cancer*** cáncer *m* de piel; ***s. complaint*** afección *f* cutánea; ***s. cream*** crema *f* para la piel; ***s. disease*** enfermedad *f* cutánea; ***s. diver*** buceador(ora) *m,f (en traje de baño)*; ***s. diving*** buceo *m (en traje de baño)*; *Fam* ***s. flick*** *(porn film)* película *f* porno; *Med* ***s. graft*** injerto *m* de piel; *Fam* ***s. mag*** revista *f* porno; ***s. patch*** parche *m* (para la piel); ***s. test*** cutirreacción *f*, dermorreacción *f*; *Fam* ***s. trade*** industria *f* pornográfica

(**b**) *(of fruit, sausage)* piel *f*; *(of potato, banana)* piel *f*, cáscara *f*; *(of onion)* capa *f* exterior, piel *f*

(**c**) *(on milk, sauce)* nata *f*

(**d**) *(of plane)* revestimiento *m*

(**e**) *(for wine)* odre *m*

(**f**) *Fam (skinhead)* cabeza *mf* rapada

(**g**) *Br Fam (cigarette paper)* papel *m* de fumar

(**h**) *US Fam (swindle)* ***s. game*** timo *m*, estafa *f*

(**i**) IDIOMS **to be nothing but** *or* **all s. and bone** estar en los huesos; *Fam* **I nearly jumped out of my s.** casi me muero del susto; *Fam* **it's no s. off my nose** me *Esp* trae *or Am* tiene sin cuidado *or* al fresco; **by the s. of one's teeth** por los pelos; **to save one's (own) s.** salvar el pellejo; *Fam* **to get under sb's s.** *(irritate)* terminar por hartar a alguien; *Fam* **I've got her under my s.** me tiene sorbido el seso; *US Fam* **gimme some s.!** ¡chócala!

2 *vt* (*pt & pp* **skinned**) (**a**) *(animal)* despellejar, desollar; IDIOM **if I find him I'll s. him alive!** ¡si lo encuentro lo voy a despellejar vivo!; PROV **there's more than one way to s. a cat** hay muchas maneras de hacer las cosas (**b**) *(tomato)* pelar (**c**) *(graze)* **to s. one's knee** arañarse la rodilla (**d**) *Fam (swindle)* timar

► **skin up** *vi Br Fam Esp* liarse *or Am* armarse un porro

skincare ['skɪnkeə(r)] *n* cuidado *m* de la piel ►► ***s. product*** producto *m* para el cuidado de la piel

skin-deep ['skɪn'di:p] *adj* superficial

skinflint ['skɪnflɪnt] *n Fam* rata *mf*, roñoso(a) *m,f*

skinful ['skɪnfʊl] *n* IDIOM *Fam* **to have had a s.** estar como una cuba *or Esp, RP* mamado(a) *or Col* caído(a) (de la perra) *or Méx* ahogado(a)

skinhead ['skɪnhed] *n* cabeza *mf* rapada, rapado(a) *m,f*

-skinned [-skɪnd] *suffix* **she's sallow-s.** tiene la de piel cetrina

skinny[1] ['skɪnɪ] *adj* (**a**) *(person, legs)* flaco(a) (**b**) *(sweater, T-shirt)* fino(a)

skinny[2] ['skɪnɪ] *n US Fam (inside information)* información *f* confidencial

skinny-dipping ['skɪnɪdɪpɪŋ] *n Fam* baño *m* en cueros; **to go s.** ir a nadar en cueros

skint [skɪnt] *adj Br Fam* **to be s.** estar sin un centavo, estar pelado(a)

skin-tight ['skɪntaɪt] *adj* muy ajustado(a)

skip[1] [skɪp] **1** *n (jump)* brinco *m* ►► *US* ***s. rope*** *Esp* comba *f*, *Am* cuerda *f* de saltar

2 *vt* (*pt & pp* **skipped**) (**a**) *(omit) (page, stage, details)* saltarse; **we decided to s. lunch/dessert** decidimos saltarnos el almuerzo/postre; **his heart skipped a beat** le dio un vuelco el corazón; *Fam* **s. it!** ¡olvídalo! (**b**) *(not turn up for) (meeting, class)* saltarse; *Fam* **to s. bail** huir durante la libertad bajo fianza

3 *vi* (**a**) *(jump) (lamb, person)* brincar; **he skipped out of the way** se apartó de un salto; *Fig* **the book keeps skipping from one subject to another** el libro va saltando de una cuestión a otra (**b**) *(with rope)* saltar a la cuerda *or Esp* comba (**c**) *Fam (go)* escaparse un momento; **we skipped across to Dublin for the weekend** hicimos una escapada a Dublín durante el fin de semana

► **skip off** *vi Fam (disappear)* largarse

► **skip over** *vt insep* saltarse, pasar por alto

skip[2] *n Br (for rubbish)* contenedor *m* (de escombros)

skipjack ['skɪpdʒæk] *n* **s. (tuna)** bonito *m* de altura, (atún *m*) listado *m*

skipper ['skɪpə(r)] **1** *n* (**a**) *(of ship)* patrón(ona) *m,f*, capitán(ana) *m,f* (**b**) *(of team)* capitán(ana) *m,f*

2 *vt* capitanear

skipping ['skɪpɪŋ] *n* **she likes s.** le gusta saltar a la cuerda *or Esp* comba ►► *Br* ***s. rope*** *Esp* comba *f*, *Am* cuerda *f* de saltar

skirmish ['skɜ:mɪʃ] **1** *n Mil* escaramuza *f*; *Fig* refriega *f*, trifulca *f*

2 *vi* pelear, luchar

skirt [skɜ:t] **1** *n* (**a**) *(garment)* falda *f*, *CSur* pollera *f* (**b**) *(part of coat)* faldón *m*, falda *f* (**c**) *very Fam (women)* titis *fpl*; *Br* **a bit of s.** una titi (**d**) *Br (cut of meat)* falda *f*, delgados *mpl*

2 *vt (village, hill)* bordear, rodear

► **skirt round,** *US* **skirt around** *vt insep (village, hill)* bordear, rodear; **to s. round** *or* **around a problem** eludir *or* evadir un problema

skirting ['skɜ:tɪŋ] *n Br* **s. (board)** zócalo *m*, rodapié *m*

skit [skɪt] *n* parodia *f*; **to do a s. on sth/sb** hacer una parodia de algo/alguien, parodiar algo/a alguien

skitter ['skɪtə(r)] *vi* (**a**) *(small animal)* moverse de forma muy ligera y rápida (**b**) *(ricochet) (stone)* rebotar

skittish ['skɪtɪʃ] *adj* (**a**) *(person)* locuelo(a), juguetón(ona) (**b**) *(of horse)* asustadizo(a)

skittle ['skɪtəl] *n* bolo *m*; **to have a game of skittles** echar una partida de bolos, jugar a los bolos ►► ***s. alley*** bolera *f*

skive [skaɪv] *Br Fam* **1** *n (easy job)* trabajo *m* fácil, *Esp* chollo *m*, *Col* camello *m* fácil, *Méx* chamba *f* fácil, *RP* laburo *m* fácil; **she's taking sociology because it's such a s.** ha escogido sociología porque es una maría

2 *vi (off school) Esp* hacer novillos, *Col* capar colegio, *Méx* irse de pinta, *RP* hacerse la rata; *(off work)* zafarse, *Esp* escaquearse

► **skive off** **1** *vt insep* **to s. off school** *Esp* hacer novillos, *Col* capar colegio, *Méx* irse de pinta, *RP* hacerse la rata; **to s. off work** escaquearse del trabajo

2 *vi Br Fam (off school)* hacer novillos, *Col* capar colegio, *Méx* irse de pinta, *RP* hacerse la rata; *(off work)* zafarse, *Esp* escaquearse

skiver ['skaɪvə(r)] *n Br Fam* holgazán(ana) *m,f*, gandul(ula) *m,f*, *Méx* flojo(a) *m,f*

skivvies ['skɪvɪz] *npl US Fam* ropa *f* interior, calzoncillos *mpl*

skivvy ['skɪvɪ] *Br Pej* **1** *n* fregona *f*, criada *f*

2 *vi* hacer de fregona

skua ['skju:ə] *n* págalo *m*

skulduggery, *US* **skullduggery** [skʌl'dʌgərɪ] *n* tejemanejes *mpl*

skulk [skʌlk] *vi (hide)* esconderse; *(move furtively)* merodear; **to s. away** *or* **off** hacer mutis por el foro

skull [skʌl] *n* cráneo *m*; **the s. and crossbones** la calavera y las tibias; *Fam* **can't you get it into your thick s. that she doesn't like you!** ¡a ver si te entra de una vez en la mollera que no le gustas!; *Fam* **to be out of one's s.** estar como una cabra ►► ***s. bone*** hueso *m* del cráneo

skullcap ['skʌlkæp] *n* casquete *m*; *(of priest)* solideo *m*

skullduggery *US* = **skulduggery**

skunk [skʌŋk] **1** *n* **(a)** *(animal)* mofeta *f* **(b)** *Fam Pej (person)* miserable *mf*, *Esp* perro *m*

2 *vt US Fam (opponent)* dar una paliza a

sky [skaɪ] *n* cielo *m*; **the s. went dark** el cielo se oscureció; *Fam* **to praise sb to the skies** poner a alguien por las nubes; IDIOM *Fam* **the s.'s the limit** el cielo es el límite, nada es imposible ►► ***s. blue*** azul *m* celeste; *US* ***s. marshal*** = policía federal de paisano cuya función es la de prevenir secuestros en aviones; *Fam* ***s. pilot*** capellán *m*

sky-blue ['skaɪ'blu:] *adj* azul celeste

skyboarding ['skaɪbɔ:dɪŋ] *n* surf *m* aéreo

sky-diver ['skaɪdaɪvə(r)] *n* = persona que practica la caída libre (en paracaídas)

sky-diving ['skaɪdaɪvɪŋ] *n* caída *f* libre (en paracaídas)

Skye terrier [skaɪ'terɪə(r)] *n* terrier *m* (de) Skye

sky-high ['skaɪ'haɪ] **1** *adj (prices, costs)* astronómico(a), desorbitado(a)

2 *adv* **to blow sth s.** hacer saltar algo por los aires; **to send sth s.** *(price, costs)* hacer que algo se dispare, poner algo por las nubes

skyjack ['skaɪdʒæk] *vt* secuestrar (en pleno vuelo)

skyjacking ['skaɪdʒækɪŋ] *n Fam* secuestro *m* aéreo

skylark ['skaɪlɑ:k] *n* alondra *f*

skylight ['skaɪlaɪt] *n* claraboya *f*

skyline ['skaɪlaɪn] *n* **(a)** *(horizon)* horizonte *m* **(b)** *(of city)* silueta *f*

skyrocket ['skaɪrɒkɪt] **1** *n (firework)* cohete *m*

2 *vi Fam (prices)* dispararse, *Esp* ponerse *or Am* irse por las nubes

skyscraper ['skaɪskreɪpə(r)] *n* rascacielos *m inv*

skyward ['skaɪwəd] **1** *adj* hacia el cielo

2 *adv* = **skywards**

skywards ['skaɪwədz] *adv* hacia el cielo

skywriting ['skaɪraɪtɪŋ] *n* = formación de palabras en el aire con la estela de un avión

slab [slæb] *n* **(a)** *(of stone, concrete)* losa *f*; *(of cake, meat)* trozo *m (grueso)*; *(of chocolate)* tableta *f* **(b)** *(in mortuary)* mesa *f* de amortajamiento

slack [slæk] **1** *n* **(a)** *(in rope)* **leave a bit of s. in the rope** deja un poco floja la cuerda; **to take up the s.** tensar la cuerda; *Fig* **to take up the s. in the economy** aprovechar al máximo la capacidad productiva de la economía; *Fig* **I'm fed up with having to take up your s.** estoy harto de tener que encargarme de tu trabajo; IDIOM *Fam* **cut me/him some s., will you?** dame/dale un respiro *or* una tregua, ¿quieres? **(b)** *(coal)* cisco *m*

2 *adj* **(a)** *(not tight)* flojo(a); **to be s.** estar flojo(a); **to go s.** aflojarse, destensarse

(b) *(demand, business)* flojo(a), parado(a); **trade is s.** el negocio está flojo; **s. periods** períodos de poca actividad

(c) *(careless)* dejado(a); **he's becoming very s. about his work/appearance** se está volviendo muy descuidado en su trabajo/aspecto personal; **she's very s. about** *or* **at getting orders ready on time** no se toma mucho interés en tener listos los pedidos a su debido tiempo

(d) *(lax) (discipline, laws, control)* relajado(a), poco severo(a)

(e) *(slow) (pace)* lento(a), tranquilo(a)

3 *vi Fam* vaguear

► **slack off** *vi (diminish)* aflojar

slacken ['slækən] **1** *vt* **(a)** *(rope, reins, grip)* aflojar **(b)** *(pace)* aflojar

2 *vi* **(a)** *(rope)* aflojarse, destensarse; *(grip)* aflojarse, soltarse un poco; *(muscles)* destensarse; relajarse **(b)** *(speed)* reducirse, disminuir; *(storm, wind)* amainar, aflojar; *(energy, enthusiasm)* atenuarse, disminuir; *(demand)* decaer, disminuir; **we must not s. in our efforts to put an end to this injustice** no debemos cejar en nuestro empeño de poner fin a esta injusticia

► **slacken off** *vi (speed)* reducirse, disminuir; *(storm, wind)* amainar, aflojar; *(energy, enthusiasm)* atenuarse, disminuir; *(demand)* decaer, disminuir

slacker ['slækə(r)] *n Fam* vago(a) *m,f*, tirado(a) *m,f*, *Méx* flojo(a) *m,f*

slackly ['slæklɪ] *adv* **(a)** *(to hang)* flojo **(b)** *(to work)* descuidadamente

slackness ['slæknɪs] *n* **(a)** *(negligence, laziness)* dejadez *f* **(b)** *(of rope)* distensión *f* **(c)** *(of business)* atonía *f*, inactividad *f*

slacks [slæks] *npl Old-fashioned (trousers)* pantalones *mpl* anchos

slag [slæg] *Br* **1** *n* **(a)** *(from coal mine, volcano)* escoria *f* ►► ***s. heap*** escorial *m* **(b)** *very Fam Pej (woman)* fulana *f*, *Esp* cualquiera *f*, *Méx* vieja *f*, *RP* reventadita *f*

2 *vt Fam* **(a)** *(criticize)* criticar, *Esp* poner a parir *or* como un trapo, *Méx* viborear **(b)** *(make fun of)* burlarse *or Esp* cachondearse de

► **slag off** *vt sep Br Fam* **(a)** *(criticize)* criticar, *Esp* poner a parir *or* como un trapo, *Méx* viborear **(b)** *(make fun of)* burlarse *or Esp* cachondearse de

slagging ['slægɪŋ] *n Br Fam* **to give sb a s.** *(make fun of)* burlarse *or Esp* cachondearse de alguien

slain [sleɪn] **1** *npl* **the s.** las bajas, los fallecidos

2 *pp of* **slay**

slake [sleɪk] *vt* **(a)** *Literary (desires)* saciar; **to s. one's thirst** apagar *or* calmar la sed **(b)** *(lime)* apagar ►► ***slaked lime*** cal *f* apagada

slalom ['slɑ:ləm] *n* eslalon *m*

slam [slæm] **1** *n* **(a)** *(of door)* portazo *m*; **the door swung shut with a s.** la puerta se cerró de un portazo **(b)** *(in bridge)* slam *m*, = contrato que exige ganar todas las bazas menos una (pequeño slam) o todas las bazas (gran slam)

2 *vt* (*pt & pp* **slammed**) **(a)** *(door, lid, drawer)* cerrar de un golpe; **to s. the door shut** cerrar la puerta de un portazo *or* de golpe; **to s. the door in sb's face** dar con la puerta en las narices a alguien; **she slammed the books on the desk** estampó los libros contra la mesa; **to s. sth down** estampar algo; **he slammed the ball into the net** incrustó la pelota en la red; **to s. on the brakes** pisar el freno de golpe

(b) *Fam (criticize)* criticar, poner verde a, *Méx* viborear, *RP* verdulear

(c) *Fam (defeat)* dar una paliza a

(d) *US Fam (have sex with)* ventilarse a

(e) *Fam (drink quickly)* ventilarse

3 *vi (door, window)* cerrarse de golpe; **the door slammed shut** la puerta se cerró de un portazo *or* de golpe

► **slam into** *vt insep* estamparse *or* estrellarse contra

slam-dunk ['slæm'dʌŋk] *n (in basketball)* mate *m*

slammer ['slæmə(r)] *n Fam Esp* chirona *f*, *Andes, Cuba, RP* cana *f*, *Méx, Ven* bote *m*

slander ['slɑ:ndə(r)] **1** *n* difamación *f*

2 *vt* difamar

slanderer ['slɑ:ndərə(r)] *n* difamador(ora) *m,f*

slanderous ['slɑ:ndərəs] *adj* difamatorio(a)

slang [slæŋ] **1** *n* argot *m*; **prison s.** lenguaje carcelario

2 *adj* argótico(a), jergal

3 *vt Fam (insult)* criticar, poner verde a, *Méx* viborear, *RP* verdulear

slanging match ['slæŋɪŋ'mætʃ] *n Br Fam* rifirrafe *m*, intercambio *m* de insultos

slangy ['slæŋɪ] *adj Fam* jergal, del argot

slant [slɑ:nt] **1** *n* **(a)** *(slope)* inclinación *f*; **the table has a s.** *or* **is on a s.** la mesa está inclinada **(b)** *(emphasis, bias)* sesgo *m*, orientación *f*; **she put a favourable s. on the information** le dio un cariz *or* sesgo favorable a la información

2 *vt* **(a)** *(set at angle)* inclinar **(b)** *(bias)* enfocar subjetivamente

3 *vi (slope)* estar inclinado(a); **a ray of sunlight slanted through the window** un rayo de sol entraba de soslayo por la ventana

slanted ['slɑ:ntɪd] *adj* **(a)** *(sloped)* inclinado(a) **(b)** *(emphasised, biased)* sesgado(a), subjetivo(a)

slant-eyed ['slɑ:ntaɪd] *adj* de ojos rasgados *or* achinados

slanting ['slɑ:ntɪŋ] *adj* inclinado(a)

slantwise ['slɑ:ntwaɪz], **slantways** ['slɑ:ntweɪz] **1** *adj* inclinado(a)

2 *adv* de forma inclinada

slap [slæp] **1** *n* **(a)** *(with hand)* bofetada *f*, cachete *m*; *also Fig* **a s. in the face** una bofetada; **a s. on the back** una palmadita en la espalda; **a s. on the wrist** *(blow)* un palmetazo en la mano *or* muñeca; *(reprimand)* un tirón de orejas; *Old-fashioned Fam* **(a bit of) s. and tickle** un revolcón **(b)** ►► ***s. shot*** *(in ice hockey)* tiro *m* de golpe **(c)** *Br Fam (make-up)* maquillaje *m*

2 *adv Fam* **I ran s. into a tree** me di de lleno contra un árbol; **s. in the middle** justo en el medio

3 *vt* (*pt & pp* **slapped**) **(a)** *(hit)* dar una palmada en; **to s. sb's face, to s. sb in the face** abofetear a alguien, dar una bofetada a alguien; **to s. sb on the back** dar a alguien una palmada en la espalda; **to s. sb's wrist** *(hit)* pegar a alguien en la mano *or* muñeca; *(reprimand)* dar un tirón de orejas a alguien; IDIOM **to s. sb down** hacer callar a alguien

(b) *(put)* **she slapped the files down on the table** puso las carpetas en la mesa dando un golpetazo; **I slapped plenty of butter on the bread** embadurné el pan con abundante mantequilla; **to s. some paint on sth** dar cuatro brochazos (de pintura) a algo; **hang on, I'll just s. some make-up on** espera, voy a untarme un poco de maquillaje; **they slapped on a 3 percent surcharge** aplicaron un recargo del 3 por ciento

▸ **slap around** *vt sep (beat)* sacudir

slap-bang ['slæp'bæŋ] *adv Fam* (**a**) *(precisely)* justo; **s. in the middle** justo en el medio, en el mismísimo centro (**b**) *(forcefully)* **he drove s. into the tree** se pegó un tortazo *or* castañazo tremendo contra el árbol

slapdash ['slæpdæʃ] *adj* chapucero(a)

slap-happy ['slæp'hæpɪ] *adj Fam* alegre, despreocupado(a)

slaphead ['slæphed] *n Br Fam* calvo *m*

slapper ['slæpə(r)] *n Br very Fam* (**a**) *(promiscuous woman)* fulana *f*, *Esp* pendón *m*, *Col* aviona *f*, *Méx* piruja *f*, *RP* reventada *f* (**b**) *Pej (woman)* piba *f*, *Esp* tía *f*, *Méx* vieja *f*, *RP* mimita *f*

slapstick ['slæpstɪk] *n* **s. (comedy)** astracanada *f*

slap-up ['slæpʌp] *adj Br Fam* ***s. meal*** comilona *f*, banquete *m*

slash [slæʃ] **1** *n* (**a**) *(cut) (with knife, sword, razor)* tajo *m*, corte *m*; *(on face)* corte *m*; *(in tyres, in cloth)* corte *m*, raja *f*; *Agr* **s. and burn** = en zonas tropicales, tala y quema de bosque o maleza para su posterior cultivo (**b**) *(act of cutting) (with knife, sword, razor)* tajo *m*, corte *m* (**c**) *Typ* barra *f* (**d**) *Br very Fam* **to have/go for a s.** echar/ir a echar una meada

2 *vt* (**a**) *(cut)* cortar; **to s. one's wrists** cortarse las venas (**b**) *(reduce)* recortar *or* reducir drásticamente; **prices slashed** *(sign)* precios por los suelos

3 *vi* **to s. at sb (with a knife)** atacar a alguien (con un cuchillo)

slasher ['slæʃə(r)] *n* ***s. movie*** *or Br* ***film*** película *f* de casquería, película *f* muy sangrienta

slashing ['slæʃɪŋ] **1** *n (attack)* acuchillamiento *m*

2 *adj (budget cut)* drástico(a)

slat [slæt] *n* (**a**) *(of blind, bench, bed)* listón *m*, tablilla *f* (**b**) *Av (on wing)* slat *m*

slate [sleɪt] **1** *n* (**a**) *(stone)* pizarra *f*; *(tile)* pizarra *f* ▸▸ ***s. grey*** gris *m* pizarra; ***s. quarry*** pizarral *m* (**b**) *(for writing)* pizarra *f* (**c**) *US Pol* lista *f* de candidatos (**d**) *(colour)* gris *m* pizarra (**e**) IDIOMS *Fam* **put it on the s.** anótalo en mi cuenta; **to wipe the s. clean** hacer borrón y cuenta nueva; *Br Fam* **to have a s. loose** tener un tornillo suelto, no estar *or* andar bien de la azotea

2 *adj* (**a**) *(made of slate)* de pizarra ▸▸ ***s. roof*** tejado *m* de pizarra (**b**) *(in colour)* gris pizarra

3 *vt* (**a**) *(cover) (roof)* empizarrar, tejar con pizarras

(**b**) *US (choose)* elegir, designar; **Magee is slated for President** Magee es la persona designada para ocupar la presidencia

(**c**) *US (expect)* **the final is slated for January** la final está prevista *or* programada para el mes de enero; **she was slated for a gold medal** *(destined)* era candidata a una medalla de oro

(**d**) *Fam (criticize)* vapulear, *Esp* poner por los suelos, *Méx* viborear, *RP* dejar por el piso

slate-grey ['sleɪt'greɪ] *adj* gris pizarra

slater ['sleɪtə(r)] *n (roofer)* pizarrero(a) *m,f*

slating ['sleɪtɪŋ] *n Fam (severe criticism)* **the play got a s. in the press** la prensa puso la obra de vuelta y media

slatted ['slætɪd] *adj* de lamas, de listones

slattern ['slætən] *n Formal* sucia harapienta *f*

slatternly ['slætənlɪ] *adj Formal (woman)* harapiento(a); *(behaviour)* desordenado(a)

slaughter ['slɔːtə(r)] **1** *n* (**a**) *(of animals)* sacrificio *m* (**b**) *(of people)* matanza *f*

2 *vt* (**a**) *(animals)* sacrificar (**b**) *(people)* matar (**c**) *Fam (defeat heavily)* dar una paliza a, *Esp* machacar

slaughtered ['slɔːtəd] *adj Br Fam (drunk)* como una cuba, *Esp, RP* mamado(a), *Col* caído(a) (de la perra), *Méx* ahogado(a)

slaughterer ['slɔːtərə(r)] *n (in abattoir)* matarife *m*

slaughterhouse ['slɔːtəhaʊs] *n* matadero *m*

Slav [slɑːv] **1** *n* eslavo(a) *m,f*

2 *adj* eslavo(a)

slave [sleɪv] **1** *n* esclavo(a) *m,f*; **he treats me like a s.** me trata como a una esclava; **a s. to fashion** un esclavo de la moda ▸▸ *Fam Fig* ***s. driver*** negrero(a) *m,f*, tirano(a) *m,f*; ***s. labour:*** **built by s. labour** construido con mano de obra esclava; **this job is s. labour!** ¡éste es un trabajo de negros!; ***s. ship*** barco *m* de esclavos *or* negrero; ***s. trade*** comercio *m or* trata *f* de esclavos; ***s. trader*** tratante *mf* de esclavos

2 *vi* trabajar como un negro; **he slaved (away) over his books all day long** se pasó todo el día estudiando como un burro; **I've been slaving over a hot stove all day!** ¡me he pasado el día bregando en la cocina!

slaver[1] ['sleɪvə(r)] *n* (**a**) *(trader)* negrero(a) *m,f* (**b**) *(ship)* barco *m* negrero

slaver[2] ['slævə(r)] **1** *n (saliva)* baba *f*

2 *vi* babear; **he slavered over the blonde who had just walked in** se le caía la baba mirando a la rubia que acababa de entrar

slavery ['sleɪvərɪ] *n* esclavitud *f*; **to be sold into s.** ser vendido(a) como esclavo(a)

Slavic ['slɑːvɪk] *adj* eslavo(a)

slavish ['sleɪvɪʃ] *adj* (**a**) *(mentality, habits)* servil; *(devotion)* ciego(a), absoluto(a) (**b**) *(imitation)* mero(a), simple

slavishly ['sleɪvɪʃlɪ] *adv* (**a**) *(to agree)* de un modo servil, servilmente (**b**) *(exactly)* **to copy sth s.** copiar algo punto por punto

Slavonian grebe [slə'vəʊnɪən'griːb] *n* zampullín *m* cuellirrojo

Slavonic [slə'vɒnɪk] **1** *n Ling* eslavo *m*

2 *adj* eslavo(a)

slaw [slɔː] *n US* = ensalada de repollo, zanahoria y cebolla con mayonesa

slay [sleɪ] (*pt* **slew** [sluː], *pp* **slain** [sleɪn]) *vt* (**a**) *Literary (kill)* dar muerte a, matar (**b**) *Fam (amuse)* **this one will really s. you** *(joke, story)* con éste(a) te vas a morir de risa; *also Ironic* **you s. me!** ¡me parto de risa contigo!

slayer ['sleɪə(r)] *n Literary* asesino(a) *m,f*

sleaze [sliːz] *n Fam* (**a**) *(of politics, politician)* corrupción *f*; **the s. factor** *Esp* las corruptelas, *Am* los chanchullos (**b**) *(of place)* sordidez *f*, *Esp* cutrez *f*

sleazebag ['sliːzbæg], **sleazeball** ['sliːzbɔːl] *n Fam* sinvergüenza *mf*, *Esp* pájaro(a) *m,f* (de cuenta)

sleaziness ['sliːzɪnɪs] *n Fam* (**a**) *(of politics, politician)* corrupción *f*, *Esp* corruptelas *fpl* (**b**) *(of place)* sordidez *f*, *Esp* cutrez *f*

sleazy ['sliːzɪ] *adj Fam* (**a**) *(place, bar, hotel)* *Esp* cutre, *Col* corroncho(a), *Méx* gacho(a), *RP* groncho(a) (**b**) *(government, politician)* corrupto(a); *(affair, reputation)* escandaloso(a) y sórdido(a)

sled = **sledge**

sledding ['sledɪŋ] *n US* **to be easy/hard s.** ser fácil/difícil

sledge [sledʒ], **sled** [sled] **1** *n* trineo *m*

2 *vi* montar en trineo; **children were sledging down the slope** los niños bajaban en trineo por la pendiente

sledgehammer ['sledʒhæmə(r)] **1** *n* mazo *m*, maza *f*; *Fam* **he's as subtle as a s.!** ¡no tiene ni pizca de delicadeza!; IDIOM **to use a s. to crack a nut** matar moscas a cañonazos

2 *adj* **s. blow** mazazo

sledging ['sledʒɪŋ] *n* (**a**) *(travel by sledge)* paseo *m* en trineo; **to go s.** ir a montar en trineo (**b**) *Sport* = intimidación del contrincante mediante repetidos insultos

sleek [sliːk] *adj* (**a**) *(hair, fur)* liso(a) y brillante; *(cat)* lustroso(a) (**b**) *(outline, contour)* elegante (**c**) *(manner)* bien plantado(a)

▸ **sleek back, sleek down** *vt sep* **to s. one's hair back** *or* **down** alisarse el pelo

sleekly ['sliːklɪ] *adv* (**a**) *(to shine)* como la seda (**b**) *(elegantly) (to dress)* elegantemente (**c**) *(to behave, smile)* empalagosamente

sleep [sliːp] **1** *n* (**a**) *(rest)* sueño *m*; **to be in a deep s.** estar profundamente dormido(a); **I need my s.** necesito mis horas de sueño; **I only got a couple of hours' s.** sólo he dormido un par de horas; **I couldn't get to s.** no conseguía dormirme; **we must try and get some s.** debemos intentar dormir un poco; **to go to s.** dormirse; **he soon went back to s.** pronto volvió a dormirse; **my foot has gone to s.** se me ha dormido el pie; **to have a s.** echarse un sueño, dormir un poco; *(in afternoon)* echarse una siesta; **did you have a good (night's) s.?** ¿dormiste bien?; **to put sb to s.** *(anaesthetize)* dormir a alguien; **to put an animal to s.** *(kill)* sacrificar a un animal *(para evitar que sufra)*; **to send sb to s.** *(cause to fall asleep)* dejar dormido(a) a alguien, dormir a alguien; *(bore)* dar sueño *or* aburrir a alguien; **to sing a child to s.** arrullar a un niño; **to walk/talk in one's s.** caminar/hablar en sueños; **I could do it in my s.!** ¡lo podría hacer con los ojos cerrados!; IDIOM **I'm not losing any s. over it** no me quita el sueño ▸▸ *Comptr* ***s. mode*** modo *m* de reposo

(**b**) *(in eye)* legañas *fpl*

2 *vi* (*pt & pp* **slept** [slept]) dormir; **I slept (for) six hours** dormí seis horas; **where did you s. last night?** ¿dónde dormiste anoche?; **the bed had not been slept in** nadie había dormido en la cama; **s. well!** ¡que duermas bien!, ¡que descanses!; **s. tight!** ¡que duermas bien!, ¡que sueñes con los angelitos!; **did you s. well?** ¿has dormido bien?, ¿has descansado?; **to s. late** dormir hasta tarde, levantarse tarde; **I'll s. on it** lo consultaré con la almohada; **to s. rough** dormir a la intemperie; IDIOM **to s. like a log** dormir como un tronco

3 *vt* (**a**) *(accommodate)* **the sofa bed sleeps two** en el sofá cama pueden dormir dos personas; **the cottage sleeps four** el chalé puede albergar a cuatro personas (**b**) *(rest)* **I haven't slept a wink all night** no he pegado ojo en toda la noche

▸ **sleep around** *vi Fam* acostarse con unos(as) y con otros(as)

▸ **sleep away** *vt sep* **he sleeps the day away** se pasa el día durmiendo

▸ **sleep in** *vi (intentionally)* quedarse durmiendo hasta tarde

▸ **sleep off** *vt sep* **he's sleeping off the effects of the journey** está durmiendo para recuperarse del viaje; **to s. off a hangover, to s. it off** dormir la mona

▸ **sleep on** *vi* seguir durmiendo; **she slept on until lunchtime** estuvo durmiendo hasta el almuerzo

▸ **sleep out** *vi* (**a**) *(away from home)* pasar la noche fuera (de casa) (**b**) *(out of doors)* dormir al aire libre

▸ **sleep over** *vi US* quedarse a pasar la noche

▸ **sleep through 1** *vt insep* **I slept through the alarm** no oí el despertador; **I slept through the whole concert** me quedé dormido durante todo el concierto

2 *vi* dormir de un tirón *or* sin interrupción

▸ **sleep together** *vi* acostarse juntos

▸ **sleep with** *vt insep (have sex with)* acostarse con

sleeper ['sli:pə(r)] *n* (**a**) *(person)* **to be a light/heavy s.** tener el sueño ligero/profundo

(**b**) *Rail (train)* tren *m* de literas; *(sleeping car)* coche *m* cama

(**c**) *Br (on railway track)* traviesa *f*

(**d**) *Br (earring)* pendiente *m* de tornillo

(**e**) *Fam (film, record, book)* = película, disco o libro de escasas ventas al principio, pero que más tarde produce beneficios inesperadamente

(**f**) *(spy)* = espía infiltrado que no actúa hasta un momento determinado; **a s. cell** *(of terrorists)* un comando legal *(no identificado)*

sleepily ['sli:pılı] *adv* somnolientamente

sleepiness ['sli:pınıs] *n* (**a**) *(of person)* somnolencia *f* (**b**) *(of town)* letargo *m*, aletargamiento *m*

sleeping ['sli:pıŋ] **1** *n* **the house has s. accommodation for ten** en la casa pueden dormir diez personas ▸▸ ***s. arrangements:* what are the s. arrangements?** ¿quién va a dormir dónde?; ***s. bag*** saco *m* de dormir, *Col, Méx* sleeping *m* (bag), *RP* bolsa *f* de dormir; ***s. car*** *(on train)* coche *m* cama; ***s. pill*** somnífero *m*, pastilla *f* para dormir; ***s. quarters*** dormitorios *mpl*; ***s. sickness*** enfermedad *f* del sueño; ***s. tablet*** somnífero *m*, pastilla *f* para dormir

2 *adj* dormido(a); IDIOM **to let s. dogs lie** no enturbiar las aguas ▸▸ ***S. Beauty*** la Bella Durmiente; *Br* ***s. partner*** *(in company)* socio(a) *m,f* capitalista *or* comanditario(a); *Br* ***s. policeman*** *(in road) Esp* resalto *m (de moderación de velocidad)*, *Arg* despertador *m*, *Méx* tope *m*

sleepless ['sli:plıs] *adj* **to have a s. night** pasar una noche en blanco

sleeplessness ['sli:plısnıs] *n* insomnio *m*

sleepover ['sli:pəʊvə(r)] *n esp US* = fiesta infantil en la que los niños pasan la noche en casa de otro niño

sleepwalk ['sli:pwɔ:k] *vi* caminar dormido(a) *or* sonámbulo(a)

sleepwalker ['sli:pwɔ:kə(r)] *n* sonámbulo(a) *m,f*

sleepwalking ['sli:pwɔ:kıŋ] *n* sonambulismo *m*

sleepwear ['sli:pweə(r)] *n* prendas *fpl* de dormir

sleepy ['sli:pı] *adj* (**a**) *(person)* adormilado(a), somnoliento(a); *(smile)* adormilado(a); *(yawn)* somnoliento(a); **to be** *or* **feel s.** tener sueño; **you look s.** tienes cara de sueño; **to make sb s.** dar sueño a alguien, dejar a alguien adormilado(a) (**b**) *(place)* **a s. little village** un pueblecito casi muerto (**c**) *(summer's day, climate)* soporífero(a), amodorrante

sleepyhead ['sli:pıhed] *n Fam* dormilón(ona) *m,f*

sleet [sli:t] **1** *n* aguanieve *f*

2 *vi* **it's sleeting** está cayendo aguanieve

sleety ['sli:tı] *adj* **s. rain** aguanieve

sleeve [sli:v] *n* (**a**) *(of shirt, jacket)* manga *f*; **he must have had something up his s.** *(magician)* seguro que tenía algo escondido en la manga; IDIOM **he's still got something up his s.** aún le queda algo escondido en la manga; IDIOM **he's got a surprise up his s.** se reserva una sorpresa (**b**) *(of record)* funda *f* ▸▸ *Br* ***s. notes*** notas *fpl* de la funda (**c**) *(of pipe)* manga *f*

sleeveless ['sli:vlıs] *adj* sin mangas

sleeving ['sli:vıŋ] *n Elec* manga *f*

sleigh [sleı] **1** *n* trineo *m* ▸▸ ***s. bell*** campanilla *f* de trineo; ***s. ride*** paseo *m* en trineo

2 *vi* montar en trineo

sleighing ['sleııŋ] *n* **to go s.** ir a montar en trineo

sleight [slaıt] *n (manual dexterity)* destreza *f* manual, habilidad *f* manual ▸▸ ***s. of hand*** trucos *mpl*, juegos *mpl* de manos; *Fig* **by s. of hand** con tejemanejes, por arte de birlibirloque

slender ['slendə(r)] *adj* (**a**) *(slim) (person, waist, figure)* esbelto(a); *(fingers)* delgado(a), fino(a); *(neck, stem)* esbelto(a), delgado(a) (**b**) *(slight) (hope)* remoto(a); *(chance)* remoto(a), mínimo(a); *(income, majority)* escaso(a); **of s. means** de pocos recursos (**c**) ***s. loris*** loris *m* esbelto

slenderize ['slendəraız] *US Fam* **1** *vt* adelgazar

2 *vi* adelgazar, perder peso

slenderly ['slendəlı] *adv* **s. built** de constitución delgada *or* esbelta

slenderness ['slendənıs] *n* (**a**) *(of person, waist, figure)* esbeltez *f*; *(of fingers)* delgadez *f*, finura *f*; *(of neck, stem)* esbeltez *f*, delgadez *f* (**b**) *(of hope)* carácter *m* remoto; *(of income, majority, means, resources)* escasez *f*

slept *pt & pp of* **sleep**

sleuth [slu:θ] *n Fam* sabueso *m*, detective *mf*

slew[1], *US* **slue** [slu:] **1** *vt (vehicle)* hacer girar *or* virar bruscamente; **he slewed the taxi around** hizo un viraje brusco con el taxi

2 *vi (skid)* patinar; **it slewed into the ditch** patinó y se metió en la zanja

3 *n Fam (large number)* **a s. of, slews of** (un) mogollón de, montones de

slew[2] *pt of* **slay**

slewed [slu:d] *adj Br Fam* como una cuba; **to be/get s.** estar/ponerse como una cuba

slice [slaıs] **1** *n* (**a**) *(piece) (of bread)* rebanada *f*; *(of cheese, ham)* loncha *f*; *(of beef)* tajada *f*; *(of salami, cucumber)* rodaja *f*; *(of cake, pizza)* trozo *m*, porción *f*; *(of melon)* raja *f*

(**b**) *(share)* parte *f*; **a s. of the profits** una parte de los beneficios; **they want a larger s. of the cake** quieren un pedazo *or* una porción mayor del pastel *or Am* de la torta; **to get a s. of the action** tomar parte

(**c**) *(utensil)* pala *f*

(**d**) *Sport (in tennis)* efecto *m* cortado

(**e**) *Sport (shot) (in golf)* slice *m*; *(in tennis)* (bola *f*) cortada *f*

2 *vt* (**a**) *(bread)* cortar *or* partir (en rebanadas); *(cheese, ham)* cortar *or* partir (en lonchas); *(beef)* cortar *or* partir (en lonchas); *(salami, cucumber)* cortar *or* partir (en rodajas); *(cake, pizza)* trocear, cortar *or* dividir (en trozos); *(melon)* cortar (en rajas); **to s. sth in two** *or* **in half** dividir algo en dos *or* por la mitad; **she sliced the melon open** abrió el melón; **to s. the top off sth** recortar algo, quitar *or Am* sacar la punta a algo; *US Fam* **any way you s. it** lo mires como lo mires

(**b**) **to s. the ball** *(in golf)* golpear la bola de slice; *(in tennis)* dar un golpe cortado a la pelota; **he sliced his drive into the rough** mandó su drive al rough pegando a la bola de slice

3 *vi* (**a**) *(be cut) (bread)* cortarse (**b**) *(cut)* **the knife sliced into the flesh** el cuchillo se hundió en la carne

▸ **slice off** *vt sep* cortar; **the machine sliced his arm off** la máquina le amputó el brazo

▸ **slice through** *vt insep* surcar

▸ **slice up** *vt sep (bread)* cortar *or* partir (en rebanadas); *(cheese, ham)* cortar *or* partir (en lonchas); *(beef)* cortar *or* partir (en lonchas); *(salami, cucumber)* cortar *or* partir (en rodajas); *(cake, pizza)* trocear, cortar *or* dividir (en trozos); *(melon)* cortar (en rajas)

sliced bread ['slaıst'bred] *n* pan *m* de molde en rebanadas, *RP* pan *m* lactal en rebanadas; IDIOM *Fam* **it's the best thing since s.** es lo mejor del mundo

slicer ['slaısə(r)] *n* máquina *f* de cortar

slick [slık] **1** *n* (**a**) **(oil) s.** marea *f* negra (**b**) *(in motor racing)* neumático *m* liso

2 *adj* (**a**) *(skilful) (campaign)* hábil; *(performance)* logrado(a) (**b**) *(cleverly made but superficial) (movie, programme)* realizado(a) con ingenio pero superficial (**c**) *Pej (excuse, reply)* ingenioso(a) pero insincero(a); **a s. salesman** un vendedor con mucha labia (**d**) *(surface, tyre)* resbaladizo(a); *(hair)* brillante y lacio(a)

▸ **slick back, slick down** *vt sep* **to s. one's hair back** *or* **down** alisarse el pelo

▸ **slick up** *vi US Fam (dress smartly)* vestir elegantemente

slicker ['slıkə(r)] *n US (raincoat)* impermeable *m*

slickly ['slıklı] *adv (marketed, organized)* hábilmente; **a s. made movie** una película hecha con ingenio pero superficial

slickness ['slɪknɪs] *n* (**a**) *(of campaign)* habilidad *f*; *(of performance)* lo logrado (**b**) *(of movie, programme)* lo ingenioso pero superficial (**c**) *Pej (of excuse, reply)* lo ingenioso pero insincero; *(of salesman)* labia *f* (**d**) *(of surface, tyre)* lo resbaladizo; *(of hair)* lisura *f*

slid *pt & pp of* **slide**

slide [slaɪd] **1** *n* (**a**) *(act of sliding)* deslizamiento *m*
(**b**) *(landslide)* desprendimiento *m*, deslizamiento *m*
(**c**) *(fall) (in prices)* caída *f*, desplome *m* (**in** de); *(in popularity, standards)* declive *m*, descenso *m* (**in** de); **this began his s. into despair/disgrace** esto marcó el comienzo de su caída en la desesperación/en desgracia
(**d**) *(in playground)* tobogán *m*
(**e**) *(photographic)* diapositiva *f* ►► ***s. projector*** proyector *m* de diapositivas; ***s. viewer*** visor *m* de diapositivas; *also Comptr* ***s. show*** proyección *f* de diapositivas
(**f**) *(for microscope)* portaobjetos *m inv*, platina *f*
(**g**) *Br (for hair)* pasador *m*
(**h**) *Math* ***s. rule*** regla *f* de cálculo
(**i**) *Mus (device for playing guitar)* vara *f* corredera; ***s. guitar*** guitarra *f* con vara corredera; ***s. trombone*** trombón *m* de varas
2 *vt* (*pt & pp* **slid** [slɪd]) pasar, deslizar; **she slid the note under the door** deslizó la nota por debajo de la puerta; **she slid him the money across the table** le acercó el dinero deslizándolo por encima de la mesa; **to s. the lid off** quitar *or Am* sacar la tapa corriéndola *or* deslizándola; **he slid the door open/shut** abrió/cerró la puerta corriéndola (a un lado)
3 *vi* (**a**) *(slip)* resbalar; **he slid down the bannisters** descendió por el pasamanos; **the door slid open** la puerta se abrió deslizándose; **to s. down a rope** deslizarse por una cuerda; **tears slid down her face** las lágrimas resbalaban por su rostro *or* sus mejillas; **the drawer slides out easily** el cajón sale (deslizándose) con facilidad; **the sheet music slid (down) behind the piano** las partituras fueron resbalando por detrás del piano; **he slid into depression** se sumió en la depresión; **she slid slowly into debt** fue endeudándose poco a poco; IDIOM **to let things s.** dejar que las cosas vayan a peor
(**b**) *(move quietly, smoothly)* deslizarse; **she slid into/out of the room** entró en/salió de la habitación sigilosamente; **the pilot slid into the cockpit** el piloto entró deslizándose en la carlinga
(**c**) *(fall) (prices, value)* caer, bajar

► **slide off** *vi* (**a**) *(lid, part)* salir, quitarse (**b**) *(fall)* caerse (**c**) *(sneak away)* escabullirse

► **slide over** *vi (move up)* correrse, apartarse

slider ['slaɪdə(r)] *n (sliding control)* mando *m (corredizo)*

sliding ['slaɪdɪŋ] *adj* corredero(a) ►► ***s. door*** puerta *f* corredera *or* corrediza; *Aut* ***s. roof*** techo *m* corredizo; ***s. scale*** escala *f* móvil

slight [slaɪt] **1** *n (affront)* agravio *m* (**on** a)
2 *adj* (**a**) *(small, unimportant)* ligero(a), pequeño(a); *(accent)* ligero(a); *(cut, graze)* leve, pequeño(a); *(accident)* leve; **he has a s. stutter/limp** tartamudea/cojea un poco; **she has a s. cold** tiene un ligero resfriado; **there's a s. problem** hay un pequeño problema; **there's a s. chance of some sunshine tomorrow** existe una ligera posibilidad de que mañana brille un poco el sol; **it was at a s. angle** estaba ligeramente torcido; **she gets angry at the slightest thing** se enfada por cualquier insignificancia *or* menudencia; **not the slightest danger/interest** ni el más mínimo peligro/interés; **I haven't the slightest idea** no tengo (ni) la menor idea; **not in the slightest** en lo más mínimo; **they weren't (in) the slightest bit interested** no tenían el más mínimo interés, no les interesaba lo más mínimo
(**b**) *(person)* menudo(a); **she is of s. build** es de constitución menuda
(**c**) *(inconsequential, lightweight) (novel, work)* intrascendente, de poco peso
3 *vt (person)* desairar; *(work, efforts)* menospreciar; **to s. sb's memory** ofender la memoria de alguien

slighting ['slaɪtɪŋ] *adj* despreciativo(a), desdeñoso(a)

slightly ['slaɪtlɪ] *adv* (**a**) *(to a small degree)* ligeramente, un poco; **this one is s. worse** éste es un poco peor; **could I have s. less?** ¿podría tomar un poco menos?; **I knew him s.** apenas lo conocía; **I was ever so s. disappointed** estaba un poquitín decepcionada (**b**) *(lightly)* **s. built** menudo(a)

slightness ['slaɪtnɪs] *n* (**a**) *(of increase, difference)* escasa importancia *f*; *(of damage)* escasa gravedad *f* (**b**) *(of build)* pequeñez *f*, lo menudo

slily = **slyly**

slim [slɪm] **1** *adj* (**a**) *(person, waist, figure)* delgado(a); *(wrist)* delgado(a), fino(a) (**b**) *(book, volume)* fino(a), delgado(a) (**c**) *(chance, hope)* pequeño(a); *(majority)* escaso(a); *(pretext)* débil
2 *vt* (*pt & pp* **slimmed**) adelgazar
3 *vi* adelgazar; **I'm slimming** estoy adelgazando

► **slim down 1** *vt sep (budget)* reducir, recortar; *(company)* reducir plantilla en; *(workforce)* reducir; *(ambitions, plans)* reducir, restringir; **a slimmed-down version of the old model** una versión simplificada del antiguo modelo
2 *vi* (**a**) *(person)* adelgazar, perder peso (**b**) *(company)* reducir plantilla

slime [slaɪm] *n* (**a**) *(mud)* lodo *m*, cieno *m* (**b**) *(sticky substance)* viscosidad *f*; *(of snail, slug)* baba *f*

slimebag ['slaɪmbæg], **slimeball** ['slaɪmbɔːl] *n Fam* baboso(a) *m,f*

sliminess ['slaɪmɪnɪs] *n* (**a**) *(of frog, snail)* viscosidad *f* (**b**) *Fam (of person)* empalago *m*, zalamería *f*

slimline ['slɪmlaɪn] *adj* (**a**) *(butter, milk, soft drink)* bajo(a) en calorías (**b**) *(slim) (dishwasher, diary, calculator)* extraplano(a); **the new s. Watson is a faster player** el nuevo Watson es ahora un jugador más veloz gracias a su régimen de adelgazamiento

slimmer ['slɪmə(r)] *n* = persona que está a régimen

slimming ['slɪmɪŋ] **1** *n* adelgazamiento *m*; **s. can be bad for you** adelgazar puede ser perjudicial ►► ***s. club*** centro *m* de adelgazamiento; ***s. diet*** régimen *m* de adelgazamiento; ***s. exercises*** ejercicios *mpl* para adelgazar; ***s. pill*** pastilla *f* para adelgazar; ***s. product*** producto *m* para adelgazar; ***s. tablet*** pastilla *f* para adelgazar
2 *adj (flattering) (dress, suit, colour)* que hace más delgado(a)

slimness ['slɪmnɪs] *n* (**a**) *(of person, waist, figure)* delgadez *f*; *(of wrist)* delgadez *f*, finura *f* (**b**) *(of book, volume)* escaso grosor *m* (**c**) *(of chance, hope)* carácter *m* remoto; *(of majority)* escasa amplitud *f*

slimy ['slaɪmɪ] *adj* (**a**) *(frog, snail)* viscoso(a), baboso(a); *(mud, substance)* viscoso(a), pegajoso(a); *(wall, surface)* pegajoso(a), gelatinoso(a) (**b**) *(person)* pegajoso(a), empalagoso(a)

sling [slɪŋ] **1** *n* (**a**) *(for injured arm)* cabestrillo *m*; **she had her arm in a s.** llevaba el brazo en cabestrillo (**b**) *(for baby)* mochila *f* portabebés (**c**) *(for loads)* eslinga *f* (**d**) *(for rifle)* portafusil *m* (**e**) *(weapon)* honda *f*
2 *vt* (*pt & pp* **slung** [slʌŋ]) (**a**) *(throw)* lanzar, arrojar; *Br Fam* **can you s. me (over) the salt?** ¿me pasas la sal?; IDIOM *Br Fam* **s. your hook!** ¡piérdete!, ¡lárgate!
(**b**) *(suspend) (hammock)* colgar (**from** de); **to s. sth over one's shoulder** echarse algo a la espalda; **the soldiers wore rifles slung across** *or* **over their shoulders** los soldados llevaban rifles colgados del hombro; **I slung the towel over the washing line** eché la toalla por encima de la cuerda del tendedero
(**c**) *(insults)* lanzar (**at** a, contra)

► **sling away** *vt sep Br Fam* tirar, *Am* botar

► **sling out** *vt sep Fam* (**a**) *(throw away)* tirar, *Am* botar (**b**) *(person)* echar (**c**) *(suggestion, plan)* rechazar

slingback ['slɪŋbæk] *n* **s. (shoe)** zapato *m* de talón abierto

slingshot ['slɪŋʃɒt] *n US* tirachinas *m inv*

slink [slɪŋk] (*pt & pp* **slunk** [slʌŋk]) *vi* **to s. off** *or* **away** marcharse subrepticiamente; **the naughty dog slunk into his kennel** el perro travieso se retiró a su caseta con el rabo entre las piernas

slinky ['slɪŋkɪ] *adj (figure)* escultural; *(walk)* sensual; **a s. dress** un vestido que marca las curvas

slip [slɪp] **1** *n* (**a**) *(fall) (of person)* resbalón *m*; IDIOM **to give sb the s.** dar esquinazo a alguien
(**b**) *(in prices, standards)* descenso *m* (**in** de)
(**c**) *(landslide)* corrimiento *m*, deslizamiento *m*
(**d**) *(error)* desliz *m*; **to make a s.** tener un desliz; **a s. of the pen** un lapsus (calami); **a s. of the tongue** un lapsus (linguae); PROV **there's many a s. twixt cup and lip** del dicho al hecho va mucho trecho
(**e**) *(form)* hoja *f*; **s. (of paper)** tira *f* de papel, hoja *f* de papel *(pequeña y alargada)*
(**f**) *Br Aut* ***s. road*** *(to join motorway)* carril *m* de incorporación *or* aceleración; *(to exit motorway)* carril *m* de salida *or* deceleración
(**g**) *(undergarment)* combinación *f*
(**h**) *(cover)* **(pillow) s.** funda *f* (de almohada)
(**i**) *(in pottery)* barbotina *f*
(**j**) *(plant cutting)* esqueje *m*
(**k**) *(slightly-built person)* **a s. of a girl** una chavalina; **a s. of a lad** un chavalín
2 *vt* (*pt & pp* **slipped**) (**a**) *(escape)* **the dog slipped its leash** el perro se soltó de la correa; **the ship slipped its moorings** el barco se soltó del amarre; **his name has slipped my mind** se me ha ido su nombre de la cabeza; **to s. sb's attention** escaparse a alguien
(**b**) *(put)* deslizar; **he slipped his shoes on/off** se puso/se quitó los zapatos; **she slipped the note into my hand** me pasó la nota con sigilo, me puso con sigilo la nota en la mano; **he slipped his hand into hers** juntó su mano con la de ella; **I slipped my arm round her waist** le pasé el brazo por la cintura; **to s. sth into the conversation** deslizar

algo en la conversación; *very Fam* **to s. it to sb,** *Br* **to s. sb a length** echarle un polvo a alguien
(**c**) *(pass)* **to s. sb sth, to s. sth to sb** pasar algo a alguien; **she slipped the waiter a dollar bill** dio un dólar al camarero disimuladamente
(**d**) *(dislocate)* **to have slipped a disc** tener una vértebra dislocada, tener una hernia discal; **she slipped a disc playing squash** se dislocó una vértebra jugando al squash ►► ***slipped disc*** hernia *f* discal
(**e**) *Aut (clutch)* mantener apretado(a)
(**f**) *(in knitting)* **to s. a stitch** saltarse un punto ►► ***s. stitch*** repulgo *m*
3 *vi* (**a**) *(slide) (person)* resbalar(se); *(knot)* soltarse, correrse; *(clutch)* patinar; **his foot slipped** le resbaló un pie; **the knife slipped and cut my finger** el cuchillo se me resbaló y me corté el dedo; **my hand slipped and I knocked it over** se me resbaló la mano y lo volqué; **she slipped down the slope** se resbaló por la pendiente; *also Fig* **to s. from sb's hands** *or* **grasp** escapársele de las manos a alguien; *Fig* **to s. through sb's fingers** escapársele de las manos a alguien
(**b**) *(go gradually)* **to s. into a depression** *(person)* sumirse en una depresión; **to s. into recession** entrar en recesión; **to s. into bad habits** caer en malos hábitos
(**c**) *(move quickly)* **to s. into** *(bed)* meterse en; *(room)* colarse en; *(clothes, shoes)* ponerse; **some misprints have slipped into the article** se han colado en el artículo algunos errores de imprenta; **to s. out of** *(bed)* salir de; *(room)* salir disimuladamente de; *(clothes)* quitarse, *Am* sacarse; **the thieves managed to s. past the roadblocks** los ladrones lograron pasar inadvertidos por los controles de carretera
(**d**) *(make mistake)* tener un desliz, cometer un error
(**e**) *(get worse) (standards, profits)* ir a peor, empeorar; **they have slipped to bottom place** han bajado al último puesto; **to let things s.** dejar que las cosas vayan a peor; **I must be slipping** debe de estar fallándome algo; **you're slipping** estás fallando
(**f**) *(escape)* **she let s. a few swear words** se le escaparon unas cuantas palabrotas; **you shouldn't let this chance s.** no deberías dejar escapar esta oportunidad; **to let one's guard s.** bajar la guardia; **to let one's concentration s.** desconcentrarse; **he let it s. that he would be resigning** se le escapó que iba a dimitir

►**slip away** *vi* (**a**) *(leave)* desaparecer, desvanecerse; **control of the party was slipping away from her** el control del partido se le estaba escapando de las manos; **the patient was slipping away** el paciente se estaba apagando *or* muriendo (**b**) *(chances)* esfumarse

►**slip by** *vi (time, years)* pasar

►**slip down** *vi (fall) (picture, socks, skirt)* caerse

►**slip in** **1** *vt sep (quotation, word)* incluir, introducir
2 *vi* (**a**) *(person)* colarse (**b**) *(mistake)* colarse

►**slip off** **1** *vt sep (garment, shoes, ring)* quitarse, *Am* sacarse
2 *vi* (**a**) *(leave)* marcharse (**b**) *(fall) (hat, book)* caerse

►**slip on** *vt sep (garment, shoes, ring)* ponerse

►**slip out** *vi* (**a**) *(escape)* escaparse (**of** de); **the glass slipped out of my hand** el vaso se me escurrió *or* escapó de las manos; **it must have slipped out of my pocket** se me ha debido de caer del bolsillo; **it just slipped out** *(remark)* se me escapó (**b**) *(leave quietly)* escabullirse (**c**) *(go quickly)* **to s. out to the shop** salir un momento a la tienda

►**slip through** **1** *vt insep (gap, security control)* colarse por; *Fig* **to s. through the net** colarse, escaparse
2 *vi (mistake, person)* colarse

►**slip up** *vi (make mistake)* tener un desliz, cometer un error; **the leaders slipped up against the second-placed team** el líder patinó frente al segundo clasificado

slipcase ['slɪpkeɪs] *n (for book)* estuche *m*

slipcover ['slɪpkʌvə(r)] *n US* (**a**) *(for furniture)* funda *f* (**b**) *(for book)* estuche *m*

slip-knot ['slɪpnɒt] *n* nudo *m* corredizo

slip-on ['slɪpɒn] **1** *n* (**a**) *(shoes)* **slip-ons** zapatos *mpl* sin cordones (**b**) *US (sweater)* suéter *m or Esp* jersey *m or Col* saco *m or RP* pulóver *m* sin botones
2 *adj* ***s. shoes*** zapatos *mpl* sin cordones

slippage ['slɪpɪdʒ] *n* (**a**) *(in value)* desplome *m*, bajón *m* (**b**) *(in standards)* empeoramiento *m*, caída *f* (**c**) *(of land)* corrimiento *m* (**d**) *Com (shortfall)* desfase *m*

slipper ['slɪpə(r)] *n* zapatilla *f*; *Br* **to give sb the s.** pegarle a alguien con la zapatilla

slipperiness ['slɪpərɪnɪs] *n* (**a**) *(of object, surface)* **the s. of the roads** el estado resbaladizo de las carreteras; **the s. of the fish** lo escurridizo que estaba el pescado (**b**) *(of person)* mañas *fpl*, artimañas *fpl* (**c**) *(of concept, issue)* ambigüedad *f*

slippery ['slɪpərɪ] *adj* (**a**) *(surface, object)* resbaladizo(a), escurridizo(a) (**b**) *(person)* tramposo(a); *Pej* **a s. customer** un pájaro de cuenta, una buena pieza; IDIOM **to be on a s. slope** ir cuesta abajo; IDIOM *Pej* **as s. as an eel** más falso(a) que Judas (**c**) *(concept, issue)* ambiguo(a), etéreo(a)

slippy ['slɪpɪ] *adj Fam (surface, object)* resbaladizo(a), escurridizo(a)

slipshod ['slɪpʃɒd] *adj* chapucero(a)

slipstream ['slɪpstri:m] **1** *n* estela *f*
2 *vi (in cycling, motor racing)* ir a rebufo

slip-up ['slɪpʌp] *n* (pequeño) error *m*, desliz *m*

slipway ['slɪpweɪ] *n Naut* grada *f*

slit [slɪt] **1** *n* (**a**) *(cut) (of dress, in paper)* corte *m*, raja *f*; **to make a s. in sth** hacer un corte a *or* en algo, rajar algo (**b**) *(crack) (in door, wall)* rendija *f*, hendidura *f* (**c**) *Vulg (vagina)* raja *f*
2 *adj* **s. skirt** falda *or RP* pollera abierta *or* con raja
3 *vt* (*pt & pp* **slit**) cortar; **the skirt is s. up the side** la falda *or RP* pollera lleva una raja al costado *or* va abierta por el costado; **to s. sth open** abrir algo rajándolo; **to s. an envelope open** abrir un sobre con un abrecartas; **to s. sb's throat** degollar a alguien; **she s. her wrists** se cortó las venas

slither ['slɪðə(r)] *vi* deslizarse; **I slithered down the tree** bajé deslizándome por el árbol; **the dog was slithering about on the ice** el perro patinaba sobre el hielo

sliver ['slɪvə(r)] *n (of ham, cheese)* lonchita *f*; *(of glass)* esquirla *f*

Sloane (Ranger) ['sləʊn('reɪndʒə(r))] *n Br Fam* niño(a) *m,f* bien, *Esp* pijo(a) *m,f*

Sloaney ['sləʊnɪ] *adj Br Fam* pijo(a)

slob [slɒb] *n Fam (untidy person)* cerdo(a) *m,f*, *Esp* guarro(a) *m,f*; *(lazy person)* dejado(a) *m,f*

►**slob about, slob around** *vi Fam* holgazanear, gandulear, *Méx* andar de flojo, *RP* hacer fiaca

slobber ['slɒbə(r)] **1** *n (dribble)* baba *f*
2 *vi* babear; **the dog slobbered all over me** el perro me llenó *or* me puso perdido de baba; *Fam* **they were slobbering over each other** *(lovers)* se estaban besuqueando; *Fam* **he was slobbering over a photo of a Porsche** se le caía la baba mirando la foto de un Porsche

slobbery ['slɒbərɪ] *adj Fam (kiss)* baboso(a)

slobbish ['slɒbɪʃ] *adj Fam (untidy)* abandonado(a), *Esp* guarro(a); *(lazy)* dejado(a), haragán(ana)

sloe [sləʊ] *n (fruit)* endrina *f*; *(tree)* endrino *m* ►► ***s. gin*** licor *m* de endrinas, ≃ pacharán *m*

slog [slɒg] *Fam* **1** *n* (**a**) *(hard task)* **it was a bit of a s.** fue un aburrimiento *or Esp* tostonazo (de trabajo); **it's a long s.** *(walk)* hay un buen trecho *or Esp* una buena tirada (**b**) *(hit)* batazo *m*
2 *vi* (*pt & pp* **slogged**) (**a**) *(work hard)* trabajar como un(a) negro(a), dar el callo; **to s. away (at sth)** trabajar como una bestia (en algo) (**b**) *(move with effort)* **to s. through snow/mud** caminar penosamente *or* trabajosamente por la nieve/el barro; **we slogged slowly up the hill** subimos la colina despacio y con gran esfuerzo
3 *vt* (**a**) *(move)* **we slogged our way through the snow** caminamos a duras penas *or* con dificultad por la nieve (**b**) *(hit) (ball, person)* golpear fuertemente; **to s. it out** *(fight)* pelear a muerte; *(argue)* discutir acaloradamente

►**slog on** *vi Fam (keep working)* seguir currando

slogan ['sləʊgən] *n (political, advertising)* eslogan *m*; *(of demonstrators)* consigna *f*

sloganeering [sləʊgə'nɪərɪŋ] *n Pej* abuso *m* de eslóganes retóricos

slo-mo ['sləʊməʊ] *adj Fam* (*abbr* **slow-motion**) a cámara lenta

sloop [slu:p] *n (ship)* balandro *m*

slop [slɒp] **1** *n* (**a**) *(pig food)* desperdicios *mpl* (para los cerdos *or* puercos) ►► ***s. bucket*** *(in prison)* cubo *m (utilizado como orinal)* (**b**) *Pej (bad food)* bazofia *f* (**c**) *Fam (sentimentality)* cursilerías *fpl*
2 *vt* (*pt & pp* **slopped**) derramar
3 *vi* derramarse; **the water slopped (over) onto the floor** el agua se derramó por el suelo

►**slop about, slop around** *vi* (**a**) *(liquid)* agitarse (**b**) *(paddle)* chapotear (**c**) *Fam (be lazy)* estar *or* andar (por ahí) tirado(a)

►**slop out** *vi Br (prisoner)* vaciar el orinal

slope [sləʊp] **1** *n* (**a**) *(of ground)* cuesta *f*, pendiente *f*; *(of roof)* inclinación *f*; *(mountainside)* ladera *f*, falda *f*; **an upward/downward s.** una cuesta *or* pendiente hacia arriba/abajo (**b**) *(for skiing)* pista *f*
2 *vi* **this table slopes** esta mesa está inclinada; **to s. backwards/forwards** *(handwriting)* inclinarse hacia atrás/delante; **to s. up/down** *(path)* ascender/descender

▸**slope off** *vi Br Fam* escabullirse

sloping ['slәʊpɪŋ] *adj* (**a**) *(roof, ground)* en pendiente, inclinado(a) (**b**) *(handwriting)* inclinado(a) (**c**) *(shoulders)* caído(a)

sloppily ['slɒpɪ] *adv* (**a**) *(to work)* chapuceramente, descuidadamente; *(to dress)* descuidadamente, desaliñadamente (**b**) *Fam (sentimental)* de un modo sensiblero

sloppiness ['slɒpɪnɪs] *n* (**a**) *(of work)* dejadez *f*, falta *f* de cuidado (**b**) *Fam (sentimentality)* sensiblería *f*

sloppy ['slɒpɪ] *adj* (**a**) *(careless) (work, worker)* chapucero(a), descuidado(a); *(essay, research)* flojo(a), pobre; *(language)* descuidado(a), empobrecido(a); **to be a s. dresser** vestir descuidadamente *or* desaliñadamente; **he was guilty of s. thinking** pecaba de falta de rigor analítico, carecía de rigor analítico (**b**) *Fam (sentimental) (person, letter)* almibarado(a), empalagoso(a); *(book, film)* sensiblero(a) (**c**) *(kiss)* baboso(a)

sloppy Joe ['slɒpɪ'dʒәʊ] *n* (**a**) *(sweater)* suéter *m or Esp* jersey *m or Col* saco *m or RP* pulóver *m* grande (**b**) *US (food)* = carne picada cocinada con salsa de tomate y especias y servida encima de un trozo de pan

slosh [slɒʃ] **1** *vt* (**a**) *Fam* **she sloshed whitewash on** *or* **over the wall** echó cal por toda la pared (**b**) *Br Fam (hit)* pegar

2 *vi* (**a**) *(liquid)* chapotear; **the water was sloshing about** *or* **around in the bottom of the bucket** el agua se agitaba ruidosamente en el fondo del cubo (**b**) *(move) (in liquid, mud)* caminar chapoteando; **children sloshing around in the puddles** niños chapoteando en los charcos

sloshed [slɒʃt] *adj Fam* **to be s.** estar como una cuba *or Esp, RP* mamado(a) *or Col* caído(a) (de la perra) *or Méx* ahogado(a); **to get s.** agarrarse un pedo

slot [slɒt] **1** *n* (**a**) *(hole) (in box, machine, computer)* ranura *f* ▸▸ ***s. machine*** *(for vending)* máquina *f* expendedora; *(for gambling)* (máquina *f*) tragaperras *f inv*; *Br* ***s. meter*** contador *m* de pago previo (**b**) *(groove)* ranura *f*, muesca *f* (**c**) *(in schedule, list)* hueco *m*; *Rad & TV* espacio *m*; *Av (for take-off)* turno *m* de despegue (**d**) *(job opening)* plaza *f*

2 *vt* (*pt & pp* **slotted**) (**a**) *(part)* introducir (**into** en) (**b**) *(find time for, fit)* hacer un hueco a (**into** en)

3 *vi* (**a**) *(part)* encajar (**into** en) (**b**) *(into timetable, schedule, team)* encajar (**into** en)

▸**slot in 1** *vt sep* (**a**) *(part)* introducir (**b**) *(into schedule)* hacer un hueco a; **I can s. him in at four o'clock** le puedo hacer un hueco a las cuatro

2 *vi (part, into team)* encajar

▸**slot together 1** *vt sep* ensamblar

2 *vi* encajar

sloth [slәʊθ] *n* (**a**) *(laziness)* pereza *f* (**b**) *(animal)* perezoso *m*

slothful ['slәʊθfʊl] *adj* perezoso(a) *m,f*

slotted ['slɒtɪd] *adj US* ***s. spatula*** pala *f*; ***s. spoon*** espumadera *f*

slouch [slaʊtʃ] **1** *n* (**a**) *(stoop)* **to have a s.** ser de hombros caídos; **to walk with a s.** caminar encorvado(a) (**b**) *Fam* **he's no s. when it comes to cooking** es un hacha en la cocina

2 *vi* (**a**) *(when standing)* encorvarse; **don't s.!** ¡ponte derecho! (**b**) *(on chair)* repantigarse (**c**) *(when moving)* **he slouched into/out of the room** entró en/salió de la habitación caminando encorvado

▸**slouch about, slouch around** *vi (laze around)* holgazanear

slough[1] [slaʊ] *n (swamp)* lodazal *m*, barrizal *m*; *Literary* **to be in a s. of despair** estar sumido(a) en la más profunda desesperación

slough[2] [slʌf] **1** *n (skin) (of snake)* piel *m*, camisa *f*; *Med* escara *f*

2 *vt (of reptile)* **to s. its skin** mudar de piel *or* de camisa

▸**slough off** *vt sep* (**a**) *(of reptile)* **to s. off its skin** mudar de piel *or* de camisa (**b**) *(responsibility)* librarse de; *(bad habit)* deshacerse de

Slovak ['slәʊvæk] **1** *n* (**a**) *(person)* eslovaco(a) *m,f* (**b**) *(language)* eslovaco *m*

2 *adj* eslovaco(a)

Slovakia [slәʊ'vækɪә] *n* Eslovaquia

Slovakian [slәʊ'vækɪәn] **1** *n* eslovaco(a) *m,f*

2 *adj* eslovaco(a)

Slovene ['slәʊviːn], **Slovenian** [slәʊ'viːnɪәn] **1** *n* (**a**) *(person)* esloveno(a) *m,f* (**b**) *(language)* esloveno *m*

2 *adj* esloveno(a)

Slovenia [slәʊ'viːnɪә] *n* Eslovenia

Slovenian = **Slovene**

slovenliness ['slʌvәnlɪnɪs] *n* (**a**) *(of appearance, dress)* desaliño *m*, dejadez *f* (**b**) *(carelessness)* carácter *m* descuidado

slovenly ['slʌvәnlɪ] *adj* (**a**) *(untidy)* desastrado(a), desaliñado(a) (**b**) *(careless)* descuidado(a)

SLOW [slәʊ] **1** *adj* (**a**) *(not fast)* lento(a); **to be s. to do sth** tardar *or Am* demorar en hacer algo; **business is s.** el negocio está flojo; **my watch is s.** mi reloj va atrasado; **my watch is ten minutes s.** mi reloj lleva diez minutos de retraso *or Am* demora; **she's a s. worker/swimmer** trabaja/nada despacio; **to be s. off the mark** *(to start)* tardar *or Am* demorar en arrancar; *(to understand)* ser un poco torpe; **it was s. going, the going was s.** iba muy lento(a); **the fog was s. to clear** la niebla escampó lentamente; PROV **s. and steady wins the race** vísteme despacio que tengo prisa; *Culin* **in a s. oven** a horno moderado; **we're making s. progress** avanzamos muy poco; **it's s. work** lleva *or* demora mucho tiempo; **she wasn't s. in accepting the cheque** no se lo pensó a la hora de aceptar el cheque; **they were s. to understand her instructions** les costó entender sus instrucciones; **she's very s. to anger** no se enfada con facilidad ▸▸ *US Fam* ***s. burn:* to do a s. burn** mosquearse, *Esp* agarrar un mosqueo; ***s. cooker*** = olla eléctrica para cocinar lentamente; ***s. handclap*** = palmas lentas de desaprobación; *Aut* ***s. lane*** carril *m* lento; ***s. loris*** loris *m inv* perezoso; *Cin & TV* **(in) s. motion** (a) cámara lenta; ***s. train*** tren *m* lento

(**b**) *(stupid)* corto(a) *or* lento(a) de entendederas

(**c**) *Sport (green, court, surface)* lento(a)

(**d**) *(dull) (evening, party)* aburrido(a); *(film)* aburrido(a), lento(a)

2 *adv* despacio, lentamente; **to go s.** *(workers)* hacer huelga de celo

3 *vt (car)* reducir la velocidad de; *(progress, growth, pace)* ralentizar; **the alcohol slowed her reactions** el alcohol redujo su capacidad de reacción; **these drugs s. the heart rate** estos medicamentos ralentizan el ritmo cardiaco; **I slowed the horse to a trot** puse el caballo al trote

4 *vi (reduce speed)* aminorar la velocidad; **traffic has slowed to a crawl** el tráfico casi se ha paralizado; **to s. to a halt** ir aminorando la velocidad hasta detenerse; **growth has slowed** el crecimiento se ha ralentizado; **the number of complaints has slowed to a trickle** las quejas llegan ahora con cuentagotas

▸**slow down, slow up 1** *vt sep* (**a**) *(reduce speed of) (car)* reducir la velocidad de; **the heart attack has slowed me down a bit** el infarto me ha hecho tomarme las cosas con más calma

(**b**) *(delay)* retrasar

2 *vi (reduce speed)* aminorar la velocidad; **s. down** *or* **up, I can't keep up (with you)/understand you!** ¡más despacio, (que) no puedo seguirte/no te entiendo!; **he has slowed down since the heart attack** se ha tomado las cosas con más calma desde el infarto; **growth slowed down in the second quarter** el crecimiento se ralentizó en el segundo trimestre

slow-acting ['slәʊ'æktɪŋ] *adj* de efecto retardado

slow-burning ['slәʊ'bɜːnɪŋ] *adj (fuse, fuel)* de combustión lenta

slowcoach ['slәʊkәʊtʃ] *n Br Fam* tortuga *f*

slowdown ['slәʊdaʊn] *n* (**a**) *US (go-slow)* huelga *f* de celo (**b**) *(in productivity, rate)* disminución *f*; *(in economy)* desaceleración *f*

slowly ['slәʊlɪ] *adv* despacio, lentamente; **s. but surely** lento, pero seguro; **he's s. realizing that...** poco a poco se está dando cuenta de que...

slow-motion ['slәʊ'mәʊʃәn] *adj* a cámara lenta ▸▸ ***s. replay*** repetición *f* a cámara lenta

slow-moving ['slәʊ'muːvɪŋ] *adj* (**a**) *(person, car, queue, river)* lento(a) (**b**) *(film, plot)* lento(a)

slowness ['slәʊnɪs] *n* lentitud *f*

slowpoke ['slәʊpәʊk] *n US Fam* tortuga *f*

slow-witted ['slәʊ'wɪtɪd] *adj* torpe, obtuso(a)

slow-worm ['slәʊwɜːm] *n* lución *m*

SLR [eselˈɑː(r)] *n Phot* (*abbr* **single-lens reflex**) cámara *f* réflex (monoobjetivo)

sludge [slʌdʒ] *n* (**a**) *(mud)* fango *m*, lodo *m* (**b**) *(in engine)* sedimento *m* (**c**) *(sewage)* aguas *fpl* residuales

slue *US* = **slew**[1]

slug [slʌg] **1** *n* (**a**) *(mollusc)* babosa *f* ▸▸ ***s. pellet*** bolita *f* de veneno para babosas (**b**) *Fam (bullet)* bala *f* (**c**) *Fam (of drink)* trago *m* (**d**) *Fam (blow)* tortazo *m*, castañazo *m* (**e**) *US (fake coin)* ficha *f*

2 *vt* (*pt & pp* **slugged**) *Fam (hit)* dar un tortazo *or* castañazo a; **to s. it out** pelear a muerte

slugfest ['slʌgfest] *n US Fam* (**a**) *(boxing match)* festival *m* de puñetazos (**b**) *(baseball game)* festival *m* de carreras

sluggard ['slʌgәd] *n* holgazán(ana) *m,f*

slugger ['slʌgə(r)] *n US Fam (boxer)* gran pegador *m*; *(in baseball)* potente bateador *m*

sluggish ['slʌgɪʃ] *adj* (**a**) *(person)* aletargado(a) (**b**) *(response)* lento(a), retardado(a); *(engine)* frío(a); *(pulse)* lento(a); *(growth, economy)* lento(a); *(business, market)* inactivo(a), flojo(a); **at a s. pace** con paso cansino

sluggishly ['slʌgɪʃlɪ] *adv* (**a**) *(to move)* lentamente, despacio (**b**) *(to respond)* con lentitud, con retardo; *(to beat)* despacio, lentamente; *(to grow)* lentamente

sluggishness ['slʌgɪʃnɪs] *n* (**a**) *(of person)* amuermamiento *m*, aletargamiento *m* (**b**) *(of response)* lentitud *f*, carácter *m* retardado; *(of engine)* enfriamiento *m*; *(of pulse)* lentitud *f*; *(of growth, economy)* lentitud *f*; *(of business, market)* inactividad *f*

sluice [slu:s] *n* (**a**) *(channel)* canal *m* (**b**) *(sluicegate)* esclusa *f*, compuerta *f* (**c**) *(wash)* **to give sth a s. (down)** lavar algo echándole agua abundante por encima

▸ **sluice down** *vt sep (wash down)* lavar algo echándole abundante agua por encima; **to s. oneself down with cold water** darse una buena ducha de agua fría

▸ **sluice out** *vt sep (rinse) (cup, pot)* enjuagar con agua abundante; **they sluiced out the stable** baldearon el suelo del establo

sluicegate ['slu:sgeɪt] *n* esclusa *f*, compuerta *f*

sluiceway ['slu:sweɪ] *n* canal *m*

slum [slʌm] **1** *n (district)* barrio *m* bajo; *(on outskirts)* arrabal *m*, suburbio *m*; *(house)* tugurio *m* ▸▸ ***s. area*** zona *f* urbana deprimida, *Esp* núcleo *m* de chabolismo; ***s. clearance*** erradicación *f Esp* del chabolismo *or Méx* las ciudades perdidas *or Arg* las villas miseria *or Urug* los cantegriles; ***s. dwelling*** tugurio *m*; ***s. landlord*** casero *m* que alquila *or Méx* renta tugurios

2 *vt (pt & pp* **slummed**) **to s. it** *(affect poverty)* ir de pobre, llevar vida de pobre; *(lower oneself)* rebajarse

slumber ['slʌmbə(r)] **1** *n* (**a**) *Literary* sueño *m* (**b**) *US* ***s. party*** = fiesta de adolescentes que se quedan a dormir en casa de quien la organiza

2 *vi Literary* dormir

slum-dweller ['slʌmdwelə(r)] *n* habitante *mf* de los barrios bajos

slummy ['slʌmɪ] *adj (area)* bajo(a)

slump [slʌmp] **1** *n* (**a**) *(in prices, sales)* desplome *m*, caída *f*; *(in popularity, interest)* bajón *m*, caída *f* (**b**) *(economic depression)* crisis *f inv*, recesión *f* (**c**) *(bad patch) (of player, team)* mala racha *f*, mal momento *m*; **she has suffered a s. in her form** ha experimentado un bajón en su forma

2 *vi* (**a**) *(physically)* desplomarse; **she slumped into an armchair** se desplomó en un sillón; **her shoulders slumped** dejó caer los hombros bruscamente; **he was found slumped over the table** lo encontraron desplomado sobre la mesa

(**b**) *(economy)* hundirse

(**c**) *(prices, sales)* desplomarse; *(popularity, interest)* caer

(**d**) *(form)* experimentar un bajón; **they have slumped to seventeenth in the table** han descendido de golpe al decimoséptimo puesto en la (tabla de) clasificación

slung *pt & pp of* **sling**

slunk *pt & pp of* **slink**

slur [slɜ:(r)] **1** *n* (**a**) *(insult)* agravio *m*, injuria *f*; **a racial s.** un insulto racista; **it's a s. on his character** es una afrenta a su personalidad; **to cast a s. on sb's reputation** manchar la reputación de alguien (**b**) *(in speech)* **she was speaking with a s.** hablaba arrastrando las palabras (**c**) *Mus (sign)* ligadura *f*

2 *vt (pt & pp* **slurred**) (**a**) *(words)* pronunciar con dificultad (**b**) *(reputation, character)* manchar, empañar (**c**) *Mus* ligar

slurp [slɜ:p] **1** *n* (**a**) *(noise)* sorbetón *m* (**b**) *Fam (sip, drink)* sorbetón *m*

2 *vt* sorber *(ruidosamente)*; **don't s. your coffee!** ¡no sorbas el café!

3 *vi* sorber *(ruidosamente)*

slurred [slɜ:d] *adj (speech)* mal articulado(a)

slurry ['slʌrɪ] *n* (**a**) *(liquid manure)* estiércol *m* líquido (**b**) *(watery cement)* lechada *f*

slush [slʌʃ] *n* (**a**) *(snow)* nieve *f* sucia *(medio derretida)* (**b**) *(drink)* granizado *m* (**c**) *Fam Pol* ***s. fund*** fondos *mpl* para corrupción *or Esp* corruptelas (**d**) *Fam (sentimentality)* sensiblería *f*

slushy ['slʌʃɪ] *adj* (**a**) *(snow)* medio derretido(a) (**b**) *(movie, book)* sensiblero(a), sentimentaloide

slut [slʌt] *n Fam* (**a**) *(promiscuous woman)* puta *f* (**b**) *(untidy, dirty woman)* marrana *f*, *Esp* guarra *f*

sluttish ['slʌtɪʃ] *adj* (**a**) *(slovenly)* desastrado(a) (**b**) *(behaviour)* de fulana

sly [slaɪ] **1** *n* **on the s.** subrepticiamente, a hurtadillas

2 *adj* (**a**) *(cunning)* astuto(a) (**b**) *(dishonest)* desaprensivo(a) (**c**) *(mischievous)* malicioso(a) (**d**) *(secretive)* **he's a s. one!** ¡qué cuco!

slyboots ['slaɪbu:ts] *n Fam* picarón(ona) *m,f*, mosquita *mf* muerta

slyly, slily ['slaɪlɪ] *adv* (**a**) *(cunningly)* astutamente (**b**) *(nastily)* de manera desaprensiva (**c**) *(mischievously)* maliciosamente

slyness ['slaɪnɪs] *n* (**a**) *(cunning)* astucia *f* (**b**) *(nastiness)* desaprensión *f* (**c**) *(mischief)* malicia *f*

SM (**a**) (*abbr* **sado-masochism**) SM, sado *m* (**b**) (*abbr* **Sergeant-Major**) sargento *mf* primero

S&M [esənd'em] *n* (**a**) *Fam* (*abbr* **sado-masochism**) SM *m*, sado *m* (**b**) (*abbr* **sales & marketing**) ventas *fpl* y marketing

smack [smæk] **1** *n* (**a**) *(blow) (on bottom)* azote *m*; *(in face)* bofetada *f*; **a s. in the face** una bofetada; **be quiet or I'll give you a s.!** ¡cállate o te doy un azote! (**b**) *(sound)* chasquido *m*; **with a s. of his lips** relamiéndose (**c**) *Fam (kiss)* besote *m*, besazo *m* (**d**) *(suggestion, hint)* **there is a s. of hypocrisy about his remarks** hay cierta hipocresía en sus comentarios (**e**) *Fam (heroin)* caballo *m* (**f**) *(boat)* barco *m* de pesca

2 *adv Fam* **to bump s. into a tree** chocar de lleno con un árbol; **it landed s. in the middle of the flowerbed** vino a caer justo en el medio del parterre

3 *vt* (**a**) *(hit) (on bottom)* dar un azote a; *(in face)* dar una bofetada a; **to s. sb's bottom** *(in punishment)* darle una azotaina a alguien; *Br Fam* **to s. sb in the mouth** darle un puñetazo *or* un mamporro en la cara a alguien

(**b**) *(put forcefully)* **she smacked the book down on the table** puso el libro enérgicamente sobre la mesa; **he smacked the ball into the back of the net** metió la pelota de un trallazo hasta el fondo de la red

(**c**) **to s. one's lips** *(in anticipation)* relamerse

4 *vi (smash)* **the ball smacked against a post** la pelota se estrelló contra un poste

▸ **smack of** *vt insep (suggest)* oler a

▸ **smack up** *vt sep Fam* dar una paliza a

smacker ['smækə(r)] *n Fam* (**a**) *(big kiss)* besote *m*, besazo *m* (**b**) **fifty smackers** *(pounds)* cincuenta libras *fpl*; *(dollars)* cincuenta dólares *mpl*

smackeroo [smækə'ru:] *n US Fam (dollar)* dólar *m*

smackhead ['smækhed] *n Fam (heroin addict)* heroinómano(a) *m,f*

SMALL [smɔ:l] **1** *n* (**a**) *(part of body)* **the s. of the back** la región lumbar, los riñones

(**b**) *Br Fam* **smalls** *(underwear)* ropa *f* interior

2 *adj* (**a**) *(not large)* pequeño(a), *Am* chico(a); **these trousers are too s. for me** estos pantalones me vienen pequeños; **to have a s. appetite** tener poco apetito; **only a very s. number of people make it** sólo un número muy reducido de gente lo consigue; **she's a conservative with a s. "c"** es de ideas conservadoras, no del Partido Conservador; **to make sth smaller** empequeñecer algo; **a s. voice** una vocecilla; **to speak in a s. voice** hablar con un hilo de voz; **on a s. scale** a pequeña escala; *Br Euph* **the smallest room** el escusado *or* excusado; **it's a s. world!** ¡el mundo es un pañuelo!; PROV **s. is beautiful** la belleza está en las cosas pequeñas ▸▸ *Journ* ***s. ads*** anuncios *mpl* breves *or* por palabras; ***s. arms*** armas *fpl* cortas; ***s. business*** pequeña empresa *f*; ***s. businessman*** pequeño empresario *m*; *Typ* ***s. caps*** versalita *f*; ***s. claims court*** = juzgado para causas de poca cuantía; *Aut* ***s. end*** pie *m* de biela; ***s. game*** caza *f* menor; ***the s. hours*** la madrugada; ***s. intestine*** intestino *m* delgado; ***s. letters*** (letras *fpl*) minúsculas *fpl*; ***s. and medium-sized business*** pequeña y mediana empresa *f*; ***the s. print*** la letra pequeña; ***the s. screen*** la pequeña pantalla

(**b**) *(not important)* pequeño(a); **it made me feel s.** hizo que me sintiera muy poca cosa *or* me avergonzara de mí mismo; **they tried to make me look s.** querían hacerme parecer insignificante; **it was s. comfort that...** de poco consuelo sirvió que...; **(it's) s. wonder that...** no es de extrañar que...; **there's the s. matter of the £150 you still owe me** todavía queda el asuntillo de las 150 libras que me debes; **it's no s. achievement** es un logro nada despreciable; **in a s. way** a pequeña escala; **I like to help, in my own s. way** me gusta ayudar, aunque sea modestamente; IDIOM *Fam* **it's s. beer** *or US* **potatoes** es una *Esp* nadería *or Am* zoncera, es cosa de niños ▸▸ ***s. change*** cambio *m*, suelto *m*, *Am* vuelto *m*, *Andes, CAm, Méx* sencillo *m*; *Fam* ***s. fry*** gente *f* de poca monta; ***s. investor*** pequeño(a) inversor(ora) *m,f*; ***s. talk*** charla *f or CAm, Méx* plática *f* insustancial; **to make s. talk** conversar sobre temas triviales

3 *adv (write)* con letra pequeña; **to chop sth up s.** cortar algo en trozos pequeños; **to start s.** comenzar con poco; **to think s.** plantearse las cosas a pequeña escala; **the cat curled itself up s.** el gato se hizo un ovillito

small-bore ['smɔːl'bɔː(r)] *adj* de pequeño calibre

smallholder ['smɔːlhəʊldə(r)] *n Br* minifundista *mf*

smallholding ['smɔːlhəʊldɪŋ] *n Br* minifundio *m*

smallish ['smɔːlɪʃ] *adj (house, town)* más bien pequeño(a); *(income)* más bien escaso(a) *or* reducido(a); *(family)* más bien reducido(a), más bien pequeño(a); *(majority)* más bien escaso(a)

small-minded [smɔːl'maɪndɪd] *adj* mezquino(a)

small-mindedness [smɔːl'maɪndɪdnɪs] *n* mezquindad *f*

smallness ['smɔːlnɪs] *n* pequeñez *f*, pequeño tamaño *m*

smallpox ['smɔːlpɒks] *n* viruela *f*

small-scale ['smɔːl'skeɪl] *adj* (**a**) *(model, map)* a pequeña escala (**b**) *(operation)* de poca envergadura

small-time ['smɔːl'taɪm] *adj Fam* de poca monta

small-town ['smɔːl'taʊn] *adj (parochial)* provinciano(a), de pueblo

smarm [smɑːm] *Pej* **1** *n* zalamería *f*

2 *vt* **to s. one's way into sth** conseguir algo a base de zalamerías *or* de dar coba

▸ **smarm up** *Pej vi* **to s. up to sb** dar coba a alguien, *Esp* hacer la pelota a alguien

smarmy ['smɑːmɪ] *adj Pej* zalamero(a)

smart [smɑːt] **1** *adj* (**a**) *(clever)* inteligente; *(sharp)* agudo(a), listo(a); **a s. move** una decisión acertada; **that wasn't very s., was it?** eso ha sido una tontería, ¿verdad?; **don't try to get s. with me** no te hagas el listo conmigo; **the s. money is on Jones to win the election** los entendidos en la materia creen que Jones ganará las elecciones ▸▸ *Fam* ***s. alec(k)*** sabelotodo *mf*, *Esp* listillo(a) *m,f*, *Méx, RP* vivo(a) *m,f*; ***s. bomb*** bomba *f* teledirigida; ***s. card*** tarjeta *f* inteligente; *Typ* ***s. quotes*** comillas *fpl* tipográficas

(**b**) *(elegant)* elegante; **you look very s. in your new suit** estás muy elegante con tu traje nuevo; **to be a s. dresser** vestir elegantemente; **the s. set** la gente guapa

(**c**) *(quick)* rápido(a); *(hit, blow)* seco(a); **give it a s. tap** dale un golpecito seco; **look s. (about it)!** ¡date prisa!, *Am* ¡apúrate!

(**d**) *Fam (excellent)* genial, *Esp* molón(ona), *Andes, CAm, Carib, Méx* chévere, *Col* tenaz, *Méx* padrísimo(a); *(pretty)* mono(a)

2 *vi* (**a**) *(wound, graze)* escocer; *(eyes)* picar, escocer; **my face was still smarting from the blow** todavía me dolía la cara del golpe (**b**) *(person)* resentirse, dolerse; **they are still smarting from the insult/defeat** todavía están escocidos del insulto/de la derrota

3 *n US Fam* **smarts** *(intelligence)* mollera *f*

4 *exclam Fam (excellent)* ¡genial!, ¡fantástico!

smart-alec(k) ['smɑːt'ælɪk], **smart-alecky** ['smɑːt'ælɪkɪ] *adj Fam (reply, comment)* de sabelotodo *or Esp* listillo(a) *or Méx, RP* vivo(a)

smartarse ['smɑːtɑːs], *US* **smartass** ['smɑːtæs] *very Fam* **1** *n* sabelotodo *mf or Esp* listillo(a) *m,f or Méx, RP* vivo(a) *m,f* de mierda

2 *adj (reply, comment)* de sabelotodo *or Esp* listillo(a) *or Méx, RP* vivo(a) de mierda

smarten ['smɑːtən]

▸ **smarten up** **1** *vt sep (place)* arreglar; **to s. oneself up** acicalarse; *Fam* **you'd better s. up your ideas** *or* **your act!** ¡a ver si (te) espabilas!

2 *vi* (**a**) *(tidy oneself up)* arreglarse (**b**) *(behave more cleverly)* espabilarse

smartly ['smɑːtlɪ] *adv* (**a**) *(cleverly)* con inteligencia, inteligentemente; *(sharply)* agudamente (**b**) *(elegantly)* elegantemente (**c**) *(quickly)* rápidamente, con rapidez; *(sharply)* secamente; **tap it s.** dale un golpecito seco

smartness ['smɑːtnɪs] *n* (**a**) *(cleverness)* inteligencia *f*; *(sharpness)* agudeza *f* (**b**) *(elegance)* elegancia *f* (**c**) *(briskness)* vivacidad *f*, rapidez *f*

smarty ['smɑːtɪ], **smarty-pants** ['smɑːtɪpænts] (*pl* **smarty-pants**) *n Fam* sabelotodo *mf*, *Esp* listillo(a) *m,f*, *Méx, RP* vivo(a)

smash [smæʃ] **1** *n* (**a**) *(noise)* estruendo *m*; **the vase fell with a s.** el jarrón cayó estrepitosamente (**b**) *(blow)* golpe *m*, batacazo *m* (**c**) *(collision)* choque *m* (**d**) *(in tennis, badminton, table-tennis)* mate *m*, smash *m* (**e**) *Fam (record, movie)* **s. (hit)** exitazo *m*

2 *vt* (**a**) *(break)* **to s. sth (to pieces)** hacer algo pedazos *or* añicos; **to s. sth against sth** destrozar algo contra algo; **to s. sth open** abrir algo de un golpetazo; **to s. down a door** derribar una puerta; **to s. a window in** hacer añicos *or* romper una ventana; *Fam* **to s. sb's face in** partirle la cara a alguien

(**b**) *(hit)* **she smashed her fist into his face** le estampó un puñetazo en la cara; **she smashed him over the head with a chair** le estrelló una silla en la cabeza; **he smashed a shot against the post** disparó un trallazo contra el poste

(**c**) *(in tennis, badminton, table-tennis)* remachar

(**d**) *(destroy) (hopes, chances, resistance)* acabar con; **to s. a drugs ring** desarticular una red de narcotraficantes; **she smashed the world record** pulverizó el récord mundial

3 *vi* (**a**) *(collide)* **to s. into sth** estrellarse contra algo (**b**) *(shatter)* **to s. (into pieces)** estallar (en mil pedazos) (**c**) *(in tennis, badminton, table-tennis)* hacer mates

4 *adv* **to go s. into a wall** estrellarse contra una pared

▸ **smash up** *vt sep* destrozar

smash-and-grab (raid) ['smæʃən'græb('reɪd)] *n* = rotura de un escaparate para robar artículos expuestos en él

smashed ['smæʃt] *adj Fam* (**a**) *(drunk)* **to be s.** estar *Esp* mamado(a) *or Méx* ahogado(a) *or RP* en pedo; **to get s.** agarrarse un pedo (**b**) *(on drugs)* **to be s.** estar colocado(a) *or Esp* pedo *or Col* trabado(a) *or RP* falopeado(a); **to get s.** agarrarse un pedo

smasher ['smæʃə(r)] *n Br Fam* **she's a s.** *(gorgeous)* es un bombón; **the goal was a s.** fue un gol de antología

smashing ['smæʃɪŋ] *adj* (**a**) *Br Fam (excellent)* genial, *Andes, CAm, Carib, Méx* chévere, *Méx* padre, *RP* bárbaro(a); **we had a s. time** nos lo pasamos genial (**b**) *(blow)* violento(a), potente

smash-up ['smæʃəp] *n Fam (traffic accident)* colisión *f*, accidente *m* de coche *or Am* carro *or CSur* auto

smattering ['smætərɪŋ] *n* (**a**) *(of knowledge)* nociones *fpl*; **she has a s. of Italian** tiene nociones de italiano (**b**) *(of people, things)* puñado *m*; **there was a s. of applause** hubo algunos aplausos

SME [esem'iː] *n* (*abbr* **small and medium-sized enterprise**) PYME *f*

smear [smɪə(r)] **1** *n* (**a**) *(stain)* mancha *f* (**b**) *(slander)* calumnia *f* (**on** contra) ▸▸ ***s. campaign*** campaña *f* de difamación; ***s. tactics*** tácticas *fpl* difamatorias (**c**) *Med (sample)* frotis *m inv* ▸▸ ***s. (test)*** citología *f*

2 *vt* (**a**) *(spread)* embadurnar, untar; **he smeared it with grease, he smeared grease over it** lo untó *or* embadurnó de grasa; **to s. paint on one's face** embadurnarse la cara de pintura; **her face was smeared with grime** tenía la cara llena de mugre (**b**) *(smudge)* emborronar (**c**) *(slander)* difamar, calumniar (**d**) *US Fam (defeat easily)* vapulear

3 *vi (make-up, ink)* correrse

smeggy ['smegɪ] *adj Br Fam* asqueroso(a)

smeghead ['smeghed] *n Br Fam* cabeza *mf* de chorlito

smegma ['smegmə] *n* esmegma *m*

smell [smel] **1** *n* (**a**) *(odour)* olor *m* (**of** a); **there's a bad s.** huele mal; **what a s.!** ¡qué mal olor!, ¡qué peste!; **there's a strong s. of gas in here** aquí dentro huele mucho a gas; **this chemical has no s.** este producto químico es inodoro; *Fig* **the s. of fear** el olor a miedo (**b**) *Fam (sniff)* **to have a s. of sth** oler algo (**c**) *(sense)* olfato *m*

2 *vt* (*pt & pp* **smelled** *or* **smelt** [smelt]) (**a**) *(notice an odour of)* oler; **I can s. burning** huele a quemado; **she could s. alcohol on his breath** podía percibir el olor a alcohol en su aliento; IDIOM **I s. a rat** aquí hay gato encerrado (**b**) *(sense) (trouble, danger)* oler(se), olfatear (**c**) *(sniff at) (of person)* oler; *(of dog)* olfatear, olisquear

3 *vi (have odour)* oler; **to s. of** *or* **like sth** oler a algo; **to s. nice/horrible** oler bien/muy mal *or Esp* fatal; **it smells stuffy in here** el ambiente está cargado aquí dentro; *Fig* **the whole affair smells of treachery** todo el asunto huele a traición

(**b**) *(stink)* apestar; **it smells in here!** ¡qué mal huele aquí!; **he smells** apesta, huele mal; **her breath smells** le huele el aliento, tiene mal aliento; **his feet s.** le huelen los pies

(**c**) *(perceive odour)* oler; **he can't s.** no huele, no puede oler

▸ **smell out** *vt sep* (**a**) *(trouble, secret, conspiracy)* olfatear, olerse (**b**) *(of dog) (hunt out)* olfatear (el rastro de) (**c**) *(stink out)* apestar

smelliness ['smelɪnɪs] *n* pestilencia *f*, tufo *m*

smelling-salts ['smelɪŋ'sɔːlts] *npl* sales *fpl* aromáticas

smelly ['smelɪ] *adj* (**a**) *(stinky)* apestoso(a), maloliente; **to be s.** oler mal, apestar; **it's a bit s. in here** aquí hay mal olor, huele mal aquí; **she has s. feet** le huelen los pies (**b**) *Br Fam (unpleasant)* apestoso(a); **you can keep your s. doll!** ¡puedes quedarte con tu muñeca apestosa!

smelt[1] [smelt] *vt (ore)* fundir

smelt[2] [smelt] *n (fish)* eperlano *m*

smelt[3] *pt & pp of* **smell**

smelter ['smeltə(r)] *n* (**a**) *(industrial plant)* fundición *f* (**b**) *(worker)* fundidor(ora) *m,f*

smew [smjuː] *n* serreta *f* chica

smidgen ['smɪdʒən] *n Fam* pizca *f*; **could I have just a s. less sauce?** ¿podría ponerme un poquitín *or Esp* pelín menos de salsa?

smile [smaɪl] **1** *n* sonrisa *f*; **"of course," he said with a s.** "por supuesto", dijo sonriente *or* sonriendo; **to give sb a s.** sonreírle a alguien; **she gave me a friendly s.** me sonrió amigablemente; **come**

on, give us a s.! ¡vamos, hombre/mujer, sonríe!; **to have a s. on one's face** estar sonriente, tener cara sonriente; **she was all smiles** *(happy)* estaba muy contenta; *(as a pretence)* se mostraba muy risueña; **to take** *or* **wipe the s. off sb's face** borrarle la sonrisa a alguien
2 *vt (approval, agreement)* mostrar con una sonrisa; **to s. a welcome to sb** obsequiar a alguien con una sonrisa de bienvenida; **she smiled a sad smile** sonrió tristemente *or* apesadumbradamente
3 *vi* sonreír; **to s. at sb** sonreírle a alguien; **she smiled at his innocence** su ingenuidad la hizo sonreír; **to s. to oneself** sonreír (uno) para sus adentros; **s.!** *(for photograph)* sonría, por favor; **keep smiling!** ¡que no decaiga el ánimo!; **fortune smiled on them** les sonrió la fortuna

smiley ['smaılı] *n Comptr Fam* emoticón *m*

smiling ['smaılıŋ] *adj* sonriente

smilingly ['smaılıŋlı] *adv* con una sonrisa

smirch [smɜːtʃ] *Literary* **1** *vt (name, reputation)* mancillar
2 *n* mácula *f* (**on** en)

smirk [smɜːk] **1** *n* sonrisa *f* complacida *(despreciativa)*
2 *vi* sonreír con satisfacción *(despreciativa)*

smite [smaıt] (*pt* **smote** [sməʊt], *pp* **smitten** ['smıtən]) *vt* (**a**) *Literary (strike)* golpear (**b**) *(affect severely)* **the city was smitten with cholera** la ciudad sufría el azote del cólera; **they were smitten with terror/remorse** les invadía el terror/remordimiento

▸ **smite down** *vt sep Literary (kill)* ajusticiar

smith [smıθ] *n* herrero *m*

smithereens [smıðəˈriːnz] *npl* **to smash/blow sth to s.** hacer algo añicos; **the house was blown to smithereens in the explosion** la explosión hizo saltar la casa en mil pedazos

smithy ['smıðı] *n (forge)* fragua *f*

smitten ['smıtən] **1** *adj* (**a**) *(in love)* locamente *or* perdidamente enamorado(a) (**with** de) (**b**) *(keen)* **he was quite s. with the idea** le seducía la idea
2 *pp of* **smite**

smock [smɒk] *n* (**a**) *(of artist, farmer)* blusón *m* (**b**) *(maternity dress)* vestido *m* premamá

smocking ['smɒkıŋ] *n* nido *m* de abeja *(en fruncido)*

smog [smɒg] *n* niebla *f* tóxica, hongo *m* de contaminación

smoggy ['smɒgı] *adj (day)* con una densa niebla tóxica; **it's s.** hay una densa niebla tóxica

smoke [sməʊk] **1** *n* (**a**) *(from fire, cigarette)* humo *m*; **to go up in s.** *(building)* ser consumido(a) por las llamas *or* el fuego; *(plans)* desbaratarse, malograrse; *(hopes)* esfumarse, desvanecerse; IDIOM *Fam* **he had s. coming out of his ears** echaba *or* estaba que echaba humo por las orejas, le salía humo por las orejas; PROV **there's no s. without fire** cuando el río suena, agua lleva ▸▸ ***s. alarm*** detector *m* de humo; ***s. bomb*** bomba *f* de humo; ***s. canister*** bote *m* de humo; ***s. detector*** detector *m* de humo; ***s. ring*** aro *m or* anillo *m* de humo; *also Fig* ***s. screen*** cortina *f* de humo; ***s. signals*** señales *fpl* de humo
(**b**) *(action)* **I went outside for a s.** salí a fumarme un cigarrillo; **to have a s.** fumarse un cigarrillo
(**c**) *Fam (cigarette)* pitillo *m*
(**d**) *Fam (cannabis cigarette)* canuto *m*, porro *m*; *(cannabis)* picadura *f* de cannabis
(**e**) *Br Fam* **the (Big) S.** *(London)* Londres
2 *vt* (**a**) *(cigarette, drug)* fumar; **to s. a pipe** fumar en pipa; **to s. twenty a day** fumarse veinte al día (**b**) *(meat, fish, cheese)* ahumar (**c**) *(glass)* ahumar
3 *vi* (**a**) *(person)* fumar; **do you mind if I smoke?** ¿le molesta que fume?; IDIOM *Fam* **to s. like a chimney** *(person)* fumar como un carretero *or Méx* un chacuaco *or RP* un escuerzo (**b**) *(chimney, oil)* echar humo; **I knew she was in because the chimney was smoking** sabía que estaba en casa porque salía humo de la chimenea *or* la chimenea echaba humo

▸ **smoke out** *vt sep* (**a**) *(insects)* ahuyentar con humo; *(fugitives, rebels)* sacar de su escondite (**b**) *(uncover) (spy, traitor, plot)* desenmascarar, destapar

▸ **smoke up** *vt sep US (room)* llenar de humo

smoked [sməʊkt] *adj (meat, fish, cheese)* ahumado(a) ▸▸ ***s. glass*** vidrio *m or Esp* cristal *m* ahumado

smoke-dried ['sməʊkdraıd] *adj* ahumado(a)

smokehouse ['sməʊkhaʊs] *n* ahumadero *m*

smokeless ['sməʊklıs] *adj* ***s. fuel*** combustible *m* que no produce humos; ***s. zone*** = zona con restricción del uso de combustibles que producen humo

smoker ['sməʊkə(r)] *n* (**a**) *(person)* fumador(ora) *m,f*; **he's a cigarette/pipe s.** fuma cigarrillos/en pipa; **to be a heavy s.** ser un/una fumador(ora) empedernido(a) ▸▸ ***s.'s cough*** tos *f* de fumador (**b**) *(train compartment)* compartimento *m* de fumadores

smokestack ['sməʊkstæk] *n (of factory, ship, steam train)* chimenea *f* ▸▸ ***s. industry*** industria *f* pesada

smokiness ['sməʊkınıs] *n* **the s. of the room** la cantidad de humo que había en el ambiente

smoking ['sməʊkıŋ] **1** *n* **s. can seriously damage your health** el tabaco perjudica seriamente la salud; **I've given up s.** he dejado de fumar, he dejado el tabaco; **no s.** *(sign)* prohibido fumar ▸▸ ***s. area*** zona *f* de fumadores; *US* ***s. car,*** *Br* ***s. carriage*** coche *m or* vagón *m* de fumadores; ***s. compartment*** compartimento *m* de fumadores; ***s. jacket*** batín *m*; ***s. room*** salón *m* de fumar
2 *adj* **s. or non-smoking?** ¿fumadores o no fumadores? ▸▸ ***s. gun*** *(clue)* pista *f* reveladora

smoky ['sməʊkı] *adj* (**a**) *(atmosphere, room)* lleno(a) de humo; **it's very s. in here** aquí dentro el ambiente está cargado de humo, aquí hay mucho humo (**b**) *(fire, lamp)* humeante (**c**) *(ceiling, wall)* descolorido(a) por el humo (**d**) *(taste)* ahumado(a) (**e**) *(in colour)* **s. grey/blue** gris/azul ahumado *or* humo

smolder, smoldering *US* = **smoulder, smouldering**

smooch [smuːtʃ] *Fam* **1** *n* (**a**) *(kiss)* **to have a s.** besuquearse (**b**) *Br (dance)* (baile *m*) agarrado *m*
2 *vi* (**a**) *(kiss)* besuquearse (**b**) *Br (dance)* bailar agarrados

smoochy ['smuːtʃı] *adj Fam* **she gave him a s. kiss** le dio un beso apasionado; **they got all s.** empezaron a besuquearse; **s. music came on** empezó a sonar música romántica para bailar agarrados

smooth [smuːð] **1** *adj* (**a**) *(not rough) (paper, fabric, skin)* liso(a), suave; *(pebble, stone)* liso(a); *(road, surface)* llano(a), liso(a); *(chin)* raso(a), lampiño(a); *(sea)* en calma; **a s. shave** un afeitado suave; **the steps were worn s.** los escalones se habían pulido con el uso; IDIOM *Br Fam* **as s. as a baby's bottom** *(skin, face)* tan suave como la piel de un niño; IDIOM **to be as s. as silk** ser suave como el terciopelo ▸▸ *Anat* ***s. muscle*** músculo *m* de fibra lisa
(**b**) *(in consistency) (sauce)* homogéneo(a)
(**c**) *(in taste) (wine, whisky)* suave
(**d**) *(movement, flow)* fluido(a); *(style)* fluido(a), suelto(a)
(**e**) *(comfortable) (flight, crossing)* tranquilo(a), cómodo(a)
(**f**) *(without problems) (transition, running)* sin contratiempos, sin problemas
(**g**) *Pej (person, manner)* meloso(a); **he's a s. talker** tiene el don de la palabra; **to be a s. operator** ser un águila, saber cómo llevarse el gato al agua
2 *vt* (**a**) *(tablecloth, sheets, skirt, hair)* alisar; **to s. one's skirt/hair** alisarse la falda/el pelo (**b**) *(wood)* cepillar, lijar (**c**) *(rub) (oil, cream)* **to s. oil into one's skin** aplicarse aceite sobre la piel con un suave masaje (**d**) *(make easier) (transition)* facilitar, allanar obstáculos en; **to s. the way for sth/sb** allanarle el camino a algo/alguien

▸ **smooth away** *vt sep* (**a**) *(wrinkles)* hacer desaparecer, eliminar (**b**) *(problems, fears)* eliminar, disipar

▸ **smooth back** *vt sep (sheet)* estirar; **to s. back one's hair** alisarse el pelo hacia atrás

▸ **smooth down** *vt sep* (**a**) *(tablecloth, sheets, skirt, hair)* alisar; **to s. down one's skirt/hair** alisarse la falda/el pelo (**b**) *(wood)* cepillar, lijar (**c**) *(person)* apaciguar, aplacar

▸ **smooth out** *vt sep* (**a**) *(map, sheets, crease)* estirar, alisar (**b**) *(difficulties)* allanar, resolver

▸ **smooth over** *vt sep* (**a**) *(gravel, sand, soil)* allanar, aplanar (**b**) *(difficulties)* allanar, resolver; **to s. things over** dulcificar las cosas

smoothie, smoothy ['smuːðı] *n* (**a**) *Fam Pej (person)* zalamero(a) *m,f* (**b**) *(drink)* = zumo de fruta con yogur

smoothly ['smuːðlı] *adv* (**a**) *(to operate, drive, move, land)* suavemente; **the engine is running s.** el motor funciona con suavidad (**b**) *(without problems)* **to go s.** transcurrir sin contratiempos; **the project is running s.** el proyecto va viento en popa *or* sobre ruedas (**c**) *Pej (to talk)* con mucha labia

smoothness ['smuːðnıs] *n* (**a**) *(of paper, fabric, pebble, stone)* suavidad *f*, lisura *f*; *(of skin)* suavidad *f*, tersura *f*; *(of road, surface)* uniformidad *f*, lisura *f*; *(of sea)* tranquilidad *f*, calma *f*
(**b**) *(of sauce)* homogeneidad *f*
(**c**) *(of wine, whisky)* suavidad *f*
(**d**) *(of action, movement)* suavidad *f*, desenvoltura *f*; *(of style)* fluidez *f*, soltura *f*; *(of flow)* fluidez *f*
(**e**) *(of transition, running)* ausencia *f* de obstáculos *or* dificultades
(**f**) *Pej (of person, manner)* hipocresía *f*, falsedad *f*

smooth-running [smu:ð'rʌnɪŋ] *adj* (**a**) *(engine, machine)* que marcha bien, que funciona perfectamente (**b**) *(business, organization)* que funciona bien *or* a la perfección

smooth-shaven [smu:ð'ʃeɪvən] *adj* bien rasurado(a)

smooth-spoken [smu:ð'spəʊkən] *adj Pej* zalamero(a)

smooth-talk ['smu:ðtɔ:k] *Pej* **1** *n* labia *f*
2 *vt* **to s. sb (into doing sth)** convencer con palabras bonitas a alguien (para que haga algo)

smooth-talking ['smu:ð'tɔ:kɪŋ], **smooth-tongued** ['smu:ð'tʌŋd] *adj Pej* con mucha labia

smoothy = **smoothie**

smorgasbord ['smɔ:gəzbɔ:d] *n* (**a**) *Culin* bufé *m* al estilo escandinavo (**b**) *(assortment)* batiburrillo *m*

smote *pt of* **smite**

smother ['smʌðə(r)] **1** *vt* (**a**) *(person)* ahogar, asfixiar; *(fire)* ahogar; *(cry, yawn, laughter)* contener, ahogar (**b**) *(scandal, criticism, opposition)* acallar, silenciar (**c**) *(emotionally)* asfixiar, no dejar respirar (**d**) *(cover)* **to s. sth in cream/sauce** cubrir algo de *Esp* nata *or Am* crema/salsa; **to s. sb with kisses/attention** colmar a alguien de besos/atenciones
2 *vi (asphyxiate)* asfixiarse

smothered ['smʌðəd] *adj (cry)* apagado(a), ensordecido(a)

smoulder, *US* **smolder** ['sməʊldə(r)] *vi (fire)* arder con rescoldo; *Fig* **to s. with anger/passion** arder de ira/pasión

smouldering, *US* **smoldering** ['sməʊldərɪŋ] *adj (fire)* humeante, con rescoldo; *(anger, passion)* ardiente, encendido(a); *(eyes, look)* encendido(a), apasionado(a)

smudge [smʌdʒ] **1** *n* mancha *f*; *(of ink)* borrón *m*; *(of lipstick)* marca *f*
2 *vt* (**a**) *(ink, paper)* emborronar; *(lipstick)* correr (**b**) *(face, hands)* mancharse (**c**) *Art (drawing)* difuminar
3 *vi (ink, lipstick)* correrse

smudgy ['smʌdʒɪ] *adj (writing, outline)* borroso(a), difuso(a); *(make-up, lipstick)* corrido(a); *(photo)* movido(a)

smug [smʌg] *adj (person)* engreído(a), petulante; **a s. grin/expression** una sonrisa/expresión llena de petulancia; **stop looking so s.** deja de darte humos *or* aires

smuggle ['smʌgəl] **1** *vt (arms, drugs)* pasar de contrabando; **to s. sth through customs** pasar algo de contrabando por la aduana; **to s. sth into/out of the country** introducir/sacar algo del país de contrabando; **to s. sb in/out** meter/sacar a alguien clandestinamente
2 *vi* contrabandear, ejercer el *or* dedicarse al contrabando

smuggled ['smʌgld] *adj (goods, arms, drugs)* de contrabando

smuggler ['smʌglə(r)] *n* contrabandista *mf*

smuggling ['smʌglɪŋ] *n* contrabando *m* ►► ***s. ring*** red *f* de contrabandistas

smugly ['smʌglɪ] *adv* con petulancia, con aires de suficiencia

smugness ['smʌgnɪs] *n* engreimiento *m*, petulancia *f*

Smurf [smɜ:f] *n* pitufo *m*

smut [smʌt] *n* (**a**) *(soot)* hollín *m*, carbonilla *f*; *(speck of dirt or soot)* tizón *m* (**b**) *(obscenity)* cochinadas *fpl*; **that book's nothing but s.** ese libro sólo contiene indecencias (**c**) *(fungus)* tizón *m*

smuttily ['smʌtɪlɪ] *adv* obscenamente

smutty ['smʌtɪ] *adj* (**a**) *(dirty)* tiznado(a) (**b**) *(obscene)* verde, cochino(a)

snack [snæk] **1** *n* (**a**) *(light meal)* tentempié *m*, *Esp* piscolabis *m inv*, *Méx* botana *f*; **to have a s.** tomarse un tentempié *or* refrigerio, comer algo ►► ***s. bar*** cafetería *f* (**b**) *(crisps, peanuts etc)* aperitivo *m*, cosa *f* de picar ►► ***s. food*** aperitivos *mpl*, cosas *fpl* de picar
2 *vi* **to s. (on sth)** tomarse un tentempié *or Esp* piscolabis (de algo)

snaffle ['snæfəl] *vt Br Fam (pinch)* levantar, afanar

►**snaffle up** *vt sep Br Fam (bargains, cakes, prizes)* arramblar con

snafu [snæ'fu:] *n esp US Fam* cagada *f*

snag [snæg] **1** *n* (**a**) *(problem)* problema *m*, inconveniente *m*; **to come across** *or* **to run into a s.** topar con un obstáculo; **that's the s.!** ¡ése es el problema!, *Esp* ¡ésa es la pega! (**b**) *(tear) (in garment, stocking)* enganchón *m*, desgarrón *m* (**c**) *(sharp protuberance)* pincho *m*, saliente *m* afilado
2 *vt* (*pt & pp* **snagged**) **to s. one's dress on sth** engancharse el vestido en *or* con algo
3 *vi* engancharse

snaggletoothed ['snægəltu:θt] *adj* con la dentadura estropeada

snail [sneɪl] *n* caracol *m*; IDIOM **at a s.'s pace** a paso de tortuga ►► *Fam Hum* ***s. mail*** correo *m* caracol, correo *m* tradicional *or* postal

snake [sneɪk] **1** *n* (**a**) *(reptile) (big)* serpiente *f*; *(small)* culebra *f*; *Br* **snakes and ladders** ≃ juego *m* de la oca; IDIOM **a s. in the grass** un judas ►► ***s. charmer*** encantador(ora) *m,f* de serpientes; ***s. pit*** nido *m* de víboras *or* serpientes (**b**) *(person)* judas *mf inv* (**c**) *Fin* serpiente *f* monetaria
2 *vi (road, river)* serpentear

snakebird ['sneɪkbɜ:d] *n* anhinga *f*

snakebite ['sneɪkbaɪt] *n* (**a**) *(of snake)* mordedura *f* de serpiente (**b**) *(drink)* = cerveza rubia con sidra

snakeskin ['sneɪkskɪn] *n* piel *f* de serpiente; **s. boots** botas de piel de serpiente

snaky ['sneɪkɪ] *adj* serpenteante

snap [snæp] **1** *n* (**a**) *(bite)* mordisco *m* al aire; **the dog made a s. at the bone** el perro trató de *or* quiso morder el hueso
(**b**) *(sound) (of fingers, whip)* chasquido *m*; **to open/close sth with a s.** abrir/cerrar algo haciendo "clac"
(**c**) *(of weather)* **cold s.** ola de frío
(**d**) *Fam (photograph)* foto *f*; **to take a s. of sb** sacar una foto a alguien
(**e**) *(card game)* = juego de naipes en el que se ganan cartas al decir "snap" primero cuando aparecen dos cartas iguales; *Fam (in identical situation)* **I'm going to Paris – s.!** me voy a París – ¿de veras? *or Esp* ¡anda!, ¡yo también!
(**f**) *Fam (energy)* brío *m*, ímpetu *m*; **put some s. into it!** ¡échale coraje!, ¡ánimo!
(**g**) *US Fam (easy task)* **it's a s.!** ¡está chupado!, ¡es pan comido!
(**h**) *(fastener)* broche *m* (presión)
(**i**) *(in American football)* saque *m* entre las piernas
2 *adj (judgement, decision)* repentino(a) súbito(a); **to call a s. election** = adelantar las elecciones para aprovechar una circunstancia favorable; **s. shot** *(in hockey, soccer)* disparo sin pensar
3 *vt* (*pt & pp* **snapped**) (**a**) *(break)* romper, partir; **to s. sth in two** romper *or* partir algo en dos
(**b**) *(crack) (whip)* restallar, chasquear; **to s. one's fingers** chasquear los dedos; **he snapped his fingers at the waiter** chasqueó los dedos para llamar la atención del camarero; **she only needs to s. her fingers and he comes running** lo tiene rendido a sus pies; **she snapped her case shut** cerró la maleta con un "clac"
(**c**) *(say sharply)* espetar
(**d**) *Fam (take photograph of)* fotografiar
4 *vi* (**a**) *(break cleanly)* romperse, partirse; *(break noisily)* quebrarse, romperse (con un chasquido); **the branch snapped in two** la rama se rompió en dos *or* por la mitad
(**b**) *(bite)* **the dog snapped at him** el perro intentó morderle; *Fig* **several new stars are snapping at the champion's heels** varias figuras noveles están pisándole los talones al campeón
(**c**) *(make cracking sound) (whip)* restallar, chasquear; *(fingers)* chasquear; **to s. shut** *(jaws, lid)* cerrarse haciendo "clac"
(**d**) *(speak abruptly)* **to s. at sb** hablar en mal tono a alguien; **there's no need to s.!** ¡no hace falta ponerse así!
(**e**) *(move quickly)* **they snapped to attention** se cuadraron al instante
(**f**) *(take photos)* tomar *or* sacar fotos
(**g**) IDIOMS **to s. out of it** *(of depression, apathy)* recuperar el ánimo; **s. out of it!** *(of sulk)* ¡alegra esa cara!, *Esp* ¡anímate, hombre!; **my patience snapped, I just snapped** perdí los estribos
5 *adv* **to go s.** partirse, romperse

►**snap back** *vi* (**a**) *(trigger, elastic)* saltar hacia atrás (**b**) *(reply brusquely)* replicar bruscamente (**at** a)

►**snap off 1** *vt sep* (**a**) *(break)* partir, arrancar (**b**) *Fam* **to s. sb's head off** *(speak sharply to)* soltarle un bufido a alguien, gruñir a alguien
2 *vi* partirse, desprenderse

►**snap up** *vt sep* (**a**) *Fam (buy, take quickly)* **the new toys were snapped up in no time** los nuevos juguetes se agotaron en un abrir y cerrar de ojos, la gente arrambló con los nuevos juguetes en un santiamén; **if we had enough money to buy that player, we'd s. him up** si tuviéramos suficiente dinero para comprar ese jugador nos haríamos con él al instante (**b**) *(seize in jaws)* agarrar, morder

snapdragon ['snæpdrægən] *n* (boca *f* de) dragón *m (planta)*

snap-fastener ['snæpfæsnə(r)] *n* broche *m* (presión)

snap-on ['snæpɒn] *adj* con broches, que se abrocha

snapper ['snæpə(r)] *n (fish)* pargo *m*

snappish ['snæpɪʃ] *adj* (**a**) *(person, reply)* arisco(a), áspero(a) (**b**) *(dog)* mordedor(ora), que pega mordiscos

snappy ['snæpɪ] *adj* (**a**) *(style, prose)* chispeante; *(slogan)* agudo(a), ingenioso(a) (**b**) *(quick) (pace, rhythm)* rápido(a), impetuoso(a); *Fam* **make it s.!** ¡rapidito! (**c**) *Fam (stylish)* **to be a s. dresser** vestirse muy bien (**d**) *(bad-tempered) (person, reply)* arisco(a), áspero(a) (**e**) *(dog)* mordedor(ora), que pega mordiscos

snapshot ['snæpʃɒt] *n* (**a**) *(photograph)* foto *f* (**b**) *(of situation)* imagen *f*, visión *f*

snare [sneə(r)] **1** *n* (**a**) *(for animals)* trampa *f* (**b**) *(trick, trap)* trampa *f* (**c**) **s. (drum)** *(in military band)* tambor *m*; *(in rock music)* caja *f*
2 *vt* (**a**) *(animal)* cazar *(con trampa)* (**b**) *(trick)* **the police snared the criminals** la policía atrapó a los delincuentes *(tendiéndoles una trampa)*

snarl [snɑ:l] **1** *n* (**a**) *(of dog)* gruñido *m*; *(of lion, person)* rugido *m* (**b**) *(in thread, wool, hair)* enredo *m*, maraña *f*; *(of traffic)* atasco *m*, embotellamiento *m*
2 *vt* (**a**) *(person)* gruñir (**b**) *(thread, rope, hair)* **the wool is all snarled** la lana está enredada *or* enmarañada
3 *vi (dog, person)* gruñir; *(lion)* rugir; **to s. at sb** *(dog, person)* gruñirle a alguien; *(lion)* rugirle a alguien

▸**snarl up 1** *vt sep* (**a**) *(thread, rope, hair)* **to get snarled up** enredarse, enmarañarse (**b**) *(traffic)* **the traffic gets snarled up at the traffic lights** se forman embotellamientos *or* atascos en los semáforos
2 *vi (thread, rope, hair)* enredarse, enmarañarse; *(traffic)* atascarse

snarl-up ['snɑ:lʌp] *n (of traffic)* atasco *m*, embotellamiento *m*; *(in system)* lío *m*, jaleo *m*

snatch [snætʃ] **1** *n* (**a**) *(of music, conversation)* fragmento *m*, retazo *m*; **to sleep in snatches** dormir a ratos (**b**) *(grab)* **to make a s. at sth** intentar agarrar *or Esp* coger algo (**c**) *Br Fam (robbery)* robo *m* (**d**) *(kidnapping)* rapto *m*, secuestro *m* (**e**) *(in weightlifting)* arrancada *f* (**f**) *Vulg (woman's genitals) Esp* coño *m*, *Col* cuca *f*, *Méx* paloma *f*, *RP* concha *f*, *Ven* cuchara *f*
2 *vt* (**a**) *(grab)* **to s. sth (from sb)** arrebatar algo (a alguien); **she snatched the document from my hands** me arrebató el documento de las manos
(**b**) *(get quickly)* **to s. something to eat** comer algo apresuradamente; **to s. some sleep** aprovechar para dormir un poco; **to s. a glance at sth/sb** tener tiempo de mirar un instante algo/a alguien
(**c**) *(opportunity)* no dejar escapar, no desaprovechar
(**d**) *(steal) (wallet, handbag)* robar (con tirón); **they snatched victory from the jaws of defeat** se hicieron con la victoria en el último instante
(**e**) *(kidnap)* secuestrar
(**f**) *Sport* **he snatched his shot** se precipitó en golpear la bola
3 *vi* **don't s.!** ¡las cosas no se quitan de las manos!; **to s. at sth** *(grab)* intentar agarrar *or Esp* coger algo; *(opportunity)* no dejar escapar algo, no desaprovechar algo; **he snatched at the shot** se precipitó en golpear la bola

▸**snatch away** *vt sep* arrebatar

snazzy ['snæzɪ] *adj Fam (clothes)* vistoso(a) y elegante, *Esp* chulo(a); **she's a s. dresser** viste muy bien, tiene mucho gusto vistiendo

sneak [sni:k] **1** *n Br Fam (telltale) Esp* chivato(a) *m,f*, *Méx* hocicón(ona) *m,f*, *RP* buchón(ona) *m,f*
2 *adj* **to get a s. preview of sth** tener un anticipo en exclusiva de algo ▸▸ ***s. thief*** ratero(a) *m,f*
3 *vt* (*pt & pp* **sneaked,** *US* **snuck** [snʌk]) **to s. sth past sb** pasar algo por delante de alguien sin que se dé cuenta; **to s. sb in/out** introducir/sacar a alguien a hurtadillas; **to s. a glance** *or* **look at sth/sb** mirar furtivamente algo/a alguien; **she sneaked her boyfriend into her bedroom** coló a su novio en su dormitorio *or Am* cuarto
4 *vi* (**a**) *Fam (tell tales)* ir con cuentos, *Esp* chivarse; **to s. on sb** *Esp* chivarse de alguien *Col* sapear a alguien, *Méx* soplar a alguien, *RP* botonear a alguien (**b**) *(move furtively)* deslizarse; **to s. in/out** entrar/salir a hurtadillas; **to s. past sb** colarse sin ser visto(a) por alguien; **to s. up/down the stairs** subir/bajar las escaleras a escondidas

▸**sneak about, sneak around** *vi (move furtively)* andar a escondidas

▸**sneak away, sneak off** *vi* escaparse, escabullirse

▸**sneak up** *vi* **to s. up (on sb)** *(attacker)* acercarse sigilosamente (a alguien); *(age, deadline)* echarse encima (a alguien)

sneaker ['sni:kə(r)] *n US (running shoe)* playera *f*, zapatilla *f* de deporte

sneakily ['sni:kɪlɪ] *adv Fam* ladinamente, con picardía

sneaking ['sni:kɪŋ] *adj* **to have a s. admiration/respect for** sentir una secreta admiración/un secreto respeto por; **I had a s. suspicion that he was guilty all along** todo el tiempo tuve una remota sospecha de que era culpable

sneaky ['sni:kɪ] *adj Fam* ladino(a), artero(a)

sneer [snɪə(r)] **1** *n (expression)* mueca *f* desdeñosa; *(remark)* comentario *m* despreciativo, burla *f*
2 *vt* decir con desprecio
3 *vi* burlarse, reírse; **to s. at sth/sb** burlarse de algo/alguien

sneering ['snɪərɪŋ] **1** *n* burlas *fpl*
2 *adj* burlón(ona)

sneeze [sni:z] **1** *n* estornudo *m*
2 *vi* estornudar; IDIOM *Fam* **it's not to be sneezed at** no es moco de pavo

sneezing ['sni:zɪŋ] *n* ***s. fit*** ataque *m* de estornudos; ***s. powder*** polvos *mpl* picapica

snick [snɪk] **1** *n (notch)* pequeña incisión *f*, muesca *f*
2 *vt (wood)* hacer una pequeña incisión *or* una muesca en

snicker ['snɪkə(r)] *US* **1** *n* risilla *f* burlona
2 *vi* burlarse, reírse (**at** de)

snide [snaɪd] *adj* malicioso(a)

snidely ['snaɪdlɪ] *adv* maliciosamente

sniff [snɪf] **1** *n* **to take a s. at sth** olfatear algo; **take three sniffs per day** realice tres inhalaciones diarias; **can I have a s.?** ¿me dejas que huela?; **with a s. of disgust** con un aire disgustado; **she didn't allow her opponent even a s. of a chance** no le brindó a su oponente (ni) la más mínima oportunidad
2 *vt* (**a**) *(smell) (of person)* oler, olfatear; *(of animal)* olisquear, olfatear; *(detect)* olfatear; **he sniffed the air and said it would rain** olió el aire y dijo que llovería (**b**) *(inhale) (air)* aspirar; *(cocaine, glue)* esnifar (**c**) *(say disdainfully)* decir con desdén
3 *vi* (**a**) *(inhale)* inspirar; *(because of cold, crying)* sorberse la nariz; **he sniffed and said that there was rain in the air** olió el aire y dijo que (éste) anunciaba agua; **to s. at sth** *(animal)* olisquear algo, olfatear algo; *(person)* oler algo, olfatear algo (**b**) *(disdainfully)* hacer un gesto de desprecio; **to s. at an idea/a suggestion** menospreciar una idea/una sugerencia; IDIOM *Fam* **it's not to be sniffed at** no es moco de pavo

▸**sniff out** *vt sep* (**a**) *(of dog)* encontrar olfateando (**b**) *(of investigator)* descubrir, dar con

sniffer dog ['snɪfədɒg] *n* perro *m* rastreador

sniffily ['snɪfɪlɪ] *adv Fam (disdainfully)* con desdén *or* desprecio

sniffle ['snɪfəl] **1** *n Fam (slight cold)* **to have a s.** *or* **the sniffles** tener un ligero resfriado
2 *vi* (**a**) *(sniff repeatedly)* sorber (**b**) *(cry quietly)* gimotear

sniffy ['snɪfɪ] *adj Fam (disdainful)* desdeñoso(a); **to be s. about sth** menospreciar algo

snifter ['snɪftə(r)] *n* (**a**) *Fam Old-fashioned (drink)* trago *m*, copita *f* (**b**) *US (glass)* copa *f* de coñac

snigger ['snɪgə(r)] **1** *n* risilla *f* burlona
2 *vi* reírse burlonamente (**at** de)

sniggering ['snɪgərɪŋ] **1** *n* risitas *fpl* burlonas
2 *adj (tone, children)* guasón(ona), burlón(ona)

snip [snɪp] **1** *n* (**a**) *(cut)* tijeretazo *m*; *Br Fam* **to have the s.** *(vasectomy)* hacerse una vasectomía (**b**) *(sound)* tijereteo *m*, sonido *m* de la(s) tijera(s) (**c**) *(small piece) (of cloth, paper)* recorte *m* (**d**) *Br Fam (bargain) Esp* chollo *m*, *Am* regalo *m*
2 *vt* (*pt & pp* **snipped**) cortar

▸**snip off** *vt sep* cortar

snipe[1] [snaɪp] (*pl* **snipe**) *n (bird)* agachadiza *f*

snipe[2] *vi (shoot)* disparar *(desde un escondite)*; **to s. at sb** disparar a alguien; *Fig (criticize)* criticar a alguien

sniper ['snaɪpə(r)] *n (rifleman)* francotirador(ora) *m,f*

sniping ['snaɪpɪŋ] **1** *n (criticism)* critiqueo *m*
2 *adj (criticism, remarks)* sarcástico(a), mordaz

snippet ['snɪpɪt] *n (of information, conversation)* fragmento *m*, retazo *m*; **a s. of news** un dato suelto

snippy ['snɪpɪ] *adj (sharp)* desabrido(a), hosco(a); *(insolent)* insolente

snit [snɪt] *n US Fam* **to be in a s.** estar hecho(a) un basilisco

snitch [snɪtʃ] *Fam* **1** *n* (**a**) *(informer) Esp* chivato(a) *m,f*, *Méx* hocicón(ona) *m,f*, *RP* buchón(ona) *m,f* (**b**) *Br (nose)* napias *fpl*
2 *vi* **to s. on sb** *Esp* chivarse de alguien, *Col* sapear a alguien, *Méx* soplar a alguien, *RP* botonear a alguien
3 *vt (steal)* birlar, *Esp* mangar

snivel ['snɪvəl] (*pt & pp* **snivelled,** *US* **sniveled**) *vi* lloriquear, gimotear

snivelling, *US* **sniveling** ['snɪvəlɪŋ] *adj* llorica

snob [snɒb] *n* presuntuoso(a) *m,f*; **don't be such a s.!** ¡no seas presuntuoso!; **she's a literary s.** presume de saber más que nadie de literatura, se las da de entendida en literatura; **his music has real s. value** su música tiene mucha aceptación entre los que se las dan de entendidos

snobbery ['snɒbərɪ] *n* presuntuosidad *f*

snobbish ['snɒbɪʃ] *adj* presuntuoso(a)

snobbishness ['snɒbɪʃnɪs] *n* presuntuosidad *f*

snobby ['snɒbɪ] *adj Fam* presuntuoso(a)

snog [snɒg] *Br Fam* 1 *n* **to have a s.** besuquearse, *Esp* morrear; **give us a s.!** ¡dame un muerdo!
2 *vt* besuquear, *Esp* morrear con
3 *vi* (*pt & pp* **snogged**) besuquearse, *Esp* morrear

snood [snu:d] *n (for outdoor wear)* redecilla *f*

snook [snu:k] *n* IDIOM **to cock a s. at sb** hacer burla a alguien con la mano

snooker ['snu:kə(r)] 1 *n (game)* snooker *m*, billar *m* inglés
2 *vt* (**a**) **to s. sb** *(in game)* = dejarle la bola blanca al rival en una posición que impide golpear directamente cualquiera de las otras bolas que tiene permitido golpear; *Fig* ahogar a alguien (**b**) *US Fam (swindle, trick)* timar, engañar

snoop [snu:p] *Fam* 1 *n* (**a**) *(person)* fisgón(ona) *m,f* (**b**) *(look)* **to have a s. (around)** fisgonear, fisgar
2 *vi* fisgonear, fisgar; **someone has been snooping (about** *or* **around) in my room** alguien ha andado fisgoneando *or* husmeando en mi habitación

snooper ['snu:pə(r)] *n Fam* fisgón(ona) *m,f*

snootily ['snu:tɪlɪ] *adv Fam* con muchos aires, con presunción

snooty ['snu:tɪ] *adj Fam* presuntuoso(a)

snooze [snu:z] *Fam* 1 *n Esp* siestecilla *f*, *Am* siestita *f*; **to have a s.** echarse una *Esp* siestecilla *or Am* siestita ▸▸ ***s. button*** *(on alarm clock)* = botón para la función de dormitar
2 *vi* echarse una *Esp* siestecilla *or Am* siestita

snore [snɔ:(r)] 1 *n* ronquido *m*
2 *vi* roncar

snoring ['snɔ:rɪŋ] *n* ronquidos *mpl*

snorkel ['snɔ:kəl] 1 *n* (**a**) *(of swimmer)* esnórkel *m*, tubo *m* para buceo (**b**) *(on submarine)* esnórkel *m*
2 *vi* (*pt & pp* **snorkelled**, *US* **snorkeled**) bucear con tubo *or* esnórkel

snorkelling ['snɔ:kəlɪŋ] *n* buceo *m* con tubo, esnórkel *m*; **to go s.** bucear con tubo *or* esnórkel

snort [snɔ:t] 1 *n* (**a**) *(of person, horse, bull)* bufido *m*, resoplido *m*; **he gave a s. of contempt** dio un resoplido de desdén (**b**) *Fam (of drug)* esnifada *f* (**c**) *Fam (drink)* trago *m*
2 *vt* (**a**) *(in derision)* **"he wants more money?" he snorted** "¿que quiere más dinero?" bufó él (**b**) *Fam (drugs)* esnifar
3 *vi (person, horse, bull)* resoplar, bufar; **to s. with laughter** soltar una carcajada *or* risotada; **to s. in derision** bufar sarcástico(a)

snorter ['snɔ:tə(r)] *n Br Fam* **her second serve was a s.** su segundo saque fue imparable; **a s. of a problem** un problema muy serio *or* muy difícil de resolver

snot [snɒt] *n Fam* (**a**) *(mucus)* mocos *mpl* (**b**) *(person)* mocoso(a) *m,f*

snotrag ['snɒtræg] *n Br Fam* moquero *m*, *RP* sacamocos *m inv*

snottily ['snɒtɪlɪ] *adv (arrogantly)* con petulancia

snotty ['snɒtɪ] *adj Fam* (**a**) *(nose, handkerchief)* con mocos (**b**) *(arrogant)* creído(a), petulante

snotty-nosed ['snɒtɪ'nəʊzd] *adj Fam* (**a**) *(child)* mocoso(a) (**b**) *(arrogant)* creído(a), petulante

snout [snaʊt] *n* (**a**) *(of animal)* hocico *m*, morro *m* (**b**) *Fam (of person)* napias *fpl* (**c**) *(of gun)* boca *f* (**d**) *Br Fam (tobacco)* tabaco *m* (**e**) *Br Fam (informer)* soplón(ona) *m,f*

snow [snəʊ] 1 *n* (**a**) *Met* nieve *f*; **heavy s. is forecast** se prevé una fuerte nevada ▸▸ ***s. blindness*** deslumbramiento *m* por la nieve; *US Fam* ***s. bunny*** = mujer joven que se dedica a zascandilear y flirtear en las estaciones de esquí; ***s. bunting*** escribano *m* nival; ***s. cannon*** cañón *m* de nieve; ***s. chain*** cadena *f* para la nieve; ***s. goose*** ganso *m* de las nieves; ***s. hole*** *(in mountaineering)* agujero *m* en la nieve; *US Fam* ***s. job:*** **to give sb a s. job** vender la moto a alguien; ***s. leopard*** pantera *f* de las nieves; ***s. line*** límite *m* de las nieves perpetuas; *US* ***s. pea*** tirabeque *m*; ***s. report*** parte *m* de nieve; *US* ***s. route*** = calle importante en una ciudad que hay que mantener despejada de coches para que pueda pasar el quitanieves; ***s. tyre*** neumático *m* para nieve
(**b**) *(on screen)* nieve *f*, interferencia *f*
(**c**) *Fam (cocaine)* nieve *f*, *Col* perica *f*, *RP* blanca *f*
2 *vi* nevar; **it's snowing** está nevando
3 *vt US Fam (charm, persuade)* **to snow sb into doing sth** vender la moto a alguien para que haga algo

▸ **snow in** *vt sep* **to be snowed in** estar aislado(a) por la nieve

▸ **snow under** *vt sep* **to be snowed under with work** estar desbordado(a) de trabajo; **to be snowed under with invitations/offers** no dar abasto para atender invitaciones/ofrecimientos

▸ **snow up** *vt sep* **to be snowed up** estar aislado(a) por la nieve

snowball ['snəʊbɔ:l] 1 *n* (**a**) *(made of snow)* bola *f* de nieve; IDIOM *Fam* **she hasn't a s.'s chance (in hell)** lo tiene muy crudo ▸▸ ***s. effect*** efecto *m* (de la) bola de nieve; ***s. fight*** guerra *f* de bolas de nieve (**b**) *(cocktail)* = cóctel con licor de huevo
2 *vt* arrojar bolas de nieve a
3 *vi (problems)* multiplicarse; *(cost)* crecer vertiginosamente

snow-blind ['snəʊblaɪnd] *adj* **to be s.** estar cegado(a) por el reflejo de la nieve

snowblower ['snəʊbləʊə(r)] *n* (máquina *f*) quitanieves *f inv*

snowboard ['snəʊbɔ:d] *n* snowboard *m*

snowboarder ['snəʊbɔ:də(r)] *n* persona *f* que practica el snowboard

snowboarding ['snəʊbɔ:dɪŋ] *n* snowboard *m*; **to go s.** hacer snowboard

snowbound ['snəʊbaʊnd] *adj* aislado(a) a causa de la nieve

snowcapped ['snəʊkæpt] *adj* cubierto(a) de nieve

snowdrift ['snəʊdrɪft] *n* nevero *m*, ventisquero *m*

snowdrop ['snəʊdrɒp] *n (flower)* campanilla *f* de invierno

snowfall ['snəʊfɔ:l] *n* (**a**) *(snow shower)* nevada *f* (**b**) *(amount)* precipitación *f* de nieve

snowfield ['snəʊfi:ld] *n* campo *m* nevado *or* de nieve

snowflake ['snəʊfleɪk] *n* copo *m* de nieve

snowman ['snəʊmæn] *n* muñeco *m* de nieve

snowmobile ['snəʊməbi:l] *n* motonieve *f*, moto *f* de nieve

snowplough, *US* **snowplow** ['snəʊplaʊ] 1 *n* (**a**) *(vehicle)* quitanieves *f inv* (**b**) *(in skiing)* cuña *f*
2 *vi (in skiing)* hacer la cuña

snowshoe ['snəʊʃu:] *n* raqueta *f (de nieve)*

snowstorm ['snəʊstɔ:m] *n* ventisca *f*, tormenta *f* de nieve

snowsuit ['snəʊsu:t] *n* traje *m* de esquí

Snow White ['snəʊ'waɪt] *n* Blancanieves; **S. and the Seven Dwarfs** Blancanieves y los siete enanitos

snow-white ['snəʊ'waɪt] *adj* blanquísimo(a), blanco(a) como la nieve

snowy ['snəʊɪ] *adj* (**a**) *(landscape, field)* nevado(a) (**b**) *(weather, day)* nevoso(a); *(climate)* nevoso(a), con abundantes nevadas; *(region)* de abundantes nevadas, donde nieva mucho; **it was very s. in January** nevó mucho en enero (**c**) *(in colour) (hair, beard)* blanco(a) como la nieve, completamente blanco(a) ▸▸ ***s. owl*** búho *m* nival

SNP [esen'pi:] *n* (*abbr* **Scottish National Party**) Partido *m* Nacionalista Escocés

Snr (*abbr* **Senior**) **Ivan Fox S.** Ivan Fox padre

snub [snʌb] 1 *n* desaire *m*
2 *adj* ***s. nose*** nariz *f* respingona y chata
3 *vt* (*pt & pp* **snubbed**) *(person)* desairar; *(offer)* desdeñar, despreciar

snub-nosed ['snʌb'nəʊzd] *adj* (**a**) *(person)* de nariz respingona y chata (**b**) *(revolver)* corto(a)

snuck *US pt & pp of* **sneak**

snuff [snʌf] 1 *n* (**a**) *(substance)* rapé *m*; **to take s.** tomar rapé (**b**) *Cin Fam* ***s. movie*** snuff movie *f*, = película que contiene escenas de torturas y asesinatos reales
2 *vt* (**a**) *(candle)* apagar (**b**) *Br Fam* **to s. it** *(die)* estirar la pata (**c**) *US Fam (murder)* cargarse a, liquidar a (**d**) *(sniff)* olisquear

▸ **snuff out** *vt sep* (**a**) *(candle)* apagar (**b**) *(life)* truncar, acabar con; *(opposition)* eliminar, acabar con; *(rebellion)* extinguir, sofocar; *(hopes)* acabar *or* terminar con

snuffbox ['snʌfbɒks] *n* tabaquera *f*, caja *f* para el rapé

snuffer ['snʌfə(r)] *n* (**a**) *(for putting out candle)* apagavelas *m inv*, matacandelas *m inv* (**b**) *(for trimming wick)* **snuffers** espabiladeras *fpl*

snuffle ['snʌfəl] 1 *n (sniff)* resoplido *m*; **to have the snuffles** tener un ligero resfriado
2 *vi (sniff)* sorber

snug [snʌg] 1 *adj* (**a**) *(cosy) (house, room, sleeping bag)* calentito(a) y confortable; **I'm nice and s. by the fire** estoy calentito y muy a gusto delante de la chimenea; **this bed's very s.** se está muy calentito y muy a gusto en esta cama; IDIOM *Fam* **to be (as) s. as a bug in a rug** estar calentito(a) y en la gloria

(**b**) *(tight-fitting)* ajustado(a), ceñido(a); **there should be a s. fit between the two pieces** las dos piezas deben quedar bien encajadas *or* ajustadas
2 *n Br (in pub)* salón *m* pequeño

snuggle ['snʌgəl] **1** *vi* acurrucarse
2 *vt (child, kitten)* acurrucar
3 *n* **to have a s.** acurrucarse, arrimarse

▸ **snuggle down** *vi* **they snuggled down under the blankets** se acurrucaron bajo las mantas

▸ **snuggle up** *vi* **to s. up to** *or* **against sb** acurrucarse contra alguien; **to s. up with a good book** sentarse acurrucado(a) a leer un buen libro

snugly ['snʌglɪ] *adv* (**a**) *(cosily)* cómodamente (**b**) *(tightly)* **the skirt fits s.** la falda queda ajustada; **the two parts fit together s.** las dos partes encajan perfectamente

SO (*abbr* **standing order**) domiciliación *f* (bancaria)

SO¹ [səʊ] **1** *adv* (**a**) *(to such an extent)* tan; **it isn't so (very) old** no es tan viejo; **I was so hungry (that) I had three helpings** tenía tantísima hambre que me serví tres veces; **what's so clever about that?** ¿qué tiene de ingenioso?; *Literary* **I have never seen so beautiful a place** nunca he visto un sitio tan bello; **don't fret so!** ¡no te preocupes tanto!; *Literary* **I love her so!** ¡la amo tanto!; **he's not so clever as she is** él no es tan listo como ella; **it is so uncommon as to be irrelevant** es tan inusual que llega a ser intranscendente; **would you be so kind as to...?** ¿sería tan amable de...?; **so few opportunities** tan pocas oportunidades; **so many children** tantos niños; **so much money** tanto dinero; **there's only so much you can do** más no se puede hacer; **it was difficult – so much so that...** ha sido difícil – tanto (es así) que...; **she wasn't so much rude as indifferent** más que grosera fue indiferente; **a little girl SO high** una niña así de alta
(**b**) *(intensive)* **it's so easy** es facilísimo, es muy fácil; **we enjoyed ourselves SO much!** ¡nos hemos divertido muchísimo!; **I was SO disappointed** me llevé una decepción enorme; **we're SO pleased you could come!** ¡qué bien que hayas podido venir!; *Fam* **I SO don't want to go there** no me apetece ir ni de coña
(**c**) *(expressing agreement)* **you're late – so I am!** llegas tarde – ¡pues sí!; **that's a Ferrari! – so it is!** ¡mira, un Ferrari! – ¡anda, es verdad!; **I'm very embarrassed – so you should be!** estoy muy avergonzado *or Andes, CAm, Carib, Méx* apenado – ¡deberías estarlo!
(**d**) *(referring to statement already mentioned)* **I hope/think/suppose so** espero/creo/supongo que sí, eso espero/creo/supongo; **I don't think so** no creo, me parece que no; **if you don't like it, say so** si no te gusta, dilo; **I told you so** te lo dije; **so I believe** eso creo; **or so I've heard** o eso he oído; **I'm not very organized – so I see!** no me organizo muy bien – ¡ya lo veo!; **so be it!** ¡así sea!; **is that so?** ¿ah, sí?, ¿de verdad?; **it is no longer so** ya no es así; **she was furious and understandably/justifiably so** estaba furiosa, y con razón; *Fam* **I didn't say that – you did so!** yo no dije eso – ¡y tanto que sí!; *Fam* **you can't do it – I can so!** ¡no puedes hacerlo – ¡ya lo creo que sí!; **if so,...** si es así,...; **she entered the room, and in so doing...** entró en la habitación, y al hacerlo...; **I told them to leave and they did so immediately** les pedí que se marcharan y lo hicieron al instante; **why** *or* **how so?** ¿y por qué?; **it was fun, more so than we had expected** fue divertido, mucho más de lo que esperábamos; **we were all delighted and none more so than Sarah** estábamos encantados, y Sarah la que más; **the same only more so** lo mismo, pero más
(**e**) *(also)* **so am I** yo también; **so do we** nosotros también; **I love cheese – so do I** me encanta el queso – a mí también; **so can they** ellos también (pueden); **so is my brother** mi hermano también; **you seem annoyed – so would you be if you'd had to wait as long as me!** pareces molesto – ¿no lo estarías tú si hubieras tenido que esperar tanto como yo?; **just as the city has changed, so too have its problems** de la misma manera en que ha cambiado la ciudad, también han cambiado sus problemas
(**f**) *(in this way)* así; **do it (like) so** hazlo así; **the tables have been so arranged as to...** las mesas han sido dispuestas de manera que...; **and so on, and so forth** y cosas así, etcétera; **it (just) so happens that...** resulta que...; **or so** más o menos; **there were thirty or so people** había una treintena de personas
2 *conj* (**a**) *(because of this)* así que; **she has a bad temper, so be careful** tiene mal genio, así que ten cuidado; **he wasn't there, so I came back again** como no estaba, me volví; **it was dark, so (that) I couldn't see** estaba oscuro, por lo que no podía ver; *Fam* **so there!** *Esp* ¡que lo sepas!, *Am* ¡para que sepas!
(**b**) *(in order that)* para que; **she sat down so I could see better** se sentó para que yo viera mejor; **we hurried so we wouldn't be late** nos dimos prisa *or Am* nos apuramos para no llegar tarde
(**c**) *(introducing remark)* **so that's what it is!** ¡así que es eso!; **so you're not coming?** entonces ¿no vienes?; **so what do we do now?** y ahora ¿qué hacemos?; **so what did you think of the movie, then?** ¿y qué te pareció la película?; **so, anyway, I opened the door...** en todo caso, abrí la puerta,...; **so, to go back to what I was saying earlier,...** bueno, volviendo a lo que estaba diciendo...; **so, here we are** pues nada, aquí estamos; **so (what)?** ¿y (qué)?; **so what if she is twenty years younger than me?** ¿y qué pasa si tiene veinte años menos que yo?
(**d**) *(in the same way)* **as 3 is to 6, so 6 is to 12** 6 es a 12 lo que 3 es a 6; **as he has lived so will he die** morirá de la misma manera que ha vivido
3 *adj* **he likes the house to be just so** le gusta que la casa esté ordenada y limpia
4 so as to *conj* para; **we hurried so as not to be late** nos dimos prisa *or Am* nos apuramos para no llegar tarde
5 so that *conj* (**a**) *(in order that)* para que; **she sat down so that I could see better** se sentó para que yo viera mejor; **we hurried so that we wouldn't be late** nos dimos prisa *or Am* nos apuramos para no llegar tarde
(**b**) *(with the result that)* por lo que, de forma que; **the crates had fallen over so that we couldn't get past** las cajas se habían caído, por lo que no pudimos pasar
6 so to speak, so to say *adv* por así decirlo

so² [səʊ] *n Mus* sol *m*

soak [səʊk] **1** *n* (**a**) *(in liquid)* **to give sth a s.** poner algo a *or* en remojo; **I had a nice long s. in the bath** estuve un buen rato sumergido plácidamente en la bañera (**b**) *Fam (drunkard)* esponja *f*, borrachín(ina) *m,f*
2 *vt* (**a**) *(leave in water)* poner en remojo; **he soaked the shirts in warm water** puso las camisas a remojar en agua tibia (**b**) *(make very wet)* empapar (**with** en *or* de) (**c**) *(immerse)* **to s. oneself in the history of a period** sumergirse en la historia de una época (**d**) *Fam (charge heavily)* clavar; *(tax heavily)* desplumar
3 *vi (food, clothes)* estar en remojo; **to leave sth to s.** dejar algo en remojo; **to s. in the bath** darse un buen baño

▸ **soak in** **1** *vt sep (atmosphere)* empaparse de, impregnarse de
2 *vi (liquid)* absorberse, empaparse

▸ **soak through** **1** *vt sep* **to be soaked through** estar empapado(a), estar calado(a) hasta los huesos
2 *vi (liquid)* calar, penetrar

▸ **soak up** *vt sep* (**a**) *(liquid)* absorber; *Fig* **to s. up the sun** tostarse al sol; *Fam Hum* **he can really s. it up** *(drink)* es una auténtica esponja (**b**) *(atmosphere, culture)* empaparse de, impregnarse de

soaked [səʊkt] *adj* empapado(a); **to be s.** estar empapado(a); **to get s.** ponerse empapado(a), calarse hasta los huesos; ponerse hecho(a) una sopa; **s. to the skin** calado(a) hasta los huesos

soaking ['səʊkɪŋ] **1** *n (of clothes)* remojo *m*; *Fam* **to get a s.** *(in rain)* ponerse como una sopa
2 *adj* calado(a), empapado(a)
3 *adv* **s. wet** calado(a), empapado(a)

so-and-so ['səʊənsəʊ] (*pl* **so-and-sos**) *n Fam* (**a**) *(unspecified person)* fulanito(a) *m,f*; **Mr/Mrs S.** don fulanito/doña fulanita de tal (**b**) *(unpleasant person)* hijo(a) *m,f* de mala madre; **you greedy old s.!** ¡qué glotón estás hecho!

soap [səʊp] **1** *n* (**a**) *(for washing)* jabón *m*; **I got her some bars of s.** *or* **some soaps** le conseguí unas pastillas de jabón ▸▸ ***s. bubble*** pompa *f* de jabón; ***s. powder*** detergente *m* en polvo (**b**) *TV* **s. (opera)** telenovela *f*, culebrón *m*
2 *vt* enjabonar

▸ **soap down** *vt sep* enjabonar bien; **to s. oneself down** enjabonarse bien

▸ **soap up** *vt sep Fam (flatter)* dar jabón *or* coba a

soapbark ['səʊpbɑːk] *n (tree)* quillay *m*

soapberry ['səʊpberɪ] *n (tree)* jaboncillo *m*

soapbox ['səʊpbɒks] *n* tribuna *f* improvisada; **get off your s.!** ¡deja de dogmatizar *or* pontificar!

soapdish ['səʊpdɪʃ] *n* jabonera *f*

soapflakes ['səʊpfleɪks] *npl* jabón *m* en escamas

soapstone ['səʊpstəʊn] *n* esteatita *f*

soapsuds ['səʊpsʌdz] *npl* espuma *f* (de jabón)

soapwort ['səʊpwɜːt] *n* jabonera *f*

soapy ['səʊpɪ] *adj* (**a**) *(water)* jabonoso(a) (**b**) *(hands, face)* enjabonado(a) (**c**) *(taste, smell)* a jabón; **this chocolate tastes s.** este chocolate sabe a jabón

soar [sɔː(r)] *vi* (**a**) *(bird, plane)* remontarse, remontar el vuelo; **the ball soared into the stands** el balón se remontó hasta las gradas
(**b**) *(building)* elevarse, alzarse; **the mountain soared above us** la montaña se elevaba *or* se alzaba sobre nosotros
(**c**) *(prices, profits, sales)* desorbitarse, dispararse; *(temperature)* subir vertiginosamente; *(hopes, ambitions)* desbordarse, desorbitarse; *(popularity)* aumentar espectacularmente; **the soldiers' spirits soared** el ánimo de los soldados se elevó por las nubes

soaring ['sɔːrɪŋ] *adj* (**a**) *(prices, profits, sales)* desorbitado(a); *(temperature)* muy elevado(a); *(hopes, ambitions)* desorbitado(a), desmesurado(a); *(popularity)* extraordinario(a), enorme (**b**) *(high) (mountain, tower)* elevado(a), eminente; **the s. flight of the eagle** el planeo del águila

s.o.b. [esəʊ'biː] *n US Fam* (*abbr* **son of a bitch**) *(person)* hijo(a) *m,f* de su madre; *(thing)* cabrón(ona) *m,f*

sob [sɒb] **1** *n* sollozo *m* ►► *Fam* ***s. story*** dramón *m*
2 *vi* (*pt & pp* **sobbed**) sollozar
3 *vt* **"I can't remember!" he sobbed** "¡no me acuerdo!", dijo sollozando; **to s. oneself to sleep** sollozar hasta quedarse dormido(a); **he was sobbing his heart out** estaba hecho un mar de lágrimas

sobbing ['sɒbɪŋ] *n* sollozos *mpl*, llanto *m*

sober ['səʊbə(r)] *adj* (**a**) *(not drunk)* sobrio(a), sereno(a) (**b**) *(sensible)* serio(a) (**c**) *(in colour, design)* sobrio(a) (**d**) *(atmosphere, occasion)* formal; *(expression, voice)* grave; *(reminder)* serio(a); **the s. fact is...** la pura verdad es...

► **sober down** **1** *vt sep (calm)* serenar
2 *vi (calm down)* serenarse

► **sober up** **1** *vt sep (drunk person)* quitar *or Am* sacar la borrachera a
2 *vi (drunk person)* **by the next day he had sobered up** al día siguiente ya se le había pasado la borrachera

sobering ['səʊbərɪŋ] *adj* **it's a s. thought** da mucho que pensar; **what she said had a s. effect on everyone** lo que dijo hizo reflexionar a todo el mundo

soberly ['səʊbəlɪ] *adv* (**a**) *(to act, speak, look)* con seriedad (**b**) *(to dress)* con sobriedad

sober-minded ['səʊbə'maɪndɪd] *adj (serious)* serio(a)

soberness ['səʊbənɪs], **sobriety** [səʊ'braɪətɪ] *n* (**a**) *(not being drunk)* sobriedad *f* (**b**) *(seriousness)* seriedad *f* (**c**) *(of colour, design)* sobriedad *f*

sobriquet ['səʊbrɪkeɪ] *n Literary* sobrenombre *m*

Soc (*abbr* **society**) asociación *f*

so-called ['səʊ'kɔːld] *adj* (**a**) *(generally known as)* (así) llamado(a) (**b**) *(wrongly known as)* mal llamado(a); **s. progress** el pretendido progreso

soccer ['sɒkə(r)] *n* fútbol *m* ►► ***s. club*** club *m* de fútbol; ***s. hooligan*** hincha *mf* violento(a); ***s. match*** partido *m* de fútbol; ***s. player*** futbolista *mf*, jugador(ora) *m,f* de fútbol

sociability [səʊʃə'bɪlətɪ] *n* sociabilidad *f*

sociable ['səʊʃəbəl] *adj* sociable; **I had a drink with them just to be s.** me tomé una copa con ellos por cortesía *or* para no mostrarme insociable ►► ***s. weaver*** republicano *m*

sociably ['səʊʃəblɪ] *adv* con amabilidad, amigablemente

social ['səʊʃəl] **1** *adj* (**a**) *(relating to society)* social; **they are not our s. equals** no son de nuestra clase (social) ►► ***s. accounting*** contabilidad *f* social; ***s. anthropologist*** antropólogo(a) *m,f* social; ***s. anthropology*** antropología *f* social; ***s. audit*** auditoría *f* social; *EU* ***S. Chapter*** capítulo *m* social *(de los acuerdos de Maastricht)*; *EU* ***S. Charter*** Carta *f* Social; ***s. class*** clase *f* social; ***s. climber*** arribista *mf*; ***s. climbing*** arribismo *m*; ***s. compact*** concertación *f* social; ***s. conscience*** conciencia *f* social; ***s. contract*** concertación *f* social; *Pol* ***s. democracy*** *(system, country)* socialdemocracia *f*; *Pol* ***s. democrat*** socialdemócrata *mf*; *Pol* ***s. democratic*** socialdemócrata; *Euph* ***s. disease*** *(venereal disease)* enfermedad *f* venérea; *(problem in society)* enfermedad *f* social; ***s. dumping*** dumping *m* social; ***s. engineering*** ingeniería *f* social, = intento de cambiar la sociedad a través de medidas políticas; ***s. exclusion*** exclusión *f* social; ***s. historian*** historiador(ora) *m,f* social; ***s. history*** historia *f* social; ***s. housing*** viviendas *fpl* sociales; ***s. insurance*** seguro *m* social; ***s. justice*** justicia *f* social; ***s. market economy*** economía *f* social de mercado; ***s. mobility*** movilidad *f* social; ***s. order*** orden *m* social; ***s. outcast*** marginado(a) *m,f*; *Ind* ***s. partners*** agentes *mpl or* interlocutores *mpl* sociales; ***s. psychology*** psicología *f* social; ***s. realism*** realismo *m* social; ***s. sciences*** ciencias *fpl* sociales; ***s. secretary*** secretario(a) *m,f* de actividades sociales; ***s. security*** seguridad *f* social; **to be on s. security** cobrar subsidios del Estado; ***s. security benefit*** prestación *f* social; ***the s. services*** los servicios sociales; ***s. studies*** (ciencias *fpl*) sociales *fpl*; ***s. welfare*** bienestar *m* social, asistencia *f or* ayuda *f* social; ***s. work*** asistencia *f or* trabajo *m* social; ***s. worker*** asistente *mf or* trabajador(ora) *m,f* social
(**b**) *(activities, engagements, event)* social; **his life is one mad s. whirl** lleva una trepidante vida social; **to pay sb a s. call** pasarse a saludar a alguien; **she's just a s. drinker** sólo bebe en compañía de otras personas ►► ***s. club*** club *m* social; ***s. life*** vida *f* social
(**c**) *(sociable)* sociable
(**d**) *(insect, animal)* social; **she has very poor s. skills** no es muy sociable
2 *n (party)* reunión *f*, fiesta *f*

socialism ['səʊʃəlɪzəm] *n* socialismo *m*

socialist ['səʊʃəlɪst] **1** *n* socialista *mf*
2 *adj* socialista ►► ***s. realism*** realismo *m* socialista

socialistic [səʊʃə'lɪstɪk] *adj Pej* socialista, socialistoide, *Esp* sociata

socialite ['səʊʃəlaɪt] *n* personaje *m* de la vida mundana

socialization [səʊʃəlaɪ'zeɪʃən] *n Pol & Psy* socialización *f*

socialize ['səʊʃəlaɪz] **1** *vt Pol & Psy* socializar
2 *vi* alternar; **to s. with sb** tener trato *or* alternar con alguien; **I don't s. much these days** últimamente no salgo mucho *or* no hago mucha vida social

socializing ['səʊʃəlaɪzɪŋ] *n* trato *m* social, relaciones *fpl* sociales; **they do a lot of s.** hacen mucha vida social

socially ['səʊʃəlɪ] *adv* (**a**) *(of society)* socialmente; **it's not s. acceptable** desde el punto de vista social *or* de la sociedad, es inaceptable; **this company is very s. aware** esta empresa está muy sensibilizada con las cuestiones sociales; **to be s. disadvantaged** pertenecer a una clase social desfavorecida
(**b**) *(relating to social life)* **we don't see each other s.** no tenemos relación fuera del trabajo; **to be s. inadequate** no ser (nada) sociable
(**c**) *(in terms of class)* **s. inferior** de (una) clase social inferior

societal [sə'saɪətəl] *adj Formal* social

society [sə'saɪətɪ] *n* (**a**) *(community, nation)* sociedad *f*; **he is a danger to s.** es una amenaza para la sociedad, es un peligro público; **Western s.** la sociedad occidental
(**b**) *(fashionable circles)* **(high) s.** la alta sociedad; **to make one's debut in s.** presentarse en sociedad ►► ***s. column*** notas *fpl* de sociedad; ***s. wedding*** boda *f* de (alta) sociedad
(**c**) *(club)* asociación *f*, sociedad *f* ►► *Rel* ***the S. of Friends*** *(Quakers)* los cuáqueros
(**d**) *Literary (company)* compañía *f*; **in polite s.** entre (la) gente bien *or* de buenas costumbres

sociocultural ['səʊsɪəʊ'kʌltʃərəl] *adj* sociocultural

socioeconomic ['səʊsɪəʊiːkə'nɒmɪk] *adj* socioeconómico(a)

sociolect [səʊsɪə'lekt] *n Ling* sociolecto *m*

sociolinguistic [səʊsɪəʊlɪŋ'gwɪstɪk] *adj* sociolingüístico(a)

sociolinguistics ['səʊsɪəʊlɪŋ'gwɪstɪks] *n* sociolingüística *f*

sociological [səʊsɪə'lɒdʒɪkəl] *adj* sociológico(a)

sociologist [səʊsɪ'ɒlədʒɪst] *n* sociólogo(a) *m,f*

sociology [səʊsɪ'ɒlədʒɪ] *n* sociología *f*

sociopath ['səʊsɪəʊpæθ] *n* (**a**) *Psy* = persona con un comportamiento antisocial patológico (**b**) *(psychopath)* psicópata *mf*

sociopolitical [səʊsɪəʊpə'lɪtɪkəl] *adj* sociopolítico(a)

sock [sɒk] **1** *n* (**a**) *(garment)* calcetín *m*; IDIOM *Br Fam* **put a s. in it!** ¡cierra el pico! (**b**) *Fam (blow)* puñetazo *m* (**c**) *(of horse)* cuartilla *f*
2 *vt Fam (hit)* **he socked him on the jaw** le arreó *or* estampó un puñetazo en la mandíbula; **I socked him one** le arreé *or* estampé un mamporro; IDIOM **s. it to them!** ¡a por ellos!, ¡valor y al toro!; IDIOM **I've got some bad news – s. it to me, then** tengo malas noticias – vamos, desembucha (de una vez)

socket ['sɒkɪt] *n* (**a**) *(for plug)* enchufe *m*, toma *f* de corriente; *(for light bulb)* casquillo *m* (**b**) *Comptr (slot)* zócalo *m* (**c**) *(of eye)* cuenca *f*; *(of limb joint)* cavidad *f*, *Spec* glena *f*; *(of tooth)* alveolo *m*; **her arm was pulled out of its s.** el brazo se le salió de su sitio, se le dislocó el brazo (**d**) *(in carpentry)* encajadura *f*, encaje *m*

socking ['sɒkɪŋ] *adv Br Fam (as intensifier)* **he had a s. great bruise!** ¡tenía una magulladura gigantesca!

Socrates ['sɒkrətiːz] *pr n* Sócrates

Socratic [sɒ'krætɪk] *adj* socrático(a)

sod[1] [sɒd] *n (of earth)* tepe *m*

sod[2] *Br very Fam* **1** *n* (**a**) *(obnoxious person)* mamón(ona) *m,f*, *Méx* mamila *mf*, *RP* choto(a) *m,f*; **the stupid s. lost the keys** el muy mamón perdió las llaves; *Br* **S.'s law** la ley de Murphy
(**b**) *Br Fam (any person)* tipo(a) *m,f*; **poor s.!** ¡pobre diablo!; **you lucky s.!** ¡eres un tipo/una tipa con suerte!

(**c**) *(thing)* plomazo *m*, *Esp* jodienda *f*, *Esp* coñazo *m*; **it's a s. of a job** es un trabajo de lo más jodido *or Esp* de lo más coñazo

(**d**) IDIOMS **I don't care** *or* **I don't give a s.** me la trae floja, me la suda; **I got s. all from them** no me dieron ni la hora; **you've done s. all today** no has dado golpe en todo el día; **they've got s. all hope of winning** todas sus esperanzas de triunfo se han ido a hacer puñetas

2 *vt* (*pt & pp* **sodded**) **s. it!** *Esp* ¡joder!, *Méx* ¡chin!, *RP* ¡la puta!; **s. you/them!** ¡vete/que se vayan a la mierda!; **s. the party, I'm tired** a la mierda la fiesta, yo estoy cansado; **s. the expense, let's just go!** a la mierda *or* a freír puñetas el dinero, ¡vámonos!

▸ **sod off** *vi Br very Fam* abrirse, *Esp, RP* pirarse; **s. off!** *Esp* ¡vete a tomar por saco!, *Méx* ¡vete a la chingada!, *RP* ¡andate a la mierda!

soda ['səʊdə] *n* (**a**) *(mixer)* **s. (water)** (agua *f* de) seltz *m*, soda *f*; **scotch and s.** whisky (escocés) con soda ▸▸ ***s. siphon*** sifón *m*

(**b**) *US (fizzy drink)* refresco *m (gaseoso)* ▸▸ ***s. fountain*** *(in shop)* = puesto *m* de helados y refrescos, *Chile, Col, Méx, Ven* fuente *f* de soda; *(siphon)* sifón *m*; *US* ***s. pop*** refresco *m* con gas

(**c**) *Culin* ***s. bread*** = pan hecho con bicarbonato sódico y suero de leche; *US* ***s. cracker*** galleta *f* salada

(**d**) *Chem* sosa *f* ▸▸ ***s. ash*** sosa *f* comercial, sosa *f* Solvay; ***s. lime*** = mezcla sólida de cal y sosa cáustica

sodden ['sɒdən] *adj* empapado(a); **to be s.** estar empapado(a)

sodding ['sɒdɪŋ] *Br very Fam* 1 *adj* puto(a), *Esp* puñetero(a), *Méx* pinche; **s. hell!** ¡puñeta!, ¡jopé!

2 *adv (for emphasis)* puñeteramente; **you can s. well do it yourself!** ¡que te den morcilla y lo haces tú solo!, *Méx* ¡pues come cuacha, lo haces tú solo!; **don't be so s. lazy!** ¡no seas tan vago, puñeta!

sodium ['səʊdɪəm] *n Chem* sodio *m* ▸▸ ***s. bicarbonate*** bicarbonato *m* sódico *or* de sodio; ***s. carbonate*** carbonato *m* sódico *or* de sodio; ***s. chloride*** cloruro *m* sódico *or* de sodio; ***s. hydroxide*** hidróxido *m* sódico *or* de sodio; ***s. lamp*** lámpara *f* de (vapor de) sodio; ***s. nitrate*** nitrato *m* sódico *or* de sodio; ***s. sulphate*** sulfato *m* sódico *or* de sodio

sodomite ['sɒdəmaɪt] *n* sodomita *mf*

sodomize ['sɒdəmaɪz] *vt* sodomizar

sodomy ['sɒdəmɪ] *n* sodomía *f*

sofa ['səʊfə] *n* sofá *m* ▸▸ ***s. bed*** sofá-cama *m*

Sofia ['səʊfɪə] *n* Sofía

soft [sɒft] *adj* (**a**) *(to touch) (fabric, skin, hair)* suave; **the cream will make your hands s.** la crema te suavizará las manos ▸▸ ***s. toy*** peluche *m (muñeco)*

(**b**) *(yielding, not firm) (pillow, mattress)* blando(a); *(ground, rock, cheese, butter)* blando(a); *(metal)* dúctil, maleable; *(wood, pencil)* blando(a); *(toothbrush)* suave; **to become** *or* **go s.** ablandarse; **this bed is too s.** esta cama es demasiado blanda ▸▸ ***s. centre*** *(of chocolate)* relleno *m* blando; ***s. coal*** carbón *m* bituminoso, hulla *f* grasa; *Br* ***s. fruit*** bayas *fpl (fresas, moras, arándanos, etc)*; *Br* ***s. furnishings***, *US* ***s. goods*** = artículos y materiales de decoración del tipo cortinas, cojines, alfombras, etc; ***s. lenses*** lentes *fpl or Esp* lentillas *fpl or Méx* pupilentes *fpl* blandas; ***s. landing*** *(of aircraft)* aterrizaje *m* suave; *(of economy)* desaceleración *f* suave; *Anat* ***s. palate*** velo *m* del paladar; *Anat* ***s. tissue*** tejido *m* blando; ***s. top*** *(car)* descapotable *m*, *Am* convertible *m*; *Aut* ***s. verges*** *(sign)* arcén *m* no estabilizado

(**c**) *(not harsh, not strong) (voice, music, rain, colour, breeze)* suave; *(accent)* suave, dulce; *(outline)* desdibujado(a), difuminado(a); *(expression, eyes)* dulce, apacible; **turn the volume up, it's a bit s.** sube el volumen, está un poco bajo ▸▸ ***s. drinks*** refrescos *mpl*; ***s. drugs*** drogas *fpl* blandas; *Phot* ***s. focus:* in s. focus** ligeramente velado(a) *or* difuminado(a); *Fin* ***s. loan*** crédito *m* blando *or* subvencionado; *US Pol* ***s. money*** = donaciones a un partido político que en principio han de servir para financiar los gastos en publicidad del mismo y no la campaña de un candidato específico; ***s. pedal*** *(on piano)* pedal *m* suave; *Fam* ***s. porn*** porno *m* blando *or Méx* ligero *or RP* liviano; *Com* ***s. sell*** venta *f* no agresiva

(**d**) *(kind) (person)* dulce, tierno(a); *(nature)* bondadoso(a), bonachón(ona); **to have a s. heart** ser bondadoso(a), tener buen corazón

(**e**) *(not strict)* blando(a); **you're too s. on him** eres demasiado blando con él; **to be s. on terrorism** ser (demasiado) indulgente *or* transigente con el terrorismo; **to take a s. line (on sth/with sb)** ser transigente (con algo/con alguien)

(**f**) *(physically weak)* debilucho(a), endeble; **you've gone s.!** ¡te has vuelto blandengue *or* demasiado delicado!; IDIOM **to have a s. spot for sb** tener *or* sentir debilidad por alguien

(**g**) *Fam (stupid)* tonto(a); IDIOM **to be s. in the head** ser un(a) tontorrón(ona) *or* bobalicón(ona); **he's going s. in his old age** está perdiendo la cabeza con los años

(**h**) *Fam (in love)* **to be s. on sb** estar colado(a) *or Méx* hasta las manitas por alguien, *RP* estar remetido(a) con alguien

(**i**) *(easy) (job, life, target)* fácil; *Fam* **to be a s. touch** ser un poco primo(a) *or Am* bobito(a) ▸▸ ***s. option*** opción *f* fácil

(**j**) *(water)* blando(a)

(**k**) *Econ (market)* débil ▸▸ ***s. currency*** divisa *f* débil

(**l**) *US Pol* ***s. money*** = fondos destinados a los partidos políticos, y no a los candidatos, durante una campaña electoral

(**m**) *Comptr* ***s. copy*** copia *f* en formato electrónico; ***s. hyphen*** guión *m* corto, guión *m* de final de renglón; ***s. return*** retorno *m* automático

(**n**) *Ling (consonant)* débil

(**o**) *(in horseracing) (going)* blando(a)

softback ['sɒftbæk] *n* libro *m* de tapa blanda *or* en rústica

softball ['sɒftbɔːl] *n* = juego parecido al béisbol jugado en un campo más pequeño y con una pelota más blanda

soft-boiled ['sɒftbɔɪld] *adj (egg)* pasado(a) por agua

soft-centred ['sɒft'sentəd] *adj* (**a**) *(chocolate)* con relleno blando (**b**) *(person)* bondadoso(a), de buen corazón

soft-core ['sɒftkɔː(r)] *adj (pornography)* blando(a)

soften ['sɒfən] 1 *vt* (**a**) *(fabric, skin, hair)* suavizar (**b**) *(wax, butter, leather)* ablandar, reblandecer (**c**) *(light, contrast, tone)* suavizar, atenuar (**d**) *(lessen) (pain, impact, shock, effect)* mitigar, atenuar; **to s. the blow** amortiguar el golpe; **the government has softened its stance on drugs** el gobierno ha flexibilizado su postura frente a las drogas (**e**) *(water)* ablandar, de(s)calcificar

2 *vi* (**a**) *(fabric, skin, hair)* suavizarse (**b**) *(wax, butter, leather)* ablandarse (**c**) *(light, contrast, tone)* suavizarse, atenuarse (**d**) *(become less severe, firm) (person)* ceder, ablandarse; *(eyes, expression)* dulcificarse; *(opinions, resolve, stance)* suavizarse

▸ **soften up** 1 *vt sep* (**a**) *(before attack)* debilitar (**b**) *(before request)* ablandar

2 *vi* **to s. up on sb** ablandarse ante alguien, ser *or* ponerse blando con alguien

softener ['sɒfnə(r)] *n (for fabric)* suavizante *m*; *(for water)* de(s)calcificador *m*

softening ['sɒfnɪŋ] *n (of attitude, expression, voice)* relajamiento *m* ▸▸ *Med* ***s. of the brain*** reblandecimiento *m* cerebral

soft-focus lens ['sɒftfəʊkəs'lenz] *n* objetivo *m* anacromático

soft-headed ['sɒft'hedɪd] *adj Fam* tontorrón(ona), bobalicón(ona)

soft-hearted ['sɒft'hɑːtɪd] *adj* bondadoso(a), de buen corazón

softie = **softy**

softly ['sɒftlɪ] *adv* (**a**) *(quietly) (to talk)* con voz suave, suavemente; *(to breathe)* suavemente; *(to walk)* sin hacer ruido; *(to move)* suavemente, sin hacer ruido; **she swore s.** juró bajito; **to be s. spoken** tener la voz suave *or* dulce (**b**) *(gently) (to blow, touch)* suavemente (**c**) *(not harshly)* **to be s. lit** tener una iluminación tenue *or* suave (**d**) *(fondly) (to smile, look)* dulcemente, con dulzura

softly-softly ['sɒftlɪ'sɒftlɪ] *adj Fam (approach, attitude)* cauteloso(a)

softness ['sɒftnɪs] *n* (**a**) *(of fabric, skin, hair)* suavidad *f*

(**b**) *(of pillow, mattress)* blandura *f*; *(of ground)* blandura *f*; *(of metal)* ductilidad *f*, maleabilidad *f*; *(of wood, pencil)* blandura *f*; *(of toothbrush)* (grado *m* de) suavidad *f*

(**c**) *(of voice, music, rain, colour)* suavidad *f*; *(of breeze)* suavidad *f*; *(of accent)* suavidad *f*, dulzura *f*; *(of outline)* carácter *m* desdibujado *or* difuminado; *(of expression, eyes)* dulzura *f*

(**d**) *(kindness) (of person, nature)* bondad *f*, dulzura *f*

(**e**) *(leniency)* debilidad *f*, indulgencia *f*

(**f**) *(weakness)* debilidad *f*, falta *f* de energía

(**g**) *(easiness) (of job, life, target)* facilidad *f*

(**h**) *(of water)* blandura *f*

soft-pedal ['sɒft'pedəl] (*pt & pp* **soft-pedalled**, *US* **soft-pedaled**) *vt (minimize)* restar importancia a

soft-soap ['sɒft'səʊp] *vt Fam* dar jabón *or* coba a

soft-spoken ['sɒft'spəʊkən] *adj* de voz suave

software ['sɒftweə(r)] *n Comptr* software *m*, soporte *m* lógico ▸▸ ***s. developer*** desarrollador(ora) *m,f* de software; ***s. engineer*** ingeniero(a) *m,f* de programas; ***s. error*** error *m* de software; ***s. package*** paquete *m* de software; ***s. piracy*** piratería *f* informática; ***s. platform*** plataforma *f* de software; ***s. tool*** herramienta *f* de software

softwood ['sɒftwʊd] *n* (**a**) *(wood)* madera *f* blanda *or* de conífera (**b**) *(tree)* conífera *f*

softy, softie ['sɒftɪ] *n Fam* (**a**) *(gentle person)* buenazo(a) *m,f* (**b**) *(coward)* gallina *mf*

soggy ['sɒgɪ] *adj (ground, clothes)* empapado(a); *(cardboard)* mojado(a); *(cake, pie)* a medio cocer, medio crudo(a); *(rice)* pasado(a); *(lettuce, tomatoes)* mustio(a)

soh [səʊ] *n Mus* sol *m*

soi-disant ['swɑːdiː'zɒŋ] *adj* autoproclamado(a)

soil [sɔɪl] **1** *n* (**a**) *(earth)* tierra *f*; **they live off the s.** viven de los productos de la tierra; **on British s.** en suelo británico; **his native s.** su tierra natal ►► ***s. science*** edafología *f* (**b**) *(sewage)* ***s. pipe*** (tubería *f* de) desagüe *m* del retrete

2 *vt* (**a**) *(clothes, sheet)* manchar, ensuciar; **to s. oneself** ensuciarse (**b**) *(reputation)* manchar, empañar; IDIOM **to s. one's hands** mancharse las manos

3 *vi (clothes, material)* ensuciarse, mancharse

soiled [sɔɪld] *adj* (**a**) *(bedlinen)* sucio(a), manchado(a) (**b**) *(goods)* manchado(a)

soirée [swɑː'reɪ] *n* velada *f*, fiesta *f* nocturna

sojourn ['sɒdʒən] **1** *n Literary Esp, Méx* estancia *f*, *Am* estadía *f*

2 *vi* pasar una temporada

sol [sɒl] *n Mus* sol *m*

solace ['sɒləs] *n Literary* consuelo *m*; **he found s. in religion** encontró consuelo en la religión

solar ['səʊlə(r)] *adj* (**a**) *(relating to the sun)* solar ►► ***s. battery*** batería *f* solar; ***s. cell*** pila *f* solar; ***s. eclipse*** eclipse *m* de sol; ***s. energy*** energía *f* solar; *Astron* ***s. flare*** fulguración *f* (cromosférica); ***s. heating*** calefacción *f* solar; ***s. panel*** panel *m or* placa *f* solar; ***s. power*** energía *f* solar; ***s. power station*** central *f* solar; ***s. system*** sistema *m* solar; *Astron* ***s. wind*** viento *m* solar (**b**) *Anat* ***s. plexus*** plexo *m* solar

solarium [sə'leərɪəm] (*pl* **solariums** *or* **solaria** [sə'leərɪə]) *n* (**a**) *(sun terrace)* solárium *m* (**b**) *(sunbed)* cama *f* de rayos UVA; *(place with sunbeds)* solárium *m*, solario *m*

solar-powered ['səʊlə'paʊəd] *adj* por energía solar, alimentado(a) por energía solar

sold *pt & pp of* **sell**

solder ['səʊldə(r)] **1** *n* soldadura *f*

2 *vt* soldar

solderer ['sɒldərə(r)] *n* soldador(ora) *m,f*

soldering-iron ['səʊldərɪŋ'aɪən] *n* soldador *m*

soldier ['səʊldʒə(r)] **1** *n* (**a**) *Mil* soldado *m*; **he wants to be a s. when he grows up** quiere ser militar de mayor; **an old s.** un veterano, un excombatiente; *Fam* **don't come** *or* **play the old s. with me** no me vengas con consejos de sabi; **to play (at) soldiers** *(children)* jugar a los soldados, jugar a la guerra; *Fam* **you poor s.!** ¡pobrecito!, ¡qué lástima! ►► ***s. of fortune*** mercenario(a) *m,f*

(**b**) *Zool* ***s. (ant)*** soldado *m*

(**c**) *Br Fam (strip of toast)* = tira fina de pan de molde para untar

2 *vi* servir como soldado

► **soldier on** *vi* seguir adelante

soldierly ['səʊldʒəlɪ] *adv* marcial, castrense

sole[1] [səʊl] **1** *n* (**a**) *(of foot)* planta *f* (**b**) *(of shoe)* suela *f*; *(of sock)* planta *f*

2 *vt (shoe)* poner suelas a

sole[2] *n (fish)* lenguado *m*

sole[3] *adj* (**a**) *(only)* único(a) (**b**) *(exclusive)* exclusivo(a); **to have s. rights on sth** tener la exclusiva *or* los derechos exclusivos de algo ►► *Com* ***s. agent*** agente *mf* en exclusiva; *US Com* ***s. proprietor*** empresario *mf* individual; *Br Com* ***s. trader*** empresario *mf* individual

solecism ['sɒlɪsɪzəm] *n* (**a**) *Gram* solecismo *m* (**b**) *Formal (blunder)* incorrección *f*

-soled [-səʊld] *suffix* **rubber-s. shoes** zapatos de suela de goma

solely ['səʊllɪ] *adv* (**a**) *(only)* únicamente (**b**) *(entirely)* exclusivamente, en su totalidad; **to be s. responsible for sth** ser el único/la única responsable de algo

solemn ['sɒləm] *adj* (**a**) *(face, expression, oath)* solemne; **she looked very s.** parecía muy seria, tenía cierto aire de gravedad (**b**) *(colours, suit)* oscuro(a), serio(a) (**c**) *(occasion, music)* solemne

solemnity [sə'lemnɪtɪ] *n* (**a**) *(of face, expression, oath)* solemnidad *f* (**b**) *(formality)* solemnidad *f* (**c**) *Literary* **solemnities** *(solemn event)* acto *m or* ceremonia *f* solemne

solemnize ['sɒləmnaɪz] *vt Formal (marriage)* celebrar

solemnly ['sɒləmlɪ] *adv* (**a**) *(gravely)* con aire de gravedad, con seriedad (**b**) *(formally)* solemnemente

solenoid ['sɒlənɔɪd] *n Phys* solenoide *m*

sol-fa [sɒl'fɑː] *n Mus* solfa *f*

solfeggio [sɒl'fedʒɪəʊ] (*pl* **solfeggi** [sɒl'fedʒiː] *or* **solfeggios**) *n Mus* solfeo *m*

solicit [sə'lɪsɪt] **1** *vt Formal (request)* solicitar; **to s. sth from sb** solicitar algo a alguien; **they came round soliciting business** vinieron a ofrecer sus servicios profesionales

2 *vi (prostitute)* abordar clientes; *(beggar)* pedir limosna, mendigar

soliciting [sə'lɪsɪtɪŋ] *n (by prostitutes)* ejercicio *m* de la prostitución en las calles

solicitor [sə'lɪsɪtə(r)] *n* (**a**) *Br Law* = abogado que hace las veces de notario para contratos de compraventa y testamentos o que actúa de procurador en los juzgados ►► ***S. General*** *(in UK)* Fiscal *m* General del Estado; *(in US)* Subsecretario(a) *m,f* de Justicia (**b**) *US (of town, city)* = asesor jurídico asignado a una unidad territorial administrativa (pueblo, ciudad, etc.)

solicitous [sə'lɪsɪtəs] *adj Formal (attentive)* solícito(a); *(showing concern)* interesado(a) (**about** por)

solicitously [sə'lɪsɪtəslɪ] *adv Formal (attentively)* solícitamente; *(showing concern)* con interés

solicitude [sə'lɪsɪtjuːd] *n Formal (attentiveness)* solicitud *f*; *(concern)* interés *m* (**about** por)

solid ['sɒlɪd] **1** *n* (**a**) *(object)* sólido *m* ►► *Comptr* ***solids modelling*** modelado *m* de sólidos (**b**) **solids** *(food)* alimentos *mpl* sólidos (**c**) *Chem* **milk solids** sólidos lácteos; **cocoa solids** sólidos *or* materia de cacao

2 *adj* (**a**) *(not liquid)* sólido(a); **to become s.** solidificarse; **it's frozen s.** está totalmente congelado ►► ***s. food*** alimentos *mpl* sólidos; ***s. fuel*** combustible *m* sólido; ***s. waste*** *(rubbish)* residuos *mpl* sólidos; *(excrement)* heces *fpl* fecales

(**b**) *(not hollow) (tyres, ball)* macizo(a) ►► ***s. rock*** roca *f* sólida

(**c**) *(of one substance)* puro(a); **my arms are s. muscle** mis brazos son puro músculo ►► ***s. gold*** oro *m* macizo; ***s. silver*** plata *f* maciza

(**d**) *(continuous)* seguido(a); *(line)* ininterrumpido(a); **I worked for twelve s. hours** trabajé (durante) doce horas seguidas; **for a s. week** durante una semana entera

(**e**) *(dense, compact)* compacto(a); **the streets were a s. mass of people** las calles estaban atestadas *or* abarrotadas de gente; **the traffic was s. all the way back to the roundabout** el tráfico de vuelta era denso hasta llegar a la rotonda

(**f**) *(physically sturdy) (structure, table)* sólido(a); **this is good, s. workmanship** éste es un trabajo sólido, bien hecho; **a man of s. build** un hombre de complexión fuerte, un hombre robusto; IDIOM **to be as s. as a rock** *(structure, table)* ser tan firme como una roca; **their defence was as s. as a rock** contaban con una férrea defensa *or* con una defensa de lo más sólida; IDIOM **to be on s. ground** pisar terreno firme

(**g**) *(reliable) (support)* fuerte, sólido(a); *(relationship, reputation)* sólido(a), firme; *(evidence, proof, argument)* sólido(a); *(advice)* sensato(a), juicioso(a); *(citizen)* cabal, íntegro(a); *(offer)* formal, en firme; **he's a s. worker** es un trabajador de fiar

(**h**) *(unanimous)* **to be s. for/against sth** estar unánimemente a favor de/en contra de algo

(**i**) *Geom* cúbico(a), tridimensional ►► ***s. geometry*** geometría *f* tridimensional

(**j**) *US Fam (excellent)* súper, fenómeno

3 *adv* **ten hours s.** diez horas seguidas; **the hall was packed s.** la sala estaba atestada de gente; **we are booked s. for the next month** estamos completos hasta final del mes que viene

solidarity [sɒlɪ'dærɪtɪ] *n* solidaridad *f* (**with** con); **they went on strike in s. with the miners** fueron a la huelga por *or* en solidaridad con los mineros

solid-fuel ['sɒlɪd'fjʊəl] *adj* de combustible sólido

solidification [səlɪdɪfɪ'keɪʃən] *n (of liquid, gas)* solidificación *f*

solidify [sə'lɪdɪfaɪ] **1** *vi* (**a**) *(liquid, gas)* solidificarse (**b**) *(system, opinion, alliance)* consolidarse

2 *vt* (**a**) *(liquid, gas)* solidificar (**b**) *(alliance)* consolidar

solidity [sə'lɪdɪtɪ] *n* solidez *f*

solidly ['sɒlɪdlɪ] *adv* (**a**) *(firmly, robustly)* sólidamente; **s. built** *(structure)* de construcción *or* edificación sólida; *(person)* de complexión fuerte, robusto(a)

(**b**) *(without interruption)* sin interrupción; **I worked s. for five hours** trabajé (durante) cinco horas seguidas

(**c**) *(thoroughly)* firmemente, sobre sólidos pilares; **a s. reasoned case** un caso razonado de forma convincente

(**d**) *(reliably)* **the defence played s.** el juego de la defensa fue sólido, la defensa jugó con solidez

(**e**) *(to vote)* unánimemente

solid-state ['sɒlɪd'steɪt] *adj* (**a**) *(circuitry, device)* de estado sólido, de componentes sólidos (**b**) *(physics)* del estado sólido

solidus ['sɒlɪdəs] (*pl* **solidi** ['sɒlɪdaɪ]) *n Typ* barra *f* oblicua

soliloquize, soliloquise [sə'lɪləkwaɪz] *vi* monologar, hablar a solas

soliloquy [sə'lɪləkwɪ] *n* soliloquio *m*

solipsism ['sɒlɪpsɪzəm] *n Phil* solipsismo *m*

solipsistic [sɒlɪp'sɪstɪk] *adj Phil* solipsista

solitaire [sɒlɪ'teə(r)] *n* (**a**) *(diamond)* solitario *m* (**b**) *(game)* solitario *m*; **to play s.** hacer un solitario

solitary ['sɒlɪtərɪ] **1** *adj* (**a**) *(alone, lonely)* solitario(a) ►► ***s. confinement*** aislamiento *m*, incomunicación *f*; **to be in s. confinement** estar incomunicado(a) (**b**) *(single)* único(a); **we found not a s. instance of this** no encontramos un solo caso de esto (**c**) *(remote) (of place)* apartado(a), retirado(a)

2 *n* (**a**) *Fam (solitary confinement)* aislamiento *m*, incomunicación *f* (**b**) *Literary (person)* solitario(a) *m,f*

solitude ['sɒlɪtjuːd] *n* soledad *f*

solo ['səʊləʊ] **1** *n* (*pl* **solos**) (**a**) *(musical)* solo *m*; **a guitar/violin s.** un solo de guitarra/violín (**b**) *(flight)* vuelo *m* en solitario (**c**) *(card game)* **s. (whist)** = juego de baraja parecido al whist en el que un solo jugador puede enfrentarse a los demás

2 *adj (performance)* en solitario ►► ***s. album*** álbum *m* en solitario; ***s. flight*** vuelo *m* en solitario; ***s. guitar*** guitarra *f* solista; ***s. voice*** voz *f* solista

3 *adv (fly, perform)* en solitario; **to go s.** *(musician)* iniciar una carrera en solitario; *(business partner)* montar el propio negocio; *Mus* **to play/sing s.** tocar/cantar en solitario

Solo® card ['səʊləʊkæd] *n* = tipo de tarjeta de débito

soloist ['səʊləʊɪst] *n* solista *mf*

Solomon ['sɒləmən] *pr n* Salomón ►► ***the S. Islands, the Solomons*** las Islas Salomón

solstice ['sɒlstɪs] *n* solsticio *m*; **the winter/summer s.** el solsticio de invierno/verano

solubility [sɒljʊ'bɪlətɪ] *n* solubilidad *f*

soluble ['sɒljʊbəl] *adj* (**a**) *(solid)* soluble (**b**) *(problem)* soluble

solute ['sɒljuːt] *n Chem* soluto *m*

solution [sə'luːʃən] *n* (**a**) *(to problem, crime, puzzle)* solución *f* (**to** a) (**b**) *(liquid)* solución *f*; **salt in s.** sal disuelta

solvable ['sɒlvəbəl] *adj* solucionable, soluble

solve [sɒlv] *vt (problem, mystery)* solucionar, resolver; *(crime)* resolver, esclarecer; *(puzzle, equation)* resolver, sacar; *(crossword clue)* resolver; **to s. a riddle** acertar una adivinanza

solvency ['sɒlvənsɪ] *n* solvencia *f*

solvent ['sɒlvənt] **1** *n* disolvente *m* ►► ***s. abuse*** inhalación *f* de disolventes *(pegamento y otros)*

2 *adj* (**a**) *(financially)* solvente (**b**) *(substance, liquid)* disolvente

solver ['sɒlvə(r)] *n (of crime)* esclarecedor(ora) *m,f*; *(of riddle)* acertante *mf*; **the first ten solvers of the crossword will get a prize** las diez primeras personas que resuelvan el crucigrama obtendrán un premio

Som (*abbr* **Somerset**) (condado *m* de) Somerset

Somali(an) [sə'mɑːlɪ(ən)] **1** *n* (**a**) *(person)* somalí *mf* (**b**) *(language)* somalí *m*

2 *adj* somalí

Somalia [sə'mɑːlɪə] *n* Somalia

Somalian = **Somali**

somatic [sə'mætɪk] *adj* somático(a)

sombre, *US* **somber** ['sɒmbə(r)] *adj* (**a**) *(colour)* oscuro(a), sombrío(a); *(place)* sombrío(a), lóbrego(a) (**b**) *(person, mood)* sombrío(a); **what are you looking so s. about?** ¿por qué tienes ese aspecto tan sombrío *or* lúgubre?

sombrely, *US* **somberly** ['sɒmbəlɪ] *adv* (**a**) *(to dress)* con tonos oscuros (**b**) *(to speak, predict)* en tono sombrío

sombreness, *US* **somberness** ['sɒmbənɪs] *n* (**a**) *(of colour)* oscuridad *f*; *(of place)* lobreguez *f* (**b**) *(of person, mood)* aspecto *m* sombrío, carácter *m* sombrío

sombrero [sɒm'breərəʊ] *n* sombrero *m* mexicano

SOME [sʌm] **1** *pron* (**a**) *(people)* algunos(as), unos(as); **s. believe that...** hay quien cree que...; **s. of my friends** algunos amigos míos; **they went off, s. one way, s. another** unos se fueron en una dirección y otros en otra

(**b**) *(a certain number)* unos(as), algunos(as); *(a certain quantity)* algo; **s. are more difficult than others** unos son más difíciles que otros; **there is s. left** queda algo; **there are s. left** quedan algunos; **give me s.** *(a few)* dame unos(as) cuantos(as); *(a bit)* dame un poco; **if you want cake, just take s.** si quieres tarta, sírvete; **would you like coffee? – no thanks, I've already had s.** ¿quieres café? – no, gracias, ya he tomado; **I've made tea, would you like s.?** he preparado té, ¿quieres?; **have s. of this cheese/these grapes** prueba este queso/estas uvas; **s. of the time** parte del tiempo; **it will probably cost about $1,000 – and then s.** probablemente costará cerca de 1.000 dólares – algo más será

2 *adj* (**a**) *(certain quantity or number of)* **there are s. apples in the kitchen** hay manzanas en la cocina; *(a few)* hay algunas *or* unas pocas manzanas en la cocina; **to drink s. water** beber agua; **I ate s. fruit** comí fruta; **can I have s. money?** ¿me das algo de dinero?; **would you like s. wine?** ¿quieres vino?; *(a bit)* ¿quieres un poco de vino?; **I've got s. good news for you** tengo buenas noticias para ti; **could you give me s. idea of when it will be ready?** ¿me podrías dar una idea de cuándo estará listo?; **I felt s. uneasiness** sentí un cierto malestar; **I hope this goes s. way towards making up for it** espero que esto te compense de alguna manera; **I've still got s. more cards to write** todavía me quedan cartas por escribir; **in s. ways** en cierto modo; **to s. extent** hasta cierto punto

(**b**) *(as opposed to other)* **s. people say...** hay quien dice...; **s. mornings he didn't come in to work at all** algunas mañanas ni siquiera se presentaba a trabajar

(**c**) *(considerable)* **s. distance away** bastante lejos; **s. miles away** a bastantes millas; **it will be s. time before we know the results** pasará un tiempo antes de que sepamos los resultados; **we waited for s. time** esperamos durante un buen rato; **for s. time I've been worried about him** llevo bastante tiempo preocupado por él; **s. years previously** unos años antes; **we discussed the matter at s. length** discutimos el asunto durante mucho tiempo

(**d**) *(unspecified)* algún(una); **he'll come s. day** algún día vendrá; **s. fool left the door open** algún idiota dejó la puerta abierta; **at s. time in the future** en algún momento futuro; **s. day or other** algún día de éstos; **for s. reason or other** por una razón u otra, por alguna razón; **in s. book or other** en no sé qué libro, en algún libro

(**e**) *Fam (for emphasis)* **that was s. storm/meal!** ¡qué *or Esp* menuda tormenta/comida!; **it would be s. achievement** sería todo un logro; *Ironic* **s. friend you are!** ¡vaya amigo estás hecho!; *Ironic* **s. hope** *or* **chance!** ¡ni lo sueñes!

3 *adv* (**a**) *(approximately)* unos(as); **s. fifteen minutes** unos quince minutos

(**b**) *US (slightly)* algo, un poco; **shall I turn it up s.?** ¿lo subo algo *or* un poco?

(**c**) *Fam (quickly)* **this bike can really go s.** esta moto corre a toda velocidad *or* que se las pela

SOMEBODY ['sʌmbədɪ], **someone** ['sʌmwʌn] **1** *n* **she thinks she's s.** se cree alguien; **I want to be s.** quiero ser alguien

2 *pron* alguien; **s. told me that...** me dijeron que...; **he's s. you can trust** se puede confiar en él; **surely s. must know the answer** alguien tiene que saber la respuesta; **ask s. else** *(question)* pregúntale a otro; *(request)* pídeselo a otro; **there's s. on the phone for you** te llaman al teléfono; **is this s.'s umbrella?** ¿es de alguien este paraguas?; **we need an electrician or s.** necesitamos un electricista o alguien así; **s. or other** alguien

somehow ['sʌmhaʊ] *adv* (**a**) *(in some way or other)* de alguna manera; **we'll get the money s. (or other)** de un modo u otro conseguiremos el dinero; **she'd s. managed to lock herself in** se las había arreglado, quién sabe cómo, para encerrarse con llave (**b**) *(for some reason or other)* por alguna razón; **s. I knew this would happen** no me preguntes cómo, pero sabía que esto iba a pasar; **it s. doesn't look right** hay algo aquí que no funciona

someone = **somebody**

someplace *US* = **somewhere**

somersault ['sʌməsɔːlt] **1** *n (of person) (jump)* salto *m* mortal; *(roll)* voltereta *f*; *(by car)* vuelta *f* de campana; **to turn** *or* **do a s.** *(person) (jump)* dar un salto mortal; *(roll)* hacer *or* dar una voltereta; *(car)* dar una vuelta de campana/vueltas de campana; **a double/triple s.** un doble/triple salto mortal

2 *vi (person) (jump)* dar un salto mortal/saltos mortales; *(roll)* hacer *or* dar una voltereta/volteretas; *(car)* dar una vuelta de campana/vueltas de campana

SOMETHING ['sʌmθɪŋ] **1** *n* (**a**) *(present)* **I've brought you a little s.** te he traído una cosilla

(**b**) *(food, drink)* **would you like a little s. (to drink)?** ¿te gustaría tomar algo (de beber)?; **would you like a little s. (to eat)?** ¿te gustaría comer algo?, *Esp* ¿te gustaría tomar algo (de comer)?

(**c**) *(important person)* **he thinks he's s.** se cree alguien (importante)

2 *pron* (**a**) *(in general)* algo; **is s. wrong?** ¿pasa algo?; **s. to drink/read** algo de beber/para leer; **s. to live for** una razón para vivir; **it's hardly s. to be proud of** no es como para estar muy orgulloso; **we'll**

think of s. ya se nos ocurrirá algo; **she has s. to do with what happened** está relacionada con lo que ocurrió; **it has s. to do with his mother** tiene que ver con su madre; **they said s. about a party** comentaron algo de una fiesta; **there's s. strange about him** tiene algo raro; **there's s. about him I don't like** hay algo en él que no me gusta; **s. tells me she'll be there** algo me dice que estará allí; **at least he apologized – that's s.!** al menos pidió disculpas – ¡eso ya es algo!; **that was quite s.!, that was s. else!** ¡fue impresionante!; **that singer has really got s.!** ¡ese cantante es genial!; **I think you've got s. there** *(you have a point)* razón no te falta; **there's s. in what you say** tienes algo de razón; **it turned out there was s. in her story after all** al final había algo de verdad en su historia; **there's s. in that idea** esa idea no deja de estar mal; **he's s. in publishing** tiene un puesto importante en el mundo editorial; **she's eighty s.** tiene ochenta y tantos años; **in this life you don't get s. for nothing** en esta vida no te van a regalar nada; *Fam* **he's got s. going with the secretary** *(relationship)* hay algo entre la secretaria y él; **in the year eleven hundred and s.** en el año mil ciento y algo; **she's got a cold or s.** tiene un resfriado o algo así; **they've got a Mercedes, or s. like that** tienen un Mercedes, o algo así

(b) *(certain degree)* **it's s. like a guinea pig** es algo así como un conejillo de Indias; **s. like** *or* **around half of all men...** algo así como la mitad de todos los hombres...; **s. over/under 200** algo por encima/por debajo de 200; **there's been s. of an improvement** se ha producido una cierta mejora; **I'm s. of an expert on the subject** soy todo un experto en el tema; **it came as s. of a shock (to me)** me sorprendió bastante

3 *adv Fam (intensifying)* **it hurt s. awful** dolía horrores *or Méx* un chorro, *Esp* dolía (una) cosa mala; *Br Fam* **he fancies her s. rotten** *Esp* le va cosa mala, *Carib, Col, Méx* le provoca harto, *Méx* le provoca un chorro, *RP* le gusta cualquier cantidad

---

sometime ['sʌmtaɪm] **1** *adv* **(a)** *(in future)* algún día, alguna vez; **give me a ring s.** llámame algún día *or* alguna vez; **see you s.** ya nos veremos; **s. next week** un día de la semana próxima; **s. before Christmas** en algún momento antes de Navidad; **s. before the end of the year** antes de que acabe el año; **s. in April** (cualquier día) en abril; **s. soon** un día de estos; **s. around the year 2025** allá por el año 2025; **s. or other** tarde o temprano

(b) *(in past)* **s. last week** un día de la semana pasada; **the last time I saw him was s. in August** la última vez que lo vi fue por el mes de agosto; **s. around 1920** allá por el año 1920

2 *adj* **(a)** *Formal (former)* antiguo(a) **(b)** *US (occasional)* ocasional

sometimes ['sʌmtaɪmz] *adv* a veces

someway ['sʌmweɪ] *US Fam* = **somehow**

somewhat ['sʌmwɒt] *adv* un poco, un tanto; **everybody came, s. to my surprise** vino todo el mundo, lo que, en cierto modo, me sorprendió; **I was in s. of a hurry to get home** tenía algo de prisa por llegar a casa; **it was s. of a failure** en cierta medida, fue un fracaso

---

SOMEWHERE ['sʌmweə(r)], *US* **someplace** ['sʌmpleɪs] *adv* **(a)** *(in some place)* en algún sitio, en alguna parte; *(to some place)* a algún sitio, a alguna parte; **it must be s. else** debe de estar en otra parte; **why don't you go s. else?** ¿por qué no te vas a otro sitio?; **we must have made a mistake s.** hemos debido cometer un error en alguna parte; **is there s. quiet where we can talk?** ¿hay algún lugar tranquilo en el que podamos hablar?; **I'm looking for s. to eat/live** busco un sitio donde comer/vivir; **s. in Spain** en (algún lugar de) España; **s. north of Chicago** (en algún lugar) al norte de Chicago; **shall we go to Paris or s.?** ¿vamos a París o algún sitio así?; IDIOM **now we're getting s.!** ¡ya parece que las cosas marchan!

(b) *(approximately)* **he is s. around fifty** tiene unos cincuenta años; **s. around four o'clock** a eso de las cuatro; **s. between 50 and 100 people** entre 50 y 100 personas; **it costs s. in the region of £500** cuesta alrededor de 500 libras

---

somnambulism [sɒm'næmbjʊlɪzəm] *n Formal* sonambulismo *m*

somnambulist [sɒm'næmbjʊlɪst] *n Formal* sonámbulo(a) *m,f*

somnolence ['sɒmnələns] *n Formal* somnolencia *f*

somnolent ['sɒmnələnt] *adj Formal* somnoliento(a)

son [sʌn] *n* **(a)** *(male offspring)* hijo *m*; **youngest/eldest s.** hijo menor/mayor; *US very Fam* **s. of a bitch** *(person)* hijo de perra, *Méx* hijo de la chingada; *(thing)* cabrón(ona), *Col, RP* puto(a), *Méx* mugre; *very Fam* **s. of a bitch!** *(expresses annoyance)* ¡hijo de perra!; *Fam* **s. of a gun** *(person)* sinvergüenza, granuja; *Fam Hum* **Tony, you old s. of a gun, how are you?** Tony, cabroncete, ¿cómo estás?; *Fam* **s. of a gun!** *(expresses surprise)* ¡su madre! ►► ***S. of God*** hijo *m* de Dios; ***S. of Man*** hijo *m* del Hombre

(b) *Fam (term of address)* hijo *m*; **how's it going (my) s.?** ¿qué tal te va, hijo (mío)?

sonar ['səʊnɑː(r)] *n* sonar *m* ►► ***s. beacon*** baliza *f* sonora

sonata [sə'nɑːtə] *n* sonata *f*

son et lumière [sɒneɪ'luːmjeə(r)] *n* espectáculo *m* de luz y sonido

song [sɒŋ] *n* **(a)** *(piece of music with words)* canción *f*; **give us a s.** anda, cántanos algo ►► ***s. book*** libro *m* de canciones; ***s. cycle*** ciclo *m* de canciones; ***the S. of Songs*** el Cantar de los Cantares; ***s. thrush*** zorzal *m* común

(b) *(songs collectively)* canción *f*; **a s. and dance act** un número de variedades

(c) *(act of singing)* **we raised our voice in s.** nos pusimos a cantar; **to burst** *or* **break into s.** ponerse a cantar

(d) *(of birds)* canto *m*

(e) IDIOMS **to buy sth for a s.** comprar algo a precio de saldo; **it's going for a s.** se vende a precio de saldo; **to make a s. and dance (about sth)** montar un número (a cuenta de algo); *Br Fam* **to be on s.** estar entonado(a)

songbird ['sɒŋbɜːd] *n* pájaro *m* cantor

songsmith ['sɒŋsmɪθ] *n* cantautor(ora) *m,f*

songster ['sɒŋstə(r)] *n Literary* **(a)** *(singer)* cantor(ora) *m,f* **(b)** *(songbird)* pájaro *m* cantor

songwriter ['sɒŋraɪtə(r)] *n* compositor(ora) *m,f*; *(of lyrics only)* letrista *mf*

sonic ['sɒnɪk] *adj* **(a)** *(of sound)* del sonido **(b)** *(of speed of sound)* sónico(a) ►► *Av* ***s. boom*** estampido *m* sónico

sonically ['sɒnɪkəlɪ] *adv* desde el punto de vista de la acústica

son-in-law ['sʌnɪnlɔː] *n* (*pl* **sons-in-law**) yerno *m*

sonnet ['sɒnɪt] *n* soneto *m*

sonny ['sʌnɪ] *n Fam* hijo *m*, pequeño *m*

sonobuoy ['səʊnəʊbɔɪ] *n* boya *f* sónica *or* acústica

sonority [sə'nɒrətɪ] *n* sonoridad *f*

sonorous ['sɒnərəs] *adj* sonoro(a)

sonorousness ['sɒnərəsnɪs] *n* sonoridad *f*

SOON [suːn] *adv* **(a)** *(within a short time)* pronto; **we will s. be moving house** nos mudaremos dentro de poco; **it will s. be Friday** pronto será viernes; **I s. realized my mistake** enseguida me di cuenta de mi error; **see you s.!** ¡hasta pronto!; **s. after(wards)** poco después; **s. after four** poco después de las cuatro; **s. after arriving** al poco de llegar; **I couldn't get home s. enough** no veía la hora de llegar a casa; **you'll find out s. enough** lo sabrás muy pronto; **as s. as he arrived, we started work** en cuanto llegó nos pusimos a trabajar; **as s. as you're better** en que te pongas bueno; **no sooner had she left than the phone rang** en cuanto se fue *or* nada más marcharse sonó el teléfono; IDIOM **no sooner said than done** dicho y hecho

(b) *(early)* pronto; **how s. can you get here?** ¿cuánto tardarás *or Am* demorarás en llegar?; **how s. will it be ready?** ¿cuándo estará listo?; **how s. can I start?** ¿cuándo podría comenzar?; **must you leave so s.?** ¿tienes que irte tan pronto?; **it's too s. to tell** aún no se puede saber; **none too s., not a moment too s.** en buena hora; **sooner than we expected** antes de lo que esperábamos; **sooner or later** tarde o temprano; **the sooner the better** cuanto antes mejor; **the sooner we start, the sooner we will finish** cuanto antes comencemos, antes acabaremos; **as s. as you can** tan pronto como puedas; **as s. as possible** lo antes posible

(c) *(expressing preference)* **I would just as s. stay** preferiría quedarme; **I would sooner do it alone** preferiría hacerlo yo solo; **I'd as s. leave as put up with that sort of treatment** antes marcharme que aguantar ese tipo de trato

---

soonish ['suːnɪʃ] *adv* en un instante

soot [sʊt] *n* hollín *m*

sooth [suːθ] *n Archaic* **in s.** en verdad

soothe [suːð] *vt* **(a)** *(pain, burn, cough)* aliviar, calmar **(b)** *(person, nerves)* calmar, tranquilizar; *(anger)* calmar, aplacar **(c)** *(fears, doubts)* desvanecer, disipar

soothing ['suːðɪŋ] *adj* **(a)** *(pain-relieving)* calmante **(b)** *(relaxing) (music)* relajante, sedante; *(bath)* relajante **(c)** *(comforting) (words, promises)* tranquilizador(ora)

soothingly ['suːðɪŋlɪ] *adv (relaxingly)* de forma relajante; **she spoke s. to him** le habló con dulzura

soothsayer ['suːθseɪə(r)] *n* adivino(a) *m,f*

soothsaying ['suːθseɪɪŋ] *n* adivinación *f*

sooty ['sʊtɪ] *adj* **(a)** *(covered in soot)* tiznado(a) **(b)** *(black)* negro(a)

sop ['sɒp] *n* (a) *(concession)* pequeña concesión *f* (to a); **she's only doing it as a s. to her conscience** sólo lo hace para que no le remuerda la conciencia (b) *Fam (weak person)* enclenque *m* (c) **sops** *(of bread)* sopas *fpl*

▸ **sop up** *vt sep (with cloth)* secar, absorber; *(with bread)* rebañar

sophism ['sɒfɪzəm] *n* sofismo *m*

sophist ['sɒfɪst] *n* (a) *(false reasoner)* sofista *mf* (b) *(in ancient Greece)* sofista *m*

sophisticate [sə'fɪstɪkət] *n Formal* sofisticado(a) *m,f*

sophisticated [sə'fɪstɪkeɪtɪd] *adj* (a) *(person, taste)* sofisticado(a) (b) *(machine, system)* avanzado(a) (c) *(subtle) (argument, novel, film)* sutil

sophistication [səfɪstɪ'keɪʃən] *n* (a) *(of person, taste)* sofisticación *f* (b) *(of machine, system)* complejidad *f*, carácter *m* avanzado (c) *(subtlety) (of argument, novel, film)* sutileza *f*

sophistry ['sɒfɪstrɪ] *n Formal* (a) *(argumentation)* sofistería *f* (b) *(argument)* sofisma *f*

sophomore ['sɒfəmɔː(r)] *n US Univ* = estudiante de segundo curso

sophomoric [sɒfə'mɔːrɪk] *adj US* inmaduro(a) y repipi

soporific [sɒpə'rɪfɪk] **1** *adj Formal* soporífero(a)
2 *n* somnífero *m*

soppiness ['sɒpɪnɪs] *n Fam (sentimentality)* sensiblería *f*, *Esp* ñoñería *f*

sopping ['sɒpɪŋ] *adj* **to be s. (wet)** estar empapado(a)

soppy ['sɒpɪ] *adj Fam* sensiblero(a), *Esp* ñoño(a); **to be s. about sb** *(in love)* caérsele a alguien la baba con alguien

soprano [sɒ'prɑːnəʊ] *(pl* **sopranos** *or* **soprani** [sɒ'prɑːniː]) **1** *n (singer)* soprano *mf*; **to sing s.** cantar de *or* como soprano
2 *adj (part)* de *or* para soprano ▸▸ ***s. saxophone*** saxofón *m* soprano; ***s. voice*** (voz *f* de) soprano *m*

sorbet ['sɔːbeɪ] *n* sorbete *m*

sorbic acid [sɔːbɪk'æsɪd] *n Chem* ácido *m* sórbico

sorbitol ['sɔːbɪtɒl] *n* sorbitol *m*

sorcerer ['sɔːsərə(r)] *n* brujo *m*, hechicero *m*

sorceress ['sɔːsərɪs] *n* bruja *f*, hechicera *f*

sorcery ['sɔːsərɪ] *n* brujería *f*, hechicería *f*

sordid ['sɔːdɪd] *adj* (a) *(base)* sórdido(a), despreciable; **spare me the s. details!** ¡ahórrate los detalles!; **they've got s. little minds** tienen mentes calenturientas (b) *(squalid)* sórdido(a)

sordidness ['sɔːdɪdnɪs] *n* (a) *(baseness)* sordidez *f*, ruindad *f* (b) *(squalor)* sordidez *f*, inmundicia *f*

sore [sɔː(r)] **1** *n (wound)* llaga *f*, úlcera *f*
2 *adj* (a) *(painful)* dolorido(a); **his feet were s.** tenía los pies doloridos; **to have a s. throat** tener dolor de garganta; **I've got a s. leg/back** me duele la pierna/espalda; **where is it s.?** ¿dónde le/te duele?; **I'm s. all over** me duele todo el cuerpo; IDIOM **it's a s. point (with him)** es un tema delicado (para él)
(b) *Fam (annoyed) esp Esp* enfadado(a) (**about** por), molesto(a) (**about** por), *esp Am* enojado(a) (**about** por); **are you still s. at me?** ¿todavía estás enfadado conmigo?; **he got s.** se molestó, se ofendió
(c) *Literary (great)* grande, fuerte; **to be in s. need of sth** necesitar algo desesperadamente
3 *adv Archaic (very)* asaz

sorehead ['sɔːhed] *n US Fam* cascarrabias *mf inv*

sorely ['sɔːlɪ] *adv (greatly)* enormemente; **she will be s. missed** se la echará muchísimo de menos, *Am* se la extrañará muchísimo; **to be s. in need of sth** necesitar algo desesperadamente; **s. tempted** enormemente tentado(a); **we are s. pressed for time** andamos muy apurados de tiempo; **to be s. troubled** estar hondamente preocupado(a)

soreness ['sɔːnɪs] *n* dolor *m*

sorghum ['sɔːgəm] *n* sorgo *m*

sorority [sə'rɒrɪtɪ] *n US Univ* = asociación femenina de estudiantes que suele funcionar como club social

sorrel ['sɒrəl] **1** *n* (a) *Bot & Culin* acedera *f* (b) *(colour)* pardo *m* rojizo, color *m* alazán (c) *(horse)* alazán *m*
2 *adj* alazán(ana)

sorrow ['sɒrəʊ] **1** *n* pena *f* (**at** *or* **for** *or* **over** por); **to my great s.** con gran pesar mío; **I am writing to express my s. at your sad loss** le escribo para expresarle mi más sentido pésame por tan irreparable pérdida; **his son's failure was a great s. to him** sintió mucho el fracaso de su hijo; **she said it more in s. than in anger** lo dijo con más pena que indignación
2 *vi Formal* sentir pena, penar (**at** *or* **for** *or* **over** por)

sorrowful ['sɒrəfʊl] *adj* afligido(a), apenado(a)

sorrowfully ['sɒrəflɪ] *adv* apenadamente, con tristeza

SORRY ['sɒrɪ] *adj* (a) *(regretful, disappointed)* **to be s. about sth** lamentar *or* sentir algo; **I'm s. about your father** siento lo de tu padre; **(I'm) s. (that) I couldn't come** siento no haber podido venir; **she's s. (that) she did it** siente mucho haberlo hecho; **I'm s. (that) I accepted, now** ahora me arrepiento de haber aceptado; *Fam* **you'll be s.!** ¡te arrepentirás!; **you'll be s. (that) you didn't try harder** ¡te arrepentirás de no haberte esforzado más!; **(I'm) s. if I seem ungrateful, but...** no querría parecer desagradecido(a), pero...; **s. to keep you waiting** siento haberle hecho esperar; **we'll be s. to see you go** sentiremos que te vayas; **I'm s. to hear (that)...** lamento saber que...; **I'm s. to say (that) you haven't been chosen** siento tener que decirte que no te han seleccionado; **most of the applicants will not, I'm s. to say, be offered a job** desafortunadamente, la mayoría de los candidatos no conseguirá un trabajo; **I'm s.** *(regretful)* lo lamento, lo siento; *(apology)* lo siento; **I'm s., but you're totally wrong** perdona, pero te equivocas por completo; **s.!** *(apology)* ¡perdón!; **s.?** *(what?)* ¿perdón?, ¿cómo dice(s)?; **s., that room is private!** ¡disculpe, esa habitación es privada!; **s., but could I ask you not to smoke?** disculpe, ¿le importaría no fumar?; **he's called Tim, s., Tom** se llama Tim, perdón, Tom; **s. about the mess!** ¡ya perdonarás el desorden!; **s. about that!** ¡lo siento!; **to say s. (to sb)** pedir perdón (a alguien); **say you are s. for being so rude** pide perdón por haber sido tan grosero
(b) *(sympathetic)* **to feel s. for sb** sentir pena *or* lástima por alguien; **he felt s. for himself** se compadecía de sí mismo; **stop feeling s. for yourself!** ¡deja de compadecerte!; **it's the children I feel s. for** los niños son los que me dan lástima
(c) *(pathetic)* lamentable, penoso(a); **to be a s. sight** ofrecer un espectáculo lamentable *or* penoso; **to be in a s. state** estar en un estado lamentable *or* penoso

---

sorry-ass(ed) ['sɔːrɪæs(t)] *adj US very Fam (miserable, contemptible)* de mierda

---

SORT [sɔːt] **1** *n* (a) *(kind)* clase *f*, tipo *m*; **what's your favourite s. of chocolate?** ¿cuál es tu tipo de chocolate favorito?; **what s. of tree is that?** ¿qué clase de árbol es éste?; **what s. of price were you thinking of?** ¿en qué franja de precios estabas pensando?; **what s. of time do you call this?** ¿qué horas piensas que son éstas?; **it was a s. of olive green** era una especie de verde oliva; **all sorts of** todo tipo de; *Fam* **they are in all sorts of trouble** tienen muchísimos problemas; **that s. of thing** ese tipo de cosas; **she's that s. of person** ella es así; **problems of one s. or another** problemas de un tipo o de otro; **something of the s.** algo por el estilo; **he is some s. of specialist** *or* **a specialist of some s.** es especialista en algo *or* no sé qué; **did you leave this window open? – I did nothing of the s.!** ¿has dejado la ventana abierta? – ¡qué va!; **you will do nothing of the s.!** ¡ni se te ocurra hacer algo así!; **he's so arrogant! – he's nothing of the s.!** ¡es tan arrogante! – ¡qué va a ser arrogante!; **coffee of a s.** *or* **of sorts** café, por llamarlo de alguna forma; **he's a writer of sorts** se le podría llamar escritor; **they're not our s. (of people)** no son como nosotros; **to be** *or* **feel out of sorts** no encontrarse muy allá
(b) *(person)* persona *f*; **she's a good s.** es buena gente; **she's not the s. to give in easily** no es de las que se rinden fácilmente; **I know your s.!** conozco a los de tu calaña; **we don't want your s. here** no queremos gente como tú por aquí; **he's not really my s.** la verdad es que no es mi tipo; *Fam Pej* **you get all sorts in that bar** en ese bar te encuentras todo tipo de gentuza; **it takes all sorts (to make a world)** de todo tiene que haber
(c) *(to organize)* **to have a s. through sth** revisar algo ▸▸ *Br* ***s. code*** *(of bank)* número *m* de sucursal
2 *vt* (a) *(classify)* ordenar, clasificar; *Comptr* ordenar; **I sorted the books into two piles** puse *or* dividí los libros en dos montones; **we sorted the good fruit from the bad** separamos la fruta buena de la mala; **to s. sth alphabetically** ordenar algo alfabéticamente
(b) *Fam (fix)* **we should get the TV sorted** tenemos que arreglar la tele; **we'll get you sorted, don't worry** no te preocupes, que nos encargamos de todo
(c) *Fam (solve) (problem)* arreglar
3 sort of *adv Fam (a little)* un poco; *(in a way)* en cierto modo; **this is s. of embarrassing** esto es un poco embarazoso; **I s. of expected it** en cierto modo ya me lo esperaba; **I s. of forgot** me he debido olvidar; **I was s. of hoping you'd invite me too** estaba como esperando que me invitaras a mí también; **do you like it? – s. of** ¿te gusta? – bueno, más o menos; **it was s. of like a big, bright sphere** era una especie de esfera grande y brillante

▸ **sort out** *vt sep* (a) *(organize)* ordenar; **she sorted out the clothes she wanted to keep** separó la ropa que no quería tirar *or Am* botar; *Fam* **I should be able to s. a room out for you** seguro que te encuentro una habitación; **you need to s. yourself out** necesitas reorganizar tu vida *or* aclararte las ideas

(**b**) *(problem)* arreglar; **it took us ages to s. out who owed what** nos llevó una eternidad determinar quién debía qué; **I'll go and s. the bill out** yo me encargo de la cuenta; **things will s. themselves out, don't worry** todo se arreglará, no te preocupes

(**c**) *Fam* **to s. sb out** *(punish)* poner a alguien en su sitio; *(beat up)* darle una paliza *or Esp* un repaso a alguien

▸ **sort through** *vt insep* revisar

sorta ['sɔːtə] *Fam* = **sort of**

sorted ['sɔːtɪd] *Br Fam* **1** *adj* (**a**) *(having everything one needs)* **if I get that pay rise, I'll be s.** si consigo ese aumento de sueldo, me daré por contento(a) *or* satisfecho(a); **to be s. for sth** *(have enough)* estar surtido(a) de algo (**b**) *(psychologically)* equilibrado(a), centrado(a); **she's the most s. person I know** es la persona más equilibrada *or* centrada que conozco

2 *exclam* ¡listo!, ¡arreglado!

sorter ['sɔːtə(r)] *n (in post office)* clasificador(ora) *m,f*

sortie ['sɔːtɪ] *n* (**a**) *Mil* incursión *f*; **30 sorties were flown today** hoy se han realizado 30 incursiones aéreas (**b**) *(outing)* incursión *f*, salida *f*; *Hum* **I sometimes make the odd s. to the pub** algunas veces hago alguna que otra escapadita al pub

sorting ['sɔːtɪŋ] *n* selección *f*, clasificación *f* ▸▸ ***s. office*** oficina *f* de clasificación de correo

sort-out ['sɔːtaʊt] *n Br Fam (tidying session)* limpieza *f* general

SOS [esəʊ'es] *n* S.O.S. *m*; **we received an S. call** *or* **message** recibimos un S.O.S.; *Fig* **aid organizations are sending out an S. for food and clothing** las organizaciones de ayuda humanitaria han hecho un llamamiento de emergencia solicitando alimentos y ropa

so-so ['səʊ'səʊ] *Fam* **1** *adj* regular; **it was only s.** fue regularcillo

2 *adv* así así, regular

sot [sɒt] *n Old-fashioned* borracho(a) *m,f*

sotto voce ['sɒtəʊ'vəʊtʃɪ] *adv* sotto voce, en voz baja, *Am* despacio

soufflé ['suːfleɪ] *n* suflé *m*; **cheese s.** suflé de queso ▸▸ ***s. dish*** fuente *f* para suflé

sough [saʊ] *Literary* **1** *n* susurro *m*, murmullo *m*

2 *vi* susurrar, murmurar

sought *pt & pp of* **seek**

sought-after ['sɔːtɑːftə(r)] *adj* solicitado(a); **a much s. award** un premio muy codiciado

souk [suːk] *n* zoco *m*

soul [səʊl] *n* (**a**) *(spirit)* alma *f*; **to sell one's s.** venderse, vender el alma; **I hope with all my s. that he is punished** deseo con toda mi alma que reciba un castigo; *Old-fashioned* **upon my s.!** ¡válgame el cielo!; *Fig* **it's good for the s.** tonifica el espíritu; **All Souls' Day** el día de (los) difuntos

(**b**) *(emotional depth)* **her singing lacks s.** a su cante le falta garra *or* sentimiento; **the building is certainly large, but it has no s.** es un edificio realmente grande, pero le falta personalidad

(**c**) *(person)* alma *f*; **not a s.** ni un alma; **I didn't tell/know a s.** no se lo dije/no conocía a nadie; **he's a good s.** es (una) buena persona; **she's a happy s.** es la alegría personificada; **poor s.!** ¡pobrecillo!

(**d**) *(epitome)* **she's the s. of discretion** es la discreción en persona

(**e**) *Mus* **s. (music)** soul *m* ▸▸ ***s. singer*** cantante *mf* de soul

(**f**) *US (referring to black people)* ***s. brother*** hermano *m* (negro); ***s. food*** = comida tradicional de los negros del sur de Estados Unidos; ***s. sister*** hermana *f* (negra)

soul-destroying ['səʊldɪstrɔɪɪŋ] *adj* desmoralizador(ora)

soulful ['səʊlfʊl] *adj* emotivo(a), conmovedor(ora)

soulfully ['səʊlfʊlɪ] *adv* conmovedoramente

soulless ['səʊllɪs] *adj* (**a**) *(person)* inhumano(a), desalmado(a) (**b**) *(place)* impersonal; *(work)* insulso(a), anodino(a)

soulmate ['səʊlmeɪt] *n* alma *f* gemela

soul-searching ['səʊlsɜːtʃɪŋ] *n* examen *m* de conciencia, reflexión *f*; **after much s. she decided to leave** tras una profunda reflexión, decidió marcharse

SOUND[1] [saʊnd] **1** *n* (**a**) *(in general)* sonido *m*; *(individual noise)* ruido *m*; **not a s. could be heard** no se oía nada; **we could hear the s. of cannons/voices in the distance** se oía el ruido de cañones/se oían voces a lo lejos; **we danced to the s. of the music** bailamos al son de la música; **don't make a s.** no hagas ni un ruido; **to turn the s. up/down** *(on TV, radio)* subir/bajar el volumen; **he likes the s. of his own voice** le gusta escucharse a sí mismo; *Fig* **I don't like the s. of it** no me gusta nada como suena; **he's angry, by** *or* **from the s. of it** parece que está *esp Esp* enfadado *or esp Am* enojado ▸▸ ***s. archives*** fonoteca *f*; ***s. barrier*** barrera *f* del sonido; ***s. bite*** frase *f* lapidaria *(en medios de comunicación)*; *Comptr* ***s. card*** tarjeta *f* de sonido; ***s. check*** prueba *f* de sonido; ***s. effects*** efectos *mpl* sonoros *or* de sonido; ***s. engineer*** ingeniero(a) *m,f* de sonido; ***s. hole*** *(of violin, viola)* ese *f*, efe *f*; *(of guitar)* boca *f*; ***s. mixer*** mezclador *m* de sonido; ***s. system*** equipo *m* de sonido; ***s. wave*** onda *f* sonora

(**b**) *Fam* **sounds** *(music)* música *f*; **the Manchester s.** la música *or* el sonido de Manchester

(**c**) *Geog (inlet)* brazo *m* de mar; *(channel)* estrecho *m*

(**d**) *Phys* sonido *m*

(**e**) *Ling* sonido *m* ▸▸ ***s. shift*** cambio *m* fonético;

(**f**) *Med (probe)* sonda *f*

2 *vt* (**a**) *(trumpet)* tocar; *Aut* **to s. one's horn** tocar el claxon *or* la bocina; **to s. the alarm** *(set off device)* hacer sonar la alarma; *Fig* dar la voz de alarma; *Fig* **to s. the retreat** batirse en retirada

(**b**) *(express)* **to s. a note of caution** llamar a la cautela; **to s. a warning** lanzar una advertencia

(**c**) *(pronounce)* pronunciar; **the "h" is not sounded** la "h" no se pronuncia

(**d**) *Naut (measure depth of)* sondar, sondear

(**e**) *Med (chest)* auscultar

3 *vi* (**a**) *(make sound) (trumpet, bell, alarm)* sonar; **it sounds hollow if you tap it** si le das golpecitos suena a hueco; **in English words are rarely spelt as they s.** en inglés las palabras rara vez se escriben como se pronuncian

(**b**) *(seem)* parecer; **you s. as if** *or* **though you could use a holiday** parece que no te irían mal unas vacaciones; **it sounds to me as if** *or* **though they're telling the truth** me parece que dicen la verdad; **that sounds like trouble!** eso suena a que puede haber problemas; **that sounds like a good idea** eso me parece muy buena idea; **from what people say, he sounds (like) a nice guy** por lo que dicen, parece buena gente *or Esp* un tío majo; **how does that s. to you?** *(referring to suggestion)* ¿a ti qué te parece?

(**c**) *(seem from voice, noise made)* sonar; **she sounds French** suena francesa; **it sounds like Mozart** suena a *or* parece Mozart; **that sounds like the postman now** parece el cartero; **he sounded pleased** sonaba contento; **you s. as if** *or* **though you've got a cold** suenas como si estuvieras resfriado

▸ **sound off** *vi Fam* despotricar (**about** de)

▸ **sound out** *vt sep* **to s. sb out (about sth)** sondear *or* tantear a alguien (acerca de algo)

sound[2] **1** *adj* (**a**) *(healthy)* sano(a); **he is of s. mind** tiene pleno uso de sus facultades mentales; IDIOM **to be s. as a bell** estar más sano(a) que una pera

(**b**) *(solid) (foundations, structure)* sólido(a); *(in good condition)* en buen estado

(**c**) *(argument, reasoning, basis)* sólido(a); *(strategy, approach)* coherente, racional; *(knowledge, understanding)* profundo(a), sólido(a); **he showed s. judgment in refusing** demostró estar en su sano juicio diciendo que no; **a s. piece of advice** un consejo sensato; **it makes good s. sense** parece de lo más razonable

(**d**) *(reliable) (investment, business)* seguro(a), sólido(a); *(person)* competente, válido(a); **is she politically s.?** ¿es una persona válida en lo que respecta a sus ideas políticas?

(**e**) *(acceptable)* aceptable; **environmentally s.** respetuoso(a) con el medio ambiente

(**f**) *(sleep)* profundo(a); **to be a s. sleeper** tener el sueño profundo

(**g**) *(severe) (hiding, thrashing)* duro(a), fuerte; *(defeat)* rotundo(a), contundente

(**h**) *Br Fam (excellent)* genial, *Esp* guay, *Andes, CAm, Carib, Méx* chévere, *Andes, RP* macanudo(a), *Méx* padre

2 *adv* **to be s. asleep** estar profundamente dormido(a)

sound-box ['saʊndbɒks] *n (of stringed instrument)* caja *f* de resonancia

-sounding [-'saʊndɪŋ] *suffix* **a foreign-s. name** un nombre que suena extranjero

sounding-board ['saʊndɪŋ'bɔːd] *n (on pulpit, stage)* tornavoz *m*; *Fig* **I used John as a s.** puse a prueba mis ideas contándoselas a John

soundings ['saʊndɪŋz] *npl Fig* **to take s.** tantear *or* sondear el terreno

soundlessly ['saʊndlɪslɪ] *adv (silently)* calladamente, en silencio

soundly ['saʊndlɪ] *adv* (**a**) *(solidly) (built)* sólidamente

(**b**) *(logically) (to say, argue)* razonablemente

(**c**) *(deeply) (to sleep)* profundamente; *Fig* **we can all sleep s. (in our beds) now that we know that the murderer has been caught** ahora que sabemos que el asesino ya no anda suelto, podremos dormir a pierna suelta (**d**) *(thoroughly)* **to thrash sb s.** dar a alguien una buena paliza; **the team was s. beaten** el equipo sufrió una rotunda *or* contundente derrota

soundness ['saʊndnɪs] *n* (**a**) *(of body, mind)* salud *m*, equilibrio *m*; *(of health)* buen estado *m* (**b**) *(solidity) (of foundations, structure)* solidez *f*; *(good condition)* buen estado *m* (**c**) *(of argument, reasoning)* solidez *f*; *(of strategy, approach)* coherencia *f*, racionalidad *f*; *(of judgement)* lo sensato, lo juicioso; *(of advice)* lo acertado (**d**) *(reliability) (of investment, business)* seguridad *f*, solidez *f*; *(of person)* competencia *f*, valía *f*

soundproof ['saʊndpru:f] **1** *adj* insonorizado(a)
2 *vt* insonorizar

soundproofing ['saʊndpru:fɪŋ] *n* insonorización *f*, aislamiento *m* acústico

soundtrack ['saʊndtræk] *n* banda *f* sonora

soup [su:p] *n* sopa *f*; IDIOM *Fam* **to be in the s.** estar en un aprieto; IDIOM *US Fam* **from s. to nuts** de cabo a rabo, de punta a cabo; ►► ***s. kitchen*** comedor *m* popular; ***s. ladle*** cucharón *m*; ***s. plate*** plato *m* hondo *or* sopero; ***s. spoon*** cuchara *f* sopera; ***s. tureen*** sopera *f*

► **soup up** *vt sep Fam (engine, car)* trucar

soupçon ['su:psɒn] *n (of salt)* pizca *f*, pellizco *m*; *(of milk)* poquitín *m*; **I detected a s. of sarcasm in her voice** detecté un asomo de *or* cierto sarcasmo en su voz

soupy ['su:pɪ] *adj (atmosphere)* denso(a), cargado(a)

sour ['saʊə(r)] **1** *adj* (**a**) *(fruit, wine)* ácido(a), agrio(a); IDIOM **it's (a case of) s. grapes** es cuestión de despecho (**b**) *(milk)* agrio(a), cortado(a); **to go** *or* **turn s.** *(milk)* cortarse, agriarse; *Fig (situation, relationship)* agriarse, echarse a perder ►► ***s. cream*** *Esp* nata *f* agria, *Am* crema *f* de leche agria (**c**) *(person, character)* agrio(a), áspero(a); *(look)* agrio(a), despreciable; *(face)* agrio(a), de mal genio
2 *vt* (**a**) *(milk)* cortar, agriar; *(wine)* avinagrar, agriar (**b**) *(atmosphere, relationship)* agriar, echar a perder; *(person, character)* agriar, amargar; **the experience soured his view of life** la experiencia le amargó su visión de la vida
3 *vi* (**a**) *(milk)* cortarse, agriarse; *(wine)* avinagrarse, agriarse (**b**) *(atmosphere, relationship)* agriarse, echarse a perder

source [sɔ:s] **1** *n* (**a**) *(of river)* nacimiento *m*
(**b**) *(origin)* fuente *f*; *(of infection, discontent)* foco *m*; **to trace the s. of sth** buscar el origen de algo; **he's a constant s. of amusement** es una fuente continua de entretenimiento; **it's our only s. of income** es nuestra única fuente de ingresos; **tax is deducted at s.** el impuesto se deduce en origen *or* en la fuente
(**c**) *(of information)* fuente *f*; **reliable/official sources** fuentes fidedignas/oficiales; **a s. close to the government** fuentes cercanas al gobierno; **I have it from a good s. that...** sé de buena tinta que...
(**d**) *(text)* **the s. of the play** la fuente de la obra ►► ***s. material*** documentación *f*
(**e**) *Comptr* ***s. code*** código *m* fuente; ***s. document*** documento *m* original; ***s. file*** archivo *m* fuente; ***s. program*** programa *f* fuente
2 *vt Com* adquirir

sourcing ['sɔ:sɪŋ] *n Com* adquisiciones *fpl*

sourdough ['saʊədəʊ] *n US* masa *f* fermentada

sour-faced ['saʊə'feɪst] *adj* con cara de vinagre *or* de pocos amigos

sourly ['saʊəlɪ] *adv (to say)* con acritud, agriamente; *(to look)* con mirada agria, agriamente

sourness ['saʊənɪs] *n* (**a**) *(of fruit, wine)* acidez *f*; *(of milk)* sabor *m* agrio (**b**) *(of person, remark)* acritud *f*, amargura *f*

sourpuss ['saʊəpʊs] *n Fam* amargado(a) *m,f*

sousaphone ['su:zəfəʊn] *n* = instrumento parecido a la tuba

sous chef ['su:ʃef] *n* subjefe(a) *m,f*

souse [saʊs] **1** *n Fam (drunkard)* borrachín(ina) *m,f*
2 *vt* (**a**) *(drench)* empapar; **he soused himself with cold water** se echó abundante agua fría (por encima) (**b**) *Culin* adobar, escabechar

soused [saʊst] *adj* (**a**) *(pickled)* **s. herrings** arenques en vinagre (**b**) *Fam (drunk)* **to be/get s.** estar/ponerse como una cuba

south [saʊθ] **1** *n* sur *m*; **to the s. (of)** al sur (de); **the S. of Spain** el sur de España; **the S.** *(region)* el Sur; *US Hist* los estados del sur; *(less affluent countries)* el Sur; **I was born in the s.** nací en el sur; **the wind is in** *or* **(coming) from the s.** el viento sopla del sur
2 *adj* (**a**) *(direction, side, wall)* (del) sur; **s. London** el sur de Londres; **the s. coast** la costa sur ►► ***s. wind*** viento *m* del sur
(**b**) *(in names)* ***S. Africa*** Sudáfrica; ***S. America*** Sudamérica, América del Sur; ***S. Australia*** Australia Meridional; ***S. Carolina*** Carolina del Sur; ***the S. China Sea*** el mar de China (meridional); ***S. Dakota*** Dakota del Sur; ***S. Island*** *(in New Zealand)* Isla del Sur; ***S. Korea*** Corea del Sur; ***the S. Pacific*** el Pacífico Sur; ***the S. Pole*** el Polo Sur; ***the S. Sea Islands*** las islas de los mares del Sur; ***the S. Seas*** los mares del Sur
3 *adv* hacia el sur, en dirección sur; **it's (3 miles) s. of here** está (a 3 millas) al sur de aquí; **they live down s.** viven en el sur; **s. by east/by west** Sur cuarta al Sudeste/Sudoeste; **to face s.** *(person)* mirar hacia el sur; *(room)* estar orientado(a) *or* mirar al sur; **to go s.** ir hacia el sur

South African [saʊθ'æfrɪkən] **1** *n* sudafricano(a) *m,f*
2 *adj* sudafricano(a)

South American [saʊθə'merɪkən] **1** *n* sudamericano(a) *m,f*
2 *adj* sudamericano(a)

southbound ['saʊθbaʊnd] *adj (train, traffic)* en dirección sur; **the s. carriageway** la calzada en dirección sur

south-east [saʊθ'i:st] **1** *n* sudeste *m*, sureste *m*; **they live in the s.** viven en el sudeste
2 *adj (side)* sudeste; *(wind)* del sudeste ►► ***S. Asia*** el sudeste asiático
3 *adv* hacia el sudeste, en dirección sudeste

south-easterly [saʊθ'i:stəlɪ] **1** *n (wind)* viento *m* del sudeste
2 *adj (wind)* del sudeste; **in a s. direction** en dirección sudeste, rumbo al sudeste

south-eastern [saʊθ'i:stən] *adj (region, accent)* del sudeste, sudoriental; **in s. France** en el sudeste de Francia, en la Francia sudoriental

southeastward [saʊθ'i:stwəd] **1** *adj* hacia el sudeste; **in a s. direction** en dirección sudeste, rumbo al sudeste
2 *adv* hacia el sudeste, en dirección sudeste

southeastwardly [saʊθ'i:stwədlɪ] **1** *adj* hacia el sudeste; **in a s. direction** en dirección sudeste, rumbo al sudeste
2 *adv* hacia el sudeste, en dirección sudeste

southeastwards [saʊθ'i:stwədz] *adv* hacia el sudeste, en dirección sudeste

southerly ['sʌðəlɪ] **1** *n (wind)* viento *m* del sur
2 *adj (wind)* del sur; **in a s. direction** en dirección sur, rumbo al sur; **the most s. point** el punto más meridional

southern ['sʌðən] *adj* (**a**) *(region, accent)* del sur, meridional; **s. Spain/Europe** el sur de España/Europa, la España/Europa meridional ►► ***s. Africa*** (el) África austral *or* meridional; *Astron* ***the S. Cross*** la Cruz del Sur; ***the s. hemisphere*** el hemisferio sur; ***the s. lights*** la aurora austral (**b**) *(in American Civil War)* sureño(a), del Sur

southerner ['sʌðənə(r)] *n* sureño(a) *m,f*

southernmost ['sʌðənməʊst] *adj* más meridional, más al sur; **the s. island of the archipelago** la isla más meridional del archipiélago

southernwood ['sʌðənwʊd] *n* abrótano *m* (macho)

south-facing ['saʊθ'feɪsɪŋ] *adj* orientado(a) al sur

South Korean [saʊθkə'rɪən] **1** *n* surcoreano(a) *m,f*
2 *adj* surcoreano(a)

southpaw ['saʊθpɔ:] *n Fam* zurdo(a) *m,f*, *Esp* zocato(a) *m,f*

south-southeast ['saʊθsaʊθ'i:st] *adv* con dirección sursudeste

south-southwest ['saʊθsaʊθ'west] *adv* con dirección sursudoeste

southward ['saʊθwəd] **1** *adj* hacia el sur; **in a s. direction** en dirección sur, rumbo al sur
2 *adv* hacia el sur, en dirección sur

southwardly ['saʊθwədlɪ] **1** *adj* hacia el sur; **in a s. direction** en dirección sur, rumbo al sur
2 *adv* hacia el sur, en dirección sur

southwards ['saʊθwədz] *adv* hacia el sur, en dirección sur

south-west [saʊθ'west] **1** *n* sudoeste *m*, suroeste *m*; **they live in the s.** viven en el sudoeste
2 *adj (side)* sudoeste; *(wind)* del sudoeste
3 *adv* hacia el sudoeste, en dirección sudoeste

south-westerly [saʊθ'westəlɪ] **1** *n (wind)* (viento *m* del) sudoeste *m*
2 *adj (wind)* del sudoeste; **in a s. direction** en dirección sudoeste, rumbo al sudoeste
3 *adv* hacia el sudoeste, en dirección sudoeste

south-western [saʊθ'westən] *adj (region, accent)* del sudoeste, sudoccidental; **in s. France** en el sudoeste de Francia, en la Francia sudoccidental

southwestward [saʊθ'westwəd] **1** *adj* hacia el sudoeste; **in a s. direction** en dirección sudoeste, rumbo al sudoeste
2 *adv* hacia el sudoeste, en dirección sudoeste

southwestwardly [saʊθ'westwədlɪ] **1** *adj* hacia el sudoeste; **in a s. direction** en dirección sudoeste, rumbo al sudoeste
2 *adv* hacia el sudoeste, en dirección sudoeste

southwestwards [saʊθ'westwədz] *adv* hacia el sudoeste, en dirección sudoeste

souvenir [suːvə'nɪə(r)] *n* recuerdo *m*; **he had a black eye as a s. of the fight** le quedó un ojo morado de *or* como recuerdo de la pelea ►► ***s. shop*** tienda *f* de recuerdos

sou'wester [saʊ'westə(r)] *n* **(a)** *(hat)* sueste *m* **(b)** *(wind)* viento *m* sudoeste

sovereign ['sɒvrɪn] **1** *n* **(a)** *(monarch)* soberano(a) *m,f* **(b)** *(coin)* soberano *m*

2 *adj* **(a)** *Pol* soberano(a) ►► ***s. state*** estado *m* soberano **(b)** *Literary (utmost) (scorn, indifference)* soberano(a)

sovereignty ['sɒvrɪntɪ] *n* soberanía *f*

Soviet ['səʊvɪet] *Formerly* **1** *n (person)* soviético(a) *m,f*; **the Soviets** los soviéticos

2 *adj* soviético(a) ►► ***the S. Bloc*** el bloque soviético; ***the S. Union*** la Unión Soviética

soviet ['səʊvɪet] *n Hist (council)* soviet *m*

sovietologist [səʊvɪə'tɒlədʒɪst] *n* sovietólogo(a) *m,f*

sow[1] [səʊ] (*pt* **sowed** [səʊd], *pp* **sown** [səʊn] *or* **sowed**) **1** *vt* **(a)** *(seeds)* sembrar; **to s. a field with wheat** sembrar trigo en un campo; IDIOM **to s. one's (wild) oats** darse la gran vida de joven **(b)** *(cause) (discord, terror)* sembrar; **to s. (the seeds of) doubt in sb's mind** sembrar la duda en la mente de alguien

2 *vi* PROV **as you s. so shall you reap** se recoge lo que se siembra, según siembres, así recogerás

sow[2] [saʊ] *n (female pig)* cerda *f*, puerca *f*, *Am* chancha *f* ►► ***s. thistle*** cerraja *f*

sower ['səʊə(r)] *n* **(a)** *(person)* sembrador(ora) *m,f* **(b)** *(machine)* sembradora *f*

sown *pp of* **sow**[1]

sox [sɒks] *npl US Fam* calcetines *mpl*, *RP* zoquetes *mpl*

soy [sɔɪ] *n esp US* soja *f* ►► ***s. bean*** semilla *f* de soja; ***s. bean oil*** aceite *m* de soja; ***s. sauce*** (salsa *f* de) soja *f*

soya ['sɔɪə] *n* soja *f* ►► ***s. bean*** semilla *f* de soja; ***s. bean oil*** aceite *m* de soja; ***s. milk*** leche *f* de soja

sozzled ['sɒzəld] *adj Fam* **to be s.** estar como una cuba *or Esp* mamado(a) *or Col* caído(a) de la perra *or Méx* ahogado(a) *or RP* en pedo; **to get s.** agarrarse un pedo

SP [es'piː] *n* (*abbr* **starting price**) *(in horse racing)* precio *m* de las apuestas a la salida; *Br Fam* **to give sb the SP on sth** contarle a alguien de qué va la película, decirle a alguien de qué va algo

spa [spɑː] *n* **(a)** *(resort)* balneario *m* **(b)** *(spring)* manantial *m* de aguas termales **(c)** *(whirlpool bath)* baño *m* de hidromasaje **(d)** *(health club)* centro *m* de salud y belleza

SPACE [speɪs] **1** *n* **(a)** *(room)* espacio *m*, sitio *m*; **the town has a lot of open s.** la ciudad tiene muchos espacios abiertos; **the house has plenty of storage s.** la casa tiene mucho espacio *or* sitio para guardar cosas; **to make s. for sth/sb** hacer sitio para algo/alguien; **to take up a lot of s.** ocupar mucho espacio *or* sitio; *Fig* **I need you to give me more s.** necesito que me des más tiempo para mí

(b) *(individual place)* sitio *m*; *(on printed form)* espacio *m* (en blanco); **leave a s. between the lines** deja un espacio entre las líneas; **a parking s.** un sitio para estacionar *or Esp* aparcar; **wide open spaces** grandes extensiones; **she cleared a s. on her desk** hizo un sitio en su mesa; **watch this s. for more details** les seguiremos informando ►► ***s. bar*** *(on keyboard)* barra *f* espaciadora; ***s. heater*** radiador *m*

(c) *(area all around)* espacio *m*; **s. and time** espacio y tiempo; **to stare into s.** mirar al vacío

(d) *(gap)* hueco *m*

(e) *(period of time)* espacio *m*, intervalo *m*; **a short s. of time** un breve espacio de tiempo; **in the s. of a year** en el espacio de un año

(f) *(outer space)* espacio *m*; **in s.** en el espacio ►► ***the s. age*** la era espacial; ***s. blanket*** manta *f* espacial; *Fam* ***s. cadet*** *or US* ***case:* he's a bit of a s. cadet** *or US* **case** está un poco colgado, está *or* anda siempre como alucinado; ***s. capsule*** cápsula *f* espacial; ***s. centre*** centro *m* espacial; ***s. exploration*** exploración *f* espacial *or* del espacio; ***s. flight*** *(travel)* viajes *mpl* espaciales *or* por el espacio; *(journey)* vuelo *m* espacial; ***S. Invaders***® marcianitos *mpl*; ***s. module*** módulo *m* espacial; ***s. platform*** plataforma *f* espacial; ***s. probe*** sonda *f* espacial; ***s. program(me)*** programa *f* espacial; ***the s. race*** la carrera espacial; ***s. rocket*** cohete *m* espacial; ***s. shuttle*** transbordador *m* espacial; ***s. sickness*** enfermedad *f* del espacio; ***s. station*** estación *f* espacial; ***s. suit*** traje *m* espacial; ***s. travel*** viajes *mpl* espaciales; ***s. walk*** paseo *m* espacial

2 *vt* espaciar; **the buildings are closely/widely spaced** los edificios están muy juntos/separados, hay muy poco/mucho espacio entre los edificios; **she has widely spaced eyes** tiene los ojos muy separados

►**space out 1** *vt sep (arrange with gaps)* espaciar, separar; **the seminars are spaced out over several weeks** los seminarios se celebrarán a lo largo de varias semanas

2 *vi (move apart)* apartarse

space-age ['speɪseɪdʒ] *adj* **(a)** *(relating to space travel)* de la era espacial **(b)** *Fam (futuristic)* futurista

spacecraft ['speɪskrɑːft] *n* nave *f* espacial, astronave *f*

spaced-out ['speɪst'aʊt] *adj Fam* **to be** *or* **feel s.** *(dazed)* estar atontado(a); *(after taking drugs)* estar colocado(a) *or* colgado(a)

space-filler ['speɪsfɪlə(r)] *n (in newspaper)* cuña *f* informativa

spacelab ['speɪslæb] *n* laboratorio *m* espacial

spaceman ['speɪsmæn] *n* **(a)** *(astronaut)* astronauta *m* **(b)** *(extraterrestrial)* hombre *m* del espacio (exterior)

space-saving ['speɪs'seɪvɪŋ] *adj* que ahorra *or* permite ahorrar espacio

spaceship ['speɪsʃɪp] *n* nave *f* espacial

space-sick ['speɪssɪk] *adj* **to be s.** padecer la enfermedad del espacio

space-time ['speɪs'taɪm] *n* espacio-tiempo *m* ►► ***s. continuum*** espacio-tiempo *m*

spacewoman ['speɪswʊmən] *n (astronaut)* astronauta *f*

spacey ['speɪsɪ] *adj Fam* **(a)** *(music)* sideral, intergaláctico(a) **(b)** *(person)* **to be s.** vivir en otro planeta

spacing ['speɪsɪŋ] *n Typ (horizontal)* espacio *m*; *(vertical)* interlineado *m*; **typed in double s.** escrito a doble espacio

spacious ['speɪʃəs] *adj (house, room, office)* espacioso(a); *(park, garden)* amplio(a), extenso(a)

spaciousness ['speɪʃəsnɪs] *n (of house, room, office)* espaciosidad *f*; *(of park, garden)* amplitud *f*, gran extensión *f*

Spackle® ['spækəl] *n US* masilla *f* (en polvo)

spackle ['spækəl] *vt US (hole, joint)* rellenar con masilla

spade [speɪd] *n* **(a)** *(tool)* pala *f*; IDIOM **to call a s. a s.** llamar a las cosas por su nombre, llamar al pan pan y al vino vino **(b)** *(in cards)* pica *f*; **spades** picas *fpl*; **ace/nine of spades** as/nueve de picas; IDIOM *Fam* **to have sth in spades** tener algo en cantidades industriales *or* a porrillo **(c)** *very Fam Old-fashioned (black person)* = término ofensivo para referirse a un negro

> **False friend:** The Spanish noun **espada** is not a translation for the English word **spade**. In Spanish the main meaning of **espada** is "sword".

spadeful ['speɪdfʊl] *n* palada *f*; *Fam* **by the s.** a punta de pala

spadework ['speɪdwɜːk] *n* trabajo *m* previo *or* preliminar

spag bol ['spæg'bɔːl] *n Br Fam (spaghetti bolognese)* espaguetis *mpl* a la boloñesa

spaghetti [spə'getɪ] *n* espaguetis *mpl*; *Fam Fig* **it's like S. Junction around here!** ¡qué tráfico más caótico hay aquí! ►► ***s. bolognese*** espaguetis *mpl* a la boloñesa; ***s. western*** spaghetti western *m*

Spain [speɪn] *n* España

spake [speɪk] *Archaic pt of* **speak**

Spam® [spæm] *n* = fiambre de cerdo en conserva ►► ***S. fritter*** = fritura de fiambre de cerdo enlatado

spam [spæm] *Comptr* **1** *n* correo *m* basura

2 *vt* enviar correo basura a

3 *vi* enviar correo basura

spammer ['spæmə(r)] *n Comptr* = persona que envía correo basura

spamming ['spæmɪŋ] *n Comptr* envío *m* de correo basura

span[1] [spæn] **1** *n* **(a)** *(of hand)* palmo *m*; *(of wing)* envergadura *f* **(b)** *(of arch)* luz *f*, vano *m*; *(of bridge)* arcada *f*, ojo *m* **(c)** *(of time)* periodo *m*, lapso *m*; **his work covers a s. of twenty years** su obra abarca un periodo de veinte años **(d)** *(of knowledge, interests)* repertorio *m*, gama *f* **(e)** *(unit of measurement)* palmo *m* **(f)** *(of horses)* tronco *m*; *(of oxen)* yunta *f*

2 *vt* (*pt & pp* **spanned**) **(a)** *(of life, knowledge)* abarcar; **his career spanned half a century** su carrera abarcó medio siglo **(b)** *(of bridge)* atravesar, cruzar **(c)** *(build bridge over)* **they spanned the river with a bridge** tendieron un puente sobre el río

span[2] *pt of* **spin**

Spandex® ['spændeks] *n* tejido *m* de poliuretano

spangle ['spæŋgəl] *n* lentejuela *f*

spangled ['spæŋgəld], **spangly** ['spæŋglɪ] *adj* de lentejuelas

Spanglish ['spæŋglɪʃ] *n* spanglish *m*

spangly = **spangled**

Spaniard ['spænɪəd] *n* español(ola) *m,f*

spaniel ['spænjəl] *n* spaniel *m*

Spanish ['spænɪʃ] **1** *npl (people)* **the S.** los españoles
2 *n (language)* español *m*, castellano *m*; **S. class/teacher** clase/profesor(ora) de español
3 *adj* español(ola) ▸▸ ***S. America*** Hispanoamérica *f*; ***S. American*** hispanoamericano(a) *m,f*; ***the S. Armada*** la Armada Invencible; ***S. broom*** retama *f* de olor; ***the S. Civil War*** la guerra civil española; ***S. fly*** *(substance)* cantaridina *f*; ***S. guitar*** guitarra *f* española; ***the S. Inquisition*** la (Santa) Inquisición; ***S. moss*** musgo *m* negro; ***S. omelette*** tortilla *f* española *or* de *Esp* patatas *or Am* papas; ***S. onion*** cebolla *f* española; ***S. pointer*** perdiguero de Burgos

Spanish-speaking ['spænɪʃspi:kɪŋ] *adj* hispanohablante

spank [spæŋk] **1** *n* **to give sb a s.** darle un azote a alguien
2 *vt (once)* dar un azote *or* una palmada a; *(several)* dar unos azotes a, azotar; **she threatened to s. his bottom** lo amenazó con calentarle el trasero

spanking ['spæŋkɪŋ] **1** *n* azotaina *f*; **to give sb a s.** dar a alguien una azotaina
2 *adj Fam (breeze)* fuerte; **to go at a s. pace** ir a galope tendido *or Esp* a toda pastilla
3 *adv Fam* **s. new** flamante; **s. clean** como los chorros del oro, reluciente; **they had a s. good time** se lo pasaron bomba *or* en grande

spanner ['spænə(r)] *n Br* llave *f* plana *(herramienta)*; IDIOM **to throw a s. in the works** fastidiar el asunto

spar[1] [spɑ:(r)] *n* **(a)** *(on ship)* palo *m*, verga *f* **(b)** *(mineral)* espato *m*

spar[2] *(pt & pp* **sparred***)* *vi* **to s. with sb** *(in boxing)* entrenar con alguien como sparring; *(argue)* discutir en tono cordial con alguien

SPARE [speə(r)] **1** *n* **(a)** *(spare part)* (pieza *f* de) recambio *m or* repuesto *m*; *(tyre)* rueda *f* de repuesto *or RP* de auxilio, *Méx* llanta *f* de refacción; **I've lost my pencil, have you got a s.?** he perdido el lápiz, ¿tienes uno de sobra?
(b) *(in bowling)* semipleno *m*
2 *adj* **(a)** *(available)* de más; *(surplus)* sobrante; **do you have a s. pencil?** ¿tienes un lápiz de sobra?; **a s. moment** un rato libre; **I always take a s. pair of socks with me** siempre llevo un par de calcetines de más; **we've got plenty of s. sheets** tenemos muchos juegos de sábanas de sobra; **is this seat s.?** ¿está libre este asiento?; **to be going s.** sobrar ▸▸ ***s. key*** llave *f* extra *or* adicional; ***s. parts*** recambios *m*, repuestos *m*, piezas *fpl* de recambio *or* repuesto; ***s. ribs*** costillas *fpl* de cerdo *or* puerco *or Am* chancho; ***s. room*** habitación *f* de invitados; ***s. time*** tiempo *m* libre; ***s. tyre*** rueda *f* de repuesto *or RP* de auxilio, *Méx* llanta *f* de refacción; *Br Fam Fig (around waist)* michelines *mpl*, *Méx* llantas *fpl*, *RP* rollos *mpl*; ***s. wheel*** rueda *f* de repuesto *or RP* de auxilio, *Méx* llanta *f* de refacción
(b) *(frugal) (meal, style, room)* sobrio(a), sencillo(a)
(c) *Literary (tall and lean) (person, build)* enjuto(a)
(d) *Br Fam (angry)* **to go s.** subirse por las paredes, *Méx* ponerse como agua para chocolate, *RP* ponerse verde; **to drive sb s.** hacer perder los estribos a alguien
3 *vt* **(a)** *(go without)* **can you s. the time?** ¿tienes tiempo?; **thank you for sparing the time to talk to me** gracias por sacar tiempo para hablar conmigo; **could you s. me some milk?** ¿puedes dejarme un poco de leche?; **can you s. me some change, please?** ¿me podría dar algo, por favor?; **I'm afraid we can't s. you next week** me temo que no podemos prescindir de ti la próxima semana; **to s. a thought for sb** acordarse de alguien; **have you got any paper to s.?** ¿no te sobrará algo de papel?; **to have no time to s.** no tener ni un minuto libre, no poder entretenerse; **they arrived with five minutes to s.** llegaron cinco minutos antes; **they won with plenty to s.** ganaron sin despeinarse; **he's got enough money and to s.** le sobra el dinero; PROV **s. the rod and spoil the child** hay que recurrir al castigo para lograr resultados
(b) *(in negative constructions)* **to s. no expense/effort** no reparar en gastos/esfuerzos; **to s. no pains (to do sth)** no ahorrar *or* escatimar esfuerzos (para hacer algo)
(c) *(save)* **to s. sb the trouble** *or* **bother of doing sth** ahorrar a alguien las molestias de hacer algo; **at least we were spared that indignity** al menos nos libramos de esa indignidad; **s. me the details!** ¡ahórrame los detalles!; **I'll s. you the rest** te ahorraré lo demás; *Br* **to s. sb's blushes** ahorrarle el bochorno a alguien
(d) *(show mercy towards)* **we begged him to s. us** le pedimos que se apiadara de nosotros; **nobody was spared** no perdonaron a nadie; **not one of the buildings was spared by the storm** ningún edificio se libró de la tormenta; **to s. sb's life** perdonarle la vida a alguien; **to s. sb's feelings** ahorrar sufrimientos a alguien

spare-part surgery ['speə'pɑ:t'sɜ:dʒərɪ] *n* cirugía *f* de transplantes

spare-time ['speə'taɪm] *adj* de ocio

sparing ['speərɪŋ] *adj* parco(a) **(with** en**)**; **to be s. with the salt** no derrochar la sal; **they've been rather s. with the marzipan on this cake** han escatimado mazapán en este pastel, a este pastel no le han puesto mucho mazapán, que digamos; **to be s. with praise** no prodigarse mucho en elogios, ser parco(a) en elogios; **the author makes s. use of metaphors** el autor hace un uso limitado *or* restringido de la metáfora

sparingly ['speərɪŋlɪ] *adv (to use)* con moderación, en pequeñas dosis; *(to eat)* con moderación, con mesura; *(to praise)* moderadamente; **apply the glue s.** aplicar una pequeña cantidad de cola

spark [spɑ:k] **1** *n* **(a)** *(electrical, from fire)* chispa *f*; IDIOM **sparks flew** salían chispas; **sparks will fly when he learns of this** va a echar chispas cuando se entere de esto
(b) *(trace) (of intelligence, enthusiasm)* chispa *f*, pizca *f*; **he hasn't a s. of imagination** no tiene ni gota *or* chispa de imaginación
(c) *(liveliness)* **he has genuine s.** tiene auténtica chispa
(d) *Aut* ***s. coil*** bobina *f* de inducción; ***s. plug*** bujía *f*
(e) *Br Fam* **sparks** *(electrician)* chispas *mf inv*
2 *vi* **(a)** *(produce sparks)* echar chispas **(b)** *(spark plug, ignition)* producir el encendido; **the game sparked into life in the second half** el partido empezó a ponerse entusiasmante en la segunda mitad

▸ **spark off** *vt sep* desencadenar

sparking plug ['spɑ:kɪŋplʌg] *n Br Aut* bujía *f*

sparkle ['spɑ:kəl] **1** *n* **(a)** *(of light, eyes, diamond)* destello *m*; **she has a s. in her eye** tiene una mirada vivaracha *or* picaresca **(b)** *(liveliness)* chispa *f*; **the s. had gone out of their marriage** su matrimonio ya no tenía ninguna chispa
2 *vi* **(a)** *(light, eyes, diamond)* destellar; **his eyes sparkled with mischief** en sus ojos brillaba un destello de picardía **(b)** *(person, conversation)* brillar, ser chispeante

sparkler ['spɑ:klə(r)] *n* **(a)** *(firework)* bengala *f* **(b)** *Fam (diamond)* diamante *m*

sparkling ['spɑ:klɪŋ] *adj* **(a)** *(light, eyes, diamond)* centelleante, brillante **(b)** *(conversation, wit)* chispeante, lleno(a) de ingenio; *(performance)* brillante, fulgurante **(c)** *(effervescent) (mineral water)* con gas; **s. wine** vino *m* espumoso

sparklingly ['spɑ:klɪŋlɪ] *adv* **(a)** *(clean)* relucientemente, resplandecientemente **(b)** *(witty)* extraordinariamente

sparring ['spɑ:rɪŋ] *n (in boxing)* pelea *f* con sparring; *(debating)* enfrentamiento *m* dialéctico amistoso, discusión *f* amistosa ▸▸ ***s. match*** *(debate)* contienda *f* dialéctica amistosa; ***s. partner*** *(in boxing)* sparring *m*; *(in debate)* adversario(a) *m,f or* contrincante *mf* dialéctico(a)

sparrow ['spærəʊ] *n* gorrión *m*

sparrowhawk ['spærəʊhɔ:k] *n* gavilán *m*

sparse [spɑ:s] *adj (vegetation)* escaso(a), exiguo(a); *(population)* disperso(a); *(crowd, audience)* escaso(a), reducido(a); *(information)* somero(a), escaso(a); *(hair)* ralo(a); *(furnishings)* escaso(a), exiguo(a)

sparsely ['spɑ:slɪ] *adv (populated)* poco, dispersamente; *(covered)* escasamente, someramente; **s. furnished** poco amueblado(a)

sparseness ['spɑ:snɪs] *n (of vegetation)* escasez *f*, exigüidad *f*; *(of population)* dispersión *f*, escasa densidad *f*; *(of crowd, audience)* lo poco nutrido; *(of information)* carácter *m* somero; *(of hair)* escasez *f*, escasa abundancia *f*; *(of furnishings)* escasez *f*, exigüidad *f*

Sparta ['spɑ:tə] *n Hist* Esparta

Spartan ['spɑ:tən] *Hist* **1** *n* espartano(a) *m,f*
2 *adj* espartano(a)

spartan ['spɑ:tən] **1** *n (ascetic person)* espartano(a) *m,f*
2 *adj (ascetic)* espartano(a)

spasm ['spæzəm] *n* **(a)** *Med* espasmo *m*; **his leg went into s.** sufrió una contractura muscular **(b)** *(fit) (of coughing, jealousy, anger)* ataque *m*; *(of activity)* arranque *m*; **she went into spasms of laughter** le dio un ataque de risa; *Br* **I tend to work in spasms** tiendo a trabajar por rachas

spasmodic [spæz'mɒdɪk] *adj* **(a)** *(irregular)* intermitente **(b)** *Med* espasmódico(a)

spasmodically [spæz'mɒdɪklɪ] *adv (irregularly)* intermitentemente

spastic ['spæstɪk] **1** *n* **(a)** *Med* enfermo(a) *m,f* de parálisis cerebral **(b)** *very Fam (idiot)* subnormal *mf*
2 *adj* **(a)** *Med* espástico(a) **(b)** *very Fam (idiotic)* (de) subnormal

spat[1] [spæt] *n* **(a)** *Fam (quarrel)* rifirrafe *m*, bronca *f* **(b)** *(worn over shoe)* polaina *f* **(c)** *(shellfish spawn)* hueva *f* de molusco *(especialmente ostra)*

spat[2] *pt & pp of* **spit**[2]

spate [speɪt] *n (of letters, crimes)* oleada *f*; **to be in full s.** *(river)* estar *or* bajar muy crecido; *(speaker)* estar en plena arenga

spatial ['speɪʃəl] *adj* espacial ►► ***s. awareness*** percepción *f* espacial, conciencia *f* del espacio

spatio-temporal [speɪʃɪəʊ'tempərəl] *adj* espaciotemporal

spatter ['spætə(r)] **1** *n* **(a)** *(stain)* salpicadura *f* **(b)** *(sound) (of rain, oil)* repiqueteo *m*; **a s. of applause rippled round the stadium** unos aplausos aislados se extendieron por el estadio

2 *vt* salpicar (**with** de); **he spattered ink on** *or* **over the table** salpicó de tinta la mesa

3 *vi* salpicar

-spattered [-'spætəd] *suffix* **blood/mud-s.** salpicado(a) de sangre/barro

spatula ['spætjʊlə] *n* **(a)** *(kitchen utensil)* espátula *f* **(b)** *Med* depresor *m*

spawn [spɔːn] **1** *n* **(a)** *(of frog, fish)* hueva *f* **(b)** *(of mushrooms)* micelio *m (de champiñón utilizado como semilla)* **(c)** *Pej (of humans)* hijos *mpl*, progenie *f*

2 *vt (give rise to)* generar

3 *vi (fish)* desovar

spawning-ground ['spɔːnɪŋ'graʊnd] *n* **(a)** *Zool* zona *f* de desove **(b)** *(for ideas, gossip)* caldo *m* de cultivo

spay [speɪ] *vt* esterilizar *(animales hembras)*

spaz [spæz], **spazzy** ['spæzɪ] *n very Fam* subnormal *mf*

SPCA [espiːsiː'eɪ] *n US* (*abbr* **Society for the Prevention of Cruelty to Animals**) ≃ Sociedad Protectora de Animales

SPCC [espiːsiː'siː] *n US* (*abbr* **Society for the Prevention of Cruelty to Children**) = asociación para la protección de la infancia

SPEAK [spiːk] **1** *vt* (*pt* **spoke** [spəʊk], *pp* **spoken** ['spəʊkən]) **(a)** *(utter)* pronunciar; **she always speaks her mind** siempre dice lo que piensa; **to s. the truth** decir la verdad; **nobody spoke a word** nadie dijo nada

(b) *(language)* hablar; **to s. Spanish** hablar español; **Spanish/English spoken** *(sign)* se habla inglés/español

2 *vi* **(a)** *(talk)* hablar, *esp Am* conversar, *Méx* platicar; **to s. to** *or* **with sb (about)** hablar *or esp Am* conversar *or Méx* platicar con alguien (de); **don't s. with your mouth full** no hables con la boca llena; **don't s. to your mother like that!** ¡no le hables así a tu madre!; **I'll s. to him about it** *(tell off)* hablaré con él al respecto; **s. to me!** ¡háblame!; **I'm not speaking to him** no me hablo con él; **they're not speaking (to each other)** no se hablan; **I know her to s. to** la conozco de haberla saludado alguna vez; **s. when you're spoken to** habla solamente cuando te dirijan la palabra; *Rel* **to s. in tongues** hablar lenguas extrañas; **to s. too soon** hablar antes de tiempo; **legally/morally speaking** (hablando) en términos legales/morales; **personally speaking...** personalmente...; **speaking as a politician** en tanto que político; **s. now or forever hold your peace** que hable ahora o calle para siempre; **so to s.** por así decirlo

(b) *(on phone)* **could I s. to Melissa?** ¿podría hablar con Melissa?; **Kate Smith speaking** soy Kate Smith, me llamo Kate Smith; **I'm speaking from Australia** llamo desde Australia, hablo desde Australia; **we spoke (on the phone) yesterday** hablamos (por teléfono) ayer; **who's speaking?** ¿de parte de quién?; **Mr Curry? – yes, speaking** ¿el señor Curry? – sí, soy yo *or* al aparato

(c) *(give a speech)* dar una charla; *(in debate, meeting)* intervenir; **the chair called upon Mrs Fox to s.** el presidente invitó a la señora Fox a que interviniese; **to s. from the floor** hablar desde el público; **to s. for/against a motion** hablar a favor de/en contra de una moción; **she spoke for over an hour** habló durante más de una hora; **he spoke on the subject of...** el tema de su charla fue...

(d) *Fig (make sound)* sonar

3 *n Pej* **computer/advertising s.** jerga informática/publicitaria

►**speak for** *vt insep* **(a)** *(talk on behalf of)* hablar en nombre de; **I'm quite capable of speaking for myself!** ¡que sé hablar!; **s. for yourself!** ¡no pluralices!; **the facts s. for themselves** los hechos hablan por sí solos *or* mismos; **the title speaks for itself** el título lo dice todo

(b) *(claim)* **the remaining places have all been spoken for** los sitios que quedan ya han sido adjudicados; **I'm spoken for** *(I have a boyfriend/girlfriend)* estoy ocupado(a)

►**speak of** *vt insep* **(a)** *(talk about)* hablar de; **speaking of holidays...** hablando de vacaciones...; **speaking of which...** hablando de lo cual...; **he always speaks well/highly of you** siempre habla muy bien de usted; **his plays are hugely popular, not to s. of his many novels** sus obras gozan de gran aceptación, por no hablar de sus muchas novelas; **you shouldn't s. ill of the dead, s. no ill of the dead** no se debe hablar mal de los muertos; **we haven't got any savings to s. of** no tenemos ningunos ahorros dignos de mención; **there was no snow to s. of** apenas había nieve; **it's not much** *or* **nothing to s. of** no es nada del otro mundo

(b) *(indicate)* **her performance speaks of a great future** su actuación anuncia un gran futuro; **his paintings s. of terrible loneliness** sus cuadros hablan de una soledad terrible

►**speak out** *vi* hablar abiertamente (**for/against** a favor de/en contra de)

►**speak up** *vi* **(a)** *(talk louder)* hablar más alto, levantar la voz

(b) *(express opinion)* hablar; **to s. up for sb** hablar en favor de alguien; **why didn't you s. up?** ¿por qué no dijiste nada?

speakeasy ['spiːkiːzɪ] *n* = bar clandestino durante la ley seca

speaker ['spiːkə(r)] *n* **(a)** *(person) (in conversation, on radio)* interlocutor(ora) *m,f*; *(at meeting)* orador(ora) *m,f*; *(at conference)* conferenciante *mf*, orador(ora) *m,f*, *Am* conferencista *mf*; **she's a good s.** es (una) buena oradora **(b)** *(of language)* hablante *mf*; **a Spanish s.** un(a) hispanohablante; **my parents are Welsh speakers** mis padres hablan galés **(c)** *Parl* **the S.** *(in UK)* el/la presidente(a) de la Cámara de los Comunes; *(in US)* el/la presidente(a) de la Cámara de Representantes **(d)** *(of hi-fi system)* bafle *m*; *(loudspeaker)* altavoz *m*, *Am* altoparlante *m*, *Am* parlante *m*, *Méx* bocina *f*

-speaking [-'spiːkɪŋ] *suffix* **(a)** *(person)* **they're both German/Spanish-s.** los dos son germanohablantes/hispanohablantes **(b)** *(country)* **French/English-s. countries** países francófonos/anglófonos

speaking ['spiːkɪŋ] **1** *n (skill)* oratoria *f*

2 *adj (doll, robot)* parlante; *Theat & Cin* **a s. part** un papel con diálogo; **she has a good s. voice** tiene buena voz para la oratoria; **to be on s. terms** *(after a quarrel)* haber hecho las paces; **we're barely on s. terms** apenas nos dirigimos la palabra ►► ***s. clock*** información *f* horaria

spear [spɪə(r)] **1** *n* **(a)** *(for thrusting)* lanza *f*; *(for throwing)* jabalina *f* **(b) asparagus spears** (puntas *fpl* de) espárragos *mpl*

2 *vt* **(a)** *(fish)* pescar con arpón, arponear **(b)** *(food)* pinchar; **he speared a piece of meat with his fork** pinchó un trozo de carne con el tenedor

speargun ['spɪəgʌn] *n* arpón *m* submarino

spearhead ['spɪəhed] **1** *n* **(a)** *(tip of spear)* punta *f* de lanza **(b)** *(of attack, campaign)* punta *f* de lanza

2 *vt (attack, campaign)* encabezar

spearmint ['spɪəmɪnt] **1** *n* **(a)** *(plant)* hierbabuena *f* **(b)** *(flavour)* menta *f*

2 *adj (toothpaste, chewing gum)* con sabor a menta, mentolado(a)

spearwort ['spɪəwɜːt] *n* flámula *f*

spec [spek] *n Fam* **(a)** *(specification)* características *fpl* técnicas **(b)** IDIOM **to do sth on s.** hacer algo por si acaso; **he bought it on s.** lo compró sin verlo

speccy ['spekɪ] *Br Fam* **1** *n* cuatro ojos *mf inv*, *Esp* gafotas *mf inv*, *Méx* cuatro lámparas *mf inv*, *RP* anteojudo(a) *m,f*

2 *adj* gafudo(a)

special ['speʃəl] **1** *n* **(a)** *(on menu)* **today's** *or* **the chef's s.** el plato del día; **the house s.** la especialidad de la casa **(b)** *(TV programme)* (programa *m*) especial *m*; *(magazine, newspaper)* número *m* extraordinario **(c)** *(train)* tren *m* especial **(d)** *(special offer)* oferta *f* especial; *US* **to be on s.** estar de *or* en oferta

2 *adj* **(a)** *(particular, specific)* especial; **pay s. attention to the details** presta especial atención a los detalles; **you need s. permission** necesitas un permiso especial; **we have no s. plans** no tenemos ningún plan en especial ►► ***s. education*** educación *f* especial; ***s. educational needs*** necesidades *fpl* educativas especiales; ***s. interest group*** grupo *m* con intereses especiales; ***s. needs*** necesidades *fpl* especiales; ***s. school*** escuela *f* para alumnos con necesidades especiales; ***s. teams*** *(in American football)* = equipos de jugadores especializados en determinadas jugadas

(b) *(important)* especial; **on s. occasions** en ocasiones especiales; **what's so s. about the 9th of November?** ¿qué tiene de especial el 9 de noviembre? ►► ***s. agent*** agente *mf* especial; ***S. Air Service*** = comando de operaciones especiales del ejército británico, *Esp* ≃ GEO *m*; ***s. assignment*** comisión *f* de servicio; **to be on s. assignment** estar en comisión de servicio; *Br* ***S. Branch*** = servicio policial de seguridad del Estado; ***s. constable*** *(in UK)* policía *mf* de reserva; ***s. correspondent*** enviado(a) *m,f* especial; ***s. delivery*** envío *m* urgente, *Esp* ≃ postal exprés *m*; **to send sth s. delivery** enviar algo por correo urgente; ***s. envoy*** enviado(a) *m,f* extraordinario(a)

(c) *(valued)* **you're very s. to me** tienes un lugar muy especial en mi corazón; **she's a very s. person** es alguien muy especial; **is there**

anyone s. in your life at the moment? ¿hay alguien especial en tu vida en este momento?

(**d**) *(privileged) (treatment)* especial, privilegiado(a) ▸▸ ***s. licence*** = licencia que permite el matrimonio sin correr las amonestaciones

(**e**) *(unusual)* especial, fuera de lo común; **we didn't do anything s.** *(on holiday, at weekend)* no hicimos nada especial *or* nada de particular; **it's nothing s.** no es nada del otro mundo; **she thinks she's something s.** se cree muy importante *or* especial ▸▸ ***s. edition*** *(of newspaper, magazine)* edición *f* extraordinaria; *Cin* ***s. effects*** efectos *mpl* especiales; ***s. offer*** oferta *f* especial; **to be on s. offer** estar en oferta especial; *Law* ***s. pleading*** alegatos *mpl* especiosos; *Pol* ***s. powers*** competencias *fpl* extraordinarias; ***s. stage*** *(in rallying)* etapa *f* especial

(**f**) *(very good)* especial, único(a); **this player is s.** este jugador es único

specialism [ˈspeʃəlɪzəm] *n (subject)* especialidad *f*

specialist [ˈspeʃəlɪst] **1** *n* (**a**) *(expert)* especialista *mf* (**b**) *Med* especialista *mf*; **heart s.** cardiólogo(a); **cancer s.** oncólogo(a)

2 *adj (knowledge, work, publication)* especializado(a) ▸▸ ***s. subject*** especialidad *f*

speciality [speʃɪˈælɪtɪ], *US* **specialty** [ˈspeʃəltɪ] *n* (**a**) *(service, product)* especialidad *f*; **the s. of the house** la especialidad de la casa; **a s. of the region** una especialidad típica de la región (**b**) *(area of study)* especialidad *f*

specialization [speʃəlaɪˈzeɪʃən] *n* (**a**) *(process)* especialización *f* (**b**) *(subject)* especialidad *f*

specialize [ˈspeʃəlaɪz] *vi* especializarse (**in** en)

specialized [ˈspeʃəlaɪzd] *adj* especializado(a)

specially [ˈspeʃəlɪ] *adv (in particular)* especialmente; **it isn't s. interesting/entertaining** no es especialmente interesante/divertido; **she had a dress s. made** le hicieron un vestido para la ocasión

specialty *US* = **speciality**

specie [ˈspiːʃɪ] *n Fin (coins)* monedas *fpl*; **in s.** con *or* en monedas

species [ˈspiːʃiːz] (*pl* **species**) *n* especie *f* ▸▸ ***s. barrier*** barrera *f* de las especies; **to cross the s. barrier** cruzar la barrera de las especies

specific [spɪˈsɪfɪk] **1** *n* (**a**) **specifics** detalles *mpl*; **let's get down to the specifics** entremos en (los) detalles (**b**) *Med* específico *m*

2 *adj* (**a**) *(particular) (case, task, sequence)* específico(a); **for no s. reason** sin ningún motivo en particular; **in this s. case** en este caso concreto; **to be s. to** ser específico(a) *or* propio(a) de; **what did he say? – nothing s.** ¿qué dijo? – nada en especial *or* de particular ▸▸ *Phys* ***s. gravity*** peso *m* específico

(**b**) *(explicit) (command, instructions)* preciso(a), concreto(a); **to be s.,...** para ser más preciso,...; **to be s. about sth** ser claro(a) respecto a algo; **could you be more s.?** ¿podrías especificar *or* concretar más?

specifically [spɪˈsɪfɪklɪ] *adv* (**a**) *(expressly)* específicamente; **I s. asked for a window seat** especifiqué que quería un asiento de ventanilla; **we were s. forbidden to tell her** nos prohibieron expresamente que le dijéramos nada (**b**) *(precisely)* precisamente, concretamente; **she's studying physics, or more s., quantum mechanics** está estudiando física, más concretamente, mecánica cuántica

specification [spesɪfɪˈkeɪʃən] *n* (**a**) *(technical details)* especificación *f*; **made to the client's s.** hecho(a) según las exigencias (específicas) del cliente; **specifications** *(of machine)* especificaciones *fpl or* características *fpl* técnicas (**b**) *(stipulation)* especificación *f*, estipulación *f*

specify [ˈspesɪfaɪ] **1** *vt* especificar; **the rules s. a 5-minute break** el reglamento estipula cinco minutos de descanso; **as specified** *(in rules, agreement)* de acuerdo con lo estipulado; **on a date to be specified** en la fecha en que se determine; **unless otherwise specified** salvo que se indique lo contrario

2 *vi* **which colour do they want? – they didn't s.** ¿qué color quieren? – no lo han especificado

specimen [ˈspesɪmɪn] *n* (**a**) *(sample) (of mineral, handwriting, blood, urine)* muestra *f* ▸▸ ***s. bottle*** frasco *m* (de recogida) de orina; ***s. copy*** ejemplar *m* de muestra; ***s. signature*** modelo *m* de firma (**b**) *(single example)* espécimen *m*, ejemplar *m*; **this butterfly is a superb s.** éste es un magnífico ejemplar de mariposa (**c**) *Fam Pej (person)* **he's an odd s.** es un bicho raro; *Hum* **he's a fine s.!** ¡es un buen ejemplar!

specious [ˈspiːʃəs] *adj Formal* especioso(a), engañoso(a)

speciousness [ˈspiːʃəsnɪs] *n Formal* carácter *m* especioso *or* engañoso

speck [spek] **1** *n* (**a**) *(particle) (of dust, dirt)* mota *f* (**b**) *(stain) (of paint, ink, blood)* salpicadura *f*, pequeña mancha *f* (**c**) *(distant dot)* **a s. on the horizon** un punto en el horizonte (**d**) *(tiny amount) (of salt, milk)* pizca *f*; **there isn't a s. of truth in the rumour** no hay ni un asomo de verdad en el rumor

2 *vt* **his trousers were specked with paint** tenía los pantalones salpicados (de pequeñas manchas) de pintura

speckle [ˈspekəl] **1** *n* mota *f*, pinta *f*

2 *vt* motear

speckled [ˈspekəld] *adj (egg)* moteado(a); *(hen)* pinto(a)

specs [speks] *npl Fam* (**a**) *(spectacles)* gafas *fpl*; **a pair of s.** unas gafas (**b**) *(of machine)* especificaciones *fpl or* características *fpl* técnicas

spectacle [ˈspektəkəl] *n* (**a**) *(show)* espectáculo *m* (**b**) *(sight)* espectáculo *m*; **he was a sorry** *or* **sad s.** dio un espectáculo lamentable; **to make a s. of oneself** dar el espectáculo, dar el número (**c**) **spectacles** *(glasses)* gafas *fpl*, *Am* lentes *fpl*, *Am* anteojos *mpl*; **a pair of spectacles** unas gafas ▸▸ ***s. case*** *(hard)* estuche *m* de gafas; *(soft)* funda *f* de gafas

spectacled [ˈspektəkld] *adj* (**a**) *(person)* con gafas (**b**) *Zool* de anteojos ▸▸ ***s. bear*** oso *m* de anteojos

spectacular [spekˈtækjʊlə(r)] **1** *n Theat* gran espectáculo *m*

2 *adj* espectacular

spectacularly [spekˈtækjʊləlɪ] *adv (improve, increase)* espectacularmente, de forma espectacular; *(big, beautiful)* espectacularmente; **to fail s.** fracasar estrepitosamente; **the movie was s. bad** la película era tremendamente mala; **the play was s. successful** la obra tuvo un éxito espectacular

spectate [spekˈteɪt] *vi* ser espectador(ora)

spectator [spekˈteɪtə(r)] *n* espectador(ora) *m,f*; **the spectators** el público, los espectadores ▸▸ ***s. sport*** deporte *m* para espectadores

specter *US* = **spectre**

spectra *pl of* **spectrum**

spectral [ˈspektrəl] *adj* espectral

spectre, *US* **specter** [ˈspektə(r)] *n* (**a**) *(ghost)* espectro *m* (**b**) *(threat)* **the s. of war/famine** el espectro de la guerra/del hambre

spectrogram [ˈspektrəgræm] *n* espectrograma *m*

spectrograph [ˈspektrəgrɑːf] *n* espectrógrafo *m*

spectrography [spekˈtrɒgrəfɪ] *n* espectrografía *f*

spectrometer [spekˈtrɒmɪtə(r)] *n* espectrómetro *m*

spectrometry [spekˈtrɒmɪtrɪ] *n* espectrometría *f*

spectroscope [ˈspektrəskəʊp] *n* espectroscopio *m*

spectroscopy [spekˈtrɒskəpɪ] *n* espectroscopia *f*

spectrum [ˈspektrəm] (*pl* **spectra** [ˈspektrə]) *n* (**a**) *Phys* espectro *m* ▸▸ ***s. analysis*** análisis *m* espectroscópico

(**b**) *(range)* espectro *m*; **the whole s. of political views** todo el espectro *or* abanico de ideas políticas; **there is agreement on this issue right across the political s.** existe unanimidad sobre este asunto en todo el espectro político; **at the other end of the s., we have the atheists** en el otro extremo del espectro se encuentran los ateos

speculate [ˈspekjʊleɪt] *vi* (**a**) *Fin* especular (**on** en); **to s. on the stock market** especular en (la) bolsa, jugar a la *or* en bolsa (**b**) *(conjecture)* especular (**about** sobre); **what her motives were, we can only s.** sólo podemos hacer especulaciones sobre cuáles fueron sus motivos; **it is widely speculated that...** se especula mucho sobre la posibilidad de que...

speculation [spekjʊˈleɪʃən] *n* (**a**) *Fin* especulación *f* (**b**) *(conjecture)* especulación *f*; **it's pure s.** no son más que conjeturas; **there's been a lot of s. in the press about her motives** se ha especulado mucho en la prensa sobre cuáles han sido sus razones

speculative [ˈspekjʊlətɪv] *adj (figures, investment)* especulativo(a); *(suggestion)* especulativo(a), teórico(a); *(shot, attempt)* aventurado(a)

speculatively [ˈspekjʊlətɪvlɪ] *adv (to invest)* de forma especulativa, haciendo especulaciones; *(to suggest)* especulativamente, de manera especulativa; *(to shoot)* aventuradamente

speculator [ˈspekjʊleɪtə(r)] *n Fin* especulador(ora) *m,f*

speculum [ˈspekjʊləm] (*pl* **specula** [ˈspekjʊlə]) *n Med* espéculo *m*

sped *pt & pp of* **speed**

speech [spiːtʃ] *n* (**a**) *(faculty)* habla *f*; **to recover one's s.** recobrar el habla; **she chose to express herself in s.** optó por expresarse verbalmente ▸▸ ***s. bubble*** bocadillo *m*; ***s. defect*** defecto *m* del habla *or* de dicción; ***s. impediment*** defecto *m* del habla *or* de dicción; *Comptr* ***s. recognition*** reconocimiento *m* del habla; ***s. synthesis*** síntesis *f* del habla; ***s. synthesizer*** sintetizador *m* de voz; ***s. therapist*** logopeda *mf*; ***s. therapy*** logopedia *f*

(**b**) *(manner of speaking)* habla *f*; **his s. was slurred** tenía un habla dificultosa

(c) *(language)* habla *f*, lenguaje *m*; **things which people say in everyday s.** cosas que se dicen en el habla cotidiana ►► ***s. pattern*** modelo *m* de dicción

(d) *(of politician, at conference)* discurso *m*; *Theat* parlamento *m*; **to give** *or* **make a s.** dar *or* pronunciar un discurso; **s.! s.!** ¡que hable!, ¡que hable! ►► *Br Sch* ***s. day*** ceremonia *f* de fin de curso

(e) *Gram* **part of s.** categoría gramatical; **direct/indirect s.** estilo directo/indirecto

(f) *Ling* ***s. act*** acto *m* de habla; ***s. community*** comunidad *f* lingüística

speechify ['spiːtʃɪfaɪ] *vi Fam* soltar un rollo, perorar

speechless ['spiːtʃlɪs] *adj* sin habla; **she was s. with admiration/anger** se quedó muda de admiración/furia; **I'm s.!** ¡me he quedado boquiabierto(a) *or* sin habla!; **to be left s.** quedarse sin habla

speechlessly ['spiːtʃlɪslɪ] *adv* estupefacto(a), con estupefacción

speechmaking ['spiːtʃmeɪkɪŋ] *n* (a) *(public speaking)* oratoria *f*, arte *m* de hablar en público (b) *Pej (speechifying)* perorata *f*

speechwriter ['spiːtʃraɪtə(r)] *n* redactor(ora) *m,f* de discursos

speed [spiːd] **1** *n* (a) *(rate of movement)* velocidad *f*; **the s. of light/of sound** la velocidad de la luz/del sonido; **typing s.** velocidad escribiendo a máquina; **to do a s. of 100 km/h** ir *or* circular a una velocidad de 100 kilómetros por hora; **what s. was he going at** *or* **doing?** ¿a qué velocidad iba?, ¿qué velocidad llevaba?; **at s.** a gran velocidad; **at top** *or* **full s.** *(to drive, work)* a toda velocidad; **you'll never finish at that s.** a ese paso no vas a terminar nunca; **to gather** *or* **pick up s.** ganar *or* cobrar velocidad; **to lose s.** perder velocidad; IDIOM *Fam* **to be up to s. on sth** estar al tanto *or* corriente de algo; IDIOM *Fam* **to bring sb up to s. (on sth)** poner al corriente *or* al día (de algo) a alguien ►► ***s. bump*** *Esp* resalto *m (de moderación de velocidad)*, *Arg* despertador *m*, *Méx* tope *m*; ***s. camera*** cámara *f* de control de velocidad; *Fam* ***s. cop*** policía *mf* de tráfico *or RP* caminera *(en carretera)*; ***s. dialling*** marcado *m* rápido; ***s. gun*** medidor *m* de velocidad, tacómetro *m*; ***s. limit*** límite *m* de velocidad; *Fam* ***s. merchant*** *(driver)* loco(a) *m,f* del volante; *(fast runner)* bala *f*; ***s. skater*** patinador(ora) *m,f* de velocidad; ***s. skating*** patinaje *m* de velocidad; ***s. trap*** control *m* de velocidad por radar

(b) *(quickness)* rapidez *f*; **the s. with which the building was completed** la rapidez con que se concluyó el edificio

(c) *(gear)* marcha *f*, velocidad *f*; **a five-s. gearbox** una caja de cambios de cinco marchas

(d) *Phot (of film)* sensibilidad *f*, velocidad *f* de la emulsión; *(of shutter)* tiempo *m* de exposición

(e) *Comptr (of processor, clock)* velocidad *f*; **a 32 s. CD-ROM** un CD-ROM de velocidad 32 x

(f) *Fam (drug)* anfetas *fpl*, speed *m*

2 *vi* (*pt & pp* **sped** [sped] *or* **speeded**) (a) *(go fast)* avanzar rápidamente; *(hurry)* precipitarse; **to s. along** ir muy rápido; **we sped across the field** atravesamos el campo a toda velocidad; **to s. away** marcharse rápidamente; **to s. past/by** pasar a toda velocidad; **the torpedo sped through the water** el torpedo avanzó velozmente por el agua

(b) *Aut (exceed speed limit)* sobrepasar el límite de velocidad; **I was caught speeding** *Esp* me cogieron conduciendo demasiado deprisa, *Am* me agarraron manejando demasiado deprisa

(c) *Fam (on drugs)* **to be speeding** estar *or* ir puesto(a) de speed

3 *vt (person)* **to s. sb on his/her way** darle la despedida a alguien, despedir a alguien

► **speed off 1** *vt sep* **they sped him off to hospital** se lo llevaron rápidamente al hospital

2 *vi* salir disparado(a)

► **speed up 1** *vt sep (process)* acelerar; *(person)* apresurar

2 *vi (car)* acelerar; *(process)* acelerarse; *(person)* apresurarse, *Am* apurarse

speedball ['spiːdbɔːl] *n Fam* speed ball *m*

speedboat ['spiːdbəʊt] *n* motora *f*, planeadora *f*

speeder ['spiːdə(r)] *n* (a) *(fast driver)* conductor(ora) *m,f* que va a toda velocidad (b) *(convicted driver)* infractor(ora) *m,f* del límite de velocidad

speedily ['spiːdɪlɪ] *adv* rápidamente; **I hope you recover s.** espero que te recuperes rápidamente

speediness ['spiːdɪnɪs] *n* rapidez *f*

speeding ['spiːdɪŋ] *n Aut* **I was stopped for s.** me pararon por exceso de velocidad ►► ***s. conviction*** sentencia *f* condenatoria por exceso de velocidad; ***s. ticket*** multa *f* por exceso de velocidad

speedo ['spiːdəʊ] (*pl* **speedos**) *n Br Fam Aut* velocímetro *m*

speedometer [spiː'dɒmɪtə(r)] *n Aut* velocímetro *m*

speedster ['spiːdstə(r)] *n Fam* (a) *(fast car)* bólido *m* (b) *(driver)* loco(a) *m,f* del volante

speed-up ['spiːdʌp] *n* aceleramiento *m*, aceleración *f* (**in** de)

speedway ['spiːdweɪ] *n* (a) *(racing)* carreras *fpl* de motos (b) *(track)* pista *f* de carreras (c) *US (expressway)* autopista *f*

speedwell ['spiːdwel] *n Bot* verónica *f*

speedy ['spiːdɪ] *adj* (a) *(fast)* rápido(a) (b) *(prompt) (answer)* pronto(a); **to wish sb a s. recovery** desearle a alguien una pronta recuperación

speleologist [spiːlɪ'ɒlədʒɪst] *n* espeleólogo(a) *m,f*

speleology [spiːlɪ'ɒlədʒɪ] *n* espeleología *f*

spell[1] [spel] *n (magic words)* conjuro *m*, fórmula *f* mágica; **to cast a s. over sb, to put a s. on sb** hechizar *or* encantar a alguien; **to say a s.** pronunciar un conjuro *or* una fórmula mágica; *Fig* **to break the s.** romper la magia del momento; *Fig* **to be under a s.** estar hechizado(a); *Fig* **to be under sb's s.** estar cautivado(a) *or* hipnotizado(a) por alguien

spell[2] *n* (a) *(period)* periodo *m*, temporada *f*; **a good/bad s.** una buena/mala racha; **it's his second s. in prison** es la segunda vez que está en la cárcel; **she did** *or* **had a s. as a reporter** trabajó una temporada como reportera

(b) *(of weather)* periodo *m*, intervalo *m*; **a cold s.** una ola de frío; **sunny spells** intervalos soleados

(c) *(turn)* turno *m*; **she offered to do a s. at the wheel** se ofreció para conducir *or Am* manejar un rato

(d) *Med* **he had a dizzy s.** le dio un mareo

spell[3] (*pt & pp* **spelt** [spelt] *or* **spelled**) **1** *vt* (a) *(write correctly)* deletrear; **how do you s. it?** ¿cómo se escribe?; **shall I s. my name for you?** ¿le deletreo mi nombre?; **C-O-U-G-H spells "cough"** la palabra "cough" se deletrea C-O-U-G-H

(b) *(signify)* suponer; **to s. disaster** suponer un desastre; **her discovery could s. success for the business** su descubrimiento podía representar *or* suponer un éxito para la empresa

2 *vi* escribir sin faltas; **he can't s.** tiene muchas faltas de ortografía

► **spell out** *vt sep* (a) *(word)* deletrear (b) *(explain explicitly)* explicar claramente; **do I have to s. it out for you?** ¿cómo te lo tengo que decir?

spellbinding ['spelbaɪndɪŋ] *adj* cautivador(ora), fascinante

spellbound ['spelbaʊnd] *adj* hechizado(a); **the movie held me s. from start to finish** la película me tuvo embelesado desde el principio hasta el fin

spell-check ['speltʃek] *Comptr* **1** *n* **to do** *or* **run a s. on a text** pasar el corrector ortográfico a un texto

2 *vt* corregir *or* revisar la ortografía de

spell-checker ['speltʃekə(r)] *n Comptr* corrector *m* ortográfico

speller ['spelə(r)] *n* (a) *(person)* **he is a good/bad s.** tiene buena/mala ortografía (b) *US (book)* manual *m* de ortografía

spelling ['spelɪŋ] *n* (a) *(correct way of writing word)* ortografía *f*; **what is the correct s. of this word?** ¿cuál es la grafía correcta de esta palabra? (b) *(ability to spell, subject)* ortografía *f*; **to be good/bad at s.** tener buena/mala ortografía ►► ***s. bee*** concurso *m* de ortografía; *Comptr* ***s. checker*** corrector *m* ortográfico; ***s. mistake*** falta *f* de ortografía; ***s. test*** prueba *f* de ortografía

spelt *pt & pp of* **spell**[3]

spelunker [spɪ'lʌŋkə(r)] *n US* espeleólogo(a) *m,f*

spelunking [spe'lʌŋkɪŋ] *n* espeleología *f*

spend [spend] (*pt & pp* **spent** [spent]) **1** *vt* (a) *(money)* gastar (**on** en); **the stadium needs a lot of money spending on it** es preciso realizar una fuerte inversión en el estadio; **I consider it money well spent** lo considero un dinero bien empleado *or* una buena inversión; IDIOM *Euph* **to s. a penny** *(go to lavatory)* hacer sus necesidades

(b) *(pass) (time)* pasar; **she spent several years in Canada** pasó varios años en Canadá; **I spent the day studying** me pasé el día estudiando; **how do you s. your weekends?** ¿qué haces *or* a qué te dedicas los fines de semana?; IDIOM **to s. the night with sb** pasar la noche con alguien

(c) *(devote) (time, effort)* dedicar; **I've spent a lot of time and effort on it** le he dedicado mucho tiempo y esfuerzo; **she spent her life helping the underprivileged** se pasó la vida ayudando a los menos privilegiados

(d) *(exhaust)* agotar; **the storm had spent its force** la tormenta había amainado; **her strength was all but spent** apenas le quedaban fuerzas

2 *vi* gastar; **with her it's just s., s., s.!** ¡no hace más que gastar y gastar!, ¡sólo sabe gastar!

3 *n Br Com (expenditure)* gasto *m*

spender ['spendə(r)] *n* **to be a high/low s.** gastar mucho/poco

spending ['spendɪŋ] *n* gasto *m*; **s. on health** el gasto sanitario; **cuts in defence s.** recortes en los gastos de defensa; **consumer s.** el gasto *or* consumo privado; **public s.** el gasto público; **to go on a s. spree** salir a gastar a lo loco ▸▸ ***s. money*** dinero *m* para gastos; ***s. power*** poder *m* adquisitivo

spendthrift ['spendθrɪft] **1** *n* despilfarrador(ora) *m,f*, manirroto(a) *m,f*

2 *adj* despilfarrador(ora), derrochador(ora)

spent [spent] **1** *adj* **(a)** *(fuel, ammunition)* usado(a) **(b)** *(exhausted)* agotado(a); **to be a s. force** estar acabado(a)

2 *pt & pp of* **spend**

sperm [spɜ:m] *n* **(a)** *(semen)* esperma *m*, semen *m* ▸▸ ***s. bank*** banco *m* de semen; ***s. count*** recuento *m* espermático *or* de espermatozoides; ***s. donor*** donante *m* de semen **(b)** *(spermatozoon)* espermatozoide *m* **(c)** *Zool* ***s. oil*** esperma *m or f* de ballena; ***s. whale*** cachalote *m*

spermaceti [spɜ:mə'setɪ] *n* esperma *m or f* de ballena

spermatozoon [spɜ:mətə'zəʊɒn] (*pl* **spermatozoa** [spɜ:mətə'zəʊə]) *n Biol* espermatozoide *m*, espermatozoo *m*

spermicidal [spɜ:mɪ'saɪdəl] *adj* espermicida

spermicide ['spɜ:mɪsaɪd] *n* espermicida *m*

spew [spju:] **1** *n Fam (vomit)* vómito *m*

2 *vt* **(a)** *(of chimney, volcano)* arrojar **(b)** *Fam (vomit)* devolver, vomitar

3 *vi* **(a)** *(pour out)* salir (a borbotones); **lava spewed everywhere** la lava salía a borbotones por todas partes **(b)** *Fam (vomit)* devolver, vomitar

▸ **spew up** *Fam* **1** *vt sep* devolver, vomitar; **to s. one's guts up** echar *or* devolver hasta la primera papilla

2 *vi* devolver, vomitar

SPF [espi:'ef] *n* (*abbr* **sun protection factor**) FPS *m*, factor *m* de protección solar

sphagnum ['sfægnəm] *n* ***s. (moss)*** musgo *m* esfagnáceo, esfagno *m*

sphenoid ['sfi:nɔɪd] *Anat* **1** *n* **s. (bone)** esfenoides *m*

2 *adj* esfenoides

sphere [sfɪə(r)] *n* **(a)** *(globe)* esfera *f* **(b)** *(of interest, activity)* esfera *f*, ámbito *m*; **that's outside my s.** eso está fuera de mi ámbito; **an important personality in the public s.** *(politics)* una importante personalidad de la vida pública; **s. of influence** ámbito *m* de influencia

spherical ['sferɪkəl] *adj* esférico(a) ▸▸ ***s. aberration*** aberración *f* de esfericidad

spheroid ['sfɪərɔɪd] *n* esferoide *m*

sphincter ['sfɪŋktə(r)] *n Anat* esfínter *m*

sphinx [sfɪŋks] *n* esfinge *f*; **the S.** la Esfinge

spic, spick [spɪk] *n US very Fam* = término ofensivo para referirse a un latino

spice [spaɪs] **1** *n* **(a)** *(seasoning)* especia *f* ▸▸ ***s. rack*** especiero *m* **(b)** *(interest, excitement)* chispa *f*; **to add s. to a story** darle *or* añadirle salsa a una historia

2 *vt* **(a)** *(food)* sazonar, especiar **(b)** *(make more exciting)* **the story is spiced with political anecdotes** la historia está aderezada con anécdotas políticas

▸ **spice up** *vt sep (make more exciting)* dar chispa a

spicebush ['spaɪsbʊʃ] *n Bot* pimienta *f* salvaje

spiciness ['spaɪsɪnɪs] *n* **(a)** *(of food)* sabor *m* picante **(b)** *(of story, adventure)* lo jugoso *or* sustancioso, lo picante

spick[1] [spɪk] *adj* **s. and span** *(room, house)* como los chorros del oro; *(appearance, person)* impecable, pulcro(a)

spick[2] = **spic**

spicy ['spaɪsɪ] *adj* **(a)** *(food) (seasoned with spices)* especiado(a), sazonado(a); *(hot)* picante **(b)** *(story, gossip)* jugoso(a), picante

spider ['spaɪdə(r)] *n* **(a)** *(animal)* araña *f* ▸▸ ***s. crab*** centollo *m*, centolla *f*; ***s. monkey*** mono *m* araña; ***s. plant*** cinta *f*; *Br* ***s.'s*** *or US* ***s. web*** tela *f* de araña, telaraña *f* **(b)** *Br (for luggage)* pulpo *m* **(c)** *Comptr* araña *f*, rastreador *m*

spiderwort ['spaɪdəwɔ:t] *n* tradescantia *f*

spidery ['spaɪdərɪ] *adj* **s. handwriting** letra de trazos largos y finos

spiel [spi:l] *n Fam* rollo *m*; **he gave me some s. about having been held up at the airport** me contó el rollo de que lo habían entretenido en el aeropuerto

spiffing ['spɪfɪŋ] *adj Br Fam Old-fashioned* fenomenal

spifflicate ['spɪflɪkeɪt] *vt Br Hum* hacer trizas, dar una soberana paliza a

spiffy ['spɪfɪ] *adj US* con estilo

spigot ['spɪgət] *n* **(a)** *(plug)* espita *f* **(b)** *(tap) Esp* grifo *m*, *Chile, Col, Méx* llave *f*, *RP* canilla *f*

spike [spaɪk] **1** *n* **(a)** *(point) (on iron railings)* barrote *m (terminado en punta)*; *(on helmet)* pincho *m*; *(on barbed wire)* púa *f*; *(on cactus)* espina *f*; *(on athletics shoe)* clavo *m*; *(for picking up paper)* pinchapapeles *m inv* **(b)** *(peak) (on graph)* pico *m* **(c)** *US (sharp increase)* subida *f* brusca (**in** en); **there was a s. in prices** los precios se dispararon brevemente **(d)** **spikes** *(running shoes)* zapatillas *fpl* de clavos **(e)** *(in volleyball)* remate *m*

2 *vt* **(a)** *(impale) (litter)* pinchar; **I spiked my arm on the railing** me clavé el brazo en la verja **(b)** *(add alcohol to)* **to s. sb's drink** añadir licor a la bebida de alguien **(c)** *(thwart) (plan)* frustrar; *(rumour)* acallar; IDIOM **to s. sb's guns** chafarle los planes a alguien

spiked [spaɪkt] *adj (shoes)* con clavos

spikenard ['spaɪknɑ:d] *n Bot* nardo *m*

spiky ['spaɪkɪ] *adj* **(a)** *(cactus, branch)* espinoso(a) **(b)** *(hair)* **he has s. hair** tiene *or* lleva el pelo punta **(c)** *Br Fam (bad-tempered)* susceptible

spill [spɪl] **1** *vt* (*pt & pp* **spilt** [spɪlt] *or* **spilled**) **(a)** *(liquid, salt)* derramar; **she spilt coffee down** *or* **over her dress** se derramó café en el vestido, se manchó el vestido de café; IDIOM **to s. blood** derramar sangre; IDIOM *Fam* **to s. the beans** descubrir el pastel, *Am* destapar la olla; IDIOM *esp US Fam* **to s. one's guts** *(under interrogation)* cantar, desembuchar

(b) *(unseat) (rider)* desmontar, derribar

2 *vi* **(a)** *(liquid, salt)* derramarse **(b)** *(audience, crowd)* **to s. onto the street** invadir la calle

3 *n* **(a)** *(of liquid)* derrame *m* **(b)** *(fall)* **to take a s.** tener una caída **(c)** *(of wood)* astilla *f*; *(of paper)* rollito *m* de papel

▸ **spill out** *vi (audience, crowd)* **to s. out onto the street** invadir la calle; **the schoolchildren spilled out of the train** los colegiales salieron del tren en tropel

▸ **spill over** *vi* **(a)** *(liquid)* derramarse; *(pan)* desbordarse **(b)** *(overflow) (conflict)* extenderse (**into** a); **the city's population has spilled over into the surrounding villages** la población de la ciudad se ha extendido a los pueblos periféricos; **her work spills over into her family life** el trabajo invade su vida familiar

spillage ['spɪlɪdʒ] *n* derrame *m*

spillway ['spɪlweɪ] *n* desagüe *m*, aliviadero *m*

spilt *pt & pp of* **spill**

spin [spɪn] **1** *n* **(a)** *(turning movement)* giro *m*; **to give sth a s.** hacer girar algo, hacer que algo dé vueltas; **to go into a s.** *(car)* empezar a dar vueltas; *(plane)* entrar en barrena; IDIOM **to go into a (flat) s.** atolondrarse

(b) *(in washing machine)* centrifugado *m*; **long/short s. (cycle)** (ciclo de) centrifugado largo/corto; **give the washing another s.** dale otro centrifugado a la ropa, centrifuga otra vez la ropa

(c) *(short drive)* **to go for a s.** ir a dar una vuelta; **would you like to give the car a s.?** ¿quiere (ir a) probar el coche *or Am* carro *or CSur* auto?

(d) *(on ball)* efecto *m*; **to put s. on a ball** dar efecto a una pelota

(e) *Pol (on news story)* sesgo *m*; **to put the right s. on a story** dar el sesgo adecuado a una noticia; **the government has been criticized for indulging in too much s.** el gobierno ha sido criticado por llevar a cabo demasiadas operaciones de maquillaje ▸▸ ***s. doctor*** asesor(ora) *m,f* político(a) *(para dar buena prensa a un partido o político)*

2 *vt* (*pt* **spun** [spʌn] *or* **span** [spæn], *pp* **spun**) **(a)** *(wool, cotton)* hilar; *Fig* **she spun some yarn about the buses being on strike** contó no sé qué cuento sobre los autobuses en huelga; *Fig* **he spins a good yarn** sabe contar historias; *Fam* **to s. sb a line about sth** contarle un cuento a alguien acerca de *or* sobre algo

(b) *(web)* tejer

(c) *(wheel, top)* (hacer) girar; **to s. a coin** tirar una moneda al aire; *(to decide something)* echar a cara o cruz *or Chile, Col* cara o sello *or Méx* águila o sol *or RP* cara o seca

(d) *(spin-dry)* centrifugar

(e) *(ball)* dar efecto a

3 *vi* **(a)** *(wheel, spinning top, dancer)* dar vueltas, girar; **my head's spinning** me da vueltas la cabeza; **these figures make your head s.** estos guarismos le ponen a uno la cabeza como un bombo; **the room's spinning** todo me da vueltas

(b) *(using spinning wheel)* hilar

(c) *(washing machine)* centrifugar

(d) *(move quickly)* **the taxi span out of control** el taxi comenzó a dar trompos; **the blow sent me spinning across the room** el golpe me mandó dando tumbos *or* bandazos de un extremo al otro de la habitación

(e) *(ball)* girar; **the ball span off a defender and into the net** el balón rebotó en un defensa y fue a parar a la red

▸ **spin off** *vt sep* (**a**) (product) comercializar como subproducto *or* derivado (**from** de) (**b**) *Fin (company)* escindir

▸ **spin out** *vt sep (speech, debate)* alargar; *(money)* estirar

▸ **spin round** 1 *vt sep (wheel)* girar (en redondo), dar la vuelta (completa); *(person)* dar *or* hacer darse la vuelta; **the Earth spins round the Sun** la Tierra gira alrededor del Sol
2 *vi (wheel)* girar (en redondo), dar la vuelta (completa); *(person)* girarse, darse la vuelta

spina bifida ['spaɪnə'bɪfɪdə] *n Med* espina *f* bífida

spinach ['spɪnɪtʃ] *n* (**a**) *(food)* espinacas *fpl* (**b**) *(plant)* espinaca *f*

spinal ['spaɪnəl] *adj Anat* espinal ▸▸ ***s. anaesthesia*** anestesia *f* epidural; ***s. column*** columna *f* vertebral; ***s. cord*** médula *f* espinal; ***s. injury*** lesión *f* de columna; *US Med* ***s. tap*** punción *f* lumbar

spindle ['spɪndəl] *n* (**a**) *Tex* huso *m* (**b**) *Tech* eje *m*

spindly ['spɪndlɪ] *adj (legs)* largo(a) y delgado(a), espigado(a); *(person)* larguirucho(a), espigado(a); *(plant, tree)* alto(a) y esbelto(a), espigado(a)

spin-drier *n* = **spin-dryer**

spin-dry ['spɪn'draɪ] *vt* centrifugar

spin-dryer ['spɪn'draɪə(r)] *n* centrifugadora *f*

spine [spaɪn] *n* (**a**) *(backbone)* columna *f* (vertebral) (**b**) *(of book)* lomo *m* (**c**) *(spike) (of plant, fish)* espina *f*; *(of hedgehog)* púa *f*

spine-chiller ['spaɪntʃɪlə(r)] *n (book)* libro *m* de terror; *(movie)* película *f* de terror

spine-chilling ['spaɪntʃɪlɪŋ] *adj* escalofriante, espeluznante

spineless ['spaɪnlɪs] *adj* (**a**) *(weak)* pusilánime, débil (**b**) *Zool* invertebrado(a)

spinelessly ['spaɪnlɪslɪ] *adv (weakly)* débilmente

spinet [spɪ'net] *n* espineta *f*

spinnaker ['spɪnəkə(r)] *n* spinnaker *m*

spinner ['spɪnə(r)] *n* (**a**) *(spin-dryer)* centrifugadora *f* (**b**) *(of textiles) (person)* hilandero(a) *m,f* (**c**) *(in angling)* cucharilla *f* (**d**) *Mktg* expositor *m* giratorio

spinney ['spɪnɪ] *n Br* bosquecillo *m*, boscaje *m*

spinning ['spɪnɪŋ] *n* (**a**) *(of wool, cotton)* hilado *m* ▸▸ ***s. jenny*** Spinny Jenny *f*, hiladora *f* mecánica; ***s. wheel*** rueca *f* (**b**) ***s. top*** peonza *f*, trompo *m*

spin-off ['spɪnɒf] *n* (**a**) *(by-product)* (producto *m*) derivado *m*, subproducto *m* (**b**) *(TV programme)* secuela *f* televisiva (**c**) *Fin (of company)* escisión *f*, constitución *f* de una nueva sociedad por escisión

spinster ['spɪnstə(r)] *n Law* soltera *f*; *Pej* solterona *f*

spinsterish ['spɪnstərɪʃ] *adj Pej* con pinta de solterona

spiny ['spaɪnɪ] *adj* espinoso(a) ▸▸ ***s. anteater*** equidna *m*; ***s. lobster*** langosta *f*

spiraea [spaɪ'ri:ə] *n Bot* espirea *f*

spiral ['spaɪrəl] 1 *n* espiral *f*; **a s. of violence** una espiral de violencia; *Econ* **the wage-price s.** la espiral de precios y salarios
2 *adj (motif)* en (forma de) espiral; *(shape)* espiral, de espiral; *(descent)* en espiral ▸▸ ***s. galaxy*** galaxia *f* espiral; ***s. notebook*** cuaderno *m* de espiral; ***s. staircase*** escalera *f* de caracol
3 *vi* (*pt & pp* **spiralled**, *US* **spiraled**) (**a**) *(smoke, stairs)* ascender en espiral (**b**) *(prices)* subir vertiginosamente; **inflation has spiralled out of control** la inflación se ha disparado por las nubes

▸ **spiral down** *vi (plane)* descender en espiral; *(leaf, feather)* caer dibujando una espiral

▸ **spiral up** *vi (smoke, stairs)* ascender en espiral; *(prices)* subir vertiginosamente

spiral-bound ['spaɪrəl'baʊnd] *adj* encuadernado(a) con canutillo de espiral ▸▸ ***s. notebook*** cuaderno *m* de espiral

spire ['spaɪə(r)] *n (of church)* aguja *f*

spirit ['spɪrɪt] *n* (**a**) *(soul)* espíritu *m*; **he is with us in s.** está con nosotros en espíritu; **the s. is willing but the flesh is weak** el espíritu está por la labor, pero la carne es débil
(**b**) *(ghost)* espíritu *m*; **evil spirits** espíritus malignos; **the s. world** el mundo de los espíritus *or* de ultratumba; **the Holy S.** el Espíritu Santo
(**c**) *(person)* alma *f*, ser *m*; **he is a generous s.** es un alma generosa
(**d**) *(mood, attitude)* espíritu *m*; **that was not the s. of the agreement** ése no era el espíritu del acuerdo; **we could do with a bit more Christmas s. round here** no nos vendría mal un poco más de espíritu navideño; **to do sth in a s. of fun** hacer algo en *or* de broma; **she entered into the s. of the occasion** se puso a tono con la ocasión, participó del acontecimiento; **to take sth in the right/wrong s.** tomar(se) algo a bien/mal; *Fam* **that's the s.!** ¡eso es!
(**e**) *(deep meaning)* **the s. of the law** el espíritu de la ley
(**f**) *(courage)* valor *m*, coraje *m*; *(energy)* brío *m*; **to show s.** mostrar valor *or* coraje; **to break sb's s.** desmoralizar a alguien; **to say sth with s.** decir algo con arrestos
(**g**) **spirits** *(mental state)* ánimo *m*, moral *f*; **to be in good/poor spirits** tener la moral alta/baja; **to be in high spirits** estar muy animado(a) *or* de muy buen ánimo; **to keep sb's spirits up** mantener elevada la moral de alguien, dar(le) ánimo *or* moral a alguien; **I kept my spirits up by humming a tune** tarareé una canción para infundirme *or* darme ánimos; **the news raised their spirits** la noticia les levantó el ánimo
(**h**) **spirits** *(drinks)* licores *mpl*; *(pure alcohol)* alcohol *m* ▸▸ ***s. lamp*** lámpara *f* de alcohol; ***s. stove*** estufa *f or* infiernillo *m* de alcohol
(**i**) ***s. level*** *(instrument)* nivel *m* de burbuja
(**j**) ***s. gum*** *(adhesive)* pegamento *m (para postizos)*

▸ **spirit away, spirit off** *vt sep* hacer desaparecer

spirited ['spɪrɪtɪd] *adj (person)* valeroso(a), con arrestos; *(horse)* brioso(a), fogoso(a); *(defence, attack, reply)* enérgico(a); *(performance) (by musician)* enérgico(a), vigoroso(a); *(by team)* lleno(a) de nervio *or* garra

spiritless ['spɪrɪtlɪs] *adj* (**a**) *(lifeless) (performance)* sin brío, sin garra (**b**) *(depressed)* deprimido(a), abatido(a) (**c**) *(cowardly)* cobarde

spiritual ['spɪrɪtjʊəl] 1 *n Mus* (**negro**) **s.** espiritual *m* negro
2 *adj* espiritual; **France is my s. home** Francia es mi patria espiritual; **the s. heir to Thatcher** el heredero espiritual de Thatcher ▸▸ ***s. adviser*** consejero(a) *m,f* espiritual

spiritualism ['spɪrɪtjʊəlɪzəm] *n Rel* espiritismo *m*

spiritualist ['spɪrɪtjʊəlɪst] *Rel* 1 *n* espiritista *mf*
2 *adj* espiritista

spirituality [spɪrɪtjʊ'ælɪtɪ] *n* espiritualidad *f*

spiritually ['spɪrɪtjʊəlɪ] *adv* espiritualmente

spirituous ['spɪrɪtʊəs] *adj Formal* espirituoso(a), espiritoso(a)

spirochaete ['spaɪərəʊki:t] *n Biol* espiroqueta *f*

spit[1] [spɪt] *n* (**a**) *(for cooking)* espetón *m*, asador *m* ▸▸ ***s. roast*** espetón *m* de carne asada (**b**) *(of land)* lengua *f*; *(of sand)* banco *m*

spit[2] 1 *n* (**a**) *(saliva)* saliva *f*; *Fam* **s. and polish** limpieza *f*, pulcritud *f* (**b**) IDIOMS **there was just a s. of rain** estaban cayendo unas gotas, estaba chispeando; *Br Fam* **to be the (very) s. of sb** ser el vivo retrato de alguien
2 *vt* (*pt & pp* **spat** [spæt], *US* **spit**) (**a**) *(blood, food)* escupir (**b**) *(say venomously)* **"I'd rather die," he spat** "preferiría morirme", espetó; **to s. curses at sb** proferir maldiciones contra alguien
3 *vi* (**a**) *(person, cat)* escupir; **to s. at sb** escupirle a alguien; **to s. in sb's face** escupirle a *or* en la cara a alguien (**b**) *(hot fat)* chisporrotear, saltar; *(fire)* chisporrotear, despedir chispas; **the sausages were spitting in the pan** las salchichas chisporroteaban en la sartén (**c**) *(rain)* **it's spitting (with rain)** está chispeando

▸ **spit out** *vt sep (food, medicine, words)* escupir; *(insults)* espetar, proferir; *Fam* **s. it out!** *(say what you want to)* ¡suéltalo!

▸ **spit up** *vt sep (blood)* expulsar, echar (por la boca)

spit-and-sawdust ['spɪtən'sɔ:dʌst] *adj Br Fam (pub, bar)* de andar por casa, sin grandes lujos

spitball ['spɪtbɔ:l] *n US* (**a**) *(paper)* pelotita *f* de papel (humedecida con saliva) (**b**) *(baseball)* = lanzamiento ilegal con mucho efecto conseguido ensalivando un lado de la pelota

spite [spaɪt] 1 *n* (**a**) *(malice)* rencor *m*; **out of** *or* **from s.** por rencor (**b**) **in s. of...** *(despite)* a pesar de...; **in s. of the fact that...** a pesar de que...; **to do sth in s. of oneself** no poder evitar hacer algo
2 *vt* fastidiar

spiteful ['spaɪtfʊl] *adj (person, character)* rencoroso(a); *(remark)* malintencionado(a), malévolo(a); **to be s. to sb** ser malévolo(a) con alguien; **to have a s. tongue** tener una lengua viperina

spitefully ['spaɪtfʊlɪ] *adv* maliciosamente

spitfire ['spɪtfaɪə(r)] *n (person)* persona *f* irascible *or* furibunda

spit-roasted ['spɪt'rəʊstɪd] *adj* asado(a) en un pincho *or* espetón

spitting ['spɪtɪŋ] *n* **no s.** *(on sign)* prohibido escupir; IDIOM *Fam* **to be in** *or* **within s. distance (of)** estar a un paso (de); IDIOM *Fam* **he's the s. image of his father** es el vivo retrato de su padre

spittle ['spɪtəl] *n* saliva *f*, baba *f*

spittoon [spɪ'tu:n] *n* escupidera *f*

spitz [spɪts] *n (dog)* perro(a) *m,f* de la raza Spitz, Spitz *mf*

spiv [spɪv] *n Br Fam (flashy person)* **he's a s.** tiene pinta de gánster

splash [splæʃ] 1 *n* (**a**) *(of liquid, mud)* salpicadura *f*; IDIOM *Fam* **to make a s.** causar sensación (**b**) *(noise)* **there was a loud s.** se oyó un fuerte ruido de algo cayendo al agua; **to fall into the water with a s.**

caer al agua salpicando (**c**) *(of colour, light)* toque *m* (**d**) **a s.** *(small amount)* un poco; *(of soda, whisky)* un chorrito
2 *vt* (**a**) *(with water, mud)* salpicar; **stop splashing me!** ¡no me salpiques!; **the bus splashed us with mud** el autobús nos salpicó de barro; **to s. water on** *or* **over sth/sb** salpicar de agua algo/a alguien; **I splashed my face with cold water** me eché agua fría en la cara
(**b**) *(stain)* **she splashed wine on** *or* **over her dress** se manchó *or* salpicó el vestido de vino
(**c**) *(in newspaper, magazine)* **a photo was splashed across the front page** publicaron una gran foto en la portada
3 *vi* (**a**) *(water, waves)* salpicar; **the tea splashed onto the floor** el té (se derramó y) salpicó el suelo (**b**) *(person)* chapotear; **he splashed through the mud** atravesó el barro chapoteando

▸**splash about, splash around** 1 *vt sep (money)* dilapidar, despilfarrar
2 *vi* chapotear

▸**splash down** *vi (spacecraft)* amerizar

▸**splash out** *Fam* 1 *vt insep* gastarse (**on** en)
2 *vi* gastarse un dineral (**on** en); **I'm really going to s. out this Christmas** estas Navidades voy a tirar la casa por la ventana

splashback ['splæʃbæk] *n* salpicadero *m*

splashdown ['splæʃdaʊn] *n* amerizaje *m*

splashguard ['splæʃgɑːd] *n US Esp, RP* guardabarros *m inv, Andes, CAm, Carib* guardafango *m, Méx* salpicadera *f*

splashy ['splæʃɪ] *adj US Fam* llamativo(a), ostentoso(a)

splat [splæt] 1 *n* **it hit the ground with a s.** hizo "plaf" al chocar contra el suelo
2 *adv* **to go s. into the wall** hacer "plaf" contra la pared

splatter ['splætə(r)] 1 *n* (**a**) *(stain)* salpicadura *f* ▸▸ *Fam* ***s. movie*** película *f* de casquería, película *f* muy sangrienta (**b**) *(sound) (of rain)* repiqueteo *m*
2 *vt* **to s. sb with mud** salpicar a alguien de barro
3 *vi (rain)* repiquetear; *(mud)* salpicar; **the tomato splattered against the wall** el tomate se despachurró *or* (se) reventó contra la pared

splay [spleɪ] 1 *vt* abrir, separar; **he splayed his legs** abrió *or* separó las piernas
2 *vi (legs)* abrirse, separarse; *(fingers)* separarse

▸**splay out** *vi* (**a**) *(feet)* separarse (**b**) *(pipe)* ensancharse

splay-footed ['spleɪ'fʊtɪd] *adj* con los pies hacia fuera

spleen [spliːn] *n* (**a**) *Anat* bazo *m* (**b**) *Formal (anger)* rabia *f*, ira *f*; **she vented her s. on him** descargó toda su rabia sobre él

splendid ['splendɪd] 1 *adj* (**a**) *(very good)* espléndido(a), magnífico(a); **we had a s. time** lo pasamos fenomenal; **that's s.!** ¡espléndido!, ¡estupendo!; **he sat in s. isolation** estaba sentado en perfecta soledad (**b**) *(beautiful, imposing) (dress, setting, decor)* suntuoso(a), magnífico(a)
2 *exclam* ¡espléndido!, ¡estupendo!

splendidly ['splendɪdlɪ] *adv* (**a**) *(very well)* estupendamente (**b**) *(beautifully, imposingly)* espléndidamente, magníficamente

splendiferous [splen'dɪfərəs] *adj Fam Hum* magnífico(a)

splendour, *US* **splendor** ['splendə(r)] *n* esplendor *m*; **to live in s.** vivir con gran esplendor; **the splendours of India** las maravillas de la India

splenetic [splɪ'netɪk] *adj* atrabiliario(a), malhumorado(a)

splenius ['spliːnɪəs] *n Anat* esplenio *m*

splice [splaɪs] 1 *n (in rope, tape)* empalme *m*
2 *vt* (**a**) *(rope, tape, movie)* empalmar (**b**) *Fam* **to get spliced** *(marry)* casarse

splicer ['splaɪsə(r)] *n* empalmadora *f*

spliff [splɪf] *n Fam* porro *m*, canuto *m*

splint [splɪnt] 1 *n (for broken limb)* tablilla *f*; **in splints** entablillado(a); **to put sb's arm in splints** entablillarle el brazo a alguien
2 *vt* entablillar

splinter ['splɪntə(r)] 1 *n (of wood, bone)* astilla *f*; *(of glass)* esquirla *f*; **I've got a s. in my finger** me he clavado una astilla en el dedo ▸▸ *Pol* ***s. group*** grupo *m* disidente *or* escindido
2 *vt* astillar
3 *vi* (**a**) *(wood, bone, glass)* astillarse (**b**) *(political party)* escindirse

splinter-proof ['splɪntəpruːf] *adj (glass)* inastillable

split [splɪt] 1 *n* (**a**) *(in wood, rock)* grieta *f*
(**b**) *(in garment) (tear)* raja *f*; *(intentional)* abertura *f*
(**c**) *(division)* división *f*, separación *f*; **the s. between rich and poor nations** la brecha entre naciones ricas y pobres; **there was a three-way s. in the voting** los votos se repartieron prácticamente por igual entre las tres fuerzas; **they suggested a fifty-fifty s. of the profits** propusieron un reparto de las ganancias al cincuenta por ciento
(**d**) *(in group, party)* escisión *f*
(**e**) *(in gymnastics)* **to do the splits** abrirse totalmente de piernas, hacer el spagat
(**f**) *(in athletics, swimming, cycling)* ***s. (time)*** tiempo *m* parcial *or* intermedio
2 *adj* (**a**) *(wood, lip)* partido(a) ▸▸ ***s. ends*** *(in hair)* puntas *fpl* abiertas; **I've got s. ends** tengo las puntas (del pelo) abiertas; *Gram* ***s. infinitive*** = intercalación de un adverbio o locución adverbial entre el "to" y la forma verbal; ***s. peas*** *Esp* guisantes *m or Méx* chícharos *mpl* secos partidos, *Am* arvejas *fpl* secas partidas; ***s. personality*** doble personalidad *f*; *Tech* ***s. pin*** chaveta *f*; ***s. screen*** pantalla *f* partida; ***s. second:*** **in a s. second** en una fracción de segundo; *Ind* ***s. shift*** turno *m* partido
(**b**) *(divided)* **the party is s. over Europe** el partido está dividido en lo que respecta a Europa ▸▸ ***s. decision*** *(in boxing)* decisión *f* no unánime
3 *vt* (*pt & pp* **split**) (**a**) *(make break in) (wood)* partir, rajar; *(stone)* partir; *(cloth)* rajar; **to s. the atom** desintegrar el átomo; **I've s. my trousers** me han estallado los pantalones, me ha estallado *or* se me ha abierto la costura del pantalón; **to s. sth in two** *or* **in half** partir algo en dos *or* por la mitad; **she s. the melon open with a knife** partió el melón por la mitad con un cuchillo; **to s. one's head open** hacerse una brecha en la cabeza; IDIOM *Fam* **to s. one's sides (laughing), to s. a gut** partirse *or* troncharse de risa; IDIOM **to s. hairs** buscarle tres pies al gato
(**b**) *(cause division in) (party, group)* dividir; **to s. the vote** dividir el voto
(**c**) *(divide) (money, profits)* dividir, repartir; **to s. the profits four ways** repartir las ganancias entre cuatro; **they decided to s. the work between them** decidieron repartirse el trabajo; **to s. a bottle** compartir *or* repartirse una botella (entre dos), beberse una botella a medias; **to s. the difference** dividir *or* repartirse la diferencia a partes iguales
4 *vi* (**a**) *(wood, stone)* partirse; *(cloth)* rajarse; **to s. in two** partirse en dos *or* por la mitad; **my trousers have s.** me han estallado los pantalones, me ha estallado *or* se me ha descosido la costura del pantalón; **the bag s. open** la bolsa estalló *or* reventó; *Fam* **my head's splitting** me va a estallar la cabeza
(**b**) *(divide) (cell)* dividirse; *(road, railway)* bifurcarse; **the hikers s. into three groups** los excursionistas se dividieron en tres grupos
(**c**) *(political party)* escindirse; *(band)* separarse
(**d**) *Fam (leave)* abrirse, *Esp, RP* pirarse, *Méx, RP* rajarse
(**e**) *Br Fam (inform)* ir con cuentos, *Esp* chivarse

▸**split away, split off** 1 *vt sep (branch, piece)* arrancar, partir

SPLIT INFINITIVE

Así se denomina al infinitivo cuando entre la preposición **to** y la forma base del verbo se introduce un adverbio o complemento adverbial, como por ejemplo en la frase:

to really get to the bottom of things *llegar de verdad al fondo del asunto*

La gramática tradicional no considera correcto este uso, quizá debido a la analogía existente con el latín, en el que el infinitivo consiste en una sola palabra y por lo tanto no puede dividirse. No obstante, este uso del infinitivo no es reciente en inglés, pues se conoce su uso ya en el siglo XVI y aparece en textos de muchos de los grandes escritores de habla inglesa, como John Donne, Samuel Johnson, Benjamin Franklin y Henry James. Es más, en ocasiones evitar esta separación del infinitivo puede dar lugar a oraciones ambiguas o poco elegantes. En la actualidad, el ejemplo más conocido de su uso es la misión encomendada a la nave de la serie "Star Trek":

to boldly go where no man has gone before.

2 *vi* (**a**) *(branch, splinter)* desprenderse (**from** de) (**b**) *(person)* separarse (**from** de); *(group)* escindirse (**from** de)

▸ **split on** *vt insep Br Fam* **to s. on sb** *Esp* chivarse de alguien, *Col* sapear a alguien, *Méx* soplar a alguien, *RP* botonear a alguien

▸ **split up 1** *vt sep* (**a**) *(money, work)* dividir; **he s. the chocolate up into small pieces** dividió el chocolate en trozos pequeños (**b**) *(people fighting)* separar; *(crowd, gathering)* dispersar, disolver
2 *vi* (**a**) *(couple, band)* separarse; **I've s. up with my boyfriend** he roto con mi novio (**b**) *(divide)* **the search party s. up into three groups** el grupo de búsqueda se dividió en tres

split-level ['splɪt'levəl] *adj (house, flat)* de dos niveles ▸▸ ***s. cooker*** cocina *f* con parrilla en la parte superior

split-second ['splɪt'sekənd] *adj (decision)* instantáneo(a); *(timing)* al milímetro

splitting ['splɪtɪŋ] **1** *n (of the atom)* desintegración *f*
2 *adj (headache)* atroz

split-up ['splɪtʌp] *n (of couple, partnership)* ruptura *f*; *(of band)* separación *f*

splodge [splɒdʒ] *n Fam* (**a**) *(stain)* manchurrón *m*, manchón *m* (**b**) *(dollop) (of cream, jam)* pegote *m*

splosh [splɒʃ] *Fam* **1** *n* **he fell into the swimming pool with a s.** sonó una fuerte zambullida cuando cayó a la piscina
2 *vi (splash) (liquid)* **the water sploshed on the floor** el agua se derramó de golpe por el suelo
3 *vt (pour) (water, disinfectant)* echar, volcar

splurge [splɜːdʒ] *Fam* **1** *n* (**a**) *(spending spree)* derroche *m*, despilfarro *m*; **to go on** *or* **have a s.** echar la casa por la ventana, despilfarrar (**b**) *(large amount)* **the book came out in a s. of publicity** el libro salió a la luz en medio de una ostentosa campaña publicitaria
2 *vt* derrochar, malgastar

splutter ['splʌtə(r)] **1** *n* (**a**) *(of person)* farfulla *f* (**b**) *(of candle)* chisporroteo *m*; *(of engine)* resoplido *m*
2 *vt* farfullar
3 *vi* (**a**) *(person)* farfullar (**b**) *(candle)* chisporrotear; *(engine)* resoplar

spluttering ['splʌtərɪŋ] **1** *n* (**a**) *(of person)* farfulla *f* (**b**) *(of candle)* chisporroteo *m*; *(of engine)* resoplido *m*
2 *adj* **a s. rage** un farfulleo de rabia

spoil [spɔɪl] **1** *vt (pt & pp* **spoilt** [spɔɪlt] *or* **spoiled**) (**a**) *(ruin)* estropear; **the bad weather spoiled our day** el mal tiempo nos aguó *or* nos echó a perder el día; **don't s. it for everyone else** no le agües la fiesta a los demás, no se lo estropees a los demás; **to s. sb's fun** aguarle la fiesta a alguien; **to s. sb's appetite** quitarle *or Am* sacarle las ganas de comer a alguien; **to s. the view** afear *or* estropear la vista; *Pol* **they spoilt their ballot papers** anularon sus papeletas de voto
(**b**) *(indulge) (person)* mimar, consentir; **to s. sb rotten** mimar *or* consentir demasiado a alguien; **I decided to s. myself and have champagne** decidí darme un capricho especial y tomar champán; **to be spoilt for choice** tener mucho donde elegir
2 *vi* (**a**) *(fruit, fish)* estropearse (**b**) IDIOM **to be spoiling for a fight** tener ganas de pelea
3 *n (earth)* escombros *mpl*

spoiled = **spoilt**

spoiler ['spɔɪlə(r)] *n* (**a**) *(on car)* spoiler *m*, alerón *m*; *(on plane)* aerofreno *m* (**b**) *(newspaper story)* maniobra *f* intencionada (para desviar la atención) (**c**) *(on Internet, in magazine)* información *f* anticipatoria

spoils [spɔɪlz] *npl (of war, crime)* botín *m*; **to claim one's share of the s.** reclamar uno una parte de su botín ▸▸ *US Pol* ***s. system*** amiguismo *m*

spoilsport ['spɔɪlspɔːt] *n Fam* aguafiestas *mf inv*

spoilt[1] [spɔɪlt], **spoiled** [spɔɪld] *adj* (**a**) *(child)* mimado(a) (**b**) *Pol* ***s. ballot*** voto *m* nulo, papeleta *f* nula, *Méx, RP* boleta *f* nula

spoilt[2], **spoiled** *pt & pp of* **spoil**

spoke[1] [spəʊk] *n (of wheel)* radio *m*; IDIOM *Br* **to put a s. in sb's wheel** poner trabas a alguien

spoke[2] *pt of* **speak**

spoken[1] ['spəʊkən] *adj (dialogue, language)* oral, hablado(a)

spoken[2] *pp of* **speak**

spokeshave ['spəʊkʃeɪv] *n* raedera *f*

spokesman ['spəʊksmən] *n* portavoz *m* (**for** de)

spokesperson ['spəʊkspɜːsən] *n* portavoz *mf* (**for** de)

spokeswoman ['spəʊkswʊmən] *n* portavoz *f* (**for** de)

spondee ['spɒndiː] *n Lit* espondeo *m*

spondulicks [spɒn'duːlɪks] *npl Fam Esp* pasta *f*, *Am* plata *f*, *Méx* lana *f*

sponge [spʌndʒ] **1** *n* (**a**) *(for bath)* esponja *f*; IDIOM **to throw in the s.** tirar la toalla ▸▸ ***s. bag*** bolsa *f* de aseo; ***s. bath*** = lavado que se practica a un paciente postrado en cama; ***s. cloth*** bayeta *f* absorbente (**b**) *Zool* esponja *f* (**c**) *(cake)* **s.** (**cake**) bizcocho *m* ▸▸ ***s. finger*** galleta *f* de bizcocho, soletilla *f*; ***s. pudding*** budín *m* de bizcocho (al baño María)
2 *vt* (**a**) *(wash)* limpiar *(con una esponja)*; **she sponged his face** le lavó la cara con una esponja (**b**) *Fam (scrounge)* **to s. sth off** *or* **from sb** gorrear *or Esp, Méx* gorronear *or RP* garronear algo a alguien
3 *vi Fam (scrounge) Esp, Méx* vivir de gorra, *RP* vivir de arriba

▸ **sponge down** *vt sep (wash)* lavar *(con una esponja)*

▸ **sponge off** *vt insep Fam (scrounge from)* vivir a costa de

▸ **sponge up** *vt sep (liquid)* absorber, secar

sponger ['spʌndʒə(r)] *n Fam* gorrero(a) *m,f*, *Esp, Méx* gorrón(ona) *m,f*, *RP* garronero(a) *m,f*

sponginess ['spʌndʒɪnɪs] *n* esponjosidad *f*

sponging ['spʌndʒɪŋ] *n Fam (scrounging) Esp, Méx* gorronería *f*, *RP* garronería *f*

spongy ['spʌndʒɪ] *adj* esponjoso(a)

sponsor ['spɒnsə(r)] **1** *n* (**a**) *(of team, exhibition, TV programme)* patrocinador(ora) *m,f* (**b**) *(for charity)* patrocinador(ora) *m,f* (**c**) *(of student, club member) (man)* padrino *m*; *(woman)* madrina *f* (**d**) *(of proposed law, bill)* ponente *mf* (**e**) *US (of godchild) (man)* padrino *m*; *(woman)* madrina *f*
2 *vt* (**a**) *(team, exhibition, TV programme)* patrocinar (**b**) *(for charity)* patrocinar; **I sponsored him to swim 10 miles** patrociné sus diez millas a nado (**c**) *(student)* subvencionar; *(club member)* recomendar, presentar (**d**) *(proposed law, bill)* presentar, proponer

sponsored ['spɒnsəd] *adj (team, TV programme, exhibition)* patrocinado(a); *(research, student)* subvencionado(a); *Br* **s. walk** = recorrido a pie con el fin de recaudar fondos para una organización benéfica

sponsorship ['spɒnsəʃɪp] *n* (**a**) *(of athlete, team, festival)* patrocinio *m*, financiación *f*, *Am* financiamiento *m*; **under the s. of** patrocinado(a) por ▸▸ ***s. deal*** *(of athlete, team)* contrato *m* con un patrocinador (**b**) *(of candidate)* apoyo *m* (**of** a) (**c**) *(of proposed law, bill)* respaldo *m*

spontaneity [spɒntə'neɪɪtɪ] *n* espontaneidad *f*

spontaneous [spɒn'teɪnɪəs] *adj* espontáneo(a) ▸▸ *Med* ***s. abortion*** aborto *m* espontáneo *or* natural; ***s. combustion*** combustión *f* espontánea; ***s. generation*** generación *f* espontánea

spontaneously [spɒn'teɪnjəslɪ] *adv (to act, answer, smile)* espontáneamente; **it s. combusted** se consumió por combustión espontánea

spoof [spuːf] **1** *n* (**a**) *(parody)* parodia *f*, burla *f* (**on** *or* **of** de) (**b**) *(hoax)* broma *f*
2 *adj (hoax)* de *or* en broma
3 *vt* (**a**) *(parody) (book, style)* parodiar (**b**) *esp US (tease) (person)* gastar una broma a, tomar el pelo a
4 *vi esp US* bromear

spook [spuːk] **1** *n* (**a**) *Fam (ghost)* fantasma *m* (**b**) *US Fam (spy)* espía *mf* (**c**) *US very Fam (black person)* = término ofensivo para referirse a un negro
2 *vt* poner los pelos de punta a

spooky ['spuːkɪ] *adj Fam* espeluznante, escalofriante; **it's really s. in the graveyard at night** la noche en el cementerio es realmente espeluznante

spool [spuːl] *n (of film, tape)* carrete *m*, rollo *m*; *(of thread)* bobina *f*; *(for fishing)* carrete *m*

spooler ['spuːlə(r)] *n Comptr* spooler *m* de impresión

spoon [spuːn] **1** *n* (**a**) *(utensil)* cuchara *f* (**b**) *(spoonful)* cucharada *f*
2 *vt* **to s. sauce onto sth** rociar salsa sobre algo con una cuchara; **he spooned the ice cream into a bowl** puso el helado en un cuenco ayudándose de una cuchara; **he spooned the soup into the child's mouth** dio la sopa al niño con una cuchara

▸ **spoon out** *vt sep (serve)* servir (ayudándose de una cuchara)

spoonbill ['spuːnbɪl] *n* espátula *f (ave)*

spoonerism ['spuːnərɪzəm] *n* = trastocamiento involuntario de las iniciales de dos palabras contiguas que produce un efecto cómico

spoon-feed ['spuːnfiːd] (*pt & pp* **spoon-fed** ['spuːnfed]) *vt* (**a**) *(baby, sick person)* dar de comer con (una) cuchara (**b**) *(help too much)* dar las cosas hechas *or* masticadas a

spoonful ['spuːnfʊl] *n* cucharada *f*

spoor [spʊə(r)] *n* rastro *m*

sporadic [spə'rædɪk] *adj* esporádico(a)

sporadically [spə'rædɪklɪ] *adv* esporádicamente

spore [spɔː(r)] *n (of fungus)* espora *f*

sporran ['spɒrən] *n* = taleguilla de piel que cuelga por delante de la falda en el traje típico escocés

sport [spɔːt] **1** *n* (**a**) *(activity)* deporte *m*; **she's keen on s.** le gusta el deporte; **to be good at s.** *or* **sports** ser buen(a) deportista; **the s. of kings** *(horse racing)* el deporte de los reyes, las carreras de caballos
(**b**) *Fam (person)* **to be a (good) s.** *Esp* ser un(a) tío(a) grande, *Am* ser buena gente; **to be a bad s.** *(bad loser)* ser mal perdedor, *Esp* tener mal perder; **go on, be a s.!** ¡vamos, pórtate *or Esp* enróllate!
(**c**) *Old-fashioned (fun)* diversión *f*; **to say sth in s.** decir algo en broma; **to make s. of sth/sb** burlarse de algo/alguien
(**d**) *Austr Fam (form of address) Esp* colega *m*, *Andes, CAm, Carib, Méx* mano *m*, *RP* flaco *m*
2 *vt (wear)* lucir, llevar
3 *vi Literary (play, frolic)* juguetear, retozar

sporting ['spɔːtɪŋ] *adj* (**a**) *(related to sport)* deportivo(a) (**b**) *(fair)* deportivo(a); **to give sb a s. chance** dar una oportunidad seria a alguien (**c**) *(kind, generous)* **it's very s. of you to let me have it** es un gesto muy bonito de tu parte el que me permitas tenerlo

sportingly ['spɔːtɪŋlɪ] *adv* (**a**) *(fairly)* deportivamente (**b**) *(kindly, generously)* amablemente, gentilmente

sports [spɔːts] **1** *npl (athletics meeting)* reunión *f* atlética
2 *adj (equipment, facilities)* deportivo(a); *(programme)* de deportes, deportivo(a) ►► ***s. bag*** bolsa *f* de deportes; ***s. bra*** sostén *m or Esp* sujetador *m or Carib, Col, Méx* brasier *m or RP* corpiño *m* deportivo; ***s. car*** coche *m or Am* carro *m or CSur* auto *m* deportivo; ***s. centre*** polideportivo *m*; ***s. club*** club *m* deportivo; ***s. commentator*** comentarista *mf* deportivo(a); *Sch* ***s. day*** día *m* dedicado a competiciones *or Am* competencias deportivas; ***s. desk*** redacción *f* de deportes; ***s. editor*** redactor(ora) *m,f* deportivo(a); ***s. ground*** campo *m* de deportes; ***s. hall*** pabellón *m* de deportes, palacio *m* de deportes; *Br* ***s. jacket*** chaqueta *f or Am* saco *m* de sport; *Journ* ***s. pages*** páginas *f or* sección *f* de deportes; ***s. reporter*** periodista *mf* deportivo(a); ***s. science*** ciencia *f* deportiva; ***s. scientist*** experto(a) *m,f* en ciencia deportiva; ***s. shoe*** zapatilla *f* deportiva *or* de deporte; ***s. shop*** tienda *f* de deportes; ***s. writer*** cronista *mf* deportivo(a)

sportscast ['spɔːtskɑːst] *n US* retransmisión *f* deportiva

sportscaster ['spɔːtskɑːstə(r)] *n US* comentarista *mf* deportivo(a)

sportsman ['spɔːtsmən] *n* (**a**) *(player of sport)* deportista *m* (**b**) *(fair person)* gentilhombre *m*, caballero *m*

sportsmanlike ['spɔːtsmənlaɪk] *adj* deportivo(a) *(cortés)*

sportsmanship ['spɔːtsmənʃɪp] *n* deportividad *f*

sportsperson ['spɔːtspɜːsən] *n* deportista *mf*

sportswear ['spɔːtsweə(r)] *n* (**a**) *(for playing sport)* ropa *f* deportiva (**b**) *(for casual wear)* ropa *f* de sport

sportswoman ['spɔːtswʊmən] *n* (**a**) *(player of sport)* deportista *f* (**b**) *(fair person)* dama *f*, señora *f*

sport-utility vehicle ['spɔːtjuː'tɪlɪtɪviːɪkəl] *n US* todoterreno *m* utilitario

sporty ['spɔːtɪ] *adj* (**a**) *(person)* deportista, aficionado(a) al deporte (**b**) *(clothes)* deportivo(a) (**c**) *(car)* deportivo(a)

spot [spɒt] **1** *n* (**a**) *(place)* lugar *m*, sitio *m*; **we found a shady s.** encontramos un lugar sombreado; **I have a tender s. on my leg** tengo un punto sensible en la pierna; **on the s.: she bought it on the s.** lo compró allí mismo; **to decide/fire sb on the s.** decidirlo/despedir a alguien en el acto; **he was killed on the s.** murió en el acto; **reporters were on the s. within ten minutes** los periodistas acudieron al lugar de los hechos en cuestión de diez minutos; **she was jogging on the s.** marchaba a trote corto sin moverse del lugar; IDIOM *Fam* **to put sb on the s.** poner a alguien en un aprieto; IDIOM *Fam* **to be in a (tight) s.** estar en un aprieto; IDIOM **that hit the s.** ¡qué bien me ha sentado! ►► *Fam* ***s. cash*** dinero *m* al contado, dinero *m* contante y sonante; ***s. check*** inspección *f* al azar; *Fin* ***s. market*** mercado *m* al contado *or* a término; *Fin* ***s. price*** precio *m* al contado; *Fin* ***s. trading*** operación *f* al contado
(**b**) *(on shirt, tie, leopard)* lunar *m*; *(on giraffe)* mancha *f*; **I've got spots before my eyes** tengo motas en la vista, veo manchas
(**c**) *(stain)* mancha *f*; **how did you get these spots of blood on your shirt?** ¿cómo te has manchado de sangre la camisa?
(**d**) *(pimple)* grano *m*; *(beauty spot)* lunar *m*; **he came out in spots** le salieron granos, le salió un sarpullido
(**e**) *(blemish) (on character, reputation)* mancha *f*
(**f**) *Br Fam (small amount) (of wine, milk)* gota *f*; **a s. of lunch** algo de comer; **a s. of bother** un problemilla; **we haven't had a s. of rain all summer** no ha caído ni una sola gota de agua en todo el verano, no ha llovido (nada) en todo el verano; **she hardly did a s. of work** apenas trabajó
(**g**) *(aspect, feature, moment)* **the only bright s. of the week** el único momento agradable de la semana, la única alegría de la semana
(**h**) *(spotlight)* foco *m*
(**i**) *TV & Rad (in schedule)* espacio *m*; *(advertisement)* anuncio *m*, spot *m*; **he has a s. on the Margie Warner show** *(as singer, comedian)* tiene un espacio en el show de Margie Warner, actúa en el show de Margie Warner
(**j**) *(in soccer)* punto *m* de penalti ►► ***s. kick*** (lanzamiento *m* de) penalti *m*
(**k**) *(in billiards, snooker)* punto *m*
(**l**) *Typ* ***s. colour*** color *m* plano *or* directo
2 *vt* (*pt & pp* **spotted**) (**a**) *(stain, mark)* salpicar
(**b**) *(notice) (person, object, mistake)* localizar, ver; *(opportunity)* encontrar, descubrir; *(winner)* pronosticar; **I spotted her in the crowd** la divisé en medio de la muchedumbre; **the missing woman was spotted in the pub** la mujer desaparecida fue vista en el bar; **can you s. the difference?** ¿te das cuenta *or* ves dónde está la diferencia?; **to s. sb doing sth** ver a alguien hacer algo; **well spotted!** ¡buena observación!; **you could s. the ending a mile off!** ¡se veía venir el final a mil leguas!
(**c**) *(place on spot) (in soccer)* colocar en el punto de penalti; *(in billiards, snooker)* colocar sobre el punto
3 *vi* (**a**) *(rain lightly)* **it's spotting (with rain)** está chispeando (**b**) *(woman)* **to be spotting** estar manchando

spot-check ['spɒttʃek] *vt* inspeccionar al azar

spotless ['spɒtlɪs] *adj* (**a**) *(room, appearance, clothes)* impecable (**b**) *(reputation)* intachable

spotlessly ['spɒtlɪslɪ] *adv* **s. clean** limpio(a) como una patena

spotlight ['spɒtlaɪt] **1** *n (in theatre)* foco *m*, reflector *m*; *(in house)* foco *m*; *Fig* **to be in the s.** estar en el candelero; *Fig* **to turn the s. on sth** centrar la atención en algo
2 *vt* (**a**) *(castle, statue)* iluminar con focos *or* reflectores (**b**) *(concentrate on) (personality, talent)* centrar la atención en, dedicar la atención a (**c**) *(pinpoint) (flaws, changes)* poner de manifiesto

spot-on ['spɒt'ɒn] *Br* **1** *adj Fam* **your guess was s.** acertaste plenamente *or* de lleno, diste en el clavo; **you were s. with your description** hiciste una descripción perfecta, lo describiste al pie de la letra
2 *adv (guess)* con toda exactitud
3 *exclam* ¡exacto!

spotted ['spɒtɪd] *adj* (**a**) *(tie, dress)* de lunares (**b**) *Zool* ***s. flycatcher*** papamoscas *m inv* gris; ***s. grouper*** cabrilla *f*; ***s. sandpiper*** andarríos *m inv* maculado (**c**) *Culin Br* ***s. dick*** = budín de pasas de Corinto cocido al vapor que se come con crema

spotter ['spɒtə(r)] *n Mil* observador(ora) *m,f* ►► ***s. plane*** avión *m* de reconocimiento

spotty ['spɒtɪ] *adj* (**a**) *(pimply)* con acné (**b**) *(fabric, tie)* moteado(a), de lunares (**c**) *(patchy) (performance)* desigual

spot-weld ['spɒtweld] **1** *n* soldadura *f* por puntos
2 *vt* soldar por puntos

spouse [spaʊs] *n* cónyuge *mf*

spout [spaʊt] **1** *n* (**a**) *(of teapot, kettle, watering can)* pitorro *m* (**b**) *(pipe) (of fountain)* caño *m*; *(of gutter)* canalón *m*, gárgola *f*; IDIOM *Br Fam* **to be up the s.** *(plans, finances)* haberse ido al garete *or Am* carajo; *(pregnant)* estar con bombo; **now we're really up the s.** ahora sí que la hemos hecho buena, ahora sí que la llevamos cruda (**c**) *(jet of liquid)* chorro *m*
2 *vt* (**a**) *(liquid)* chorrear; *(fire, smoke)* arrojar, lanzar bocanadas de (**b**) *Fam (speech, nonsense)* soltar
3 *vi* (**a**) *(liquid)* chorrear; *(fire, smoke)* salir bocanadas de (**b**) *Fam (person)* largar, enrollarse

sprain [spreɪn] **1** *n (injury)* torcedura *f*, esguince *m*
2 *vt* **to s. one's ankle/wrist** torcerse el tobillo/la muñeca

sprained [spreɪnd] *adj (ankle, wrist)* torcido(a)

sprang *pt of* **spring**

sprat [spræt] *n (fish)* espadín *m*; IDIOM **to use a s. to catch a mackerel** dar poco para obtener mucho a cambio

sprawl [sprɔːl] **1** *n* (**a**) *(position)* **he lay in an ungainly s.** estaba tendido todo despatarrado (**b**) *(of city)* aglomeración *f*
2 *vi* (**a**) *(person)* despatarrarse; **she was sprawling in the armchair/on the bed** estaba toda despatarrada en el sillón/la cama; **the blow sent him sprawling** el golpe lo dejó tumbado (**b**) *(town, plant)* extenderse

sprawling ['sprɔːlɪŋ] *adj* (**a**) *(person)* despatarrado(a) (**b**) *(town)* desperdigado(a) (**c**) *(handwriting)* desgarbado(a)

spray[1] [spreɪ] *n (of flowers)* ramo *m*

spray[2] **1** *n* (**a**) *(liquid)* rociada *f*; *(from sea)* rocío *m* del mar, roción *m* (**b**) *(act of spraying)* rociada *f*; **to give sth a s.** *(flowers, crops)* rociar algo; *(room)* rociar algo con ambientador; **I'll just give my hair a quick s.** voy a echarme un poco de laca en el pelo
(**c**) *(device)* aerosol *m*, spray *m*; *(for perfume)* atomizador *m* ►► ***s. can*** aerosol *m*, spray *m*; ***s. gun*** *(for paint)* pistola *f* (pulverizadora); ***s. paint*** pintura *f* en aerosol
2 *vt* (**a**) *(liquid, room, crops)* rociar (**with** de); **he sprayed the deodorant under his arms** se echó desodorante en las axilas; **three layers of paint are sprayed onto the metal** el metal lleva tres capas de pintura pulverizada; **a slogan sprayed on a wall** una pintada con espray en una pared (**b**) *(with bullets)* **he sprayed the room with bullets** acribilló la habitación a balazos
3 *vi (liquid)* salpicar; **the water sprayed onto the floor** el agua salpicó por el suelo; **the oil sprayed over them** el aceite les salpicó

sprayer ['spreɪə(r)] *n* (**a**) *(for perfume)* pulverizador *m*, atomizador *m*; *(spray gun)* pistola *f* pulverizadora (**b**) *Agr (machine)* aspersor *m*, equipo *m* de aspersión; *(plane)* avión *m* fumigador

spray-on ['spreɪɒn] *adj* en aerosol

spray-paint ['spreɪ'peɪnt] *vt (with spray can)* pintar con aerosol; *(with spray gun)* pintar a pistola

SPREAD [spred] **1** *n* (**a**) *(of wings, sails)* envergadura *f*
(**b**) *(range) (of products, ages)* gama *f*; *(of opinions)* gama *f*, variedad *f*; *(of investments)* abanico *m* ►► ***s. betting*** = sistema de apuestas por el que las ganancias son proporcionales a la precisión de la predicción
(**c**) *(of disease, fire)* propagación *f*; *(of doctrine, technology)* difusión *f*; **they fear the s. of unrest to other cities** temen que los disturbios se propaguen a otras ciudades
(**d**) *Fam (big meal)* banquete *m*, comilona *f*
(**e**) *(in newspaper)* **a full-page s.** una plana entera; **a two-page s.** una página doble
(**f**) *(paste)* **cheese s.** queso para untar; **chocolate s.** crema de cacao; **low-fat s.** margarina baja en grasas
(**g**) *US (ranch)* rancho *m*
(**h**) *(for bed)* colcha *f*, cubrecama *m*
(**i**) *St Exch* diferencial *m*
2 *vt* (*pt & pp* **spread**) (**a**) *(extend) (map, newspaper, wings)* desplegar, extender; *(sail)* desplegar; *(fingers)* estirar; *(rug)* tender; **she s. a tablecloth on the table** extendió un mantel sobre la mesa; **to s. one's arms/legs** extender los brazos/las piernas; IDIOM **to s. one's wings** emprender el vuelo
(**b**) *(distribute) (sand, straw)* extender, esparcir; *(disease, fire)* propagar; *(news, doctrine, gossip)* difundir; *(terror, panic)* sembrar; **he s. his papers on the desk** esparció sus papeles sobre el escritorio; **take your shoes off, you're spreading dirt everywhere!** ¡quítate los zapatos, lo estás dejando todo perdido!; **the explosion s. debris over a large area** la explosión desperdigó escombros por un amplio radio; **the votes were evenly s.** los votos se distribuyeron uniformemente; **we'll s. the work across the different departments** repartiremos el trabajo entre los diferentes departamentos; **to s. payments over several months** distribuir los pagos a lo largo de varios meses; **to s. the load** repartir el trabajo; **to s. the word** correr la voz; IDIOM *Br Fam* **to s. it** *or* **oneself around** *or* **about** *(be sexually promiscuous)* acostarse con unos y con otros
(**c**) *(apply) (butter, ointment)* untar; *(glue, paint)* extender; **s. the bread with butter, s. butter on the bread** untar el pan con mantequilla; **to s. a surface with sth** untar algo en una superficie; **to s. the paint evenly** extender la pintura de manera uniforme; **their troops are s. too thinly to be effective** sus tropas están demasiado desperdigadas como para que puedan actuar con eficacia; IDIOM **to s. oneself too thinly** intentar abarcar demasiado
3 *vi* (**a**) *(extend) (forest, oil slick, stain)* extenderse; *(disease, fire, species)* propagarse; *(news, doctrine, gossip)* difundirse; *(terror, panic)* cundir; **a smile s. across his face** una sonrisa recorrió su cara; **the infection has s. to her lungs** la infección se ha extendido a los pulmones; **the custom s. to the rest of Europe** la costumbre se extendió por el resto de Europa; **the suburbs continue to s.** los suburbios continuan creciendo; **he feels embarrassed about his spreading waistline** le da vergüenza *or Andes, CAm, Carib, Méx* pena que se le esté ensanchando la cintura; **their correspondence spreads over 20 years** hace más de 20 años que mantienen correspondencia
(**b**) *(butter)* extenderse
4 *adj Ling (vowel)* pronunciado(a) con los labios extendidos

►**spread out** **1** *vt sep (map, newspaper)* desplegar, extender; **to s. oneself out** *(on sofa)* estirarse
2 *vi* (**a**) *(person) (on floor, bed)* estirarse
(**b**) *(search party)* desplegarse
(**c**) *(city, oil slick)* extenderse

spread-eagle ['spred'iːgəl] *vt (knock flat)* tumbar, dejar tumbado (despatarrado)

spread-eagled ['spred'iːgəld] *adj* despatarrado(a), con los miembros extendidos

spreader ['spredə(r)] *n* (**a**) *(for fertilizer, manure)* máquina *f* esparcidora, distribuidora *f* de abono (**b**) *(for putty, plaster)* espátula *f*

spreadsheet ['spredʃiːt] *n Comptr* hoja *f* de cálculo

spree [spriː] *n Fam* **to go on a s.** *(go drinking)* ir de juerga *or* parranda; **to go on a shopping/spending s.** salir a comprar/gastar a lo loco; **a killing s.** una carnicería, una matanza

sprig [sprɪg] *n* ramita *f*

sprightliness ['spraɪtlɪnɪs] *n (of person)* vivacidad *f*; *(of tune)* alegría *f*

sprightly ['spraɪtlɪ] *adj (person)* vivaz, vivaracho(a); *(tune)* alegre

spring [sprɪŋ] **1** *n* (**a**) *(of water)* manantial *m*; **hot** *or* **thermal springs** fuentes termales, manantial de aguas termales ►► ***s. water*** agua *f* de manantial
(**b**) *(season)* primavera *f*; **in (the) s.** en primavera; IDIOM *Fam* **he's no s. chicken** ya no es ningún niño *or Esp* mozo; IDIOM **s. is in the air** la primavera la sangre altera ►► ***s. fever*** fiebre *f* primaveral *or* de primavera; *Br* ***s. greens*** hojas *fpl* de col jóvenes; ***s. onion*** cebolleta *f*, *RP* cebolla *f* de verdeo; ***s. roll*** rollo *m or* rollito *m* de primavera, *RP* arrollado *m or* arrolladito *m* primavera; ***s. tide*** marea *f* viva *(de primavera)*
(**c**) *(metal coil)* muelle *m*; *(in watch)* resorte *m*; *(in car)* ballesta *f* ►► ***s. balance*** dinamómetro *m*; ***s. lock*** cerradura *f* de golpe *or* resbalón; ***s. mattress*** colchón *m* de muelles
(**d**) *(leap)* brinco *m*, salto *m*
(**e**) *(elasticity)* elasticidad *f*; **he walked with a s. in his step** caminaba con paso alegre
2 *vt* (*pt* **sprang** [spræŋ], *pp* **sprung** [sprʌŋ]) (**a**) *(reveal unexpectedly)* **to s. sth on sb** soltarle algo a alguien; **he doesn't like people springing surprises on him** no le gusta que le den sorpresas
(**b**) *(develop)* **to s. a leak** *(container)* empezar a tener una fuga; *(boat)* empezar a hacer agua
(**c**) *(trap) (of animal)* hacer saltar, accionar; **to s. a trap on sb** sorprender con una trampa a alguien
(**d**) *Fam (free)* **to s. sb out of jail** ayudar a alguien a escapar de la cárcel
(**e**) *(jump over) (hedge, brook)* saltar por encima de
3 *vi* (**a**) *(jump)* brincar, saltar; **to s. at sb** *(dog, attacker)* abalanzarse sobre alguien; **she sprang back in horror** retrocedió de un brinco horrorizada; **the branch sprang back** la rama retrocedió de golpe a su posición inicial, la rama saltó hacia atrás; **the lid sprang open/shut** la tapa se abrió/cerró de golpe; **the cat sprang out of the armchair** el gato saltó del sillón; **he sprang out of the way just in time** se quitó de en medio de un salto justo a tiempo; **to s. to attention** ponerse firme; **to s. to one's feet** levantarse de un brinco; **to s. into action** entrar inmediatamente en acción; **to s. to sb's defence** lanzarse a la defensa de alguien; **the engine sprang to** *or* **into life** el motor arrancó de golpe; **to s. to mind** venir(se) a la cabeza
(**b**) *(originate, come into being)* **to s. from** provenir de, proceder de; **to s. into existence** aparecer de pronto; *Fam* **where did you s. from?** ¿de dónde has salido?

►**spring up** *vi* (**a**) *(jump to one's feet)* levantarse de un brinco (**b**) *(appear suddenly) (town, factory, company)* aparecer, surgir (de la noche a la mañana); *(plants)* brotar, nacer; *(doubt, rumour, friendship)* surgir, aparecer; *(breeze)* levantarse (**c**) *(grow in size, height)* **hasn't Lisa sprung up this year!** ¡qué estirón ha pegado Lisa!

springboard ['sprɪŋbɔːd] *n* (**a**) *Sport* trampolín *m* (**b**) *(starting point)* trampolín *m* (**for** para)

springbok ['sprɪŋbɒk] *n* springbok *m*; *Sport* **the Springboks** = la selección de rugby de Sudáfrica

spring-clean ['sprɪŋ'kliːn] **1** *n* limpieza *f* a fondo
2 *vt (house)* limpiar a fondo
3 *vi* hacer limpieza a fondo

spring-cleaning ['sprɪŋ'kliːnɪŋ] *n* limpieza *f* a fondo; **to do the s.** hacer una limpieza a fondo

springer spaniel ['sprɪŋə'spænjəl] *n* springer spaniel *m*

springiness ['sprɪŋɪnɪs] *n (of material, ground, mattress, hair)* elasticidad *f*

springlike ['sprɪŋlaɪk] *adj (weather, day)* primaveral

springtail ['sprɪŋteɪl] *n* colémbolo *m*

springtide ['sprɪŋtaɪd] *n Literary* primavera *f*

springtime ['sprɪŋtaɪm] *n* primavera *f*

springy ['sprɪŋɪ] *adj* (**a**) *(material)* elástico(a); *(ground, mattress)* mullido(a), flexible; *(of hair)* flexible (**b**) *(step)* ligero(a)

sprinkle ['sprɪŋkəl] **1** *n (of rain)* gotas *fpl* de lluvia, llovizna *f*
2 *vt* (**a**) *(with liquid)* rociar (**with** con); **he sprinkled vinegar on** *or* **over his chips** roció las *Esp* patatas *or Am* papas fritas con vinagre
(**b**) *(with salt, flour)* espolvorear (**with** con); **to s. sth over sth** espolvorear algo por encima de algo; **I sprinkled sugar on** *or* **over my cereal, I sprinkled my cereal with sugar** espolvoreé los cereales con azúcar, les eché azúcar por encima a los cereales
(**c**) *(strew, dot)* **the sky was sprinkled with stars** el cielo estaba tachonado de estrellas; **a speech sprinkled with metaphors** un discurso salpicado de metáforas
3 *vi (rain)* lloviznar, chispear

sprinkler ['sprɪŋklə(r)] *n* (**a**) *(for lawns, fields)* aspersor *m* (**b**) *(to extinguish fires)* rociador *m* contra incendios ▸▸ ***s. system*** sistema *m* de rociadores contra incendios (**c**) *(for sugar)* azucarero *m*, dosificador *m* de azúcar (**d**) ***s. (head)*** *(of shower, watering can)* alcachofa *f*

sprinkling ['sprɪŋklɪŋ] *n (small quantity) (of sugar, salt)* pizca *f*, poco *m*; *(of rain)* gotas *fpl*; *(of snow)* copos *mpl*; **there was a s. of new faces** había unas cuantas caras nuevas; **her speech contained a liberal s. of witty references** su discurso estuvo abundantemente salpicado de ingeniosas alusiones

sprint [sprɪnt] **1** *n* (**a**) *(fast run)* carrera *f*; *(in cycling)* esprint *m*; **to break into a s.** echar a correr; **to make a s. for sth** echar una carrera hasta algo; **he was overtaken in the s. for the line** lo adelantaron en el esprint final ▸▸ ***s. finish*** *(of race)* final *m* al esprint; *(of athlete)* esprint *m* final (**b**) *(running race)* carrera *f or* prueba *f* de velocidad; **the 60 metre s.** los 60 metros lisos
2 *vt (run fast)* cubrir *or* recorrer a toda velocidad
3 *vi* (**a**) *(run fast)* correr a toda velocidad; *(in cycling)* esprintar, hacer un esprint; **he sprinted after her** corrió tras ella a toda velocidad; **to s. off** salir corriendo a toda velocidad (**b**) *(in athletics)* correr al esprint

sprinter ['sprɪntə(r)] *n (athlete, cyclist)* velocista *mf*, esprínter *mf*

sprite [spraɪt] *n (in folklore)* duendecillo(a) *m,f*

spritsail ['sprɪtseɪl] *n Naut* cebadera *f*

spritzer ['sprɪtsə(r)] *n* vino *m* blanco con soda

sprocket ['sprɒkɪt] *n* (**a**) *(cog)* diente *m* (de engranaje) ▸▸ ***s. holes*** *(in film)* perforación *f* lateral (**b**) ***s. (wheel)*** rueda *f* dentada

sprog [sprɒg] *n Br Fam Hum (child)* mocoso(a) *m,f*; **to drop a s.** echar al mundo un churumbel

sprout [spraʊt] **1** *n* (**a**) *(of plant)* brote *m* (**b**) *(vegetable)* **(Brussels) sprouts** coles *fpl or CSur* repollitos *mpl* de Bruselas
2 *vt* (**a**) *(leaves)* echar (**b**) *(grow)* **he's starting to s. a beard** *(for first time)* le está saliendo barba; **the ram is sprouting horns** al carnero le están saliendo los cuernos; **the town centre has sprouted several new cafés** han aparecido de repente varias cafeterías nuevas en el centro de la ciudad
3 *vi* (**a**) *(grow) (leaves, hair)* brotar (**b**) *(germinate) (bean, seed, onion)* germinar (**c**) *(appear suddenly)* aparecer de repente

▸**sprout up** *vi (plant, child)* crecer rápidamente; *(new buildings, businesses)* surgir (de la noche a la mañana)

spruce[1] [spru:s] *n* (**a**) *(tree)* picea *f* (**b**) *(wood)* (madera *f* de) picea *f*

spruce[2] *adj (tidy)* pulcro(a); *(smart)* elegante

▸**spruce up** *vt sep (room)* adecentar; **to s. oneself up** arreglarse, acicalarse

sprucely ['spru:slɪ] *adv (dressed)* impecablemente

sprung [sprʌŋ] **1** *adj (mattress)* de muelles
2 *pp of* **spring**

spry [spraɪ] *adj* vivaz, vivaracho(a)

spud [spʌd] *n Br Fam (potato) Esp* patata *f*, *Am* papa *f*

spud-bashing ['spʌd'bæʃɪŋ] *n Br Fam* = castigo aplicado en el ejército y consistente en pelar *Esp* patatas *or Am* papas

spume [spju:m] *n Literary* espuma *f*

spun [spʌn] **1** *adj* ***s. glass*** vidrio *m* hilado, lana *f* de vidrio; ***s. gold*** hilo *m* de oro; ***s. silk*** hilado *m* de seda; ***s. sugar*** caramelo *m* hilado
2 *pt & pp of* **spin**

spunk [spʌŋk] *n* (**a**) *Fam (courage)* agallas *fpl*, arrestos *mpl* (**b**) *Br Vulg (semen)* leche *f*, *Esp* lefa *f*

spunky ['spʌŋkɪ] *adj Fam (performance)* valiente, con agallas; **he's a s. character** es un tipo con agallas, tiene agallas

spur [spɜ:(r)] **1** *n* (**a**) *(for riding)* espuela *f*; IDIOM **he won his spurs** demostró su valía (**b**) *(stimulus)* acicate *m*, incentivo *m*; **the s. of competition drove her to new heights** el estímulo de la competición la llevó a superar listones cada vez más altos; **on the s. of the moment** sin pararse a pensar (**c**) *(of cock)* espolón *m* (**d**) *(of land, rock)* estribación *f* (**e**) *Rail (branch line)* ramal *m*
2 *vt* (*pt & pp* **spurred**) (**a**) *(horse)* espolear (**b**) *(stimulate)* **to s. sb (on) to do sth** espolear a alguien para que haga algo; **he was spurred on by the crowd** fue espoleado por la muchedumbre; **to s. sb into action** hacer que alguien pase a la acción

spurge [spɜ:dʒ] *n* tártago *m* ▸▸ ***s. laurel*** lauréola *f*, adelfilla *f*

spurious ['spjʊərɪəs] *adj* (**a**) *(ill-founded) (argument, reasoning, objection)* falso(a), espurio(a) (**b**) *(insincere) (enthusiasm, sympathy, compliment)* fingido(a), falso(a)

spuriously ['spjʊərɪəslɪ] *adv (to argue, object)* sin fundamentos legítimos

spuriousness ['spjʊərɪəsnɪs] *n* (**a**) *(of argument, reasoning, objection)* falta *f* de fundamentos legítimos (**b**) *(of enthusiasm, sympathy, compliment)* carácter *m* fingido, falsedad *f*

spurn [spɜ:n] *vt* desdeñar

spurned [spɜ:nd] *adj* desdeñado(a)

spur-of-the-moment ['spɜ:əvðə'məʊmənt] *adj (purchase, phone call, decision)* impensado(a), indeliberado(a)

spurt [spɜ:t] **1** *n* (**a**) *(of liquid)* chorro *m*; *(of flame)* llamarada *f*; *(of gunfire)* ráfaga *f* (**b**) *(of action, energy)* arranque *m*; *(of speed)* arrancada *f*; **to put on a s.** acelerar; **her inspiration came in spurts** le llegaban ráfagas repentinas de inspiración
2 *vt (liquid)* lanzar chorros de
3 *vi* (**a**) *(liquid)* chorrear; *(flames)* salir despedido(a) (**b**) *(go quickly)* apretar el paso, acelerar

sputter ['spʌtə(r)] *vi (fire, flame, candle)* crepitar; *(motor)* pegar explosiones; **he sputtered angrily** barbotó furioso

sputum ['spju:təm] *n Med* expectoración *f*, esputo *m*

spy [spaɪ] **1** *n* espía *mf* ▸▸ ***s. plane*** avión *m* espía *or* de espionaje; ***s. ring*** red *f* de espionaje; ***s. satellite*** satélite *m* espía *or* de espionaje; ***s. story*** historia *f* de espías *or* de espionaje
2 *vt (notice)* ver; **she had spied a flaw in his reasoning** había captado un error en su razonamiento
3 *vi* espiar (**for** para); **to s. on sb** espiar a alguien

▸**spy out** *vt sep* **to s. out the land** reconocer el terreno

spycatcher ['spaɪkætʃə(r)] *n Fam* contraespía *mf*

spyglass ['spaɪglɑ:s] *n* catalejo *m*

spyhole ['spaɪhəʊl] *n* mirilla *f*

spying ['spaɪɪŋ] *n* espionaje *m*

Sq (*abbr* **Square**) Pl.

sq *Math* (*abbr* **square**) cuadrado(a)

sq. ft. (*abbr* **square foot** *or* **feet**) pie(s) *m(pl)* cuadrado(s)

SQL [eskju:'el] *n Comptr* (*abbr* **structured query language**) SQL *m*

squab [skwɒb] *n (young pigeon)* pichón *m*

squabble ['skwɒbəl] **1** *n* riña *f*, pelea *f*
2 *vi* reñir, pelear (**over** *or* **about** por)

squabbling ['skwɒblɪŋ] *n* riñas *fpl*, peleas *fpl*

squacco ['skwækəʊ] *n* **s. (heron)** garcilla *f* cangrejera

squad [skwɒd] *n* (**a**) *(of athletes, players)* plantilla *f*; **the first-team s.** el primer equipo; **he's been included in the England s. for Saturday's match** ha sido incluido en la plantilla de la selección inglesa para el partido del sábado; **they are taking a thirty-man s. to Australia** la plantilla que viajará a Australia está compuesta por treinta jugadores
(**b**) *(of soldiers)* escuadra *f*
(**c**) *(of police force)* brigada *f* ▸▸ ***s. car*** coche *m* patrulla
(**d**) *(of workmen)* brigada *f*, cuadrilla *f*

squaddie ['skwɒdɪ] *n Br Fam* soldado *m* raso

squadron ['skwɒdrən] *n Mil* (**a**) *(of planes)* escuadrón *m* ▸▸ ***s. leader*** comandante *mf* de aviación (**b**) *(of ships)* escuadra *f* (**c**) *(in armoured regiment, cavalry)* escuadrón *m*

squalid ['skwɒlɪd] *adj* (**a**) *(dirty)* mugriento(a), inmundo(a) (**b**) *(sordid) (details, affair)* sórdido(a)

squall [skwɔ:l] **1** *n* (**a**) *(of wind)* turbión *m*, ventarrón *m*; *(rain shower)* aguacero *m* (**b**) *(cry)* berrido *m* (**c**) *(argument)* tempestad *f*, borrasca *f*
2 *vi (cry)* berrear

squalling ['skwɔ:lɪŋ] *adj (child)* berreón(ona), chillón(ona)

squally ['skwɔ:lɪ] *adj (weather, day)* borrascoso(a), ventoso(a); *(showers)* tormentoso(a)

squalor ['skwɒlə(r)] *n* (**a**) *(dirtiness)* inmundicia *f*; **to live in s.** vivir en la miseria (**b**) *(sordidness) (of details, affair)* sordidez *f*

squander ['skwɒndə(r)] *vt (money, time, talents)* despilfarrar, malgastar; *(opportunity)* desperdiciar

square [skweə(r)] **1** *n* (**a**) *(shape)* cuadrado *m*; **he folded the napkin into a s.** dobló la servilleta formando un cuadrado
(**b**) *(of chocolate)* onza *f*; *(of paper, material)* (trozo *m*) cuadrado *m*; **cut the cake into squares** parte el pastel en (trozos) cuadrados
(**c**) *(on chessboard)* escaque *m*; *(in crossword)* casilla *f*; *(on map)* recuadro *m*; IDIOM **to be back at** *or* **to s. one** haber vuelto al punto de partida
(**d**) *Math (of number)* cuadrado *m*
(**e**) *(of town, village)* plaza *f*; *(smaller)* plazoleta *f*; *Mil (parade ground)* patio *m*
(**f**) *(instrument)* escuadra *f*
(**g**) *Fam (unfashionable person)* carca *mf*
2 *adj* (**a**) *(in shape)* cuadrado(a); **to have s. shoulders** estar cuadrado(a) de hombros; **to have a s. jaw** tener la mandíbula cuadrada; IDIOM *Hum* **you'll get s. eyes if you keep watching TV all day** se te van a poner los ojos cuadrados si sigues viendo la tele todo el día; IDIOM **she felt like a s. peg in a round hole** se sentía fuera de lugar ▸▸ ***s. bracket*** corchete *m*; ***s. dance*** baile *m* de figuras *or* en cuadrilla; ***the S. Mile*** = el barrio financiero y bursátil de Londres; ***s. sail*** vela *f* cuadra
(**b**) *(forming right angle)* **the shelves aren't s.** la estantería no está cuadrada con la pared, la estantería no está en ángulo recto con la pared; **to be s. with** *or* **to sth** estar cuadrado(a) *or* en ángulo recto con algo ▸▸ ***s. corner*** esquina *f* en ángulo recto
(**c**) *Math* cuadrado(a); **10 s. kilometres** 10 kilómetros cuadrados; **the room is 5 metres s.** la habitación mide 5 x 5 metros ▸▸ ***s. root*** raíz *f* cuadrada
(**d**) *Fam (unfashionable)* carca
(**e**) *(honest, fair)* **to be s. with sb** ser claro(a) con alguien; **a s. deal** un trato justo
(**f**) *(even)* **the teams are (all) s.** los equipos van empatados *or* igualados; **we're s.** *(having settled debt)* estamos en paz; **to get s. with sb** *(get revenge)* desquitarse *or* tomarse la revancha con alguien
(**g**) *(satisfying)* **a s. meal** una buena comida
(**h**) *(in soccer) (defence, player)* alineado(a), en línea; *(pass, ball)* lateral
(**i**) *US Fam* ***s. shooter*** *(person)* persona *f* de fiar, *Esp* tío(a) *m,f* legal
3 *adv* (**a**) *(directly)* directamente; **she hit him s. on the jaw** le dio de lleno en la mandíbula; **he hit the ball s. in the middle of the racket** le dio a la pelota de lleno con la raqueta; **to look sb s. in the eye** mirar a alguien fijamente a los ojos
(**b**) *(in soccer) (pass)* lateralmente; **their defence was caught s.** sorprendió a la defensa del equipo contrario alienada *or* en línea
4 *vt* (**a**) *(make square)* cuadrar; **to s. one's shoulders** ponerse recto(a); IDIOM **it's like trying to s. the circle** es como intentar la cuadratura del círculo *or* como intentar cuadrar el círculo
(**b**) *Math (number)* elevar al cuadrado; **three squared is nine** tres (elevado) al cuadrado es nueve
(**c**) *(settle)* **to s. accounts with sb** arreglar cuentas con alguien
(**d**) *(reconcile)* casar, hacer encajar (**with** con); **how do you s. it with your convictions/conscience?** ¿cómo lo haces encajar con tus convicciones/conciencia?
(**e**) *Sport (level) (match, series)* nivelar, igualar
(**f**) *(in soccer)* **to s. the ball** hacer un pase lateral
5 *vi (agree)* cuadrar, concordar; **his story doesn't s. with the facts** su historia no cuadra con los hechos

▸ **square off** *vt sep* (**a**) *(piece of paper)* cuadricular (**b**) *(corner, log)* cuadrar

▸ **square up** *vi* (**a**) *(settle debts)* hacer *or* saldar cuentas (**with** con) (**b**) *(fighters)* ponerse en guardia; *Fig* **to s. up to a problem/an opponent** hacer frente a un problema/un adversario

square-bashing ['skweə'bæʃɪŋ] *n Fam* instrucción *f* en el patio de armas

squared [skweəd] *adj (paper)* cuadriculado(a)

square-eyed ['skweəraɪd] *adj Fam Hum* teleadicto(a), con los ojos cuadrados de ver tanta tele

square-eyes ['skweəraɪz] *n Fam Hum* teleadicto(a) *m,f*; **come on s.! never mind the television** ¡apaga la tele, que se te van a poner los ojos cuadrados!

squarely ['skweəlɪ] *adv* (**a**) *(directly)* directamente; **to look sb s. in the eye** mirar a alguien fijamente a los ojos; **she hit the ball s. in the middle of the racket** le dio a la pelota de lleno con la raqueta; **the blow landed s. on his nose** el golpe le dio de lleno *or* plano en la nariz; **the responsibility for the disaster rests s. on their shoulders** la responsabilidad del desastre recae directamente sobre sus hombros
(**b**) *(honestly)* con franqueza

square-rigged ['skweə'rɪgd] *adj* con aparejo de cruz

square-shouldered ['skweə'ʃəʊldəd] *adj* de hombros cuadrados, cuadrado(a) de hombros

square-toed ['skweə'təʊd] *adj (shoes)* con las puntas cuadradas, de puntera cuadrada

squash[1] [skwɒʃ] **1** *n* (**a**) *(crush)* apretones *mpl*; **it was a s., but everyone got into the taxi** nos tuvimos que apretar, pero entramos todos en el taxi
(**b**) *Br (drink)* **orange/lemon s.** (bebida a base de) concentrado de naranja/limón
(**c**) *(sport)* squash *m* ▸▸ ***s. ball*** pelota *f* de squash; ***s. club*** club *m* de squash; ***s. court*** pista *f or* cancha *f* de squash; ***s. racket*** raqueta *f* de squash; *Br* ***s. rackets*** *(game)* squash *m*
2 *vt* (**a**) *(crush)* aplastar; **you're squashing me!** ¡me estás estrujando!; **we were squashed in the hold like sardines** íbamos en la bodega como sardinas en lata; **I can s. one more person in the back** cabe una persona más atrás (si todos se aprietan un poco)
(**b**) *(objection, opposition)* acallar; *(hopes)* dar al traste con; *(rebellion)* aplastar; **I felt utterly squashed by her contemptuous dismissal** me dejó totalmente chafado con aquel rechazo desdeñoso
3 *vi* **to s. into a room/a taxi** apretujarse en una habitación/un taxi

▸ **squash in** *vi (people)* meterse apretujándose

▸ **squash together 1** *vt sep* apretar
2 *vi (people)* apretujarse, apretarse

▸ **squash up** *vi* apretujarse, apretarse

squash[2] *n US (vegetable)* cucurbitácea *f*

squashy ['skwɒʃɪ] *adj (ground, fruit)* blando(a)

squat [skwɒt] **1** *n* (**a**) *Br (illegally occupied dwelling)* casa *f* ocupada *(ilegalmente)* (**b**) *(crouch)* postura *f* en cuclillas ▸▸ ***s. thrust*** *(exercise)* flexión *f or* estiramiento *m* en cuclillas (**c**) *US Fam (nothing)* **I didn't get s.** no conseguí ni un pimiento
2 *adj (person)* chaparro(a), achaparrado(a); *(object, building)* muy bajo(a)
3 *vi (pt & pp* **squatted**) (**a**) *(crouch down)* agacharse, ponerse de cuclillas (**b**) *(occupy dwelling illegally)* ocupar una vivienda ilegalmente

▸ **squat down** *vi* agacharse, ponerse de cuclillas

squatter ['skwɒtə(r)] *n* ocupante *mf* ilegal

squaw [skwɔː] *n* = mujer india norteamericana

squawk [skwɔːk] **1** *n* (**a**) *(of bird)* graznido *m* (**b**) *US Fam (complaint)* queja *f*
2 *vi* (**a**) *(bird)* graznar (**b**) *Fam (person, baby)* chillar

squeak [skwiːk] **1** *n (of animal, person)* chillido *m*; *(of door, wheel)* chirrido *m*; *(of floorboard)* crujido *m*; *(of shoes)* crujido *m*; **to let out** *or* **to give a s. of pleasure** pegar un chillido de alegría; *Fam* **I don't want to hear another s. out of you** no quiero oírte decir ni pío; *Fam* **have you heard from her? – not a s.** ¿sabes algo de ella? – nada en absoluto
2 *vt (say in high voice)* chillar
3 *vi* (**a**) *(animal, person)* chillar (**with** de); *(door, wheel)* chirriar, rechinar; *(floorboard)* crujir; *(shoes)* crujir (**b**) *Fam (succeed narrowly)* **the team squeaked into the semi-finals** el equipo se metió en las semifinales por los pelos

▸ **squeak through** *vi Fam* (**a**) *(pass through)* pasar por los pelos (**b**) *(succeed narrowly)* pasar por los pelos

squeaky ['skwiːkɪ] *adj (voice)* chillón(ona); *(door, wheel)* chirriante; *(floorboard)* que cruje; *(shoes)* que crujen; **s. clean** *(person, image)* impoluto(a)

squeal [skwiːl] **1** *n (of person, animal)* chillido *m*; *(of tyres, brakes)* chirrido *m*; **squeals of laughter** grandes carcajadas
2 *vt* chillar
3 *vi* (**a**) *(person, animal)* chillar; *(tyres, brakes)* chirriar; **to s. with pain** chillar de dolor; **to s. with laughter** reír(se) con estridentes carcajadas (**b**) *Fam (complain)* **to s. (about sth)** quejarse (de algo) (**c**) *Fam (inform)* **to s. (on sb)** dar el soplo (sobre alguien), *Col* sapear (a alguien), *Méx* soplar (a alguien), *RP* botonear (a alguien)

squealer ['skwiːlə(r)] *n Fam* soplón(ona) *m,f*, *Esp* chivato(a) *m,f*

squeamish ['skwiːmɪʃ] *adj* (**a**) *(physically)* aprensivo(a); **to be s. about sth** ser (muy) aprensivo(a) con algo; **I'm very s. about blood** la sangre me da mucha aprensión (**b**) *(morally)* **we cannot afford to be s. about sacking them** no podemos andarnos con escrúpulos a la hora de despedirlos

squeamishness ['skwiːmɪʃnɪs] *n* (**a**) *(physical)* aprensión *f* (**b**) *(moral)* escrúpulos *mpl*

squeegee ['skwiːdʒiː] *n* escobilla *f* de goma ▸▸ *Fam* ***s. merchant*** limpiacristales *mf inv* de semáforo

squeeze [skwi:z] 1 *n* (a) *(pressure)* apretón *m*, apretujón *m*; **to give sth a s.** apretar algo, dar un apretón a algo; **he gave my hand a s.** me apretó la mano; **to give sb a s.** *(hug)* dar un achuchón a alguien; *Fam* **we all got in but it was a tight s.** cupimos *or* entramos todos, pero tuvimos que apretujarnos bastante; IDIOM *Fam* **to put the s. on sb** *(pressurize)* apretarle las tuercas a alguien; IDIOM **to feel the s.** sentir la presión
(b) *(restriction)* reducción *f*; **credit/profits s.** reducción del crédito/ de los beneficios
(c) *(small amount)* **a s. of lemon** un chorrito de limón; **a s. of toothpaste** un poquito de dentífrico
(d) *Fam (difficult situation)* apuro *m*, situación *f* apurada; **in a s. you can always stay at my place** si te ves en un apuro, siempre puedes quedarte en mi casa
(e) *Fam (boyfriend, girlfriend)* novio(a) *m,f*, noviete(a) *m,f*
2 *vt* (a) *(press) (tube, trigger)* apretar; *(sponge)* estrujar; *(lemon)* exprimir; *(spot)* sacar; *(pimple)* reventar; **to s. sb's hand** apretar la mano de alguien; **I kept my eyes squeezed tight shut** mantuve los ojos fuertemente cerrados
(b) *(extract)* **I squeezed some toothpaste onto the brush** puse un poquito de dentífrico en el cepillo de dientes; **to s. money out of sb** sacarle dinero a alguien
(c) *(fit)* **to s. sth into a box** meter algo en una caja apretando; **they're squeezing more and more circuits onto microchips** cada vez consiguen meter más circuitos en un microchip; **twenty men were squeezed into one small cell** hacinaron a veinte hombres en una pequeña celda; **he squeezed his way under the fence** consiguió colarse por debajo de la cerca
(d) *(put pressure on)* presionar; **profits have been squeezed by foreign competition** los beneficios se han visto mermados por la competencia extranjera
3 *vi* (a) *(press)* apretar (b) *(fit)* **to s. into a place** meterse a duras penas en un sitio; **try and s. into these trousers** intenta ponerte estos pantalones; **to s. through a gap** lograr colarse *or* deslizarse por un hueco; **the ball squeezed past the keeper and into the net** el balón encontró un resquicio entre el palo y el portero y se coló en la red

▶ **squeeze in** 1 *vi (get in)* **I had to s. in past six people to reach my seat** tuve que pasar apretujándome entre seis personas hasta llegar a mi asiento; **I think I can just s. in if they move up a bit** creo que quepo si se aprietan un poco *or* me hacen un pequeño hueco
2 *vt sep (in schedule)* **she's hoping to s. in a trip to Rome too** espera encontrar también un hueco en su agenda para hacer una escapadita a Roma; **I think we can just s. you in** creo que te podemos hacer un hueco

▶ **squeeze out** *vt sep* (a) *(juice)* exprimir; **to s. the juice out of a lemon** exprimir un limón, sacarle el jugo a un limón; **to s. the water out of a sponge** exprimir una esponja (b) *(sponge, wet clothes)* exprimir, escurrir (c) *(exclude)* excluir; **he was squeezed out in the race for the presidency** lograron dejarlo fuera de la carrera presidencial

▶ **squeeze up** *vi* **tell them to s. up a bit** diles que se aprieten *or* corran un poco

squeeze-box ['skwi:zbɒks] *n Fam* acordeón *m*

squeezer ['skwi:zə(r)] *n* exprimidor *m*

squelch [skweltʃ] 1 *n* chapoteo *m*
2 *vt US Fam (idea, creativity)* acabar con, silenciar
3 *vi* (a) *(person)* chapotear; **to s. through the mud** atravesar el lodo chapoteando (b) *(water, mud)* chapaletear; **I heard something soft s. beneath my foot** sentí algo blando despachurrarse bajo mi pie

squelchy ['skweltʃɪ] *adj (ground, carpet)* empapado(a); *(sound)* de chapoteo

squib [skwɪb] *n (firework)* petardo *m*

squid [skwɪd] (*pl* **squid**) *n (animal)* calamar *m*; *(as food)* calamares *mpl*

squidgy ['skwɪdʒɪ] *adj* blando(a) y húmedo(a)

squiffy ['skwɪfɪ] *adj Br Old-fashioned Fam* alegre, *Esp* piripi

squiggle ['skwɪgəl] *n* (a) *(scrawl, doodle)* garabato *m* (b) *(wavy line)* línea *f* serpenteante

squiggly ['skwɪglɪ] *adj* ondulante, serpenteante

squillions ['skwɪljənz] *npl Br Fam Hum* tropecientos(as) mil *m,fpl*, *Méx* chorrocientos(as) mil *m,fpl*, *RP* chiquicientos(as) mil *m,fpl*

squint [skwɪnt] 1 *n* (a) *(eye defect)* **to have a s.** tener estrabismo, ser estrábico(a) (b) *Br Fam (quick look)* ojeada *f*, vistazo *m*; **to have a s. at sth** echar una ojeada a algo
2 *vi* (a) *(have an eye defect)* tener estrabismo (b) *(narrow one's eyes)* entrecerrar *or* entornar los ojos; **to s. at sth/sb** *(look sideways)* mirar algo/a alguien de reojo

squint-eyed ['skwɪntaɪd] *adj* estrábico(a), bizco(a)

squire ['skwaɪə(r)] *n* (a) *(landowner)* terrateniente *m* (b) *Hist* escudero *m* (c) *Br Fam (term of address)* **evening, s.!** ¡buenas tardes, jefe!

squirm [skwɜ:m] *vi* (a) *(wriggle)* retorcerse; **he squirmed out of my grasp** se me escapó de las manos; **to s. out of doing sth** escabullirse *or Esp* escaquearse de hacer algo; **don't try to s. out of it!** ¡no te escaquees ahora!, ¡no escurras el bulto ahora!
(b) *(feel embarrassed)* **to s. (with embarrassment)** sentirse violento(a); **his speech was so bad it made me s.** su discurso fue tan malo que sentí vergüenza ajena

squirrel ['skwɪrəl, *US* 'skwɜ:rəl] *n* ardilla *f* ▸▸ ***s. monkey*** mono *m* ardilla

▶ **squirrel away** (*pt & pp* **squirrelled**) *vt sep* acumular, ir poniendo a buen recaudo

squirrelly ['skwɜ:rəlɪ] *adj US Fam* tocado(a) del ala, *Esp* majara

squirt [skwɜ:t] 1 *n* (a) *(of liquid)* chorro *m* (b) *Fam (insignificant person)* mequetrefe *mf*
2 *vt (liquid)* lanzar un chorro de; **to s. sb with sth** echar un chorro de algo a alguien; **s. some oil on the hinges** engrasa las bisagras
3 *vi (liquid)* chorrear; **some lemon juice squirted into my eye** me entró un chorro de limón en el ojo

squish [skwɪʃ] *vt Fam (crush)* despachurrar; **the cake got all squished** el pastel se despachurró entero

squishy ['skwɪʃɪ] *adj (ground)* empapado(a); *(fruit, mess)* blando(a) y húmedo(a); *(sound)* de chapoteo

squit [skwɪt] *n Br Fam* (a) *(unpleasant, insignificant person)* pelagatos *mf inv* (b) **to have the squits** *(diarrhoea)* tener cagaleras

Sr (a) (*abbr* **Senior**) **Thomas Smith, S.** Thomas Smith, padre (b) (*abbr* **Sister**) sor *f*, hermana *f*

Sri Lanka [sri:'læŋkə] *n* Sri Lanka

Sri Lankan [sri:'læŋkən] 1 *n* ceilandés(esa) *m,f*
2 *adj* ceilandés(esa), de Sri Lanka

SRN [esɑ:r'en] *n Br* (*abbr* **State Registered Nurse**) = enfermera británica con la máxima cualificación profesional

SS [es'es] *n* (a) (*abbr* **steamship**) (buque *m* de) vapor *m* (b) *Hist* (*abbr* **Schutzstaffel**) **the SS** las S.S.; **an SS officer** un oficial de las S.S. (c) *Rel* (*abbr* **Saints**) santos

SSE (*abbr* **south-southeast**) SSE

ssh [ʃ] *exclam* ¡chis!

SSL [eses'el] *n Comptr* (*abbr* **secure sockets layer**) SSL *m*

SSM (*abbr* **surface-to-surface missile**) misil *m* superficie-superficie *or* tierra-tierra

SSW (*abbr* **south-southwest**) SSO

St (a) (*abbr* **Street**) c/ (b) (*abbr* **Saint**) S./Sto./Sta.; **St Kitts and Nevis** *(island group)* San Cristóbal y Nieves; **St Lucia** *(island)* Santa Lucía; **St Petersburg** San Petersburgo; **St Vincent and the Grenadines** *(island group)* San Vicente y las Granadinas

st *Br* (*abbr* **stone**) = unidad de peso equivalente a 6,35 kg

stab [stæb] 1 *n* (a) *(with knife)* cuchillada *f*; *(with dagger)* puñalada *f*; **he made a s. at me with the broken bottle** trató de apuñalarme con la botella rota; **he had received several s. wounds (to the chest)** había recibido varias puñaladas (en el pecho); *Fig* **it was a s. in the back** fue una puñalada por la espalda
(b) *(of pain, envy)* punzada *f*
(c) *(attempt) Fam* **to have a s. at (doing) sth** intentar (hacer) algo; **a s. in the dark** una respuesta al azar *or* a(l) voleo
2 *vt* (*pt & pp* **stabbed**) (a) *(with knife)* acuchillar; *(with dagger)* apuñalar; *(food)* pinchar, ensartar; **he stabbed me in the arm** me clavó un arma en el brazo; **to s. sb to death** matar a alguien a puñaladas; *also Fig* **to s. sb in the back** darle a alguien una puñalada por la espalda
(b) *(thrust, jab)* **to s. one's finger at sth** señalar algo con el dedo; **I stabbed my finger in his eye** le clavé *or* hundí el dedo en el ojo; **he stabbed his fork into the sausage** pinchó la salchicha con el tenedor
3 *vi* **she stabbed at him with a knife** intentó clavarle un cuchillo, intentó acuchillarlo; **he stabbed at the map with his finger** señaló el mapa clavando el dedo en él

stabbing ['stæbɪŋ] 1 *n (attack)* apuñalamiento *m*
2 *adj (pain)* punzante

stability [stə'bɪlɪtɪ] *n* estabilidad *f*

stabilization [steɪbɪlaɪ'zeɪʃən] *n* estabilización *f* ▸▸ *Econ* ***s. policy*** política *f* de estabilización

stabilize ['steɪbɪlaɪz] 1 *vt* estabilizar
2 *vi* estabilizarse

stabilizer ['steɪbɪlaɪzə(r)] *n* (a) *(on bicycle)* estabilizador *m*, ruedín *m* *(para bicicleta infantil)* (b) *(on plane, ship)* estabilizador *m* (c) *(in processed food)* estabilizante *m*, estabilizador *m*

stable[1] ['steɪbəl] **1** *n* **(a)** *(for horses)* cuadra *f*, establo *m*; IDIOM **to lock the s. door after the horse has bolted** tomar medidas demasiado tarde ►► ***s. boy*** mozo *m* de cuadra; ***s. girl*** moza *f* de cuadra; ***s. lad*** mozo *m* de cuadra **(b)** *(of sports people, actors)* escuela *f*

2 *vt (keep in stable)* guardar en cuadra

stable[2] *adj* **(a)** *(marriage, job, situation)* estable **(b)** *(person)* equilibrado(a) **(c)** *(object, structure)* fijo(a), seguro(a) **(d)** *(medical condition)* estacionario(a); **the patient** *or* **the patient's condition is s.** el paciente permanece estable *or* está estabilizado, el estado del paciente se ha estabilizado **(e)** *Chem & Phys* estable

stablemate ['steɪbəlmeɪt] *n* **(a)** *(horse)* compañero(a) *m,f* de cuadra **(b)** *(person)* compañero(a) *m,f* de escuela

staccato [stə'kɑːtəʊ] **1** *adj* **(a)** *Mus* en staccato **(b)** *(voice)* entrecortado(a)

2 *adv Mus* en staccato

stack [stæk] **1** *n* **(a)** *(of wood, plates)* pila *f*, montón *m*; *(of hay)* almiar *m*; *(of rifles)* pabellón *m*; *(of planes)* = aviones que se mantienen en espera para aterrizar sobrevolando el aeropuerto a diferente altura

(b) *Fam (large amount)* **stacks of time/money** un montón de tiempo/dinero

(c) *(chimney)* chimenea *f*

(d) *(hi-fi system)* equipo *m* de música

(e) *(in library)* **the stack(s)** = los estantes en los que se guardan los libros y a los que no tiene acceso el público

(f) *Comptr* pila *f*

2 *vt* **(a)** *(wood, plates)* apilar; **the shelves were stacked with cans of film** en los estantes se apilaban las latas de películas

(b) *(planes)* = asignar distintas alturas a los aviones que esperan para aterrizar en un aeropuerto

(c) *(deck of cards)* colocar *(haciendo trampa)*; **the odds** *or* **cards were stacked against them** tenían todo en contra de ellos; **the elections are heavily stacked against the smaller parties** los partidos más pequeños no tienen muchas posibilidades de éxito *or* están en una situación desventajosa en las elecciones

► **stack up 1** *vt sep* apilar

2 *vi* **(a)** *(chairs, boxes)* apilarse **(b)** *(mount up)* **the evidence was stacking up against him** se iban amontonando pruebas contra él **(c)** *(compare)* **how does he s. up against** *or* **with the other candidates?** ¿qué tal es con respecto a los otros candidatos?; **our product stacks up well against theirs** nuestro producto compite a un buen nivel respecto del suyo

stacked [stækt] *adj* **(a)** *(shoe heels)* reforzado(a) **(b)** *very Fam (woman)* **she's s.** está jamona

stacker ['stækə(r)] *n (in supermarket)* repositor(ora) *m,f*

stadium ['steɪdɪəm] *n* estadio *m* ►► ***s. rock*** rock *m* para grandes estadios; ***s. rocker*** cantante *mf* de macroconciertos

staff[1] [stɑːf] **1** *n* **(a)** *(personnel)* personal *m*; **we have ten lawyers on the s.** tenemos diez abogados en plantilla; **teaching/nursing s.** personal docente/de enfermería; **is he a member of s.?** ¿forma parte del *or* pertenece al personal?, ¿es miembro del personal?; **the s./student ratio** la relación profesorado/alumnado ►► ***s. association*** asociación *f* del personal; ***s. meeting*** reunión *f* del personal; *Med* ***s. nurse*** enfermero(a) *m,f*; *Sch* ***s. room*** sala *f* de profesores; ***s. training*** formación *f* del personal

(b) *Mil* Estado *m* Mayor ►► ***s. college*** academia *f or* escuela *f* militar superior; ***s. corps*** cuerpo *m* de oficiales; ***s. officer*** oficial *m* del Estado Mayor; *Br* ***s. sergeant*** sargento *mf* primero

2 *vt* proveer de personal; **the office is staffed by volunteers** el personal de la oficina está formado por voluntarios; **the desk is staffed at all times** el mostrador está atendido en todo momento; **the shop is well staffed** la tienda está bien dotada de personal

staff[2] **(a)** (*pl* **staffs** *or* **staves** [steɪvz]) *(stick)* bastón *m*; *(of shepherd)* cayado *m*; *(of bishop)* báculo *m*; *(of flag)* asta *f*; **the s. of life** *(bread)* el pan nuestro de cada día **(b)** *Mus* (*pl* **staves** [steɪvz]) pentagrama *m*

staffer ['stɑːfə(r)] *n Fam* empleado(a) *m,f*

staffing ['stɑːfɪŋ] *n (recruiting)* dotación *f* de personal, contratación *f* (de personal); **the delay is due to s. difficulties** el retraso se debe a problemas de personal ►► ***s. levels*** número *m* de empleados

Staffs (*abbr* **Staffordshire**) (condado *m* de) Staffordshire

stag [stæg] *n* **(a)** *(animal)* ciervo *m* ►► ***s. beetle*** ciervo *m* volante; ***s. night*** despedida *f* de soltero; ***s. party*** despedida *f* de soltero **(b)** *Br St Exch* especulador(ora) *m,f* ciervo

stage [steɪdʒ] **1** *n* **(a)** *(platform) (in theatre)* escenario *m*; *(more generally)* estrado *m*; **the s.** *(profession, activity)* el (mundo del) teatro; *Theat* **to exit/enter s. left/right** salir de/entrar en escena por la izquierda/derecha; **I never feel nervous on s.** nunca me pongo nervioso(a) en el escenario; **to come/go on s.** subir al escenario, salir a escena; **to go on the s.** *(become actor)* hacerse actor/actriz; **he first appeared on the s. in 1920** la primera vez que actuó en un escenario fue en 1920; *Fig* **on the world s.** en el plano internacional; IDIOM **to set the s. for sth** preparar el terreno para algo; IDIOM **the s. is set (for)** se dan todas las condiciones (para) ►► ***s. adaptation*** adaptación *f* teatral *or* para la escena; ***s. business*** pirueta *f* escénica; ***s. design*** escenografía *f*; ***s. designer*** escenógrafo(a) *m,f*; ***s. directions*** acotaciones *fpl*; ***s. door*** entrada *f* de artistas; ***s. fright*** miedo *m* escénico; ***s. manager*** director(ora) *m,f* de escena, regidor(ora) *m,f*; ***s. name*** nombre *m* artístico; ***s. presence*** presencia *f* en el escenario; *Theat* ***s. setting*** decorado *m*; ***s. whisper*** aparte *m*

(b) *(phase)* etapa *f*, fase *f*; **the conflict is still in its early stages** el conflicto se encuentra todavía en su fase inicial *or* en su primera fase; **at an early s.** en un primer momento, en una primera fase; **at a later s.** más adelante; **at one s. it looked like he was going to win** en cierto momento pareció que iba a ganar; **at some s.** en algún momento; **at this s. of the negotiations** en esta fase de las negociaciones; **at this s. it's too early to tell if she'll recover** en este momento es demasiado pronto para poder decir si se recuperará o no; **there's nothing we can do at this late s.** no hay nada que podamos hacer a estas alturas; **by that s.** por entonces; **I'd reached the s. where I didn't care any more** había llegado a tal punto que ya nada me importaba; **to do sth in stages** hacer algo por etapas

(c) *(in cycling)* etapa *f* ►► ***s. race*** carrera *f* por etapas

(d) *(of space rocket)* fase *f*

(e) *(stagecoach)* diligencia *f*

2 *vt* **(a)** *(play)* llevar a escena, representar; **Macbeth was very well staged** la puesta en escena de Macbeth fue muy buena

(b) *(demonstration, invasion, coup)* llevar a cabo; *(festival, ceremony)* organizar; **the team staged a remarkable comeback** el equipo llevó a cabo una espectacular remontada

(c) *(fake)* fingir; **the murder was staged to look like a suicide** el asesinato se presentó de forma que pareciese un suicidio

stagecoach ['steɪdʒkəʊtʃ] *n* diligencia *f*

stagecraft ['steɪdʒkrɑːft] *n Theat* arte *m* escénico

stagehand ['steɪdʒhænd] *n Theat* tramoyista *mf*, sacasillas *mf inv*

stage-manage ['steɪdʒ'mænɪdʒ] *vt* **(a)** *Theat* dirigir **(b)** *(event, demonstration)* orquestar

stage-struck ['steɪdʒstrʌk] *adj Theat* **to be s.** estar enamorado(a) de las tablas

stagey, stagy ['steɪdʒɪ] *adj (mannerisms)* teatral; *(performance)* efectista

stagflation [stæg'fleɪʃən] *n Econ* estanflación *f*

stagger ['stægə(r)] **1** *n (totter)* **he got up with a s.** se tambaleó al ponerse en pie

2 *vt* **(a)** *(astound)* dejar anonadado(a) **(b)** *(work, holidays)* escalonar; **employees' vacation times are staggered over the summer months** las vacaciones de los empleados se distribuyen escalonadamente a lo largo de los meses de verano

3 *vi (stumble)* tambalearse; **to s. along** ir tambaleándose; **to s. to one's feet** levantarse tambaleándose

staggered ['stægəd] *adj* **(a)** *(amazed)* atónito(a), estupefacto(a); **I was s. to learn of his decision** me quedé pasmado(a) al oír su decisión **(b)** *(in stages)* escalonado(a) ►► *Sport* ***s. start*** salida *f* escalonada

staggering ['stægərɪŋ] *adj* asombroso(a); **the price is a s. $500,000** cuesta la friolera de 500.000 dólares

staggers ['stægəz] *n (animal disease)* modorra *f*

staginess ['steɪdʒɪnɪs] *n (of mannerisms)* teatralidad *f*; *(of performance)* efectismo *m*

staging ['steɪdʒɪŋ] *n* **(a)** *Theat* montaje *m*, puesta *f* en escena **(b)** *(scaffolding)* andamiaje *m* **(c)** ***s. post*** *(on journey, route)* escala *f*

stagnancy ['stægnənsɪ] *n* **(a)** *(of water, pond, air)* estancamiento *m* **(b)** *(of economy, career, society)* estancamiento *m*

stagnant ['stægnənt] *adj* **(a)** *(water, pond, air)* estancado(a) **(b)** *(economy, career, society)* estancado(a)

stagnate [stæg'neɪt] *vi* **(a)** *(water, pond, air)* estancarse **(b)** *(economy, career, society)* estancarse

stagnation [stæg'neɪʃən] *n* **(a)** *(of water, pond, air)* estancamiento *m* **(b)** *(of economy, career, society)* estancamiento *m*

stagy = **stagey**

staid [steɪd] *adj (person)* formal, estirado(a); *(colours, clothes)* austero(a), serio(a)

staidness ['steɪdnɪs] *n (of person)* formalidad *f*; *(of colours, clothes)* austeridad *f*, seriedad *f*

stain [steɪn] **1** *n* (**a**) *(mark)* mancha *f* ►► ***s. remover*** quitamanchas *m inv* (**b**) *(blemish)* **it was a s. on her character** aquello manchó *or* empañó su reputación (**c**) *(dye)* tinte *m*
2 *vt* (**a**) *(mark)* manchar; **smoking stains your teeth** (el) fumar mancha los dientes (**b**) *(character, reputation)* manchar, empañar (**c**) *(dye) (wood, cell specimen)* teñir
3 *vi* (**a**) *(liquid)* dejar mancha, manchar (**b**) *(fabric)* mancharse

-stained [-steɪnd] *suffix* **nicotine/sweat-s.** manchado(a) de nicotina/sudor

stained-glass ['steɪnd'glɑːs] *n* vidrio *m* de colores ►► ***s. window*** vidriera *f*

stainless ['steɪnlɪs] *n* (**a**) *(rust-resistant)* ***s. steel*** acero *m* inoxidable (**b**) *(character, reputation)* intachable, sin tacha

stair [steə(r)] *n* (**a**) *(single step)* escalón *m*, peldaño *m*
(**b**) *(staircase)* escalera *f*; *Fam* **she lives on our s.** vive en nuestra escalera ►► ***s. carpet*** alfombra *f* de escalera; ***s. rod*** varilla *f* para alfombra de escalera
(**c**) *(flight)* **stairs** escalera(s) *f(pl)*; **to run up/down the stairs** subir/bajar las escaleras corriendo, correr escaleras arriba/abajo; **at the top of the stairs** en lo alto de las escaleras

staircase ['steəkeɪs] *n* escalera *f*

stairway ['steəweɪ] *n* escalera *f*

stairwell ['steəwel] *n* hueco *m* de la escalera

stake [steɪk] **1** *n* (**a**) *(piece of wood, metal)* estaca *f*; *(for plant)* guía *f*, rodrigón *m*; **to die** *or* **be burned at the s.** morir quemado(a) en la hoguera
(**b**) *(bet)* apuesta *f*; **the stakes are high** hay mucho en juego; **the two multinationals are playing for high stakes** ambas multinacionales tienen mucho en juego *or* se juegan mucho; **to be at s.** estar en juego; **she has a lot at s.** se juega mucho, es mucho lo que se juega
(**c**) *(share)* **to have a s. in sth** *(interest)* tener intereses en algo; *(shareholding)* tener una participación (accionarial) en algo; **she has a 10 percent s. in the company** tiene una participación del 10 por ciento en la sociedad; **we all have a s. in the education of the young** a todos nos concierne la educación de los jóvenes
(**d**) **stakes** *(horse race)* = carrera en la que los propietarios de los caballos que compiten contribuyen al premio en metálico; *Fig* **the party is riding high in the popularity stakes** el partido mantiene un elevado índice de popularidad
2 *vt* (**a**) *(bet) (money)* apostar (**on** a); *(one's reputation, job)* jugarse (**on** en); **I'd s. my life on it** pondría la mano en el fuego
(**b**) *(register)* **to s. a claim (to sth)** reivindicar el derecho (a algo); **with this novel she stakes her claim to being one of the greatest writers of the century** con esta novela reivindica el derecho a figurar entre los mejores escritores del siglo
(**c**) *(mark out with stakes) (piece of land)* estacar, señalar (el límite de) *or* delimitar con estacas
(**d**) *(fasten) (boat)* amarrar a un madero; *(animal)* atar a un poste
(**e**) *(support) (plant, vine)* arrodrigonar, enrodrigonar

► **stake out** *vt insep* (**a**) *(piece of land)* estacar, señalar (el límite de) *or* delimitar con estacas; *Fig* **she was quick to s. out her intentions on this issue** no tardó en dejar bien claro cuáles eran sus intenciones en este asunto (**b**) *(home, suspect)* tener vigilado(a)

stakeholder ['steɪkhəʊldə(r)] *n (in company)* parte *f* interesada, partícipe *mf*; **the stakeholders in a project** las personas con interés en un proyecto ►► *Br* ***s. pension*** = plan de pensiones regulado por el gobierno británico para complementar el estatal; ***s. society*** sociedad *f* cooperativa *or* participativa

stakeholding ['steɪkhəʊldɪŋ] *n* participación *f*

stakeout ['steɪkaʊt] *n* vigilancia *f*; **to be on s.** montar vigilancia

stalactite ['stæləktaɪt] *n* estalactita *f*

stalagmite ['stæləgmaɪt] *n* estalagmita *f*

stale [steɪl] *adj* (**a**) *(bread)* rancio(a), duro(a); *(cake)* rancio(a), echado(a) a perder; *(cheese, butter, smell)* rancio(a); *(beer)* pasado(a), sin fuerza; *(air)* viciado(a); *(breath)* podrido(a), maloliente; **to go s.** *(bread)* ponerse rancio(a) *or* duro(a); *(cake)* ponerse rancio(a), echarse a perder; *(cheese, butter)* ponerse rancio(a); *(beer)* perder la fuerza
(**b**) *(ideas, jokes)* manido(a); *(social life, relationship)* anquilosado(a); **to get s.** *(person)* anquilosarse

stalemate ['steɪlmeɪt] **1** *n* (**a**) *(in chess)* tablas *fpl* (**b**) *(impasse) (in negotiations)* punto *m* muerto, estancamiento *m*; **to reach a s.** llegar a un punto muerto; **the announcement broke the s. in the negotiations** el anuncio puso fin a la fase de paralización que habían alcanzado las negociaciones; **the match ended in s.** el partido acabó en empate
2 *vt* (**a**) *(in chess)* forzar a acabar en tablas a (**b**) *(negotiations)* llevar a un punto muerto, paralizar

staleness ['steɪlnɪs] *n* (**a**) *(of bread, cake, cheese, butter)* rancidez *f*, ranciedad *f*; *(of beer)* falta *f* de fuerza, poca fuerza *f*; *(of air)* lo viciado; *(of breath)* lo podrido, lo maloliente (**b**) *(of ideas, jokes)* lo manido; *(of social life, relationship)* anquilosamiento *m*

Stalin ['stɑːlɪn] *pr n* Stalin

Stalinism ['stɑːlɪnɪzəm] *n* estalinismo *m*

Stalinist ['stɑːlɪnɪst] **1** *n* estalinista *mf*
2 *adj* estalinista

stalk[1] [stɔːk] **1** *vt* (**a**) *(hunt) (of person, animal)* acechar, estar al acecho de (**b**) *(track) (of private detective)* seguir con sigilo (**c**) *(obsessively) (of stalker)* seguir obsesivamente a, vigilar obsesivamente a
2 *vi (walk angrily)* **she stalked out of the room** salió *esp Esp* enfadada *or esp Am* enojada de la habitación; **to s. off** marcharse airadamente

stalk[2] *n (of plant, flower)* tallo *m*; *(of fruit)* rabo *m*; *(of cabbage, cauliflower)* troncho *m*

stalker ['stɔːkə(r)] *n* = persona que sigue o vigila obsesivamente a otra

stalking ['stɔːkɪŋ] *n (of person)* acecho *m*, = seguimiento o vigilancia obsesiva de una persona

stalking-horse ['stɔːkɪŋ'hɔːs] *n (in political contest)* candidato(a) *m,f* de paja; *(pretext)* tapadera *f*, pretexto *m*

stall [stɔːl] **1** *n* (**a**) *(in market)* puesto *m*; *(at fair, exhibition)* caseta *f*, stand *m*; **I bought some tulips at a flower s.** compré algunos tulipanes en un puesto de flores (**b**) *(in stable)* casilla *f* (**c**) *(in horseracing)* **the (starting) stalls** los cajones de salida (**d**) *Br Cin & Theat* **the stalls** el patio de butacas, la platea (**e**) *(in church)* **the (choir) stalls** la sillería (del coro)
2 *vt* (**a**) *(car, engine) Esp* calar
(**b**) *(campaign, talks)* paralizar, estancar; **the negotiations have been stalled for weeks** las negociaciones llevan semanas paralizadas *or* estancadas
(**c**) *(hold off)* entretener, distraer; **I'll s. her in the lobby while you grab a taxi** la entretendré en el vestíbulo mientras te subes a un taxi; **I can't s. them (off) for much longer** no puedo seguir entreteniéndolos por mucho más tiempo
3 *vi* (**a**) *(car, engine)* calarse, pararse; *(plane)* entrar en pérdida (**b**) *(campaign, negotiations)* estancarse, quedarse estancado(a) (**c**) *(delay)* **to s. (for time)** intentar ganar tiempo; **stop stalling and tell me the truth** deja de andarte por las ramas y cuéntame la verdad

stallholder ['stɔːlhəʊldə(r)] *n* dueño(a) *m,f* de un puesto, *Am* puestero(a) *m,f*

stalling ['stɔːlɪŋ] *n* evasivas *fpl*, rodeos *mpl* ►► ***s. tactics*** tácticas *fpl* dilatorias

stallion ['stæljən] *n* (**a**) *(horse)* (caballo *m*) semental *m* (**b**) *Fam (man)* semental *m*

stalwart ['stɔːlwət] **1** *n* incondicional *mf*
2 *adj* (**a**) *(supporter, believer)* acérrimo(a); *(faith)* inquebrantable (**b**) *(strongly built) (person)* robusto(a), rollizo(a)

stamen ['steɪmən] *n Bot* estambre *m*

stamina ['stæmɪnə] *n* resistencia *f*, aguante *m*; **I don't have the s. to study law** no tengo la capacidad de esfuerzo necesaria para estudiar Derecho

stammer ['stæmə(r)] **1** *n* tartamudeo *m*; **to have** *or* **speak with a (bad) s.** tartamudear (mucho)
2 *vt* balbucir, farfullar
3 *vi* tartamudear

► **stammer out** *vt sep* balbucir, farfullar

stammerer ['stæmərə(r)] *n* tartamudo(a) *m,f*

stamp [stæmp] **1** *n* (**a**) *(on letter)* sello *m*, *Am* estampilla *f*, *CAm, Méx* timbre *m* ►► ***s. album*** álbum *m* de sellos; ***s. book*** *(of postage stamps)* libreta *f* de sellos; *(for trading stamps)* libreta *f* de puntos; ***s. collecting*** filatelia *f*; ***s. collector*** coleccionista *mf* de sellos; ***s. hinge*** fijasellos *m inv*; ***s. machine*** máquina *f* expendedora de sellos
(**b**) *(mark)* sello *m*; **he has an Israeli s. in his passport** tiene un sello de Israel en el pasaporte; *Fig* **s. of approval** aprobación, beneplácito; *Fig* **to bear the s. of genius** tener el sello *or* la marca inconfundible del genio; *Fig* **poverty has left its s. on him** la pobreza lo ha dejado marcado
(**c**) *(device)* tampón *m*, sello *m*; *(for metal)* cuño *m*
(**d**) *(on legal documents)* póliza *f*, timbre *m* ►► *Fin* ***s.*** *Br* ***duty*** *or US* ***tax*** póliza *f* = impuesto de transmisiones patrimoniales
(**e**) *(voucher) (for free food)* cupón *m*
(**f**) *(type, ilk)* **we need more teachers of her s.** necesitamos más profesores como ella, necesitamos más profesores de su talla
(**g**) *(noise) (of boots)* **he heard the s. of boots** oyó el estampido de

unas botas; **"no!" he cried with a s. of his foot** "¡no!" gritó dando un zapatazo

2 *vt* **(a)** *(letter)* **a stamped addressed envelope** un sobre franqueado y con el domicilio

(b) *(put mark on)* estampar; *(passport)* sellar; **he stamped the firm's name on each document** le puso el sello de la empresa a cada uno de los documentos

(c) *(imprint) (leather, metal)* estampar, grabar; **a design is stamped on the butter** la mantequilla lleva un sello estampado *or* grabado en relieve; *Fig* **as editor she stamped her personality on the magazine** como directora le imprimió a la revista su sello personal; **recent events have stamped the president as indecisive** los últimos acontecimientos han hecho que se tilde al presidente de indeciso

(d) *(hit on ground)* **to s. one's foot** patear; **he stamped the snow off his boots** se sacudió la nieve de las botas dando zapatazos *or* golpes en el suelo con los pies

3 *vi* **(a)** *(in one place) (person)* patear, dar zapatazos; *(horse)* piafar **(b)** *(walk)* **to s. upstairs** subir ruidosamente las escaleras; **he stamped off in a rage** se marchó *esp Esp* enfadado *or esp Am* enojado

> **False friend**: The Spanish noun **estampa** is not a translation for the English word **stamp**. In Spanish **estampa** means "illustration", "appearance" or "image".

▸ **stamp down** *vt sep (loose earth, snow)* apisonar, aplastar con el pie

▸ **stamp on** *vt insep* **(a)** *(step on)* pisotear, pisar; **she stamped on my foot** me dio un pisotón **(b)** *(dissent, opponents, rebellion)* aplastar

▸ **stamp out** *vt sep* **(a)** *(fire)* apagar con el pie **(b)** *(resistance, dissent, corruption, crime)* acabar *or* terminar con **(c)** *(hole, pattern)* troquelar

stampede [stæm'pi:d] **1** *n (of animals)* estampida *f*, desbandada *f* **(b)** *(of people)* desbandada *f*, huida *f* precipitada; **there was a s. for the door** hubo una desbandada hacia la puerta

2 *vt* **(a)** *(animals)* hacer salir en estampida **(b)** *(pressurize)* **to s. sb into doing sth** empujar *or* impulsar a alguien a hacer algo

3 *vi* **(a)** *(animals)* salir de estampida **(b)** *(people)* salir en desbandada, huir precipitadamente; **the crowd stampeded for the exit** el gentío huyó precipitadamente en busca de la salida, el gentío salió en desbandada en busca de la salida

stamping-ground ['stæmpɪŋgraʊnd] *n Fam* lugar *m* predilecto

stance [stæns] *n* **(a)** *(physical position)* postura *f* **(b)** *(view)* postura *f*; **they have changed their s. on abortion** han cambiado su postura con respecto al aborto **(c)** *Scot (in bus station)* andén *m*

stanch *US* = **staunch**

stanchion ['stænʃən] *n* puntal *m*; *(of soccer goal)* palo *m* trasero

STAND [stænd] **1** *n* **(a)** *(view)* postura *f* **(on** sobre); **to take a s.** adoptar una postura

(b) *(of lamp)* soporte *m*; *(for books, postcards)* expositor *m*; *(for sheet music)* atril *m*; *(for coats)* perchero *m*

(c) *(stall) (in open air)* puesto *m*, tenderete *m*; *(at exhibition)* stand *m*, puesto *m*; *(in market)* puesto *m*; **newspaper s.** quiosco (de periódicos)

(d) *(at stadium)* **stand(s)** gradas *fpl*, *Esp* graderío *m*

(e) *US (witness box)* estrado *m*; **to take the s.** subir al estrado

(f) *(taxi rank)* parada *f* de taxis

(g) *(battle, resistance)* **they made their last s. on the bridge** presentaron batalla por última vez en el puente; **to make a s.** resistir al enemigo; **to make a s. against an abuse** alzar la voz frente a un abuso

2 *vt* (*pt & pp* **stood** [stʊd]) **(a)** *(place)* colocar; **he stood the ladder against the wall** apoyó la escalera contra la pared; **he stood the boy on a chair** puso al niño de pie en una silla; *Fig* **this discovery stands previous theories on their head** este descubrimiento invalida por completo las teorías previas

(b) *(endure)* soportar, aguantar; **he can't s. her** no la soporta *or* aguanta; **built to s. rough treatment/high temperatures** construido para soportar un trato duro/altas temperaturas; **I can't s. people calling me that** no soporto *or* aguanto que me llamen eso; **I've had as much of this as I can s.!** ¡ya no puedo soportarlo más!; **to s. comparison with** poder compararse con; **the allegation does not s. closer examination** la acusación no se sostiene ante un análisis detallado; **to s. one's ground** mantenerse firme

(c) *(pay for)* **to s. sb a drink** invitar a alguien a una copa

(d) *(have)* **to s. a chance (of doing sth)** tener posibilidades (de hacer algo); **he doesn't s. a chance!** ¡no tiene ninguna posibilidad!

(e) *Law* **to s. trial** ser procesado(a)

3 *vi* **(a)** *(person) (get up)* ponerse de pie, levantarse, *Am* pararse; *(be upright)* estar de pie *or Am* parado(a); *(remain upright)* quedarse de pie *or Am* parado(a); **I could hardly s.** casi no me tenía en pie; **we had to s. the whole way** tuvimos que ir de pie *or Am* parados todo el trayecto; **we couldn't see anything from where we were standing** desde donde estábamos no se veía nada; *Fig* **it sounds like a good idea from where I'm standing** desde mi perspectiva parece una buena idea; **don't just s. there!** ¡no te quedes ahí parado(a)!; **we stood there shivering** estábamos ahí de pie *or Am* parados tiritando; **we stood and watched the plane take off** nos quedamos ahí de pie *or Am* parados y vimos despegar el avión; **they were standing against the wall** estaban de pie *or Am* parados contra la pared; **he was standing at the door** estaba junto a la puerta; **s. in a line!** ¡pónganse en fila!; *US* **to s. in line** hacer cola; **to s. in sb's way** *(obstruct)* estorbar a alguien; *(try to stop)* ponerse delante de alguien; **a picture of them standing on the beach** una foto de ellos ahí de pie *or Am* parados en la playa; **I can reach it if I s. on a chair** lo alcanzo si me subo a una silla; **he stood on my foot** me pisó; **to s. still** *(person)* quedarse quieto(a); *(time)* detenerse; **we cannot afford to s. still whilst our competitors catch us up** no podemos cruzarnos de brazos mientras nuestros competidores nos ganan terreno; **he stands two metres tall** mide dos metros; **s. and deliver!** ¡la bolsa o la vida!; *Fig* **the government will s. or fall by the success of its policies** el futuro del gobierno dependerá del éxito o fracaso de sus políticas; **I had to s. on my toes to see** me tuve que poner de puntillas para poder ver; **to s. fast** *or* **firm** mantenerse firme; **to s. on one's hands** hacer el pino *(sin apoyar la cabeza en el suelo)*; **to s. on one's head** hacer el pino *(apoyando la cabeza en el suelo)*; IDIOM **I could do it standing on my head!** ¡lo podría hacer con los ojos vendados!; IDIOM **the boss didn't s. on his dignity and helped us move the filing cabinets** el hecho de que fuera el jefe no impidió que nos ayudara a mover los archivadores; IDIOM **to s. on one's own two feet** ser autosuficiente, valerse (uno) por sí mismo; IDIOM **we're standing right behind you** estamos de tu lado

(b) *(be situated) (building)* estar situado(a) *or* ubicado(a); *(object)* estar colocado(a); **there's a taxi standing outside the entrance** hay un taxi esperando a la entrada; **the house stands on a hill** la casa se encuentra en una colina; **a vase stood on the table** había un jarrón en la mesa; **a wardrobe stood against one wall** había un armario de pared; **the train now standing at platform 11** el tren estacionado en la vía 11; *US* **no standing** *(sign)* = prohibido detenerse

(c) *(remain upright) (building, tree)* **not a single tree was left standing** no quedó en pie ni un árbol; **the house is still standing** la casa todavía está en pie

(d) *(be in situation)* **as things s.** tal y como están las cosas; **just print the text as it stands** imprime el texto tal y como está; **to know how things s.** saber cómo están las cosas; **I don't know where I s.** no sé a qué atenerme; **you always know where you s. with him** con él sabes a qué atenerte; **inflation/the debt stands at...** la inflación/la deuda asciende a *or* se sitúa en...; **the Mavericks are currently standing third in the table** los Mavericks están clasificados actualmente en tercera posición; **nothing stood between her and victory** nada se interpuso en su camino hacia la victoria; **his theory stood unchallenged for a decade** su teoría prevaleció durante una década; **to s. accused of sth** ser acusado(a) de algo; **I s. corrected** corrijo lo dicho; **the house is standing empty** la casa está vacía; **the machine has been standing idle** la máquina ha estado inactiva; **I've got a taxi standing ready** tengo un taxi esperándome; **to s. alone: she stands alone in advocating this approach** es la única que aboga por este enfoque; **we s. united** estamos unidos(as); **they s. very high in our esteem** los tenemos en gran estima; **you s. in danger of getting killed** corres el peligro de que te maten; **to s. in need of...** tener necesidad de...; **you s. to lose/gain $5,000** puedes perder/ganar 5.000 dólares; **it stands to reason that...** se cae por su propio peso que...

(e) *(remain motionless) (liquid, mixture)* reposar

(f) *(contest elections)* **to s. for Parliament/the presidency** presentarse (como candidato) a las elecciones parlamentarias/a la presidencia; **to s. against sb (in an election)** enfrentarse a alguien (en unas elecciones)

(g) *(be valid) (argument, verdict, objection)* mantenerse; **the offer still stands** la oferta sigue en pie

(h) *(have opinion)* **where do you s. on this issue?** ¿cuál es tu postura ante este tema?

▸ **stand about, stand around** *vi* **we were standing about** *or* **around chatting** estábamos ahí de pie *or Am* parados charlando *or CAm, Méx* platicando; **they just s. about** *or* **around all day doing nothing** se pasan todo el día sin hacer nada; **I'm not going to s. about** *or* **around waiting for you to decide!** no voy a quedarme parado esperando a que te decidas

▸ **stand apart from** *vt sep (be different to)* **what makes our candidate s. apart from the rest** lo que diferencia *or* distingue a nuestro candidato del resto

► **stand aside** *vi (move aside)* hacerse a un lado; *(withdraw opposition)* retirarse

► **stand back** *vi* (**a**) *(move away)* alejarse (**from** de); **s. back!** ¡atrás!; **s. back from the doors!** ¡no se acerquen a las puertas! (**b**) *(in order to reflect)* distanciarse (**c**) *(be set back)* estar apartado(a)

► **stand by** 1 *vt insep* (**a**) *(friend)* apoyar
(**b**) *(promise, prediction)* mantener
2 *vi* (**a**) *(be ready)* estar preparado(a) (**for** para); **the police/ambulances are standing by** la policía/las ambulancias están en alerta; **s. by for takeoff!** ¡preparados para el despegue *orAm* decolaje!
(**b**) *(not get involved)* mantenerse al margen; *(do nothing)* quedarse sin hacer nada; **I stood by helplessly** me quedé parado sin poder hacer nada

► **stand down** *vi* (**a**) *(retire)* retirarse; **he stood down in favour of a younger candidate** se retiró para dejar paso a un candidato más joven
(**b**) *(leave witness box)* bajar del estrado
(**c**) *Mil (of troops)* **he ordered the troops to stand down** puso fin al estado de alerta de las tropas

► **stand for** *vt insep* (**a**) *(mean)* significar, querer decir; *(represent)* representar **I detest everything they s. for!** aborrezco todo lo que representan
(**b**) *(tolerate)* tolerar; *(bear)* aguantar; **I'm not going to s. for it!** ¡no lo voy a tolerar!; **I've stood for his nonsense long enough** he aguantado sus tonterías demasiado tiempo

► **stand in for** *vt insep* sustituir a

► **stand off** *vt insep (coast, island)* **they have an aircraft carrier standing off Aden** tienen un portaaviones a la espera cerca de Adén

► **stand out** *vi* (**a**) *(protrude) (ledge)* sobresalir; **the veins in his neck stood out** se le marcaban las venas del cuello
(**b**) *(be prominent)* destacar; **she stood out from the other candidates** destacaba del resto de los candidatos; *Fam* **it stands out a mile!** ¡se nota *or* se ve a la legua!
(**c**) *(show opposition)* **to s. out against sth** oponerse a algo; **they stood out for a better deal** aguantaron para conseguir un trato más provechoso

► **stand over** 1 *vt insep* **there's no need for you to s. over me while I do it** no hace falta que estés ahí vigilándome mientras lo hago
2 *vi* **we have two items standing over from the last meeting** tenemos dos asuntos pendientes de la última reunión; **we can let the matter s. over till next week** podemos aplazar el asunto hasta la semana que viene

► **stand to** *Mil* 1 *vt sep* poner en alerta a
2 *vi* entrar en alerta; **s. to!** ¡a sus puestos!

► **stand together** *vi (agree)* estar de acuerdo (**on** en)

► **stand up** 1 *vt sep* (**a**) *(set upright)* poner de pie
(**b**) *Fam* **to s. sb up** *(on date)* dar plantón a alguien
2 *vi* (**a**) *(get up)* levantarse, ponerse de pie, *Am* pararse; *(be upright)* estar de pie; *(remain upright)* quedarse de pie *orAm* parado(a); *Fig* **to s. up and be counted** *(express opinion)* hacerse oír
(**b**) *(be upright)* **his hair stands up** tiene el pelo de punta; **the candle won't s. up straight** la vela no se quedará de pie
(**c**) *(argument, theory)* sostenerse; **the allegation does not s. up to closer examination** la acusación no resiste un análisis detallado; **his confession will never s. up in court** su confesión no serviría como prueba en un juicio; **they stood up well under intense pressure** aguantaron bien bajo la intensa presión

► **stand up for** *vt insep* defender; **to s. up for oneself** defenderse

► **stand up to** *vt insep* (**a**) *(not be intimidated by)* hacer frente a
(**b**) *(withstand)* resistir; **it won't s. up to that sort of treatment** no resistirá ese tipo de tratamiento

---

stand-alone ['stændələʊn] *adj Comptr* independiente, autónomo(a)

standard ['stændəd] 1 *n* (**a**) *(norm) (for weight, measurement)* norma *f*; *(to judge performance, success)* criterio *m*; **we have high safety standards** disponemos de excelentes medidas de seguridad; **we apply the same standards to all candidates** medimos con el mismo rasero a todos los candidatos; *Fin* **gold/dollar s.** patrón oro/dólar; **their salaries are low by European standards** sus salarios están por debajo de los niveles europeos; **it was a success by any standards** fue un éxito de todas todas, fue a todas luces un éxito
(**b**) *(required level)* nivel *m*; **to be up to/below s.** estar al nivel/por debajo del nivel exigido; **to have high/low standards** *(at work)* ser muy/poco exigente; *(morally)* tener muchos/pocos principios; **he sets high standards for himself** se pone alto el listón, se exige mucho; **her performance has set the s. for all the other competitors** su actuación ha colocado el listón bien alto a los demás competidores; **this vehicle sets a new s. for its class** este vehículo marca un nuevo hito dentro de su clase
(**c**) *(quality)* calidad *f*; **the s. of the workmanship was excellent** la calidad del trabajo era excelente; **to be of a high s.** ser de excelente calidad ►► ***s. of living*** nivel *m* de vida
(**d**) *(moral principle)* **young people don't have any standards any more** hoy día la juventud carece de valores (morales); **I won't do it, I have my standards!** no lo haré, ¡tengo mis principios!
(**e**) *(flag)* estandarte *m* ►► *also Fig* ***s. bearer*** abanderado(a) *m,f*
(**f**) *(pole) (for flag)* mástil *m*; *(for lamp)* pie *m* ►► ***s. lamp*** lámpara *f* de pie
(**g**) *(tune)* clásico *m*
2 *adj* (**a**) *(normative) (length, width, measure)* estándar; *(pronunciation, spelling)* estándar; **it's the s. work on the subject** es la obra de referencia clásica sobre el tema ►► ***S. English*** inglés *m* normativo; *Rail* ***s. gauge*** (ancho *m* de) vía *f* normal; *Scot Educ* ***S. grade*** = examen de grado medio tras el cuarto curso de enseñanza secundaria; ***s. size*** tamaño *m* estándar *or* normal; ***s. time*** hora *f* oficial
(**b**) *(usual) (method, procedure, reaction)* habitual; **the s. model has 64 MB memory** el modelo estándar *or* corriente tiene 64 MB de memoria; **the s. return fare is $500** el precio normal de ida y vuelta es de 500 dólares; **headrests are fitted as s.** viene equipado con reposacabezas de serie; **it is s. practice** es la práctica habitual; **we got the s. response** nos dieron la respuesta habitual en estos casos
(**c**) *(ordinary, average)* corriente, común; **it was just a s. hotel room** era una habitación de hotel normal y corriente; **the food is fairly s.** la comida es bastante normalita ►► *Br* ***s. class*** *(on train)* segunda *f* clase
(**d**) *(in statistics)* ***s. deviation*** desviación *f* típica *or* estándar; ***s. error*** error *m* típico
(**e**) *Comptr* ***s. memory*** memoria *f* estándar

standardization [stændədaɪ'zeɪʃən] *n* normalización *f*, estandarización *f*

standardize ['stændədaɪz] *vt* normalizar, estandarizar

stand-by ['stændbaɪ] 1 *n* (**a**) *(money, fuel, food)* reserva *f*; *(person)* suplente *mf*; **eggs are a great s. in the kitchen** es muy socorrido tener siempre huevos en la cocina; **to have sth as a s.** tener algo de reserva; **to be on s.** *(troops, emergency services)* estar en alerta; **troops are on 24-hour s.** las tropas están en alerta permanente; **to be on s. duty** *(doctor, emergency repairman)* estar de guardia ►► ***s. generator*** generador *m* auxiliar; *Comptr* ***s. mode*** modo *m* de reposo, modo *m* de suspensión del sistema
(**b**) *(for air travel) (passenger)* pasajero(a) *m,f* en lista de espera *or* stand-by; **to be on s.** estar en lista de espera *or* stand-by ►► ***s. passenger*** pasajero(a) *m,f* en lista de espera *or* stand-by; ***s. ticket*** *Esp* billete *m orAm* boleto *m orAm* pasaje *m* de lista de espera *or* stand-by
2 *adv (to travel)* mediante el sistema de lista de espera, con tarifas "standby"

standee [stæn'di:] *n US (in theatre)* espectador(ora) *m,f* sin derecho a asiento; *(in public transport)* pasajero(a) *m,f* sin derecho a asiento

stand-in ['stændɪn] 1 *n (substitute)* suplente *mf*, sustituto(a) *m,f*; *(stunt person)* doble *mf*
2 *adj* suplente

standing ['stændɪŋ] 1 *n* (**a**) *(position)* posición *f*; *(status)* reputación *f*; **an economist of considerable s.** un economista de reconocido prestigio; **people of lower/higher social s.** personas de posición social inferior/superior; **enquiries were made into his financial s.** se investigó su posición económica; **in good s. (with)** con reputación (entre)
(**b**) *(duration)* **friends of long s.** amigos de hace mucho tiempo; **an agreement of long s.** un acuerdo que viene de lejos; **an employee of ten years' s.** un empleado con diez años de antigüedad
(**c**) *(ranking)* **her s. in the opinion polls is at its lowest yet** su posición en las encuestas de opinión es la más baja hasta la fecha; **the latest standings show that he has moved up to fourth in the world** las últimas listas de clasificación indican que ha subido al cuarto puesto mundial
2 *adj* (**a**) *(upright)* vertical, derecho(a); **there was s. room only** *(on train, bus, in room)* no quedaban asientos ►► ***s. count*** *(in boxing)* = cuenta realizada a un púgil que ya se ha levantado; ***s. jump*** salto *m* sin carrera; ***s. ovation*** ovación *f* cerrada (del público puesto) en pie; **the audience gave her a s. ovation** el público la ovacionó en pie; ***s. start*** *Sport* salida *f* de pie *or* en posición vertical; *Aut* **it accelerates to 100 km/h from a s. start in four seconds** se pone de cero a cien en cuatro segundos; ***s. stone*** menhir *m*
(**b**) *(permanent)* permanente; **you have a s. invitation** estás invitado a venir cuando quieras; **it's a s. joke in the office** es una de las bromas de siempre en la oficina ►► ***s. army*** ejército *m* permanente; ***s.***

committee comisión *f* permanente; *Br Fin* ***s. order*** domiciliación *f* (bancaria); **I pay my gas bill by s. order** tengo domiciliado el recibo del gas; ***s. order(s)*** *(of body, committee)* reglamento *m*

(c) *(stagnant) (water)* estancado(a)

stand-off ['stændɒf] *n* (a) *(deadlock)* punto *m* muerto; **the s. between the two armies didn't last long** la tregua entre los dos ejércitos no duró mucho tiempo (b) *(in rugby)* ***s. (half)*** medio *m* (de) apertura (c) *US Sport (tie)* empate *m*

stand-offish ['stænd'ɒfɪʃ] *adj* distante

stand-offishness [stænd'ɒfɪʃnɪs] *n* postura *f* distante

standout ['stændaʊt] 1 *n* **the third track is a real s.** el tercer tema del disco es el mejor con diferencia

2 *adj* excelente, superior

standpipe ['stændpaɪp] *n (in street)* = surtidor provisional de agua instalado en la calle

standpoint ['stændpɔɪnt] *n* punto *m* de vista

standstill ['stændstɪl] *n* **to be at a s.** estar paralizado(a); **to bring sth to a s.** paralizar algo; **to come to a s.** pararse, detenerse; **the country came to a s.** el país se paralizó

stand-up ['stændʌp] 1 *n* **s. (comedy)** monólogos *mpl* de humor

2 *adj* (a) *(comedian)* **s. comic** *or* **comedian** humorista *mf (de monólogos)*, monologuista *mf* (b) *(meal)* de pie (c) *(collar)* alto(a), subido(a) (d) *(passionate)* **a s. argument** una violenta discusión; **a s. fight** una batalla campal, una pelea salvaje (e) *US (decent, honest)* decente

stank *pt of* **stink**

Stanley knife® ['stænlɪnaɪf] *n* cúter *m*

stanza ['stænzə] *n* (a) *(in poetry)* estrofa *f* (b) *US Sport* cuarto *m*

stapes ['steɪpi:z] *n Anat* estribo *m*

staphylococcus ['stæfɪlə'kɒkəs] *n Biol* estafilococo *m*

staple[1] ['steɪpəl] 1 *n* (a) *(for paper)* grapa *f*, *Chile* corchete *m*, *Col* gancho *m*, *RP* ganchito *m* ▸▸ ***s. gun*** grapadora *f* industrial; ***s. remover*** quitagrapas *m inv* (b) *(for cables)* grapa *f*

2 *vt* grapar, *Chile* corchetear, *Méx* engrapar, *RP* abrochar; **to s. sth together** grapar *or Chile* corchetear *or Méx* engrapar *or RP* abrochar algo

staple[2] 1 *n* (a) *(basic food)* alimento *m* básico; *(raw material)* materia *f* prima (b) *Com & Econ (main product)* producto *m* básico *or* de primera necesidad (c) *(regular element)* **such stories are a s. of the tabloid press** esas historias son el pan de cada día en la prensa amarilla (d) *(fibre)* ***s. (fibre)*** fibra *f* cortada

2 *adj (food, commodity)* básico(a), de primera necesidad; *(diet)* básico(a); *(export, crop)* básico(a); **violence is a s. feature of the sport** la violencia es un elemento característico de ese deporte

stapler ['steɪplə(r)] *n* grapadora *f*, *Chile* corchetera *f*, *RP* abrochadora *f*

star [stɑ:(r)] 1 *n* (a) *(heavenly body)* estrella *f*; **to sleep (out) under the stars** dormir al relente, dormir bajo el manto de las estrellas; IDIOM **his s. is rising/on the wane** su estrella está empezando a brillar/apagarse; IDIOM **to have stars in one's eyes** estar lleno(a) de sueños e ilusiones; IDIOM **to reach for the stars** *(aspire)* apuntar al cielo; IDIOM **to see stars** *(after blow to head)* ver las estrellas ▸▸ *Astron* ***s. cluster*** cúmulo *m* de estrellas, asociación *f* de estrellas; ***the Stars and Stripes*** las barras y estrellas, = la bandera estadounidense; ***s. system*** *(in space)* galaxia *f*, sistema *m* estelar; *Mil* ***S. Wars*** la Guerra de las Galaxias

(b) *(shape)* estrella *f* ▸▸ ***s. anise*** anís *m* estrellado; ***S. of David*** estrella *f* de David; ***s. jump*** *(exercise)* = salto en el que se estiran los brazos y las piernas semejando una estrella; *Comptr* ***s. network*** red *f* en estrella

(c) *(actor, singer, sportsperson)* estrella *f*; **movie** *or Br* **film s.** estrella de cine; **she's my s. student** es mi mejor alumna, es la más brillante de mis alumnas; **thanks for your help, you're a s.!** ¡gracias por tu ayuda, campeón! ▸▸ ***s. attraction*** atracción *f* estelar; ***s. billing*** rango *m* de estrella; ***s. player*** estrella *f or* figura *f* del equipo; ***s. prize*** premio *m* estrella; ***s. quality*** madera *f or* hechuras *fpl* de estrella; ***s. system*** *(in Hollywood)* star-system *m*, promoción *f* de estrellas de cine; ***s. turn*** atracción *f* principal, actuación *f* estelar; ***s. witness*** principal testigo *mf*

(d) *Fam* **stars** *(horoscope)* horóscopo *m*; **I like reading my stars in the paper** me gusta leer mi horóscopo en el periódico; **it's (written) in the stars** lo dicen las estrellas ▸▸ ***s. chart*** carta astral; ***s. sign*** signo *m* del zodiaco

(e) *(as indicator of quality)* estrella *f*; *Sch* estrella *f*; **a five-s. hotel** un hotel de cinco estrellas; *Br* **four-s. petrol** gasolina *or RP* nafta súper

(f) *(symbol)* estrella *f* ; *(asterisk)* asterisco *m*

2 *vt* (*pt & pp* **starred**) *(of movie)* estar protagonizado(a) por; **Casablanca, starring Humphrey Bogart and Ingrid Bergman** Casablanca, protagonizada por Humphrey Bogart e Ingrid Bergman

3 *vi* **to s. in a movie** protagonizar una película; **he's starring in a new TV serial** protagoniza una nueva serie de televisión; **he starred as a gangster in The Godfather** protagonizó El Padrino haciendo de gángster

starboard ['stɑ:bəd] 1 *n Naut* estribor *m*; **vessel to s.!** ¡barco a estribor!

2 *adj* de estribor

starch [stɑ:tʃ] 1 *n* (a) *(for shirts)* almidón *m* (b) *(in food)* fécula *f*, almidón *m*; **you eat too much s.** tomas demasiada fécula *or* demasiado almidón

2 *vt (shirt)* almidonar

starchily ['stɑ:tʃɪlɪ] *adv (to reply, react)* con rigidez

starch-reduced ['stɑ:tʃrɪ'dju:st] *adj (bread, diet)* de bajo contenido en almidón *or* fécula

starchy ['stɑ:tʃɪ] *adj* (a) *(food)* feculento(a) (b) *Fam (person, manner)* estirado(a), rígido(a)

star-crossed ['stɑ:krɒst] *adj* malhadado(a), infortunado(a)

stardom ['stɑ:dəm] *n* estrellato *m*; **to achieve s.** alcanzar el estrellato

stardust ['stɑ:dʌst] *n* quimeras *fpl*, ilusiones *fpl*; **to have s. in one's eyes** hacerse grandes ilusiones

stare [steə(r)] 1 *n* mirada *f* fija; **to give sb a hostile/an incredulous s.** quedarse mirando a alguien con ojos hostiles/de incredulidad

2 *vt* **her steely eyes stared him into submission** lo subyugó clavándole sus ojos acerados; **the answer was staring me in the face** tenía la solución delante de las narices; **ruin was staring us in the face** nos enfrentábamos a la ruina

3 *vi* **to s. (at sth/sb)** mirar fijamente (algo/a alguien); **she stared at me in disbelief** se me quedó mirando con ojos incrédulos; **what are you staring at?** *(as challenge)* ¿y tú qué miras?; **stop it, people are staring!** ¡estate quieto(a), la gente nos está mirando *or* no deja de mirarnos!; **he stared straight ahead** dirigió la mirada al frente, miró al frente; **I stared into his eyes** lo miré a los ojos, clavé mi mirada en la suya; **to s. into the distance** mirar al vacío; **it's rude to s.** es de mala educación quedarse mirando (con descaro)

▸ **stare down, stare out** *vt sep* hacer apartar la vista a

starfish ['stɑ:fɪʃ] *n* estrella *f* de mar

starfruit ['stɑ:fru:t] *n* carambola *f (fruto)*

stargazer ['stɑ:geɪzə(r)] *n* (a) *(astronomer)* astrónomo(a) *m,f* (b) *(astrologer)* astrólogo(a) *m,f* (c) *(daydreamer)* soñador(ora) *m,f*

stargazing ['stɑ:geɪzɪŋ] *n* (a) *(astronomy)* astronomía *f* (b) *(astrology)* astrología *f* (c) *(daydreaming)* ensoñación *f*

staring ['steərɪŋ] *adj* **he had s. eyes** tenía los ojos fuera de las órbitas

stark [stɑ:k] 1 *adj* (a) *(light, colours)* frío(a); *(landscape)* desolado(a); *(beauty)* austero(a), sobrio(a)

(b) *(truth, facts)* crudo(a); *(contrast, warning, reminder)* claro(a), inequívoco(a); *(choice)* difícil, arduo(a); **the s. reality is we have no choice** la cruda realidad es que no tenemos elección; **the s. simplicity of the plan** la brutal simplicidad del plan

(c) *(utter) (brutality, terror, poverty)* puro(a), absoluto(a); **his remarks today are in s. contrast to what he said last week** sus comentarios de hoy chocan radicalmente con lo que dijo la semana pasada

2 *adv* **s. naked** completamente desnudo(a); **s. raving** *or* **staring mad** completamente loco(a)

starkers ['stɑ:kəz] *adj Br Fam* en pelotas, en cueros, *Chile* pilucho(a)

starkly ['stɑ:klɪ] *adv* (a) *(lit)* fríamente; *(beautiful)* austeramente, sobriamente (b) *(to tell, demonstrate)* claramente, inequívocamente; *(deny)* categóricamente, rotundamente; **this contrasts s. with what she said last week** esto choca radicalmente con lo que dijo la semana pasada

starkness ['stɑ:knɪs] *n* (a) *(of light, colours)* frialdad *f*; *(of landscape)* desolación *f*; *(of beauty)* austeridad *f*, sobriedad *f* (b) *(of choice)* dificultad *f*, lo arduo (c) *(of brutality, terror, poverty)* carácter *m* absoluto; *(of contrast)* claridad *f*

starless ['stɑ:lɪs] *adj* sin estrellas

starlet ['stɑ:lɪt] *n (young actress)* actriz *f* incipiente

starlight ['stɑ:laɪt] *n* luz *f* de las estrellas; **by s.** a la luz de las estrellas

starling ['stɑ:lɪŋ] *n* estornino *m* (pinto)

starlit ['stɑ:lɪt] *adj* iluminado(a) por las estrellas

starry ['stɑ:rɪ] *adj (night, sky)* estrellado(a)

starry-eyed ['stɑ:rɪ'aɪd] *adj (idealistic, naive)* cándido(a), idealista; *(lovers)* embelesado(a), embobado(a); **the children stood s. in front of the Christmas tree** los niños se quedaron extasiados delante del árbol de Navidad

Star-Spangled Banner ['stɑːspæŋgəld'bænə(r)] *n* **the S.** *(anthem)* el himno estadounidense; *(flag)* las barras y estrellas, = la bandera estadounidense

star-studded ['stɑːstʌdɪd] *adj (sky)* cuajado(a) de estrellas, tachonado(a) de estrellas; **a s. cast** un reparto estelar, un reparto plagado de estrellas

START [stɑːt] **1** *n* **(a)** *(beginning)* principio *m*, comienzo *m*; *(starting place, of race)* salida *f*; **our team had a good/bad s.** nuestro equipo tuvo un buen/mal comienzo; **it's a s.** por algo se empieza; **at the s.** al principio; **at the s. of the month** a principios de mes; **for a s.** para empezar; **from the s.** desde el principio; **from s. to finish** de principio a fin; **the evening got off to a good/bad s.** la noche empezó bien/mal; **he lent her £500 to give her a s.** le prestó 500 libras para ayudarla a empezar; **to give sb a good s. in life** dar a alguien una buena base para el futuro; **to give sb a 60 metre(s)/ten minute(s) s.** dar a alguien una ventaja de 60 metros/diez minutos; **she has made a promising s. in her new job** ha tenido un comienzo prometedor en su nuevo trabajo; **we want to make an early s.** *(to journey)* queremos salir temprano; **to make a s. on sth** empezar con algo; **she has a two hour s. on us** nos lleva dos horas de ventaja ►► ***s. hut*** *(in skiing)* caseta *f* de salida

(b) *(sudden movement)* sobresalto *m*; **to wake with a s.** despertarse sobresaltado(a); **I gave a s.** me sobresalté; **to give sb a s.** *(frighten)* sobresaltar a alguien, dar un susto a alguien

2 *vt* **(a)** *(begin)* empezar, comenzar; *(conversation, talks)* entablar, iniciar; **to s. school** empezar el colegio; **to s. work** *(work for first time)* empezar *or* comenzar a trabajar; *(begin working day)* empezar *or* comenzar *or* entrar a trabajar; **frogs s. life as tadpoles** las ranas comienzan siendo renacuajos; **the restaurant started life as a café** el restaurante empezó *or* comenzó como cafetería; **to s. a family** empezar a tener hijos; **to s. doing sth, to s. to do sth** empezar *or* comenzar a hacer algo; **it's just started raining** acaba de ponerse a *or* empezar a llover; **they've started shouting again** han vuelto a ponerse a gritar; **to get started** empezar, comenzar; **here's $10 to get you started** aquí tienes 10 dólares para que vayas comenzando; **I need a coffee to get me started in the morning** por las mañanas necesito un café que me ponga en marcha

(b) *(cause to begin) (campaign, war)* empezar, comenzar; *(club, fund)* crear, formar; *(fashion)* comenzar; *(rumour)* poner en circulación; *(fire, avalanche)* provocar, ocasionar; *(a business)* montar; **to s. a fight (with sb)** empezar *or* comenzar una pelea (con alguien); **his comment started me thinking** su comentario me hizo ponerme a pensar; *Fam* **are you trying to s. something?** ¿buscas algo?; **it started her crying/laughing** le hizo llorar/reír; **if you s. him on this subject he'll never stop** como le des pie a que hable del asunto, después no hay quien lo pare; *Fam* **you started it!** ¡has empezado tú!

(c) *(cause to work) (machine, engine, car)* arrancar, poner en marcha

(d) *(give signal to begin) (race)* dar la salida a

3 *vi* **(a)** *(begin)* empezar, comenzar; **please s.!** *(begin eating)* ¡comiencen a comer, por favor!; **she had started as a doctor** había comenzado trabajando como médica; **to s. at the beginning** empezar por el principio; **the neutral zone starts at the river** la zona neutral comienza en el río; **I s. on $500 a week** empiezo con 500 dólares a la semana; **prices s. at** *or* **from £20** *(in advert)* precios desde 20 libras; **to s. by doing sth** comenzar haciendo algo; **to s. again** *or* **afresh** comenzar de nuevo; **I didn't know where to s.** no sabía por dónde empezar; **you have 60 seconds starting from now** tienes 60 segundos empezando a contar desde ya; **starting (from) next week** a partir de la semana que viene; **to s. with** *(in the first place)* para empezar; *(at the beginning)* al comienzo *or* principio; **what would you like to s. (with)?** *(in restaurant) Esp* ¿qué tomarán para empezar?, *Am* ¿qué se van a servir para empezar?; **now don't YOU s.!** ¡no empieces (otra vez)!, ¡no empecemos (otra vez)!

(b) *(make sudden movement)* sobresaltarse (**at** con); **I started from my seat** me levanté de mi asiento sobresaltado; **to s. out of one's sleep** despertarse sobresaltado(a)

(c) *(begin journey)* salir, partir; **the tour starts at** *or* **from the main square** la visita comienza en la plaza mayor; **I'll have to s. for the airport soon** pronto tendré que salir hacia el aeropuerto; **she started along the path** comenzó a caminar por el sendero; *Fig* **we're back where we started** hemos vuelto al punto de partida

(d) *(car, engine)* arrancar

(e) *(gush)* **tears started to his eyes** se le comenzaron a saltar las lágrimas

► **start back** *vi* **(a)** *(begin to return)* **we'd better s. back soon** sería mejor que vayamos volviendo

(b) *(start again)* **the children s. back at school tomorrow** los niños comienzan las clases mañana

► **start off 1** *vt sep (argument, debate)* suscitar, provocar; **to s. sb off** *(in business)* dar un primer empujón a alguien; *(on a subject)* dar cuerda a alguien; **she started the meeting off with introductions** inició la reunión con las presentaciones; **he gave me some coins to start my collection off** me dio unas monedas para que comenzara mi colección; **what started them off laughing?** ¿qué les hizo ponerse a reír?; **if you mention it it'll only s. her off again** como lo menciones, ya la tienes otra vez

2 *vi (begin)* empezar, comenzar; *(on journey)* salir; **we started off down the road** nos pusimos en camino; **to s. off by doing sth** comenzar haciendo algo; **I started off agreeing with him** al principio estaba de acuerdo con él

► **start on 1** *vt insep (begin)* empezar; **after they'd searched the vehicle they started on the luggage** cuando acabaron de registrar el vehículo, se pusieron con el equipaje; **don't s. on me, I'm not to blame!** conmigo no te metas que yo no tengo la culpa

2 *vt sep* **they've started me on a special diet** me han puesto una dieta especial

3 *vi Fam (complain)* **my mother started on at me about not cleaning my room** mi madre empezó a darme la lata *or Col, Méx* dar lata por no haber limpiado mi habitación

► **start out** *vi* **(a)** *(begin)* empezar; **she started out as a secretary** empezó de secretaria

(b) *(on journey)* salir, partir

(c) *(intend)* **he started out to write a novel** al empezar tenía la intención de escribir una novela

► **start over** *vi US* volver a empezar

► **start up 1** *vt sep (car, machine)* arrancar, poner en marcha; *(computer)* arrancar; *(club, fund)* crear, formar; *(business)* montar, poner

2 *vi (begin)* empezar, comenzar; *(engine)* arrancar, ponerse en marcha; *(computer)* arrancar; **the applause started up again** comenzaron a sonar aplausos de nuevo; **to s. up in business** poner *or* montar un negocio

starter ['stɑːtə(r)] *n* **(a)** *(competitor) (person)* competidor(ora) *m,f*; *(horse)* caballo *m* que comienza una carrera

(b) *(official)* juez *mf* de salida; **they're under s.'s orders, and they're off** *(in horseracing)* están esperando la orden de salida del juez, y allá van; **s.'s gun** *(signal)* pistoletazo de salida

(c) *(person)* **to be a late s.** *(child)* llevar retraso *or Am* demora (en el aprendizaje); **to be a slow s.** tardar *or Am* demorar en ponerse en marcha ►► *Br* ***s. home*** primera vivienda *f*; *Comptr* ***s. pack*** *(for Internet connection)* kit *m* de conexión

(d) *(device)* **s. (motor)** motor *m* de arranque

(e) *(in meal)* entrada *f*, entrante *m*, primer plato *m*; **for starters** *(in meal)* de primero; *Fig (for a start)* para empezar

starting ['stɑːtɪŋ] *n* **(a)** *(beginning)* ***s. place*** punto *m* de partida; ***s. point*** punto *m* de partida; ***s. salary*** salario *m or* sueldo *m* inicial

(b) *Sport* ***s. block*** *(in athletics)* tacos *mpl or* puesto *m* de salida; *(in swimming)* podio *m* de salida; ***s. gate*** *(in horseracing)* puerta *f* de los cajones de salida; ***s. grid*** *(in motor racing)* parrilla *f* de salida; ***s. line*** línea *f* de salida; ***s. line-up*** alineación *f*; ***s. pistol*** pistola *f* para dar la salida; ***s. post*** *(in horseracing)* poste *m* de salida; ***s. price*** *(in betting)* precio *m* de las apuestas a la salida; *(at auction)* precio *m* de salida (a subasta); ***s. stalls*** *(in horseracing)* cajones *mpl* de salida

startle ['stɑːtəl] *vt* sobresaltar; **I didn't mean to s. you** no pretendía asustarte; **the noise startled him out of his reverie** el ruido lo hizo bajar repentinamente de las nubes

startled ['stɑːtəld] *adj (look, cry)* de sobresalto; *(silence)* sobrecogedor(ora); **to look/seem s.** parecer sobresaltado(a)

startling ['stɑːtlɪŋ] *adj* **(a)** *(noise)* que sobresalta; *(news, event)* sorprendente **(b)** *(contrast, resemblance)* llamativo(a), asombroso(a)

start-up ['stɑːtʌp] *n* **(a)** *Com* puesta *f* en marcha ►► ***s. company*** empresa *f* de reciente creación, nueva empresa *f*; ***s. costs*** gastos *mpl* de puesta en marcha; ***s. loan*** préstamo *m* para la puesta en marcha de un negocio **(b)** *Comptr* arranque *m* ►► ***s. disk*** disco *m* de arranque; ***s. screen*** pantalla *f* de arranque

starvation [stɑː'veɪʃən] *n* inanición *f*; **to die of s.** morir de inanición *or* hambre ►► ***s. diet*** dieta *f* miserable; ***s. wages*** salario *m* mísero

starve [stɑːv] **1** *vt* **(a)** *(not give food)* privar de alimentos; **he starved himself to feed his child** se quitaba el pan de la boca para dar de comer a su hijo; **to s. sb to death** matar a alguien de inanición; **to s. sb into surrender** hacer rendirse a alguien por el hambre; *Fam* **I'm starved!** ¡me muero de hambre!

(b) *(deprive)* **to be starved of sth** estar privado(a) de algo; **the club**

has been starved of success for many years el club se ha visto privado de éxito durante muchos años

2 *vi (lack food)* pasar mucha hambre; **to s. (to death)** morir de inanición *or* hambre

▸ **starve out** *vt sep (rebels, people in garrison)* obligar a rendirse por hambre a

starving ['stɑːvɪŋ] *adj* famélico(a), hambriento(a); *Fam* **I'm s.** me muero de hambre

stash [stæʃ] *Fam* 1 *n* (a) *(hidden supply)* reserva *f*; *(of drugs)* alijo *m*, cargamento *m*; **a s. of money** dinero escondido (b) *(hiding place)* escondrijo *m*

2 *vt (hide)* **it was stashed (away) under the bed** estaba muy bien escondido debajo de la cama; **he's got a lot of money stashed (away) in an offshore bank account** tiene mucho dinero bien guardado en una cuenta bancaria en el extranjero

stasis ['steɪsɪs] *n* (a) *Med* estasis *f* (b) *Formal (total inactivity)* estasis *f*

STATE [steɪt] 1 *n* (a) *(condition, situation)* estado *m*; **look at the s. of this room!** ¡qué desastre de habitación!; *Fam* **my hair's (in) a s.!** ¡tengo el pelo hecho un revoltijo *or Esp* follón!; **s. of affairs** situación; **given the current s. of affairs** dadas las actuales circunstancias; **it's an embarrassing s. of affairs** es una situación embarazosa; **the married s.** el matrimonio; **the single s.** la soltería, el celibato; **chlorine in its gaseous/liquid s.** cloro en estado gaseoso/líquido; **the s. of the art** el último grito, lo último *or* más moderno; **a s. of emergency** un estado de emergencia; **s. of health** estado de salud; **s. of mind** estado anímico; **s. of play** *(situation)* situación; **to be in a good/poor s. of repair** estar en buen/mal estado; **he was in a s. of confusion/panic** estaba sumido en la confusión/el pánico; **in a s. of shock** en estado de shock; **a s. of siege** un estado de sitio; **the country is in a s. of terror** el país vive aterrorizado; **I am not in a fit s. to travel** no estoy en condiciones de viajar; **to be in a good/terrible s.** estar en buen estado/en un estado terrible; *Fam* **she was in a real s.** *(upset)* estaba hecha un manojo de nervios; *Fam* **I got into a s. about my exams** los exámenes me pusieron nerviosísimo ▸▸ *US* ***the S. of the Union address*** el discurso sobre el estado de la nación

(b) *(country, administrative region)* estado *m*; **a s. within a s.** un estado dentro del Estado; *Fam* **the States** *(the USA)* (los) Estados Unidos

(c) *(ceremony)* pompa *f*, boato *m*; **to lie in s.** *(before funeral)* yacer en la capilla ardiente; **to travel in s.** viajar con mucho ceremonial ▸▸ ***s. funeral*** funeral *m* de estado; ***s. occasion*** ceremonia *f* de gala; ***the s. opening of Parliament*** = apertura anual del parlamento británico presidida por la reina; ***s. visit*** viaje *m* oficial *or* de Estado

2 *adj* (a) *(of country)* estatal, del estado ▸▸ ***s. capitalism*** capitalismo *m* de estado; ***s. church*** iglesia *f* del estado; *Pol* ***S. Department*** Departamento *m* de Estado, = Ministerio de Asuntos *or Am* Relaciones Exteriores estadounidense; ***s. education*** enseñanza *f* pública; ***s. school*** colegio *m* estatal *or* público; ***s. secret*** secreto *m* de Estado; ***s. sector*** sector *m* público; ***s. socialism*** socialismo *m* de estado; *Br* ***the s. system*** el sistema público

(b) *(of administrative region)* estatal, del estado ▸▸ *US* ***s. attorney*** fiscal *mf* de distrito; *US* ***s. bank*** banco *f* del estado, banco *m* estatal; *US* ***s. control*** control *m* estatal; *US* ***State's evidence:*** **to turn State's evidence** = inculpar a un cómplice ante un tribunal a cambio de recibir un trato indulgente; *US* ***s. highway*** ≃ carretera *f* nacional; *US* ***s. line*** frontera *f* interestatal; *US* ***s. prison*** prisión *m* estatal; ***states' rights*** = derechos de los que goza cada estado de Estados Unidos; *US* ***s. trooper*** policía *m* estatal

3 *vt (declare)* declarar; *(one's name and address)* indicar; *(reason, demand, objection, opinion)* exponer; *(intention)* dar a conocer; **s. the figure as a percentage** exprese la cifra en porcentaje; **she stated her case** expuso sus argumentos; **s. the nature of the problem** indique la naturaleza del problema; **s. why you are applying for the post** exponga por qué solicita el puesto; **to s. (that)...** declarar que...; **it states in paragraph six that...** en el párrafo seis se dice que...; **to s. the obvious** decir una obviedad; **as stated earlier/above** como se hizo constar antes/más arriba

state-controlled ['steɪtkən'trəʊld] *adj (industry, company)* estatal, controlado(a) por el Estado

statecraft ['steɪtkrɑːft] *n (political skill)* arte *m* de gobernar, habilidad *f* política

stated ['steɪtɪd] *adj* (a) *(intentions)* **our s. aim is to cut inflation by three percent** nuestro objetivo manifiesto es reducir la inflación en un tres por ciento (b) *(purpose, amount, dose)* indicado(a); *(date, price)* fijado(a)

statehood ['steɪthʊd] *n* condición *f* de estado

stateless ['steɪtlɪs] *adj* apátrida

stateliness ['steɪtlɪnɪs] *n* majestuosidad *f*

stately ['steɪtlɪ] *adj* imponente, majestuoso(a); **she proceeded at a s. pace** avanzó con paso majestuoso ▸▸ ***s. home*** casa *f* solariega

statement ['steɪtmənt] *n* (a) *(of opinion)* declaración *f*; **to make a s.** *(spokesperson)* hacer una declaración; **punks were making a s. by the way they dressed** la forma de vestir de los punkis decía mucho de ellos; **his actions are a political s.** sus actos son una declaración política

(b) *Law* declaración *f*; **to make a s.** *(witness)* prestar declaración; **to take sb's s.** tomar declaración a alguien

(c) *(act of stating) (of theory, opinions, aims)* manifestación *f*, exposición *f*; **a s. of the facts** una exposición de los hechos

(d) *(from bank)* extracto *m* (bancario)

(e) *Fin* ***s. of accounts*** *(of company)* estado *m* de cuentas; *(of client)* extracto *m* de cuenta

state-of-the-art ['steɪtəvðɪ'ɑːt] *adj* de vanguardia; **the equipment we use is s.** el equipo que utilizamos es de lo más moderno ▸▸ ***s. technology*** tecnología *f* punta

state-owned ['steɪt'əʊnd] *adj* público(a), estatal

stateroom ['steɪtruːm] *n* (a) *(on ship)* camarote *m* de lujo (b) *(in palace)* salón *m* principal

state-run ['steɪt'rʌn] *adj* estatal

Stateside ['steɪtsaɪd] *adv Fam (to be)* en Estados Unidos, en América; **to go S.** ir a Estados Unidos *or* América

statesman ['steɪtsmən] *n* estadista *m*, hombre *m* de Estado

statesmanlike ['steɪtsmənlaɪk] *adj (behaviour, speech)* digno(a) de un gran hombre de Estado; **he's not very s.** le falta la gravedad propia de un hombre de Estado

statesmanship ['steɪtsmənʃɪp] *n* (a) *(art)* arte *m* de gobernar (b) *(political skill)* **he showed great s. in dealing with the problem** demostró una gran habilidad política en la forma en que abordó el problema

statesperson ['steɪtspɜːsən] *n* estadista *mf*

stateswoman ['steɪtswʊmən] *n* estadista *f*

state-wide ['steɪtwaɪd] *US* 1 *adj (support, protest, celebration)* de ámbito estatal, a escala estatal

2 *adv* en *or* por todo el estado

static ['stætɪk] 1 *n* (a) *(electricity)* electricidad *f* estática (b) *(on radio, TV)* interferencias *fpl* (c) *US Fam (complaints, objections)* **you can expect plenty of s. from mom** ya verás como mamá te va a dar la lata

2 *adj* (a) *(stationary, unchanging)* estático(a); **prices have remained s.** los precios no se han alterado, los precios han permanecido inalterables (b) *Elec* estático(a) ▸▸ ***s. electricity*** electricidad *f* estática

station ['steɪʃən] 1 *n* (a) *(for trains, buses)* estación *f* ▸▸ *US* ***s. wagon*** *(car)* ranchera *f*

(b) *(establishment, building)* **(police) s.** comisaría *f* (de policía); **they took me to the s. for questioning** me llevaron a comisaría para interrogarme ▸▸ *US* ***s. house*** *(of police)* comisaría *f*; *(of fire department)* parque *m or* cuartel *m* de bomberos

(c) *(channel)* **(radio) s.** emisora *f* (de radio); **(television) s.** canal *m* (de televisión)

(d) *Mil (post)* puesto *m*; **to take up one's s.** ocupar uno su puesto, apostarse

(e) *(social condition)* posición *f*; **to marry above/below one's s.** casarse con alguien de posición social superior/inferior a la de uno; **to have ideas above one's s.** tener demasiadas aspiraciones

(f) *Rel* **the Stations of the Cross** el vía crucis

2 *vt* (a) *(position) (person)* colocar; *(soldier, guard)* apostar; **to s. oneself** apostarse (b) *Mil (garrison)* destacar

stationary ['steɪʃənərɪ] *adj* (a) *(not moving)* inmóvil; *(vehicle)* parado(a); **to remain s.** permanecer inmóvil (b) *(fixed)* fijo(a), anclado(a)

stationer ['steɪʃənə(r)] *n* **s.'s (shop)** papelería *f*

stationery ['steɪʃənərɪ] *n* (a) *(writing materials)* artículos *mpl* de papelería (b) *(writing paper)* papel *m* de carta (c) *Br* ***the S. Office*** = imprenta del Estado

stationmaster ['steɪʃənmɑːstə(r)] *n* jefe *m* de estación

statism ['steɪtɪzəm] *n* estatismo *m*

statist ['steɪtɪst] *adj* propio(a) del estatismo

statistic [stə'tɪstɪk] *n* dato *m* (estadístico); **statistics** *(facts)* estadísticas, datos estadísticos; *(science)* estadística; **he may be just another s. to the police, but he was my brother** puede que para la policía no sea más que otro número en las estadísticas, pero era mi hermano

statistical [stə'tɪstɪkəl] *adj* estadístico(a); **it's a s. certainty** se trata de un hecho estadístico, es un hecho estadísticamente comprobado

statistically [stəˈtɪstɪklɪ] *adv* estadísticamente; **a s. insignificant number** un número insignificante en términos estadísticos, un número estadísticamente insignificante; **it has been s. proven that...** se ha demostrado por medio de estadísticas que..., está estadísticamente comprobado que...

statistician [stætɪsˈtɪʃən] *n* estadístico(a) *m,f*

stative [ˈsteɪtɪv] *adj* ***s. verb*** verbo *m* de estado

stats [stæts] *n Fam (facts)* estadísticas *fpl*, datos *mpl* (estadísticos); *(subject)* estadística *f*

statuary [ˈstætʃʊərɪ] *n* (**a**) *(statues)* estatuas *fpl* (**b**) *(art)* estatuaria *f*

statue [ˈstætju:] *n* estatua *f* ►► ***the S. of Liberty*** la estatua de la libertad

statuesque [stætjʊˈesk] *adj* escultural

statuette [stætjʊˈet] *n* estatuilla *f*

stature [ˈstætjə(r)] *n* (**a**) *(physical build)* estatura *f* (**b**) *(reputation)* talla *f*, estatura *f*; **she is a politician of s.** es una renombrada *or* prestigiosa política; **he has grown** *or* **increased in s. during the tournament** ha mejorado su categoría a lo largo del torneo

status [ˈsteɪtəs] *n* (**a**) *(in society, profession)* categoría *f*, posición *f*; **she enjoys celebrity s.** goza de popularidad, es un personaje famoso

(**b**) *(prestige)* categoría *f*, prestigio *m* ►► ***s. symbol*** símbolo *f* de prestigio *or* estatus

(**c**) *(situation, condition)* situación *f*, estado *m*; **what is their financial s.?** ¿cuál es su situación económica?; **is his HIV s. positive or negative?** ¿es seropositivo o seronegativo? ►► ***s. enquiry*** *(about creditworthiness)* petición *f* de informe sobre la capacidad de endeudamiento; ***s. report*** informe *m* de la situación

(**d**) *Law* estado *m*; **it has no legal/official s.** carece de validez legal/oficial

(**e**) *Comptr* ***s. bar*** barra *f* de estado; ***s. line*** línea *f* de estado

status quo [ˈsteɪtəsˈkwəʊ] *n* statu quo *m*

statute [ˈstætju:t] *n* ley *f*; **by s.** por ley; **the club's statutes say that...** los estatutos del club establecen que... ►► ***s. book*** legislación *f*, código *m* de leyes; **to reach the s. book** convertirse en ley; ***s. law*** derecho *m* escrito; *Law* ***s. of limitations*** (estatuto *m* de) prescripción *f* legal; ***s. mile*** milla *f* terrestre

statutorily [ˈstætjʊtərɪlɪ] *adv* según (lo establecido por) la ley, de acuerdo *or* conformidad con (lo establecido por) la ley

statutory [ˈstætjʊtərɪ] *adj* legal; **the s. regulations say that...** la normativa jurídica establece que...; **the s. penalty for this offence is a £100 fine** la multa reglamentaria es de 100 libras; **this is a s. offence** éste es un delito castigado por la ley; **it is a s. requirement for all dog owners to have a licence** es un requisito marcado por la ley que los propietarios de perros posean una licencia ►► ***s. duty*** obligación *f* legal; ***s. holidays*** días *mpl* festivos oficiales; *US Law* ***s. rape*** relaciones *fpl* sexuales con un/una menor; ***s. rights*** derechos *mpl* legales; ***s. sick pay*** subsidio *m* por enfermedad

staunch[1] [stɔ:ntʃ], *US* **stanch** [stɑ:ntʃ] *vt (blood, flow)* cortar; *(wound)* restañar

staunch[2] *adj (supporter, ally)* fiel, leal; *(socialist, Catholic)* fervoroso(a), comprometido(a)

staunchly [ˈstɔ:ntʃlɪ] *adv* firmemente, fielmente

staunchness [ˈstɔ:ntʃnɪs] *n (of support)* lealtad *f*, firmeza *f*

stave [steɪv] *n* (**a**) *(of barrel)* duela *f* (**b**) *Mus* pentagrama *m* (**c**) *(stanza)* estrofa *f*

► **stave in** (*pt & pp* **staved** *or* **stove** [stəʊv]) *vt sep* romper, quebrar

► **stave off** *vt sep* (**a**) *(postpone) (problem, disaster)* aplazar, retrasar; **to s. off one's hunger** espantar el hambre (**b**) *(avoid) (defeat, illness, questions)* evitar, impedir

staves *Mus pl of* **staff**[2]

STAY [steɪ] **1** *n* (**a**) *(visit) Esp, Méx* estancia *f*, *Am* estadía *f*; **we hope you enjoyed your s.** esperamos que haya disfrutado de su *Esp, Méx* estancia *or Am* estadía; **an overnight s. in hospital** (una estancia de) una noche en el hospital (**b**) *Law* ***s. of execution*** aplazamiento *m* de sentencia (**c**) *(for mast, flagpole)* estay *m* (**d**) **stays** *(corset)* corsé *m*

2 *vt* (**a**) *(endure)* **to s. the course** *or* **distance** aguantar hasta el final (**b**) *Literary (stop)* detener; **to s. sb's hand** detener a alguien; **to s. one's hand** contenerse

3 *vi* (**a**) *(remain in place)* quedarse; **s. where you are!** ¡no te muevas de donde estás!; **s.!** *(to dog)* ¡quieto!; **she stayed late at work** se quedó en el trabajo hasta tarde; **I can't s. long** no puedo quedarme mucho tiempo; **to s. for** *or* **to dinner** quedarse a cenar; **it looks like mobile phones are here to s.** parece que los teléfonos móviles no son una moda pasajera

(**b**) *(remain in state)* permanecer, quedarse; **it stays dark here until at least 9 o'clock in the morning** aquí está oscuro hasta las nueve de la mañana; **the weather stayed fine/wet all week** hizo buen tiempo/llovió toda la semana; *Fam* **to s. put** no moverse; **to s. still** quedarse quieto(a), permanecer inmóvil; **s. still!** ¡no te muevas!; **the picture won't s. straight** el cuadro no se quiere quedar derecho; **to s. awake** permanecer despierto(a); *Fam* **s. cool!** ¡tranqui!; **to s. fit** mantenerse en forma; **I hope we can s. friends** ojalá sigamos siendo amigos; **we s. open all night** estamos abiertos toda la noche; **it will s. sunny all day** el sol seguirá brillando todo el día; **s. tuned!** ¡siga con nosotros!; **we have stayed within our budget** nos hemos ajustado al presupuesto

(**c**) *(reside temporarily)* quedarse; **how long are you staying in New York?** ¿cuánto tiempo te quedarás en Nueva York?; **we have some friends coming to s.** unos amigos van a venir a quedarse con nosotros; **to s. overnight** *or* **the night** quedarse por la noche *or* a pasar la noche; **I'm staying at a hotel** estoy (alojado) en un hotel; **to s. with sb** estar (alojado) en casa de alguien; **I usually s. with my sister over New Year** normalmente paso el Año Nuevo en casa de mi hermana

(**d**) *Scot (live)* vivir

(**e**) *Literary (stop, pause)* detenerse

► **stay ahead** *vi* mantenerse por delante

► **stay away** *vi* **s. away from the fire!** ¡no te acerques al fuego!; **I'd s. away from him if I were you** yo de ti no me acercaría a él; **s. away from my wife!** ¡no te acerques a mi mujer!; **spectators stayed away from the match** los espectadores dieron la espalda al partido

► **stay behind** *vi* quedarse

► **stay down** *vi* (**a**) *(remain crouched)* quedarse agachado(a); *(remain lying)* quedarse estirado(a)

(**b**) *(of hair, lid)* **my hair won't s. down** el pelo no se me queda en su sitio

(**c**) *Br Sch* **she had to s. down a year** tuvo que repetir curso

(**d**) *(of food)* **I do eat, but nothing will s. down** sí como, pero no retengo nada

► **stay in** *vi* (**a**) *(stay at home)* quedarse en casa

(**b**) *(be kept in after school)* quedarse castigado(a)

(**c**) *(not fall out)* **I can't get this nail to s. in** no consigo fijar este clavo

► **stay off** **1** *vt insep* (**a**) *(keep away from) (main roads, private property)* no acercarse a; *(alcohol, drugs)* no tomar, no tocar

(**b**) *(not attend) (school, work)* faltar a

2 *vi (bad weather)* **we're hoping the rain will s. off** esperamos que no llegue la lluvia

► **stay on** *vi* (**a**) *(remain longer)* quedarse; **more pupils are staying on at school after 16** un mayor número de alumnos continuan en el colegio tras cumplir los 16; **he's staying on as product manager** se queda de jefe de producto

(**b**) *(remain in place)* quedarse en su sitio

► **stay out** *vi* (**a**) *(stay outside)* quedarse *or* permanecer fuera; **to s. out all night** estar fuera toda la noche; **get out and s. out!** ¡lárgate y no vuelvas!

(**b**) *(strikers)* permanecer en huelga

(**c**) *(not interfere)* **to s. out of sth** mantenerse al margen de algo; **to s. out of trouble** no meterse en líos; **s. out of this!** ¡no te metas en esto!

► **stay over** *vi* (**a**) *(stay overnight)* pasar la noche

(**b**) *(stay longer)* quedarse

► **stay up** *vi* (**a**) *(not go to bed)* quedarse levantado(a); **we stayed up all night talking** nos quedamos hablando toda la noche;

(**b**) *(remain in place) (building, mast)* seguir en pie; *(socks, trousers)* no caerse; *(pictures, decorations, shelf)* quedarse en su sitio

► **stay with** *vt insep Fam* **just s. with it, you can do it!** no te rindas, tú puedes

stay-at-home [ˈsteɪəthəʊm] **1** *n Br Fam Pej* persona *f* casera *or* hogareña, ermitaño(a) *m,f*

2 *adj* ermitaño(a)

stayer [ˈsteɪə(r)] *n* (**a**) *Sport* **this runner/horse is a s.** es un atleta de fondo/un caballo para carreras de fondo (**b**) *(person who perseveres)* **she's a real s.** es una persona con verdadero tesón

staying power [ˈsteɪɪŋˈpaʊə(r)] *n* resistencia *f*

staysail [ˈsteɪseɪl] *n* vela *f* de estay

STD [esti:ˈdi:] (**a**) *Med* (*abbr* **sexually transmitted disease**) enfermedad *f* de transmisión sexual (**b**) *Br* (*abbr* **subscriber trunk dialling**) = línea directa de larga distancia sin necesidad de operadora ►► ***S. code*** prefijo *m*, indicativo *m*

stead [sted] *n* **it will stand you in good s.** te será de gran utilidad; **I went in his s.** fui en su lugar

steadfast ['stedfɑːst] *adj* (a) *(support, determination)* firme; *(refusal, opposition)* rotundo(a), firme; **to be s. in adversity** mantenerse incólume ante las adversidades (b) *(gaze)* fijo(a)

steadfastly ['stedfɑːstlɪ] *adv* (a) *(to support, refuse)* con firmeza; *(opposed)* rotundamente (b) *(to gaze)* fijamente

steadfastness ['stedfɑːstnɪs] *n* (a) *(of support, determination)* firmeza *f*; *(of refusal, opposition)* rotundidad *f*, firmeza *f* (b) *(of gaze)* fijeza *f*

Steadicam® ['stedɪkæm] *n Cin* steadycam® *f*

steadily ['stedɪlɪ] *adv* (a) *(at regular rate) (change, grow)* constantemente; *(to work)* a buen ritmo; *(to breathe)* con regularidad; **her health grew s. worse** su salud empeoraba irremisiblemente; **a s. falling number of jobs** un índice de empleo en continuo descenso (b) *(non-stop) (to rain)* sin parar, ininterrumpidamente (c) *(firmly) (to walk)* con paso firme; *(to look)* fijamente

steadiness ['stedɪnɪs] *n* (a) *(stability) (of ladder, chair)* estabilidad *f* (b) *(calmness) (of voice, gaze)* serenidad *f*; *(of nerves)* imperturbabilidad *f* (c) *(regularity) (of rate, growth, pace, pulse)* regularidad *f*; *(of progress)* continuidad *f*; *(of breathing)* ritmo *m* constante (d) *(reliability) (of worker, character)* formalidad *f*

steady ['stedɪ] **1** *adj* (a) *(stable)* firme, estable; **try to keep the camera s.** intenta que no se mueva la cámara; **hold the ladder s. for me** sujétame firmemente la escalera; **to be s. on one's feet** caminar *or Esp* andar con paso firme; **to have a s. hand** tener buen pulso; IDIOM **to be s. as a rock** ser firme como una roca

(b) *(calm) (gaze)* sereno(a), imperturbable; *(nerves)* imperturbable, templado(a); **in a s. voice** con voz tranquila

(c) *(regular) (rate, growth, pace)* constante; *(progress)* continuo(a); *(income)* regular; *(pulse)* constante, regular; *(breathing)* constante; **s. girlfriend/boyfriend** novia/novio estable; **to have a s. job** tener un trabajo fijo; **to drive at a s. 50 mph** ir a una velocidad constante de 50 mph; **we have received a s. stream of enquiries** hemos recibido un incesante flujo de preguntas ▸▸ *Astron* ***s. state theory*** teoría *f* del estado estacionario *or* de la creación continua

(d) *(non-stop) (rain)* ininterrumpido(a)

(e) *(reliable) (worker, character)* formal, responsable

2 *adv* **go s. on the salt** no te excedas con la sal; **they are going s.** son novios formales

3 *vt* (a) *(stabilize)* estabilizar, afianzar; **I reached out to s. the vase** me apresuré a sujetar el jarrón para que no se tambalease; **to s. oneself** *(physically)* afianzarse; *(mentally)* reunir fuerzas; IDIOM **to s. the ship** controlar la situación (b) *(calm)* **marriage has steadied him** su matrimonio lo ha vuelto más sosegado; **drink this, it'll s. your nerves** bébete esto, te tranquilizará

4 *vi* (a) *(pulse, breathing)* estabilizarse (b) *(prices, stock market)* estabilizarse

5 *exclam* ¡tranquilo!; *Fam* **s. (on)!** ¡calma!

steadying ['stedɪɪŋ] *adj* **to have a s. influence on sb** ejercer una influencia tranquilizadora en *or* sobre una persona

steak [steɪk] *n* (a) *(piece of beef)* filete *m*, bistec *m*, *RP* bife *m* ▸▸ ***s. knife*** cuchillo *m* de carne; ***s. tartare*** steak tartare *m*, bistec *m* tártaro *or* a la tártara (b) *(beef) (for stews, casseroles)* trozos *mpl* de carne ▸▸ ***s. and kidney pie*** empanada *f* de ternera y riñones; ***s. and kidney pudding*** pastel *m or Col, CSur* torta *f* de ternera y riñones (c) *(of fish)* filete *m*; *(of gammon)* loncha *f* a la plancha

steakhouse ['steɪkhaʊs] *n* parrilla *f*, *RP* churrasquería *f*

steal [stiːl] **1** *vt* (*pt* **stole** [stəʊl], *pp* **stolen** ['stəʊlən]) (a) *(money, property, idea)* robar; **to s. sth from sb** robar algo a alguien; **I've had my purse stolen** me han robado el monedero; **she stole my boyfriend off me!** ¡me robó el novio!

(b) IDIOMS **to s. a glance at sb** dirigir una mirada furtiva a alguien; **to s. sb's heart** robarle *or* arrebatarle el corazón a alguien; **to s. a kiss** *(lovers)* darse un beso furtivo; **to s. a kiss from sb** robarle un beso a alguien, darle a alguien un beso furtivo; **to s. a march on sb** ganar por la mano a alguien; **to s. the show** acaparar toda la atención; **to s. sb's thunder** arrebatarle todo el protagonismo a alguien

2 *vi* (a) *(rob)* robar (**from** a)

(b) *(move quietly)* **to s. away/in/out** alejarse/entrar/salir furtivamente; **he stole in between the two central defenders to score** se coló entre los dos defensas centrales y marcó; **to s. over sb** *(tiredness, feeling)* invadir a alguien; **to s. up on sb** acercarse furtivamente a alguien; **middle age steals up on you** cuando te quieres dar cuenta, eres una persona de mediana edad

3 *n* (a) *Fam* **to be a s.** *(very cheap)* ser baratísimo(a), estar tirado(a) de precio (b) *Sport (in basketball)* recuperación *f*

stealing ['stiːlɪŋ] *n* robo *m*

stealth [stelθ] *n* sigilo *m*; **to do sth by s.** hacer algo sigilosamente *or* con sigilo ▸▸ ***s. bomber*** avión *m or* bombardero *m* invisible

stealthily ['stelθɪlɪ] *adv* subrepticiamente, furtivamente

stealthiness ['stelθɪnɪs] *n* sigilo *m*

stealthy ['stelθɪ] *adj* subrepticio(a), furtivo(a)

steam [stiːm] **1** *n* (a) *(vapour)* vapor *m*; *(on window, mirror)* vaho *m*; **to get up** *or* **to pick up s.** *(vehicle)* calentar calderas, coger velocidad; *(campaign)* despegar, empezar a tomar impulso ▸▸ ***s. bath*** baño *m* de vapor; ***s. boiler*** caldera *f* de vapor; ***s. engine*** máquina *f* de vapor; ***s. iron*** plancha *f* de vapor; ***s. power*** energía *f* de vapor; ***s. shovel*** excavadora *f*; ***s. turbine*** turbina *f* de vapor

(b) IDIOMS **to let off s.** desfogarse; **to run out of s.** *(lose momentum)* perder fuelle; **she did it under her own s.** lo hizo por sus propios medios

2 *vt* (a) *Culin* cocinar al vapor (b) *(unstick with steam)* **to s. open an envelope** abrir un sobre exponiéndolo al vapor; **s. the stamps off the envelope** despega los sellos del sobre con *or* por medio de vapor

3 *vi* (a) *(give off steam)* despedir vapor

(b) *(travel under steam power)* **the liner steamed into the harbour** el transatlántico entró en el puerto echando vapor

(c) *(move quickly)* **we were steaming along at 180 km/h** íbamos a todo gas, manteniendo una velocidad de 180 kilómetros por hora; **he steamed past the athlete in front of him** adelantó en dos zancadas al atleta que le precedía, adelantó a toda marcha al atleta que le precedía; **our party has steamed ahead in the polls** nuestro partido se ha colocado rápidamente a la cabeza de las encuestas

(d) *Culin* cocer al vapor

▸**steam up 1** *vt sep* (a) *(window, glasses)* empañar (b) *Fam (infuriate)* **what's he all steamed up about?** ¿por qué está echando *or* que echa humo?, ¿qué tripa se le ha roto ahora?; **to get all steamed up (about sth)** acalorarse (con algo)

2 *vi (window, glasses)* empañarse

steamboat ['stiːmbəʊt] *n* barco *m* de vapor

steam-driven ['stiːmdrɪvən] *adj* de *or* a vapor, accionado(a) por vapor de agua

steamed [stiːmd] *adj (vegetables)* al vapor ▸▸ ***s. pudding*** budín *m* al vapor

steamer ['stiːmə(r)] *n* (a) *(ship)* barco *m* de vapor (b) *Culin (pot)* olla *f* para cocinar al vapor; *(basket inside pan)* rejilla *f* para cocción al vapor

steaming ['stiːmɪŋ] **1** *n* (a) *Culin* cocción *f* al vapor (b) *Br Fam (crime)* = robo a mano armada perpetrado en los transportes públicos por bandas de delincuentes juveniles

2 *adj* (a) *(very hot)* humeante (b) *Br Fam (drunk)* como una cuba, *Esp* cocido(a), *Col* caído(a) (de la perra), *Méx* ahogado(a), *RP* en pedo (c) *US Fam (angry)* que echa humo

3 *adv* **s. hot** ardiendo, humeante

steamroller ['stiːmrəʊlə(r)] **1** *n Constr* apisonadora *f*; *Fig* **to use s. tactics** aplicar el rodillo

2 *vt* **to s. sb into doing sth** forzar a alguien a hacer algo; **to s. a bill through Parliament** aprobar un proyecto de ley aplicando el rodillo parlamentario

steamship ['stiːmʃɪp] *n* barco *m* de vapor

steamy ['stiːmɪ] *adj* (a) *(room)* lleno(a) de vapor; *(window, mirror)* empañado(a) (b) *Fam (novel, movie)* erótico(a); *(relationship)* ardiente, apasionado(a)

steed [stiːd] *n Literary* corcel *m*

steel [stiːl] **1** *n* (a) *(metal)* acero *m*; **nerves of s.** nervios de acero; **the s. industry** la industria del acero ▸▸ ***s. band*** *(musical)* = grupo de percusión caribeño que utiliza bidones de metal; ***s. blue*** azul *m* acero; ***s. engraving*** grabado *m* en acero; ***s. grey*** gris *m* acero; ***s. guitar*** guitarra *f* hawaiana; ***s. mill*** fundición *f* de acero; ***s. wool*** estropajo *m* de acero

(b) *(for sharpening knives)* afilador *m*

(c) *(resoluteness)* temple *m* (de acero)

(d) *Literary (sword)* acero *m*

2 *adj (made of steel)* de acero

3 *vt* **to s. oneself to do sth** armarse de valor para hacer algo; **to s. oneself against sth** armarse de valor para enfrentarse con algo; **I had steeled myself for the worst** me había preparado para lo peor

steel-blue ['stiːl'bluː] *adj* azul acerado

steel-grey ['stiːl'greɪ] *adj* gris acerado

steel-plated ['stiːl'pleɪtɪd] *adj* chapado(a) en acero

steelworker ['stiːlwɜːkə(r)] *n* trabajador(ora) *m,f* del acero

steelworks ['stiːlwɜːks] *n* acería *f*

steely ['stiːlɪ] *adj (glint)* acerado(a); *(glare)* duro(a); *(determination)* férreo(a), inflexible; **s. blue/grey** azul/gris acerado

steelyard ['stiːljɑːd] *n* romana *f*

steely-eyed ['sti:lɪ'aɪd] *adj (person)* de ojos acerados, de mirada acerada; *(gaze)* acerado(a), inflexible

steenbok ['sti:nbɒk] *n* raficero *m* común

steep[1] [sti:p] *adj* (**a**) *(path, hill, climb, staircase)* empinado(a); **the plane went into a s. dive** el avión comenzó a descender en *Esp* picado *or Am* picada (**b**) *(rise, fall)* pronunciado(a) (**c**) *Fam (expensive)* abusivo(a) (**d**) *Fam (unreasonable)* **it's a bit s. asking us to do all that work by Friday** ¡se ha pasado al pedirnos que hagamos todo ese trabajo para el viernes!

steep[2] **1** *vt (clothes)* dejar en remojo; *(food)* macerar; **to be steeped in history/tradition** rezumar historia/tradición; **a culture that is steeped in prejudice** una cultura impregnada de prejuicios
2 *vi (clothes)* estar en remojo

steepen ['sti:pən] *vi (path)* empinarse

steeple ['sti:pəl] *n (of church)* torre *f*

steeplechase ['sti:pəltʃeɪs] *n Sport* carrera *f* de obstáculos

steeplechaser ['sti:pəltʃeɪsə(r)] *n* (**a**) *(horse)* caballo *m* (para carreras) de obstáculos (**b**) *(runner)* corredor(ora) *m,f* (de carreras) de obstáculos; *(jockey)* jinete *mf* de carreras de obstáculos

steeplejack ['sti:pəldʒæk] *n* = persona que arregla torres y chimeneas

steeply ['sti:plɪ] *adv* (**a**) *(to rise)* pronunciadamente; **s. banked** con pronunciados *or* abruptos terraplenes; **the field slopes s. down to the lake** el terreno desciende abruptamente hasta el lago (**b**) *(to increase, decrease)* acusadamente, de forma pronunciada; **prices rose s.** los precios experimentaron una acusada *or* pronunciada subida

steepness ['sti:pnɪs] *n* (**a**) *(of slope, hill)* **the s. of the descent/rise** lo empinado del descenso/ascenso (**b**) *(of increase, decrease)* lo acusado, lo pronunciado

steer[1] [stɪə(r)] **1** *vt* (**a**) *(car) Esp* conducir, *Am* manejar; *(ship)* gobernar; **she nearly steered the taxi into a tree** por poco dio con el taxi contra un árbol; **he steered the boat away from the reef** alejó el barco del arrecife; **she steered her way through the crowd** se abrió paso entre la multitud; *Fig* **it's a dangerous course you're steering** vas por un camino bastante peligroso
(**b**) *(guide)* **she steered me over to the sofa** me condujo hasta el sofá; **to s. sb out of trouble** sacar a alguien de un aprieto; **he steered us towards a more expensive model** trató de vendernos un modelo más caro; **she steered the conversation away from such sensitive subjects** llevó la conversación a terrenos menos espinosos
2 *vi* (**a**) *(person) (in car)* conducir, *Am* manejar; *(in boat)* timonear, manejar el timón; **I steered carefully into the garage** metí el coche *or Am* carro *or CSur* auto en el garaje con cuidado; **to s. for sth** *(boat)* llevar rumbo a algo; IDIOM **to s. clear of sth/sb** evitar algo/a alguien (**b**) *(ship, car)* manejarse

steer[2] *n (bull)* buey *m*

steerage ['stɪərɪdʒ] *n* tercera clase *f*

steering ['stɪərɪŋ] *n (mechanism)* dirección *f*; **there's something wrong with the s.** a la dirección le pasa algo ►► *Aut* ***s. column*** columna *f* de dirección; *Pol* ***s. committee*** comisión *f* directiva; ***s. lock*** *Aut (turning circle)* ángulo *m* de giro; *(antitheft device)* inmovilizador *m* antirrobo, antirrobo *m* de volante; *Aut* ***s. wheel*** volante *m*, *Andes* timón *m*

steersman ['stɪəzmən] (*pl* **steersmen** ['stɪəzmən]) *n* timonel *m*

stegosaurus [stegə'sɔ:rəs] *n* estegosaurio *m*

stein [staɪn] *n* jarra *f* de cerveza de barro cocido

stellar ['stelə(r)] *adj* (**a**) *Astron* estelar (**b**) *(cast, performance)* estelar

stem [stem] **1** *n* (**a**) *(of plant, flower)* tallo *m*; *(of fruit)* rabo *m*, rabillo *m*; *(of leaf)* pedúnculo *m* ►► ***s. ginger*** trozos *mpl* cristalizados de jengibre
(**b**) *(of glass)* pie *m*; *(of tobacco pipe)* tubo *m*
(**c**) *(vertical stroke) (of letter)* trazo *m* vertical, palito *m*; *(of musical note)* plica *f*
(**d**) *(on watch winder)* tija *f*, eje *m*
(**e**) *(of word)* raíz *f*
(**f**) *(of ship)* **from s. to stern** de proa a popa
(**g**) ***s. turn*** *(in skiing)* media cuña *f*
(**h**) *US Fam* **stems** *(legs)* piernas *fpl*
(**i**) *Biol* ***s. cell*** célula *f* madre
2 *vt* (*pt & pp* **stemmed**) *(halt) (bleeding)* cortar, detener; *(spread, flooding)* contener; *(increase)* frenar, contener; **they are trying to s. the tide of protest** están intentando frenar *or* contener la oleada de protestas
3 *vi* **to s. from** derivarse de

-stemmed [-stemd] *suffix* **a long/short-s. plant** una planta de tallo largo/corto; **a long/short-s. glass** una copa de pie alto/bajo

stench [stentʃ] *n* hedor *m*, tufo *m* (**of** a); *Fig* **the s. of corruption pervaded the organization** el hedor *or* tufo a corrupción había invadido la organización

stencil ['stensəl] **1** *n* (**a**) *Art* plantilla *f* (**b**) *(for typing)* cliché *m*, clisé *m*
2 *vt* (*pt & pp* **stencilled**, *US* **stenciled**) estarcir

Sten gun ['stengʌn] *n* metralleta *f* ligera

steno ['stenəʊ] (*pl* **stenos**) *n US Fam* (**a**) *(stenographer)* taquígrafo(a) *m,f* (**b**) *(stenography)* taquigrafía *f*

stenographer [stə'nɒgrəfə(r)] *n US* taquígrafo(a) *m,f*

stenography [stə'nɒgrəfɪ] *n* taquigrafía *f*

stentorian [sten'tɔ:rɪən] *adj Literary (voice)* estentóreo(a)

STEP [step] **1** *n* (**a**) *(movement, sound)* paso *m*; **to take a s.** dar un paso; **at** *or* **with every s.** a cada paso; **every s. of the way** en todo momento; **s. by s., one s. at a time** paso a paso; **it's only a (short) s. to the shops** hay tiendas a la vuelta de la esquina; **the different steps in the manufacturing process** las diferentes etapas del proceso de fabricación; **to keep (in) s.** *(in dance)* seguir el ritmo; **to march in s.** llevar el paso; **I fell into s. with the rest of the troop** me puse al ritmo del resto de la tropa; **he was walking out of s. with the others** no llevaba el paso de los otros; **the government is in/out of s. with public opinion** el gobierno sigue/no sigue los dictados de la opinión pública; **supply is out of s. with demand** la oferta no se corresponde con la demanda; *also Fig* **to watch one's s.** andarse con cuidado; *Fig* **a s. backwards/forwards** un paso atrás/adelante; **to stay one s. ahead of the competition** mantenerse por delante de la competencia; IDIOM **one s. forward, two steps back** un paso adelante y dos para atrás, como los cangrejos ►► ***s. change*** cambio *m* radical
(**b**) *Literary (gait)* **with weary s.** con paso cansino
(**c**) *(action, measure)* medida *f*; **to take steps (to do sth)** tomar medidas (para hacer algo); **the next s. is to...** el siguiente paso es...; **a s. in the right direction** un paso en la dirección correcta
(**d**) *(of staircase)* escalón *m*, peldaño *m*; *(of stepladder)* peldaño *m*; *(on outside of building)* escalón *m*; **(flight of) steps** (tramo *m* de) escalera *f*; *Br* **steps** *(stepladder)* escalera *f* de tijera; **we were standing on the front steps** estábamos en las escaleras de delante; **mind the s.** cuidado con el escalón; *Fig* **the new job is a s. up for me** el nuevo trabajo me supone un ascenso
(**e**) *(exercise)* **s. (aerobics)** step *m*, aerobic *m* con escalón ►► ***s. class*** clase *f* de step
(**f**) *US Mus* tono *m*
2 *vi* (*pt & pp* **stepped**) *(take a step)* dar un paso; *(walk)* caminar; **s. this way** pasa por aquí; **I stepped down from the ladder** bajé de la escalera; **I stepped in a puddle** pisé un charco; **I stepped into the boat** subí al barco; **she stepped into the room** entró en la habitación; **to s. on sb's foot** pisarle un pie a alguien; **I stepped onto/off the train** subí al/bajé del tren; **we stepped out into the street** salimos a la calle; **he stepped through the door** entró por la puerta; **I stepped up onto the stage** subí al escenario; IDIOM *Fam* **to s. on it** *(hurry up)* aligerar, darse prisa, *Am* apurarse; *(driver)* pisar a fondo; IDIOM **to s. out of line** saltarse las normas

► **step aside** *vi (move aside)* hacerse a un lado; *(resign)* dimitir

► **step back** *vi* (**a**) *(move away)* alejarse (**from** de); **s. back!** ¡atrás! (**b**) *(in order to reflect)* **to s. back from a situation** dar un paso atrás para considerar una situación objetivamente

► **step down** **1** *vt sep (production, efforts)* reducir
2 *vi* (**a**) *(descend)* bajar (**from** de)
(**b**) (resign) dimitir

► **step forward** *vi (volunteer)* presentarse, ofrecerse

► **step in** *vi (intervene)* intervenir

► **step into** *vt insep (role)* asumir; **to s. into sb's shoes** tomar el relevo de alguien

► **step out** *vi* (**a**) *(go out of doors)* salir; (**b**) *Old-fashioned (court)* salir (**with** con) (**c**) *(walk quickly)* apretar el paso

► **step up** **1** *vt sep (production, efforts, pressure)* aumentar; *(pace)* aumentar, acelerar
2 *vi* **to s. up to sb/sth** acercarse a alguien/algo

stepbrother ['stepbrʌðə(r)] *n* hermanastro *m*

step-by-step ['stepbaɪ'step] *adj (guide, explanation)* paso a paso; *(approach)* progresivo(a), gradual

stepchild ['steptʃaɪld] *n* hijastro(a) *m,f*; **stepchildren** hijastros

stepdaughter ['stepdɔ:tə(r)] *n* hijastra *f*

step-down transformer ['stepdaʊntrænz'fɔ:mə(r)] *n* transformador *m* reductor (de voltaje)

stepfather ['stepfɑ:ðə(r)] *n* padrastro *m*

Stephen ['sti:vən] *pr n* **S. I/II** Esteban I/II

stepladder ['steplædə(r)] *n* escalera *f* de tijera

stepmother ['stepmʌðə(r)] *n* madrastra *f*

step-parent ['steppeərənt] *n (man)* padrastro *m*; *(woman)* madrastra *f*; **step-parents** padrastros *mpl*

steppe [step] *n* estepa *f* ▸▸ ***s. eagle*** águila *f* esteparia *or* de las estepas

stepping-stone ['stepɪŋ'stəʊn] *n* **(a)** *(in river)* (piedra *f*) pasadera *f* **(b)** *(aid)* **a s. to success** un trampolín hacia el éxito

stepsister ['stepsɪstə(r)] *n* hermanastra *f*

stepson ['stepsʌn] *n* hijastro *m*

step-up transformer ['stepʌptrænz'fɔ:mə(r)] *n* transformador *m* elevador (de voltaje)

stereo ['sterɪəʊ] **1** *n* (*pl* **stereos**) **(a)** *(equipment)* equipo *m* de música **(b)** *(sound)* estéreo *m*, sonido *m* estereofónico; **in s.** en estéreo

2 *adj* estéreo, estereofónico(a)

stereogram ['sterɪəgræm] *n Br Old-fashioned* equipo *m* estereofónico

stereophonic [sterɪə'fɒnɪk] *adj* estereofónico(a)

stereoscope ['sterɪəʊskəʊp] *n* estereoscopio *m*

stereoscopic [sterɪə'skɒpɪk] *adj (vision)* estereoscópico(a)

stereotype ['sterɪətaɪp] **1** *n* estereotipo *m*

2 *vt* estereotipar

stereotyped ['sterɪətaɪpt] *adj* estereotipado(a)

stereotypical [sterɪə'tɪpɪkəl] *adj* estereotipado(a); **a s. reaction** una reacción típica

sterile ['steraɪl] *adj* **(a)** *(germ-free)* estéril **(b)** *(unable to have babies)* estéril **(c)** *(barren) (land)* estéril **(d)** *(unoriginal) (ideas, imagination)* estéril

sterility [stə'rɪlɪtɪ] *n* **(a)** *(absence of germs)* esterilidad *f* **(b)** *(inability to have babies)* esterilidad *f* **(c)** *(of land)* esterilidad *f* **(d)** *(of ideas, imagination)* esterilidad *f*

sterilization [sterɪlaɪ'zeɪʃən] *n* **(a)** *(to remove germs)* esterilización *f* **(b)** *(of man, woman, animal)* esterilización *f*

sterilize ['sterɪlaɪz] *vt* **(a)** *(remove germs from)* esterilizar **(b)** *(man, woman, animal)* esterilizar

sterilized ['sterəlaɪzd] *adj (germ-free)* esterilizado(a)

sterilizer ['sterɪlaɪzə(r)] *n* esterilizador *m*

sterling ['stɜ:lɪŋ] **1** *n (British currency)* libra *f* esterlina; **s. rose against the dollar** la libra esterlina subió con respecto al dólar; **to pay in s.** pagar en libras (esterlinas); **twenty thousand pounds s.** veinte mil libras (esterlinas)

2 *adj* **(a)** *(silver)* de ley **(b)** *(relating to British currency) (reserves)* de libras esterlinas; *(traveller's cheques)* en libras esterlinas **(c)** *(effort, quality)* admirable, excelente; **he has done his country s. service as a diplomat** ha prestado un admirable *or* excelente servicio a su país como diplomático

stern[1] [stɜ:n] *adj (person, look, measure, punishment)* severo(a), duro(a); *(warning)* muy serio(a); **we are made of sterner stuff** somos duros de pelar

stern[2] *n Naut* popa *f*

sternly ['stɜ:nlɪ] *adv (to reprimand, look)* severamente, duramente; *(to warn)* muy seriamente

sternness ['stɜ:nnɪs] *n (of person, look, measure, punishment)* severidad *f*, dureza *f*; *(of warning)* seriedad *f*

sternum ['stɜ:nəm] *n Anat* esternón *m*

steroid ['sterɔɪd] *n* esteroide *m*

stertorous ['stɜ:tərəs] *adj Formal (breathing)* estertóreo(a)

stet [stet] *Typ* **1** *n* vale *m*

2 *vt* dejar como estaba

stethoscope ['steθəskəʊp] *n Med* fonendoscopio *m*, estetoscopio *m*

stetson ['stetsən] *n* **s. (hat)** sombrero *m* vaquero

stevedore ['sti:vədɔ:(r)] *n* estibador *m*

stew [stju:] **1** *n Culin* guiso *m*; **fish s.** guiso de pescado; IDIOM *Fam* **to be/get in a s. (about sth)** estar/ponerse hecho(a) un manojo de nervios (por algo)

2 *vt (meat)* guisar, cocer; *(fruit)* hacer compota de

3 *vi* **(a)** *(meat)* guisarse, cocer; *(fruit)* hacerse compota **(b)** *Br (tea)* **don't let the tea s.** no dejes que el té repose demasiado **(c)** IDIOMS *Fam* **to let sb s. (in his/her own juice)** dejar a alguien que sufra; *Br Fam* **it's stewing in here** *(very hot)* hace un calor que te asas

steward ['stju:əd] *n* **(a)** *(on estate)* administrador *m* **(b)** *(on plane)* auxiliar *m* de vuelo; *(on ship)* camarero *m* **(c)** *(at concert, demonstration, in motor racing)* auxiliar *mf* de la organización **(d)** *(in athletics)* juez *mf* **(e)** *Br (in horseracing)* juez(a) *m,f*

stewardess [stju:ə'des] *n (on plane)* auxiliar *f* de vuelo, azafata *f*, *Am* aeromoza *f*; *(on ship)* camarera *f*

stewardship ['stju:ədʃɪp] *n* administración *f*, gestión *f*; **only through sensible s. of the environment will we save the planet** sólo por medio de una gestión adecuada del medio ambiente podremos salvar el planeta

stewed [stju:d] *adj* **this tea is s.** este té ha reposado demasiado; *Fam* **s. (to the gills)** como una cuba, *Esp, RP* mamado(a), *Col* caído(a) (de la perra), *Méx* ahogado(a) ▸▸ ***s. beef*** carne *f* de vaca guisada; ***s. fruit*** compota *f*

stewing steak ['stju:wɪŋ'steɪk] *n* carne *f* de vaca para guisar

St. Ex. (*abbr* **stock exchange**) Bolsa *f*

stg (*abbr* **sterling**) esterlina

stick[1] [stɪk] *n* **(a)** *(of wood, for kindling)* palo *m*; *(for walking)* bastón *m*; *(for drum)* baqueta *f*, palillo *m*; *(for lollipop)* palo *m*; **a few sticks of furniture** unos cuantos muebles; **she had legs like sticks** tenía las piernas como palillos; *Fig* **the threat of redundancy has become a s. with which industry beats the unions** la amenaza del despido se ha convertido en una baza con la que la industria ataca a los sindicatos; IDIOM *Fam* **to get (hold of) the wrong end of the s.** coger el rábano por las hojas; PROV **sticks and stones may break my bones (but names will never hurt me)** a palabras necias oídos sordos ▸▸ ***s. insect*** insecto *m* palo; ***s. man*** muñeco *m* hecho con palotes

(b) *(of chewing gum, glue, deodorant, rock, liquorice)* barra *f*; *(of dynamite)* cartucho *m*; *(of celery, rhubarb)* tallo *m*, rama *f*; *(of cinnamon)* rama *f*; **a s. of chalk** una tiza, un trozo de tiza

(c) *(for hockey, ice hockey)* stick *m*, bastón *m*

(d) *US Aut* ***s. shift*** *(system)* palanca *f* de cambio manual; *(vehicle)* vehículo *m* con cambio manual

(e) *Fam* **the sticks** el campo; **he lives out in the sticks** vive en el quinto infierno *or Esp* pino

(f) *Br Fam (criticism)* **to give sb s. for sth** poner verde a alguien por algo; **to get** *or* **take a lot of s.** llevarse muchos palos *or* críticas

(g) *Br Fam (teasing)* **to give sb s. about sth** burlarse de alguien por algo, *Esp, Carib, Méx* vacilar a alguien por algo; **to get a lot of s. about sth** recibir mucha caña por algo; **I got a lot of stick about my new haircut/girlfriend** me metieron mucha caña con mi nuevo corte de pelo/nueva novia

(h) *Br Fam Old-fashioned (person)* tipo(a) *m,f*; **he's a dry old s.** es un poco soso, el pobre

(i) IDIOM *Br Fam* **to be up the s.** *(pregnant)* llevar un bombo, estar preñada

STICK[2] (*pt & pp* **stuck** [stʌk]) **1** *vt* **(a)** *(insert, jab)* **to s. sth in(to) sth** clavar *or* hincar algo en algo; **he stuck his elbow in my ribs** me dio un codazo en las costillas; **she stuck the revolver in his back** le clavó la pistola en la espalda; **he stuck a skewer through the meat** atravesó la carne con un pincho

(b) *Fam (put)* poner; **I'll just s. it in my suitcase** lo meto en la maleta; **s. your things over there** pon tus bártulos por ahí; **she stuck her head round the door** asomó *or* sacó la cabeza por la puerta; **they stuck another £100 on the price** subieron el precio otras 100 libras; **s. it on my bill** póngalo en mi cuenta; IDIOM *Vulg* **s. it up your** *Br* **arse** *or US* **ass!** ¡metételo por el culo!; IDIOM *Fam* **you can s. your job!** ¡métete el trabajo por donde te quepa!; IDIOM *very Fam* **she told me where I could s. it, she told me to s. it where the sun don't shine** me ha dicho que me lo meta por donde me quepa

(c) *(attach with glue)* pegar (**on** a); **make sure you s. the edges down** asegúrate de que pegas bien los bordes; **I stuck the photo in my album** pegué la foto en mi álbum; **s. no bills** *(sign)* prohibido fijar carteles

(d) *Fam (endure)* aguantar, soportar; **I can't s. him** no lo aguanto *or* soporto

(e) *Fam (with chore, burden)* **to s. sb with a fine/the blame** endosarle una multa/la culpa a alguien

(f) *(pig) (slaughter)* degollar; *(as sport)* lancear

2 *vi* **(a)** *(adhere)* pegarse (**to** a); **my shirt was sticking to my back** tenía la camisa pegada a la espalda; **the butterfly had stuck to the flypaper** la mariposa quedó pegada en el papel atrapamoscas; *Fig* **they couldn't make the charges s.** no consiguieron que los cargos contra ella se mantuvieran; *Fig* **the name stuck** el nombre tuvo éxito, se quedó con el nombre; *Fam* **have some stew, that'll s. to your ribs!** toma un poco de estofado, ya verás como te llena

(b) *(become jammed)* atascarse; **his words stuck in my mind** sus palabras se me quedaron grabadas en la memoria; **she has the kind of face that sticks in your memory** tiene una de esas caras que no se te olvidan; IDIOM **it sticks in my throat** se me atraganta

(**c**) *(be embedded)* **there's something sticking into my toe** tengo algo que se me está clavando en el dedo del pie; **don't leave the spade sticking in the ground** no dejes la pala clavada en la tierra; **they had straw sticking in their hair** tenían paja en el pelo

(**d**) *(protrude)* **the point was sticking through the lining** la punta salía por el forro; **I could see his head sticking over the fence** vi cómo asomaba la cabeza por encima de la valla

(**e**) *(in cards)* plantarse

► **stick around** *vi Fam* quedarse

► **stick at** *vt insep* (**a**) *(persevere with)* perseverar en (**b**) *(stop) Fam* **to s. at nothing** no reparar en nada

► **stick away** *vt sep Fam (object)* meter; **they stuck him away in a lunatic asylum** lo metieron en un manicomio

► **stick by** *vt insep (friend)* apoyar; *(promise, statement)* mantener

► **stick down** **1** *vt sep* (**a**) *(flap, envelope)* pegar; **make sure you s. the edges down** asegúrate de que pegas bien los bordes

(**b**) *Fam (write down)* poner

(**c**) *Fam (place)* poner

2 *vi (flap, envelope)* pegar

► **stick in** **1** *vt sep* (**a**) *(knife, needle, spade)* clavar

(**b**) *(insert)* meter; **I stuck my hand in to test the water temperature** metí la mano para comprobar la temperatura del agua

(**c**) *(glue in)* pegar

2 *vi* (**a**) *(dart, arrow, spear)* clavar

(**b**) *Fam (persevere)* **s. in there!** ¡aguanta!

► **stick on** **1** *vt sep* (**a**) *(fasten on)* pegar (**b**) *Fam (clothes)* ponerse

2 *vi* pegarse

► **stick out** **1** *vt sep* (**a**) *(cause to protrude)* sacar; **she stuck her head out of the window** asomó *or* sacó su cabeza por la ventana; **he stuck a leg out and tripped me up** extendió una pierna y me puso la zancadilla; **she stuck her tongue out at me** me sacó la lengua; **to s. one's chest out** sacar pecho; *Fam* **to s. one's neck out** arriesgar el pellejo

(**b**) *Fam (endure)* **to s. it out** aguantar

2 *vi* (**a**) *(protrude)* sobresalir; **his legs were sticking out from under the table** sus piernas sobresalían por debajo de la mesa; **my teeth/ears s. out** tengo los dientes salidos/las orejas salidas; **only her head was sticking out of the water** sólo le salía la cabeza del agua

(**b**) *Fam (be noticeable)* verse a la legua, *Esp* cantar; IDIOM **it sticks out a mile** se ve a la legua; IDIOM **it sticks out like a sore thumb** se ve a la legua, *Esp* canta un montón

► **stick out for** *vt insep* insistir en conseguir

► **stick to** *vt insep* (**a**) *(stay close to) (person)* seguir, pegarse a; *(path, road)* seguir; **s. close to the house** no te alejes de la casa, quédate cerca de la casa

(**b**) *(restrict oneself to) (rules, budget)* atenerse a; **I'll s. to wine, thanks** seguiré con el vino, gracias; **to s. to the basics** centrarse en lo esencial; **to s. to the facts** atenerse a los hechos; **to s. to the point** no salirse del tema

(**c**) *(not abandon) (beliefs, story, promise, decision)* ser fiel a; *(plan)* seguir con; **I s. to what I said** me mantengo en lo que dije; **the author would be better off sticking to journalism** más le valdría al autor limitarse al periodismo; **she stuck to her principles** fue fiel a sus principios; IDIOM **to s. to one's guns** mantenerse en sus trece

► **stick together** **1** *vt sep* pegar

2 *vi* (**a**) *(with glue)* pegarse; **the pages have stuck together** se han pegado las hojas

(**b**) *(friends) (stay close to each other)* mantenerse unidos(as); *(support each other)* apoyarse

► **stick up** **1** *vt sep* (**a**) *(sign, poster)* pegar; **to s. one's hand up** levantar la mano; *Fam* **s. 'em up!** ¡manos arriba!

(**b**) *Fam (rob)* atracar

2 *vi (point upwards) (building, shoots)* sobresalir; **her hair sticks up** tiene el pelo de punta

► **stick up for** *vt insep (person, rights)* defender; **to s. up for oneself** defenderse

► **stick with** *vt insep* (**a**) *(not give up)* seguir con

(**b**) *(remain with) (person)* seguir con; **his words have stuck with me ever since** sus palabras se me quedaron grabadas desde entonces

---

stickball ['stɪkbɔːl] *n US* béisbol *m* callejero

sticker ['stɪkə(r)] *n* (**a**) *(with information, price)* etiqueta *f* (**b**) *(with slogan, picture)* pegatina *f* (**c**) *Fam (determined person)* **she's a s.** es tenaz

stickiness ['stɪkɪnɪs] *n* (**a**) *(of material)* pegajosidad *f* (**b**) *(of weather)* bochorno *m*

sticking-plaster ['stɪkɪŋ'plɑːstə(r)] *n Br (to cover wound) Esp* tirita® *f*, *Am* curita *m or f*; *(to keep bandage in place)* esparadrapo *m*

sticking-point ['stɪkɪŋ'pɔɪnt] *n* escollo *m*

stick-in-the-mud ['stɪkɪnðəmʌd] *n Fam* carroza *mf*

stickleback ['stɪkəlbæk] *n* espinoso *m* (de agua dulce)

stickler ['stɪklə(r)] *n* **to be a s. for detail/discipline/tradition** estar obsesionado con el detalle/la disciplina/la tradición

stick-on ['stɪkɒn] *adj* adhesivo(a)

stickpin ['stɪkpɪn] *n US* (**a**) *(tie-pin)* alfiler *m* de corbata (**b**) *(for woman)* prendedor *m*

stick-up ['stɪkʌp] *n Fam (robbery)* atraco *m* (a mano armada); **this is a s.!** ¡esto es un atraco!

sticky ['stɪkɪ] *adj* (**a**) *(substance, hands, fingers, surface)* pegajoso(a); *(label)* adhesivo(a); IDIOM *Fam* **to have s. fingers** *(steal things)* tener la mano muy larga ►► *Fam* ***s. bun*** bollo *m* dulce; ***s. tape*** cinta *f* adhesiva; ***s. toffee pudding*** = postre a base de bizcocho mojado en caramelo

(**b**) *(climate, weather)* bochornoso(a)

(**c**) *(sweaty) (person)* sudoroso(a)

(**d**) *Fam (awkward)* problemático(a); **to come to a s. end** tener un final sangriento; **to be in a s. situation** estar en una situación delicada, estar en un brete; **their relationship is going through a s. patch** su relación está pasando por un mal momento; IDIOM *Br* **to be (batting) on a s. wicket** estar en un atolladero

sticky-fingered ['stɪkɪ'fɪŋgəd] *adj* (**a**) *(children)* con dedos pegajosos (**b**) *Fam (thieving)* ratero(a), *Esp* chorizo(a)

stiff [stɪf] **1** *adj* (**a**) *(rigid)* tieso(a), rígido(a); **a s. brush** un cepillo de cerdas duras; IDIOM **as s. as a board** tieso(a) como un palo; IDIOM **to keep a s. upper lip** mantenerse incólume

(**b**) *(paste)* consistente; *(egg whites)* a punto de nieve

(**c**) *(joint)* agarrotado(a), anquilosado(a); **to be s.** *(after exercise) Esp* tener agujetas; **I'm s. from sitting at my desk all morning** necesito estirarme después pasar toda la mañana sentado a la mesa; **I have a s. back** *(in general)* tengo la espalda dolorida; *(after exercise) Esp* tengo agujetas en la espalda; **to have a s. neck** tener tortícolis

(**d**) *(handle, hinge, drawer)* duro(a); **the lock is rather s.** la cerradura está un poco dura, la cerradura se atasca un poco

(**e**) *(severe) (fine, competition, prison sentence)* duro(a); *(exam, test)* difícil; **to encounter s. resistance** enfrentarse a una fuerte oposición, encontrar gran resistencia

(**f**) *(strong) (breeze, drink)* fuerte; **she poured herself a s. whisky** se sirvió un buen vaso de whisky

(**g**) *(formal) (person, manner)* rígido(a), estirado(a); *(bow)* rígido(a); *(smile, style)* forzado(a)

(**h**) *US Fam (drunk)* como una cuba, *Esp, RP* mamado(a), *Col* caído(a) (de la perra), *Méx* ahogado(a)

(**i**) *(high) (price, bill)* caro(a)

2 *adv* **to be bored/scared/frozen s.** estar muerto(a) de aburrimiento/miedo/frío; **to be worried s.** estar tremendamente preocupado

3 *n Fam* (**a**) *(corpse)* fiambre *m* (**b**) *US (tramp)* vagabundo(a) *m,f* (**c**) *US (worker)* trabajador(ora) *m,f*, *Esp* currante *mf*

4 *vt US Fam (not pay)* **the customer stiffed me!** ¡el cliente se largó sin pagar!

stiffen ['stɪfən] **1** *vt* (**a**) *(fabric, paper)* aprestar, endurecer; *(collar)* almidonar (**b**) *(paste, sauce)* espesar (**c**) *(resolve, resistance)* reforzar

2 *vi* (**a**) *(limb, joint, person)* agarrotarse (**b**) *(paste, egg whites, sauce)* espesar (**c**) *(corpse)* ponerse rígido(a) (**d**) *(tense, stop moving)* ponerse tenso(a); **everybody in the room suddenly stiffened** de repente todo el mundo que había en la habitación se puso tenso (**e**) *(become stronger) (opposition)* endurecerse; *(breeze)* hacerse más fuerte

stiffener ['stɪfənə(r)] *n* (**a**) *(in shirt collar)* varilla *f* (**b**) *(substance)* apresto *m* (**c**) *Br Fam (drink)* pelotazo *m* para coger ánimos

stiffening ['stɪfənɪŋ] **1** *n (in garment)* entretela *f*

2 *adj (resistance, opposition)* creciente

stiffly ['stɪflɪ] *adv* (**a**) *(to move)* con rigidez; **the soldier stood s. to attention** el soldado se puso rígidamente firme; **he rose s. from his chair** se levantó de la silla con rigidez (**b**) *(to bow)* con rigidez; *(to answer, greet, smile)* forzadamente

stiff-necked ['stɪf'nekt] *adj (stubborn) (person)* obstinado(a); *(opposition)* tenaz

stiffness ['stɪfnɪs] *n* (**a**) *(of fabric, paper, collar)* rigidez *f* (**b**) *(of egg whites)* punto *m* de nieve (**c**) *(of muscles)* agarrotamiento *m*; *(of joints)* anquilosamiento *m* (**d**) *(of manner, person)* rigidez *f*; *(of bow)* rigidez *m*, poca flexibilidad *f*; *(of smile, style)* rigidez *f* (**e**) *(of fine, competition, prison sentence)* dureza *f*; *(of exam, test)* dificultad *f*

stiffy ['stɪfɪ] *n Br Vulg* **he got a s.** se le puso dura, *Esp* se le empalmó; **to have a s.** tenerla dura, *Esp* estar empalmado

stifle ['staɪfəl] **1** *vt* (**a**) *(suffocate) (person)* ahogar, asfixiar (**b**) *(cries, yawn)* ahogar, reprimir; *(laughter)* contener; *(flames)* sofocar, apagar; *(anger)* reprimir, contener (**c**) *(rebellion)* sofocar; *(creativity)* reprimir; *(progress)* detener; **all this bureaucracy stifles innovation** tanta burocracia acaba con cualquier intento de innovación

2 *vi* asfixiarse, ahogarse

stifled ['staɪfəld] *adj (cry)* entrecortado(a)

stifling ['staɪflɪŋ] *adj* (**a**) *(heat)* bochornoso(a); **open the window, it's s. in here!** ¡abre la ventana, hay mucho bochorno!; **it was a s. hot day** hacía un día bochornoso (**b**) *(oppressive) (atmosphere)* cargado(a)

stigma ['stɪgmə] *n* (**a**) *(disgrace)* estigma *m*, deshonra *f* (**b**) *(of flower)* estigma *m*

stigmata [stɪg'mɑːtə] *npl (of saint)* estigmas *mpl*

stigmatize ['stɪgmətaɪz] *vt* estigmatizar; **she was stigmatized as a traitor** le colgaron el sambenito de traidora

stile [staɪl] *n (in fence, hedge)* escalones *mpl*

stiletto [stɪ'letəʊ] (*pl* **stilettos**) *n* (**a**) *(dagger)* estilete *m* (**b**) *(shoe)* zapato *m* de tacón *or Am* taco de aguja ►► ***s. heels*** tacones *mpl or Am* tacos *mpl* de aguja

still[1] [stɪl] **1** *n* (**a**) *(calm)* **in the s. of the night** en el silencio de la noche (**b**) *Cin* fotograma *m*

2 *adj* (**a**) *(motionless)* quieto(a); PROV **s. waters run deep** tras una fachada silenciosa se ocultan fuertes emociones ►► *Art* ***s. life*** bodegón *m*, naturaleza *f* muerta (**b**) *(calm)* sereno(a); *(silent)* silencioso(a); *(air, day)* sin viento (**c**) *(uncarbonated) (orange juice)* natural; *(mineral water)* sin gas

3 *adv* **to be/sit/stand s.** estar quieto(a); **be s.!** ¡estate quieto!; **try to hold the camera s.** intenta no mover la cámara; **just hold s. a moment** estese quieto un momento; **keep s.!** ¡no te muevas!

4 *vt Formal* (**a**) *(calm) (person)* calmar, tranquilizar; **to s. sb's fears** ahuyentar los temores de alguien (**b**) *(silence)* acallar, silenciar

STILL[2] *adv* (**a**) *(up to given point in time)* todavía, aún, *Am* siempre; **I s. have $50** aún me quedan 50 dólares; **he's s. not here** todavía no ha llegado; **is it s. raining?** ¿sigue lloviendo?; **it's stuck – s.?** está pegado – ¿todavía?; **I s. can't see what was wrong with my suggestion** sigo sin ver qué hay de malo en mi propuesta; **it is s. to be decided whether...** está por decidir si...; **I s. think/say that...** sigo creyendo/diciendo que...

(**b**) *(even)* aún, incluso, todavía; **s. more/better** aún *or* incluso *or* todavía más/mejor; **better s., we could watch a movie** mejor aún *or* incluso *or* todavía, podríamos ver una película; **s. further, further s.** aún más; **she could be injured or, worse s., dead** podría estar herida o, peor aún *or* incluso *or* todavía, muerta; **the sea was getting s. rougher** el mar continuaba embraveciéndose

(**c**) *(nonetheless)* de todas formas, aún así; **she's s. your mother, despite everything** sigue siendo tu madre, a pesar de todo; **are you s. coming to the party?** ¿sigues pensando *or Am* siempre piensas venir a la fiesta?; **I missed the train, s., never mind** perdí el tren, en fin, no importa

still[3] *n (distilling equipment)* alambique *m*

stillage ['stɪlɪdʒ] *n* base *m* de madera

stillbirth ['stɪlbɜːθ] *n* nacimiento *m* de un niño muerto; **the number of stillbirths has risen** el número de bebés nacidos muertos se ha incrementado

stillborn ['stɪlbɔːn] *adj* **the child was s.** el niño nació muerto; *Fig* **the project was s.** el proyecto estaba condenado a fracasar

stillness ['stɪlnɪs] *n* (**a**) *(motionlessness)* silencio *m* (**b**) *(calm)* calma *f*, quietud *f*

stilt [stɪlt] *n* (**a**) *(for walking)* zanco *m*; **to walk on stilts** andar con zancos (**b**) *(for building)* poste *m*, pilote *m* (**c**) *(bird)* **black-winged s.** cigüeñela *f*

stilted ['stɪltɪd] *adj (style, manner)* forzado(a); *(language)* artificioso(a), rebuscado(a); *(delivery, acting)* falto(a) de naturalidad

Stilton ['stɪltən] *n* **S. (cheese)** queso *m* Stilton

stimulant ['stɪmjʊlənt] *n* (**a**) *(substance, drug)* estimulante *m* (**b**) *(stimulus)* estímulo *m*

stimulate ['stɪmjʊleɪt] *vt* (**a**) *(organism, circulation)* estimular (**b**) *(person, mind, appetite)* estimular; **to s. sb to do sth** animar a alguien a hacer algo (**c**) *(enthusiasm, interest)* suscitar; *(production, demand)* estimular

stimulating ['stɪmjʊleɪtɪŋ] *adj* (**a**) *(work, conversation, experience)* estimulante (**b**) *(medicine, drug)* estimulante

stimulation [stɪmjʊ'leɪʃən] *n* (**a**) *(action)* estimulación *f* (**b**) *(result)* estímulo *m* (**c**) *(stimulus)* estímulo *m*

stimulus ['stɪmjʊləs] (*pl* **stimuli** ['stɪmjʊlaɪ]) *n* estímulo *m*

sting [stɪŋ] **1** *n* (**a**) *(organ) (of bee, scorpion)* aguijón *m*

(**b**) *(wound) (of bee, scorpion, nettle)* picadura *f*

(**c**) *(sensation)* escozor *m*, quemazón *f*; **he felt the s. of the whip on his back** sintió la quemazón del látigo en la espalda; **the s. of remorse** la quemazón del remordimiento

(**d**) *Fam (swindle) Esp* timo *m*, *Am* chanchullo *m*; *(robbery)* golpe *m*

(**e**) *Fam (police operation)* operación *f* policial

(**f**) IDIOMS **to have a s. in the tail** *(story)* tener un final sorpresa muy fuerte; **to take the s. out of sth** hacer algo menos traumático(a)

2 *vt* (*pt & pp* **stung** [stʌŋ]) (**a**) *(of bee, scorpion, jellyfish)* picar; *(of nettle)* pinchar

(**b**) *(of vinegar, acid)* quemar; *(of disinfectant)* hacer escocer; *(of whip)* quemar; **the whip stung his back** el látigo le quemó la espalda; **the rain stung our faces** la lluvia nos hacía daño en la cara; **the smoke stung my eyes** me picaban los ojos del humo

(**c**) *(of remark)* herir; **she was stung by their criticisms** se sintió herida por sus críticas; IDIOM **to s. sb into action** espolear a alguien para que pase a la acción

(**d**) *Fam (swindle)* timar; **I got stung** me timaron; **they stung him for £10** le clavaron 10 libras

3 *vi* (**a**) *(bee, scorpion, jellyfish, nettle)* picar (**b**) *(vinegar, acid)* quemar; *(disinfectant)* escocer (**c**) *(eyes, skin)* escocer; **my eyes are stinging** me escuecen los ojos (**d**) *(blow)* hacer daño; **the blow to his face really stung** el puñetazo que le dieron le hizo daño de verdad (**e**) *(remark, criticism)* **her remarks really stung** sus comentarios lo hirieron de verdad

stingily ['stɪndʒɪlɪ] *adv* con tacañería *or* racanería

stinginess ['stɪndʒɪnɪs] *n (of person, budget)* tacañería *f*, racanería *f*; *(of portions)* miseria *f*

stinging ['stɪŋɪŋ] *adj* (**a**) *(insect)* que pica (**b**) *(pain)* punzante ►► ***s. nettle*** ortiga *f* (**c**) *(remark, criticism)* hiriente, despiadado(a)

stingray ['stɪŋreɪ] *n* (raya *f*) pastinaca *f*

stingy ['stɪndʒɪ] *adj (person)* tacaño(a), rácano(a); *(portion)* mísero(a), raquítico(a); **to be s. with food/praise** ser tacaño(a) con la comida/los elogios

stink [stɪŋk] **1** *n* (**a**) *(smell)* peste *f*, hedor *m*; *Fam* **what a s.!** ¡qué peste! ►► ***s. bomb*** bomba *f* fétida (**b**) *Fam (scandal, fuss)* **there was a terrible s. about it** se armó un fenomenal escándalo con eso; **to raise** *or* **make** *or Br* **kick up a s. (about sth)** montar un escándalo (por algo)

2 *vi* (*pt* **stank** [stæŋk] *or* **stunk** [stʌŋk], *pp* **stunk**) (**a**) *(smell bad)* apestar (**of** a); **to s. to the heavens** apestar, oler a rayos; *Fig* **to s. of corruption** apestar *or* oler a corrupción (**b**) *Fam (be very bad)* **this movie stinks!** ¡esta película no vale un pimiento *or Am* nada!; **this town stinks!** ¡esta ciudad es un churro!

►**stink out, stink up** *vt sep (fill with a bad smell)* apestar, dejar mal olor en

stinker ['stɪŋkə(r)] *n Fam* (**a**) *(unpleasant person)* mamón(ona) *m,f*, *Méx* mamila *mf*, *RP* choto(a) *m,f* (**b**) *(unpleasant thing)* hueso *m*; **to be a real s.** *(question, exam)* ser muy *Esp* chungo(a) *or Am* feo(a); **to have a s. of a cold** tener un resfriado de mil demonios *or Esp* de (tres pares de) narices (**c**) *(worthless thing)* **the film/match was a s.** la película/el partido fue un churro

stinkhorn ['stɪŋkhɔːn] *n (fungus)* falo *m* hediondo

stinking ['stɪŋkɪŋ] **1** *adj* (**a**) *(smelly)* apestoso(a) (**b**) *Fam (very bad, disgusting)* asqueroso(a); **a s. cold** un resfriado espantoso; **I'm going to leave this s. town!** ¡me voy de esta ciudad de mierda!

2 *adv Fam* **to be s. rich** estar podrido(a) de dinero, *Méx* tener un chorro de lana; **to be s. drunk** estar como una cuba

stinkweed ['stɪŋkwiːd] *n* estramonio *m*

stinky ['stɪŋkɪ] *adj Fam (smelly)* apestoso(a)

stint[1] [stɪnt] **1** *n* (**a**) *(period)* periodo *m*; **to take a s. at the wheel** tomar el relevo al volante; **he had a two-year s. in the army** sirvió por un período de dos años en el ejército (**b**) *(share)* **we expect everybody to do their s.** esperamos que todos colaboren con la parte que les toca (**c**) *Formal (limitation)* **without s.** *(give, spend)* sin restricciones

2 *vt* escatimar; **to s. oneself** privarse de algunas cosas *(en beneficio de otras personas)*
3 *vi* **to s. on sth** escatimar algo

stint² *n* correlimos *m inv*; **little s.** correlimos menudo; **long-toed s.** correlimos chico

stipend ['staɪpend] *n Rel & Univ* estipendio *m*

stipendiary [staɪ'pendɪərɪ] *adj* estipendiario(a), estipendial ▸▸ ***s. magistrate*** magistrado(a) *m,f* estipendiario(a)

stipple ['stɪpəl] *vt* puntear, motear

stippled ['stɪpəld] *adj* salpicado(a) (**with** de)

stipulate ['stɪpjʊleɪt] 1 *vt* estipular
2 *vi Formal* **to s. for sth** estipular algo

> En inglés culto o elevado, y especialmente en inglés americano, **stipulate** puede ir seguido de **that** más un verbo en subjuntivo (ver el panel SUBJUNCTIVE):
> **the regulations stipulate that any unused supplies be returned**
> *las normas estipulan que se devuelvan los suministros que no sean usados*
> Lo mismo también podría decirse del siguiente modo:
> **the regulations stipulate that any unused supplies should be returned**

stipulation [stɪpjʊ'leɪʃən] *n* estipulación *f*

stir [stɜ:(r)] 1 *n* (**a**) *(action)* **to give sth a s.** remover *or* revolver algo (**b**) *(excitement)* **to cause** *or* **create** *or* **make a s.** causar (un gran) revuelo (**c**) *Fam (prison)* **to be in s.** estar en *Esp* chirona *or Andes, Col, RP* la cana *or Méx* el bote
2 *vt* (*pt & pp* **stirred**) (**a**) *(liquid, mixture)* remover, revolver; **s. the flour into the sauce** añadir la harina a la salsa removiendo
(**b**) *(move) (leaves)* agitar; *Fam* **s. yourself!** ¡muévete!
(**c**) *(move emotionally) (person)* conmover, emocionar
(**d**) *(arouse) (emotion)* provocar; *(curiosity, sympathy)* despertar; **to s. sb to do sth** mover a alguien a hacer algo; **to s. sb into action** incitar a alguien a actuar
(**e**) *Br Fam* **she's just stirring it!** *(making trouble)* ¡solo está metiendo cizaña!
3 *vi* (**a**) *(move)* moverse; **the audience were stirring in their seats** el público se movía impaciente en sus asientos; **nobody stirred until well into the afternoon** nadie se movió hasta bien entrada la tarde; **I shan't s. from my bed until midday** no me sacan de la cama hasta el mediodía
(**b**) *(be roused) (feeling, anger)* despertar; **he felt new emotions stirring within him** sentía como se le despertaban nuevos sentimientos
(**c**) *Fam (make trouble)* meter cizaña *or RP* púa

▸ **stir up** *vt sep* (**a**) *(dust, leaves)* levantar
(**b**) *(incite) (rebellion, dissent, anger)* provocar; *(workers, crowd)* agitar; **to s. it** *or* **things up** meter cizaña
(**c**) *(awaken) (memories)* resucitar, traer de nuevo; *(emotions)* despertar, traer de nuevo; **seeing her again stirred up old memories** verla otra vez le resucitó *or* trajo viejos recuerdos; **seeing her again stirred up emotions which had lain dormant for several years** verla otra vez le despertó *or* le trajo de nuevo emociones que habían estado dormidas durante años

stir-crazy ['stɜ:kreɪzɪ] *adj Fam* **to be/go s.** estar/volverse loco *or Esp* majara

stir-fry ['stɜ:fraɪ] *Culin* 1 *n* = salteado de (carne y) verduras típico de la cocina china
2 *adj* salteado(a)
3 *vt* saltear, rehogar a fuego vivo

stirrer ['stɜ:rə(r)] *n Fam (trouble-maker)* cizañero(a) *m,f*, *RP* metepúas *mf inv*

stirring ['stɜ:rɪŋ] 1 *n* **the first stirrings of...** los primeros indicios de...; **he felt vague stirrings of guilt** empezó a notar un ligero remordimiento
2 *adj (speech, movie)* conmovedor(ora), emocionante; **the movie is s. stuff** la película es muy emocionante

stirrup ['stɪrəp] *n* (**a**) *(on saddle)* estribo *m* ▸▸ ***s. iron*** estribo *m*; ***s. leather*** correa *f* del estribo (**b**) *Anat* **s. (bone)** *(in ear)* estribo *m* (**c**) ***s. pump*** *(for water)* bomba *f* de mano (**d**) *Med* **stirrups** soportes *mpl*

stitch [stɪtʃ] 1 *n* (**a**) *(individual) (in sewing)* puntada *f*; *(in knitting)* punto *m*; *(style)* punto *m*; *Fam* **she didn't have a s. on** estaba en cueros *or* en pelotas; PROV **a s. in time saves nine** una puntada a tiempo ahorra ciento
(**b**) *Med* punto *m* (de sutura); **she had to have ten stitches in her face** le tuvieron que dar diez puntos en la cara
(**c**) *(sharp pain)* **to have a s.** tener flato; **I got a s. and I had to stop** me dio *or* entró flato y tuve que parar
(**d**) *US Fam (amusing person, thing)* **to be a s.** ser muy gracioso(a), *Esp* ser la monda
(**e**) IDIOMS *Fam* **we were in stitches** *(laughing)* nos partíamos (de risa); **she had us in stitches** nos partíamos (de risa) con ella
2 *vt* (**a**) *(clothing)* coser; **he stitched the button back on his shirt** cosió el botón que se le había caído a su camisa (**b**) *Med* suturar, coser
3 *vi (sew)* coser

▸ **stitch up** *vt sep* (**a**) *(material, shirt, hem)* coser (**b**) *Med* coser (**c**) *Fam (falsely incriminate)* **they stitched him up** hicieron un montaje para que cargara con el muerto (**d**) *Fam (deal)* cerrar

stitching ['stɪtʃɪŋ] *n* (**a**) *(in sewing) (stitches)* cosido *m*; *(ornamental)* costura *f*; **the s.'s come undone on my hem** se ha soltado la costura del dobladillo, se me ha descosido el dobladillo (**b**) *(of book)* cosido *m*

stoat [stəʊt] *n* armiño *m*

stocious ['stəʊʃəs] *adj Scot Fam* **to be s.** estar cargado(a); **to get s.** cargarse

stock [stɒk] 1 *n* (**a**) *(supply)* reservas *fpl*; **fish stocks are declining** la población de peces está disminuyendo; **the housing s.** el número de viviendas; **we got in a s. of food for the holiday** hicimos acopio de comida para las vacaciones; **she always has a wonderful s. of funny stories** siempre cuenta con un fantástico repertorio de divertidas historias
(**b**) *Com* existencias *fpl*, stock *m*; **the red ones are in s.** tenemos los rojos en almacén *or* en stock; **we keep a wide range of books in s.** tenemos una amplia gama de libros en almacén *or* en stock; **the red ones are out of s.** los rojos están agotados; **I'm afraid we're out of s. (of red ones)** lo siento, en estos momentos no nos quedan (de los rojos); *Fig* **to take s.** hacer balance; **I've been taking s. of my life** he estado haciendo un repaso a mi vida; **we took s. of the situation** hicimos balance de la situación ▸▸ ***s. check*** balance *m* de inventario; ***s. control*** control *m* de existencias *or* stock; ***s. items*** artículos *mpl* en stock; ***s. list*** inventario *m*; ***s. size*** talla *f* de muestra; ***s. take*** balance *m* de inventario
(**c**) *(livestock)* ganado *m* ▸▸ ***s. breeder*** ganadero(a) *m,f*; ***s. breeding*** ganadería *f*; ***s. farm*** explotación *f* ganadera; ***s. farmer*** ganadero(a) *m,f*; ***s. farming*** ganadería *f*
(**d**) *Fin (share)* valor *m*; *(total share value)* (capital *m* en) acciones *fpl*; **he owns 27 percent of the company's s.** es el propietario del 27 por ciento de las acciones de la empresa; **stocks and shares** valores; *Fig* **her s. is going up/down** está ganando/perdiendo crédito ▸▸ *US* ***s. certificate*** título *m* de acción; *US* ***s. company*** sociedad *f* anónima; ***s. exchange*** bolsa *f* (de valores); **he lost a fortune on the s. exchange** perdió una fortuna en la bolsa; ***s. market*** mercado *m* bursátil *or* de valores; **he lost a fortune on the s. market** perdió una fortuna en la bolsa; ***s. market index*** índice *m* bursátil
(**e**) *(descent)* ascendencia *f*, origen *m*; **she's of German s.** es de origen alemán; **he is** *or* **comes of good s.** es de buena familia
(**f**) *(of rifle)* culata *f*
(**g**) *(of whip, fishing rod)* mango *m*
(**h**) **stocks** *(for punishment)* picota *f*
(**i**) *(in cooking)* caldo *m*; **chicken/vegetable s.** caldo de pollo/verduras ▸▸ ***s. cube*** pastilla *f or* cubito *m* de caldo (concentrado); ***s. pot*** olla *f*
(**j**) *Bot (flower)* alhelí *m*
(**k**) *(tree trunk)* tronco *m*
(**l**) *(stem receiving graft)* patrón *m*; *(plant from which graft is taken)* planta *f* madre
(**m**) *(in card games)* montón *m*
(**n**) *Sport* ***s. car*** stock-car *m*, = automóvil adaptado para carreras en pista de tierra con muchos choques; ***s. car racing*** carreras *fpl* de stock-cars
(**o**) *US Theat (repertory)* repertorio *m* ▸▸ ***s. company*** compañía *f* de repertorio
(**p**) *Zool* ***s. dove*** paloma *f* zurita
2 *adj (argument, excuse)* tópico(a); *(question, answer)* habitual; *(phrase, expression)* típico(a) ▸▸ *Cin* ***s. footage*** imágenes *fpl* de archivo; ***s. phrase*** tópico *m*, cliché *m*
3 *vt* (**a**) *(have in stock) (goods)* **I'm afraid we don't s. that item any more** lo siento, pero ya no vendemos ese artículo (**b**) *(supply) (shop)* surtir, abastecer (**with** de); **the shop is well stocked** la tienda está bien surtida *or* abastecida; **they have a well stocked wine cellar** tienen una bodega bien abastecida (**c**) *(lake) (with fish)* repoblar

▸ **stock up** *vi* aprovisionarse (**with** *or* **on** de)

stockade [stɒ'keɪd] *n* (**a**) *(enclosure)* empalizada *f* (**b**) *US (military prison)* prisión *f* militar

stockbroker ['stɒkbrəʊkə(r)] *n Fin* corredor(ora) *m,f* de bolsa ►► *Br Fam* ***s. belt*** = cinturón formado por zonas residenciales exclusivas que rodean una gran ciudad

stockbroking ['stɒkbrəʊkɪŋ] *n* correduría *f* de bolsa

stockfish ['stɒkfɪʃ] *n* pescado *m* seco y salado

stockholder ['stɒkhəʊldə(r)] *n Fin* accionista *mf*

Stockholm ['stɒkhəʊm] *n* Estocolmo

stockily ['stɒkɪlɪ] *adv* **s. built** bajo(a) y robusto(a)

stockiness ['stɒkɪnɪs] *n* constitución *f* baja y robusta

stockinet, stockinette [stɒkɪ'net] *n (fabric)* punto *m* de media

stocking ['stɒkɪŋ] *n* media *f*; **a pair of stockings** un par de medias; **stockings and suspenders** medias y liguero ►► *Br* ***s. filler*** regalito *m* de Navidad; ***s. mask*** máscara *f* de media; ***s. stitch*** punto *m* de media

stockinged ['stɒkɪŋd] *adj* **in one's s. feet** sin zapatos, descalzo(a)

stock-in-trade ['stɒkɪn'treɪd] *n (speciality)* especialidad *f*; **charm is part of a politician's s.** el encanto forma parte de las armas de un político

stockist ['stɒkɪst] *n Com* distribuidor(ora) *m,f*

stockjobber ['stɒkdʒɒbə(r)] *n Fin* (**a**) *Br Formerly* agente *mf* (libre) de Bolsa (**b**) *US Pej* corredor(ora) *m,f* de Bolsa

stockman ['stɒkmən] (*pl* **stockmen** ['stɒkmən]) *n (cowherd)* mozo *m*; *(breeder)* ganadero *m*

stock-market ['stɒkmɑːkɪt] *adj (crash, prices)* bursátil

stockpile ['stɒkpaɪl] **1** *n* reservas *fpl*; **America's nuclear s.** la reserva nuclear de Estados Unidos

2 *vt* acumular, hacer acopio de

stockroom ['stɒkruːm] *n* almacén *m*

stock-still ['stɒk'stɪl] *adv* **to stand s.** quedarse inmóvil

stocktaking ['stɒkteɪkɪŋ] *n* (**a**) *Com* inventario *m*, balance *m* de existencias; **to do the s.** hacer inventario; **closed for s.** *(sign)* cerrado por inventario (**b**) *(evaluation)* **to do some s.** hacer balance

stocky ['stɒkɪ] *adj* bajo(a) y robusto(a)

stockyard ['stɒkjɑːd] *n* corral *m* (de ganado)

stodge [stɒdʒ] *n Fam* (**a**) *(food)* mazacote *m* (**b**) *(writing)* pesadez *f*, *Esp* muermo *m*

stodgy ['stɒdʒɪ] *adj Fam* (**a**) *(food)* pesado(a) (**b**) *(book, style, person)* pesado(a)

stogie, stogy ['stəʊgɪ] (*pl* **stogies**) *n US Fam* puro *m*

stoic ['stəʊɪk] **1** *n* estoico(a) *m,f*

2 *adj* estoico(a)

stoical ['stəʊɪkəl] *adj* estoico(a)

stoically ['stəʊɪklɪ] *adv* estoicamente

stoicism ['stəʊɪsɪzəm] *n* estoicismo *m*

stoke [stəʊk] *vt* (**a**) *(add fuel to)* alimentar (**b**) *(emotions, anger, controversy)* alimentar

► **stoke up 1** *vt sep* = **stoke**

2 *vi Br Fam (fill one's stomach)* **to s. up (on** *or* **with sth)** llenarse la barriga (de algo)

stokehold ['stəʊkhəʊld] *n* cuarto *m* de calderas

stoke-hole ['stəʊkhəʊl] *n* (**a**) *(opening in furnace)* boca *f*, *Spec* tragante *m* (**b**) = **stokehold**

stoker ['stəʊkə(r)] *n* fogonero(a) *m,f*

stole[1] [stəʊl] *n* (**a**) *(worn by woman)* estola *f* (**b**) *(worn by priest)* estola *f*

stole[2] *pt of* **steal**

stolen ['stəʊlən] **1** *adj* (**a**) *(car, property)* robado(a) (**b**) *(kiss, moment)* furtivo(a)

2 *pp of* **steal**

stolid ['stɒlɪd] *adj* imperturbable

stolidly ['stɒlɪdlɪ] *adv* imperturbablemente

stolidness ['stɒlɪdnɪs] *n* imperturbabilidad *f*

stomach ['stʌmək] **1** *n* (**a**) *(internal organ)* estómago *m*; **on an empty s.** con el estómago vacío; **to have an upset s.** tener mal el estómago; **I have a pain in my s.** me duele el estómago; **it turns my s.** me revuelve el estómago; IDIOM **to have no s. for sth** no tener el ánimo para algo ►► ***s. infection*** infección *f* estomacal; ***s. pains*** dolores *mpl* en el estómago; ***s. pump*** sonda *f* gástrica; ***s. ulcer*** úlcera *f* gástrica *or* de estómago; ***s. upset*** molestias *fpl* estomacales, trastorno *m* gástrico; **to have a s. upset** tener mal el estómago

(**b**) *(belly)* vientre *m*, tripa *f*, barriga *f*; **to be lying on one's s.** estar tendido(a) boca abajo; **to punch sb in the s.** dar un puñetazo en la tripa a alguien ►► ***s. muscles*** músculos *mpl* del abdomen

2 *vt* (**a**) *(tolerate)* soportar; **I can't s. his sister** no soporto a su hermana (**b**) *(digest)* digerir

stomach-ache ['stʌməkeɪk] *n* **to have (a) s.** tener dolor de estómago

stomp [stɒmp] *vi* dar fuertes pisadas; **to s. about** ir *or* andar por ahí dando fuertes pisotones; **to s. in/out** entrar/salir airadamente

stone [stəʊn] **1** *n* (**a**) *(material)* piedra *f*; *Fig* **are you made of s.?** ¿es que estás hecho de piedra? ►► ***the S. Age*** la Edad de Piedra; ***s. curlew*** alcaraván *m*; ***s. marten*** garduña *f*; ***s. pine*** pino *m* piñonero; ***s. quarry*** cantera *f* de piedra

(**b**) *(piece of rock)* piedra *f*; **the plane fell out of the sky like a s.** el avión se desplomó; IDIOM **to leave no s. unturned** no dejar piedra por mover; IDIOM **a s.'s throw from here** a un tiro de piedra (de aquí) ►► ***s. circle*** crómlech *m*, crónlech *m*

(**c**) *(on grave)* lápida *f*

(**d**) *(gem)* piedra *f*

(**e**) *(of fruit)* hueso *m*, *RP* carozo *m*

(**f**) *(in kidney)* piedra *f*

(**g**) *(British unit of weight)* = unidad de peso equivalente a 6,35 kg

2 *adj* de piedra

3 *vt* (**a**) *(fruit, olive)* deshuesar (**b**) *(person)* apedrear; **he was stoned to death** murió lapidado; *Fam Old-fashioned* **s. me!, s. the crows!** ¡caramba!, *Méx* ¡ándale!, *RP* ¡mirá vos!

Stone-Age ['stəʊneɪdʒ] *adj* de la Edad de Piedra

stone-blind ['stəʊn'blaɪnd] *adj* totalmente ciego(a)

stone-broke ['stəʊn'brəʊk] *adj US Fam* **to be s.** estar sin un centavo *or Esp* duro

stonechat ['stəʊntʃæt] *n* tarabilla *f* (común)

stone-cold ['stəʊn'kəʊld] **1** *adj* helado(a)

2 *adv* **to be s. sober** estar totalmente sobrio(a)

stonecrop ['stəʊnkrɒp] *n Bot* uva *f* de gato

stone-cutter ['stəʊnkʌtə(r)] *n (person)* cantero(a) *m,f*, picapedrero(a) *m,f*

stoned [stəʊnd] *adj* (**a**) *Fam (on drugs)* colocado(a); **to be s.** estar colocado(a); **to get s.** colocarse (**b**) *Fam Old-fashioned (drunk)* trompa (**c**) *(fruit)* con hueso

stone-dead ['stəʊn'ded] *adj Fam* **to be s.** estar tieso(a) *or* seco(a); **to kill sb s.** dejar a alguien tieso(a) *or* seco(a); *Fig* **this revelation killed the proposal s.** esta revelación acabó de seco con la propuesta

stone-deaf ['stəʊn'def] *adj Fam* sordo(a) como una tapia; **to be s.** estar sordo(a) como una tapia

stonefish ['stəʊnfɪʃ] *n* pez *m* piedra

stoneground ['stəʊngraʊnd] *adj (flour)* molido(a) artesanalmente

stonemason ['stəʊnmeɪsən] *n* cantero(a) *m,f (que labra la piedra)*

stonewall ['stəʊnwɔːl] *vi* (**a**) *(in inquiry)* entorpecer, andarse con evasivas (**b**) *(in game)* jugar a la defensiva

stonewalling [stəʊn'wɔːlɪŋ] *n (in inquiry)* entorpecimiento *m*

stoneware ['stəʊnweə(r)] *n* (cerámica *f* de) gres *m*

stonewashed ['stəʊnwɒʃt] *adj (denim)* lavado(a) a la piedra

stonework ['stəʊnwɜːk] *n* obra *f* de cantería

stonily ['stəʊnɪlɪ] *adv* con frialdad, fríamente

stoning ['stəʊnɪŋ] *n (of person)* lapidación *f*

stonker ['stɒŋkə(r)] *n Br Fam* **their new album's a s.!** ¡su nuevo disco es *Esp* una pasada *or Andes, CAm, Carib, Méx* super chévere *or Méx* padrísimo *or RP* bárbaro!

stonking ['stɒŋkɪŋ] *adv Fam* **s. big** gigantesco(a); **we had a s. good time** lo pasamos en grande, lo pasamos bomba *or Esp* teta

stony ['stəʊnɪ] *adj* (**a**) *(ground, beach)* pedregoso(a); IDIOM **to fall on s. ground** caer en saco roto (**b**) *(look, silence)* glacial; *(reception)* frío(a)

stony-broke ['stəʊnɪ'brəʊk] *adj Br Fam* **to be s.** estar sin un centavo *or Esp* duro

stony-faced ['stəʊnɪ'feɪst] *adj* impertérrito(a), impasible

stony-hearted ['stəʊnɪ'hɑːtɪd] *adj* insensible

stood *pt & pp of* **stand**

stooge [stuːdʒ] *n Fam* (**a**) *(comedian's fall-guy)* comparsa *mf* (**b**) *(minion)* títere *m*, secuaz *mf*

stook [stʊk] **1** *n* gavillas *fpl*, garbera *f*

2 *vt* hacer gavillas con

stool [stuːl] *n* (**a**) *(seat)* banqueta *f*; *(with short legs)* taburete *m*; IDIOM **to fall between two stools** quedarse nadando entre dos aguas ►► *Fam* ***s. pigeon*** *(informer)* soplón(ona) *m,f* (**b**) *Med (faeces)* **stools** heces *fpl*; **he examined my s.** examinó mis heces

stoolie ['stuːlɪ] *n Fam* soplón(ona) *m,f*

stoop[1] [stu:p] 1 *n* **to have a s.** ser cargado(a) de espaldas; **to walk with a s.** caminar encorvado(a)

2 *vi* (a) *(bend down)* agacharse, agachar el cuerpo; **she stooped to pick up her pen** se agachó para recoger la pluma (b) *(stand, walk with a stoop)* encorvarse (c) *(abase oneself)* **to s. to (doing) sth** rebajarse a (hacer) algo; **she would s. to anything** no le importa rebajarse y hacer lo que sea; **I never thought they'd s. so low (as to...)** nunca pensé que caerían tan bajo (como para...)

3 *vt* **he stooped his head to go through the door** agachó la cabeza para poder pasar por la puerta

stoop[2] *n US (verandah)* porche *m*

stooped [stu:pt] *adj* encorvado(a)

stooping ['stu:pɪŋ] *adj (back, shoulders, figure)* encorvado(a)

STOP [stɒp] 1 *n* (a) *(halt)* parada *f*; **she brought the vehicle to a s.** detuvo el vehículo; **our first s. was Brussels** *(on bus, train)* la *or* nuestra primera parada era Bruselas; *(on flight)* la primera escala era Bruselas; **my whole career has been full of stops and starts** mi trayectoria profesional ha ido siempre a trompicones; **to come to a s.** detenerse; **to put a s. to sth** poner fin a algo; **without a s.** sin descanso ▸▸ *Aut* ***s. sign*** (señal *f* de) stop *m*

(b) *(pause) (in work, journey)* parada *f*; *(of plane)* escala *f*; **to make a s.** parar, detenerse; **ten minutes' s.** una parada de diez minutos

(c) *(stopping place) (of bus, train)* parada *f*

(d) *Sport (save)* parada *f*

(e) *(full stop)* punto *m*; *(in telegram)* stop *m*

(f) *Mus (on organ)* registro *m*; IDIOM **to pull out all the stops** tocar todos los registros

(g) *Phot (aperture setting)* posición *f* del número f ▸▸ ***s. bath*** baño *m* de paro *or* parada

(h) *(blocking device)* tope *m*

(i) *Ling* **s. consonant** (consonante *f*) oclusiva *f*

2 *vt* (*pt & pp* **stopped**) (a) *(halt) (person, vehicle, machine)* parar, detener; *(taxi)* parar; *(conversation)* interrumpir; *(spread, advance, bleeding)* detener; *(corruption, abuse)* poner fin a; *(cheque)* bloquear; *(wages, aid, funding)* suspender; *(standing order, subscription)* cancelar; *(fire)* extinguir; **once he starts there's no stopping him** cuando se pone, no hay quien lo pare; **the referee stopped the fight** el árbitro detuvo la pelea; **he stopped his opponent after two rounds** noqueó a su contrincante en dos asaltos; **remember to s. the newspaper** no te olvides de pedir que no te manden el periódico; *Mil* **all leave is stopped** se han suspendido todos los permisos; **to s. sb short** hacer que se detenga alguien súbitamente; *Fam* **to s. a bullet** *(bodyguard)* hacer de escudo humano

(b) *(cease)* parar; **I s. work at five** acabo de trabajar a las cinco; **we stopped what we were doing** dejamos lo que estábamos haciendo; **s. it** *or* **that!** ¡basta ya!, *Esp* ¡vale ya!; **to s. doing sth** dejar de hacer algo; **to s. smoking/drinking** dejar de fumar/beber *or Am* tomar; **she couldn't s. crying** no podía dejar de llorar; **it hasn't stopped raining all day** no ha dejado de llover en todo el día; **I wish they'd s. that noise!** ¡a ver si dejan de hacer ruido!

(c) *(prevent)* impedir; **to s. sb (from) doing sth** impedir que alguien haga algo; **taking these tablets stops me (from) getting seasick** estas pastillas evitan que me maree; **the only thing that stopped me (from) hitting him was...** la única razón por la que no le pegué fue...; **there's nothing to s. you (from) asking** nada te impide preguntar; **what's stopping you?** ¿qué te lo impide?; **I couldn't s. myself** no podía contenerme; **nothing can s. us now** nada nos detendrá

(d) *(fill in) (hole, gap)* taponar, tapar; **to s. one's ears** taparse las orejas

(e) *Sport (save)* parar

(f) *Br (deduct)* deducir

3 *vi* (a) *(halt) (moving person, vehicle)* parar(se), detenerse; *(watch)* pararse; *(heart)* pararse, dejar de latir; **s., who goes there?** ¡alto!, ¿quién va ahí?; **this train stops at all stations to Durham** este tren va a Durham y para en todas las estaciones; **to s. to do sth** parar para hacer algo; *Fig* **we never stopped to think what might happen** nunca nos paramos a pensar lo que podría pasar; **we can s. for tea on the way** podemos parar a *or* para tomar té de camino; **without stopping** sin parar; *Naut* **to s. at a port** hacer escala; **to s. short** *or* **dead** pararse en seco; **they stopped short of actually harming him** no le hicieron daño, pero les faltó un pelo; **s., thief!** ¡al ladrón!

(b) *(cease) (speaker, worker)* parar; *(road)* acabarse, terminar; *(music, shouting)* terminar, cesar; **the rain has stopped** ha dejado de llover; **the pain has stopped** ya no me duele; **I used to play soccer but I stopped last year** antes jugaba a fútbol pero lo dejé el año pasado; **the road stops a few miles east of Alice Springs** la carretera se acaba unas millas al este de Alice Springs; **our responsibility stops there** nuestra responsabilidad llega hasta ahí; **he doesn't know when to s.** *(when drinking)* no sabe decir basta; **this has got to s.** esto tiene que acabarse; **she did not s. at that** no se contentó con eso; **he'll s. at nothing** no se detendrá ante nada; **to s. short** *or* **dead** pararse en seco

(c) *(stay)* quedarse; **we can't s.** no podemos quedarnos; **which hotel did you s. at?** ¿en qué hotel te quedaste?

> Hay una serie de verbos en inglés que pueden ir seguidos tanto como de infinitivo como de gerundio sin que apenas cambie su significado; por ejemplo **begin**, **bother**, **continue**, **hate**, **like** o **try**. Sin embargo, **stop** es uno de los pocos verbos en los que existe una clara diferencia entre ambas opciones:
> **they stopped to have lunch**
> *pararon para almorzar*
> **he soon stopped writing to us**
> *pronto dejó de escribirnos*

▸ **stop away** *vi Br Fam* **many people were stopping away because of the bad publicity** mucha gente ni se acercaba por la mala publicidad

▸ **stop by** 1 *vt insep (visit briefly)* pasarse por

2 *vi (visit briefly)* pasarse; **I'll s. by at your place tomorrow** me pasaré mañana por tu casa

▸ **stop down** *vi Phot* reducir la apertura del diafragma

▸ **stop in** *vi* (a) *(visit briefly)* pasarse (**at** por)

(b) *Br (stay in)* quedarse en casa

▸ **stop off** *vi (stay briefly)* parar, hacer una parada; **could you s. off at the baker's for me?** ¿podrías hacerme el favor de pasarte por el panadero?

▸ **stop out** *vi Br (stay out)* quedarse *or* permanecer fuera; **to s. out all night** estar fuera toda la noche

▸ **stop over** *vi* (a) *Av* hacer escala (b) *Br (spend the night)* pasar la noche

▸ **stop round** *vi* pasarse

▸ **stop up** 1 *vt sep (hole)* taponar, tapar; *(sink, pipe)* atascar

2 *vi Br (stay up)* quedarse levantado(a)

stop-and-go *US* = **stop-go**

stop-and-search [stɒpən'sɜ:tʃ] *adj* **the police have been given special s. powers** la policía ha recibido poderes especiales para detener y registrar

stopcock ['stɒpkɒk] *n* llave *f* de paso

stopgap ['stɒpgæp] *n (thing)* recambio *m*, repuesto *m (provisional)*; *(person)* sustituto(a) *m,f (temporal)* ▸▸ ***s. measure*** medida *f* provisional

stop-go ['stɒp'gəʊ], *US* **stop-and-go** [stɒpən'gəʊ] *adj Econ* de frenado y aceleración

stoplight ['stɒplaɪt] *n US* (a) *(traffic light)* semáforo *m* (b) *(brake light)* luz *f* del freno, luz *f* de frenado

stop-off ['stɒpɒf] *n* parada *f*

stop-out ['stɒpaʊt] *n Br Hum Fam* **dirty s.** crápula *mf*, calavera *mf*

stopover ['stɒpəʊvə(r)] *n (break in any journey)* parada *f*; *(in journey by plane)* escala *f*

stoppage ['stɒpɪdʒ] *n* (a) *(of flow, traffic)* retención *f*, detención *f*; *(of work)* interrupción *f*; *Sport* interrupción *f* del juego ▸▸ *Sport* ***s. time*** tiempo *m* de descuento (b) *(strike)* paro *m* (c) *(blockage) (in pipe, intestine)* obstrucción *f* (d) *Fin (deduction)* retención *f*

stopper ['stɒpə(r)] 1 *n* tapón *m*

2 *vt* poner el tapón a

stopping ['stɒpɪŋ] *n Aut* ***s. distance*** distancia *f* de frenado; ***s. place*** sitio *m* para parar; *Br* ***s. train*** tren *m* con paradas en todas las estaciones

stop-press ['stɒppres] *Journ* 1 *n* noticias *fpl* de última hora

2 *adj* **s. news** noticias de última hora

stopwatch ['stɒpwɒtʃ] *n* cronómetro *m*

storage ['stɔ:rɪdʒ] *n* (a) *(putting into store)* almacenamiento *m*, almacenaje *m*; **the goods were damaged in s.** las mercancías sufrieron daños en el almacén; **our furniture is in s.** tenemos todas nuestras cosas en un guardamuebles; **to put sth into s.** almacenar algo ▸▸ *Elec* ***s. battery*** acumulador *m*; ***s. charges*** gastos *mpl* de almacenaje; ***s. heater*** acumulador *m* de calor; ***s. room*** trastero *m*; ***s. space*** sitio *m or* espacio *m* para guardar cosas; ***s. tank*** depósito *m*

(b) *Comptr* almacenamiento *m* ▸▸ ***s. capacity*** capacidad *f* de almacenamiento; ***s. device*** dispositivo *m* de almacenamiento; ***s. media*** sistemas *mpl* de almacenamiento

(c) *(costs)* almacenaje *m*

store [stɔː(r)] **1** *n* **(a)** *(supply) (of goods, food)* reserva *f*, provisión *f*; *(of knowledge, wisdom)* caudal *m*, cúmulo *m*; *(jokes)* repertorio *m*; **we keep a s. of tins in case of emergency** guardamos una provisión de latas en caso de emergencia; **to hold** *or* **keep sth in s.** tener algo guardado(a) *or* reservado(a); **we should get in** *or* **lay in a s. of coal** deberíamos hacernos con una buena reserva de carbón; **stores** *(supplies)* reservas *fpl*; *Mil* reserva *f*

(b) *(warehouse)* almacén *m*; **our furniture is in s.** tenemos los muebles en un almacén; **to put sth into s.** almacenar algo ▸▸ ***s. cupboard*** almacén *m* con estanterías

(c) *esp US (shop)* tienda *f*

(d) *(large shop)* **(department) s.** grandes almacenes *mpl*, *Am* grandes tiendas *fpl* ▸▸ ***s. card*** tarjeta *f* de compra (a crédito); ***s. detective*** vigilante *m* de paisano *(de establecimiento comercial)*; ***s. manager*** director(ora) *m,f* del establecimiento

(e) IDIOMS **I have a surprise in s. for her** le tengo reservada *or* guardada una sorpresa; **who knows what's in s. for us?** ¿quién sabe lo que nos espera *or Esp* aguarda?; **to set** *or* **lay great s. by sth** dar mucha importancia a algo

2 *vt* **(a)** *(put in storage)* almacenar; *(facts, ideas)* almacenar **(b)** *(keep)* guardar; **s. in a cool place** consérvese en lugar fresco; **to s. sth away** guardar algo **(c)** *Comptr* almacenar **(d)** *(electricity, heat)* almacenar; **the body stores energy in the form of fat** el cuerpo almacena energía en forma de grasa **(e)** *(fill with provisions)* llenar **(with** de)

3 *vi (goods)* conservarse

▸ **store up** *vt sep* acumular; **he's just storing up trouble for himself by keeping silent** al permanecer callado se está metiendo en un lío

store-bought [ˈstɔːbɔːt] *adj US (cake)* comprado(a); *(clothes)* de confección

storefront [ˈstɔːfrʌnt] *n US* fachada *f (de tienda)* ▸▸ ***s. church*** = iglesia en una zona comercial

storehouse [ˈstɔːhaʊs] *n* **(a)** *(warehouse)* almacén *m* **(b)** *(of information)* mina *f*

storekeeper [ˈstɔːkiːpə(r)] *n US (shopkeeper)* tendero(a) *m,f*

storeman [ˈstɔːmən] *n* almacenista *mf*, almacenero(a) *m,f*

storeroom [ˈstɔːruːm] *n (in office, shop, factory)* almacén *m*; *(at home)* trastero *m*; *Naut* bodega *f*

storey, *US* **story** [ˈstɔːrɪ] *(pl* **storeys,** *US* **stories)** *n* piso *m*, planta *f*; **a single-s./four-s. building** un edificio de una planta *or* un piso/de cuatro plantas *or* pisos

-storeyed, *US* **-storied** [ˈstɔːrɪd] *suffix* **a single-s./four-s. building** un edificio de una planta *or* un piso/de cuatro plantas *or* pisos

stork [stɔːk] *n* cigüeña *f*

storm [stɔːm] **1** *n* **(a)** *(bad weather)* tormenta *f*; IDIOM **a s. in a teacup** una tormenta en un vaso de agua ▸▸ *US* ***s. cellar*** refugio *m* para ciclones; ***s. clouds*** nubes *fpl* de tormenta; *Fig* **the s. clouds are gathering over the peace process** unos nubarrones de tormenta se ciernen sobre el proceso de paz; ***s. cock*** zorzal *m* charlo, cagaaceite *m*; ***s. damage*** daños *mpl* causados por el temporal; ***s. door*** doble puerta *f*, contrapuerta *f*; ***s. lantern*** farol *m*; ***s. petrel*** paíño *m* europeo; ***s. warning*** aviso *m* de tormenta; ***s. window*** contraventana *f*

(b) *(scandal)* tormenta *f*; *(of insults, protest, criticism)* aluvión *m*; **the arms deal caused a political s.** el acuerdo armamentístico causó una tormenta política; **she left the stage to a s. of applause** dejó el escenario bajo una salva de aplausos

(c) *Mil (frontal attack)* **to take a town/a fortress by s.** tomar una ciudad/una fortaleza por asalto; *Fig* **the show took Broadway by s.** el espectáculo arrasó en Broadway ▸▸ ***s. troops*** tropas *fpl* de asalto

2 *vt* **(a)** *(town, fortress)* asaltar; *(house)* invadir **(b)** *(shout angrily)* **"get out!" he stormed** "¡fuera!" vociferó

3 *vi* **(a)** *(be angry)* enfurecerse; **to s. at sb** gritar a alguien

(b) *(go angrily)* **to s. in/out** entrar/salir furiosamente; **she stormed off without saying a word** se marchó enfurecida y sin decir una palabra; **she was storming about the place like a madwoman** iba de un sitio para otro hecha una furia

(c) *(move quickly)* **he stormed past the defender and scored** pasó como una flecha por delante del defensa y marcó

(d) *(wind, gale)* arreciar

stormbound [ˈstɔːmbaʊnd] *adj (airport)* cerrado(a) por el temporal; *(town)* aislado(a) por el temporal

stormily [ˈstɔːmɪlɪ] *adv* de manera violenta

storminess [ˈstɔːmɪnɪs] *n* **(a)** *(of weather)* lo tormentoso **(b)** *(of relationship, meeting, career)* tempestuosidad *f*

storming [ˈstɔːmɪŋ] **1** *n (attack, capture)* asalto *m*; **the s. of the Bastille** la toma de la Bastilla

2 *adj Fam (performance, speech)* arrollador(ora)

stormproof [ˈstɔːmpruːf] *adj* a prueba de temporales

storm-tossed [ˈstɔːmtɒst] *adj* zarandeado(a) por el vendaval

stormtrooper [ˈstɔːmtruːpə(r)] *n* soldado *m* (de las tropas) de asalto

stormy [ˈstɔːmɪ] *adj* **(a)** *(weather, day, sky)* tormentoso(a); *(sea)* tempestuoso(a); **it's s. today** hoy hay tormentas **(b)** *(of relationship, meeting, career)* tempestuoso(a)

story[1] [ˈstɔːrɪ] *n* **(a)** *(account) (fictional)* cuento *m*; *(factual)* historia *f*; **a ghost/murder s.** un relato de fantasmas/crímenes; **the book/movie tells the s. of...** el libro/la película narra la historia de...; **the witness changed his s.** el testigo cambió su declaración; **that's not the whole s., that's only part of the s.** eso no es todo; **there's a s. behind** *or* **attached to every exhibit in the museum** cada objeto expuesto en el museo tiene una historia detrás; **that's (quite) another s.** eso ya es otra cosa; **it's the same old s.** es la historia de siempre; **he told us his life s.** nos contó la historia de su vida; *Fam* **it's the s. of my life!** ¡siempre me pasa lo mismo!; **it's a long s.** es muy largo de contar; **to cut a long s. short,...** para resumir,...; **end of s.** y no hay más que hablar; **that's my s. and I'm sticking to it** así pasó y así lo cuento; **let me tell you my side of the s.** deja que te cuente mi versión de los hechos; **these bruises tell their own s.** estos moratones hablan por sí mismos

(b) *(plot) (of novel, play)* argumento *m*; **the s. is set in wartime London** la historia se desarrolla en el Londres de la guerra

(c) *(joke)* chiste *m*

(d) *(in newspaper)* artículo *m*; **the paper is running a s. on corruption** el periódico publica un artículo sobre la corrupción; **what's the s.?** ¿qué ha pasado aquí?

(e) *(rumour)* rumor *m*; **there's a s. going about that...** circula el rumor de que...; **the s. goes that...** se dice *or* cuenta que...

(f) *(lie)* cuento *m*; **to tell stories** contar cuentos

story[2] *US* = **storey**

storyboard [ˈstɔːrɪbɔːd] *n Cin* storyboard *m*, = dibujo de los planos que se van a rodar

storybook [ˈstɔːrɪbʊk] *n* libro *m* de cuentos; **a s. ending** un final de cuento

storyline [ˈstɔːrɪlaɪn] *n (of book, play, movie)* argumento *m*

storyteller [ˈstɔːrɪtelə(r)] *n* **(a)** *(narrator)* narrador(ora) *m,f*; **to be a good/bad s.** ser buen/mal contador de historias **(b)** *(liar)* cuentista *mf*

stoup [stuːp] *n* pila *f* de agua bendita

stout [staʊt] **1** *n (beer)* cerveza *f* negra

2 *adj* **(a)** *(fat) (person)* rechoncho(a) **(b)** *(solid) (door, shoes, stick)* resistente **(c)** *(brave) (person, resistance)* valeroso(a); *(support)* firme

stouthearted [ˈstaʊtˈhɑːtɪd] *adj Literary* denodado(a), valeroso(a)

stoutly [ˈstaʊtlɪ] *adv* **(a)** *(to resist)* denodadamente; *(to support)* firmemente **(b)** *(to maintain, deny)* a toda costa **(c)** *(solidly) (built)* sólidamente; *(made)* resistentemente

stoutness [ˈstaʊtnɪs] *n* **(a)** *(of person, figure)* rechonchez *f* **(b)** *(of door, shoes, stick)* solidez *f* **(c)** *(of person, resistance)* aguante *m*; *(of support)* firmeza *f*

stove[1] [stəʊv] *n* **(a)** *(for cooking)* cocina *f*, *Col, Méx, Ven* estufa *f* **(b)** *(for heating)* estufa *f*

stove[2] *pt & pp of* **stave**

stovepipe [ˈstəʊvpaɪp] *n* **(a)** *(on stove)* tubo *m* de estufa **(b)** *Fam* **s. (hat)** chistera *f*

stow [stəʊ] *vt (put away)* guardar; *Naut* estibar; **he stowed the keys behind the clock** *(hid)* escondió las llaves detrás del reloj; IDIOM *Br Fam* **s. it!** *(stop)* ¡para ya!; *(shut up)* ¡calla ya!

▸ **stow away** **1** *vt (hide)* esconder

2 *vi (on ship)* ir *or* viajar de polizón

stowage [ˈstəʊɪdʒ] *n* **(a)** *(of goods)* almacenamiento *m*; *Naut* estiba *f* **(b)** *(space)* sitio *m or* espacio *m* para guardar cosas; *Naut* bodega *f*

stowaway [ˈstəʊəweɪ] *n* polizón *m*

straddle [ˈstrædəl] *vt* **(a)** *(horse, wall)* sentarse a horcajadas en

(b) *(span)* **the bridge straddles the river** el puente une las dos orillas del río; **their empire straddled the Mediterranean** su imperio alcanzaba a todo el Mediterráneo; **his career has straddled the worlds of politics and the stage** su carrera se ha desarrollado a caballo entre la política y el teatro

(c) *US Fam* **to s. the fence** *(be noncommittal)* no pronunciarse, nadar entre dos aguas

strafe [streɪf] *vt (with machine guns)* ametrallar desde el aire

straggle [ˈstrægəl] *vi* **(a)** *(lag behind)* rezagarse; **she was straggling behind all the others** se estaba quedando rezagada del resto; **to s. in/out** entrar/salir poco a poco (**b**) *(spread untidily) (roots, creepers)* extenderse desordenadamente; **her hair straggled over her forehead** le caían mechones sueltos de pelo sobre la frente; **the houses s. along the river** las casas están diseminadas a lo largo del río

straggler ['strægl ə(r)] *n* rezagado(a) *m,f*

straggly ['strægl ɪ] *adj (hair)* desgreñado(a); *(beard)* muy descuidada; *(roots, creepers)* extendido(a) desordenadamente; **a s. line of refugees** una cola caótica de refugiados

STRAIGHT [streɪt] **1** *n* (**a**) *(level)* **to be out of s.** estar torcido(a); IDIOM **to keep to the s. and narrow** seguir por el buen camino

(**b**) *(in sport)* recta *f*; **the final** *or* **home s.** la recta final

(**c**) *Fam (heterosexual)* heterosexual *mf*

(**d**) *US Fam (conventional person)* persona *f* convencional; **don't be such a s.!** ¡no seas tan convencional!

(**e**) *(in card game)* escalera *f*

2 *adj* (**a**) *(not curved) (line, back, skirt)* recto(a); *(hair)* liso(a); **in a s. line** en línea recta; **to keep a s. face** contener la sonrisa; IDIOM **s. as a ramrod** tieso(a) como una vela *or* palo ►► ***s. angle*** ángulo *m* llano; *US* ***s. razor*** navaja *f* de barbero

(**b**) *(level, not sloping) (picture, tie)* derecho(a)

(**c**) *(tidy) (room)* arreglado(a), en orden; **to put one's hair s.** arreglarse el pelo; **to put** *or* **set s.** *(room, one's affairs)* poner en orden

(**d**) *(clear)* **let me get this s.** a ver si te entiendo; **now just you get this s.!** ¡a ver si te enteras de una vez!; **next time, get your facts s. before you start criticizing** la próxima vez procura informarte bien antes de criticar; **to put** *or* **set things s.** aclarar las cosas; **to put** *or* **set sb s.** aclararle las cosas a alguien

(**e**) *(simple) (choice, swap)* simple; **it's a s. fight between Mitchell and Davies** es una lucha entre dos, Mitchell y Davies

(**f**) *(basic, plain)* ordinario(a)

(**g**) *(undiluted)* solo(a); *(pure, utter)* puro(a); **to drink s. vodkas** beber vodka a palo seco; **it's just s. propaganda** es pura propaganda ►► *US Pol* ***a s. ticket*** una lista cerrada

(**h**) *(consecutive)* consecutivo(a); **three s. wins** tres victorias consecutivas; **to win in s. sets** ganar sin ceder un solo set; **I got s. As in my exams** saqué sobresaliente en todos mis exámenes ►► ***s. flush*** *(in cards)* escalera *f* de color

(**i**) *(honest) (person, answer)* franco(a); **to be s. with sb** ser franco(a) con alguien; **he's always been s. in his dealings with me** siempre ha dejado las cosas claras cuando ha tratado conmigo; **to do some s. talking** hablar sin tapujos; IDIOM **to be as s. as an arrow** *or* **a die** actuar sin dobleces ►► *US Fam* ***s. arrow*** tipo(a) *m,f* convencional; *US Fam* ***s. shooter*** persona *f* de fiar, *Esp* tío(a) *m,f* legal; ***s. talk:*** **teenagers appreciate s. talk about drug issues** a los adolescentes les gusta que les hablen sin rodeos sobre las drogas

(**j**) *(conventional)* convencional

(**k**) *Theat (role)* serio(a) ►► ***s. man*** *(in comedy act)* = en una pareja, el cómico con el papel serio

(**l**) *Fam* **to be s.** *(not criminal)* estar limpio(a)

(**m**) *Fam (heterosexual)* heterosexual

(**n**) *Fam (of addict)* **I'm s. now** *(not on drugs)* ya no me drogo; *(I don't drink)* ya no bebo *or Am* tomo

(**o**) *Fam (not owing money)* **are we s. now?** ¿estamos en paz?

3 *adv* (**a**) *(in straight line)* recto, en línea recta; **sit up s.!** ¡siéntate derecho!; **I can't walk s.** no puedo caminar recto *or* en línea recta; **it's s. ahead, it's s. in front of us** está justo delante de nosotros; **to look s. ahead** mirar hacia adelante; **go s. on** sigue todo recto *or* derecho; **he was coming s. towards me** venía derecho hacia mí; **the rocket shot s. up** el cohete salió disparado hacia arriba; IDIOM **to go s.** *(criminal)* reformarse

(**b**) *(level)* recto(a); **have I hung the picture s.?** ¿he colgado el cuadro recto?; **to shoot s.** disparar recto

(**c**) *(clearly)* **to see/think s.** ver/pensar con claridad

(**d**) *(honestly)* **tell me s. (out)** cuéntamelo sin rodeos; *Fam* **to let sb have it s.** soltarle la verdad a alguien; *Fam* **I'm giving it to you s.** te estoy diciendo la verdad; *Br Fam* **s. up** en serio

(**e**) *(immediately)* inmediatamente, en seguida; **s. after(wards)** inmediatamente después; **s. away** *or* **off** inmediatamente; **to get s. down to business** ponerse a trabajar inmediatamente *or* en seguida

(**f**) *(directly)* directamente; **he looked me s. in the eye** me miró (directamente) a los ojos; **to drink s. from the bottle** beber de la botella; **I'll come s. back** vuelvo en seguida; **come s. home** ven directamente a casa; **she walked s. past me** pasó por delante de mí sin detenerse; **to come** *or* **get s. to the point** ir directamente al grano; **s. through: to cut/go s. through sth** atravesar algo; **we drove s. through Burgos** pasamos Burgos de largo; **to read a book s. through** *(from beginning to end)* leer un libro entero; *(without stopping)* leer un libro de un tirón; **to come s. out with sth** decir algo sin rodeos; IDIOM **s. from the shoulder** sin ambages

(**g**) *(continuously)* **for 24 hours s.** durante 24 horas ininterrumpidas

(**h**) *(neat)* **to drink whisky s.** tomar el whisky solo

(**i**) *(straightforwardly)* **to play it s.** *(actor)* actuar sin histrionismos

straight-arm ['streɪtɑːm] **1** *adj* **s. tackle** placaje *m* con el brazo estirado

2 *vt* placar con el brazo estirado a

straightaway ['streɪtəweɪ] **1** *adv* inmediatamente, *Méx* ahorita, *Andes, RP* al tiro

2 *n US* recta *f*

straightedge ['streɪtedʒ] *n (ruler)* regla *f*

straighten ['streɪtən] **1** *vt* (**a**) *(bent nail, rod)* enderezar; *(wheel)* enderezar; *(hair)* peinar; *(picture, tie, hat)* poner derecho(a); *(hem)* igualar; *(sheets, tablecloth)* alisar; **to s. one's back** enderezar la espalda; **she's having her teeth straightened** le están enderezando los dientes

(**b**) *(tidy) (room, papers, desk)* ordenar

2 *vi (person)* ponerse derecho(a); *(road)* hacerse recto(a)

► **straighten out** **1** *vt sep* (**a**) *(leg, arm)* estirar; *(bent object)* enderezar; *(sheets, tablecloth)* alisar (**b**) *(problem)* resolver; *(mess, confusion)* esclarecer; *(misunderstanding)* aclarar; *(one's affairs)* poner en orden (**c**) *Fam (help)* poner bien a; *(punish)* poner firme a; **I'll soon s. her out!** ¡a ésa sí que la voy a poner firme pronto!

2 *vi (road)* hacerse recto(a); *(hair)* alisarse

► **straighten up** **1** *vt sep* (**a**) *(room, papers)* ordenar (**b**) *(affairs)* poner en orden

2 *vi* (**a**) *(person)* ponerse derecho(a) (**b**) *(tidy up)* recoger

straight-faced ['streɪt'feɪst] *adj* con la cara seria

straightforward [streɪt'fɔːwəd] *adj* (**a**) *(honest)* franco(a); **it's impossible to get a s. answer out of her** es imposible sacarle una respuesta directa (**b**) *(simple)* sencillo(a)

straightforwardly [streɪt'fɔːwədlɪ] *adv* (**a**) *(honestly)* con franqueza, claramente (**b**) *(simply)* de forma sencilla, con sencillez; **the meeting did not go off quite as s. as hoped** la reunión no se desarrolló con la facilidad que habíamos esperado

straightforwardness [streɪt'fɔːwədnɪs] *n* (**a**) *(honesty)* franqueza *f* (**b**) *(simplicity)* sencillez *f*

straight-out ['streɪtaʊt] *adj esp US Fam* (**a**) *(answer)* sin rodeos; *(refusal)* rotundo(a) (**b**) *(utter) (liar, hypocrite)* profesional; *(lie, dishonesty)* evidente; *(opponent, supporter)* acérrimo(a)

straight-to-video ['streɪttə'vɪdɪəʊ] *adv Cin* **it went s.** fue comercializado directamente en *Esp* vídeo *or Am* video

strain[1] [streɪn] **1** *n* (**a**) *(on beam, rope) (from pressure, pushing)* presión *f*; *(from tension, pulling)* tensión *f*; **the rope snapped under the s.** la cuerda se rompió por la presión; **the weight put too much s. on the rope** la carga puso la cuerda demasiado tensa; **the girder isn't designed to take so much s.** la viga no está preparada para aguantar tanta presión *or* peso; **this prop takes the s. off the girder** este puntal reduce la presión de la viga

(**b**) *(on economy)* tensión *f*; *(on friendship)* tirantez *f*; **to put a s. on** *(economy, friendship)* crear tensiones en; **watching so much TV is a s. on the eyes** ver tanta televisión cansa la vista; **the war is putting a great s. on the country's resources** la guerra está llevando al límite los recursos del país

(**c**) *(mental pressure)* agobio *m*; **to be under a lot of s.** estar muy agobiado(a); **to put sb under a lot of s.** someter a alguien a mucha presión; **he's beginning to feel/show the s. of working such late hours** está empezando a sentir/mostrar el estrés que le causa trabajar hasta tan tarde; **the arrival of a new secretary took the s. off me** la llegada de la nueva secretaria me quitó el estrés de encima; **the s. of making polite conversation** la tensión de mantener una conversación formal; **he can't take the s. anymore** no puede soportar más la presión

(**d**) *(of muscle)* distensión *f*; *(of ankle)* torcedura *f*

2 *vt* (**a**) *(put strain on) (beam, rope)* ejercer presión sobre

(**b**) *(economy, friendship)* crear tensiones en; *(resources, budget)* llevar al límite a; **to s. sb's patience** agotar la paciencia de alguien; **it would be straining the truth to call the play a masterpiece** sería forzar la verdad llamar a esto una obra maestra

(**c**) *(force)* **he strained his ears to hear what they were saying** aguzó al máximo el oído para oír lo que decían; **to s. one's eyes to see sth** afinar la vista para ver algo; **to s. every nerve** *or* **sinew to do sth** hacer todo lo imposible por conseguir hacer algo

(**d**) *(hurt, damage)* **to s. a muscle** distenderse un músculo; **to s. one's ankle** torcerse el tobillo; **to s. one's back** hacerse daño en la espalda; **reading small print strains your eyes** leer la letra pequeña cansa la vista; **mind you don't s. yourself lifting that desk** ten cuidado, no te hagas daño al levantar el escritorio; *Ironic* **don't s. yourself!** ¡ten cuidado, no te vayas a herniar *or* quebrar!

(**e**) *Culin (liquid)* colar; *(vegetables)* escurrir; **to s. sth off** colar algo

3 *vi* (**a**) *(pull)* **to s. at a rope/door** tirar de una cuerda/puerta; *Fig* **to be straining at the leash (to do sth)** estar impaciente (por hacer algo)

(**b**) *(struggle)* **the beam strained under the weight** la viga se combó por el peso; **she was straining under the weight of the rucksack** apenas podía con el peso de la mochila

(**c**) *(strive)* **to s. to do sth** hacer un esfuerzo por hacer algo; **he tends to s. after** *or* **for effect** tiende a emplear recursos demasiado efectistas

strain[2] *n* (**a**) *(variety) (of virus)* cepa *f*; *(of plant)* variedad *f* (**b**) *(streak)* **a s. of madness** un toque de locura; **there's a strong s. of fantasy in his novels** hay un importante componente de fantasía en sus novelas (**c**) *(style)* **in the same s.** en la misma línea (**d**) **strains** *(of music)* compases *mpl*

strained [streɪnd] *adj* (**a**) *(muscle)* distendido(a); **to have a s. ankle** tener un tobillo torcido; **to have a s. neck** tener tortícolis (**b**) *(tired) (eyes)* cansado(a) (**c**) *(tense) (atmosphere, conversation, relations)* tenso(a), tirante; *(expression)* cansado(a) (**d**) *(forced) (humour, smile, laugh, style)* forzado(a) (**e**) *Culin (yoghurt)* espeso(a); *(baby food)* pasado(a) por el pasapurés

strainer ['streɪnə(r)] *n* colador *m*

strait [streɪt] *n* estrecho *m*; **to be in dire** *or* **desperate straits** *(in serious difficulty)* estar en serios aprietos ▸▸ ***the Strait(s) of Gibraltar*** el estrecho de Gibraltar; ***the Strait(s) of Magellan*** el estrecho de Magallanes

straitened ['streɪtənd] *adj Formal* **to be in s. circumstances** pasar calamidades *or* estrecheces

straitjacket ['streɪtdʒækɪt] *n* camisa *f* de fuerza; *Fig* **the financial s. imposed by the government** las restricciones económicas impuestas por el gobierno

straitlaced ['streɪt'leɪst] *adj* mojigato(a)

strand[1] [strænd] *vt (ship)* varar; **to be stranded** quedar varado(a); **a whale was stranded on the beach** una ballena quedó varada en la playa; **we were stranded at Laguardia for 15 hours** nos quedamos atrapados en Laguardia durante 15 horas; **we were left stranded in the middle of nowhere** nos dejaron tirados en mitad de la nada

strand[2] *n* (**a**) *(of rope)* cabo *m*; *(of cotton)* hebra *f*; *(of wire)* hilo *m*; *(of hair)* pequeño mechón *m* (**b**) *(of plot)* hilo *m* (argumental) (**c**) *Literary (beach)* playa *f*

strange [streɪndʒ] *adj* (**a**) *(odd) (person, behaviour)* raro(a), extraño(a); **he didn't tell his wife – how s.!** no se lo contó a su mujer – ¡qué raro *or* extraño!; **it felt s. to be back in Canada** se hacía raro estar de nuevo en Canadá; **it's bound to feel a little s. at first** seguramente se te hará raro *or* extraño al principio; **it's s. he hasn't phoned** es raro que no haya llamado, me extraña que no haya llamado; **the s. thing is, I'm sure she recognized me** lo raro es que estoy seguro de que me reconoció; **the strangest thing happened to me today** hoy me ha pasado una cosa extrañísima; **for some s. reason I can't seem to remember her name** por alguna extraña razón parece que no puedo acordarme de su nombre; **s. as it may seem,...** por extraño que parezca,..., aunque parezca mentira,...; **s. to say, I've never been there** aunque suene extraño, nunca he estado allí

(**b**) *(unfamiliar) (person, place)* desconocido(a), extraño(a); **I was surrounded by s. faces** estaba rodeado de caras desconocidas *or* extrañas; **I woke up to find a s. man in my room** me desperté y encontré un extraño en mi habitación; **she awoke in a s. bed** se despertó en una cama extraña; **he is still s. to city life** todavía se le hace rara la vida en la ciudad

(**c**) *(unwell)* **I feel rather s.** me siento un poco raro

(**d**) *Phys (particle)* extraño(a) ▸▸ ***s. attractor*** atractor *m* extraño

strangely ['streɪndʒlɪ] *adv (to behave, dress)* de modo extraño; **s. familiar** extrañamente familiar; **s. enough,...** aunque parezca raro *or* extraño,...

strangeness ['streɪndʒnɪs] *n* (**a**) *(oddness)* rareza *f* (**b**) *(unfamiliarity)* lo desconocido (**c**) *Phys* extrañeza *f*

stranger ['streɪndʒə(r)] *n* (**a**) *(unknown person)* desconocido(a) *m,f*, extraño(a) *m,f*; **a perfect s.** un perfecto desconocido; **we are complete strangers** no nos conocemos en absoluto; **she is no s. to controversy** la polémica no le es ajena, la polémica le acompaña; **I'm something of a s. to the subject** el tema me es bastante desconocido; *Fam* **hello s.!** ¡dichosos los ojos!

(**b**) *(person from other place)* forastero(a) *m,f*; **I'm a s. here myself** yo tampoco soy de aquí

strangle ['stræŋgəl] *vt* (**a**) *(person)* estrangular; **he should have been strangled at birth** mejor que no hubiera nacido, maldita sea la hora en que nació (**b**) *(economy)* estrangular; *(opposition, originality)* acabar con

strangled ['stræŋgəld] *adj (voice, cry)* ahogado(a)

stranglehold ['stræŋgəlhəʊld] *n* (**a**) *(in wrestling, fight)* llave *f* al cuello; **to have sb in a s.** tener a alguien inmovilizado(a) con una llave al cuello (**b**) *(control)* **to have a s. on sth/sb** tener un control absoluto sobre algo/alguien; **he is hoping to break Sampras' s. on the singles title** espera acabar con el dominio de Sampras en la categoría de individuales

strangler ['stræŋglə(r)] *n* estrangulador(ora) *m,f*

strangling ['stræŋglɪŋ] *n* (**a**) *(asphyxiation)* asfixia *f* (**b**) *(case of murder by strangulation)* estrangulamiento *m*

strangulated ['stræŋgjʊleɪtɪd] *adj (cry)* ahogado(a) ▸▸ *Med* ***s. hernia*** hernia *f* estrangulada

strangulation [stræŋgjʊ'leɪʃən] *n* estrangulamiento *m*

strap [stræp] **1** *n* (**a**) *(of watch, bag)* correa *f*; *(of shoe)* tira *f*; *(on dress, bra)* tirante *m*, *Am* bretel *m*; *(for helmet)* correa *f* (**b**) *(as punishment)* **to give sb the s.** dar a alguien con la correa; **to get the s.** ser castigado con la correa (**c**) *(on bus, underground)* agarradera *f*

2 *vt* (*pt & pp* **strapped**) (**a**) *(tie with straps)* **to s. sth to sth** sujetar algo con correas a algo (**b**) *(wound)* vendar

▸ **strap down** *vt sep* sujetar con correas

▸ **strap in** *vt sep* **to s. oneself in** abrocharse *or* ponerse el cinturón (de seguridad); **he strapped the child in** le abrochó *or* puso el cinturón (de seguridad) al niño

▸ **strap up** *vt sep (wound)* vendar

strap-hanger ['stræphæŋə(r)] *n Fam* usuario(a) *m,f* del transporte público

strap-hanging ['stræphæŋɪŋ] *n Fam* = viajar de pie en el transporte público

strapless ['stræplɪs] *adj (dress, bra)* sin tirantes *or Am* breteles

strap-on ['stræpɒn] *adj* con correaje

strapped [stræpt] *adj Fam* **to be s. (for cash)** estar sin un centavo, estar pelado(a)

strapping ['stræpɪŋ] *adj* fornido(a)

Strasbourg ['stræzbɜːg] *n* Estrasburgo

strata *pl of* **stratum**

stratagem ['strætədʒəm] *n* estratagema *f*

strategic [strə'tiːdʒɪk] *adj* estratégico(a) ▸▸ ***s. business unit*** unidad *f* estratégica de negocio; ***S. Defense Initiative*** Iniciativa *f* de Defensa Estratégica

strategically [strə'tiːdʒɪklɪ] *adv* estratégicamente; **our company is s. placed to benefit from this development** nuestra compañía está estratégicamente situada para aprovechar este cambio

strategist ['strætədʒɪst] *n* estratega *mf*

strategy ['strætədʒɪ] *n* estrategia *f*

stratification [strætɪfɪ'keɪʃən] *n* estratificación *f*

stratified ['strætɪfaɪd] *adj* (**a**) *(rock)* estratificado(a) (**b**) *(society)* estamental, estratificado(a) ▸▸ ***s. sample*** muestra *f* estratificada

stratify ['strætɪfaɪ] **1** *vt* estratificar

2 *vi* estratificarse

stratocumulus [strætəʊ'kjuːmjʊləs] (*pl* **stratocumuli** [strætəʊ'kjuːmjʊlaɪ]) *n Met* estratocúmulo *m*

stratosphere ['strætəsfɪə(r)] *n* estratosfera *f*

stratospheric [strætə'sferɪk] *adj* **her popularity has reached s. heights** su popularidad ha alcanzado cotas estratosféricas

stratum ['strɑːtəm] (*pl* **strata** ['strɑːtə]) *n* (**a**) *(of rock)* estrato *m* (**b**) *(of society)* estamento *m*, estrato *m*

stratus ['streɪtəs] (*pl* **strati** ['streɪtaɪ]) *n Met* estrato *m*

straw [strɔː] *n* (**a**) *(dry stalks)* paja *f* ▸▸ ***s. hat*** sombrero *m* de paja; *Fig* ***s. man*** hombre *m* de paja; ***s. mat*** felpudo *m*; ***s. mattress*** colchón *m* de paja; ***s. poll*** sondeo *m* informal

(**b**) *(for drinking)* pajita *f*, *Méx* popote *m*

(**c**) IDIOMS **it's a s. in the wind** puede ser un indicio de cómo van a ser las cosas; **to clutch** *or* **grasp at straws** agarrarse a un clavo ardiendo; **that's the last s.!** ¡es el colmo!; **the s. that broke the camel's back** la gota que colmó el vaso

strawberry ['strɔːbərɪ] *n (fruit, plant)* fresa *f*, *CSur* frutilla *f*; **s. jam** mermelada de fresa *or CSur* frutilla ▸▸ ***s. blonde*** rubio(a) *m,f* bermejo(a); ***s. field*** fresal *m*; ***s. mark*** antojo *m* (en la piel)

straw-coloured ['strɔːkʌləd] *adj* pajizo(a)

stray [streɪ] **1** *n* (**a**) *(dog)* perro *m* callejero; *(cat)* gato *m* callejero (**b**) *(child)* golfillo(a) *m,f*

2 *adj* (**a**) *(dog, cat)* callejero(a); *(cow, sheep)* descarriado(a) (**b**) *(bullet)* perdido(a); *(memory)* aislado(a), desconectado(a); **a few s. birds flew by** pasó algún que otro pájaro (**c**) *(curl, hair)* suelto(a)

3 *vi* (**a**) *(move)* desviarse; **some sheep had strayed onto the railway line** algunas ovejas se habían descarriado y estaban en la vía del tren; **to s. onto sb's property** meterse sin querer en la propiedad de alguien; **to s. from** *(person)* desviarse de; *(animal)* descarriarse de; **her thoughts strayed (back) to her days in Japan** sus pensamientos vagaron hasta (remontarse a) sus días en Japón

(**b**) *(digress)* **to s. from the point** divagar

streak [stri:k] **1** *n* (**a**) *(stripe)* raya *f*, lista *f*; *(in hair)* mecha *f*; *(in marble, of ore)* vena *f*, veta *f*; *(of dirt, blood, paint)* tira *f*, chorro *m*; **a s. of lightning** un rayo

(**b**) *(run)* **a s. of luck** una racha de suerte; **to be on a winning/losing s.** tener una buena/mala racha

(**c**) *(character trait)* vena *f*; **to have a cruel s.** tener una vena de crueldad; **there's a s. of Indian blood in the family** hay gotas de sangre india en la familia

(**d**) *Fam (naked dash)* **to do a s.** correr desnudo(a)

2 *vt* **streaked with dirt** manchado(a) *(con tiras o chorros de suciedad)*; **streaked with tears** cubierto(a) de lágrimas; **his hair is streaked with silver** tiene mechones grises; **marble streaked with red** mármol veteado de *or* en rojo; **to have one's hair streaked** hacerse mechas en el pelo

3 *vi* (**a**) *(move quickly)* **to s. in/out** entrar/salir a toda prisa; **to s. off** salir disparado(a); **to s. past** pasar a toda velocidad (**b**) *Fam (run naked)* correr desnudo(a)

streaker ['stri:kə(r)] *n Fam* = espontáneo que irrumpe corriendo desnudo en un espectáculo público

streaking ['stri:kɪŋ] *n Fam* streaking *m*, = acto de exhibirse corriendo desnudo en un espectáculo público

streaky ['stri:kɪ] *adj (surface, pattern)* veteado(a); **her make-up had gone s.** se le había corrido el maquillaje ▸▸ ***s. bacon*** tocino *m or Esp* bacon *m* entreverado

stream [stri:m] **1** *n* (**a**) *(brook)* arroyo *m*, riachuelo *m*

(**b**) *(current)* corriente *f*; *(of thoughts, ideas)* corriente *f*; *Fig* **to go with/against the s.** dejarse llevar por/nadar contra la corriente

(**c**) *(of light, blood, water)* chorro *m*; *(of lava)* flujo *m*; *(of tears, insults)* torrente *m*; *(of people)* oleada *f*; *(of traffic)* oleada *f*, torrente *m*; *(of applications, complaints)* alud *m*; **there was a continuous s. of visitors** había un continuo torrente de visitantes; **to come on s.** *(industrial plant)* entrar en funcionamiento ▸▸ ***s. of consciousness*** *Lit* monólogo *m* interior; *Psy* flujo *m* de la consciencia

(**d**) *Br Sch* = cada una de las divisiones del alumnado en grupos por niveles de aptitud

2 *vt* (**a**) *(spurt) (blood)* chorrear; **her eyes were streaming tears** sus ojos chorreaban lágrimas (**b**) *Br Sch* **to s. pupils** dividir en grupos a los alumnos según su capacidad

3 *vi* (**a**) *(flow)* **the water streamed out** el agua salía a chorros; **blood streamed from his wounds** le chorreaba *or* manaba la sangre de las heridas; **people streamed into the stadium** la gente entraba en masa al estadio; **the light streamed in through the window** la luz entraba a raudales por la ventana; **his eyes were streaming** le lloraban los ojos; **the walls were streaming with water** las paredes estaban chorreando de agua, las paredes chorreaban agua; **tears streamed down her cheeks** le resbalaban las lágrimas por las mejillas

(**b**) *(hair, banner)* ondear

streamer ['stri:mə(r)] *n* (**a**) *(paper decoration)* serpentina *f* (**b**) *(banner)* banderola *f* (**c**) *(in newspaper)* gran titular *m*

streamertail ['stri:məteɪl] *n* colibrí *m* gallardete

streaming ['stri:mɪŋ] **1** *n Br Sch* = sistema de división del alumnado en grupos por niveles de aptitud

2 *adj* **to have a s. cold** tener un fuerte resfriado

streamline ['stri:mlaɪn] *vt* (**a**) *(vehicle)* hacer más aerodinámico(a) (**b**) *(system, department, industry)* racionalizar

streamlined ['stri:mlaɪnd] *adj* (**a**) *(vehicle)* aerodinámico(a) (**b**) *(system, department, industry)* racionalizado(a)

street [stri:t] *n* (**a**) *(road)* calle *f*; **it's on** *or Br* **in Main S.** está en la calle Main Street; **on** *or Br* **in the s.** en la calle; **at s. level** (al) nivel de la calle; **the whole s. knows about it** toda la calle lo sabe; **thousands of protesters took to the streets** miles de manifestantes salieron a la calle ▸▸ ***s. art*** arte *m* callejero; ***s. atlas*** plano *m* de calles; ***s. cleaner*** *(person)* barrendero(a) *m,f*; *(machine)* camión *m* barrecalles; ***s. corner*** esquina *f*; ***s. directory*** plano *m* de calles; ***s. door*** puerta *f* principal; ***s. fighting*** peleas *fpl* callejeras; ***s. furniture*** mobiliario *m* urbano; ***s. guide*** plano *m* de calles; ***s. hockey*** hockey *m* callejero; ***s. lighting*** alumbrado *m* público; ***s. map*** plano *m* de calles; *(book)* callejero *m*; ***s. market*** mercado *m* en la calle; ***s. musician*** músico *m* callejero; ***s. party*** fiesta *f* en la calle; ***s. plan*** plano *m* de calles; ***s. sweeper*** barrendero(a) *m,f*; ***s. theatre*** teatro *m* callejero; *Old-fashioned* ***s. urchin*** golfillo(a) *m,f*; ***s. value*** *(of drugs)* valor *m* en la calle; *US* ***s. vendor*** vendedor(ora) *m,f* callejero(a)

(**b**) IDIOMS *Fam* **to be on the s.** *or* **streets** *(homeless person)* estar en la calle, no tener un techo; *(prostitute)* hacer la calle; **to put** *or* **turn sb out into the s.** echar a alguien de casa; **to walk the streets** *(prostitute)* hacer la calle; **the man in the s.** el hombre de la calle; **to be streets ahead: she's streets ahead of the rest of the class at French** da cien vueltas al resto de la clase en francés; **the company is streets ahead of the competition** la empresa está muy por delante de la competencia; *Fam* **that's right up my s.** eso es lo mío, *Esp* eso es lo que me va; *Fam* **the band hasn't lost their s. credibility** el grupo no ha perdido nada de su carisma; *Fam* **wear a jacket like that and there goes your s. cred!** ponte una chaqueta como ésa y vas a perder enteros

streetcar ['stri:tkɑ:(r)] *n US* tranvía *m*

streetlamp ['stri:tlæmp], **streetlight** ['stri:tlaɪt] *n* farola *f*

streetwalker ['stri:twɔ:kə(r)] *n Old-fashioned* prostituta *f*

streetwise ['stri:twaɪz] *adj* espabilado(a), *RP* canchero(a)

strength [streŋθ] *n* (**a**) *(physical power) (of person, animal, muscle)* fuerza *f*; **I don't have the s. to lift these boxes** no me veo con fuerzas para levantar estas cajas; **she doesn't know her own s.** no se da cuenta de la fuerza que tiene; **I pushed the door with all my s.** empujé la puerta con todas mis fuerzas; **to get one's s. back** *(after illness)* recobrar las fuerzas; **his s. failed him** le fallaron las fuerzas; **I'm saving my s. for later** estoy reservando fuerzas para más tarde; IDIOM **to go from s. to s.** ir cada vez mejor

(**b**) *(of emotion)* intensidad *f*; *(of faith, opinion, determination)* firmeza *f*; **she showed great s. of character** mostró una gran firmeza; **they have great s. of purpose** tienen una gran determinación; **s. of will** fuerza de voluntad; **give me s.!** ¡Señor, dame fuerzas!

(**c**) *(of alcohol)* graduación *f*; *(of solution)* concentración *f*; **the cheese is graded into five strengths** el queso está graduado en una escala de cinco niveles del más suave al más fuerte; **maximum-s.** extrafuerte

(**d**) *(of light, sound)* intensidad *f*; *(of earthquake, wind)* intensidad *f*; *(of voice, lens, magnet)* potencia *f*; *(of current)* fuerza *f*

(**e**) *(resistance, durability) (of nail, rope)* resistencia *f*

(**f**) *(of currency, economy)* fortaleza *f*; *(of claim, position, relationship)* solidez *f*; *(of argument, protest)* validez *f*; **on the s. of...** atendiendo a...

(**g**) *(strong point)* punto *m* fuerte

(**h**) *(full number)* **the current s. of the workforce is 20,000** en este momento, el número total de empleados es de 20.000; **to be at full s.** *(department, regiment)* tener el cupo completo; *(team)* disponer de todos los jugadores; **to be below full** *or* **under s.** *(department, regiment)* estar por debajo del cupo; *(team)* no disponer de todos los jugadores; **in s.** en gran número

strengthen ['streŋθən] **1** *vt* (**a**) *(body, muscles)* fortalecer; *(voice, eyesight, hearing)* mejorar; *Fig* **he has strengthened his grip on the country** ha reforzado su control del país

(**b**) *(wall, building, material)* reforzar

(**c**) *(company, nation, team)* reforzar, fortalecer; *(friendship, relationship, links)* consolidar; *(determination)* reafirmar; *(position)* reforzar, afianzar; *(belief, argument)* reafirmar; **I felt strengthened by the experience** aquella experiencia me hizo más fuerte

(**d**) *(currency, economy)* fortalecer

(**e**) *(increase concentration of) (solution)* condensar

2 *vi* (**a**) *(body, muscles)* fortalecerse; *Fig* **his grip on the country has strengthened** su control del país se ha reforzado (**b**) *(emotion)* aumentar; *(friendship)* consolidarse; *(determination)* reafirmarse; *(faith)* reafirmarse (**c**) *(wind, current)* incrementarse (**d**) *(currency, economy)* fortalecerse

strenuous ['strenjʊəs] *adj* (**a**) *(activity, exercise, lifestyle)* agotador(ora); **it was a long, s. climb** fue una larga y ardua escalada (**b**) *(opposition)* enérgico(a); *(denial)* tajante; *(protests)* vehemente; **to make s. efforts to do sth** esforzarse denodadamente por hacer algo

strenuously ['strenjʊəslɪ] *adv* (**a**) *(to campaign)* enérgicamente (**b**) *(to oppose, resist)* enérgicamente; *(to deny)* tajantemente; *(to protest)* con vehemencia

strep throat ['strep'θrəʊt] *n US Fam* inflamación *f* de garganta

streptococcus [streptə'kɒkəs] (*pl* **streptococci** [streptə'kɒkaɪ]) *n* estreptococo *m*

streptomycin [streptə'maɪsɪn] *n* estreptomicina *f*

stress [stres] **1** *n* **(a)** *(nervous tension)* estrés *m*; **to suffer from s.** sufrir de estrés; **she's been under a lot of s. lately** últimamente ha estado sometida a mucho estrés; **it puts our relationship under s.** pone nuestra relación bajo tensión; **how does he react under s.?** ¿cómo reacciona en situaciones de estrés?; **I always play better under s.** siempre juego mejor bajo presión; **a s. factor** un factor de estrés; **the stresses and strains of city life** el estrés de la vida urbana ►► ***s. management*** control *m* del estrés

(b) *(physical pressure)* presión *f*; **can the girders take the s.?** ¿resistirán la presión las vigas? ►► *Med* ***s. fracture*** fractura *f* por presión

(c) *(emphasis)* énfasis *m*; **to put** *or* **lay s. on sth** hacer hincapié en algo

(d) *Ling* acento *m*; **the s. is** *or* **falls on the third syllable** el acento cae en la tercera sílaba ►► ***s. mark*** signo *m* de acento fonético

2 *vt* **(a)** *(emphasize)* subrayar, hacer hincapié en; **she stressed that no decision had yet been taken** subrayó que todavía no se había tomado ninguna decisión; **this point cannot be stressed enough** este punto es de vital importancia **(b)** *Ling* acentuar; **it's stressed on the second syllable** lleva acento en la segunda sílaba **(c)** *(concrete, metal)* ejercer presión sobre

3 *vi Fam* estresarse

► **stress out** *vt sep Fam* **to s. sb out** agobiar *or* estresar a alguien

stressed [strest] *adj* **(a)** *(person)* estresado(a) **(b)** *Ling* acentuado(a)

stressed-out ['strest'aʊt] *adj Fam* agobiado(a), estresado(a)

stressful ['stresfʊl] *adj* estresante

stress-related ['stresrɪ'leɪtɪd] *adj* relacionado(a) con el estrés

---

STRETCH [stretʃ] **1** *n* **(a)** *(of body)* **to have a s.** estirarse; **to give one's legs a s.** estirar las piernas; *Fig* **by no s. of the imagination** de ningún modo; IDIOM **by a long s.** de largo; IDIOM **not by a long s.** ni por asomo ►► ***s. marks*** estrías *fpl*

(b) *(of material)* elasticidad *f* ►► ***s. fabric*** tejido *m* elástico; *Fam* ***s. limo*** limusina *f* ampliada

(c) *(of water, land)* extensión *f*; *(of road, river, coast)* tramo *m*, trecho *m*; *(of countryside)* trozo *m*; *(of text)* fragmento *m*; *(of time, silence)* período *m*; **the final s.** *(in race)* la recta final; **for ten hours at a s.** durante diez horas seguidas; **the cabin will sleep ten at a s.** en la cabaña caben diez como mucho, en la cabaña caben diez justitos

(d) *(capacity)* **to be at full s.** *(factory)* estar a pleno rendimiento; *(player, team)* emplearse a fondo

(e) *Fam (term of imprisonment)* temporada *f*; **he did a five-year s.** pasó cinco años a la sombra

2 *vt* **(a)** *(extend) (elastic, belt)* estirar; *(arm, hand)* estirar, extender; *(lead, advantage)* aumentar; **we stretched the banner across the road** desplegamos la pancarta a lo ancho de la carretera; **to s. one's legs** estirar las piernas; **to s. oneself** estirarse; **we are stretching the limits of what is possible** estamos apurando los límites de lo posible; **a novel that stretches the imagination** una novela que pone a prueba la imaginación; **to s. a point** *(make exception)* hacer una excepción; **it's stretching a point to call him a lawyer** llamarle abogado es pasarse un poco; **to s. the rules** ser flexible en la interpretación de las reglas; **to s. it** *or* **the truth** apurar *or* forzar las cosas

(b) *(pull, strain) (muscle)* **I've stretched my calf muscle** me he estirado un gemelo; **s. the rope tight** tensa la cuerda; **to s. sth out of shape** deformar algo

(c) *(put demands on) (person)* exigir mucho a; *(resources)* mermar mucho; *(sb's patience)* abusar de; **we're fully stretched at the moment** en este momento estamos trabajando al límite (de nuestras posibilidades); **his schoolwork never really stretched him** el trabajo escolar nunca le obligó a esforzarse; **I didn't have to s. myself** no tuve que esforzarme demasiado; **our budget is stretched to the limit** nuestro presupuesto está estirado al máximo; **the police are stretched too thin at the moment** en estos momentos la policía tiene recursos insuficientes

(d) *(make last) (income, supplies)* estirar; **we should be able to s. the food until the weekend** la comida nos tiene que llegar hasta el fin de semana

3 *vi* **(a)** *(rope, elastic)* estirarse; *(clothing)* estirarse, dar de sí; **my T-shirt stretched in the wash** mi camiseta se estiró al lavarla; **the shoes will s. with wear** los zapatos darán de sí con el uso; **my sweater has stretched out of shape** se me ha deformado el jersey

(b) *(person)* estirarse; *(when warming up)* hacer estiramientos; **she stretched across me to get the salt** alargó el brazo por delante de mí para agarrar la sal

(c) *(road, time)* extenderse; **the desert stretches for several hundred miles** el desierto se extiende por varios cientos de millas; **minutes stretched into hours** los minutos se hicieron horas; **her unbeaten run stretches back to January** su racha triunfal se remonta a enero

(d) *(resources, budget)* dar de sí (**to** para); *Fam* **could you s. to $20?** ¿podrías subir hasta 20 dólares?; **my salary won't s. to a bigger house** con mi salario no me llega para comprar una casa más grande

> **False friend**: The Spanish verb **estrechar** is not a translation for the English word **stretch**. In Spanish **estrechar** means "to narrow", "to make closer" or "to squeeze".

► **stretch out 1** *vt sep* **(a)** *(extend)* **to s. out one's arm** estirar el brazo; **to s. out one's hand** tender la mano; **she lay stretched out in front of the television** estaba tumbada delante del televisor **(b)** *(resources, budget)* estirar; *(payments)* extenderse; **she'll have to s. her thesis out a bit for publication** tendrá que alargar un poco la tesis para su publicación

2 *vi* **(a)** *(person)* tenderse; **he stretched out and took the salt from the next table** estiró el brazó y agarró la sal de la mesa de al lado **(b)** *(road, time)* extenderse; **a barren future stretched out ahead of her** le esperaba un futuro yermo

---

stretcher ['stretʃə(r)] *n* **(a)** *Med* camilla *f* ►► ***s. case*** *(wounded person)* herido(a) *m,f*/enfermo(a) *m,f* trasladado(a) en camilla **(b)** *(for shoes)* horma *f*; *(for gloves)* ensanchador *m* **(c)** *(brick)* ladrillo *m* colocado a soga

► **stretcher off** *vt sep Sport* **to s. sb off** sacar a alguien en camilla *(del terreno de juego)*

stretcher-bearer ['stretʃə(r)'beərə(r)] *n* camillero(a) *m,f*

stretchy ['stretʃɪ] *adj* elástico(a)

strew [stru:] (*pp* **strewed** *or* **strewn** [stru:n]) *vt* **(a)** *(objects)* dispersar (**over** *or* **around** por); **the guests strewed confetti over the bride** los invitados tiraron confeti a la novia **(b)** *(surface)* cubrir (**with** de); **the path was strewn with leaves/litter** el camino estaba cubierto de hojas/desperdicios

strewth [stru:θ] *exclam Austr, Br Fam* ¡por Dios!, ¡madre mía!

striated [straɪ'eɪtɪd] *adj Geol* estriado(a)

-stricken [-'strɪkən] *suffix* **grief-s.** afligido(a); **terror-s.** aterrado(a)

stricken ['strɪkən] *adj* **(a)** *(with grief, guilt)* afligido(a) (**with** por); *(with illness, by disaster)* gravemente afectado(a) (**with** *or* **by** por) **(b)** *(damaged) (ship, convoy)* dañado(a); **our s. economy** nuestra maltrecha economía; **the s. city may never be rebuilt** puede que la devastada ciudad nunca sea reconstruida **(c)** *(sad, grieving)* **to look s.** parecer muy desolado(a)

strict [strɪkt] *adj* **(a)** *(person, instruction, discipline)* estricto(a); **s. morals** moral estricta; **a s. Moslem** un musulmán ortodoxo; **she's a s. vegetarian** es vegetariana estricta; **you have to be very s. with them** tienes que ser muy estricto con ellos; **I gave s. orders not to be disturbed** di órdenes estrictas de que no me molestaran; **I'm on a s. diet** sigo una dieta estricta

(b) *(precise) (meaning, minimum)* estricto(a); **in the s. sense of the word** en el sentido estricto de la palabra

(c) *(absolute) (accuracy, hygiene)* absoluto(a); **to tell sb sth in strictest confidence** contar algo a alguien en el más riguroso secreto; **the meeting took place in s. secrecy** la reunión se celebró en el más absoluto secreto

strictly ['strɪktlɪ] *adv* **(a)** *(severely) (to treat, bring up)* estrictamente **(b)** *(exactly)* rigurosamente; **the rules must be s. observed** las normas deben ser cumplidas rigurosamente; **s. speaking** en un sentido estricto

(c) *(absolutely)* **s. confidential** estrictamente confidencial; **s. forbidden** terminantemente prohibido(a); **it was s. a business meeting** era estrictamente una reunión de negocios; **not s. true** no del todo *or* rigurosamente cierto; **s. between you and me** exclusivamente entre tú y yo

strictness ['strɪktnɪs] *n* **(a)** *(of discipline, rules)* rigor *m*; *(of person, upbringing)* severidad *f* **(b)** *(of criteria, definition)* rigurosidad *f*

stricture ['strɪktʃə(r)] *n* **(a)** *(criticism)* invectiva *f* (**on** contra), censura *f* (**on** a) **(b)** *(restriction)* prohibición *f* **(c)** *Med* estrictura *f*

stride [straɪd] **1** *n* **(a)** *(step)* zancada *f*; **in a single s.** de una zancada; **to shorten/lengthen one's s.** acortar/alargar la zancada; **she recognized him by his purposeful s.** lo reconoció por sus decididas zancadas

(b) *Austr, Br Fam* **strides** *(trousers)* pantalones *mpl*

(c) IDIOMS **to get into** *or* **hit one's s.** agarrar *or Esp* coger el ritmo; **to make great strides** progresar a pasos agigantados; **to put sb off their s.** hacer perder la concentración a alguien; **to take sth in one's s.** asumir algo bien; **she takes everything in her s.** no deja que nada la perturbe

2 *vi* (*pt* **strode** [strəʊd], *pp* **stridden** ['strɪdən]) **to s. in/out/off** entrar/salir/alejarse a grandes zancadas

3 *vt (streets, fields, deck)* recorrer a grandes zancadas

stridency ['straɪdənsɪ] *n* (**a**) *(of voice, sound)* estridencia *f* (**b**) *(of colour)* estridencia *f* (**c**) *(of protests, demands)* clamor *m*

strident ['straɪdənt] *adj* (**a**) *(voice, sound)* estridente (**b**) *(colour)* chillón(ona) (**c**) *(protests, demands)* clamoroso(a)

stridently ['straɪdəntlɪ] *adv* (**a**) *(to cry, sing, ring)* con estridencia (**b**) *(to protest, demand)* clamorosamente

strife [straɪf] *n* conflictos *mpl*; **the cause of much domestic s.** la causa de muchos conflictos domésticos

---

STRIKE [straɪk] **1** *n* (**a**) *Ind* huelga *f*; **teachers'/miners' s.** huelga de profesores/de mineros; **to be on s.** estar en huelga; **to go on s.** declararse en huelga ►► ***s. action*** huelga *f*; **to threaten s. action** amenazar con ir a la huelga; ***s. ballot*** = voto para decidir si se va a la huelga; ***s. fund*** caja *f* de resistencia; ***s. pay*** subsidio *m* de huelga

(**b**) *(discovery) (of ore, oil)* descubrimiento *m*

(**c**) *Mil* ataque *m* ►► *Mil* ***s. force*** fuerza *f* de combate

(**d**) *Sport (shot)* golpe *m*

(**e**) *(in baseball)* strike *m*

(**f**) *(in bowling)* pleno *m*, strike *m*

(**g**) *(impact)* golpe *m*, impacto *m*

(**h**) *(sound of clock)* campanada *f*; **at the s. of midnight** al dar la medianoche

2 *vt (pt & pp* **struck** [strʌk]) (**a**) *(hit)* golpear; **to s. sb in the face** golpear a alguien en la cara; **he struck me with his fist** me arreó un puñetazo; **to s. sb/sth a blow** pegar un golpe a alguien/algo; *Fig* **to s. a blow for freedom** romper una lanza a favor de la libertad; **to s. a shot** disparar

(**b**) *(collide with)* chocar contra; *(of missile, bomb)* dar en, alcanzar; *(of bullet)* alcanzar; *(of light)* caer sobre; **her head struck the floor** su cabeza chocó contra el suelo; **she struck her head on** *or* **against a branch** se dio *or* golpeó en la cabeza con una rama; **he was struck by a car** lo atropelló un coche *or Am* carro *or CSur* auto; **the tree was struck by lightning** el árbol fue alcanzado por un rayo

(**c**) *(a match)* encender, *Am* prender; *Br Old-fashioned Fam* **s. a light!** ¡recórcholis!

(**d**) *(mint) (coin, medal)* acuñar

(**e**) *(make sound)* **the clock struck ten/the hour** el reloj dio las diez/la hora; **she struck a few notes on the piano** le arrancó unas notas al piano; *Fig* **her remarks struck a false note** hizo unos comentarios fuera de todo; IDIOM **to s. the right note** *(speech, remark)* calar hondo; IDIOM **to s. the wrong note** *(speech, remark)* dar una nota discordante

(**f**) *(impress, surprise)* chocar, sorprender; **I was struck by her voice** lo que me chocó mucho fue su voz; **I was struck by his calm** me llamó la atención su calma; *Fam* **I wasn't very struck with her boyfriend** su novio no me hizo demasiada gracia

(**g**) *(occur to)* **it strikes me that...** se me ocurre que...; **I was struck by the thought that...** se me ocurrió que...; **only later did it s. me as unusual** no fue hasta más tarde cuando reparé en que era extraño; **it suddenly struck him how little had changed** de repente se dio cuenta que había cambiado muy poco

(**h**) *(seem to)* parecer; **it doesn't s. me as being very difficult** no me parece muy difícil; **he strikes me as a reasonable person** me da la impresión de que es una persona razonable; **how does their reaction s. you?** ¿qué te parece su reacción?; **we could all meet up later, how does that s. you?** ¿qué te parece si quedamos todos más tarde?

(**i**) *(discover) (gold, oil)* descubrir; *Fig* **to s. gold** *(find source of wealth)* descubrir una mina; *(win gold medal)* conquistar el oro; *Fam* **to s. it lucky** tener un golpe de suerte; *Fam* **to s. it rich** hacerse rico(a)

(**j**) *(cause to be)* **he was struck dead by a heart attack** murió de un ataque cardíaco fulminante; **the news struck us speechless with horror** el horror de la noticia nos dejó atónitos; **to be struck dumb** quedarse mudo(a), no poder articular palabra; **to s. terror into sb** aterrorizar a alguien

(**k**) *(affect) (of disaster, earthquake, disease)* sacudir; **the pain struck her as she tried to get up** le dio una punzada de dolor cuando intentó levantarse

(**l**) *(reach)* **to s. a balance** encontrar un equilibrio; **to s. a bargain** *or* **deal** hacer un trato

(**m**) *(adopt) (pose, attitude)* adoptar

(**n**) *(delete)* tachar (**from** de); **that remark must be struck** *or US* **stricken from the record** que no conste en acta el comentario

(**o**) *(take down)* **to s. camp** levantar el campamento; *Naut* **to s. the flag** *or* **the colours** arriar la bandera

(**p**) *Bot* **to s. roots** echar raíces

3 *vi* (**a**) *(attack) (enemy, criminal, animal)* atacar; *(earthquake, illness, disease)* sobrevenir; *(lightning)* caer; **the murderer struck again** el asesino actuó de nuevo; **she struck at me with her umbrella** me golpeó con el paraguas; **disaster struck** sobrevino un desastre; *Fig* **to s. at the heart of sth** atacar directamente a algo; **to s. home** *(missile, blow)* dar en el blanco; *(comment, message)* dar en la diana; IDIOM **s. while the iron is hot** aprovecha ahora que estás a tiempo

(**b**) *Sport (score)* marcar

(**c**) *(clock)* dar las horas; **midnight struck** dieron las doce de la medianoche

(**d**) *(go on strike)* hacer huelga, declararse en huelga; *(be on strike)* estar en huelga; **to s. against/for sth** estar en huelga contra/por algo

(**e**) *(collide)* **to s. against sth** golpear contra algo

(**f**) *(travel, head)* **to s. across country** ir campo a través; **they then struck west** después se dirigieron hacia el oeste

► **strike back** *vi* (**a**) *(retaliate)* devolver el ataque

(**b**) *Sport (score in response)* **they struck back within minutes of conceding a goal** respondieron marcando a los pocos minutos de encajar un gol

► **strike down** *vt sep* (**a**) *(of disease)* abatir, abatirse sobre; *(of lightning, bullet)* alcanzar; **she was struck down by cancer** *(killed)* un cáncer acabó con ella (**b**) *US Law* revocar

► **strike off** **1** *vt sep* (**a**) *(doctor, lawyer)* inhabilitar; **to s. sb off a list** tachar a alguien de una lista

(**b**) *(sever)* cortar

(**c**) *Typ* imprimir

2 *vi (go)* **to s. off to the left** desviarse a la izquierda; **we struck off into the forest** nos adentramos en el bosque

► **strike on, strike upon** *vt insep (idea, plan, solution)* dar con

► **strike out** **1** *vt sep* (**a**) *(delete)* tachar

(**b**) *(in baseball)* eliminar a *(por cometer tres strikes), Am* ponchar

2 *vi* (**a**) *(hit out)* **to s. out at sb** arremeter contra alguien; **he struck out in all directions** arremetió en todas direcciones

(**b**) *(leave)* partir (**for** hacia); *(start swimming)* ponerse a nadar (**for** hacia); **she struck out across the fields** se marchó por entre los campos; **to s. out in a new direction** tomar un nuevo rumbo; **to s. out on one's own** independizarse

(**c**) *(in baseball)* quedar eliminado(a) *(por cometer tres strikes), Am* poncharse

(**d**) *US Fam (fail)* estrellarse

► **strike through** *vt sep (cross out)* tachar

► **strike up** **1** *vt insep (song)* arrancar con; *(friendship, conversation)* trabar, iniciar

2 *vi (band, orchestra)* empezar a tocar

► **strike upon** = **strike on**

---

strikebound ['straɪkbaʊnd] *adj* paralizado(a) por una huelga

strikebreaker ['straɪkbreɪkə(r)] *n* esquirol *mf*

strikeout ['straɪkaʊt] *n (in baseball)* strikeout *m*

striker ['straɪkə(r)] *n* (**a**) *(striking worker)* huelguista *mf* (**b**) *(in soccer)* delantero(a) *m,f* centro, ariete *mf*

strike-through ['straɪkθru:] *n Comptr* **s. mode** efecto *m* de tachado

striking ['straɪkɪŋ] *adj* (**a**) *(noticeable, surprising)* chocante, sorprendente; *(impressive)* deslumbrante; **it bears a s. resemblance to...** guarda un parecido increíble *or* asombroso con...; **a s. example of Baroque architecture** un ejemplo deslumbrante de arquitectura barroca; **the s. thing about this is...** lo chocante del asunto es...; **the most s. feature of his work is...** el rasgo más notable de su obra es...; **she's very s.** es una mujer (de una belleza) fuera de lo común

(**b**) *(worker)* en huelga

(**c**) IDIOMS **she lives within s. distance of London** vive a un tiro de piedra de Londres; **they are within s. distance of finding a solution** tienen la solución al alcance de la mano

strikingly ['straɪkɪŋlɪ] *adv (obvious, similar, original)* sorprendentemente; **a s. beautiful woman** una mujer increíblemente hermosa

strimmer ['strɪmə(r)] *n* desbrozadora *f*

Strine [straɪn] *n Hum* argot *m* australiano

string [strɪŋ] **1** *n* (**a**) *(substance)* cuerda *f*; **a (piece of) s.** una cuerda ►► ***s. bag*** bolsa *f* de red; *US* ***s. tie*** lazo *m*; *Br* ***s. vest*** camiseta *f* interior de rejilla

(**b**) *(of puppet)* hilo *m*; *(on apron, pyjamas)* tira *f*, cordón *m*; IDIOM *Fam* **to have sb on a s.** tener a alguien a los pies; IDIOM **with no strings attached** sin compromiso; IDIOM **to pull strings** mover hilos

(**c**) *(of tennis racket, archer's bow)* cuerda *f*

(**d**) *Mus (of violin, guitar)* cuerda *f*; **the strings** la sección de cuerda, las cuerdas; IDIOM **to have more than one s. to one's bow** tener varios recursos ►► ***s. band*** *(of popular music)* rondalla *f*; ***s. instrument*** instrumento *m* de cuerda; ***s. orchestra*** orquesta *f* de cuerda; ***s. quartet*** cuarteto *m* de cuerda; ***s. section*** sección *f* de cuerda

(**e**) *(row) (of garlic, onions, sausages)* ristra *f*; *(of pearls, beads)* sarta *f*; *(of lights)* guirnalda *f*; *(of islands)* rosario *m*

(**f**) *(series) (of words, defeats, mistakes)* serie *f*; *(of wins)* racha *f*; *(of insults, lies)* retahíla *f*, sarta *f*; **we have had a s. of visitors over the past few weeks** en las últimas semanas hemos recibido una visita tras otra

(**g**) *(group) (of shops)* grupo *m*; *(of racehorses)* cuadra *f*

(**h**) *Comptr (of characters)* cadena *f*

(**i**) *(of plant, bean)* hebra *f* ▸▸ ***s. bean*** *Esp* judía *f* verde, *Bol, RP* chaucha *f*, *Chile* poroto *m* verde, *Carib, Col* habichuela *f*, *Méx* ejote *m*

(**j**) *Phys* cuerda *f* ▸▸ ***s. theory*** teoría *f* de cuerdas

2 *vt* (*pp & pt* **strung** [strʌŋ]) (**a**) *(violin, guitar, tennis racket, bow)* encordar; **I like my tennis racket tightly strung** me gusta que mi raqueta tenga el cordaje muy tenso

(**b**) *(pearls, beads)* ensartar

(**c**) *(hang)* **Christmas lights had been strung across the street** habían colgado las luces de Navidad de un lado a otro de la calle; **they strung him from a lamppost** lo colgaron de una farola

(**d**) *(beans)* deshebrar

▸ **string along** *Fam* **1** *vt sep* dar falsas esperanzas a

2 *vi (tag along)* **do you mind if I s. along (with you)?** ¿te importa si me apunto?

▸ **string out** *vt sep* (**a**) *(in space)* **the houses are strung out along the roadside** las casas se extienden alineadas a lo largo de la carretera (**b**) *(in time)* prolongar, alargar; **the TV series was strung out over six weeks** alargaron la serie de televisión seis semanas

▸ **string together** *vt sep* **they have finally managed to s. a couple of wins together** al fin han conseguido encadenar un par de victorias consecutivas; **I was so drunk, I couldn't s. two sentences together** estaba tan borracho que apenas podía hilvanar una frase; *Fam* **he can't s. two words together** *(in foreign language)* no sabe ni jota, no puede hilar dos palabras

▸ **string up** *vt sep* (**a**) *(lights)* colgar (**b**) *Fam (criminal)* ahorcar

-stringed [-strɪŋd] *suffix* **a five-s. instrument** un instrumento de cinco cuerdas

stringed [strɪŋd] *adj (instrument)* de cuerda

stringency ['strɪndʒənsɪ] *n* (**a**) *(severity)* rigor *m*, severidad *f* (**b**) *Econ* rigor *m*, austeridad *f*

stringent ['strɪndʒənt] *adj* (**a**) *(rules)* riguroso(a), estricto(a) (**b**) *Econ (measures, conditions)* riguroso(a), austero(a); **in today's s. economic climate** en el actual clima de austeridad económica

stringently ['strɪndʒəntlɪ] *adv (to test, enforce)* rigurosamente

stringer ['strɪŋə(r)] *n* (**a**) *(beam)* riostra *f* (**b**) *Journ* coresponsal *mf* local *or* de zona

string-pulling ['strɪŋpʊlɪŋ] *n Esp* enchufismo *m*, *Am* palanca *f*

stringy ['strɪŋɪ] *adj* (**a**) *(meat)* fibroso(a); *(vegetable)* con muchas hebras (**b**) *(hair)* lacio(a)

strip[1] [strɪp] *n* (**a**) *(of cloth, paper, metal)* tira *f*; *(of land)* franja *f*; *(of water)* brazo *m*; *Av (landing strip)* pista *f* de aterrizaje; **tear the paper into strips** rompe el papel en tiras; IDIOM *Fam* **to tear sb off a s., to tear a s. off sb** echar un rapapolvo a alguien, *Méx* repelar a alguien, *RP* pegar un levante a alguien ▸▸ ***s. light*** fluorescente *m*; ***s. lighting*** iluminación *f* con fluorescentes; ***s. mining*** explotación *f* minera a cielo abierto

(**b**) *Br (of sports team)* indumentaria *f*, equipaje *m*

(**c**) **s. (cartoon)** tira *f* cómica

strip[2] **1** *n* **to do a s.** *(undress)* hacer un striptease ▸▸ ***s. club*** club *m* de striptease; *Fam* ***s. joint*** club *m* de striptease; ***s. poker*** strip póquer *m*; ***s. show*** (espectáculo *m* de) striptease *m*

2 *vt* (*pt & pp* **stripped**) (**a**) *(undress) (person)* desnudar; **they were stripped to the waist** los desnudaron de cintura para arriba; **to s. sb naked** desnudar a alguien

(**b**) *(paint, wallpaper)* rascar, quitar, *Am* sacar; *(door, furniture, walls)* raspar; *(bed)* deshacer *(quitando las sábanas)*; *(house, room)* vaciar; **the ants had stripped the tree of its bark/leaves** las hormigas habían dejado el árbol sin corteza/hojas; **thieves have stripped the house bare** los ladrones han vaciado la casa

(**c**) *(deprive)* **to s. sb of sth** *(rank, honour)* despojar a alguien de algo; **stripped of its captain, the team lacked cohesion** privado de su capitán, el equipo carecía de cohesión

(**d**) *(dismantle) (engine, gun)* desmontar

(**e**) *(damage) (gear)* dejar desgranado(a)

(**f**) *(sell off) (assets)* vender, liquidar

3 *vi* (**a**) *(undress)* desnudarse; **to s. to the waist** desnudarse de cintura para arriba (**b**) *(do striptease)* hacer striptease

▸ **strip down** *vt sep (car engine)* desmontar

▸ **strip off** **1** *vt sep* (**a**) *(clothes)* quitar, *Am* sacar; **he stripped off his shirt** se quitó la camisa (**b**) *(paint, wallpaper)* rascar, quitar, *Am* sacar; **the ants stripped the bark/leaves off the tree** las hormigas dejaron el árbol sin corteza/hojas

2 *vi* (**a**) *(undress)* desnudarse, desvestirse (**b**) *(paint)* desconcharse

▸ **strip out** *vt sep (wiring)* quitar

stripe [straɪp] *n* (**a**) *(on cloth, animal's coat)* raya *f*, lista *f* (**b**) *(indicating rank)* galón *m*; **to get/lose one's stripes** ganarse/perder los galones (**c**) *(kind)* **they are of the same political s.** tienen las mismas ideas políticas

striped [straɪpt] *adj* a rayas; **s. with blue** a rayas azules

stripling ['strɪplɪŋ] *n* mozalbete *m*

strippagram, strippergram ['strɪpəgræm] *n* = regalo consistente en contratar a un/una artista de striptease que actúe para la persona homenajeada

stripped [strɪpt] *adj (pine)* natural, sin barnizar

stripped-down ['strɪpt'daʊn] *adj* desmontado(a); **a s. version** una versión simplificada *or* básica

stripper ['strɪpə(r)] *n* (**a**) *(striptease artist)* artista *mf* de striptease (**b**) *(for paint) (liquid)* aguarrás *m inv*; *(tool)* rascador *m*

strippergram = **strippagram**

strip-search ['strɪp'sɜːtʃ] **1** *n* registro *m* integral

2 *vt* **to s. sb** someter a alguien a un registro integral

striptease ['strɪptiːz] *n* strip-tease *m* ▸▸ ***s. artist*** artista *mf* de striptease

stripy ['straɪpɪ] *adj* a *or* de rayas; **its coat is s.** tiene el pelaje a rayas

strive [straɪv] (*pt* **strove** [strəʊv], *pp* **striven** ['strɪvən]) *vi* esforzarse; **to s. to do sth** esforzarse por hacer algo; **to s. for** *or* **after sth** luchar por algo; **to s. for effect** buscar el efecto a toda costa; **to s. against sth** luchar contra algo

strobe [strəʊb] *n* (**a**) *(in disco)* **s. (light)** luz *f* estroboscópica ▸▸ ***s. lighting*** luces *fpl* estroboscópicas (**b**) *(stroboscope)* estroboscopio *m*

stroboscope ['strəʊbəskəʊp] *n* estroboscopio *m*

strode *pt of* **stride**

stroganoff, stroganov ['strɒgənɒf] *n* **(beef) s.** ternera *f* strogonoff

stroke [strəʊk] **1** *n* (**a**) *(tennis shot, in golf)* golpe *m* ▸▸ ***s. index*** *(in golf)* índice *m* de golpes

(**b**) *(movement in swimming)* brazada *f*; *(swimming style)* estilo *m*

(**c**) *(in rowing) (movement)* palada *f*; *(oarsman)* cabo *mf*; IDIOM **to put sb off their s.** desconcentrar a alguien ▸▸ ***s. rate*** número *m* de brazadas por minuto

(**d**) *(blow)* golpe *m*; **he was given 50 strokes** le dieron 50 azotes; **a s. of lightning** un rayo

(**e**) *(of clock, bell)* campanada *f*; **on the s. of nine** al dar las nueve

(**f**) *(of brush) Art* pincelada *f*; *(of decorator)* brochazo *m*; *(of pen)* trazo *m*; *(of letter, character)* rabo *m*

(**g**) *(of piston)* tiempo *m*

(**h**) *Typ (oblique)* barra *f* inclinada

(**i**) *(piece, example)* **a s. of genius** una genialidad; **a s. of luck** un golpe de suerte; **by a s. of luck, she had remembered to take the key** por suerte, se había acordado de coger la llave; **she hasn't done a s. of work** no ha dado ni golpe; **at a s.** de un golpe

(**j**) *(caress)* caricia *f*; **to give sth/sb a s.** acariciar algo/a alguien

(**k**) *Med* derrame *m* cerebral, apoplejía *f*; **to have a s.** sufrir un derrame cerebral

2 *vt* (**a**) *(caress)* acariciar; **he stroked his chin pensively** se acarició la barbilla pensativamente; *Fig* **to s. sb's ego** alimentar el ego de alguien (**b**) *(ball) (in soccer)* tocar; *(in tennis, golf)* golpear con suavidad

strokeplay ['strəʊkpleɪ] *n (in golf)* stroke play *m*, juego *m* por golpes

stroll [strəʊl] **1** *n* paseo *m*; **to go for a s.** ir a dar un paseo

2 *vi* caminar; **I strolled down to the beach** fui caminando tranquilamente a la playa; **to s. in/out** entrar/salir tranquilamente; **she strolled up to me and asked if I was all right** se me acercó tranquilamente y me preguntó cómo estaba

stroller ['strəʊlə(r)] *n* (**a**) *(walker)* paseante *mf* (**b**) *US* silla *f* *or* sillita *f* de paseo

STRONG [strɒŋ] **1** *adj* (**a**) *(physically or mentally powerful)* fuerte; *(friendship)* sólido(a), estrecho(a); *(links)* estrecho(a); **he's the s., silent type** es de esos tipos fuertes y callados; **you'll have to be s. now** *(when consoling or encouraging)* ahora tienes que ser fuerte; **you've got to be s. and say "no"** tienes que ser fuerte y decir "no"; **to have a s. will** tener mucha voluntad; **to have a s. stomach** tener buen estómago; **you need a s. stomach to watch this film** hay que tener mucho estómago para ver esta película; IDIOM **to be as s. as a horse** *or* **an ox** ser *or* estar fuerte como un toro (**b**) *(healthy) (person, heart)* sano(a), fuerte; **she has a s. constitution** es de constitución fuerte; **I feel much stronger now** ahora me siento mucho más fuerte

(**c**) *(intense) (colour, light)* intenso(a); *(smell, drink, taste, medicine)* fuerte; *(glasses, lens, magnet)* potente; *(emotions, desire)* intenso(a); *(belief, support)* firme; *(protest, measures, language, impact, temptation)* fuerte; **I feel a s. sense of responsibility towards her** me siento muy responsable por lo que le pueda pasar

(**d**) *(forceful) (wind, current, character)* fuerte; *(opinions)* firme; **to have a s. personality** tener mucha personalidad; **he is a s. supporter of privatisation** es un ferviente partidario de las privatizaciones; **to have s. feelings on** *or* **about sth** tener una opinión muy clara sobre algo; **I wrote him a s. letter** le escribí una carta contundente; **the book is s. stuff** es un libro muy fuerte; **he expressed himself in the strongest terms** utilizó términos tajantes *or* contundentes ▸▸ *Phys* ***s. nuclear force*** fuerza *f* nuclear fuerte

(**e**) *(durable) (rope, cloth, shoes)* fuerte, resistente; *(nerves)* de acero

(**f**) *(pronounced) (nose, chin)* pronunciado(a); *(resemblance, accent, tendency)* marcado(a), fuerte; **there is a s. possibility that he will resign** es muy probable que dimita; **there is a s. element of truth in what you say** hay mucho de verdad en lo que dices

(**g**) *(convincing) (evidence, argument, reasons)* convincente

(**h**) *(good) (team, currency, economy)* fuerte; *(eyesight, memory)* muy bueno(a); **several s. candidates applied** se presentaron varios candidatos muy bien preparados; **he's a s. swimmer** es un buen nadador; **she's s. at physics** se le da muy bien la física; **the film was s. on style but weak on content** la película tenía un estilo conseguido pero un contenido flojo; **they have a s. case** *(in trial)* tienen una defensa/acusación muy sólida; *(in argument, debate)* tienen unos argumentos muy sólidos; **they are in a s. position (to win the league)** están en una posición muy favorable (para ganar la liga) ▸▸ ***s. point*** (punto *m*) fuerte *m*; ***s. suit*** (punto *m*) fuerte *m*

(**i**) *(referring to number)* **the group is thirty s.** el grupo cuenta con treinta miembros

(**j**) *Ling (verb)* irregular

2 *adv* **to be still going s.** *(person)* estar todavía en forma; *(company, institution)* seguir funcionando muy bien; **the favourite was going s. as they turned into the home straight** cuando tomaron la recta final el favorito venía muy fuerte

3 *npl* **the s.** los fuertes

---

strongarm ['strɒŋɑːm] **1** *adj* implacable, inflexible; **to use s. tactics** emplear mano dura

2 *vt* **to s. sb into doing sth** obligar por la fuerza a alguien a hacer algo

strongbox ['strɒŋbɒks] *n* caja *f* fuerte

stronghold ['strɒŋhəʊld] *n* (**a**) *(fortress)* fortaleza *f* (**b**) *(of political party, religion)* baluarte *m*, bastión *m*

strongly ['strɒŋlɪ] *adv* (**a**) *(robustly)* fuertemente; **s. built** *(wall, structure)* sólidamente construido(a); *(person)* de complexión robusta

(**b**) *(forcefully) (to oppose, endorse)* rotundamente, fuertemente; *(to attack, criticize)* con vehemencia; *(to deny)* categóricamente, tajantemente; **I cannot emphasize s. enough how important this is** no me cansaré de repetir lo importante que es esto; **a s. worded letter** una carta escrita en un tono fuerte; **wearing a seatbelt is s. recommended** se recomienda encarecidamente llevar el cinturón de seguridad abrochado; **I s. advise you to reconsider** le ruego encarecidamente que recapacite; **I s. disagree with you** estoy totalmente en desacuerdo contigo; **to be s. in favour of sth** estar completamente a favor de algo; **to argue s. for** apoyar sin reservas; **to argue s. against** oponerse totalmente a

(**c**) *(deeply) (to believe)* firmemente; *(to regret)* de veras; **he feels very s. about it** (es un tema que) le preocupa mucho

(**d**) *(intensely)* **the kitchen smelt s. of bleach** la cocina despedía un fuerte olor a lejía; **he smelled s. of drink** despedía un fuerte aliento a alcohol; **it's s. reminiscent of his earlier work** recuerda mucho a sus primeras obras; **I am s. tempted to say yes** tengo la enorme tentación de decir que sí; **I am s. attracted to him** me siento enormemente atraída hacia él

(**e**) *(prominently)* **rail travel features s. in the government's transport plan** el ferrocarril figura de manera destacada en el plan de transportes del gobierno

strongman ['strɒŋmæn] *n* (**a**) *(in circus)* forzudo *m* (**b**) *(dictator)* caudillo *m*

strong-minded ['strɒŋ'maɪndɪd] *adj* decidido(a), resuelto(a)

strong-mindedly [strɒŋ'maɪndɪdlɪ] *adv* resueltamente

strongroom ['strɒŋruːm] *n* cámara *f* acorazada

strong-willed ['strɒŋ'wɪld] *adj* tenaz, tozudo(a)

strontium ['strɒntɪəm] *n Chem* estroncio *m*

strop [strɒp] **1** *n* (**a**) *(leather strap)* asentador *m* (**b**) *Br Fam (bad temper)* **to be in a s.** estar de mal humor *or Esp* de mal café

2 *vt (razor)* afilar

stroppy ['strɒpɪ] *adj Br Fam* **to be s.** *(by nature)* tener mal genio *or Esp* mal café; *(in a mood)* estar de mal humor *or Esp* de mal café; **there's no need to get s. about it!** ¡no hay por qué ponerse así!

strove *pt of* **strive**

struck *pt & pp of* **strike**

structural ['strʌktʃərəl] *adj* estructural; **we are making some s. improvements to the house** estamos mejorando la estructura de la casa ▸▸ *Econ* ***s. adjustment programme*** programa *m* de ajuste estructural; ***s. damage*** daños *mpl* estructurales; ***s. engineer*** ingeniero(a) *m,f* estructural; *EU* ***s. funds*** fondos *mpl* estructurales; ***s. linguistics*** lingüística *f* estructural; ***s. survey*** peritaje *m or* tasación *f* de estructuras; ***s. unemployment*** desempleo *m or Esp* paro *m* estructural

structuralism ['strʌktʃərəlɪzəm] *n* estructuralismo *m*

structuralist ['strʌktʃərəlɪst] **1** *n* estructuralista *mf*

2 *adj* estructuralista

structurally ['strʌktʃərəlɪ] *adv (similar, well written)* estructuralmente; **there's nothing wrong with the house s., the house is s. sound** no hay ningún problema con la estructura de la casa

structure ['strʌktʃə(r)] **1** *n* (**a**) *(composition)* estructura *f* (**b**) *(building, monument)* construcción *f*

2 *vt* estructurar, articular

structured ['strʌktʃəd] *adj* estructurado(a) ▸▸ *Comptr* ***s. query language*** lenguaje *m* estructurado de consulta

strudel ['struːdəl] *n* strudel *m*, = rollo de hojaldre relleno de pasas y fruta y espolvoreado con canela

struggle ['strʌgəl] **1** *n (effort)* lucha *f* (**for** por); *(physical fight)* forcejeo *m*; **armed s.** lucha armada; **life is a s.** la vida es una lucha constante; **it was a s. to get there on time** nos costó mucho llegar allí a tiempo; **without a s.** sin oponer resistencia; **I finally succeeded but not without a s.** al final lo conseguí, pero me costó lo mío; **she won't give up without a s.** no dará su brazo a torcer fácilmente; **to put up a s.** ofrecer resistencia

2 *vi* (**a**) *(try hard)* luchar (**for** por); **to s. to do sth** luchar por hacer algo

(**b**) *(move with effort)* **to s. free** forcejear hasta lograr liberarse; **he struggled back up onto the raft** consiguió a duras penas volver a subir a la balsa; **to s. to one's feet** levantarse a duras penas; **they struggled through the gap** pasaron por la abertura no sin esfuerzo; **he struggled into his clothes** se hizo un lío al ponerse la ropa

(**c**) *(fight physically)* forcejear (**with** con); **to s. with one's conscience** luchar con la conciencia de uno

(**d**) *(have difficulty)* **he struggled with the lock** tuvo problemas con la cerradura; **to be struggling** *(person, company)* estar pasándolo muy mal; **he was struggling to finish the assignment** le estaba costando mucho terminar la tarea; **he was obviously struggling for** *or* **to find the right word** obviamente le costaba encontrar la palabra adecuada

▸**struggle along** *vi (in life, with work)* ir tirando

▸**struggle on** *vi (keep trying)* perseverar

▸**struggle through** *vi (in difficult situation)* apañárselas

struggling ['strʌglɪŋ] *adj* (**a**) *(in difficulty) (company, team)* en apuros (**b**) *(hard up) (painter, writer)* sin recursos

strum [strʌm] *(pt & pp* **strummed**) **1** *vt (guitar)* rasguear; **to s. a tune** rasguear una melodía (a la guitarra)

2 *vi* **she started strumming on her guitar** se puso a rasguear la guitarra; **to s. along to a melody** acompañar una melodía rasgueando la guitarra

strumpet ['strʌmpɪt] *n Old-fashioned or Hum* cualquiera *f*, mujer *f* de vida alegre

strung *pt & pp of* **string**

strung-out ['strʌŋ'aʊt] *adj Fam* (**a**) *(addicted)* enganchado(a) (**on** a) (**b**) *(tense)* tenso(a), agobiado(a)

strung-up ['strʌŋ'ʌp] *adj Fam (tense)* tenso(a), agobiado(a)

strut[1] [strʌt] *n* (**a**) *(for building, roof)* puntal *m* (**b**) *Av* montante *m*

strut[2] *(pt & pp* **strutted**) **1** *vt* IDIOM *Fam* **to s. one's stuff** *(dancer, model)* menearse con sensualidad

2 *vi* pavonearse; **he struts about as if he owns the place** se pasea de aquí para allá todo ufano como si fuera el rey del mambo; **to s. in/out** entrar/salir pavoneándose

strychnine ['strɪkniːn] *n* estricnina *f*

Stuart ['stjʊət] *pr n* **the Stuarts** los Estuardo

stub [stʌb] **1** *n* **(a)** *(of pencil)* punta *f* final; *(of cigarette)* colilla *f*; *(of candle)* cabo *m* **(b)** *(of cheque, ticket)* matriz *f*
2 *vt* *(pt & pp* **stubbed)** **to s. one's toe (on** *or* **against sth)** darse un golpe en el dedo gordo (contra algo)

▸ **stub out** *vt sep (cigarette)* apagar, aplastar

stubble ['stʌbəl] *n* **(a)** *(in field)* rastrojo *m* **(b)** *(on face)* barba *f* incipiente

stubbly ['stʌblɪ] *adj (beard)* de unos días; *(chin)* con barba incipiente

stubborn ['stʌbən] *adj* **(a)** *(person)* testarudo(a), terco(a); *(animal)* terco(a); *(determination, resistance, refusal)* obstinado(a), pertinaz; *(silence)* obstinado(a); IDIOM **as s. as a mule** terco(a) como una mula **(b)** *(stain, cold, cough)* persistente

stubbornly ['stʌbənlɪ] *adv (obstinately) (of person)* testarudamente, tercamente; *(of animal)* tercamente; **she was s. determined to finish** se obstinaba *or* se empeñaba en terminar; **he s. refused to listen to me** se negó testarudamente a escucharme; **the stain s. refuses to wash out** la mancha se empeña en no desaparecer

stubbornness ['stʌbənnɪs] *n* **(a)** *(of person)* testarudez *f*; *(of animal)* terquedad *f*; *(of determination, resistance, refusal)* obstinación *f* **(b)** *(of cold, cough)* persistencia *f*

stubby ['stʌbɪ] *adj (person, finger)* regordete(a); *(tail)* corto(a); *(pencil)* gastado(a)

stucco ['stʌkəʊ] **1** *n* estuco *m*; **a s. ceiling** un techo de estuco
2 *vt* estucar

stuccoed ['stʌkəʊd] *adj* estucado(a)

stuck [stʌk] **1** *adj* **(a)** *(jammed, immobile)* atascado(a); **the window was s.** la ventana estaba atascada; **to get s.** atascarse; **he got his hand s. inside the jar** se le quedó la mano atascada en el tarro; *Fig* **I got s. on the last question** me quedé atascado en la última pregunta; **to be s. at home** estar metido(a) en casa sin poder salir; **to be s. in traffic** estar atrapado(a) en un atasco; **they were** *or* **they got s. at the airport overnight** tuvieron que pasar la noche en el aeropuerto; *Fig* **to be s. in a boring job** estar atrapado(a) en un trabajo aburrido
(b) *Fam (without)* **he's never s. for an answer** tiene respuestas para todo; **to be s. for cash** *Esp* estar sin blanca, *Am* andar sin plata; **to be s. for something to say/do** no saber qué decir/hacer
(c) *Fam (lumbered)* **to be s. with sth/sb** tener que cargar con algo/alguien; **it's not a very good plan but we're s. with it** no es muy buen plan, pero tendremos que apañarnos
(d) *Fam (fond, keen)* **to be s. on sb** estar loco(a) por alguien; **I'm not exactly s. on the idea** no me entusiasma la idea
(e) IDIOMS *Fam* **to get s. into sb** *(physically) Esp* emprenderla a golpes con alguien, *Am* empezar a los golpes con alguien; *(verbally)* arremeter contra alguien; *Fam* **to get s. into sth** darle a algo; *Fam* **get s. in!** ¡al ataque!
2 *pt & pp of* **stick**[2]

stuck-up ['stʌk'ʌp] *adj Fam* creído(a), engreído(a)

stud[1] [stʌd] **1** *n* **(a)** *(fastener) (for collar, shirt)* automático *m*, corchete *m* **(b)** *(for decoration)* tachón *m* **(c)** *(on soccer, rugby boots) Esp* taco *m*, *RP* tapón *m* **(d)** *(earring) Esp* pendiente *m*, *Am* arete *m*
2 *vt (shoes, belt, door, chest)* tachonar; *Fig* **stars studded the night sky** el cielo estaba tachonado de estrellas

stud[2] *n* **(a)** *(farm)* **s. (farm)** cuadra *f* **(b)** *(stallion)* semental *m* **(c)** *Fam (man)* semental *m* ▸▸ *US Fam* ***s. muffin*** buen mozo *m* **(d)** *(card game)* ***s. poker*** póquer *m* descubierto

studbook ['stʌdbʊk] *n* libro *m* de registro de pedigrí

-studded [-'stʌdɪd] *suffix* **diamond-s.** incrustado(a) de diamantes; **star-s.** *(sky)* tachonado(a) de estrellas; **a star-s. cast** un reparto estelar, un reparto plagado de estrellas

studded ['stʌdɪd] *adj (jacket, belt)* tachonado(a); **to be s. with** estar tachonado(a) con *or* de

student ['stju:dənt] *n (at university)* estudiante *mf*; *(at school)* alumno(a) *m,f*, estudiante *mf*; **law/medical s.** estudiante de derecho/medicina; **in her s. days** en sus días de estudiante; **a s. of human nature** un estudioso de la naturaleza humana ▸▸ *esp US* ***the s. body*** el cuerpo estudiantil; ***s. card*** carné *m* de estudiante; *US* ***s. driver*** conductor(ora) *m,f* en prácticas; ***s. grant*** beca *f* de estudios; ***s. life*** la vida estudiantil; ***s. loan*** préstamo *m* para estudiantes; ***s. nurse*** estudiante *mf* de enfermería; ***s. teacher*** profesor(ora) *m,f* en prácticas; ***students' union*** *(association)* = en una universidad, asociación que organiza actividades, asesora y representa a los estudiantes; *(place)* = edificio para los estudiantes que cuenta con bares, discoteca, servicios y oficinas

studentship ['stju:dəntʃɪp] *n Br (scholarship)* beca *f*

studenty ['stju:dəntɪ] *adj Fam (area, bar)* de estudiantes, estudiantil

studhorse ['stʌdhɔ:s] *n* semental *m*

studied ['stʌdi:d] *adj (manner, politeness, ease)* estudiado(a)

studio ['stju:dɪəʊ] *(pl* **studios)** *n* **(a)** *(of TV, movie company)* estudio *m*, plató *m* ▸▸ *TV* ***s. audience*** público *m* en estudio **(b)** *(for recording music)* estudio *m* **(c)** *(of artist, photographer)* estudio *m* **(d)** *(flat, apartment)* **s. (apartment** *or Br* **flat)** (apartamento *m*) estudio *m* ▸▸ ***s. couch*** sofá *m* cama

studious ['stju:dɪəs] *adj* **(a)** *(diligent)* estudioso(a) **(b)** *(deliberate) (avoidance, indifference)* deliberado(a), cuidadoso(a) **(c)** *(painstaking) (attention, effort)* concienzudo(a)

studiously ['stju:dɪəslɪ] *adv* **(a)** *(diligently)* afanosamente, diligentemente **(b)** *(deliberately) (to ignore, avoid)* deliberadamente, cuidadosamente; **he remained s. indifferent to her offer** se mostró deliberadamente indiferente ante su oferta

studiousness ['stju:djəsnɪs] *n (eagerness to study)* estudiosidad *f*

study ['stʌdɪ] **1** *n* **(a)** *(academic work)* estudio *m*; **she devotes most evenings to s.** dedica casi todas las tardes al estudio; **how are your studies going?** ¿cómo te van los estudios? ▸▸ ***s. group*** grupo *m* de estudio; *US* ***s. hall*** *(room)* sala *f* de estudio *or* estudios; *(period)* hora *f* de estudio; ***s. period*** hora *f* de estudio; ***s. room*** sala *f* de estudio *or* estudios; ***s. tour*** viaje *m* de estudio; ***s. trip*** excursión *f* de estudios
(b) *(investigation)* estudio *m*, investigación *f*; *(written report)* estudio *m*, informe *m*, *CAm, Méx* reporte *m*; **to make a s. of sth** realizar un estudio sobre algo; **the plan is under s.** el plan se está estudiando; **business studies** (ciencias) empresariales; **peace studies** estudios sobre la paz
(c) *(by artist)* estudio *m*; *Fig* **her face was a s. in disbelief** su cara era la viva imagen de la incredulidad
(d) *(room)* (cuarto *m* de) estudio *m*
2 *vt* **(a)** *(at school, university)* estudiar; **I'm studying French** estudio francés **(b)** *(investigate)* estudiar; **the problem hasn't been studied very much** el problema no se ha estudiado en detalle **(c)** *(examine) (plan, evidence, situation)* estudiar, analizar; *(expression, reactions)* estudiar, observar con detenimiento
3 *vi* estudiar; **to s. for an exam** prepararse un examen, estudiar para un examen; **he's studying for a degree in history** está estudiando para ser licenciado en historia; **to s. to be a lawyer** estudiar para abogado; **she studied under Messiaen** estudió con Messiaen

STUFF [stʌf] **1** *n* **(a)** *Fam (substance)* cosa *f*; **what's this s.?** ¿qué es esto?; **what's that black s. on your trousers?** ¿qué es eso negro que tienes en los pantalones?; **I've got a lot of s. to do tonight** tengo que hacer un montón de cosas esta noche; **he reads all that intellectual s.** se dedica a leer todas esas cosas de intelectuales; **there was some s. about unions on the news** dijeron algo de los sindicatos en las noticias; **do you call that s. art/music?** ¿y a eso lo llamas arte/música?; **he's the s. that heroes are made of** tiene madera de héroe; **marriage and all that s.** el matrimonio y todo ese rollo; **don't give me (all) that s. about the good of the nation!** ¡no me vengas con el rollo ese del bien de la nación!; **...and s. (like that)** ...y cosas por el estilo; **caviar? I hate the s.** ¿caviar?, me da asco; **this wine is good s.** este vino es del bueno; **she writes good s.** escribe bien; **good s.!** ¡genial!, *Andes, CAm, Carib, Méx* ¡chévere!, *Méx* ¡padrísimo!, *RP* ¡bárbaro!; **he knows his s.** conoce bien el tema; **go on, do your s.!** ¡vamos, tú, a lo tuyo!; **s. and nonsense!** ¡déjate de lloriqueos!; IDIOM **that's the s.!** ¡sí señor!, ¡eso es!; IDIOM *Fam* **I don't** *or* **couldn't give a s.!** ¡me importa un carajo!
(b) *Fam (objects, possessions)* cosas *fpl*; **where's my shaving/fishing s.?** ¿dónde están mis cosas de afeitar/pescar?
(c) *Formal (topic, matter)* **this is the very s. of politics** en esto consiste la política; **his ability to take his drink was the s. of legend** su capacidad para beber *or Am* tomar era legendaria
(d) *Old-fashioned (cloth)* tejido *m*
(e) *Fam (drugs)* material *m*, mandanga *f*, *RP* merca *f*
(f) *Br very Fam (female)* **she's a nice bit of s.** está muy buena
(g) *US Sport (spin)* efecto *m*
2 *vt* **(a)** *(fill) & Culin* rellenar **(with** con); *(cushion)* forrar, rellenar **(with** con); *(pockets)* llenar **(with** de); *(dead animal)* disecar; **a suitcase stuffed with clothes** una maleta *or Am* valija hasta arriba de ropa; **their house is stuffed with souvenirs from India** tienen la casa abarrotada de recuerdos de la India; **his teachers stuffed his head with a load of political nonsense** sus profesores le llenaron la cabeza de absurdas ideas políticas; *Fam* **to s. oneself** *or* **one's face (with sth)** atiborrarse (de algo), ponerse las botas (con algo)
(b) *(shove)* **to s. sth into sth** meter algo dentro de algo; **he stuffed the papers into his pocket** se apretujó los papeles en el bolsillo; *Fam* **just s. everything under the bed** apíñalo todo debajo de la cama
(c) *(plug) (gap, hole)* taponar
(d) *Fam (defeat heavily)* dar una paliza *or Esp* un repaso a

(e) *Br very Fam (expressing anger)* **s. him/them!** ¡que le/les den!; **s. it, we can do it tomorrow!** ¡a la mierda *or Esp* a tomar por saco, lo haremos mañana!; **you can s. your money!** ¡te puedes meter tu dinero por donde te quepa!; **get stuffed!, s. you!** ¡que te den!

(f) *Vulg (have sex with) Esp* follarse a, *Am* cogerse a, *Méx* chingarse a

(g) *US Pol (ballot box)* **to s. ballot boxes** rellenar con votos fraudulentos las urnas electorales

▶ **stuff up** *vt sep (block)* **my nose is all stuffed up, I'm all stuffed up** tengo la nariz taponada *or* bloqueada

---

stuffed [stʌft] *adj* (a) *(pepper, mushroom, olive)* relleno(a) (b) *(toy)* de peluche (c) *(animal)* disecado(a) (d) *Fam (full)* **I'm s.!** ¡estoy llenísimo(a)!, ¡no me cabe más! (e) *Fam Fig* ***s. shirt*** *(pompous person)* petulante *mf*, estirado(a) *m,f*

stuffily [ˈstʌfɪlɪ] *adv (to say, reply)* petulantemente, altaneramente

stuffiness [ˈstʌfɪnɪs] *n* (a) *(of room)* ambiente *m* cargado (b) *(of person)* carácter *m* retrógrado

stuffing [ˈstʌfɪŋ] *n* (a) *(for furniture, toys)* relleno *m*; IDIOM *Fam* **to knock the s. out of sb** *(blow)* dejar hecho(a) polvo a alguien; *(news, disappointment)* dejar a alguien con la moral por los suelos, *Am* dejar a alguien los ánimos por el piso (b) *(for chicken)* relleno *m*

stuffy [ˈstʌfɪ] *adj* (a) *(room)* cargado(a); **it's a bit s. in here** está un poco cargado el ambiente (b) *(person)* retrógrado(a), anticuado(a); *(atmosphere)* altanero(a); *(remark)* petulante (c) *(nose)* taponado(a), tapado(a); **my nose is s.** tengo la nariz tapada

stultify [ˈstʌltɪfaɪ] *vt Formal* (a) *(make stupid) (person, mind)* idiotizar (b) *(stifle) (creativity, talent)* atrofiar

stultifying [ˈstʌltɪfaɪɪŋ] *adj Formal* tedioso(a)

stumble [ˈstʌmbəl] 1 *n* tropezón *m*

2 *vi* (a) *(when walking)* tropezar; **to s. along** ir tropezando, ir a trompicones; **to s. into sth/sb** tropezar *or* toparse con algo/alguien; **he stumbled over the toys in the hall** tropezó con los juguetes que había en el recibidor; **he was stumbling about in the dark** iba tropezando con todo en la oscuridad

(b) *(when speaking)* trastabillar (**over** con); **he managed to s. through his lecture** consiguió acabar la conferencia a trancas y barrancas

▶ **stumble across, stumble (up)on** *vt insep (find)* tropezar con, toparse con

stumbling-block [ˈstʌmblɪŋblɒk] *n* escollo *m*

stump [stʌmp] 1 *n* (a) *(of tree)* tocón *m*; *(of arm, leg)* muñón *m*; *(of tail)* muñón *m*; *(of tooth)* raíz *f*; *(of pencil)* punta *f* final; *(of candle)* cabo *m* (b) *(in cricket)* estaca *f* (c) *US Pol* **to be on the s.** estar de campaña electoral

2 *vt* (a) *(baffle)* dejar perplejo(a); **I'm stumped** *(don't know answer)* no tengo ni idea; *(don't know what to do)* no se me ocurre nada; **to be stumped for an answer** no saber qué contestar (b) *US Pol (constituency, state)* recorrer en campaña electoral

3 *vi (move heavily)* **to s. off** marcharse dando grandes pisotones; **to s. in/out** entrar/salir airadamente

▶ **stump up** *Br Fam* 1 *vt insep* **to s. up the money (for sth)** poner *or Esp* apoquinar el dinero (para algo)

2 *vi (pay)* poner dinero, *Esp* apoquinar; **come on, s. up!** ¡vamos, a poner dinero!, *Esp* ¡venga, a apoquinar!

stumpy [ˈstʌmpɪ] *adj (person)* rechoncho(a); *(arms, legs)* regordete(a); *(pencil)* gastado(a)

stun [stʌn] (*pt & pp* **stunned**) *vt* (a) *(make unconscious)* dejar sin sentido ▶▶ ***s. grenade*** granada *f* aturdidora; ***s. gun*** pistola *f* inmovilizadora (b) *(shock)* dejar de piedra; **we were stunned by the news of their death** la noticia de su muerte nos dejó de piedra

stung *pt & pp of* **sting**

stunk *pp of* **stink**

stunned [stʌnd] *adj (person, expression)* atónito(a); **I was too s. to reply** me quedé tan atónito que no supe qué responder; **they watched in s. silence** miraban en silencio, estupefactos

stunner [ˈstʌnə(r)] *n Br Fam (person)* bombón *m*; *(car)* cochazo *m*; **the goal was a s.** fue un golazo

stunning [ˈstʌnɪŋ] *adj* (a) *(blow)* contundente; *Fig* **this has dealt a s. blow to the party** esto ha asestado un duro golpe al partido (b) *(performance, goal)* soberbio(a); *(woman, figure, outfit)* imponente; *(news, event)* sensacional; *(success, victory)* espectacular; **the model is absolutely s.** la modelo es absolutamente despampanante; **you look s. in that dress** estás preciosa en ese vestido

stunningly [ˈstʌnɪŋlɪ] *adv* **a s. good-looking man/beautiful woman** un hombre/una mujer imponente; **s. beautiful countryside** una campiña sobrecogedoramente hermosa; **a s. simple idea** una idea de una sencillez pasmosa

stunt[1] [stʌnt] *vt (person, growth)* atrofiar; *(intelligence)* afectar irreversiblemente

stunt[2] *n* (a) *(in movie)* escena *f* peligrosa; **to do a s.** rodar una escena peligrosa ▶▶ ***s. double*** doble *mf*; ***s. man*** especialista *m*, doble *m*; ***s. woman*** especialista *f*, doble *f* (b) *(in plane)* acrobacia *f* aérea ▶▶ ***s. pilot*** piloto *mf* acrobático (c) *(trick)* truco *m*; *(for publicity)* truco *m* publicitario; *Fam* **to pull a s. (on sb)** gastar una broma pesada (a alguien)

stunted [ˈstʌntɪd] *adj (person)* raquítico(a); *(growth)* truncado(a); *(plant)* esmirriado(a)

stupefaction [stjuːpɪˈfækʃən] *n* estupefacción *f*

stupefied [ˈstjuːpɪfaɪd] *adj* (a) *(tired, bored)* hastiado(a) (b) *(amazed)* estupefacto(a)

stupefy [ˈstjuːpɪfaɪ] *vt* (a) *(of alcohol, drugs, tiredness, blow)* aturdir (b) *(of behaviour)* dejar perplejo(a); *(of news)* dejar sobrecogido(a)

stupefying [ˈstjuːpɪfaɪɪŋ] *adj* (a) *(boring)* embotante (b) *(amazing)* asombroso(a)

stupendous [stjuːˈpendəs] *adj* extraordinario(a), impresionante; **we had a s. time** nos lo pasamos en grande

stupendously [stjuːˈpendəslɪ] *adv* extraordinariamente

stupid [ˈstjuːpɪd] 1 *adj* (a) *(person, suggestion)* estúpido(a), tonto(a); **don't be s.!** ¡no seas estúpido!; **how s. of me!** ¡qué tonto soy!; **you s. idiot!** ¡idiota!; **I was s. enough to believe her** fui tan tonto que la creí; **it was s. of me to forget** fue una estupidez que se me olvidara; **he's always saying/doing s. things** siempre está diciendo/haciendo tonterías; **what a s. thing to do!** ¡menuda estupidez!; **don't do anything s., will you?** no hagas ninguna tontería, ¿de acuerdo?; **to make sb feel/look s.** dejar en ridículo a alguien, hacer que alguien se sienta/parezca un imbécil; **I look s. in this dress** estoy ridícula en este vestido

(b) *Fam (expressing irritation)* dichoso(a), condenado(a); **take your s. book!** ¡toma tu dichoso *or* maldito libro!

(c) *(unconscious)* **to knock sb s.** dejar a alguien inconsciente; **to drink oneself s.** beber hasta perder el conocimiento; **I was bored s.** me aburría como una ostra

2 *n Fam* **I'm only joking, s.!** ¡lo digo en broma, tonto!

3 *adv* **to talk s.** decir tonterías

stupidity [stjuːˈpɪdɪtɪ] *n* estupidez *f*, imbecilidad *f*

stupidly [ˈstjuːpɪdlɪ] *adv (to grin, gawp)* tontamente; **I s. forgot to phone them** tonto de mí, olvidé llamarlos; **he had s. left the gas on** el muy burro se había dejado el gas encendido

stupor [ˈstjuːpə(r)] *n* aturdimiento *m*

sturdily [ˈstɜːdɪlɪ] *adv* (a) *(solidly)* **to be s. built** *(person)* ser robusto(a) *or* fornido(a); *(furniture)* ser resistente *or* sólido(a); *(house)* ser sólido(a) (b) *(firmly) (to deny, refuse, oppose)* categóricamente, tajantemente

sturdiness [ˈstɜːdɪnɪs] *n* (a) *(of person, limbs)* robustez *f*; *(of table, tree, shoes)* resistencia *f*, solidez *f* (b) *(of opposition, resistance)* firmeza *f*, solidez *f*

sturdy [ˈstɜːdɪ] *adj* (a) *(person, limbs)* robusto(a), fornido(a); *(table, tree, shoes)* resistente, sólido(a) (b) *(opposition, resistance)* firme, sólido(a); **with s. determination** inasequible al desaliento

sturgeon [ˈstɜːdʒən] *n* esturión *m*

stutter [ˈstʌtə(r)] 1 *n* tartamudeo *m*; **to have** *or* **speak with a s.** tartamudear

2 *vi (person)* tartamudear; *Fig* **the engine stuttered into life** el motor traqueteó hasta ponerse en marcha

3 *vt* balbucear; **she stuttered (out) an apology** balbuceó unas disculpas

stutterer [ˈstʌtərə(r)] *n* tartamudo(a) *m,f*

stuttering [ˈstʌtərɪŋ] 1 *n* tartamudeo *m*

2 *adj* (a) *(person, apology)* balbuceante (b) *(inconsistent) (start, performance)* titubeante, vacilante

stutteringly [ˈstʌtərɪŋlɪ] *adv (to say, apologize)* balbuceantemente

STV [estiːˈviː] *n* (*abbr* **single transferable vote**) voto *m* personal transferible (por listas)

St Valentine's Day [seɪntˈvæləntaɪnzdeɪ] *n* día *m* de San Valentín, día *m* de los enamorados

sty[1] [staɪ] *n* (a) *(pigsty)* pocilga *f* (b) *Fam (dirty place)* pocilga *f*

sty[2], **stye** [staɪ] *n (eye infection)* orzuelo *m*

Stygian [ˈstɪdʒɪən] *adj Literary* estigio(a)

-style [-staɪl] *suffix* **a sixties'-s. haircut** un corte de pelo al estilo de los (años) sesenta

style [staɪl] **1** *n* **(a)** *(manner)* estilo *m*; **he has a more aggressive management s.** tiene un estilo de dirección más agresivo; **I like your s.** me gusta tu estilo; **lying isn't his s.** mentir no es propio de él; **this is entertainment, nineties s.** esto es espectáculo, al estilo de los 90
(b) *(of writer, artist, musician)* estilo *m*; **in the s. of Rubens** al estilo *or* a la manera de Rubens
(c) *(design)* diseño *m*; *(hairstyle)* peinado *m*; **a new s. of dress** un nuevo estilo de vestido; **the boots come in two styles** hay dos modelos de estas botas
(d) *(fashion)* moda *f*; **to be dressed in the latest s.** estar vestido(a) a la última (moda); **to be in s.** estar de moda; **to go out of s.** pasarse de moda; **to come back into s.** volver a estar de moda; **that dress isn't your s.** ese vestido no te pega
(e) *(sophistication)* estilo *m*; **she has s.** tiene estilo; **to celebrate in s.** celebrar a lo grande *or* por todo lo alto; **to live/travel in s.** vivir/viajar con lujo; **he won the race in s.** ganó la carrera de calle; **he keeps me in the s. to which I am accustomed** él me mantiene en el lujo al que estoy acostumbrada
(f) *Typ (in editing)* estilo *m*; **house s.** estilo (editorial) de la casa ►► ***s. book*** libro *m* de estilo
(g) *Comptr* estilo *m* ►► ***s. sheet*** hoja *f* de estilos
(h) *Bot* estilo *m*
2 *vt* **(a)** *(design)* diseñar; *(hair)* peinar **(b)** *Formal (name)* denominar; **...as it is now styled** ...como se le llama *or* denomina ahora; **she styles herself "countess"** se hace llamar "condesa"

stylechecker ['staɪltʃekə(r)] *n Comptr* corrector *m* de estilo

style-conscious ['staɪl'kɒnʃəs] *adj* preocupado(a) por la moda

styling ['staɪlɪŋ] *n (of dress, car)* diseño *m* ►► ***s. brush*** rizador *m*; ***s. gel*** gel *m* moldeador; ***s. mousse*** espuma *f* (moldeadora)

stylish ['staɪlɪʃ] *adj (person, clothes, hotel, area)* elegante; *(book, film)* efectista; **he's a s. dresser** se viste con mucho estilo

stylishly ['staɪlɪʃlɪ] *adv (to dress)* elegantemente, con estilo; *(to live)* a todo lujo; *(written, filmed)* de manera efectista

stylishness ['staɪlɪʃnɪs] *n (of person, clothes, hotel, area)* elegancia *f*; *(of book, film)* efectismo *m*

stylist ['staɪlɪst] *n* **(a)** *(hairdresser)* peluquero(a) *m,f*, estilista *mf* **(b)** *(designer)* diseñador(ora) *m,f* **(c)** *(writer)* estilista *mf*

stylistic [staɪ'lɪstɪk] *adj* estilístico(a)

stylistically [staɪ'lɪstɪklɪ] *adv* desde el punto de vista estilístico

stylistics [staɪ'lɪstɪks] *n Ling* estilística *f*

stylization [staɪlaɪ'zeɪʃən] *n* carácter *m* convencional *or* estereotipado

stylized ['staɪlaɪzd] *adj* estilizado(a)

stylus ['staɪləs] *n* **(a)** *(for engraving)* estilo *m*, punzón *m* **(b)** *(on record player)* aguja *f*

stymie ['staɪmɪ] *vt* **(a)** *(in golf)* obstaculizar **(b)** *Fam (obstruct)* bloquear; **their refusal to help stymied our efforts** su negativa a cooperar truncó *or* frustró todos nuestros esfuerzos; **now we're really stymied!** ¡ahora sí que estamos apañados!

styptic ['stɪptɪk] **1** *n* astringente *m*
2 *adj* astringente ►► ***s. pencil*** barrita *f* astringente

Styrofoam® ['staɪrəfəʊm] *n esp US* espuma *f* de poliestireno

Styx [stɪks] *n (in mythology)* **the (River) S.** el río Estigio, la laguna Estigia

suave [swɑːv] *adj* **(a)** *(polite, charming)* fino(a), cortés; *Pej (smooth)* zalamero(a), lisonjero(a) **(b)** *(elegant) (clothes, dress sense)* elegante

> **False friend**: The Spanish word **suave** is not a translation for the English word **suave**. In Spanish **suave** means "soft", "mild", "smooth" or "gentle".

suavely ['swɑːvlɪ] *adv* **(a)** *(politely, charmingly)* cortésmente; *Pej (smoothly)* con zalamería **(b)** *(elegantly) (dressed)* elegantemente

suaveness ['swɑːvnɪs], **suavity** ['swɑːvətɪ] *n* **(a)** *(politeness, charm)* finura *f*, cortesía *f*; *Pej (smoothness)* zalamería *f* **(b)** *(elegance) (of dress)* elegancia *f*

sub- [sʌb-] *prefix* sub-; **to run a s.-four minute mile** correr la milla por debajo de los cuatro minutos

sub [sʌb] *Fam* **1** *n* **(a)** *(to newspaper, magazine)* suscripción *f*; *(to club, trade union)* cuota *f*; **to pay one's subs** *(to newspaper, magazine)* pagar la cuota (de suscripción); *(to club, trade union)* pagar la cuota
(b) *(substitute)* suplente *mf*; **to be on the subs' bench** estar en el banquillo de suplentes
(c) *(submarine)* submarino *m*
(d) *Journ* redactor(ora) *m,f*
(e) *Br Fam (small loan)* préstamo *m or Méx* prestamiento *m* pequeño; *(advance payment)* anticipo *m*
(f) *US (sandwich) Esp* flauta *f*, = *Esp* bocadillo *or Am* sándwich hecho con una barra de pan larga y estrecha
2 *vt* (*pt & pp* **subbed**) **(a)** *Journ* corregir **(b)** *Br Fam (lend)* prestar; **can you s. me a fiver?** ¿me prestas un billete de cinco?
3 *vi (substitute)* **to s. for sb** reemplazar *or* sustituir a alguien

subalpine [sʌb'ælpaɪn] *adj* subalpino(a) ►► ***s. warbler*** curruca *f* carrasqueña

subaltern ['sʌbəltən] *n Br Mil* (oficial *m*) subalterno *m (por debajo de capitán)*

subaqua [sʌb'ækwə] *adj (club, gear)* de submarinismo ►► ***s. diving*** submarinismo *m*

subaquatic [sʌbə'kwætɪk] *adj* subacuático(a)

subarctic [sʌb'ɑːktɪk] *adj Geog* subártico(a)

sub-assembly ['sʌbəsemblɪ] *n* subensamblaje *m*

subatomic [sʌbə'tɒmɪk] *adj* subatómico(a) ►► *Phys* ***s. particle*** partícula *f* subatómica

subbasement ['sʌbbeɪsmənt] *n* subsótano *m*

subcategory ['sʌbkætəgərɪ] *n* subcategoría *f*

subclass ['sʌbklɑːs] *n Biol* subclase *f*

subclause ['sʌbklɔːz] *n (in contract)* subcláusula *f*

subclavian [sʌb'kleɪvɪən], **subclavicular** [sʌbklə'vɪkjʊlə(r)] *adj Anat* subclavicular

subclinical [sʌb'klɪnɪkəl] *adj Med* en fase latente, subclínico(a)

subcommittee ['sʌbkəmɪtɪ] *n* subcomité *m*

subcompact [sʌbkəm'pækt] *n US* miniutilitario *m*

subconscious [sʌb'kɒnʃəs] **1** *n* subconsciente *m*
2 *adj* subconsciente; **the s. mind** el subconsciente

subconsciously [sʌb'kɒnʃəslɪ] *adv* inconscientemente, subconscientemente

subcontinent [sʌb'kɒntɪnənt] *n* subcontinente *m*; **the (Indian) S.** el subcontinente asiático *or* indio

subcontract **1** *n* [sʌb'kɒntrækt] subcontrato *m*
2 *vt* ['sʌbkən'trækt] subcontratar; **they s. some of the work (out) to local firms** subcontratan parte del trabajo a empresas locales

subcontractor ['sʌbkən'træktə(r)] *n* subcontratista *mf*

subcortex [sʌb'kɔːteks] *n Anat* subcórtex *m*

subcortical [sʌb'kɔːtɪkəl] *adj Anat* subcortical

subcritical [sʌb'krɪtɪkəl] *adj* subcrítico(a)

subculture ['sʌbkʌltʃə(r)] *n* subcultura *f*; **the drugs s.** la subcultura de las drogas

subcutaneous [sʌbkjʊ'teɪnɪəs] *adj* subcutáneo(a)

subcutaneously [sʌbkjuː'teɪnjəslɪ] *adv* por vía subcutánea

subdirectory ['sʌbdɪrektərɪ] *n Comptr* subdirectorio *m*

subdivide [sʌbdɪ'vaɪd] **1** *vt* subdividir
2 *vi* subdividirse

subdivision ['sʌbdɪvɪʒən] *n* subdivisión *f*

subdominant [sʌb'dɒmɪnənt] *n Mus* subdominante *f*

subdue [səb'djuː] *vt* **(a)** *(enemy, rebels, nation)* someter, subyugar; *(resistance)* doblegar **(b)** *(emotions)* dominar, controlar

subdued [səb'djuːd] *adj* **(a)** *(person, audience, mood)* apagado(a); **you're very s., what's the matter?** te veo muy apagado, ¿qué te pasa? **(b)** *(voice, tone, colours)* apagado(a) **(c)** *(light, sound)* tenue

subedit [sʌb'edɪt] *vt Journ* corregir

subediting [sʌb'edɪtɪŋ] *n Journ* correcciones *fpl*

subeditor [sʌb'edɪtə(r)] *n Journ* redactor(ora) *m,f*

subentry [sʌb'entrɪ] *n Typ* subentrada *f*

subfamily ['sʌbfæməlɪ] *n* **(a)** *Biol* subfamilia *f* **(b)** *Ling* subfamilia *f*

subfolder ['sʌbfəʊldə(r)] *n Comptr* subcarpeta *f*

subgenus [sʌb'dʒiːnəs] *n Biol* subgénero *m*

subglacial [sʌb'gleɪsɪəl] *adj Geog* subglacial

subgroup ['sʌbgruːp] *n* subgrupo *m*

subharmonic [sʌbhɑː'mɒnɪk] *n* subarmónico *m*

subhead(ing) ['sʌbhed(ɪŋ)] *n* subtítulo *m*

subhuman ['sʌb'hjuːmən] **1** *n* bestia *mf*
2 *adj* infrahumano(a)

subject ['sʌbdʒɪkt] **1** *n* **(a)** *(topic) (of conversation, book, picture)* tema *m*; *(of e-mail message)* asunto *m*; **s.: recruitment of new staff** *(on letter or memo)* asunto: contratación de nuevo personal; **it was the s. of much debate** fue objeto de un intenso debate; **a paper on the s. of string theory** un trabajo sobre la teoría de cuerdas; **on the s. of**

money, I hope you haven't forgotten that you owe me ten dollars hablando de dinero, espero que no te hayas olvidado de que me debes diez dólares; **while we are on the s.,...** ya que hablamos del tema,...; **to change the s.** cambiar de tema; **let's come** *or* **get back to the s.** volvamos al tema; **to keep off** *or* **avoid the s.** no tocar el tema, eludir hablar del asunto ►► ***s. catalogue*** *(of books)* catálogo *m* temático *or* por materias; ***s. heading*** *(in catalogue, index)* epígrafe *m*; ***s. index*** *(in book)* índice *m* por materias; ***s. matter*** *(of letter, book)* tema *m*, asunto *m*

(**b**) *(at school, university)* asignatura *f*, materia *f*

(**c**) *Gram* sujeto *m*

(**d**) *(of artist, photographer)* sujeto *m*

(**e**) *(of experiment, test)* sujeto *m*

(**f**) *Med (patient)* sujeto *m*

(**g**) *(of monarch)* súbdito(a) *m,f*; **she is a British s.** es súbdita británica

2 *adj* (**a**) *(prone)* **to be s. to illness/jealousy/depression** ser propenso(a) a las enfermedades/los celos/la depresión; **to be s. to delay/a fine of £50** estar sujeto(a) a retrasos *orAm* demoras/una multa de 50 libras; **the terms are s. to alteration without notice** los términos están sujetos a cambios sin previo aviso; **the price is s. to a handling charge** el precio está sujeto a una tarifa por gastos de gestión

(**b**) **s. to** *(dependent on)* sujeto(a) a; **s. to your passing the exam** siempre y cuando apruebes el examen

(**c**) *(subordinate) (state, country)* sometido(a); **they are s. to my authority** están sometidos a mi autoridad

3 *vt* [səb'dʒekt] (**a**) *(subjugate) (people, nation)* someter, subyugar (**b**) *(force to undergo)* **to s. sb to sth** someter a alguien a algo; **their plans were subjected to much criticism** sus planes fueron objeto de muchas críticas

subjection [səb'dʒekʃən] *n* (**a**) *(act of subjecting)* sometimiento *m* (**b**) *(subjugation)* sometimiento *m*; **we lived in s. to his wishes** vivíamos sometidos a sus deseos

subjective [səb'dʒektɪv] *adj* (**a**) *(not impartial)* subjetivo(a) (**b**) *Gram (pronoun, case)* subjetivo(a)

subjectively [səb'dʒektɪvlɪ] *adv* subjetivamente

subjectivism [səb'dʒektɪvɪzəm] *n* subjetivismo *m*

subjectivity [sʌbdʒek'tɪvɪtɪ] *n* subjetividad *f*

sub judice ['sʌb'dʒu:dɪsɪ] *adj Law* sub iudice, sub júdice

subjugate ['sʌbdʒʊgeɪt] *vt* (**a**) *(people, nation)* someter, subyugar (**b**) *(feelings)* reprimir

subjugation [sʌbdʒʊ'geɪʃən] *n* (**a**) *(of people, nation)* sometimiento *m*, subyugación *f* (**b**) *(feelings)* represión *f*

subjunctive [səb'dʒʌŋktɪv] *Gram* **1** *n* subjuntivo *m*; **in the s.** en subjuntivo

2 *adj* subjuntivo(a) ►► ***the s. mood*** el modo subjuntivo

sublease ['sʌb'li:s] *vt* realquilar, subarrendar

sub-lessee ['sʌble'si:] *n* subarrendatario(a) *m,f*

sub-lessor ['sʌble'sɔ:(r)] *n* subarrendador(ora) *m,f*

sublet ['sʌb'let] (*pt & pp* **sublet**) **1** *vt* realquilar, subarrendar

2 *vi* subarrendar (**from** de)

3 *n (apartment, house)* subarriendo *m*; **our house is a s.** nuestra casa es subarrendada

sub-letting ['sʌb'letɪŋ] *n* subarrendamiento *m*

sublieutenant ['sʌblef'tenənt] *n* alférez *mf* de navío

sublimate 1 *n* ['sʌblɪmət] *Chem* sublimado *m*

2 *vt* ['sʌblɪmeɪt] *(desire)* sublimar

sublimation [sʌblɪ'meɪʃən] *n (of desire)* sublimación *f*

sublime [sə'blaɪm] **1** *n* **from the s. to the ridiculous** de lo sublime a lo ridículo

2 *adj* (**a**) *(beauty)* sublime; **you look s.** estás divina (**b**) *(very good) (performance, goal, food)* sublime (**c**) *Ironic (ignorance)* supino(a); *(indifference)* absoluto(a); *(contempt)* olímpico(a)

sublimely [sə'blaɪmlɪ] *adv* (**a**) *(extremely)* **s. beautiful** divinamente hermoso(a) (**b**) *(very well) (to perform, flavour)* extraordinariamente (**c**) *(utterly) (ignorant, indifferent)* completamente; *(contemptuous)* olímpicamente

subliminal [səb'lɪmɪnəl] *adj Psy* subliminal ►► ***s. advertising*** publicidad *f* subliminal

submachine gun ['sʌbmə'ʃi:ngʌn] *n* metralleta *f*

submarine [sʌbmə'ri:n] **1** *n* (**a**) *(vessel)* submarino *m* (**b**) *US* **s. (sandwich)** *Esp* flauta *f*, = *Esp* bocadillo *orAm* sándwich hecho con una barra de pan larga y estrecha

2 *adj (cable, volcano)* submarino(a)

submariner [səb'mærɪnə(r)] *n* tripulante *mf* de submarino, submarinista *mf*

SUBJUNCTIVE

El subjuntivo en inglés tiene la misma forma que el indicativo, con la excepción de la tercera persona del singular, a la que no se le añade "**s**". Sólo el verbo **to be** presenta una forma distinta a la del indicativo: **be** en presente y **were** en pasado. En la actualidad es poco frecuente fuera del ámbito la lengua formal o culta, especialmente en inglés británico, aunque sí aparece en frases hechas como las siguientes:

if I were you... *yo que tú...*
long live the King! *¡viva el rey!*
come rain or shine *llueva o haga sol*
be that as it may... *en cualquier caso...*
as it were *por así decirlo*

En inglés formal hablado o escrito el subjuntivo se usa normalmente para referirse a hechos que pueden no ocurrir o que no son ciertos:

If he were to spend less money on clothes he wouldn't be asking us for loans all the time
si gastara menos dinero en ropa no nos estaría pidiendo siempre préstamos

were I to tell them everything I know, they would be horrified
si yo les dijera todo lo que sé, se horrorizarían

También se usa, especialmente en inglés americano, con una serie de verbos que expresan esperanzas, deseos y órdenes en relación a acontecimientos futuros.

I suggested that he think it over *le sugerí que lo pensara*
they begged that she show mercy *le rogaron que mostrara piedad*
he commanded that we be silent *nos ordenó que nos calláramos*
the doctor recommended that they operate at once *el médico recomendó que lo operaran inmediatamente*

También se usa tras la estructura **it is** + ADJETIVO + **that,** cuando hace referencia a un posible hecho futuro que se desea o se ordena:

it is vital that all communications be unambiguous
es vital que no haya ambigüedad en las comunicaciones

it is important that he understand the implications of this decision
es importante que entienda las implicaciones de esta decisión

submenu ['sʌbmenju:] *n Comptr* submenú *m*

submerge [səb'mɜ:dʒ] **1** *vt* **(a)** *(immerse)* sumergir; *Fig* **to s. oneself in one's work** encerrarse en el trabajo **(b)** *(flood, cover)* inundar; **the rocks were soon submerged by the tide** la marea cubrió rápidamente las rocas

2 *vi (submarine, diver)* sumergirse

submerged [səb'mɜ:dʒd] *adj (field)* anegado(a); *(submarine)* sumergido(a); *(reef, volcano)* submarino(a)

submersible [səb'mɜ:sɪbəl] **1** *n* sumergible *m*

2 *adj* sumergible

submersion [səb'mɜ:ʃən] *n* **(a)** *(in liquid, of submarine)* inmersión *f* **(b)** *(flooding)* anegamiento *m*

submicroscopic [səbmaɪkrə'skɒpɪk] *adj* submicroscópico(a)

submission [səb'mɪʃən] *n* **(a)** *(to person's will, authority)* sumisión *f*; **to starve sb into s.** someter a alguien dejándole sin comer; **to beat sb into s.** someter a alguien a golpes

(b) *(submissiveness)* sumisión *f*

(c) *(in wrestling)* rendición *f*

(d) *(handing in) (of documents)* entrega *f*

(e) *(report)* ponencia *f*

(f) *(proposal, competition entry)* propuesta *f*; *Law* alegato *m*

(g) *Formal (opinion)* parecer *m*; **it is my s. that...** sostengo que...

submissive [səb'mɪsɪv] *adj* sumiso(a)

submissively [səb'mɪsɪvlɪ] *adv* de forma sumisa

submissiveness [səb'mɪsɪvnɪs] *n* sumisión *f*

submit [səb'mɪt] **1** *vt* **(a)** *(present)* presentar; **to s. sth for approval/inspection** presentar algo para su aprobación/inspección **(b)** *(yield)* **to s. oneself to sth/sb** someterse a algo/alguien **(c)** *Formal (argue, contend)* **to s. that...** sostener que...

2 *vi (to person, authority)* someterse (**to** a); **they refused to s.** se negaban a rendirse; **we shall never s. to such demands** jamás cederemos ante tales exigencias

subnet ['sʌbnet] *n Comptr* subred *f*

subnormal ['sʌb'nɔ:məl] *adj* **(a)** *(person)* subnormal; **educationally s. children** niños subnormales **(b)** *(temperatures)* por debajo de lo normal

subnotebook ['sʌb'nəʊtbʊk] *n Comptr* miniordenador *m or Am* minicomputadora *f* portátil

suborbital ['sʌb'ɔ:bɪtəl] *adj Anat* suborbital

suborder ['sʌbɔ:də(r)] *n Biol* suborden *m*

subordinate [sə'bɔ:dɪnət] **1** *n* subordinado(a) *m,f*

2 *adj* **(a)** *(rank, role)* inferior; **to be s. to sb** estar subordinado(a) a alguien; **that is s. to the main problem** eso es secundario con respecto al problema principal **(b)** *Gram* subordinado(a) ▸▸ ***s. clause*** oración *f* subordinada

3 *vt* [sə'bɔ:dɪneɪt] subordinar; **we must s. speed to safety** la velocidad debe estar subordinada a la seguridad, debemos anteponer la seguridad a la velocidad

subordinating conjunction [sə'bɔ:dɪneɪtɪŋkən'dʒʌŋkʃən] *n Gram* conjunción *f* subordinada

subordination [səbɔ:dɪ'neɪʃən] *n* subordinación *f* (**to** a)

suborn [sə'bɔ:n] *vt Formal* sobornar

sub-paragraph [sʌb'pærəgræf] *n* subpárrafo *m*

subplot ['sʌbplɒt] *n* trama *f* secundaria

subpoena [sə'pi:nə] *Law* **1** *n* citación *f*

2 *vt* citar

sub-polar [sʌb'pəʊlə(r)] *adj Geog* subpolar

sub-post-office [sʌb'pəʊstɒfɪs] *n Br* = oficina de correos que no ofrece todos los servicios y suele hallarse dentro de una tienda

subprogram ['sʌbprəʊgræm] *n Comptr* subprograma *m*

subrogate ['sʌbrəgeɪt] *vt Law* subrogar

subrogation [sʌbrə'geɪʃən] *n Law* subrogación *f*

sub rosa [sʌb'rəʊzə] *adv* en secreto

subroutine ['sʌbru:ti:n] *n Comptr* subrutina *f*

sub-Saharan ['sʌbsə'hɑ:rən] *adj* subsahariano(a)

subscribe [səb'skraɪb] **1** *vi* **(a)** **to s. to** *(newspaper, magazine)* suscribirse a; *(telephone, Internet service)* abonarse a; *(charity)* dar donativos a; **I s. to several magazines** estoy suscrito a varias revistas **(b)** *Formal* **to s. to** *(opinion, theory)* suscribir; **I don't s. to that view** yo no suscribo esa opinión **(c)** *Fin* **to s. for shares in a company** suscribir acciones de una compañía

2 *vt* **(a)** *(donate)* donar **(b)** *(apply for)* **a heavily subscribed share issue** una emisión de acciones con muchas solicitudes; **I'm afraid this course is already fully subscribed** me temo que la matrícula para este curso ya está al completo **(c)** *Formal (sign) (name, signature)* adherir; *(document)* firmar

subscriber [səb'skraɪbə(r)] *n* **(a)** *(to newspaper, magazine)* suscriptor(ora) *m,f*; *(to telephone)* abonado(a) *m,f*; *(to Internet service)* usuario(a) *m,f*, cliente *mf*; *(to charity)* donador(ora) *m,f* ▸▸ *Br* ***s. trunk dialling*** = línea directa de larga distancia sin necesidad de operadora **(b)** *Fin (for shares)* solicitante *mf* **(c)** *Formal (to opinion, belief)* adepto(a) *m,f*, partidario(a) *m,f*

subscript ['səbskrɪpt] *n Typ* subíndice *m*; **s. "a"** "a" escrita como subíndice

subscription [səb'skrɪpʃən] *n (to newspaper, magazine)* suscripción *f*; *(to club)* cuota *f*; *(to Internet service)* cuota *f* de conexión; *(to charity)* donativo *m*; **to take out a s. to a magazine** suscribirse a una revista ▸▸ ***s. fee*** *(to newspaper, magazine)* suscripción *f*; *(to club)* cuota *f*; *(to Internet service)* cuota *f* de conexión; *(for share purchase)* tarifa *f* de reserva; ***s. form*** boletín *m* de suscripción

subsection ['sʌbsekʃən] *n (of document)* apartado *m*

subsequent ['sʌbsɪkwənt] *adj* posterior; **s. to this,...** con posterioridad a esto,...

subsequently ['sʌbsɪkwəntlɪ] *adv* posteriormente

subservience [sʌb'sɜ:vɪəns] *n* **(a)** *(servility)* servilismo *m* (**to** hacia) **(b)** *(subjugation)* sometimiento *m*

subservient [sʌb'sɜ:vɪənt] *adj* **(a)** *(servile)* servil (**to** hacia) **(b)** *(subjugated)* sometido(a) (**to** a) **(c)** *(secondary)* accesorio(a) (**to** a)

subset ['sʌbset] *n* subconjunto *m*

subside [səb'saɪd] *vi* **(a)** *(ground, building)* hundirse

(b) *(water)* bajar (de nivel); *(blister, bump)* bajar, deshincharse

(c) *(storm)* amainar; *(excitement, fever, pain, anger)* calmarse; *(fever)* remitir; *(anger)* aplacarse; *(shooting, laughter, applause)* ir apagándose

(d) *(person)* **I subsided into the nearest armchair** me dejé caer en el primer sillón que vi; **we subsided into helpless laughter** no pudimos contener ya la risa

subsidence [səb'saɪdəns] *n* **(a)** *(of ground, building)* hundimiento *m* **(b)** *(of water)* bajada *f*

subsidiarity [səbsɪdɪ'ærɪtɪ] *n* subsidiariedad *f*

subsidiary [səb'sɪdɪərɪ] **1** *n (company)* filial *f*

2 *adj* **(a)** *(secondary)* secundario(a) ▸▸ ***s. company*** filial *f* **(b)** *(supplementary) (income)* adicional

subsidization [sʌbsɪdaɪ'zeɪʃən] *n* subvenciones *f*

subsidize ['sʌbsɪdaɪz] *vt* subvencionar; **why should I carry on subsidizing your extravagant lifestyle?** ¿por qué tengo que pagarte yo tu vida de derroche?

subsidized ['sʌbsɪdaɪzd] *adj* subvencionado(a)

subsidy ['sʌbsɪdɪ] *n* subvención *f*

subsist [səb'sɪst] *vi* **(a)** *(survive) (person)* subsistir; **to s. on** subsistir a base de **(b)** *Formal (remain in existence) (custom)* pervivir

subsistence [səb'sɪstəns] *n* subsistencia *f* ▸▸ *Com* ***s. allowance*** dietas *fpl*; ***s. crop*** cultivo *m* de subsistencia; ***s. economy*** economía *f* de subsistencia; ***s. farming*** agricultura *f* de subsistencia; ***s. level*** nivel *m* mínimo de subsistencia; **to live at s. level** vivir en el nivel mínimo de subsistencia; ***s. wage*** salario *m* exiguo

subsoil ['sʌbsɔɪl] *n Geol* subsuelo *m*

subsonic ['sʌb'sɒnɪk] *adj* subsónico(a)

subspecies ['sʌbspi:ʃi:z] *n Biol* subespecie *f*

substance ['sʌbstəns] *n* **(a)** *(matter)* sustancia *f* ▸▸ *Formal* ***s. abuse*** abuso *m* de narcóticos

(b) *(essential element) (of article, argument)* esencia *f*; **in s., that is what he said** en esencia, eso es lo que dijo; **I agree in s.** esencialmente, estoy de acuerdo

(c) *(physical solidity)* consistencia *f*; **the meal lacked s.** a la comida le faltaba sustancia

(d) *(significance, weight)* substancia *f*; **these developments add s. to our hypothesis** estos acontecimientos dan peso a nuestra hipótesis; **the accusations lack s.** las acusaciones no tienen fundamento; **there is little of s. in the book** el libro no tiene mucha enjundia *or* sustancia; **it is a case of style over s.** es un ejemplo de estilo por encima de contenido

(e) *Literary (wealth)* **a woman of s.** una mujer acaudalada

substandard ['sʌb'stændəd] *adj* **(a)** *(work, meal, goods, housing)* deficiente **(b)** *Ling* no estándar *inv*

substantial [səb'stænʃəl] *adj* **(a)** *(significant) (progress, difference)* sustancial, significativo(a); *(reason, evidence)* de peso; **a s. number of...** una cantidad considerable de...; **for a s. sum** por una suma

considerable; **we have reached s. agreement on the matter** hemos alcanzado un acuerdo sustancial en este asunto
(**b**) *(sum of money, profit)* sustancioso(a), considerable
(**c**) *(meal)* abundante; **I need something s. to eat** necesito comer algo sustancioso
(**d**) *(solid) (structure, building, furniture)* sólido(a)
(**e**) *(book)* enjundioso(a)
(**f**) *Literary (rich)* acaudalado(a)

substantially [səb'stænʃəlɪ] *adv* (**a**) *(considerably) (better, worse)* significativamente, considerablemente; **taxes have been cut s.** se han reducido los impuestos considerablemente (**b**) *(for the most part)* esencialmente; **the accusations are s. true** las acusaciones son en esencia *or* en su mayor parte verdaderas (**c**) *(solidly)* firmemente; **he is s. built** es de complexión sólida

substantiate [səb'stænʃɪeɪt] *vt (statement, claim)* probar

substantiation [səbstænʃɪ'eɪʃən] *n (proof)* prueba *f*

substantive [səb'stæntɪv] **1** *n Gram* sustantivo *m*
2 *adj (measures, issue, role)* significativo(a); *(proof, evidence)* fehaciente; *(reason)* de peso

substation ['sʌbsteɪʃən] *n Elec* subestación *f*

substitute ['sʌbstɪtjuːt] **1** *n* (**a**) *(person)* sustituto(a) *m,f*; *Sport* suplente *mf*; **he's no s. for our previous teacher** no está a la altura de nuestro anterior profesor; *Sport* **to be on the substitutes' bench** estar en el banquillo (de los suplentes) ►► ***s. goalkeeper*** portero *m* suplente; *US, Irish* ***s. teacher*** profesor(ora) *m,f* suplente *or* interino(a)
(**b**) *(thing)* sustituto *m*; **coffee/milk s.** sucedáneo de café/leche; **there's no s. for the real thing** como lo auténtico no hay nada, nada puede reemplazar a lo auténtico; **tapes are a poor s. for live music** las cintas no pueden sustituir a la música en directo; **accept no s.** rechace imitaciones
2 *vt* (**a**) *(thing)* sustituir, reemplazar (**for** por); **margarine may be substituted for butter** se puede sustituir la mantequilla por margarina (**b**) *Sport* sustituir, cambiar
3 *vi* **to s. for sth/sb** sustituir *or* reemplazar a algo/alguien

substitution [sʌbstɪ'tjuːʃən] *n* (**a**) *(of one thing for another)* sustitución *f*; **the s. of the old system by a new one** la sustitución del viejo sistema por uno nuevo (**b**) *Sport* sustitución *f*, cambio *m*; **to make a s.** hacer una sustitución *or* un cambio

substrate ['sʌbstreɪt] *n* sustrato *m*

substratum ['sʌb'strɑːtəm] (*pl* **substrata** ['sʌb'strɑːtə]) *n* sustrato *m*

substructure ['sʌbstrʌktʃə(r)] *n* (**a**) *Constr* subestructura *f* (**b**) *(of society, organization)* subestructura *f*

subsume [səb'sjuːm] *vt Formal* englobar, incluir (**into** *or* **under** en *or* bajo)

subsystem ['sʌbsɪstəm] *n* subsistema *m*

subteen [sʌb'tiːn] *n US* preadolescente *mf*

subtenancy [sʌb'tenənsɪ] *n* subarrendamiento *m*

subtenant ['sʌbtenənt] *n* subarrendatario(a) *m,f*

subtend [səb'tend] *vt Geom* subtender

subterfuge ['sʌbtəfjuːdʒ] *n* (**a**) *(trickery)* subterfugios *mpl*; **to achieve sth by s.** lograr algo mediante subterfugios (**b**) *(trick)* subterfugio *m*

subterranean [sʌbtə'reɪnɪən] *adj* subterráneo(a)

subtext ['sʌbtekst] *n* trasfondo *m*

subtitle ['sʌbtaɪtəl] **1** *n* subtítulo *m*
2 *vt* subtitular

subtitled ['sʌbtaɪtəld] *adj (film)* subtitulado(a)

subtitling ['sʌbtaɪtlɪŋ] *n* subtitulación *f*

subtle ['sʌtəl] *adj* (**a**) *(delicate, gentle)* sutil; **a s. flavour** un delicado sabor; **a s. shade of blue** un discreto tono azul (**b**) *(not obvious)* sutil, fino(a); **a s. distinction** una sutil distinción (**c**) *(indirect, tactful)* sutil, discreto(a); **that wasn't very s. of you** no fue muy sutil de tu parte; **to drop sb a s. hint** lanzar una sutil indirecta a alguien (**d**) *(ingenious)* sutil, perspicaz

subtlety ['sʌtəltɪ] *n* (**a**) *(delicacy, gentleness)* sutileza *f*; **the s. of the flavour** la delicadeza del sabor (**b**) *(lack of obviousness)* sutileza *f*, sutilidad *f* (**c**) *(indirectness, tact)* sutilidad *f*, discreción *f* (**d**) *(ingenuity)* sutileza *f*, perspicacia *f*; **to lack s.** *(person)* carecer de sutileza *or* perspicacia; *(book, movie)* carecer de sutileza (**e**) *(detail, distinction)* pormenor *m*

subtly ['sʌtlɪ] *adv* (**a**) *(delicately, gently)* sutilmente (**b**) *(not obviously)* sutilmente; **they are s. different** hay una sutil diferencia entre ellos (**c**) *(indirectly, tactfully)* sutilmente, discretamente (**d**) *(ingeniously)* con sutileza, con perspicacia

subtonic [sʌb'tɒnɪk] *n Mus* subtónica *f*

subtotal ['sʌbtəʊtəl] **1** *n* subtotal *m*
2 *vt* subtotalizar

subtract [səb'trækt] **1** *vt* restar, sustraer; **to s. five from ten** restarle a diez cinco, restarle cinco a diez
2 *vi* restar

subtraction [səb'trækʃən] *n* resta *f*, sustracción *f*

subtropical ['sʌb'trɒpɪkəl] *adj* subtropical

subtype ['sʌbtaɪp] *n* subtipo *m*

suburb ['sʌbɜːb] *n* = zona residencial en la periferia de una ciudad; **the suburbs** las zonas residenciales de la periferia

> **False friend**: Although **suburbio** and **suburb** both refer to a residential district outside the centre of a city, they suggest quite different ideas. A **suburbio** would be where poorer people live, rather than the middle-classes of the **suburb**.

suburban [sə'bɜːbən] *adj* (**a**) *(area)* periférico(a); *(population)* del área periférica ►► ***s. train*** tren *m* de cercanías (**b**) *Pej (attitudes, life)* aburguesado(a)

suburbanite [sə'bɜːbənaɪt] *n* habitante *mf* de barrio residencial (periférico)

suburbia [sə'bɜːbɪə] *n* zonas *fpl* residenciales de la periferia

subvention [səb'venʃən] *n Formal Fin* subvención *f*

subversion [səb'vɜːʃən] *n* subversión *f*

subversive [səb'vɜːsɪv] **1** *n* subversivo(a) *m,f*
2 *adj* subversivo(a)

subvert [səb'vɜːt] *vt* (**a**) *(established order)* subvertir; *(government)* minar (**b**) *(belief, loyalty)* quebrantar

subway ['sʌbweɪ] *n* (**a**) *Br (underpass)* paso *m* subterráneo (**b**) *US (underground railway)* metro *m*, *RP* subte *m* ►► ***s. station*** estación *f* de metro; ***s. train*** tren *m* de metro

subzero ['sʌbzɪərəʊ] *adj* bajo cero; **s. temperatures** temperaturas bajo cero

succeed [sək'siːd] **1** *vt (follow)* suceder a; **I succeeded him as editor** lo sucedí en el cargo de editor; *Literary* **as month succeeded month** mientras un mes sucedía a otro mes
2 *vi* (**a**) *(be successful) (person)* tener éxito; *(plan)* tener éxito, funcionar; *(in life)* triunfar; **to s. in business** triunfar en los negocios; **the first attack did not s.** el primer ataque no tuvo éxito; **I tried to convince her, but didn't s.** intenté convencerla, pero no lo conseguí; **to s. in doing sth** conseguir *or* lograr hacer algo; **he succeeded in annoying everyone** consiguió *or* logró enojar a todo el mundo; PROV **nothing succeeds like success** el éxito llama al éxito; PROV **if at first you don't s., try again** en la perseverancia está el éxito
(**b**) *(monarch)* **to s. to the throne** suceder al *or* en el trono

succeeding [sək'siːdɪŋ] *adj* (**a**) *(following) (weeks, years)* siguiente; **each s. year saw their number fall** con cada año que pasaba, su número disminuía (**b**) *(future) (generations)* venidero(a)

success [sək'ses] *n* (**a**) *(good result)* éxito *m*; **s. in your career isn't everything** el éxito profesional no lo es todo; **did you have any s. in finding him?** ¿conseguiste *or* lograste encontrarlo?; **we have had a lot of s. with this approach** hemos tenido muy buenos resultados con este enfoque; **to meet with** *or* **achieve s.** tener éxito; **without s.** sin éxito; **I wish you every s. in your new job** te deseo mucho éxito en tu nuevo trabajo; **the school has a high s. rate at getting pupils through exams** la escuela posee un alto índice *or* porcentaje de aprobados ►► ***s. story*** éxito *m*
(**b**) *(successful thing, person)* éxito *m*; **to be a s.** *(plan, product)* ser un éxito; *(person)* tener éxito; **the canapés were a great s. with the guests** los canapés tuvieron mucho éxito con los invitados; **to make a s. of sth** tener éxito con algo

> **False friend**: The Spanish noun **suceso** is not a translation for the English word **success**. In Spanish **suceso** means "event", "crime" or "incident".

successful [sək'sesfʊl] *adj* (**a**) *(thriving) (project, movie, novel)* de éxito, exitoso(a); **to be s.** tener éxito; **she's a s. businesswoman** es una empresaria de éxito; **one of the most s. British authors** uno de los autores británicos de más éxito
(**b**) *(achieving desired result) (attempt, negotiations, partnership, meeting, day)* fructífero(a); *(plan, operation, experiment)* exitoso(a); *(outcome)* positivo(a); **s. applicants** los candidatos elegidos; **I tried to convince her – and were you s.?** intenté convencerla – ¿y lo conseguiste?; **to be s. in doing sth** conseguir *or* lograr hacer algo; **she was not s. in her application for the post** no tuvo éxito con su candidatura para el puesto; **she was able to bring the project to a s. conclusion** al final consiguió llevar el proyecto a buen puerto

successfully [sək'sesfəlɪ] *adv* con éxito; **I s. avoided the issue** conseguí evitar el asunto; **students who s. complete the course are awarded a certificate** a los alumnos que aprueban el curso se les entrega un certificado

succession [sək'seʃən] *n* (a) *(sequence, series)* sucesión *f*; **a s. of disasters/visitors** una serie de desastres/de visitantes; **we won three years in s.** ganamos durante tres años seguidos; **for two years in s.** durante dos años consecutivos; **in quick** *or* **rapid s.** inmediatamente uno tras otro

(b) *(to throne)* sucesión *f*; **she's first in s. (to the throne)** es la primera en la línea de sucesión (al trono)

successive [sək'sesɪv] *adj (attempts, generations, governments)* sucesivo(a); **on four s. days** durante cuatro días consecutivos; **with each s. year the problem gets worse** cada año que pasa el problema se agrava

successively [sək'sesɪvlɪ] *adv* sucesivamente; **s. more right-wing governments** gobiernos cada vez más de derechas

successor [sək'sesə(r)] *n* sucesor(ora) *m,f*

succinct [sək'sɪŋkt] *adj* sucinto(a), escueto(a)

succinctly [sək'sɪŋktlɪ] *adv* de forma sucinta, escuetamente

succinctness [sək'sɪŋktnɪs] *n* concisión *f*

succor *US* = **succour**

succotash ['sʌkətæʃ] *n* = plato de la cocina india de Norteamérica consistente en maíz y alubias con pimientos o cerdo

succour, *US* **succor** ['sʌkə(r)] *Formal* 1 *n* socorro *m*, auxilio *m*; **to give s. to sb** socorrer *or* auxiliar a alguien

2 *vt* socorrer, auxiliar

succubus ['sʌkjʊbəs] (*pl* **succubi** ['sʌkjʊbaɪ]) *n* súcubo *m*

succulence ['sʌkjʊləns] *n* jugosidad *f*

succulent ['sʌkjʊlənt] 1 *n Bot* planta *f* carnosa *or* suculenta

2 *adj* (a) *(juicy)* suculento(a) (b) *Bot (plant, leaves)* carnoso(a)

succumb [sə'kʌm] *vi* sucumbir (**to** a)

SUCH [sʌtʃ] 1 *pron* **if s. were the case** en tal caso; **s. is the role of men in the nineties** tal es el papel del hombre de los noventa; **s. is life!** ¡así es la vida!; **and s.** y otros(as) por el estilo; *Formal* **s. was not my intention** ese no era mi propósito; **philosophy as s. is not taught in our schools** la filosofía, como tal (asignatura), no se enseña en nuestros colegios; **the text as s. is fine but...** el texto en sí está bien pero...; **she doesn't get a salary as s.** no tiene un salario *or* sueldo propiamente dicho; **I wasn't scared as s.** asustado, lo que se dice asustado, no estaba; **she is a criminal and should be dealt with as s.** es una criminal y se la debería tratar como tal; **have they offered you more money? – well, not as s.** ¿te han ofrecido más dinero? – bueno, no del todo

2 *adj* tal; **s. a man** un hombre así, semejante hombre; **books s. as these** *or* **s. books as these** los libros como estos *or* de este tipo; **s. ignorance** tamaña *or* semejante ignorancia; **how can you tell s. lies?** ¿cómo puedes mentir de esa manera?; **in s. situations** en situaciones así; **in s. detail** en tal detalle; **we will take s. steps as are considered necessary** tomaremos las medidas que consideremos oportunas; *Formal* **we took with us s. possessions as we were able to rescue** nos llevamos tantas cuantas posesiones pudimos rescatar; **how will they cope with s. a setback as this?** ¿cómo se las arreglarán ante este revés?; **did you ever see s. a thing!** ¿has visto alguna vez algo parecido *or* semejante?; **do you have s. a thing as a screwdriver?** ¿no tendrás un destornillador?; **we can't afford s. things (as caviar)** no podemos permitirnos cosas tales (como el caviar); **he called me an idiot, or some s. thing** me llamó idiota, o algo por el estilo; **their problems are s. that...** sus problemas son tales *or* de tal calibre que...; **their timetable is s. that we never see them** con el horario que tienen nunca los vemos; **he speaks in s. a way as to be incomprehensible to ordinary people** habla de tal forma que a la gente normal le resulta incomprensible; **the lion, the tiger and other s. animals** el león, el tigre, y otros animales similares; **animals s. as the lion or the tiger** animales (tales) como el león y el tigre; **there are several alternatives – s. as?** hay varias alternativas – ¿como cuáles?; **there's the church, s. as it is** ahí está la iglesia, que *or* aunque no es gran cosa; **there is no s. thing** eso no existe; **there's no s. thing as a unicorn** el unicornio no existe; **he will do no s. thing!** ¡no lo hará!; **I said no s. thing** yo no dije tal cosa *or* nada de eso; **in s. a way that...** de tal forma que..., de forma tal que...; **on s. and s. a day** tal día; *Formal* **until s. time as may be convenient** en tanto resulte conveniente

3 *adv* tan; **I had never seen s. a big house** nunca había visto una casa tan grande; **he was in s. pain that he fainted** le dolía tanto que se desmayó; **I'm not s. a fool as to believe him!** ¡no soy tan tonta como para creerle!; **draw a triangle s. that...** trace un triángulo en el cual...; **you're s. an idiot!** ¡mira que eres idiota!; **I had never heard s. good music** nunca había escuchado una música tan buena; **it was s. a long time ago** pasó hace tanto tiempo; **it's s. a long way away** está tan lejos; **we had s. a good time!** ¡nos lo pasamos tan bien!; **they have s. a lot of money!** ¡tienen tantísimo dinero!

such-and-such ['sʌtʃənsʌtʃ] 1 *pron* tal y tal

2 *adj* tal (y tal); **you'll be told to turn up on s. a day at s. a time** te dirán que vengas tal día a tal hora

suchlike ['sʌtʃlaɪk] *Fam* 1 *pron* **frogs, toads and s.** ranas, sapos y tal

2 *adj* **paella, risotto and s. dishes** paella, risotto y platos por el estilo

suck [sʌk] 1 *vt* (a) *(lollipop, finger)* chupar; *(liquid)* succionar; *(mother's milk)* mamar; *(air) (of machine)* aspirar; *(blood) (of insect, leech)* succionar, chupar; **she was sucking water through a straw** bebía agua con una pajita; **to s. the poison out of a wound** chupar el veneno de una herida; **to s. one's thumb** chuparse el dedo; *Fig* **it's a case of s. it and see** es un ejemplo de probar y ver qué pasa; *Fig* **to s. sb dry** exprimir a alguien; *US Fam* **to s. face** *(kiss)* besuquearse

(b) *(pull)* succionar; **the pump sucks the water out of the tank** la bomba succiona el agua del depósito; **the whirlpool sucked him to the bottom of the sea** el remolino lo arrastró al fondo del mar; *Fig* **we found ourselves sucked into the conflict against our will** nos vimos arrastrados al conflicto contra nuestra voluntad

2 *vi* (a) *(to draw in air, liquid)* **to s. on** *or* **at** *(straw, pipe)* chupar; *(tube)* aspirar por; **the child was sucking at her breast** el bebé estaba mamando de su pecho (b) *esp US very Fam* **that movie/idea sucks!** ¡esa película/idea es una mierda!; **I've got to work all weekend – that sucks!** tengo que trabajar todo el fin de semana – ¡vaya mierda!

3 *n* chupada *f*; **to have a s. at sth** chupar algo; **to give s. to** *(baby)* dar de mamar a

► **suck down** *vt sep (quicksand, whirlpool)* tragarse; **the quicksand sucked him down** las arenas movedizas se lo tragaron

► **suck in** *vt sep* (a) *(gas)* aspirar; *(liquid)* succionar; *Fig* **we tried to avoid getting sucked in** intentamos que no nos metieran en ese asunto (b) *(one's cheeks, stomach)* encoger; **he sucked his stomach in** metió el estómago

► **suck off** *vt sep Vulg* chupársela a, *Esp* hacer una mamada a

► **suck up** 1 *vt sep (liquid)* succionar; *(dust)* aspirar

2 *vi Fam* **to s. up to sb** *Esp* hacer la pelota a *or Col* pasar el cepillo a *or Méx* lambisconear a *or RP* chuparle las medias a alguien

sucker ['sʌkə(r)] 1 *n* (a) *(of octopus, leech)* ventosa *f*; *(made of rubber)* ventosa *f*

(b) *(of plant)* chupón *m*, vástago *m*

(c) *Fam (gullible person)* pringado(a) *m,f*, primo(a) *m,f*; **he's a s. for blondes/fancy chocolates** las rubias/los bombones caros le chiflan; **you really are a s. for punishment, aren't you?** eres un poco masoquista, ¿no?; *Fig* **they fell for the s. punch** cayeron en la trampa más vieja del mundo

(d) *US Fam (object)* cachivache *m*

(e) *US (lollipop)* piruleta *f*

2 *vt US Fam (trick, swindle)* timar, estafar; **she suckered him out of $300** le estafó 300 dólares

sucking pig ['sʌkɪŋ'pɪg] *n* lechón *m*

suckle ['sʌkəl] 1 *vt (child, young)* amamantar

2 *vi (baby, animal)* mamar

suckling ['sʌklɪŋ] 1 *n (animal)* cría *f* de leche; *(child)* bebé *mf* lactante

2 *adj* ***s. pig*** lechón *m*

Sucre ['suːkreɪ] *n* Sucre

sucrose ['suːkrəʊs] *n* sacarosa *f*

suction ['sʌkʃən] *n* succión *f* ►► ***s. cup*** ventosa *f*; ***s. pad*** ventosa *f*; ***s. pump*** bomba *f* aspirante *or* de succión; ***s. valve*** válvula *f* de aspiración *or* succión

Sudan [suː'dɑːn] *n* Sudán

Sudanese [suːdə'niːz] 1 *n* sudanés(esa) *m,f*

2 *adj* sudanés(esa)

sudden ['sʌdən] *adj* repentino(a), súbito(a); **don't make any s. moves** no hagas ningún movimiento brusco; **she had a s. change of heart** cambió de opinión repentinamente *or* súbitamente; **there's nothing s. about this decision** esta decisión no tiene nada de precipitado; **all of a s.** de repente; **this is all very s.!** ¿por qué tan de repente? ►► ***s. death*** *(in match, contest)* muerte *f* súbita; ***s. death play-off*** *(in golf)* play-off *m* a muerte súbita; *Med* ***s. infant death syndrome*** muerte *f* súbita (infantil)

suddenly ['sʌdənlɪ] *adv* (**a**) *(all of a sudden)* de repente, de pronto; **s., she was no longer there** de repente, ya no estaba allí (**b**) *(unexpectedly)* inesperadamente; **he died s. in the night** murió durante la noche repentinamente (**c**) *(quickly)* **it happened so s.** todo sucedió tan deprisa

suddenness ['sʌdənnɪs] *n* (**a**) *(unexpectedness)* **the s. of her death/decision** lo repentino de su muerte/decisión (**b**) *(speed)* **the s. of the attack surprised us** la rapidez del ataque nos sorprendió

suds [sʌdz] *npl* (**a**) *(of soap)* espuma *f* (de jabón) (**b**) *(soapy water)* agua *f* con jabón (**c**) *US Fam (beer)* birra *f*

sue [su:] **1** *vt Law* demandar (**for** por); **he's being sued for libel** lo han demandado por libelo; **she's suing him for divorce** le ha presentado una demanda de divorcio

2 *vi* (**a**) *Law* ir a juicio; **to s. for divorce** solicitar el divorcio (**b**) *(request)* **to s. for peace** pedir la paz

suede [sweɪd] *n* ante *m*; **a s. jacket** una chaqueta de ante

suet ['su:ɪt] *n* sebo *m*, unto *m* ▸▸ ***s. pudding*** = budín con base de sebo y relleno dulce o salado

Suez ['su:ez] *n* **the S. Canal** el Canal de Suez

Suff (*abbr* **Suffolk**) (condado *m* de) Suffolk

suffer ['sʌfə(r)] **1** *vt* (**a**) *(loss, defeat, consequences, setback, decline)* sufrir; *(pain, sorrow)* sufrir, padecer; *(hunger, thirst)* pasar; **we suffered great hardship during the war** sufrimos grandes penalidades durante la guerra

(**b**) *(tolerate)* aguantar, soportar; **she doesn't s. fools gladly** no les da ningún cuartel a los tontos

(**c**) *Formal (allow)* **he wouldn't s. them to touch him** no les permitía tocarlo

2 *vi* (**a**) *(experience pain, punishment)* sufrir (**for** por); **someone is going to s. for this!** ¡alguien va a pagar muy caro por esto!; **I'll make you s. for this!** ¡me las pagarás por lo que has hecho!; **he drank too much and suffered for it the next day** bebió demasiado y al día siguiente pagó las consecuencias; **she has no choice but to s. in silence** no puede hacer más que aguantarse y callar

(**b**) *(from illness)* sufrir, padecer (**from** de); **to s. from rheumatism/diabetes** ser reumático(a)/diabético(a); **she was taken to hospital suffering from shock** la llevaron al hospital en estado de shock; **she suffers from an inferiority complex** tiene complejo de inferioridad; *Fig* **he is suffering from a severe case of self-delusion** sufre de un serio caso de autoengaño

(**c**) *(be affected)* **the low-paid will be the first to s.** los que tienen los sueldos más bajos serán los primeros en verse afectados; **the garden is suffering from neglect** este jardín necesita un poco más de cuidado; **the industry suffers from a lack of skilled workers** la industria necesita más trabajadores cualificados

(**d**) *(deteriorate) (profits, sales)* resentirse, verse afectado(a); **your health/work will s.** se resentirá tu salud/trabajo

(**e**) *(be disadvantaged)* **this film suffers by comparison with his earlier work** esta película no llega a la altura de sus anteriores trabajos

sufferance ['sʌfərəns] *n* **you are only here on s.** tolero tu presencia, pero nada más; **to admit sb on s.** tolerar la presencia de alguien

sufferer ['sʌfərə(r)] *n* enfermo(a) *m,f*; **a cancer s.** un enfermo de cáncer; **an arthritis s.** un artrítico

suffering ['sʌfərɪŋ] *n* sufrimiento *m*

suffice [sə'faɪs] *Formal* **1** *vt* **that should s. us** con eso nos será suficiente

2 *vi* bastar, ser suficiente; **s. (it) to say that...** baste decir que...

sufficiency [sə'fɪʃənsɪ] *n Formal* cantidad *f* suficiente; **the country already had a s. of oil** el país tenía suficiente petróleo

sufficient [sə'fɪʃənt] *adj* suficiente; **to be s.** bastar, ser suficiente; **this will be quite s. for my purposes** con esto tengo más que suficiente, con esto tengo de sobra; **$5 should be s.** debería bastar con 5 dólares

sufficiently [sə'fɪʃəntlɪ] *adv* suficientemente, bastante; **to be s. big** ser (lo) suficientemente *or* lo bastante grande; **she has improved s. to turn professional** ha mejorado lo bastante para pasar a ser profesional

suffix ['sʌfɪks] *n Gram* sufijo *m*

suffocate ['sʌfəkeɪt] **1** *vt* (**a**) *(kill)* asfixiar (**b**) *(repress, inhibit)* sofocar

2 *vi* asfixiarse; *Fig* **open the window, I'm suffocating in here!** ¡abre la ventana, que me ahogo!

suffocating ['sʌfəkeɪtɪŋ] *adj* (**a**) *(heat, smoke, fumes)* asfixiante; *Fig* **it's s. in here** hace un calor asfixiante aquí dentro (**b**) *(love, relationship, atmosphere)* asfixiante

suffocation [sʌfə'keɪʃən] *n* asfixia *f*; **to die from s.** morir asfixiado(a)

suffragan ['sʌfrəgən] *n* **s. (bishop)** obispo *m* sufragáneo

suffrage ['sʌfrɪdʒ] *n Pol* sufragio *m*, derecho *m* de voto; **universal/women's s.** sufragio universal/femenino

suffragette [sʌfrə'dʒet] *n Hist* sufragista *f*

suffuse [sə'fju:z] *vt Literary* **suffused with light** bañado(a) de luz; **the clouds were suffused with a rosy glow** las nubes estaban teñidas de un fulgor rosáceo

sugar ['ʃʊgə(r)] **1** *n* (**a**) *(food)* azúcar *m or f*; **two sugars, please** dos cucharaditas/terrones de azúcar, por favor ▸▸ ***s. almond*** peladilla *f*; *Br* ***s. basin*** azucarero *m*; ***s. beet*** remolacha *f* (azucarera), *Méx* betabel *m* (azucarero); ***s. bowl*** azucarero *m*; ***s. candy*** azúcar *m* cande *or* candi; ***s. cane*** caña *f* de azúcar; ***s. cube*** terrón *m* de azúcar, azucarillo *m*; *Fam* ***s. daddy*** = hombre maduro que tiene una joven mantenida; ***s. industry*** industria *f* azucarera; ***s. loaf*** pan *m* de azúcar; ***s. lump*** terrón *m* de azúcar, azucarillo *m*; ***s. maple*** arce *m* sacarino; ***s. pea*** = variedad de tirabeque; ***s. plantation*** plantación *f* de azúcar; ***s. refinery*** azucarera *f*, refinería *f* de azúcar; ***s. snap pea*** = variedad de tirabeque; ***s. soap*** jabón *m* decapante; ***s. tongs*** pinzas *fpl* para el azúcar

(**b**) *Fam (term of address)* cielo *m*, cariño *m*

2 *vt (coffee, tea)* echar azúcar a; IDIOM **to s. the pill** dorar la píldora

3 *exclam Br Fam Euph* ¡miércoles!

sugar-coated ['ʃʊgə'kəʊtɪd] *adj (pills, sweets)* azucarado(a)

sugared ['ʃʊgəd] *adj* (**a**) *Culin* **s. almonds** peladillas (**b**) *(voice, tones)* almibarado(a)

sugar-free ['ʃʊgə'fri:] *adj* sin azúcar

sugar-plum ['ʃʊgəplʌm] *n* (**a**) *(sweet)* confite *m* (**b**) *(term of endearment)* cielito *m*, corazón *m*

sugary ['ʃʊgərɪ] *adj* (**a**) *(of drink, food)* azucarado(a); *(of taste)* dulzón(ona) (**b**) *(smile, tone)* almibarado(a); *(sentimentality)* empalagoso(a)

suggest [sə'dʒest] *vt* (**a**) *(propose)* sugerir; **to s. (that)...** sugerir que...; **I s. (that) we discuss it tomorrow** sugiero que lo discutamos mañana; **what do you s. we do about it?** ¿qué sugieres *or* propones que hagamos al respecto?; **I suggested an alternative plan** propuse un plan alternativo; **I suggested going for a pizza** propuse que nos comiéramos una pizza; **can you s. someone for the job?** ¿se te ocurre a alguien para el puesto?; **can you s. where we might find one?** ¿se te ocurre dónde podríamos encontrar uno?; **might I s. that they are taking advantage of you** no te ofendas, pero creo que se están aprovechando de ti; **no easy solution suggests itself to me** no se me ocurre ninguna solución sencilla

(**b**) *(insinuate, imply)* insinuar; **just what are you suggesting?** ¿qué insinúas?; **are you suggesting (that) I lied to you?** ¿insinúas que te mentí?

(**c**) *(indicate)* indicar; **this suggests that it was an accident** esto indica que fue un accidente; **her expression suggested a lack of interest** su expresión denotaba falta de interés; **these marks s. you haven't been trying** estas notas dan a entender *or* indican que no te has esforzado

(**d**) *(evoke)* sugerir, hacer pensar en; **what does this picture s. to you?** ¿qué te sugiere este dibujo?; **the music suggests a sense of elation** la música sugiere *or* comunica una sensación de euforia

> En inglés culto o elevado, y especialmente en inglés americano, **suggest** puede ir seguido de **that** más un verbo en subjuntivo (ver el panel SUBJUNCTIVE):
> **I suggest that he make sure the details are correct**
> *sugiero que se asegure de que los detalles son correctos*
> Lo mismo también podría decirse del siguiente modo:
> **I suggest that he should make sure the details are correct**
> **I suggest that he makes sure the details are correct**

suggestibility [sədʒestə'bɪlətɪ] *n* sugestionabilidad *f*

suggestible [sə'dʒestɪbəl] *adj* sugestionable

suggestion [sə'dʒestʃən] *n* (**a**) *(proposal)* sugerencia *f*; **to make a s.** hacer una sugerencia; **to be open to suggestions** estar abierto(a) a sugerencias; **have you any suggestions about how to help him?** ¿se te ocurre cómo podemos ayudarle?; **my s. would be to ignore them** yo sugeriría que no les hicieras caso; **at your s.** a sugerencia tuya, a instancias tuyas; **suggestions box** buzón de sugerencias

(**b**) *(insinuation, hint)* insinuación *f*

(**c**) *(indication)* **there is no s. that he might be guilty** no hay indicios de que pueda ser culpable; **her expression gave no s. of what she was really thinking** por la expresión de su cara era imposible saber qué pensaba en realidad; **she has just a s. of a foreign accent** tiene un ligerísimo acento extranjero; **there's just the faintest s. of garlic** hay un levísimo saborcillo a ajo

(**d**) *Psy* sugestión *f*; **the power of s.** el poder de la sugestión

suggestive [sə'dʒestɪv] *adj* (**a**) *(reminiscent)* sugerente; **to be s. of sth** sugerir algo (**b**) *(thought-provoking)* sugerente (**c**) *(erotic)* insinuante

> **False friend:** The Spanish word **sugestivo** is not a translation for the English word **suggestive**. In Spanish **sugestivo** means "attractive".

suggestively [sə'dʒestɪvlɪ] *adv* de forma insinuante

suggestiveness [sə'dʒestɪvnɪs] *n* (**a**) *(evocativeness) (of picture, image)* poder *m* de evocación (**b**) *(erotic nature)* tono *m* insinuante

suicidal [su:ɪ'saɪdəl] *adj also Fig* suicida; **to be s.** *(person)* tener tendencias suicidas; *(action, policy)* ser un suicidio *or* una locura, ser suicida potencial; **to feel s.** tener ganas de suicidarse; **a s. policy/idea** una política/idea suicida

suicide ['su:ɪsaɪd] *n* (**a**) *(act)* suicidio *m*; **to commit s.** suicidarse; *Fig* **to commit commercial s.** cometer un suicidio económico; *Fig* **it would be s. to do that** sería un suicidio hacer eso ►► ***s. attempt*** tentativa *f* de suicidio; ***s. bombing*** atentado *m* suicida con bomba; ***s. mission*** misión *f* suicida; ***s. note*** = nota que deja un suicida; ***s. pact*** = pacto para cometer un suicidio colectivo; ***s. squad*** comando *m* suicida

(**b**) *Literary (person)* suicida *mf*

sui generis [su:i:'dʒenərɪs] *adj Formal* **to be s.** ser único(a)

suit [su:t] **1** *n* (**a**) *(clothing)* traje *m*, *Andes, RP* terno *m* ►► ***s. of armour*** armadura *f*

(**b**) *(in cards)* palo *m*; **to follow s.** *(in cards)* seguir el palo; *Fig (do likewise)* seguir el ejemplo; IDIOM **politeness is not his strong s.** la amabilidad no es su fuerte

(**c**) *Law* pleito *m*, demanda *f*; **to bring** *or* **file a s. against sb** presentar una demanda contra alguien

(**d**) *Fam Pej (person)* oficinista *mf* de corbata

(**e**) *Literary (courtship)* cortejo *m*; *(appeal)* petición *f*; **I decided to press** *or* **plead my s.** *(ask to marry her)* decidí pedirle la mano

2 *vt* (**a**) *(of clothes, colours)* sentar bien a; **blue/this hat suits you** el azul/este sombrero te sienta bien; **black clothes s. his pale complexion** la ropa negra le sienta bien a su tez pálida

(**b**) *(of arrangement, time, job)* convenir a, venir bien a; **would next Friday s. you?** ¿le viene bien el viernes próximo?; **that doesn't s. me at all** eso no me viene nada bien; **tomorrow would s. me best** mañana es cuando mejor me viene; *Fam* **that suits me down to the ground** (eso) me viene a pedir de boca; **if they want to do all the work, that suits me fine** si quieren hacer ellos todo el trabajo, por mí, estupendo; **s. yourself** haz lo que quieras

(**c**) *(agree with)* **life in the country obviously suits her** está claro que la vida en el campo le sienta muy bien

(**d**) *(be appropriate)* **the role suits her perfectly** ese papel está hecho a su medida; **clothes to s. all tastes** ropas para (satisfacer) todos los gustos; **to be suited to** *or* **for sth** *(purpose, job)* ser indicado(a) para algo; **they are well suited (to each other)** están hechos el uno para el otro

(**e**) *(adapt)* **to s. sth to sth** adecuar algo a algo

3 *vi (be satisfactory)* **would some time next week s.?** ¿le iría bien la semana que viene?

► **suit up** *vt sep* **to get suited up** *(diver, astronaut)* ponerse el traje

suitability [su:tə'bɪlɪtɪ] *n* (**a**) *(convenience) (of arrangement)* conveniencia *f* (**b**) *(appropriateness) (of comment, dress)* conveniencia *f*; **they doubt his s. for the post** dudan que sea la persona adecuada para el puesto

suitable ['su:təbəl] *adj* (**a**) *(convenient)* conveniente; **would Friday be s. (for you)?** ¿le viene bien el viernes?

(**b**) *(appropriate)* adecuado(a), apropiado(a); **these shoes are s. for all occasions** estos zapatos son para todas las ocasiones; **the movie is not s. for children** la película no es apta para menores; **this is hardly a s. time to bring that subject up** éste no es el mejor momento para sacar a relucir ese asunto; **the most s. person for the job** la persona más adecuada *or* indicada para el trabajo; **that young ruffian is not s. for our daughter** ese rufián no es conveniente para nuestra hija

suitably ['su:təblɪ] *adv (to behave, dress)* adecuadamente; **I tried to look s. surprised** intenté parecer tan sorprendido como correspondía; **she was s. impressed** estaba impresionada como correspondía

suitcase ['su:tkeɪs] *n* maleta *f*, *Am* valija *f*

suite [swi:t] *n* (**a**) *(of rooms)* suite *f* (**b**) *(of furniture)* **(three-piece) s.** tresillo *m*, conjunto *m* de sofá y (dos) sillones; **bedroom s.** juego de dormitorio; **bathroom s.** = conjunto de bañera, lavabo e inodoro (**c**) *Mus* suite *f* (**d**) *Comptr (of software)* paquete *m* integrado (**e**) *(staff, followers)* séquito *m*

suited ['su:tɪd] *adj (wearing a suit)* con traje

suiting ['su:tɪŋ] *n* tela *f* de traje

suitor ['su:tə(r)] *n* (**a**) *Literary (admirer)* pretendiente *m* (**b**) *Law* demandante *mf*

sukiyaki [su:kɪ'jækɪ] *n Culin* sukiyaki *m*, = plato japonés de carne con verduras rehogadas

sulfa, sulfate *US* = **sulpha, sulphate**

sulfide, sulphite *US* = **sulphide, sulphite**

sulfonamide *US* = **sulphonamide**

sulfur, sulfuric, sulfurous *US* = **sulphur, sulphuric, sulphurous**

sulk [sʌlk] **1** *n* **to be in a s.** estar enfurruñado(a); *Fam* **to have the sulks** haber cogido un berrinche *or* una rabieta

2 *vi* enfurruñarse; **stop sulking!** ¡déjate de rabietas!

sulkily ['sʌlkɪlɪ] *adv* enrabietadamente

sulkiness ['sʌlkɪnɪs] *n* berrinches *mpl*

sulky ['sʌlkɪ] *adj (expression, reply, voice)* enfurruñado(a), enrabietado(a); **to be s.** *(person) (temporarily)* tener un berrinche *or* una rabieta; *(permanent characteristic)* estar siempre de mal humor

sullen ['sʌlən] *adj* (**a**) *(person, look, silence, remark)* huraño(a), hosco(a) (**b**) *(clouds, sky)* amenazador(ora), hosco(a)

sullenly ['sʌlənlɪ] *adv* hoscamente

sullenness ['sʌlənnɪs] *n (of person, look, silence, remark)* hosquedad *f*

sully ['sʌlɪ] *vt Literary (reputation)* manchar; *Fig* **to s. one's hands (with sth)** mancharse las manos (con algo)

sulpha, *US* **sulfa** ['sʌlfə] *n Pharm* sulfamida *f*

sulphate, *US* **sulfate** ['sʌlfeɪt] *n Chem* sulfato *m*

sulphide, *US* **sulfide** ['sʌlfaɪd] *n Chem* sulfuro *m*

sulphite, *US* **sulfite** ['sʌlfaɪt] *n* sulfito *m*

sulphonamide, *US* **sulfonamide** [sʌl'fɒnəmaɪd] *n Pharm* sulfamida *f*

sulphur, *US* **sulfur** ['sʌlfə(r)] *n Chem* azufre *m* ►► ***s. dioxide*** dióxido *m* de azufre

sulphuric, *US* **sulfuric** [sʌl'fjʊərɪk] *adj Chem* sulfúrico(a) ►► ***s. acid*** ácido *m* sulfúrico

sulphurous, *US* **sulfurous** ['sʌlfərəs] *adj (smell)* sulfúreo(a)

sultan ['sʌltən] *n* sultán *m*

sultana [sʌl'tɑ:nə] *n* (**a**) *esp Br (raisin)* pasa *f* sultana, pasa *f* de Esmirna (**b**) *(woman)* sultana *f*

sultanate ['sʌltəneɪt] *n* sultanato *m*

sultriness ['sʌltrɪnɪs] *n* (**a**) *(of weather)* bochorno *m*, sofoco *m* (**b**) *(of look, smile, person)* sensualidad *f*

sultry ['sʌltrɪ] *adj* (**a**) *(heat, weather)* bochornoso(a), sofocante (**b**) *(look, smile, person)* sensual

sum [sʌm] **1** *n* (**a**) *(amount of money)* suma *f*; **it's going to cost us a considerable s. (of money)** nos va a costar una suma considerable (de dinero) ►► *Fin* ***s. at risk*** *(in term insurance)* capital *m* asegurado

(**b**) *(mathematical problem)* suma *f*; **to do sums** hacer cuentas; **he's very weak at sums** se le dan mal los números; **the government will need to get its sums right** el gobierno tendrá que hacer bien las cuentas

(**c**) *(total)* suma *f*, total *m*; **the s. of my efforts** el resultado *or* la suma de mis esfuerzos; **in s.** en suma; **one medal was the s. total of our achievements at the Olympics** la suma total de nuestros logros en los juegos olímpicos es una medalla; **is that the s. total of what you've done today?** ¿eso es todo lo que has hecho hoy?

2 *vt (add)* **to s. two totals together** sumar dos totales

► **sum up** (*pt & pp* **summed**) **1** *vt sep* (**a**) *(summarize)* resumir; **one word sums the matter up: corruption** el asunto se resume en una palabra: corrupción (**b**) *(assess quickly)* evaluar

2 *vi (summarize)* resumir; *(in debate, trial)* recapitular; **to s. up I would say that...** a modo de recapitulación, diré que...

sumac(h) ['su:mæk] *n Bot* zumaque *m*

Sumatra [sʊ'mɑ:trə] *n* Sumatra

summa cum laude ['sʌməkʊm'laʊdeɪ] *adv US* **to graduate s.** = licenciarse con la nota más alta en la escala de calificaciones

summarily ['sʌmərɪlɪ] *adv* sumariamente

summarize ['sʌməraɪz] **1** *vt* resumir

2 *vi* resumir; **to s., then...** resumiendo,..., en resumen,...

summary ['sʌmərɪ] **1** *n* resumen *m*; *TV & Rad* **news s.** resumen de noticias

2 *adj* (**a**) *(trial, execution)* sumario(a) ►► ***s. dismissal*** despido *m* inmediato; *Law* ***s. offence*** falta *f* (**b**) *(brief) (description)* sumario(a)

summation [sʌ'meɪʃən] *n* (**a**) *Law (summing-up)* conclusiones *fpl* (**b**) *Formal (addition)* suma *f* (**c**) *Formal (final result)* resultado *m*; **the book is a s. of her life's work** el libro es el resultado de una vida de trabajo

summer ['sʌmə(r)] **1** *n* verano *m*; **in (the) s.** en verano; **we spend our summers there** veraneamos allí; **a summer('s) day** un día de verano; **we basked in the s. sun** nos tumbamos al sol veraniego; *Literary* **a youth of fifteen summers** un mancebo de quince primaveras ►► ***s. camp*** colonia *f* de verano; ***s. holidays*** vacaciones *fpl* de verano; ***s. job*** trabajo *m* de verano; ***s. resort*** lugar *m* de veraneo; ***s. school*** escuela *f* de verano; ***s. season*** temporada *f* de verano, estación *f* veraniega; ***s. solstice*** solsticio *m* de verano; ***s. term*** tercer trimestre *m*; ***s. time*** *(by clock)* horario *m* de verano
2 *vi (people)* veranear; *(birds)* pasar el verano

summerhouse ['sʌməhaʊs] *n (in garden)* glorieta *f*, cenador *m*

summertime ['sʌmətaɪm] *n (summer)* verano *m*; **in (the) s.** en verano

summery ['sʌmərɪ] *adj (dress, weather, day)* veraniego(a); **you look very s. in that dress** vas muy veraniega con ese vestido

summing-up ['sʌmɪŋ'ʌp] *n Law* recapitulación *f*, conclusiones *fpl*

summit ['sʌmɪt] *n* (**a**) *(of mountain)* cima *f*, cumbre *f* (**b**) *(of career, power)* cima *f*, cumbre *f*; **he is a player at the s. of his powers** es un jugador en la cima de sus facultades (**c**) *(meeting)* cumbre *f*; **to hold a s.** celebrar una (reunión en la) cumbre ►► ***s. conference*** (conferencia *f* en la) cumbre *f*; ***s. meeting*** cumbre *f*

summon ['sʌmən] *vt* (**a**) *(police, doctor, waiter, servant)* llamar; *(help)* pedir; **we were summoned to the headmaster's office** nos llamaron al despacho del director (**b**) *(meeting)* convocar (**c**) *Law (witness)* citar (**d**) *(courage)* armarse de; **I couldn't s. the strength to stand up** no tenía fuerzas para levantarme

► **summon up** *vt sep* (**a**) *(courage)* armarse de; *(support)* reunir; *(interest)* despertar; **to s. up one's strength** hacer acopio de fuerzas; **I couldn't s. up the courage to ask her out** me faltó valor para pedirle salir (**b**) *(evoke) (memories, thoughts)* evocar (**c**) *(spirits)* invocar

summons ['sʌmənz] **1** *n* (*pl* **summonses** ['sʌmənzɪz]) *Law* citación *f*; **he received** *or* **got a s. for speeding** recibió una citación por exceso de velocidad; *Fig* **I received a s. from the chief executive** fui convocado al despacho del director general; **to serve sb with a s., to serve a s. on sb** hacer entrega a alguien de una citación
2 *vt Law* citar

sumo ['su:məʊ] *n* sumo *m* ►► ***s. wrestler*** luchador *m* de sumo; ***s. wrestling*** sumo *m*

sump [sʌmp] *n* (**a**) *Aut* cárter *m* inferior (**b**) *(in mining)* sumidero *m* (**c**) *(cesspool)* pozo *m* negro

sumptuous ['sʌmptjʊəs] *adj* suntuoso(a)

sumptuously ['sʌmptjʊəslɪ] *adv* suntuosamente

sumptuousness ['sʌmptʃʊəsnɪs] *n* suntuosidad *f*

Sun (*abbr* **Sunday**) dom.

sun [sʌn] **1** *n* (**a**) *(in heavens)* sol *m*; **the s. is shining** brilla el sol; **in the s.** al sol; **don't stay out in the s. too long** no estés mucho tiempo al sol; **let's get out of the s.** vayamos a la sombra; **you've caught the s.** te ha dado el sol; **the living room gets the s. in the afternoon** el sol entra en el salón por la tarde; **the s. is in my eyes** me da el sol en los ojos ►► ***s. bear*** oso *m* malayo; ***s. bittern*** ave *f* sol; ***s. bonnet*** cofia *f*, papalina *f*; ***s. cream*** crema *f* solar; ***s. dress*** vestido *m* (corto) de tirantes *or Am* breteles; ***s. god*** dios *m* sol; ***the S. King*** el Rey Sol; ***s. lamp*** lámpara *f* de rayos UVA; ***s. lotion*** loción *f* bronceadora; ***s.*** *Br* ***lounge*** *or US* ***parlor*** solárium *m*; *Aut* ***s. shield*** parasol *m*; *Aut* ***s. visor*** parasol *m*
(**b**) IDIOMS **I've tried everything under the s.** he intentado todo lo habido y por haber; **every species under the s.** todas las especies conocidas; **every subject under the s.** todos los temas imaginables; **there's nothing new under the s.** no queda nada por descubrir; *Fam* **she thinks the s. shines out of him** lo tiene en un pedestal; *Vulg* **he thinks the s. shines out of his arse** se cree el rey del mambo, *Méx* se cree el gran chingón
2 *vt* (*pt & pp* **sunned**) **to s. oneself** *(person)* tomar el sol; *(animal)* estar tumbado(a) al sol

sunbaked ['sʌnbeɪkt] *adj* abrasado(a), agostado(a)

sunbathe ['sʌnbeɪð] *vi* tomar el sol

sunbather ['sʌnbeɪðə(r)] *n* **there were hundreds of sunbathers on the beach** había cientos de personas tomando el sol en la playa

sunbathing ['sʌnbeɪðɪŋ] *n* baños *mpl* de sol; **I like s.** me gusta tomar el sol; **to do some s.** tomar el sol

sunbeam ['sʌnbi:m] *n* rayo *m* de sol

sunbed ['sʌnbed] *n* (**a**) *(for tanning)* cama *f* de rayos UVA (**b**) *(sun-lounger)* tumbona *f*

Sunbelt ['sʌnbelt] *n* **the S.** = los estados del sur y suroeste de Estados Unidos

sunbird ['sʌnbɜ:d] *n* nectarínido *m*, nectarinia *f*

sunblind ['sʌnblaɪnd] *n Br* toldo *m*

sunblock ['sʌnblɒk] *n* pantalla *f* solar, crema *f* solar de protección total

sunburn ['sʌnbɜ:n] *n* quemaduras *fpl* (por el sol)

sunburnt ['sʌnbɜ:nt], **sunburned** ['sʌnbɜ:nd] *adj* quemado(a) (por el sol); **I get s. easily** el sol me quema en seguida

sunburst ['sʌnbɜ:st] *n* (**a**) *(through cloud)* rayo *m* de sol (**b**) *(design)* motivo *m* en forma de rayos solares

sundae ['sʌndeɪ] *n* = copa de helado con fruta y nueces

Sunday ['sʌndeɪ] *n (day)* domingo *m*; *Br* **the Sundays** *(newspapers)* los dominicales ►► ***S. best*** traje *m* de los domingos; **they were wearing their S. best** llevaban el traje de los domingos; *Pej* ***S. driver*** (conductor(ora) *m,f*) dominguero(a) *m,f*; ***S. opening*** apertura *f* de las tiendas en domingo; ***S. painter*** pintor(ora) *m,f* aficionado(a); ***S. paper*** periódico *m* dominical *or* del domingo; ***S. roast*** = el rosbif que se come tradicionalmente los domingos; *Rel* ***S. school*** catequesis *f inv* dominical; ***S. supplement*** suplemento *m* dominical; ***S. trading*** apertura *f* de comercios en domingos; ***S. trading laws*** normativa *f* sobre la apertura de comercios en domingos; *see also* **Saturday**

sundeck ['sʌndek] *n (on ship)* cubierta *f* superior

sunder ['sʌndə(r)] *vt Literary* desgajar

sundew ['sʌndju:] *n Bot* rosela *f*, rosolí *m*

sundial ['sʌndaɪəl] *n* reloj *m* de sol

sundown ['sʌndaʊn] *n* puesta *f* de sol, atardecer *m*; **at s.** al atardecer

sundowner ['sʌndaʊnə(r)] *n* (**a**) *Br Fam (drink)* = bebida alcohólica tomada con la puesta de sol (**b**) *Austr (tramp)* vagabundo(a) *m,f*

sun-drenched ['sʌndrenʃt] *adj* bañado(a) de sol

sun-dried ['sʌndraɪd] *adj* secado(a) al sol ►► ***s. tomatoes*** tomates *mpl or Méx* jitomates *mpl* secos

sundry ['sʌndrɪ] **1** *n* (**a**) **all and s.** *(everyone)* propios y extraños; **she told all and s. about it** se lo contó a propios y extraños (**b**) *Com* **sundries** *(items)* artículos *mpl* varios; *(costs)* gastos *mpl* diversos
2 *adj* diversos(as)

sunfish ['sʌnfɪʃ] *n* pez *m* luna

sunflower ['sʌnflaʊə(r)] *n* girasol *m* ►► ***s. oil*** aceite *m* de girasol; ***s. seeds*** pipas *fpl* de girasol

sung *pp of* **sing**

sunglasses ['sʌnglɑ:sɪz] *npl* gafas *fpl or Am* anteojos *mpl* de sol

sunhat ['sʌnhæt] *n* pamela *f*

sunk [sʌŋk] **1** *adj Fam* **if she finds out, we're s.** como se entere, se va todo al carajo
2 *pp of* **sink**[2]

sunken ['sʌŋkən] *adj* (**a**) *(in water) (ship, treasure)* hundido(a); *(rock)* sumergido(a) (**b**) *(in hollow) (eyes, cheeks)* hundido(a) ►► ***s. garden*** jardín *m* a un nivel más bajo

sun-kissed ['sʌnkɪst] *adj (beach)* bañado(a) por el sol

sunlight ['sʌnlaɪt] *n* (luz *f* del) sol *m*; **in the s.** al sol

sunlit ['sʌnlɪt] *adj* soleado(a)

sun-lounger ['sʌnlaʊndʒə(r)] *n Br* tumbona *f*

Sunni ['sʊnɪ] *n* (**a**) *(religion)* sunnismo *m* (**b**) *(person)* sunnita *mf*

sunnily ['sʌnɪlɪ] *adv (to remark, smile)* radiantemente

Sunnite ['sʌnaɪt] *n* sunnita *mf*

sunny ['sʌnɪ] *adj* (**a**) *(day, place)* soleado(a); **it's s.** hace sol; **there will be s. intervals** *or* **periods** habrá intervalos de sol; **s. side** *(of street)* lado donde da el sol; **to look on the s. side (of things)** buscar el lado bueno (de las cosas); **s. side up** *(eggs)* frito(a) sólo por debajo de la yema (**b**) *(face, personality)* radiante; **she has a s. disposition** es de un carácter muy jovial

sunray lamp ['sʌnreɪ'læmp] *n* lámpara *f* de rayos UVA

sunrise ['sʌnraɪz] *n* amanecer *m*; **at s.** al amanecer ►► *Econ* ***s. industry*** industria *f* de tecnología punta

sunroof ['sʌnru:f] *n Aut* techo *m* solar

sunscreen ['sʌnskri:n] *n* pantalla *f* solar, crema *f* solar de protección total

sunseeker ['sʌnsi:kə(r)] *n* amante *mf* del sol

sunset ['sʌnset] *n* puesta *f* de sol, atardecer *m*; **at s.** al atardecer

sunshade ['sʌnʃeɪd] *n* (**a**) *(for table)* sombrilla *f* (**b**) *(over shop window)* toldo *m*

sunshine ['sʌnʃaɪn] *n* (**a**) *(sunlight)* sol *m*; **five hours' s.** cinco horas de sol; **to lie in the s.** estar tumbado(a) al sol; (**b**) *Br Fam (term of address)* querido(a) *m,f*, nene(a) *m,f*; **watch it, s.!** ¡cuidado, nene *or* chico!

sun-soaked ['sʌnsəʊkt] *adj (beach)* bañado(a) por el sol

sunspot ['sʌnspɒt] *n* (**a**) *Astron* mancha *f* solar (**b**) *Fam (holiday resort)* lugar *m* (costero) de veraneo

sunstroke ['sʌnstrəʊk] *n Med* insolación *f*; **to have/get s.** padecer/coger una insolación

suntan ['sʌntæn] *n* bronceado *m*; **to get a s.** broncearse ▸▸ ***s. lotion*** loción *f* bronceadora; ***s. oil*** aceite *m* bronceador

sun-tanned ['sʌntænd] *adj* bronceado(a)

suntrap ['sʌntræp] *n* solana *f*, solanera *f (lugar)*

sun-up ['sʌnʌp] *n US* amanecer *m*; **at s.** al amanecer

sun-worshipper ['sʌnwɜːʃɪpə(r)] *n (sunbather)* amante *mf* del sol

sup [sʌp] *(pt & pp* **supped**) **1** *vt (drink)* beber a sorbos
2 *vi Old-fashioned (have supper)* tomar la cena; **they supped on** *or* **off some leftovers** cenaron restos

▸ **sup up** *vi (drink up)* ir terminando

super ['suːpə(r)] **1** *n* (**a**) *(petrol)* (gasolina *f or RP* nafta *f*) súper *f* (**b**) *US (of apartment building)* portero(a) *m,f* (**c**) *Fam (police superintendent)* subinspector(ora) *m,f* jefe
2 *adj Fam (excellent)* genial, *Andes, CAm, Carib, Méx* chévere, *Méx* padre, *RP* bárbaro(a); **we had a s. time** lo pasamos bomba *or* en grande; **that's s., thanks** estupendo *or CAm, Carib, Col, Méx* chévere *or RP* bárbaro(a), gracias, *Méx* qué padre, gracias; **it was s. of them to help** fue todo un detalle *or Esp* un detallazo por su parte que echaran una mano ▸▸ ***S. Bowl*** Superbowl *f*, = la final de la temporada de fútbol americano; ***s. Giant*** *or* ***G*** *(in skiing)* súper gigante *m*; *Br* ***S. League*** *(in rugby league)* = la primera división del rugby a trece británico
3 *adv Fam (very)* **his family is s. rich** su familia es superrica
4 *exclam Fam* ¡estupendo!, *CAm, Carib, Col, Méx* ¡chévere!, *RP* ¡bárbaro!

superabundance [suːpərə'bʌndəns] *n* superabundancia *f*

superabundant [suːpərə'bʌndənt] *adj* superabundante

superannuate [suːpər'ænjʊeɪt] *vt (person)* jubilar

superannuated [suːpər'ænjʊeɪtɪd] *adj* (**a**) *(job, post)* con plan de jubilación incluido (**b**) *(obsolete)* anticuado(a), obsoleto(a)

superannuation [suːpərænjʊ'eɪʃən] *n (pension)* pensión *f* (de jubilación) ▸▸ ***s. contribution*** cotización *f* a la pensión; ***s. scheme*** plan *m* de jubilación

superb [suː'pɜːb] *adj* magnífico(a), maravilloso(a) ▸▸ ***s. lyrebird*** ave *f* lira real

superbly [suː'pɜːblɪ] *adv* de maravilla; **they did s. well in their exams** los exámenes les salieron de maravilla; **a s. made movie** una película magníficamente realizada; **the team performed s.** el equipo jugó de maravilla; **a s. clever solution** una solución extraordinariamente ingeniosa

superbrat ['suːpəbræt] *n Fam* (**a**) *(child)* niño(a) *m,f* super mimado(a) (**b**) *(adult)* enfant *m* terrible

superbug ['suːpəbʌg] *n* supermicrobio *m*

supercargo ['suːpəkɑːgəʊ] *(pl* **supercargoes** *or* **supercargos**) *n* sobrecargo *m*

supercharge ['suːpətʃɑːdʒ] *vt (engine)* sobrealimentar

supercharged ['suːpətʃɑːdʒd] *adj* (**a**) *(engine)* sobrealimentado(a) (**b**) *(atmosphere)* muy caldeado(a)

supercharger ['suːpətʃɑːdʒə(r)] *n (in car, plane)* sobrealimentador *m*

supercilious [suːpə'sɪlɪəs] *adj* arrogante, altanero(a)

superciliously [suːpə'sɪlɪəslɪ] *adv* con arrogancia *or* altanería

superciliousness [suːpə'sɪlɪəsnɪs] *n* arrogancia *f*, altanería *f*

supercomputer ['suːpəkəmpjuːtə(r)] *n Comptr Esp* superordenador *m*, *Am* supercomputador *m*

superconductive [suːpəkʌn'dʌktɪv] *adj Phys* superconductor(ora)

superconductor ['suːpəkəndʌktə(r)] *n Phys* superconductor *m*

supercontinent [suːpə'kɒntɪnənt] *n* supercontinente *m*

supercool ['suːpə'kuːl] *vt Phys (liquid)* sobreenfriar, someter a subfusión

supercooled ['suːpə'kuːld] *adj Phys (liquid)* sobreenfriado(a)

super-duper ['suːpə'duːpə(r)] *adj Fam* genial, *Esp* superguay, *Andes, Carib* cheverísimo(a), *Méx* padrísimo(a), *RP* regenial

superego ['suːpəriːgəʊ] *(pl* **superegos**) *n Psy* superyó *m*, superego *m*

superficial [suːpə'fɪʃəl] *adj* (**a**) *(wound, burn, damage)* superficial (**b**) *(knowledge, differences)* superficial; **it bears a s. resemblance to...** se parece un poco a... (**c**) *(cursory) (inspection, glance)* superficial, por encima (**d**) *(person)* superficial

superficiality [suːpəfɪʃɪ'ælɪtɪ] *n* (**a**) *(of knowledge, differences)* superficialidad *f* (**b**) *(of person)* superficialidad *f*

superficially [suːpə'fɪʃəlɪ] *adv* (**a**) *(to wound, burn, damage)* superficialmente (**b**) *(to know, learn, differ, resemble)* superficialmente (**c**) *(to inspect, glance)* superficialmente, por encima

superfine ['suːpəfaɪn] *adj* (**a**) *(quality, product)* superfino(a) (**b**) *(distinction)* muy sutil

superfluity [suːpə'flʊətɪ] *n* (**a**) *(superfluousness)* superfluidad *f* (**b**) *(excess)* superabundancia *f*

superfluous [suː'pɜːflʊəs] *adj* superfluo(a); **it is s. to say that...** huelga decir que...; **I'm starting to feel a bit s.** comienzo a sentirme un poco innecesario

superfluously [suː'pɜːflʊəslɪ] *adv* superfluamente

superfluousness [suː'pɜːflʊəsnɪs] *n* superfluidad *f*

supergiant ['suːpədʒaɪənt] *n Astron* supergigante *f*

superglue ['suːpəgluː] **1** *n* pegamento *m* rápido
2 *vt* pegar con pegamento rápido

supergrass ['suːpəgrɑːs] *n Br Fam* supersoplón(ona) *m,f*, *Méx* hocicón(ona) *m,f*, *RP* buchón(ona) *m,f*

supergroup ['suːpəgruːp] *n* supergrupo *m*

superheat ['suːpə'hiːt] *vt* sobrecalentar

superheavyweight [suːpə'hevɪweɪt] **1** *adj (in boxing)* del peso superpesado
2 *n (in boxing)* peso *m* superpesado

superhero ['suːpəhɪərəʊ] *n* superhéroe *m*

superhighway ['suːpə'haɪweɪ] *n* (**a**) *US (motorway)* autopista *f* (**b**) *Comptr* **(information) s.** autopista *f* de la información

superhuman [suːpə'hjuːmən] *adj* sobrehumano(a)

superimpose [suːpərɪm'pəʊz] *vt* superponer (**on** a)

superintend [suːpərɪn'tend] *vt* supervisar

superintendent [suːpərɪn'tendənt] *n* (**a**) *(supervisor) (of institution)* supervisor(ora) *m,f*, director(ora) *m,f*; *(of swimming pool)* supervisor(ora) *m,f* ▸▸ ***s. of schools*** = administrador a cargo de todas las escuelas de un distrito (**b**) *(police officer) (in UK)* comisario(a) *m,f*; *(in US)* comisario(a) *m,f* jefe (**c**) *US (of apartment building)* portero(a) *m,f*

superior [suː'pɪərɪə(r)] **1** *n* (**a**) *(senior)* superior *m*; **to be sb's s.** ser el superior de alguien (**b**) *(in ability)* **to be sb's s.** ser mejor que alguien
2 *adj* (**a**) *(more senior)* superior; **his s. officer** su (oficial) superior; **I am s. to him** soy su superior
(**b**) *(better)* superior; **a s. wine** un vino (de calidad) superior; **s. in numbers/quality** superior en número/calidad; **of s. quality** de primera (calidad), de calidad superior; **it's far s. (to)** es muy superior (a)
(**c**) *Pej (supercilious) (person)* engreído(a); **stop being so s.!** ¡no seas tan creído!; **a s. smile** una sonrisa (con aires) de superioridad
(**d**) *(upper)* superior

superiority [suːpɪərɪ'ɒrɪtɪ] *n* (**a**) *(higher amount, worth)* superioridad *f*; **their s. in numbers was beginning to tell** su superioridad numérica comenzaba a pasar factura (**b**) *Pej (superciliousness)* engreimiento *m* ▸▸ ***s. complex*** complejo *m* de superioridad

superlative [suː'pɜːlətɪv] **1** *n* (**a**) *Gram* superlativo *m*; **in the s.** en superlativo (**b**) *(when praising)* superlativo *m*; **she always speaks in superlatives** siempre habla con superlativos
2 *adj* (**a**) *(excellent)* excelente; **workmanship of s. quality** trabajo de calidad suprema (**b**) *(overwhelming) (indifference, joy)* absoluto(a); *(ignorance)* supino(a) (**c**) *Gram* superlativo(a)

superlatively [suː'pɜːlətɪvlɪ] *adv (good, efficient)* extremadamente, extraordinariamente; **the team played s. (well)** el equipo jugó extraordinariamente (bien)

Superman ['suːpəmæn] *n (comic book hero)* Supermán

superman ['suːpəmæn] *n (very strong, skilful man)* superhombre *m*

supermarket ['suːpəmɑːkɪt] *n* supermercado *m* ▸▸ ***s. trolley*** carrito *m* de supermercado

supermodel ['suːpəmɒdəl] *n* supermodelo *f*, top model *f*

supernatural [suːpə'nætʃərəl] **1** *n* **the s.** lo sobrenatural
2 *adj* sobrenatural

supernova [suːpə'nəʊvə] *n Astron* supernova *f*; **to go s.** explotar y convertirse en una (estrella) supernova

supernumerary [su:pə'nju:mərərı] *Formal* **1** *n* (**a**) *(actor) Theat* figurante *mf*; *Cin & TV* extra *mf* (**b**) *(worker)* trabajador(ora) *m,f* temporal; *(in army)* reservista *mf*
2 *adj (additional)* extra, adicional

superordinate [su:pə'rɔ:dınət] **1** *n* término *m* genérico
2 *adj* superior

superposition [su:pəpə'zıʃən] *n* (**a**) *Geol* superposición *f* (**b**) *Phys* ***s. of states*** superposición *f* de estados

superpower ['su:pəpaʊə(r)] *n* superpotencia *f*

supersaturated ['su:pə'sætʃəreıtıd] *adj (liquid, vapour)* sobresaturado(a)

superscript ['su:pəskrıpt] *n Typ* superíndice *m*; **s. "a"** "a" escrita como superíndice

supersede [su:pə'si:d] *vt* sustituir; **these methods have been superseded** estos métodos han sido superados

supersonic [su:pə'sɒnık] *adj Av* supersónico(a)

superstar ['su:pəstɑ:(r)] *n* superestrella *f*

superstardom ['su:pəstɑ:dəm] *n* superestrellato *m*

superstition [su:pə'stıʃən] *n* superstición *f*

superstitious [su:pə'stıʃəs] *adj* supersticioso(a) (**about** respecto a)

superstitiously [su:pə'stıʃəslı] *adv* supersticiosamente

superstore ['su:pəstɔ:(r)] *n Com* hipermercado *m*, gran superficie *f*

superstring ['sʊ:pəstrıŋ] *n Phys* supercuerda *f* ▸▸ ***s. theory*** teoría *f* de la supercuerda

superstructure ['su:pəstrʌktʃə(r)] *n* superestructura *f*

supertanker ['su:pətæŋkə(r)] *n Naut* superpetrolero *m*

supertax ['su:pətæks] *n* impuesto *m* adicional

supertitle = **surtitle**

supervene [su:pə'vi:n] *vi Formal* advenir

supervise ['su:pəvaız] *vt* (**a**) *(children)* vigilar (**b**) *(work, workers)* supervisar (**c**) *(research student)* dirigir

supervision [su:pə'vıʒən] *n* (**a**) *(of children)* vigilancia *f*; **the children must be under the s. of qualified staff at all times** los niños tienen que estar en todo momento bajo la supervisión de personal cualificado ▸▸ *Br Law* ***s. order*** = orden de acogimiento bajo la tutela de una institución (**b**) *(of work, workers)* supervisión *f* (**c**) *(of research student)* dirección *f*

supervisor ['su:pəvaızə(r)] *n* (**a**) *(of work, workers)* supervisor(ora) *m,f* (**b**) *(of research student)* director(ora) *m,f* (de tesis)

supervisory [su:pə'vaızərı] *adj (body, post)* de supervisión; **in a s. capacity** en calidad de supervisor(ora)

superwoman ['su:pəwʊmən] *n Fam* supermujer *f*

supine ['su:paın] **1** *n Gram* supino *m*
2 *adj Formal* (**a**) *(on one's back)* **to be (lying) in a s. position** estar tendido(a) en decúbito supino (**b**) *Pej (passive)* apático(a)
3 *adv Formal* **to lie s.** yacer de espaldas

supper ['sʌpə(r)] *n* (**a**) *(evening meal)* cena *f*; **to have s.** cenar; **we had fish for s.** cenamos pescado; **you can stay to s. if you like** si quieres, puedes quedarte a cenar (**b**) *(snack before going to bed)* = refrigerio que se toma antes de ir a la cama

suppertime ['sʌpətaım] *n* la hora de cenar

supplant [sə'plɑ:nt] *vt (theory, method)* desbancar; **she supplanted her rival** arrebató el puesto a su rival

supple ['sʌpəl] *adj (person, limbs)* ágil; *(leather)* flexible; *(mind)* flexible

supplement **1** *n* ['sʌplımənt] (**a**) *(addition)* complemento *m*; **a small s. to my income** un pequeño complemento a mis ingresos; **a vitamin s.** un suplemento vitamínico (**b**) *(extra charge)* suplemento *m* (**c**) *(of newspaper, book)* suplemento *m*
2 *vt* ['sʌplıment] complementar; **he supplements his diet with vitamins** complementa su dieta con vitaminas

supplementary [sʌplı'mentərı] *adj* complementario(a), suplementario(a) ▸▸ *Formerly Br* ***s. benefit*** = subsidio estatal dado a personas con bajos ingresos, sustituido en 1988 por el "income support"

suppleness ['sʌpəlnıs] *n (of person, limbs)* agilidad *f*; *(of leather)* flexibilidad *f*; *(of mind)* flexibilidad *f*

suppletion [sə'pli:ʃən] *n Ling* supleción *f*

suppliant ['sʌplıənt], **supplicant** ['sʌplıkənt] *Literary* **1** *n* suplicante *mf*
2 *adj* suplicante

supplicate ['sʌplıkeıt] *Formal* **1** *vt (forgiveness, mercy)* suplicar; **to s. sb to do sth** suplicar a alguien que haga algo
2 *vi* **to s. for forgiveness/mercy** suplicar perdón/piedad

supplication [sʌplı'keıʃən] *n Formal* súplica *f*

supplier [sə'plaıə(r)] *n* proveedor *m*

supply [sə'plaı] **1** *n* (**a**) *(provision)* abastecimiento *m*, suministro *m*; **they won a contract for the s. of 10,000 computers to schools** consiguieron un contrato para proveer a las escuelas de 10.000 ordenadores; **the domestic hot water s.** el suministro de agua caliente a las casas ▸▸ *Mil* ***s. lines*** líneas *fpl* de abastecimiento; *Naut* ***s. ship*** buque *m* nodriza; *Br Sch* ***s. teacher*** profesor(ora) *m,f* suplente; *Br Sch* ***s. teaching:*** **to do s. teaching** hacer suplencias de profesor(ora)
(**b**) *(stocks)* reservas *fpl*; *(of food)* provisiones *fpl*; **a week's/month's s. (of sth)** reservas (de algo) para una semana/un mes; **our supplies of ammunition/food are running low** se nos están acabando las reservas de munición/comida; **we urgently need more medical supplies** necesitamos urgentemente más provisiones médicas; **we have a limited s. of this special edition model** tenemos existencias limitadas de este modelo especial; **he has an endless s. of funny stories** es una fuente inagotable de historias divertidas; **water is in short s.** escasea el agua
(**c**) *Econ* oferta *f*; **s. and demand** la oferta y la demanda
2 *vt* **to s. sb with sth, to s. sth to sb** suministrar algo a alguien; **she supplied us with vital information** nos proporcionó información de vital importancia; **they s. all the local retailers** abastecen a todos los pequeños comerciantes locales; **all toys are supplied with batteries** todos los juguetes vienen con las pilas incluidas; **to s. sb's needs** satisfacer las necesidades de alguien

supply-side [sə'plaısaıd] *adj Econ* de la oferta

support [sə'pɔ:t] **1** *n* (**a**) *(backing)* apoyo *m*, respaldo *m* (**for** a); **he looked towards me for s.** me miró buscando apoyo; **the s. from the crowd was terrific** el apoyo de la hinchada fue magnífico; **to give sb emotional s.** dar apoyo emocional a alguien; **there is no s. for this measure** esta medida carece de apoyo, nadie apoya *or* respalda esta medida; **there is growing s. for this policy** esta política recibe cada vez mayor apoyo *or* respaldo; **they are striking in s. of the miners** están haciendo huelga en apoyo *or* favor de los mineros; **to speak in s. of a motion** hablar a favor de una moción; **to give** *or* **provide s. to sth/sb, to lend one's s. to sth/sb** apoyar *or* respaldar algo/a alguien; **you have my full s. on this matter** tienes mi apoyo incondicional en este asunto ▸▸ ***s. band*** *Mus* (grupo *m*) telonero *m*; ***s. group*** *(for victims)* grupo *m* de apoyo; *Mus* (grupo *m*) telonero *m*
(**b**) *(financial)* ayuda *f*; **a concert in s. of the war orphans** un concierto a beneficio de los huérfanos de guerra; **my son is my only means of s.** mi hijo es mi único sostén económico ▸▸ ***s. price*** precio *m* subvencionado
(**c**) *(holding up)* soporte *m*; **I was holding his arm for s.** me agarraba de su brazo para sostenerme; **this bra gives good s.** este sostén *or Esp* sujetador da una buena sujeción ▸▸ ***s. hose*** medias *fpl* de compresión
(**d**) *(corroboration)* argumento *m*; **the investigation found no s. for this view** la investigación no encontró ninguna base para esa hipótesis; **another piece of evidence in s. of this theory is...** otro argumento en favor de esta teoría es...
(**e**) *(person, thing supporting)* soporte *m*; **the steel supports had buckled** los soportes de acero se habían combado; **she's been a great s. to me** ella ha estado en todo momento a mi lado
(**f**) *Med (device)* soporte *m* elástico; *(strapping)* venda *f* elástica
(**g**) *(supporters)* **the home/away s.** la hinchada local/visitante
(**h**) *(for a product)* servicio *m* post-venta; **we provide 24-hour technical s.** ofrecemos un servicio de asistencia técnica las 24 horas del día ▸▸ ***s. line*** línea *f* de asistencia técnica
(**i**) *(in rugby, soccer)* apoyo *m*
(**j**) *Mil* refuerzos *mpl* ▸▸ ***s. troops*** tropas *fpl* de apoyo
(**k**) *Comptr* soporte *m*
2 *vt* (**a**) *(hold up)* sostener, soportar; **I supported him with my arm** lo sujeté con mi brazo; **she held on to the table to s. herself** se agarró a la mesa para poder sostenerse; **to s. the weight of sth** aguantar *or* resistir el peso de algo
(**b**) *(back, aid)* apoyar; **I can't s. their decision** no puedo apoyar su decisión; **she supports the Labour Party** vota al Partido Laborista; **his wife has supported him through all his difficulties** su esposa le ha estado apoyando mientras atravesaba dificultades; **the star was ably supported by a talented cast** el actor principal estaba muy bien respaldado por un excelente reparto; *Mus* **Oasis were supported by a band from Liverpool** Oasis tuvo como telonero a un grupo de Liverpool
(**c**) *(financially) (family)* mantener; *(company, project)* financiar; **his parents supported him through college** sus padres lo mantuvieron durante sus estudios universitarios; **to s. oneself** ganarse la vida, mantenerse
(**d**) *(sustain)* sustentar; **the atmosphere on the planet could not s.**

life la atmósfera en el planeta no podría sostener la vida

(e) *Sport* **he supports Lazio** es del Lazio; **which team do you s.?** ¿de qué equipo eres?

(f) *(corroborate) (theory, claim)* respaldar, corroborar

(g) *Comptr* soportar; **this package is supported by all workstations** este paquete se puede utilizar en todas las estaciones de trabajo; **56K supported** con acceso a 56k

(h) *Fin (price, currency)* apoyar

supporter [sə'pɔːtə(r)] *n* (a) *(of opinion, party)* partidario(a) *m,f* (b) *(of team)* seguidor(ora) *m,f*; **I'm a Leeds s.** soy del Leeds

supporting [sə'pɔːtɪŋ] *adj* (a) *Mus* ***s. act*** teloneros *mpl*; *Cin* ***s. actor*** actor *m* secundario *or* de reparto; ***s. actress*** actriz *f* secundaria *or* de reparto; ***s. band*** teloneros *mpl*; *Cin & Theat* ***s. cast*** actores *mpl* secundarios *or* de reparto; *Cin* ***s. programme*** pase *m* previo (b) *(wall, pillar)* maestro(a); *(structure)* de soporte (c) *(evidence)* fehaciente

supportive [sə'pɔːtɪv] *adj* **he was s. (of)** apoyó mucho (a), fue muy comprensivo (con); **I have very s. parents** tengo unos padres que siempre me apoyan

supportively [sə'pɔːtɪvlɪ] *adv* en señal de apoyo

supportiveness [sə'pɔːtɪvnɪs] *n* apoyo *m*

SUPPOSE [sə'pəʊz] *vt* (a) *(assume)* suponer; **he's gone, I s.** imagino que se ha ido; **the theory supposes a balanced budget** la teoría presupone que el presupuesto cuadra; **I s. so** supongo (que sí); **I s. not, I don't s. so** supongo que no; **I s. you won't be coming** supongo que no vendrás; **I s. you think that's clever** supongo que te parece inteligente; **it was easier than I had supposed** fue más fácil de lo que había supuesto; **let us s. that...** supongamos que...; **s.** *or* **supposing he came back** supongamos *or* suponiendo que volviera; **I'm worried about granny, s.** *or* **supposing she falls over?** me preocupa la abuelita, imagina que se cae; **s.** *or* **supposing they find out?** ¿y qué pasa si se enteran?; **s. we change the subject?** ¿qué te parece si cambiamos de tema?; **s.** *or* **supposing you say please?** ¿y qué tal si lo pides por favor?; **I don't s. you'd consider sharing it?** ¿no te importaría compartirlo?; **I don't s. you could help me?** ¿no te importaría ayudarme?, ¿no me podrías ayudar?

(b) *(think)* creer; **I s. it must be three years since I last saw her** creo que debe de hacer tres años que no la veo; **you don't s. she could be angry with me, do you?** no estará *esp Esp* enfadada *or esp Am* enojada conmigo, ¿verdad?; **when do you s. they'll arrive?** ¿cuándo crees que llegarán?; **who do you s. I saw?** ¿a que no te imaginas a quién vi?; **what sort of way to behave do you s. this is?** ¿pero qué manera de comportarte te has creído que es ésta?

(c) *Formal (require)* suponer; **a plan of this nature would s. a major investment** un plan de este género supondría una inversión de primer orden

---

supposed [sə'pəʊzd] *adj* (a) *(expressing duty)* **to be s. to do sth** tener que hacer algo; **you were s. to wash the dishes** tenías que fregar los platos; **you're not s. to smoke in here** aquí dentro no se puede fumar; **you're not s. to do it that way, it can damage the engine** no debes hacerlo de esa forma, puedes estropear el motor

(b) *(meant, intended)* **there's s. to be a meeting today** se supone que hoy hay reunión; **there is s. to be a well in the garden** tendría que haber un pozo en el jardín; **it's s. to be a house** se supone que es una casa; **this wasn't s. to happen** esto no estaba previsto que ocurriera; **the engine's not s. to make a noise like that** no es normal que el motor haga ese ruido; **what's that s. to mean?** ¿qué quieres decir con eso?; **how am I s. to know?** ¿cómo quieres que lo sepa?; **how am I s. to work in conditions like these!** ¡cómo puedo trabajar en estas condiciones?; **am I s. to understand all that?** ¿se supone que tengo que entender todo eso?

(c) *(reputed)* **the film's s. to be very good** se supone que es una película muy buena; **it's s. to be good for you** dicen que es bueno para la salud; **you're s. to be my friend!** pensaba que eras mi amigo

(d) *(alleged)* supuesto(a); **the s. advantages** las supuestas ventajas

supposedly [sə'pəʊzɪdlɪ] *adv* supuestamente

supposing [sə'pəʊzɪŋ] *conj* **s. he came back** supongamos *or* suponiendo que volviera; **we'll invite him, s. he still wants to go, of course** lo invitaremos, suponiendo que todavía quiera venir; **s. you're wrong, what then?** ¿y si no tienes razón, qué?; **s. you tried being nice for a change** ¿qué tal si, para variar, intentas ser simpático?; **...always s. he arrives in time** ...siempre y cuando llegue a la hora; **even s. she does come** aun suponiendo que venga; **just s., (for the sake of argument)...** pongamos por caso que..., digamos, es un suponer, que...

supposition [sʌpə'zɪʃən] *n* suposición *f*; **the s. is that...** se supone que...; **it's pure s.** no son más que suposiciones; **on the s. that...** dando por supuesto que...

suppository [sə'pɒzɪtrɪ] *n Med* supositorio *m*

suppress [sə'pres] *vt* (a) *(put an end to) (revolt, dissent)* reprimir, sofocar (b) *(ban) (newspaper)* prohibir (c) *(conceal) (fact, evidence, scandal)* ocultar; *(report)* prohibir (d) *(delete) (passage of text, scene)* suprimir (e) *(feelings, emotions, smile)* reprimir; *(cough)* ahogar; *(sneeze, yawn)* reprimir

suppressant [sə'presənt] *n* inhibidor *m*

suppressed [sə'prest] *adj (emotion)* reprimido(a)

suppression [sə'preʃən] *n* (a) *(of revolt, dissent)* represión *f* (b) *(of newspaper)* prohibición *f* (c) *(of fact, evidence, scandal)* ocultación *f*; *(of report)* prohibición *f* (d) *(of passage of text, scene)* supresión *f* (e) *(of feelings, emotions)* represión *f*

suppressor [sə'presə(r)] *n Elec* supresor *m*

suppurate ['sʌpjʊreɪt] *vi Med* supurar

suppuration [sʌpjʊ'reɪʃən] *n Med* supuración *f*

supra- ['suːprə] *prefix* supra-

supranational ['suːprə'næʃənəl] *adj* supranacional

suprarenal [suːprə'riːnəl] *adj Anat* **s. gland** glándula suprarrenal

supremacist [sə'preməsɪst] *n* = persona que cree en la supremacía racial, sexual, etc., de un grupo; **white s.** racista blanco(a)

supremacy [sə'preməsɪ] *n* supremacía *f*; **to achieve air s.** conseguir la supremacía aérea

supreme [suː'priːm] *adj* supremo(a); **her s. ambition was to...** su mayor ambición era...; **to make a s. effort** hacer un esfuerzo supremo; **it would be an act of s. folly to do that now** sería una soberana estupidez hacer eso ahora; **she handles politicians with s. skill** maneja a los políticos con suma habilidad; **to reign s.** *(person)* no tener rival; *(justice, ideology)* imperar; IDIOM **to make the s. sacrifice** dar *or* entregar la vida ►► *Rel* ***the S. Being*** el Ser Supremo; *Mil* ***S. Commander*** comandante *m* en jefe; *US Law* ***S. Court*** Tribunal *m* Supremo, *Am* Corte *f* Suprema; ***S. Soviet*** soviet *m* supremo

supremely [suː'priːmlɪ] *adv* sumamente; **she was s. indifferent to their plight** era completamente indiferente a su sufrimiento

supremo [suː'priːməʊ] (*pl* **supremos**) *n Fam* mandamás *mf*, jefazo(a) *m,f*

Supt (*abbr* **superintendent**) inspector(ora) *m,f* jefe

surcharge ['sɜːtʃɑːdʒ] 1 *n* recargo *m*

2 *vt* cobrar con recargo a

surd [sɜːd] *n Math* número *m* irracional

SURE [ʃʊə(r)] 1 *adj* (a) *(certain, convinced)* seguro(a); **to be s. of** *or* **about sth** estar seguro(a) de algo; **I'm s. of it** estoy segura; **is there anything you're not s. of** *or* **about?** ¿hay algo que no te quede claro?; **are you s. of** *or* **about your facts?** ¿estás seguro de que tienes la información correcta?; **I won't have any more, thanks – are you s.?** no quiero más, gracias – ¿estás seguro?; **I'm s. (that) I didn't tell them** estoy seguro de que no se lo dije; **I can't be s., but I think it was at two o'clock** no estoy seguro pero me parece que era a las dos; **I'm not s. when they're coming/what he wants** no estoy seguro de cuándo vienen/de qué quiere; **I'm not s. how to tell you this** no sé cómo decirte esto; **I'm not s. whether** *or* **if I'll be able to come** no estoy seguro de que pueda venir; **I feel s. (that) it's the right decision** estoy convencido de que es la decisión adecuada; **for s.** *(for certain)* con (toda) seguridad; *US (expressing agreement)* claro que sí; **they won't be happy, that's for s.** no les va a gustar, de eso puedes estar seguro; **one thing's for s., he won't call you stupid again** al menos puedes estar seguro de que no te volverá a llamar estúpido; **to be s.** *(undoubtedly)* sin duda alguna

(b) *(confident)* seguro(a); **I'm not very s. about him** no sé muy bien qué pensar de él; **you can be s. of Tony** puedes confiar en Tony; **you can be s. of good service in this restaurant** en este restaurante la buena atención está garantizada; **we cannot be s. of arriving on time** no podemos garantizar que lleguemos puntuales; **she is very s. of herself** está muy segura de sí misma; **what makes you so s. (that) I'll accept it?** ¿qué te hace estar tan seguro de que voy a aceptarlo?; **I wouldn't be so s. about that!** ¡yo no estaría tan seguro (al respecto)!

(c) *(guaranteed, infallible)* **it's a s. sign of old age** es un signo claro de la vejez; **it's a s. way of getting noticed** es una manera muy efectiva de atraer la atención; **it's a s. bet he'll be late** fijo que llega tarde; **they are s. of a place in the final** se han asegurado un lugar en la final; **she's s. to win** ganará sin duda; **you are s. to find something to your taste** seguro que encontrarás algo que te guste; **they're s. to get caught** *(by police)* seguro que los atrapan; *(by teacher)* seguro que los pillan; **be s. not to lose it, be s. that you don't lose it** mira de no perderlo; **be s. to tell us how you get on** no te olvides de contarnos qué tal te va; **to make s. of sth** asegurarse de algo; **to make s.**

(that)... asegurarse de que...; *Fam* **s. thing!** ¡desde luego!; *Fam* **to be a s. thing** ser una apuesta segura

(d) *(secure, firm)* **to have a s. hold** estar agarrado(a) firmemente; **with a s. hand** con mano firme; **to have a s. touch** tener un pulso firme; **to have a s. understanding** *or* **grasp of sth** tener sólidos conocimientos de algo

2 *adv* (a) *US Fam (certainly)* **it s. is cold** qué frío que hace; **are you tired? – I s. am** ¿estás cansado? – ya lo creo *or* y tanto; **she s. can cook!** ¡vaya si sabe cocinar!; **it s. seems so** ya lo creo; **I s. don't want to have to do that again!** ¡por nada del mundo querría hacer eso de nuevo!; **s., it seems like a good idea now, but...** ya, *or Esp* vale, ahora parece una buena idea, pero...; **I s. as hell won't let her do that again!** ¡te juro por Dios que no se lo volveré a dejar hacer!

(b) *(yes)* claro; **do you like it? – s. I do** ¿te gusta? – pues sí; **can I make a phone call? – s. (you can)!** ¿puedo llamar por teléfono? – ¡desde luego!; *Ironic* **I think I can win – oh, s.!** creo que puedo ganar – ¡seguro que sí!

(c) *(as intensifier)* **(as) s. as...: as s. as my name is Jones** como que me llamo Jones; **as s. as I'm standing here** está más claro que el agua

(d) *US Fam (it's a pleasure)* **thanks – s.** gracias – de nada

3 sure enough *adv* **s. enough he was there** efectivamente estaba allí; **it's whisky s. enough** ¡vaya si es whisky!

---

surface ['sɜːfɪs]

sure-fire ['ʃʊəfaɪə(r)] *adj (success)* asegurado(a); *(winner)* seguro(a); *(method)* infalible

surefooted ['ʃʊə'fʊtɪd] *adj* **to be s.** *(when walking)* moverse con paso seguro; *(politician, performance)* ser convincente

surely ['ʃʊəlɪ] *adv* (a) *(expressing doubt, disbelief)* **they s. can't have forgotten** me imagino que no se habrán olvidado, ¿no?; **you're s. not suggesting it was my fault?** supongo que no estarás insinuando que fue culpa mía; **s. it's more complex than that?** tiene que ser más complicado que eso, ¿no?; **s. it's better if you do it this way?** me imagino que es mejor hacerlo así, ¿no?; **s. you don't believe that!** ¡no me digas que te crees eso!; **s. not!** ¡no me digas!

(b) *(certainly)* seguramente, sin duda; **they will s. win** sin duda van a ganar

(c) *(in a sure manner)* **slowly but s.** lento pero seguro

(d) *(of course)* **can I have one? – s.!** ¿me das uno? – ¡pues claro!; *US* **are you interested? – I s. am!** ¿te interesa? – ¡claro que sí!

sureness ['ʃʊənɪs] *n* (a) *(certainty)* certeza *f*, certidumbre *f* (b) *(steadiness) (of aim)* lo certero; *Fig* **he handled the problem with great s. of touch** se enfrentó al problema con gran aplomo

surety ['ʃʊərətɪ] *n Law* (a) *(money)* fianza *f*, garantía *f* (b) *(person)* fiador(ora) *m,f*, garante *mf*; **to stand s. (for sb)** ser fiador(ora) *or* garante (de alguien)

surf [sɜːf] **1** *n* (a) *(waves)* oleaje *m* (b) *(foam)* espuma *f* (c) *Culin* **s. and turf** = plato consistente en un bistec con gambas (d) *Mus* **s. (music)** música *f* surf

2 *vt Comptr* **to s. the Net** navegar por Internet

3 *vi* (a) *(on surfboard)* hacer surf (b) *Comptr* navegar

surface ['sɜːfɪs] **1** *n* (a) *(exterior, face)* superficie *f*; **the road s.** el pavimento; **the submarine/diver came to the s.** el submarino/buceador salió a la superficie; **all the old tensions came** *or* **rose to the s. when they met** todas las viejas rencillas salieron a la superficie cuando se encontraron ▸▸ ***s. feeder*** *(duck)* pato *m* nadador; ***s. mail: by s. mail*** por correo por superficie; *Comptr* ***s. modelling*** modelado *m* de superficies; ***s. noise*** *(on record player)* ruido *m* de superficie; *Ling* ***s. structure*** estructura *f* superficial; ***s. temperature*** temperatura *f* de la superficie; *Phys* ***s. tension*** tensión *f* superficial; ***s. water*** aguas *fpl* superficiales

(b) *(area)* área *f*, superficie *f* ▸▸ ***s. area*** área *f*, superficie *f*

(c) *(outward appearance)* apariencia *f*; **on the s., it seems like a simple problem to solve** a primera vista, parece un problema de fácil solución; **on the s. she seems nice enough** en apariencia, es bastante simpática; **there was a feeling of anxiety lying beneath** *or* **below the s.** había un sentimiento de preocupación bajo una aparente normalidad

2 *vt (road)* pavimentar, revestir

3 *vi* (a) *(submarine, whale, diver)* salir a la superficie (b) *(emotion)* surgir, aparecer; *(rumour)* surgir (c) *(person) (appear, reappear)* surgir, aparecer; **he surfaced again after many years of obscurity** reapareció de nuevo tras muchos años de anonimato; *Fam* **he didn't s. till 11 o'clock** no se levantó hasta las 11

surface-mounted ['sɜːfɪs'maʊntɪd] *adj Comptr (chips)* montado(a) en superficie

surface-to-air missile ['sɜːfɪstə'eə'mɪsaɪl] *n Mil* misil *m* superficie-aire *or* tierra-aire

surface-to-surface missile ['sɜːfɪstə'sɜːfɪs'mɪsaɪl] *n Mil* misil *m* superficie-superficie *or* tierra-tierra

surfactant [sɜː'fæktənt] *n Chem* agente *m* tensioactivo *or* de superficie

surfboard ['sɜːfbɔːd] *n* tabla *f* de surf

surfboarder ['sɜːfbɔːdə(r)] *n* surfista *mf*

surfboarding ['sɜːfbɔːdɪŋ] *n* surf *m*; **to go s.** hacer surf

surfeit ['sɜːfɪt] *n* exceso *m* **(of** de**)**; **there is a s. of imported goods** hay un exceso de importaciones

surfer ['sɜːfə(r)] *n* surfista *mf*

surfing ['sɜːfɪŋ] *n* surf *m*; **I like s.** me gusta el surf; **to go s.** ir a hacer surf

surge [sɜːdʒ] **1** *n* (a) *(of electricity)* sobrecarga *f* (temporal) ▸▸ ***s. protector*** protector *m* de sobrecarga

(b) *(of enthusiasm, support, hatred)* oleada *f*; **a s. in demand** un incremento repentino de la demanda; **he felt a s. of pride at the sight of his novel in the bookshop** se sintió lleno de orgullo cuando vio su novela en la librería

(c) *(rush, stampede)* tropel *m*; **there was a sudden s. for the exit** hubo una inmediata avalancha hacia la salida

2 *vi* (a) *(electricity)* experimentar una sobrecarga (temporal)

(b) *(demand, support)* incrementarse repentinamente

(c) *(rise suddenly) (sea)* encresparse; **anger surged (up) inside her** empezó a hervir de rabia

(d) *(move forward) (crowd)* abalanzarse; **to s. past/through sth** pasar en tropel por delante de/a través de algo; **to s. into the lead** *(runner, competitor)* avanzar con fuerza hasta la primera posición; **to s. forward** *(crowd)* avanzar en tropel

> **False friend**: The Spanish verb **surgir** is not a translation for the English word **surge**. In Spanish **surgir** means "to emerge", "to appear" or "to arise".

surgeon ['sɜːdʒən] *n* cirujano(a) *m,f* ▸▸ ***s. fish*** pez *m* cirujano; ***S. General*** *(in USA)* director(ora) *m,f* general de sanidad pública; ***s.'s mask*** mascarilla *f* (quirúrgica)

surgery ['sɜːdʒərɪ] *n* (a) *(surgical treatment, field of medicine)* cirugía *f*; **he'll need major/minor s.** necesitará una intervención quirúrgica importante/sin importancia; **to have brain/heart s.** ser intervenido(a) quirúrgicamente en el cerebro/el corazón; **to perform s. on sb** realizar una operación a alguien; **to undergo s.** ser intervenido(a) quirúrgicamente

(b) *Br (of doctor, dentist, vet) (premises)* consultorio *m*, consulta *f*; *(consultation time)* consulta *f*; **the doctor holds his s. in the afternoons** el doctor pasa consulta por las tardes ▸▸ ***s. hours*** horas *fpl* de consulta

(c) *Br Pol* = tiempo que los miembros del Parlamento dedican cada semana para hablar en persona con sus electores sobre los problemas de éstos

surgical ['sɜːdʒɪkəl] *adj* (a) *(medical)* quirúrgico(a) ▸▸ ***s. appliance*** aparato *m* ortopédico; ***s. collar*** collarín *m*; ***s. corset*** faja *f* ortopédica; ***s. dressing*** gasa *f* esterilizada; ***s. instruments*** instrumental *m* quirúrgico; ***s. mask*** máscara *f* quirúrgica; ***s. spirit*** alcohol *m* desinfectante; ***s. stocking*** media *f* ortopédica

(b) *(precise)* **with s. precision** con una precisión milimétrica ▸▸ *Mil* ***s. strike*** ataque *m* controlado *(de objetivos específicos)*

surgically ['sɜːdʒɪklɪ] *adv* quirúrgicamente

Surinam(e) [sʊərɪ'næm] *n* Surinam

Surinamese [sʊərɪnæ'miːz] **1** *n (person)* surinamés(esa) *m,f*; **the S.** los surinameses

2 *adj* surinamés(esa)

surliness ['sɜːlɪnɪs] *n* hosquedad *f*

surly ['sɜːlɪ] *adj* hosco(a), arisco(a)

surmise [sɜː'maɪz] *Formal* **1** *vt* presumir, figurarse

2 *n* conjetura *f*

surmount [sɜː'maʊnt] *vt* (a) *(obstacle, difficulty)* vencer, superar (b) *Archit* **the building is surmounted by a large dome** el edificio está coronado por una gran cúpula

surmountable [sɜː'maʊntəbəl] *adj* superable

surname ['sɜːneɪm] *n* apellido *m*

surpass [sɜː'pɑːs] *vt* (a) *(rival)* aventajar, sobrepasar; **you've really surpassed yourself this time!** *(doing well)* ¡esta vez te has superado a ti misma!; *Ironic (doing badly)* ¡esta vez sí que la has hecho buena! (b) *(expectation, record)* superar; *(understanding)* estar *or* ir más allá de

surpassing [sə'pɑːsɪŋ] *adj Literary* **a woman of s. beauty** una mujer de indescriptible belleza

surplice ['sɜːplɪs] *n Rel* sobrepelliz *f*

surplus ['sɜːpləs] **1** *n Econ (of goods)* excedente *m*; *(of trade, budget)* superávit *m inv*

2 *adj (items)* excedente; **pour off any s. liquid** vierta todo el líquido sobrante; **to be s. to requirements** sobrar ►► ***s. stock*** excedentes *mpl*; ***s. value*** plusvalía *f*

surprise [sə'praɪz] **1** *n* **(a)** *(unexpected event, experience)* sorpresa *f*; **it was** *or* **came as no s.** no fue ninguna sorpresa; **to come as a s. (to sb)** ser *or* suponer una sorpresa (para alguien); **to give sb a s.** dar una sorpresa a alguien; **what a s.!** ¡qué sorpresa!; **you're in for (a bit of) a s.!** te espera una buena sorpresa; *Ironic* **s. s.!** ¡mira por dónde!, ¡sorpresa sorpresa!

(b) *(astonishment)* sorpresa *f*; **he looked at me in s.** me miró sorprendido; **imagine my s. when she offered me the job** imagina cómo me sorprendí cuando me ofreció el trabajo; **to my great s., much to my s.** para gran sorpresa mía

(c) *(catching unawares)* sorpresa *f*; **the element of s. is on our side** tenemos la baza del factor sorpresa; **to take sb by s.** *Esp* coger *or Am* agarrar a alguien por sorpresa

2 *adj (attack)* (por) sorpresa; *(defeat, victory)* sorprendente; *(announcement)* inesperado(a) ►► ***s. party*** fiesta *f* sorpresa

3 *vt* **(a)** *(astonish)* sorprender; **you seem surprised** pareces sorprendida; **I was pleasantly surprised** me sorprendió gratamente; **I'm not surprised that...** no me extraña que...; **it wouldn't s. me if they lost** no me extrañaría que perdieran; **don't be surprised if she doesn't come** no te extrañe que no venga; **I surprised myself by how calm I was** yo mismo me sorprendí de lo tranquilo que estaba; **you'd be surprised at how difficult it was** te sorprenderías de lo difícil que era; **I'm surprised at you!** ¡me sorprendes!, ¡me dejas sorprendido!

(b) *(catch unawares) Esp* coger *or Am* agarrar por sorpresa

surprised [sə'praɪzd] *adj (look, expression)* sorprendido(a)

surprising [sə'praɪzɪŋ] *adj* sorprendente; **it's not** *or* **it's hardly s. (that) he left** no es de extrañar que se fuera; **it would be s. if they didn't feel that way** lo raro sería que no se sintieran así

surprisingly [sə'praɪzɪŋlɪ] *adv* sorprendentemente; **it's s. easy to make this mistake** es sorprendente lo fácil que resulta cometer este error; **s., he was the first to finish** sorprendentemente, fue el primero en acabar; **s. enough** sorprendentemente; **not s.** como era de esperar

surreal [sə'rɪəl] **1** *n* **the s.** el surrealismo

2 *adj* surrealista

surrealism [sə'rɪəlɪzəm] *n* surrealismo *m*

surrealist [sə'rɪəlɪst] **1** *n* surrealista *mf*

2 *adj* surrealista

surrealistic [sərɪə'lɪstɪk] *adj* surrealista

surrender [sə'rendə(r)] **1** *n* **(a)** *(of army)* rendición *f*; **the government's s. to the unions** la capitulación del gobierno ante los sindicatos; **no s.!** ¡no nos rendiremos! **(b)** *(of weapons, documents)* entrega *f*; *(of right, possessions)* renuncia *f* ►► *Law* ***s. of property*** cesión *f* de bienes **(c)** *(of insurance policy)* rescate *m* ►► ***s. value*** valor *m* de rescate

2 *vt* **(a)** *(fortress, town)* rendir, entregar **(b)** *(weapons, documents)* entregar; *(right, possessions)* renunciar a; *(advantage)* perder; **to s. control of sth** entregar el control de algo; **to s. oneself to sth** sucumbir a algo **(c)** *(hand in) (ticket, coupon)* entregar

3 *vi (to enemy)* rendirse **(to** a); *(to police)* entregarse; *Fig* **to s. to temptation** caer en la tentación

surreptitious [sʌrəp'tɪʃəs] *adj* subrepticio(a), clandestino(a)

surreptitiously [sʌrəp'tɪʃəslɪ] *adv* subrepticiamente, clandestinamente

surrogacy ['sʌrəgəsɪ] *n Med* alquiler *m* de úteros

surrogate ['sʌrəgət] **1** *n* **(a)** *(substitute)* sustituto(a) *m,f* **(b)** *Br Rel* obispo *m* auxiliar

2 *adj (parents, family)* sustituto(a) ►► ***s. mother*** madre *f* de alquiler; ***s. motherhood*** maternidad *f* de alquiler

surround [sə'raʊnd] **1** *n* **(a)** *(border, edging)* marco *m* **(b)** *Mus* ***s. sound*** sonido *m* envolvente

2 *vt* rodear; **surrounded by...** rodeado(a) de *or* por...; **the president surrounded himself with advisers** el presidente se rodeó de consejeros; **there is a great deal of controversy surrounding the budget cuts** hay una gran polémica acerca de los recortes presupuestarios

surrounding [sə'raʊndɪŋ] *adj (countryside, mountains)* circundante

surroundings [sə'raʊndɪŋz] *npl* **(a)** *(environment)* entorno *m*; **to be in familiar s.** estar en un entorno conocido; **he was brought up in beautiful s.** se crió en medio de hermosos parajes **(b)** *(surrounding area)* **the s. of the village/school** los alrededores de la aldea/escuela

surtax ['sɜːtæks] *Fin* **1** *n* impuesto *m* adicional

2 *vt* aplicar un impuesto adicional a

surtitle ['sʌrtaɪtəl], **supertitle** ['suːpətaɪtəl] *n Theat* sobretítulo *m (en ópera)*

surveillance [sɜː'veɪləns] *n* vigilancia *f*; **under s.** bajo vigilancia

survey 1 *n* ['sɜːveɪ] **(a)** *(study) (of subject, situation)* estudio *m*; *(of opinions)* encuesta *f*; **according to a recent s.,...** según una encuesta reciente,... **(b)** *(overview)* visión *f* **(c)** *(of building) (inspection)* inspección *f*, peritaje *m*; *(report)* informe *m*, peritaje *m*; **to have a s. done** encargar un peritaje **(d)** *(of land)* estudio *m* topográfico

2 *vt* [sə'veɪ] **(a)** *(topic, subject)* estudiar; *(in opinion poll)* encuestar **(b)** *(give overview of)* analizar **(c)** *(building)* tasar, peritar **(d)** *(land)* medir **(e)** *Literary (look at)* contemplar

surveying [sə'veɪɪŋ] *n* **(a)** *(of building)* tasación *f*, peritaje *m* **(b)** *(of land)* agrimensura *f*

surveyor [sə'veɪə(r)] *n* **(a)** *(of building)* tasador(ora) *m,f or* perito(a) *m,f* de la propiedad **(b)** *(of land)* agrimensor(ora) *m,f* ►► ***s.'s cross*** escuadra *f* de agrimensor

survival [sə'vaɪvəl] *n* **(a)** *(continued existence)* supervivencia *f*; **what are their chances of s.?** ¿cuántas *or* qué posibilidades tienen de sobrevivir?; **the s. of the fittest** la supervivencia del más apto ►► ***s. bag*** manta *f* térmica *or* de supervivencia; ***s. instinct*** instinto *m* de supervivencia; ***s. kit*** equipo *m* de supervivencia; ***s. skills*** técnicas *fpl* de supervivencia **(b)** *(relic)* vestigio *m*

survive [sə'vaɪv] **1** *vt* **(a)** *(live through) (accident, illness, experience, war)* sobrevivir a; **few of the soldiers survived the battle** pocos soldados sobrevivieron a la batalla

(b) *(withstand)* resistir; **few buildings survived the earthquake intact** pocos edificios quedaron intactos tras el terremoto

(c) *(cope with, get through)* superar; **I never thought I'd s. the evening!** ¡no sé cómo soporté aquella noche!

(d) *(outlive)* **she is survived by her husband and two sons** deja un marido y dos hijos, le sobreviven un marido y dos hijos

2 *vi* **(a)** *(remain alive)* sobrevivir

(b) *(continue in existence)* sobrevivir; **the custom survives to this day** la costumbre ha perdurado *or* se ha mantenido hasta hoy; **those toys wouldn't s. two minutes with our kids** con nuestros hijos, esos juguetes no durarían ni dos minutos

(c) *(manage)* sobrevivir; **my pay is barely enough to s. on** mi sueldo apenas llega para sobrevivir; **I survived on (a diet of) rice** sobrevivía *or* me mantenía a base de arroz; *Fam* **how's things? – I'm surviving** ¿qué tal te va? – voy tirando; *Fam* **is the injury serious? – he'll s.** ¿es una herida seria? – sobrevivirá

surviving [sə'vaɪvɪŋ] *adj* superviviente; **her only s. relative** su único pariente vivo; **one of the few s. examples of his work** uno de los pocos ejemplos que sobreviven de su obra

survivor [sə'vaɪvə(r)] *n* superviviente *mf*; *Fam* **he's a real s.** siempre sale adelante, *Esp* es absolutamente incombustible

susceptibility [səseptɪ'bɪlɪtɪ] *n* **(a)** *(to illness, infection)* propensión *f* **(to** a); *(to criticism, pressure, noise, flattery)* sensibilidad *f* **(to** a) **(b) susceptibilities** *(feelings)* sensibilidad *f*

susceptible [sə'septɪbəl] *adj (to criticism, pressure, noise)* sensible **(to** a); *(to illness, infection)* propenso(a) **(to** a); **he's not s. to flattery** con él la adulación no funciona; *Formal* **her decisions are s. of modification** sus decisiones son susceptibles de ser modificadas

sushi ['suːʃɪ] *n* sushi *m* ►► ***s. bar*** bar *m* de sushi

suspect ['sʌspekt] **1** *n (person)* sospechoso(a) *m,f*; **the cause of death is unclear, but a stroke is the prime s.** se desconoce la causa de su muerte, pero se sospecha que fue un derrame cerebral

2 *adj* sospechoso(a); **his ankle is still rather s.** tiene el tobillo un poco débil todavía

3 *vt* [sə'spekt] **(a)** *(person)* sospechar de; **to s. sb of having done sth** sospechar que alguien ha hecho algo; **to be suspected of sth** ser sospechoso(a) de algo

(b) *(mistrust) (motives)* recelar de

(c) *(have intuition of)* **does your husband s. anything?** ¿sospecha algo tu marido?; **to s. the truth** sospechar (cuál es) la verdad

(d) *(consider likely)* **arson is suspected** se sospecha que el incendio pudo ser provocado; **I suspected there would be trouble** sospechaba que habría problemas; **I s. you're right** sospecho que tienes razón; **I suspected as much!** ¡ya me lo imaginaba!; **(it's) just as I suspected!** ¡(es) justo lo que yo pensaba!

suspected [sə'spektɪd] *adj* supuesto(a); **a s. murderer/terrorist** un presunto asesino/terrorista; **he's undergoing tests for a s. tumour** le están haciendo pruebas porque se sospecha que puede tener un tumor

suspend [sə'spend] *vt* (**a**) *(hang)* suspender, colgar (**from** de); **particles of radioactive dust were suspended in the atmosphere** quedaron suspendidas en el aire partículas de polvo radioactivo
(**b**) *(service, employee)* suspender; **he was suspended from school** lo expulsaron temporalmente del colegio
(**c**) *(discontinue) (licence, hostilities, work)* suspender
(**d**) *(defer)* **to s. judgement (until)** aplazar *or* posponer el veredicto (hasta); **to s. one's disbelief** dejar de *or* a un lado la incredulidad

suspended [sə'spendɪd] *adj (service, employee)* suspendido(a); *(schoolchild)* expulsado(a) temporalmente; *Law* **to give sb a s. sentence** conceder a alguien una suspensión condicional de la pena ►► ***s. animation*** muerte *f* aparente; **the scheme is in a state of s. animation** el proyecto está en estado de animación suspendida

suspender [sə'spendə(r)] *n* (**a**) *Br (for stocking, sock)* liga *f* ►► ***s. belt*** liguero *m* (**b**) *US* **suspenders** *(for trousers)* tirantes *mpl*, *Am* breteles *mpl*

suspense [sə'spens] *n (uncertainty)* incertidumbre *f*; *(in movie) Esp* suspense *m*, *Am* suspenso *m*; **to keep sb in s.** tener a alguien en suspenso; *Fam* **the s. is killing me!** ¡me muero por saberlo! ►► *Fin* ***s. account*** cuenta *f* transitoria

suspenseful [sə'spensfʊl] *adj (uncertain)* de incertidumbre; *(movie)* lleno(a) de *Esp* suspense *or Am* suspenso

suspension [sə'spenʃən] *n* (**a**) *(of car)* suspensión *f*
(**b**) *(hanging)* suspensión *f* ►► ***s. bridge*** puente *m* colgante; ***s. file*** archivo *m* colgante
(**c**) *(of service, employee)* suspensión *f*; **s. on full pay** suspensión de empleo
(**d**) *(from school)* expulsión *f* (temporal)
(**e**) *(discontinuation) (of licence, hostilities, work)* suspensión *f* ►► ***s. of payments*** suspensión *f* de pagos
(**f**) *(liquid, gas)* suspensión *f*; **in s.** en suspensión
(**g**) *esp US* ***s. points*** puntos *mpl* suspensivos

suspicion [sə'spɪʃən] *n* (**a**) *(belief of guilt)* sospecha *f*; **to be under s.** estar bajo sospecha; **to be above** *or* **beyond s.** estar libre de sospecha; **he was arrested on s. of drug trafficking** lo arrestaron bajo sospecha de tráfico de drogas; **I have my suspicions about him** tengo mis sospechas sobre él; **to arouse s.** despertar sospechas
(**b**) *(notion, feeling)* presentimiento *m*; **I had a s. you'd be here** tenía el presentimiento de que estarías aquí
(**c**) *(small amount)* asomo *m*; **there was a s. of a smile on her lips** tenía un asomo de sonrisa en los labios

suspicious [sə'spɪʃəs] *adj* (**a**) *(arousing suspicion) (fact, behaviour, circumstances)* sospechoso(a); **it is s. that she didn't phone the police** es sospechoso que no llamara a la policía
(**b**) *(having suspicions) (person, mind)* receloso(a) (**of** *or* **about** de); *(look)* desconfiado(a); **I'm s. of his motives** desconfío de sus motivos; **she became s. when he refused to give his name** comenzó a sospechar de él cuando se negó a dar su nombre; **his behaviour made me s.** su comportamiento me hizo sospechar

suspiciously [sə'spɪʃəslɪ] *adv* (**a**) *(to behave)* sospechosamente; **she was s. keen to leave** estaba sospechosamente impaciente por irse; **s. similar** sospechosamente similares; **it looks s. like malaria** mucho me temo que es malaria (**b**) *(to watch, ask)* recelosamente, con suspicacia

suss [sʌs] *Br Fam* **1** *n* **to arrest sb on s.** detener a alguien bajo sospecha
2 *vt* (**a**) *(suspect, sense)* olerse (**b**) *(work out)* enterarse de; **to have (got) sb sussed** tener calado(a) a alguien; **to have (got) sth sussed** *Esp* haber cogido el truco *or* el tranquillo a algo, *Am* haber agarrado la onda a algo

►**suss out** *vt sep Br Fam (person)* calar; *(system)* enterarse de; **I haven't sussed out how it works yet** todavía no me he enterado *or Esp* coscado de cómo funciona

sussed [sʌst] *adj Br Fam (astute)* listo(a); **he's pretty s.** es la mar de listo, se las sabe todas

sustain [sə'steɪn] *vt* (**a**) *(weight, growth, life)* sostener; *(conversation)* mantener; *(efforts, pressure)* mantener; **to s. (one's) interest in sth** mantener el interés por algo
(**b**) *(nourish)* mantener; **they had only fruit and water to s. them** sólo tenían fruta y agua para mantenerse
(**c**) *(suffer) (loss, attack, damage, injury)* sufrir; **he sustained a serious blow to the head** sufrió un fuerte golpe en la cabeza
(**d**) *Law (motion, claim)* admitir; **objection sustained** se admite la protesta
(**e**) *Mus (note)* sostener

sustainability [səsteɪnə'bɪlɪtɪ] *n* sostenibilidad *f*

sustainable [sə'steɪnəbəl] *adj* sostenible ►► ***s. development*** desarrollo *m* sostenible

sustained [sə'steɪnd] *adj* (**a**) *(efforts, growth, pressure)* continuo(a), sostenido(a); **s. applause** aplauso prolongado (**b**) *Mus (note)* alargado(a)

sustain(ing) pedal [sə'steɪn(ɪŋ)'pedəl] *n (on piano)* pedal *m* derecho

sustenance ['sʌstɪnəns] *n* sustento *m*; **there is little s. in such foods** ese tipo de comida no alimenta; **means of s.** medio de vida

suture ['suːtʃə(r)] *Med* **1** *n* (**a**) *(stitch)* sutura *f* (**b**) *(thread)* hilo *m*
2 *vt* suturar

SUV [esjuː'viː] *n US* (*abbr* **sport-utility vehicle**) todoterreno *m*

Suva ['suːvə] *n* Suva

suzerain ['suːzəreɪn] *n* (**a**) *(feudal overlord)* señor *m* (**b**) *(state)* estado *m* protector

suzerainty ['suːzəreɪntɪ] *n Pol* protectorado *m*

svelte [svelt] *adj* esbelto(a)

SVGA [esviːdʒiː'eɪ] *Comptr* (*abbr* **super video graphics array**) SVGA

SW (**a**) (*abbr* **south west**) SO (**b**) *Rad* (*abbr* **Short Wave**) SW, OC

swab [swɒb] **1** *n Med* (**a**) *(cotton wool)* torunda *f* (**b**) *(sample)* muestra *f (en torunda)* (**c**) *(mop)* fregona *f*
2 *vt* (*pt & pp* **swabbed**) (**a**) *(wound)* limpiar (**b**) *(floor)* fregar

swacked [swækt] *adj US Fam (drunk)* piripi; **to be/get s.** estar/ponerse piripi

swaddle ['swɒdəl] *vt* envolver (**in** en *or* con)

swaddling clothes ['swɒdlɪŋkləʊðz] *npl Literary* pañales *mpl*

swag [swæg] *n Fam (of thief)* botín *m*

swagger ['swægə(r)] **1** *n* pavoneo *m*; **he entered the room with a s.** entró pavoneándose en la habitación ►► ***s. stick*** bastón *m* de mando
2 *vi (strut)* pavonearse; **to s. in/out** entrar/salir pavoneándose

swaggering ['swægərɪŋ] *adj (gait, attitude)* presuntuoso(a); *(person)* fanfarrón(ona)

swagman ['swægmæn] *n Austr* temporero *m*

Swahili [swə'hiːlɪ] **1** *n (language)* suahili *m*
2 *adj* suahili

swain [sweɪn] *n* (**a**) *Literary (peasant youth)* mozo *m* (**b**) *Hum (suitor)* pretendiente *m*

SWALK [swɔːlk] *adj* (*abbr* **sealed with a loving kiss**) *Fam* sellado(a) con un beso

swallow[1] ['swɒləʊ] **1** *n (of drink)* trago *m*; *(of food)* bocado *m*
2 *vt* (**a**) *(food, drink)* tragar, tragarse; **to s. sth whole** tragar algo sin masticar; **to s. one's tongue** tragarse la lengua; *Fig* **to s. one's words** tragarse las palabras
(**b**) *Fam (believe)* tragarse; **she swallowed the story whole** se tragó toda la historia
(**c**) *(accept unprotestingly)* **I find it hard to s.** me cuesta aceptarlo y quedarme de brazos cruzados
(**d**) *(repress) (anger, disappointment)* reprimir, contener; **to s. one's pride** tragarse el orgullo
(**e**) *(absorb)* **they were soon swallowed by the crowd** la multitud se los tragó rápidamente
3 *vi* tragar; **to s. hard** *(when nervous, afraid)* tragar saliva

►**swallow up** *vt sep (company, country)* absorber; *(budget, savings)* tragarse; **they were swallowed up in the crowd** se los tragó la multitud

swallow[2] *n (bird)* golondrina *f*; PROV **one s. doesn't make a summer** una golondrina no hace verano ►► *Br* ***s. dive*** salto *m* del ángel

swallowtail ['swɔːləʊteɪl] *n* (**a**) *(butterfly)* macaón *m* (**b**) *(coat)* levita *f*

swam *pt of* **swim**

swami ['swɑːmɪ] *n* = título honorífico concedido a un maestro religioso hindú

swamp [swɒmp] **1** *n (of freshwater)* pantano *m (generalmente tropical)*; *(of seawater)* marisma *f (generalmente tropical)* ►► ***s. fever*** *(malaria)* paludismo *m*, malaria *f*; *(horse disease)* anemia *f* infecciosa equina
2 *vt* (**a**) *(flood)* anegar, inundar; **the boat was swamped by the waves** *(sank)* las olas se tragaron al barco (**b**) *(overwhelm)* **we were swamped with calls** nos inundaron con llamadas; **to be swamped with work** estar desbordado(a) de trabajo; **we were swamped by applications/offers of help** nos llovían las solicitudes/los ofrecimientos de ayuda

swampland ['swɒmplænd] *n (of freshwater)* zona *f* pantanosa *(generalmente tropical); (of seawater)* marismas *fpl (generalmente tropical)*

swampy ['swɔːmpɪ] *adj* pantanoso(a)

swan [swɒn] **1** *n* cisne *m* ▸▸ *US* ***s. dive*** salto *m* del ángel; *Fig* ***s. song*** canto *m* de(l) cisne

2 *vi* (*pt & pp* **swanned**) *Fam* **to s. in/out** entrar/salir despreocupadamente; **they spent a year swanning round Europe** pasaron un año vagando por Europa; **you can't just go swanning off to the pub, we're too busy** no puedes irte al bar tan tranquilo, tenemos mucho que hacer

▸ **swan about, swan around** *vi Fam* pasearse (por ahí) a la buena de Dios

swank [swæŋk] *Fam* **1** *n* (**a**) *(ostentation)* fanfarronería *f* (**b**) *(ostentatious person)* fanfarrón(ona) *m,f,* figurón *m*

2 *vi* fanfarronear

swanky ['swæŋkɪ] *adj Fam* (**a**) *(person) (boastful)* fanfarrón(ona); *(posh) Esp* pijo(a), *Méx* fresa, *RP* (con)cheto(a), *Ven* sifrino(a) (**b**) *(restaurant, hotel)* fastuoso(a), pomposo(a)

swansdown ['swɒnzdaʊn] *n* (**a**) *(feathers)* plumón *m* (**b**) *(fabric)* fustán *m*, bombasí *m*

swap, swop [swɒp] **1** *n* (**a**) *(exchange)* trueque *m*, intercambio *m*; **to do a s.** hacer un trueque (**b**) *(duplicate) (stamp)* sello *m* repetido; *(picture card)* cromo *m* repetido (**c**) *Fin* swap *m*, permuta *f* financiera

2 *vt* (*pt & pp* **swapped**) **to s. sth for sth** cambiar algo por algo; **I'll s. you this marble for one of your toy soldiers** te cambio esta canica por uno de tus soldaditos; **to s. partners** *(in game, dance)* cambiar de pareja; *(in relationship)* hacer un intercambio de parejas; **to s. places with sb** *(change seat)* cambiarse de sitio con alguien; *(change roles)* intercambiar papeles con alguien; **to s. insults/ideas** intercambiar insultos/ideas

3 *vi* hacer un intercambio; **my seat's better than yours, do you want to s.?** mi asiento es mejor que el tuyo, ¿quieres que cambiemos?

▸ **swap over, swap round 1** *vt sep* cambiar de sitio; **she swapped their glasses over** *or* **round when he left the room** cuando él salió, ella cambió los vasos de sitio

2 *vi* **do you mind swapping over** *or* **round so I can sit next to Max?** ¿te importaría cambiarme el sitio para que pueda sentarme al lado de Max?

sward [swɔːd] *n Literary* prado *m*

swarf [swɔːf] *n* virutas *fpl*

swarm [swɔːm] **1** *n* (**a**) *(of bees)* enjambre *m*; *(of mosquitoes)* nube *f*; **a s. of ants** una marbunta (**b**) *(of people)* nube *f*, enjambre *m*

2 *vi* (**a**) *(bees)* volar en enjambre

(**b**) *(people)* apelotonarse, ir en masa; **Oxford was swarming with tourists** Oxford era un hervidero de turistas; **the place was swarming with flies** el sitio estaba plagado de moscas; **they swarmed up the ramp** subieron la rampa en tropel; **children were swarming round the ice cream van** los niños se arremolinaban alrededor del camión de los helados

(**c**) *(climb)* **she swarmed up the tree** trepó al árbol

swarthiness ['swɔːðɪnɪs] *n* morenez *f*

swarthy ['swɔːðɪ] *adj* moreno(a)

swashbuckler ['swɒʃbʌklə(r)] *n (adventurer)* aventurero *m* espadachín

swashbuckling ['swɒʃbʌklɪŋ] *adj (hero)* intrépido(a); *(movie, story)* de espadachines

swastika ['swɒstɪkə] *n* esvástica *f*, cruz *f* gamada

SWAT [swɒt] *n US* (*abbr* **Special Weapons and Tactics**) = unidad armada de la policía estadounidense especializada en intervenciones peligrosas, *Esp* ≃ GEO *m*

swat [swɒt] (*pt & pp* **swatted**) **1** (**a**) *(device)* matamoscas *m inv* (**b**) *(swipe)* **he took a s. at the fly** intentó aplastar la mosca de un golpe

2 *vt (insect)* aplastar; *Fig* **he swatted the ball past his opponent** superó a su oponente con un golpe fortísimo a la pelota

3 *vi* **to s. at sth (with sth)** tratar de darle a algo (con algo)

swatch [swɔːtʃ] *n* (**a**) *(sample)* muestra *f* (**b**) *(book of samples)* muestrario *m*

swath [swɔːθ] *n* = **swathe**

swathe [sweɪð] **1** *n (strip of cloth, land)* faja *f*, banda *f*; **great swathes of the country have been affected by the problem** grandes áreas del país se han visto afectadas por el problema; *Fig* **the cannons had cut great swathes through the troops** los cañones hicieron estragos en las tropas; *Fig* **he cut a s. through their defence** cruzó la defensa como una exhalación

2 *vt* **to s. sth in bandages** vendar algo, envolver algo en vendajes; **the town was swathed in mist** la ciudad estaba envuelta en brumas

swatter ['swɒtə(r)] *n* matamoscas *m inv*

sway [sweɪ] **1** *n* (**a**) *(movement)* vaivén *m*, balanceo *m* (**b**) *(control, power)* dominio *m*; **he was under her s.** estaba bajo su yugo; **to hold s. over** ejercer dominio sobre; **the economic theories that hold s. today** las teorías económicas que predominan actualmente

2 *vt* (**a**) *(move) (hips, body)* balancear (**b**) *(influence, persuade)* hacer cambiar (de opinión); **to refuse to be swayed** negarse a cambiar de postura; **don't be swayed by his charm** no dejes que su encanto te influya

3 *vi* balancearse; **to s. from side to side** balancearse de un lado a otro; **the poplars swayed in the wind** los álamos se balanceaban al viento; **he swayed towards her** se le acercó haciendo eses; *Fig* **opinion was swaying towards the Liberals** la opinión pública se iba decantando por los liberales

swaying ['sweɪɪŋ] *adj (motion)* balanceante

Swazi ['swɑːzɪ] **1** *n* (**a**) *(person)* suazi *mf* (**b**) *(language)* suazi *m*

2 *adj* suazi

Swaziland ['swɑːzɪlænd] *n* Suazilandia

swear [sweə(r)] (*pt* **swore** [swɔː(r)], *pp* **sworn** [swɔːn]) **1** *vt* (**a**) *(vow)* jurar; **to s. allegiance to the King** jurar lealtad al Rey; *Law* **to s. an oath** prestar juramento; **I s. I'll never do it again!** ¡juro que no lo volveré a hacer!; **he swears he's never seen her before** jura que nunca la había visto; **I could have sworn I'd seen him somewhere before** hubiera jurado que ya lo había visto antes en alguna parte; **to s. to do sth** jurar hacer algo; **to s. blind that...** jurar por lo más sagrado que...

(**b**) *(make sb pledge)* **to s. sb to secrecy** hacer prometer a alguien que guardará el secreto

2 *vi* (**a**) *(use swearwords)* jurar, decir palabrotas; **to s. at sb** insultar a alguien; **they started swearing at each other** empezaron a insultarse; IDIOM *Fam* **to s. like a trooper** jurar como un carretero

(**b**) *(take oath)* **he swore on the Bible** juró sobre la Biblia

(**c**) *(solemnly assert)* **to s. to sth** jurar algo; **I wouldn't s. to it, but I think it was him** creo que fue él, pero no pondría la mano en el fuego

▸ **swear by** *vt insep* (**a**) *(invoke)* jurar por; **he swore by his honour** juró por su honor (**b**) *(have total confidence in)* confiar ciegamente en

▸ **swear in** *vt sep (jury, witness, president)* tomar juramento a; **the new president will be sworn in tomorrow** mañana se tomará juramento al nuevo presidente

▸ **swear off** *vt insep (alcohol, cigarettes)* prometer renunciar a

swearing ['sweərɪŋ] *n* palabrotas *fpl*; **s. is rude** decir palabrotas es de mala educación; **there's too much s. in the book** hay demasiadas palabrotas en el libro, el libro posee un lenguaje demasiado vulgar

swearing-in ['sweərɪŋ'ɪn] *n (of jury, witness, president)* juramento *m*

swearword ['sweəwɜːd] *n* palabrota *f*, *Esp* taco *m*

sweat [swet] **1** *n (perspiration)* sudor *m*; **she awoke in a s.** se despertó empapada en sudor; *Fam* **no s.!** ¡no hay problema!; IDIOM **by the s. of one's brow** con el sudor de la frente ▸▸ ***s. gland*** glándula *f* sudorípara; ***s. pants*** pantalón *m* de deporte *or Esp* de chándal

(**b**) *Br Fam (anxious state)* **to be in a s. about sth** estar apurado(a) por algo; **there's no need to get into a s. about it!** ¡no hay por qué apurarse por eso!

(**c**) *Fam (hard task)* currada *f*; **picking strawberries is a real s.** recoger fresas es una currada

(**d**) *(on wall, surface)* condensación *f*

(**e**) *Br Old-fashioned Fam* **(old) s.** *(veteran)* veterano(a) *m,f*

2 *vt* (**a**) *(exude)* sudar; IDIOM *Fam* **to s. buckets** sudar a chorros *or* la gota gorda; IDIOM **to s. blood (over sth)** sudar tinta (con algo) (**b**) *Culin* rehogar

3 *vi* (**a**) *(perspire)* sudar; IDIOM *Fam* **to s. like a pig** sudar como un cerdo (**b**) *Fam (worry)* sufrir, angustiarse; **I'm going to make him s.** voy a dejarlo que sufra (**c**) *(work hard)* sudar tinta (**d**) *(walls, surface)* transpirar; *(cheese)* sudar

▸ **sweat off** *vt insep (excess weight)* adelgazar sudando

▸ **sweat out** *vt sep* (**a**) *(cold, fever)* sudar (**b**) *(wait uncomfortably)* **they'll have to s. it out until the rescuers arrive** tendrán que aguantar hasta que llegue el equipo de rescate; **let's leave him to s. it out** vamos a dejarlo que sufra

sweatband ['swetbænd] *n* (**a**) *Sport (on head)* banda *f (para la frente)*; *(on wrist)* muñequera *f* (**b**) *(in hat)* cinta *f* para la cabeza

sweated ['swetɪd] *adj* **s. labour** *(staff)* mano de obra explotada; *(work)* trabajo forzado

sweater ['swetə(r)] *n* suéter *m*, *Esp* jersey *m*, *Col* saco *m*, *RP* pulóver *m*

sweatiness ['swetɪnɪs] *n* transpiración *f*, sudoración *f*

sweating ['swetɪŋ] *n* transpiración *f*, sudoración *f*

sweatshirt ['swetʃɜːt] *n* sudadera *f*, *Col, CSur* buzo *m*

sweatshop ['swetʃɒp] *n* = fábrica donde se explota al trabajador

sweatsuit ['swetsu:t] *n US Esp* chándal *m*, *Méx* pants *mpl*, *RP* jogging *m*

sweaty ['swetɪ] *adj* (a) *(person, face, hands, feet)* sudoroso(a); *(clothes)* sudado(a); **to be s.** *(person)* estar sudoroso(a); *(clothes)* estar sudado(a); **a s. smell** un olor a sudor (b) *(weather, place)* caluroso(a) (c) *(cheese)* que suda (d) *(work, climb)* fatigoso(a)

Swede [swi:d] *n (person)* sueco(a) *m,f*

swede [swi:d] *n esp Br (vegetable)* colinabo *m*

Sweden ['swi:dən] *n* Suecia

Swedish ['swi:dɪʃ] **1** *npl (people)* **the S.** los suecos
2 *n (language)* sueco *m*
3 *adj* sueco(a)

sweep [swi:p] **1** *n* (a) *(action)* barrido *m*, *Am* barrida *f*; **to give the floor a s.** barrer el suelo; *Fig* **at one s.** de una pasada
(b) *(movement)* **with a s. of the arm** moviendo el brazo extendido; **he cut his head off with a s. of his sword** le cortó la cabeza de un sablazo
(c) *(search) (of radar, searchlight)* barrido *m*; **the police made a s. of the area** la policía peinó la zona; **her eyes made a s. of the room** recorrió la habitación con la mirada
(d) *(of road, river)* curva *f*; **from there we could see the whole s. of the bay** desde allí se podía ver toda la curva de la bahía
(e) *(extent, range) (of land, knowledge)* extensión *f*; *(of opinion)* porcentaje *m*, proporción *f*; **the vast s. of the work** el enorme alcance de la obra
(f) *Fam (chimney sweep)* deshollinador(ora) *m,f*
(g) *Fam (sweepstake)* porra *f (juego)*
2 *vt* (*pt & pp* **swept** [swept]) (a) *(with brush, broom) (floor, street)* barrer; *(chimney)* deshollinar; **she swept the leaves into a corner** fue barriendo las hojas hacia un rincón; **I swept the broken glass into the dustpan** recogí los *Esp* cristales *or Am* vidrios rotos con el recogedor; IDIOM **to s. sth under the carpet** *or US* **rug** soterrar algo
(b) *(with hand)* **he swept the crumbs off the table** despejó la mesa de migas con la mano; **she swept the coins off the table into her bag** arrastró las monedas hasta el borde de la mesa y las dejó caer en el bolso; **he wears his long hair swept back** lleva el pelo recogido por detrás
(c) *(brush lightly)* **her dress swept the ground** su vestido rozaba el suelo
(d) *(move through, over)* **the storms which are sweeping the country** las tormentas que asolan el país; **the flu epidemic which swept Europe in 1919** la epidemia de gripe que asoló Europa en 1919; **the latest craze to s. the country** la última moda que está haciendo furor en todo el país; IDIOM **to s. the board** *(in competition)* arrasar
(e) *(carry)* **the wind swept his hat into the river** el viento se llevó su sombrero al río; **a wave swept him overboard** lo arrastró una ola y cayó al mar; **they were swept out to sea** se los llevó el mar; *Fig* **he was swept to power on a wave of popular discontent** una ola de descontento generalizado lo llevó hasta el poder; *Fig* **the victorious army swept all before it** el ejército vencedor arrasó con todo lo que le salió al paso; *Fig* **he swept her off to Paris for the weekend** la sorprendió llevándosela a París para el fin de semana; IDIOM **he swept her off her feet** se enamoró perdidamente de él
(f) *(scan, survey) (of police, radar, searchlight)* barrer; **to s. the sky with a telescope** barrer el cielo con un telescopio; **her eyes swept the room** recorrió la habitación con la mirada
(g) *(mines, sea, channel)* barrer
(h) *(win easily) (election, tournament)* barrer en
3 *vi* (a) *(with broom)* barrer
(b) *(move rapidly)* **fierce winds swept across the planet's surface** vientos huracanados barrían la superficie del planeta; **to s. in/out** *(person)* entrar/salir con gallardía; **to s. through sth** atravesar a toda velocidad algo; **the fire swept through the upper floors** el fuego se propagó por los pisos superiores; **a wave of nationalism swept through the country** una ola de nacionalismo recorrió el país; **to s. to power** subir al poder de forma arrasadora
(c) *(curve)* describir una curva; **the fields s. down to the lake** los campos describen una pronunciada curva en su descenso hasta el lago

▶**sweep aside** *vt sep* (a) *(opposition)* barrer; *(criticism)* hacer caso omiso de (b) *(defeat easily)* barrer

▶**sweep away** *vt sep* (a) *(with brush, broom) (dust, snow)* barrer (b) *(of wind, tide, crowd)* arrastrar, llevarse; **she was swept away by a huge wave** fue arrastrada por una ola enorme; *Fig* **I was swept away by her enthusiasm** me arrastró su entusiasmo (c) *(usher away)* llevar *or* conducir apresuradamente

▶**sweep up** **1** *vt sep* (a) *(dust, leaves)* barrer; **he swept the leaves up into a pile** barrió las hojas hasta hacer un montón (b) *(pick up)* **she swept up her two babies in her arms and left** recogió rápidamente a un bebé con cada brazo y se fue (c) *(hair)* **she wears her hair swept up in a bun** lleva el pelo recogido en un moño
2 *vi (clean up)* barrer

sweeper ['swi:pə(r)] *n* (a) *(device) (for streets)* camión *m or* vehículo *m* de limpieza; **(carpet) s.** cepillo *m* mecánico (b) *(person)* barrendero(a) *m,f* (c) *(in soccer)* líbero *m* (d) *(in cycle race)* **s. van** coche *m* escoba

sweeping ['swi:pɪŋ] *adj* (a) *(gesture)* amplio(a); *(view)* panorámico(a) (b) *(statement)* (demasiado) generalizador(ora); *(generalization)* desmesurado(a) (c) *(changes, reforms)* radical (d) *(gains, cuts)* significativo(a)

sweepings ['swi:pɪŋz] *npl (dirt)* basura *f*

sweepstake ['swi:psteɪk] *n* (a) *(lottery)* porra *f (juego)* (b) *(horse race)* = carrera de caballos en la que el ganador se lleva todo el dinero de las apuestas

sweet [swi:t] **1** *n* (a) *Br (confectionery)* dulce *m*, caramelo *m* ▸▸ ***s. shop*** confitería *f* (b) *Br (dessert)* postre *m* ▸▸ ***s. trolley*** carro *m or* carrito *m* de (los) postres (c) *(term of address)* **my s.** cariño
2 *adj* (a) *(in taste) (honey, tea, fruit, wine)* dulce; **this tea is too s. for me** este té es demasiado dulce para mí; **to taste s.** saber dulce; **he eats too many s. things** come demasiado dulce; IDIOM **as s. as honey** dulce como la miel; IDIOM **to have a s. tooth** ser goloso(a) ▸▸ ***s. basil*** albahaca *f* fina; ***s. brier*** eglantina *f*; ***s. cherry*** cereza *f* dulce; ***s. chestnut*** castaño *m*; *US* ***s. cider*** *(unfermented apple juice) Esp* zumo *m or Am* jugo *m* de manzana; ***s. flag*** cálamo *m*; *Bot* ***s. pea*** *Esp* guisante *m or Am* arveja *f or Méx* chícharo *m* de olor; ***s. pepper*** pimiento *m* morrón, *RP* ají *m*; ***s. potato*** batata *f*, *Esp, Cuba, Urug* boniato *m*, *CAm, Méx* camote *m*; *Bot* ***s. william*** minutisa *f*
(b) *(pleasant) (smell)* fragante; *(water)* refrescante; *(sound, voice)* agradable; **the roses smell so s.!** ¡qué bien huelen las rosas!; **s. dreams!** ¡que sueñes con los angelitos!; IDIOM **the s. smell of success** las mieles del éxito
(c) *(cute) (baby, dress)* rico(a), mono(a); **how s.!** ¡qué mono!
(d) *(kind, generous) (person, nature)* amable, dulce; **that's very s. of you** eres muy amable; **to keep sb s.** tener contento(a) a alguien; **to whisper s. nothings to sb** susurrar palabras de amor a alguien ▸▸ ***s. talk*** coba *f*
(e) *(satisfying) (victory, revenge)* dulce
(f) *(good, well executed) (shot, forehand)* preciso(a), limpio(a) ▸▸ ***s. spot*** *(on golf club, tennis racket)* punto *m* ideal (de contacto)
(g) *Fam (in love)* **to be s. on sb** estar colado(a) por alguien
(h) *Fam (for emphasis)* **he'll please his own s. self** hará lo que le dé la real gana; **s. Jesus!** ¡Jesús!; *Br Fam* **s. fanny adams, s. FA** nada de nada, *Esp* nasti de plasti

sweet-and-sour ['swi:tən'saʊə(r)] *adj (sauce, pork)* agridulce

sweetbreads ['swi:tbredz] *npl* mollejas *fpl*

sweetcorn ['swi:tkɔ:n] *n* maíz *m* tierno, *Andes, RP* choclo *m*, *Méx* elote *m*

sweeten ['swi:tən] *vt* (a) *(food, drink)* endulzar (b) *(improve smell of) (air)* perfumar; *(breath)* refrescar (c) *(mollify, soften) (person)* ablandar; **to s. sb's temper** aplacar el mal humor de alguien (d) *Fam (bribe)* untar (e) *(make more pleasant) (process, task)* endulzar, dorar; *(offer)* hacer más atractivo(a)

▶**sweeten up** *vt sep* ablandar

sweetener ['swi:tnə(r)] *n* (a) *(in food)* edulcorante *m* (b) *Fam (bribe)* propina *f*

sweetheart ['swi:thɑ:t] *n* (a) *Old-fashioned (girlfriend, boyfriend)* novio(a) *m,f*; **he married his childhood s.** se casó con su amor de la infancia (b) *(form of address)* corazón *m*, cariño *m* (c) *Ind* ***s. agreement*** *or* ***contract*** *or* ***deal*** *(between union and management)* = acuerdo interesado entre patronal y sindicatos que puede no ser del todo favorable para los trabajadores

sweetie ['swi:tɪ] *n Fam* (a) *Br (confectionery)* golosina *f* (b) *(darling)* cariño *m*; **he's such a s.** es un encanto

sweetie-pie ['swi:tɪ'paɪ] *n Fam (term of address)* cariño *m*

sweetly ['swi:tlɪ] *adv* (a) *(kindly) (to smile)* con dulzura; **he very s. agreed to help us** accedió muy amablemente a ayudarnos (b) *(to sing, play)* con dulzura (c) *(smoothly) (to hit ball)* suavemente; **a s. struck penalty** un penalti ejecutado con gran precisión

sweetmeat ['swi:tmi:t] *n Old-fashioned* dulce *m*

sweet-natured ['swi:t'neɪtʃəd] *adj* amable, dulce

sweetness ['swi:tnɪs] *n* (**a**) *(in taste)* dulzura *f*, dulzor *m* (**b**) *(of smell)* fragancia *f*; *(of water)* frescura *f*; *(of sound, voice)* suavidad *f*, dulzura *f* (**c**) *(kindness, generosity) (of person, nature)* amabilidad *f*, dulzura *f*; IDIOM **to be all s. and light** estar de lo más amable

sweet-scented ['swi:t'sentɪd] *adj* fragante

sweet-smelling ['swi:t'smelɪŋ] *adj* fragante

sweet-talk ['swi:t'tɔ:k] *vt Fam* **to s. sb into doing sth** engatusar a alguien para que haga algo

sweet-tempered ['swi:t'tempəd] *adj* apacible

sweet-toothed ['swi:t'tu:θt] *adj* goloso(a)

swell [swel] **1** *n* (**a**) *(of sea)* oleaje *m* (**b**) *(bulge) (of sails, belly, breasts)* redondez *f* (**c**) *(increase) (in numbers)* aumento *m*; *(of anger, opposition, sympathy)* incremento *m* (**d**) *Mus (crescendo)* crescendo *m* diminuendo; *(device)* caja *f* de expresión (**e**) *Fam Old-fashioned (dandy)* petimetre *m*

2 *vt* (*pp* **swollen** ['swəʊlən] *or* **swelled**) (**a**) *(distend)* hinchar; **her eyes were swollen with tears** tenía los ojos hinchados de llorar; **the wind swelled the sails** el viento hinchaba las velas (**b**) *(increase) (numbers, crowd)* aumentar; **he is now swelling the ranks of the unemployed** ha pasado a engrosar las listas de desempleados *or Esp* parados (**c**) *(river)* hacer subir el caudal de

3 *vi* (**a**) *(distend) (part of body, lentils)* hincharse; *(wood)* abombarse; **his leg swelled** se le hinchó la pierna; **to s. with pride** henchirse de orgullo (**b**) *(increase) (number, crowd)* aumentar, crecer (**c**) *(river)* tener una crecida (**d**) *(grow louder)* **the applause/music swelled to a crescendo** la ovación/la música fue subiendo in *or* en crescendo

4 *adj US Fam (excellent)* genial, *Andes, CAm, Carib, Méx* chévere, *Méx* padre, *RP* bárbaro(a); **we had a s. time** nos lo pasamos genial

5 *exclam US Fam* ¡genial!

► **swell up** *vi (part of body)* hincharse; **her leg had swollen up** se le había hinchado la pierna

swellhead ['swelhed] *n US Fam* creído(a) *m,f*, engreído(a) *m,f*

swellheaded [swel'hedɪd] *adj US Fam* creído(a), engreído(a)

swelling ['swelɪŋ] *n* hinchazón *f*

swelter ['sweltə(r)] *vi* sofocarse (de calor), achicharrarse

sweltering ['sweltərɪŋ] *adj (day, heat)* asfixiante, sofocante; **it's s. in here!** hace un calor asfixiante aquí dentro

swelteringly ['sweltərɪŋlɪ] *adv* **a s. hot day** un día (de un calor) asfixiante

swept *pt & pp of* **sweep**

sweptback ['sweptbæk] *adj* (**a**) *(hair)* peinado(a) hacia atrás (**b**) *Av (wing)* en flecha

sweptwing ['sweptwɪŋ] *adj Av* de alas en flecha

swerve [swɜ:v] **1** *n (of car)* giro *m or* desplazamiento *m* brusco; *(on ball)* efecto *m*; *(of player)* regate *m*

2 *vt (car)* girar bruscamente; *(ball)* golpear con efecto

3 *vi (car, driver)* desplazarse bruscamente; *(player)* regatear; *(ball)* ir con efecto; **I had to s. to avoid the cyclist** tuve que girar bruscamente para no arrollar al ciclista

swift [swɪft] **1** *n (bird)* vencejo *m*

2 *adj* (**a**) *(runner, horse)* veloz, rápido(a) (**b**) *(reaction, reply)* rápido(a), pronto(a); **she was s. to reply** respondió rápidamente; **the government was s. to deny the rumours** el gobierno se apresuró a desmentir los rumores; *Br Fam* **do you fancy a s. pint?** ¿te apetece una cerveza rapidita?

swift-flowing ['swɪft'fləʊɪŋ] *adj (river)* torrencial

swift-footed ['swɪft'fʊtɪd] *adj* rápido(a)

swiftly ['swɪftlɪ] *adv* (**a**) *(to run, move)* velozmente, rápidamente; **the meeting moved s. to its conclusion** se dio rápidamente por concluida la reunión (**b**) *(to react, reply)* con rapidez, con prontitud

swiftness ['swɪftnɪs] *n* (**a**) *(of movement, runner)* rapidez *f* (**b**) *(of reaction, reply)* rapidez *f*, prontitud *f*

swig [swɪg] *Fam* **1** *n* trago *m*; **he took a s. from the bottle** dio un trago de la botella

2 *vt* (*pt & pp* **swigged**) *Esp* pimplar, *Am* tomar

swill [swɪl] **1** *n* (**a**) *(food) (for pigs)* sobras *fpl* para los cerdos *or* puercos *or Am* chanchos; *Pej (for people)* bazofia *f*, bodrio *m* (**b**) *(rinse)* **to give sth a s.** dar un enjuague a algo

2 *vt* (**a**) *(wash)* **he swilled the floor (down)** echó un cubo de agua por el suelo; **go and s. the glass under the tap** vete a enjuagar el vaso (**b**) *Fam (drink) Esp* tragar, *Am* tomar

► **swill about, swill around** *vi (liquid)* agitarse

► **swill out** *vt sep (rinse)* enjuagar, *Esp* aclarar

swim [swɪm] **1** *n* baño *m*; **to go for** *or* **have a s.** ir a nadar, ir a darse un baño; **it's a good 20-minute s. out to the island** se tarda por lo menos 20 minutos en nadar hasta la isla; **that was her fastest s. this year** ése fue el mejor tiempo de la nadadora este año; IDIOM *Fam* **to be in/out of the s. (of things)** estar/no estar al día ►► ***s. bladder*** vejiga *f* natatoria

2 *vt* (*pt* **swam** [swæm], *pp* **swum** [swʌm]) *(distance, length)* nadar; **to s. the breaststroke** *Esp* nadar a braza, *Am* nadar pecho; **to s. the Channel** atravesar el Canal de la Mancha a nado

3 *vi* (**a**) *(in water) (person, fish)* nadar; **I can't s.!** ¡no sé nadar!; **to go swimming** ir a nadar; **to s. across a river** atravesar un río a nado; **to s. for the shore** nadar hacia la costa; **he managed to s. to safety** consiguió nadar hasta ponerse a salvo; **the raft sank and they had to s. for it** la balsa se hundió y tuvieron que nadar para salvarse; IDIOM **to s. with the tide** seguir la corriente; IDIOM **to s. against the tide** nadar contra corriente

(**b**) *(be soaked, flooded)* **the floor was swimming with water** el suelo estaba anegado *or* inundado de agua; **the sausages were swimming in grease** las salchichas nadaban en grasa

(**c**) *(be dizzy)* **my head is swimming** me da vueltas la cabeza

swimmer ['swɪmə(r)] *n* nadador(ora) *m,f*; **I'm a strong/weak s.** nado bien/mal

swimming ['swɪmɪŋ] *n* natación *f*; **I like s.** me gusta la natación; **to go s.** ir a nadar ►► ***s. bath(s)*** *Br* piscina *f or Méx* alberca *f or RP* pileta *f* cubierta; ***s. cap*** gorro *m* de baño *or* de piscina; ***s. costume*** bañador *m*, traje *m* de baño, *RP* malla *f*; ***s. gala*** concurso *m* de natación; ***s. hat*** gorro *m* de baño; ***s. instructor*** monitor(ora) *m,f* de natación; ***s. lesson*** clase *f* de natación; ***s. pool*** piscina *f*, *Méx* alberca *f*, *RP* pileta *f*; ***s. trunks*** traje *m* de baño *(de hombre)*, *Esp* bañador *m (de hombre)*, *RP* malla *f (de hombre)*

swimmingly ['swɪmɪŋlɪ] *adv Fam (to get on)* estupendamente; **everything's going s.** todo va viento en popa

swimsuit ['swɪmsu:t] *n* traje *m* de baño, *Esp* bañador *m*, *RP* malla *f*

swimwear ['swɪmweə(r)] *n* moda *f* de baño

swindle ['swɪndəl] **1** *n* timo *m*, estafa *f*

2 *vt* timar, estafar; **to s. sb out of sth** estafarle algo a alguien

swindler ['swɪndlə(r)] *n* timador(ora) *m,f*, estafador(ora) *m,f*

swine [swaɪn] (*pl* **swine**) *n* (**a**) *(pig)* cerdo *m*, puerco *m*, *Am* chancho *m* ►► ***s. fever*** peste *f* porcina (**b**) *Fam (unpleasant person)* cerdo(a) *m,f*, canalla *mf*; **he's a lazy s.!** ¡es un vago asqueroso! (**c**) *Fam (difficult thing)* tarea *f* de titanes; **it's a s. of a job** es una currada

swineherd ['swaɪnhɜ:d] *n Old-fashioned* porquero(a) *m,f*

swing [swɪŋ] **1** *n* (**a**) *(movement) (of rope, chain)* vaivén *m*, balanceo *m*; *(of pendulum)* oscilación *f*; **he released the ball with a s. of his arm** lanzó la pelota balanceando la mano; IDIOM **to be in full s.** ir a toda marcha; IDIOM *Fam* **everything went with a s.** todo fue sobre ruedas; IDIOM *Fam* **to get into the s. of things** agarrar *or Esp* coger el ritmo ►► ***s. bin*** cubo *m* de la basura con tapa oscilante; ***s. bridge*** puente *m* giratorio; ***s. door*** puerta *f* pendular *or* basculante; *US Fam* ***s. shift*** *(work period, people)* turno *m* de tarde y noche

(**b**) *(in golf)* swing *m*

(**c**) *(arc)* **the plane came round in a wide s.** el avión se acercó describiendo un gran arco

(**d**) *Fam (attempted punch)* **to take a s. at sb** intentar darle un golpe a alguien

(**e**) *(change) (in opinion, mood)* cambio *m* repentino (**in** de); **a s. to the left/against the government** un giro a la izquierda/en contra del gobierno; **the swings of the stock market** los altibajos del mercado de valores; **the party needs a 10 percent s. to win the election** el partido necesita arrancar un 10 por ciento de votos a sus rivales para ganar las elecciones

(**f**) *(in playground) (object)* columpio *m*; **can I have a s.?** ¿puedo columpiarme un rato?; IDIOM **it's swings and roundabouts, what you lose on the swings you gain on the roundabouts** lo que se pierde aquí, se gana allá

(**g**) *(rhythm)* ritmo *m*

(**h**) *(style of jazz)* swing *m* ►► ***s. band*** banda *f* de swing

2 *vt* (*pt & pp* **swung** [swʌŋ]) (**a**) *(move in a curve) (racket, bat, axe)* balancear; **he swung a rope over the branch** hizo pasar una cuerda sobre la rama; **to s. sth/sb onto one's shoulder** echarse algo/a alguien al hombro; **he swung the suitcase onto the bed** echó la maleta *or Am* valija encima de la cama; **I swung myself (up) into the saddle** me monté en la silla; **she swung the door shut** cerró la puerta

(**b**) *(cause to sway)* balancear; **he walked along swinging his arms** caminaba balanceando los brazos; **to s. one's hips** menear las caderas; IDIOM *Old-fashioned* **to s. the lead** acudir a un subterfugio

(**c**) *(turn) (steering wheel, vehicle)* hacer girar

(**d**) *(cause to change)* **that swung the decision our way/against us** eso cambió la decisión en nuestro favor/nuestra contra; **to s. the vote** alterar el sentido del voto

(**e**) *Fam (arrange)* **to s. it so that...** agenciárselas para que...; **to s. a deal** cerrar un trato

3 *vi* (**a**) *(move to and fro)* balancearse; *(pendulum)* oscilar; *(on playground swing)* columpiarse; **he walked along with his arms swinging** caminaba balanceando los brazos; **the gate was swinging in the wind** el viento abría y cerraba la puerta; **a long rope swung from the ceiling** una larga cuerda se balanceaba colgada del techo; *Fam* **he should s. for this** *(be hanged)* deberían colgarlo por esto; IDIOM *Fam* **to s. both ways** *(be bisexual)* ser bisexual

(**b**) *(pivot)* **to s. open/shut** *(door)* abrirse/cerrarse; **the boom swung round and hit me in the face** la botavara giró y me dio en la cara

(**c**) *(move along)* **to s. from tree to tree** columpiarse de árbol en árbol; **I swung into the saddle** me monté en la silla; *Fig* **to s. into action** entrar en acción

(**d**) *(change direction)* girar, torcer; **the car swung left** el coche *or Am* carro *or CSur* auto giró a la izquierda

(**e**) *(change opinion, mood)* **to s. to the left/right** *(electorate, public opinion)* virar a la izquierda/derecha; **she swings between depression and elation** oscila entre la depresión y el júbilo

(**f**) *(hit out, aim blow)* **to s. for** *or* **at sb** tratar de pegar a alguien; **he swung at the ball but missed** intentó dar a la pelota, pero falló

(**g**) *Fam (musician, music)* tener ritmo

(**h**) *Fam (be lively) (club, disco)* estar muy animado(a); **the party was really swinging** la fiesta estaba muy animada

(**i**) *Fam (exchange sexual partners)* hacer intercambio de parejas

▸**swing round** **1** *vt sep (vehicle)* dar media vuelta a; *(person)* dar la vuelta a (**b**) *(change) (public opinion)* dar un vuelco a; **he managed to s. her round to his point of view** consiguió hacerla adoptar su punto de vista

2 *vi* (**a**) *(turn round) (person)* dar media vuelta; *(vehicle)* dar un giro de 180 grados (**b**) *(public opinion, person)* dar un vuelco

swingboat ['swɪŋbəʊt] *n* góndola *f*, = columpio de feria en forma de barca

swingeing ['swɪndʒɪŋ] *adj Br (cuts, rise, fall)* drástico(a); *(criticism)* demoledor(ora); *(victory, majority)* abrumador(ora)

swinger ['swɪŋə(r)] *n Fam* (**a**) *(sociable person) Esp* marchoso(a) *m,f*, *Am* parrandero(a) *m,f* (**b**) *(who swaps sexual partners)* = persona que participa en intercambios de pareja

swinging ['swɪŋɪŋ] *adj* (**a**) *(motion)* oscilante; *(gait)* saltarín(ina) (**b**) *Fam (trendy) Esp* marchoso(a), *Am* parrandero(a) ▸▸ ***s. London*** = el Londres efervescente de los años sesenta; ***the s. sixties*** los locos *or* febriles años sesenta

swing-wing ['swɪŋ'wɪŋ] *adj Av* de geometría variable

swinish ['swaɪnɪʃ] *adj* canallesco(a)

swipe [swaɪp] **1** *n (with fist, stick)* **to take a s. at sb** intentar dar un golpe a alguien; *Fig* **the programme takes a s. at the rich and famous** el programa arremete contra los ricos y famosos ▸▸ ***s. card*** tarjeta *f* con banda magnética

2 *vt* (**a**) *Fam (hit)* dar un golpe a, *Esp* atizar (**b**) *Fam (steal)* afanar, birlar, *Méx* bajar (**c**) *(card)* pasar

3 *vi* **to s. at sth/sb** intentar dar un golpe a algo/alguien

swirl [swɜːl] **1** *n (of cream)* rizo *m*; *(of smoke)* voluta *f*; *(of leaves, dust, water)* remolino *m*

2 *vt* revolver

3 *vi (leaves, dust, person, skirt)* arremolinarse

swirling ['swɜːlɪŋ] *adj (leaves, dust)* arremolinado(a)

swish [swɪʃ] **1** *n* (**a**) *(sound) (of cane, whip)* silbido *m*; *(of dress, silk)* frufrú *m*, (sonido *m* del) roce *m*; *(of water)* susurro *m*; *(of scythe)* sonido *m* cortante (**b**) *(movement)* **the cow flicked the flies away with a s. of its tail** la vaca sacudió el rabo para espantar las moscas (**c**) *US Fam (effeminate homosexual)* mariquita *m*

2 *adj Fam* (**a**) *(elegant, smart)* distinguido(a), refinado(a) (**b**) *US (effeminate)* mariquita

3 *vt (cane, whip)* hacer silbar; **to s. its tail** *(animal)* menear *or* agitar la cola

4 *vi (dress, silk)* sonar al rozar; *(cane, whip)* silbar; *(water)* susurrar

swishy ['swɪʃɪ] *adj US Fam (effeminate)* mariquita

Swiss [swɪs] **1** *n* suizo(a) *m,f*

2 *npl* **the S.** los suizos

3 *adj* suizo(a) ▸▸ ***S. army knife*** navaja *f* (suiza) multiusos; ***S. chard*** acelga *f*; ***S. cheese*** queso *m* suizo; ***S. cheese plant*** costilla *f* de hombre; ***S. Guard*** *(Pope's bodyguards)* Guardia *f* Suiza; *(person)* guardia *m* suizo; *Br* ***S. roll*** brazo *m* de gitano

Swiss-French [swɪs'frentʃ] **1** *n (dialect)* dialecto *m* suizo del francés

2 *adj* franco-suizo(a)

Swiss-German [swɪs'dʒɜːmən] **1** *n (dialect)* dialecto *m* suizo del alemán

2 *adj* suizo-alemán(ana)

Switch® [swɪtʃ] *n Br* **to pay by S.** pagar con tarjeta Switch ▸▸ ***S. card*** = tipo de tarjeta de débito

switch [swɪtʃ] **1** *n* (**a**) *(electrical)* interruptor *m*; **is the s. on/off?** ¿está encendido/apagado el interruptor?

(**b**) *(changeover) (to new system, position)* cambio *m*; *(in policy, opinion)* cambio *m*, viraje *m*; **the s. to the new equipment went very smoothly** el cambio al nuevo equipamiento se produjo sin ningún problema; **to make a s.** hacer un cambio; **the country has successfully made the s. from totalitarianism to democracy** el país ha realizado con éxito la transición de un sistema totalitario a la democracia

(**c**) *(swap)* cambiazo *m*; **to make a s.** dar el cambiazo

(**d**) *(stick)* vara *f*; *(riding crop)* fusta *f*

(**e**) *US Rail* agujas *fpl*

(**f**) *(hairpiece)* postizo *m*

2 *vt* (**a**) *(change)* cambiar; **he switched channels/jobs** cambió de canal/trabajo; **the fixture has been switched to next Wednesday** han cambiado la fecha del partido al miércoles que viene; **the government has switched its policy from prevention to cure** el gobierno ha pasado de una política de prevención a una de cura

(**b**) *(exchange)* intercambiar; **the two employees asked to s. jobs** los dos empleados solicitaron intercambiar sus puestos; **to s. seats with sb** cambiarse de asiento con alguien; **somebody had switched their drinks** alguien les había cambiado las bebidas; **he switched the case with the banknotes for an empty one** cambió el maletín con los billetes por uno vacío

(**c**) *(transfer)* trasladar (**to** a); **he's been switched to another department** lo han trasladado a otro departamento; **they switched their attention to something else** dirigieron su atención a otra cosa

(**d**) *Elec* **s. the heater to "low"** pon el calentador al mínimo

(**e**) *US Rail* **the train was switched to another track** cambiaron el tren de vía

3 *vi* (**a**) *(change)* cambiar (**to** a); **to s. to a new system** cambiar *or* cambiarse a un sistema nuevo; **can I s. to another channel?** ¿puedo cambiar de canal?; *Comptr* **press this key to s. between screens** pulse esta tecla para moverse entre pantallas; **to s. from gas to electricity** cambiar el gas por la electricidad, pasarse del gas a la electricidad; **he switches effortlessly from one language to another** pasa de una lengua a otra sin ningún esfuerzo; **the player switched from defence to midfield** el jugador pasó de la defensa al mediocampo

(**b**) *(exchange)* cambiarse

(**c**) *(be transferred)* trasladarse

▸**switch around** = **switch round**

▸**switch back** *vi (revert to)* **to s. back from electricity to gas** volver a pasar de la electricidad al gas; **to s. back to BBC2** volver a cambiar a la BBC2

▸**switch off** **1** *vt sep (appliance, heating, light, engine)* apagar; **the printer switches itself off after half an hour** la impresora se desconecta automáticamente después de media hora

2 *vi* (**a**) *(appliance, heating, light)* apagarse (**b**) *Br (TV viewer, radio listener)* apagar (**c**) *Fam (stop paying attention)* desconectar

▸**switch on** **1** *vt sep (appliance, heating, light, engine)* encender, *Am* prender; **it switches itself on** se enciende *or Am* prende solo; *Fig* **to s. on the charm** ponerse encantador(ora)

2 *vi* (**a**) *(appliance, heating, light)* encenderse, *Am* prenderse (**b**) *(TV viewer)* encender *or Am* prender la televisión; *(radio listener)* sintonizar

▸**switch over** *vi* (**a**) *(change TV or radio channel)* cambiar de cadena/emisora (**b**) *(change)* **to s. over to gas** pasarse *or* cambiar al gas

▸**switch round** **1** *vt sep* (**a**) *(swap round)* cambiar de sitio (**b**) *(rearrange) (furniture)* cambiar de sitio; **the manager has switched the team round again** el entrenador ha vuelto a cambiar la alineación

2 *vi (two people)* cambiarse

switchback ['swɪtʃbæk] *n* (**a**) *(road)* carretera *f* en zigzag (**b**) *Br (rollercoaster)* montaña *f* rusa

switchblade ['swɪtʃbleɪd] *n US* navaja *f* automática

switchboard ['swɪtʃbɔːd] *n* centralita *f*, *Am* conmutador *m* ▸▸ ***s. operator*** telefonista *mf*

switched-on [swɪtʃt'ɒn] *adj Fam (aware of fashion)* a la última

switcher ['swɪtʃə(r)] *n US TV & Cin (person)* ingeniero(a) *m,f* de imagen; *(machine)* mezclador *m* de imagen

switchgear ['swɪtʃgɪə(r)] *n* dispositivo *m* de distribución

switch-hitter ['swɪtʃhɪtə(r)] *n US* (**a**) *(in baseball)* bateador(ora) *m,f* ambidextro(a) (**b**) *very Fam (bisexual)* bisexual *mf*, *RP* bi *mf*

switchman ['swɪtʃmən] *n US Rail* guardagujas *m inv*
switchover ['swɪtʃəʊvə(r)] *n (to different method, system)* cambio *m* (**from/to** de/a)
switchyard ['swɪtʃjɑːd] *n US* patio *m* de maniobras
swither ['swɪðə(r)] *vi (hesitate)* vacilar, titubear (**about** *or* **over** sobre)
Switzerland ['swɪtsələnd] *n* Suiza
swivel ['swɪvəl] **1** *n* cabeza *f* giratoria ►► ***s. chair*** silla *f* giratoria
2 *vt* (*pt & pp* **swivelled**, *US* **swiveled**) hacer girar
3 *vi* girar; **he swivelled (round) and shot** giró sobre sí mismo y disparó
swizz [swɪz] *n Br Fam* timo *m*; **what a s.!** ¡qué timo!
swizzle ['swɪzəl] *n* ***s. stick*** agitador *m*, varilla *f* de cóctel
swollen ['swəʊlən] **1** *pp of* **swell**
2 *adj* (**a**) *(foot, ankle)* hinchado(a); *(gland)* inflamado(a); **her eyes were red and s. with crying** tenía los ojos rojos e hinchados de llorar; *Fig* **to have a s. head** ser un(a) creído(a) (**b**) *(river)* crecido(a)
swollen-headed ['swəʊlən'hedɪd] *adj Fam* creído(a), engreído(a)
swoon [swuːn] **1** *n Literary (fainting fit)* desmayo *m*, desvanecimiento *m*; **to go** *or* **fall into a s.** desmayarse, desvanecerse
2 *vi* (**a**) *Literary (faint)* desmayarse, desvanecerse (**b**) *(become ecstatic)* derretirse
► **swoon over** *vt insep* deshacerse con, derretirse por
swoop [swuːp] **1** *n* (**a**) *(of bird, plane)* (vuelo *m* en) picado *m* (**b**) *(of police)* redada *f*
2 *vi (bird, plane)* volar en *Esp* picado *or Am* picada; **the hawk swooped down on its prey** el halcón se lanzó en *Esp* picado *or Am* picada sobre su presa; *Fig* **critics were quick to s. on his mistake** los críticos no tardaron en echarse encima suyo por su error (**b**) *(police)* hacer una redada (**on** en)
swoosh [swuːʃ] **1** *n* silbido *m*
2 *vi* silbar, cortar el aire; **the express train swooshed past** el expreso pasó cortando el aire
3 *adv* **to go s.** silbar, cortar el aire
swop = **swap**
sword [sɔːd] *n* espada *f*; **to put sb to the s.** pasar a alguien por las armas; IDIOM **to beat** *or* **turn swords into ploughshares** forjar de las espadas azadones, abrazar la paz; PROV **those that live by the s. shall die by the s.** quien a hierro mata, a hierro muere ►► ***s. of Damocles*** espada *f* de Damocles; ***s. dance*** danza *f* del sable; ***s. fight*** duelo *m* de espadas
sword-and-sandals ['sɔːdən'sændəlz] *adj Fam (film)* de romanos
swordbill ['sɔːdbɪl] *n* colibrí *m* pico de espada
swordcraft ['sɔːdkrɑːft] *n* esgrima *f*
swordfish ['sɔːdfɪʃ] *n* pez *m* espada
swordplay ['sɔːdpleɪ] *n* esgrima *f*
swordsman ['sɔːdzmən] *n* espadachín *m*
swordsmanship ['sɔːdzmənʃɪp] *n* destreza *f* en el manejo de la espada
swordstick ['sɔːdstɪk] *n* bastón *m* de estoque
sword-swallower ['sɔːd'swɒləʊə(r)] *n* tragaespadas *mf inv*
swordtail ['sɔːdteɪl] *n* xifo *m*
swore *pt of* **swear**
sworn [swɔːn] **1** *adj* (**a**) *(committed)* ***s. enemy*** enemigo(a) *m,f* encarnizado(a) (**b**) *Law* ***s. statement*** declaración *f* jurada
2 *pp of* **swear**
swot [swɒt] *Br Fam* **1** *n Pej (studious pupil) Esp* empollón(ona) *m,f*, *Méx* matado(a) *m,f*, *RP* traga *mf*
2 *vi* (*pt & pp* **swotted**) *(study hard)* matarse estudiando, *Esp* empollar, *RP* tragar (**for** para)
► **swot up on** *vt insep Br Fam (subject)* matarse estudiando, *Esp* empollarse, *RP* tragarse
SWOT analysis ['swɒtə'næləsɪs] *n Econ* análisis *m inv* de las fuerzas, debilidades, oportunidades y amenazas
swotting ['swɒtɪŋ] *n Br Fam* **to do some s. (for sth)** empollar (para algo)
swum *pp of* **swim**
swung [swʌŋ] **1** *adj Typ* ***s. dash*** tilde *f*, virgulilla *f*
2 *pt & pp of* **swing**
sybarite ['sɪbəraɪt] *n Literary* sibarita *mf*
sybaritic [sɪbə'rɪtɪk] *adj Literary* sibarita
sycamore ['sɪkəmɔː(r)] *n* (**a**) *Br (maple)* plátano *m* falso, sicomoro *m* (**b**) *US (plane tree)* plátano *m*
sycophancy ['sɪkəfænsɪ] *n Pej* adulación *f*
sycophant ['sɪkəfənt] *n Pej* adulador(ora) *m,f*
sycophantic [sɪkə'fæntɪk] *adj Pej* adulador(ora)
Sydney ['sɪdnɪ] *n* Sidney
syllabic [sɪ'læbɪk] *adj* silábico(a)
syllable ['sɪləbəl] *n* sílaba *f*; *Fig* **I had to explain it to him in words of one s.** se lo tuve que explicar de forma muy clarita
syllabub ['sɪləbʌb] *n* = postre dulce de crema o leche batida y vino
syllabus ['sɪləbəs] *n* plan *m* de estudios, programa *m* de estudios
syllogism ['sɪlədʒɪzəm] *n* silogismo *m*
syllogistic [sɪlə'dʒɪstɪk] *adj* silogístico(a)
sylph [sɪlf] *n* (**a**) *(mythical being)* sílfide *f* (**b**) *Literary (slender woman)* sílfide *f*
sylph-like ['sɪlflaɪk] *adj Literary (woman)* esbelto(a); *(figure)* de sílfide; *Hum* **you're looking positively s., my dear** estás hecha una sílfide, cariño
sylvan ['sɪlvən] *adj Literary* silvano(a)
symbiosis [sɪmbaɪ'əʊsɪs] *n* simbiosis *f inv*
symbiotic [sɪmbaɪ'ɒtɪk] *adj* simbiótico(a)
symbol ['sɪmbəl] *n* símbolo *m*
symbolic [sɪm'bɒlɪk] *adj* simbólico(a); **to be s. of sth** simbolizar algo ►► ***s. logic*** lógica *f* simbólica
symbolically [sɪm'bɒlɪklɪ] *adv* simbólicamente, de forma simbólica
symbolism ['sɪmbəlɪzəm] *n* (**a**) *(use of symbols)* simbolismo *m* (**b**) *(artistic movement)* simbolismo *m*
symbolist ['sɪmbəlɪst] *Art* **1** *n* simbolista *mf*
2 *adj* simbolista
symbolize ['sɪmbəlaɪz] *vt* simbolizar
symmetrical [sɪ'metrɪkəl] *adj* simétrico(a)
symmetrically [sɪ'metrɪklɪ] *adv* simétricamente
symmetry ['sɪmɪtrɪ] *n* (**a**) *Math* simetría *f* (**b**) *(harmony)* simetría *f*
sympathetic [sɪmpə'θetɪk] *adj* (**a**) *(understanding)* comprensivo(a); *(compassionate)* compasivo(a); **they weren't very s. (towards me)** no se compadecieron mucho (de mí)
(**b**) *(favourably inclined)* **to be s. to** *or* **towards a proposal/cause** simpatizar con una propuesta/causa; **he was s. to my request for a loan** se mostró abierto *or* dispuesto a concederme un préstamo; **a s. audience** un público bien dispuesto
(**c**) *(character in novel, movie)* **I thought the doctor was the most s. character** el personaje del médico era el que más se ganó mi simpatía
(**d**) *(favourable) (environment, atmosphere)* propicio(a)
(**e**) *Anat* simpático(a)

False friend: The most common senses of the English adjective **sympathetic** are not translated by the Spanish word **simpático**. In Spanish **simpático** means "likeable", "agreeable" or "amusing".

sympathetically [sɪmpə'θetɪklɪ] *adv* (**a**) *(with understanding)* comprensivamente; *(with compassion)* compasivamente (**b**) *(in favourable light)* con indulgencia; **she received his request s.** accedió a su petición con indulgencia
sympathize ['sɪmpəθaɪz] *vi* (**a**) *(show sympathy)* compadecerse (**with** de); **poor Emma, I really s. with her!** ¡pobre Emma!, la comprendo perfectamente (**b**) *(understand)* **to s. (with sth/sb)** comprender (algo/a alguien) (**c**) *(support)* **to s. (with sth/sb)** simpatizar (con algo/alguien); **I cannot s. with that point of view** no puedo estar de acuerdo con esa opinión
sympathizer ['sɪmpəθaɪzə(r)] *n (political)* simpatizante *mf*; **a communist s.** un simpatizante comunista
sympathy ['sɪmpəθɪ] *n* (**a**) *(pity, compassion)* compasión *f*; *(understanding)* comprensión *f*; **to feel s. for sb** simpatizar con alguien; **I have nothing but s. for you** te comprendo perfectamente; **if you do break your leg don't expect any s. from me!** ¡si te partes la pierna, luego no me vengas llorando!; **he showed no s. for the children** no mostró ninguna compasión por los niños
(**b**) *(condolences)* **our sympathies are with the families of the dead** enviamos nuestro pésame a las familias de los fallecidos; *Formal* **you have my deepest s.** le doy mi más sincero pésame ►► ***s. card*** tarjeta *f* de condolencia
(**c**) *(support)* apoyo *m*, solidaridad *f*; **I have no s. for** *or* **with terrorism** estoy en contra del terrorismo; **to come out in s. with sb** *(workers)* declararse en huelga de solidaridad con alguien ►► *Ind* ***s. strike*** huelga *f* de solidaridad *or* apoyo
(**d**) **sympathies** *(leanings)* inclinación *f*; **she has strong left-wing sympathies** es muy de izquierdas
(**e**) *(affinity)* afinidad *f*
(**f**) *Anat* simpatía *f*

False friend: The most common sense of the English noun **sympathy** (i.e. "compassion, understanding") is not translated by the Spanish word **simpatía**. The most common sense of **simpatía** is "friendliness".

symphonic [sɪm'fɒnɪk] *adj* sinfónico(a) ►► ***s. poem*** poema *m* sinfónico

symphony ['sɪmfənɪ] *n Mus* sinfonía *f* ►► ***s. orchestra*** orquesta *f* sinfónica

symposium [sɪm'pəʊzɪəm] (*pl* **symposia** [sɪm'pəʊzɪə]) *n* simposio *m*

symptom ['sɪm(p)təm] *n* (**a**) *Med* síntoma *m* (**b**) *(sign)* síntoma *m*; **the team is showing symptoms of decline** el equipo muestra síntomas de declive

symptomatic [sɪm(p)tə'mætɪk] *adj* sintomático(a) (**of** de)

synaesthesia, *US* **synesthesia** [sɪnɪs'θi:zjə] *n Psy* sinestesia *f*

synagogue ['sɪnəgɒg] *n* sinagoga *f*

synapse ['saɪnæps] *n Anat* sinapsis *f inv*

synaptic [sɪ'næptɪk] *adj Anat* sináptico(a)

sync(h) [sɪŋk] *n Fam* sincronización *f*; **to be in/out of s. with** *Cin & TV* estar/no estar sincronizado(a) con; *(with person, electorate)* estar/no estar en sintonía con, *RP* sintonizar/no sintonizar el mismo canal que

synchromesh ['sɪnkrəʊmeʃ] *n Aut* sincronizador *m* (de velocidades) ►► ***s. gears*** transmisión *f* sincronizada

synchronic [sɪŋ'krɒnɪk] *adj Ling* sincrónico(a)

synchronicity [sɪŋkrə'nɪsɪtɪ] *n* sincronicidad *f*

synchronization [sɪŋkrənaɪ'zeɪʃən] *n* sincronización *f*

synchronize ['sɪŋkrənaɪz] **1** *vt* sincronizar

2 *vi* estar sincronizado(a) (**with** con)

synchronized ['sɪŋkrənaɪzd] *adj* sincronizado(a) ►► ***s. swimming*** natación *f* sincronizada

synchronous ['sɪŋkrənəs] *adj* (**a**) *(simultaneous)* sincrónico(a) (**b**) *Comptr* sincrónico(a)

synchrotron ['sɪŋkrətrɒn] *n Phys* sincrotrón *m*

syncopate ['sɪŋkəpeɪt] *vt Mus* sincopar

syncopated ['sɪŋkəpeɪtɪd] *adj Mus* sincopado(a)

syncopation [sɪŋkə'peɪʃən] *n Mus* síncopa *f*

syncope ['sɪŋkəpɪ] *n* (**a**) *Med* síncope *m* (**b**) *Ling* síncopa *f*

syncretism ['sɪŋkrɪtɪzəm] *n Phil* sincretismo *m*

syndicalism ['sɪndɪkəlɪzəm] *n Pol* sindicalismo *m* (revolucionario)

syndicate **1** *n* ['sɪndɪkət] (**a**) *Com* agrupación *f*; *(in lottery)* peña *f*; **crime s.** organización criminal (**b**) *Journ* agencia *f* de noticias

2 *vt* ['sɪndɪkeɪt] *Journ* **her column is syndicated to all the major newspapers** su columna aparece en los principales periódicos; **syndicated columnist** = columnista que publica simultáneamente en varios medios

syndication [sɪndɪ'keɪʃən] *n Journ* = producción independiente para su publicación conjunta por diferentes medios

syndrome ['sɪndrəʊm] *n* (**a**) *Med* síndrome *m* (**b**) *(symptoms)* síndrome *m*

synecdoche [sɪ'nekdəkɪ] *n Lit* sinécdoque *f*

synergy ['sɪnədʒɪ] *n* sinergia *f*

synesthesia *US* = **synaesthesia**

synod ['sɪnəd] *n Rel* sínodo *m*

synonym ['sɪnənɪm] *n* sinónimo *m*; **her name is a s. for professionalism** su nombre es sinónimo de profesionalidad

synonymous [sɪ'nɒnɪməs] *adj* sinónimo(a) (**with** de); **her name is s. with professionalism** su nombre es sinónimo de profesionalidad

synonymy [sɪ'nɒnəmɪ] *n* sinonimia *f*

synopsis [sɪ'nɒpsɪs] (*pl* **synopses** [sɪ'nɒpsi:z]) *n* sinopsis *f inv*, resumen *m*

synoptic [sɪ'nɒptɪk] *adj* sinóptico(a)

synovial [saɪ'nəʊvɪəl] *adj Anat* sinovial ►► ***s. fluid*** líquido *m* sinovial

synovitis ['saɪnəvaɪtɪs] *n Med* sinovitis *f inv*

syntactic(al) [sɪn'tæktɪk(əl)] *adj* sintáctico(a)

syntagm ['sɪntæm] *n Ling* sintagma *m*

syntax ['sɪntæks] *n Ling* sintaxis *f inv* ►► *Comptr* ***s. error*** error *m* de sintaxis

synth [sɪnθ] *n Fam* sintetizador *m* ►► ***s. pop*** pop *m* electrónico

synthesis ['sɪnθɪsɪs] (*pl* **syntheses** ['sɪnθɪsi:z]) *n* síntesis *f inv*

synthesize ['sɪnθəsaɪz] *vt* sintetizar

synthesizer ['sɪnθəsaɪzə(r)] *n* sintetizador *m*

synthetic [sɪn'θetɪk] **1** *npl* **synthetics** fibras *fpl* sintéticas

2 *adj* (**a**) *(fibre, rubber)* sintético(a) ►► ***s. drug*** droga *f* sintética (**b**) *(electronically produced) (speech)* sintético(a) (**c**) *Pej (food)* sintético(a) (**d**) *Ling* sintético(a) (**e**) *Phil* sintético(a)

synthetically [sɪn'θetɪklɪ] *adv* sintéticamente

syphilis ['sɪfɪlɪs] *n* sífilis *f inv*

syphilitic [sɪfɪ'lɪtɪk] **1** *n* sifilítico(a) *m,f*

2 *adj* sifilítico(a)

syphon = **siphon**

Syria ['sɪrɪə] *n* Siria

Syrian ['sɪrɪən] **1** *n* sirio(a) *m,f*

2 *adj* sirio(a)

syringa [sɪ'rɪŋgə] *n* celinda *f*, jeringuilla *f*

syringe [sɪ'rɪndʒ] **1** *n* jeringuilla *f*

2 *vt (ears)* destaponar

syrup ['sɪrəp] *n* (**a**) *(of sugar)* almíbar *m* (**b**) *(medicinal)* jarabe *m* ►► ***s. of figs*** jarabe *m* de higos

syrupy ['sɪrəpɪ] *adj* (**a**) *(liquid, mixture)* espeso(a) (**b**) *(smile, music)* almibarado(a)

SYSADMIN ['sɪsədmɪn] *n Comptr* (*abbr* **Systems Administrator**) administrador(ora) *m,f* del sistema

SYSOP ['sɪsɒp] *n Comptr* (*abbr* **Systems Operator**) operador(ora) *m,f* del sistema

system ['sɪstəm] *n* (**a**) *(structure)* sistema *m*; **the education s.** el sistema educativo

(**b**) *(method)* sistema *m*; **there's no s. to it** no sigue ningún método, no es nada sistemático

(**c**) **the S.** *(established order)* el sistema; **you can't beat the s.** no hay forma de burlar al sistema

(**d**) *Anat & Physiol* sistema *m*; **digestive s.** aparato digestivo; **nervous s.** sistema nervioso; IDIOM *Fam* **to get sth/sb out of one's s.** quitarse *or Am* sacarse algo/a alguien de la cabeza

(**e**) *(equipment, devices)* sistema *m*; **he's got a new (hi-fi) s.** tiene un nuevo equipo (de alta fidelidad); **all systems go** ¡allá vamos!, ¡vamos allá! ►► ***systems engineer*** ingeniero(a) *m,f* de sistemas; ***system(s) engineering*** ingeniería *f* de sistemas

(**f**) *Comptr* sistema *m* ►► ***systems analysis*** análisis *m inv* de sistemas; ***systems analyst*** analista *mf* de sistemas; ***s. date*** fecha *f* del sistema; ***s. disk*** disco *m* de sistema; ***s. error*** error *m* del sistema; ***s. failure*** *Esp* fallo *m or Am* falla *f* del sistema; ***s. file*** archivo *m* del sistema; ***s. folder*** carpeta *f* del sistema; ***s. program*** programa *m* del sistema; ***s. software*** software *m* de sistema

(**g**) *(in gambling)* sistema *m*

(**h**) *Astron* sistema *m*

systematic [sɪstə'mætɪk] *adj* sistemático(a)

systematically [sɪstə'mætɪklɪ] *adv* sistemáticamente

systematization [sɪstɪmətaɪ'zeɪʃən] *n* sistematización *f*

systematize ['sɪstəmətaɪz] *vt* sistematizar

systemic [sɪs'temɪk] *adj Biol & Med* sistémico(a)

systole ['sɪstəlɪ] *n Physiol* sístole *f*

systolic [sɪ'stɒlɪk] *adj Physiol* sistólico(a)

T, t

T, t [tiː] *n* (a) *(letter)* T, t *f* (b) IDIOM **that's you to a T** *(of impersonation)* es clavado a ti; **it suits me to a T** me viene como anillo al dedo

t (*abbr* **ton(s)**) tonelada(s) *f(pl) (Br = 1.016 kilos, US = 907 kilos)*

TA [tiː'eɪ] *n Br* (*abbr* **Territorial Army**) = cuerpo militar de reservistas voluntarios que reciben instrucción en su tiempo libre

ta [tɑː] *exclam Br Fam* gracias; **ta very much!** muchas gracias

tab [tæb] **1** *n* (a) *(on garment) (label)* etiqueta *f*; *(on file)* ceja *f*; *(on cassette, diskette)* pestaña *f*; IDIOM **to keep tabs on sth/sb** vigilar de cerca algo/a alguien

(b) *US (on can)* anilla *f*

(c) *(on typewriter, word processor)* tabulador *m*; **t. (key)** tecla *f* de tabular, tabulador *m* ►► ***t. character*** tabulador *m*

(d) *US Fam (bill)* cuenta *f*; **put it on my t.** apúntemelo en la cuenta; **to pick up the t.** *(at restaurant)* pagar (la cuenta); *(company)* correr con los gastos; *Fig* **we have had to pick up the t. for their mismanagement** hemos tenido que pagar el pato por su mala administración

(e) *Fam (of LSD)* pasti *f*, pastilla *f*, *RP* pepa *f*

2 *vt (text)* tabular

tabard ['tæbəd] *n* tabardo *m*

Tabasco® [tə'bæskəʊ] *n* **T. (sauce)** tabasco *m*

tabbouleh [tæ'buːleɪ] *n* tabule *m*, = ensalada de trigo, hierbabuena, perejil y pepino, procedente de Oriente Próximo

tabby ['tæbɪ] *n* **t. (cat)** gato *m* atigrado

tab-delimited ['tæbdiː'lɪmɪtɪd] *adj Comptr* separado(a) por tabuladores

tabernacle ['tæbənækəl] *n* (a) *(church)* tabernáculo *m* (b) *(on altar)* sagrario *m*

table ['teɪbəl] **1** *n* (a) *(furniture)* mesa *f*; **to clear the t.** recoger la mesa; **to lay** *or* **set the t.** poner la mesa; **at t.** a la mesa; **it's rude to yawn at the t.** es de mala educación bostezar en la mesa ►► ***t. dancing*** striptease *m (en el que las bailarinas se acercan a las mesas)*; *Br* ***t. football*** fútbol *m* de mesa, *Esp* futbolín *m*, *Arg* metegol *m*, *Chile* taca-taca *m*, *Méx, Urug* futbolito *m*; ***t. knife*** cuchillo *m* de mesa; ***t. lamp*** lámpara *f* de mesa; ***t. leg*** pata *f* de la mesa; ***t. licence*** = permiso para la venta de bebidas alcohólicas sólo con la comida; ***t. linen*** mantelería *f*; ***t. manners*** modales *mpl* (en la mesa); ***t. mat*** salvamanteles *m inv*; ***t. napkin*** servilleta *f*; ***t. salt*** sal *f* de mesa; ***t. talk*** conversación *f* ligera; ***t. tennis*** ping-pong *m*, tenis *m* de mesa; *Br* ***t. tennis bat*** pala *f* de ping-pong; *US* ***t. tennis paddle*** pala *f* de ping-pong; ***t. tennis player*** jugador(ora) *m,f* de ping-pong; ***t. top*** tablero *m*; **give the t. top a wipe down** limpia la mesa; ***t. wine*** vino *m* de mesa

(b) *(people seated)* mesa *f*

(c) *Formal (food)* menú *m*; **she keeps an excellent t.** en su casa se come excelentemente

(d) *(of facts, figures)* tabla *f*; *Br* **(league) t.** (tabla *f* de) clasificación *f* (de la liga); **they are currently top/bottom of the t.** van a la cabeza/cola de la clasificación; **t. of contents** tabla de materias, índice; *Math* **twelve times t.** tabla (de multiplicar) del doce

(e) *Geog (plateau)* meseta *f* ►► ***T. Mountain*** Montaña *f* de la Tabla

(f) IDIOMS **the offer is still on the t.** la oferta está aún sobre la mesa; **they put a better offer on the t.** pusieron una oferta mejor sobre la mesa; **now that we have all the different parties around the (negotiating) t.** ahora que tenemos a todos los partidos sentados a la mesa (de negociaciones); *Fam* **to drink sb under the t.** dejar a alguien tumbado(a) bebiendo *or Am* tomando, aguantar la bebida mucho más que alguien; *Fam* **two drinks and I'm under the t.** dos copas y ya no me tengo en pie; **he offered me £100 under the t.** me ofreció 100 libras bajo mano; **to turn the tables on sb** cambiarle *or* volverle las tornas a alguien

2 *vt* (a) *Pol* **to t. a motion/proposal** *Br (present)* someter a discusión una moción/propuesta; *US (postpone)* posponer la discusión de una moción/propuesta (b) *(schedule)* **the discussion is tabled for 4 o'clock** el debate está programado para las 4

tableau ['tæbləʊ] *n* cuadro *m*, escena *f* ►► ***t. vivant*** cuadro *m* vivo

tablecloth ['teɪbəlklɒθ] *n* mantel *m*

table d'hôte menu [tæblə'dəʊt'menjuː] *n* menú *m* del día

table-hop ['teɪbəlhɒp] (*pt & pp* **table-hopped**) *vi US* ir de mesa en mesa

tableland ['teɪbəllænd] *n Geog* meseta *f*, altiplano *m*

tablespoon ['teɪbəlspuːn] *n* (a) *(utensil)* cuchara *f* de servir (b) *(measurement)* cucharada *f* (grande)

tablespoonful ['teɪbəlspuːnfʊl] *n* cucharada *f* (grande)

tablet ['tæblɪt] *n* (a) *(pill)* comprimido *m*, pastilla *f* (b) *(of stone) (inscribed)* lápida *f*; *(for writing on)* tablilla *f*; IDIOM **to be set in** *or* **written on tablets of stone** ser inamovible (c) *(of paper) (small notepad)* taco *m* de notas; *(loose-leaf pad)* bloc *m* de anillas (d) *Br (bar) (of soap)* pastilla *f*; *(of chocolate)* tableta *f* (e) *Comptr* tableta *f*

tableware ['teɪbəlweə(r)] *n* servicio *m* de mesa, vajilla *f*

tabloid ['tæblɔɪd] *n (newspaper)* diario *m* popular *or* sensacionalista *(de formato tabloide)*; **the t. press, the tabloids** la prensa popular *or* sensacionalista; *Pej* **t. journalism** periodismo sensacionalista

taboo [tə'buː] **1** *n* (*pl* **taboos**) tabú *m*

2 *adj* tabú; **these subjects are t.** estos temas son tabú *or* intocables

tabular ['tæbjʊlə(r)] *adj* **in t. form** en forma tabular

tabulate ['tæbjʊleɪt] *vt (arrange in table)* tabular

tabulation [tæbjʊ'leɪʃən] *n (arranging into tables)* tabulación *f*

tabulator ['tæbjʊleɪtə(r)] *n* tabulador *m* ►► ***t. key*** (tecla *f* del) tabulador *m*

tache [tæʃ] *n Fam* (*abbr* **moustache**) bigote *m*

tachograph ['tækəgrɑːf] *n Aut* tacógrafo *m*

tachometer [tæ'kɒmɪtə(r)] *n Aut* tacómetro *m*

tachycardia [tækɪ'kɑːdɪə] *n Med* taquicardia *f*

tachymeter [tæ'kɪmɪtə(r)] *n* taquímetro *m*

tacit ['tæsɪt] *adj* tácito(a)

tacitly ['tæsɪtlɪ] *adv* tácitamente

taciturn ['tæsɪtɜːn] *adj* taciturno(a), retraído(a)

taciturnity [tæsɪ'tɜːnɪtɪ] *n* taciturnidad *f*

tack[1] [tæk] **1** *n* (a) *(small nail)* tachuela *f* (b) *(thumbtack) Esp* chincheta *f*, *Am* chinche *m* (c) *(in sewing)* hilván *m* (d) *Naut* bordada *f* (e) *(direction)* **to change t.** cambiar de enfoque; **let's try a different t.** vamos a probar con otro enfoque; **he went off on a quite different t.** cambió de tema por completo (f) *Fam (tacky things)* cosas *fpl* de mal gusto, *Esp* horteradas *fpl*, *RP* mersadas *fpl*

2 *vt* (a) *(fasten) (with nail)* clavar; *(with thumbtack)* sujetar con *Esp* chincheta *or Am* chinche; *Fig* **to t. sth on** *(add)* añadir algo a posteriori (b) *(in sewing)* **to t. up a hem** hilvanar un dobladillo

3 *vi Naut* dar bordadas

tack[2] *n (saddle, harness, bridle)* arreos *mpl*

tackily ['tækɪlɪ] *adv Fam (decorated)* con mal gusto

tackiness ['tækɪnɪs] *n* (a) *(stickiness)* pegajosidad *f* (b) *Fam (tastelessness)* chabacanería *f*, mal gusto *m*

tacking ['tækɪŋ] *n (in sewing)* hilvanes *mpl* ►► ***t. stitch*** hilvanado *m*; ***t. thread*** hilo *m* de hilvanar

tackle ['tækəl] **1** *n* (a) *(equipment)* equipo *m*; **(fishing) t.** aparejos *mpl* de pesca

(b) *(ropes and pulleys) (for lifting)* aparejo *m*

(c) *Naut (rigging)* aparejos *mpl*

(d) *(challenge) (in soccer, hockey)* entrada *f*; *(in rugby, American football)* placaje *m*, *Am* tackle *m*; **sliding t.** *(in soccer)* entrada en plancha; **late t.** *(in soccer)* entrada a destiempo; **t. from behind** *(in soccer)* entrada por detrás

(e) *(position in American football)* tackle *m*

(f) *Br Fam Hum* **(wedding) t.** las vergüenzas

2 *vt* (a) *(deal with) (task, issue, problem)* abordar; **I'm going to t.**

"War and Peace" during the holidays voy a meterle mano a "Guerra y paz" durante las vacaciones; **he tried to t. the blaze on his own** intentó apagar el fuego él solo
(**b**) *(confront)* enfrentarse a; **to t. sb about sth** plantear algo a alguien, abordar a alguien para tratar algo; **if you're not happy with his work, you ought to t. him about it** si su trabajo no te parece bien, deberías planteárselo
(**c**) *(in soccer, hockey)* entrar a, *Méx* taclear; *(in rugby, American football)* hacer un placaje a, *Am* tacklear
3 *vi (in soccer, hockey)* hacer una entrada; *(in rugby, American football)* hacer un placaje, *Am* hacer un tackle

tackler ['tæklə(r)] *n* (**a**) *(in soccer, hockey)* **he's a good t.** es bueno robando pelotas (**b**) *(in rugby, American football)* placador(ora) *m,f*, *Am* tackleador(ora) *m,f*

tacky ['tækɪ] *adj* (**a**) *(sticky)* pegajoso(a) (**b**) *Fam (tasteless)* chabacano(a), ordinario(a), *Esp* hortera, *Méx* gacho(a), *RP* mersa

taco ['tækəʊ] *n Culin* taco *m*

tact [tækt] *n* tacto *m*, discreción *f*

tactful ['tæktfʊl] *adj* discreto(a), diplomático(a); **she's a very t. person** es una persona con mucho tacto; **the t. thing would have been to say nothing** lo más adecuado hubiera sido no decir nada

tactfully ['tæktfʊlɪ] *adv* discretamente, con tacto; **I t. said nothing** fui discreto y no dije nada

tactic ['tæktɪk] *n* táctica *f*; **tactics** táctica; **to change one's tactics** cambiar de táctica

tactical ['tæktɪkəl] *adj* táctico(a) ►► ***t. (nuclear) weapons*** armamento *m* táctico (nuclear); *Pol* ***t. voting*** el voto útil

tactically ['tæktɪklɪ] *adv* tácticamente; **the home team was t. superior** la táctica del equipo de casa fue mejor

tactician [tæk'tɪʃən] *n Mil & Sport* estratega *mf*

tactile ['tæktaɪl] *adj* táctil; **the French are very t.** a los franceses les gusta mucho el contacto físico

tactless ['tæktlɪs] *adj* falto(a) de tacto, indiscreto(a); **he's a very t. person** es una persona con muy poco tacto; **what a t. thing to say/do!** ¡qué falta de tacto decir/hacer eso!

tactlessly ['tæktlɪslɪ] *adv* indiscretamente, sin tacto alguno

tactlessness ['tæktlɪsnɪs] *n* indiscreción *f*, falta *f* de tacto

tad [tæd] *n Fam (small bit)* **a t.** un poquitín, *Esp* un pelín, *Am* un chiquitín; **a t. short** un poquitín *or Esp* pelín *or Am* chiquitín corto

tadger ['tædʒə(r)] *n Br Fam (penis)* pito *m*, pilila *f*

tadpole ['tædpəʊl] *n* renacuajo *m*

Tadzhik, Tajik [tɑː'dʒiːk] **1** *n (person)* tayiko(a) *m,f*
2 *adj* tayico(a)

Tadzhiki [tɑː'dʒiːkɪ] **1** *n (language)* tayico *m*
2 *adj* tayico(a)

Tadzhikistan, Tajikistan [tædʒɪkɪ'stɑːn] *n* Tayikistán

taekwondo [taɪkwɒn'dəʊ] *n* taekwondo *m*

taffeta ['tæfɪtə] *n* tafetán *m*

Taffy ['tæfɪ] *n Br Fam (Welshman)* galés *m*

taffy ['tæfɪ] *n US* caramelo *m* de melaza

tag [tæg] **1** *n* (**a**) *(label)* etiqueta *f*
(**b**) *(on shoelace)* herrete *m*
(**c**) *(for offender)* dispositivo *m* electrónico de control *(para personas que cumplen condena fuera de un recinto penitenciario)*
(**d**) *Comptr (code)* etiqueta *f*
(**e**) *(game)* **to play t.** jugar a pillarse *or* al corre que te pillo
(**f**) *Gram* interrogación *f* de confirmación ►► ***t. question*** cláusula *f* final interrogativa
(**g**) *Fam (piece of graffiti)* firma *f*
(**h**) *US* ***t. line*** frase *f* característica, muletilla *f*
2 *vt* (*pt & pp* **tagged**) (**a**) *(fix label to)* etiquetar; *US* **it was tagged at $39.95** la etiqueta marcaba 39,95 dólares
(**b**) *(offender)* colocar un dispositivo electrónico de control a
(**c**) *Comptr* etiquetar
(**d**) *(brand)* **he was tagged as a troublemaker** lo tildaron de alborotador
(**e**) *US (follow)* seguir
(**f**) *(in baseball)* = eliminar entre bases a un jugador tocándolo con la bola
(**g**) *Fam (leave graffiti on)* firmar

► **tag along** *vi* pegarse; **to t. along with sb** pegarse a alguien; **do you mind if I t. along?** ¿te importa si me apunto?

► **tag on 1** *vt sep* añadir (a posteriori)
2 *vi* **to t. on to sb** pegarse a alguien

Tagalog [tə'gɑːlɒg] *n (language)* tagalo *m*

tagger ['tægə(r)] *n Fam (graffiti artist)* graffitero(a) *m,f*

tagliatelle [tæglɪə'telɪ] *n* tallarines *mpl*

Tagus ['teɪgəs] *n* **the (River) T.** el (río) Tajo

tahini [tə'hiːnɪ] *n* tahín *m*, = pasta de semillas de sésamo

Tahiti [tə'hiːtɪ] *n* Tahití

Tahitian [tə'hiːʃən] **1** *n* tahitiano(a) *m,f*
2 *adj* tahitiano(a)

tai chi [taɪ'tʃiː] *n* tai-chi *m*

taiga ['taɪgə] *n* taiga *f*

tail [teɪl] **1** *n* (**a**) *(of birds, fish, most mammals)* cola *f*; *(of bull, lizard)* rabo *m* ►► ***t. end*** *(of conversation, movie, summer)* final *m*; *(of procession)* cola *f*; *(of storm)* final *m*; ***t. feather*** pluma *f* de la cola
(**b**) *(of plane)* cola *f* ►► ***t. assembly*** ensamble *m* de la cola
(**c**) *(of shirt)* faldón *m*; *(of coat)* cola *f*; **he was wearing tails** llevaba un frac ►► ***t. coat*** frac *m*
(**d**) *(of comet)* cola *f*
(**e**) *(of procession, queue)* cola *f*
(**f**) **tails** *(of coin)* cruz *f*, *Chile, Col* sello *m*, *Méx* sol *m*, *RP* ceca *f*
(**g**) *Fam (person following)* perseguidor(ora) *m,f*; **to put a t. on sb** hacer seguir a alguien
(**h**) *Fam (buttocks)* trasero *m*; **he worked his t. off** sudó la gota gorda
(**i**) *US very Fam (woman)* **a piece of t.** *Esp* una chorba, *Méx* una vieja, *RP* una piba; **he's looking for some t.** está buscando un chocho
(**j**) IDIOMS **with his t. between his legs** con el rabo entre las piernas; **to be on sb's t.** pisarle los talones a alguien; *Fam* **to turn t.** salir corriendo *or Esp* por piernas; **it's a case of the t. wagging the dog** es una situación en la que el que menos pinta es el que tiene la sartén por el mango
2 *vt Fam (follow)* seguir; **I think we're being tailed** creo que nos están siguiendo

► **tail away** = **tail off**

► **tail back** *vi Br (traffic)* formar caravana; **the traffic tailed back for 10 miles** había retenciones de más de 10 millas

► **tail off** *vi (attendance)* decrecer; *(performance)* decaer; *(demand, interest)* disminuir; *(voice)* desvanecerse

tailback ['teɪlbæk] *n Br Aut* caravana *f*

tailboard ['teɪlbɔːd] *n Aut* puerta *f* trasera

-tailed [teɪld] *suffix* **short/long-t.** de cola corta/larga

tailender [teɪl'endə(r)] *n (in race)* rezagado(a) *m,f*

tailgate ['teɪlgeɪt] *Aut* **1** *n esp US* puerta *f* trasera ►► *US* ***t. party*** = fiesta previa a un partido de fútbol americano celebrada en el parking del estadio
2 *vt Esp* conducir *or Am* manejar pegado a, pisar los talones a

tailings ['teɪlɪŋz] *npl (from mining)* ganga *f*

tailless ['teɪllɪs] *adj* sin cola

tail-light ['teɪllaɪt] *n US Aut* luz *f* trasera

tailor ['teɪlə(r)] **1** *n* sastre *m*; **t.'s (shop)** sastrería *f* ►► ***t.'s chalk*** jaboncillo *m* (de sastre); ***t.'s dummy*** maniquí *m*
2 *vt* (**a**) *(suit)* confeccionar (**b**) *(adapt)* adaptar (**to** a); **this product can be tailored to our customer's specific requirements** este producto puede ser adaptado a los requerimientos específicos de nuestro cliente

tailored ['teɪləd] *adj* (**a**) *(tailor-made)* hecho(a) a medida (**b**) *(fitted)* entallado(a)

tailor-made ['teɪləmeɪd] *adj* (**a**) *(suit)* hecho(a) a medida (**b**) *(product)* diseñado(a) a medida *or* ex profeso; **the job was t. for her** el trabajo parecía hecho a su medida

tailpiece ['teɪlpiːs] *n* (**a**) *(of plane)* cola *f* (**b**) *(of stringed instrument)* cordal *m* (**c**) *(concluding part)* coletilla *f*, colofón *m*

tailpipe ['teɪlpaɪp] *n US Aut* tubo *m* de escape

tailplane ['teɪlpleɪn] *n Av* plano *m* de cola

tailspin ['teɪlspɪn] *n Av* barrena *f*; *Fig* **to go into a t.** entrar en barrena

tailwind ['teɪlwɪnd] *n* viento *m* de cola

taint [teɪnt] **1** *n* (**a**) *(contamination)* impureza *f*, contaminación *f* (**b**) *(of sin, corruption)* mancha *f*
2 *vt* (**a**) *(contaminate)* contaminar (**b**) *(reputation)* manchar; **his personal life is tainted with scandal** su vida privada está marcada por el escándalo

tainted ['teɪntɪd] *adj* (**a**) *(contaminated)* contaminado(a) (**b**) *(reputation)* manchado(a); **a t. politician** un político con la reputación manchada

Taipei [taɪ'peɪ] *n* Taipei

Taiwan [taɪ'wɑːn] *n* Taiwán

Taiwanese [taɪwə'ni:z] **1** *n* taiwanés(esa) *m,f*
2 *adj* taiwanés(esa)

Tajik = **Tadzhik**

Tajikistan = **Tadzhikistan**

TAKE [teɪk] **1** *vt* (*pt* **took** [tʊk], *pp* **taken** ['teɪkən]) **(a)** *(grasp)* tomar, agarrar, *Esp* coger; **let me t. your coat** dame el abrigo; **to t. hold of sth** agarrar algo; **to t. sb's arm, to t. sb by the arm** agarrar *or Esp* coger a alguien del brazo; **to t. sb's hand** agarrarle *or Esp* cogerle la mano a alguien; **to t. sb in one's arms** agarrar *or Esp* coger en brazos a alguien; **he took the ball on his chest** paró la pelota con el pecho; **to t. the opportunity to do sth** aprovechar la oportunidad para hacer algo

(b) *(remove, steal)* sacar, *Esp* coger; **to t. sth from sb** quitarle *or Am* sacarle algo a alguien; **she took an envelope from her pocket** sacó un sobre del bolsillo; **someone's taken my wallet** me han robado la cartera; **the music is taken from an opera by Puccini** la música está sacada de una ópera de Puccini; *Math* **t. six from ten** resta seis a diez; **to t. sth out of sth** sacar algo de algo; **to t. the credit for sth** apuntarse el mérito de algo, *RP* anotarse los puntos de algo

(c) *(capture) (town)* tomar; *Pol (seat)* conquistar; *(chess piece)* comer(se); **to t. first prize/the first set** ganar el primer premio/el primer set; **to t. power** hacerse con el poder, tomar el poder; **to t. sb prisoner** hacer prisionero a alguien; **to t. sb alive** capturar *or* atrapar con vida a alguien

(d) *(record) (temperature, notes)* tomar; **to t. sb's details** tomar los datos a alguien; **to t. a letter** tomar nota de una carta; **to t. sb's pulse** tomar el pulso a alguien

(e) *(earn) (money)* hacer; **the bookstore takes about $3,000 a day** la librería hace unos 3.000 dólares de caja al día

(f) *(bring, lead, carry)* llevar; **don't forget to t. your keys (with you)** no te olvides de llevar *or Esp* coger las llaves; **she took some towels upstairs/downstairs** subió/bajó unas toallas; **the ambulance took him to hospital** la ambulancia se lo llevó al hospital; **he took the matter to his boss** le planteó el asunto a su jefe; **to t. flowers to sb, to t. sb flowers** llevarle flores a alguien; **to t. sb home/to a restaurant** llevar a alguien a casa/a un restaurante; **this road will t. you to their house** esta carretera va *or* te llevará hasta su casa; *Fam* **I can't t. you anywhere** no se te puede llevar a ningún sitio *or* sacar de casa; **to t. oneself to bed** irse a la cama; **the record took her to number one in the charts** el disco la llevó al número uno de las listas; **I will t. my business elsewhere** no volveré a comprar aquí; **she took me shopping** me llevó de compras; **to t. the dog for a walk** sacar a pasear al perro; **her job takes her all over the world** su trabajo la hace viajar por todo el mundo; **to t. sb to court** llevar a alguien a juicio; **this takes the total to 250** esto sube el total a 250; **if you can get the money we'll t. it from there** si consigues el dinero, entonces veremos; IDIOM **you can't t. it with you** *(money when you die)* no te lo puedes llevar al otro mundo

(g) *(tolerate) (heat, pressure)* soportar, aguantar; **he can/can't t. his drink** sabe/no sabe beber *or Am* tomar; **she can't t. criticism/a joke** no sabe aguantar *or* aceptar una crítica/broma; **I can't t. being treated like this** no soporto que me traten así; **I can't t. (it) any more** no (lo) aguanto más; **it won't t. your weight** no soportará tu peso

(h) *(accept)* aceptar; *(blame, responsibility, consequences)* asumir; **will you t. a cheque?** ¿se puede pagar con cheque?, ¿aceptan cheques?; **does this machine t. pound coins?** ¿esta máquina acepta monedas de una libra?; **it only takes diesel** sólo funciona con gasoil; **this bus takes fifty passengers** en este autobús caben cincuenta pasajeros; **t. my advice and don't do it** sigue mi consejo y no lo hagas; **she is unable to t. your call** ahora no puede contestarle *or* atenderlo; **he took the blow on his arm** recibió el golpe en el brazo; **do you want milk? – I'll t. it as it comes** ¿quieres leche? – me da igual, como te venga mejor; **I t. people as they come** *or* **as I find them** acepto a las personas tal como son; **t. it or leave it!** ¡lo tomas o lo dejas!; **you can t. it from me that...** créeme cuando te digo que...; **t. that!** *(when hitting sb)* ¡toma ésa!

(i) *(react to)* **to t. sth well/badly** tomarse algo bien/mal; **to t. sth/sb seriously** tomar algo/a alguien en serio; **to t. sth the wrong way** malinterpretar algo; **don't t. that literally** no lo tomes al pie de la letra; **how did she t. the questioning?** ¿cómo se tomó el interrogatorio?; **I don't know how to t. her** no sé qué pensar de ella

(j) *(assume)* **I t. it that...** supongo que...; **can I t. it (that) you no longer need me?** ¿debo suponer que ya no me necesitas?; **you'll be leaving early, I t. it** *Esp* te irás pronto, imagino, *Am* me imagino que te vas a ir temprano; **we took her to be your sister** pensábamos que era tu hermana; **he is generally taken to be the favourite for the job** se supone que es el favorito para conseguir el trabajo

(k) *(require) (effort, dedication, strength)* requerir; **it took four of us to carry him** hicimos falta cuatro para llevarlo; **it takes courage/patience to...** hace falta valor *or Am* coraje/paciencia para...; **how long does it t.?** ¿cuánto tiempo lleva *or Am* demora?; **learning a language takes a long time** aprender un idioma lleva mucho tiempo; **it took me an hour to get here** tardé *or Am* demoré una hora en llegar; **I won't t. long** no tardaré *or Am* demoraré mucho; **this verb takes the subjunctive** este verbo lleva subjuntivo; **that will t. some explaining** eso va a ser complicado de explicar; **he didn't t. much convincing** no costó mucho convencerlo; **he's got what it takes** tiene lo que hay que tener; **one glance was all it took** con un vistazo fue suficiente; IDIOM *Fam Pej* **it takes one to know one!** ¡mira quién fue a hablar!

(l) *(consume) (tablet, medicine)* tomar; **to t. drugs** tomar drogas; **not to be taken (internally)** *(on packaging)* para uso externo; **to be taken twice a day** *(on packaging)* tómese dos veces al día; **do you t. sugar in your tea?** ¿tomas el té con azúcar?; *Formal* **we will t. tea in the garden** tomaremos el té en el jardín

(m) *(wear) (shoe size)* calzar; *(dress size)* usar

(n) *(buy)* comprar; **I'll t. the red one** me quedo con el rojo; **we t. the "Guardian"** compramos el "Guardian"

(o) *Br (rent) (holiday home, apartment)* alquilar, *Méx* rentar

(p) *(get on) (bus, train, plane, road)* tomar, *esp Esp* coger; **I decided not to t. the train** decidí no ir en tren, *esp Esp* decidí no coger el tren; **t. the first turning on the left** gira *or* dobla *or* tuerce por la primera a la izquierda; *US* **t. a right** gira a la izquierda

(q) *(adopt) (precautions, measures)* tomar; **to t. legal advice** consultar a un abogado; **I t. the view that...** yo soy de la opinión de que...

(r) *(use as example)* **t. the Germans...** los alemanes, por ejemplo...; **to t. sth as an example** tomar algo como ejemplo

(s) *(have)* **to t. a bath** darse un baño; **to t. a break** descansar; **to t. a holiday** tomarse unas vacaciones; **to t. a look at sth** echar un vistazo a algo; **to t. a seat** sentarse, tomar asiento; **to t. a walk** dar un paseo

(t) *Educ (subject, course)* hacer; *(exam)* hacer, *RP* rendir; *Br* **he takes them for English** *(teaches them)* les da inglés; **she took her degree last year** se licenció or graduó el año pasado; **the assistant director took the rehearsals** el ayudante de dirección se hizo cargo de los ensayos

(u) *Sport (penalty)* lanzar; *(corner)* lanzar, botar; **to t. a throw-in** *Esp, CAm, Méx* sacar *or* lanzar de banda, *Andes, RP* sacar de costado

(v) *(make)* **to t. a photograph of sth/sb** hacer *or* sacar una fotografía a algo/alguien

(w) *(negotiate) (bend)* tomar; *(fence)* saltar

(x) *(start to suffer from)* **to t. fright** asustarse; **to be taken ill, to t. sick** ponerse enfermo(a)

(y) *(show)* **to t. an interest in sth/sb** interesarse por algo/alguien; **to t. pity on sb** apiadarse *or* compadecerse de alguien

(z) *(have sex with)* poseer

2 *vi (be successful) (fire)* prender; *(plant cutting)* arraigar, *RP* prender; *(dye)* agarrar, *Esp* coger; *(innovation)* cuajar; **the graft didn't take** el injerto fue rechazado *or RP* no prendió

3 *n* **(a)** *(recording) (of film, music)* toma *f*; **t. six** toma (número) seis **(b)** *(money)* recaudación *f*; IDIOM *Fam* **to be on the t.** llenarse los bolsillos, *Esp* engordar el bolsillo **(c)** *(interpretation)* **what's your t. on events?** ¿cuál es tu versión de los hechos? **(d)** *(in hunting)* captura *f*

► **take aback** *vt sep* sorprender

► **take after** *vt insep (resemble)* parecerse a

► **take against** *vt insep (come to dislike)* tomar *or Esp* coger manía a

► **take along** *vt sep* llevar

► **take apart** *vt* **(a)** *(dismantle) (machine, engine)* desmontar; *Fig* **they took the room apart looking for evidence** pusieron la habitación patas arriba en busca de pruebas **(b)** *(criticize) (argument)* destrozar; *(person)* vapulear **(c)** *(defeat easily)* destrozar

► **take aside** *vt sep* llevar a un aparte

► **take away 1** *vt sep (remove)* quitar, *Am* sacar; *Math* restar (**from** de); **to t. sth away from sb** quitar *or Am* sacar algo a alguien; **his work took him away from his family for long periods** se alejaba de su familia durante largos periodos de tiempo por trabajo; **not to be taken away** *(on library book)* exento de préstamo; **nine t. away six is three** nueve menos seis es tres; **guards, t. him away!** ¡guardias, llévenselo!

2 *vi* **(a)** *Br (food)* **is it to eat in or to t. away?** ¿es para comer aquí o para llevar? **(b)** *(detract)* **to t. away from the pleasure/value of sth** restar placer/valor a algo

► **take back** *vt sep* **(a)** *(return)* devolver; **I'll t. you back to your house** te llevaré de vuelta a tu casa; **t. it back to the shop** devuélvelo (a la tienda); **that takes me back to my childhood** eso me hace volver a la infancia; **that photo takes me back** esa foto me trae muchos recuerdos

(**b**) *(accept again) (former employee)* readmitir; *(faulty goods)* admitir (devolución de); **she's a fool to t. him back** es tonta por dejarle volver

(**c**) *(withdraw) (remark)* retirar; **t. that back!** ¡retira eso!

▸ **take down** *vt sep* (**a**) *(remove) (from shelf)* bajar; *(poster, curtains)* quitar, *Am* sacar (**b**) *(lower)* **to t. down one's trousers** bajarse los pantalones (**c**) *(dismantle) (tent, scaffolding)* desmontar; *(wall, barricade)* desmantelar; *(decorations, Christmas tree)* quitar, *Am* sacar (**d**) *(lengthen) (hem)* sacar; *(skirt)* alargar (**e**) *(record)* anotar, apuntar; *(notes)* tomar

▸ **take for** *vt sep* (**a**) *(imagine to be)* **I took him for somebody else** lo tomé por *or* lo confundí con otro; **what do you t. me for?** ¿por quién me tomas?; **do you t. me for an idiot?** ¿te crees que soy idiota?

(**b**) *Fam (cheat)* **they took him for every penny (he had)** le estafaron hasta el último céntimo (que tenía)

▸ **take in** *vt sep* (**a**) *(lead, carry) (person)* conducir dentro; *(harvest, washing)* recoger; *Naut* **to t. in a sail** arriar una vela; **she takes in ironing/laundry** plancha/lava para afuera

(**b**) *(orphan)* acoger; *(lodgers)* admitir; **the police have taken him in for questioning** la policía se lo ha llevado para interrogarlo

(**c**) *(garment)* meter

(**d**) *(include)* abarcar, cubrir; **the tour takes in all the major sights** el recorrido cubre todos los principales puntos de interés

(**e**) *(understand, perceive)* asimilar; **to t. in the situation** hacerse cargo de la situación; **he was taking it all in** lo estaba captando todo; **it's a lot to t. in all at once** es mucho como para asimilarlo todo de golpe

(**f**) *US (watch) (movie, play)* ir a ver

(**g**) *(deceive)* engañar, embaucar; **he was completely taken in** lo engañaron por completo

(**h**) *(ingest) (food, liquid)* ingerir

▸ **take off** 1 *vt sep* (**a**) *(remove) (lid, sheets)* quitar, *Am* sacar; **to t. off one's clothes/make-up** quitarse *or Am* sacarse la ropa/el maquillaje; **to t. sth off sb** quitar *or Am* sacar algo a alguien; **t. your feet off the table!** ¡quita *or Am* saca los pies de la mesa!; **the contaminated product was taken off the shelves** retiraron el producto contaminado de las tiendas; **he never took his eyes off us** no apartó la mirada de nosotros; **he took £10 off (the price)** rebajó 10 libras (del precio); **to t. sth off sb's hands** quitar *or Am* sacar algo de las manos a alguien; **to t. years off sb** *(clothes, diet)* quitar *or Am* sacarle a alguien años de encima

(**b**) *(lead) (person)* llevar; **to t. oneself off** *(leave)* retirarse; **she took herself off to Italy** se marchó a Italia; **the injured man was taken off the ship by helicopter** evacuaron al herido del barco en helicóptero

(**c**) *(mimic)* imitar

(**d**) *(not work)* **to t. the day off** tomarse el día libre; **he suggested that I t. some time off work** me sugirió que me tomara unos días de vacaciones

(**e**) *Sport (player)* sustituir; **to t. a player off** sustituir a un jugador

(**f**) *(discontinue) (transport service, programme)* suspender

2 *vi* (**a**) *(leave) (aircraft)* despegar, *Am* decolar; *Fam (person)* marcharse, irse; **they took off for Heathrow** despegaron *or Am* decolaron con destino a Heathrow (**b**) *Fam (succeed)* empezar a cuajar; **it never took off** nunca cuajó

▸ **take on** 1 *vt sep* (**a**) *(accept) (task, responsibility, work)* aceptar; **she took it on herself to tell him** asumió la responsabilidad de decírselo (ella misma);

(**b**) *(confront) (problem, opponent)* enfrentarse a; **I'll t. you on at chess!** ¡te desafío a una partida de ajedrez!

(**c**) *(load up) (supplies)* reponer; *(fuel)* repostar; *(passengers)* recoger

(**d**) *(hire) (worker)* contratar

(**e**) *(acquire)* tomar, adquirir; **her face took on an anxious expression** su cara adquirió una expresión de ansiedad

2 *vi Fam (fret)* **don't t. on so!** no te lo tomes tan a pecho

▸ **take out** *vt sep* (**a**) *(remove)* sacar; **he took a gun out of his pocket** sacó una pistola del bolsillo; **to t. money out of one's account** sacar dinero de la cuenta; **it takes the fun out of it** le quita toda la gracia; IDIOM **her job really takes it out of her** su trabajo la deja totalmente agotada; IDIOM **to t. it out on sb** pagarla *or* desahogarse con alguien; IDIOM *Br* **I tried to t. him out of himself** *(cheer up)* intenté animarle

(**b**) *(invite) (person)* sacar; **to t. sb out for a meal/to a restaurant** llevar a alguien a comer/a un restaurante

(**c**) *(delete) (passage of text)* suprimir

(**d**) *(destroy)* liquidar, eliminar; *Fam (kill)* asesinar a, cepillarse a

(**e**) *(obtain) (licence)* sacarse; *(patent)* registrar; *(insurance policy, mortgage)* contratar, suscribir; *(advert)* poner; *(injunction)* obtener; **to t. out a subscription** suscribirse; **I had to t. out a loan to pay for my studies** tuve que pedir un préstamo para pagarme los estudios

▸ **take over** 1 *vt sep* (**a**) *(become responsible for)* hacerse cargo de; **I'll t. over the driving if you like** ya conduciré *or Am* manejaré yo si quieres (**b**) *(take control of) (place)* tomar; *(company)* absorber, adquirir; *(government, country)* apoderarse de; **fast-food restaurants have taken over the city centre** los restaurantes de comida rápida se han apoderado del centro de la ciudad

2 *vi* (**a**) *(assume power)* tomar el poder; *(in job)* tomar posesión (**b**) *(relieve)* tomar el relevo (**from** de); **compact discs have taken over from records** los discos compactos han tomado el relevo de los convencionales

▸ **take through** *vt sep (explain)* **to t. sb through sth** explicar algo a alguien

▸ **take to** 1 *vt insep* (**a**) *(go to)* **to t. to one's bed** meterse en la cama; **to t. to the hills** echarse al monte; **protesters took to the streets** los manifestantes se echaron a la calle

(**b**) *(adopt habit of)* **to t. to doing sth** adquirir la costumbre de hacer algo, empezar a hacer algo; **to t. to drink** darse a la bebida

(**c**) *(like)* **I took to them** me cayeron bien; **I've taken to Canada** le he tomado *or Esp* cogido cariño a Canadá; **I don't t. kindly to that sort of treatment** no me sabe nada bien que me traten así

2 *vt sep (use on)* **he took an axe to the door** arremetió contra la puerta con un hacha; **his father took a stick to him** su padre arremetió contra él con un bastón

▸ **take up** *vt sep* (**a**) *(carry)* subir; **the lift took us up to the 25th floor** el ascensor nos subió hasta la planta 25

(**b**) *(lead) (person)* llevar, subir

(**c**) *(pick up, take hold of)* agarrar, *Esp* coger

(**d**) *(lift) (carpet, floorboards, paving stones)* levantar; **they're taking up the street** están levantando la calle;

(**e**) *(shorten) (skirt, hem)* subir, acortar

(**f**) *(accept) (challenge, offer, suggestion)* aceptar; **to t. sb up on an offer** aceptar una oferta de alguien; **I'll t. you up on that!** ¡te tomo la palabra!

(**g**) *(address) (subject, problem)* discutir (**with** con); *(cause)* adoptar; **I am taking the matter up with the authorities** voy a informar *or CAm, Méx* reportar del asunto a las autoridades; **can I t. you up on that last point?** ¿podría pedirle que me explicara con más detalle ese último punto?

(**h**) *(assume) (position)* tomar; *(post, duties)* asumir

(**i**) *(continue with) (tune, song)* retomar; **she paused and I took up the story** hizo una pausa y yo continué con la historia; **we t. up the story just after...** retomamos la historia justo después de...; **she took up her knitting again** se puso a hacer punto de nuevo

(**j**) *(hobby, studies)* **she's taken up fencing/psychology** ha empezado a practicar esgrima/estudiar psicología

(**k**) *(occupy) (space, time, attention)* ocupar; **most of the document is taken up with tables of statistics** la mayor parte del documento está lleno de tablas estadísticas; **moving took up the whole day** nos llevó todo el día mudarnos

(**l**) *Fin (option)* ejecutar

▸ **take upon** *vt sep* **she took it upon herself to tell him my secret** decidió por su cuenta contarle mi secreto

▸ **take up with** *vt insep (become friendly with)* trabar amistad con

---

takeaway ['teɪkəweɪ] *Br* 1 *n* (**a**) *(restaurant)* establecimiento *m* de comida para llevar (**b**) *(meal)* comida *f* para llevar; **shall we go out for dinner, or just phone for a t.?** ¿salimos a cenar o encargamos algo para llevar?

2 *adj (food)* para llevar ▸▸ ***t. restaurant*** establecimiento *m* de comida para llevar

take-home pay ['teɪkhəʊm'peɪ] *n* paga *f* neta

taken ['teɪkən] 1 *adj* (**a**) *(occupied)* **is this seat t.?** ¿está ocupado este asiento? (**b**) *(impressed)* **I was very t. with him/it** me impresionó mucho

2 *pp of* **take**

takeoff ['teɪkɒf] *n* (**a**) *(imitation)* imitación *f*; **to do a t. of sb** imitar a alguien (**b**) *(of plane)* despegue *m*, *Am* decolaje *m*; **keep your seatbelts fastened during t.** mantengan los cinturones de seguridad abrochados durante el despegue *or Am* decolaje (**c**) *(of economy, campaign)* despegue *m* (**d**) *(of high-jumper, long-jumper)* impulso *m*

takeout ['teɪkaʊt] *US* 1 *n (meal)* comida *f* para llevar

2 *adj (food)* para llevar ▸▸ ***t. restaurant*** establecimiento *m* de comida para llevar

takeover ['teɪkəʊvə(r)] *n* (**a**) *Com (of company)* absorción *f*, adquisición *f* ▸▸ ***t. bid*** oferta *f* pública de adquisición (de acciones), OPA *f* (**b**) *(of power)* usurpación *f* del poder; **there has been a military t. in Rwanda** ha habido un golpe militar en Ruanda

taker ['teɪkə(r)] *n* (**a**) *(of suggestion, offer)* **there were no takers** nadie aceptó la oferta; **any takers?** ¿hay alguien interesado? (**b**) *(user)* **takers of drugs are the highest-risk group** los consumidores de drogas son el grupo de mayor riesgo

take-up ['teɪkʌp] *n* (**a**) *(of share offer)* grado *m* de aceptación; *(of benefits)* número *m* de solicitudes; **t. of the new benefit has been poor** la nueva prestación social ha tenido muy poca demanda; **there has been a 10 percent t. of the grants** se han otorgado el 10 por ciento de las becas (**b**) *(on tape recorder)* ***t. spool*** carrete *m* de rebobinado

taking ['teɪkɪŋ] *n* (**a**) *(of city)* toma *f*; **the job is yours for the t.** el trabajo es para ti, si lo quieres; **the game was hers for the t., but she blew it** el partido ya era suyo *or* ya tenía el partido en sus manos, pero lo echó todo a perder (**b**) *Br Com* **takings** recaudación *f*

talc [tælk] *n* talco *m*

talcum powder ['tælkəm'paʊdə(r)] *n* polvos *mpl* de talco

tale [teɪl] *n* (**a**) *(story)* historia *f*; *(legend)* cuento *m*; **he told us the t. of his escape** nos contó cómo se escapó; **she lived to tell the t.** vivió para contarlo; **the scars on his back tell their own t.** las cicatrices de su espalda hablan por sí mismas; **how did you come to possess this elephant's tusk? – ah, thereby hangs a t.!** ¿cómo conseguiste este colmillo de elefante? – bueno, es una larga historia; **she told me her t. of woe** me contó sus penas

(**b**) *(lie)* cuento *m*, patraña *f*; **to tell tales (about** *or* **on sb)** contar patrañas (sobre alguien)

talent ['tælənt] *n* (**a**) *(ability)* talento *m*, dotes *fpl* (**for** para); **she has a t. for music** tiene talento *or* dotes para la música; *Ironic* **he has a t. for saying the wrong thing** tiene el don de decir lo que no debe; **I see you have hidden talents!** ¡qué callado lo tenías!

(**b**) *(person with ability)* talento *m*; *(people with ability)* gente *f* con talento ▸▸ *Mus & Sport* ***t. scout*** cazatalentos *mf inv*; *Mus & Sport* ***t. spotter*** cazatalentos *mf inv*

(**c**) *Br Fam (attractive people)* ganado *m*; **he's gone to a nightclub to check out the t.** ha ido a una discoteca a ver cómo está el ganado

talented ['tæləntɪd] *adj* con talento; **she's really t.** tiene mucho talento; **one of our most t. musicians** uno de nuestros músicos con más talento

Taliban ['tælɪbæn] **1** *n* talibán *m*; **the T.** los talibanes

2 *adj* talibán

talisman ['tælɪzmən] *n* talismán *m*

talismanic [tælɪz'mænɪk] *adj* talismánico(a)

TALK [tɔːk] **1** *n* (**a**) *(conversation)* conversación *f*, charla *f*, *CAm, Méx* plática *f*; **to have a t. with sb** hablar con alguien; **we had a long t.** hablamos largo y tendido; **there is a lot of t. in the background** hay muchas voces de fondo; **it's women's t.** son cosas de mujeres; **that's the sort of t. we usually hear from the government** esa es la típica forma de hablar del gobierno; **all this t. is getting us nowhere** tanto hablar no nos lleva a ninguna parte; **I don't believe what they said, I think it's just t.** no me creo lo que dijeron, no son más que habladurías; IDIOM *Fam* **to be all t. (and no action)** hablar mucho (y no hacer nada) ▸▸ *TV & Rad* ***t. show*** programa *m* de entrevistas

(**b**) **talks** *(negotiations)* conversaciones *fpl*; **so far there have only been talks about talks** aún no se ha pasado de la primera toma de contacto

(**c**) *(gossip)* habladurías *fpl*; *(speculation)* especulaciones *fpl*; **his behaviour is causing a lot of t.** su comportamiento está dando mucho de qué hablar; **there is some t. of his returning** se dice que va a volver; **it's the t. of the town** es la comidilla local

(**d**) *(lecture)* conferencia *f*, charla *f*

2 *vt* (**a**) *(speak) (a language)* hablar; *Fam* **we're talking serious money** hablamos de un montón de *Esp* pasta *or Am* plata; **to t. nonsense** *or Br* **rubbish** decir tonterías; **to t. politics** hablar de política; **to t. (common) sense** hablar con sensatez *or* con sentido común; **to t. (some) sense into sb** hacer entrar en razón a alguien; **to t. the t.** saber cómo venderse; **she can t. her way out of anything** sabe salir con palabras de cualquier situación; IDIOM *US* **to t. a blue streak** hablar como una cotorra; IDIOM *US Fam* **to t. turkey** hablar de cosas serias

(**b**) *(convince)* **to t. sb into/out of doing sth** persuadir a alguien para que haga/para que no haga algo; **she talked me into it** me convenció; **she wanted to tell them, but I talked her out of it** quería contárselo, pero la convencí para que no lo hiciera; **to t. oneself out of trouble** salir del paso con buenas palabras

3 *vi* (**a**) *(speak)* hablar, *esp Am* conversar, *Méx* platicar (**to** *or* **with/about** *or* **of** con/de); **can we t. a moment?** ¿podríamos hablar *or esp Am* conversar *or Méx* platicar un momento?; **it was the first time we had talked together** era la primera vez que hablábamos; **we're not talking (to each other)** *(have fallen out)* no nos hablamos; **she didn't t. to me the whole evening** no me dirigió la palabra en toda la noche; **they were talking in Chinese** hablaban en chino; **once we got talking, I started to like her** una vez que empezamos a hablar *or esp Am* conversar *or Méx* platicar, comenzó a gustarme; **what are you talking about?** ¡pero qué dices!; **I don't know what you're talking about** no sé de qué me hablas; **she knows what she's talking about** sabe de lo que habla; **t. about stupid/luck!** ¡qué estúpido/suerte!; **to t. of** *or* **about doing sth** hablar de hacer algo; **talking of embarrassing situations...** hablando de situaciones embarazosas...; **I'm talking to you, young man!** ¡le hablo a usted, jovencito!; **don't you t. to me like that!** ¡no te dirijas a mí de esa forma!; **to t. to oneself** hablar solo; *Fam* **now you're talking!** ¡así se habla!; *Fam* **YOU can t.!, look who's talking!, you're a fine one to t.!** ¡mira quién fue a hablar!; **to t. big** farolear; **to t. dirty** decir obscenidades; **to t. tough** hablar con contundencia

(**b**) *(gossip)* murmurar, *Esp* cotillear (**about** sobre); **people will t. if we do that** si hacemos eso la gente murmurará; **he got himself talked about** consiguió que se hablase de él

(**c**) *(give lecture)* dar una conferencia (**on** sobre)

(**d**) *(reveal secrets)* hablar; **someone must have talked** alguien ha debido de hablar; **to make a prisoner t.** hacer hablar a un prisionero

▸ **talk around**, *Br* **talk round** **1** *vt insep (problem, issue)* eludir

2 *vt sep (convince)* convencer

▸ **talk at** *vt insep* **he doesn't so much t. TO you as AT you** más que hablarte, te suelta su monólogo

▸ **talk away** **1** *vi* charlar

2 *vt sep* **to t. the night away** quedarse toda la noche charlando

▸ **talk back** *vi* responder, replicar; **don't you t. back to me!** ¡a mí no me respondas *or* repliques!

▸ **talk down** **1** *vt sep* (**a**) *(detract from)* menospreciar (**b**) *(coax)* **air traffic control talked him down** la torre de control le dio instrucciones por radio sobre cómo aterrizar; **the policeman talked him down from the top of the building** el policía le convenció para que no saltara desde lo alto del edificio (**c**) *(silence)* acallar; **he tried to object but they talked him down** trató de protestar pero lo acallaron

2 *vi* **to t. down to sb** hablar con aires de superioridad a alguien

▸ **talk out** *vt sep* (**a**) *(resolve)* **we need to t. out our problems** tenemos que hablar hasta encontrar una solución a nuestros problemas (**b**) *Parl* **to t. out a bill** = prolongar en exceso el debate sobre un proyecto de ley para que no dé tiempo a someterlo a votación

▸ **talk over** *vt sep* hablar de, tratar de; **to t. things over** discutir

▸ **talk round** = **talk around**

▸ **talk through** **1** *vt insep* IDIOM *Fam* **he was talking through his hat** *or* **the back of his neck** no sabía de lo que hablaba

2 *vt sep* (**a**) *(explain)* **to t. sb through sth** explicarle algo a alguien (**b**) *(discuss in detail)* discutir en detalle

▸ **talk up** *vt sep (chances, possibility)* exagerar

talkative ['tɔːkətɪv] *adj* hablador(ora), locuaz; **you're not very t., what's wrong?** estás muy callado, ¿qué es lo que pasa?

talkativeness ['tɔːkətɪvnɪs] *n* locuacidad *f*

talker ['tɔːkə(r)] *n* hablador(ora) *m,f*; **he's not much of a t.** no habla mucho, es más bien reservado; **she's a brilliant t.** habla muy bien (en público), es buena comunicadora

talkie ['tɔːkɪ] *n Fam Old-fashioned* película *f* sonora; **the talkies** el cine sonoro

talking ['tɔːkɪŋ] **1** *n* **there's too much t.** se habla demasiado; **leave the t. to me** deja que hable yo; **he did all the t.** él se encargó de hablar; **no t.!** *(sign)* ¡silencio!

2 *adj* ***t. book*** audiolibro *m*, = cinta grabada con la lectura de un libro; *TV* ***t. head*** busto *m* parlante; ***t. pictures*** cine *m* sonoro; ***t. point*** tema *m* de conversación; *Br Fam* ***t. shop*** = sitio u organización donde se habla mucho y se hace poco

talking-to ['tɔːkɪŋtuː] (*pl* **talking-tos**) *n Fam* sermón *m*, *Esp* rapapolvo *m*; **to give sb a t.** echarle a alguien un buen sermón *or Esp* rapapolvo

tall [tɔːl] **1** *adj (person, building, tree, grass)* alto(a); **how t. are you?** ¿cuánto mides?; **how t. is that building?** ¿cuánto mide ese edificio?; **I'm six foot t.** mido un metro ochenta; **the building is sixty metres t.** el edificio mide sesenta metros de altura; **I'm two centimetres taller than her** le saco dos centímetros de altura, mido dos centímetros más que ella; **she's grown a lot taller in the past year** ha crecido mucho

durante el ultimo año; IDIOM **that's a t. order** eso es mucho pedir; **a t. story** un cuento chino ►► ***t. ship*** gran velero *m*
2 *adv* **to walk** *or* **stand t.** ir *or* andar con la cabeza bien alta

tallboy ['tɔːlbɔɪ] *n* cómoda *f* alta

Tallin ['tælɪn] *n* Tallin

tallness ['tɔːlnɪs] *n (of person, tree, building, grass)* altura *f*

tallow ['tæləʊ] *n* sebo *m*

tally ['tælɪ] **1** *n* **(a)** *(record)* cuenta *f*; **to keep a t. of sth** llevar la cuenta de algo; **to keep a t. of the score** llevar la cuenta de los puntos ►► *Naut* ***t. clerk*** medidor(ora) *m,f*, controlador(ora) *m,f* de carga **(b)** *(total) (of goals, points)* total *m*
2 *vt* hacer el recuento (final) de
3 *vi (figures, report)* encajar, concordar

tally-ho ['tælɪ'həʊ] *exclam* ¡hala! *(en caza)*

Talmud ['tælmʊd] *n* **the T.** el Talmud

talon ['tælən] *n* **(a)** *(of animal)* garra *f* **(b)** *(of person)* uña *f* extremadamente larga

> **False friend:** The Spanish noun **talón** is not a translation for the English word **talon**. In Spanish **talón** means "heel" or "cheque".

talus ['teɪləs] *n* **(a)** *Geol* talud *m* **(b)** *Anat* hueso *m* del talón

tamable = **tameable**

tamale [tə'mɑːlɪ] *n Culin* tamal *m*

tamarind ['tæmərɪnd] *n* tamarindo *m*

tamarisk ['tæmərɪsk] *n* tamarisco *m*

tambour ['tæmbʊə(r)] *n (in sewing)* tambor *m*

tambourine [tæmbə'riːn] *n Mus* pandereta *f*

tame [teɪm] **1** *adj* **(a)** *(lion, tiger)* manso(a); *(birds, squirrels)* dócil; **the lion had become t. in captivity** el león se había amansado en cautividad **(b)** *(unadventurous)* soso(a); **the team's t. capitulation in the second half** la dócil capitulación del equipo en la segunda parte
2 *vt* **(a)** *(lion, tiger)* domar **(b)** *(person)* domar **(c)** *(emotion, passion)* dominar, controlar **(d)** *(nature)* domesticar; *(river)* controlar

tameable, tamable ['teɪməbəl] *adj (animal)* domable

tamely ['teɪmlɪ] *adv (to accept, agree to)* dócilmente; *(to give up, capitulate)* sin ofrecer resistencia; **t. worded** pusilánime, blando(a); **the novel ends t.** la novela tiene un final insulso

tameness ['teɪmnɪs] *n* **(a)** *(of lion, tiger)* mansedumbre *f*; *(of bird, squirrel)* docilidad *f* **(b)** *(of ending, style, movie, party)* falta *f* de emoción, insulsez *f*; **the t. of the team's capitulation** la dócil capitulación del equipo

tamer ['teɪmə(r)] *n* domador(ora) *m,f*

Tamil ['tæmɪl] **1** *n* **(a)** *(person)* tamil *mf* **(b)** *(language)* tamil *m*
2 *adj* tamil

tam-o'-shanter [tæmə'ʃæntə(r)] *n* boina *f* tradicional escocesa

tamp [tæmp] *vt* **to t. (down)** *(earth)* apisonar; *(tobacco)* apretar

Tampax® ['tæmpæks] *n* támpax® *m*

tamper ['tæmpə(r)]

► **tamper with** *vt insep* **(a)** *(lock)* intentar forzar; *(brakes, machinery)* manipular; *(documents, records)* manipular, falsear; *(product)* manipular; *(system)* modificar **(b)** *US (witness, jury)* manipular

tamper-evident [tæmpər'evɪdənt] *adj* a prueba de manipulación, inviolable

tamper-proof ['tæmpəpruːf] *adj* imposible de manipular

tampon ['tæmpɒn] *n* tampón *m*

tam-tam ['tæmtæm] *n* tam-tam *m*

tan[1] [tæn] *n Math (abbr* **tangent**) tangente *f*

tan[2] **1** *n* **(a)** *(from sun)* bronceado *m*, *Esp* moreno *m*; **I came back from my trip with a good t.** volví de viaje con un buen bronceado; **to lose one's t.** perder el bronceado **(b)** *(colour)* marrón *m* claro
2 *adj (colour)* marrón claro
3 *vt (pt & pp* **tanned**) **(a)** *(leather)* curtir; IDIOM *Fam* **to t. sb, to t. sb's hide** dar una paliza a alguien, *Esp* zurrarle a alguien la badana **(b)** *(of sun) (skin)* broncear, tostar
4 *vi (person, skin)* broncearse, ponerse moreno(a)

tanager ['tænədʒə(r)] *n* **magpie t.** tangará *m* overo; **scarlet t.** tangará *m* escarlata

tandem ['tændəm] **1** *n* **(a)** *(bicycle)* tándem *m* **(b)** IDIOM **to do sth in t. (with sb)** hacer algo en conjunto *or Esp* al alimón (con alguien); **the two devices work in t.** los dos dispositivos funcionan complementariamente
2 *adv* **to ride t.** montar en tándem

tandoori [tæn'dʊərɪ] *n* tandori *m*, = método indio de asar la carne en un horno de barro ►► ***t. chicken*** pollo *m* (al) tandori

tang [tæŋ] *n* **(a)** *(strong taste)* sabor *m* fuerte; *(acid taste)* acidez *f*, sabor *m* ácido **(b)** *(smell)* olor *m* penetrante

tanga ['tæŋgə] *n* tanga *m*

tangent ['tændʒənt] *n Math* tangente *f*; IDIOM **to go off at** *or* **on a t.** irse por las ramas

tangential [tæn'dʒenʃəl] *adj* **(a)** *Math* tangencial **(b)** *Astron* tangencial **(c)** *Formal (secondary)* tangencial (**to** a)

tangentially [tæn'dʒenʃəlɪ] *adv Formal* tangencialmente, de manera tangencial

tangerine [tændʒə'riːn] **1** *n* **(a)** *(fruit)* mandarina *f* **(b)** *(tree)* mandarino *m* **(c)** *(colour)* mandarina *m*
2 *adj (colour)* naranja, mandarina

tangible ['tændʒɪbəl] *adj* **(a)** *(object)* tangible ►► *Fin* ***t. assets*** (activo *m*) tangible *m* **(b)** *(substantial) (proof)* tangible, palpable; *(difference)* palpable

tangibly ['tændʒɪblɪ] *adv* claramente

Tangier(s) [tæn'dʒɪə(z)] *n* Tánger

tanginess ['tæŋɪnɪs] *n (strong taste)* sabor *m* fuerte; *(acid taste)* acidez *f*, sabor *m* ácido

tangle ['tæŋgəl] **1** *n* **(a)** *(of threads, hair)* maraña *f*, lío *m*; **this wool is in an awful t.** esta lana está totalmente enmarañada *or* hecha un lío; **my hair got into a t.** se me enredó el pelo **(b)** *(muddle)* lío *m*; **to be in a t.** estar hecho(a) un lío; **I got into a t. over my accounts** me hice un lío con las cuentas **(c)** *Fam (disagreement)* follón *m*
2 *vt* **(a)** *(wire, wool)* enmarañar, hacer un lío con; *(hair)* enredar; **to get tangled (in sth)** quedarse enredado(a) (en algo)
3 *vi* **(a)** *(wire)* enmarañarse, hacerse un lío; *(hair)* enredarse **(b)** *Fam (fight, argue)* liarla

► **tangle up** *vt sep* **(a)** *(wire, wool)* enmarañar, hacer un lío con; *(hair)* enredar; **to get tangled up (in sth)** quedarse enredado(a) (en algo); **she had got tangled up in some barbed wire** se enredó en una alambrada de púas
(b) *(involve)* **to get tangled up (in sth)** verse involucrado(a) (en algo)
(c) *(confuse)* **I got very tangled up trying to understand the system** me hice un auténtico lío tratando de entender el sistema

► **tangle with** *vt insep Fam (quarrel, fight with)* buscarse un lío con

tangled ['tæŋgəld] *adj* **(a)** *(wire, wool)* enmarañado(a), liado(a); *(hair)* enredado(a) **(b)** *(complex) (story, love life)* complicado(a), enmarañado(a)

tangleweed ['tæŋgəlwiːd] *n* alga *f* parda, feofita *f*

tango ['tæŋgəʊ] **1** *n (pl* **tangos**) *(dance)* tango *m*
2 *vi* bailar el tango; IDIOM *Fam* **he may have started it, but it takes two to t.** puede que haya empezado él, pero tiene que haber sido cosa de dos

tangy ['tæŋɪ] *adj* **(a)** *(taste) (strong)* fuerte; *(acid)* ácido(a) **(b)** *(smell)* penetrante

tank [tæŋk] **1** *n* **(a)** *(container)* depósito *m*; *(on truck, train)* cisterna *f*; **(*Br* petrol *or US* gas) t.** depósito *m*, tanque *m* de gasolina; **(fish) t.** pecera *f* ►► *US Rail* ***t. car*** vagón *m* cisterna; *Rail* ***t. engine*** locomotora *f* cisterna; *Br Rail* ***t. wagon*** vagón *m* cisterna
(b) *(tankful) (of petrol)* **how much does a t. of petrol cost?** ¿cuánto cuesta llenar el depósito *or* tanque?
(c) *Mil* tanque *m*, carro *m* de combate; IDIOM *Fam* **to be built like a t.** estar cuadrado(a), ser una mula ►► ***t. regiment*** regimiento *m* de tanques
(d) *(clothing)* ***t. top*** *Br (sweater)* chaleco *m* de lana; *US (shirt)* camiseta *f* de tirantes *or* sin mangas
(e) *US Fam (jail)* cárcel *f*, *Esp* chirona *f*, *Andes, RP* cana *f*, *Méx* bote *m*
2 *vt Fam (defeat heavily)* aplastar

► **tank along** *vi Fam* ir a toda máquina *or Esp* pastilla

► **tank up** *vi* **(a)** *Aut* llenar el depósito *or* tanque **(b)** *Fam (with alcohol)* darle a la botella, empinar el codo

tankard ['tæŋkəd] *n* jarra *f*, bock *m*

tanked (up) ['tæŋkt('ʌp)] *adj Fam* **to get t.** agarrarse *or Esp* cogerse un pedo, *Méx* ponerse una peda

tanker ['tæŋkə(r)] *n* **(a)** *(ship) (in general)* buque *m* cisterna; *(for oil)* petrolero *m*; *(for gas)* metanero *m* **(b)** *(truck)* (camión *m*) cisterna *f* **(c)** *(train wagon)* vagón *m* cisterna **(d)** *(plane)* avión *m* cisterna

tankful ['tæŋkfʊl] *n* **(a)** *(of petrol)* depósito *m* lleno; **half a t.** medio depósito **(b)** *(of water)* tanque *m* (entero), depósito *m* (entero)

tanned [tænd] *adj* **(a)** *(person, face, complexion)* moreno(a), bronceado(a); **to be t.** estar moreno(a) *or* bronceado(a) **(b)** *(leather)* curtido(a)

tanner ['tænə(r)] *n* **(a)** *(of leather)* curtidor(ora) *m,f* **(b)** *Br Fam Formerly (sixpence)* = antigua moneda de seis peniques

tannery ['tænərı] *n* curtiduría *f*, tenería *f*

tannic acid ['tænık'æsıd] *n* tanino *m*

tannin ['tænın] *n* tanino *m*

tanning ['tænıŋ] *n* **(a)** *(of skin)* bronceado *m* ►► ***t. lotion*** crema *f* bronceadora; ***t. studio*** salón *m* de bronceado, solarium *m* **(b)** *(of hides)* curtido *m* **(c)** *Fam Old-fashioned (beating)* zurra *f*; **to give sb a t.** dar una zurra a alguien

tannoy® ['tænɔı] *n Br* (sistema *m* de) megafonía *f*; **over the t.** por megafonía

tansy ['tænzı] *n* tanaceto *m*

tantalize ['tæntəlaız] *vt* **(a)** *(excite)* incitar (**with** con) **(b)** *(torment)* atormentar (**with** con)

tantalizing ['tæntəlaızıŋ] *adj (smell, sight)* sugerente, estimulante; *(offer, prospect)* atractivo(a), prometedor(ora)

tantalizingly ['tæntəlaızıŋlı] *adv* **the cool water was t. near** la proximidad del agua fresca era una tortura; **they came t. close to winning** estuvieron a punto de *or* en un tris de ganar

tantalum ['tæntələm] *n Chem* tantalio *m*

tantamount ['tæntəmaʊnt] *adj* equivalente; **to be t. to** equivaler a

tantrum ['tæntrəm] *n* rabieta *f*; **to have** *or* **throw a t.** agarrar *or Esp* coger una rabieta

Tanzania [tænzə'nıə] *n* Tanzania

Tanzanian [tænzə'nıən] **1** *n* tanzano(a) *m,f*

2 *adj* tanzano(a)

Taoiseach ['ti:ʃəχ] *n* primer(era) ministro(a) *m,f (de Irlanda)*

Taoism ['taʊızəm, 'daʊızəm] *n* taoísmo *m*

Taoist ['taʊıst, 'daʊıst] **1** *n* taoísta *mf*

2 *adj* taoísta

tap[1] [tæp] **1** *n* **(a)** *Br (for water) Esp* grifo *m*, *Chile, Col, Méx* llave *f*, *RP* canilla *f*; *(for gas)* llave *f* (de paso); *(on barrel)* espita *f*, *Esp* grifo *m*; **the hot/cold t.** *Esp* el grifo *or Chile, Col, Méx* la llave *or RP* la canilla del agua caliente/fría; **to leave the t. running** dejar *Esp* el grifo abierto *or Chile, Col, Méx* la llave *or RP* la canilla abierta; **on t.** *(beer)* de barril; *Fig* **to be on t.** *(available)* estar disponible; **they seem to have funds on t.** parece que sus fondos no se acaban ►► ***t. water*** agua *f* del *Esp* grifo *or Chile, Col, Méx* de la llave *or RP* de la canilla

(b) *(listening device)* **to put a t. on the phone** intervenir *or* pinchar el teléfono; **who authorized the t.?** ¿quién ha autorizado a intervenir *or* pinchar el teléfono?

(c) *Med* punción *f*, drenaje *m*

2 *vt* (*pt & pp* **tapped**) **(a)** *(tree)* sangrar

(b) *(liquid) (from barrel, cask)* sacar (con una espita)

(c) *(gas, water main)* hacer una toma de

(d) *(resources)* aprovechar, explotar; *Fam* **to t. sb for money** tratar de sacar dinero a alguien, tratar de dar un sablazo a alguien; *Fam* **to t. sb for information** intentar sonsacar información a alguien

(e) *(phone)* intervenir, pinchar; **the phones are tapped** los teléfonos están intervenidos *or* pinchados

(f) *Med* hacer una punción en, drenar

tap[2] **1** *n* **(a)** *(light blow)* golpecito *m*; **to give sth a t.** darle un golpecito a algo; **to give sb a t. on the shoulder** darle un golpecito en el hombro a alguien; **we heard a t. at the door** alguien llamó con suavidad a la puerta **(b)** *(dancing)* **t. (dance** *or* **dancing)** claqué *m* ►► ***t. dancer*** bailarín(ina) *m,f* de claqué **(c)** *(on shoe)* tapa *f*

2 *vt* (*pt & pp* **tapped**) **(a)** *(strike lightly)* dar un golpecito a; **I tapped him on the shoulder** le di un golpecito en el hombro **(b)** *(drum)* **she was tapping her fingers on the table** tamborileaba con los dedos sobre la mesa; **he tapped his feet to the rhythm** seguía el ritmo con los pies

3 *vi* **to t. at** *or* **on the door** llamar suavemente a la puerta; **to t. on the window** dar unos golpecitos en la ventana; **she was tapping away at the computer** estaba a teclear en *Esp* el ordenador *orAm* la computadora

► **tap in** *vt sep Comptr* introducir

► **tap out** *vt sep* **(a)** *(pipe)* **to t. out one's pipe** vaciar la pipa con unos golpecitos **(b)** *(rhythm)* reproducir dando golpes; **he tapped out a message in Morse** envió un mensaje en morse

tapas ['tæpəs] *npl Culin* raciones *fpl*, tapas *fpl* ►► ***t. bar*** = restaurante especializado en raciones de comida española y mediterránea

tap-dance ['tæp'dɑ:ns] *vi* bailar claqué

tape [teıp] **1** *n* **(a)** *(ribbon)* cinta *f*; **(adhesive** *or Fam* **sticky) t.** cinta adhesiva; *Sport* **the (finishing) t.** la (cinta de) meta; **t. (measure)** cinta *f* métrica

(b) *(for recording)* cinta *f* (magnetofónica); *(cassette, recording)* cinta *f*; **on t.** en cinta; **to do a t. for sb** grabar una cinta a alguien; **will you do me a t. of that album?** ¿me puedes grabar una cinta de ese disco? ►► *Comptr* ***t. backup*** copia *f* de seguridad en cinta; *Comptr* ***t. backup system*** sistema *m* de copia de seguridad en cinta; ***t. deck*** pletina *f*, platina *f*, *Am* casetera *f*; ***t. head*** cabezal *m* (de casete *or* cinta); ***t. recorder*** grabadora *f*, casete *m*; ***t. recording*** grabación *f* (magnetofónica); ***t. unit*** unidad *f* de cinta

2 *vt* **(a)** *(stick with tape)* pegar con cinta adhesiva (**to** a); IDIOM **I've got him/it taped** lo tengo controlado *or Esp* pillado **(b)** *(record)* grabar; **would you t. me that album?** ¿me puedes grabar ese album?

3 *vi* grabar

► **tape together** *vt sep (fix)* pegar con cinta adhesiva

► **tape up** *vt sep* **(a)** *(fasten) (parcel)* sellar con cinta adhesiva **(b)** *(close) (letterbox, hole)* sellar *or* tapar con cinta adhesiva **(c)** *US (bandage up)* poner una venda a, vendar

taper ['teıpə(r)] **1** *n* **(a)** *(candle)* cerillo *m*, vela *f* delgada **(b)** *(for lighting fires) (of wood)* astilla *f* **(c)** *(decrease in diameter)* ángulo *m* de estrechamiento

2 *vi* estrecharse; **to t. to a point** acabar en punta

► **taper off** *vi* **(a)** *(object)* estrecharse **(b)** *(production, numbers, demand)* disminuir progresivamente *or* paulatinamente; *(noise)* desaparecer progresivamente *or* paulatinamente; *(conversation)* apagarse progresivamente *or* paulatinamente

tape-record ['teıprıkɔ:d] *vt* grabar (en cinta)

tapered ['teıpəd] *adj (table leg, stick)* en punta; *(fingers)* afilado(a); *(clothes)* estrecho(a)

tapestried ['tæpıstrıd] *adj* con tapices

tapestry ['tæpıstrı] *n* **(a)** *(wall hanging)* tapiz *m* **(b)** *(art)* tapicería *f* **(c)** *(of fields)* manto *m*, tapiz *m*; *(of characters)* cuadro *m*; **life's rich t.** las cosas de la vida

tapeworm ['teıpwɜ:m] *n* tenia *f*, solitaria *f*

tapioca [tæpı'əʊkə] *n* tapioca *f* ►► ***t. pudding*** = postre elaborado a base de tapioca y leche

tapir ['teıpıə(r)] *n* tapir *m*

tappet ['tæpıt] *n Aut* taqué *m*

tapping ['tæpıŋ] *n (sound)* golpeteo *m*

taproom ['tæprʊm] *n Br* bar *m*

taproot ['tæpru:t] *n* raíz *f* principal *or* primaria

taps [tæps] *n US Mil (at funeral)* toque *m* de difuntos; *(at night)* toque *m* de retreta

tar [tɑ:(r)] **1** *n* **(a)** *(substance) (for roads, in cigarettes)* alquitrán *m*; *(for ships, in soap)* brea *f* ►► *US* ***t. paper*** papel *m* de alquitrán **(b)** *Fam Old-fashioned (sailor)* marinero *m*

2 *vt* (*pt & pp* **tarred**) *(road, roof)* alquitranar; *(boat)* brear; **to t. and feather sb** emplumar a alguien; IDIOM **we have all been tarred with the same brush** nos han metido a todos en el mismo saco

taramasalata [tærəmæsə'lɑ:tə] *n* taramasalata *f*, = paté de huevas de pescado, especialmente bacalao, de color rosado

tarantella [tærən'telə] *n* tarantela *f*

tarantula [tə'ræntjʊlə] *n* tarántula *f*

tardily ['tɑ:dılı] *adv Formal* **(a)** *(late)* tardíamente **(b)** *(slowly)* lentamente

tardiness ['tɑ:dınıs] *n Formal* **(a)** *(delay)* tardanza *f*, *Am* demora *f* **(b)** *(slowness)* lentitud *f*

tardy ['tɑ:dı] *adj Formal* **(a)** *(late)* tardío(a) **(b)** *(slow)* lento(a)

tare [teə(r)] *n Com (weight of vehicle)* tara *f*

target ['tɑ:gıt] **1** *n* **(a)** *(in archery, shooting)* diana *f*, blanco *m* ►► ***t. practice*** prácticas *fpl* de tiro; ***t. shooting*** tiro *m* al blanco

(b) *(in soccer, hockey)* **his shot was on/off t.** su disparo iba/no iba dirigido a portería *orAm* al arco; **he should at least have hit the t.** su disparo al menos tendría que haber ido (dirigido) a portería *orAm* al arco

(c) *(of attack, joke, criticism)* blanco *m*, objetivo *m*; **he had become an easy t. for the press** se había convertido en un blanco fácil para la prensa; **she was right on t. with her criticisms** acertó con sus críticas, sus críticas fueron muy acertadas

(d) *(aim, goal)* objetivo *m*, meta *f*; **sales t.** objetivo(s) de ventas; **to set oneself a t.** trazarse una meta; **my t. weight is 65 kilos** me he propuesto quedarme en 65 kilos; **sales are on t.** las ventas van según lo previsto; **to be on t. to do sth** ir camino de hacer algo ►► *TV, Rad & Com* ***t. audience*** audiencia *f* a la que está orientada la emisión; *Comptr* ***t. disk*** disco *m* de destino; ***t. group*** = sector o grupo al que va destinado algo; *Ling* ***t. language*** lengua *f* de destino *or* llegada; *Com* ***t. market*** mercado *m* objeto *or* objetivo; ***t. price*** objetivo *m* de precio; ***t. readership:*** **what is the t. readership of the newspaper?** ¿a qué lectores va dirigido el periódico?

2 *vt* **(a)** *(aim)* **to t. sth at sth** *(missile)* apuntar algo hacia *or* a algo; *(campaign, TV programme, benefits)* destinar algo a algo

(b) *(aim at)* apuntar a, tener como objetivo; **she has been targeted as the best person for the job** ha sido elegida *or* designada como la persona ideal para el puesto; **they have targeted the government's environmental policy as a possible weakness** han encontrado en la política medioambiental un posible punto débil del gobierno

targeted ['tɑːgɪtɪd] *adj* específico(a)

targeting ['tɑːgɪtɪŋ] *n (of funds, resources, benefits)* selección *f or* fijación *f* de objetivo(s)

tariff ['tærɪf] *n* **(a)** *(tax)* arancel *m* ►► ***t. barrier*** barrera *f* arancelaria; ***t. wall*** barrera *f* arancelaria **(b)** *(price list)* tarifa *f* **(c)** *Br (rate) (of gas, electricity)* tarifa *f*

tarmac® ['tɑːmæk] **1** *n* **(a)** *(asphalt)* asfalto *m* **(b)** *(runway)* pista *f*; *(road)* asfalto *m*, piso *m*

2 *vt (pt & pp* **tarmacked***)* asfaltar

tarmacadam® ['tɑːmə'kædəm] *n* asfalto *m*

tarn [tɑːn] *n* laguna *f* (de montaña)

tarnish ['tɑːnɪʃ] **1** *vt* **(a)** *(metal)* quitar el brillo a, deslucir **(b)** *(reputation)* empañar

2 *vi (metal)* empañarse, deslucirse

tarnished ['tɑːnɪʃt] *adj* **(a)** *(metal)* sin brillo, deslucido(a) **(b)** *(reputation)* empañado(a)

tarot ['tærəʊ] *n* tarot *m* ►► ***t. card*** carta *f* de(l) tarot

tarp [tɑːp] *n US Fam* lona *f* (recauchutada)

tarpaulin [tɑː'pɔːlɪn] *n* **(a)** *(material)* lona *f* recauchutada **(b)** *(sheet)* lona *f* (recauchutada)

tarpon ['tɑːpɒn] *n* tarpón *m*

tarragon ['tærəgən] *n* estragón *m*

tarry¹ ['tærɪ] *vi Literary* **(a)** *(delay)* demorarse **(b)** *(remain)* quedarse

tarry² ['tɑːrɪ] *adj* **(a)** *(like tar)* alquitranado(a) **(b)** *(covered or stained with tar)* lleno(a) de alquitrán

tarsus ['tɑːsəs] *n Anat* tarso *m*

tart [tɑːt] **1** *n* **(a)** *(cake) (large)* tarta *f*; *(small)* pastelillo *m* **(b)** *Fam Pej (promiscuous woman, prostitute)* fulana *f*

2 *adj* **(a)** *(in taste)* agrio(a) **(b)** *(in tone) (remark)* áspero(a)

►**tart up** *vt sep Br Fam (room, building)* retocar, hacer retoques en; **to t. oneself up** emperifollarse; **it's just a tarted up version of the old model** no es más que una versión retocada del antiguo modelo

tartan ['tɑːtən] *n* **(a)** *(fabric)* tartán *m*, tela *f* de cuadros escoceses; **t. tie** corbata de cuadros escoceses **(b)** *(design)* tartán *m*, diseño *m* de tartán

Tartar, Tatar ['tɑːtə(r)] *n* tártaro(a) *m,f*

tartar ['tɑːtə(r)] *n* **(a)** *(on teeth)* sarro *m* **(b)** *Br (fearsome person)* fiera *f*

tartar(e) sauce ['tɑːtə'sɔːs] *n* salsa *f* tártara

tartaric acid [tɑː'tærɪk'æsɪd] *n* ácido *m* tartárico

tartlet ['tɑːtlɪt] *n Br* tartaleta *f*

tartly ['tɑːtlɪ] *adv* ásperamente

tartness ['tɑːtnɪs] *n* **(a)** *(of flavour)* acidez *f* **(b)** *(of remark)* aspereza *f*, acritud *f*

tarty ['tɑːtɪ] *adj Fam (clothes)* de fulana; **to look t.** parecer una fulana

Tarzan ['tɑːzæn] *pr n* Tarzán

Tashkent [tæʃ'kent] *n* Tashkent

task [tɑːsk] **1** *n* **(a)** *(job)* tarea *f*; **convincing them will be no easy t.** convencerlos no será tarea fácil; **to take sb to t. for (doing) sth** reprender a alguien por (haber hecho) algo **(b)** *Comptr* tarea *f*

2 *vt Com* **to t. sb to do sth** *or* **with doing sth** encomendar a alguien la tarea de hacer algo

taskbar ['tɑːskbɑː(r)] *n Comptr* barra *f* de tareas

taskforce ['tɑːskfɔːs] *n* **(a)** *Mil* destacamento *m*; **a naval t.** un destacamento naval **(b)** *(committee)* grupo *m* de trabajo

taskmaster ['tɑːskmɑːstə(r)] *n* **he's a hard t.** es muy exigente

Tasmania [tæz'meɪnɪə] *n* Tasmania

Tasmanian [tæz'meɪnɪən] **1** *n* tasmano(a) *m,f*

2 *adj* tasmano(a) ►► ***T. devil*** diablo *m* de Tasmania

Tasman Sea ['tæzmən'siː] *n* **the T.** el Mar de Tasmania

tassel ['tæsəl] *n* borla *f*

tasselled ['tæsəld] *adj* con borlas

TASTE [teɪst] **1** *n* **(a)** *(flavour)* sabor *m*, gusto *m* (**of** a); **(sense of) t.** (sentido *m* del) gusto *m*; **to be sweet/salty to the t.** tener un sabor *or* gusto dulce/salado; **this cheese doesn't have much t.** este queso es bastante insípido; IDIOM **it left a bad** *or* **bitter t. in my mouth** me dejó un mal sabor de boca ►► *Anat* ***t. bud*** papila *f* gustativa

(b) *(sample)* **to have a t. of sth** probar algo; **I'll just have a t. of the ice cream** sólo quiero un poquito de helado; **now that I've had a t. of success, I want more** ahora que ya he saboreado el éxito, quiero más; **he's already had a t. of prison life** ya sabe *or* ha probado lo que es la vida en la cárcel; **a t. of things to come** una muestra de lo que vendrá; IDIOM **to give sb a t. of their own medicine** pagar a alguien con su misma moneda

(c) *(liking, preference)* afición *f*, gusto *m* (**for** por); **to acquire** *or* **develop a t. for sth** aficionarse a algo; **to have a t. for sth** ser aficionado(a) a algo; **I've lost my t. for sweet things** ha dejado de gustarme el *or* lo dulce; **her t. in furniture/men** su gusto en cuestión de muebles/hombres; **add sugar to t.** añada azúcar a (su) gusto; **it's a matter of t.** es una cuestión de gustos; **I have expensive tastes** tengo gustos caros; **he's a bit short for my t.** es un poco bajo para mi gusto; **classical music is more to my t.** me gusta *or Esp* va más la música clásica; **violent films are not to my t.** las películas violentas no son de mi gusto

(d) *(judgement)* gusto *m*; **she has good t. (in clothes/men)** tiene buen gusto; **they don't have much t. when it comes to art** en lo referente al arte no tienen demasiado buen gusto; **they have awful** *or* **no t.** tienen un gusto malísimo *or* espantoso; **it's bad t. to ask personal questions** es de mal gusto hacer preguntas personales; **in bad** *or* **poor t.** de mal gusto; **everything was in the best possible t.** todo era de un gusto exquisito

2 *vt* **(a)** *(detect flavour of)* notar (un sabor a); **I've never tasted oysters before** nunca he comido ostras; **can you t. the thyme?** ¿notas el (sabor a) tomillo?; **I can't t. my food because of my cold** con este *Esp, CAm, Carib, Méx* resfriado *or Andes, RP* resfrío la comida no me sabe a nada

(b) *(sample)* probar; *(of expert taster)* degustar; *(wine)* catar

(c) *(experience)* **to t. success/despair** probar el éxito/la desesperación; **to t. freedom** disfrutar de la libertad

3 *vi* saber, tener sabor (**of** *or* **like** a); **to t. good/bad** tener buen/mal sabor; **it tastes delicious** sabe delicioso; **it tastes fine to me** a mí me sabe bien; **it doesn't t. of anything** no sabe a nada, es insípido

tasteful ['teɪstfʊl] *adj* de buen gusto

tastefully ['teɪstfəlɪ] *adv* con buen gusto

tastefulness ['teɪstfʊlnɪs] *n* buen gusto *m*

tasteless ['teɪstlɪs] *adj* **(a)** *(food)* insípido(a) **(b)** *(remark)* de mal gusto **(c)** *(clothes, decor)* con poco gusto

tastelessly ['teɪstlɪslɪ] *adv (decorated)* con poco gusto

tastelessness ['teɪstlɪsnɪs] *n* **(a)** *(of food)* falta *f* de sabor, insipidez *f* **(b)** *(of remark)* mal gusto *m*; *(of clothes, decor)* falta *f* de gusto

taster ['teɪstə(r)] *n* **(a)** *(person)* catador(ora) *m,f* **(b)** *(sample)* **would you like a t.?** ¿te gustaría probarlo? **(c)** *(foretaste)* muestra *f*, anticipo *m*

tastiness ['teɪstɪnɪs] *n (of food)* **he complimented her on the t. of the meal** la felicitó por lo rica *or* buena que estaba la comida

tasting ['teɪstɪŋ] *n* degustación *f*; **wine t.** cata de vinos

tasty ['teɪstɪ] *adj* **(a)** *(delicious)* sabroso(a), rico(a); **these pies are really t.** estos pasteles están muy sabrosos *or* ricos **(b)** *(gossip)* jugoso(a) **(c)** *Fam (good-looking)* **she's really t.** está muy buena, está como un tren

tat [tæt] *n Fam* porquerías *fpl*, *Esp* chorradas *fpl*

ta-ta [tə'tɑː] *exclam Br Fam* ¡chao!, *Am* ¡chau!

Tatar = **Tartar**

tater ['teɪtə(r)] *n Fam Esp* patata *f*, *esp Am* papa *f*

tattered ['tætəd] *adj (person, clothes)* andrajoso(a); *(page)* hecho(a) pedazos; *(reputation)* arruinado(a)

tatters ['tætəz] *npl (rags)* harapos *mpl*; **to be in t.** *(clothes)* estar hecho(a) jirones; *(reputation, plan)* haber quedado arruinado(a); *(defence)* haber quedado desmembrado(a)

tattie ['tætɪ] *n esp Scot Fam (potato) Esp* patata *f*, *esp Am* papa *f*

tatting ['tætɪŋ] *n* encaje *m*

tattle ['tætəl] **1** *n (gossip)* habladurías *fpl*, chismes *mpl*

2 *vi* **(a)** *(gossip)* chismorrear, *Am* chismear, *Col, Méx* chismosear **(b)** *(tell tales)* **now don't t. to my parents** no le vayas con el cuento a mis padres **(c)** *(chat)* charlar

tattler ['tætlə(r)] *n (gossip)* chismoso(a) *m,f*

tattoo¹ [tə'tuː] *(pl* **tattoos***) n* **(a)** *(on drum)* retreta *f* **(b)** *(military show)* = espectáculo con bandas militares

tattoo[2] 1 *n* (*pl* **tattoos**) *(design)* tatuaje *m*; **to get a t.** hacerse un tatuaje
2 *vt* tatuar

tattooist [tə'tu:ɪst] *n* tatuador(ora) *m,f*

tatty ['tætɪ] *adj Fam (furniture, clothes)* gastado(a); *(book)* manoseado(a)

taught [tɔ:t] 1 *adj (course)* con profesor
2 *pt & pp of* **teach**

taunt [tɔ:nt] 1 *n (words)* pulla *f*
2 *vt* mofarse de, hacer mofa de; **they taunted him with his speech defect** se mofaban *or* burlaban de él porque tenía un defecto al hablar

taunting ['tɔ:ntɪŋ] 1 *n* pullas *fpl*
2 *adj* hiriente, burlón(ona)

tauntingly ['tɔ:ntɪŋlɪ] *adv* en tono de mofa *or* burla

taupe [təʊp] 1 *n* taupe *m*
2 *adj* taupe

Taurean [tɔ:'rɪən] *Astrol* 1 *n* **to be a T.** ser Tauro
2 *adj* Tauro

Taurus ['tɔ:rəs] *n* **(a)** *(sign of zodiac)* Tauro *m*; **to be (a) T.** ser Tauro **(b)** *(constellation)* Tauro *m*

taut [tɔ:t] *adj* **(a)** *(rope, muscles, string)* tenso(a), tirante; *(skin)* tirante **(b)** *(nervous) (situation, person, face)* tenso(a) **(c)** *(firm) (legs, thighs)* firme **(d)** *(style, writing)* conciso(a)

tauten ['tɔ:tən] 1 *vt* tensar
2 *vi* **(a)** *(rope, muscles)* tensarse, ponerse tirante; *(skin)* ponerse tirante **(b)** *(nerves)* ponerse tenso(a)

tautness ['tɔ:tnɪs] *n* **(a)** *(of rope, muscles, string)* tensión *f*, tirantez *f*; *(of skin)* tirantez *f* **(b)** *(nervousness) (of situation, person, face)* tensión *f* **(c)** *(firmness) (of legs, thighs)* firmeza *f* **(d)** *(of style, writing)* concisión *f*

tautological [tɔ:tə'lɒdʒɪkəl], **tautologous** [tɔ:'tɒləgəs] *adj* tautológico(a)

tautology [tɔ:'tɒlədʒɪ] *n* tautología *f*

tavern ['tævən] *n Literary* taberna *f*

tawdriness ['tɔ:drɪnɪs] *n* **(a)** *(of decor)* chabacanería *f*; *(of jewellery)* carácter *m* oropelesco **(b)** *(of conduct, motive)* sordidez *f*

tawdry ['tɔ:drɪ] *adj* **(a)** *(decor)* chabacano(a); *(jewellery)* de oropel, oropelesco(a) **(b)** *(conduct, motive)* sórdido(a)

tawny ['tɔ:nɪ] *adj* leonado(a) ►► ***t. owl*** cárabo *m*; ***t. pipit*** bisbita *m* campestre; ***t. port*** oporto *m* tawny

tax [tæks] 1 *n* **(a)** *(levy)* impuesto *m*, tributo *m*; *(taxation)* impuestos *mpl*; **to levy** *or* **to put a 10 percent t. on sth** gravar algo con un 10 por ciento de impuestos; **baby food is free of t.** los alimentos para recién nacidos están libres de impuestos; **I have to keep receipts for t. purposes** tengo que guardar los recibos para la declaración de la renta; **to pay t.** ser un/una contribuyente, pagar impuestos; **I don't pay much t.** no pago muchos impuestos; **I paid over $5,000 in t.** he pagado más de 5.000 dólares de impuestos; **before/after t.** antes/después de impuestos ►► *Br* ***t. allowance*** exención *f* tributaria *or* fiscal; ***t. avoidance*** elusión *f* fiscal; ***t. base*** *(people)* contribuyentes *mpl*; *(money)* recaudación *f* tributaria; ***t. benefit*** ventaja *f* fiscal; ***t. bill*** cotización *f* a Hacienda; ***t. bracket*** banda *f* impositiva, tramo *m* impositivo; ***t. break*** ventaja *f* fiscal; ***t. burden*** presión *f* fiscal; ***t. ceiling*** máxima cantidad *f* a abonar en impuestos; ***t. code*** código *m* impositivo; ***t. collection*** recaudación *f* de impuestos; ***t. collector*** recaudador(ora) *m,f* de impuestos; ***t. consultant*** asesor(ora) *m,f* fiscal; ***t. cut*** reducción *f* fiscal; *Br* ***t. disc*** *(on vehicle)* pegatina *f* del impuesto de circulación; *Fam* ***t. dodge*** trampa *f* para engañar a Hacienda; *Fam* ***a t. dodger*** un defraudador fiscal; ***t. evasion*** fraude *m or* evasión *f* fiscal; ***t. exemption*** exención *f* fiscal; ***t. exile*** *(person)* exiliado(a) *m,f* fiscal; ***t. form*** declaración *f* de la renta; ***t. haven*** paraíso *m* fiscal; ***t. holiday*** periodo *m* de exención fiscal, vacaciones *fpl* fiscales; ***t. incentive*** incentivo *m* fiscal; *Br* ***t. inspector*** inspector(ora) *m,f* de Hacienda; ***t. law*** derecho *m* fiscal; ***t. liability*** *(of person)* deuda *f* fiscal, impuesto *m* a pagar; *US* ***t. lien*** embargo *m* fiscal; ***t. loophole*** laguna *f* fiscal; ***t. offence*** delito *m* fiscal; ***t. office*** oficina *f* de Hacienda; ***t. rate*** tipo *m* impositivo; ***t. rebate*** devolución *f* fiscal; ***t. refund*** devolución *f* fiscal; ***t. relief*** desgravación *f* fiscal; **to claim t. relief on sth** desgravar algo; ***t. return*** declaración *f* de la renta; ***t. revenue*** cantidad *f* recaudada por Hacienda; ***t. shelter*** refugio *m or* amparo *m* fiscal; ***t. system*** régimen *m* fiscal; ***t. year*** año *m* fiscal
(b) *(strain) (on strength, resources)* pesada carga *f* (**on** para); **it was a t. on even her patience** puso a prueba incluso su paciencia
2 *vt* **(a)** *Fin (goods, income)* gravar; *(people)* cobrar impuestos a; *(company)* imponer una carga fiscal a; **the rich should be more heavily taxed** los que más tienen deberían pagar más impuestos; **luxury goods are taxed at 28 percent** los artículos de lujo tienen una carga fiscal del 28 por ciento; **our wages are taxed at source** nos descuentan los impuestos de la nómina; **companies are being taxed out of business** los elevados impuestos están haciendo que cierren algunas empresas
(b) *BrAut* **to t. one's car** pagar el impuesto de circulación
(c) *(resources, patience, knowledge, strength)* poner a prueba
(d) *Formal (accuse)* **he was taxed with having lied** se le imputó haber mentido

taxable ['tæksəbəl] *adj* gravable, imponible ►► ***t. income*** ingresos *mpl* sujetos a gravamen, ≃ base *f* imponible

taxation [tæk'seɪʃən] *n* **(a)** *(system)* fiscalidad *f*, sistema *m* fiscal *or* tributario **(b)** *(taxes)* **an increase in t.** un aumento de los impuestos

tax-deductible ['tæksdɪ'dʌktɪbəl] *adj* desgravable

taxeme ['tæksi:m] *n Ling* taxema *f*

tax-exempt [tæksɪg'zempt] *adj (goods, income, savings)* exento(a) de impuestos

tax-free ['tæks'fri:] 1 *adj* libre de impuestos ►► ***t. shop*** tienda *f* exenta de impuestos
2 *adv* sin pagar impuestos

taxi ['tæksɪ] 1 *n* taxi *m* ►► ***t. driver*** taxista *mf*; *Br* ***t. rank*** parada *f* de taxis; *US* ***t. stand*** parada *f* de taxis
2 *vi (aircraft)* rodar

taxicab ['tæksɪkæb] *n* taxi *m*

taxidermist ['tæksɪdɜ:mɪst] *n* taxidermista *mf*

taxidermy ['tæksɪdɜ:mɪ] *n* taxidermia *f*

taximeter ['tæksɪmi:tə(r)] *n* taxímetro *m*

taxing ['tæksɪŋ] *adj* difícil, arduo(a); **a physically/mentally t. task** una tarea que conlleva un importante esfuerzo físico/mental

taxiway ['tæksɪweɪ] *n Av* pista *f* de rodaje

taxman ['tæksmæn] *n* **the t.** *(tax authority)* el fisco, Hacienda

taxonomic [tæksə'nɒmɪk] *adj* taxonómico(a)

taxonomist [tæk'sɒnəmɪst] *n* taxonomista *mf*

taxonomy [tæk'sɒnəmɪ] *n* taxonomía *f*

taxpayer ['tækspeɪə(r)] *n* contribuyente *mf*

TB [ti:'bi:] *n (tuberculosis)* tuberculosis *f inv* ►► *Fam* ***TB jab*** vacuna *f* de la tuberculosis

TBA (*abbr* **to be announced**) se comunicará próximamente

T-bar (lift) ['ti:bɑ:(r)(lɪft)] *n (for skiers)* telesquí *m*, telearrastre *m*

T-bone (steak) ['ti:bəʊn('steɪk)] *n* chuleta *f (con hueso en forma de T)*, *RP* costilla *f*

tbs, tbsp (*abbr* **tablespoon** *or* **tablespoonful**) cucharada *f* (grande)

T-cell ['ti:sel] *n Med* linfocito *m or* célula *f* T

TCP® [ti:si:'pi:] *n* (*abbr* **trichlorophenylmethyliodosalicyl**) = compuesto antiséptico y desinfectante, utilizado para pequeñas heridas, limpieza de la boca, etc.

TCP/IP *n Comptr* (*abbr* **transmission control protocol/Internet protocol**) TCP/IP *m*

TD [ti:'di:] *n* (*abbr* **touchdown**) ensayo *m*

te [ti:] *n Mus* si *m*

tea [ti:] *n* **(a)** *(plant, drink)* té *m*; **I prefer t. to coffee** prefiero el té al café; IDIOM **not for all the t. in China** ni por todo el oro del mundo; IDIOM **t. and sympathy** una taza de té y un poco de comprensión ►► ***t. bag*** bolsita *f* de té; *Br* ***t. break*** descanso *m* para el té; ***t. caddy*** lata *f* de té; *US* ***t. cart*** carrito *m*, *Esp* camarera *f*; ***t. chest*** caja *f* para embalaje; *Br* ***t. cloth*** trapo *m or* paño *m* de cocina, *RP* repasador *m*; *Br* ***t. cosy*** cubretetera *m*; *US* ***t. cozy*** cubretetera *m*; ***t. dance*** = baile con merienda a media tarde; *Br* ***t. lady*** = señora encargada de preparar y servir el té; *Br Fam* ***t. leaf*** *(thief)* ladrón(ona) *m,f*, *Esp* chorizo(a) *m,f*; ***t. leaves*** *(dry)* hojas *fpl* de té; *(in bottom of cup)* posos *mpl* de té; ***a t. party*** una reunión para tomar el té; ***t. plantation*** plantación *f or* campo *m* de té; ***t. rose*** rosa *f* de té; ***t. service*** servicio *m* de té; ***t. set*** servicio *m* de té; ***t. strainer*** colador *m (pequeño)*; *Br* ***t. towel*** trapo *m or* paño *m* de cocina, *RP* repasador *m*; ***t. tray*** bandeja *f* para el té; *Br* ***t. trolley*** carrito *m*, *Esp* camarera *f*; ***t. urn*** tetera *f* enorme (de uso industrial); *US* ***t. wagon*** carrito *m*, *Esp* camarera *f*
(b) *(cup of tea)* (taza *f* de) té *m*
(c) *(herbal infusion)* infusión *f*, té *m*; **camomile t.** manzanilla
(d) *Br (evening meal)* cena *f*; **to have (one's) t.** cenar, tomar la cena; **to ask sb to t.** invitar a alguien a cenar
(e) *(afternoon meal)* **(afternoon) t.** ≃ merienda *f*; **to have** *or Formal* **take t.** ≃ merendar

teacake ['ti:keɪk] *n Br* bollito *m* de pasas

teach [ti:tʃ] (*pt & pp* **taught** [tɔ:t]) **1** *vt* (**a**) *(in class)* enseñar; **to t. sb sth, to t. sth to sb** enseñar algo a alguien; **I t. Spanish** enseño español, doy clases de español; **he taught me Spanish at school** me daba clases de español en el colegio; **she teaches primary school children** es maestra de escuela (primaria); **this course is taught by an eminent professor** este curso lo imparte un ilustre catedrático; **she taught herself French/to play the piano** aprendió francés/a tocar el piano ella sola; *US* **to t. school** ser profesor(ora); *Fig* **to t. sb a lesson** darle una lección a alguien

(**b**) *(show by example)* enseñar; **to t. sb (how) to do sth** enseñarle a alguien a hacer algo; **didn't anyone ever t. you not to interrupt people?** ¿nadie te ha enseñado a no interrumpir a los demás cuando están hablando?; **I'll t. you to be rude to your elders!** *(as threat)* ¡yo te voy a enseñar a responder así a tus padres!; **that'll t. him!** ¡así aprenderá!; **that'll t. you to go around telling lies!** ¡eso te enseñará a ir por ahí contando mentiras!; **to t. sb a thing or two** *(advise)* enseñarle a alguien alguna que otra cosa; *(punish)* darle una buena lección a alguien; IDIOM **to t. one's grandmother to suck eggs** enseñar a orar a un monje, darle lecciones al que se las sabe todas

2 *vi (be a teacher, give classes)* dar clase(s); **what do you do? – I t.** ¿a qué te dedicas? – soy profesor *or* doy clases

teacher ['ti:tʃə(r)] *n* profesor(ora) *m,f*; *(at primary school)* maestro(a) *m,f*; **she's a good t.** sabe enseñar, es una buena profesora; **French t.** profesor(ora) de francés; **teachers are threatening to strike** los profesores amenazan con ir a la huelga; **t.-pupil ratio** proporción profesor-alumno ►► *US* ***t.'s college*** escuela *f* de magisterio; ***t.'s pet*** favorito(a) *m,f* del profesor; ***t. training*** formación *f* pedagógica *or* de profesorado; *Br* ***t. training college*** escuela *f* de magisterio

teach-in ['ti:tʃɪn] *n* seminario *m*

teaching ['ti:tʃɪŋ] *n* (**a**) *(profession)* enseñanza *f*, docencia *f*; **to go into t.** dedicarse a la enseñanza ►► ***the t. profession*** la enseñanza; ***t. staff*** profesorado *m*, personal *m* docente

(**b**) *(action)* enseñanza *f*; **the t. at that school is very poor** el nivel (de enseñanza) en este colegio es muy malo ►► ***t. aid*** ayuda *f* pedagógica, herramienta *f* pedagógica; ***t. hospital*** hospital *m* clínico *or* universitario; ***t. material*** material *m* pedagógico; ***t. practice*** prácticas *fpl* de enseñanza

(**c**) *(hours taught)* clase *f*; **she only does a few hours' t. a week** sólo da unas cuantas horas de clase a la semana

(**d**) *(doctrine)* enseñanza *f*; **the teachings of the Church on this matter** las enseñanzas *or* la doctrina de la Iglesia en esta materia

teach-yourself book ['ti:tʃjə'self'bʊk] *n* libro *m* de autoenseñanza

teacup ['ti:kʌp] *n* taza *f* de té

tea-drinker ['ti:drɪŋkə(r)] *n* bebedor(ora) *m,f* de té

teahouse ['ti:haʊs] *n* salón *m* de té

teak [ti:k] *n* teca *f*; **t. furniture** mobiliario de (madera de) teca

teal [ti:l] *n* (**a**) *(duck)* cerceta *f*; **blue-winged t.** cerceta aliazul (**b**) *(colour)* azul *m* ánade *(verdoso)*

team [ti:m] **1** *n* (**a**) *(of players, workers)* equipo *m*; **a t. effort** una labor de equipo; **we make a good t.** formamos un buen equipo ►► ***t. classification*** *(in cycling)* clasificación *f* por equipos; ***t. game*** juego *m* de equipo; ***t. member*** miembro *mf or* integrante *mf* de un equipo; ***t. player*** buen(a) trabajador(ora) *m,f* en equipo; ***t. pursuit*** *(in cycling)* persecución *f* por equipos; ***t. spirit*** espíritu *m* de equipo; *Sport* ***t. talk*** charla *f (con todo el equipo)*; ***t. time trial*** *(in cycling)* contrarreloj *f* por equipos

(**b**) *(of horses)* tiro *m*; *(of oxen)* yunta *f*

2 *vt (workers, players)* **to t. sb with sb** agrupar *or* poner a alguien con alguien

► **team up 1** *vt sep (workers, players)* poner (**with** con); **the manager has teamed Adams up with Campbell in central defence** el entrenador ha puesto a Adams con Campbell en el centro de la defensa

2 *vi* unirse (**with** a)

team-mate ['ti:mmeɪt] *n Sport* compañero(a) *m,f* de equipo

teamster ['ti:mstə(r)] *n US* camionero(a) *m,f*; **the Teamsters (Union)** = sindicato norteamericano de camioneros

teamwork ['ti:mwɜ:k] *n* trabajo *m* en *or* de equipo

teapot ['ti:pɒt] *n* tetera *f*

tear[1] [tɪə(r)] *n (when crying)* lágrima *f*; **to be in tears** estar llorando; **to burst into tears** echar(se) *or* romper a llorar; **she was crying tears of joy** lloraba de alegría; **he had tears** *or* **there were tears in his eyes** tenía lágrimas en los ojos; **it brought tears to his eyes** hizo que se le saltaran las lágrimas; **it will end in tears** acabará mal; **I was moved to tears by her performance** se me saltaron las lágrimas con su representación ►► *Anat* ***t. duct*** conducto *m* lacrimal; ***t. gas*** gas *m* lacrimógeno

tear[2] [teə(r)] **1** *n (in material)* desgarrón *m*; *(of muscle)* desgarro *m*; **this page has a t. in it** esta página está rota *or* rasgada

2 *vt* (*pt* **tore** [tɔ:(r)], *pp* **torn** [tɔ:n]) (**a**) *(rip)* rasgar; **to t. sth in two** *or* **in half** romper algo en dos; **I tore (a hole in) my jacket on a nail** me rasgué *or* rompí la chaqueta *or* me hice un roto en la chaqueta con un clavo; **he tore a hole in the paper** hizo un agujero en el papel; **to t. a muscle** tener un desgarro muscular; **the lion was tearing the meat from the zebra's carcass** el león arrancaba con sus garras la carne de la cebra; **I managed to t. myself from his grasp** conseguí librarme de sus garras; **she tore open the letter/wrapping** abrió la carta (rasgándola)/abrió el regalo (rasgando el envoltorio); *also Fig* **to t. sth to pieces** *or* **shreds** hacer trizas algo; **the fox was torn to pieces by the hounds** los perros de caza destrozaron al zorro; *Fig* **to t. sb to pieces** *or* **shreds** hacer trizas a alguien; IDIOM *Br Fam* **that's torn it!** ¡estamos *Esp* apañados *or Am* fritos!

(**b**) *(divide)* **the party was torn by infighting** el partido se hallaba dividido por las luchas internas; **a nation torn by civil war** una nación dividida por la guerra civil; **she was torn between going and staying** tenía unas dudas tremendas sobre si irse o quedarse; **he is torn between his job and his family** tiene que elegir entre su trabajo y su familia

(**c**) *(snatch)* arrancar; **she tore the bag out of his hands** le arrancó la bolsa de las manos; **the door had been torn from its hinges by the wind** el viento había arrancado la puerta de cuajo; *Fig* **sorry to t. you from your reading, but I need your help** perdona que te saque de tu lectura, pero necesito que me ayudes

3 *vi* (**a**) *(material)* rasgarse; *(muscle)* desgarrarse

(**b**) *(person)* **to t. at sth** desgarrar algo; **t. along the dotted line** *(on form)* rásguese *or* sepárese *or* recórtese por la línea de puntos; **I managed to t. free from his grasp** me las apañé para escapar de sus garras

(**c**) *(move quickly)* **to t. along/past/away** ir/pasar/alejarse muy deprisa; **the dog tore after the rabbit** el perro salió tras el conejo como una exhalación; **she came tearing into the garden** entró en el jardín como una exhalación

(**d**) *(hurry)* **he tore through the book/report** le dio una pasada rápida al libro/informe

► **tear apart** *vt sep* (**a**) *(rip to pieces) (of wild animal)* hacer pedazos, destrozar; *Fig* **the thieves tore the place apart looking for the diamond** los ladrones lo pusieron todo patas arriba *or* manga por hombro buscando el diamante (**b**) *(emotionally) (person)* partir el alma a (**c**) *(divide) (party, country)* desmembrar; *(two people)* dividir (**d**) *(criticize)* poner *or* tirar por los suelos

► **tear away** *vt sep* (**a**) *(remove by tearing)* arrancar (**b**) *(move away)* **to t. oneself away from sth** despegarse de algo; **I couldn't t. him away from the television** no lograba despegarlo del televisor

► **tear down** *vt sep* (**a**) *(building, statue)* derribar (**b**) *(poster)* arrancar

► **tear into** *vt insep* (**a**) *(attack)* **to t. into sb** *(physically)* arrojarse sobre alguien; *(verbally)* arremeter contra alguien; **the boxers tore into each other** los boxeadores la emprendieron a golpes (**b**) *(of teeth, saw)* clavarse en

► **tear off 1** *vt sep (detach by tearing)* arrancar; **he tore off his trousers and jumped into the water** se quitó los pantalones de un tirón y saltó al agua; **he had had one of his arms torn off by a machine** una máquina le había arrancado un brazo

2 *vi (run away)* salir pitando

► **tear out** *vt sep* arrancar; *Fig* **to t. one's hair out** tirarse de los pelos

► **tear up** *vt sep* (**a**) *(document, photo)* romper, rasgar; *Fig* **the two sides have torn up the peace agreement** las dos partes han roto *or* anulado el acuerdo de paz (**b**) *(plant, floorboards)* arrancar

tearaway ['teərəweɪ] *n Fam* alborotador(ora) *m,f*, *Esp* elemento(a) *m,f*

teardrop ['tɪədrɒp] *n* lágrima *f*

tearful ['tɪəfʊl] *adj* (**a**) *(expression, voice)* lloroso(a), sollozante; **I'm feeling a bit t.** se me saltan las lágrimas (**b**) *(goodbye, reunion)* lacrimoso(a)

tearfully ['tɪəfəlɪ] *adv* entre lágrimas, lacrimosamente

tearing ['teərɪŋ] *adj Fam* **to be in a t. hurry** tener muchísima prisa, *Am* tener muchísimo apuro

tearjerker ['tɪədʒɜ:kə(r)] *n Fam* **it's a real t.** *(movie, book)* es lacrimógeno *or Chile* cebollero a más no poder

tearjerking ['tɪədʒɜ:kɪŋ] *adj Fam* lacrimógeno(a), *Chile* cebollero(a)

tear-off ['teərɒf] *adj (reply slip, coupon)* recortable ►► ***t. calendar*** calendario *m* de taco; *Comptr* ***t. menu*** menú *m* flotante

tearoom ['ti:ru:m] *n* salón *m* de té

tearstained ['tɪəsteɪnd] *adj* **her face was t.** tenía un rastro de lágrimas en la cara

tease [ti:z] **1** *n* **(a)** *(person) (joking)* guasón(ona) *m,f*, bromista *mf*; *(sexually)* coqueto(a) *m,f* **(b)** *(behaviour)* **to do sth for a t.** hacer algo en broma

2 *vt* **(a)** *(person) (joking)* tomar el pelo a (**about** por); *(sexually)* coquetear con, provocar **(b)** *(animal)* provocar, hacer rabiar a **(c)** *(fabric, wool)* cardar **(d)** *(coax)* **he teased the wire through the hole** consiguió meter el alambre por el agujero **(e)** *US (hair)* cardar

3 *vi* bromear; **I was only teasing!** ¡sólo era una broma!

▸**tease out** *vt sep* **(a)** *(untangle) (hair, wool)* sacar con cuidado **(b)** *(information)* sonsacar, extraer

teasel ['ti:zəl] *n* **(a)** *Bot* cardencha *f* **(b)** *Tex* carda *f*

teaser ['ti:zə(r)] *n* **(a)** *Fam (problem)* rompecabezas *m inv* **(b)** *(person) (joking)* guasón(ona) *m,f*, bromista *mf*; *(sexually)* coqueto(a) *m,f* **(c)** *(advertisement)* enigma *m*

teashop ['ti:ʃɒp] *n* salón *m* de té, tetería *f*

teasing ['ti:zɪŋ] **1** *n* burlas *fpl*, pitorreo *m*

2 *adj* burlón(ona)

teasingly ['ti:zɪŋlɪ] *adv* de broma, en tono burlón

teaspoon ['ti:spu:n] *n* **(a)** *(utensil)* cucharilla *f* **(b)** *(measurement)* cucharadita *f (de las de café)*

teaspoonful ['ti:spu:nfʊl] *n* cucharadita *f* (de las de café)

teat [ti:t] *n* **(a)** *(of animal)* teta *f* **(b)** *(of feeding bottle, dummy)* tetina *f*

teatime ['ti:taɪm] *n esp Br (in afternoon)* hora *f* del té; *(in evening)* hora *f* de la cena *or* de cenar

TEC [tek] *n* (*abbr* **Training and Enterprise Council**) = organismo encargado de la formación y apoyo a la iniciativa empresarial de los jóvenes en Inglaterra y Gales

tech [tek] *n Fam* **(a)** *Br* (*abbr* **technical college**) centro *m* de formación profesional *(a partir de los 16 años)* **(b)** *US (technician)* técnico(a) *m,f*, chispas *mf inv*

techie ['tekɪ] *n Fam* **(a)** *Comptr (person)* experto(a) *m,f* en informática **(b)** *US (technician)* técnico(a) *m,f*, chispas *mf inv*

technical ['teknɪkəl] *adj* técnico(a); **I'll try not to get too t. in my explanation** intentaré no utilizar demasiados tecnicismos *or* detalles técnicos; **he was acquitted on a t. point** lo absolvieron por un defecto de forma; **it is not possible for t. reasons** no es posible por motivos técnicos ▸▸ *Br Educ* ***t. college*** centro *m* de formación profesional *(a partir de los 16 años)*; *Sch* ***t. drawing*** dibujo *m* técnico; ***t. foul*** *(in basketball)* (falta *f*) técnica *f*; ***t. hitch*** *Esp* fallo *m* técnico, *Am* falla *f* técnica; ***t. knockout*** *(in boxing)* K.O. *m* técnico; ***t. merit*** *(in ice skating)* mérito *m* técnico; *Comptr* ***t. support*** servicio *m* de asistencia técnica

technicality [teknɪ'kælɪtɪ] *n* **(a)** *(detail)* detalle *m* técnico; **he was acquitted on a t.** lo absolvieron por un defecto de forma **(b)** *(technical nature)* carácter *m* técnico

technically ['teknɪklɪ] *adv* **(a)** *(in technical terms)* técnicamente; **to be t. minded** ser bueno(a) para las cuestiones técnicas **(b)** *(in terms of technique)* técnicamente; **a t. superb player** un intérprete técnicamente genial *or* con un genial dominio de la técnica **(c)** *(in theory)* estrictamente hablando; **t., they are still married** estrictamente hablando, siguen casados

technician [tek'nɪʃən] *n* técnico(a) *m,f*

Technicolor® ['teknɪkʌlə(r)] *n* tecnicolor® *m*; **in T.** en tecnicolor®

technicolour yawn ['teknɪkʌlə'jɔ:n] *n Br Fam Hum* **to have a t.** echar la pota

technique [tek'ni:k] *n* técnica *f*

techno ['teknəʊ] *n (music)* tecno *m*

technobabble ['teknəʊbæbəl] *n Fam* jerga *f* tecnológica, *Esp* palabros *mpl* técnicos

technocracy [tek'nɒkrəsɪ] *n* tecnocracia *f*

technocrat ['teknəkræt] *n* tecnócrata *mf*

technocratic [teknə'krætɪk] *adj* tecnocrático(a)

technofreak ['teknəʊfri:k] *n Fam* obseso(a) *m,f* de las nuevas tecnologías

technological [teknə'lɒdʒɪkəl] *adj* tecnológico(a)

technologically [teknə'lɒdʒɪklɪ] *adv* tecnológicamente

technologist [tek'nɒlədʒɪst] *n* tecnólogo(a) *m,f*

technology [tek'nɒlədʒɪ] *n* tecnología *f* ▸▸ ***t. park*** parque *m* tecnológico; ***t. transfer*** transferencia *f* de tecnología

technophile ['teknəfaɪl] *n* partidario(a) *m,f* de las nuevas tecnologías

technophobe ['teknəfəʊb] *n* enemigo(a) *m,f* de las nuevas tecnologías

technophobia [teknə'fəʊbɪə] *n* rechazo *m* de las nuevas tecnologías

technothriller ['teknəʊθrɪlə(r)] *n* tecnothriller *m*, = thriller que utiliza elementos de alta tecnología y ciencia ficción

tectonic [tek'tɒnɪk] *adj Geol* tectónico(a) ▸▸ ***t. plates*** placas *fpl* tectónicas

tectonics [tek'tɒnɪks] *n Geol* tectónica *f*

ted [ted] *n Br Fam (teddy boy)* teddy-boy *m*, gamberro *m* agresivo

teddy ['tedɪ] *n* **(a)** *(toy)* **t. (bear)** osito *m* de peluche **(b)** *(underwear)* body *m* **(c)** *Br (person)* ***t. boy*** teddy-boy *m*

tedious ['ti:dɪəs] *adj (activity, speech, journey)* pesado(a), tedioso(a); *(person)* pesado(a)

tediously ['ti:dɪəslɪ] *adv* de forma pesada *or* tediosa; **the journey was t. long** el viaje fue largo y pesado

tediousness ['ti:dɪəsnɪs] *n (of activity, speech, journey)* pesadez *f*, tedio *m*

tedium ['ti:dɪəm] *n* tedio *m*

tee [ti:] *n* **(a)** *(peg)* tee *m* ▸▸ ***t. peg*** tee *m* **(b)** *(area)* salida *f* (del hoyo), tee *m*; **on the t.** en el tee ▸▸ ***t. shot*** golpe *m* de salida

▸**tee off 1** *vi* **(a)** *(in golf)* dar el primer golpe **(b)** *(begin)* tomar como punto de partida

2 *vt sep US Fam (annoy)* mosquear, poner negro(a); **to be teed off about sth** estar mosqueado(a) por algo

▸**tee up 1** *vt sep (in golf)* colocar en el tee; *(in soccer)* preparar, colocar

2 *vi* colocar la bola en el tee

tee-hee ['ti:'hi:] *exclam Fam* ¡ja, ja, ja!

teem [ti:m] *vi* **(a)** *(rain)* **it was teeming (down)** llovía a cántaros **(b)** **to t. with** *(insects, ideas)* rebosar de; **the streets were teeming (with people)** las calles estaban atestadas *or* repletas de gente

teeming ['ti:mɪŋ] *adj (streets)* atestado(a); *(crowds)* numeroso(a)

teen [ti:n] **1** *n* adolescente *mf*

2 *adj* (de) adolescente ▸▸ ***t. idol*** ídolo *m* juvenil

teenage ['ti:neɪdʒ] *adj (person)* adolescente; *(fashion, literature)* juvenil; **t. boys and girls** (chicos y chicas) adolescentes; **t. pregnancies** embarazos de adolescentes; **in my t. years** en (los años de) mi adolescencia

teenager ['ti:neɪdʒə(r)] *n* adolescente *mf*

teens [ti:nz] *npl* adolescencia *f*; **to be in one's t.** ser (un) adolescente; **she's in her early/late t.** está al principio/al final de la adolescencia

teen(s)y ['ti:n(z)ɪ] *adj Fam* chiquitín(ina), *Esp* pequeñín(ina); **a t. bit of...** un poquitín *or Am* un chiquitín de...

teen(s)y-ween(s)y ['ti:n(z)ɪ'wi:n(z)ɪ] *adj Fam* chiquitín(ina), *Esp* pequeñín(ina); **a t. bit of...** un poquitín *or Am* un chiquitín de...

teenybopper ['ti:nɪbɒpə(r)] *n Fam* = quinceañera seguidora de la música pop y sus modas

teepee = **tepee**

teeshirt ['ti:ʃɜ:t] *n* camiseta *f*, *Chile* polera *f*, *RP* remera *f*

teeter ['ti:tə(r)] *vi* tambalearse; *Fig* **to t. on the brink of war/a nervous breakdown** estar al borde de la guerra/una crisis nerviosa

teeter-totter ['ti:tətɒtər] *n US* balancín *m*, subibaja *m*

teeth *pl of* **tooth**

teethe [ti:ð] *vi* **to be teething** estar echando los dientes

teething ['ti:ðɪŋ] *n* dentición *f* ▸▸ ***t. ring*** mordedor *m*; ***t. troubles*** *(of project)* problemas *mpl* de partida

teetotal [ti:'təʊtəl] *adj (person)* abstemio(a); *(organization)* antialcohólico(a); *(party)* sin alcohol

teetotalism [ti:'təʊtəlɪzəm] *n* abstinencia *f*

teetotaller, *US* **teetotaler** [ti:'təʊtələ(r)] *n* abstemio(a) *m,f*

TEFL ['tefəl] *n* (*abbr* **Teaching English as a Foreign Language**) enseñanza *f* del inglés como lengua extranjera

Teflon® ['teflɒn] *n* teflón® *m*; *Fig Hum* **a T. politician** un(a) político(a) acorazado(a)

Tegucigalpa [təgu:sɪ'gælpə] *n* Tegucigalpa

Teh(e)ran [teə'rɑ:n] *n* Teherán

tel (*abbr* **telephone**) tel.

Tel Aviv ['telə'vi:v] *n* Tel Aviv

telebanking ['telɪbæŋkɪŋ] *n* banca *f* telefónica, telebanca *f*

telecast ['telɪkɑ:st] **1** *n* emisión *f* (televisiva)

2 *vt* televisar, emitir por televisión

telecom(s) ['telɪkɒm(z)] *n* (*abbr* **telecommunications**) telecomunicaciones *fpl*

telecommunications ['telɪkəmju:nɪ'keɪʃənz] *n* telecomunicaciones *fpl* ▸▸ ***the t. industry*** la industria *or* el sector de las telecomunicaciones; ***t. satellite*** satélite *m* de telecomunicaciones

telecommute ['telɪkəmju:t] *vi* teletrabajar

telecommuter ['telɪkəmju:tə(r)] *n* teletrabajador(ora) *m,f*

telecommuting ['telɪkə'mju:tɪŋ] *n* teletrabajo *m*

telecoms = **telecom**

teleconference ['telɪ'kɒnfərəns] *n* teleconferencia *f*

teleconferencing ['telɪ'kɒnfərənsɪŋ] *n* teleconferencias *fpl*

telecottage ['telɪkɒtɪdʒ] *n Br* = casa en el campo usada por teletrabajadores

telefax ['telɪfæks] *n* fax *m inv*, telefax *m inv*

telegenic [telɪ'dʒenɪk] *adj* telegénico(a)

telegram ['telɪgræm] *n* telegrama *m*

telegraph ['telɪgrɑ:f] **1** *n* **(a)** *(system)* telégrafo *m* ▸▸ ***t. pole*** poste *m* telegráfico; ***t. post*** poste *m* telegráfico; ***t. wire*** tendido *m* telegráfico **(b)** *(message)* telegrama *m*

2 *vt* **(a)** *(news)* telegrafiar; *(money)* girar; **she telegraphed us to say she couldn't come** nos telegrafió *or* mandó un telegrama para decir que no podía venir **(b)** *Sport* **he telegraphed his pass** fue un pase muy inocente

telegrapher [tə'legrəfə(r)] *n* telegrafista *mf*

telegraphese [telɪgrə'fi:z] *n* estilo *m* telegráfico

telegraphic [telɪ'græfɪk] *adj* **(a)** *Tel* telegráfico(a) **(b)** *(style, speech)* telegráfico(a)

telegraphist [tə'legrəfɪst] *n* telegrafista *mf*

telegraphy [tə'legrəfɪ] *n* telegrafía *f*

telekinesis ['telɪkɪ'ni:sɪs] *n* telequinesia *f*, telequinesis *f*

telemark ['telɪmɑ:k] *n* ***t. landing*** *(in ski jumping)* posición *f* de telemark; ***t. skiing*** telemark *m*; ***t. skis*** esquís *mpl* de telemark

telemarketing ['telɪmɑ:kɪtɪŋ] *n Com* telemarketing *m*, ventas *fpl* por teléfono

telematics [telɪ'mætɪks] *n* telemática *f*

Telemessage® ['telɪmesɪdʒ] *n Br* = teletipo enviado por télex o por teléfono

telemeter [tə'lemɪtə(r)] *n* telémetro *m*

telemetry [tɪ'lemɪtrɪ] *n* telemetría *f*

teleology [telɪ'ɒlədʒɪ] *n* teleología *f*

telepath ['telɪpæθ] *n* telépata *mf*

telepathic [telɪ'pæθɪk] *adj* telepático(a); **they have a t. understanding** tienen telepatía; **I must be t.!** ¡debo de tener telepatía!

telepathically [telɪ'pæθɪklɪ] *adv (to communicate)* por telepatía, telepáticamente

telepathy [tɪ'lepəθɪ] *n* telepatía *f*

telephone ['telɪfəʊn] **1** *n* teléfono *m*; **to be on the t.** *(talking)* estar al teléfono; *(have a telephone)* tener teléfono; **the boss is on the t. for you** tienes al jefe al teléfono, te llama el jefe; **to get sb on the t.** contactar con alguien por teléfono; **to get on the t. to sb** llamar a alguien por teléfono; **to discuss sth on** *or* **over the t.** discutir algo por teléfono; **you're wanted on the t.** te llaman por teléfono ▸▸ ***t. answering machine*** contestador *m* automático; *Com* ***t. banking*** telebanca *f*, banca *f* telefónica; ***t. bill*** factura *f* del teléfono; ***t. book*** guía *f* telefónica, listín *m* de teléfonos, *Am* directorio *m* de teléfonos; ***t. booking*** reserva *f* telefónica *or* por teléfono; ***t. booth*** cabina *f* telefónica; *Br* ***t. box*** cabina *f* telefónica; ***t. call*** llamada *f* telefónica, *Am* llamado *m* telefónico; ***t. conversation*** conversación *f* telefónica *or* por teléfono; ***t. directory*** guía *f* telefónica, listín *m* de teléfonos, *Am* directorio *m* de teléfonos; ***t. exchange*** central *f* telefónica; ***t. interview*** encuesta *f* telefónica; *Br* ***t. kiosk*** cabina *f* telefónica; ***t. line*** línea *f* de teléfono; ***t. manner*** trato *m* por teléfono; **a good t. manner is essential for somebody working in a call centre** para trabajar de teleoperador es imprescindible ser amable por teléfono; ***t. message*** mensaje *m* telefónico; ***t. number*** número *m* de teléfono; *Fig* **his salary is a t. number** tiene un sueldo astronómico; ***t. operator*** telefonista *mf*, operador(ora) *m,f*; ***t. order*** pedido *m* por teléfono; *US* ***t. pole*** poste *m* de telégrafos; ***t. receiver*** auricular *m*, *RP, Ven* tubo *m*; ***t. sales*** venta *f* telefónica, televenta *f*, telemarketing *m*; ***t. sex*** sexo *m* telefónico *or* por teléfono; ***t. sex line*** línea *f* erótica *o* caliente, teléfono *m* erótico; ***t. subscriber*** abonado(a) *m,f* al teléfono; ***t. tapping*** escuchas *fpl* telefónicas

2 *vt* **to t. sb** telefonear a alguien, llamar a alguien (por teléfono); **to t. the United States/home** telefonear a Estados Unidos/a casa, llamar (por teléfono) a Estados Unidos/a casa

3 *vi* telefonear, llamar (por teléfono); **shall I t. for a taxi?** ¿llamo a un taxi?

telephonic [telə'fɒnɪk] *adj* telefónico(a)

telephonist [tɪ'lefənɪst] *n Br* telefonista *mf*

telephony [tɪ'lefənɪ] *n* telefonía *f*

telephoto lens ['telɪfəʊtəʊ'lenz] *n* teleobjetivo *m*

teleplay ['telɪpleɪ] *n* guión *m* televisivo *or* de televisión

teleport ['telɪpɔ:t] *vt* teletransportar

teleprinter ['telɪprɪntə(r)] *n* teletipo *m*, teleimpresor *m*

teleprocessing [telɪ'prəʊsesɪŋ] *n Comptr* teleproceso *m*, tratamiento *m* de datos a distancia

Teleprompter® ['telɪprɒmptə(r)] *n US* teleapuntador *m*

telesales ['telɪseɪlz] *npl Com* televenta *f*, venta *f* telefónica, telemarketing *m*

telesalesperson [telɪ'seɪlzpɜ:sən] *n Com* televendedor(ora) *m,f*

telescope ['telɪskəʊp] **1** *n Astron* telescopio *m*; *Naut* catalejo *m*

2 *vt (condense) (description, report)* resumir, condensar (**into** en)

3 *vi* plegarse (como un telescopio)

telescopic [telɪ'skɒpɪk] *adj* **(a)** *(relating to vision)* telescópico(a) ▸▸ ***t. lens*** lente *f* telescópica; ***t. sight*** *(of rifle)* mira *f* telescópica **(b)** *(expanding) (ladder)* extensible; *(aerial)* telescópico(a); *(umbrella)* plegable

telescopy [tɪ'leskəpɪ] *n Astron* técnica *f* telescópica

teleshopping ['telɪʃɒpɪŋ] *n Com* telecompra *f*

teletext ['telɪtekst] *n TV* teletexto *m*

telethon ['telɪθɒn] *n* maratón *m* benéfico televisivo

Teletype® ['telɪtaɪp] *n* teletipo *m*

teletypewriter [telɪ'taɪpraɪtə(r)] *n US* teletipo *m*, teleimpresor *m*

televangelism [telɪ'vændʒəlɪzəm] *n* predicación *f* evangelista por televisión

televangelist [telɪ'vændʒəlɪst] *n* telepredicador(ora) *m,f* (evangelista)

televise ['telɪvaɪz] *vt* televisar; **we will be televising the game live** el partido será retransmitido *or* televisado en directo

television [telɪ'vɪʒən] *n* **(a)** *(system, broadcasts)* televisión *f*; **on (the) t.** en *or* por (la) televisión; **I was on (the) t. yesterday** salí en *or* por (la) televisión ayer; **to watch t.** ver la televisión; **it makes/doesn't make good t.** es muy/poco televisivo; **the t. industry** el sector de la televisión, la industria televisiva ▸▸ ***t. advertisement*** anuncio *m* de televisión, spot *m* (publicitario); ***t. advertising*** publicidad *f* televisiva; ***t. broadcast*** retransmisión *f* por televisión; ***t. broadcaster*** presentador(ora) *m,f* de televisión; ***t. camera*** cámara *f* de televisión; ***t. channel*** cadena *f* de televisión, canal *m* de televisión; ***t. commercial*** anuncio *m* de televisión, spot *m* (publicitario); ***t. drama*** programa *m* dramático; ***t. film*** telefilme *m*, telefilm *m*; ***t. guide*** guía *f* de la programación (de televisión); ***t. interview*** entrevista *f* por televisión; ***t. journalist*** periodista *mf* de televisión; *Br* ***t. licence*** = certificado de haber pagado el impuesto que autoriza a ver la televisión, con el que se financian las cadenas públicas; ***t. lounge*** sala *f* de televisión; ***t. movie*** telefilme *m*, telefilm *m*; ***t. network*** cadena *f* de televisión; ***t. news*** noticias *fpl* de la televisión; ***t. personality*** figura *f* de la televisión; ***t. programme*** programa *m* de televisión; ***t. rights*** derechos *mpl* de retransmisión (por televisión); ***t. room*** sala *f* de televisión; ***t. show*** programa *m* de televisión; ***t. studio*** estudio *m* de televisión; ***t. viewer*** telespectador(ora) *m,f*, televidente *mf*

(b) *(set)* televisor *m*, (aparato *m* de) televisión *f* ▸▸ ***t. screen*** pantalla *f* de televisión; ***t. set*** televisor *m*, (aparato *m* de) televisión *f*; ***t. tube*** tubo *m* de imagen

(c) *(industry)* televisión *f*; **I want a career in t.** quiero dedicarme a la televisión *or* a hacer televisión

televisual [telɪ'vɪʒʊəl] *adj* televisivo(a)

teleworker ['telɪwɜ:kə(r)] *n* teletrabajador(ora) *m,f*

teleworking ['telɪwɜ:kɪŋ] *n* teletrabajo *m*

telex ['teleks] **1** *n* télex *m inv*

2 *vt (message)* enviar por télex; **we telexed her as soon as we found out** le enviamos *or* pusimos un télex tan pronto como lo supimos

TELL [tel] (*pt & pp* **told** [təʊld]) **1** *vt* **(a)** *(say to, inform)* decir; **to t. sb sth, to t. sth to sb** contarle algo a alguien; **I told him the answer/what I thought** le dije la respuesta/lo que pensaba; **I told him what to do in case of an emergency** le expliqué lo que tenía que hacer en caso de emergencia; **I am delighted to be able to t. you that you have passed** tengo el placer de comunicarle que ha aprobado; **I told myself not to worry** me dije que no tenía que preocuparme; **to t. sb about sth** contar algo a alguien; *Formal* **to t. sb of sth** relatar algo a alguien; **to t. sb how to do sth** decir *or* explicar a alguien cómo hacer algo; **to t. sb (that)...** decir *or* contar a alguien que...; **can you t. me the way to the station?** ¿me puede decir cómo se va a la estación?; **a sign**

telling us where the exit is un cartel indicando dónde está la salida; **his expression told us the answer** la expresión de su cara nos reveló la respuesta; **what does this reaction t. us about her character?** ¿qué nos revela su reacción sobre su personalidad?; **to t. the time** *(clock)* indicar *or* dar la hora; **she hasn't learned to t. the time yet** todavía no ha aprendido a leer las horas; **they t. the time using sundials** utilizan relojes de sol para saber la hora; **to t. sb the time** *(person)* decir la hora a alguien; **we are told that...** se dice que...; **so I've been told** es lo que me han dicho; **t. me, do you come here often?** dime, ¿vienes mucho por aquí?; **are you telling me (that) you spent £50 on THAT?** ¿quieres decir que te has gastado 50 libras en eso?; **it's not so easy, let me t. you!** te aseguro que no es fácil; **didn't I t. you?, what did I t. you!** ¿qué te dije?; **I told you so!** ¡te lo dije!; **I can't t. you how grateful I am** no sabes lo agradecido que estoy; **don't t. me you've forgotten!** ¡no me digas que te has olvidado!; **don't t. me, she's late** no hace falta que me lo digas, no ha llegado todavía; **I'll t. you one thing** *or* **something...** te voy a decir una cosa...; **you're telling me!** ¡a mí me lo vas a contar!; **let me t. you, I was frightened!** te confieso que estaba asustado; *Fam Ironic* **t. me about it!** *(I know)* ¡dímelo a mí!; *Fam* **(I'll) t. you what, let's have a cup of tea** oye *or Méx* ándale *or RP* dale, vamos a tomarnos un té; *Fam* **t. you what** mira, verás; IDIOM **if I've told you once, I've told you a thousand times!** si no te lo he dicho mil veces, no te lo he dicho ninguna

(**b**) *(story, joke, secret)* contar; **to t. the truth/a lie** decir la verdad/una mentira; **to t. (you) the truth...** a decir verdad...; **she tells it like it is** dice las cosas claramente; **he had heard t. that...** había oído decir que...; *Fam Ironic* **t. me another!** ¡no me vengas con cuentos!, *Esp* ¡a otro perro con ese hueso!

(**c**) *(order)* **to t. sb to do sth** decir a alguien que haga algo; **do as you are told!** ¡haz lo que te dicen *or* mandan!; **you can't t. me what to do!** no tienes derecho a decirme qué tengo que hacer; **I told them not to interrupt** les pedí que no interrumpieran; **a sign telling us not to enter** un cartel prohibiéndonos la entrada; **I'm not asking you, I'm telling you!** no es una petición *or Am* pedido, ¡es una orden!; **she wouldn't be told** no hacía caso de lo que le decían

(**d**) *(discern) (attitude, mood)* ver, saber; **can you t. what this says?** ¿puedes leer lo que pone aquí?; **can you t. how long it will take?** ¿sabes cuánto te llevará?; **we couldn't t. if he was angry or not** no se sabía si estaba *esp Esp* enfadado *or esp Am* enojado o no; **I can t. it from the look in your eyes** se te ve en la mirada; **you can t. (that) she's lived abroad** se nota que ha vivido en el extranjero; **there's no telling what she'll do next** no hay manera de saber qué hará a continuación; **as** *or* **so far as I can t.** por lo que yo sé

(**e**) *(distinguish)* distinguir (**from** de); **to t. two people/things apart** distinguir entre dos personas/cosas; **to t. right from wrong** distinguir lo que está bien de lo que está mal; **I can't t. the difference** no veo la diferencia

(**f**) *Pol (count)* escrutar; *Fig* **all told** en total

2 *vi* (**a**) *(reveal secret)* **please don't t.!** ¡no te chives!; **I'm not telling!** ¡no te lo voy a contar!; **that would be telling!** ¡eso sería contar demasiado!; **more than words can t.** más de lo que se puede expresar con palabras

(**b**) *(discern)* **how can you t.?** ¿cómo lo sabes?; **it's difficult** *or* **hard to t.** es difícil de saber; **it's too early to t.** es demasiado pronto para saberlo; **you could t. by** *or* **from her expression that she was annoyed** se veía que estaba *esp Esp* enfadada *or esp Am* enojada por su cara; **you never can t.** nunca se sabe

(**c**) *(have effect)* hacerse notar; **his inexperience told against him** su inexperiencia le perjudicó; **the hard work was starting to t. on her** el intenso trabajo comenzaba a afectarla

(**d**) *Literary (speak)* **he told of distant lands** nos habló de tierras distantes; **I've heard t. of phantom ships** he oído hablar de barcos fantasmas

(**e**) *Literary (bear witness)* **his face told of a hard life** su rostro era el testimonio de una vida dura

► **tell off** *vt sep Fam (scold)* **to t. sb off (about/for)** echar una reprimenda *or Esp* bronca a alguien (por), dar *Méx* una jalada *or RP* un rezongo a alguien (por)

► **tell on** *vt insep Fam (inform on) Esp* chivarse de, *Méx* soplar a, *RP* botonear a

---

teller ['telə(r)] *n* (**a**) *(in bank)* cajero(a) *m,f* (**b**) *(of votes)* escrutador (ora) *m,f* (**c**) *(of story)* narrador(ora) *m,f*

telling ['telɪŋ] **1** *n (of story)* narración *f*, relato *m*; **it loses nothing in the t.** no pierde nada al contarlo

2 *adj* (**a**) *(blow, contribution)* decisivo(a); *(argument)* contundente (**b**) *(revealing)* revelador(ora)

tellingly ['telɪŋlɪ] *adv* (**a**) *(decisively)* de forma decisiva (**b**) *(revealingly)* de forma reveladora

telling-off ['telɪŋ'ɒf] *n Fam* reprimenda *f*, *Esp* bronca *f*, *Méx* jalada *f*, *RP* rezongo *m*; **to give sb a t.** echar una reprimenda *or Esp* bronca a alguien, dar *Méx* una jalada *or RP* un rezongo a alguien

telltale ['telteɪl] **1** *n (person)* acusica *mf*, *Esp* chivato(a) *m,f*

2 *adj (sign, odour)* revelador(ora)

tellurium [te'ljʊərɪəm] *n Chem* telurio *m*, teluro *m*

telly ['telɪ] *n Br Fam* tele *f*; **on (the) t.** en *or* por la tele ►► ***t. addict*** teleadicto(a) *m,f*

telnet ['telnet] *n Comptr* telnet *m*

temazepam® [tə'mæzəpæm] *n* temazepán *m*

temblor ['temblɔː(r)] *n* terremoto *m*, temblor *m* de tierra

temerity [tɪ'merɪtɪ] *n* osadía *f*, atrevimiento *m*; **to have the t. to do sth** tener la osadía de hacer algo

temp[1] [temp] *Fam* **1** *n* trabajador(ora) *m,f* temporal (administrativo(a)); **to be a t.** hacer trabajo temporal de administrativo(a)

2 *vi* hacer trabajo temporal de administrativo(a)

temp[2] (*abbr* **temperature**) temp.

temper ['tempə(r)] **1** *n* (**a**) *(character)* carácter *m*; **to have an even t.** ser pacífico(a) *or* tranquilo(a), tener un carácter pacífico *or* tranquilo; **to have a quick** *or* **hot t.** tener mal genio

(**b**) *(mood)* humor *m*; **to be in a good/bad t.** estar de buen/mal humor

(**c**) *(bad mood)* mal humor; **to be in a t.** estar de mal humor; **to fly into a t.** ponerse hecho(a) una furia; **tempers were rising** los ánimos se estaban caldeando ►► ***t. tantrum*** rabieta *f*

(**d**) *(calm, patience)* **to keep one's t.** mantener la calma; **to lose one's t.** perder los estribos; **I finally lost my t. with him** al final me hizo perder los estribos; **to have a short t.** tener mal genio; *Fam* **t., t.!** ¡calma, calma!

(**e**) *(of metal)* temple *m*

2 *vt* (**a**) *(steel)* templar (**b**) *(action)* moderar; *(passions, enthusiasm)* atemperar; *(suffering)* mitigar

tempera ['tempərə] *n* témpera *f*

temperament ['temprəmənt] *n* (**a**) *(character)* temperamento *m* (**b**) *(moodiness)* mal genio *m*, temperamento *m* difícil

temperamental [temprə'mentəl] *adj* (**a**) *(person)* temperamental (**b**) *(machine)* **this TV is a bit t.** este televisor funciona cuando quiere; **his knee has been a bit t. since his accident** desde el accidente, la rodilla le ha seguido molestando a ratos (**c**) *(relating to one's character)* natural, innato(a)

temperamentally [temprə'mentəlɪ] *adv* (**a**) *(to behave)* caprichosamente; **the TV has been behaving rather t. recently** últimamente la televisión funciona cuando quiere

(**b**) *(in terms of character)* temperamentalmente, por temperamento; **to be t. unsuited to sth** no tener el temperamento adecuado para algo; **they were t. unsuited** *(couple)* por su carácter no congeniaban

temperance ['tempərəns] *n* (**a**) *(moderation)* moderación *f*, sobriedad *f* (**b**) *(abstinence from alcohol)* abstinencia *f* (del alcohol) ►► *Hist* ***t. movement*** liga *f* antialcohólica

temperate ['tempərət] *adj* (**a**) *(climate, zone)* templado(a) ►► ***t. zones*** zonas *fpl* templadas (**b**) *(language, criticism, person)* moderado(a), mesurado(a)

temperately ['tempərətlɪ] *adv* con moderación, moderadamente

temperature ['temprətʃə(r)] *n* (**a**) *(heat, cold)* temperatura *f*; **what t. is the swimming pool?** ¿a qué temperatura está la piscina?, ¿qué temperatura hay en la piscina?; **temperatures will be in the low twenties** las temperaturas se mantendrán ligeramente por encima de los veinte grados; *Fig* **her contribution certainly raised the t. of the debate** su intervención caldeó bastante el debate ►► ***t. gauge*** indicador *m* de temperatura

(**b**) *(of body)* temperatura *f*; **to take sb's t.** tomar la temperatura a alguien; **to have** *or* **to run a t.** tener fiebre; **to have a t. of 100** tener casi 38 de fiebre ►► ***t. chart*** gráfica *f* de temperaturas

tempered ['tempəd] *adj* (**a**) *(steel)* templado(a) (**b**) *Mus (scale)* temperado(a)

tempest ['tempɪst] *n Literary* tempestad *f*; *US* **it was a t. in a teapot** fue una tormenta en un vaso de agua

tempestuous [tem'pestjʊəs] *adj* (**a**) *(relationship, meeting)* tempestuoso(a), tormentoso(a) (**b**) *Literary (weather, night)* tempestuoso(a); *(seas)* proceloso(a), tempestuoso(a)

temping ['tempɪŋ] *n* trabajo *m* temporal (administrativo) ►► ***t. agency*** empresa *f* de trabajo temporal, ETT *f*

template ['templeɪt] *n* (**a**) *(pattern)* plantilla *f* (**b**) *Comptr* plantilla *f*

temple[1] ['tempəl] *n (place of worship)* templo *m*

temple[2] *n (side of head)* sien *f*

templet ['templɪt] *n* plantilla *f*

tempo ['tempəʊ] (*pl* **tempos** *or* **tempi** ['tempi:]) *n* (**a**) *Mus* tempo *m* (**b**) *(speed)* ritmo *m*; **to up the t.** incrementar el ritmo

temporal ['tempərəl] *adj* (**a**) *(power)* temporal, terrenal (**b**) *Gram* temporal (**c**) *(relating to time)* temporal (**d**) *Anat* ***t. lobe*** lóbulo *m* temporal

temporarily [tempə'rerılı] *adv* temporalmente, *Am* temporariamente

temporary ['tempərərı] *adj (employment)* temporal, *Am* temporario(a); *(office, arrangement, repairs)* provisional, *Am* temporario(a); **to employ sb on a t. basis** hacer un contrato temporal *or* contratar temporalmente a alguien; **he suffered t. hearing loss** sufrió una pérdida de audición transitoria *or* temporal ►► ***t. contract*** contrato *m* temporal; ***t. file*** archivo *m* temporal; ***t. job*** trabajo *m* temporal; *Comptr* ***t. storage*** almacenamiento *m* temporal; ***t. surface*** *(of road)* firme *m* provisional; ***t. work*** trabajo *m* temporal *or* eventual; ***t. worker*** trabajador(ora) *m,f* temporal

temporize ['tempəraız] *vi Formal* procurar ganar tiempo

tempt [tem(p)t] *vt* tentar; **to t. sb to do sth** *or* **into doing sth** tentar a alguien a hacer algo; **I'm tempted to accept** me siento tentado de aceptar; **did you hit him? – no, but I was sorely tempted** ¿le pegaste? – no, pero ganas me dieron *or* no me faltaron; **can I t. you to** *or* **with a piece of cake?** ¿te apetece un trozo de tarta?; *Hum* **you should tell him what you think of him – don't t. me!** deberías decirle lo que opinas de él – ¡no me tientes!; **a rival company tried to t. him away** una empresa rival le hizo proposiciones para que se fuera con ellos; **to t. fate** *or* **providence** tentar (a) la suerte

temptation [tem(p)'teıʃən] *n* tentación *f*; **to give in to t.** caer en la tentación; **she couldn't resist the t. to make a nasty remark** no pudo resistir la tentación de soltar una pulla; **lead us not into t.** *(in the Lord's Prayer)* no nos dejes caer en la tentación

tempter ['temptə(r)] *n (person)* seductor *m*; *Fam (thing)* tentación *f*; **the offer was a real t.** la oferta era verdaderamente tentadora; **the T.** *(Satan)* el Tentador, el diablo

tempting ['tem(p)tıŋ] *adj* tentador(ora); **it's t. to suggest that he had it coming** uno se siente tentado de decir que se lo andaba buscando

temptingly ['tem(p)tıŋlı] *adv* de un modo tentador; **it looks t. easy** parece tan fácil que dan ganas de probar

temptress ['tem(p)trıs] *n Literary* seductora *f*, mujer *f* fatal

tempura ['tempərə] *n Culin* tempura *m or f*, témpura *m or f*, = plato japonés de marisco o verdura rebozados y fritos

ten [ten] **1** *n* (**a**) *(number)* diez *m*; **tens of thousands of refugees** decenas de miles de refugiados (**b**) IDIOMS **they're t. a penny** los hay a patadas; **t. to one he'll find out** me apuesto el cuello a que lo descubrirá

2 *adj* diez; **the T. Commandments** los Diez Mandamientos; *see also* **eight**

tenable ['tenəbəl] *adj* (**a**) *(argument, position)* defendible, sostenible (**b**) *(post)* ostentable; **the appointment is t. for a five-year period** la duración del cargo será de cinco años

tenacious [tə'neıʃəs] *adj* tenaz

tenaciously [tə'neıʃəslı] *adv* tenazmente, con tenacidad

tenacity [tə'næsıtı] *n* tenacidad *f*

tenancy ['tenənsı] *n Law* (**a**) *(right)* arrendamiento *m*, alquiler *m* ►► ***t. agreement*** contrato *m* de alquiler *or* arrendamiento (**b**) *(period)* periodo *m* de alquiler; **during my t. of the house** mientras estuve de alquiler *or* de inquilino en la casa (**c**) *(property)* **a council t.** una vivienda municipal de alquiler

tenant ['tenənt] *n (of house)* inquilino(a) *m,f*; *(of land)* arrendatario(a) *m,f* ►► ***t. farmer*** agricultor(ora) *m,f* arrendatario(a), ≃ aparcero(a) *m,f*; ***t. farming*** arrendamiento *m* agrícola, ≃ aparcería *f*

tench [tentʃ] *n* tenca *f*

tend[1] [tend] *vt (look after) (person, sheep)* cuidar (de), atender; *(garden)* ocuparse de, atender; **to t. sb's wounds** curar las heridas a alguien; *US* **to t. bar** atender en el bar

► **tend to** *vt insep (look after) (wounds)* curar; *(business, guests)* atender; **she tended to his every wish** sus palabras eran órdenes para ella

tend[2] *vi* (**a**) *(be inclined)* tender (**towards** a *or* hacia); **his writings t. towards exoticism** sus escritos tienden *or* tienen tendencia al exotismo; **to t. to do sth** soler hacer algo, tender a hacer algo; **the number of road accidents tends to increase in summer** el número de accidentes de tráfico tiende a *or* suele incrementarse en verano; **some people like that kind of movie, but I t. not to** hay gente a la que le gusta esa clase de cine, pero en general no es mi caso; **that does t. to be the case** efectivamente, eso suele ocurrir; **I t. to agree (with you)** yo me inclino a pensar lo mismo (que usted); **I t. to think (that)...** me inclino a pensar (que)...

(**b**) *(colour)* **red tending to orange** rojo tirando a naranja

tendency ['tendənsı] *n* (**a**) *(inclination)* tendencia *f*, inclinación *f*; **to have a t. to (do) sth** tener tendencia a (hacer) algo; **he has suicidal/criminal tendencies** tiene inclinaciones suicidas/delictivas, tiene propensión al suicidio/delito (**b**) *(trend)* tendencia *f*; **an upward t. in prices** una tendencia alcista de los precios (**c**) *Pol* tendencia *f*, corriente *f*

tendentious [ten'denʃəs] *adj Formal* tendencioso(a)

tendentiously [ten'denʃəslı] *adv Formal* de manera tendenciosa, tendenciosamente

tendentiousness [ten'denʃəsnıs] *n Formal* tendenciosidad *f*

tender[1] ['tendə(r)] *n* (**a**) *Naut* barcaza *f* (**b**) *Rail* ténder *m*

tender[2] *adj* (**a**) *(gentle, affectionate) (person, smile, look)* cariñoso(a), tierno(a); **I need a bit of t. loving care** me hace falta un poquito de mimo *or* cariño; IDIOM *Ironic* **I left him to the t. mercies of the schoolmaster** lo dejé a merced del profesor

(**b**) *(sensitive) (part of body)* dolorido(a); *(subject)* delicado(a); **is it t. when I touch you here?** ¿si te toco aquí te duele?

(**c**) *(meat, vegetables)* tierno(a), blando(a)

(**d**) *(young)* **a boy of his t. years** un niño de tan corta edad; **at the t. age of...** a la tierna edad de...

tender[3] **1** *n Com (bid)* oferta *f*, licitación *f*; **to make** *or* **put in a t. (for sth)** presentarse a concurso con una oferta (para algo), licitar (por algo); **to put sth out to t., to invite tenders for sth** sacar a concurso algo

2 *vt Formal (offer) (one's services, apologies)* ofrecer; **to t. one's thanks** dar las gracias; **to t. one's resignation** presentar la dimisión; **please t. the exact fare** *(sign)* se ruega abonar el importe exacto

3 *vi Com* **to t. for a contract** presentarse a una licitación de contrata

tenderfoot ['tendəfʊt] *n US (novice)* novato(a) *m,f*, principiante *mf*

tenderhearted [tendə'hɑ:tıd] *adj* bondadoso(a)

tenderheartedness [tendə'hɑ:tıdnıs] *n* bondad *f*, buen corazón *m*

tenderize ['tendəraız] *vt (meat)* ablandar

tenderizer ['tendəraızə(r)] *n* (**a**) *(instrument)* maja *f*, maza *f (para ablandar la carne)* (**b**) *(substance)* ablandador *m*

tenderloin ['tendəlɔın] *n (of beef, pork)* solomillo *m*

tenderly ['tendəlı] *adv (affectionately)* con ternura, cariñosamente

tenderness ['tendənıs] *n* (**a**) *(affection) (of person, smile, look)* ternura *f*, cariño *m* (**b**) *(soreness)* **there's still some t.** todavía duele un poco (**c**) *(of vegetables)* blandura *f*; **he complimented me on the t. of the meat** me felicitó por lo tierna que estaba la carne

tendinitis, tendonitis [tendə'naıtıs] *n Med* tendinitis *f inv*

tendon ['tendən] *n Anat* tendón *m*

tendonitis = **tendinitis**

tendril ['tendrıl] *n Bot* zarcillo *m*

tenebrism ['tenəbrızəm] *n Art* tenebrismo *m*

tenebrous ['tenıbrəs] *adj Literary* tenebroso(a)

tenement ['tenımənt] *n* **t. (building)** bloque *m* de apartamentos *or Esp* pisos *or Arg* departamentos ►► ***t. flat*** apartamento *m*, *Esp* piso *m*, *Arg* departamento *m*

Tenerife [tenə'ri:f] *n* Tenerife

tenet ['tenıt] *n* principio *m*, postulado *m*

tenfold ['tenfəʊld] **1** *adj* **there has been a t. increase in applications** se ha multiplicado por diez el número de solicitudes

2 *adv* por diez, diez veces; **to increase t.** multiplicarse por diez

ten-gallon hat ['tengælən'hæt] *n* sombrero *m* de vaquero (de copa alta)

Tenn. (*abbr* **Tennessee**) Tennessee

tenner ['tenə(r)] *n Fam* (**a**) *Br (ten-pound note)* billete *m* de diez libras; **it cost me a t.** me costó diez libras (**b**) *US (ten-dollar note)* billete *m* de diez dólares

Tennessee [tenı'si:] *n* Tennessee

tennis ['tenıs] *n* tenis *m*; **to play t.** jugar al tenis ►► ***t. ball*** pelota *f* de tenis; ***t. club*** club *m* de tenis; ***t. court*** pista *f or* cancha *f* de tenis; *Med* ***t. elbow*** codo *m* de tenista; ***t. player*** tenista *mf*; ***t. racket*** raqueta *f* de tenis; ***t. racquet*** raqueta *f* de tenis; ***t. shoe*** zapatilla *f* de tenis; ***t. whites*** ropa *f* blanca *or* uniforme *m* blanco de tenis

tenon ['tenən] *n* espiga *f* ►► ***t. saw*** serrucho *m* (de costilla)

tenor ['tenə(r)] **1** *n* (**a**) *Mus* tenor *m*; **I sing t. in the choir** canto de tenor en el coro (**b**) *(content, sense)* tenor *m*

2 *adj Mus (part, voice)* de tenor; *(aria)* para tenor ►► ***t. clef*** clave *f* de do en cuarta; ***t. sax(ophone)*** saxo *m* tenor

tenosynovitis ['tenəʊsaɪnə'vaɪtɪs] *n Med* tenosinovitis *f inv*

tenpence ['tenpəns] *n Br Old-fashioned* diez peniques *mpl*

tenpin bowling ['tenpɪn'bəʊlɪŋ] *n Br* bolos *mpl*; **to go t.** ir a jugar a los bolos

tenpins ['tenpɪnz] *n US* bolos *mpl*

tense[1] [tens] *n Gram* tiempo *m*; **in the present/future t.** en (tiempo) presente/futuro

tense[2] **1** *adj* **(a)** *(nervous) (person, atmosphere, situation)* tenso(a); *(smile)* nervioso(a), tenso(a); **the audience was t. with excitement** entre el público había una tensa emoción; **her voice was t. with emotion** tenía la voz agarrotada por la emoción; **things were getting t. at the meeting** la cosa se puso tensa en la reunión

(b) *(taut) (person, muscles)* tenso(a); *(wire, rope)* tenso(a), tirante; **my neck was very t.** tenía el cuello muy tenso; **his muscles became t.** se le tensaron *or* se le pusieron tensos los músculos

2 *vt* tensar; **to t. oneself** ponerse tenso(a)

3 *vi* tensarse, ponerse tenso(a)

► **tense up** *vi* ponerse tenso(a)

tensely ['tenslɪ] *adv (nervously)* tensamente

tenseness ['tensnɪs] *n (of person, atmosphere, situation, smile)* tensión *f*

tensile strength ['tensaɪl'streŋθ] *n Phys* resistencia *f* a la tracción, resistencia *f* última

tension ['tenʃən] *n* **(a)** *(of person, atmosphere, situation, smile)* tensión *f* ►► ***t. headache*** dolor *m* de cabeza (de carácter) nervioso, jaqueca *f* nerviosa **(b)** *(of muscles)* tensión *f*; *(of wire, rope)* tensión *f*, tirantez *f* **(c)** *Elec* tensión *f* **(d)** *(in knitting)* tensión *f*

tensor ['tensə(r)] *n* **(a)** *Anat* (músculo *m*) tensor *m* **(b)** *Math* tensor *m*

ten-spot ['tenspɒt] *n US Fam* billete *m* de diez dólares

tent [tent] *n* tienda *f* de campaña, *Am* carpa *f* ►► ***t. peg*** piqueta *f*, clavija *f*; ***t. pole*** mástil *m* (de tienda *or Am* carpa)

tentacle ['tentəkəl] *n* tentáculo *m*

tentative ['tentətɪv] *adj* **(a)** *(uncertain) (person)* vacilante, titubeante; *(steps)* inseguro(a), vacilante; *(smile)* tímido(a); **could I make a t. suggestion?** ¿me permites (hacerte) una pequeña sugerencia? **(b)** *(provisional) (arrangement, conclusions, offer)* provisional

tentatively ['tentətɪvlɪ] *adv* **(a)** *(hesitantly) (to behave, say)* con vacilación, con titubeo; *(to smile)* tímidamente; *(to walk)* de modo inseguro, con paso vacilante; **he t. stuck his head above the parapet** con precaución *or* cuidado asomó la cabeza por encima del parapeto; **could I t. suggest a different approach?** ¿puedo sugerir, si se me permite, un enfoque distinto?

(b) *(provisionally)* provisionalmente

tenterhooks ['tentəhʊks] *npl* **to be on t.** estar sobre ascuas; **to keep sb on t.** tener a alguien sobre ascuas

tenth [tenθ] **1** *n* **(a)** *(fraction)* décimo *m*, décima parte *f* **(b)** *(in series)* décimo(a) *m,f* **(c)** *(of month)* diez *m* **(d)** *Mus* (intervalo *m* de) décima *f*

2 *adj* décimo(a); *see also* **eighth**

tenth-rate ['tenθ'reɪt] *adj Fam* de tres al cuarto, de poca monta

tenuous ['tenjʊəs] *adj* **(a)** *(connection, link)* vago(a), tenue; *(argument)* flojo(a), débil; *(evidence)* poco concluyente, endeble; *(comparison)* traído(a) por los pelos; **I have only a t. grasp of the subject** tengo un conocimiento bastante somero del tema **(b)** *(thread)* tenue; *(voice)* tenue

tenuously ['tenjʊəslɪ] *adv (connected, linked)* vagamente, tenuemente; **her remarks were only t. connected with the discussion** sus comentarios sólo tenían una vaga relación con lo que se discutía

tenuousness ['tenjʊəsnɪs] *n* **(a)** *(of connection, link)* vaguedad *f*; *(of argument, evidence)* falta *f* de solidez; *(of comparison)* falta *f* de conexión **(b)** *(of thread)* finura *f*, consistencia *f* tenue; *(of voice)* debilidad *f*, tenuidad *f*

tenure ['tenjə(r)] *n* **(a)** *(of land)* arriendo *m* **(b)** *(of office)* ocupación *f*; **during his t. as chairman** durante su mandato como presidente **(c)** *Univ* titularidad *f*; **to have t.** ser profesor(ora) numerario(a) *or* titular

tenured ['tenjəd] *adj Univ (post)* permanente, de (profesor) titular

tepee, teepee ['ti:pi:] *n* tipi *m*

tepid ['tepɪd] *adj* **(a)** *(of water)* tibio(a), templado(a); **to be t.** estar tibio(a) *or* templado(a) **(b)** *(welcome, thanks, reaction)* tibio(a), poco caluroso(a)

tepidity [te'pɪdɪtɪ], **tepidness** ['tepɪdnɪs] *n* **(a)** *(of water)* tibieza *f* **(b)** *(of welcome, thanks, reaction)* tibieza *f*, falta *f* de entusiasmo

tepidly ['tepɪdlɪ] *adv (to welcome, thank, react)* tibiamente, sin demasiado entusiasmo

tepidness = **tepidity**

tequila [tə'ki:lə] *n* tequila *m or f* ►► ***t. slammer*** coscorrón *m* de tequila, *Méx* muppet *m*; ***t. sunrise*** tequila sunrise *m*

Ter (*abbr* **terrace**) = abreviatura escrita en las direcciones de una calle compuesta por una hilera de casas adosadas

terabyte ['terəbaɪt] *n Comptr* terabyte *m*

terbium ['tɜ:bɪəm] *n Chem* terbio *m*

tercentenary [tɜ:sen'ti:nərɪ] *n* tricentenario *m*

tercet ['tɜ:sɪt] *n* terceto m

teriyaki [terɪ'jækɪ] *n Culin* teriyaki *m*, = plato japonés de pescado o carne en adobo y a la plancha

---

TERM [tɜ:m] **1** *n* **(a)** *(word, expression)* término *m*; **a medical/legal t.** un término médico/legal; **she spoke of you in very flattering terms** se refirió a ti de forma halagadora; **a t. of abuse** un insulto; **a t. of endearment** un apelativo cariñoso; **I must object in the strongest terms** quiero hacer constar mi más enérgica protesta; **I told her in no uncertain terms** se lo dije en términos muy claros

(b) *(perspective)* **in economic/real terms** en términos económicos/reales; **in personal terms, it was a disaster** desde el punto de vista personal fue desastroso; **in terms of salary/pollution** en cuanto a salario/contaminación; **consider it in terms of the environmental damage it will cause** considera el daño medioambiental que causará; **I was thinking in terms of around £30,000** estaba pensando en algo en la región de las 30.000 libras; **in his terms, this is unacceptable** según su manera de ver las cosas, esto es inaceptable

(c) *(relations)* **I'm on good/bad terms with her** me llevo bien/mal con ella; **we're on good/bad terms** nos llevamos bien/mal; **to be on friendly terms with sb** llevarse bien con alguien, estar en buenos términos con alguien; **they aren't on speaking terms** no se hablan

(d) *(conditions)* **terms** *(of contract)* términos *mpl*, condiciones *fpl*; **he offered me favourable terms** me ofreció unas condiciones favorables; **terms of employment** condiciones de contrato; **terms of payment** condiciones de pago; **terms of reference** *(of commission)* competencias; *(of report)* ámbito; **I'll do it, but on my (own) terms** lo haré, pero yo fijaré las condiciones; **to compete on equal** *or* **the same terms** competir en condiciones de igualdad; **to come to** *or* **make terms with sb** llegar a un acuerdo con alguien; **to come to terms with sth** llegar a aceptar algo; **to dictate terms to sb** imponer condiciones a alguien; **on easy terms** *(loan, hire-purchase)* con facilidades de pago; **weekly terms** *(in hotel)* tarifas *fpl* semanales ►► *Econ* ***terms of trade*** balanza *f* comercial

(e) *(period)* **a t. of imprisonment, a prison t.** un periodo de reclusión; **he was given a five-year prison t.** fue condenado a cinco años de reclusión; **t. (of office)** *(of politician)* mandato *m*; **the president is elected for a four-year t.** el presidente es elegido por un periodo de cuatro años; **her pregnancy has reached (full) t.** ha salido de cuentas, *RP* está con un embarazo a término; **in the long/short/medium t.** a largo/corto/medio plazo ►► *Fin* ***t. insurance*** seguro *m* de vida limitado al plazo contratado

(f) *Sch & Univ (of three months)* trimestre *m*; *(of four months)* cuatrimestre *m*; **in** *or* **during t. (time)** durante el curso; **spring/winter t.** el trimestre de primavera/de invierno ►► *US Univ* ***t. paper*** trabajo *m* trimestral

(g) *Math* término *m*

(h) *Law (duration of contract)* vigencia *f*

2 *vt* denominar, llamar; **I would t. their remarks irrelevant** yo calificaría sus comentarios de irrelevantes

---

terminal ['tɜ:mɪnəl] **1** *n* **(a)** *Elec (of battery)* polo *m* **(b)** *(for train, bus, at airport)* terminal *f*; **smoking is not permitted inside the t. building** está prohibido fumar dentro (del edificio) de la terminal **(c)** *Comptr* terminal *m* ►► ***t. emulation*** emulación *f* de terminal; ***t. server*** servidor *m* de terminales

2 *adj* **(a)** *Med (phase)* terminal; *(illness, patient)* (en fase) terminal; *Fig* **an industry in t. decline** una industria en vías de desaparecer *or* en fase de desaparición; *Fam Hum* **I think I'm suffering from t. boredom** creo que lo que pasa es que me aburro como una ostra **(b)** *(final)* **t. station** fin de trayecto, final de línea, estación terminal **(c)** *Phys* ***t. velocity*** velocidad *f* terminal *or* límite **(d)** *Fin* ***t. bonus*** bonificación *f* a vencimiento de póliza

terminally ['tɜ:mɪnəlɪ] *adv* **he is t. ill** está en fase terminal, es un enfermo terminal; **she's t. ill with cancer** tiene cáncer en fase terminal; **t. ill patient** enfermo(a) terminal

terminate ['tɜ:mɪneɪt] **1** *vt* **(a)** *(contract)* rescindir; *(project)* suspender; *(relationship, conversation, meeting)* poner fin a; **his employment with the company has been terminated as of today** con fecha de hoy causa baja como empleado de la empresa **(b)** *(pregnancy)* interrumpir **(c)** *(make redundant) (employee)* prescindir de los servicios de (**d**) *Fam (kill)* eliminar, liquidar

2 *vi* (**a**) *(contract)* finalizar, cumplir; *(relationship, conversation, meeting, project)* terminar, concluir; **his employment with us terminated last year** causó baja en nuestra empresa el año pasado (**b**) *(bus, train)* **the train terminates here/at Glasgow** ésta/Glasgow es la última parada del tren

termination [tɜːmɪˈneɪʃən] *n* (**a**) *(of contract)* rescisión *f*; *(of project)* suspensión *f* ►► ***t. of employment*** despido *m* (**b**) *Med* **t. (of pregnancy)** interrupción *f* (voluntaria) del embarazo; **to have a t.** abortar

terminator [ˈtɜːmɪneɪtə(r)] *n Comptr* terminador *m*

terminological [tɜːmɪnəˈlɒdʒɪkəl] *adj* terminológico(a)

terminologist [tɜːmɪˈnɒlədʒɪst] *n* terminólogo(a) *m,f*

terminology [tɜːmɪˈnɒlədʒɪ] *n* terminología *f*

terminus [ˈtɜːmɪnəs] *n* (**a**) *(final stop) (of bus)* última parada *f*, final *m* de trayecto; *(of train)* estación *f* terminal (**b**) *(building) (of bus, train)* (estación *f*) terminal *f*

termite [ˈtɜːmaɪt] *n* termes *m inv*, termita *f*

termtime [ˈtɜːmtaɪm] *n* periodo *m* lectivo; **her t. address** su dirección durante el curso

tern [tɜːn] *n* charrán *m* (común)

ternary [ˈtɜːnərɪ] *adj Math* ternario(a)

Terr (*abbr* **terrace**) = abreviatura escrita en las direcciones de una calle compuesta por una hilera de casas adosadas

terrace [ˈterɪs] **1** *n* (**a**) *(outside cafe, hotel)* terraza *f* (**b**) *(on hillside)* terraza *f* (**c**) *Br* **the terraces** *(in sports ground)* las gradas (**d**) *Br (of houses)* hilera *f* de casas adosadas ►► ***t. house*** casa *f* adosada

2 *vt (hillside)* hacer terrazas en

terraced [ˈterɪst] *adj* (**a**) *(hillside)* en terrazas (**b**) *Br (house, row)* adosado(a)

terracotta [ˈterəˈkɒtə] **1** *n* (**a**) *(earthenware)* terracota *f*, barro *m* cocido (**b**) *(colour)* color *m* terracota, rojo *m* arcilloso

2 *adj* (**a**) *(pottery)* de terracota, de barro cocido (**b**) *(colour)* rojo(a) arcilloso(a)

terra firma [ˈterəˈfɪrmə] *n* tierra *f* firme

terrain [təˈreɪn] *n* terreno *m*

Terramycin® [terəˈmaɪsɪn] *n Pharm* terramicina *f*

terrapin [ˈterəpɪn] *n* galápago *m*, tortuga *f* acuática

terrarium [təˈreərɪəm] *n (for plants, reptiles)* terrario *m*

terrazzo [təˈrætsəʊ] *n* terrazo *m*

terrestrial [tɪˈrestrɪəl] *adj* terrestre ►► ***t. globe*** esfera *f* terrestre; ***t. television*** *or* ***TV*** televisión *f* (por vía) terrestre

terrible [ˈterɪbəl] *adj* (**a**) *(severe) (accident, storm, heat, pain)* terrible, tremendo(a); *(shock)* tremendo(a); **it caused t. damage** causó destrozos terribles *or* tremendos; **it was a t. blow** fue un golpe terrible *or* muy duro

(**b**) *(very bad) (meal, performance, smell, conditions)* horrible, espantoso(a); *(headache, cold)* terrible, espantoso(a); *(mistake)* terrible, tremendo(a); **she has a t. memory** tiene una memoria horrible, tiene muy mala memoria; **I'm t. at French, my French is t.** se me da muy mal *or Esp* fatal el francés; **what a t. thing to say/do!** ¡está muy feo decir/hacer eso!; **to feel t.** *(ill)* encontrarse muy mal *or Esp* fatal; **I feel t. about leaving them on their own** me sabe muy mal dejarlos solos, *Esp* me siento fatal dejándolos solos; **I've had a t. week at work** he tenido una semana horrible en el trabajo; **I had a t. time** lo pasé horrible *or Esp* fatal; **to look t.** *(ill, unhappy, unattractive)* tener muy mal aspecto; **to smell t.** oler horrible *or Esp* fatal; **we only get two weeks holiday – that's t.!** sólo nos dan dos semanas de vacaciones – ¡qué mal!; *Fam* **the t. twos** la edad crítica de los dos años

(**c**) *(shocking) (noise, sight)* tremendo(a), horrible

(**d**) *(for emphasis)* **it's a t. shame!** ¡es una verdadera *or* auténtica pena!; **he's a t. gossip** es tremendamente chismoso; **the food was a t. disappointment** la comida fue verdaderamente decepcionante; **he's had t. trouble with his washing machine** ha tenido muchísimos problemas con su lavadora

(**e**) *Literary (frightening) (person, gaze)* temible, amedrentador

terribly [ˈterɪblɪ] *adv* (**a**) *(badly) (to perform, play, behave)* tremendamente mal, *Esp* fatal

(**b**) *(very)* tremendamente; **I'm t. sorry** no sabes cuánto lo siento, lo siento en el alma; **I'm not t. interested** no es que me interese demasiado; **that's t. kind of you** es muy amable de *or* por tu parte; **the food here is t. good** aquí la comida es buenísima *or* extraordinaria; **I've been t. ill** he estado muy enfermo; **she did t. well in her exams** le salieron muy bien los exámenes; **our plan went t. wrong** el plan nos salió tremendamente mal *or Esp* fatal

(**c**) *(a lot)* **I'll miss you t.** te voy a echar muchísimo de menos; **his wound hurt t.** la herida le dolía muchísimo

terrier [ˈterɪə(r)] *n* (**a**) *(dog)* terrier *m* (**b**) *(persistent person)* batallador(ora) *m,f*

terrific [təˈrɪfɪk] *adj* (**a**) *Fam (very good) (food, book, weather, performance)* estupendo(a), genial, *Andes, CAm, Carib, Méx* chévere, *Méx* padre, *RP* bárbaro(a); **you look t. in that dress** estás fantástica con ese vestido; **we had a t. time** lo pasamos genial *or* estupendamente; **I've got tickets for the concert – (that's) t.!** tengo entradas para el concierto – ¡estupendo *or* genial!; *Ironic* **that's just t.!** ¡mira qué bien!, *Esp* ¡pues sí que estamos apañados!

(**b**) *(very great) (amount, size, speed, bang, shock)* tremendo(a); **it was a t. disappointment to lose in the semi-final** la decepción por perder en la semifinal fue tremenda *or* mayúscula

terrifically [təˈrɪfɪklɪ] *adv Fam* (**a**) *(very)* tremendamente; **t. exciting** superemocionante; **t. fast** superrápido(a); **it was t. hot** hacía un calor tremendo (**b**) *(very well) (to sing, act)* estupendamente, genial; **you did t. just to finish the race** que terminaras la carrera fue ya todo un logro; **they get along t. (well)** se llevan estupendamente *or* fantásticamente

terrified [ˈterɪfaɪd] *adj* aterrorizado(a), aterrado(a); **to be t. of sth/sb** tener terror a algo/alguien; **to be t. of doing sth** tener terror a hacer algo; **he was t. of offending his father** le daba terror el que pudiera ofender a su padre; **I was t. that he might never return** me aterraba la idea de que no regresara

terrify [ˈterɪfaɪ] *vt* aterrar, aterrorizar; **it terrifies me to think that it could have been me instead of him** me aterra pensar que yo podría haber estado en su lugar

terrifying [ˈterɪfaɪɪŋ] *adj* aterrador(ora); **what a t. thought!** ¡qué horrible!, ¡qué horror *or* espanto!

terrifyingly [ˈterɪfaɪɪŋlɪ] *adv* aterradoramente

terrine [təˈriːn] *n* terrina *f*, tarrina *f*

territorial [terɪˈtɔːrɪəl] **1** *n Br* **the Territorials** = cuerpo militar de reservistas voluntarios que reciben instrucción en su tiempo libre

2 *adj* (**a**) *Pol* territorial ►► *Sport* ***t. advantage*** superioridad *f* territorial; *Br* ***the T. Army*** = cuerpo militar de reservistas voluntarios que reciben instrucción en su tiempo libre; ***t. waters*** aguas *fpl* territoriales *or* jurisdiccionales (**b**) *(animal, person)* **it's very t.** tiene un gran sentido de la territorialidad; **he's very t.** no le gusta nada que invadan su terreno

territory [ˈterɪtərɪ] *n* (**a**) *(land)* territorio *m*

(**b**) *(dependency)* territorio *m*

(**c**) *(of animal)* territorio *m*; *(of salesperson)* zona *f*

(**d**) *Sport* **in terms of t., Wales had the advantage** Gales gozó de superioridad territorial

(**e**) *(area of activity)* ámbito *m*; **I'm afraid customer relations isn't really my t.** me temo que la atención al cliente cae fuera de mi responsabilidad; **the book covers what will be familiar t. for his regular readers** el libro se adentra en terreno ya conocido por sus lectores habituales; **late nights go with the t. in this job** en este trabajo ya se sabe que hay que trasnochar

terror [ˈterə(r)] *n* (**a**) *(fear)* terror *m*; **she cried out in t.** gritó aterrorizada; **the whole country was living in t.** el país entero vivía aterrorizado; **to live in t. of (doing) sth** tener terror a (hacer) algo, vivir aterrorizado(a) pensando en la posibilidad de (hacer) algo; **she was in t. of her life** temía por su propia vida; **I have a t. of flying** me da pánico volar; **a reign of t.** un imperio del terror ►► ***t. group*** grupo *m* terrorista

(**b**) *(frightening thing)* **the terrors of the night** los horrores de la noche; **to hold no terrors for sb** no inspirar ningún miedo a alguien

(**c**) *Fam (person)* **that child is a t.** ese niño es un demonio *or* diablo

terrorism [ˈterərɪzəm] *n* terrorismo *m*

terrorist [ˈterərɪst] **1** *n* terrorista *mf*

2 *adj* terrorista; **a t. attack/group** un atentado/grupo terrorista

terrorize [ˈterəraɪz] *vt* aterrorizar; **they terrorized the local people into leaving their homes** hicieron que los lugareños huyeran despavoridos de sus casas

terror-stricken [ˈterəstrɪkən], **terror-struck** [ˈterəstrʌk] *adj* aterrado(a); **to be t.** estar aterrado(a)

terry [ˈterɪ] *n* **t. (towelling** *or US* **cloth)** *(material)* toalla *f* de rizo ►► *Br* ***t. nappy*** pico *m*, pañal *m* lavable *(de toalla)*

terse [tɜːs] *adj* seco(a)

tersely [ˈtɜːslɪ] *adv* con sequedad; **a t. worded statement** unas declaraciones secas y escuetas

terseness [ˈtɜːsnɪs] *n* sequedad *f*

tertiary ['tɜːʃərɪ] **1** *n Geol* **the T.** el Terciario
2 *adj* **(a)** *Br Educ* superior ►► ***t. education*** enseñanza *f* superior **(b)** *Ind* terciario(a), de servicios **(c)** *Geol* **T.** terciario(a)

Terylene® ['terɪliːn] *n Br* fibra *f* Terilene; **a T. shirt** una camiseta de fibra Terilene

TESL ['tesəl] *n* (*abbr* **teaching English as a second language**) enseñanza *f* del inglés como segunda lengua

TESOL ['tiːsəl] *n* (*abbr* **Teaching English to Speakers of Other Languages**) enseñanza *f* del inglés a hablantes de otras lenguas

TESSA ['tesə] *n Br Fin* (*abbr* **tax-exempt special savings account**) = plan de ahorro que permite unos máximos anuales de inversión y de capitalización de intereses exentos de tributación fiscal

tessellated ['tesəleɪtɪd] *adj* teselado(a), de teselas

tessellation [tesɪ'leɪʃən] *n (mosaic)* (mosaico *m*) teselado *m*, mosaico *m* de teselas

test [test] **1** *n* **(a)** *Sch* examen *m*, control *m*; *(for job)* prueba *f*; **French t.** examen *or* control de francés; **all applicants have to complete a written t.** todos los solicitantes deberán realizar una prueba escrita; **there was a general knowledge t. in the paper** en el examen había un test de cultura general; **I had to do** *or* **sit** *or* **take a t. at the interview** tuve que hacer una prueba durante la entrevista ►► ***t. paper*** *(exam)* examen *m*
(b) *Aut* **(driving) t.** examen *m* de *Esp* conducir *or Am* manejar; **have you passed your t. yet?** ¿has aprobado ya el examen de *Esp* conducir *or Am* manejar?
(c) *Med* análisis *m inv*, prueba *f*; **blood t.** análisis de sangre; **eye t.** revisión de la vista; **he is still undergoing tests** aún le están haciendo pruebas ►► ***t. battery*** batería *f* de pruebas
(d) *(of equipment, product, quality)* prueba *f*; **to carry out tests on sth** realizar pruebas con algo ►► ***t. ban*** suspensión *f or* prohibición *f* de pruebas *or* ensayos nucleares; ***t. ban treaty*** tratado *m* de prohibición de pruebas *or* ensayos nucleares; *Br* ***t. card*** *(on television)* carta *f* de ajuste; *Law* ***t. case*** resolución *f or* precedente *m* judicial que sienta jurisprudencia; ***t. drive*** prueba *f* en carretera; **to go for a t. drive** hacer una prueba en carretera; ***t. flight*** vuelo *m* de prueba; *Chem* ***t. paper*** papel *m* indicador *or* reactivo; *US* ***t. pattern*** carta *f* de ajuste; ***t. pilot*** piloto *mf* de pruebas; ***t. run*** *(trial)* prueba *f*, ensayo *m*; ***t. tube*** tubo *m* de ensayo
(e) *(of character, endurance, resolve)* prueba *f*; **the strike will be a t. of union solidarity** la huelga pondrá a prueba la solidaridad sindical; **the game will be a good t. of how far the team has progressed** el partido servirá de piedra de toque para comprobar los progresos del equipo; **to pass the t.** superar la prueba; **to put sth/sb to the t.** poner algo/a alguien a prueba; **to stand the t. of time** resistir la prueba del tiempo
(f) *Sport* **t. (match)** *(in cricket)* encuentro *m* internacional de cinco días; *(in rugby)* encuentro *m or* partido *m* internacional ►► ***t. team*** equipo *m or* selección *f* nacional
2 *vt* **(a)** *(examine) (pupil)* examinar; *(job applicant)* hacer una prueba a; **to t. sb's knowledge/ability** poner a prueba los conocimientos/ la capacidad de alguien; **she was tested on her knowledge of plants** le hicieron una prueba de sus conocimientos sobre plantas; **would you t. me on my Latin verbs?** ¿me preguntas los verbos en latín?
(b) *Med (sight, hearing)* revisar; *(blood, urine)* analizar; *(reflexes)* probar, hacer una prueba de; **to have one's eyes tested** hacerse una revisión de la vista; *Fam Fig* **you need your eyes testing!** que Dios te conserve el oído, porque lo que es la vista...; **to t. sb for drugs/AIDS** hacer a alguien la prueba antidoping/del sida
(c) *(equipment, product, quality)* probar; *(pressure, suspension)* revisar, comprobar; *(weapon, drug)* probar, hacer pruebas con; *(soil, water)* analizar; **none of our products are tested on animals** ninguna prueba experimental de nuestros productos se realiza con animales; **the water was tested for phosphates** se analizó el agua en busca de fosfatos; IDIOM **to t. the water(s)** tantear el terreno
(d) *(character, endurance, patience, resolve)* poner a prueba; **it tested our friendship to the limit** aquello puso verdaderamente a prueba nuestra amistad
3 *vi* **(a)** *(make examination)* **to t. for Aids** hacerse la prueba del sida; **we are testing for phosphates in the water** estamos analizando el agua en busca de fosfatos; **we will be testing for an ability to work under pressure** se harán pruebas para comprobar la capacidad de trabajar sometido a presión; *Fam Hum* **just testing!** ¡sólo lo decía por si las moscas!
(b) *(show test result)* **to t. positive/negative (for drugs/AIDS)** dar positivo/negativo (en la prueba antidoping/del sida)
(c) *Rad & Tel* **testing, testing!** ¡probando, probando!

► **test out** *vt sep (idea, scheme)* poner a prueba

testament ['testəmənt] *n* **(a)** *Law (will)* testamento *m* **(b)** *(tribute)* testimonio *m*; **to be a t. to** dar testimonio de **(c)** *Rel* **the Old/New T.** el Antiguo/ Nuevo Testamento

testate ['testeɪt] *adj Law* testado(a); **to die t.** morir testado(a)

testator [te'steɪtə(r)] *n Law* testador(ora) *m,f*

testatrix [te'steɪtrɪks] *n Law* testadora *f*

test-bed ['testbed] *n* banco *m* de pruebas

test-drive ['testdraɪv] *vt Aut* probar en carretera

tester ['testə(r)] *n* **(a)** *(person)* verificador(ora) *m,f*, comprobador(ora) *m,f*; *(quality controller)* técnico(a) *m,f* de control de calidad; *(machine)* tester *m* **(b)** *(sample)* muestra *f* **(c)** *(difficult thing)* prueba *f* de fuego

testes *pl of* **testis**

test-fly ['testflaɪ] *vt (plane)* hacer un vuelo de prueba a

testicle ['testɪkəl] *n Anat* testículo *m*

testicular [tes'tɪkjʊlə(r)] *adj* testicular ►► ***t. cancer*** cáncer *m* de testículo(s) *or* testicular

testify ['testɪfaɪ] *Law* **1** *vt* **to t. that...** testificar *or* atestiguar que...
2 *vi* testificar, declarar (**for/against** a favor de/en contra de); *Fig* **to t. to sth** *(be proof of)* atestiguar algo

testily ['testɪlɪ] *adv* irritadamente, con irritación

testimonial [testɪ'məʊnɪəl] *n* **(a)** *(character reference)* referencias *fpl* **(b)** *Sport* **t. (match)** partido *m* de homenaje

testimony ['testɪmənɪ] *n* **(a)** *Law* testimonio *m* **(b)** *(proof)* testimonio *m* (**to** *or* **of** de); **to bear t. to sth** atestiguar algo

testiness ['testɪnɪs] *n (of person, mood, manner)* susceptibilidad *f*, irritabilidad *f*; *(of tone)* irritación *f*

testing ['testɪŋ] **1** *n (of machine, bridge)* prueba *f*; *(of weapons)* pruebas *fpl*, ensayos *mpl* ►► ***t. ground*** campo *m* de pruebas
2 *adj (problem)* difícil, arduo(a); **these have been t. times** han sido tiempos difíciles; **he had a t. time of it at full back** pasó muchos apuros en el lateral de la defensa

testis ['testɪs] (*pl* **testes** ['testiːz]) *n Anat* testículo *m*

test-market ['testmɑːkɪt] *vt* hacer pruebas de mercado a

testosterone [tes'tɒstərəʊn] *n Biol* testosterona *f*

test-tube baby ['tes'tjuːb'beɪbɪ] *n* niño(a) *m,f* probeta

testy ['testɪ] *adj (person, mood, manner)* susceptible, irritable; *(tone)* irritado(a); **to be t.** *(by nature)* ser susceptible *or* irritable; *(temporarily)* estar irritado(a) *or* irritable

tetanus ['tetənəs] *n Med* tétanos *m inv* ►► ***t. injection*** (vacuna *f*) antitetánica *f*

tetchily ['tetʃɪlɪ] *adv* irritadamente, con irritación

tetchiness ['tetʃɪnɪs] *n* susceptibilidad *f*, irritabilidad *f*

tetchy ['tetʃɪ] *adj* susceptible, irritable; **to be t.** estar susceptible *or* irritable

tête-à-tête ['tetə'tet] *n* conversación *f* a solas

tether ['teðə(r)] **1** *n (for tying animal)* correa *f*, atadura *f*
2 *vt (animal)* atar

tetra ['tetrə] *n* tetra *m (pez tropical de colores)*

tetrachloromethane [tetrəklɔːrəʊ'miːθeɪn] *n Chem* tetracloruro *m* de carbono, tetraclorometano *m*

tetracycline [tetrə'saɪkliːn] *n Pharm* tetraciclina *f*

tetrahedron [tetrə'hiːdrən] *n Geom* tetraedro *m*

tetralogy [te'trælədʒɪ] *n* tetralogía *f*

tetrameter [te'træmɪtə(r)] *n* tetrámetro *m*

tetraplegia [tetrə'pliːdʒɪə] *n* tetraplejía *f*, tetraplejia *f*

tetraplegic [tetrə'pliːdʒɪk] **1** *n* tetrapléjico(a) *m,f*
2 *adj* tetrapléjico(a)

Teutonic [tjuː'tɒnɪk] *adj* teutón(ona)

Tex (*abbr* **Texas**) Texas, Tejas

Texan ['teksən] **1** *n* tejano(a) *m,f*
2 *adj* tejano(a)

Texas ['teksəs] *n* Texas, Tejas

Tex-Mex ['teks'meks] **1** *n* **(a)** *(food)* comida *f* tex-mex **(b)** *(music)* (música *f*) tex-mex *m*
2 *adj* tex-mex, tejano-mejicano(a)

text [tekst] **1** *n* **(a)** *(writing, piece of writing, contents)* texto *m*; **the t. of his speech was published in the newspapers** el texto de su discurso fue publicado por la prensa ►► *Comptr* ***t. editing*** edición *f* de textos; *Comptr* ***t. editor*** editor *m* de textos; *Comptr* ***t. field*** campo *m* de texto; *Comptr* ***t. file*** archivo *m* de texto; ***t. message*** *(sent by mobile phone)* mensaje *m* de texto; ***t. messaging*** *(on mobile phones)* envío *m* de mensajes de texto; *Comptr* ***t. mode*** modo *m* (de) texto; *Comptr* ***t. processing*** procesado *m or* tratamiento *m* de textos; *Comptr* ***t. wrap*** contorneo *m* de texto

(**b**) *(textbook)* (libro *m* de) texto *m*

(**c**) *Rel (from Bible)* pasaje *m*

2 *vt (send text message to)* enviar un mensaje de texto a

3 *vi (send text messages)* enviar mensajes de texto

textbook ['tekstbʊk] *n* libro *m* de texto; *Fig* **a t. example** un ejemplo modélico *or* de libro; *Fig* **that was a t. backhand smash** ha sido un mate de revés como mandan los cánones *or* de libro

textile ['tekstaɪl] 1 *n* tejido *m*; **the t. industry** la industria textil

2 *adj* textil

texting ['tekstɪŋ] *n Fam (on mobile phones)* envío *m* de mensajes de texto

textual ['tekstjʊəl] *adj* textual ►► ***t. analysis*** comentario *m* de texto

texture ['tekstʃə(r)] *n* textura *f*

textured ['tekstʃəd] *adj* texturizado(a) ►► ***t. vegetable protein*** proteína *f* vegetal texturizada, = alimento proteínico a base de soja texturizada que se utiliza como sustituto de la carne

TFT [ti:ef'ti:] *n Comptr* (*abbr* **thin film transistor**) TFT *m* ►► ***T. display*** pantalla *f* TFT; ***T. screen*** pantalla *f* TFT

T&G ['ti:ən'dʒi:] *n* (*abbr* **Transport and General Workers' Union**) = sindicato británico compuesto por trabajadores de diversos sectores del transporte y la industria

TGIF [ti:dʒi:aɪ'ef] *n Fam Hum* (*abbr* **thank God it's Friday!**) ¡por fin es viernes!

Thai [taɪ] 1 *n* (**a**) *(person)* tailandés(esa) *m,f* (**b**) *(language)* tailandés *m*

2 *adj* tailandés(esa) ►► ***T. boxing*** boxeo *m* tailandés

Thailand ['taɪlænd] *n* Tailandia

thalamus ['θæləməs] *n Anat* tálamo *m*

thalassotherapy [θæləsəʊ'θerəpɪ] *n* talasoterapia *f*

thali ['tɑ:lɪ] *n Culin* = plato variado de comida india

thalidomide [θə'lɪdəmaɪd] *n Pharm* talidomida *f* ►► ***t. baby*** = bebé expuesto a la talidomida

thallium ['θælɪəm] *n Chem* talio *m*

Thames [temz] *n* **the (River) T.** el (río) Támesis

THAN [ðæn, *unstressed* ðən] 1 *conj (in general)* que; *(with numbers, amounts)* de; **he's taller t. me** es más alto que yo; **he was taller t. I had expected** era más alto de lo que me esperaba; **she stands a better chance of winning t. she did last year** tiene más posibilidades de ganar (de las) que (tuvo) el año pasado; **I'd rather** *or* **sooner die t. admit that** antes morirme que admitir eso; **no sooner had I arrived t. I realized she wasn't there** nada más llegar *or RP* en cuanto llegué me di cuenta de que no estaba allí; **he is more t. a friend** es más que un amigo; **more/less t. ten** más/menos de diez; **more t. once** más de una vez

2 *prep US* **different t.** diferente de

thank [θæŋk] *vt* dar las gracias a; **I thanked everybody** se lo agradecí a todo el mundo; **to t. sb for sth** agradecer algo a alguien, dar las gracias a alguien por algo; **to t. sb for doing sth** agradecer a alguien que haya hecho algo, dar gracias a alguien por haber hecho algo; **she thanked us for coming** nos dio las gracias por haber ido, nos agradeció que hubiéramos ido; **I can't t. you enough for what you've done** te estoy agradecidísimo por lo que has hecho, no sabes cuánto te agradezco lo que has hecho; **how can I ever t. you for your help?** ¿cómo podré agradecerte tu ayuda?; **t. God!** ¡gracias a Dios!; **t. God** *or* **goodness** *or* **heaven(s) they didn't see us!** ¡menos mal que no nos vieron!; **t. you** gracias; **t. you very much** muchas gracias; **no, t. you** no, gracias; **t. you for coming** gracias por venir; **t. you for all your help** gracias por tu ayuda; **to say t. you to sb** dar las gracias a alguien; *Ironic* **I'll t. you to mind your own business!** te agradecería que te ocuparas de tus asuntos; **we have Michael to t. for this** esto se lo tenemos que agradecer a Michael; *Ironic* esto ha sido cosa de Michael, la culpa de esto la tiene Michael; *Ironic* **you have only yourself to t. for that!** ¡tú te lo has buscado!, ¡la culpa no es más que tuya!; **he won't t. you for that** eso le va a sentar muy mal; **he won't t. you for disturbing him** le va a sentar muy mal que lo molestes, como lo molestes se va a acordar de ti

thankful ['θæŋkfʊl] *adj* agradecido(a); **to be t. to sb for sth** estar agradecido(a) a alguien por algo; **we are very t. to you for your help** te estamos muy agradecidos por tu ayuda; **to be t. that...** dar gracias de que...; **you should be t. for what you have got** deberías dar gracias por lo que tienes; **I'm t. not to have to go back** menos mal que no tengo que volver

thankfully ['θæŋkfəlɪ] *adv* (**a**) *(with gratitude)* agradecidamente (**b**) *(fortunately)* afortunadamente

thankfulness ['θæŋkfʊlnɪs] *n* agradecimiento *m*

thankless ['θæŋklɪs] *adj* ingrato(a)

thanks [θæŋks] 1 *npl* gracias *fpl*; **I'd like to express my t. to...** me gustaría expresar mi agradecimiento *or* gratitud a...; **words of t.** palabras de agradecimiento; **received with t.** *(on statement)* recibí; **to give t. to sb for sth** darle a alguien las gracias por algo; **give him my t.** dale las gracias de mi parte; **I save his life, and this is (all) the t. I get!** ¡le salvé la vida y mira cómo me lo agradece!; *Rel* **t. be to God** te alabamos, Señor; **t. to him/to his help** gracias a él/a su ayuda; **no t. to you/them!** a pesar de ti/ellos

2 *exclam* ¡gracias!; **t. very much** muchas gracias; **t. a million** muchísimas gracias, un millón de gracias; **many t.** muchas gracias; **t. for all your help** gracias por tu ayuda; **no t.** no, gracias; **t. for coming** gracias por venir; *Ironic* **t. for nothing!** ¡gracias por nada!; *Ironic* **t. a lot** *or* **a bunch** *or* **a bundle!** ¡muchas gracias!

thanksgiving [θæŋks'gɪvɪŋ] *n* agradecimiento *m*; *US* **T. (Day)** día *m* de acción de gracias

thank you ['θæŋkju:] *n* agradecimiento *m*; **I have a few thank yous to say** debo expresar mi agradecimiento a varias personas; **I'd like to say a special t. to Jenny** quisiera expresar mi agradecimiento de manera especial a Jenny; **she left without so much as a t.** se marchó sin dar ni las gracias ►► ***t. letter*** carta *f* de agradecimiento; *see also* **thank**

THAT [ðæt] 1 *demonstrative adj* (*pl* **those** [ðəʊz]) *(masculine)* ese; *(further away)* aquel; *(feminine)* esa; *(further away)* aquella; **t. man standing in front of you** ese hombre (que está) delante de ti; **t. man right at the back** aquel hombre del fondo; **compare t. edition with these two** compara esa edición con estas dos; **later t. day** ese mismo día (más tarde); **t. woman I met** esa mujer que conocí; **we went to t. restaurant by the river** fuimos a ese restaurante que hay al lado del río; **t. one** *(masculine)* ése; *(further away)* aquél; *(feminine)* ésa; *(further away)* aquélla; **at t. time** en aquella época; **t. fool of a teacher** ese *or* aquel profesor tan tonto; *Fam* **t. sister of yours is nothing but trouble** esa hermana tuya no da más que problemas; *Fam*

THAT, WHO, WHOM, WHICH

Omisión del pronombre relativo

Una de las principales diferencias entre el inglés y el español en cuanto al uso de los pronombres relativos es que **that**, **who**, **whom** y **which** pueden omitirse a menudo, mientras que en español esto no ocurre nunca. En inglés pueden omitirse cuando funcionan como objeto de la oración subordinada, por ejemplo:

I brought the money (that/which) we discussed at our last meeting
traje el dinero del que hablamos en la última reunión

he met the woman (who/whom/that) they had warned him against
conoció a la mujer sobre la que le habían advertido

Cuando el pronombre funciona como sujeto de la oración subordinada no puede omitirse:

he visited the place that/which had haunted his dreams for years
visitó el lugar con el que había soñado muchas veces durante años

he met the woman who would become his wife
conoció a la mujer que sería su mujer

well, how's t. leg of yours? a ver, ¿cómo va esa pierna?; **what about t. drink you owe me?** ¿qué pasa con esa copa que me debes?

2 *demonstrative pron* (*pl* **those**) *(in near to middle distance) (indefinite)* eso; *(masculine)* ése; *(feminine)* ésa; *(further away) (indefinite)* aquello; *(masculine)* aquél; *(feminine)* aquélla; **give me t.** dame eso; **this is new and t.'s old** éste es nuevo y ése es viejo; **t.'s my husband over there** ése es mi marido; **what's t.?** ¿qué es eso?; **who's t.?** *(pointing)* ¿quién es ése/ésa?; *(who are you?)* ¿quién es?; **who's t. at the back in the blue coat?** ¿quién es aquél del fondo con el abrigo azul?; **is t. all the luggage you're taking?** ¿es ése todo el equipaje que llevas?; **is t. you, Julie?** *(on phone)* ¿eres tú, Julie?; **is t. you screaming, John?** ¿eres tú el que grita, John?; **t.'s where he lives** ahí es donde vive; **t.'s why we lost** por eso perdimos; **you say you disagree... why is t.?** dices que no estás de acuerdo... ¿por qué?; **so THAT'S how it works!** ¡conque es así como funciona!; **t. was a delicious meal!** ¡qué comida más deliciosa!; **1967, t. was a great year** 1967, ¡qué año aquél!; **t. was two years ago** eso fue hace dos años; **is she intelligent? – t. she is!** ¿es lista? – ¡ya lo creo!; *Fam* **good stuff, t.!** ¡no veas lo bueno que está!; **I've got some gloves like t.** tengo unos guantes como ésos; *Formal* **a storm like t. of ten years ago** una tormenta como la de hace diez años; *Formal* **t. which has no explanation** aquello que no tiene explicación; **t.'s strange/terrible!** ¡qué raro/terrible!, ¡es extraño/terrible!; **t.'s true** es verdad; **take your medicine, t.'s a good boy!** sé bueno y tómate la medicina; **t.'s the French (for you)!** ¡así son los franceses!; **t. is (to say)** esto es; **t.'s all** eso es todo; **t.'s enough of t.!** ¡ya basta!; **t.'s more like it!** ¡así está mejor!; **t.'s it** *(it's over)* eso es todo; **t.'s it, I'm leaving!** *(expressing anger)* ¡ya no aguanto más, me marcho!; **t.'s right!, t.'s it!** *(that's correct)* ¡eso es!; **t.'s t.!** ¡ya está!; **we locked the door, and t. was t.** cerramos la puerta, y eso fue todo; **all t. about my family** lo de *or* aquello de mi familia; *Fam* **they were very friendly and (all) t.** fueron muy amables y todo eso; **for all t. I still love her...** por mucho que la quiera...; **can you run as fast as t.?** ¿puedes correr así de deprisa?; **it was a long journey and a tedious one at t.** fue un viaje largo y, encima, tedioso; **what do you mean by t.?** ¿qué quieres decir con eso?; **with t. she turned and left** con eso, dio media vuelta y se marchó

3 *adv* (**a**) *(in comparisons)* así de; **t. high** así de alto; **can you run t. fast?** ¿puedes correr así de deprisa?; **t. many** tantos(as); **t. much** tanto

(**b**) *(so, very)* tan; **it isn't t. good** no es tan bueno; **is she t. tall?** ¿tan alta es?; **I'm not t. keen on it** no me entusiasma demasiado; *Fam* **he's t. stupid (t.) he...** es tan estúpido que...; **there weren't t. many there** no había muchos; **I haven't played this game t. much** no he jugado demasiado a este juego

4 *[unstressed* ðət*] relative pron*

El pronombre relativo **that** puede omitirse salvo cuando es sujeto de la oración subordinada.

(**a**) *(introducing subordinate clause)* que; **the letter t. came yesterday** la carta que llegó ayer; **the letters t. I sent you** las cartas que te envié; **you're the only person t. can help me** eres la única persona que puede ayudarme; **the reason t. I'm telling you** la razón por la que te lo digo

(**b**) *(with following preposition)* que; **the envelope t. I put it in** el sobre en que lo guardé; **the woman t. we're talking about** la mujer de quien *or* de la que estamos hablando; **the person t. I gave it to** la persona a quien *or* a la que se lo di; **the people t. I work with** la gente con la que trabajo

(**c**) *(when)* que; **the last time t. I saw him** la última vez que lo vi; **the day t. I left** el día (en) que me fui

5 *[unstressed* ðət*] conj*

that se puede omitir cuando introduce una oración subordinada.

(**a**) *(introducing subordinate clause)* que; **she said t. she would come** dijo que vendría; **I'll see to it t. everything is ready** me ocuparé de que todo esté listo; **my opinion is t. you should stay** opino que debes quedarte; **the fact t. he told you** el hecho de que te lo contara

(**b**) *Formal (so that)* **let's explain, t. she might understand our actions** expliquémonos para que así comprenda nuestras acciones; **he died t. we might live** dio la vida para que pudiésemos sobrevivir

(**c**) *Literary (in exclamations)* **t. it should have come to this!** ¡que hayamos tenido que llegar a esto!; **oh t. it were possible!** ¡ojalá fuese posible!

6 **that way** *adv* (**a**) *(in that manner)* así; **t. way you'll only make things worse** así sólo conseguirás empeorar las cosas

(**b**) *Fam (in that respect)* **she's funny t. way** para eso es muy suya; **I didn't know he was t. way inclined** no sabía que tenía esas inclinaciones; IDIOM *US* **to be t. way about sb/sth** estar prendado(a) de alguien/algo

thatch [θætʃ] **1** *n* (**a**) *(on roof)* paja *f* (**b**) *Fam (of hair)* mata *f*

2 *vt (roof)* cubrir con paja

thatched [θætʃt] *adj* **t. cottage** casa de campo con techo de paja; **t. roof** techo de paja

thatcher ['θætʃə(r)] *n* techador(ora) *m,f*, chamicero(a) *m,f*

Thatcherism ['θætʃərɪzəm] *n* thatcherismo *m*

Thatcherite ['θætʃəraɪt] **1** *n* thatcherista *mf*

2 *adj* thatcherista

thatching ['θætʃɪŋ] *n* (**a**) *(material)* paja *f* para techumbre, chamiza *f* (**b**) *(skill)* techado *m* con paja *or* chamiza

that's [ðæts] = **that is, that has**

thaw [θɔː] **1** *n* deshielo *m*; *Fig* **a t. in relations** una mejora de las relaciones

2 *vt* (**a**) *(snow, ice)* fundir, derretir (**b**) *(food)* descongelar

3 *vi* (**a**) *(to melt) (snow, ice)* derretirse, fundirse; **it's beginning to t.** está empezando el deshielo (**b**) *(food)* descongelarse (**c**) *(get warmer) (hands, feet)* entrar en calor (**d**) *(person, manner, atmosphere)* relajarse; *(relations)* distenderse; **she seems finally to be thawing towards me** parece que por fin me trata con más cariño

▸ **thaw out 1** *vt sep* (**a**) *(food)* descongelar (**b**) *(feet, hands)* hacer entrar en calor a

2 *vi* (**a**) *(lake)* deshelarse (**b**) *(food)* descongelarse (**c**) *(person) (in front of fire)* entrar en calor

THE *[before consonant sounds* ðə, *before vowel sounds* ðɪ, *stressed* ðiː*] definite article* (**a**) *(singular) (masculine)* el; *(feminine)* la; *(plural) (masculine)* los; *(feminine)* las; **t. book** el libro; **t. table** la mesa; **t. books** los libros; **t. tables** las mesas; **t. cold water** el agua fría; **t. same thing** la misma cosa, lo mismo; **to/from t. airport** al/del aeropuerto; **t. good/beautiful** *(as concepts)* lo bueno/bello; **t. impossible** lo imposible; **I'll see him in t. summer** lo veré en verano; **later in t. week** esta semana (más adelante), *RP* más entrada la semana; **she's got t. measles/t. flu** tiene (el) sarampión/(la) gripe *or Col, Méx* gripa; **I've been t. president of this company for many years** he sido (el) presidente de esta compañía durante muchos años; **t. best** el/la mejor; **t. longest** el/la más largo(a); **I like this one t. most** éste es el que más me gusta

(**b**) *(specifying)* **t. reason I asked is...** el motivo de mi pregunta es...; **I was absent at t. time** yo no estaba en ese momento; **t. Europe of today** la Europa actual; **t. minute I saw her** en cuanto la vi; **it hit me on t. head** me golpeó en la cabeza; *Fam* **how's t. knee?** ¿qué tal esa rodilla?; *Fam* **t. wife's been ill** la *Esp* parienta *or Am* vieja *or RP* patrona ha estado enferma

(**c**) *(denoting class, group)* **t. poor/blind** los pobres/ciegos; **t. French** los franceses; **t. tiger is threatened with extinction** el tigre está en peligro de extinción; **t. Wilsons** los Wilson

(**d**) *(with musical instruments)* **to play t. piano** tocar el piano

(**e**) *(with titles)* **Edward t. Eighth** *(written Edward VIII)* Eduardo Octavo *(escrito Eduardo VIII)*; **Catherine t. Great** Catalina la Grande

(**f**) *(proportions, rates)* **to be paid by t. hour** cobrar por hora(s); **15 kilometres to t. litre** 15 kilómetros por *or* el litro; **20 pesos to t. pound** 20 pesos por libra

(**g**) *(in exclamations)* **t. arrogance/stupidity of it!** ¡qué arrogancia/estupidez!; **t. lucky devil!** ¡qué suertudo(a)!; **she's giving up her job – t. woman's mad!** va a dejar su empleo – ¡esta mujer está loca!; *Fam* **he's gone and borrowed my bike, t. cheeky so-and-so!** ¡el muy caradura se ha ido y se ha llevado mi bicicleta!

(**h**) *[stressed* ðiː*]* **not THE Professor Brown?** ¿no será el famosísimo Profesor Brown?; **it's THE car for the young professional** es el coche de los jóvenes profesionales; **for him Bach is THE composer** para él Bach es el compositor por excelencia; **it's THE place to be seen** es el lugar de moda

(**i**) *(in comparisons)* **t. sooner t. better** cuanto antes, mejor; **t. less we argue, t. more work we'll get done** cuanto menos discutamos, más trabajaremos; **I was all t. more puzzled by his calmness** lo que más me extrañaba era su tranquilidad; **she felt all t. better for having told him** se sentía mucho mejor por habérselo dicho; **I feel none t. worse for t. experience** a pesar de la experiencia me siento perfectamente

(**j**) *(with dates)* **t. ninth of June** el nueve de junio; **t. sixties** los sesenta; **t. eighteen hundreds** el siglo diecinueve; **she arrived on t. Friday** llegó el viernes

(**k**) *(enough)* **she hasn't got t. time/money to do it** no tiene (el) dinero/(el) tiempo para hacerlo

theatre, *US* **theater** ['θɪətə(r)] *n* (**a**) *(building)* teatro *m*; **to go to the t.** ir al teatro ▸▸ ***t. ticket*** entrada *f or Col, Méx* boleto *m* para el teatro

(**b**) *(art)* teatro *m*; **Greek/modern t.** teatro griego/moderno; **the t. of**

the absurd el teatro del absurdo ►► ***t. company*** compañía *f* de teatro; ***t. critic*** crítico(a) *m,f* teatral *or* de teatro

(**c**) *(profession)* teatro *m*; **he has spent his life in the t.** ha consagrado su vida al (mundo del) teatro

(**d**) *US (for movies)* cine *m*

(**e**) *Br Med* **(operating) t.** quirófano *m*

(**f**) *(lecture hall)* aula *f*

(**g**) *Mil* **t. of war** escenario de guerra

theatre-goer, *US* **theater-goer** [ˈθɪətəgəʊə(r)] *n* aficionado(a) *m,f* al teatro

theatre-going, *US* **theater-going** [ˈθɪətəgəʊɪŋ] 1 *n* afición *f* al teatro; **my pastimes include t. and crosswords** entre mis pasatiempos están el teatro y los crucigramas

2 *adj* **the t. public** los aficionados al teatro, los espectadores de teatro

theatre-in-the-round [ˈθɪətəɪnðəˈraʊnd] *n* teatro *m* con escenario central

theatrical [θɪˈætrɪkəl] 1 *n* **theatricals** *Theat* montajes *mpl or* representaciones *fpl* teatrales; *(exaggerated behaviour)* teatralidad *f*; **amateur t.** teatro aficionado

2 *adj* (**a**) *Theat* teatral ►► ***t. agency*** empresa *f* de contratación artística; ***t. agent*** agente *mf* teatral; ***t. company*** compañía *f* teatral (**b**) *(exaggerated) (gesture, behaviour)* teatral; **why do you always have to be so t. about everything?** ¿por qué siempre tienes que echarle tanto teatro a todo?

theatricality [θɪætrɪˈkælɪtɪ] *n* teatralidad *f*

theatrically [θɪˈætrɪklɪ] *adv* (**a**) *Theat* teatralmente (**b**) *(in exaggerated fashion)* teatralmente; **to behave t.** hacer mucho teatro

theatrics [θɪˈætrɪks] *npl* (**a**) *Theat* teatro *m* (**b**) *(contrived effects)* tramoya *f*, golpes *mpl* de efecto

thee [ðiː] *pron* (**a**) *Literary* te; *(after preposition)* ti (**b**) *Rel* te; *(after preposition)* ti

theft [θeft] *n* robo *m*; *(less serious)* hurto *m*

theftproof [ˈθeftpruːf] *adj (vehicle, door)* a prueba de robo, antirrobo

---

THEIR [ðeə(r)] *possessive adj* (**a**) *(singular)* su; *(plural)* sus; **t. dog** su perro; **t. parents** sus padres; **we went to t. house** *(not yours or ours)* fuimos a su casa; **it wasn't THEIR idea!** ¡la idea no fue de ellos!; **we were upset at t. mentioning it** nos disgustó que lo mencionaran; **t. understanding was that we would share the cost** ellos habían entendido que compartiríamos los costos

(**b**) *(for parts of body, clothes) (translated by definite article)* **t. eyes are blue** tienen los ojos azules; **they both forgot t. hats** los dos se olvidaron el sombrero; **they washed t. faces** se lavaron la cara; **they put t. hands in t. pockets** se metieron las manos en los bolsillos; **someone stole t. clothes** alguien les robó la ropa

(**c**) *(indefinite use)* su; **somebody called but they didn't leave t. name** ha llamado alguien, pero no ha dejado su nombre; **someone's left t. umbrella** alguien se ha dejado el paraguas

---

theirs [ðeəz] *possessive pron* (**a**) *(singular)* el suyo *m*, la suya *f*; *(plural)* los suyos *mpl*, las suyas *fpl*; **our house is big but t. is bigger** nuestra casa es grande, pero la suya es mayor; **he didn't have a book so we gave him t.** como no tenía libro le dimos el de ellos; **it must be one of t.** debe de ser uno de los suyos; **it wasn't my fault, it was THEIRS** la culpa no fue mía sino suya *or* de ellos; **t. is the work she admires most** el trabajo que más admira es el de ellos *or* suyo

(**b**) *(used attributively) (singular)* suyo(a); *(plural)* suyos(as); **this book is t.** este libro es suyo; **a friend of t.** un amigo suyo; **that wretched dog of t.** ese maldito perro que tienen

(**c**) *(indefinite use)* **if anyone hasn't got t. they can use mine** si alguien no tiene el suyo, puede usar el mío

theism [ˈθiːɪzəm] *n Rel* teísmo *m*

theist [ˈθiːɪst] 1 *n* teísta *mf*

2 *adj* teísta

theistic [θiːˈɪstɪk] *adj* teísta

THEM [ðem, *unstressed* ðəm] 1 *pron* (**a**) *(direct object)* los *mpl*, las *fpl*; **I hate t.** los odio; **I like t.** me gustan; **kill t.!** ¡mátalos!; **I can forgive their son but not THEM** puedo perdonar a su hijo, pero no a ellos

(**b**) *(indirect object)* les; **I gave t. the book** les di el libro; **I gave it to t.** se lo di; **give it to t.** dáselo

(**c**) *(after preposition)* ellos *mpl*, ellas *fpl*; **I'm thinking of t.** estoy pensando en ellos; **it was meant for you, not for THEM** iba dirigido a ti, no a ellos; **we must avoid seeing things in terms of t. and us** debemos evitar ver las cosas en términos de ellos por un lado y nosotros por el otro

(**d**) *(as complement of verb "to be")* ellos *mpl*, ellas *fpl*; **it's t.!** ¡son ellos!; **it was t. who did it** fueron ellos los que lo hicieron; **the décor isn't really t.** la decoración no va *or* pega mucho con ellos

(**e**) *(indefinite use)* **if anyone comes, tell t....** si viene alguien, dile que...

2 *adj Fam (considered incorrect) (those)* esos; **give us one of t. sweets** dame uno de esos caramelos

---

thematic [θɪˈmætɪk] *adj* temático(a)

thematically [θɪˈmætɪklɪ] *adv* por temas, temáticamente

theme [θiːm] *n* (**a**) *(subject)* tema *m*, asunto *m* ►► ***t. park*** parque *m* temático; ***t. pub*** bar *m* temático (**b**) *(in literature, music)* tema *m* ►► ***t. music*** tema *m* (musical); ***t. song*** sintonía *f*; ***t. tune*** sintonía *f* (**c**) *Ling* tema *m*

themed [θiːmd] *adj (restaurant, bar, evening)* temático(a)

themselves [ðəmˈselvz] *pron* (**a**) *(reflexive)* se; **they've hurt t.** se han hecho daño; **they introduced t.** se presentaron; **they bought t. some flowers** se compraron unas flores; **they consider t. lucky** se consideran afortunados; **they could see t. reflected in the water** vieron su imagen reflejada *or* se vieron reflejados en el agua

(**b**) *(unaided, alone)* ellos *mpl* solos, ellas *fpl* solas; **they can do it t.** (ellos) pueden hacerlo solos, pueden hacerlo ellos solos; **did they do all the work t.?** ¿hicieron todo el trabajo ellos solos?

(**c**) *(emphatic)* ellos *mpl* mismos, ellas *fpl* mismas; **they told me t.** me lo dijeron ellos mismos; **they t. saw him leave** ellos mismos lo vieron salir

(**d**) *(their usual selves)* **they'll soon feel t. again** en breve *or* pronto se volverán a sentir los de siempre; **they don't seem t. today** hoy no se les ve nada bien; **they should just be t.** *(act naturally)* deberían comportarse tal como son

(**e**) *(after preposition)* **they were talking about t.** estaban hablando de sí mismos; **they shared the money among t.** se repartieron el dinero; **they sorted it out among t.** lo arreglaron entre ellos; **they did it by t.** lo hicieron ellos mismos *or* ellos solos; **they were all by t.** estaban ellos solos; **they live by t.** viven solos; **they bought it for t.** se lo compraron para ellos; **they kept the best seats for t.** se quedaron con los mejores asientos

(**f**) *(replacing "them")* **it is meant for people like t.** está pensado para gente como ellos

---

THEN [ðen] 1 *adv* (**a**) *(at that time)* entonces, *Am* en aquel momento *or* entonces; **it was better t.** era mejor entonces *or* aquella época; **I'll be back on Monday – I'll see you t.** volveré el lunes – nos veremos entonces; **before t.** antes (de eso); **by t.** para entonces; **from t. on** desde entonces, a partir de entonces, de ahí en adelante; **just** *or* **right t.** justo entonces, justo en ese momento; **since/until t.** desde/hasta entonces; **Marilyn, or Norma Jean as she was t. known** Marilyn, o Norma Jean como se la conocía (por aquel) entonces; **I decided to tell them t. and there** decidí decírselo en aquel momento; **he was sacked t. and there** lo despidieron en el acto

(**b**) *(next)* luego; **do your homework first, t. you can watch TV** primero haz los deberes y después podrás ver la televisión; **what t.?** y luego *or* después, ¿qué?

(**c**) *(in addition)* luego; **and t. there's the cost** y luego está el costo; **it must have cost a million and t. some** debe de haber costado un millón largo *or* y pico; **t. again, but t.** pero por otra parte

(**d**) *(in that case)* entonces; **t. stop complaining** pues deja de quejarte; **if you don't like it, t. choose another one** si no te gusta, elige otro; **all right, t.** bueno, *Esp* vale *or Arg* está bien *or Méx* órale

(**e**) *(so, therefore)* entonces; **are you coming, t.?** entonces ¿qué?, ¿vas a venir?, *RP* ¿y?, ¿venís o no?; **you already knew, t.?** entonces, ¿ya lo sabías?; **its significance, t., is twofold** por lo tanto su importancia es doble; **if x = 2, t. y = 6** si x = 2, y = 6

2 *adj* **the t. President** el entonces presidente

---

thence [ðens] *adv Formal* (**a**) *(from there)* de allí, de ahí; **we went to Paris and t. to Rome** fuimos a París y de ahí a Roma (**b**) *(because of that)* de ahí

thenceforth [ðensˈfɔːθ], **thenceforward** [ðensˈfɔːwəd] *adv Formal* desde entonces (en adelante)

theocracy [θiːˈɒkrəsɪ] *n* teocracia *f*

theocratic [θɪəˈkrætɪk] *adj* teocrático(a)

theodolite [θiːˈɒdəlaɪt] *n* teodolito *m*

theologian [θiːəˈləʊdʒən] *n* teólogo(a) *m,f*

theological [θiːəˈlɒdʒɪkəl] *adj* teológico(a) ►► ***t. college*** seminario *m*

theologically [θiːəˈlɒdʒɪklɪ] *adv* teológicamente, desde el punto de vista teológico

theology [θiːˈɒlədʒɪ] *n* teología *f*

theorem [ˈθɪərəm] *n Math* teorema *m*

theoretical [θiːəˈretɪkəl] *adj* (**a**) *(physics, course)* teórico(a) (**b**) *(hypothetical)* teórico(a)

theoretically [θiːəˈretɪklɪ] *adv* (**a**) *(relating to theory)* en la teoría, teóricamente (**b**) *(hypothetically)* en teoría, teóricamente; **it's t. possible** en teoría es posible

theoretician [θiːərɪˈtɪʃən] *n* teórico(a) *m,f*

theorist [ˈθiːərɪst] *n* teórico(a) *m,f*

theorize [ˈθiːəraɪz] **1** *vt* formular como teoría
2 *vi* teorizar (**about** sobre)

theorizing [ˈθiːəraɪzɪŋ] *n* teorías *fpl*, especulaciones *fpl*

theory [ˈθiːərɪ] *n* teoría *f*; **in t.** en teoría; **my t. is that he never wanted you to succeed** mi teoría es que nunca quiso que triunfaras; **she's studying musical t.** estudia teoría musical ►► ***the t. of evolution*** la teoría de la evolución; ***the t. of relativity*** la teoría de la relatividad

theosophy [θɪˈɒsəfɪ] *n* teosofía *f*

therapeutic [θerəˈpjuːtɪk] *adj* (**a**) *Med* terapéutico(a) ►► ***t. abortion*** aborto *m* terapéutico (**b**) *(relaxing)* terapéutico(a)

therapeutically [θerəˈpjuːtɪklɪ] *adv* con fines terapéuticos

therapeutics [θerəˈpjuːtɪks] *n* terapéutica *f*

therapist [ˈθerəpɪst] *n* terapeuta *mf*

therapy [ˈθerəpɪ] *n* terapia *f*; **to be in t.** *(psychotherapy)* recibir tratamiento psíquico

---

THERE [ðeə(r), *unstressed* ðə(r)] **1** *pron* **t. is/are** hay; **t. was/were** había; **t.'s that girl I was telling you about before** esa es la chica de la que te hablaba antes; *Fam* **t.'s a few things I'm not happy with** hay unas cuantas cosas con las que no estoy muy contento; **t. was plenty of food** había mucha comida; **t. was a bang** hubo una explosión; **t.'s a bus coming** viene un autobús; **t. was singing and dancing** la gente cantó y bailó; **t. were no apples** no había manzanas; **t. were several explosions** hubo varias explosiones; **t. will be** habrá; **t. must be a reason** tiene que haber una razón; **t.'s a page missing** falta una página; **t. are** *or Fam* **t.'s two apples left** quedan dos manzanas; **t. isn't any – yes, t. is!** no hay – sí que hay; **t. are four of us** somos cuatro; **t.'s no doubt that...** no cabe duda de que...; **I don't want t. to be any arguing** no quiero que discutamos; **t.'s no denying it...** no se puede negar...; **t.'s no going back now** ya no podemos dar marcha atrás; **now t.'s a surprise!** ¡vaya *or* qué sorpresa!; **t.'s a good dog!** ¡qué buen perro!; **close the window for me, t.'s a dear!** sé bueno y cierra la ventana; **t. appears** *or* **seems to be a problem** parece que hay un problema; **t. comes a time when...** llega un momento en que...; **t. followed a period of calm** siguió un periodo de calma; **t. remains the prospect of...** queda la posibilidad de...; **t. once lived** *or* **was a princess...** *(in children's stories)* érase una vez una princesa...

2 *adv* (**a**) *(referring to place)* ahí; *(more distant) (at precise point)* allí, *esp Am* allá; *(more vaguely)* allá; **we're t.!** *(we've arrived)* ¡ya hemos llegado!; **give me that book t.** dame ese libro de ahí; **those bicycles t.** aquellas bicicletas de allí; **your friend t.** tu amigo aquel; **I'm going t. tomorrow** voy para allá mañana; **I've never been t.** no he estado nunca (allí); **when will we get t.?** *(arrive)* ¿cuándo llegaremos?; **you'll get t. eventually** *(succeed)* al final lo conseguirás; *(understand)* al final lo entenderás; **we went to Paris and from t. to Rome** fuimos a París, y de allí a Roma; **somewhere near t.** por allí cerca; **out/in t.** allí fuera/dentro, *Am* allá afuera/adentro; **put it over t.** ponlo ahí; **up/down t.** ahí arriba/abajo; **do we have time to get t. and back?** ¿tenemos tiempo de ir (allí *or Am* allá) y volver?; **it's ten miles t. and back** hay diez millas entre la ida y la vuelta; **I decided to tell them t. and then** decidí decírselo en aquel momento; **he was sacked t. and then** lo despidieron en el acto; **so t. we were/I was** y en esas estábamos/estaba; **she just sat/stood t.** ni se inmutó; *Fig* **I've been t. (before)** *(experienced that)* ya sé lo que es eso; **move along t., please!** ¡circulen, por favor!

(**b**) *(present)* **most of my family were t.** estaba (ahí) la mayoría de mi familia; **they're not t.** no están (ahí); **the opportunity is t. if we can take it** la oportunidad está ahí, si sabemos aprovecharla; **is anybody t.?** ¿hay alguien ahí?; **who's t.?** *(after knock on door)* ¿quién es?; **is Paul t.?** *(on phone)* ¿está Paul?; *Fam* **he's not all t.** no está bien de la cabeza; **she was t. for me when I needed her** estuvo a mi lado *or Am* conmigo cuando la necesité

(**c**) *(at that point, on that subject)* **we'll stop t. for today** lo dejamos aquí por hoy; **I'll have to ask you to stop t.** tengo que pedirle que lo deje ahí; **as for the food, I've no complaints t.** no me puedo quejar de la comida; **you're wrong t.** en eso estás equivocada; **t.'s the difficulty** ahí está la dificultad; **I agree with you t.** en ese punto estoy de acuerdo contigo; *Fam* **t. you have me!, you've got me t.!** *(I don't know the answer) Esp* ¡ahí me has pillado!, *Am* ¡ahí me agarraste!

(**d**) *(emphasizing, pointing out) Fam* **hi, t.!** ¡hola!; **hey! you t.!** ¡oye, tú!, *RP* ¡che, vos!; **t. they are!** ¡ahí están!; **t. she goes!** ¡por ahí va!, ¡allá va!; **t. he goes again, complaining about the food!** ¡ya está otra vez quejándose de la comida!; **t. goes the phone again!** ¡otra vez el teléfono!; **t. go our chances of winning!** ¡adiós a nuestras oportunidades de ganar!; **I lost, but t. you go** perdí, pero qué le vamos a hacer; **t. you go** *or* **are!** *(when giving sb sth)* ¡ahí tienes!; **just press the button and t. you are** *or* **go!** pulsa el botón y listo; **t. (you go** *or* **are), I told you so** ¿ves?, ya te lo dije

3 *exclam* **t. now, that's done!** *Esp* ¡hala, ya está!, *Am* ¡bueno, está pronto!; **t., that wasn't so bad, was it?** ¡lo ves!, no era para tanto, ¿verdad?; **t., now you've made me lose count!** ¡hala!, ya me has hecho perder la cuenta; **t., t.! don't worry!** *Esp* ¡venga, no te preocupes!, *Am* ¡bueno, no te preocupes!

4 there again *adv* por otra parte

---

thereabouts [ˈðeərəˈbaʊts], *US* **thereabout** [ˈðeərəˈbaʊt] *adv* (**a**) *(with place)* **(or) t.** (o) por ahí (**b**) *(with number, quantity, distance)* **50 people, or t.** más o menos 50 personas, 50 personas o por ahí (**c**) *(with time)* **at 10 p.m. or t.** a eso de las diez de la noche

thereafter [ðeərˈɑːftə(r)] *adv Formal* (**a**) *(in time)* en lo sucesivo, a partir de ahí (**b**) *(in document)* en adelante; **in paragraph 6 and the paragraphs t.** en el párrafo 6 y párrafos subsiguientes

thereby [ˈðeəbaɪ] *adv Formal* así, de ese modo; IDIOM **t. hangs a tale!** y el asunto tiene miga

therefore [ˈðeəfɔː(r)] *adv* por (lo) tanto, por consiguiente; *Math* **x = 10, t. y = 5** x = 10, luego y = 5; **I think, t. I am** pienso, luego existo

therein [ðeəˈrɪn] *adv* (**a**) *Formal (inside)* dentro (**b**) *Law* dentro (**c**) *Formal (in that point)* ahí; **t. lies the problem** ahí radica el problema

thereof [ðeəˈrɒv] *adv Formal* de éste/ésta/esto; **the principal disadvantage t. is...** la principal desventaja de esto es...; **the republic and all the citizens t.** la república y todos sus ciudadanos *or* todos los ciudadanos de ésta

thereon [ðeəˈrɒn] *adv Formal & Law* en él/ella/ello; **the property and all the buildings t.** el terreno y todos los inmuebles sitos en él

there's [ðeəz] = **there is, there has**

thereto [ðeəˈtuː] *adv* (**a**) *Formal* a él/ella/ello (**b**) *Law* a él/ella/ello

thereunder [ðeəˈrʌndə(r)] *adv* (**a**) *Formal* bajo él/ella/ello (**b**) *Law* bajo él/ella/ello

thereupon [ðeərəˈpɒn] *adv Formal* (**a**) *(then)* acto seguido (**b**) *(on that subject)* sobre el/la mismo(a), al respecto

therm [θɜːm] *n Phys* termia *f*

thermal [ˈθɜːməl] **1** *n* (**a**) *Met* corriente *f* de aire ascendente, (corriente *f*) térmica *f* (**b**) *Fam* **thermals** *(thermal underwear)* ropa *f* interior térmica
2 *adj* térmico(a) ►► ***t. baths*** baños *mpl* termales; *Phys* ***t. conductivity*** conductividad *f* or conductancia *f* calorífica; ***t. energy*** energía *f* térmica; ***t. imaging*** imagen *f* or visualización *f* térmica; *Comptr* ***t. paper*** papel *m* térmico; *Comptr* ***t. printer*** impresora *f* térmica; ***t. reactor*** reactor *m* (nuclear) térmico; *Geol* ***t. springs*** manantial *m* de aguas termales; ***t. underwear*** ropa *f* interior térmica

thermionic [θɜːmaɪˈɒnɪk] *adj Phys* term(o)iónico(a) ►► ***t.*** *Br* ***valve*** *or US* ***tube*** válvula *f* term(o)iónica, tubo *m* term(o)iónico

thermobaric [θɜːməʊˈbærɪk] *n Phys* termobárico(a) ►► *Mil* ***t. weapon*** arma *f* termobárica

thermocouple [ˈθɜːməʊkʌpəl] *n Phys* termopar *m*

thermodynamic [θɜːməʊdaɪˈnæmɪk] *adj Phys* termodinámico(a)

thermodynamics [θɜːməʊdaɪˈnæmɪks] *n Phys* termodinámica *f*

thermoelectric [θɜːməʊɪˈlektrɪk] *adj Phys* termoeléctrico(a)

thermometer [θəˈmɒmɪtə(r)] *n* termómetro *m*

thermonuclear [θɜːməʊˈnjuːklɪə(r)] *adj* termonuclear

thermopile [ˈθɜːməʊpaɪl] *n Phys* termopila *f*, pila *f* termoeléctrica

thermoplastic [θɜːməʊˈplæstɪk] **1** *n* termoplástico *m*
2 *adj* termoplástico(a)

Thermos® [ˈθɜːməs] *n* **T. (flask)** termo *m*

thermosetting [ˈθɜːməʊsetɪŋ] *adj* termoendurecible

thermostat [ˈθɜːməstæt] *n* termostato *m*

thermostatic [θɜːməˈstætɪk] *adj* termostático(a)

thermostatically [θɜːməʊˈstætɪklɪ] *adv* por termostato

thesaurus [θɪˈsɔːrəs] *n* (**a**) *(book) (thematic)* diccionario *m* ideológico *or* de ideas afines; *(alphabetical)* diccionario *m* de sinónimos (**b**) *Comptr* diccionario *m* de sinónimos

THESE [ðiːz] 1 *adj* estos(as); **t. ones** éstos(as); **t. ones here** éstos de aquí *or Am* acá; *Fam* **I met t. Germans** conocí a unos alemanes; *Fam* **he used to wear t. funny trousers** solía llevar unos pantalones bien raros
2 *pron* éstos(as); **t. are the ones I want** éstos son los que quiero; **t. here** éstos de aquí *or Am* acá

thesis ['θiːsɪs] (*pl* **theses** ['θiːsiːz]) *n* (**a**) *(for doctorate)* tesis *f inv* (**b**) *Formal (theory)* tesis *f inv*, teoría *f*

thespian ['θespɪən] *Literary or Hum* 1 *n* actor *m*, actriz *f*, farandulero(a) *m,f*
2 *adj* teatral, dramático(a); **his t. friends** sus amigos faranduleros *or* de la farándula

theurgy ['θiːɜːdʒɪ] *n (divine intervention)* obra *f* divina

THEY [ðeɪ] *pron* (**a**) *(personal use)* ellos *mpl*, ellas *fpl (usually omitted in Spanish, except for contrast)*; **they're Scottish** son escoceses; **t. like red wine** les gusta el vino tinto; **who are t.?** *(pointing)* ¿quiénes son ésos?; **THEY haven't got it!** ¡ellos no lo tienen!; **t. alone know** sólo ellos lo saben
(**b**) *(indefinite use)* **nobody ever admits they've lied** la gente nunca reconoce que ha mentido; **they're going to cut interest rates** van a reducir los tipos *or Am* las tasas de interés; **t. say (that)...** dicen que...

they'd [ðeɪd] = **they had, they would**

they'll [ðeɪl] = **they will, they shall**

they're [ðeə(r)] = **they are**

they've [ðeɪv] = **they have**

thiamin ['θaɪəmɪn], **thiamine** ['θaɪəmiːn] *n* tiamina *f*

thick [θɪk] 1 *n* **in the t. of the forest** en la espesura del bosque; **he was always to be found in the t. of the fighting** siempre se encontraba allá donde la lucha era más encarnizada; **in the t. of it** *or* **of things** en primera línea; IDIOM **to stand by sb through t. and thin** estar con alguien a las duras y a las maduras *or* para lo bueno y para lo malo
2 *adj* (**a**) *(in size)* grueso(a); **the wall is a metre t.** el muro tiene un metro de espesor *or* grosor; **how t. is the wall?** ¿qué espesor *or* grosor tiene la pared?; **he has t. lips** tiene labios gruesos *or* carnosos; **the boots have a t. fur lining** las botas llevan un tupido forro de piel; IDIOM **to have a t. skin** tener mucha correa *or* mucho aguante *(ante críticas o insultos)*; IDIOM *Fam* **to give sb a t. ear** dar a alguien un coscorrón
(**b**) *(dense) (forest)* espeso(a); *(hair)* tupido(a), abundante; *(beard, eyebrows)* poblado(a), tupido(a); *(fur, carpet)* tupido(a); **to have t. hair** tener mucho pelo; **the snow was t. on the ground** había una espesa capa de nieve (en el suelo); *Fig* **to be t. on the ground** *(plentiful)* ser abundante
(**c**) *(mist, smoke)* denso(a); **the air is rather t. in here** el ambiente está muy cargado aquí dentro
(**d**) *(full)* **the air was t. with smoke** un humo espeso invadía el aire; **the shelves were t. with dust** los estantes estaban llenos de polvo; **the streets were t. with police** las calles estaban abarrotadas de policía, en la calle había policía por todas partes
(**e**) *(soup, paint, sauce)* espeso(a)
(**f**) *(accent)* acusado(a), marcado(a)
(**g**) *(of voice) (after drinking)* pastoso(a); *(from tiredness, fear)* confuso(a); **a voice t. with emotion** una voz quebrada por la emoción
(**h**) *Fam (stupid)* corto(a), lerdo(a); IDIOM **to be as t. as two short planks** *or* **a brick** no tener dos dedos de frente; IDIOM *Vulg* **to be as t. as shit** ser tonto(a) del culo, ser más burro(a) que un arado
(**i**) *Br Fam (unreasonable)* **that's a bit t.!** ¡eso es un poco fuerte!; **it's a bit t. expecting us to take them to the airport!** ¡me parece demasiado *or* el colmo que esperen que los llevemos al aeropuerto!
(**j**) *Fam (intimate)* **he's very t. with the boss** es uña y carne con el jefe, está a partir un piñón con el jefe; **they're as t. as thieves** son uña y carne, están a partir un piñón
3 *adv* **to cut the bread t.** cortar el pan en rebanadas gruesas; **to spread the butter t.** untar mucha mantequilla; **arrows started falling t. and fast around them** empezaron a lloverles flechas por todas partes; **to come t. and fast** llegar a raudales; *Fam* **to lay it on a bit t.** cargar las tintas

thicken ['θɪkən] 1 *vt (sauce)* espesar
2 *vi (fog, smoke, sauce)* espesarse; *(bushes, forest)* hacerse más espeso(a); *(crowd)* apiñarse; IDIOM *Hum* **the plot thickens** la cosa se complica

thickener ['θɪknə(r)] *n* espesante *m*

thicket ['θɪkɪt] *n* matorral *m*

thickhead ['θɪkhed] *n Fam* burro(a) *m,f*, tarugo(a) *m,f*

thick-headed [θɪk'hedɪd] *adj Fam* (**a**) *(stupid)* burro(a), tarugo(a) (**b**) *(groggy)* atontado(a)

thickie ['θɪkɪ], **thicko** ['θɪkəʊ] *n Fam* burro(a) *m,f*, tarugo(a) *m,f*

thick-lipped ['θɪk'lɪpt] *adj* de labios gruesos *or* carnosos

thickly ['θɪklɪ] *adv* (**a**) *(in thick pieces)* **t. cut slices of cheese** lonchas de queso gruesas; **to spread butter t.** untar una gruesa capa de mantequilla (**b**) *(densely)* **a t. wooded area** una zona de espesos bosques; **t. populated** densamente poblado(a); **the snow fell t.** nevaba intensamente (**c**) *(to speak)* con la voz quebrada

thickness ['θɪknɪs] *n* (**a**) *(of wall, layer)* grosor *m*, espesor *m*; *(of lips)* grosor, carnosidad *f* (**b**) *(layer)* capa *f*; **wrap it in three thicknesses of paper** envuélvalo en una capa triple *or* en tres capas de papel (**c**) *(of forest, hair, beard)* espesura *f*; *(of fur, carpet)* lo tupido (**d**) *(of mist, smoke)* densidad *f* (**e**) *(of sauce)* consistencia *f* (**f**) *(of accent)* carácter *m* marcado

thicko = **thickie**

thickset ['θɪk'set] *adj (person)* corpulento(a), fornido(a)

thick-skinned ['θɪk'skɪnd] *adj Fig* **to be t.** tener mucha correa *or* mucho aguante *(ante críticas o insultos)*

thick-sliced ['θɪk'slaɪst] *adj (bread)* en rebanadas gruesas

thief [θiːf] (*pl* **thieves** [θiːvz]) *n* ladrón(ona) *m,f*; **stop t.!** ¡al ladrón!; PROV **set a t. to catch a t.** = nadie como el ladrón sabe cómo atrapar a otro ladrón

thieve [θiːv] 1 *vt* robar
2 *vi* robar

thieving ['θiːvɪŋ] 1 *n* robo *m*
2 *adj* ladrón(ona); *Fam* **keep your t. hands off my piece of cake!** ¡las manos quietas, que ese trozo de tarta es mío!

thigh [θaɪ] *n* muslo *m*

thighbone ['θaɪbəʊn] *n* fémur *m*

thigh-length ['θaɪleŋθ] *adj (dress)* corto(a); **a t. coat** un chaquetón ▸▸ ***t. boots*** botas *fpl* altas (de medio muslo)

thimble ['θɪmbəl] *n* dedal *m*

thimbleful ['θɪmbəlfʊl] *n* dedal *m*, chorrito *m*; **just a t. of whisky for me, please** para mí un dedito *or* una gotita de whisky, por favor

thin [θɪn] 1 *adj* (**a**) *(not thick) (slice, layer, wire)* fino(a), delgado(a); *(blanket, clothing)* ligero(a), fino(a); *(carpet)* fino(a), poco grueso(a); **my jacket is wearing t. at the elbows** me empiezan a clarear los codos de la chaqueta, tengo los codos de la chaqueta muy desgastados
(**b**) *(not fat) (person, face, arm)* delgado(a); *(lips)* fino(a), delgado(a); **to get** *or* **grow** *or* **become thinner** *(person)* adelgazar
(**c**) *(sparse) (hair, beard)* ralo(a), escaso(a); *(crowd, vegetation)* escaso(a), disperso(a); *Fam* **he's getting a bit t. on top** se está quedando calvo
(**d**) *(fog, mist)* ligero(a), tenue; **the higher up the mountain you go, the thinner the air gets** cuanto más se asciende por la montaña, más se enrarece el aire
(**e**) *(soup)* claro(a); *(paint, sauce)* aguado(a), de consistencia líquida
(**f**) *(voice, sound)* flojo(a), apagado(a)
(**g**) *(feeble) (smile)* desganado(a), tibio(a); *(excuse, argument)* pobre, endeble; *(storyline, plot)* flojo(a), endeble
(**h**) *(profits)* escaso(a), exiguo(a)
(**i**) IDIOMS **to be as t. as a rake** estar como un *or* hecho(a) un palillo; **he had vanished into t. air** había desaparecido como por arte de magia; **she managed to conjure a meal out of t. air** se las apañó para hacer una comida prácticamente de la nada; **they saw this demand as the t. end of the wedge** consideraron que esta demanda era sólo el principio (y luego pedirían más); **to have a t. skin** ser muy susceptible; **to have a t. time (of it)** estar en horas bajas; **to be t. on the ground** *(scarce)* ser escaso(a)
2 *adv* **to slice sth t.** cortar algo en rodajas finas; **to spread sth t.** *(butter, jam)* untar una capa fina de algo; **our resources are spread very t.** nuestros recursos se hallan demasiado repartidos
3 *vt* (*pt & pp* **thinned**) (**a**) *(sauce)* aclarar, aguar; *(paint)* diluir, aclarar (**b**) *(plants)* aclarar, entresacar
4 *vi (crowd)* dispersarse; *(fog, mist)* despejarse; **his hair is thinning** está empezando a perder pelo

▸ **thin down** 1 *vt sep (sauce)* aclarar, aguar; *(paint)* diluir, aclarar
2 *vi (person)* adelgazar

▸ **thin out** 1 *vt sep (plants)* aclarar, entresacar
2 *vi (traffic)* disminuir; *(crowd)* dispersarse; *(trees)* hacerse menos denso(a); **my hair is starting to t. out** estoy empezando a quedarme calvo *or* perder pelo

thine [ðaɪn] *Literary & Rel* 1 *adj* tu
2 *pron (singular)* tuyo(a) *m,f*; *(plural)* tuyos(as) *m,fpl*

THING [θɪŋ] *n* (**a**) *(object)* cosa *f*; *Fam* **what's that t.?** ¿qué es eso *or* ese chisme *or CAm, Carib, Col* esa vaina *or RP* esa cosa?; **I don't like sweet things** no me gusta el dulce; **he kept his painting things in a box** guardaba sus cosas de pintar en una caja; **let's wash up the breakfast things** vamos a lavar las cosas *or Esp* los cacharros *or Andes, CAm, Carib, Méx* los trastes del desayuno; *Fam* **we need one of those modem things** necesitamos un módem de esos *or RP* uno de esos módems; **my/your things** *(clothes)* mi/tu ropa; *(belongings)* mis/tus cosas; **he bought me a spade, of all things!** me regaló una pala, ¡tiene cada ocurrencia!; **to be just the t.** *or* **the very t.** venir de perlas *or* como anillo al dedo; IDIOM *Hum* **things that go bump in the night** fantasmas, *RP* mengues

(**b**) *(action, remark, fact)* cosa *f*; **that's a t. I very rarely do** eso es algo que yo casi nunca hago; **a terrible t. has happened** ha ocurrido algo terrible; **that was a nice t. to do/say!** ¡qué amable!; **that was a silly t. to do/say** hacer/decir eso fue una tontería; **the things you say!** ¡qué cosas dices!; **of all the stupid things to do!** ¡a quién se le ocurre hacer una cosa así!; **it's not an easy t. to do** no es fácil de hacer, no es fácil hacerlo; **the important t. is that...** lo importante es que...; **the first/next t. we need to do is...** lo primero/lo siguiente que tenemos que hacer es...; **it's the only t. we can do** es lo único que podemos hacer; **he did the right/wrong t.** hizo lo que debía/lo que no debía; **let's forget the whole t.** olvidémoslo, dejémoslo así; **the t. to do/realize is...** lo que hay que hacer/entender es...; **the t. that annoys me is...** lo que me da rabia es...; *Fam* **he's obsessed with this abseiling t.** está obsesionado con eso del rappel; **and another t., why were you late?** y, otra cosa, ¿por qué llegaste tarde?; **that's quite another t.** *or* **another t. altogether** eso es algo completamente distinto; **it's the done t. to curtsy** se hace una reverencia, hay que hacer una reverencia; **smoking at work isn't the done t.** en el trabajo no se fuma; **that's now a t. of the past** eso ha pasado a la historia; **it's just one of those things** son cosas que pasan; **all things considered,** *Br* **taking one t. with another** teniendo todo en cuenta; **all (other) things being equal** en condiciones normales; **in all things** siempre, en toda ocasión; *Fam* **they tortured us and things** nos torturaron y eso; **for one t.** para empezar; **if there's one t. you should avoid...** lo que hay que evitar a toda costa...; **it's one t. to admire him, quite another to vote for him** una cosa es admirarlo y otra muy distinta votar por él; **what with one t. and another** entre unas cosas y otras; **it's been one t. after another** *(we've been busy)* no hemos parado; *(we've had lots of problems)* hemos tenido miles de problemas; **if it's not one t. it's another** cuando no es una cosa, es otra; **the t. is...** el caso es que..., lo que pasa es que...; **the t. about** *or* **with her is...** lo que pasa con ella es que...; **you're imagining things** eso son imaginaciones *or RP* ideas tuyas; **to know a t. or two (about)** saber bastante (de); **I could teach** *or* **show him a t. or two (about)** a ése podría enseñarle yo unas cuantas cosas (de); **there's no need to make a (big) t. out of** *or* **about it** no es para tanto, no hay que darle tanta importancia; **let's take one t. at a time** tomémonos las cosas con calma, vamos por partes, *RP* despacito por las piedras

(**c**) **things** *(situation)* las cosas; **things are going badly** las cosas van mal; **the way things are at the moment** tal y como están las cosas; *Fam* **how are things (with you)?, how's things?** ¿qué tal van las cosas?, ¿cómo te va?; **things aren't what they used to be** las cosas ya no son lo que eran; **I can make things difficult/easy for you if...** te puedo hacer la vida imposible/más fácil si...; **you take things too seriously** te tomas las cosas demasiado en serio; **I feel rather out of things** me siento un poco perdido

(**d**) *(anything)* **they didn't eat a t.** no comieron nada; **I don't have a t. to wear** no tengo qué *or* nada que ponerme; **she hadn't got a t. on** no llevaba nada puesto; **she didn't say/couldn't see a t.** no dijo/veía nada; **I don't know a t. about algebra** no tengo ni idea de álgebra; **I didn't understand a t. she said** no entendí ni jota de lo que dijo; **it doesn't mean a t. to me** *(I don't understand it, I don't recognize it)* no me dice nada; *(it doesn't matter to me)* ni me va ni me viene; **there isn't a t. we can do about it** no podemos hacer nada

(**e**) *Fam (person, animal)* **(the) poor t.!** ¡(el) pobre!; **she's a clever little t.** es una chica muy lista; **there wasn't a living t. around** no había ni un ser vivo; **you lucky t.!** ¡vaya suerte que tienes!; **you silly t.!** ¡qué bobo(a) eres!

(**f**) *(monster)* cosa *f*, monstruo *m*

(**g**) *Fam (strong feelings)* **she has a t. about...** *(likes)* le encanta..., *Esp* le mola cantidad *or* le priva..., *RP* le copa pila...; *(dislikes)* le tiene manía a..., *RP* la mata...; **she's got a t. about tidiness/punctuality** es muy maniática con la limpieza/puntualidad; **it's a bit of a t. with me** es una manía mía

(**h**) *(fashion)* **the latest t. in shoes** lo último en zapatos; **these hats are quite the t. at the moment** estos sombreros están muy de moda

(**i**) *(interest)* **classical music is my t.** lo mío es la música clásica; **she usually does her own t.** normalmente va a *or* se ocupa de lo suyo

(**j**) *(relationship)* **to have a t. (going) with sb** estar liado(a) con alguien

(**k**) *Fam (penis)* pito *m*, cola *f*, *Chile* pico *m*, *Méx* pájaro *m*

thingumabob [ˈθɪŋəmɪbɒb], **thingumajig** [ˈθɪŋəmɪdʒɪg], **thingummy** [ˈθɪŋəmɪ], **thingy** [ˈθɪŋɪ] *n Fam (object)* chisme *m*, *CAm, Carib, Col* vaina *f*, *RP* coso *m*; *(person)* fulanito(a) *m,f*, mengano(a) *m,f*

THINK [θɪŋk] **1** *n* **to have a t. about sth** pensarse algo; **I'll have a t. and let you know tomorrow** me lo pensaré y te lo diré mañana; IDIOM *Fam* **you've got another t. coming!** ¡estás muy equivocado!

2 *vt (pt & pp* **thought** [θɔːt]) (**a**) *(have in mind)* **to t. (that)...** pensar que...; **what are you thinking?** ¿en qué estás pensando?; **to t. evil/kind thoughts** tener pensamientos malévolos/benévolos; **"what an idiot," I thought (to myself)** "menudo idiota", pensé (para mis adentros); **I kept thinking "why me?"** no dejaba de preguntarme "¿por qué yo?"; **let me t. what I can do to help** a ver (que piense) cómo podría ayudar; **I can't t. what his name is** no recuerdo ahora cómo se llama; **I can't t. who could have done it** no se me ocurre quién puede haberlo hecho; **did you t. to bring any money?** ¿se te ha ocurrido traer algo de dinero?

(**b**) *(believe, have as opinion)* creer, pensar; **to t. (that)...** creer que...; **he thinks (that) he knows everything** se cree que lo sabe todo; **I thought I heard a noise** me pareció haber oído un ruido; **I t. (that) I'll have a nap** creo que me voy a echar una siesta; **do you t. (that) I could borrow your bike?** ¿me prestas tu bici?; **more tea? – I don't t. I will, thank you** ¿más té? – la verdad es que no, gracias; **I thought we could maybe watch a movie** ¿qué te parece la idea de ver una película?; **she's upstairs, I t.** creo que está arriba; **all this is very sad, don't you t.?** todo esto es muy triste, ¿no crees?; **what do you t., should I accept?** ¿tú qué crees?, ¿debería aceptar?; **I don't know what to t.** no sé qué pensar; **what will people t.?** ¿qué va a pensar la gente?; **that's what YOU t.!** eso es lo que tú te crees; **I t. so** creo que sí; **I t. not** no creo; **he hadn't arrived, or so I thought** no había llegado, o así lo creía yo; **I thought so, I thought as much** ya me lo figuraba; **we'll be there by nine, I should t.** yo creo que estaremos allí a las nueve; **I should t. so** me parece que sí; **I shouldn't t. so** no creo; **anyone would t. she was asleep** cualquiera hubiera creído que está dormida; **what do you t. you are doing?** pero, ¿qué haces?; **who does she t. she's kidding?** ¿a quién pretende engañar?; **who do you t. you are?** ¿quién te has creído que eres?; **I thought it (to be) a bit expensive** me pareció un poco caro; **we t. the rule unfair** creemos que la norma es injusta; **I t. it important to remember that...** considero importante recordar que...; **do you t. me a fool?** ¿me tomas por tonto?; **it is thought that...** se cree que...; **he is thought to have escaped through the window** se cree que escapó por una ventana; **they were thought to be rich** se les creía *or* consideraba ricos

(**c**) *(imagine)* imaginarse; **t. what we could do with all that money!** ¡imagínate lo que podríamos hacer con todo ese dinero!; **I (really) can't t. what/where/why...** no se me ocurre qué/dónde/por qué...; **it's better than I had thought possible** es mejor de lo que creía posible; **who'd have thought it!** ¡quién lo hubiera pensado!; **to t. (that) he's only twenty!** ¡y pensar que sólo tiene veinte años!

(**d**) *(expect)* creer, esperarse; **it was easier than I thought** fue más fácil de lo que creía *or* me esperaba; **I didn't t. to find you here** no esperaba encontrarte aquí; *Formal* **I little thought I would see him again** no podía imaginar que lo volvería a ver; **you'd t.** *or* **you would have thought they'd have waited!** ¡podían haber esperado!; **I should t. so too!** ¡faltaría más!

(**e**) *(taking as theme)* **designers are thinking pink this season** los diseñadores apuestan por el rosa esta temporada

3 *vi* pensar; **let me t....** déjame que piense..., a ver...; **I did it without thinking** lo hice sin darme cuenta; **sorry, I didn't t.** *or* **wasn't thinking** perdona, no me di cuenta; **you just don't t., do you!** *(are inconsiderate, careless)* ¡es que haces las cosas sin pensar!; **she has to learn to t. for herself** tiene que aprender a pensar por sí misma; **we would ask you to t. again** le pediríamos que reconsiderase su decisión; **if you t. I'll help you do it, you can t. again!** ¡vas listo si crees que te voy a ayudar!; **to t. ahead** planear con anticipación; **to t. aloud** pensar en voz alta; **she thinks as I do** piensa igual que yo; **do as you t. best** haz lo que te parezca mejor; **I was going to protest, but thought better of it** iba a protestar, pero después lo pensé mejor; *Fam* **to t. big** ser ambicioso(a); **to t. on one's feet** improvisar, discurrir sobre la marcha; **to t. (long and) hard about sth** pensarse algo muy bien; **I wasn't thinking straight** no estaba yo en mis cabales; **it makes you t.** da que pensar; **just t., you might have married him!** imagínatelo, ¡podrías haber acabado casándote con él!; *Ironic* **oh, he's so honest, (and) I don't t.!** sí, honesto, y un cuerno; IDIOM **I could hardly** *or* **couldn't hear myself t.** el ruido era ensordecedor

▸ **think about** *vt insep* (**a**) *(consider, reflect upon)* pensar en; **to t. about a problem** reflexionar sobre un problema; **to t. about doing sth** pensar en hacer algo; **it's not a bad idea, if** *or* **when you t. about it** bien mirado, no es mala idea; **it's quite cheap when you t. about it** si lo piensas bien, sale bastante barato; **thinking about it, you may be right** ahora que lo pienso, puede que tengas razón; **I'll t. about it** me lo pensaré; **all she ever thinks about is men** sólo piensa en los hombres; **I'd t. twice** *or* **again about that, if I were you** yo, en tu lugar, me lo pensaría dos veces; **that will give them something to t. about** eso les dará qué pensar

(**b**) *(take into account)* tener en cuenta; **I've got my family to t. about** debo tener en cuenta a mi familia

(**c**) *(have opinion about)* opinar de, pensar de; **what do you t. about my new dress?** ¿qué te parece mi vestido nuevo?

▸ **think back** *vi* **thinking back** *or* **when I t. back, I don't know how I managed** la verdad es que no sé cómo pude hacerlo; **to t. back to sth** recordar algo

▸ **think of** **1** *vt insep* (**a**) *(consider, reflect upon)* **come to t. of it, I DID see her that night** ahora que caigo *or* que lo pienso, sí que la vi aquella noche; **just t. of it... a holiday in the Caribbean!** ¡imagínate... unas vacaciones en el Caribe!; **when I t. of what might have happened!** cuando pienso en lo que podría haber pasado; **I wouldn't t. of it!** ¡jamás se me ocurriría!

(**b**) *(have in mind)* pensar en; **to t. of doing sth** pensar en hacer algo; **what were you thinking of giving her?** ¿qué estabas pensando regalarle?; **what (on earth) were you thinking of when you said that?** ¿cómo (demonios) se te ocurrió decir una cosa así?

(**c**) *(take into account)* pensar en, tener en cuenta; **I have my family to t. of** tengo que mirar por *or* pensar en mi familia; **you've thought of everything!** ¡has pensado en todo!; **I can't t. of everything!** ¡no puedo ocuparme de *or* estar en todo!

(**d**) *(recall)* recordar; **I can't t. of the answer** no se me ocurre cuál es la respuesta

(**e**) *(find, come up with) (idea, solution, excuse, name)* **t. of a number** piensa un número; **try every method you can t. of** prueba todos los métodos que se te ocurran; **I can't t. of anyone who could help** no se me ocurre quién podría ayudar; **I hadn't thought of that** no se me había ocurrido; **whatever will they t. of next!** ¡qué se les ocurrirá ahora!

(**f**) *(have opinion about)* opinar de, pensar de; **what do you t. of my new dress?** ¿qué te parece mi vestido nuevo?; **to t. well/badly of sb** tener buena/mala opinión de alguien; **I told her what I thought of her** le dije lo que pensaba de ella; **as a doctor she is very well thought of** como doctora está muy bien considerada; **I t. of you as a friend** te considero un amigo; **he thinks of himself as an artist** se tiene a sí mismo por artista; **I t. of it as my duty** lo considero mi obligación

2 *vt sep* **I try to t. the best of people** trato de ver el lado bueno de la gente; **I t. an awful lot of you** me pareces una persona fantástica; **to t. a great deal of oneself, to t. too much of oneself** tener mucha autoestima; **I don't t. much of the idea** la idea no me parece muy buena; **I didn't t. much of her behaviour** su comportamiento no me pareció nada bien

▸ **think out** *vt sep* meditar; **their strategy has been well thought out** han meditado mucho su estrategia; **he likes to t. things out for himself** prefiere formarse sus propias opiniones

▸ **think over** *vt sep* reflexionar sobre, pensar sobre; **I'll t. it over** me lo pensaré; **I need some time to t. things over** necesito tiempo para reflexionar

▸ **think through** *vt sep* pensar *or* meditar bien; **the scheme has not been properly thought through** no han reflexionado lo suficiente respecto al proyecto

▸ **think up** *vt sep* idear; *(excuse)* inventar; **where did you get that idea? – I just thought it up** ¿de dónde has sacado esa idea? – se me ocurrió así por las buenas

---

thinkable ['θɪŋkəbəl] *adj* **it is scarcely** *or* **barely t. that...** resulta poco menos que inimaginable *or* inconcebible que...

thinker ['θɪŋkə(r)] *n* pensador(ora) *m,f*

thinking ['θɪŋkɪŋ] **1** *n* (**a**) *(process of thought)* pensamiento *m*; **to do some t.** pensar un poco; **I've done some serious** *or* **hard t. about the situation** he pensado *or* reflexionado detenidamente sobre la situación; **his life was saved thanks to the nurse's quick t.** la rapidez de ideas de la enfermera le salvó la vida; **good t.!** ¡buena idea!, ¡bien pensado!

(**b**) *(opinion)* opinión *f*, parecer *m*; **the government's current t. on this issue** la postura *or* línea actual del gobierno en lo referente a este asunto; **to my (way of) t....** en mi opinión...; **she finally came round to my way of t.** terminó siendo de la misma opinión *or* pensando igual que yo

2 *adj (person)* inteligente, con cerebro; **the t. man's cover girl** una belleza con cerebro; **the novel is the t. man's answer to pulp fiction** la novela es la réplica intelectual a la literatura de consumo; IDIOM **to put on one's t. cap** estrujarse el cerebro, devanarse los sesos

think-tank ['θɪŋktæŋk] *n* grupo *m* de expertos, equipo *m* de cerebros

thin-lipped ['θɪn'lɪpt] *adj (person)* de labios finos; **she looked at him in t. disapproval** lo miró frunciendo los labios en un gesto de desaprobación

thinly ['θɪnlɪ] *adv* (**a**) *(in thin amounts)* **to spread sth t.** extender una capa fina de algo; **to slice sth t.** cortar algo en rodajas finas (**b**) *(not densely)* **t. populated** escasamente poblado(a) (**c**) *(to smile)* con desgana, tibiamente (**d**) *(poorly)* **t. disguised** *(criticism, description)* sin tapujos; *(emotions)* apenas disimulado(a)

thinner ['θɪnə(r)] *n* disolvente *m*

thinness ['θɪnnɪs] *n* (**a**) *(of slice, layer, wire)* finura *f*, delgadez *f*; *(of blanket, clothing)* ligereza *f*; *(of carpet)* poco grosor *m*

(**b**) *(of person, face, arms)* delgadez *f*; *(of lips)* finura *f*, delgadez *f*

(**c**) *(of hair, beard)* escasez *f*; *(of crowd, vegetation)* escasez *f*

(**d**) *(of fog, mist)* poca densidad *f*; *(of air)* enrarecimiento *m*

(**e**) *(of soup)* fluidez *f*; *(of paint, sauce)* consistencia *f* líquida

(**f**) *(of voice, sound)* falta *f* de fuerza, flojedad *f*

(**g**) *(of smile)* desgana *f*, tibieza *f*; *(of excuse, argument)* pobreza *f*, endeblez *f*; *(of storyline, plot)* endeblez *f*, falta *f* de solidez

thin-skinned ['θɪn'skɪnd] *adj* **to be t.** ser muy susceptible

third [θɜːd] **1** *n* (**a**) *(fraction)* tercio *m*; **two thirds of the Earth's surface/the people surveyed** dos tercios *or* dos terceras partes de la superficie terrestre/los encuestados

(**b**) *(in series)* tercero(a) *m,f*; **Edward the T.** *(written)* Eduardo III; *(spoken)* Eduardo tercero

(**c**) *(of month)* tres *m*; **the t. of May** el tres de mayo; **we're leaving on the t.** nos vamos el (día) tres

(**d**) *Mus* tercera *f*

(**e**) *Aut (third gear)* tercera *f*; **in t.** en tercera

(**f**) *Br Univ* **to get a t.** *(in degree)* = licenciarse con la nota mínima en la escala de calificaciones

(**g**) *Sport (of pitch)* tercio *m* (del terreno de juego)

2 *adj* tercero(a); *(before masculine singular noun)* tercer; **the t. century** el siglo tercero *or* tres; **I was t. in the race** llegué el tercero en la carrera; IDIOM *Fam* **to give sb the t. degree** someter a alguien a un duro interrogatorio; PROV **t. time lucky** a la tercera va la vencida ▸▸ ***the T. Age*** la tercera edad, los ancianos; *Med* ***t. degree burns*** quemaduras *fpl* de tercer grado; ***t. estate*** estado *m* llano, tercer estado *m*; *Aut* ***t. gear*** tercera *f* (marcha *f*); *Law* ***t. party*** tercero *m*; ***t. party cover*** seguro *m* a terceros; ***t. party insurance*** seguro *m* a terceros; *Gram* ***t. person*** tercera persona *f*; **in the t. person** en tercera persona; ***t. quarter*** *(of financial year)* tercer trimestre *m*; *(of American football game)* tercer cuarto *m*; ***the T. Reich*** el tercer Reich; *Br Pol* ***the T. Way*** la tercera vía; ***the T. World*** el Tercer Mundo

3 *adv (thirdly)* en tercer lugar, tercero

third-class [θɜːd'klɑːs] **1** *adj* (**a**) *US* **t. mail** = clase económica de correo que se emplea sobre todo para enviar publicidad (**b**) *Formerly (ticket, travel, seats)* de tercera (clase) (**c**) *Br Univ* **to get a t. degree** = licenciarse con la nota mínima en la escala de calificaciones (**d**) *Pej (inferior)* de tercera (clase)

2 *adv* (**a**) *US (mail)* = mediante la clase económica de correo que se emplea sobre todo para enviar publicidad (**b**) *Formerly (to travel)* en tercera (clase)

thirdly ['θɜːdlɪ] *adv* en tercer lugar

third-rate ['θɜːd'reɪt] *adj (mediocre)* de tercera (categoría)

third-world ['θɜːd'wɜːld] *adj* del tercer mundo, tercermundista

thirst [θɜːst] **1** *n* (**a**) *(for drink)* sed *f*; **all that hard work has given me a t.** con tanto trabajo me ha entrado sed (**b**) *(desire)* **the t. for knowledge** la sed de conocimientos

2 *vi* (**a**) *(for drink)* **he was thirsting for a beer** tenía unas ganas enormes de tomarse una cerveza (**b**) *(have desire) (for knowledge, revenge)* tener sed (**for** de)

thirstily ['θɜːstɪlɪ] *adv* con avidez

thirst-quenching ['θɜːstkwentʃɪŋ] *adj* **a t. drink** una bebida que quita la sed

thirsty ['θɜːstɪ] *adj* (**a**) *(for drink)* **to be t.** tener sed; **I feel very t.** tengo mucha sed, estoy sediento; **she felt t.** le entró sed; **salted peanuts make you t.** los cacahuetes salados dan mucha sed

(**b**) *(causing thirst)* **all this talking is t. work** tanto hablar da sed

(**c**) *(plant, soil)* necesitado(a) de agua, sediento(a); **those plants look t.** a esas plantas parece que les hace falta agua
(**d**) *(for knowledge, adventure, revenge)* sediento(a), ávido(a) (**for** de)
(**e**) *Fam (car)* **my motorbike is very t.** mi moto chupa mucha gasolina

thirteen [θɜː'tiːn] **1** *n* trece *m*
2 *adj* trece; *see also* **eight**

thirteenth [θɜː'tiːnθ] **1** *n* (**a**) *(fraction)* treceavo *m*, treceava parte *f* (**b**) *(in series)* decimotercero(a) *m,f* (**c**) *(of month)* trece *m*
2 *adj* decimotercero(a); *(before masculine singular noun)* decimotercer; *see also* **eleventh**

thirties ['θɜːtiːz] *npl* **the t.** los (años) treinta; *see also* **eighties**

thirtieth ['θɜːtɪɪθ] **1** *n* (**a**) *(fraction)* treceavo *m*, treceava parte *f* (**b**) *(in series)* trigésimo(a) *m,f* (**c**) *(of month)* treinta *m*; **(on) the t. of May** el treinta de mayo; **we're leaving on the t.** nos vamos el (día) treinta
2 *adj* trigésimo(a)

thirty ['θɜːtɪ] **1** *n* treinta *m*
2 *adj* treinta; *see also* **eighty**

thirty-first ['θɜːtɪ'fɜst] **1** *n* (**a**) *(in series)* trigésimo(a) *m,f* primero(a) (**b**) *(of month)* treinta y uno *m*
2 *adj* trigésimo(a) primero(a); *(before masculine singular noun)* trigésimo primer

thirty-one ['θɜːtɪ'wʌn] **1** *n* treinta y uno *m*
2 *adj* treinta y uno(a); *(before masculine noun)* treinta y un

thirty-second note [θɜːtɪ'sekənd'nəʊt] *n US Mus* fusa *f*

thirty-something ['θɜːtɪ'sʌmθɪŋ] *n* = persona treintañera con un buen empleo y una buena posición económica

THIS [ðɪs] **1** *demonstrative adj* (*pl* **these** [ðiːz]) este(a); **t. one** éste(a); **t. book** este libro; **t. question** esta pregunta; **t. book here** este libro de aquí; **I saw him t. morning** lo vi esta mañana; **the meeting is t. Tuesday** la reunión es este martes; **stop that t. instant!** ¡para ahora mismo!; **by t. time, it was already too late** para entonces ya era demasiado tarde; *Fam* **t. leg of mine is killing me!** ¡esta pierna me está matando!; *Fam* **I met t. German** conocí a un tipo alemán; *Fam* **he used to wear t. funny hat** llevaba *or Am* usaba siempre un sombrero muy raro
2 *demonstrative pron* (*pl* **these**) éste(a); *(indefinite)* esto; **what's t.?** ¿qué es esto?; **who's t.?** ¿quién es éste?; **t. is Jason Wallace** *(introducing another person)* te presento a Jason Wallace; *(introducing self on telephone)* soy Jason Wallace; *(said by news reporter)* **t. is Jason Wallace for CNN** Jason Wallace para la CNN; **t. is Radio Four** Radio Cuatro; **t. is ridiculous!** ¡esto es ridículo!; **t. is what she told me** eso es lo que ella me dijo; **t. is where I live** aquí es donde vivo, vivo aquí; **t. is why I'm worried** por eso estoy preocupado; **t. is it!** *(when arriving somewhere)* ¡ya estamos aquí!, *Am* ¡llegamos!; *(before doing sth)* ¡ha llegado el momento de la verdad!; *(expressing agreement)* ¡exacto!; **is t. all the luggage you're taking?** ¿es éste todo el equipaje que llevas?; **listen to t.** escucha esto; **drink some of t.** toma un poco (de esto); **what's (all) t. I hear about you resigning?** ¿qué es eso de que vas a dimitir?; **they seem disappointed... why is t.?** parecen decepcionados, ¿por qué será?; **at t., he started laughing** entonces *or* ante esto empezó a reírse; **we had expected to finish before t.** esperábamos terminar antes; **I've got some gloves like t.** tengo unos guantes como estos; **do it like t.** hazlo así; **in a case like t.** en un caso así; *Fam* **we talked about t. and that** *or* **t., that and the other** hablamos de todo un poco
3 *adv* **t. high/far** tan alto/lejos; *(gesturing with hands)* así de alto/lejos; **about t. much** más o menos así; **it was t. much bigger** era un tanto así más grande; **t. much is certain...** esto es cierto *or* seguro...; **I can tell you t. much...** una cosa es segura...

thistle ['θɪsəl] *n* cardo *m*

thistledown ['θɪsəldaʊn] *n* vilano *m* (de cardo)

thither ['ðɪðə(r)] *adv Literary* allá; **to run hither and t.** correr de aquí para allá

thitherto [ðɪðə'tuː] *adv Literary* hasta entonces

tho' [ðəʊ] = **though**

thole [θəʊl], **tholepin** ['θəʊlpɪn] *n* tolete *m*, escálamo *m*

thong [θɒŋ] *n* (**a**) *(for fastening)* correa *f* (**b**) *(underwear, swimming costume)* tanga *m* (**c**) *Austr, US (sandal)* chancleta *f*, chancla *f*

thoracic [θɔ'ræsɪk] *adj Anat* torácico(a)

thorax ['θɔːræks] *n Anat* tórax *m inv*

thorium ['θɔːrɪəm] *n Chem* torio *m*

thorn [θɔːn] *n* (**a**) *(prickle)* espina *f*; *Fig* **to be a t. in sb's flesh** *or* **side** no dar tregua a alguien ►► ***t. apple*** estramonio *m* (**b**) *(tree, shrub)* espino *m*, zarza *f*

thornback ['θɔːnbæk] *n* raya *f* (de clavos) *(pez)*

thornbill ['θɔːnbɪl] *n* colibrí *m* pico espina

thornbush ['θɔːnbʊʃ] *n* espino *m*, zarza *f*

thorny ['θɔːnɪ] *adj* (**a**) *(plant, bush)* espinoso(a) (**b**) *(problem, issue)* espinoso(a)

thorough ['θʌrə] *adj* (**a**) *(search, work)* minucioso(a), concienzudo(a); *(worker)* meticuloso(a), concienzudo(a); *(cross-examination, revision)* exhaustivo(a), a fondo; *(knowledge)* profundo(a); **to give sth a t. cleaning** limpiar algo a fondo *or* a conciencia; **to do** *or* **make a t. job of it** hacerlo con mucho esmero; **they were given a t. telling-off** les cayó una buena reprimenda
(**b**) *(for emphasis)* **a t. scoundrel** un perfecto canalla; **what a t. bore this book is!** ¡este libro es un auténtico *or* verdadero tostón!; **to make a t. nuisance of oneself** ponerse de lo más pesado(a)

thoroughbred ['θʌrəbred] **1** *n* (**a**) *(horse)* purasangre *m* (**b**) *(person)* fuera de serie *mf*, superclase *mf*
2 *adj* (**a**) *(horse)* purasangre (**b**) *(person)* nato(a), fuera de serie

thoroughfare ['θʌrəfeə(r)] *n* vía *f* (pública); **no t.** *(sign) (no entry)* prohibido el paso; *(cul-de-sac)* calle sin salida

thoroughgoing ['θʌrəgəʊɪŋ] *adj (search, revision, inspection)* minucioso(a), concienzudo(a); *(knowledge)* profundo(a); *(selfishness)* puro(a); **he's a t. nuisance** es un auténtico *or* verdadero pelmazo

thoroughly ['θʌrəlɪ] *adv* (**a**) *(with care, in detail) (to search, work)* minuciosamente, concienzudamente; *(to cross-examine, revise)* exhaustivamente, a fondo; *(to clean, rinse, wash)* a fondo, bien; *(to mix)* bien; **make sure the meat is t. cooked** asegúrate de que la carne esté *or* quede bien hecha; **read all the questions t.** lea detenidamente *or* con atención todas las preguntas
(**b**) *(entirely)* completamente; **it's t. disgraceful** es una auténtica vergüenza *or* un verdadero escándalo; **I can t. recommend it** lo recomiendo de todo corazón; **I t. enjoyed myself** (me) lo pasé estupendamente

thoroughness ['θʌrənɪs] *n (of search, work)* minuciosidad *f*; *(of worker)* meticulosidad *f*; *(of cross-examination, revision)* exhaustividad *f*; *(of knowledge)* profundidad *f*

THOSE [ðəʊz] (*plural of* **that**) **1** *adj* esos(as); *(further away)* aquellos(as); **t. ones** ésos(as); *(further away)* aquéllos(as); **t. ones over there** aquellos de allí *or esp Am* allá; **t. men in front of you** esos hombres que están delante de ti; **t. men right at the back** aquellos hombres del fondo; **t. parcels that were at the bottom of the bag got crushed** los paquetes del fondo de la bolsa se aplastaron; *Fam* **t. sisters of yours are nothing but trouble** esas hermanas tuyas no dan más que problemas; *Fam* **how are t. eyes of yours?** ¿cómo van esos ojos?
2 *pron* ésos(as); *(further away)* aquéllos(as); **t. over there** aquéllos de allá; **t. are my children over there** aquéllos de allá son mis hijos; **what are t.?** ¿qué son esos?; **t. requiring assistance should stay here** los que *or* quienes necesiten ayuda, que se queden aquí; **there are t. who believe that...** los hay que creen *or* piensan que...; **I'm not one of t. who** no soy de los que...; **their leader was amongst t. killed** su jefe se encontraba entre los fallecidos; **the hardest years were t. after the war** los años más duros fueron los que siguieron a la guerra; **I've got some gloves like t.** tengo unos guantes como esos; *Formal* **floods like t. of ten years ago** (unas) inundaciones como las de hace diez años; **t. of us who remember the war** aquéllos *or* los que recordamos la guerra; **t. of us who were present** los que estuvimos presentes; **t. were the days** ¡qué tiempos aquellos!

thou[1] [ðaʊ] *pron* (**a**) *Literary* tú (**b**) *Rel* tú

thou[2] [θaʊ] *n Fam* (*abbr* **thousand**) mil del ala

though [ðəʊ] **1** *conj* aunque; **t. young, she's very mature** aunque joven *or* a pesar de su juventud, es muy madura; **it's an excellent book, t. I say so myself** es un libro excelente, aunque no esté bien que yo lo diga; **kind t. she was, we never really got on** aunque era muy amable, nunca nos llevamos bien; **strange t. it may seem** aunque parezca raro; **even t. you'll laugh at me** aunque te rías de mí; **as t.** como si
2 *adv* **it's nice, t., isn't it?** pero está bueno, ¿no?; **he's not very clever – he's rich, t.** no es muy listo – pero es rico; *Fam* **did she like it? – did she t.!** ¿le gustó? – ¡ya lo creo que le gustó!

thought [θɔːt] **1** *n* (**a**) *(act of thinking)* pensamiento *m*; **he hadn't given my proposal a single t.** no había pensado en mi propuesta ni por un momento; **I didn't give it another** *or* **a second t.** no me lo pensé dos veces; **don't give it another t.** no lo pienses más, no le des más vueltas; **without a t. for his own safety** sin reparar *or* sin pararse a pensar en su propia seguridad; **his first t. was for her safety** lo primero que le preocupó era si le había pasado algo a ella; **my thoughts went back to the time I had spent in Tunisia** me vinieron a la mente recuerdos de la época que pasé en Túnez; **my thoughts were elsewhere** estaba pensando en otra cosa; **our thoughts are with you at this difficult time** pensamos mucho en ti en este difícil trance

(**b**) *(idea)* idea *f*; **the mere t. of it** sólo (de) pensar en ello; **I've had a t., why don't we have a party?** se me acaba de ocurrir una idea, ¿por qué no hacemos una fiesta?; **the t. had crossed my mind** ya se me había pasado por la cabeza; **that's** *or* **there's a t.!** ¡qué buena idea!; **it's quite a t.!** *(pleasant)* ¡sería genial!; *(unpleasant)* ¡sería horrible!; **that's a nice** *or* **happy t.** ¡qué gusto (de sólo pensar en ello)!; **what a kind t.!** ¡qué detalle tan amable!; **it's just a t., but what if we went tomorrow instead?** sólo es una idea, pero ¿y si (en lugar de eso) vamos mañana?; **I can't bear the t. that...** no puedo soportar la idea de que..., no soporto pensar que...; **the t. occurred to me that you might like to come** se me ocurrió que tal vez quisieras venir

(**c**) *(reflection)* reflexión *f*; **a decision that requires careful t.** una decisión que merece cierta reflexión; **are animals capable of t.?** ¿tienen capacidad de raciocinio *or* son capaces de razonar los animales?; **after much t.** tras mucho reflexionar; **to give a great deal of t. to sth** reflexionar mucho sobre algo; **I've never given the matter much t.** nunca me he parado a pensar en el asunto; **we gave some t. to the matter** reflexionamos sobre el asunto; **he just did it without giving any t. to the consequences** lo hizo sin pararse a pensar en las consecuencias; **she put a lot of t. into his present** se estuvo pensando mucho qué regalarle; **she was deep** *or* **lost in t.** estaba sumida en sus pensamientos ►► ***t. process*** proceso *m* mental

(**d**) *(opinion)* **what are your thoughts on the matter?** ¿qué es lo que piensas del asunto?; **she keeps her thoughts to herself** se calla lo que piensa, se reserva sus opiniones

(**e**) *(intention)* **I had no t. of offending you** no tenía intención de ofenderte; **her one t. was to reach the summit before nightfall** lo único que tenía en mente *or* su única idea era alcanzar la cima antes del anochecer; **you must give up all thought(s) of seeing him** olvida la idea de verlo; **it's the t. that counts** la intención es lo que cuenta

(**f**) *(doctrine, ideology)* pensamiento *m*; **according to contemporary political t.** según el pensamiento político contemporáneo

2 *pt & pp of* **think**

thoughtful ['θɔːtfʊl] *adj* (**a**) *(pensive) (person)* pensativo(a), meditabundo(a) (**b**) *(considerate)* considerado(a), atento(a); **it was very t. of them to send the flowers** fueron muy atentos al mandar flores, fue todo un detalle por su parte mandar flores (**c**) *(book)* serio(a), meditado(a); *(writer)* serio(a), reflexivo(a)

thoughtfully ['θɔːtfəlɪ] *adv* (**a**) *(pensively)* pensativamente, con aire pensativo *or* meditabundo (**b**) *(considerately)* consideradamente; **she very t. offered to help** tuvo la consideración *or* el detalle de ofrecer su ayuda (**c**) *(with careful thought)* **it's a t. written article** es un artículo muy serio *or* meditado

thoughtfulness ['θɔːtfʊlnɪs] *n* (**a**) *(consideration)* consideración *f*; **she was touched by his t. in remembering her birthday** le llegó al alma que tuviera el detalle de acordarse de su cumpleaños (**b**) *(pensiveness)* aire *m* pensativo *or* meditabundo (**c**) *(careful reasoning) (of book, writer)* seriedad *f*

thoughtless ['θɔːtlɪs] *adj* (**a**) *(inconsiderate)* desconsiderado(a); **that was really t. of her** fue una falta de consideración por su parte; **what a t. thing to do!** ¡qué poca consideración! (**b**) *(rash) (decision, action)* irreflexivo(a), precipitado(a); *(person)* irreflexivo(a), atropellado(a)

thoughtlessly ['θɔːtlɪslɪ] *adv* (**a**) *(inconsiderately)* desconsideradamente; **he very t. left the door locked** sin consideración alguna, dejó la puerta cerrada (**b**) *(rashly)* sin pensar, precipitadamente

thoughtlessness ['θɔːtlɪsnɪs] *n* (**a**) *(lack of consideration)* falta *f* de consideración, desconsideración *f* (**b**) *(rashness) (of decision, action, person)* irreflexión *f*, precipitación *f*

thought-out ['θɔːt'aʊt] *adj* **well/poorly t.** *(plan, scheme)* bien/mal meditado(a)

thought-provoking ['θɔːtprəvəʊkɪŋ] *adj* intelectualmente estimulante

thousand ['θaʊzənd] 1 *n* **a** *or* **one t.** mil; **three t.** tres mil; **in the year two t.** en el (año) dos mil *or* 2000; **a t. and one** mil uno; *Fig* **to have a t. and one things to do** tener mil cosas que hacer; **thousands of people** millares *or* miles de personas; **in thousands** a millares; *Fig* **she's one in a t.** hay pocas como ella

2 *adj* mil; *Fig* **I've told you a t. times** te lo he dicho mil veces *or* miles de veces; **a t. years** mil años ►► ***T. Island dressing*** salsa *f* rosa

thousandfold ['θaʊzəndfəʊld] 1 *adj* **a t. increase (in)** un aumento por mil (de)

2 *adv* por mil, mil veces; **to increase a t.** multiplicarse por mil

thousandth ['θaʊzənθ] 1 *n* (**a**) *(fraction)* milésima *f*, milésima parte *f* (**b**) *(in series)* milésimo(a) *m,f*

2 *adj* milésimo(a)

thraldom, *US* **thralldom** ['θrɔːldəm] *n Literary* esclavitud *f*, cautiverio *m*

thrall [θrɔːl] *n Literary* (**a**) *(state)* **to be in t. to sth/sb** ser esclavo(a) de algo/alguien; **to hold sb in t.** tener a alguien esclavizado(a) (**b**) *(person)* esclavo(a) *m,f*

thrash [θræʃ] 1 *vt* (**a**) *(hit)* golpear; *(as punishment)* dar una paliza a; **he threatened to t. us within an inch of our lives** nos amenazó con darnos una paliza que no olvidáramos en nuestra vida (**b**) *Fam (defeat)* dar una paliza a, vapulear (**c**) *(move vigorously)* **to t. one's arms/legs** agitar con violencia los brazos/las piernas (**d**) *Br Fam (car) Esp* conducir *or Am* manejar a lo bestia

2 *n* (**a**) *(music)* ***t. (metal)*** thrash *m* (**b**) *Br Fam (party)* fiestón *m*, jolgorio *m*

► **thrash about, thrash around** 1 *vt sep* **to t. one's arms and legs about** agitar con violencia los brazos y las piernas

2 *vi (move furiously)* agitarse *or* revolverse (con violencia)

► **thrash out** *vt sep* (**a**) *(agree on) (solution)* alcanzar por fin (**b**) *(try to agree on)* **they are still thrashing out an agreement** todavía están luchando por alcanzar un acuerdo

thrasher ['θræʃə(r)] *n (bird)* cuitlacoche *m*

thrashing ['θræʃɪŋ] *n* (**a**) *(beating)* **to give sb a t.** dar una paliza a alguien; **to get a t.** llevarse una paliza (**b**) *Fam (defeat)* paliza *f*; **to give sb a t.** dar una paliza a alguien; **to get a t.** recibir una paliza

thread [θred] 1 *n* (**a**) *(of cotton, nylon)* hilo *m*; **a (piece of) t.** un hilo; **polyester t.** hilo *or* fibra de poliéster; IDIOM **to hang by a t.** pender de un hilo

(**b**) *(of spider)* hilo *m*, hebra *f*

(**c**) *(of screw, bolt)* rosca *f*

(**d**) *(sequence) (of argument, reasoning)* hilo *m*; **to lose the t. of the conversation/of what one was saying** perder el hilo de la conversación/de lo que uno estaba diciendo; **she gradually began to pick up the threads of her life again** poco a poco comenzó a rehacer su vida

(**e**) *Comptr (in newsgroup)* hilo *m* de discusión

2 *vt* (**a**) *(needle)* enhebrar; *(beads)* ensartar; **she threaded the cotton through the needle** introdujo *or* ensartó el hilo de algodón por el agujero de la aguja, enhebró la aguja con el hilo de algodón; **you have to t. the elastic through the loops** hay que introducir *or* colar el elástico por las trabillas; **to t. one's way between the desks** avanzar sorteando las mesas; **he threaded a pass between the two central defenders** coló *or* introdujo un pase entre los dos centrales

(**b**) *(screw)* roscar

3 *vi (pass)* **the tape threads through the slot** la cinta se introduce por la ranura

threadbare ['θredbeə(r)] *adj* (**a**) *(clothes, carpet)* raído(a) (**b**) *(argument, joke)* trillado(a)

threads [θredz] *npl Fam (clothes)* trapos *mpl*; *(man's suit)* traje *m*

threadworm ['θredwɜːm] *n* lombriz *f* (intestinal), *Spec* oxiuro *m*

threat [θret] *n* amenaza *f*; **he's a t. to our society** es una amenaza para nuestra sociedad; **to make threats against sb** amenazar a alguien, lanzar amenazas contra alguien; **to be under t.** estar *or* verse amenazado(a)

threaten ['θretən] 1 *vt* (**a**) *(make threats against) (person)* amenazar; **the government threatened drastic measures** el gobierno amenazó con tomar medidas drásticas; **to t. to do sth** amenazar con hacer algo; **to t. sb with sth** amenazar a alguien con algo; **we were threatened with the sack** se nos amenazó con el despido *or* con despedirnos

(**b**) *(endanger)* amenazar, poner en peligro; **our jobs are threatened** nuestros empleos corren peligro; **the threatened strike didn't come off** la amenaza de huelga no se llevó a cabo; **the species is threatened with extinction** la especie está amenazada de extinción *or* en peligro de extinción; **the factory is threatened with closure** la fábrica corre peligro de cierre

(**c**) *(show signs of)* **it's threatening to snow** parece que va a nevar; **the election is threatening to become a farce** las elecciones amenazan con convertirse en una farsa

2 *vi (danger, storm)* amenazar

threatened ['θretənd] *adj* **to feel t. (by sb/sth)** sentirse amenazado(a) (por alguien/algo)

threatening ['θretənɪŋ] *adj (gesture, look, letter)* amenazador(ora), amenazante; *(behaviour)* intimidatorio(a); *(clouds, sky)* amenazador(ora), amenazante

threateningly ['θretənɪŋlɪ] *adv (to look)* con aire amenazador; *(to say)* en tono amenazador; *(to behave)* intimidatoriamente

three [θriː] 1 *n* tres *m inv*
2 *adj* tres; **t. cheers for...** tres hurras por... ►► ***the T. Kings*** los Reyes Magos; ***the t. Rs*** la lectura, la escritura y la aritmética; *US Fam* ***t. strikes law*** = ley que penaliza con cadena perpetua la comisión de un tercer delito grave; ***the T. Wise Men*** los Reyes Magos; *see also* **eight**

three-act ['θriːækt] *adj (play)* en tres actos

three-button mouse ['θriːbʌtən'maʊs] *n Comptr Esp* ratón *m or Am* mouse *m* de tres botones

three-card trick ['θriːkɑːd'trɪk] *n* trile(s) *m(pl) (con cartas)*

three-colour(ed), *US* **three-color(ed)** ['θriː'kʌləd] *adj* de tricromía, a tres tintas; **t. printing** tricromía

three-cornered ['θriː'kɔːnəd] *adj* triangular ►► ***t. hat*** sombrero *m* de tres picos

three-course meal ['θriːkɔːs'miːl] *n* comida *f* con primer y segundo platos, y postre

three-D ['θriː'diː] 1 *n* **in t.** en tres dimensiones
2 *adj* tridimensional, en 3-D

three-day event ['θriːdeɪə'vent] *n Sport* prueba *f or* concurso *m* de tres días

three-dimensional ['θriːdaɪ'menʃənəl] *adj* tridimensional

threefold ['θriːfəʊld] 1 *adj* triplicado(a); **a t. increase (in)** un aumento por tres (de)
2 *adv* por tres, tres veces; **to increase t.** triplicarse

three-legged ['θriː'legɪd] *adj (stool)* de tres patas ►► ***t. race*** = carrera por parejas con un pie atado

three-line whip ['θriːlaɪn'wɪp] *n Br Parl* = despacho enviado a un diputado por su portavoz de grupo en el que le recuerda la gran importancia de determinada votación y la obligatoriedad de su asistencia a la misma

threepence ['θrepəns] *n Br Formerly* tres peniques *mpl* (antiguos)

threepenny ['θrepənɪ] *adj Br Formerly (stamp)* de tres peniques (antiguos) ►► ***t. bit*** moneda *f* (antigua) de tres peniques; ***t. piece*** moneda *f* (antigua) de tres peniques

three-phase ['θriːfeɪz] *adj Elec* ***t. current*** corriente *f* trifásica

three-piece ['θriːpiːs] 1 *n (band)* trío *m*
2 *adj* ***t. band*** trío *m*; ***t. suit*** terno *m*; ***t. suite*** tresillo *m*, sofá *m* y dos sillones

three-pin ['θriːpɪn] *adj* ***t. plug*** enchufe *m* (macho) de tres clavijas *or* patillas

three-ply ['θriːplaɪ] 1 *n (wood)* contrachapado *m* de tres capas
2 *adj (wood)* de tres capas; *(wool)* de tres hebras

three-point ['θriːpɔɪnt] *n* **(a)** *Aut* ***t. turn*** cambio *m* de sentido con marcha atrás **(b)** ***t. line*** *(in basketball)* línea *f* de seis veinticinco

three-pointer ['θriː'pɔɪntə(r)] *n (in basketball)* triple *m*

three-quarter-length [θriː'kwɔːtəleŋθ] *adj* ***t. coat*** tres cuartos *m inv*; ***t. sleeve*** manga *f* (de) tres cuartos

three-quarters [θriː'kwɔːtəz] 1 *pron (amount)* tres cuartos *mpl*, tres cuartas partes *fpl*; **t. of voters voted against** tres cuartas partes del electorado votaron en contra; **it took me t. of an hour** me llevó tres cuartos de hora
2 *npl (in rugby)* tres cuartos *mfpl*
3 *adv* **t. full/finished** lleno(a)/terminado(a) en sus tres cuartas partes

three-ring circus ['θriːrɪŋ'sɜːkəs] *n US (confusing situation)* **it's a real t. in here** es un auténtico desbarajuste, aquí no hay quien se aclare

threescore ['θriːskɔː(r)] *adj Literary* sesenta; **t. (years) and ten** setenta (años)

three-sided ['θriːsaɪdɪd] *adj (shape)* de tres lados, *Spec* trilátero(a)

threesome ['θriːsəm] *n* **(a)** *(group)* trío *m*; **we went as a t.** fuimos los tres juntos **(b)** *(in golf)* threesome *m*, partido *m* a tres; *(in cards)* partida *f* de tres (jugadores) **(c)** *(for sex)* ménage à trois *m*, trío *m*

three-speed ['θriːspiːd] *adj (gears)* de tres marchas *or* velocidades

three-star ['θriːstɑː(r)] *adj (hotel)* de tres estrellas

three-way ['θriːweɪ] *adj (division)* en tres partes; *(discussion)* a tres bandas, entre tres; *(switch)* de tres posiciones ►► ***t. calling*** llamada *f* a tres

three-wheeler [θriː'wiːlə(r)] *n (car)* automóvil *m* de tres ruedas; *(tricycle)* triciclo *m*

threnody ['θrenədɪ] *n (ode)* elegía *f*; *(song)* canto *m* fúnebre, *Spec* treno *m*

thresh [θreʃ] *vt* trillar

thresher ['θreʃə(r)] *n* **(a)** *(person)* trillador(ora) *m,f* **(b)** *(machine)* trilladora *f* **(c) t. (shark)** zorro *m* marino

threshing ['θreʃɪŋ] *n* trilla *f* ►► ***t. floor*** era *f*; ***t. machine*** trilladora *f*

threshold ['θreʃhəʊld] *n* **(a)** *(doorway)* umbral *m*; **to cross the t.** franquear el umbral
(b) *(verge)* **to be on the t. (of)** estar en el umbral *or* en puertas (de)
(c) *(limit)* umbral *m*, límite *m*; **the government has raised tax thresholds** el gobierno ha elevado los umbrales impositivos; **to have a low/high pain t.** tener un umbral de dolor bajo/alto, soportar poco/mucho dolor; **to have a low boredom t.** aburrirse a la mínima ►► ***t. price*** precio *m* umbral; *Br Ind* ***t. (wage) agreement*** acuerdo *m* de actualización *or* revalorización salarial automática

threw *pt of* **throw**

thrice [θraɪs] *adv Literary* tres veces

thrift [θrɪft] *n* **(a)** *(care with money)* ahorro *m*, frugalidad *f* ►► *US* ***t. institution*** ≃ caja *f* de ahorros; *US* ***t. shop*** = tienda perteneciente a una entidad benéfica en la que normalmente se venden artículos de segunda mano; *US* ***t. store*** = tienda perteneciente a una entidad benéfica en la que normalmente se venden artículos de segunda mano
(b) *US (savings bank)* ≃ caja *f* de ahorros
(c) *Bot* armeria *f* (de mar)

thriftiness ['θrɪftmɪs] *n* ahorro *m*, frugalidad *f*

thriftless ['θrɪftlɪs] *adj* derrochador(ora)

thrifty ['θrɪftɪ] *adj (person)* ahorrativo(a); *(meal, habits)* frugal

thrill [θrɪl] 1 *n* **(a)** *(excitement)* emoción *f*; **it was a real t. to meet the president** fue verdaderamente emocionante conocer al presidente, me hizo mucha ilusión conocer al presidente; **he gets a t. out of ordering people about** disfruta dando órdenes a la gente; **to do sth for the t. of it** hacer algo por gusto; **thrills and spills** emoción y aventura
(b) *(trembling)* estremecimiento *m*; **the touch of his hand sent a t. through her** el contacto de su mano le hizo estremecerse; **a t. of excitement went down his spine** sintió un estremecimiento que le recorría la espalda
2 *vt* encantar, entusiasmar
3 *vi Literary* estremecerse (**to** con)

thrilled [θrɪld] *adj* encantado(a), contentísimo(a); **he was t. with his present** estaba encantado *or* contentísimo con su regalo; **I'm t. for you** me alegro muchísimo por ti; **I'm not exactly t. at the prospect** no es que la idea me vuelva loco precisamente; *Fam* **to be t. to bits** estar loco(a) de contento

thriller ['θrɪlə(r)] *n* **(a)** *(novel)* novela *f* de *Esp* suspense *or Am* suspenso, thriller *m*; *(movie)* thriller *m*, película *f* de *Esp* suspense *or Am* suspenso **(b)** *(exciting game)* encuentro *m* emocionantísimo *or* no apto para cardiacos

thrilling ['θrɪlɪŋ] *adj* apasionante, emocionante; *Ironic* **today we will be looking at sales figures – t.!** hoy nos ocuparemos de las cifras de ventas – ¡oh, qué apasionante! *or* ¡oh, qué ilusión!

thrillingly ['θrɪlɪŋlɪ] *adv* apasionantemente, emocionantemente

thrips [θrɪps] *n* trips *m inv*

thrive [θraɪv] (*pt* **thrived** *or* **throve** [θrəʊv]) *vi (business, person)* prosperar; *(plant)* crecer muy bien; **the plants t. in peaty soil** las plantas crecen muy bien *or* lozanas en mantillo de turba; **young children t. on a diet of milk** los lácteos son muy buenos para el desarrollo de los niños; **how's she getting on in her new job? – she's thriving** ¿cómo le va en su nuevo trabajo? – (le va) mejor que nunca *or* como nunca; **to t. on other people's misfortunes** aprovecharse de las desgracias ajenas; **some people t. on stress** algunas personas se crecen con el estrés

thriving ['θraɪvɪŋ] *adj (plant)* lozano(a); *(business)* próspero(a), floreciente

thro' [θruː] *Literary* = **through**

throat [θrəʊt] *n* **(a)** *(gullet)* garganta *f*; *(neck)* cuello *m*; **to cut sb's t.** degollar a alguien, cortar el cuello a alguien; **to grab sb by the t.** agarrar a alguien por el cuello; **to clear one's t.** carraspear, aclararse la garganta; *Hum* **get this drink down your t.!** ¡métete esto entre pecho y espalda!
(b) IDIOMS *Fam* **he never misses the chance to ram** *or* **shove his success down my t.** nunca pierde ocasión de pasarme *or* restregarme *or* refregarme su éxito por las narices; *Fam* **there's no need to jump**

down my t.! ¡no hay motivo para que me eches así los perros!; *Fam* **they're always at each other's throats** siempre se están tirando los trastos (a la cabeza)

throaty ['θrəʊtɪ] *adj (cough, voice)* ronco(a); *(chuckle)* cavernoso(a), gutural

throb [θrɒb] **1** *n* **(a)** *(of heart)* palpitación *f*, latido *m* **(b)** *(of engine)* zumbido *m*; *(of drums)* vibración *f*

2 *vi* (*pt & pp* **throbbed**) **(a)** *(heart)* palpitar, latir; **my head/finger is throbbing** me dan punzadas (de dolor) en la cabeza/el dedo **(b)** *(engine)* zumbar; *(drums)* vibrar; **the city was throbbing with activity** la ciudad era un hervidero, la ciudad bullía de actividad

throbbing ['θrɒbɪŋ] *adj* **(a)** *(rhythm)* vibrante, palpitante; *(engine, machine)* vibrante **(b)** *(heart)* palpitante **(c)** *(pain)* punzante; **I've got a t. headache** me dan punzadas en la cabeza

throes [θrəʊz] *npl* **the t. of death, death t.** la agonía de la muerte, los últimos estertores; **a country in the t. of revolution** un país en plena revolución, un país sumido en una revolución; **he's in the t. of a divorce** está pasando por el trance de divorciarse; **we're in the t. of moving house** estamos pasando la agonía de mudarnos de casa

thrombosis [θrɒm'bəʊsɪs] *n Med* trombosis *f inv*

thrombus ['θrɒmbəs] (*pl* **thrombi** ['θrɒmbaɪ]) *n* trombo *m*

throne [θrəʊn] *n* trono *m*; **he had designs on the French t.** aspiraba a hacerse con el trono francés *or* la corona francesa; **to be on the t.** *(monarch)* reinar, ocupar el trono; *Fam Euph (on toilet)* estar en el trono, *Esp* haber ido a visitar al señor Roca; **to come to** *or* **ascend** *or* **mount the t.** acceder *or* subir al trono ►► ***t. room*** sala *f* del trono

throng [θrɒŋ] **1** *n* muchedumbre *f*, gentío *m*; **throngs of people were doing their Christmas shopping** había multitud de gente haciendo las compras de Navidad

2 *vt* atestar, abarrotar; **demonstrators thronged the streets** las calles estaban atestadas *or* abarrotadas de manifestantes

3 *vi (gather)* aglomerarse, apelotonarse; **to t. round sb** apiñarse en torno a alguien; **crowds of supporters thronged towards the stadium** multitud de aficionados iban en tropel *or* en masa hacia el estadio; **people thronged to see the procession** la gente acudió en masa a presenciar la procesión

thronging ['θrɒŋɪŋ] *adj* **the crowd was a t. mass** la multitud era un torbellino de gente apiñada

throttle ['θrɒtəl] **1** *n (grip)* gas *m*; *(valve)* estrangulador *m*; *(in plane)* palanca *f* de gases; **to step on the t.** pisar el acelerador; **to open/close the t.** abrir/soltar el gas; IDIOM **at full t.** a toda velocidad

2 *vt (strangle)* estrangular; *Fam Fig* **I could have throttled her!** ¡la hubiera estrangulado allí mismo!

►**throttle back, throttle down**

1 *vt sep* **to t. back** *or* **down the engine** decelerar, desacelerar

2 *vi (in vehicle)* decelerar, desacelerar

THROUGH [θru:] **1** *prep* **(a)** *(with place)* a través de; **to go t. a tunnel** atravesar un túnel, pasar a través de un túnel; **to go t. a door** pasar por una puerta; **we went t. Belgium** fuimos atravesando Bélgica; **he swam quickly through the water** nadó rápidamente; **they went** *or* **drove t. a red light** se saltaron *or RP* comieron un semáforo (en rojo); **the bullet went t. his heart** el proyectil le atravesó el corazón; **what was going t. your mind?** ¿en qué estabas pensando?; **she came in/looked t. the window** entró/miró por la ventana; **can you see t. the glass?** ¿el cristal es transparente?; **I can't see much t. the fog** apenas veo por entre la niebla; **she cut t. the rope** cortó la cuerda; **I fell t. the ice into the freezing water** el hielo se rompió y caí al agua helada; **the ball flew t. the air** la pelota voló por los aires; **it took ages to get t. the crowd** nos llevó siglos atravesar la muchedumbre; **he wouldn't let me t. the door** no me dejaba pasar por la puerta; **the bull had a ring t. its nose** el toro tenía un aro en el hocico; **to make a hole t. sth** hacer un agujero en algo; **to look t. a hole** mirar por un agujero; **put your finger t. this loop** mete el dedo por este agujero; **we walked t. the fields** atravesamos los campos a pie; **I wandered t. the streets** vagué por las calles

(b) *(from start to finish of)* **she looked after me t. those years** me cuidó (durante) aquellos años; **all t. his life** durante toda su vida; **t. the ages** a lo largo de los siglos; **halfway t. a book/a movie** a *or RP* en mitad de un libro/una película; **three quarters of the way t. the race** a los tres cuartos de carrera, cuando llevaba recorridas tres cuartas partes de la carrera; **she cried right the way** *or* **the whole way t. the movie** lloró durante toda la película; **she maintained her dignity t. it all** mantuvo la dignidad de principio a fin; **to get t. sth** *(finish)* terminar algo; *(exams)* aprobar algo; **I don't know how I got t. those years** no sé cómo sobreviví aquellos años; **I'll have a look t. it** le echaré un vistazo; **they searched t. the files** revisaron los archivos; *Fam* **he's been t. a lot** ha pasado mucho

(c) *(by means of)* por; **to send sth t. the mail** mandar algo por correo; **I found out t. my brother** me enteré por mi hermano; **I got the job t. a friend** conseguí el trabajo por medio de un amigo; **they won t. sheer effort** ganaron a base de puro esfuerzo

(d) *(because of)* por; **t. ignorance/carelessness** por ignorancia/descuido; **I was late, but t. no fault of my own** llegué tarde, pero no fue por culpa mía; **it all came about t. a misunderstanding** ocurrió debido a un malentendido

(e) *US (until)* **Tuesday t. Thursday** desde el martes hasta el jueves inclusive

2 *adv* **(a)** *(to other side)* **please come t.** pase, por favor; **the emergency services couldn't get t.** los servicios de emergencia no pudieron llegar hasta allí; **to get t. to the front** llegar hasta la parte de delante *or Am* adelante; **to get t. to the final** llegar *or* pasar a la final; **to go t.** *(bullet, nail)* traspasar, pasar al otro lado; **I went t. into the living room** pasé a la sala de estar; **this train goes t. to Cambridge** este tren va hasta Cambridge; **to let sb t.** dejar pasar a alguien; **her trousers are t. at the knees** tiene los pantalones agujereados por las rodillas

(b) *(from start to finish)* **to sleep all night t.** dormir de un tirón; **we had to stop halfway t.** tuvimos que parar a mitad de camino; **to read a book right t.** leerse un libro de principio a fin; **she cried right the way** *or* **the whole way t.** no paró de llorar en todo el camino; **I've only had a quick look t.** sólo le he echado un vistazo; **I worked t. until midnight** trabajé sin parar hasta las 12 de la noche

(c) *(completely)* **to be wet t.** estar calado(a); **t. and t.** de pies a cabeza, de cabo a rabo

(d) *(in contact)* **to get t. to sb** *(on phone)* conseguir contactar *or Esp* comunicar con alguien; *Fam (make oneself understood)* comunicarse con alguien; **can you put me t. to Elaine/extension 363?** ¿me puede pasar con Elaine/la extensión *or RP* el interno 363?; **I'll put you t. to him** *(on phone)* le comunico *or* paso *or Esp* pongo con él

3 *adj* **(a)** *(finished)* **to be t. (with sth/sb)** haber terminado (con algo/alguien); **I'm not t. with you yet!** ¡todavía no he acabado (contigo)!; **I'll be t. reading the newspaper in a minute** sólo me falta un momento para acabar de leer el periódico; **I'm t. with being helpful to everyone** se ha acabado el mostrarme servicial con todo el mundo; **we're t.** *(no longer a couple)* lo nuestro se acabó

(b) *(direct) Br* **no t. road,** *US* **no t. traffic** *(sign)* = señal de tráfico que indica carretera sin salida ►► ***t. ticket*** billete *m or Am* boleto *m or esp Am* pasaje *m* directo; ***t. traffic*** tráfico *m* de paso; ***t. train*** tren *m* directo

throughout [θru:'aʊt] **1** *prep* **(a)** *(place)* por todo(a); **t. the country** por todo el país **(b)** *(time)* durante todo(a), a lo largo de todo(a); **t. her life** durante toda su vida; **t. the year** a lo largo del año

2 *adv* **(a)** *(place)* en su totalidad; **the house has been repainted t.** la casa se ha vuelto a pintar en su totalidad *or* de arriba abajo **(b)** *(time)* en todo momento; **she was silent t.** estuvo callada en todo momento *or* todo el tiempo

throughput ['θru:pʊt] *n* **(a)** *(total production) (of factory)* (volumen *m* de) producción *f* **(b)** *Comptr* rendimiento *m*, capacidad *f* de procesamiento

throughway = **thruway**

throve *pt of* **thrive**

THROW [θrəʊ] **1** *n* **(a)** *(of dice, darts)* tirada *f*; *(of ball, javelin, discus)* lanzamiento *m*; *(in wrestling)* derribo *m*; **it's my t.** *(in dice)* me toca tirar (a mí) **(b)** *(cloth, cover)* = tela decorativa que se coloca sobre camas, sillones, etc. **(c)** *Fam (item)* **they're £10 a t.** están a 10 libras

2 *vt* (*pt* **threw** [θru:], *pp* **thrown** [θrəʊn]) **(a)** *(with hands) (in general)* tirar, *Am* aventar; *(ball, javelin)* lanzar; **the rioters began throwing stones** los alborotadores empezaron a arrojar piedras; **she threw a six** *(with dice)* sacó un seis; **he threw 120/a bull's-eye** *(in darts)* hizo 120 puntos/diana; **to t. sb sth, to t. sth to sb** lanzar *or* pasar algo a alguien; **could you t. me my lighter?** ¿me pasas *or* tiras mi encendedor?; **to t. sth at sth/sb** lanzar *or* tirar algo a algo/alguien; **to t. a punch (at sb)** dar un puñetazo (a alguien); *Fig* **we won't solve the problem just by throwing money at it** no solucionaremos el problema sólo con dinero

(b) *(hurl)* lanzar; **I was thrown across the room by the explosion** la explosión me lanzó al otro lado de la habitación; **she was thrown clear** *(in car accident)* salió despedida; **she threw her arms around him** le echó los brazos al cuello; **to t. (sb) forwards/backwards** lanzar (a alguien) hacia delante/atrás; **they threw us in a dungeon** nos echaron en una mazmorra; **to t. sth in sb's face** arrojar algo a alguien en la cara; *Fig* echar en cara algo a alguien; **she threw her clothes on the floor** tiró *or Am* botó su ropa al suelo; **she threw a few**

clothes into a suitcase lanzó unas cuantas prendas en la maleta *orAm* valija; **he threw her to the ground** la tiró al suelo; **to t. oneself off a bridge/under the table** tirarse de un puente/debajo de la mesa; **to t. oneself into** *(river)* tirarse a; *(chair)* tirarse en; *Fig (undertaking, work)* entregarse a; *Fig* **she threw herself at him** prácticamente se echó en sus brazos; *Fig* **she threw herself at his feet** se echó a sus pies; **to t. oneself on sb's mercy** ponerse a merced de alguien; *Fig* **to t. sth back in sb's face** echarle algo en cara a alguien; **we were thrown back on our own resources** tuvimos que valernos de nuestros recursos; *Fig* **to t. good money after bad** tirar el dinero por la ventana; **to t. sb into confusion/a panic** sumir a alguien en la confusión/el pánico; *Fig* **to t. sth overboard** tirar *orAm* botar algo por la borda

(c) *Sport (in wrestling)* derribar; **the horse threw its rider** el caballo desmontó al jinete

(d) *(glance)* lanzar (**at** a)

(e) *(project) (image, shadow, voice)* proyectar; *Fig* **to t. doubt on sth** poner algo en duda; *Fig* **to t. light on sth** arrojar luz sobre algo

(f) *(turn on)* **to t. a switch** dar al interruptor

(g) *(have)* **to t. a fit** *(get angry)* ponerse hecho(a) una furia; **to t. a party** dar una fiesta

(h) *Fam (disconcert)* desconcertar; **I was completely thrown for a few seconds** me quedé desconcertado unos segundos

(i) *Fam (lose intentionally)* **he threw the game/fight** se dejó ganar

(j) *(in pottery)* tornear

(k) *(of cat, pig)* **to t. a litter** parir

(l) *Constr* **to t. a bridge over a river** tender un puente sobre un río

3 *vi* tirar, *Am* aventar; *(with ball, javelin)* lanzar; **I can't t. straight** no sé tirar/lanzar recto; **it's your turn to t.** te toca tirar; **he threw for 240 yards** *(in American football)* dio pases sumando un total de 240 yardas

▸ **throw about, throw around** *vt sep* **the kids were throwing a ball about** los niños estaban jugando con una pelota; **stop throwing your toys around** deja ya de tirar los juguetes por todas partes; **to be thrown about** ser sacudido(a); **she was throwing her arms about wildly** hacía aspavientos con los brazos; *Fig* **to t. money around** despilfarrar el dinero

▸ **throw aside** *vt sep (unwanted object)* tirar; *Fig* **he threw me aside when he came into money** se desentendió de mí cuando tuvo dinero

▸ **throw away** *vt sep* **(a)** *(discard)* tirar, *Am* botar **(b)** *(opportunity, life, money)* desperdiciar; **don't t. yourself away on someone like him** no eches a perder *or* desperdicies tu vida con alguien como él **(c)** *(remark)* dejar caer

▸ **throw back** *vt sep* **(a)** *(return) (ball)* devolver; *(fish)* devolver al agua; *Fig* **to t. sth back in sb's face** echarle algo en cara a alguien; IDIOM **we were thrown back on our own resources** tuvimos que valernos de nuestros recursos **(b)** *(move backwards) (hair, shoulders, head)* echar hacia atrás **(c)** *(open) (curtains)* descorrer; *(shutters)* abrir; **to t. back the bedclothes** destaparse

▸ **throw down** *vt sep* **(a)** *(object)* tirar; **they threw down their weapons** soltaron las armas; **to t. oneself down on the ground** tirarse al suelo **(b)** *(challenge)* lanzar

▸ **throw in 1** *vt sep* **(a)** *(into a place)* echar, tirar; IDIOM **to t. in one's hand** *or* **one's cards** *or* **the towel** tirar la toalla; *Fig* **he threw in his lot with the rebels** unió su destino al de los rebeldes **(b)** *(add)* añadir; *(include as extra)* incluir (como extra) **(c)** *Sport (ball)* sacar de banda, poner en juego

2 *vi US* **to t. in with sb** asociarse con alguien

▸ **throw off** *vt sep* **(a)** *(cold)* librarse de, deshacerse de **(b)** *(pursuer)* despistar; **he managed to t. the dogs off the trail** consiguió despistar a los perros **(c)** *(clothing)* quitarse rápidamente **(d)** *(write hastily) (poem, letter)* escribir de un tirón

▸ **throw on** *vt sep (clothes)* ponerse

▸ **throw open** *vt sep (door, window)* abrir de par en par; *Fig* **the House of Commons has been thrown open to television cameras** han abierto las puertas de la Cámara de los Comunes a las cámaras de televisión

▸ **throw out** *vt sep* **(a)** *(eject) (person)* echar; *(thing)* tirar; **to t. sb out of work** echar a alguien del trabajo **(b)** *(reject) (proposal)* rechazar; *Law* **the judge threw out the charges** el juez desestimó *or* rechazó los cargos **(c)** *(emit) (light, heat)* despedir **(d)** *(extend) (arms, leg)* estirar; **to t. out one's chest** sacar pecho **(e)** *(make) (remark, suggestion)* soltar; **to t. out a challenge** lanzar un reto **(f)** *(upset) (calculation, results)* desvirtuar

▸ **throw over** *vt sep (partner)* abandonar

▸ **throw together** *vt sep (assemble or gather hurriedly)* juntar a la carrera; *(make hurriedly)* pergeñar; **chance had thrown us together** el azar quiso que nos conociéramos; **he managed to t. a meal together** se las ingenió para pergeñar una comida

▸ **throw up 1** *vt sep* **(a)** *(raise) (dust, dirt)* levantar; **can you t. me up my towel?** ¿me puedes pasar la toalla?; **to t. up one's hands** *(in horror, dismay)* echarse las manos a la cabeza **(b)** *(reveal) (facts, information)* poner de manifiesto; **the discussion threw up some new ideas** la discusión aportó algunas ideas nuevas **(c)** *(abandon) (career, studies)* abandonar; *(opportunity)* desperdiciar **(d)** *Pej (building)* **the buildings were thrown up overnight** los edificios salieron como setas de la noche a la mañana **(e)** *Fam (vomit)* devolver

2 *vi Fam (vomit)* devolver, echar la papilla

---

throwaway ['θrəʊəweɪ] *adj* **(a)** *(disposable)* desechable; **we live in a t. culture** *or* **society** vivimos en la sociedad consumista del usar y tirar **(b)** *(casual) (line, remark)* insustancial, pasajero(a)

throwback ['θrəʊbæk] *n* **(a)** *Biol* regresión *f*, salto *m* atrás; **he's a t. to his great-grandfather** *(strongly resembles)* es la viva imagen de su bisabuelo, es clavado a su bisabuelo **(b)** *(of fashion, custom)* regreso *m*, vuelta *f*; **those new hats are a t. to the 1930s** esos nuevos sombreros suponen un regreso *or* una vuelta a los años treinta

throw-in ['θrəʊɪn] *n (in soccer)* saque *m* de banda, *Andes, RP* saque *m* de costado; **to take a t.** sacar de banda, *Andes, RP* sacar de costado

thrown *pp of* **throw**

thru [θruː] **1** *prep US Fam* = **through**

2 *adv US Fam* = **through**

thrum [θrʌm] **1** *vt (guitar)* rasguear

2 *vi (engine, machine)* ronronear; *(rain)* repiquetear

thrush[1] [θrʌʃ] *n (bird)* tordo *m*, zorzal *m*

thrush[2] *n (disease)* candidiasis *f inv*

thrust [θrʌst] **1** *n* **(a)** *(with knife)* cuchillada *f*; *(in fencing)* estocada *f* **(b)** *(attack) (of army)* ofensiva *f*; *Sport* incursión *f*, penetración *f* **(c)** *(of campaign, policy)* objetivo *m*; *(of argument)* sentido *m*, objetivo *m*; **the main t. of his argument was that...** lo que pretendía demostrar con su argumento era que... **(d)** *Av* empuje *m*

2 *vt* (*pt & pp* **thrust**) *(push, shove) (sword, stick, finger)* clavar, hundir (**into** en); **I t. the stick into the sand** clavé *or* hinqué el palo en la arena; **he t. his hands into his pockets** hundió las manos en los bolsillos; **she t. the letter into my hands** me echó la carta en las manos; **he t. his head out of the window** sacó *or* asomó la cabeza de golpe por la ventana; **she t. me to the front of the crowd** me fue arrimando hasta las primeras filas; **he t. her into the cell** la arrojó al calabozo de un empujón; **she t. the money towards him** le tendió el dinero con brusquedad; **he was suddenly t. into a position of responsibility** se vio de repente en un puesto de responsabilidad

3 *vi* **(a)** *(with sword, knife)* **to t. at sth/sb (with a knife)** lanzar una cuchillada a algo/alguien **(b)** *(move)* **to t. past sb** *(rudely)* pasar apartando a alguien de un empujón; *(quickly)* sortear *or* rebasar con rapidez a alguien

▸ **thrust aside** *vt sep* **(a)** *(person, thing)* apartar de un empujón **(b)** *(suggestion)* rechazar, descartar

▸ **thrust forward** *vt sep (push forward)* empujar (hacia delante); **to t. oneself forward** *(for job, to gain attention)* hacerse notar

▸ **thrust on** *vt sep* **fame was t. on him** la fama le cayó encima; **the job was t. on me** el trabajo me vino impuesto; **he t. himself on them** tuvieron que cargar con él

▸ **thrust out** *vt sep (one's arm, leg)* extender de golpe; **to t. out one's chest** sacar pecho

▸ **thrust upon** = **thrust on**

thrusting ['θrʌstɪŋ] *adj Br* agresivamente ambicioso(a)

thruway, throughway ['θruːweɪ] *n US Aut* autopista *f*

thud [θʌd] **1** *n* golpe *m* sordo

2 *vi* (*pt & pp* **thudded**) hacer un ruido sordo; **we could hear the cannon thudding in the distance** se oía el retumbar del cañón en la lejanía; **his fist thudded into my stomach** su puñetazo me alcanzó el estómago con un golpe sordo; **my heart was thudding** el corazón me latía *or* palpitaba con fuerza; **we could hear him thudding about** se oía el ruido sordo de sus pisadas

thug [θʌg] *n* matón *m*

thuggery ['θʌgərɪ] *n* matonismo *m*, chulería *f*

thuggish ['θʌgɪʃ] *adj* de matón, chulesco(a)

thulium ['θuːlɪəm] *n Chem* tulio *m*

thumb [θʌm] **1** *n* (**a**) *(digit)* pulgar *m* ▸▸ ***t. index*** uñero *m*, índice *m* recortado (**b**) IDIOMS **she's got him under her t., he's under her t.** lo tiene completamente dominado; *Fam* **he's all (fingers and) thumbs** es un torpe *or* manazas; *Fam* **to give sth/sb the thumbs up** dar el visto bueno a algo/alguien; *Fam* **to give sth/sb the thumbs down** no dar el visto bueno a algo/alguien

2 *vt* (**a**) *(book)* hojear; **a well thumbed book** un libro manoseado; IDIOM **to t. one's nose at sb** hacerle burla a alguien (**b**) *Fam (hitch)* **to t. a lift** *or* **ride** hacer dedo, *CAm, Méx, Perú* pedir aventón; **I thumbed a ride to Chicago** fui a Chicago a dedo

3 *vi* **to t. through sth** hojear algo

thumbnail ['θʌmneɪl] *n* (**a**) *(of finger)* uña *f* del pulgar ▸▸ ***t. sketch*** reseña *f*, descripción *f* somera (**b**) *Typ* miniatura *f*

thumbprint ['θʌmprɪnt] *n* huella *f* del pulgar

thumbscrew ['θʌmskruː] *n* (**a**) *Hist* empulgueras *fpl* (**b**) *(screw)* tornillo *m* de mariposa

thumbtack ['θʌmtæk] *n US Esp* chincheta *f*, *Am* chinche *m*

thump [θʌmp] **1** *n* (**a**) *(blow)* porrazo *m* (**b**) *(sound)* ruido *m* seco

2 *vt* (**a**) *(hit)* dar un porrazo a; **he thumped me in the stomach** me dio un puñetazo en el estómago; **to t. sb on the back** palmotear a alguien en la espalda, dar fuertes palmadas a alguien en la espalda; **he thumped his fist on the table** dio un puñetazo en la mesa; **he thumped his bag down on the floor** soltó la bolsa de golpe en el suelo (**b**) *Fam (defeat heavily)* machacar, dar una paliza *or* un palizón a

3 *vi* (**a**) *(hit)* **to t. on the door/table** aporrear la puerta/mesa (**b**) *(make loud noise)* **I could hear him thumping around upstairs** lo oía dar fuertes pisadas en el apartamento *or Esp* piso de arriba (**c**) *(heart)* **my heart was thumping** el corazón me latía con fuerza

▸ **thump out** *Fam* **1** *vt sep* **to t. out a tune on the piano** tocar una canción aporreando el piano

2 *vi (music)* sonar a todo volumen

thumping ['θʌmpɪŋ] *Fam* **1** *n (heavy defeat)* paliza *f*, palizón *m*

2 *adj (very large)* enorme, tremendo(a)

3 *adv* **a t. great book/house** un pedazo de libro/casa, un libro/una casa de aquí te espero; **that was a t. good show!** ¡ha sido un pedazo de espectáculo!

thunder ['θʌndə(r)] **1** *n* (**a**) *Met* truenos *mpl*; **there was a lot of t. last night** anoche hubo *or* se oyeron muchos truenos; **a clap of t.** un trueno; **t. and lightning** aparato eléctrico; IDIOM **with a face like t.** con el rostro encendido por la ira (**b**) *(of applause)* estallido *m*; *(of engine, traffic, waves, hooves)* estruendo *m*; *(of guns)* estallido *m*, estampido *m*

2 *vt (order, threat)* vociferar; *(applause)* estallar *or* prorrumpir en; **"damn them!" he thundered** "¡malditos sean!", vociferó *or* rugió él

3 *vi* (**a**) *(during storm)* tronar; **it's thundering** hay truenos, está tronando

(**b**) *(guns, waves)* retumbar; **applause thundered from the crowd as he finished his performance** al terminar su actuación el público estalló *or* prorrumpió en aplausos; **the tanks/cavalry thundered past** los tanques pasaron/la caballería pasó con gran estruendo; **to t. along** *(train, lorry)* pasar con estrépito

(**c**) *(speaker)* tronar, vociferar

thunderbolt ['θʌndəbəʊlt] *n* (**a**) *Met* rayo *m* (**b**) *(news)* mazazo *m*

thunderclap ['θʌndəklæp] *n* trueno *m*

thundercloud ['θʌndəklaʊd] *n* nube *f* de tormenta

thundering ['θʌndərɪŋ] **1** *adj* (**a**) *Old-fashioned (very large)* tremendo(a), enorme; **to be in a t. rage** estar hecho(a) una furia (**b**) *(very powerful)* **a t. shot** un cañonazo, un trallazo; **a t. goal** un gol de fuerte *or* potente disparo

2 *adv Old-fashioned* **it's a t. good read** da gusto leerlo, es un pedazo de libro

thunderous ['θʌndərəs] *adj (voice, applause)* atronador(ora)

thunderstorm ['θʌndəstɔːm] *n* tormenta *f*

thunderstruck ['θʌndəstrʌk] *adj* pasmado(a), atónito(a); **she was t. by the news** la noticia la dejó pasmada *or* atónita

thunderthighs ['θʌndəθaɪz] *n Br Fam Hum* foca *f*, vaca *f*

thundery ['θʌndərɪ] *adj Met (weather, showers)* tormentoso(a); *(storms)* con aparato eléctrico

Thur, Thurs (*abbr* **Thursday**) jves., J.

Thursday ['θɜːzdeɪ] *n* jueves *m inv*; *see also* **Saturday**

thus [ðʌs] *adv Formal* (**a**) *(in this way)* así, de este modo; **put your hands on your head, t.** ponga las manos sobre la cabeza de este modo; **it was ever t.** siempre ha sido así (**b**) *(therefore)* por consiguiente; **he resigned, t. provoking great panic** dimitió, generando así los consiguientes ataques de pánico (**c**) **t. far** *(up to now)* hasta el momento; *(up to here)* hasta aquí

thwack [θwæk] **1** *n (blow, sound)* golpetazo *m*

2 *vt (hit)* dar un golpetazo a, *Esp* atizar; **the player thwacked the ball into the crowd** el jugador estrelló el balón contra el público

thwart [θwɔːt] *vt (person, plan)* frustrar; **I was thwarted in my attempts to leave the country** mis intentos de abandonar el país se vieron frustrados

thy [ðaɪ] *adj* (**a**) *Literary* tu (**b**) *Rel* tu; **love t. neighbour** amarás al prójimo

thyme [taɪm] *n* tomillo *m*

thymus ['θaɪməs] *n Anat* **t. (gland)** timo *m*

thyroid ['θaɪrɔɪd] *Anat* **1** *n* **t. (gland)** (glándula *f*) tiroides *m inv*

2 *adj* tiroideo(a)

thyself [ðaɪ'self] *pron* (**a**) *Literary* tú mismo(a); **for t.** para ti mismo (**b**) *Rel* tú mismo(a)

ti [tiː] *n Mus* si *m*

tiara [tɪ'ɑːrə] *n (jewellery)* diadema *f*; *(of Pope)* tiara *f*

Tibet [tɪ'bet] *n* (el) Tíbet

Tibetan [tɪ'betən] **1** *n* (**a**) *(person)* tibetano(a) *m,f* (**b**) *(language)* tibetano *m*

2 *adj* tibetano(a)

tibia ['tɪbɪə] *n Anat* tibia *f*

tic [tɪk] *n* tic *m*; **a nervous t.** un tic nervioso

tick[1] [tɪk] *n (parasite)* garrapata *f*

tick[2] *n Br Fam (credit)* **to buy sth on t.** comprar algo fiado

tick[3] **1** *n* (**a**) *(of clock)* tictac *m*

(**b**) *Br Fam (moment)* momentín *m*, segundo *m*; **just a t.!** ¡un momentín *or* segundo!; **I'll be with you in (half) a t.** *or* **in two ticks!** ¡estoy contigo en un momentín *or* segundo!

(**c**) *(mark)* marca *f*, señal *f* de visto bueno; **put a t. against the name of your preferred candidate** marque con una señal el nombre del candidato elegido

(**d**) *Tex (for mattress, pillow)* funda *f*; *(ticking)* terliz *m*, cutí *m (para colchones)*

2 *vi (clock)* hacer tictac; **the minutes are ticking by** *or* **away** los minutos pasan; IDIOM **I don't know what makes him t.** no sé qué es lo que le mueve

3 *vt (mark) (name, answer, box)* marcar (con una señal); *Sch* marcar con una señal de visto bueno, marcar como corregido(a)

▸ **tick off** *vt sep* (**a**) *(on list)* marcar con una señal de visto bueno (**b**) *(count) (reasons, chapters)* enumerar (**c**) *Br Fam (reprimand)* echar regañina (**d**) *US Fam (irritate)* fastidiar, mosquear; **to be ticked off (with sb)** estar mosqueado(a) (con alguien)

▸ **tick over** *vi* (**a**) *(engine)* estar al ralentí (**b**) *(business)* ir tirando; **it keeps my brain ticking over** mantiene mi mente fresca *or* despierta

ticker ['tɪkə(r)] *n* (**a**) *Fam (heart)* corazón *m* (**b**) *US (printer)* teletipo *m* *or* teleimpresor *m* de cotizaciones (bursátiles)

ticker tape ['tɪkəteɪp] *n* cinta *f* de cotizaciones (bursátiles); **a t. parade** un desfile de recibimiento multitudinario

ticket ['tɪkɪt] **1** *n* (**a**) *(for train, bus, plane)* billete *m*, *Am* boleto *m*, *esp Am* pasaje *m*; *(for theatre, cinema, museum, game)* entrada *f*, *Col, Méx* boleto *m*; *(for lottery)* billete *m*, boleto *m*; *(to car park)* tíquet *m*, ticket *m*; *(for left luggage, from cloakroom, dry cleaner's, pawnshop)* resguardo *m*, tíquet *m*, ticket *m*; IDIOM *Fam* **it was just the t.!** ¡era justo lo que necesitaba! ▸▸ ***t. agency*** *(for theatre, pop concerts)* punto *m or* agencia *f* de venta de entradas *or Col, Méx* boletos; ***t. barrier*** *(at train station, airport)* (puesto *m* de) control *m* de billetes *or Am* boletos *or esp Am* pasajes; ***t. collector*** revisor(ora) *m,f*; ***t. desk*** *(at airport)* mostrador *m* de venta de billetes *or Am* boletos *or esp Am* pasajes; ***t. holder*** *(for train, bus, plane)* poseedor(ora) *m,f* de billete *or Am* boleto *or esp Am* pasaje; *(for theatre, cinema, museum, game)* poseedor(ora) *m,f* de entrada *or Col, Méx* boleto; *Br* ***t. inspector*** revisor(ora) *m,f*; ***t. machine*** *(at train station, airport)* máquina *f* expendedora de billetes *or Am* boletos *or esp Am* pasajes; ***t. office*** taquilla *f*, *Esp* despacho *m* de billetes, *Am* boletería *f*; *Br* ***t. tout*** reventa *mf*; ***t. window*** ventanilla *f*

(**b**) *(for membership) (of library)* carné *m or* carnet *m* (de socio)

(**c**) *(fine) (for parking illegally, speeding)* multa *f*; **I got a (parking) t.** me pusieron una multa (de estacionamiento)

(**d**) *(label)* **(price) t.** etiqueta *f* (de precio)

(**e**) *Pol (list of candidates)* candidatura *f*; **his vice-presidential running mate on the Democratic t.** su número dos y candidato a la vicepresidencia por los demócratas; **she ran on an anti-corruption t.** se presentó bajo la bandera de la anticorrupción

2 *vt* (**a**) *(goods)* etiquetar (**b**) *US (fine)* multar, poner una multa a

ticketless ['tɪkɪtlɪs] *adj* ***t. travel*** viaje *m* sin billete *or Am* boleto *or esp Am* pasaje

tickety-boo [tɪkɪtɪ'buː] *adj Br Fam* **everything's t.** todo va de perlas *or* sobre ruedas

ticking ['tɪkɪŋ] *n* **(a)** *(of clock)* tictac *m* **(b)** *Tex* terliz *m*, cutí *m (para colchones)*

ticking-off ['tɪkɪŋ'ɒf] *n Br Fam (reprimand) Esp* rapapolvo *m*, *Am* regaño *m*; **to give sb a t.** echar *Esp* un rapapolvo *or Am* un regaño a alguien

tickle ['tɪkəl] **1** *n* cosquillas *fpl*; **to give sb a t.** hacer cosquillas a alguien; **to have a t. in one's throat** tener picor de garganta

2 *vt* **(a)** *(of person, garment)* hacer cosquillas a; **don't t. my feet!** ¡no me hagas cosquillas en los pies!; IDIOM *Hum* **to t. the ivories** darle a las teclas, tocar el piano **(b)** *(amuse)* divertir; IDIOM **to t. sb's fancy** atraer *or Esp* apetecer *or Carib, Col, Méx* provocar *or Méx* antojársele a alguien; IDIOM **to be tickled pink** estar encantado(a) **(c)** *(arouse) (curiosity)* picar, despertar

3 *vi (wool, material)* picar; **stop tickling!** ¡deja de hacerme cosquillas!

tickler ['tɪklə(r)] *n* **(a)** *Br Fam (tricky problem)* problemón *m*, papeleta *f*; **it's a bit of a t.** el asunto tiene miga(s) **(b)** *US (memorandum book)* bloc *m* de notas *(para recordatorios)*

tickling ['tɪklɪŋ] *adj* **I felt a t. sensation in my feet** sentía cosquilleo en los pies

ticklish ['tɪklɪʃ] *adj* **(a)** *(person)* **to be t.** tener cosquillas; **I have t. feet** tengo cosquillas en los pies **(b)** *Fam (situation, problem)* delicado(a), peliagudo(a), *Méx* pelón(ona) **(c)** *Fam (touchy) (person)* picajoso(a), susceptible

tickly ['tɪklɪ] *adj Fam* **a t. blanket/beard** una manta/barba que pica; **I've got a t. throat** tengo la garganta tomada, me pica la garganta

tick-tack-toe [tɪktæk'təʊ] *n US* tres en raya *m*

ticktock ['tɪktɒk] *n (of clock)* tictac *m*

ticky-tacky ['tɪkɪtækɪ] *US Fam* **1** *n* materiales *mpl* baratos

2 *adj* **(a)** *(dull)* soso(a) **(b)** *(cheaply made)* de chichinabo, de chicha y nabo

tidal ['taɪdəl] *adj (estuary, river)* con mareas; *(current, force)* de las mareas; **the river is t. as far as Newtown** la marea llega hasta Newtown ►► ***t. basin*** dársena *f* de marea; ***t. energy*** energía *f* mareomotriz; ***t. wave*** *(tsunami)* maremoto *m*; *(of protest, sympathy)* oleada *f*, avalancha *f*

tidbit *US* = **titbit**

tiddler ['tɪdlə(r)] *n Br Fam* **(a)** *(small fish)* pececillo *m* **(b)** *(child)* renacuajo(a) *m,f*, *Méx* cosita *f*, *RP* piojo *m*

tiddly ['tɪdlɪ] *adj Br Fam* **(a)** *(small)* minúsculo(a) **(b)** *(tipsy)* achispado(a)

tiddlywinks ['tɪdlɪwɪŋks] *n* (juego *m* de la) pulga *f*

tide [taɪd] *n* **(a)** *(of sea)* marea *f*; **high/low t.** marea alta/baja; **at high/low t.** con la marea alta/baja, en pleamar/bajamar; **the t. is in/out** ha subido/bajado la marea ►► ***t. table*** tabla *f or* anuario *m* de mareas

(b) *(of events)* rumbo *m*, curso *m*; **the rising t. of discontent** la creciente ola de descontento; **to go** *or* **swim against the t.** ir contra (la) corriente; **to go** *or* **drift with the t.** dejarse llevar (por la corriente); **to swim with the t.** seguir la corriente; **the t. has turned** se han vuelto las tornas; **the t. of public opinion has turned against the government** la corriente de opinión se ha vuelto contra el gobierno; **you cannot turn back the t. of progress** es imposible frenar la máquina del progreso

► **tide over** *vt sep* **to t. sb over** *(of money)* sacar a alguien del apuro; **I lent him some money to t. him over till payday** le presté un poco de dinero para que llegara hasta el día de cobro; **to t. sb over a difficult patch** ayudar a alguien a superar un bache *or* una mala racha

tideless ['taɪdlɪs] *adj* sin mareas

tidemark ['taɪdmɑːk] *n* **(a)** *(mark left by tide)* línea *f* de la marea **(b)** *Br Fam (in bath)* marca *f* de suciedad

tidewater ['taɪdwɔːtə(r)] *n* **(a)** *Br (water)* agua *f* de (la) marea **(b)** *US (land)* marisma *f*

tideway ['taɪdweɪ] *n* zona *f* de mareas

tidily ['taɪdɪlɪ] *adv* ordenadamente

tidiness ['taɪdɪnɪs] *n (of room, habits)* orden *m*; *(of garden)* aspecto *m* cuidado; *(of appearance)* pulcritud *f*, aseo *m*; *(of hair)* buen arreglo *m*; *(of schoolwork, writing)* pulcritud *f*, esmero *m*

tidings ['taɪdɪŋz] *npl Literary* nuevas *fpl*, noticias *fpl*

tidy ['taɪdɪ] **1** *adj* **(a)** *(room, habits)* ordenado(a); *(garden)* cuidado(a); *(appearance)* arreglado(a), aseado(a); *(hair)* arreglado(a); *(schoolwork, writing)* pulcro(a), esmerado(a) **(b)** *(mind)* metódico(a) **(c)** *Fam (considerable) (sum)* bonito(a); *(profit)* bueno(a), considerable

2 *vt (room, desk)* ordenar; *(garden, hair)* arreglar

3 *n* **(a)** *(receptacle)* = recipiente con compartimentos para utensilios de escritorio **(b)** *(clean)* limpieza *f*; **I'm just going to give my bedroom a quick t.** voy a arreglar *or* ordenar un poco la habitación

► **tidy away** *vt sep* recoger; **I tidied the books away in a cupboard** guardé los libros en un armario

► **tidy out** *vt sep (drawer, wardrobe, garden shed)* hacer limpieza en, ordenar

► **tidy up** **1** *vt sep* **(a)** *(room, desk, clothes)* ordenar; **t. your things up** *(put them away)* recoge tus cosas **(b)** *(in appearance)* **to t. oneself up** arreglarse

2 *vi* **(a)** *(in room)* ordenar **(b)** *(in appearance)* arreglarse

tidy-up ['taɪdɪʌp] *n Fam* limpieza *f*; **to have a t.** hacer limpieza, ordenar

tie [taɪ] **1** *n* **(a)** *(item of clothing)* corbata *f* ►► ***t. clip*** pasador *m* de corbata, pasacorbatas *m inv*; *US* ***t. tack*** alfiler *m* de corbata

(b) *(fastener) (for closing bag)* atadura *f*, = cierre flexible de alambre plastificado para bolsas de plástico, cables enrollados, etc.; *(for curtain)* alzapaño *m (cinta)*; *(on apron)* cinta *f*, lazo *m*

(c) *(link)* lazo *m*, vínculo *m*; **he has no ties to the place** no hay nada que lo una *or* lo ligue al lugar

(d) *(restriction)* atadura *f*; **pets can be a t.** los animales de compañía pueden ser una atadura *or* pueden atar mucho

(e) *Sport (draw)* empate *m*; **the game ended in a t.** el partido acabó en *or* con empate

(f) *Sport (game)* eliminatoria *f*, partido *m* de clasificación; **their fourth round (cup) t. against Wolves was postponed** su eliminatoria *or* partido de copa contra los Wolves fue aplazado

(g) *US Rail* traviesa *f*

(h) *Constr* ***t. beam*** tirante *m*

(i) *Mus* ligadura *f*

2 *vt* **(a)** *(shoelace, piece of string)* atar; **to t. a knot (in sth)** atar *or* hacer un nudo (a *or* en algo); **to t. one's shoelaces** atarse (los cordones de) los zapatos; **to t. a scarf round one's neck** anudarse *or* atarse un pañuelo al cuello; **she tied the ribbon in a bow** hizo un lazo con la cinta; **they tied his hands and feet** lo ataron *or* amarraron de pies y manos; **she tied a ribbon in her hair** se ató un lazo al pelo; **to t. sth to sth** atar algo a algo; **they tied him to a tree** lo ataron *or* amarraron a un árbol; IDIOM **to have one's hands tied** *(have no alternative)* tener las manos atadas

(b) *(restrict)* **they're tied to** *or* **by the conditions of the contract** se deben atener a las condiciones del contrato; **she's tied to the house because of the children** se pasa el día encerrada en casa por los niños; **she felt tied by a sense of duty** se sentía obligada por sentido del deber; **he was tied to his desk** estaba atado a su trabajo

(c) *(link)* **to be tied to sth** ir ligado(a) a algo, estar vinculado(a) a algo

(d) *Sport (game)* empatar

3 *vi* **(a)** *(be fastened)* **the dress ties at the back** el vestido se ata por detrás **(b)** *(in race, contest)* empatar; **they tied for third place** quedaron empatados en tercer lugar

► **tie back** *vt sep (hair, curtains)* recoger; **her hair was tied back in a bun** llevaba el pelo recogido en un moño

► **tie down** *vt sep* **(a)** *(with string, rope)* atar

(b) *(restrict)* **children t. you down** los hijos atan mucho; **she doesn't want to feel tied down** no quiere ataduras, no quiere sentirse atada

(c) *(commit)* **try and t. him down to a specific date** intenta que se comprometa a una fecha concreta; **I don't want to be tied down** *or* **to t. myself down to a specific date** no quiero comprometerme a una fecha concreta

► **tie in** **1** *vt sep* relacionar; **how is this tied in with your previous experiments?** ¿cómo encaja esto con tus experimentos anteriores?, ¿qué relación guarda con tus experimentos anteriores?; **she's trying to t. her work experience in with her research** trata de que su experiencia laboral esté relacionada *or* guarde relación con sus investigaciones

2 *vi (facts, story)* encajar, concordar; **this ties in with what I said before** esto concuerda *or* viene al hilo de lo que dije antes

► **tie on** *vt* **(a)** *(attach)* atar **(b)** *US Fam* **to t. one on** *(get drunk)* agarrarse una buena (curda), *Méx* ponerse una peda

► **tie together** **1** *vt sep (papers, sticks)* atar; **to t. sb's hands/feet together** atar las manos/los pies a alguien

2 *vi (make sense)* cuadrar, encajar; **it all ties together** todo encaja *or* cuadra *or* concuerda

► **tie up** **1** *vt sep* **(a)** *(prisoner, animal, parcel)* atar; *(boat)* amarrar; **to t. up one's shoelaces** atarse (los cordones de) los zapatos

(b) *(finalize) (deal)* cerrar; **I'd like to get everything tied up before the holidays** me gustaría dejarlo todo (atado y) bien atado antes de las vacaciones (**c**) *(money)* **my capital is tied up in property** tengo mi capital metido *or* invertido en bienes inmuebles; **her inheritance is tied up until her 21st birthday** su herencia está inmovilizada hasta que cumpla veintiún años

(**d**) *(connect)* **to be tied up with sth** estar íntimamente ligado(a) a algo

(**e**) *(busy)* **to be tied up** estar muy ocupado(a); **he's tied up in a meeting until 5** está reunido *or* tiene una reunión hasta las 5

(**f**) *(impede) (traffic)* congestionar; *(progress, production)* paralizar

2 *vi* (**a**) *(be connected)* relacionarse, estar relacionado(a) (**with** con); **it's all beginning to t. up** todo empieza a encajar *or* cuadrar (**b**) *Naut* atracar, echar amarras

tieback ['taɪbæk] *n (for curtain)* alzapaño *m (cordón, cinta)*

tie-break(er) ['taɪbreɪk(ər)] *n (in tennis)* tie-break *m*, muerte *f* súbita; *(in quiz, competition)* desempate *m*

tied [taɪd] *adj* (**a**) *Sport* **to be t.** *(players)* estar *or* ir empatados(as); *(game)* estar empatado(a); **they are t. for the lead** van empatados en cabeza

(**b**) *(by obligation, duties)* atado(a); **he doesn't want to feel t.** no quiere tener ataduras, no quiere sentirse atado ▸▸ *Br* ***t. cottage*** = casa de campo alquilada por un agricultor a sus trabajadores; *Br* ***t. house*** *(pub)* = "pub" británico que pertenece a una cervecera y vende principalmente su cerveza

(**c**) *Mus (note)* ligado(a)

tied-up ['taɪdʌp] *adj* ***t. capital*** capital *m* inmovilizado

tie-dyed ['taɪdaɪd] *adj* teñido(a) con nudos

tie-in ['taɪɪn] *n* (**a**) *(link)* relación *f* (**with** con) (**b**) *Com* **a movie/TV t.** = un producto a veces promocional relacionado con una nueva película/un programa televisivo

tie-on ['taɪɒn] *adj (label)* de *or* para colgar, colgante

tie-pin ['taɪpɪn] *n* alfiler *m* de corbata

tier [tɪə(r)] *n* (**a**) *(of theatre)* fila *f*; *(of stadium)* grada *f*; **we arranged the seats in tiers** colocamos los asientos escalonados *or* en gradas (**b**) *(of wedding cake)* piso *m* (**c**) *(administrative)* nivel *m*; *Pej* **a two-t. health service** un sistema sanitario que distingue entre ciudadanos de primera y de segunda clase

tiered ['tɪəd] *adj* (**a**) *(seating) (in theatre)* escalonado(a), sobre gradas; **t. seating** *(in stadium)* gradas, *Esp* graderío (**b**) *(of wedding cake)* **a three-t. cake** una tarta de tres pisos (**c**) *(system, approach)* de varios niveles, multilateral

tie-up ['taɪʌp] *n* (**a**) *(connection)* nexo *m* (de unión), vínculo *m* (**b**) *Com (joint venture)* empresa *f* conjunta (**c**) *US (traffic jam)* atasco *m*, embotellamiento *m*

TIFF [tɪf] *n Comptr* (*abbr* **tagged image file format**) TIFF *m*

tiff [tɪf] *n Fam* riña *f*, desavenencia *f*; **they had a lover's t.** tuvieron una pelea *or* riña de novios

tig [tɪg] *n (game)* **to play t.** jugar a pillarse *or* al corre que te pillo

tiger ['taɪgə(r)] *n* tigre *m*; **to fight like a t.** luchar como una fiera *or* con uñas y dientes ▸▸ ***t. cub*** cachorro *m* de tigre; ***t. economy*** tigre *m* asiático; ***t. lily*** lirio *m* naranja, azucena *f* atigrada; ***t. moth*** mariposa *f* tigre; ***t. prawn*** langostino *m* tigre *or* rayado *or* jumbo; ***t. shark*** tiburón *m* tigre

tigerish ['taɪgərɪʃ] *adj (performance)* esforzado(a); *(tackling)* duro(a); *(sportsman)* batallador(ora), peleón(ona)

tiger's-eye ['taɪgəzaɪ] *n (stone)* ojo *m* de tigre

tight [taɪt] **1** *adj* (**a**) *(clothes) (close-fitting)* ajustado(a), ceñido(a); *(uncomfortable)* justo(a), prieto(a), estrecho(a); **she likes wearing t. trousers** le gusta llevar pantalones ajustados; **these shoes are a bit t.** estos zapatos me quedan un poco justos *or* me aprietan un poco; **my tie was too t.** llevaba la corbata demasiado apretada *or* prieta; **to be a t. fit** *(clothes)* quedar muy justo(a); **there was just enough room in the car, but it was a t. squeeze** cabíamos en el coche, pero íbamos muy apretados *or* apiñados

(**b**) *(stiff) (screw, lid)* apretado(a), prieto(a)

(**c**) *(taut) (rope)* tenso(a), tirante; *(knot)* apretado(a), prieto(a); **her face looked t. and drawn** tenía el rostro tenso y demacrado; **my chest is feeling t.** siento una opresión en el pecho

(**d**) *(firm) (grip, embrace)* fuerte, firme; **to keep a t. hold on sth** tener algo bien agarrado; *Fig* **we need to keep a t. hold on expenditure** hay que ejercer un riguroso *or* estricto control de los gastos; **they huddled together in a t. bunch** se agruparon formando una piña; *Fig* **the dictator kept a t. grip on power** el dictador detentaba el poder con mano firme

(**e**) *(hermetic) (seal)* hermético(a)

(**f**) *(bend)* cerrado(a)

(**g**) *(strict) (restrictions)* severo(a); *(control)* riguroso(a), estricto(a); **there will be t. security at the summit** habrá fuertes *or* estrictas medidas de seguridad durante la cumbre

(**h**) *(limited) (budget)* justo(a), limitado(a); **money's a bit t. at the moment** ahora estoy un poco justo de dinero; **we're a bit t. for time** vamos un poco cortos *or* justos de tiempo

(**i**) *(close) (race, finish)* reñido(a)

(**j**) *(schedule)* apretado(a); **to work to a t. schedule** trabajar con un calendario estricto; **it was t. but I made it in time** apenas tenía margen, pero llegué a tiempo

(**k**) *Fam (miserly)* agarrado(a), roñoso(a)

(**l**) *Fam (drunk)* alegre, *Esp* piripi; **to get t.** ponerse alegre *or Esp* piripi

(**m**) *Mus (band, playing)* sólido(a), conjuntado(a)

(**n**) *Sport* ***t. end*** *(in American football)* tight end *m*; ***t. head prop*** *(in rugby)* pilar *mf* derecho(a), cabeza *mf* cerrada

(**o**) IDIOMS **to be in a t. spot** *or* **corner** estar en un aprieto; **to run a t. ship** llevar el timón con mano firme

2 *adv (to hold, squeeze)* con fuerza; *(to seal, shut)* bien; **pull the thread t.** pon el hilo bien tirante; **make sure you screw the lid on t.** deja la tapa bien cerrada *or* apretada; **hold t.!** ¡agárrate fuerte!; **the stands were packed t.** las gradas estaban abarrotadas *or* a rebosar de gente, la gente se apelotonaba en las gradas; **sleep t.!** ¡que descanses!

tight-arsed ['taɪt'ɑːst], *US* **tight-assed** ['taɪt'æst] *adj very Fam (repressed)* estrecho(a)

tighten ['taɪtən] **1** *vt* (**a**) *(screw, knot)* apretar (**b**) *(rope)* tensar; *(belt, strap)* apretar; **to t. one's grip on** *(rope, handle)* asir con más fuerza; *Fig* **he tightened his grip on the organization** incrementó su control sobre la organización; *Fig* **to t. one's belt** apretarse el cinturón (**c**) *(restrictions, security)* intensificar, incrementar; *(conditions, rules)* endurecer

2 *vi* (**a**) *(knot)* apretarse (**b**) *(rope, muscles)* tensarse; **his throat/stomach tightened** se le hizo un nudo en la garganta/el estómago (**c**) *(restrictions, security)* intensificarse, incrementarse; *(rules)* endurecerse

▸**tighten up** **1** *vt sep* (**a**) *(screw)* apretar (**b**) *(restrictions, security)* intensificar, incrementar; *(law, regulations)* endurecer

2 *vi* (**a**) *(become stricter)* ponerse más duro(a) *or* severo(a) (**on** con) (**b**) *(runner)* flaquear, desfallecer

tightening ['taɪtnɪŋ] *n (of restrictions, security)* intensificación *f*

tight-fisted ['taɪt'fɪstɪd] *adj Fam* agarrado(a), rata

tight-fitting ['taɪt'fɪtɪŋ] *adj (item of clothing)* ajustado(a), ceñido(a); **you need a t. lid for the saucepan** te hace falta una tapa que encaje *or* ajuste bien en la cacerola

tight-knit ['taɪt'nɪt] *adj (community)* muy integrado(a)

tight-lipped ['taɪt'lɪpt] *adj* **to be t. (about sth)** *(silent)* no soltar prenda (sobre algo); *(angry)* estar enfurruñado(a) (por algo); **she sat in t. silence** estaba sentada en silencio sin decir esta boca es mía

tightly ['taɪtlɪ] *adv* (**a**) *(to hold, squeeze)* con fuerza; *(to seal, close)* bien; **he held his daughter t. to him** abrazó fuertemente *or* firmemente a su hija contra sí; **we held on t. to the rail** nos agarramos con fuerza *or* firmemente a la baranda; **make sure you screw the lid on t.** deja la tapa bien cerrada *or* apretada; **keep your eyes t. shut** mantenga los ojos bien cerrados; **the lecture hall was t. packed** el salón de actos estaba abarrotado

(**b**) *(to control)* rigurosamente, de manera estricta

tightness ['taɪtnɪs] *n* (**a**) *(of clothing) (close-fitting design)* carácter *m* ceñido *or* ajustado; *(uncomfortable nature)* estrechez *f*

(**b**) *(of screw, lid)* dureza *f*; **the t. of the lid meant she couldn't get it off** la tapa estaba tan ajustada que no podía abrirla

(**c**) *(of rope, knot)* tirantez *f*; *(in chest)* opresión *f*

(**d**) *(of grip, embrace)* fuerza *f*, firmeza *f*

(**e**) *(of bend)* ángulo *m* cerrado

(**f**) *(of restrictions)* severidad *f*; *(of control, security)* rigurosidad *f*, carácter *m* estricto

(**g**) *(of budget, resources)* escasez *f*

(**h**) *(of schedule)* **the t. of the president's schedule** la apretada agenda del presidente

tightrope ['taɪtrəʊp] *n* cuerda *f* floja; *Fig* **to be walking a t.** estar en la cuerda floja ▸▸ ***t. walker*** funambulista *mf*

tights [taɪts] *npl* (**a**) *Br (nylon, silk)* medias *fpl*, pantis *mpl* (**b**) *(woollen)* leotardos *mpl*, *Col* medias *fpl* veladas, *RP* cancanes *mpl*

tightwad ['taɪtwɒd] *n Fam* rata *mf*, roñoso(a) *m,f*

tigress ['taɪgrɪs] *n* tigresa *f*

tikka ['tiːkə] *n Culin* **chicken t.** pollo *m* (al estilo) tikka, = pollo troceado, adobado con yogur, pimentón y especias, y hecho al horno

'til [tɪl] = **until**

tilbury ['tɪlbərɪ] *n (carriage)* tílburi *m*

tilde ['tɪldə] *n* tilde *f (sobre la ñ)*

tile [taɪl] **1** *n (on roof)* teja *f*; *(on floor)* baldosa *f*; *(on wall)* azulejo *m*
2 *vt* (**a**) *(put tiles on) (roof)* tejar; *(floor)* embaldosar; *(walls)* poner azulejos en, *Esp* alicatar (**b**) *Comptr (windows)* poner en mosaico

tiled [taɪld] *adj (floor)* embaldosado(a); *(wall)* con azulejos, *Esp* alicatado(a); **a t. roof** un tejado

tiler ['taɪlə(r)] *n (of roof)* techador(ora) *m,f*; *(of floor)* solador(ora) *m,f*; *(of wall)* = albañil que coloca azulejos, *Esp* alicatador(ora) *m,f*

tiling ['taɪlɪŋ] *n (tiles) (on floor)* embaldosado *m*; *(on wall)* azulejos *mpl*, *Esp* alicatado *m*

till[1] [tɪl] *vt (field, soil)* labrar

till[2] *n (cash register)* caja *f* (registradora); **please pay at the t.** *(sign)* los productos se abonan en caja; IDIOM **to be caught with one's hand** *or* **fingers in the t.** ser atrapado(a) haciendo un desfalco ►► ***t. receipt*** recibo *m* de caja, tíquet *m* de compra

till[3] = **until**

tiller ['tɪlə(r)] *n (on boat)* caña *f* del timón

tilt [tɪlt] **1** *n* (**a**) *(angle)* inclinación *f*; **she wore her hat at a t.** llevaba el sombrero ladeado; **I'm sure that picture's on a t.** estoy seguro de que ese cuadro está torcido (**b**) *(speed)* **at full t.** a toda marcha; **he ran full t. into the door** se estrelló contra la puerta (**c**) *Hist (jousting tournament)* justa *f*, torneo *m*; *(thrust with lance)* lanzada *f*; *Fig* **to have a t. at sb** arremeter contra alguien *(de palabra)*
2 *vt* inclinar; **to t. one's head** inclinar la cabeza; **to t. one's chair (back)** inclinarse hacia atrás en la silla; *Fig* **this may t. the odds in our favour** esto puede inclinar la balanza a nuestro favor
3 *vi* (**a**) *(incline)* inclinarse; **to t. forwards/backwards** inclinarse hacia delante/hacia atrás; **don't t. back on your chair** no inclines la silla hacia atrás, no te inclines hacia atrás en la silla ►► *Comptr* ***t. and swivel base*** *(of monitor)* base *f* inclinable y giratoria (**b**) IDIOM **to t. at windmills** arremeter contra molinos de viento

► **tilt over** *vi* (**a**) *(lean)* inclinarse (**b**) *(overturn)* volcarse

tilting ['tɪltɪŋ] *adj (window, seat)* basculante; *(computer screen)* desplegable

timbale [tæm'bæl] *n Culin* timbal *m*; *(mould)* (molde *m* de) timbal *m*

timber ['tɪmbə(r)] *n* (**a**) *(wood)* madera *f* (de construcción) ►► *Br* ***t. merchant*** maderero *m*; ***the t. trade*** el sector maderero, la industria maderera
(**b**) *(trees)* árboles *mpl* (madereros *or* maderables); **to fell t.** talar árboles; **t.!** ¡árbol va! ►► ***t. line*** límite *m* superior de la vegetación arbórea; ***t. wolf*** lobo *m* gris
(**c**) *(beam) (in house)* viga *f* de madera, madero *m*; *(in ship)* cuaderna *f*
(**d**) IDIOM **to be presidential/managerial t.** tener madera de presidente/jefe

timbered ['tɪmbəd] *adj (house)* de madera; *(land)* arbolado(a)

timbering ['tɪmbərɪŋ] *n (of mine shaft)* entibado *m*, entibación *f*

timberland ['tɪmbəlænd] *n US* bosques *mpl* madereros *or* maderables

timberyard ['tɪmbəjɑːd] *n Br* almacén *m* maderero, maderería *f*, *RP* barraca *f* maderera

timbre ['tæmbə(r)] *n Mus* timbre *m*

Timbuktu [tɪmbʌk'tuː] *n Geog* Tombuctú; *Fig* **they might as well live in T.** es como si vivieran en la Conchinchina

TIME [taɪm] **1** *n* (**a**) *(in general)* tiempo *m*; **space and t.** el espacio y el tiempo; **t. is getting on** no queda mucho tiempo; **I spend most of my t. filling in forms** paso casi todo el tiempo rellenando impresos *or* formularios *or Méx* formas; **he wants some t. to himself** quiere tener tiempo para él; **now that my t. is my own** ahora que tengo todo el tiempo del mundo; **it's only a matter** *or* **question of t.** tan solo es cuestión de tiempo; **t.'s up!** ¡se acabó el tiempo!; **as t. goes by** *or* **on I find myself becoming more and more intolerant** a medida que pasa el tiempo me vuelvo más intolerante; *Literary* **for all t.** por siempre jamás; **in t.** *(eventually)* con el tiempo; **in t. for sth/to do sth** a tiempo para algo/para hacer algo; **I was just in t. to see it** llegué justo a tiempo para verlo; **in good t.** *(early)* con tiempo; **all in good t.!** cada cosa a su (debido) tiempo, *Esp* todo se andará; **she'll do it in her own good t.** lo hará a su ritmo; **he did it in his own t.** *(out of working hours)* lo hizo fuera de las horas de trabajo; *(at his own pace)* lo hizo a su ritmo *or Esp* aire; **in no t. at all, in next to** *or* **less than no t.** en un abrir y cerrar de ojos; **she is the greatest tennis player of all t.** es la mejor tenista de todos los tiempos; **over** *or* **with t.** con el tiempo; **given t., I'll succeed** si me dan tiempo lo conseguiré; **to have (the) t. to do sth** tener tiempo para hacer algo; **when I have** *or* **I've got (the) t.** cuando tenga tiempo; **to have all the t. in the world** tener todo el tiempo del mundo; **I've a lot of t. for him** me cae muy bien; **I've no t. for him** no me cae nada bien; **I've a lot of/no t. for her novels** me encantan/no me gustan sus novelas; **there's no t. to lose** no hay tiempo que perder; **to put in t. (doing sth)** invertir tiempo (en hacer algo); **I've taken a lot of t. over it** le he dedicado mucho tiempo; **she took her t. (doing it)** se tomó su tiempo (para hacerlo); **take your t.!** ¡tómate tu tiempo!; **you took your t.!** ¡has tardado *or Am* demorado mucho!; **it takes t.** lleva su tiempo; **to take t. off work** tomarse tiempo libre; **to take t. out (from sth/to do sth)** sacar tiempo (de algo/para algo); **she took t. out from her studies** interrumpió sus estudios; *Fam* **to do** *or* **serve t.** *(go to prison)* pasar una temporada a la sombra; **to have t. on one's hands** tener tiempo de sobra; **we have t. on our side, t. is on our side** tenemos el tiempo a nuestro favor, el tiempo está de nuestro lado; **if I had my t. over again** si pudiera vivir otra vez; **(only) t. will tell** el tiempo lo dirá; **t. is of the essence** hay que actuar rápidamente; PROV **t. is a great healer, t. heals all wounds** el tiempo todo lo cura; PROV **t. is money** el tiempo es oro; PROV **t. flies** el tiempo vuela; PROV **t. flies when you're having fun** el tiempo vuela cuando lo estás pasando bien; PROV **t. and tide wait for no man** el paso del tiempo es inexorable ►► ***t. bomb*** bomba *f* de relojería *or Am* tiempo; *Fig* **to be sitting on a t. bomb** estar (sentado(a)) sobre un volcán; *Gram* ***t. clause*** oración *f* (subordinada) temporal; ***t. machine*** máquina *f* del tiempo; ***t. off*** tiempo *m* libre; ***t. travel*** viaje *m* en el tiempo; **t. warp: to be in a t. warp** seguir anclado(a) en el pasado
(**b**) *(period)* **during their t. in office** durante el tiempo que pasaron en el poder; **part** *or* **some of the t.** parte del tiempo; **after my t. in Italy** después de estar en Italia, *Am* después de mi estadía en Italia; **there were more good times than bad times** hubo más épocas buenas que malas; **to take a long t. over sth/to do sth** tomarse mucho tiempo *or Am* demorarse mucho para algo/para hacer algo; **a long t. ago** hace mucho tiempo; **some t. ago** hace algún tiempo; **a short t. later** poco (tiempo) después; **after a t.** después de un tiempo; **all the t.** *(frequently)* constantemente, todo el rato; *(all along)* en todo momento, *Am* todo el tiempo; **for a t.** durante un tiempo; **for a long t.** durante mucho tiempo; **I waited for a long t.** esperé mucho tiempo; **I had to wait for a short t.** tuve que esperar un rato; **the fighting lasted only a short t.** la pelea duró poco tiempo; **that's the best meal I've had for** *or* **in a long t.** es lo mejor que he comido en mucho tiempo, *Esp* es la mejor comida que he tomado en mucho tiempo; **to make** *or* **find t. for sth/sb** encontrar tiempo para algo/alguien; *US Fam* **to make t. with sb** *(chat up)* intentar ligar con alguien, *Col, RP, Ven* intentar levantar a alguien; *(embrace, pet) Esp* darse el lote con alguien, *Am* manosear a alguien, *RP* amasijar con alguien; **for some t.** durante bastante tiempo; **I've been coming here for some t. now** vengo aquí desde hace algún tiempo; **it won't start for some t. yet** todavía falta rato para que empiece; **for the t. being** por ahora, por el momento; **in a short t.** *(soon)* dentro de poco; *(quickly)* en poco tiempo; **in three weeks' t.** dentro de tres semanas; **in record t.** *(very quickly)* en un tiempo récord; **most of the t.** la mayor parte del tiempo, casi todo el tiempo; **the whole t.** todo el tiempo
(**c**) *(age)* época *f*; **at the t. of the First World War** en la época de la Primera Guerra Mundial; **in Roman times** en tiempos de los romanos; **in times gone by/to come** en tiempos *Esp* pretéritos *or Am* pasados/futuros; **in times of war** en tiempos de guerra; **she is one of the best artists of our time(s)** es una de las mejores artistas de nuestra época; **times are changing** los tiempos están cambiando; **times were hard in those days** aquellos fueron tiempos duros; **to be ahead of one's t.** estar por delante de su tiempo, ser un adelantado de su tiempo; **the invention was ahead of its t.** ese invento se adelantó a su tiempo; **to be behind the times** no andar con los tiempos; **that was before my t.** *(before I was born)* eso fue antes de nacer yo; *(my arrival)* eso fue antes de mi llegada; **he grew old before his t.** envejeció antes de tiempo *or* prematuramente; **she was a good singer in her t.** en sus tiempos fue una gran cantante; **she's seen a few things in her t.** ha visto unas cuantas cosas en su vida; **it won't happen in our t.** nosotros no lo viviremos; **since** *or* **from t. out of mind** desde tiempos inmemoriales; **to move with the times** ir con los tiempos; **t. was when...** hubo un tiempo en que... ►► ***t. capsule*** = recipiente que contiene objetos propios de una época y que se entierra para que futuras generaciones puedan conocer cómo se vivía entonces
(**d**) *(moment)* momento *m*; **at that t.** en aquel momento *or* entonces; **at that t. of (the) year** por aquellas fechas, a esa altura del año; **it's cold for the t. of year** hace frío para esa época del año; **at this t. of night** a estas horas de la noche; **I didn't know it at the t.** en aquel momento *or* entonces no lo sabía; **at the present t., at this t.** en el momento presente; **this t. last week** hace ahora una semana; **at the same t.** al mismo tiempo; **we arrived at the wrong t.** llegamos en un momento inoportuno; **at all times** en todo momento; **smoking is not allowed at any t.** está prohibido fumar (en todo momento); **at any**

one *or* **given t.** en un momento dado; **at no t.** en ningún momento; **at one t., it was different** hubo un tiempo en que era distinto; **at some t. or other** alguna vez; **at my t. of life** a mi edad; **any t. now** en cualquier momento; **some t. next month** en algún momento del mes que viene; **now is the t. to invest** ahora es el momento de invertir; **by that t.** para entonces; **by the t. we arrived** (para) cuando llegamos; **from that t. (onwards)** desde entonces (en adelante); **from the t. we arrived to the t. we left** desde que llegamos hasta que nos fuimos; **this t. next year** el año que viene por estas fechas; **it's t. for a change** es hora de cambiar; **the t. is ripe for...** es un momento propicio para...; **the t. for talking is past** la ocasión de hablar ya ha pasado; **the t. has come to...** ha llegado la hora de...; **when the t. comes (to...)** cuando llegue el momento (de...), llegado el momento (de...); **our t. has come** ha llegado nuestra hora; **and about t. too!, not before t.!** ¡ya era hora!; **it's about** *or* **high t.!** ¡ya era hora!; **it's about** *or* **high t. (that) you told her!** ¡ya era hora de que se lo dijeras!; **this is neither the t. nor the place for such remarks** no es ni el lugar ni el momento para ese tipo de comentarios; **this is no t.** *or* **hardly the t. to have second thoughts** este no es momento para volverse atrás; **there's no t. like the present** no dejes para mañana lo que puedas hacer hoy

(**e**) *(on clock)* hora *f*; **what's the t.?, what t. is it?** ¿qué hora es?, *Am* ¿qué horas son?; **what t. does it start?** ¿a qué hora empieza?; **what t. (of day) suits you?** ¿a qué hora te viene bien?; **what t. do you** *Br* **make it** *or US* **have?** ¿qué hora tienes?; **the t. is six o'clock** son las seis (en punto); **it's 6.30 local t.** son las 6:30, hora local; *Fam* **is that the t.!, look at the t.!** ¡qué tarde es!, ¡qué tarde se me ha hecho!; **it's t. for bed/to get up** es hora de irse a la cama/de levantarse; **it's t. we left** es hora de que nos vayamos; **have you got the t. (on you)?** ¿tienes hora?; **this t. tomorrow** mañana a estas horas; **see you next week, same t., same place** nos vemos la semana que viene, en el mismo lugar, a la misma hora; **between times** el resto del tiempo; **on t.** a la hora en punto; **to be on t.** llegar a la hora; **we're a bit ahead of/behind t.** vamos algo avanzados/retrasados; *Br* **t., please!** *(in pub)* ¡vamos a cerrar!; **to keep good t.** *(clock)* estar siempre en hora; IDIOM **I wouldn't give him the t. of day** a él no le daría ni la hora *or* ni los buenos días; PROV **there's a t. and a place for everything** todo tiene su momento y su lugar ►► *Ind* ***t. card*** tarjeta *f (para fichar)*; ***t. check*** *(in cycling, skiing, motor racing)* control *m* (de tiempos parciales); **there's a t. check every five minutes** *(on radio)* dan la hora cada cinco minutos; *Ind* ***t. clock*** reloj *m (de fichar)*; ***t. code*** *(on photograph, video)* código *m* de tiempo; ***t. difference*** diferencia *f* horaria; *Phot* ***t. exposure*** tiempo *m* de exposición; ***t. frame*** plazo *m* de tiempo; ***t. lag*** lapso *m*; ***t. lapse*** lapso *m* (de tiempo); ***t. limit:* there's a t. limit of three weeks** hay un plazo de tres semanas; **there's no t. limit** no hay límite de tiempo; ***t. lock*** sistema *m* de apertura retardada; *Ind* ***t. sheet*** ficha *f* de horas trabajadas; ***t. signal*** señal *f* horaria; ***t. slot*** *(in TV schedule)* franja *f* horaria; ***t. switch*** temporizador *m*; ***t. trial*** *(in cycling)* contrarreloj *f*; *(in rallying)* prueba *f* cronometrada; ***t. trial specialist*** *(in cycling)* contrarrelojista *mf*; ***t. zone*** huso *m* horario, franja *f* horaria

(**f**) *(occasion)* vez *f*; **do you remember the t. I broke my leg?** te acuerdas de la vez que me rompí la pierna?; **there are times when I wish I had never been born** hay ocasiones en las que desearía no haber nacido; **you can borrow it any t.** tómalo prestado cuando quieras; *Fam* **thanks – any t.** gracias – para eso estamos; **at times** a veces; **one at a t., please** de uno en uno, por favor, *RP* de a uno, por favor; **he went down the stairs three at a t.** bajó las escaleras de tres en tres, *RP* bajó las escaleras de a tres escalones; **let's look at your comments one at a t.** examinemos tus comentarios uno por uno *or RP* de a uno; **I often heard nothing from her for months at a t.** a menudo pasaban meses enteros sin que supiera nada de ella; **he does the same thing every t.** siempre hace lo mismo; **every** *or* **each t. she looks at me** cada vez que me mira; *Br Fam* **the times I've told you not to do that!** ¿cuántas veces te tengo que decir que no hagas eso?; **I don't like these foreign cheeses, give me cheddar every t.** no me gustan esos quesos extranjeros, donde esté el cheddar que se quite todo lo demás *or* prefiero mil veces el cheddar; **from t. to t.** de vez en cuando, de cuando en cuando; **(the) last t. I was here...** la última vez que estuve aquí...; **next t.** la próxima vez; **the t. before** la vez anterior; **I had to tell him a second t.** se lo tuve que repetir; **I'll let you off this t.** (por) esta vez no te castigaré; **the one t. I'm winning, he wants to stop playing** una vez que iba ganando y quiere dejar de jugar; **why now of all times?** ¿por qué precisamente ahora?; **t. and (t.) again, t. after t.** una y otra vez; **third t. lucky** a la tercera va la vencida, *RP* la tercera es la vencida

(**g**) *(time required for something)* **the flying t. to Madrid is two hours** el tiempo de vuelo a Madrid es de dos horas; **the cooking t. is two hours** el tiempo de cocción son dos horas

(**h**) *(experience)* **to give sb a hard** *or* **rough** *or* **tough t.** hacer pasar a alguien un mal rato; **to have a good/bad t.** pasarlo bien/mal; **I had a hard t. convincing them** me costó mucho convencerlos; **to have the t. of one's life** pasarlo en grande

(**i**) *(in race)* tiempo *m*; **she recorded the fastest t. in the world this year** hizo el tiempo récord de este año

(**j**) *Ind* **to get paid t. and a half** cobrar una vez y media el sueldo normal

(**k**) *Rad & TV (airtime)* tiempo *m* de emisión; **to buy/sell t. on television** comprar/vender espacios publicitarios en televisión

(**l**) *(in multiplication)* **four times two is eight** cuatro por dos son ocho; **three times as big (as)** tres veces mayor (que); *Fig* **the food here is ten times better than it used to be** la comida de aquí es diez veces mejor que antes

(**m**) *Mus* tiempo *m*, compás *m*; **in 3/4 t.** *Esp* al *or Am* en compás de tres por cuatro; **to sing in t. to** *or* **with the music** cantar al compás de la música; **to sing out of t.** cantar descompasadamente; **the drums are out of t.** la batería está descompasada; **to beat t.** llevar *or RP* marcar el ritmo *or* compás; **to keep t.** seguir el ritmo *or* compás ►► ***t. signature*** compás *m*

2 *vt* (**a**) *(person, race)* cronometrar; **the winner was timed at 9.87 seconds** el ganador hizo un tiempo de 9,87 segundos; **he timed his speech to last 20 minutes** cronometró su discurso para que durase 20 minutos; **I timed how long it took to get there** cronometré el tiempo que llevó llegar hasta allí

(**b**) *(meeting, visit, schedule)* programar; **the bomb was timed to go off at 7.30** la bomba estaba programada para estallar a las 7:30; **I timed my holidays to coincide with the World Cup** programé mis vacaciones para que coincidieran con el mundial

(**c**) *(remark, action)* **well timed** oportuno(a); **badly timed** inoportuno(a); **he timed his entrance well** calculó muy bien el momento de su entrada; **she timed the punch line beautifully** la pausa que hizo dio un gran efecto al chiste; **he timed his pass perfectly** hizo el pase en el momento exacto; **she timed her backhand beautifully** conectó un revés impecable

(**d**) *(synchronize)* **she tried to t. her steps to the music** trataba de ir al compás de la música

► **time out** *vi Comptr* **the connection timed out** el tiempo de conexión ha expirado

---

time-and-motion study [taɪmən'məʊʃən'stʌdɪ] *n* = estudio del aprovechamiento del tiempo en una empresa para mejorar la productividad

time-consuming ['taɪmkənsjuːmɪŋ] *adj* **a t. task** una tarea que lleva mucho tiempo; **to be t.** llevar mucho tiempo

time-critical ['taɪm'krɪtɪkəl] *adj* **this project is absolutely t.** el tiempo es un factor crucial en este proyecto

time-honoured ['taɪmɒnəd] *adj (ancient)* ancestral; *(long-standing)* antiguo(a); **a t. tradition** una tradición de gran raigambre; **they greeted their guest in the t. manner** saludaron a su invitado a la manera tradicional

timekeeper ['taɪmkiːpə(r)] *n* (**a**) *Sport* cronometrador(ora) *m,f* (**b**) *(clock, watch)* **to be a good t.** ser preciso(a) (**c**) *(person)* **I have always been a good/bad t.** siempre/nunca he sido muy puntual

timekeeping ['taɪmkiːpɪŋ] *n* (**a**) *Ind (in factory)* control *m* de puntualidad (**b**) *Br (punctuality)* puntualidad *f*; **good/poor t.** mucha/poca puntualidad; **your t. needs to improve** hay que ser más puntual *or* tener mayor puntualidad

time-lapse ['taɪmlæps] *adj* ***t. photography*** = montaje cinematográfico formado por planos tomados a intervalos regulares para mostrar procesos lentos como el crecimiento de una planta

timeless ['taɪmlɪs] *adj* **a t. classic** un clásico imperecedero; **a t. summer afternoon** una tarde de verano en la que el tiempo parecía haberse detenido

timelessness ['taɪmlɪsnɪs] *n (of music, writing)* intemporalidad *f*, atemporalidad *f*

timeliness ['taɪmlɪnɪs] *n* oportunidad *f*

timely ['taɪmlɪ] *adj* oportuno(a)

time-out [taɪm'aʊt] *n Sport* tiempo *m* muerto; *Fig* **to take a t.** tomarse un descanso

timepiece ['taɪmpiːs] *n* reloj *m*

timer ['taɪmə(r)] *n* (**a**) *(for cooking time) (on oven, microwave)* reloj *m* automático, temporizador *m*; *(clockwork)* temporizador *m* (**b**) *(for central heating, lighting)* programador *m*, temporizador *m*; *(on video)* programador *m*; *(on bomb)* temporizador *m*, mecanismo *m or* dispositivo *m* de relojería

time-saver ['taɪmseɪvə(r)] *n* **the dishwasher is a great t.** el lavavajillas (te) ahorra mucho tiempo

time-saving ['taɪmseɪvɪŋ] *adj (device, method)* que ahorra tiempo

timescale ['taɪmskeɪl] *n* plazo *m* (de tiempo)

time-served ['taɪmsɜːvd] *adj (trained)* formado(a), experto(a)

timeserver ['taɪmsɜːvə(r)] *n* oportunista *mf*

time-share ['taɪmʃeə(r)] *n* (**a**) *(system)* multipropiedad *f* (**b**) *(holiday home)* (vivienda *f* en) multipropiedad *f*

time-sharing ['taɪmʃeərɪŋ] *n* (**a**) *(of holiday home)* multipropiedad *f* (**b**) *Comptr* tiempo *m* compartido

timespan ['taɪmspæn] *n* plazo *m*

timetable ['taɪmteɪbəl] **1** *n* (**a**) *(for buses, trains, school)* horario *m* (**b**) *(for event, project)* programa *m*; *(for talks, reform)* calendario *m*; **the government has set a five-year t. for Britain to join the euro** el gobierno ha establecido un calendario *or* programa de cinco años para adherirse al euro; **she has a very busy t.** tiene una agenda muy apretada; **to work to a t.** trabajar con unos plazos determinados
2 *vt* programar

timewaster ['taɪmweɪstə(r)] *n* **no timewasters, please** *(in advertisement)* por favor, abstenerse curiosos

time-wasting ['taɪmweɪstɪŋ] *n* (**a**) *(messing around)* pérdida *f* de tiempo; **that's enough t.!** ¡vale ya de perder el tiempo! (**b**) *Sport* pérdida *f* de tiempo

timeworn ['taɪmwɔːn] *adj (custom, phrase)* gastado(a); *(person, face)* desgastado(a)

timid ['tɪmɪd] *adj* tímido(a)

timidity [tɪ'mɪdɪtɪ] *n* timidez *f*

timidly ['tɪmɪdlɪ] *adv* tímidamente

timidness ['tɪmɪdnɪs] *n* timidez *f*

timing ['taɪmɪŋ] *n* (**a**) *(of announcement, election)* (elección *f* del) momento *m*, oportunidad *f*; **the t. of the visit was unfortunate** la fecha de la visita fue desafortunada
(**b**) *(of remark, action)* **how's that for t.! we've finished one day before the deadline** ¡qué precisión! hemos terminado un día antes de la fecha límite; **that was good t., we needed an extra hand!** ¡qué oportuno! *or* ¡qué a tiempo!, justo ahora nos hacía falta una mano; **her remarks were good/bad t.** sus comentarios vinieron en buen/mal momento
(**c**) *(of musician)* compás *m*, (sentido *m* del) ritmo *m*; *(of playing)* compás *m*; *(of tennis player, shot)* coordinación *f*; **the comedian's t. was perfect** el humorista hizo un uso perfecto de las pausas y del ritmo
(**d**) *(timekeeping)* cronometraje *m* ►► ***t. device*** *(for bomb)* temporizador *m*, mecanismo *m or* dispositivo *m* de relojería; *(for lights)* programador *m*, temporizador *m*; ***t. gear*** engranaje *m* de distribución; ***t. mechanism*** *(for bomb)* mecanismo *m or* dispositivo *m* de relojería, temporizador *m*

timorous ['tɪmərəs] *adj* timorato(a), temeroso(a)

timpani, tympani ['tɪmpənɪ] *npl Mus* timbales *mpl*

timpanist, tympanist ['tɪmpənɪst] *n Mus* timbalero(a) *m,f*

tin [tɪn] **1** *n* (**a**) *(metal)* estaño *m*; *(tin plate)* hojalata *f*; **the t.** *(of squash court)* la chapa; IDIOM *esp US* **he's got a t. ear** no tiene oído (para la música) ►► ***t. can*** lata *f*; *Pej* ***t. god*** endiosado(a) *m,f*, engreído(a) *m,f*; ***t. hat*** *(of soldier)* casco *m* (de acero); *US (of worker)* casco *m* (protector); *Fam Old-fashioned* ***t. lizzie*** cafetera *f*, cacharro *m*; ***t. mine*** mina *f* de estaño; ***T. Pan Alley*** = la industria de la música pop; ***t. plate*** hojalata *f*; ***t. soldier*** soldadito *m* de plomo; ***t. whistle*** flautín *m*
(**b**) *esp Br (can)* lata *f*; **to live out of tins** comer (comida) de lata, alimentarse a base de latas ►► ***t. opener*** abrelatas *m inv*
(**c**) *(for storing)* (caja *f* de) lata *f*, bote *m*
(**d**) *(mould)* molde *m*; **cake t.** molde *(para bizcocho, plum-cake, etc.)*
2 *vt* (**a**) *(can) (food)* enlatar (**b**) *(plate)* revestir de estaño, estañar

tinamou ['tɪnəmuː] *n* tinamú *m*

tincture ['tɪŋktʃʊə(r)] *n* (**a**) *Med* tintura *f* ►► ***t. of iodine*** tintura *f* de yodo (**b**) *(trace) (of colour, flavour)* toque *m*

tinder ['tɪndə(r)] *n* yesca *f*

tinderbox ['tɪndəbɒks] *n* (**a**) *(box)* caja *f* de la yesca (**b**) *(explosive situation)* **the country is a t.** el país es un polvorín

tinder-dry ['tɪndə'draɪ] *adj* más seco(a) que la mojama

tine [taɪn] *n (of fork)* diente *m*; *(of antler)* candil *m*, asta *f* (terminal)

tinea ['tɪnɪə] *n Med* tiña *f*

tinfoil ['tɪnfɔɪl] *n* papel *m* (de) aluminio

ting [tɪŋ] **1** *n* tintineo *m*
2 *vi* tintinear

ting-a-ling ['tɪŋəlɪŋ] **1** *n* tilín *m*
2 *adv* tilín

tinge [tɪndʒ] **1** *n (of colour, emotion)* matiz *m*
2 *vt* **tinged with** *(colour)* con un matiz de; *(emotion)* teñido(a) de

tingle ['tɪŋgəl] **1** *n (physical sensation)* hormigueo *m*; *(of fear, excitement)* estremecimiento *m*
2 *vi* **my hands are tingling** siento un hormigueo en las manos; **my whole body was tingling after my swim in the cold lake** la sangre me bullía por todo el cuerpo después de nadar en las aguas frías del lago; **to t. with fear/excitement** estremecerse de miedo/emoción

tingling ['tɪŋglɪŋ] **1** *n (physical sensation)* hormigueo *m*; *(of fear, excitement)* estremecimiento *m*
2 *adj* **a t. sensation** *(physical)* una sensación de hormigueo, un hormigueo; *(from fear, excitement)* un estremecimiento

tingly ['tɪŋglɪ] *adj* **a t. sensation** *(physical)* una sensación de hormigueo, un hormigueo; *(from fear, excitement)* un estremecimiento; **my fingers have gone all t.** me ha entrado un hormigueo en los dedos; **the cold shower made me feel t. all over** la ducha fría me entonó el cuerpo

tinhorn ['tɪnhɔːn] *US Fam* **1** *n* fanfarrón(ona) *m,f*, *Esp* fantasma *mf*
2 *adj* fanfarrón(ona), *Esp* fantasma

tininess ['taɪnɪnɪs] *n* pequeñez *f*

tinker ['tɪŋkə(r)] **1** *n* (**a**) *(pot mender)* calderero(a) *m,f*, quincallero(a) *m,f*; *(gypsy)* gitano(a) *m,f*; IDIOM *Fam* **he doesn't give a t.'s damn** *or Br* **cuss** le importa un rábano (**b**) *Br Fam Old-fashioned (child)* perillán(ana) *m,f*, pillastre *mf*
2 *vi* **to t. with sth** *(adjust, modify)* retocar *or* reajustar algo; *(interfere)* enredar con algo; **he has been tinkering with his drive to try and improve it** ha estado probando con su drive *or* reajustando su drive para mejorarlo; **he wastes hours tinkering with that bike** se pasa horas enredando con la moto; **so far you've only been tinkering with the problem** hasta ahora lo único que has hecho es ponerle parches al problema

► **tinker about** *vi Pej* enredar (**with** con)

tinkle ['tɪŋkəl] **1** *n* (**a**) *(of bell)* tintineo *m*; *Br Fam* **I'll give you a t.** *(on phone)* te daré un toque *or* telefonazo, *Méx* te pego un grito (**b**) *Br Fam (act of urinating)* **to go for** *or* **have a t.** hacer pipí
2 *vi* (**a**) *(bell)* tintinear (**b**) *Br Fam (urinate)* hacer pipí

tinkling ['tɪŋklɪŋ] **1** *n (of bell)* tintineo *m*
2 *adj (bell)* tintineante; *(water)* cantarín(ina)

tinkly ['tɪŋklɪ] *adj* tintineante

tinned [tɪnd] *adj (food)* de lata; **t. meat/fruit** carne/fruta en conserva *or* en lata

tinnitus ['tɪnɪtəs] *n Med* zumbido *m* de oídos

tinny ['tɪnɪ] *adj Pej* (**a**) *(sound)* a lata, metálico(a) (**b**) *(taste)* a lata (**c**) *Fam (poor quality)* de pacotilla, de tres al cuarto

tinpot ['tɪnpɒt] *adj Fam (dictator, regime, company)* de pacotilla, de tres al cuarto

tinsel ['tɪnsəl] *n* (**a**) *(for Christmas tree)* espumillón *m* (**b**) *(false glamour)* oropel *m*, relumbrón *m*

Tinseltown ['tɪnsəltaʊn] *n Fam* Hollywood

tinsmith ['tɪnsmɪθ] *n* hojalatero(a) *m,f*

tint [tɪnt] **1** *n* (**a**) *(colour)* matiz *m* (**b**) *(in hair)* tinte *m*
2 *vt* (**a**) *(colour)* **blue-tinted walls** paredes con tonalidad azul *or* con un tono azulado (**b**) *(hair)* teñir; **she tints her hair** lleva el pelo teñido, se tiñe el pelo

tinted ['tɪntɪd] *adj (glass, lenses)* tintado(a)

tinware ['tɪnweə(r)] *n* objetos *mpl or* cacharros *mpl* de hojalata

tiny ['taɪnɪ] *adj* diminuto(a), minúsculo(a); **a t. bit** un poquitín ►► ***t. tot*** pequeñín(ina) *m,f*

tip[1] [tɪp] **1** *n (end)* punta *f*; *(on walking stick, umbrella)* contera *f*; *(on snooker cue)* suela *f*; **the northernmost t. of the island** el extremo septentrional de la isla; **to stand on the tips of one's toes** ponerse de puntillas; **I scrubbed him down from t. to toe** lo lavé (bien) de pies a cabeza; *Fig* **the t. of the iceberg** la punta del iceberg; IDIOM **to have sth on the t. of one's tongue** tener algo en la punta de la lengua; IDIOM **to be honest to the tips of one's fingers** ser honrado(a) a carta cabal
2 *vt* (*pt & pp* **tipped**) **it was tipped with steel** tenía la punta de acero; **arrows tipped with poison** flechas envenenadas *or* con la punta envenenada

tip[2] **1** *n* (**a**) *(payment)* propina *f*; **she gave me a generous t.** me dio una buena *or* generosa propina; **how much t. shall I leave?** ¿cuánto dejo de propina?, ¿cuánta propina dejo?
(**b**) *(piece of advice)* consejo *m*; *(for horse race)* pronóstico *m*, favorito *m*, *RP* fija *f*; **my t. for the 3.45 is Orlando** mi favorito para la carrera de las 3:45 es Orlando; **take a t. from me and don't accept**

the job hazme caso *or* sigue mi consejo y no aceptes ese empleo

2 *vt (pt & pp* **tipped**) (**a**) *(give money to)* dar (una) propina a; **she tipped him $5** le dio 5 dólares de propina, le dio una propina de 5 dólares; **how much should I t.?** ¿cuánto doy *or* cuánto se da de propina?

(**b**) *(predict)* **to t. a winner** *(person)* pronosticar quién será el ganador; *(horse)* pronosticar qué caballo será el ganador; **our racing expert has tipped Orlando to win the 2.30** (el pronóstico de) nuestro experto en carreras hípicas da como favorito *or RP* fija a Orlando para la de las 2:30; **to t. sb for promotion** pronosticar que alguien será ascendido(a); **he is strongly tipped to become Home Secretary** figura en todos los pronósticos como el próximo *or* futuro ministro de Interior

3 *vi (give money)* dar *or* dejar propina

tip[3] 1 *n Br (dump) (for rubbish, coal)* vertedero *m*; *Fam* **this room's a t.!** ¡esta habitación es una pocilga *or Méx* un mugrero *or RP* un chiquero!

2 *vt (pt & pp* **tipped**) (**a**) *(tilt, lean)* **she tipped her head to one side** ladeó la cabeza, inclinó la cabeza hacia un lado; **don't t. your chair back!** ¡no te inclines hacia atrás en la silla!, ¡no inclines la silla hacia atrás!; **to t. one's hat to sb** saludar a alguien con el sombrero; **to t. the scales at 95 kg** *(weigh)* pesar 95 kg; IDIOM **to t. the scales** *or* **balance (in sb's favour)** inclinar la balanza (a favor de alguien)

(**b**) *(pour)* verter; **she tipped the sugar into the bowl** vertió *or* echó el azúcar en el cuenco

(**c**) *(upset, overturn)* **I was tipped off my stool** me tiraron del taburete inclinándolo *or* volcándolo

3 *vi* (**a**) *(tilt)* **to t. forwards** inclinarse hacia delante; **to t. to the left** inclinarse *or* ladearse hacia la izquierda (**b**) *(overturn)* volcarse (**c**) *Br (rubbish)* **no tipping** *(sign)* prohibido verter *or* arrojar basura(s)

▸ **tip down** *Fam* 1 *vt sep* **it's tipping it down** están cayendo chuzos de punta, *Méx* está lloviendo duro, *RP* están cayendo soretes de punta

2 *vi* **it's tipping down** están cayendo chuzos de punta, *Méx* está lloviendo duro, *RP* están cayendo soretes de punta

▸ **tip in** *vt sep* (**a**) *(in basketball)* palmear (**b**) *Typ* cortar y pegar

▸ **tip off** *vt sep (warn)* avisar, prevenir

▸ **tip out** *vt sep (container)* vaciar *(volcando)*; **he tipped out the suitcase onto the bed** vació la maleta volcándola sobre la cama; **she tipped the coins out into my hand** me echó las monedas en la mano

▸ **tip over** 1 *vt sep* volcar

2 *vi* volcarse

▸ **tip up** 1 *vt sep* (**a**) *(seat, table)* plegar (**b**) *(turn upside down) (bottle, barrel)* poner boca abajo, dar la vuelta a

2 *vi (cinema seat)* plegarse

tip-in ['tɪpɪn] *n (in basketball)* palmeo *m*

tip-off ['tɪpɒf] *n* (**a**) *(warning)* soplo *m*; **to give sb a t.** dar a alguien el soplo (**b**) *(in basketball)* salto *m* inicial

tipped [tɪpt] *adj (cigarette)* con boquilla

-tipped [tɪpt] *suffix* **a steel-t. cane** un bastón con (la) contera de acero; **the bird has black-t. wings** el pájaro tiene alas de puntas negras, el pájaro tiene las alas negras por los extremos

tipper ['tɪpə(r)] *n* (**a**) *(vehicle)* **t. (truck)** volquete *m* (**b**) *(customer)* **he's a generous t.** siempre da *or* deja buenas propinas

Tipp-Ex® ['tɪpeks] 1 *n* Tipp-Ex® *m*, corrector *m*

2 *vt* **to T. sth out** borrar algo con Tipp-Ex®

tipple ['tɪpəl] *Fam* 1 *n* (**a**) *(drink)* **he likes a t. now and then** le gusta tomarse una copa *or* copita de vez en cuando; **what's your t.?** ¿qué bebes *or Am* tomas? (**b**) *(favourite drink)* bebida *f* preferida

2 *vi* beber, empinar el codo, *Am* tomar

tippler ['tɪplə(r)] *n Fam* **he's quite a t.** se toma sus copitas

tippy-toe ['tɪpɪtəʊ] *US Fam* = **tiptoe**

tipsily ['tɪpsɪlɪ] *adv Fam* **he got t. to his feet** medio borracho, se puso en pie

tipstaff ['tɪpstɑːf] *n Br Law (person)* alguacil *mf*

tipster ['tɪpstə(r)] *n* pronosticador(ora) *m,f*

tipsy ['tɪpsɪ] *adj* achispado(a); **to be t.** estar achispado(a); **to get t.** achisparse ▸▸ *Br* ***t. cake*** (bizcocho *m*) borracho *m*

tiptoe ['tɪptəʊ] 1 *n* **to walk/stand on t.** caminar *or* andar/ponerse de puntillas

2 *vi* caminar *or* andar de puntillas; **to t. in/out** entrar/salir de puntillas

tiptop ['tɪptɒp] *adj* inmejorable, perfecto(a); **in t. condition** en inmejorables condiciones

tip-up ['tɪpʌp] *adj (seat)* plegable

TIR [tiːaɪ'ɑː(r)] *n (abbr* **transports internationaux routiers**) TIR *m*, transporte *m* internacional por carretera

tirade [taɪ'reɪd] *n* invectiva *f*, diatriba *f*

Tirana, Tiranë [tɪ'rɑːnə] *n* Tirana

tire[1] *US* = **tyre**

tire[2] ['taɪə(r)] 1 *vt* (**a**) *(exhaust)* cansar, fatigar (**b**) *(bore)* cansar, aburrir

2 *vi* (**a**) *(become exhausted)* cansarse, fatigarse; **she tires easily** se cansa *or* se fatiga con facilidad (**b**) *(become bored)* **to t. of (doing) sth** cansarse de (hacer) algo; **he never tires of teasing me** no se cansa jamás de tomarme el pelo

▸ **tire out** *vt sep (exhaust)* agotar; **you'll t. yourself out moving all those boxes** te vas a agotar *or* quedar agotado de mover tantas cajas

tired ['taɪəd] *adj* (**a**) *(exhausted)* cansado(a), fatigado(a); **to be** *or* **feel t.** estar cansado(a) *or* fatigado(a); **to get t.** cansarse, fatigarse; **you look t.** pareces cansado; **I'm t. out!** ¡estoy agotado *or* cansadísimo!; **my eyes are t.** tengo los ojos cansados *or* cargados; **in a t. voice** con voz cansina; *Br Hum Euph* **t. and emotional** *(drunk)* beodo(a), bebido(a)

(**b**) *(fed up)* **to be t. of (doing) sth** estar cansado(a) *or* harto(a) de (hacer) algo; **I'm t. of you and your complaining** estoy cansado *or* harto de ti y de tus quejas; **I'm t. of telling them not to do it** estoy cansado *or* harto de decirles que no lo hagan; **I got rather t. of playing cards** me harté *or* cansé de jugar a las cartas

(**c**) *(hackneyed)* **a t. old cliché** un lugar común muy manido

(**d**) *(old) (lettuce, vegetables)* mustio(a); *(upholstery, springs)* gastado(a)

tiredly ['taɪədlɪ] *adv (to say)* con voz cansina, cansinamente; *(to move)* pesadamente; *(to walk)* con paso cansino; *(to smile, nod)* con aire cansado

tiredness ['taɪədnɪs] *n* (**a**) *(fatigue)* cansancio *m*, fatiga *f* (**b**) *(of style, image, idea)* falta *f* de originalidad

tireless ['taɪəlɪs] *adj (worker, campaigner)* incansable, infatigable; *(efforts)* incesante, inagotable

tirelessly ['taɪəlɪslɪ] *adv* incansablemente, infatigablemente

tiresome ['taɪəsəm] *adj* pesado(a); **how t.!** ¡qué fastidio!

tiresomely ['taɪəsəmlɪ] *adv* de la manera más pesada

tiring ['taɪərɪŋ] *adj* cansado(a), pesado(a); **it's t. work** cansa mucho

tiro = **tyro**

Tirol, Tirolean = **Tyrol, Tyrolean**

'tis [tɪz] *Literary* = **it is**

tissue ['tɪʃuː] *n* (**a**) *Biol* tejido *m* ▸▸ ***t. culture*** cultivo *m* de tejidos; *Med* ***t. typing*** tipificación *f* de tejidos (**b**) *(paper handkerchief)* kleenex® *m inv*, pañuelo *m* de papel; *Fig* **a t. of lies** una sarta de mentiras (**c**) *(for wrapping, decoration)* **t. (paper)** papel *m* de seda

tit[1] [tɪt] *n (bird)* paro *m (carbonero o herrerillo)*

tit[2] *n* **t. for tat** donde las dan, las toman; **to give sb t. for tat** pagar a alguien con la misma moneda

tit[3] *n very Fam* (**a**) *(breast)* teta *f*, *Esp* dominga *f*, *Méx* chichi *f*, *RP* lola *f*; IDIOM *Br* **to get on sb's tits** hincharle las pelotas a alguien (**b**) *Br (idiot) Esp* gilipollas *mf inv*, *Am* pendejo(a) *m,f*, *RP* boludo(a) *m,f*

titan ['taɪtən] *n (person, company)* coloso *m*, titán *m*, gigante *m*

titanic [taɪ'tænɪk] *adj (conflict, struggle)* titánico(a), descomunal

titanium [taɪ'teɪnɪəm] *n Chem* titanio *m*

titbit ['tɪtbɪt], *US* **tidbit** ['tɪdbɪt] *n* (**a**) *(snack)* tentempié *m*, refrigerio *m* (**b**) *(small piece)* **a t. of gossip** un chismorreo *or Esp* cotilleo; **a t. of information** una noticia jugosa

titch [tɪtʃ] *n Br Fam (small person)* renacuajo(a) *m,f*

titchy ['tɪtʃɪ] *adj Br Fam* diminuto(a), minúsculo(a)

titfer ['tɪtfə(r)] *n Br Fam Old-fashioned* chapeo *m*, *Esp* chapiri *m*

tit-for-tat ['tɪtfə'tæt] *adj (killing, expulsion)* en represalia

tithe [taɪð] *n Hist* diezmo *m*

titillate ['tɪtɪleɪt] 1 *vt* excitar

2 *vi* excitar, provocar excitación

titillating ['tɪtɪleɪtɪŋ] *adj* excitante

titillation [tɪtɪ'leɪʃən] *n* excitación *f*

titivate ['tɪtɪveɪt] *vt Fam (person, room)* arreglar; **to t. oneself** arreglarse, acicalarse

titivation [tɪtɪ'veɪʃən] *n Fam* arreglo *m*

title ['taɪtəl] 1 *n* (**a**) *(of book, chapter)* título *m* ▸▸ *Comptr* ***t. bar*** barra *f* de título; ***t. page*** portada *f (página interior)*; *Cin & Theat* ***t. role:*** **she plays the t. role in the movie** interpreta el personaje que da título a la película; *Mus* ***t. track*** *(of album)* canción *f* que da título al disco

(**b**) *(of person)* título *m*; *(of noble)* título *m* nobiliario; *(form of address)* tratamiento *m*
(**c**) *Sport* título *m*; **he holds the world heavyweight boxing t.** tiene el título de campeón mundial de boxeo de los pesos pesados ►► ***t. fight*** combate *m* por el título
(**d**) *(book)* título *m*
(**e**) *Law (to property)* título *m* de propiedad ►► ***t. deed*** escritura *f*, título *m* de propiedad
(**f**) *Cin & TV* **the titles** los títulos (de crédito)
2 *vt* titular; **the first chapter is titled "Alpha"** el primer capítulo se titula "Alpha"

titled ['taɪtəld] *adj (person)* con título nobiliario

titleholder ['taɪtəlhəʊldə(r)] *n Sport* campeón(ona) *m,f*

titmouse ['tɪtmaʊs] (*pl* **titmice**) *n* paro *m (carbonero o herrerillo)*

titrate ['taɪtreɪt] *vt Chem* valorar, titular

titration [taɪ'treɪʃən] *n Chem* valoración *f*, titulación *f*, análisis *m* volumétrico

titre, *US* **titer** ['taɪtə(r)] *n Chem (concentration)* título *m*, concentración *f* volumétrica

titter ['tɪtə(r)] **1** *n* risilla *f*
2 *vi* reírse tontamente

tittle ['tɪtəl] *n (small amount)* **not one jot or t.** ni un ápice, ni lo más mínimo

tittle-tattle ['tɪtəltætəl] *Fam* **1** *n* habladurías *fpl*, chismes *mpl*
2 *vi* chismorrear, *Am* chismear, *Col, Méx* chismosear

titty ['tɪtɪ] *n very Fam* teta *f*, *Esp* dominga *f*, *Méx* chichi *f*, *RP* lola *f*

titular ['tɪtjʊlə(r)] *adj* nominal

Titus ['taɪtəs] *pr n* Tito

tizz [tɪz], **tizzy** ['tɪzɪ] *n Fam* **to be in a t. (about sth)** estar histérico(a) (con *or* por algo); **to get into a t.** ponerse histérico(a)

T-joint ['tiːdʒɔɪnt] *n* junta *f or* empalme *m* en T

T-junction ['tiːdʒʌŋkʃən] *n Br* intersección *f* en forma de T

TKO [tiːkeɪ'əʊ] *n* (*abbr* **technical knockout**) *(in boxing)* K.O. *m* técnico

TLC [tiːel'siː] *n Fam* (*abbr* **tender loving care**) mimo *m*, cariño *m*

T-lymphocyte ['tiː'lɪmfəsaɪt] *n Med* linfocito *m or* célula *f* T

TM [tiː'em] *n* (**a**) (*abbr* **trademark**) marca *f* registrada (**b**) (*abbr* **transcendental meditation**) meditación *f* trascendental

T-man ['tiːmæn] *n US Fam* agente *mf* del Tesoro *or* de delitos fiscales

TN (*abbr* **Tennessee**) Tennessee

tnpk *US* (*abbr* **turnpike**) autopista de peaje

TNT [tiːen'tiː] *n Chem* (*abbr* **trinitrotoluene**) TNT *m*

TO [tuː, *unstressed* tə] **1** *prep* (**a**) *(towards)* a; **to go to France** ir a Francia; **to go to church/to school** ir a misa/a la escuela; **to go to bed/to the toilet** ir a la cama/al baño; **to point to sth** señalar algo; **the road to Rome** la carretera a *or Esp* de Roma; **to the front** al *or Esp* hacia el frente; **to the left/right** a la izquierda/derecha; **to the north/south** al norte/sur; **she had her back to us** nos daba la espalda; **to travel from country to country** viajar de un país a otro
(**b**) *(touching)* **to stick sth to sth** pegar algo a algo; **he held her to his breast** la apretó contra su pecho; **she put her ear to the wall** pegó la oreja a la pared, puso la oreja contra la pared
(**c**) *(until)* hasta; **open from 9 to 5** abierto de 9 a 5; **from here to the capital** de aquí a la capital; **everything from paintbrushes to easels** de todo, desde pinceles hasta caballetes; **to this day** hasta el día de hoy; **a year to the day** hoy hace exactamente un año; **to count (up) to ten** contar hasta diez; **the total has risen to fifty** el total ha ascendido hasta cincuenta; **there were twenty to thirty people there** había entre veinte y treinta *or* de veinta a treinta personas; **they starved to death** murieron de hambre; **she nursed me back to health** sus cuidados me devolvieron la salud; **it drove me to despair** me llevó a la desesperación; **it was smashed to pieces** se rompió en pedazos
(**d**) *Br (when telling the time)* **it's ten to (six)** *Esp, RP* son (las seis) menos diez, *Andes, CAm, Carib, Méx* faltan diez (para las seis)
(**e**) *(with indirect object)* a; **to give sth to sb** dar algo a alguien; **give it to me** dámelo; **what did he do to you?** ¿qué te hizo?; **to be nice to sb** ser amable con alguien; **to speak to sb** hablar con alguien; **a threat to us** una amenaza para nosotros
(**f**) *(regarding)* **how did they react to that?** ¿cómo reaccionaron ante eso?; *Fam* **what's it to you?** ¿y a ti qué?, *RP* ¿y vos qué te metés?
(**g**) *(with result)* **to my surprise/joy** para mi sorpresa/alegría; **to my horror, I discovered that...** cuál no sería mi horror al descubrir que...; **it is to our advantage** redunda en beneficio nuestro; **is it to your liking?** ¿es de su agrado?
(**h**) *(in opinion of)* para; **to me, she's telling the truth** para mí que dice la verdad; **it seems to me that...** me parece (a mí) que...; **$1,000 is nothing to her** para ella mil dólares no son nada
(**i**) *(compared with)* **that's nothing to what it was last year** eso no es nada comparado con cómo fue el año pasado; **they had ten players to our eleven** ellos tenían diez jugadores, mientras que nosotros teníamos once
(**j**) *(expressing a proportion)* a; **by six votes to four** por seis votos a cuatro; **forty miles to the gallon** cuarenta millas por galón (de combustible), ≃ 7 litros a los 100 km; **there are 10 pesos to the dollar** un dólar equivale a 10 pesos
(**k**) *(at the same time as)* **to dance to music** bailar al compás de la música; **she entered to the sound of cheers** fue recibida con ovaciones
(**l**) *(for)* para; **suppliers to the Royal Family** proveedores de la Casa Real; **he has a whole desk to himself** tiene una mesa entera para él; **To Sue** *(on envelope)* (Para) Sue
(**m**) *(of)* **the key to the front door** la llave de la puerta de entrada; **it has a dangerous look to it** tiene aspecto peligroso; **I can't see the funny side to it** no le veo la gracia
(**n**) *(involved in)* **there's an element of danger to it** tiene un elemento de peligro; **there's a lot to the book** es un libro con mucha enjundia; **there's nothing to it** es facilísimo
(**o**) *(in invitations)* a; **to invite sb to dinner** invitar a alguien a cenar
(**p**) *(in honour of)* **a toast to sb** un brindis por alguien; **dedicated to...** dedicado(a) a...
(**q**) *(in betting odds)* **twelve to one** doce a uno
2 *adv* **to push the door to** cerrar la puerta del todo; **to and fro** de aquí para allá; **to go to and fro** ir y venir (de un lado para otro)
3 *particle* (**a**) *(with the infinitive)* **to go** ir; **I have a lot to do** tengo mucho que hacer; **I have nothing to do** no tengo nada que hacer; **there's also the expense to consider** también hay que considerar el gasto que supone; **I have/want to go** tengo que/quiero ir; **I want him to know** quiero que lo sepa; **I was the first person to do it** yo fui la primera persona que lo hizo; **to be honest...** sinceramente...; **I hope to be finished by tomorrow** espero terminar mañana; **I hope I live to see it finished** espero vivir para verlo terminado; **I woke up to find myself in a cell** al despertar me encontré en una celda; **she's old enough to go to school** ya tiene edad para ir al colegio; **it's too hot to drink** está demasiado caliente para beberlo; **I was reluctant to ask her** me resistía a preguntarle; **it's unlikely to happen** es improbable que ocurra; **an attempt to do sth** un intento de hacer algo; **to have reason to do sth** tener motivos para hacer algo; **to be betrayed like that, it's so upsetting!** una traición así... ¡me ha dolido tanto!
(**b**) *(representing verb)* **I want to** quiero (hacerlo); **you ought to** deberías hacerlo; **I was told to** me dijeron que lo hiciera; **have you phoned them? – I've tried to** ¿los has llamado? – lo he intentado; **will you be going? – I hope to** ¿irás allí? – eso espero; **can you come to my party? – I'd love to** ¿quieres venir a mi fiesta? – me encantaría
(**c**) *(in order to)* para; **he came to help me** vino a ayudarme; **I'm going to visit my aunt** voy a visitar a mi tía; **it is designed to save fuel** está diseñado para ahorrar combustible
(**d**) *(forming future tense)* **wages are to be cut** se van a recortar los salarios; **he was never to be seen again** nunca se lo volvió a ver; **government to cut interest rates** *(newspaper headline)* el gobierno recortará los tipos *or Am* las tasas de interés
(**e**) *(in orders)* **I told them to do it** les dije que lo hicieran; **you are not to do that** no debes hacer eso

toad [təʊd] *n* (**a**) *(animal)* sapo *m* (**b**) *Fam Pej (person)* gusano *m*; **you lying t.!** ¡embustero!, ¡rata mentirosa! (**c**) *Br Culin* **t. in the hole** = masa al horno compuesta de salchichas rebozadas en harina, huevo y leche

toadflax ['təʊdflæks] *n Bot* linaria *f*

toadstool ['təʊdstuːl] *n Esp* seta *f* venenosa, *Am* hongo *m* venenoso

toady ['təʊdɪ] *Fam* **1** *n Esp* pelotillero(a) *m,f*, *Am* arrastrado(a) *m,f*, *Col* cepillero(a) *m,f*, *Méx* lambiscón(ona) *m,f*, *RP* chupamedias *mf inv*
2 *vi* **to t. to sb** *Esp* hacer la pelota a alguien, *Col* pasar el cepillo a alguien, *Méx* lambisconear a alguien, *RP* chupar las medias a alguien

toadying ['təʊdɪɪŋ] *n Fam* adulación *f*, *Esp* peloteo *m*, *Méx* lambisconeo *m*

toast [təʊst] **1** *n* (**a**) *(toasted bread)* pan *m* tostado; **a slice** *or* **piece of t.** una tostada; **don't burn the t.** que no se te quemen las tostadas; **cheese on t.** tostada de queso (fundido); IDIOM *Fam* **you're t.!** *(in big trouble)* ¡se te va a caer el pelo! ►► ***t. rack*** portatostadas *m inv*
(**b**) *(tribute)* brindis *m inv*; **to drink a t. to sb** hacer un brindis a la salud de alguien; **I'd like to propose a t. to the bride and groom** quisiera proponer *or* hacer un brindis por los novios

(c) *(person)* **tonight, the actress is the t. of Hollywood** esta noche, la actriz es la reina de Hollywood

2 *vt* (a) *(bread)* tostar; **toasted cheese** tostada de queso (fundido); **toasted sandwich** sándwich (caliente); *Fig* **he was toasting his feet by the fire** se estaba calentando los pies junto al fuego (b) *(pay tribute to) (person)* brindar a la salud de, brindar por; *(success, win)* brindar por; **they toasted her victory in champagne** celebraron su triunfo con champán

toaster ['təʊstə(r)] *n* tostador(ora) *m,f*

toastie ['təʊstɪ] *n Br Fam* sándwich *m* (caliente)

toasting-fork ['təʊstɪŋfɔːk] *n* = tenedor largo para tostar

toastmaster ['təʊstmɑːstə(r)] *n* maestro *m* de ceremonias

toasty ['təʊstɪ] *adj Fam (warm)* **it's t. in here** ¡qué calorcito hace aquí!, ¡qué calentito se está aquí!

tobacco [tə'bækəʊ] *n* (a) *(for smoking)* tabaco *m* ►► ***t. industry*** industria *f* tabacalera *or* del tabaco; ***t. pouch*** petaca *f*; ***t. tin*** lata *f* de tabaco, tabaquera *f* (b) *(plant)* (planta *f* del) tabaco *m* ►► ***t. leaf*** hoja *f* de tabaco; ***t. plantation*** tabacal *m*, plantación *f* de tabaco

tobacconist [tə'bækənɪst] *n* estanquero(a) *m,f*; **t.'s (shop)** estanco *m*, *CSur* quiosco *m*, *Méx* estanquillo *m*

Tobago [tə'beɪgəʊ] *n* Tobago

-to-be [tə'biː] *suffix* **mother-t.** futura madre; **father-t.** futuro padre

toboggan [tə'bɒgən] 1 *n* tobogán *m (trineo)* ►► ***t. run*** (pista *f* de) tobogán *m*

2 *vi* tirarse en tobogán *(en pista de nieve)*

tobogganing [tə'bɒgənɪŋ] *n* **to go t.** tirarse en tobogán *(en pista de nieve)*

toby jug ['təʊbɪdʒʌg] *n* = jarra de cerveza con forma de hombre gordo con un sombrero de tres picos

toccata [tə'kɑːtə] *n Mus* tocata *f*

tocsin ['tɒksɪn] *n Literary* **to sound the t.** tocar a rebato

tod [tɒd] *n Br Fam* **to be on one's t.** estar solateras, *RP* estar solitari

today [tə'deɪ] 1 *n* (a) *(this day)* hoy *m*; **what day is it t.?** ¿a qué estamos hoy?, ¿qué día es hoy?; **a week from t.** dentro de una semana; **as from t.** a partir de hoy; **t.'s date/paper** la fecha/el periódico de hoy (b) *(this era)* hoy *m*; **the youth of t., t.'s youth** los jóvenes de hoy

2 *adv* (a) *(on this day)* hoy; **t. is Tuesday, it's Tuesday t.** hoy es martes; **he resigned earlier t.** ha presentado su dimisión hoy; **she's arriving a week t.** llega dentro de una semana *or* de aquí a una semana; **a week ago t.** hace (hoy) una semana; **why did you have to do it t. of all days?** ¿por qué tenías que hacerlo precisamente hoy?; **many new bands are here t. and gone tomorrow** muchos nuevos grupos son flor de un día

(b) *(in this era)* hoy

toddle ['tɒdəl] *vi* (a) *(infant)* dar los primeros pasos; **he managed to t. across the room** con paso vacilante logró cruzar la habitación (b) *Fam (go)* **could you just t. down to the shops for me?** ¿me harías el favor de acercarte a la tienda?; **he toddled off** se largó

toddler ['tɒdlə(r)] *n* niño(a) *m,f* pequeño(a) *(que aprende a caminar)*

toddy ['tɒdɪ] *n* **(hot) t.** = ponche hecho con una bebida alcohólica, azúcar, agua caliente, zumo de limón y especias

to-die-for [tə'daɪfɔː(r)] *adj Fam* **it's t.** está que te mueres; **the food was t.** la comida estaba de muerte; **her shoes were t.** llevaba unos zapatos monísimos

to-do [tə'duː] *(pl* **to-dos***) n Fam* escandalera *f*; **she made a great t. about it** armó una escandalera por eso

toe [təʊ] 1 *n* (a) *(of foot)* dedo *m* del pie; **big t.** dedo gordo del pie; **little t.** meñique del pie; **to stand on one's toes** ponerse de puntillas ►► ***t. loop*** *(in figure skating)* toe loop *m*, bucle *m* picado

(b) *(of sock, shoe)* puntera *f*

(c) IDIOMS **to be on one's toes** estar alerta; **to keep sb on his/her toes** no dar tregua a alguien; **to make sb's toes curl** *(with embarrassment)* hacer que alguien se muera de vergüenza *or Am* pena; *(with pleasure)* hacer que alguien se derrita de gusto; **to tread** *or* **step on sb's toes** meterse en el terreno de alguien

2 *vt* (a) *(ball)* dar de puntera a, tocar con la puntera (b) IDIOMS **to t. the line** acatar las normas, portarse como es debido; **he is not the sort of politician to t. the party line** no es de esa clase de políticos que siguen a rajatabla la disciplina de partido

toecap ['təʊkæp] *n* puntera *f*

-toed [təʊd] *suffix* **six-t.** de seis dedos *(en el pie)*; **square-t. shoes** de puntera cuadrada

toehold ['təʊhəʊld] *n (in climbing)* punto *m* de apoyo; *Fig* **to gain a t. in the market** lograr introducirse en el mercado

toenail ['təʊneɪl] *n* uña *f* del pie ►► ***t. clipper(s)*** cortaúñas *m inv*

toepoke ['təʊpəʊk] *Sport* 1 *n* punterazo *m*

2 *vt* dar un punterazo a

toerag ['təʊræg] *n Br Fam* sinvergüenza *mf*

toff [tɒf] *n Br Fam Esp* pijo(a) *m,f*, *Méx* fresa *mf*, *RP* copetudo(a) *m,f*

toffee ['tɒfɪ] *n* (a) *(small sweet)* (caramelo *m* de) tofe *m* (b) *(substance)* caramelo *m*; IDIOM *Br Fam* **he can't sing/act for t.** no tiene ni idea de cantar/actuar ►► ***t. apple*** manzana *f* de caramelo

toffee-nosed ['tɒfɪ'nəʊzd] *adj Br Fam* presumido(a), engreído(a)

tofu ['tɒfuː] *n Culin* tofu *m*

tog [tɒg] *n (of duvet)* = unidad de medida del grado de aislamiento térmico

► **tog out, tog up** *(pt & pp* **togged***) vt sep Fam* trajear, emperifollar; **he hates getting togged up for special occasions** odia tener que trajearse *or* emperifollarse para las grandes ocasiones; **to t. oneself out** *or* **up** trajearse, emperifollarse

toga ['təʊgə] *n* toga *f* ►► ***t. party*** = fiesta juvenil a la que se acude envuelto en una sábana a modo de toga sin apenas ropa debajo

TOGETHER [tə'geðə(r)] 1 *adv* (a) *(in general)* juntos(as); **t., we earn over $120,000** entre los dos ganamos más de 120.000 dólares; **t. we can change things** juntos podemos cambiar las cosas; **we're all in this t.!** nos afecta a todos; **even taken t., their efforts don't amount to much** incluso mirados en conjunto, sus esfuerzos no son gran cosa; **t. with** junto(a) con; **all t.** todos(as) juntos(as); **we were t. at university** íbamos juntos a la universidad; **are they t.?** *(a couple)* ¿son pareja?; *(in one group)* ¿vienen juntos?; **to act t.** obrar al unísono; **to add/mix two things t.** sumar/mezclar dos cosas; **to bang two things t.** hacer chocar dos cosas; **to get t. again** *(couple, partners)* volver a juntarse; **to get it** *or* **one's act t.** ponerse manos a la obra; **the spectators were packed t. inside the stadium** los espectadores abarrotaban el estadio; **to stick sth back t.** volver a pegar algo

(b) *(at the same time)* al mismo tiempo, a un tiempo; **pull both levers t.** acciona las dos palancas al mismo tiempo; **all t. now!** *(when singing)* ¡todos juntos!; *(when pulling, pushing)* ¡todos a una!

(c) *(consecutively)* **for 12 hours t.** (durante) doce horas seguidas

2 *adj Fam (well-balanced)* equilibrado(a)

togetherness [tə'geðənɪs] *n* unidad *f*, unión *f*

toggle ['tɒgəl] 1 *n* (a) *(on coat)* botón *m* de trenca (b) *Comptr* ***t. key*** = tecla o botón que permite activar o desactivar una función; *Comptr* ***t. switch*** = tecla o botón que permite activar o desactivar una función (c) *Naut* cazonete *m*

2 *vi Comptr* = activar o desactivar una función con la misma tecla; **you can t. between the two applications** puedes pasar de una aplicación a otra pulsando una tecla

► **toggle off** *vt sep Comptr* desactivar utilizando una tecla

► **toggle on** *vt sep Comptr* activar utilizando una tecla

Togo ['təʊgəʊ] *n* Togo

Togolese [təʊgə'liːz] 1 *n* togolés(esa) *m,f*

2 *adj* togolés(esa)

togs [tɒgz] *npl Fam (clothes)* ropa *f*; **don't forget your swimming t.** ¡no te olvides del traje de baño!

toil [tɔɪl] 1 *n Literary* esfuerzo *m*

2 *vi* (a) *(work hard)* trabajar arduamente; **to t. away at sth** esforzarse mucho en algo; **he spent years toiling over his novel** pasó años trabajando arduamente en su novela (b) *(go with difficulty)* **to t. up a hill** escalar penosamente una montaña; **they toiled on over the rough ground** siguieron avanzando con dificultad por aquel áspero terreno

toile [twɑːl] *n (fabric)* = tela fina de lino o algodón

toiler ['tɔɪlə(r)] *n* trabajador(ora) *m,f* incansable

toilet ['tɔɪlɪt] *n* (a) *Br (room) (in house)* cuarto *m* de baño, retrete *m*; *(in public place)* baño(s) *m(pl)*, *Esp* servicio(s) *m(pl)*, *CSur* toilette *f*; **he's on the t.** está en el cuarto de baño; **to go to the t.** *(in house)* ir al baño; *(in public place)* ir al baño *or Esp* al servicio *or CSur* a la toilette; **the nearest (public) toilets are in the park** los servicios (públicos) más cercanos están en el parque; **Toilets** *(sign)* Servicio(s), Aseo(s) ►► ***t. humour*** humor *m* escatológico; ***t. paper*** papel *m* higiénico *or Chile* confort; ***t. roll*** rollo *m* de papel higiénico; ***t. roll holder*** portarrollos *m inv* (de baño); ***t. tissue*** papel *m* higiénico *or Chile* confort

(b) *(object)* váter *m*, inodoro *m*; **the t. won't flush** no funciona la cisterna; **he threw it down the t.** lo tiró al váter *or* por el váter ►► ***t. bowl*** taza *f* (del váter *or* retrete); ***t. seat*** asiento *m* del váter; ***t. training*** aprendizaje *m* de ir solo al baño

(c) *Fam (dirty place)* pocilga *f*, agujero *m* inmundo

(d) *Old-fashioned (washing and dressing)* toilette *f*, aseo *m* personal;

to be at one's t. estar haciéndose la toilette ▸▸ ***t. bag*** bolsa *f* de aseo; ***t. soap*** jabón *m* de tocador; ***t. water*** (agua *f* de) colonia *f*

(e) IDIOMS *Br Fam* **to go down the t.** *(plan, career, work)* irse al garete; *Br Fam* **that's our holidays down the t.!** ¡nuestras vacaciones a la porra *or Am* por el piso *or RP* a la miércoles!

toiletries ['tɔɪlɪtrɪz] *npl* artículos *mpl* de tocador

toilette [twɑː'let] *n Old-fashioned* toilette *f*, aseo *m*; **to perform one's t.** hacerse la toilette, asearse

toilet-train ['tɔɪlɪttreɪn] *vt* enseñar a ir al baño

toilsome ['tɔɪlsəm] *adj* laborioso(a), arduo(a)

to-ing and fro-ing [tuːɪŋən'frəʊɪŋ] *n (activity)* trasiego *m*, idas y venidas *fpl*

toke [təʊk] *Fam* **1** *n Esp* calada *f*, *Am* pitada *f (a un porro)*; **to have** *or* **take a t. on a joint** dar una *Esp* calada *or Am* pitada a un porro

2 *vi* **to t. on a joint** dar *Esp* caladas *or Am* pitadas a un porro

token ['təʊkən] **1** *n* (a) *(indication)* señal *f*, muestra *f*; **as a t. of respect** como señal *or* muestra de respeto; **a love t.** una prenda de amor; **by the same t.** de la misma manera (b) *(for vending machine)* ficha *f*; *(paper)* vale *m*; **a record t.** un vale para discos (c) *(souvenir)* recuerdo *m*

2 *adj (resistance, effort, gesture)* simbólico(a); **I don't want to be the t. woman on the committee** no quiero estar en la comisión para cubrir el porcentaje femenino; **the prime minister made a t. appearance at the event** el primer ministro hizo una aparición testimonial en el acto

tokenism ['təʊkənɪzəm] *n* **the appointment of a woman to the board was nothing but t.** el nombramiento de una mujer para el consejo fue un mero formulismo *or* un hecho meramente testimonial

Tokyo ['təʊkɪəʊ] *n* Tokio

tolbooth = **tollbooth**

told *pt & pp of* **tell**

tolerable ['tɒlərəbəl] *adj* (a) *(pain, discomfort)* soportable, tolerable (b) *(behaviour, effort)* aceptable; *(food)* pasable

tolerably ['tɒlərəblɪ] *adv* aceptablemente; **t. well** aceptablemente *or* razonablemente bien; **they were t. pleased with the results** se hallaban razonablemente contentos con los resultados

tolerance ['tɒlərəns] *n* (a) *(of behaviour, beliefs, opinions)* tolerancia *f*; **they showed great t. towards us** se mostraron muy tolerantes con nosotros (b) *(to drug, alcohol)* tolerancia *f*; **to have a high/low t. to sth** tolerar bien/mal algo, tener un alto/bajo nivel de tolerancia a algo (c) *Tech* (margen *m* de) tolerancia *f*

tolerant ['tɒlərənt] *adj* (a) *(of person, attitudes, society)* tolerante (**of** con) (b) *(to drug, alcohol)* **to be t. to sth** tolerar algo

tolerantly ['tɒlərəntlɪ] *adv* con tolerancia

tolerate ['tɒləreɪt] *vt* (a) *(put up with, accept) (behaviour, views)* tolerar (b) *(stand) (heat, pain)* soportar (c) *(drug, alcohol)* tolerar

toleration [tɒlə'reɪʃən] *n* tolerancia *f*

toll[1] [tɒl] *n* (a) *(charge)* peaje *m*, *Méx* cuota *f* ▸▸ ***t. road*** carretera *f* de peaje *or Méx* cuota; ***t. tunnel*** túnel *m* de peaje *or Méx* cuota

(b) *US Tel* ***t. call*** llamada *f or Am* llamado *m* de larga distancia, *Esp* conferencia *f*

(c) *(of dead, injured)* **the death t. has risen to 100** el número de víctimas ha ascendido a 100; **the disease had taken its** *or* **a heavy t.** la enfermedad había hecho estragos; **the years have taken their t. on him** los años le han pasado factura

toll[2] **1** *n (of bell)* tañido *m*; **the first t. of the bell** la primera campanada

2 *vt (bell)* tañer; **the church clock tolled midday** el reloj de la iglesia dio las doce

3 *vi (bell)* doblar; **to t. for the dead** tocar a muerto, doblar por un difunto

tol(l)booth ['tɒlbuːθ] *n* cabina *f (donde se paga el peaje)*

tollbridge ['tɒlbrɪdʒ] *n* puente *m* de peaje *or Méx* cuota

toll-free [tɒl'friː] *US* **1** *adj* ***t. number*** (número *m* de) teléfono *m* gratuito

2 *adv (to call)* gratuitamente

tollgate ['tɒlgeɪt] *n* control *m* de peaje *or Méx* cuota

tollway ['tɒlweɪ] *n US* autopista *f* de peaje *or Méx* cuota

toluene ['tɒljʊiːn] *n Chem* tolueno *m*

Tom [tɒm] *n* IDIOM *Fam* **every** *or Br* **any T., Dick or Harry** cualquier mequetrefe ▸▸ ***T. Collins*** *(drink)* Tom Collins *m inv*, = cóctel hecho con ginebra, limón, soda y azúcar

tom [tɒm] *n Fam* gato *m* (macho)

tomahawk ['tɒməhɔːk] *n* hacha *f* india

tomato [tə'mɑːtəʊ, *US* tə'meɪtəʊ] (*pl* **tomatoes**) *n* (a) *(fruit)* tomate *m*, *Méx* jitomate *m*; *(plant)* tomatera *f* ▸▸ ***t. juice*** *Esp* zumo *m or Am* jugo *m* de tomate *or Méx* jitomate; ***t. ketchup*** ketchup *m*, catchup *m*; ***t. plant*** tomatera *f*; ***t. purée*** concentrado *m* de tomate *or Méx* jitomate; ***t. salad*** ensalada *f* de tomate; ***t. sauce*** *(for pasta)* (salsa *f* de) tomate *m or Méx* jitomate *m*; *(ketchup)* (tomate) ketchup *m*, catchup *m*; ***t. soup*** crema *f* de tomate *m or Méx* jitomate *m*

(b) *US Fam (beautiful woman)* **she's a real t.** está buenísima

tomb [tuːm] *n* tumba *f*

tombola [tɒm'bəʊlə] *n* tómbola *f*

tomboy ['tɒmbɔɪ] *n* marimacho *m*

tomboyish ['tɒmbɔɪɪʃ] *adj* marimacho(a)

tombstone ['tuːmstəʊn] *n* lápida *f*

tomcat ['tɒmkæt] *n* gato *m* (macho)

tome [təʊm] *n Formal (book)* tomo *m*, volumen *m*; *Hum* **that's a hefty t. you're reading!** ¡menudo tocho *or* libraco te estás leyendo!

tomfool ['tɒmfʊl] *adj (idea, suggestion)* tonto(a)

tomfoolery [tɒm'fuːlərɪ] *n Fam* tonterías *fpl*, niñerías *fpl*

Tommy ['tɒmɪ] *n Br Fam Old-fashioned* soldado *m* raso (británico)

tommygun ['tɒmɪgʌn] *n* metralleta *f*

tommy-rot ['tɒmɪrɒt] *n Br Fam Old-fashioned* tonterías *fpl*, disparates *mpl*; **t.!** ¡tonterías!, ¡qué tontería!

tomography [tə'mɒgrəfɪ] *n Med* tomografía *f*

tomorrow [tə'mɒrəʊ] **1** *n* (a) *(day after today)* mañana *m*; **there's just time for a look at t.'s newspaper headlines** nos queda el tiempo justo para echar un vistazo a los titulares de la prensa de mañana; **what's t.'s date?** ¿qué fecha es mañana?, ¿a qué (fecha) estamos mañana?; **the day after t.** pasado mañana; **a week from t.** en una semana a partir de mañana; **t. is another day** mañana será otro día; **t. may never come** no dejes para mañana lo que puedas hacer hoy; IDIOM *Fam* **she was eating like there was no t.** comía como si se fuese a acabar el mundo; PROV **never put off till t. what you can do today** no dejes para mañana lo que puedas hacer hoy

(b) *(future)* mañana *m*, futuro *m*; **she is one of the stars of t.** es una de las estrellas del mañana *or* futuro

2 *adv* (a) *(on day after today)* mañana; **see you t.** ¡hasta mañana!; **t. morning/evening** mañana por la mañana/tarde; **they will arrive a week t.** llegarán en una semana a partir de mañana (b) *(in future)* mañana; **what will the world be like t.?** ¿cómo será el mundo en el futuro?

tomtit ['tɒmtɪt] *n (blue tit)* herrerillo *m* (común)

tom-tom ['tɒmtɒm] *n Mus* tam-tam *m inv*

ton [tʌn] *n* (a) *(weight)* tonelada *f* (aproximada) *(Br = 1.016 kilos, US = 907 kilos)*; *Fam* **this suitcase weighs a t.** esta maleta pesa una tonelada *or* un quintal; *Fam* **tons of...** *(lots of)* montones de...; *Fam* **this one is tons better than the old one** este es mejor que el antiguo con diferencia; IDIOM **to come down on sb like a t. of bricks** poner firme a alguien, cantarle las cuarenta a alguien

(b) *Fam (100 mph)* **he was doing a t.** iba a cien millas por hora

tonal ['təʊnəl] *adj* (a) *Mus* tonal (b) *(of colour)* tonal

tonality [tə'nælɪtɪ] *n* (a) *Mus* tonalidad *f* (b) *(of colour)* tonalidad *f*

tone [təʊn] **1** *n* (a) *(sound)* tono *m*; **t. of voice** tono de voz; **to raise/lower the t. of one's voice** alzar/bajar la voz *or* el tono de voz; **don't talk to me in that t. of voice!** ¡no me hables en ese tono!; **I don't like your t.!** ¡no me gusta (que me hables en) ese tono!

(b) *(quality of sound)* timbre *m*; **the rich bass tones of his voice** la sonoridad de su voz en las notas bajas ▸▸ ***t. arm*** *(on record player)* brazo *m* (del tocadiscos); ***t. control*** *(on radio, stereo)* mando *m* de graves y agudos

(c) *(on phone)* señal *f*, tono *m*; **speak after the t.** hable después de la señal

(d) *(colour)* tono *m*

(e) *(mood)* tono *m*; **to raise/lower the t.** *(of place, occasion)* elevar/bajar el tono; **this set the t. for the whole debate** esto marcó la tónica *or* pauta de todo el debate

(f) *Mus (interval)* tono *m* ▸▸ *Mus* ***t. poem*** poema *m* sinfónico

(g) *US Mus (note)* nota *f*

(h) *(of muscles)* tono *m* (muscular)

(i) *Ling* tono *m* ▸▸ ***t. language*** lengua *f* tonal

2 *vt (muscles, body)* tonificar, entonar; *(skin)* tonificar

3 *vi (harmonize)* ir bien, armonizar (**with** con)

▸ **tone down** *vt sep* (a) *(colour)* rebajar el tono de (b) *(remarks, criticisms)* bajar el tono de; *(views, language)* moderar

▸ **tone in** *vi (harmonize)* ir bien, armonizar (**with** con)

▸ **tone up** *vt sep (muscles, body)* tonificar, entonar

tone-deaf [təʊn'def] *adj* **to be t.** tener mal oído
toneless ['təʊnlɪs] *adj (voice)* monótono(a)
tonelessly ['təʊnlɪslɪ] *adv (to say, speak)* con tono monótono
toner ['təʊnə(r)] *n* (**a**) *(for printer)* tóner *m* ►► ***t. cartridge*** cartucho *m* de tóner (**b**) *(for skin)* tónico *m*
Tonga ['tɒŋgə] *n* Tonga
Tongan ['tɒŋgən] **1** *n* (**a**) *(person)* tongano(a) *m,f* (**b**) *(language)* tongano *m*
2 *adj* de Tonga, tongano(a)
tongs [tɒŋz] *npl (for coal, heavy objects)* tenazas *fpl*; *(for food, smaller objects)* pinzas *fpl*; **a pair of t.** unas tenazas/pinzas; **(curling) t.** *(for hair)* tenacillas *fpl* de rizar
tongue [tʌŋ] *n* (**a**) *(in mouth)* lengua *f*; **to stick one's t. out (at sb)** sacar la lengua (a alguien); **his t. was practically hanging out** *(in eagerness)* se le caía la baba ►► ***t. depressor*** depresor *m* de lengua; ***t. twister*** trabalenguas *m inv*
(**b**) *Culin* lengua *f*
(**c**) *(of land)* lengua *f*; *(of shoe)* lengüeta *f*; *(of bell)* badajo *m*
(**d**) *(of flame)* lengua *f*
(**e**) *(language)* idioma *m*, lengua *f*
(**f**) IDIOMS **he seems to have found his t. again** parece que ha recuperado el habla; **to get one's t. round** *or* **around sth** llegar a pronunciar algo; **she has a cruel t.** tiene una lengua viperina; **hold your t.!** ¡cierra la boca!; **try to keep a civil t. in your head!** intenta que no se te vaya la lengua; **have you lost your t.?** ¿se te ha comido la lengua el gato?; **to say sth t. in cheek** decir algo en broma; *Fam* **tongues will wag** van a correr rumores; **the news set tongues wagging** la noticia hizo que se soltaran las malas lenguas
tongue-and-groove (joint) ['tʌŋən'gru:v(dʒɔɪnt)] *n* machihembrado *m*
tongue-in-cheek ['tʌŋɪn'tʃi:k] *adj (remark, article)* en broma
tongue-lashing ['tʌŋlæʃɪŋ] *n* reprimenda *f*; **to give sb a t.** echar una reprimenda a alguien
tongue-tied ['tʌŋtaɪd] *adj* mudo(a); **to be t.** quedarse mudo(a); **I get t. when he's there** se me traba la lengua *or* me corto delante de él
tonguing ['tʌŋɪŋ] *n Mus* lengüeo *m*
tonic ['tɒnɪk] **1** *n* (**a**) *(medicine)* tónico *m*, reconstituyente *m*; *Fig* **it was a real t. to see her again** fue tonificante volver a verla (**b**) *(drink)* **t. (water)** (agua *f*) tónica *f* (**c**) *Mus* tónica *f*
2 *adj* (**a**) *(healthy)* **the sea air had a t. effect on her** la brisa del mar tuvo un efecto tonificante en ella *or* le dio nuevas fuerzas (**b**) *Mus* tónico(a) (**c**) *Ling* tónico(a)
tonight [tə'naɪt] **1** *n* esta noche; **t.'s headlines** los titulares del día *or* de hoy
2 *adv* esta noche; **the game kicks off at seven o'clock t.** el partido (de hoy) empieza a las siete de la tarde
tonnage ['tʌnɪdʒ] *n Naut (of ship)* tonelaje *m*
tonne [tʌn] *n* tonelada *f* (métrica)
-tonner ['tʌnə(r)] *suffix* **a 10-t.** *(lorry)* un camión de 10 toneladas; **a 700-t.** *(ship)* un 700 toneladas
tonsil ['tɒnsəl] *n* amígdala *f*; **to have one's tonsils out** operarse de las amígdalas
tonsillectomy [tɒnsɪ'lektəmɪ] *n Med* amigdalectomía *f*
tonsillitis [tɒnsɪ'laɪtɪs] *n Med* amigdalitis *f inv*
tonsorial [tɒn'sɔ:rɪəl] *adj Hum* barberil
tonsure ['tɒnsjʊə(r)] *n* tonsura *f*
tony ['təʊnɪ] *adj US Fam* fino(a), distinguido(a)

TOO [tu:] *adv* (**a**) *(excessively)* demasiado; **it's t. difficult** es demasiado difícil; **that's t. bad** *(a shame)* es una pena *or* lástima; *(not my problem)* qué se le va hacer; **t. many** demasiados(as); **I've got one t. many** tengo uno de más; **t. much** demasiado; **he gave me $5 t. much/little** me dio cinco dólares de más/de menos; **t. little money** demasiado poco dinero; **t. few people** demasiada poca gente; **she's t. tired to go out** está demasiado cansada (como) para salir; **you're t. kind** es usted muy amable; **I know her all** *or* **only t. well** la conozco demasiado bien; **I'd be only t. pleased to help** estaré encantado de ayudar; *Fam* **t. right!, t. true!** ¡desde luego!
(**b**) *(also)* también
(**c**) *(moreover)* además; **it was a great performance, and by a beginner, t.!** fue una actuación brillante, sobre todo para un principiante
(**d**) *(very, especially)* demasiado, muy; **he's not t. well today** no se encuentra muy *or* demasiado bien hoy; **I'm not t. sure about it** no estoy seguro del todo *or* del todo seguro
(**e**) *Fam (for emphasis)* **I'm not a nationalist! – you are t.!** ¡no soy nacionalista! – ¡claro que sí!; **he got a heavy fine – and quite right t.!** le han puesto una multa elevada – ¡se lo tiene bien merecido!; **and about time, t.!** ¡ya era hora!; *US* **you will t. behave!** ¡ya lo creo que te vas a portar bien!

toodle-oo [tu:dəl'u:] *exclam Br Fam Hum or Old-fashioned* ¡adiosito!
took *pt of* **take**
tool [tu:l] **1** *n* (**a**) *(implement)* herramienta *f*; **(set of) tools** (juego *m* de) herramientas *fpl*; **gardening tools** útiles de jardinería; **the tools of the trade** las herramientas de trabajo ►► ***t. bag*** bolsa *f* de herramientas; *Comptr* ***t. bar*** barra *f* de herramientas; ***t. belt*** cinturón *m* de herramientas; *Comptr* paleta *f* de herramientas; ***t. kit*** juego *m* de herramientas; *Comptr* ***tools menu*** menú *m* de herramientas; ***t. shed*** cobertizo *m* para los aperos
(**b**) *(means, instrument)* instrumento *m*; **this scheme is a useful t. for fighting unemployment** este programa es una herramienta útil en la lucha contra el desempleo; **he was nothing but a t. of the government** no era más que un instrumento del gobierno
(**c**) *very Fam (penis)* nabo *m*, *Chile* pico *m*, *Méx* pájaro *m*, *RP* pija *f*
(**d**) *very Fam (idiot)* mamón *m*
(**e**) *Br Fam (gun)* pipa *f*, *Am* fierro *m*
2 *vt* labrar
► **tool along** *vi Fam* **we were tooling along at 160 km/h when the tyre burst** conducíamos alegremente a 160 km/h cuando se reventó el neumático
► **tool around** *vi Fam* perder el tiempo
► **tool up** *vt sep* (**a**) *(factory)* equipar (**b**) *Br Fam* **to be tooled up** *(carrying gun)* ir armado(a)
toolbox ['tu:lbɒks] *n* caja *f* de herramientas
tooled [tu:ld] *adj (leather, book cover)* labrado(a)
tooling ['tu:lɪŋ] *n* (**a**) *(on leather, book cover)* labrado *m* (**b**) *(equipping)* equipamiento *m*
toolmaker ['tu:lmeɪkə(r)] *n* fabricante *m* de herramientas
toolroom ['tu:lrʊm] *n* almacén *m* de herramientas
toot [tu:t] **1** *n* (**a**) *(on horn)* bocinazo *m*; *(on trumpet)* trompetazo *m* (**b**) *Fam (of cocaine)* raya *f* (**c**) *US Fam (drinking spree)* **to go out on a t.** ir de copas
2 *vt (horn, trumpet)* tocar
3 *vi (car)* tocar la bocina *or* el claxon, pitar; *(train)* pitar; *(driver)* tocar la bocina *or* el claxon, pitar; *(horn, trumpet)* sonar; **he tooted at me** me tocó la bocina *or* el claxon, me pitó
tooth [tu:θ] (*pl* **teeth** [ti:θ]) *n* (**a**) *(of person)* diente *m*; *(molar)* muela *f*; **(set of) teeth** dentadura *f*; **our son is cutting his teeth** a nuestro hijo le están saliendo los dientes, nuestro hijo está echando los dientes; **to have good/bad teeth** tener buena/mala dentadura; **he had a t. out** le sacaron una muela ►► ***t. decay*** caries *f inv*; ***the t. fairy*** ≃ el ratoncito Pérez; ***t. glass*** vaso *m* (para el cepillo de dientes); ***t. mug*** vaso *m* de plástico (para el cepillo de dientes)
(**b**) *(of comb)* púa *f*; *(of saw)* diente *m*; *(of gear wheel)* piñón *m*
(**c**) IDIOMS **armed to the teeth** armado(a) hasta los dientes; **the government implemented the plan in the teeth of fierce opposition** el gobierno puso en marcha el plan pese a la fortísima oposición; *Br Fam* **I'm fed up** *or* **sick to the back teeth with him** estoy hasta la coronilla de él; **I cut my teeth on the more straightforward tasks** me curtí en las tareas más simples, empecé haciendo las tareas más simples; **to fight t. and nail** luchar con uñas y dientes; **to get one's teeth into sth** hincar el diente a algo; **the play gives you nothing to get your teeth into** la obra carece de sustancia; **the amendment will give the law some teeth** la enmienda hará que la ley sea efectiva; **the new regulation has no teeth** la nueva normativa carece de medios para que sea cumplida; **to lie through one's teeth** mentir como un(a) bellaco(a); **to set sb's teeth on edge** *(noise)* dar dentera a alguien; *(habit, behaviour)* poner enfermo(a) a alguien
toothache ['tu:θeɪk] *n* dolor *m* de muelas; **I've got t.** me duelen las muelas
toothbrush ['tu:θbrʌʃ] *n* cepillo *m* de dientes ►► ***t. moustache*** bigote *m* de cepillo
toothed [tu:θt] *adj (wheel)* dentado(a)
toothless ['tu:θlɪs] *adj* (**a**) *(person, animal, grin)* desdentado(a) (**b**) *(law, organization)* inoperante, ineficaz; *(team)* sin poder ofensivo; **their t. attack** su falta de poder ofensivo
toothpaste ['tu:θpeɪst] *n* dentífrico *m*, pasta *f* de dientes ►► ***t. tube*** tubo *m* del dentífrico *or* de la pasta de dientes
toothpick ['tu:θpɪk] *n* palillo *m* (de dientes)
toothpowder ['tu:θpaʊdə(r)] *n* polvo *m* dentífrico
toothsome ['tu:θsəm] *adj Hum (food, dish)* sabroso(a), apetitoso(a)

toothy ['tu:θɪ] *adj* **a t. grin** una sonrisa que enseña todos los dientes

tootle ['tu:təl] *vi Fam* **(a)** *(on trumpet, flute)* **she was tootling away on a trumpet** estaba tocando la trompeta **(b)** *(go)* **I'm going to t. into town** voy a acercarme al centro; **well, I'll t. along now** bueno, me largo ya

toots [tu:ts] *n Fam (term of address)* cariño *m*

tootsy, tootsie ['tu:tsi:] *n Fam* **(a)** *(in children's language) (toe)* dedito *m* del pie **(b)** *(term of address)* cariño *m*

top¹ [tɒp] *n (spinning toy)* peonza *f*, trompo *m*

TOP² 1 *n* **(a)** *(highest part)* parte *f* superior, parte *f* de arriba; *(of tree)* copa *f*; *(of mountain)* cima *f*; *(of sb's head)* coronilla *f*; *(of bus)* piso *m* superior; *(of list)* cabeza *f*; *(of table, bed)* cabecera *f*; **at the t. of the page** en la parte superior de la página; **at the t. of the stairs/building** en lo alto de la escalera/del edificio; **at the t. of the street** al final de la calle; **right at the t.** arriba del todo; **to be (at the) t. of the class/league** ser el primero/la primera de la clase/liga; **to be (at the) t. of the list of things to do** encabezar la lista de cosas que hacer; **the t. of the milk** la *Esp* nata *or Am* crema de la leche; *Irish* **t. of the morning!** ¡buenos días!; **she is at the t. of her profession** se encuentra en la cima de su profesión; **at the t. of one's voice** a grito pelado; **from t. to bottom** de arriba abajo; **from t. to toe** de la cabeza a los pies; **let's take it from the t.!** desde el principio; **fill my glass up right to the t.** lléname el vaso hasta el borde *or* hasta arriba; **the corruption goes right to the t.** la corrupción se extiende hasta los más altos niveles; **off the t. of my/his** *etc* **head** *(at a guess)* a ojo; *(without thinking)* así de repente; *(without preparation)* improvisadamente; **I can't say off the t. of my head** así de repente no sabría decir; *Fig* **to make it to** *or* **reach the t.** llegar a la cumbre; IDIOM *Br* **to be at the t. of the tree** haber llegado a la cima; IDIOM **life at the t.** la vida en las altas esferas; IDIOM **over the t.** *(excessive)* exagerado(a); **to go over the t.** *Mil* entrar en acción; *Fig* pasarse de la raya; IDIOM *Fam* **he's got nothing up t.** es un cabeza de chorlito *or* un cabeza hueca; **he's got plenty up t.** es más listo que el hambre

(b) *(lid)* tapa *f*; *(of bottle, tube)* tapón *m*; *(of pen)* capucha *f*

(c) *(upper surface)* superficie *f*

(d) *(garment) (T-shirt)* camiseta *f*, *Chile* polera *f*, *Méx* playera *f*, *RP* remera *f*; *(blouse)* blusa *f*; *(of pyjamas, bikini)* parte *f* de arriba

(e) *(of vegetable)* parte *f* de arriba

(f) *Fam (topspin)* = efecto que se obtiene al golpear la pelota por la parte de arriba

(g) *(in baseball)* **at the t. of the fifth (inning)** en la primera parte del quinto turno de bateo

(h) *Fam Old-fashioned* **it's (the) tops** *(excellent)* es pistonudo(a)

2 *adj* **(a)** *(highest)* de más arriba, más alto(a); *(in pile)* de encima; *(layer)* superior; *(rung)* último(a); **the t. part of sth** la parte superior de algo; **the t. right-hand corner of the page** la esquina superior derecha de la página; **they are in the t. half of the league** se encuentran en la primera mitad de la clasificación de la liga; **our t. priority** nuestra prioridad absoluta; *Fig* **out of the t. drawer** *(upper-class)* de alta extracción social; *(top-quality)* de primera (clase); *Fig* **the t. rung of the ladder** el nivel más alto del escalafón ►► ***t. copy*** original *m*; *Br* ***t. deck*** *(of bus)* piso *m* superior *or* de arriba; *(of ship)* cubierta *f* A, cubierta *f* superior; ***t. floor*** último piso *m*; *Br Aut* ***t. gear*** *(fourth)* cuarta *f*, directa *f*; *(fifth)* quinta *f*, directa *f*; *Fig* **the Bulls moved into t. gear** los Bulls metieron la directa; ***t. hat*** sombrero *m* de copa; *Fin* ***t. rate*** tipo *m* impositivo más alto; *Sport* ***t. scorer*** *(in basketball, American football, rugby)* máximo(a) anotador(ora) *m,f*; *(in soccer, hockey)* máximo(a) goleador(ora) *m,f*; *Br* ***t. security prison*** cárcel *f* de alta seguridad; ***t. sheet*** sábana *f* encimera; ***t. speed*** velocidad *f* máxima; *also Fig* **at t. speed** a toda velocidad

(b) *(best)* mejor; *(major)* más importante; **t. quality products** productos de primera calidad; **a t. sprinter** un esprínter de primera línea; **t. executive** alto(a) ejecutivo(a); **a t. job** un alto puesto; **one of London's t. restaurants** uno de los mejores restaurantes de Londres; **one of America's t. earners** una de las personas que más dinero gana de América; **to get t. marks** obtener *or* sacar las mejores notas; **my t. choice** mi primera opción; **the t. people** *(in society)* la flor y nata; *(in an organization)* los jefes; **the t. ten** *(in general)* los diez mejores; *(in music charts)* el top diez, los diez primeros; **she came t. in history** fue la mejor en historia; *US Fam* **to pay t. dollar (for sth)** pagar *Esp* un pastón *or Méx* un chorro de lana *or RP* un vagón de guita (por algo); **to be on t. form** estar en plena forma; *Br Fam* **to pay/earn t. whack** pagar/ganar lo máximo (posible); IDIOM *Fam* **to be t. dog** *or US* **t. banana** ser el mandamás ►► *Fam* ***the t. brass*** *(army officers)* los altos mandos; ***t. management*** los altos directivos; *Br* ***the t. table*** la mesa de honor

3 *vt* (*pt & pp* **topped**) **(a)** *(place on top of)* cubrir (**with** de); **ice cream topped with hazelnuts** helado con avellanas por encima; **mountains topped with snow** montañas con las cumbres nevadas

(b) *(exceed)* superar, sobrepasar; *(an offer)* mejorar; **production is expected to t. last year's figures** se prevé que la producción superará las cifras del año pasado; **t. that!** ¡toma ya!; **to t. it all** para colmo

(c) *(be at top of) (list, class)* encabezar; **to t. the bill** encabezar el cartel; **to t. the charts** *(of record, singer)* estar *or* ir a la cabeza de las listas de éxitos

(d) *Br (cut ends off)* **to t. and tail vegetables** cortarle los extremos a las verduras

(e) *Br Fam (kill)* asesinar a, *Esp* cargarse a; **to t. oneself** matarse

(f) *Literary (reach summit of) (hill, rise)* coronar

4 on top *adv* encima; *Fam Fig* **he's getting a bit thin on t.** se está quedando calvo; IDIOM **to be on t.** dominar el juego; IDIOM **to come out on t.** salir victorioso(a)

5 on top of *prep* **(a)** *(above)* encima de, sobre; *(in addition to)* además de; **on t. of everything else** encima de todo **(b)** IDIOMS **to be on t. of sth** tener algo bajo control; **to be** *or* **feel on t. of the world** estar en la gloria; **you mustn't let things get on t. of you** no debes dejar que las cosas te agobien

6 tops *adv Fam (at the most)* como máximo, como mucho

► **top off** *vt sep (round off)* poner la guinda a

► **top out** *vi (finish building)* colocar la última piedra

► **top up** *vt sep (glass, tank)* rellenar, llenar; *(battery)* recargar; *(sum of money)* complementar; **can I t. your beer up for you?** ¿te pongo más cerveza?; *Fam* **shall I t. you up?** ¿te lleno?

---

topaz ['təʊpæz] *n* topacio *m*

top-class ['tɒp'klɑ:s] *adj* de primera (categoría)

topcoat ['tɒpkəʊt] *n* **(a)** *Old-fashioned (clothing)* sobretodo *m* **(b)** *(of paint)* última mano *f*

top-down ['tɒp'daʊn] *adj* **a t. management style** un estilo de dirección jerárquico; **t. processing** proceso descendente

top-drawer ['tɒp'drɔ:(r)] *adj (excellent)* de primera (clase)

top-dressing ['tɒp'dresɪŋ] *n (fertilizer)* fertilizante *m* superficial

topee = **topi**

toper ['təʊpə(r)] *n Old-fashioned* borracho(a) *m,f*

top-flight ['tɒpflaɪt] *adj* de primera (categoría)

topgallant [tɒp'gælənt, tə'gælənt] *n Naut* **(a)** *(mast)* mastelero *m* de juanete **(b)** *(sail)* juanete *m*

top-heavy ['tɒp'hevɪ] *adj* **(a)** *(structure)* sobrecargado(a) en la parte superior **(b)** *(organization)* **the company is t.** la empresa cuenta con demasiados altos cargos **(c)** *Fam (woman)* **to be t.** tener mucha delantera, tener mucho de arriba

top-hole ['tɒp'həʊl] *exclam Br Fam Old-fashioned* fenómeno

topi ['təʊpɪ] *n* **(a)** *(pith helmet)* salacot *m* **(b)** *(antelope)* damalisco *m*

topiary ['təʊpɪərɪ] *n* poda *f* ornamental *(de setos y arbustos)*

topic ['tɒpɪk] *n* tema *m*, asunto *m*; **t. of conversation** tema *m* de conversación

> **False friend:** The Spanish noun **tópico** is not a translation for the English word **topic**. In Spanish **tópico** means "cliché".

topical ['tɒpɪkəl] *adj* **(a)** *(relating to present)* actual, de actualidad; **it's a very t. issue** es un tema de actualidad **(b)** *Med* tópico(a)

topicality [tɒpɪ'kælɪtɪ] *n* actualidad *f*

topically ['tɒpɪklɪ] *adv* **(a)** *(relating to present)* **...he said t.** ...dijo con una referencia muy de actualidad **(b)** *Med* tópicamente

topknot ['tɒpnɒt] *n (hairstyle)* moño *m*, *Méx* chongo *m*, *RP* rodete *m*

topless ['tɒplɪs] *adj (person)* en topless; *(beach, bar)* de topless; **to go t.** hacer topless

top-level ['tɒp'levəl] *adj* de alto nivel

top-loader ['tɒpləʊdə(r)] *n (washing machine)* lavadora *f* de carga superior

topmast ['tɒpmɑ:st] *n Naut* mastelero *m*

topmost ['tɒpməʊst] *adj* superior, más alto(a); *(in pile)* de encima

top-notch ['tɒp'nɒtʃ] *adj* de primera

top-of-the-range ['tɒpəvðə'reɪndʒ], *US* **top-of-the-line** ['tɒpəvðə'laɪn] *adj* de gama alta; **it is our t. model** es el modelo más alto de la gama

topographer [tə'pɒgrəfə(r)] *n* topógrafo(a) *m,f*

topographic(al) [tɒpə'græfɪk(əl)] *adj* topográfico(a)

topography [tə'pɒgrəfɪ] *n* topografía *f*

topological [tɒpə'lɒdʒɪkəl] *adj Geom* topológico(a)

topology [tə'pɒlədʒɪ] *n Geom* topología *f*

toponymy [tə'pɒnəmɪ] *n* toponimia *f*

topper ['tɒpə(r)] *n Fam (hat)* sombrero *m* de copa

topping ['tɒpɪŋ] **1** *n (for pizza)* ingrediente *m*; **cake with cream t.** pastel con *Esp* nata *or Am* crema de leche encima; **ice cream with raspberry t.** helado con frambuesa líquida por encima
2 *adj Br Fam Old-fashioned* excelente

topple ['tɒpəl] **1** *vt* (**a**) *(cause to fall) (structure)* derribar, derrumbar; *(person)* derribar (**b**) *(government)* derribar
2 *vi* (**a**) *(fall) (pile)* venirse abajo, derrumbarse; **he toppled over the edge of the cliff** perdió el equilibrio y se cayó precipicio abajo (**b**) *(government)* derrumbarse

▸**topple over** *vi (pile, person)* venirse abajo

top-quality ['tɒp'kwɒlətɪ] *adj* de primera (clase)

top-ranking ['tɒp'ræŋkɪŋ] *adj* de alto nivel

topsail ['tɒpseɪl] *n Naut* gavia *f*

top-secret ['tɒp'si:krɪt] *adj* altamente confidencial

top-security ['tɒpsɪ'kjʊərɪtɪ] *adj (prison, prisoner)* de alta seguridad

top-shelf ['tɒpʃelf] *adj Br Euph (magazine)* para adultos

topside ['tɒpsaɪd] *n* (**a**) *(cut of beef)* redondo *m* (**b**) *(part of ship)* obra *f* muerta

topsoil ['tɒpsɔɪl] *n* (capa *f* superficial del) suelo *m*

topspin ['tɒpspɪn] **1** *n* efecto *m* liftado; **she puts a lot of t. on the ball** lifta mucho la pelota, golpea la pelota muy liftada
2 *adj* liftado(a); **t. lob** globo *or* lob liftado

topsy-turvy [tɒpsɪ'tɜ:vɪ] *adj* (**a**) *(untidy)* manga por hombro (**b**) *(confused)* enrevesado(a); **the whole world's turned t.** el mundo entero está patas arriba

top-up ['tɒpʌp] *n Br (for drink)* **can I give you a t.?** ¿quieres que te lo llene? ▸▸ ***t. card*** *(for mobile phone)* tarjeta *f* de recarga; ***t. loan*** *(for students)* préstamo *m* suplementario

tor [tɔ:(r)] *n* peñasco *m*

Torah ['tɔ:rə] *n Rel* **the T.** la tora

torch [tɔ:tʃ] **1** *n* (**a**) *(burning stick)* antorcha *f*; **to put a t. to sth** prender fuego a algo; *Fig* **the movement has carried the t. of democracy throughout the dictatorship** el movimiento ha mantenido viva la democracia a lo largo de la dictadura; IDIOM *Old-fashioned* **to carry a t. for sb** estar enamorado(a) *or* prendado(a) de alguien ▸▸ ***t. song*** canción *f* romántica popular, ≃ copla *f*
(**b**) *Br (electric light)* linterna *f*
(**c**) *(for welding, soldering)* quemador *m*
2 *vt* prender fuego a

torchbearer ['tɔ:tʃbeərə(r)] *n* portador(ora) *m,f* de la antorcha; *Fig (leader)* abanderado(a) *m,f*

torchlight ['tɔ:tʃlaɪt] *n* **by t.** con luz de linterna ▸▸ ***t. procession*** procesión *f* de antorchas

tore *pt of* **tear**

toreador ['tɒrɪədɔ:(r)] *n* torero *m*

tori *pl of* **torus**

torment 1 *n* ['tɔ:ment] (**a**) *(suffering)* tormento *m*; **to be in t.** sufrir (**b**) *(ordeal)* **the torments of love** los sufrimientos del amor (**c**) *(pest)* **that child is a real t.** ese niño es un auténtico tormento
2 *vt* [tɔ:'ment] (**a**) *(cause suffering to)* atormentar; **he was tormented by doubt** la duda lo atormentaba (**b**) *(annoy, harass)* hacer rabiar a

tormentil ['tɔ:məntɪl] *n Bot* tormentil(l)a *f*

tormentor [tɔ:'mentə(r)] *n* torturador(ora) *m,f*

torn *pp of* **tear**

tornado [tɔ:'neɪdəʊ] (*pl* **tornadoes**) *n* tornado *m*

Toronto [tə'rɒnteʊ] *n* Toronto

torpedo [tɔ:'pi:dəʊ] **1** *n* (*pl* **torpedoes**) (**a**) *Mil* torpedo *m* ▸▸ ***t. boat*** lancha *f* torpedera, torpedero *m*; ***t. tube*** tubo *m* lanzatorpedos (**b**) *US Fam (sandwich) Esp* flauta *f*, = bocadillo hecho con una barra de pan larga y estrecha
2 *vt* (**a**) *Mil* torpedear (**b**) *(plans, negotiations)* echar por tierra, torpedear

torpid ['tɔ:pɪd] *adj Formal* aletargado(a)

torpor ['tɔ:pə(r)] *n* letargo *m*

torque [tɔ:k] *n* (**a**) *Phys* par *m* de torsión; *Aut* par *m* motor ▸▸ ***t. wrench*** llave *f* dinamométrica *or* de torsión (**b**) *(necklace)* torque *m*, torques *f inv*

torrent ['tɒrənt] *n* torrente *m*; **it's raining in torrents** llueve torrencialmente; *Fig* **a t. of abuse** un torrente de insultos

torrential [tə'renʃəl] *adj* torrencial; **we've had t. rain all week** hemos tenido lluvias torrenciales toda la semana

torrentially [tə'renʃəlɪ] *adv* torrencialmente, de forma torrencial

torrid ['tɒrɪd] *adj* (**a**) *(weather)* tórrido(a) ▸▸ *Geog* ***t. zone*** zona *f* tórrida (**b**) *(affair)* ardiente, apasionado(a) (**c**) *Br (very difficult)* **to give sb a t. time** hacer pasar por un aprieto a alguien, poner a alguien en apuros

torsion ['tɔ:ʃən] *n Tech* torsión *f* ▸▸ ***t. balance*** balance *m* de torsión; ***t. bar*** barra *f* de torsión

torso ['tɔ:səʊ] (*pl* **torsos**) *n* (**a**) *(of person)* torso *m* (**b**) *(statue)* torso *m*

tort [tɔ:t] *n Law* agravio *m*, acto *m* civil ilícito

torte [tɔ:t] *n* tarta *f*

tortellini [tɔ:tə'li:nɪ] *npl Culin* tortellini *mpl*

tortilla [tɔ:'ti:jə] *n* tortilla *f* ▸▸ ***t. chips*** chips *mpl* de tortilla

tortoise ['tɔ:təs] *n* tortuga *f* (terrestre)

tortoiseshell ['tɔ:təsʃel] *n* (**a**) *(substance)* carey *m* ▸▸ ***t. glasses*** gafas *fpl* de carey (**b**) *(animal)* **t. (cat)** = gato con manchas negras y marrones (**c**) *(butterfly)* ninfálida *f*

tortuous ['tɔ:tjʊəs] *adj* (**a**) *(path)* tortuoso(a) (**b**) *(explanation)* enrevesado(a); *(argument, mind)* retorcido(a)

tortuously ['tɔ:tjʊəslɪ] *adv* (**a**) *(to wind) (path)* tortuosamente (**b**) *(to explain, argue)* enrevesadamente

torture ['tɔ:tʃə(r)] **1** *n* tortura *f*; **the prisoners were subjected to t.** los prisioneros fueron torturados *or* sufrieron torturas; *Fig* **it was sheer t.!** ¡fue una auténtica tortura!, ¡fue un tormento! ▸▸ ***t. chamber*** cámara *f* de torturas
2 *vt* (**a**) *(inflict pain on)* torturar (**b**) *(torment)* atormentar; **she was tortured by remorse** la atormentaba *or* no la dejaban vivir los remordimientos; **stop torturing yourself, there's nothing you could have done** deja de torturarte, no hubieras podido hacer nada

torturer ['tɔ:tʃərə(r)] *n* torturador(ora) *m,f*

torus ['tɔ:rəs] (*pl* **tori** ['tɔ:raɪ]) *n* (**a**) *Geom* toro *m* (**b**) *Phys* toro *m*

Tory ['tɔ:rɪ] *Br* **1** *n* tory *mf*, miembro *mf* del partido conservador británico
2 *adj* tory, del partido conservador británico

Toryism ['tɔ:rɪɪzəm] *n Br* conservadurismo *m*

tosh [tɒʃ] *n Br Fam Esp* chorradas *fpl*, *Am* güevadas *fpl*; **don't talk t.!** ¡no digas *Esp* chorradas *or Am* güevadas!

toss [tɒs] **1** *n* (**a**) *(of ball)* lanzamiento *m* (**b**) *(of coin)* **to decide sth on the t. of a coin** decidir algo a cara o cruz *or Chile, Col* cara o sello *or Méx* águila o sol *or RP* cara o seca; *Sport* **our team won/lost the t.** nuestro equipo ganó/perdió el sorteo inicial (**c**) *(of head)* sacudida *f* (**d**) IDIOMS *Br* **to argue the t.** discutir inútilmente; *Br very Fam* **he couldn't give a t.** le importa un carajo, *Méx* le vale madre
2 *vt* (**a**) *(throw) (ball)* lanzar; **to t. sth to sb** echar algo a alguien; **I tossed some herbs into the soup** le eché unas hierbas a la sopa; **the horse nearly tossed its rider into the ditch** el caballo casi tiró al jinete a la cuneta; **he was tossed by the bull** el toro lo zarandeó en el aire; IDIOM *US Fam* **to t. one's cookies** *(vomit)* echar la pota
(**b**) *(spin)* **to t. a coin** tirar una moneda al aire; *(to decide something)* echar a cara o cruz *or Chile, Col* cara o sello *or Méx* águila o sol *or RP* cara o seca; **who's going to pay? – I'll t. you for it** ¿quién paga? – lo echaremos a suertes; **to t. a pancake** dar la vuelta a una crepe lanzándola por el aire
(**c**) *(salad)* remover; **pasta tossed in olive oil** pasta aderezada con aceite de oliva
(**d**) *(shake)* **to t. one's head** sacudir la cabeza; **the ship was tossed by the sea** el mar sacudía *or* zarandeaba el barco
3 *vi* (**a**) *(with coin)* **to t. for sth** jugarse algo a cara o cruz *or Chile, Col* cara o sello *or Méx* águila o sol *or RP* cara o seca (**b**) *(move around)* **to t. and turn (in bed)** dar vueltas en la cama; **the boat was pitching and tossing in the storm** el barco cabeceaba y daba bandazos con la tormenta

▸**toss about, toss around** *vt sep* (**a**) *(ship)* zarandear (**b**) *(ball)* pasarse, lanzarse (**c**) *(ideas, figures)* barajar

▸**toss aside, toss away** *vt sep* (**a**) *(throw away)* tirar (**b**) *(person)* deshacerse de

▸**toss off 1** *vt sep* (**a**) *Fam (write quickly)* escribir rápidamente (**b**) *Br Vulg (masturbate)* **to t. oneself off** hacerse una *or Am* la paja; **to t. sb off** hacer una *or Am* la paja a alguien
2 *vi Br Vulg (masturbate)* hacerse una *or Am* la paja; **t. off!** ¡vete a la mierda!

▸**toss out** *vt sep* tirar

▸**toss up 1** *vt sep (throw up)* **she tossed the ball up into the air** lanzó la pelota al aire
2 *vi (with coin)* **to t. up for sth** jugarse algo a cara o cruz *or Chile, Col* cara o sello *or Méx* águila o sol *or RP* cara o seca

tosser ['tɒsə(r)], **tosspot** ['tɒspɒt] *n Br very Fam Esp* gilipollas *mf inv, Am* pendejo(a) *m,f, RP* boludo(a) *m,f*

toss-up ['tɒsʌp] *n* **(a)** *(with coin)* **to have a t.** decidir a cara o cruz *or Chile, Col* cara o sello *or Méx* águila o sol *or RP* cara o seca
(b) *Fam (fifty-fifty situation)* **it's a t. between the bar and the cinema** igual vamos al bar que vamos al cine; **it's a t. whether he'll say yes or no** lo mismo dice que sí o dice que no; **it's a t. as to which of the two teams will win** los dos equipos tienen las mismas posibilidades de ganar

tot [tɒt] *n* **(a)** *(child)* pequeñín(ina) *m,f* **(b)** *(of whisky, rum)* chupito *m*

▸ **tot up** *(pt & pp* **totted)** **1** *vt sep* sumar; **I'll t. up your bill** yo te haré la cuenta
2 *vi* **that tots up to $30** eso suma 30 dólares

total ['təʊtəl] **1** *n* total *m*; **in t.** en total; **she wrote a t. of ten books** escribió un total de diez libros; **that comes to a t. of £25** eso hace un total de 25 libras
2 *adj* **(a)** *(number, amount)* total; **the t. cost of the damage will be over a million dollars** los daños ascenderán a un total de más de un millón de dólares
(b) *(complete)* total; **she had t. recall of the events** recordaba los acontecimientos con detalle; **a t. ban on exports** una prohibición total de exportar; **his translation was a t. mess** su traducción era un lío tremendo; **he was a t. stranger to me** era un perfecto desconocido para mí; **it was a t. failure** fue un rotundo fracaso; **that's t. nonsense!** ¡eso es una enorme tontería!; **it's a t. waste of money** es un auténtico desperdicio de dinero ▸▸ *Astron* ***t. eclipse*** eclipse *m* total
3 *vt (pt & pp* **totalled,** *US* **totaled)** **(a)** *(amount to)* ascender a; **prizes totalling $5,000** premios por un total de *or* que ascienden a un total de 5.000 dólares; **his collection now totals 500 CDs** tiene una colección de 500 CDs **(b)** *(count up)* sumar **(c)** *US Fam (car)* cargarse, *Esp* jeringar, *Méx* dar en la madre, *RP* hacer bolsa

▸ **total up** *vt sep* sumar

totalitarian [təʊtælɪ'teərɪən] *adj* totalitario(a)

totalitarianism [təʊtælɪ'teərɪənɪzəm] *n* totalitarismo *m*

totality [təʊ'tælɪtɪ] *n* **(a)** *(completeness)* totalidad *f*, conjunto *m*; **in its t.** en su totalidad **(b)** *Astron* (fase *f* de) totalidad *f*

Totalizator ['təʊtəlaɪzeɪtə(r)] *n Br (in betting)* totalizador *m*

totally ['təʊtəlɪ] *adv* totalmente, completamente; **I'm not t. happy with it** no estoy del todo contento con ello; **what she said was t. without justification** lo que dijo estaba totalmente injustificado

tote[1] [təʊt] *n (in betting)* totalizador *m*

tote[2] **1** *n US* ***t. bag*** bolsa *f* (de la compra)
2 *vt Fam (carry)* pasear, cargar con; *(gun)* portar

totem ['təʊtəm] *n* **(a)** *(in Native American culture)* tótem *m* ▸▸ ***t. pole*** tótem *m* **(b)** *(symbol)* símbolo *m*

totemic [təʊ'temɪk] *adj (symbolic)* simbólico(a)

totter ['tɒtə(r)] *vi* **(a)** *(person, pile, vase)* tambalearse, bambolearse; **to t. in/out** entrar/salir tambaleándose **(b)** *(government)* tambalearse

tottering ['tɒtərɪŋ] *adj* **(a)** *(steps, building)* poco seguro(a) **(b)** *(government)* inestable

totty ['tɒtɪ] *n Br Fam (attractive women)* tipazas *fpl*, *Esp* tías *fpl* buenas, *Méx* viejas *fpl* bien buenas

toucan ['tu:kæn] *n* tucán *m*

TOUCH [tʌtʃ] **1** *n* **(a)** *(act of touching)* toque *m*; *(lighter)* roce *m*; **I felt a t. on my arm** noté que me tocaban el brazo; **at the t. of a button** con sólo apretar un botón; **it was t. and go whether...** no era seguro si...; **it was t. and go for a while, but eventually they won** durante un rato parecía que iban a perder, pero al final ganaron ▸▸ ***t. football*** = modalidad de fútbol americano en la que en lugar de placar, basta con tocar al contrario; ***t. rugby*** = modalidad de rugby en la que en lugar de placar, basta con tocar al contrario; *Comptr* ***t. screen*** pantalla *f* táctil
(b) *(sense, feel)* tacto *m*; **I found the light switch by t.** encontré el interruptor de la luz al tacto; **hard/soft to the t.** duro(a)/blando(a) al tacto
(c) *(finesse, skill)* **he has great t.** juega con mucha finura; **she writes with a light t.** escribe con un estilo ágil; **the house needed a woman's t.** le hacía falta un toque femenino a la casa; **he's lost his t.** ha perdido facultades
(d) *(detail)* toque *m*; **there were some nice touches in the movie** la película tenía algunos buenos detalles
(e) *(small amount)* toque *m*, pizca *f*; **a t. (too) strong/short** un poquito fuerte/corto; **to add a t. of class to sth** dar un toque de distinción a algo; **a t. of flu/frost** una ligera gripe *or Am* gripa/helada; **there was a t. of irony in his voice** había una nota de ironía en su voz
(f) *(communication)* **to be/get in t. with sb** estar/ponerse en contacto con alguien; **to keep** *or* **stay in/lose t. with sb** mantener/perder el contacto con alguien; **he put me in t. with the manager** me puso en contacto con el gerente; **we'll be in t.** estaremos en contacto; **I'm in t. with my feelings** estoy en contacto con mis sentimientos; **to be in t./out of t. with public opinion** estar/no estar al corriente de la opinión del hombre de la calle; **to be in t./out of t. with events** estar/no estar al corriente de los acontecimientos; **the government are out of t.** el gobierno ha perdido el contacto con los ciudadanos; **to keep sb in t. with a situation** mantener a alguien informado de una situación; **to lose t. with reality** desconectarse de la realidad
(g) *(in soccer, rugby)* **the ball has gone into t.** la pelota ha salido a lateral; **to find t., to kick the ball into t.** *(in rugby)* sacar la pelota a lateral; **to kick for t.** *(in rugby)* patear a lateral; **first t.** *(in soccer)* primer toque; **he controlled the ball with his first t.** controló la pelota al primer toque ▸▸ ***t. judge*** *(in rugby)* juez *m* de lateral; ***t. kick*** *(in rugby)* puntapié *m* a lateral
2 *vt* **(a)** *(physically)* tocar; *(more lightly)* rozar; **she touched my arm, she touched me on the arm** me tocó (en) el brazo; **can you t. your toes?** ¿puedes tocarte los dedos de los pies?; **I didn't t. him!** ¡no lo toqué!; *Fig* **a smile touched her lips** sus labios esbozaron una ligera sonrisa; **he touched his hat to her** la saludó tocando el ala de su sombrero; **I never t. wine** nunca pruebo el vino; *Fig* **we won't t. stuff like that** no nos vamos a acercar a ese tipo de cosas; **she didn't even t. her dinner** ni tocó la cena; *Fig* **everything he touches turns to gold** convierte en oro todo lo que toca; **to be touched with genius** tener momentos geniales; **to t. bottom** *(ship, economy)* tocar fondo; IDIOM **to t. a (raw) nerve** poner el dedo en la llaga; IDIOM *Br Fam* **t. wood!** ¡toquemos madera!
(b) *(affect)* afectar; **the war didn't t. this area** la guerra no afectó a esta zona; **it's a problem that touches us all** es un problema que nos atañe a todos; **the law can't t. her** la ley no puede tocarla
(c) *(emotionally)* conmover
(d) *(equal)* **his paintings can't t. those of Miró** sus cuadros no son comparables a los de Miró; **there's nothing to t. it** no tiene rival
(e) *(reach) (speed, level)* llegar a, alcanzar
(f) *Fam* **to t. sb for sth** sacar algo a alguien; **can I t. you for $10?** ¿me dejas 10 dólares?
3 *vi* **(a)** *(be in contact)* rozarse; **our legs were touching** nuestras piernas se rozaban **(b)** *(with hands)* **don't t.!** ¡no toques eso! **(c)** *Naut* **the ship touches at Hong Kong** el barco hace escala en Hong Kong

▸ **touch down** **1** *vi* **(a)** *(plane)* aterrizar **(b)** *(in rugby) (score try)* marcar un ensayo
2 *vt sep (in rugby)* **to t. the ball down** apoyar el balón (en el suelo)

▸ **touch off** *vt sep (cause to start)* desencadenar

▸ **touch on** *vt insep* tocar, mencionar

▸ **touch up** *vt sep* **(a)** *(picture, make-up, paintwork)* retocar **(b)** *Br Fam (molest)* manosear, sobar

▸ **touch upon** *vt insep* = **touch on**

---

touchback ['tʌtʃbæk] *n (in American football)* touchback *m*

touchdown ['tʌtʃdaʊn] *n* **(a)** *(of plane) (on land)* aterrizaje *m*; *(on sea)* amerizaje *m* **(b)** *(in American football)* ensayo *m*

touché [tu:'ʃeɪ] *exclam (in fencing)* ¡touché!; *Hum & Fig* ¡touché!, ¡es verdad!

touched [tʌtʃt] *adj* **(a)** *(emotionally moved)* conmovido(a) **(b)** *Fam (mad) Esp* tocado(a) del ala, *Am* zafado(a)

touchily ['tʌtʃɪlɪ] *adv (to say, answer)* con susceptibilidad

touchiness ['tʌtʃɪnɪs] *n* **(a)** *(of person)* susceptibilidad *f* **(b)** *(of subject)* carácter *m* espinoso *or* peliagudo

touching ['tʌtʃɪŋ] **1** *adj (moving)* conmovedor(ora)
2 *prep Formal* en lo tocante a

touchingly ['tʌtʃɪŋlɪ] *adv* de un modo conmovedor; **t., he always remembered her birthday** era conmovedor cómo siempre se acordaba de su cumpleaños

touch-in goal ['tʌtʃɪn'gəʊl] *n (in rugby)* anulada *f*, *Arg* touch in goal *m*

touchline ['tʌtʃlaɪn] *n (in soccer, rugby, hockey)* línea *f* de banda

touchpaper ['tʌtʃpeɪpə(r)] *n* mecha *f (de fuego artificial)*

touch-sensitive ['tʌtʃ'sensɪtɪv] *adj Comptr* táctil ▸▸ ***t. screen*** pantalla *f* táctil

touchstone ['tʌtʃstəʊn] *n* **(a)** *(standard)* piedra *f* de toque **(b)** *(stone)* piedra *f* de toque

touch-tone telephone ['tʌtʃtəʊn'teləfəʊn] *n* teléfono *m* de tonos *or* de marcado por tonos

touch-type ['tʌtʃtaɪp] *vi* mecanografiar al tacto

touch-typing ['tʌtʃtaɪpɪŋ] *n* mecanografía *f* al tacto

touch-up ['tʌtʃʌp] *n (improvement)* retoque *m*

touchy ['tʌtʃɪ] *adj* **(a)** *(person)* susceptible; **she's t. about her height** le molesta que le mencionen la altura **(b)** *(subject)* espinoso(a), peliagudo(a)

touchy-feely ['tʌtʃɪfi:lɪ] *adj Fam Pej (overly sensitive) (person)* **my counsellor is very t.** mi psicólogo es un tipo supercomprensivo que no deja de toquetearte

tough [tʌf] **1** *n* matón *m*

2 *adj* **(a)** *(material)* resistente, fuerte; *(meat, skin)* duro(a); IDIOM *Fam* **the steak was as t. as old boots** el filete estaba más duro que una piedra

(b) *(person) (resilient)* resistente, fuerte; *(hard, violent)* duro(a); **she's a t. competitor** es una dura oponente; **a t. guy** un tipo duro; *Fam* **to be as t. as old boots** *(person)* ser fuerte como un roble, ser duro(a) como el acero

(c) *(harsh) (rule, policy)* duro(a); *(boss)* duro(a), exigente; *(negotiations)* duro(a), difícil; **to be t. on sb** ser duro(a) con alguien; **to get t. (with sb)** ponerse duro (con alguien); **the boss takes a t. line with people who are late** el jefe se pone duro con los que llegan tarde; **there was some t. talking** hubo palabras muy duras ►► ***t. love*** = el amor que en ocasiones requiere dureza en beneficio de la persona amada

(d) *(difficult)* difícil; **she had a t. life** llevaba una vida dura; **we had a t. time convincing her to agree** nos costó Dios y ayuda convencerla; **she made it t. for him** se lo puso difícil; **he's a t. act to follow** ha dejado el listón muy alto; **I find the work t. going** me parece que el trabajo es duro

(e) *(unfair)* injusto(a); **it's t. on you** no es justo; *Fam* **t. luck!** ¡mala suerte!; *very Fam* **t. titty!** ¡a aguantarse (tocan)!; *Vulg* **t. shit!** ¡te jodes *or Méx* chingas!

3 *adv* **to act t.** hacerse el/la duro(a); **the government has been talking t. on drugs** el gobierno ha hecho unas declaraciones muy duras sobre las drogas

4 *exclam Fam* ¡mala suerte!

► **tough out** *vt sep (crisis, period of time)* aguantar, resistir; **to t. it out** capear el temporal

toughen ['tʌfən] **1** *vt* **(a)** *(metal, leather)* hacer más resistente; **toughened glass** vidrio reforzado **(b)** *(person)* hacer más fuerte **(c)** *(stance, rules)* endurecer

2 *vi* **(a)** *(metal, leather)* hacerse más resistente **(b)** *(stance, rules)* endurecerse

► **toughen up** **1** *vt sep* **(a)** *(person)* hacer más fuerte **(b)** *(stance, rules)* endurecer

2 *vi (person)* hacerse más fuerte

toughened ['tʌfənd] *adj (glass)* reforzado(a)

toughie ['tʌfɪ] *n Fam* **(a)** *(person)* matón(ona) *m,f* **(b)** *(question)* **that's a bit of a t.** qué pregunta más difícil

toughly ['tʌflɪ] *adv* **to battle t.** oponer una gran resistencia

tough-minded ['tʌf'maɪndɪd] *adj (person)* que no se deja llevar por los sentimientos; **we need to adopt a t. approach** no debemos dejarnos llevar por los sentimientos

toughness ['tʌfnɪs] *n* **(a)** *(of material)* resistencia *f*; *(of meat, skin)* dureza *f* **(b)** *(of person) (resilience)* fortaleza *f*; *(hardness, violence)* dureza *f* **(c)** *(of rule, policy, boss)* dureza *f*; *(of negotiations)* dificultad *f*, dureza *f* **(d)** *(difficulty)* dureza *f*

toupee ['tu:peɪ] *n* bisoñé *m*

tour [tʊə(r)] **1** *n* **(a)** *(of country, region)* recorrido *m*, viaje *m*; **to go on a t.** hacer un recorrido turístico; **we're going on a t. of Eastern Europe** vamos a hacer un recorrido *or* viaje por Europa del Este; **they're off on a world t.** están dando la vuelta al mundo; **the president went on a t. of the area hit by the earthquake** el presidente visitó la zona afectada por el terremoto ►► ***t. guide*** *(person)* guía *mf* turístico(a); *(book)* guía *f* turística; ***t. of inspection*** (recorrido *m* de) inspección *f*; ***t. operator*** tour operador *m*, operador *m* turístico

(b) *(short visit) (of castle, factory)* visita *f*; **would you like a t. of the garden?** ¿quieres que te de una vuelta *or* te enseñe el jardín?; **we went on a guided t. of the city** hicimos un recorrido turístico con guía por la ciudad, hicimos una visita guiada por la ciudad

(c) *(by entertainer, sports team)* gira *f*; **to be/go on t.** estar/irse de gira; **she's taking the play on t.** van a hacer una gira con la obra ►► *Sport* ***t. manager*** organizador(ora) *m,f* de la gira

(d) *Mil* ***t. of duty*** periodo *m* de servicio en el extranjero

(e) *Sport (circuit)* circuito *m*; **the European t.** *(in golf)* el circuito europeo

(f) *(in cycling)* vuelta *f*; **the T. de France** el Tour de Francia; **the T. of Italy** el Giro de Italia; **the T. of Spain** la Vuelta (ciclista) a España

2 *vt* **(a)** *(country)* recorrer; **they're touring Italy** están recorriendo Italia **(b)** *(hospital, factory)* recorrer **(c)** *(of entertainer, sports team)* ir de gira por; **the orchestra is touring the north of the country** la orquesta está haciendo una gira por el norte del país

3 *vi* **(a)** *(tourist)* hacer turismo **(b)** *(entertainer, sports team)* estar de gira; **we spent the whole summer touring** pasamos todo el verano de gira

tour de force ['tʊədə'fɔ:s] *n* tour de force *m*, creación *f* magistral

tourer ['tʊərə(r)] *n* vehículo *m* descapotable

Tourette's syndrome [tʊə'rets'sɪndrəʊm] *n Med* síndrome *m* de Tourette

touring ['tʊərɪŋ] **1** *n* **(a)** *(of tourist)* **we're going to do a bit of t. in Portugal** vamos a hacer un recorrido por Portugal **(b)** *(of sports team, theatre company)* giras *fpl*; **I enjoy t.** me gustan las giras

2 *adj (sports team, theatre company)* de gira; *(exhibition, play)* itinerante ►► ***t. bicycle*** bicicleta *f* de paseo; *Sport* ***t. car*** turismo *m* de competición; *Theat* ***t. company*** compañía *f* itinerante; *Sport* ***the t. party*** los seleccionados para ir de gira

tourism ['tʊərɪzəm] *n* turismo *m*

tourist ['tʊərɪst] *n* **(a)** *(holidaymaker)* turista *mf* ►► ***t. attraction*** atracción *f* turística; ***t. board*** patronato *m* de turismo; *Av* ***t. class*** clase *f* turista; ***t. destination*** destino *m* turístico; ***t. guide*** *(person)* guía *mf* turístico(a); *(book)* guía *f* turística; ***the t. industry*** la industria del turismo, el sector turístico; ***t. information centre, t. (information) office*** oficina *f* de (información y) turismo; ***t. resort*** centro *m* turístico; ***t. route*** ruta *f* turística; ***t. season*** temporada *f* turística; ***the t. trade*** el sector turístico; *Fam* ***t. trap:*** **that restaurant is a t. trap** ese restaurante es sólo para turistas

(b) *Sport* **the tourists won 27-15** el equipo visitante ganó 27 a 15

touristy ['tʊərɪstɪ] *adj Fam (place)* muy turístico(a); *(activity)* típico(a) de turistas

tournament ['tʊənəmənt] *n* **(a)** *Sport* torneo *m*; **the t. favourite** el/la favorito(a) del torneo **(b)** *Hist* torneo *m*

tournedos ['tʊənədəʊ] *n Culin* tournedós *m inv*

tourney ['tʊənɪ] *n* **(a)** *US Sport* torneo *m* **(b)** *Hist* torneo *m*

tourniquet ['tʊənɪkeɪ] *n Med* torniquete *m*

tousle ['taʊzəl] *vt (hair)* alborotar

tousled ['taʊzəld] *adj (hair)* alborotado(a)

tout [taʊt] **1** *n* **(a)** *Br* **(ticket) t.** reventa *mf* **(b)** *(for bar, hotel, timeshare)* buscador(ora) *m,f* de clientes **(c)** *(in racing)* = persona que vende información privilegiada sobre las apuestas en las carreras de caballos

2 *vt* **(a)** *(goods)* tratar de vender; *Br (tickets)* revender; **she had touted her article around all the newspapers** tuvo que ir ofreciendo su artículo de periódico en periódico **(b)** *(promote)* **he is being touted as a future prime minister** lo están promocionando como futuro primer ministro

3 *vi* **(a)** *(solicit)* **to t. for custom** tratar de captar clientes **(b)** *(in racing)* captar información relacionada con las apuestas de caballos

tow [təʊ] **1** *n* **(a)** *(action)* **to give sth/sb a t.** remolcar algo/a alguien; *Br* **on** *or US* **in** *or* **under t.** *(sign)* vehículo remolcado; **he took us in t.** nos llevó a remolque, nos remolcó; *Fam* **to have someone in t.** llevar a alguien detrás ►► ***t. truck*** grúa *f (automóvil)* **(b)** *Tex* estopa *f*

2 *vt* remolcar, llevar a remolque; **the vehicle was towed away** la grúa se llevó el vehículo

towage ['təʊɪdʒ] *n (fee)* costo *m or Esp* coste *m* de la retirada del vehículo

TOWARD(S) [tə'wɔ:d(z)] *prep* **(a)** *(in the direction of)* hacia; **to point t. sth** señalar hacia algo; **she had her back t. him** le daba la espalda; **there has been some progress t. an agreement** se ha avanzado hacia la consecución de un acuerdo; **we are working t. this goal** estamos trabajando para conseguir ese objetivo; **T. a New Humanism** *(title)* Hacia un nuevo humanismo

(b) *(respecting)* **his attitude t. this issue** su actitud con respecto a este asunto; **her feelings t. me** sus sentimientos por *or* hacia mí; **they behaved strangely t. us** se comportaron de un modo extraño con nosotros

(c) *(as contribution)* **to contribute t. the cost of...** contribuir a costear...; **it counts t. your final mark** cuenta para la nota final; **15 percent of the budget will go** *or* **be directed t. improving safety** el 15 por ciento del presupuesto estará dedicado a mejoras en la seguridad; **this money can go t. your new bicycle** aquí tienes una contribución para tu nueva bicicleta; **it went a long way t. appeasing them** contribuyó en gran medida a calmarlos (**d**) *(near)* **we're getting t. spring** ya falta poco para la primavera; **t. the end of his life** hacia el final de su vida; **t. the middle** hacia el centro

---

towaway zone ['təʊəweɪ'zəʊn] *n US* = zona de estacionamiento prohibido de la que se retiran los vehículos

towbar ['təʊbɑː(r)] *n (on car)* barra *f* de remolque

towel ['taʊəl] **1** *n* toalla *f*; IDIOM **to throw in the t.** tirar la toalla ▸▸ *US **t. bar*** toallero *m*; *Br **t. rail*** toallero *m*; ***t. ring*** toallero *m (en forma de anilla)*

2 *vt* (*pt & pp* **towelled**, *US* **toweled**) **to t. sb/oneself (down** *or* **dry)** secar a alguien/secarse (con la toalla)

towel-head ['taʊəlhed] *n Fam Esp* moro(a) *m,f*, *Andes, CSur, Ven* turco(a) *m,f*

towelling, *US* **toweling** ['taʊəlɪŋ] *n* (tejido *m* de) toalla *f*; **t. bathrobe** albornoz

tower ['taʊə(r)] **1** *n* (**a**) *(building, pile)* torre *f*; **church t.** torre de iglesia; IDIOM **she's a t. of strength** es un apoyo sólido como una roca ▸▸ ***the T. of Babel*** la torre de Babel; *Br **t. block*** torre *f*, bloque *m* alto *(edificio)* (**b**) *Comptr* **t. (system)** torre *f*

2 *vi* **to t. above** *or* **over sth** elevarse por encima de algo; **to t. above** *or* **over sb** ser mucho más alto que alguien; *Fig* **she towers above** *or* **over her contemporaries** destaca por encima de *or* entre todos sus contemporáneos

towering ['taʊərɪŋ] *adj* (**a**) *(very tall) (building, tree, figure)* imponente (**b**) *(achievement)* enorme (**c**) *(very strong)* **he was in a t. rage** montaba en cólera

tow-headed ['taʊhedɪd] *adj* rubio(a)

towline ['təʊlaɪn] *n* cuerda *f* para remolcar

town [taʊn] *n (big)* ciudad *f*; *(smaller)* pueblo *m*; **they do the best pizzas in t.** hacen las mejores pizzas de la ciudad; **he is back in t.** ha vuelto a la ciudad; **to go into t.** ir al centro (de la ciudad); **it's situated out of t.** está en las afueras (de la ciudad); **he's out of t.** está fuera (de la ciudad); **the whole t. was opposed to the bypass** toda la ciudad estaba en contra de la circunvalación; **t. and gown** los lugareños y la gente de la universidad; IDIOM *Fam* **to be/go out on the t.** estar/ir de fiesta *or* juerga; IDIOM *Fam* **to go to t.** *(in celebration)* tirar la casa por la ventana; *(in explanation, description)* explayarse ▸▸ ***t. centre*** centro *m* urbano; ***t. clerk*** secretario(a) *m,f* del municipio *or* ayuntamiento; *Br **t. council*** municipio *m*, ayuntamiento *m*; *Br **t. councillor*** concejal(ala) *m,f*; ***t. crier*** pregonero(a) *m,f*; ***t. hall*** municipio *m*, ayuntamiento *m*; ***t. house*** *(terraced house)* casa *f* adosada; *(not in country)* casa *f* de la ciudad; *US **t. meeting*** = asamblea de vecinos que se reúne para discutir asuntos de interés público; ***t. planner*** urbanista *mf*; ***t. planning*** urbanismo *m*

town-dweller ['taʊndwelə(r)] *n Br* habitante *mf* de ciudad, urbanita *mf*

townee, townie ['taʊniː] *n Fam* urbanita *mf*, *RP* bicho *m* de ciudad

townscape ['taʊnskeɪp] *n* paisaje *m* urbano

townsfolk ['taʊnzfəʊk] *npl* habitantes *mpl*, ciudadanos *mpl*

township ['taʊnʃɪp] *n* (**a**) *(in US)* ≃ municipio *m* (**b**) *Formerly (in South Africa)* = área urbana reservada para la población negra

townsman ['taʊnzmən] *n* ciudadano *m*

townspeople ['taʊnzpiːpəl] *npl* ciudadanos *mpl*; **my fellow t.** mis conciudadanos

townswoman ['taʊnzwʊmən] *n* ciudadana *f*

towpath ['təʊpɑːθ] *n* camino *m* de sirga

towrope ['təʊrəʊp] *n* cuerda *f* para remolcar

toxaemia, *US* **toxemia** [tɒk'siːmɪə] *n Med* toxemia *f*

toxic ['tɒksɪk] *adj* tóxico(a) ▸▸ *Med **t. shock syndrome*** síndrome *m* del shock tóxico; ***t. waste*** residuos *mpl* tóxicos

toxicity [tɒk'sɪsɪtɪ] *n* toxicidad *f*

toxicological [tɒksɪkə'lɒdʒɪkəl] *adj* toxicológico(a)

toxicologist [tɒksɪ'kɒlədʒɪst] *n* toxicólogo(a) *m,f*

toxicology [tɒksɪ'kɒlədʒɪ] *n* toxicología *f*

toxin ['tɒksɪn] *n* toxina *f*

toy [tɔɪ] **1** *n* juguete *m* ▸▸ ***t. car*** coche *m or Am* carro *m or CSur* auto *m* de juguete; ***t. dog*** perro *m* faldero, perrito *m*; ***t. gun*** pistola *f* de juguete; ***t. poodle*** caniche *m* enano; ***t. shop*** juguetería *f*; ***t. soldier*** soldadito *m* de juguete; ***t. train*** tren *m* de juguete

2 *vi* **to t. with one's food** juguetear con la comida; **to t. with sb** jugar con alguien; **to t. with an idea** darle vueltas a una idea; **to t. with sb's affections** jugar con los sentimientos de alguien

toyboy ['tɔɪbɔɪ] *n Br Fam* amiguito *m*, = amante muy joven

TQM [tiːkjuː'em] *n Com* (*abbr* **total quality management**) gestión *f* de calidad total

trace [treɪs] **1** *n* (**a**) *(sign)* rastro *m*, pista *f*; **they found no traces of life on the Moon's surface** no encontraron ningún rastro de vida sobre la superficie de la Luna; **there was no t. of them when we got there** no había ni rastro de ellos cuando llegamos; **the ship had sunk without t.** el barco se había hundido sin dejar ningún resto; **the fraudster disappeared** *or* **vanished without t.** el timador desapareció sin dejar rastro; **we've lost all t. of her** le hemos perdido completamente la pista

(**b**) *(small amount)* rastro *m*, resto *m*; **traces of cocaine were found in his blood** le encontraron restos de cocaína en la sangre; **she didn't even show a t. of nervousness** no mostró ni la más mínima señal de nerviosismo; **there was the t. of a smile on her face** su rostro esbozaba una ligera sonrisa ▸▸ *Chem **t. element*** oligoelemento *m*

(**c**) *(on screen, graph)* traza *f*

(**d**) *Tel* **to put a t. on a call** averiguar de dónde procede una llamada

2 *vt* (**a**) *(draw)* trazar; *(with tracing paper)* calcar

(**b**) *(track) (person)* seguir la pista *or* el rastro a; *(phone call)* localizar; **they traced the murder to him** las investigaciones del asesinato llevaron hasta él; **we eventually traced the problem to a computer error** al final averiguamos que el problema se debía a un error informático

(**c**) *(find)* localizar; **they traced the lost shipment** localizaron el cargamento desaparecido

(**d**) *(development, history)* trazar; **the movie traces her rise to power** la película reconstruye su ascenso al poder

▸ **trace back** *vt sep* **this practice can be traced back to medieval times** esta costumbre se remonta a tiempos medievales; **she has traced her ancestry back to the 15th century** su árbol genealógico se remonta hasta el siglo XV; **the cause of the epidemic was traced back to an infected water supply** la causa de la epidemia fue localizada en una fuente de agua infectada

traceable ['treɪsəbəl] *adj* localizable

tracer ['treɪsə(r)] *n* (**a**) *Mil* **t. (bullet)** bala *f* trazadora ▸▸ ***t. fire*** fuego *m* de balas trazadoras (**b**) *Med* trazador *m* radiactivo

tracery ['treɪsərɪ] *n* (**a**) *Archit* tracería *f* (**b**) *(pattern)* filigrana *f*

trachea [trə'kiːə] (*pl* **tracheae** [trə'kɪiː]) *n Anat* tráquea *f*

tracheotomy [trækɪ'ɒtəmɪ] *n Med* traqueotomía *f*; **to perform a t. (on sb)** hacer una traqueotomía (a alguien)

trachoma [trə'kəʊmə] *n Med* tracoma *m*

tracing ['treɪsɪŋ] *n (picture, process)* calco *m* ▸▸ ***t. paper*** papel *m* de calcar *or* de calco

track [træk] **1** *n* (**a**) *(single mark)* huella *f*; *(set of marks)* rastro *m*; **tyre tracks** rodada; **the terrorists had covered their tracks well** los terroristas no habían dejado ningún rastro; **to keep t. of sb** seguirle la pista a alguien; **I want to keep t. of developments** quiero estar al corriente de lo que vaya ocurriendo; **we'll have to keep t. of the time** tendremos que estar al tanto *or* pendientes de la hora; **I've lost t. of her** le he perdido la pista; **don't lose t. of those files** no te olvides de dónde están estos ficheros; **I've lost t. of how much money I've spent** he perdido la cuenta del dinero que llevo gastado; **I lost t. of the time** no me daba cuenta de qué hora era; **he lost t. of what he was saying** perdió el hilo de lo que estaba diciendo; IDIOM *Fam* **to make tracks** largarse, *Esp, RP* pirarse; **to put** *or* **throw sb off the t.** despistar a alguien; **to stop sb in his tracks** hacer que alguien se pare en seco

(**b**) *(path)* senda *f*, camino *m*; *(of planet, missile, storm)* trayectoria *f*; *Fig* **to be on the right/wrong t.** ir por (el) buen/mal camino; **we're back on t. to finish the project by May** volvemos a estar en condiciones de acabar el proyecto en mayo

(**c**) *(for race)* pista *f*; *Br* **motor-racing t.** circuito de carreras ▸▸ ***t. cycling*** ciclismo *m* en pista; ***t. events*** atletismo *m* en pista, carreras *fpl* de atletismo; ***t. and field*** atletismo *m*; *US **t. meet*** reunión *f* atlética; ***t. racing*** *(in cycling)* carrera *f* en pista; ***t. record*** *(previous performance)* historial *m*, antecedentes *mpl*; **a company with a good/poor t. record in winning export orders** una empresa con buen/mal historial en cuanto al número de pedidos de exportación; ***t. shoes*** zapatillas *fpl* de deporte; ***t. star*** estrella *f* de la pista

(**d**) *(on record, CD) (song)* tema *m*, canción *f*; *(for recording)* pista *f*

(**e**) *Comptr* pista *f*

(**f**) *(of tank, tractor)* oruga *f*; *(distance between wheels)* distancia *f* entre ejes

(**g**) *(railway line)* vía *f*; **six miles of t. had to be relaid** tuvieron que volver a tender seis millas de vía; IDIOM **from the wrong side of the tracks** de origen humilde ▸▸ ***t. bed*** asiento *m* de la vía

(**h**) *(for curtain, spotlight)* riel *m*

(**i**) *US Sch* = cada una de las divisiones del alumnado en grupos por niveles de aptitud

(**j**) *Fam* **tracks** *(injection marks)* marcas *fpl* de jeringuillas

2 *vt* (**a**) *(follow) (animal, person)* seguir la pista de; *(rocket)* seguir la trayectoria de; **to t. sb's movements** seguir los movimientos de alguien (**b**) *US (bring on shoes)* **don't t. mud into the house!** ¡no dejes barro por la casa!

3 *vi* (**a**) *Cin* hacer un travelling (**b**) *(stylus)* seguir los surcos

▸ **track back** *vi (in soccer)* recuperar la posición

▸ **track down** *vt sep (locate)* localizar, encontrar

▸ **track in** *vi Cin* acercar la cámara

▸ **track out** *vi Cin* alejar la cámara

trackball ['trækbɔːl] *n Comptr* trackball *f*, seguibola *f*

tracked [trækt] *adj (vehicle)* de oruga

tracker ['trækə(r)] *n (person)* rastreador(ora) *m,f* ▸▸ ***t. dog*** perro *m* rastreador; *Br Fin* ***t. fund*** fondo *m* indexado *or* índice

tracking ['trækɪŋ] *n* (**a**) *(following) (of person, plane, satellite)* seguimiento *m* ▸▸ ***t. device*** dispositivo *m* de seguimiento; *Cin* ***t. shot*** travelling *m*; ***t. station*** *(for satellites)* estación *f* de seguimiento (**b**) *US Sch* = sistema de división del alumnado en grupos por niveles de aptitud (**c**) *Comptr* tracking *m*, espacio *m* entre palabras (**d**) *Aut* alineación *f*

tracklaying ['træklеɪɪŋ] *adj* ***t. vehicle*** vehículo *m* oruga

trackless ['træklɪs] *adj (jungle, desert)* sin pistas *or* caminos

tracklist ['træklɪst] *n (of CD, cassette)* lista *f* de temas *or* canciones

trackpad ['trækpæd] *n Comptr* trackpad *m*

tracksuit ['træks(j)uːt] *n Esp* chándal *m*, *Méx* pants *mpl*, *RP* jogging *m* ▸▸ ***t. bottoms*** pantalones *mpl* de *Esp* chándal *or RP* jogging, *Méx* pants *mpl*; ***t. trousers*** pantalones *mpl* de *Esp* chándal *or RP* jogging, *Méx* pants *mpl*

tract[1] [trækt] *n* (**a**) *(of land)* tramo *m*; **vast tracts of forest have been felled** enormes extensiones de bosque han sido taladas (**b**) *Anat* **respiratory t.** vías respiratorias; **digestive t.** tubo digestivo (**c**) *US* ***t. house*** = casa en una urbanización en la que todas las viviendas son iguales

tract[2] *n (pamphlet)* panfleto *m*

tractable ['træktəbəl] *adj Formal* (**a**) *(person, animal)* dócil, manejable; *(problem)* de fácil solución (**b**) *(metal)* maleable, dúctil

traction ['trækʃən] *n* (**a**) *(force)* tracción *f* ▸▸ ***t. engine*** locomotora *f* de tracción (**b**) *Med* **to have one's leg in t.** tener la pierna en alto *(por lesión)*

tractor ['træktə(r)] *n* (**a**) *(vehicle)* tractor *m* (**b**) *Comptr* ***t. feed*** alimentación *f* automática de papel *(por arrastre)*

tractor-drawn ['træktədrɔːn] *adj* arrastrado(a) por un tractor

tractor-trailer ['træktə'treɪlə(r)] *n US* camión *m* articulado

trad [træd] *n* **t. (jazz)** jazz *m* tradicional

trade [treɪd] **1** *n* (**a**) *(commerce)* comercio *m* (**in** de); **domestic/foreign t.** el comercio interior/exterior; **t. has been brisk this Christmas** las ventas han sido muy buenas estas Navidades; **the warm weather is good for t.** el buen tiempo es bueno para las ventas; **they've been doing a good** *or* **roaring t.** han hecho buen negocio últimamente ▸▸ ***t. agreement*** acuerdo *m* comercial; ***t. ban*** embargo *m* comercial; ***t. barriers*** barreras *fpl* comerciales; ***t. cycle*** ciclo *m* económico; ***t. deficit*** déficit *m* comercial; *Br* ***T. Descriptions Act*** = ley que prohíbe a las empresas hacer uso de la publicidad engañosa; *Br Fig Hum* **calling this a strawberry tart is against the T. Descriptions Act, there are hardly any strawberries in it!** llamar a esto tarta de fresas es una estafa *or* tomadura de pelo ¡si apenas hay fresas!; ***t. discount*** descuento *m* comercial; ***t. embargo*** embargo *m* comercial; ***t. fair*** feria *f* (de muestras); ***t. figures*** cifras *fpl* comerciales; ***t. gap*** déficit *m* de la balanza comercial; ***t. name*** *(of product)* nombre *m* comercial; *(of company)* razón *f* social; *Br* ***t. plates*** *(for car)* matrícula *f or* placa *f* temporal; ***t. policy*** política *f* comercial; ***t. price*** precio *m* al por mayor; ***t. restrictions*** restricciones *fpl* comerciales; ***t. route*** *(of ship)* ruta *f* comercial; ***t. secret*** *Com* secreto *m* profesional; *Fig Hum (of person)* secreto *m* profesional; ***t. war*** guerra *f* comercial; *Geog* ***t. winds*** vientos *mpl* alisios

(**b**) *(industry)* sector *m*, industria *f*; **the building/hotel t.** el sector *or* la industria de la construcción/hostelería; **the drug/arms t.** el tráfico de drogas/armas; **the retail/wholesale t.** el comercio al por menor/mayor ▸▸ ***t. association*** asociación *f* gremial; ***t. directory*** guía *f* por profesiones; ***t. journal*** publicación *f* gremial *or* del sector; ***t. press*** prensa *f* del sector

(**c**) *(profession)* oficio *m*; **he's an electrician by t.** su oficio es el de electricista; **people in the t.** la gente del oficio, los profesionales; **as we say in the t.** como decimos los del oficio ▸▸ ***t. union*** sindicato *m*; *Br* ***the Trades Union Congress*** = confederación nacional de sindicatos británicos; ***t. unionism*** sindicalismo *m*; ***t. unionist*** sindicalista *mf*

(**d**) *(people in the industry)* **we only sell to the t.** solo vendemos al por mayor

(**e**) *(customers)* **most of our sales come from passing t.** la mayoría de nuestras ventas son a clientes no habituales *or* que vienen de paso

(**f**) *(swap)* intercambio *m*; **to do a t. (with sb)** hacer un intercambio (con alguien)

2 *vt* **to t. sth (for sth)** intercambiar algo (por algo); **to t. places with sb** cambiarse de sitio con alguien; **to t. insults/blows** intercambiar insultos/golpes; *US* **to t. gossip (with sb/about sth)** chismorrear *or Esp* cotillear (con alguien/sobre algo)

3 *vi* (**a**) *(buy and sell)* comerciar; **the firm ceased trading a year ago** la empresa cerró *or* se dio de baja hace un año; **we do not t. with this country** no tenemos relaciones comerciales con ese país; **farmers have been forced to t. at a loss** han obligado a los agricultores a vender con pérdidas; **he trades in clothing** se dedica a la compraventa de ropa; **what name does the company t. under?** ¿bajo qué nombre funciona la empresa?

(**b**) *(exchange)* intercambiar, trocar

(**c**) *(be sold) (shares, commodity)* cotizar (**at** a)

▸ **trade in** *vt sep* entregar como parte del pago

▸ **trade off** *vt sep* sacrificar (**against** por)

▸ **trade on** *vt insep (exploit)* aprovecharse de

▸ **trade up** *vi (car owner)* **buy the cheapest model, and t. up later** compra el modelo más barato, y cámbialo por uno mejor más adelante

traded option ['treɪdɪd'ɒpʃən] *n Fin* = opción negociada en un mercado financiero

trade-in ['treɪdɪn] *n Com* = artículo usado que se entrega como parte del pago; **they took my old refrigerator as a t.** se quedaron con el frigorífico antiguo como parte del pago ▸▸ ***t. price*** = cantidad que se recibe por un artículo viejo al comprar uno nuevo; ***t. value*** = valor que se le da a un artículo viejo al comprar uno nuevo

trademark ['treɪdmɑːk] *n* (**a**) *Com* marca *f* comercial *or* registrada (**b**) *(of person)* sello *m* personal; **he was there with his t. cigar** estaba ahí con su característico puro

trade-off ['treɪdɒf] *n* **there is a t. between speed and accuracy** al aumentar la velocidad se sacrifica la precisión, y viceversa; **the slightly higher cost is an acceptable t. for the increase in quality** vale la pena pagar un poco más porque, a cambio, la calidad es superior

trader ['treɪdə(r)] *n* (**a**) *(of goods)* comerciante *mf* (**b**) *(on stock exchange)* operador(ora) *m,f* de bolsa (**c**) *(ship)* mercante *m*

tradescantia [trædɪ'skæntɪə] *n* tradescantia *f*

tradesfolk ['treɪdzfəʊk], **tradespeople** ['treɪdzpiːpəl] *npl* comerciantes *mpl*

tradesman ['treɪdzmən] *n* (**a**) *(shopkeeper)* pequeño comerciante *m*, tendero *m* (**b**) *(electrician, plumber)* trabajador(ora) *m,f* manual; **t.'s entrance** *(in building)* entrada de servicio; *Br Vulg* **he went in the t.'s entrance** se la metió *or Esp* endiñó por detrás

tradeswoman ['treɪdzwʊmən] *n (shopkeeper)* pequeña comerciante *f*, tendera *f*

trading ['treɪdɪŋ] *n* (**a**) *Com* comercio *m* ▸▸ ***t. account*** cuenta *f* de explotación; *Br* ***t. estate*** polígono *m* industrial; ***t. hours*** horario *m* comercial; ***t. links*** relaciones *fpl* comerciales; ***t. loss*** pérdidas *fpl* comerciales; ***t. partner*** socio(a) *m,f* comercial; ***t. post*** = establecimiento comercial en zonas remotas o de colonos; ***t. profit*** beneficios *mpl* comerciales; ***t. results*** resultados *mpl* comerciales; ***t. stamp*** cupón *m*, vale *m*; ***t. standards authority*** = organismo que vela por el cumplimiento de la normativa comercial

(**b**) *(on stock exchange)* compraventa *f* de acciones; **t. was heavy today** el volumen de negocio ha sido muy alto hoy ▸▸ ***t. floor*** parquet *m*

tradition [trə'dɪʃən] *n* tradición *f*; **t. has it that you get a present when you leave the firm** la costumbre es dar un regalo a los que se van de la empresa; **a comedian in the t. of Chaplin** un cómico que sigue la tradición de Charlot; **this year's event was in the best t. of office parties** el acto de este año seguía la línea de las fiestas de oficina por excelencia

traditional [trə'dɪʃənəl] *adj* tradicional; **it is t. to sing a song together** es tradición cantar juntos una canción

traditionalism [trə'dɪʃənəlɪzəm] *n* tradicionalismo *m*

traditionalist [trə'dɪʃənəlɪst] **1** *n* tradicionalista *mf*

2 *adj* tradicionalista

traditionally [trə'dɪʃənəlɪ] *adv* tradicionalmente

traduce [trə'dju:s] *vt Formal* calumniar, difamar

traffic ['træfɪk] *n* **1** (**a**) *(vehicles)* tráfico *m*; **road/air t.** tráfico rodado/aéreo; **the t. is heavy/light** el tráfico es muy denso/fluido; **watch out for t. when crossing the road!** ¡cuidado con el tráfico al cruzar la calle!; **eastbound t. is moving slowly** el tráfico en dirección este avanza muy lentamente ►► ***t. accident*** accidente *m* de tráfico; *US* ***t. block*** atasco *m*; ***t. calming (measures)*** medidas *fpl* para reducir la velocidad del tráfico; *US* ***t. circle*** rotonda *f*, *Esp* glorieta *f*; ***t. cone*** cono *m* de señalización; *Fam* ***t. cop*** policía *m or Esp* guardia *mf* de tráfico; ***t. island*** refugio *m*, isleta *f*; ***t. jam*** atasco *m*, embotellamiento *m*; ***t. lights*** semáforo *m*; ***t. offence*** infracción *f* de tráfico; ***t. police*** policía *f* de tráfico; ***t. policeman*** policía *m* de tráfico; ***t. sign*** señal *f* de tráfico; *US* ***t. violation*** infracción *f* de tráfico; *Br* ***t. warden*** = agente que pone multa por estacionamiento indebido
(**b**) *(trade) (in drugs, slaves)* tráfico *m* (**in** de)
2 *vt* traficar con
3 *vi* traficar (**in** en)

trafficker ['træfɪkə(r)] *n* traficante *mf* (**in** de)

trafficking ['træfɪkɪŋ] *n* tráfico *m* (**in** de)

tragacanth ['trægəkænθ] *n* tragacanto *m*

tragedian [trə'dʒi:dɪən] *n* (**a**) *(actor)* (actor *m*) trágico *m* (**b**) *(writer)* trágico(a) *m,f*, dramaturgo(a) *m,f*

tragedienne [trədʒi:dɪ'en] *n (actress)* (actriz *f*) trágica *f*

tragedy ['trædʒɪdɪ] *n* (**a**) *(tragic event)* tragedia *f*; **the t. of the whole affair is that...** lo trágico de todo este asunto es que... (**b**) *Theat* tragedia *f*

tragic ['trædʒɪk] *adj* (**a**) *(very sad)* trágico(a) (**b**) *Theat (actor, actress)* trágico(a) ►► ***t. hero*** héroe *m* trágico; ***t. irony*** ironía *f* trágica (**c**) *Fam (very bad)* horroroso(a)

tragically ['trædʒɪklɪ] *adv* trágicamente; **the mission went t. wrong** la misión acabó en tragedia; **he died at a t. early age** fue una tragedia que muriera tan joven

tragicomedy [trædʒɪ'kɒmədɪ] *n* tragicomedia *f*

tragicomic [trædʒɪ'kɒmɪk] *adj* tragicómico(a)

tragopan ['trægəpæn] *n* tragopán *m*

trail [treɪl] **1** *n* (**a**) *(of animal, person)* rastro *m*, huellas *fpl*; **to be on the t. of sth/sb** estar sobre la pista de algo/alguien; **to pick up the t.** encontrar el rastro; **to put** *or* **throw sb off the t.** despistar a alguien, dar pistas falsas a alguien
(**b**) *(of smoke, blood)* rastro *m*; **they had left a t. of footprints in the snow** habían dejado un rastro *or* sendero de huellas sobre la nieve; **the storm left a t. of destruction** la tormenta dejó una estela de destrucción; **she leaves a t. of broken hearts behind her wherever she goes** va rompiendo corazones allí donde va
(**c**) *(path)* camino *m*, senda *f*; *Fig* **he hit the campaign t.** emprendió la campaña electoral ►► ***t. bike*** moto *f* de trial *or* motocross; *US* ***t. hiker*** excursionista *mf*; ***t. mix*** mezcla *f* de frutos secos; ***t. riding*** trail *m*
2 *vt* (**a**) *(drag)* arrastrar; **he was trailing a sack of coal behind him** iba arrastrando *or* tirando de un saco de carbón; **she trailed her hand through the water** iba cortando el agua con la mano
(**b**) *(bring on shoes)* **they trailed mud all over the carpet** dejaron restos de barro por toda la alfombra
(**c**) *(follow)* seguir la pista de
(**d**) *(in competition, game)* ir por detrás de; **they were trailing the Liberals by fifteen points** iban quince puntos por delante del partido liberal
3 *vi* (**a**) *(drag)* arrastrar; **your skirt is trailing (on the ground)** te arrastra la falda (por el suelo)
(**b**) *(move in line)* **smoke trailed from the chimney** una columna de humo salía de la chimenea
(**c**) *(move slowly)* avanzar con paso cansino; **to t. in and out** entrar y salir con desgana; **the British athlete trailed in in last place** el atleta británico consiguió alcanzar la meta en ultimo lugar
(**d**) *(be losing)* ir perdiendo; **they are trailing in the polls** van por detrás *or* perdiendo en las encuestas
(**e**) *(vine, plant)* trepar

►**trail along** *vi (walk slowly)* caminar con desgana

►**trail away, trail off** *vi (voice, sound)* ir debilitándose; **he trailed off in mid sentence** perdió el hilo en mitad de la frase

trailblazer ['treɪlbleɪzə(r)] *n* innovador(ora) *m,f*, pionero(a) *m,f*

trailblazing ['treɪlbleɪzɪŋ] *adj* innovador(ora), pionero(a)

trailer ['treɪlə(r)] *n* (**a**) *(vehicle)* remolque *m*, tráiler *m* (**b**) *US (caravan)* caravana *f*, roulotte *f* ►► ***t. park*** camping *m* para caravanas *or* roulottes; *Fam Pej* ***t. trash*** = personas de clase humilde que viven en campings para caravanas (**c**) *(for movie)* avance *m*, tráiler *m*, *Arg* cola *f*; *(for TV programme)* avance *m*

trailing ['treɪlɪŋ] *adj (long garment)* que arrastra; *(plant)* rastrero(a) ►► ***t. edge*** *(of plane wing)* borde *m* de ataque

train [treɪn] **1** *n* (**a**) *(means of transport)* tren *m*; **to go/travel by t.** ir/viajar en tren; **to transport goods by t.** transportar mercancías en tren *or* por ferrocarril; **I met a friend on the t.** me encontré con un amigo en el tren; **the t. times** el horario de trenes; **the t. journey took three hours** el viaje en tren duró tres horas ►► ***t. crash*** accidente *m* ferroviario; *Br* ***t. driver*** conductor(ora) *m,f* del tren, maquinista *mf*; ***t. fare*** precio *m* del billete *or Am* boleto *or Am* pasaje de tren; ***t. service*** servicio *m* de trenes; ***t. set*** tren *m* de juguete; ***t. station*** estación *f* de tren; ***t. timetable*** guía *f* de ferrocarriles
(**b**) *(series) (of events)* serie *f*; **t. of thought** pensamientos; **I can't quite follow your t. of thought** no entiendo tu razonamiento; **I lost my t. of thought** me he perdido; *Formal* **to set sth in t.** poner algo en marcha
(**c**) *(retinue)* séquito *m*; *(of mules)* reata *f*; *(of camels)* caravana *f*; *Formal* **the famine brought disease in its t.** el hambre vino acompañada de las enfermedades; *Formal* **the evils that follow in the t. of war** los males que acarrea la guerra
(**d**) *(of dress)* cola *f*
(**e**) *(of gears)* tren *m*
(**f**) *(of gunpowder)* reguero *m*
2 *vt* (**a**) *(person)* dar formación a, formar; *(animal)* adiestrar; *(voice, ear)* educar; *(soldier)* dar instrucción a; *(in sport)* entrenar; **to t. sb for sth/to do sth** adiestrar a alguien para algo/para hacer algo; **we've trained the dog to go for the paper** hemos enseñado al perro a que recoja el periódico; **I was trained in Germany** *(studied)* recibí mi formación en Alemania; **our troops are trained to resist interrogation** nuestras tropas están preparadas para resistir un interrogatorio; **he had trained his mind** *or* **himself to block out distractions** se había preparado mentalmente para no sufrir distracciones; **he has been trained in the use of explosives** ha sido entrenado para manejar explosivos; **to t. sb in a trade/a new skill** formar a alguien en un oficio/una técnica
(**b**) *(gun, telescope)* dirigir (**on** hacia); **she kept the gun trained on us while we spoke** nos apuntaba con el arma mientras nos hablaba; **the TV cameras were all trained on the star** las cámaras de televisión enfocaban al protagonista
(**c**) *(plant)* dirigir el crecimiento de
(**d**) *Fam (travel by train)* **to t. it** ir en tren
3 *vi* (**a**) *(study)* estudiar; **to t. as a nurse/teacher** estudiar para (ser) enfermero(a)/maestro(a); **I trained as an electrician** aprendí el oficio de electricista (**b**) *Sport* entrenar(se) (**for** para)

►**train up** *vt sep* capacitar

trained [treɪnd] *adj (person)* cualificado(a); *(animal)* entrenado(a); *(voice)* educado(a); **he's not t. for this job** no está preparado para este trabajo; **our workers are t. in a wide range of skills** nuestros trabajadores están formados en una amplia variedad de técnicas; **her t. eye spotted the mistake** su ojo experto detectó el error; *Hum* **her husband is very well t.!** ¡tiene muy bien enseñado a su marido!

trainee [treɪ'ni:] *n (in trade)* aprendiz(iza) *m,f*, aprendiz *mf*; *(in profession)* persona *f* en formación; *(at lawyer's)* pasante *mf*; *(at accountant's) Esp* contable *mf or Am* contador(ora) *m,f* en prácticas; **a t. hairdresser** un(a) aprendiz de peluquería; **a t. translator/manager** un traductor/gerente en formación

traineeship [treɪ'ni:ʃɪp] *n (in trade)* aprendizaje *m*; *(in profession)* formación *f*; *(at lawyer's)* pasantía *f*; *(at accountant's)* prácticas *fpl*

trainer ['treɪnə(r)] *n* (**a**) *(of athletes, racehorses)* entrenador(ora) *m,f*; *(of sports team)* preparador(ora) *m,f* físico(a) (**b**) *(teacher) (on training scheme)* tutor(ora) *m,f*, instructor(ora) *m,f* (**c**) *(in circus)* domador (ora) *m,f* (**d**) *Av* **t. (aircraft)** avión *m* de entrenamiento (**e**) *Br (shoe)* zapatilla *f* de deporte

training ['treɪnɪŋ] *n* (**a**) *(for job)* formación *f*; **he is a lawyer by t.** tiene el título de abogado, estudió derecho; *Mil* **to do one's basic t.** hacer la instrucción; *Fig* **it's good t. for when you're a parent** te sirve de preparación para cuando tengas un hijo ►► *Mil* ***t. camp*** campamento *m* de instrucción; ***t. centre*** centro *m* de formación; *Br* ***t. college*** *(for pilots)* centro *m* de formación de vuelo; *(for teachers)* escuela *f* de magisterio; ***t. course*** cursillo *m* de formación; ***t. manual*** manual *m* de formación; ***t. officer*** jefe(a) *m,f* de formación; ***t. programme*** programa *m* de formación; ***t. scheme*** programa *m* de formación; ***t. ship*** buque *m* escuela; ***t. of trainers*** formación *f* de instructores; ***t. video*** vídeo *m or Am* video *m* de formación
(**b**) *(in sport)* entrenamiento *m*; **to be in t. (for sth)** estar entrenando (para algo); **to be out of t.** estar desentrenado(a), no estar en forma ►► ***t. camp*** lugar *m* de concentración; ***t. ground*** campo *m* de entrenamiento; ***t. shoes*** zapatillas *fpl* de deporte

trainload ['treɪnləʊd] *n* **a t. of...** un tren cargado *or* lleno de...; **supporters were arriving by the t.** llegaron varios trenes llenos de seguidores

trainman ['treɪnmæn] *n US* ferroviario *m*, empleado *m* del tren

trainspotter ['treɪnspɒtə(r)] *n Br* (**a**) *(rail enthusiast)* = aficionado a los trenes que se dedica a apuntar y coleccionar el número del modelo de las locomotoras (**b**) *Fam (boring, pedantic person)* petardo(a) *m,f*

trainspotting ['treɪnspɒtɪŋ] *n Br* = afición consistente en apuntar y coleccionar números de modelos de locomotoras

traipse [treɪps] **1** *n* **it's quite a t. to the castle** hay un buen trecho hasta el castillo

2 *vi Fam* **they traipsed from one museum to another** fueron de un museo a otro de mala gana; **we all traipsed off to school** fuimos al colegio sin ganas; **to t. round the shops** patearse las tiendas

trait [treɪt] *n* rasgo *m*

traitor ['treɪtə(r)] *n* traidor(ora) *m,f*; **you're a t. to your country/the cause** eres un traidor a tu país/a la causa

traitorous ['treɪtərəs] *adj Literary* traicionero(a)

traitress ['treɪtrɪs] *n* traidora *f*

trajectory [trə'dʒektərɪ] *n* trayectoria *f*

tram [træm] *n Br* (**a**) *(in street)* tranvía *m*; **to go by t.** ir en tranvía ►► ***t. driver*** conductor(ora) *m,f* del tranvía (**b**) *(in mine)* vagoneta *f*

tramcar ['træmkɑː(r)] *n Br* tranvía *m*

tramline ['træmlaɪn] *n* (**a**) *Br (track)* carril *m* de tranvía; *(route)* línea *f* de tranvía (**b**) *(in tennis)* **tramlines** líneas *fpl* laterales (**c**) *Fam (on arm)* **tramlines** marcas *fpl* de jeringuillas

trammel ['træməl] **1** *n Literary* **the trammels of society** las trabas sociales; **the trammels of routine** las obligaciones impuestas por la rutina

2 *vt* (*pt & pp* **trammelled**, *US* **trammeled**) *(hinder)* obstaculizar, poner trabas a

tramp [træmp] **1** *n* (**a**) *(vagabond)* vagabundo(a) *m,f* (**b**) *US Fam (promiscuous woman)* fulana *f*, *Méx* piruja *f*, *RP* reventada *f* (**c**) *(boat)* **t. (steamer)** carguero *m* (**d**) *(long walk)* caminata *f* (**e**) *(sound of feet)* pisada *f* fuerte

2 *vt* **to t. the streets** recorrer a pie las calles

3 *vi* caminar con pasos pesados, marchar; **she tramped up the road** subió la carretera caminando con pasos pesados; **they had tramped all over the carpet in their muddy shoes** habían pisoteado toda la alfombra con los zapatos llenos de barro

> **False friend:** The Spanish noun **trampa** is not a translation for the English word **tramp**. In Spanish the main meanings of **trampa** are "trap" or "trick".

► **tramp down** *vt sep (earth)* apelmazar *(a pisotones)*

trample ['træmpəl] *vt* (**a**) *(stamp on)* pisotear; **they were trampled to death** murieron pisoteados (**b**) *(feelings, rights)* hacer caso omiso de, ignorar

► **trample on** *vt insep* (**a**) *(stamp on)* pisotear (**b**) *(feelings, rights, objections)* hacer caso omiso de, ignorar

► **trample over** *vt insep* **he trampled over anyone who opposed him** pasaba por encima de cualquiera que se le opusiera

trampoline [træmpə'liːn] *n* cama *f* elástica

> **False friend:** The Spanish noun **trampolín** is not a translation for the English word **trampoline**. In Spanish **trampolín** means "diving board", "springboard" or "ski jump".

trampolining [træmpə'liːnɪŋ] *n* saltos *mpl* en cama elástica; **to go t.** hacer saltos en cama elástica

tramway ['træmweɪ] *n Br* (**a**) *(track)* carril *m* de tranvía (**b**) *(system)* (línea *f* de) tranvía *m*

trance [trɑːns] *n* (**a**) *(state)* trance *m*; **to go into a t.** entrar en trance; **the hypnotist put me into a t.** el hipnotizador me hizo entrar en trance (**b**) *Mus* **t. (music)** (música *f*) trance *m*

tranche [trɒnʃ] *n Fin (of shares)* paquete *m*; *(of loan)* tramo *m*

trannie, tranny ['trænɪ] *n Fam* (**a**) *Br* (*abbr* **transistor radio**) radio *f* (**b**) (*abbr* **transvestite, transexual**) travesti *mf*, *Esp* travestí *mf*

tranquil ['træŋkwɪl] *adj* tranquilo(a)

tranquillity, *US* **tranquility** [træŋ'kwɪlɪtɪ] *n* tranquilidad *f*

tranquillize, *US* **tranquilize** ['træŋkwɪlaɪz] *vt (with drug)* sedar

tranquillizer, *US* **tranquilizer** ['træŋkwɪlaɪzə(r)] *n* tranquilizante *m*

tranquilly ['træŋkwɪlɪ] *adv* tranquilamente

transact [træn'zækt] *vt (deal)* realizar, llevar a cabo; **to t. business with sb** llevar a cabo negocios con alguien

transaction [træn'zækʃən] *n* (**a**) *(financial operation)* transacción *f*; **there is a charge for credit card transactions** hay un cargo por las transacciones *or* operaciones realizadas con la tarjeta de crédito

(**b**) *(act of transacting)* **the t. of government business** el ejercicio de las funciones del gobierno; **we are open for the t. of business from 9 a.m.** la negociación comienza a las nueve de la mañana

(**c**) *(of learned society)* **transactions** actas *fpl*

transalpine [trænz'ælpaɪn] *adj* transalpino(a)

transaminase [trænz'æmɪneɪz] *n Biochem* transaminasa *f*

transatlantic [trænzət'læntɪk] *adj* transatlántico(a); *Br Hum* **our t. cousins** nuestros vecinos del otro lado del Atlántico

transceiver [træn'siːvə(r)] *n Comptr* transceptor *m*

transcend [træn'send] *vt* ir más allá de, superar

transcendence [træn'sendəns], **transcendency** [træn'sendənsɪ] *n* trascendencia *f*

transcendent [træn'sendənt] *adj* trascendente

transcendental [trænsen'dentəl] *adj* trascendental ►► ***t. meditation*** meditación *f* trascendental

transcendentalism [trænsen'dentəlɪzəm] *n* trascendentalismo *m*

transcontinental [trænzkɒntɪ'nentəl] *adj* transcontinental

transcribe [træn'skraɪb] *vt* (**a**) *(write exact copy of)* transcribir, copiar; **to t. sth phonetically** transcribir algo fonéticamente (**b**) *(in shorthand)* taquigrafiar (**c**) *Mus* transcribir (**d**) *(audio recording)* transcribir

transcript ['trænskrɪpt] *n* (**a**) *(of speech, tapes)* transcripción *f* (**b**) *US Sch & Univ* expediente *m* académico

transcription [træns'krɪpʃən] *n* transcripción *f*

transducer [trænz'djuːsə(r)] *n Elec* transductor *m*

transect [træn'sekt] *vt* cortar transversalmente

transept ['trænsept] *n* nave *f* lateral del crucero

transexual [træn'sekʃʊəl] **1** *n* transexual *mf*

2 *adj* transexual

transfer **1** *n* ['trænsfɜː(r)] (**a**) *(move) (of employee, department, prisoners)* traslado *m*; *(of passengers)* transporte *m*, traslado *m*; *(of sports player)* fichaje *m*; *(of money, funds)* transferencia *f*; *(of ownership, property)* transmisión *f*; **t. of power** traspaso de poderes; **he has asked for a t.** *(employee, prisoner)* ha pedido un traslado; *(player)* ha pedido que lo traspasen; *Sport* **to be on the t. list** ser transferible ►► *Sport* ***t. deadline*** cierre *m* del plazo de fichajes; ***t. desk*** *(at airport)* mostrador *m* para pasajeros en tránsito; *Sport* ***t. fee*** fichaje *m*; ***t. lounge*** *(in airport)* sala *f* de tránsito; *Sport* ***t. market*** mercado *m* de fichajes; ***t. passengers*** pasajeros *mpl* en tránsito *or* de paso; *Comptr* ***t. rate*** velocidad *f* de transferencia; *Comptr* ***t. speed*** velocidad *f* de transmisión

(**b**) *(sticker)* calcomanía *f*

(**c**) *US (ticket)* = billete válido para efectuar un transbordo a otro autobús, tren, etc.

2 *vt* [træns'fɜː(r)] (**a**) *(employee, department, prisoners)* trasladar; *(passengers)* transportar, llevar; *(sports player)* traspasar; *(funds)* transferir; *(ownership, property)* transmitir; *(power, responsibility)* traspasar, transferir; *(attention, affection)* trasladar; **t. the mixture to a greased baking tin** pase *or* traspase la mezcla a una fuente de horno previamente engrasada; **can this ticket be transferred to another airline?** ¿se puede utilizar este pasaje con otra línea aérea?; **the disease can be transferred from one species to another** la enfermedad se puede transmitir de una especie a otra; **we have been transferring our film archives to digital media** hemos estado transfiriendo nuestros archivos filmados a un soporte digital; **they transferred their allegiance to another candidate** han trasladado su lealtad a otro candidato

(**b**) *(phone call)* pasar, transferir; **I'll t. you** *(caller)* le paso

3 *vi* (**a**) *(within organization)* trasladarse; **she transferred to another school** se trasladó a otro colegio; **I'm transferring to a different course** me voy a cambiar de asignatura (**b**) *(between planes, trains)* hacer transbordo; **we had to t. from the train to a bus** nos pasaron de un tren a un autobús

transferable [trænz'fɜːrəbəl] *adj* transferible ►► *Pol* ***t. vote*** voto *m* transferible

transference [trænz'fɜːrəns] *n* (**a**) *(of money, funds)* transferencia *f*; **t. of power** traspaso *m* de poderes (**b**) *Psy* transferencia *f*

transfer-listed ['trænzfɜːlɪstɪd] *adj Br Sport* **to be t.** estar en la lista de traspasos

transfiguration [trænzfɪgə'reɪʃən] *n Formal* transfiguración *f*; *Rel* **the T.** la transfiguración

transfigure [trænz'fɪgə(r)] *vt Formal* transfigurar

transfix [træn'fɪks] *vt* (**a**) *(pierce)* atravesar (**b**) *(paralyze)* **they were transfixed with fear** estaban paralizados por el miedo

transform [trænz'fɔːm] *vt* (**a**) *(change)* transformar; **to t. sth into sth** transformar algo en algo; **she was completely transformed by her experience** la experiencia la transformó completamente; **the new manager has transformed the team's fortunes** el nuevo seleccionador ha hecho que cambie la suerte del equipo (**b**) *Elec* transformar (**c**) *Math* transformar

transformation [trænzfə'meɪʃən] *n* (**a**) *(change)* transformación *f*; **the new manager has brought about a t. in the team's fortunes** el nuevo seleccionador ha traído consigo una transformación en la suerte del equipo (**b**) *Math* transformación *f* (**c**) *Ling* transformación *f*

transformational [trænzfɔː'meɪʃənəl] *adj Ling (rule)* transformacional ▸▸ ***t. grammar*** gramática *f* transformacional

transformer [trænz'fɔːmə(r)] *n Elec* transformador *m*

transfuse [træns'fjuːz] *vt* (**a**) *(blood)* transfundir (**b**) *(permeate)* **in a voice transfused with emotion** con una voz impregnada de emoción

transfusion [trænz'fjuːʒən] *n* **(blood) t.** transfusión *f* (de sangre); **they gave him a (blood) t.** le hicieron una transfusión (de sangre)

transgenic [trænz'dʒiːnɪk] *adj* transgénico(a)

transgress [trænz'gres] *Formal* **1** *vt (law)* transgredir, infringir
2 *vi* (**a**) *(violate law)* infringir la ley (**b**) *(sin)* pecar

transgression [trænz'greʃən] *n Formal* (**a**) *(violation of law)* transgresión *f* (**b**) *(sin)* pecado *m*

transgressor [trænz'gresə(r)] *n Formal* (**a**) *(of law)* transgresor(ora) *m,f* (**b**) *(sinner)* pecador(ora) *m,f*

transience ['trænzɪəns] *n* transitoriedad *f*

transient ['trænzɪənt] **1** *n* (**a**) *US (tramp)* sin techo *mf* (**b**) *(temporary resident)* residente *mf* temporal (**c**) *Elec* transiente *m*
2 *adj* pasajero(a), transitorio(a)

transistor [træn'zɪstə(r)] *n* (**a**) *Elec* transistor *m* (**b**) **t. (radio)** transistor *m*

transistorized [træn'zɪstəraɪzd] *adj* transistorizado(a)

transit ['trænzɪt] *n* (**a**) *(passing)* tránsito *m*; **in t.** en tránsito; **goods lost in t.** mercancías perdidas durante el traslado ▸▸ ***t. camp*** campo *m* provisional; ***t. lounge*** *(at airport)* sala *f* de tránsito; ***t. passenger*** pasajero(a) *m,f* en tránsito; ***t. visa*** visado *m or Am* visa *f* de tránsito (**b**) *US (transport)* transporte *m* (**c**) *(airport transfer vehicle)* monorraíl *m* de conexión

transition [træn'zɪʃən] *n* transición *f*; **the t. to democracy** la transición a la democracia; **the country has made the t. from dictatorship to democracy** el país ha superado la transición de la dictadura a la democracia ▸▸ *Chem* ***t. element*** elemento *m* de transición; ***t. period*** periodo *m* de transición

transitional [træn'zɪʃənəl] *adj* de transición

transitive ['trænzɪtɪv] *adj Gram* transitivo(a)

transitively ['trænzɪtɪvlɪ] *adv Gram* transitivamente

transitory ['trænzɪtərɪ] *adj* transitorio(a)

translatable [trænz'leɪtəbəl] *adj* traducible

translate [trænz'leɪt] **1** *vt* (**a**) *(language, word, text)* traducir (**from/ into** de/a); **to t. sth from Spanish into English** traducir algo del español al inglés; **how do you t. "hunger"?** ¿cómo se traduce "hunger"?, ¿qué traducción tiene "hunger"?; **the title has been translated as...** el título se ha traducido como...
(**b**) *(convert)* **I'll attempt to t. these figures into an easily understandable graph** intentaré pasar estas cifras a un gráfico de fácil comprensión; **how will we t. these ideas into action?** ¿cómo podemos llevar estas ideas a la práctica?
(**c**) *Rel (cleric, relics)* trasladar
2 *vi* (**a**) *(person)* traducir (**b**) *(word, expression)* traducirse (**as** por); **this word doesn't t.** esta palabra no tiene traducción (**c**) *(convert)* **these savings t. into a 5 percent rise in profitability** estos ahorros dan un 5 por ciento de beneficios

translation [trænz'leɪʃən] *n* (**a**) *(of word, text, book)* traducción *f*; **to read sth in t.** leer la traducción de algo; **the text loses something in (the) t.** el texto pierde algo en la traducción ▸▸ ***t. agency*** agencia *f* de traducción (**b**) *Rel (of cleric, relics)* traslado *m*

translator [trænz'leɪtə(r)] *n* traductor(ora) *m,f*

transliterate [trænz'lɪtəreɪt] *vt Ling* transliterar

transliteration [trænzlɪtə'reɪʃən] *n Ling* transliteración *f*

translucence [trænz'luːsəns] *n* translucidez *f*

translucent [trænz'luːsənt] *adj* traslúcido(a)

transmigrate [trænzmaɪ'greɪt] *vi (soul)* transmigrar

transmigration [trænzmaɪ'greɪʃən] *n (of souls)* transmigración *f*

transmissible [trænz'mɪsəbəl] *adj* transmisible

transmission [trænz'mɪʃən] *n* (**a**) *(of information, disease)* transmisión *f* (**b**) *(broadcasting)* transmisión *f* (**c**) *(broadcast) (on TV, radio)* transmisión *f*, emisión *f* (**d**) *Aut* transmisión *f* ▸▸ ***t. shaft*** árbol *m* de transmisión

transmit [trænz'mɪt] **1** *vt* (**a**) *(information, disease, sense of unease)* transmitir (**to** a) (**b**) *TV & Rad (TV, radio programme)* transmitir
2 *vi* transmitir

transmitter [trænz'mɪtə(r)] *n (emitter)* emisora *f*; *(relay station)* repetidor *m*

transmogrify [trænz'mɒgrɪfaɪ] *vt Hum* transformar (como por arte de magia)

transmutable [trænz'mjuːtəbəl] *adj* transmutable

transmutation [trænzmjuː'teɪʃən] *n* (**a**) *Formal (transformation)* transmutación *f*, transformación *f* (**b**) *(by alchemy)* transmutación *f* (**c**) *Phys* transmutación *f*

transmute [trænz'mjuːt] *vt* (**a**) *Formal (transform)* transmutar, transformar (**b**) *(by alchemy)* transmutar

transnational ['trænznæʃənəl] *adj* transnacional ▸▸ ***t. company*** compañía *f* multinacional

transoceanic [trænzəʊsɪ'ænɪk] *adj (flight, voyage)* transoceánico(a)

transom ['trænsəm] *n (above door)* dintel *m*, travesaño *m*; **t. (window)** montante *m*

transparency [trænz'pærənsɪ] *n* (**a**) *(of material)* transparencia *f* (**b**) *(of process, accounts)* transparencia *f* (**c**) *(photographic slide)* diapositiva *f* (**d**) *(for overhead projector)* transparencia *f*

transparent [træns'pærənt] *adj* (**a**) *(of material)* transparente (**b**) *(of process, accounts)* transparente (**c**) *(of person)* **you're so t.!** ¡se te ve a la legua!; **a t. lie** una mentira flagrante; **a t. attempt to deceive us** un intento descarado de engañarnos

transparently [trænz'pærəntlɪ] *adv* **it's t. obvious that...** está clarísimo que...; **a t. mendacious reply** una respuesta de una mendacidad flagrante

transpiration [trænspɪ'reɪʃən] *n (of plant, person)* transpiración *f*

transpire [træns'paɪə(r)] **1** *vt* (**a**) *(become apparent)* **it transpired that...** se supo que... (**b**) *(of plant, person)* transpirar
2 *vi* (**a**) *(happen)* ocurrir, pasar (**b**) *(plant, person)* transpirar

transplant **1** *n* ['trænsplɑːnt] *(operation)* trasplante *m*; **she's had a kidney t.** le hicieron un trasplante de riñón ▸▸ ***t. operation*** (operación *f* de) trasplante *m*; ***t. patient*** *(after operation)* paciente *mf* trasplantado(a); ***t. surgery*** cirugía *f* de trasplantes
2 *vt* [trænz'plɑːnt] (**a**) *(organ)* trasplantar (**b**) *(plant)* trasplantar (**c**) *(population)* trasladar

transplantation [trænsplɑːn'teɪʃən] *n* (**a**) *(organ)* trasplante *m* (**b**) *(of plant)* trasplante *m*

transponder [træns'pɒndə(r)] *n* transponedor *m*

transport **1** *n* ['trænspɔːt] (**a**) *(of people, goods)* transporte *m*; **road/ rail t.** transporte por carretera/ferrocarril; **have you got t. for tonight?** ¿tienes forma de ir/venir esta noche?; **you need your own t. for the job** se necesita vehículo propio para el empleo ▸▸ ***t. authority*** = organismo que gestiona el transporte; *Br* ***t. café*** ≃ bar *m* de carretera; ***t. costs*** gastos *mpl* de transporte; ***t. plane*** avión *m* de transporte; ***t. ship*** buque *m* de transporte; ***t. system*** sistema *m* de transportes
(**b**) *Literary (rapture)* **to be in a t.** *or* **transports of delight** no caber en sí de gozo; **it sent him into a t. of rage** lo sacó de quicio
(**c**) *(ship)* buque *m* de transporte; *(plane)* avión *m* de transporte
2 *vt* [træns'pɔːt] (**a**) *(people, goods)* transportar (**b**) *Hist (as punishment)* deportar (**c**) *(take)* **the music transports you to a different world** la música te transporta a un mundo diferente; **I was transported back in time** me llevaron atrás en el tiempo (**d**) *Literary (with emotion)* **I was transported with delight** estaba extasiado

transportable [træns'pɔːtəbəl] *adj* transportable

transportation [trænspɔː'teɪʃən] *n* (**a**) *(of people, goods)* transporte *m* (**b**) *Hist (as punishment)* deportación *f*

transporter [træns'pɔːtə(r)] *n (for cars)* camión *m* para el transporte de vehículos

transpose [træns'pəʊz] *vt* (**a**) *(words)* invertir (**b**) *Typ* transponer (**c**) *(music)* transportar

transposition [trænspə'zɪʃən] *n* (**a**) *(of words)* trasposición *f* (**b**) *(of music)* trasposición *f*

transputer [træns'pjuːtə(r)] *n Comptr* transputador *m*

transsexual [trænz'sekʃʊəl] 1 *n* transexual *mf*
2 *adj* transexual

transsexuality [trænzsekʃʊ'ælɪtɪ] *n* transexualidad *f*

transshipment [trænz'ʃɪpmənt] *n* transbordo *m*

transubstantiation [trænsəbstænʃɪ'eɪʃən] *n Rel* transubstanciación *f*

transuranic [trænzjʊ'rænɪk] *adj* transuránico(a)

transversal [trænz'vɜːsəl] *n Geom* transversal *f*

transverse ['trænzvɜːs] *adj* transversal ►► *Med* ***t. colon*** colon *m* transverso; ***t. flute*** flauta *f* travesera; *Phys* ***t. wave*** onda *f* transversal

transvestism [trænz'vestɪzəm] *n* travestismo *m*

transvestite [trænz'vestaɪt] *n* travestido(a) *m,f*, travesti *mf*, *Esp* travestí *mf*

trap [træp] 1 *n* (a) *(in hunting)* trampa *f*; **they set a t. for the foxes** tendieron *or* pusieron una trampa para zorros
(b) *(trick) (for person)* trampa *f*; **to set a t. for sb** tender *or* poner una trampa a alguien; **to fall** *or* **walk straight into the t.** caer en la trampa; **we mustn't fall into the t. of underestimating them** no debemos caer en la trampa de subestimarlos
(c) *Fam (mouth)* **shut your t.!** ¡cierra el pico!; **to keep one's t. shut** no decir ni mu, mantener cerrado el pico
(d) *(vehicle)* carrito *m*, carretón *m*
(e) *(in clay pigeon shooting)* lanzaplatos *m inv* ►► ***t. shooting*** tiro *m* al plato
(f) *(in greyhound racing)* cajón *m* de salida
(g) *(in golf)* búnker *m*
(h) *(in drain)* sifón *m*
2 *vt* (*pt & pp* **trapped**) (a) *(animal)* atrapar
(b) *(catch, immobilize) (person)* atrapar; **they got trapped in the lift** quedaron atrapados en el ascensor; **they were trapped in the rubble** estaban atrapados entre los escombros; **I trapped my leg** *or* **my leg got trapped under the table** se me quedó la pierna pillada debajo de la mesa; **she trapped her fingers in the door** se pilló los dedos con la puerta; **some air was trapped in the pipe** se formó una cámara de aire en la tubería; **she was/felt trapped in a loveless marriage** estaba/se sentía atrapada en un matrimonio sin amor
(c) *(trick)* **to t. sb into saying/doing sth** engañar a alguien para que diga/haga algo
(d) *(hold back) (water, gas, heat)* retener
(e) *(in soccer) (ball)* controlar el balón *(pisándolo)*

trapdoor ['træpdɔː(r)] *n* trampilla *f* ►► ***t. spider*** migala *f or* migale *f* albañil

trapeze [trə'piːz] *n* trapecio *m* ►► ***t. artist*** trapecista *mf*

trapezium [trə'piːzɪəm] (*pl* **trapeziums** *or* **trapezia** [trə'piːzɪə]) *n Geom* (a) *Br (with two parallel sides)* trapecio *m* (b) *US (with no parallel sides)* trapezoide *m*

trapezius [trə'piːzɪəs] *n Anat* (músculo *m*) trapecio *m* ►► ***t. muscle*** músculo *m* trapecio

trapezoid ['træpəzɔɪd] *n* (a) *Br (with no parallel sides)* trapezoide *m* (b) *US (with two parallel sides)* trapecio *m*

trapper ['træpə(r)] *n (hunter)* trampero *m*

trappings ['træpɪŋz] *npl* (a) *(of power, success)* parafernalia *f*; **she had all the t. of power, but wielded little real influence** tenía todos los atributos del poder, pero ejercía muy poca influencia real (b) *(harness)* jaeces *mpl*

Trappist ['træpɪst] 1 *n* trapense *mf*
2 *adj (monastery, beer)* trapense ►► ***T. monk*** monje *m* trapense

trash [træʃ] 1 *n* (a) *(worthless objects)* bazofia *f*, basura *f*; **the products they sell are a load of t.** los productos que venden no son más que basura; **that book/movie is a load of t.** ese libro/esa película es pura bazofia
(b) *(nonsense)* bobadas *fpl*; **he's talking t.** no dice más que bobadas *or* estupideces
(c) *US (refuse)* basura *f*; **to put sth in the t.** tirar algo a la basura ►► ***t. can*** cubo *m* de la basura; *Comptr* papelera *f* (de reciclaje); ***t. heap*** vertedero *m*
(d) *Fam (people)* gentuza *f* (baja); **he's just t.** no es más que escoria
2 *vt Fam* (a) *(vandalize)* destrozar (b) *(criticize) (book, movie, ideas)* poner *or* dejar por los suelos, *Esp* poner a parir, *Méx* viborear, *RP* dejar por el piso

trashed [træʃt] *adj Fam (drunk) Esp, Méx* pedo *inv*, *Col* caído(a), *RP* en pedo; *(on drugs)* colocado(a), *Esp* ciego(a), *Col* trabado(a), *Méx* pingo(a), *RP* falopeado(a)

trashman ['træʃmæn] *n US* basurero *m*

trashy ['træʃɪ] *adj Fam (magazine, book, programme)* de pacotilla, *Esp* cutre, *Méx* gacho(a), *RP* groncho(a)

trauma ['trɔːmə] *n* (a) *Med* traumatismo *m* (b) *(psychological, emotional)* trauma *m*

traumatic [trɔː'mætɪk] *adj* traumático(a)

traumatism ['trɔːmətɪzəm] *n* traumatismo *m*

traumatize ['trɔːmətaɪz] *vt* traumatizar

travail ['træveɪl] *n Literary* penalidad *f*

travel ['trævəl] 1 *n* (a) *(journeys)* viajes *mpl*; **foreign t. is increasingly popular** los viajes al extranjero tienen cada vez mayor demanda; **can I invoice them for t. to and from the airport?** ¿les puedo presentar factura por los desplazamientos del aeropuerto?; **what do you spend on t. to work?** ¿cuánto te gastas en transporte para ir al trabajo?; **it's two days' t. from here** desde aquí son dos días de viaje; **t. broadens the mind** viajando se amplían horizontes, viajando se hace uno más abierto; **on my travels** en mis viajes; **the team has yet to win on its travels** el equipo todavía tiene que ganar fuera de casa *or* a domicilio ►► ***t. agency*** agencia *f* de viajes; ***t. agent*** empleado(a) *m,f* de una agencia de viajes; ***t. agent's*** agencia *f* de viajes; ***t. bag*** bolsa *f* de viaje; ***t. book*** libro *m* de viajes; ***t. brochure*** folleto *m* turístico; ***t. bureau*** agencia *f* de viajes; ***t. clock*** despertador *m* de viaje; ***t. company*** tour operador *m*, operador *m* turístico; ***t. documents*** documentación *f* para el viaje; ***t. expenses*** gastos *mpl* de viaje; ***t. grant*** bolsa *f* de viaje; ***t. insurance*** seguro *m* de (asistencia en) viaje; ***t. news*** noticias *fpl* para los viajeros; *Br* ***t. pass*** bono *m* (de viaje); ***t. rug*** manta *f* de viaje; ***t. sickness*** mareo *m*; ***t. writer*** autor(ora) *m,f* de libros de viajes
(b) *(of piston)* recorrido *m*
2 *vt* (*pt & pp* **travelled**, *US* **traveled**) *(road, country)* viajar por; **they had to t. a long way** tuvieron que viajar desde muy lejos; **I travelled 50 kilometres to get here** recorrí 50 kilómetros para llegar hasta aquí
3 *vi* (a) *(journey) (person, animal)* viajar; **to t. by air** *or* **by plane** viajar en avión; **we decided to t. there by train/boat** decidimos ir allí en tren/barco; **to t. by land/sea** viajar por tierra/por mar; **to t. overland** viajar por tierra; **passengers travelling to Chicago, please go to gate 8** los pasajeros con destino Chicago, por favor procedan por la puerta 8; **after graduating she travelled around South America** después de acabar los estudios, viajó por América del Sur; **to t. round the world** viajar por todo el mundo, dar la vuelta al mundo; **to t. light** viajar ligero(a) de equipaje; **let's t. back in time to 1940** regresemos en el tiempo hasta 1940
(b) *(move) (aircraft)* volar, ir; *(car)* circular, ir; *(train, boat)* ir; *(sound, light, electricity)* propagarse; *(piston)* recorrer; **we were travelling at an average speed of 90 km/h** íbamos a una (velocidad) media de 90 km/h; **the electricity travels along this wire** la electricidad circula *or* se desplaza por este cable; **the Earth travels round the Sun** la Tierra gira alrededor del Sol; **news travels fast round here** por aquí las noticias vuelan
(c) *(wine, humour)* **it doesn't t. well** no es fácilmente exportable
(d) *(sports team)* **they don't t. well** no juegan bien fuera de casa
(e) *Fam (go fast) Esp* ir a toda pastilla *or Méx* hecho(a) la raya *or RP* a todo lo que da; **this car certainly travels!** ¡este coche sí que corre!
(f) *(in basketball)* hacer pasos

travelator, travolator ['trævəleɪtə(r)] *n* tapiz *m* deslizante, pasillo *m* móvil

travelled, *US* **traveled** ['trævəld] *adj* **he's a widely t. man** es un hombre que ha viajado mucho; **this is a much t. road** esta carretera está muy transitada

traveller, *US* **traveler** ['trævələ(r)] *n* (a) *(in general)* viajero(a) *m,f*; **I'm not a good t.** no me sientan bien los viajes; **rail travellers** usuarios del ferrocarril ►► *Br* ***t.'s cheque,*** *US* ***t.'s check*** cheque *m* de viaje; *Bot* ***t.'s joy*** hierba *f* de los pordioseros
(b) *(salesman)* viajante *mf* (de comercio)
(c) *Br* **(New Age) t.** = persona que vive en una tienda o caravana sin lugar fijo de residencia y que lleva un estilo de vida contrario al de la sociedad convencional

travelling, *US* **traveling** ['trævəlɪŋ] 1 *n* (a) *(in general)* viajes *mpl*; **I do a lot of t.** hago muchos viajes, viajo mucho; **I love t.** me encanta viajar ►► ***t. bag*** bolsa *f* de viaje; ***t. companion*** compañero(a) *m,f* de viaje; ***t. expenses*** gastos *mpl* de viaje; ***t. rug*** manta *f* de viaje (b) *(in basketball)* pasos *mpl*
2 *adj (theatre company, exhibition, preacher)* itinerante ►► ***t. folk*** gentes *fpl* itinerantes; ***t. people*** gentes *fpl* itinerantes; ***t. salesman*** viajante *mf* (de comercio)

travelogue, *US* **travelog** ['trævəlɒg] *n (film)* documental *m* sobre viajes

travel-sick ['trævəlsɪk] *adj Br* mareado(a); **to be** *or* **feel t.** estar mareado(a); **I get t. on buses** me mareo en los autobuses

travel-weary ['trævəlwɪərɪ] *adj* cansado(a) por el viaje

traverse [trə'vɜːs] **1** *n (in mountaineering, skiing) (path)* travesía *f*
2 *vt* **(a)** *Literary (cross)* atravesar, cruzar **(b)** *(in skiing, mountaineering)* cruzar transversalmente
3 *vi (in skiing, mountaineering)* **to t. across a slope** cruzar una ladera transversalmente

travesty ['trævəstɪ] **1** *n* farsa *f*, parodia *f* burda; **the trial was a t. of justice** el juicio fue una auténtica farsa
2 *vt* parodiar (burdamente)

> **False friend:** The Spanish noun **travesti** is not a translation for the English word **travesty**. In Spanish **travesti** means "transvestite" or "drag artist".

travolator = **travelator**

trawl [trɔːl] **1** *n* **(a)** *(net)* red *f* de arrastre **(b)** *(search)* rastreo *m*; **he had a t. through the records** hizo un rastreo de los archivos
2 *vt* **(a)** *(sea)* hacer pesca de arrastre en (**for** de) **(b)** *(search through)* rastrear, rebuscar; **to t. sth for** *or* **in search of sth** rastrear algo en busca de algo
3 *vi* **(a)** *(fish)* hacer pesca de arrastre (**for** de) **(b)** *(search)* **to t. through sth** rebuscar en *or* rastrear algo

trawler ['trɔːlə(r)] *n* **(a)** *(ship)* (barco *m*) arrastrero *m* **(b)** *(fisherman)* arrastrero(a) *m,f*, pescador *m* de arrastre

trawling ['trɔːlɪŋ] *n* (pesca *f* de) arrastre *m*

trawl-net ['trɔːlnet] *n* red *f* de arrastre, traína *f*

tray [treɪ] *n* **(a)** *(for carrying)* bandeja *f* **(b)** *(for papers, mail)* bandeja *f*; *(of printer)* bandeja *f* **(c)** *(in box of chocolates)* bandeja *f*

treacherous ['tretʃərəs] *adj* **(a)** *(person)* traicionero(a); *(action)* traidor(ora) **(b)** *(road, ice, water)* traicionero(a); **driving conditions are t.** es peligroso conducir en estas condiciones

treacherously ['tretʃərəslɪ] *adv* **(a)** *(to act)* a traición, traicioneramente **(b)** *(dangerously)* peligrosamente; **the currents are t. strong** las corrientes son fuertes y traicioneras

treachery ['tretʃərɪ] *n* traición *f*; **it was an act of t.** fue una traición

treacle ['triːkəl] *n* melaza *f* ►► *Br* ***t. pudding*** dulce *m* de melaza; *Br* ***t. tart*** tarta *f* de melaza

treacly ['triːklɪ] *adj* **(a)** *(sweet)* meloso(a) **(b)** *(sentimental)* meloso(a), sensiblero(a)

tread [tred] **1** *n* **(a)** *(sound of footsteps)* pisadas *fpl*, pasos *mpl* **(b)** *(footstep)* **to walk with a heavy t.** caminar fatigosamente **(c)** *(of tyre)* banda *f* de rodadura, dibujo *m*; *(of shoe)* dibujo *m* **(d)** *(of stair)* peldaño *m*, escalón *m*
2 *vt* (*pt* **trod** [trɒd], *pp* **trodden** ['trɒdən]) **(a)** *(trample) (ground, grapes)* pisar; **a path had been trodden through the grass** había un camino de hierba pisada; **to t. sth underfoot** pisotear algo; **to t. dirt into the carpet** ensuciar la *Esp* moqueta *or Am* alfombra con suciedad pegada al zapato; **to t. water** *(when swimming)* flotar moviendo las piernas; *(be going nowhere)* estar en un punto muerto
(b) *(walk) (path)* recorrer; *(streets)* patear, recorrer; *Fig* **this path has been trodden by previous governments** esta vía ya la han probado los gobiernos anteriores; *Fig* **he is treading a fine line between aggression and foul play** está en el límite de la agresión y el juego sucio; IDIOM **to t. the boards** *(appear on stage)* pisar las tablas
3 *vi* caminar; **t. lightly so you don't disturb the wildlife** camine con cuidado para no molestar a los animales; **they trod wearily home** con paso cansino regresaron a casa; **to t. on/in sth** pisar algo; *Fig* **to t. on sb's heels** ir a la zaga de alguien; **to t. on sb's toes** pisar (el pie) a alguien; *Fig* meterse en los asuntos de alguien; *Fig* **to t. carefully** *or* **warily** ir *or* andar con pies de plomo

► **tread down** *vt sep* pisar

treadle ['tredəl] *n* pedal *m*

treadmill ['tredmɪl] *n* **(a)** *(in gym)* tapiz *m* rodante, cinta *f* de footing *or* de correr **(b)** *Hist (in prison)* noria *f*; IDIOM **to be on a t.** sentirse esclavizado(a) por la rutina

treason ['triːzən] *n* traición *f*

treasonable ['triːzənəbəl] *adj (offence, act)* de alta traición

treasure ['treʒə(r)] **1** *n* **(a)** *(gold, silver, jewels, etc)* tesoro *m*; **buried t.** tesoro enterrado ►► ***t. hunt*** juego *m* de las pistas, caza *f* del tesoro
(b) *(valuable thing)* tesoro *m*, joya *f*; *(valuable person)* joya *f*; **the museum has many treasures of Renaissance art** el museo tiene muchas joyas del Renacimiento; **his works are a t. house of language** sus obras son una mina *or* un tesoro de la lengua
(c) *Fam (term of address)* tesoro *m*, cielo *m*
2 *vt (friendship, gift, memory, moment)* apreciar de verdad; **my most treasured possession** mi bien más preciado

treasurer ['treʒərə(r)] *n* tesorero(a) *m,f*

treasure-trove ['treʒətrəʊv] *n* **(a)** *Law* tesoro *m* encontrado **(b)** *(museum, shop)* descubrimiento *m*

treasury ['treʒərɪ] *n* **(a)** *(in castle, church, palace)* tesorería *f*, sala *f* del tesoro
(b) *Pol* **the T.** *(in UK)* el tesoro (público), ≃ (el Ministerio de) Economía; **the Department of the T.** *(in US)* el tesoro (público), ≃ (el Ministerio de) Hacienda ►► *Br* ***T. bench*** escaños *mpl* del gobierno, *Esp* ≃ banco *m* azul; ***T. bill*** letra *f* del tesoro; ***T. bond*** bono *m* del tesoro; ***T. note*** pagaré *m* del tesoro

treat [triːt] **1** *n* **(a)** *(pleasure)* alegría *f*; **it's a t. for us to see you looking so happy** para nosotros es una alegría verte tan contenta; **to give oneself a t.** darse un capricho; **you've got a real t. in store** te espera algo bueno; **watching this team play is a real t.** ver jugar a este equipo es un gustazo; IDIOM *Br Fam* **the renovation of our house is coming on a t.** la reforma de la casa va que da gusto; IDIOM *Br Fam* **this beer is going down a t.** esta cerveza sienta de maravilla; IDIOM *Br Fam* **it worked a t.** *(plan)* funcionó a las mil maravillas
(b) *(gift)* regalo *m*; **as a special t. we were taken to the zoo** como premio nos llevaron al zoo; **I bought him tickets to go and see his favourite band as a birthday t.** le compré entradas para que fuera a ver a su grupo favorito como regalo de cumpleaños; **it's my t.** *(I'm paying)* invito yo
2 *vt* **(a)** *(deal with) (person)* tratar; **to t. sb well/badly** tratar bien/mal a alguien; **to t. sb like an idiot** tomar a alguien por imbécil, tratar a alguien como a un(a) imbécil; **the hostages said that they had been well treated** los rehenes dijeron que los habían tratado bien; **you t. this place like a hotel!** ¡te comportas como si esto fuera un hotel!; **how's life been treating you?** ¿cómo te va?
(b) *(handle) (substance, object)* manejar; **the weedkiller needs to be treated with great care** los herbicidas deben ser manejados con mucho cuidado
(c) *(consider) (problem, question, situation)* tratar; **to t. sth as a joke** tomarse algo a broma; **she treated the subject rather superficially** trató *or* abordó el tema bastante superficialmente; **they treated my offer with suspicion/contempt** acogieron mi oferta con recelo/desdén; **police are treating this as a very serious matter** la policía le está dando mucha importancia a este asunto
(d) *(patient, illness)* tratar; **to t. sb for sth** tratar a alguien de algo; **she was treated for minor cuts and bruises** la atendieron para curarle pequeñas heridas y golpes; **the condition can be treated successfully using antibiotics** la enfermedad se puede curar con antibióticos
(e) *(material, timber, crops, sewage)* tratar; **the land has been treated with fertilizer** la tierra ha sido tratada *or* abonada con fertilizantes
(f) *(give as a present)* **to t. sb to sth** invitar a alguien a algo; **I'll t. you** te invito; **to t. oneself to sth** darse el capricho de comprarse algo; **go on, t. yourself!** ¡vamos *or Esp* venga, date el gusto!; *Ironic* **she treated us to one of her tantrums** nos deleitó con una de sus rabietas
3 *vi Formal* **(a)** *(negotiate)* negociar (**with** con) **(b)** *(be about)* **the book treats of love** el libro versa sobre el amor

treatable ['triːtəbəl] *adj* tratable, curable

treatise ['triːtɪz] *n* tratado *m* (**on** sobre)

treatment ['triːtmənt] *n* **(a)** *(behaviour towards) (of prisoner, animal)* trato *m*; **his t. of the prisoners** el trato que daba a los prisioneros; **I got very good t.** me trataron muy bien; **preferential t.** trato de favor; IDIOM *Fam* **to give sb the (full) t.** *(treat well)* nos trataron como reyes; *(beat up)* dar una paliza *or Esp* un buen repaso a alguien
(b) *Med (of patient)* tratamiento *m*; **she was sent to Toronto for t.** la enviaron a Toronto para el tratamiento; **to be given** *or* **undergo t.** recibir tratamiento; **he is not responding to t.** no está respondiendo al tratamiento; **he spent most of the year on the t. table** pasó la mayor parte del año en recuperación
(c) *(of problem, question, situation)* tratamiento *m*; **the government was criticized for its t. of the matter** el gobierno fue criticado por el tratamiento que le dieron al asunto; **Cézanne's t. of colour** la forma de tratar el color de Cézanne
(d) *(of material, timber, crops, sewage)* tratamiento *m*

treaty ['triːtɪ] *n* tratado *m*; **the Maastricht T.** el Tratado de Maastricht ►► ***the T. of Rome*** el Tratado de Roma

treble ['trebəl] **1** *n* **(a)** *Mus (person, voice)* soprano *m*, tiple *m* **(b)** *(on hi-fi)* agudos *mpl* **(c)** *(in darts)* triple *m* **(d)** *Br (in soccer)* **to do the t.** hacer *or* conseguir el triplete **(e)** *(bet)* = apuesta acumulada a tres caballos de diferentes carreras
2 *adj* **(a)** *(triple)* triple; *Br* **t. six** *(when reading numbers)* seis seis seis ►► *Br* ***t. chance*** triple apuesta *f* **(b)** *Mus (part, voice)* de soprano *or* tiple ►► ***t. clef*** clave *f* de sol

3 *vt (value, number)* triplicar
4 *vi* triplicarse
5 *adv* **t. the amount** el triple, tres veces la cantidad

tree [tri:] *n* (**a**) *(plant)* árbol *m*; **a pear t.** un peral; **a plum t.** un ciruelo; **an oak t.** un roble; IDIOM **to get to the top of the t.** llegar a lo más alto; IDIOM *Fam* **to be out of one's t.** *(crazy)* estar como una cabra; *(drunk)* estar como una cuba; *(on drugs)* tener un buen colocón ►► ***t. fern*** helecho *m* arbóreo; ***t. fox*** zorro *m* gris; ***t. frog*** rana *f* de San Antonio; ***t. house*** cabaña *f* en (la copa de) un árbol; *Fam Pej* ***t. hugger*** *(environmentalist)* verde *mf*; ***the t. of knowledge*** el árbol de la ciencia; ***t. of life*** árbol *m* de la vida; ***t. line*** límite *m* superior de la vegetación arbórea; ***t. pipit*** bisbita *m* arbóreo; ***t. snake*** serpiente *f* arborícola; ***t. sparrow*** gorrión *m* molinero; ***t. stump*** tocón *m* (de árbol); ***t. surgeon*** arboricultor(ora) *m,f*; ***t. trunk*** tronco *m* (de árbol)
(**b**) *Comptr* árbol *m*
(**c**) *Math & Ling* ***t. diagram*** (diagrama *m* en) árbol *m*

treecreeper ['tri:kri:pə(r)] *n* agateador *m* norteño ►► ***short-toed t.*** agateador *m*

treeless ['tri:lɪs] *adj* sin árboles

tree-lined ['tri:laɪnd] *adj* bordeado(a) de árboles

treetop ['tri:tɒp] *n* copa *f* de árbol; **in the treetops** en las copas *or* en lo alto de los árboles

trefoil ['trefɔɪl] *n* (**a**) *Bot* trébol *m* (**b**) *Archit* trifolio *m*

trek [trek] **1** *n (long walk)* caminata *f*; *(long journey)* largo camino *m*; *Fam* **it's quite a t. into town** hasta el centro hay un buen trecho *or Esp* una buena tirada
2 *vi* **to t. over the hills** recorrer las montañas; **to t. home** recorrer el largo camino hasta casa; *Fam* **to t. to the shops** darse una caminata hasta las tiendas

Trekkie ['trekɪ] *n Fam* trekkie *mf*, fan *mf* de "Star Trek"

trekking ['trekɪŋ] *n* senderismo *m*, excursionismo *m*; **to go t.** hacer senderismo *or* excursionismo

trellis ['trelɪs] *n* espaldar *m*, guía *f*

trellis-work ['trelɪswɜ:k] *n* enrejado *m*

trematode ['tremətəʊd] *n* trematodo *m*

tremble ['trembəl] **1** *n* temblor *m*; *Br* **to be all of a t.** estar temblando como un flan
2 *vi (vibrate)* temblar; **his hands were trembling** le temblaban las manos; **to t. with fear** temblar de miedo; **her voice trembled with emotion** la voz le temblaba de la emoción; *Fig* **she trembled at the thought of what they might get up to** temblaba con pensar lo que estarían tramando

trembling ['tremblɪŋ] *adj (body, hands)* tembloroso(a); **she spoke in a t. voice** hablaba con (la) voz temblorosa ►► ***t. poplar*** álamo *m* temblón

tremendous [trɪ'mendəs] *adj* (**a**) *(big) (amount, size, noise)* tremendo(a); **it was a t. success** fue un éxito tremendo, fue todo un éxito; **you've been a t. help** has sido de una enorme ayuda
(**b**) *(excellent) (book, holiday, writer)* extraordinario(a), estupendo(a), *Andes, CAm, Carib, Méx* chévere, *Méx* padre, *RP* bárbaro(a); **we had a t. time** lo pasamos de maravilla *or* estupendamente; **she looks t. in black** el negro le sienta estupendamente; **he scored a t. goal** marcó un gol de antología

tremendously [trɪ'mendəslɪ] *adv* (**a**) *(very)* enormemente, tremendamente; **he did t. well** le fue estupendamente (bien); **I'm not t. keen on his plays** no me vuelve loco su obra teatral; **you've been t. kind** has sido muy amable (**b**) *(very much)* **we enjoyed it t.** nos gustó muchísimo

tremolo ['treməlәʊ] *n Mus* trémolo *m* ►► ***t. arm*** (palanca *f* de) trémolo *m*

tremor ['tremə(r)] *n* (**a**) *(of person)* temblor *m*; **she spoke with a t. in her voice** hablaba con (la) voz temblorosa; **a t. of anticipation ran through the audience** se notaba entre el público la emoción de que se acercaba el momento (**b**) *(earthquake)* temblor *m* de tierra

tremulous ['tremjʊləs] *adj Literary* (**a**) *(quivering) (person, hands, voice)* trémulo(a) (**b**) *(timid) (person, manner, smile)* apocado(a)

tremulously ['tremjʊləslɪ] *adv Literary* (**a**) *(to answer, sing)* de forma trémula (**b**) *(to smile)* apocadamente

trench [trentʃ] *n* (**a**) *(ditch)* zanja *f* (**b**) *Mil* trinchera *f* ►► ***t. coat*** trinchera *f*; ***t. fever*** fiebre *f* de las trincheras; ***t. foot*** = afección de los pies producida por la estancia prolongada en terreno húmedo; ***t. warfare*** guerra *f* de trincheras

trenchant ['trentʃənt] *adj* mordaz

trenchantly ['trentʃəntlɪ] *adv* mordazmente

trencherman ['trentʃəmən] *n Hum* tragaldabas *mf inv*

trend [trend] **1** *n* tendencia *f*; **the latest trends in fashion** las últimas tendencias de la moda; **the t. is towards decentralization** se tiende a la descentralización; **there is a t. away from going abroad for holidays** las vacaciones en el extranjero están disminuyendo; **house prices are on an upward t. again** la tendencia de los precios de la vivienda está otra vez al alza; **to set/start a t.** establecer/iniciar una tendencia
2 *vi (prices)* tender; *(opinion)* inclinarse

trendily ['trendɪlɪ] *adv (to dress)* a la última (moda)

trendiness ['trendɪnɪs] *n (of clothes, style, idea)* lo moderno, estilo *m* a la última (moda); *(of person)* modernidad *f*; *(of bar, district)* lo moderno

trendsetter ['trendsetə(r)] *n* **he's a t. for the young** marca estilo entre los jóvenes

trendsetting ['trendsetɪŋ] *adj* rompedor(ora); **a t. idea** una idea rompedora

trendy ['trendɪ] **1** *n Br Fam Pej (person)* modernillo(a) *m,f*, *RP* modernoso(a) *m,f*; **the bar was full of trendies** el bar estaba lleno de gente que iba de moderna
2 *adj (clothes, style)* de moda; *(person, idea)* moderno(a); *(bar, district)* de moda; **it's very t. to do that** está muy de moda hacer eso; **he's a very t. dresser** viste a la última *or* muy a la moda ►► *Pej* ***t. lefty*** progre *mf*

trepan [trɪ'pæn] *Med* **1** *n* trépano *m*
2 *vt* trepanar

trepidation [trepɪ'deɪʃən] *n Formal* inquietud *f*, miedo *m*; **he stood there in t. before the headmaster** estaba atemorizado ante el director; **it was with some t. that I entered the room** entré con un cierto temor en la habitación

trespass ['trespəs] **1** *vi* (**a**) *Law* entrar sin autorización; **no trespassing** *(sign)* prohibido el paso (**b**) *Rel* **to t. against sb** ofender a alguien
2 *n* (**a**) *Law* entrada *f* no autorizada (**b**) *Rel* **forgive us our trespasses** perdona nuestras ofensas *or* deudas

> **False friend**: The Spanish verb **traspasar** is not a translation for the English word **trespass**. In Spanish **traspasar** means "to go through", "to go through" or "to transfer".

► **trespass on** *vt insep* (**a**) *(sb's property)* invadir, entrar sin autorización en; **you're trespassing on my property** estás invadiendo mi propiedad
(**b**) *(encroach on) (sb's privacy, business)* inmiscuirse en; **I don't want to t. on your time** no quiero quitarte tu tiempo; **he's trespassing on my area of responsibility** se está inmiscuyendo *or* entrometiendo en mis responsabilidades; **to t. on sb's rights** violar los derechos de alguien

trespasser ['trespəsə(r)] *n Law* intruso(a) *m,f*; **trespassers will be prosecuted** *(sign)* prohibido el paso (bajo sanción)

tress [tres] *n Literary (lock of hair)* mechón *m*; **tresses** *(hair)* melena *f*, cabellera *f*

trestle ['tresəl] *n* caballete *m* ►► ***t. bridge*** puente *m* de caballete; ***t. table*** mesa *f* de caballetes

trews [tru:z] *npl* = pantalones ceñidos de tela escocesa

tri- [traɪ] *prefix* tri-

triable ['traɪəbəl] *adj Law* enjuiciable, procesable

triad ['traɪæd] *n* (**a**) *(trio)* tríada *f*, terna *f* (**b**) *Mus* tríada *f* (**c**) *Chem* tríada *f* (**d**) *(Chinese secret society)* **T. (Society)** tríada *f* china

triage ['tri:ɑ:ʒ] *n* selección *f* de prioridades *(en la atención a víctimas de guerra, catástrofes, etc.)*

trial ['traɪəl] **1** *n* (**a**) *Law* juicio *m*; **to be on t. (for)** estar siendo juzgado(a) (por); **he is still awaiting t.** está todavía en espera de juicio; **to bring sb to t., to put sb on t.** llevar a alguien a juicio; **to come** *or* **go to t.** ir a juicio; **to give sb a fair t.** dar a alguien un juicio justo; **to go on t. for sth** ir a juicio por algo ►► ***t. by jury*** juicio *m* con jurado; *Fam Pej* ***t. by television*** juicio *m* paralelo (en los medios)
(**b**) *(test)* ensayo *m*, prueba *f*; **the new drug is still undergoing trials** el nuevo fármaco está todavía a prueba; **to give sb a t.** *(for a job)* tener a alguien a prueba; **it was a t. of strength between the government and the unions** fue una prueba de fuerza entre el gobierno y los sindicatos; **we are using the system on a t. basis** tenemos el sistema a prueba; **on t.** a prueba; **t. and error** ensayo y error, tanteo; **we found the right amount by t. and error** dimos con la cantidad adecuada después de hacer varias pruebas ►► *Fin* ***t. balance*** balance *m* de comprobación; ***t. flight*** vuelo *m* de prueba; ***t. offer*** *(of product)* oferta *f* especial de lanzamiento; ***t. period*** periodo *m* de prueba; ***t. run*** ensayo *m*; ***t. separation*** *(of married couple)* separación *f* de prueba
(**c**) *Sport (with club)* periodo *m* de prueba; **trials** *(competition)*

pruebas *fpl* de selección ►► ***trials riding*** trial *m*

(**d**) *(ordeal)* suplicio *m*, calvario *m*; **the trials of married life** las dificultades de la vida de casado; **my boss is a real t.!** ¡aguantar a mi jefe es un verdadero suplicio *or* calvario!; **the child is a real t. to his parents** el niño es un auténtico martirio para sus padres; **trials and tribulations** penas y desventuras, tribulaciones

2 *vt (test)* probar; **the product is still being trialled** el producto está todavía a prueba

trialist ['traɪəlɪst] *n Sport* deportista *mf* en periodo de prueba

triangle ['traɪæŋgəl] *n* (**a**) *(shape)* triángulo *m*; **a t. of cheese** un quesito, una porción de queso (**b**) *Mus* triángulo *m* (**c**) *US Math (set square) (with angles of 45, 45 and 90°)* escuadra *f*; *(with angles of 30, 60 and 90°)* cartabón *m*

triangular [traɪ'æŋgjʊlə(r)] *adj* triangular

triangulate [traɪ'æŋgjʊleɪt] *vt* triangular

triangulation [traɪæŋgjʊ'leɪʃən] *n Geog* triangulación *f* ►► ***t. pillar*** vértice *m* geodésico; ***t. point*** vértice *m* geodésico

Triassic [traɪ'æsɪk] **1** *n* **the T.** el triásico

2 *adj* triásico(a)

triathlete [traɪ'æθliːt] *n* triatleta *mf*

triathlon [traɪ'æθlɒn] *n* triatlón *m*

tribal ['traɪbəl] *adj* tribal

tribalism ['traɪbəlɪzəm] *n Pol* tribalismo *m*

tribally ['traɪbəlɪ] *adv* por tribus

tribe [traɪb] *n* (**a**) *(social group)* tribu *f* (**b**) *Biol* tribu *f* (**c**) *Fam (family)* tribu *f*, gente *f*

tribesman ['traɪbzmən] *n* miembro *m* de una tribu; **a Tutsi t.** un tutsi

tribespeople ['traɪbzpiːpəl] *n* miembros *mpl* de una tribu

tribeswoman ['traɪbzwʊmən] *n* mujer *f* de una tribu; **a Tutsi t.** una tutsi

tribulation [trɪbjʊ'leɪʃən] *n Formal* tribulación *f*

tribunal [tr(a)ɪ'bjuːnəl] *n* (**a**) *(court)* tribunal *m* (**b**) *Br (committe)* comisión *f* investigadora

tribune ['trɪbjuːn] *n Hist* ***t. of the people*** tribuno *m* (de la plebe)

tributary ['trɪbjʊtərɪ] **1** *n* (**a**) *(of river)* afluente *m* (**b**) *(state)* estado *m* tributario

2 *adj (stream)* tributario(a)

tribute ['trɪbjuːt] *n* (**a**) *(homage)* tributo *m*; **to pay t. to** rendir tributo a; **to be a t. to sth** *(indication of)* hacer honor a algo, ser el mejor testimonio de algo; **that the project succeeded is a t. to his organizational skills** el éxito del proyecto hace honor a su talento organizativo ►► ***t. band*** grupo *m* de imitación (**b**) *Hist (payment)* tributo *m*

trice [traɪs] *n* **in a t.** en un santiamén

tricentenary [traɪsen'tiːnərɪ], *US* **tricentennial** [traɪsen'tenɪəl] *n* tricentenario *m*

triceps ['traɪseps] *n Anat* tríceps *m inv*

triceratops [traɪ'serətɒps] *n* triceratops *m inv*

trichinosis [trɪkɪ'nəʊsɪs] *n Med* triquinosis *f inv*

trichloride [traɪ'klɔːraɪd] *n Chem* tricloruro *m*

trichloroethylene [traɪklɔːrəʊ'eθɪliːn] *n Chem* tricloroetileno *m*

trick [trɪk] **1** *n* (**a**) *(ruse, deceitful behaviour)* artimaña *f*; **it was just a t. to get you to open the door** fue una artimaña para que abrieras la puerta; **to obtain sth by a t.** conseguir algo con engaños; **a t. of the light made her look like my mother** con el efecto de la luz se parecía a mi madre ►► ***t. cyclist*** acróbata *mf* del monociclo; *Fam (psychiatrist)* psiquiatra *mf*; ***t. photograph*** fotografía *f* trucada; ***t. photography*** fotografía *f* trucada, montaje *m* fotográfico; ***t. question*** pregunta *f* con trampa

(**b**) *(practical joke)* broma *f*; **to play a t. on sb** gastar una broma a alguien; **my memory is/my eyes are playing tricks on me** la memoria/la vista me juega malas pasadas; **a nasty t.** una jugarreta; *US* **t. or treat** = frase que pronuncian los niños que van de casa en casa en la noche de Halloween cuando se les abre la puerta

(**c**) *(by magician)* truco *m*; **a t. spider/finger** una araña/un dedo de plástico *or* de mentira

(**d**) *(piece of skill)* truco *m*; **we've taught the dog to do tricks** hemos enseñado al perro a hacer algunas cosas; **he performed a few tricks with a football** hizo unas cuantas virguerías con el balón ►► ***t. shot*** *(in pool, snooker)* trick shot *m*

(**e**) *(knack, system)* truquillo *m*; **there's a special t. to it** tiene su truquillo; **the t. is not to add too much water** el truco *or* secreto está en no añadir demasiada agua

(**f**) *(habit)* **he has a t. of always being in the right place at the right time** tiene el don de estar en el momento preciso en el lugar adecuado

(**g**) *(in card game)* mano *f*, baza *f*; **to take** *or* **make a t.** ganar una mano *or* una baza

(**h**) *Fam (prostitute's client)* cliente *m*; **to turn a t.** hacer una carrera; **to turn tricks** hacer la calle

(**i**) IDIOMS **he's been up to his old tricks again** ha vuelto a las andadas, ha vuelto a hacer de las suyas; **that should do the t.** esto debería servir; **that glass of brandy really did the t.** esa copa de coñac me vino *or* sentó muy bien; **she knows all the tricks** se las sabe todas; **the tricks of the trade** los trucos del oficio; **every t. in the book** todos los trucos habidos y por haber, toda clase de estratagemas; **that's the oldest t. in the book** ése es el viejo truco; **she doesn't miss a t.** no se le escapa una; *Fam* **how's tricks?** ¿qué pasa?, *Esp* ¿cómo lo llevas?

2 *vt (person)* engañar; **to t. sb into doing sth** engañar a alguien para que haga algo; **to t. sb out of sth** quitar *orAm* sacarle algo a alguien a base de engaños; **to t. sth out of sb** *(admission, information)* sacar algo a alguien con malas artes

3 *adj US (weak) (knee, leg)* débil, delicado(a)

► **trick out, trick up** *vt sep Literary* engalanar

trickery ['trɪkərɪ] *n* (**a**) *(deceit)* engaños *mpl*, trampas *fpl*; **by t.** con malas artes (**b**) *(skill)* virguería(s) *f(pl)*, destreza *f* en el juego

trickiness ['trɪkɪnɪs] *n (of task, situation, subject)* lo delicado; *(of question)* dificultad *f*

trickle ['trɪkəl] **1** *n* (**a**) *(of blood, water) (thin stream)* hilo *m*, reguero *m*; *(drops)* goteo *m* (**b**) *(of complaints, letters)* goteo *m*; **the new attraction has received little more than a t. of visitors** los visitantes que ha recibido la nueva atracción han venido con cuentagotas; **enquiries have slowed to a t.** ya sólo se atienden unas pocas consultas (**c**) *Aut* ***t. charger*** cargador *m* de goteo

2 *vt (liquid)* derramar un hilo de; **to t. sand through one's fingers** dejar caer la arena por entre los dedos

3 *vi* (**a**) *(liquid)* **water/sweat trickled down my face** me corrían unas gotas de agua/sudor por la cara (**b**) *(move slowly)* **to t. in/out** *(people)* ir entrando/saliendo poco a poco; **the ball trickled into the net** la pelota llegó mansamente hasta el fondo de la red; **news is beginning to t. through** la noticia está empezando a filtrarse

► **trickle away** *vi* (**a**) *(liquid)* **the water trickled away down the plughole** el agua se iba colando por el desagüe (**b**) *(money, savings)* **our savings had gradually trickled away** nuestros ahorros se habían ido consumiendo

trickle-down theory ['trɪkəl'daʊnθɪərɪ] *n* = teoría según la cual la riqueza de unos pocos termina por revertir en toda la sociedad

trickster ['trɪkstə(r)] *n* timador(ora) *m,f*

tricksy ['trɪksɪ] *adj* (**a**) *(mischievous)* bromista; **she's very t.** le gusta mucho gastar bromas (**b**) *(sly)* astuto(a)

tricky ['trɪkɪ] *adj* (**a**) *(task, situation, subject)* delicado(a); *(question)* difícil; **this is where things start to get t.** aquí es donde la cosa empieza a complicarse; **conditions were t.** las condiciones eran difíciles (**b**) *(sly)* **he's a t. customer** es un elemento de cuidado *or* un pájaro (de cuenta)

tricolour, *US* **tricolor** ['trɪkələ(r)] *n* bandera *f* tricolor

tricorn(e) ['traɪkɔːn] *n* **t. (hat)** tricornio *m*

tricycle ['traɪsɪkəl] *n* triciclo *m*

tricyclic [traɪ'saɪklɪk] *n* (antidepresivo *m*) tricíclico *m*

trident ['traɪdənt] *n* tridente *m*

tried-and-tested ['traɪdən'testɪd] *adj* probado(a)

triennial [traɪ'enɪəl] **1** *n* trienio *m*

2 *adj* trienal

triennially [traɪ'enjəlɪ] *adv* cada tres años

trier ['traɪə(r)] *n Fam* **to be a t.** tener mucho tesón

trifle ['traɪfəl] *n* (**a**) *(insignificant thing)* nadería *f*; **she doesn't worry over trifles like money** no se preocupa por nimiedades de ésas; **I bought it for a t.** lo compré por muy poco; **$500 is a mere t. to them** 500 dólares no es nada para ellos; **a t. wide/short** un poquito ancho(a)/corto(a) (**b**) *esp Br Culin* = postre de frutas en gelatina y bizcocho cubiertas de crema y nata

► **trifle with** *vt insep (affections)* jugar con; **a person not to be trifled with** una persona con la que no se puede jugar

trifling ['traɪflɪŋ] *adj* insignificante; *Ironic* **the t. sum of £10,000** la insignificante cantidad de 10.000 libras

trifoliate [traɪ'fəʊlɪɪt] *adj Bot* trifoliado(a)

trig [trɪg] *n* (**a**) *Math Fam* trigonometría *f* (**b**) *Geog* ***t. point*** vértice *m* geodésico

trigger ['trɪgə(r)] **1** *n* (**a**) *(of gun)* gatillo *m*; **to pull the t.** apretar el gatillo; *Fam* **to be t. happy** tener el gatillo demasiado ligero ►► ***t. finger*** *(index finger)* (dedo *m*) índice *m*; *(medical problem)* dedo *m*

engatillado (**b**) *(of change, decision)* factor *m* desencadenante, detonante *m*; **the strike was the t. for nationwide protests** la huelga provocó una cadena de protestas por toda la nación
2 *vt (reaction)* desencadenar; *(revolution, protest)* hacer estallar
▸ **trigger off** *vt sep* desencadenar
triggerfish ['trɪgəfɪʃ] *n* pez *m* gatillo
triglyceride [traɪ'glɪsəraɪd] *n Chem* triglicérido *m*
trigonometric [trɪgənə'metrɪk] *adj* trigonométrico(a)
trigonometry [trɪgə'nɒmɪtrɪ] *n* trigonometría *f*
trike [traɪk] *n Fam (tricycle)* triciclo *m*
trilateral [traɪ'lætərəl] *adj* (**a**) *(figure)* de tres caras, trilátero(a) (**b**) *(talks)* trilateral
trilby ['trɪlbɪ] *n Br* sombrero *m* de fieltro
trilingual [traɪ'lɪŋgwəl] *adj* (**a**) *(person)* trilingüe (**b**) *(document, conference)* trilingüe, en tres idiomas
trill [trɪl] **1** *n* (**a**) *(of bird)* trino *m* (**b**) *Mus* trino *m* (**c**) *Ling* vibración *f*
2 *vt* (**a**) *Mus* hacer vibrar (**b**) *(say in high-pitched voice)* gorjear (**c**) *Ling (consonant)* hacer vibrar
3 *vi (bird)* trinar
trillion ['trɪljən] *n* (10^{12}) billón *m*; *Br* (10^{18}) trillón *m*; *Fam* **I've got trillions of things to do!** ¡tengo millones de cosas que hacer!
trilogy ['trɪlədʒɪ] *n* trilogía *f*
trim [trɪm] **1** *n* (**a**) *(of hedge)* recorte *m*; *(of beard)* arreglo *m*; **to give sth a t.** recortar algo; **to give sb a t.** cortar las puntas del pelo a alguien; **just a t., please** sólo (un poco por) las puntas, por favor
(**b**) *(fit condition)* **to be/keep in t.** estar/mantenerse en forma; **to get in** *or* **into t.** ponerse en forma
(**c**) *(neat state)* **to be in good t.** estar *or* conservarse en buen estado
(**d**) *(decoration, finish) (on clothes)* ribetes *mpl*; *(on car)* embellecedores *mpl*, *Chile* tapas *fpl*, *RP* tazas *fpl*
(**e**) *very Fam (women)* nenas *fpl*, *Esp* pavas *fpl*, *Arg* pibas *fpl*; **that's his new bit of t.** esa es la nena *or Esp* pava *or Arg* piba con la que sale ahora
2 *adj* (**a**) *(neat) (of person)* aseado(a); *(of beard)* recortado(a); *(of garden)* cuidado(a) (**b**) *(svelte)* **to have a t. figure** tener buen tipo
3 *vt* (*pt & pp* **trimmed**) (**a**) *(cut) (hedge)* recortar; *(beard)* arreglar; *(wick)* cortar; *(meat)* quitar *or Am* sacar la grasa a; *(paper, photo)* recortar; **to have one's hair trimmed** cortarse las puntas del pelo; **to t. one's nails** cortarse las uñas; **t. the edges off the material** recorta los bordes de la tela
(**b**) *(reduce) (text, expenditure)* recortar
(**c**) *(decorate) (hat, dress)* adornar (**with** con); *(on edges)* ribetear (**with** con)
(**d**) *(sails)* orientar; *(ship)* equilibrar; IDIOM **to t. one's sails** apretarse el cinturón
▸ **trim away** *vt sep* recortar, quitar
▸ **trim down** *vt sep* (**a**) *(wick)* cortar (**b**) *(text, expenditure)* recortar; *(company)* racionalizar
▸ **trim off** *vt sep (edge)* recortar; *(fat)* quitar; **the vet trimmed off the fur around the injury** el veterinario recortó el pelo alrededor de la herida; **she trimmed just under a second off the world record** consiguió rebajar el récord del mundo en poco menos de un segundo
trimaran ['traɪməræn] *n* trimarán *m*
trimester ['traɪmestə(r)] *n* trimestre *m*
trimmer ['trɪmə(r)] *n* (**a**) *(tool) (for hedges)* máquina *f* de podar (**b**) *Fam (person)* oportunista *mf*, *Esp* chaquetero(a) *m,f*
trimming ['trɪmɪŋ] *n* (**a**) *(on clothes)* adorno *m*; *(on edge)* ribete *m* (**b**) *Culin* **turkey with all the trimmings** pavo con la guarnición clásica *(patatas asadas, coles de bruselas, caldo de carne, etc.)* (**c**) *(cutting)* **trimmings** recortes
Trinidad and Tobago ['trɪnɪdædəntə'beɪgəʊ] *n* Trinidad y Tobago
Trinidadian [trɪnɪ'dædɪən] **1** *n* trinidense *mf*
2 *adj* de Trinidad, trinidense
Trinitarian [trɪnɪ'teərɪən] **1** *n* trinitario(a) *m,f*
2 *adj* trinitario(a)
trinitrotoluene [traɪnaɪtrəʊ'tɒljʊi:n] *n* trinitrotolueno *m*
Trinity ['trɪnɪtɪ] *n Rel* **the (Holy) T.** la (Santísima) Trinidad ▸▸ ***T. Sunday*** (día *m* de la) Trinidad *f*; *Br Univ* ***T. term*** último trimestre *m*
trinket ['trɪŋkɪt] *n* baratija *f*, chuchería *f*
trio ['tri:əʊ] (*pl* **trios**) *n* (**a**) *Mus* trío *m* (**b**) *(group of three)* trío *m*
trip [trɪp] **1** *n* (**a**) *(journey)* viaje *m*; **a train t.** un viaje en tren; **a t. round the world** una vuelta al mundo; **it took several trips for us to move everything** tuvimos que hacer varios viajes para llevarlo todo; **I'm going on a long t.** voy a hacer un largo viaje
(**b**) *(excursion)* excursión *f*; **a t. to the beach** una excursión *or* salida a la playa; **to go on a birdwatching t.** hacer una excursión para observar las aves
(**c**) *(outing)* **a t. into town/to the theatre** una salida al centro (de la ciudad)/al teatro; **I have to make a t. to the dentist's tomorrow** tengo que ir mañana al dentista
(**d**) *(stumble)* tropezón *m*
(**e**) *(causing stumble)* zancadilla *f*; **he was booked for a t. on the winger** fue sancionado por ponerle la zancadilla al extremo ▸▸ *Tech* ***t. hammer*** martinete *m*; ***t. switch*** interruptor *m* diferencial; ***t. wire*** = cable tendido para hacer tropezar a quien pase
(**f**) *Fam (on drugs)* viaje *m*, *Esp* flipe *m*; **to have a good/bad t.** tener un buen/mal viaje
(**g**) *Fam (experience)* **to be on a guilt t.** sentirse muy culpable; **to be on a power t.** estar ebrio de poder
(**h**) *Mus* ***t. hop*** trip hop *m*
2 *vt* (*pt & pp* **tripped**) (**a**) *(cause to stumble)* poner la zancadilla a; **the coil of rope on the floor tripped me** tropecé con el rollo de cuerda que había en el suelo (**b**) *(switch, alarm)* hacer saltar (**c**) IDIOM *Hum* **to t. the light fantastic** mover el esqueleto
3 *vi* (**a**) *(stumble)* tropezar; **I tripped on a pile of books on the floor** tropecé con un montón de libros que había en el suelo
(**b**) *(step lightly)* brincar, danzar; **to t. in/out** entrar/salir con paso ligero; *Fig* **to t. off the tongue** *(word, name)* pronunciarse fácilmente; *Fig* **her name doesn't exactly t. off the tongue** su nombre no es precisamente fácil de pronunciar
(**c**) *Fam (on drugs)* **to be tripping on acid** ir de tripi
▸ **trip along** *vi* caminar a saltitos
▸ **trip out** *vi Fam (after taking drugs)* ir puesto(a), *Esp* ir colocado(a), *Col* ir pingo(a), *Méx* ir trabado(a), *RP* ir falopeado(a)
▸ **trip over** **1** *vt insep* tropezar con
2 *vi* tropezar
▸ **trip up** **1** *vt sep* (**a**) *(cause to fall)* poner la zancadilla a; **the coil of rope tripped me up** tropecé con el rollo de cuerda (**b**) *(cause to make mistake)* hacer caer; **a trick question designed to t. people up** una pregunta con trampa para hacer caer a la gente
2 *vi* (**a**) *(stumble)* tropezar (**b**) *(make a mistake)* equivocarse, meter la pata
tripartite [traɪ'pɑ:taɪt] *adj* tripartito(a)
tripe [traɪp] *n* (**a**) *Culin* mondongo *m*, *Esp* callos *mpl*, *Chile* chunchules *mpl* (**b**) *Fam (nonsense)* tonterías *fpl*, bobadas *fpl*; **what a load of t.!** ¡qué montón de tonterías!; **the film is absolute t.!** ¡la película es una porquería!
triphthong ['trɪfθɒŋ] *n* triptongo *m*
triplane ['traɪpleɪn] *n* triplano *m*
triple ['trɪpəl] **1** *n (in baseball)* triple *m*
2 *adj* triple; **the organization serves a t. purpose** la organización tiene tres propósitos *or* cometidos; **a t. whisky** un whisky triple ▸▸ ***t. axle*** *(in figure skating)* triple axle *m*; *Br* ***T. Crown*** *(in rugby)* triple corona *f*; ***t. crown*** *(Pope's tiara)* tiara *f* pontificia; ***t. glazing*** triple acristalamiento *m*; ***t. jump*** triple salto *m*; ***t. jumper*** saltador(ora) *m,f* de triple salto; *Mus* ***t. time*** compás *m* ternario; ***t. vaccine*** vacuna *f* triple
3 *adv* **t. the amount (of)** el triple (de)
4 *vt* triplicar, multiplicar por tres
5 *vi* triplicarse, multiplicarse por tres
triplet ['trɪplɪt] *n* (**a**) *(child)* trillizo(a) *m,f* (**b**) *Mus* tresillo *m* (**c**) *Lit* terceto *m*
triplicate ['trɪplɪkət] **1** *n* **in t.** por triplicado
2 *adj (copies)* triplicado(a)
triply ['trɪplɪ] *adv* triplemente
tripod ['traɪpɒd] *n* trípode *m*
Tripoli ['trɪpəlɪ] *n* Trípoli
tripper ['trɪpə(r)] *n Br* excursionista *mf*
trippy ['trɪpɪ] *adj Fam* (**a**) *(music, special effects)* psicodélico(a) (**b**) *(strange)* rarísimo(a)
triptych ['trɪptɪtʃ] *n Art* tríptico *m*
trireme ['trɪri:m] *n* trirreme *m*
trisect [traɪ'sekt] *vt* trisecar
trishaw ['traɪʃɔ:] *n* rickshaw *m* de tres ruedas
trisyllabic [traɪsɪ'læbɪk] *adj* trisílabo(a), trisilábico(a)
trisyllable [traɪ'sɪləbəl] *n* trisílabo *m*
trite [traɪt] *adj* manido(a)
tritely ['traɪtlɪ] *adv* de forma poco original
tritium ['trɪtɪəm] *n Chem* tritio *m*

Triton ['traɪtən] *n* **(a)** *(in mythology)* Tritón **(b)** *Astron* Tritón

triton *n* ['traɪtən] *(marine animal)* tritón *m*

triumph ['traɪəmf] **1** *n* **(a)** *(victory)* triunfo *m*; **she gave him a look of t.** lo miró con aire triunfal; **the t. of reason over passion** el triunfo de la razón sobre la pasión; **to return in t.** regresar triunfalmente; **the musical was an absolute t.** el musical fue un auténtico éxito **(b)** *(in ancient Rome)* desfile *m* triunfal

2 *vi* triunfar (**over** sobre); **to t. over adversity** vencer a la adversidad

triumphal [traɪ'ʌmfəl] *adj* triunfal ►► ***t. arch*** arco *m* de triunfo

triumphalism [traɪ'ʌmfəlɪzəm] *n* triunfalismo *m*

triumphalist [traɪ'ʌmfəlɪst] *adj* triunfalista

triumphant [traɪ'ʌmfənt] *adj* **(a)** *(victorious) (team, army)* triunfador(ora), victorioso(a); *(return)* triunfal **(b)** *(proud) (look, smile)* triunfante **(c)** *(success)* clamoroso(a)

triumphantly [traɪ'ʌmfəntlɪ] *adv* **(a)** *(victoriously) (to march, return)* triunfalmente **(b)** *(to look, smile, say)* con aire triunfal

triumvir [traɪ'ʌmvɜː(r)] *n* triunviro *m*

triumvirate [traɪ'ʌmvɪrɪt] *n* triunvirato *m*

trivalent [traɪ'veɪlənt] *adj Chem* trivalente

trivet ['trɪvɪt] *n (on table)* salvamanteles *m inv (de metal)*

trivia ['trɪvɪə] *npl* trivialidades *fpl* ►► ***t. quiz*** concurso *m* de preguntas triviales

trivial ['trɪvɪəl] *adj* **(a)** *(insignificant) (sum, reason, offence, problem)* insignificante, trivial **(b)** *(banal) (story, duty)* banal **(c)** *(superficial) (person)* superficial

triviality [trɪvɪ'ælɪtɪ] *n* **(a)** *(insignificance) (of sum, reason, offence, problem)* insignificancia *f*, trivialidad *f* **(b)** *(insignificant thing)* nimiedad *f*, trivialidad *f*

trivialize ['trɪvɪəlaɪz] *vt* trivializar

trochaic [trəʊ'keɪɪk] *adj* trocaico(a)

trochanter [trəʊ'kæntə(r)] *n Anat* trocánter *m*

trochee ['trəʊkiː] *n* troqueo *m*

trod *pt of* **tread**

trodden *pp of* **tread**

troglodyte ['trɒglədaɪt] *n* troglodita *mf*

troika ['trɔɪkə] *n* **(a)** *(carriage)* troika *f*, troica *f* **(b)** *Pol* troika *f*, troica *f*

Trojan ['trəʊdʒən] *Hist* **1** *n* troyano(a) *m,f*; IDIOM **to work like a T.** trabajar como una mula

2 *adj* troyano(a) ►► ***T. Horse*** *Hist* caballo *m* de Troya; *Comptr* troyano *m*; ***the T. War*** la guerra de Troya

troll [trəʊl] *n* troll *m*, trasgo *m*

trolley ['trɒlɪ] *n* **(a)** *Br (in supermarket, for luggage)* carro *m*; *(for food, drinks)* carrito *m*; IDIOM *Fam* **to be off one's t.** *(mad)* estar chalado(a) *or Col, Méx* zafado(a) *or RP* rayado(a) ►► *Br Fam Hum* ***t. dolly*** *(air hostess)* azafata *f*, *Am* aeromoza *f* **(b)** *(in mine)* vagoneta *f* **(c)** *Br (in hospital) (bed)* camilla *f* **(d)** *US* ***t. (car)*** tranvía *m*

trolleybus ['trɒlɪbʌs] *n* trolebús *m*

trollop ['trɒləp] *n Old-fashioned or Hum (promiscuous woman)* fulana *f*, *Esp* pendón *m*

trombone [trɒm'bəʊn] *n Mus* trombón *m*

trombonist [trɒm'bəʊnɪst] *n Mus* trombonista *mf*

trompe l'oeil ['trɔ̃plœːj] *n* ilusión *f* óptica

troop [truːp] **1** *n* **(a)** *Mil (unit) (of cavalry)* escuadrón *m*; *(of armoured cars)* batería *f*; **troops** *(soldiers)* tropas *fpl*; **Britain has sent 1,000 troops to the area** el Reino Unido ha enviado 1.000 soldados a la zona ►► ***t. carrier*** vehículo *m* para el transporte de tropas; ***t. ship*** buque *m* de transporte militar; ***t. train*** tren *m* para el transporte de tropas

(b) *(of people)* grupo *m*, batallón *m*

(c) *(of Scouts)* tropa *f*

2 *vt Br* **to t. the colour** desfilar ceremonialmente con la bandera

3 *vi* **to t. in/out** entrar/salir en tropel; **the children trooped off to school** los niños se dirigieron en grupo hacia el colegio

trooper ['truːpə(r)] *n* **(a)** *(soldier)* soldado *m (de caballería o división acorazada)* **(b)** *US (policeman)* policía *mf*

trooping ['truːpɪŋ] *n Br* **T. the Colour** = ceremonia de presentación de la bandera a la Reina en su cumpleaños

trope [trəʊp] *n Lit* tropo *m*

trophic ['trɒfɪk] *adj* trófico(a)

trophy ['trəʊfɪ] *n* trofeo *m* ►► ***t. cabinet*** vitrina *f* de trofeos; *Fam* ***t. wife*** = esposa joven de un hombre maduro de la que éste hace ostentación

tropic ['trɒpɪk] *n* trópico *m*; **the tropics** *(region)* el trópico, los trópicos ►► ***T. of Cancer*** trópico *m* de Cáncer; ***T. of Capricorn*** trópico *m* de Capricornio

tropical ['trɒpɪkəl] *adj* **(a)** *(region, climate, medicine)* tropical ►► ***t. rainforest*** selva *f* tropical **(b)** *Fam (hot)* tropical

tropicbird ['trɒpɪkbɜːd] *n* ***yellow-billed t.*** rabijunco *m*

troposphere ['trɒpəsfɪə(r)] *n* troposfera *f*

Trot [trɒt] *n Br Fam Pej Pol* trosco(a) *m,f*

trot [trɒt] **1** *n* trote *m*; **to go/set off at a t.** ir/salir al trote; **to break into a t.** echar a trotar; *Fam* **to go for a t.** *(run)* ir a correr; IDIOM *Br Fam* **on the t.: they have won ten matches on the t.** han ganado diez partidos seguidos; **for six years on the t.** por sexto año consecutivo

2 *vi* (*pt & pp* **trotted**) **(a)** *(horse)* trotar **(b)** *(person)* ir a paso de trote; **I'll just t. over to the office with this** voy un momento a la oficina con esto

3 *vt (horse)* hacer trotar

► **trot along** *vi* **(a)** *(horse)* trotar **(b)** *Fam (person) (leave)* largarse; **I must be trotting along** me tengo que ir

► **trot out** *vt sep Fam (excuses, information)* salir con

► **trot over** *vi Fam (person)* **why don't you t. over to see me some time?** ¿por qué no te pasas un día a verme?

troth [trəʊθ] *n Old-fashioned* **by my t.!** ¡doy mi palabra!

trots [trɒts] *npl Fam* **to have the t.** estar suelto(a), tener *Esp* cagalera *or RP* cagadera

Trotskyist ['trɒtskiɪst], **Trotskyite** ['trɒtskiaɪt] **1** *n* trotskista *mf*

2 *adj* trotskista

trotter ['trɒtə(r)] *n Culin* **(pig's) trotters** manitas *fpl or* pies *mpl* (de cerdo)

troubadour ['truːbədɔː(r)] *n Hist* trovador *m*

TROUBLE ['trʌbəl] **1** *n* **(a)** *(problem)* problema *m*; *(problems)* problemas *mpl*; **what's** *or* **what seems to be the t.?** ¿cuál es el problema?; **the plane developed engine t.** el avión tuvo problemas con el motor; **I've had back t.** he tenido problemas de espalda; *Fam* **man/woman t.** mal de amores; **her troubles are over** se han acabado sus problemas; **the t. is that...** el problema es que...; **the t. with answerphones/Jane is that...** el problema de los contestadores/con Jane es que...; **he won without too much t.** no tuvo demasiados problemas para ganar; **to have t. with sth/sb** tener problemas con algo/alguien; **to have t. doing sth** tener dificultades para hacer algo; **I had t. convincing them** me costó convencerlos; **it has been nothing but t.** no ha traído (nada) más que problemas; **to be in t.** *(in difficulty)* tener problemas; **I'm in t. with the police** tengo problemas con la policía; **I'm in t. with my dad** mi padre está muy *esp Esp* enfadado *or esp Am* enojado conmigo; **you'll be in t.** *or* **there will be t. if they find out** *Esp* como se enteren, te la vas a ganar, *Am* si se enteran, vas a tener problemas; **that's asking for t.** está/estás/*etc.* buscando problemas; **to cause t.** crear *or* dar *or* causar problemas; **to get into t.** meterse en líos; **to get sb into t.** *(cause to be in bad situation)* meter a alguien en un lío; *Old-fashioned Euph (make pregnant)* dejar a alguien en estado; **to get out of t.** salir de un apuro; **to get sb out of t.** sacar a alguien de un apuro; **my leg has been giving me t.** la pierna me ha estado molestando; **you're heading for t.** vas a tener problemas; **to keep** *or* **stay out of t.** no meterse en líos; **to keep sb out of t.** evitar que alguien se salga del buen camino; **to make t.** causar problemas; **to make t. for oneself** buscarse problemas; **to give sb t.** darle problemas a alguien; **to mean t. (for sb)** traer problemas (a alguien); *Fam* **here comes t.!** ¡mira quién está aquí!; PROV **a t. shared is a t. halved** contando las cosas uno se siente mejor ►► *Br Fam Hum* ***t. and strife*** esposa *f*, *Esp* parienta *f*, *CSur* patrona *f*

(b) *(inconvenience)* molestia *f*; **I don't want to be any t.** no quiero ser un incordio; **(it's) no t.** no es molestia; **the dog is no t.** el perro no es ninguna molestia; **if it isn't too much t.** si no es demasiada molestia; **nothing is too much t. for her** nada le resulta una molestia; **it's more t. than it's worth** no merece la pena el esfuerzo; **it's not worth the t.** no merece la pena; **to go to the t. of doing sth** tomarse la molestia de hacer algo; **you shouldn't have gone to all that** *or* **to so much t.** no deberías haberte tomado tantas molestias; **to put sb to a lot of t.** causarle muchas molestias a alguien; **to take the t. to do sth** tomarse la molestia de hacer algo; **to take a lot of t. over sth** esmerarse en algo

(c) *(disorder, violence)* conflictos *mpl*; **we don't want any t.** no queremos problemas; **there's some sort of t. down at the mine** tienen algún tipo problema en la mina; **to be looking for t.** estar buscando pelea; **crowd t.** disturbios; **the Troubles** *(in Northern Ireland)* = el conflicto político en Irlanda del Norte desde 1968 ►► ***t. spot*** punto *m* conflictivo

2 *vt* (**a**) *(worry, disturb)* preocupar, inquietar; **to t. oneself about sth** preocuparse por algo; **her conscience was troubling her** tenía remordimientos de conciencia; *Literary* **a slight breeze troubled the surface of the lake** una ligera brisa agitó la superficie del lago

(**b**) *(inconvenience, bother)* molestar; **to be troubled by an injury** sufrir *or* sentir molestias debido a una lesión; **I won't t. you with the details just now** no te molestaré con los detalles ahora; **don't t. yourself!** no te molestes; **to t. oneself to do sth** tomarse la molestia de hacer algo

(**c**) *(cause pain to)* dar problemas a; **his back is troubling him** la espalda le está dando problemas

(**d**) *Formal (in requests)* **may I t. you for a match** *or* **to give me a match?** ¿sería tan amable de darme un fósforo?; **I'm sorry to t. you, but could you pass me the newspaper?** perdone, pero ¿sería tan amable de acercarme el periódico?

3 *vi* **to t. to do sth** tomarse la molestia de hacer algo

---

troubled ['trʌbəld] *adj* (**a**) *(worried) (person, look)* preocupado(a), inquieto(a); *(conscience, mind)* intranquilo(a) (**b**) *(psychologically disturbed) (person)* traumatizado(a); *(childhood)* traumático(a) (**c**) *(period, region)* agitado(a); *(relationship)* turbulento(a); **we live in t. times** vivimos tiempos difíciles (**d**) *(sleep, night, breathing)* agitado(a)

trouble-free ['trʌbəlfri:] *adj (installation, operation)* sencillo(a), sin complicaciones; *(stay, holiday, period)* tranquilo(a)

troublemaker ['trʌbəlmeɪkə(r)] *n* alborotador(ora) *m,f*

troubleshooter ['trʌbəlʃu:tə(r)] *n* (**a**) *(for organizational problems)* = experto contratado para localizar y resolver problemas financieros, estructurales, etc. (**b**) *(for machines)* técnico(a) *m,f* (en averías)

troubleshooting ['trʌbəlʃu:tɪŋ] *n* (**a**) *(for organizational problems)* localización *f* de problemas (**b**) *(for machines)* reparación *f* de averías (**c**) *Comptr* resolución *f* de problemas

troublesome ['trʌbəlsəm] *adj (person, child, situation)* problemático(a); *(cough, toothache)* molesto(a); *(job, task)* difícil

troubling ['trʌblɪŋ] *adj (worrying)* preocupante

trough [trɒf] *n* (**a**) *(for food)* comedero *m*; *(for drink)* abrevadero *m* (**b**) *(of wave)* seno *m*; *(in land)* hoya *f* (**c**) *(on graph)* depresión *f* (**d**) *(in weather front)* banda *f* de bajas presiones (**e**) *(low point)* mala racha *f*

trounce [traʊns] *vt* aplastar, arrollar

troupe [tru:p] *n (of actors, dancers)* compañía *f*; *(in circus)* troupe *f*

trouper ['tru:pə(r)] *n Theat* miembro *mf* de una compañía (de teatro); IDIOM *Fam* **he's a real t.** siempre da la cara, se puede contar con él

trouser ['traʊzə(r)] *n* ***t. leg*** pierna *f* del pantalón; ***t. pocket*** bolsillo *m* del pantalón; ***t. press*** prensa *f* para pantalones, percha *f* planchadora; ***t. suit*** traje *m* de chaqueta y pantalón *(para mujer)*

trousers ['traʊzəz] *npl* (**a**) *(garment)* pantalones *mpl*; **a pair of t.** unos pantalones; **I need some new t.** necesito unos pantalones nuevos (**b**) IDIOMS *Fam* **she's the one who wears the t.** ella es la que lleva los pantalones en casa; *Fam* **he was caught with his t. down** lo pillaron en bragas

trousseau ['tru:səʊ] *n* ajuar *m*

trout [traʊt] (*pl* **trout**) *n* (**a**) *(fish)* trucha *f* ▸▸ ***t. farm*** criadero *m* de truchas; ***t. fishing*** pesca *f* de la trucha (**b**) *Br Fam (woman)* **(old) t.** (vieja) bruja *f*

trowel ['traʊəl] *n (for gardening)* pala *f* de jardinero, desplantador *m*; *(for building)* llana *f*, paleta *f*

Troy [trɔɪ] *n* Troya

troy [trɔɪ] *n* **t. (weight)** sistema *m* troy (de pesos)

truancy ['tru:ənsɪ] *n* ausentismo *m or Esp* absentismo *m* escolar

truant ['tru:ənt] *n* niño(a) *m,f* que hace novillos *or Col* capa clase *or Méx* se va de pinta *or RP* se hace la rabona; **to play t.** faltar a clase, *Esp* hacer novillos, *Col* capar clase, *Méx* irse de pinta, *RP* hacerse la rabona

truce [tru:s] *n also Fig* tregua *f*; **to call a t.** hacer una tregua

truck [trʌk] **1** *n* (**a**) *(lorry)* camión *m* ▸▸ ***t. driver*** camionero(a) *m,f*; ***t. stop*** bar *m* de carretera

(**b**) *Br (rail wagon)* vagón *m* de mercancías

(**c**) *(trolley)* carretilla *f*

(**d**) *US (produce)* productos *mpl* ▸▸ ***t. farm*** explotación *f* agrícola; ***t. farmer*** horticultor(ora) *m,f*; ***t. farming*** horticultura *f*; ***t. garden*** huerto *m*

(**e**) *Fam (dealings)* **I'll have no t. with him/it** no pienso tener nada que ver con él/ello

2 *vt (goods)* transportar en camión

3 *vi US (drive a truck) Esp* conducir *or Am* manejar un camión; *Fam* **keep on trucking!** ¡sigue dándole!

trucker ['trʌkə(r)] *n US (lorry driver)* camionero(a) *m,f*

trucking ['trʌkɪŋ] *n* transporte *m* en *or* por carretera ▸▸ ***t. company*** empresa *f* de transporte en *or* por carretera

truckle ['trʌkəl] **1** *n* (**a**) ***t. bed*** carriola *f (cama)* (**b**) *(cheese)* queso *m* entero *(con forma de tambor)*

2 *vi Literary* **to t. to sb** someterse a alguien; **to t. to sth** ceder ante algo

truckload ['trʌkləʊd] *n* **a t. of...** un camión cargado de...; *Fam* **by the t.** *(in large amounts)* en cantidades industriales

truculence ['trʌkjʊləns] *n* agresividad *f*

truculent ['trʌkjʊlənt] *adj* agresivo(a)

> **False friend**: The Spanish adjective **truculento** is not a translation for the English word **truculent**. In Spanish **truculento** means "gruesome".

truculently ['trʌkjʊləntlɪ] *adv* con agresividad

trudge [trʌdʒ] **1** *n (long walk)* caminata *f*

2 *vt (streets, land)* patear, recorrer fatigosamente

3 *vi* caminar fatigosamente; **to t. along/through/over** marchar/cruzar/pasar fatigosamente

---

TRUE [tru:] **1** *adj* (**a**) *(factually correct)* cierto(a); **is that t.?** ¿de verdad?; **it is t. that...** es cierto *or* verdad que...; **is it t. about Michael?** ¿es cierto lo de Michael?; **it can't be t.** no puede ser (cierto); **this is especially t. of boys** esto es especialmente cierto en el caso de los chicos; **the same is** *or* **holds t. of other countries** lo mismo ocurre en otros países; **if t.** en caso de ser cierto(a); **how** *or* **too t.!** ¡cuánta razón tienes *or Esp* llevas!; **she has no experience – t., but...** no tiene experiencia – cierto *or* es verdad, pero...; **t. or false?** ¿verdadero o falso?; **to come t.** *(dream, prophecy)* cumplirse *(wish)* hacerse realidad, cumplirse; **this holds** *or* **is t. for...** esto vale para...; **as long as this remains t....** mientras siga siendo el caso; *Fam* **he's so stupid it's not t.** es tonto como él solo; PROV **there's many a t. word spoken in jest** a veces las cosas más serias se dicen en broma ▸▸ ***t. story*** historia *f* real

(**b**) *(real) (reason, feelings, owner)* verdadero(a); **the t. horror of his crimes** el verdadero horror de sus crímenes; **she discovered her t. self** se descubrió a sí misma; **in t. British style, he said he didn't mind** en un estilo genuinamente británico dijo que no le importaba ▸▸ ***t. love*** amor *m* verdadero; ***t. north*** norte *m* geográfico

(**c**) *(genuine)* verdadero(a); **a t. friend/gentleman** un verdadero amigo/caballero; **it is not a t. vegetable** no es realmente una verdura; **spoken like a t. soldier/Spaniard/Marxist!** ¡has hablado como un verdadero soldado/español/marxista!

(**d**) *(faithful)* leal, fiel; **a t. believer** un creyente fiel; **to be t. to sb** ser leal a alguien; **to be t. to oneself** ser fiel a sí mismo; **she was t. to her principles** era fiel a sus principios; **he was t. to his word** cumplió su palabra *or* lo prometido; **t. to life** fiel a la realidad; **t. to form** *or* **type** como era de esperar

(**e**) *(accurate)* exacto(a); *(picture, reflection)* acertado(a); **his aim was t.** acertó, dio en el blanco; **he's not a genius in the t. sense of the word** no es un genio en el sentido literal de la palabra; **to get a t. idea of the situation** hacerse una idea real de la situación; **a t. likeness** un verdadero parecido ▸▸ ***t. copy*** copia *f* fiel

(**f**) *(level, straight)* derecho(a)

2 *n* **out of t.** torcido(a)

3 *adv* (**a**) *(aim, shoot)* con precisión

(**b**) *Literary (truly)* **tell me t.** dime la verdad, sé sincero

---

true-blue ['tru:blu:] *Br* **1** *n* conservador(ora) *m,f* acérrimo(a)

2 *adj (loyal)* leal; **a t. Tory** un conservador acérrimo

trueborn ['tru:bɔ:n] *adj (Englishman)* de pura cepa; *(gentleman)* auténtico(a)

truebred ['tru:bred] *adj (racehorse)* de raza

true-false ['tru:'fɔ:ls] *adj (question, test)* de verdadero o falso

truehearted [tru:'hɑ:tɪd] *adj Literary* leal, fiel

true-life ['tru:laɪf] *adj (story)* real

truelove ['tru:lʌv] *n Literary* amado(a) *m,f*

truffle ['trʌfəl] *n* (**a**) *(fungus)* trufa *f* (**b**) *(chocolate)* trufa *f*

trug [trʌg] *n Br* canastillo *m*

truism ['tru:ɪzəm] *n* tópico *m*, lugar *m* común

truly ['tru:lɪ] *adv* (a) *(really)* verdaderamente, realmente; **I'm t. sorry** lo siento en el alma, de verdad que lo siento; **do you t. love me?** ¿me quieres de verdad?; **can we t. say that this is the case?** ¿verdaderamente podemos decir que se trata de eso?

(b) *(as intensifier) (delicious, amazing)* verdaderamente, realmente; **it was a t. awful movie** fue una película verdaderamente *or* realmente horrorosa

(c) *(sincerely)* **yours t.** *(at end of letter)* atentamente; *Fam (myself)* este menda, un servidor

trump [trʌmp] 1 *n (in cards)* **t. (card)** triunfo *m*; **what's trumps?** ¿(en) qué pintan?; **spades are trumps** pintan picas; **to play a t.** jugar un triunfo; IDIOM **she played her t. card** jugó su mejor baza *or* el as que escondía en la manga; IDIOM *Fam* **to come** *or Br* **turn up trumps** cumplir

2 *vt* (a) *(in cards) (card)* matar *(con un triunfo)* (b) *(surpass)* superar

▸ **trump up** *vt sep (invent) (excuse, charge)* inventar

trumped-up ['trʌmptʌp] *adj* falso(a)

trumpet ['trʌmpɪt] 1 *n* (a) *(instrument)* trompeta *f* ▸▸ ***t. call*** toque *m* de trompeta; *Fig* llamamiento *m* a la movilización (b) *(trumpeter)* trompeta *mf* (c) *(of elephant)* barrito *m*

2 *vt (success, achievements)* pregonar

3 *vi (elephant)* barritar

trumpeter ['trʌmpɪtə(r)] *n* trompetista *mf* ▸▸ ***t. finch*** camachuelo *m* trompetero; ***t. swan*** cisne *m* trompetero

truncate [trʌŋ'keɪt] *vt* (a) *(make shorter)* truncar (b) *Comptr* truncar

truncated [trʌŋ'keɪtɪd] *adj* truncado(a); **it was published in a t. form** fue publicado en una versión abreviada ▸▸ ***t. cone*** cono *m* truncado, tronco *m* de cono

truncation [trʌŋ'keɪʃən] *n* (a) *(shortening)* truncamiento *m* (b) *Comptr* truncamiento *m*

truncheon ['trʌn(t)ʃən] *n Br* porra *f*

trundle ['trʌndəl] 1 *vt (push)* empujar lentamente; *(pull)* tirar lentamente de; **he trundled the barrel across the courtyard** cruzó el patio haciendo rodar el barril lentamente

2 *vi* (a) *(vehicle)* rodar; **the lorries trundled past** los camiones circulaban lenta y ruidosamente (b) *Fam (person)* arrastrarse; **I have to t. off home now** ahora me toca pegarme la caminata hasta casa; **the athlete trundled in in last place** al atleta le costó llegar en el último lugar

▸ **trundle out** *vt sep (theory, excuse)* salir con; **they trundled out a few war heroes to lend dignity to the occasion** sacaron a unos cuantos héroes de guerra para dar un poco de dignidad a la ocasión

trunk [trʌŋk] *n* (a) *(of tree)* tronco *m* ▸▸ *Br Tel* ***t. call*** llamada *f or Am* llamado *m* de larga distancia, *Esp* conferencia *f*; ***t. line*** *Br Tel* línea *f* principal; *Rail* línea *f* troncal; *BrAut* ***t. road*** carretera *f* troncal (b) *(of body)* tronco *m* (c) *(case)* baúl *m* (d) *US (of car)* maletero *m*, *CAm, Méx* cajuela *f*, *RP* baúl *m* (e) *(of elephant)* trompa *f* (f) **trunks** *(swimming costume)* traje *m* de baño *(de hombre)*, *Esp* bañador *m (de hombre)*, *RP* malla *f (de hombre)*

truss [trʌs] 1 *n* (a) *Med* braguero *m* (b) *(for roof, bridge)* apuntalamiento *m*, armadura *f* (c) *(of hay)* haz *m*; *(of fruit)* racimo *m*

2 *vt* (a) *(tie up) (person, poultry)* atar (b) *(roof, bridge)* apuntalar

▸ **truss up** *vt sep (person)* atar

trust [trʌst] 1 *n* (a) *(belief)* confianza *f*; **I have complete t. in them** tengo plena confianza en ellos; **he put** *or* **placed his t. in them** depositó su confianza en ellos; **to take sth on t.** dar por cierto algo

(b) *(responsibility)* **a position of t.** un puesto de confianza *or* responsabilidad

(c) *(care)* **to give** *or* **place sth into sb's t.** confiar algo a alguien

(d) *Law (agreement)* fideicomiso *m*; *(organization)* fundación *f*; **a charitable t.** una fundación benéfica; **in t.** en fideicomiso; **the money was held in t. until her eighteenth birthday** el dinero se mantuvo en fideicomiso hasta que cumplió los dieciocho años ▸▸ ***t. account*** cuenta *f* de fideicomiso *o* de custodia; ***t. company*** compañía *f* fiduciaria; ***t. deed*** contrato *m or* escritura *f* de fideicomiso; ***t. fund*** fondo *m* fiduciario *or* de fideicomiso

(e) *Com (group of companies)* trust *m*

(f) *Br Med* **t. hospital** = hospital estatal con autonomía económica

2 *vt* (a) *(believe in)* confiar en; **I don't t. her/the data** no me fío de ella/de los datos; **you can t. me** puedes confiar en mí; **to t. sb's judgement** fiarse de la opinión de alguien; **to t. one's instincts** fiarse de los propios instintos; **he can't be trusted** no se puede uno fiar de él, no es de fiar; **to t. sb to do sth** confiar en que alguien haga algo; **I'm trusting you to tell me if you need help** confío que me pedirás ayuda si la necesitas; **you can't t. this motorbike to start first time** no es seguro que esta moto arranque a la primera; **I couldn't t. myself not to say anything** no estoy seguro de que pueda contenerme; *Fam* **t. him to say/do that!** ¡típico de él!; *Fam* **I'm afraid I deleted the file by accident – t. you!** me temo que he borrado el fichero sin darme cuenta –¡hombre, cómo no!; IDIOM *Fam* **I wouldn't t. him as far as I could throw him** yo no me fío de él (ni) un pelo

(b) *(entrust)* **to t. sb with sth** confiar algo a alguien; **I would t. him with my life** tengo plena confianza en él; **she can't be trusted with a credit card** tiene mucho peligro con las tarjetas de crédito

(c) *Formal (hope)* **to t. (that)...** confiar en que...; **I t. (that) you arrived home safely** confío en que llegaste bien a casa; **will they arrive late? – I t. not** ¿llegarán tarde? – confío en que no

3 *vi* **to t. in sth/sb** tener confianza *or* confiar en algo/alguien; **to t. to luck** confiar en la suerte

trusted ['trʌstɪd] *adj (friend, adviser, method)* de confianza ▸▸ *Comptr* ***t. third party*** *(for Internet transactions)* tercero *m* de confianza

trustee [trʌs'ti:] *n* (a) *(of fund, property)* fideicomisario(a) *m,f*, administrador(ora) *m,f* fiduciario(a) (b) *(of charity, institution)* miembro *m* del consejo de administración

trusteeship [trʌs'ti:ʃɪp] *n* (a) *(of fund, property)* fideicomiso *m*, administración *f* fiduciaria (b) *(of charity, institution)* administración *f* fiduciaria

trustful ['trʌstfʊl], **trusting** ['trʌstɪŋ] *adj* confiado(a); **he's too t. of people** se fía demasiado de la gente, es demasiado confiado

trustfully ['trʌstfʊlɪ], **trustingly** ['trʌstɪŋlɪ] *adv* con confianza; **she smiled at me t.** me sonrió confiada

trustworthiness ['trʌstwɜ:ðɪnɪs] *n (of person)* honradez *f*, *Am* confiabilidad *f*; *(of source, information, data)* fiabilidad *f*, *Am* confiabilidad *f*

trustworthy ['trʌstwɜ:ðɪ] *adj (person)* fiable, de confianza, *Am* confiable; *(source, information, data)* fidedigno(a), fiable, *Am* confiable

trusty ['trʌstɪ] 1 *n (prisoner)* recluso(a) *m,f* de confianza

2 *adj Literary or Hum* fiel, leal

truth [tru:θ] *n* verdad *f*; **to tell the t.** decir la verdad; **to tell you the t., I can't remember** a decir verdad *or* si quieres que te diga la verdad, no me acuerdo; **the t. is (that) I don't care** la verdad es que me da igual; **is there any t. in the allegations?** ¿hay algo de verdad en las alegaciones?; **there isn't a grain** *or* **an ounce of t. in what he says** no hay ni un ápice de verdad en lo que dice; **there is no t. in the rumour** no hay nada de cierto en el rumor; **there's some t. in what she says** lleva parte de razón; **if the t. be told,...** a decir verdad,..., para ser sinceros,...; *Literary* **t. to tell, in t.** a decir verdad; **the t. will out** la verdad siempre se descubre; **he learned some fundamental truths** descubrió ciertas verdades fundamentales; *Law* **I swear to tell the t., the whole t., and nothing but the t.** juro decir la verdad, toda la verdad y nada más que la verdad; PROV **t. is stranger than fiction** la realidad supera a la ficción ▸▸ *Fam* ***t. drug*** suero *m* de la verdad

truthful ['tru:θfʊl] *adj (person)* sincero(a); *(answer, statement)* veraz; *(story)* veraz, verídico(a); *(portrait)* fiel; **I wasn't entirely t. with you** no fui totalmente sincero contigo

truthfully ['tru:θfʊlɪ] *adv* con sinceridad, sinceramente; **I can t. say that...** puedo asegurar, sin temor a equivocarme, que...

truthfulness ['tru:θfʊlnɪs] *n (of answer, statement)* veracidad *f*; *(of story)* veracidad *f*, lo verídico; *(of portrait)* fidelidad *f*; **in all t.** con toda sinceridad

TRY [traɪ] 1 *n* (a) *(attempt)* intento *m*; **good t., you nearly did it!** ¡bien, casi lo conseguiste!; **to give sth a t.** intentar algo; **to have a t. at doing sth** probar a hacer algo; **it's worth a t.** merece la pena intentarlo

(b) *(test, trial)* **to give sth a t.** probar algo; **let's give that new bar a t.** a ver qué tal está ese nuevo bar; **to give sb a t.** probar a alguien, darle una oportunidad a alguien; **do you want a t. on my bike?** ¿quieres probar mi moto?

(c) *(in rugby)* ensayo *m*; **to score a t.** anotar un ensayo ▸▸ ***t. line*** línea *f* de marca

2 *vt* (a) *(sample)* probar; **I'll t. anything once** estoy dispuesto a probar todo una vez; **have you tried acupuncture?** ¿has probado la acupuntura?

(b) *(attempt)* intentar; **to t. to do sth** tratar de *or* intentar hacer algo; **she tried not to think about it** trató de no pensar en ello; **I tried hard to understand** me esforcé para entenderlo; **t. putting it here** prueba a ponerlo aquí; **you should t. being nice to people for once** deberías intentar ser amable con la gente por una vez; **have you tried the drugstore?** ¿has probado en la farmacia?; **have you tried Steve?** ¿le has preguntado a Steve?; **t. him again** *(on telephone)* llámalo otra vez; **t. the number again** *(on telephone)* vuelve a probar el número otra vez; **I tried my best** *or* **hardest** lo hice lo mejor que pude; *Fam* **it's trying to rain** parece que quiere llover

(c) *(attempt to open) (door, window, lock)* probar a abrir

(**d**) *Law (case)* ver; *(person)* juzgar; **he was tried for murder** lo juzgaron por asesinato

(**e**) *(test) (person, patience)* poner a prueba; **the method has been tried and tested** el método está probado; **he has been tried and found wanting** lo han puesto a prueba pero no ha dado la talla; **to t. one's strength against sb** medir las fuerzas con alguien; **I've decided to t. my luck at acting** he decidido probar suerte como actriz; **this machine would t. the patience of a saint!** ¡con esta máquina hay que tener más paciencia que un santo!; **t. this for size** *(garment, shoe)* pruébeselo para saber la talla; *Fig* aquí tenemos una muestra; *Fam* **(just) t. me!** ponme a prueba

3 *vi* intentarlo; *Fam* **to t. and do sth** tratar de *or* intentar hacer algo; **he didn't really t.** no lo intentó de veras; **the Rangers weren't trying very hard** los Rangers no estaban esforzándose mucho; **you must t. harder** debes esforzarte más; **I'll t. again later** *(on phone)* volveré a intentarlo más tarde; **we can but t.** habrá que intentarlo; **just you t.!** ¡inténtalo y verás!; *Fam* **you couldn't do it if you tried!** ¡no podrías hacerlo en la vida!; **t. as I might, I couldn't do it** por mucho que lo intenté, no pude hacerlo

▸ **try for** *vt insep (job, scholarship)* intentar conseguir; **we're trying for a baby** estamos intentando tener un hijo

▸ **try on** *vt sep* (**a**) *(clothes)* probarse; **why don't you t. this skirt on for size?** ¿por qué no te pruebas esta falda a ver si te queda bien?; *Fig* **t. this on for size** *(idea)* ¿qué te parece?

(**b**) *Fam* **the children tried it on with their teacher** los niños pusieron a prueba al profesor; **stop trying it on with me!** ¡conmigo eso no va a colar!; **she's just trying it on** está probando a ver si cuela

▸ **try out** *vt sep (method, machine)* probar; **to t. sth out on sb** probar algo con alguien

▸ **try out for** *vt insep US (team)* ser seleccionado(a) para

---

trying ['traɪɪŋ] *adj (experience)* difícil; **these are t. times** corren tiempos difíciles; **he can be really t.** a veces pone a prueba la paciencia de cualquiera

try-on ['traɪɒn] *n Br Fam* vacilada *f*, tomadura *f* de pelo

try-out ['traɪaʊt] *n* prueba *f*; **he was given a t.** le hicieron una prueba

trypanosome ['trɪpənəsəʊm] *n* tripanosoma *m*

tryst [trɪst] *n Literary* (**a**) *(arrangement to meet)* cita *f* (amorosa) (**b**) *(place)* rincón *m* (de encuentro)

tsar [zɑ:(r)] *n* zar *m*

tsarina [zɑ:'ri:nə] *n* zarina *f*

tsarist ['zɑ:rɪst] 1 *n* zarista *mf*

2 *adj* zarista

tsetse ['t(s)etsɪ] *n* **t. (fly)** mosca *f* tse-tsé

T-shaped ['ti:ʃeɪpt] *adj* en forma de T

T-shirt ['ti:ʃɜ:t] *n* camiseta *f*, *Chile* polera *f*, *RP* remera *f*; *Hum* **been there, done that, got the T.** ya he pasado por ésas

tsk [təsk] *exclam* ¡vaya (por Dios)!

tsp (*abbr* **teaspoon(ful)**) cucharadita *f* (de las de café)

T-square ['ti:skweə(r)] *n* escuadra *f* en forma de T

tsunami [su:'nɑ:mɪ] *n* tsunami *m*

TT ['ti:'ti:] 1 *n* (*abbr* **teetotaller**) abstemio(a) *m,f*

2 *adj* (*abbr* **teetotal**) abstemio(a)

TTP [ti:ti:'pi:] *n Comptr* (*abbr* **trusted third party**) tercero *m* de confianza

TU [ti:'ju:] *n* (*abbr* **trade union**) sindicato *m*

tub [tʌb] *n* (**a**) *(for washing clothes)* tina *f*; *(for liquids)* cuba *f* (**b**) *(bath)* bañera *f*, *Am* tina *f*, *Am* bañadera *f* (**c**) *(for ice cream, margarine)* tarrina *f* (**d**) *Fam (boat)* cascarón *m*

tuba ['tju:bə] *n Mus* tuba *f* ▸▸ ***t. player*** tuba *m*

tubal ['tju:bəl] *adj Med (pregnancy)* tubárico(a) ▸▸ ***t. ligation*** ligadura *f* de trompas

tubby ['tʌbɪ] *adj Fam (person)* rechoncho(a)

tube [tju:b] *n* (**a**) *(pipe)* tubo *m*; IDIOM *Fam* **to go down the tubes** irse a pique; **that's £500 down the tubes** ¡qué manera de tirar *or* malgastar 500 libras! ▸▸ *US* ***t. top*** = top ajustado sin mangas ni tirantes

(**b**) *(container) (of glue, toothpaste, paint)* tubo *m*

(**c**) *Anat* **(Fallopian) t.** trompa *f* (de Falopio); **I've had my tubes tied** me han hecho una ligadura de trompas

(**d**) *(in tyre)* cámara *f*

(**e**) *(cathode-ray tube)* tubo *m* de imagen *or* catódico

(**f**) *Fam (TV)* **the t.** la tele

(**g**) *Br Fam* **the t.** *(underground railway)* el metro, *RP* el subte; **to go by t., to take the t.** ir en metro, tomar el metro ▸▸ ***t. map*** plano *m* del metro; ***t. station*** estación *f* de metro *or RP* subte; ***t. train*** metro *m*, *RP* subte *m*

tubeless ['tju:blɪs] *adj (tyre)* sin cámara

tuber ['tju:bə(r)] *n Bot* tubérculo *m*

tubercle ['tju:bəkəl] *n* (**a**) *(on lung)* tubérculo *m* ▸▸ ***t. bacillus*** bacilo *m* tuberculoso *or* de Koch (**b**) *(on skin, bone, plant)* tubérculo *m*

tubercular [tjʊ'bɜ:kjʊlə(r)] *adj Med* tuberculoso(a)

tuberculin [tjʊ'bɜ:kjʊlɪn] *n Med* tuberculina *f*

tuberculin-tested [tjʊ'bɜ:kjʊlɪn'testɪd] *adj* que ha pasado la prueba de la tuberculina

tuberculosis [tjʊbɜ:kjʊ'ləʊsɪs] *n Med* tuberculosis *f inv*

tuberculous [tjʊ'bɜ:kjʊləs] *adj Med* tuberculoso(a)

tuberose ['tju:bərəʊs] *n Bot* nardo *m*, tuberosa *f*

tuberous ['tju:bərəs] *adj Bot (root)* tuberoso(a)

tubing ['tju:bɪŋ] *n (tubes)* tuberías *fpl*; **a piece of rubber/glass t.** un trozo de tubo de goma/vidrio

tub-thumper ['tʌbθʌmpə(r)] *n* demagogo(a) *m,f*

tub-thumping ['tʌbθʌmpɪŋ] 1 *n* demagogia *f*

2 *adj (speech)* demagógico(a)

tubular ['tju:bjʊlə(r)] *adj* (**a**) *(tube-shaped)* tubular ▸▸ *Mus* ***t. bells*** campanas *fpl* tubulares (**b**) *US Fam (excellent)* genial, *Esp* dabuten, *Andes, CAm, Carib, Méx* chévere, *Col* tenaz, *Méx* padrísimo(a)

tubule ['tju:bju:l] *n Anat* túbulo *m*

TUC [ti:ju:'si:] *n* (*abbr* **Trades Union Congress**) = confederación nacional de sindicatos británicos

tuck [tʌk] 1 *n* (**a**) *(in sewing)* pinza *f*, pliegue *m*; **to put** *or* **to make a t. in sth** hacer un pliegue a algo (**b**) *Br Fam (food)* chucherías *fpl*, golosinas *fpl* ▸▸ ***t. box*** fiambrera *f*; ***t. shop*** *(in school)* puesto *m* de golosinas (**c**) *(in diving)* **a triple somersault with t.** un salto mortal con el cuerpo encogido (**d**) *(cosmetic surgery)* retoque *m*

2 *vt* (**a**) *(put)* **to t. one's trousers into one's socks** remeterse los pantalones en los calcetines; **she tucked the sheets under the mattress** remetió las sábanas por debajo del colchón; **he tucked his briefcase under his arm** se encajó la cartera bajo el brazo; **to t. sth into a drawer** guardar algo en un cajón (**b**) *(in sewing)* hacer un pliegue a, alforzar

▸ **tuck away** *vt sep* (**a**) *(hide)* esconder; **the house was tucked away in the hills** la casa estaba oculta entre los montes (**b**) *(put away) (money)* guardar, reservar; **he tucked the contract away in his pocket** se guardó el contrato en el bolsillo (**c**) *Fam (eat)* manducar, *Esp, Ven* papear; **she really can t. it away!** ¡no sé dónde le cabe! (**d**) *(in soccer) (chance, penalty)* aprovechar bien

▸ **tuck in** 1 *vt sep* (**a**) *(sheets)* remeter; **t. your shirt in** (re)métete la camisa por dentro (**b**) *(children in bed)* arropar (**c**) *(stomach)* meter

2 *vi Fam (eat)* manducar *or Esp, Ven* papear sin cortarse; **t. in!** ¡come, come!

▸ **tuck into** *vt insep Fam (meal)* manducar *or Esp, Ven* papear con ganas

▸ **tuck up** *vt sep* **to t. sb up in bed** arropar a alguien en la cama

tucker ['tʌkə(r)] *n Austr, NZ Fam (food)* papeo *m*, *Méx, RP* papa *f*, *RP* morfi *m*

▸ **tucker out** *vt sep US Fam (exhaust)* rendir, moler

tuckered-out [tʌkə'daʊt] *adj US Fam (exhausted)* rendido(a), molido(a)

tuck-in ['tʌkɪn] *n Br Fam* **we had a good t.** nos dimos un atracón

Tudor ['tju:də(r)] 1 *n Hist* **the Tudors** los Tudor ▸▸ ***T. rose*** rosa *f* de los Tudor

2 *adj* Tudor

Tue(s) (*abbr* **Tuesday**) mart.

Tuesday ['tju:zdeɪ] *n* martes *m inv*; *see also* **Saturday**

tufa ['tju:fə] *n* toba *f*

tuft [tʌft] *n (of hair)* mechón *m*; *(of feathers)* cresta *f*; *(of grass)* mata *f*

tufted duck ['tʌftɪd'dʌk] *n* porrón *m* moñudo

tug [tʌg] 1 *n* (**a**) *(pull)* tirón *m*; **to give sth a t.** dar un tirón a algo ▸▸ *Fam* ***t. of love*** enfrentamiento *m* por amor; ***t. of war*** *(game)* = juego en el que dos equipos tiran de una soga; *Fig* lucha *f* a brazo partido (**b**) *(attraction)* **the t. of the sea was too strong for him to resist** no pudo resistirse a la llamada del mar (**c**) *Naut* remolcador *m*

2 *vt* (*pt & pp* **tugged**) (**a**) *(rope, handle)* tirar de; **he tugged the heavy crate along the path** iba arrastrando la pesada caja por el camino (**b**) *Naut* remolcar

3 *vi* **to t. at** *or* **on sth** dar un tirón a algo

tugboat ['tʌgbəʊt] *n* remolcador *m*
tuition [tjʊ'ɪʃən] *n* (**a**) *(instruction)* clases *fpl* (**in** de) (**b**) *Univ* **t. (fees)** matrícula *f*
tulip ['tju:lɪp] *n* tulipán *m* ►► ***t. tree*** tulipero *m*
tulle [tju:l] *n* tul *m*
tum [tʌm] *n (in children's language)* tripita *f*, barriga *f*, *Chile* guata *f*
tumble ['tʌmbəl] **1** *n (fall) (accidental)* caída *f*, revolcón *m*; *(of gymnast, acrobat)* volteretas *fpl*; **to take a t.** *(person)* caer, caerse; *(prices)* caer en *Esp* picado *orAm* picada ►► ***t. turn*** *(in swimming)* vuelta *f* de campana, giro *m* sobre sí mismo(a)
2 *vt (knock down, push) (person)* derribar; **she tumbled me into the pool** me empujó para que cayera a la piscina
3 *vi* (**a**) *(fall) (accidentally)* caer, caerse; *(gymnast, acrobat)* dar volteretas; **he tumbled down the stairs** cayó rodando por las escaleras; **he reluctantly tumbled out of bed** se dejó caer de la cama sin ganas; **the clothes tumbled out of the cupboard when I opened it** la ropa se cayó a la vez del armario al abrirlo; **the barrel went tumbling down the hill** el barril fue rodando cuesta abajo; **the pile of books tumbled over** la pila de libros se vino abajo; **her long golden hair tumbled across her face** sus largos cabellos dorados se dejaban caer sobre su cara
(**b**) *(prices)* caer en *Esp* picado *orAm* picada
(**c**) *(rush)* **the kids tumbled out of the bus** los niños salieron del autobús en tropel
►**tumble down** *vi (wall, building)* desmoronarse; *Fig* **his whole business empire came tumbling down** todo su imperio comercial se desmoronó
►**tumble to** *vt insep Fam* caer en (la cuenta de), percatarse de
tumbledown ['tʌmbəldaʊn] *adj (house)* ruinoso(a), en ruinas
tumble-drier [tʌmbəl'draɪə(r)] *n* secadora *f*
tumble-dry [tʌmbəl'draɪ] *vt* secar (en la secadora)
tumbler ['tʌmblə(r)] *n* (**a**) *(glass)* vaso *m* (**b**) *(acrobat)* volteador(ora) *m,f* (**c**) *(in lock)* gacheta *f*, fiador *m* (**d**) *(tumble-drier)* secadora *f* (**e**) *(pigeon)* pichón *m* volteador
tumbleweed ['tʌmbəlwi:d] *n* planta *f* rodadora
tumefaction [tju:mɪ'fækʃən] *n* tumefacción *f*
tumescent [tjʊ'mesənt] *adj Formal* tumefacto(a)
tumid ['tju:mɪd] *adj Med* tumefacto(a)
tummy ['tʌmɪ] *n Fam* tripita *f*, barriga *f*, *Chile* guata *f*; **to have (a) t. ache** tener dolor de tripa *or* de barriga *or Chile* de guata ►► *Br* ***t. button*** ombligo *m*
tumour, *US* **tumor** ['tju:mə(r), *US* 'tu:mər] *n Med* tumor *m*
tumuli *pl of* **tumulus**
tumult ['tju:mʌlt] *n* tumulto *m*; **my thoughts were in a t.** estaba confusa
tumultuous [tjʊ'mʌltjʊəs] *adj (crowd, noise)* tumultuoso(a); **t. applause** aplausos enfervorecidos
tumulus ['tju:mjʊləs] (*pl* **tumuli** ['tju:mjʊlaɪ]) *n* túmulo *m*
tun [tʌn] *n* tonel *m*
tuna ['tju:nə, *US* 'tu:nə] *n* atún *m* ►► ***t. fish*** atún *m*; *US* ***t. melt*** = tostada de atún con queso fundido por encima

> **False friend**: The Spanish noun **tuna** is not a translation for the English word **tuna**. In Spanish **tuna** means "group of student minstrels" or (in Latin America) "prickly pear".

tundra ['tʌndrə] *n* tundra *f*
tune [tju:n] **1** *n* (**a**) *(melody)* melodía *f*; **the song's cheerful t. contrasts with the sad words** la alegre melodía de la canción contrasta con la letra triste; **jazz music has no t. to it** el jazz no tiene mucha melodía; **give us a t. on the mouth organ** tócanos algo con la armónica; **they marched to the t. of the national anthem** marchaban al ritmo del himno nacional
(**b**) *(correct pitch)* **I can't sing in t.** desafino al cantar; **the violins are not in t. with the piano** los violines desentonan con el piano; **to be out of t.** *(instrument)* estar desafinado(a); *(person)* desafinar; **to sing out of t.** desafinar (al cantar)
(**c**) IDIOMS **to be in t. with one's surroundings** estar a tono con el entorno; **he is completely in t. with public opinion** está totalmente en sintonía con la opinión pública; **the minister was out of t. with the rest of his party** el ministro no sintonizaba con el resto del partido; **to call the t.** llevar la batuta; **to the t. of** por valor de; **we have received EU funds to the t. of £50,000** hemos recibido fondos de la UE por valor de 50.000 libras esterlinas
2 *vt* (**a**) *(musical instrument)* afinar (**b**) *(engine)* poner a punto (**c**) *(TV, radio)* sintonizar; **we can't t. our TV to that channel** no podemos sintonizar ese canal en nuestro televisor; **stay tuned!** permanezcan en nuestra sintonía (**d**) *(adapt, tailor)* ajustar, adaptar
►**tune in 1** *vt sep* **to be tuned in to sb's needs/way of thinking** sintonizar con las necesidades/con la manera de pensar de alguien
2 *vi Rad & TV* **to t. in to sth** sintonizar (con) algo; **make sure you t. in next week** vuelva a sintonizarnos la próxima semana
►**tune out** *US* **1** *vt sep (ignore)* desconectar de
2 *vi (stop listening)* desconectar
►**tune up 1** *vt sep* (**a**) *Mus* afinar (**b**) *(engine)* poner a punto
2 *vi Mus* afinar
tuneful ['tju:nfʊl] *adj* melodioso(a)
tunefully ['tju:nfʊlɪ] *adv* melodiosamente
tuneless ['tju:nlɪs] *adj* sin melodía
tunelessly ['tju:nlɪslɪ] *adv* sin melodía, desafinadamente
tuner ['tju:nə(r)] *n* (**a**) *Rad & TV* sintonizador *m* (**b**) *(of piano) (person)* afinador(ora) *m,f*
tune-up ['tju:nʌp] *n (of engine)* puesta *f* a punto
tungsten ['tʌŋstən] *n Chem* tungsteno *m* ►► ***t. lamp*** lámpara *f* de tungsteno; ***t. steel*** acero *m* de tungsteno
tunic ['tju:nɪk] *n* túnica *f*
tuning ['tju:nɪŋ] *n* (**a**) *(of musical instrument)* afinamiento *m*, afinación *f* ►► ***t. fork*** diapasón *m*; ***t. key*** llave *f* de afinación (**b**) *Rad & TV* sintonización *f* ►► ***t. dial*** dial *m*; ***t. knob*** sintonizador *m* (**c**) *(of car engine)* puesta *f* a punto
Tunis ['tju:nɪs] *n* Túnez *(ciudad)*
Tunisia [tju:'nɪzɪə] *n* Túnez *(país)*
Tunisian [tju:'nɪzɪən] **1** *n* tunecino(a) *m,f*
2 *adj* tunecino(a)
tunnel ['tʌnəl] **1** *n* túnel *m*; *(underpass)* paso *m* subterráneo; *(in stadium)* túnel *m* de vestuarios; *(in mine)* galería *f*; *(of mole, badger)* túnel *m* ►► *Phys* ***t. effect*** efecto *m* túnel; ***t. vision*** *Med* visión *f* en túnel; *Fig* estrechez *f* de miras
2 *vt* (*pt & pp* **tunnelled,** *US* **tunneled**) **to t. one's way out of prison** escapar de la cárcel haciendo un túnel; **a secret passage tunnelled by the prisoners** un túnel secreto excavado por los prisioneros
3 *vi* abrir un túnel; **to t. through/under sth** abrir un túnel a través de/por debajo de algo
tunny ['tʌnɪ] *n* atún *m* ►► ***t. fish*** atún *m*
tuppence, twopence ['tʌpəns] *n Br* (**a**) *(coin)* moneda *f* de dos peniques (**b**) IDIOMS *Fam* **it isn't worth t.** no vale un pimiento, no vale nada; *Fam Old-fashioned* **she doesn't give** *or* **care t.** le importa un comino
tuppenny, twopenny ['tʌpənɪ] *adj Br* de dos peniques; IDIOM *Fam* **I couldn't give a t. damn** me importa un comino
turban ['tɜ:bən] *n* turbante *m*
turbid ['tɜ:bɪd] *adj* turbio(a)
turbine ['tɜ:baɪn] *n* turbina *f* ►► ***t. engine*** motor *m* de turbina
turbo ['tɜ:bəʊ] (*pl* **turbos**) **1** *n* (**a**) *(car)* turbo *m* (**b**) *(turbocharger)* turbo *m*
2 *adj* (**a**) *(of car)* turbo *inv* (**b**) *Fam (more powerful) (version, model)* turbo *inv*
turbo-charged ['tɜ:bəʊtʃɑ:dʒd] *adj* turbo *inv*
turbo-charger ['tɜ:bəʊtʃɑ:dʒə(r)] *n* turbo *m*, turbocompresor *m*
turbodiesel ['tɜ:bəʊdi:zəl] *adj (engine)* turbodiesel
turboelectric [tɜ:bəʊɪ'lektrɪk] *adj* turboeléctrico(a)
turbofan ['tɜ:bəʊfæn] *n* turboventilador *m*
turbogenerator [tɜ:bəʊ'dʒenəreɪtə(r)] *n* turbogenerador *m*
turbojet ['tɜ:bəʊdʒet] *n (engine, plane)* turborreactor *m*
turboprop ['tɜ:bəʊprɒp] *n (engine)* turbopropulsor *m*, turbohélice *f*; *(plane)* avión *m* turbopropulsado
turbosupercharger [tɜ:bəʊ'su:pətʃɑ:dʒə(r)] *n* turbosobrealimentador *m*
turbot ['tɜ:bət] *n* rodaballo *m*
turbulence ['tɜ:bjʊləns] *n* (**a**) *(in air)* turbulencia *f*; **some t.** turbulencias (**b**) *Phys* turbulencia *f* (**c**) *(unrest)* turbulencia *f*
turbulent ['tɜ:bjʊlənt] *adj* (**a**) *(crowd, period, emotions)* turbulento(a) (**b**) *(air, sea)* turbulento(a)
turd [tɜ:d] *n very Fam* (**a**) *(excrement)* cagada *f*, mierda *f* (**b**) *(person)* *Esp* gilipollas *mf inv*, *Am* pendejo(a) *m,f*, *RP* boludo(a) *m,f*
tureen [tjʊə'ri:n] *n* sopera *f*

turf [tɜːf] **1** *n* **(a)** *(surface)* césped *m*; **a piece of t.** un tepe; *Fig* **they are very hard to beat on their own t.** son muy difíciles de batir en su propio campo **(b)** *(peat)* (tepe *m* de) turba *f* **(c)** *Fam (territory) (of gang)* territorio *m* **(d) the t.** *(horse racing)* las carreras de caballos ►► *Br* ***t. accountant*** corredor *m* de apuestas
2 *vt* **(a)** *(with grass)* cubrir de césped **(b)** *Br Fam (throw)* tirar

► **turf out** *vt sep Br Fam* **(a)** *(person)* echar **(b)** *(unwanted item)* tirar, *Am* botar

turgid [ˈtɜːdʒɪd] *adj (style)* ampuloso(a)

turgidly [ˈtɜːdʒɪdlɪ] *adv (written)* de forma ampulosa

Turin [tjʊəˈrɪn] *n* Turín

Turk [tɜːk] *n* turco(a) *m,f*

Turkestan, Turkistan [tɜːkɪˈstɑːn] *n* Turquestán

Turkey [ˈtɜːkɪ] *n* Turquía

turkey [ˈtɜːkɪ] *n* **(a)** *(bird)* pavo *m*, *Méx* guajolote *m*; IDIOM *Fam* **to talk t.** ir al grano ►► ***t. buzzard*** gallinazo *m* común; ***t. cock*** pavo *m*, *Méx* guajolote *m*; ***t. hen*** pava *f*; ***t. vulture*** gallinazo *m* común **(b)** *(meat)* pavo *m* **(c)** *Fam (bad play, movie)* fracaso *m* **(d)** *Fam (person)* pavo(a) *m,f*

Turkish [ˈtɜːkɪʃ] **1** *n (language)* turco *m*
2 *adj* turco(a) ►► ***T. bath*** baño *m* turco; ***T. carpet*** alfombra *f* turca; ***T. coffee*** café *m* turco; ***T. delight*** delicias *fpl* turcas, = dulce gelatinoso recubierto de azúcar en polvo

Turkistan = **Turkestan**

Turkmenistan [tɜːkmenɪˈstɑːn] *n* Turkmenistán

turmeric [ˈtɜːmərɪk] *n* cúrcuma *f*

turmoil [ˈtɜːmɔɪl] *n* (estado *m* de) confusión *f or* agitación *f*; **the country is in (a) t.** reina la confusión en el país; **his mind was in (a) t.** tenía la mente trastornada

TURN [tɜːn] **1** *n* **(a)** *(of wheel, screw)* vuelta *f*; **he gave the handle a t.** giró el pomo; **with a t. of the wrist** con un golpe de muñeca; **the meat is done to a t.** la carne está en su punto
(b) *(change of direction)* giro *m*; *(in road, river)* curva *f*; **to make a left t.** girar a la derecha; **no right t.** *(on sign)* prohibido girar a la derecha; **at the t. of the year/century** a principios de año/siglo; *Fig* **at every t.** a cada paso; **he was by turns charming and rude** se mostraba alternativamente encantador y maleducado; **the tide is on the t.** está cambiando la marea; **this milk is on the t.** la leche se está cortando; **my luck is on the t.** mi suerte está cambiando; **to take a t. for the better/worse** comenzar a mejorar/empeorar; **events took an unexpected t.** los acontecimientos tomaron un cariz *or* rumbo inesperado; **a dangerous t. of events** un giro peligroso de los acontecimientos; *Br* **he has a good t. of speed** tiene una buena punta de velocidad; **the t. of the tide** el cambio de marea; *Fig* el punto de inflexión ►► *US Aut* ***t. signal*** intermitente *m*
(c) *(in game, sequence)* turno *m*; **it's my t.** me toca a mí; **whose t. is it?** *(in queue, game)* ¿a quién le toca?; **it's his t. to do the dishes** le toca a él lavar los platos; **to miss a t.** *(in game)* perder un turno; **you can take** *or* **have your t. on the video game first** puedes jugar tú primero con el videojuego; **to take turns (at doing sth),** *Br* **to take it in turns (to do sth)** turnarse (para hacer algo); **t. and t. about** por turnos; **I, in t., told her** yo, a mi vez, se lo dije a ella; **they asked each of us in t. our name** nos preguntaron el nombre a uno detrás de otro; **to play out of t.** saltarse el turno; **to speak** *or* **talk out of t.** decir una inconveniencia
(d) *Fam (fit)* ataque *m*; **it gave me quite a t.** *(fright)* me dio un buen susto; **she had a funny t.** *(felt faint)* le dio un mareo
(e) *Theat* número *m*
(f) *(service)* **to do sb a good t.** hacer un favor a alguien; **I've done my good t. for the day** he hecho la buena obra del día; **to do sb a bad t.** hacerle un pobre favor a alguien; PROV **one good t. deserves another** amor con amor se paga
(g) *(tendency)* **people of a religious t. of mind** personas con tendencias religiosas ►► ***t. of phrase*** modo *m* de expresión
(h) *Old-fashioned (stroll)* **to take a t. in the park** dar un paseo por el parque
2 *vt* **(a)** *(cause to move) (wheel, handle, dial)* girar; *(page)* pasar; *(key, omelette)* dar la vuelta a; **t. the sofa to face the door** gira el sofá y déjalo mirando hacia la puerta; **t. the control to "off"** pon el mando en la posición "apagado"; **t. the knob to the right** gira el pomo a la derecha; **he turned the taxi into the alleyway** enfiló el callejón en el taxi; **to t. one's head/eyes** volver la cabeza/la vista; IDIOM **to t. sb's stomach** revolver el estómago a alguien; IDIOM **success has turned her head** el éxito se le ha subido a la cabeza; IDIOM **she was the sort of woman who turned heads** era un monumento de mujer
(b) *(direct)* **I turned my gaze on them** dirigí la mirada hacia ellos; *also Fig* **to t. one's back on sb** volver la espalda a alguien; **we turned our steps homeward** dimos media vuelta y nos dirigimos hacia casa; **they turned their guns on us** nos apuntaron con sus armas; **they turned their anger on us** dirigieron su ira hacia nosotros; **I turned my attention/thoughts** *or* **mind to...** centré mi atención/mis pensamientos en...; **to t. the conversation to...** encauzar la conversación hacia...; **their votes could t. the election in his favour** sus votos podrían darle la vuelta a las elecciones en su favor; **he would not be turned from his decision to resign** no hubo modo de que se volviera atrás en su decisión de dimitir; **research workers have turned the theory to practical use** los investigadores han puesto la teoría en práctica
(c) *(send away)* **he turned the beggar from his door** echó al mendigo de su portal; **they turned the poachers off their land** echaron a los cazadores furtivos de sus tierras
(d) *(go round, past)* **to t. the corner** doblar *orAm* voltear la esquina; *Fig* superar la crisis; **she's turned forty** ha cumplido cuarenta años; **it has just turned six o'clock** acaban de dar las seis (en punto)
(e) *(twist)* **to t. one's ankle** torcerse un tobillo
(f) *(change, convert)* **to t. sth into sth** convertir algo en algo; **to t. sth green/black** poner *or* volver algo verde/negro; **she turned the remark into a joke** convirtió el comentario en un chiste; **they're turning the book into a film** van a adaptar el libro al cine
(g) *(perform) (cartwheel, somersault)* dar, hacer
(h) *(on lathe)* tornear
(i) *Com* **to t. a profit** sacar *or* tener beneficios
3 *vi* **(a)** *(rotate) (wheel, planet, key)* girar; **the earth turns on its axis** la Tierra gira sobre su eje; IDIOM **to make sb's stomach t.** hacer que se le revuelva el estómago a alguien
(b) *(change direction) (person)* volverse; *(tide)* empezar a bajar/subir; *(wind)* cambiar de dirección; **the car turned into/up/down a side street** el vehículo se metió por una calle lateral; **to t. (to the) right/left** *(person, car)* girar *or* torcer *or* doblar a la derecha/izquierda; *(road, path)* girar a la derecha/izquierda; *St Exch* **the market turned downwards/upwards** el mercado comenzó a caer/subir; **t. to page 12** *(said by teacher)* vayan a la página 12; *(on page)* continúa en la página 12; **she turned to** *or* **towards me, she turned to face me** se volvió hacia mí; **to t. to sb (for help/advice)** acudir a alguien (en búsqueda *or* busca de ayuda/consejo); **I had no one to t. to** no tenía a quién acudir *or* recurrir; *Fig* **I don't know where** *or* **which way to t.** no sé qué dirección tomar *or* qué hacer; **he turned to drugs** se refugió en las drogas; **we now t. to the issue of funding** vamos a pasar al tema de la financiación; **my thoughts often t. to this subject** pienso en este asunto a menudo; *Fig* **he can t. on a** *Br* **sixpence** *or US* **dime** tiene muy buen golpe de cintura, es capaz de girar muy bruscamente
(c) *(change) (weather, luck)* cambiar; *(leaves)* cambiar de color; *(game)* dar un giro; **the rain turned to snow** la lluvia se volvió nieve; **the mood turned from optimism to despair** los ánimos pasaron del optimismo a la desesperación; **our optimism turned to despair** nuestro optimismo se tornó en desesperación
(d) *(become)* **to t. blue** *(change colour)* ponerse azul; **her fingers had turned blue (with cold)** se le habían puesto los dedos azules (de frío); **it has turned cold** *(weather)* hace más frío; **to t. nasty** *(person)* ponerse agresivo(a); *(situation, weather)* ponerse feo(a); **to t. pale** empalidecer; **to t. professional** hacerse profesional; **to t. red** *(sky, water)* ponerse rojo(a), enrojecer; *(person)* ponerse colorado(a); **to t. sour** *(milk)* cortarse, agriarse; *(relationship)* deteriorarse; **the whole family turned Muslim** toda la familia se convirtió al islamismo *or* islam; **he turned traitor and told the enemy their plan** les traicionó contando su plan al enemigo; **he's an actor turned politician** es un actor que se metió a político
(e) *(milk)* cortarse, agriarse

► **turn about** *vi* girar

► **turn against** **1** *vt insep* volverse contra
2 *vt sep* volver contra; **you've turned my whole family against me** has puesto a toda mi familia en mi contra; **we turned his joke against him** volvimos la broma en su contra

► **turn around** = **turn round**

► **turn aside** **1** *vt* desviar
2 *vi* retirarse, apartarse

► **turn away** **1** *vt sep* **(a)** *(avert)* apartar; **she turned her head away** giró la cabeza **(b)** *(refuse entry)* prohibir la entrada a; *(reject)* rechazar; **we had to t. business away** tuvimos que rechazar trabajo
2 *vi* **she turned away from him** *(rotated whole body)* le volvió la espalda; *(looked away)* desvió la mirada; **to t. away from sth/sb** *(reject, abandon)* volver la espalda a algo/alguien

► **turn back** **1** *vt sep* **(a)** *(person)* hacer volver **(b)** *(reset)* **to t. the clocks back** atrasar los relojes; *Fig* retroceder en el tiempo, regresar al pasado (c) *(sheets, blankets)* **to t. back the covers** abrir la cama

2 *vi* volver; **t. back to page 12** *(said by teacher)* vayan a la página 12; *(on page)* continúa en la página 12; *Fig* **we can't t. back now** ahora no podemos volvernos atrás

▸ **turn down** *vt sep* (a) *(volume, radio, heat)* bajar (b) *(fold)* **to t. one's collar down** bajarse el cuello; **to t. down the corner of a page** doblar la esquina de una página; **to t. down the bed** preparar la cama (c) *(request, application, person, job)* rechazar

▸ **turn forward** *vt sep (clocks)* adelantar

▸ **turn in** 1 *vt sep* (a) *(lost property)* entregar; *(person)* entregar a la policía; **to t. oneself in** entregarse (b) *(results)* dar; **she turned in a fantastic performance** tuvo una actuación brillante (c) *(fold in)* **t. in the edges** doble las puntas

2 *vi* (a) *(point inwards)* **my feet t. in** tengo las puntas de los pies hacia dentro; IDIOM **to t. in on oneself** volverse introvertido(a) (b) *(off road)* **he turned in at the gate** giró y entró por la verja (c) *Fam* irse a dormir

▸ **turn into** *vt insep (become)* convertirse en; **autumn turned into winter** al otoño siguió el invierno

▸ **turn off** 1 *vt insep (leave) (road, path)* salir de

2 *vt sep* (a) *(water, gas)* cerrar; *(light, TV, engine)* apagar (b) *Fam (cause to lose excitement)* cortar el rollo a; **it really turns me off** me corta el rollo totalmente

3 *vi* (a) *(leave road, path)* salir (b) *(switch off)* apagarse

▸ **turn on** 1 *vt sep* (a) *(water, gas)* abrir; *(light, TV, engine)* encender, *Am* prender; *Pej* **to t. the charm on** hacerse el(la) encantador(ora); **she knows how to t. the tears on** puede ponerse a llorar cuando le conviene; **Ríos really turned it on in the second set** Ríos sacó todo su talento a relucir en el segundo set

(b) *Fam (excite)* entusiasmar; *(sexually)* excitar, *Esp, Méx* poner cachondo(a) a; **whatever turns you on** sobre gustos no hay nada escrito, si eso le/te/*etc.* hace ilusión

2 *vt insep* (a) *(attack)* volverse contra (b) *(depend on)* **it all turns on...** todo depende de...

3 *vi* (a) *(switch on)* encenderse, *Am* prenderse (b) *Fam (take drugs)* drogarse

▸ **turn out** 1 *vt sep* (a) *(eject) (person)* echar; **he turned his daughter out of the house** echó a su hija de casa (b) *(empty) (pocket, container)* vaciar; **t. the jelly out onto a plate** volcar la gelatina en un plato (c) *(light)* apagar; *(gas)* cerrar (d) *(produce)* producir; **few colleges t. out the kind of people we need** pocas escuelas dan la formación que requerimos (e) *(dress)* **to be well turned out** *(person)* ir muy arreglado(a) (f) *(police, troops)* enviar (g) *(clean and tidy)* arreglar

2 *vi* (a) *(appear, attend)* acudir, presentarse; **the doctor had to t. out in the middle of the night** el médico tuvo que acudir *or* presentarse de madrugada (b) *(result)* salir; **to t. out well/badly** salir bien/mal; **it has turned out nice today** hoy hace un buen día; **he turned out to be a cousin of mine** resultó ser primo mío; **it turns out that...** resulta que...; **as it turns out...** resulta que... (c) *(point outwards)* **my feet t. out** tengo las puntas de los pies hacia afuera

▸ **turn over** 1 *vt sep* (a) *(flip over)* dar la vuelta a; *(vehicle, boat)* hacer volcar; *(page)* volver; **to t. sth over (in one's mind)** dar vueltas a algo; *Agr* **to t. over the soil** remover la tierra; IDIOM **to t. over a new leaf** hacer borrón y cuenta nueva

(b) *(hand over)* **to t. sth/sb over to sb** entregar algo/a alguien a alguien

(c) *Fam (rob)* **our house got turned over** nos entraron a robar en casa

(d) *(change)* **he's turning the land over to cattle farming** está reconvirtiendo la tierra para la cría de ganado

(e) *Fin* facturar

2 *vi* (a) *(person)* darse la vuelta; *(car)* volcar(se); *(boat)* volcar (b) *Aut* **keep the engine turning over** deja el motor encendido *or Am* prendido (c) *(move to next page)* pasar la página (d) *(change TV channels)* cambiar de cadena

▸ **turn round** 1 *vt sep* (a) *(car, table)* dar la vuelta a; *(head)* volver, girar (b) *(economy, situation, company)* enderezar (c) *(question, sentence)* dar la vuelta a (d) *(finish, get done)* terminar, hacer; *Com* **to t. round an order** procesar un pedido

2 *vi (wheel)* girar, dar vueltas; *(car)* dar la vuelta; *(person)* darse la vuelta; *Fig* **you can't just t. round and say you're not interested any more** no puedes agarrar *or Esp* coger y decirme que ya no te interesa; *Fig* **before you could t. round** en un santiamén

▸ **turn up** 1 *vt sep* (a) *(trousers)* meter (de abajo); **to t. one's collar up** subirse el cuello (b) *(volume, radio, heat)* subir; **she turned the oven up** subió la temperatura del horno (c) *(discover)* encontrar; **her research turned up some interesting new facts** su investigación arrojó unos datos interesantes

2 *vi (person)* presentarse, aparecer; *(lost object)* aparecer; *(opportunity, job)* presentarse; **to t. up late** llegar *or* presentarse tarde; **something is sure to t. up** seguro que algo aparecerá

---

turnabout ['tɜ:nəbaʊt] *n (in situation, opinion)* vuelco *m*, giro *m*

turnaround ['tɜ:nəraʊnd] *n* (a) *(in situation, opinion)* vuelco *m*, giro *m* (b) *(improvement)* mejoría *f* radical (c) *(of ship, plane) (loading time)* tiempo *m* de carga y descarga (d) *Com* ***t. time*** tiempo *m* de respuesta

turn-around ['tɜ:nəraʊnd] *adj* **t. jump shot** *(in basketball)* tiro a la media vuelta

turncoat ['tɜ:nkəʊt] *n Esp* chaquetero(a) *m,f*, *Am* oportunista *mf*, *RP* camaleón *m*

turned-down ['tɜ:ndaʊn] *adj (collar)* vuelto(a) (hacia abajo)

turned-up ['tɜ:ndʌp] *adj (collar)* subido(a); *(nose)* respingón(ona)

turner ['tɜ:nə(r)] *n (lathe operator)* tornero(a) *m,f*

turning ['tɜ:nɪŋ] *n* (a) *(off road) (in country)* giro *m*, desviación *f*; *(in town)* bocacalle *f*; **take the third t. on the right** tome la tercera bocacalle a la derecha; **we must have missed the t.** se nos debe de haber pasado la calle, nos debemos haber pasado de calle (b) *Aut* ***t. circle*** (capacidad *f* de) giro *m* (c) *(change)* ***t. point*** punto *m* de inflexión, momento *m* decisivo

turnip ['tɜ:nɪp] *n* nabo *m*

turnkey ['tɜ:nki:] 1 *n Old-fashioned (jailer)* carcelero(a) *m,f*

2 *adj (project, factory)* llave en mano *inv*

turn-off ['tɜ:nɒf] *n* (a) *(on road)* salida *f*, desvío *m*; **we must have missed the t.** se nos debe de haber pasado la salida *or* el desvío (b) *Fam* **it's a t.** me corta el rollo, *Méx* es un bajón, *RP* es una pálida, *Ven* es un aguaje

turn-on ['tɜ:nɒn] *n Fam* **it's a t. for him** *(sexually)* le vuelve loco, *Esp* le pone a cien

turnout ['tɜ:naʊt] *n* (a) *(attendance)* concurrencia *f*, asistencia *f*; **there was a good t. at the meeting** la reunión tuvo un alto nivel de asistencia (b) *(for election)* (índice *m* de) participación *f* (c) *Br (clearout)* **we had a good t. of the attic** hicimos una limpieza a fondo en el desván (d) *US (off road)* apartadero *m*

turnover ['tɜ:nəʊvə(r)] *n* (a) *Com* facturación *f*, volumen *m* de negocio (b) *(of stock)* movimiento *m* (c) *(of staff)* rotación *f*; *(of tenants)* rotación *f*, movimiento *m* (d) *Culin* **apple t.** = especie de empanada de hojaldre rellena de compota de manzana (e) *(in basketball, American football)* pérdida *f*

turnpike ['tɜ:npaɪk] *n* (a) *US (road)* autopista *f* de peaje (b) *Hist (barrier)* barrera *f* de portazgo

turnround ['tɜ:nraʊnd] *esp US* = **turnaround**

turnstile ['tɜ:nstaɪl] *n* torniquete *m*, torno *m* (de entrada); **the number of people going through the turnstiles has fallen** el número de personas que acuden al estadio ha disminuido

turnstone ['tɜ:nstəʊn] *n* vuelvepiedras *m inv*

turntable ['tɜ:nteɪbəl] *n* (a) *(part of record player)* plato *m*, giradiscos *m inv*; *(record player)* plato *m* (b) *(in microwave oven)* plato *m* giratorio (c) *Rail* placa *f* giratoria

turn(-)up ['tɜ:nʌp] *n* (a) *Br (on trousers)* vuelta *f* (b) *Fam* **what a t. (for the books)!** ¡eso sí que es una sorpresa!

turpentine ['tɜ:pəntaɪn] *n* trementina *f*

turpitude ['tɜ:pɪtju:d] *n Formal* bajeza *f*, vileza *f*

turps [tɜ:ps] *n Fam* trementina *f*

turquoise ['tɜ:kwɔɪz] 1 *n* (a) *(colour)* (azul *m*) turquesa *m* (b) *(stone)* turquesa *f*

2 *adj* (a) *(bracelet, ring)* de turquesa (b) *(in colour)* turquesa

turret ['tʌrɪt] *n* (a) *(on building)* torrecilla *f* (b) *(on tank, warship)* **(gun) t.** torreta *f*

turtle ['tɜ:təl] *n* (a) *(aquatic animal)* tortuga *f* (marina); IDIOM **to turn t.** *(ship)* volcar ▸▸ ***t. soup*** sopa *f* de tortuga (b) *US (tortoise)* tortuga *f* (c) *Comptr* tortuga *f*

turtledove [tɜ:təl'dʌv] *n* tórtola *f*

turtleneck ['tɜ:təlnek] *n (collar)* cuello *m* alto; **t. (sweater)** suéter *m or Esp* jersey *m* de cuello alto

Tuscan ['tʌskən] 1 *n* (a) *(person)* toscano(a) *m,f* (b) *(dialect)* toscano *m*

2 *adj* toscano(a)

Tuscany ['tʌskənɪ] *n* (la) Toscana

tush [tʊʃ] *n esp US Fam (buttocks)* trasero *m*

tusk [tʌsk] *n* colmillo *m*

tussle ['tʌsəl] *also Fig* **1** *n* pelea *f*; **to have a t. with sb** tener una pelea con alguien
2 *vi* **to t. (with sb for sth)** pelearse (con alguien por algo)

tussock ['tʌsək] *n* mata *f*

tut [tʌt] **1** *vi* quejarse *(con un chasquido de la lengua)*; **she tutted with disapproval** chasqueó la lengua en señal de desaprobación
2 *exclam* ¡vaya (por Dios)!

tutelage ['tju:təlɪdʒ] *n Formal* tutela *f*

tutor ['tju:tə(r)] **1** *n* **(a)** *Br (at university)* tutor(ora) *m,f* **(b)** *(private teacher)* **(private) t.** profesor(ora) *m,f* particular
2 *vt* **to t. sb in French** dar clases particulares de francés a alguien

tutorial [tjʊ'tɔ:rɪəl] *n* **(a)** *Br Univ* seminario *m* **(b)** *Comptr* tutorial *m* ►► ***t. program*** tutorial *m*

tutti-frutti ['tu:tɪ'fru:tɪ] **1** *n (flavour)* tutti-frutti *m*
2 *adj (ice cream)* de tutti frutti

tut-tut [tʌt'tʌt] **1** *vi* (*pt & pp* **tut-tutted**) quejarse *(con un chasquido de la lengua)*; **she tut-tutted with disapproval** chasqueó la lengua en señal de desaprobación
2 *exclam* ¡vaya (por Dios)!

tutu ['tu:tu:] *n* tutú *m*

Tuvalu [tu:'vɑ:lu:] *n* (las islas) Tuvalu

tu-whit tu-whoo [tu:'wɪttə'wu:] *exclam* = canto del búho

tux [tʌks] *n US Fam* esmoquin *m*

tuxedo [tʌk'si:dəʊ] (*pl* **tuxedos**) *n* esmoquin *m*

TV [ti:'vi:] *n* **(a)** *(system, broadcasts)* televisión *f*; **on (the) TV** en *or* por (la) televisión; **to watch TV** ver la televisión; **it makes/doesn't make good TV** es muy/poco televisivo; **the TV industry** el sector de la televisión, la industria televisiva ►► ***TV advertisement*** anuncio *m* de televisión, spot *m* (publicitario); ***TV advertising*** publicidad *f* en televisión; ***TV broadcast*** retransmisión *f* por televisión; ***TV broadcaster*** presentador(ora) *m,f* de televisión; ***TV camera*** cámara *f* de televisión; **he always performs well in front of the TV cameras** siempre sale muy bien delante de las cámaras; ***TV channel*** cadena *f* de televisión, canal *m* de televisión; ***TV commercial*** anuncio *m* de televisión, spot *m* (publicitario); ***TV on demand*** televisión *f* a la carta; ***TV dinner*** = menú completo precocinado y congelado que sólo necesita calentarse en el mismo envase; ***TV drama*** programa *m* dramático; ***TV film*** telefilme *m*, telefilm *m*; ***TV guide*** guía *f* de la programación (de televisión); ***TV interview*** entrevista *f* por televisión; ***TV journalist*** periodista *mf* de televisión; *Br* ***TV licence*** = certificado de haber pagado el impuesto que autoriza a ver la televisión, con el que se financian las cadenas públicas; ***TV lounge*** sala *f* de televisión; ***TV movie*** telefilme *m*, telefilm *m*; ***TV news*** noticias *fpl* de la televisión; ***TV personality*** figura *f* de la televisión; ***TV programme*** programa *m* de televisión; ***TV rights*** derechos *mpl* de retransmisión (por televisión); ***TV room*** sala *f* de televisión; ***TV show*** programa *m* de televisión; ***TV studio*** estudio *m* de televisión; ***TV viewer*** telespectador(ora) *m,f*, televidente *mf*
(b) *(set)* televisor *m*, (aparato *m* de) televisión *f* ►► ***TV screen*** pantalla *f* de televisión; ***TV set*** televisor *m*, (aparato *m* de) televisión *f*
(c) *(industry)* televisión *f*; **I want a career in TV** quiero dedicarme a la televisión
(d) *Fam* (*abbr* **transvestite**) travesti *mf*, travestido(a) *m,f*

TVA [ti:vi:'eɪ] *n* (*abbr* **Tennessee Valley Authority**) = organismo responsable de la construcción y gestión de presas hidroeléctricas en el estado de Tennessee

TVP [ti:vi:'pi:] *n Culin* (*abbr* **textured vegetable protein**) proteína *f* vegetal texturizada, = alimento proteínico a base de soja texturizada que se utiliza como sustituto de la carne

twaddle ['twɒdəl] *n Fam* tonterías *fpl*, sandeces *fpl*; **what she said was a load of t.** lo que dijo no fueron más que tonterías *or* sandeces

twain [tweɪn] *n Literary* dos *m*; IDIOM **...and ne'er the t. shall meet** ...y están condenados a no entenderse

twang [twæŋ] **1** *n* **(a)** *(of string, guitar)* sonido *m* gangoso; **the t. of country guitar** el sonido gangoso de la guitarra country **(b)** *(of voice)* **a nasal t.** una entonación nasal; **he has a slight Australian t.** tiene un ligero deje australiano
2 *vt (string)* pulsar; *(guitar, banjo)* tañer, pulsar las cuerdas de
3 *vi (string)* producir un sonido gangoso

'twas [twɒz] *Literary* = **it was**

twat [twæt] *n Vulg* **(a)** *(woman's genitals) Esp* conejo *m*, *Col* cuca *f*, *Méx* paloma *f*, *RP* concha *f*, *Ven* cuchara *f* **(b)** *(person) Esp* gilipollas *mf inv*, *Am* pendejo(a) *m,f*, *RP* boludo(a) *m,f*

tweak [twi:k] **1** *n* **(a) to give sb's ear a t.** dar a alguien un tirón de orejas **(b)** *(to text, computer programme)* **to give sth a t.** hacer un pequeño ajuste en algo
2 *vt* **(a)** *(nose, ear)* pellizcar **(b)** *(text, computer programme)* ajustar

twee [twi:] *adj Br Fam Pej* cursi

tweed [twi:d] *n* **(a)** *(cloth)* tweed *m*; **a t. skirt** una falda de tweed **(b) tweeds** *(suit)* traje *m* de tweed

tweedy ['twi:dɪ] *adj Fam (liking outdoor pursuits)* = aristocrático, que viste de tweed para ir de caza al campo

'tween [twi:n] *Literary* = **between**

tweenager ['twi:neɪdʒə(r)], **tweeny** ['twi:nɪ] *n Fam (pre-teen)* preadolescente *mf*

tweet [twi:t] **1** *n* pío *m*, gorjeo *m*
2 *vi* piar, gorjear

tweeter ['twi:tə(r)] *n (hi-fi speaker)* altavoz *m* de agudos

tweezers ['twi:zəz] *npl* pinzas *fpl*; **a pair of t.** unas pinzas

twelfth [twelfθ] **1** *n* **(a)** *(fraction)* doceavo *m*, doceava parte *f* **(b)** *(in series)* duodécimo(a) *m,f* **(c)** *(of month)* doce *m*
2 *adj* duodécimo(a) ►► ***T. Night*** noche *f* de Reyes; *see also* **eleventh**

twelve [twelv] **1** *n* doce *m*
2 *adj* doce; *see also* **eight**

twelve-hour clock ['twelvaʊəklɒk] *n* reloj *m* de doce horas

twelve-inch ['twelvɪntʃ] *n (record)* maxisingle *m*

twelvemonth ['twelvmʌnθ] *n Br Literary* año *m*

twelve-string guitar ['twelvstrɪŋgɪ'tɑ:(r)] *n* guitarra *f* de doce cuerdas

twelve-tone ['twelvtəʊn] *adj Mus* dodecafónico(a)

twenties ['twenti:z] *npl* **the t.** los (años) veinte; *see also* **eighties**

twentieth ['twentɪɪθ] **1** *n* **(a)** *(fraction)* veinteavo *m*, vigésima parte *f* **(b)** *(in series)* vigésimo(a) *m,f* **(c)** *(of month)* veinte *m*
2 *adj* vigésimo(a); *see also* **eleventh**

twenty ['twentɪ] **1** *n* veinte *m*
2 *adj* veinte; *see also* **eighty**

twenty-first ['twentɪ'fɜ:st] **1** *n* **(a)** *(in series)* vigésimo(a) primero(a) *m,f* **(b)** *(of month)* veintiuno *m* **(c)** *Fam (birthday, celebration)* vigésimo primer cumpleaños *m*; **it's Jim's t.** Jim cumple veintiuno
2 *adj* vigésimo(a) primero(a); *(before masculine singular noun)* vigésimo primer; *see also* **eleventh**

twenty-four-hour clock [twentɪ'fɔ:raʊə'klɒk] *n* reloj *m* de veinticuatro horas

twenty-four/seven ['twentɪfɔ:sevən] *adv Fam* las veinticuatro horas del día

twenty-one ['twentɪ'wʌn] **1** *n* **(a)** *(number)* veintiuno *m* **(b)** *US (card game)* veintiuna *f*
2 *adj* veintiuno(a); *(before masculine singular noun)* veintiún

twenty-twenty vision ['twentɪ'twentɪ'vɪʒən] *n* **to have t.** tener una vista perfecta

twerp, twirp [twɜ:p] *n Fam* lerdo(a) *m,f*, *Esp* memo(a) *m,f*

twice [twaɪs] *adv* dos veces; **t. as big as...** el doble de grande que...; **t. as slow** el doble de lento(a); **it would cost t. as much** *or* **t. the price** costaría el doble; **he's t. your age** te dobla en edad, tiene el doble de años que tú; **he's almost t. your height** es casi el doble de alto que tú; **t. 3 is 6** 2 por 3 son 6; **the programme is shown t. a week** *or* **t. weekly** el programa se emite dos veces a la semana; **t. over** dos veces; **to think t. before doing sth** pensárselo dos veces antes de hacer algo; **he didn't have to be asked t.** no hubo que pedírselo dos veces; **he's t. the man you are!** ¡es el doble de hombre que tú!

twiddle ['twɪdəl] **1** *n* **give the knob a t.** gira un poco el mando
2 *vt (knob, dial)* dar vueltas a, girar; **to t. one's thumbs** *(move thumbs in circle)* girar los pulgares; **I had to sit there twiddling my thumbs for an hour** tuve que estar allí sentado una hora de brazos cruzados
3 *vi* **to t. with sth** juguetear *or* trastear con algo

twig[1] [twɪg] *n (small branch)* ramita *f*; **we gathered some twigs to make a fire** recogimos unas ramitas para hacer un fuego

twig[2] (*pt & pp* **twigged**) *Br Fam* **1** *vt (realize)* darse cuenta de, coscarse
2 *vi (realize)* darse cuenta, coscarse; **to t. to sth** darse cuenta de algo, coscarse de algo

twiglet ['twɪglɪt] *n Br (small twig)* ramita *f* pequeña

twilight ['twaɪlaɪt] *n* **(a)** *(time of day)* crepúsculo *m*; **at t.** al ponerse el sol ►► *Med* ***t. sleep*** estado *m* crepuscular; ***t. world*** mundo *m* nebuloso; ***t. zone*** *(of city)* barrio *m* marginal; *Fig* mundo *m* nebuloso (**b**) *(half-light)* penumbra *f*; **I could hardly see you in the t.** apenas podía verte en la penumbra (**c**) *(last stages, end)* **he is in the t. of his career** está en el ocaso de su carrera profesional

twilit ['twaılıt] *adj* en penumbra

twill [twıl] *n* sarga *f*

twin [twın] **1** *n (identical)* gemelo(a) *m,f*; *(non-identical)* mellizo(a) *m,f*

2 *adj* (**a**) *(child, sibling)* **they have t. boys/girls** *(identical)* tienen gemelos/gemelas; *(non-identical)* tienen mellizos/mellizas ►► ***t. brother*** *(identical)* hermano *m* gemelo; *(non-identical)* hermano *m* mellizo; ***t. sister*** *(identical)* hermana *f* gemela; *(non-identical)* hermana *f* melliza

(**b**) *(paired) (aims, evils)* dos; **the t. towers overlooking the bay** las dos torres con vistas a la bahía ►► ***t. beds*** camas *fpl* gemelas; ***t. town*** ciudad *f* hermanada; ***t. tub*** *(washing machine)* lavadora *f* de doble tambor

3 *vt* (*pt & pp* **twinned**) *(towns)* hermanar; **Glasgow is twinned with...** Glasgow está hermanada con...

twin-bedded ['twın'bedıd] *adj (room)* con *or* de dos camas

twin-cam ['twınkæm] *adj Aut* de doble árbol de levas

twin-cylinder ['twın'sılındə(r)] *adj (engine)* de dos cilindros

twine [twaın] **1** *n (string)* (hilo *m* de) bramante *m*

2 *vt* **the creeper had twined itself round the tree** la enredadera se había enroscado *or* enrollado alrededor del árbol; **to t. one's arms around sth/sb** rodear algo/a alguien con los brazos

3 *vi* (**a**) *(stem, ivy)* enroscarse (**around** alrededor de) (**b**) *(path, river)* serpentear

twin-engine(d) ['twın'endʒın(d)] *adj* ***t. aircraft*** (avión *m*) bimotor *m*

twinge [twındʒ] *n (of pain)* punzada *f*; **a t. of conscience** un remordimiento (de conciencia); **a t. of envy** una punzada de envidia; **a t. of guilt** una sensación de culpa

twinjet ['twındʒet] *n* birreactor *m*

twinkie ['twıŋkı] *n US Fam (homosexual)* marica *m*

twinkle ['twıŋkəl] **1** *n* (**a**) *(of stars, lights)* parpadeo *m* (**b**) *(of eyes)* brillo *m*; IDIOM *Hum* **when he was just a t. in his father's eye** cuando ni siquiera lo había encargado

2 *vi* (**a**) *(star, light)* parpadear (**b**) *(eyes)* brillar

twinkling ['twıŋklıŋ] *n* IDIOM **in the t. of an eye** en un abrir y cerrar de ojos

twinky ['twıŋkı] *n US Fam* (**a**) *(homosexual)* marica *m* (**b**) *(attractive person)* pimpollo *m*

twinning ['twınıŋ] *n (of towns)* hermanamiento *m*

twinset ['twınset] *n Br* conjunto *m* de suéter y rebeca

twirl [twɜːl] **1** *n (movement)* giro *m*, vuelta *f*; *Fam* **give us a t.!** ¡date la vuelta, que te veamos!

2 *vt* girar; **she twirled her parasol as she walked along** giraba la sombrilla al caminar; **he twirled his moustache** se retorció el bigote

3 *vi (person)* **to t. round** dar vueltas sobre sí mismo(a)

twirly ['twɜːlı] *adj* retorcido(a)

twirp = **twerp**

twist [twıst] **1** *n* (**a**) *(action)* **to give sth a t.** retorcer algo; **with a t. of the wrist** con un giro de muñeca ►► *Tech* ***t. drill*** broca *f* helicoidal; ***t. grip*** *(accelerator)* puño *m* del acelerador; *(gear change)* palanca *f* de cambios

(**b**) *(bend) (in river, staircase, rope, wire)* curva *f*; **there's a t. in the tape** la cinta se ha doblado; **twists and turns** *(of road)* vueltas y revueltas; *(of events)* avatares; IDIOM *Br Fam* **to be round the t.** estar *Esp* majara *or Col, Méx* zafado(a) *or RP* rayado(a); IDIOM *Br Fam* **to go round the t.** *Esp* volverse majara, *Col, Méx* zafarse, *RP* rayarse; IDIOM *Br Fam* **to drive sb round the t.** volver loco(a) *or Esp* majara a alguien; IDIOM **to get (oneself) into a t. about sth** *(get angry)* salirse de sus casillas por algo; *(get agitated)* ponerse nervioso(a) por algo

(**c**) *(in story, plot)* giro *m* inesperado; **the book gives a new t. to the old story** el libro da un nuevo giro a la vieja historia; **by a strange t. of fate...** por una de esas vueltas que da la vida...

(**d**) *(piece)* **a t. of lemon** un trozo de peladura de limón retorcida; **a t. of paper** un envoltorio de papel retorcido en los extremos; **a t. of thread** un torzal de hilo; **a t. of tobacco** una cuerda de tabaco

(**e**) *(dance)* twist *m*; **to do the t.** bailar el twist

(**f**) *(in diving)* giro *m*

2 *vt* (**a**) *(thread, rope, wire)* retorcer; **to get twisted** *(rope, cable)* retorcerse; **the railings were twisted out of shape** la valla quedó completamente retorcida; **she twisted her hair into a bun** se recogió el pelo en un moño; *Fig* **her face was twisted with pain** tenía el rostro retorcido de dolor; **to t. sb's arm** retorcerle el brazo a alguien; *Fig* presionar a alguien

(**b**) *(turn) (lid, handle)* girar, dar vueltas a; **you have to t. the lid clockwise** tienes que girar la tapa hacia la derecha; IDIOM **to t. the knife (in the wound)** remover la herida

(**c**) *(injure)* **to t. one's ankle/wrist** torcerse el tobillo/la muñeca

(**d**) *(wrench)* **he twisted the keys from my hand** me arrancó las llaves de la mano; **he twisted himself free** se retorció hasta que pudo escapar

(**e**) *(distort) (sb's words, meaning of text)* tergiversar

3 *vi* (**a**) *(bend) (road)* torcer; *(smoke)* elevarse en espirales; **the road twists back on itself** la carretera gira en redondo; **to t. and turn** *(road)* serpentear

(**b**) *(turn)* girar; **to t. and turn** *(person)* ir cambiando bruscamente de dirección

(**c**) *(wrench)* **she managed to t. free of him** se retorció hasta que pudo escapar de él; **his mouth twisted into a grimace** torció la boca en una mueca

(**d**) *(dance)* bailar el twist

(**e**) *(in pontoon)* **t.!** ¡carta!

► **twist off** **1** *vt sep (lid)* desenroscar; *(branch)* arrancar retorciendo

2 *vi (lid)* desenroscarse

twisted ['twıstıd] *adj* (**a**) *(piece of metal, string)* retorcido(a) ►► *Comptr* ***t. pair*** par *m* trenzado (**b**) *(smile, grin, features)* torcido(a) (**c**) *(mind, logic, argument)* retorcido(a)

twister ['twıstə(r)] *n* (**a**) *Br Fam (dishonest person)* marrullero(a) *m,f* (**b**) *esp US Fam (tornado)* tornado *m*

twisting ['twıstıŋ] *adj (path)* sinuoso(a)

twist-off ['twıstɒf] *adj* de rosca

twit [twıt] *n Br Fam* lerdo(a) *m,f*, *Esp* memo(a) *m,f*

twitch [twıtʃ] **1** *n* (**a**) *(pull)* tirón *m* (**b**) *(tic)* **to have a nervous t.** tener un tic nervioso

2 *vt* (**a**) *(pull)* dar un tirón a (**b**) *(contract) (nose)* contraer; *(ears)* menear

3 *vi (nose)* contraerse; *(ears, tail)* menearse; **his hands twitched nervously** contraía las manos nerviosamente; **his right eye twitches** tiene un tic en el ojo derecho

twitcher ['twıtʃə(r)] *n Fam* entusiasta *mf* de la ornitología

twitchy ['twıtʃı] *adj Fam* tenso(a), nervioso(a); **to get t.** ponerse tenso(a) *or* nervioso(a)

twite [twaıt] *n* pardillo *m* piquigualdo

twitter ['twıtə(r)] **1** *n* (**a**) *(of birds)* gorjeo *m* (**b**) *Fam (of person)* parloteo *m*; IDIOM **to be in a t.** estar agitado(a)

2 *vi* (**a**) *(bird)* gorjear (**b**) *Fam (person)* parlotear; **to t. on** *or* **away** no parar de darle a la lengua

twittery ['twıtərı] *adj Fam* **to go all t.** ponerse como unas Pascuas *or* como unas castañuelas

'twixt [twıkst] *prep Literary* entre

two [tuː] **1** *n* (*pl* **twos**) dos *m*; **to break/fold sth in t.** romper/doblar algo en dos; **to walk in twos, to walk t. by t.** caminar de dos en dos; *Fam* **that makes t. of us** ya somos dos; **it takes t. to start a fight/an argument** no hay pelea/discusión si dos no quieren; IDIOM **to be t. of a kind** ser tal para cual; IDIOM **to put t. and t. together** atar cabos; **she put t. and t. together, and made five** fue atando cabos y llegó a la conclusión equivocada; PROV **t.'s company, three's a crowd** dos son compañía, tres son multitud

2 *adj* dos; **a drink or t.** alguna que otra copa, un par de copas; IDIOM **for t. pins** de buena gana; **for t. pins I'd let the whole thing drop** de buena gana lo dejaba todo; IDIOM **he doesn't care t. pins about it** le importa tres pepinos; IDIOM **there are no t. ways about it** *(there's no argument)* no hay más que hablar; *(there's no avoiding it)* no hay vuelta de hoja ►► ***t. pairs*** *(in poker)* doble pareja *f*; *see also* **eight**

two-bit ['tuː'bıt] *adj US Fam (insignificant)* de tres al cuarto, *RP* de morondanga

two-by-four ['tuːbaı'fɔː(r)] *n* tablón *m* alargado de dos por cuatro *(pulgadas de grosor y anchura respectivamente)*

two-colour ['tuː'kʌlə(r)] *adj* de dos colores

two-cycle ['tuː'saıkəl] *adj US (engine)* de dos tiempos

two-cylinder ['tuː'sılındə(r)] *adj (engine)* de dos cilindros

two-dimensional ['tuːdaı'menʃənəl] *adj* (**a**) *(shape)* bidimensional (**b**) *Pej (character, film)* superficial, plano(a)

two-door ['tuː'dɔː(r)] *adj (car)* de *or* con dos puertas

two-edged ['tuːedʒd] *adj* (**a**) *(blade)* de doble filo (**b**) *(remark)* de doble filo; IDIOM **to be a t. sword** ser un arma de doble filo

two-faced ['tuː'feıst] *adj Fam* falso(a)

twofold ['tu:fəʊld] 1 *adj* doble; **a t. plan** un doble plan; **a t. rise** una subida del doble, una duplicación
2 *adv* por dos, dos veces; **to increase t.** duplicarse

two-handed ['tu:'hændɪd] *adj* (**a**) *(sword, axe)* para dos manos (**b**) *(saw)* con dos mangos (**c**) *(in tennis)* con las dos manos; **a t. volley** una volea con las dos manos

two-horse race ['tu:hɔ:s'reɪs] *n esp Br Fig* mano a mano *m*

two-legged ['tu:'legɪd] *adj* bípedo(a)

two-one ['tu:'wʌn] *n Br Univ* **to get a t.** = licenciarse con la segunda nota más alta en la escala de calificaciones

two-party ['tu:'pɑ:tɪ] *adj (coalition, system)* bipartidista

twopence = **tuppence**

twopenny = **tuppenny**

two-phase ['tu:'feɪz] *adj Elec* ***t. current*** corriente *f* de dos fases

two-piece ['tu:pi:s] *adj* ***t. (suit)*** traje *m*; ***t. (swimsuit)*** biquini *m*

two-pin ['tu:pɪn] *adj (plug, socket)* de dos clavijas

two-ply ['tu:plaɪ] 1 *n (wood)* madera *f* de dos capas
2 *adj (wood, tissue)* de dos capas; *(wool)* de dos hebras

two-point ['tu:pɔɪnt] *adj* ***t. basket*** *(in basketball)* tiro *m* de dos (puntos)

two-seater ['tu:'si:tə(r)] 1 *n* (**a**) *(plane)* (avión *m*) biplaza *m* (**b**) *(car)* biplaza *m*
2 *adj* biplaza *inv*

two-sided ['tu:'saɪdɪd] *adj* (**a**) *(problem, argument)* de doble vertiente *or* dos vertientes (**b**) *(photocopy)* por las dos caras

twosome ['tu:səm] *n* (**a**) *(pair, couple)* dúo *m* (**b**) *(in golf)* partido *m* a dos

two-speed ['tu:spi:d] *adj* **a t. Europe** una Europa de dos velocidades

two-star ['tu:stɑ:(r)] 1 *adj* (**a**) *(hotel)* de dos estrellas (**b**) *Br (petrol)* normal
2 *n Br (petrol)* normal *f*

two-step ['tu:step] *n (dance)* = baile de salón con un ritmo de 2 por 4

two-stroke ['tu:strəʊk] *adj (engine)* de dos tiempos

two-time ['tu:taɪm] *vt Fam* **to t. sb** engañar *or Esp* pegársela a alguien

two-timer [tu:'taɪmə(r)] *n Fam* infiel *mf*

two-timing ['tu:taɪmɪŋ] *adj Fam* **that t. boyfriend of hers** ese novio que la está engañando con otra *or Esp* que se la está pegando con otra

two-tone ['tu:təʊn] 1 *n (musical style)* ska *m*
2 *adj* (**a**) *(in colour)* bicolor, de dos colores (**b**) *(in sound)* de dos notas (**c**) *(of musical style)* ska *inv*

two-two ['tu:'tu:] *n Br Univ* **to get a t.** = licenciarse con una nota media

'twould [twʊd] *Literary* = **it would**

two-way ['tu:weɪ] *adj (agreement, process)* mutuo(a) ►► ***t. mirror*** espejo *m* espía; ***t. radio*** aparato *m* emisor y receptor de radio; ***t. street*** calle *f* de doble sentido; ***t. switch*** conmutador *m* de dos vías

TX (*abbr* **Texas**) Texas, Tejas

tycoon [taɪ'ku:n] *n* magnate *m*

tyke [taɪk] *n* (**a**) *(dog)* chucho *m* (**b**) *Br Fam (rough person)* bruto(a) *m,f*, *Esp* basto(a) *m,f* (**c**) *US Fam (naughty child)* pilluelo(a) *m,f*, *Esp* pillastre(a) *m,f* (**d**) *Br Fam (person from Yorkshire)* = persona de Yorkshire

tympani, tympanist = **timpani, timpanist**

tympanum ['tɪmpənəm] *n Anat* tímpano *m*

type [taɪp] 1 *n* (**a**) *(kind)* tipo *m*, clase *f*; **a cream suitable for all skin types** una crema adecuada para todo tipo de piel; **a new t. of mobile phone** un nuevo tipo de teléfono móvil; **it's not my t. of movie** no me gusta mucho ese tipo de películas; **that t. of thing** ese tipo de cosas; **it's a t. of big sparrow** es una especie de gorrión grande; **you know the t. of thing I mean** ya sabes a lo que me refiero
(**b**) *(person)* **an athletic/intellectual t.** un individuo atlético/intelectual; **she's the thoughtful t.** es de esa (clase de) gente (que es) atenta; **she's not that t. (of person)** no es de esa clase de personas; **he's not the t. to complain** no es de los que se quejan; **I know their t.** conozco a los de su calaña; *Fam* **he's not my t.** no es mi tipo
(**c**) *(typical example)* **he's the very t. of the punctilious bureaucrat** es el burócrata puntilloso por excelencia; **he was cast against t.** le dieron un papel opuesto al que acostumbra a representar
(**d**) *Typ* tipo *m*, letra *f*; **in large/small t.** en letra grande/pequeña; **in bold t.** en negrita ►► ***t. size*** tamaño *m* de la letra
2 *vt* (**a**) *(with typewriter)* escribir a máquina, mecanografiar; *(with word processor)* escribir *or* introducir en *Esp* el ordenador *or Am* la computadora; **to t. a letter on the computer** escribir una carta en *Esp* el ordenador *or Am* la computadora (**b**) *Med (blood sample)* clasificar
3 *vi* escribir a máquina, mecanografiar

►**type out** *vt sep* escribir a máquina

►**type up** *vt sep (with typewriter)* escribir a máquina; *(with word processor)* escribir en *Esp* el ordenador *or Am* la computadora

typecast ['taɪpkɑ:st] (*pt & pp* **typecast**) *vt* encasillar; **he is always t. as a villain** siempre lo encasillan en el papel de malo

typeface ['taɪpfeɪs] *n* tipo *m*, letra *f*

typeover ['taɪpəʊvə(r)] *n Comptr* **t. mode** modo sobreescribir

typescript ['taɪpskrɪpt] *n* copia *f* mecanografiada

typeset ['taɪpset] *vt* componer

typesetter ['taɪpsetə(r)] *n* (**a**) *(person)* tipógrafo(a) *m,f* (**b**) *Comptr* filmadora *f*

typesetting ['taɪpsetɪŋ] *n* composición *f* (tipográfica)

typewriter ['taɪpraɪtə(r)] *n* máquina *f* de escribir

typewriting ['taɪpraɪtɪŋ] *n* mecanografía *f*

typewritten ['taɪprɪtən] *adj* escrito(a) a máquina, mecanografiado(a)

typhoid ['taɪfɔɪd] *n Med* **t. (fever)** fiebre *f* tifoidea

typhoon [taɪ'fu:n] *n* tifón *m*

typhus ['taɪfəs] *n Med* tifus *m inv*

typical ['tɪpɪkəl] *adj* típico(a) (**of** de); **this dog is t. of the breed** este perro es un ejemplar típico de su raza; **on a t. day** en un día normal; **isn't that t. (of him/her)!** ¡típico (en él/ella)!; **your letter took six days to get here – t.!** tu carta tardó seis días en llegar aquí – ¡para variar!; **in t. fashion** como es costumbre, como de costumbre

typically ['tɪpɪklɪ] *adv* (**a**) *(characteristically)* **to act t.** comportarse como de costumbre; **t., she changed her mind at the last minute** como de costumbre, en el último minuto cambió de opinión (**b**) *(usually)* normalmente; **t., this would cost around $500** normalmente esto costaría unos 500 dólares

typify ['tɪpɪfaɪ] *vt* (**a**) *(exemplify)* tipificar (**b**) *(embody)* representar

typing ['taɪpɪŋ] *n (by typewriter)* mecanografía *f*; *(by word processor)* introducción *f* (de datos) en *Esp* el ordenador *or Am* la computadora; **his t. isn't very good** no escribe muy bien a máquina; **I'll help you once I've finished this t.** en cuanto haya pasado esto a máquina, te ayudo ►► ***t. error*** error *m* mecanográfico; ***t. paper*** papel *m* para escribir a máquina; ***t. pool*** sección *f* de mecanografía; ***t. speed*** velocidad *f* de mecanografiado

typist ['taɪpɪst] *n* mecanógrafo(a) *m,f*

typo ['taɪpəʊ] *n Fam* error *m* tipográfico

typographer [taɪ'pɒgrəfə(r)] *n* tipógrafo(a) *m,f*

typographic(al) [taɪpə'græfɪk(əl)] *adj* tipográfico(a)

typography [taɪ'pɒgrəfɪ] *n* tipografía *f*

typological [taɪpə'lɒdʒɪkəl] *adj* tipológico(a)

typology [taɪ'pɒlədʒɪ] *n* tipología *f*

tyrannical [tɪ'rænɪkəl] *adj* tiránico(a)

tyrannize ['tɪrənaɪz] 1 *vt* tiranizar
2 *vi* **to t. over sb** tiranizar a alguien

tyrannosaurus [tɪrænə'sɔ:rəs] *n* tiranosaurio *m*

tyrannous ['tɪrənəs] *adj* tiránico(a)

tyranny ['tɪrənɪ] *n* tiranía *f*

tyrant ['taɪrənt] *n* tirano(a) *m,f*

tyre, *US* **tire** ['taɪə(r)] *n* neumático *m*, *Am* llanta *f*, *Arg* goma *f* ►► ***t. chain*** cadena *f (para la nieve)*; ***t. gauge*** manómetro *m*; ***t. marks*** rodada *f*; ***t. pressure*** presión *f* de los neumáticos *or* de las ruedas; ***t. valve*** válvula *f* de neumático

tyro, tiro ['taɪrəʊ] *n* principiante *mf*

Tyrol, Tirol [tɪ'rɒl] *n* Tirol

Tyrolean, Tirolean [tɪrə'lɪən] 1 *n* tirolés(esa) *m,f*
2 *adj* tirolés(esa) ►► ***T. hat*** sombrero *m* tirolés

tzar, tzarina *etc* = **tsar, tsarina** *etc*

tzatziki [tsæt'si:ki:] *n Culin* tzatziki *m*, = crema griega hecha con yogur, pepino, ajo y menta

U, u

U, u [juː] *n (letter)* U, u *f* ▸▸ ***U bend*** sifón *m*; ***U boat*** submarino *m (alemán)*

U [juː] *adj Br* (**a**) *Cin* (*abbr* **universal**) ≃ (apta) para todos los públicos (**b**) *Br Fam (upper-class) (expression, activity)* finolis *inv*

UAE [juːeɪ'iː] *n* (*abbr* **United Arab Emirates**) EAU *mpl*

UAW [juːeɪ'dʌbəljuː] *n US* (*abbr* **United Automobile Workers**) UAW *m or f*, = sindicato de trabajadores del sector automovilístico

UB40 [juːbiː'fɔːtɪ] *n Br* (*abbr* **Unemployment Benefit form 40**) ≃ cartilla *f* de desempleado, *Esp* ≃ cartilla *f* del paro

ubiquitous [juː'bɪkwɪtəs] *adj* omnipresente, ubicuo(a); **a u. TV personality** un personaje de la televisión omnipresente; **there is no escape from the u. mobile phone** es imposible escapar del omnipresente teléfono móvil

ubiquitousness [juː'bɪkwɪtəsnɪs], **ubiquity** [juː'bɪkwɪtɪ] *n Formal* ubicuidad *f*, omnipresencia *f*

UCAS ['juːkæs] *n Br* (*abbr* **Universities and Colleges Admissions Service**) = centro de admisiones y matriculaciones universitarias

UDA [juːdiː'eɪ] *n* (*abbr* **Ulster Defence Association**) UDA *f*, Asociación *f* para la Defensa del Ulster, = organización paramilitar norirlandesa partidaria de la permanencia en el Reino Unido

udder ['ʌdə(r)] *n* ubre *f*

UEFA [juː'eɪfə] *n* (*abbr* **Union of European Football Associations**) UEFA *f* ▸▸ ***the U. Cup*** la Copa de la UEFA

UFO ['juːfəʊ, juːef'əʊ] (*pl* **UFOs**) *n* (*abbr* **unidentified flying object**) OVNI *m*

ufologist [juː'fɒlədʒɪst] *n* ufólogo(a) *m,f*

ufology [juː'fɒlədʒɪ] *n* ufología *f*

Uganda [juː'gændə] *n* Uganda

Ugandan [juː'gændən] **1** *n* ugandés(esa) *m,f*
2 *adj* ugandés(esa)

ugh [ʌχ] *exclam* ¡puaj!

ugli (fruit)® ['ʌglɪ(fruːt)] *n* = tipo de cítrico caribeño híbrido de pomelo, naranja y mandarina

uglify ['ʌglɪfaɪ] *vt Fam (city, building)* afear

ugliness ['ʌglɪnɪs] *n* (**a**) *(in appearance)* fealdad *f* (**b**) *(of mood, situation)* carácter *m* desagradable

ugly ['ʌglɪ] *adj* (**a**) *(in appearance) (person, building, place)* feo(a); IDIOM **as u. as sin** más feo(a) que Picio ▸▸ ***u. duckling*** *(person)* patito *m* feo; ***the U. Sisters*** *(in Cinderella)* las hermanastras (de Cenicienta) (**b**) *(unpleasant) (wound, custom)* feo(a), desagradable; *(rumour)* siniestro(a); **there were u. scenes at the airport** hubo escenas muy desagradables en el aeropuerto; **things were taking an u. turn** las cosas se estaban poniendo muy feas; **to be in an u. mood** estar de muy mal humor; **the u. truth is...** la verdad, por desagradable que parezca, es...; **he's an u. customer** es un tipo peligroso

UHF [juːeɪtʃ'ef] *n Rad* (*abbr* **ultrahigh frequency**) UHF *m or f*

uh-huh [ʌ'hʌ] *exclam Fam (yes)* ajá

UHT [juːeɪtʃ'tiː] *adj* (*abbr* **ultra heat treated**) ***U. milk*** leche *f* uperisada *or* UHT

uh-uh ['ʌʌ] *exclam Fam (no)* tch tch

UK [juː'keɪ] (*abbr* **United Kingdom**) **1** *n* Reino *m* Unido; **in the UK** en el Reino Unido; **the UK representative** el representante del Reino Unido
2 *adj* del Reino Unido

UKAEA [juːkeɪeɪiː'eɪ] (*abbr* **United Kingdom Atomic Energy**) = consejo de seguridad nuclear británico

ukelele = **ukulele**

Ukraine [juː'kreɪn] *n* **(the) U.** Ucrania

Ukrainian [juː'kreɪnɪən] **1** *n* (**a**) *(person)* ucraniano(a) *m,f* (**b**) *(language)* ucraniano *m*
2 *adj* ucraniano(a)

ukulele [juːkə'leɪlɪ], **ukelele** [juːkə'leɪlɪ] *n* ukelele *m*

Ulan-Bator [uːlɑːn'bɑːtɔː(r)] *n* Ulan-Bator

ulcer ['ʌlsə(r)] *n (in stomach)* úlcera *f*; *(in mouth, on body)* úlcera *f*, llaga *f*

ulcerate ['ʌlsəreɪt] **1** *vt (stomach)* ulcerar; *(mouth, skin)* ulcerar, llagar
2 *vi (stomach)* ulcerarse; *(mouth, skin)* ulcerarse, llagarse

ulcerated ['ʌlsəreɪtɪd] *adj (stomach)* ulcerado(a); *(mouth, skin)* ulcerado(a), llagado(a)

ulceration [ʌlsə'reɪʃən] *n* ulceración *f*

ulcerous ['ʌlsərəs] *adj* ulceroso(a)

ulna ['ʌlnə] *n Anat* cúbito *m*

Ulster ['ʌlstə(r)] *n* el Ulster ▸▸ ***the U. Defence Association*** Asociación *f* para la Defensa del Ulster, = organización paramilitar norirlandesa partidaria de la permanencia en el Reino Unido; ***the U. Democratic Unionist Party*** el Partido Unionista Democrático del Ulster; ***the U. Unionists*** el Partido Unionista del Ulster; ***the U. Volunteer Force*** la Fuerza de Voluntarios del Ulster

Ulsterman ['ʌlstəmən] *n* = hombre del Ulster

Ulsterwoman ['ʌlstəwʊmən] *n* = mujer del Ulster

ulterior [ʌl'tɪərɪə(r)] *adj* **u. motive** motivo encubierto

ultimate ['ʌltɪmət] **1** *n Fam* **the u. in hi-fi equipment** lo mejor en *or Esp* el no va más en equipos de alta fidelidad; **for the u. in comfort, try our special new beds** si busca el máximo confort, pruebe nuestras nuevas camas especiales
2 *adj* (**a**) *(eventual, final) (responsibility, decision, objective)* final; **her tragic illness and u. death** su trágica enfermedad y posterior fallecimiento; **I believe in the party's u. victory** tengo fe en que, un día, nuestro partido ganará
(**b**) *(basic, fundamental) (cause, source, constituent)* último(a); **the u. meaning of life** el sentido último de la vida; **the u. deterrent** la medida disuasoria *or Am* disuasiva definitiva
(**c**) *(supreme) (authority)* máximo(a); **the u. hi-fi** lo mejor en *or Esp* el no va más en alta fidelidad; **the u. holiday** las vacaciones más especiales; **the u. humiliation** la mayor de las humillaciones, el colmo de la humillación; **the u. stupidity** el colmo de la estupidez; **she made the u. sacrifice** realizó el sacrificio supremo
(**d**) *Literary (furthest)* último(a)

ultimately ['ʌltɪmətlɪ] *adv* (**a**) *(finally)* en última instancia; **a solution will u. be found** en última instancia se hallará una solución; **responsibility u. lies with you** en última instancia la responsabilidad es tuya (**b**) *(basically)* básicamente; **u. it's a question of how much we can afford** en esencia se trata de cuánto podemos permitirnos

ultimatum [ʌltɪ'meɪtəm] *n* ultimátum *m*; **to deliver** *or* **issue an u. (to sb)** dar un ultimátum (a alguien)

ultra- ['ʌltrə] *prefix* ultra-

ultraconservative [ʌltrəkən'sɜːvətɪv] *adj (in politics)* ultraconservador(ora), muy de derechas; *(in morals, dress)* muy tradicional

ultra-fashionable ['ʌltrə'fæʃnəbəl] *adj* de ultimísima moda

ultrahigh frequency ['ʌltrəhaɪ'friːkwənsɪ] *n Rad & Phys* frecuencia *f* ultraalta

ultralight **1** *n* ['ʌltrəlaɪt] ultraligero *m*
2 *adj* [ʌltrə'laɪt] ultraligero(a)

ultramarine [ʌltrəmə'riːn] **1** *n* azul *m* de ultramar
2 *adj* azul de ultramar

ultramodern [ʌltrə'mɒdən] *adj* ultramoderno(a)

ultrasensitive [ʌltrə'sensɪtɪv] *adj* ultrasensible

ultrashort [ʌltrə'ʃɔːt] *adj Phys* ultracorto(a)

ultrasonic [ʌltrə'sɒnɪk] *adj Phys & Med* ultrasónico(a)

ultrasound ['ʌltrəsaʊnd] *n Phys & Med* ultrasonido *m* ▸▸ ***u. scan*** ecografía *f*; ***u. scanner*** ecógrafo *m*

ultraviolet [ʌltrə'vaɪələt] *adj* ultravioleta

ululate ['ju:ljʊleɪt] *vi Literary (wolf, dog)* ulular

um [ʌm] *Fam* **1** *exclam* ee, *Esp* esto, *Méx, RP, Ven* este
2 *vi* **to um and aah** titubear

umbelliferous [ʌmbe'lɪfərəs] *adj* umbelífero(a)

umber ['ʌmbə(r)] **1** *n* (**a**) *(pigment)* tierra *f* de sombra (**b**) *(colour)* pardo *m* oscuro
2 *adj* pardo(a) oscuro(a)

umbilical cord [ʌm'bɪlɪkəl'kɔ:d] *n* cordón *m* umbilical

umbilicus [ʌm'bɪlɪkəs] *n Anat* ombligo *m*

umbra ['ʌmbrə] *n Astron* umbra *f*

umbrage ['ʌmbrɪdʒ] *n* **to take u. (at sth)** sentirse ofendido(a) (por algo)

umbrella [ʌm'brelə] *n* (**a**) *(against rain)* paraguas *m inv*, *Col* sombrilla *f*; *Fig* **under the u. of...** al amparo de..., bajo la protección de... ►► ***u. bird*** pájaro *m* paraguas; ***u. plant*** paraguas *m inv*; ***u. stand*** paragüero *m* (**b**) *(body)* **u. (group** *or* **organization)** organización *f* aglutinante (**c**) *Mil* cortina *f* de protección

umlaut ['ʊmlaʊt] *n (mark)* umlaut *m*

umpire ['ʌmpaɪə(r)] **1** *n (in tennis)* juez *mf* de silla; *(in cricket, baseball)* árbitro(a) *m,f*
2 *vt* arbitrar
3 *vi (in tennis, cricket, baseball)* dirigir

umpteen [ʌmp'ti:n] *adj Fam* **to have u. things to do** tener montones de cosas que hacer; **I've told you u. times** te lo he dicho mil veces

umpteenth [ʌmp'ti:nθ] *adj Fam* enésimo(a); **for the u. time** por enésima vez

UMW [ju:em'dʌbəlju:] *n US* (*abbr* **United Mineworkers of America**) UMW *m or f*, = sindicato de mineros de EE.UU.

UN [ju:'en] *n* (*abbr* **United Nations**) **the UN** la ONU ►► ***UN peacekeeping forces*** fuerzas *fpl* de paz de las Naciones Unidas *or* de la ONU; ***UN resolution*** resolución *f* de las Naciones Unidas *or* de la ONU; ***UN Security Council*** Consejo *m* de Seguridad de las Naciones Unidas *or* de la ONU

'un [ʌn] *pron Fam* **the little 'uns** los pequeñajos; **this horse is a good 'un** este caballo vale

unabashed [ʌnə'bæʃt] *adj* descarado(a); **to be u. (by** *or* **at)** no sentir vergüenza *or Am* pena (de *or* por); **to carry on u.** seguir impasible

unabated [ʌnə'beɪtɪd] *adj* **the noise continued u. for most of the night** el ruido continuó sin descanso casi toda la noche; **their enthusiasm was u.** su entusiasmo no se enfrió

unable [ʌn'eɪbəl] *adj* **to be u. to do sth** *(owing to lack of skill, knowledge)* ser incapaz de hacer algo; *(owing to lack of time, money)* no poder hacer algo; **children who are u. to read/swim** niños que no saben leer/nadar; **I'm u. to understand why we can't do as I suggest** soy incapaz de entender por qué no hacemos lo que he sugerido

unabridged [ʌnə'brɪdʒd] *adj* íntegro(a)

unacademic [ʌnækə'demɪk] *adj (approach, piece of research)* poco riguroso(a)

unaccented [ʌnək'sentɪd] *adj* (**a**) *Ling (syllable)* átono(a), inacentuado(a) (**b**) *Mus (beat)* débil

unacceptability [ʌnək'septəbɪlɪtɪ] *n* inadmisibilidad *f*

unacceptable [ʌnək'septəbəl] *adj* inadmisible, inaceptable

unacceptably [ʌnək'septəblɪ] *adv* inadmisiblemente; **the movie was u. violent** la violencia de la película era inadmisible *or* inaceptable; **to behave u.** comportarse de una manera inadmisible *or* inaceptable

unaccommodating [ʌnə'kɒmədeɪtɪŋ] *adj (person)* poco dispuesto(a) a ayudar

unaccompanied [ʌnə'kʌmpənɪd] **1** *adj* (**a**) *(child)* no acompañado(a) (**b**) *(violin, singer)* solo(a), sin acompañamiento
2 *adv* (**a**) **to travel u.** viajar solo(a) (**b**) **to play/sing u.** tocar/cantar sin acompañamiento

unaccomplished [ʌnə'kʌmplɪʃt] *adj (unimpressive)* mediocre

unaccountable [ʌnə'kaʊntəbəl] *adj* (**a**) *Formal (not answerable)* **to be u. (to sb)** no tener que rendir cuentas (a alguien) (**b**) *(puzzling)* inexplicable; **for some u. reason** por alguna razón inexplicable

unaccountably [ʌnə'kaʊntəblɪ] *adv* inexplicablemente

unaccounted for [ʌnə'kaʊntɪd'fɔ:(r)] *adj* (**a**) *(money)* sin contabilizar; **that leaves a further $2,000 still u.** con eso nos quedan aún 2.000 dólares que no aparecen (**b**) *(person)* **there are several people still u.** siguen sin aparecer varias personas

unaccredited [ʌnə'kredɪtɪd] *adj* no acreditado(a)

unaccustomed [ʌnə'kʌstəmd] *adj* (**a**) *(unused)* **to be u. to sth** no estar acostumbrado(a) a algo (**b**) *(not usual)* inusual, desacostumbrado(a)

unachievable [ʌnə'tʃi:vəbəl] *adj* inalcanzable

unacknowledged [ʌnək'nɒlɪdʒd] **1** *adj* no reconocido(a)
2 *adv* **to go u.** *(talent, achievement)* no ser reconocido(a); *(letter)* no recibir respuesta

unacquainted [ʌnə'kweɪntɪd] *adj* **to be u. with sth** estar familiarizado(a) con algo; **to be u. with sth** no conocer a alguien; **we are not u. with the phenomenon** no desconocemos el fenómeno

unaddressed [ʌnə'drest] *adj (letter, envelope)* sin dirección

unadjusted [ʌnə'dʒʌstɪd] *adj (figures)* no corregido(a)

unadopted [ʌnə'dɒptɪd] *adj Br (road)* = cuya reparación no corre a cargo de las autoridades locales, sino de los usuarios

unadorned [ʌnə'dɔ:nd] *adj* (**a**) *(beauty)* sin adornos (**b**) *(truth)* sin tapujos

unadulterated [ʌnə'dʌltəreɪtɪd] *adj* (**a**) *(food)* natural, no adulterado(a) (**b**) *(absolute) (joy)* absoluto(a); **that book is u. rubbish!** ¡ese libro es una verdadera porquería!

unadventurous [ʌnəd'ventʃərəs] *adj (person)* poco atrevido(a), convencional; *(decision, choice, player)* poco arriesgado(a); *(performance)* sin riesgos, poco arriesgado(a); **she is an u. cook** es una cocinera poco innovadora

unadvertised [ʌn'ædvətaɪzd] *adj (appearance, visit)* no anunciado(a)

unadvisable [ʌnəd'vaɪzəbəl] *adj* desaconsejable

unaffected [ʌnə'fektɪd] *adj* (**a**) *(sincere) (person, style)* poco afectado(a), natural; *(joy)* espontáneo(a) (**b**) *(not touched, damaged)* **he was u.** no se vio afectado; **most of the city was u. by the earthquake** la mayor parte de la ciudad no se vio afectada por el terremoto (**c**) *(resistant)* **this material is u. by heat** a este material no le afecta el calor

unaffectionate [ʌnə'fekʃənət] *adj (person, kiss)* poco afectuoso(a)

unaffiliated [ʌnə'fɪlɪeɪtɪd] *adj* no afiliado(a)

unaffordable [ʌnə'fɔ:dəbəl] *adj* inasequible

unafraid [ʌnə'freɪd] *adj* **to be u. of sth/sb** no temer algo/a alguien; **he was quite u.** no tuvo miedo

unaided [ʌn'eɪdɪd] *adv* sin ayuda

unalarmed [ʌnə'lɑ:md] *adj (not anxious)* **to be u.** no preocuparse

unalike [ʌnə'laɪk] *adj* **the two sisters are quite u.** las dos hermanas no se parecen en nada

unallocated [ʌn'æləkeɪtɪd] *adj (money, grants)* no asignado(a); *(places)* vacante

unalloyed [ʌnə'lɔɪd] *adj Formal* puro(a)

unalterable [ʌn'ɔ:ltərəbəl] *adj (fact, truth)* inmutable; *(decision)* irrevocable

unaltered [ʌn'ɔ:ltəd] *adj* **to remain u.** *(weather, opinion)* permanecer igual; **her appearance was u.** su aspecto no había cambiado en lo más mínimo

unambiguous [ʌnæm'bɪgjʊəs] *adj* inequívoco(a); **she was u. in the way she told him** la forma en que se lo dijo no dejaba lugar a dudas

unambiguously [ʌnæm'bɪgjʊəslɪ] *adv* inequívocamente, de forma inequívoca

unambitious [ʌnæm'bɪʃəs] *adj (person, project)* poco ambicioso(a)

unamended [ʌnə'mendɪd] *adj* sin enmiendas

un-American [ʌnə'merɪkən] *adj (not typical of America)* poco americano(a); *(against America)* antiamericano(a) ►► *Pol* ***u. activities*** actividades *fpl* antiamericanas

unamused [ʌnə'mju:zd] *adj* **he was u.** no le hizo gracia

unanimity [ju:nə'nɪmɪtɪ] *n* unanimidad *f*

unanimous [ju:'nænɪməs] *adj* unánime; **passed by a u. vote** aprobado por unanimidad; **they were u. in condemning the plan** condenaron unánimemente el plan

unanimously [ju:'nænɪməslɪ] *adv* unánimemente; **she was elected u.** fue elegida por unanimidad

unannounced [ʌnə'naʊnst] **1** *adj (arrival)* no anunciado(a)
2 *adv* **to turn up** *or* **arrive u.** llegar sin previo aviso

unanswerable [ʌn'ɑ:nsərəbəl] *adj (argument)* incontestable, irrefutable; **the question is u. without further information** sin más datos la pregunta es imposible de contestar

unanswered [ʌn'ɑ:nsəd] **1** *adj* (**a**) *(question, letter)* sin contestar; **I left two questions u. in the exam** dejé dos preguntas del examen sin contestar (**b**) *(mystery, puzzle)* sin resolver
2 *adv* **to go u.** *(question, letter)* quedar sin respuesta

unanticipated [ʌnæn'tɪsɪpeɪtɪd] *adj* inesperado(a)

unapologetic [ʌnəpɒlə'dʒetɪk] *adj* **to be u. (about sth)** no tener intención de disculparse (por algo)

unappealing [ʌnə'pi:lɪŋ] *adj* poco atractivo(a)

unappetizing [ʌn'æpɪtaɪzɪŋ] *adj* (**a**) *(food)* poco apetitoso(a) (**b**) *(prospect)* poco halagüeño(a)

unappreciated [ʌnə'pri:ʃieɪtɪd] **1** *adj (effort, contribution)* no reconocido(a); **to feel u.** sentirse poco valorado(a)
2 *adv* **his efforts went u.** no se valoraron sus esfuerzos

unappreciative [ʌnə'pri:ʃiətɪv] *adj (audience, response)* poco agradecido(a); **to be u. of sth** no valorar algo

unapproachable [ʌnə'prəʊtʃəbəl] *adj* (**a**) *(person, manner)* inaccesible (**b**) *(place)* inaccesible

unarguable [ʌn'ɑ:gjʊəbəl] *adj* indiscutible

unarguably [ʌn'ɑ:gjʊəblɪ] *adv* indiscutiblemente

unarmed [ʌn'ɑ:md] *adj* desarmado(a) ►► ***u. combat*** combate *m* sin armas

unashamed [ʌnə'ʃeɪmd] *adj (curiosity, greed, lie)* descarado(a); **he was completely u. about it** no le dio ninguna vergüenza *orAm* pena; **I sighed with u. relief** suspiré con un alivio no disimulado

unashamedly [ʌnə'ʃeɪmɪdlɪ] *adv (brazenly)* descaradamente; *(openly)* abiertamente; **he was u. in favour of taking tough measures** estaba abiertamente a favor de tomar medidas más duras

unasked [ʌn'ɑ:skt] *adj (advice)* no solicitado(a); **to do sth u.** hacer algo por propia iniciativa, hacer algo sin que se lo pidan a uno; **the question remained u.** la pregunta seguía sin formularse

unassailable [ʌnə'seɪləbəl] *adj* (**a**) *(castle, position)* inexpugnable; **she had built up an u. lead** había cobrado una ventaja inalcanzable (**b**) *(argument, theory)* irrebatible; *(reputation)* intachable

unassisted [ʌnə'sɪstɪd] **1** *adj* en solitario
2 *adv* sin ayuda

unassuming [ʌnə'sju:mɪŋ] *adj* modesto(a)

unassumingly [ʌnə'sju:mɪŋlɪ] *adv* modestamente

unattached [ʌnə'tætʃt] *adj* (**a**) *(loose)* suelto(a) (**b**) *(without a partner)* **to be u.** no tener pareja

unattainable [ʌnə'teɪnəbəl] *adj* inalcanzable

unattended [ʌnə'tendɪd] *adj* desatendido(a); **to leave sth u.** dejar algo desatendido(a); **to leave sb u.** dejar solo(a) a alguien; **please do not leave your luggage u.** les rogamos no se separen de su equipaje; **she was always leaving customers u.** siempre hacía esperar a los clientes

unattractive [ʌnə'træktɪv] *adj* poco atractivo(a)

unattractiveness [ʌnə'træktɪvnɪs] *n* falta *f* de atractivo

unauthenticated [ʌnɔ:'θentɪkeɪtɪd] *adj* no verificado(a)

unauthorized [ʌn'ɔ:θəraɪzd] *adj* no autorizado(a) ►► *Comptr* ***u. access*** acceso *m* no autorizado

unavailable [ʌnə'veɪləbəl] *adj* (**a**) *(information, services)* no disponible; *(product)* agotado(a), no disponible; **to be u.** *(telephone number)* no estar disponible
(**b**) *(person)* no disponible; **Mr Fox is u. at the moment, shall I get him to call you back?** Mr Fox no está disponible en este momento, ¿quiere que le diga que lo llame más tarde?; **the minister was u. for comment** el ministro no quiso hacer declaraciones

unavailing [ʌnə'veɪlɪŋ] *adj Formal (effort)* inútil, vano(a)

unavailingly [ʌnə'veɪlɪŋlɪ] *adv Formal* vanamente, en vano

unavoidable [ʌnə'vɔɪdəbəl] *adj* inevitable

unavoidably [ʌnə'vɔɪdəblɪ] *adv* inevitablemente; **we were u. delayed** nos fue imposible llegar a la hora

unaware [ʌnə'weə(r)] *adj* (**a**) *(ignorant)* **to be u. of sth** no ser consciente de algo, ignorar algo; **we are not u. of the need for reform** somos conscientes de *or* no ignoramos la necesidad de reforma; **I was u. that they had arrived** no me había dado cuenta de que habían llegado; **he seemed quite u. that he was being watched** no parecía darse cuenta de que lo estaban mirando
(**b**) *(uninformed)* **to be politically/environmentally u.** no estar concienciado políticamente/medioambientalmente, no tener conciencia política/medioambiental

unawares [ʌnə'weəz] *adv* (**a**) *(by surprise)* **to catch sb u.** agarrar *or Esp* coger a alguien desprevenido(a) (**b**) *Literary (without realizing)* inadveridamente

unbalance [ʌn'bæləns] *vt* desequilibrar

unbalanced [ʌn'bælənst] *adj* (**a**) *(mentally)* desequilibrado(a) (**b**) *(report)* sesgado(a), parcial (**c**) *(diet)* poco equilibrado(a) (**d**) *Fin* **u. accounts** cuentas que no cuadran

unbandage [ʌn'bændɪdʒ] *vt* quitar la venda a

unbar [ʌn'bɑ:(r)] *(pt & pp* **unbarred**) *vt (door, gate)* desatrancar; *Fig* **the decision could u. the way to a lasting solution** la decisión podría abrir las puertas a una solución duradera

unbearable [ʌn'beərəbəl] *adj* insoportable

unbearably [ʌn'beərəblɪ] *adv (to behave)* de forma insoportable; **he's u. arrogant** es de una arrogancia insoportable; **it's u. hot** hace un calor insoportable

unbeatable [ʌn'bi:təbəl] *adj* (**a**) *(team, position)* invencible, imbatible (**b**) *(product, value, price)* insuperable

unbeaten [ʌn'bi:tən] *adj* **they remained u. for the rest of the season** siguieron sin perder un partido hasta el final de la temporada; **his u. record stretches back to 1999** sigue imbatible desde 1999

unbecoming [ʌnbɪ'kʌmɪŋ] *adj Old-fashioned* (**a**) *(behaviour)* impropio(a) (**to** de) (**b**) *(dress)* poco favorecedor(ora)

unbefitting [ʌnbɪ'fɪtɪŋ] *adj Formal* **he behaved in a manner u. a member of parliament** se comportó de manera impropia en un parlamentario

unbeknown(st) [ʌnbɪ'nəʊn(st)] *adv* **u. to me** sin mi conocimiento, sin que yo lo supiera

unbelief ['ʌnbɪli:f] *n Formal (religious)* descreimiento *m*

unbelievable [ʌnbɪ'li:vəbəl] *adj* (**a**) *(extraordinary)* increíble; **that was an u. piece of good fortune** aquello fue un golpe de suerte increíble; **you're u.!** ¡eres el colmo! (**b**) *(implausible)* increíble; **his story was totally u.** su historia no había quien se la creyera

unbelievably [ʌnbɪ'li:vəblɪ] *adv (extraordinarily)* increíblemente; **u., he didn't even say hello** fue increíble, ni siquiera saludó; **we were u. lucky** tuvimos una suerte increíble

unbeliever [ʌnbɪ'li:və(r)] *n Formal (religious)* no creyente *mf*, descreído(a) *m,f*

unbelieving [ʌnbɪ'li:vɪŋ] *adj (listeners, eyes)* incrédulo(a)

unbend [ʌn'bend] **1** *vt (fork, wire)* enderezar
2 *vi (person)* relajarse

unbending [ʌn'bendɪŋ] *adj (person, attitude)* inflexible; *(will)* férreo(a)

unbias(s)ed [ʌn'baɪəst] *adj* imparcial

unbidden [ʌn'bɪdən] *adv Formal* sin querer, de forma espontánea; **they arrived u.** vinieron sin ser invitados

unbind [ʌn'baɪnd] *(pt & pp* **unbound** [ʌn'baʊnd]) *vt (prisoner)* desatar

unbleached [ʌn'bli:tʃt] *adj (fabric, T-shirt, paper, flour)* sin blanquear

unblemished [ʌn'blemɪʃt] *adj* (**a**) *(skin)* sin defectos (**b**) *(reputation)* intachable; **the team has an u. record so far this year** hasta ahora el equipo ha tenido una trayectoria impecable

unblinking [ʌn'blɪŋkɪŋ] *adj* impasible

unblock [ʌn'blɒk] *vt* (**a**) *(sink, pipe)* desatascar (**b**) *(road)* desbloquear (**c**) *(nose, ear)* destapar

unblushing [ʌn'blʌʃɪŋ] *adj* declarado(a)

unbolt [ʌn'bəʊlt] *vt (door)* abrir el cerrojo de

unborn [ʌn'bɔ:n] *adj* **generations yet u.** generaciones venideras ►► ***u. child*** niño *m* (aún) no nacido

unbosom [ʌn'bʊzəm] *vt Literary (secret)* confesar; *(emotions)* desahogar; **to u. oneself to sb** desahogarse con alguien

unbothered [ʌn'bɒðəd] *adj* (**a**) *(not disturbed)* **I was u. by the noise** el ruido no le molestaba (**b**) *(indifferent)* **I'm u. about it** me trae sin cuidado

unbound [ʌn'baʊnd] **1** *adj* (**a**) *(untied)* desatado(a), suelto(a) (**b**) *(book, pages)* sin encuadernar
2 *pt & pp of* **unbind**

unbounded [ʌn'baʊndɪd] *adj* ilimitado(a), sin límites

unbowed [ʌn'baʊd] *adj (head)* erguido(a); **their heads remained u.** mantuvieron la cabeza erguida *or* bien alta; **they emerged from the struggle, bloody but u.** salieron maltrechos de la lucha pero con la moral intacta

unbreakable [ʌn'breɪkəbəl] *adj* (**a**) *(plate, toy)* irrompible (**b**) *(spirit, alliance)* inquebrantable

unbreathable [ʌn'bri:ðəbəl] *adj (air)* irrespirable

unbridgeable [ʌn'brɪdʒəbəl] *adj (gap)* insalvable

unbridled [ʌn'braɪdəld] *adj (passion, aggression)* desatado(a); *(enthusiasm, optimism)* desbocado(a)

un-British [ʌn'brɪtɪʃ] *adj* poco británico(a)

unbroken [ʌn'brəʊkən] *adj* (**a**) *(intact) (crockery, seal)* intacto(a); *(record)* imbatido(a) (**b**) *(uninterrupted) (line, expanse, peace, tradition)* ininterrumpido(a) (**c**) *(undefeated)* **their spirit remains u.** mantienen la moral alta (**d**) *(horse)* sin domar

unbuckle [ʌn'bʌkəl] *vt* desabrochar (la hebilla de)

unburden [ʌn'bɜːdən] *vt* (**a**) *Formal (of load)* **can I u. you of your bags?** ¿le ayudo con las bolsas? (**b**) *(of emotions)* **to u. one's conscience** descargar la conciencia; **to u. oneself** *or* **one's heart to sb** desahogarse con alguien

unburied [ʌn'berɪd] *adj* sin enterrar

unbusinesslike [ʌn'bɪznɪslaɪk] *adj* poco profesional

unbutton [ʌn'bʌtən] *vt* desabrochar, desabotonar; **to u. one's shirt** desabrocharse la camisa

unbuttoned [ʌn'bʌtənd] *adj* (**a**) *(shirt)* desabrochado(a), desabotonado(a) (**b**) *(relaxed, informal)* informal, desenfadado(a)

uncalled-for [ʌn'kɔːldfɔː(r)] *adj* **to be u.** *(behaviour, remark)* estar fuera de lugar; **that was totally u.!** ¡eso estaba totalmente fuera de lugar!, ¡eso fue una salida de tono!

uncannily [ʌn'kænɪlɪ] *adv* asombrosamente; **u. accurate** de una precisión asombrosa

uncanny [ʌn'kænɪ] *adj (coincidence, similarity, resemblance)* asombroso(a), extraño(a); *(knack, ability)* inexplicable; **it's u. how she always seems to know what I'm about to say** no me explico cómo siempre parece saber lo que voy a decir

uncap [ʌn'kæp] *vt (pen)* quitar *or Am* sacar la capucha a

uncapped [ʌn'kæpt] *adj (player)* debutante

uncared-for [ʌn'keədfɔː(r)] *adj (house, garden, child)* abandonado(a), descuidado(a); *(appearance)* descuidado(a)

uncaring [ʌn'keərɪŋ] *adj* desafecto(a), indiferente; **an u. mother** una madre poco afectuosa

uncarpeted [ʌn'kɑːpɪtɪd] *adj Esp, RP* sin enmoquetar, *Am* sin alfombrar

uncashed [ʌn'kæʃt] *adj (cheque)* sin cobrar

uncatalogued [ʌn'kætəlɒgd] *adj* sin catalogar

unceasing [ʌn'siːsɪŋ] *adj* incesante

unceasingly [ʌn'siːsɪŋlɪ] *adv* incesantemente, sin cesar

uncensored [ʌn'sensəd] *adj* sin censurar, íntegro(a)

unceremonious [ʌnserə'məʊnɪəs] *adj* brusco(a), poco ceremonioso(a)

unceremoniously [ʌnserə'məʊnɪəslɪ] *adv* sin contemplaciones

uncertain [ʌn'sɜːtən] *adj* (**a**) *(doubtful, unclear)* incierto(a); **to be u. about sth** no estar seguro(a) de algo; **they were u. how to begin** no estaban seguros de cómo empezar; **I feel u. about him** tengo mis dudas sobre él; **it is u. if...** no se sabe si...; **it is u. whether they will succeed** no es seguro *or* no está claro que vayan a lograrlo; **the minister's future is u.** el futuro del ministro es incierto; **in no u. terms** en términos bien claros

(**b**) *(unconfident) (voice, steps)* inseguro(a), vacilante; **to be u. of oneself** no estar seguro(a) de sí mismo(a)

(**c**) *(unknown)* **the cause of her death is still u.** todavía se desconocen las causas de su muerte

(**d**) *(undecided) (plans)* sin decidir

uncertainly [ʌn'sɜːtənlɪ] *adv (to smile, enter)* de forma vacilante; **...he said u.** ...dijo vacilante *or* inseguro

uncertainty [ʌn'sɜːtəntɪ] *n* incertidumbre *f*; **today's statement put an end to the u. about her future** la declaración de hoy ha puesto fin a la incertidumbre sobre su futuro; **there's still some u. as to what was actually said** todavía no se sabe con certeza qué fue lo que dijeron en realidad; **I am in some u. as to whether I should tell him** estoy en duda sobre si debería decírselo; **despite this clarification a number of uncertainties remain** a pesar de esta aclaración quedan ciertas dudas ►► *Phys* ***u. principle*** principio *m* de indeterminación *or* incertidumbre

unchain [ʌn'tʃeɪn] *vt* desencadenar

unchallengeable [ʌn'tʃælɪndʒəbəl] *adj (argument, right)* incuestionable; *(evidence, proof)* irrefutable; **he has built up an u. lead** ya nadie puede disputarle el liderazgo

unchallenged [ʌn'tʃælɪndʒd] **1** *adj* (**a**) *(authority, leader)* **his position as party leader is u.** nadie le disputa su puesto como líder del partido; **her authority remains u.** nadie le disputa aún su autoridad (**b**) *(assumption)* no cuestionado(a); **he did not want to leave the accusations u.** no quiso dejar las acusaciones sin desmentir

2 *adv* **her decisions always go u.** nunca se cuestionan sus decisiones; **he let this claim pass u.** dejó pasar esa afirmación sin cuestionarla

unchanged [ʌn'tʃeɪndʒd] *adj* igual, sin cambios; **he was completely u. by his experience** aquella experiencia no le cambió en absoluto; **to remain u.** no haber cambiado

unchanging [ʌn'tʃeɪndʒɪŋ] *adj* inmutable

uncharacteristic [ʌnkærəktə'rɪstɪk] *adj* atípico(a), poco característico(a) (**of** de); **it's u. for her to make a mistake like that** no es normal en ella cometer un error como ése

uncharacteristically [ʌnkærəktə'rɪstɪklɪ] *adv* **he was u. generous/cheerful** mostraba una generosidad/alegría atípica *or* poco normal en él; **to behave u.** comportarse de una manera atípica *or* rara

uncharitable [ʌn'tʃærɪtəbəl] *adj* mezquino(a)

uncharitably [ʌn'tʃærɪtəblɪ] *adv* sin conmiseración

uncharted [ʌn'tʃɑːtɪd] *adj (region, forest, ocean)* inexplorado(a), sin explorar; *Fig* **these are u. waters for us** para nosotros es un territorio inexplorado

unchastened [ʌn'tʃeɪsənd] *adj* no escarmentado(a); **he was u. by his experience** no escarmentó con la experiencia

unchecked [ʌn'tʃekt] **1** *adj* (**a**) *(not restrained) (growth, expansion, anger)* incontrolado(a) (**b**) *(not verified)* sin comprobar

2 *adv* **to go u.** *(corruption, epidemic)* avanzar sin control; **if left u., this outbreak could turn into an epidemic** si no se controla a tiempo, este brote podría convertirse en una epidemia

unchivalrous [ʌn'ʃɪvəlrəs] *adj* descortés, poco caballeroso(a)

unchristian [ʌn'krɪstʃən] *adj* poco cristiano(a)

uncircumcised [ʌn'sɜːkəmsaɪzd] *adj (penis, person)* incircunciso(a)

uncivil [ʌn'sɪvəl] *adj* maleducado(a), descortés; **to be u. to sb** ser maleducado(a) con alguien

uncivilized [ʌn'sɪvɪlaɪzd] *adj* (**a**) *(tribes, peoples)* primitivo(a), sin civilizar; *(regions)* sin civilizar (**b**) *(behaviour)* poco civilizado(a), incivilizado(a) (**c**) *(inconvenient)* **at an u. hour** a una hora intempestiva

unclaimed [ʌn'kleɪmd] **1** *adj (money, baggage, prize)* no reclamado(a) ►► *Law* ***u. estate*** herencia *f* yacente

2 *adv* **to go u.** *(money, baggage, prize)* no ser reclamado por nadie

unclasp [ʌn'klɑːsp] *vt (buckle, brooch)* desabrochar; *(hands)* descruzar

unclassifiable [ʌnklæsɪ'faɪəbəl] *adj* inclasificable

unclassified [ʌn'klæsɪfaɪd] *adj* (**a**) *(not secret)* desclasificado(a), no confidencial (**b**) *(uncategorized)* sin clasificar

uncle ['ʌŋkəl] *n* tío *m*; **all my uncles and aunts were there** todos mis tíos estaban allí ►► *US* ***U. Sam*** el Tío Sam; *Fam Pej* ***U. Tom*** = persona de raza negra que muestra una actitud sumisa ante los blancos

unclean [ʌn'kliːn] *adj* (**a**) *(dirty)* sucio(a); **to feel u.** sentirse sucio(a) (**b**) *(sinful) (thoughts, food)* impuro(a)

unclear [ʌn'klɪə(r)] *adj* (**a**) *(confused, ambiguous) (thinking, instructions, reason)* confuso(a), poco claro(a); **I'm still u. about what happened** todavía no tengo muy claro lo que pasó (**b**) *(uncertain) (future, outcome)* incierto(a); **it's still u. who will win** aún no está claro quién va a ganar (**c**) *(indistinct) (sound, speech)* confuso(a), poco claro(a)

unclearly [ʌn'klɪəlɪ] *adv* (**a**) *(to describe, explain, think)* de forma confusa *or* poco clara (**b**) *(to hear, speak)* de forma confusa *or* poco clara

unclench [ʌn'klentʃ] *vt (fist, teeth)* relajar

uncloak [ʌn'kləʊk] *vt (mystery, plans)* revelar; *(impostor)* descubrir

unclog [ʌn'klɒg] *vt* desatascar

unclothed [ʌn'kləʊðd] *adj* desvestido(a), desnudo(a)

unclouded [ʌn'klaʊdɪd] *adj* (**a**) *(sky)* despejado(a) (**b**) *(thinking, vision)* despejado(a); **a future u. by financial worries** un futuro no ensombrecido por preocupaciones económicas

uncluttered [ʌn'klʌtə(d)] *adj* (**a**) *(room, desk)* despejado(a); *(design, layout)* no recargado(a) (**b**) *(mind, thinking)* claro(a)

uncoil [ʌn'kɔɪl] **1** *vt* desenrollar

2 *vi* desenrollarse

uncollected [ʌnkə'lektɪd] *adj (tax)* no recaudado(a)

uncoloured, *US* **uncolored** [ʌn'kʌləd] *adj (impartial)* imparcial

uncombed [ʌn'kəʊmd] *adj* despeinado(a)

uncomfortable [ʌn'kʌmftəbəl] *adj* (**a**) *(physically) (person, bed, clothes)* incómodo(a); **to be** *or* **feel u.** estar incómodo(a)

(**b**) *(uneasy)* **to be** *or* **feel u.** sentirse incómodo(a) *or* violento(a); **I'd feel u. (about) asking my parents for money** me sentiría incómodo *or* violento si tuviera que pedir dinero a mis padres; **there was an u. silence** se produjo un silencio incómodo *or* violento; **I've an u. feeling this isn't going to work** tengo la desagradable sensación de que esto

no va a salir bien; **to make life** *or* **things u. for sb** complicar la vida a alguien
(**c**) *(unpleasant) (fact, truth)* incómodo(a)

uncomfortably [ʌn'kʌmftəblɪ] *adv* (**a**) *(physically) (to lie, sit, stand)* incómodamente; **to be u. dressed** llevar una ropa incómoda; **it was u. hot** hacía un calor incómodo; **the train was u. crowded** el tren era incómodo por lo abarrotado que estaba
(**b**) *(uneasily)* incómodamente, violentamente; **I was u. aware of him watching me** me sentía incómoda *or* violenta al saber que me estaba mirando
(**c**) *(worryingly)* **this sounds u. close to...** esto tiene un alarmante parecido con...; **we came u. close to losing** es preocupante lo cerca que estuvimos de perder

uncommercial [ʌnkə'mɜːʃəl] *adj* poco comercial

uncommitted [ʌnkə'mɪtɪd] *adj* (**a**) *(voter)* indeciso(a) (**b**) *(funds)* no comprometido(a)

uncommon [ʌn'kɒmən] *adj* (**a**) *(rare, unusual)* poco frecuente; **it's not u. for this sort of thing to happen** no es raro que ocurran cosas como ésta (**b**) *Formal (exceptional)* singular

uncommonly [ʌn'kɒmənlɪ] *adv* (**a**) *(infrequently)* con poca frecuencia; **not u.** con relativa frecuencia (**b**) *Formal (extremely)* extraordinariamente; **the food was u. good** la comida estaba absolutamente exquisita

uncommunicative [ʌnkə'mjuːnɪkətɪv] *adj* reservado(a), poco comunicativo(a)

uncompetitive [ʌnkəm'petɪtɪv] *adj* (**a**) *(product, company, economy)* poco competitivo(a) (**b**) *(person)* poco competitivo(a), sin espíritu competitivo

uncomplaining [ʌnkəm'pleɪnɪŋ] *adj* **she accepted the extra work with u. resignation** aceptó el trabajo extra resignada y sin quejarse

uncomplainingly [ʌnkəm'pleɪnɪŋlɪ] *adv* sin quejarse

uncompleted [ʌnkəm'pliːtɪd] *adj* incompleto(a)

uncomplicated [ʌn'kɒmplɪkeɪtɪd] *adj* sencillo(a)

uncomplimentary [ʌnkɒmplɪ'mentərɪ] *adj* crítico(a); **to be u. about sth/sb** ser crítico(a) con algo/alguien

uncomprehending [ʌnkɒmprɪ'hendɪŋ] *adj* **to be u. of sth** no entender algo; **with an u. look** con cara de no haber comprendido

uncomprehendingly [ʌnkɒmprɪ'hendɪŋlɪ] *adv* con aire *or* un gesto de incomprensión

uncompromising [ʌn'kɒmprəmaɪzɪŋ] *adj (inflexible)* intransigente; *(resolute)* inquebrantable; **we took an u. stance on the proposals** no transigimos ante las propuestas; **an u. defense of free speech** una defensa sin concesiones de la libertad de expresión; **the documentary takes an u. look at the subject** el documental enfoca el tema sin concesiones

uncompromisingly [ʌnkɒmprə'maɪzɪŋlɪ] *adv* sin concesiones, de manera inquebrantable; **to be u. honest** ser de una honradez inquebrantable

unconcealed [ʌnkən'siːld] *adj* indisimulado(a), manifiesto(a)

unconcern [ʌnkən'sɜːn] *n* (**a**) *(indifference)* indiferencia *f* (**b**) *(lack of worry)* despreocupación *f*, tranquilidad *f*

unconcerned [ʌnkən'sɜːnd] **1** *adj* (**a**) *(indifferent)* indiferente; **he seemed quite u. about their problems** parecía indiferente a sus problemas (**b**) *(unworried)* **to be u. about sth** no inquietarse *or* preocuparse por algo; **she seemed u. by the danger** parecía no inquietarle *or* preocuparle el peligro
2 *adv* **to watch/wait u.** mirar/esperar con indiferencia

unconcernedly [ʌnkən'sɜːnɪdlɪ] *adv* (**a**) *(indifferently)* con indiferencia (**b**) *(calmly)* despreocupadamente

unconditional [ʌnkən'dɪʃənəl] *adj* incondicional ►► *Law* ***u. discharge*** libertad *f* incondicional; ***u. surrender*** rendición *f* incondicional

unconditionally [ʌnkən'dɪʃənəlɪ] *adv (to support)* incondicionalmente; *(to surrender, accept)* sin condiciones; **to agree u. to sb's terms** aceptar sin condiciones los términos impuestos por alguien

unconditioned [ʌnkən'dɪʃənd] *adj* ***u. response*** respuesta *f* incondicionada

unconfident [ʌn'kɒnfɪdənt] *adj (not self-assured)* inseguro(a)

unconfirmed [ʌnkən'fɜːmd] *adj* no confirmado(a)

uncongenial [ʌnkən'dʒiːnjəl] *adj (surroundings, atmosphere)* poco agradable; *(person, personality)* poco amigable

unconnected [ʌnkə'nektɪd] *adj* inconexo(a), sin relación; **two u. facts** dos hechos inconexos *or* sin relación; **to be u. (with sth)** no estar relacionado(a) (con algo); **the two incidents are not u.** hay una relación entre ambos incidentes

unconscionable [ʌn'kɒnʃənəbəl] *adj Formal* (**a**) *(amount, demand)* desmesurado(a), desorbitado(a) (**b**) *(liar)* redomado(a)

unconscious [ʌn'kɒnʃəs] **1** *n Psy* **the u.** el inconsciente
2 *adj* (**a**) *(not awake)* inconsciente; **to be u.** estar inconsciente; **to become u.** quedarse inconsciente; **to knock sb u.** dejar a alguien inconsciente de un golpe (**b**) *(unaware)* **to be u. of sth** no ser consciente de algo; **I was u. of having offended you** no era consciente de haberte ofendido (**c**) *(unintentional)* inintencionado(a) (**d**) *Psy* inconsciente; **the u. mind** el inconsciente

unconsciously [ʌn'kɒnʃəslɪ] *adv* inconscientemente

unconsciousness [ʌn'kɒnʃəsnɪs] *n Med* inconsciencia *f*; **he lapsed into u.** perdió el conocimiento, se quedó inconsciente

unconsidered [ʌnkən'sɪdəd] *adj* (**a**) *(action, remark)* irreflexivo(a) (**b**) *Formal (insignificant)* sin importancia

unconstitutional [ʌnkɒnstɪ'tjuːʃənəl] *adj* inconstitucional, anticonstitucional

unconstitutionally [ʌnkɒnstɪ'tjuːʃənəlɪ] *adv* inconstitucionalmente, anticonstitucionalmente

unconstrained [ʌnkən'streɪnd] *adj (laughter, joy)* incontenible

unconstricted [ʌnkən'strɪktɪd] *adj (breathing, movement)* sin restricciones

unconsummated [ʌn'kɒnsəmeɪtɪd] *adj (marriage)* no consumado(a)

uncontaminated [ʌnkən'tæmɪneɪtɪd] *adj* sin contaminar

uncontested [ʌnkən'testɪd] *adj (right, superiority)* indisputado(a); *Pol* **u. seat** escaño con un solo candidato

uncontrollable [ʌnkən'trəʊləbəl] *adj (rage, excitement, situation)* incontrolable; *(desire, urge)* irrefrenable; *(laughter)* incontenible; **their children are quite u.** a sus hijos no hay forma de controlarlos

uncontrollably [ʌnkən'trəʊləblɪ] *adv* incontrolablemente; **they laughed u.** no podían parar de reírse; **prices are rising u.** los precios están aumentando de forma incontrolable

uncontrolled [ʌnkən'trəʊld] *adj* (**a**) *(fall, rise, emotion)* incontrolado(a), sin control (**b**) *(experiment)* incontrolado(a), sin control

uncontroversial [ʌnkɒntrə'vɜːʃəl] *adj* anodino(a), nada polémico(a)

unconventional [ʌnkən'venʃənəl] *adj* poco convencional

unconventionally [ʌnkən'venʃənəlɪ] *adv* de forma poco convencional

unconvinced [ʌnkən'vɪnst] *adj* **to be u. (of sth)** no estar convencido(a) (de algo); **I remain u.** sigo sin convencerme

unconvincing [ʌnkən'vɪnsɪŋ] *adj* poco convincente

unconvincingly [ʌnkən'vɪnsɪŋlɪ] *adv (to argue, lie, perform)* de forma poco convincente; **they won u.** su victoria no fue convincente

uncooked [ʌn'kʊkt] *adj* crudo(a)

uncool [ʌn'kuːl] *adj Fam* (**a**) *(unfashionable)* poco enrollado(a), *Méx* nada suave, *RP* nada copado(a), *Ven* aguado(a); **what an u. thing to do!** ¡qué *Esp* mal rollo *orAm* mala onda! (**b**) *(not accepted)* **I think it's a bit u. to smoke in here** creo que no está bien visto fumar aquí

uncooperative [ʌnkəʊ'ɒpərətɪv] *adj* **to be u.** no estar dispuesto(a) a cooperar

uncoordinated [ʌnkəʊ'ɔːdɪneɪtɪd] *adj* (**a**) *(efforts)* descoordinado(a) (**b**) *(person, movements)* falto(a) de coordinación, torpe

uncork [ʌn'kɔːk] *vt* descorchar

uncorrected [ʌnkə'rektɪd] *adj (exercise, proof, error)* sin corregir

uncorroborated [ʌnkə'rɒbəreɪtɪd] *adj* no confirmado(a)

uncountable [ʌn'kaʊntəbəl] *adj Gram* incontable

uncouple [ʌn'kʌpəl] *vt (railway carriage)* desenganchar

uncouth [ʌn'kuːθ] *adj* basto(a)

uncover [ʌn'kʌvə(r)] *vt* (**a**) *(remove cover from)* destapar (**b**) *(unearth) (buried treasure)* descubrir (**c**) *(discover) (evidence, plot)* descubrir

uncovered [ʌn'kʌvəd] *adj* (**a**) *(food, pot)* destapado(a) (**b**) *(uninsured) (person)* **to be u.** no estar cubierto(a)

uncritical [ʌn'krɪtɪkəl] *adj* poco crítico(a); **to be u. of sth/sb** no ser crítico(a) con algo/alguien

uncross [ʌn'krɒs] *vt* **to u. one's legs** descruzar las piernas

uncrossed [ʌn'krɒst] *adj Br (cheque)* sin cruzar

uncrowded [ʌn'kraʊdɪd] *adj* sin aglomeraciones

uncrowned [ʌn'kraʊnd] *adj* sin corona; **the u. king of movie directors** el rey sin corona de los directores de cine

UNCTAD ['ʌŋktæd] *n* (*abbr* **United Nations Conference on Trade and Development**) UNCTAD *f*

unction ['ʌŋkʃən] *n* (**a**) *Formal (of manner)* untuosidad *f*, empalago *m* (**b**) *Rel* unción *f*

unctuous ['ʌŋktjʊəs] *adj Pej* untuoso(a), empalagoso(a)

unctuously [ˈʌŋktjʊəslɪ] *adv Pej* con maneras untuosas, empalagosamente

unctuousness [ˈʌŋktjʊəsnɪs] *n Pej* untuosidad *f*, maneras *fpl* untuosas

uncultivated [ʌnˈkʌltɪveɪtɪd] *adj* (**a**) *(land)* sin cultivar (**b**) *(person, manners)* inculto(a)

uncultured [ʌnˈkʌltʃəd] *adj* inculto(a)

uncured [ʌnˈkjʊəd] *adj (meat, fish)* fresco(a)

uncurl [ʌnˈkɜːl] 1 *vt (rope)* desenrollar; **to u. one's fingers** estirar los dedos
2 *vi (leaf)* desenrollarse; *(cat, snake)* desenroscarse

uncut [ʌnˈkʌt] *adj* (**a**) *(grass, hair, nails)* sin cortar; *(wheat)* sin segar (**b**) *(gem)* en bruto (**c**) *(pages)* sin cortar (**d**) *(text, movie)* íntegro(a) (**e**) *(drugs)* sin cortar

undamaged [ʌnˈdæmɪdʒd] *adj* intacto(a)

undamped [ʌnˈdæmpt] *adj* **their enthusiasm was u. by this minor setback** este pequeño contratiempo no les había desalentado

undated [ʌnˈdeɪtɪd] *adj* no fechado(a)

undaunted [ʌnˈdɔːntɪd] *adj* imperturbable; **he carried on u.** continuó imperturbable; **to be u. by sth** no amilanarse *or* arredrarse por algo

undead [ʌnˈded] *npl* **the u.** *(the living)* los vivos; *(zombies, vampires)* los muertos vivientes

undeceive [ʌndəˈsiːv] *vt Formal* desengañar

undecided [ʌndɪˈsaɪdɪd] *adj* (**a**) *(question, problem)* sin resolver; **that's still u.** todavía está por decidir (**b**) *(person)* indeciso(a); **to be u. about sth** estar indeciso(a) sobre algo; **he is u. whether to stay or go, he is u. as to whether he should stay or go** está indeciso sobre si irse o quedarse

undecipherable [ʌndɪˈsaɪfərəbəl] *adj (writing)* indescifrable

undeclared [ʌndɪˈkleəd] *adj (war, income, payment)* no declarado(a); *(love)* secreto(a), no declarado(a)

undefeated [ʌndɪˈfiːtɪd] *adj* invicto(a); **she is u. in twenty matches** lleva veinte partidos invicta

undefended [ʌndɪˈfendɪd] *adj (fort, town)* indefenso(a); *(goal)* desguarnecido(a), vacío(a)

undefinable [ʌndɪˈfaɪnəbəl] *adj* indefinible

undefined [ʌndɪˈfaɪnd] *adj (feeling)* vago(a), indefinido(a)

undelete [ʌndɪˈliːt] *vt Comptr* restaurar

undelivered [ʌndɪˈlɪvəd] *adj (letter)* **if u. please return to...** en caso de no encontrarse el destinatario, devolver a...

undemanding [ʌndɪˈmɑːndɪŋ] *adj (job)* fácil, que exige poco esfuerzo; *(person)* poco exigente

undemocratic [ʌndeməˈkrætɪk] *adj* antidemocrático(a)

undemonstrative [ʌndɪˈmɒnstrətɪv] *adj* reservado(a)

undeniable [ʌndɪˈnaɪəbəl] *adj* innegable

undeniably [ʌndɪˈnaɪəblɪ] *adv* innegablemente; **it is u. true that...** es innegable que...

UNDER [ˈʌndə(r)] 1 *prep* (**a**) *(beneath)* debajo de, bajo, *Am* abajo de; *(with verbs of motion)* bajo, abajo; **u. the table/the stairs** debajo *or* abajo de la mesa/las escaleras; **to walk u. a ladder** pasar por debajo *or* abajo de una escalera; **he staggered u. his heavy load** se tambaleaba bajo tanto peso; **to look at sth u. the microscope** mirar algo al microscopio; *Fig* escudriñar algo; **I was born u. Aries** nací bajo el signo de Aries
(**b**) *(less than)* menos de; **in u. ten minutes** en menos de diez minutos; **a number u. ten** un número menor que diez; **he's u. thirty** tiene menos de treinta años; **children u. (the age of) five** niños menores de cinco años; **he's two u. par** *(in golf)* está dos bajo par
(**c**) *(controlled by)* **he has a hundred men u. him** tiene cien hombres a su cargo; **Spain u. Franco** la España de Franco; **u. the Conservatives** bajo el gobierno conservador; **u. fascism, many organizations were outlawed** durante el fascismo muchas organizaciones fueron ilegalizadas; **I work u. a German** mi jefe es alemán; **she came u. his influence** él empezó a influenciarla; **he studied u. Foxworth** fue discípulo de Foxworth
(**d**) *(subject to)* **to be u. anaesthetic** estar bajo los efectos de la anestesia; **to be u. the impression that...** tener la impresión de que...; **to be u. orders to do sth** tener órdenes de hacer algo; **to be u. pressure** estar bajo presión; **to be u. suspicion** ser sospechoso(a); **to be u. threat** estar amenazado(a); **u. these conditions/circumstances** en estas condiciones/circunstancias; **u. the new law, all this will change** con la nueva ley todo (esto) cambiará; **u. this system, the President has little real power** en este sistema el presidente apenas tiene poder real
(**e**) *(in the process of)* **he's u. attack** están atacándolo; **u. construction/observation** en construcción/observación; **the matter is u. investigation** se está investigando el asunto; **to be u. treatment (for)** estar en tratamiento (contra); **to be u. way** *(meeting, campaign)* estar en marcha; **to get u. way** *(meeting, campaign)* ponerse en marcha, arrancar
(**f**) *(as a result of)* **it snapped u. the strain** se rompió por la presión
(**g**) *(according to)* según; **u. the terms of the agreement** según el acuerdo
(**h**) *(using)* **u. a false name** con un nombre falso; **published u. the title of...** publicado con el título de...
(**i**) *(in classifications)* **this item comes u. overheads** esta cifra va con los gastos generales; **I filed it u. "pending"** lo archivé bajo el epígrafe de "asuntos pendientes"
(**j**) *Agr* **u. wheat/barley** de trigo/cebada
2 *adv* (**a**) *(underneath)* debajo, *Am* abajo; *(underwater)* bajo el agua, debajo *or Am* abajo del agua; **to go u.** *(ship, company)* hundirse; IDIOM **when I'm six feet u.** cuando esté criando malvas
(**b**) *(less)* **for £5 or u.** por 5 libras o menos; **children of seven and u.** niños menores de ocho años; **he's two u.** *(in golf)* está dos bajo par
(**c**) *(anaesthetized)* anestesiado(a), bajo los efectos de la anestesia

under-21 [ˈʌndətwentɪˈwʌn] 1 *n* **the under-21s** los sub-21
2 *adj* sub-21

underachieve [ʌndərəˈtʃiːv] *vi* tener un bajo rendimiento

underachievement [ʌndərəˈtʃiːvmənt] *n* bajo rendimiento *m*

underachiever [ʌndərəˈtʃiːvə(r)] *n* = persona que rinde por debajo de sus posibilidades

under-age [ʌndəˈreɪdʒ] *adj* **to be u.** ser menor de edad ►► ***u. drinking*** consumo *m* de alcohol de los menores; ***u. sex*** relaciones *fpl* sexuales entre menores

underarm [ˈʌndərɑːm] 1 *adj* (**a**) *(hair)* de las axilas; *(deodorant)* para las axilas (**b**) *Sport* ***u. serve*** saque *m* de cuchara
2 *adv* **to throw a ball u.** = lanzar una pelota con el brazo extendido hacia abajo; **to serve a ball u.** servir una pelota de cuchara

underbelly [ˈʌndəbelɪ] *n* (**a**) *(of animal, fish)* panza *f*, vientre *m* (**b**) *(vulnerable part)* bajo vientre *m*; **the soft u. of Europe/the economy** el punto flaco de Europa/la economía

underblanket [ˈʌndəblæŋkɪt] *n (non-electric)* cubrecolchones *m inv*; *(electric)* manta *f* eléctrica

underbody [ˈʌndəbɔːdɪ] *n* (**a**) *(of animal)* parte *f* inferior (**b**) *(of car)* bajos *mpl*

underbrush [ˈʌndəbrʌʃ] *n US* maleza *f*

undercapitalization [ʌndəkæpɪtəlaɪˈzeɪʃən] *n Fin* descapitalización *f (parcial)*

undercapitalized [ʌndəˈkæpɪtəlaɪzd] *adj Fin* descapitalizado(a) *(parcialmente)*

undercarriage [ˈʌndəkærɪdʒ] *n Av* tren *m* de aterrizaje

undercharge [ʌndəˈtʃɑːdʒ] *vt* cobrar de menos; **she undercharged him by $6** le cobró 6 dólares de menos

underclass [ˈʌndəklɑːs] *n* clase *f* marginal

underclothes [ˈʌndəkləʊðz] *npl* ropa *f* interior

underclothing [ˈʌndəkləʊðɪŋ] *n* ropa *f* interior

undercoat [ˈʌndəkəʊt] *n* (**a**) *(of paint)* primera mano *f (de pintura)* (**b**) *(type of paint)* pintura *f* base

undercook [ʌndəˈkʊk] *vt* dejar poco hecho(a); **to be undercooked** no estar lo suficientemente hecho(a)

undercover 1 *adj* [ˈʌndəkʌvə(r)] *(agent, investigation)* secreto(a)
2 *adv* [ʌndəˈkʌvə(r)] **to work u.** trabajar de incógnito

undercurrent [ˈʌndəkʌrənt] *n* (**a**) *(in sea)* corriente *f* submarina (**b**) *(of emotion, unrest)* corriente *f* subyacente

undercut [ˈʌndəkʌt] *(pt & pp* **undercut**) *vt* (**a**) *Com* **to u. the competition** vender a precios más baratos que los de la competencia; **they u. us by £500** hicieron un presupuesto 500 libras más barato que el nuestro (**b**) *(undermine) (efforts)* socavar

underdeveloped [ʌndədɪˈveləpt] *adj* (**a**) *(economy, country)* subdesarrollado(a) (**b**) *(body, muscles, foetus)* poco desarrollado(a) (**c**) *(argument, idea)* poco desarrollado(a) (**d**) *(film, print)* subrevelado(a)

underdevelopment [ʌndədɪˈveləpmənt] *n* (**a**) *(of economy, country)* subdesarrollo *m* (**b**) *(of body, muscles, foetus)* falta *f* de desarrollo

underdog [ˈʌndədɒg] *n* (**a**) *(in contest)* = jugador o equipo considerado probable perdedor; **England are the underdogs** Inglaterra no sale como favorita; **the underdogs won 5-2** los que no eran favoritos ganaron 5-2 (**b**) *(in society)* **the u.** los débiles y oprimidos

underdone [ʌndəˈdʌn] *adj* poco hecho(a)

underdressed [ʌndəˈdrest] *adj* no lo suficientemente elegante; **I felt distinctly u. in my shorts** con aquellos pantalones cortos tenía la sensación de no ir vestido para la ocasión

underemphasize [ʌndəˈremfəsaɪz] *vt* restar importancia a

underemployed [ʌndərɪmˈplɔɪd] *adj* (**a**) *(skills, resources)* infrautilizado(a) (**b**) *(worker)* subempleado(a)

underemployment [ʌndərɪmˈplɔɪmənt] *n* (**a**) *(of skills, resources)* infrautilización *f* (**b**) *(of workers)* subempleo *m*

underestimate 1 *n* [ʌndəˈrestɪmɪt] **to say $200 was a huge u.** decir que iban a ser 200 dólares era subestimarlo mucho

2 *vt* [ʌndəˈrestɪmeɪt] *(difficulty, strength, time)* subestimar; *(person)* infravalorar; **we underestimated the size of the problem** subestimamos la magnitud del problema; **they seriously underestimated the cost of the repairs** subestimaron gravemente el costo de las reparaciones

underestimation [ʌndərestɪˈmeɪʃən] *n* infravaloración *f*

underexposed [ʌndərɪkˈspəʊzd] *adj Phot* subexpuesto(a)

underexposure [ʌndərɪkˈspəʊʒə(r)] *n Phot* subexposición *f*

underfed [ʌndəˈfed] *adj* desnutrido(a), malnutrido(a)

underfeed [ʌndəˈfiːd] (*pt & pp* **underfed** [ʌndəˈfed]) *vt* subalimentar

underfelt [ˈʌndəfelt] *n Br* = protección de fieltro colocada debajo de las moquetas

underfinanced [ʌndəˈfaɪnænst] *adj (scheme, service)* **to be u.** no tener la financiación necesaria

underfloor [ˈʌndəflɔː(r)] *adj* **u. pipes** tuberías que van bajo el suelo ▸▸ ***u. heating*** calefacción *f* por debajo del suelo

underfoot [ʌndəˈfʊt] 1 *adj* **the u. conditions are slippery** el terreno está resbaladizo

2 *adv* **it's wet u.** el suelo está mojado; **to trample sth u.** pisotear algo

underfunded [ʌndəˈfʌndɪd] *adj* infradotado(a), sin suficientes fondos

underfunding [ʌndəˈfʌndɪŋ] *n* financiación *f* insuficiente

undergarment [ˈʌndəgɑːmənt] *n Formal* prenda *f* (de ropa) interior; **she removed her undergarments** se quitó la ropa interior

undergo [ʌndəˈgəʊ] (*pt* **underwent** [ʌndəˈwent], *pp* **undergone** [ʌndəˈgɒn]) *vt* (**a**) *(experience) (change, revival)* experimentar; *(pain)* sufrir (**b**) *(test, operation)* ser sometido(a) a; *(training)* recibir; **to u. treatment** *(patient)* recibir tratamiento; **the rail network is undergoing modernization** la red ferroviaria está siendo modernizada

undergrad [ˈʌndəgræd] *n Fam* universitario(a) *m,f (sin licenciatura)*

undergraduate [ʌndəˈgrædjʊɪt] 1 *n* estudiante *mf* universitario(a) *(sin licenciatura)*; **she was an u. at Manchester** hizo la carrera en Mánchester

2 *adj (course, life, accommodation, studies)* universitario(a) ▸▸ ***u. student*** estudiante *mf* universitario(a) *(sin licenciatura)*

underground [ˈʌndəgraʊnd] 1 *n* (**a**) *Br (railway system)* metro *m*, *RP* subte *m* ▸▸ ***u. station*** estación *f* de metro *or RP* subte; ***u. train*** tren *m* del metro *or RP* subte (**b**) *(resistance movement)* resistencia *f* (clandestina) (**c**) *(avant-garde) (in literature, music, theatre)* underground *m*, vanguardia *f*

2 *adj* (**a**) *(cables, passage, car park, lake)* subterráneo(a) (**b**) *(movement, newspaper)* clandestino(a) (**c**) *(avant-garde) (literature, music, theatre)* underground *inv*, de vanguardia

3 *adv* (**a**) *(to work, live)* bajo tierra (**b**) *(in hiding)* **to go u.** pasar a la clandestinidad

undergrowth [ˈʌndəgrəʊθ] *n* maleza *f*

underhand(ed) [ʌndəˈhænd(ɪd)] *adj (behaviour, scheme, trick)* turbio(a), poco honrado(a); *(person)* poco honrado(a)

underhandedly [ʌndəˈhændɪdlɪ] *adv* poco honradamente

underinsured [ʌndərɪnˈʃɔːd] *adj* **to be u.** no tener el seguro suficiente

underinvestment [ʌndərɪnˈvestmənt] *n* inversión *f* insuficiente

underlay [ˈʌndəleɪ] *n (for carpet)* refuerzo *m (debajo de las moquetas)*

underlie [ʌndəˈlaɪ] (*pt* **underlay** [ʌndəˈleɪ], *pp* **underlain** [ʌndəˈleɪn]) *vt* subyacer bajo

underline [ʌndəˈlaɪn] *vt* (**a**) *(text, word)* subrayar (**b**) *(emphasize)* subrayar

underling [ˈʌndəlɪŋ] *n Pej* subordinado(a) *m,f*

underlining [ʌndəˈlaɪnɪŋ] *n* subrayado *m*

underlying [ʌndəˈlaɪɪŋ] *adj* subyacente ▸▸ *Econ* ***u. inflation*** inflación *f* subyaciente

undermanned [ʌndəˈmænd] *adj (factory)* sin personal suficiente, escaso(a) de personal; *(ship)* con tripulación insuficiente

undermanning [ʌndəˈmænɪŋ] *n (of factory)* insuficiencia *f* de personal

undermentioned [ˈʌndəmenʃənd] *adj Formal* abajo mencionado(a) *or* citado(a)

undermine [ʌndəˈmaɪn] *vt (authority, health, confidence)* minar, socavar

undermost [ˈʌndəməʊst] *adj (in heap)* de abajo del todo; *(in depth)* más profundo(a)

undernamed [ʌndəˈneɪmd] *Formal* 1 *adj* abajo citado(a)

2 *n* **the u.** los/las abajo citados(as)

underneath [ʌndəˈniːθ] 1 *n* parte *f* inferior *or* de abajo

2 *prep* debajo de, bajo; *(with verbs of motion)* bajo; **he crawled u. the fence** se arrastró por debajo de la valla

3 *adv* debajo; **I've got a shirt on u.** llevo una camisa debajo; *Fig* **u., he's quite shy** en el fondo es muy tímido

undernourished [ʌndəˈnʌrɪʃt] *adj* desnutrido(a)

undernourishment [ʌndəˈnʌrɪʃmənt] *n* desnutrición *f*

underpaid [ʌndəˈpeɪd] *adj* mal pagado(a)

underpants [ˈʌndəpænts] *npl* calzoncillos *mpl*, *Chile* fundillos *mpl*, *Col* pantaloncillos *mpl*, *Méx* calzones *mpl*; **a pair of u.** unos calzoncillos *or Chile* fundillos *or Col* pantaloncillos *or Méx* calzones

underparts [ˈʌndəpɑːts] *npl (of animal)* parte *f* inferior; *(of car)* bajos *mpl*

underpass [ˈʌndəpɑːs] *n (for cars, pedestrians)* paso *m* subterráneo

underpay [ʌndəˈpeɪ] *vt* pagar mal

underpayment [ʌndəˈpeɪmənt] *n* pago *m* insuficiente

underperform [ʌndəpəˈfɔːm] *vi* (**a**) *(person, team)* rendir por debajo de sus posibilidades (**b**) *(shares)* tener un bajo rendimiento

underperformance [ʌndəpəˈfɔːməns] *n* (**a**) *(of person, team)* bajo rendimiento *m* (**b**) *(of shares)* bajo rendimiento *m*

underpin [ʌndəˈpɪn] (*pt & pp* **underpinned**) *vt* (**a**) *Constr* apuntalar (**b**) *(support) (theory, policy)* sustentar

underpinning [ʌndəˈpɪnɪŋ] *n Constr* apuntalamiento *m*

underplay [ʌndəˈpleɪ] *vt* restar importancia a; **to u. the importance of sth** restar importancia a algo; IDIOM **to u. one's hand** quitarse importancia

underpopulated [ʌndəˈpɒpjʊleɪtɪd] *adj* poco poblado(a)

underprepared [ʌndəprɪˈpeəd] *adj* poco preparado(a)

underpriced [ʌndəˈpraɪst] *adj* demasiado barato(a)

underprivileged [ʌndəˈprɪvɪlɪdʒd] 1 *npl* **the u.** los (sectores) desfavorecidos

2 *adj* desfavorecido(a)

underproduction [ʌndəprəˈdʌkʃən] *n Econ* producción *f* insuficiente

underqualified [ʌndəˈkwɒlɪfaɪd] *adj* **to be u.** no estar suficientemente cualificado(a)

underquote [ʌndəˈkwəʊt] *vt (competitor)* presupuestar más barato que

underrate [ʌndəˈreɪt] *vt* subestimar, infravalorar

underrated [ʌndəˈreɪtɪd] *adj* infravalorado(a)

under-rehearsed [ʌndərɪˈhɜːst] *adj Mus & Theat (play)* poco ensayado(a); **they were u.** no habían ensayado suficiente

underrepresented [ʌndəreprəˈzentɪd] *adj* infrarrepresentado(a)

underripe [ʌndəˈraɪp], **underripened** [ʌndəˈraɪpənd] *adj* verde, poco maduro(a)

underscore [ʌndəˈskɔː(r)] *vt* (**a**) *(word, text)* subrayar (**b**) *(emphasize)* subrayar, poner de relieve

undersea 1 *adj* [ˈʌndəsiː] submarino(a)

2 *adv* [ʌndəˈsiː] bajo el mar

underseal [ˈʌndəsiːl] *n Br Aut* anticorrosivo *m*

under-secretary [ʌndəˈsekrətrɪ] *n* (**a**) *(in UK)* viceministro(a) *m,f* (**b**) *(in US)* subsecretario(a) *m,f*

undersell [ʌndəˈsel] *vt* (**a**) *(product, goods)* malvender; *(competitor)* vender más barato que; **they claimed they were never undersold** aseguraban que vendían más barato que nadie (**b**) *(be too modest about)* **to u. oneself** ser demasiado modesto(a)

undersexed [ʌndəˈsekst] *adj* con la libido baja

undersheet [ˈʌndəʃiːt] *n* cubrecolchón *m*

undershirt [ˈʌndəʃɜːt] *n US* camiseta *f*

undershoot [ʌndəˈʃuːt] *vt Av* **to u. the runway** aterrizar antes del comienzo de la pista; *Fig* **we undershot our sales target by $50,000** nos hemos quedado a 50.000 dólares de nuestro objetivo de ventas

undershorts [ˈʌndəʃɔːts] *npl US* bóxer *m*

underside [ˈʌndəsaɪd] *n* parte *f* inferior

undersigned [ʌndəˈsaɪnd] **1** *adj* abajo firmante
2 *n* **we the u.** los abajo firmantes

undersized [ʌndəˈsaɪzd] *adj* demasiado pequeño(a)

underskirt [ˈʌndəskɜːt] *n* enaguas *fpl*

undersoil [ˈʌndəsɔɪl] *n* subsuelo *m* ►► ***u. heating*** calefacción *f* subterránea

underspend [ʌndəˈspend] **1** *n Fin* superávit *m* (de gastos)
2 *vt* gastar por debajo de

understaffed [ʌndəˈstɑːft] *adj* **to be u.** no tener suficiente personal

understaffing [ʌndəˈstɑːfɪŋ] *n* escasez *f* de personal

UNDERSTAND [ʌndəˈstænd] (*pt & pp* **understood** [ʌndəˈstʊd]) **1** *vt* **(a)** *(comprehend)* entender, comprender; *(language)* entender; **they u. each other** se entienden mutuamente; **I can u. her being upset** entiendo que esté molesta; **what do you u. by this word?** ¿qué entiendes por esta palabra?; **I don't u. a thing about economics** no entiendo nada de economía **I can't u. it!** ¡no lo entiendo!; **he says his wife doesn't u. him** dice que su esposa no le entiende; **what I can't u. is why...** lo que no llego a entender es por qué...; **as I u. it, there's nothing to pay** por lo que he entendido, no hay que pagar nada; **is that understood?, do you u.?** ¿entendido?; **I tried to make myself understood** intenté hacerme entender; **do I make myself understood?** *(as threat)* ¿me explico?
(b) *(believe, assume)* entender; **I u. that...** tengo entendido que...; **are we to u. that...?** ¿quiere eso decir *or* eso quiere decir que...?, ¿debemos entender (con eso) que...?; **it was understood that few of us would survive** se entendía *or* se daba por sabido que pocos sobreviviríamos; **I understood her to mean that...** yo entendí que lo que quería decir era...; **he is understood to have left her his fortune** se entiende que le dejó a ella su fortuna; **we were given to u. that he was ill** se nos dio a entender que estaba enfermo; **as I u. it...** según yo lo entiendo,...; **so I u.** eso parece; **to give sb to u. that...** dar a entender a alguien que...
(c) *(leave implicit)* **she let it be understood that she wanted to be alone** dio a entender que quería estar sola; *Gram* **the object of the sentence is understood** el objeto *or* complemento de la oración se sobreentiende
2 *vi* entender, comprender; **if you do that once more you're out, u.?** como lo vuelvas a hacer, se acabó, ¿comprendido?; **they don't u. about these things at their age** a su edad no entienden *or* comprenden estas cosas

---

understandable [ʌndəˈstændəbəl] *adj* **(a)** *(speech, writing, theory)* comprensible; **easily u.** fácil de entender **(b)** *(natural)* lógico(a); **their u. reluctance to participate** su lógica falta de disposición a tomar parte; **they refused to help – that's u.** se negaron a ayudar – es lógico; **it's u. that they should be annoyed** es lógico que se enfadaran

understandably [ʌndəˈstændəblɪ] *adv* **(a)** *(to speak, write)* comprensiblemente **(b)** *(naturally)* **u. (enough), he was very annoyed, he was u. very annoyed** como es lógico *or* natural, estaba muy enojado

understanding [ʌndəˈstændɪŋ] **1** *n* **(a)** *(comprehension)* comprensión *f*, entendimiento *m*; **she has a good u. of electronics** entiende mucho de electrónica; **we now have a better u. of the physics of black holes** ahora entendemos mejor la física de los agujeros negros; **they have little u. of what the decision involves** apenas llegan a entender lo que implica esa decisión; **it's beyond all u.** no tiene ninguna lógica, es incomprensible
(b) *(interpretation)* interpretación *f*; **that wasn't my u. of what we agreed** no era así como yo interpretaba lo que habíamos acordado; **my u. of the matter is that he's resigned** a mi modo de ver, lo que ha hecho es dimitir
(c) *(belief)* **it is our u. that they have now left the country** tenemos entendido que han abandonado el país
(d) *(sympathy)* comprensión *f*; **we work to promote international u.** trabajamos para fomentar el entendimiento internacional
(e) *(agreement)* acuerdo *m*; **to come to** *or* **to reach an u. (about sth/with sb)** llegar a un acuerdo (sobre algo/con alguien); **to have an u. with sb** tener un acuerdo con alguien; **on the u. that...** a condición de que...
2 *adj (person, smile)* comprensivo(a)

understandingly [ʌndəˈstændɪŋlɪ] *adv* **he smiled at me u.** me sonrió comprensivo

understate [ʌndəˈsteɪt] *vt* minimizar (la importancia de); **he understated the size of the problem** minimizó la magnitud del problema; **to say she has done well would be to u. her achievement** decir que lo ha hecho bien es quedarse corto

understated [ʌndəˈsteɪtɪd] *adj (clothes, design)* discreto(a); *(performance)* sobrio(a), *Esp* comedido(a)

understatement [ʌndəˈsteɪtmənt] *n* **that's an u.!** ¡eso es quedarse corto!; **it would be an u. to call it bad** llamarlo malo es quedarse corto, malo es poco: era más que malo; **he is a master of u.** es un maestro del comedimiento en la expresión; **with typical British u., he said it wasn't bad** con la mesura típica de los británicos, dijo que no estaba mal

understocked [ʌndəˈstɒkt] *adj* **to be u.** *(shop)* tener poco stock *or* pocas existencias

understood *pt & pp of* **understand**

understudy [ˈʌndəstʌdɪ] **1** *n Theat* (actor(triz) *m,f*) suplente *mf*
2 *vt* **to u. a role** prepararse un papel para una posible sustitución; **to u. an actor** prepararse el papel de un actor para una posible sustitución

undersubscribed [ʌndəsəbˈskraɪbd] *adj* **the share issue was u.** la emisión de acciones no fue suscrita en su totalidad; **the course was heavily u.** muy poca gente se matriculó para el curso

undertake [ʌndəˈteɪk] (*pt* **undertook** [ʌndəˈtʊk], *pp* **undertaken** [ʌndəˈteɪkən]) *vt Formal* **(a)** *(project, journey)* emprender; *(experiment)* poner en marcha; **we will u. repairs on most makes of vehicle** realizamos reparaciones en vehículos de casi todas las marcas; **to u. responsibility for sth** asumir la responsabilidad de algo **(b)** *(agree, promise)* **to u. to do sth** encargarse de hacer algo

undertaker [ˈʌndəteɪkə(r)] *n* encargado(a) *m,f* de funeraria; **the u.'s** *(company)* la funeraria

undertaking [ʌndəˈteɪkɪŋ] *n* **(a)** *(enterprise)* empresa *f*, proyecto *m* **(b)** *(promise)* compromiso *m*; **she gave an u. that she wouldn't intervene** se comprometió a no intervenir; **we had their solemn u. that they would do it** se comprometieron solemnemente a realizarlo

under-the-counter [ˈʌndəðəˈkaʊntə(r)] **1** *adj* ilícito(a)
2 *adv (to sell)* bajo cuerda, de forma ilícita

underthings [ˈʌndəθɪŋz] *npl* ropa *f* interior

undertone [ˈʌndətəʊn] *n* **(a)** *(low voice)* voz *f* baja; **in an u.** en voz baja **(b)** *(hint, suggestion)* tono *m*; **the situation had distinctly comic undertones** la situación tenía unos visos claramente cómicos **(c)** *(in colour)* viso *m*

undertook *pt of* **undertake**

undertow [ˈʌndətəʊ] *n* resaca *f*

underuse 1 *n* [ʌndəˈjuːs] infrautilización *f*
2 *vt* [ʌndəˈjuːz] infrautilizar

underused [ʌndəˈjuːzd] *adj* infrautilizado(a)

underutilize [ʌndəˈjuːtɪlaɪz] *vt* infrautilizar

underutilized [ʌndəˈjuːtɪlaɪzd] *adj* infrautilizado(a)

undervalue [ʌndəˈvæljuː] *vt* **(a)** *(property, goods, currency)* infravalorar **(b)** *(person, contribution)* infravalorar, minusvalorar

underwater 1 *adj* [ˈʌndəwɔːtə(r)] submarino(a)
2 *adv* [ʌndəˈwɔːtə(r)] **to swim u.** bucear; **to film sth u.** filmar algo bajo el agua; **I can stay u. for up to three minutes** yo puedo aguantar hasta tres minutos bajo el agua

underwear [ˈʌndəweə(r)] *n* ropa *f* interior

underweight [ʌndəˈweɪt] *adj* **(a)** *(person)* **to be u.** estar muy delgado(a); **I'm five kilos u.** peso cinco kilos menos de lo que debería **(b)** *(goods)* **to be u.** pesar menos de lo indicado

underwent *pt of* **undergo**

underwhelmed [ʌndəˈwelmd] *adj Hum* **I was distinctly u. by the film** la película no me emocionó que digamos

underwhelming [ʌndəˈwelmɪŋ] *adj Hum* **it was distinctly u.** no me emocionó que digamos

underwired [ʌndəˈwaɪəd] *adj (bra)* de aros

underworld [ˈʌndəwɜːld] **1** *n* **(a)** *(in mythology)* **the U.** el Hades **(b)** *(of criminals)* **the u.** el hampa, los bajos fondos
2 *adj (boss, character)* del hampa, de los bajos fondos

underwrite [ˈʌndəraɪt] (*pt* **underwrote** [ʌndəˈrəʊt], *pp* **underwritten** [ʌndəˈrɪtən]) *vt* **(a)** *(insure)* asegurar **(b)** *(share issue)* subscribir **(c)** *(pay for) (project, scheme)* financiar

underwriter [ˈʌndəraɪtə(r)] *n* **(a)** *(in insurance)* asegurador(ora) *m,f* **(b)** *(of share issue)* subscriptor(ora) *m,f*

undeserved [ʌndɪˈzɜːvd] *adj* inmerecido(a)

undeservedly [ʌndɪˈzɜːvɪdlɪ] *adv* inmerecidamente

undeserving [ʌndɪ'zɜːvɪŋ] *adj* **to be u. of sth** no merecer algo; **he seems an u. candidate for the award** no parece un candidato merecedor del premio *or* que merezca el premio; **the u. poor** los pobres indignos de ayuda

undesirable [ʌndɪ'zaɪərəbəl] **1** *n* indeseable *mf*
2 *adj* indeseable; **it has u. side-effects** tiene efectos secundarios no deseados

undesired [ʌndɪ'zaɪəd] *adj* no deseado(a)

undetected [ʌndɪ'tektɪd] **1** *adj* no detectado(a)
2 *adv* **to go u.** no ser detectado(a); **to remain u.** seguir sin ser detectado(a)

undetermined [ʌndɪ'tɜːmɪnd] *adj* indeterminado(a); **to be u.** *(cause)* no estar determinado(a)

undeterred [ʌndɪ'tɜːd] **1** *adj* **to be u. by sth** no desanimarse por algo; **u. by the weather, he went out for a walk** salió a dar un paseo, sin importarle el mal tiempo
2 *adv* **he carried on u.** siguió sin arredrarse

undeveloped [ʌndɪ'veləpt] *adj* **(a)** *(unexploited) (resources, potential)* sin explotar; **u. land** tierra sin explotar **(b)** *(muscles, organs)* no desarrollado(a) **(c)** *Phot* sin revelar

undid *pt of* **undo**

undies ['ʌndɪz] *npl Fam* ropa *f* interior

undigested [ʌnd(a)ɪ'dʒestɪd] *adj also Fig* no digerido(a)

undignified [ʌn'dɪgnɪfaɪd] *adj* poco digno(a), indecoroso(a); **he made an u. exit from the government** salió del gobierno por la puerta de atrás

undiluted [ʌndaɪ'luːtɪd] *adj* **(a)** *(liquid)* no diluido(a) **(b)** *(pleasure, malice)* puro(a), absoluto(a); **the film was u. rubbish** la película es una absoluta porquería

undiminished [ʌndɪ'mɪnɪʃt] *adj* no disminuido(a); **to remain u.** no haber disminuido

undiplomatic [ʌndɪplə'mætɪk] *adj* poco diplomático(a)

undiscerning [ʌndɪ'sɜːnɪŋ] *adj* poco entendido(a)

undischarged [ʌndɪs'tʃɑːdʒd] *adj (bankrupt)* no rehabilitado(a); *(debt)* no saldado(a), no liquidado(a)

undisciplined [ʌn'dɪsɪplɪnd] *adj* indisciplinado(a)

undisclosed [ʌndɪs'kləʊzd] *adj* no revelado(a)

undiscovered [ʌndɪs'kʌvəd] **1** *adj* sin descubrir
2 *adv* **to go/remain u.** estar/permanecer sin descubrir

undiscriminating [ʌndɪs'krɪmɪneɪtɪŋ] *adj (person, taste)* poco entendido(a); **to be u.** no hacer distinciones, no distinguir

undisguised [ʌndɪs'gaɪzd] *adj* no disimulado(a)

undismayed [ʌndɪs'meɪd] *adj* **he seemed quite u. by his defeat** su derrota no parecía haberle desmoralizado

undisputed [ʌndɪs'pjuːtɪd] *adj (truth, fact)* indiscutible; **the u. champion** *(in general)* el campeón indiscutible; *(in boxing)* el campeón absoluto

undistinguished [ʌndɪs'tɪŋgwɪʃt] *adj* mediocre

undistributed [ʌndɪs'trɪbjʊtɪd] *adj (profits, earnings)* no distribuido(a)

undisturbed [ʌndɪs'tɜːbd] *adj* **(a)** *(uninterrupted) (sleep)* tranquilo(a); **I want to be left u. for a while** quiero que me dejen tranquilo un rato
(b) *(untroubled)* **she was u. by the news** la noticia no la preocupó; **village life has gone on here u. for centuries** la vida de este pueblo apenas ha cambiado a través de los siglos
(c) *(untouched)* **the tomb had lain u. for centuries** la tumba había permanecido intacta durante siglos; **she left his papers u.** dejó sus papeles tal como estaban

undivided [ʌndɪ'vaɪdɪd] *adj (loyalty)* completo(a); **my u. love** todo mi amor; **he gave me his u. attention** me prestó toda su atención

undo [ʌn'duː] (*pt* **undid** [ʌn'dɪd], *pp* **undone** [ʌn'dʌn]) *vt* **(a)** *(knot, bow, knitting)* deshacer; *(button, dress, buckle)* desabrochar; *(parcel, zip)* abrir; *(shoelaces)* desatar **(b)** *(mistake)* corregir; *(damage)* reparar **(c)** *(ruin)* echar a perder; **your carelessness has undone all our hard work** con tu falta de atención has echado a perder todo nuestro trabajo **(d)** *Comptr (command)* deshacer; **u. changes** *(instruction)* deshacer los cambios; **u. last** *(instruction)* deshacer el último cambio

undock [ʌn'dɒk] **1** *vt (spacecraft)* desacoplar
2 *vi (spacecraft)* desacoplarse

undoing [ʌn'duːɪŋ] *n* perdición *f*; **greed was his u.** la codicia fue su perdición

undone [ʌn'dʌn] *adj* **(a)** *(jacket, buttons)* desabrochado(a); *(shoelaces)* desatado(a); *(zip, flies)* abierto(a); **to come u.** *(jacket, buttons)* desabrocharse; *(shoelaces)* desatarse; *(zip, flies)* abrirse; *(bow, knot)* deshacerse **(b)** *(incomplete)* sin hacer; **to leave sth u.** dejar algo sin hacer

undoubted [ʌn'daʊtɪd] *adj* indudable

undoubtedly [ʌn'daʊtɪdlɪ] *adv* indudablemente

undramatic [ʌndrə'mætɪk] *adj* poco dramático(a)

undrawn [ʌn'drɔːn] *adj (curtains)* abierto(a); **they had left the curtains u.** se habían dejado las cortinas abiertas

undreamed-of [ʌn'driːmdɒv], **undreamt-of** [ʌn'dremtɒv] *adj* inimaginable

undress [ʌn'dres] **1** *n* **in a state of u.** desvestido(a), desnudo(a)
2 *vt* desvestir, desnudar
3 *vi* desvestirse, desnudarse

undressed [ʌn'drest] *adj* **(a)** *(person)* desnudo(a), desvestido(a); **to get u.** desvestirse, desnudarse **(b)** *(wound)* sin vendar **(c)** *(salad)* sin aderezar *or* aliñar

undrinkable [ʌn'drɪŋkəbəl] *adj (unpleasant-tasting)* imbebible; *(unfit for human consumption)* no potable

undue [ʌn'djuː] *adj* excesivo(a) ►► *Law* **u. *influence*** influencia *f* indebida

undulate ['ʌndjʊleɪt] *vi* ondular

undulating ['ʌndjʊleɪtɪŋ] *adj* ondulante

undulation [ʌndjʊ'leɪʃən] *n* ondulación *f*

unduly [ʌn'djuːlɪ] *adv* excesivamente; **it wasn't u. difficult** no fue excesivamente difícil

undyed [ʌn'daɪd] *adj (fabric, wool)* sin teñir

undying [ʌn'daɪɪŋ] *adj* eterno(a)

unearned [ʌn'ɜːnd] *adj* **(a)** *(reward, fame, punishment)* inmerecido(a) **(b)** *Fin* **u. *income*** rendimientos *mpl* del capital, renta *f* no salarial

unearth [ʌn'ɜːθ] *vt* **(a)** *(buried object)* desenterrar **(b)** *(information, secret)* descubrir

unearthly [ʌn'ɜːθlɪ] *adj* **(a)** *(presence, silence, beauty)* sobrenatural **(b)** *Fam (ridiculous, extreme)* **at an u. hour** a una hora intempestiva; **an u. din** *or* **racket** un ruido espantoso; **for some u. reason** por algún motivo incomprensible

unease [ʌn'iːz], **uneasiness** [ʌn'iːzɪnɪs] *n* **(a)** *(nervousness)* inquietud *f*, desasosiego *m*; **there was an air of u. in the room** se respiraba cierta inquietud *or* cierto desasosiego en la sala **(b)** *(unrest)* malestar *m*; **there was some u. at the announcement of the new appointment** el anuncio del nuevo nombramiento ha generado cierto malestar

uneasily [ʌn'iːzɪlɪ] *adv* con inquietud; **they eyed each other u. across the room** se miraron inquietos *or* incómodos cada uno desde un lado de la habitación

uneasy [ʌn'iːzɪ] *adj* **(a)** *(troubled) (person)* inquieto(a); *(conscience)* intranquilo(a); **to be u. (about sth)** estar inquieto(a) (por algo); **I was u. about leaving all the work to them** no me quedaba tranquilo dejándoles todo el trabajo; **he seemed u. with this decision** no parecía conforme con esta decisión; **I've got an u. feeling that the plan is going to go wrong** tengo la desagradable sensación de que va a salir mal el plan
(b) *(disturbed) (sleep)* agitado(a)
(c) *(embarrassed) (person, silence)* violento(a), tenso(a)
(d) *(uncertain)* **an u. peace** una paz precaria

uneatable [ʌn'iːtəbəl] *adj* **(a)** *(not edible)* incomestible **(b)** *(unpalatable)* incomible

uneaten [ʌn'iːtən] *adj* sin comer; **he left his meal u.** no probó bocado de la comida

uneconomic [ʌniːkə'nɒmɪk] *adj (unprofitable)* carente de rentabilidad, antieconómico(a)

uneconomical [ʌniːkə'nɒmɪkəl] *adj (wasteful, inefficient)* ineficaz desde el punto de vista económico, poco rentable

unedifying [ʌn'edɪfaɪɪŋ] *adj (unpleasant)* nada edificante

unedited [ʌn'edɪtɪd] *adj (text)* sin editar

uneducated [ʌn'edjʊkeɪtɪd] *adj (person)* sin estudios; *(accent, speech)* popular

unelectable [ʌnɪ'lektəbəl] *adj (party, person)* inelegible

unelected [ʌnɪ'lektɪd] *adj* no electo(a)

unemancipated [ʌnɪ'mænsɪpeɪtɪd] *adj (woman)* no emancipada; *(man, attitudes)* machista

unembarrassed [ʌnɪm'bærəst] *adj* **he was u. by the experience** la experiencia no le había resultado violenta; **she gave me an u. grin** me sonrió ampliamente sin sentirse violenta

unembellished [ʌnɪm'belɪʃt] *adj (account, story)* sin adornos

unemotional [ʌnɪ'məʊʃənəl] *adj (person)* frío(a), insensible; *(reaction)* frío(a); *(account, style)* desapasionado(a); **..., she said in her u. voice** ..., dijo sin transmitir ninguna emoción en su voz

unemotionally [ʌnɪ'məʊʃənəlɪ] *adv* fríamente; **he watched u.** miró sin transmitir ninguna emoción

unemployable [ʌnɪm'plɔɪəbəl] *adj* **to be u.** no ser apto(a) para trabajar

unemployed [ʌnɪm'plɔɪd] **1** *npl* **the u.** los desempleados, *Esp* los parados, *Am* los desocupados

2 *adj* **(a)** *(person)* desempleado(a), *Esp* parado(a), *Am* desocupado(a); **to be u.** estar desempleado(a) *or Esp* en (el) paro *or Am* desocupado(a) **(b)** *(resources)* sin utilizar, sin emplear

unemployment [ʌnɪm'plɔɪmənt] *n* desempleo *m*, *Esp* paro *m*, *Am* desocupación *f*; **u. stands at 10 percent** la tasa de desempleo *or Esp* de paro *or Am* la desocupación se sitúa en el 10 por ciento ►► ***u. benefit*** subsidio *m* de desempleo *or Am* de desocupación; *US* ***u. compensation*** subsidio *m* de desempleo *or Am* de desocupación; *US* ***u. insurance*** seguro *m* de desempleo *or Am* de desocupación

unencumbered [ʌnɪn'kʌmbəd] *adj* **he was u. by children or a mortgage** no tenía hijos ni una hipoteca que lo atase

unending [ʌn'endɪŋ] *adj* interminable

unendurable [ʌnɪn'djʊərəbəl] *adj* insoportable

unenforceable [ʌnɪn'fɔːsəbəl] *adj (rule, law)* imposible de hacer cumplir

un-English [ʌn'ɪŋglɪʃ] *adj* poco inglés(esa)

unenjoyable [ʌnɪn'dʒɔɪəbəl] *adj* poco agradable

unenlightened [ʌnɪn'laɪtənd] *adj* **(a)** *(backward) (person, decision)* retrógrado(a) **(b)** *(unclear)* **I remained completely u. by her explanation** su explicación no me aclaró nada

unenlightening [ʌnɪn'laɪtnɪŋ] *adj* poco ilustrativo(a)

unenterprising [ʌn'entəpraɪzɪŋ] *adj (person, approach)* poco emprendedor(ora); *(measure)* poco ambicioso(a); *(player, team)* conservador(ora)

unenthusiastic [ʌnɪnθjuːzɪ'æstɪk] *adj (reaction, response)* tibio(a), poco entusiasta; *(person)* poco entusiasmado(a) (**about** por)

unenthusiastically [ʌnɪnθjuːzɪ'æstɪklɪ] *adv* sin entusiasmo

unenviable [ʌn'envɪəbəl] *adj* desagradable, nada envidiable

unequal [ʌn'iːkwəl] *adj* **(a)** *(uneven) (amounts, sizes, contest)* desigual; **an u. struggle** una lucha desigual **(b)** *(incapable)* **he was u. to the challenge** no estuvo a la altura de lo exigido

unequalled, *US* **unequaled** [ʌn'iːkwəld] *adj* sin par

unequally [ʌn'iːkwəlɪ] *adv (to divide, share out)* desigualmente; **to be u. matched** no estar de igual a igual, tener niveles muy distintos

unequivocal [ʌnɪ'kwɪvəkəl] *adj Formal* inequívoco(a); **she was completely u.** no dejó lugar a dudas

unequivocally [ʌnɪ'kwɪvəklɪ] *adv Formal* inequívocamente, de modo inequívoco

unerring [ʌn'ɜːrɪŋ] *adj (aim, accuracy, judgement)* infalible

UNESCO [juː'neskəʊ] *n* (*abbr* **United Nations Educational, Scientific and Cultural Organization**) UNESCO *f*

unessential [ʌnɪ'senʃəl] *adj* prescindible, no esencial

unethical [ʌn'eθɪkəl] *adj* poco ético(a)

unethically [ʌn'eθɪklɪ] *adv* de forma poco ética

uneven [ʌn'iːvən] *adj* **(a)** *(not level) (surface, road, teeth)* irregular; **the floorboards are u.** los tablones del suelo están desnivelados **(b)** *(not regular) (breathing, pulse)* irregular **(c)** *(not consistent) (performance, quality)* irregular **(d)** *(unequal) (distribution, contest)* desigual

unevenly [ʌn'iːvənlɪ] *adv* **(a)** *(not level)* de forma irregular **(b)** *(irregularly) (to breathe, beat)* irregularmente, de forma irregular **(c)** *(inconsistently) (to perform)* de forma irregular **(d)** *(unequally) (divided, spread)* de forma desigual; **to be u. matched** no estar de igual a igual, tener niveles muy distintos

unevenness [ʌn'iːvənnɪs] *n* **(a)** *(of surface, road, ground)* irregularidad *f* **(b)** *(of breathing, pulse)* irregularidad *f* **(c)** *(of performance, quality)* irregularidad *f* **(d)** *(of distribution, contest)* desigualdad *f*

uneventful [ʌnɪ'ventfʊl] *adj (without unfortunate incidents)* sin incidentes; *(without unusual incidents)* sin acontecimientos de interés; **she led an u. life** hubo pocos acontecimientos de interés en su vida

uneventfully [ʌnɪ'ventfʊlɪ] *adv* **the week went by u.** *(without unfortunate incidents)* la semana transcurrió sin incidentes; *(without unusual incidents)* la semana transcurrió sin que ocurriera nada de interés

unexceptionable [ʌnɪk'sepʃənəbəl] *adj* irreprochable

unexceptional [ʌnɪk'sepʃənəl] *adj* mediocre; **to be u.** no tener nada de especial

unexcited [ʌnɪk'saɪtɪd] *adj* no muy animado(a) (**about** con)

unexciting [ʌnɪk'saɪtɪŋ] *adj* anodino(a), insulso(a)

unexpected [ʌnɪks'pektɪd] **1** *adj* inesperado(a); **this is all so u.!** ¡esto sí que no me lo esperaba!

2 *n* **the u.** lo inesperado

unexpectedly [ʌnɪks'pektɪdlɪ] *adv* inesperadamente, de forma inesperada; **her parents arrived u.** sus padres se presentaron de improviso; **an u. high number of...** un número sorprendentemente elevado de...

unexplained [ʌnɪks'pleɪnd] *adj* inexplicado(a); **the reason for their decision remains u.** se desconocen aún las causas de su decisión; **we cannot allow mistakes like this to go u.** no podemos permitir que no se den explicaciones a errores como éste

unexploded [ʌnɪk'spləʊdɪd] *adj* sin explotar, sin estallar

unexploited [ʌnɪks'plɔɪtɪd] *adj* sin explotar

unexplored [ʌnɪks'plɔːd] *adj* **(a)** *(place)* inexplorado(a) **(b)** *(solution, possibility)* sin investigar

unexposed [ʌnɪks'pəʊzd] *adj (film)* virgen

unexpressed [ʌnɪk'sprest] *adj* tácito(a)

unexpurgated [ʌn'ekspəgeɪtɪd] *adj* sin expurgar

unfailing [ʌn'feɪlɪŋ] *adj (hope, courage)* firme, inconmovible; *(punctuality)* infalible; *(patience, good humour, supply)* inagotable; *(loyalty, support)* inquebrantable

unfailingly [ʌn'feɪlɪŋlɪ] *adv* indefectiblemente

unfair [ʌn'feə(r)] *adj* injusto(a); **it was u. of them to do that** fue una injusticia que hicieran eso; **it's so u.!** ¡no es justo!; **it's u. on us** para nosotros es injusto; **to be u. to sb** ser injusto(a) con alguien; **he has been put at an u. disadvantage** lo han puesto en una situación injusta de desventaja ►► *Com* ***u. competition*** competencia *f* desleal; *Ind* ***u. dismissal*** despido *m* improcedente *(que viola los derechos de los trabajadores)*

unfairly [ʌn'feəlɪ] *adv* injustamente; *Com* **they were accused of competing u.** los acusaron de competencia desleal; *Ind* **to be u. dismissed** ser despedido(a) injustamente *or* de forma improcedente

unfairness [ʌn'feənɪs] *n* injusticia *f*

unfaithful [ʌn'feɪθfʊl] *adj (spouse)* infiel; **to be u. (to sb)** ser infiel (a alguien)

unfaithfulness [ʌn'feɪθfʊlnɪs] *n* infidelidad *f*

unfaltering [ʌn'fɔːltərɪŋ] *adj (speech, steps, gaze)* decidido(a); *(support, optimism)* inquebrantable; **she was u. in her support of the reform** dio su apoyo inquebrantable a la reforma

unfalteringly [ʌn'fɔːltərɪŋlɪ] *adv (to speak, walk, gaze)* con decisión; *(to support)* sin fisuras; **she is u. optimistic** es de un optimismo inquebrantable

unfamiliar [ʌnfə'mɪlɪə(r)] *adj* **(a)** *(face, person, surroundings)* extraño(a), desconocido(a) **(b)** *(unacquainted)* **to be u. with sth** no estar familiarizado(a) con algo; **I'm u. with that theory** desconozco esa teoría

unfamiliarity [ʌnfəmɪlɪ'ærɪtɪ] *n* **(a)** *(strangeness)* **the u. of their surroundings** lo desconocido del entorno **(b)** *(lack of knowledge)* desconocimiento *m* (**with** de), falta *f* de familiarización (**with** con)

unfancied [ʌn'fænsɪd] *adj (player, team, racehorse)* no favorito(a)

unfashionable [ʌn'fæʃənəbəl] *adj* **(a)** *(clothes, ideas)* pasado(a) de moda; **to be u.** no estar de moda; **to become u.** pasar de moda **(b)** *(area, restaurant, writer)* **to be u.** no estar de moda

unfashionably [ʌn'fæʃənəblɪ] *adv* **to dress u.** llevar ropa que no está de moda; **he has u. liberal attitudes** su actitud liberal no se lleva hoy en día

unfasten [ʌn'fɑːsən] *vt (dress, button, buckle)* desabrochar; *(knot)* desatar, deshacer; *(door)* abrir; **to u. one's belt** desabrocharse el cinturón

unfathomable [ʌn'fæðəməbəl] *adj* **(a)** *(depths)* insondable **(b)** *(inexplicable)* **why he did it is quite u.** por qué lo hizo es algo totalmente inexplicable

unfathomed [ʌn'fæðəmd] *adj (mystery)* sin resolver

unfavourable, *US* **unfavorable** [ʌn'feɪvərəbəl] *adj* **(a)** *(weather, conditions)* desfavorable, poco favorable; **the conditions were u. for sailing** las condiciones eran desfavorables *or* no eran favorables para la navegación

(b) *(review, reaction)* desfavorable, poco favorable; **the week's events have shown the minister in a very u. light** los sucesos de esta semana han sido muy desfavorables para la imagen del ministro

unfavourably, *US* **unfavorably** [ʌn'feɪvərəblɪ] *adv* desfavorablemente; **the play was received u.** la obra tuvo una acogida negativa; **they reacted u. to my suggestion** reaccionaron negativamente a mi propuesta; **this novel compares u. with her previous one** su última novela sale perdiendo en comparación con la anterior

unfazed [ʌn'feɪzd] *adj Fam* **he was u. by the experience** la experiencia no le afectó lo más mínimo

unfeasible [ʌn'fi:zɪbəl] *adj (plan, suggestion)* inviable

unfeeling [ʌn'fi:lɪŋ] *adj (person)* insensible; *(remark, attitude)* falto(a) de sensibilidad

unfeigned [ʌn'feɪnd] *adj* no fingido(a), real

unfeminine [ʌn'femɪnɪn] *adj* poco femenino(a)

unfermented [ʌnfə'mentɪd] *adj* sin fermentar

unfertilized [ʌn'fɜ:tɪlaɪzd] *adj (egg)* no fertilizado(a)

unfettered [ʌn'fetəd] *adj (person)* desembarazado(a) (**by** de); *(imagination)* desbocado(a)

unfinished [ʌn'fɪnɪʃt] *adj* (**a**) *(incomplete)* inacabado(a); **to leave sth u.** dejar algo sin terminar; **u. business** asunto(s) pendiente(s); **the U. Symphony** la Sinfonía Inacabada (**b**) *(rough) (furniture, wood)* sin pulir

unfit [ʌn'fɪt] *adj* (**a**) *(unsuitable)* inadecuado(a), inapropiado(a); **he's an u. person to be left in charge of children** es una persona a la que no se puede confiar el cuidado de un niño; **she is u. to hold such an important position** no es la persona apropiada para ostentar un cargo de tanta importancia; **to be u. for sth** no ser apto(a) para algo; **u. for human consumption** no apto(a) para el consumo humano; **this house is u. for habitation** esta casa no reúne las condiciones de habitación necesarias

(**b**) *(in poor physical condition)* bajo(a) de forma; *(injured)* lesionado(a); **three of our players have been declared u.** tres de nuestros jugadores no han pasado el examen físico

unfitness [ʌn'fɪtnɪs] *n (unsuitability)* **u. for public office** no apto(a) para un cargo público

unfitted [ʌn'fɪtɪd] *adj (unsuitable)* **to be u. for sth/to do sth** no reunir las condiciones para algo/para hacer algo

unfitting [ʌn'fɪtɪŋ] *adj (remarks, behaviour)* inapropiado(a)

unflagging [ʌn'flægɪŋ] *adj (enthusiasm, support)* infatigable; *(interest)* inagotable

unflappable [ʌn'flæpəbəl] *adj* impasible, imperturbable

unflattering [ʌn'flætərɪŋ] *adj (clothes)* poco favorecedor(ora); *(description, remark)* poco halagüeño(a); **the programme shows him in an u. light** el programa da una imagen poco favorecedora de él

unflatteringly [ʌn'flætərɪŋlɪ] *adv (to dress)* de forma poco favorecedora; *(to portray, speak)* en términos poco halagüeños; **she was u. dressed in baggy trousers** llevaba unos pantalones amplios que no la favorecían

unfledged [ʌn'fledʒd] *adj* (**a**) *(bird)* sin plumas (**b**) *(person)* novato(a), bisoño(a)

unflinching [ʌn'flɪntʃɪŋ] *adj (resolve, courage)* a toda prueba; *(loyalty, support)* inquebrantable; **he was u. in his support of the prime minister** dio su apoyo inquebrantable al primer ministro

unflinchingly [ʌn'flɪntʃɪŋlɪ] *adv (to support)* sin reservas; **she took the injection u.** recibió la inyección sin inmutarse

unflustered [ʌn'flʌstəd] *adj* imperturbable

unfocus(s)ed [ʌn'fəʊkəst] *adj* (**a**) *(discussion, project, person)* descentrado(a) (**b**) *(eyes, gaze)* perdido(a)

unfold [ʌn'fəʊld] **1** *vt* (**a**) *(newspaper, map)* desdoblar (**b**) *(wings)* desplegar; **she unfolded her arms** descruzó los brazos (**c**) *(story, proposal)* revelar

2 *vi* (**a**) *(wings)* desplegarse (**b**) *(story, events)* desarrollarse; **a spectacular view unfolded before us** ante nosotros se abría un paisaje espectacular

unforced [ʌn'fɔ:st] *adj (natural)* espontáneo(a) ▸▸ *Sport* ***u. error*** error *m* no forzado

unforeseeable [ʌnfə'si:əbəl] *adj* imprevisible

unforeseen [ʌnfɔ:'si:n] *adj* imprevisto(a)

unforgettable [ʌnfə'getəbəl] *adj* inolvidable

unforgettably [ʌnfə'getəblɪ] *adv* inolvidablemente; **an u. moving experience** una experiencia conmovedora difícil de olvidar

unforgivable [ʌnfə'gɪvəbəl] *adj* imperdonable

unforgivably [ʌnfə'gɪvəblɪ] *adv* imperdonablemente; **an u. stupid mistake** un error estúpido e imperdonable

unforgiving [ʌnfə'gɪvɪŋ] *adj* implacable

unformatted [ʌn'fɔ:mætɪd] *adj (disk)* sin formatear

unformed [ʌn'fɔ:md] *adj* (**a**) *(idea, plan)* sin formar (**b**) *(limb)* sin formar

unforthcoming [ʌnfɔ:θ'kʌmɪŋ] *adj (person)* reservado(a); **to be u. with information/assistance** ser reacio(a) a dar información/prestar ayuda; **to be u. about sth** no dar muchos detalles sobre algo

unfortunate [ʌn'fɔ:tʃənət] **1** *n* desdichado(a) *m,f*

2 *adj* (**a**) *(unlucky) (person, mistake)* desafortunado(a); *(accident, event)* desgraciado(a); **he's been extremely u.** ha tenido muy mala fortuna; **she was u. enough to be caught in the storm** tuvo la mala fortuna de que la pillara la tormenta

(**b**) *(regrettable)* **it is u. that things turned out this way** es una lástima que las cosas hayan salido así; **how u.!** ¡qué lástima!

(**c**) *(inappropriate) (choice, remark)* desafortunado(a); *(moment)* poco oportuno(a); **he has an u. turn of phrase** se expresa de una forma poco afortunada

unfortunately [ʌn'fɔ:tʃənətlɪ] *adv* (**a**) *(regrettably)* desgraciadamente, por desgracia; **u. not** desgraciadamente, no (**b**) *(unluckily)* desafortunadamente; **u. for him** por desgracia para él (**c**) *(inappropriately) (worded, phrased)* de forma poco afortunada

unfounded [ʌn'faʊndɪd] *adj* infundado(a)

unframed [ʌn'freɪmd] *adj* sin marco

unfreeze [ʌn'fri:z] **1** *vt* (**a**) *(defrost)* descongelar (**b**) *Fin (prices, wages)* descongelar

2 *vi* descongelarse

unfrequented [ʌnfrɪ'kwentɪd] *adj* poco frecuentado(a)

unfriendliness [ʌn'frendlɪnɪs] *n (of person)* antipatía *f*; *(of reception, tone, voice)* hostilidad *f*

unfriendly [ʌn'frendlɪ] *adj (person)* arisco(a), antipático(a); *(reception, tone, voice)* hostil; **to be u. to** *or* **towards sb** ser antipático(a) con alguien

unfrock [ʌn'frɒk] *vt (priest)* expulsar del sacerdocio

unfruitful [ʌn'fru:tfʊl] *adj (efforts, search)* infructuoso(a)

unfulfilled [ʌnfʊl'fɪld] *adj (promise)* incumplido(a); *(desire, ambition)* insatisfecho(a); *(potential)* desaprovechado(a); **to feel u.** sentirse insatisfecho(a)

unfunny [ʌn'fʌnɪ] *adj* **to be u.** no tener ninguna gracia

unfurl [ʌn'fɜ:l] **1** *vt (flag, sails)* desplegar

2 *vi* desplegarse

unfurnished [ʌn'fɜ:nɪʃt] *adj* sin amueblar ▸▸ ***u. accommodation*** vivienda *f* sin amueblar

unfussy [ʌn'fʌsɪ] *adj* sencillo(a)

ungainly [ʌn'geɪnlɪ] *adj* desgarbado(a)

ungallant [ʌn'gælənt] *adj (person, behaviour)* poco galante

ungenerous [ʌn'dʒenərəs] *adj* (**a**) *(allowance, person)* mezquino(a); **the offer was not u.** era una oferta nada desdeñable (**b**) *(criticism, remark)* mezquino(a)

ungentlemanly [ʌn'dʒentəlmənlɪ] *adj (attitude, conduct, remark)* poco caballeroso(a)

unget-at-able [ʌnget'ætəbəl] *adj Fam (place, person)* inaccesible

unglamorous [ʌn'glæmərəs] *adj* (**a**) *(unalluring) (person, clothes)* poco atractivo(a) (**b**) *(unexciting) (lifestyle, career, place)* poco glamoroso(a)

unglazed [ʌn'gleɪzd] *adj* (**a**) *(window)* sin *Esp* cristal *or Am* vidrio (**b**) *(paper, print)* mate (**c**) *(porcelain, brick)* sin vidriar

ungloved [ʌn'glʌvd] *adj* sin guantes

ungodly [ʌn'gɒdlɪ] *adj* (**a**) *(immoral)* impío(a) (**b**) *(noise)* infernal; *Hum* **at an u. hour** a una hora intempestiva

ungovernable [ʌn'gʌvənəbəl] *adj* (**a**) *(people, country)* ingobernable (**b**) *(feelings)* incontrolable

ungracious [ʌn'greɪʃəs] *adj (impolite)* descortés; *(unwilling)* displicente; **it would be u. not to go** sería una descortesía no ir; **I was surprised by his u. acceptance of the trophy** me sorprendió el que aceptara el trofeo tan de mala gana

ungraciously [ʌn'greɪʃəslɪ] *adv (impolitely)* descortésmente; *(unwillingly)* con displicencia, de mala gana

ungrammatical [ʌngrə'mætɪkəl] *adj (sentence, construction)* incorrecto(a) (gramaticalmente)

ungrateful [ʌn'greɪtfʊl] *adj (person)* desagradecido(a); **to be u. to sb** ser desagradecido(a) con alguien

ungratefully [ʌn'greɪtfʊlɪ] *adv* con desagradecimiento

ungrudging [ʌn'grʌdʒɪŋ] *adj* sincero(a); **to be u. in one's praise/support** no escatimar elogios/apoyo

ungrudgingly [ʌn'grʌdʒɪŋlɪ] *adv* con franqueza, abiertamente

unguarded [ʌn'gɑːdɪd] *adj* (**a**) *(place)* desprotegido(a); *(prisoner)* no vigilado(a) (**b**) *(fire)* desatendido(a); *(machinery, mechanism)* sin protección (de seguridad) (**c**) *(remark)* imprudente; **in an u. moment** en un momento de despiste

ungulate ['ʌŋgjʊleɪt] 1 *adj* ungulado(a)
2 *n* ungulado *m*

unhallowed [ʌn'hæləʊd] *adj Rel (ground)* no consagrado(a)

unhampered [ʌn'hæmpəd] *adj (movement)* libre, sin trabas; **the press is u. by censorship** la prensa no tiene las trabas de la censura

unhand [ʌn'hænd] *vt Literary* soltar; **u. me, sir!** ¡suélteme, señor!

unhappily [ʌn'hæpɪlɪ] *adv* (**a**) *(sadly)* tristemente; **they're u. married** su matrimonio tiene problemas (**b**) *(unfortunately)* por desgracia

unhappiness [ʌn'hæpɪnɪs] *n* (**a**) *(sadness)* infelicidad *f*, desdicha *f*; **her departure caused me great u.** su partida me causó gran tristeza (**b**) *(dissatisfaction)* descontento *m*

unhappy [ʌn'hæpɪ] *adj* (**a**) *(sad) (person, childhood)* infeliz, desdichado(a); *(day, ending, face)* triste; **after years in an u. marriage** tras años de infelicidad en su matrimonio; **I've been very u. recently** lo he pasado muy mal últimamente; **it makes me so u.** me pone tan triste, me da tanta pena; **a deeply u. childhood** una niñez muy desdichada
(**b**) *(worried)* **I'm u. about leaving the child alone** me preocupa dejar al niño solo
(**c**) *(not pleased, not satisfied)* **to be u. about** *or* **with sth** estar descontento(a) *or* no estar contento(a) con algo; **she was u. about me spending so much money** no le gustaba que yo gastara tanto dinero
(**d**) *(unfortunate) (choice, remark)* desafortunado(a), poco atinado(a); **an u. turn of phrase** una frase poco afortunada; **it's a most u. state of affairs** es una situación lamentable

unharmed [ʌn'hɑːmd] *adj (person)* indemne, ileso(a); *(object)* intacto(a); **to escape u.** escapar ileso(a)

unharness [ʌn'hɑːnɪs] *vt (remove harness from)* quitar los arneses a; *(unhitch)* desenganchar

unhatched [ʌn'hætʃt] *adj (egg)* sin eclosionar

UNHCR [juːeneɪtʃsiː'ɑː(r)] *n* (*abbr* **United Nations High Commission for Refugees**) ACNUR *m*

unhealthily [ʌn'helθɪlɪ] *adv* de forma poco saludable; **to be u. thin/pale** ser de una delgadez/palidez enfermiza

unhealthiness [ʌn'helθɪnɪs] *n* (**a**) *(of person)* mala salud *f*; *(of complexion)* aspecto *m* enfermizo (**b**) *(conditions, climate)* insalubridad *f*; **because of the u. of their diet/lifestyle** por tener una dieta/un estilo de vida tan poco saludable *or* sano (**c**) *(unwholesome nature) (of curiosity, interest)* naturaleza *f* malsana *or* enfermiza; *(of influence, relationship)* naturaleza *f* malsana, nocividad *f*

unhealthy [ʌn'helθɪ] *adj* (**a**) *(ill) (person, appearance)* enfermizo(a); **to have an u. complexion** tener un cutis de aspecto enfermizo
(**b**) *(diet, lifestyle)* poco saludable, poco sano(a); *(conditions, surroundings, climate)* insalubre; **it's u. to stay indoors all day** no es sano estar encerrado en casa todo el día
(**c**) *(unwholesome) (curiosity, interest)* malsano(a), enfermizo(a); *(influence, relationship)* malsano(a), nocivo(a)

unheard [ʌn'hɜːd] *adj* (**a**) *(not heard)* **a previously u. recording** una grabación nunca escuchada antes (**b**) *(not heeded)* **his cries for help went u.** nadie escuchó sus gritos de socorro; **the opinions of the immigrant population go u.** no se escuchan las opiniones de la población inmigrante

unheard-of [ʌn'hɜːdɒv] *adj* (**a**) *(unknown)* desconocido(a); **several previously u. painters** varios pintores hasta ahora desconocidos; **foreign holidays were u. in my youth** ir de vacaciones al extranjero era impensable cuando yo era joven (**b**) *(unprecedented)* insólito(a), inaudito(a); **such an occurrence is quite u.** un hecho como éste es totalmente insólito *or* inaudito

unheated [ʌn'hiːtɪd] *adj (food)* sin calentar; *(room, house)* sin calefacción

unheeded [ʌn'hiːdɪd] *adj* desoído(a), desatendido(a); **to go u.** ser desoído(a), caer en saco roto

unhelpful [ʌn'helpfʊl] *adj* (**a**) *(unwilling to help)* **I find the staff very u.** el personal me parece muy poco dispuesto a ayudar (**b**) *(of little use)* **to be u.** *(person)* no ayudar mucho; *(criticism, advice, map)* no servir de mucho

unhelpfully [ʌn'helpfʊlɪ] *adv* **"I haven't got a clue," he said u.** "no tengo ni idea", dijo poco dispuesto a ayudar; **u., no date is given** no aparece ninguna fecha, lo cual no ayuda mucho

unheralded [ʌn'herəldɪd] *adj (unannounced)* no anunciado(a); *(unexpected)* inesperado(a)

unheroic [ʌnhɪ'rəʊɪk] *adj (person, behaviour)* poco heroico(a)

unhesitating [ʌn'hezɪteɪtɪŋ] *adj (support)* decidido(a); *(reply)* inmediato(a); *(belief)* firme, inquebrantable

unhesitatingly [ʌn'hezɪteɪtɪŋlɪ] *adv* con decisión, decididamente

unhindered [ʌn'hɪndəd] *adj* **to work u.** trabajar sin estorbos; **to travel u. by heavy luggage** viajar sin el estorbo que supone un equipaje pesado

unhinged [ʌn'hɪndʒd] *adj (mad)* trastornado(a)

unhip [ʌn'hɪp] *adj Fam Esp* nada enrollado(a), *Méx* nada suave, *RP* nada copado(a), *Ven* aguado(a)

unhitch [ʌn'hɪtʃ] *vt (unfasten)* desenganchar

unholy [ʌn'həʊlɪ] *adj* (**a**) *(evil)* profano(a); *(words)* blasfemo(a); *(thoughts)* impuro(a) ▸▸ ***u. alliance*** alianza *f* contra natura (**b**) *Fam* **an u. mess/noise** un desorden/ruido espantoso

unhook [ʌn'hʊk] *vt* (**a**) *(trailer)* desenganchar; *(window)* abrir (**b**) *(garment)* desabrochar

unhoped-for [ʌn'həʊptfɔː(r)] *adj* inesperado(a)

unhorse [ʌn'hɔːs] *vt* derribar

UNHRC [juːeneɪtʃɑː'siː] *n* (*abbr* **United Nations Human Rights Commission**) UNHRC *f*

unhurried [ʌn'hʌrɪd] *adj (person, manner)* pausado(a)

unhurt [ʌn'hɜːt] *adj* ileso(a); **to be u.** *(after accident)* salir ileso; **to escape u.** escapar ileso(a)

unhygienic [ʌnhaɪ'dʒiːnɪk] *adj* antihigiénico(a)

unhyphenated [ʌn'haɪfəneɪtɪd] *adj* sin guión

uni ['juːnɪ] *n Br Fam* uni *f*

unicameral [juːnɪ'kæmərəl] *adj* unicameral

UNICEF ['juːnɪsef] *n* (*abbr* **United Nations International Children's Emergency Fund**) UNICEF *m or f*

unicellular [juːnɪ'seljʊlə(r)] *adj Biol* unicelular

unicorn ['juːnɪkɔːn] *n* unicornio *m*

unicycle ['juːnɪsaɪkəl] *n* monociclo *m*

unidentifiable [ʌnaɪdentɪ'faɪəbəl] *adj* imposible de identificar

unidentified [ʌnaɪ'dentɪfaɪd] *adj* no identificado(a) ▸▸ ***u. flying object*** objeto *m* volador no identificado

unidirectional [juːnɪdɪ'rekʃənəl] *adj* unidireccional

unification [juːnɪfɪ'keɪʃən] *n* unificación *f* ▸▸ ***U. Church*** Iglesia *f* de la Unificación

uniform ['juːnɪfɔːm] 1 *n* uniforme *m*; **to be in u.** ir de uniforme; **in school u.** con el uniforme escolar; **to wear u.** llevar uniforme
2 *adj (colour, size)* uniforme; *(temperature)* constante

uniformed ['juːnɪfɔːmd] *adj* uniformado(a)

uniformity [juːnɪ'fɔːmɪtɪ] *n* uniformidad *f*

uniformly ['juːnɪfɔːmlɪ] *adv* uniformemente

unify ['juːnɪfaɪ] 1 *vt* unificar
2 *vi* unificarse

unilateral [juːnɪ'lætərəl] *adj* unilateral ▸▸ ***u. disarmament*** desarme *m* unilateral

unilateralism [juːnɪ'lætərəlɪzəm] *n* política *f* de desarme unilateral

unilaterally [juːnɪ'lætərəlɪ] *adv* unilateralmente

unimaginable [ʌnɪ'mædʒɪnəbəl] *adj* inimaginable

unimaginative [ʌnɪ'mædʒɪnətɪv] *adj* **to be u.** *(person)* tener poca imaginación, ser poco imaginativo(a); *(book, meal, choice)* ser muy poco original, ser poco imaginativo(a)

unimaginatively [ʌnɪ'mædʒɪnətɪvlɪ] *adv* con poca imaginación, poco imaginativamente

unimpaired [ʌnɪm'peəd] *adj* **his health was u.** se conservaba en perfecta salud; **her eyesight/faculties remained u.** no había perdido vista/facultades

unimpeachable [ʌnɪm'piːtʃəbəl] *adj (character, reputation)* irreprochable; *(source)* fidedigno(a); *(evidence)* fehaciente

unimpeded [ʌnɪm'piːdɪd] *adj* libre, sin trabas

unimportant [ʌnɪm'pɔːtənt] *adj* poco importante; **to be u.** no importar

unimpressed [ʌnɪm'prest] *adj* **to be u. by sth** no quedar convencido(a) con algo

unimpressive [ʌnɪm'presɪv] *adj (performance)* mediocre; *(person)* insignificante; **their record is u.** su trayectoria es más bien mediocre

unimproved [ʌnɪm'pruːvd] *adj* (**a**) *(condition)* **to be u.** no haber mejorado (**b**) *(land)* agreste

uninflected [ʌnɪn'flektɪd] *adj Gram* no flexivo(a)

uninformative [ʌnɪn'fɔːmətɪv] *adj (book, leaflet, bulletin)* poco informativo(a); **he was most u.** me dio muy poca información

uninformed [ʌnɪnˈfɔːmd] *adj (person)* desinformado(a); **to be u. about sth** no estar informado(a) de algo; **contrary to u. opinion** en contra de lo que opinan los poco informados

uninhabitable [ʌnɪnˈhæbɪtəbəl] *adj* inhabitable

uninhabited [ʌnɪnˈhæbɪtɪd] *adj* desierto(a)

uninhibited [ʌnɪnˈhɪbɪtɪd] *adj (person, behaviour, reaction, laughter)* desinhibido(a)

uninitialized [ʌnɪˈnɪʃəlaɪzd] *adj (disk)* sin inicializar

uninitiated [ʌnɪˈnɪʃɪeɪtɪd] **1** *npl* **to the u.** para los profanos (en la materia)

2 *adj* no iniciado(a), profano(a)

uninjured [ʌnˈɪndʒəd] *adj (person)* ileso(a); **miraculously she was u.** salió milagrosamente ilesa

uninspired [ʌnɪnˈspaɪəd] *adj* poco inspirado(a)

uninspiring [ʌnɪnˈspaɪərɪŋ] *adj* anodino(a), mediocre

uninstall [ʌnɪnˈstɑːl] *vt Comptr* desinstalar

uninsured [ʌnɪnˈʃʊəd] *adj* no asegurado(a) (**against** contra)

unintelligent [ʌnɪnˈtelɪdʒənt] *adj* poco inteligente; **he's not an u. lad** no le falta inteligencia al chico

unintelligible [ʌnɪnˈtelɪdʒɪbəl] *adj* ininteligible

unintelligibly [ʌnɪnˈtelɪdʒɪblɪ] *adv* ininteligiblemente

unintended [ʌnɪnˈtendɪd] *adj* no deseado(a)

unintentional [ʌnɪnˈtenʃənəl] *adj* no intencionado(a); **any implied criticism was u.** no fue nuestra intención insinuar una crítica

unintentionally [ʌnɪnˈtenʃənəlɪ] *adv* sin querer; **the scene is u. comic** la escena resulta cómica sin pretenderlo

uninterested [ʌnˈɪntrestɪd] *adj* poco interesado(a); **to be u. in sth/sb** no estar interesado(a) en algo/alguien; **he was completely u.** no le interesaba en absoluto

uninteresting [ʌnˈɪntrestɪŋ] *adj (subject, book, person)* falto(a) de interés, sin interés

uninterrupted [ʌnɪntəˈrʌptɪd] *adj* ininterrumpido(a); **their affair continued u. for several years** su aventura continuó varios años sin interrupción; **to work u.** trabajar sin interrupciones *or* sin ser interrumpido(a)

uninterruptible [ʌnɪntəˈrʌptəbəl] *adj Comptr* ***u. power supply*** sistema *m* de alimentación ininterrumpida

uninvited [ʌnɪnˈvaɪtɪd] **1** *adj (comment, advice)* no solicitado(a); **there were a few u. guests** algunos de los presentes no habían sido invitados

2 *adv* **to arrive u.** llegar sin haber sido invitado(a)

uninviting [ʌnɪnˈvaɪtɪŋ] *adj (place)* inhóspito(a); *(food)* nada apetitoso(a); *(prospect)* desagradable

union [ˈjuːnjən] *n* (**a**) *(of countries)* unión *f*; **the U.** *(in US)* los estados de la Unión; *Formerly* **the U. of South Africa** la Unión de Sudáfrica ►► ***U. flag, U. Jack*** bandera *f* del Reino Unido

(**b**) *(marriage)* enlace *m*

(**c**) *Ind* sindicato *m*; **unions and management** los sindicatos y la patronal ►► ***u. card*** carnet *m* de sindicato; ***u. official*** sindicalista *mf*, dirigente *mf* sindical; ***u. shop*** = empresa o fábrica en que la afiliación sindical es obligatoria

(**d**) *(at university)* **(students') u.** sindicato *m* de estudiantes

unionism [ˈjuːnjənɪzəm] *n* (**a**) *(trade unionism)* sindicalismo *m* (**b**) *(in Northern Ireland)* unionismo *m*

unionist [ˈjuːnjənɪst] *n* (**a**) *(trade unionist)* sindicalista *mf* (**b**) *(in Northern Ireland)* unionista *mf*

unionize [ˈjuːnjənaɪz] **1** *vt* sindicar

2 *vi* sindicarse

unionized [ˈjuːnjənaɪzd] *adj* sindicado(a)

unique [juːˈniːk] *adj* (**a**) *(sole, exclusive)* único(a); **to be u. to** ser exclusivo(a) de (**b**) *(exceptional)* único(a), excepcional; **his work is quite u.** su obra no tiene parangón

uniquely [juːˈniːklɪ] *adv* excepcionalmente; **a u. talented individual** un individuo de un talento único *or* excepcional; **he is u. placed to get this information** está en una situación privilegiada para conseguir esta información

uniqueness [juːˈniːknɪs] *n* singularidad *f*

unisex [ˈjuːnɪseks] *adj* unisex

UNISON [ˈjuːnɪsən] *n* = sindicato británico de funcionarios

unison [ˈjuːnɪsən] *n* **in u.** al unísono

unit [ˈjuːnɪt] *n* (**a**) *(subdivision)* unidad *f*; **the course is divided into six units** el curso consta de seis unidades *or* partes; **family u.** unidad familiar ►► *Fin* ***u. of account*** unidad *f* de cuenta; *Br Fin* ***u. trust*** fondo *m* de inversión mobiliaria

(**b**) *(in amounts, measurement)* unidad *f*; **u. of length/time** unidad de longitud/tiempo; **a glass of wine equals one u. of alcohol** una copa de vino equivale a una unidad de alcohol ►► ***u. of currency*** unidad *f* monetaria; ***u. of measurement*** unidad *f* de medida

(**c**) *(section) (in hospital, university)* unidad *f*; *(in army)* unidad *f*, sección *f*; **office units** módulos de oficina

(**d**) *(item of furniture)* **(kitchen) u.** módulo *m* (de cocina)

(**e**) *Com (item)* unidad *f* ►► ***u. cost*** costo *m or Esp* coste *m* unitario; ***u. price*** precio *m* por unidad; ***u. pricing*** precio *m* al peso

Unitarian [juːnɪˈteərɪən] **1** *n Rel* unitario(a) *m,f*

2 *adj Rel* unitario(a)

Unitarianism [juːnɪˈteərɪənɪzəm] *n Rel* unitarismo *m*

unitary [ˈjuːnɪtərɪ] *adj* unitario(a)

unite [juːˈnaɪt] **1** *vt* (**a**) *(join, link) (forces)* unir (**b**) *(unify) (country, party)* unir; **more unites us than separates us** nos unen más cosas de las que nos separan; **common interests that u. two countries** intereses comunes que unen a dos países (**c**) *(bring together) (people, relatives)* unir (**d**) *Formal (marry)* unir

2 *vi* unirse; **the two countries united in opposing oppression** los dos países se unieron para enfrentarse a la opresión; **they united in their efforts to defeat the enemy** aunaron esfuerzos para derrotar al enemigo

united [juːˈnaɪtɪd] *adj* (**a**) *(joined)* unido(a); **to be u. against sth/sb** estar unido(a) contra algo/alguien; **to present a u. front** presentar un frente común; **to be u. in grief** estar unidos por el dolor; PROV **u. we stand, divided we fall** unidos venceremos

(**b**) *(in proper names)* ***the U. Arab Emirates*** los Emiratos Árabes Unidos; ***the U. Kingdom (of Great Britain and Northern Ireland)*** el Reino Unido (de Gran Bretaña e Irlanda del Norte); ***the U. Nations*** las Naciones Unidas; ***the U. States (of America)*** los Estados Unidos (de América)

unit-linked [ˈjuːnɪtˈlɪŋkt] *adj Br Fin* de renta variable

unity [ˈjuːnɪtɪ] *n* (**a**) *(union)* unidad *f*; **national/political u.** unidad nacional/política; **to have u. of purpose** estar unidos por el mismo objetivo; PROV **u. is strength** la unión hace la fuerza (**b**) *Theat* **the dramatic unities** las unidades dramáticas

universal [juːnɪˈvɜːsəl] *adj* universal; **a u. truth** una verdad universal; **topics of u. interest** temas de interés universal; **the bombing met with u. condemnation** el atentado fue condenado de forma unánime; **this practice is now almost u.** esta práctica es hoy prácticamente generalizada ►► ***u. coupling*** junta *f* universal; ***U. Declaration of Human Rights*** declaración *f* universal de los derechos humanos; *Phys* ***u. gravitation*** gravitación *f* universal; ***u. joint*** junta *f* universal; ***u. suffrage*** sufragio *m* universal

universality [juːnɪvɜːˈsælətɪ] *n* universalidad *f*

universalize, -ise [juːnɪˈvɜːsəlaɪz] *vt* universalizar

universally [juːnɪˈvɜːsəlɪ] *adv* universalmente; **a u. held opinion** una opinión mantenida por todos; **he is u. liked/admired** es querido/admirado por todos

universe [ˈjuːnɪvɜːs] *n* universo *m*

university [juːnɪˈvɜːsɪtɪ] *n* universidad *f*; **to be** *Br* **at** *or US* **at the u.** estar en la universidad; **to go to u.** ir a la universidad; *Fig* **I studied at the u. of life** aprendí en la escuela de la calle ►► ***u. degree*** título *m* universitario; ***u. education*** enseñanza *f* universitaria; **to have (had) a u. education** tener estudios universitarios; ***u. graduate*** titulado(a) *m,f* superior; ***u. professor*** *Br* catedrático(a) *m,f* de universidad; *US* profesor(ora) *m,f* de universidad; ***u. student*** (estudiante *mf*) universitario(a) *m,f*; ***u. town*** ciudad *f* universitaria

UNIX [ˈjuːnɪks] *n Comptr* (*abbr* **Uniplexed Information and Computing System**) UNIX *m*

unjam [ʌnˈdʒæm] *vt* desatascar

unjust [ʌnˈdʒʌst] *adj* injusto(a); **to be u. to sb** ser injusto(a) con alguien

unjustifiable [ʌnˈdʒʌstɪfaɪəbəl] *adj* injustificable

unjustifiably [ʌnˈdʒʌstɪfaɪəblɪ] *adv* injustificablemente, sin justificación

unjustified [ʌnˈdʒʌstɪfaɪd] *adj (optimism, accusation, criticism)* injustificado(a)

unjustly [ʌnˈdʒʌstlɪ] *adv* injustamente

unkempt [ʌnˈkem(p)t] *adj (hair)* revuelto(a); *(beard, appearance)* descuidado(a)

unkind [ʌnˈkaɪnd] *adj (unpleasant)* antipático(a), desagradable; *(uncharitable)* cruel; *(thought, remark)* mezquino(a); **to be u. (to sb)** ser antipático(a) *or* desagradable (con alguien); **to say u. things to sb**

decir cosas feas *or* desagradables a alguien; **the years since his death have been u. to his reputation** en los años transcurridos desde su muerte su reputación se ha visto mermada

unkindly [ʌn'kaɪndlɪ] *adv (harshly)* con dureza, duramente; **to behave u. towards sb** estar desagradable con alguien; **it wasn't meant u.** no iba con mala intención

unkindness [ʌn'kaɪndnɪs] *n (of person)* antipatía *f*; *(of comment, manner)* mezquindad *f*

unknot [ʌn'nɒt] *(pt & pp* **unknotted**) *vt* desanudar

unknowingly [ʌn'nəʊɪŋlɪ] *adv* inconscientemente, inadvertidamente

unknown [ʌn'nəʊn] **1** *n* (**a**) *(person)* desconocido(a) *m,f* (**b**) **the u.** *(place, things)* lo desconocido (**c**) *Math* la incógnita

2 *adj* (**a**) *(not known)* desconocido(a); **such cases are not u.** esos casos se dan; *Law* **murder by person or persons u.** asesinato por parte de persona o personas desconocidas; IDIOM **he's an u. quantity** es una incógnita ►► ***the U. Soldier*** el soldado desconocido (**b**) *(obscure) (cause, place, actor)* desconocido(a)

3 *adv* **u. to the rest of us** sin que lo supiéramos los demás

unlabelled [ʌn'leɪbəld] *adj (item, luggage)* sin etiqueta

unlace [ʌn'leɪs] *vt* desatar

unladylike [ʌn'leɪdɪlaɪk] *adj (behaviour)* impropio(a) de una señorita/señora; **she's very u.** su comportamiento es impropio de una señorita/señora

unlamented [ʌnlə'mentɪd] *adj* no lamentado(a); **his death was u., he died u.** nadie lamentó su muerte

unlatch [ʌn'lætʃ] *vt (door)* descorrer el pestillo de; **the door had been left unlatched** la puerta no tenía el pestillo echado

unlawful [ʌn'lɔːfʊl] *adj* ilegal, ilícito(a) ►► *Law* ***u. arrest*** detención *f or* arresto *m* ilegal; *Law* ***u. assembly*** reunión *f* ilícita; *Law* ***u. entry*** violación *f* de domicilio; *Law* ***u. killing*** homicidio *m*

unlawfully [ʌn'lɔːfʊlɪ] *adv* ilegalmente, ilícitamente

unleaded [ʌn'ledɪd] **1** *n* gasolina *f or RP* nafta *f* sin plomo

2 *adj* **u.** *Br* ***petrol*** *or US* ***gasoline*** gasolina *f or RP* nafta *f* sin plomo

unlearn [ʌn'lɜːn] *(pt & pp* **unlearned** *or* **unlearnt** [ʌn'lɜːnt]) *vt* desaprender

unleash [ʌn'liːʃ] *vt* (**a**) *(dog)* soltar (**b**) *Fig (forces, criticism, anger)* desencadenar

unleavened [ʌn'levənd] *adj* ***u. bread*** pan *m* ácimo *or* ázimo

unless [ʌn'les] *conj* a no ser que, a menos que; **don't move u. I tell you to** no te muevas a no ser que *or* a menos que yo te lo mande; **u. I hear to the contrary** a no ser que *or* a menos que me digan lo contrario; **u. otherwise stated** a no ser que *or* a menos que se indique lo contrario; **u. I'm mistaken** si no me equivoco

unlet [ʌn'let] *adj (house, flat)* sin alquilar, no alquilado(a)

unliberated [ʌn'lɪbəreɪtɪd] *adj (attitudes)* poco liberal; **the u. woman** la mujer no emancipada

unlicensed [ʌn'laɪsənst] *adj (parking, sale)* sin autorización; *(fishing, hunting)* sin licencia *or* permiso; *(premises)* sin licencia para vender bebidas alcohólicas

unlike [ʌn'laɪk] **1** *prep* **to be u. sth/sb** no parecerse a algo/alguien; **he's not u. his sister** se parece bastante a su hermana; **it's u. him to do such a thing** no es propio de él hacer algo así; **it's u. you to turn down the offer of a free meal** tú no eres de los que rechazan una invitación a comer; **u. his father,...** a diferencia de su padre,...

2 *adj* distinto(a), diferente

unlikelihood [ʌn'laɪklɪhʊd] *n* improbabilidad *f*

unlikely [ʌn'laɪklɪ] *adj* (**a**) *(not likely to happen)* improbable; **it's u. to happen** no es probable que suceda; **it's very u.** *or* **most u. that it will rain** es muy improbable que llueva; **he's u. to do it** no es probable que lo haga; **in the u. event of an accident** en el caso improbable de un accidente

(**b**) *(not likely to be true)* inverosímil; **u. as it may seem,...** aunque parezca inverosímil,...

(**c**) *(bizarre)* **an u. couple** una extraña pareja; **the director chose the most u. person to run the department** el director puso al frente del departamento a la persona más insospechada; **we found the ring in a very u. place** encontramos el anillo en un lugar insospechado; **he seems an u. choice to lead the party** no parece la persona apropiada para dirigir el partido

unlimited [ʌn'lɪmɪtɪd] *adj* (**a**) *(supply, funds, patience, power, time)* ilimitado(a); **to be u.** no tener límite; **with u. mileage** *(of hired car)* sin límite de kilometraje; **this pass gives you u. travel in twenty countries** con este abono se puede hacer un número ilimitado de viajes en veinte países (**b**) *Br Com (liability)* ilimitado(a); *(company)* de responsabilidad ilimitada

unlined [ʌn'laɪnd] *adj* (**a**) *(paper)* sin rayas *or* pautas (**b**) *(garment)* sin forro (**c**) *(face)* sin arrugas *or* líneas de expresión

unlisted [ʌn'lɪstɪd] *adj* (**a**) *Fin* ***u. company*** compañía *f* que no cotiza en bolsa; ***u. securities*** títulos *mpl* no cotizados (**b**) *US (phone number)* que no figura en la guía (telefónica)

unlit [ʌn'lɪt] *adj (fire, cigarette)* sin encender, *Am* sin prender; *(place)* sin iluminar

unload [ʌn'ləʊd] **1** *vt (boat, gun, goods, film)* descargar; **have you unloaded the washing machine?** ¿has vaciado ya la lavadora?; *Fig* **he always unloads his problems onto me** siempre me viene con sus problemas

2 *vi (lorry, ship)* descargar

unloaded [ʌn'ləʊdɪd] *adj (gun)* descargado(a)

unlock [ʌn'lɒk] **1** *vt (door)* abrir; *Comptr (file, diskette)* desbloquear; *Fig (mystery)* desvelar; **the door was unlocked** la puerta no estaba cerrada con llave *or* no tenía echada la llave

2 *vi (door)* abrirse

unlooked-for [ʌn'lʊktfɔː(r)] *adj (unexpected)* inesperado(a), imprevisto(a)

unloose [ʌn'luːs], **unloosen** [ʌn'luːsən] *vt* aflojar; **he unloosened his tie** se aflojó la corbata

unlovable [ʌn'lʌvəbəl] *adj* desagradable

unloved [ʌn'lʌvd] *adj* **to feel u.** no sentirse querido(a)

unlovely [ʌn'lʌvlɪ] *adj* poco atractivo(a), nada agraciado(a)

unluckily [ʌn'lʌkɪlɪ] *adv* por desgracia, desgraciadamente; **u. for us, it rained** por desgracia para nosotros, llovió

unlucky [ʌn'lʌkɪ] *adj (person)* sin suerte; *(coincidence)* desafortunado(a); *(day)* funesto(a), aciago(a); *(number, colour)* que trae *or* da mala suerte; **to be u.** *(have bad luck)* tener mala suerte; *(bring bad luck)* traer *or* dar mala suerte; **I was u. enough to miss the train** tuve la mala suerte de perder el tren; **it was u. for him that she arrived just at that moment** tuvo la mala suerte de que ella llegara justo en ese momento; **to be u. in love** tener mala suerte en cuestiones amorosas; **it's supposed to be u. to break a mirror** dicen que romper un espejo trae mala suerte

unmade ['ʌnmeɪd] *adj (bed)* deshecho(a), sin hacer

unmanageable [ʌn'mænɪdʒəbəl] *adj (person)* rebelde, díscolo(a); *(situation)* ingobernable; *(hair)* rebelde

unmanly [ʌn'mænlɪ] *adj (effeminate)* poco viril; *(cowardly)* pusilánime

unmanned [ʌn'mænd] *adj (spacecraft)* no tripulado(a); *(lighthouse)* automático(a); **the switchboard was u.** no había operador en la centralita

unmannerly [ʌn'mænəlɪ] *adj (person, behaviour)* descortés

unmapped [ʌn'mæpt] *adj* sin cartografiar; **we are now entering u. territory** entramos ahora en territorio sin explorar

unmarked [ʌn'mɑːkt] *adj* (**a**) *(without scratches, cuts) (person)* incólume; *(object, surface)* inmaculado(a) (**b**) *(unidentified) (grave)* sin lápida; *(police car)* camuflado(a) (**c**) *(uncorrected)* sin corregir (**d**) *Br Sport (player)* desmarcado(a)

unmarketable [ʌn'mɑːkɪtəbəl] *adj* no comercializable

unmarried [ʌn'mærɪd] *adj (person)* soltero(a); **an u. couple** una pareja no casada, una pareja de hecho ►► ***u. mother*** madre *f* soltera

unmask [ʌn'mɑːsk] *vt (criminal)* desenmascarar; *(plot)* descubrir

unmatched [ʌn'mætʃt] *adj* inigualable; **she is u. as a novelist** como novelista es inigualable

unmatured [ʌnmə'tʃʊəd] *adj (wine, spirits)* no envejecido(a); *(cheese)* sin madurar

unmemorable [ʌn'memərəbəl] *adj* poco memorable

unmentionable [ʌn'menʃənəbəl] *adj (subject)* vedado(a), innombrable

unmerciful [ʌn'mɜːsɪfʊl] *adj* inmisericorde; **to be u. to** *or* **towards sb** no tener piedad con alguien

unmercifully [ʌn'mɜːsɪfʊlɪ] *adv* sin piedad, despiadadamente

unmerited [ʌn'merɪtɪd] *adj* inmerecido(a)

unmet [ʌn'met] *adj (target, requirement)* no cumplido(a); *(quota)* no cubierto(a)

unmindful [ʌn'maɪndfʊl] *adj Formal* **to be u. of sth** *(unaware)* no ser consciente de algo; *(uncaring)* hacer caso omiso de algo; **we are not u. of the risk you are undertaking** somos conscientes del riesgo que corres

unmissable [ʌn'mɪsəbəl] *adj* imprescindible; **this movie is u.** nadie debe perderse esta película

unmistakable [ʌnmɪs'teɪkəbəl] *adj (smell, sound, symptom)* inconfundible

unmistakably [ʌnmɪs'teɪkəblɪ] *adv* indudablemente, sin lugar a dudas; **an u. Russian accent** un acento ruso inconfundible

unmitigated [ʌn'mɪtɪgeɪtɪd] *adj (disaster, failure)* completo(a), absoluto(a)

unmolested [ʌnmə'lestɪd] *adj* tranquilo(a), sin problemas; **to leave sb u.** *(not bother)* dejar a alguien tranquilo(a)

unmotivated [ʌn'məʊtɪveɪtɪd] *adj (act)* sin motivo; *(person)* sin motivación; **his actions were u. by any desire for personal glory** la búsqueda de gloria personal no motivó sus actos

unmourned [ʌn'mɔ:nd] *adj* **he died u.** nadie lamentó *or* lloró su muerte

unmoved [ʌn'mu:vd] **1** *adj* **she was u. by his appeal** sus súplicas no la conmovieron; **the music left me u.** la música no me emocionó
2 *adv* **to watch/listen u.** observar/escuchar impertérrito(a)

unmusical [ʌn'mju:zɪkəl] *adj* **(a)** *(sound)* poco melodioso(a) **(b)** *(person)* sin talento para la música

unnamed [ʌn'neɪmd] *adj* no mencionado(a)

unnatural [ʌn'nætʃərəl] *adj* **(a)** *(abnormal)* anormal; **it's u. to...** no es normal...; **it's u. for a boy of his age to spend all his time at home** no es normal que un chico de su edad pase tanto tiempo en casa **(b)** *(affected) (manner, tone, smile)* forzado(a), poco natural **(c)** *(perverse) (love, passion)* antinatural

unnaturally [ʌn'nætʃərəlɪ] *adv* **(a)** *(abnormally)* anormalmente; **she was u. quiet that evening** aquella noche estaba más callada de lo normal; **not u., he decided to resign** naturalmente, decidió de renunciar **(b)** *(affectedly)* sin naturalidad

unnecessarily [ʌnnesɪ'serɪlɪ] *adv* innecesariamente; **we don't want to worry them u.** no queremos preocuparles sin necesidad; **they died u.** murieron en vano

unnecessary [ʌn'nesɪsərɪ] *adj* innecesario(a); **it's quite u.** *(declining help, favour)* no hace falta; **don't go to any u. trouble** no te molestes más de lo estrictamente necesario

unneighbourly, *US* **unneighborly** [ʌn'neɪbəlɪ] *adj* **to be u.** no mostrar consideración con los vecinos

unnerve [ʌn'nɜ:v] *vt* poner nervioso(a), desconcertar

unnerving [ʌn'nɜ:vɪŋ] *adj (event, experience)* inquietante

unnervingly [ʌn'nɜ:vɪŋlɪ] *adv* inquietantemente; **there was something u. quiet about the village** la calma que reinaba en el pueblo tenía algo de inquietante

unnoticed [ʌn'nəʊtɪst] **1** *adj* inadvertido(a)
2 *adv* **to pass** *or* **go u.** pasar desapercibido(a) *or* inadvertido(a)

UNO [ju:en'əʊ] *n* (*abbr* **United Nations Organization**) ONU *f*

unobservant [ʌnəb'zɜ:vənt] *adj* **to be u.** ser poco observador(ora); **you're so u.!** ¡qué poca atención pones!

unobserved [ʌnəb'zɜ:vd] *adv* **to do sth u.** hacer algo sin ser visto(a); **to pass** *or* **go u.** pasar desapercibido(a)

unobstructed [ʌnəb'strʌktɪd] *adj (exit, view)* despejado(a)

unobtainable [ʌnəb'teɪnəbəl] *adj* **to be u.** *(product)* no poderse obtener, ser inasequible; *(on phone)* no estar disponible

unobtrusive [ʌnəb'tru:sɪv] *adj* discreto(a)

unobtrusively [ʌnəb'tru:sɪvlɪ] *adv* discretamente

unoccupied [ʌn'ɒkjʊpaɪd] *adj* **(a)** *(person)* desocupado(a) **(b)** *(seat)* libre; *(house)* desocupado(a) **(c)** *Mil (territory)* no ocupado(a)

unofficial [ʌnə'fɪʃəl] *adj* extraoficial; **to be u.** no ser oficial; **in an u. capacity** extraoficialmente, de forma oficiosa; **from an u. source** de fuentes extraoficiales *or* oficiosas ▸▸ *Ind* ***u. strike*** huelga *f* no apoyada por los sindicatos

unofficially [ʌnə'fɪʃəlɪ] *adv* extraoficialmente, de forma no oficial

unopened [ʌn'əʊpənd] *adj* sin abrir

unopposed [ʌnə'pəʊzd] **1** *adj* **to be u.** no tener oposición
2 *adv* **to go u.** no encontrar oposición; **to be elected u.** salir elegido(a) sin oposición

unorganized [ʌn'ɔ:gənaɪzd] *adj* **(a)** *(disorganized)* desorganizado(a) **(b)** *(workforce, labour)* sin sindicar

unoriginal [ʌnə'rɪdʒənəl] *adj* poco original

unorthodox [ʌn'ɔ:θədɒks] *adj* poco ortodoxo(a)

unostentatious [ʌnɒsten'teɪʃəs] *adj (person, behaviour, house, party)* discreto(a), poco ostentoso(a); *(dress)* discreto(a)

unpack [ʌn'pæk] **1** *vt (suitcase)* deshacer, *esp Am* desempacar; *(contents)* desembalar; **I have six boxes to u.** tengo que sacar las cosas de seis cajas; **to get unpacked** *(after travelling)* deshacer las maletas, *esp Am* desempacar; *(after moving)* desembalar
2 *vi (after travelling)* deshacer las maletas, *esp Am* desempacar; *(after moving)* desembalar

unpaid [ʌn'peɪd] *adj* **(a)** *(work, volunteer)* no retribuido(a) ▸▸ ***u. leave*** baja *f* no retribuida *or* sin sueldo **(b)** *(bill, debt)* impagado(a); **the money is still u.** aún no se ha pagado

unpalatable [ʌn'pælətəbəl] *adj* **(a)** *(food)* intragable **(b)** *(truth, idea)* desagradable, difícil de aceptar

unparalleled [ʌn'pærəleld] *adj (growth, decline, disaster)* sin precedentes; *(success)* sin igual; **a place of u. beauty** un lugar de una belleza incomparable

unpardonable [ʌn'pɑ:dənəbəl] *adj* imperdonable

unparliamentary [ʌnpɑ:lɪ'mentərɪ] *adj (behaviour, language)* contrario(a) a la cortesía parlamentaria

unpasteurized [ʌn'pɑ:stʃəraɪzd] *adj (milk, beer)* sin pasteurizar

unpatriotic [ʌnpeɪtrɪ'ɒtɪk] *adj* antipatriótico(a)

unpaved [ʌn'peɪvd] *adj (street)* sin pavimentar

unperceptive [ʌnpə'septɪv] *adj (person)* poco perspicaz; *(remark)* poco atinado(a)

unperturbed [ʌnpə'tɜ:bd] **1** *adj* **she seemed u. by the news** no parecieron afectarla las noticias
2 *adv* **to remain u.** permanecer impasible

unpick [ʌn'pɪk] *vt (stitches, hem)* descoser

unpin [ʌn'pɪn] *vt (sewing)* quitar los alfileres a; *(label)* quitar

unplaced [ʌn'pleɪst] *adj (in race) (horse, dog)* no colocado(a); *(athlete)* fuera de los puestos de honor

unplanned [ʌn'plænd] *adj (result, visit)* imprevisto(a); **an u. pregnancy** un embarazo no planeado

unplayable [ʌn'pleɪəbəl] *adj (shot, ball)* imposible de golpear; *(serve)* imposible de restar; **the pitch was u.** el terreno de juego no estaba en condiciones

unpleasant [ʌn'plezənt] *adj* desagradable; **there's no need to be so u. about it!** ¡no hace falta ponerse así (de desagradable *or* antipático) por eso!

unpleasantly [ʌn'plezəntlɪ] *adv* desagradablemente; **it was u. hot** hacía un calor desagradable; **the wine was u. sweet** el vino tenía un dulzor desagradable

unpleasantness [ʌn'plezəntnɪs] *n* **the u. of...** lo desagradable de...; **to cause u.** crear una situación desagradable; **I could have done without the u. over the tickets** no hacía falta ponerse así (de desagradable *or* antipático) por lo de las entradas

unplug [ʌn'plʌg] (*pt & pp* **unplugged**) *vt* desenchufar

unplugged [ʌn'plʌgd] *adj (acoustic)* desenchufado(a), acústico(a)

unplumbed [ʌn'plʌmd] *adj (depths of knowledge)* insondable

unpolished [ʌn'pɒlɪʃt] *adj* **(a)** *(shoes, surface)* deslustrado(a) **(b)** *(imperfect) (performance)* deslucido(a); *(style)* tosco(a); *(manners)* no refinado(a), tosco(a)

unpolluted [ʌnpə'lu:tɪd] *adj* no contaminado(a), limpio(a)

unpopular [ʌn'pɒpjʊlə(r)] *adj (politician, decision)* impopular; **an u. child** un niño con pocos amigos; **he was u. with his colleagues** sus compañeros no le tenían mucho aprecio; **to make oneself u.** granjearse enemistades; **an u. make of car** una marca de automóviles que se vende poco; **this style is u. with the younger generation** este estilo no se lleva entre los más jóvenes

unpopularity [ʌnpɒpjʊ'lærɪtɪ] *n* impopularidad *f*

unpractical [ʌn'præktɪkəl] *adj* poco práctico(a)

unpractised, *US* **unpracticed** [ʌn'præktɪst] *adj* con poca experiencia; **to be u. in the art of public speaking** tener poca experiencia en el arte de hablar en público; **to the u. ear/eye** para el oído/ojo no acostumbrado

unprecedented [ʌn'presɪdentɪd] *adj* sin precedente(s); **to an u. degree** hasta un punto inusitado; **such a situation is u.** una situación así no tiene precedentes

unpredictability [ʌnprɪdɪktə'bɪlətɪ] *n* **the u. of** lo imprevisible *or* impredecible de

unpredictable [ʌnprɪ'dɪktəbəl] *adj (person, mood, weather)* imprevisible, impredecible

unpredictably [ʌnprɪ'dɪktəblɪ] *adv* de manera imprevisible *or* impredecible

unprejudiced [ʌn'predʒʊdɪst] *adj (unbigoted)* sin prejuicios, libre de prejuicios; *(unbiased)* imparcial; **to be u.** *(unbigoted)* no tener prejuicios; *(unbiased)* ser imparcial

unpremeditated [ʌnpriː'medɪteɪtɪd] *adj* sin premeditación; **to be u.** no ser premeditado(a)

unprepared [ʌnprɪ'peəd] *adj (speech)* improvisado(a); **to be u. for sth** *(not ready, not expecting)* no estar preparado(a) para algo

unprepossessing [ʌnpriːpə'zesɪŋ] *adj (person, appearance, place)* poco atractivo(a)

unpresentable [ʌnprɪ'zentəbəl] *adj* impresentable

unpretentious [ʌnprɪ'tenʃəs] *adj (person, tastes, house)* sin pretensiones, modesto(a)

unprincipled [ʌn'prɪnsɪpəld] *adj (person)* sin principios; **to be u.** no tener principios; **they were criticized for their u. behaviour during the elections** les criticaron su falta de principios durante las elecciones

unprintable [ʌn'prɪntəbəl] *adj (offensive)* impublicable

unproblematic(al) [ʌnprɒblə'mætɪk(əl)] *adj* no problemático(a); **to be u.** no ser problemático(a)

unproductive [ʌnprə'dʌktɪv] *adj (land, work)* improductivo(a); *(meeting, conversation, effort)* infructuoso(a)

unprofessional [ʌnprə'feʃənəl] *adj* poco profesional

unprofessionally [ʌnprə'feʃənəlɪ] *adv* con poca profesionalidad

unprofitable [ʌn'prɒfɪtəbəl] *adj (company, industry)* no rentable; *(meeting)* infructuoso(a), poco productivo(a); **coalmining became u.** el carbón dejó de ser rentable

unpromising [ʌn'prɒmɪsɪŋ] *adj* poco prometedor(ora); **that's an u. start** no es un comienzo prometedor

unprompted [ʌn'prɒmptɪd] *adj (action, words)* espontáneo(a); **his actions were quite u. by any self-interest** no le movía ningún interés personal en sus acciones

unpronounceable [ʌnprə'naʊnsəbəl] *adj* impronunciable

unprotected [ʌnprə'tektɪd] *adj* desprotegido(a) ►► ***u. sex*** sexo *m* sin protección *or* sin preservativo

unproved, unproven [ʌn'pruːvd, ʌn'pruːvən] *adj* (**a**) *(not proved) (accusation, allegation)* no probado(a); *(theory)* no demostrado(a), no probado(a) (**b**) *(untried) (product, procedure)* no probado(a)

unprovoked [ʌnprə'vəʊkt] *adj* espontáneo(a), no provocado(a)

unpublished [ʌn'pʌblɪʃt] *adj (manuscript, book, author)* no publicado(a), inédito(a)

unpunctual [ʌn'pʌŋktʃʊəl] *adj* impuntual, poco puntual

unpunctuality [ʌnpʌŋktʃʊ'ælɪtɪ] *n* impuntualidad *f*, falta *f* de puntualidad

unpunished [ʌn'pʌnɪʃt] **1** *adj* impune
2 *adv* **to go u.** quedar impune

unputdownable [ʌnpʊt'daʊnəbəl] *adj Fam (book)* absorbente, que se lee de una sentada

unqualified [ʌn'kwɒlɪfaɪd] *adj* (**a**) *(doctor, teacher)* sin titulación; **I'm quite u. to talk about it** no estoy cualificado para hablar de ello (**b**) *(support, praise)* incondicional; *(success, disaster)* completo(a), sin paliativos

unquenchable [ʌn'kwentʃəbəl] *adj (curiosity, desire, thirst)* insaciable

unquestionable [ʌn'kwestʃənəbəl] *adj* indiscutible, indudable

unquestionably [ʌn'kwestʃənəblɪ] *adv* indiscutiblemente, indudablemente

unquestioning [ʌn'kwestʃənɪŋ] *adj (trust, obedience)* ciego(a); *(support)* incondicional

unquestioningly [ʌn'kwestʃənɪŋlɪ] *adv (to trust, obey)* ciegamente; *(to support)* incondicionalmente

unquiet [ʌn'kwaɪət] *adj Literary (mind)* intranquilo(a); *(period)* turbulento(a); **he lies in an u. grave** no reposa en paz

unquote [ʌn'kwəʊt] *adv* **quote u.** entre comillas

unquoted [ʌn'kwəʊtɪd] *adj Fin* **u. shares/company** acciones que no cotizan/empresa que no cotiza en bolsa

unravel [ʌn'rævəl] *(pt & pp* **unravelled**, *US* **unraveled**) **1** *vt* (**a**) *(wool)* desenredar (**b**) *(plot, mystery)* desentrañar
2 *vi* (**a**) *(wool)* desenredarse; *(garment)* deshilacharse (**b**) *(plan)* desbaratarse; *(mystery)* desentrañarse

unread [ʌn'red] *adj* (**a**) *(book, leaflet)* sin leer; **he left the magazine on the table u.** dejó la revista sin leer sobre la mesa (**b**) *(person)* inculto(a), poco leído(a)

unreadable [ʌn'riːdəbəl] *adj* (**a**) *(handwriting, signature)* ilegible; *(book, author)* de difícil lectura, incomprensible (**b**) *Comptr (file, data)* no leíble

unreal [ʌn'rɪəl] *adj* (**a**) *(illusory, imaginary)* irreal (**b**) *Fam (unbelievable)* increíble; **this is u.!** ¡esto es de lo que no hay! (**c**) *Fam (excellent) Esp* guay, *Andes, CAm, Carib, Méx* chévere, *Méx* padre, *RP* bárbaro(a)

unrealistic [ʌnrɪə'lɪstɪk] *adj* poco realista; **it's u. to expect any news so soon** no sería realista esperar que hubiera noticias tan pronto

unreality [ʌnrɪ'ælɪtɪ] *n* irrealidad *f*

unrealized [ʌn'rɪəlaɪzd] *adj* (**a**) *(wish, ambition)* insatisfecho(a); **her hopes remain u.** sus esperanzas no se han hecho realidad (**b**) *Fin (capital)* no realizado(a)

unreasonable [ʌn'riːzənəbəl] *adj* (**a**) *(person)* poco razonable, irrazonable; **he was being totally u.** no estaba siendo razonable; **it's not u. to expect that...** es razonable esperar que... (**b**) *(demand, price)* poco razonable

unreasonably [ʌn'riːzənəblɪ] *adv (to behave)* de forma poco razonable; **they argue, not u., that...** arguyen, no sin razón, que...; **the price is u. high** el precio es excesivo

unreceptive [ʌnrɪ'septɪv] *adj (audience, student)* poco receptivo(a); **to be u. to sth** ser poco receptivo(a) a algo

unreciprocated [ʌnrɪ'sɪprəkeɪtɪd] *adj (love, feelings)* no correspondido(a)

unrecognizable [ʌnrekəg'naɪzəbəl] *adj* irreconocible

unrecognized [ʌn'rekəgnaɪzd] **1** *adj (talent, government)* no reconocido(a)
2 *adv* **to go u.** *(talent, famous person)* pasar desapercibido(a)

unrecorded [ʌnrɪ'kɔːdɪd] *adj* **many of these crimes go u.** de muchos de estos delitos no queda constancia

unredeemed [ʌnrɪ'diːmd] *adj* (**a**) *Rel (unsaved)* irredento(a) (**b**) *(uncompensated)* **the movie is u. by the slightest flicker of humour** no asoma el más leve atisbo de humor que logre salvar a la película (**c**) *Fin (bond)* sin cobrar; *(pawned item)* sin desempeñar

unreel [ʌn'riːl] *vt* desenrollar

unrefined [ʌnrɪ'faɪnd] *adj* (**a**) *(sugar, oil)* sin refinar (**b**) *(person, taste)* poco refinado(a)

unreflective [ʌnrɪ'flektɪv] *adj* (**a**) *(mind, person)* irreflexivo(a) (**b**) *(surface)* no reflectante

unreformed [ʌnrɪ'fɔːmd] *adj (person, system, law)* no reformado(a)

unregenerate [ʌnrɪ'dʒenərət] *Formal* **1** *n* persona *f* contumaz *or* incorregible
2 *adj* contumaz, incorregible

unregistered [ʌn'redʒɪstəd] *adj (worker, immigrant)* sin papeles; *(voter)* no inscrito(a); *(birth)* no registrado(a)

unregulated [ʌn'regjʊleɪtɪd] *adj (access, market, economy, competition)* no regulado(a)

unrehearsed [ʌnrɪ'hɜːst] *adj* (**a**) *(improvised)* improvisado(a) (**b**) *Mus & Theat* sin ensayar, no ensayado(a)

unrelated [ʌnrɪ'leɪtɪd] *adj* (**a**) *(events)* inconexo(a); **the two incidents are u.** no existe relación entre los dos hechos (**b**) *(people)* no emparentado(a)

unreleased [ʌnrɪ'liːst] *adj (song, record)* inédito(a); *(movie)* sin estrenar

unrelenting [ʌnrɪ'lentɪŋ] *adj (criticism, pressure, persecution)* implacable; *(struggle)* sin tregua; **the rain was u.** la lluvia era incesante

unreliability ['ʌnrɪlaɪə'bɪlətɪ] *n (of method, machine, statistics)* falta *f* de fiabilidad; *(of person)* informalidad *f*

unreliable [ʌnrɪ'laɪəbəl] *adj (machine, equipment, method)* poco fiable; *(memoirs, statistics, source of information)* poco fidedigno(a), poco fiable; *(person)* informal

unrelieved [ʌnrɪ'liːvd] *adj (boredom, ugliness, gloom)* absoluto(a); *(pain)* sin alivio

unremarkable [ʌnrɪ'mɑːkəbəl] *adj* corriente

unremitting [ʌnrɪ'mɪtɪŋ] *adj (activity)* incesante; *(efforts)* infatigable; *(demands, opposition)* sin tregua

unremittingly [ʌnrɪ'mɪtɪŋlɪ] *adv (to work, rain)* sin cesar; **to be u. opposed to sth** oponerse a algo sin tregua

unremunerative [ʌnrɪ'mjuːnərətɪv] *adj (work, industry, sector)* poco remunerativo(a)

unrepeatable [ʌnrɪ'piːtəbəl] *adj* (**a**) *(words)* irrepetible, irreproducible (**b**) *(offer)* irrepetible

unrepentant [ʌnrɪ'pentənt] *adj (sinner)* impenitente; **to die u.** morir sin arrepentirse; **to be u. (about)** no arrepentirse (de)

unreported [ʌnrɪ'pɔːtɪd] 1 *adj* **an u. incident/problem** un incidente/problema del que no se ha informado *or CAm, Méx* reportado
2 *adv* **many crimes go u.** muchos delitos no se denuncian *or CAm, Méx* reportan

unrepresentative [ʌnreprɪ'zentətɪv] *adj* no representativo(a) (**of** de); **it's completely u. of the style of the period** no es nada representativo del estilo de la época

unrepresented [ʌnreprɪ'zentɪd] *adj* no representado(a), sin representación

unrequited ['ʌnrɪkwaɪtɪd] *adj (love)* no correspondido(a)

unreserved [ʌnrɪ'zɜːvd] *adj* (**a**) *(praise, support)* sin reservas; **she was u. in her praise** no escatimó elogios (**b**) *(seat, table)* libre, no reservado(a)

unreservedly [ʌnrɪ'zɜːvɪdlɪ] *adv (to recommend, praise, support)* sin reservas; *(to apologize)* profusamente

unresolved [ʌnrɪ'zɒlvd] *adj (issue, problem)* sin resolver

unresponsive [ʌnrɪ'spɒnsɪv] *adj* (**a**) *(showing no reaction) (person, audience)* indiferente (**to** ante); **the patient was u. to the treatment** el paciente no respondió al tratamiento (**b**) *(sexually)* indiferente

unrest [ʌn'rest] *n (unease)* malestar *m*; *(disturbances)* desórdenes *mpl*, disturbios *mpl*; *(in labour relations)* conflictividad *f*; **social u.** desórdenes sociales

unrestrained [ʌnrɪ'streɪnd] *adj (anger, growth, joy)* desmedido(a); **the u. use of force** el uso desmedido de la fuerza

unrestricted [ʌnrɪ'strɪktɪd] *adj (access, power, growth)* ilimitado(a), sin restricciones

unrewarded [ʌnrɪ'wɔːdɪd] *adj* **to be** *or* **go u.** no verse recompensado(a)

unrewarding [ʌnrɪ'wɔːdɪŋ] *adj (financially)* poco rentable; *(intellectually)* poco gratificante

unrig [ʌn'rɪg] *vt* desmantelar

unripe [ʌn'raɪp] *adj* verde; **to be u.** estar verde

unrivalled, *US* **unrivaled** [ʌn'raɪvəld] *adj (person, brilliance, beauty)* incomparable; **to be u.** ser inigualable

unroll [ʌn'rəʊl] 1 *vt* desenrollar
2 *vi* desenrollarse

unromantic [ʌnrə'mæntɪk] *adj* poco romántico(a)

unruffled [ʌn'rʌfəld] *adj (person, manner)* sereno(a), imperturbable; *(water surface)* en calma; **she appeared to be u. by the experience** no parecía afectada por la experiencia

unruliness [ʌn'ruːlɪnɪs] *n (of children, mob, behaviour)* rebeldía *f*, falta *f* de disciplina

unruly [ʌn'ruːlɪ] *adj (children, mob, behaviour)* revoltoso(a); *(hair)* rebelde

unsaddle [ʌn'sædəl] *vt (horse)* desensillar

unsafe [ʌn'seɪf] *adj* (**a**) *(dangerous)* peligroso(a); **it's u. to eat** no se puede comer (**b**) *(at risk)* inseguro(a), en peligro (**c**) *Law (conviction, verdict)* infundado(a)

unsaid [ʌn'sed] *adj* **to leave sth u.** no decir algo; **it's better left u.** es mejor no decirlo

unsalaried [ʌn'sælərɪd] *adj (person)* no asalariado(a); *(post)* no remunerado(a)

unsalted [ʌn'sɔːltɪd] *adj* sin sal

unsatisfactory [ʌnsætɪs'fæktərɪ] *adj (situation, outcome, performance)* insatisfactorio(a), poco satisfactorio(a); **this result was u. for all concerned** el resultado no satisfizo a ninguna de las partes; **an u. explanation** una explicación poco convincente

unsatisfied [ʌn'sætɪsfaɪd] *adj* insatisfecho(a); **to be u. with sth** no estar satisfecho(a) con algo

unsatisfying [ʌn'sætɪsfaɪɪŋ] *adj (explanation)* insatisfactorio(a); *(ending, meal)* decepcionante; *(experience)* poco gratificante

unsaturated [ʌn'sætʃəreɪtɪd] *adj Chem* insaturado(a), no saturado(a) ►► ***u. fats*** grasas *fpl* no saturadas

unsavoury, *US* **unsavory** [ʌn'seɪvərɪ] *adj (person)* indeseable; *(reputation)* dudoso(a)

unsay [ʌn'seɪ] *vt* desdecirse de, retractarse de

unscathed [ʌn'skeɪðd] *adj* (**a**) *(person) (physically)* ileso(a); *(reputation)* indemne, intacto(a); **luckily he emerged u. from the experience** por suerte la experiencia no lo marcó (**b**) *(building)* intacto(a); **the city survived the bombing relatively u.** la ciudad quedó relativamente intacta del bombardeo

unscented [ʌn'sentɪd] *adj (soap)* sin perfume

unscheduled [ʌn'ʃedjuːld, *US* ʌn'skedjuːld] *adj* no programado(a), imprevisto(a)

unschooled [ʌn'skuːld] *adj Formal (person)* sin escolarizar, no escolarizado(a); **he is u. in such matters** es lego en la materia

unscientific [ʌnsaɪən'tɪfɪk] *adj (method, approach)* poco científico(a)

unscramble [ʌn'skræmbəl] *vt* (**a**) *(decode) (code, message)* descifrar; *(TV signals)* descodificar (**b**) *Fam (thoughts)* desenmarañar

unscrew [ʌn'skruː] 1 *vt* (**a**) *(remove screws from)* desatornillar, destornillar (**b**) *(twist off)* desenroscar
2 *vi (lid, cap)* desenroscarse

unscripted [ʌn'skrɪptɪd] *adj (speech, remark)* improvisado(a)

unscrupulous [ʌn'skruːpjʊləs] *adj (person, behaviour, methods)* sin escrúpulos

unscrupulously [ʌn'skruːpjʊləslɪ] *adv* sin escrúpulos

unseal [ʌn'siːl] *vt (letter)* abrir

unsealed [ʌn'siːld] *adj* abierto(a)

unseasonable [ʌn'siːzənəbəl] *adj* atípico(a) para la época del año

unseasonably [ʌn'siːzənəblɪ] *adv* **an u. cold night** una noche anormalmente fría para la época del año

unseasoned [ʌn'siːzənd] *adj* (**a**) *(food)* sin condimentar *or* sazonar (**b**) *(wood)* verde, no estacionado(a)

unseat [ʌn'siːt] *vt* (**a**) *(rider)* derribar (**b**) *(government, ruler)* derrocar, derribar; **he was unseated in the last election** perdió su escaño en las últimas elecciones

unsecured [ʌnsɪ'kjʊəd] *adj* (**a**) *(door, window) (unlocked)* sin candar; *(open)* mal cerrado(a) (**b**) *Fin (loan, overdraft)* no garantizado(a), sin garantía ►► ***u. creditor*** acreedor *m* común *or* no garantizado; ***u. debt*** deuda *f* sin garantía

unseeded [ʌn'siːdɪd] *adj Sport* que no es cabeza de serie

unseemly [ʌn'siːmlɪ] *adj (behaviour, language)* inapropiado(a)

unseen [ʌn'siːn] *adj* **u. by the guards** sin ser visto por los guardias ►► *Br Sch* ***u. translation*** traducción *f* directa sin preparación

unselfconscious [ʌnself'kɒnʃəs] *adj (person, manner)* natural; *(laughter)* espontáneo(a), natural; **he's got a birth mark on his face but he's quite u. about it** tiene una mancha de nacimiento en la cara pero no le preocupa para nada

unselfconsciously [ʌnself'kɒnʃəslɪ] *adv (to speak, behave)* con naturalidad; *(to laugh)* con espontaneidad *or* naturalidad

unselfish [ʌn'selfɪʃ] *adj (person, act)* desinteresado(a), generoso(a)

unselfishly [ʌn'selfɪʃlɪ] *adv* desinteresadamente, con generosidad

unselfishness [ʌn'selfɪʃnɪs] *n* generosidad *f*

unsentimental [ʌnsentɪ'mentəl] *adj* poco sentimental; **the novel is an u. account of family life** la novela describe la vida familiar sin sentimentalismos

unserviceable [ʌn'sɜːvɪsəbəl] *adj (aircraft, vehicle, machine)* inutilizable

unsettle [ʌn'setəl] *vt* (**a**) *(make nervous)* desasosegar, intranquilizar (**b**) *(make sick) (stomach)* revolver

unsettled [ʌn'setəld] *adj* (**a**) *(restless) (person)* inquieto(a) (**b**) *(unstable) (conditions, situation, weather)* inestable (**c**) *(unresolved) (issue, dispute)* sin resolver (**d**) *(unpaid) (account, bill)* sin pagar (**e**) *(sick) (stomach)* revuelto(a)

unsettling [ʌn'setlɪŋ] *adj (news, experience, prospect)* desestabilizador(ora)

unsexy [ʌn'seksɪ] *adj (person, underwear)* nada sexy; **to be u.** no ser sexy

unshackle [ʌn'ʃækəl] *vt* desencadenar; *Fig* liberar

unshak(e)able [ʌn'ʃeɪkəbəl] *adj (belief, determination, faith)* inquebrantable

unsheathe [ʌn'ʃiːð] *vt (sword)* desenvainar

unshockable [ʌn'ʃɒkəbəl] *adj* imperturbable

unshod [ʌn'ʃɒd] *adj* (**a**) *(horse)* sin herrar (**b**) *(person)* descalzo(a)

unsightliness [ʌn'saɪtlɪnɪs] *n* fealdad *f*

unsightly [ʌn'saɪtlɪ] *adj* feo(a)

unsigned [ʌn'saɪnd] *adj* (**a**) *(contract)* sin firmar (**b**) *(band)* sin contrato

unsinkable [ʌn'sɪŋkəbəl] *adj* **to be u.** *(ship)* no poder hundirse; *Fig (person)* ser invencible

unskilful, *US* **unskillful** [ʌn'skɪlfʊl] *adj* torpe, desmañado(a)

unskilled [ʌn'skɪld] *adj (worker)* no cualificado(a); *(job, work)* no especializado(a); **he is u. at such work** se le da mal ese tipo de trabajos

unskillful *US* = **unskilful**

unsling [ʌn'slɪŋ] (*pt & pp* **unslung** [ʌn'slʌŋ]) *vt (gun, bow, hammock)* descolgar

unsmiling [ʌn'smaɪlɪŋ] *adj (person, face)* serio(a), adusto(a); **she stood there u.** siguió allí de pie sin sonreír

unsmoked [ʌn'sməʊkt] *adj* fresco(a), sin ahumar

unsociable [ʌn'səʊʃəbəl] *adj* insociable; **don't be so u.!** ¡no seas tan poco sociable!

unsocial [ʌn'səʊʃəl] *adj Br* **to work u. hours** trabajar a deshoras

unsold [ʌn'səʊld] *adj* sin vender; **to remain u.** seguir sin venderse

unsolicited [ʌnsə'lɪsɪtɪd] *adj (comment, contribution, application)* no solicitado(a); **the advice was u.** nadie había pedido ese consejo

unsolved [ʌn'sɒlvd] *adj (mystery, problem)* sin resolver; **the crime remains u.** el crimen sigue sin resolverse

unsophisticated [ʌnsə'fɪstɪkeɪtɪd] *adj* (**a**) *(person) (in dress, tastes, attitudes)* sencillo(a) (**b**) *(method, technology)* simple, sencillo(a) (**c**) *(novice, inexperienced)* inexperimentado(a)

unsound [ʌn'saʊnd] *adj* (**a**) *(health)* frágil; *Law* **to be of u. mind** no estar en plena posesión de las facultades mentales
(**b**) *(building)* poco sólido(a); **it's structurally u.** el edificio tiene problemas estructurales
(**c**) *(decision, advice)* poco sensato(a); *(argument)* poco sólido(a); *Fin (investment)* poco seguro(a); **to be scientifically u.** ser poco científico(a); **he was regarded as politically u.** no le consideraban una persona de confianza políticamente; **this method of waste disposal is environmentally u.** este método para la eliminación de desechos puede ser nocivo para el medio ambiente

unsparing [ʌn'speərɪŋ] *adj* **to be u. of one's time/efforts** no escatimar tiempo/esfuerzo

unspeakable [ʌn'spi:kəbəl] *adj (conditions, squalor)* atroz; *(pain)* atroz, indecible

unspeakably [ʌn'spi:kəblɪ] *adv (rude, cruel, arrogant)* indeciblemente

unspecified [ʌn'spesɪfaɪd] *adj* sin especificar

unspoiled [ʌn'spɔɪld], **unspoilt** [ʌn'spɔɪlt] *adj (countryside, beach)* virgen; **they were u. by fame** la fama no se les había subido a la cabeza

unspoken [ʌn'spəʊkən] *adj (fear)* oculto(a), no expresado(a); *(threat)* velado(a); *(agreement)* tácito(a); **although his name remained u....** aunque no se mencionó su nombre...

unsporting [ʌn'spɔ:tɪŋ], **unsportsmanlike** [ʌn'spɔ:tsmənlaɪk] *adj* antideportivo(a); **it was u. of him just to quit like that** abandonar así fue muy poco deportivo

unstable [ʌn'steɪbəl] *adj* (**a**) *(structure, government)* inestable (**b**) *(person)* inestable (**c**) *(currency, prices)* inestable (**d**) *Chem (compound)* inestable

unstatesmanlike [ʌn'steɪtsmənlaɪk] *adj (behaviour)* impropio(a) de un estadista *or* un hombre de estado

unsteadily [ʌn'stedɪlɪ] *adv (to move, walk)* con paso inseguro; *(to speak)* con voz temblorosa

unsteadiness [ʌn'stedɪnɪs] *n (of table, chair)* inestabilidad *f*; *(voice, hand)* temblor *m*; *(of step)* inseguridad *f*

unsteady [ʌn'stedɪ] *adj (table, chair)* inestable, inseguro(a); *(hand, voice)* tembloroso(a); **he was u. on his feet** andaba inseguro *or* con paso vacilante

unsterilized [ʌn'sterɪlaɪzd] *adj* no esterilizado(a), sin esterilizar

unstinting [ʌn'stɪntɪŋ] *adj (praise, effort)* generoso(a); **to be u. in one's praise (of sth/sb)** no escatimar elogios (a algo/alguien); **the firm has been u. in its efforts to help us** la empresa no ha escatimado esfuerzos para ayudarnos

unstitch [ʌn'stɪtʃ] *vt* descoser; **to come unstitched** descoserse

unstoppable [ʌn'stɒpəbəl] *adj (force, ambition, drive)* incontenible; *(flow, rise)* imparable, incontenible

unstrap [ʌn'stræp] (*pt & pp* **unstrapped**) *vt* desabrochar

unstreamed [ʌn'stri:md] *adj Br Educ (schoolchildren)* = que no están divididos en grupos según sus niveles de aptitud

unstressed [ʌn'strest] *adj Ling* no acentuado(a), sin acento

unstructured [ʌn'strʌktʃəd] *adj (essay, plan)* deslavazado(a), poco estructurado(a); *(meeting)* poco estructurado(a)

unstuck [ʌn'stʌk] *adj* **to come u.** *(stamp, label)* despegarse; *Fig (person)* fracasar, darse un batacazo; *(plan)* fallar

unstudied [ʌn'stʌdɪd] *adj (natural)* natural, espontáneo(a)

unstuff [ʌn'stʌf] *vt Comptr* descomprimir

unsubsidized [ʌn'sʌbsɪdaɪzd] *adj (industry, sector)* no subvencionado(a)

unsubstantiated [ʌnsəb'stænʃɪeɪtɪd] *adj (accusation, rumour)* no probado(a)

unsubtle [ʌn'sʌtəl] *adj (person, humour)* poco sutil; **she's so u.!** ¡qué falta de sutileza!

unsuccessful [ʌnsək'sesfʊl] *adj* (**a**) *(not achieving desired result) (attempt)* fallido(a); *(candidate)* no elegido(a); **to be u.** *(operation)* no tener éxito, fracasar; **your application has been u.** no ha sido seleccionado para el puesto (**b**) *(not flourishing) (project, company, writer)* sin éxito; **to be u.** no tener éxito

unsuccessfully [ʌnsək'sesfəlɪ] *adv* sin éxito

unsuitability [ʌns(j)u:tə'bɪlɪtɪ] *n* **the u. of** *(arrangement, behaviour, language, climate)* lo inadecuado *or* inapropiado de; **she commented on the u. of his clothes** comentó que la ropa que llevaba no era adecuada *or* apropiada; **this seems proof of his u. for the job** esto parece demostrar que no es la persona adecuada *or* apropiada para el puesto

unsuitable [ʌn's(j)u:təbəl] *adj (arrangement, behaviour, language, climate)* inadecuado(a), inapropiado(a) (**for** para); *(time)* inoportuno(a) (**for** para); **he's u. for the job** no es la persona adecuada *or* apropiada para el trabajo; **this movie is u. for children** esta película no es apta para menores; **the land is u. for farming** la tierra no es apta para la agricultura

unsuitably [ʌn's(j)u:təblɪ] *adv* inadecuadamente

unsuited [ʌn's(j)u:tɪd] *adj* **to be u. to sth** *(of person)* no servir para algo; *(of machine, tool)* no ser adecuado(a) para algo; **he's u. to politics/teaching** no sirve para la política/dar clases; **as a couple they seem totally u. (to each other)** como pareja son incompatibles

unsullied [ʌn'sʌlɪd] *adj Literary (reputation)* inmaculado(a), incólume; **he was u. by fame** la fama no lo había contaminado

unsung [ʌn'sʌŋ] *adj* **to go u.** no ser reconocido(a), no tener ningún eco; **u. hero** héroe olvidado

unsupervised [ʌn'su:pəvaɪzd] *adj* **they were u. for an hour** no los supervisó nadie durante una hora; **to leave sb u.** dejar solo(a) a alguien; **u. minors not admitted** *(sign)* no se admiten menores sin la supervisión de un adulto

unsupported [ʌnsə'pɔ:tɪd] *adj* (**a**) *(statement, charges)* sin pruebas de apoyo; **the theories were u. by any evidence** las teorías no estaban corroboradas por pruebas (**b**) *(structure)* **to be u.** no tener apoyo; **to walk u.** *(invalid)* caminar sin ayuda (**c**) *Fig (person) (financially, emotionally)* **to be u.** no recibir ayuda económica

unsure [ʌn'ʃʊə(r)] *adj* inseguro(a); **to be u. of** *or* **about sth** no estar seguro(a) de algo; **to be u. of oneself** no tener seguridad en uno(a) mismo(a), sentirse inseguro(a)

unsurpassed [ʌnsə'pɑ:st] *adj* sin igual, insuperable; **to be u. (in** *or* **at sth)** ser insuperable (en algo)

unsurprising [ʌnsə'praɪzɪŋ] *adj* comprensible, poco sorprendente

unsurprisingly [ʌnsə'praɪzɪŋlɪ] *adv* **u., this suggestion was rejected** lógicamente *or* como era de esperar, la sugerencia fue rechazada

unsuspected [ʌnsəs'pektɪd] *adj* insospechado(a); **her treason was u. by her superiors** sus superiores nunca sospecharon de su traición

unsuspecting [ʌnsəs'pektɪŋ] *adj* **to be quite u. (of)** no sospechar nada (de)

unsweetened [ʌn'swi:tənd] *adj (without sugar)* sin azúcar; *(without sweeteners)* sin edulcorantes

unswerving [ʌn'swɜ:vɪŋ] *adj (devotion, loyalty, determination)* inquebrantable, sin fisuras

unswervingly [ʌn'swɜ:vɪŋlɪ] *adv* **to be u. loyal** ser de una lealtad inquebrantable *or* sin fisuras; **to support a party u.** apoyar a un partido sin vacilaciones

unsympathetic [ʌnsɪmpə'θetɪk] *adj* (**a**) *(lacking sympathy)* poco comprensivo(a) (**to** con) (**b**) *(not favourable)* **they are u. to such requests** no ven ese tipo de peticiones con mucha simpatía; **to be u. to a cause** no simpatizar con una causa (**c**) *(unlikable)* antipático(a)

unsympathetically [ʌnsɪmpə'θetɪklɪ] *adv (to speak, behave, react)* de forma poco comprensiva

unsystematic [ʌnsɪstə'mætɪk] *adj* poco sistemático(a)

untainted [ʌn'teɪntɪd] *adj (water)* no contaminado(a); *(reputation)* intachable; **to be u. by corruption** no estar contaminado(a) por la corrupción

untalented [ʌn'tæləntɪd] *adj* sin talento

untamed [ʌn'teɪmd] *adj* (**a**) *(animal)* salvaje; *(wilderness)* agreste (**b**) *Fig (person, spirit)* indomable

untangle [ʌn'tæŋgəl] *vt (hair, ropes)* desenredar, desenmarañar; *(mystery)* desentrañar; *(confusion)* aclarar

untapped [ʌn'tæpt] *adj (resources, talent, market)* sin explotar

untarnished [ʌn'tɑ:nɪʃt] *adj (silver)* no deslucido(a); *Fig (reputation)* intachable

untaxed [ʌn'tækst] *adj (items)* libre *or* exento(a) de impuestos; *(income)* no gravado(a), exento(a) de impuestos

untempered [ʌn'tempəd] *adj* sin templar

untenable [ʌn'tenəbəl] *adj* insostenible

untenanted ['ʌn'tenəntɪd] *adj Literary* sin inquilinos, vacío(a)

untended [ʌn'tendɪd] *adj (sick person, garden)* desatendido(a)

untested [ʌn'testɪd] *adj (employee, method, theory, product)* no puesto(a) a prueba; **to be u.** no haber sido puesto(a) a prueba

unthinkable [ʌn'θɪŋkəbəl] **1** *n* **the u.** lo impensable, lo inimaginable; **to think the u.** pensar lo impensable
 2 *adj* impensable

unthinking [ʌn'θɪŋkɪŋ] *adj* irreflexivo(a)

unthinkingly [ʌn'θɪŋkɪŋlɪ] *adv* irreflexivamente, de forma irreflexiva

unthought-of [ʌn'θɔːtɒv] *adj* **an u. possibility** una posibilidad en la que no se había pensado

unthreatening ['ʌn'θretənɪŋ] *adj (person, manner, atmosphere, environment)* no intimidatorio(a)

untidily [ʌn'taɪdɪlɪ] *adv* desordenadamente; **he was u. dressed** iba muy desaliñado *or* descuidado

untidiness [ʌn'taɪdɪnɪs] *n (of place, work)* desorden *m*; **he was well-known for his u.** tenía fama de ser muy desordenado

untidy [ʌn'taɪdɪ] *adj (person, place, desk, work)* desordenado(a); **u. appearance** aspecto desaliñado *or* descuidado

untie [ʌn'taɪ] *vt* desatar

until [ʌn'tɪl] **1** *prep* hasta; **u. ten o'clock** hasta las diez; **open from 9 u. 5** abierto de 9 a 5; **u. now/then** hasta ahora/entonces; **not u. tomorrow** hasta mañana, no
 2 *conj* hasta que; **u. she gets back** hasta que vuelva; **we waited u. the rain stopped** esperamos a que escampara; **he won't come u. he's invited** no vendrá mientras no lo invitemos; **can I leave? – not u. the bell rings** ¿puedo irme? – cuando suene el timbre; **I laughed u. I cried** lloré de la risa

untimely [ʌn'taɪmlɪ] *adj* **(a)** *(inopportune) (remark, visit)* intempestivo(a), inoportuno(a) **(b)** *(premature) (death)* prematuro(a); **to meet** *or* **come to an u. end** tener un final prematuro

untiring [ʌn'taɪərɪŋ] *adj* incansable

untitled ['ʌn'taɪtəld] *adj (painting)* sin título

unto ['ʌntuː] *prep Literary* **(a)** *(to)* a; **and he said u. them** y les dijo **(b)** *(until)* hasta; **u. death** hasta la muerte

untogether [ʌntə'geðə(r)] *adj Fam (disorganized)* desordenado(a), desorganizado(a); *(emotionally unstable)* inestable

untold [ʌn'təʊld] *adj (wealth)* inconmensurable; *(beauty)* indecible; *(suffering)* indecible; **u. millions were lost in such speculation** se perdieron millones incontables con aquella especulación

untouchable [ʌn'tʌtʃəbəl] **1** *n* intocable *mf*
 2 *adj* intocable

untouched [ʌn'tʌtʃt] *adj* **(a)** *(undisturbed) (meal)* intacto(a); *(countryside, beach)* virgen; **u. by human hand** no tocado(a) por la mano del hombre; **he left the meal u.** dejó la comida intacta **(b)** *(unaffected)* **to be u. by the influence of television** no haber sufrido la influencia de la televisión

untoward [ʌntə'wɔːd] *adj Formal (unlucky)* desafortunado(a); *(unusual)* inusual, fuera de lo común; **I hope nothing u. has happened** espero que no haya sucedido ninguna desgracia

untrained [ʌn'treɪnd] *adj* **(a)** *(person)* sin preparación; **to the u. eye/ear** para el ojo/oído poco avezado **(b)** *(animal)* sin adiestrar

untrammelled, *US* **untrammeled** [ʌn'træməld] *adj Literary* sin trabas; **u. by convention** no atado(a) por las convenciones sociales

untranslatable [ʌntrænz'leɪtəbəl] *adj* intraducible

untreatable ['ʌn'triːtəbəl] *adj (condition, illness)* intratable

untreated ['ʌn'triːtɪd] *adj* **(a)** *(unprocessed) (food, wood, sewage)* sin tratar **(b)** *(infection, tumour)* sin tratar; **her condition will worsen if left u.** su estado empeorará si no se la trata

untried [ʌn'traɪd] *adj* **(a)** *(untested)* **to be u.** *(system, person)* no haber sido puesto(a) a prueba **(b)** *Law (person, case)* pendiente de juicio

untroubled [ʌn'trʌbəld] *adj* tranquilo(a), despreocupado(a); **to be u. (by)** no estar afectado(a) (por)

untrue [ʌn'truː] *adj* **(a)** *(false)* falso(a) **(b)** *(unfaithful)* desleal (**to** a); **he has been u. to his principles** no ha sido fiel a sus principios; **to be u. to one's spouse** ser infiel al cónyuge, no serle fiel al cónyuge

untrustworthy [ʌn'trʌstwɜːðɪ] *adj (person)* indigno(a) de confianza; *(information)* poco fiable

untruth [ʌn'truːθ] *n Formal* falsedad *f*

untruthful [ʌn'truːθfʊl] *adj (person)* embustero(a), mentiroso(a); *(story, reply)* falso(a)

untruthfully [ʌn'truːθfʊlɪ] *adv* con mentiras, con falsedad

untuned [ʌn'tjuːnd] *adj (instrument)* desafinado(a)

untutored [ʌn'tjuːtəd] *adj (person)* sin estudios; *(eye)* no avezado(a)

untypical [ʌn'tɪpɪkəl] *adj* atípico(a) (**of** de); **it's very u. of her (to be so sulky)** es muy raro en ella (estar de tan mal humor)

untypically [ʌn'tɪpɪklɪ] *adv* **it was u. sunny** hacía más sol de lo normal; **the streets were u. quiet** en las calles había un silencio que no era normal; **u., he didn't have anything to say** en contra de lo habitual, no tenía nada que decir

unusable [ʌn'juːzəbəl] *adj* inutilizable, inservible

unused [ʌn'juːzd] *adj* **(a)** *(not in use)* sin usar **(b)** *(never yet used)* sin estrenar **(c)** [ʌn'juːst] **to be u. to sth** no estar acostumbrado(a) a algo

unusual [ʌn'juːʒʊəl] *adj (not common)* poco corriente, inusual; *(strange)* raro(a); **it's u. to have snow at this time of year** no es normal que nieve en esta época del año; **an u. occurrence** un hecho poco corriente; **it's not u. for him to take two hours for lunch** no es nada raro que se tome dos horas para almorzar; **it's u. of her not to notice** es raro que no se dé cuenta

unusually [ʌn'juːʒʊəlɪ] *adv* **(a)** *(abnormally)* **she was u. dressed** iba vestida de una forma rara; **his speech was u. long** su discurso fue más largo de lo normal; **she slept for an u. long time** durmió mucho más de lo normal; **u. for him, he hesitated** dudó, algo que es poco frecuente en él **(b)** *(very)* extraordinariamente; **she was u. intelligent** su inteligencia era excepcional

unutterable [ʌn'ʌtərəbəl] *adj Formal* indescriptible

unvaried [ʌn'veərɪd] *adj* monótono(a), uniforme

unvarnished [ʌn'vɑːnɪʃt] *adj* sin barnizar; *Fig* **the u. truth** la verdad desnuda

unveil [ʌn'veɪl] *vt (statue, plaque)* descubrir; *Fig (product, plan)* revelar, desvelar

unveiling [ʌn'veɪlɪŋ] *n (of statue, plaque)* descubrimiento *m*, inauguración *f*; *Fig (of product, plan)* revelación *f* ►► ***u. ceremony*** inauguración *f*

unverifiable [ʌnverɪ'faɪəbəl] *adj* inverificable

unversed [ʌn'vɜːst] *adj* poco ducho(a) *or* versado(a) (**in** en)

unvoiced [ʌn'vɔɪst] *adj* **(a)** *Ling* sordo(a) **(b)** *(unspoken)* no expresado(a); **an u. fear** un temor oculto

unwaged [ʌn'weɪdʒd] *Br* **1** *npl* **the u.** los desempleados, *Am* los desocupados
 2 *adj (not earning money)* desempleado(a), *Am* desocupado(a)

unwanted [ʌn'wɒntɪd] *adj (baby, pregnancy)* no deseado(a); **he was given an u. responsibility** le dieron una responsabilidad que él no quería; **we accept donations of u. clothes or toys** aceptamos donaciones de ropa o juguetes usados; **to remove u. hair** eliminar el vello superfluo; **to feel u.** sentirse rechazado(a)

unwarrantable [ʌn'wɒrəntəbəl] *adj Formal* injustificable

unwarranted [ʌn'wɒrəntɪd] *adj* injustificado(a)

unwary [ʌn'weərɪ] *adj* incauto(a)

unwashed [ʌn'wɒʃt] *adj* sucio(a), sin lavar; *Hum* **the great u.** la plebe

unwatchable [ʌn'wɒtʃəbəl] *adj* insoportable

unwavering [ʌn'weɪvərɪŋ] *adj (loyalty, support)* inquebrantable, sin fisuras; *(gaze)* fijo(a); *(concentration)* intenso(a)

unwaveringly [ʌn'weɪvərɪŋlɪ] *adv (to believe, support)* sin vacilaciones; *(to look, stare)* sin parpadear, fijamente

unwelcome [ʌn'welkəm] *adj (visit, visitor)* inoportuno(a); *(news)* desagradable; *(attention)* no deseado(a); **to make sb feel u.** hacer que alguien se sienta incómodo(a); **the extra money was not u.** el dinero extra no vino mal

unwelcoming [ʌn'welkəmɪŋ] *adj (place)* muy poco acogedor(ora); *(person)* frío(a), hostil

unwell [ʌn'wel] *adj* indispuesto(a), enfermo(a); **to be u.** estar indispuesto(a) *or* enfermo(a); **to look u.** tener mal aspecto

unwholesome [ʌn'həʊlsəm] *adj (food, climate)* insalubre; *(activity, habits, thoughts)* malsano(a)

unwieldy [ʌn'wiːldɪ] *adj (tool)* poco manejable; *(object, system)* aparatoso(a)

unwilling [ʌn'wɪlɪŋ] *adj* reacio(a); **I was their u. accomplice** fui su cómplice a pesar mío; **to be u. to do sth** ser reacio(a) a hacer algo

unwillingly [ʌn'wɪlɪŋlɪ] *adv* de mala gana

unwillingness [ʌn'wɪlɪŋnɪs] *n* reticencia *f*

unwind [ʌn'waɪnd] *(pt & pp* **unwound** [ʌn'waʊnd]) **1** *vt* desenrollar
2 *vi* **(a)** *(string, wool)* desenrollarse **(b)** *Fam (relax)* relajarse

unwise [ʌn'waɪz] *adj* imprudente; **an u. choice** una mala elección; **it would be u. to ignore this advice** no sería prudente desoír este consejo

unwisely [ʌn'waɪzlɪ] *adv* imprudentemente, con mal criterio

unwitting [ʌn'wɪtɪŋ] *adj (accomplice, victim, ally)* involuntario(a)

unwittingly [ʌn'wɪtɪŋlɪ] *adv* sin querer, involuntariamente

unwonted [ʌn'waʊntɪd] *adj Formal (not customary)* desacostumbrado(a), inusitado(a)

unworkable [ʌn'wɜːkəbəl] *adj* impracticable

unworldly [ʌn'wɜːldlɪ] *adj* **(a)** *(spiritual)* espiritual **(b)** *(naive)* ingenuo(a)

unworried [ʌn'wʌrɪd] *adj* despreocupado(a)

unworthiness [ʌn'wɜːðɪnɪs] *n* **I was conscious of my u.** era consciente de que no lo merecía

unworthy [ʌn'wɜːðɪ] *adj* indigno(a) **(of** de); **such behaviour is u. of you!** semejante actitud no es digna de ti; **the subject is u. of further attention** el tema no merece mayor atención

unwound *pt & pp of* **unwind**

unwrap [ʌn'ræp] *(pt & pp* **unwrapped**) *vt* desenvolver

unwritten [ʌn'rɪtən] *adj (language, law)* no escrito(a); *(agreement)* tácito(a), verbal; **an u. rule** una regla no escrita

unyielding [ʌn'jiːldɪŋ] *adj (person, attitude)* inflexible; *(opposition)* férreo(a); *(resistance)* pertinaz

unyoke [ʌn'jəʊk] *vt* quitar el yugo a, desuncir; *Fig* liberar

unzip [ʌn'zɪp] *(pt & pp* **unzipped**) *vt* **(a)** *(clothes, bag)* abrir la cremallera *or Am* el cierre de; **to u. one's trousers** bajarse la cremallera *or Am* el cierre de los pantalones **(b)** *Comptr* descomprimir

---

UP [ʌp] **1** *adv* **(a)** *(with motion)* hacia arriba; **to come/go up** subir; **the sun has come up** ha salido el sol; **prices have gone up** los precios han subido; **to go up north** ir hacia el norte; **to go up to Canada** subir *or* ir a Canadá; **the bird flew up into the sky** el pájaro se elevó en el cielo; **up you get!** ¡levántate!; **she jumped up** se levantó de un salto; **the path leads up into the forest** el camino lleva al bosque; **to pick sth up** recoger algo; **to put one's hand up** levantar la mano; **to put a poster up** pegar un cartel; **I ran up** subí corriendo; **could you take this suitcase up?** *(upstairs)* ¿podrías subir esta maleta?; **we took the** *Br* **lift** *or US* **elevator up** subimos en ascensor; *Fig* **the economy is on its way up again** la economía está recuperándose; **to jump up and down** pegar brincos *or* saltos; **she was pacing up and down** caminaba de arriba a abajo; *Fig* **I've been a bit up and down since the divorce** he tenido bastantes altibajos después del divorcio

(b) *(with position)* arriba; **up above** arriba; **up here/there** aquí/allí arriba; **up in the sky/mountains** en el cielo/las montañas; *Fam* **people are friendlier up North** la gente del norte es más simpática; **further up** más arriba; **from 3,000 metres up** a partir de 3.000 metros de altitud; **place it bottom up** colócalo boca abajo; **which way up does it go?** ¿cuál es la parte de arriba?; **it's up there with the best performances of all time** se encuentra entre las mejores interpretaciones de todos los tiempos; IDIOM *Fam* **he's a bit funny up there** está un poco tocado del ala *or Am* zafado

(c) *(ahead)* **to be one goal/five points up** ir ganando por *or Esp* de un gol/cinco puntos; **to be three up with two to play** *(in golf)* ir ganando por tres hoyos cuando quedan dos por jugar; **he went two sets up** se puso dos sets por delante

2 *prep* **(a)** *(with motion)* **to climb up a hill** subir una colina; **to go up the stairs** subir las escaleras; **I ran up the hill** subí la colina corriendo; **we swam up the river** nadamos río arriba; **to walk up the street** caminar *or Esp* andar por la calle; **I got water up my nose** me entró agua por la nariz; **he stuffed the cushion up his sweater** se metió el almohadón bajo el suéter; **she paced up and down the corridor** recorría el pasillo de arriba a abajo; **supermarkets up and down the country** los supermercados de todo el país; *Vulg* **up yours!** vete a la mierda!

(b) *(with position)* **up a tree/ladder** en lo alto de un árbol/una escalera; **my room is up the stairs** mi habitación está arriba; **halfway up the mountain** a mitad de camino hacia la cumbre de la montaña; **she lives up the street from me** vive en la misma calle que yo

3 *adj* **(a)** *(higher)* **prices/sales are up** los precios/las ventas han subido; **unemployment is at 10 percent, up 1 percent on last year** la tasa de desempleo es del diez por ciento, un uno por ciento mayor que la del año pasado

(b) *(out of bed)* **he isn't up** no está levantado, no se ha levantado; **I was up all night** pasé toda la noche levantado; **I was up at six** me levanté a las seis; **to be up and about** *(in morning)* estar levantado(a); *(after illness)* estar recuperado(a)

(c) *(visible)* **the sun is up** ya ha salido el sol

(d) *(optimistic)* **she seemed quite up when I saw her** parecía de bastante buen humor cuando la vi

(e) *(tied)* **I prefer you with your hair up** me gustas más con el pelo recogido

(f) *Fam (wrong)* **what's up?** ¿qué pasa?; **what's up with you/him?** ¿qué te/le pasa?; **something's up** algo pasa *or* ocurre; **there's something up with the TV** le pasa algo a la tele

(g) *Fam* **what's up?** *(what's happening)* ¿qué pasa?; *US (as greeting)* ¿qué (te) cuentas?

(h) *(finished)* **your time's up** se te ha terminado el tiempo; **the two weeks were nearly up** ya casi habían transcurrido las dos semanas

(i) *(functioning)* **how long before the network's up again?** ¿cuándo va a volver a funcionar la red?; **to be up and running** *(machine, project)* estar en marcha

(j) *Br (being repaired)* **the road is up at the moment** la carretera está en obras

(k) *Fam (on trial)* **he was up before the magistrate on Wednesday** el juez vio su causa el miércoles; **he was up for theft** lo juzgaron por robo

(l) *Fam (informed)* **to be (well) up on sth** estar (muy) enterado de algo

(m) *Fam (ready)* **tea's up!** ¡el té está listo!

(n) *(intended, available)* **that is not up for negotiation** eso no es negociable; **to be up for re-election** presentarse a la reelección; **to be up for sale** estar en venta; *Br Fam* **I'm up for it if you are** si tú te apuntas yo también; *Br very Fam* **to be up for it** *(sexually eager)* estar caliente

(o) *(level)* **to be up with the leaders** estar entre los líderes; **we're currently up to target** de momento estamos cumpliendo nuestros objetivos

(p) *Comptr* ***u. arrow*** flecha *f* arriba; ***u. arrow key*** tecla *f* de flecha arriba

4 *n* **life's ups and downs** los altibajos de la vida; IDIOM **to be on the up and up** *Br (improving)* ir a mejor; *US Fam (honest)* ser *Esp* legal *or Am* recto(a)

5 *vt* (*pt & pp* **upped**) **(a)** *Fam (increase) (price)* subir; *(offer)* mejorar; **to up the tempo** acelerar el ritmo **(b)** IDIOM *Fam* **to u. stakes** *or* **sticks** *(move house)* levantar el campamento

6 *vi Fam* **to up and leave** *or* **go** *Esp* coger y marcharse, *Am* agarrar e irse

7 *exclam Br* **up the Rovers!** ¡ánimo Rovers!, *Esp* ¡aúpa Rovers!, *Am* ¡dale Rovers!

8 up against *prep* **put it up against the wall** colócalo *or Am* páralo contra la pared; **to be up against sth** *(confronted with)* enfrentarse a algo; **they came up against stiff opposition** encontraron una fuerte oposición; IDIOM **to be up against it** tenerlo muy difícil

9 up to *prep* **(a)** *(until, as far as)* hasta; **up to now** hasta ahora; **up to £100 a week** hasta 100 libras semanales; **up to the age of seven** hasta los siete años; **up to fifty people may have died** pueden haberse producido hasta cincuenta muertes; **the water came up to their necks** el agua les llegaba hasta el cuello; **to go up to sb** acercarse a alguien; **I'm up to here (with sth)** *(work, things to do)* estoy hasta arriba (de algo); *(fed up)* estoy hasta la coronilla (de algo)

(b) *(equal to)* **he's not up to the job** no está a la altura del puesto; **I don't feel up to it** no me siento en condiciones de hacerlo; **it's not up to its usual standard** no está tan bueno como de costumbre; *Fam* **it's not up to much** *(not very good)* no es gran cosa

(c) *(doing)* **what have you been up to?** ¿qué has estado haciendo?; **I'm sure he's up to something!** ¡estoy seguro de que prepara algo!; **what are the children up to?** ¿qué están tramando los niños?

(d) *(indicating responsibility, decision)* **it's up to you to do it** te corresponde a ti hacerlo; **it's up to you whether you tell her** depende de ti si se lo dices o no; **shall we tell her? – it's up to you** ¿se lo decimos? – como tú quieras; **if it was up to me, I'd sell it** si dependiera de mí, lo vendería

10 up until *prep* hasta

---

up-and-coming ['ʌpənd'kʌmɪŋ] *adj* **an u. athlete/novelist** un atleta/novelista prometedor; **the u. generation of politicians** la nueva generación de políticos

upbeat 1 *n* ['ʌpbiːt] *Mus* último tiempo *m* del compás
2 *adj* [ʌp'biːt] *(optimistic)* optimista

upbraid [ʌp'breɪd] *vt Formal* recriminar; **to u. sb for sth** recriminar algo a alguien

upbringing ['ʌpbrɪŋɪŋ] *n* educación *f*

upchuck ['ʌptʃʌk] *vi Fam* devolver, echar la papilla

upcoming ['ʌpkʌmɪŋ] *adj (event)* próximo(a); *(book, movie)* próximo(a), de próxima aparición

up-country 1 *adj* ['ʌpkʌntrɪ] del interior
2 *adv* [ʌp'kʌntrɪ] *(to go, move)* al interior, tierra adentro; *(to live)* en el interior, tierra adentro

update 1 *n* ['ʌpdeɪt] (**a**) *(new information)* **to give sb an u. on sth** poner a alguien al corriente *or* al día de algo; **our reporter has an u. on the crisis** nuestro reportero tiene nueva información sobre la crisis (**b**) *Comptr* actualización *f*
2 *vt* [ʌp'deɪt] (**a**) *(records)* actualizar, poner al día; **to u. sb on sth** poner a alguien al corriente *or* al día de algo (**b**) *Comptr* actualizar

up-draught, *US* **up-draft** ['ʌpdrɑːft] *n Av* corriente *f* ascendente

upend [ʌp'end] *vt* (**a**) *(turn upside down)* poner boca abajo; **she upended the contents of the box over the table** derramó el contenido de la caja sobre la mesa (**b**) *(knock over)* derribar

upfront [ʌp'frʌnt] 1 *adj* (**a**) *Fam (frank)* claro(a), franco(a); **he's very u. about the whole thing** habla sin tapujos del tema (**b**) *Com (costs)* inicial
2 *adv (to pay)* por adelantado

upgradable [ʌp'greɪdəbəl] *adj Comptr (hardware, system)* actualizable; *(memory)* ampliable

upgrade 1 *n* ['ʌpgreɪd] (**a**) *Comptr (of hardware, system)* actualización *f*; *(of memory)* ampliación *f* ►► ***u. kit*** kit *m* de actualización (**b**) *US (slope)* subida *f*
2 *vt* [ʌp'greɪd] (**a**) *(improve)* mejorar; **they plan to u. the facilities at the airport** tienen pensado mejorar las instalaciones del aeropuerto (**b**) *(promote) (officer, employee)* ascender; **the department has been upgraded to a ministry** el departamento ha ascendido de categoría y ha pasado a ser un ministerio; **I was upgraded to business class** *(on plane)* me pasaron a clase business (**c**) *Comptr (hardware, system)* actualizar; *(memory)* ampliar

upheaval [ʌp'hiːvəl] *n* trastorno *m*, conmoción *f*; **moving from the country to the city was a great u. for the family** mudarse del campo a la ciudad fue un verdadero trastorno *or* una verdadera conmoción para la familia; **emotional u.** tensión emocional; **a time of great political u.** una época de mucha agitación *or* gran convulsión política

upheld *pt & pp of* **uphold**

uphill 1 *adj* ['ʌphɪl] *(road)* cuesta arriba; **it's u. all the way** es todo cuesta arriba; *Fig* es una lucha continua; **it was an u. struggle to convince him** nos costó Dios y ayuda convencerle
2 *adv* [ʌp'hɪl] cuesta arriba

uphold [ʌp'həʊld] (*pt & pp* **upheld** [ʌp'held]) *vt* (**a**) *(opinion, principle)* defender; **to u. the law** hacer respetar la ley (**b**) *Law (decision, verdict)* confirmar

upholstered [ʌp'həʊlstəd] *adj* tapizado(a); *Hum* **to be well u.** tener buenas sentaderas

upholsterer [ʌp'həʊlstərə(r)] *n* tapicero(a) *m,f*

upholstery [ʌp'həʊlstərɪ] *n* (**a**) *(filling)* relleno *m*; *(covering)* tapicería *f* (**b**) *(craft, trade)* tapicería *f*

UPI [juːpiː'aɪ] (*abbr* **United Press International**) UPI *f*, United Press *f*

upkeep ['ʌpkiːp] *n (of property)* mantenimiento *m*; **he paid nothing towards the u. of the children** no pasó dinero alguno para los gastos de manutención de los hijos

upland ['ʌplənd] 1 *n* **the upland(s)** las tierras altas
2 *adj* de las tierras altas

uplift 1 *n* ['ʌplɪft] subida *f* de ánimo; **to give sth/sb an u.** animar algo/a alguien ►► ***u. bra*** sostén *m or Esp* sujetador *m or Carib, Col, Méx* brasier *m or RP* corpiño *m* armado
2 *vt* [ʌp'lɪft] *(emotionally)* animar, levantar el espíritu a

uplifted [ʌp'lɪftɪd] *adj* (**a**) *(morally, spiritually)* **he felt u. by the music** la música le había levantado el espíritu (**b**) *(face)* vuelto(a) hacia arriba

uplifting [ʌp'lɪftɪŋ] *adj* **an u. experience/story** una experiencia/historia que levanta el espíritu; **I found the music very u.** la música me levantó el espíritu

uplighter ['ʌplaɪtə(r)] *n* = lámpara o luz que ilumina hacia arriba

upload ['ʌpləʊd] *Comptr* 1 *n* carga *f*
2 *vt* cargar, subir

upmarket ['ʌpmɑːkɪt] 1 *adj (neighbourhood, restaurant)* elegante; *(newspaper, program)* dirigido(a) a un público selecto
2 *adv* **this place has gone u. since I was last here** este local ha subido de categoría desde la última vez que estuve aquí; **the newspaper wants to move u.** el periódico quiere atraer a un público más selecto

upmost = **uppermost**

upon [ə'pɒn] *prep* (**a**) *(on)* en, sobre; **u. the table** sobre la mesa; **the ring u. her finger** el anillo que llevaba en el dedo; **she had a sad look u. her face** su rostro tenía un aire triste; **suddenly, the dogs were u. us** de pronto, teníamos a los perros encima; IDIOM *Old-fashioned* **u. my word!** ¡caramba!
(**b**) *(indicating imminence)* **autumn is nearly u. us** ya casi estamos en otoño, tenemos el otoño encima
(**c**) *Formal (immediately after)* **u. our arrival in Rome** a nuestra llegada a Roma; **u. realizing what had happened...** al darse cuenta de lo ocurrido...
(**d**) *(indicating large amount)* **thousands u. thousands** miles y miles; **mile u. mile of desert** kilómetros y kilómetros de desierto

upper ['ʌpə(r)] 1 *n* (**a**) *(of shoe)* empeine *m*; IDIOM *Br Fam* **to be on one's uppers** estar sin un centavo *or Esp* duro (**b**) *Fam (drug)* estimulante *m*, excitante *m*
2 *adj* superior; **the u. echelons of society/the army** los escalones más altos del escalafón social/militar; **the u. reaches** *or* **waters of the Nile** el curso alto del Nilo; **temperatures are in the u. 30s** las temperaturas están cerca de 40 grados; **models at the u. end of the range** los modelos más altos de gama; IDIOM **to gain the u. hand** tomar la delantera; IDIOM **to have the u. hand** llevar ventaja ►► *Met* ***u. atmosphere*** atmósfera *f* superior; *Typ* ***u. case*** mayúsculas *fpl*; ***u. class*** clase *f* alta; ***u. deck*** *(of bus)* piso *m* superior *or* de arriba; *(of ship)* cubierta *f* superior; *Pol* ***the U. House*** la cámara alta; ***u. limit*** límite *m* superior, tope *m*; *Comptr* ***u. memory*** memoria *f* superior; ***u. middle class*** clase *f* media alta; *Educ* ***u. sixth*** = el segundo de los dos últimos cursos del bachillerato en Inglaterra, Gales e Irlanda del Norte

upper-case [ʌpə'keɪs] *adj* en mayúsculas

upper-class [ʌpə'klɑːs] *adj* de clase alta

upper-crust [ʌpə'krʌst] *adj Fam (person, accent)* de clase alta, de postín

uppercut ['ʌpəkʌt] *n (in boxing)* uppercut *m*; **left/right u.** uppercut de izquierda/derecha

uppermost ['ʌpəməʊst], **upmost** ['ʌpməʊst] *adj (in position)* superior; *Fig* **it was u. in my mind** era una cuestión prioritaria para mí

uppity ['ʌpɪtɪ] *adj Fam* creído(a), engreído(a); **to get u.** darse aires

upright ['ʌpraɪt] 1 *n (beam) (of door, bookshelf)* montante *m*; *(of goal post)* poste *m*
2 *adj* (**a**) *(vertical)* vertical, derecho(a) ►► ***u. freezer*** congelador *m* vertical; ***u. piano*** piano *m* vertical; ***u. vacuum cleaner*** aspiradora *f* vertical (**b**) *(honest)* honrado(a)
3 *adv* (**a**) *(to put)* vertical, derecho(a); **to put/place sth u.** poner/colocar algo vertical *or* derecho (**b**) *(to sit, stand)* derecho(a), erguido(a); **he sat bolt u.** se sentó bien derecho *or* erguido

uprising ['ʌpraɪzɪŋ] *n* levantamiento *m*

upriver ['ʌp'rɪvə(r)] 1 *adj* río arriba
2 *adv (to be, move, swim)* río arriba

uproar ['ʌprɔː(r)] *n (noise)* alboroto *m*; *(protest)* escándalo *m*; **the meeting was in an u.** se armó un gran alboroto en la reunión; **his speech caused quite an u.** su discurso provocó un escándalo

uproarious [ʌp'rɔːrɪəs] *adj (noisy)* escandaloso(a); *(funny)* divertidísimo(a)

uproariously [ʌp'rɔːrɪəslɪ] *adv (to laugh)* a carcajadas; **u. funny** divertidísimo(a), hilarante

uproot [ʌp'ruːt] *vt (plant)* arrancar de raíz, desarraigar; *(person)* desarraigar

UPS [juːpiː'es] *n* (**a**) *Comptr* (*abbr* **uninterruptible power supply**) SAI *m* (**b**) (*abbr* **United Parcel Service**) = empresa estadounidense de paquetería

ups-a-daisy ['ʌpsədeɪzɪ] *exclam Fam* ¡epa!

upset 1 *n* ['ʌpset] (**a**) *(disturbance)* trastorno *m*; **the result caused a major political u.** el resultado causó un importante trastorno político (**b**) *(surprise)* resultado *m* inesperado (**c**) *US* ***u. price*** precio *m* mínimo de subasta
2 *vt* [ʌp'set] (*pt & pp* **upset**) (**a**) *(liquid)* tirar, derramar; *(container, chair)* tirar, volcar; *(boat)* volcar
(**b**) *(person)* disgustar; **the least thing upsets him** se disgusta por cualquier cosa; **to u. oneself** disgustarse; **it's not worth upsetting yourself over** no vale la pena disgustarse por eso
(**c**) *(plans, schedule)* trastornar, alterar
(**d**) *(make ill)* **seafood always upsets my stomach** los mariscos siempre me sientan *or* caen mal
3 *adj* [ʌp'set] (**a**) *(unhappy)* disgustado(a) (**about** por); **what are you**

so u. about? ¿por qué estás tan disgustada?; **she was u. by the pictures** las imágenes la impresionaron; **to get u. (about sth)** disgustarse (por algo) **(b) to have an u. stomach** tener el estómago mal

upsetting [ʌp'setɪŋ] *adj* **being criticized in public can be very u.** puede ser demoledor que te critiquen en público; **he found it u. that they hadn't even bothered to phone him** le dolió que ni siquiera le llamasen; **viewers might find some of these scenes u.** algunas escenas pueden herir la sensibilidad de los espectadores

upshot ['ʌpʃɒt] *n* resultado *m*; **the u. of it all was that he resigned** el resultado de todo fue que él dimitió; **what was the u. of it all?** ¿cómo terminó *or* acabó la cosa?, ¿en qué quedó la cosa?

upside down ['ʌpsaɪd'daʊn] **1** *adj (cup, glass, picture)* al *or* del revés
2 *adv* **to hang u.** *(person, animal)* colgar cabeza abajo; **to turn sth u.** *(object)* poner algo al *or* del revés; *Fig (house, room)* poner algo patas arriba; *(life, world)* dar un vuelco a algo

upstage [ʌp'steɪdʒ] **1** *adv Theat (to move)* hacia el fondo del escenario; *(to enter, exit)* por el fondo del escenario; **to be** *or* **stand u. of sb** estar en segundo plano respecto a alguien
2 *vt Theat & Fig* dejar en segundo plano

upstairs 1 *adj* ['ʌpsteəz] *(room, window, neighbour)* de arriba; **the u. apartment/bathroom** el apartamento/cuarto de baño de arriba
2 *adv* [ʌp'steəz] **(a)** *(ascending stairs)* arriba; **to come/go u.** subir (la escalera) **(b)** *(on upper floor)* **he lives u.** vive en el apartamento *or Esp* piso de arriba; **I'll take your bags u.** te llevo las maletas arriba; IDIOM *Fam* **he hasn't got much u.** tiene la cabeza llena de serrín *or Am* aserrín **(c)** *Old-fashioned (in house with masters and servants)* arriba
3 *n* ['ʌpsteəz] **(a)** *(of house)* **we rent out the u.** alquilamos la parte de arriba **(b)** *Old-fashioned (in house with masters and servants)* los de arriba, los amos

upstanding [ʌp'stændɪŋ] *adj* **(a)** *(honest)* honrado(a), recto(a) **(b)** *Formal (on one's feet)* **would you please be u.** en pie, por favor

upstart ['ʌpstɑːt] *n* advenedizo(a) *m,f*

upstate *US* **1** *adj* ['ʌpsteɪt] del norte del estado; **u. New York** el norte del estado de Nueva York
2 *adv* [ʌp'steɪt] al norte del estado; **to go upstate** ir al norte del estado

upstream ['ʌpstriːm] **1** *adv* **(a)** *(to live, row, swim)* río arriba; **u. of the village** aguas arriba del pueblo **(b)** *Ind* en una fase previa, aguas arriba
2 *adj (on river)* río arriba

upstroke ['ʌpstrəʊk] *n* **(a)** *(in engine)* movimiento *m* ascendente, *Spec* carrera *f* ascendente **(b)** *(in writing)* trazo *m* hacia arriba

upsurge ['ʌpsɜːdʒ] *n* aumento *m* **(in** de)

upswing ['ʌpswɪŋ] *n* **(a)** *(movement)* alza *f* **(b)** *(improvement)* mejora *f*, alza *f* **(in** en); **the stock market is on the u.** la bolsa está en alza

uptake ['ʌpteɪk] *n* **(a)** IDIOM *Fam* **to be quick/slow on the u.** ser/no ser muy espabilado(a) **(b)** *Physiol (of oxygen, nutrients)* asimilación *f* **(c)** *Br (of offer, allowance)* **they want to improve the u. of these benefits** quieren animar a más gente que tiene derecho a estas prestaciones a que la pidan

uptight [ʌp'taɪt] *adj Fam* **(a)** *(nervous)* tenso(a) **(about** por); **he gets so u. whenever I mention it** se pone muy tenso cuando lo menciono **(b)** *(strait-laced)* puritano(a); **to be u. about sex** ser puritano(a) en cuestiones sexuales

up-to-date [ʌptə'deɪt] *adj (news, information)* reciente, actualizado(a); *(method, approach)* moderno(a); **to bring sb u. (on sth)** poner a alguien al día (sobre algo); **they brought the reports u.** actualizaron los informes; **I try to keep u. on the news** intento estar informado *or* al día de lo que pasa

up-to-the-minute ['ʌptəðə'mɪnɪt] *adj (modern, fashionable)* a la última; *(recent)* al día

uptown ['ʌptaʊn] *US* **1** *n* zona *f* residencial
2 *adj (area)* residencial; **u. New York** las zonas residenciales de Nueva York; **u. traffic** el tráfico que sale del centro
3 *adv* [ʌp'taʊn] *(to be, live)* fuera del centro

upturn ['ʌptɜːn] *n* mejora *f* **(in** de)

upturned ['ʌptɜːnd] *adj* **(a)** *(bucket, box) (face down)* boca abajo; *(on its side)* volcado(a) **(b)** *(facing upwards)* **u. faces** caras vueltas hacia arriba **(c)** *(nose)* respingón(ona)

upward ['ʌpwəd] **1** *adj (direction, movement, path)* ascendente; **the figures show an u. trend** las cifras muestran una tendencia al alza ▸▸ *Comptr* ***u. compatibility*** compatibilidad *f* con versiones anteriores; ***u. mobility*** ascenso *m* en la escala social
2 *adv* = **upwards**

upward-compatible ['ʌpwədkəm'pætɪbəl] *adj Comptr* compatible con versiones anteriores

upwardly mobile ['ʌpwədlɪ'məʊbaɪl] *adj* = que va ascendiendo en la escala social

upward(s) ['ʌpwəd(z)] *adv* **(a)** *(to move, look)* hacia arriba; **we will have to revise our estimates u.** tendremos que revisar al alza nuestros cálculos; **prices are climbing u.** los precios van en aumento
(b) *(facing up)* **she placed the photos (face) u. on the table** puso las fotos boca arriba sobre la mesa
(c) *(onwards)* **from 15 years u.** a partir de los 15 años; **from $100 u.** a partir de 100 dólares; **u. of** más de, por encima de

upwind 1 *adj* ['ʌpwɪnd] **luckily, the village is u. of the factory** por suerte el viento no sopla desde la fábrica en dirección al pueblo
2 *adv* [ʌp'wɪnd] contra el viento

Urals ['jʊərəlz] *npl* **the U.** los Urales

uranium [jʊ'reɪnɪəm] *n Chem* uranio *m*

Uranus [jʊ'reɪnəs, 'jʊrənəs] *n (planet)* Urano

urban ['ɜːbən] *adj (area, community)* urbano(a); **u. life** la vida en la ciudad ▸▸ *Br* ***u. district*** distrito *m* urbano; *Br Formerly* ***u. district council*** = municipio que corresponde a varios centros urbanos; ***u. guerrilla*** guerrillero(a) *m,f* urbano(a); ***u. legend*** leyenda *f* urbana; ***u. myth*** leyenda *f* urbana; ***u. renewal*** renovación *f* urbana; ***u. sprawl*** aglomeración *f* urbana

urbane [ɜː'beɪn] *adj* muy bien educado(a)

urbanely [ɜː'beɪnlɪ] *adv* con muy buena educación

urbanity [ɜː'bænɪtɪ] *n Formal* urbanidad *f*

urbanization [ɜːbənaɪ'zeɪʃən] *n (process)* urbanización *f*

urbanized ['ɜːbənaɪzd] *adj* urbanizado(a)

urchin ['ɜːtʃɪn] *n (child)* pilluelo(a) *m,f*, golfillo(a) *m,f* ▸▸ ***u. cut*** corte *m* a lo garçon

Urdu ['ʊəduː] *n* urdu *m*

urea [jʊ'rɪə] *n Biochem* urea *f*

ureter [jʊ'riːtə(r)] *n Anat* uréter *m*

urethra [jʊ'riːθrə] *n Anat* uretra *f*

urethritis [jʊrɪ'θraɪtɪs] *n Med* uretritis *f inv*

urge [ɜːdʒ] **1** *n* impulso *m*, deseo *m* irresistible; **to have** *or* **feel an u. to do sth** sentir la necesidad de hacer algo; **sexual urges** impulsos sexuales
2 *vt* **(a)** *(encourage)* **to u. sb to do sth** instar a alguien a hacer algo; **she urged us to take advantage of the opportunity** nos instó a que aprovecháramos la oportunidad; **I u. you to reconsider** le ruego encarecidamente que recapacite
(b) *(recommend)* **they urged the need for new schools** insistieron en la necesidad de construir nuevas escuelas; **they urged acceptance of the treaty** insistieron en que se aceptara el tratado; **she urged caution** instó a ser cautos
(c) *(goad, incite)* **he urged his men into battle** incitó a sus hombres a entrar en batalla; **to u. a horse forward** espolear a un caballo
3 *vi* **to u. for sth** instar a algo; **he urged against a hasty decision** instó a no tomar una decisión apresurada; **he needed no urging** no hizo falta que le insistieran mucho

> En inglés culto o elevado, y especialmente en inglés americano, **urge** puede ir seguido de **that** más un verbo en subjuntivo (ver el panel SUBJUNCTIVE):
> **I urge that you be more careful in future**
> *le ruego encarecidamente que tengas más cuidado en el futuro*
> Lo mismo también podría decirse del siguiente modo:
> **I urge you to be more careful in future**

▸ **urge on** *vt sep (person, troops)* alentar, animar; **to u. sb on to do sth** alentar *or* animar a alguien a hacer algo

urgency ['ɜːdʒənsɪ] *n* urgencia *f*; **there was a note of u. in his voice** había un tono apremiante en su voz; **it's a matter of u.** es muy urgente; **as a matter of u.** urgentemente, con la mayor urgencia; **there's no great u.** no es muy urgente

urgent ['ɜːdʒənt] *adj (matter, need, message)* urgente; **it needs some u. repairs** necesita repararse urgentemente; **in an u. tone of voice** con un tono de voz apremiante; **to be in u. need of sth** necesitar algo urgentemente; **this is u.** es urgente

urgently ['ɜːdʒəntlɪ] *adv* urgentemente; **supplies are u. needed** se necesitan provisiones con urgencia *or* urgentemente

uric ['jʊrɪk] *adj Biochem* úrico(a) ▸▸ ***u. acid*** ácido *m* úrico

urinal [jə'raɪnəl] *n* urinario *m*

urinary ['jʊərɪnərɪ] *adj Anat* urinario(a) ▸▸ ***u. infection*** infección *f* urinaria; ***u. tract*** vías *fpl* urinarias

urinate ['jʊərɪneɪt] *vi* orinar

urination [jʊərɪˈneɪʃən] *n* micción *f*

urine [ˈjʊərɪn] *n* orina *f*; **u. analysis/sample** análisis/muestra de orina

urinogenital [jʊərɪnəʊˈdʒenɪtəl] *adj Physiol* urogenital

URL [juːɑːˈrel] *n Comptr* (*abbr* **uniform resource locator**) URL *m*

urn [ɜːn] *n* (a) *(decorative)* urna *f* (b) *(for ashes)* urna *f* (cineraria) (c) *(for tea)* = recipiente grande de metal con un grifo para el té

urogenital [jʊərəʊˈdʒenɪtəl] *adj Physiol* urogenital

urologist [jʊˈrɒlədʒɪst] *n* urólogo(a) *m,f*

urology [jʊˈrɒlədʒɪ] *n Med* urología *f*

urticaria [ɜːtɪˈkeərɪə] *n Med* urticaria *f*

Uruguay [ˈjʊərəgwaɪ] *n* Uruguay

Uruguayan [jʊərəˈgwaɪən] 1 *n* uruguayo(a) *m,f*
2 *adj* uruguayo(a)

US [juːˈes] (*abbr* **United States**) 1 *n* EE.UU. *mpl*
2 *adj* estadounidense

US [ʌs, *unstressed* əs] 1 *pron* (a) *(direct object)* nos; **they hate us** nos odian; **they like us** les gustamos; **she forgave our son but not US** perdonó a nuestro hijo, pero no a nosotros
(b) *(indirect object)* nos; **she gave us the book** nos dio el libro; **she gave it to us** nos lo dio; **give it to us** dánoslo
(c) *(after preposition)* nosotros; **they are thinking of us** están pensando en nosotros; **it was meant for them, not for US** iba dirigido a ellos, no a nosotros; **all four of us went** fuimos los cuatro; **there are three of us** somos cuatro
(d) *(as complement of verb "to be")* nosotros; **it's us!** ¡somos nosotros!; **it was us who did it** fuimos nosotros los que lo hicimos; **the décor isn't really us** la decoración no va *or* pega mucho con nosotros
(e) *Br Fam (me)* **lend us a fiver** préstame cinco libras; **let's have a go** déjame probar
(f) *US Fam* **let's go and get us some guns/ice cream** vamos a ver si nos hacemos con unas pistolas/un poco de helado
2 *n Fam* **is there still an us?** *(in relationship)* ¿lo nuestro continúa?

USA [juːesˈeɪ] *n* (a) (*abbr* **United States of America**) EE.UU. (b) (*abbr* **United States Army**) ejército *m* de los Estados Unidos

usable [ˈjuːzəbəl] *adj* utilizable; **it's no longer u.** ya no sirve

USAF [juːeseɪˈef] *n* (*abbr* **United States Air Force**) fuerzas *fpl* aéreas de los Estados Unidos

usage [ˈjuːsɪdʒ] *n* (a) *(use)* uso *m* (b) *(custom)* uso *m*, costumbre *f* (c) *Gram* uso *m*; **correct u.** uso correcto

USB [juːesˈbiː] *n Comptr* (*abbr* **Universal Serial Bus**) USB *m*

USCG [juːessiːˈdʒiː] *n* (*abbr* **United States Coast Guard**) = guardacostas de Estados Unidos

USDA [juːesdiːˈeɪ] *n* (*abbr* **United States Department of Agriculture**) = ministerio de agricultura de Estados Unidos

USDAW [ˈʌzdɔː] (*abbr* **Union of Shop, Distributive and Allied Workers**) = sindicato británico de trabajadores del sector secundario

USE 1 *n* [juːs] (a) *(utilization)* uso *m*; *(consumption) (of water, resources)* consumo *m*; **drug u.** consumo de drogas; **to wear out with u.** gastarse con el uso; **the dishes are for everyday u.** estos platos son para uso diario; **ready for u.** listo(a) para usar; **to make (good) u. of sth** hacer (buen) uso de algo, aprovechar algo; **to put sth to (good) u.** dar (buen) uso a algo, aprovechar algo; **for staff u. only** sólo para empleados; **for u. in case of emergency** *(sign)* usar en caso de emergencia; **it is intended for u. as an analgesic** está pensado para usarse como analgésico; **to be in u.** *(machine, system, phrase)* estar en uso, usarse; **to come into u.** empezar a usarse; **not to be in u., to be out of u.** *(machine, system)* no usarse; **the word is no longer in u.** esta palabra ha caído en desuso; **to go out of u.** dejar de usarse; **directions** *or* **instructions for u.** instrucciones de uso; *Med* **for external/internal u. only** *(on packaging)* para uso externo/interno
(b) *(ability, permission to use)* **he lost the u. of his arm** se le quedó un brazo inutilizado; **he only has the u. of one arm** sólo puede usar un brazo; **she has full u. of her faculties** está en plena posesión de sus facultades; **to have the u. of the bathroom** poder usar el cuarto de baño
(c) *(usefulness)* **to be of u.** ser útil; **can I be of any u. to you?** ¿te puedo ser útil en algo?; *Ironic* **a lot of u. you were!** ¡sí que ayudaste mucho!; **it's not much u.** no sirve de mucho; **he's not much u. as a secretary** como secretario no sirve de mucho; **it's (of) no u.** no sirve de nada; **it's (of) no u. to me** no me sirve para nada; **it's no u., I can't do it!** ¡es inútil, no puedo hacerlo!; **it's** *or* **there's no u. crying** llorar no sirve de nada; *Fam* **he's no u.** es un inútil; **they were no u. at all during the move** no ayudaron nada en la mudanza; **to have no u. for sth** no tener necesidad de algo; **we have no u. for lazy workers here** aquí no nos hacen falta holgazanes; **being able to do karate must be nice – it has its uses** ¡qué bien, saber hacer kárate! – tiene su utilidad; *Hum* **your husband's well-trained, making us a cup of tea – he has his uses** tienes bien amaestrado a tu marido, nos ha preparado el té – sí, no es tan malo como parece; **what's the u. of** *or* **what u. is worrying?** ¿de qué sirve preocuparse?; *Fam* **oh, what's the u.?** ¿para qué insistir?; IDIOM **to be no u. to man nor beast** ser un inútil completo
(d) *(practical application)* uso *m*; **this tool has many uses** esta herramienta tiene muchos usos; **do you have any u. for that box?** ¿usas esa caja para algo?; **we'll find a u. for it** ya le encontraremos alguna utilidad *or* uso; *Hum* **I have my uses** alguna cosilla sé hacer
(e) *(sense) (of word)* uso *m*; **that's an old-fashioned u.** es un uso anticuado
(f) *Rel* rito *m*
2 *vt* [juːz] (a) *(utilize)* usar, utilizar; **to explain to sb how to u. sth** explicar a alguien cómo usar algo; **this cup has been used** esta taza está sucia; **is anyone using this book?** ¿alguien está usando este libro?; **can I u. the** *Br* **toilet** *or US* **bathroom?** ¿puedo ir al cuarto de baño?; **I always u. public transport** siempre uso el transporte público; **we u. this room as an office** usamos esta habitación de oficina; **I'd like to u. my language skills more** me gustaría usar más los idiomas; **to u. force/diplomacy** hacer uso de la fuerza/la diplomacia; **he used his influence to get me a job** empleó su influencia para conseguirme un trabajo; **he used every means at his disposal** empleó todos los medios a su alcance; **it may be used in evidence against you** se puede utilizar como prueba contra usted; **u. a bit of imagination!** ¡échale un poco de imaginación!; **u. your head!** ¡piensa un poco!; *Fam* **I could u. some help carrying these boxes** me vendría bien que alguien me ayudara a cargar estas cajas; *Fam* **I could u. some sleep** me vendría bien dormir un poco
(b) *(make the most of) (opportunity)* aprovechar; **he used the time well** aprovechó bien el tiempo
(c) *(exploit)* utilizar; **to u. sth to one's advantage** emplear algo en favor de uno; **I feel I've been used** me siento utilizado
(d) *(consume) (drugs)* consumir; **the bike's using a lot of oil** la moto consume mucho aceite
(e) *(run on) (petrol, electricity)* usar
(f) *(finish)* **have you used all the shampoo?** ¿has usado todo el champú?; **u. by Nov 2003** *(on packaging)* consumir antes del fin de nov. 2003
(g) *Formal (treat)* tratar; **I consider I was ill used** considero que me han tratado mal
3 *vi Fam (take drugs)* ponerse
4 **used to** *v aux* [ˈjuːstə]

Como verbo auxiliar, aparece siempre en pasado. Se traduce al español por el verbo principal en pretérito imperfecto, o por el pretérito imperfecto de **soler** más infinitivo.

we used to live abroad antes vivíamos en el extranjero; **you used to be able to leave your door unlocked all night** antes se podía dejar la puerta sin cerrojo toda la noche; **it used to be true** antes era cierto; **she never used to smoke** antes no fumaba; **did he u. to visit her?** ¿solía visitarla?; **I used not to** *or* **didn't u. to like him** antes no me caía bien; **I used to eat there a lot** solía comer *or* comía allí muy a menudo; **do you travel much? – I used to** ¿viajas mucho? – antes sí; **people don't tip like they used to** la gente ya no da tanta propina como antes; **things aren't what they used to be** las cosas ya no son lo que eran

▸ **use up** *vt sep (food, fuel, soap)* acabar; *(money)* gastar; *(resources, energy, ideas)* agotar; **she used up the leftovers in a soup** con las sobras hizo una sopa

use-by date [ˈjuːzbaɪdeɪt] *n Com* fecha *f* de caducidad

used [juːzd] *adj* (a) *(second-hand)* usado(a); *(car, book)* usado(a), de ocasión
(b) *(exploited)* **to feel u.** sentirse utilizado(a)
(c) [juːst] *(accustomed)* **to be u. to (doing) sth** estar acostumbrado(a) a (hacer) algo; **I'm not u. to being told what to do** no estoy acostumbrado a que me digan lo que tengo que hacer; **to be u. to sb** estar acostumbrado(a) a alguien; **to get u. to sth/sb** acostumbrarse a algo/alguien; **it takes a bit of getting u. to** cuesta un poco acostumbrarse

useful [ˈjuːsfʊl] *adj (person, addition, accessory)* útil; *(discussion, advice, experience)* útil, provechoso(a); *Br* **it will come in very u.** va a venir muy bien; **he could be u. to us** podría sernos útil; **does it serve any u. purpose?** ¿tiene alguna utilidad?; **she's a u. person to know** puede venir bien conocerla; *Fam* **to be u. with one's fists** saber valerse con los puños; *Fam* **he's a very u. player** es un jugador muy versátil; **to make oneself u.: he makes himself u. about the house** ayuda en casa; **make yourself u. and clean the sink** haz algo, limpia el fregadero ▸▸ ***u. life*** vida *f* útil

usefully ['ju:sfəlɪ] *adv (profitably)* provechosamente; **you could u. spend more time on the introduction** sería útil que le dedicaras más tiempo a la introducción; **his free time is u. employed** aprovecha su tiempo libre

usefulness ['ju:sfʊlnɪs] *n* utilidad *f*; **it has outlived its u.** ha dejado de ser útil

useless ['ju:slɪs] *adj* **(a)** *(not useful)* inservible; **to be u.** *(system, method)* no servir para nada **(b)** *(incompetent)* **to be u. (at sth)** ser un(a) negado(a) (para algo); **to be u. when it comes to spelling** ser un(a) negado(a) para la ortografía **(c)** *(futile)* inútil; **it would be u. to try** de nada serviría intentarlo, sería inútil intentarlo

uselessly ['ju:slɪslɪ] *adv* inútilmente

uselessness ['ju:slɪsnɪs] *n* inutilidad *f*; **his general u.** lo inútil que es

Usenet ['ju:znet] *n Comptr* Usenet *f*

user ['ju:zə(r)] *n* **(a)** *(of road, public service, dictionary)* usuario(a) *m,f* **(b)** *Comptr* usuario(a) *m,f* ▸▸ ***u. agent*** agente *m* de usuario; ***u. group*** grupo *m* de usuarios; ***u. ID*** nombre *m* de usuario; ***u. interface*** interfaz *m or f* de usuario; ***u. language*** lenguaje *m* de usuario; ***u. manual*** manual *m* del usuario; ***u. name*** nombre *m* de usuario; ***u. network*** red *f* de usuarios; ***u. support*** soporte *m* de usuario **(c)** *Fam (of drugs)* consumidor(ora) *m,f*

user-definable [ju:zədɪ'faɪnəbəl] *adj Comptr* definible por el usuario

user-friendliness [ju:zə'frendlɪnɪs] *n also Comptr* facilidad *f* de manejo

user-friendly [ju:zə'frendlɪ] *adj also Comptr* de fácil manejo

usher ['ʌʃə(r)] **1** *n* **(a)** *(in theatre, cinema)* acomodador *m* **(b)** *(in court)* ujier *m* **(c)** *(at wedding)* = persona encargada de indicar a los invitados dónde deben sentarse

2 *vt* **to u. sb in** hacer pasar a alguien; **to u. sb out** acompañar a alguien afuera; **I ushered them to their seats** los acompañé hasta sus asientos; *Fig* **to u. sth in** abrir las puertas a algo

usherette [ʌʃə'ret] *n (in cinema, theatre)* acomodadora *f*

USIA [ju:esaɪ'eɪ] *n* (*abbr* **United States Information Agency**) = organismo encargado de promover la cultura estadounidense en el extranjero

USM [ju:es'em] *n* **(a)** (*abbr* **United States Mail**) = servicio estadounidense de correos **(b)** (*abbr* **United States Mint**) = organismo estadounidense encargado de la fabricación de billetes y monedas, *Esp* ≃ Fábrica *f* Nacional de Moneda y Timbre

USMC [ju:esem'si:] *n* (*abbr* **United States Marine Corps**) = cuerpo de infantería de marina de Estados Unidos

USN [ju:es'en] *n* (*abbr* **United States Navy**) armada *f* estadounidense

USO [ju:es'əʊ] *n* (*abbr* **United Service Organization**) = organización de apoyo a los militares estadounidenses y sus familias en el extranjero

USP [ju:es'pi:] *n Com* (*abbr* **unique selling point** *or* **proposition**) rasgo *m* distintivo (del producto)

USPGA [ju:espi:dʒi:'eɪ] *n* (*abbr* **United States Professional Golfers Association**) *(organization)* PGA *f* estadounidense; *(tournament)* torneo *m* de la PGA estadounidense

USPHS [ju:espi:eɪtʃ'es] *n US* (*abbr* **United States Public Health Service**) = servicio de salud pública de EE.UU.

USS [ju:es'es] *n Naut* (*abbr* **United States Ship**) = título que precede a los nombres de buques de la marina estadounidense

USSR [ju:eses'ɑ:(r)] *n Formerly* (*abbr* **Union of Soviet Socialist Republics**) URSS *f*

usual ['ju:ʒʊəl] **1** *n Fam (in bar)* **the u.** lo de siempre

2 *adj* habitual, acostumbrado(a); **it's the u. problem** es el problema de siempre; **at the u. time/place** a la hora/en el sitio de siempre *or* costumbre; *Hum* **the u. suspects** los de siempre, los sospechosos habituales; **you're not your u. cheery self today** hoy no estás tan alegre como de costumbre; **she's her u. self again** vuelve a ser ella misma; **it's not u. for him to be this late** no suele llegar tan tarde; **it's u. to pay in advance** se suele pagar por adelantado; **earlier/later than u.** más pronto/tarde de lo normal; **more/less than u.** más/menos que de costumbre; **as is u. in these cases** como suele ocurrir en estos casos; **as u.** como de costumbre; *Fam* **as per u.** como de costumbre

usually ['ju:ʒʊəlɪ] *adv* habitualmente, normalmente; **I'm u. in bed by ten** normalmente *or* habitualmente estoy en la cama antes de las diez, suelo estar en la cama antes de las diez; **are they u. this late?** ¿llegan siempre así de tarde?; **he was more than u. polite** estuvo más amable que de costumbre

usufruct ['ju:zjʊfrʌkt] *n Law* usufructo *m*

usurer ['ju:ʒərə(r)] *n* usurero(a) *m,f*

usurious [ju:'zjʊərɪəs] *adj* de usura, abusivo(a)

usurp [ju:'zɜ:p] *vt* usurpar

usurper [jʊ'zɜ:pə(r)] *n* usurpador(ora) *m,f*

usury ['ju:ʒʊrɪ] *n* usura *f*

UT (*abbr* **Utah**) Utah

Utah ['ju:tɑ:] *n* Utah

ute [ju:t] *n Austr Fam* camioneta *f*

utensil [ju:'tensɪl] *n* utensilio *m*; **kitchen utensils** utensilios de cocina

uterine ['ju:təraɪn] *adj Anat* uterino(a)

uterus ['ju:tərəs] *n Anat* útero *m*

utilitarian [ju:tɪlɪ'teərɪən] **1** *n (in philosophy)* utilitarista *mf*

2 *adj* **(a)** *(approach)* pragmático(a); *(design)* funcional, práctico(a) **(b)** *(in philosophy)* utilitarista

utilitarianism [ju:tɪlɪ'teərɪənɪzəm] *n* utilitarismo *m*

utility [ju:'tɪlɪtɪ] *n* **(a)** *(usefulness)* utilidad *f* ▸▸ *US* ***u. man*** *(in company)* empleado *m* de mantenimiento; *(in theatre)* = persona que desempeña funciones de utilero y actor de reparto de papeles pequeños; *Sport* ***u. player*** jugador(ora) *m,f* comodín *or* polivalente; *Comptr* ***u. program*** utilidad *f*; ***u. room*** = cuarto utilizado para planchar, lavar, etc; *Austr* ***u. truck*** camioneta *f*; *Austr* ***u. vehicle*** camioneta *f* **(b)** *(company)* **(public) u.** servicio *m* público **(c)** *US* **utilities** *(service charges)* servicio *m*

utilization [ju:tɪlaɪ'zeɪʃən] *n* utilización *f*, empleo *m*

utilize ['ju:tɪlaɪz] *vt* utilizar

utmost ['ʌtməʊst], **uttermost** ['ʌtəməʊst] **1** *n* **to the u.** al máximo; **she did her u. to persuade them** hizo todo lo que pudo para convencerlos

2 *adj* **(a)** *(greatest)* sumo(a); **with the u. contempt** con el mayor desprecio; **it is of the u. importance that...** es de suma importancia que...; **with the u. ease** con suma facilidad **(b)** *(furthest)* **the u. ends of the earth** los últimos confines de la tierra

utopia [ju:'təʊpɪə] *n* utopía *f*

utopian [ju:'təʊpɪən] **1** *n* utópico(a) *m,f*

2 *adj* utópico(a)

utter[1] ['ʌtə(r)] *adj* total, completo(a); **it's u. madness** es una auténtica locura; **the movie is u. garbage** la película es una verdadera porquería; **to her u. amazement** para su completo desconcierto

utter[2] *vt* **(a)** *(cry)* lanzar, dar; *(word)* decir, pronunciar; **he didn't u. a sound for the rest of the journey** no dijo esta boca es mía durante el resto del viaje **(b)** *Law (libel)* difundir; *(counterfeit money)* poner en circulación

utterance ['ʌtərəns] *n* **(a)** *(act)* **to give u. to sth** manifestar *or* expresar algo **(b)** *(words spoken)* expresión *f*; **the child's first utterances** las primeras palabras del niño **(c)** *Ling* enunciado *m*

utterly ['ʌtəlɪ] *adv* completamente, totalmente; **I u. detest it** lo odio con toda mi alma

uttermost = **utmost**

U-turn ['ju:tɜ:n] *n (in car)* cambio *m* de sentido; *Fig* giro *m* radical *or* de 180 grados; **to do** *or* **make a U.** *(in car)* cambiar de sentido, dar la *or* media vuelta; *Fig* dar un giro radical *or* de 180 grados; **the government were accused of doing** *or* **making a U. on health policy** se acusó al gobierno de haber dado un giro de 180 grados en sanidad

UV [ju:'vi:] *adj Phys* (*abbr* **ultra-violet**) ultravioleta ▸▸ ***UV radiation*** radiación *f* ultravioleta; ***UV rays*** rayos *mpl* ultravioleta

UVF [ju:vi:'ef] *n* (*abbr* **Ulster Volunteer Force**) Fuerza *f* de Voluntarios del Ulster, = organización paramilitar norirlandesa partidaria de la permanencia en el Reino Unido

uvula ['ju:vjələ] *n Anat* úvula *f*

uvular ['ju:vjələ(r)] *adj Anat, Ling* uvular

uxorious [ʌk'sɔ:rɪəs] *adj Formal* **he's u.** *(devoted to his wife)* siente excesiva devoción por su esposa; *(dominated by his wife)* está excesivamente sometido a su esposa

uxoriousness [ʌk'sɔ:rɪəsnɪs] *n Formal* **his u.** *(devotion to his wife)* la excesiva devoción que le profesa a su esposa; *(submission to his wife)* el excesivo sometimiento a su esposa

Uzbek ['ʊzbek] **1** *n* **(a)** *(person)* uzbeko(a) *m,f* **(b)** *(language)* uzbeko *m*

2 *adj* uzbeko(a)

Uzbekistan [ʊzbekɪ'stɑ:n] *n* Uzbekistán

V, v

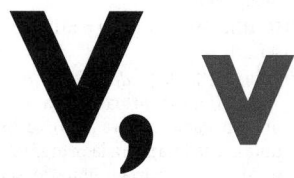

V, v [viː] *n (letter)* V, v *f* ▸▸ ***V sign*** *(for victory)* uve *f* de la victoria; *Br (as insult)* = gesto ofensivo que se forma mostrando el dorso de los dedos índice y corazón en forma de uve a la persona insultada

V *Elec* (*abbr* **volt**) V; **240 V.** 240 V

v [viː] (**a**) (*abbr* **very**) muy (**b**) (*abbr* **versus**) contra (**c**) (*abbr* **verse**) (*pl* **vv**) versículo *m* (**d**) (*abbr* **vide**) vid.

VA *n* (**a**) [viː'eɪ] *US* (*abbr* **Veterans Administration**) = organismo estadounidense que se ocupa de los veteranos de guerra (**b**) (*abbr* **Virginia**) Virginia

vac [væk] *n Br Fam Univ* vacaciones *fpl*

vacancy ['veɪkənsɪ] *n* (**a**) *(position, job)* (puesto *m*) vacante *f*; **to fill a v.** cubrir una vacante (**b**) *(at hotel)* habitación *f* libre; **no vacancies** *(sign)* completo (**c**) *(lack of intelligence)* vacuidad *f* (**d**) *(emptiness)* vacío *m*

vacant ['veɪkənt] *adj* (**a**) *(job)* vacante; **an administrative job became** *or* **fell v.** quedó vacante un puesto administrativo (**b**) *(seat, space, house, room)* libre; **to be v.** *(seat, space)* estar libre ▸▸ *US* ***v. lot*** solar *m* (sin edificar); *Br* ***v. possession*** propiedad *f* desocupada *or* libre de inquilinos (**c**) *(expression, look)* vacío(a), inexpresivo(a)

vacantly ['veɪkəntlɪ] *adv (absentmindedly)* distraídamente; *(expressionlessly)* sin expresión

vacate [və'keɪt] *vt Formal (seat, apartment)* dejar libre; *(room, building)* desalojar; *(one's post)* dejar vacante

vacation [və'keɪʃən] **1** *n* (**a**) *US (holiday)* vacaciones *fpl*; **to take a v.** tomarse unas vacaciones; **to be on v.** estar de vacaciones; **to go on v.** irse de vacaciones ▸▸ ***v. resort*** centro *m* turístico, lugar *m* de veraneo (**b**) *Univ* vacaciones *fpl*; *Br Law* periodo *m* vacacional ▸▸ ***v. course*** curso *m* de verano; ***v. work*** empleo *m or* trabajo *m* de vacaciones

2 *vi US* pasar las vacaciones; *(in summer)* veranear

vacationer [və'keɪʃənə(r)] *n US* turista *mf*; *(in summer)* veraneante *mf*

vaccinate ['væksɪneɪt] *vt Med* vacunar (**against** contra)

vaccination [væksɪ'neɪʃən] *n Med* (**a**) *(act of vaccinating)* vacunación *f*; **to have a v.** vacunarse (**b**) *(vaccine)* vacuna *f*

vaccine ['væksiːn] *n Med* vacuna *f*; **smallpox v.** vacuna de la viruela

vaccinee [væksɪ'niː] *n US* vacunado(a) *m,f*

vacillate ['væsɪleɪt] *vi* vacilar, titubear

vacillation [væsɪ'leɪʃən] *n* vacilación *f*, titubeos *mpl*

vacuity [və'kjuːɪtɪ], **vacuousness** ['vækjʊəsnɪs] *n Formal* vacuidad *f*

vacuous ['vækjʊəs] *adj (person, remark, book)* vacuo(a), vacío(a); *(look, expression)* vacío(a), vago(a)

vacuum ['vækjʊm] **1** *n* (**a**) *(void)* vacío *m*; **his death left a v. in my life** su muerte dejó un vacío en mi vida; **a political v.** un vacío político; **it doesn't exist in a v.** no tiene lugar aisladamente

(**b**) *Phys* vacío *m* ▸▸ *US* ***v. bottle*** termo *m*; ***v. brake*** freno *m* de vacío; *Br* ***v. flask*** termo *m*; ***v. pump*** bomba *f* de vacío; *Elec* ***v. tube*** tubo *m* de vacío

(**c**) *(when cleaning)* **I gave the room a quick v.** pasé la aspiradora rápidamente por la habitación ▸▸ ***v. cleaner*** aspiradora *f*, aspirador *m*

2 *vt* pasar la aspiradora por, aspirar

3 *vi* pasar la aspiradora, aspirar

vacuum-clean ['vækjʊm'kliːn] *vt* pasar la aspiradora por

vacuum-packed ['vækjʊm'pækt] *adj* envasado(a) al vacío

vade mecum [vɑːdɪ'meɪkʊm] (*pl* **vade mecums**) *n* vademécum *m*

Vaduz [væ'dʊts] *n* Vaduz

vagabond ['vægəbɒnd] *n* vagabundo(a) *m,f*

vagaries ['veɪgərɪz] *npl* **the v. of...** los avatares *or* caprichos de...

vagina [və'dʒaɪnə] *n* vagina *f*

vaginal [və'dʒaɪnəl] *adj* vaginal ▸▸ ***v. discharge*** flujo *m* vaginal; ***v. mucus*** moco *m* vaginal; ***v. smear*** frotis *m inv* vaginal

vaginitis [vædʒɪ'naɪtɪs] *n Med* vaginitis *f inv*

vagrancy ['veɪgrənsɪ] *n Law* vagabundeo *m*

vagrant ['veɪgrənt] *n* mendigo(a) *m,f*, vagabundo(a) *m,f*

vague [veɪg] *adj* (**a**) *(ill-defined, unclear) (feeling, recollection, statement)* vago(a); *(instructions, description)* impreciso(a), poco preciso(a); *(shape, outline)* vago(a), borroso(a); **I haven't the vaguest idea** no tengo ni la más remota idea; **he was rather v. about it** no precisó mucho; **to bear a v. resemblance to sth/sb** parecerse *or* recordar vagamente a algo/alguien (**b**) *(person, expression)* distraído(a)

vaguely ['veɪglɪ] *adv* (**a**) *(not clearly)* vagamente; **I v. remember him** lo recuerdo vagamente; **it tastes v. of coffee** tiene un dejo a café; **she v. resembles her aunt** recuerda *or* se parece vagamente a su tía (**b**) *(absent-mindedly)* distraídamente; **he looked v. around him** miró distraídamente a su alrededor

vagueness ['veɪgnɪs] *n* (**a**) *(of feeling, recollection, statement)* vaguedad *f*; *(of instructions, description)* imprecisión *f* (**b**) *(absent-mindedness)* distracción *f*

vain [veɪn] **1** *n* **in v.** en vano; **thou shalt not take my name in v.** no tomarás mi nombre en vano; *Hum* **are you taking my name in v. again?** ¡me vais a gastar el nombre!

2 *adj* (**a**) *(conceited)* vanidoso(a), vano(a); **he's very v. about his looks** es muy presumido (**b**) *(futile)* vano(a) (**c**) *Literary (empty, worthless)* vano(a)

vainglorious [veɪn'glɔːrɪəs] *adj Literary* vanaglorioso(a)

vainly ['veɪnlɪ] *adv* (**a**) *(conceitedly)* vanidosamente, con vanidad (**b**) *(unsuccessfully)* en vano

vainness ['veɪnnɪs] *n (futility)* inutilidad *f*

valance ['væləns] *n (round bed frame)* doselera *f*; *(round shelf, window)* cenefa *f*

vale [veɪl] *n Literary* valle *m*; *Fig* **a v. of tears** un valle de lágrimas

valediction [vælɪ'dɪkʃən] *n Formal* (**a**) *(farewell)* despedida *f* (**b**) *(speech)* alocución *f or* discurso *m* de despedida

valedictory [vælɪ'dɪktərɪ] **1** *n US Univ* discurso *m* de despedida

2 *adj Formal (speech)* de despedida

valence *US* = **valency**

Valencia [və'lensɪə] *n* Valencia

Valencian [və'lensɪən] **1** *n* valenciano(a) *m,f*

2 *adj* valenciano(a)

valency ['veɪlənsɪ], *US* **valence** ['veɪləns] *n Chem* valencia *f*

valentine ['væləntaɪn] *n* (**a**) **Saint V.** san Valentín (**b**) *(beloved)* **will you be my v.?** = fórmula que se emplea en las tarjetas de San Valentín para expresar los sentimientos hacia alguien ▸▸ ***V.'s Day*** día *m* de San Valentín, día *m* de los enamorados (**c**) *(card)* **v. (card)** = tarjeta para el día de los enamorados

valerian [və'lɪərɪən] *n* valeriana *f*

valet **1** *n* ['væleɪ] (**a**) *(manservant)* ayuda *m* de cámara (**b**) *(in hotel)* valet *m*, mozo *m* de hotel ▸▸ ***v. parking*** servicio *m* de aparcacoches; ***v. service*** servicio *m* de planchado

2 *vt* ['vælɪt] (**a**) *(car)* lavar y limpiar (**b**) *(clothes)* planchar

Valetta [və'letə] *n* La Valetta

valetudinarian [vælɪtjuːdɪ'neərɪən] *Literary* **1** *adj* valetudinario(a)

2 *n* valetudinario(a) *m,f*

Valhalla [væl'hælə] *n* Valhala

valiant ['vælɪənt] *adj Literary* valeroso(a), valiente; **she made a v. effort to pull herself together** hizo un enorme esfuerzo por recobrar la compostura

valiantly ['vælɪəntlɪ] *adv* valerosamente, con valor

valid ['vælɪd] *adj (excuse, argument, reason)* válido(a), legítimo(a); *(licence)* en vigor; *(contract)* legal; **v. for six months** válido *or* valedero(a) durante seis meses; **no longer v.** caducado(a)

validate ['vælɪdeɪt] *vt* (**a**) *(theory, claim, argument)* validar (**b**) *(document, ticket)* dar validez a (**c**) *(contract)* validar, dar validez a

validation [vælɪ'deɪʃən] *n* validación *f*

validity [və'lɪdɪtɪ] *n* validez *f*

validly ['vælɪdlɪ] *adv* legítimamente

valise [væ'li:z] *n US (small suitcase)* maleta *f* de fin de semana

Valium® ['vælɪəm] *n* valium® *m*; **to be on V.** tomar valium®

Valkyrie [væl'kɪərɪ] *n* valquiria *f*

Valletta [və'letə] *n* La Valeta

valley ['vælɪ] *n* valle *m*

valor *US* = **valour**

valorous ['vælərəs] *adj Literary* valeroso(a)

valour, *US* **valor** ['vælə(r)] *n Literary* valor *m*

valuable ['væljʊəbəl] **1** *n* **valuables** objetos *mpl* de valor
2 *adj* valioso(a)

valuation [væljʊ'eɪʃən] *n* (**a**) *(act)* tasación *f*; valoración *f*; **to get a v. of sth** hacer tasar *or* valorar algo (**b**) *(price)* valoración *f*, tasación *f*

value ['vælju:] **1** *n* (**a**) *(monetary worth)* valor *m*; **to the v. of...** hasta un valor de...; **of great/little v.** muy/poco valioso(a); **of no v.** sin valor; **to be of v.** tener valor; **to be good/poor v. (for money)** tener buena/mala relación calidad-precio; **to increase/decrease in v.** aumentar/disminuir de valor; **to set** *or* **put a v. on sth** poner precio a algo; **they put a v. of £90,000 on the house** valoraron *or* tasaron la casa en 90.000 libras ►► ***v. judgement*** juicio *m* de valor; **to make a v. judgement** hacer un juicio de valor
(**b**) *(merit, importance)* valor *m*, importancia *f*; **they place a high v. on punctuality** valoran mucho la puntualidad, le dan mucha importancia a la puntualidad
(**c**) *(principle)* **values** valores *mpl*; **a sense of values** una escala de valores; **moral values** valores morales
(**d**) *Ling, Math & Mus* valor *m*
2 *vt* (**a**) *(evaluate)* valorar, tasar; **to get sth valued** pedir una valoración de algo (**b**) *(appreciate)* apreciar; **he values your friendship highly** valora (en) mucho tu amistad

value-added tax ['vælju:ædɪd'tæks] *n Br* impuesto *m* sobre el valor añadido *or Am* agregado

valued ['vælju:d] *adj (friend)* estimado(a), apreciado(a); *(contribution)* valioso(a)

valueless ['væljʊlɪs] *adj* sin valor

valuer ['væljʊə(r)] *n* tasador(ora) *m,f*

valve [vælv] *n* (**a**) *Anat & Tech* válvula *f* (**b**) *Mus* pistón *m* (**c**) *Bot & Zool* valva *f* (**d**) *Br Elec* válvula *f*

vamoose [və'mu:s] *vi US Fam* **v.!** ¡largo *or* fuera (de aquí)!

vamp [væmp] **1** *n* (**a**) *(woman) Fam* vampiresa *f* (**b**) *(of shoe)* empeine *m*
2 *vt (of woman) (man)* encandilar
3 *vi (improvise)* improvisar

►**vamp up** *vt sep* (**a**) *Br (refurbish)* arreglar, redecorar; *(story, music)* retocar, hacer arreglos a (**b**) *(of woman)* **to v. it up** hacer *or* ir de mujer fatal *or* vampiresa

vampire ['væmpaɪə(r)] *n* vampiro *m* ►► ***v. bat*** vampiro *m*

van[1] [væn] *n* (**a**) *Aut* camioneta *f*, furgoneta *f* ►► ***v. driver*** conductor(ora) *m,f* de camioneta (**b**) *Br Rail* furgón *m*

van[2] [væn] *n* (**a**) *Mil (vanguard)* vanguardia *f*; **in the v.** en la vanguardia (**b**) *(cutting edge)* **in the v. of abstract art** en la vanguardia del arte abstracto

vanadium [və'neɪdɪəm] *n Chem* vanadio *m*

vandal ['vændəl] *n (hooligan)* vándalo *m*, *Esp* gamberro(a) *m,f*

vandalism ['vændəlɪzəm] *n* vandalismo *m*, *Esp* gamberrismo *m*

vandalize ['vændəlaɪz] *vt* destrozar adrede

vane [veɪn] *n* (**a**) *(for indicating wind direction)* **(weather) v.** veleta *f* (**b**) *(of propeller, turbine)* paleta *f* (**c**) *(of feather)* barba *f*

vanguard ['vængɑ:d] *n* vanguardia *f*; **to be in the v.** ir en vanguardia, estar a la vanguardia

vanilla [və'nɪlə] *n* vainilla *f*; **v. ice cream** helado de vainilla ►► ***v. pod*** vainilla *f (fruto)*

vanish ['vænɪʃ] *vi* desaparecer; **to v. into thin air** esfumarse

vanishing ['vænɪʃɪŋ] *adj* IDIOM **to do a v. act** *(disappear)* desaparecer ►► *Old-fashioned* ***v. cream*** crema *f* (hidratante) de día; ***v. point*** punto *m* de fuga; **profits have dwindled to v. point** los beneficios han disminuido hasta casi desaparecer

vanity ['vænɪtɪ] *n* (**a**) *(conceit)* vanidad *f* ►► ***v. bag*** bolsa *f* de aseo, neceser *m*; ***v. case*** bolsa *f* de aseo, neceser *m*; ***v. mirror*** espejo *m* de cortesía; *US* ***v. plate*** matrícula *f* personalizada; ***v. publishing*** edición *f* propia *(costeada por el autor)*; *Br* ***v. unit*** lavabo *m or Am* lavamanos *m inv* empotrado (**b**) *Literary (futility)* vanidad *f*; **all is v.** todo es vanidad

vanload ['vænləʊd] *n* **a v. of...** una camioneta *or* furgoneta cargada de...

vanquish ['væŋkwɪʃ] *vt Literary* vencer, derrotar

vantage point ['vɑ:ntɪdʒ'pɔɪnt] *n* atalaya *f*; *Fig* posición *f* ventajosa

Vanuatu [vænu:'ætu:] *n* Vanuatú

vapid ['væpɪd] *adj (person)* insulso(a); *(conversation, remark)* insustancial

vapidity [və'pɪdətɪ] *n (of conversation, remark)* insustancialidad *f*; *(of person)* insulsez *f*

vapor *US* = **vapour**

vaporize ['veɪpəraɪz] **1** *vt* evaporar
2 *vi* evaporarse

vaporizer ['veɪpəraɪzə(r)] *n* (**a**) *(for water)* vaporizador *m*; *(for perfume, spray)* pulverizador *m*, vaporizador *m* (**b**) *Med (inhaler)* inhalador *m*; *(for throat)* espray *m* para la garganta

vapour, *US* **vapor** ['veɪpə(r)] *n* vapor *m*; IDIOM **to have (an attack of) the vapours** ponerse de los nervios ►► ***v. trail*** *(from plane)* estela *f*

variability [veərɪə'bɪlɪtɪ] *n* variabilidad *f*

variable ['veərɪəbəl] **1** *n* variable *f*
2 *adj* variable ►► *Com* ***v. costs*** costos *mpl or Esp* costes *mpl* variables; *Fin* ***v. interest rate*** tipo *m or* tasa *f* de interés variable; *Astron* ***v. star*** estrella *f* variable

variable-interest ['veərɪəbəl'ɪntrest] *adj Fin (securities, shares)* de renta variable; *(mortgage)* (con tipo *or* tasa) de interés variable

variance ['veərɪəns] *n* (**a**) *(difference)* discrepancia *f*; **to be at v. with sth/sb** discrepar de algo/alguien (**b**) *(in statistics)* varianza *f*

variant ['veərɪənt] **1** *n* (**a**) variante *f* (**b**) *Ling* variante *f*
2 *adj* (**a**) *(different)* alternativo(a), distinto(a) (**b**) *Ling (form, pronunciation)* alternativo(a); **v. spelling** variante *f* ortográfica

variation [veərɪ'eɪʃən] *n* (**a**) *(discrepancy, difference)* variación *f*; **there is considerable v. between individuals** hay gran variación *or* grandes diferencias de un individuo a otro (**b**) *(different version)* variación *f*, variedad *f*; **variations on a theme** variaciones sobre un tema *or* sobre el mismo tema (**c**) *Mus* variación *f* (**d**) *Biol* variación *f*, mutación *f*

varicose vein ['værɪkəʊs'veɪn] *n Med* variz *f*, vena *f* varicosa

varied ['veərɪ:d] *adj* variado(a)

variegated ['veərɪgeɪtɪd] *adj (leaf)* moteado(a), jaspeado(a); *(plant)* colorido(a); *(foliage, plumage)* abigarrado(a), colorido(a)

variety [və'raɪətɪ] *n* (**a**) *(number, assortment)* variedad *f*; **a v. of reasons** diversos motivos; **in a v. of ways** de diversas maneras; **the dresses come in a v. of sizes** tenemos los vestidos en varias tallas *or RP* varios talles; **there is a wide v. of colours/styles to choose from** hay una amplia variedad de colores/estilos para elegir
(**b**) *(diversity)* variedad *f*; **for v.** para variar; **he needs more v. in his diet** necesita una dieta más variada; **the work lacks v.** el trabajo es muy monótono; **meeting lots of different people adds v. to the job** conocer a mucha gente diferente hace el trabajo más entretenido; PROV **v. is the spice of life** en la variedad está el gusto
(**c**) *(of plant, species)* variedad *f*
(**d**) *Theat & TV* variedades *fpl* ►► ***v. show*** espectáculo *m* de variedades

varifocals [veərɪ'fəʊkəlz] *npl* lentes *fpl* progresivas

various ['veərɪəs] *adj (different)* diversos(as), diferentes; *(several)* varios(as); **at v. times** en distintas *or* diversas ocasiones

variously ['veərɪəslɪ] *adv* **v. described as a hero and a bandit** descrito por unos como héroe y por otros como bandido; **he was v. known as soldier, king and emperor** según el caso, fue conocido como soldado, como rey y como emperador; **the number of cases has been v. estimated at between 2,000 and 8,000** se han hecho estimaciones muy diversas sobre el número de casos, que van desde el 2.000 a 8.000

varlet ['vɑ:lɪt] *n* (**a**) *Archaic (servant)* valet *m* (**b**) *Pej Literary* villano *m*, bellaco *m*

varmint ['vɑ:rmɪnt] *n US Fam (animal)* bicho *m*; *(person)* sabandija *f*

varnish ['vɑ:nɪʃ] **1** *n* (**a**) *(for wood, oil painting)* barniz *m* (**b**) *Br (for nails)* esmalte *m* (de uñas)
2 *vt* (**a**) *(wood, painting)* barnizar (**b**) *Br* **to v. one's nails** darse esmalte en las uñas

►**varnish over** *vt sep Fig* maquillar, disfrazar

varsity ['vɑːsɪtɪ] *n* (**a**) *US (university team)* equipo *m* universitario (**b**) *Br Fam Old-fashioned* universidad *f* ►► ***v. match*** encuentro *m* universitario

vary ['veərɪ] **1** *vt* variar

2 *vi* variar (**in** de); **opinions v.** hay diversas opiniones; **the students v. considerably in ability** el nivel de los alumnos varía notablemente; **attitudes v. greatly** las actitudes varían mucho; **his routine never varies** su rutina nunca cambia; **how often do you go? – it varies** ¿con qué frecuencia va? – depende

varying ['veərɪŋ] *adj* diverso(a); **with v. degrees of success** con mayor o menor éxito

vascular ['væskjʊlə(r)] *adj Biol* vascular ►► ***v. disease*** enfermedad *f* vascular

vas deferens ['væs'defərənz] *n Anat* conducto *m or* vaso *m* deferente

vase [vɑːz, *US* veɪs] *n* jarrón *m*

vasectomy [və'sektəmɪ] *n Med* vasectomía *f*; **to have a v.** hacerse una vasectomía

Vaseline® ['væsəliːn] *n* vaselina *f*

vasoconstrictor [veɪzəʊkən'strɪktə(r)] *n Med* vasoconstrictor *m*

vasodilator [veɪzəʊdaɪ'leɪtə(r)] *n Med* vasodilatador *m*

vassal ['væsəl] *n* (**a**) *Hist* vasallo(a) *m,f* (**b**) *(dependent person)* súbdito(a) *m,f*; *(dependent nation)* estado *m* satélite ►► ***v. state*** estado *m or* país *m* satélite

vast [vɑːst] *adj* (**a**) *(area)* vasto(a); **it's a v. country** es un país inmenso (**b**) *(majority, number)* inmenso(a); *(experience, improvement)* enorme; *(difference)* abismal; **it's a v. improvement on his last performance** su rendimiento ha mejorado enormemente con respecto a la última vez; **v. sums of money** enormes *or* incalculables sumas de dinero

vastly ['vɑːstlɪ] *adv* enormemente; **his books are v. overrated** sus libros están enormemente sobrevalorados; **it's v. different/superior** es infinitamente distinto/superior

vastness ['vɑːstnɪs] *n* inmensidad *f*

VAT [viːeɪ'tiː, væt] *n Br* (*abbr* **value-added tax**) IVA *m*

vat [væt] *n (container)* tina *f*, cuba *f*

Vatican ['vætɪkən] *n* **the V.** el Vaticano ►► ***V. City*** Ciudad *f* del Vaticano

vaudeville ['vɔːdəvɪl] *n US Theat* vodevil *m*

vault[1] [vɔːlt] *n* (**a**) *Archit* bóveda *f*; *Literary* **the v. of heaven** la bóveda celeste (**b**) *(cellar)* sótano *m* (**c**) *(for burial)* cripta *f*; **the family v.** el panteón familiar (**d**) *(of bank)* cámara *f* acorazada, *Am* bóveda *f* de seguridad

vault[2] **1** *n (in gymnastics) (event)* salto *m* de caballo; *(jump)* salto *m*

2 *vt* saltar

3 *vi* saltar; **to v. over sth** saltar por encima de algo

vaulted ['vɔːltɪd] *adj (ceiling)* abovedado(a)

vaulting ['vɔːltɪŋ] **1** *n Archit* abovedado *m*

2 *adj* (**a**) *Sport (pole)* de salto ►► ***v. horse*** plinto *m*, caballo *m* sin arcos (**b**) *Fig Literary (arrogance, ambition)* desmesurado(a), desmedido(a)

vaunt [vɔːnt] *vt Formal* alardear de, hacer alarde de; **his much vaunted reputation as...** su tan cacareada reputación de...

VC [viː'siː] *n* (**a**) (*abbr* **Vice-Chairman**) vicepresidente(a) *m,f* (**b**) *Br Mil* (*abbr* **Victoria Cross**) = la más alta condecoración militar británica (**c**) *US Mil Fam* (*abbr* **Vietcong**) Vietcong *m*

V-chip ['viːtʃɪp] *n Comptr & TV* chip *m* antiviolencia, = dispositivo que bloquea la recepción de programas con escenas de sexo o violencia

VCR [viːsiː'ɑː(r)] *n* (*abbr* **video cassette recorder**) (aparato *m* de) vídeo *m or Am* video *m*

VD [viː'diː] *n* (*abbr* **venereal disease**) enfermedad *f* venérea

VDT [viːdiː'tiː] *n Comptr* (*abbr* **visual display terminal**) monitor *m*

VDU [viːdiː'juː] *n Comptr* (*abbr* **visual display unit**) monitor *m* ►► ***V. operator*** persona *f* trabajando en pantalla

veal [viːl] *n* ternera *f* (blanca)

vector ['vektə(r)] *n* (**a**) *Math* vector *m* ►► ***v. space*** espacio *m* vectorial (**b**) *Med* vector *m* (**c**) *Comptr* ***v. graphics*** gráficos *mpl* vectoriales

VE day [viː'iːdeɪ] *n* = fecha que marca el triunfo aliado en Europa el 8 de mayo de 1945

veep [viːp] *n US Fam* vicepresidente(a) *m,f*

veer ['vɪə(r)] *vi* (**a**) *(vehicle, road)* torcer, girar; *(ship)* virar; *(wind)* cambiar de dirección, *Spec* rolar; **to v. to the left/right** *(road)* torcer a la izquierda/derecha; **the taxi veered off into the ditch** el taxi dio un viraje y cayó en la zanja; **the ship veered off course** el barco se desvió de su rumbo; **the wind has veered (round) to the east** el viento ha cambiado *or Spec* rolado al este

(**b**) *Fig* **the party has veered to the left** el partido ha dado un giro a la izquierda; **the speaker kept veering off the subject** el disertante se salía del tema constantemente; **her mood veers between euphoria and black depression** su estado de ánimo va de la euforia a la depresión más absoluta

► **veer round** *vi (wind)* cambiar de dirección, *Spec* rolar

veg [vedʒ] *n Br Fam* verduras *fpl*; **meat and two v.** carne con dos tipos de verdura

► **veg out** *vi Fam* rascarse la barriga, *Esp* tocarse las narices

vegan ['viːgən] **1** *n* vegetaliano(a) *m,f*, vegetalista *mf*, = vegetariano estricto que no come ningún producto de origen animal

2 *adj* vegetaliano(a), vegetalista

vegeburger ['vedʒɪbɜːgə(r)] *n* hamburguesa *f* vegetariana

vegetable ['vedʒtəbəl] *n* (**a**) *(plant)* hortaliza *f*; **vegetables** verdura *f*, verduras *fpl*; **eat up your vegetables** cómete la verdura ►► ***v. fat*** grasa *f* vegetal; ***v. garden*** huerto *m*; ***v. kingdom*** reino *m* vegetal; ***v. marrow*** = especie de calabacín *or CSur* zapallito *or Méx* calabacita de gran tamaño; ***v. matter*** materia *f* vegetal; ***v. oil*** aceite *m* vegetal; ***v. patch*** huerto *m*; ***v. soup*** sopa *f* de verduras (**b**) *(brain-damaged person)* vegetal *m*

vegetarian [vedʒɪ'teərɪən] **1** *n* vegetariano(a) *m,f*

2 *adj* vegetariano(a)

vegetarianism [vedʒɪ'teərɪənɪzəm] *n* vegetarianismo *m*

vegetate ['vedʒɪteɪt] *vi* vegetar

vegetation [vedʒɪ'teɪʃən] *n* vegetación *f*

vegetative ['vedʒɪtətɪv] *adj Med (condition)* vegetativo(a)

veggie, veggy ['vedʒɪ] *n Fam* (**a**) *(vegetarian)* vegetariano(a) *m,f* (**b**) *(vegetable)* **veggies** verdura *f*, verduras *fpl*

vehemence ['viːɪməns] *n* vehemencia *f*

vehement ['viːɪmənt] *adj* vehemente; **she launched a v. attack on the government** lanzó un furibundo ataque contra el gobierno

vehemently ['viːɪməntlɪ] *adv (to speak)* vehementemente, con vehemencia; *(to deny)* rotundamente; *(to gesticulate)* ostensiblemente; *(to attack)* con furia

vehicle ['viːɪkəl] *n* (**a**) *(transport)* vehículo *m* ►► *Br* ***V. Registration Document*** permiso *m* de circulación (**b**) *Fig (means)* vehículo *m*; **the movie was conceived as a v. for his comic talent** la película se concibió como un escaparate para su talento cómico; **the newspaper is merely a v. for state propaganda** el periódico no es más que un vehículo *or* medio de propaganda oficial

vehicular [vɪ'hɪkjʊlə(r)] *adj* de vehículos ►► ***v. access*** acceso *m* para vehículos; *US* ***v. homicide*** homicidio *m* por atropello; ***v. traffic*** tráfico *m* de vehículos *or* rodado

veil [veɪl] **1** *n* velo *m*; **a v. of smoke** una cortina de humo; *Rel* **to take the v.** tomar los hábitos, hacerse monja; *Fig* **under a v. of secrecy** rodeado(a) de un halo de secreto *or* misterio; IDIOM **to draw a v. over sth** correr un tupido velo sobre algo

2 *vt* (**a**) *(person)* cubrir con un velo (**b**) *(truth, feelings, intentions)* velar, ocultar; **veiled in secrecy** rodeado(a) de un halo de secreto *or* misterio

veiled [veɪld] *adj* (**a**) *(wearing veil)* con velo; **to be v.** llevar velo (**b**) *(threat, allusion)* velado(a); **thinly v. hostility** hostilidad apenas disimulada

vein [veɪn] *n* (**a**) *Anat (in body)* vena *f*; **she has Polish blood in her veins** tiene sangre polaca, lleva sangre polaca en sus venas (**b**) *(of leaf)* nervio *m* (**c**) *(in rock)* filón *m*, veta *f*; *(in wood, marble)* veta *f*; **a rich v. of irony runs through the book** el libro tiene una fuerte carga de ironía (**d**) IDIOMS **in a lighter v.** en un tono más ligero; **in a similar v.** en la misma línea, en el mismo tono

veined [veɪnd] *adj* (**a**) *(hand, skin)* venoso(a), de venas marcadas (**b**) *(leaf)* nervado(a) (**c**) *(cheese, stone)* veteado(a); **green-v. marble** mármol de vetas verdes

velar ['viːlə(r)] *adj Anat & Ling* velar

Velcro® ['velkrəʊ] *n* velcro® *m*

veld(t) [velt] *n* veld *m*, = altiplano estepario sudafricano

vellum ['veləm] *n* pergamino *m*, vitela *f* ►► ***v. paper*** papel *m* pergamino

velocity [vɪ'lɒsɪtɪ] *n* velocidad *f*

velodrome ['velədrəʊm] *n* velódromo *m*

velour [və'lʊə(r)] **1** *n* veludillo *m*, velvetón *m*

2 *adj* de veludillo, de velvetón

velum ['viːləm] *n Anat* velo *m* del paladar

velvet ['velvɪt] *n* terciopelo *m*; **as smooth as v.** *(skin)* suave como el terciopelo, aterciopelado(a); **v. jacket** chaqueta de terciopelo; *Fam Fig* **to be on v.** estar de maravilla *or* a las mil maravillas; IDIOM **an iron fist** *or* **hand in a v. glove** mano dura bajo un manto de aparente bondad

velveteen ['velvɪti:n] *n* pana *f* lisa

velvety ['velvɪtɪ] *adj* aterciopelado(a)

venal ['vi:nəl] *adj Formal* venal, corrupto(a)

venality [vi:'nælɪtɪ] *n Formal* venalidad *f*

vendetta [ven'detə] *n* vendetta *f*; **to carry on** *or* **wage a v. against sb** llevar a cabo una campaña para destruir a alguien

vending machine ['vendɪŋmə'ʃi:n] *n* máquina *f* expendedora

vendor ['vendɔ:(r)] *n* vendedor(ora) *m,f*; *Law* parte *f* vendedora

veneer [və'nɪə(r)] *n* **(a)** *(of wood)* laminado *m*, chapa *f*, enchapado *m* **(b)** *Fig (appearance)* pátina *f*, barniz *m*

venerable ['venərəbəl] *adj* venerable

venerate ['venəreɪt] *vt* venerar

veneration [venə'reɪʃən] *n* veneración *f*

venereal [vɪ'nɪərɪəl] *adj* venéreo(a) ►► ***v. disease*** enfermedad *f* venérea

Venetian [vɪ'ni:ʃən] **1** *n* veneciano(a) *m,f*
2 *adj* veneciano(a) ►► ***V. blind*** persiana *f* veneciana; ***V. glass*** cristal *m* de Murano

Venezuela [venə'zweɪlə] *n* Venezuela

Venezuelan [venə'zweɪlən] **1** *n* venezolano(a) *m,f*
2 *adj* venezolano(a)

vengeance ['vendʒəns] *n* venganza *f*; **to take** *or* **wreak v. on sb** vengarse de alguien; **to seek v. for sth** buscar venganza por algo; *Fig* **the problem has returned with a v.** el problema se ha presentado de nuevo con agravantes; **by then it was raining with a v.** para entonces llovía con ganas *or* fuerza; **to work with a v.** trabajar denodadamente

vengeful ['vendʒfʊl] *adj* vengativo(a)

venial ['vi:nɪəl] *adj (sin)* venial; *(error)* leve

Venice ['venɪs] *n* Venecia

venison ['venɪsən] *n* (carne *f* de) venado *m*

Venn diagram ['ven'daɪəgræm] *n Math* diagrama *m* de Venn

venom ['venəm] *n also Fig* veneno *m*

venomous ['venəməs] *adj* venenoso(a); *(look, criticism)* envenenado(a), ponzoñoso(a); **he has a v. tongue** tiene una lengua viperina

venous ['vi:nəs] *adj Med* venoso(a)

vent [vent] **1** *n* **(a)** *(opening)* orificio *m* de ventilación, respiradero *m*; *(duct)* conducto *m* de ventilación; *(in chimney)* tiro *m*; *(in volcano)* chimenea *f*; **to give v. to sth: she gave v. to her feelings** se desahogó, dio rienda suelta a sus sentimientos; **he gave full v. to his anger** descargó toda su ira **(b)** *(in jacket, skirt)* abertura *f* **(c)** *(of bird, fish)* cloaca *f*, ano *m*
2 *vt* **she vented her anger on him** descargó su ira sobre él

ventilate ['ventɪleɪt] *vt* **(a)** *(room)* ventilar; *Med (blood)* oxigenar; **a well/badly ventilated room** una habitación bien/mal ventilada **(b)** *(subject)* airear

ventilation [ventɪ'leɪʃən] *n* ventilación *f* ►► ***v. shaft*** *(in mine)* pozo *m* de ventilación

ventilator ['ventɪleɪtə(r)] *n* **(a)** *(in building)* ventilador *m* **(b)** *Med* respirador *m*; **to be on a v.** estar conectado a un respirador, estar con respiración asistida

ventral ['ventrəl] *adj* ventral ►► ***v. fin*** aleta *f* pelviana *or* abdominal

ventricle ['ventrɪkəl] *n Anat* ventrículo *m*

ventriloquism [ven'trɪləkwɪzəm] *n* ventriloquía *f*

ventriloquist [ven'trɪləkwɪst] *n* ventrílocuo(a) *m,f* ►► ***v.'s dummy*** muñeco *m* de ventrílocuo

venture ['ventʃə(r)] **1** *n* **(a)** *(undertaking)* aventura *f*, iniciativa *f*; **it's his first v. into politics/fiction** es su primera incursión en política/la literatura de ficción ►► *Br* ***V. Scout*** = scout de entre 16 y 20 años, ≃ pionero(a) *m,f* **(b)** *(in business)* empresa *f*, operación *f* ►► *Fin* ***v. capital*** capital *m* de riesgo
2 *vt* **(a)** *(stake, life)* arriesgar; **to v. to do sth** aventurarse *or* atreverse a hacer algo; **he ventured to contradict her** se atrevió a contradecirla; PROV **nothing ventured, nothing gained** el que no se arriesga no pasa la mar **(b)** *(comment)* aventurar; **to v. a suggestion** aventurarse a sugerir algo; **if I may v. a guess/an opinion** si se me permite aventurar una hipótesis/opinión
3 *vi* aventurarse; **he ventured into the woods** se aventuró en el interior del bosque; **I wouldn't v. out of doors in this weather** yo no me aventuraría a salir con este tiempo; **the government has ventured on a new defence policy** el gobierno se ha embarcado en una nueva política de defensa; **to v. into politics** aventurarse en política

► **venture forth** *vi Literary* aventurarse

► **venture on, venture upon** *vt insep* aventurarse en, meterse en

► **venture out** *vi* aventurarse a salir

venturesome ['ventʃəsəm] *adj Literary (person)* audaz; *(action)* arriesgado(a)

venue ['venju:] *n* **(a)** *(for meeting)* lugar *m*; *(for concert)* local *m* (de conciertos), sala *f* (de conciertos); *(for sports game)* estadio *m*; **they've changed the v. for tonight's meeting** han cambiado de sitio *or* lugar la reunión de esta noche; **the band have played at all of the biggest London venues** la banda ha tocado en las salas (de conciertos) más importantes de Londres **(b)** *Law* jurisdicción *f*

Venus ['vi:nəs] *n* **(a)** *(goddess)* Venus *f* **(b)** *(planet)* Venus *m* **(c)** ***V. flytrap*** dionea *f*, atrapamoscas *f inv*

veracity [və'ræsɪtɪ] *n Formal* veracidad *f*

veranda(h) [və'rændə] *n* porche *m*, galería *f*

verb [vɜ:b] *n* verbo *m* ►► *Ling* ***v. phrase*** sintagma *m* verbal

verbal ['vɜ:bəl] **1** *adj* **(a)** *(oral) (account, confession)* oral; *(promise, agreement)* verbal ►► ***v. abuse*** insultos *mpl*; *Fam* ***v. diarrhoea*** verborrea *f*; **to have v. diarrhoea** hablar por los codos, enrollarse como las persianas; ***v. skills*** expresión *f* verbal **(b)** *Ling* verbal
2 *n Br Fam (insults)* insultos *mpl*, improperios *mpl*; **to give sb some v.** poner a alguien de vuelta y media, poner a alguien como un trapo

verbalize ['vɜ:bəlaɪz] *vt* expresar con palabras

verbally ['vɜ:bəlɪ] *adv* **(a)** *(orally)* de palabra, verbalmente; **to be v. abused** ser insultado(a) **(b)** *Ling* verbalmente, con función verbal *or* de verbo

verbatim [vɜ:'beɪtɪm] **1** *adj* literal
2 *adv* literalmente

verbena [vɜ:'bi:nə] *n* verbena *f (planta)*

verbiage ['vɜ:bɪɪdʒ] *n* palabrería *f*, verborrea *f*

verbose [vɜ:'bəʊs] *adj* verboso(a), prolijo(a)

verbosity [vɜ:'bɒsɪtɪ] *n* verbosidad *f*, verborrea *f*

verdant ['vɜ:dənt] *adj Literary* verde

verdict ['vɜ:dɪkt] *n Law & Fig* veredicto *m*; **to return a v. of guilty/not guilty** pronunciar un veredicto de culpabilidad/inocencia; **to reach a v.** llegar a un veredicto final; **what's your v. on the play?** ¿qué le ha parecido la obra?, ¿qué opinión le merece la obra?

verdigris ['vɜ:dɪgri:] *n* cardenillo *m*, verdín *m*

verdin ['vɜ:dɪn] *n* pájaro *m* moscón verde

verdure ['vɜ:djə(r)] *n Literary* verdor *m*

verge [vɜ:dʒ] *n* **(a)** *(edge)* borde *m*, margen *m* **(b)** *Br (of road)* borde *m*; **grass v.** *(beside road)* franja *f* de hierba *or* césped **(c)** *(threshold)* **on the v. of...** al borde de...; **to be on the v. of bankruptcy/a nervous breakdown** estar al borde de la quiebra/una crisis nerviosa; **to be on the v. of tears** estar a punto de echarse a llorar; **to be on the v. of doing sth** estar a punto de hacer algo

► **verge on** *vt insep* rayar en; **verging on...** rayano(a) *or* rayando en; **they were verging on hysteria** estaban al borde de la histeria; **she's verging on forty** está a punto de cumplir los cuarenta; **green verging on blue** verde casi azul, verde tirando a azul

verger ['vɜ:dʒə(r)] *n* sacristán *m (de la Iglesia anglicana)*

verifiable [verɪ'faɪəbəl] *adj* verificable

verification [verɪfɪ'keɪʃən] *n (confirmation)* corroboración *f*, confirmación *f*; *(checking)* verificación *f*, comprobación *f*

verify ['verɪfaɪ] *vt (confirm)* corroborar, confirmar; *(check)* verificar, comprobar

verisimilitude [verɪsɪ'mɪlɪtju:d] *n Formal* verosimilitud *f*

veritable ['verɪtəbəl] *adj Formal* verdadero(a)

verity ['verɪtɪ] *n Literary* verdad *f*; **the eternal verities** las verdades eternas

vermicelli [vɜ:mɪ'tʃelɪ] *n* fideos *mpl*

vermilion [və'mɪljən] **1** *n* bermellón *m*
2 *adj* bermejo(a) ►► ***v. flycatcher*** churrinche *m*

vermin ['vɜ:mɪn] *npl* **(a)** *(insects)* bichos *mpl*, sabandijas *fpl*; *(bigger animals)* alimañas *fpl* **(b)** *Pej (people)* escoria *f*, gentuza *f*

verminous ['vɜ:mɪnəs] *adj* **(a)** *(infested) (person)* piojoso(a); *(clothes, mattress)* lleno(a) de pulgas/piojos/chinches **(b)** *(disgusting)* detestable

Vermont [vɜ:'mɒnt] *n* Vermont

vermouth ['vɜ:məθ] *n* vermú *m*, vermut *m*

vernacular [və'nækjʊlə(r)] **1** *n* (**a**) *Ling* lengua *f* vernácula; *(spoken language)* lenguaje *m* de la calle; **in the local v.** en el habla local (**b**) *(jargon)* jerga *f*; **the sporting v.** la jerga deportiva (**c**) *Archit* arquitectura *f* local

2 *adj (language)* vernáculo(a); *(architecture)* local; *(literature)* en lengua vernácula; **in v. speech** en lenguaje cotidiano, en el habla corriente

vernal ['vɜːnəl] *adj Astron* ***v. equinox*** equinoccio *m* de primavera *or Spec* vernal

veronica [və'rɒnɪkə] *n Bot* verónica *f*

verruca [və'ruːkə] *n Med* verruga *f (especialmente en las plantas de los pies)*

Versailles [vɜː'saɪ] *n* Versalles

versatile ['vɜːsətaɪl] *adj (person)* polifacético(a), versátil; *(mind)* abierto(a), flexible; *(object)* polivalente, multiuso(s) *inv*; *(dress, jacket)* versátil, que da mucho juego; *(ingredient)* polivalente, con múltiples aplicaciones; **a v. player** un jugador polivalente

versatility [vɜːsə'tɪlɪtɪ] *n (of person)* versatilidad *f*, carácter *m* polifacético; *(of object, ingredient)* versalitidad *f*, polivalencia *f*

verse [vɜːs] *n* (**a**) *(poetry)* poesía *f*, verso *m*; **written in v.** escrito en verso ►► ***v. drama*** teatro *m* en verso; ***v. translation*** traducción *f* en verso (**b**) *(stanza)* estrofa *f* (**c**) *(of Bible)* versículo *m*

versed [vɜːst] *adj* **to be (well) v. in sth** estar (muy) versado(a) *or* ducho(a) en algo

version ['vɜːʃən] *n* (**a**) *(account)* versión *f*; **he gave us his v. of events** nos dio su versión de los hechos (**b**) *(model)* modelo *m*; **the deluxe/economy v.** *(of car, computer)* el modelo de lujo/económico; *Fig* **he looks like a younger v. of his father** es igual(ito) que su padre cuando era joven (**c**) *(form) (of book, song)* versión *f*; **the screen** *or* **film v. of the book** la versión fílmica del libro

verso ['vɜːsəʊ] *n Typ (of page)* verso *m*

versus ['vɜːsɪz] *prep* (**a**) *Law & Sport (against)* contra (**b**) *(compared with)* frente a, en contraposición a

vertebra ['vɜːtɪbrə] (*pl* **vertebrae** ['vɜːtɪbriː]) *n Anat* vértebra *f*

vertebral column ['vɜːtɪbrəl'kɒləm] *n Anat* columna *f* vertebral

vertebrate ['vɜːtɪbrət] **1** *n* vertebrado(a) *m,f*

2 *adj* vertebrado(a)

vertex ['vɜːteks] (*pl* **vertices** ['vɜːtɪsiːz]) *n Math* vértice *m*

vertical ['vɜːtɪkəl] **1** *n* vertical *f*

2 *adj* vertical; **there was a v. drop to the sea below** había una caída en vertical hasta el mar ►► *Com* ***v. integration*** integración *f* vertical; *Comptr* ***v. justification*** justificación *f* vertical; *Comptr* ***v. orientation*** orientación *f* vertical; *Av* ***v. take-off (and landing)*** despegue *m or Am* decolaje *m* (y aterrizaje) vertical

vertically ['vɜːtɪklɪ] *adv* verticalmente; *Com* **v. integrated** de integración vertical

vertiginous [vɜː'tɪdʒɪnəs] *adj Formal* vertiginoso(a)

vertigo ['vɜːtɪgəʊ] *n Med* vértigo *m*

verve [vɜːv] *n* nervio *m*, energía *f*

Very ['verɪ] *n* ***V. light*** bengala *f* (de color) Very; ***V. pistol*** pistola *f* de bengalas (de color) Very

VERY ['verɪ] **1** *adv* (**a**) *(extremely)* muy; **v. good/little** muy bueno/poco, buenísimo/poquísimo; **v. few** muy pocos(as); **v. few people** muy poca gente; **v. many** muchos(as); **it isn't v. difficult** no es muy difícil; **I'm v. sorry** lo siento mucho; **there's nothing v. special about it** no tiene nada demasiado especial; **v. good** *or* **well!** *(expressing agreement, consent)* muy bien; **that's all v. well but...** todo eso está muy bien pero...; **you can't v. well expect me to do that** no esperarás que vaya a hacer eso; **v. much** mucho; **I v. much hope you'll come and visit us** espero de verdad que vengas a visitarnos; **it v. much depends** depende mucho; **did you like it? – v. much so** ¿te gustó? – muchísimo; **was it good? – yes, v./not v.** ¿fue bueno? – sí, mucho/no mucho; **are you hungry? – yes, v./not v.** ¿tienes hambre? – sí, mucha/no mucha; **how v. annoying/stupid!** ¡qué fastidio/estupidez más grande!; *Rel* **the V. Reverend John Green** el reverendo John Green ►► *Rad* ***v. high frequency*** frecuencia *f* muy alta

(**b**) *(emphatic use)* **the v. first/best** el primero/el mejor de todos; **I did my v. best** me esforcé al máximo; **we're the v. best of friends** somos amiguísimos; **the v. latest technology** lo ultimísimo en tecnología; **the v. next day** precisamente el día siguiente; **the v. same day** justo ese mismo día; **my v. own bike** una bici sólo para mí; **I v. nearly died** estuve a punto de morir; **at the v. least/latest** como muy poco/tarde; **at the v. most** como máximo; **I'm telling you for the v. last time** esta es la última vez que te lo digo

2 *adj* (**a**) *(extreme)* **at the v. top of the mountain** en lo más alto de la montaña; **at the v. back** al fondo; **at the v. beginning** al principio del todo; **at the v. end** al final; **she's the v. opposite of me** es opuesta a mí en todo

(**b**) *(exact)* **those were his v. words** esas fueron sus palabras exactas; **in this v. house** en esta misma casa; **you're the v. person I was looking for** eres precisamente la persona a quien estaba buscando; **this is the v. thing for the job** esto es precisamente lo que necesitábamos; **by its v. nature** por su propia naturaleza

(**c**) *(emphatic use)* **the v. fact that you lied to me** precisamente el hecho de que me mintieras; **the v. thought of it was enough to turn my stomach** sólo de pensarlo se me revolvía el estómago; **before my/your v. eyes** ante mis/tus propios ojos; **the v. idea!** ¡ni en sueños!

vesicle ['vesɪkəl] *n Med* vesícula *f*

vespers ['vespəz] *n Rel* vísperas *fpl*

vessel ['vesəl] *n* (**a**) *Naut* buque *m*, navío *m* (**b**) *(receptacle)* vasija *f*, recipiente *m* (**c**) *Anat* vaso *m*

vest [vest] **1** *n* (**a**) *Br (sleeveless shirt)* camiseta *f* de tirantes *or Am* breteles (**b**) *Sport* camiseta *f* (de tirantes *or Am* breteles) (**c**) *US (waistcoat)* chaleco *m*

2 *vt Formal* **to v. sth in sb** conferir algo a alguien; **legislative authority is vested in Parliament** el poder legislativo se hace recaer sobre el parlamento; **by the power vested in me...** por los poderes que me han sido conferidos...; **to v. sb with sth** investir a alguien con *or* de algo

vestal virgin ['vestəl'vɜːdʒɪn] *n* vestal *f*

vested ['vestɪd] *adj* **to have a v. interest in sth** *(personal involvement)* tener un interés personal en algo; *(money invested)* tener dinero invertido en algo; **v. interests** *(advantages, privileges)* intereses *mpl* creados; **the v. interests in society** *(privileged groups)* los poderes establecidos de la sociedad *or* del sistema; **there are v. interests in industry opposed to reform** hay (grupos con) intereses creados en el sector industrial que se oponen a la reforma

vestibule ['vestɪbjuːl] *n* (**a**) vestíbulo *m* (**b**) *Anat* vestíbulo *m* (**c**) *US Rail* fuelle *m* de conexión

vestige ['vestɪdʒ] *n* (**a**) *(remnant)* vestigio *m*; **there's not a v. of evidence that he was involved in the conspiracy** no existe el menor indicio de que estuviera involucrado en la conspiración; **not a v. of the original building remains** no queda el menor rastro *or* vestigio del edificio original (**b**) *Anat & Zool* rudimento *m*, vestigio *m*; **the v. of a tail** el vestigio de una cola, una cola rudimentaria *or* vestigial

vestigial [ves'tɪdʒɪəl] *adj* (**a**) *Formal (remaining)* residual; **some v. sense of decency prevented him from doing it** algún vestigio de decencia que le quedaba le impidió hacerlo (**b**) *Biol (tail)* rudimentario(a), vestigial

vestments ['vestmənts] *npl Rel* vestiduras *fpl* (sacerdotales)

vest-pocket ['vest'pɒkɪt] *adj US* (**a**) *(book, camera, pistol)* de bolsillo (**b**) *(small) (farm, park)* minúsculo(a)

vestry ['vestrɪ] *n Rel* sacristía *f*

Vesuvius [və'suːvɪəs] *n* **(Mount) V.** el Vesubio

vet[1] [vet] *n* veterinario(a) *m,f*

vet[2] (*pt & pp* **vetted**) *vt (person)* someter a investigación; *(application)* investigar; *(book, speech)* revisar, examinar; *(claims, figures)* revisar, contrastar

vet[3] *n US Mil Fam (veteran)* excombatiente *mf*, veterano(a) *m,f*

vetch [vetʃ] *n* arveja *f*

veteran ['vetərən] **1** *n Mil* excombatiente *mf*, veterano(a) *m,f*; *Fig* veterano(a) *m,f*

2 *adj* veterano(a) ►► ***v. car*** coche *m* antiguo *or* de época *(fabricado antes de 1905)*; *US* ***Veterans' Day*** día *m* del Armisticio

veterinarian [vetərɪ'neərɪən] *n US* veterinario(a) *m,f*

veterinary ['vetərɪnərɪ] *adj* veterinario(a) ►► ***v. medicine*** veterinaria *f*; *Br* ***v. surgeon*** veterinario(a) *m,f*

veto ['viːtəʊ] **1** *n* (*pl* **vetoes**) veto *m*; **right** *or* **power of v.** derecho de veto; **to use one's v.** hacer uso del derecho de veto; **to impose a v. on sth** vetar algo

2 *vt* vetar

vetting ['vetɪŋ] *n* investigación *f* (del historial) personal

vex [veks] *vt (annoy)* molestar, disgustar; *(anger) esp Esp* enfadar, *esp Am* enojar

vexation [vek'seɪʃən] *n (annoyance)* disgusto *m*, molestia *f*; *(anger) esp Esp* enfado *m*, *esp Am* enojo *m*

False friend: The Spanish noun **vejación** is not a translation for the English word **vexation**. In Spanish **vejación** means "humiliation".

vexatious [vek'seɪʃəs] *adj Formal* molesto(a), enojoso(a)

vexed [vekst] *adj* (**a**) *(annoyed)* molesto(a), disgustado(a); *(angry) esp Esp* enfadado(a), *esp Am* enojado(a); **to become v.** *esp Esp* enfadarse, *esp Am* enojarse; **to be v. with sb** estar *esp Esp* enfadado *or esp Am* enojado con alguien; **she was v. at his behaviour** estaba muy disgustada por su comportamiento (**b**) *(much debated)* **a v. question** una cuestión controvertida

vexing ['veksɪŋ] *adj (annoying)* molesto(a); *(infuriating)* enojoso(a)

VGA [viːdʒiː'eɪ] *Comptr* (*abbr* **video graphics array**) VGA; **Super V.** Super VGA

VHF [viːeɪtʃ'ef] *adj Rad* (*abbr* **very high frequency**) VHF

VHS [viːeɪtʃ'es] *n* (*abbr* **video home system**) VHS *m*

via ['vaɪə] *prep* (**a**) *(travel)* vía, por (**b**) *(using)* a través de; **v. satellite** vía *or* por satélite

viability [vaɪə'bɪlɪtɪ] *n* viabilidad *f*

viable ['vaɪəbəl] *adj* viable

viaduct ['vaɪədʌkt] *n* viaducto *m*

Viagra® [vaɪ'ægrə] *n* Viagra® *m or f*

vial ['vaɪəl] *n Pharm* ampolla *f*, vial *m*; *(of perfume)* frasquito *m*

viands ['vaɪəndz] *npl Archaic or Literary* viandas *fpl*

vibes [vaɪbz] *npl Fam* (**a**) *(feelings)* vibraciones *fpl*, *Esp* rollo *m*, *Am* onda *f*; **I got good/bad v. from that place** aquel lugar me daba buenas/malas vibraciones *or Esp* buen/mal rollo *or Am* buenas/malas ondas (**b**) *(vibraphone)* vibráfono *m*

vibrancy ['vaɪbrənsɪ] *n (of sound, voice)* vibración *f*, sonoridad *f*; *(of colours)* viveza *f*, brillo *m*; *(of scene, city, atmosphere)* animación *f*; *(of personality)* pujanza *f*

vibrant ['vaɪbrənt] *adj (sound, voice)* vibrante, sonoro(a); *(colour)* vivo(a), brillante; *(scene, city, atmosphere)* vibrante, lleno(a) de animación; *(personality)* pujante

vibraphone ['vaɪbrəfəʊn] *n* vibráfono *m*

vibrate [vaɪ'breɪt] *vi* vibrar

vibration [vaɪ'breɪʃən] *n* (**a**) *(motion)* vibración *f* (**b**) *Fam* **vibrations** *(feelings)* vibraciones *fpl*

vibrato [vɪ'brɑːtəʊ] *n Mus* vibrato *m*

vibrator [vaɪ'breɪtə(r)] *n* vibrador *m*

vicar ['vɪkə(r)] *n (in Church of England)* párroco *m* ►► ***V. of Christ*** *(pope)* vicario *m* de Cristo

vicarage ['vɪkərɪdʒ] *n (in Church of England)* casa *f* del párroco

vicarious [vɪ'keərɪəs] *adj* indirecto(a); **cinema allows us to gain v. experience of extreme situations** el cine constituye una forma indirecta *or* pasiva de experimentar situaciones extremas; **reading travel guides can be a form of v. travel** leer guías de viajes puede ser un sucedáneo de viajar; **to get v. pleasure from sth** disfrutar de algo de forma indirecta, disfrutar de algo sin tomar parte en ello

vicariously [vɪ'keərɪəslɪ] *adv* indirectamente

vice[1] [vaɪs] *n (immorality)* vicio *m*; *Hum* **it's my only v.** es el único vicio que tengo ►► ***v. ring*** red *f* de delincuencia; ***the V. Squad*** la brigada antivicio

vice[2], *US* **vise** *n (for wood or metalwork)* torno *m or* tornillo de banco

vice-chairman [vaɪs'tʃeəmən] *n* vicepresidente *m*

vice-chairwoman [vaɪs'tʃeəwʊmən] *n* vicepresidenta *f*

vice-chancellor [vaɪs'tʃɑːnsələ(r)] *n Br (of university)* ≃ rector(ora) *m,f*

vice-consul [vaɪs'kɒnsəl] *n* vicecónsul *mf*

vicelike ['vaɪslaɪk] *adj* **held in a v. grip** sujeto(a) con mucha fuerza, fuertemente aferrado(a) *or* atenazado(a)

vice-premier [vaɪs'premɪə(r)] *n* viceprimer(era) ministro(a) *m,f*

vice-president [vaɪs'prezɪdənt] *n* (**a**) *(of country)* vicepresidente(a) *m,f* (**b**) *US Com (of company)* vicepresidente(a) *m,f*

vice-presidential [vaɪs'prezɪ'denʃəl] *adj* vicepresidencial ►► ***v. candidate*** el candidato a la vicepresidencia

viceroy ['vaɪsrɔɪ] *n* virrey *m*

vice versa [vaɪs'vɜːsə] *adv* viceversa

vicinity [vɪ'sɪnɪtɪ] *n Formal* (**a**) *(surrounding area, neighbourhood)* cercanías *fpl*, inmediaciones *fpl*; **in the v.** en las cercanías; **he's somewhere in the v.** está por aquí cerca; **in the v. of the town centre** en las inmediaciones del centro de la ciudad

(**b**) *(proximity)* proximidad *f*, cercanía *f*; **one good thing about the house is its v. to the station** una de las ventajas de la casa es su proximidad a la estación

(**c**) *(approximate figures, amounts)* **a sum in the v. of £25,000** una cantidad que ronda las 25.000 libras

vicious ['vɪʃəs] *adj* (**a**) *(violent) (person)* brutal, cruel; *(animal, struggle)* feroz; *(blow, attack)* brutal; **she has a v. temper** tiene un carácter terrible (**b**) *(malicious, cruel) (comment, criticism)* despiadado(a); *(gossip)* malintencionado(a); *(person)* cruel; **he has a v. tongue** tiene una lengua viperina; **a v. circle** un círculo vicioso

> **False friend**: The most common senses of the English adjective **vicious** are not translated by the Spanish word **vicioso**. In Spanish **vicioso** means "depraved" or "addicted".

viciously ['vɪʃəslɪ] *adv (to attack, kick)* brutalmente, con saña; *(to criticize)* despiadadamente; *(to gossip)* con mala intención

viciousness ['vɪʃəsnɪs] *n* (**a**) *(violence) (of person, attack)* brutalidad *f*, saña *f*; *(of animal)* ferocidad *f*, fiereza *f* (**b**) *(cruelty, malice) (of criticism)* crueldad *f*; *(of gossip)* mala intención *f*

vicissitude [vɪ'sɪsɪtjuːd] *n Formal* vicisitud *f*

victim ['vɪktɪm] *n* víctima *f*; **victims of cancer, cancer victims** víctimas del cáncer; **the flood/earthquake victims** *(casualties)* las víctimas de la inundación/del terremoto; *(survivors)* los damnificados por la inundación/el terremoto; **to be the v. of** ser víctima de; **he was a v. of his own success** fue víctima de su propio éxito; **to fall v. to sth** *(disease, recession)* ser víctima de algo; **to fall v. to sb's charms** caer rendido(a) ante los encantos de alguien

victimization [vɪktɪmaɪ'zeɪʃən] *n* persecución *f*, trato *m* injusto

victimize ['vɪktɪmaɪz] *vt* perseguir, tratar injustamente; **he was victimized at school** en la escuela se metían con él; **this law victimizes the lower-paid** esta ley castiga a aquellos con los sueldos más bajos

victimless ['vɪktɪmlɪs] *adj* ***v. crime*** delito *m* sin víctima *or* sin dolo

victor ['vɪktə(r)] *n* vencedor(ora) *m,f*

Victoria [vɪk'tɔːrɪə] *pr n* **(Queen) V.** (la reina) Victoria ►► ***V. Cross*** = la más alta condecoración militar británica; ***V. sandwich*** bizcocho *m* relleno

Victorian [vɪk'tɔːrɪən] **1** *n* victoriano(a) *m,f*

2 *adj* victoriano(a); **a return to V. values** una vuelta a los valores victorianos

Victoriana [vɪktɔːrɪ'ɑːnə] *npl* antigüedades *fpl* de la época victoriana

victorious [vɪk'tɔːrɪəs] *adj* victorioso(a); **to be v. over sb** triunfar sobre alguien; **to emerge v.** salir victorioso

victory ['vɪktərɪ] *n* victoria *f*; **a v. for common sense** un triunfo del sentido común; **to gain** *or* **win a v. over sb** vencer a alguien, triunfar sobre alguien ►► ***v. celebrations*** celebración *f* de la victoria; ***v. sign*** señal *f* de la victoria

victualler ['vɪtlə(r)] *n* **(licensed) v.** = dueño/encargado de un bar con licencia para la venta y consumo de bebidas alcóholicas

victuals ['vɪtəlz] *npl Old-fashioned (food)* vituallas *fpl*

videlicet [vɪ'diːlɪset] *adv Formal* a saber

video ['vɪdɪəʊ] **1** *n* (*pl* **videos**) (**a**) *(medium)* vídeo *m*, *Am* video *m*; **to have sth on v.** tener algo (grabado) en vídeo *or Am* video ►► ***v. arcade*** sala *f* (recreativa) de videojuegos; ***v. art*** arte *m* en vídeo *or Am* video, videoarte *m*; ***v. camera*** cámara *f* de vídeo *or Am* video, videocámara *f*; ***v. clip*** videoclip *m*, vídeo *m*, *Am* video *m*; ***v. console*** videoconsola *f*; ***v. disc*** videodisco *m*; ***v. game*** videojuego *m*; ***v. game console*** consola *f* de videojuegos; ***v. installation*** videoinstalación *f*; *Fam* ***v. nasty*** = vídeo de violencia extrema; ***v. recording*** grabación *f* en vídeo *or Am* video, videograbación *f*

(**b**) *(cassette)* vídeo *m*, *Am* video *m* ►► ***v. cassette*** cinta *f* de vídeo *or Am* video, videocinta *f*; ***v. library*** videoteca *f*; ***v. piracy*** piratería *f* de vídeos *or Am* videos; ***v. player*** aparato *m or* reproductor *m* de vídeo *or Am* video; ***v. shop*** videoclub *m*; *US* ***v. store*** videoclub *m*

(**c**) *(recorder)* vídeo *m*, *Am* video *m*; **have you set the v.?** ¿has programado el vídeo *or Am* video? ►► ***v. (cassette) recorder*** (aparato *m or* reproductor *m* de) vídeo *m or Am* video *m*

(**d**) *Comptr* vídeo *m*, *Am* video *m* ►► ***v. accelerator*** acelerador *m* de vídeo *or Am* video; ***v. adapter*** adaptador *m* de vídeo *or Am* video; ***v. board*** placa *f* de vídeo *or Am* video; ***v. card*** tarjeta *f* de vídeo *or Am* video; ***v. RAM*** memoria *f* de vídeo *or Am* video

2 *vt* (**a**) *(with VCR)* grabar (en vídeo *or Am* video) (**b**) *(with camera)* hacer un vídeo *or Am* video de

videoconference ['vɪdɪəʊkɒnfrəns] *n* videoconferencia *f*

videoconferencing ['vɪdɪəʊkɒnfrənsɪŋ] *n* videoconferencias *fpl*

video-on-demand ['vɪdɪəʊɒndə'mɑːnd] *n* vídeo *m or Am* video *m* a la carta

videophone ['vɪdɪəʊfəʊn] *n* videoteléfono *m*

videotape ['vɪdɪəʊteɪp] **1** *n* cinta *f* de vídeo *or Am* video, videocinta *f*

2 *vt* (**a**) *(record)* grabar (en vídeo *or Am* video) (**b**) *(film)* hacer un vídeo *or Am* video de

videotext [ˈvɪdɪəʊtekst] *n* videotexto *m* ►► ***v. terminal*** terminal *m* videotexto

video-wall [ˈvɪdɪəʊwɔːl] *n* panel *m* de pantallas de vídeo *or Am* video

vie [vaɪ] (*pt & pp* **vied** [vaɪd], *continuous* **vying**) *vi* **to v. with sb (for sth/ to do sth)** rivalizar con alguien (por algo/para hacer algo); **the two children vied with each other for attention** los dos niños pugnaban por acaparar la atención; **several companies were vying with each other to sponsor the event** varias empresas competían *or* rivalizaban por patrocinar el acontecimiento; **to v. for control of sth** disputarse el control de algo, competir por hacerse con el control de algo

Vienna [vɪˈenə] *n* Viena

Viennese [vɪəˈniːz] **1** *n* vienés(esa) *m,f*
2 *adj* vienés(esa)

Vietnam [vɪetˈnæm] *n* Vietnam ►► ***the V. War*** la guerra de Vietnam

Vietnamese [vɪetnəˈmiːz] **1** *n* (**a**) *(person)* vietnamita *mf* (**b**) *(language)* vietnamita *m*
2 *npl* **the V.** los vietnamitas
3 *adj* vietnamita

view [vjuː] **1** *n* (**a**) *(sight)* vista *f*; **to come into v.** empezar a verse, aparecer; **to disappear from v.** dejar de verse, perderse de vista; **to be hidden from v.** estar escondido(a), no estar a la vista; **the house was hidden from v. by the trees** los árboles no dejaban ver la casa; **in v.** a la vista; **in full v. of** delante de, a la vista de; **on v.** *(painting)* expuesto(a) al público; **out of v.** fuera de la vista
(**b**) *(scene, prospect)* vista *f*; **a room with a v.** una habitación con vistas; **you're blocking my v.** no me dejas ver; **to have a good v. of sth** *(in general)* ver bien algo; *(scenery, landscape)* tener una buena vista de algo; **you get a better v. from here** desde aquí verás mejor; **a side v. of the building** una vista lateral del edificio
(**c**) *(opinion)* opinión *f*; **what is your v. on the matter?** ¿qué opina *or* cuál es su opinión sobre el asunto?; **to take the v. that...** ser de la opinión de que...; **I don't take that v.** no comparto esa opinión; **in my v.** en mi opinión, a mi parecer, bajo mi punto de vista
(**d**) *(way of considering)* visión *f*, perspectiva *f*; **I take a very serious v. of this matter** me tomo este asunto muy en serio; **she took a poor** *or* **dim v. of his behaviour** su comportamiento le merecía una pobre opinión; **to take the long v. of sth** mirar algo desde una perspectiva amplia; **in v. of...** en vista de..., teniendo en cuenta...; **in v. of the fact that...** en vista de que..., teniendo en cuenta que...
(**e**) *(intention)* **with this in v.** con esto en mente, con este propósito; **there appears to be no solution in v.** no parece vislumbrarse una solución; **with a v. to doing sth** con vistas a hacer algo; **they bought the house with a v. to their retirement** compraron la casa pensando en su jubilación
(**f**) *(picture, photograph)* imagen *f*, vista *f*; **views of Venice** imágenes de Venecia; **an aerial v. of New York** una vista aérea de Nueva York
2 *vt* (**a**) *(inspect, look at)* ver; **the house may be viewed at weekends only** la casa sólo se puede ver los fines de semana
(**b**) *(consider)* ver, considerar; **she viewed it as a mistake** lo veía *or* consideraba un error; **viewed in this light, his behaviour seems more understandable** (visto) desde esta perspectiva, su forma de actuar se entiende un poco más; **he was viewed with some suspicion by the leadership** la directiva no se fiaba de él; **to v. sth with horror/delight** contemplar algo con horror/placer
(**c**) *Comptr (codes, document)* visualizar

viewable area [ˈvjuːəbəlˈeərɪə] *n Comptr (of monitor)* área *f* visible

viewdata [ˈvjuːdeɪtə] *n* videotexto *m*

viewer [ˈvjuːə(r)] *n* (**a**) *TV* telespectador(ora) *m,f*, televidente *mf* (**b**) *(for slides)* visor *m* (**c**) *Comptr* visualizador *m*

viewfinder [ˈvjuːfaɪndə(r)] *n Phot* visor *m*

viewing [ˈvjuːɪŋ] *n* (**a**) *(of movie, TV programme)* **the movie stands up to repeated v.** la película no pierde cuando se ve en repetidas ocasiones; **for home v.** para ver en casa; **this programme is essential v.** no te debes/se debe perder este programa ►► ***v. figures*** índices *mpl* de audiencia, rating *m*; ***v. hours:*** **during peak v. hours** en horario de máxima audiencia; ***v. public*** televidentes *mpl*, público *m* telespectador (**b**) *(of house)* visita *f*

viewpoint [ˈvjuːpɔɪnt] *n* punto *m* de vista; **from another v.** desde otro punto de vista

vigil [ˈvɪdʒɪl] *n* vigilia *f*; **to keep v.** *Rel* observar la vigilia; *(guard, watch)* estar en vela, velar

vigilance [ˈvɪdʒɪləns] *n* vigilancia *f*; **to escape sb's v.** *(person)* escapar del control de alguien; *(mistake)* escapársele a alguien; **to relax one's v.** bajar la guardia ►► *US* ***v. committee*** patrulla *f* vecinal

vigilant [ˈvɪdʒɪlənt] *adj* alerta

vigilante [vɪdʒɪˈlæntɪ] *n* miembro *m* de una patrulla vecinal ►► ***v. group*** patrulla *f* vecinal

vigilantly [ˈvɪdʒɪləntlɪ] *adv* atentamente

vignette [vɪnˈjet] *n Phot* viñeta *f*; *Fig (picture)* escena *f*; *(in writing)* estampa *f*

vigor *US* = **vigour**

vigorous [ˈvɪgərəs] *adj* (**a**) *(strong and healthy)* vigoroso(a) (**b**) *(energetic)* enérgico(a); *(lifestyle)* dinámico(a); *(exercise)* intenso(a) (**c**) *(forceful) (opposition, protest, criticism)* fuerte, enérgico(a); *(campaign)* intenso(a), enérgico(a); *(support, denial)* rotundo(a)

vigorously [ˈvɪgərəslɪ] *adv* (**a**) *(healthily) (to grow)* vigorosamente (**b**) *(energetically) (to exercise)* intensamente; **he nodded his head v.** asintió enérgicamente *or* vigorosamente con la cabeza (**c**) *(forcefully) (to oppose, protest, campaign)* enérgicamente; *(to support, deny)* rotundamente

vigour, *US* **vigor** [ˈvɪgə(r)] *n* (**a**) *(health, strength) (of person)* vigor *m* (**b**) *(energy)* intensidad *f* (**c**) *(forcefulness) (of criticism)* rotundidad *f*, fuerza *f*; *(of denial)* rotundidad *f*

Viking [ˈvaɪkɪŋ] **1** *n* vikingo(a) *m,f*
2 *adj* vikingo(a)

vile [vaɪl] *adj* (**a**) *(despicable)* vil; **a v. deed** una vileza, un acto vil (**b**) *(awful)* horroroso(a), espantoso(a); **it smells/tastes v.!** ¡huele/sabe horrible!; **to be in a v. temper** estar de un humor de perros

vileness [ˈvaɪlnɪs] *n* (**a**) *(of deed, accusation)* vileza *f*, bajeza *f* (**b**) *(of smell, taste)* repugnancia *f*; *(of weather)* pésimo estado *m*

vilification [vɪlɪfɪˈkeɪʃən] *n Formal* vilipendio *m*

vilify [ˈvɪlɪfaɪ] *vt Formal* vilipendiar, denigrar

villa [ˈvɪlə] *n* (**a**) *(in ancient Rome)* villa *f* (**b**) *(residential) (in country)* chalé *m*, casa *f* de campo; *(in town)* chalé *m* (**c**) *(luxurious holiday home)* chalé *m*

village [ˈvɪlɪdʒ] *n* pueblo *m*; *(smaller)* aldea *f* ►► ***v. green*** espacio *m* verde comunal; ***v. hall*** = centro cultural y social de un pueblo; ***v. idiot*** tonto(a) *m,f* del pueblo; ***v. life*** la vida en el pueblo; ***v. weaver*** *(bird)* tejedor *m* familiar

villager [ˈvɪlɪdʒə(r)] *n* lugareño(a) *m,f*

villain [ˈvɪlən] *n* (**a**) *(scoundrel)* canalla *mf*, villano(a) *m,f* (**b**) *Theat & Cin* malo(a) *m,f*; *Hum* **the v. of the piece** el malo de la película (**c**) *Br Fam (criminal)* maleante *mf*

villainous [ˈvɪlənəs] *adj* vil, infame

villainy [ˈvɪlənɪ] *n Formal* villanía *f*, infamia *f*

Vilnius [ˈvɪlnɪəs] *n* Vilna, Vilnius

vim [vɪm] *n Fam* brío *m*, ganas *fpl*; **full of v. (and vigour)** lleno(a) de vitalidad

vinaigrette [vɪnəˈgret] *n* (salsa *f*) vinagreta *f*

vindaloo [vɪndəˈluː] *n* vindaloo *m*, = plato indio muy picante y especiado a base de carne o pescado

vindicate [ˈvɪndɪkeɪt] *vt* (**a**) *(decision, action)* justificar (**b**) *(person, regime)* (re)vindicar, defender

vindication [vɪndɪˈkeɪʃən] *n* (**a**) *(of decision, action)* justificación *f* (**b**) *(of person, regime)* (re)vindicación *f*, defensa *f*

vindictive [vɪnˈdɪktɪv] *adj* vengativo(a)

vindictively [vɪnˈdɪktɪvlɪ] *adv* de un modo vengativo, con afán de venganza

vindictiveness [vɪnˈdɪktɪvnɪs] *n* afán *m* de venganza; **that was sheer v.!** ¡eso no eran más que ganas de vengarse!

vine [vaɪn] *n (in vineyard)* vid *f*; *(decorative)* parra *f* ►► ***v. leaf*** hoja *f* de parra

vinegar [ˈvɪnɪgə(r)] *n* vinagre *m* ►► ***v. fly*** mosca *f* de la fruta

vinegary [ˈvɪnəgərɪ] *adj (taste)* a vinagre, avinagrado(a); *(wine)* avinagrado(a)

vineyard [ˈvɪnjəd] *n* viñedo *m*

vino [ˈviːnəʊ] *n Fam* vinito *m*, *Esp* morapio *m*

vintage [ˈvɪntɪdʒ] **1** *n* (**a**) *(crop)* cosecha *f*; **1986 was an excellent v.** la de 1986 fue una cosecha excelente; **this claret is an excellent v.** este burdeos es de una cosecha excelente; *Fig* **a v. year for comedy** un año excepcional en cuanto a comedias
(**b**) *(period)* época *f*; **an old radio of pre-war v.** una vieja radio de antes de la guerra; *Hum* **our parents are of the same v.** nuestros padres son de la misma quinta ►► ***v. car*** coche *m* antiguo *or* de época *(especialmente de entre 1919 y 1930)*
2 *adj* (**a**) *(wine, port, champagne)* de buena cosecha (**b**) *(classic, superior)* excelente; **a season of v. films** un ciclo de clásicos del cine; **it was v. Agatha Christie** era un clásico exponente de la mejor Agatha Christie (**c**) *Fam (old)* prehistórico(a), del año de la polca

vintner ['vɪntnə(r)] *n Formal* vinatero(a) *m,f*

vinyl ['vaɪnəl] *n* vinilo *m*

viola [vɪ'əʊlə] *n* viola *f*

violate ['vaɪəleɪt] *vt* (**a**) *(law, treaty, right)* violar, vulnerar; *(frontier, property)* violar, invadir; **to v. a country's territorial waters** violar las aguas territoriales de un país (**b**) *(peace, silence)* romper, perturbar; **to v. sb's privacy** violar *or* invadir la intimidad de alguien (**c**) *(tomb, sanctuary)* violar, profanar (**d**) *Formal (rape)* violar, ultrajar

violation [vaɪə'leɪʃən] *n* (**a**) *(of law, treaty, right)* violación *f*, vulneración *f*; *(of frontier, property)* violación *f*, invasión *f*; **to be in v. of sth** violar algo; **v. of territorial waters** violación de aguas territoriales
(**b**) *(of peace, silence)* perturbación *f*
(**c**) *(of tomb, sanctuary)* violación *f*, profanación *f*
(**d**) *US Law* infracción *f*; **traffic v.** infracción de tráfico
(**e**) *(in basketball)* violación *f*; **three-second v.** violación *f* de los tres segundos
(**f**) *Formal (rape)* violación *f*, ultraje *m*

violence ['vaɪələns] *n* (**a**) *(physical)* violencia *f*; **acts/scenes of v.** actos/escenas de violencia; **to resort to v.** recurrir a la violencia; **the men of v.** *(terrorists)* los terroristas, los violentos; *Law* **crimes of v.** delitos con violencia; IDIOM **to do v. to sth** dañar algo (**b**) *(of language, passion, storm)* violencia *f*

violent ['vaɪələnt] *adj* (**a**) *(place, person, movie)* violento(a); **to get** *or* **become v.** *(person, situation)* ponerse violento(a); **to die a v. death** tener una muerte violenta; **an increase in v. crime** un aumento en la cantidad de delitos con violencia
(**b**) *(emotions, passion, storm)* violento(a); *(language)* fuerte, violento(a); **to be in a v. temper** estar fuera de sí; **to take a v. dislike to sb** tomar *or Esp* coger una enorme antipatía a alguien; **to have a v. headache/toothache** tener un dolor de cabeza/de muelas terrible

violently ['vaɪələntlɪ] *adv* violentamente; **to disagree v.** estar fuertemente en desacuerdo; **to be v. ill** vomitar muchísimo

violet ['vaɪələt] **1** *n* (**a**) *(plant)* violeta *f* (**b**) *(colour)* violeta *m*
2 *adj* **v.(-coloured)** (de color) violeta

violin [vaɪə'lɪn] *n* violín *m* ►► ***v. case*** estuche *m* de violín

violinist [vaɪə'lɪnɪst] *n* violinista *mf*

violoncellist [vaɪəlɪn'tʃelɪst] *n* violonchelista *mf*

violoncello [vaɪəlɪn'tʃeləʊ] *n* violonchelo *m*

VIP [viːaɪ'piː] *n* (*abbr* **very important person**) VIP *mf*; **to get V. treatment** recibir tratamiento de persona importante ►► ***V. box*** *(in theatre, stadium)* palco *m* de autoridades; ***V. lounge*** sala *f* VIP

viper ['vaɪpə(r)] *n* víbora *f*; IDIOM **a v.'s nest** un nido de víboras; IDIOM **to be nurturing a v. in one's bosom** estar alimentando a un monstruo

viperish ['vaɪpərɪʃ] *adj* viperino(a)

virago [vɪ'rɑːgəʊ] *n Literary* virago *f*

viral ['vaɪrəl] *adj Med* vírico(a), viral ►► ***v. marketing*** marketing *m* viral

virgin ['vɜːdʒɪn] **1** *n* virgen *mf*; **the (Blessed) V.** la (Santísima) Virgen ►► ***the V. Birth:*** **they believe in the V. Birth of Christ** creen que Cristo nació de Virgen; ***the V. Islands*** las Islas Vírgenes; ***the V. Mary*** la Virgen María
2 *adj* virgen ►► ***v. forest*** selva *f* virgen; ***v. snow*** nieve *f* virgen, nieve *f* sin tocar; ***v. territory*** territorio *m* virgen; *Fig* **this market is v. territory for the company** este mercado es nuevo *or* desconocido para la compañía; ***v. wool*** lana *f* virgen

virginal ['vɜːgɪnəl] *adj* virginal

Virginia [və'dʒɪnɪə] *n* Virginia ►► ***V. creeper*** parra *f or* hiedra *f* virgen; ***V. tobacco*** tabaco *m* de Virginia, tabaco *m* rubio

virginity [və'dʒɪnɪtɪ] *n* virginidad *f*; **to lose/keep one's v.** perder/conservar la virginidad

Virgo ['vɜːgəʊ] *n (sign of zodiac)* virgo *m*; **to be (a) V.** ser virgo

virile ['vɪraɪl] *adj* viril

virility [vɪ'rɪlɪtɪ] *n* virilidad *f*

virologist [vɪ'rɒlədʒɪst] *n Med* virólogo(a) *m,f*

virology [vaɪ'rɒlədʒɪ] *n Med* virología *f*

virtual ['vɜːtjʊəl] *adj* (**a**) *(near total)* virtual; **the v. extinction of the wild variety** la práctica desaparición de la variedad silvestre; **it's a v. impossibility** es virtualmente *or* prácticamente imposible; **it's a v. dictatorship** es una dictadura de hecho; **the organization was in a state of v. collapse** la organización se hallaba prácticamente al borde del hundimiento
(**b**) *Comptr (disk, image)* virtual ►► ***v. memory*** memoria *f* virtual; ***v. reality*** realidad *f* virtual; ***v. reality game*** juego *m* de realidad virtual

virtually ['vɜːtjʊəlɪ] *adv* prácticamente, virtualmente; **it's v. finished** está prácticamente terminado; **I'm v. certain** estoy casi seguro; **v. nothing is known about the origins of the virus** prácticamente no se sabe nada acerca de los orígenes del virus

virtue ['vɜːtjuː] **1** *n* virtud *f*; **it has the added v. of being quicker** cuenta con la virtud añadida de ser más rápido(a); **she at least has the v. of being discreet** ella tiene al menos el don de la discreción; IDIOM **to make a v. of necessity** hacer de la necesidad una virtud; PROV **v. is its own reward** la satisfacción del deber cumplido es en sí misma una recompensa
2 by virtue of *prep* en virtud de; **by v. of her age** en virtud de su edad; **by v. of being the eldest** en virtud de ser el mayor

virtuosity [vɜːtjʊ'ɒsɪtɪ] *n* virtuosismo *m*

virtuoso [vɜːtjʊ'əʊzəʊ] (*pl* **virtuosos** *or* **virtuosi** [vɜːtjʊ'əʊziː]) *n Mus* virtuoso(a) *m,f*; *also Fig* **a v. performance** una actuación digna de un virtuoso

virtuous ['vɜːtjʊəs] *adj* virtuoso(a)

virulence ['vɪr(j)ʊləns] *n (of disease, attack, hatred)* virulencia *f*

virulent ['vɪr(j)ʊlənt] *adj* virulento(a)

virus ['vaɪrəs] *n Med & Comptr* virus *m inv* ►► *Comptr* ***v. check*** detección *f* de virus; *Comptr* ***v. detector*** detector *m* de virus

virus-free ['vaɪrəsfriː] *adj Comptr* sin virus

visa ['viːzə] *n* visado *m*, *Am* visa *f*

visage ['vɪzɪdʒ] *n Literary* rostro *m*, semblante *m*

vis-à-vis ['viːzɑːviː] **1** *n* (**a**) *(person or thing opposite)* = persona o cosa que se tiene enfrente (**b**) *(counterpart)* colega *mf*, homólogo(a) *m,f*
2 *prep (in comparison with)* en comparación con, frente a; *(in relation to)* en relación con, con relación *or* respecto a

viscera ['vɪsərə] *npl Anat* vísceras *fpl*

visceral ['vɪsərəl] *adj Formal* visceral

viscose ['vɪskəʊs] *n* viscosa *f*

viscosity [vɪs'kɒsɪtɪ] *n* viscosidad *f*

viscount ['vaɪkaʊnt] *n* vizconde *m*

viscountess ['vaɪkaʊntɪs] *n* vizcondesa *f*

viscous ['vɪskəs] *adj* viscoso(a)

vise *US* = **vice**

visibility [vɪzɪ'bɪlɪtɪ] *n* visibilidad *f*; **good/poor v.** buena/mala visibilidad; **v. was down to a few yards** no se veía más allá de unos pocos metros

visible ['vɪzɪbəl] *adj* (**a**) *(able to be seen)* visible; **clearly v. to the naked eye** visible a simple vista; **only v. under a microscope** sólo visible *or* observable al microscopio; **the beach is not v. from the road** la playa no se ve desde la carretera ►► *Fam* ***v. panty line*** marca *f* de las bragas; *Phys* ***v. spectrum*** espectro *m* visible
(**b**) *(evident)* evidente; **his nervousness was clearly v.** su nerviosismo era más que evidente; **it serves no v. purpose** no cumple ningún propósito claro; **with no v. means of support** sin ingresos conocidos, sin medios económicos aparentes ►► *Econ* ***v. exports*** exportaciones *fpl* visibles

visibly ['vɪzɪblɪ] *adv* visiblemente

vision ['vɪʒən] *n* (**a**) *(eyesight)* visión *f*, vista *f*; **to have good/poor v.** estar bien/mal de la vista
(**b**) *(plan)* **he presented his v. for the company** presentó sus planes de futuro para la empresa
(**c**) *(image, idea)* visión *f*; **a v. of a future without poverty** una visión del futuro donde no exista la pobreza
(**d**) *(perception)* **a man/woman of v.** un hombre/una mujer con visión de futuro; **a player of great v.** un jugador con mucha visión de juego
(**e**) *(apparition)* visión *f*, aparición *f*; **to have a v.** tener una visión; **she claimed to have had a v. of the Virgin Mary** aseguraba que se le había aparecido la Virgen María; **to have** *or* **see visions** ver visiones; **I had visions of being left homeless** ya me veía sin un techo y durmiendo en la calle; *Fig* **she was a v. in white lace** estaba hermosa vestida con encaje blanco
(**f**) *Br TV & Cin* **sound and v.** imagen y sonido ►► ***v. mixer*** *(person)* ingeniero(a) *m,f* de imagen; *(machine)* mezclador *m* de imagen

visionary ['vɪʒənərɪ] **1** *n* visionario(a) *m,f*
2 *adj* visionario(a)

visit ['vɪzɪt] **1** *n* visita *f*; **I had a v. from your aunt last week** la semana pasada me hizo una visita *or* me vino a ver tu tía; **you should make regular visits to your dentist** debería visitar *or* acudir a su dentista con regularidad; **this is my first v. to New York** esta es la primera vez que vengo a Nueva York; **to pay sb a v.** hacer una visita a alguien; **you must pay them a return v.** debes devolverles la visita; **I haven't paid a**

v. to the cathedral yet aún no he visitado la catedral, aún no he ido a ver la catedral; **to be on a v.** estar de visita; **she's on a v. to her aunt's** está de visita en casa de su tía; **she's on a v. to Amsterdam** está visitando Amsterdam; **the President is on an official v. to Australia** el presidente se halla de *or* en visita oficial por Australia

2 *vt* (**a**) *(go to see)* visitar; **to v. the doctor** ir al médico; **she went to v. her aunt in hospital** fue a visitar a su tía al hospital; **to v. a museum/the sick** visitar un museo/a los enfermos

(**b**) *Literary (inflict)* infligir (**on** *or* **upon** a); **the city was visited by the plague in the 17th century** la ciudad fue asolada por la peste en el siglo XVII; **the sins of the fathers are visited upon their sons** los hijos cargan con los pecados de los padres

3 *vi* **to be visiting** estar de visita

▸**visit on** *vt sep Literary* **to v. sth on sb** infligir algo a alguien

▸**visit with** 1 *vt insep US* charlar *or CAm, Méx* platicar con

2 *vt sep Literary* **to v. sb with sth** castigar a alguien con algo

visitant ['vɪzɪtənt] *n* (**a**) *Literary (ghost)* aparición *f* (**b**) *(bird)* ave *f* de paso

visitation [vɪzɪ'teɪʃən] *n Formal* (**a**) *(official visit)* visita *f* oficial; *Hum* **we're having a v. from the managing director next week** la semana próxima nos hará una de sus visitas el director general (**b**) *(of vengeance, punishment)* azote *m*, castigo *m* (**c**) *(supernatural)* aparición *f*

visiting ['vɪzɪtɪŋ] 1 *n* **I want to do some v. while I'm in Madrid** mientras estoy en Madrid quiero hacer unas visitas; **hospital v.** visitas a hospitales ▸▸ ***v. card*** tarjeta *f* de visita; *Hum Euph* **the dog left its v. card** el perro dejó su regalito; ***v. hours*** horas *fpl* de visita, horario *m* de visita(s); *Law* ***v. rights*** *(of divorced parent)* derecho *m* de visita (a los hijos)

2 *adj (team)* visitante ▸▸ *US Fam Hum* ***v. fireman*** visitante *mf or* visita *f* importante *(a quien hay que agradar)*; ***v. lecturer*** profesor(ora) *m,f* invitado(a); *US* ***v. nurse*** = enfermera de un hospital o de los servicios sociales que realiza visitas a enfermos

visitor ['vɪzɪtə(r)] *n (guest, in hospital)* visita *f*; *(tourist)* turista *mf*, visitante *mf*; **you have a v.** tienes (una) visita; **we have visitors next weekend** la semana que viene tenemos invitados; **they are not allowed any visitors after 10 p.m.** no les permiten recibir visitas después de las diez de la noche; **this species is a winter v. to Britain** esta especie migratoria pasa el invierno en Gran Bretaña ▸▸ ***visitors' book*** libro *m* de visitas; ***v. centre*** *(in park, at tourist attraction)* centro *m* de atención al visitante; *Br Formerly* ***v.'s passport*** pasaporte *m* provisional

visor ['vaɪzə(r)] *n (of helmet, cap)* visera *f*

> **False friend:** The Spanish noun **visor** is not a translation for the English word **visor**. In Spanish **visor** means "viewfinder", "sight" or "file tab".

vista ['vɪstə] *n* vista *f*, panorama *m*; *Fig* horizonte *m*; **to open up new vistas** abrir nuevos horizontes, ampliar el horizonte

visual ['vɪʒʊəl] *adj* visual ▸▸ ***v. aids*** medios *mpl* visuales; ***the v. arts*** las artes plásticas; *Comptr* ***v. display unit*** monitor *m*; ***v. field*** campo *m* visual; ***v. handicap*** deficiencia *f or* discapacidad *f* visual; ***v. memory*** memoria *f* visual

visualize ['vɪʒʊəlaɪz] *vt* (**a**) *(picture)* visualizar, imaginar; **I remember the name but I can't v. his face** recuerdo el nombre pero no su cara (**b**) *(foresee)* prever; **I don't v. any major changes** no creo que se vayan a dar grandes cambios

visually ['vɪʒʊəlɪ] *adv* visualmente; **the v. handicapped** *or* **impaired** las personas con discapacidades visuales

vital ['vaɪtəl] *adj* (**a**) *(essential)* vital; *Fig* **the v. ingredient** el ingrediente esencial; **to play a v. role** jugar un papel vital *or* decisivo; **their involvement is v. to the success of the operation** su participación es vital para el éxito de la operación; **of v. importance (to...)** de vital importancia (para...); **tonight's game is v.** el partido de esta noche es crucial ▸▸ ***v. organ*** órgano *m* vital; *Med* ***v. signs*** constantes *fpl* vitales; ***v. statistics*** *(of country)* datos *mpl* demográficos; *Hum (of woman)* medidas *fpl*

(**b**) *(vigorous)* vital, lleno(a) de vida

vitality [vaɪ'tælɪtɪ] *n* vitalidad *f*

vitally ['vaɪtəlɪ] *adv* **supplies are v. needed** se necesitan suministros urgentemente; **v. important** de vital importancia

vitamin ['vɪtəmɪn, *US* 'vaɪtəmɪn] *n* vitamina *f*; **with added vitamins** enriquecido(a) con vitaminas ▸▸ ***v. complex*** complejo *m* vitamínico; ***v. content*** aporte *m* vitamínico; ***v. deficiency*** insuficiencia *f* vitamínica; ***v. pill*** píldora *f or* pastilla *f* de vitaminas; ***v. supplement*** suplemento *m* vitamínico; ***v. tablet*** comprimido *m* vitamínico

vitiate ['vɪʃɪeɪt] *vt Formal* (**a**) *(spoil quality, effect)* menoscabar, perjudicar (**b**) *(make invalid)* viciar

viticulture ['vɪtɪkʌltʃə(r)] *n* viticultura *f*

vitreous ['vɪtrɪəs] *adj* ***v. enamel*** esmalte *m* (vítreo); *Anat* ***v. humour*** humor *m* vítreo

vitrify ['vɪtrɪfaɪ] 1 *vt* vitrificar

2 *vi* vitrificarse

vitriol ['vɪtrɪəl] *n* (**a**) *(acid)* vitriolo *m* (**b**) *(vicious remarks)* causticidad *f*; **a stream of v.** un torrente de comentarios cáusticos *or* corrosivos

vitriolic [vɪtrɪ'ɒlɪk] *adj* cáustico(a), corrosivo(a)

vituperate [vɪ'tju:pəreɪt] *Formal vi* lanzar vituperios, injuriar; **to v. against sth/sb** vituperar algo/a alguien

vituperation [vɪtju:pə'reɪʃən] *n Formal* vituperios *mpl*

vituperative [vɪ'tju:pərətɪv] *adj Formal* injurioso(a)

viva = **viva voce**

vivacious [vɪ'veɪʃəs] *adj* vivaracho(a), vivaz

vivacity [vɪ'væsɪtɪ] *n* vivacidad *f*

vivarium [vaɪ'veərɪəm] (*pl* **vivariums** *or* **vivaria** [vaɪ'veərɪə]) *n (with earth)* terrario *m*; *(with water)* vivero *m*

viva (voce) ['vaɪvə('vəʊtʃɪ)] *n Univ (of thesis)* defensa *f* de la tesis; *(after written exam)* examen *m* oral

vivid ['vɪvɪd] *adj (description, memory, impression)* vívido(a); *(imagination)* muy vivo(a); *(colour)* vivo(a), intenso(a); **he paints a v. picture of 18th century life** retrata muy vívidamente la vida en el siglo XVIII

vividly ['vɪvɪdlɪ] *adv (to remember, describe)* vívidamente; **v. coloured** de vivos *or* llamativos colores

vividness ['vɪvɪdnɪs] *n (of colour)* viveza *f*, intensidad *f*; *(of description, image, memory)* carácter *m* vívido

viviparous [vɪ'vɪpərəs] *adj Zool* vivíparo(a)

vivisection [vɪvɪ'sekʃən] *n* vivisección *f*

vivisectionist [vɪvɪ'sekʃənɪst] *n* (**a**) *(practitioner)* vivisector(ora) *m,f* (**b**) *(advocate)* partidario(a) *m,f* de la vivisección

vixen ['vɪksən] *n* (**a**) *Zool* zorra *f* (**b**) *Pej (woman)* arpía *f*

Viyella® [vaɪ'elə] *n* viyela® *f*

viz [vɪz] *adv* (*abbr* **videlicet**) a saber

vizier [vɪ'zɪə(r)] *n* visir *m*

VJ day [vi:'dʒeɪdeɪ] *n* = fecha que marca la victoria aliada sobre Japón el 15 de agosto de 1945

VLF [vi:el'ef] *adj Rad* (*abbr* **very low frequency**) VLF

VLSI [vi:eles'aɪ] *n Comptr* (*abbr* **very large-scale integration**) integración *f* a muy gran escala

V-neck ['vi:nek] 1 *n (of garment)* cuello *m* de pico, escote *m* en pico; *(pullover)* suéter *m or Esp* jersey *m or Col* saco *m or RP* pulóver *m* de (cuello de) pico

2 *adj* **V-neck(ed)** de (cuello de) pico

VOA [vi:əʊ'eɪ] *n* (*abbr* **Voice of America**) = cadena de radio exterior estadounidense

vocab ['vəʊkæb] *n Fam* vocabulario *m*

vocabulary [və'kæbjʊlərɪ] *n* vocabulario *m*

vocal ['vəʊkəl] 1 *n Mus* **vocals** voces *fpl*; **on vocals** como vocalista

2 *adj* (**a**) *(music)* vocal ▸▸ *Anat* ***v. cords*** cuerdas *fpl* vocales (**b**) *(outspoken)* vehemente, explícito(a); **a v. minority** una minoría muy ruidosa; **to be very v. in one's criticism** expresar las críticas muy a las claras

vocalic [vəʊ'kælɪk] *adj Ling* vocálico(a)

vocalist ['vəʊkəlɪst] *n Mus* vocalista *mf*

vocalize ['vəʊkəlaɪz] *vt* expresar, manifestar

vocally ['vəʊkəlɪ] *adv* (**a**) *(vehemently)* vehementemente, explícitamente (**b**) *(with the voice)* vocalmente; **he did not express his thoughts v.** no expresó sus pensamientos con la voz

vocation [vəʊ'keɪʃən] *n* vocación *f*; **to have a v. (for sth)** tener vocación (para algo); **he has no v. for acting** no tiene vocación de actor; **you missed your v.!** ¡te equivocaste de profesión!

vocational [vəʊ'keɪʃənəl] *adj (course, qualification)* de formación profesional ▸▸ ***v. guidance*** orientación *f* profesional; ***v. training*** formación *f* profesional

vocationally [vəʊ'keɪʃənəlɪ] *adv* **v. oriented** de formación profesional; **v. relevant subjects** materias relacionadas con el mundo profesional

vocative ['vɒkətɪv] *Gram* 1 *n* vocativo *m*

2 *adj* vocativo(a)

vociferous [və'sɪfərəs] *adj* ruidoso(a), vehemente; **to be v. in one's criticism of sth** criticar fuertemente algo

vociferously [və'sɪfərəslɪ] *adv* ruidosamente, vehementemente

vodka ['vɒdkə] *n* vodka *m or f*

vogue [vəʊg] *n* moda *f* (**for** de); **to be in v.** estar de moda *or* en boga; **to come into v.** ponerse de moda ►► ***v. word*** palabra *f* de moda

voice [vɔɪs] **1** *n* (**a**) *(of person)* voz *f*; **we heard the sound of voices** oímos (ruido de) voces; **in a low/loud v.** en voz baja/alta; **to raise/lower one's v.** levantar/bajar la voz; **don't you raise your v. at me!** ¡a mí no me levantes la voz!; **keep your voices down!** ¡hablen en voz baja!, ¡bajen la voz!; **at the top of one's v.** a voz en grito; *also Fig* **to make one's v. heard** hacerse oír; **to be in fine v.** *(of singer)* tener bien la voz; **to hear voices** *(gen)* & *Rel* escuchar voces; **to lose one's v.** quedarse afónico(a) ►► ***v. box*** laringe *f*; ***v. mail*** buzón *m* de voz; *Comptr* ***v. recognition*** reconocimiento *m* de voz; *Comptr* ***v. synthesizer*** sintetizador *m* de voz

(**b**) *(say)* opinión *f*, voz *f*; **we have no v. in the matter** en ese tema no tenemos voz; **proportional representation would give small parties a greater v.** la representación proporcional daría a los partidos minoritarios mayor participación

(**c**) *Gram* **active/passive v.** voz activa/pasiva

(**d**) IDIOMS **the v. of reason** la voz de la razón; **with one v.** unánimemente; **to give v. to one's feelings** expresar *or* manifestar los sentimientos; **he likes the sound of his own v.** le encanta escucharse a sí mismo, le encanta el sonido de su propia voz

2 *vt* (**a**) *(opinion, feelings)* expresar (**b**) *Ling (consonant)* sonorizar

voice-activated ['vɔɪs'æktɪveɪtɪd] *adj* activado(a) por la voz

voiced [vɔɪst] *adj Ling* sonoro(a)

voiceless ['vɔɪslɪs] *adj Ling* sordo(a)

voice-over ['vɔɪs'əʊvə(r)] *n Cin & TV* voz *f* en off

voiceprint ['vɔɪsprɪnt] *n* espectrograma *m*

void [vɔɪd] **1** *n* vacío *m*; **to fill a v.** llenar un vacío; **her husband's death left an aching v. in her life** la muerte de su marido dejó en su vida un vacío difícil de llenar

2 *adj* (**a**) *(empty)* **v. of** carente de (**b**) *Law (deed, contract)* (**null and**) **v.** nulo(a) y sin valor (**c**) *(in cards)* **to be v. in hearts** no tener ningún corazón

3 *vt* (**a**) *Formal (empty)* **to v. one's bowels** evacuar (**b**) *Law* invalidar, anular

voile [vwɑːl] *n* gasa *f*

vol *n* (*abbr* **volume**) (**a**) *(sound)* vol. (**b**) *(book)* vol.

volatile ['vɒlətaɪl] *adj* (**a**) *(person)* temperamental, de carácter voluble; **he has a v. temper** tiene un pronto muy fuerte, salta a la mínima (**b**) *(situation, economy, market)* inestable, volátil (**c**) *Chem* volátil (**d**) *Comptr* ***v. memory*** memoria *f* volátil

volatility [vɒlə'tɪlɪtɪ] *n* (**a**) *(of person)* carácter *m* temperamental *or* voluble (**b**) *(of situation, economy, market)* inestabilidad *f*, volatilidad *f* (**c**) *Chem* volatilidad *f*

vol-au-vent ['vɒləʊvɒŋ] *n* volován *m*

volcanic [vɒl'kænɪk] *adj* volcánico(a)

volcano [vɒl'keɪnəʊ] (*pl* **volcanoes**) *n* volcán *m*

volcanologist [vɒlkə'nɒlədʒɪst] *n* vulcanólogo(a) *m,f*

volcanology [vɒlkə'nɒlədʒɪ] *n* vulcanología *f*

vole [vəʊl] *n* ratón *m* de campo

volition [və'lɪʃən] *n Formal* **of one's own v.** por propia voluntad

volley ['vɒlɪ] **1** *n* (**a**) *(of gunfire)* ráfaga *f*; *(of blows, stones)* lluvia *f*; *(of insults)* torrente *m*; *(of applause)* salva *f*, lluvia *f* (**b**) *(in tennis, soccer)* volea *f*

2 *vt (in tennis, soccer)* volear, golpear de volea; **to v. the ball** golpear la pelota de volea

volleyball ['vɒlɪbɔːl] *n* voleibol *m*, balonvolea *m*

volt [vəʊlt] *n Elec* voltio *m*

voltage ['vəʊltɪdʒ] *n Elec* voltaje *m* ►► ***v. drop*** caída *f* de tensión

volte-face ['vɒltfɑːs] *n* viraje *m or* giro *m* radical

voltmeter ['vəʊltmiːtə(r)] *n Elec* voltímetro *m*

volubility [vɒljʊ'bɪlɪtɪ] *n* locuacidad *f*

voluble ['vɒljʊbəl] *adj* locuaz

> **False friend:** The Spanish adjective **voluble** is not a translation for the English word **voluble**. In Spanish **voluble** means "changeable, fickle".

volubly ['vɒljʊblɪ] *adv* con locuacidad

volume ['vɒljuːm] *n* (**a**) *Phys* volumen *m*

(**b**) *(capacity)* capacidad *f*

(**c**) *(amount) (of trade, traffic)* volumen *m*; **to increase in v.** aumentar en volumen; **the v. of traffic has greatly increased** el volumen *or* la intensidad del tráfico se ha incrementado enormemente; **a huge v. of work** un enorme volumen de trabajo; **the v. of business/imports** el volumen de negocio/importaciones

(**d**) *(of sound)* volumen *m*; **to turn the v. up/down** *(on TV, radio)* subir/bajar el volumen; **at full v.** a todo volumen ►► ***v. control*** mando *m* del volumen

(**e**) *(book)* volumen *m*; *(one of series)* tomo *m*, volumen *m*; IDIOM **to speak volumes (for)** decir mucho (de); **the look on her face spoke volumes** su rostro hablaba por sí solo; **it speaks volumes for his discretion** deja bien a las claras su discreción

(**f**) *Comptr* volumen *m*

voluminous [və'ljuːmɪnəs] *adj* voluminoso(a)

voluntarily [vɒlən'terɪlɪ] *adv* voluntariamente

voluntary ['vɒləntərɪ] *adj* voluntario(a) ►► ***v. muscle*** músculo *m* de contracción voluntaria; ***v. redundancy*** despido *m* voluntario, baja *f* voluntaria *or* incentivada; *Br* ***V. Service Overseas*** = agencia de voluntariado para la cooperación con países en vías de desarrollo; ***v. work*** voluntariado *m*, trabajo *m* voluntario; **to do v. work** trabajar como voluntario(a); ***v. worker*** voluntario(a) *m,f*

volunteer [vɒlən'tɪə(r)] **1** *n* voluntario(a) *m,f*; **can I have a v. from the audience?** ¿algún voluntario entre el público?

2 *vt* (**a**) *(information, advice)* ofrecer (voluntariamente); **he volunteered his services** ofreció sus servicios; **to v. to do sth** ofrecerse a hacer algo (**b**) *(suggest)* **"he might be at home," someone volunteered** "puede que esté en casa", se atrevió a sugerir alguien

3 *vi* ofrecerse (voluntariamente) (**for** para); **to v. for the Marines** alistarse como voluntario en la infantería de marina

voluptuous [və'lʌptjʊəs] *adj* voluptuoso(a)

voluptuously [və'lʌptjʊəslɪ] *adv* voluptuosamente

vomer ['vəʊmə(r)] *n Anat* vómer *m*

vomit ['vɒmɪt] **1** *n* vómito *m*

2 *vt* vomitar

3 *vi* vomitar

voodoo ['vuːduː] **1** *n* vudú *m*

2 *adj* de vudú

voracious [və'reɪʃəs] *adj (eater, appetite)* voraz; **he's a v. reader** lee todo lo que cae en sus manos

voraciously [və'reɪʃəslɪ] *adv (to eat)* vorazmente; *(to read)* ávidamente

voracity [və'ræsɪtɪ] *n* voracidad *f*

vortex ['vɔːteks] (*pl* **vortices** ['vɔːtɪsiːz]) *n* torbellino *m*, remolino *m*; *Fig* vorágine *f*

votary ['vəʊtərɪ] *n* (**a**) *Rel* devoto(a) *m,f* (**b**) *Formal (follower, enthusiast)* incondicional *mf*

vote [vəʊt] **1** *n* (**a**) *(choice)* voto *m*; *(voting)* votación *f*; **votes in favour/against** votos afirmativos *or* a favor/negativos *or* en contra; **to put sth to the v., to take a v. on sth** someter algo a votación; **they got 52 percent of the v.** obtuvieron un *or* el 52 por ciento de los votos; **the v. went in the government's favour/against the government** el resultado de la votación fue favorable/desfavorable para el gobierno; **they've got my v.** voy a votarlos a ellos, cuentan con mi voto; **to count the votes** contar los votos, realizar el escrutinio (de los votos); **one member, one v.** un voto por miembro ►► ***v. of confidence*** voto *m* de confianza; ***v. of no confidence*** voto *m* de censura; ***v. of thanks:* to propose a v. of thanks for sb** pedir el agradecimiento para alguien; ***v. rigging*** fraude *m* electoral

(**b**) *(suffrage)* sufragio *m*, elección *f*; **to have the v.** tener el derecho a votar *or* al voto; **to get the v.** obtener el derecho al voto; **to give the v. to sb** otorgar a alguien el derecho a votar *or* al voto

2 *vt* (**a**) *(in ballot)* **to v. Communist** votar a los comunistas; **v. Malone!** ¡vote a Malone!; **to v. yes/no** votar a favor/en contra, votar sí/no; **to v. to do sth** votar hacer algo; **to v. a proposal down** rechazar una propuesta en votación

(**b**) *(elect, depose)* **to v. sb in** elegir a alguien (en votación); **to v. sb out** rechazar a alguien (en votación); **to v. sb into office** votar a alguien para que ocupe un cargo; **to v. sb out of office** votar para que alguien sea relevado de su cargo; **she was voted president** fue elegida presidenta; **to v. sb off a committee** expulsar a alguien de un comité por votación

(**c**) *(propose)* **I v. (that) we go** voto por ir, voto (por) que vayamos

(**d**) *(declare)* **they voted the holiday a success** coincidieron en que las vacaciones habían sido un éxito

3 *vi* votar (**for/against** por/en contra de); **to v. on sth** someter algo a votación; **to v. in favour of/against sth** votar a favor/en contra de algo; **Spain is voting this weekend** este fin de semana España acude a las urnas; **to v. by a show of hands** votar levantando la mano, votar a mano alzada; IDIOM **to v. with one's feet** desmarcarse, hacer boicot

voter ['vəʊtə(r)] *n* votante *mf* ►► ***v. registration*** inscripción *f* en el padrón *or* censo electoral

voting ['vəʊtɪŋ] **1** *n* votación *f*; **v. takes place on Sunday** las elecciones son el domingo ►► ***v. booth*** cabina *f* electoral; ***v. paper*** papeleta *f* (de voto), voto *m*, *Col* tarjetón *m*, *Méx, RP* boleta *f*
2 *adj (member)* con voto

votive ['vəʊtɪv] *adj Rel* votivo(a) ►► ***v. offering*** exvoto *m*

vouch [vaʊtʃ]

► **vouch for** *vt insep (person)* responder de; *(quality, truth)* dar fe de

voucher ['vaʊtʃə(r)] *n* **(a)** *Br (for restaurant, purchase, petrol)* vale *m*, cupón *m*; **(gift) v.** vale *m* de regalo **(b)** *(receipt)* comprobante *m*, resguardo *m*

vouchsafe [vaʊtʃ'seɪf] *vt Literary* conceder; **to v. to do sth** dignarse a hacer algo; **to v. an answer** dignarse a dar una respuesta

vow [vaʊ] **1** *n* **(a)** *Rel* voto *m*; **to take a v. of chastity/poverty/silence** hacer voto de castidad/pobreza/silencio; **to take one's vows** hacer *or* tomar los votos **(b)** *(promise)* promesa *f*; **to make a v. to do sth** prometer solemnemente hacer algo
2 *vt* prometer solemnemente, jurar; **to v. to do sth** jurar hacer algo; **she vowed never to return** *or* **that she would never return** juró que nunca volvería, juró no volver nunca; **to v. revenge on sb** jurarle venganza a alguien

vowel ['vaʊəl] *n* vocal *f* ►► ***v. shift*** cambio *m* vocálico; ***v. sound*** sonido *m* vocálico

vox pop ['vɒks'pɒp] *n Br Fam* encuesta *f* en la calle

voyage ['vɔɪɪdʒ] **1** *n* travesía *f*, viaje *m (largo, marítimo o espacial)*; **to go on a v.** embarcarse en una travesía *or* un viaje; *Fig* **great voyages of discovery** grandes viajes (en busca) de descubrimientos
2 *vi* viajar; **they voyaged across the Atlantic** cruzaron el Atlántico; **to v. round the world** dar la vuelta al mundo navegando

voyager ['vɔɪɪdʒə(r)] *n Literary* viajero(a) *m,f*

voyeur [vɔɪ'jɜː(r)] *n* voyeur *mf*

voyeuristic [vɔɪjɜː'rɪstɪk] *adj* voyeurista

VP (*abbr* **Vice-President**) vicepresidente(a) *m,f*

VPL [viːpiː'el] *n Fam Hum* (*abbr* **visible panty line**) marca *f* de las bragas

VR [viː'ɑː(r)] *n* (*abbr* **virtual reality**) VR

VRAM ['viːræm] *n Comptr* (*abbr* **video random access memory**) VRAM *f*

VRML [viːɑːrem'el] *n Comptr* (*abbr* **virtual reality modelling language**) VRML *m*

vs (*abbr* **versus**) contra

v-shaped ['viːʃeɪpt] *adj* en forma de V *or* de cuña

VSO [viːes'əʊ] *n Br* (*abbr* **Voluntary Service Overseas**) = agencia de voluntariado para la cooperación con países en vías de desarrollo

VT (*abbr* **Vermont**) Vermont

VTOL [viːtiːəʊ'el] *n Av* (*abbr* **vertical take-off and landing**) despegue *m or Am* decolaje *m* (y aterrizaje) vertical

VTR [viːtiː'ɑː(r)] *n* (*abbr* **video tape recorder**) (aparato *m* de) vídeo *m or Am* video *m*

vulcanize ['vʌlkənaɪz] *vt* vulcanizar ►► ***vulcanized rubber*** caucho *m* vulcanizado

vulgar ['vʌlgə(r)] *adj* **(a)** *(rude)* vulgar, grosero(a); **don't be v.!** ¡no seas grosero! **(b)** *(in poor taste)* vulgar, ordinario(a), chabacano(a) **(c)** *Math* ***v. fraction*** fracción *f*, quebrado *m* **(d)** *(popular)* ***V. Latin*** latín *m* vulgar; ***the v. tongue*** la lengua vulgar *or* vernácula

vulgarian [vʌl'geərɪən] *n* chabacano(a) *m,f*, ordinario(a) *m,f*

vulgarism ['vʌlgərɪzəm] *n* **(a)** *(coarse expression)* palabra *f* vulgar *or* malsonante, palabrota *f* **(b)** *(mistaken usage)* vulgarismo *m*

vulgarity [vʌl'gærɪtɪ] *n* **(a)** *(rudeness)* vulgaridad *f*, grosería *f* **(b)** *(poor taste)* vulgaridad *f*, ordinariez *f*, chabacanería *f*

vulgarization [vʌlgəraɪ'zeɪʃən] *n* vulgarización *f*

vulgarize ['vʌlgəraɪz] *vt* vulgarizar

vulgarly ['vʌlgəlɪ] *adv* **(a)** *(coarsely)* vulgarmente, groseramente **(b)** *(popularly)* vulgarmente

vulnerability [vʌlnərə'bɪlɪtɪ] *n* vulnerabilidad *f*

vulnerable ['vʌlnərəbəl] *adj* **(a)** vulnerable (**to** a); **this left them v. on their eastern border** esto los hizo vulnerables en su frontera oriental **(b)** *(in bridge)* vulnerable

vulpine ['vʌlpaɪn] *adj* **(a)** *(foxlike)* zorruno(a) **(b)** *(crafty)* ladino(a), artero(a)

vulture ['vʌltʃə(r)] *n* buitre *m*

vulturine guinea fowl ['vʌltʃəraɪn'gɪnɪfaʊl] *n* pintada *f* vulturina

vulva ['vʌlvə] *n* vulva *f*

vv **(a)** (*abbr* **versus**) contra **(b)** (*abbr* **vice versa**) viceversa

W, w

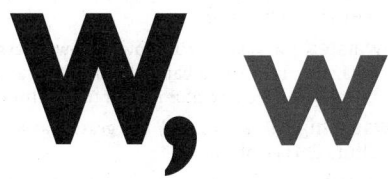

W, w ['dʌbəljuː] *n* **(a)** *(letter)* W, w *f* **(b)** *(abbr* **west**) O

W *Elec* (*abbr* **watt(s)**) W

W2 ['dʌbəljuː'tuː] *n US (form)* certificado *m* (anual) de ingresos y retenciones impositivas

W3 *n Comptr* (*abbr* **World Wide Web**) W3 *f*, WWW *f*

WA **(a)** (*abbr* **Washington**) Washington **(b)** (*abbr* **Western Australia**) Australia Occidental

WAAC [wæk] *n Hist* (*abbr* **Women's Army Auxiliary Corps**) = sección femenina del ejército británico durante la Segunda Guerra Mundial

WAAF [wæf] *n Hist* (*abbr* **Women's Auxiliary Air Force**) = sección femenina de las fuerzas aéreas británicas durante la Segunda Guerra Mundial

wackiness ['wækɪnɪs] *n Fam (of person, behaviour)* extravagancia *f*, excentricidad *f*; *(of sense of humour, comedian)* excentricidad *f*, carácter *m* estrambótico

wacko, whacko ['wækəʊ] *Fam* **1** *n* pirado(a) *m,f*, *Am* zafado(a) *m,f*, *RP* rayado(a) *m,f*
2 *adj* pirado(a), *Am* zafado(a), *RP* rayado(a)

wacky, whacky ['wækɪ] *adj Fam (person, behaviour, dress sense)* estrafalario(a); *(sense of humour, comedian)* estrambótico(a) ►► *Hum* ***w. baccy*** *(marijuana)* maría *f*, hierba *f*; *(hashish)* chocolate *m*, costo *m*

wad [wɒd] *n* **(a)** *(of cotton)* bolita *f* **(b)** *(of paper)* taco *m* **(c)** *(of tobacco, chewing gum)* bola *f*

wadding ['wɒdɪŋ] *n (for packing)* relleno *m*

waddle ['wɒdəl] *vi (duck)* caminar, *Esp* andar; *(person)* caminar *or Esp* andar como un pato, anadear; **he waddled along the street** caminaba como un pato por la calle; **he waddled into the room** entró en la sala con paso torpe y pesado

wade [weɪd] *vi (in water)* caminar en el agua; **to w. across a stream** vadear un riachuelo; **she waded out to the boat** caminó por el agua hasta el bote; *Fig* **to w. in** entrometerse

► **wade into** *vt insep Fig (task)* acometer; *(person)* arremeter contra

► **wade through** *vt insep* **(a)** *(water)* caminar por **(b)** *Fig (paperwork)* leerse

wader ['weɪdə(r)] *n* **(a)** *(bird)* (ave *f*) zancuda *f* **(b) waders** *(boots)* botas *fpl* altas de agua

wadi ['wɒdɪ] *n* uadi *m*, = en Arabia y Norteáfrica río seco todo el año salvo en la estación de lluvias

wading pool ['weɪdɪŋ'puːl] *n US* piscina *f or Méx* alberca *f or RP* pileta *f* para niños

wafer ['weɪfə(r)] *n* **(a)** *(biscuit)* barquillo *m* **(b)** *Rel* hostia *f* **(c)** *Comptr & Tech* oblea *f or* disco *m* de silicio **(d)** *(seal)* oblea *f*

wafer-thin ['weɪfə'θɪn] *adj* muy fino(a); *Fig (majority)* ajustadísimo(a)

waffle[1] ['wɒfəl] *n (food) Esp* gofre *m*, *Am* wafle *m* ►► ***w. iron*** *Esp* gofrera *f*, *Am* waflera *f*

waffle[2] *Br Fam* **1** *n (wordiness)* verborrea *f*, palabrería *f*; *(in written text)* paja *f*, *Am* palabrerío *m*; **it's just a load of w.** es pura palabrería
2 *vi* enrollarse

► **waffle on** *vi* enrollarse; **he waffled on for ages about his thesis** se enrolló a hablar de su tesis y no paraba

waft [wɒft] **1** *vt* llevar, hacer flotar
2 *vi* flotar; **a delicious smell wafted into the room** un delicioso aroma se deslizó en la habitación; **her voice wafted gently down the stairs** su voz llegaba suave desde la parte de arriba

wag[1] [wæg] **1** *n (action)* meneo *m*; **with a w. of its tail** meneando la cola
2 *vt* (*pt & pp* **wagged**) menear, agitar; **to w. one's finger at sb** advertir a alguien con el dedo
3 *vi* menearse

wag[2] *n Fam (joker)* bromista *mf*, guasón(ona) *m,f*

wage [weɪdʒ] **1** *n (pay)* **wage(s)** salario *m*, sueldo *m*; **daily w.** jornal; **his employers took it out of his wages** sus jefes se lo descontaron de su sueldo; *Fig (in bible)* **the wages of sin is death** el pecado se paga con la muerte ►► ***w. agreement*** convenio *m or* acuerdo *m* salarial; ***w. claim*** reivindicación *f or* demanda *f* salarial; ***w. cut*** recorte *m* salarial; ***w. differential*** diferencia *f* salarial; ***w. earner*** asalariado(a) *m,f*; **they are both w. earners** trabajan los dos; ***w. freeze*** congelación *f* salarial; ***w. packet*** *(envelope)* sobre *m* de la paga; *(money)* salario *m*; ***w. rise*** incremento *m or* aumento *m* salarial; ***w. scale*** escala *f* salarial; ***w. settlement*** convenio *m or* acuerdo *m* salarial; ***w. slave*** *(in Marxism)* esclavo(a) *m,f* del trabajo; *Ironic* **I'm fed up with being a w. slave** estoy harto de estar esclavizado al trabajo; ***w. slip*** nómina *f*, recibo *m* de sueldo
2 *vt* **to w. war (on)** librar una guerra (contra); **to w. a campaign against smoking** emprender una campaña contra el tabaco

wager ['weɪdʒə(r)] *Formal* **1** *n* apuesta *f*; **to make** *or* **lay a w.** hacer una apuesta
2 *vt* apostar; **I'll w. £10 that he'll come** te apuesto 10 libras a que viene

wageworker ['weɪdʒwɜːkə(r)] *n US* asalariado(a) *m,f*

waggish ['wægɪʃ] *adj (sense of humour, remark)* jocoso(a); *(person)* guasón(ona)

waggle ['wægəl] *Fam* **1** *vt* mover
2 *vi* menearse

waggly ['wæglɪ] *adj Fam (tooth)* medio suelto(a), flojo(a)

wag(g)on ['wægən] *n* **(a)** *(horse-drawn)* carro *m* ►► ***w. train*** caravana *f* de carretas **(b)** *Br Rail* vagón *m* **(c)** *US (drinks trolley)* carrito *m* **(d)** IDIOMS *Fam* **to be on the w.** *(alcoholic)* haber dejado de beber *or Am* tomar; *Fam* **to be off** *or* **have fallen off the w.** haber vuelto a beber *or Am* tomar, *RP* haber volcado

wagoner ['wægənə(r)] *n* carretero(a) *m,f*

wagonload ['wægənləʊd] *n* vagón *m* (cargado)

wagtail ['wægteɪl] *n* lavandera *f*

wah-wah ['wɑːwɑː] *n Mus* wah-wah *m* ►► ***w. pedal*** pedal *m* del wah-wah

waif [weɪf] *n* niño(a) *m,f* abandonado(a); **waifs and strays** criaturas desamparadas

waif-like ['weɪflaɪk] *adj* frágil

wail [weɪl] **1** *n (of person)* gemido *m*, lamento *m*; *(of siren)* sonido *m*, aullido *m*; *(of wind)* aullido *m*
2 *vt* gemir; **"you've broken it!" she wailed** "¡lo has roto!", protestó ella con un gemido
3 *vi (person)* gemir; *(siren)* sonar, aullar; *(wind)* aullar

wailing ['weɪlɪŋ] **1** *n (of people, children)* gemidos *mpl*, lamentos *mpl*; *(of siren, wind)* aullido *m*
2 *adj* **w. children** niños gimiendo; **w. sirens** sirenas aullando ►► ***the W. Wall*** el Muro de *Esp* las Lamentaciones *or Am* los Lamentos

wainscot ['weɪnskɒt], **wainscotting** ['weɪnskɒtɪŋ] *n* zócalo *m* de madera

WAIS ['dʌbəljuːeɪaɪ'es] *n Comptr* (*abbr* **wide area information search**) = sistema de búsquedas en Internet basado en UNIX

waist [weɪst] *n (of person, garment)* cintura *f*, talle *m*; **he measures 80 cm around the w., his w. measures 80 cm** de cintura mide *or* tiene 80 cm; **he put his arm around her w.** le rodeó la cintura *or* el talle con el brazo; **it's too tight at** *or* **round the w.** está muy apretado *or* ceñido de cintura; **he was up to the** *or* **his w. in water** el agua le llegaba a la cintura

waistband ['weɪstbænd] *n* cinturilla *f*

waistcoat ['weɪstkəʊt] *n Br* chaleco *m*

waist-deep ['weɪst'di:p] *adj* **to be w. in mud** estar metido(a) en el barro hasta la cintura

-waisted ['weɪstɪd] *suffix* **a low/high-w. dress** un vestido de cintura baja/alta, un vestido bajo/alto de cintura; **to be slim/thick-w.** ser estrecho/ancho de cintura, tener una cintura estrecha/ancha

waist-high ['weɪst'haɪ] *adj* **the grass was w.** la hierba llegaba a (la altura de) la cintura

waistline ['weɪstlaɪn] *n* cintura *f*; **to watch one's w.** cuidar la línea

WAIT [weɪt] **1** *n* espera *f*; **we had a long w.** esperamos mucho; **it was worth the w.** mereció la pena esperar; **to lie in w. for sb** acechar a alguien

2 *vt* (**a**) *(wait for)* **I'm waiting my chance** estoy esperando mi oportunidad; **you must w. your turn** debes esperar tu turno (**b**) *US (serve at)* **to w. table(s)** servir mesas (**c**) *US Fam (delay)* **don't w. dinner for me** no me esperes para cenar

3 *vi* (**a**) *(in general)* esperar; **I'm waiting to use the phone** estoy esperando para llamar por teléfono; **I've been waiting for half an hour** hace media hora que espero, llevo esperando media hora; **to w. for sth/sb** esperar algo/a alguien; **w. for me!** ¡espérame!; **a parcel was waiting for me when I got back** cuando volví había un paquete esperándome; **to w. for sth to happen** esperar a que ocurra algo; **to w. for sb to do sth** esperar que alguien haga algo; **he didn't w. to be told twice** no esperó a que se lo repitieran; **we're waiting to be seated** esperamos a que nos sentaran; **it was worth waiting for** merecía la pena esperar; **what are you waiting for, ask him!** ¿a qué esperas? ¡pregúntale!; **what are we waiting for, let's start!** ¿a qué esperamos? ¡empecemos!; *Fam* **w. for it!** *(before sth happens)* ¡espera!; *(before saying sth)* ¡agárrate!; **to keep sb waiting** tener a alguien esperando, hacer esperar a alguien; **w. a minute** *or* **second!** ¡espera un momento!; **we must w. and see** tendremos que esperar a ver (qué pasa); **I can't w. to see her** estoy impaciente por verla; *also Ironic* **I can hardly w.** estoy impaciente; **I can hardly w. till they get here** estoy impaciente por que lleguen; **w. till you hear what I just did!** ¿a que no adivinas lo que acabo de hacer?; **(just) you w.!** ¡espera y verás!; **repairs while you w.** *(sign)* arreglos en el acto; PROV **everything comes to him** *or* **he who waits** la paciencia es la madre de la ciencia, no se tomó Zamora en una hora

(**b**) *(be postponed)* **it can't w.** es urgente; **can't it w.?** ¿no puede esperar?; **it will have to w. until tomorrow** tendrá que esperar hasta mañana

(**c**) *(serve) Br* **to w. at table** servir mesas

▸ **wait about, wait around** *vi* esperar; **I can't stand all this waiting about** no soporto tanta espera

▸ **wait behind** *vi* quedarse atrás

▸ **wait in** *vi Br* quedarse en casa esperando, esperar en casa

▸ **wait on** *vt insep* (**a**) *(serve)* servir; **to w. on sb hand and foot** traérselo todo en bandeja a alguien (**b**) *Scot (wait for)* esperar (**c**) *US (in restaurant)* **to w. on tables** servir mesas

▸ **wait out** *vt sep* **we waited out the storm** esperamos a que pasara la tormenta

▸ **wait up** *vi* (**a**) *(stay up)* **to w. up for sb** esperar a alguien levantado(a) (**b**) *US (hold on)* **w. up!** ¡un momento!

▸ **wait upon** *vt insep* servir; **to w. upon sb hand and foot** traérselo todo en bandeja a alguien

wait-and-see [weɪtænd'si:] *adj* **w. approach** *or* **policy** política *f* de esperar y ver qué pasa

waiter ['weɪtə(r)] *n* camarero *m*, *Andes, RP* mozo *m*, *Chile, Ven* mesonero *m*, *Col, Guat, Méx, Salv* mesero *m*

waiting ['weɪtɪŋ] *n* (**a**) espera *f*; **after two hours of w.** después de dos horas de espera; *Br Aut* **no w.** *(sign)* = prohibido detenerse; **they are playing a w. game** están dejando que transcurra el tiempo a ver qué pasa ▸▸ ***w. list*** lista *f* de espera; **he's on the w. list** está en lista de espera; ***w. room*** sala *f* de espera (**b**) *Formal (attendance)* **to be in w. on sb** estar al servicio de alguien

waitlist ['weɪtlɪst] *vt US* colocar en lista de espera; **I'm waitlisted for the next flight** estoy en lista de espera para el próximo vuelo

waitress ['weɪtrɪs] *n* camarera *f*, *Andes, RP* moza *f*, *Chile, Ven* mesonera *f*, *Col, Guat, Méx, Salv* mesera *f*

waive [weɪv] *vt* (**a**) *(rights, claim)* renunciar a (**b**) *(rule, requirement)* obviar, pasar por alto

waiver ['weɪvə(r)] *n* (**a**) *(document)* renuncia *f*; **to sign a w.** firmar una renuncia, renunciar por escrito (**b**) *(of right, claim)* renuncia *f* (**c**) *(of rule, requirement)* exención *f*

wake[1] [weɪk] *n (of ship)* estela *f*; *Fig* **in the w. of sth** a raíz de algo; **famine followed in the w. of the drought** a la sequía le siguió la hambruna; **the destruction left in the w. of the storm** la destrucción que la tormenta dejó a su paso; **the war brought chaos and misery in its w.** la guerra dejó tras de sí un rastro *or* una estela de caos y penuria; **he left the other athletes trailing in his w.** dejó atrás *or* rezagados a los demás atletas; *Fig* **to follow in sb's w.** seguir los pasos de alguien

wake[2] *n (on night before funeral)* velatorio *m*, *Am* velorio *m*

wake[3] (*pt* **woke** [wəʊk], *pp* **woken** ['wəʊkən]) **1** *vt* despertar; **the noise was enough to w. the dead** había un ruido infernal

2 *vi* despertarse, despertar; **he woke to the news that war had broken out** despertó con la noticia de que había estallado la guerra; **they woke to find themselves famous** amanecieron famosos

▸ **wake up 1** *vt sep* (**a**) *(rouse from sleep)* despertar (**b**) *(make alert)* despertar; **a little exercise will w. you up!** ¡un poco de ejercicio te despertará *or* espabilará!; **the accident woke us up to the dangers of nuclear power** el accidente nos hizo tomar conciencia de los peligros de la energía nuclear

2 *vi* (**a**) *(from sleep)* despertarse, despertar (**b**) *(become alert)* **w. up!** ¡espabila!; **to w. up to the truth** abrir los ojos a la realidad; **it took him a long time to w. up to what was going on** tardó mucho en darse cuenta *or* tomar conciencia de lo que pasaba

wakeful ['weɪkfʊl] *adj* (**a**) *(sleepless)* desvelado(a); **to be w.** estar desvelado(a); **to have a w. night** pasar la noche en vela (**b**) *(vigilant)* alerta; **to be w.** estar alerta

waken ['weɪkən] **1** *vt* despertar

2 *vi* despertar

wake-up call ['weɪkʌp'kɔ:l] *n* (**a**) *(on phone)* **I asked the operator for a w.** le pedí a la operadora que me despertara (**b**) *(warning)* llamada *f or Am* llamado *m* de atención

wakey ['weɪkɪ] *exclam Br Fam* **w., w.!** ¡despierta ya!, ¡arriba!

waking ['weɪkɪŋ] *adj* **w. hours** horas que uno pasa despierto

Wales [weɪlz] *n* (País *m* de) Gales

WALK [wɔ:k] **1** *n* (**a**) *(short)* paseo *m*; *(long)* caminata *f*; **it's a ten-minute w. away** está a diez minutos a pie (de aquí); **to go for** *or* **take a w.** (ir a) dar un paseo; **to go on a w.** hacer una marcha; **to take the children/dog for a w.** sacar a los niños de paseo/sacar a pasear al perro; IDIOM *Fam* **it was a w. in the park** *(very easy)* fue pan comido *or* un paseo, fue coser y cantar; *US Fam* **take a w.!** ¡vete a paseo!

(**b**) *(gait)* andares *mpl*, manera *f* de caminar *or Esp* andar

(**c**) *(speed)* **at a w.** al paso, paseando; **to slow to a w.** reducir el paso *(y continuar caminando)*

(**d**) *(path)* paseo *m*, sendero *m*; **there's an interesting forest w. there** hay una ruta de senderismo interesante en ese bosque

(**e**) *(profession, condition)* **people from all walks of life** gente de toda condición

(**f**) *Sport* marcha *f*

(**g**) *(in baseball)* paso *m* a primera base *(caminando)*

2 *vt* (**a**) *(cover on foot)* caminar, *Esp* andar, recorrer caminando *or* a pie *or Esp* andando; **I walked the three miles to the station** caminé las tres millas que hay hasta la estación; **to w. it** *(go on foot)* ir a pie; **the baby can w. a few steps** el niño da algunos pasos; **to w. the plank** = caminar por un tablón colocado sobre la borda hasta caer al mar; **to w. the streets** caminar por las calles; *Euph (prostitute)* hacer la calle; IDIOM **to w. the talk** cumplir

(**b**) *(accompany)* **to w. sb home** acompañar a alguien a casa; **to w. the dog** sacar *or* pasear al perro; *Br Fam* **she has walked me off my feet** me ha hecho caminar tanto que no me tengo en pie

(**c**) *Br Fam (win easily)* ganar con mucha facilidad *or Esp* de calle; *(exam)* aprobar con facilidad *or Esp* con la gorra *or RP* de taquito; **to w. it** *(win easily)* llevárselo con mucha facilidad *or Esp* de calle; *(in exam)* aprobar con facilidad *or Esp* con la gorra *or RP* de taquito

(**d**) *(move)* **we walked the wardrobe into the room** llevamos el armario a la habitación adelantando un lado y después el otro

3 *vi* (**a**) *(move on foot)* caminar, *Esp* andar; *(for exercise, pleasure)* pasear, caminar; **let's w. instead of taking the train** vamos caminando *or Esp* andando en lugar de en tren; **we walked back** volvimos caminando; **he walked across the street** cruzó la calle; **I was walking down the street** iba caminando *or Esp* andando por la calle; **to w. home** ir caminando *or Esp* andando a casa; **she walked right past me** pasó por mi lado; **he walks in his sleep** es sonámbulo; **to w. on one's hands** caminar haciendo la vertical; **to w. up** *or* **over to sb** acercarse a alguien; *US* **w.** *(sign)* = señal que autoriza a los peatones a cruzar; *US*

don't w. *(sign)* = señal que prohíbe cruzar a los peatones; IDIOM **you have to (learn to) w. before you can run** hay que aprender poco a poco; IDIOM **to w. on water: as far as the faithful are concerned, he can w. on water** para sus seguidores es un dios; IDIOM **to be walking on air** estar en el séptimo cielo, estar más feliz que unas castañuelas

(**b**) *(in baseball)* = avanzar a una base cuando el pítcher comete cuatro bolas

(**c**) *Fam (go free)* salir libre

(**d**) *Fam (disappear, be stolen)* esfumarse, desaparecer; **the money seems to have walked** parece que el dinero se ha esfumado *or* ha desaparecido

▸ **walk about, walk around** *vi* pasear

▸ **walk away** *vi* irse (caminando *or Esp* andando); *Fig* **she walked away (unharmed) from the accident** salió ilesa del accidente; *Fig* **you can't just w. away from the problem** no puedes lavarte las manos así; *Fig* **to w. away with a prize** salir premiado(a), llevarse un premio; *Fig* **they walked away with the championship** se hicieron con el título de campeones

▸ **walk by** *vi* pasarse

▸ **walk in** *vi* entrar

▸ **walk in on** *vt insep* **I walked in on them** los pillé *orAm* agarré

▸ **walk into** *vt insep* (**a**) *(enter)* entrar en; *(difficult situation)* meterse en; *Fig (trap)* caer en; *Fam* **you walked right into that one!** ¡te metiste (en eso) de cabeza! (**b**) *(collide with)* chocar con (**c**) *(obtain easily) (job)* conseguir fácilmente

▸ **walk off 1** *vt sep* **we walked off our dinner** fuimos a dar un paseo para bajar la cena; **I'm going to see if I can w. off my headache** voy a dar un paseo a ver si se me quita *orAm* saca el dolor de cabeza

2 *vi* marcharse; **to w. off with sth** *(steal, win easily)* llevarse algo

▸ **walk out** *vi* salir; *Ind (go on strike)* ponerse *or* declararse en huelga; **they walked out of the talks** abandonaron la mesa de negociaciones; **to w. out on sb** *(leave)* dejar *or* abandonar a alguien; **to w. out on a deal** abandonar un pacto

▸ **walk out with** *vt insep Br Old-fashioned* salir con

▸ **walk over** *vt insep Fam* **to w. all over sb** *(treat badly)* pisotear a alguien; *(defeat easily)* dar una paliza a

▸ **walk through 1** *vt insep* (**a**) *(practise)* practicar, ensayar (**b**) *Fam* **you'll w. through the exam** el examen será un paseo para ti

2 *vt sep* **to w. sb through sth** *(show how to do)* enseñar algo a alguien paso a paso

---

walkabout ['wɔːkəbaʊt] *n Br (of politician)* paseo *m* entre la gente; **to go on a w.** caminar entre la gente

walkaway ['wɔːkəweɪ] *n US Fam* paseo *m* (triunfal); **the race was a w. for him** la carrera fue pan comido *or* un paseo (triunfal) para él

walker ['wɔːkə(r)] *n* caminante *mf*; *Sport* marchador(ora) *m,f*; **are you a keen w.?** ¿te gusta caminar?; **she's a fast/slow w.** camina rápido/lento

walkies ['wɔːkɪz] *npl Br Fam* **to go (for) w.** *(with dog)* sacar a pasear al perro

walkie-talkie [wɔːkɪ'tɔːkɪ] *n Rad* walkie-talkie *m*

walk-in ['wɔːkɪn] **1** *n* (**a**) *(customer in hotel)* cliente(a) *m,f* sin reserva; *esp US (patient)* paciente *mf* sin cita previa (**b**) *US Fam (victory)* paseo *m* triunfal, triunfo *m* (electoral) aplastante

2 *adj (safe)* lo bastante grande para meterse dentro; *Br* **the house is in w. condition** la casa se puede ocupar *or* habitar de inmediato, la casa está para entrar ▸▸ *US* ***w. apartment*** apartamento *m or Esp* piso *m or Arg* departamento *m* con acceso directo a la calle; ***w. cupboard*** *(for clothes)* armario *m* vestidor; *(for food)* despensa *f*

walking ['wɔːkɪŋ] **1** *n* (**a**) **I like w.** me gusta caminar; **we do a lot of w.** caminamos *or Esp* andamos mucho; **w. is the best form of exercise** caminar es el mejor ejercicio; **it's within w. distance** se puede ir caminando *or* a pie *or Esp* andando; **within five minutes' w. distance** a cinco minutos a pie; IDIOM *Fam* **to give sb their w. papers** *(employee)* poner a alguien de patitas en la calle; *(lover)* mandar a paseo a alguien; **he got his w. papers** *(employee)* lo pusieron de patitas en la calle; *(lover)* lo mandó a paseo ▸▸ ***w. boots*** botas *fpl* de montaña *or* senderismo; ***w. frame*** andador *m*; ***w. shoes*** botas *fpl* (de senderismo); ***w. stick*** *(cane)* bastón *m*; *US (insect)* insecto *m* palo

(**b**) *Sport* marcha *f* atlética

2 *adj* **at w. pace** al paso, paseando; **a w. holiday** unas vacaciones con excursiones a pie; *Fam* **she's a w. encyclopedia** es una enciclopedia ambulante *or* andante; **the w. wounded** los heridos que aún pueden caminar

Walkman® ['wɔːkmən] *n* walkman® *m*

walk-on (part) ['wɔːkɒn('pɑːt)] *n Cin & Theat* papel *m* de figurante

walkout ['wɔːkaʊt] *n (strike)* huelga *f*, plante *m*; *(from meeting)* abandono *m (en señal de protesta)*; **to stage a w.** *(workers)* abandonar el puesto de trabajo *or* realizar un plante en señal de protesta; *(negotiators, students)* abandonar la sala en señal de protesta

walkover ['wɔːkəʊvə(r)] *n* (**a**) *Fam (easy win)* paseo *m*; **it was a w.** fue un paseo *or* pan comido (**b**) *(win by default)* victoria *f* por incomparecencia (del contrario)

walk-through ['wɔːkθruː] *n* (**a**) *Theat* ensayo *m* (**b**) *Comptr* explicación *f* paso a paso

walkup ['wɔːkʌp] *n US (building)* edificio *m* sin ascensor

walkway ['wɔːkweɪ] *n (between buildings)* pasadizo *m*, pasaje *m*

wall [wɔːl] *n* (**a**) *(interior)* pared *f*; *(exterior, freestanding)* muro *m*; *(partition)* tabique *m*; *(of garden, around building)* tapia *f*; *(of town, city)* muralla *f*; **within/outside the city walls** dentro/fuera de la ciudad, intramuros/extramuros; *Fig* **a w. of silence** un muro de silencio; *Fig* **a w. of fire** una cortina de fuego; **the prisoners went over the w.** los prisioneros escaparon trepando el muro; **people like him should be put up against a w. and shot** a la gente como él habría que llevarla al paredón (y fusilarla) ▸▸ ***w. bars*** espalderas *fpl*; ***w. chart*** (gráfico *m*) mural *m*; ***w. cupboard*** alacena *f*; ***w. hanging*** tapiz *m*; ***w. lamp*** aplique *m* (de luz); ***w. light*** aplique *m* (de luz); ***w. painting*** pintura *f* mural; ***W. Street*** Wall Street; *Hist* ***the W. Street Crash*** el crack *or* crash de 29; ***w. unit*** mueble *m* mural

(**b**) *(of artery, stomach)* pared *f*

(**c**) *(in soccer)* barrera *f*

(**d**) IDIOMS **to go to the w.** irse al traste; *Fam* **to be up the w.** estar como una cabra, *Esp* estar majareta; *Fam* **to drive sb up the w.** hacer que alguien se suba por las paredes; **walls have ears** las paredes oyen; **this is between you, me and the four walls** que esto quede entre nosotros (y estas cuatro paredes)

▸ **wall in** *vt sep (surround with wall)* tapiar; *(enclose)* encerrar, rodear; **the park was walled in by high buildings** el parque estaba cercado por altos edificios

▸ **wall off** *vt sep* separar con un muro

▸ **wall up** *vt sep* condenar, tapiar

wallaby ['wɒləbɪ] *n* wallaby *m*, valabí *m*

wallah ['wɔːlə] *n Br Old-fashioned Fam* señor *m*

walled [wɔːld] *adj (garden, enclosure)* tapiado(a); *(city)* amurallado(a)

wallet ['wɒlɪt] *n* (**a**) *(for money, cards)* cartera *f* (**b**) *(for documents)* carpeta *f*

walleyed ['wɔːlaɪd] *adj* (**a**) *(with clouded eye)* con leucoma (**b**) *(with squint)* bizco(a), estrábico(a)

wallflower ['wɔːlflaʊə(r)] *n (plant)* alhelí *m*; IDIOM **to be a w.** no tener con quien bailar

wall-mounted ['wɔːlmaʊntɪd] *adj (clock, telephone)* de pared

Walloon [wɒ'luːn] **1** *n* valón(ona) *m,f*

2 *adj* valón(ona)

wallop ['wɒləp] *Fam* **1** *n* (**a**) *(blow)* tortazo *m*, trompazo *m*, *Méx* madrazo *m*; **to give sth/sb a w.** dar un tortazo a algo/alguien (**b**) *(impact)* **she fell down with a w.** se dio un porrazo *or* trompazo al caer (**c**) *Br (beer)* cerveza *f*

2 *vt* (**a**) *(hit)* dar un tortazo *or* trompazo a (**b**) *(defeat)* dar una buena paliza a

walloping ['wɒləpɪŋ] *Fam* **1** *n* (**a**) *(beating)* paliza *f* (**b**) *(defeat)* paliza *f*

2 *adv (for emphasis)* **a w. great pay rise** *Esp* una subida de sueldo de aquí te espero, *Am* un aumento de sueldo que para qué te cuento

wallow ['wɒləʊ] **1** *n* **to have a w. in sth** *(bath, mud)* revolcarse en algo; *(self-pity)* recrearse *or* regodearse en algo

2 *vi* revolcarse; **to w. in self-pity** recrearse *or* regodearse en la autocompasión

wallpaper ['wɔːlpeɪpə(r)] **1** *n* (**a**) *(on walls)* papel *m* pintado (**b**) *Comptr* papel *m* tapiz

2 *vt* empapelar

wall-to-wall ['wɔːltəwɔːl] *adj* ***w. carpeting*** *Esp* enmoquetado *m*, *Esp* moqueta *f*, *Am* alfombra *f*; *Fig* ***w. coverage*** cobertura *f* total

wally ['wɒlɪ] *n Br Fam (idiot)* idiota *mf*, imbécil *mf*, *Esp* chorra *mf*; **I felt a bit of a w.** me sentí como un auténtico idiota *or* imbécil

walnut ['wɔːlnʌt] *n* (**a**) *(nut)* nuez *f* ▸▸ ***w. cake*** pastel *m* de nueces (**b**) *(tree, wood)* nogal *m*

walrus ['wɔːlrəs] *n* morsa *f* ▸▸ ***w. moustache*** mostacho *m*

waltz [wɔːls] **1** *n* vals *m*

2 *vt (dance)* llevar (a alguien) al compás de un vals; **he waltzed her round the room** la llevó por todo el salón al compás de un vals

3 *vi* bailar el vals; *Fam* **she waltzed into the room** entró en la habitación como si tal cosa; *Fam* **to w. off with sth** llevarse algo

▸ **waltz through** *vt insep (exam, interview)* pasar sin problema

waltzer ['wɔːltsə(r)] *n (fairground ride)* látigo *m*

WAN ['dʌbəljuːeɪ'en] *n Comptr* (*abbr* **wide area network**) red *f* de área extensa

wan [wɒn] *adj (face, person)* macilento(a), pálido(a); *(smile)* lánguido(a); *(light, star)* tenue

wand [wɒnd] *n* varita *f*

wander ['wɒndə(r)] **1** *n* vuelta *f*; **to go for a w.** ir a dar una vuelta
2 *vt (streets, world)* vagar por
3 *vi* (**a**) *(roam) (directionless)* deambular, vagar (**around** por); *(casually)* pasear (**around** por); **she wandered into a café** entró en un café; **she had wandered from the path** se había alejado del camino; **to w. off** alejarse, apartarse; **don't w. too far, the bus will be here in ten minutes** no te vayas muy lejos, el autobús estará aquí en diez minutos
(**b**) *(verbally, mentally)* distraerse; **to w. from the subject** desviarse del tema, divagar; **my thoughts were wandering** mi mente empezaba a divagar, tenía la cabeza en otro sitio; **I can't concentrate, my mind keeps wandering** no me puedo concentrar, no hago más que distraerme; **my mind wandered back to when we first met** me volvió a la mente el momento en que nos conocimos; **his eyes wandered over the scene** su mirada recorría la escena
(**c**) *(become confused)* desvariar; **her mother's mind** *or* **her mother has begun to w.** su madre ha empezado a desvariar un poco

wanderer ['wɒndərə(r)] *n* trotamundos *mf inv*; IDIOM **the w. returns!** ¡vuelve el hijo pródigo!

wandering ['wɒndərɪŋ] *adj (person, life)* errante, errabundo(a); *(tribe)* nómada; *(path, stream)* sinuoso(a); IDIOM *Hum* **to have w. hand trouble** ser un pulpo ▸▸ ***w. albatross*** albatros *m* viajero; ***w. Jew*** *(plant)* tradescantia *f*; ***the W. Jew*** *(person)* el judío errante

wanderlust ['wɒndəlʌst] *n* pasión *f* por viajar

wane [weɪn] **1** *n* **to be on the w.** *(moon)* estar menguando; *(popularity, enthusiasm, power)* ir decayendo; *(empire, civilization)* estar en decadencia; *(beauty)* ir desapareciendo
2 *vi* (**a**) *(moon)* menguar (**b**) *(popularity, enthusiasm, power)* decaer; *(empire, civilization)* estar en decadencia; *(beauty)* ir desapareciendo

wangle ['wæŋgəl] *vt Fam* agenciarse; **he wangled it so that...** se las arregló *or Esp* apañó para que...; **could you w. me a ticket?** ¿podrías comprarme *or Esp* pillarme una entrada?; **he wangled his way into the job** se las arregló *or Esp* apañó para conseguir el empleo

waning ['weɪnɪŋ] **1** *n (of moon)* menguante *m*; *(of interest, power)* pérdida *f*; *(of empire)* decadencia *f*
2 *adj (moon)* menguante; *(interest, power)* cada vez menor, decreciente; *(empire)* en decadencia, decadente

wank [wæŋk] *Br Vulg* **1** *n* **to have a w.** hacerse una *or Am* la paja
2 *vi* hacerse una *or Am* la paja

▸ **wank off** *Br Vulg* **1** *vt sep* **to w. sb off** hacer una *or Am* la paja a alguien; **to w. oneself off** hacerse una *or Am* la paja
2 *vi* hacerse una *or Am* la paja

wanker ['wæŋkə(r)] *n Br Vulg Esp* gilipollas *mf inv*, *Am* pendejo(a) *m,f*, *RP* pelotudo(a) *m,f*

wanna *Fam* ['wɒnə] (**a**) = **want to** (**b**) = **want a**

wannabe ['wɒnəbiː] *n Fam* aprendiz(iza) *m,f*; **Brad Pitt wannabes** Brad Pitts de pacotilla

---

WANT [wɒnt] **1** *n* (**a**) *(need)* necesidad *f*; **I have few wants, my wants are few** me arreglo con bien poco, no necesito gran cosa; *Formal* **to be in w. of sth** carecer de algo ▸▸ *US* ***w. ad*** demanda *f*
(**b**) *(poverty)* necesidad *f*; **to live in w.** vivir en la necesidad, pasar necesidades
(**c**) *(lack)* falta *f*, carencia *f* (**of** de); **a w. of generosity/goodwill** falta de generosidad/buena voluntad; **for w. of anything better to do** a falta de algo mejor que hacer; **for w. of a better word** a falta de una palabra mejor; **it wasn't for w. of trying** no será porque no lo intentamos
2 *vt* (**a**) *(wish, desire)* querer; **to w. to do sth** querer hacer algo; **I w. to say how grateful I am** deseo expresar mi gratitud; **to w. sb to do sth** querer que alguien haga algo; **I don't w. you watching** no quiero que mires; **I w. the room cleaned by tomorrow** quiero la habitación limpia mañana; *Fam* **w. a drink?** ¿quieres una bebida?; **she knows what she wants** sabe lo que quiere; **that's the last thing we w.!** ¡sólo nos faltaba eso!; **I w. my money back** quiero que me devuelvan mi dinero; **how much do you w. for the book?** ¿cuánto quieres por el libro?; **what do you w. in a man/out of life?** ¿qué buscas en los hombres/la vida?; **what does he w. with** *or* **of me?** ¿qué quiere de mí?; **what do you w. with an exercise bike?** ¿para qué quieres una bicicleta estática?
(**b**) *(need)* necesitar; **it wants a bit more salt** necesita un poco más de sal; **the lawn wants cutting** hay que cortar el césped; **this coat wants cleaning very badly** este abrigo está pidiendo a gritos una limpieza; **she wants taking down a peg or two** necesita que le bajen los humos; *Fam* **you w. your head seeing to!** ¡tú estás mal de la cabeza!; **you w. to be careful with him** deberías tener cuidado con él; *Fam* **you don't w. to do that** es mejor que no hagas eso
(**c**) *(seek)* **she's wanted by the police (for questioning)** la busca la policía (para interrogarla); **the boss wants you in her office** el jefe te llama a su despacho; **you're wanted on the phone** te llaman por teléfono; **will I be wanted tomorrow?** ¿me necesitarán mañana?; **I know when I'm not wanted** sé perfectamente cuándo estoy de más; **wanted, a good cook** *(advertisement)* se necesita buen cocinero; **wanted** *(sign above photo of criminal)* se busca
(**d**) *(wish to have sex with)* desear
(**e**) *Formal (lack) (food, shelter)* carecer de
3 *vi* **he wants for nothing** no le falta de nada

▸ **want in** *vi Fam* (**a**) *(wish to come in)* querer entrar (**b**) *(wish to participate)* querer participar (**on** en)

▸ **want out** *vi Fam* (**a**) *(wish to go out)* querer salir (**b**) *(no longer wish to participate)* querer salirse (**of** de)

---

wanted ['wɒntɪd] *adj (criminal)* buscado(a) por la policía

wanting ['wɒntɪŋ] *adj* **he is w. in intelligence** le falta inteligencia; **to be found w.** *(person)* no dar la talla; *(technology, theory, argument)* ser deficiente, tener carencias

wanton ['wɒntən] *adj* (**a**) *(unjustified)* injustificado(a), sin sentido; *(cruelty)* gratuito(a) (**b**) *Old-fashioned (licentious)* licencioso(a) (**c**) *(unrestrained)* descontrolado(a)

wantonly ['wɒntənlɪ] *adv* (**a**) *(without good reason)* gratuitamente, de manera injustificada (**b**) *Old-fashioned (licentiously)* licenciosamente

wantonness ['wɒntənnɪs] *n* (**a**) *(of insult, destruction)* falta *f* de justificación, gratuidad *f* (**b**) *Old-fashioned (licentiousness)* licenciosidad *f*

WAP [wæp] *n Comptr* (*abbr* **Wireless Application Protocol**) WAP *m* ▸▸ ***W. phone*** teléfono *m* WAP

war [wɔː(r)] *n* guerra *f*; **to be at w. (with)** estar en guerra (con); **to go to w. (with/over)** entrar en guerra (con/por); **he fought in the w.** estuvo *or* luchó en la guerra; **the w. to end all wars** la guerra que pondría fin a todas las guerras; **to have a good w.** *(soldier)* salir victorioso(a) de la guerra; *(businessman)* hacer negocio con la guerra; **a w. of nerves** una guerra de nervios; *Fig* **the w. on crime/drugs** la batalla *or* lucha contra la delincuencia/la droga; *Fig* **a w. of words** una batalla dialéctica, un combate verbal; IDIOM *Fam* **you look as if you've been in the wars** parece que volvieras de la guerra; *Fam Hum* **that carpet (looks like it) has been through the wars!** ¡a esa alfombra se le ha dado ya mucho trote! ▸▸ ***w. baby*** niño(a) *m,f* de la guerra; ***w. cabinet*** gabinete *m* de guerra; ***w. chest*** *US Pol* fondos *mpl* recaudados para la campaña electoral; *Fig* fondos *mpl* especiales; ***w. correspondent*** corresponsal *mf* de guerra; ***w. crime*** crimen *m* de guerra; ***w. criminal*** criminal *mf* de guerra; ***w. cry*** grito *m* de guerra; ***w. dance*** danza *f* de guerra; ***the w. effort*** el esfuerzo bélico; ***w. games*** *Mil* maniobras *fpl*; *(with model soldiers)* juegos *mpl* de estrategia (militar); ***w. memorial*** monumento *m* a los caídos (en la guerra); ***w. toys*** juguetes *mpl* bélicos; ***w. widow*** viuda *f* de guerra; ***w. zone*** zona *f* de guerra

warble ['wɔːbəl] **1** *n* trino *m*
2 *vi* trinar

warbler ['wɔːblə(r)] *n* ***garden w.*** curruca *f* mosquitera; ***melodious w.*** zarcero *m* común; ***reed w.*** carricero *m* común; ***thick-billed w.*** carricero *m* picogordo

ward [wɔːd] *n* (**a**) *(in hospital)* sala *f*; **cancer w.** sala de oncología ▸▸ ***w. round*** ronda *f* de visitas (**b**) *(electoral division)* distrito *m* electoral ▸▸ *US Fam Pej* ***w. heeler*** = adepto que hace campaña para un candidato (**c**) *Law (person)* tutelado(a) *m,f*; *(guardianship)* custodia *f*, tutela *f*; **to be in w.** estar bajo tutela ▸▸ ***w. of court*** pupilo(a) *m,f* bajo tutela (judicial)

▸ **ward off** *vt sep (blow)* rechazar, parar; *(danger, evil spirits)* ahuyentar; *(illness)* prevenir

warden ['wɔːdən] *n* (**a**) *(of park)* guarda *mf* (**b**) *(of institution, hostel)* guardián(ana) *m,f*, vigilante *mf* (**c**) *US (of prison)* director(ora) *m,f*, alcaide(esa) *m,f* (**d**) *Br Univ* rector(ora) *m,f*

warder ['wɔːdə(r)] *n Br (in prison)* vigilante *mf*

wardrobe ['wɔːdrəʊb] *n* (**a**) *(cupboard)* armario *m*, ropero *m* (**b**) *(clothes)* guardarropa *m*; **to have a large w.** tener un amplio guardarropa (**c**) *Cin & Theat (costumes)* vestuario *m*; **Elizabeth Taylor's w. by...** el vestuario de Elizabeth Taylor es de... ▸▸ ***w. master*** (encargado *m* del) guardarropa *m*; ***w. mistress*** (encargada *f* del) guardarropa *f*

wardroom ['wɔːdruːm] *n Naut* sala *f* de oficiales

warehouse ['weəhaʊs] *n* almacén *m* ►► ***w. club*** = almacén de venta al por mayor en el que sólo pueden comprar los socios; ***w. party*** fiesta *f* en una nave

warehouseman ['weəhaʊsmən] *n (employee, owner)* almacenista *mf*, almacenero(a) *m,f*; *(manager)* jefe(a) *m,f* de almacén

warehousing ['weəhaʊzɪŋ] *n (of goods)* almacenaje *m*; *(of goods in bond)* depósito *m*

wares [weəz] *npl* mercaderías *fpl*, mercancías *fpl*

warfare ['wɔːfeə(r)] *n* guerra *f*; **modern/guerrilla w.** la guerra moderna/de guerillas; **class/psychological w.** guerra de clases/psicológica; **open w.** guerra abierta

warhead ['wɔːhed] *n* cabeza *f* explosiva, ojiva *f*

warhorse ['wɔːhɔːs] *n Fig* **an old w.** un veterano, un perro viejo

warily ['weərɪlɪ] *adv* cautelosamente; **they eyed the newcomer w.** miraban al recién llegado con recelo *or* desconfianza; **to tread w.** proceder con cautela, ir con pies de plomo

wariness ['weərɪnɪs] *n* cautela *f*, precaución *f*

warlike ['wɔːlaɪk] *adj* agresivo(a), belicoso(a)

warlock ['wɔːlɒk] *n* brujo *m*

warlord ['wɔːlɔːd] *n* señor *m* de la guerra

warm [wɔːm] **1** *adj* (**a**) *(iron, oven, bath)* caliente; *(water)* templado(a); *(weather)* cálido(a); *(garment)* de abrigo; **it's w.** *(weather)* hace calor; **to be w.** *(person)* tener calor; *(water)* estar templado(a); *(house)* ser caliente; **it's nice and w. in here** aquí se está calentito; **the weather is w.** hace calor; **this soup is barely w.** esta sopa está medio fría; **are you w. enough?** ¿vas bien abrigado?; **does that jacket keep you w.?** ¿te abriga esa chaqueta?; **to get w.** *(person)* entrar en calor; *(room, water)* calentarse; **the weather is getting warmer** está haciendo más calor; **you're getting warmer** *(in guessing game)* ¡caliente, caliente! ►► *Comptr* ***w. boot*** arranque *m* en caliente; *Met* ***w. front*** frente *m* cálido

(**b**) *(welcome, applause)* caluroso(a), cálido(a); *(greeting)* caluroso(a), cordial; *(person)* afectuoso(a); **give my warmest wishes to your wife** haga llegar mis más cordiales saludos a su esposa

(**c**) *(colour)* cálido(a)

2 *vt* calentar; **to w. oneself by the fire** calentarse junto al fuego; **she warmed her hands by the fire** se calentó las manos con el fuego

3 *vi* **to w. to sb** *(take liking to)* tomar afecto *or* cariño a alguien; **you'll soon w. to the idea** la idea pronto te parecerá interesante, ya te irá seduciendo la idea; **the speaker began to w. to his subject** el disertante hablaba del tema cada vez con mayor vehemencia

4 *n* **come into the w.** ven, que aquí se está calentito; **to give sth a w.** calentar algo

► **warm over** *vt sep US* (**a**) *(food)* recalentar (**b**) *Pej (idea)* hacer un refrito de

► **warm up 1** *vt sep (food, room)* calentar; **this will w. you up** esto te hará entrar en calor, esto hará que entres en calor

2 *vi* (**a**) *(dancer, athlete)* calentar (**b**) *(engine room)* calentarse (**c**) *(party)* animarse

warm-blooded [wɔːm'blʌdɪd] *adj* de sangre caliente

warm-hearted [wɔːm'hɑːtɪd] *adj* cariñoso(a), amable

warming pan ['wɔːmɪŋpæn] *n* calentador *m* (de cama)

warmly ['wɔːmlɪ] *adv* (**a**) *(retaining heat)* **w. dressed** abrigado(a) (**b**) *Fig (to applaud, welcome)* calurosamente; *(to thank)* de todo corazón; **his suggestion was not w. welcomed** su propuesta no fue muy bien recibida; **the film was w. received by the critics** la película tuvo muy buena acogida entre la crítica

warmonger ['wɔːmʌŋgə(r)] *n* belicista *mf*

warmongering ['wɔːmʌŋgərɪŋ] **1** *n (activities)* actividad *f* bélica; *(attitude)* belicismo *m*

2 *adj* belicista

warmth [wɔːmθ] *n* (**a**) *(heat)* calor *m*; **we huddled together for w.** nos acurrucamos los unos contra los otros en busca de calor (**b**) *(of welcome, applause)* calidez *f*, calor *m*; *(of greeting)* cordialidad *f*; *(of person's character)* calidez *f*, afectuosidad *f*; *(affection)* cariño *m* (**c**) *(of colour)* calidez *f*

warm-up ['wɔːmʌp] *n (of dancer, athlete)* calentamiento *m* ►► ***w. exercises*** ejercicios *mpl* de (pre)calentamiento; ***w. lap*** *(in motor racing)* vuelta *f* de calentamiento

warn [wɔːn] *vt* (**a**) *(caution)* advertir; **to w. sb about sth** advertir a alguien de algo; **he warned her not to go** le advirtió que no fuese; **stop that, I'm warning you!** ¡te lo advierto, basta ya!; **you have been warned!** ¡quedas advertido!

(**b**) *(alert, inform)* avisar, advertir; **she warned them that she would be late** les avisó que llegaría tarde; **I did w. you that this might happen** ya te advertí que esto podía pasar; **she had been warned in advance** la habían avisado de antemano

► **warn against 1** *vt insep* **to w. against (doing) sth** desaconsejar (hacer) algo; **he warned against complacency at such a critical time** previno a todos del peligro de caer en la autocomplacencia en momentos tan cruciales

2 *vt sep* **to w. sb against sth** prevenir a alguien contra *or* sobre algo; **to w. sb against doing sth** prevenir a alguien contra algo; **people have been warned against travelling to the region** se ha advertido a la gente que no viaje a la región, se ha desaconsejado viajar a la región

► **warn of** *vt insep* avisar de; **I warned them of the danger** les previne *or* avisé (acerca) del peligro

► **warn off** *vt sep* **we wanted to go there last summer but a friend warned us off** queríamos ir allí el verano pasado pero un amigo nos quitó la idea de la cabeza; **he warned them off his land** les advirtió que se fueran de su tierra; **the doctor has warned him off alcohol** el médico le advirtió que dejara de beber; **to w. sb off doing sth** tratar de disuadir a alguien de hacer algo, advertir a alguien que deje de hacer algo

warning ['wɔːnɪŋ] *n* (**a**) *(caution)* advertencia *f*, aviso *m*; **to give sb a w.** hacer una advertencia a alguien, dar un toque de atención a alguien; **to issue a w. against sth** hacer pública una advertencia acerca de algo; **there was a note of w. in her voice** la manera en que lo dijo tenía cierto tono de advertencia; **let that be a w. to you** que esto te sirva de advertencia; **this is your last w.** *(to child)* es la última vez que te lo digo; *(to worker)* es el último aviso ►► ***w. light*** chivato *m*; ***w. shot*** disparo *m* de aviso *or* advertencia; ***w. sign*** señal *f* de alarma; *Aut* ***w. triangle*** triángulo *m* de peligro

(**b**) *(advance notice)* aviso *m*; **we need a few day's w.** necesitamos que nos avisen con unos días de antelación; **without w.** sin previo aviso

warp [wɔːp] **1** *n* (**a**) *Tex (of yarn)* urdimbre *f* (**b**) *(fault) (in wood)* alabeo *m*, comba *f*; *(in metal, plastic)* comba *f*; **there's a slight w. in the door** la puerta está un poco combada

2 *vt* (**a**) *(wood, metal)* alabear, combar (**b**) *(person, mind)* corromper, pervertir

3 *vi (wood, metal)* alabearse, combarse

warpaint ['wɔːpeɪnt] *n* (**a**) *(of warrior)* pintura *f* de guerra (**b**) *Fam Hum (make-up)* pintura *f*, maquillaje *m*

warpath ['wɔːpɑːθ] *n* IDIOM **to be on the w.** *(ready for battle)* estar en pie de guerra; *Fam (angry, belligerent)* estar con ganas de guerra, estar con un humor de perros

warped [wɔːpt] *adj* (**a**) *(wood, metal)* alabeado(a), combado(a) (**b**) *(person, mind)* degenerado(a), pervertido(a); *(sense of humour)* retorcido(a)

warplane ['wɔːpleɪn] *n* avión *m* de guerra

warrant ['wɒrənt] **1** *n* (**a**) *Law* mandamiento *m or* orden *f* judicial; **a w. for sb's arrest** una orden de detención *or* arresto contra alguien; **there's a w. out for his arrest** hay una orden de detención *or* arresto contra él, sobre él pesa una orden de detención *or* arresto

(**b**) *Mil* ***w. officer*** ≃ subteniente *mf*

(**c**) *Com & Fin (for payment)* comprobante *m*, resguardo *m*; *(guarantee)* garantía *f*; *(for shares)* bono *m* de suscripción, warrant *m*

(**d**) *Formal (justification)* justificación *f*

2 *vt* (**a**) *(justify)* justificar; *(deserve)* merecer (**b**) *Old-fashioned (declare with certainty)* garantizar; **I'll w. (you) that's the last we see of her** te puedo garantizar que es la última vez que la vemos

warrantable ['wɒrəntəbəl] *adj Formal (justifiable)* justificable; **to be w.** estar justificado(a)

warrantee [wɒrən'tiː] *n Com* titular *mf* de una garantía

warrantor [wɒrən'tɔː(r)] *n Com* garante *mf*

warranty ['wɒrəntɪ] *n (document)* garantía *f*; **this printer has a five-year w.** esta impresora tiene cinco años de garantía; **under w.** en garantía; **on-site w.** garantía in situ; **return-to-base w.** garantía de reparación en el taller del proveedor ►► ***w. certificate*** certificado *m* de garantía

warren ['wɒrən] *n (of rabbit)* red *f* de madrigueras *or* conejeras; *Fig* laberinto *m*

warring ['wɔːrɪŋ] *adj (nations, tribes)* en guerra; *(couple, family)* enfrentado(a); **w. factions within the Labour Party** facciones enfrentadas *or* antagónicas en el seno del partido laborista

warrior ['wɒrɪə(r)] *n* guerrero(a) *m,f*

Warsaw ['wɔːsɔː] *n* Varsovia ►► *Formerly* ***W. Pact*** Pacto *m* de Varsovia

warship ['wɔːʃɪp] *n* buque *m or* barco *m* de guerra

wart [wɔ:t] *n* verruga *f*; IDIOM **warts and all: he loves me, warts and all** me quiere tal como soy, con todos mis defectos; **a biography of Margaret Thatcher, warts and all** una biografía de Margaret Thatcher que muestra lo bueno y lo malo

warthog ['wɔ:thɒg] *n* facóquero *m*, jabalí *m* verrugoso

wartime ['wɔ:taɪm] *n* tiempos *mpl* de guerra; **in w.** en tiempos de guerra; **w. London** Londres durante la guerra

war-torn ['wɔ:tɔ:n] *adj* desvastado(a) por la guerra

wary ['weərɪ] *adj (person, attitude)* cauteloso(a), precavido(a); *(look)* cauteloso(a); **to be w. of sth/sb** recelar de algo/alguien; **the people were w. of the new regime** el pueblo desconfiaba del nuevo régimen; **I'm w. about employing people like that** no me convence del todo la idea de contratar a ese tipo de gente; **he kept a w. eye on the dog** miraba al perro con desconfianza

was *pt of* **be**

Wash (*abbr* **Washington**) Washington

wash [wɒʃ] **1** *n* (**a**) *(action)* lavado *m*; **to have a w.** lavarse; **to give sth a w.** lavar algo; **give the floor a good w.** friega bien el suelo; **this floor needs a good w.** a este suelo le hace falta un buen fregado; **give your hands a w.** lávate las manos; **to do a w.** lavar la ropa, *Esp* hacer la colada; **your shirt is in the w.** *(is going to be washed)* tu camisa está para lavar; *(is being washed)* tu camisa está lavándose; **the stain came out in the w.** la mancha salió con el lavado; IDIOM **it will all come out in the w.** *(become known)* todo se aclarará; *(be all right)* todo se arreglará ►► ***w. cycle*** programa *m* de lavado
(**b**) *(from boat)* estela *f*
(**c**) *(sound of waves)* batir *m*
(**d**) *Art* = capa fina de agua o acuarela ►► ***w. drawing*** aguada *f*
(**e**) *(of paint)* mano *m*
2 *vt* (**a**) *(clean)* lavar; *(floor)* fregar; **to w. oneself** lavarse; **to w. one's face/one's hands** lavarse la cara/las manos; **to w. one's hair** lavarse la cabeza *or* el pelo; **to w. the dishes** fregar *or* lavar los platos; **w. in cold/hot water** *(on clothing label)* lavar en agua fría/caliente
(**b**) *(carry)* **the cargo was washed ashore** el mar arrastró el cargamento hasta la costa; **he was washed overboard** un golpe de mar lo tiró *or Am* botó del barco
(**c**) *(paint)* dar una mano de pintura a
(**d**) *Min (gold, ore)* lavar
(**e**) IDIOMS **to w. one's hands of sth/sb** desentenderse de algo/alguien, lavarse las manos en relación con algo/alguien; **to w. one's dirty linen in public** sacar a relucir los trapos sucios
3 *vi* (**a**) *(wash oneself)* lavarse; IDIOM *Fam* **that won't w.!** *(won't be believed)* ¡eso no se lo cree nadie!, *Esp* ¡eso no va a colar!; **his story doesn't w. with me!** ¡a mí no me la da con esa historia! (**b**) *(do dishes)* **you w. and I'll dry** tú lavas y yo seco (**c**) *(sea, tide)* **to w. against sth** batir *or* romper contra algo; **I let the music w. over me** me dejé llevar por la música

► **wash away** *vt sep* (**a**) *(bridge, house)* arrastrar, llevarse (por delante); *(road)* arrasar (**b**) *(dirt)* quitar, *Am* sacar; *Fig* **to w. one's sins away** lavar los pecados

► **wash down** *vt sep* (**a**) *(clean with water)* lavar bien (**b**) *(food)* regar, acompañar; **roast beef washed down with Burgundy wine** carne asada regada con borgoña

► **wash off 1** *vt sep* lavar, quitar *or Am* sacar lavando
2 *vi* salir, quitarse

► **wash out 1** *vt sep* (**a**) *(cup, bottle)* enjuagar (**b**) *(cause to be cancelled)* provocar la suspensión de; **the game was washed out** el partido tuvo que ser suspendido por la lluvia
2 *vi* (**a**) *(disappear)* salir, quitarse (**b**) *US Fam (fail to qualify) Esp* catear, *Am* reprobar, *Méx* tronar, *RP* desaprobar; **he washed out of college** le fue mal en la facultad

► **wash over** *vt insep (of waves)* batir contra; **anything I say just washes over her** cualquier cosa que diga le entra por una oreja y le sale por la otra

► **wash up 1** *vt sep* (**a**) *Br (clean)* fregar, lavar (**b**) *(bring ashore) (of sea)* arrastrar hasta la costa
2 *vi* (**a**) *Br (do dishes)* fregar *or* lavar los platos (**b**) *US (have a wash)* lavarse

washable ['wɒʃəbəl] *adj* lavable

wash-and-wear ['wɒʃən'weə(r)] *adj* que no necesita plancha

washbasin ['wɒʃbeɪsən] *n (sink)* lavabo *m*, *Am* lavamanos *m inv*; *(basin)* palangana *f*

washboard ['wɒʃbɔ:d] *n* tabla *f* de lavar

washbowl ['wɒʃbəʊl] *n US* palangana *f*

washcloth ['wɒʃklɒθ] *n US (face cloth)* toallita *f* (para la cara)

washday ['wɒʃdeɪ] *n* día *m* de lavar la ropa *or Esp* de la colada

washed-out [wɒʃt'aʊt] *adj* (**a**) *(person)* extenuado(a) (**b**) *(fabric)* descolorido(a) (**c**) *(sports event)* suspendido(a) por el mal tiempo

washed-up [wɒʃt'ʌp] *adj Fam* **to be (all) w.** *(person)* estar acabado(a); *(plan)* haberse ido al traste *or* al garete

washer ['wɒʃə(r)] *n* (**a**) *(washing machine)* lavadora *f*, *RP* lavarropas *m inv* (**b**) *(for screw)* arandela *f*; *(rubber)* zapata *f*, junta *f*

washer-dryer ['wɒʃə'draɪə(r)] *n* lavadora-secadora *f*

washerwoman ['wɒʃəwʊmən] *n* lavandera *f*

washhouse ['wɒʃhaʊs] *n* lavadero *m*

washing ['wɒʃɪŋ] *n* (**a**) *(action)* **to do the w.** lavar la ropa, *Esp* hacer la colada ►► *Br* ***w. line*** cuerda *f* de tender la ropa; *Br* ***w. liquid*** detergente *m*; ***w. machine*** lavadora *f*, *RP* lavarropas *m inv*; ***w. powder*** jabón *m or* detergente *m* (en polvo); ***w. soda*** sosa *f* para lavar (**b**) *(dirty clothes)* ropa *f* sucia; *(clean clothes)* ropa *f* limpia

Washington ['wɒʃɪŋtən] *n* (**a**) *(city)* **W. (DC)** Washington (DC) (**b**) *(state)* Washington

washing-up [wɒʃɪŋ'ʌp] *n Br* **to do the w.** fregar *or* lavar los platos ►► ***w. bowl*** palangana *f or Esp* barreño *m* (para lavar los platos); ***w. liquid*** lavavajillas *m inv (detergente)*

washout ['wɒʃaʊt] *n* (**a**) *Fam (fiasco)* fiasco *m*, desastre *m* (**b**) *US Fam (failed student) Esp* suspenso(a) *m,f*, *Am* reprobado(a) *m,f*

washrag ['wɒʃræg] *n US (face cloth)* toallita *f* (para la cara)

washroom ['wɒʃru:m] *n US* baño *m*, *Esp* servicios *mpl*, *CSur* toilette *f*

washstand ['wɒʃstænd] *n* aguamanil *m*, palanganero *m*

washtub ['wɒʃtʌb] *n (for laundry)* tina *f* de lavar

wasn't [wɒznt] = **was not**

WASP [wɒsp] *n* (*abbr* **white Anglo-Saxon Protestant**) WASP *mf*, = persona de raza blanca, origen anglosajón y protestante

wasp [wɒsp] *n* avispa *f*; **wasps' nest** avispero ►► ***w. waist*** cintura *f* de avispa

waspish ['wɒspɪʃ] *adj (person, mood, remark)* mordaz, hiriente

wasp-waisted [wɒsp'weɪstɪd] *adj* con cintura de avispa

wassail ['wɒseɪl] *Archaic or Literary* **1** *n* (**a**) *(drink) (beer)* = bebida ceremonial hecha con cerveza; *(wine)* = bebida ceremonial dulce hecha con vino aromatizado, manzana asada y especias (**b**) *(festivity)* parranda *f* (**c**) *(toast)* brindis *m inv*
2 *vi* festejar; **to go wassailing** irse de parranda

wastage ['weɪstɪdʒ] *n (of material, heat, time)* desperdicio *m*; *(of money)* despilfarro *m* ►► ***w. rate*** tasa *f or* índice *m* de abandonos *(en universidad, profesión)*

waste [weɪst] **1** *n* (**a**) *(of money, time)* pérdida *f*, derroche *m*; *(of effort)* desperdicio *m*; **to go to w.** desperdiciarse; **what a w.!** ¡qué desperdicio!; **that book was a complete w. of money** comprar ese libro fue tirar el dinero; **it's a w. of time talking to her** hablar con ella es perder el tiempo; **what a w. of time!** ¡qué manera de perder el tiempo!; *Fam* **to be a w. of space** ser un/una inútil
(**b**) *(unwanted material)* desechos *mpl*; *(radioactive, toxic)* residuos *mpl*; **household w.** basura ►► *Br* ***w. bin*** balde *m or Esp* cubo *m* de la basura; ***w. collection*** recogida *f* de basura; ***w. disposal*** eliminación *f* de residuos; *Br* ***w. disposal unit*** trituradora *f* de basuras; ***w. dumping*** vertido *m* de residuos; ***w. incinerator*** (planta *f*) incineradora *f*; ***w. pipe*** tubo *m* de desagüe; ***w. segregation*** selección *f or* separación *f* de residuos reciclables
(**c**) **wastes** *(desert)* erial *m*, desierto *m*; **the snowy wastes of Alaska** las vastas extensiones de terreno nevado de Alaska ►► ***w. ground*** descampado *m*, (terreno *m*) baldío *m*
2 *adj (heat, water)* residual; *(fuel)* de desecho ►► ***w. material*** material *m* de desecho; ***w. matter*** residuos *mpl*; ***w. paper*** papel *m* usado; ***w. product*** *Ind* producto *m or* material *m* de desecho; *Physiol* excrementos *mpl*
3 *vt* (**a**) *(squander) (money, energy)* malgastar, derrochar; *(time)* perder; *(opportunity, talent, food)* desperdiciar; **this wine would be wasted on them** no sabrían apreciar este vino; **stop wasting my time!** ¡deja ya de hacerme perder el tiempo!; **she wasted no time (in) telling me** le faltó tiempo para decírmelo; **he felt that he had wasted his life** sintió que había desperdiciado su vida; **you're wasting your breath!** estás gastando saliva; **don't w. your breath trying to convince them** no gastes saliva intentando convencerlos; PROV **w. not, want not** no malgastes y nada te faltará
(**b**) *(wear away) (limb, muscle)* atrofiar; *(body, person)* consumir; **her body was completely wasted by cancer** estaba consumida por el cáncer
(**c**) *Fam (kill) Esp* cargarse, *Am* sacar de en medio a

► **waste away** *vi* consumirse

wastebasket ['weɪstbɑːskɪt] *n* (**a**) *(for paper etc)* papelera *f*, cesto *m* de los papeles, *Arg, Méx* cesto *m*, *Méx* bote *m* (**b**) *Comptr* papelera *f*

wasted ['weɪstɪd] *adj* (**a**) *(effort, opportunity)* desperdiciado(a), desaprovechado(a) (**b**) *Fam (drunk) Esp, Méx* pedo *inv*, *Esp, RP* mamado(a), *Col* caído(a); *(on drugs)* colocado(a), *Esp* ciego(a), *Col* trabado(a), *Méx* pingo(a), *RP* falopeado(a) (**c**) *(emaciated) (limb)* atrofiado(a); *(figure, person)* consumido(a)

wasteful ['weɪstfʊl] *adj* **to be w.** *(method)* ser un derroche; *(person)* ser despilfarrador(ora); **w. expenditure** despilfarro; **a w. use of natural resources** un uso indiscriminado *or* un derroche de los recursos naturales

wastefully ['weɪstfʊlɪ] *adv* de manera poco económica; **to spend money w.** derrochar dinero; **we spend our time so w.** perdemos el tiempo demasiado, usamos muy mal nuestro tiempo

wastefulness ['weɪstfʊlnɪs] *n* despilfarro *m*

wasteland ['weɪstlænd] *n (disused land)* terreno *m* baldío; *(uncultivated land)* erial *m*; *Fig* **a cultural w.** un páramo cultural

wastepaper [weɪst'peɪpə(r)] *n* papel *m* usado ►► ***w. basket*** papelera *f*, cesto *m* de los papeles, *Arg, Méx* cesto *m*, *Méx* bote *m*; ***w. bin*** papelera *f*, cesto *m* de los papeles, *Arg, Méx* cesto *m*, *Méx* bote *m*

waster ['weɪstə(r)] *n Fam (idle person)* inútil *mf*

wasting ['weɪstɪŋ] *adj Fin* ***w. asset*** activo *m* amortizable, posesión *f* que genera pérdidas; ***w. disease*** = enfermedad debilitante que consume los tejidos

wastrel ['weɪstrəl] *n Literary* holgazán(ana) *m,f*

WATCH [wɒtʃ] **1** *n* (**a**) *(timepiece)* reloj *m*; **it's 6 o'clock by my w.** según mi reloj son las seis ►► ***w. battery*** pila *f* (de) botón; ***w. chain*** correa *f* de reloj

(**b**) *(period of guard duty)* turno *m* de vigilancia; *(guard)* guardia *f*; **to keep w.** hacer la guardia; **we kept him under close w.** lo teníamos bien vigilado; **to keep a close w. on sth/sb** vigilar de cerca algo/a alguien; **to be on w.** estar de guardia; **make sure you're on the w. for** *or* **you keep a w. out for any houses for sale** estate al tanto por si ves alguna casa en venta; *Literary* **the slow watches of the night** las largas horas en vela

2 *vt* (**a**) *(observe)* mirar, observar; *(movie, game, programme, video)* ver; **to w. television** ver la televisión; **w. this!** ¡mira!; *Fam* **I don't believe you'll do it – just w. me!** no me creo que lo vayas a hacer – ¿que no?, ¡mira!; **we are being watched** nos están observando; **to w. sb doing** *or* **do sth** ver *or* observar a alguien hacer algo; **I watched her prepare the meal** la miraba mientras preparaba la comida; **w. her run!** ¡mira cómo corre!; **I spent the afternoon watching the clock** me pasé la tarde mirando el reloj; **w. this space for more details** les seguiremos informando; **we have to w. the time** tenemos que estar al tanto de la hora; PROV **a watched pot never boils** = no por mucho madrugar amanece más temprano

(**b**) *(keep an eye on) (children, luggage)* vigilar; **I'll have to w. myself, to make sure I don't tell them** tendré que tener cuidado para que no se me escape delante de ellos

(**c**) *(be careful of)* tener cuidado con; **w. (that) you don't get your clothes dirty!** ¡ten cuidado de no mancharte la ropa!; **w. what you're doing with that knife!** ¡a ver qué haces con ese cuchillo!; **w. where you're going!** ¡mira por dónde vas!; **w. your head!** ¡cuidado con la cabeza!; **you'd better w. your back** ándate con cuidado; **w. your language!** ¡cuidado con ese lenguaje!; **I've been watching my weight recently** últimamente he estado vigilando mi peso; *Fam* **w. it!** ¡ojo (con lo que haces)!; *Fam* **w. yourself!** *(be careful)* ¡ten cuidado!; *also Fig* **w. your step** ¡ve con cuidado!

3 *vi* (**a**) *(observe)* mirar, observar; **you w., they'll never agree to it** ya verás como no acceden; **I watched to see how she would react** la observé para ver su reacción

(**b**) *(keep vigil)* **his mother watched by his bedside** su madre lo velaba junto a la cama

► **watch for** *vt insep (opportunity)* esperar, aguardar

► **watch out** *vi* tener cuidado; **w. out!** ¡cuidado!; **to w. out for sth** estar al tanto de algo; **w. out for sharp bends in the road** ten cuidado que en la carretera hay curvas cerradas; **w. out for this horse in tomorrow's race** al tanto con ese caballo en la carrera de mañana

► **watch over** *vt insep* vigilar; **God watches over us all** Dios nos protege

watchable ['wɒtʃəbəl] *adj* (**a**) *(viewable)* **some scenes are barely w.** hay escenas que apenas se pueden ver (**b**) *Fam (enjoyable)* **it's quite w.** se deja ver muy bien

watchband ['wɒtʃbænd] *n US* correa *f* de reloj

watchcase ['wɒtʃkeɪs] *n* estuche *m* de reloj

watchdog ['wɒtʃdɒg] *n* (**a**) *(dog)* perro *m* guardián (**b**) *(organization)* organismo *m* regulador (**c**) *Comptr* ***w. program*** programa *m* de vigilancia *or* control

watcher ['wɒtʃə(r)] *n* observador(ora) *m,f*; *(spectator)* espectador(ora) *m,f*; *(idle onlooker)* curioso(a) *m,f*; **CIA/Kremlin watchers** observadores de la CIA/del Kremlin

watchful ['wɒtʃfʊl] *adj* vigilante, alerta; **under the teacher's w. eye** bajo la atenta mirada del profesor; **to keep a w. eye on sth/sb** observar algo/a alguien atentamente, vigilar algo/a alguien de cerca

watching ['wɒtʃɪŋ] *adj* ***w. brief*** *Law* = seguimiento de un caso por una parte no interesada; *Fig* papel *m* de observador(ora)

watchmaker ['wɒtʃmeɪkə(r)] *n* relojero(a) *m,f*

watchman ['wɒtʃmən] *n* vigilante *m*

watchnight ['wɒtʃnaɪt] *n Rel* ***w. service*** *(on Christmas Eve)* misa *f* del gallo; *(on New Year's Eve)* = misa oficiada a medianoche el 31 de diciembre

watchout ['wɒtʃaʊt] *n US* **to keep a w. for sth/sb** cuidar algo/a alguien

watchspring ['wɒtʃsprɪŋ] *n* muelle *m* real, resorte *m* principal

watchstrap ['wɒtʃstræp] *n Br* correa *f* de reloj

watchtower ['wɒtʃtaʊə(r)] *n* atalaya *f*

watchword ['wɒtʃwɜːd] *n* (**a**) *(slogan)* consigna *f* (**b**) *(password)* contraseña *f*

WATER ['wɔːtə(r)] **1** *n* (**a**) *(liquid, element)* agua *f*; **to be under w.** *(flooded)* estar inundado(a); **they held his head under w.** le metieron la cabeza en el agua; **turn on the w.** *(at main)* abre el agua; *(at tap)* abre *Esp* el grifo *or Chile, Col, Méx* la llave *or RP* la canilla; *Formal* **to pass w.** *(urinate)* orinar ►► ***w. beetle*** escarabajo *m* de agua; ***w. bird*** ave *f* acuática; ***w. biscuit*** galleta *f* sin sal; ***w. blister*** ampolla *f*; *Br* ***w. board*** = organismo responsable del suministro de agua; ***w. boatman*** chinche *f* acuática *or* de agua; ***w. bottle*** cantimplora *f*; *Med* ***w. on the brain*** hidrocefalia *f*; ***w. buffalo*** búfalo *m* de agua; *Br* ***w. butt*** contenedor *m (para recoger el agua de lluvia)*; ***w. cannon*** cañón *m* de agua; ***w. carrier*** *(person)* aguador(ora) *m,f*; *Astrol* ***the W. Carrier*** el Aguador; ***w. chestnut*** castaña *f* de agua; ***w. chute*** *(in swimming pool)* tobogán *m*; ***w. clock*** clepsidra *f*, reloj *m* de agua; *Old-fashioned* ***w. closet*** retrete *m*; ***w. cooler*** refrigerador *m* del agua; ***w. cooler show*** programa *m* que causa furor; ***w. flea*** pulga *f* de agua; ***w. fountain*** *(for drinking)* fuente *f*; ***w. gauge*** indicador *m* del nivel del agua; ***w. hammer*** golpe *m* de ariete; ***w. heater*** calentador *m* de agua; *Br Old-fashioned* ***w. ice*** *(sorbet)* sorbete *m*; ***w. jump*** *(in horse-racing, athletics)* ría *f*; *Med* ***w. on the knee*** líquido *m* en la rodilla, *Spec* derrame *m* sinovial (en la rodilla); ***w. level*** nivel *m* del agua; ***w. lily*** nenúfar *m*; ***w. main*** cañería *f* principal; ***w. meadow*** = prado en la proximidad de un río que se inunda con frecuencia; ***w. meter*** contador *m* del agua; ***w. mill*** molino *m* de agua; *US* ***w. moccasin*** mocasín *m* de agua; ***w. nymph*** náyade *f*; ***w. pipe*** *(tube)* tubería *f or* cañería *f* del agua; *(hookah)* narguile *m*; ***w. pipit*** bisbita *m* ribereño alpino; ***w. pistol*** pistola *f* de agua; ***w. pollution*** contaminación *f* del agua; ***w. polo*** waterpolo *m*; ***w. power*** energía *f* hidráulica; ***w. pump*** bomba *f* de agua; ***w. purification plant*** (planta *f*) depuradora *f* (de aguas); ***w. rat*** rata *f* de agua; *Br* ***w. rates*** tarifa *f* del agua; ***w. resources*** recursos *mpl* hídricos; ***w. shortage*** escasez *f* de agua; *Astrol* ***w. sign*** signo *m* de agua; ***w. snake*** serpiente *f* de agua; ***w. softener*** descalcificador *m*; ***w. spider*** araña *f* de agua; ***w. sports*** *(water-skiing, windsurfing etc)* deportes *mpl* acuáticos *or* náuticos; *Vulg* lluvia *f* dorada; ***w. supply*** suministro *m* de agua; ***w. table*** nivel *m* freático, capa *f* freática; ***w. tank*** depósito *m* de agua; ***w. torture*** = tortura consistente en dejar caer gotas de agua sobre la cabeza de la víctima; ***w. tower*** depósito *m* de agua; ***w. treatment*** purificación *f* del agua; ***w. turbine*** turbina *f* hidráulica; ***w. vapour*** vapor *m* de agua; ***w. vole*** rata *f* de agua; ***w. wheel*** noria *f*; ***w. wings*** manguitos *mpl*, flotadores *mpl*

(**b**) *(body of water)* **waters** *(of country, river, lake)* aguas *fpl*; **the children played at the w.'s edge** los niños jugaban al borde del agua; **they sent the goods by w.** *(by sea)* enviaron la mercancía por mar; **in Japanese waters** en aguas japonesas; *Fig* **to enter uncharted waters** navegar por mares desconocidos

(**c**) *(of spring)* **to take the waters** tomar las aguas

(**d**) *(tide)* **at high/low w.** con la marea alta/baja

(**e**) *(of pregnant woman)* **her waters broke** rompió aguas

(**f**) *(of fabric)* aguas *fpl*

(**g**) IDIOMS **it's like w. off a duck's back** por un oído le entra y por el otro le sale; **to spend money like w.** gastar dinero a manos llenas; **the wine flowed like w.** corrieron ríos de vino; **that's all w. under the bridge now** todo eso es agua pasada; **a lot of w. has passed** *or* **flowed under the bridge since then** ha llovido mucho desde entonces; *Br*

Formal **he's an artist of the first w.** es un artista de primera línea; **the argument doesn't hold w.** ese argumento no se tiene en pie; **to keep one's head above w.** mantenerse a flote

2 *vt* (**a**) *(fields, plants)* regar; **the land here is watered by the Ebro** el Ebro baña las tierras de esta zona (**b**) *(horse)* dar de beber a (**c**) *(dilute)* aguar, diluir

3 *vi (eyes)* llorar, empañarse; **my eyes are watering** me lloran los ojos; **it makes my mouth w.** me hace la boca agua

▸ **water down** *vt sep (dilute)* aguar, diluir; *Fig (criticism, legislation)* atenuar, dulcificar

---

water-based ['wɔːtəbeɪst] *adj* al agua

waterbed ['wɔːtəbed] *n* cama *f* de agua

waterborne ['wɔːtəbɔːn] *adj* (**a**) *(goods) (by sea)* transportado(a) por mar; *(by river)* transportado(a) por río (**b**) *(disease)* transmitido(a) por el agua

watercolour ['wɔːtəkʌlə(r)] **1** *n Art* acuarela *f*; **painted in watercolours** pintado(a) con *or* a la acuarela

2 *adj (paint)* a la acuarela; *(landscape, portrait)* en acuarela

watercolourist ['wɔːtəkʌlərɪst] *n* pintor(ora) *m,f* de acuarelas, acuarelista *mf*

water-cooled ['wɔːtəkuːld] *adj* refrigerado(a) por agua

watercourse ['wɔːtəkɔːs] *n (river)* curso *m* de agua

watercress ['wɔːtəkres] *n* berros *mpl*

water-diviner ['wɔːtədɪvaɪnə(r)] *n Br* zahorí *mf*

watered-down ['wɔːtəd'daʊn] *adj Fig* descafeinado(a), light *inv*

waterfall ['wɔːtəfɔːl] *n (small)* cascada *f*, salto *m* de agua; *(larger)* catarata *f*

waterfinder ['wɔːtəfaɪndə(r)] *n US* zahorí *mf*

waterfowl ['wɔːtəfaʊl] (*pl* **waterfowl**) *n* ave *f* acuática

waterfront ['wɔːtəfrʌnt] *n (promenade)* paseo *m* marítimo; **on the w.** *(at harbour)* en los muelles; *(on seafront)* a la orilla del mar; **a w. development** = viviendas u oficinas ubicadas junto al mar, a un río o a un lago

waterhole ['wɔːtəhəʊl] *n* abrevadero *m*, bebedero *m*

wateriness ['wɔːtərɪnɪs] *n* (**a**) *(of soup, beer)* lo aguado (**b**) *(of colour)* palidez *f*, claridad *f*

watering ['wɔːtərɪŋ] *n* (**a**) *(of garden, fields, plants)* riego *m*; **azaleas need daily w.** las azaleas hay que regarlas a diario ▸▸ ***w. can*** regadera *f* (**b**) *(of animals)* abrevado *m* ▸▸ ***w. hole*** *(for animals)* abrevadero *m*, bebedero *m*; *Fam (bar)* bar *m*; ***w. place*** *Br (spa)* balneario *m*; *(seaside resort)* balneario *m* marítimo, centro *m* turístico costero; *(waterhole)* abrevadero *m*, bebedero *m*

waterline ['wɔːtəlaɪn] *n* (**a**) *Naut* línea *f* de flotación (**b**) *(left by river)* marca *f* del nivel del agua; *(left by tide)* marca *f* de la marea

waterlogged ['wɔːtəlɒgd] *adj (shoes, clothes)* empapado(a); *(land)* anegado(a); *(pitch)* (totalmente) encharcado(a)

Waterloo [wɔːtə'luː] *n* IDIOM *Br* **to meet one's W.** conocer el amargo sabor de la derrota

watermark ['wɔːtəmɑːk] *n* (**a**) *(in paper)* filigrana *f* (**b**) *(left by river)* marca *f* del nivel de agua; *(left by tide)* marca *f* de la marea

watermelon ['wɔːtəmelən] *n* sandía *f*

watermill ['wɔːtəmɪl] *n* molino *m* de agua

waterproof ['wɔːtəpruːf] **1** *n* impermeable *m*; **he was wearing waterproofs** llevaba ropa impermeable

2 *adj (fabric, garment)* impermeable; *(watch)* sumergible

3 *vt* impermeabilizar

water-repellent ['wɔːtərəpelənt] *adj* hidrófugo(a)

water-resistant ['wɔːtərɪzɪstənt] *adj (watch)* sumergible; *(fabric)* impermeable

watershed ['wɔːtəʃed] *n* (**a**) *Geog* (línea *f*) divisoria *f* de aguas (**b**) *(turning point)* punto *m* de inflexión (**c**) *Br TV* **the (nine o'clock) w.** = las nueve de la noche, hora antes de la cual no se recomienda la emisión de programas no aptos para niños

waterside ['wɔːtəsaɪd] **1** *n* orilla *f*; **on the w.** en la orilla

2 *adj (house)* junto al mar/río/lago, a la orilla del mar/río/lago; *(path, resident)* ribereño(a)

water-ski ['wɔːtəskiː] *vi* hacer esquí acuático *or* náutico

water-skier ['wɔːtəskiːə(r)] *n* esquiador(ora) *m,f* acuático(a) *or* náutico(a)

water-skiing ['wɔːtəskiːɪŋ] *n* esquí *m* acuático *or* náutico; **to go w.** hacer esquí acuático *or* náutico

water-soluble ['wɔːtə'sɒljʊbəl] *adj* soluble en agua

waterspout ['wɔːtəspaʊt] *n* tromba *f* marina

watertight ['wɔːtətaɪt] *adj* (**a**) *(seal)* hermético(a); *(compartment)* estanco(a) (**b**) *(argument, alibi)* irrefutable

waterway ['wɔːtəweɪ] *n* vía *f* fluvial, curso *m* de agua navegable

waterworks ['wɔːtəwɜːks] *n* (**a**) *(for treating water)* central *f* de abastecimiento de agua (**b**) *Br Euph (urinary system)* **how are the w.?** ¿tiene problemas al orinar? (**c**) IDIOM *Fam* **to turn on the w.** *(cry)* ponerse a llorar (con ganas)

watery ['wɔːtərɪ] *adj* (**a**) *(like water)* acuoso(a); **he ended in a w. grave** se lo llevó el mar, el mar fue su tumba (**b**) *(soup, beer)* aguado(a) (**c**) *(eyes)* lloroso(a), acuoso(a) (**d**) *(colour)* pálido(a), claro(a); *(light)* tenue

watt [wɒt] *n Elec* vatio *m*

wattage ['wɒtɪdʒ] *n Elec* potencia *f* en vatios

wattle ['wɒtəl] *n* zarzo *m* ▸▸ ***w. and daub*** cañas *fpl* y adobe *m*

wave [weɪv] **1** *n* (**a**) *(of water)* ola *f*; IDIOM **to make waves** alborotar, armar jaleo ▸▸ ***w. energy*** energía *f* de las olas; ***w. power*** energía *f* de las olas

(**b**) *(gesture)* saludo *m* (con la mano); **to give sb a w.** *(in greeting)* saludar con la mano a alguien; *(in farewell)* decir adiós a alguien con la mano; **with a w. of the hand** con un gesto de *or* con la mano; **with a w. of her magic wand** con un movimiento de su varita mágica

(**c**) *(rush, movement) (of troops, refugees, crime)* oleada *f*; *(of emotion)* arranque *m*; **a w. of attacks/strikes** una ola de atentados/huelgas

(**d**) *(in hair)* onda *f*; **her hair has a natural w. to it** su cabello es ondulado

(**e**) *Phys* onda *f* ▸▸ ***w. mechanics*** mecánica *f* ondulatoria; ***w. motion*** movimiento *m* ondulatorio *or* de ondulación

2 *vt* (**a**) *(flag, stick)* agitar; **to w. one's arms about** agitar los brazos; **to w. goodbye to sb** decir adiós a alguien con la mano; **he waved his magic wand over the box** agitó su varita mágica sobre la caja; **the policeman waved us through the crossroads** el policía nos hizo señas en el cruce para que pasáramos (**b**) **to have one's hair waved** ondularse el pelo

3 *vi* (**a**) *(person)* saludar (con la mano); **to w. to sb** *(in greeting)* saludar a alguien con la mano; *(in farewell)* decir adiós a alguien con la mano; **he waved vaguely towards the door** hizo un gesto vago con la mano hacia la puerta (**b**) *(flag)* ondear; *(branches)* agitarse

▸ **wave aside** *vt insep (objection, criticism)* rechazar, desechar

▸ **wave down** *vt sep* **to w. sb down** *(car driver)* hacer señas *or* señales con la mano a alguien para que se detenga

▸ **wave off** *vt sep* despedir (diciendo adiós con la mano)

▸ **wave on** *vt sep* **to w. sb on** hacer señas *or* señales con la mano a alguien para que continúe (la marcha)

waveband ['weɪvbænd] *n Rad* banda *f* de frecuencias

waveform ['weɪvfɔːm], **waveshape** ['weɪvʃeɪp] *n Phys* forma *f* de onda

wavelength ['weɪvleŋθ] *n Rad* longitud *f* de onda; IDIOM **we're not on the same w.** no estamos en la misma onda

wavelike ['weɪvlaɪk] *adj* ondulado(a)

waver ['weɪvə(r)] *vi* (**a**) *(person)* vacilar, titubear; *(courage)* flaquear (**b**) *(voice)* temblar; *(flame, shadow)* oscilar

waverer ['weɪvərə(r)] *n* indeciso(a) *m,f*

wavering ['weɪvərɪŋ] *adj* (**a**) *(person)* vacilante; *(confidence, courage)* que flaquea (**b**) *(voice)* tembloroso(a); *(flame, shadow)* oscilante; *(temperature)* cambiante

waviness ['weɪvɪnɪs] *n (of hair)* ondulación *f*

wavy ['weɪvɪ] *adj* ondulado(a)

wax[1] [wæks] **1** *n* (**a**) *(for candles, polishing, skis)* cera *f* ▸▸ ***w. crayon*** lápiz *m* de cera; ***w. museum*** museo *m* de cera; ***w. paper*** papel *m* de cera (**b**) *(in ear)* cera *f*, cerumen *m*

2 *vt* (**a**) *(polish) (floor, furniture)* encerar (**b**) *(skis)* encerar (**c**) **to have one's legs waxed** hacerse la cera en las piernas, depilarse las piernas *(con cera)*

wax[2] *vi* (**a**) *(moon)* crecer; **to w. and wane** tener altibajos (**b**) *(become)* **to w. lyrical (about)** ponerse lírico(a) *or* poético(a) (hablando de)

waxbill ['wæksbɪl] *n* estrilda *f* ondulada

waxed [wækst] *adj (cloth, paper)* encerado(a); **a w. jacket** una chaqueta impermeable de algodón

waxen ['wæksən] *adj* (**a**) *(resembling wax) (complexion)* céreo(a) (**b**) *(made of wax) (candle, figure)* de cera

waxwing ['wækswɪŋ] *n* ampelis *m inv*

waxwork ['wækswɜːk] *n* **w. (dummy)** figura *f* de cera; **waxworks** museo *m* de cera

waxy ['wæksɪ] *adj* céreo(a)

WAY [weɪ] 1 *n* **(a)** *(route) also Fig* camino *m*; **the w. to the station** el camino a *or Esp* de la estación; **could you tell me the w. to the station?** ¿me podría decir dónde queda la estación?; **we went back the w. we came** volvimos por donde habíamos venido; **investment is the w. forward for our company** la inversión es el futuro de nuestra empresa; **the w. in** la entrada; **the w. out** la salida; **to ask the w.** preguntar cómo se va, preguntar el camino; **we couldn't find a w. across the river** no encontramos un lugar por donde vadear el río; **to find one's w. to a place** encontrar el camino (para llegar) a un sitio; **how did this book find its w. here?** ¿cómo ha venido a parar aquí este libro?; *Fig* **to find a w. out of** *or* **around a problem** encontrar la solución a un problema; *BrAut* **give w.** *(sign)* ceda el paso; *BrAut* **to give w. to sth/sb** ceder el paso a algo/alguien; *(give in)* ceder ante algo/alguien; **our excitement gave w. to nervousness** nuestra ilusión dio paso al nerviosismo; **to give w.** *(break)* ceder; **to go the wrong w.** equivocarse de camino; **I'm going your w., I'll give you a ride** voy en la misma dirección que tú, te llevo; *Fig* **she can go her own (sweet) w.** puede hacer lo que le venga en gana, puede hacer lo que se le antoje; **the two companies have decided to go their separate ways** las dos empresas han decidido irse cada una por su lado; **my girlfriend and I have gone our separate ways** mi novia y yo lo hemos dejado; **their latest plan went the w. of all the others** su último plan corrió la misma suerte que los demás; **to know one's w. about** *or* **around** *(area)* conocer la zona; *(job, subject)* conocer el tema; **to lead the w.** mostrar el camino; *Fig* marcar la pauta; **to lose one's w.** perderse; *Fig* despistarse; **to make one's w. to a place** dirigirse a un lugar; **we made our own w. there** fuimos cada uno por nuestra cuenta; **to make one's w. through the crowd** abrirse paso entre la multitud; *Fig* **to make one's w. in the world** abrirse camino en el mundo; *also Fig* **to make w. for sth/sb** dejar vía libre a algo/alguien; **to show sb the w.** indicar el camino a alguien; **he ate his w. through two loaves of bread** devoró dos barras de pan; *also Fig* **to be in the w.** estar en medio, *Am* estar en el medio del camino; **am I in your w.?** ¿te estorbo?; **that table is in the w. of the door** esa mesa bloquea la puerta; **a barrier blocked our w.** una barrera nos impedía el paso; *also Fig* **to get in the w.** ponerse en medio, *Am* ponerse en el medio del camino; **to stand in sb's w.** cerrar el paso a alguien; *Fig* interponerse en el camino de alguien; **I won't let anything stand** *or* **get in the w. of our victory** no dejaré que nada se interponga en nuestro camino hacia la victoria; **on the w.** *(during journey)* en el camino; **we saw them on the w. to the station** los vimos camino de la estación; **I can take you there, it's on my w.** te puedo llevar, me queda de camino; **I'm on my w.!** ¡(ya) voy!; **he was on his w. to Seville** iba camino *Esp* de *or Am* a Sevilla; **I bought a paper on my w. home** compré un periódico camino *Esp* de *or Am* a casa; **close the door on your w. out** cierra la puerta cuando salgas; **monetarist ideas are on the** *or* **their w. out** las ideas monetaristas están pasando de moda; **he reached the final, beating two former champions on** *or* **along the w.** alcanzó la final, derrotando a dos antiguos campeones en *or* por el camino; **they've got a baby on the w.** van a tener un bebé; **elections are on the w.** va a haber elecciones; **there's a postcard on its w. to you** te he mandado una postal; **he's on the w. to recovery** se está recuperando; **she is well on the w. to success** va camino del éxito; **we're well on the w. to finishing the project** el proyecto está bien avanzado; **I must be on my w.** debo irme ya; **we were soon on our w. again** nos pusimos en camino al poco rato; **out of the w.** *(isolated)* retirado(a), apartado(a); **it's out of my w., but I'll take you there** no me queda de camino, pero te llevaré, *RP* me queda trasmano, pero te llevo; *also Fig* **to get out of the w.** quitarse de en medio, *RP* salir del medio; **get out of my w.!** ¡quítate de en medio!, *RP* ¡salí del medio!; **I'd rather get the hard part out of the w. first** preferiría quitarme *or Am* sacarme de en medio primero la parte difícil; *also Fig* **to keep out of the w.** mantenerse alejado(a); **stay out of my w.** mantente alejado(a) de mí; *Fig* **he went out of his w. to help her** se esforzó por ayudarla; IDIOM **to go the w. of all flesh** pasar a mejor vida; *Hum* **love will find a w.** el amor prevalecerá ►► *Rel* ***W. of the Cross*** vía crucis *m inv*; *US Rail* ***w. station*** apeadero *m*

(b) *(distance)* **it's quite a w. to the station** hay un buen camino hasta la estación; **to go a part of/all the w.** hacer parte del/todo el camino; **a quarter of the w. through the movie** al cuarto de película; **move a little w. forwards** muévete un poco hacia delante; **we've walked a long w. today** hemos caminado mucho hoy; **to be a long w. from...** estar muy lejos de...; *Fig* **we have come a long w. since then** hemos progresado mucho desde entonces; **we've still got a long w. to go, we have a w. to go yet** todavía nos queda mucho camino por delante; **a little of this polish goes a long w.** este betún rinde *or Esp* cunde mucho; **you have to go a long w. back to find a better player** habría que remontarse a muchos años atrás para encontrar un jugador mejor; **to be a little/long w. off** *(in distance)* estar un poco/muy lejos; *(when guessing)* ir un poco/muy desencaminado(a); **my birthday is still a long w. off** todavía queda mucho tiempo para mi cumpleaños; **her apology went a long w. towards healing the rift** sus disculpas contribuyeron en buena medida a cerrar la brecha; **it is the best, by a long w.** es, con mucho, el mejor; **she has come all the w. from Australia** ha venido ni más ni menos que desde Australia; **I've come all this w. for nothing** he recorrido todo este camino para nada *or* en balde; **he ran all the w. to the top** subió corriendo hasta arriba del todo; **she took her complaint all the w. to the president** llevó su queja hasta el mismísimo presidente; **I read the article all the w. through** leí el artículo de principio a fin; **they range all the w. from Catholics to Buddhists** hay desde católicos hasta budistas; *Fam* **did you go all the w.** *or* **the whole w.?** *(have sex)* ¿llegaste a hacerlo?; IDIOM **I'm with you all the w.** tienes todo mi apoyo

(c) *(direction)* dirección *f*; **this/that w.** por aquí/allí; **which w....?** ¿en qué dirección...?; **which w. is the station?** ¿por dónde *or* cómo se va a la estación?; **which w. did you come here?** ¿por dónde viniste?; **it is unclear which w. they will vote in the presidential elections** no está claro por quién votarán en las elecciones presidenciales; **which w. up does it go?** ¿se pone hacia arriba o hacia abajo?; **your sweater is the wrong w. round** llevas el suéter del *or* al revés; **you've put the slides in the wrong w. round** has puesto las diapositivas al revés; **turn it the other w. round** dale la vuelta, *RP* dalo vuelta; **to look the other w.** *(in opposite direction)* mirar hacia el otro lado; *(ignore something)* hacer la vista gorda; *Fam* **down our w.** donde vivo yo; **if the chance comes your w.** si se te presenta la ocasión; **I don't like the w. things are going** no me gusta cómo van las cosas; **things are going our w.** las cosas nos están saliendo bien; **I was expected to win but the vote went the other w.** se esperaba que ganara yo, pero ganó el otro candidato; **we split the money three ways** dividimos el dinero en tres partes

(d) *(manner, method)* manera *f*, modo *m*, forma *f*; **he spoke to me in a threatening w.** me habló de modo *or* de forma amenazante; **in the same/this w.** de la misma/de esta manera; **in such a w. that...** de tal manera *or* modo *or* forma que...; **this/that w.** así; **to find a w. of doing sth** hallar la manera de hacer algo; **to go about sth the wrong w.** hacer algo de forma equivocada; **do it the w. I told you** hazlo (tal y) como te dije; **I don't like the w. he interrupts me all the time** no me gusta que me interrumpa todo el tiempo; **it's fascinating the w. it can change colour** es fascinante cómo cambia de color; **that's always the w. with young children** esto pasa siempre con niños pequeños; **that's the w.!** ¡así se hace!; **she prefers to do things her (own) w.** prefiere hacer las cosas a su manera; **let's try it your w.** hagámoslo a tu manera; **have it your w., then!** *Esp* venga pues *or Am* está bien, como tú quieras; **you can't have it all your (own) w.** no te puedes salir siempre con la tuya; **in her own w. she's quite nice** a su manera es buena chica; **trust should work both ways** la confianza debe ser mutua; **you can't have it both ways** o una cosa o la otra, pero no puedes tenerlo todo; **there's no w. of knowing** no hay forma de saberlo, *Esp* no se puede saber; **there's no w. I can help** me es imposible ayudar; **that's no w. to treat your brother!** ¡no trates así a tu hermano!; **one w. and another** se mire como se mire; **one w. or another** *(somehow or other)* de un modo u otro; **I don't mind one w. or the other** me da igual; **it's old and unreliable, but I wouldn't have it any other w.** es viejo y poco fiable, pero no lo cambiaría por nada; **w. of life** *(lifestyle)* estilo de vida; **it has become a w. of life to them** se ha convertido en un hecho cotidiano para ellos; **to my w. of thinking, the w. I see it** para mí, a mi parecer; **he doesn't mean to be rude, it's just his w.** no pretende ser grosero, es simplemente su manera de ser; *US Fam* **w. to go!** ¡bien hecho! ►► ***ways and means*** métodos *mpl*; **there are ways and means of...** existen maneras de...; *US Pol* ***ways and means committee*** = comisión presupuestaria de la Cámara de Representantes estadounidense

(e) *(habit, custom)* **the ways of our ancestors** las costumbres de nuestros antepasados; **I don't like her and her city ways** no me gustan ni ella ni sus costumbres urbanas; **to change one's ways** enmendarse, enmendar la plana; **to get used to sb's ways** acostumbrarse a la manera de ser de alguien; **to get into the w. of doing sth** acostumbrarse a hacer algo; **these things have a w. of happening to me** estas cosas siempre me pasan a mí; **as is the w. with these events...** como suele ocurrir en estos acontecimientos...; IDIOM **that's the w. of the world** este mundo va así

(f) *(street)* calle *f*; **over** *or* **across the w.** enfrente

(g) *(respect)* sentido *m*; **in a w.** en cierto sentido; **in every w.** en todos los sentidos; **in more ways than one** en más de un sentido; **in many ways** en muchos sentidos; **in no w.** de ningún modo; **in one w.** en cierto sentido; **in some ways** en cierto sentido, *Esp* en ciertos sentidos; **I hope I have helped, in some small w.** espero haber ayudado de alguna manera o de otra; **there are no two ways about it** no hay duda alguna *or* lugar a dudas (**h**) *(state, condition)* **to be in a good/bad w.** *(business)* marchar bien/mal; **to be in a bad w.** *(person)* estar mal; **given the w. things are** dadas las circunstancias; **we left the flat the w. it was** dejamos el piso tal y como estaba; **is he staying here? – it looks that w.** ¿se aloja aquí? – eso parece; **I'm in charge and I'm going to keep it that w.** aquí mando yo y eso pienso seguir haciendo

(**i**) *(skill, talent)* **he has a w. with children** se le dan bien los niños, se lleva muy bien con los niños; **she has a w. with words** tiene facilidad de palabra, *Esp* tiene un pico de oro; **she has a (certain) w. with her** tiene ese algo especial; **trouble has a w. of showing up when least expected** los problemas se presentan cuando menos te los esperas

(**j**) *(wish)* **he got his (own) w.** se salió con la suya; **if I had my w....** si por mi fuera...; *Fam* **to have one's (wicked) w. with sb** hacer el amor *or Esp* hacérselo *or RP* fifar con alguien

(**k**) *US Fam (distance)* **it's a ways from here** está a una buena tirada de aquí

2 *adv Fam* mucho; **w. ahead/behind** mucho más adelante/atrás; **the German is w. ahead/behind** el alemán va muy destacado/retrasado; **their technology is w. ahead of/behind ours** su tecnología está mucho más avanzada/retrasada que la nuestra; **w. back in the 1920s** allá en los años 20; **we go w. back** nos conocemos desde hace mucho (tiempo); **w. down south** muy al sur; **w. off in the distance** muy a lo lejos; **your guess was w. out** ibas muy desencaminado; **it's w. past my bedtime** normalmente a estas horas ya llevaría dormido un buen rato; **it was w. too easy** fue exageradamente fácil; **she drinks w. too much** bebe *or Am* toma en exceso; **he's w. crazy** ¡está como una regadera!; *US* **it's about w. high** *(with gesture)* es así de alto

3 by the way *adv* a propósito, por cierto; **I bring up this point by the w.** menciono este punto de pasada; **that point is quite by the w.** ese punto apenas tiene importancia

4 by way of *prep* (**a**) *(via)* por, vía; **we went by w. of Amsterdam** fuimos por *or* vía Amsterdam, pasamos por Amsterdam (**b**) *(serving as)* **by w. of an introduction/a warning** a modo de introducción/advertencia

5 in the way of *prep* **we don't have much in the w. of food** no tenemos mucha comida; **what do you have in the w. of desserts?** ¿qué postres tienen?

6 no way *adv Fam* **can I borrow it? – no w.!** ¿me lo dejas? – ¡ni hablar! *or Esp* ¡de eso nada!; *US* **we're getting married – no w.!** *(expressing surprise)* nos vamos a casar – ¡no me digas *or Esp* fastidies!; **there's no w. that's Antonio Banderas!** ¡ese no es Antonio Banderas ni de broma!; **no w. am I going to help them** ni de casualidad les voy a ayudar; *Fam* **no w., José!** de eso nada, monada

---

waybill ['weɪbɪl] *n (in road transport)* hoja *f* de ruta; *(in air or sea transport)* conocimiento *m* de embarque (aéreo/marítimo)

wayfarer ['weɪfeərə(r)] *n Literary* caminante *mf*

wayfaring ['weɪfeərɪŋ] *adj Literary* caminante, viajero(a); **a w. life** una vida errante

waylay [weɪ'leɪ] (*pt & pp* **waylaid** [weɪ'leɪd]) *vt (attack)* atracar, asaltar; *Fig (stop)* abordar, detener; **sorry I'm late, I got waylaid** perdón por el retraso *or* la demora, pero es que me han entretenido

way-out [weɪ'aʊt] *adj Fam* extravagante

wayside ['weɪsaɪd] *n* borde *m* de la carretera; IDIOM **to fall by the w.** irse a paseo

wayward ['weɪwəd] *adj* rebelde, desmandado(a)

waywardness ['weɪwədnɪs] *n* rebeldía *f*

WBA ['dʌbəlju:bi:'eɪ] *n* (*abbr* **World Boxing Association**) AMB *f*, Asociación *f* Mundial de Boxeo

WBC ['dʌbəlju:bi:'si:] *n* (*abbr* **World Boxing Council**) CMB *m*, Consejo *m* Mundial de Boxeo

WBO ['dʌbəlju:bi:'əʊ] *n* (*abbr* **World Boxing Organization**) OMB *f*, Organización *f* Mundial de Boxeo

WC ['dʌbəlju:'si:] *n* (*abbr* **water closet**) váter *m*, retrete *m*

WCC ['dʌbəlju:si:'si:] (*abbr* **World Council of Churches**) = asamblea ecuménica de iglesias, excluida la católica romana

---

WE [wi:] *pron* (**a**) *(first person plural)* nosotros(as) *(usually omitted in Spanish, except for contrast)*; **we're Scottish** somos escoceses; **we like red wine** nos gusta el vino tinto; **WE haven't got it!** ¡nosotros no lo tenemos!; **w. alone know** sólo lo sabemos nosotros; **as we say in Canada** como decimos en Canadá; **as we saw in Chapter 5** como vimos en el capítulo 5; **we Spanish are...** (nosotros) los españoles somos...

(**b**) *Formal (first person singular) (used by royalty)* nos; **we do not agree** no estamos de acuerdo; *Hum* **I hope he was using the royal "we"** espero que estuviera hablando en primera persona, espero que no nos estuviera incluyendo a todos nosotros

(**c**) *Fam (second person singular)* **we don't want you getting your clothes dirty, do we?** no te vayas a ensuciar la ropa, ¿eh?; **and how are we today?** ¿cómo estamos hoy?

WEA ['dʌbəlju:i:'eɪ] *n Br* (*abbr* **Workers' Educational Association**) = asociación para la educación de adultos

weak [wi:k] *adj* (**a**) *(physically) (person)* débil; *(structure)* endeble, frágil; **to grow w.** debilitarse; **to have a w. heart** estar mal del corazón; **she managed a w. smile** pudo esbozar una débil *or* tímida sonrisa; **she answered in a w. voice** contestó débilmente, contestó con un hilo de voz; *Old-fashioned* **the weaker sex** el sexo débil; *Fig* **she went w. at the knees** le empezaron a temblar las piernas; **he's the w. link in the chain** es el eslabón más débil de la cadena; **he has a w. chin** tiene el mentón poco marcado ►► *also Fig* ***w. spot*** punto *m* débil *or* flaco

(**b**) *(emotionally, intellectually)* débil; **to be w. in the head** ser corto(a) de entendederas; **one of the weaker students in the class** uno de los alumnos más flojos de la clase; **to be w. at physics** estar flojo en física; **in a w. moment** en un momento de debilidad ►► ***w. point*** punto *m* débil *or* flaco

(**c**) *(excuse, reasoning, case)* flojo(a), pobre; *(army, government, institution, leader)* débil

(**d**) *(tea)* flojo(a); *(beer)* suave; *(alcoholic drink, coffee)* poco(a) cargado(a)

(**e**) *Econ (currency, economy)* débil

(**f**) *Gram & Ling (verb)* regular; *(syllable)* átono(a)

weaken ['wi:kən] **1** *vt* (**a**) *(person, health, structure, government)* debilitar; **to w. sb's hold on power** socavar la posición de poder de alguien; **this weakens your case** esto hace que tu argumentación se tambalee; **to w. sb's resolve** hacer flaquear a alguien (**b**) *Econ (currency, economy)* debilitar

2 *vi* (**a**) *(person, health, determination)* debilitarse; **to w. in one's resolve (to do sth)** flaquear (a la hora de hacer algo) (**b**) *Econ (currency, economy)* debilitarse; **the dollar has weakened against the euro** el dólar ha perdido terreno *or* se ha debilitado frente al euro

weakening ['wi:kənɪŋ] *adj* (**a**) *(debilitating)* debilitante (**b**) *(losing strength) (powers)* en declive; *(resolve)* menguante

weak-kneed [wi:k'ni:d] *adj Fig* débil de carácter, pusilánime

weakling ['wi:klɪŋ] *n* enclenque *mf*, canijo(a) *m,f*

weakly ['wi:klɪ] *adv (to speak)* débilmente, con un hilo de voz; *(to smile)* débilmente, tímidamente; *(to protest)* sin convicción

weak-minded ['wi:k'maɪndɪd] *adj* (**a**) *(simple-minded)* corto(a) de entendederas (**b**) *(lacking willpower)* con poco carácter

weakness ['wi:knɪs] *n* (**a**) *(lack of strength) (of person)* debilidad *f*; *(of structure, defences)* endeblez *f*, fragilidad *f* (**b**) *(of leadership)* fragilidad *f*, debilidad *f*; **w. of character** falta de personalidad; **in a moment of w.** en un momento de debilidad (**c**) *(of argument, reasoning)* pobreza *f* (**d**) *(weak point)* punto *m* débil, defecto *m*; **to have a w. for sth/sb** *(liking)* sentir *or* tener debilidad por algo/alguien

weak-willed ['wi:k'wɪld] *adj* sin fuerza de voluntad

weal [wi:l] *n* (**a**) *(mark on skin)* señal *f*, verdugón *m* (**b**) *Archaic or Literary (wellbeing)* bienestar *m*; **the common** *or* **public w.** el bien común

wealth [welθ] *n* (**a**) *(riches)* riqueza *f*; **a man of great w.** un hombre muy rico *or* con una gran fortuna ►► ***w. creation*** generación *f* de riqueza; ***w. tax*** impuesto *m* sobre el patrimonio (**b**) *(large quantity)* (gran) abundancia *f*, profusión *f*; **he provided them with a w. of information about the area** les facilitó un amplio caudal de información sobre la zona

wealthy ['welθɪ] **1** *npl* **the w.** los ricos

2 *adj (person, family)* rico(a), pudiente; *(country, city)* rico(a)

wean [wi:n] *vt (baby)* destetar; *Fig* **a generation of children weaned on Hollywood movies** una generación de niños que ha crecido *or* que se ha criado viendo películas de Hollywood; *Fig* **to w. sb from** *or* **off a bad habit** quitar *or Am* sacarle una mala costumbre a alguien; **he was trying to w. himself off cigarettes** estaba intentando dejar el tabaco

weapon ['wepən] *n* arma *f*; **weapons of mass destruction** armas de destrucción masiva; *Fig* **high interest rates are seen as a w. against inflation** los tipos de interés altos se tienen por herramientas para combatir la inflación

weaponry ['wepənrɪ] *n* armamento *m*

WEAR [weə(r)] **1** *n* (**a**) *(clothing)* ropa *f*; **for everyday w.** para llevar a diario; **women's/children's w.** ropa de mujer/de niño; **evening/casual w.** ropa de noche/de esport

(**b**) *(use)* uso *m*; **it still has a bit more w. left in it** todavía debería durar una temporada; **to get a lot of w. out of sth** aprovechar mucho algo

(**c**) *(damage)* **w. (and tear)** deterioro *m*, desgaste *m*; **fair** *or* **normal**

w. and tear desgaste natural por el uso; **the sheets are beginning to show signs of w.** las sábanas comienzan a desgastarse

2 *vt* (*pt* **wore** [wɔː(r)], *pp* **worn** [wɔːn]) (**a**) *(garment, glasses, seat belt, watch)* llevar (puesto(a)); *(perfume, make-up)* llevar; **what are you going to w. (to the wedding)?** ¿qué te vas a poner (para la boda)?; **I've got nothing to w. to the wedding** no tengo nada que ponerme para la boda; **she wore a ribbon in her hair** llevaba un lazo en el pelo; **to w. black** ir de negro; **to w. a beard** llevar barba; **to w. one's hair long** llevar el pelo largo

(**b**) *(expression)* **she wore a frown** fruncía el ceño; **he wore a bemused expression** tenía una expresión de perplejidad

(**c**) *(erode)* desgastar; **to w. a hole in sth** terminar haciendo un agujero en algo; **a path had been worn across the lawn** se había ido formando un camino en el césped *(por el paso de la gente)*; IDIOM **to w. oneself to a frazzle** deslomarse, deriñonarse

(**d**) *Br Fam (accept)* **she won't w. it** por ahí no va a pasar

3 *vi* (**a**) *(become damaged through use)* **this sweater is starting to w. at the elbows** este suéter está comenzado a desgastarse en los codos; **to w. thin** *(clothes)* gastarse, desgastarse; **that excuse is wearing thin** esa excusa ya no sirve; **that joke is wearing thin** esa broma ha dejado de tener gracia; **my patience is wearing thin** se me está acabando la paciencia

(**b**) *(endure, last)* durar; **it's worn well** *(clothing)* ha durado mucho; *(movie)* ha aguantado (bien) el paso del tiempo; **he's worn well** se conserva muy bien; **the movie has not worn well** la película no ha aguantado el paso del tiempo

(**c**) *Literary (time)* **as morning wore into afternoon** conforme se acercaba la tarde; **as the year wore to its close** conforme se acababa el año

▸ **wear away** 1 *vt sep* gastar, desgastar

2 *vi* desgastarse

▸ **wear down** 1 *vt sep* (**a**) *(erode)* gastar, desgastar (**b**) *(tire)* agotar, extenuar; **he tried to w. his opponent down** intentó agotar a su rival

2 *vi (erode)* desgastarse

▸ **wear off** *vi* (**a**) *(pain, effect)* pasar; *(enthusiasm, excitement, novelty)* desvanecerse; **when the anaesthetic wears off** cuando pase el efecto de la anestesia (**b**) *(design)* desgastarse

▸ **wear on** *vi (time)* transcurrir, pasar

▸ **wear out** 1 *vt sep* (**a**) *(clothes)* gastar, desgastar; *(batteries)* gastar; *(machinery)* deteriorar (**b**) *(person, patience, reserves)* agotar; **to w. oneself out** agotarse; IDIOM **to w. out one's welcome** hacerse pesado(a)

2 *vi (clothes)* gastarse, desgastarse; *(batteries)* gastarse; *(machinery)* deteriorarse

▸ **wear through** 1 *vt sep* agujerear

2 *vi* agujerearse; **my sweater has worn through at the elbows** se me han agujereado los codos del suéter

---

wearer ['weərə(r)] *n* **wearers of glasses** los que llevan gafas *or Am* anteojos *or Am* lentes; **these gloves protect the w. from getting burned** estos guantes protegen al que los lleva puestos de quemaduras

wearily ['wɪərɪlɪ] *adv (to walk)* cansinamente; *(to lean, sit down)* con aire de cansancio; *(to sigh)* fatigosamente

weariness ['wɪərɪnɪs] *n (tiredness)* fatiga *f*, cansancio *m*; *(boredom)* hastío *m*, cansancio *m*

wearing ['weərɪŋ] *adj (tiring)* fatigoso(a); *(annoying)* exasperante; **to be w. on the nerves** sacar de quicio

wearisome ['wɪərɪsəm] *adj (boring)* tedioso(a); *(tiring)* fatigoso(a); *(annoying)* exasperante

weary ['wɪərɪ] 1 *adj (physically tired)* fatigado(a), cansado(a) (**of** de); *(bored)* hastiado(a), cansado(a) (**of** de); **to grow w. of sth** hastiarse *or* cansarse de algo

2 *vt (tire)* fatigar, cansar; *(annoy)* hastiar

3 *vi* hartarse, cansarse (**of** de)

wearying ['wɪərɪɪŋ] *adj* **I find her/city life quite w.** ella/la vida en la ciudad me cansa *or* hastía

weasel ['wiːzəl] *n* comadreja *f*; *Pej (person)* zorrón(ona) *m,f* ▸▸ *Fam Pej* ***w. words*** términos *mpl* ambiguos

weather ['weðə(r)] 1 *n* tiempo *m*; **what's the w. like?** ¿qué (tal) tiempo hace?; **the w. is good/bad** hace buen/mal tiempo; **in this w.** con este tiempo; **in hot w.** con calor, cuando hace calor; **in all weathers** haga frío o calor; **w. permitting** si el tiempo lo permite; IDIOM **to keep a w. eye open for sth** estar atento(a) a algo; IDIOM **I'll keep a w. eye on the kids** no perderé de vista a los niños; IDIOM **to make heavy w. of sth** hacer una montaña de algo; IDIOM **to be/feel under the w.** *(ill)* estar/encontrarse pachucho(a) ▸▸ ***w. balloon*** globo *m* sonda; *US* ***w. bureau*** servicio *m or* instituto *m* meteorológico; ***w. conditions*** condiciones *fpl* atmosféricas *or* meteorológicas; ***w. forecast*** pronóstico *m* del tiempo, boletín *m or* parte *m* meteorológico; ***w. forecaster*** meteorólogo(a) *m,f*; ***w. map*** mapa *m* del tiempo; ***w. report*** pronóstico *m* del tiempo, boletín *m or* parte *m* meteorológico; ***w. station*** estación *f* meteorológica, observatorio *m* meteorológico; ***w. vane*** veleta *f*

2 *vt (rock)* erosionar; *Fig (crisis, scandal)* capear; **to w. the storm** capear el temporal

3 *vi (rock)* erosionarse

weatherbeaten ['weðəbiːtən] *adj (person, face)* curtido(a); *(cliff, rock)* erosionado(a)

weatherboard ['weðəbɔːd] *n* tabla *f* superpuesta

weather-bound ['weðəbaʊnd] *adj (ships, planes, people)* detenido(a) por el mal tiempo; *(port, town, airport)* paralizado(a) por el mal tiempo

weathercock ['weðəkɒk] *n* (**a**) *(weather vane)* veleta *f* (**b**) *(changeable person)* veleta *mf*

weathered ['weðəd] *adj (face)* curtido(a); *(wall)* deteriorado(a) por las inclemencias del tiempo

weathergirl ['weðəgɜːl] *n* mujer *f* del tiempo

weathering ['weðərɪŋ] *n Geol* erosión *f*

weatherlady ['weðəleɪdɪ] *n* mujer *f* del tiempo

weatherman ['weðəmæn] *n* hombre *m* del tiempo

weatherproof ['weðəpruːf] *adj (paint, building, windows)* resistente (a las inclemencias del tiempo); *(clothing)* impermeable

weather-worn ['weðəwɔːn] *adj (features, visage)* curtido(a); *(house)* deteriorado(a) por las inclemencias del tiempo

weave [wiːv] 1 *n (pattern)* tejido *m*

2 *vt* (*pt* **weaved** *or* **wove** [wəʊv], *pp* **weaved** *or* **woven** ['wəʊvən]) *(cloth, web, basket)* tejer; *(garland)* hacer; **to w. the threads together** entretejer los hilos; *Fig* **a skilfully woven plot** una trama muy bien urdida; **he managed to w. all the facts together in his report** logró relacionar todos los datos en su informe; **political elements have been woven into the plot** en el argumento se han intercalado cuestiones políticas

3 *vi* (**a**) *(make cloth)* tejer (**b**) *(move)* **to w. through the traffic** avanzar zigzagueando entre el tráfico

weaver ['wiːvə(r)] *n* tejedor(ora) *m,f* ▸▸ ***w. bird*** tejedor *m*

weaving ['wiːvɪŋ] *n* tejeduría *f*

web [web] *n* (**a**) *(of spider)* telaraña *f*, tela *f* de araña; *Fig (of lies, intrigue)* trama *f* (**b**) *(of duck, frog)* membrana *f* interdigital (**c**) *Comptr* **the W.** la Web ▸▸ ***w. address*** dirección *f* web; ***w. authoring*** creación *f* de páginas web; ***w. browser*** navegador *m*; ***w. cam*** cámara *f* web; ***w. design agency*** agencia *f* de diseño de páginas web; ***w. designer*** diseñador(ora) *m,f* de páginas web; ***w. hosting*** hospedaje *m* de páginas web; ***w. page*** página *f* web; ***w. server*** servidor *m* web; ***w. space*** espacio *m* web

webbed [webd] *adj (foot)* palmeado(a)

webbing ['webɪŋ] *n (on chair, bed)* cinchas *fpl*

web-footed [web'fʊtɪd] *adj (bird)* palmípedo(a); *(animal)* con membrana interdigital

Webmaster ['webmɑːstə(r)] *n Comptr* administrador(ora) *m,f* de (sitio) web, webmaster *mf*

website ['websaɪt] *n Comptr* sitio *m* web

webzine ['webziːn] *n Comptr* webzine *m*, ciberrevista *f*

Wed (*abbr* **Wednesday**) mier.

wed [wed] (*pt & pp* **wedded**) 1 *vt* (**a**) *(marry) (of bride, groom)* casarse con; *(of priest)* desposar, casar; **lawfully wedded wife** legítima esposa; **lawfully wedded husband** legítimo esposo; **the newly wedded couple** los recién casados

(**b**) *(combine, link)* **to w. sth to sth** casar *or* enlazar algo con algo; **to be wedded to** *(principle, cause, one's work)* estar entregado(a) en cuerpo y alma a; **the fate of the project was wedded to that of the Chairman** la suerte del proyecto estaba ligada directamente a la del presidente; **intelligence wedded to beauty** inteligencia aliada con *or* acompañada de belleza

2 *vi* casarse, desposarse

we'd [wiːd] = **we had, we would**

wedding ['wedɪŋ] *n* boda *f*, *Andes* matrimonio *m*, *RP* casamiento *m*; **to have a church w.** casarse por la iglesia, *Andes, RP* casarse por iglesia; **we had a quiet w.** la boda se celebró en la intimidad ▸▸ ***w. anniversary*** aniversario *m* de boda *or Andes* matrimonio *or RP* casamiento; ***w. breakfast*** banquete *m* de bodas *or Andes* matrimonio *or RP* casamiento; ***w. cake*** tarta *f or* pastel *m* de boda, *Andes* torta *f* de matrimonio, *RP* torta *f* de casamiento; ***w. day*** día *m* de la boda *or Andes* del matrimonio *or RP* del casamiento; ***w. dress*** traje *m or* vestido *m* de novia; ***w. invitation*** invitación *f* de boda *or Andes* matrimonio *or RP* casamiento; ***w. list*** lista *f* de boda *or Andes* matrimonio *or RP* casamiento; ***w. march*** marcha *f* nupcial; ***w. night*** noche *f* de bodas; ***w. reception*** banquete *m* de boda *or Andes* matrimonio *or RP* casamiento; ***w. ring*** alianza *f*, anillo *m* de boda *or Andes* matrimonio *or RP* casamiento; *Fam Hum* ***w. tackle*** *(man's genitals)* las vergüenzas

wedge [wedʒ] **1** *n* **(a)** *(for door, wheel)* cuña *f*, calzo *m*; *(for splitting stone, wood)* cuña *f*; IDIOM **it has driven a w. between them** los ha enemistado **(b)** *(of cake, pie)* trozo *m* grande; *(of cheese)* trozo *m* **(c)** *(golf club)* cucharilla *f* **(d)** *(shoe heel)* alza *f*, tacón *m* de cuña, *Andes, RP* taco *m* chino **(e)** *Br Fam (money) Esp, RP* guita *f*, *Am* plata *f*, *Méx* lana *f*

2 *vt (insert)* encajar; **to w. a door open** calzar una puerta para dejarla abierta; **he wedged his foot in the door** puso un pie en la puerta para que no se cerrara; **to be wedged between two things** estar encajado(a) *or* encajonado(a) entre dos cosas; **she sat wedged between her two aunts** se sentaba apretujada entre sus dos tías; **to be wedged into sth** estar encajado(a) en algo

wedgie [wedʒɪ] *n Fam* **to give sb a w.** = tirarle a alguien para arriba de los pantalones/la ropa interior como broma (para que se le remetan por la entrepierna)

wedlock ['wedlɒk] *n Law* matrimonio *m*; **to be born out of w.** nacer fuera del matrimonio

Wednesday ['wenzdɪ] *n* miércoles *m inv*; *see also* **Saturday**

wee[1] [wi:] *adj Irish, Scot Fam* pequeño(a), chiquito(a); **a w. bit** un poquito; **a w. boy** un niñito, un chavalín; **the w. small hours** la madrugada

wee[2] *Br Fam* **1** *n* **to do** *or* **have a w.** *(urinate)* hacer pipí

2 *vi* hacer pipí

weed [wi:d] **1** *n* **(a)** *(plant)* mala hierba *f* **(b)** *Br Fam (weak person) (physically)* debilucho(a) *m,f*; *(lacking character)* blandengue *mf* **(c)** *Fam* **the w.** *(tobacco)* el tabaco, *Esp* el fumeque **(d)** *Fam (marijuana)* hierba *f*, maría *f*

2 weeds *npl* (ropa *f* de) luto *m*; **in widow's weeds** vestida de luto

3 *vt (garden)* escardar

▸**weed out** *vt sep Fig (people, applications)* descartar; *(mistakes)* eliminar

weeding ['wi:dɪŋ] *n* escarda *f*, limpieza *f* de las malas hierbas; **to do the w.** escardar, limpiar las malas hierbas

weedkiller ['wi:dkɪlə(r)] *n* herbicida *m*

weedy ['wi:dɪ] *adj Fam (person)* enclenque

week [wi:k] *n* semana *f*; **next w.** la semana que viene; **last w.** la semana pasada; **every w.** todas las semanas; **during the w.** *(not at weekend)* entre semana; **yesterday w., a w. yesterday** hace ayer una semana; **Monday w., a w. on Monday** una semana a partir del lunes, este lunes no, el otro; **once/twice a w.** una vez/dos veces a la *or* por semana; **a three/four day w.** una semana laboral de tres/cuatro días; **the working w.** la semana laboral; **within a w.** en el plazo de una semana; **in a w., in a w.'s time** dentro de una semana; **I haven't seen her for** *or* **in weeks** no la he visto desde hace semanas; **w. in w. out, w. after w.** semana tras semana; **tomorrow/Tuesday w.** de mañana/del martes en ocho días

weekday ['wi:kdeɪ] *n* día *m* entre semana, día *m* laborable; **weekdays only** sólo laborables; **on w. mornings** entre semana *or* los días laborables por la mañana

weekend [wi:k'end] *n* fin *m* de semana; *Br* **at** *or US* **on the w.** el fin de semana; **have a good w.!** ¡(que tengas un) buen fin de semana!; **a long w.** un fin de semana largo, ≃ un puente ▸▸ ***w. break*** vacaciones *fpl* de fin de semana

weekender [wi:k'ende(r)] *n* visitante *mf* de fin de semana

weekly ['wi:klɪ] **1** *adj* semanal; **these incidents were an almost w. occurrence** este tipo de incidentes tenía lugar casi todas las semanas

2 *adv* semanalmente; **twice w.** dos veces por semana *or* a la semana

3 *n (newspaper)* semanario *m*

weeknight ['wi:knaɪt] *n* noche *f* de entre semana

weenie ['wi:nɪ], **wiener** ['wi:nə(r)] *n US Fam* **(a)** *(frankfurter)* salchicha *f* (de Fráncfort) **(b)** *(penis)* pito *m*, pilila *f*

weeny ['wi:nɪ] *adj Fam* chiquitín(ina), chiquitito(a)

weep [wi:p] **1** *n* **to have a good w.** desahogarse llorando

2 *vt* (*pt & pp* **wept** [wept]) **to w. tears of joy/anger** llorar de alegría/rabia; **she wept bitter tears** lloró lágrimas de amargura

3 *vi* **(a)** *(person)* llorar (**for/over** por); **it's enough to make you w.** es como para echarse a llorar; **to w. with joy** llorar de alegría **(b)** *(wound, sore)* supurar

weeping ['wi:pɪŋ] **1** *n* llanto *m*

2 *adj* lloroso(a) ▸▸ ***w. willow*** sauce *m* llorón

weepy ['wi:pɪ] *Fam* **1** *n (book, film)* obra *f* lacrimógena *or Chile* cebollera

2 *adj (book, film, ending)* lacrimógeno(a), *Chile* cebollero(a); **to be w.** *(person)* estar lloroso(a)

weevil ['wi:vɪl] *n* gorgojo *m*

wee(-)wee ['wi:wi:] *n Fam* **to do a w.** *(urinate)* hacer pipí

wef *Com* (*abbr* **with effect from**) a partir de

weft [weft] *n Tex* trama *f*

weigh [weɪ] **1** *vt* **(a)** *(measure)* pesar; **to w. oneself** pesarse

(b) *(consider)* sopesar; **he weighed his words carefully** midió bien sus palabras; **to w. one thing against another** sopesar una cosa frente a otra, contraponer una cosa a otra; **to w. the consequences** estudiar *or* sopesar las consecuencias

(c) *Naut* **to w. anchor** levar anclas

2 *vi* pesar; **it weighs 2 kilos** pesa 2 kilos; **how much do you w.?** ¿cuánto pesas?; **it's weighing on my conscience** me remuerde la conciencia; **her experience weighed in her favour** su experiencia inclinó la balanza a su favor; **the evidence weighs heavily against him** las pruebas están claramente en su contra

▸**weigh down** *vt sep* cargar; **the branches were weighed down with snow** las ramas estaban dobladas bajo el peso de la nieve; **all the extra equipment was weighing me down** todo el equipo adicional me pesaba mucho; *Fig* **to be weighed down with grief** estar abrumado(a) por la pena

▸**weigh in** *vi* **(a)** *(boxer, jockey)* pesarse; **to w. in at...** dar un peso de... **(b)** *Fam (join in)* tomar parte

▸**weigh out** *vt sep* pesar

▸**weigh up** *vt sep (situation, chances)* sopesar; **to w. up the pros and cons** sopesar los pros y los contras

weighbridge ['weɪbrɪdʒ] *n* báscula *f* de puente

weigh-in ['weɪɪn] *n (in boxing, horse racing)* pesaje *m*

weight [weɪt] **1** *n* **(a)** *(of person, object)* peso *m*; **they're the same w.** pesan lo mismo; **what a w.!** ¡cómo *or* cuánto pesa!; **that case must be quite a w.** esa maleta debe de pesar mucho; **to lose w.** adelgazar, perder peso; **to put on** *or* **gain w.** engordar, ganar peso; **to have a w. problem** tener problemas de peso; **she's watching her w.** está cuidándose para no engordar; *Hum* **take the w. off your feet** siéntate y descansa

(b) *(for scales, of clock)* pesa *f*; **weights and measures** pesos y medidas; **to lift weights** levantar pesas; **don't lift any heavy weights** no levante cosas pesadas ▸▸ ***w. training*** gimnasia *f* con pesas

(c) *(load)* peso *m*, carga *f*

(d) IDIOMS **that's a w. off my mind** me he quitado *or Am* sacado un peso de encima; **to carry w.** influir, tener peso; **to lend w. to an argument** dar consistencia a un argumento; **to take the w. off one's feet** descansar un rato; **she tends to throw her w. about** *or* **around** tiende a abusar de su autoridad; **she threw her w. behind the candidate/project** utilizó su influencia para apoyar al candidato/el proyecto; **she's worth her w. in gold** vale su peso en oro

2 *vt* **(a)** *(make heavier)* cargar **(b)** *(bias)* **the system is weighted in his favour** el sistema juega a su favor *or* le favorece; **the electoral system is weighted against them** el sistema electoral juega en su contra *or* los perjudica

▸**weight down** *vt sep* sujetar *(con un peso)*

weighted ['weɪtɪd] *adj (mean, average)* ponderado(a)

weighting ['weɪtɪŋ] *n Br Fin* ponderación *f*; **London w.** *(in salary)* = compensación salarial que sirve para equilibrar el coste de la vida en Londres

weightless ['weɪtlɪs] *adj* ingrávido(a)

weightlessness ['weɪtlɪsnɪs] *n* ingravidez *f*

weightlifter ['weɪtlɪftə(r)] *n* levantador(ora) *m,f* de pesas

weightlifting ['weɪtlɪftɪŋ] *n* halterofilia *f*, levantamiento *m* de pesas; **to do w.** levantar pesas

weightwatcher ['weɪtwɒtʃə(r)] *n* persona *f* a dieta

weighty ['weɪtɪ] *adj* **(a)** *(load, object)* pesado(a) **(b)** *(problem, matter)* grave; *(reason)* de peso

weir [wɪə(r)] *n* presa *f*

weird [wɪəd] *adj* (**a**) *Fam (odd)* raro(a), extraño(a); **one of his w. and wonderful schemes** uno de sus descabellados y maravillosos planes; **it felt w. to be back in his home town again** le parecía extraño estar en su pueblo natal otra vez (**b**) *(eerie, uncanny) (atmosphere, figure)* fantasmagórico(a), misterioso(a)

weirdly ['wɪədlɪ] *adv* (**a**) *Fam (oddly)* extrañamente; **she was w. dressed** iba vestida de forma extravagante (**b**) *(eerily, uncannily)* fantasmagóricamente

weirdness ['wɪədnɪs] *n* extravagancia *f*, rareza *f*

weirdo ['wɪədəʊ] (*pl* **weirdos**) *n Fam* bicho *m* raro

welch = **welsh**

welcome ['welkəm] 1 *n* bienvenida *f*; **she said a few words of w.** pronunció unas palabras de bienvenida; **they gave him a warm w.** le dieron una calurosa bienvenida *or* un caluroso recibimiento, lo recibieron calurosamente

2 *adj* (**a**) *(person)* bienvenido(a); *(news, change)* grato(a); **I don't feel w. here** siento que no soy bienvenido(a) aquí; **a cold beer is always w. on a day like this** una cerveza bien fresca siempre sienta bien en días así; **that would be most w.** *(food, drink etc)* vendría muy bien, sería muy de agradecer; **to make sb w.** ser hospitalario(a) con alguien; **to give sth/sb a warm w.** dar una calurosa acogida a algo/alguien; **thank you very much – you're w.!** muchas gracias – de nada *or* no hay de qué; **you're always w.** siempre serás bienvenido; **you're w. to borrow it** tómalo *or Esp* cógelo prestado cuando quieras; **he's w. to it** es todo suyo; **that's w. news** es una buena noticia; **it's a w. change from housework/proofreading!** ¡cómo se agradece dejar un poco las tareas domésticas/la corrección de pruebas! ▸▸ *Comptr* ***w. message*** mensaje *m* de bienvenida

(**b**) *(in greetings)* **w. home!** ¡bienvenido(a) a casa!; **w. to Mexico!** ¡bienvenido(a) a México!

3 *vt (person)* dar la bienvenida a; *(news, change)* acoger favorablemente; **she welcomed them warmly** les dio una calurosa bienvenida *or* un caluroso recibimiento, los recibió calurosamente; **we welcomed him with open arms** lo recibimos con los brazos abiertos; **would you please w. Tiger Woods!** *(to audience)* ¡les pido un fuerte aplauso para Tiger Woods!; **we w. this change** este cambio nos parece muy positivo; **we w. the opportunity to work with a new company** nos complace poder trabajar con una nueva empresa; **she welcomed any comments on her presentation** invitó a los presentes a aportar comentarios sobre su presentación; **his comments weren't welcomed** sus comentarios no fueron bien recibidos

▸**welcome back** *vt sep* recibir de nuevo, dar la bienvenida a; **we welcomed her back after her illness** le dimos la bienvenida después de su enfermedad; *Rad & TV* **I am pleased to w. back Billy Bragg** me complace recibir una vez más *or* dar de nuevo la bienvenida a Billy Bragg

welcoming ['welkəmɪŋ] *adj (person, attitude)* afable, hospitalario(a); **a w. party met them at the airport** un grupo de personas los recibió *or* les dio la bienvenida en el aeropuerto ▸▸ ***w. committee*** comité *m* de bienvenida

weld [weld] 1 *n* soldadura *f*

2 *vt* soldar; **to w. parts together** soldar piezas; **a set of policies that will w. the party into a united political force** un programa político que aúne *or* unifique al partido

welder ['weldə(r)] *n* soldador(ora) *m,f*

welding ['weldɪŋ] *n* soldadura *f*

welfare ['welfeə(r)] *n* (**a**) bienestar *m*; **I am concerned about** *or* **for her w.** me preocupa su bienestar ▸▸ ***w. officer*** trabajador(ora) *m,f* social; ***the w. state*** el estado del bienestar; ***w. work*** trabajo *m* social; ***w. worker*** trabajador(ora) *m,f* social

(**b**) *US (social security)* **to be on w.** recibir un subsidio del estado; **people on w.** las personas que reciben un subsidio del estado ▸▸ *US* ***w. check*** cheque *m* del subsidio del estado; ***w. payment*** subsidio *m* del estado

welfare-to-work ['welfeə(r)tu:'wɜ:k] *n Pol* = trabajos para la comunidad o cursos de formación de carácter obligatorio para desempleados con subsidio

well[1] [wel] *n* (**a**) *(for water, oil)* pozo *m* (**b**) *(for lift, stairs)* hueco *m*

▸**well up** *vi (tears)* brotar

WELL[2] (*comparative* **better** ['betə(r)], *superlative* **best** [best]) 1 *adj* (**a**) *(in health)* **to be w.** estar bien; **I don't feel w.** no me encuentro bien; **to get w.** ponerse bien; **get w. soon** *(on card)* que te mejores; **you're looking** *or* **you look w.** tienes buen aspecto; **he's not a w. man** no está bien, no se encuentra bien; **how are you? – w., thank you** ¿cómo estás? – bien, gracias

(**b**) *(good, satisfactory)* **all is not w. with them** las cosas no les van demasiado bien; **it is just as w.** menos mal; **that's all very w., but...** todo eso está muy bien, pero...; **it's all very w. pretending you don't care, but...** me parece bien *or* perfecto que finjas que no te importa, pero...

2 *adv* (**a**) *(satisfactorily)* bien; **to speak w. of sb** hablar bien de alguien; **I did as w. as I could** lo hice lo mejor que pude; **to be doing w.** *(after operation)* ir recuperándose; **w. done!** ¡bien hecho!; **to do w. by sb** mirar por el bien de alguien; **she's done w. for herself** le han ido bien las cosas; **to do well out of sth** salir beneficiado(a) de algo; **you would do w. to say nothing** harías bien en no decir nada; **to come out of sth w.** salir bien parado(a) de algo; **to go w.** ir bien; **to go w. with sth** ir bien con algo; **I like him w. enough** no me cae mal; **w. said!** ¡bien dicho!; **very w.!** *(OK)* ¡muy bien!, *Esp* ¡vale!, *Méx* ¡órale!

(**b**) *(easily, readily)* **you may w. be right** bien puede ser que tengas razón; **I can w. believe it** no me extraña nada; **he apologized, as w. he might** se disculpó, y no era para menos

(**c**) *(thoroughly)* bien; **shake/stir w.** agítese/remuévase bien; **w. cooked** *or* **done** muy hecho; **I know her w.** la conozco bien; **I know only too w. how hard it is** de sobra sé lo difícil que es; **I am w. aware of that** soy perfectamente consciente de eso

(**d**) *(for emphasis)* bien; **it is w. known that...** todo el mundo sabe que..., es bien sabido que...; **it's w. worth trying** bien vale la pena intentarlo; **she's w. able to look after herself** es perfectamente capaz de valerse por sí misma; **w. before/after** mucho antes/después; **it's w. above/within the limit** está muy por encima/debajo de límite; **let me know w. in advance** avísame con tiempo (de sobra); **the fashion lasted w. into the 1960s** la moda duró hasta bien entrada la década de los sesenta; **he's w. on in years** está bien entrado en años; **she's w. rid of him/it!** menos mal que se ha librado de él/eso; **to leave w. alone** dejar las cosas como están; **w. and truly** totalmente; **we got w. and truly soaked** nos empapamos hasta los huesos

(**e**) *(also)* **as w.** también; **as w. as** *(in addition to)* además de

(**f**) *Br Fam (very)* **the club was w. cool** la disco era supergenial *or Esp* superguay *or Méx* de poca; **he's w. hard** es superduro

(**g**) IDIOMS *Br Fam* **he was w. away** *(drunk)* estaba borracho como una cuba, *Arg* estaba re-dado vuelta; **to be w. in with sb** codearse con alguien; **to be w. up on sth** estar empapado(a) de algo

3 *exclam* **w., who was it?** ¿y bien?, ¿quién era?; **w., here we are (at last)!** bueno, ¡por fin hemos llegado!; **w., as I was saying...** pues, como decía...; **I've known her for ages, w. at least three years** hace siglos que la conozco, bueno, al menos tres años; **you remember John? w. I saw him yesterday** ¿te acuerdas de John?, pues lo vi ayer; **he was, w., rather unpleasant really** fue, no sé cómo decirlo, bastante desagradable; **are you ready? – w., I should really stay in and work** ¿estás lista? – esto, en realidad debería quedarme a trabajar; **w., really!** ¡ya está bien!; **oh w., it can't be helped** pues, qué se le va a hacer; **w., w.!** ¡vaya, vaya!; **w. I never!** ¡caramba!; **w., that's life!** en fin, ¡así es la vida!

---

we'll [wi:l] = **we will, we shall**

well-acquainted [welə'kweɪntɪd] *adj* muy familiarizado(a) (**with** con); **they are w. (with one another)** se conocen bien

well-adjusted [welə'dʒʌstɪd] *adj (person)* equilibrado(a)

well-advised [welәd'vaɪzd] *adj* sensato(a), prudente; **you'd be w. to stay indoors today** hoy lo mejor sería no salir de casa

well-aimed [wel'eɪmd] *adj (shot, criticism, remark)* certero(a)

well-appointed [welə'pɔɪntɪd] *adj Br Formal (house, room)* bien acondicionado(a)

well-argued [wel'ɑ:gju:d] *adj* bien argumentado(a)

well-attended [welə'tendɪd] *adj* muy concurrido(a); **the meeting was w.** a la reunión acudió *or* asistió mucha gente; **the classes were not w.** no iban muchos asistentes a las clases

well-balanced [wel'bælənst] *adj (person, diet)* equilibrado(a)

well-behaved [welbɪ'heɪvd] *adj* (bien) educado(a); **to be w.** portarse bien

wellbeing [wel'bi:ɪŋ] *n* bienestar *m*; **he felt a sense of w.** sintió cierto bienestar

well-born [wel'bɔ:n] *adj* de buena familia, de noble cuna

well-bred [wel'bred] *adj* (bien) educado(a)

well-built [wel'bɪlt] *adj (building)* bien construido(a); *(person)* fornido(a)

well-chosen [wel'tʃəʊzən] *adj* acertado(a)

well-connected ['welkə'nektɪd] *adj* bien relacionado(a), con buenos contactos; **to be w.** tener buenos contactos

well-defined [weldɪ'faɪnd] *adj (outline, shape)* nítido(a); *(fear, problem, features, types)* bien definido(a); *(path)* bien marcado(a)

well-deserved [weldɪ'zɜːvd] *adj* (bien) merecido(a)
well-designed [weldɪ'zaɪnd] *adj* bien diseñado(a)
well-developed [weldɪ'veləpt] *adj (muscles, body, person)* muy desarrollado(a)
well-disposed [weldɪs'pəʊzd] *adj* **to be w. towards sb** tener buena disposición hacia alguien
well-done [wel'dʌn] *adj (steak)* muy hecho(a)
well-dressed [wel'drest] *adj* elegante; **to be w.** ir bien vestido(a)
well-earned [wel'ɜːnd] *adj* (bien) merecido(a)
well-educated [wel'edjʊkeɪtɪd] *adj* culto(a), instruido(a)
well-endowed [welɪn'daʊd] *adj Fam Hum (woman)* pechugona, con una buena delantera; *(man)* muy bien dotado
well-equipped [welɪ'kwɪpt] *adj* bien equipado(a), con los medios necesarios; **to be w. to do sth** estar bien equipado(a) *or* contar con los medios necesarios para hacer algo
well-established [welɪ'stæblɪʃt] *adj (principle, procedure)* establecido(a); *(custom, tradition)* arraigado(a); *(company)* de sólida reputación
well-favoured [wel'feɪvəd] *adj Old-fashioned* bien plantado(a), bien parecido(a)
well-fed [wel'fed] *adj* bien alimentado(a)
well-fixed [wel'fɪksd] *adj US Fam* ricachón(ona), forrado(a), *Esp* con pelas, *Am* con plata; **to be w.** estar forrado(a), tener *Esp* muchas pelas *or Am* mucha plata
well-formed [wel'fɔːmd] *adj Ling* bien construido(a)
well-founded [wel'faʊndɪd] *adj (suspicion, fear)* fundado(a)
well-groomed [wel'gruːmd] *adj (person, hair)* arreglado(a); *(horse, lawn)* (bien) cuidado(a)
wellhead ['welhed] *n* manantial *m*
well-heeled [wel'hiːld] *adj Fam* ricachón(ona), forrado(a), *Esp* con pelas, *Am* con plata; **to be w.** estar forrado(a), tener *Esp* muchas pelas *or Am* mucha plata
well-hung [wel'hʌŋ] *adj very Fam (man)* bien dotado, *Esp* con un buen paquete, *RP* bien armado
wellie = **welly**
well-informed [welɪn'fɔːmd] *adj* (bien) informado(a) (**about** de); **he's very w. about current affairs** está muy al tanto *or* al corriente de los temas de actualidad
wellington ['welɪŋtən] *n Br* **wellingtons, w. boots** botas *fpl* de agua *or* de goma *or Méx, Ven* de caucho
well-intentioned [welɪn'tenʃənd] *adj* bienintencionado(a)
well-judged [wel'dʒʌdʒd] *adj (remark, performance)* acertado(a); *(shot)* medido(a), bien calculado(a)
well-kept [wel'kept] *adj* (**a**) *(nails, hair)* (bien) arreglado(a), *RP* prolijo(a); *(garden, house)* (bien) cuidado(a) (**b**) *(secret)* bien guardado(a)
well-known [wel'nəʊn] *adj* conocido(a), famoso(a); **it is w.** *or* **it is a w. fact that she disagrees with the policy** es bien sabido *or* es de todos sabido que no está de acuerdo con esta política; **what is less w. is that she's an accomplished actress** lo que ya no se conoce tanto es que es una excelente actriz
well-liked [wel'laɪkt] *adj* querido(a), apreciado(a)
well-loved [wel'lʌvd] *adj* muy querido(a)
well-made [wel'meɪd] *adj* bien hecho(a)
well-mannered [wel'mænəd] *adj* con buenos modales, educado(a)
well-matched [wel'mætʃt] *adj (opponents)* igualado(a); **they're a w. couple** hacen buena pareja
well-meaning [wel'miːnɪŋ] *adj* bienintencionado(a); **these people are w., but naive** esta gente tiene buenas intenciones, pero pecan de inocentes
well-meant [wel'ment] *adj* bienintencionado(a)
well-nigh ['welnaɪ] *adv* casi, prácticamente
well-off [wel'ɒf] **1** *adj (wealthy)* acomodado(a), rico(a); *Fig* **you don't know when you're w.** no sabes lo afortunado que eres
2 *npl* **the w.** la gente acomodada *or* de dinero; **the less w.** los que tienen menos, los pobres
well-oiled [wel'ɔɪld] *adj* (**a**) *(machinery)* bien engrasado(a); *Fig* **the party's w. electoral machine** la perfecta maquinaria electoral del partido (**b**) *Fam (drunk)* como una cuba, *Méx, RP* remamado(a)
well-ordered [wel'ɔːdəd] *adj* ordenado(a)
well-padded [wel'pædɪd] *adj Fam Euph* rellenito(a), rechoncho(a)
well-paid [wel'peɪd] *adj* bien pagado(a)
well-placed [wel'pleɪst] *adj* bien situado(a); **to be w. to do sth** estar en una buena posición para hacer algo; **she's not very w. to criticize the government** no está en condiciones de criticar al gobierno
well-preserved [welprɪ'zɜːvd] *adj (object, building)* bien conservado(a); *Fig* **to be w.** *(person)* conservarse bien
well-proportioned [wel'prə'pɔːʃnd] *adj (building, room, person)* bien proporcionado(a), con buenas proporciones
well-read [wel'red] *adj* leído(a), culto(a); **she's very w.** es una persona muy leída
well-rounded [wel'raʊndɪd] *adj* (**a**) *(figure)* torneado(a), curvilíneo(a) (**b**) *(education)* completo(a); *(personality)* equilibrado(a)
well-spoken [wel'spəʊkən] *adj* bienhablado(a)
well-spoken-of [wel'spəʊkənɒv] *adj* **she's very w. in business circles** se habla muy bien de ella en círculos empresariales
wellspring ['welsprɪŋ] *n* (**a**) *(spring, fountain)* manantial *m* (**b**) *Literary* fuente *f* inagotable
well-stacked [wel'stækt] *adj Fam* **she's w.** está jamona
well-stocked [wel'stɒkt] *adj (cupboard, shop)* bien surtido(a)
well-thought-of [wel'θɔːtɒv] *adj* prestigioso(a)
well-thumbed [wel'θʌmd] *adj (book)* manoseado(a), ajado(a)
well-timed [wel'taɪmd] *adj* oportuno(a)
well-to-do ['weltədu:] *adj* acomodado(a), próspero(a)
well-travelled, *US* **well-traveled** [wel'trævəld] *adj (person)* que ha viajado mucho
well-trodden [wel'trɒdən] *adj also Fig* (muy) trillado(a)
well-turned [wel'tɜːnd] *adj (phrase)* bien construido(a); *(ankle)* proporcionado(a)
well-upholstered [welʌp'həʊlstəd] *adj Fam (plump)* rellenito(a), rechoncho(a)
well-versed [wel'vɜːst] *adj* **to be w. in sth** estar muy versado(a) en algo, ser docto(a) en algo
well-wisher ['welwɪʃə(r)] *n* simpatizante *mf*, admirador(ora) *m,f*; **the family received thousands of messages of support from well-wishers** la familia recibió miles de mensajes de apoyo y solidaridad
well-woman clinic ['wel'wʊmən'klɪnɪk] *n Br* = clínica de atención y orientación sanitaria y ginecológica para la mujer
well-worn [wel'wɔːn] *adj* (**a**) *(garment)* gastado(a) (**b**) *(argument)* manido(a); *(phrase)* manido(a), trillado(a)
well-written [wel'rɪtən] *adj* bien escrito(a)
welly ['welɪ] *n Br Fam* (**a**) **w.(-boot)** bota *f* de agua *or* de goma *or Méx, Ven* de caucho (**b**) *(effort)* **give it some w.!** ¡con ganas!, ¡échale ganas!
Welsh [welʃ] **1** *npl (people)* **the W.** los galeses
2 *n (language)* galés *m*
3 *adj* galés(esa) ►► ***the W. Assembly*** el parlamento autónomo de Gales; ***W. dresser*** aparador *m*; ***W. rarebit*** tostada *f* de queso fundido
welsh, welch [welʃ] *vi* imcumplir
►**welsh on, welch on** *vt insep Br Fam (debt)* no pagar; *(agreement)* imcumplir
Welshman ['welʃmən] *n* galés *m*
Welshwoman ['welʃwʊmən] *n* galesa *f*
welt [welt] *n (mark on skin)* señal *f*, verdugón *m*
welter ['weltə(r)] *n* **a w. of...** un aluvión de..., una ingente cantidad de...
welterweight ['weltəweɪt] *n Sport* (peso *m*) welter *m*
wen [wen] *n* (**a**) *Med* quiste *m* sebáceo (**b**) *Br Literary* **the Great W.** la gran urbe londinense
wench [wentʃ] *n Old-fashioned or Hum* moza *f*
wend [wend] *vt Literary* **they wended their way homewards** con paso lento pusieron rumbo a casa
Wendy house ['wendɪhaʊs] *n Br* casita *f* de juguete *(para meterse dentro)*
went *pt of* **go**
wept *pt & pp of* **weep**
we're [wɪə(r)] = **we are**
were *pt of* **be**
weren't [wɜːnt] = **were not**
werewolf ['wɪəwʊlf] *n* hombre *m* lobo
west [west] **1** *n* oeste *m*; **to the w. (of)** al oeste (de); **in the w. of Canada** en el oeste de Canadá; **the W. of Spain** el oeste de España; **the W.** *(direction, region)* el oeste; *(as opposed to Asia or the former Soviet Bloc)* Occidente; **the wind is in** *or* **(coming) from the w.** el viento sopla *or* viene del oeste

2 *adj* (**a**) *(direction, side)* oeste, occidental; **the w. coast** la costa oeste; **w. London** la parte oeste *or* el oeste de Londres ►► ***w. wind*** viento *m* de poniente *or* del oeste

(**b**) *(in names)* ***W. Africa*** África Occidental; ***W. African*** africano(a) *m,f* occidental; ***the W. Bank*** Cisjordania; *Formerly* ***W. Berlin*** Berlín oeste *or* occidental; ***the W. Country*** el suroeste de Inglaterra; ***the W. End*** *(of London)* = zona de Londres famosa por sus comercios y teatros; *Formerly* ***W. German*** alemán(ana) *m,f or* germano(a) *m,f* occidental; *Formerly* ***W. Germany*** Alemania Occidental; ***W. Highland terrier*** terrier *m* blanco escocés; ***W. Indian*** antillano(a) *m,f*; ***the W. Indies*** las Antillas; ***the W. Midlands*** el oeste de la región de Midlands *(en el centro de Inglaterra)*; ***the W. Side*** = el barrio oeste de Manhattan; ***W. Virginia*** Virginia Occidental

3 *adv* hacia el oeste, en dirección oeste; **it's (3 miles) w. of here** está (a 3 millas) al oeste de aquí; **they live out w.** viven en el oeste; **drive west until you come to a main road** continúe hacia el oeste hasta que llegue a una carretera principal; **w. by north/by south** oeste cuarta al noroeste/suroeste; **to face w.** dar *or* mirar al oeste; **to go w.** ir hacia el oeste; *Fig (TV, car)* romperse, estropearse

westbound ['westbaʊnd] *adj (train, traffic)* en dirección oeste; **the w. carriageway** el carril que va hacia el oeste

westerly ['westəlɪ] 1 *n (wind)* viento *m* de poniente *or* del oeste

2 *adj (direction)* hacia el oeste; **in a w. direction** en dirección oeste, rumbo al oeste; **the most w. point** el punto más occidental; **w. wind** viento de poniente *or* del oeste; **a room with a w. aspect** una habitación que da al oeste

western ['westən] 1 *n (movie)* película *f* del oeste, western *m*; *(novel)* novela *f* del oeste

2 *adj* occidental; **the w. side of the city** la parte oeste de la ciudad; **w. Spain** la España occidental ►► ***W. Australia*** Australia Occidental; ***W. Europe*** Europa occidental; ***the w. hemisphere*** el hemisferio occidental; ***the W. Isles*** *(of Scotland)* las Hébridas; ***W. Sahara*** el Sáhara Occidental; ***W. Samoa*** Samoa Occidental; ***W. Samoan*** samoano(a) *m,f* occidental; ***the W. world*** el mundo occidental, Occidente

westerner ['westənə(r)] *n* occidental *mf*

westernization [westənaɪ'zeɪʃən] *n* occidentalización *f*

westernize ['westənaɪz] *vt* occidentalizar

westernized ['westənaɪzd] *adj* occidentalizado(a); **to become w.** occidentalizarse

westernmost ['westənməʊst] *adj* más occidental, más al oeste; **the w. island of the archipelago** la isla más occidental *or* al oeste del archipiélago

Westminster [west'mɪnstə(r)] *n (as seat of administration)* Westminster, el parlamento británico

west-northwest ['westnɔːθ'west] 1 *adj (direction)* al oesnoroeste; *(wind)* del oesnoroeste

2 *adv* al oesnoroeste

west-southwest ['westsaʊθ'west] 1 *adj (direction)* al oesuroeste; *(wind)* del oesuroeste

2 *adv* al oesuroeste

westward ['westwəd] 1 *adj* hacia el oeste

2 *adv* hacia el oeste

westwards ['westwədz] *adv* hacia el oeste

wet [wet] 1 *adj* (**a**) *(damp)* húmedo(a); *(soaked)* mojado(a); **to be w.** *(damp)* estar húmedo(a); *(soaked)* estar mojado(a); *(ink, paint)* estar fresco(a); **to get w.** mojarse; **I got my feet w.** se me mojaron los pies; **to be w. through** *(person)* estar calado(a) (hasta los huesos), estar empapado(a); *(clothes, towel)* estar empapado(a); **w. paint** *(sign)* recién pintado; IDIOM **to be w. behind the ears** *(inexperienced)* estar un poco verde, ser novato(a) ►► *US* ***w. bar*** bar *m or* barra *f (con fregadero)*; *Fig* ***w. blanket*** aguafiestas *mf inv*; *Fam* ***w. dream*** polución *f* nocturna, *Am* orgasmo *m* nocturno; ***w. fish*** pescado *m* fresco; ***w. nurse*** nodriza *f*, ama *f* de cría *or* de leche; ***w. suit*** traje *m* de buzo *or* de submarinismo

(**b**) *(rainy)* lluvioso(a); **it's w. outside** fuera está lloviendo; **a w. weekend** un fin de semana pasado por agua; IDIOM *Fam* **to look like a w. weekend** estar *Esp* amuermado(a) *or Méx* apachurrado(a) *or RP* embolado(a) *or Ven* aguado(a)

(**c**) *Br Fam (feeble)* blandengue, soso(a); **he thinks it's w. to discuss emotions** piensa que hablar de sentimientos es de blandengues

(**d**) *US Fam (wrong, misguided)* **to be all w.** equivocarse de medio a medio, estar totalmente equivocado(a)

(**e**) *Br Pol* conservador(ora) moderado(a)

(**f**) *US (state, town)* no prohibicionista

2 *vt (pt & pp* **wet** *or* **wetted**) *(dampen)* humedecer; *(soak)* mojar; **to w. one's lips** humedecerse los labios; **to w. the bed** mojar la cama, orinarse en la cama; *Fam* **to w. oneself** mearse (encima); *Fam* **I nearly w. myself laughing!** ¡casi me meo de la risa!; IDIOM *Fam* **to w. one's whistle** mojarse el gaznate

3 *n* (**a**) *(dampness)* humedad *f*; *(rain)* lluvia *f*; **come in out of the w.** pasa, no te quedes ahí, que está lloviendo (**b**) *Br Pol* conservador(ora) *m,f* moderado(a) (**c**) *Br Fam (feeble person)* pusilánime *mf*, soso(a) *m,f*

wetback ['wetbæk] *n US Fam Pej* espalda *mf* mojada, *Méx* mojado(a) *m,f*

wetland ['wetlænd] 1 *n* **wetlands** terreno *m* pantanoso, *Spec* humedal(es) *m(pl)*

2 *adj* de los pantanos, *Spec* de los humedales

wet-look ['wetlʊk] *adj (fabric)* satinado(a); *(hair gel)* brillante

wetness ['wetnɪs] *n* (**a**) *(of weather, climate)* humedad *f*, carácter *m* lluvioso (**b**) *(of surface, clothes)* humedad *f*

WEU ['dʌbəljuːiː'juː] *n (abbr* **Western European Union**) UEO *f*

we've [wiːv] = **we have**

whack [wæk] 1 *n* (**a**) *(blow)* porrazo *m*, *Méx* madrazo *m*

(**b**) *Fam (attempt)* intento *m*; **to have a w. at sth** intentar algo, probar suerte con algo

(**c**) *Fam (share)* parte *f*; **he paid more than his w.** pagó más de lo que le correspondía

(**d**) *Fam (amount, rate)* **you're already earning the top w. for this job** ya estás ganando un dineral con este trabajo; **they charge top w.** cobran un riñón, cobran muchísimo

(**e**) *US Fam* **to be out of w.** *(out of shape)* estar deformado(a); *(out of order)* estar estropeado(a) *or Esp* cascado(a), no funcionar; **to be out of w. with sth** no ir a la par *or* no estar en sincronía con algo

2 *vt* (**a**) *(hit) (person)* dar un porrazo *or Méx* madrazo a; *(ball)* golpear, dar un golpe a; **he whacked the ball across the tennis court** pasó la pelota al otro lado de la pista de un raquetazo; **to w. sb on** *or* **over the head** dar un tortazo *or Esp* porrazo *or Méx* madrazo a alguien en la cabeza

(**b**) *US Fam (murder)* liquidar, *Esp* cepillarse, *Esp* cargarse

► **whack off** *vi Vulg (masturbate)* hacerse una paja

whacked [wækt] *adj Fam (exhausted)* reventado(a), molido(a)

whacking ['wækɪŋ] 1 *n* (**a**) *(beating)* paliza *f*, tunda *f*; **his father gave him a w.** su padre le dio una paliza *or* tunda; **to get a w.** recibir una paliza (**b**) *(defeat)* **we gave them a w.** los ganamos, les dimos una paliza; **to get a w.** ser derrotado *or* vencido

2 *adv Fam* **a w. great increase/fine** un subida/una multa descomunal

whacko = **wacko**

whacky = **wacky**

whale [weɪl] *n* (**a**) *(mammal)* ballena *f* ►► ***w. oil*** aceite *m* de ballena; ***w. shark*** tiburón *m* ballena (**b**) *Fam (as intensifier)* **we had a w. of a time** nos lo pasamos bomba

whalebone ['weɪlbəʊn] *n* ballena *f (material)*

whaler ['weɪlə(r)] *n (vessel)* ballenero *m*; *(person)* ballenero(a) *m,f*

whale-watching ['weɪlwɒtʃɪŋ] *n* observación *f* de ballenas; **to go w.** ir a observar ballenas

whaling ['weɪlɪŋ] *n* caza *f* de ballenas; **to go w.** ir a cazar ballenas ►► ***w. industry*** industria *f* ballenera; ***w. ship*** (barco *m*) ballenero *m*

wham [wæm] *Fam* 1 *vt (pt & pp* **whammed**) estampar, pegar un golpe con

2 *vi* estamparse, pegarse un golpe

3 *exclam* ¡zas! IDIOM **it was w., bam, thank you ma'am** fue aquí te pillo aquí te mato, fue sólo un polvo de una noche

wharf [wɔːf] (*pl* **wharves** [wɔːvz]) *n* embarcadero *m*

WHAT [wɒt] 1 *adj* (**a**) *(in questions)* qué; **w. sort do you want?** ¿qué tipo quieres?; **tell me w. books you want** dime qué libros quieres; **w. colour/size is it?** ¿de qué color/talla *or RP* talle es?; **w. good is that?** ¿de qué sirve eso?; **w. time are they arriving?** ¿a qué hora llegarán?

(**b**) *(in relative constructions)* **he took w. little I had left** se llevó lo poco que me quedaba; **I'll give you w. money I have** te daré todo el dinero que tengo; **I gave her w. comfort I could** traté de consolarla como mejor pude

2 *pron* (**a**) *(in questions)* qué; **w. do you want?** ¿qué quieres?; **he asked her w. she wanted** le preguntó qué quería; **w. are you doing here?** ¿qué haces aquí?; **w.'s that?** ¿qué es eso?; **w.'s your phone number?** ¿cuál es tu (número de) teléfono?; **w. are the main reasons?** ¿cuáles son las principales razones?; **w.'s to be done about this problem?** ¿qué podemos hacer para resolver este problema?; **w. did I tell you?** ¿qué te dije?; **w. will people say?** ¿qué va a decir la gente?;

w. do I care? ¿y a mí qué me importa?; **w. did it cost?** ¿cuánto costó?; **w.'s she called?** ¿cómo se llama?; **w.'s the Spanish for "dog"?** ¿cómo se dice "dog" en español?; **w.'s he/she/it like?** ¿cómo es?; *Fam* **w.'s in it for me?** ¿y yo qué gano con eso?; *Fam* **w.?** *(pardon?)* ¿qué?; **I'm resigning – w.?** voy a dimitir *or* renunciar – ¿qué (dices)?; *Fam* **w.'s up?** ¿qué pasa?; *US (as greeting)* ¡qué tal!; **they bought WHAT?** ¿que compraron qué?; **she must be, w., 50?** debe de tener unos cincuenta (años); **that's an increase of, w., 50 percent** es un incremento de, vamos a ver, el 50 por ciento; **w. about the money I lent you?** ¿y el dinero que te presté?; **w. about me?** ¿y yo qué?; **we've bought all her presents, now w. about his?** hemos comprado todos los regalos de ella, ¿qué hacemos con los de él?; **w. about a game of bridge?** ¿*Esp* te apetece *or Carib, Col, Méx* te provoca *or Méx* se te antoja echar una partida de bridge?, *CSur* ¿querés jugar una partida de bridge?; **w. about this shirt here?** ¿qué te parece esta otra camisa?; **w. if they find out?** ¿y qué pasa si se enteran?; **w. if I come too?** ¿y qué tal si voy yo también?; **if that doesn't work, w. then?** y si eso no funciona, ¿qué?; *Fam* **d'you think I'm mad or w.?** ¿te crees que estoy loco o qué?; *Fam* **now is that clever or w.?** no está nada mal, ¿eh?; *Fam* **so w.?, w. of** *or* **about it?** ¿y qué?; *Fam* **you w.?** *(pardon?)* ¿qué?; *(expressing surprise, indignation)* ¿qué (dices)?, ¿que qué?; **I sold it – you did w.?** lo vendí – ¿hiciste qué? *or* ¿que qué?; *Fam* **paper, pens, pencils, and w. not** *or* **w. have you** papel, bolígrafos, lápices y todo *or* y toda la pesca *or RP* y la mar en coche

(**b**) *(relative)* qué; **I don't know w. has happened** no sé qué ha pasado; **they can't decide w. to do** no consiguen decidir qué hacer; **she told me w. she knew** me contó lo que sabía; **it is w. is known as an aneurism** es lo que se conoce como aneurisma; **w. is more,...** (lo que) es más,...; **w. is most remarkable is that...** lo más sorprendente es que...; **w. I like is a good detective story** lo que más me gusta son las novelas policíacas; **guess w.!** ¡adivina qué!, *RP* ¿adiviná lo que pasó?; **I know w., let's watch a video** tengo una idea, pongamos un vídeo *orAm* video; **I'll tell you w., why don't we go out for a meal?** escucha, ¿por qué no salimos a comer?; **I'll tell you w., it may be expensive, but it will never let you down** te voy a decir una cosa, puede que sea caro, pero no te fallará; **w. with having to look after the children and everything...** entre (tener que) cuidar a los niños y todo eso...; **w. with one thing and another I never got there** entre una cosa y otra acabé por no llegar; IDIOM *Fam* **he knows w.'s w.** tiene la cabeza *Esp* sobre los hombros *orAm* bien puesta

(**c**) **w. for?** *(for what purpose)* ¿para qué?; *(why)* ¿por qué?; **w.'s that for?** ¿para qué es eso?; **w. did he do that for?** ¿por qué hizo eso?; **tell me w. you're crying for** dime por qué lloras; IDIOM *Fam* **to give sb w. for** *(verbally)* cantarle a alguien las cuarenta; *(physically)* darle una zurra a alguien

(**d**) *(in exclamations)* **w. an idea!** ¡menuda idea!, ¡qué idea!; **w. a fool he is!** ¡qué tonto es!; **w. a lot of people!** ¡cuánta gente!; **w. a shame!** ¡qué vergüenza *or CAm, Carib, Col, Méx* pena!; **w. a beautiful view!** ¡qué vista tan bonita!; **w. an odd thing to say!** ¿por qué habrá dicho eso?; **w. nonsense!** ¡tonterías!, ¡qué tontería!

(**e**) *Br Fam Old-fashioned (inviting agreement)* **an interesting book, w.?** un libro interesante, ¿verdad?

3 *exclam* **w., you didn't check the dates?** ¿qué? ¿que no comprobaste las fechas?; **w., aren't you interested?** ¿qué (pasa)?, ¿no te interesa?; **w. next (I ask myself)!** ¡(me pregunto) con qué saldrán ahora!

---

what-d'ye-call-her ['wɒtjəkɔːlə(r)] *n Fam (person)* fulanita *f*, menganita *f*

what-d'ye-call-him ['wɒtjəkɔːlɪm] *n Fam (person)* fulanito *m*, menganito *m*

what-d'ye-call-it ['wɒtjəkɔːlɪt] *n Fam (thing)* chisme *m*, *CAm, Carib, Col* vaina *f*, *RP* coso *m*

whatever [wɒt'evə(r)] 1 *pron* **do w. you like** haz lo que quieras; **give him w. he wants** dale lo que quiera; **w. it is, w. it may be** sea lo que sea; **w. happens** pase lo que pase; **w. you do, don't tell Eric** hagas lo que hagas, no llames a Eric; **it's a quasar, w. that is** es un cuásar, pero no me preguntes más *or* sea lo que sea eso; **w. you say** *(expressing acquiescence)* lo que tú digas; **w. I say, he always disagrees** siempre está en desacuerdo con cualquier cosa que yo diga; **w. you may think, I am telling the truth** pienses lo que pienses, estoy diciendo la verdad; **w. does that mean?** ¿y eso qué significa?; **w. are they doing?** ¿qué es lo que hacen?; **w. the reason** cualquiera que sea *or* sea cual sea la razón; **w. next!** ¡lo que faltaba!

2 *adj* (**a**) *(no matter what)* **I regret w. harm I may have done** pido disculpas por el daño que pueda haber ocasionado; **w. doubts I had were gone** todas mis dudas se habían disipado, las pocas dudas que me quedaban se habían disipado; **he gave up w. ambitions he still had** abandonó cualquier *or* toda ambición que pudiera quedarle; **pay w. price they ask** paga el precio que sea; **if, for w. reason,...** si por cualquier razón *or* motivo,..., si por la razón *or* el motivo que sea,...

(**b**) *(emphatic)* **for no reason w.** sin motivo alguno; **none/nothing w.** absolutamente ninguno(a)/nada

3 *exclam* lo que tú digas, sí, lo que sea

whatnot ['wɒtnɒt] *n* (**a**) *Fam* **...and w.** ...y cosas así, ...y cosas por el estilo (**b**) *(ornament shelf)* rinconera *f*

what's-her-face ['wɒtsəfeɪs], **what's-his-face** ['wɒtsɪzfeɪs], **what's-its-face** ['wɒtsɪtsfeɪs] *n Fam* = **what-d'ye-call-her/him/it**

what's-her-name ['wɒtsəneɪm], **what's-his-name** ['wɒtsɪzneɪm], **what's-its-name** ['wɒtsɪtsneɪm] *n Fam* = **what-d'ye-call-her/him/it**

whatsit ['wɒtsɪt] *n Fam* chisme *m*, *CAm, Carib, Col* vaina *f*, *RP* coso *m*

whatsoever [wɒtsəʊ'evə(r)] *adj* **for no reason w.** sin motivo alguno; **none/nothing w.** absolutamente ninguno(a)/nada

wheat [wiːt] *n* trigo *m*; IDIOM **to separate** *or* **sort out the w. from the chaff** separar la paja del grano *or* las churras de las merinas ►► ***w. germ*** germen *m* de trigo

wheatear ['wiːtiə(r)] *n* collalba *f* gris ►► ***black-eared w.*** collalba *f* rubia

wheaten ['wiːtən] *adj (loaf, roll)* de trigo

wheatfield ['wiːtfiːld] *n* trigal *m*

wheatsheaf ['wiːtʃiːf] *n* gavilla *f* de trigo

wheedle ['wiːdəl] *vt* **to w. sth out of sb** sacar algo a alguien con halagos; **to w. sb into doing sth** hacer zalamerías a alguien para que haga algo; **he wheedled his way into the old lady's confidence** se ganó *or* se granjeó la confianza de la anciana

wheedling ['wiːdlɪŋ] 1 *n* zalamerías *fpl*

2 *adj* zalamero(a), adulador(ora)

wheel [wiːl] 1 *n* (**a**) *(on vehicle, in mechanism)* rueda *f*; **the w. of fortune** la rueda de la fortuna ►► ***w. clamp*** cepo *m*; ***w. clamping*** inmovilización *f* de vehículos con cepo

(**b**) *(for steering) (of car)* volante *m*, *Andes* timón *m*; *(of boat)* timón *m*; **to be at** *or* **behind the w.** ir al volante

(**c**) IDIOMS **to set the wheels in motion** ponerse manos a la obra; **the w. has come full circle** volvemos a estar donde empezamos; **there are wheels within wheels** hay muchos entresijos

2 **wheels** *npl Fam (car)* coche *m*, *Am* carro *m*, *CSur* auto *m*; **have you got wheels?** ¿tienes coche *orAm* carro *or CSur* auto?

3 *vt (push) (bicycle, cart)* empujar, hacer rodar; **she wheeled the baby around the park** paseaba al bebé por el parque

4 *vi* (**a**) *(turn)* girar, dar vueltas; *(vultures)* volar en círculo; *(marching soldiers)* girar en redondo (**b**) *Fam* **to w. and deal** *(scheme, negotiate)* andarse con chanchullos *or* tejemanejes

►**wheel about, wheel around** 1 *vi* (**a**) *(turn)* dar media vuelta, girar sobre los talones; *(procession, birds)* cambiar de repente de dirección; *(horse)* dar media vuelta; **she wheeled around to face him** se dio la vuelta para mirarlo de frente (**b**) *(circle)* **vultures wheeling about in the sky** buitres volando en círculo

2 *vt sep (turn)* hacer girar en círculo a; *(dancing partner)* hacer dar vueltas como un trompo a

►**wheel in** *vt sep* (**a**) *(trolley, person in wheelchair)* meter (**b**) *Fam (produce)* sacar

►**wheel out** *vt sep* (**a**) *(trolley, person in wheelchair)* sacar (**b**) *Fam (produce)* echar mano de; **he wheeled out the same old excuses** echó mano de las excusas de siempre

►**wheel round** *vi* dar media vuelta, girar sobre los talones

wheelbarrow ['wiːlbærəʊ] *n* carretilla *f*

wheelbase ['wiːlbeɪs] *n Aut* distancia *f* entre ejes, batalla *f*

wheelchair ['wiːltʃeə(r)] *n* silla *f* de ruedas; **she'll be in a w. (for) the rest of her life** tendrá que ir en silla de ruedas el resto de su vida ►► ***w. access*** acceso *m* para minusválidos

-wheeled [wiːld] *suffix* **two/three/***etc* **-w.** de dos/tres/*etc.* ruedas

wheeler-dealer ['wiːlə'diːlə(r)] *n Fam* chanchullero(a) *m,f*, trapichero(a) *m,f*

wheeler-dealing ['wiːlə'diːlɪŋ] *n Fam* chanchullos *mpl*, tejemanejes *mpl*

wheelhouse ['wiːlhaʊs] *n (on boat)* timonera *f*, caseta *f* del timón

wheelie ['wiːlɪ] *n Fam* **to do a w.** *(on bicycle, motorbike)* hacer el caballito ►► ***w. bin*** contenedor *m* de basura

wheeling ['wiːlɪŋ] *n Fam* **w. and dealing** chanchullos, tejemanejes

wheelspin ['wiːlspɪn] *n* **the system prevents w.** el sistema evita que las ruedas patinen

wheelwright ['wiːlraɪt] *n* carretero(a) *m,f*

wheeze [wi:z] **1** *n* (**a**) *(noise)* resuello *m*, resoplido *m* (**b**) *Br Fam (trick)* truco *m*, trampa *f*
2 *vt* **"call the doctor," he wheezed** "llama al médico", dijo con la respiración entecortada
3 *vi (breathe heavily)* resollar, resoplar

wheezily ['wi:zɪlɪ] *adv* resollando

wheezy ['wi:zɪ] *adj (voice)* jadeante, con resuello; *(cough)* con silbido; **he had a w. chest** le sonaba el pecho (al respirar)

whelk [welk] *n* bu(c)cino *m*

whelp [welp] **1** *n* (**a**) *(dog)* cachorro *m* (**b**) *(person)* mocoso(a) *m,f*
2 *vi* tener cachorros

WHEN [wen] **1** *adv* cuándo; **w. will you come?** ¿cuándo vienes?; **w. was the Renaissance?** ¿en qué época tuvo lugar el Renacimiento?; **w. do you use the subjunctive?** ¿cuándo se utiliza el subjuntivo?; **w. is the best time to call?** ¿cuándo es el mejor momento para llamar?; **tell me w. it happened** dime cuándo ocurrió; **w. will it be ready?** ¿(para) cuándo estará listo?; **since w. do you tell me what to do?** ¿desde cuándo me das órdenes?; **until w. can you stay?** ¿hasta cuándo te puedes quedar?; *Fam* **say w.!** *(when pouring drink)* dime basta
2 *conj* (**a**) *(with time)* cuando; **I had just gone to bed w. the phone rang** acababa de acostarme cuando sonó el teléfono; **tell me w. you've finished** avísame cuando hayas terminado; **the day w. Kennedy was shot** el día en que mataron a Kennedy; **w. I was a boy...** cuando era un niño..., de niño...; **what's the good of talking w. you never listen?** ¿de qué sirve hablarte si nunca escuchas?; **w. using this device, care must be taken to...** al utilizar este aparato hay que tener cuidado de...; **w. finished, it will be the highest building in Lima** una vez terminado, será el edificio más alto de Lima; **w. compared with other children of his age** comparado con otros niños de su edad
(**b**) *(whereas)* cuando; **she said it was black, w. it was really white** dijo que era negro, cuando en realidad era blanco
(**c**) *(considering that)* cuando; **how can you say that w. you don't even know me?** ¿cómo puedes decir eso cuando ni siquiera *or* si ni siquiera me conoces?

whence [wens] *adv Literary* de dónde

whenever [wen'evə(r)] **1** *conj* (**a**) *(every time that)* cada vez que, siempre que; **I go w. I can** voy siempre que puedo; **w. possible** siempre que sea posible (**b**) *(no matter when)* **come w. you like** ven cuando quieras; **you can leave w. you're ready** en cuanto estén listos pueden marcharse; **on her birthday, w. that is** en su cumpleaños, que no sé cuando cae
2 *adv (referring to unspecified time)* cuando sea; **Sunday, Monday, or w.** el domingo, el lunes o cuando sea (**b**) *(in questions)* cuándo; **w. did you find the time to do all that?** ¿de dónde sacaste tiempo para hacer todo eso?

WHERE [weə(r)] **1** *adv (in questions)* dónde; **w. are you going?** ¿adónde *or* dónde vas?; **w. does he come from?** ¿de dónde es?; **w. should I start?** ¿por dónde empiezo?; **w. am I?** ¿dónde estoy?; **tell me w. she is** dime dónde está; **tell me w. to go** dime adónde ir; **w. did I go wrong?** ¿en qué *or* dónde me equivoqué?; **w. do you see the company in ten years' time?** ¿dónde crees que estará la compañía dentro de diez años?; **w. did you get that idea?** ¿de dónde has sacado esa idea?; **w. would we be if...?** ¿dónde estaríamos si...?; **now, w. was I?** veamos, ¿por dónde iba?
2 *conj* (**a**) *(in general)* donde; **I'll stay w. I am** me quedaré donde estoy; **go w. you like** ve a donde quieras; **the house w. I was born** la casa donde *or* en que nací; **near w. I live** cerca de donde vivo; **they went to Paris, w. they stayed a week** fueron a París, donde permanecieron una semana; **that is w. you are mistaken** ahí es donde te equivocas; **I've reached the point w. I no longer care** he llegado a un punto en el que ya no me importa; **I can see w. this line of argument is leading** ya veo adónde nos lleva esta lógica; **I am prepared to fire people w. necessary** estoy dispuesto a despedir gente cuando haga falta; **w. there is disagreement, seek legal advice** en caso de disputa, pide asesoría jurídica *or* asesoramiento jurídico
(**b**) *(whereas)* mientras (que); **w. most people see a cruel dictator, she sees a man who cares about his country** mientras (que) la mayoría de la gente ve a un dictador cruel, ella ve a un hombre que se preocupa por su país
(**c**) *Math* **w. x equals y** donde x es igual a y
3 *n* **the w. and the when** el dónde y el cuándo; *Fam* **any old w.** en/a cualquier parte

whereabouts 1 *npl* ['weərəbaʊts] *(location)* **nobody knows her w., her w. are unknown** está en paradero desconocido
2 *adv* [weərə'baʊts] *(where)* dónde; **w. in Los Angeles do you live?** ¿en qué parte de Los Ángeles vives?

whereas [weə'ræz] *conj* (**a**) *(on the other hand)* mientras que (**b**) *Law* considerando que

whereat [weə'ræt] *conj Formal* **the bell rang, w. he rose to leave** sonó la campana y se dispuso a salir

whereby [weə'baɪ] *adv Formal* por el/la cual, en virtud del/de la cual; **the rules w. social conduct is regulated** las reglas que rigen el comportamiento *or* la conducta social; **the means w. society can be transformed** los medios a través de los cuales se puede transformar la sociedad

wherefore [weə'fɔ:(r)] *Formal* **1** *conj* por qué
2 *n* **the whys and wherefores** el cómo y el porqué

wherein [weə'rɪn] *adv Formal* donde; **the issue w. they found most agreement** el asunto en el que más de acuerdo estaban

whereof [weə'rɒf] *pron Formal* del que, de la que

wheresoever [weəsəʊ'evə(r)] *adv Formal* allá donde, dondequiera que

whereupon [weərə'pɒn] *conj Literary* tras lo cual

wherever [weə'revə(r)] **1** *conj* (**a**) *(everywhere that)* allá donde, dondequiera que; **I see him w. I go** vaya donde vaya, siempre lo veo; **w. we went, he complained about the food** en todos los sitios adonde íbamos, se quejaba de la comida; **I corrected the mistakes w. I could** corregí los errores que pude; **w. possible** (allá) donde sea posible (**b**) *(no matter where)* dondequiera que; **we'll go w. you want** iremos donde quieras; **he takes work w. he can find it** acepta trabajo venga de donde venga; **w. there is poverty there are social problems** (allá) donde hay pobreza, hay problemas sociales
2 *adv* (**a**) *(referring to unknown or unspecified place)* en cualquier parte; **at home, in the office, or w.** en casa, en la oficina o donde sea; **it's in Antananarivo, w. that is** está en Antananarivo, dondequiera que quede eso (**b**) *(in questions)* **w. can he be?** ¿dónde puede estar?; **w. has he gone?** ¿adónde ha ido?; **w. did you get that idea?** ¿de dónde has sacado esa idea?

wherewithal ['weərwɪðɔ:l] *n* **the w. (to do sth)** los medios (para hacer algo)

whet [wet] (*pt & pp* **whetted**) *vt* (**a**) *(tool, blade)* afilar (**b**) *(appetite)* despertar, abrir; *Fig* **to w. sb's appetite (for sth)** despertar el interés de alguien (por algo); **her few days holiday only whetted her appetite for more** esos pocos días de vacaciones no hicieron más que despertarle las ganas de repetir

WHETHER ['weðə(r)] *conj* (**a**) *(referring to doubt, choice)* si; **I don't know w. it's true** no sé si es verdad; **I was unsure w. to go or stay** no estaba seguro de si ir o quedarme; **the decision w. to go or stay is yours** la decisión de ir o quedarte es tuya; **I doubt w. they'll agree** dudo que vayan a estar de acuerdo; **I don't know w. or not to tell them** no sé si contárselo o no
(**b**) *(no matter if)* **w. it's you or me doesn't matter** no importa que seas tú o que sea yo; **she won't come, w. you ask her or I do** no vendrá, se lo pidas tú o se lo pida yo; **w. she comes or not, we shall leave** nos iremos, venga ella o no; **w. or not this is true** sea eso verdad o no

> En inglés elevado, tanto hablado como escrito, en ocasiones se usa el subjuntivo en oraciones que empiezan por **whether**:
> **whether they be British or foreign, they will all find the weather harsh**
> *sean británicos o extranjeros, a todos les parecerá duro el clima*
> si bien en este caso también sería aceptable decir:
> **whether they are British or foreign, they will all find the weather harsh**

whetstone ['wetstəʊn] *n* piedra *f* de afilar

whew [hju:] *exclam* (**a**) *(expressing relief, fatigue)* ¡uf! (**b**) *(expressing astonishment)* ¡hala!

whey [weɪ] *n* suero *m*

whey-faced ['weɪfeɪst] *adj* pálido(a)

WHICH [wɪtʃ] **1** *adj* (**a**) *(in questions)* qué; **w. colour do you like best?** ¿qué color te gusta más?; **w. books have you read?** ¿qué libros has leído?; **w. way do we go?** ¿hacia dónde vamos?; **w. country would you rather go to?** ¿a qué país preferirías ir?; **he asked her w. colour she preferred** le preguntó qué color prefería; **w. one?** ¿cuál?; **w. ones?** ¿cuáles?
(**b**) *(in relative constructions)* **I was there for a week, during w. time...** estuve allí una semana, durante la cual...; **she came at noon, by w. time I had left** llegó a mediodía, pero para entonces yo ya me había marchado *or* ido

2 *pron* **(a)** *(in questions) (singular)* cuál; *(plural)* cuáles; **w. have you chosen?** ¿cuál/cuáles has escogido?; **w. of the two is prettier?** ¿cuál de las dos es más bonita?; **w. of you is going?** ¿cuál de *Esp* vosotros *or Am* ustedes va?; **he asked her w. she preferred** le preguntó cuál prefería; **it's red or blue, but I've forgotten w.** es rojo o azul, ya no me acuerdo de cuál; **I can never remember w. is w.** nunca me acuerdo (de) cuál es cuál

(b) *(relative)* que; **the house w. is for sale** la casa que está en venta; **this is the one w. I mentioned** éste es el que mencioné; **the house, w. has been empty for years** la casa, que lleva años vacía

(c) *(referring back to whole clause)* lo cual; **he's getting married, w. surprises me** se va a casar, lo cual *or* cosa que me sorprende; **she was back in London, w. annoyed me** estaba de vuelta en Londres, y eso me molestaba; **I met an old school friend, w. was nice** me encontré con un antiguo compañero de colegio, *Esp* lo que estuvo bien *or Am* lo cual fue muy bueno; **she said she'd be on time, w. I doubt** dijo que llegaría a la hora *or RP* en hora, lo que dudo

(d) *(with prepositions)* **the house of w. I am speaking** la casa de la que estoy hablando; **the countries w. we are going to** los países a los que vamos a ir; **the town w. we live in** la ciudad en (la) que vivimos; **I have three exams, the first of w. is tomorrow** tengo tres exámenes, el primero de los cuales es mañana; **I made several suggestions, most of w. were rejected** hice varias sugerencias, la mayoría de las cuales fueron rechazadas; **I was shocked by the anger with w. she said this** me sorprendió el *esp Esp* enfado *or esp Am* enojo con (el) que dijo esto; **after w. he went out** tras lo cual, salió

Ver nota en la entrada **that** para una explicación de cuándo se puede omitir **which.**

whichever [wɪtʃ'evə(r)] **1** *adj* **(a)** *(indicating the specified choice or preference)* **take w. book you like best** toma *or Esp* coge el libro que prefieras; **we'll travel by w. train is fastest** viajaremos en el tren que sea más rápido

(b) *(no matter what)* **w. job you take, it will mean a lot of travelling** cualquiera que sea el empleo que aceptes, supondrá viajar mucho; **w. party is in power** cualquiera que sea el partido que gobierne; **w. way we do it there'll be problems** lo hagamos como lo hagamos habrá problemas; **w. way you look at it** lo mires como lo mires

2 *pron* **(a)** *(the one that)* el que, la que; **take w. you prefer** toma el que prefieras; **will w. of you arrives first turn on the heating?** el que llegue primero, que haga el favor de encender la calefacción; **the 30th or the last Friday, w. comes first** el día 30 o el último viernes, lo que venga antes

(b) *(no matter which one)* **w. you choose, it will be a bargain** elijas el que elijas, será una ganga; **w. of the houses you buy it will be a good investment** cualquiera que sea la casa que compres, será una buena inversión

whiff [wɪf] *n* **(a)** *(smell)* olorcillo *m* (**of** a); **she caught a w. of it** le llegó el olorcillo; *Fig* **a w. of scandal/hypocrisy** un tufillo a escándalo/hipocresía; **a w. of failure has clung to him since his involvement in this fiasco** el fracaso le ha perseguido desde que se vio envuelto en este fiasco

(b) *(inhalation)* **one w. of this gas could kill you!** una mínima inhalación de este gas podría matarte; **take a w. of this!** ¡huele esto!

whiffy ['wɪfɪ] *adj Fam* maloliente, apestoso(a); **it's a bit w. in here, don't you think?** qué mal huele aquí *or Arg* qué baranda, ¿no?

WHILE [waɪl] **1** *n* **(a)** *(time) (minutes, hours)* rato *m*; *(days, months, years)* tiempo *m*; **a short** *or* **little w.** un rato/tiempo; **a good w., quite a w.** un buen rato/tiempo; **it happened a w. ago** ocurrió hace bastante tiempo; **it took me a w. to realize what she meant** tardé un rato en comprender qué quería decir; **after a w.** después de un rato/tiempo; **all the w.** todo el rato/tiempo; **for a w.** (durante) un rato/tiempo; **I haven't been there for a w.** hace tiempo que no voy por allí; **in a w.** dentro de un rato; **it's the first time in a w. that I've had the chance** es la primera vez en mucho tiempo que he tenido la oportunidad; **once in a w.** de vez en cuando

(b) *(effort)* **it's not worth my w.** no (me) merece la pena; **I'll make it worth your w.** te recompensaré

2 *conj* **(a)** *(during the time that)* mientras; **I fell asleep w. reading** me quedé dormido mientras leía; **I met her w. in Spain** la conocí (cuando estaba) en España; **it won't happen w. I'm in charge!** ¡esto no ocurrirá mientras yo esté al cargo!; **if you're going to the shop, could you get me some apples w. you're there?** ya que vas a la tienda, ¿por qué no me traes unas manzanas?; **you may as well clean the bathroom w. you're at it** ya que estás en ello podrías aprovechar para limpiar el baño

(b) *(although)* si bien; **w. I admit it's difficult,...** si bien admito que es difícil,...; **the exam, w. difficult, was not impossible** el examen, aunque difícil, no fue imposible

(c) *(whereas)* mientras que; **one wore white, w. the other was all in black** uno iba de blanco, mientras que el otro vestía todo de negro

▸ **while away** *vt sep (hours, evening)* entretener; **he whiled away the hours reading until his wife returned** entretuvo las horas leyendo hasta que su esposa regresó; **to w. away the time** matar *or* pasar el rato

whilst [waɪlst] *conj Br* = **while**

whim [wɪm] *n* capricho *m*; **to do sth on a w.** hacer algo por capricho; **it's just one of his little whims** es sólo uno de sus caprichos; **she indulges his every w.** le consiente todos los caprichos; **arrangements are altered at the w. of the king** los planes se modifican a capricho del rey

whimbrel ['wɪmbrəl] *n* zarapito *m* trinador

whimper ['wɪmpə(r)] **1** *n* gimoteo *m*; *Fig* **without a w.** sin rechistar; **I don't want to hear a w. out of you** no te quiero oír (más)

2 *vi* gemir, gimotear

whimpering ['wɪmpərɪŋ] **1** *n* gimoteo *m*, lloriqueo *m*; **stop your w.!** ¡deja ya de gimotear *or* lloriquear!

2 *adj (voice)* sollozante; *(person)* que gimotea *or* lloriquea

whimsical ['wɪmzɪkəl] *adj (person, behaviour)* caprichoso(a); *(remark, story)* curioso(a), inusual

whimsically ['wɪmzɪklɪ] *adv (capriciously)* caprichosamente; *(playfully)* juguetonamente; *(to smile)* de una manera enigmática, enigmáticamente

whimsy ['wɪmzɪ] *n* capricho *m*; **a piece of pure w.** no es nada más que un capricho *or* una extravagancia

whinchat ['wɪntʃæt] *n* tarabilla *f* norteña

whine [waɪn] **1** *n* **(a)** *(of person, animal)* gemido *m* **(b)** *(of machine)* chirrido *m*

2 *vt (of person)* decir gimiendo; *(of child)* decir lloriqueando; **"I'm hungry," she whined** "tengo hambre", rezongó *or* se quejó

3 *vi* **(a)** *(dog)* gemir, aullar **(b)** *(in pain)* gimotear **(c)** *(complain)* quejarse (**about** de)

whinge [wɪndʒ] *vi Br Fam (complain)* quejarse (**about** de)

whinger ['wɪndʒə(r)] *n Br Esp* quejica *mf*, *Méx, RP* quejoso(a) *m,f*

whining ['waɪnɪŋ] **1** *n* **(a)** *(of person)* quejidos *mpl*; *(of dog)* gemidos *mpl*, aullidos *mpl*; **I've had enough of your w.!** ¡estoy harto de tus quejas! **(b)** *(of machinery, engine)* chirrido *m*

2 *adj (person)* quejumbroso(a), quejoso(a); *(voice)* quejumbroso(a); *(dog)* que gime *or* aúlla lastimeramente

whinny ['wɪnɪ] **1** *n* relincho *m*

2 *vi* relinchar

whiny ['waɪnɪ] *adj (voice)* quejumbroso(a)

whip [wɪp] **1** *n* **(a)** *(for punishment)* látigo *m*; *(for horse)* fusta *f*; IDIOM **to have the w. hand** tener la sartén por el mango; **to have the w. hand over sb** tener control sobre alguien

(b) *Pol (person)* = encargado de mantener la disciplina de un partido político en el parlamento

(c) *Br Parl (document)* = despacho enviado a un diputado por su portavoz de grupo en el que se le insta a asistir al parlamento para votar en un asunto determinado; **to break the w.** romper la disciplina de voto

2 *vt* (*pt & pp* **whipped**) **(a)** *(lash, hit)* azotar; *(horse)* fustigar; *Fig* **he whipped the crowd into a frenzy** exaltó al gentío; *Fig* **I'll soon w. the team into shape** en poco tiempo pondré en forma al equipo

(b) *Culin (egg whites, cream)* batir; **whipped cream** *Esp* nata montada, *Am* crema batida

(c) *Fam (defeat)* dar una soberana paliza a

(d) *Fam (steal)* afanar, *Esp* mangar

(e) *(move quickly)* **she whipped it out of sight** lo hizo desaparecer en un abrir y cerrar de ojos; **she was whipped into hospital** se la llevaron rápidamente al hospital

3 *vi (move quickly)* moverse rápidamente; **the taxi whipped along the road** el taxi pasó a toda velocidad por la calle; **she whipped around the corner** dobló rápidamente la esquina; **the sound of bullets whipping through the air** el sonido de las balas que atravesaban el aire; **the ball whipped past him into the net** la pelota pasó junto a él como una exhalación y se estrelló en la red; **I'll just w. down to the shop** voy corriendo *or* en un momento a la tienda

▸ **whip off** *vt sep (cover, tablecloth)* quitar, *Am* sacar; *(one's clothes)* quitarse, *Am* sacarse

▸**whip out** *vt sep* sacar rápidamente; **she whipped out a gun** de pronto sacó una pistola

▸**whip round** *vi Br (turn quickly)* darse la vuelta rápidamente, *Méx* voltearse rápidamente

▸**whip through** *vt insep Fam (book)* echar una rápida ojeada a; *(task)* despachar por la vía rápida

▸**whip up** *vt sep* **(a)** *(provoke)* **to w. up one's audience** entusiasmar al público; **to w. up support (for sth)** recabar apoyo (para algo); **they found it hard to w. up interest in the subject** les costaba mucho despertar interés en el tema **(b)** *Fam (meal)* **I'll w. you up something to eat** te prepararé algo de comer

whipcord ['wɪpkɔːd] *n* **(a)** *(cloth)* pana *f (diagonal)* **(b)** *(cord)* tralla *f*

whiplash ['wɪplæʃ] *n Med* **w. (injury)** esguince *m* cervical

whipper-in [wɪpə'rɪn] *n (in hunting)* montero(a) *m,f* de traílla

whippersnapper ['wɪpəsnæpə(r)] *n Fam* mocoso(a) *m,f*

whippet ['wɪpɪt] *n* lebrel *m*

whipping ['wɪpɪŋ] *n* azotes *mpl*; **to give sb a w.** *(punish)* azotar a alguien; *Fam (defeat)* dar una soberana paliza a alguien ▸▸ ***w. boy*** cabeza *mf* de turco; ***w. cream*** *Esp* nata *f or Am* crema *f* de leche líquida para montar

whippoorwill ['wɪpəwɪl] *n* chotacabras *m or f inv* americano(a)

whipround ['wɪpraʊnd] *n Br Fam* **to have a w. (for sb)** hacer una colecta (para alguien)

whipsaw ['wɪpsɔː] **1** *n* sierra *f* abrazadera, sierra *f* cabrilla

2 *vt* **(a)** *(cut with saw)* aserrar **(b)** *US (on stock market)* **he was whipsawed by the volatile market** se llevó un duro golpe por la volatilidad del mercado **(c)** *US Fam (damage)* reventar *or* hacer trizas por partida doble; **the candidate whipsawed his opponent** el candidato reventó *or* hizo trizas por partida doble a su oponente

whir = **whirr**

whirl [wɜːl] **1** *n* remolino *m*; **a w. of activity** un torbellino de actividad; **the social w.** el torbellino de la vida social; **my head's in a w.** tengo una gran confusión mental; *Fam* **let's give it a w.** probémoslo

2 *vt* **to w. sth/sb around** hacer girar algo/a alguien

3 *vi (dust, smoke, leaves)* arremolinarse; *(person)* girar vertiginosamente; **snowflakes whirled past the window** los copos de nieve pasaban arremolinados frente a la ventana; **my head's whirling** me da vueltas la cabeza

▸**whirl along** *vi (car, train)* avanzar rápidamente

▸**whirl round** *vi* volverse *or* darse la vuelta rápidamente

whirligig ['wɜːlɪgɪg] *n Br* **(a)** *(top)* peonza *f*, trompo *m*; *(toy windmill)* molinillo *m*, molinete *m* **(b)** *(merry-go-round)* tiovivo *m*, carrusel *m*, *RP* calesita *f* ▸▸ ***w. beetle*** escribano *m* de(l) agua

whirlpool ['wɜːlpuːl] *n* remolino *m* ▸▸ ***w. bath*** bañera *f* de hidromasaje

whirlwind ['wɜːlwɪnd] *n* torbellino *m*; *Fig* **he went through the office accounts like a w.** revisó volando las cuentas de la oficina; **he came into the room like a w.** entró en la habitación como un torbellino ▸▸ ***w. romance*** romance *m* arrebatado; ***w. tour*** *(of city, museum)* visita *f* relámpago

whirlybird ['wɜːlɪbɜːd] *n Fam Old-fashioned* helicóptero *m*

whir(r) [wɜː(r)] **1** *n (of helicopter, fan, machine)* zumbido *m*, runrún *m*; *(of bird's wings)* (sonido *m* del) aleteo *m*

2 *vi (helicopter, fan, machine)* zumbar; *(bird's wings)* aletear

whisk [wɪsk] **1** *n* **(a)** *Culin* batidor *m* (manual) **(b)** **(fly) w.** matamoscas *m inv* **(c)** *(of tail)* sacudida *f*; *(of broom)* golpe *m*; **the horse gave a w. of its tail** el caballo sacudió la cola

2 *vt* **(a)** *(eggs, cream, egg whites)* batir; **w. in the cream** agregue crema sin dejar de batir; **w. the egg whites until stiff** bata las claras a punto de nieve **(b)** *(move quickly)* **she whisked the crumbs onto the floor** sacudió las migas al suelo; **he was whisked into hospital** lo llevaron apresuradamente *or* a toda prisa al hospital

3 *vi (move quickly)* **she whisked past me** pasó zumbando a mi lado

▸**whisk away, whisk off** *vt sep* llevarse rápidamente; **the president was whisked away in a helicopter** al presidente se lo llevaron rápidamente en helicóptero; **a car whisked us away to the embassy** un coche nos trasladó rápidamente a la embajada

whisker ['wɪskə(r)] *n* **(a)** *(hair)* **whiskers** *(of cat, mouse)* bigotes *mpl*; *(of man)* patillas *fpl* **(b)** IDIOMS *Fam* **to win by a w.** ganar por un pelo; **within a w. (of)** a punto (de), en un tris (de)

whisky, *US, Irish* **whiskey** ['wɪskɪ] *n* whisky *m*; **a w. and soda** un whisky con soda; **a w. on the rocks** un whisky con hielo *or* on the rocks

whisper ['wɪspə(r)] **1** *n* **(a)** *(of voice)* susurro *m*; **to speak in a w.** hablar en voz baja *or Am* despacio; **and remember, not a w. of it to anyone!** y recuerda, ¡ni una palabra a nadie! **(b)** *(of leaves, wind)* murmullo *m*, susurro *m*, rumor *m* **(c)** *Br (rumour)* rumor *m*; **I've heard whispers that...** he oído rumores de que...

2 *vt* **(a)** *(person)* susurrar; **to w. sth to sb** susurrar algo a alguien **(b)** *Br (rumour)* **it is being whispered that...** se rumorea que...

3 *vi* **(a)** *(speak in low voice)* susurrar; **stop whispering at the back of the class!** ¡basta ya de cuchichear ahí atrás! **(b)** *(wind)* **the wind was whispering in the trees** el viento susurraba entre los árboles

whispering ['wɪspərɪŋ] *n* **(a)** *(of people, voices)* cuchicheo *m* ▸▸ ***w. campaign*** campaña *f* de difamación; *Archit* ***w. gallery*** galería *f* con eco **(b)** *(of leaves, water, wind)* murmullo *m*, susurro *m*, rumor *m*

whist [wɪst] *n* whist *m* ▸▸ *Br* ***w. drive*** torneo *m* de whist

whistle ['wɪsəl] **1** *n* **(a)** *(noise) (of person, bird)* silbido *m*; *(of kettle, train)* silbido *m*, pitido *m* **(b)** *(musical instrument)* pífano *m*, flautín *m*; *(of referee, policeman)* silbato *m*, pito *m*; **to blow a w.** hacer sonar un silbato; IDIOM **as clean as a w.** *(place)* (limpio(a)) como una patena; *(person)* con un historial intachable

2 *vt (tune)* silbar

3 *vi (person, bird)* silbar; *(kettle, train)* silbar, pitar; **if you need me, just w.** si me necesitas, sólo tienes que silbar; **the porter whistled for a taxi** el portero llamó a un taxi con un silbido; **he whistles at all the girls** les silba a todas las muchachas; **the audience booed and whistled** el público abucheaba y silbaba; **the bullet whistled past his ear** la bala le pasó silbando junto al oído; IDIOM *Fam* **he can w. for his money** puede esperar sentado su dinero

▸**whistle up** *vt sep Br* **(a)** *(by whistling)* llamar con un silbido; **I'll w. up a cab** llamaré a un taxi (de un silbido) **(b)** *(find)* conseguir; **I managed to w. up a van for the move** conseguí una camioneta para la mudanza; **I can't w. up the money just like that!** no puedo reunir el dinero como por arte de magia

whistle-blower ['wɪsəlbləʊə(r)] *n (in company, government)* denunciante *mf (de ilegalidades o corruptelas)*

whistle-stop ['wɪsəlstɒp] **1** *n* **(a)** *(brief appearance)* visita *f or* aparición *f* relámpago ▸▸ ***w. tour:* a w. tour of Europe** un recorrido rápido *or* una gira relámpago por Europa **(b)** *US (station)* apeadero *m*; *(town)* pueblo *m* con apeadero

2 *vi US Pol* = hacer campaña electoral en tren deteniéndose a dar mitines en todas las estaciones

Whit [wɪt] *n* Pentecostés *m* ▸▸ ***W. Sunday*** domingo *m* de Pentecostés

whit [wɪt] *n* **not a w.** ni pizca; **he hasn't changed a w.** no ha cambiado un ápice; **I don't care a w. what people think** me tiene sin cuidado lo que la gente piense; **it won't make a w. of a difference** va a dar exactamente igual

white [waɪt] **1** *n* **(a)** *(colour)* blanco *m*; **the bride wore w.** la novia iba (vestida) de blanco; **he was dressed all in w.** estaba *or* iba vestido de blanco **(b)** *(person)* blanco(a) *m,f* **(c)** *(of egg)* clara *f* **(d)** *(of eyes)* blanco *m* **(e)** *(in chess)* (las) blancas

2 whites *npl (sportswear)* equipo *m* blanco, ropa *f* blanca (de deporte); *(linen)* ropa *f* blanca

3 *adj* blanco(a); **to turn** *or* **go w.** ponerse blanco(a), empalidecer; IDIOM **(to show the) w. feather** (demostrar) falta de agallas; **w. with fear** pálido(a) de miedo; IDIOM **w. as a ghost** *or* **sheet** blanco(a) como la nieve ▸▸ ***w. admiral*** *(butterfly)* ninfa *f* de bosque; ***w. ant*** termita *f*, hormiga *f* blanca; ***w. blood cell*** glóbulo *m* blanco, leucocito *m*; ***w. chocolate*** chocolate *m* blanco; ***w. Christmas*** Navidades *fpl* blancas; ***w. coffee*** café *m* con leche; *Physiol* ***w. corpuscle*** glóbulo *m* blanco, leucocito *m*; *Astron* ***w. dwarf*** enana *f* blanca; *Fig* ***w. elephant*** mamotreto *m* inútil; *Br* ***w. elephant stall*** puesto *m* de venta de objetos usados; ***W. Ensign*** = bandera de los barcos de la marina británica; *Br Hist* ***w. feather*** = pluma blanca utilizada como símbolo de cobardía en Gran Bretaña durante la Primera Guerra Mundial; **to show the w. feather** actuar con cobardía; ***w. fish*** pescado *m* blanco; ***w. flag*** bandera *f* blanca; ***w. flour*** harina *f* (refinada); ***W. Friar*** monje *m* carmelita(no); ***w. gold*** oro *m* blanco; ***w. goods*** *(linen)* ropa *f* blanca *or* de cama; *(kitchen appliances)* línea *f* blanca (de electrodomésticos); ***w. heat*** calor *m* blanco, rojo *m* blanco; ***w. hope*** gran esperanza *f*; **he's the great w. hope of British car racing** es la gran esperanza *or* promesa del automovilismo británico; ***w. horses*** *(on wave)* cabrillas *fpl*; *US* ***the W. House*** la Casa Blanca; *Com* ***w. knight*** caballero *m* blanco, = persona o entidad que salva a una empresa de la quiebra o de ser absorbida; ***w. lead*** albayalde *m*; ***w. lie*** mentira *f* piadosa; ***w. light*** luz *f* blanca; ***w. magic*** magia *f* blanca; ***a w. man*** un hombre blanco; ***w. meat*** carne *f* blanca; ***w. noise*** ruido *m* blanco; *US* ***W. Out***® líquido *m* corrector; *US* ***the W. Pages*** la guía telefónica, las páginas blancas; *Parl* ***w. paper*** libro *m* blanco; ***w. pepper*** pimienta *f* blanca; ***w.***

pudding = morcilla blanca a base de sebo y avena; *Hist* ***W. Russian*** ruso(a) *m,f* blanco(a); ***w. sauce*** (salsa *f*) bechamel *f, Col, CSur* salsa *f* blanca; ***w. slave trade*** trata *f* de blancas; ***w. slavery*** trata *f* de blancas; *Br* ***w. spirit*** aguarrás *m*; ***w. stick*** bastón *m* de ciego; ***w. stork*** cigüeña *f* blanca; ***w. sugar*** azúcar *f* blanquilla; ***w. supremacist*** defensor(ora) *m,f* de la supremacía (de la raza) blanca; ***w. supremacy*** supremacía *f* (de la raza) blanca; ***w. tie*** *(formal dress)* frac *m* y *Esp* pajarita blanca *or Méx* corbata de moño blanca *or RP* moñito blanco; *US Fam Pej* ***w. trash*** gentuza *f* blanca; ***w. water*** aguas *fpl* bravas; ***w. water rafting*** descenso *m* de aguas bravas; ***w. wedding*** boda *f or Andes* matrimonio *m or RP* casamiento *m* de blanco; ***w. whale*** beluga *f*; ***w. wine*** vino *m* blanco; ***w. witch*** bruja *f* buena *or* blanca

▸**white out** *vt sep (word, sentence, text)* borrar con líquido corrector

whitebait ['waɪtbeɪt] *n* pescadito *m*; **deep-fried w.** pescadito frito

whitebeam ['waɪtbiːm] *n* serbal *m* (de montaña)

whiteboard ['waɪtbɔːd] *n* pizarra *f* blanca

white-collar ['waɪt'kɒlə] *adj (job)* de oficina, administrativo(a) ▸▸ ***w. worker*** oficinista *mf*

whited ['waɪtɪd] *adj Literary* ***w. sepulchre*** sepulcro *m* blanqueado

whitefaced ['waɪtfeɪst] *adj* pálido(a)

whitefly ['waɪtflaɪ] *n* mosca *f or* mosquita *f* blanca

white-haired ['waɪt'heəd] *adj* canoso(a), de pelo cano ▸▸ *US Fig* ***w. boy*** niño *m* bonito *or* mimado, favorito *m*

white-headed ['waɪt'hedɪd] *adj (person)* canoso(a), de pelo cano; *(animal, bird)* de cabeza blanca ▸▸ *US Fig* ***w. boy*** niño *m* bonito *or* mimado, favorito *m*

Whitehall ['waɪthɔːl] *n* = nombre de la calle de Londres donde se encuentra la administración central británica

white-hot ['waɪt'hɒt] *adj* candente

white-knuckle [waɪt'nʌkəl] *adj* ***w. ride*** atracción *f* que pone los pelos de punta

whiten ['waɪtən] **1** *vt* blanquear

2 *vi (hair)* encanecer, ponerse blanco(a); *(face)* palidecer, ponerse pálido(a) *or* blanco(a); *(sky)* clarear

whitener ['waɪtnə(r)] *n* (**a**) *(in toothpaste, detergent)* blanqueador *m* (**b**) *(for tea, coffee)* sucedáneo *m* de leche

whiteness ['waɪtnɪs] *n* blancura *f*

white-out ['waɪtaʊt] *n* = pérdida total de visibilidad durante una tormenta de nieve

whitethroat ['waɪtθrəʊt] *n* curruca *f* zarcera

whitewash ['waɪtwɒʃ] **1** *n* (**a**) *(paint)* cal *f*, lechada *f* (**b**) *Fam (cover-up)* encubrimiento *m*

2 *vt* (**a**) *(wall, fence)* encalar (**b**) *Fam (cover up)* echar tierra sobre, tapar

whitewashed ['waɪtwɒʃt] *adj (wall, house)* encalado(a), blanqueado(a)

whitewood ['waɪtwʊd] *n* madera *f* blanca

whitey ['waɪtɪ] *n Fam Pej* blanco(a) *m,f*

whither ['wɪðə(r)] *adv Literary* adónde; **w. Christianity?** *(in headlines, titles)* ¿adónde va el cristianismo?; **I shall go w. fate leads me** iré donde me lleve el destino

whiting ['waɪtɪŋ] *n* (**a**) *(fish)* pescadilla *f* (**b**) *(chalk)* blanco *m* (de) España

whitish ['waɪtɪʃ] *adj* blancuzco(a), blanquecino(a)

whitlow ['wɪtləʊ] *n Med* panadizo *m*

Whitsun ['wɪtsən] *n* Pentecostés *m*

whittle ['wɪtəl] *vt (carve)* tallar; *(sharpen)* sacar punta a, pelar

▸**whittle away** **1** *vt sep* **his savings had been gradually whittled away** sus ahorros se habían visto mermados gradualmente; **their rights were being whittled away** poco a poco les iban despojando de sus derechos

2 *vi* **inflation had whittled away at their savings** la inflación había ido mermando sus ahorros

▸**whittle down** *vt sep* **to w. sth down** ir reduciendo algo; **we've whittled down the number of candidates to four** hemos reducido hasta cuatro el número de candidatos; **to be whittled down to** quedar reducido(a) a

whizz [wɪz] **1** *n* (**a**) *(hissing sound)* silbido *m*, zumbido *m* (**b**) *Fam (expert)* genio *m* (**at** de); **a computer w.** un genio de la informática ▸▸ ***w. kid*** joven *mf* prodigio (**c**) *Br Fam (amphetamines)* anfetas *fpl*

2 *vi (bullet)* silbar, zumbar; *(person, car)* ir corriendo, ir zumbando; **a bullet whizzed past her ear** una bala le pasó silbando junto a la oreja; **to w. past** pasar zumbando; **the holiday has just whizzed by** las vacaciones se pasaron volando; **he whizzed through the work** hizo el trabajo a toda velocidad

WHO ['dʌbəljuːeɪtʃ'əʊ] *n* (*abbr* **World Health Organization**) OMS *f*

WHO [huː] *pron* (**a**) *(in questions) (singular)* quién; *(plural)* quiénes; **w. is it?** ¿quién es?; **w. are they?** ¿quiénes son?; **w. with?** ¿con quién?; **w. is it for?** ¿para quién es?; **I asked w. it was for** pregunté para quién era; **w. should I ask?** ¿a quién debo preguntar?; **w. am I to criticize?** ¿quién so yo para criticar?; **why did she do it? – w. knows?** ¿por qué lo hizo? – ¿quién sabe?, *RP* andá a saber; **w. did you say was there?** ¿quién has dicho que estaba allí?; **I met someone called Paul Major – Paul w.?** conocí a alguien llamado Paul Major – ¿Paul qué?; **w. does he think he is?** ¿quién se cree que es?; **I haven't quite worked out w.'s w. in the office yet** todavía no tengo muy claro quién es quién en la oficina; **Who's W.** *(book)* = libro que contiene información sobre gente famosa; **the meeting was like a Who's W. of British politics** la reunión concentró a todos los que son alguien en la política británica

(**b**) *(relative)* que; **the people w. came yesterday** las personas que vinieron ayer; **it is I w. did it** fui yo el que lo hizo; **those w. have already paid can leave** los que ya hayan pagado pueden marcharse *or* irse; **Louise's father, w. is a doctor, was there** el padre de Louise, que es médico, estaba allí

> Ver nota en la entrada **that** para una explicación de cuándo se puede omitir **who**.

whoa [wəʊ] *exclam (to horse)* ¡so!; *(to person)* ¡quieto(a)!

whodun(n)it [huː'dʌnɪt] *n Fam (book)* novela *f* de *Esp* suspense *or Am* suspenso *(centrada en la resolución de un caso de asesinato)*; *(film)* película *f* de *Esp* suspense *or Am* suspenso *(centrada en la resolución de un caso de asesinato)*

whoever [huː'evə(r)] *pron* (**a**) *(anyone that) (singular)* quienquiera; *(plural)* quienesquiera; **w. finds it may keep it** quienquiera que lo encuentre *or* quien lo encuentre, puede quedarse con ello; **invite w. you like** invita a quien quieras; **I'll give it to w. needs it most** se lo daré a quien más lo necesite

(**b**) *(the person or people who)* **w. wrote that letter** el que escribió esa carta; **w. is responsible will be punished** sea quien sea el responsable será castigado

(**c**) *(no matter who)* **tell w. you like** díselo a quien quieras *or* a quien te dé la gana; **w. you are, speak!** habla, quienquiera que seas; **w. it is, don't let them in** sea quien sea, no le abras; **it's by George Eliot, w. he was** es de un tal George Eliot, que no sé quien fue; *Fam* **ask Simon or Chris or w.** pregúntale a Simon, a Chris o a quien sea

(**d**) *(in questions)* **w. can that be?** ¿quién puede ser?; **w. heard such nonsense!** ¡habráse visto tamaña tontería!

WHOLE [həʊl] **1** *n* totalidad *f*; **the w. of the village/month** todo el pueblo/el mes; **the w. is greater than the sum of the parts** el todo es más grande que la suma de sus partes; **as a w.** en conjunto; **on the w.** en general

2 *adj* (**a**) *(entire, intact)* entero(a); **he swallowed it w.** se lo tragó entero; **to last a w. week** durar toda una semana *or* una semana entera; **we have a w. range of products** tenemos toda una gama de productos; **the w. day** todo el día, el día entero; **that's the w. point** de eso se trata; **that's not the w. story** ahí no acaba la historia *or* todo; **I find the w. affair most worrying** me parece todo muy preocupante; **all she does is complain the w. time** no hace otra cosa que quejarse todo el tiempo; **to tell the w. truth** decir toda la verdad; **the w. world** todo el mundo ▸▸ ***w. milk*** leche *f* entera; *US Mus* ***w. note*** semibreve *f*, *Am* redonda *f*; *Math* ***w. number*** número *m* entero; *US* ***w. wheat flour*** harina *f* de trigo integral

(**b**) *Fam* **the w. lot of them** todos ellos; **for a w. lot of reasons** por un montón de razones; **it's a w. lot better than the last one** es mucho mejor que el último

3 *adv (completely)* completamente; **it gives a w. new meaning to the word "charity"** concede un significado completamente nuevo a la palabra "caridad"

wholefood ['həʊlfuːd] *n* alimentos *mpl* integrales ▸▸ ***w. restaurant*** restaurante *m* macrobiótico; ***w. shop*** tienda *f* naturista, ≃ herbolario *m*

wholegrain ['həʊlgreɪn] *adj (bread, flour)* integral

wholehearted [həʊl'hɑːtɪd] *adj (support, agreement)* incondicional, sin reservas; **he is a w. supporter of their cause** apoya su causa de manera incondicional

wholeheartedly [həʊl'hɑːtɪdlɪ] *adv (to support, agree)* incondicionalmente, sin reservas; **I agree w.** estoy plenamente de acuerdo; **he flung himself w. into his new job** se metió de lleno y sin reservas en su nuevo trabajo

wholemeal ['həʊlmiːl] *adj Br* ***w. bread*** pan *m* integral; ***w. flour*** harina *f* integral

wholesale ['həʊlseɪl] 1 *n Com* venta *f* al por mayor, *Am* mayoreo *m*; **w. and retail** (ventas) al por mayor y al por menor
2 *adj* (a) *(price, dealer)* al por mayor; **the w. sector** el sector de la compraventa al por mayor (b) *(rejection)* rotundo(a); *(slaughter)* indiscriminado(a); **the w. destruction of the rainforests** la destrucción a gran escala de las selvas tropicales
3 *adv* (a) *Com* al por mayor (b) *(to reject)* rotundamente; **villages have been destroyed w.** pueblos enteros han sido destruidos

wholesaler ['həʊlseɪlə(r)] *n* mayorista *mf*

wholesome ['həʊlsəm] *adj (food, life, environment)* sano(a), saludable; **a w. family image** una imagen de familia feliz

wholewheat ['həʊlwiːt] *adj* integral ►► ***w. bread*** pan *m* integral

wholly ['həʊllɪ] *adv* enteramente, completamente

whom [huːm] *pron Formal*

En la actualidad, sólo aparece en contextos formales. **Whom** se puede sustituir por **who** en todos los casos salvo cuando va después de preposición.

(a) *(in questions) (singular)* quién; *(plural)* quiénes; **w. did you see?** ¿a quién viste?; **to w. were you speaking?** ¿con quién estabas hablando?; **to w. it may concern** *(in letter)* a quien corresponda
(b) *(relative)* que; **the woman w. you saw** la mujer que viste; **the man to w. you gave the money** el hombre al que diste el dinero; **somebody to w. he could talk** alguien con quien pudiera hablar; **the person of w. we were speaking** la persona de la que hablábamos; **the men, both of w. were quite young,...** los dos hombres, que eran bastante jóvenes,...

whomever [huː'mevə(r)] *pron Formal* quienquiera; **I will contact w. we need for this** hablaré con quien sea necesario para esto

whoop [wuːp] 1 *n* grito *m*, alarido *m*; **whoops of delight came from the audience** del público llegaban gritos de regocijo
2 *vi (shout)* gritar

whoopee *Fam* 1 *n* ['wʊpiː] *US Old-fashioned* **to make w.** *(have fun)* pasarlo genial *or Esp* teta *or Méx* de pelos; *(have sex)* echar un polvo *or* casquete ►► ***w. cushion*** = cojín de goma que emite el sonido de una ventosidad
2 *exclam* [wʊ'piː] ¡yupi!, ¡yuju!

whooper ['huːpə(r)] *n* **w. (swan)** cisne *m* cantor

whooping ['huːpɪŋ] *n* (a) ***w. cough*** tos *f* ferina (b) ***w. crane*** grulla *f* cantora

whoops [wʊps] *exclam* ¡huy!

whoops-a-daisy ['wʊpsədeɪzɪ] *exclam* ¡huy!

whoosh [wʊʃ] 1 *n (of plane)* zumbido *m*; *(of air)* ráfaga *f*; *(of water)* chorro *m*; **there was a w. of flame** hubo una fuerte llamarada
2 *vi (plane)* pasar zumbando; *(water)* salir a chorro; **the taxi whooshed through the puddles** el taxi pasó velozmente por los charcos salpicando

whopper ['wɒpə(r)] *n Fam* (a) *(huge thing)* enormidad *f*, *Esp* pasada *f* (de grande); **what a w.!** ¡qué grande!; **he's got a w. of a nose** tiene un buen narigón *or* unas buenas napias; **he caught a real w.** *(fish)* pescó uno enorme (b) *(lie)* cuento *m*, bola *f*

whopping ['wɒpɪŋ] *adj Fam* **w. (great)** enorme

whore [hɔː(r)] *Fam* 1 *n* puta *f*
2 *vi (frequent prostitutes)* ir(se) de putas; *(prostitute oneself)* hacer la calle; **to go whoring** ir(se) de putas

►**whore after** *vt sep* ir *or* andar detrás de

whorehouse ['hɔːhaʊs] *n Fam* casa *f* de putas, burdel *m*

whoremonger ['hɔːmʌŋgə(r)] *n Archaic* putero *m*, putañero *m*

whorl [wɔːl] *n* (a) *(on leaf)* verticilo *m* (b) *(on shell)* espira *f* (c) *(on finger)* espiral *f*

whortleberry ['wɜːtəlberɪ] *n* arándano *m*

whose [huːz] 1 *possessive pron (in questions) (singular)* de quién; *(plural)* de quiénes; **w. are these gloves?** ¿de quién son estos guantes?; **tell me w. they are** dime de quién son
2 *possessive adj* (a) *(in questions) (singular)* de quién; *(plural)* de quiénes; **w. daughter are you?** ¿de quién eres hija?; **w. fault is it?** ¿de quién es la culpa? (b) *(relative)* cuyo(a); **the pupil w. work I showed you** el alumno cuyo trabajo te enseñé; **the man to w. wife I gave the money** el hombre a cuya esposa entregué el dinero; **the girl, both of w. parents had died, lived with her aunt** la chica, cuyos padres habían fallecido, vivía con su tía

whosoever [huːsəʊ'evə(r)] *pron Formal (singular)* quienquiera; *(plural)* quienesquiera

WHY [waɪ] 1 *adv* (a) *(in questions)* por qué; **w. didn't you say so?** ¿por qué no lo dijiste?; **w. not?** ¿por qué no?; **w. not tell him?** ¿por qué no se lo dices?; **w. get angry?** ¿para qué *esp Esp* enfadarse *or esp Am* enojarse?; **w. the sad face?** ¿a qué viene *or* se debe esa cara de tristeza?; **give me that! – w. should I?** ¡dame eso! – ¿por qué?; **w. is it (that) you're always late?** ¿por qué (razón) llegas siempre tarde?; **answer the phone, Rob – w. me?** contesta el teléfono, Rob – ¿por qué yo?; **w. oh w. didn't you say so earlier?** ¡pero por qué no lo has dicho antes!
(b) *(in suggestions)* por qué; **w. don't you phone him?** ¿por qué no lo llamas?; **w. don't I come with you?** ¿y si voy contigo?
2 *conj (relative)* por qué; **I'll tell you w. I don't like her** te diré por qué no me gusta; **that is w. I didn't say anything** (es) por eso (por lo que) no dije nada; **I'm not coming, and this is w.** no voy, y éste es el porqué; **she's an Aries, which is w. she's so impulsive** es *Esp* Aries *or Am* de Aries, por eso es tan impulsiva; **the reason w. she can't come** la razón por la que no puede venir; **tell me the reason w.** dime la razón *or* por qué
3 *npl* **the whys and wherefores (of sth)** el cómo y el porqué (de algo)
4 *exclam* **w., it's** *or* **if it isn't David!** ¡vaya, si es David!; **w., certainly!** ¡claro que sí!; **w., it's so easy!** ¡pero si es muy fácil!; **w., he's an impostor!** ¡es un impostor!

WI *n* (a) ['dʌbəljuː'aɪ] *Br* (*abbr* **Women's Institute**) = asociación de mujeres del medio rural que organiza diversas actividades (b) (*abbr* **Wisconsin**) Wisconsin

wick [wɪk] *n* (a) *(of lamp, candle)* pabilo *m* (b) IDIOMS *Br Fam* **he gets on my w.** me saca de mis casillas; *very Fam* **to dip one's w.** mojar (el churro), meterla en caliente, *RP* mojar el bizcocho

wicked ['wɪkɪd] 1 *adj* (a) *(evil)* perverso(a), malo(a); *(dreadful)* horroroso(a), horrible; **w. witch** bruja malvada; **it was a w. thing to do** esas cosas no se hacen, fue una mala pasada; IDIOM *Hum* **to have one's w. way with sb** llevar a alguien al huerto, seducir a alguien
(b) *Fam (appalling)* asqueroso(a); **he's got a w. temper** tiene muy malas pulgas; **prices have gone up something w.** los precios han subido una barbaridad
(c) *(mischievous) (smile, wink)* pícaro(a); **a w. sense of humour** un sentido del humor con mucha picardía *or* retranca
(d) *Fam (excellent)* genial, *Esp* guay, *Andes, CAm, Carib, Méx* chévere, *Col* tenaz, *Méx* muy padre, *Ven* arrecho(a), *RP* bárbaro(a)
2 *exclam Fam (excellent)* ¡genial!, *Esp* ¡guay!, *Andes, CAm, Carib, Méx* ¡chévere!, *Col* ¡tenaz!, *Méx* ¡muy padre!, *RP* ¡bárbaro!
3 *npl* IDIOM **(there's) no peace** *or* **rest for the w.!** ¡a trabajar tocan!

wickedness ['wɪkɪdnɪs] *n* maldad *f*, perversidad *f*; **he spoke of the w. in the world** habló de la maldad *or* del mal en el mundo

wicker ['wɪkə(r)] *n* mimbre *m*; **w. chairs** sillas de mimbre

wickerwork ['wɪkəwɜːk] *n (baskets)* cestería *f*

wicket ['wɪkɪt] *n* (a) *(in cricket) (stumps)* palos *mpl*; *(pitch)* = parte del terreno de juego comprendida entre el lugar de bateo y el de lanzamiento; IDIOM *Br* **to be on a sticky w.** verse en un apuro *or* aprieto (b) *(gate)* portillo *m* (c) *US (window)* ventanilla *f*

wicketkeeper ['wɪkɪtkiːpə(r)] *n (in cricket)* cátcher *mf*

wide [waɪd] 1 *adj* (a) *(broad)* ancho(a); *(plain, area)* amplio(a); *(ocean)* vasto(a); *(grin, smile)* amplio(a); **it's 4 metres w.** tiene 4 metros de ancho; **how w. is it?** ¿qué ancho tiene?, ¿cuánto mide de ancho?; **to get wider** ensancharse; **they're making the street wider** están ensanchando la calle; **in the whole w. world** en todo el ancho mundo; **her eyes were w. with surprise** los ojos se le pusieron como platos de la sorpresa ►► *Comptr* ***w. area network*** red *f* de área extensa; *Br Fam* ***w. boy*** pájaro *m* de cuenta, vivales *m inv*; ***w. receiver*** *(in American football)* receptor(ora) *m,f*, receiver *mf*; *Cin & TV* ***w. screen*** pantalla *f* ancha
(b) *(range, experience, gap)* amplio(a), extenso(a); *(variation)* amplio(a); *(support, publicity, appeal)* generalizado(a); *(aims)* muy diversos(as); **to take a wider view** tomar una perspectiva más amplia; **there are wider issues at stake here** aquí hay cosas más importantes en juego; **I'm using the word in its widest sense** estoy usando la palabra en su más amplio significado; **he has very w. interests** tiene intereses muy diversos; **she has a w. knowledge of music/politics** sabe mucho *or* tiene amplios conocimientos de música/política; **the model is available in a w. variety of colours** el modelo viene en una amplia variedad de colores

(**c**) *(off target)* **to be w.** ir *or* salir desviado(a)

2 *adv* (**a**) *(fully)* **to open sth w.** *(eyes, mouth)* abrir algo mucho; *(door)* abrir algo de par en par; **open w.!** *(said by dentist)* ¡abra bien la boca!; **his mouth was w. open** se quedó boquiabierto(a); **the tournament is still w. open** el torneo sigue muy abierto; **to be w. open to criticism** estar muy expuesto(a) a la crítica; **he spread his arms w.** extendió del todo los brazos; **w. apart** muy separado(a); **she stood with her legs w. apart** estaba de pie *or Am* parado(a) con las piernas muy abiertas; **to be w. awake** estar completamente despierto(a)

(**b**) *(off target)* **the shot went w.** el tiro salió desviado; **his guess was w. of the mark** su conjetura iba totalmente descaminada

wide-angle ['waɪd'æŋgəl] *adj Phot* ***w. lens*** gran angular *m*; *Cin & TV* ***w. shot*** toma *f* con gran angular

wide-bodied ['waɪd'bɒdɪd] *adj (aircraft)* de fuselaje ancho

wide-eyed ['waɪdaɪd] *adj* con los ojos muy abiertos *or* como platos; **he looked at me in w. astonishment** me miró con los ojos como platos (de asombro)

widely ['waɪdlɪ] *adv* (**a**) *(generally)* en general; **she is w. expected to resign** la opinión generalizada es que dimitirá; **w. known** ampliamente conocido; **the drug is now w. available** ahora el medicamento se consigue fácilmente; **this herb is w. used in cooking** esta hierba se utiliza mucho para cocinar; **it is w. believed that...** existe la creencia generalizada de que...

(**b**) *(at a distance)* **w. spaced** muy espaciado(a)

(**c**) *(a lot)* **to read w.** leer de todo; **a w. read author/newspaper** un autor/diario muy leído; **to travel w.** viajar mucho; **opinions differ w.** hay muchas y muy diversas opiniones; **the students came from w. differing backgrounds** los estudiantes provenían de orígenes *or* medios muy diversos

wide-mouthed [waɪd'maʊðd] *adj* de boca ancha

widen ['waɪdən] **1** *vt (road, garment)* ensanchar, ampliar; *(influence, limits)* ampliar, extender; *(scope)* ampliar; **this policy will w. the gap between rich and poor** esta política ampliará la brecha existente entre los ricos y los pobres

2 *vi (river)* ensancharse; *(gap)* acrecentarse

▸ **widen out** *vi* ensancharse

widening ['waɪdənɪŋ] **1** *n* (**a**) *(of road, channel)* ensanchamiento *m* (**b**) *(of influence)* aumento *m*, ampliación *f*

2 *adj (gap)* creciente; **a w. range of options** una creciente gama de opciones, una gama de opciones cada vez mayor *or* más amplia

wide-open ['waɪd'əʊpən] *adj (door, window, mouth)* bien abierto(a); **the w. spaces of Australia** los grandes espacios abiertos de Australia

wide-ranging [waɪd'reɪndʒɪŋ] *adj (report, survey, reforms)* amplio(a), de gran alcance; **he has w. interests** tiene intereses muy diversos

widescreen ['waɪdskriːn] *adj Cin* de pantalla ancha ▸▸ ***w. TV*** televisor *m* panorámico *or* de pantalla ancha

widespread ['waɪdspred] *adj* extendido(a), generalizado(a); **to become w.** extenderse, generalizarse

widgeon = **wigeon**

widget ['wɪdʒɪt] *n* (**a**) *(in beer can)* = mecanismo adherido al fondo de una lata de cerveza que hace que tenga espuma al servirla (**b**) *Fam (manufactured item)* cacharro *m*, chisme *m*, *CAm, Carib, Col* vaina *f*, *RP* coso *m*

widow ['wɪdəʊ] **1** *n* (**a**) *(person)* viuda *f*; **she was left a w. at the age of thirty** quedó viuda a los treinta (años) ▸▸ *Literary* ***the w.'s mite*** el óbolo de la viuda; ***w.'s peak*** *(hair)* = pico de pelo en la frente; ***w.'s pension*** pensión *f* de viudedad; ***w.'s weeds*** luto *m* (**b**) *Typ* viuda *f*

2 *vt* **to be widowed** enviudar, quedarse viudo(a); **she is twice widowed** ha enviudado dos veces

widowed ['wɪdəʊd] *adj* viudo(a)

widower ['wɪdəʊə(r)] *n* viudo *m*

widowhood ['wɪdəʊhʊd] *n* viudez *f*, viudedad *f*

width [wɪdθ] *n* (**a**) *(dimension)* anchura *f*; **the room was ten metres in w.** la sala tenía diez metros de ancho (**b**) *(in swimming pool)* ancho *m*

widthways ['wɪdθweɪz], **widthwise** ['wɪdθwaɪz] **1** *adj* a lo ancho

2 *adv* a lo ancho

wield [wiːld] *vt* (**a**) *(sword)* blandir, empuñar; *(pen)* manejar (**b**) *(power, influence)* ejercer

wiener = **weenie**

Wiener schnitzel ['viːnə'ʃnɪtsəl] *n* escalope *m* (de ternera) a la milanesa

wienerwurst ['wiːnərwʊərst] *n US (frankfurter)* salchicha *f* (de Fráncfort)

wife [waɪf] (*pl* **wives** [waɪvz]) *n* mujer *f*, esposa *f*; *Fam* **the w.** *Esp* la parienta, *Am* la vieja, *RP* la doña

wifely ['waɪflɪ] *adj* de esposa, conyugal

wife-swapping ['waɪfswɒpɪŋ] *n Fam* intercambio *m* de parejas

wig [wɪg] *n* peluca *f*

▸ **wig out** *vi* (*pt & pp* **wigged**) *US Fam (be angry)* ponerse hecho(a) un basilisco *or* una furia; *(be enthusiastic)* ponerse como unas castañuelas *or* loco(a) de contento

wigeon, widgeon ['wɪdʒən] *n* ánade *m* silbón

wigging ['wɪgɪŋ] *n Br (scolding)* regañina *f*

wiggle ['wɪgəl] **1** *n* meneo *m*

2 *vt (toes)* menear, mover; *(hips)* contonear

3 *vi (toes)* menearse, moverse; *(hips)* contonearse

wiggly ['wɪgəlɪ] *adj Fam (line)* ondulado(a)

wigmaker ['wɪgmeɪkə(r)] *n* fabricante *mf* de pelucas

wigwam ['wɪgwæm] *n* tipi *m*, tienda *f* india

wilco ['wɪlkəʊ] *exclam Tel* ¡enterado!

WILD [waɪld] **1** *n* **in the w.** *(animal)* en estado salvaje; **in the wilds of Alaska** en los remotos parajes de Alaska

2 *adj* (**a**) *(not domesticated) (plant)* silvestre; *(animal)* salvaje; *(countryside)* agreste; **w. beast** fiera, bestia salvaje; IDIOM **(to send sb on) a w. goose chase** (enviar a alguien a hacer) una búsqueda inútil; IDIOM *Fam* **w. horses wouldn't drag it out of me** no me lo sacarán *Esp* ni a tiros *or Am* ni que me maten ▸▸ ***w. boar*** jabalí *m*; ***w. flowers*** flores *fpl* silvestres; ***w. goat*** cabra *f* montés; ***w. mushroom*** *Esp* seta *f or esp Am* hongo *m* silvestre; ***w. oats*** avena *f* loca; ***w. rice*** arroz *m* salvaje *or* silvestre; ***w. rose*** *(dog rose)* escaramujo *m*, rosa *f* silvestre; *(sweetbrier)* eglantina *f*; ***the W. West*** el salvaje oeste (americano)

(**b**) *(unrestrained) (fury, passion)* salvaje; *(enthusiasm, applause, life)* descontrolado(a), desenfrenado(a); *(person)* descontrolado(a); *(party)* desenfrenado(a), loco(a); *(tackle)* violento(a); *(shot)* alocado(a); *(hair)* rebelde; *(promise, rumour, accusation)* descabellado(a); *(imagination)* desbordante; *(fluctuations)* extremo(a); **w. eyes** ojos desorbitados; **she has a w. look in her eyes** tiene una mirada rebelde; **to drive sb w.** poner a alguien fuera de sí; **to go w.** *(get angry)* ponerse hecho(a) una furia; **the audience went w. (with excitement)** el público se desmelenó *or* enfervorizó; **to be w. with grief** sentir una tremenda aflicción; **we had some w. times together!** juntos hicimos muchas locuras; *Fam* **w. and woolly** *(idea, plan)* descabellado(a); **it is beyond my wildest dreams** es mejor de lo que jamás habría soñado

(**c**) *(stormy) (wind)* furioso(a); *(weather, day, night)* borrascoso(a)

(**d**) *(random) (estimate)* descabellado(a); **it was just a w. guess** fue un intento de acertar al tuntún

(**e**) *(in cards)* **sevens are w.** los siete son comodines ▸▸ ***w. card*** *Comptr* comodín *m*; *Sport (player)* = deportista invitado a tomar parte en una competición a pesar de no haberse clasificado; *(in American football)* = equipo que se clasifica para la fase final sin ganar su grupo

(**f**) *Fam (enthusiastic)* **to be w. about sth/sb** estar loco(a) por algo/alguien; **I'm not w. about it** no me entusiasma mucho

(**g**) *Fam (excellent)* alucinante

(**h**) *Fam (strange, unusual)* **(that's) w.!** ¡(qué) alucinante!

3 *adv* **to grow w.** *(plant)* crecer silvestre; **the deer live w. in the hills** los ciervos viven en estado salvaje en las colinas; **to run w.** *(children, criminals)* descontrolarse; **they allowed the garden to run w.** descuidaron el jardín; **she allowed her imagination to run w.** dio rienda suelta a su imaginación

---

wildcat ['waɪldkæt] *n* (**a**) *(animal)* gato *m* montés; *Fig* **she's a real w.** es una mujer de armas tomar (**b**) *Ind* ***w. strike*** huelga *f* salvaje

wildebeest ['wɪldəbiːst] (*pl* **wildebeest** *or* **wildebeests**) *n* ñu *m*

wilderness ['wɪldənɪs] *n* desierto *m*, yermo *m*; **a w. of snow and ice** un páramo de hielo y nieve; **his warnings came like a voice in the w.** sus advertencias eran como predicar en el desierto; *Fig* **she's been relegated to the political w.** ha sido relegada (fuera) de la vida política; *Fig* **his years in the w.** los años que pasó en el ostracismo; *Fig* **a cultural w.** un páramo *or* desierto cultural

wildfire ['waɪldfaɪə(r)] *n* **to spread like w.** extenderse como un reguero de pólvora

wildfowl ['waɪldfaʊl] (*pl* **wildfowl**) *n* aves *fpl* de caza

wildlife ['waɪldlaɪf] *n* flora *f* y fauna *f* ▸▸ ***w. park*** parque *m* natural; *TV* ***w. programme*** programa *m* sobre naturaleza; ***w. sanctuary*** reserva *f or* santuario *m* natural

wildly ['waɪldlɪ] *adv* (**a**) *(to behave)* descontroladamente; *(to cheer, applaud)* enfervorizadamente, vehementemente; **to rush about w.** ir de aquí para allá como un/una loco(a); **exchange rates fluctuated w.** los tipos de cambio fluctuaban dramáticamente

(b) *(at random)* al azar; **"you're a Scorpio, aren't you?" I said, guessing w.** "eres escorpio, ¿no?", dije un poco al tuntún

(c) *(for emphasis) (expensive, funny, enthusiastic)* enormemente, tremendamente; **w. inaccurate** disparatado(a); **w. exaggerated** exageradísimo(a); **to be w. jealous/happy** ser increíblemente celoso(a)/ inmensamente feliz

wildness ['waɪldnɪs] *n* (a) *(of country, landscape)* carácter *m* agreste; *(of animal)* estado *m* salvaje (b) *(of applause)* fervor *m*, vehemencia *f*; *(of ideas, words)* extravagancia *f*, excentricidad *f* (c) *(of wind, waves, storm)* furia *f*, violencia *f*

wiles [waɪlz] *npl* artimañas *fpl*, engaños *mpl*; **he fell victim to her feminine w.** cayó en la trampa de sus encantos femeninos

wilful, *US* **willful** ['wɪlfʊl] *adj* (a) *(stubborn)* obstinado(a), tozudo(a) (b) *(deliberate)* premeditado(a), deliberado(a) ▸▸ *Law* ***w. murder*** asesinato *m* premeditado

wilfully, *US* **willfully** ['wɪlfəlɪ] *adv* (a) *(stubbornly)* obstinadamente, tozudamente (b) *(deliberately)* deliberadamente

wilfulness, *US* **willfulness** ['wɪlfʊlnɪs] *n* (a) *(stubbornness)* obstinación *f*, tozudez *f* (b) *(deliberateness)* premeditación *f*, deliberación *f*

will[1] [wɪl] 1 *n* (a) *(resolve, determination)* voluntad *f*; **the w. to live** las ganas de vivir; **to show good w.** demostrar buena voluntad; **with the best w. in the world** con la mejor voluntad del mundo; **he imposed his w. on them** les impuso su voluntad; **it is the w. of the people that...** es (la) voluntad del pueblo que...; **this computer has a w. of its own** *Esp* este ordenador *or Am* esta computadora hace lo que le da la gana; **he had to do it against his w.** tuvo que hacerlo contra su voluntad; **at w.** a voluntad, libremente; **to fire at w.** abrir fuego *or* disparar a discreción; PROV **where there's a w. there's a way** quien la sigue, la consigue

(b) *Law* testamento *m*; **the last w. and testament of...** la última voluntad de...; **to leave sb sth in one's w.** dejar algo en herencia a alguien; **to make one's w.** hacer testamento

2 *vt* (a) *(urge)* **he was willing her to win** deseaba con todas sus fuerzas que ganara; **I could feel the crowd willing me on** podía sentir al público dándome fuerzas; **she was willing herself to do it** apeló a toda su fuerza de voluntad para hacerlo (b) *Formal (wish)* desear (c) *(leave in one's will)* **to w. sth to sb** legar algo a alguien

3 *vi Formal* **as you w.** como guste; **if you w.** si lo prefiere

WILL[2] *modal aux v*

En el inglés hablado, y en el escrito en estilo coloquial, el verbo **will** se contrae de manera que **I/you/he** *etc* **will** se transforman en **I'll, you'll, he'll** *etc*. La forma negativa **will not** se transforma en **won't**.

(a) *(expressing future tense)* **I'll do it tomorrow** lo haré mañana; **it won't take long** no llevará *or Am* demorará mucho tiempo; **I'll be forty tomorrow** mañana cumpliré cuarenta; **persuading my parents w. be difficult** va a ser difícil convencer a mi padres; **the programme w. have finished by then** el programa ya habrá acabado para entonces; **you won't forget, w. you?** no te olvides, por favor; **w. you be there? – yes I w./no I won't** ¿vas a ir? – sí/no; **w. anyone be there? – I w.** ¿habrá alguien allí? – yo sí

(b) *(expressing wish, determination)* **I won't allow it! – oh yes you w.** ¡no lo permitiré! – ya lo creo que sí; **you w. stop shouting at once!** ¡cállate ahora mismo!; *Fam* **w. do!** ¡por descontado!; **she won't let me see him** no me deja verlo; **it won't open** no se abre; **be quiet for a minute, w. you?** estate callado un momento, ¿quieres?; **she WILL insist on doing everything herself, so it's hardly surprising she's exhausted** no me sorprende nada que esté agotada, siempre insiste en hacerlo todo ella; **WILL you go away!** ¡quieres hacer el favor de irte!

(c) *(in requests, invitations)* **w. you help me?** ¿me ayudas?; **won't you sit down?** ¿no se quiere sentar?; **w. you have another chocolate?** ¿quiere otro bombón?; **you'll write to me, won't you?** me escribirás, ¿verdad?; **you won't forget, w. you?** no te olvides, por favor; *Formal* **if you w. come with me** si es tan amable de acompañarme

(d) *(expressing general truth)* **the restaurant w. seat a hundred people** el restaurante puede albergar a cien personas; **the male w. usually return to the nest within hours** el macho acostumbra a volver al nido a las pocas horas; **one moment she'll be angry, the next she'll be all smiles** en un instante pasa de estar *esp Esp* enfadada *or esp Am* enojada a muy contenta; **the truth w. out** la verdad siempre se descubre; **accidents w. happen** le puede pasar a cualquiera; **these things w. happen** son cosas que pasan

(e) *(conjecture)* **you'll be tired** debes de estar cansado; **they'll be home by now** ya deben de haber llegado a casa; **that'll be the electrician** debe de ser el electricista; **you w./won't have heard the news** has/no has debido de oír las noticias

(f) *(when saying price)* **that'll be £15, please** son 15 libras, por favor

(g) *(indicating habitual action)* **she'll play in the park for hours** se pasa horas jugando en el parque

willful, willfully *etc US* = **wilful, willfully** *etc*

William ['wɪljəm] *pr n* **W. I/II** Guillermo I/II; **W. the Conqueror** Guillermo I el Conquistador; **W. of Orange** Guillermo III (de Nassau)

willie ['wɪlɪ] *n Br Fam (penis)* pito *m*, pilila *f*

willies ['wɪlɪz] *npl Fam* **to have the w.** tener canguelo *or Col* culillo *or Méx* mello *or RP* cagazo; **this place gives me the w.** este lugar me da canguelo *or Col* culillo *or Méx* mello *or RP* cagazo

willing ['wɪlɪŋ] *adj (assistant)* muy dispuesto(a); *(accomplice)* voluntario(a); **she was a w. participant** participó de muy buena gana; **to be w. to do sth** estar dispuesto(a) a hacer algo; **they were more than w. to help** tenían muchas ganas de ayudar; **God w.** si Dios quiere; **to show w.** mostrar buena disposición

willingly ['wɪlɪŋlɪ] *adv* (a) *(happily)* de buena gana, gustosamente; **I would w. help** ayudaría gustoso (b) *(voluntarily)* por propia voluntad

willingness ['wɪlɪŋnɪs] *n* buena disposición *f*; **w. to compromise** disposición a alcanzar un compromiso; **the soldiers were surprised at the enemy's w. to fight** los soldados se sorprendieron de las ganas de pelear que tenía el enemigo; **he admired her w. to sacrifice her own happiness** él admiraba que estuviera dispuesta a sacrificar su propia felicidad

will-o'the-wisp [wɪləðə'wɪsp] *n* (a) *(light)* fuego *m* fatuo (b) *(elusive aim)* quimera *f*

willow ['wɪləʊ] *n* **w. (tree)** sauce *m* ▸▸ ***w. grouse*** lagópodo *m* escandinavo; ***w. pattern*** *(on pottery)* = diseño de cerámica en colores azules sobre fondo blanco en el que suele aparecer un paisaje chino con un sauce; ***w. tit*** carbonero *m* sibilino; ***w. warbler*** mosquitero *m* musical

willowy ['wɪləʊɪ] *adj (person, figure)* esbelto(a)

willpower ['wɪlpaʊə(r)] *n* fuerza *f* de voluntad; **he lacks w.** le falta fuerza de voluntad; **she succeeded through sheer w.** consiguió triunfar sólo con su fuerza de voluntad

willy ['wɪlɪ] *n Br Fam (penis)* pito *m*, pilila *f*

willy-nilly ['wɪlɪ'nɪlɪ] *adv* (a) *(like it or not)* a la fuerza, quieras o no (b) *(haphazardly)* a la buena de Dios

wilt [wɪlt] *vi* (a) *(plant)* marchitarse (b) *(person)* desfallecer, flaquear; **he wilted under her fierce gaze** él se arrugaba ante su fiera mirada

Wilts (*abbr* **Wiltshire**) (condado *m* de) Wiltshire

wily ['waɪlɪ] *adj* astuto(a), taimado(a)

WIMP [wɪmp] *Comptr n* (*abbr* **windows, icons, menus and pointing device** *or* **pointer**) **W. (interface)** interfaz *f* WIMP

wimp [wɪmp] *n Fam (physically)* debilucho(a) *m,f*; *(lacking character)* blandengue *mf*; **don't be such a w.!** ¡no seas blandengue!, ¡no te arrugues!

▸**wimp out** *vi Fam* rajarse; **to w. out of sth/doing sth** rajarse de algo/de hacer algo

wimpish ['wɪmpɪʃ], **wimpy** ['wɪmpɪ] *adj Fam* blandengue

wimple ['wɪmpəl] *n* griñón *m*

wimpy = **wimpish**

WIN [wɪn] 1 *n* victoria *f*, triunfo *m*; **my lottery w. changed my life** ganar la lotería cambió mi vida

2 *vt* (*pt & pp* **won** [wʌn]) (a) *(battle, race, prize, election)* ganar; *(contract, order, scholarship)* obtener, conseguir; *(parliamentary seat)* obtener, sacar; **he won first prize** ganó el primer premio; **he won £100 at poker** ganó 100 libras jugando al poker; **to w. an argument** salir victorioso(a) en una discusión; **w. yourself a dream holiday!** ¡gane unas vacaciones de ensueño!; **his determination won him the race** su determinación le permitió ganar la carrera; **to w. money off** *or* **from sb** ganarle dinero a alguien; **they won the seat from Labour** le arrebataron el escaño a los laboristas; *Fam* **you can't w. them all, you w. some you lose some** a veces se gana y a veces se pierde

(b) *(acquire, secure) (friendship, confidence, love)* conseguir, ganarse; *(sympathy, popularity, recognition)* ganarse, granjearse; **to w. sb's heart** conquistar el corazón de alguien; *Old-fashioned* **to w. sb's hand** ganarse la mano de alguien; **to w. the right to do sth** obtener el derecho de hacer algo; **it won us a lot of friends** nos hizo ganar un montón de amigos; **she was desperate to w. his favour** trataba desesperadamente de congraciarse con él; **intransigence has won him many enemies** su intransigencia le ha granjeado muchos enemigos; **his impartiality has won him the respect of his colleagues** con su imparcialidad se ha ganado el respeto de sus compañeros; **he has**

finally won recognition for his work finalmente ha conseguido que le reconozcan su trabajo

(c) *Formal or Literary (reach)* ganar

3 *vi* ganar; **Chile are winning 2-0** Chile gana por dos a cero; **she always wins at chess** siempre gana al ajedrez; **he won by only one point** ganó por sólo un punto; **to let sb w.** dejar ganar a alguien; *Fam* **you (just) can't w.** no hay forma de salir ganando; *Fam* **I can't w., if I do it my way she gets annoyed, if I do it her way she accuses me of copying her** con ella es imposible ganar, si lo hago a mi manera se *esp Esp* enfada *or esp Am* enoja, si lo hago a la suya me acusa de copiarle; **OK, you w.!** de acuerdo *or Esp* vale, tú ganas

▸**win back** *vt sep* recuperar; **they were determined to w. back the Cup from the Australians** estaban decididos a volver a ganar la copa que los australianos les arrebataron; **he wanted to w. back their trust** quería volver a ganarse su confianza

▸**win out** *vi (succeed)* triunfar (**over** frente a)

▸**win over, win round** *vt sep* convencer, ganarse (el apoyo de); **I won him over** *or* **round to my point of view** lo convencí de que yo tenía razón; **the report won her over to the protesters' cause** el informe ganó su apoyo para con los manifestantes

▸**win through** *vi (succeed)* triunfar; **they won through against impossible odds** triunfaron contra todo pronóstico

▸**win through to** *vt insep (qualify for)* clasificarse para

---

wince [wɪns] 1 *n (of pain)* mueca *f* de dolor; *(of embarrassment)* cara *f* de vergüenza

2 *vi (with pain)* hacer una mueca de dolor; *(with embarrassment)* poner cara de vergüenza

winch [wɪntʃ] 1 *n* torno *m*, cabrestante *m*; *Naut* manubrio *m*

2 *vt* levantar con un torno *or* cabrestante; **to w. sth/sb up** alzar algo/a alguien con un torno; **the survivors were winched to safety** un torno alzó a los supervivientes hasta un lugar seguro

Winchester disk ['wɪntʃestə'dɪsk] *n* disco *m* Winchester

wind[1] [wɪnd] 1 *n* (a) *(air current)* viento *m*; **to sail into** *or* **against the w.** navegar contra el viento; *Fig* **with a fair w.** si los hados nos son favorables; **the cold w. of recession** los vientos de recesión ▸▸ ***w. chimes*** móvil *m* sonoro; ***w. cone*** manga *f* (catavientos); ***w. energy*** energía *f* eólica; ***w. farm*** parque *m* eólico, central *f* eólica; ***w. gauge*** anemómetro *m*; ***w. machine*** ventilador *m* (de atrezo); ***w. pollination*** polinización *f* anemófila; ***w. power*** energía *f* eólica; ***w. pump*** bomba *f* eólica; ***w. tunnel*** túnel *m* aerodinámico; ***w. turbine*** aerogenerador *m*, turbina *f* eólica

(b) *(breath)* aliento *m*, resuello *m*; **let me get my w. back** deja que recupere el aliento; **to get one's second w.** recobrar fuerzas, recuperarse

(c) *(abdominal)* gases *mpl*; **to break w.** soltar una ventosidad; **the boy's got w.** el niño tiene gases

(d) *Mus* **the w. (section)** la sección de viento, los vientos; **the w. is** *or* **are too loud** los vientos suenan demasiado fuerte ▸▸ *Mus* ***w. instrument*** instrumento *m* de viento

(e) IDIOMS *Fam* **to put the w. up sb** meter miedo a alguien; **to sail close to the w.** lindar con lo prohibido; **to take the w. out of sb's sails** bajar la moral a alguien; **to wait and see which way the w. is blowing** esperar a ver por dónde van los tiros; **to get w. of sth** enterarse de algo; **a w. of change** nuevos aires, aires de cambio; **to be in the w.** avecinarse; **to be scattered to the four winds** estar diseminado(a) por todas partes *or* en todas direcciones

2 *vt* (a) **to w. sb** *(with punch)* dejar a alguien sin respiración; **to be winded** *(after falling)* quedarse sin respiración (b) *(baby)* hacer eructar, sacar el aire

wind[2] [waɪnd] (*pt & pp* **wound** [waʊnd]) 1 *n* (a) *(turn)* **give the clock/watch a w.** dar cuerda al reloj; **she gave the handle another w.** le dio otra vuelta al picaporte (b) *(bend) (of road, river)* curva *f*, recodo *m*

2 *vt* (a) *(thread, string)* enrollar; **to w. sth into a ball** hacer un ovillo con algo (b) *(handle)* dar vueltas a; *(clock, watch)* dar cuerda a; **to w. a tape on/back** pasar rápidamente/rebobinar una cinta

3 *vi (path, river)* serpentear, zigzaguear; **the road winds up/down the hill** la carretera sube/baja la colina haciendo eses

▸**wind around** = **wind round**

▸**wind down** 1 *vt sep* (a) *(car window)* bajar, abrir (b) *(reduce) (production)* ir reduciendo; *(company)* ir reduciendo la actividad de

2 *vi* (a) *(party, meeting)* perder animación (b) *Fam (person)* relajarse

▸**wind round** *vt sep* **to w. sth round sth** enrollar algo alrededor de algo; **she wound the scarf round her neck** se enrolló la bufanda al cuello; IDIOM *Fam* **she's got him wound round her little finger** lo tiene en un puño, hace con él lo que quiere

▸**wind up** 1 *vt sep* (a) *(car window)* subir, cerrar (b) *(toy, clock)* dar cuerda a (c) *(bring to an end) (meeting)* concluir; *(company)* liquidar, disolver (d) *Br Fam (tease)* tomar el pelo a, *Esp, Carib, Méx* vacilar; *(annoy)* mosquear

2 *vi* (a) *(end speech, meeting)* concluir (b) *Fam (end up)* acabar, terminar; **we wound up in the same bar** acabamos en el mismo bar

windbag ['wɪndbæg] *n Fam* charlatán(ana) *m,f*

windborne ['wɪndbɔːn] *adj (pollen, seeds)* transportado(a) por el viento

windbreak ['wɪndbreɪk] *n* pantalla *f* contra el viento

windburn ['wɪndbɜːn] *n* enrojecimiento *m* de la piel por el viento; **her face showed signs of w.** tenía la cara algo quemada por el viento

windcheater ['wɪndtʃiːtə(r)] *n (jacket)* cazadora *f*, *CSur* campera *f*, *Méx* chamarra *f*

windchill factor ['wɪndtʃɪlfæktə(r)] *n* = bajada de la temperatura producida por el viento

winder ['waɪndə(r)] *n* (a) *(on watch)* cuerda *f* (b) *(on car door)* manivela *f*

windfall ['wɪndfɔːl] *n* (a) *(of fruit)* fruta *f* caída (b) *(of money)* dinero *m* caído del cielo ▸▸ *Fin* ***w. profits*** *(of company)* beneficio *m* inesperado; ***w. tax*** = impuesto sobre ingresos extraordinarios

winding ['waɪndɪŋ] *adj (path, stream)* serpenteante, zigzagueante ▸▸ ***w. staircase*** escalera *f* de caracol

winding-sheet ['waɪndɪŋʃiːt] *n Literary* sudario *m*, mortaja *f*

winding-up ['waɪndɪŋʌp] *n (of meeting)* conclusión *f*; *(of company)* liquidación *f*, disolución *f*

windlass ['wɪndləs] *n* torno *m*, molinete *m*

windmill ['wɪndmɪl] *n* molino *m* de viento

window ['wɪndəʊ] *n* (a) *(of house)* ventana *f*; *(of vehicle)* ventana *f*, ventanilla *f*; *(of shop)* escaparate *m*, *Am* vidriera *f*, *Chile, Col, Méx* vitrina *f*; *(at bank, ticket office)* ventanilla *f*; **he jumped out of the w.** se tiró por la ventana; **she looked out of the w.** miró por la ventana ▸▸ ***w. box*** jardinera *f*; ***w. cleaner*** *(person)* limpiacristales *mf inv*; *(liquid)* limpiacristales *m inv*; ***w. frame*** marco *m* de ventana; ***w. ledge*** alféizar *m*, antepecho *m*; ***w. seat*** *(in room)* asiento *m* junto a una ventana; *(on train, plane)* asiento *m* de ventana; *Aut* ***w. winder*** *(handle)* manivela *f* de la ventanilla; *(electric)* elevalunas *m inv*

(b) *Comptr* ventana *f*

(c) *(on envelope)* ventanilla *f*

(d) IDIOMS **to provide a w. on sth** dar una idea de algo; **a w. of opportunity** una ocasión *or* oportunidad única; *Fam* **that's my holiday out of the w.** ya puedo decir adiós a *or* despedirme de las vacaciones

window-dresser ['wɪndəʊdresə(r)] *n (in shop)* escaparatista *mf*

window-dressing ['wɪndəʊdresɪŋ] *n* (a) *(in shop)* escaparatismo *m* (b) *(ornamentation)* decoración *f* (c) *Fig (pretence, facade)* fachada *f*; **that's just w.** eso es pura fachada; **no amount of w. can hide the fact that they are in crisis** por mucho que intenten dar una buena imagen no pueden ocultar que están en crisis

windowpane ['wɪndəʊpeɪn] *n* vidrio *m or Esp* cristal *m* (de ventana)

window-shopper ['wɪndəʊʃɒpə(r)] *n* **the streets were full of window-shoppers** las calles estaban llenas de gente mirando escaparates

window-shopping ['wɪndəʊʃɒpɪŋ] *n* **to go w.** ir a mirar escaparates

windowsill ['wɪndəʊsɪl] *n* alféizar *m*, antepecho *m*

windpipe ['wɪndpaɪp] *n* tráquea *f*

windscreen ['wɪndskriːn], *US* **windshield** ['wɪndʃiːld] *n* parabrisas *m inv* ▸▸ ***w. wiper*** limpiaparabrisas *m inv*

windsock ['wɪndsɒk] *n* manga *f* (catavientos)

windstorm ['wɪndstɔːm] *n* vendaval *m*

windsurf ['wɪndsɜːf] *vi* hacer windsurf

windsurfer ['wɪndsɜːfə(r)] *n (board)* tabla *f* de windsurf; *(person)* windsurfista *mf*

windsurfing ['wɪndsɜːfɪŋ] *n* windsurf *m*; **to go w.** ir a hacer windsurf

windswept ['wɪndswept] *adj (hillside, scene)* azotado(a) por el viento; **w. hair** pelo revuelto por el viento

wind-up ['waɪndʌp] 1 *n Br Fam* vacilada *f*, tomadura *f* de pelo; **this has to be a w.!** ¡esto no puede ir en serio!

2 *adj (mechanism)* **a w. toy/watch** un juguete/reloj de cuerda

windward ['wɪndwəd] 1 *n* **to w.** hacia *or* a barlovento

2 *adj* de barlovento ▸▸ ***the W. Islands*** las Islas de Barlovento

windy[1] ['wɪndɪ] *adj* (a) *(day)* ventoso(a); *(place)* expuesto(a) al viento; **it's w.** hace viento; **it's a very w. place** hace mucho viento en ese sitio (b) *(rhetoric, speech)* lleno(a) de verborrea

windy[2] ['waɪndɪ] *adj (road)* serpenteante, zigzagueante

wine [waɪn] **1** *n* vino *m*; **red/white w.** vino tinto/blanco ▸▸ ***w. bar*** bar *m (especializado en vinos y con una pequeña carta de comidas)*; ***w. bottle*** botella *f* de vino; ***w. cellar*** bodega *f*; ***w. cooler*** refrescador *m* de vino; ***w. glass*** copa *f* de vino; ***w. grower*** viticultor(ora) *m,f*; ***w. gum*** pastilla *f* de goma, *Esp* ≃ gominola *f*; ***w. list*** carta *f* de vinos; ***w. merchant*** *(shopkeeper)* bodeguero(a) *m,f*, vinatero(a) *m,f*; *(wholesaler)* mayorista *mf* de vinos; ***w. rack*** botellero *m*; ***w. snob*** = persona que se las da de entendida en vinos; ***w. tasting*** cata *f* de vinos; ***w. vinegar*** vinagre *m* de vino; ***w. waiter*** sumiller *m*, som(m)elier *m*
2 *vt* **to w. and dine sb** agasajar a alguien

wineglass ['waɪnglɑːs] *n* copa *f* de vino

winepress ['waɪnpres] *n* lagar *m*

winery ['waɪnərɪ] *n US* bodega *f*

wineskin ['waɪnskɪn] *n Hist* odre *m*, pellejo *m* de vino

wing [wɪŋ] **1** *n* **(a)** *(of bird, plane)* ala *f*; **on the w.** en vuelo; *Literary* **to take w.** alzar el vuelo; *Fig Literary* **desire/fear gave** *or* **lent him wings** el deseo/miedo le dio alas; IDIOM **to take sb under one's w.** poner a alguien bajo la propia tutela, apadrinar a alguien; IDIOM **to spread** *or* **stretch one's wings** emprender el vuelo; IDIOM **on a w. and a prayer** a la buena de Dios, encomendándose a todos los santos ▸▸ ***w. case*** *(of insect)* élitro *m*; ***w. chair*** sillón *m* de orejas; ***w. collar*** cuello *m* de esmoquin; ***w. commander*** ≃ teniente *mf* coronel de aviación; ***w. nut*** palomilla *f*, tuerca *f* de mariposa
(b) *Br (of car)* aleta *f* ▸▸ ***w. mirror*** (espejo *m*) retrovisor *m* lateral
(c) *(of building, hospital)* ala *f*; **the west w.** el ala oeste
(d) *(in soccer, hockey, rugby) (area)* banda *f*; *(player)* extremo *mf*, lateral *mf* ▸▸ ***w. back*** *(in soccer)* carrilero(a) *m,f*; ***w. forward*** *(in rugby)* ala *m* delantero
(e) *(in theatre)* **the wings** los bastidores; **to be waiting in the wings** *(actor)* esperar entre bastidores; *Fig* esperar la ocasión *or* oportunidad
(f) *Pol* **the left/right w.** la izquierda/derecha; **the political w. of the IRA** el brazo político del IRA
(g) *Br (in RAF)* **a fighter/bomber w.** un ala de cazas/bombarderos
(h) *Av & Mil (insignia)* alas *fpl or* insignia *f* de piloto; **to win one's wings** obtener la categoría de piloto
2 *vt* **(a)** *(injure) (bird)* herir en el ala; *(person)* herir en el brazo **(b)** *Fam (improvise)* **to w. it** improvisar **(c)** *(fly) (of bird)* **to w. its way towards** volar hacia; *Fig* **my report should be winging its way towards you** mi informe *or CAm, Méx* reporte ya está en camino
3 *vi Literary (fly)* **the plane winged over the mountains** el avión sobrevoló las montañas

wingding ['wɪŋdɪŋ] *n US Fam* fiestorro *m*, *Am* pachanga *f*

winged [wɪŋd] *adj (insect)* con alas, alado(a)

winger ['wɪŋə(r)] *n (in soccer, rugby)* extremo *mf*

wingless ['wɪŋlɪs] *adj (insect)* sin alas

wingspan ['wɪŋspæn] *n* envergadura *f* (de alas)

wink [wɪŋk] **1** *n* guiño *m*; **to give sb a w.** guiñarle un ojo a alguien; *Fam* **I didn't sleep a w.** no pegué ojo; **in the w. of an eye, as quick as a w.** en un abrir y cerrar de ojos; IDIOM **to tip sb the w.** poner sobre aviso a alguien
2 *vi* **(a)** *(eye)* guiñar, hacer un guiño; IDIOM **it's as easy as winking** es facilísimo **(b)** *(star, light)* titilar

▸ **wink at** *vt insep (person)* guiñar a, hacer un guiño a; *Fig (abuse, illegal practice)* hacer la vista gorda ante

winker ['wɪŋkə(r)] *n Br Aut* (luz *f*) intermitente *m*

winkle ['wɪŋkəl] *n* **(a)** *(mollusc)* bígaro *m* **(b)** *Br Fam (penis)* pito *m*, pilila *f*

▸ **winkle out** *vt sep Fam* **to w. sth out of sb** sacarle *or* extraerle algo a alguien

winkle-picker ['wɪŋkəlpɪkə(r)] *n Br Fam* zapato *m* puntiagudo

winnable ['wɪnəbəl] *adj* **to be w.** poderse ganar

winner ['wɪnə(r)] *n (of prize)* ganador(ora) *m,f*; *(of lottery)* acertante *mf*; *(of competition)* vencedor(ora) *m,f*, ganador(ora) *m,f*; **this book will be a w.** este libro será un éxito; **there will be neither winners nor losers in this war** no habrá vencedores ni vencidos en esta guerra; **to be on to a w.** tener un éxito entre manos; **to back a w.** *(in horse-racing)* apostar por un favorito; *Fig* apostar por algo seguro; **to score the w.** anotar el tanto de la victoria; **w. takes all** el que gana se lo lleva todo ▸▸ *Br* ***w.'s enclosure*** *(at racecourse)* recinto *m* de ganadores

winning ['wɪnɪŋ] **1** *adj* **(a)** *(victorious) (team, person)* ganador(ora), vencedor(ora); *(goal)* de la victoria; *(ticket, number)* premiado(a) ▸▸ ***w. post*** meta *f*; ***w. streak*** racha *f* de suerte; **to be on a w. streak** tener una buena racha, estar en racha **(b)** *(attractive)* encantador(ora); **she has a very w. manner** es una persona encantadora
2 *npl* **winnings** ganancias *fpl*

winnow ['wɪnəʊ] *vt (grain)* aventar; *Fig* **to w. out fact from fiction** separar la realidad de la ficción

wino ['waɪnəʊ] (*pl* **winos**) *n Fam (alcoholic)* borracho(a) *m,f* (indigente)

winsome ['wɪnsəm] *adj Literary* encantador(ora), atractivo(a)

winter ['wɪntə(r)] **1** *n* invierno *m*; **a cold w.'s day** un frío día de invierno; **in (the) w.** en invierno ▸▸ ***w. break*** vacaciones *fpl* de invierno; ***w. clothing*** ropa *f* de invierno; *Br* ***the w. of discontent*** = el invierno de 1978, época en que Gran Bretaña sufrió una oleada de huelgas y que supuso la derrota del partido laborista en las siguientes elecciones; ***w. garden*** jardín *m* de invierno; ***the W. Olympics*** los Juegos Olímpicos de invierno; ***w. solstice*** solsticio *m* de invierno; ***w. sports*** deportes *mpl* de invierno
2 *vi* pasar el invierno

wintergreen ['wɪntəgriːn] *n* gaulteria *f*; **oil of w.** aceite de gaulteria

winterize ['wɪntəraɪz] *vt US (car, home)* preparar para el invierno

wintertime ['wɪntətaɪm] *n* invierno *m*

wint(e)ry ['wɪntərɪ] *adj* **(a)** *(weather)* invernal **(b)** *(smile)* gélido(a)

wipe [waɪp] **1** *n* **(a)** *(action)* **to give sth a w.** limpiar algo con un paño, pasar el paño a algo **(b)** *(moist tissue)* toallita *f* húmeda
2 *vt* **(a)** *(table, plate)* pasar un paño por *or* a; **to w. one's nose** limpiarse la nariz; **he wiped his hands on the towel** se secó las manos con la toalla; **to w. one's feet** *or* **shoes on the mat** limpiarse los zapatos en el felpudo; **she wiped the sweat from his brow** le limpió *or* enjugó el sudor de la frente; **he wiped his knife clean** limpió el cuchillo con un paño; **she wiped the plate dry** secó el plato (limpio) con un paño; IDIOM *Fam Br* **to w. the floor with sb,** *US* **to w. up the floor with sb** dar un buen repaso *or* una buena paliza a alguien
(b) *(recording tape)* borrar

▸ **wipe away** *vt sep (tears)* enjugar; *(mark)* limpiar, quitar, *Am* sacar

▸ **wipe down** *vt sep* pasar un trapo a, limpiar

▸ **wipe off 1** *vt sep* limpiar; **she wiped the oil off her hands** se limpió *or* quitó *or Am* sacó el aceite de las manos; IDIOM *Fam* **w. that smile** *or* **grin off your face!** ¡deja ya de sonreír así!; **that'll w. the smile off his face!** ¡eso le borrará la sonrisa de la cara!
2 *vi (stain)* irse, quitarse

▸ **wipe out** *vt sep* **(a)** *(erase) (memory)* borrar; *(debt)* saldar; *(lead)* hacer desaparecer, borrar **(b)** *(destroy) (family)* acabar con; *(species)* hacer desaparecer, exterminar; *(disease)* erradicar; *(enemy)* aniquilar; *Fam* **he was wiped out in the last financial crash** lo perdió todo con la última crisis financiera **(c)** *Fam (exhaust)* **I was** *or* **felt wiped out** estaba molido

▸ **wipe up** *vt sep* limpiar

wipeout ['waɪpaʊt] *n Fam* **(a)** *(in surfing)* caída *f* **(b)** *(failure)* debacle *f*

wiper ['waɪpə(r)] *n Aut* limpiaparabrisas *m inv*

wire ['waɪə(r)] **1** *n* **(a)** *(in general)* alambre *m*; *(electrical)* cable *m* ▸▸ ***w. brush*** cepillo *m* de púas metálicas; ***w. fence*** alambrada *f*; ***w. mesh*** tela *f* metálica; ***w. netting*** tela *f* metálica; ***w. rope*** cable *m* (de alambre); ***w. wool*** estropajo *m* de aluminio
(b) *US (telegram)* telegrama *m*
(c) *US Fam (hidden microphone)* micrófono *m* oculto
(d) IDIOMS *Fam* **we got our wires crossed** tuvimos un cruce de cables y no nos entendimos; **the contest went right down to the w.** el desenlace del concurso no se decidió hasta el último momento; **he got his application in just under the w.** entregó la solicitud justo en el último momento
2 *vt* **(a)** *(house)* cablear, tender el cableado de; *(plug, appliance)* conectar el cable a; **to w. sth to sth** *(connect electrically)* conectar algo a algo (con un cable); *(attach with wire)* sujetar algo a algo con un alambre **(b)** *(send telegram to)* mandar un telegrama a; **to w. money to sb** mandar un giro telegráfico a alguien **(c)** *US Fam (police officer, detective)* colocar un micrófono oculto a

▸ **wire up** *vt sep* **(a)** *(connect)* cablear **(b)** *US Fam (make nervous)* poner histérico(a); **he gets all wired up before exams** se pone hecho un manojo de nervios antes de los exámenes

wirecutters ['waɪəkʌtəz] *npl* cizallas *fpl*; **a pair of w.** unas cizallas

wired [waɪəd] *adj Fam* **(a)** *(highly strung)* histérico(a), hecho(a) un manojo de nervios **(b)** *(after taking drugs)* muy acelerado(a), *Esp* espídico(a)

wireframe modelling, *US* **wireframe modeling** ['waɪəfreɪm'mɒdəlɪŋ] *n Comptr* modelado *m* de alambres

wire-haired ['waɪə'heəd] *adj (dog)* de pelaje duro *or* áspero

wireless ['waɪəlɪs] *n Old-fashioned* **w. (set)** radio *f*

wirepulling ['waɪəpʊlɪŋ] *n US Fam* enchufismo *m*; **he did some w. for me** él medio me enchufó

wirestripper ['waɪəstrɪpə(r)] *n* pelacables *m inv*

wiretap ['waɪətæp] *US* **1** *n* escucha *f* telefónica
2 *vt* (*pt & pp* **wiretapped**) *(telephone)* intervenir

wiretapping ['waɪətæpɪŋ] *n US* intervención *f* de la línea

wiring ['waɪərɪŋ] *n (electrical)* instalación *f* eléctrica

wiry ['waɪərɪ] *adj* **(a)** *(hair)* basto(a) y rizado(a) *or Méx* quebrado(a) **(b)** *(person)* fibroso(a)

Wis (*abbr* **Wisconsin**) Wisconsin

Wisconsin [wɪs'kɒnsɪn] *n* Wisconsin

wisdom ['wɪzdəm] *n* **(a)** *(knowledge)* sabiduría *f*; *(judgement)* sensatez *f*, cordura *f*; *Hum* **Donald, in his w., decided we should cancel** Donald decidió, sabe Dios por qué, que debíamos suspenderlo ▸▸ ***w. tooth*** muela *f* del juicio
(b) *(of action, behaviour, decision)* carácter *m* acertado; **he questioned the w. of this decision** puso en duda lo acertado de esta decisión; **I have my doubts about the w. of moving house this year** tengo mis dudas sobre si será una buena idea mudarnos este año

wise [waɪz] **1** *adj* **(a)** *(knowledgeable)* sabio(a); **a w. man** un sabio; *Fam Pej* **a w. guy** un sabelotodo; *Fam* **so who's the w. guy who left the door open?** ¿y quién ha sido el listo que se ha dejado la puerta abierta?; **the Three W. Men** los Reyes Magos; **to be none the wiser** quedarse igual; **do it while he's out, he'll be none the wiser** hazlo cuando no esté, no se va a enterar; IDIOM **to be w. after the event** verlo todo claro a posteriori
(b) *(sensible)* sensato(a), prudente; **you'd be w. to take my advice** sería sensato *or* prudente que siguieras mi consejo; **it wouldn't be w. to do it** no sería aconsejable hacerlo; **the president made a w. move in dismissing the attorney general** el presidente tomó una decisión acertada al destituir al ministro de justicia; **she decided that the wisest course of action was to apologize** decidió que pedir disculpas era la medida más sensata a tomar
(c) *Fam (aware)* **to be w. to sth** conocer algo; **to get w. to a fact** percatarse de un hecho; **to get w. to sb** calar a alguien; **to put sb w. to sth** poner a alguien al corriente de algo; **to put sb w. to sb** advertir a alguien sobre alguien
2 *n Literary (way)* modo *m*, manera *f*; **he is in no w.** *or* **not in any w. satisfied with his new position** no está en absoluto satisfecho con su nuevo puesto

▸ **wise up** *vi Fam* **to w. up to sb** calar a alguien; **to w. up to the fact that...** darse cuenta de que...; **w. up!** ¡espabílate!

-wise [waɪz] *suffix Fam (with reference to)* **health/salary-w.** en cuanto a la salud/al sueldo

wiseacre ['waɪzeɪkə(r)] *n* sabelotodo *mf*, sabihondo(a) *m,f*

wiseass ['waɪzæs] *n US very Fam* sabelotodo *mf or Esp* listillo(a) *m,f* de mierda

wisecrack ['waɪzkræk] *Fam* **1** *n* chiste *m*, salida *f* ingeniosa
2 *vi* soltar un chiste, tener una salida ingeniosa

wisecracking ['waɪzkrækɪŋ] *adj Fam* chistoso(a), con muchas salidas (ingeniosas)

wisely ['waɪzlɪ] *adv (sensibly)* sensatamente

WISH [wɪʃ] **1** *n* **(a)** *(desire)* deseo *m*; **my greatest w. is...** mi mayor deseo es...; **his last** *or* **dying w.** su última voluntad; **I got my w.** conseguí mi deseo; **to have no w. to do sth** no tener ningún deseo de hacer algo; **I've no great w. to see them suffer** no tengo ganas particulares de verles sufrir; **to make a w.** pedir un deseo; **to grant sb a w.** conceder un deseo a alguien; **to do sth against sb's wishes** hacer algo en contra de los deseos de alguien; *Hum* **your w. is my command** tus deseos son órdenes; **number one on my w. list would be...** lo que más desearía sería... ▸▸ ***w. fulfilment*** satisfacción *f* de deseos
(b) *(greeting)* **they send you their best wishes** te envían saludos *or CAm, Col, Ecuad* saludes; **give your parents my best wishes** dale recuerdos a tus padres de mi parte; **best wishes for the coming year** te deseo lo mejor para el año que viene; **(with) best wishes** *(in letter, on card)* un saludo cordial *or* afectuoso
2 *vt* **(a)** *(want)* desear, querer; **to w. to do sth** desear *or* querer hacer algo; **those people wishing to leave early should inform me** aquéllos que deseen salir antes deben informarme; **I don't w. to sound greedy, but...** no quiero parecer codicioso, pero...; **do you w. me to leave?** ¿desea que me vaya?; **I wished myself somewhere else** deseé haber estado en alguna otra parte; **it is to be wished that she succeeds** sería deseable que tuviera éxito; **to w. sb luck/a pleasant journey** desear a alguien suerte/un buen viaje; **I don't w. you any harm** no te deseo ningún mal; **wishing you a Merry Christmas** *(on card)* Felices Navidades; **he wished us good day** nos dio los buenos días; **to w. sb well** desear a alguien lo mejor; **to w. sb dead** desearle la muerte a alguien; **I wouldn't w. that on anyone** no se lo deseo a nadie; **I w. you joy of it** que lo disfrutes con salud
(b) *(want something impossible, unlikely)* **I w. (that) I had seen it!** ¡ojalá lo hubiera visto!; **I w. (that) I hadn't left so early** ojalá no me hubiera marchado tan pronto; **when will it be ready? – I w. I knew!** ¿cuándo estará listo? – ¡ojalá lo supiera!; **I w. (that) I was younger** ¡ojalá fuera más joven!; **I w. I were a bird!** ¡ojalá fuera un pájaro!; **I w. (that) you were going to be there** ¡ojalá pudieras estar allí!; **I w. you'd stop doing that!** ¡quieres hacer el favor de dejar eso!; **I w. you'd pay attention!** ¿por qué no prestas atención?; **she wishes (that) she had told them earlier** se arrepiente de no habérselo dicho antes; **I wished (that) I would never have to see him again** deseé no tener que volver a verle nunca más; **w. you were here!** *(on postcard)* te echo de menos, *Am* te extraño
3 *vi* **to w. for sth** *(want)* desear algo; *(by magic)* pedir algo; **it was the best birthday I could have wished for** fue el mejor cumpleaños que podría haber soñado nunca; **what more could you w. for?** ¿qué más se puede pedir *or* desear?; **as you w.** como quieras; **if you w.** si usted quiere; *Fam* **I think she fancies me – you w.!** creo que le voy – ¡ya te gustaría!

▸ **wish away** *vt sep* **you can't just w. your problems away** no puedes esperar que desaparezcan tus problemas como por arte de magia

---

wishbone ['wɪʃbəʊn] *n* espoleta *f (hueso de ave)*

wishful ['wɪʃfʊl] *adj* **that's just w. thinking** no son más que ilusiones

wish-fulfilment ['wɪʃfʊlfɪlmənt] *n Psy* realización *f* de deseos subconscientes

wishing well ['wɪʃɪŋwel] *n* pozo *m* de los deseos

wishy-washy ['wɪʃɪ'wɒʃɪ] *adj Fam* vacilante

wisp [wɪsp] *n (of straw)* brizna *f*; *(of hair, wool)* mechón *m*; *(of smoke)* voluta *f*; *(of cloud)* jirón *m*; *Fig* **a w. of a girl** un suspiro de niña; **there wasn't a w. of cloud** no había ni rastro de nubes

wispy ['wɪspɪ] *adj (hair)* ralo(a), a mechones; *(clouds)* tenue

wisteria [wɪs'tɪərɪə] *n* glicinia *f*

wistful ['wɪstfʊl] *adj* nostálgico(a)

wistfully ['wɪstfʊlɪ] *adv* con nostalgia

wit [wɪt] **1** *n* **(a)** *(intelligence, presence of mind)* inteligencia *f*, lucidez *f*; **he hasn't the w. to see it** no tiene la lucidez suficiente *or* las luces suficientes para verlo; **to have quick wits** tener rapidez mental; **to have lost one's wits** haber perdido la razón; **to have/keep one's wits about one** ser/estar espabilado(a); **to collect** *or* **gather one's wits** poner en orden las ideas; **to be at one's w.'s end** estar al borde de la desesperación; **to live by one's wits** ser un pícaro; **to scare sb out of his wits** dar un susto de muerte a alguien
(b) *(humour)* ingenio *m*, agudeza *f*; **to have a quick** *or* **ready w.** ser muy ingenioso(a) *or* agudo(a)
(c) *(witty person)* ingenioso(a) *m,f*
2 *vi Law or Formal* **to w.,...** a saber,...

witch [wɪtʃ] *n* **(a)** *(sorceress)* bruja *f* ▸▸ ***a w.'s brew*** una pócima *or* un brebaje (de bruja); ***w. doctor*** hechicero *m*, curandero *m*; ***w. hazel*** *(tree)* ocozol *m* americano; *(lotion)* liquidámbar *m*; ***w.'s sabbath*** aquelarre *m* **(b)** *Fam (unpleasant woman)* bruja *f*

witchcraft ['wɪtʃkrɑːft] *n* brujería *f*, hechicería *f*

witch-hunt ['wɪtʃhʌnt] *n* caza *f* de brujas

witching hour ['wɪtʃɪŋaʊə(r)] *n Literary* **the w. hour** la hora de las brujas, medianoche

---

WITH [wɪð, wɪθ] *prep* con; **w. me** conmigo; **w. you** contigo; **w. himself/herself** consigo; **does it have all the software w. it?** ¿viene con todo el software?; **to travel/work w. sb** viajar/trabajar con alguien; **he is staying w. friends** se queda con *or* en casa de unos amigos; **Humphrey Bogart starred w. Lauren Bacall in the movie** Humphrey Bogart protagonizó la película junto con Lauren Bacall; **she came in w. a suitcase** entró con una maleta en la mano; **he's in bed w. a cold** está en cama con un *Esp, CAm, Carib, Méx* resfriado *or Andes, RP* resfrío; **a girl w. blue eyes** una chica de ojos azules; **the man w. the beard** el hombre de la barba; **a house w. no garden** una casa sin jardín; **covered w. snow** cubierto de nieve; **she was trembling w. cold** temblaba de frío; **payments vary w. age** los pagos varían con *or* según la edad; **he greeted them w. a smile** los recibió con una sonrisa *or* sonriendo; **I've been w. the company for ten years** llevo *or Am* tengo diez años en la compañía; **we're w. Chemical Bank** tenemos nuestras cuentas en el Chemical Bank; **to part w. sth** desprenderse de algo; **I was left w. nobody to talk to** me quedé sin nadie con quien hablar; **I started off w. nothing** cuando comencé no tenía nada; **w. the elections only a week away...** a una semana de las elecciones...; **w. Brazil out of the competition, Italy are now favourites** con Brasil eliminado, Italia es la favorita; **w. all her faults, I still love**

her a pesar de todos sus defectos, sigo queriéndola; **it improves w. age** mejora con la edad; **w. that, she left** y con eso, se marchó *or* se fue; **away w. them!** ¡que se los lleven!; **off to bed w. you!** ¡a la cama!; **this problem will always be w. us** siempre tendremos este problema; **the wind is w. us** tenemos el viento a favor; **I'm w. you** *(I support you)* estoy contigo; **they voted w. the government** votaron con el gobierno; **I'm not w. you** *(I don't understand)* no te sigo; **how are things w. you?** ¿qué tal te van las cosas?, *RP* ¿qué tal te va?; *Fam* **what's w. you today?** *(what's wrong?)* ¿qué te pasa hoy?; *Fam* **what's w. the long face?** ¿a qué viene esa cara tan larga?; *Fam* **to be w. it** *(fashionable) (person)* ser enrollado(a) *or Méx* suave *or RP* copado(a); *(clothing)* estar en la onda; *Fam* **I'm not really w. it today** *(alert)* hoy no estoy muy allá *or RP* demasiado avispado; **to get w. it** espabilar

withdraw [wɪð'drɔː] (*pt* **withdrew** [wɪð'druː], *pp* **withdrawn** [wɪð'drɔːn]) **1** *vt* (**a**) *(troops, offer, support)* retirar; *(product)* retirar del mercado; *(statement, accusation)* retirar, retractarse de; **he withdrew his hand from his pocket** (se) sacó la mano del bolsillo; **it has been withdrawn from sale** ya no se vende (**b**) *(money)* sacar, retirar (**from** de)

2 *vi* retirarse; **to w. in favour of sb** dejar paso a alguien; **he has decided to w. from politics** ha decidido retirarse de la política; **she withdrew into herself** se encerró en sí misma

withdrawal [wɪð'drɔːəl] *n* (**a**) *(of troops, offer, support, statement)* retirada *f*; *(of product)* retirada *f* del mercado ►► ***w. method*** coitus *m inv* interruptus, marcha *f* atrás

(**b**) *(from bank)* reintegro *m*, *Esp* retirada *f*, *Am* retiro *m*; **to make a w.** efectuar un reintegro ►► ***w. slip*** justificante *m* de reintegro

(**c**) *Psy* introversión *f*, retraimiento *m*; **the boy is showing signs of w.** el niño se muestra muy retraído

(**d**) *Med (from drugs)* síndrome *m* de abstinencia; **to experience w.** tener el síndrome de abstinencia ►► ***w. symptoms*** síndrome *m* de abstinencia

withdrawn [wɪð'drɔːn] **1** *adj (person)* retraído(a)

2 *pp of* **withdraw**

withdrew *pt of* **withdraw**

wither ['wɪðə(r)] *vi (plant)* marchitarse; *(limb)* atrofiarse; **to w. away** marchitarse; IDIOM **to w. on the vine** quedar(se) en agua de borrajas

withered ['wɪðəd] *adj (plant)* marchito(a); *(limb)* atrofiado(a)

withering ['wɪðərɪŋ] *adj (look)* fulminante; *(tone)* mordaz

withers ['wɪðəz] *npl (of horse)* cruz *f*

withhold [wɪð'həʊld] (*pt & pp* **withheld** [wɪð'held]) *vt (consent, help)* negar (**from** a); *(money)* retener (**from** a); *(payment)* aplazar, suspender (**from** a); *(information, evidence)* ocultar (**from** a)

withholding [wɪð'həʊldɪŋ] *n* (**a**) *(of help, aid)* denegación *f*; *(of loan, taxes)* retención *f* (**b**) *(of information, facts)* ocultación *f* ►► *Fin* ***w. tax*** *(on non-resident's income)* retención *f* (fiscal) a no residentes; *US* retención *f* a cuenta

within [wɪð'ɪn] **1** *prep* (**a**) *(inside)* dentro de; **the man's role w. the family is changing** el papel del hombre en la familia está cambiando; **problems w. the party** problemas en el seno del partido; **a play w. a play** una obra de teatro dentro de otra

(**b**) *(not beyond)* **he lives w. a few kilometres of the city centre** vive a pocos kilómetros del centro; **w. a radius of ten miles** en un radio de diez millas; **it's w. walking distance (of)** se puede ir caminando *or Esp* andando (desde); **accurate to w. 20 cm** con un margen de precisión de 20 cm; **it is well w. her abilities** es más que capaz de hacerlo, puede hacerlo de sobra; **w. the law** dentro de la legalidad; **w. limits** dentro de un orden, hasta cierto punto; **to live w. one's means** vivir dentro de sus posibilidades; **w. reason** dentro de lo razonable; **w. sight** a la vista; IDIOM *Fam* **to come w. an inch of doing sth** estar a punto de *or* en un tris de hacer algo

(**c**) *(time)* en menos de; **w. an** *or* **the hour** en menos de una hora; **w. hours of the announcement** a las pocas horas del anuncio; **w. twenty-four hours** en las siguientes veinticuatro horas, en el plazo de veinticuatro horas; **use w. two days of purchase** *(on packaging)* consúmase antes de dos días después de la compra; **w. the past few minutes we have learnt that...** en los últimos minutos hemos sabido que...; **w. the next five years** *(during) (in future)* durante los próximos cinco años; *(in past)* durante los cinco años siguientes; *(before end of)* dentro de un plazo de cinco años; **they died w. a few days of each other** murieron con pocos días de diferencia

2 *adv* **from w.** desde dentro

WITHOUT [wɪð'aʊt] **1** *prep* (**a**) *(lacking)* sin; **you look better w. a beard** estás *or* quedas mejor sin barba; **w. any money/difficulty** sin dinero/dificultad; **a journey w. end** un viaje sin fin; **w. doing sth** sin hacer algo; **I did it w. their knowledge** lo hice sin que lo supieran; **I took it w. them** *or* **their realizing** me lo llevé sin que se dieran cuenta; **w. wishing to sound ungrateful,...** sin querer parecer un desagradecido,...; **it's hard enough as it is, w. you distracting me** ya es lo suficientemente difícil para que encima me distraigas; **it's not w. its attractions** no deja de tener sus atractivos; **he left w. so much as a goodbye** se marchó sin (ni) siquiera decir adiós; **I wouldn't be w. my mobile phone** no podría pasar sin mi teléfono móvil; **to do** *or* **go w. sth** pasar *or* arreglárselas sin algo; **it goes w. saying that...** huelga decir que...

(**b**) *Archaic or Literary (outside)* fuera de

2 *adv* (**a**) *(not having)* **do you want milk in your coffee? – I prefer it w.** ¿quieres leche en el café? – mejor no; **those w. will be left to fend for themselves** los que se queden sin nada tendrán que valerse por sí mismos (**b**) *Formal (outside)* **from w.** desde fuera *or Am* afuera

with-profits ['wɪθ'prɒfɪts] *adj Br Fin* con participación en los beneficios

withstand [wɪð'stænd] (*pt & pp* **withstood** [wɪð'stʊd]) *vt* soportar, aguantar; **to w. the test of time** aguantar bien el paso del tiempo

witless ['wɪtlɪs] *adj (person, remark)* necio(a), simple; **to scare sb w.** helar la sangre en las venas a alguien

witness ['wɪtnɪs] **1** *n* (**a**) *(in trial)* testigo *mf*; **to call sb as w.** llamar a alguien a testificar; **w. for the defence/prosecution** testigo de descargo/de cargo ►► ***w. box*** estrado *m* del testigo; ***w. stand*** estrado *m* del testigo

(**b**) *(to marriage, contract)* testigo *mf*; **two people must be witnesses to my signature/will** dos personas deben figurar como testigos de mi firma/en mi testamento

(**c**) *(testimony)* **to bear w. (to sth)** *(person)* dar testimonio (de algo); *(facts)* dar fe *or* cuenta (de algo); *Rel* **to bear false w.** levantar falso testimonio

2 *vt (scene)* ser testigo de, presenciar; **did she w. the accident?** ¿presenció *or* vio el accidente?; **I witnessed the whole thing** yo fui testigo de todo, yo lo vi todo; **the house has witnessed many changes** la casa ha sido testigo de muchos cambios; **recent years have witnessed a rapid growth in exports** en los últimos años se ha visto un rápido crecimiento de las exportaciones; **to w. sb's signature** firmar en calidad de testigo de alguien

3 *vi Law* **to w. to sth** dar testimonio de algo; **she witnessed to finding the body** ella dio testimonio de haber encontrado el cadáver

witter ['wɪtə(r)] *vi Fam* **to w. (on)** no parar de hablar; **he's always wittering on about his time in the army** se pasa el día hablando de cuando estuvo en el ejército

witticism ['wɪtɪsɪzəm] *n* ocurrencia *f*, agudeza *f*

wittily ['wɪtɪlɪ] *adv* ingeniosamente

wittiness ['wɪtɪnɪs] *n (of person, joke)* ingenio *m*, agudeza *f*

wittingly ['wɪtɪŋlɪ] *adv (intentionally)* adrede, intencionadamente

witty ['wɪtɪ] *adj (person, remark)* ingenioso(a), agudo(a)

wives *pl of* **wife**

wizard ['wɪzəd] **1** *n* (**a**) *(sorcerer)* brujo *m*, mago *m* (**b**) *Fam (genius)* genio *m*; **a financial/political w.** un genio de las finanzas/la política (**c**) *Comptr* asistente *m*

2 *exclam Br Old-fashioned Fam* ¡formidable!

wizardry ['wɪzədrɪ] *n* (**a**) *(sorcery)* brujería *f*, magia *f* (**b**) *Fam (skill)* genialidad *f*; **financial w.** genio *m* para las finanzas; **that was sheer w. with the ball** eso fue una auténtica genialidad *or* floritura con el balón

wizened ['wɪzənd] *adj* marchito(a), arrugado(a)

wiz(z) [wɪz] *n Fam* genio *m* (**at** de)

wk (*abbr* **week**) semana *f*

WNW (*abbr* **west-north-west**) ONO

WO (*abbr* **Warrant Officer**) ≃ subteniente *mf*

woad [wəʊd] *n* (**a**) *(plant)* glasto *m*, (hierba *f*) pastel *m* (**b**) *(dye)* = tinte semejante al añil, que se obtiene del glasto

wobble ['wɒbəl] **1** *n* tambaleo *m*; **the chair has got a bit of a w.** la silla cojea *or* baila *or* se tambalea un poco

2 *vi (chair, table)* cojear, bailar; *(pile of objects, cyclist)* tambalearse; *(jelly)* temblar, agitarse; *(voice)* temblar; **the stone wobbled as I stood on it** la piedra se movió cuando la pisé

wobbly ['wɒblɪ] **1** *n* IDIOM *Br Fam* **to throw a w.** ponerse como una fiera *or* hecho(a) un basilisco *or Méx* como agua para el chocolate

2 *adj* (**a**) *(chair, table)* cojo(a); *(shelf, ladder)* tambaleante; *(jelly)* temblón(ona) (**b**) *(hand, voice)* tembloroso(a); **to be w. (on one's legs)** tambalearse, caminar con paso inseguro; **I feel a bit w.** me siento un poco inseguro al andar

wodge [wɒdʒ] *n* (**a**) *(of paper, banknotes)* fajo *m* (**b**) *(of bread, cake)* cacho *m*

woe [wəʊ] *n Literary* infortunio *m*, desdicha *f*; **he gave me a tale of w.** me contó una sarta de desgracias; *Old-fashioned* **w. betide you** ¡ay de ti!; **w. is me!** ¡ay de mí!

woebegone ['wəʊbɪgɒn] *adj (look, expression)* desconsolado(a)

woeful ['wəʊfʊl] *adj* (**a**) *(sad) (person, look)* apesadumbrado(a), desconsolado(a); *(news)* aciago(a) (**b**) *(terrible)* penoso(a), deplorable; **w. ignorance** ignorancia supina

woefully ['wəʊfʊlɪ] *adv* (**a**) *(sadly)* apesadumbradamente, con pesadumbre (**b**) *(extremely)* terriblemente, extremadamente; **our funds are w. inadequate** la absoluta insuficiencia de nuestros fondos es deplorable

wog [wɒg] *n Br very Fam* = término ofensivo para referirse a una persona que no es de raza blanca, especialmente afrocaribeña

wok [wɒk] *n* wok *m*, = sartén china con forma de cuenco

woke *pt of* **wake**

woken *pp of* **wake**

wold [wəʊld] *n* llanura *f* ondulada

wolf [wʊlf] (*pl* **wolves** [wʊlvz]) *n* (**a**) *(animal)* lobo *m* ▸▸ ***w. cub*** lobezno *m*, lobato *m*; ***w. pack*** jauría *f* de lobos; ***w. spider*** licosa *f*, araña *f* corredora; ***w. whistle*** silbido *m (como piropo)*

(**b**) IDIOMS **to earn enough to keep the w. from the door** ganar lo suficiente como para ir tirando; **to throw sb to the wolves** arrojar a alguien a las fieras; **a w. in sheep's clothing** un lobo con piel de cordero; **to cry w.** dar una falsa voz de alarma

▸ **wolf down** *vt sep* tragar, engullir

wolfhound ['wʊlfhaʊnd] *n* perro *m* lobo

wolfish ['wʊlfɪʃ] *adj (appearance)* lobuno(a); *(appetite)* feroz

wolverine ['wʊlvəri:n] *n* glotón *m*

woman ['wʊmən] (*pl* **women** ['wɪmɪn]) *n* (**a**) *(adult female)* mujer *f*; **a young w.** una chica; **an old w.** una señora mayor, una anciana; **don't be such an old w.!** *(said to man)* ¡no seas tan quejica!; **I'm a busy/lucky w.** soy una mujer muy ocupada/afortunada; *Fam* **I can't stand the w. myself** a ésa es que no la aguanto; *Br Old-fashioned* **my (dear** *or* **good) w.!** ¡mi querida señorita!; **a w.'s hat/bicycle** un sombrero/una bicicleta de mujer; **a w.'s watch** un reloj de señora; **the women's 100 metres** los 100 metros femeninos; *Old-fashioned* **a w. of the streets** *(prostitute)* una mujer de la calle; **a w. of the world** una mujer de mundo, una mujer con mucho mundo; **a w. of the people** una mujer del pueblo; **she's a w. of her word** es una mujer de palabra; **she's a w. of few words** es mujer de pocas palabras; **she's just the w. for the job** es la mujer indicada (para el trabajo); **they have a w. who comes in to clean once a week** tienen una mujer que viene a limpiar una vez por semana; **the w. of the moment** la figura del momento; **to be one's own w.** ser dueña de sí misma; **she's a working/career w.** es una mujer trabajadora/con una carrera profesional; **women and children first** las mujeres y los niños primero; PROV **a w.'s work is never done** una mujer nunca acaba su jornada ▸▸ ***w. driver*** conductora *f*; *Br* ***Women's Institute*** ≃ Instituto *m* de la Mujer; ***women's lib*** *or* ***liberation*** la liberación de la mujer; ***women's magazine*** revista *f* femenina; ***the women's movement*** el movimiento feminista; ***women's page*** páginas *fpl* femeninas; *Euph* ***women's problems*** *(gynaecological)* problemas *mpl* femeninos; ***women's refuge*** centro *m* de acogida para mujeres (maltratadas); ***women's rights*** los derechos de la mujer; *US* ***women's room*** lavabo *m or Esp* servicio *m* de señoras

(**b**) *(wife)* mujer *f*; *Fam (girlfriend)* novia *f*; *Fam* **to have w. trouble** tener problemas de faldas *or RP* polleras; **the w. in my life** la mujer de mi vida

womanhood ['wʊmənhʊd] *n* (**a**) *(maturity)* edad *f* adulta *(de mujer)*; **to reach w.** hacerse mujer (**b**) *(femininity)* femin(e)idad *f* (**c**) *(women collectively)* las mujeres

womanish ['wʊmənɪʃ] *adj (typical of women)* mujeril; *(effeminate)* afeminado(a)

womanizer ['wʊmənaɪzə(r)] *n* mujeriego *m*

womankind [wʊmən'kaɪnd] *n* las mujeres, la mujer

womanly ['wʊmənlɪ] *adj* femenino(a)

womb [wu:m] *n* matriz *f*, útero *m*

wombat ['wɒmbæt] *n* wombat *m*

women *pl of* **woman**

womenfolk ['wɪmɪnfəʊk] *n* mujeres *fpl*

won *pt & pp of* **win**

WONDER ['wʌndə(r)] **1** *n* (**a**) *(miracle)* milagro *m*; **to work** *or* **do wonders** hacer milagros; **it has worked** *or* **done wonders for my confidence** ha mejorado muchísimo mi seguridad en mí mismo; **it's a w. (that) he hasn't lost it** es un milagro *or* es increíble que no lo haya perdido; **the w. (of it) is that...** lo increíble (del asunto) es que...; **no w. the plan failed, it's little** *or* **small w. (that) the plan failed** no es de extrañar que el plan haya fracasado; **is it any w. that he got lost?** ¿acaso es de extrañar que se perdiera?; **I broke it – no w.!** lo rompí – ¡no me sorprende *or* extraña!; **the Seven Wonders of the World** las Siete Maravillas del Mundo; *Fam* **the band were a one-hit w.** fue un grupo de un solo éxito; **ah, the wonders of modern technology!** ¡ah!, ¡qué maravilla la tecnología moderna!; IDIOM *Hum* **wonders will never cease!** ¡vivir para ver! ▸▸ ***w. child*** niño(a) *m,f* prodigio; ***w. drug*** droga *f* milagrosa

(**b**) *Fam (person)* **thanks, you're a w.!** ¡gracias, eres una maravilla!

(**c**) *(astonishment)* asombro *m*; **they were filled with w.** se quedaron asombrados; **in w.** con asombro, asombrado(a)

2 *vt* (**a**) *(ask oneself)* preguntarse; **I often w. that myself** con frecuencia me lo pregunto; **I w. how they did it/what she means** me pregunto cómo lo hicieron/qué quiere decir; **it made me w. if** *or* **whether she was telling the truth** me hizo cuestionarme si decía o no la verdad; **one wonders whether...** me pregunto si...

(**b**) *(in polite requests)* **I w. if** *or* **whether I could ask you a favour?** ¿te importaría hacerme un favor?, ¿podrías hacerme un favor?; **I w. if** *or* **whether you could help me?** ¿te importaría ayudarme?, ¿podrías ayudarme?; **I was wondering if** *or* **whether you were free tonight** ¿por (alguna) casualidad no estarás libre esta noche?

(**c**) *(be surprised that)* **I w. (that) they didn't ring earlier** me sorprende que no hayan llamado antes; **I don't w. (that) they got into trouble** no me sorprende que se hayan metido en líos; **I shouldn't w. if he were already married** no me extrañaría que ya estuviese casado

3 *vi* (**a**) *(be curious)* **will she come, I w.?** me pregunto si vendrá; **can they win? – I w.** ¿tienen posibilidades de ganar? – eso mismo me pregunto yo; **it will soon be over – I w.** pronto se habrá acabado – no sé, no sé; **why do you ask? – I was just wondering** ¿por qué lo preguntas? – por curiosidad; **it makes you w.** te hace pensar; **it set me wondering** me dio que pensar; **where are they? – in the garden, I shouldn't w.** ¿dónde están? – en el jardín, imagino; **to w. about sth** *(motives)* preguntarse por algo; **I've been wondering about what to do** me he estado preguntando qué debo hacer; **I w. about her sometimes** *(don't understand her)* hay veces que no la entiendo; *(don't trust her)* a veces no sé si fiarme de ella; **some players have wondered out loud about the decision** algunos jugadores han expresado abiertamente sus dudas sobre la decisión

(**b**) *(be amazed)* asombrarse (**at** de); **you can't help but w. at their sheer cheek** no deja de asombrar su descaro

---

wonderful ['wʌndəfʊl] *adj* maravilloso(a); **to have a w. time** pasárselo de maravilla; **you passed? that's w.!** ¿aprobaste? ¡qué bien!; **what w. news!** ¡qué buena *or* estupenda noticia!; **she has some w. ideas** tiene unas ideas estupendas; **you look w.** estás estupenda *or* maravillosa

wonderfully ['wʌndəfʊlɪ] *adv* de maravilla, maravillosamente; **he looks w. well** se lo ve de maravilla

wondering ['wʌndərɪŋ] *adj* pensativo(a)

wonderingly ['wʌndərɪŋlɪ] *adv* **"so what he said was true after all," he said w.** "o sea, que lo que dijo resultó ser verdad", dijo pensativo

wonderland ['wʌndəlænd] *n* paraíso *m*; **Alice in W.** Alicia en el país de las maravillas

wonderment ['wʌndəmənt] *n* asombro *m*; **to watch in w.** observar asombrado(a) *or* con asombro

wondrous ['wʌndrəs] *adj* maravilloso(a)

wonk [wɒŋk] *n Fam* (**a**) *(student) Esp* empollón(ona) *m,f*, *Méx* matado(a) *m,f*, *RP* traga *mf* (**b**) *(expert)* experto(a) *m,f*

wonky ['wɒŋkɪ] *adj Br Fam (wheel, floorboards)* flojo(a); *(table)* cojo(a), *Am* chueco(a); **this sentence is a bit w.** esta frase no suena bien

wont [wəʊnt] *Formal* **1** *n* costumbre *f*; **as is his w.** como acostumbra
2 *adj* **to be w. to do sth** ser dado(a) a hacer algo

won't [wəʊnt] = **will not**

wonted ['wəʊntɪd] *adj Formal (customary)* acostumbrado(a)

woo [wu:] *vt* (**a**) *(woman)* cortejar (**b**) *(supporters, investors)* atraer; **they tried to w. the voters with promises of lower taxes** intentaron captar votantes con la promesa de bajar los impuestos

wood [wʊd] *n* (**a**) *(material)* madera *f*; *(for fire)* leña *f*; **made of w.** de madera ▸▸ ***w. alcohol*** alcohol *m* metílico; ***w. carving*** *(object)* talla *f* (en madera); ***w. engraving*** xilografía *f* (a contrafibra); ***w. pulp*** pasta *f* de papel; ***w. stain*** tinte *m* para la madera (**b**) *(forest)* bosque *m*; **the woods** el bosque ▸▸ ***w. anemone*** anémona *f* de los bosques; ***w. nymph*** ninfa *f* de los bosques, dríada *f*; ***w. sandpiper*** andarríos *m inv* bastardo; ***w. stork*** tántalo *m* americano; ***w. warbler*** mosquitero *m* silbador

(**c**) *(in golf)* madera *f*; **a 3/5 w.** una madera del 3/5

(**d**) *(in bowls)* bolo *m*

(**e**) *(casks, barrels)* **matured in the w.** envejecido(a) en barrica; **drawn from the w.** de barril, sacado(a) del barril

(**f**) IDIOMS **she can't see the w. for the trees** los árboles no le dejan ver el bosque; **we're not out of the woods yet** todavía no hemos salido del túnel; *Vulg* **he got w.** *(had an erection)* se le puso dura, empalmó

woodbine ['wʊdbaɪn] *n (plant) (honeysuckle)* madreselva *f*; *US (Virginia creeper)* parra *f or* hiedra *f* virgen

woodblock ['wʊdblɒk] *n (for parquet floor)* tablilla *f or* lámina *f* de madera; **a w. floor** un suelo de parqué *or* parquet

woodchat ['wʊdtʃæt] *n* **w. (shrike)** alcaudón *m*

woodchip ['wʊdtʃɪp] *n* = papel pintado con trocitos de madera para dar textura

woodchuck ['wʊdtʃʌk] *n* marmota *f* de Norteamérica

woodcock ['wʊdkɒk] *n* chocha *f* perdiz

woodcut ['wʊdkʌt] *n (print)* grabado *m* en madera, xilografía *f*; *(wood block)* plancha *f* de madera grabada

woodcutter ['wʊdkʌtə(r)] *n* leñador(ora) *m,f*

wooded ['wʊdɪd] *adj* cubierto(a) de árboles, boscoso(a)

wooden ['wʊdən] *adj* (**a**) *(made of wood)* de madera ▸▸ ***w. horse*** caballo *m* de madera; **the W. Horse of Troy** el caballo de Troya; ***w. leg*** pata *f* de palo; *Fam Hum* ***w. overcoat*** *(coffin)* traje *m* de madera; ***w. spoon*** cuchara *f* de palo; *Sport* cuchara *f* de madera; *Sport* **to get the w. spoon** ser el farolillo rojo (**b**) *(actor, performance)* acartonado(a)

wooden-headed ['wʊdən'hedɪd] *adj Fam* estúpido(a)

woodenly ['wʊdənlɪ] *adv (unexpressively)* envaradamente

woodland ['wʊdlənd] **1** *n* bosque *m*

2 *adj (fauna)* del bosque; **w. walks** paseos por el bosque

woodlark ['wʊdlɑːk] *n* totovía *f*

woodlouse ['wʊdlaʊs] (*pl* **woodlice** ['wʊdlaɪs]) *n* cochinilla *f*, *RP* bicho *m* bolita

woodman = **woodsman**

woodpecker ['wʊdpekə(r)] *n* pájaro *m* carpintero ▸▸ ***great spotted w.*** pico *m* picapinos; ***lesser spotted w.*** pico *m* menor

woodpigeon ['wʊdpɪdʒən] *n* paloma *f* torcaz

woodpile ['wʊdpaɪl] *n* montón *m* de leña

woodruff ['wʊdrʌf] *n* asperilla *f*, reina *f* de los bosques

woodscrew ['wʊdskruː] *n* tornillo *m* para madera

woodshed ['wʊdʃed] *n* leñera *f*

wood(s)man ['wʊd(z)mən] *n (woodcutter)* leñador *m*; *(forest officer)* guarda *m* forestal; *(inhabitant)* hombre *m* del bosque

woodsy ['wʊdzɪ] *adj US Fam (smell)* a madera; *(area)* de bosques

woodwind ['wʊdwɪnd] *n Mus (section of orchestra)* sección *f* de (instrumentos de) viento de madera ▸▸ ***w. instrument*** instrumento *m* de viento de madera

woodwork ['wʊdwɜːk] *n* (**a**) *(craft)* carpintería *f* (**b**) *(of house, room)* madera *f*, carpintería *f*; **they hit the w. three times** *(in soccer)* estrellaron tres disparos contra los palos; IDIOM **to come** *or* **crawl out of the w.** salir de las sombras, surgir de la nada

woodworm ['wʊdwɜːm] *n* carcoma *f*; **the sideboard has got w.** el aparador está carcomido

woody ['wʊdɪ] *adj* (**a**) *(countryside)* boscoso(a), arbolado(a) (**b**) *(plant)* leñoso(a) ▸▸ ***w. nightshade*** dulcamara *f* (**c**) *(taste, smell)* a madera

woof [wʊf] *exclam (of dog)* ¡guau!

woofer ['wʊfə(r)] *n (hi-fi speaker)* altavoz *m or Am* altoparlante *m or Méx* bocina *f* de graves

wool [wʊl] **1** *n* lana *f*; **pure new w.** pura lana virgen; IDIOM *Fam* **to pull the w. over sb's eyes** embaucar *or Esp* dar el pego a alguien

2 *adj (jacket)* de lana

wooliness *US* = **woolliness**

woollen ['wʊlən] **1** *adj (dress)* de lana ▸▸ ***w. mill*** fábrica *f* de lana

2 woollens *npl* prendas *fpl* de lana

woolliness, *US* **wooliness** ['wʊlɪnɪs] *n (of reasoning, style)* carácter *m* farragoso; *(of ideas, theories)* vaguedad *f*, carácter *m* confuso

woolly ['wʊlɪ] **1** *adj* (**a**) *(sweater)* de lana; *(sheep)* lanudo(a); *Fig (clouds)* aborregado(a) (**b**) *(idea, theory)* confuso(a), vago(a); *(reasoning, style)* farragoso(a)

2 *n Br Fam (jumper)* suéter *m or Esp* jersey *m or Col* saco *m or RP* pulóver *m* de lana; **woollies** ropa *f or* prendas *fpl* de lana

Woolsack ['wʊlsæk] *n Br* **the W.** = escaño que ocupa el presidente de la cámara de los lores

woozy ['wuːzɪ] *adj Fam (dazed)* aturdido(a), atontado(a)

wop [wɒp] *n very Fam* = término despectivo para referirse a personas de origen italiano, *RP* tano(a) *m,f*

Worcester(shire) sauce ['wʊstə(ʃə)'sɔːs] *n* salsa *f* Perrins®

WORD [wɜːd] **1** *n* (**a**) *(in general)* palabra *f*; **what's the w. for "bottle" in German?** ¿cómo se dice "botella" en alemán?; **the Japanese don't have a w. for it** los japoneses no tienen un término para eso; **I didn't understand/believe a w. (of it)** no entendí/(me) creí ni una (sola) palabra; **it is written as one w.** se escribe (todo) junto; **in a w.** en una palabra; **in other words** en otras palabras; **in the words of Shelley...** como dijo Shelley...; **she said it in her own words** lo dijo con sus propias palabras; **not in so many words** no con esas palabras; **she told me in so many words that I was a liar** me dijo con estas mismas palabras que era un mentiroso; **I had to explain it to him in words of one syllable** se lo tuve que explicar muy clarito; **I can't put it into words** no lo puedo expresar con palabras; **he's a man of few words** es hombre de pocas palabras; **without a w.** sin mediar palabra; **w. for w.** *(to repeat, quote)* al pie de la letra; *(to translate)* palabra por palabra; **I couldn't get a w. in (edgeways)** no pude meter baza *or RP* pasar ni un aviso; **don't say** *or* **breathe a w. about it** no digas ni una palabra; **it was too ridiculous for words** no se puede imaginar nada más ridículo; **I'm too disappointed for words** no te puedes imaginar lo decepcionado que estoy; *Old-fashioned* **(upon) my w.!** ¡Virgen Santa!; **are you nervous? – nervous isn't the w.!** ¿estás nervioso? – ¡nervioso es poco!; **he's very easy-going – idle would be a better w.** es un tipo tranquilo – un vago sería más atinado; **he's mad, there's no other w. for it** está loco, esa es la palabra exacta; **there's a w. for people like you... it's "thief"** a los de tu calaña se les llama ladrones; **the W. (of God)** la palabra de Dios, la palabra divina; **the printed/written w.** la palabra impresa/escrita ▸▸ ***w. association*** asociación *f* de ideas a través de las palabras; *Comptr* ***w. count*** cuenta *f or Am* conteo *m* de palabras; ***w. game*** juego *m or* pasatiempo *m* a base de palabras; *Gram* ***w. order*** orden *m* de las palabras; ***w. play*** juegos *mpl* de palabras; *Comptr* ***w. processing*** tratamiento *m or* procesamiento *m* de textos; *Comptr* ***w. processor*** procesador *m* de textos; *Comptr* ***w. wrap*** salto *m* de línea automático

(**b**) *(remarks, conversation)* **with these words he left** con aquellas palabras se marchó; **to have a w.** *or* **a few words with sb** hablar con alguien; **could I have a quick w.?** ¿podríamos hablar un momento?; *Fam* **to have words with sb** *(argue)* discutir con alguien; **to have a w. in sb's ear** hablar con alguien en privado; **I'd like to say a w. about punctuality** querría hacer un comentario sobre la puntualidad; **you're putting words in(to) my mouth** me estás atribuyendo cosas que no he dicho; **you've taken the words (right) out of my mouth** me has quitado *or Am* sacado la palabra de la boca; **she wants a w. with you** quiere hablar contigo; **he never has a good w. for anyone** nunca tiene buenas palabras para nadie; **to put in a good w. for sb** decir algo en favor de alguien; **a w. of advice, a w. to the wise** un consejo; **a w. of caution** un consejo; **a w. of encouragement** unas palabras de aliento; **to say a w. of thanks to sb** decir unas palabras de agradecimiento a alguien; **a w. of warning** una advertencia

(**c**) *(news)* **w. of the scandal was leaked to the press** se filtraron a la prensa noticias del escándalo; **we got w. of the decision from an inside source** nos enteramos de la decisión por una fuente interna; **I left w. with reception that I'd be back late** dejé dicho *or Col, Méx, Ven* razón en recepción que volvería tarde; **to put the w. about** *or* **around** *or* **out that...** hacer circular la voz de que...; **to receive** *or* **have w. from sb** tener noticias de alguien; **we have received** *or* **had no w. from them** no hemos sabido nada de ellos, no hemos tenido noticias suyas; **to send sb w. of sth** avisar a alguien de algo; **they sent w. to say that they were safe** enviaron un mensaje *or Col, Méx, Ven* mandaron razón diciendo que estaban a salvo; **to spread** *or* **pass the w.** correr la voz; **the w. is that..., w. has it that...** se rumorea que...; **the w. is out that Bob and Liz are to divorce** se rumorea que Bob y Liz se van a divorciar; **w. got around that there were going to be redundancies** corrió la voz de que iba a haber despidos; **by w. of mouth** de palabra, de boca en boca

(**d**) *(promise, assurance)* palabra *f*; **we only have his w. for it** sólo tenemos su palabra; **it's your w. against mine** es tu palabra contra la mía; **he broke** *or* **went back on his w.** no cumplió con su palabra; **I give you my w., you have my w.** te doy mi palabra; **I give you my w.**

that I won't tell anyone te doy mi palabra de que no se lo diré a nadie; **I always keep my w.** yo siempre mantengo mi palabra; **we held** *or* **kept her to her w.** le hicimos cumplir con su palabra; **take my w. for it** te lo aseguro; **I'll take your w. for it** daré por cierto lo que (me) dices; **I took him at his w.** me fié de su palabra; **w. of honour** palabra de honor

(e) *(command)* **do it as soon as you receive w. from headquarters** hazlo tan pronto como recibas órdenes del cuartel general; **to give sb the w.** avisar a alguien; **just say the w. and I'll do it** no tienes más que pedirlo, y lo haré; **start running at my w.** comienza a correr cuando te lo diga

(f) words *(lyrics)* letra *f*; **I'm learning my words** estoy aprendiendo mi papel; **he forgot his words** se olvidó de lo que tenía que decir

2 *vt* expresar; *(in writing)* redactar; **a carefully-worded letter** una carta muy (bien) medida; **we sent a strongly worded letter of protest** le enviamos una carta de protesta con tono contundente

word-blind ['wɜːdblaɪnd] *adj* con trastornos de lectura

word-blindness ['wɜːdblaɪndnɪs] *n* trastornos *mpl* de lectura

wordfinder ['wɜːdfaɪndə(r)] *n* **(a)** *(puzzle)* sopa *f* de letras **(b)** *(word index)* diccionario *m* de sinónimos

word-for-word [wɜːdfə'wɜːd] *adj* literal

wording ['wɜːdɪŋ] *n* **to change the w. of sth** redactar algo de otra forma; **the w. was ambiguous** estaba escrito de forma ambigua

word-of-mouth [wɜːdəv'maʊθ] *adj* boca a boca ▸▸ *Mktg* ***w. advertising*** publicidad *f* boca a boca

word-perfect [wɜːd'pɜːfɪkt] *adj* al dedillo

word-process ['wɜːdprəʊses] **1** *vi* procesar textos

2 *vt (text)* procesar

wordsearch ['wɜːdsɜːtʃ] *n (puzzle)* sopa *f* de letras

wordsmith ['wɜːdsmɪθ] *n* artífice *mf* de la palabra

wordy ['wɜːdɪ] *adj* verboso(a)

wore *pt of* **wear**

WORK [wɜːk] **1** *n* **(a)** *(labour)* trabajo *m*; **w. in progress** *(sign)* trabajos en curso; **to be at w. (on sth)** estar trabajando (en algo); **to be at w.** *(workplace)* estar en el trabajo; **men at w.** *(sign)* obras; **you can see his Cubist influences at w. in this painting** en este cuadro se observan *or* se ponen de manifiesto sus influencias cubistas; **to get to w.** *(begin working)* ponerse a trabajar; *(arrive at workplace)* llegar al trabajo; **to go to w.** *(begin working)* ponerse a trabajar; *(go to workplace)* ir al trabajo; **she put** *or* **set them to w. cleaning the kitchen** los puso a trabajar limpiando la cocina; **when do you start/finish w.?** ¿cuándo comienzas a/acabas de trabajar?; **they have finished w. on the new bus station** ya han acabado las obras de la nueva estación de autobuses; **the house needs a lot of w.** la casa necesita muchas reformas; PROV **all w. and no play (makes Jack a dull boy)** no conviene obsesionarse con el trabajo ▸▸ ***w. camp*** campo *m* de trabajo; ***w. clothes*** ropa *f* de trabajo; ***the w. ethic*** la ética del trabajo; ***w. study*** estudio *m* de trabajo; ***w. surface:* there aren't enough w. surfaces in this kitchen** no hay suficientes superficies para trabajar en esta cocina

(b) *(employment)* trabajo *m*, empleo *m*; **to look for/find w.** buscar/encontrar empleo *or* trabajo; **I'm looking for secretarial w.** busco (un) trabajo de secretaria; **I started w. at the age of sixteen** comencé a trabajar a los dieciséis (años); **he's a friend from w.** es un amigo del trabajo; **to be in w.** tener trabajo; **to be out of w.** no tener trabajo, *Esp* estar parado(a) ▸▸ ***w. contract*** contrato *m* laboral *or* de trabajo; ***w. experience*** *(previous employment)* experiencia *f* laboral; *Br (placement)* prácticas *fpl* (laborales); ***w. permit*** permiso *m* de trabajo; *US* ***w. week*** semana *f* laboral

(c) *(effort)* esfuerzo *m*; **to put a lot of w. into sth** poner mucho esfuerzo en algo; **it will take a lot of w.** costará mucho trabajo; **take the w. out of doing the washing-up!** ¡olvídese del trabajo de fregar!

(d) *(tasks)* trabajo *m*; **to have w. to do** tener trabajo (que hacer); **wait until the medicine has done its w.** espera hasta que el medicamento haga *or* surja efecto; **let's get down to w.!** ¡manos a la obra!; IDIOM **to have one's w. cut out** tenerlo bastante difícil; IDIOM **to make quick** *or* **short w. of sth** despachar algo en seguida; IDIOM **it's all in a day's w.** es el pan nuestro de cada día

(e) *(product, achievement)* obra *f*; **a w. of art** una obra de arte; **very detailed/delicate w.** una obra minuciosa/delicada; **a new w. on Portugal** una nueva obra sobre Portugal; **the works of Shakespeare** las obras de Shakespeare; **is this all your own w.?** ¿lo has hecho todo tú mismo?; **this is the w. of a professional killer** ha sido obra de un asesino a sueldo; **good** *or* **nice w.!** ¡buen trabajo!

(f) *(papers, material being worked on)* trabajo *m*; **to take w. home** llevarse trabajo a casa

(g) *(deed)* obra *f*; **charitable works** obras de caridad

(h) *(research)* trabajo *m*

(i) *Ind* **a cement works** una fábrica *orAm* planta de cemento, una cementera; **£300 ex works** 300 libras más gastos de envío; **works outing** excursión anual (de los trabajadores de una empresa) ▸▸ ***works council*** comité *m* de empresa

(j) works *(construction)* obras *fpl*

(k) works *(mechanism)* mecanismo *m*

(l) *Fam* **the works** *(everything)* todo; **to give sb the works** *(beating)* dar una paliza a alguien; *(luxury treatment)* tratar a alguien a cuerpo de rey

(m) *Fam* **works** *(drug paraphernalia)* material *m* (para ponerse)

(n) *Phys* trabajo *m*

2 *vt* **(a)** *(hours, days)* trabajar; **I w. a six-day week** trabajo seis días a la semana; **I worked my way through college** trabajaba mientras hacía la carrera; **to w. one's passage** pagarse el pasaje trabajando en el barco

(b) *(cause to do labour)* **to w. sb hard** hacer trabajar mucho a alguien; **to w. sb/oneself to death** matar a alguien/matarse a trabajar

(c) *(operate) (machine)* manejar, hacer funcionar; **the machine is worked by turning this handle** la máquina se acciona girando esta manivela; **do you know how to w. this VCR?** ¿sabes manejar este vídeo *orAm* video?

(d) *(bring about) (miracle, cure)* hacer, obrar; **to w. a change on sth/sb** operar un cambio en algo/alguien; **the landscape soon worked its magic on us** el paisaje no tardó *orAm* demoró en cautivarnos; **she has worked wonders with the children** ha hecho milagros con los niños; **she worked the audience into a frenzy** puso al público frenético; **to w. oneself into a rage** ponerse hecho una furia; **I'll w. it** *or* **things so that they pay in advance** lo arreglaré de forma que paguen por adelantado

(e) *(move)* **to w. one's hands free** lograr soltarse las manos; **I worked the handle up and down** moví la palanca de arriba abajo; **he worked his way to the front of the crowd** se abrió paso hasta el frente de la multitud; **to w. one's way through a book** ir avanzando en la lectura de un libro; **she worked her way up through the company** fue ascendiendo en la escalafón de la empresa

(f) *(do work in)* **I w. the north of the town** cubro la zona norte de la ciudad; **all the staff were working the phones** todo el personal estaba atendiendo los teléfonos; *Fig* **the candidate worked the crowd** el candidato se trabajó a la multitud

(g) *(exploit) (mine, quarry)* explotar; *(land)* labrar

(h) *(shape) (clay, metal, dough)* trabajar; **to w. sth into sth** transformar algo en algo

3 *vi* **(a)** *(person)* trabajar; **I w. as a translator** trabajo de *or* como traductor; **to w. for sb** trabajar para alguien; **to w. for oneself** trabajar por cuenta propia; **to w. for world peace** trabajar por la paz mundial; **he works in wood/oils** trabaja la madera/en óleo; **to w. towards an agreement** trabajar para alcanzar un acuerdo; **she works with disabled people** trabaja con discapacitados; *Ind* **to w. to rule** hacer huelga de celo; **we worked until we dropped** trabajamos hasta el agotamiento

(b) *(function) (machine, system)* funcionar; **my brain was working frantically** mi cerebro estaba trabajando a tope; **this relationship isn't working** esta relación no funciona; **the acid works as a catalyst** el ácido hace de catalizador; **it works off** *or* **on solar power** funciona con energía solar

(c) *(have effect) (medicine)* hacer efecto; *(plan, method)* funcionar; **the sax solo doesn't really w.** el solo de saxo no queda nada bien; IDIOM **to w. like magic** *or* **a charm** funcionar de maravilla

(d) *(count)* **her age works against her/in her favour** la edad juega en su contra/en su favor

(e) *(move)* **the screw worked loose** el tornillo se soltó

▸**work around** = **work round**

▸**work at** *vt insep (try to improve)* intentar mejorar

▸**work in** *vt sep (include)* añadir, incluir; **w. the butter in slowly** ve incorporando la mantequilla poco a poco; **he worked in a few sly remarks about the boss** incluyó algunos comentarios maliciosos referidos al jefe

▸**work into** *vt sep (include)* añadir, incluir; **w. the butter into the flour** mezcla la mantequilla con la harina; **gently w. the cream into your skin** suavemente aplique la crema frotándola sobre la piel

▸**work off** *vt sep* **(a)** *(get rid of)* **he worked off 5 kilos** con el esfuerzo perdió 5 kilos; **she worked off her frustration** desahogó su frustración **(b)** *(debt)* trabajar para amortizar

▸**work on 1** *vt insep* **(a)** *(try to improve)* **to w. on sth** trabajar en algo; **have you got any ideas about who did it? – I'm working on it** ¿tienes idea de quién lo hizo? – estoy en ello **(b)** *(try to influence)*

I'll w. on my brother to see if I can get him to help us trabajaré a mi hermano para que nos ayude (**c**) *(base oneself on)* **to w. on the assumption that...** partir de la base de que...
2 *vi (continue to work)* seguir trabajando

▸**work out** 1 *vt sep* (**a**) *(cost, total)* calcular; *(plan)* elaborar; *(compromise)* llegar a; *(details)* precisar; **to w. out the answer** dar con la solución; **she won't tell us the answer, so we'll have to w. it out for ourselves** no quiere decirnos la respuesta, por lo que la tendremos que sacar por nosotros mismos; **to w. out how to do sth** dar con la manera de hacer algo; **I finally worked out what was going on** al final conseguí entender lo que pasaba; **we need to w. out who does what** necesitamos establecer quién hace qué; **I can't w. out where I went wrong** no consigo descubrir dónde me he equivocado; **we need to w. out a way of letting them know** tenemos que idear una manera de decírselo; **I've got it all worked out** lo tengo todo planeado; **I'm sure we can w. this thing out** estoy seguro de que lo podemos arreglar; **I can't w. her out** no consigo entenderla
(**b**) *(solve)* **it'll all w. itself out** todo se arreglará
(**c**) *(complete)* **I can't start my new job until I've worked out my notice** no puedo empezar mi nuevo trabajo hasta que no cumpla mis obligaciones contractuales con el que tengo ahora
(**d**) *(mine, well)* agotar
2 *vi* (**a**) *(problem, situation)* **it all** *or* **things worked out in the end** al final todo salió bien; **to w. out well/badly (for sb)** salir bien/mal (a alguien); **how are things working out with your new boyfriend?** ¿qué tal te van las cosas con tu nuevo novio?; **she worked out fine as personnel director** se desenvolvió muy bien de directora de personal; **my new job isn't really working out** mi nuevo trabajo no está resultando
(**b**) *(total)* salir; **it works out a bit more expensive** sale un poco más caro; **it works out at $150 each** sale a 150 dólares por cabeza
(**c**) *(exercise)* hacer ejercicios

▸**work over** *vt sep Fam (beat up)* dar una paliza a

▸**work round** 1 *vi* (**a**) *(wind)* cambiar (**b**) *(in conversation)* **he finally worked round to the subject of housing** finalmente se decidió a abordar el asunto de la vivienda
2 *vt sep (bring round)* **I worked the conversation round to my salary** saqué a colación el tema de mi salario

▸**work through** *vt insep* (**a**) *(continue to work)* **she worked through lunch** siguió trabajando durante la hora de la comida
(**b**) *(resolve)* **he worked through his emotional problems** superó sus problemas emocionales

▸**work up** 1 *vt sep* (**a**) *(acquire, build up)* **to w. up enthusiasm/interest for sth** ir entusiasmándose con/interesándose por algo; **to w. up the courage to do sth** reunir el valor para hacer algo; **I've worked up an appetite after all that walking** después de tanto caminar me ha entrado el apetito; **I worked up a sweat on the exercise bike** sudé mucho en la bicicleta estática; *Fig* **he won the competition without working up a sweat** ganó el campeonato sin despeinarse
(**b**) *(upset)* **to be worked up (about sth)** estar alterado(a) (por algo); **to get worked up (about sth), to w. oneself up (about sth)** alterarse (por algo); **to w. oneself up into a frenzy** ponerse frenético(a)
(**c**) *(develop)* **she worked the notes up into an article** convirtió las notas en un artículo
2 *vi (clothing)* salirse; **his shirt had worked up at the back** se le había salido la camisa por detrás

▸**work up to** 1 *vt insep* prepararse *or Am* alistarse para
2 *vt sep* **I'm working myself up to asking her out** me estoy mentalizando para pedirle salir

---

workable ['wɜːkəbəl] *adj* (**a**) *(solution, plan, proposal)* viable, factible (**b**) *(mine)* explotable; *(field)* cultivable

workaday ['wɜːkədeɪ] *adj (clothes)* de diario; *(routine)* diario(a), de todos los días

workaholic [wɜːkə'hɒlɪk] *n Fam* **to be a w.** estar obsesionado(a) con el trabajo

workbag ['wɜːkbæg] *n* bolsa *f* de la labor

workbasket ['wɜːkbɑːskɪt] *n* cesta *f* de la labor, costurero *m*

workbench ['wɜːkbentʃ] *n* banco *m* de carpintero

workbook ['wɜːkbʊk] *n* libro *m* de ejercicios

workbox ['wɜːkbɒks] *n* cesta *f* de la labor, costurero *m*

workday ['wɜːkdeɪ] *n US* jornada *f* laboral

worked [wɜːkt] *adj* trabajado(a), elaborado(a); **a w. example** *(in textbook)* un ejemplo resuelto

worker ['wɜːkə(r)] *n* trabajador(ora) *m,f*; **skilled workers** mano *f* de obra cualificada; **to be a fast/slow w.** trabajar rápido/lento; **he's a hard w.** es muy trabajador ▸▸ ***w. ant*** hormiga *f* obrera; ***w. bee*** abeja *f* obrera; ***w. participation*** = participación de los trabajadores en la gestión de la empresa; ***w. priest*** sacerdote *m or* cura *m* obrero

workfare ['wɜːkfeə(r)] *n US* = trabajos para la comunidad o cursos de formación de carácter obligatorio para desempleados con subsidio

workforce ['wɜːkfɔːs] *n* (**a**) *(working population)* población *f* activa (**b**) *(employees)* trabajadores *mpl*, mano *f* de obra

workhorse ['wɜːkhɔːs] *n* (**a**) *(horse)* caballo *m* de tiro (**b**) *(person)* burro *m* de carga; *(machine)* principal herramienta *f*

workhouse ['wɜːkhaʊs] *n Hist* = institución pública en la que los pobres trabajaban a cambio de comida y albergue

work-in ['wɜːkɪn] *n (by employees)* encierro *m*

working ['wɜːkɪŋ] 1 *n* (**a**) *(operation) (of machine)* funcionamiento *m* (**b**) **workings** *(mechanism)* mecanismo *m*, maquinaria *f*; *Fig (of government, system)* funcionamiento *m*; **it's difficult to understand the workings of his mind** es difícil entender los entresijos de su mente
2 *adj* (**a**) *(person)* trabajador(ora); **a relaxed w. environment** un ambiente de trabajo tranquilo; **we have a close w. relationship** nos compenetramos bien en el trabajo ▸▸ ***the w. class*** la clase trabajadora *or* obrera; ***w. clothes*** ropa *f* de trabajo; ***w. conditions*** condiciones *fpl* de trabajo; ***w. day*** *(hours of work in a day)* jornada *f* laboral; *(not holiday)* día *m* laborable; *Euph* ***w. girl*** *(prostitute)* chica *f* de la calle; ***w. hours*** horario *m* laboral *or* de trabajo; ***w. life*** vida *f* laboral; ***w. lunch*** almuerzo *m* de trabajo; *Br* ***w. men's club*** club *m* social de trabajadores; ***w. population*** población *f* activa; ***w. week*** semana *f* laboral
(**b**) *(functioning) (farm, factory)* en funcionamiento; **to be in w. order** funcionar bien; **to have a w. knowledge of French** tener un conocimiento básico de francés ▸▸ ***w. agreement*** acuerdo *m* tácito; *Fin* ***w. capital*** capital *m* circulante; ***w. hypothesis*** hipótesis *f inv* de trabajo; ***w. majority*** mayoría *f* suficiente; ***w. model*** prototipo *m*; ***w. party*** comisión *f* de trabajo

working-class ['wɜːkɪŋ'klɑːs] *adj (person, accent)* de clase trabajadora *or* obrera; *(community, district)* obrero(a); **he's w.** es de clase obrera

workload ['wɜːkləʊd] *n* cantidad *f* de trabajo; **he has a very heavy w.** tiene mucho trabajo

workman ['wɜːkmən] *n* obrero *m*; PROV **a bad w. always blames his tools** el mal trabajador siempre le echa la culpa a sus herramientas

workmanlike ['wɜːkmənlaɪk] *adj* competente, profesional

workmanship ['wɜːkmənʃɪp] *n* confección *f*, factura *f*; **a fine piece of w.** un trabajo de excelente factura; **many of the problems can be traced back to poor w.** muchos de los problemas pueden tener su origen en la falta de profesionalidad *or* el trabajo mal hecho

workmate ['wɜːkmeɪt] *n Br* compañero(a) *m,f* de trabajo

work-out ['wɜːkaʊt] *n* sesión *f* de ejercicios

workplace ['wɜːkpleɪs] *n* lugar *m* de trabajo

workroom ['wɜːkruːm] *n* taller *m*

worksharing ['wɜːkʃeərɪŋ] *n* reparto *m* del trabajo

worksheet ['wɜːkʃiːt] *n (detailing work plan)* hoja *f* de trabajo; *(of exercises)* hoja *f* de ejercicios

workshop ['wɜːkʃɒp] *n* (**a**) *(for repairs)* taller *m* (**b**) *(study group)* taller *m*

workshy ['wɜːkʃaɪ] *adj* perezoso(a)

workspace ['wɜːkspeɪs] *n* espacio *m* de trabajo

workstation ['wɜːksteɪʃən] *n Comptr* estación *f* de trabajo

worktable ['wɜːkteɪbəl] *n* mesa *f* de trabajo

worktop ['wɜːktɒp] *n (in kitchen)* encimera *f*

work-to-rule [wɜːktə'ruːl] *n Ind* huelga *f* de celo

workwear ['wɜːkweə(r)] *n* ropa *f* de trabajo

WORLD [wɜːld] 1 *n* (**a**) *(the earth)* mundo *m*; **the best/biggest in the w.** el mejor/más grande del mundo; **workers of the w., unite!** proletarios del mundo, ¡uníos!; **to go round the w.** dar la vuelta al mundo; **to sail round the w.** circunnavegar el mundo; **to see the w.** ver mundo; **the w. over, all over the w.** en todas partes; **people from all over the w.** gente de todas partes; **throughout the w.** por todo el mundo; **since the w. began** desde el principio de los tiempos, desde que el mundo es mundo ▸▸ ***the W. Bank*** el Banco Mundial; ***w. champion*** campeón(ona) *m,f* mundial; ***w. championship(s)*** campeonato *m* mundial, campeonatos *mpl* mundiales; ***W. Council of Churches*** Consejo *m* Mundial de Iglesias; ***the W. Cup*** *(of soccer)* el Mundial (de fútbol), los Mundiales (de fútbol); *(of cricket, rugby, basketball)* el Mundial, el Campeonato del Mundo; ***w. domination*** dominación *f* mundial; *US* ***w.'s fair*** exposición *f* universal; ***W. Health Organization*** Organización *f* Mundial de la Salud; ***w. language*** lenguaje *m* universal; ***w. map*** mapamundi *m*; ***w. music*** música *f* étnica; ***w. power*** *(country)* potencia *f* mundial; ***w. record*** récord *m* mundial *or* del mundo; ***W. Series*** Serie *f* Mundial, = final a siete partidos entre los dos campeones de las ligas de béisbol en Estados Unidos; ***W. Service*** *(of BBC)* = división de la BBC que emite programas para el extranjero; ***w. tour*** gira *f* mundial; ***w. trade*** el comercio mundial; ***W. Trade Organization*** Organización *f* Mundial del Comercio; ***w. war*** guerra *f* mundial; ***W. War One*** la Primera Guerra Mundial; ***W. War Two*** la Segunda Guerra Mundial; ***the W. Wide Web*** la (World Wide) Web; ***W. Wildlife Fund*** Fondo *m* Mundial para la Naturaleza

(**b**) *(realm)* mundo *m*; **the Arab/Spanish-speaking w.** el mundo árabe/hispanohablante; **the literary/business w.** el mundo literario/de los negocios; **the animal/plant w.** el mundo animal/vegetal; **a nightmare/fantasy w.** un mundo de pesadilla/fantasía

(**c**) *(society)* **to create a better w.** crear un mundo mejor; **to be alone in the w.** estar solo(a) en el mundo; **to come down in the w.** venir a menos; **to go up in the w.** prosperar; **a man of the w.** un hombre de mundo; **the w. at large** el mundo en general ►► ***w. view*** visión *f* del mundo

(**d**) *(for emphasis)* **he is the w.'s worst photographer** como fotógrafo no vale nada; **we don't want the whole w. to know** no queremos que se entere todo el mundo; **there's a w. of difference between the two parties** hay una diferencia abismal *or* enorme entre los dos partidos; **that will do you the** *or* **a w. of good** te vendrá la mar de bien; **I'd give the w. to...** daría cualquier cosa *or* lo que fuera por...; **you mean (all) the w. to me** lo eres todo para mí; **she thinks the w. of him** lo quiere como a nada en el mundo; **they carried on for all the w. as if nothing had happened** siguieron tranquilamente como si nada hubiera pasado; **I wouldn't do that for anything in** *or* **all the w.** no lo haría ni por todo el oro del mundo; **nothing in the w. can stop them** nada en el mundo los detendrá; **what/where/who in the w.....?** ¿qué/dónde/quién demonios...?

(**e**) IDIOMS *Fam Hum* **all the w. and his wife** *or* **her husband were there** todo Dios estaba allí; **to watch the w. go by** ver a la gente pasar; **they are worlds apart** media un abismo entre ellos/ellas; **he's not long for this w.** le queda poco, está con un pie en la tumba; **the w. is your oyster** el mundo es tuyo; **to bring a child into the w.** traer un niño al mundo; *Literary* **to come into the w., to enter this w.** venir al mundo; **what is the w. coming to?** ¿adónde vamos a ir a parar?; **he wants to have the best of both worlds** quiere estar en misa y repicando, quiere nadar y guardar la ropa; **he's got the w. at his feet** tiene el mundo a sus pies; **she lives in a w. of her own** vive en su propio mundo; **her w. came crashing down (about her** *or* **her ears)** se le vino el mundo abajo; **love makes the w. go round** el amor lo puede todo; **to set the w. alight** *or* **on fire** causar sensación; **in the next w.** en el otro mundo; **in this w. and the next** en esta y en la próxima vida; **multinationals like the General Motors of this w.** las multinacionales como la General Motors; *Fam* **it's out of this w.** es una maravilla

2 *adj (peace, economy, statesman)* mundial; *(history)* del mundo, universal; *(religion)* del mundo; **on a w. scale** a escala mundial

---

world-beater ['wɜːldbiːtə(r)] *n (sportsperson)* fuera de serie *mf*; *(product)* producto *m* fuera de serie

world-class ['wɜːldklɑːs] *adj Sport* de talla mundial *or* internacional; *Ironic* de marca mayor

world-famous ['wɜːld'feɪməs] *adj* mundialmente famoso(a)

worldliness ['wɜːldlɪnɪs] *n* sofisticación *f*, mundanería *f*

worldly ['wɜːldlɪ] *adj (person)* mundano(a); *(pleasure)* mundano(a), terrenal; **she was very w. for one so young** había visto mucho mundo para alguien de su edad ►► ***w. goods*** bienes *mpl* terrenales; ***w. wisdom*** gramática *f* parda

worldly-wise ['wɜːldlɪ'waɪz] *adj* **to be w.** tener mucha experiencia de *or* en la vida

world-shattering ['wɜːldʃætərɪŋ], **world-shaking** ['wɜːldʃeɪkɪŋ] *adj* extraordinariamente trascendental

world-weariness ['wɜːld'wɪərɪnɪs] *n* hastío *m* de la vida *or* del mundo

world-weary ['wɜːldwɪərɪ] *adj* hastiado(a) de la vida *or* del mundo

worldwide ['wɜːldwaɪd] **1** *adj* mundial

2 *adv* en todo el mundo

worm [wɜːm] **1** *n* (**a**) *(in general)* gusano *m*; *(earthworm)* lombriz *f* (de tierra); **to have worms** *(intestinal)* tener lombrices (**b**) *Comptr* gusano *m* (**c**) IDIOMS **he's a w.** es un miserable *or* un gusano; **the w. has turned!** ¡finalmente el perro enseña los dientes!; **a w.'s eye view** una visión humilde de las cosas

2 *vt* (**a**) *(cat, dog)* administrar vermífugos a (**b**) *(wriggle)* **she wormed her way out of the situation** se las ingenió para salir del paso; *Pej* **to w. oneself into sb's favour/confidence** apañárselas para ganarse el favor/la confianza de alguien (**c**) *(extract)* **to w. a secret out of sb** sonsacar un secreto a alguien

WORM [wɜːm] *Comptr* (*abbr* **write once read many times**) WORM

wormcast ['wɜːmkɑːst] *n* = cúmulo dejado por una lombriz de tierra

worm-eaten ['wɜːmiːtən] *adj (wood)* carcomido(a); *(fruit)* agusanado(a)

wormhole ['wɜːmhəʊl] *n* (**a**) *(in wood, fruit)* agujero *m* de gusano (**b**) *Astron* agujero *m* de gusano

wormwood ['wɜːmwʊd] *n* (**a**) *(plant)* ajenjo *m* (**b**) *Literary (bitterness)* amargura *f*

worn 1 *pp of* **wear**

2 *adj* (**a**) *(shoes, rug, tyre)* gastado(a) (**b**) *(weary) (person)* agotado(a)

worn out [wɔːn'aʊt] *adj* (**a**) *(person)* rendido(a), extenuado(a) (**b**) *(object)* gastado(a); *(idea)* trillado(a)

worried ['wʌrɪd] *adj (person)* preocupado(a); **a w. expression/look** una expresión/mirada de preocupación; **I'm w. that I won't remember** me preocupa que se me olvide; **to be w. (about)** estar preocupado(a) (por); **I'm w. about the future** me preocupa el futuro; **to be w. sick** *or* **to death** estar muerto(a) de preocupación; **they are w. for his safety** están preocupados por su seguridad, les preocupa su seguridad; **you had me w. for a minute** por un momento me llegaste a preocupar

worriedly ['wʌrɪdlɪ] *adv* con preocupación

worrier ['wʌrɪə(r)] *n* **to be a w.** preocuparse por todo; **he's a born w.** siempre se ha preocupado demasiado por todo

worrisome ['wʌrɪsəm] *adj* preocupante

worry ['wʌrɪ] **1** *n* (**a**) *(anxiety)* preocupación *f*; **it's causing me a lot of w.** me tiene muy preocupado; **money is a constant source of w.** el dinero es una fuente constante de preocupaciones

(**b**) *(concern, problem)* preocupación *f*; **he doesn't seem to have any worries** no parece tener ninguna preocupación; **her sons are a constant w. to her** sus hijos son una preocupación constante para ella; **that's the least of my worries** eso es lo que menos me preocupa ►► ***w. beads*** = sarta de cuentas que se manipula para calmar los nervios

2 *vt* (**a**) *(cause anxiety to)* preocupar; **it doesn't w. me** no me preocupa; **he was worried by her sudden disappearance** estaba preocupado por su repentina desaparición, su repentina desaparición lo tenía preocupado; **it doesn't seem to w. you if other people get killed** parece que te trae sin cuidado que otros puedan morir; **to w. oneself sick (about sth)** angustiarse (por algo)

(**b**) *(of dog) (sheep)* perseguir, acosar; *(bone)* roer

3 *vi* preocuparse (**about** de *or* por); **what's the use of worrying?** ¿de qué sirve preocuparse?; **don't (you) w. about me** no te preocupes por mí; **I w. about him finding out** me preocupa que se entere; **I'll pay it back next week – no, don't w. about it!** te lo pago la semana que viene – ¡no te preocupes!; **there's** *or* **it's nothing to w. about** no hay de qué *or* por qué preocuparse; **not to w.!** ¡no pasa nada!; **they'll be found, don't you w.** los encontrarán, ya lo verás; *Ironic* **YOU should w.!** ¡mira quién fue a preocuparse!, ¡tú no tienes problema!

►**worry at** *vt insep (bone)* roer; *(scab)* tocarse; *(problem)* darle vueltas a

worrying ['wʌrɪɪŋ] *adj* preocupante; **the w. thing is that it could happen again** lo preocupante es que podría volver a pasar

worryingly ['wʌrɪɪŋlɪ] *adv* de forma preocupante, preocupantemente; **w., there has been no improvement** es muy preocupante que no haya habido ninguna mejora; **even more w.,...** lo que es aún más preocupante es que...

worrywart ['wʌrɪwɔːt] *n US Fam Esp* angustias *mf inv*, *Am* angustiado(a) *m,f*

WORSE [wɜːs] **1** *n* **there was w. to come, w. was to follow** lo peor no había llegado aún; **I've seen w.** he visto cosas peores; **a change for the w.** un cambio a *or* para peor

2 *adj (comparative of "bad")* peor (**than** que); **there's nothing w. than...** no hay nada peor que...; **it's w. than we thought** es peor de lo que pensábamos; **it's now w. than useless** ya no sirve *or* vale para nada; **to get w.** empeorar; **the wind got w.** el viento comenzó a soplar con más fuerza; **the rain got w.** comenzó a llover más fuerte; **it could have been w.** podría haber sido peor; **rubbing your eyes will only make them w.** frotándote los ojos no arreglas nada; **it only made things** *or* **matters w.** sólo empeoró las cosas; **and, to make matters w., I lost my camera** y, para colmo de males, perdí mi cámara; **to go**

from bad to w. ir de mal en peor; **I'm none the w. for the experience** me siento perfectamente a pesar de la experiencia; **he's lost a couple of kilos but he's none the w. for it** ha perdido un par de kilos y le ha sentado muy bien; **so much the w. for them!** ¡peor para ellos!; **she was the w. for drink** estaba bastante bebida; *Fam* **to be the w. for wear** estar para tirar, estar para el arrastre; *Fam* **it was none the w. for wear** tampoco estaba tan mal; **and, what's w.,...** y, lo que es peor,...; *Fam* **I can't go, w. luck!** ¡no puedo ir, por desgracia!; PROV **w. things happen at sea** más se perdió en la guerra (de Cuba), hay cosas peores

3 *adv (comparative of "badly")* peor; **you could do (a lot) w. than accept their offer** harías bien en aceptar su oferta; **he may not be terribly handsome, but you could do (a lot) w.** puede que no sea muy atractivo, pero los hay peores; **I don't think any w. of her for it** no tengo peor concepto de ella por eso; **he is w. off than before** *(in less advantageous situation)* las cosas le van peor que antes; *(poorer)* está peor económicamente que antes; **I'm $100 w. off than before** tengo 100 dólares menos que antes; **the country is no w. off for having a coalition government** el país no ha salido perdiendo con la coalición en el gobierno

---

worsen ['wɜːsən] 1 *vt* empeorar

2 *vi* empeorar

worse-off [wɜːs'ɒf] *n* **the w.** los menos favorecidos

Worship ['wɜːʃɪp] *n* **His/Her W.** *(referring to judge)* Su Señoría; **His W. the Mayor** el excelentísimo señor alcalde

worship ['wɜːʃɪp] 1 *n (of deity)* adoración *f* (**of** de), culto *m* (**of** a); *(of person)* adoración *f* (**of** por); **freedom of w.** libertad de culto; **place of w.** templo; **an act of w.** un rito religioso, una ceremonia religiosa; **the rock star has become an object of w.** las estrellas del rock se han convertido en personajes de culto; **the w. of wealth and power** el culto a la riqueza y al poder

2 *vt (pt & pp* **worshipped**, *US* **worshiped**) *(deity)* adorar, rendir culto a; *(person)* adorar; *(money)* rendir culto a; **they worshipped the ground she walked on** besaban el suelo que ella pisaba

3 *vi* rezar; **the church where she worshipped for ten years** la iglesia adonde acudió (a rezar) durante diez años; **they worshipped at the temple of Apollo** eran devotos del templo de Apolo

worshipper, *US* **worshiper** ['wɜːʃɪpə(r)] *n* (**a**) *(of deity)* fiel *mf*, devoto(a) *m,f*; **thousands of worshippers came to the shrine** miles de fieles acudieron al santuario (**b**) *(of person)* admirador(ora) *m,f*; **worshippers of material possessions** los que rinden culto a los bienes materiales

---

WORST [wɜːst] 1 *n* **the w.** lo peor; *(plural)* los peores; **he's the w. of them all** es el peor de todos; **the ones that refuse to cooperate are the w.** los que se niegan a cooperar son los peores; **that's the w. I've ever played** nunca había jugado tan mal; **the w. that could happen** lo peor que podría suceder; **the w. of it is that...** lo peor de todo es que...; **that's the w. of cheap shoes** eso es lo peor de los zapatos baratos; **and that's not the w. of it!** ¡y eso no es lo peor!; **he's prepared for the w.** está preparado para lo peor; **the w. is yet to come** lo peor aún está por llegar; **the w. is over** ya ha pasado lo peor; **she's at her w. in the mornings** la mañana es su peor momento del día; **an example of communism at its w.** un ejemplo de lo peor del comunismo; **when things** *or* **matters were at their w.** cuando las cosas estaban peor (que nunca); **even at her w. she is still a brilliant player** incluso en sus peores actuaciones continúa siendo una jugadora excepcional; **at (the) w.** en el peor de los casos; **he brings out the w. in me** hace aflorar lo peor de mí mismo; *Fam Hum* **do your w.!** ¡aquí te espero!, *Esp* ¡ven a por mí si puedes!; **we have taken all possible precautions, so let the hurricane do its w.!** hemos tomado todas las precauciones posibles, ¡ya puede venir el huracán!; **she got** *or* **had the w. of it** *(in quarrel, fight)* se llevó la peor parte; IDIOM **if it** *or* **the w. comes to the w.** en el peor de los casos

2 *adj (superlative of "bad")* peor; **the w. book** el peor libro; **the w. movie** la peor película; **his w. mistake** su error más grave; **it happened at the w. possible time** sucedió en el momento más inoportuno, sucedió en el peor momento; **the fighting was w. near the border** la lucha era más encarnecida cerca de la frontera; **the w. one** el/la peor; **the w. ones** los/las peores; **the w. thing was...** lo peor fue...; **this is a w. case scenario** esto es lo que ocurriría en el peor de los casos

3 *adv (superlative of "badly")* peor; **the North has been w. hit by the storms** el Norte ha sufrido los peores efectos de las tormentas; **the w. affected** los más afectados; **w. of all,...** y lo que es peor,...; **the elderly are the w. off** *(in least advantageous situation)* los ancianos son los que peor están; *(poorest)* los ancianos son los que menos dinero tienen; **he came off w.** se llevó la peor parte, fue quien salió peor parado

4 *vt Old-fashioned* derrotar

---

worsted ['wɜːstɪd] *n Tex* estameña *f*

WORTH [wɜːθ] 1 *n* valor *m*; **give me $30 w. of gasoline** póngame 30 dólares de gasolina *or RP* nafta; **a week's w. of fuel** combustible para una semana; **men of such w. are few and far between** hombres tan valiosos se pueden contar con los dedos de una mano; **to get one's money's w.** sacar partido al *or* del dinero; **he always wants to get his money's w.** siempre quiere sacarle el máximo partido a su dinero; **you should know your own w.** deberías saber lo que vales; **she has proved** *or* **shown her w.** ha desmostrado su valía

2 *prep* (**a**) *(having a value of)* **to be w. £150/a lot of money** valer 150 libras/mucho dinero; **how much is it w.?** ¿qué valor tiene?; **prizes w. $10,000** premios por valor de 10.000 dólares; **is it really w. all that money?** ¿vale la pena pagar ese precio?; **it was (well) w. the money we paid for it** justificó el dinero que pagamos por él; **it must be w. a fortune** debe costar *or* valer una fortuna; **this watch/your friendship is w. a lot to me** me aprecio mucho este reloj/tu amistad; *Fam* **can I borrow your bike? – what's it w.?** ¿me prestas tu bici? – ¿a cambio de qué?; *Fam* **he's w. at least 50 million** tiene por lo menos 50 millones; **she's w. ten of you** vale muchísimo más que tú; **he was pulling for all he was w.** tiraba con todas sus fuerzas; **we exploited the loophole for all it was w.** aprovechamos el vacío legal al máximo; **that's my opinion, for what it's w.** esa es mi opinión, si sirve de algo; **for what it's w., we wouldn't have won anyway** total, para lo que importa, no hubiéramos ganado de ninguna manera; IDIOM **it's not w. the paper it's written on** no vale siquiera el papel en el que está escrito, *Esp* es papel mojado; IDIOM **you're w. your weight in gold** vales tu peso en oro

(**b**) *(meriting)* **it's w. it** merece *or* vale la pena; **it isn't w. it** no merece *or* vale la pena; **her achievement was w. a mention in the local paper** su logro mereció una mención en el periódico local; **it was w. a try** mereció *or* valió la pena intentarlo; **the museum is w. a visit** merece *or* vale la pena visitar el museo; **it was (well) w. the effort** el esfuerzo (ciertamente) mereció *or* valió la pena; **this book is not w. buying** no merece *or* vale la pena comprar este libro; **without you life wouldn't be w. living** sin ti no valdría la pena vivir; **he isn't w. crying about** no merece *or* vale la pena que llores por él; **it's w. reading the instructions first** conviene leer primero las instrucciones; **it's w. remembering/mentioning that...** cabe recordar/mencionar que...; **it's w. thinking about** es algo a tener en cuenta

---

worthiness ['wɜːðɪnɪs] *n (of person)* valía *f*; *(of cause, project, contribution)* mérito *m*

worthless ['wɜːθlɪs] *adj* **to be w.** *(thing)* no valer nada, no tener ningún valor; *(advice, suggestion)* no servir para nada; **he's completely w.** es un perfecto inútil

worthlessness ['wɜːθlɪsnɪs] *n (of thing)* insignificancia *f*; *(of advice, person)* inutilidad *f*

worthwhile [wɜːθ'waɪl] *adj* **to be w.** merecer *or* valer la pena; **this makes it all w.** esto hace que valga la pena; **all the hard work was well w.** todas las horas de trabajo merecieron la pena

worthy ['wɜːðɪ] 1 *n* **the town worthies** los notables *or* las fuerzas vivas de la ciudad

2 *adj (person, life)* virtuoso(a); *(winner)* digno(a), merecido(a); **it's for a w. cause** es para una causa justa; **to be w. of sth** ser digno de algo; **w. of respect** digno(a) de respeto; **other features w. of mention are...** otras características dignas de mención son...; **her remarks are w. of contempt** sus comentarios no merecen otra cosa que desprecio; **the town has no museum w. of the name** la ciudad no tiene un museo digno de tal nombre; **it isn't w. of him** eso le desmerece; **he's not w. of her** él no se la merece, él no es digno de ella

wotcha ['wɒtʃə], **wotcher** ['wɒtʃə(r)] *exclam Br Fam* ¡qué tal!, ¡qué pasa!, *CAm, Col, Méx* ¡qué hubo!

WOULD [wʊd] 1 *modal aux v*

> En el inglés hablado, y en el escrito en estilo coloquial, el verbo **would** se contrae de manera que **I/you/he** *etc* **would** se transforman en **I'd**, **you'd**, **he'd** *etc*. La forma negativa **would not** se transforma en **wouldn't**.

(**a**) *(expressing conditional tense)* **she w. come if you invited her** si la invitases, vendría; **had he let go** *or* **if he had let go, he w. have fallen** si (se) hubiera soltado, se habría caído; **he w. have been 60 today, had he lived** si viviera habría cumplido 60 años hoy; **it w. be too dangerous** sería demasiado peligroso; **they w. never agree to such conditions** nunca aceptarían unas condiciones así; **w. you do it? – yes I w./no I wouldn't** ¿lo harías? – sí/no; **you wouldn't do it, w. you?** tú no lo harías, ¿verdad?; **I wouldn't do that if I were you** yo que tú no haría eso; **I w. if I could** lo haría si pudiera

(**b**) *(in reported speech)* **she told me she w. be there** me dijo que estaría allí; **I said I w. do it** dije que lo haría; **I asked him to leave, and he said he w./but he said he wouldn't** le pedí que se marchara, y dijo que sí/pero dijo que no

(**c**) *(expressing wish, determination)* **I wouldn't do it for anything** no lo haría por nada del mundo; **I w. like to know** me gustaría saberlo; *Literary* **w. to God she were still alive!** ¡cómo desearía que aún siguiese con vida!; **she wouldn't let me speak to him** no me dejaba hablar con él; **they wouldn't say who did it** no querían decir quién lo había hecho; **what w. you have me do?** ¿qué quieres que haga?; **the wound wouldn't heal** la herida no cicatrizaba

(**d**) *(in polite requests)* **w. you pass the mustard please?** ¿me pasas la mostaza, por favor?; **w. you let me know as soon as possible?** ¿me lo podrías decir cuanto antes?; **w. you like a drink?** ¿ *Esp* te apetece *or Carib, Col, Méx* te provoca *or Méx* se te antoja *or CSur* tenés ganas de tomar algo?; **w. you mind if I smoked?** ¿te importaría que fumara?; **be quiet, w. you!** haz el favor de callarte, ¿quieres?; **you wouldn't let me borrow your bike, w. you?** ¿no te importaría dejarme prestada tu moto, no?; **I'll do it – w. you?** lo haré yo – ¿no te importa?

(**e**) *(expressing polite opinion)* **I w. suggest that...** yo sugeriría que...; **it's not what I w. have hoped for** no es lo que había esperado; **I w. have thought you w. know the answer** alguien como tú debería saber la respuesta; **you wouldn't think she was 50, w. you?** ¡cualquiera diría que tiene 50 años!; **I wouldn't have said that was the way to do it, actually** me parece que esa no es la manera de hacerlo

(**f**) *(expressing preference)* **I'd rather go later** preferiría ir más tarde; **I'd sooner** *or* **just as soon not tell them** preferiría no contárselo

(**g**) *(expressing advice)* **I'd let the boss know about it** yo se lo diría al jefe; **I wouldn't take any notice of her** yo no le haría ningún caso

(**h**) *(expressing conjecture)* **why w. he say such a thing?** ¿por qué habrá dicho algo así?; **w. that be my pencil you're using?** ¿no será ese lápiz que estás usando el mío?; **he was a tall man with a red beard – that w. be Phil** era un hombre alto con barba roja – debió ser Phil; **that w. have been before your time** eso debe de haber sido antes de tu época; **I wouldn't know** no sé

(**i**) *(for emphasis)* **you WOULD insist on going!** ¡pero tú tenías que insistir en ir!; **it WOULD have to happen today of all days!** ¡y precisamente tenía que ocurrir hoy!; **I forgot – you WOULD** se me olvidó – ¡cómo no!; **they WOULD say that!** ¡qué iban a decir si no!

(**j**) *(expressing past habit)* **she w. often return home exhausted** solía volver agotada a casa; **there w. always be some left over** siempre sobraba algo

2 would that *conj Literary* ¡ojalá!; **w. that she were mine!** ¡ojalá fuera mía!

---

would-be ['wʊdbi:] *adj* **a w. actor/politician** un aspirante a actor/político

wouldn't [wʊdənt] = **would not**

wound[1] [wu:nd] **1** *n* (**a**) *(physical)* herida *f*; **a bullet/knife w.** una herida de bala/navaja; **he had serious head wounds** tenía graves heridas en la cabeza (**b**) *(emotional)* herida *f*; **he was still suffering from deep psychological wounds** aún tenía profundas heridas psicológicas; **to reopen an old w.** abrir una vieja herida

2 *vt* (**a**) *(physically)* herir; **she was wounded in the shoulder** estaba herida en el hombro (**b**) *(emotionally)* herir; **he was deeply wounded by their criticism** sus críticas lo afectaron *or* hirieron profundamente; **to w. sb's pride** herir el orgullo de alguien

wound[2] *pt & pp of* **wind**[2]

wounded ['wu:ndɪd] **1** *npl* **the w.** los heridos

2 *adj (person, animal, pride)* herido(a); **to be w.** estar herido(a)

wounding ['wu:ndɪŋ] *adj* hiriente

wove *pt of* **weave**

woven *pp of* **weave**

wow [waʊ] *Fam* **1** *vt* encandilar, deslumbrar

2 *exclam* ¡hala!, *RP* ¡uau!

WP ['dʌbəlju:'pi:] *n Comptr* (**a**) (*abbr* **word processor**) procesador *m* de textos (**b**) (*abbr* **word processing**) tratamiento *m* de textos

WPC ['dʌbəlju:pi:'si:] *n Br* (*abbr* **woman police constable**) agente *f* de policía

wpm ['dʌbəlju:pi:'em] (*abbr* **words per minute**) palabras *fpl* por minuto

WRAC [ræk] *n Br* (*abbr* **Women's Royal Army Corps**) = sección femenina del ejército británico

WRAF [ræf] (*abbr* **Women's Royal Air Force**) = sección femenina de las fuerzas aéreas británicas

wraith [reɪθ] *n Literary* espectro *m*

wraithlike ['reɪθlaɪk] *adj Literary* fantasmagórico(a), espectral

wrangle ['ræŋgəl] **1** *n* disputa *f*; **a long legal w. over the amount of damages** una larga disputa legal por la cantidad a percibir en concepto de daños

2 *vt US (cattle, horses)* arrear

3 *vi* pelear, reñir (**about** *or* **over** por)

wrangler ['ræŋglə(r)] *n US (cowboy)* vaquero *m*

wrangling ['ræŋglɪŋ] *n* riñas *fpl*, disputas *fpl*; **there was a lot of w. over who to give the job to** hubo mucho tira y afloja acerca de a quién debía dársele el puesto

wrap [ræp] **1** *n* (**a**) *(shawl)* chal *m* (**b**) *(cover)* envoltorio *m*; IDIOM **to keep sth under wraps** mantener algo en secreto; IDIOM **to take the wraps off** sacar a la luz (**c**) *Cin* **it's a w.** se acabó (**d**) *(sandwich)* = tipo de *Esp* bocadillo o *Am* sándwich doblado por la mitad (**e**) *Fam (of drugs)* papelina *f*

2 *vt* (*pt & pp* **wrapped**) envolver (**in** en *or* con); **the baby was wrapped in a blanket** el bebé iba envuelto en una manta; **he wrapped the vase in tissue paper** envolvió el jarrón con papel de seda; **she had a towel wrapped around her head** llevaba la cabeza envuelta en *or* con una toalla; **she wrapped the bandage round his head** le puso la venda alrededor de la cabeza; **she wrapped her arms around him** lo estrechó entre sus brazos, lo rodeó con sus brazos; **she wrapped her legs around him** lo rodeó con sus piernas; **would you like it wrapped?** ¿quiere que se lo envuelva?, ¿se lo envuelvo?, *Arg* ¿es para regalo?; *Fig* **wrapped in mystery** rodeado(a) de misterio; *Fam Fig* **he wrapped the car round a tree** estrelló el auto contra un árbol

►**wrap up 1** *vt sep* (**a**) *(parcel, present)* envolver; *Fig* **to be wrapped up in sth** *(absorbed)* estar embebido(a) en algo; **she's very wrapped up in herself** piensa demasiado en sí misma

(**b**) *Fam (bring to an end)* finiquitar, poner punto final a; **that wraps up business for today** con esto terminamos por hoy

(**c**) *US (summarize)* resumir; **she wrapped up her talk with three points** resumió su charla en tres puntos

2 *vi* (**a**) *(dress warmly)* abrigarse (**b**) *Br Fam (be quiet)* callarse; **w. up!** ¡cállate (la boca)!

wraparound ['ræpəraʊnd] **1** *n* (**a**) *(skirt)* falda *f or RP* pollera *f* cruzada; *(blouse)* blusa *f* cruzada (**b**) *Comptr* contorneo *m*

2 *adj (skirt, blouse)* cruzado(a) ►► ***w. sunglasses*** gafas *fpl* de sol aerodinámicas, *Am* anteojos *mpl* de sol aerodinámicos

wrapper ['ræpə(r)] *n* (**a**) *(of sweet, parcel, cigar)* envoltorio *m* (**b**) *(cover) (on book)* sobrecubierta *f*; *(on magazine, newspaper)* faja *f* (**c**) *US (dressing-gown)* salto *m* de cama

wrapping ['ræpɪŋ] *n* envoltura *f*, envoltorio *m* ►► ***w. paper*** *(for gifts)* papel *m* de regalo; *(for parcels, packages)* papel *m* de embalar *or* embalaje

wrath [rɒθ] *n Literary* ira *f*, cólera *f*

wrathful ['rɒθfʊl] *adj Literary* iracundo(a), colérico(a)

wrathfully ['rɒθfʊlɪ] *adv Literary* coléricamente, de manera iracunda

wreak [ri:k] *vt* **to w. havoc (on)** causar estragos (en); **the strike wreaked havoc with my holiday plans** la huelga hizo trizas mis planes para las vacaciones; **to w. vengeance on sb** vengarse de alguien

wreath [ri:θ] *n* (**a**) *(of flowers)* corona *f* (de flores); **the President laid a w. at the war memorial** el presidente depositó una corona de flores en el monumento a los caídos (**b**) *(of mist, smoke)* espiral *f*, columna *f*

wreathe [ri:ð] *vt* rodear con una corona; **the pulpit was wreathed with holly** el púlpito estaba adornado con una corona de acebo; **to be wreathed in mist/cloud** estar envuelto(a) en bruma/nubes; **to be wreathed in smiles** ser todo sonrisas

wreck [rek] **1** *n* (**a**) *(remains) (of ship)* restos *mpl* del naufragio; *(of car, train, plane)* restos *mpl* del accidente; **the car was a w.** el auto era un montón de chatarra; **the burnt-out w. of a bus** los restos calcinados de un autobús

(**b**) *(destruction) (of ship)* naufragio *m*, hundimiento *m*; *(of career)* ruina *f*; *(of hopes)* derrumbe *m*

(**c**) *US (accident)* accidente *m*; **a train w.** un accidente ferroviario *or* de tren

(**d**) *(person)* **to be a physical w.** estar destrozado(a) físicamente; *Fig* **to be a nervous w.** tener los nervios destrozados; **I must look a w.** debo de estar hecho un desastre

2 *vt (ship)* hundir; *(car, room, house)* destrozar; *(plans, hopes, happiness)* dar al traste con; *(marriage, career)* destruir, arruinar; **to w. one's health** destrozarse la salud

wreckage ['rekɪdʒ] *n (of ship)* restos *mpl* del naufragio; *(of car, train, plane)* restos *mpl* del accidente; **the w. of the plane** los restos del avión siniestrado

wrecked [rekt] *adj Fam* (**a**) *(exhausted)* molido(a), hecho(a) polvo (**b**) *(drunk) Esp, Méx* pedo *inv, Esp, RP* mamado(a), *Col* caído(a); **to get w.** agarrarse un pedo (**c**) *(on drugs)* colocado(a), *Esp* ciego(a), *Col* trabado(a), *Méx* pingo(a), *RP* falopeado(a)

wrecker ['rekə(r)] *n* (**a**) *US (salvage vehicle)* grúa *f* (**b**) *(saboteur)* saboteador(ora) *m,f*

wrecking ['rekɪŋ] *n* (**a**) *(destruction) (of ship)* naufragio *m* ►► ***w. ball*** bola *f* de demolición (**b**) *(of relationship, hopes)* derrumbamiento *m* (**c**) *US (salvaging)* rescate *m* de barcos naufragados/vehículos siniestrados

wren [ren] *n* chochín *m*

wrench [rentʃ] **1** *n* (**a**) *(pull)* tirón *m*; *(to ankle, shoulder)* torcedura *f*; **to give sth a w.** darle un tirón a algo, tirar fuerte de algo; *Fig* **it was a w. to leave** me partía el corazón *or* era muy doloroso tener que irme (**b**) *(spanner)* llave *f*; *(adjustable spanner)* llave *f* inglesa; IDIOM *US* **he threw a w. into the works** lo arruinó todo, lo echó todo a perder

2 *vt* (**a**) *(pull)* dar un tirón a; **to w. sth out of sb's hands** arrancarle algo a alguien de las manos; **she wrenched the door open** abrió la puerta de un tirón; **to w. one's ankle/shoulder** torcerse un tobillo/hombro

(**b**) *Fig* **I couldn't w. my gaze (away) from the horrible sight** no podía quitar *or* apartar la vista de aquel horrible espectáculo; **nothing could w. her away from her book** no había nada que la arrancara del libro

► **wrench away** *vt sep* arrancar, despegar

wrest [rest] *vt* **to w. sth from sb** arrebatar *or* arrancar algo a alguien; **they are trying to w. control of the party** están intentando hacerse con el control del partido; *Fig* **he wrested the truth from her** le arrancó la verdad

wrestle ['resəl] **1** *vt* **to w. sb to the floor** *or* **ground** tumbar *or* derribar a alguien

2 *vi* (**a**) *(fight, in sport)* luchar (**with** con) (**b**) *(struggle)* **to w. with a problem** lidiar con un problema; **to w. with one's conscience** batallar *or* debatirse con la conciencia

wrestler ['reslə(r)] *n* luchador(ora) *m,f* (de lucha libre)

wrestling ['reslɪŋ] *n* lucha *f* libre ►► ***w. match*** combate *m* de lucha libre; *Fig* combate *m*

wretch [retʃ] *n* (**a**) *(unfortunate person)* miserable *mf*, desgraciado(a) *m,f* (**b**) *Literary or Hum (scoundrel)* sinvergüenza *mf*; **the w. who stole my suitcase** el desgraciado que me robó la maleta (**c**) *(child)* pillo(a) *m,f*; **you little w.!** ¡pillín(ina)!

wretched ['retʃɪd] *adj* (**a**) *(very bad) (weather, state, conditions)* horrible, pésimo(a); *(life, childhood)* miserable, desdichado(a); **what w. luck!** ¡qué desgracia!; **to feel w.** *(ill)* sentirse muy mal; *(depressed)* estar muy deprimido(a); **she felt w. about what she had done** se sentía muy mal por lo que había hecho (**b**) *(unhappy)* abatido(a) (**c**) *(for emphasis)* **I can't find the w. umbrella!** ¡no encuentro el maldito paraguas!

wretchedly ['retʃɪdlɪ] *adv* (**a**) *(poorly) (to live, dress)* miserablemente, de manera miserable (**b**) *(unhappily) (to cry, look)* desconsoladamente, amargamente; **he was w. lonely/unhappy** se sentía terriblemente solo/infeliz (**c**) *(abominably) (to behave, play, perform)* pésimamente, horriblemente mal; **a w. small amount** una cantidad nimia *or* insignificante

wretchedness ['retʃɪdnɪs] *n* (**a**) *(of surroundings)* inmundicia *f*, miseria *f*; *(of life, childhood)* desdicha *f*; *(of weather)* pésimo estado *m*; **they lived in conditions of such w. that disease was rife** vivían en medio de tal miseria que las enfermedades eran moneda corriente (**b**) *(unhappiness)* abatimiento *m*

wriggle ['rɪgəl] **1** *n* **to give a w.** *(snake)* serpentear; *(fish)* serpentear; *(person)* menearse, retorcerse; **with a w. the rabbit shook itself free from the trap** el conejo se liberó de la trampa con un movimiento

2 *vt* (**a**) *(toes)* menear (**b**) *(manoeuvre)* **to w. one's way out of a situation** lograr escurrir el bulto (de una situación); **I'd like to see him w. his way out of that!** me gustaría ver cómo se libra *or* zafa de ésta

3 *vi* **to w. (about)** menearse, retorcerse; **to w. along** *(worm, snake)* deslizarse serpenteando; **stop wriggling!** ¡quédate quieto!; **to w. through a hole** conseguir colarse por un agujero; **to w. out of (doing) sth: he wriggled out of paying the fine** se las ingenió para no pagar la multa; **he should have been held responsible but he managed to w. out of it** debería haber cargado con la responsabilidad pero logró escurrir el bulto

wriggly ['rɪglɪ] *adj* serpenteante

wring [rɪŋ] (*pt & pp* **wrung** [rʌŋ]) *vt (clothes)* escurrir, estrujar; **he wrung the towel dry** escurrió la toalla; **to w. one's hands** retorcerse las manos; **it's no use sitting there wringing your hands** de nada sirve que te quedes ahí lamentándote sin hacer nada; *Fam* **I'd like to w. his neck** me gustaría retorcerle el pescuezo; *Fig* **to w. sth from sb** lograr sacarle algo a alguien; **to w. sb's heart** partir el corazón a alguien

► **wring out** *vt sep (clothes)* escurrir, estrujar; **to w. the water out of sth** escurrir el agua a algo; **to w. a confession/the truth out of sb** lograr sacarle una confesión/la verdad a alguien

wringer ['rɪŋə(r)] *n* escurridor *m* de rodillos; IDIOM *Fam* **to put sb through the w.** hacer pasar un mal trago *or* las de Caín a alguien; **after the interrogation he really felt he had been put through the w.** tras el interrogatorio, verdaderamente se sentía como si lo hubieran puesto a prueba

wringing ['rɪŋɪŋ] *adj* **to be w. (wet)** estar empapado(a)

wrinkle ['rɪŋkəl] **1** *n* (**a**) *(in cloth, skin)* arruga *f*; *Fig* **there are still some wrinkles in the plan which need ironing out** aún hay que pulir algunos aspectos del plan (**b**) *Fam (tip, hint)* truquillo *m*

2 *vt* (**a**) *(nose)* arrugar; *(brow)* fruncir (**b**) *(cloth, paper)* arrugar

3 *vi* arrugarse

wrinkled ['rɪŋkəld] *adj* arrugado(a); **to get w.** arrugarse

wrinkly ['rɪŋklɪ] **1** *n Br Fam (old person)* vejestorio *m*, pureta *mf*, *Méx* ruco(a) *m,f*

2 *adj* arrugado(a)

wrist [rɪst] *n* muñeca *f* ►► *Comptr* ***w. rest*** apoyamuñecas *m inv*, reposamuñecas *m inv*

wristband ['rɪstbænd] *n (on sleeve)* puño *m*; *(sweatband)* muñequera *f*

wristwatch ['rɪstwɒtʃ] *n* reloj *m* (de pulsera)

writ [rɪt] **1** *n Law* mandato *m* judicial; **to serve a w. on sb** entregar un mandato judicial a alguien ►► ***w. of attachment*** (orden *f* de) embargo *m*; ***w. of execution*** auto *m* de ejecución; ***w. of habeas corpus*** procedimiento *m* de hábeas corpus; ***w. of possession*** auto *m* de posesión, orden *f* de desahucio; ***w. of subpoena*** citación *f*

2 *adj* **w. large** *(taken to an extreme)* llevado(a) a sus últimas consecuencias; *(on a large scale)* a gran escala; **astonishment was w. large on everybody's face** el asombro era evidente en el rostro de todos

WRITE [raɪt] (*pt* **wrote** [rəʊt], *pp* **written** ['rɪtən]) **1** *vt* (**a**) *(answer, letter, software, music)* escribir; *(will)* redactar; **to w. a letter to sb, to w. sb a letter** escribir una carta a alguien; **to w. (sb) a cheque/prescription** extender un cheque/una receta (a nombre de alguien); **shall I w. you a cheque?** ¿te hago *or* extiendo un cheque?; **he wrote that he was getting married** escribió para decir que se iba a casar; **it is written in the Bible "thou shalt love thy neighbour as thyself"** la Biblia dice "ama al prójimo como a ti mismo"; **she had guilt written all over her face** su rostro era el vivo retrato de la culpabilidad

(**b**) *US (send letter to)* **to w. sb** escribir a alguien

(**c**) *Comptr (CD-ROM)* grabar; **w. the changes to disk** guarda los cambios en el disco duro

2 *vi* escribir; **I am writing regarding the matter of my pension** *(in letter)* me dirijo a usted en relación a mi pensión; **this pen doesn't w. very well** este bolígrafo no escribe bien; **I w. (for a living)** soy escritor(ora); **to w. to thank/invite sb** escribir para dar las gracias a/invitar a alguien; **to w. on** *or* **about sth** escribir sobre algo; **to w. for a newspaper** escribir *or* colaborar en un periódico; **I've written for a catalogue** he escrito pidiendo un catálogo; **to w. in ink/pencil** escribir con tinta/a lápiz; *Br* **to w. to sb** escribir a alguien; IDIOM *Fam* **it's/he's nothing to w. home about** no es nada del otro mundo; IDIOM *US Fam* **that was all she wrote** se acabó lo que se daba; IDIOM *US Fam* **he wrote the book on that** es un maestro en eso

► **write away for** *vt insep* **to w. away (to sb) for sth** escribir (a alguien) pidiendo algo

► **write back** *vi* responder, contestar *(por carta)*

► **write down** *vt sep* (**a**) *(make note of)* escribir, anotar (**b**) *Fin* rebajar, amortizar

► **write in 1** *vt sep* (**a**) *(name, answer)* escribir (**b**) *US Pol* = en las elecciones, votar por un candidato que no aparece en la papeleta escribiendo su nombre

2 *vi (send letter)* escribir; **hundreds of listeners wrote in to complain** cientos de oyentes escribieron quejándose

► **write into** *vt sep* **this speech was written into the play specially for her** este parlamento fue añadido a la obra especialmente para ella; **he has a guarantee written into his contract that...** su contrato incorpora una garantía que...

► **write off 1** *vt sep* (**a**) *(debt)* condonar (**b**) *Fam (car)* cargarse, *Méx* dar en la madre, *RP* hacer bolsa (**c**) *(person)* descartar; **we wrote the plan off as a waste of time** descartamos el plan por ser una pérdida de tiempo; **to w. sb off as a has-been** considerar que alguien está acabado

2 *vi* **to w. off (to sb) for sth** escribir (a alguien) pidiendo algo

▸ **write out** *vt sep* (**a**) *(instructions, recipe)* escribir, copiar; *(cheque)* extender; **w. it out neatly** pásalo a limpio; **can you w. the amount out in full, please?** exprese la cantidad en letras, por favor (**b**) *(remove from script)* **to w. sb out of a programme** eliminar a alguien de un programa

▸ **write up** *vt sep* (**a**) *(notes, thesis)* redactar; *(diary, journal)* poner al día (**b**) *(review)* **the movie was written up in the paper** la película fue reseñada en el periódico

---

write-off ['raɪtɒf] *n* (**a**) *(of debt)* condonación *f* (**b**) *Fam (car)* siniestro *m* total

write-protect ['raɪtprə'tekt] *vt Comptr* proteger contra escritura

write-protected ['raɪtprə'tektɪd] *adj Comptr* protegido(a) contra escritura

writer ['raɪtə(r)] *n (by profession)* escritor(ora) *m,f*; *(of article, book)* autor(ora) *m,f* ▸▸ ***w.'s block*** bloqueo *m* mental *(al escribir)*; ***w.'s cramp*** calambre *m* en la muñeca *(de escribir)*

write-up ['raɪtʌp] *n (review)* crítica *f*; *(report)* artículo *m*, informe *m*, *CAm, Méx* reporte *m*; **the play got a good w.** la obra recibió buenas críticas

writhe [raɪð] *vi* retorcerse; **to w. in agony** *or* **pain** retorcerse de dolor; **to w. with embarrassment** morirse de vergüenza *or Am* pena; **her remarks made him w.** *(in disgust)* sus comentarios le parecieron de lo peor; *(in embarrassment)* sus comentarios le hicieron sentir vergüenza ajena

writing ['raɪtɪŋ] *n* (**a**) *(action)* **at the time of w.** en el momento de escribir estas líneas; **the thesis was five years in the w.** escribir la tesis llevó cinco años ▸▸ ***w. case*** recado *m* de escribir; ***w. desk*** escritorio *m*; ***w. materials*** material *m* de papelería, artículos *mpl* de escritorio; ***w. pad*** bloc *m* de notas; ***w. paper*** papel *m* de escribir; ***w. skills*** expresión *f* escrita
(**b**) *(handwriting)* letra *f*, escritura *f*; **her w. is terrible** tiene muy mala letra; **I can't read his w.** no entiendo su letra
(**c**) *(written words)* escritura *f*; **there's some w. on the side of the box** hay algo escrito en un lateral de la caja; **the w. has rubbed off** se ha borrado lo que decía; **in w.** por escrito; **legally, you are required to have permission in w.** de acuerdo con la ley, necesitas un permiso (por) escrito; **to put sth in w.** poner algo por escrito; IDIOM **the w. on the wall: the w. is on the wall for him** tiene los días contados; **he saw the w. on the wall** vio lo que se avecinaba
(**d**) *(literature)* literatura *f*; **I enjoy his w.** me gusta cómo escribe, me gusta lo que escribe; **it's a good piece of w.** es un trabajo bien escrito; **his later writings** sus últimos escritos; **the collected writings of...** las obras completas de...

written ['rɪtən] **1** *adj (text, examination)* escrito(a); *(confirmation, consent)* escrito(a), por escrito; **her w. Spanish is not as good as her oral Spanish** su español escrito no es tan bueno como el oral, no escribe español tan bien como lo habla ▸▸ ***w. accent*** acento *m* gráfico *or* ortográfico; ***the w. word*** la palabra escrita
2 *pp of* **write**

WRNS [renz] *n Br* (*abbr* **Women's Royal Naval Service**) = sección femenina de la marina británica

---

WRONG [rɒŋ] **1** *n (immoral action)* mal *m*; **we have suffered many wrongs** hemos sufrido muchos males; **to know right from w.** distinguir el bien del mal; **he can do no w.** lo hace todo bien; **I have done no w.** no he hecho ningún mal; **to do sb (a) w.** agraviar a alguien; **to right a w.** deshacer un entuerto; **to be in the w.** tener la culpa; **to put sb in the w.** contradecir a alguien; PROV **two wrongs don't make a right** vengándose no se consigue nada
2 *adj* (**a**) *(morally bad)* malo(a); **stealing is w.** robar está mal; **what's w. with that?** ¿qué tiene de malo?; **there's nothing w. with it** no tiene nada de malo; **it was w. of you not to tell me** hiciste mal en no decírmelo; **it's w. that their work should go unrewarded** no está bien *or* no es justo que no se recompense su trabajo; **I hope you're not marrying me for the w. reasons** espero que tengas buenos motivos para casarte conmigo
(**b**) *(incorrect, mistaken)* erróneo(a), incorrecto(a); **to be w.** *(person)* estar equivocado(a); *(answer)* ser erróneo(a); **my watch is w.** mi reloj va *or* está mal; **I was w. about the date/her** me equivoqué con respecto a la fecha/a ella; **you are w. in thinking** *or* **to think that...** te equivocas si piensas que...; **that's the w. one, it's this one** no es ése, es éste; **you chose the w. one** elegiste mal; **that's the w. answer** *(in quiz)* respuesta incorrecta; *(that's not what I wanted to hear)* mal contestado; **they came on the w. day** vinieron en el día equivocado; **to take the w. road/train** equivocarse de carretera/tren; **they made the w. decision** tomaron la decisión equivocada; **don't get the w. idea** no te equivoques; **you have the w. number** *(on phone)* se ha equivocado (de número); **they kidnapped the w. person** los secuestradores se equivocaron de víctima; **to drive on the w. side of the road** conducir *or Am* manejar por el lado contrario de la carretera; **I did/said the w. thing** hice/dije lo que no debía; **we took a w. turning** nos equivocamos de giro, *RP* doblamos mal *or* en la esquina equivocada; **it went down the w. way** *(food, drink)* se me/le/*etc.* atragantó; **to go about it the w. way** hacerlo mal; **they took what I said the w. way** se tomaron a mal lo que dije; IDIOM **to back the w. horse** apostar por el perdedor; IDIOM **to catch sb on the w. foot** *Esp* coger *or Am* agarrar a alguien desprevenido(a); IDIOM **to start** *or* **get off on the w. foot** empezar con mal pie *or RP* con el pie izquierdo
(**c**) *(inappropriate) (place, climate)* inadecuado(a); **you chose the w. moment** no escogiste *or* elegiste el momento oportuno; **he's the w. person for this job** no es la persona adecuada *or* indicada para este trabajo; **doing that would send out the w. signal** si hiciéramos eso daríamos una impresión equivocada; **it's the w. time of year to go skiing** no es la época del año para ir a esquiar; **it wasn't her fault, she was just in the w. place at the w. time** no fue culpa suya, simplemente estaba en el lugar y momento equivocados
(**d**) *(amiss)* **what's w.?** ¿qué pasa?; **what's w. with you?** ¿qué te pasa?; **what's w. with liking jazz?** ¿qué tiene de malo que me/te/*etc* guste el jazz?; **is anything w.?** ¿pasa algo?; **I hope there's nothing w.** espero que no pase nada malo; **there's nothing w. with you** a Ud. no le pasa nada; **there's nothing w. with the motor** el motor está perfectamente bien; **there's nothing w. with liking jazz** no tiene nada de malo que me/te/*etc* guste el jazz; **there's something w. with this machine** a este aparato le pasa algo; **he has something w. with his heart** su corazón no está bien; **something feels w.** da la impresión de que algo está mal; IDIOM *Fam* **to be w. in the head** estar chiflado(a) *or Am* zafado(a) *or RP* rayado(a)
(**e**) *(undesirable)* **to live on the w. side of town** vivir en uno de los barrios malos de la ciudad; **to mix with the w. people** mezclarse con malas compañías; **we don't want this information to fall into the w. hands** no queremos que esta información caiga en malas manos
3 *adv* (**a**) *(morally)* mal; **he admitted he had done w. to...** admitió que había hecho mal en...
(**b**) *(incorrectly)* mal; **I got the date w.** me equivoqué de fecha; **sorry, I got it w., it's on Tuesday** perdona, me equivoqué, es el martes; **you've got it w., I never said that** te equivocas, no dije eso; **you've got it all w., it's just a joke** lo has entendido mal, no es más que una broma; **you've got her all w.** te equivocas con ella completamente; **don't get me w., I like her** no me malentiendas, (ella) me cae bien; **to go w.** *(machine, watch)* estropearse, romperse; *(plan)* salir mal; *(make mistake)* equivocarse; **something has gone w. with the TV** le pasa algo a la tele; **it's simple, you can't go w.** es sencillo, no te puedes equivocar; **you can't go w. with a good book** *(to pass time)* no hay nada como un buen libro; *(as present)* con un buen libro siempre quedas bien; **things started to go w. that morning** las cosas comenzaron a estropearse *or* a andar mal aquella mañana; **where did our relationship go w.?** ¿dónde ha fallado nuestra relación?; **to guess w.** no acertar, equivocarse; **if you thought that, you thought w.** si pensaste eso, pensaste mal
4 *vt* agraviar, tratar injustamente

---

wrongdoer ['rɒŋdu:ə(r)] *n* malhechor(ora) *m,f*

wrongdoing ['rɒŋdu:ɪŋ] *n (immoral actions)* desmanes *mpl*; *(crime)* delincuencia *f*; **he denies any w.** niega haber hecho nada malo

wrong-foot [rɒŋ'fʊt] *vt* (**a**) *(in tennis, soccer) Esp* coger *or Am* agarrar a contrapié a (**b**) *(opponent, critic)* despistar

wrongful ['rɒŋfʊl] *adj* injusto(a) ▸▸ ***w. arrest*** detención *f* ilegal; ***w. dismissal*** despido *m* improcedente *(que incumple el contrato)*; ***w. imprisonment*** encarcelamiento *m* ilegal

wrongfully ['rɒŋfʊlɪ] *adv (accused)* injustamente; *(dismissed)* de forma improcedente

wrong-headed [rɒŋ'hedɪd] *adj* empecinado(a)

wrongly ['rɒŋlɪ] *adv* (**a**) *(unjustly)* injustamente (**b**) *(incorrectly)* erróneamente; **to be w. informed** estar mal informado; **this word is spelt w.** esta palabra está mal escrita

wrote *pt of* **write**

wrought [rɔ:t] *Literary or Old-fashioned* **1** *adj* **the damage w. by the hurricane** los daños acarreados *or* ocasionados por el huracán; **the changes w. by the weather** los cambios originados por el estado del tiempo ▸▸ ***w. iron*** hierro *m* forjado
2 *pt & pp of* **work**

wrought-iron ['rɔ:t'aɪən] *adj* de hierro forjado

wrought-up ['rɔ:t'ʌp] *adj* **to be w. (about sth)** estar muy alterado(a) (por algo)

WRULD ['dʌbəlju:ɑ:ju:el'di:] *n Med* (*abbr* **work-related upper limb disorder**) trastorno *m* musculoesquelético de origen laboral de las extremidades superiores

wrung *pt & pp of* **wring**

WRVS ['dʌbəlju:ɑ:vi:'es] *n* (*abbr* **Women's Royal Voluntary Service**) = organización británica de voluntarias para ayuda a los necesitados y en estados de emergencia

wry [raɪ] *adj (comment, humour)* irónico(a), socarrón(ona); *(smile, joke)* irónico(a), sarcástico(a); **she made a w. face** puso mala cara, hizo un gesto de desagrado

wrybill ['raɪbɪl] *n* chorlito *m* piquivuelto

wryly ['raɪlɪ] *adv* irónicamente

WSW (*abbr* **west-south-west**) OSO

wt (*abbr* **weight**) peso *m*

WTO ['dʌbəlju:ti:'əʊ] (*abbr* **World Trade Organization**) OMC *f*

wunderkind ['wʌndəkɪnd] *n* niño(a) *m,f* prodigio

wuss [wʊs] *n Fam (physically)* debilucho(a) *m,f*; *(lacking character)* blandengue *mf*

WV (*abbr* **West Virginia**) Virginia Occidental

WW (*abbr* **World War**) **WWI/II** la Primera/Segunda Guerra Mundial

WWF ['dʌbəlju:dʌbəlju:'ef] *n* (*abbr* **World Wildlife Fund, Worldwide Fund for Nature**) WWF *m*

WWW *n Comptr* (*abbr* **World Wide Web**) WWW *f*

WY (*abbr* **Wyoming**) Wyoming

Wyoming [waɪ'əʊmɪŋ] *n* Wyoming

WYSIWYG ['wɪzɪwɪg] *n Comptr* (*abbr* **what you see is what you get**) WYSIWYG, = se imprime lo que ves

X, x

X, x [eks] *n (letter)* X, x *f*; **for x number of years** durante un número x de años, durante x años; **Mr X** el señor X, fulano; *Br Formerly* **X (certificate) film** película *f* para mayores de 18 años

x-axis ['eksæksɪs] *n Math* eje *m* de abscisas, abcisa *f*

X-chromosome ['ekskrəʊməsəʊm] *n Biol* cromosoma *m* X

xenon ['zenɒn] *n Chem* xenón *m*

xenophile ['zenəfaɪl] *n* xenófilo(a) *m,f*

xenophilic [zenə'fɪlɪk] *adj* xenófilo(a)

xenophobe ['zenəfəʊb] *n* xenófobo(a) *m,f*

xenophobia [zenə'fəʊbɪə] *n* xenofobia *f*

xenophobic [zenə'fəʊbɪk] *adj* xenófobo(a)

xenotransplant ['zenəʊtrænsplɑːnt] *n Med* xenotrasplante *m*

xenotransplantation ['zenəʊtrænsplɑːn'teɪʃən] *n Med* xenotrasplante *m*

xerography [zɪə'rɒgrəfɪ] *n* xerografía *f*

xerophilous [zɪə'rɒfɪləs] *adj Bot* xerófilo(a)

xerophthalmia [zɪərəʊ'θælmɪə] *n Med* xeroftalmia *f*

xerophytic [zɪərəʊ'fɪtɪk] *adj Bot* xerófito(a)

Xerox® ['zɪərɒks] **1** *n* fotocopia *f*, xerocopia *f*
2 *vt* fotocopiar

xiphoid ['zɪfɔɪd] *n Anat* ***x. cartilage*** xifoides *m*; ***x. process*** xifoides *m*

XL (*abbr* **extra large**) XL, (talla *f*) muy grande

Xmas ['krɪsməs, 'eksməs] *n* (*abbr* **Christmas**) Navidad *f*

XML [eksem'el] *n Comptr* (*abbr* **extensible markup language**) XML *m*

X-rated ['eksreɪtɪd] *adj Fam* fuerte; **X. movie** *or Br* **film** *(pornographic)* película *f* X; *Formerly (with adult certificate)* película *f* para mayores de 18 años

X-ray ['eksreɪ] **1** *n (radiation)* rayo *m* X; *(picture)* radiografía *f*; **to have an X.** hacerse una radiografía; **to take an X. of sth** tomar *or* hacer una radiografía de algo ►► ***X. examination*** examen *m* por rayos X; ***X. eyes*** vista *f* de rayos X
2 *vt* radiografiar

xylene ['zaɪliːn] *n* xileno *m*, xilol *m*

xylophagous [zaɪ'lɒfəgəs] *adj Zool* xilófago(a)

xylophone ['zaɪləfəʊn] *n* xilófono *m*, xilofón *m*

Y, y

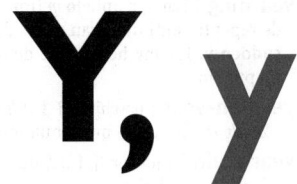

Y, y [waɪ] *n (letter)* Y, y *f*

yacht [jɒt] *n (sailing boat)* velero *m*; *(large private boat)* yate *m* ▸▸ ***y. club*** club *m* náutico; ***y. race*** regata *f*

yachting ['jɒtɪŋ] *n* (navegación *f* a) vela *f*; **to go y.** practicar la vela, hacer vela

yachtsman ['jɒtsmən] *n (in race)* tripulante *m*; *(round-the-world)* navegante *m*

yachtswoman ['jɒtswʊmən] *n (in race)* tripulante *f*; *(round-the-world)* navegante *f*

yack [jæk] *Fam* **1** *n* **to have a y.** charlar, *Esp* cascar, *CAm, Méx* platicar

2 *vi* charlar, *Esp* cascar, *CAm, Méx* platicar

yackety-yak [jækətɪ'jæk] *Fam* **1** *vi* charlar, *Esp* cascar, *CAm, Méx* platicar

2 *adv* **to go y.** charlar, *Esp* cascar, *CAm, Méx* platicar

yah [jɑː] *exclam Br Fam* ¡sí!

yahoo [jɑː'huː] *exclam Fam* ¡yupi!

yak[1] [jæk] *n (animal)* yak *m*, yac *m*

yak[2] = **yack**

Yale® [jeɪl] *n* ***Y. key*** llave *f* plana; ***Y. lock*** cerradura *f* de cilindro

yam [jæm] *n* **(a)** *(vegetable)* ñame *m* **(b)** *US (sweet potato)* batata *f*, *Esp* boniato *m*, *Am* camote *m*

yammer ['jæmə(r)] *vi Fam (whine)* gimotear, quejarse; *(chatter)* parlotear

Yank [jæŋk] *n Br Fam* yanqui *mf*, gringo(a) *m,f*

yank [jæŋk] *Fam* **1** *n* **to give sth a y.** dar un tirón a algo

2 *vt* **to y. the door open** abrir la puerta de un tirón; **to y. sth out/off** sacar/arrancar algo de un tirón; **he was yanked to his feet** lo pusieron de pie de un tirón; IDIOM *US Fam* **to y. sb's chain** *(tease)* tomar el pelo a alguien; *(bring under control)* cortar las alas a alguien

Yankee ['jæŋkɪ] *Fam* **1** *n* **(a)** *Br (person from the USA)* yanqui *mf*, gringo(a) *m,f* **(b)** *US (person from north-eastern USA)* = estadounidense del nordeste **(c)** *US Hist (soldier)* (soldado *m*) yanqui *m* **(d)** ***Y. Doodle*** *(song)* = canción considerada como típicamente nacional de Estados Unidos

2 *adj Br* yanqui, gringo(a)

Yaoundé [jæ'ʊndeɪ] *n* Yaoundé, Yaundé

yap [jæp] (*pt & pp* **yapped**) *vi* **(a)** *(dog)* ladrar *(de forma aguda)* **(b)** *Fam (person)* parlotear

yappy ['jæpɪ] *adj* **a y. dog** un perro que da labridos agudos

yard[1] [jɑːd] *n (measurement)* yarda *f (0,914 m)*; **it was about ten yards away** estaba como a nueve metros de distancia ▸▸ ***y. of ale*** *(container)* = recipiente estrecho y alargado de cristal que se utiliza en los concursos de beber cerveza

yard[2] *n* **(a)** *(of house, school)* patio *m*; *(of farm)* corral *m* **(b)** *US (garden)* jardín *m* ▸▸ ***y. sale*** = venta de objetos particulares en el jardín de una casa **(c)** *(for working)* taller *m (al aire libre)*; **(ship) y.** astillero *m* **(d)** *(for storage)* almacén *m*, depósito *m (al aire libre)*; **(builder's) y.** almacén *m* de materiales de construcción **(e)** *Br Fam* **the Y.** Scotland Yard

yardarm ['jɑːdɑːm] *n Naut* penol *m*; *Hum Fam* **the sun's over the y.** ya es buena hora para tomar una copa

Yardie ['jɑːdɪ] *n* gán(g)ster *mf* jamaicano(a)

yardstick ['jɑːdstɪk] *n (standard)* patrón *m* (de medida)

yarmulka, yarmulke [jɑː'mʊlkə] *n* kipá *f*, kipa *f*

yarn [jɑːn] *n* **(a)** *Tex* hilo *m* **(b)** *Fam (story)* batallita *f*, historia *f*

yarrow ['jærəʊ] *n* milenrama *f*

yashmak ['jæʃmæk] *n* velo *m* musulmán

yaw [jɔː] *vi (ship, aircraft)* guiñar, hacer una guiñada

yawl [jɔːl] *n* **(a)** *(sailing boat)* yola *f* (a vela) **(b)** *(carried on ship)* bote *m or* yola *f* de remos

yawn [jɔːn] **1** *n* **(a)** *(of tiredness, boredom)* bostezo *m*; **to give a big y.** dar un gran bostezo **(b)** *Fam (boring thing)* plomazo *m*; **what a y.!** ¡qué plomazo!

2 *vt (utter with yawn)* decir bostezando; *Fam* **she was yawning her head off** no paraba de bostezar

3 *vi* **(a)** *(person)* bostezar **(b)** *(chasm)* abrirse

yawning ['jɔːnɪŋ] *adj* **(a)** *(person)* que bosteza **(b)** *(gap, chasm, hole)* enorme

yaws [jɔːz] *n* frambesia *f*, pian *m*

y-axis ['waɪæksɪs] *n Math* eje *m* de ordenadas, ordenada *f*

Y-chromosome ['waɪkrəʊməsəʊm] *n Biol* cromosoma *m* Y

yds (*abbr* **yards**) yardas *fpl*

ye [jiː] **1** *pron Literary* = **you**

2 *definite article Hum* = **the**

yea [jeɪ] **1** *n* **yeas and nays** votos *mpl* a favor y en contra; **y. or nay** sí o no

2 *adv Archaic or Literary* **(a)** = **yes** **(b)** *(truly)* en verdad

yeah [jeə] *Fam* **1** *adv* sí; **oh y.?** *(in disbelief, challenging)* ¿ah, sí?

2 *exclam* ¡sí!; *Ironic* **y., right!** ¡sí, claro!, ¡ya, claro!

year [jɪə(r)] *n* **(a)** *(of calendar)* año *m*; **in the y. 1931** en el año 1931; **this y.** este año; **last y.** el año pasado; **next y.** el año que viene; **the y. after next** el año que viene no, el otro; **every y.** todos los años; **twice a y.** dos veces al año; **to earn $30,000 a y.** ganar 30.000 dólares al año; **he got five years** *(prison sentence)* le cayeron cinco años; **for (many) years** durante (muchos) años; **y. after y.** año tras año, todos los años; **y. in, y. out** año tras año; **over the years** con el paso de los años; **years ago** hace años; **in years to come** en los años sucesivos *or* venideros; **1996 was a good y. for the team** 1996 fue un buen año para el equipo; **after thirty years in politics he has decided to retire** después de treinta años en política, ha decidido retirarse; **in all my years as a social worker** en todos mis años (de experiencia) como trabajador(ora) social; *Rel or Old-fashioned* **y. of grace** *or* **our Lord** año de gracia *or* de nuestro Señor; **it's years since I saw him, I haven't seen him for** *or* **in years** hace años que no lo veo; *Comptr* **y. 2000 compliant** adaptado(a) al *or* a prueba del efecto 2000; IDIOM *Fam* **since the y. dot** desde tiempos de Maricastaña, desde el año de la pera *or* polca *or* nana

(b) *(in age)* año *m*; **to be ten years old** tener diez años; **to look years older/younger** parecer mucho más mayor/joven; **from his earliest years** desde temprana edad; **she's old for her years** *(child)* es muy madura para la edad que tiene *or* para su edad; *(adult)* está avejentada; **it takes years off you** *(dress, hairstyle)* te quita *or Am* saca años de encima, te hace parecer más joven; **smoking can take years off your life** fumar puede quitarte años de vida; **it put years on him** lo avejentó, le echó años encima; **to be getting on in years** empezar a hacerse viejo(a); **she died in her seventieth y.** murió a la edad de setenta (años)

(c) *(at school, university)* curso *m*; **she was in the y. above/below me** iba un curso por encima/por debajo de mí

yearbook ['jɪəbʊk] *n* **(a)** *(of club, society)* anuario *m* **(b)** *US (from high school)* anuario *m (con la fotografías de los estudiantes de una escuela)*

year-end [jɪə'end] **1** *n* final *m or* fin *m* de año; **at the y.** al final del año, a final(es) de año

2 *adj Fin (accounts)* de cierre de ejercicio; *(profits, losses)* al final del año, al cierre del ejercicio

yearling ['jɪəlɪŋ] *n* **(a)** *(animal)* añal *m* **(b)** *(in horse racing)* potranco(a) *m,f*

yearlong ['jɪəlɒŋ] *adj* de un año; **a y. wait** una espera de un año

yearly ['jɪəlɪ] **1** *adj* anual

2 *adv* anualmente, cada año; **twice y.** dos veces al año; **two/three-y.** cada dos/tres años

yearn [jɜːn] *vi* **to y. for sth/to do sth** anhelar algo/hacer algo; **he yearned for sleep** anhelaba poder dormir; **he yearned for home** añoraba su casa

yearning ['jɜːnɪŋ] *n* anhelo *m* (**for** de); **I felt a sudden y. for company** de repente sentí una gran necesidad de estar acompañado(a); **I felt a sudden y. for my hometown** de repente sentí una gran añoranza de mi pueblo

year-on-year ['jɪərɒnjɪə(r)] 1 *adj* interanual
2 *adv (to increase)* interanualmente

year-round ['jɪəraʊnd] 1 *adj* de todo el año
2 *adv* todo el año

yeast [jiːst] *n* levadura *f* ►► *US* ***y. cake*** torta *f* de levadura; *Culin* ***y. extract*** extracto *m* de levadura

yeasty ['jiːstɪ] *adj* (**a**) *(taste, smell)* a levadura (**b**) *(frothy)* espumoso(a)

yell [jel] 1 *n* grito *m*, chillido *m*; **to give a y.** dar un grito
2 *vt* gritar, chillar; *Fam* **he was yelling his head off** gritaba *or* chillaba como un loco
3 *vi* gritar, chillar; **to y. in** *or* **with pain** gritar de dolor; **to y. at sb** gritarle *or* chillarle a alguien; **to y. at the top of one's voice** desgañitarse gritando *or* chillando

yelling ['jelɪŋ] *n* griterío *m*, chillidos *mpl*; **stop that y.!** ¡deja ya de gritar *or* chillar!

yellow ['jeləʊ] 1 *n* amarillo *m*
2 *adj* (**a**) *(in colour)* amarillo(a); **to turn** *or* **go y.** amarillear, ponerse amarillo ►► ***y. card*** *(in soccer, rugby)* tarjeta *f* amarilla; *Med* ***y. fever*** fiebre *f* amarilla; ***y. flag*** *(plant)* lirio *m* de agua; ***y. iris*** lirio *m* de agua; ***the y. jersey*** *(in cycling)* el maillot amarillo; ***y. line*** *(on road)* línea *f* amarilla; **to park on a y. line** estacionar *or Esp* aparcar sobre la línea amarilla *(de estacionamiento restringido)*; ***y. ochre*** ocre *m* amarillo; *Tel* ***the Y. Pages*** las páginas amarillas; *Old-fashioned* ***the Y. Peril*** la amenaza amarilla; *Old-fashioned* ***the y. press*** la prensa sensacionalista *or* amarilla; *US* ***y. ribbon*** = cinta amarilla que simboliza la bienvenida a los que regresan sanos y salvos a casa; ***the Y. River*** el río Amarillo; ***the Y. Sea*** el mar Amarillo; ***y. wagtail*** lavandera *f* boyera
(**b**) *Fam (cowardly)* gallina, cagueta; IDIOM **to have a y. streak** ser un(a) gallina *or Esp* cagueta
3 *vi* amarillear, ponerse amarillo(a)

yellow-bellied ['jeləʊbelɪd] *adj Fam* gallina, cagón(ona), cagueta

yellow-belly ['jeləʊbelɪ] *n Fam* gallina *mf*, cagón(ona) *m,f*, cagueta *mf*

yellowhammer ['jeləʊhæmə(r)] *n* escribano *m* cerillo

yellowish ['jeləʊɪʃ], **yellowy** ['jeləʊɪ] *adj* amarillento(a)

yellowness ['jeləʊnɪs] *n (colour)* color *m* amarillo, amarillez *f*; *(of person, complexion)* tono *m* amarillento, amarillez *f*

yelp [jelp] 1 *n (of dog, person)* chillido *m*, aullido *m*
2 *vi (dog, person)* chillar, aullar

Yemen ['jemən] *n* Yemen

Yemeni ['jemənɪ] 1 *n* yemení *mf*
2 *adj* yemení

yen[1] [jen] (*pl* **yen**) *n (Japanese currency)* yen *m*

yen[2] *n Fam* **to have a y. for sth/to do sth** tener muchas ganas de algo/de hacer algo

yeoman ['jəʊmən] *n Hist* (**a**) **y. (farmer)** = pequeño propietario rural (**b**) *(soldado)* = soldado del regimiento de voluntarios de caballería británico ►► ***y. of the guard*** = alabardero de la casa real británica

yeomanry ['jəʊmənrɪ] *n* (**a**) *Hist (farmers)* = pequeños propietarios rurales (**b**) *Mil* = regimiento de voluntarios de caballería británico

yep [jep] *exclam Fam* ¡sí!

Yerevan [jerə'væn] *n* Ereván, Yereván

yes [jes] 1 *n* sí *m*
2 *adv* sí; **he said y.** dijo que sí; **didn't you hear me? – y., I did** ¿no me has oído? – sí; **you didn't give it to me – y., I did!** a mí no me lo diste – sí que te lo di; **y.?** *(to sb waiting to speak)* ¿sí?; *(answering phone)* ¿sí?, *Esp* ¿diga?, *Esp* ¿dígame?, *Am* ¿aló?, *Carib, RP* ¿oigo?, *Méx* ¿bueno?, *RP* ¿hola?; **did they enjoy the cruise? – oh, y.!** ¿les gustó el crucero? – ¡(sí,) mucho!; **I went to see the new Woody Allen movie on Saturday – oh y.?** el sábado fui a ver la última película de Woody Allen – ah, ¿sí?; **I won't go – oh y. you will!** no voy a ir – ¡sí que vas a ir *or* claro que vas a ir!; **do you like him? – well, y. and no** ¿te cae bien? – pues, sí y no

yes-man ['jesmæn] *n* adulador(ora) *m,f*, cobista *mf*

yesterday ['jestədeɪ] 1 *n* ayer *m*; *Fam* **he's y.'s man** está acabado(a)
2 *adv* ayer; **the day before y.** anteayer; **y. morning/evening** ayer por la mañana/por la tarde; **a week (ago) y.**, *Br* **y. week** hace ayer una semana; **it seems like (only) y.** parece que fue ayer; IDIOM **I wasn't born y.** yo no nací ayer, yo no me he caído de un guindo

yesteryear ['jestəjɪə(r)] *n Formal & Literary* el ayer; **of y.** de antaño

---

YET [jet] 1 *adv* (**a**) *(still, up to now)* todavía, aún; **I haven't finished (just) y.** todavía *or* aún no he terminado; **don't go (just) y.** no te vayas todavía *or* aún; **it'll be some time y. before we finish** todavía *or* aún tardaremos *or Am* demoraremos en acabar; **there are another ten miles/minutes to go y.** todavía quedan diez millas/minutos; **it may y. happen** puede que todavía *or* aún ocurra, *Am* todavía *or* aún puede suceder; **it's the best y.** es el mejor hasta el momento; **our worst result y.** nuestro peor resultado por *or* hasta el momento; **they have y. to be convinced** todavía *or* aún están sin convencer, *Am* todavía *or* aún falta convencerlos; **the best is y. to come** todavía *or* aún no hemos visto lo mejor; **I'll catch her y.!** ¡ya la atraparé!; **there's hope for me y.!** ¡todavía *or* aún me quedan esperanzas!; **as y.** hasta ahora, por el momento; **not (just) y.** todavía *or* aún no; **y. again** una vez más; **y. more** todavía *or* aún más; **y. another mistake** otro error más
(**b**) *(in questions)* ya; **have they decided y.?** ¿han decidido ya?; *US* **did you go to the zoo y.?** ¿ya has ido al zoo?
2 *conj* aunque, sin embargo; **they had no income y. they still had to pay taxes** aunque no tenían ingresos debían pagar impuestos; **small y. strong** pequeño aunque fuerte; **and y. I like him** y, sin embargo, me gusta

---

yeti ['jetɪ] *n* yeti *m*

yew [juː] *n* **y. (tree)** tejo *m*

Y-fronts® ['waɪfrʌnts] *n* slip *m*, eslip *m*

YHA [waɪeɪtʃ'eɪ] (*abbr* **Youth Hostels Association**) Asociación *f* de Albergues Juveniles

Yid [jɪd] *n Fam* = término ofensivo para referirse a un judío, *RP* ruso(a) *m,f*

Yiddish ['jɪdɪʃ] 1 *n* yiddish *m*
2 *adj* yiddish

yield [jiːld] 1 *n* (**a**) *(of field)* cosecha *f*; *(of mine, interest)* rendimiento *m* (**b**) *Fin (profit)* beneficio *m*
2 *vt* (**a**) *(results)* proporcionar; *(crop)* dar, producir; *(interest)* rendir, producir; **to y. a profit** proporcionar beneficios; **their research has yielded some interesting results** su investigación ha dado (como fruto) algunos resultados interesantes; **these remarks y. an insight into his motives** esos comentarios permiten entender algo mejor sus motivos (**b**) *(territory)* ceder; *(right)* conceder
3 *vi* (**a**) *(surrender)* ceder (**to** ante), rendirse (**to** a); **to y. to temptation** ceder a la tentación; **to y. to pressure/blackmail** ceder ante la presión/el chantaje; **I had to y. to them on that point** en ese punto tuve que ceder ante ellos; **as the train approached London the countryside yielded to suburbia** a medida que el tren se acercaba a Londres, el paisaje rural daba *or* dejaba paso a los barrios residenciales
(**b**) *(break, bend)* ceder; **the ice yielded under his weight** el hielo cedió bajo su peso; **the door began to y. under the pressure** la puerta comenzó a ceder ante la presión
(**c**) *US* **y.** *(traffic sign)* ceda el paso

►**yield up** *vt sep Br* (**a**) *(surrender) (town, prisoner)* entregar; **he yielded himself up to the police** se entregó a la policía (**b**) *(reveal) (secret)* revelar; **divers have made the ocean y. up its treasures** los submarinistas han hecho que el océano nos revele *or* descubra sus tesoros

yin and yang ['jɪnənd'jæŋ] *n* el yin y el yang

yippee [jɪ'piː] *exclam* ¡yupi!, ¡viva!

yips ['jɪps] *npl Fam* **the y.** *(in golf)* = nerviosismo que hace que un jugador falle en el momento decisivo

YMCA [waɪemsiː'eɪ] *n* (*abbr* **Young Men's Christian Association**) ACJ *f*, Asociación *f* Cristiana de Jóvenes *(que regenta hostales económicos)*

yo [jəʊ] *exclam Fam* ¡hola!, ¡qué pasa!

yob [jɒb], **yobbo** ['jɒbəʊ] *n Br Fam* vándalo *m*, *Esp* gamberro *m*, *Perú, RP* patotero *m*

yobbish ['jɒbɪʃ] *adj Br Fam (behaviour)* vandálico(a), *Esp* gamberro(a), *Perú, RP* patotero(a)

yodel ['jəʊdəl] *vi* cantar a la tirolesa

yoga ['jəʊgə] *n* yoga *m*

yog(h)urt ['jɒgət] *n* yogur *m*

yoke [jəʊk] **1** *n* (**a**) *(for oxen)* yugo *m* (**b**) *(for carrying)* balancín *m* (**c**) *Fig (burden, domination)* yugo *m*; **under the y. of tyranny/imperialism** bajo el yugo de la tiranía/del imperialismo; **a country struggling to cast off the y. of foreign domination** un país que lucha por liberarse del yugo extranjero

2 *vt (oxen)* uncir (al yugo); *Fig* **to be yoked to...** estar uncido al yugo de...

yokel ['jəʊkəl] *n Pej or Hum* palurdo(a) *m,f*, *Esp* paleto(a) *m,f*

yolk [jəʊk] *n* yema *f* (de huevo) ►► *Zool* ***y. sac*** saco *m* vitelino, membrana *f* vitelina

Yom Kippur [jɒmkɪ'pʊə(r)] *n Rel* Yom Kippur *m*

yonder ['jɒndə(r)] *Literary* **1** *adv* **(over) y.** allá; IDIOM **to disappear into the wide blue y.** esfumarse sin dejar rastro

2 *adj* **y. tree** aquel árbol, el árbol aquel

yonks [jɒŋks] *npl Br Fam* **I haven't done that for y.** hace un montón de tiempo que no hago eso; **y. ago** hace la tira *or Méx* un chorro *or RP* un toco (de tiempo)

yoo-hoo ['ju:hu:] *exclam* ¡eh!, ¡yuju!

yore [jɔ:(r)] *n Literary* **in days of y.** antaño

Yorkie ['jɔ:kɪ] *n* Yorkshire terrier *m*

Yorks (*abbr* **Yorkshire**) (condado *m* de) Yorkshire

Yorkshire ['jɔ:kʃə(r)] *n* Yorkshire ►► ***Y. pudding*** = masa horneada de harina, huevos y leche que se sirve con el rosbif; ***Y. terrier*** Yorkshire terrier *m*

YOU [ju:] *pron*

In Spanish, the formal form **usted** takes a third person singular verb and **ustedes** takes a third person plural verb. In Latin America, **ustedes** is the standard form of the second person plural both in formal and non-formal contexts, while the informal form **vos** can be used as an alternative to **tu**. This is the norm in the River Plate area, but **vos** is found elsewhere, for example in Central America and in the Andean region.

(**a**) *(subject) (usually omitted in Spanish, except for contrast) (singular)* tú, *esp RP* vos, *Formal* usted; *(plural) Esp* vosotros(as), *Am or Formal* ustedes; **y. seem happy** *(singular)* pareces feliz, *Formal* parece feliz; *(plural) Esp* parecéis felices, *Am or Formal* parecen felices; **do y. like red wine?** *(singular)* ¿te gusta el vino tinto?, *Formal* ¿le gusta el vino tinto?; *(plural) Esp* ¿os gusta el vino tinto?, *Am or Formal* ¿les gusta el vino tinto?; **have YOU got it?** *(singular)* ¿lo tienes tú?, *Formal* ¿lo tiene usted?; *(plural) Esp* ¿lo tenéis vosotros?, *Am or Formal* ¿lo tienen ustedes?; **y. alone know** *(singular)* sólo lo sabes tú, *Formal* sólo lo sabe usted; *(plural) Esp* sólo lo sabéis vosotros, *Am or Formal* sólo lo saben ustedes; **y. French are...** *Esp* vosotros los franceses sois..., *Am or Formal* ustedes los franceses son...; **come here, y. two!** *Esp* ¡venid aquí, vosotros dos!, *Am* ¡vengan acá, ustedes dos!

(**b**) *(direct object) (singular)* te, *Formal* lo(la); *(plural) Esp* os, *Am or Formal* los(las); **they hate y.** *(singular)* te odian, *Formal* lo odian; *(plural) Esp* os odian, *Am or Formal* los odian; **I can understand your son but not YOU** *(singular)* a tu hijo lo entiendo, pero a ti no, *Formal* a su hijo lo entiendo, pero a usted no; *(plural) Esp* a vuestro hijo lo entiendo, pero a vosotros no, *Am or Formal* a su hijo lo entiendo, pero a ustedes no

(**c**) *(indirect object) (singular)* te, *Formal* le; *(plural) Esp* os, *Am or Formal* les; **I gave y. the book** *(singular)* te di el libro, *Formal* le di el libro; *(plural) Esp* os di el libro, *Am or Formal* les di el libro; **I told y.** *(singular)* te lo dije, *Formal* se lo dije; *(plural) Esp* os lo dije, *Am or Formal* se lo dije

(**d**) *(after preposition) (singular)* ti, *Formal* usted; *(plural) Esp* vosotros(as), *Am or Formal* ustedes; **I'm thinking of y.** *(singular)* pienso en ti, *Formal* pienso en usted; *(plural) Esp* pienso en vosotros, *Am or Formal* pienso en ustedes; **with y.** *(singular)* contigo, *Formal* con usted; *(plural) Esp* con vosotros, *Am or Formal* con ustedes

(**e**) *(impersonal)* **y. don't do that kind of thing** esas cosas no se hacen; **y. never know** nunca se sabe; **this account gives y. a higher rate of interest** esta cuenta da más intereses; **exercise is good for y.** es bueno hacer ejercicio; **y. have to be careful with him** hay que *or* uno tiene que tener cuidado con él

(**f**) *(as complement of verb "to be")* **oh, it's y.!** *(singular)* ¡ah, eres tú!, *Formal* ¡ah, es usted!; *(plural) Esp* ¡ah, sois vosotros!, *Am or Formal* ¡ah, son ustedes!; **it was y. who did it** *(singular)* fuiste tú quien lo hiciste, *Formal* fue usted quien lo hizo; *(plural) Esp* fuisteis vosotros quienes lo hicisteis, *Am or Formal* fueron ustedes quienes lo hicieron; *Fam* **that hat's not really y.** ese sombrero no va contigo

(**g**) *(with interjections)* **poor old y.!** ¡pobrecito!; **y. idiot!** ¡idiota!; **hey, y. with the beard!** ¡eh, tú, el de la barba!; **don't y. forget!** ¡no te olvides!

(**h**) *(in apposition)* **y. men are all the same!** ¡todos los hombres *Esp* sois *or Am* son iguales!

(**i**) *(with imperative)* **y. sit down here** *(singular)* tú siéntate aquí; *(plural) Esp* vosotros sentaos aquí, *Am* ustedes siéntense acá; **don't y. dare!** ¡ni se te ocurra!

you'd [ju:d] = **you had, you would**

you-know-what [ju:nəʊ'wɒt] *n Fam Euph* **does he know about the y.?** ¿está al corriente de... ya sabes?; **they were doing y.** estaban haciendo ya sabes qué *or* lo que te dije

you-know-who [ju:nəʊ'hu:] *n* **he was talking to y.** estaba hablando ya sabes con quién

you'll [ju:l] = **you will, you shall**

young [jʌŋ] **1** *npl* (**a**) *(people)* **the y.** los jóvenes; **a game suitable for y. and old alike** un juego apto tanto para chicos como para grandes (**b**) *(animals)* crías *fpl*; **to be with y.** estar preñada

2 *adj* (**a**) *(person, animal)* joven; **she's (two years) younger than me** es (dos años) menor que yo; **y. man** chico, joven; **now listen to me, y. man!** ¡escúchame bien, jovencito!; **y. woman** chica, joven; **the y. men and women of today** los jóvenes de hoy; **y. lady** joven; **now listen to me, y. lady!** ¡escúchame bien, jovencita!; **she's quite the y. lady now** ya es toda una señorita; **y. people** los jóvenes, la gente joven; **when I was a y. man** cuando era joven; **my younger brother** mi hermano menor; **the younger generation** la nueva generación; **y. in spirit** *or* **at heart** joven de espíritu; **in his younger days** en su juventud; **he's y. for his age** *(immature, youthful)* parece más joven *or* aparenta ser más joven de lo que es; **she's y. for her year** *(at school, university)* va adelantada de curso; **you're only y. once** sólo se es joven una vez en la vida; **I'm not getting any younger** me estoy haciendo mayor; **the night is y.!** ¡la noche es joven! ►► *Fig* ***y. blood*** savia *f* nueva; ***y. offender*** delincuente *mf* juvenil; ***y. turk*** radical *mf*

(**b**) *(appearance, style)* juvenil

(**c**) *(recent) (vegetables, wine)* joven; **a y. country/company** un país/una compañía joven

youngish ['jʌŋɪʃ] *adj* más bien joven

youngster ['jʌŋstə(r)] *n* joven *mf*

YOUR [jɔ:(r)] *possessive adj* (**a**) *(of one person)* tu, *Formal* su; **y. house** tu casa, *Formal* su casa; **y. books** tus libros, *Formal* sus libros; **what's y. name?** ¿cómo te llamas?, *Formal* ¿cómo se llama?; **it wasn't YOUR idea!** ¡no fue idea tuya!, *Formal* ¡no fue idea suya!; **we were upset at y. mentioning it** nos disgustó que lo mencionaras, *Formal* nos disgustó que lo mencionara; **what was y. understanding?** ¿cómo lo interpretaste?, *Formal* ¿cómo lo interpretó?

(**b**) *(of more than one person) Esp* vuestro(a), *Am or Formal* su; **y. house** *Esp* vuestra casa, *Am or Formal* su casa; **y. books** *Esp* vuestros libros, *Am or Formal* sus libros; **what are y. names?** *Esp* ¿cómo os llamáis?, *Am or Formal* ¿cómo se llaman?; **it wasn't YOUR idea!** *Esp* ¡no fue idea vuestra!, *Am or Formal* ¡no fue idea suya *or* de ustedes!; **we were upset at y. mentioning it** *Esp* nos disgustó que lo mencionarais, *Am or Formal* nos disgustó que lo mencionaran; **what was y. understanding?** *Esp* ¿cómo lo interpretasteis?, *Am or Formal* ¿cómo lo interpretaron?

(**c**) *(for parts of body, clothes) (translated by definite article)* **you forgot y. hat** te olvidaste el sombrero, *Formal* se olvidó el sombrero; **why did you put y. hand in y. pocket?** ¿por qué te metiste la mano en el bolsillo?, *Formal* ¿por qué se metió la mano en el bolsillo?; **someone stole y. clothes** *(singular)* te han robado la ropa, *Formal* le han robado la ropa; *(plural) Esp* os han robado la ropa, *Am or Formal* les han robado la ropa; **y. eyes are beautiful** tienes unos ojos preciosos, *Formal* tiene unos ojos preciosos

(**d**) *(impersonal)* **you should buy y. ticket first** hay que comprar la entrada antes; **you have to take y. chances** hay que aprovechar las oportunidades; **smoking is bad for y. health** el tabaco perjudica la salud; *Fam* **y. average Frenchman** el francés medio; *Fam* **it was not y. usual holiday in the sun** no fueron las típicas vacaciones al sol

(**e**) *(in titles)* **Y. Highness** Su Alteza; **Y. Majesty** Su Majestad

you're [jɔ:(r)] = **you are**

yours [jɔ:z] *possessive pron*

In Spanish, the forms **tuyo(a)**, **suyo(a)** and **vuestro(a)** require a definite article in the singular and in the plural when they are the subject of the phrase.

(**a**) *(of one person) (singular)* tuyo(a), *Formal* suyo(a); *(plural)* tuyos(as), *Formal* suyos(as); **my house is big but y. is bigger** mi casa es grande, pero la tuya/suya es mayor; **this book is y.** este libro es tuyo/suyo; **these books are y.** estos libros son tuyos/suyos; **she didn't have a book so we gave her y.** ella no tenía libro, así que le dimos el tuyo/suyo; **it must be one of y.** debe de ser uno de los tuyos/suyos; **it wasn't our fault, it was YOURS** no fue culpa nuestra, sino tuya/suya; **y. is the work I admire most** tu/su obra es la que más admiro; **a friend of y.** un amigo tuyo/suyo; **where's that brother of y.?** ¿dónde está *or* anda ese hermano tuyo/suyo?; **that wretched dog of y.** ese maldito perro tuyo/suyo; **it's all y.!** ¡todo tuyo/suyo!; **y.** *(at end of letter)* saludos; **y. sincerely, y. faithfully** atentamente, le saluda muy atentamente

(**b**) *(of more than one person) (singular) Esp* vuestro(a), *Am or Formal* suyo(a); *(plural) Esp* vuestros(as), *Am or Formal* suyos(as); **this book is y.** *Esp* este libro es vuestro, *Am or Formal* este libro es suyo; **these books are y.** *Esp* estos libros son vuestros, *Am or Formal* estos libros son suyos

yourself [jɔː'self] *pron* (**a**) *(reflexive)* te, *Formal* se; **have you hurt y.?** ¿te has hecho daño?, *Formal* ¿se ha hecho daño?; **you can introduce y.** te puedes presentar, *Formal* se puede presentar; **buy y. some flowers** cómprate unas flores, *Formal* cómprese unas flores; **you can see y. reflected in the water** puedes verte reflejado *or* ver tu imagen reflejada en el agua, *Formal* puede verse reflejado *or* ver su imagen reflejada en el agua

(**b**) *(unaided, alone)* tú solo(a), *Formal* usted solo(a); **you can do it y.** lo puedes hacer tú solo, *Formal* lo puede hacer usted solo; **did you do all the work y.?** ¿has hecho todo el trabajo tú solo?, *Formal* ¿ha hecho todo el trabajo usted solo?

(**c**) *(emphatic)* tú mismo(a), *Formal* usted mismo(a); **you told me y.** me lo dijiste tú mismo, *Formal* me lo dijo usted mismo; **you y. don't have to go** no hace falta que vayas tú, *Formal* no hace falta que vaya usted

(**d**) *(your usual self)* **you'll soon feel y. again** en breve te volverás a sentir el/la de siempre, *Formal* en breve se volverá a sentir el/la de siempre; **you don't seem y. today** hoy no se te nota nada bien, *Formal* hoy no se le nota nada bien; **just be y.** *(act naturally)* sé tú mismo, actúa con naturalidad, *Formal* sea usted mismo, actúe con naturalidad

(**e**) *(after preposition)* ti, *Formal* usted; **you shouldn't talk about y.** no deberías hablar de ti, *Formal* no debería hablar de usted; **did you do this by y.?** ¿lo has hecho tú solo?, *Formal* ¿lo ha hecho usted solo?; **do you live by y.?** ¿vives solo?, *Formal* ¿vive solo?; **were you all by y.?** ¿estabas completamente solo?, *Formal* ¿estaba completamente solo?; **did you buy it for y.?** ¿te lo has comprado para ti?, *Formal* ¿se lo ha comprado para usted?; **did I hear you talking to y.?** ¿estabas hablando solo?, *Formal* ¿estaba hablando solo?

(**f**) *(replacing "you")* **it is meant for people like y.** es para gente como tú, *Formal* es para gente como usted; *Fam* **I'll have a brandy... and y.?** yo voy a tomar un coñac... ¿y tú?

(**g**) *Fam (oneself)* **you can hurt y. doing that** te puedes hacer daño al hacer eso

yourselves [jɔː'selvz] *pron*

> In Latin America, **se/ustedes** is the standard form of the second person plural and is not considered formal. The peninsular Spanish informal forms **os/vosotros** are occasionally found in religious liturgy, but would sound quaint and old-fashioned elsewhere.

(**a**) *(reflexive) Esp* os, *Am or Formal* se; **have you hurt y.?** *Esp* ¿os habéis hecho daño?, *Am or Formal* ¿se han hecho daño?; **you can introduce y.** *(to each other, to the others) Esp* podéis presentaros, *Am or Formal* pueden presentarse; **you can see y. reflected in the water** *Esp* podéis veros reflejados en el agua, *Am or Formal* pueden verse reflejados en el agua

(**b**) *(unaided, alone) Esp* vosotros(as) solos(as), *Am or Formal* ustedes solos(as); **did you do all the work y.?** *Esp* ¿hicisteis todo el trabajo vosotros solos?, *Am or Formal* ¿hicieron todo el trabajo ustedes solos?

(**c**) *(emphatic) Esp* vosotros(as) mismos(as), *Am or Formal* ustedes mismos(as); **you told me y.** *Esp* me lo dijisteis vosotros, *Am or Formal* me lo dijeron ustedes

(**d**) *(your usual selves)* **you'll soon feel y. again** *Esp* en breve os volveréis a sentir los de siempre, *Am or Formal* en breve se volverán a sentir los de siempre; **you don't seem y. today** *Esp* hoy no se os nota nada bien, *Am or Formal* hoy no se les nota nada bien; **just be y.** *(act naturally) Esp* sed vosotros mismos, actuad con naturalidad, *Am or Formal* sean ustedes mismos, actúen con naturalidad

(**e**) *(after preposition) Esp* vosotros(as), *Am or Formal* ustedes; **you shouldn't talk about y.** *Esp* no deberíais hablar de vosotros, *Am or Formal* no deberían hablar de ustedes; **share the money among y.** *Esp* repartíos el dinero, *Am or Formal* repártanse el dinero; **sort it out among y.** *Esp* arregladlo entre vosotros, *Am or Formal* arréglenlo entre ustedes; **did you do this by y.?** *Esp* ¿lo habéis hecho vosotros solos?, *Am or Formal* ¿lo han hecho ustedes solos?; **were you all by y.?** *Esp* ¿estabais completamente solos?, *Am or Formal* ¿estaban completamente solos?; **did you buy it for y.?** *Esp* ¿os lo habéis comprado para vosotros?, *Am or Formal* ¿se lo han comprado para ustedes?; **you've kept the best seats for y.** *Esp* os habéis quedado con los mejores asientos, *Am or Formal* se han quedado con los mejores asientos

(**f**) *(replacing you)* **it is meant for people like y.** es para gente como *Esp* vosotros *or Am or Formal* ustedes; *Fam* **we're having the lamb... and y.?** nosotros vamos a comer cordero, ¿y *Esp* vosotros *or Am* ustedes?

youth [juːθ] *n* (**a**) *(period)* juventud *f*; **in his early y.** en su (primera) juventud; **he is no longer in his first y.** ya no es tan joven

(**b**) *(young man)* joven *m*

(**c**) *(young people)* juventud *f*; **the y. of today** los jóvenes *or* la juventud de hoy ▸▸ ***y. club*** club *m* juvenil; ***y. culture*** la cultura juvenil; *Br* ***y. custody centre*** = centro preventivo y de formación para delincuentes juveniles; ***y. hostel*** albergue *m* juvenil *or* de juventud; ***y. hostel card*** carné *m* de alberguista; ***y. hosteller*** alberguista *mf*; ***y. hostelling:*** **to go y. hostelling** ir de viaje parando en albergues juveniles; ***y. unemployment*** desempleo *m* juvenil; ***y. worker*** asistente *mf* social para la juventud

youthful ['juːθfʊl] *adj (person)* joven; *(looks, enthusiasm)* juvenil; **to look y.** tener un aspecto juvenil, parecer joven; **y. good looks** aspecto juvenil y atractivo; **he is a y. fifty-two** es un joven de 52

youthfulness ['juːθfʊlnɪs] *n* juventud *f*

you've [juːv] = **you have**

yowl [jaʊl] **1** *n* aullido *m*, chillido *m*

2 *vi* aullar, chillar

yo-yo ['jəʊjəʊ] (*pl* **yo-yos**) *n* yoyó *m*; **to go up and down like a y.** no parar de subir y bajar

yr (*abbr* **year**) año *m*

yrs (**a**) (*abbr* **years**) años *mpl* (**b**) *Fam* (*abbr* **yours**) *(in letter writing)* saludos

ytterbium [ɪ'tɜːbɪəm] *n Chem* iterbio *m*

yttrium ['ɪtrɪəm] *n Chem* itrio *m*

yuan [juː'æn] *n (Chinese currency)* yuan *m*

Yucatan [juːkə'tɑːn] *n* Yucatán

yucca ['jʌkə] *n* yuca *f*

yuck [jʌk] *exclam Fam* ¡puaj!, ¡aj!

yucky ['jʌkɪ] *adj Fam* asqueroso(a)

Yugoslav ['juːgəʊslɑːv] **1** *n* yugoslavo(a) *m,f*

2 *adj* yugoslavo(a)

Yugoslavia [juːgəʊ'slɑːvɪə] *n* Yugoslavia

Yugoslavian [juːgəʊ'slɑːvɪən] *adj* yugoslavo(a)

yuk [jʌk] *exclam Fam* ¡puaj!, ¡aj!

yukky ['jʌkɪ] *adj Fam* asqueroso(a)

Yule [juːl] *n Old-fashioned or Literary* Natividad *f*, Navidad *f*

yuletide ['juːltaɪd] *n* Navidad *f*

yum(-yum) [jʌm('jʌm)] *exclam Fam* ¡ñam, ñam!, *RP* ¡miam, miam!

yummy ['jʌmɪ] *adj Fam* rico(a)

yup [jʌp] *exclam Fam* ¡sí!

yuppie, yuppy ['jʌpɪ] **1** *n Fam* yupi *mf*; **a y. restaurant** un restaurante de yupis ▸▸ ***y. flu*** la gripe *or Am* gripa del yupi *(encefalomielitis miálgica)*

2 *adj (lifestyle)* de yupi; *(area)* yuppie, yupi

yuppification [jʌpɪfɪ'keɪʃən] *n Fam* transformación *f* en yuppie *or* yupi

yuppify ['jʌpɪfaɪ] *vt Fam (place)* convertir en yuppie *or* yupi

YWCA [waɪ'dʌbəljuːsiː'eɪ] *n* (*abbr* **Young Women's Christian Association**) ACJ *f*, Asociación *f* Cristiana de Jóvenes *(que regenta hostales económicos)*

Z, z

Z, z [zed, *US* zi:] *n (letter)* Z, z *f*; IDIOM *US Fam* **to get** *or* **score some z's** echar una cabezada *or* un sueñecito, echarse una siestecita

Zaire [zɑ:'ɪə(r)] *n Formerly* Zaire

Zairean [zɑ:'ɪərɪən] **1** *n* zaireño(a) *m,f*
2 *adj* zaireño(a)

Zambezi [zæm'bi:zɪ] *n* **the Z.** el Zambeze

Zambia ['zæmbɪə] *n* Zambia

Zambian ['zæmbɪən] **1** *n* zambiano(a) *m,f*
2 *adj* zambiano(a)

zaniness ['zeɪnɪnɪs] *n Fam (of humour, movie)* carácter *m* disparatado; *(of person)* chifladura *f*

zany ['zeɪnɪ] *adj Fam (humour, movie)* disparatado(a); *(person)* chiflado(a), *Am* zafado(a), *RP* rayado(a)

Zanzibar ['zænzɪbɑ:(r)] *n* Zanzíbar

zap [zæp] (*pt & pp* **zapped**) *Fam* **1** *vt* (**a**) *(destroy, disable)* fulminar (**b**) *Comptr (delete)* borrar
2 *vi* (**a**) *(change TV channels)* zapear, hacer zapping (**b**) *(go quickly)* ir a todo correr *or* a toda mecha *or Esp* a toda pastilla; **I'll z. over to see her** voy corriendo *or* disparado a verla

zapper ['zæpə(r)] *n Fam (TV remote control)* mando *m* a distancia, telemando *m*

zappy ['zæpɪ] *adj Br Fam* brioso(a)

z-axis ['zedæksɪs] *n Math* eje *m* Z

Z-car ['zedkɑ:(r)] *n Br Old-fashioned* coche *m* patrulla, *Esp* zeta *m*

zeal [zi:l] *n* celo *m*; **political/religious z.** fervor político/religioso; **her z. for reform/justice** su afán reformista/por la justicia

zealot ['zelət] *n* fanático(a) *m,f*

zealotry ['zelətrɪ] *n* fanatismo *m*

zealous ['zeləs] *adj* celoso(a); **the authorities have been overly z. in their application of this law** las autoridades han aplicado la ley con un exceso de celo

zealously ['zeləslɪ] *adv* celosamente

zebra ['zi:brə, 'zebrə] *n* cebra *f* ►► *Br Aut* ***z. crossing*** paso *m* de cebra

zed [zed], *US* **zee** [zi:] *n* (**a**) *(letter)* zeta *f* (**b**) IDIOM *Fam* **to catch some** *Br* **zeds** *or US* **zees** echar una cabezada *or* un sueñecito, echarse una siestecita

Zeitgeist ['zaɪtgaɪst] *n* espíritu *m*

Zen [zen] *n* zen *m* ►► ***Z. Buddhism*** budismo *m* zen

zenith ['zenɪθ] *n Astron & Fig* cenit *m*; **at the z. of his fame** en el apogeo de su fama; **she was at the z. of her influence** su influencia estaba en el punto más alto

zephyr ['zefə(r)] *n Literary* céfiro *m*

zeppelin ['zepəlɪn] *n* zepelín *m*

zero ['zɪərəʊ] **1** *n* (*pl* **zeros** *or* **zeroes**) (**a**) *(number)* cero *m*; **22 degrees below z.** 22 grados bajo cero; *Fam* **his chances are z.** no tiene ninguna posibilidad ►► *Astron* ***z. gravity*** gravedad *f* cero, ingravidez *f*; *Mil* ***z. hour*** hora *f* cero *or* H; *Mil* ***z. option*** opción *f* cero; ***z. tolerance*** tolerancia *f* cero, inflexibilidad *f* absoluta; **to have a z. tolerance approach to crime/vagrancy** tener una política de tolerancia cero *or* ser absolutamente inflexible con el delito/la mendicidad
(**b**) *US Fam (person)* cero *m* a la izquierda
2 *adj Fam* nulo(a); **to have z. charm** no tener el más mínimo encanto
3 *vi* **to z. in on sth** *(weapon)* apuntar hacia algo; *(person)* centrarse en algo

zero-rated ['zɪərəʊreɪtɪd] *adj Fin (for VAT)* con una tasa de IVA del 0 por ciento

zest [zest] *n* (**a**) *(eagerness)* entusiasmo *m*; **her z. for life** sus ganas de vivir *or* disfrutar de la vida; **he set about the task with real z.** emprendió la tarea con muchas ganas *or* con mucho brío; **to add z. to sth** dar emoción a algo (**b**) *Culin (of orange, lemon)* peladura *f*

zestful ['zestfʊl] *adj (enthusiastic)* brioso(a), entusiasta

zesty ['zestɪ] *adj* (**a**) *(piquant)* fuerte (**b**) *(enthusiastic)* brioso(a), entusiasta

zeugma ['zju:gmə] *n Gram* zeugma *m*

Zeus [zju:s] *n Mythol* Zeus

ziggurat ['zɪgʊræt] *n* zigurat *m*

zigzag ['zɪgzæg] **1** *n* zigzag *m*
2 *adj (path, line)* en zigzag, zigzagueante; *(pattern)* en zigzag
3 *vi* (*pt & pp* **zigzagged**) zigzaguear; **the road zigzags through the valley** la carretera atraviesa el valle haciendo zigzag

zilch [zɪltʃ] *n Fam* nada de nada; **there's z. on TV** no hay nada de nada en la tele

zillion ['zɪljən] *n Fam Hum* millón *m*, montón *m*; **I have told you a z. times** te lo he dicho tropecientas *or Méx* chorrocientas *or RP* chiquicientas mil veces; **zillions of** montones de, *Esp* mogollón de

Zimbabwe [zɪm'bɑ:bweɪ] *n* Zimbabue

Zimbabwean [zɪm'bɑ:bweɪən] **1** *n* zimbabuense *mf*
2 *adj* zimbabuense

Zimmer frame ['zɪməfreɪm] *n* andador *m* ortopédico

zinc [zɪŋk] *n Chem* cinc *m*, zinc *m* ►► ***z. ointment*** ungüento *m* de cinc; ***z. oxide*** óxido *m* de cinc; ***z. white*** blanco *m* de cinc

zing [zɪŋ] **1** *n* (**a**) *(sound)* silbido *m* (**b**) *Fam (vitality)* chispa *f*
2 *vt US Fam (tease)* tomar el pelo a
3 *vi (of projectile)* silbar; **the bullet zinged past me** la bala pasó silbando junto a mí

zinnia ['zɪnɪə] *n Bot* cinnia *f*

Zion ['zaɪɒn] *n* Zión

Zionism ['zaɪənɪzəm] *n* sionismo *m*

Zionist ['zaɪənɪst] **1** *n* sionista *mf*
2 *adj* sionista

zip [zɪp] **1** *n* (**a**) *Br* **z. (fastener)** cremallera *f*, *Am* cierre *m* (**b**) *Fam (vigour)* nervio *m*, brío *m* (**c**) *US* ***z. code*** código *m* postal (**d**) *Comptr* ***Zip® disk*** disco *m* Zip® (**e**) *US Fam (nothing)* nada de nada; **the score was already four-z.** ya iban cuatro a cero (**f**) *(sound) (of bullets)* silbido *m*
2 *vt* (*pt & pp* **zipped**) (**a**) *(with zip fastener)* **to z. sth open/shut** abrir/cerrar la cremallera *or Am* el cierre de algo; **I zipped myself into my sleeping bag** me metí en el saco de dormir y cerré la cremallera (**b**) *Comptr* comprimir (**c**) *Fam* **z. it!** *(keep quiet)* ¡cállate!, ¡cierra el pico!
3 *vi* **to z. past** *(car, bullet)* pasar zumbando; **she zipped out to get a paper** salió corriendo a comprar un periódico

► **zip through** *vt insep Fam* **I zipped through the last chapters** me liquidé los últimos capítulos en un periquete

► **zip up** **1** *vt sep (clothes, bag)* cerrar la cremallera *or Am* el cierre de; **can you z. me up?** ¿me puedes subir la cremallera *or Am* el cierre?
2 *vi* cerrarse con cremallera *or Am* cierre

zipper ['zɪpə(r)] *n US* cremallera *f*, *Am* cierre *m*

zippy ['zɪpɪ] *adj Fam* animado(a)

zip-up ['zɪpʌp] *adj (bag, coat)* con cremallera *or Am* cierre

zircon ['zɜ:kɒn] *n Geol* circón *m*

zirconium [zɜ:'kəʊnɪəm] *n Chem* circonio *m*

zit [zɪt] *n Fam* grano *m*

zither ['zɪðə(r)] *n Mus* cítara *f*

zodiac ['zəʊdɪæk] *n* zodiaco *m*, zodíaco *m*

zombie ['zɒmbɪ] *n* zombi *mf*; **he walks about like a z.** anda por ahí como un zombi

zonal ['zəʊnəl] *adj* por zonas, zonal

zone [zəʊn] **1** *n* (**a**) *(area, sector)* zona *f*; *Mil* **the occupied z.** la zona ocupada; *Mil* **battle/war z.** zona de combate/guerra ►► ***z. defence*** *(in basketball)* defensa *f* en zona (**b**) *Fam Sport* **to be in the z.** estar totalmente concentrado(a) (**c**) *US Fam* **to be in a z.** *(dazed)* estar atontado(a); *(after taking drugs)* estar con el bajón

2 *vt (town, area)* dividir en zonas; *US (administratively)* zonificar; **they zoned the area for industrial development** la zona fue calificada como área industrial

zonked (out) [zɒŋkt('aʊt)] *adj Fam* **to be z.** *(exhausted)* estar molido(a) *or* hecho(a) polvo; *(drugged)* colocado(a), *Esp* flipado(a), *Col* trabado(a), *Méx* pingo(a), *RP* falopeado(a); *(drunk)* estar mamado(a) *or* pedo

zoo [zu:] (*pl* **zoos**) *n* zoo *m*, zoológico *m*

zookeeper ['zu:ki:pə(r)] *n* guardián(ana) *m,f* de zoológico

zoological [zʊə'lɒdʒɪkəl] *adj* zoológico(a) ►► ***z. garden(s)*** parque *m* zoológico

zoologist [zʊ'ɒlədʒɪst] *n* zoólogo(a) *m,f*

zoology [zʊ'ɒlədʒɪ] *n* zoología *f*

zoom [zu:m] **1** *n* (**a**) *(noise)* zumbido *m* (**b**) *Phot* ***z. lens*** zoom *m* (**c**) *Comptr* ***z. box*** cuadro *m* de zoom

2 *vi* **to z. along/past** pasar zumbando *or* a toda velocidad; **inflation zoomed upwards** la inflación se disparó

► **zoom in** *vi Cin & TV* enfocar en primer plano (**on** a)

► **zoom off** *vi* salir pitando

► **zoom out** *vi Cin & TV* cambiar de primer plano a plano general

zoot suit ['zu:tsu:t] *n Fam* traje *m* años cuarenta *(con chaqueta larga de hombreras)*

Zoroastrian [zɒrəʊ'æstrɪən] *Rel* **1** *n* zoroastra *mf*, zoroástrico(a) *m,f*

2 *adj* zoroástrico(a)

zowie ['zaʊi:] *exclam US Fam* ¡atiza!

zucchini [zu:'ki:nɪ] (*pl* **zucchini** *or* **zucchinis**) *n US* calabacín *m*

Zulu ['zu:lu:] **1** *n* zulú *mf*

2 *adj* zulú

Zululand ['zu:lu:lænd] *n* Zululandia

Zurich ['zʊərɪk] *n* Zurich, Zúrich

zygomatic [zaɪgəʊ'mætɪk] *adj Anat* cigomático(a)

zygote ['zaɪgəʊt] *n Biol* zigoto *m*, cigoto *m*

zymogen ['zaɪməʊdʒen] *n Biol* cimógeno *m*, zimógeno *m*

zymotic [zaɪ'mɒtɪk] *adj* (**a**) *(relating to fermentation)* de la fermentación, zimótico(a) (**b**) *Old-fashioned Med* cimótico(a)

SPANISH VERB TABLES

This guide to Spanish verbs opens with the three regular conjugations (verbs ending in **-ar**, **-er** and **-ir**) followed by the two most common auxiliary verbs: "**haber**", which is used to form the perfect tenses, and "**ser**", which is used to form the passive. These are followed by a list of Spanish irregular verbs, numbered 3–74. A number refers you to these tables after irregular verbs on the Spanish-English side of the dictionary.

The numbers 1, 2, 3 to the left of the each verb form indicate the first, second and third person forms of the verb. In each block the second 1, 2, 3 are the plural forms.

Note that the second person pronouns "**usted**" (formal address) and "**ustedes**" (formal address in Spain and standard in Latin America) – "you" in the singular and plural – are used with the third person of the verb. In the imperative, the plural form is therefore not the "**-d**" form (i.e. "**hablad**") but instead the same as the third person plural of the present subjunctive (i.e. "**hablen**").

The pluperfect subjunctive is shown with the "**hubiera**" form of the auxiliary. The alternative "**hubiese**" form can also be used – see "**haber**" (verb table 1) for the full conjugation.

HABLAR

	PRESENT	IMPERFECT	PRETERITE	FUTURE	**CONDITIONAL** PRESENT	PAST
1	hablo	hablaba	hablé	hablaré	hablaría	habría hablado
2	hablas	hablabas	hablaste	hablarás	hablarías	habrías hablado
3	habla	hablaba	habló	hablará	hablaría	habría hablado
1	hablamos	hablábamos	hablamos	hablaremos	hablaríamos	habríamos hablado
2	habláis	hablabais	hablasteis	hablaréis	hablaríais	habríais hablado
3	hablan	hablaban	hablaron	hablarán	hablarían	habrían hablado

	PERFECT	PLUPERFECT	PAST ANTERIOR	FUTURE PERFECT	**INFINITIVE**	**PARTICIPLE**
1	he hablado	había hablado	hube hablado	habré hablado	PRESENT	PRESENT
2	has hablado	habías hablado	hubiste hablado	habrás hablado	hablar	hablando
3	ha hablado	había hablado	hubo hablado	habrá hablado		
1	hemos hablado	habíamos hablado	hubimos hablado	habremos hablado	PAST	PAST
2	habéis hablado	habíais hablado	hubisteis hablado	habreis hablado	haber hablado	hablado
3	han hablado	habían hablado	hubieron hablado	habrán hablado		

	SUBJUNCTIVE PRESENT	IMPERFECT	PERFECT	PLUPERFECT	**IMPERATIVE**
1	hable	habl-ara/ase	haya hablado	hubiera hablado	
2	hables	habl-aras/ases	hayas hablado	hubieras hablado	(tú) habla
3	hable	habl-ara/ase	hayan hablado	hubiera hablado	(Vd) hable
1	hablemos	habl-áramos/ásemos	hayamos hablado	hubiéramos hablado	(nosotros) hablemos
2	habléis	habl-arais/aseis	hayais hablado	hubierais hablado	(vosotros) hablad
3	hablen	habl-aran/asen	hayan hablado	hubieran hablado	(Vds) hablen

COMER

	PRESENT	IMPERFECT	PRETERITE	FUTURE	**CONDITIONAL** PRESENT	PAST
1	como	comía	comí	comeré	comería	habría comido
2	comes	comías	comiste	comerás	comerías	habrías comido
3	come	comía	comió	comerá	comería	habría comido
1	comemos	comíamos	comimos	comeremos	comeríamos	habríamos comido
2	coméis	comíais	comisteis	comeréis	comeríais	habríais comido
3	comen	comían	comieron	comerán	comerían	habrían comido

	PERFECT	PLUPERFECT	PAST ANTERIOR	FUTURE PERFECT	**INFINITIVE**	**PARTICIPLE**
1	he comido	había comido	hube comido	habré comido	PRESENT	PRESENT
2	has comido	habías comido	hubiste comido	habrás comido	comer	comiendo
3	ha comido	había comido	hubo comido	habrá comido		
1	hemos comido	habíamos comido	hubimos comido	habremos comido	PAST	PAST
2	habéis comido	habíais comido	hubisteis comido	habréis comido	haber comido	comido
3	han comido	habían comido	hubieron comido	habrán comido		

	SUBJUNCTIVE PRESENT	IMPERFECT	PERFECT	PLUPERFECT	**IMPERATIVE**
1	coma	com-iera/iese	haya comido	hubiera comido	
2	comas	com-ieras/ieses	hayas comido	hubieras comido	(tú) come
3	coma	com-iera/iese	haya comido	hubiera comido	(Vd) coma
1	comamos	com-iéramos/iésemos	hayamos comido	hubiéramos comido	(nosotros) comamos
2	comáis	com-ierais/ieseis	hayáis comido	hubierais comido	(vosotros) comed
3	coman	com-ieran/iesen	hayan comido	hubieran comido	(Vds) coman

VIVIR

	PRESENT	IMPERFECT	PRETERITE	FUTURE	**CONDITIONAL** PRESENT	PAST
1	vivo	vivía	viví	viviré	viviría	habría vivido
2	vives	vivías	viviste	vivirás	vivirías	habrías vivido
3	vive	vivía	vivió	vivirá	viviría	habría vivido
1	vivimos	vivíamos	vivimos	viviremos	viviríamos	habríamos vivido
2	vivís	vivíais	vivisteis	viviréis	viviríais	habríais vivido
3	viven	vivían	vivieron	vivirán	vivirían	habrían vivido

	PERFECT	PLUPERFECT	PAST ANTERIOR	FUTURE PERFECT	**INFINITIVE**	**PARTICIPLE**
1	he vivido	había vivido	hube vivido	habré vivido	PRESENT	PRESENT
2	has vivido	habías vivido	hubiste vivido	habrás vivido	vivir	viviendo
3	ha vivido	había vivido	hubo vivido	habrá vivido		
1	hemos vivido	habíamos vivido	hubimos vivido	habremos vivido	PAST	PAST
2	habéis vivido	habíais vivido	hubisteis vivido	habréis vivido	haber vivido	vivido
3	han vivido	habían vivido	hubieron vivido	habrán vivido		

	SUBJUNCTIVE PRESENT	IMPERFECT	PERFECT	PLUPERFECT	**IMPERATIVE**
1	viva	viv-iera/iese	haya vivido	hubiera vivido	
2	vivas	viv-ieras/ieses	hayas vivido	hubieras vivido	(tú) vive
3	viva	viv-iera/iese	haya vivido	hubiera vivido	(Vd) viva
1	vivamos	viv-iéramos/iésemos	hayamos vivido	hubiéramos vivido	(nosotros) vivamos
2	viváis	viv-ierais/ieseis	hayáis vivido	hubierais vivido	(vosotros) vivid
3	vivan	viv-ieran/iesen	hayan vivido	hubieran vivido	(Vds) vivan

1 HABER

PRESENT	IMPERFECT	FUTURE
1. he	había	habré
2. has	habías	habrás
3. ha/hay	había	habrá
1. hemos	habíamos	habremos
2. habéis	habíais	habréis
3. han	habían	habrán
PRETERITE	**PERFECT**	**PLUPERFECT**
1. hube		
2. hubiste		
3. hubo	ha habido	había habido
1. hubimos		
2. hubisteis		
3. hubieron		
PAST ANTERIOR	**FUTURE PERFECT**	
hubo habido etc	habrá habido etc	
CONDITIONAL		***IMPERATIVE***
PRESENT	PAST	
1. habría		
2. habrías		
3. habría	habría habido	
1. habríamos		
2. habríais		
3. habrían		
SUBJUNCTIVE		
PRESENT	IMPERFECT	PLUPERFECT
1. haya	hub-iera/iese	
2. hayas	hub-ieras/ieses	
3. haya	hub-iera/iese	hubiera habido
1. hayamos	hub-iéramos/iésemos	
2. hayáis	hub-ierais/ieseis	
3. hayan	hub-ieran/iesen	

PERFECT haya habido etc

INFINITIVE	*PARTICIPLE*
PRESENT	PRESENT
haber	habiendo
PAST	PAST
haber habido	habido

2 SER

PRESENT	IMPERFECT	FUTURE
1. soy	era	seré
2. eres	eras	serás
3. es	era	será
1. somos	éramos	seremos
2. sois	erais	seréis
3. son	eran	serán
PRETERITE	**PERFECT**	**PLUPERFECT**
1. fui	he sido	había sido
2. fuiste	has sido	habías sido
3. fue	ha sido	había sido
1. fuimos	hemos sido	habíamos sido
2. fuisteis	habéis sido	habíais sido
3. fueron	han sido	habían sido
PAST ANTERIOR	**FUTURE PERFECT**	
hube sido etc	habré sido etc	
CONDITIONAL		***IMPERATIVE***
PRESENT	PAST	
1. sería	habría sido	
2. serías	habrías sido	(tú) sé
3. sería	habría sido	(Vd) sea
1. seríamos	habríamos sido	(nosotros) seamos
2. seríais	habríais sido	(vosotros) sed
3. serían	habrían sido	(Vds) sean
SUBJUNCTIVE		
PRESENT	IMPERFECT	PLUPERFECT
1. sea	fu-era/ese	hubiera sido
2. seas	fu-eras/eses	hubieras sido
3. sea	fu-era/ese	hubiera sido
1. seamos	fu-éramos/ésemos	hubiéramos sido
2. seáis	fu-erais/eseis	hubierais sido
3. sean	fu-eran/esen	hubieran sido

PERFECT haya sido etc

INFINITIVE	*PARTICIPLE*
PRESENT	PRESENT
ser	siendo
PAST	PAST
haber sido	sido

3 ACERTAR

PRESENT	IMPERFECT	FUTURE
1. acierto	acertaba	acertaré
2. aciertas	acertabas	acertarás
3. acierta	acertaba	acertará
1. acertamos	acertábamos	acertaremos
2. acertáis	acertábais	acertaréis
3. aciertan	acertaban	acertarán
PRETERITE	**PERFECT**	**PLUPERFECT**
1. acerté	he acertado	había acertado
2. acertaste	has acertado	habías acertado
3. acertó	ha acertado	había acertado
1. acertamos	hemos acertado	habíamos acertado
2. acertasteis	habéis acertado	habíais acertado
3. acertaron	han acertado	habían acertado
PAST ANTERIOR	**FUTURE PERFECT**	
hube acertado etc	habré acertado etc	
CONDITIONAL		***IMPERATIVE***
PRESENT	PAST	
1. acertaría	habría acertado	
2. acertarías	habrías acertado	(tú) acierta
3. acertaría	habría acertado	(Vd) acierte
1. acertaríamos	habríamos acertado	(nosotros) acertemos
2. acertaríais	habríais acertado	(vosotros) acertad
3. acertarían	habrían acertado	(Vds) acierten
SUBJUNCTIVE		
PRESENT	IMPERFECT	PLUPERFECT
1. acierte	acert-ara/ase	hubiera acertado
2. aciertes	acert-aras/ases	hubieras acertado
3. acierte	acert-ara/ase	hubiera acertado
1. acertemos	acert-áramos/ásemos	hubiéramos acertado
2. acertéis	acert-árais/áseis	hubierais acertado
3. acierten	acert-aran/asen	hubieran acertado

PERFECT haya acertado etc

INFINITIVE	*PARTICIPLE*
PRESENT	PRESENT
acertar	acertando
PAST	PAST
haber acertado	acertado

4 ACTUAR

PRESENT	IMPERFECT	FUTURE
1. actúo	actuaba	actuaré
2. actúas	actuabas	actuarás
3. actúa	actuaba	actuará
1. actuamos	actuábamos	actuaremos
2. actuáis	actuabais	actuaréis
3. actúan	actuaban	actuarán
PAST HISTORIC	**PERFECT**	**PLUPERFECT**
1. actué	he actuado	había actuado
2. actuaste	has actuado	habías actuado
3. actuó	ha actuado	había actuado
1. actuamos	hemos actuado	habíamos actuado
2. actuasteis	habéis actuado	habíais actuado
3. actuaron	han actuado	habían actuado
PAST ANTERIOR	**FUTURE PERFECT**	
hube actuado etc	habré actuado etc	
CONDITIONAL		***IMPERATIVE***
PRESENT	PAST	
1. actuaría	habría actuado	
2. actuarías	habrías actuado	(tú) actúa
3. actuaría	habría actuado	(Vd) actúe
1. actuaríamos	habríamos actuado	(nosotros) actuemos
2. actuaríais	habríais actuado	(vosotros) actuad
3. actuarían	habrían actuado	(Vds) actúen
SUBJUNCTIVE		
PRESENT	IMPERFECT	PLUPERFECT
1. actúe	actu-ara/ase	hubiera actuado
2. actúes	actu-aras/ases	hubieras actuado
3. actúe	actu-ara/ase	hubiera actuado
1. actuemos	actu-áramos/ásemos	hubiéramos actuado
2. actuéis	actu-arais/aseis	hubierais actuado
3. actúen	actu-aran/asen	hubieran actuado

PERFECT haya actuado etc

INFINITIVE	*PARTICIPLE*
PRESENT	PRESENT
actuar	actuando
PAST	PAST
haber actuado	actuado

5 ADQUIRIR

PRESENT	IMPERFECT	FUTURE
1. adquiero	adquiría	adquiriré
2. adquieres	adquirías	adquirirás
3. adquiere	adquiría	adquirirá
1. adquirimos	adquiríamos	adquiriremos
2. adquirís	adquiríais	adquiriréis
3. adquieren	adquirían	adquirirán
PRETERITE	PERFECT	PLUPERFECT
1. adquirí	he adquirido	había adquirido
2. adquiriste	has adquirido	habías adquirido
3. adquirió	ha adquirido	había adquirido
1. adquirimos	hemos adquirido	habíamos adquirido
2. adquiristeis	habéis adquirido	habíais adquirido
3. adquirieron	han adquirido	habían adquirido
PAST ANTERIOR	FUTURE PERFECT	
hube adquirido etc	habré adquirido etc	
CONDITIONAL		*IMPERATIVE*
PRESENT	PAST	
1. adquiriría	habría adquirido	
2. adquirirías	habrías adquirido	(tú) adquiere
3. adquiriría	habría adquirido	(Vd) adquiera
1. adquiriríamos	habríamos adquirido	(nosotros) adquiramos
2. adquiriríais	habríais adquirido	(vosotros) adquirid
3. adquirirían	habrían adquirido	(Vds) adquieran
SUBJUNCTIVE		
PRESENT	IMPERFECT	PLUPERFECT
1. adquiera	adquir-iera/iese	hubiera adquirido
2. adquieras	adquir-ieras/ieses	hubieras adquirido
3. adquiera	adquir-iera/iese	hubiera adquirido
1. adquiramos	adquir-iéramos/iésemos	hubiéramos adquirido
2. adquiráis	adquir-ierais/ieseis	hubierais adquirido
3. adquieran	adquir-ieran/iesen	hubieran adquirido
PERFECT	haya adquirido etc	
INFINITIVE	*PARTICIPLE*	
PRESENT	PRESENT	
adquirir	adquiriendo	
PAST	PAST	
haber adquirido	adquirido	

6 AGORAR

PRESENT	IMPERFECT	FUTURE
1. agüero	agoraba	agoraré
2. agüeras	agorabas	agorarás
3. agüera	agoraba	agorará
1. agoramos	agorábamos	agoraremos
2. agoráis	agorabais	agoraréis
3. agüeran	agoraban	agorarán
PRETERITE	PERFECT	PLUPERFECT
1. agoré	he agorado	había agorado
2. agoraste	has agorado	habías agorado
3. agoró	ha agorado	había agorado
1. agoramos	hemos agorado	habíamos agorado
2. agorasteis	habéis agorado	habíais agorado
3. agoraron	han agorado	habían agorado
PAST ANTERIOR	FUTURE PERFECT	
hube agorado etc	habré agorado etc	
CONDITIONAL		*IMPERATIVE*
PRESENT	PAST	
1. agoraría	habría agorado	
2. agorarías	habrías agorado	(tú) agüera
3. agoraría	habría agorado	(Vd) agüere
1. agoraríamos	habríamos agorado	(nosotros) agoremos
2. agoraríais	habríais agorado	(vosotros) agorad
3. agorarían	habrían agorado	(Vds) agüeren
SUBJUNCTIVE		
PRESENT	IMPERFECT	PLUPERFECT
1. agüere	agor-ara/ase	hubiera agorado
2. agüeres	agor-aras/ases	hubieras agorado
3. agüere	agor-ara/ase	hubiera agorado
1. agoremos	agor-áramos/ásemos	hubiéramos agorado
2. agoréis	agor-arais/aseis	hubierais agorado
3. agüeren	agor-aran/asen	hubieran agorado
PERFECT	haya agorado etc	
INFINITIVE	*PARTICIPLE*	
PRESENT	PRESENT	
agorar	agorando	
PAST	PAST	
haber agorado	agorado	

7 ANDAR

PRESENT	IMPERFECT	FUTURE
1. ando	andaba	andaré
2. andas	andabas	andarás
3. anda	andaba	andará
1. andamos	andábamos	andaremos
2. andáis	andabais	andaréis
3. andan	andaban	andarán
PRETERITE	PERFECT	PLUPERFECT
1. anduve	he andado	había andado
2. anduviste	has andado	habías andado
3. anduvo	ha andado	había andado
1. anduvimos	hemos andado	habíamos andado
2. anduvisteis	habéis andado	habíais andado
3. anduvieron	han andado	habían andado
PAST ANTERIOR	FUTURE PERFECT	
hube andado etc	habré andado etc	
CONDITIONAL		*IMPERATIVE*
PRESENT	PAST	
1. andaría	habría andado	
2. andarías	habrías andado	(tú) anda
3. andaría	habría andado	(Vd) ande
1. andaríamos	habríamos andado	(nosotros) andemos
2. andaríais	habríais andado	(vosotros) andad
3. andarían	habrían andado	(Vds) anden
SUBJUNCTIVE		
PRESENT	IMPERFECT	PLUPERFECT
1. ande	anduv-iera/iese	hubiera andado
2. andes	anduv-ieras/ieses	hubieras andado
3. ande	anduv-iera/iese	hubiera andado
1. andemos	anduv-iéramos/iésemos	hubiéramos andado
2. andéis	anduv-ierais/ieseis	hubierais andado
3. anden	anduv-ieran/iesen	hubieran andado
PERFECT	haya andado etc	
INFINITIVE	*PARTICIPLE*	
PRESENT	PRESENT	
andar	andando	
PAST	PAST	
haber andado	andado	

8 ARGÜIR

PRESENT	IMPERFECT	FUTURE
1. arguyo	argüía	argüiré
2. arguyes	argüías	argüirás
3. arguye	argüía	argüirá
1. argüimos	argüíamos	argüiremos
2. argüís	argüíais	argüiréis
3. arguyen	argüían	argüirán
PRETERITE	PERFECT	PLUPERFECT
1. argüí	he argüido	había argüido
2. argüiste	has argüido	habías argüido
3. arguyó	ha argüido	había argüido
1. argüimos	hemos argüido	habíamos argüido
2. argüisteis	habéis argüido	habíais argüido
3. arguyeron	han argüido	habían argüido
PAST ANTERIOR	FUTURE PERFECT	
hube argüido etc	habré argüido etc	
CONDITIONAL		*IMPERATIVE*
PRESENT	PAST	
1. argüiría	habría argüido	
2. argüirías	habrías argüido	(tú) arguye
3. argüiría	habría argüido	(Vd) arguya
1. argüiríamos	habríamos argüido	(nosotros) arguyamos
2. argüiríais	habríais argüido	(vosotros) argüid
3. argüirían	habrían argüido	(Vds) arguyan
SUBJUNCTIVE		
PRESENT	IMPERFECT	PLUPERFECT
1. arguya	argu-yera/yese	hubiera argüido
2. arguyas	argu-yeras/yeses	hubieras argüido
3. arguya	argu-yera/yese	hubiera argüido
1. arguyamos	argu-yéramos/yésemos	hubiéramos argüido
2. arguyáis	argu-yerais/yeseis	hubierais argüido
3. arguyan	argu-yeran/yesen	hubieran argüido
PERFECT	haya argüido etc	
INFINITIVE	*PARTICIPLE*	
PRESENT	PRESENT	
argüir	arguyendo	
PAST	PAST	
haber argüido	argüido	

9 ASIR

PRESENT	IMPERFECT	FUTURE
1. asgo	asía	asiré
2. ases	asías	asirás
3. ase	asía	asirá
1. asimos	asíamos	asiremos
2. asís	asíais	asiréis
3. asen	asían	asirán
PRETERITE	**PERFECT**	**PLUPERFECT**
1. así	he asido	había asido
2. asiste	has asido	habías asido
3. asió	ha asido	había asido
1. asimos	hemos asido	habíamos asido
2. asisteis	habéis asido	habíais asido
3. asieron	han asido	habían asido
PAST ANTERIOR	**FUTURE PERFECT**	
hube asido etc	habré asido etc	

CONDITIONAL PRESENT	PAST	*IMPERATIVE*
1. asiría	habría asido	
2. asirías	habrías asido	(tú) ase
3. asiría	habría asido	(Vd) asga
1. asiríamos	habríamos asido	(nosotros) asgamos
2. asiríais	habríais asido	(vosotros) asid
3. asirían	habrían asido	(Vds) asgan

SUBJUNCTIVE PRESENT	IMPERFECT	PLUPERFECT
1. asga	as-iera/iese	hubiera asido
2. asgas	as-ieras/ieses	hubieras asido
3. asga	as-iera/iese	hubiera asido
1. asgamos	as-iéramos/iésemos	hubiéramos asido
2. asgáis	as-ierais/ieseis	hubierais asido
3. asgan	as-ieran/iesen	hubieran asido

PERFECT haya asido etc

INFINITIVE	*PARTICIPLE*
PRESENT	PRESENT
asir	asiendo
PAST	PAST
haber asido	asido

10 AVERGONZAR

PRESENT	IMPERFECT	FUTURE
1. avergüenzo	avergonzaba	avergonzaré
2. avergüenzas	avergonzabas	avergonzarás
3. avergüenza	avergonzaba	avergonzará
1. avergonzamos	avergonzábamos	avergonzaremos
2. avergonzáis	avergonzabais	avergonzaréis
3. avergüenzan	avergonzaban	avergonzarán
PRETERITE	**PERFECT**	**PLUPERFECT**
1. avergoncé	he avergonzado	había avergonzado
2. avergonzaste	has avergonzado	habías avergonzado
3. avergonzó	ha avergonzado	había avergonzado
1. avergonzamos	hemos avergonzado	habíamos avergonzado
2. avergonzasteis	habéis avergonzado	habíais avergonzado
3. avergonzaron	han avergonzado	habían avergonzado
PAST ANTERIOR	**FUTURE PERFECT**	
hube avergonzado etc	habré avergonzado etc	

CONDITIONAL PRESENT	PAST	*IMPERATIVE*
1. avergonzaría	habría avergonzado	
2. avergonzarías	habrías avergonzado	(tú) avergüénzate
3. avergonzaría	habría avergonzado	(Vd) avergüéncese
1. avergonzaríamos	habríamos avergonzado	(nosotros) avergoncémonos
2. avergonzaríais	habríais avergonzado	(vosotros) avergonzaos
3. avergonzarían	habrían avergonzado	(Vds) avergüéncense

SUBJUNCTIVE PRESENT	IMPERFECT	PLUPERFECT
1. avergüence	avergonz-ara/ase	hubiera avergonzado
2. avergüences	avergonz-aras/ases	hubieras avergonzado
3. avergüence	avergonz-ara/ase	hubiera avergonzado
1. avergoncemos	avergonz-áramos/ásemos	hubiéramos avergonzado
2. avergoncéis	avergonz-arais/aseis	hubierais avergonzado
3. avergüencen	avergonz-aran/asen	hubieran avergonzado

PERFECT haya avergonzado etc

INFINITIVE	*PARTICIPLE*
PRESENT	PRESENT
avergonzarse	avergonzándose
PAST	PAST
haberse avergonzado	avergonzado

11 AVERIGUAR

PRESENT	IMPERFECT	FUTURE
1. averiguo	averiguaba	averiguaré
2. averiguas	averiguabas	averiguarás
3. averigua	averiguaba	averiguará
1. averiguamos	averiguábamos	averiguaremos
2. averiguáis	averiguabais	averiguaréis
3. averiguan	averiguaban	averiguarán
PRETERITE	**PERFECT**	**PLUPERFECT**
1. averigüé	he averiguado	había averiguado
2. averiguaste	has averiguado	habías averiguado
3. averiguó	ha averiguado	había averiguado
1. averiguamos	hemos averiguado	habíamos averiguado
2. averiguasteis	habéis averiguado	habíais averiguado
3. averiguaron	han averiguado	habían averiguado
PAST ANTERIOR	**FUTURE PERFECT**	
hube averiguado etc	habré averiguado etc	

CONDITIONAL PRESENT	PAST	*IMPERATIVE*
1. averiguaría	habría averiguado	
2. averiguarías	habrías averiguado	(tú) averigua
3. averiguaría	habría averiguado	(Vd) averigüe
1. averiguaríamos	habríamos averiguado	(nosotros) averigüemos
2. averiguaríais	habríais averiguado	(vosotros) averiguad
3. averiguarían	habrían averiguado	(Vds) averigüen

SUBJUNCTIVE PRESENT	IMPERFECT	PLUPERFECT
1. averigüe	averigu-ara/ase	hubiera averiguado
2. averigües	averigu-aras/ases	hubieras averiguado
3. averigüe	averigu-ara/ase	hubiera averiguado
1. averigüemos	averigu-áramos/ásemos	hubiéramos averiguado
2. averigüéis	averigu-arais/aseis	hubierais averiguado
3. averigüen	averigu-aran/asen	hubieran averiguado

PERFECT haya averiguado etc

INFINITIVE	*PARTICIPLE*
PRESENT	PRESENT
averiguar	averiguando
PAST	PAST
haber averiguado	averiguado

12 CABER

PRESENT	IMPERFECT	FUTURE
1. quepo	cabía	cabré
2. cabes	cabías	cabrás
3. cabe	cabía	cabrá
1. cabemos	cabíamos	cabremos
2. cabéis	cabíais	cabréis
3. caben	cabían	cabrán
PRETERITE	**PERFECT**	**PLUPERFECT**
1. cupe	he cabido	había cabido
2. cupiste	has cabido	habías cabido
3. cupo	ha cabido	había cabido
1. cupimos	hemos cabido	habíamos cabido
2. cupisteis	habéis cabido	habíais cabido
3. cupieron	han cabido	habían cabido
PAST ANTERIOR	**FUTURE PERFECT**	
hube cabido etc	habré cabido etc	

CONDITIONAL PRESENT	PAST	*IMPERATIVE*
1. cabría	habría cabido	
2. cabrías	habrías cabido	(tú) cabe
3. cabría	habría cabido	(Vd) quepa
1. cabríamos	habríamos cabido	(nosotros) quepamos
2. cabríais	habríais cabido	(vosotros) cabed
3. cabrían	habrían cabido	(Vds) quepan

SUBJUNCTIVE PRESENT	IMPERFECT	PLUPERFECT
1. quepa	cup-iera/iese	hubiera cabido
2. quepas	cup-ieras/ieses	hubieras cabido
3. quepa	cup-iera/iese	hubiera cabido
1. quepamos	cup-iéramos/iésemos	hubiéramos cabido
2. quepáis	cup-ierais/ieseis	hubierais cabido
3. quepan	cup-ieran/iesen	hubieran cabido

PERFECT haya cabido etc

INFINITIVE	*PARTICIPLE*
PRESENT	PRESENT
caber	cabiendo
PAST	PAST
haber cabido	cabido

13 CAER

PRESENT	IMPERFECT	FUTURE
1. caigo	caía	caeré
2. caes	caías	caerás
3. cae	caía	caerá
1. caemos	caíamos	caeremos
2. caéis	caíais	caeréis
3. caen	caían	caerán
PRETERITE	PERFECT	PLUPERFECT
1. caí	he caído	había caído
2. caíste	has caído	habías caído
3. cayó	ha caído	había caído
1. caímos	hemos caído	habíamos caído
2. caísteis	habéis caído	habíais caído
3. cayeron	han caído	habían caído
PAST ANTERIOR	FUTURE PERFECT	
hube caído etc	habré caído etc	
CONDITIONAL		*IMPERATIVE*
PRESENT	PAST	
1. caería	habría caído	
2. caerías	habrías caído	(tú) cae
3. caería	habría caído	(Vd) caiga
1. caeríamos	habríamos caído	(nosotros) caigamos
2. caeríais	habríais caído	(vosotros) caed
3. caerían	habrían caído	(Vds) caigan
SUBJUNCTIVE		
PRESENT	IMPERFECT	PLUPERFECT
1. caiga	ca-yera/yese	hubiera caído
2. caigas	ca-yeras/yeses	hubieras caído
3. caiga	ca-yera/yese	hubiera caído
1. caigamos	ca-yéramos/yésemos	hubiéramos caído
2. caigáis	ca-yerais/yeseis	hubierais caído
3. caigan	ca-yeran/yesen	hubieran caído
PERFECT	haya caído etc	
INFINITIVE	*PARTICIPLE*	
PRESENT	PRESENT	
caer	cayendo	
PAST	PAST	
haber caído	caído	

14 CAZAR

PRESENT	IMPERFECT	FUTURE
1. cazo	cazaba	cazaré
2. cazas	cazabas	cazarás
3. caza	cazaba	cazará
1. cazamos	cazábamos	cazaremos
2. cazáis	cazabais	cazaréis
3. cazan	cazaban	cazarán
PRETERITE	PERFECT	PLUPERFECT
1. cacé	he cazado	había cazado
2. cazaste	has cazado	habías cazado
3. cazó	ha cazado	había cazado
1. cazamos	hemos cazado	habíamos cazado
2. cazasteis	habéis cazado	habíais cazado
3. cazaron	han cazado	habían cazado
PAST ANTERIOR	FUTURE PERFECT	
hube cazado etc	habré cazado etc	
CONDITIONAL		*IMPERATIVE*
PRESENT	PAST	
1. cazaría	habría cazado	
2. cazarías	habrías cazado	(tú) caza
3. cazaría	habría cazado	(Vd) cace
1. cazaríamos	habríamos cazado	(nosotros) cacemos
2. cazaríais	habríais cazado	(vosotros) cazad
3. cazarían	habrían cazado	(Vds) cacen
SUBJUNCTIVE		
PRESENT	IMPERFECT	PLUPERFECT
1. cace	caz-ara/ase	hubiera cazado
2. caces	caz-aras/ases	hubieras cazado
3. cace	caz-ara/ase	hubiera cazado
1. cacemos	caz-áramos/ásemos	hubiéramos cazado
2. cacéis	caz-arais/aseis	hubierais cazado
3. cacen	caz-aran/asen	hubieran cazado
PERFECT	haya cazado etc	
INFINITIVE	*PARTICIPLE*	
PRESENT	PRESENT	
cazar	cazando	
PAST	PAST	
haber cazado	cazado	

15 COCER

PRESENT	IMPERFECT	FUTURE
1. cuezo	cocía	coceré
2. cueces	cocías	cocerás
3. cuece	cocía	cocerá
1. cocemos	cocíamos	coceremos
2. cocéis	cocíais	coceréis
3. cuecen	cocían	cocerán
PRETERITE	PERFECT	PLUPERFECT
1. cocí	he cocido	había cocido
2. cociste	has cocido	habías cocido
3. coció	ha cocido	había cocido
1. cocimos	hemos cocido	habíamos cocido
2. cocisteis	habéis cocido	habíais cocido
3. cocieron	han cocido	habían cocido
PAST ANTERIOR	FUTURE PERFECT	
hube cocido etc	habré cocido etc	
CONDITIONAL		*IMPERATIVE*
PRESENT	PAST	
1. cocería	habría cocido	
2. cocerías	habrías cocido	(tú) cuece
3. cocería	habría cocido	(Vd) cueza
1. coceríamos	habríamos cocido	(nosotros) cozamos
2. coceríais	habríais cocido	(vosotros) coced
3. cocerían	habrían cocido	(Vds) cuezan
SUBJUNCTIVE		
PRESENT	IMPERFECT	PLUPERFECT
1. cueza	coc-iera/iese	hubiera cocido
2. cuezas	coc-ieras/ieses	hubieras cocido
3. cueza	coc-iera/iese	hubiera cocido
1. cozamos	coc-iéramos/iésemos	hubiéramos cocido
2. cozáis	coc-ierais/ieseis	hubierais cocido
3. cuezan	coc-ieran/iesen	hubieran cocido
PERFECT	haya cocido etc	
INFINITIVE	*PARTICIPLE*	
PRESENT	PRESENT	
cocer	cociendo	
PAST	PAST	
haber cocido	cocido	

16 COLGAR

PRESENT	IMPERFECT	FUTURE
1. cuelgo	colgaba	colgaré
2. cuelgas	colgabas	colgarás
3. cuelga	colgaba	colgará
1. colgamos	colgábamos	colgaremos
2. colgáis	colgabais	colgaréis
3. cuelgan	colgaban	colgarán
PRETERITE	PERFECT	PLUPERFECT
1. colgué	he colgado	había colgado
2. colgaste	has colgado	habías colgado
3. colgó	ha colgado	había colgado
1. colgamos	hemos colgado	habíamos colgado
2. colgasteis	habéis colgado	habíais colgado
3. colgaron	han colgado	habían colgado
PAST ANTERIOR	FUTURE PERFECT	
hube colgado etc	habré colgado etc	
CONDITIONAL		*IMPERATIVE*
PRESENT	PAST	
1. colgaría	habría colgado	
2. colgarías	habrías colgado	(tú) cuelga
3. colgaría	habría colgado	(Vd) cuelgue
1. colgaríamos	habríamos colgado	(nosotros) colguemos
2. colgaríais	habríais colgado	(vosotros) colgad
3. colgarían	habrían colgado	(Vds) cuelguen
SUBJUNCTIVE		
PRESENT	IMPERFECT	PLUPERFECT
1. cuelgue	colg-ara/ase	hubiera colgado
2. cuelgues	colg-aras/ases	hubieras colgado
3. cuelgue	colg-ara/ase	hubiera colgado
1. colguemos	colg-áramos/ásemos	hubiéramos colgado
2. colguéis	colg-arais/aseis	hubierais colgado
3. cuelguen	colg-aran/asen	hubieran colgado
PERFECT	haya colgado etc	
INFINITIVE	*PARTICIPLE*	
PRESENT	PRESENT	
colgar	colgando	
PAST	PAST	
haber colgado	colgado	

17 COMENZAR

PRESENT	IMPERFECT	FUTURE
1. comienzo	comenzaba	comenzaré
2. comienzas	comenzabas	comenzarás
3. comienza	comenzaba	comenzará
1. comenzamos	comenzábamos	comenzaremos
2. comenzáis	comenzabais	comenzaréis
3. comienzan	comenzaban	comenzarán
PRETERITE	PERFECT	PLUPERFECT
1. comencé	he comenzado	había comenzado
2. comenzaste	has comenzado	habías comenzado
3. comenzó	ha comenzado	había comenzado
1. comenzamos	hemos comenzado	habíamos comenzado
2. comenzasteis	habéis comenzado	habíais comenzado
3. comenzaron	han comenzado	habían comenzado
PAST ANTERIOR	FUTURE PERFECT	
hube comenzado etc	habré comenzado etc	
CONDITIONAL		*IMPERATIVE*
PRESENT	PAST	
1. comenzaría	habría comenzado	
2. comenzarías	habrías comenzado	(tú) comienza
3. comenzaría	habría comenzado	(Vd) comience
1. comenzaríamos	habríamos comenzado	(nosotros) comencemos
2. comenzaríais	habríais comenzado	(vosotros) comenzad
3. comenzarían	habrían comenzado	(Vds) comiencen
SUBJUNCTIVE		
PRESENT	IMPERFECT	PLUPERFECT
1. comience	comenz-ara/ase	hubiera comenzado
2. comiences	comenz-aras/ases	hubieras comenzado
3. comience	comenz-ara/ase	hubiera comenzado
1. comencemos	comenz-áramos/ásemos	hubiéramos comenzado
2. comencéis	comenz-arais/aseis	hubierais comenzado
3. comiencen	comenz-aran/asen	hubieran comenzado
PERFECT	haya comenzado etc	
INFINITIVE	*PARTICIPLE*	
PRESENT	PRESENT	
comenzar	comenzando	
PAST	PAST	
haber comenzado	comenzado	

18 CONDUCIR

PRESENT	IMPERFECT	FUTURE
1. conduzco	conducía	conduciré
2. conduces	conducías	conducirás
3. conduce	conducía	conducirá
1. conducimos	conducíamos	conduciremos
2. conducís	conducíais	conduciréis
3. conducen	conducían	conducirán
PRETERITE	PERFECT	PLUPERFECT
1. conduje	he conducido	había conducido
2. condujiste	has conducido	habías conducido
3. condujo	ha conducido	había conducido
1. condujimos	hemos conducido	habíamos conducido
2. condujisteis	habéis conducido	habíais conducido
3. condujeron	han conducido	habían conducido
PAST ANTERIOR	FUTURE PERFECT	
hube conducido etc	habré conducido etc	
CONDITIONAL		*IMPERATIVE*
PRESENT	PAST	
1. conduciría	habría conducido	
2. conducirías	habrías conducido	(tú) conduce
3. conduciría	habría conducido	(Vd) conduzca
1. conduciríamos	habríamos conducido	(nosotros) conduzcamos
2. conduciríais	habríais conducido	(vosotros) conducid
3. conducirían	habrían conducido	(Vds) conduzcan
SUBJUNCTIVE		
PRESENT	IMPERFECT	PLUPERFECT
1. conduzca	conduj-era/ese	hubiera conducido
2. conduzcas	conduj-eras/eses	hubieras conducido
3. conduzca	conduj-era/ese	hubiera conducido
1. conduzcamos	conduj-éramos/ésemos	hubiéramos conducido
2. conduzcáis	conduj-erais/eseis	hubierais conducido
3. conduzcan	conduj-eran/esen	hubieran conducido
PERFECT	haya conducido etc	
INFINITIVE	*PARTICIPLE*	
PRESENT	PRESENT	
conducir	conduciendo	
PAST	PAST	
haber conducido	conducido	

19 CONOCER

PRESENT	IMPERFECT	FUTURE
1. conozco	conocía	conoceré
2. conoces	conocías	conocerás
3. conoce	conocía	conocerá
1. conocemos	conocíamos	conoceremos
2. conocéis	conocíais	conoceréis
3. conocen	conocían	conocerán
PRETERITE	PERFECT	PLUPERFECT
1. conocí	he conocido	había conocido
2. conociste	has conocido	habías conocido
3. conoció	ha conocido	había conocido
1. conocimos	hemos conocido	habíamos conocido
2. conocisteis	habéis conocido	habíais conocido
3. conocieron	han conocido	habían conocido
PAST ANTERIOR	FUTURE PERFECT	
hube conocido etc	habré conocido etc	
CONDITIONAL		*IMPERATIVE*
PRESENT	PAST	
1. conocería	habría conocido	
2. conocerías	habrías conocido	(tú) conoce
3. conocería	habría conocido	(Vd) conozca
1. conoceríamos	habríamos conocido	(nosotros) conozcamos
2. conoceríais	habríais conocido	(vosotros) conoced
3. conocerían	habrían conocido	(Vds) conozcan
SUBJUNCTIVE		
PRESENT	IMPERFECT	PLUPERFECT
1. conozca	conoc-iera/iese	hubiera conocido
2. conozcas	conoc-ieras/ieses	hubieras conocido
3. conozca	conoc-iera/iese	hubiera conocido
1. conozcamos	conoc-iéramos/iésemos	hubiéramos conocido
2. conozcáis	conoc-ierais/ieseis	hubierais conocido
3. conozcan	conoc-ieran/iesen	hubieran conocido
PERFECT	haya conocido etc	
INFINITIVE	*PARTICIPLE*	
PRESENT	PRESENT	
conocer	conociendo	
PAST	PAST	
haber conocido	conocido	

20 DAR

PRESENT	IMPERFECT	FUTURE
1. doy	daba	daré
2. das	dabas	darás
3. da	daba	dará
1. damos	dábamos	daremos
2. dais	dabais	daréis
3. dan	daban	darán
PRETERITE	PERFECT	PLUPERFECT
1. di	he dado	había dado
2. diste	has dado	habías dado
3. dio	ha dado	había dado
1. dimos	hemos dado	habíamos dado
2. disteis	habéis dado	habíais dado
3. dieron	han dado	habían dado
PAST ANTERIOR	FUTURE PERFECT	
hube dado etc	habré dado etc	
CONDITIONAL		*IMPERATIVE*
PRESENT	PAST	
1. daría	habría dado	
2. darías	habrías dado	(tú) da
3. daría	habría dado	(Vd) dé
1. daríamos	habríamos dado	(nosotros) demos
2. daríais	habríais dado	(vosotros) dad
3. darían	habrían dado	(Vds) den
SUBJUNCTIVE		
PRESENT	IMPERFECT	PLUPERFECT
1. dé	di-era/ese	hubiera dado
2. des	di-eras/eses	hubieras dado
3. dé	di-era/ese	hubiera dado
1. demos	di-éramos/ésemos	hubiéramos dado
2. deis	di-erais/eseis	hubierais dado
3. den	di-eran/esen	hubieran dado
PERFECT	haya dado etc	
INFINITIVE	*PARTICIPLE*	
PRESENT	PRESENT	
dar	dando	
PAST	PAST	
haber dado	dado	

21 DECIR

PRESENT	IMPERFECT	FUTURE
1. digo	decía	diré
2. dices	decías	dirás
3. dice	decía	dirá
1. decimos	decíamos	diremos
2. decís	decíais	diréis
3. dicen	decían	dirán
PRETERITE	**PERFECT**	**PLUPERFECT**
1. dije	he dicho	había dicho
2. dijiste	has dicho	habías dicho
3. dijo	ha dicho	había dicho
1. dijimos	hemos dicho	habíamos dicho
2. dijisteis	habéis dicho	habíais dicho
3. dijeron	han dicho	habían dicho
PAST ANTERIOR	**FUTURE PERFECT**	
hube dicho etc	habré dicho etc	

CONDITIONAL		*IMPERATIVE*
PRESENT	PAST	
1. diría	habría dicho	
2. dirías	habrías dicho	(tú) di
3. diría	habría dicho	(Vd) diga
1. diríamos	habríamos dicho	(nosotros) digamos
2. diríais	habríais dicho	(vosotros) decid
3. dirían	habrían dicho	(Vds) digan

SUBJUNCTIVE		
PRESENT	IMPERFECT	PLUPERFECT
1. diga	dij-era/ese	hubiera dicho
2. digas	dij-eras/eses	hubieras dicho
3. diga	dij-era/ese	hubiera dicho
1. digamos	dij-éramos/ésemos	hubiéramos dicho
2. digáis	dij-erais/eseis	hubierais dicho
3. digan	dij-eran/esen	hubieran dicho

PERFECT haya dicho etc

INFINITIVE	*PARTICIPLE*
PRESENT	PRESENT
decir	diciendo
PAST	PAST
haber dicho	dicho

22 DELINQUIR

PRESENT	IMPERFECT	FUTURE
1. delinco	delinquía	delinquiré
2. delinques	delinquías	delinquirás
3. delinque	delinquía	delinquirá
1. delinquimos	delinquíamos	delinquiremos
2. delinquís	delinquíais	delinquiréis
3. delinquen	delinquían	delinquirán
PRETERITE	**PERFECT**	**PLUPERFECT**
1. delinquí	he delinquido	había delinquido
2. delinquiste	has delinquido	habías delinquido
3. delinquió	ha delinquido	había delinquido
1. delinquimos	hemos delinquido	habíamos delinquido
2. delinquisteis	habéis delinquido	habíais delinquido
3. delinquieron	han delinquido	habían delinquido
PAST ANTERIOR	**FUTURE PERFECT**	
hube delinquido etc	habré delinquido etc	

CONDITIONAL		*IMPERATIVE*
PRESENT	PAST	
1. delinquiría	habría delinquido	
2. delinquirías	habrías delinquido	(tú) delinque
3. delinquiría	habría delinquido	(Vd) delinca
1. delinquiríamos	habríamos delinquido	(nosotros) delincamos
2. delinquiríais	habríais delinquido	(vosotros) delinquid
3. delinquirían	habrían delinquido	(Vds) delincan

SUBJUNCTIVE		
PRESENT	IMPERFECT	PLUPERFECT
1. delinca	delinqu-iera/iese	hubiera delinquido
2. delincas	delinqu-ieras/ieses	hubieras delinquido
3. delinca	delinqu-iera/iese	hubiera delinquido
1. delincamos	delinqu-iéramos/iésemos	hubiéramos delinquido
2. delincáis	delinqu-ierais/ieseis	hubierais delinquido
3. delincan	delinqu-ieran/iesen	hubieran delinquido

PERFECT haya delinquido etc

INFINITIVE	*PARTICIPLE*
PRESENT	PRESENT
delinquir	delinquiendo
PAST	PAST
haber delinquido	delinquido

23 DESOSAR

PRESENT	IMPERFECT	FUTURE
1. deshueso	desosaba	desosaré
2. deshuesas	desosabas	desosarás
3. deshuesa	desosaba	desosará
1. desosamos	desosábamos	desosaremos
2. desosáis	desosabais	desosaréis
3. deshuesan	desosaban	desosarán
PAST HISTORIC	**PERFECT**	**PLUPERFECT**
1. desosé	he desosado	había desosado
2. desosaste	has desosado	habías desosado
3. desosó	ha desosado	había desosado
1. desosamos	hemos desosado	habíamos desosado
2. desosasteis	habéis desosado	habíais desosado
3. desosaron	han desosado	habían desosado
PAST ANTERIOR	**FUTURE PERFECT**	
hube desosado etc	habré desosado etc	

CONDITIONAL		*IMPERATIVE*
PRESENT	PAST	
1. desosaría	habría desosado	
2. desosarías	habrías desosado	(tú) deshuesa
3. desosaría	habría desosado	(Vd) deshuese
1. desosaríamos	habríamos desosado	(nosotros) desosemos
2. desosaríais	habríais desosado	(vosotros) desosad
3. desosarían	habrían desosado	(Vds) deshuesen

SUBJUNCTIVE		
PRESENT	IMPERFECT	PLUPERFECT
1. deshuese	desos-ara/ase	hubiera desosado
2. deshueses	desos-aras/ases	hubieras desosado
3. deshuese	desos-ara/ase	hubiera desosado
1. desosemos	desos-áramos/ásemos	hubiéramos desosado
2. desoséis	desos-arais/aseis	hubierais desosado
3. deshuesen	desos-aran/asen	hubieran desosado

PERFECT haya desosado etc

INFINITIVE	*PARTICIPLE*
PRESENT	PRESENT
desosar	desosando
PAST	PAST
haber desosado	desosado

24 DIRIGIR

PRESENT	IMPERFECT	FUTURE
1. dirijo	dirigía	dirigiré
2. diriges	dirigías	dirigirás
3. dirige	dirigía	dirigirá
1. dirigimos	dirigíamos	dirigiremos
2. dirigís	dirigíais	dirigiréis
3. dirigen	dirigían	dirigirán
PRETERITE	**PERFECT**	**PLUPERFECT**
1. dirigí	he dirigido	había dirigido
2. dirigiste	has dirigido	habías dirigido
3. dirigió	ha dirigido	había dirigido
1. dirigimos	hemos dirigido	habíamos dirigido
2. dirigisteis	habéis dirigido	habíais dirigido
3. dirigieron	han dirigido	habían dirigido
PAST ANTERIOR	**FUTURE PERFECT**	
hube dirigido etc	habré dirigido etc	

CONDITIONAL		*IMPERATIVE*
PRESENT	PAST	
1. dirigiría	habría dirigido	
2. dirigirías	habrías dirigido	(tú) dirige
3. dirigiría	habría dirigido	(Vd) dirija
1. dirigiríamos	habríamos dirigido	(nosotros) dirijamos
2. dirigiríais	habríais dirigido	(vosotros) dirigid
3. dirigirían	habrían dirigido	(Vds) dirijan

SUBJUNCTIVE		
PRESENT	IMPERFECT	PLUPERFECT
1. dirija	dirig-iera/iese	hubiera dirigido
2. dirijas	dirig-ieras/ieses	hubieras dirigido
3. dirija	dirig-iera/iese	hubiera dirigido
1. dirijamos	dirig-iéramos/iésemos	hubiéramos dirigido
2. dirijáis	dirig-ierais/ieseis	hubierais dirigido
3. dirijan	dirig-ieran/iesen	hubieran dirigido

PERFECT haya dirigido etc

INFINITIVE	*PARTICIPLE*
PRESENT	PRESENT
dirigir	dirigiendo
PAST	PAST
haber dirigido	dirigido

25 DISCERNIR

PRESENT	IMPERFECT	FUTURE
1. discierno	discernía	discerniré
2. disciernes	discernías	discernirás
3. discierne	discernía	discernirá
1. discernimos	discerníamos	discerniremos
2. discernís	discerníais	discerniréis
3. disciernen	discernían	discernirán
PRETERITE	PERFECT	PLUPERFECT
1. discerní	he discernido	había discernido
2. discerniste	has discernido	habías discernido
3. discernió	ha discernido	había discernido
1. discernimos	hemos discernido	habíamos discernido
2. discernisteis	habéis discernido	habíais discernido
3. discernieron	han discernido	habían discernido
PAST ANTERIOR	FUTURE PERFECT	
hube discernido etc	habré discernido etc	
CONDITIONAL		*IMPERATIVE*
PRESENT	PAST	
1. discerniría	habría discernido	
2. discernirías	habrías discernido	(tú) discierne
3. discerniría	habría discernido	(Vd) discierna
1. discerniríamos	habríamos discernido	(nosotros) discirnamos
2. discerniríais	habríais discernido	(vosotros) discernid
3. discernirían	habrían discernido	(Vds) disciernan
SUBJUNCTIVE		
PRESENT	IMPERFECT	PLUPERFECT
1. discierna	discirn-iera/iese	hubiera discernido
2. disciernas	discirn-ieras/ieses	hubieras discernido
3. discierna	discirn-iera/iese	hubiera discernido
1. discirnamos	discirn-iéramos/iésemos	hubiéramos discernido
2. discirnáis	discirn-ierais/ieseis	hubierais discernido
3. disciernan	discirn-ieran/iesen	hubieran discernido
PERFECT	haya discernido etc	
INFINITIVE	*PARTICIPLE*	
PRESENT	PRESENT	
discernir	discirniendo	
PAST	PAST	
haber discernido	discernido	

26 DISTINGUIR

PRESENT	IMPERFECT	FUTURE
1. distingo	distinguía	distinguiré
2. distingues	distinguías	distinguirás
3. distingue	distinguía	distinguirá
1. distinguimos	distinguíamos	distinguiremos
2. distinguís	distinguíais	distinguiréis
3. distinguen	distinguían	distinguirán
PRETERITE	PERFECT	PLUPERFECT
1. distinguí	he distinguido	había distinguido
2. distinguiste	has distinguido	habías distinguido
3. distinguió	ha distinguido	había distinguido
1. distinguimos	hemos distinguido	habíamos distinguido
2. distinguisteis	habéis distinguido	habíais distinguido
3. distinguieron	han distinguido	habían distinguido
PAST ANTERIOR	FUTURE PERFECT	
hube distinguido etc	habré distinguido etc	
CONDITIONAL		*IMPERATIVE*
PRESENT	PAST	
1. distinguiría	habría distinguido	
2. distinguirías	habrías distinguido	(tú) distingue
3. distinguiría	habría distinguido	(Vd) distinga
1. distinguiríamos	habríamos distinguido	(nosotros) distingamos
2. distinguiríais	habríais distinguido	(vosotros) dintinguid
3. distinguirían	habrían distinguido	(Vds) distingan
SUBJUNCTIVE		
PRESENT	IMPERFECT	PLUPERFECT
1. distinga	distingu-iera/iese	hubiera distinguido
2. distingas	distingu-ieras/ieses	hubieras distinguido
3. distinga	distingu-iera/iese	hubiera distinguido
1. distingamos	distingu-iéramos/iésemos	hubiéramos distinguido
2. distingáis	distingu-ierais/ieseis	hubierais distinguido
3. distingan	distingu-ieran/iesen	hubieran distinguido
PERFECT	haya distinguido etc	
INFINITIVE	*PARTICIPLE*	
PRESENT	PRESENT	
distinguir	distinguiendo	
PAST	PAST	
haber distinguido	distinguido	

27 DORMIR

PRESENT	IMPERFECT	FUTURE
1. duermo	dormía	dormiré
2. duermes	dormías	dormirás
3. duerme	dormía	dormirá
1. dormimos	dormíamos	dormiremos
2. dormís	dormíais	dormiréis
3. duermen	dormían	dormirán
PRETERITE	PERFECT	PLUPERFECT
1. dormí	he dormido	había dormido
2. dormiste	has dormido	habías dormido
3. durmió	ha dormido	había dormido
1. dormimos	hemos dormido	habíamos dormido
2. dormisteis	habéis dormido	habíais dormido
3. durmieron	han dormido	habían dormido
PAST ANTERIOR	FUTURE PERFECT	
hube dormido etc	habré dormido etc	
CONDITIONAL		*IMPERATIVE*
PRESENT	PAST	
1. dormiría	habría dormido	
2. dormirías	habrías dormido	(tú) duerme
3. dormiría	habría dormido	(Vd) duerma
1. dormiríamos	habríamos dormido	(nosotros) durmamos
2. dormiríais	habríais dormido	(vosotros) dormid
3. dormirían	habrían dormido	(Vds) duerman
SUBJUNCTIVE		
PRESENT	IMPERFECT	PLUPERFECT
1. duerma	durm-iera/iese	hubiera dormido
2. duermas	durm-ieras/ieses	hubieras dormido
3. duerma	durm-iera/iese	hubiera dormido
1. durmamos	durm-iéramos/iésemos	hubiéramos dormido
2. durmáis	durm-ierais/ieseis	hubierais dormido
3. duerman	durm-ieran/iesen	hubieran dormido
PERFECT	haya dormido etc	
INFINITIVE	*PARTICIPLE*	
PRESENT	PRESENT	
dormir	durmiendo	
PAST	PAST	
haber dormido	dormido	

28 ERGUIR

PRESENT	IMPERFECT	FUTURE
1. yergo/irgo	erguía	erguiré
2. yergues/irgues	erguías	erguirás
3. yergue/irgue	erguía	erguirá
1. erguimos	erguíamos	erguiremos
2. erguís	erguíais	erguiréis
3. yerguen/irguen	erguían	erguirán
PRETERITE	PERFECT	PLUPERFECT
1. erguí	he erguido	había erguido
2. erguiste	has erguido	habías erguido
3. irguió	ha erguido	había erguido
1. erguimos	hemos erguido	habíamos erguido
2. erguisteis	habéis erguido	habíais erguido
3. irguieron	han erguido	habían erguido
PAST ANTERIOR	FUTURE PERFECT	
hube erguido etc	habré erguido etc	
CONDITIONAL		*IMPERATIVE*
PRESENT	PAST	
1. erguiría	habría erguido	
2. erguirías	habrías erguido	(tú) yergue/irgue
3. erguiría	habría erguido	(Vd) yerga/irga
1. erguiríamos	habríamos erguido	(nosotros) yergamos/ irgamos
2. erguiríais	habríais erguido	(vosotros) erguid
3. erguirían	habrían erguido	(Vds) yergan/irgan
SUBJUNCTIVE		
PRESENT	IMPERFECT	PLUPERFECT
1. yerga/irga	irgu-iera/iese	hubiera erguido
2. yergas/irgas	irgu-ieras/ieses	hubieras erguido
3. yerga/irga	irgu-iera/iese	hubiera erguido
1. yergamos/irgamos	irgu-iéramos/iésemos	hubiéramos erguido
2. yergáis/irgáis	irgu-ierais/ieseis	hubierais erguido
3. yergan/irgan	irgu-ieran/iesen	hubieran erguido
PERFECT	haya erguido etc	
INFINITIVE	*PARTICIPLE*	
PRESENT	PRESENT	
erguir	irguiendo	
PAST	PAST	
haber erguido	erguido	

NOTE The "yer-" forms are more common than the "ir-" forms.

29 ERRAR

PRESENT	IMPERFECT	FUTURE
1. yerro	erraba	erraré
2. yerras	errabas	errarás
3. yerra	erraba	errará
1. erramos	errábamos	erraremos
2. erráis	errabais	erraréis
3. yerran	erraban	errarán
PRETERITE	PERFECT	PLUPERFECT
1. erré	he errado	había errado
2. erraste	has errado	habías errado
3. erró	ha errado	había errado
1. erramos	hemos errado	habíamos errado
2. errasteis	habéis errado	habíais errado
3. erraron	han errado	habían errado
PAST ANTERIOR	FUTURE PERFECT	
hube errado etc	habré errado etc	
CONDITIONAL		*IMPERATIVE*
PRESENT	PAST	
1. erraría	habría errado	
2. errarías	habrías errado	(tú) yerra
3. erraría	habría errado	(Vd) yerre
1. erraríamos	habríamos errado	(nosotros) erremos
2. erraríais	habríais errado	(vosotros) errad
3. errarían	habrían errado	(Vds) yerren
SUBJUNCTIVE		
PRESENT	IMPERFECT	PLUPERFECT
1. yerre	err-ara/ase	hubiera errado
2. yerres	err-aras/ases	hubieras errado
3. yerre	err-ara/ase	hubiera errado
1. erremos	err-áramos/ásemos	hubiéramos errado
2. erréis	err-arais/aseis	hubierais errado
3. yerren	err-aran/asen	hubieran errado
PERFECT	haya errado etc	
INFINITIVE	*PARTICIPLE*	
PRESENT	PRESENT	
errar	errando	
PAST	PAST	
haber errado	errado	

30 ESTAR

PRESENT	IMPERFECT	FUTURE
1. estoy	estaba	estaré
2. estás	estabas	estarás
3. está	estaba	estará
1. estamos	estábamos	estaremos
2. estáis	estabais	estaréis
3. están	estaban	estarán
PRETERITE	PERFECT	PLUPERFECT
1. estuve	he estado	había estado
2. estuviste	has estado	habías estado
3. estuvo	ha estado	había estado
1. estuvimos	hemos estado	habíamos estado
2. estuvisteis	habéis estado	habíais estado
3. estuvieron	han estado	habían estado
PAST ANTERIOR	FUTURE PERFECT	
hube estado etc	habré estado etc	
CONDITIONAL		*IMPERATIVE*
PRESENT	PAST	
1. estaría	habría estado	
2. estarías	habrías estado	(tú) está
3. estaría	habría estado	(Vd) esté
1. estaríamos	habríamos estado	(nosotros) estemos
2. estaríais	habríais estado	(vosotros) estad
3. estarían	habrían estado	(Vds) estén
SUBJUNCTIVE		
PRESENT	IMPERFECT	PLUPERFECT
1. esté	estuv-iera/iese	hubiera estado
2. estés	estuv-ieras/ieses	hubieras estado
3. esté	estuv-iera/iese	hubiera estado
1. estemos	estuv-iéramos/iésemos	hubiéramos estado
2. estéis	estuv-ierais/ieseis	hubierais estado
3. estén	estuv-ieran/iesen	hubieran estado
PERFECT	haya estado etc	
INFINITIVE	*PARTICIPLE*	
PRESENT	PRESENT	
estar	estando	
PAST	PAST	
haber estado	estado	

31 FORZAR

PRESENT	IMPERFECT	FUTURE
1. fuerzo	forzaba	forzaré
2. fuerzas	forzabas	forzarás
3. fuerza	forzaba	forzará
1. forzamos	forzábamos	forzaremos
2. forzáis	forzabais	forzaréis
3. fuerzan	forzaban	forzarán
PRETERITE	PERFECT	PLUPERFECT
1. forcé	he forzado	había forzado
2. forzaste	has forzado	habías forzado
3. forzó	ha forzado	había forzado
1. forzamos	hemos forzado	habíamos forzado
2. forzasteis	habéis forzado	habíais forzado
3. forzaron	han forzado	habían forzado
PAST ANTERIOR	FUTURE PERFECT	
hube forzado etc	habré forzado etc	
CONDITIONAL		*IMPERATIVE*
PRESENT	PAST	
1. forzaría	habría forzado	
2. forzarías	habrías forzado	(tú) fuerza
3. forzaría	habría forzado	(Vd) fuerce
1. forzaríamos	habríamos forzado	(nosotros) forcemos
2. forzaríais	habríais forzado	(vosotros) forzad
3. forzarían	habrían forzado	(Vds) fuercen
SUBJUNCTIVE		
PRESENT	IMPERFECT	PLUPERFECT
1. fuerce	forz-ara/ase	hubiera forzado
2. fuerces	forz-aras/ases	hubieras forzado
3. fuerce	forz-ara/ase	hubiera forzado
1. forcemos	forz-áramos/ásemos	hubiéramos forzado
2. forcéis	forz-arais/aseis	hubierais forzado
3. fuercen	forz-aran/asen	hubieran forzado
PERFECT	haya forzado etc	
INFINITIVE	*PARTICIPLE*	
PRESENT	PRESENT	
forzar	forzando	
PAST	PAST	
haber forzado	forzado	

32 GUIAR

PRESENT	IMPERFECT	FUTURE
1. guío	guiaba	guiaré
2. guías	guiabas	guiarás
3. guía	guiaba	guiará
1. guiamos	guiábamos	guiaremos
2. guiáis	guiabais	guiaréis
3. guían	guiaban	guiarán
PAST HISTORIC	PERFECT	PLUPERFECT
1. guié	he guiado	había guiado
2. guiaste	has guiado	habías guiado
3. guió	ha guiado	había guiado
1. guiamos	hemos guiado	habíamos guiado
2. guiasteis	habéis guiado	habíais guiado
3. guiaron	han guiado	habían guiado
PAST ANTERIOR	FUTURE PERFECT	
hube guiado etc	habré guiado etc	
CONDITIONAL		*IMPERATIVE*
PRESENT	PAST	
1. guiaría	habría guiado	
2. guiarías	habrías guiado	(tú) guía
3. guiaría	habría guiado	(Vd) guíe
1. guiaríamos	habríamos guiado	(nosotros) guiemos
2. guiaríais	habríais guiado	(vosotros) guiad
3. guiarían	habrían guiado	(Vds) guíen
SUBJUNCTIVE		
PRESENT	IMPERFECT	PLUPERFECT
1. guíe	gui-ara/ase	hubiera guiado
2. guíes	gui-aras/ases	hubieras guiado
3. guíe	gui-ara/ase	hubiera guiado
1. guiemos	gui-áramos/ásemos	hubiéramos guiado
2. guiéis	gui-arais/aseis	hubierais guiado
3. guíen	gui-aran/asen	hubieran guiado
PERFECT	haya guiado etc	
INFINITIVE	*PARTICIPLE*	
PRESENT	PRESENT	
guiar	guiando	
PAST	PAST	
haber guiado	guiado	

33 HACER

PRESENT	IMPERFECT	FUTURE
1. hago	hacía	haré
2. haces	hacías	harás
3. hace	hacía	hará
1. hacemos	hacíamos	haremos
2. hacéis	hacíais	haréis
3. hacen	hacían	harán
PRETERITE	PERFECT	PLUPERFECT
1. hice	he hecho	había hecho
2. hiciste	has hecho	habías hecho
3. hizo	ha hecho	había hecho
1. hicimos	hemos hecho	habíamos hecho
2. hicisteis	habéis hecho	habíais hecho
3. hicieron	han hecho	habían hecho
PAST ANTERIOR	FUTURE PERFECT	
hube hecho etc	habré hecho etc	

CONDITIONAL		*IMPERATIVE*
PRESENT	PAST	
1. haría	habría hecho	
2. harías	habrías hecho	(tú) haz
3. haría	habría hecho	(Vd) haga
1. haríamos	habríamos hecho	(nosotros) hagamos
2. haríais	habríais hecho	(vosotros) haced
3. harían	habrían hecho	(Vds) hagan

SUBJUNCTIVE		
PRESENT	IMPERFECT	PLUPERFECT
1. haga	hic-iera/iese	hubiera hecho
2. hagas	hic-ieras/ieses	hubieras hecho
3. haga	hic-iera/iese	hubiera hecho
1. hagamos	hic-iéramos/iésemos	hubiéramos hecho
2. hagáis	hic-ierais/ieseis	hubierais hecho
3. hagan	hic-ieran/iesen	hubieran hecho
PERFECT	haya hecho etc	

INFINITIVE	*PARTICIPLE*
PRESENT	PRESENT
hacer	haciendo
PAST	PAST
haber hecho	hecho

34 HUIR

PRESENT	IMPERFECT	FUTURE
1. huyo	huía	huiré
2. huyes	huías	huirás
3. huye	huía	huirá
1. huimos	huíamos	huiremos
2. huís	huíais	huiréis
3. huyen	huían	huirán
PRETERITE	PERFECT	PLUPERFECT
1. huí	he huido	había huido
2. huiste	has huido	habías huido
3. huyó	ha huido	había huido
1. huimos	hemos huido	habíamos huido
2. huisteis	habéis huido	habíais huido
3. huyeron	han huido	habían huido
PAST ANTERIOR	FUTURE PERFECT	
hube huido etc	habré huido etc	

CONDITIONAL		*IMPERATIVE*
PRESENT	PAST	
1. huiría	habría huido	
2. huirías	habrías huido	(tú) huye
3. huiría	habría huido	(Vd) huya
1. huiríamos	habríamos huido	(nosotros) huyamos
2. huiríais	habríais huido	(vosotros) huid
3. huirían	habrían huido	(Vds) huyan

SUBJUNCTIVE		
PRESENT	IMPERFECT	PLUPERFECT
1. huya	hu-yera/yese	hubiera huido
2. huyas	hu-yeras/yeses	hubieras huido
3. huya	hu-yiera/yese	hubiera huido
1. huyamos	hu-yéramos/yésemos	hubiéramos huido
2. huyáis	hu-yerais/yeseis	hubierais huido
3. huyan	hu-yeran/yesen	hubieran huido
PERFECT	haya huido etc	

INFINITIVE	*PARTICIPLE*
PRESENT	PRESENT
huir	huyendo
PAST	PAST
haber huido	huido

35 IR

PRESENT	IMPERFECT	FUTURE
1. voy	iba	iré
2. vas	ibas	irás
3. va	iba	irá
1. vamos	íbamos	iremos
2. vais	ibais	iréis
3. van	iban	irán
PRETERITE	PERFECT	PLUPERFECT
1. fui	he ido	había ido
2. fuiste	has ido	habías ido
3. fue	ha ido	había ido
1. fuimos	hemos ido	habíamos ido
2. fuisteis	habéis ido	habíais ido
3. fueron	han ido	habían ido
PAST ANTERIOR	FUTURE PERFECT	
hube ido etc	habré ido etc	

CONDITIONAL		*IMPERATIVE*
PRESENT	PAST	
1. iría	habría ido	
2. irías	habrías ido	(tú) ve
3. iría	habría ido	(Vd) vaya
1. iríamos	habríamos ido	(nosotros) vamos
2. iríais	habríais ido	(vosotros) id
3. irían	habrían ido	(Vds) vayan

SUBJUNCTIVE		
PRESENT	IMPERFECT	PLUPERFECT
1. vaya	fu-era/ese	hubiera ido
2. vayas	fu-eras/eses	hubieras ido
3. vaya	fu-era/ese	hubiera ido
1. vayamos	fu-éramos/ésemos	hubiéramos ido
2. vayáis	fu-erais/eseis	hubierais ido
3. vayan	fu-eran/esen	hubieran ido
PERFECT	haya ido etc	

INFINITIVE	*PARTICIPLE*
PRESENT	PRESENT
ir	yendo
PAST	PAST
haber ido	ido

36 JUGAR

PRESENT	IMPERFECT	FUTURE
1. juego	jugaba	jugaré
2. juegas	jugabas	jugarás
3. juega	jugaba	jugará
1. jugamos	jugábamos	jugaremos
2. jugáis	jugabais	jugaréis
3. juegan	jugaban	jugarán
PRETERITE	PERFECT	PLUPERFECT
1. jugué	he jugado	había jugado
2. jugaste	has jugado	habías jugado
3. jugó	ha jugado	había jugado
1. jugamos	hemos jugado	habíamos jugado
2. jugasteis	habéis jugado	habíais jugado
3. jugaron	han jugado	habían jugado
PAST ANTERIOR	FUTURE PERFECT	
hube jugado etc	habré jugado etc	

CONDITIONAL		*IMPERATIVE*
PRESENT	PAST	
1. jugaría	habría jugado	
2. jugarías	habrías jugado	(tú) juega
3. jugaría	habría jugado	(Vd) juegue
1. jugaríamos	habríamos jugado	(nosotros) juguemos
2. jugaríais	habríais jugado	(vosotros) jugad
3. jugarían	habrían jugado	(Vds) jueguen

SUBJUNCTIVE		
PRESENT	IMPERFECT	PLUPERFECT
1. juegue	jug-ara/ase	hubiera jugado
2. juegues	jug-aras/ases	hubieras jugado
3. juegue	jug-ara/ase	hubiera jugado
1. juguemos	jug-áramos/ásemos	hubiéramos jugado
2. juguéis	jug-arais/aseis	hubierais jugado
3. jueguen	jug-aran/asen	hubieran jugado
PERFECT	haya jugado etc	

INFINITIVE	*PARTICIPLE*
PRESENT	PRESENT
jugar	jugando
PAST	PAST
haber jugado	jugado

37 LEER

PRESENT	IMPERFECT	FUTURE
1. leo	leía	leeré
2. lees	leías	leerás
3. lee	leía	leerá
1. leemos	leíamos	leeremos
2. leéis	leíais	leeréis
3. leen	leían	leerán
PRETERITE	PERFECT	PLUPERFECT
1. leí	he leído	había leído
2. leíste	has leído	habías leído
3. leyó	ha leído	había leído
1. leímos	hemos leído	habíamos leído
2. leísteis	habéis leído	habíais leído
3. leyeron	han leído	habían leído
PAST ANTERIOR	FUTURE PERFECT	
hube leído etc	habré leído etc	
CONDITIONAL		*IMPERATIVE*
PRESENT	PAST	
1. leería	habría leído	
2. leerías	habrías leído	(tú) lee
3. leería	habría leído	(Vd) lea
1. leeríamos	habríamos leído	(nosotros) leamos
2. leeríais	habríais leído	(vosotros) leed
3. leerían	habrían leído	(Vds) lean
SUBJUNCTIVE		
PRESENT	IMPERFECT	PLUPERFECT
1. lea	le-yera/yese	hubiera leído
2. leas	le-yeras/yeses	hubieras leído
3. lea	le-yera/yese	hubiera leído
1. leamos	le-yéramos/yésemos	hubiéramos leído
2. leáis	le-yerais/yeseis	hubierais leído
3. lean	le-yeran/yesen	hubieran leído
PERFECT	haya leído etc	
INFINITIVE	*PARTICIPLE*	
PRESENT	PRESENT	
leer	leyendo	
PAST	PAST	
haber leído	leído	

38 LLEGAR

PRESENT	IMPERFECT	FUTURE
1. llego	llegaba	llegaré
2. llegas	llegabas	llegarás
3. llega	llegaba	llegará
1. llegamos	llegábamos	llegaremos
2. llegáis	llegabais	llegaréis
3. llegan	llegaban	llegarán
PRETERITE	PERFECT	PLUPERFECT
1. llegué	he llegado	había llegado
2. llegaste	has llegado	habías llegado
3. llegó	ha llegado	había llegado
1. llegamos	hemos llegado	habíamos llegado
2. llegasteis	habéis llegado	habíais llegado
3. llegaron	han llegado	habían llegado
PAST ANTERIOR	FUTURE PERFECT	
hube llegado etc	habré llegado etc	
CONDITIONAL		*IMPERATIVE*
PRESENT	PAST	
1. llegaría	habría llegado	
2. llegarías	habrías llegado	(tú) llega
3. llegaría	habría llegado	(Vd) llegue
1. llegaríamos	habríamos llegado	(nosotros) lleguemos
2. llegaríais	habríais llegado	(vosotros) llegad
3. llegarían	habrían llegado	(Vds) lleguen
SUBJUNCTIVE		
PRESENT	IMPERFECT	PLUPERFECT
1. llegue	lleg-ara/ase	hubiera llegado
2. llegues	lleg-aras/ases	hubieras llegado
3. llegue	lleg-ara/ase	hubiera llegado
1. lleguemos	lleg-áramos/ásemos	hubiéramos llegado
2. lleguéis	lleg-arais/aseis	hubierais llegado
3. lleguen	lleg-aran/asen	hubieran llegado
PERFECT	haya llegado etc	
INFINITIVE	*PARTICIPLE*	
PRESENT	PRESENT	
llegar	llegando	
PAST	PAST	
haber llegado	llegado	

39 LUCIR

PRESENT	IMPERFECT	FUTURE
1. luzco	lucía	luciré
2. luces	lucías	lucirás
3. luce	lucía	lucirá
1. lucimos	lucíamos	luciremos
2. lucís	lucíais	luciréis
3. lucen	lucían	lucirán
PRETERITE	PERFECT	PLUPERFECT
1. lucí	he lucido	había lucido
2. luciste	has lucido	habías lucido
3. lució	ha lucido	había lucido
1. lucimos	hemos lucido	habíamos lucido
2. lucisteis	habéis lucido	habíais lucido
3. lucieron	han lucido	habían lucido
PAST ANTERIOR	FUTURE PERFECT	
hube lucido etc	habré lucido etc	
CONDITIONAL		*IMPERATIVE*
PRESENT	PAST	
1. luciría	habría lucido	
2. lucirías	habrías lucido	(tú) luce
3. luciría	habría lucido	(Vd) luzca
1. luciríamos	habríamos lucido	(nosotros) luzcamos
2. luciríais	habríais lucido	(vosotros) lucid
3. lucirían	habrían lucido	(Vds) luzcan
SUBJUNCTIVE		
PRESENT	IMPERFECT	PLUPERFECT
1. luzca	luc-iera/iese	hubiera lucido
2. luzcas	luc-ieras/ieses	hubieras lucido
3. luzca	luc-iera/iese	hubiera lucido
1. luzcamos	luc-iéramos/iésemos	hubiéramos lucido
2. luzcáis	luc-ierais/ieseis	hubierais lucido
3. luzcan	luc-ieran/iesen	hubieran lucido
PERFECT	haya lucido etc	
INFINITIVE	*PARTICIPLE*	
PRESENT	PRESENT	
lucir	luciendo	
PAST	PAST	
haber lucido	lucido	

40 MECER

PRESENT	IMPERFECT	FUTURE
1. mezo	mecía	meceré
2. meces	mecías	mecerás
3. mece	mecía	mecerá
1. mecemos	mecíamos	meceremos
2. mecéis	mecíais	meceréis
3. mecen	mecían	mecerán
PAST HISTORIC	PERFECT	PLUPERFECT
1. mecí	he mecido	había mecido
2. meciste	has mecido	habías mecido
3. meció	ha mecido	había mecido
1. mecimos	hemos mecido	habíamos mecido
2. mecisteis	habéis mecido	habíais mecido
3. mecieron	han mecido	habían mecido
PAST ANTERIOR	FUTURE PERFECT	
hube mecido etc	habré mecido etc	
CONDITIONAL		*IMPERATIVE*
PRESENT	PAST	
1. mecería	habría mecido	
2. mecerías	habrías mecido	(tú) mece
3. mecería	habría mecido	(Vd) meza
1. meceríamos	habríamos mecido	(nosotros) mezamos
2. meceríais	habríais mecido	(vosotros) meced
3. mecerían	habrían mecido	(Vds) mezan
SUBJUNCTIVE		
PRESENT	IMPERFECT	PLUPERFECT
1. meza	mec-iera/iese	hubiera mecido
2. mezas	mec-ieras/ieses	hubieras mecido
3. meza	mec-iera/iese	hubiera mecido
1. mezamos	mec-iéramos/iésemos	hubiéramos mecido
2. mezáis	mec-ierais/ieseis	hubierais mecido
3. mezan	mec-ieran/iesen	hubieran mecido
PERFECT	haya mecido etc	
INFINITIVE	*PARTICIPLE*	
PRESENT	PRESENT	
mecer	meciendo	
PAST	PAST	
haber mecido	mecido	

41 MOVER

PRESENT	IMPERFECT	FUTURE
1. muevo	movía	moveré
2. mueves	movías	moverás
3. mueve	movía	moverá
1. movemos	movíamos	moveremos
2. movéis	movíais	moveréis
3. mueven	movían	moverán
PRETERITE	**PERFECT**	**PLUPERFECT**
1. moví	he movido	había movido
2. moviste	has movido	habías movido
3. movió	ha movido	había movido
1. movimos	hemos movido	habíamos movido
2. movisteis	habéis movido	habíais movido
3. movieron	han movido	habían movido
PAST ANTERIOR	**FUTURE PERFECT**	
hube movido etc	habré movido etc	

CONDITIONAL		*IMPERATIVE*
PRESENT	PAST	
1. movería	habría movido	
2. moverías	habrías movido	(tú) mueve
3. movería	habría movido	(Vd) mueva
1. moveríamos	habríamos movido	(nosotros) movamos
2. moveríais	habríais movido	(vosotros) moved
3. moverían	habrían movido	(Vds) muevan

SUBJUNCTIVE		
PRESENT	IMPERFECT	PLUPERFECT
1. mueva	mov-iera/iese	hubiera movido
2. muevas	mov-ieras/ieses	hubieras movido
3. mueva	mov-iera/iese	hubiera movido
1. movamos	mov-iéramos/iésemos	hubiéramos movido
2. mováis	mov-ierais/ieseis	hubierais movido
3. muevan	mov-ieran/iesen	hubieran movido
PERFECT	haya movido etc	

INFINITIVE	*PARTICIPLE*
PRESENT	PRESENT
mover	moviendo
PAST	PAST
haber movido	movido

42 NACER

PRESENT	IMPERFECT	FUTURE
1. nazco	nacía	naceré
2. naces	nacías	nacerás
3. nace	nacía	nacerá
1. nacemos	nacíamos	naceremos
2. nacéis	nacíais	naceréis
3. nacen	nacían	nacerán
PRETERITE	**PERFECT**	**PLUPERFECT**
1. nací	he nacido	había nacido
2. naciste	has nacido	habías nacido
3. nació	ha nacido	había nacido
1. nacimos	hemos nacido	habíamos nacido
2. nacisteis	habéis nacido	habíais nacido
3. nacieron	han nacido	habían nacido
PAST ANTERIOR	**FUTURE PERFECT**	
hube nacido etc	habré nacido etc	

CONDITIONAL		*IMPERATIVE*
PRESENT	PAST	
1. nacería	habría nacido	
2. nacerías	habrías nacido	(tú) nace
3. nacería	habría nacido	(Vd) nazca
1. naceríamos	habríamos nacido	(nosotros) nazcamos
2. naceríais	habríais nacido	(vosotros) naced
3. nacerían	habrían nacido	(Vds) nazcan

SUBJUNCTIVE		
PRESENT	IMPERFECT	PLUPERFECT
1. nazca	nac-iera/iese	hubiera nacido
2. nazcas	nac-ieras/ieses	hubieras nacido
3. nazca	nac-iera/iese	hubiera nacido
1. nazcamos	nac-iéramos/iésemos	hubiéramos nacido
2. nazcáis	nac-ierais/ieseis	hubierais nacido
3. nazcan	nac-ieran/iesen	hubieran nacido
PERFECT	haya nacido etc	

INFINITIVE	*PARTICIPLE*
PRESENT	PRESENT
nacer	naciendo
PAST	PAST
haber nacido	nacido

43 NEGAR

PRESENT	IMPERFECT	FUTURE
1. niego	negaba	negaré
2. niegas	negabas	negarás
3. niega	negaba	negará
1. negamos	negábamos	negaremos
2. negáis	negabais	negaréis
3. niegan	negaban	negarán
PRETERITE	**PERFECT**	**PLUPERFECT**
1. negué	he negado	había negado
2. negaste	has negado	habías negado
3. negó	ha negado	había negado
1. negamos	hemos negado	habíamos negado
2. negasteis	habéis negado	habíais negado
3. negaron	han negado	habían negado
PAST ANTERIOR	**FUTURE PERFECT**	
hube negado etc	habré negado etc	

CONDITIONAL		*IMPERATIVE*
PRESENT	PAST	
1. negaría	habría negado	
2. negarías	habrías negado	(tú) niega
3. negaría	habría negado	(Vd) niegue
1. negaríamos	habríamos negado	(nosotros) neguemos
2. negaríais	habríais negado	(vosotros) negad
3. negarían	habrían negado	(Vds) nieguen

SUBJUNCTIVE		
PRESENT	IMPERFECT	PLUPERFECT
1. niegue	neg-ara/ase	hubiera negado
2. niegues	neg-aras/ases	hubieras negado
3. niegue	neg-ara/ase	hubiera negado
1. neguemos	neg-áramos/ásemos	hubiéramos negado
2. neguéis	neg-arais/aseis	hubierais negado
3. nieguen	neg-aran/asen	hubieran negado
PERFECT	haya negado etc	

INFINITIVE	*PARTICIPLE*
PRESENT	PRESENT
negar	negando
PAST	PAST
haber negado	negado

44 OÍR

PRESENT	IMPERFECT	FUTURE
1. oigo	oía	oiré
2. oyes	oías	oirás
3. oye	oía	oirá
1. oímos	oíamos	oiremos
2. oís	oíais	oiréis
3. oyen	oían	oirán
PRETERITE	**PERFECT**	**PLUPERFECT**
1. oí	he oído	había oído
2. oíste	has oído	habías oído
3. oyó	ha oído	había oído
1. oímos	hemos oído	habíamos oído
2. oísteis	habéis oído	habíais oído
3. oyeron	han oído	habían oído
PAST ANTERIOR	**FUTURE PERFECT**	
hube oído etc	habré oído etc	

CONDITIONAL		*IMPERATIVE*
PRESENT	PAST	
1. oiría	habría oído	
2. oirías	habrías oído	(tú) oye
3. oiría	habría oído	(Vd) oiga
1. oiríamos	habríamos oído	(nosotros) oigamos
2. oiríais	habríais oído	(vosotros) oíd
3. oirían	habrían oído	(Vds) oigan

SUBJUNCTIVE		
PRESENT	IMPERFECT	PLUPERFECT
1. oiga	o-yera/yese	hubiera oído
2. oigas	o-yeras/yeses	hubieras oído
3. oiga	o-yera/yese	hubiera oído
1. oigamos	o-yéramos/yésemos	hubiéramos oído
2. oigáis	o-yerais/yeseis	hubierais oído
3. oigan	o-yeran/yesen	hubieran oído
PERFECT	haya oído etc	

INFINITIVE	*PARTICIPLE*
PRESENT	PRESENT
oír	oyendo
PAST	PAST
haber oído	oído

45 OLER

PRESENT	IMPERFECT	FUTURE
1. huelo	olía	oleré
2. hueles	olías	olerás
3. huele	olía	olerá
1. olemos	olíamos	oleremos
2. oléis	olíais	oleréis
3. huelen	olían	olerán
PRETERITE	**PERFECT**	**PLUPERFECT**
1. olí	he olido	había olido
2. oliste	has olido	habías olido
3. olió	ha olido	había olido
1. olimos	hemos olido	habíamos olido
2. olisteis	habéis olido	habíais olido
3. olieron	han olido	habían olido
PAST ANTERIOR	**FUTURE PERFECT**	
hube olido etc	habré olido etc	
CONDITIONAL		*IMPERATIVE*
PRESENT	PAST	
1. olería	habría olido	
2. olerías	habrías olido	(tú) huele
3. olería	habría olido	(Vd) huela
1. oleríamos	habríamos olido	(nosotros) olamos
2. oleríais	habríais olido	(vosotros) oled
3. olerían	habrían olido	(Vds) huelan
SUBJUNCTIVE		
PRESENT	IMPERFECT	PLUPERFECT
1. huela	ol-iera/iese	hubiera olido
2. huelas	ol-ieras/ieses	hubieras olido
3. huela	ol-iera/iese	hubiera olido
1. olamos	ol-iéramos/iésemos	hubiéramos olido
2. oláis	ol-ierais/ieseis	hubierais olido
3. huelan	ol-ieran/iesen	hubieran olido
PERFECT	haya olido etc	
INFINITIVE	*PARTICIPLE*	
PRESENT	PRESENT	
oler	oliendo	
PAST	PAST	
haber olido	olido	

46 PARECER

PRESENT	IMPERFECT	FUTURE
1. parezco	parecía	pareceré
2. pareces	parecías	parecerás
3. parece	parecía	parecerá
1. parecemos	parecíamos	pareceremos
2. parecéis	parecíais	pareceréis
3. parecen	parecían	parecerán
PRETERITE	**PERFECT**	**PLUPERFECT**
1. parecí	he parecido	había parecido
2. pareciste	has parecido	habías parecido
3. pareció	ha parecido	había parecido
1. parecimos	hemos parecido	habíamos parecido
2. parecisteis	habéis parecido	habíais parecido
3. parecieron	han parecido	habían parecido
PAST ANTERIOR	**FUTURE PERFECT**	
hube parecido etc	habré parecido etc	
CONDITIONAL		*IMPERATIVE*
PRESENT	PAST	
1. parecería	habría parecido	
2. parecerías	habrías parecido	(tú) parece
3. parecería	habría parecido	(Vd) parezca
1. pareceríamos	habríamos parecido	(nosotros) parezcamos
2. pareceríais	habríais parecido	(vosotros) pareced
3. parecerían	habrían parecido	(Vds) parezcan
SUBJUNCTIVE		
PRESENT	IMPERFECT	PLUPERFECT
1. parezca	parec-iera/iese	hubiera parecido
2. parezcas	parec-ieras/ieses	hubieras parecido
3. parezca	parec-iera/iese	hubiera parecido
1. parezcamos	parec-iéramos/iésemos	hubiéramos parecido
2. parezcáis	parec-ierais/ieseis	hubierais parecido
3. parezcan	parec-ieran/iesen	hubieran parecido
PERFECT	haya parecido etc	
INFINITIVE	*PARTICIPLE*	
PRESENT	PRESENT	
parecer	pareciendo	
PAST	PAST	
haber parecido	parecido	

47 PEDIR

PRESENT	IMPERFECT	FUTURE
1. pido	pedía	pediré
2. pides	pedías	pedirás
3. pide	pedía	pedirá
1. pedimos	pedíamos	pediremos
2. pedís	pedíais	pediréis
3. piden	pedían	pedirán
PRETERITE	**PERFECT**	**PLUPERFECT**
1. pedí	he pedido	había pedido
2. pediste	has pedido	habías pedido
3. pidió	ha pedido	había pedido
1. pedimos	hemos pedido	habíamos pedido
2. pedisteis	habéis pedido	habíais pedido
3. pidieron	han pedido	habían pedido
PAST ANTERIOR	**FUTURE PERFECT**	
hube pedido etc	habré pedido etc	
CONDITIONAL		*IMPERATIVE*
PRESENT	PAST	
1. pediría	habría pedido	
2. pedirías	habrías pedido	(tú) pide
3. pediría	habría pedido	(Vd) pida
1. pediríamos	habríamos pedido	(nosotros) pidamos
2. pediríais	habríais pedido	(vosotros) pedid
3. pedirían	habrían pedido	(Vds) pidan
SUBJUNCTIVE		
PRESENT	IMPERFECT	PLUPERFECT
1. pida	pid-iera/iese	hubiera pedido
2. pidas	pid-ieras/ieses	hubieras pedido
3. pida	pid-iera/iese	hubiera pedido
1. pidamos	pid-iéramos/iésemos	hubiéramos pedido
2. pidáis	pid-ierais/ieseis	hubierais pedido
3. pidan	pid-ieran/iesen	hubieran pedido
PERFECT	haya pedido etc	
INFINITIVE	*PARTICIPLE*	
PRESENT	PRESENT	
pedir	pidiendo	
PAST	PAST	
haber pedido	pedido	

48 PLACER

PRESENT	IMPERFECT	FUTURE
1. plazgo	placía	placeré
2. places	placías	placerás
3. place	placía	placerá
1. placemos	placíamos	placeremos
2. placéis	placíais	placeréis
3. placen	placían	placerán
PAST HISTORIC	**PERFECT**	**PLUPERFECT**
1. plací	he placido	había placido
2. placiste	has placido	habías placido
3. plació/plugo	ha placido	había placido
1. placimos	hemos placido	habíamos placido
2. placisteis	habéis placido	habíais placido
3. placieron/pluguieron	han placido	habían placido
PAST ANTERIOR	**FUTURE PERFECT**	
hube placido etc	habré placido etc	
CONDITIONAL		*IMPERATIVE*
PRESENT	PAST	
1. placería	habría placido	
2. placerías	habrías placido	(tú) place
3. placería	habría placido	(Vd) plazca
1. placeríamos	habríamos placido	(nosotros) plazcamos
2. placeríais	habríais placido	(vosotros) placed
3. placerían	habrían placido	(Vds) plazcan
SUBJUNCTIVE		
PRESENT	IMPERFECT	PLUPERFECT
1. plazca	plac-iera/iese	hubiera placido
2. plazcas	plac-ieras/ieses	hubieras placido
3. plazca/plegue	plac-iera/iese *or* plugu-iera/iese	hubiera placido
1. plazcamos	plac-iéramos/iésemos	hubiéramos placido
2. plazcáis	plac-ierais/ieseis	hubierais placido
3. plazcan	plac-ieran/iesen	hubieran placido
PERFECT	haya placido etc	
INFINITIVE	*PARTICIPLE*	
PRESENT	PRESENT	
placer	placiendo	
PAST	PAST	
haber placido	placido	

49 PODER

PRESENT	IMPERFECT	FUTURE
1. puedo	podía	podré
2. puedes	podías	podrás
3. puede	podía	podrá
1. podemos	podíamos	podremos
2. podéis	podíais	podréis
3. pueden	podían	podrán
PRETERITE	**PERFECT**	**PLUPERFECT**
1. pude	he podido	había podido
2. pudiste	has podido	habías podido
3. pudo	ha podido	había podido
1. pudimos	hemos podido	habíamos podido
2. pudisteis	habéis podido	habíais podido
3. pudieron	han podido	habían podido
PAST ANTERIOR	**FUTURE PERFECT**	
hube podido etc	habré podido etc	

CONDITIONAL		*IMPERATIVE*
PRESENT	PAST	
1. podría	habría podido	
2. podrías	habrías podido	(tú) puede
3. podría	habría podido	(Vd) pueda
1. podríamos	habríamos podido	(nosotros) podamos
2. podríais	habríais podido	(vosotros) poded
3. podrían	habrían podido	(Vds) puedan

SUBJUNCTIVE		
PRESENT	IMPERFECT	PLUPERFECT
1. pueda	pud-iera/iese	hubiera podido
2. puedas	pud-ieras/ieses	hubieras podido
3. pueda	pud-iera/iese	hubiera podido
1. podamos	pud-iéramos/iésemos	hubiéramos podido
2. podáis	pud-ierais/ieseis	hubierais podido
3. puedan	pud-ieran/iesen	hubieran podido

PERFECT haya podido etc

INFINITIVE	*PARTICIPLE*
PRESENT	PRESENT
poder	pudiendo
PAST	PAST
haber podido	podido

50 PONER

PRESENT	IMPERFECT	FUTURE
1. pongo	ponía	pondré
2. pones	ponías	pondrás
3. pone	ponía	pondrá
1. ponemos	poníamos	pondremos
2. ponéis	poníais	pondréis
3. ponen	ponían	pondrán
PRETERITE	**PERFECT**	**PLUPERFECT**
1. puse	he puesto	había puesto
2. pusiste	has puesto	habías puesto
3. puso	ha puesto	había puesto
1. pusimos	hemos puesto	habíamos puesto
2. pusisteis	habéis puesto	habíais puesto
3. pusieron	han puesto	habían puesto
PAST ANTERIOR	**FUTURE PERFECT**	
hube puesto etc	habré puesto etc	

CONDITIONAL		*IMPERATIVE*
PRESENT	PAST	
1. pondría	habría puesto	
2. pondrías	habrías puesto	(tú) pon
3. pondría	habría puesto	(Vd) ponga
1. pondríamos	habríamos puesto	(nosotros) pongamos
2. pondríais	habríais puesto	(vosotros) poned
3. pondrían	habrían puesto	(Vds) pongan

SUBJUNCTIVE		
PRESENT	IMPERFECT	PLUPERFECT
1. ponga	pus-iera/iese	hubiera puesto
2. pongas	pus-ieras/ieses	hubieras puesto
3. ponga	pus-iera/iese	hubiera puesto
1. pongamos	pus-iéramos/iésemos	hubiéramos puesto
2. pongáis	pus-ierais/ieseis	hubierais puesto
3. pongan	pus-ieran/iesen	hubieran puesto

PERFECT haya puesto etc

INFINITIVE	*PARTICIPLE*
PRESENT	PRESENT
poner	poniendo
PAST	PAST
haber puesto	puesto

51 PREDECIR

PRESENT	IMPERFECT	FUTURE
1. predigo	predecía	predeciré
2. predices	predecías	predecirás
3. predice	predecía	predecirá
1. predecimos	predecíamos	predeciremos
2. predecís	predecíais	predeciréis
3. predicen	predecían	predecirán
PAST HISTORIC	**PERFECT**	**PLUPERFECT**
1. predije	he predicho	había predicho
2. predijiste	has predicho	habías predicho
3. predijo	ha predicho	había predicho
1. predijimos	hemos predicho	habíamos predicho
2. predijisteis	habéis predicho	habíais predicho
3. predijeron	han predicho	habían predicho
PAST ANTERIOR	**FUTURE PERFECT**	
hube predicho etc	habré predicho etc	

CONDITIONAL		*IMPERATIVE*
PRESENT	PAST	
1. predeciría	habría predicho	
2. predecirías	habrías predicho	(tú) di
3. predeciría	habría predicho	(Vd) diga
1. predeciríamos	habríamos predicho	(nosotros) digamos
2. predeciríais	habríais predicho	(vosotros) decid
3. predecirían	habrían predicho	(Vds) digan

SUBJUNCTIVE		
PRESENT	IMPERFECT	PLUPERFECT
1. prediga	predij-era/ese	hubiera predicho
2. predigas	predij-eras/eses	hubieras predicho
3. prediga	predij-era/ese	hubiera predicho
1. predigamos	predij-éramos/ésemos	hubiéramos predicho
2. predigáis	predij-erais/eseis	hubierais predicho
3. predigan	predij-eran/esen	hubieran predicho

PERFECT haya predicho etc

INFINITIVE	*PARTICIPLE*
PRESENT	PRESENT
predecir	prediciendo
PAST	PAST
haber predicho	predicho

52 PROTEGER

PRESENT	IMPERFECT	FUTURE
1. protejo	protegía	protegeré
2. proteges	protegías	protegerás
3. protege	protegía	protegerá
1. protegemos	protegíamos	protegeremos
2. protegéis	protegíais	protegeréis
3. protegen	protegían	protegerán
PRETERITE	**PERFECT**	**PLUPERFECT**
1. protegí	he protegido	había protegido
2. protegiste	has protegido	habías protegido
3. protegió	ha protegido	había protegido
1. protegimos	hemos protegido	habíamos protegido
2. protegisteis	habéis protegido	habíais protegido
3. protegieron	han protegido	habían protegido
PAST ANTERIOR	**FUTURE PERFECT**	
hube protegido etc	habré protegido etc	

CONDITIONAL		*IMPERATIVE*
PRESENT	PAST	
1. protegería	habría protegido	
2. protegerías	habrías protegido	(tú) protege
3. protegería	habría protegido	(Vd) proteja
1. protegeríamos	habríamos protegido	(nosotros) protejamos
2. protegeríais	habríais protegido	(vosotros) proteged
3. protegerían	habrían protegido	(Vds) protejan

SUBJUNCTIVE		
PRESENT	IMPERFECT	PLUPERFECT
1. proteja	proteg-iera/iese	hubiera protegido
2. protejas	proteg-ieras/ieses	hubieras protegido
3. proteja	proteg-iera/iese	hubiera protegido
1. protejamos	proteg-iéramos/iésemos	hubiéramos protegido
2. protejáis	proteg-ierais/ieseis	hubierais protegido
3. protejan	proteg-ieran/iesen	hubieran protegido

PERFECT haya protegido etc

INFINITIVE	*PARTICIPLE*
PRESENT	PRESENT
proteger	protegiendo
PAST	PAST
haber protegido	protegido

53 QUERER

PRESENT	IMPERFECT	FUTURE
1. quiero	quería	querré
2. quieres	querías	querrás
3. quiere	quería	querrá
1. queremos	queríamos	querremos
2. queréis	queríais	querréis
3. quieren	querían	querrán
PRETERITE	**PERFECT**	**PLUPERFECT**
1. quise	he querido	había querido
2. quisiste	has querido	habías querido
3. quiso	ha querido	había querido
1. quisimos	hemos querido	habíamos querido
2. quisisteis	habéis querido	habíais querido
3. quisieron	han querido	habían querido
PAST ANTERIOR	**FUTURE PERFECT**	
hube querido etc	habré querido etc	
CONDITIONAL		*IMPERATIVE*
PRESENT	**PAST**	
1. querría	habría querido	
2. querrías	habrías querido	(tú) quiere
3. querría	habría querido	(Vd) quiera
1. querríamos	habríamos querido	(nosotros) queramos
2. querríais	habríais querido	(vosotros) quered
3. querrían	habrían querido	(Vds) quieran
SUBJUNCTIVE		
PRESENT	**IMPERFECT**	**PLUPERFECT**
1. quiera	quis-iera/iese	hubiera querido
2. quieras	quis-ieras/ieses	hubieras querido
3. quiera	quis-iera/iese	hubiera querido
1. queramos	quis-iéramos/iésemos	hubiéramos querido
2. queráis	quis-ierais/ieseis	hubierais querido
3. quieran	quis-ieran/iesen	hubieran querido
PERFECT	haya querido etc	
INFINITIVE	*PARTICIPLE*	
PRESENT	**PRESENT**	
querer	queriendo	
PAST	**PAST**	
haber querido	querido	

54 RAER

PRESENT	IMPERFECT	FUTURE
1. raigo/rayo/rao	raía	raeré
2. raes	raías	raerás
3. rae	raía	raerá
1. raemos	raíamos	raeremos
2. raéis	raíais	raeréis
3. raen	raían	raerán
PAST HISTORIC	**PERFECT**	**PLUPERFECT**
1. raí	he raído	había raído
2. raíste	has raído	habías raído
3. rayó	ha raído	había raído
1. raímos	hemos raído	habíamos raído
2. raísteis	habéis raído	habíais raído
3. rayeron	han raído	habían raído
PAST ANTERIOR	**FUTURE PERFECT**	
hube raído etc	habré raído etc	
CONDITIONAL		*IMPERATIVE*
PRESENT	**PAST**	
1. raería	habría raído	
2. raerías	habrías raído	(tú) rae
3. raería	habría raído	(Vd) raiga/raya
1. raeríamos	habríamos raído	(nosotros) raigamos
2. raeríais	habríais raído	(vosotros) raed
3. raerían	habrían raído	(Vds) raigan/rayan
SUBJUNCTIVE		
PRESENT	**IMPERFECT**	**PLUPERFECT**
1. raiga/raya	ra-yera/yese	hubiera raído
2. raigas/rayas	ra-yeras/yeses	hubieras raído
3. raiga/raya	ra-yera/yese	hubiera raído
1. raigamos/rayamos	ra-yéramos/yésemos	hubiéramos raído
2. raigáis/rayáis	ra-yerais/yeseis	hubierais raído
3. raigan/rayan	ra-yeran/yesen	hubieran raído
PERFECT	haya raído etc	
INFINITIVE	*PARTICIPLE*	
PRESENT	**PRESENT**	
raer	rayendo	
PAST	**PAST**	
haber raído	raído	

55 REGIR

PRESENT	IMPERFECT	FUTURE
1. rijo	regía	regiré
2. riges	regías	regirás
3. rige	regía	regirá
1. regimos	regíamos	regiremos
2. regís	regíais	regiréis
3. rigen	regían	regirán
PAST HISTORIC	**PERFECT**	**PLUPERFECT**
1. regí	he regido	había regido
2. registe	has regido	habías regido
3. rigió	ha regido	había regido
1. regimos	hemos regido	habíamos regido
2. registeis	habéis regido	habíais regido
3. rigieron	han regido	habían regido
PAST ANTERIOR	**FUTURE PERFECT**	
hube regido etc	habré regido etc	
CONDITIONAL		*IMPERATIVE*
PRESENT	**PAST**	
1. regiría	habría regido	
2. regirías	habrías regido	(tú) rige
3. regiría	habría regido	(Vd) rija
1. regiríamos	habríamos regido	(nosotros) rijamos
2. regiríais	habríais regido	(vosotros) regid
3. regirían	habrían regido	(Vds) rijan
SUBJUNCTIVE		
PRESENT	**IMPERFECT**	**PLUPERFECT**
1. rija	rig-iera/iese	hubiera regido
2. rijas	rig-ieras/ieses	hubieras regido
3. rija	rig-iera/iese	hubiera regido
1. rijamos	rig-iéramos/iésemos	hubiéramos regido
2. rijáis	rig-ierais/ieseis	hubierais regido
3. rijan	rig-ieran/iesen	hubieran regido
PERFECT	haya regido etc	
INFINITIVE	*PARTICIPLE*	
PRESENT	**PRESENT**	
regir	rigiendo	
PAST	**PAST**	
haber regido	regido	

56 REÍR

PRESENT	IMPERFECT	FUTURE
1. río	reía	reiré
2. ríes	reías	reirás
3. ríe	reía	reirá
1. reímos	reíamos	reiremos
2. reís	reíais	reiréis
3. ríen	reían	reirán
PRETERITE	**PERFECT**	**PLUPERFECT**
1. reí	he reído	había reído
2. reíste	has reído	habías reído
3. rió	ha reído	había reído
1. reímos	hemos reído	habíamos reído
2. reísteis	habéis reído	habíais reído
3. rieron	han reído	habían reído
PAST ANTERIOR	**FUTURE PERFECT**	
hube reído etc	habré reído etc	
CONDITIONAL		*IMPERATIVE*
PRESENT	**PAST**	
1. reiría	habría reído	
2. reirías	habrías reido	(tú) ríe
3. reiría	habría reído	(Vd) ría
1. reiríamos	habríamos reído	(nosotros) riamos
2. reiríais	habríais reído	(vosotros) reíd
3. reirían	habrían reído	(Vds) rían
SUBJUNCTIVE		
PRESENT	**IMPERFECT**	**PLUPERFECT**
1. ría	ri-era/ese	hubiera reído
2. rías	ri-eras/eses	hubieras reído
3. ría	ri-era/ese	hubiera reído
1. riamos	ri-éramos/ésemos	hubiéramos reído
2. riáis	ri-erais/eseis	hubierais reído
3. rían	ri-eran/esen	hubieran reído
PERFECT	haya reído etc	
INFINITIVE	*PARTICIPLE*	
PRESENT	**PRESENT**	
reír	riendo	
PAST	**PAST**	
haber reído	reído	

57 REUNIR

PRESENT	IMPERFECT	FUTURE
1. reúno	reunía	reuniré
2. reúnes	reunías	reunirás
3. reúne	reunía	reunirá
1. reunimos	reuníamos	reuniremos
2. reunís	reuníais	reuniréis
3. reúnen	reunían	reunirán
PRETERITE	**PERFECT**	**PLUPERFECT**
1. reuní	he reunido	había reunido
2. reuniste	has reunido	habías reunido
3. reunió	ha reunido	había reunido
1. reunimos	hemos reunido	habíamos reunido
2. reunisteis	habéis reunido	habíais reunido
3. reunieron	han reunido	habían reunido
PAST ANTERIOR	**FUTURE PERFECT**	
hube reunido etc	habré reunido etc	

CONDITIONAL PRESENT	PAST	*IMPERATIVE*
1. reuniría	habría reunido	
2. reunirías	habrías reunido	(tú) reúne
3. reuniría	habría reunido	(Vd) reúna
1. reuniríamos	habríamos reunido	(nosotros) reunamos
2. reuniríais	habríais reunido	(vosotros) reunid
3. reunirían	habrían reunido	(Vds) reúnan

SUBJUNCTIVE PRESENT	IMPERFECT	PLUPERFECT
1. reúna	reun-iera/iese	hubiera reunido
2. reúnas	reun-ieras/ieses	hubieras reunido
3. reúna	reun-iera/iese	hubiera reunido
1. reunamos	reun-iéramos/iésemos	hubiéramos reunido
2. reunáis	reun-ierais/ieseis	hubierais reunido
3. reúnan	reun-ieran/iesen	hubieran reunido
PERFECT	haya reunido etc	

INFINITIVE PRESENT	*PARTICIPLE* PRESENT
reunir	reuniendo
PAST	**PAST**
haber reunido	reunido

58 ROER

PRESENT	IMPERFECT	FUTURE
1. roo/roigo/royo	roía	roeré
2. roes	roías	roerás
3. roe	roía	roerá
1. roemos	roíamos	roeremos
2. roéis	roíais	roeréis
3. roen	roían	roerán
PRETERITE	**PERFECT**	**PLUPERFECT**
1. roí	he roído	había roído
2. roíste	has roído	habías roído
3. royó	ha roído	había roído
1. roímos	hemos roído	habíamos roído
2. roísteis	habéis roído	habíais roído
3. royeron	han roído	habían roído
PAST ANTERIOR	**FUTURE PERFECT**	
hube roído etc	habré roído etc	

CONDITIONAL PRESENT	PAST	*IMPERATIVE*
1. roería	habría roído	
2. roerías	habrías roído	(tú) roe
3. roería	habría roído	(Vd) roa
1. roeríamos	habríamos roído	(nosotros) roamos
2. roeríais	habríais roído	(vosotros) roed
3. roerían	habrían roído	(Vds) roan

SUBJUNCTIVE PRESENT	IMPERFECT	PLUPERFECT
1. roa/roiga/roya	ro-yera/yese	hubiera roído
2. roas	ro-yeras/yeses	hubieras roído
3. roa	ro-yera/yese	hubiera roído
1. roamos	ro-yéramos/yésemos	hubiéramos roído
2. roáis	ro-yerais/yeseis	hubierais roído
3. roan	ro-yeran/yesen	hubieran roído
PERFECT	haya roído etc	

INFINITIVE PRESENT	*PARTICIPLE* PRESENT
roer	royendo
PAST	**PAST**
haber roído	roído

59 SABER

PRESENT	IMPERFECT	FUTURE
1. sé	sabía	sabré
2. sabes	sabías	sabrás
3. sabe	sabía	sabrá
1. sabemos	sabíamos	sabremos
2. sabéis	sabíais	sabréis
3. saben	sabían	sabrán
PRETERITE	**PERFECT**	**PLUPERFECT**
1. supe	he sabido	había sabido
2. supiste	has sabido	habías sabido
3. supo	ha sabido	había sabido
1. supimos	hemos sabido	habíamos sabido
2. supisteis	habéis sabido	habíais sabido
3. supieron	han sabido	habían sabido
PAST ANTERIOR	**FUTURE PERFECT**	
hube sabido etc	habré sabido etc	

CONDITIONAL PRESENT	PAST	*IMPERATIVE*
1. sabría	habría sabido	
2. sabrías	habrías sabido	(tú) sabe
3. sabría	habría sabido	(Vd) sepa
1. sabríamos	habríamos sabido	(nosotros) sepamos
2. sabríais	habríais sabido	(vosotros) sabed
3. sabrían	habrían sabido	(Vds) sepan

SUBJUNCTIVE PRESENT	IMPERFECT	PLUPERFECT
1. sepa	sup-iera/iese	hubiera sabido
2. sepas	sup-ieras/ieses	hubieras sabido
3. sepa	sup-iera/iese	hubiera sabido
1. sepamos	sup-iéramos/iésemos	hubiéramos sabido
2. sepáis	sup-ierais/ieseis	hubierais sabido
3. sepan	sup-ieran/iesen	hubieran sabido
PERFECT	haya sabido etc	

INFINITIVE PRESENT	*PARTICIPLE* PRESENT
saber	sabiendo
PAST	**PAST**
haber sabido	sabido

60 SACAR

PRESENT	IMPERFECT	FUTURE
1. saco	sacaba	sacaré
2. sacas	sacabas	sacarás
3. saca	sacaba	sacará
1. sacamos	sacábamos	sacaremos
2. sacáis	sacabais	sacaréis
3. sacan	sacaban	sacarán
PRETERITE	**PERFECT**	**PLUPERFECT**
1. saqué	he sacado	había sacado
2. sacaste	has sacado	habías sacado
3. sacó	ha sacado	había sacado
1. sacamos	hemos sacado	habíamos sacado
2. sacasteis	habéis sacado	habíais sacado
3. sacaron	han sacado	habían sacado
PAST ANTERIOR	**FUTURE PERFECT**	
hube sacado etc	habré sacado etc	

CONDITIONAL PRESENT	PAST	*IMPERATIVE*
1. sacaría	habría sacado	
2. sacarías	habrías sacado	(tú) saca
3. sacaría	habría sacado	(Vd) saque
1. sacaríamos	habríamos sacado	(nosotros) saquemos
2. sacaríais	habríais sacado	(vosotros) sacad
3. sacarían	habrían sacado	(Vds) saquen

SUBJUNCTIVE PRESENT	IMPERFECT	PLUPERFECT
1. saque	sac-ara/ase	hubiera sacado
2. saques	sac-aras/ases	hubieras sacado
3. saque	sac-ara/ase	hubiera sacado
1. saquemos	sac-áramos/ásemos	hubiéramos sacado
2. saquéis	sac-arais/aseis	hubierais sacado
3. saquen	sac-aran/asen	hubieran sacado
PERFECT	haya sacado etc	

INFINITIVE PRESENT	*PARTICIPLE* PRESENT
sacar	sacando
PAST	**PAST**
haber sacado	sacado

61 SALIR

PRESENT	IMPERFECT	FUTURE
1. salgo	salía	saldré
2. sales	salías	saldrás
3. sale	salía	saldrá
1. salimos	salíamos	saldremos
2. salís	salíais	saldréis
3. salen	salían	saldrán
PRETERITE	PERFECT	PLUPERFECT
1. salí	he salido	había salido
2. saliste	has salido	habías salido
3. salió	ha salido	había salido
1. salimos	hemos salido	habíamos salido
2. salisteis	habéis salido	habíais salido
3. salieron	han salido	habían salido
PAST ANTERIOR	FUTURE PERFECT	
hube salido etc	habré salido etc	
CONDITIONAL		*IMPERATIVE*
PRESENT	PAST	
1. saldría	habría salido	
2. saldrías	habrías salido	(tú) sal
3. saldría	habría salido	(Vd) salga
1. saldríamos	habríamos salido	(nosotros) salgamos
2. saldríais	habríais salido	(vosotros) salid
3. saldrían	habrían salido	(Vds) salgan
SUBJUNCTIVE		
PRESENT	IMPERFECT	PLUPERFECT
1. salga	sal-iera/iese	hubiera salido
2. salgas	sal-ieras/ieses	hubieras salido
3. salga	sal-iera/iese	hubiera salido
1. salgamos	sal-iéramos/iésemos	hubiéramos salido
2. salgáis	sal-ierais/ieseis	hubierais salido
3. salgan	sal-ieran/iesen	hubieran salido
PERFECT	haya salido etc	
INFINITIVE	*PARTICIPLE*	
PRESENT	PRESENT	
salir	saliendo	
PAST	PAST	
haber salido	salido	

62 SEGUIR

PRESENT	IMPERFECT	FUTURE
1. sigo	seguía	seguiré
2. sigues	seguías	seguirás
3. sigue	seguía	seguirá
1. seguimos	seguíamos	seguiremos
2. seguís	seguíais	seguiréis
3. siguen	seguían	seguirán
PRETERITE	PERFECT	PLUPERFECT
1. seguí	he seguido	había seguido
2. seguiste	has seguido	habías seguido
3. siguió	ha seguido	había seguido
1. seguimos	hemos seguido	habíamos seguido
2. seguisteis	habéis seguido	habíais seguido
3. siguieron	han seguido	habían seguido
PAST ANTERIOR	FUTURE PERFECT	
hube seguido etc	habré seguido etc	
CONDITIONAL		*IMPERATIVE*
PRESENT	PAST	
1. seguiría	habría seguido	
2. seguirías	habrías seguido	(tú) sigue
3. seguiría	habría seguido	(Vd) siga
1. seguiríamos	habríamos seguido	(nosotros) sigamos
2. seguiríais	habríais seguido	(vosotros) seguid
3. seguirían	habrían seguido	(Vds) sigan
SUBJUNCTIVE		
PRESENT	IMPERFECT	PLUPERFECT
1. siga	sigu-iera/iese	hubiera seguido
2. sigas	sigu-ieras/ieses	hubieras seguido
3. siga	sigu-iera/iese	hubiera seguido
1. sigamos	sigu-iéramos/iésemos	hubiéramos seguido
2. sigáis	sigu-ierais/ieseis	hubierais seguido
3. sigan	sigu-ieran/iesen	hubieran seguido
PERFECT	haya seguido etc	
INFINITIVE	*PARTICIPLE*	
PRESENT	PRESENT	
seguir	siguiendo	
PAST	PAST	
haber seguido	seguido	

63 SENTIR

PRESENT	IMPERFECT	FUTURE
1. siento	sentía	sentiré
2. sientes	sentías	sentirás
3. siente	sentía	sentirá
1. sentimos	sentíamos	sentiremos
2. sentís	sentíais	sentìreis
3. sienten	sentían	sentirán
PRETERITE	PERFECT	PLUPERFECT
1. sentí	he sentido	había sentido
2. sentiste	has sentido	habías sentido
3. sintió	ha sentido	había sentido
1. sentimos	hemos sentido	habíamos sentido
2. sentisteis	habéis sentido	habíais sentido
3. sintieron	han sentido	habían sentido
PAST ANTERIOR	FUTURE PERFECT	
hube sentido etc	habré sentido etc	
CONDITIONAL		*IMPERATIVE*
PRESENT	PAST	
1. sentiría	habría sentido	
2. sentirías	habrías sentido	(tú) siente
3. sentiría	habría sentido	(Vd) sienta
1. sentiríamos	habríamos sentido	(nosotros) sintamos
2. sentiríais	habríais sentido	(vosotros) sentid
3. sentirían	habrían sentido	(Vds) sientan
SUBJUNCTIVE		
PRESENT	IMPERFECT	PLUPERFECT
1. sienta	sint-iera/iese	hubiera sentido
2. sientas	sint-ieras/ieses	hubieras sentido
3. sienta	sint-iera/iese	hubiera sentido
1. sintamos	sint-iéramos/iésemos	hubiéramos sentido
2. sintáis	sint-ierais/ieseis	hubierais sentido
3. sientan	sint-ieran/iesen	hubieran sentido
PERFECT	haya sentido etc	
INFINITIVE	*PARTICIPLE*	
PRESENT	PRESENT	
sentir	sintiendo	
PAST	PAST	
haber sentido	sentido	

64 SONAR

PRESENT	IMPERFECT	FUTURE
1. sueno	sonaba	sonaré
2. suenas	sonabas	sonarás
3. suena	sonaba	sonará
1. sonamos	sonábamos	sonaremos
2. sonáis	sonabais	sonaréis
3. suenan	sonaban	sonarán
PRETERITE	PERFECT	PLUPERFECT
1. soné	he sonado	había sonado
2. sonaste	has sonado	habías sonado
3. sonó	ha sonado	había sonado
1. sonamos	hemos sonado	habíamos sonado
2. sonasteis	habéis sonado	habíais sonado
3. sonaron	han sonado	habían sonado
PAST ANTERIOR	FUTURE PERFECT	
hube sonado etc	habré sonado etc	
CONDITIONAL		*IMPERATIVE*
PRESENT	PAST	
1. sonaría	habría sonado	
2. sonarías	habrías sonado	(tú) suena
3. sonaría	habría soñado	(Vd) suene
1. sonaríamos	habríamos sonado	(nosotros) sonemos
2. sonaríais	habríais sonado	(vosotros) sonad
3. sonarían	habrían sonado	(Vds) suenen
SUBJUNCTIVE		
PRESENT	IMPERFECT	PLUPERFECT
1. suene	son-ara/ase	hubiera sonado
2. suenes	son-aras/ases	hubieras sonado
3. suene	son-ara/ase	hubiera sonado
1. sonemos	son-áramos/ásemos	hubiéramos sonado
2. sonéis	son-arais/aseis	hubierais sonado
3. suenen	son-aran/asen	hubieran sonado
PERFECT	haya sonado etc	
INFINITIVE	*PARTICIPLE*	
PRESENT	PRESENT	
sonar	sonando	
PAST	PAST	
haber sonado	sonado	

65 TAÑER

PRESENT	IMPERFECT	FUTURE
1. taño	tañía	tañeré
2. tañes	tañías	tañerás
3. tañe	tañía	tañerá
1. tañemos	tañíamos	tañeremos
2. tañéis	tañíais	tañeréis
3. tañen	tañían	tañerán
PRETERITE	PERFECT	PLUPERFECT
1. tañí	he tañido	había tañido
2. tañiste	has tañido	habías tañido
3. tañó	ha tañido	había tañido
1. tañimos	hemos tañido	habíamos tañido
2. tañisteis	habéis tañido	habíais tañido
3. tañeron	han tañido	habían tañido
PAST ANTERIOR	FUTURE PERFECT	
hube tañido etc	habré tañido etc	
CONDITIONAL		*IMPERATIVE*
PRESENT	PAST	
1. tañería	habría tañido	
2. tañerías	habrías tañido	(tú) tañe
3. tañería	habría tañido	(Vd) taña
1. tañeríamos	habríamos tañido	(nosotros) tañamos
2. tañeríais	habríais tañido	(vosotros) tañed
3. tañerían	habrían tañido	(Vds) tañan
SUBJUNCTIVE		
PRESENT	IMPERFECT	PLUPERFECT
1. taña	tañ-era/ese	hubiera tañido
2. tañas	tañ-eras/eses	hubieras tañido
3. taña	tañ-era/ese	hubiera tañido
1. tañamos	tañ-éramos/ésemos	hubiéramos tañido
2. tañáis	tañ-erais/eseis	hubierais tañido
3. tañan	tañ-eran/esen	hubieran tañido
PERFECT	haya tañido etc	
INFINITIVE	*PARTICIPLE*	
PRESENT	PRESENT	
tañer	tañendo	
PAST	PAST	
haber tañido	tañido	

66 TENDER

PRESENT	IMPERFECT	FUTURE
1. tiendo	tendía	tenderé
2. tiendes	tendías	tenderás
3. tiende	tendía	tenderá
1. tendemos	tendíamos	tenderemos
2. tendéis	tendíais	tenderéis
3. tienden	tendían	tenderán
PAST HISTORIC	PERFECT	PLUPERFECT
1. tendí	he tendido	había tendido
2. tendiste	has tendido	habías tendido
3. tendió	ha tendido	había tendido
1. tendimos	hemos tendido	habíamos tendido
2. tendisteis	habéis tendido	habíais tendido
3. tendieron	han tendido	habían tendido
PAST ANTERIOR	FUTURE PERFECT	
hube tendido etc	habré tendido etc	
CONDITIONAL		*IMPERATIVE*
PRESENT	PAST	
1. tendería	habría tendido	
2. tenderías	habrías tendido	(tú) tiende
3. tendería	habría tendido	(Vd) tienda
1. tenderíamos	habríamos tendido	(nosotros) tendamos
2. tenderíais	habríais tendido	(vosotros) tended
3. tenderían	habrían tendido	(Vds) tiendan
SUBJUNCTIVE		
PRESENT	IMPERFECT	PLUPERFECT
1. tienda	tend-iera/iese	hubiera tendido
2. tiendas	tend-ieras/ieses	hubieras tendido
3. tienda	tend-iera/iese	hubiera tendido
1. tendamos	tend-iéramos/iésemos	hubiéramos tendido
2. tendáis	tend-ierais/ieseis	hubierais tendido
3. tiendan	tend-ieran/iesen	hubieran tendido
PERFECT	haya tendido etc	
INFINITIVE	*PARTICIPLE*	
PRESENT	PRESENT	
tender	tendiendo	
PAST	PAST	
haber tendido	tendido	

67 TENER

PRESENT	IMPERFECT	FUTURE
1. tengo	tenía	tendré
2. tienes	tenías	tendrás
3. tiene	tenía	tendrá
1. tenemos	teníamos	tendremos
2. tenéis	teníais	tendréis
3. tienen	tenían	tendrán
PRETERITE	PERFECT	PLUPERFECT
1. tuve	he tenido	había tenido
2. tuviste	has tenido	habías tenido
3. tuvo	ha tenido	había tenido
1. tuvimos	hemos tenido	habíamos tenido
2. tuvisteis	habéis tenido	habíais tenido
3. tuvieron	han tenido	habían tenido
PAST ANTERIOR	FUTURE PERFECT	
hube tenido etc	habré tenido etc	
CONDITIONAL		*IMPERATIVE*
PRESENT	PAST	
1. tendría	habría tenido	
2. tendrías	habrías tenido	(tú) ten
3. tendría	habría tenido	(Vd) tenga
1. tendríamos	habríamos tenido	(nosotros) tengamos
2. tendríais	habríais tenido	(vosotros) tened
3. tendrían	habrían tenido	(Vds) tengan
SUBJUNCTIVE		
PRESENT	IMPERFECT	PLUPERFECT
1. tenga	tuv-iera/iese	hubiera tenido
2. tengas	tuv-ieras/ieses	hubieras tenido
3. tenga	tuv-iera/iese	hubiera tenido
1. tengamos	tuv-iéramos/iésemos	hubiéramos tenido
2. tengáis	tuv-ierais/ieseis	hubierais tenido
3. tengan	tuv-ieran/iesen	hubieran tenido
PERFECT	haya tenido etc	
INFINITIVE	*PARTICIPLE*	
PRESENT	PRESENT	
tener	teniendo	
PAST	PAST	
haber tenido	tenido	

68 TRAER

PRESENT	IMPERFECT	FUTURE
1. traigo	traía	traeré
2. traes	traías	traerás
3. trae	traía	traerá
1. traemos	traíamos	traeremos
2. traéis	traíais	traeréis
3. traen	traían	traerán
PRETERITE	PERFECT	PLUPERFECT
1. traje	he traído	había traído
2. trajiste	has traído	habías traído
3. trajo	ha traído	había traído
1. trajimos	hemos traído	habíamos traído
2. trajisteis	habéis traído	habíais traído
3. trajeron	han traído	habían traído
PAST ANTERIOR	FUTURE PERFECT	
hube traído etc	habré traído etc	
CONDITIONAL		*IMPERATIVE*
PRESENT	PAST	
1. traería	habría traído	
2. traerías	habrías traído	(tú) trae
3. traería	habría traído	(Vd) traiga
1. traeríamos	habríamos traído	(nosotros) traigamos
2. traeríais	habríais traído	(vosotros) traed
3. traerían	habrían traído	(Vds) traigan
SUBJUNCTIVE		
PRESENT	IMPERFECT	PLUPERFECT
1. traiga	traj-era/ese	hubiera traído
2. traigas	traj-eras/eses	hubieras traído
3. traiga	traj-era/ese	hubiera traído
1. traigamos	traj-éramos/ésemos	hubiéramos traído
2. traigáis	traj-erais/eseis	hubierais traído
3. traigan	traj-eran/esen	hubieran traído
PERFECT	haya traído etc	
INFINITIVE	*PARTICIPLE*	
PRESENT	PRESENT	
traer	trayendo	
PAST	PAST	
haber traído	traído	

69 TROCAR

PRESENT	IMPERFECT	FUTURE
1. trueco	trocaba	trocaré
2. truecas	trocabas	trocarás
3. trueca	trocaba	trocará
1. trocamos	trocábamos	trocaremos
2. trocáis	trocabais	trocaréis
3. truecan	trocaban	trocarán
PAST HISTORIC	PERFECT	PLUPERFECT
1. troqué	he trocado	había trocado
2. trocaste	has trocado	habías trocado
3. trocó	ha trocado	había trocado
1. trocamos	hemos trocado	habíamos trocado
2. trocasteis	habéis trocado	habíais trocado
3. trocaron	han trocado	habían trocado
PAST ANTERIOR	FUTURE PERFECT	
hube trocado etc	habré trocado etc	
CONDITIONAL		*IMPERATIVE*
PRESENT	PAST	
1. trocaría	habría trocado	
2. trocarías	habrías trocado	(tú) trueca
3. trocaría	habría trocado	(Vd) trueque
1. trocaríamos	habríamos trocado	(nosotros) troquemos
2. trocaríais	habríais trocado	(vosotros) trocad
3. trocarían	habrían trocado	(Vds) truequen
SUBJUNCTIVE		
PRESENT	IMPERFECT	PLUPERFECT
1. trueque	troc-ara/ase	hubiera trocado
2. trueques	troc-aras/ases	hubieras trocado
3. trueque	troc-ara/ase	hubiera trocado
1. troquemos	troc-áramos/ásemos	hubiéramos trocado
2. troquéis	troc-arais/aseis	hubierais trocado
3. truequen	troc-aran/asen	hubieran trocado
PERFECT	haya trocado etc	
INFINITIVE	*PARTICIPLE*	
PRESENT	PRESENT	
trocar	trocando	
PAST	PAST	
haber trocado	trocado	

70 VALER

PRESENT	IMPERFECT	FUTURE
1. valgo	valía	valdré
2. vales	valías	valdrás
3. vale	valía	valdrá
1. valemos	valíamos	valdremos
2. valéis	valíais	valdréis
3. valen	valían	valdrán
PRETERITE	PERFECT	PLUPERFECT
1. valí	he valido	había valido
2. valiste	has valido	habías valido
3. valió	ha valido	había valido
1. valimos	hemos valido	habíamos valido
2. valisteis	habéis valido	habíais valido
3. valieron	han valido	habían valido
PAST ANTERIOR	FUTURE PERFECT	
hube valido etc	habré valido etc	
CONDITIONAL		*IMPERATIVE*
PRESENT	PAST	
1. valdría	habría valido	
2. valdrías	habrías valido	(tú) vale
3. valdría	habría valido	(Vd) valga
1. valdríamos	habríamos valido	(nosotros) valgamos
2. valdríais	habríais valido	(vosotros) valed
3. valdrían	habrían valido	(Vds) valgan
SUBJUNCTIVE		
PRESENT	IMPERFECT	PLUPERFECT
1. valga	val-iera/iese	hubiera valido
2. valgas	val-ieras/ieses	hubieras valido
3. valga	val-iera/iese	hubiera valido
1. valgamos	val-iéramos/iésemos	hubiéramos valido
2. valgáis	val-ierais/ieseis	hubierais valido
3. valgan	val-ieran/iesen	hubieran valido
PERFECT	haya valido etc	
INFINITIVE	*PARTICIPLE*	
PRESENT	PRESENT	
valer	valiendo	
PAST	PAST	
haber valido	valido	

71 VENIR

PRESENT	IMPERFECT	FUTURE
1. vengo	venía	vendré
2. vienes	venías	vendrás
3. viene	venía	vendrá
1. venimos	veníamos	vendremos
2. venís	veníais	vendréis
3. vienen	venían	vendrán
PRETERITE	PERFECT	PLUPERFECT
1. vine	he venido	había venido
2. viniste	has venido	habías venido
3. vino	ha venido	había venido
1. vinimos	hemos venido	habíamos venido
2. vinisteis	habéis venido	habíais venido
3. vinieron	han venido	habían venido
PAST ANTERIOR	FUTURE PERFECT	
hube venido etc	habré venido etc	
CONDITIONAL		*IMPERATIVE*
PRESENT	PAST	
1. vendría	habría venido	
2. vendrías	habrías venido	(tú) ven
3. vendría	habría venido	(Vd) venga
1. vendríamos	habríamos venido	(nosotros) vengamos
2. vendríais	habríais venido	(vosotros) venid
3. vendrían	habrían venido	(Vds) vengan
SUBJUNCTIVE		
PRESENT	IMPERFECT	PLUPERFECT
1. venga	vin-iera/iese	hubiera venido
2. vengas	vin-ieras/ieses	hubieras venido
3. venga	vin-iera/iese	hubiera venido
1. vengamos	vin-iéramos/iésemos	hubiéramos venido
2. vengáis	vin-ierais/ieseis	hubierais venido
3. vengan	vin-ieran/iesen	hubieran venido
PERFECT	haya venido etc	
INFINITIVE	*PARTICIPLE*	
PRESENT	PRESENT	
venir	viniendo	
PAST	PAST	
haber venido	venido	

72 VER

PRESENT	IMPERFECT	FUTURE
1. veo	veía	veré
2. ves	veías	verás
3. ve	veía	verá
1. vemos	veíamos	veremos
2. veis	veíais	veréis
3. ven	veían	verán
PRETERITE	PERFECT	PLUPERFECT
1. vi	he visto	había visto
2. viste	has visto	habías visto
3. vio	ha visto	había visto
1. vimos	hemos visto	habíamos visto
2. visteis	habéis visto	habíais visto
3. vieron	han visto	habían visto
PAST ANTERIOR	FUTURE PERFECT	
hube visto etc	habré visto etc	
CONDITIONAL		*IMPERATIVE*
PRESENT	PAST	
1. vería	habría visto	
2. verías	habrías visto	(tú) ve
3. vería	habría visto	(Vd) vea
1. veríamos	habríamos visto	(nosotros) veamos
2. veríais	habríais visto	(vosotros) ved
3. verían	habrían visto	(Vds) vean
SUBJUNCTIVE		
PRESENT	IMPERFECT	PLUPERFECT
1. vea	v-iera/iese	hubiera visto
2. veas	v-ieras/ieses	hubieras visto
3. vea	v-iera/iese	hubiera visto
1. veamos	v-iéramos/iésemos	hubiéramos visto
2. veáis	v-ierais/ieseis	hubierais visto
3. vean	v-ieran/iesen	hubieran visto
PERFECT	haya visto etc	
INFINITIVE	*PARTICIPLE*	
PRESENT	PRESENT	
ver	viendo	
PAST	PAST	
haber visto	visto	

73 YACER

PRESENT	IMPERFECT	FUTURE
1. yazgo/yago/yazco	yacía	yaceré
2. yaces	yacías	yacerás
3. yace	yacía	yacerá
1. yacemos	yacíamos	yaceremos
2. yacéis	yacíais	yaceréis
3. yacen	yacían	yacerán
PRETERITE	**PERFECT**	**PLUPERFECT**
1. yací	he yacido	había yacido
2. yaciste	has yacido	habías yacido
3. yació	ha yacido	había yacido
1. yacimos	hemos yacido	habíamos yacido
2. yacisteis	habéis yacido	habíais yacido
3. yacieron	han yacido	habían yacido
PAST ANTERIOR	**FUTURE PERFECT**	
hube yacido etc	habré yacido etc	

CONDITIONAL / *IMPERATIVE*

PRESENT	PAST	
1. yacería	habría yacido	
2. yacerías	habrías yacido	(tú) yace
3. yacería	habría yacido	(Vd) yazga
1. yaceríamos	habríamos yacido	(nosotros) yazgamos
2. yaceríais	habríais yacido	(vosotros) yaced
3. yacerían	habrían yacido	(Vds) yazgan

SUBJUNCTIVE

PRESENT	IMPERFECT	PLUPERFECT
1. yazga	yac-iera/iese	hubiera yacido
2. yazgas	yac-ieras/ieses	hubieras yacido
3. yazga	yac-iera/iese	hubiera yacido
1. yazgamos	yac-iéramos/iésemos	hubiéramos yacido
2. yazgáis	yac-ierais/ieseis	hubierais yacido
3. yazgan	yac-ieran/iesen	hubieran yacido

PERFECT haya yacido etc

INFINITIVE	*PARTICIPLE*
PRESENT	PRESENT
yacer	yaciendo
PAST	PAST
haber yacido	yacido

NOTE Present subjunctive: The following forms are also found: yazca/yazcas etc

74 ZURCIR

PRESENT	IMPERFECT	FUTURE
1. zurzo	zurcía	zurciré
2. zurces	zurcías	zurcirás
3. zurce	zurcía	zurcirá
1. zurcimos	zurcíamos	zurciremos
2. zurcís	zurcíais	zurciréis
3. zurcen	zurcían	zurcirán
PRETERITE	**PERFECT**	**PLUPERFECT**
1. zurcí	he zurcido	había zurcido
2. zurciste	has zurcido	habías zurcido
3. zurció	ha zurcido	había zurcido
1. zurcimos	hemos zurcido	habíamos zurcido
2. zurcisteis	habéis zurcido	habíais zurcido
3. zurcieron	han zurcido	habían zurcido
PAST ANTERIOR	**FUTURE PERFECT**	
hube zurcido etc	habré zurcido etc	

CONDITIONAL / *IMPERATIVE*

PRESENT	PAST	
1. zurciría	habría zurcido	
2. zurcirías	habrías zurcido	(tú) zurce
3. zurciría	habría zurcido	(Vd) zurza
1. zurciríamos	habríamos zurcido	(nosotros) zurzamos
2. zurciríais	habríais zurcido	(vosotros) zurcid
3. zurcirían	habrían zurcido	(Vds) zurzan

SUBJUNCTIVE

PRESENT	IMPERFECT	PLUPERFECT
1. zurza	zurc-iera/iese	hubiera zurcido
2. zurzas	zurc-ieras/ieses	hubieras zurcido
3. zurza	zurc-iera/iese	hubiera zurcido
1. zurzamos	zurc-iéramos/iésemos	hubiéramos zurcido
2. zurzáis	zurc-ierais/ieseis	hubierais zurcido
3. zurzan	zurc-ieran/iesen	hubieran zurcido

PERFECT haya zurcido etc

INFINITIVE	*PARTICIPLE*
PRESENT	PRESENT
zurcir	zurciendo
PAST	PAST
haber zurcido	zurcido

VERBOS IRREGULARES INGLESES

INFINITIVO	*PASADO*	*PARTICIPIO*
arise	arose	arisen
awake	awoke	awoken
awaken	awoke, awakened	awakened, awoken
be	were/was	been
bear	bore	borne
beat	beat	beaten
become	became	become
begin	began	begun
bend	bent	bent
beseech	besought, beseeched	besought, beseeched
bet	bet, betted	bet, betted
bid	bade, bid	bidden, bid
bind	bound	bound
bite	bit	bitten
bleed	bled	bled
blow	blew	blown
break	broke	broken
breed	bred	bred
bring	brought	brought
build	built	built
burn	burnt, burned	burnt, burned
burst	burst	burst
bust	bust, busted	bust, busted
buy	bought	bought
cast	cast	cast
catch	caught	caught
chide	chided, chid	chided, chidden
choose	chose	chosen
cleave	cleaved, cleft, clove	cleaved, cleft, cloven
cling	clung	clung
clothe	clad, clothed	clad, clothed
come	came	come
cost	cost	cost
creep	crept	crept
crow	crowed, crew	crowed
cut	cut	cut
deal	dealt	dealt
dig	dug	dug
dive	dived, *US* dove	dived
do	did	done
draw	drew	drawn
dream	dreamt, dreamed	dreamt, dreamed
drink	drank	drunk
drive	drove	driven
dwell	dwelt	dwelt
eat	ate	eaten
fall	fell	fallen
feed	fed	fed
feel	felt	felt
fight	fought	fought
find	found	found
flee	fled	fled
fling	flung	flung
fly	flew	flown
forget	forgot	forgotten

INFINITIVO	*PASADO*	*PARTICIPIO*
forgive	forgave	forgiven
forsake	forsook	forsaken
freeze	froze	frozen
get	got	got, *US* gotten
gild	gilded, gilt	gilded, gilt
gird	girded, girt	girded, girt
give	gave	given
go	went	gone
grind	ground	ground
grow	grew	grown
hang	hung/hanged	hung/hanged
have	had	had
hear	heard	heard
hew	hewed	hewn, hewed
hide	hid	hidden
hit	hit	hit
hold	held	held
hurt	hurt	hurt
keep	kept	kept
kneel	knelt	knelt
knit	knitted, knit	knitted, knit
know	knew	known
lay	laid	laid
lead	led	led
lean	leant, leaned	leant, leaned
leap	leapt, leaped	leapt, leaped
learn	learnt, learned	learnt, learned
leave	left	left
lend	lent	lent
let	let	let
lie	lay	lain
light	lit	lit
lose	lost	lost
make	made	made
mean	meant	meant
meet	met	met
mow	mowed	mown
pay	paid	paid
plead	pleaded, *US* pled	pleaded, *US* pled
prove	proved	proved, proven
put	put	put
quit	quit, quitted	quit, quitted
read [ri:d]	read [red]	read [red]
rend	rent	rent
rid	rid	rid
ride	rode	ridden
ring	rang	rung
rise	rose	risen
run	ran	run
saw	sawed	sawn, sawed
say	said	said
see	saw	seen
seek	sought	sought
sell	sold	sold
send	sent	sent
set	set	set
sew	sewed	sewn
shake	shook	shaken
shear	sheared	shorn, sheared
shed	shed	shed
shine	shone	shone
shit	shitted, shat	shitted, shat
shoe	shod	shod
shoot	shot	shot
show	showed	shown

INFINITIVO	*PASADO*	*PARTICIPIO*
shrink	shrank	shrunk
shut	shut	shut
sing	sang	sung
sink	sank	sunk
sit	sat	sat
slay	slew	slain
sleep	slept	slept
slide	slid	slid
sling	slung	slung
slink	slunk	slunk
slit	slit	slit
smell	smelled, smelt	smelled, smelt
smite	smote	smitten
sneak	sneaked, *US* snuck	sneaked, *US* snuck
sow	sowed	sown, sowed
speak	spoke	spoken
speed	sped, speeded	sped, speeded
spell	spelt, spelled	spelt, spelled
spend	spent	spent
spill	spilt, spilled	spilt, spilled
spin	span	spun
spit	spat, *US* spit	spat, *US* spit
split	split	split
spoil	spoilt, spoiled	spoilt, spoiled
spread	spread	spread
spring	sprang	sprung
stand	stood	stood
stave in	staved in, stove in	staved in, stove in
steal	stole	stolen
stick	stuck	stuck
sting	stung	stung
stink	stank, stunk	stunk
strew	strewed	strewed, strewn
stride	strode	stridden
strike	struck	struck
string	strung	strung
strive	strove	striven
swear	swore	sworn
sweep	swept	swept
swell	swelled	swollen, swelled
swim	swam	swum
swing	swung	swung
take	took	taken
teach	taught	taught
tear	tore	torn
tell	told	told
think	thought	thought
thrive	thrived, throve	thrived
throw	threw	thrown
thrust	thrust	thrust
tread	trod	trodden
wake	woke	woken
wear	wore	worn
weave	wove, weaved	woven, weaved
weep	wept	wept
wet	wet, wetted	wet, wetted
win	won	won
wind	wound	wound
wring	wrung	wrung
write	wrote	written

HARRAP'S
SPANISH
DICTIONARY

Harrap's Spanish Dictionary is the culmination of several years' work by a large team of experienced lexicographers and translators. This top-of-the-range dictionary offers a fantastic breadth of coverage and level of detail in an attractive and accessible format.

As with all Harrap's dictionaries, there is excellent coverage of **slang** and everyday colloquial language. This is supplemented by extensive treatment of **terminology** from computing to sports, and from business and law to journalism and politics.

The **many varieties of Spanish**, from Spain and Latin America, are covered in considerable detail. North American and British varieties of English are of course given detailed attention, but the user will also find words and expressions typical of Australian, Canadian, Scottish and Irish varieties of English.

A special feature of this dictionary is the inclusion of boxes warning about **false friends**, as well as a number of **usage and grammar panels** for both English and Spanish speakers, which give full and clear explanations of important areas that can cause difficulties.

The central colour supplement features detailed **communication guides** for Spanish and English, covering a wide range of contexts and with lots of practical information.

From the beginning Harrap has published language books and its commitment to producing educational but accessible books of the highest quality has remained unchanged throughout its over 100-year history. Today Harrap publishes bilingual dictionaries in Spanish, French, German, Italian and Portuguese. Alongside its renowned range of dictionaries for general use, it also publishes a number of specialist slang and business dictionaries.

Harrap's Pardon my Spanish!

This new pocket-sized Spanish slang dictionary gives thorough treatment of the most common words and phrases in current use. More than just a list of "rude words", it shows how these words function in racy and colourful idiomatic speech.

ISBN 0245 60721 8
£5.99

Harrap's Computers and the Internet Dictionary English-Spanish – Español-Inglés

With over 6,000 words and phrases and the most up-to-date Internet vocabulary, as well as an invaluable supplement full of practical information on writing e-mails in Spanish.

ISBN 0245 60712 9
£9.99

Harrap's Concise Spanish Dictionary

Unrivalled coverage of contemporary Spanish, with particular attention given to Latin-American Spanish. With over 245,000 translations, in-depth treatment of the most common words in both languages, and notes on false friends.

ISBN 0245 60695 5
£15.99

Abbreviations Used in this Dictionary

Abreviaturas utilizadas en este diccionario

abbreviation	*abbr/abrev*	abreviatura
accounting	*Acct*	contabilidad
adjective	*adj*	adjetivo
adverb	*adv*	adverbio
agriculture	*Agr*	agricultura
Latin American Spanish	*Am*	español de América
anatomy	*Anat*	anatomía
architecture	*Archit*	arquitectura
Argentinian Spanish	*Arg*	español de Argentina
architecture	*Arquit*	arquitectura
art	*Art*	arte
article	*art*	artículo
astrology	*Astrol*	astrología
astronomy	*Astron*	astronomía
Australian English	*Austr*	inglés de Australia
cars	*Aut*	automoción
auxiliary	*aux*	auxiliar
aviation	*Av*	aviación
biochemistry	*Biochem*	bioquímica
biology	*Biol*	biología
biochemistry	*Bioquím*	bioquímica
Bolivian English	*Bol*	español de Bolivia
botany	*Bot*	botánica
British English	*Br*	inglés británico
Central American Spanish	*CAm*	español centroamericano
Canadian English	*Can*	inglés de Canadá
Caribbean Spanish (Cuba, Puerto Rico, Dominican Republic, Venezuela)	*Carib*	español caribeño (Cuba, Puerto Rico, República Dominicana, Venezuela)
chemistry	*Chem*	química
cinema	*Cin*	cine
Colombian Spanish	*Col*	español de Colombia
commerce	*Com*	comercio
computing	*Comptr*	informática
conjunction	*conj*	conjunción
construction	*Constr*	construcción
accounting	*Cont*	contabilidad
Costa Rican Spanish	*CRica*	español de Costa Rica
Cono Sur Spanish (Argentina, Chile, Paraguay, Uruguay)	*CSur*	español del Cono Sur (Argentina, Chile, Paraguay, Uruguay)
cooking	*Culin*	cocina
sport	*Dep*	deporte
law	*Der*	derecho
economics	*Econ*	economía
Ecuadorian Spanish	*Ecuad*	español de Ecuador
education	*Educ*	educación
electricity and electronics	*Elec*	electricidad y electrónica
Peninsular Spanish	*Esp*	español de España
especially	*esp*	*especialmente*
specialist term	*Espec*	término especializado
European Union	*EU*	Unión Europea
euphemism	*Euph/Euf*	eufemismo
exclamation	*exclam*	interjección
Spanish idiom(s)	EXPR	expresión (o expresiones) idiomática(s)
feminine	*f*	femenino
informal	*Fam*	familiar
pharmacy	*Farm*	farmacia
rail	*Ferroc*	ferrocarril
figurative	*Fig*	sentido figurado
finance	*Fin*	finanzas
physics	*Fís*	física
physiology	*Fisiol*	fisiología
photography	*Fot*	fotografía
geography	*Geog*	geografía
geology	*Geol*	geología
geometry	*Geom*	geometría
grammar	*Gram*	gramática
Guatemalan Spanish	*Guat*	español de Guatemala
history	*Hist*	historia
Honduran Spanish	*Hond*	español de Honduras
humorous	*Hum*	humorístico
industry	*Ind*	industria
computing	*Informát*	informática
interjection	*interj*	interjección
invariable	*inv*	invariable
journalism	*Journ*	periodismo
law	*Law*	derecho
linguistics	*Ling*	lingüística
literature	*Lit*	literatura
adjectival phrase	*loc adj*	locución adjetiva
adverbial phrase	*loc adv*	locución adverbial
conjunctive phrase	*loc conj*	locución conjuntiva
prepositional phrase	*loc prep*	locución prepositiva